BUTTERWORTHS
EMPLOYMENT LAW
HANDBOOK

BUTTERWORTHS EMPLOYMENT LAW HANDBOOK

Sixteenth edition

Editor

PETER WALLINGTON QC

Barrister, 11 KBW Chambers
Sometime Professor of Law at the University of Lancaster and Brunel University
A Part-time Employment Judge

LexisNexis®

Members of the LexisNexis Group worldwide

United Kingdom	LexisNexis, a Division of Reed Elsevier (UK) Ltd, Halsbury House, 35 Chancery Lane, London, WC2A 1EL, and London House, 20–22 East London Street, Edinburgh EH7 4BQ
Australia	LexisNexis Butterworths, Chatswood, New South Wales
Austria	LexisNexis Verlag ARD Orac GmbH & Co KG, Vienna
Benelux	LexisNexis Benelux, Amsterdam
Canada	LexisNexis Canada, Markham, Ontario
China	LexisNexis China, Beijing and Shanghai
France	LexisNexis SA, Paris
Germany	LexisNexis Deutschland GmbH, Munster
Hong Kong	LexisNexis Hong Kong, Hong Kong
India	LexisNexis India, New Delhi
Italy	Giuffrè Editore, Milan
Japan	LexisNexis Japan, Tokyo
Malaysia	Malayan Law Journal Sdn Bhd, Kuala Lumpur
New Zealand	LexisNexis NZ Ltd, Wellington
Poland	Wydawnictwo Prawnicze LexisNexis Sp, Warsaw
Singapore	LexisNexis Singapore, Singapore
South Africa	LexisNexis Butterworths, Durban
USA	LexisNexis, Dayton, Ohio

Published by LexisNexis

This is a Butterworths title

A CIP Catalogue record for this book is available from the British Library.

ISBN: 978 1 4057 2879 9

Typeset by Columns Design Ltd, Reading, England
Printed in the UK by CPI William Clowes Beccles NR34 7TL
Visit LexisNexis at www.lexisnexis.co.uk

EDITOR'S INTRODUCTION TO THE SIXTEENTH EDITION

The established practice of annual publication of this Handbook is continued with this, the sixteenth edition. The pace of legislative change remains such that annual updating has for some time been essential. The reasonably well established (if not always observed) policy of government that legislative changes affecting employment relations should take place on two fixed dates each year, 6 April and 1 October, has also enabled the publishers to standardise the publishing cycle so that each edition is up to date to 6 April, and published as soon as practicable thereafter.

In terms of changes to legislation, the year covered by this edition may prove to be the lull before the storm. The Employment Bill is expected to receive Royal Assent in October 2008, with implementation of its main provisions likely in April 2009 (with associated changes such as a new ACAS Discipline and Grievance Code). Furthermore, in May 2008 it was announced that the long-awaited Equality Bill, a major restatement of discrimination law, will form part of the Government's 2008–09 legislative programme. That is not to suggest that little has changed since the cut-off date for the fifteenth edition. The principal new materials included in this edition, or incorporated as amendments to existing materials, are as follows:

- The Corporate Manslaughter and Corporate Homicide Act 2007.
- Changes introduced by the Tribunals, Courts and Enforcement Act 2007 to the administration of employment tribunals and the Employment Appeal Tribunal.
- The Working Time (Amendment) Regulations 2007, extending statutory holiday rights.
- Amendments to the Sex Discrimination Act 1975 made by the Sex Discrimination Act 1975 (Amendment) Regulations 2008 (further implementing the requirements of EU Directives) and the Sex Discrimination (Amendment of Legislation) Regulations 2008 (doing the same in the fields covered by Part III of the 1975 Act).
- The new Codes of Practice issued by the Border and Immigration Agency to provide guidance on the implementation of the changes made by the Immigration, Asylum and Nationality Act 2006 in employers' obligations to avoid the employment of workers not entitled to work in the UK.
- New EAT Procedure Practice Direction (May 2008).
- Repeals, amendments and transitional provisions for the implementation of the Equality Act 2006 and of the major part of the Companies Act 2006 affecting directors' rights and duties.

In addition, and as has become a feature of every new edition of this Handbook, there are numerous detailed amendments to the standing text, derived from a wide variety of sources.

The format of this Handbook is as in previous editions. Part 1 contains statutes, in chronological order and printed as amended and in force at the time of going to press. Amendments are indicated using the house style of the Handbooks series as follows: repeals are indicated by three dots; insertions and substitutions are in square brackets; and prospective repeals or substitutions are in italics, with the text to be substituted set out in the notes. Details of the provenance of changes are given in the notes, together with the effective date (unless this was before 6 April 2003).

Part 2 contains Statutory Instruments, in similar format and with similar annotations. Part 3 is European material, covering relevant Treaty provisions and Directives and

Recommendations, with subsequent amendments annotated. Part 4 consists of statutory Codes of Practice and the Statutory Guidance on the meaning of disability under the Disability Discrimination Act 1995. Part 5 (miscellaneous materials) includes international materials, Practice Directions, the non-statutory Age Diversity Guide for Business, the Cabinet Office Statement of Practice on Staff Transfers in the Public Sector (as reissued in November 2007), Employment Tribunal Claim and Response Forms, and useful addresses.

All the materials in this Handbook apply equally to England and Wales and Scotland unless otherwise stated in the annotations. Since it would not be practicable, for reasons of space, to include equivalent Northern Ireland legislation (nearly all of which is separate, if largely similar), no attempt is made to cover Northern Ireland, and this book is not suitable for researching Northern Ireland domestic legislation; nor does it indicate whether particular materials extend to Northern Ireland.

The materials reproduced are as in force on 6 April 2008, though later developments have been noted where possible. The text of new legislation, and amendments to existing legislation, available at that date but not due to come into force until later, is included with appropriate annotations.

I am grateful to those, sadly too numerous to name individually, who have contributed, wittingly or otherwise, to the development of the Handbook over the past 28 years, and to this edition in particular. I include those who have drawn my attention to materials or supplied copies and those who have helpfully commented on coverage and format (even those whose suggestions to enliven the content have not proved practicable). I am particularly grateful to LexisNexis for its organisational support and commitment, and especially to its editorial staff for their efficiency and forbearance in the face of the demanding schedule for publication. Responsibility for the selection and annotation of contents is mine.

Peter Wallington QC

11 KBW Chambers
11 King's Bench Walk
Temple
London EC4

May 2008

CONTENTS

PART 2 STATUTORY INSTRUMENTS

SECTION B. REGULATIONS, DIRECTIVES AND RECOMMENDATIONS

PART 4 STATUTORY CODES OF PRACTICE

PART 5 MISCELLANEOUS MATERIALS

(A) INTERNATIONAL LAW MATERIALS

(B) EMPLOYMENT APPEAL TRIBUNAL PRACTICE DIRECTION AND PRACTICE STATEMENT, ETC

(C) CLAIM AND RESPONSE FORMS FOR TRIBUNAL CLAIMS

(D) CODES OF PRACTICE, ETC

(E) CABINET OFFICE STATEMENT OF PRACTICE

(F) USEFUL ADDRESSES

PART 1
STATUTES

APPORTIONMENT ACT 1870

(1870 c 35)

An Act for the better Apportionment of Rents and other periodical Payments

[1 August 1870]

NOTES

See *Harvey* B1(B), B3(6).

1 Short title

This Act may be cited for all purposes as "The Apportionment Act 1870".

[1]

2 Rents, etc to be apportionable in respect of time

... All rents, annuities, dividends, and other periodical payments in the nature of income (whether reserved or made payable under an instrument in writing or otherwise) shall, like interest on money lent, be considered as accruing from day to day, and shall be apportionable in respect of time accordingly.

[2]

NOTES

Words omitted repealed by the Statute Law Revision (No 2) Act 1893.

3, 4 (*Outside the scope of this work.*)

5 Interpretation

In the construction of this Act—

The word "rents" includes rent service, rentcharge, and rent seck, and also tithes and all periodical payments or renderings in lieu of or in the nature of rent or tithe.

The word "annuities" includes salaries and pensions.

The word "dividends" includes (besides dividends strictly so called) all payments made by the name of dividend, bonus or otherwise out of the revenue of trading or other public companies, divisible between all or any of the members of such respective companies, whether such payments shall be usually made or declared, at any fixed times or otherwise; and all such divisible revenue shall, for the purposes of this Act, be deemed to have accrued by equal daily increment during or within the period for or in respect of which the payment of the same revenue shall be declared or expressed to be made, but the said word "dividend" does not include payments in the nature of a return or reimbursement of capital.

[3]

6 (*Outside the scope of this work.*)

7 Nor where stipulation made to the contrary

The provisions of this Act shall not extend to any case in which it is or shall be expressly stipulated that no apportionment shall take place.

[4]

EQUAL PAY ACT 1970

(1970 c 41)

ARRANGEMENT OF SECTIONS

An Act to prevent discrimination, as regards terms and conditions of employment between men and women

[29 May 1970]

NOTES

Application, etc: the Pensions Act 1995, s 62 (equal treatment rules in occupational pension schemes) at **[890]**, is to be construed as one with s 1 of this Act, and ss 2, 2A have effect for the purposes of that provision subject to certain modifications; see the Pensions Act 1995, s 63(4) at **[891]**. See also s 63(5) (regulations may make provision for this Act to have effect, in relation to the equal treatment rule, with prescribed modifications). The Occupational Pension Schemes (Equal Treatment) Regulations 1995, SI 1995/3183 and the Occupational Pension Schemes (Equal Treatment) (Amendment) Regulations 2005, SI 2005/1923 provide for extensive modifications of this Act in the circumstances to which the those Regulations apply. As these modifications are complex, and for ease of reference, the 1995 and 2005 Regulations are printed in full at **[2305]** and **[3320]**, and should be referred to for the text of the modified versions of provisions of this Act.

Employment Appeal Tribunal: an appeal lies to the Employment Appeal Tribunal on any question of law arising from any decision of, or in any proceedings before, an employment tribunal under or by virtue of this Act; see the Employment Tribunals Act 1996, s 21(1)(a) at **[978]**.

Codes of practice: as to the power of the Commission for Equality and Human Rights to issue a code of practice in connection with any matter addressed by this Act, see the Equality Act 2006, s 14 at **[1657]**. For the current code of practice (issued by the Equal Opportunities Commission under the Sex Discrimination Act 1975, s 56A (repealed) and continued in force by the Equality Act 2006, s 42(3)), see **[4648]**.

Transfer of functions: as to the transfer of the functions of the Secretary of State for Trade and Industry under this Act to the Secretary of State for Communities and Local Government, see the Secretary of State for Communities and Local Government Order 2006, SI 2006/1926, arts 7(1), (2), (3)(a), 8. Note also that by the Transfer of Functions (Equality) Order 2007, SI 2007/2914, art 3(1), (2)(a), the functions of the Secretary of State under this Act are transferred to the Lord Privy Seal (as from 12 October 2007).

See *Harvey* K, L1, Q.

1 Requirement of equal treatment for men and women in same employment

[(1) If the terms of a contract under which a woman is employed at an establishment in Great Britain do not include (directly or by reference to a collective agreement or otherwise) an equality clause they shall be deemed to include one.

(2) An equality clause is a provision which relates to terms (whether concerned with pay or not) of a contract under which a woman is employed (the "woman's contract"), and has the effect that—

(a) where the woman is employed on like work with a man in the same employment—

(i) if (apart from the equality clause) any term of the woman's contract is or becomes less favourable to the woman than a term of a similar kind in the contract under which that man is employed, that term of the woman's contract shall be treated as so modified as not to be less favourable, and

(ii) if (apart from the equality clause) at any time the woman's contract does not include a term corresponding to a term benefiting that man included in the contract under which he is employed, the woman's contract shall be treated as including such a term;

(b) where the woman is employed on work rated as equivalent with that of a man in the same employment—

(i) if (apart from the equality clause) any term of the woman's contract determined by the rating of the work is or becomes less favourable to the woman than a term of a similar kind in the contract under which that man is employed, that term of the woman's contract shall be treated as so modified as not to be less favourable, and

(ii) if (apart from the equality clause) at any time the woman's contract does not include a term corresponding to a term benefiting that man included in the contract under which he is employed and determined by the rating of the work, the woman's contract shall be treated as including such a term;

[(c) where a woman is employed on work which, not being work in relation to which paragraph (a) or (b) above applies, is, in terms of the demands made on her (for instance under such headings as effort, skill and decision), of equal value to that of a man in the same employment—

(i) if (apart from the equality clause) any term of the woman's contract is or becomes less favourable to the woman than a term of a similar kind in the contract under which that man is employed, that term of the woman's contract shall be treated as so modified as not to be less favourable, and

(ii) if (apart from the equality clause) at any time the woman's contract does not include a term corresponding to a term benefiting that man included in the contract under which he is employed, the woman's contract shall be treated as including such a term];

[(d) where—

(i) any term of the woman's contract regulating maternity-related pay provides for any of her maternity-related pay to be calculated by reference to her pay at a particular time,

(ii) after that time (but before the end of the statutory maternity leave period) her pay is increased or would have increased had she not been on statutory maternity leave, and

(iii) the maternity-related pay is neither what her pay would have been had she not been on statutory maternity leave nor the difference between what her pay would have been had she not been on statutory maternity leave and any statutory maternity pay to which she is entitled,

if (apart from the equality clause) the terms of the woman's contract do not provide for the increase to be taken into account for the purpose of calculating the maternity-related pay, the term mentioned in sub-paragraph (i) above shall be treated as so modified as to provide for the increase to be taken into account for that purpose;

(e) if (apart from the equality clause) the terms of the woman's contract as to—

(i) pay (including pay by way of bonus) in respect of times before she begins to be on statutory maternity leave,

(ii) pay by way of bonus in respect of times when she is absent from work in consequence of the prohibition in section 72(1) of the Employment Rights Act 1996 (compulsory maternity leave), or

(iii) pay by way of bonus in respect of times after she returns to work following her having been on statutory maternity leave,

do not provide for such pay to be paid when it would be paid but for her having time off on statutory maternity leave, the woman's contract shall be treated as including a term providing for such pay to be paid when ordinarily it would be paid;

(f) if (apart from the equality clause) the terms of the woman's contract regulating her pay after returning to work following her having been on statutory maternity leave provide for any of that pay to be calculated without taking into account any amount by which her pay would have increased had she not been on statutory maternity leave, the woman's contract shall be treated as including a term providing for the increase to be taken into account in calculating that pay].]

[(3) [An equality clause falling within subsection (2)(a), (b) or (c) above shall not] operate in relation to a variation between the woman's contract and the man's contract if the employer proves that the variation is genuinely due to a material factor which is not the difference of sex and that factor—

(a) in the case of an equality clause falling within subsection (2)(a) or (b) above, must be a material difference between the woman's case and the man's; and

(b) in the case of an equality clause falling within subsection (2)(c) above, may be such a material difference.]

(4) A woman is to be regarded as employed on like work with men if, but only if, her work and theirs is of the same or a broadly similar nature, and the differences (if any) between the things she does and the things they do are not of practical importance in relation to terms and conditions of employment; and accordingly in comparing her work with theirs regard shall be had to the frequency or otherwise with which any such differences occur in practice as well as to the nature and extent of the differences.

(5) A woman is to be regarded as employed on work rated as equivalent with that of any men if, but only if, her job and their job have been given an equal value, in terms of the demand made on a worker under various headings (for instance effort, skill, decision), on a

study undertaken with a view to evaluating in those terms the jobs to be done by all or any of the employees in an undertaking or group of undertakings, or would have been given an equal value but for the evaluation being made on a system setting different values for men and women on the same demand under any heading.

[(5A) For the purposes of subsection (2)(d) to (f) above—

(a) "maternity-related pay", in relation to a woman, means pay (including pay by way of bonus) to which she is entitled as a result of being pregnant or in respect of times when she is on statutory maternity leave, except that it does not include any statutory maternity pay to which she is entitled;

(b) "statutory maternity leave period", in relation to a woman, means the period during which she is on statutory maternity leave;

(c) an increase in an amount is taken into account in a calculation if in the calculation the amount as increased is substituted for the unincreased amount.

(5B) For the purposes of subsections (2)(d) to (f) and (5A) above, "on statutory maternity leave" means absent from work—

(a) in exercise of the right conferred by section 71(1) or 73(1) of the Employment Rights Act 1996 (ordinary or additional maternity leave), or

(b) in consequence of the prohibition in section 72(1) of that Act (compulsory maternity leave).]

(6) Subject to the following subsections, for purposes of this section—

(a) "employed" means employed under a contract of service or of apprenticeship or a contract personally to execute any work or labour, and related expressions shall be construed accordingly;

(b) …

(c) two employers are to be treated as associated if one is a company of which the other (directly or indirectly) has control or if both are companies of which a third person (directly or indirectly) has control,

[and men shall be treated as in the same employment with a woman if they are men employed by her employer or any associated employer at the same establishment or at establishments in Great Britain which include that one and at which common terms and conditions of employment are observed either generally or for employees of the relevant classes].

[(6A) This section applies to—

(a) the holding of an office or post to which persons are appointed to discharge functions personally under the direction of another person, and in respect of which they are entitled to remuneration, or

(b) any office or post to which appointments are made by (or on the recommendation of or subject to the approval of) a Minister of the Crown, a government department, the National Assembly for Wales or any part of the Scottish Administration,

as it applies to employment by a private person, and shall so apply as if references to a contract of employment included references to the terms of appointment, and as if references to the employer included references to the person responsible for paying any remuneration that a holder of the office or post is entitled to in respect of the office or post.

(6B) For the purposes of subsection (6A), the holder of an office or post—

(a) is to be regarded as discharging her functions under the direction of another person if that other person is entitled to direct her as to when and where she discharges those functions;

(b) is not to be regarded as entitled to remuneration merely because she is entitled to payments—

(i) in respect of expenses incurred by her in carrying out the functions of the office or post, or

(ii) by way of compensation for the loss of income or benefits she would or might have received from any person had she not been carrying out the functions of the office or post.

(6C) For the purposes of subsection (6A)—

(a) "office or post" does not include a political office (see section 1A), and

(b) appointment to an office or post does not include election to an office or post.]

(7) …

[(8) This section shall apply to—

(a) service for purposes of a Minister of the Crown or government department, other than service of a person holding a statutory office, or

(b) service on behalf of the Crown for purposes of a person holding a statutory office or purposes of a statutory body,

as it applies to employment by a private person, and shall so apply as if references to a contract of employment included references to the terms of service.

(9) …

(10) In this section "statutory body" means a body set up by or in pursuance of an enactment [(including an enactment comprised in, or in an instrument made under, an Act of the Scottish Parliament)], and "statutory office" means an office so set up; and service "for purposes of" a Minister of the Crown or government department does not include service in any office in Schedule 2 (Ministerial offices) to the House of Commons Disqualification Act 1975 as for the time being in force.]

[(10A) This section applies in relation to service as a relevant member of the House of Commons staff as in relation to service for the purposes of a Minister of the Crown or government department, and accordingly applies as if references to a contract of employment included references to the terms of service of such a member.

In this subsection "relevant member of the House of Commons staff" has the same meaning as in [section 195 of the Employment Rights Act 1996]; and [subsections (6) to (12)] of that section (person to be treated as employer of House of Commons staff) apply, with any necessary modifications, for the purposes of this section.]

[(10B) This section applies in relation to employment as a relevant member of the House of Lords staff as in relation to other employment.

In this subsection "relevant member of the House of Lords staff" has the same meaning as in [section 194 of the Employment Rights Act 1996]; and [subsection (7)] of that section applies for the purposes of this section.]

[(11) For the purposes of this Act it is immaterial whether the law which (apart from this subsection) is the [law applicable to] a contract is the law of any part of the United Kingdom or not.

(12) In this Act "Great Britain" includes such of the territorial waters of the United Kingdom as are adjacent to Great Britain.

(13) Provisions of this section and [sections 2 [to 2A]] below framed with reference to women and their treatment relative to men are to be read as applying equally in a converse case to men and their treatment relative to women.]

[5]

NOTES

Sub-s (1): substituted, together with sub-s (2), by the Sex Discrimination Act 1975, s 8(1).

Sub-s (2): substituted as noted above; para (c) added by the Equal Pay (Amendment) Regulations 1983, SI 1983/1794, reg 2(1); paras (d)–(f) added by the Employment Equality (Sex Discrimination) Regulations 2005, SI 2005/2467, reg 36(1), (2), as from 1 October 2005.

Sub-s (3): substituted by SI 1983/1794, reg 2(2); words in square brackets substituted by SI 2005/2467, reg 36(1), (3), as from 1 October 2005.

Sub-ss (5A), (5B): inserted by SI 2005/2467, reg 36(1), (4), as from 1 October 2005.

Sub-s (6): para (b) repealed, and words in square brackets added, by the Sex Discrimination Act 1975, s 8(6), Sch 1, Pt I, para 1(1).

Sub-ss (6A)–(6C): inserted by SI 2005/2467, reg 35(1), (2), as from 1 October 2005.

Sub-s (7): repealed by the Sex Discrimination Act 1975, s 8(6), Sch 1, Pt I, para 1(2).

Sub-s (8): substituted, together with sub-ss (9), (10) for original sub-s (8), by the Sex Discrimination Act 1975, s 8(1), (6), Sch 1, Pt I.

Sub-s (9): substituted as noted above; repealed by the Armed Forces Act 1996, ss 24(1), 35(2), Sch 7, Pt III.

Sub-s (10): substituted as noted above; words in square brackets inserted by the Scotland Act 1998 (Consequential Modifications) Order 2000, SI 2000/2040, arts 1(1), 2(1), Schedule, Pt I, para 4.

Sub-s (10A): inserted by the Trade Union and Labour Relations (Consolidation) Act 1992, s 300(2), Sch 2, para 3(1), (2); words in square brackets substituted by the Employment Rights Act 1996, s 240, Sch 1.

Sub-s (10B): inserted by the Trade Union Reform and Employment Rights Act 1993, s 49(1), Sch 7, para 8; words in square brackets substituted by the Employment Rights Act 1996, s 240, Sch 1.

Sub-s (11): added, together with sub-ss (12), (13), by the Sex Discrimination Act 1975, s 8(6), Sch 1, Pt I, para 1(4); words in square brackets substituted by the Contracts (Applicable Law) Act 1990, s 5, Sch 4, para 1.

Sub-s (12): added as noted above.

Sub-s (13): added as noted above; words in first (outer) pair of square brackets substituted by SI 1983/1794, reg 3(2); words in second (inner) pair of square brackets substituted by the Equal Pay Act 1970 (Amendment) Regulations 2003, SI 2003/1656, reg 10, as from 19 July 2003.

Application, etc: see the note preceding this section.

[1A Meaning of "political office" in section 1(6C)(a)

The following are political offices for the purposes of section 1(6C)(a)—

(a) any office of the House of Commons held by a member of it,

(b) a life peerage within the meaning of the Life Peerages Act 1958, or any office of the House of Lords held by a member of it,

(c) any office mentioned in Schedule 2 (Ministerial offices) to the House of Commons Disqualification Act 1975,

(d) the offices of Leader of the Opposition, Chief Opposition Whip or Assistant Opposition Whip within the meaning of the Ministerial and other Salaries Act 1975,

(e) any office of the Scottish Parliament held by a member of it,

(f) a member of the Scottish Executive within the meaning of section 44 of the Scotland Act 1998, or a junior Scottish Minister within the meaning of section 49 of that Act,

(g) any office of the National Assembly for Wales held by a member of it,

(h) in England, any office of a county council, a London borough council, a district council or a parish council held by a member of it,

(i) in Wales, any office of a county council, a county borough council or a community council held by a member it,

(j) in relation to a council constituted under section 2 of the Local Government etc (Scotland) Act 1994, or a community council established under section 51 of the Local Government (Scotland) Act 1973, any office of such a council held by a member of it,

(k) any office of the Greater London Authority held by a member of it,

(l) any office of the Common Council of the City of London held by a member of it,

(m) any office of the Council of the Isles of Scilly held by a member of it, and

(n) any office of a political party.]

[5A]

NOTES

Commencement: 1 October 2005.

Inserted by the Employment Equality (Sex Discrimination) Regulations 2005, SI 2005/2467, reg 35(1), (3), as from 1 October 2005.

2 Disputes as to, and enforcement of, requirement of equal treatment

[(1) Any claim in respect of the contravention of a term modified or included by virtue of an equality clause, including a claim for arrears of remuneration or damages in respect of the contravention, may be presented by way of a complaint to an [employment tribunal].

(1A) Where a dispute arises in relation to the effect of an equality clause the employer may apply to an [employment tribunal] for an order declaring the rights of the employer and the employee in relation to the matter in question.]

(2) Where it appears to the [Minister] that there may be a question whether the employer of any women is or has been [contravening a term modified or included by virtue of their equality clauses], but that it is not reasonable to expect them to take steps to have the question determined, the question may be referred by him [as respects all or any of them] to an [employment tribunal] and shall be dealt with as if the reference were of a claim by the women [or woman] against the employer.

(3) Where it appears to the court in which any proceedings are pending that a claim or counter-claim in respect of the operation of an [equality clause] could more conveniently be disposed of separately by an [employment tribunal], the court may direct that the claim or counter-claim shall be struck out; and (without prejudice to the foregoing) where in proceedings before any court a question arises as to the operation of an [equality clause], the court may on the application of any party to the proceedings or otherwise refer that question, or direct it to be referred by a party to the proceedings, to an [employment tribunal] for determination by the tribunal, and may stay or sist the proceedings in the meantime.

[(4) No determination may be made by an employment tribunal in the following proceedings—
(a) on a complaint under subsection (1) above,
(b) on an application under subsection (1A) above, or
(c) on a reference under subsection (2) above,

unless the proceedings are instituted on or before the qualifying date (determined in accordance with section 2ZA below).]

[(5) A woman shall not be entitled, in proceedings brought in respect of a contravention of a term modified or included by virtue of an equality clause (including proceedings before an employment tribunal), to be awarded any payment by way of arrears of remuneration or damages—
(a) in proceedings in England and Wales, in respect of a time earlier than the arrears date (determined in accordance with section 2ZB below), and
(b) in proceedings in Scotland, in respect of a time before the period determined in accordance with section 2ZC below.]

[(5A) In this section "employer", in relation to the holder of an office or post to which section 1 above applies by virtue of subsection (6A) of that section, shall be construed in accordance with that subsection.]

(6), (7) …

[6]

NOTES

Sub-s (1): substituted by the Sex Discrimination Act 1975, s 8(6), Sch 1, Pt I, para 2(1); words in square brackets substituted by the Employment Rights (Dispute Resolution) Act 1998, s 1(2)(a).

Sub-s (1A): inserted by the Sex Discrimination Act 1975, s 8(6), Sch 1, Pt I, para 2(2); words in square brackets substituted by the Employment Rights (Dispute Resolution) Act 1998, s 1(2)(a).

Sub-s (2): word in first pair of square brackets substituted by the Transfer of Functions (Equality) Order 2007, SI 2007/2914, art 8, Schedule, para 3(a), as from 12 October 2007; words in second and third pairs of square brackets substituted, and words in final pairs of square brackets inserted, by the Sex Discrimination Act 1975, s 8(6), Sch 1, Pt I, para 2(3)(a); words in fourth pair of square brackets substituted by the Employment Rights (Dispute Resolution) Act 1998, s 1(2)(a).

Sub-s (3): words in first and third pairs of square brackets substituted by the Sex Discrimination Act 1975, s 8(6), Sch 1, Pt I, para 6(1); words in second and final pairs of square brackets substituted by the Employment Rights (Dispute Resolution) Act 1998, s 1(2)(a).

Sub-s (4): substituted by the Equal Pay Act 1970 (Amendment) Regulations 2003, SI 2003/1656, reg 3(1), (2), as from 19 July 2003, with effect in accordance with reg 2(1)(a), (2)–(4) of those Regulations (see **[2939]**). See also the first note at the beginning of this Act. It is unclear whether the substitution of sub-s (4) by SI 2003/1656 affects the substituted sub-s (4) applicable in pensions cases by virtue of s 63(4) of the 1995 Act.

Sub-s (5): substituted by SI 2003/1656, reg 3(1), (3), as from 19 July 2003, in relation to proceedings instituted on or after that date (see **[2939]**).

Sub-s (5A): inserted by the Employment Equality (Sex Discrimination) Regulations 2005, SI 2005/2467, reg 35(1), (4), as from 1 October 2005.

Sub-s (6): repealed by the Sex Discrimination Act 1975, s 8(6), Sch 1, Pt I, para 2(4).

Sub-s (7): repealed by the Employment Protection (Consolidation) Act 1978, s 159(3), Sch 17.

Application, etc: see the note preceding s 1 at **[5]**.

Conciliation: employment tribunal proceedings and claims which could be the subject of employment tribunal proceedings under sub-s (1) above are proceedings to which the Employment Tribunals Act 1996, s 18 applies; see s 18(1)(a)(i) of that Act at **[975]**.

Tribunal jurisdiction: the Employment Act 2002, ss 31, 32, 38 at **[1493]**, **[1494]**, **[1496]** apply to proceedings before the employment tribunal relating to a claim under this section; see ss 31(1), 32(1), 38(1) of, and Schs 3–5 to, the 2002 Act at **[1508]**–**[1510]**.

For the circumstances in which the normal time limit for presenting a complaint under this section is extended for a period of three months, see the Employment Act 2002 (Dispute Resolution) Regulations 2004, SI 2004/752, regs 15 and 18 at **[3096]** and **[3098]**.

[2ZA "Qualifying date" under section 2(4)

(1) This section applies for the purpose of determining the qualifying date, in relation to proceedings in respect of a woman's employment, for the purposes of section 2(4) above.

(2) In this section—

"concealment case" means a case where—
(a) the employer deliberately concealed from the woman any fact (referred to in this section as a "qualifying fact")—
(i) which is relevant to the contravention to which the proceedings relate, and

(ii) without knowledge of which the woman could not reasonably have been expected to institute the proceedings, and

(b) the woman did not discover the qualifying fact (or could not with reasonable diligence have discovered it) until after—

(i) the last day on which she was employed in the employment, or

(ii) the day on which the stable employment relationship between her and the employer ended,

(as the case may be);

"disability case" means a case where the woman was under a disability at any time during the six months after—

(a) the last day on which she was employed in the employment,

(b) the day on which the stable employment relationship between her and the employer ended, or

(c) the day on which she discovered (or could with reasonable diligence have discovered) the qualifying fact deliberately concealed from her by the employer (if that day falls after the day referred to in paragraph (a) or (b) above, as the case may be),

(as the case may be);

"stable employment case" means a case where the proceedings relate to a period during which a stable employment relationship subsists between the woman and the employer, notwithstanding that the period includes any time after the ending of a contract of employment when no further contract of employment is in force;

"standard case" means a case which is not—

(a) a stable employment case,

(b) a concealment case,

(c) a disability case, or

(d) both a concealment and a disability case.

(3) In a standard case, the qualifying date is the date falling six months after the last day on which the woman was employed in the employment.

(4) In a case which is a stable employment case (but not also a concealment or a disability case or both), the qualifying date is the date falling six months after the day on which the stable employment relationship ended.

(5) In a case which is a concealment case (but not also a disability case), the qualifying date is the date falling six months after the day on which the woman discovered the qualifying fact in question (or could with reasonable diligence have discovered it).

(6) In a case which is a disability case (but not also a concealment case), the qualifying date is the date falling six months after the day on which the woman ceased to be under a disability.

(7) In a case which is both a concealment and a disability case, the qualifying date is the later of the dates referred to in subsections (5) and (6) above.]

[7]

NOTES

Commencement: 19 July 2003

Inserted by the Equal Pay Act 1970 (Amendment) Regulations 2003, SI 2003/1656, reg 4, as from 19 July 2003, with effect in accordance with reg 2(1)(b), (2)–(4) of those Regulations (see **[2939]**).

[2ZB "Arrears date" in proceedings in England and Wales under section 2(5)

(1) This section applies for the purpose of determining the arrears date, in relation to an award of any payment by way of arrears of remuneration or damages in proceedings in England and Wales in respect of a woman's employment, for the purposes of section 2(5)(a) above.

(2) In this section—

"concealment case" means a case where—

(a) the employer deliberately concealed from the woman any fact—

(i) which is relevant to the contravention to which the proceedings relate, and

(ii) without knowledge of which the woman could not reasonably have been expected to institute the proceedings, and

(b) the woman instituted the proceedings within six years of the day on which she discovered the fact (or could with reasonable diligence have discovered it);

"disability case" means a case where—

(a) the woman was under a disability at the time of the contravention to which the proceedings relate, and

(b) the woman instituted the proceedings within six years of the day on which she ceased to be under a disability;

"standard case" means a case which is not—

(a) a concealment case,

(b) a disability case, or

(c) both.

(3) In a standard case, the arrears date is the date falling six years before the day on which the proceedings were instituted.

(4) In a case which is a concealment or a disability case or both, the arrears date is the date of the contravention.]

[8]

NOTES

Commencement: 19 July 2003

Inserted, together with s 2ZC, by the Equal Pay Act 1970 (Amendment) Regulations 2003, SI 2003/1656, reg 5, as from 19 July 2003, in relation to proceedings instituted on or after that date (see **[2939]**).

[2ZC Determination of "period" in proceedings in Scotland under section 2(5)

(1) This section applies, in relation to an award of any payment by way of arrears of remuneration or damages in proceedings in Scotland in respect of a woman's employment, for the purpose of determining the period mentioned in section 2(5)(b) above.

(2) Subject to subsection (3) below, that period is the period of five years which ends on the day on which the proceedings were instituted, except that the five years shall not be regarded as running during—

(a) any time when the woman was induced, by reason of fraud on the part of, or error induced by the words or conduct of, the employer or any person acting on his behalf, to refrain from commencing proceedings (not being a time after she could with reasonable diligence have discovered the fraud or error), or

(b) any time when she was under a disability.

(3) If, after regard is had to the exceptions in subsection (2) above, that period would include any time more than twenty years before the day mentioned in that subsection, that period is instead the period of twenty years which ends on that day.]

[9]

NOTES

Commencement: 19 July 2003

Inserted as noted to s 2ZB at **[8]**.

[2A Procedure before tribunal in certain cases

(1) Where on a complaint or reference made to an [employment tribunal] under section 2 above, a dispute arises as to whether any work is of equal value as mentioned in section 1(2)(c) above the tribunal [may either—

(a) proceed to determine that question; or

(b) … require a member of the panel of independent experts to prepare a report with respect to that question;

…]

[(1A) Subsections (1B) and (1C) below apply in a case where the tribunal has required a member of the panel of independent experts to prepare a report under paragraph (b) of subsection (1) above.

(1B) The tribunal may—

(a) withdraw the requirement, and

(b) request the member of the panel of independent experts to provide it with any documentation specified by it or make any other request to him connected with the withdrawal of the requirement.

(1C) If the requirement has not been withdrawn under paragraph (a) of subsection (1B) above, the tribunal shall not make any determination under paragraph (a) of subsection (1) above unless it has received the report.]

[(2) Subsection (2A) below applies in a case where—
(a) a tribunal is required to determine whether any work is of equal value as mentioned in section 1(2)(c) above, and
(b) the work of the woman and that of the man in question have been given different values on a study such as is mentioned in section 1(5) above].

[(2A) The tribunal shall determine that the work of the woman and that of the man are not of equal value unless the tribunal has reasonable grounds for suspecting that the evaluation contained in the study—
(a) was (within the meaning of subsection (3) below) made on a system which discriminates on grounds of sex, or
(b) is otherwise unsuitable to be relied upon.]

(3) An evaluation contained in a study such as is mentioned in section 1(5) above is made on a system which discriminates on grounds of sex where a difference, or coincidence, between values set by that system on different demands under the same or different headings is not justifiable irrespective of the sex of the person on whom those demands are made.

(4) [In this section a] reference to a member of the panel of independent experts is a reference to a person who is for the time being designated by the Advisory, Conciliation and Arbitration Service for the purposes of that paragraph as such a member, being neither a member of the Council of that Service nor one of its officers or servants.]

[10]

NOTES

Inserted by the Equal Pay (Amendment) Regulations 1983, SI 1983/1794, reg 3(1).

Sub-s (1): words in first pair of square brackets substituted by the Employment Rights (Dispute Resolution) Act 1998, s 1(2)(a); words in second pair of square brackets substituted by the Sex Discrimination and Equal Pay (Miscellaneous Amendments) Regulations 1996, SI 1996/438, reg 3(1), (2); words omitted repealed by the Equal Pay Act 1970 (Amendment) Regulations 2004, SI 2004/2352, reg 2(1), (2), as from 1 October 2004, in relation to proceedings instituted on or after that date (see further the final note below).

Sub-ss (1A)–(1C): inserted by SI 2004/2352, reg 2(1), (3), as from 1 October 2004, in relation to proceedings instituted on or after that date (see further the final note below).

Sub-s (2): substituted by SI 2004/2352, reg 2(1), (4), as from 1 October 2004, in relation to proceedings instituted on or after that date.

Sub-s (2A): inserted by SI 2004/2352, reg 2(1), (5), as from 1 October 2004, in relation to proceedings instituted on or after that date.

Sub-s (4): words in square brackets substituted by SI 2004/2352, reg 2(1), (6), as from 1 October 2004, in relation to proceedings instituted on or after that date (see further the final note below).

Application, etc: see the note preceding s 1 at **[5]**.

Note: the Equal Pay Act 1970 (Amendment) Regulations 2004, SI 2004/2352, reg 1(3) provides that the amendments made by reg 2(2), (3), (6) of the 2004 Regulations (ie, the amendments to sub-ss (1), (4) and the insertion of sub-ss (1A)–(1C) as noted above) also apply to proceedings instituted before 1 October 2004 if, before that date, an employment tribunal in proceedings before it has not required a member of the panel of independent experts (within the meaning of sub-s (4) above) to prepare a report under sub-s (1)(b) of this section.

3–5 *(S 3 repealed by the Sex Discrimination Act 1986, s 9, Schedule, Pt II (for savings, see s 9(3)); s 4 repealed by the Wages Act 1986, s 32(2), Sch 5, Pt II; s 5 (agricultural wages orders) outside the scope of this work.)*

6 Exclusion from ss 1 to 5 of pensions etc

[(1) [An equality clause shall not] operate in relation to terms—
(a) affected by compliance with the laws regulating the employment of women, or
(b) affording special treatment to women in connection with pregnancy or childbirth.]

[(1AA) Subsection (1)(b) does not affect the operation of an equality clause falling within section 1(2)(d), (e) or (f).]

[(1B) An equality clause shall not operate in relation to terms relating to a person's membership of, or rights under, an occupational pension scheme, being terms in relation to which, by reason only of any provision made by or under sections 62 or 64 of the Pensions Act 1995 (equal treatment), an equal treatment rule would not operate if the terms were included in the scheme.

(1C) In subsection (1B), "occupational pension scheme" has the same meaning as in the Pension Schemes Act 1993 and "equal treatment rule" has the same meaning given by section 62 of the Pensions Act 1995.]

[11]–[15]

NOTES

Sub-s (1): substituted, together with sub-s (1A), by the Sex Discrimination Act 1975, s 8(6), Sch 1, Pt I, para 3; words in square brackets substituted by the Sex Discrimination Act 1986, s 9(1), (3), Schedule, Pt II.

Sub-s (1AA): inserted by the Employment Equality (Sex Discrimination) Regulations 2005, SI 2005/2467, reg 36(1), (5), as from 1 October 2005.

Sub-ss (1B), (1C): substituted for sub-s (1A) (as substituted as noted above) and sub-s (2) by the Pensions Act 1995, s 66(1). A further amendment to the substituted sub-s (1A) made by the Social Security Act 1989, s 23, Sch 5, Pt II, para 13, was never brought into effect and has now been superseded.

7A–7AC (*Provisions relating to members of the armed forces: outside the scope of this work.*)

[7B Questioning of Employer

(1) For the purposes of this section—

(a) a person who considers that she may have a claim under section 1 above is referred to as "the complainant", and

(b) a person against whom the complainant may decide to make, or has made, a complaint under section 2(1) or 7A(3) above is referred to as "the respondent".

(2) With a view to helping a complainant to decide whether to institute proceedings and, if she does so, to formulate and present her case in the most effective manner, the [Minister] shall by order prescribe—

(a) forms by which the complainant may question the respondent on any matter which is or may be relevant, and

(b) forms by which the respondent may if he so wishes reply to any questions.

(3) Where the complainant questions the respondent (whether in accordance with an order under subsection (2) above or not), the question and any reply by the respondent (whether in accordance with such an order or not) shall, subject to the following provisions of this section, be admissible as evidence in any proceedings under section 2(1) or 7A(3) above.

(4) If in any proceedings under section 2(1) or 7A(3) above it appears to the employment tribunal that the complainant has questioned the respondent (whether in accordance with an order under subsection (2) above or not) and that—

(a) the respondent deliberately and without reasonable excuse omitted to reply within such period as the [Minister] may by order prescribe, or

(b) the respondent's reply is evasive or equivocal,

it may draw any inference which it considers it just and equitable to draw, including an inference that the respondent has contravened a term modified or included by virtue of the complainant's equality clause or corresponding term of service.

(5) Where the [Minister] questions an employer in relation to whom he may decide to make, or has made, a reference under section 2(2) above, the question and any reply by the employer shall, subject to the following provisions of this section, be admissible as evidence in any proceedings under that provision.

(6) If in any proceedings on a reference under section 2(2) above it appears to the employment tribunal that the [Minister] has questioned the employer to whom the reference relates and that—

(a) the employer deliberately and without reasonable excuse omitted to reply within such period as the [Minister] may by order prescribe, or

(b) the employer's reply is evasive or equivocal,

it may draw any inference which it considers it just and equitable to draw, including an inference that the employer has contravened a term modified or included by virtue of the equality clause of the woman, or women, as respects whom the reference is made.

(7) The [Minister] may by order—

(a) prescribe the period within which questions must be duly served in order to be admissible under subsection (3) or (5) above, and

(b) prescribe the manner in which a question, and any reply, may be duly served.

(8) This section is without prejudice to any other enactment or rule of law regulating interlocutory and preliminary matters in proceedings before an employment tribunal, and has effect subject to any enactment or rule of law regulating the admissibility of evidence in such proceedings.

(9) Power to make orders under this section is exercisable by statutory instrument subject to annulment in pursuance of a resolution of either House of Parliament.

(10) An order under this section may make different provision for different cases.]

[16]

NOTES

Commencement: 6 April 2003.

Inserted by the Employment Act 2002, s 42, as from 6 April 2003.

Sub-ss (2), (4)–(7): words in square brackets substituted by the Transfer of Functions (Equality) Order 2007, SI 2007/2914, art 8, Schedule, para 3(c), as from 12 October 2007.

Orders: the Equal Pay (Questions and Replies) Order 2003, SI 2003/722 at **[2895]**.

8 (*Repealed by the Sex Discrimination Act 1975, s 8(6), Sch 1, Pt I, para 4.*)

9 Commencement

(1) … the foregoing provisions of this Act shall come into force on the 29th December 1975 and references in this Act to its commencement shall be construed as referring to the coming into force of those provisions on that date.

(2)–(5) …

[17]

NOTES

Sub-s (1): words omitted repealed by the Sex Discrimination Act 1975, s 8(6), Sch 1, Pt I, para 5.

Sub-ss (2)–(5): repealed by the Sex Discrimination Act 1975, s 8(6), Sch 1, Pt I, para 5.

10 (*Repealed by the Sex Discrimination Act 1986, s 9, Schedule, Pt II (for savings, see s 9(3)).*)

11 Short title, interpretation and extent

(1) This Act may be cited as the Equal Pay Act 1970.

(2) In this Act the expression "man" and "woman" shall be read as applying to persons of whatever age.

[(2A) For the purposes of this Act a woman is under a disability—

(a) in the case of proceedings in England and Wales, if she is a minor or of unsound mind (which has the same meaning as in section 38(2) of the Limitation Act 1980); or

(b) in the case of proceedings in Scotland, if she has not attained the age of sixteen years or is incapable within the meaning of the Adults with Incapacity (Scotland) Act 2000.]

[(2B) In this Act "the Minister" means the Lord Privy Seal.]

(3) This Act shall not extend to Northern Ireland.

[18]

NOTES

Sub-s (2A): inserted by the Equal Pay Act 1970 (Amendment) Regulations 2003, SI 2003/1656, reg 9, as from 19 July 2003.

Sub-s (2B): inserted by the Transfer of Functions (Equality) Order 2007, SI 2007/2914, art 8, Schedule, para 2, as from 12 October 2007.

EUROPEAN COMMUNITIES ACT 1972

(1972 c 68)

ARRANGEMENT OF SECTIONS

PART I
GENERAL PROVISIONS

An Act to make provision in connection with the enlargement of the European Communities to include the United Kingdom, together with (for certain purposes) the Channel Islands, the Isle of Man and Gibraltar

[17 October 1972]

NOTES

The Parts of this Act which have been reproduced here are those which govern the status in UK law of the European Community Treaties and legislation, and empower the incorporation of Community legislation into UK law.

PART I
GENERAL PROVISIONS

1 Short title and interpretation

(1) This Act may be cited as the European Communities Act 1972.

(2) In this Act … —

"the Communities" means the European Economic Community, the European Coal and Steel Community and the European Atomic Energy Community;

"the Treaties" or "the Community Treaties" means, subject to subsection (3) below, the pre-accession treaties, that is to say, those described in Part I of Schedule 1 to this Act, taken with—

(a) the treaty relating to the accession of the United Kingdom to the European Economic Community and to the European Atomic Energy Community, signed at Brussels on the 22nd January 1972; and

(b) the decision, of the same date, of the Council of the European Communities relating to the accession of the United Kingdom to the European Coal and Steel Community; [and

(c) the treaty relating to the accession of the Hellenic Republic to the European Economic Community and to the European Atomic Energy Community, signed at Athens on 28th May 1979; and

(d) the decision, of 24th May 1979, of the Council relating to the accession of the Hellenic Republic to the European Coal and Steel Community;] [and

[(e) the decisions of the Council of 7th May 1985, 24th June 1988, 31st October 1994, 29th September 2000 and 7th June 2007 on the Communities' system of own resources;]]

[(g) the treaty relating to the accession of the Kingdom of Spain and the Portuguese Republic to the European Economic Community and to the European Atomic Energy Community, signed at Lisbon and Madrid on 12th June 1985; and

(h) the decision, of 11th June 1985, of the Council relating to the accession of the Kingdom of Spain and the Portuguese Republic to the European Coal and Steel Community;] [and

(j) the following provisions of the Single European Act signed at Luxembourg and The Hague on 17th and 28th February 1986, namely Title II (amendment of the treaties establishing the Communities) and, so far as they relate to any of the Communities or any Community institution, the preamble and Titles I (common provisions) and IV (general and final provisions);] [and

(k) Titles II, III and IV of the Treaty on European Union signed at Maastricht on 7th February 1992, together with the other provisions of the Treaty so far as they relate to those Titles, and the Protocols adopted at Maastricht on that date and annexed to the Treaty establishing the European Community with the exception of the Protocol on Social Policy on page 117 of Cm 1934] [and

(l) the decision, of 1st February 1993, of the Council amending the Act concerning the election of the representatives of the European Parliament by direct universal suffrage annexed to Council Decision 76/787/ECSC, EEC, Euratom of 20th September 1976] [and

(m) the Agreement on the European Economic Area signed at Oporto on 2nd May 1992 together with the Protocol adjusting that Agreement signed at Brussels on 17th March 1993] [and

(n) the treaty concerning the accession of the Kingdom of Norway, the Republic of Austria, the Republic of Finland and the United Kingdom of Sweden to the European Union, signed at Corfu on 24th June 1994;] [and

(o) the following provisions of the Treaty signed at Amsterdam on 2nd October 1997 amending the Treaty on European Union, the Treaties establishing the European Communities and certain related Acts—

(i) Articles 2 to 9,

(ii) Article 12, and

(iii) the other provisions of the Treaty so far as they relate to those Articles,

and the Protocols adopted on that occasion other than the Protocol on Article J.7 of the Treaty on European Union;] [and

(p) the following provisions of the Treaty signed at Nice on 26th February 2001 amending the Treaty on European Union, the Treaties establishing the European Communities and certain related Acts—

(i) Articles 2 to 10, and

(ii) the other provisions of the Treaty so far as they relate to those Articles,

and the Protocols adopted on that occasion;] [and

(q) the treaty concerning the accession of the Czech Republic, the Republic of Estonia, the Republic of Cyprus, the Republic of Latvia, the Republic of Lithuania, the Republic of Hungary, the Republic of Malta, the Republic of Poland, the Republic of Slovenia and the Slovak Republic to the European Union, signed at Athens on 16th April 2003;] [and

(r) the treaty concerning the accession of the Republic of Bulgaria and Romania to the European Union, signed at Luxembourg on 25th April 2005;]

and any other treaty entered into by any of the Communities, with or without any of the member States, or entered into, as a treaty ancillary to any of the Treaties, by the United Kingdom;

and any expression defined in Schedule 1 to this Act has the meaning there given to it.

(3) If Her Majesty by Order in Council declares that a treaty specified in the Order is to be regarded as one of the Community Treaties as herein defined, the Order shall be conclusive that it is to be so regarded; but a treaty entered into by the United Kingdom after the 22nd January 1972, other than a pre-accession treaty to which the United Kingdom accedes on terms settled on or before that date, shall not be so regarded unless it is so specified, nor be so specified unless a draft of the Order in Council has been approved by resolution of each House of Parliament.

(4) For purposes of subsections (2) and (3) above, "treaty" includes any international agreement, and any protocol or annex to a treaty or international agreement.

[19]

NOTES

Sub-s (2): words omitted repealed by the Interpretation Act 1978, s 25(1), Sch 3; in definition ""the Treaties" or "the Community Treaties"" para (c) and word immediately preceding it, and para (d), inserted by the European Communities (Greek Accession) Act 1979, s 1; para (e) and word immediately preceding it originally inserted (together with para (f)) by the European Communities (Finance) Act 1985, s 1, and substituted, together with the word immediately preceding it, (for paras (e), (f)) by the European Communities (Finance) Act 2001, s 1, as from 4 December 2001; para (e) further substituted by the European Communities (Finance) Act 2008, s 1, as from 19 February 2008; para (g) and word immediately preceding it and para (h) inserted by the European Communities (Spanish and Portuguese Accession) Act 1985, s 1; para (j) and word immediately preceding it inserted by the European Communities (Amendment) Act 1986, s 1; para (k) and word immediately preceding it inserted by the European Communities (Amendment) Act 1993, s 1(1); para (l) and word immediately preceding it inserted by the European Parliamentary Elections Act 1993, s 3(2); para (m) and word immediately preceding it inserted by the European Economic Area Act 1993, s 1; para (n) and word immediately preceding it added by the European Union (Accessions) Act 1994, s 1; para (o) and word immediately preceding it added by the European Communities (Amendment) Act 1998, s 1; para (p) and word immediately preceding it added by the European Communities (Amendment) Act 2002, s 1(1); para (q) and word immediately preceding it added by the European Union (Accessions) Act 2003, s 1(1), as from 13 November 2003; para (r) and word immediately preceding it added by the European Union (Accessions) Act 2006, s 1(1), as from 16 February 2006.

The reference in sub-s (2)(n) to Norway was superseded by the subsequent decision of Norway not to accede to the Union.

Orders in Council made under this section: omitted as outside the scope of this work.

2 General implementation of Treaties

(1) All such rights, powers, liabilities, obligations and restrictions from time to time created or arising by or under the Treaties, and all such remedies and procedures from time to time provided for by or under the Treaties, as in accordance with the Treaties are without further enactment to be given legal effect or used in the United Kingdom shall be recognised and available in law, and be enforced, allowed and followed accordingly; and the expression "enforceable Community right" and similar expressions shall be read as referring to one to which this subsection applies.

(2) Subject to Schedule 2 to this Act, at any time after its passing Her Majesty may by Order in Council, and any designated Minister or department may [by order, rules, regulations or scheme], make provision—

(a) for the purpose of implementing any Community obligation of the United Kingdom, or enabling any such obligation to be implemented, or of enabling any rights enjoyed or to be enjoyed by the United Kingdom under or by virtue of the Treaties to be exercised; or

(b) for the purpose of dealing with matters arising out of or related to any such obligation or rights or the coming into force, or the operation from time to time, of subsection (1) above;

and in the exercise of any statutory power or duty, including any power to give directions or to legislate by means of orders, rules, regulations or other subordinate instrument, the person entrusted with the power or duty may have regard to the objects of the Communities and to any such obligation or rights as aforesaid.

In this subsection "designated Minister or department" means such Minister of the Crown or government department as may from time to time be designated by Order in Council in relation to any matter or for any purpose, but subject to such restrictions or conditions (if any) as may be specified by the Order in Council.

(3) There shall be charged on and issued out of the Consolidated Fund or, if so determined by the Treasury, the National Loans Fund the amounts required to meet any Community obligation to make payments to any of the Communities or member States, or any Community obligation in respect of contributions to the capital or reserves of the European Investment Bank or in respect of loans to the Bank, or to redeem any notes or obligations issued or created in respect of any such Community obligation; and, except as otherwise provided by or under any enactment,—

(a) any other expenses incurred under or by virtue of the Treaties or this Act by any Minister of the Crown or government department may be paid out of moneys provided by Parliament; and

(b) any sums received under or by virtue of the Treaties or this Act by any Minister of the Crown or government department, save for such sums as may be required for disbursements permitted by any other enactment, shall be paid into the Consolidated Fund or, if so determined by the Treasury, the National Loans Fund.

(4) The provision that may be made under subsection (2) above includes, subject to Schedule 2 to this Act, any such provision (of any such extent) as might be made by Act of Parliament, and any enactment passed or to be passed, other than one contained in this Part of this Act, shall be construed and have effect subject to the foregoing provisions of this section; but, except as may be provided by any Act passed after this Act, Schedule 2 shall have effect in connection with the powers conferred by this and the following sections of this Act to make Orders in Council [or orders, rules, regulations or schemes].

(5), (6) (*Relate to Northern Ireland, the Channel Islands and the Isle of Man.*)

[20]

NOTES

Sub-ss (2), (4): words in square brackets substituted by the Legislative and Regulatory Reform Act 2006, s 27(1), as from 8 January 2007.

Transfer of functions and modification in relation to Scotland: various functions under this section are, in so far as exercisable in or as regards Scotland, transferred to the Scottish Minsters by the Scotland Act 1998 (Transfer of Functions to the Scottish Ministers etc) Order 1999, SI 1999/1750, the Scotland Act 1998 (Transfer of Functions to the Scottish Ministers etc) Order 2005, SI 2005/849, and the Scotland Act 1998 (Transfer of Functions to the Scottish Ministers etc) Order 2006, SI 2006/304. References in this section to a statutory power or duty include a power or duty conferred by an Act of the Scottish Parliament or an instrument made under such an Act, and references to an enactment include an enactment within the meaning of the Scotland Act 1998: see the Scotland Act 1998, s 125, Sch 8, para 15(1), (2). In relation to any order, rules, regulations or scheme made by the Scottish Ministers, or an Order in Council made on the recommendation of the First Minister, the word "designated" in the first sentence of sub-s (2), and the second sentence of that subsection, are to be disregarded, and references to an Act of Parliament are to be read as references to an Act of the Scottish Parliament: see the Scotland Act 1998, s 125, Sch 8, para 15(1), (3) (as amended by the Legislative and Regulatory Reform Act 2006, s 27(4)).

See also the Government of Wales Act 2006, s 59(1) which provides that the power to designate a Minister of the Crown or government department under this section may be exercised to so designate the Welsh Ministers.

The number of Orders and Regulations made under this section is so numerous that references are omitted for reasons of space.

3 Decisions on, and proof of, Treaties and Community instruments, etc

(1) For the purposes of all legal proceedings any question as to the meaning or effect of any of the Treaties, or as to the validity, meaning or effect of any Community instrument, shall be treated as a question of law (and, if not referred to the European Court, be for determination as such in accordance with the principles laid down by and any relevant [decision of the European Court or any court attached thereto)].

(2) Judicial notice shall be taken of the Treaties, of the Official Journal of the Communities and of any decision of, or expression of opinion by, the European Court [or any court attached thereto] on any such question as aforesaid; and the Official Journal shall be admissible as evidence of any instrument or other act thereby communicated of any of the Communities or of any Community institution.

(3) Evidence of any instrument issued by a Community institution, including any judgment or order of the European Court [or any court attached thereto], or of any document in the custody of a Community institution, or any entry in or extract from such a document, may be given in any legal proceedings by production of a copy certified as a true copy by an official of that institution; and any document purporting to be such a copy shall be received in evidence without proof of the official position or handwriting of the person signing the certificate.

(4) Evidence of any Community instrument may also be given in any legal proceedings—

(a) by production of a copy purporting to be printed by the Queen's Printer;

(b) where the instrument is in the custody of a government department (including a department of the Government of Northern Ireland), by production of a copy certified on behalf of the department to be a true copy by an officer of the department generally or specially authorised so to do;

and any document purporting to be such a copy as is mentioned in paragraph (b) above of an instrument in the custody of a department shall be received in evidence without proof of the official position or handwriting of the person signing the certificate, or of his authority to do so, or of the document being in the custody of the department.

(5) In any legal proceedings in Scotland evidence of any matter given in a manner authorised by this section shall be sufficient evidence of it.

[21]

NOTES

Sub-s (1): words in square brackets substituted by the European Communities (Amendment) Act 1986, s 2.

Sub-ss (2), (3): words in square brackets inserted by the European Communities (Amendment) Act 1986, s 2.

Modification in relation to Scotland: references in sub-s (4) to a government department include any part of the Scottish Administration: see the Scotland Act 1998, s 125, Sch 8, para 15(1), (4).

4–12 *(Ss 4–6, 11, 12 outside the scope of this work; s 7(1), (2) repealed by the Agriculture (Miscellaneous Provisions) Act 1976, s 26(3), Sch 4, Pt I; s 7(3), (4) repealed by the Food Act 1984, s 134, Sch 11; s 8 repealed by the Films Act 1985, s 7(1), Sch 2; s 9 repealed by the Companies Consolidation (Consequential Provisions) Act 1985, s 29, Sch 1; s 10 repealed by the Restrictive Trade Practices Act 1976, s 44(6), Sch 6.)*

SCHEDULES

SCHEDULE 1
DEFINITIONS RELATING TO COMMUNITIES

Section 1

PART I
THE PRE-ACCESSION TREATIES

1. The "ECSC Treaty", that is to say, the Treaty establishing the European Coal and Steel Community, signed at Paris on the 18th April 1951.

2. The "EEC Treaty", that is to say, the Treaty establishing the European Economic Community, signed at Rome on the 25th March 1957.

3. The "Euratom Treaty", that is to say, the Treaty establishing the European Atomic Energy Community, signed at Rome on the 25th March 1957.

4. The Convention on certain Institutions common to the European Communities, signed at Rome on the 25th March 1957.

5. The Treaty establishing a single Council and a single Commission of the European Communities, signed at Brussels on the 8th April 1965.

6. The Treaty amending certain Budgetary Provisions of the Treaties establishing the European Communities and of the Treaty establishing a single Council and a single Commission of the European Communities, signed at Luxembourg on the 22nd April 1970.

7. Any treaty entered into before the 22nd January 1972 by any of the Communities (with or without any of the member States) or, as a treaty ancillary to any treaty included in this Part of this Schedule, by the member States (with or without any other country).

[22]

PART II
OTHER DEFINITIONS

"Economic Community", "Coal and Steel Community" and "Euratom" mean respectively the European Economic Community, the European Coal and Steel Community and the European Atomic Energy Community.

"Community customs duty" means, in relation to any goods, such duty of customs as may from time to time be fixed for those goods by directly applicable Community provision as the duty chargeable on importation into member States.

"Community institution" means any institution of any of the Communities or common to the Communities; and any reference to an institution of a particular Community shall include one common to the Communities when it acts for that Community, and similarly with references to a committee, officer or servant of a particular Community.

"Community instrument" means any instrument issued by a Community institution.

"Community obligation" means any obligation created or arising by or under the Treaties, whether an enforceable Community obligation or not.

"Enforceable Community right" and similar expressions shall be construed in accordance with section 2(1) of this Act.

"Entry date" means the date on which the United Kingdom becomes a member of the Communities.

"European Court" means the Court of Justice of the European Communities [or the Court of First Instance, and any reference to a court attached to the European Court is a reference to a judicial panel attached to the Court of First Instance].

"Member", in the expression "member State", refers to membership of the Communities.

[23]

NOTES

In definition "European Court" words in square brackets inserted by the European Communities (Amendment) Act 2002, s 2.

SCHEDULE 2
PROVISIONS AS TO SUBORDINATE LEGISLATION

Section 2

1.—(1) The powers conferred by section 2(2) of this Act to make provision for the purposes mentioned in section 2(2)(a) and (b) shall not include power—

(a) to make any provision imposing or increasing taxation; or

(b) to make any provision taking effect from a date earlier than that of the making of the instrument containing the provision; or

(c) to confer any power to legislate by means of orders, rules, regulations or other subordinate instrument, other than rules of procedure for any court or tribunal; or

(d) to create any new criminal offence punishable with imprisonment for more than two years or punishable on summary conviction with imprisonment for more than *three months* or with a fine of more than [level 5 on the standard scale] (if not calculated on a daily basis) or with a fine of more than [£100 a day].

(2) Sub-paragraph (1)(c) above shall not be taken to preclude the modification of a power to legislate conferred otherwise than under section 2(2), or the extension of any such power to purposes of the like nature as those for which it was conferred; and a power to give directions as to matters of administration is not to be regarded as a power to legislate within the meaning of sub-paragraph (1)(c).

[(3) In sub-paragraph (1)(d), "the prescribed term" means—

(a) in relation to England and Wales, where the offence is a summary offence, 51 weeks;

(b) in relation to England and Wales, where the offence is triable either way, twelve months;

(c) in relation to Scotland and Northern Ireland, three months.]

[1A.—(1) Where—

(a) subordinate legislation makes provision for a purpose mentioned in section 2(2) of this Act,

(b) the legislation contains a reference to a Community instrument or any provision of a Community instrument, and

(c) it appears to the person making the legislation that it is necessary or expedient for the reference to be construed as a reference to that instrument or that provision as amended from time to time,

the subordinate legislation may make express provision to that effect.

2.—(1) Subject to paragraph 3 below, where a provision contained in any section of this Act confers power to make [any order, rules, regulations or scheme] (otherwise than by modification or extension of an existing power), the power shall be exercisable by statutory instrument.

(2) Any statutory instrument containing an Order in Council or [any order, rules, regulations or scheme] made in the exercise of a power so conferred, if made without a draft having been approved by resolution of each House of Parliament, shall be subject to annulment in pursuance of a resolution of either House.

[2A.—(1) This paragraph applies where, pursuant to paragraph 2(2) above, a draft of a statutory instrument containing provision made in exercise of the power conferred by section 2(2) of this Act is laid before Parliament for approval by resolution of each House of Parliament and—

(a) the instrument also contains provision made in exercise of a power conferred by any other enactment; and

(b) apart from this paragraph, any of the conditions in sub-paragraph (2) below applies in relation to the instrument so far as containing that provision.

(2) The conditions referred to in sub-paragraph (1)(b) above are that—

(a) the instrument, so far as containing the provision referred to in sub-paragraph (1)(a) above, is by virtue of any enactment subject to annulment in pursuance of a resolution of either House of Parliament;

(b) the instrument so far as containing that provision is by virtue of any enactment required to be laid before Parliament after being made and to be approved by resolution of each House of Parliament in order to come into or remain in force;

(c) in a case not falling within paragraph (a) or (b) above, the instrument so far as containing that provision is by virtue of any enactment required to be laid before Parliament after being made;

(d) the instrument or a draft of the instrument so far as containing that provision is not by virtue of any enactment required at any time to be laid before Parliament.

(3) Where this paragraph applies in relation to the draft of a statutory instrument—

(a) the instrument, so far as containing the provision referred to in sub-paragraph (1)(a) above, may not be made unless the draft is approved by a resolution of each House of Parliament;

(b) in a case where the condition in sub-paragraph (2)(a) above is satisfied, the instrument so far as containing that provision is not subject to annulment in pursuance of a resolution of either House of Parliament;

(c) in a case where the condition in sub-paragraph (2)(b) above is satisfied, the instrument is not required to be laid before Parliament after being made (and accordingly any requirement that the instrument be approved by each House of Parliament in order for it to come into or remain in force does not apply); and

(d) in a case where the condition in sub-paragraph (2)(c) above is satisfied, the instrument so far as containing that provision is not required to be laid before Parliament after being made.

(4) In this paragraph, references to an enactment are to an enactment passed or made before or after the coming into force of this paragraph.

2B.—(1) This paragraph applies where, pursuant to paragraph 2(2) above, a statutory instrument containing provision made in exercise of the power conferred by section 2(2) of this Act is laid before Parliament under section 5 of the Statutory Instruments Act 1946 (instruments subject to annulment) and—

(a) the instrument also contains provision made in exercise of a power conferred by any other enactment; and

(b) apart from this paragraph, either of the conditions in sub-paragraph (2) below applies in relation to the instrument so far as containing that provision.

(2) The conditions referred to in sub-paragraph (1)(b) above are that—

(a) the instrument so far as containing the provision referred to in sub-paragraph (1)(a) above is by virtue of any enactment required to be laid before Parliament after being made but—

(i) is not subject to annulment in pursuance of a resolution of either House of Parliament; and

(ii) is not by virtue of any enactment required to be approved by resolution of each House of Parliament in order to come into or remain in force;

(b) the instrument or a draft of the instrument so far as containing that provision is not by virtue of any enactment required at any time to be laid before Parliament.

(3) Where this paragraph applies in relation to a statutory instrument, the instrument, so far as containing the provision referred to in sub-paragraph (1)(a) above, is subject to annulment in pursuance of a resolution of either House of Parliament.

(4) In this paragraph, references to an enactment are to an enactment passed or made before or after the coming into force of this paragraph.

2C. Paragraphs 2A and 2B above apply to a Scottish statutory instrument containing provision made in the exercise of the power conferred by section 2(2) of this Act (and a draft of any such instrument) as they apply to any other statutory instrument containing such provision (or, as the case may be, any draft of such an instrument), but subject to the following modifications—

(a) references to Parliament and to each or either House of Parliament are to be read as references to the Scottish Parliament;

(b) references to an enactment include an enactment comprised in, or in an instrument made under, an Act of the Scottish Parliament; and

(c) the reference in paragraph 2B(1) to section 5 of the Statutory Instruments Act 1946 is to be read as a reference to article 11 of the Scotland Act 1998 (Transitory and Transitional Provisions) (Statutory Instruments) Order 1999 (SI 1999/1096).]

3. Nothing in paragraph 2 above shall apply to any Order in Council made by the Governor of Northern Ireland or to any [any order, rules, regulations or scheme] made by a Minister or department of the Government of Northern Ireland; but where a provision contained in any section of this Act confers power to make such an Order in Council or [any order, rules, regulations or scheme], then any Order in Council or [any order, rules, regulations or scheme] made in the exercise of that power, if made without a draft having been approved by resolution of each House of the Parliament of Northern Ireland, shall be subject to negative resolution within the meaning of section 41(6) of the Interpretation Act (Northern Ireland) 1954 as if the Order or [any order, rules, regulations or scheme] were a statutory instrument within the meaning of that Act.

4, 5. *(Outside the scope of this work.)*

[24]

NOTES

Para 1: for the words in italics in sub-para (1)(d) there are substituted the words "the prescribed term", and sub-para (3) is added, by the Criminal Justice Act 2003, s 283, Sch 27, para 3, as from a day to be appointed; first-mentioned maximum fine in sub-para (1)(d) increased and converted to a level on the standard scale by the Criminal Justice Act 1982, ss 37, 40, 46; words in second pair of square brackets in sub-para (1)(d) substituted by the Criminal Law Act 1977, s 32(3).

Paras 1A, 2A–2C: inserted by the Legislative and Regulatory Reform Act 2006, ss 28, 29, as from 8 January 2007.

Paras 2, 3: words in square brackets substituted by the Legislative and Regulatory Reform Act 2006, s 27(2), as from 8 January 2007.

Modification in relation to Scotland: para 2(2) has effect in relation to regulations made by Scottish Ministers, or an Order in Council made on the recommendation of the First Minister, under s 2 of this Act, as if the references to each, or either, House of Parliament were to the Scottish Parliament: see the Scotland Act 1998, s 125, Sch 8, para 15(3)(c).

Welsh Ministers: see the note to s 2 at **[20]** with regard to the Government of Wales Act 2006, s 59(1). Note also s 59(4) of the 2006 Act which disapplies para 2(2) above in relation to any statutory instrument made by the Welsh Ministers in certain circumstances.

EMPLOYMENT AGENCIES ACT 1973

(1973 c 35)

ARRANGEMENT OF SECTIONS

Prohibition orders

Conduct of employment agencies and employment businesses

Supplementary provisions

An Act to regulate employment agencies and businesses; and for connected purposes
[18 July 1973]

NOTES

Disapplication of Act: this Act does not apply to an employment agency or an employment business in so far as its activities consist of activities for which a licence is required under the Gangmasters (Licensing) Act 2004; see s 27 of that Act at **[1613]**.

Regulatory functions: the regulatory functions conferred by, or under, this Act are subject to the Legislative and Regulatory Reform Act 2006, ss 21, 22 at **[1783]**, **[1784]**; see the Legislative and Regulatory Reform (Regulatory Functions) Order 2007, SI 2007/3544 (made under s 24(2) of the 2006 Act) for details.

1–3 *(Repealed by the Deregulation and Contracting Out Act 1994, ss 35, 81(1), Sch 10, para 1(1), (2), Sch 17.)*

[Prohibition orders

3A Power to make orders

(1) On application by the Secretary of State, an [employment tribunal] may by order prohibit a person from carrying on, or being concerned with the carrying on of—

(a) any employment agency or employment business; or

(b) any specified description of employment agency or employment business.

(2) An order under subsection (1) of this section (in this Act referred to as "a prohibition order") may either prohibit a person from engaging in an activity altogether or prohibit him from doing so otherwise than in accordance with specified conditions.

(3) A prohibition order shall be made for a period beginning with the date of the order and ending—

(a) on a specified date, or

(b) on the happening of a specified event,

in either case, not more than ten years later.

(4) Subject to subsections (5) and (6) of this section, an [employment tribunal] shall not make a prohibition order in relation to any person unless it is satisfied that he is, on account of his misconduct or for any other sufficient reason, unsuitable to do what the order prohibits.

(5) An [employment tribunal] may make a prohibition order in relation to a body corporate if it is satisfied that—

(a) any director, secretary, manager or similar officer of the body corporate,

(b) any person who performs on behalf of the body corporate the functions of a director, secretary, manager or similar officer, or

(c) any person in accordance with whose directions or instructions the directors of the body corporate are accustomed to act,

is unsuitable, on account of his misconduct or for any other sufficient reason, to do what the order prohibits.

(6) An [employment tribunal] may make a prohibition order in relation to a partnership if it is satisfied that any member of the partnership, or any manager employed by the partnership, is unsuitable, on account of his misconduct or for any other sufficient reason, to do what the order prohibits.

(7) For the purposes of subsection (4) of this section, where an employment agency or employment business has been improperly conducted, each person who was carrying on, or concerned with the carrying on of, the agency or business at the time, shall be deemed to have been responsible for what happened unless he can show that it happened without his connivance or consent and was not attributable to any neglect on his part.

(8) A person shall not be deemed to fall within subsection (5)(c) of this section by reason only that the directors act on advice given by him in a professional capacity.

(9) In this section—

"director", in relation to a body corporate whose affairs are controlled by its members, means a member of the body corporate; and

"specified", in relation to a prohibition order, means specified in the order.]

[25]

NOTES

Inserted, together with ss 3B–3D, by the Deregulation and Contracting Out Act 1994, s 35, Sch 10, para 1(1), (3).

Sub-ss (1), (4)–(6): words in square brackets substituted by the Employment Rights (Dispute Resolution) Act 1998, s 1(2)(a).

[3B Enforcement

Any person who, without reasonable excuse, fails to comply with a prohibition order shall be guilty of an offence and liable on summary conviction to a fine not exceeding level 5 on the standard scale.]

[26]

NOTES

Inserted as noted to s 3A at **[25]**.

[3C Variation and revocation of orders

(1) On application by the person to whom a prohibition order applies, an [employment tribunal] may vary or revoke the order if the tribunal is satisfied that there has been a material change of circumstances since the order was last considered.

(2) An [employment tribunal] may not, on an application under this section, so vary a prohibition order as to make it more restrictive.

(3) The Secretary of State shall be a party to any proceedings before an [employment tribunal] with respect to an application under this section, and be entitled to appear and be heard accordingly.

(4) When making a prohibition order or disposing of an application under this section, an [employment tribunal] may, with a view to preventing the making of vexatious or frivolous applications, by order prohibit the making of an application, or further application, under this section in relation to the prohibition order before such date as the tribunal may specify in the order under this subsection.]

[27]

NOTES

Inserted as noted to s 3A at **[25]**.

Words in square brackets substituted by the Employment Rights (Dispute Resolution) Act 1998, s 1(2)(a).

[3D Appeals

(1) An appeal shall lie to the Employment Appeal Tribunal on a question of law arising from any decision of, or arising in proceedings before, an [employment tribunal] under section 3A or 3C of this Act.

(2) No other appeal shall lie from a decision of an [employment tribunal] under section 3A or 3C of this Act; and section 11 of the Tribunals and Inquiries Act 1992 (appeals from certain tribunals to High Court or Court of Session) shall not apply to proceedings before an [employment tribunal] under section 3A or 3C of this Act.]

[28]

NOTES

Inserted as noted to s 3A at **[25]**.

Words in square brackets substituted by the Employment Rights (Dispute Resolution) Act 1998, s 1(2)(a).

4 (*S 4 was substituted (together with s 3) by a new s 3 only by the Employment Protection Act 1975, s 114, Sch 13, para 4 (s 3 was subsequently repealed as noted ante).*)

Conduct of employment agencies and employment businesses

5 General regulations

(1) The Secretary of State may make regulations to secure the proper conduct of employment agencies and employment businesses and to protect the interests of persons availing themselves of the services of such agencies and businesses, and such regulations may in particular make provision—

(a) requiring persons carrying on such agencies and businesses to keep records;
(b) prescribing the form of such records and the entries to be made in them;
(c) prescribing qualifications appropriate for persons carrying on such agencies and businesses;
(d) regulating advertising by persons carrying on such agencies and businesses;
(e) safeguarding client's money deposited with or otherwise received by persons carrying on such agencies and businesses;
[(ea) restricting the services which may be provided by persons carrying on such agencies and businesses;
(eb) regulating the way in which and the terms on which services may be provided by persons carrying on such agencies and businesses;
(ec) restricting or regulating the charging of fees by persons carrying on such agencies and businesses].

[(1A) A reference in subsection (1)(ea) to (ec) of this section to services includes a reference to services in respect of—

(a) persons seeking employment outside the United Kingdom;
(b) persons normally resident outside the United Kingdom seeking employment in the United Kingdom.]

(2) Any person who contravenes or fails to comply with any regulation made under this section shall be guilty of an offence and liable on summary conviction to a fine not exceeding [level 5 on the standard scale].

[28A]

NOTES

Sub-s (1): paras (ea)–(ec) substituted, for original paras (f), (g) and the subsequent proviso, by the Employment Relations Act 1999, s 31, Sch 7, paras 1, 2(1), (2).

Sub-s (1A): inserted by the Employment Relations Act 1999, s 31, Sch 7, paras 1, 2(1), (3).

Sub-s (2): maximum fine increased and converted to a level on the standard scale by the Criminal Justice Act 1982, ss 37, 38, 46.

Regulations: the Conduct of Employment Agencies and Employment Businesses Regulations 2003, SI 2003/3319 at **[3048]**.

6 Restriction on charging persons seeking employment, etc

[(1) Except in such cases or classes of case as the Secretary of State may prescribe—

(a) a person carrying on an employment agency shall not request or directly or indirectly receive any fee from any person for providing services (whether by the provision of information or otherwise) for the purpose of finding him employment or seeking to find him employment;

(b) a person carrying on an employment business shall not request or directly or indirectly receive any fee from an employee for providing services (whether by the provision of information or otherwise) for the purpose of finding or seeking to find another person, with a view to the employee acting for and under the control of that other person;

(c) a person carrying on an employment business shall not request or directly or indirectly receive any fee from a second person for providing services (whether by the provision of information or otherwise) for the purpose of finding or seeking to find a third person, with a view to the second person becoming employed by the first person and acting for and under the control of the third person.]

(2) Any person who contravenes this section shall be guilty of an offence and liable on summary conviction to a fine not exceeding [level 5 on the standard scale].

[28B]

NOTES

Sub-s (1): substituted by the Employment Relations Act 1999, s 31, Sch 7, paras 1, 3, as from 1 April 2004.

Sub-s (2): maximum fine increased and converted to a level on the standard scale by the Criminal Justice Act 1982, ss 37, 38, 46.

Regulations: the Conduct of Employment Agencies and Employment Businesses Regulations 2003, SI 2003/3319 at **[3048]**.

7 *(Repealed by the Deregulation and Contracting Out Act 1994, s 81(1), Sch 17.)*

Supplementary provisions

8–11, 11A, 11B *(S 8 repealed by the Employment Protection Act 1975, ss 114, 125(3), Sch 13, para 5, Sch 18; ss 9–11, 11A, 11B outside the scope of this work.)*

12 Regulations and orders

(1) Subject to the next following subsection, the Secretary of State shall have power to make regulations for prescribing anything which under this Act is to be prescribed.

(2) The Secretary of State shall not make any regulations under this Act except after consultation with such bodies as appear to him to be representative of the interests concerned.

(3) Regulations under this Act may make different provision in relation to different cases or classes of case.

(4) The power of the Secretary of State to make regulations and orders under this Act shall be exercisable by statutory instrument.

[(5) Regulations under section 5(1) or 6(1) of this Act shall not be made unless a draft has been laid before, and approved by resolution of, each House of Parliament.

(6) Regulations under section 13(7)(i) of this Act or an order under section 14(3) shall be subject to annulment in pursuance of a resolution of either House of Parliament.]

[28C]

NOTES

Sub-ss (5), (6): substituted, for original sub-s (5), by the Employment Relations Act 1999, s 31, Sch 7, paras 1, 6.

13 Interpretation

(1) In this Act—

…

"employment" includes—

(a) employment by way of a professional engagement or otherwise under a contract for services;

(b) the reception in a private household of a person under an arrangement whereby that person is to assist in the domestic work of the household in consideration of receiving hospitality and pocket money or hospitality only;

and "worker" and "employer" shall be construed accordingly;

"employment agency" has the meaning assigned by subsection (2) of this section but does not include any arrangements, services, functions or business to which this Act does not apply by virtue of subsection (7) of this section;

"employment business" has the meaning assigned by subsection (3) of this section but does not include any arrangements, services, functions or business to which this Act does not apply by virtue of subsection (7) of this section;

"fee" includes any charge however described;

…

…

"local authority", in relation to England …, means a county council, …, the Common Council of the City of London, a district council or a London borough council [and in relation to Wales, means a county council or a county borough council,] and, in relation to Scotland means a [council constituted under section 2 of the Local Government etc (Scotland) Act 1994];

"organisation" includes an association of organisations;

"organisation of employers" means an organisation which consists wholly or mainly of employers and whose principal objects include the regulation of relations between employers and workers or organisations of workers

"organisation of workers" means an organisation which consists wholly or mainly of workers and whose principal objects include the regulation of relations between workers and employers or organisations of employers;

"prescribed" means prescribed by regulations made under this Act by the Secretary of State;

["prohibition order" has the meaning given by section 3A(2) of this Act;]

…

(2) For the purposes of this Act "employment agency" means the business (whether or not carried on with a view to profit and whether or not carried on in conjunction with any other business) of providing services (whether by the provision of information or otherwise) for the purpose of finding [persons] employment with employers or of supplying employers with [persons] for employment by them.

(3) For the purposes of this Act "employment business" means the business (whether or not carried on with a view to profit and whether or not carried on in conjunction with any other business) of supplying persons in the employment of the person carrying on the business, to act for, and under the control of, other persons in any capacity.

(4) The reference in subsection (2) of this section to providing services does not include a reference—

(a) to publishing a newspaper or other publication unless it is published wholly or mainly for the purpose mentioned in that subsection;

(b) to the display by any person of advertisements on premises occupied by him otherwise than for the said purpose; [or

(c) to providing a programme service (within the meaning of the Broadcasting Act 1990)].

(5) For the purposes of section 269 of the Local Government Act 1972, this Act shall be deemed to have been passed after 1st April 1974.

(6) In this Act, except where the context otherwise requires, references to any enactment shall be construed as references to that enactment as amended, extended or applied by or under any other enactment.

(7) This Act does not apply to—

(a) any business which is carried on exclusively for the purpose of obtaining employment for—

(i) persons formerly members of Her Majesty's naval, military or air forces; or

(ii) persons released from a [custodial sentence passed by a criminal court in the United Kingdom, the Channel Islands or the Isle of Man;]

and which is certified annually by or on behalf of the Admiralty Board of the Defence Council, the Army Board of the Defence Council or the Air Force Board of the Defence Council or by the Secretary of State (as the case may be) to be properly conducted;

(b) *any agency for the supply of nurses as defined in section 8 of the Nurses Agencies Act 1957 or section 32 of the Nurses (Scotland) Act 1951;*

(c) *the business carried on by any county or district nursing association or other similar organisation, being an association or organisation established and existing wholly or mainly for the purpose of providing patients with the services of a nurse to visit them in their own homes without herself taking up residence there;*

(d) services which are ancillary to the letting upon hire of any aircraft, vessel, vehicle, plant or equipment;

(e) …

(f) the exercise by a local authority[, a police authority established under [section 3 of the Police Act 1996]][…][… or a joint authority established by Part IV of the Local Government Act 1985] of any of their functions;

[(fza) the exercise by an authority established for an area in England under section 207 of the Local Government and Public Involvement in Health Act 2007 (joint waste authorities) of any of its functions;]

[(fa) the exercise by the Metropolitan Police Authority of any of its functions;]

[(ff) the exercise by the Broads Authority of any of its functions;]

[(fg) the exercise by a National Park authority of any of its functions;]

[(fh) the exercise by the London Fire and Emergency Planning Authority of any of its functions;]

(g) services provided by any organisation of employers or organisation of workers for its members;

[(ga) services provided in pursuance of arrangements made, or a direction given, under section 10 of the Employment and Training Act 1973;]

(h) services provided by an appointments board or service controlled by—

(i) one or more universities;

(ii) a central institution as defined in section 145 of the Education (Scotland) Act 1962 or a college of education as defined in the said section 145;

[(i) any prescribed business or service, or prescribed class of business or service or business or service carried on or provided by prescribed persons or classes of person]:

Provided that paragraph (b) of this subsection shall not be taken as exempting from the provisions of this Act any other business carried on in conjunction with an agency for the supply of nurses.

(8) *Subsection (7)(c) of this section shall have effect in its application to Scotland as if at the end there were added the words "or mainly or substantially supported by voluntary subscriptions and providing patients with the services of a nurse whether or not the nurse takes up residence in the patient's house".*

[28D]

NOTES

Sub-s (1) is amended as follows:

First, second and final definitions omitted repealed, and definition "prohibition order" inserted, by the Deregulation and Contracting Out Act 1994, ss 35, 81, Sch 10, para 1(5), Sch 17.

Third definition omitted repealed by the Employment Protection Act 1975, ss 114, 125(3), Sch 13, para 7, Sch 18.

In definition "local authority" first words omitted repealed, and words in first pair of square brackets inserted, by the Local Government (Wales) Act 1994, s 66(6), (8), Sch 16, para 41, Sch 18; second words omitted repealed by the Local Government Act 1985, s 102, Sch 17; words in second pair of square brackets substituted by the Local Government etc (Scotland) Act 1994, s 180(1), Sch 13, para 90.

Sub-s (2): words in square brackets substituted by the Employment Relations Act 1999, s 31, Sch 7, paras 1, 7, as from 6 July 2004.

Sub-s (4): words in square brackets substituted by the Broadcasting Act 1990, s 203(1), Sch 20, para 18.

Sub-s (7) is amended as follows:

Words in square brackets in para (a)(ii) substituted by the Criminal Justice Act 1988, s 123(6), Sch 8, para 7.

Paras (b), (c) and the proviso repealed by the Care Standards Act 2000, ss 111(2), 117(2), Sch 6, as from 1 April 2003 (in relation to England) and 2 October 2003 (in relation to Wales) (the italicised paragraphs remain in force for Scotland).

Para (e) repealed by the Deregulation and Contracting Out Act 1994, ss 35, 81, Sch 10, para 4, Sch 17.

In para (f), words in first (outer) pair of square brackets inserted by the Police and Magistrates' Courts Act 1994, s 43, Sch 4, Pt II, para 50; words in second (inner) pair of square brackets substituted by the

Police Act 1996, s 103, Sch 7, para 1(2)(i); first words omitted (as originally inserted by the Police Act 1997, s 134(1), Sch 9, para 26) repealed by the Serious Organised Crime and Police Act 2005, ss 59, 174(2), Sch 4, para 19, Sch 17, Pt 2, as from 1 April 2006; words in final pair of square brackets inserted by the Local Government Act 1985, s 84, Sch 14, para 50, and words omitted therefrom repealed by the Education Reform Act 1988, s 237, Sch 13, Pt I.

Sub-s (7): para (fza) inserted by the Local Government and Public Involvement in Health Act 2007, s 209(2), Sch 13, Pt 2, para 30, as from 1 April 2008.

Paras (fa), (fh) inserted by the Greater London Authority Act 1999, ss 325, 328, Sch 27, para 37, Sch 29, Pt I, para 22.

Para (ff) inserted by the Norfolk and Suffolk Broads Act 1988, s 21, Sch 6.

Para (fg) inserted by the Environment Act 1995, s 78, Sch 10, para 11.

Para (ga) inserted by the Trade Union Reform and Employment Rights Act 1993, s 49(2), Sch 8, para 4.

Para (i) substituted by the Employment Relations Act 1999, s 31, Sch 7, paras 1, 8.

Sub-s (8): substituted by the Care Standards Act 2000, s 111(2), as from a day to be appointed, as follows (as amended by the Regulation of Care (Scotland) Act 2001, s 79, Sch 3, para 6)—

"(8) This Act, in its application to Scotland, does not apply to—

(a) [a nurse agency as defined in section 2(6) of the Regulation of Care (Scotland) Act 2001 (asp 8)] (but excluding any other business carried on in conjunction with such an agency);

(b) the business carried on by any county or district nursing association or other similar organisation, being an association or organisation within paragraph (a) or (b) of that definition.".

Regulations: the Employment Agencies Act 1973 (Exemption) Regulations 1976, SI 1976/710; the Employment Agencies Act 1973 (Exemption) (No 2) Regulations 1979, SI 1979/1741; the Employment Agencies Act 1973 (Exemption) (No 2) Regulations 1984, SI 1984/978 (all made under sub-s (7)(i)).

14 Short title, repeals, commencement and extent

(1) This Act may be cited as the Employment Agencies Act 1973.

(2) The enactments specified in the Schedule to this Act are hereby repealed to the extent specified in the third column of that Schedule.

(3) The Secretary of State may, after consultation with such bodies as appear to him to be concerned, by order repeal any provision of any local Act, being a provision which is not specified in Part II of the said Schedule and which appears to him to be unnecessary having regard to the provisions of this Act, or to be inconsistent with the provisions of this Act, and may by that order make such amendments of that or any other local Act as appear to him to be necessary in consequence of the repeal and such transitional provision as appears to him to be necessary or expedient in connection with the matter.

(4) This Act shall come into force on such date as the Secretary of State may by order appoint, and different dates may be appointed for different provisions and for different purposes.

(5) This Act does not extend to Northern Ireland.

[29]

NOTES

Orders: the Employment Agencies Act 1973 (Commencement) Order 1976, SI 1976/709; the Employment Agencies Act 1973 (Local Act Repeals) Order 1976, SI 1976/711.

(*Schedule (repeals) outside the scope of this work.*)

HEALTH AND SAFETY AT WORK ETC ACT 1974

(1974 c 37)

ARRANGEMENT OF SECTIONS

PART I
HEALTH, SAFETY AND WELFARE IN CONNECTION WITH WORK, AND CONTROL OF DANGEROUS SUBSTANCES AND CERTAIN EMISSIONS INTO THE ATMOSPHERE

Preliminary

General duties

The Health and Safety Executive

Health and safety regulations and approved codes of practice

Enforcement

Obtaining and disclosure of information

Provisions as to offences

Financial provisions

Miscellaneous and supplementary

PART IV
MISCELLANEOUS AND GENERAL

SCHEDULES:

An Act to make further provision for securing the health, safety and welfare of persons at work, for protecting others against risks to health or safety in connection with the activities of persons at work, for controlling the keeping and use and preventing the unlawful acquisition, possession and use of dangerous substances, and for controlling certain emissions into the atmosphere; to make further provision with respect to the employment medical advisory service; to amend the law relating to building regulations, and the Building (Scotland) Act 1959; and for connected purposes

[31 July 1974]

NOTES

Section 5 was repealed by the Environmental Protection Act 1990, ss 162(2), 164(3), Sch 16, Pt I. Sections 29–32 and Sch 4 were repealed by the Employment Protection Act 1975, ss 116, 125(3), Sch 15, Pt I, Sch 18. Sections 61–74, 76 and Schs 5, 6 were repealed by the Building Act 1984, s 133(2), Sch 7. Section 75 was repealed by the Building (Scotland) Act 2003, s 58, Sch 6, para 9 (as from 1 May 2005). Section 77 and Sch 7 were repealed by the Health Protection Agency Act 2004, s 11(2), Sch 4 (as from 1 April 2005). Section 78 and Sch 8 were repealed by the Regulatory Reform (Fire Safety) Order 2005, SI 2005/1541 and the Fire (Scotland) Act 2005 (Consequential Modifications and Savings) Order 2006, SSI 2006/475 (as from 1 October 2006). Section 79 was repealed by the Companies Consolidation (Consequential Provisions) Act 1985, s 29, Sch 1. Section 83 and Schs 9, 10 were repealed by the Statute Law (Repeals) Act 1993.

Sections 55–60 (the Employment Medical Advisory Service) are outside the scope of this work. The rest of the Act is printed in full.

The Act confers extensive powers to make subordinate legislation. Considerations of space preclude reference to all Orders made under the Act, for details of which specialist works on Health and Safety should be consulted.

As to the transfer of railway safety functions to the Office of Rail Regulation and for transitional provisions in connection with the transfer, see the Railways Act 2005, s 2, Schs 1, 3. See also the Health and Safety (Enforcing Authority for Railways and Other Guided Transport Systems) Regulations 2006, SI 2006/557, which provide that the ORR shall be responsible for the enforcement of the relevant statutory provisions (within the meaning of s 53) to the extent that they relate to the operation of a railway, the operation of a tramway, and the operation of any other system of guided transport.

Disapplication: as to the disapplication of this Act in relation to premises to which the Regulatory Reform (Fire Safety) Order 2005, SI 2005/1541 applies, see art 47 of the 2005 Order. See also the Fire (Scotland) Act 2005, s 70 (Consequential restriction of application of Part I of the Health and Safety at Work etc Act 1974).

As to the transfer of the functions of the Minister for the Civil Service to the Treasury, see the Transfer of Functions (Minister for the Civil Service and Treasury) Order 1981, SI 1981/1670.

Regulatory functions: the regulatory functions conferred by, or under, this Act are subject to the Legislative and Regulatory Reform Act 2006, ss 21, 22 at **[1783]**, **[1784]**; see the Legislative and Regulatory Reform (Regulatory Functions) Order 2007, SI 2007/3544 (made under s 24(2) of the 2006 Act) for details.

Health and Safety Commission; Health and Safety Executive: as to the abolition of these bodies (with effect from 1 April 2008) and their replacement with a single Health and Safety Executive exercising the combined functions of those bodies, see the Legislative Reform (Health and Safety Executive) Order 2008, SI 2008/960 (at **[3474L]**), and the amendments made by that Order to this Act (see, in particular, ss 10–13 at **[38]** et seq). For transitional provisions in relation to the abolition of the former bodies and the establishment of the new Health and Safety Executive, see art 21 of, and Sch 2 to, the 2008 Order at **[3474N]**, **[3474O]**.

See *Harvey* N.

PART I
HEALTH, SAFETY AND WELFARE IN CONNECTION WITH WORK, AND CONTROL OF DANGEROUS SUBSTANCES AND CERTAIN EMISSIONS INTO THE ATMOSPHERE

NOTES

The general purposes of this Part of this Act are extended by the Offshore Safety Act 1992, ss 1(1), 2(1), the Consumer Protection Act 1987, s 36, and the Railways Act 1993, s 117(2), (6), (7).

Preliminary

1 Preliminary

(1) The provisions of this Part shall have effect with a view to—

(a) securing the health, safety and welfare of persons at work;

(b) protecting persons other than persons at work against risks to health or safety arising out of or in connection with the activities of persons at work;

(c) controlling the keeping and use of explosive or highly flammable or otherwise dangerous substances, and generally preventing the unlawful acquisition, possession and use of such substances; …

(d) …

(2) The provisions of this Part relating to the making of health and safety regulations … and the preparation and approval of codes of practice shall in particular have effect with a view to enabling the enactments specified in the third column of Schedule 1 and the regulations, orders and other instruments in force under those enactments to be progressively replaced by a system of regulations and approved codes of practice operating in combination with the other provisions of this Part and designed to maintain or improve the standards of health, safety and welfare established by or under those enactments.

(3) For the purposes of this Part risks arising out of or in connection with the activities of persons at work shall be treated as including risks attributable to the manner of conducting an undertaking, the plant or substances used for the purposes of an undertaking and the condition of premises so used or any part of them.

(4) References in this Part to the general purposes of this Part are references to the purposes mentioned in subsection (1) above.

[30]

NOTES

Sub-s (1): words omitted repealed by the Environmental Protection Act 1990, s 162(2), Sch 16, Pt I.

Sub-s (2): words omitted repealed by the Employment Protection Act 1975, ss 116, 125(3), Sch 15, para 1, Sch 18.

Dangerous substances: for certain purposes, the reference to dangerous substances in sub-s (1)(c) above is extended to include environmentally hazardous substances; see the Health and Safety at Work etc Act 1974 (Application to Environmentally Hazardous Substances) Regulations 2002, SI 2002/282.

Regulations: Regulations made under this section are outside the scope of this work.

General duties

2 General duties of employers to their employees

(1) It shall be the duty of every employer to ensure, so far as is reasonably practicable, the health, safety and welfare at work of all his employees.

(2) Without prejudice to the generality of an employer's duty under the preceding subsection, the matters to which that duty extends include in particular—

(a) the provision and maintenance of plant and systems of work that are, so far as is reasonably practicable, safe and without risks to health;

(b) arrangements for ensuring, so far as is reasonably practicable, safety and absence of risks to health in connection with the use, handling, storage and transport of articles and substances;

(c) the provision of such information, instruction, training and supervision as is necessary to ensure, so far as is reasonably practicable, the health and safety at work of his employees;

(d) so far as is reasonably practicable as regards any place of work under the employer's control, the maintenance of it in a condition that is safe and without risks to health and the provision and maintenance of means of access to and egress from it that are safe and without such risks;

(e) the provision and maintenance of a working environment for his employees that is, so far as is reasonably practicable, safe, without risks to health, and adequate as regards facilities and arrangements for their welfare at work.

(3) Except in such cases as may be prescribed, it shall be the duty of every employer to prepare and as often as may be appropriate revise a written statement of his general policy with respect to the health and safety at work of his employees and the organisation and arrangements for the time being in force for carrying out that policy, and to bring the statement and any revision of it to the notice of all his employees.

(4) Regulations made by the Secretary of State may provide for the appointment in prescribed cases by recognised trade unions (within the meaning of the regulations) of safety representatives from amongst the employees, and those representatives shall represent the employees in consultations with the employers under subsection (6) below and shall have such other functions as may be prescribed.

(5) …

(6) It shall be the duty of every employer to consult any such representatives with a view to the making and maintenance of arrangements which will enable him and his employees to co-operate effectively in promoting and developing measures to ensure the health and safety at work of the employees, and in checking the effectiveness of such measures.

(7) In such cases as may be prescribed it shall be the duty of every employer, if requested to do so by the safety representatives mentioned in [subsection (4)] above, to establish, in accordance with regulations made by the Secretary of State, a safety committee having the function of keeping under review the measures taken to ensure the health and safety at work of his employees and such other functions as may be prescribed.

[31]

NOTES

Sub-s (5): repealed by the Employment Protection Act 1975, ss 116, 125(3), Sch 15, para 2, Sch 18.

Sub-s (7): words in square brackets substituted by the Employment Protection Act 1975, ss 116, 125(3), Sch 15, para 2, Sch 18.

Exclusion or modification: see s 15(3)(b) and (6)(c) at **[43]**.

Regulations: the Employers' Health and Safety Policy Statements (Exceptions) Regulations 1975, SI 1975/1584 (which exempt employers with fewer than 5 employees from the requirements of sub-s (3)); the Safety Representatives and Safety Committees Regulations 1977, SI 1977/500 at **[2034]**; the Police (Health and Safety) Regulations 1999, SI 1999/860 at **[2505]**.

3 General duties of employers and self-employed to persons other than their employees

(1) It shall be the duty of every employer to conduct his undertaking in such a way as to ensure, so far as is reasonably practicable, that persons not in his employment who may be affected thereby are not thereby exposed to risks to their health or safety.

(2) It shall be the duty of every self-employed person to conduct his undertaking in such a way as to ensure, so far as is reasonably practicable, that he and other persons (not being his employees) who may be affected thereby are not thereby exposed to risks to their health or safety.

(3) In such cases as may be prescribed, it shall be the duty of every employer and every self-employed person, in the prescribed circumstances and in the prescribed manner, to give to persons (not being his employees) who may be affected by the way in which he conducts his undertaking the prescribed information about such aspects of the way in which he conducts his undertaking as might affect their health or safety.

[32]

NOTES

Exclusion or modification: see s 15(3)(b) and (6)(c) at **[43]**.

4 General duties of persons concerned with premises to persons other than their employees

(1) This section has effect for imposing on persons duties in relation to those who—

(a) are not their employees; but

(b) use non-domestic premises made available to them as a place of work or as a place where they may use plant or substances provided for their use there,

and applies to premises so made available and other non-domestic premises used in connection with them.

(2) It shall be the duty of each person who has, to any extent, control of premises to which this section applies or of the means of access thereto or egress therefrom or of any plant or substance in such premises to take such measures as it is reasonable for a person in his position to take to ensure, so far as is reasonably practicable, that the premises, all means of access thereto or egress therefrom available for use by persons using the premises, and any plant or substance in the premises or, as the case may be, provided for use there, is or are safe and without risks to health.

(3) Where a person has, by virtue of any contract or tenancy, an obligation of any extent in relation to—

(a) the maintenance or repair of any premises to which this section applies or any means of access thereto or egress therefrom; or

(b) the safety of or the absence of risks to health arising from plant or substances in any such premises;

that person shall be treated, for the purposes of subsection (2) above, as being a person who has control of the matters to which his obligation extends.

(4) Any reference in this section to a person having control of any premises or matter is a reference to a person having control of the premises or matter in connection with the carrying on by him of a trade, business or other undertaking (whether for profit or not).

[33]

NOTES

Exclusion or modification: see s 15(3)(b) and (6)(c) at **[43]**.

5 *(Repealed by the Environmental Protection Act 1990, ss 162(2), 164(3), Sch 16, Pt I.)*

6 General duties of manufacturers etc as regards articles and substances for use at work

[(1) It shall be the duty of any person who designs, manufactures, imports or supplies any article for use at work or any article of fairground equipment—

(a) to ensure, so far as is reasonably practicable, that the article is so designed and constructed that it will be safe and without risks to health at all times when it is being set, used, cleaned or maintained by a person at work;

(b) to carry out or arrange for the carrying out of such testing and examination as may be necessary for the performance of the duty imposed on him by the preceding paragraph;

(c) to take such steps as are necessary to secure that persons supplied by that person with the article are provided with adequate information about the use for which the article is designed or has been tested and about any conditions necessary to ensure that it will be safe and without risks to health at all such times as are mentioned in paragraph (a) above and when it is being dismantled or disposed of; and

(d) to take such steps as are necessary to secure, so far as is reasonably practicable, that persons so supplied are provided with all such revisions of information provided to them by virtue of the preceding paragraph as are necessary by reason of its becoming known that anything gives rise to a serious risk to health or safety.

(1A) It shall be the duty of any person who designs, manufactures, imports or supplies any article of fairground equipment—

(a) to ensure, so far as is reasonably practicable, that the article is so designed and constructed that it will be safe and without risks to health at all times when it is being used for or in connection with the entertainment of members of the public;

(b) to carry out or arrange for the carrying out of such testing and examination as may be necessary for the performance of the duty imposed on him by the preceding paragraph;

(c) to take such steps as are necessary to secure that persons supplied by that person with the article are provided with adequate information about the use for which the article is designed or has been tested and about any conditions necessary to ensure that it will be safe and without risks to health at all times when it is being used for or in connection with the entertainment of members of the public; and

(d) to take such steps as are necessary to secure, so far as is reasonably practicable, that persons so supplied are provided with all such revisions of information provided to them by virtue of the preceding paragraph as are necessary by reason of its becoming known that anything gives rise to a serious risk to health or safety.]

(2) It shall be the duty of any person who undertakes the design or manufacture of any article for use at work [or of any article of fairground equipment] to carry out or arrange for the carrying out of any necessary research with a view to the discovery and, so far as is reasonably practicable, the elimination or minimisation of any risks to health or safety to which the design or article may give rise.

(3) It shall be the duty of any person who erects or installs any article for use at work in any premises where that article is to be used by persons at work [or who erects or installs any article of fairground equipment] to ensure, so far as is reasonably practicable, that nothing about the way in which [the article is erected or installed makes it unsafe or a risk to health at any such time as is mentioned in paragraph (a) of subsection (1) or, as the case may be, in paragraph (a) of subsection (1) or (1A) above].

[(4) It shall be the duty of any person who manufactures, imports or supplies any substance—

(a) to ensure, so far as is reasonably practicable, that the substance will be safe and without risks to health at all times when it is being used, handled, processed, stored or transported by a person at work or in premises to which section 4 above applies;

(b) to carry out or arrange for the carrying out of such testing and examination as may be necessary for the performance of the duty imposed on him by the preceding paragraph;

(c) to take such steps as are necessary to secure that persons supplied by that person with the substance are provided with adequate information about any risks to health or safety to which the inherent properties of the substance may give rise, about the results of any relevant tests which have been carried out on or in connection with the substance and about any conditions necessary to ensure that the substance will be safe and without risks to health at all such times as are mentioned in paragraph (a) above and when the substance is being disposed of; and

(d) to take such steps as are necessary to secure, so far as is reasonably practicable, that persons so supplied are provided with all such revisions of information provided to them by virtue of the preceding paragraph as are necessary by reason of its becoming known that anything gives rise to a serious risk to health or safety.]

(5) It shall be the duty of any person who undertakes the manufacture of any [substance] to carry out or arrange for the carrying out of any necessary research with a view to the

discovery and, so far as is reasonably practicable, the elimination or minimisation of any risks to health or safety to which the substance may give rise [at all such times as are mentioned in paragraph (a) of subsection (4) above].

(6) Nothing in the preceding provisions of this section shall be taken to require a person to repeat any testing, examination or research which has been carried out otherwise than by him or at his instance, in so far as it is reasonable for him to rely on the results thereof for the purposes of those provisions.

(7) Any duty imposed on any person by any of the preceding provisions of this section shall extend only to things done in the course of a trade, business or other undertaking carried on by him (whether for profit or not) and to matters within his control.

(8) Where a person designs, manufactures, imports or supplies an article [for use at work or an article of fairground equipment and does so for or to another] on the basis of a written undertaking by that other to take specified steps sufficient to ensure, so far as is reasonably practicable, that the article will be safe and without risks to health [at all such times as are mentioned in paragraph (a) of subsection (1) or, as the case may be, in paragraph (a) of subsection (1) or (1A) above], the undertaking shall have the effect of relieving the first-mentioned person from the duty imposed [by virtue of that paragraph] above to such extent as is reasonable having regard to the terms of the undertaking.

[(8A) Nothing in subsection (7) or (8) above shall relieve any person who imports any article or substance from any duty in respect of anything which—

(a) in the case of an article designed outside the United Kingdom, was done by and in the course of any trade, profession or other undertaking carried on by, or was within the control of, the person who designed the article; or

(b) in the case of an article or substance manufactured outside the United Kingdom, was done by and in the course of any trade, profession or other undertaking carried on by, or was within the control of, the person who manufactured the article or substance.]

(9) Where a person ("the ostensible supplier") supplies any [article or substance] to another ("the customer") under a hire-purchase agreement, conditional sale agreement or credit-sale agreement, and the ostensible supplier—

(a) carries on the business of financing the acquisition of goods by others by means of such agreements; and

(b) in the course of that business acquired his interest in the article or substance supplied to the customer as a means of financing its acquisition by the customer from a third person ("the effective supplier"),

the effective supplier and not the ostensible supplier shall be treated for the purposes of this section as supplying the article or substance to the customer, and any duty imposed by the preceding provisions of this section on suppliers shall accordingly fall on the effective supplier and not on the ostensible supplier.

[(10) For the purposes of this section an absence of safety or a risk to health shall be disregarded in so far as the case in or in relation to which it would arise is shown to be one the occurrence of which could not reasonably be foreseen; and in determining whether any duty imposed by virtue of paragraph (a) of subsection (1), (1A) or (4) above has been performed regard shall be had to any relevant information or advice which has been provided to any person by the person by whom the article has been designed, manufactured, imported or supplied or, as the case may be, by the person by whom the substance has been manufactured, imported or supplied.]

[34]

NOTES

Sub-ss (1), (1A): substituted, for original sub-s (1), by the Consumer Protection Act 1987, s 36, Sch 3, para 1(1), (2).

Sub-ss (2), (3), (5), (8), (9): words in square brackets inserted or substituted by the Consumer Protection Act 1987, s 36, Sch 3, para 1(1), (3), (4), (6), (7), (9).

Sub-ss (4), (10): substituted by the Consumer Protection Act 1987, s 36, Sch 3, para 1(1), (5), (10).

Sub-s (8A): inserted by the Consumer Protection Act 1987, s 36, Sch 3, para 1(1), (8).

Exclusion or modification: see s 15(3)(b) and (6)(c) at **[43]**.

Enforcing authority: the ORR is the enforcing authority for the purposes of this section in so far as it relates to articles designed, manufactured, imported or supplied (or substances manufactured, imported or supplied), to be used exclusively or primarily in the operation of railways, tramways and certain other systems of guided transport (or, in the case of sub-s (3)), in so far as it relates to the erection or installation of articles for use at work in the operation of such systems of transport); see the Health and Safety (Enforcing Authority for Railways and Other Guided Transport Systems) Regulations 2006, SI 2006/557.

PART 1

7 General duties of employees at work

It shall be the duty of every employee while at work—

(a) to take reasonable care for the health and safety of himself and of other persons who may be affected by his acts or omissions at work; and

(b) as regards any duty or requirement imposed on his employer or any other person by or under any of the relevant statutory provisions, to co-operate with him so far as is necessary to enable that duty or requirement to be performed or complied with.

[35]

NOTES

Exclusion or modification: see s 15(3)(b) and (6)(c) at **[43]**.

8 Duty not to interfere with or misuse things provided pursuant to certain provisions

No person shall intentionally or recklessly interfere with or misuse anything provided in the interests of health, safety or welfare in pursuance of any of the relevant statutory provisions.

[36]

NOTES

Exclusion or modification: see s 15(3)(b) and (6)(c) at **[43]**.

9 Duty not to charge employees for things done or provided pursuant to certain specific requirements

No employer shall levy or permit to be levied on any employee of his any charge in respect of anything done or provided in pursuance of any specific requirement of the relevant statutory provisions.

[37]

NOTES

Exclusion or modification: see s 15(3)(b) and (6)(c) at **[43]**.

The Health and Safety Executive

[10 Establishment of the Executive

(1) There shall be a body corporate to be known as the Health and Safety Executive (in this Act referred to as "the Executive").

(2) The provisions of Schedule 2 shall have effect with respect to the Executive.

(3) The functions of the Executive and of its officers and servants shall be performed on behalf of the Crown.

(4) For the purpose of any civil proceedings arising out of those functions—

(a) in England and Wales and Northern Ireland, the Crown Proceedings Act 1947 shall apply to the Executive as if it were a government department within the meaning of that Act, and

(b) in Scotland, the Crown Suits (Scotland) Act 1857 shall apply to the Executive as if it were a public department within the meaning of that Act.]

[38]

NOTES

Commencement: 1 April 2008.

Substituted by the Legislative Reform (Health and Safety Executive) Order 2008, SI 2008/960, arts 3, 4, as from 1 April 2008 (for transitional provisions in relation to the abolition of the Health and Safety Commission and the Health and Safety Executive and their replacement with a single Health and Safety Executive, see art 21 of, and Sch 2 to, that Order at **[3474N]**, **[3474O]**).

Note: the Legislative Reform (Health and Safety Executive) Order 2008, SI 2008/960 does not amend the heading immediately before this section. However, in light of the other amendments made by that Order, and in light of the abolition of the HSC by art 2 of that Order, the heading has been changed from "The Health and Safety Commission and the Health and Safety Executive" to "The Health and Safety Executive".

[11 Functions of the Executive

(1) It shall be the general duty of the Executive to do such things and make such arrangements as it considers appropriate for the general purposes of this Part.

(2) In connection with the general purposes of this Part, the Executive shall—

(a) assist and encourage persons concerned with matters relevant to those purposes to further those purposes;

(b) make such arrangements as it considers appropriate for the carrying out of research and the publication of the results of research and the provision of training and information, and encourage research and the provision of training and information by others;

(c) make such arrangements as it considers appropriate to secure that the following persons are provided with an information and advisory service on matters relevant to those purposes and are kept informed of and are adequately advised on such matters—

(i) government departments,
(ii) local authorities,
(iii) employers,
(iv) employees,
(v) organisations representing employers or employees, and
(vi) other persons concerned with matters relevant to the general purposes of this Part.

(3) The Executive shall submit from time to time to the Secretary of State such proposals as the Executive considers appropriate for the making of regulations under any of the relevant statutory provisions.

(4) In subsections (1) to (3)—

(a) references to the general purposes of this Part do not include references to the railway safety purposes; and

(b) the reference to the making of regulations under the relevant statutory provisions does not include a reference so far as the regulations are made for the railway safety purposes.

(5) It shall be the duty of the Executive—

(a) to submit to the Secretary of State from time to time particulars of what it proposes to do for the purpose of performing of its functions;

(b) to ensure that its activities are in accordance with proposals approved by the Secretary of State; and

(c) to give effect to any directions given to it by the Secretary of State.

(6) The Executive shall provide a Minister of the Crown on request—

(a) with information about its activities in connection with any matter with which the Minister is concerned; and

(b) with advice on any matter with which he is concerned, where relevant expert advice is obtainable from any of the officers or servants of the Executive, but which is not relevant to the general purposes of this Part.]

[39]

NOTES

Commencement: 1 April 2008.

Ss 11–13 substituted by the Legislative Reform (Health and Safety Executive) Order 2008, SI 2008/960, arts 3, 5, as from 1 April 2008 (for transitional provisions in relation to the abolition of the Health and Safety Commission and the Health and Safety Executive and their replacement with a single Health and Safety Executive, see art 21 of, and Sch 2 to, that Order at **[3474N]**, **[3474O]**).

[12 Control of the Executive by the Secretary of State

(1) The Secretary of State may approve any proposals submitted to him under section 11(5)(a) with or without modifications.

(2) The Secretary of State may at any time give to the Executive—
- (a) such directions as he thinks fit with respect to its functions, or
- (b) such directions as appear to him requisite or expedient to give in the interests of the safety of the State.

(3) The Secretary of State may not under subsection (2) give any directions with regard to the enforcement of the relevant statutory provisions in any particular case.

(4) The reference to directions in subsection (2)(a)—
- (a) includes directions modifying the Executive's functions, but
- (b) does not include directions conferring functions on the Executive other than any functions of which it was deprived by previous directions given under subsection (2)(a).]

[40]

NOTES
Commencement: 1 April 2008.
Substituted as noted to s 11 at **[39]**.

[13 Powers of the Executive

(1) Subject to subsection (2), the Executive shall have power to do anything which is calculated to facilitate, or is conducive or incidental to, the performance of its functions, including a function conferred on it under this subsection.

(2) The power in subsection (1) shall not include the power to borrow money.

(3) The Executive may make agreements with a government department or other person for that department or person to perform any of its functions, with or without payment.

(4) Subject to subsections (5) and (6), the Executive may make agreements with a Minister of the Crown, with a government department or with a public authority to perform functions exercisable by that Minister, department or authority, with or without payment.

(5) The functions referred to in subsection (4)—
- (a) in the case of a Minister of the Crown, include functions not conferred by an enactment;
- (b) shall be functions which the Secretary of State considers can be appropriately performed by the Executive; and
- (c) do not include any power to make regulations or other instruments of a legislative character.

(6) The Executive may provide services or facilities, with or without payment, otherwise than for the general purposes of this Part, to a government department or public authority in connection with the exercise of that department's or authority's functions.

(7) The Executive may appoint persons or committees of persons to provide it with advice in connection with any of its functions and, without prejudice to subsection (8), it may remunerate these persons.

(8) The Executive may, in connection with the performance of its functions, pay to any person—
- (a) travelling and subsistence allowances, and
- (b) compensation for loss of remunerative time.

(9) Any amounts paid under subsections (7) and (8) shall be such as may be determined by the Secretary of State, with the approval of the Minister for the Civil Service.

(10) The Executive may—
- (a) carry out, arrange for, or make payments for the carrying out of, research into any matter connected with its functions, and
- (b) disseminate or arrange for or make payments for the dissemination of information derived from this research.

(11) The Executive may include, in any arrangements made for the provision of services or facilities under subsection (6), provision for the making of payments to the Executive, or any person acting on its behalf, by other parties to the arrangements and by persons using those services or facilities.]

[41]

NOTES

Commencement: 1 April 2008.

Substituted as noted to s 11 at **[39]**.

14 Power of [the Executive] to direct investigations and inquiries

(1) This section applies to the following matters, that is to say any accident, occurrence, situation or other matter whatsoever which [the Executive] thinks it necessary or expedient to investigate for any of the general purposes of this Part or with a view to the making of regulations for those purposes; and for the purposes of this subsection—

[(a) those general purposes shall be treated as not including the railway safety purposes; but

(b) it is otherwise]

immaterial whether the Executive is or is not responsible for securing the enforcement of such (if any) of the relevant statutory provisions as relate to the matter in question.

[(2) The Executive may at any time—

(a) investigate and make a special report on any matter to which this section applies; or

(b) authorise another person to investigate and make a special report into any such matter.

(2A) The Executive may at any time, with the consent of the Secretary of State, direct an inquiry to be held into any matter to which this section applies.]

(3) Any inquiry held by virtue of [subsection (2A)] above shall be held in accordance with regulations made for the purposes of this subsection by the Secretary of State, and shall be held in public except where or to the extent that the regulations provide otherwise.

(4) Regulations made for the purposes of subsection (3) above may in particular include provision—

(a) conferring on the person holding any such inquiry, and any person assisting him in the inquiry, powers of entry and inspection;

(b) conferring on any such person powers of summoning witnesses to give evidence or produce documents and power to take evidence on oath and administer oaths or require the making of declarations;

(c) requiring any such inquiry to be held otherwise than in public where or to the extent that a Minister of the Crown so directs.

[(5) In the case of a special report made by virtue of subsection (2), or a report made by the person holding an inquiry by virtue of subsection (2A), the Executive may cause the report, or so much of it as the Executive thinks fit, to be made public at such time and in such manner as it thinks fit.]

(6) [The Executive]—

(a) in the case of an investigation and special report made by virtue of [subsection (2)] above (otherwise than by an officer or servant of the Executive), may pay to the person making it such remuneration and expenses as the Secretary of State may, with the approval of the Minister for the Civil Service, determine;

(b) in the case of an inquiry held by virtue of [subsection (2A)] above, may pay to the person holding it and to any assessor appointed to assist him such remuneration and expenses, and to persons attending the inquiry as witnesses such expenses, as the Secretary of State may, with the like approval, determine; and

(c) may, to such extent as the Secretary of State may determine, defray the other costs, if any, of any such investigation and special report or inquiry.

(7) Where an inquiry is directed to be held by virtue of [subsection (2A)] above into any matter to which this section applies arising in Scotland, being a matter which causes the death of any person, no inquiry with regard to that death shall, unless the Lord Advocate otherwise directs, be held in pursuance of the Fatal Accidents [and Sudden Deaths Inquiry (Scotland) Act 1976]. **[42]**

NOTES

Sub-s (1): words in first pair of square brackets substituted by the Legislative Reform (Health and Safety Executive) Order 2008, SI 2008/960, arts 3, 6(1), (2), as from 1 April 2008 (for transitional provisions in relation to the abolition of the Health and Safety Commission and the Health and Safety Executive and their replacement with a single Health and Safety Executive, see art 21 of, and Sch 2 to, that Order at **[3474N]**, **[3474O]**); words in second pair of square brackets substituted by the Railways Act 2005, s 2, Sch 3, para 4(5), as from 1 April 2006.

Sub-ss (2), (2A): substituted, for original sub-s (2), by SI 2008/960, arts 3, 6(1), (3), as from 1 April 2008 (for transitional provisions see the note above).

Sub-ss (3), (6): words in square brackets substituted by SI 2008/960, arts 3, 6(1), (4), (6), as from 1 April 2008 (for transitional provisions see the note above).

Sub-s (5): substituted by SI 2008/960, arts 3, 6(1), (5), as from 1 April 2008 (for transitional provisions see the note above).

Sub-s (7): words in first pair of square brackets substituted by SI 2008/960, arts 3, 6(1), (7), as from 1 April 2008 (for transitional provisions see the note above); words in second pair of square brackets substituted by the Fatal Accidents and Sudden Deaths Inquiry (Scotland) Act 1976, s 8(1), Sch 1, para 4.

Note: the Legislative Reform (Health and Safety Executive) Order 2008, SI 2008/960 does not amend the title of this section. However, in light of the other amendments made by that Order, and in light of the abolition of the HSC by art 2 of that Order, the title of this section has been changed from "Power of the Commission to direct investigations and inquiries" to "Power of the Executive to direct investigations and inquiries".

Regulations: the Health and Safety Inquiries (Procedure) Regulations 1975, SI 1975/335.

Health and safety regulations and approved codes of practice

15 Health and safety regulations

[(1) Subject to the provisions of section 50, the Secretary of State … shall have power to make regulations under this section for any of the general purposes of this Part (and regulations so made are in this Part referred to as "health and safety regulations").]

(2) Without prejudice to the generality of the preceding subsection, health and safety regulations may for any of the general purposes of this Part make provision for any of the purposes mentioned in Schedule 3.

(3) Health and safety regulations—

(a) may repeal or modify any of the existing statutory provisions;

(b) may exclude or modify in relation to any specified class of case any of the provisions of sections 2 to 9 or any of the existing statutory provisions;

(c) may make a specified authority or class of authorities responsible, to such extent as may be specified, for the enforcement of any of the relevant statutory provisions.

(4) Health and safety regulations—

(a) may impose requirements by reference to the approval of [the Executive] or any other specified body or person;

(b) may provide for references in the regulations to any specified document to operate as references to that document as revised or re-issued from time to time.

(5) Health and safety regulations—

(a) may provide (either unconditionally or subject to conditions, and with or without limit of time) for exemptions from any requirement or prohibition imposed by or under any of the relevant statutory provisions;

(b) may enable exemptions from any requirement or prohibition imposed by or under any of the relevant statutory provisions to be granted (either unconditionally or subject to conditions, and with or without limit of time) by any specified person or by any person authorised in that behalf by a specified authority.

(6) Health and safety regulations—

(a) may specify the persons or classes of persons who, in the event of a contravention of a requirement or prohibition imposed by or under the regulations, are to be guilty of an offence, whether in addition to or to the exclusion of other persons or classes of persons;

(b) may provide for any specified defence to be available in proceedings for any offence under the relevant statutory provisions either generally or in specified circumstances;

(c) may exclude proceedings on indictment in relation to offences consisting of a contravention of a requirement or prohibition imposed by or under any of the existing statutory provisions, sections 2 to 9 or health and safety regulations;

(d) may restrict the punishments [(other than the maximum fine on conviction on indictment)] which can be imposed in respect of any such offence as is mentioned in paragraph (c) above.

[(e) in the case of regulations made for any purpose mentioned in section 1(1) of the Offshore Safety Act 1992, may provide that any offence consisting of a contravention of the regulations, or of any requirement or prohibition imposed by or under them, shall be punishable on conviction on indictment by imprisonment for a term not exceeding two years, or a fine, or both.]

(7) Without prejudice to section 35, health and safety regulations may make provision for enabling offences under any of the relevant statutory provisions to be treated as having been committed at any specified place for the purpose of bringing any such offence within the field of responsibility of any enforcing authority or conferring jurisdiction on any court to entertain proceedings for any such offence.

(8) Health and safety regulations may take the form of regulations applying to particular circumstances only or to a particular case only (for example, regulations applying to particular premises only).

(9) If an Order in Council is made under section 84(3) providing that this section shall apply to or in relation to persons, premises or work outside Great Britain then, notwithstanding the Order, health and safety regulations shall not apply to or in relation to aircraft in flight, vessels, hovercraft or offshore installations outside Great Britain or persons at work outside Great Britain in connection with submarine cables or submarine pipelines except in so far as the regulations expressly so provide.

(10) In this section "specified" means specified in health and safety regulations.

[43]

NOTES

Sub-s (1): substituted by the Employment Protection Act 1975, s 116, Sch 15, para 6; words omitted repealed by the Ministry of Agriculture, Fisheries and Food (Dissolution) Order 2002, SI 2002/794, art 5(2), Sch 2.

Sub-s (4): words in square brackets substituted by the Legislative Reform (Health and Safety Executive) Order 2008, SI 2008/960, arts 3, 7, as from 1 April 2008 (for transitional provisions in relation to the abolition of the Health and Safety Commission and the Health and Safety Executive and their replacement with a single Health and Safety Executive, see art 21 of, and Sch 2 to, that Order at **[3474N]**, **[3474O]**).

Sub-s (6): words in square brackets in para (d) inserted by the Criminal Law Act 1977, s 65(4), Sch 12; para (e) added by the Offshore Safety Act 1992, s 4(1), (6).

See further, for additional provision as to the power to make regulations under this section: the Offshore Safety Act 1992, ss 1(2), 2(2), the Railways Act 1993, s 117(3), (4), and the Coal Industry Act 1994, s 55; for the Secretary of State's power to repeal or revoke any provision of regulations, see the Deregulation and Contracting Out Act 1994, s 37(1)(b).

A very large number of regulations has been made under this section, and specialist Health and Safety publications should be consulted for a full list. Among the most important currently in force are: the Safety Representatives and Safety Committees Regulations 1977, SI 1977/500 at **[2034]**; the Health and Safety (First-Aid) Regulations 1981, SI 1981/917; the Electricity at Work Regulations 1989, SI 1989/635; the Health and Safety Information for Employees Regulations 1989, SI 1989/682 at **[2154]**; the Health and Safety (Display Screen Equipment) Regulations 1992, SI 1992/2792; the Manual Handling Operations Regulations 1992, SI 1992/2793; the Personal Protective Equipment at Work Regulations 1992, SI 1992/2966; the Workplace (Health, Safety and Welfare) Regulations 1992, SI 1992/3004; the Reporting of Injuries, Diseases and Dangerous Occurrences Regulations 1995, SI 1995/3163; the Health and Safety (Enforcing Authority) Regulations 1998, SI 1998/494; the Provision and Use of Work Equipment Regulations 1998, SI 1998/2306; the Lifting Operations and Lifting Equipment Regulations 1998, SI 1998/2307; the Control of Major Accident Hazards Regulations 1999, SI 1999/743; the Police (Health and Safety) Regulations 1999, SI 1999/860 at **[2505]**; the Railway Safety Regulations 1999, SI 1999/2244; the Ionising Radiations Regulations 1999, SI 1999/3232; the Management of Health and Safety at Work Regulations 1999, SI 1999/3242 at **[2526]**; the Control of Lead at Work Regulations 2002, SI 2002/2676; the Control of Substances Hazardous to Health Regulations 2002, SI 2002/2677; the Work at Height Regulations 2005, SI 2005/735; the Manufacture and Storage of Explosives Regulations 2005, SI 2005/1082; the Control of Vibration at Work Regulations 2005, SI 2005/1093; the Control of Noise at Work Regulations 2005, SI 2005/1643; the Health and Safety (Enforcing Authority for Railways and Other Guided Transport Systems) Regulations 2006, SI 2006/557; the Control of Asbestos Regulations 2006, SI 2006/2739; the Construction (Design and Management) Regulations 2007, SI 2007/320; the Carriage of Dangerous Goods and Use of Transportable Pressure Equipment Regulations 2007, SI 2007/1573; the Coal Mines (Control of Inhalable Dust) Regulations 2007, SI 2007/1894.

16 Approval of codes of practice by [the Executive]

(1) For the purpose of providing practical guidance with respect to the requirements of any provision of [any of the enactments or instruments mentioned in subsection (1A) below], [the Executive] may, subject to the following subsection … —

(a) approve and issue such codes of practice (whether prepared by it or not) as in its opinion are suitable for that purpose;

(b) approve such codes of practice issued or proposed to be issued otherwise than by [the Executive] as in its opinion are suitable for that purpose.

[(1A) Those enactments and instruments are—

(a) sections 2 to 7 above;

(b) health and safety regulations, except so far as they make provision exclusively in relation to transport systems falling within paragraph 1(3) of Schedule 3 to the Railways Act 2005; and

(c) the existing statutory provisions that are not such provisions by virtue of section 117(4) of the Railways Act 1993.]

(2) [The Executive] shall not approve a code of practice under subsection (1) above without the consent of the Secretary of State, and shall, before seeking his consent, consult—

(a) any government department or other body that appears to [the Executive] to be appropriate (and, in particular, in the case of a code relating to electro-magnetic radiations, [the Health Protection Agency]); and

(b) such government departments and other bodies, if any, as in relation to any matter dealt with in the code, [the Executive] is required to consult under this section by virtue of directions given to it by the Secretary of State.

(3) Where a code of practice is approved by [the Executive] under subsection (1) above, [the Executive] shall issue a notice in writing—

(a) identifying the code in question and stating the date on which its approval by [the Executive] is to take effect; and

(b) specifying for which of the provisions mentioned in subsection (1) above the code is approved.

(4) [The Executive] may—

(a) from time to time revise the whole or any part of any code of practice prepared by it in pursuance of this section;

(b) approve any revision or proposed revision of the whole or any part of any code of practice for the time being approved under this section;

and the provisions of subsections (2) and (3) above shall, with the necessary modifications, apply in relation to the approval of any revision under this subsection as they apply in relation to the approval of a code of practice under subsection (1) above.

(5) [The Executive] may at any time with the consent of the Secretary of State withdraw its approval from any code of practice approved under this section, but before seeking his consent shall consult the same government departments and other bodies as it would be required to consult under subsection (2) above if it were proposing to approve the code.

(6) Where under the preceding subsection [the Executive] withdraws its approval from a code of practice approved under this section, [the Executive] shall issue a notice in writing identifying the code in question and stating the date on which its approval of it is to cease to have effect.

(7) References in this part to an approved code of practice are references to that code as it has effect for the time being by virtue of any revision of the whole or any part of it approved under this section.

(8) The power of [the Executive] under subsection (1)(b) above to approve a code of practice issued or proposed to be issued otherwise than by [the Executive] shall include power to approve a part of such a code of practice; and accordingly in this Part "code of practice" may be read as including a part of such a code of practice.

[44]

NOTES

Words "the Executive" in square brackets in each place they occur substituted by the Legislative Reform (Health and Safety Executive) Order 2008, SI 2008/960, arts 3, 8, as from 1 April 2008 (for transitional provisions in relation to the abolition of the Health and Safety Commission and the Health and Safety Executive and their replacement with a single Health and Safety Executive, see art 21 of, and Sch 2 to, that Order at **[3474N]**, **[3474O]**).

Other amendments to this section are as follows:

Sub-s (1): words in first pair of square brackets substituted by the Railways Act 2005, s 2, Sch 3, para 9(1), as from 1 April 2006; words omitted repealed by the Employment Protection Act 1975, ss 116, 125(3), Sch 15, para 7, Sch 18.

Sub-s (1A): inserted by the Railways Act 2005, s 2, Sch 3, para 9(2), as from 1 April 2006.

Sub-s (2): words in third pair of square brackets substituted by the Health Protection Agency Act 2004, s 11(1), Sch 3, para 5(1), (2), as from 1 April 2005.

For reasons of space the only Codes of Practice made under this section which are reproduced in this work are Safety Representatives and Safety Committees (1978) and Time off for the Training of Safety Representatives (1978) at **[4501]** and **[4502]**.

17 Use of approved codes of practice in criminal proceedings

(1) A failure on the part of any person to observe any provision of an approved code of practice shall not of itself render him liable to any civil or criminal proceedings; but where in any criminal proceedings a party is alleged to have committed an offence by reason of a contravention of any requirement or prohibition imposed by or under any such provision as is mentioned in section 16(1) being a provision for which there was an approved code of practice at the time of the alleged contravention, the following subsection shall have effect with respect to that code in relation to those proceedings.

(2) Any provision of the code of practice which appears to the court to be relevant to the requirement or prohibition alleged to have been contravened shall be admissible in evidence in the proceedings; and if it is proved that there was at any material time a failure to observe any provision of the code which appears to the court to be relevant to any matter which it is necessary for the prosecution to prove in order to establish a contravention of that requirement or prohibition, that matter shall be taken as proved unless the court is satisfied that the requirement or prohibition was in respect of that matter complied with otherwise than by way of observance of that provision of the code.

(3) In any criminal proceedings—

(a) a document purporting to be a notice issued by [the Executive] under section 16 shall be taken to be such a notice unless the contrary is proved; and

(b) a code of practice which appears to the court to be the subject of such a notice shall be taken to be the subject of that notice unless the contrary is proved.

[45]

NOTES

Sub-s (3): words in square brackets substituted by the Legislative Reform (Health and Safety Executive) Order 2008, SI 2008/960, arts 3, 9, as from 1 April 2008 (for transitional provisions in relation to the abolition of the Health and Safety Commission and the Health and Safety Executive and their replacement with a single Health and Safety Executive, see art 21 of, and Sch 2 to, that Order at **[3474N]**, **[3474O]**).

Enforcement

18 Authorities responsible for enforcement of the relevant statutory provisions

(1) It shall be the duty of the Executive to make adequate arrangements for the enforcement of the relevant statutory provisions except to the extent that some other authority or class of authorities is by any of those provisions or by regulations under subsection (2) below made responsible for their enforcement.

(2) The Secretary of State may by regulations—

(a) make local authorities responsible for the enforcement of the relevant statutory provisions to such extent as may be prescribed;

(b) make provision for enabling responsibility for enforcing any of the relevant statutory provisions to be, to such extent as may be determined under the regulations—

(i) transferred from the Executive to local authorities or from local authorities to the Executive; or

(ii) assigned to the Executive or to local authorities for the purpose of removing any uncertainty as to what are by virtue of this subsection their respective responsibilities for the enforcement of those provisions;

and any regulations made in pursuance of paragraph (b) above shall include provision for securing that any transfer or assignment effected under the regulations is brought to the notice of persons affected by it.

(3) Any provision made by regulations under the preceding subsection shall have effect subject to any provision made by health and safety regulations … in pursuance of section 15(3)(c).

(4) It shall be the duty of every local authority—

(a) to make adequate arrangements for the enforcement within their area of the relevant statutory provisions to the extent that they are by any of those provisions or by regulations under subsection (2) above made responsible for their enforcement; and

(b) to perform the duty imposed on them by the preceding paragraph and any other functions conferred on them by any of the relevant statutory provisions in accordance with such guidance as [the Executive] may give them.

[(4A) Before the Executive gives guidance under subsection (4)(b) it shall consult the local authorities.

(4B) It shall be the duty of the Executive and the local authorities—

(a) to work together to establish best practice and consistency in the enforcement of the relevant statutory provisions;

(b) to enter into arrangements with each other for securing cooperation and the exchange of information in connection with the carrying out of their functions with regard to the relevant statutory provisions; and

(c) from time to time to review those arrangements and to revise them when they consider it appropriate to do so.]

(5) Where any authority other than … the Executive or a local authority is by any of the relevant statutory provisions … made responsible for the enforcement of any of those provisions to any extent, it shall be the duty of that authority—

(a) to make adequate arrangements for the enforcement of those provisions to that extent; and

(b) [except where that authority is the Office of Rail Regulation,] to perform the duty imposed on the authority by the preceding paragraph and any other functions conferred on the authority by any of the relevant statutory provisions in accordance with such guidance as [the Executive] may give to the authority.

(6) Nothing in the provisions of this Act or of any regulations made thereunder charging any person in Scotland with the enforcement of any of the relevant statutory provisions shall be construed as authorising that person to institute proceedings for any offence.

(7) In this Part—

(a) "enforcing authority" means the Executive or any other authority which is by any of the relevant statutory provisions or by regulations under subsection (2) above made responsible for the enforcement of any of those provisions to any extent; and

(b) any reference to an enforcing authority's field of responsibility is a reference to the field over which that authority's responsibility for the enforcement of those provisions extends for the time being;

but where by virtue of [subsection (3) of section 13] the performance of any function of … the Executive is delegated to a government department or person, references to … the Executive (or to an enforcing authority where that authority is the Executive) in any provision of this Part which relates to that function shall, so far as may be necessary to give effect to any agreement under [that subsection], be construed as references to that department or person; and accordingly any reference to the field of responsibility of an enforcing authority shall be construed as a reference to the field over which that department or person for the time being performs such a function.

[46]

NOTES

Sub-s (3): words omitted repealed by the Employment Protection Act 1975, ss 116, 125(3), Sch 15, para 8, Sch 18.

Sub-s (4): words in square brackets substituted by the Legislative Reform (Health and Safety Executive) Order 2008, SI 2008/960, arts 3, 10(1), (2), as from 1 April 2008 (for transitional provisions in relation to the abolition of the Health and Safety Commission and the Health and Safety Executive and their replacement with a single Health and Safety Executive, see art 21 of, and Sch 2 to, that Order at **[3474N]**, **[3474O]**).

Sub-ss (4A), (4B): inserted by SI 2008/960, arts 3, 10(1), (3), as from 1 April 2008 (for transitional provisions see the note above).

Sub-s (5): first words omitted repealed by the Employment Protection Act 1975, ss 116, 125(3), Sch 15, para 8, Sch 18; second words omitted repealed by the Railways Act 2005, s 59(6), Sch 13, Pt 1, as from 8 June 2005; words in first pair of square brackets in para (b) inserted by the Railways Act 2005, s 2, Sch 3, para 10(3), as from 1 April 2006; words in second pair of square brackets in para (b) substituted by SI 2008/960, arts 3, 10(1), (4), as from 1 April 2008 (for transitional provisions see the note above).

Sub-s (7): words omitted repealed, and words in square brackets substituted, by SI 2008/960, arts 3, 10(1), (5), as from 1 April 2008 (for transitional provisions see the note above).

See also the Health and Safety (Enforcing Authority for Railways and Other Guided Transport Systems) Regulations 2006, SI 2006/557, which provides that the ORR shall be responsible for the enforcement of the relevant statutory provisions to the extent that they relate to the operation of a railway, the operation of a tramway, and the operation of any other system of guided transport.

Regulations: the Petroleum (Consolidation) Act 1928 (Enforcement) Regulations 1979, SI 1979/427; the Railway Safety (Miscellaneous Provisions) Regulations 1997, SI 1997/553; the Health and Safety (Enforcing Authority) Regulations 1998, SI 1998/494; the Ammonium Nitrate Materials (High Nitrogen Content) Safety Regulations 2003, SI 2003/1082; the Adventure Activities (Enforcing Authority) Regulations 2004, SI 2004/1359; the Railways and Other Guided Transport Systems (Safety) Regulations 2006, SI 2006/599; the Control of Asbestos Regulations 2006, SI 2006/2739; the Manufacture and Storage of Explosives and the Health and Safety (Enforcing Authority) (Amendment and Supplementary Provisions) Regulations 2007, SI 2007/2598.

19 Appointment of inspectors

(1) Every enforcing authority may appoint as inspectors (under whatever title it may from time to time determine) such persons having suitable qualifications as it thinks necessary for carrying into effect the relevant statutory provisions within its field of responsibility, and may terminate any appointment made under this section.

(2) Every appointment of a person as an inspector under this section shall be made by an instrument in writing specifying which of the powers conferred on inspectors by the relevant statutory provisions are to be exercisable by the person appointed; and an inspector shall in right of his appointment under this section—

- (a) be entitled to exercise only such of those powers as are so specified; and
- (b) be entitled to exercise the powers so specified only within the field of responsibility of the authority which appointed him.

(3) So much of an inspector's instrument of appointment as specifies the powers which he is entitled to exercise may be varied by the enforcing authority which appointed him.

(4) An inspector shall, if so required when exercising or seeking to exercise any power conferred on him by any of the relevant statutory provisions, produce his instrument of appointment or a duly authenticated copy thereof.

[47]

20 Powers of inspectors

(1) Subject to the provisions of section 19 and this section, an inspector may, for the purpose of carrying into effect any of the relevant statutory provisions within the field of responsibility of the enforcing authority which appointed him, exercise the powers set out in subsection (2) below.

(2) The powers of an inspector referred to in the preceding subsection are the following, namely—

- (a) at any reasonable time (or, in a situation which in his opinion is or may be dangerous, at any time) to enter any premises which he has reason to believe it is necessary for him to enter for the purpose mentioned in subsection (1) above;
- (b) to take with him a constable if he has reasonable cause to apprehend any serious obstruction in the execution of his duty;
- (c) without prejudice to the preceding paragraph, on entering any premises by virtue of paragraph (a) above to take with him—
  - (i) any other person duly authorised by his (the inspector's) enforcing authority; and
  - (ii) any equipment or materials required for any purpose for which the power of entry is being exercised;
- (d) to make such examination and investigation as may in any circumstances be necessary for the purpose mentioned in subsection (1) above;
- (e) as regards any premises which he has power to enter, to direct that those premises or any part of them, or anything therein, shall be left undisturbed (whether generally or in particular respects) for so long as is reasonably necessary for the purpose of any examination or investigation under paragraph (d) above;
- (f) to take such measurements and photographs and make such recordings as he considers necessary for the purpose of any examination or investigation under paragraph (d) above;

(g) to take samples of any articles or substances found in any premises which he has power to enter, and of the atmosphere in or in the vicinity of any such premises;

(h) in the case of any article or substance found in any premises which he has power to enter, being an article or substance which appears to him to have caused or to be likely to cause danger to health or safety, to cause it to be dismantled or subjected to any process or test (but not so as to damage or destroy it unless this is in the circumstances necessary for the purpose mentioned in subsection (1) above);

(i) in the case of any such article or substance as is mentioned in the preceding paragraph, to take possession of it and detain it for so long as is necessary for all or any of the following purposes, namely—

  (i) to examine it and do to it anything which he has power to do under that paragraph;

  (ii) to ensure that it is not tampered with before his examination of it is completed;

  (iii) to ensure that it is available for use as evidence in any proceedings for an offence under any of the relevant statutory provisions or any proceedings relating to a notice under section 21 or 22;

(j) to require any person whom he has reasonable cause to believe to be able to give any information relevant to any examination or investigation under paragraph (d) above to answer (in the absence of persons other than a person nominated by him to be present and any persons whom the inspector may allow to be present) such questions as the inspector thinks fit to ask and to sign a declaration of the truth of his answers;

(k) to require the production of, inspect, and take copies of or of any entry in—

  (i) any books or documents which by virtue of any of the relevant statutory provisions are required to be kept; and

  (ii) any other books or documents which it is necessary for him to see for the purposes of any examination or investigation under paragraph (d) above;

(l) to require any person to afford him such facilities and assistance with respect to any matters or things within that person's control or in relation to which that person has responsibilities as are necessary to enable the inspector to exercise any of the powers conferred on him by this section;

(m) any other power which is necessary for the purpose mentioned in subsection (1) above.

(3) The Secretary of State may by regulations make provision as to the procedure to be followed in connection with the taking of samples under subsection (2)(g) above (including provision as to the way in which samples that have been so taken are to be dealt with).

(4) Where an inspector proposes to exercise the power conferred by subsection (2)(h) above in the case of an article or substance found in any premises, he shall, if so requested by a person who at the time is present in and has responsibilities in relation to those premises, cause anything which is to be done by virtue of that power to be done in the presence of that person unless the inspector considers that its being done in that person's presence would be prejudicial to the safety of the State.

(5) Before exercising the power conferred by subsection (2)(h) above in the case of any article or substance, an inspector shall consult such persons as appear to him appropriate for the purpose of ascertaining what dangers, if any, there may be in doing anything which he proposes to do under that power.

(6) Where under the power conferred by subsection (2)(i) above an inspector takes possession of any article or substance found in any premises, he shall leave there, either with a responsible person or, if that is impracticable, fixed in a conspicuous position, a notice giving particulars of that article or substance sufficient to identify it and stating that he has taken possession of it under that power; and before taking possession of any such substance under that power an inspector shall, if it is practicable for him to do so, take a sample thereof and give to a responsible person at the premises a portion of the sample marked in a manner sufficient to identify it.

(7) No answer given by a person in pursuance of a requirement imposed under subsection (2)(j) above shall be admissible in evidence against that person or the [spouse or civil partner] of that person in any proceedings.

(8) Nothing in this section shall be taken to compel the production by any person of a document of which he would on grounds of legal professional privilege be entitled to

withhold production on an order for discovery in an action in the High Court or, as the case may be, on an order for the production of documents in an action in the Court of Session. **[48]**

NOTES

Sub-s (7): words in square brackets substituted by the Civil Partnership Act 2004, s 261(1), Sch 27, para 49, as from 5 December 2005.

Regulations: the Ammonium Nitrate Materials (High Nitrogen Content) Safety Regulations 2003, SI 2003/1082.

21 Improvement notices

If an inspector is of the opinion that a person—

(a) is contravening one or more of the relevant statutory provisions; or

(b) has contravened one or more of those provisions in circumstances that make it likely that the contravention will continue or be repeated,

he may serve on him a notice (in this Part referred to as "an improvement notice") stating that he is of that opinion, specifying the provision or provisions as to which he is of that opinion, giving particulars of the reasons why he is of that opinion, and requiring that person to remedy the contravention or, as the case may be, the matters occasioning it within such period (ending not earlier than the period within which an appeal against the notice can be brought under section 24) as may be specified in the notice. **[49]**

22 Prohibition notices

(1) This section applies to any activities which are being or are [likely] to be carried on by or under the control of any person, being activities to or in relation to which any of the relevant statutory provisions apply or will, if the activities are so carried on, apply.

(2) If as regards any activities to which this section applies an inspector is of the opinion that, as carried on or [likely] to be carried on by or under the control of the person in question, the activities involve or, as the case may be, will involve a risk of serious personal injury, the inspector may serve on that person a notice (in this Part referred to as "a prohibition notice").

(3) A prohibition notice shall—

(a) state that the inspector is of the said opinion;

(b) specify the matters which in his opinion give or, as the case may be, will give rise to the said risk;

(c) where in his opinion any of those matters involves or, as the case may be, will involve a contravention of any of the relevant statutory provisions, state that he is of that opinion, specify the provision or provisions as to which he is of that opinion, and give particulars of the reasons why he is of that opinion; and

(d) direct that the activities to which the notice relates shall not be carried on by or under the control of the person on whom the notice is served unless the matters specified in the notice in pursuance of paragraph (b) above and any associated contraventions of provisions so specified in pursuance of paragraph (c) above have been remedied.

[(4) A direction contained in a prohibition notice in pursuance of subsection (3)(d) above shall take effect—

(a) at the end of the period specified in the notice; or

(b) if the notice so declares, immediately.] **[50]**

NOTES

Sub-ss (1), (2): words in square brackets substituted by the Consumer Protection Act 1987, s 36, Sch 3, para 2(a).

Sub-s (4): substituted by the Consumer Protection Act 1987, s 36, Sch 3, para 2(b).

23 Provisions supplementary to ss 21 and 22

(1) In this section "a notice" means an improvement notice or a prohibition notice.

(2) A notice may (but need not) include directions as to the measures to be taken to remedy any contravention or matter to which the notice relates; and any such directions—

(a) may be framed to any extent by reference to any approved code of practice; and

(b) may be framed so as to afford the person on whom the notice is served a choice between different ways of remedying the contravention or matter.

(3) Where any of the relevant statutory provisions applies to a building or any matter connected with a building and an inspector proposes to serve an improvement notice relating to a contravention of that provision in connection with that building or matter, the notice shall not direct any measures to be taken to remedy the contravention of that provision which are more onerous than those necessary to secure conformity with the requirements of any building regulations for the time being in force to which that building or matter would be required to conform if the relevant building were being newly erected unless the provision in question imposes specific requirements more onerous than the requirements of any such building regulations to which the building or matter would be required to conform as aforesaid.

In this subsection "the relevant building", in the case of a building, means that building, and, in the case of a matter connected with a building, means the building with which the matter is connected.

(4) Before an inspector serves in connection with any premises used or about to be used as a place of work a notice requiring or likely to lead to the taking of measures affecting the means of escape in case of fire with which the premises are or ought to be provided, he shall consult the [fire and rescue authority].

In this subsection "[fire and rescue authority]"[, in relation to premises, means—

(a) where the Regulatory Reform (Fire Safety) Order 2005 applies to the premises, the enforcing authority within the meaning given by article 25 of that Order;

(b) in any other case, the fire and rescue authority under the Fire and Rescue Services Act 2004 for the area where the premises are (or are to be) situated].

(5) Where an improvement notice or a prohibition notice which is not to take immediate effect has been served—

(a) the notice may be withdrawn by an inspector at any time before the end of the period specified therein in pursuance of section 21 or section 22(4) as the case may be; and

(b) the period so specified may be extended or further extended by an inspector at any time when an appeal against the notice is not pending.

(6) In the application of this section to Scotland—

(a) in subsection (3) for the words from "with the requirements" to "aforesaid" there shall be substituted the words—

"(a) to any provisions of the building standards regulations to which that building or matter would be required to conform if the relevant building were being newly erected; or

(b) where the sheriff, on an appeal to him under section 16 of the Building (Scotland) Act 1959—

(i) against an order under section 10 of that Act requiring the execution of operations necessary to make the building or matter conform to the building standards regulations, or

(ii) against an order under section 11 of that Act requiring the building or matter to conform to a provision of such regulations,

has varied the order, to any provisions of the building standards regulations referred to in paragraph (a) above as affected by the order as so varied,

unless the relevant statutory provision imposes specific requirements more onerous than the requirements of any provisions of building standards regulations as aforesaid or, as the case may be, than the requirements of the order as varied by the sheriff.";

(b) after subsection (5) there shall be inserted the following subsection—

"(5A) In subsection (3) above "building standards regulations" has the same meaning as in section 3 of the Building (Scotland) Act 1959.".

[51]

NOTES

Sub-s (4): words in first and second pairs of square brackets substituted, in relation to England and Wales only, by the Fire and Rescue Services Act 2004, s 53(1), Sch 1, para 44, as from 1 October 2004 (in relation to England), and as from 10 November 2004 (in relation to Wales); words in third pair of square brackets substituted, in relation to England and Wales only, by the Regulatory Reform (Fire Safety) Order 2005, SI 2005/1541, art 53(1), Sch 2, para 9 as from 6 April 2006. Note that this subsection has also been amended, in relation to Scotland only, by the Fire (Scotland) Act 2005 (Consequential Modifications and Amendments) Order 2005, SSI 2005/383, art 2(1), Sch 1, para 4 (as from 2 August 2005), and by the Fire (Scotland) Act 2005 (Consequential Modifications and Savings) Order 2006, SSI 2006/475, art 2(1), Sch 1, para 6 (as from 1 October 2006). In relation to Scotland, this subsection now reads as follows—

"(4) Before an inspector serves in connection with any premises used or about to be used as a place of work a notice requiring or likely to lead to the taking of measures affecting the means of escape in case of fire with which the premises are or ought to be provided, he shall consult—

[(a) where Part 3 of the Fire (Scotland) Act 2005 (asp 5) applies in relation to the premises, the enforcing authority (as defined in section 61(9) of that Act);

(b) in any other case, the relevant authority (as defined in section 6 of that Act) for the area where the premises are (or are to be) situated.]".

24 Appeal against improvement or prohibition notice

(1) In this section "a notice" means an improvement notice or a prohibition notice.

(2) A person on whom a notice is served may within such period from the date of its service as may be prescribed appeal to an [employment tribunal]; and on such an appeal the tribunal may either cancel or affirm the notice and, if it affirms it, may do so either in its original form or with such modifications as the tribunal may in the circumstances think fit.

(3) Where an appeal under this section is brought against a notice within the period allowed under the preceding subsection, then—

(a) in the case of an improvement notice, the bringing of the appeal shall have the effect of suspending the operation of the notice until the appeal is finally disposed of or, if the appeal is withdrawn, until the withdrawal of the appeal;

(b) in the case of a prohibition notice, the bringing of the appeal shall have the like effect if, but only if, on the application of the appellant the tribunal so directs (and then only from the giving of the direction).

(4) One or more assessors may be appointed for the purposes of any proceedings brought before an [employment tribunal] under this section.

[52]

NOTES

Sub-ss (2), (4): words in square brackets substituted by the Employment Rights (Dispute Resolution) Act 1998, s 1(2)(a).

Regulations: the Employment Tribunals (Constitution and Rules of Procedure) Regulations 2004, SI 2004/1861 at **[3151]**. For the procedure on appeal, including the time limit prescribed for the purpose of sub-s (2), see reg 16(3)(b) of, and Sch 4 to, those Regulations at **[3166]** and **[3174]**.

25 Power to deal with cause of imminent danger

(1) Where, in the case of any article or substance found by him in any premises which he has power to enter, an inspector has reasonable cause to believe that, in the circumstances in which he finds it, the article or substance is a cause of imminent danger of serious personal injury, he may seize it and cause it to be rendered harmless (whether by destruction or otherwise).

(2) Before there is rendered harmless under this section—

(a) any article that forms part of a batch of similar articles; or

(b) any substance,

the inspector shall, if it is practicable for him to do so, take a sample thereof and give to a responsible person at the premises where the article or substance was found by him a portion of the sample marked in a manner sufficient to identify it.

(3) As soon as may be after any article or substance has been seized and rendered harmless under this section, the inspector shall prepare and sign a written report giving particulars of the circumstances in which the article or substance was seized and so dealt with by him, and shall—

(a) give a signed copy of the report to a responsible person at the premises where the article or substance was found by him; and

(b) unless that person is the owner of the article or substance, also serve a signed copy of the report on the owner;

and if, where paragraph (b) above applies, the inspector cannot after reasonable enquiry ascertain the name or address of the owner, the copy may be served on him by giving it to the person to whom a copy was given under the preceding paragraph.

[53]

[25A Power of customs officer to detain articles and substances

(1) A customs officer may, for the purpose of facilitating the exercise or performance by any enforcing authority or inspector of any of the powers or duties of the authority or inspector under any of the relevant statutory provisions, seize any imported article or imported substance and detain it for not more than two working days.

(2) Anything seized and detained under this section shall be dealt with during the period of its detention in such manner as the Commissioners of Customs and Excise may direct.

(3) In subsection (1) above the reference to two working days is a reference to a period of forty-eight hours calculated from the time when the goods in question are seized but disregarding so much of any period as falls on a Saturday or Sunday or on Christmas Day, Good Friday or a day which is a bank holiday under the Banking and Financial Dealings Act 1971 in the part of Great Britain where the goods are seized.]

[54]

NOTES

Inserted by the Consumer Protection Act 1987, s 36, Sch 3, para 3.

Commissioners of Customs and Excise: a reference to the Commissioners of Customs and Excise is now to be taken as a reference to the Commissioners for Her Majesty's Revenue and Customs; see the Commissioners for Revenue and Customs Act 2005, s 50(1), (7).

26 Power of enforcing authorities to indemnify their inspectors

Where an action has been brought against an inspector in respect of an act done in the execution or purported execution of any of the relevant statutory provisions and the circumstances are such that he is not legally entitled to require the enforcing authority which appointed him to indemnify him, that authority may, nevertheless, indemnify him against the whole or part of any damages and costs or expenses which he may have been ordered to pay or may have incurred, if the authority is satisfied that he honestly believed that the act complained of was within his powers and that his duty as an inspector required or entitled him to do it.

[55]

Obtaining and disclosure of information

27 Obtaining of information by … the Executive, enforcing authorities etc

(1) For the purpose of obtaining—

(a) any information which [the Executive] needs for the discharge of its functions; or

(b) any information which an enforcing authority needs for the discharge of the authority's functions,

[the Executive] may, with the consent of the Secretary of State, serve on any person a notice requiring that person to furnish to [the Executive] or, as the case may be, to the enforcing authority in question such information about such matters as may be specified in the notice, and to do so in such form and manner and within such time as may be so specified.

In this subsection "consent" includes a general consent extending to cases of any stated description.

(2) Nothing in section 9 of the Statistics of Trade Act 1947 (which restricts the disclosure of information obtained under that Act) shall prevent or penalise—

(a) the disclosure by a Minister of the Crown to … the Executive of information obtained under that Act about any undertaking within the meaning of that Act, being information consisting of the names and addresses of the persons carrying on the undertaking, the nature of the undertaking's activities, the numbers of persons of different descriptions who work in the undertaking, the addresses or places where activities of the undertaking are or were carried on, the nature of the activities carried on there, or the numbers of persons of different descriptions who work or worked in the undertaking there; …

(b) …

[(3) In the preceding subsection, any reference to a Minister of the Crown or the Executive includes respectively a reference to an officer of that person or of that body and also, in the case of a reference to the Executive, includes a reference to—

(a) a person performing any functions of the Executive on its behalf by virtue of section 13(3);

(b) an officer of a body which is so performing any such functions; and

(c) an adviser appointed under section 13(7).]

(4) A person to whom information is disclosed in pursuance of subsection (2) above shall not use the information for a purpose other than a purpose … of the Executive.

[56]

NOTES

Sub-s (1): words in square brackets substituted by the Legislative Reform (Health and Safety Executive) Order 2008, SI 2008/960, arts 3, 11(1), (2), as from 1 April 2008 (for transitional provisions in relation to the abolition of the Health and Safety Commission and the Health and Safety Executive and their replacement with a single Health and Safety Executive, see art 21 of, and Sch 2 to, that Order at **[3474N]**, **[3474O]**).

Sub-s (2): first words omitted repealed by SI 2008/960, arts 3, 11(1), (3), as from 1 April 2008 (for transitional provisions see the note above); other words omitted repealed by the Employment Act 1989, s 29(3), (4), Sch 6, para 10, Sch 7, Pt I.

Sub-s (3): substituted by SI 2008/960, arts 3, 11(1), (4), as from 1 April 2008 (for transitional provisions see the note above).

Sub-s (4): words omitted repealed by SI 2008/960, arts 3, 11(1), (5), as from 1 April 2008 (for transitional provisions see the note above).

Note: the Legislative Reform (Health and Safety Executive) Order 2008, SI 2008/960 does not amend the title of this section. However, in light of the other amendments made by that Order, and in light of the abolition of the HSC by art 2 of that Order, the title of this section has been changed from "Obtaining of information by the Commission, the Executive, enforcing authorities etc" to "Obtaining of information by the Executive, enforcing authorities etc".

[[27A Information communicated by Commissioners for Revenue and Customs]

(1) If they think it appropriate to do so for the purpose of facilitating the exercise or performance by any person to whom subsection (2) below applies of any of that person's powers or duties under any of the relevant statutory provisions, [the Commissioners for Her Majesty's Revenue and Custom] may authorise the disclosure to that person of any information obtained [or held] for the purposes of the exercise [by Her Majesty's Revenue and Customs] of their functions in relation to imports.

(2) This subsection applies to an enforcing authority and to an inspector.

(3) A disclosure of information made to any person under subsection (1) above shall be made in such manner as may be directed by [the Commissioners for Her Majesty's Revenue and Customs] and may be made through such persons acting on behalf of that person as may be so directed.

(4) Information may be disclosed to a person under subsection (1) above whether or not the disclosure of the information has been requested by or on behalf of that person.]

[57]

NOTES

Inserted by the Consumer Protection Act 1987, s 36, Sch 3, para 4.

Section heading: substituted by the Commissioners for Revenue and Customs Act 2005, s 50(6), Sch 4, para 18(1), (4), as from 18 April 2005.

Sub-s (1): words in first and third pairs of square brackets substituted, and words in second pair of square brackets inserted, by the Commissioners for Revenue and Customs Act 2005, s 50(6), Sch 4, para 18(1), (2), as from 18 April 2005.

Sub-s (3): words in square brackets substituted by the Commissioners for Revenue and Customs Act 2005, s 50(6), Sch 4, para 18(1), (3), as from 18 April 2005.

28 Restrictions on disclosure of information

(1) In this and the two following subsections—

(a) "relevant information" means information obtained by a person under section 27(1) or furnished to any person [under section 27A above[, by virtue of section 43A(6) below] or] in pursuance of a requirement imposed by any of the relevant statutory provisions; and

(b) "the recipient", in relation to any relevant information, means the person by whom that information was so obtained or to whom that information was so furnished, as the case may be.

(2) Subject to the following subsection, no relevant information shall be disclosed without the consent of the person by whom it was furnished.

(3) The preceding subsection shall not apply to—

(a) disclosure of information to ... the Executive, [the Environment Agency, the Scottish Environment Protection Agency,] a government department or any enforcing authority;

(b) without prejudice to paragraph (a) above, disclosure by the recipient of information to any person for the purpose of any function conferred on the recipient by or under any of the relevant statutory provisions;

(c) without prejudice to paragraph (a) above, disclosure by the recipient of information to—

(i) an officer of a local authority who is authorised by that authority to receive it,

[(ii) an officer ... of a water undertaker, sewerage undertaker, water authority or water development board who is authorised by that ... undertaker, authority or board to receive it,]

(iii) ...

(iv) a constable authorised by a chief officer of police to receive it;

(d) disclosure by the recipient of information in a form calculated to prevent it from being identified as relating to a particular person or case;

(e) disclosure of information for the purposes of any legal proceedings or any investigation or inquiry held by virtue of [section 14(2) or (2A)], or for the purposes of a report of any such proceedings or inquiry or of a special report made by virtue of [section 14(2) or (2A)];

[(f) any other disclosure of information by the recipient, if—

(i) the recipient is, or is acting on behalf of a person who is, a public authority for the purposes of the Freedom of Information Act 2000, and

(ii) the information is not held by the authority on behalf of another person].

[(4) In the preceding subsection, any reference to the Executive, the Environment Agency, the Scottish Environment Protection Agency, a government department or an enforcing authority includes respectively a reference to an officer of that body or authority (including, in the case of an enforcing authority, any inspector appointed by it), and also, in the case of a reference to the Executive, includes a reference to—

(a) a person performing any functions of the Executive on its behalf by virtue of section 13(3);

(b) an officer of a body which is so performing any such functions; and

(c) an adviser appointed under section 13(7).]

(5) A person to whom information is disclosed in pursuance of [any of paragraphs (a) to (e) of] subsection (3) above shall not use the information for a purpose other than—

(a) in a case falling within paragraph (a) of that subsection, a purpose ... of the Executive or [of the Environment Agency or of the Scottish Environment Protection Agency or] of the government department in question, or the purposes of the enforcing authority in question in connection with the relevant statutory provisions, as the case may be;

(b) in the case of information given to an officer of a [body which is a local authority, ... a water undertaker, a sewerage undertaker, a water authority, a river purification board or a water development board, the purposes of the body] in connection with the relevant statutory provisions or any enactment whatsoever relating to public health, public safety or the protection of the environment;

(c) in the case of information given to a constable, the purposes of the police in connection with the relevant statutory provisions or any enactment whatsoever relating to public health, public safety or the safety of the State.

[(6) References in subsections (3) and (5) above to a local authority include ... a joint authority established by Part IV of the Local Government Act 1985[, an authority established for an area in England by an order under section 207 of the Local Government and Public Involvement in Health Act 2007 (joint waste authorities)] [and the London Fire and Emergency Planning Authority].]

(7) A person shall not disclose any information obtained by him as a result of the exercise of any power conferred by section 14(4)(a) or 20 (including, in particular, any information with respect to any trade secret obtained by him in any premises entered by him by virtue of any such power) except—

(a) for the purposes of his functions; or

(b) for the purposes of any legal proceedings or any investigation or inquiry held by virtue of [section 14(2) or (2A)] or for the purposes of a report of any such proceedings or inquiry or of a special report made by virtue of [section 14(2) or (2A)]; or

(c) with the relevant consent.

In this subsection "the relevant consent" means, in the case of information furnished in pursuance of a requirement imposed under section 20, the consent of the person who furnished it, and, in any other case, the consent of a person having responsibilities in relation to the premises where the information was obtained.

(8) Notwithstanding anything in the preceding subsection an inspector shall, in circumstances in which it is necessary to do so for the purpose of assisting in keeping persons (or the representatives of persons) employed at any premises adequately informed about matters affecting their health, safety and welfare, give to such persons or their representatives the following descriptions of information, that is to say—

(a) factual information obtained by him as mentioned in that subsection which relates to those premises or anything which was or is therein or was or is being done therein; and

(b) information with respect to any action which he has taken or proposes to take in or in connection with those premises in the performance of his functions;

and, where an inspector does as aforesaid, he shall give the like information to the employer of the first-mentioned persons.

[(9) Notwithstanding anything in subsection (7) above, a person who has obtained such information as is referred to in that subsection may furnish to a person who appears to him to be likely to be a party to any civil proceedings arising out of any accident, occurrence, situation or other matter, a written statement of relevant facts observed by him in the course of exercising any of the powers referred to in that subsection.]

[(9A) Subsection (7) above does not apply if—

(a) the person who has obtained any such information as is referred to in that subsection is, or is acting on behalf of a person who is, a public authority for the purposes of the Freedom of Information Act 2000, and

(b) the information is not held by the authority on behalf of another person.]

[(10) The Broads Authority and every National Park authority shall be deemed to be local authorities for the purposes of this section.]

[58]

NOTES

Sub-s (1): words in first (outer) pair of square brackets inserted by the Consumer Protection Act 1987, s 36, Sch 3, para 5; words in second (inner) pair of square brackets inserted by the Railways and Transport Safety Act 2003, s 105(2), as from 10 September 2003.

Sub-s (3) is amended as follows:

Words omitted from para (a) repealed by the Legislative Reform (Health and Safety Executive) Order 2008, SI 2008/960, arts 3, 12(1), (2)(a), as from 1 April 2008 (for transitional provisions in relation to the abolition of the Health and Safety Commission and the Health and Safety Executive and their replacement with a single Health and Safety Executive, see art 21 of, and Sch 2 to, that Order at **[3474N]**, **[3474O]**).

Words in square brackets in para (a) inserted by the Environment Act 1995, s 120(1), (3), Sch 22, para 30(1), (6)(a).

Para (c)(ii) substituted by the Water Act 1989, s 190, Sch 25, para 46, in relation to England and Wales only; words omitted from that paragraph repealed by the Environment Act 1995, s 120(1), (3), Sch 22, para 30(1), (6)(b).

Para (c)(ii), as it applies to Scotland, was substituted by the Environment Act 1995, s 120(1), (3), Sch 22, para 30(1), (6)(c), and further amended by the Water Industry (Scotland) Act 2002 (Consequential Modifications) Order 2004, SI 2004/1822, art 2, Schedule, Pt 1, para 8(a), as from 14 July 2004, and now reads as follows—

"(ii) an officer of a water undertaker, sewerage undertaker [or Scottish Water] who is authorised by [that undertaker or, as the case may be, Scottish Water] to receive it,".

Para (c)(iii) repealed by the Environment Act 1995, s 120(1), (3), Sch 22, para 30(1), (6)(d).

Words in square brackets in para (e) substituted by SI 2008/960, arts 3, 12(1), (2)(b), as from 1 April 2008 (for transitional provisions see the note above).

Para (f) added by the Freedom of Information (Removal and Relaxation of Statutory Prohibitions on Disclosure of Information) Order 2004, SI 2004/3363, art 5(1), (2), as from 1 January 2005.

Sub-s (4): substituted by SI 2008/960, arts 3, 12(1), (3), as from 1 April 2008 (for transitional provisions see the note above).

Sub-s (5) is amended as follows:

Words in first pair of square brackets inserted by SI 2004/3363, art 5(1), (3), as from 1 January 2005.

Words omitted from para (a) repealed by SI 2008/960, arts 3, 12(1), (4), as from 1 April 2008 (for transitional provisions see the note above).

Words in square brackets in para (a) inserted by the Environment Act 1995, s 120(1), (3), Sch 22, para 30(1), (6)(f).

Words in square brackets in para (b) substituted by the Water Act 1989, s 190, Sch 25, para 46; words omitted from that paragraph repealed by the Environment Act 1995, s 120(1), (3), Sch 22, para 30(6)(f).

The words from the beginning of para (b) to "in connection" were substituted by the Environment Act 1995, s 120(1), (3), Sch 22, para 30(1), (6)(f), in relation to Scotland only, and that paragraph was further amended (in relation to Scotland only) by SI 2004/1822, art 2, Schedule, Pt 1, para 8(b), as from 14 July 2004. Para (b), as it applies to Scotland, now reads as follows—

"(b) [in the case of information given to an officer of a body which is a local authority, a water undertaker [or a sewerage undertaker or to an officer of Scottish Water,] the purposes of the [authority, undertaker or, as the case may be, Scottish Water] in connection] with the relevant statutory provisions or any enactment whatsoever relating to public health, public safety or the protection of the environment;".

Sub-s (6): substituted by the Local Government Act 1985, s 84, Sch 14, para 52; words omitted repealed by the Education Reform Act 1988, s 237, Sch 13, Pt I; words in first pair of square brackets inserted by the Local Government and Public Involvement in Health Act 2007, s 209(2), Sch 13, Pt 2, para 32, as from 1 April 2008; words in second pair of square brackets added by the Greater London Authority Act 1999, s 328(8), Sch 29, Pt I, para 23.

Sub-s (7): words in square brackets substituted by SI 2008/960, arts 3, 12(1), (5), as from 1 April 2008 (for transitional provisions see the note above).

Sub-s (9): inserted by the Employment Protection Act 1975, s 116, Sch 15, para 9.

Sub-s (9A): inserted by SI 2004/3363, art 5(1), (4), as from 1 January 2005.

Sub-s (10): inserted by the Norfolk and Suffolk Broads Act 1988, s 21, Sch 6, para 13; substituted by the Environment Act 1995, s 78, Sch 10, para 12.

Disclosure: sub-s (7) has effect in relation to the disclosure of information by or on behalf of a public authority as if the purposes for which disclosure is authorised included the purposes mentioned in the Anti-terrorism, Crime and Security Act 2001, s 17; see Sch 4, Pt 1 to that Act.

29–32 *(Repealed by the Employment Protection Act 1975, ss 116, 125(3), Sch 15, para 10, Sch 18.)*

Provisions as to offences

33 Offences

(1) It is an offence for a person—

(a) to fail to discharge a duty to which he is subject by virtue of sections 2 to 7;

(b) to contravene section 8 or 9;

(c) to contravene any health and safety regulations ... or any requirement or prohibition imposed under any such regulations (including any requirement or prohibition to which he is subject by virtue of the terms of or any condition or restriction attached to any licence, approval, exemption or other authority issued, given or granted under the regulations);

(d) to contravene any requirement imposed by or under regulations under section 14 or intentionally to obstruct any person in the exercise of his powers under that section;

(e) to contravene any requirement imposed by an inspector under section 20 or 25;

(f) to prevent or attempt to prevent any other person from appearing before an inspector or from answering any question to which an inspector may by virtue of section 20(2) require an answer;

(g) to contravene any requirement or prohibition imposed by an improvement notice or a prohibition notice (including any such notice as modified on appeal);

(h) intentionally to obstruct an inspector in the exercise or performance of his powers or duties [or to obstruct a customs officer in the exercise of his powers under section 25A];

(i) to contravene any requirement imposed by a notice under section 27(1);

(j) to use or disclose any information in contravention of section 27(4) or 28;

(k) to make a statement which he knows to be false or recklessly to make a statement which is false where the statement is made—

(i) in purported compliance with a requirement to furnish any information imposed by or under any of the relevant statutory provisions; or

(ii) for the purpose of obtaining the issue of a document under any of the relevant statutory provisions to himself or another person;

(l) intentionally to make a false entry in any register, book, notice or other document required by or under any of the relevant statutory provisions to be kept, served or given or, with intent to deceive, to made use of any such entry which he knows to be false;

(m) with intent to deceive, to … use a document issued or authorised to be issued under any of the relevant statutory provisions or required for any purpose thereunder or to make or have in his possession a document so closely resembling any such document as to be calculated to deceive;

(n) falsely to pretend to be an inspector;

(o) to fail to comply with an order made by a court under section 42.

[(1A) Subject to any provision made by virtue of section 15(6)(d), a person guilty of an offence under subsection (1)(a) above consisting of failing to discharge a duty to which he is subject by virtue of sections 2 to 6 shall be liable—

(a) on summary conviction, to a fine not exceeding £20,000;

(b) on conviction on indictment, to a fine.]

(2) A person guilty of an offence under paragraph (d), (f), (h) or (n) of subsection (1) above, or of an offence under paragraph (e) of that subsection consisting of contravening a requirement imposed by an inspector under section 20, shall be liable on summary conviction to a fine not exceeding [level 5 on the standard scale];

[(2A) A person guilty of an offence under subsection (1)(g) or (o) above shall be liable—

(a) on summary conviction, to imprisonment for a term not exceeding six months, or a fine not exceeding £20,000, or both;

(b) on conviction on indictment, to imprisonment for a term not exceeding two years, or a fine, or both.]

(3) Subject to any provision made by virtue of section 15(6)(d) [or (e)] or by virtue of paragraph 2(2) of Schedule 3, a person guilty of [an offence under subsection (1) above not falling within subsection (1A), (2) or (2A) above], or of an offence under any of the existing statutory provisions, being an offence for which no other penalty is specified, shall be liable—

(a) on summary conviction, to a fine not exceeding [the prescribed sum];

(b) on conviction on indictment—

(i) if the offence is one to which this sub-paragraph applies, to imprisonment for a term not exceeding two years, or a fine, or both;

(ii) if the offence is not one to which the preceding sub-paragraph applies, to a fine.

(4) Subsection (3)(b)(i) above applies to the following offences—

(a) an offence consisting of contravening any of the relevant statutory provisions by doing otherwise than under the authority of a licence issued by the Executive … something for the doing of which such a licence is necessary under the relevant statutory provisions;

(b) an offence consisting of contravening a term of or a condition or restriction attached to any such licence as is mentioned in the preceding paragraph;

(c) an offence consisting of acquiring or attempting to acquire, possessing or using an explosive article or substance (within the meaning of any of the relevant statutory provisions) in contravention of any of the relevant statutory provisions;

(d) …

(e) an offence under subsection (1)(j) above.

(5), (6) …

[59]

NOTES

Sub-s (1): words omitted from para (c) repealed by the Employment Protection Act 1975, ss 116, 125(3), Sch 15, para 11, Sch 18; words in square brackets in para (h) added by the Consumer Protection Act 1987, s 36, Sch 3, para 6; words omitted from para (m) repealed by the Forgery and Counterfeiting Act 1981, s 30, Schedule, Pt I.

Sub-ss (1A), (2A): inserted by the Offshore Safety Act 1992, s 4(2), (3), (6).

Sub-s (2): maximum fine increased by the Criminal Law Act 1977, s 31, Sch 6, and converted to a level on the standard scale by the Criminal Justice Act 1982, ss 37, 46 (for England and Wales) and the Criminal Procedure (Consequential Provisions) (Scotland) Act 1995, s 3(2), Sch 2 (for Scotland).

Sub-s (3): words in first pair of square brackets inserted, and words in second pair of square brackets substituted, by the Offshore Safety Act 1992, s 4(4), (6); words in third pair of square brackets substituted by the Magistrates' Courts Act 1980, s 32(2).

Sub-s (4): words omitted from para (a) repealed by the Employment Protection Act 1975, ss 116, 125(3), Sch 15, para 11, Sch 18; para (d) repealed by the Offshore Safety Act 1992, ss 4(5), (6), 7(2), Sch 2.

Sub-s (5): repealed by the Offshore Safety Act 1992, ss 4(5), (6), 7(2), Sch 2.

Sub-s (6): repealed by the Forgery and Counterfeiting Act 1981, s 30, Schedule, Pt I.

34 Extension of time for bringing summary proceedings

(1) Where—

(a) a special report on any matter to which section 14 of this Act applies is made by virtue of subsection [(2)] of that section; or

(b) a report is made by the person holding an inquiry into any such matter by virtue of subsection [(2A)]) of that section; or

(c) a coroner's inquest is held touching the death of any person whose death may have been caused by an accident which happened while he was at work or by a disease which he contracted or probably contracted at work or by any accident, act or omission which occurred in connection with the work of any person whatsoever; or

(d) a public inquiry into any death that may have been so caused is held under the Fatal Accidents Inquiry (Scotland) Act 1895 or the Fatal Accidents and Sudden Deaths Inquiry (Scotland) Act 1906,

and it appears from the report or, in a case falling within paragraph (c) or (d) above, from the proceedings at the inquest or inquiry, that any of the relevant statutory provisions was contravened at a time which is material in relation to the subject-matter of the report, inquest or inquiry, summary proceedings against any person liable to be proceeded against in respect of the contravention may be commenced at any time within three months of the making of the report or, in a case falling within paragraph (c) or (d) above, within three months of the conclusion of the inquest or inquiry.

(2) Where an offence under any of the relevant statutory provisions is committed by reason of a failure to do something at or within a time fixed by or under any of those provisions, the offence shall be deemed to continue until that thing is done.

(3) Summary proceedings for an offence to which this subsection applies may be commenced at any time within six months from the date on which there comes to the knowledge of a responsible enforcing authority evidence sufficient in the opinion of that authority to justify a prosecution for that offence; and for the purposes of this subsection—

(a) a certificate of an enforcing authority stating that such evidence came to its knowledge on a specified date shall be conclusive evidence of that fact; and

(b) a document purporting to be such a certificate and to be signed by or on behalf of the enforcing authority in question shall be presumed to be such a certificate unless the contrary is proved.

(4) The preceding subsection applies to any offence under any of the relevant statutory provisions which a person commits by virtue of any provision or requirement to which he is subject as the designer, manufacturer, importer or supplier of any thing; and in that subsection "responsible enforcing authority" means an enforcing authority within whose field of responsibility the offence in question lies, whether by virtue of section 35 or otherwise.

(5) In the application of subsection (3) above to Scotland—

(a) for the words from "there comes" to "that offence" there shall be substituted the words "evidence, sufficient in the opinion of the enforcing authority to justify a report to the Lord Advocate with a view to consideration of the question of prosecution, comes to the knowledge of the authority";

(b) at the end of paragraph (b) there shall be added the words "and

(c) [section 331(3) of the Criminal Procedure (Scotland) Act 1975] (date of commencement of proceedings) shall have effect as it has effect for the purposes of that section".

[(6) In the application of subsection (4) above to Scotland, after the words "applies to" there shall be inserted the words "any offence under section 33(1)(c) above where the health and safety regulations concerned were made for the general purpose mentioned in section 18(1) of the Gas Act 1986 and".]

[60]

NOTES

Sub-s (1): figures in square brackets substituted by the Legislative Reform (Health and Safety Executive) Order 2008, SI 2008/960, arts 3, 13, as from 1 April 2008 (for transitional provisions in relation to the abolition of the Health and Safety Commission and the Health and Safety Executive and their replacement with a single Health and Safety Executive, see art 21 of, and Sch 2 to, that Order at **[3474N]**, **[3474O]**).

Sub-s (5): words in square brackets in para (b) substituted by the Criminal Procedure (Scotland) Act 1975, s 461(1), Sch 9, para 51.

Sub-s (6): added by the Gas Act 1986, s 67(1), Sch 7, para 18.

Criminal Procedure (Scotland) Act 1975: repealed by Criminal Procedure (Consequential Provisions) (Scotland) Act 1995, s 6, Sch 5. S 331 of the 1975 Act is replaced by s 136 of the Criminal Procedure (Scotland) Act 1995.

Fatal Accidents and Sudden Deaths Inquiry (Scotland) Act 1906; Fatal Accidents Inquiry (Scotland) Act 1895: repealed by the Fatal Accidents and Sudden Deaths Inquiry (Scotland) Act 1976, s 8(2), Sch 2.

Gas Act 1986, s 18(1): repealed by the Offshore Safety Act 1992, ss 3(3)(a), 7(2), Sch 2.

35 Venue

An offence under any of the relevant statutory provisions committed in connection with any plant or substance may, if necessary for the purpose of bringing the offence within the field of responsibility of any enforcing authority or conferring jurisdiction on any court to entertain proceedings for the offence, be treated as having been committed at the place where that plant or substance is for the time being.

[61]

36 Offences due to fault of other person

(1) Where the commission by any person of an offence under any of the relevant statutory provisions is due to the act or default of some other person, that other person shall be guilty of the offence, and a person may be charged with and convicted of the offence by virtue of this subsection whether or not proceedings are taken against the first-mentioned person.

(2) Where there would be or have been the commission of an offence under section 33 by the Crown but for the circumstance that that section does not bind the Crown, and that fact is due to the act or default of a person other than the Crown, that person shall be guilty of the offence which, but for that circumstance, the Crown would be committing or would have committed, and may be charged with and convicted of that offence accordingly.

(3) The preceding provisions of this section are subject to any provision made by virtue of section 15(6).

[62]

NOTES

The Crown: references to the Crown in this section shall be treated as including the Assembly Commission; see the National Assembly for Wales Commission (Crown Status) (No 2) Order 2007, SI 2007/1353, art 2.

37 Offences by bodies corporate

(1) Where an offence under any of the relevant statutory provisions committed by a body corporate is proved to have been committed with the consent or connivance of, or to have been attributable to any neglect on the part of, any director, manager, secretary or other similar officer of the body corporate or a person who was purporting to act in any such capacity, he as well as the body corporate shall be guilty of that offence and shall be liable to be proceeded against and punished accordingly.

(2) Where the affairs of a body corporate are managed by its members, the preceding subsection shall apply in relation to the acts and defaults of a member in connection with his functions of management as if he were a director of the body corporate.

[63]

38 Restriction on institution of proceedings in England and Wales

Proceedings for an offence under any of the relevant statutory provisions shall not, in England and Wales, be instituted except by an inspector or [the Environment Agency or] by or with the consent of the Director of Public Prosecutions.

[64]

NOTES

Words in square brackets inserted by the Environment Act 1995, s 120(1), Sch 22, para 30(1), (7).

39 Prosecutions by inspectors

(1) An inspector, if authorised in that behalf by the enforcing authority which appointed him, may, although not of counsel or a solicitor, prosecute before a magistrates' court proceedings for an offence under any of the relevant statutory provisions.

(2) This section shall not apply to Scotland.

[65]

40 Onus of proving limits of what is practicable etc

In any proceedings for an offence under any of the relevant statutory provisions consisting of a failure to comply with a duty or requirement to do something so far as is practicable or so far as is reasonably practicable, or to use the best practicable means to do something, it shall be for the accused to prove (as the case may be) that it was not practicable or not reasonably practicable to do more than was in fact done to satisfy the duty or requirement, or that there was no better practicable means than was in fact used to satisfy the duty or requirement.

[66]

41 Evidence

(1) Where an entry is required by any of the relevant statutory provisions to be made in any register or other record, the entry, if made, shall, as against the person by or on whose behalf it was made, be admissible as evidence or in Scotland sufficient evidence of the facts stated therein.

(2) Where an entry which is so required to be so made with respect to the observance of any of the relevant statutory provisions has not been made, that fact shall be admissible as evidence or in Scotland sufficient evidence that that provision has not been observed.

[67]

42 Power of court to order cause of offence to be remedied or, in certain cases, forfeiture

(1) Where a person is convicted of an offence under any of the relevant statutory provisions in respect of any matters which appear to the court to be matters which it is in his power to remedy, the court may, in addition to or instead of imposing any punishment, order him, within such time as may be fixed by the order, to take such steps as may be specified in the order for remedying the said matters.

(2) The time fixed by an order under subsection (1) above may be extended or further extended by order of the court on an application made before the end of that time as originally fixed or as extended under this subsection, as the case may be.

(3) Where a person is ordered under subsection (1) above to remedy any matters, that person shall not be liable under any of the relevant statutory provisions in respect of those matters in so far as they continue during the time fixed by the order or any further time allowed under subsection (2) above.

(4) Subject to the following subsection, the court by or before which a person is convicted of an offence such as is mentioned in section 33(4)(c) in respect of any such explosive article or substance as is there mentioned may order the article or substance in question to be forfeited and either destroyed or dealt with in such other manner as the court may order.

(5) The court shall not order anything to be forfeited under the preceding subsection where a person claiming to be the owner of or otherwise interested in it applies to be heard by the court, unless an opportunity has been given to him to show cause why the order should not be made.

[68]

Financial provisions

43 Financial provisions

(1) It shall be the duty of the Secretary of State to pay to [the Executive] such sums as are approved by the Treasury and as he considers appropriate for the purpose of enabling [the Executive] to perform its functions; …

(2) Regulations may provide for such fees as may be fixed by or determined under the regulations to be payable for or in connection with the performance by or on behalf of any authority to which this subsection applies of any function conferred on that authority by or under any of the relevant statutory provisions.

(3) Subsection (2) above applies to the following authorities, namely … the Executive, the Secretary of State, … every enforcing authority, and any other person on whom any function is conferred by or under any of the relevant statutory provisions.

(4) Regulations under this section may specify the person by whom any fee payable under the regulations is to be paid; but no such fee shall be made payable by a person in any of the following capacities, namely an employee, a person seeking employment, a person training for employment, and a person seeking training for employment.

(5) Without prejudice to section 82(3), regulations under this section may fix or provide for the determination of different fees in relation to different functions, or in relation to the same function in different circumstances.

[(6) The power to make regulations under this section shall be exercisable by the Secretary of State …]

(7) …

(8) In subsection (4) above the references to a person training for employment and a person seeking training for employment shall include respectively a person attending an industrial rehabilitation course provided by virtue of the Employment and Training Act 1973 and a person seeking to attend such a course.

(9) For the purposes of this section the performance by an inspector of his functions shall be treated as the performance by the enforcing authority which appointed him of functions conferred on that authority by or under any of the relevant statutory provisions.

[69]–[72]

NOTES

Sub-s (1): words in square brackets substituted, and words omitted repealed, by the Legislative Reform (Health and Safety Executive) Order 2008, SI 2008/960, arts 3, 14(a), as from 1 April 2008 (for transitional provisions in relation to the abolition of the Health and Safety Commission and the Health and Safety Executive and their replacement with a single Health and Safety Executive, see art 21 of, and Sch 2 to, that Order at **[3474N]**, **[3474O]**).

Sub-s (3): first words omitted repealed by SI 2008/960, arts 3, 14(b), as from 1 April 2008 (for transitional provisions see the note above); second words omitted repealed by the Employment Protection Act 1975, ss 116, 125(3), Sch 15, para 12, Sch 18.

Sub-s (6): substituted, for original sub-ss (6), (7), by the Employment Protection Act 1975, s 116, Sch 15, para 12; words omitted repealed by the Ministry of Agriculture, Fisheries and Food (Dissolution) Order 2002, SI 2002/794, art 5(2), Sch 2.

Fees: the current Regulations prescribing fees are the Health and Safety (Fees) Regulations 2008, SI 2008/736.

Regulations: other regulations made under this section are outside the scope of this work.

43A (*S 43A (Railway safety levy) outside the scope of this work.*)

Miscellaneous and supplementary

44, 45 (*S 44 (Appeals in connection with licensing provisions in the relevant statutory provisions), s 45 (Default powers) outside the scope of this work.*)

46 Service of notices

(1) Any notice required or authorised by any of the relevant statutory provisions to be served on or given to an inspector may be served or given by delivering it to him or by leaving it at, or sending it by post to, his office.

(2) Any such notice required or authorised to be served on or given to a person other than an inspector may be served or given by delivering it to him, or by leaving it at his proper address, or by sending it by post to him at that address.

(3) Any such notice may—

(a) in the case of a body corporate, be served on or given to the secretary or clerk of that body;

(b) in the case of a partnership, be served on or given to a partner or a person having the control or management of the partnership business or, in Scotland, the firm.

(4) For the purposes of this section and of section 26 of the Interpretation Act 1889 (service of documents by post) in its application to this section, the proper address of any person on or to whom any such notice is to be served or given shall be his last known address, except that—

(a) in the case of a body corporate or their secretary or clerk, it shall be the address of the registered or principal office of that body;

(b) in the case of a partnership or a person having the control or the management of the partnership business, it shall be the principal office of the partnership;

and for the purposes of this subsection the principal office of a company registered outside the United Kingdom or of a partnership carrying on business outside the United Kingdom shall be their principal office within the United Kingdom.

(5) If the person to be served with or given any such notice has specified an address within the United Kingdom other than his proper address within the meaning of subsection (4) above as the one at which he or someone on his behalf will accept notices of the same description as that notice, that address shall also be treated for the purposes of this section and section 26 of the Interpretation Act 1889 as his proper address.

(6) Without prejudice to any other provision of this section, any such notice required or authorised to be served on or given to the owner or occupier of any premises (whether a body corporate or not) may be served or given by sending it by post to him at those premises, or by addressing it by name to the person on or to whom it is to be served or given and delivering it to some responsible person who is or appears to be resident or employed in the premises.

(7) If the name or the address of any owner or occupier of premises on or to whom any such notice as aforesaid is to be served or given cannot after reasonable inquiry be ascertained, the notice may be served or given by addressing it to the person on or to whom it is to be served or given by the description of "owner" or "occupier" of the premises (describing them) to which the notice relates, and by delivering it to some responsible person who is or appears to be resident or employed in the premises, or, if there is no such person to whom it can be delivered, by affixing it or a copy of it to some conspicuous part of the premises.

(8) The preceding provisions of this section shall apply to the sending or giving of a document as they apply to the giving of a notice.

[73]

NOTES

Interpretation Act 1889, s 26: see now the Interpretation Act 1978, s 7, Sch 2, para 3.

47 Civil Liability

(1) Nothing in this Part shall be construed—

(a) as conferring a right of action in any civil proceedings in respect of any failure to comply with any duty imposed by sections 2 to 7 or any contravention of section 8; or

(b) as affecting the extent (if any) to which breach of a duty imposed by any of the existing statutory provisions is actionable; or

(c) as affecting the operation of section 12 of the Nuclear Installations Act 1965 (right to compensation by virtue of certain provisions of that Act).

(2) Breach of a duty imposed by health and safety regulations … shall, so far as it causes damage, be actionable except in so far as the regulations provide otherwise.

(3) No provision made by virtue of section 15(6)(b) shall afford a defence in any civil proceedings, whether brought by virtue of subsection (2) above or not; but as regards any duty

imposed as mentioned in subsection (2) above health and safety regulations … may provide for any defence specified in the regulations to be available in any action for breach of that duty.

(4) Subsections (1)(a) and (2) above are without prejudice to any right of action which exists apart from the provisions of this Act, and subsection (3) above is without prejudice to any defence which may be available apart from the provisions of the regulations there mentioned.

(5) Any term of an agreement which purports to exclude or restrict the operation of subsection (2) above, or any liability arising by virtue of that subsection shall be void, except in so far as health and safety regulations … provide otherwise.

(6) In this section "damage" includes the death of, or injury to, any person (including any disease and any impairment of a person's physical or mental condition).

[74]

NOTES

Sub-ss (2), (3), (5): words omitted repealed by the Employment Protection Act 1975, ss 116, 125(3), Sch 15, para 14, Sch 18.

48 Application to Crown

(1) Subject to the provisions of this section, the provisions of this Part, except sections 21 to 25 and 33 to 42, and of regulations made under this Part shall bind the Crown.

(2) Although they do not bind the Crown, sections 33 to 42 shall apply to persons in the public service of the Crown as they apply to other persons.

(3) For the purposes of this Part and regulations made thereunder persons in the service of the Crown shall be treated as employees of the Crown whether or not they would be so treated apart from this subsection.

(4) Without prejudice to section 15(5), the Secretary of State may, to the extent that it appears to him requisite or expedient to do so in the interests of the safety of the State or the safe custody of persons lawfully detained, by order exempt the Crown either generally or in particular respects from all or any of the provisions of this Part which would, by virtue of subsection (1) above, bind the Crown.

(5) The power to make orders under this section shall be exercisable by statutory instrument, and any such order may be varied or revoked by a subsequent order.

(6) Nothing in this section shall authorise proceedings to be brought against Her Majesty in her private capacity, and this subsection shall be construed as if section 38(3) of the Crown Proceedings Act 1947 (interpretation of references in that Act to Her Majesty in her private capacity) were contained in this Act.

[75]–[76]

NOTES

The Crown: references to the Crown in sub-ss (1)–(4) shall be treated as including the Assembly Commission; see the National Assembly for Wales Commission (Crown Status) (No 2) Order 2007, SI 2007/1353, art 2.

Secretary of State: the power of the Secretary of State under sub-s (4) above includes power to provide for exemptions in relation to designated premises within the meaning of the Atomic Weapons Establishment Act 1991, or activities carried on by a contractor at such premises; see s 3(1) of, and the Schedule, paras 1, 7(1) to, that Act.

49 (*S 49* (*Adaptation of enactments to metric units or appropriate metric units*) *outside the scope of this work.*)

50 Regulations under the relevant statutory provisions

[(1) Where any power to make regulations under any of the relevant statutory provisions is exercisable by the Secretary of State, that power may be exercised either—

(a) so as to give effect (with or without modifications) to proposals submitted by the Executive under section 11(3); or

(b) subject to subsection (1AA), independently of such proposals.

(1AA) The Secretary of State shall not exercise the power referred to in subsection (1) independently of proposals from the Executive unless he has consulted the Executive and such other bodies as appear to him to be appropriate.]

[(1A) Subsection (1) does not apply to the exercise of a power to make regulations so far as it is exercised—

(a) for giving effect (with or without modifications) to proposals submitted by the Office of Rail Regulation under paragraph 2(5) of Schedule 3 to the Railways Act 2005; or

(b) otherwise for or in connection with the railway safety purposes.]

(2) Where the [authority who is to exercise any such power as is mentioned in subsection (1) above proposes to exercise that power] so as to give effect to any such proposals as are there mentioned with modifications, he shall, before making the regulations, consult [the Executive].

(3) Where [the Executive] proposes to submit [under section [11(3)]] any such proposals as are mentioned in subsection (1) above except proposals for the making of regulations under section 43(2), it shall, before so submitting them, consult—

(a) any government department or other body that appears to [the Executive] to be appropriate (and, in particular, in the case of proposals for the making of regulations under section 18(2), any body representing local authorities that so appears, and, in the case of proposals for the making of regulations relating to electro-magnetic radiations, [the Health Protection Agency]);

(b) such government departments and other bodies, if any, as, in relation to any matter dealt with in the proposals, [the Executive] is required to consult under this subsection by virtue of directions given to it by the Secretary of State.

(4), (5) …

[77]

NOTES

Sub-ss (1), (1AA): substituted, for sub-s (1), by the Legislative Reform (Health and Safety Executive) Order 2008, SI 2008/960, arts 3, 16(1), (2), as from 1 April 2008 (for transitional provisions in relation to the abolition of the Health and Safety Commission and the Health and Safety Executive and their replacement with a single Health and Safety Executive, see art 21 of, and Sch 2 to, that Order at **[3474N]**, **[3474O]**).

Sub-s (1A): inserted by the Railways Act 2005, s 2, Sch 3, para 13, as from 1 April 2006.

Sub-s (2): words in first pair of square brackets substituted by the Employment Protection Act 1975, s 116, Sch 15, para 16(2); words in second pair of square brackets substituted by SI 2008/960, arts 3, 16(1), (3), as from 1 April 2008 (for transitional provisions see the note above).

Sub-s (3): words in first, third (inner), fourth and final pairs of square brackets substituted by SI 2008/960, arts 3, 16(1), (4), as from 1 April 2008 (for transitional provisions see the note above); words in second (outer) pair of square brackets substituted by the Employment Protection Act 1975, s 116, Sch 15, para 16(3); words in fifth pair of square brackets substituted by the Health Protection Agency Act 2004, s 11(1), Sch 3, para 5(1), (3), as from 1 April 2005.

Sub-ss (4), (5): repealed by the Employment Protection Act 1975, ss 116, 125(3), Sch 15, para 16(4), Sch 18.

Minister of Agriculture, Fisheries and Food: functions transferred to the Secretary of State for Environment, Food and Rural Affairs (see the Ministry of Agriculture, Fisheries and Food (Dissolution) Order 2002, SI 2002/794) but no consequential amendment was made to this section.

51 Exclusion of application to domestic employment

Nothing in this Part shall apply in relation to a person by reason only that he employs another, or is himself employed, as a domestic servant in a private household.

[78]

[51A Application of Part to police

(1) For the purposes of this Part, a person who, otherwise than under a contract of employment, holds the office of constable or an appointment as police cadet shall be treated as an employee of the relevant officer.

(2) In this section "the relevant officer"—

(a) in relation to a member of a police force or a special constable or police cadet appointed for a police area, means the chief officer of police,

[(b) in relation to a member of a police force seconded to the Serious Organised Crime Agency to serve as a member of its staff, means that Agency, and]

(c) in relation to any other person holding the office of constable or an appointment as police cadet, means the person who has the direction and control of the body of constables or cadets in question.

[(2A) For the purposes of this Part the relevant officer, as defined by subsection (2)(a) or (c) above, shall be treated as a corporation sole.

(2B) Where, in a case in which the relevant officer, as so defined, is guilty of an offence by virtue of this section, it is proved—

(a) that the officer-holder personally consented to the commission of the offence,
(b) that he personally connived in its commission, or
(c) that the commission of the offence was attributable to personal neglect on his part,

the office-holder (as well as the corporation sole) shall be guilty of the offence and shall be liable to be proceeded against and punished accordingly.

(2C) In subsection (2B) above "the office-holder", in relation to the relevant officer, means an individual who, at the time of the consent, connivance or neglect—

(a) held the office or other position mentioned in subsection (2) above as the office or position of that officer; or
(b) was for the time being responsible for exercising and performing the powers and duties of that office or position.

(2D) The provisions mentioned in subsection (2E) below (which impose the same liability for unlawful conduct of constables on persons having their direction or control as would arise if the constables were employees of those persons) do not apply to any liability by virtue of this Part.

(2E) Those provisions are—

(a) section 39 of the Police (Scotland) Act 1967;
(b) section 88(1) of the Police Act 1996;
(c), (d) …
(e) paragraph 14(1) of Schedule 3 to the Criminal Justice and Police Act 2001;
(f) section 28 of the Serious Organised Crime and Police Act 2005;
[(g) paragraph 20 of Schedule 1 to the Police and Justice Act 2006].

(2F) In the application of this section to Scotland—

(a) subsection (2A) shall have effect as if for the words "corporation sole" there were substituted "distinct juristic person (that is to say, as a juristic person distinct from the individual who for the time being is the office-holder)";
(b) subsection (2B) shall have effect as if for the words "corporation sole" there were substituted "juristic person"; and
(c) subsection (2C) shall have effect as if for the words "subsection (2B)" there were substituted "subsections (2A) and (2B)".]

(3) For the purposes of regulations under section 2(4) above—

(a) the Police Federation for England and Wales shall be treated as a recognised trade union recognised by each chief officer of police in England and Wales,
(b) the Police Federation for Scotland shall be treated as a recognised trade union recognised by each chief officer of police in Scotland, and
(c) any body recognised by the Secretary of State for the purposes of section 64 of the Police Act 1996 shall be treated as a recognised trade union recognised by each chief officer of police in England, Wales and Scotland.

(4) Regulations under section 2(4) above may provide, in relation to persons falling within subsection (2)(b) or (c) above, that a body specified in the regulations is to be treated as a recognised trade union recognised by such person as may be specified.]

[79]

NOTES

Inserted by the Police (Health and Safety) Act 1997, s 1.

Sub-s (2): para (b) substituted by the Serious Organised Crime and Police Act 2005, s 59, Sch 4, para 20, as from 1 April 2006.

Sub-ss (2A), (2B)–(2D), (2F): inserted, together with sub-s (2E), by the Serious Organised Crime and Police Act 2005, s 158(1), (5), as from 7 April 2005, with effect for the purposes of any proceedings in or before a court or tribunal that are commenced on or after that date as if this insertion had come into force on 1 July 1998.

Sub-s (2E): inserted as noted above; paras (c), (d) repealed, and para (g) added, by the Police and Justice Act 2006, ss 1(3), 52, Sch 1, Pt 7, para 54, Sch 15, Pt 1, as from 1 April 2007.

Note: this section was amended by the Police Reform Act 2002, s 95, as from a day to be appointed. Those amendments lapsed following the repeal of that section without being brought into force, by the Serious Organised Crime and Police Act 2005, ss 158(4)(a), 174(2), Sch 17, Pt 1, as from 7 April 2005.

Regulations: the Police (Health and Safety) Regulations 1999, SI 1999/860 at **[2505]**.

52 Meaning of work and at work

(1) For the purposes of this Part—

(a) "work" means work as an employee or as a self-employed person;

(b) an employee is at work throughout the time when he is in the course of his employment, but not otherwise;

[(bb) a person holding the office of constable is at work throughout the time when he is on duty, but not otherwise; and]

(c) a self-employed person is at work throughout such time as he devotes to work as a self-employed person;

and, subject to the following subsection, the expressions "work" and "at work", in whatever context, shall be construed accordingly.

(2) Regulations made under this subsection may—

(a) extend the meaning of "work" and "at work" for the purposes of this Part; and

(b) in that connection provide for any of the relevant statutory provisions to have effect subject to such adaptations as may be specified in the regulations.

[(3) The power to make regulations under subsection (2) above shall be exercisable by the Secretary of State …]

[80]

NOTES

Sub-s (1): para (bb) substituted for original word "and" following para (b) by the Police (Health and Safety) Act 1997, s 2.

Sub-s (3): substituted, for original sub-ss (3), (4), by the Employment Protection Act 1975, s 116, Sch 15, para 17; words omitted repealed by the Ministry of Agriculture, Fisheries and Food (Dissolution) Order 2002, SI 2002/794, art 5(2), Sch 2.

Modifications: in accordance with sub-s (2) above, the definitions "work" and "at work" are modified, inter alia, by the Health and Safety (Training for Employment) Regulations 1990, SI 1990/1380, which extend the definitions of "work" and "at work" to cover persons engaged in specified training.

Regulations: Regulations made under this section are outside the scope of this work.

53 General interpretation of Part I

(1) In this Part, unless the context otherwise requires—

…

"article for use at work" means—

(a) any plant designed for use or operation (whether exclusively or not) by persons at work, and

(b) any article designed for use as a component in any such plant;

["article of fairground equipment" means any fairground equipment or any article designed for use as a component in any such equipment;]

"code of practice" (without prejudice to section 16(8)) includes a standard, a specification and any other documentary form of practical guidance;

…

"conditional sale agreement" means an agreement for the sale of goods under which the purchase price or part of it is payable by instalments, and the property in the goods is to remain in the seller (notwithstanding that the buyer is to be in possession of the goods) until such conditions as to the payment of instalments or otherwise as may be specified in the agreement are fulfilled;

"contract of employment" means a contract of employment or apprenticeship (whether express or implied and, if express, whether oral or in writing);

"credit-sale agreement" means an agreement for the sale of goods, under which the purchase price or part of it is payable by instalments, but which is not a conditional sale agreement;

["customs officer" means an officer within the meaning of the Customs and Excise Management Act 1979;]

"domestic premises" means premises occupied as a private dwelling (including any garden, yard, garage, outhouse or other appurtenance of such premises which is not used in common by the occupants of more than one such dwelling), and "non-domestic premises" shall be construed accordingly;

"employee" means an individual who works under a contract of employment [or is treated by section 51A as being an employee], and related expressions shall be construed accordingly;

"enforcing authority" has the meaning assigned by section 18(7);

"the Executive" has the meaning assigned by section [10(1)];

"the existing statutory provisions" means the following provisions while and to the extent that they remain in force, namely the provisions of the Acts mentioned in Schedule 1 which are specified in the third column of that Schedule and of the regulations, orders or other instruments of a legislative character made or having effect under any provision so specified;

…

["fairground equipment" means any fairground ride, any similar plant which is designed to be in motion for entertainment purposes with members of the public on or inside it or any plant which is designed to be used by members of the public for entertainment purposes either as a slide or for bouncing upon, and in this definition the reference to plant which is designed to be in motion with members of the public on or inside it includes a reference to swings, dodgems and other plant which is designed to be in motion wholly or partly under the control of, or to be put in motion by, a member of the public;]

"the general purposes of this Part" has the meaning assigned by section 1;

"health and safety regulations" has the meaning assigned by section 15(1);

"hire-purchase agreement" means an agreement other than a conditional sale agreement, under which—

(a) goods are bailed or (in Scotland) hired in return for periodical payments by the person to whom they are bailed or hired; and

(b) the property in the goods will pass to that person if the terms of the agreement are complied with and one or more of the following occurs—

(i) the exercise of an option to purchase by that person;

(ii) the doing of any other specified act by any party to the agreement;

(iii) the happening of any other event;

and "hire-purchase" shall be construed accordingly;

"improvement notice" means a notice under section 21;

"inspector" means an inspector appointed under section 19;

…

"local authority" means—

(a) in relation to England … , a county council, … , a district council, a London borough council, the Common Council of the City of London, the Sub-Treasurer of the Inner Temple or the Under-Treasurer of the Middle Temple,

[(aa) in relation to Wales, a county council or a county borough council,]

(b) in relation to Scotland, a [council constituted under section 2 of the Local Government etc (Scotland) Act 1994] except that before 16th May 1975 it means a town council or county council;

["micro-organism" includes any microscopic biological entity which is capable of replication;]

"offshore installation" means any installation which is intended for underwater exploitation of mineral resources or exploration with a view to such exploitation;

"personal injury" includes any disease and any impairment of a person's physical or mental condition;

"plant" includes any machinery, equipment or appliance;

"premises" includes any place and, in particular, includes—

(a) any vehicle, vessel, aircraft or hovercraft,

(b) any installation on land (including the foreshore and other land intermittently covered by water), any offshore installation, and any other installation (whether floating, or resting on the seabed or the subsoil thereof, or resting on other land covered with water or the subsoil thereof), and

(c) any tent or movable structure;

"prescribed" means prescribed by regulations made by the Secretary of State;

"prohibition notice" means a notice under section 22;

["railway safety purposes" has the same meaning as in Schedule 3 to the Railways Act 2005;]

…

"the relevant statutory provisions" means—

(a) the provisions of this Part and of any health and safety regulations … ; and

(b) the existing statutory provisions;

"self-employed person" means an individual who works for gain or reward otherwise than under a contract of employment, whether or not he himself employs others;

"substance" means any natural or artificial substance [(including micro-organisms)], whether in solid or liquid form or in the form of a gas or vapour;

…

"supply", where the reference is to supplying articles or substances, means supplying them by way of sale, lease, hire or hire-purchase, whether as principal or agent for another.

(2)–(6) …

[81]

NOTES

Sub-s (1): definitions "article of fairground equipment", "customs officer", "fairground equipment" and "micro-organism" inserted by the Consumer Protection Act 1987, s 36, Sch 3, para 7; definition "the Commission" (omitted) repealed, and figure in square brackets in definition "the Executive" substituted, by the Legislative Reform (Health and Safety Executive) Order 2008, SI 2008/960, arts 3, 17, as from 1 April 2008 (for transitional provisions in relation to the abolition of the Health and Safety Commission and the Health and Safety Executive and their replacement with a single Health and Safety Executive, see art 21 of, and Sch 2 to, that Order at **[3474N]**, **[3474O]**); in definition "employee" words in square brackets inserted by the Police (Health and Safety) Act 1997, s 6(1); definition "railway safety purposes" inserted by the Railways Act 2005, s 2, Sch 3, para 15(3), as from 1 April 2006; in definition "substance", words in square brackets inserted by the Consumer Protection Act 1987, s 36, Sch 3, para 7; definition "substance for use at work" (omitted) repealed by the Consumer Protection Act 1987, s 48, Sch 5; in definition "local authority", second words omitted repealed by the Local Government Act 1985, s 102, Sch 17, first words omitted from that definition repealed, and para (aa) inserted, by the Local Government (Wales) Act 1994, ss 22(3), 66(8), Sch 9, para 9, Sch 18, and words in square brackets in para (b) of that definition substituted by the Local Government etc (Scotland) Act 1994, s 180(1), Sch 13, para 93(3); other words and definitions omitted repealed by the Employment Protection Act 1975, ss 116, 125(3), Sch 15, para 18, Sch 18.

Sub-ss (2)–(6): repealed by the Employment Protection Act 1975, ss 116, 125(3), Sch 15, para 18, Sch 18.

54 Application of Part I to Isles of Scilly

This Part, in its application to the Isles of Scilly, shall apply as if those Isles were a local government area and the Council of those Isles were a local authority.

[82]

55–76 *(Ss 55–60 (Pt II: Employment Medical Advisory Service) outside the scope of this work; Pt III (ss 61–76) repealed as follows: ss 61–74, 76 repealed by the Building Act 1984, s 133(2), Sch 7; s 75 repealed by the Building (Scotland) Act 2003, s 58, Sch 6, para 9, as from 1 May 2005.)*

PART IV
MISCELLANEOUS AND GENERAL

77–79 *(S 77 repealed by the Health Protection Agency Act 2004, s 11(2), Sch 4, as from 1 April 2005; s 78 repealed by the Regulatory Reform (Fire Safety) Order 2005, SI 2005/1541 and the Fire (Scotland) Act 2005 (Consequential Modifications and Savings) Order 2006, SSI 2006/475, as from 1 October 2006; s 79 repealed by the Companies Consolidation (Consequential Provisions) Act 1985, s 29, Sch 1.)*

80 General power to repeal or modify Acts and instruments

(1) Regulations made under this subsection may repeal or modify any provision to which this subsection applies if it appears to the authority making the regulations that the repeal or, as the case may be, the modification of that provision is expedient in consequence of or in connection with any provision made by or under Part I.

(2) Subsection (1) above applies to any provision, not being among the relevant statutory provisions, which—

(a) is contained in this Act or in any other Act passed before or in the same Session as this Act; or

(b) is contained in any regulations, order or other instrument of a legislative character which was made under an Act before the passing of this Act; or

(c) applies, excludes or for any other purpose refers to any of the relevant statutory provisions and is contained in any Act not falling within paragraph (a) above or in any regulations, order or other instrument of a legislative character which is made under an Act but does not fall within paragraph (b) above.

[(2A) Subsection (1) above shall apply to provisions in [the Employment Rights Act 1996 or the Trade Union and Labour Relations (Consolidation) Act 1992 which derive from provisions of the Employment Protection (Consolidation) Act 1978 which re-enacted] provisions previously contained in the Redundancy Payments Act 1965, the Contracts of Employment Act 1972 and the Trade Union and Labour Relations Act 1974 as it applies to provisions contained in Acts passed before or in the same session as this Act.]

(3) Without prejudice to the generality of subsection (1) above, the modifications which may be made by regulations thereunder include modifications relating to the enforcement of provisions to which this section applies (including the appointment of persons for the purpose of such enforcement, and the powers of persons so appointed).

[(4) The power to make regulations under subsection (1) above shall be exercisable by the Secretary of State ... ; but the authority who is to exercise the power shall, before exercising it, consult such bodies as appear to him to be appropriate.

(5) In this section "the relevant statutory provisions" has the same meaning as in Part I.]

[83]

NOTES

Sub-s (2A): inserted by the Employment Protection (Consolidation) Act 1978, s 159(2), Sch 16, para 17; words in square brackets substituted by the Employment Rights Act 1996, s 240, Sch 1, para 5.

Sub-ss (4), (5): substituted, for original sub-ss (4)–(6), by the Employment Protection Act 1975, s 116, Sch 15, para 19; words omitted from sub-s (4) repealed by the Ministry of Agriculture, Fisheries and Food (Dissolution) Order 2002, SI 2002/794, art 5(2), Sch 2.

Employment Protection (Consolidation) Act 1978: repealed by the Trade Union and Labour Relations (Consolidation) Act 1992, s 300(1), Sch 1, and the Employment Rights Act 1996, s 242, Sch 3, Pt I.

Redundancy Payments Act 1965; Contracts of Employment Act 1972; Trade Union and Labour Relations Act 1974: the relevant provisions previously contained in those Acts were repealed by the Employment Protection (Consolidation) Act 1978, s 159(3), Sch 17.

Regulations: Regulations made under this section are outside the scope of this work.

81 Expenses and receipts

There shall be paid out of money provided by Parliament—

(a) any expenses incurred by a Minister of the Crown or government department for the purposes of this Act; and

(b) any increase attributable to the provisions of this Act in the sums payable under any other Act out of money so provided;

and any sums received by a Minister of the Crown or government department by virtue of this Act shall be paid into the Consolidated Fund.

[84]

82 General provisions as to interpretation and regulations

(1) In this Act—

(a) "Act" includes a provisional order confirmed by an Act;

(b) "contravention" includes failure to comply, and "contravene" has a corresponding meaning;

(c) "modifications" includes additions, omissions and amendments, and related expressions shall be construed accordingly;

(d) any reference to a Part, section or Schedule not otherwise identified is a reference to that Part or section of, or Schedule to, this Act.

(2) Except in so far as the context otherwise requires, any reference in this Act to an enactment is a reference to it as amended, and includes a reference to it as applied, by or under any other enactment, including this Act.

(3) Any power conferred by Part I or II or this Part to make regulations—

(a) includes power to make different provision by the regulations for different circumstances or cases and to include in the regulations such incidental, supplemental and transitional provisions as the authority making the regulations considers appropriate in connection with the regulations; and

(b) shall be exercisable by statutory instrument, which [(unless subsection (4) applies)] shall be subject to annulment in pursuance of a resolution of either House of Parliament.

[(4) The first regulations under section 43A(1) shall not be made unless a draft has been laid before and approved by resolution of each House of Parliament.]

[85]

NOTES

Sub-s (3): words in square brackets in para (b) inserted by the Railways and Transport Safety Act 2003, s 105(3)(a), as from 10 September 2003.

Sub-s (4): added by the Railways and Transport Safety Act 2003, s 105(3)(b), as from 10 September 2003.

83 (*Repealed by the Statute Law (Repeals) Act 1993.*)

84 Extent, and application of Act

(1) This Act, except—

(a) Part I and this Part so far as may be necessary to enable regulations under section 15 … to be made and operate for the purpose mentioned in paragraph 2 of Schedule 3; and

(b) paragraph … 3 of Schedule 9,

does not extend to Northern Ireland.

(2) Part III, except section 75 and Schedule 7, does not extend to Scotland.

(3) Her Majesty may by order in Council provide that the provisions of Parts I and II and this Part shall, to such extent and for such purposes as may be specified in the Order, apply (with or without modification) to or in relation to persons, premises, work, articles, substances and other matters (of whatever kind) outside Great Britain as those provisions apply within Great Britain or within a part of Great Britain so specified.

For the purposes of this subsection "premises", "work" and "substance" have the same meanings as they have for the purposes of Part I.

(4) An Order in Council under subsection (3) above—

(a) may make different provision for different circumstances or cases;

(b) may (notwithstanding that this may affect individuals or bodies corporate outside the United Kingdom) provide for any of the provisions mentioned in that subsection, as applied by such an Order, to apply to individuals whether or not they are British subjects and to bodies corporate whether or not they are incorporated under the law of any part of the United Kingdom;

(c) may make provision for conferring jurisdiction on any court or class of courts specified in the Order with respect to offences under Part I committed outside Great Britain or with respect to causes of action arising by virtue of section 47(2) in respect of acts or omissions taking place outside Great Britain, and for the determination, in accordance with the law in force in such part of Great Britain as may be specified in the Order, of questions arising out of such acts or omissions;

(d) may exclude from the operation of section 3 of the Territorial Waters Jurisdiction Act 1878 (consents required for prosecutions) proceedings for offences under any provision of Part I committed outside Great Britain;

(e) may be varied or revoked by a subsequent Order in Council under this section;

and any such Order shall be subject to annulment in pursuance of a resolution of either House of Parliament.

(5) …

(6) Any jurisdiction conferred on any court under this section shall be without prejudice to any jurisdiction exercisable apart from this section by that or any other court.

[86]

NOTES

Sub-s (1): words omitted from para (a) repealed by the Employment Protection Act 1975, ss 116, 125(3), Sch 15, para 20; words omitted from para (b) repealed by the House of Commons Disqualification Act 1975, s 10(2), Sch 3.

Sub-s (5): repealed by the Offshore Safety Act 1992, ss 3(1)(b), 7(2), Sch 2.
Orders: the Health and Safety at Work etc Act 1974 (Application outside Great Britain) Order 2001, SI 2001/2127, revoking and replacing SI 1995/263, which applies ss 1–59 and 80–82 of the Act, with appropriate modifications, to various offshore activities.

85 Short title and commencement

(1) This Act may be cited as the Health and Safety at Work etc Act 1974.

(2) This Act shall come into operation on such day as the Secretary of State may by order made by statutory instrument appoint, and different days may be appointed under this subsection for different purposes.

(3) An order under this section may contain such transitional provisions and savings as appear to the Secretary of State to be necessary or expedient in connection with the provisions thereby brought into force, including such adaptations of those provisions or any provision of this Act then in force as appear to him to be necessary or expedient in consequence of the partial operation of this Act (whether before or after the day appointed by the order).

[87]

NOTES

Orders: six commencement orders have been made under this section (outside the scope of this work).

SCHEDULES

SCHEDULE 1
EXISTING ENACTMENTS WHICH ARE RELEVANT STATUTORY PROVISIONS
Sections 1, 53

Chapter	*Short title*	*Provisions which are relevant statutory provisions*
1875 c 17	The Explosives Act 1875	The whole Act except sections *30 to 32, 80 and* 116 to 121.
1882 c 22	The Boiler Explosions Act 1882	The whole Act.
1890 c 35	The Boiler Explosions Act 1890	The whole Act.
1906 c 14	The Alkali, &c Works Regulation Act 1906	The whole Act.
1909 c 43	The Revenue Act 1909	Section 11.
…	…	…
1920 c 65	The Employment of Women, Young Persons and Children Act 1920	The whole Act.
1922 c 35	The Celluloid and Cinematograph Film Act 1922	The whole Act.
…	…	…
1926 c 43	The Public Health (Smoke Abatement) Act 1926	The whole Act.
1928 c 32	The Petroleum (Consolidation) Act 1928	The whole Act.
1936 c 22	The Hours of Employment (Conventions) Act 1936	The whole Act except section 5.
1936 c 27	The Petroleum (Transfer of Licences) Act 1936	The whole Act.
1937 c 45	The Hydrogen Cyanide (Fumigation) Act 1937	The whole Act.

Chapter	*Short title*	*Provisions which are relevant statutory provisions*
1945 c 19	The Ministry of Fuel and Power Act 1945	Section 1(1) so far as it relates to maintaining and improving the safety, health and welfare of persons employed in or about mines and quarries in Great Britain.
1946 c 59	The Coal Industry Nationalisation Act 1946	Section 42(1) and (2).
1948 c 37	The Radioactive Substances Act 1948	Section 5(1)(a).
1951 c 21	The Alkali, &c Works Regulations (Scotland) Act 1951	The whole Act.
…	…	…
1952 c 60	The Agriculture (Poisonous Substances) Act 1952	The whole Act.
…	…	…
[…	…	…]
1954 c 70	The Mines and Quarries Act 1954	The whole Act except section 151.
1956 c 49	The Agriculture (Safety, Health and Welfare Provisions) Act 1956	The whole Act.
1961 c 34	The Factories Act 1961	The whole Act except section 135.
1961 c 64	The Public Health Act 1961	Section 73.
1962 c 58	The Pipe-lines Act 1962	Sections 20 to 26, 33, 34 and 42, Schedule 5.
1963 c 41	The Offices, Shops and Railway Premises Act 1963	The whole Act.
1965 c 57	The Nuclear Installations Act 1965	Sections 1, 3 to 6, 22 and [24A], Schedule 2.
1969 c 10	The Mines and Quarries (Tips) Act 1969	Sections 1 to 10.
1971 c 20	The Mines Management Act 1971	The whole Act.
1972 c 28	The Employment Medical Advisory Service Act 1972	The whole Act except sections 1 and 6 and Schedule 1.

[88]

NOTES

In entry relating to the Explosives Act 1875 words in italics repealed by the Fireworks Act 2003, s 15, Schedule, as from a day to be appointed; entry relating to "The Anthrax Prevention Act 1919" repealed by the Anthrax Prevention Order 1971 etc (Revocation) Regulations 2005, SI 2005/228, reg 2(2), as from 1 April 2005; entries relating to "The Explosives Act 1923", "The Fireworks Act 1951" and "The Emergency Laws (Miscellaneous Provisions) Act 1953" repealed by the Manufacture and Storage of Explosives Regulations 2005, SI 2005/1082, reg 28(1), (2), Sch 5, Pt 1, para 14, Sch 6, Pt 1, as from 26 April 2005; entry relating to the "Baking Industry (Hours of Work) Act 1954" originally inserted by the Sex Discrimination Act 1975, s 23(3), Sch 5, para 3, and repealed by the Sex Discrimination Act 1986, s 9, Schedule, Pt III; in the entry relating to the Nuclear Installations Act 1965, figure in square brackets substituted by the Atomic Energy Act 1989, s 6(3).

Existing enactments that are relevant statutory provisions: (i) as to the power of the Secretary of State to repeal or revoke any provision which is an existing statutory provision for the purposes of Pt I of this Act, see the Deregulation and Contracting Out Act 1994, s 37(1)(a); (ii) Pt I of the Act has effect subject to modifications by the Offshore Safety Act 1992, ss 1(1), 2(1), the Railways Act 1993, s 117(1), (4), and the Gas Act 1995, s 16(1), Sch 4, para 10. These Acts specify that a variety of sector related enactments are relevant statutory provisions within the meaning of this Part.

Boiler Explosions Act 1882; Boiler Explosions Act 1890; Alkali, &c Works Regulation Act 1906; Revenue Act 1909, s 11; Public Health (Smoke Abatement) Act 1926; Hours of Employment (Conventions) Act 1936; Hydrogen Cyanide (Fumigation) Act 1937; Coal Industry Nationalisation Act 1946, s 42(1), (2); Radioactive Substances Act 1948, s 5(1)(a); Agriculture (Poisonous Substances) Act 1952; Pipe-lines Act 1962, ss 20–26, 33, 34, 42, Sch 5; Nuclear Installations Act 1965, Sch 2; Mines and Quarries (Tips) Act 1969, ss 8, 9; Mines Management Act 1971: all repealed.

Ministry of Fuel and Power Act 1945, s 1(1): repealed, in so far as it is a relevant statutory provision.

[SCHEDULE 2
ADDITIONAL PROVISIONS RELATING TO THE CONSTITUTION ETC OF THE HEALTH AND SAFETY EXECUTIVE

Section 10

The Health and Safety Executive

1. The Executive shall consist of—
   (a) the Chair of the Executive, and
   (b) at least seven and no more than eleven other members (referred to in this Schedule as "members").

2.—(1) The Secretary of State shall appoint the Chair of the Executive.

(2) The Secretary of State shall appoint the other members of the Executive according to sub-paragraph (3).

(3) The Secretary of State—
   (a) shall appoint three members after consulting such organisations representing employers as he considers appropriate;
   (b) shall appoint three members after consulting such organisations representing employees as he considers appropriate;
   (c) shall appoint one member after consulting such organisations representing local authorities as he considers appropriate; and
   (d) may appoint up to four other members after consulting, as he considers appropriate—
      (i) the Scottish Ministers,
      (ii) the Welsh Ministers, or
      (iii) such organisations as he considers appropriate, including professional bodies, whose activities are concerned with matters relating to the general purposes of this Part.

(4) Service as the Chair or as another member of the Executive is not service in the civil service of the State.

(5) The Secretary of State, with the approval of the Chair, may appoint one of the other members appointed under sub-paragraph (2) to be the deputy chair of the Executive.

Terms of Appointment of the Executive

3. Subject to paragraphs 4 and 5, a person shall hold and vacate office as the Chair or as another member according to the terms of the instrument appointing him to that office.

4. The Chair or any other member of the Executive may at any time resign his office by giving notice in writing to the Secretary of State.

5. The Secretary of State may remove a Chair or other member who—
   (a) has been absent from meetings of the Executive for a period longer than six months without the permission of the Executive;
   (b) has become bankrupt or has made an arrangement with his creditors;
   (c) in Scotland, has had his estate sequestrated or has made a trust deed for creditors or a composition contract;
   (d) has become incapacitated by physical or mental illness; or
   (e) is otherwise, in the opinion of the Secretary of State, unable or unfit to carry out his functions.

Remuneration of Members

6.—(1) The Executive shall pay to each member such remuneration and such travelling and other allowances as may be determined by the Secretary of State.

(2) The Executive shall pay to, or in respect of, any member, such sums by way of pension, superannuation allowances and gratuities as the Secretary of State may determine.

(3) Where a person ceases to be a member otherwise than on the expiry of his term of office, and the Secretary of State determines that there are special circumstances which make it right that he should receive compensation, the Executive shall pay to him such amount by way of compensation as the Secretary of State may determine.

Proceedings of the Executive

7.—(1) The Executive may regulate its own procedure.

(2) The validity of any proceedings of the Executive shall not be affected by any vacancy among the members or by any defect in the appointment of a member.

(3) The Executive shall consult with the Secretary of State before making or revising its rules and procedures for dealing with conflicts of interest.

(4) The Executive shall from time to time publish a summary of its rules and procedures.

Staff

8.—(1) The Executive shall, with the consent of the Secretary of State, appoint a person to act as Chief Executive on such terms and conditions as the Secretary of State may determine.

(2) The Executive shall appoint such other staff to the service of the Executive as it may determine, with the consent of the Secretary of State as to numbers of persons appointed and as to the terms and conditions of their service.

(3) The Executive shall pay to the Minister for the Civil Service at such times as that Minister may direct, such sums as the Minister may determine in respect of any increase attributable to this paragraph in the sums payable out of monies provided by Parliament under the Superannuation Act 1972.

(4) A person appointed to the staff of the Executive may not at the same time be a member of the Executive.

(5) Service as a member of staff of the Executive is service in the civil service of the State.

Performance of functions

9.—(1) Subject to sub-paragraphs (2) to (4), anything authorised or required to be done by the Executive (including exercising the powers under this paragraph) may be done by—

- (a) such members of the Executive or members of staff of the Executive as the Executive considers fit to authorise for that purpose, whether generally or specifically; or
- (b) any committee of the Executive which has been so authorised.

(2) Sub-paragraph (1)(b) does not apply to a committee whose members include a person who is neither a member of the Executive nor a member of staff of the Executive.

(3) The Executive—

- (a) shall authorise such of its members of staff as it considers fit to authorise for that purpose, to perform on its behalf those of its functions which consist of the enforcement of the relevant statutory provisions in any particular case; but
- (b) shall not authorise any member or committee of the Executive to make decisions concerning the enforcement of the relevant statutory provisions in any particular case.

(4) The Executive shall not authorise any person to legislate by subordinate instrument.

(5) The Executive shall publish any authorisations which it makes under this paragraph.

Accounts and Reports

10.—(1) It shall be the duty of the Chief Executive—

(a) to keep proper accounts and proper records in relation to the accounts;

(b) to prepare in respect of each accounting year a statement of accounts in such form as the Secretary of State may direct with the approval of the Treasury; and

(c) to send copies of the statement to the Secretary of State and the Comptroller and Auditor General before the end of November next following the accounting year to which the statement relates.

(2) The Comptroller and the Auditor General shall examine, certify and report on each statement referred to in sub-paragraph (1)(c) and shall lay copies of each statement and his report before each House of Parliament.

(3) As soon as possible after the end of the accounting year, the Executive shall make to the Secretary of State a report on the performance of the Executive's functions during the year.

(4) The Secretary of State shall lay the report referred to in sub-paragraph (3) before each House of Parliament.

(5) In this paragraph, "accounting year" means the period of 12 months ending with 31st March in any year; but the first accounting year of the Executive shall, if the Secretary of State so directs, be of such other period not exceeding 2 years as may be specified in the direction.

Supplemental

11. The Secretary of State shall not make any determination or give his consent under paragraph 6 or 8 of this Schedule except with the approval of the Minister for the Civil Service.

12.—(1) The fixing of the common seal of the Executive shall be authenticated by the signature of the Chair or some other person authorised by the Executive to act for that purpose.

(2) A document purporting to be duly executed under the seal of the Executive shall be received in evidence and shall be deemed to be so executed unless the contrary is proved.

(3) This paragraph does not apply to Scotland.]

[89]

NOTES

Commencement: 1 April 2008.

Substituted by the Legislative Reform (Health and Safety Executive) Order 2008, SI 2008/960, arts 3, 16(1), (2), as from 1 April 2008 (for transitional provisions in relation to the abolition of the Health and Safety Commission and the Health and Safety Executive and their replacement with a single Health and Safety Executive, see art 21 of, and Sch 2 to, that Order at **[3474N]**, **[3474O]**).

SCHEDULE 3
SUBJECT-MATTER OF HEALTH AND SAFETY REGULATIONS

Section 15

1.—(1) Regulating or prohibiting—

(a) the manufacture, supply or use of any plant;

(b) the manufacture, supply, keeping or use of any substance;

(c) the carrying on of any process or the carrying out of any operation.

(2) Imposing requirements with respect to the design, construction, guarding, siting, installation, commissioning, examination, repair, maintenance, alteration, adjustment, dismantling, testing or inspection of any plant.

(3) Imposing requirements with respect to the marking of any plant or of any articles used or designed for use as components in any plant, and in that connection regulating or restricting the use of specified markings.

(4) Imposing requirements with respect to the testing, labelling or examination of any substance.

(5) Imposing requirements with respect to the carrying out of research in connection with any activity mentioned in sub-paragraphs (1) to (4) above.

2.—(1) Prohibiting the importation into the United Kingdom or the landing or unloading there of articles or substances of any specified description, whether absolutely or unless conditions imposed by or under the regulations are complied with.

(2) Specifying, in a case where an act or omission in relation to such an importation, landing or unloading as is mentioned in the preceding sub-paragraph constitutes an offence under a provision of this Act and of [the Customs and Excise Acts 1979], the Act under which the offence is to be punished.

3.—(1) Prohibiting or regulating the transport of articles or substances of any specified description.

(2) Imposing requirements with respect to the manner and means of transporting articles or substances of any specified description, including requirements with respect to the construction, testing and marking of containers and means of transport and the packaging and labelling of articles or substances in connection with their transport.

4.—(1) Prohibiting the carrying on of any specified activity or the doing of any specified thing except under the authority and in accordance with the terms and conditions of a licence, or except with the consent or approval of specified authority.

(2) Providing for the grant, renewal, variation, transfer and revocation of licences (including the variation and revocation of conditions attached to licences).

5. Requiring any person, premises or thing to be registered in any specified circumstances or as a condition of the carrying on of any specified activity or the doing of any specified thing.

6.—(1) Requiring, in specified circumstances, the appointment (whether in a specified capacity or not) of persons (or persons with specified qualifications or experience, or both) to perform specified functions, and imposing duties or conferring powers on persons appointed (whether in pursuance of the regulations or not) to perform specified functions.

(2) Restricting the performance of specified functions to persons possessing specified qualifications or experience.

7. Regulating or prohibiting the employment in specified circumstances of all persons or any class of persons.

8.—(1) Requiring the making of arrangements for securing the health of persons at work or other persons, including arrangements for medical examinations and health surveys.

(2) Requiring the making of arrangements for monitoring the atmospheric or other conditions in which persons work.

9. Imposing requirements with respect to any matter affecting the conditions in which persons work, including in particular such matters as the structural condition and stability of premises, the means of access to and egress from premises, cleanliness, temperature, lighting, ventilation, overcrowding, noise, vibrations, ionising and other radiations, dust and fumes.

10. Securing the provision of specified welfare facilities for persons at work, including in particular such things as an adequate water supply, sanitary conveniences, washing and bathing facilities, ambulance and first-aid arrangements, cloakroom accommodation, sitting facilities and refreshment facilities.

11. Imposing requirements with respect to the provision and use in specified circumstances of protective clothing or equipment, including affording protection against the weather.

12. Requiring in specified circumstances the taking of specified precautions in connection with the risk of fire.

13.—(1) Prohibiting or imposing requirements in connection with the emission into the atmosphere of any specified gas, smoke or dust or any other specified substance whatsoever.

(2) Prohibiting or imposing requirements in connection with the emission of noise, vibrations or any ionising or other radiations.

(3) Imposing requirements with respect to the monitoring of any such emission as is mentioned in the preceding sub-paragraphs.

14. Imposing requirements with respect to the instruction, training and supervision of persons at work.

15.—(1) Requiring, in specified circumstances, specified matters to be notified in a specified manner to specified persons.

(2) Empowering inspectors in specified circumstances to require persons to submit written particulars of measures proposed to be taken to achieve compliance with any of the relevant statutory provisions.

16. Imposing requirements with respect to the keeping and preservation of records and other documents, including plans and maps.

17. Imposing requirements with respect to the management of animals.

18. The following purposes as regards premises of any specified description where persons work, namely—

(a) requiring precautions to be taken against dangers to which the premises or persons therein are or may be exposed by reason of conditions (including natural conditions) existing in the vicinity;

(b) securing that persons in the premises leave them in specified circumstances.

19. Conferring, in specified circumstances involving a risk of fire or explosion, power to search a person or any article which a person has with him for the purpose of ascertaining whether he has in his possession any article of a specified kind likely in those circumstances to cause a fire or explosion, and power to seize and dispose of any article of that kind found on such a search.

20. Restricting, prohibiting or requiring the doing of any specified thing where any accident or other occurrence of a specified kind has occurred.

21. As regards cases of any specified class, being a class such that the variety in the circumstances of particular cases within it calls for the making of special provision for particular cases, any of the following purposes, namely—

(a) conferring on employers or other persons power to make rules or give directions with respect to matters affecting health or safety;

(b) requiring employers or other persons to make rules with respect to any such matters;

(c) empowering specified persons to require employers or other persons either to make rules with respect to any such matters or to modify any such rules previously made by virtue of this paragraph; and

(d) making admissible in evidence without further proof, in such circumstances and subject to such conditions as may be specified, documents which purport to be copies of rules or rules of any specified class made under this paragraph.

22. Conferring on any local or public authority power to make byelaws with respect to any specified matter, specifying the authority or person by whom any byelaws made in the exercise of that power need to be confirmed, and generally providing for the procedure to be followed in connection with the making of any such byelaws.

Interpretation

23.—(1) In this Schedule "specified" means specified in health and safety regulations.

(2) It is hereby declared that the mention in this Schedule of a purpose that falls within any more general purpose mentioned therein is without prejudice to the generality of the more general purpose.

[90]

NOTES

Para 2: words in square brackets in sub-para (2) substituted by the Customs and Excise Management Act 1979, s 177(1), Sch 4, para 12, Table, Pt I.

Regulations: see the note to s 15 at **[35]**.

(Sch 4 repealed by the Employment Protection Act 1975, ss 116, 125(3), Sch 15, para 21, Sch 18; Schs 5, 6 repealed by the Building Act 1984, s 133(2), Sch 7; Sch 7 repealed by the Building (Scotland) Act 2003, s 58, Sch 6, para 9, as from 1 May 2005; Sch 8 repealed by the Regulatory Reform (Fire Safety) Order 2005, SI 2005/1541 and the Fire (Scotland) Act 2005 (Consequential Modifications and Savings) Order 2006, SSI 2006/475, as from 1 October 2006; Schs 9, 10 repealed by the Statute Law (Repeals) Act 1993.)

REHABILITATION OF OFFENDERS ACT 1974

(1974 c 53)

ARRANGEMENT OF SECTIONS

An Act to rehabilitate offenders who have not been reconvicted of any serious offence for periods of years, to penalise the unauthorised disclosure of their previous convictions, to amend the law of defamation, and for purposes connected therewith

[31 July 1974]

NOTES

See *Harvey* DI.

1 Rehabilitated persons and spent convictions

(1) Subject to subsection (2) below, where an individual has been convicted, whether before or after the commencement of this Act, of any offence or offences, and the following conditions are satisfied, that is to say—

(a) he did not have imposed on him in respect of that conviction a sentence which is excluded from rehabilitation under this Act; and

(b) he has not had imposed on him in respect of a subsequent conviction during the rehabilitation period applicable to the first-mentioned conviction in accordance with section 6 below a sentence which is excluded from rehabilitation under this Act;

then, after the end of the rehabilitation period so applicable (including, where appropriate, any extension under section 6(4) below of the period originally applicable to the first-mentioned conviction) or, where that rehabilitation period ended before the commencement of this Act, after the commencement of this Act, that individual shall for the purposes of this Act be treated as a rehabilitated person in respect of the first-mentioned conviction and that conviction shall for those purposes be treated as spent.

(2) A person shall not become a rehabilitated person for the purposes of this Act in respect of a conviction unless he has served or otherwise undergone or complied with any

PART 1

sentence imposed on him in respect of that conviction; but the following shall not, by virtue of this subsection, prevent a person from becoming a rehabilitated person for those purposes—

(a) failure to pay a fine or other sum adjudged to be paid by or imposed on a conviction, or breach of a condition of a recognizance or of a bond of caution to keep the peace or be of good behaviour;

(b) breach of any condition or requirement applicable in relation to a sentence which renders the person to whom it applies liable to be dealt with for the offence for which the sentence was imposed, or, where the sentence was a suspended sentence of imprisonment, liable to be dealt with in respect of that sentence (whether or not, in any case, he is in fact so dealt with);

(c) failure to comply with any requirement of a suspended sentence supervision order;

[(d) breach of any condition of a release supervision order made under section 16 of the Crime (Sentences) Act 1997.]

[(2A) Where in respect of a conviction a person has been sentenced to imprisonment with an order under section 47(1) of the Criminal Law Act 1977, he is to be treated for the purposes of subsection (2) above as having served the sentence as soon as he completes service of so much of the sentence as was by that order required to be served in prison.]

[(2B) In subsection (2)(a) above the reference to a fine or other sum adjudged to be paid by or imposed on a conviction does not include a reference to an amount payable under a confiscation order made under Part 2 or 3 of the Proceeds of Crime Act 2002.]

(3) In this Act "sentence" includes any order made by a court in dealing with a person in respect of his conviction of any offence or offences, other than—

[(za) a surcharge imposed under section 161A of the Criminal Justice Act 2003;]

(a) an order for committal or any other order made in default of payment of any fine or other sum adjudged to be paid by or imposed on a conviction, or for want of sufficient distress to satisfy any such fine or other sum;

(b) an order dealing with a person in respect of a suspended sentence of imprisonment.

[(3A) In subsection (3)(a), the reference to want of sufficient distress to satisfy a fine or other sum includes a reference to circumstances where—

(a) there is power to use the procedure in Schedule 12 to the Tribunals, Courts and Enforcement Act 2007 to recover the fine or other sum from a person, but

(b) it appears, after an attempt has been made to exercise the power, that the person's goods are insufficient to pay the amount outstanding (as defined by paragraph 50(3) of that Schedule).]

(4) In this Act, references to a conviction, however expressed, include references—

(a) to a conviction by or before a court outside Great Britain; and

(b) to any finding (other than a finding linked with a finding of insanity) in any criminal proceedings … that a person has committed an offence or done the act or made the omission charged;

and notwithstanding anything in section 9 of the Criminal Justice (Scotland) Act 1949 or [section 14 of the Powers of Criminal Courts (Sentencing) Act 2000] [or section 187 of the Armed Forces Act 2006] (conviction of a person … discharged to be deemed not to be a conviction) a conviction in respect of which an order is made [discharging the person concerned] absolutely or conditionally shall be treated as a conviction for the purposes of this Act and the person in question may become a rehabilitated person in respect of that conviction and the conviction a spent conviction for those purposes accordingly.

[91]

NOTES

Sub-s (2): para (d) added by the Crime (Sentences) Act 1997, s 55(1), Sch 4, para 9(1), as from a day to be appointed.

Sub-s (2A): inserted by the Criminal Law Act 1977, s 47, Sch 9, para 11.

Sub-s (2B): inserted by the Proceeds of Crime Act 2002, s 456, Sch 11, paras 1, 7.

Sub-s (3): para (za) inserted by the Domestic Violence, Crime and Victims Act 2004, s 58(1), Sch 10, para 9, as from 1 April 2007.

Sub-s (3A): inserted by the Tribunals, Courts and Enforcement Act 2007, s 62(3), Sch 13, para 38, as from a day to be appointed.

Sub-s (4): first words omitted repealed by the Children Act 1989, s 108(7), Sch 15; words in first pair of square brackets substituted by the Powers of Criminal Courts (Sentencing) Act 2000, s 165(1), Sch 9, para 47; words in second pair of square brackets inserted by the Armed Forces Act 2006, s 378(1),

Sch 16, para 63, as from a day to be appointed; second words omitted repealed, and words in third pair of square brackets substituted, by the Criminal Justice Act 1991, ss 100, 101(2), Sch 11, para 20, Sch 13.

The reference in sub-s (2)(a) to a fine or other sum adjudged to be paid by or imposed on a conviction does not include a reference to an amount payable under a confiscation order made under the Criminal Justice (Scotland) Act 1987, the Criminal Justice Act 1988, or the Drug Trafficking Act 1994. See, respectively, the Criminal Justice (Scotland) Act 1987, s 45(2), the Criminal Justice Act 1988, s 170(1), Sch 15, para 47, and the Drug Trafficking Act 1994, s 65(2).

Criminal Law Act 1977, s 47(1): repealed by the Criminal Justice Act 1991.

2, 3 (*S 2* (*Rehabilitation of persons dealt with in service disciplinary proceedings*), *s 3* (*Special provision with respect to certain disposals by children's hearings under the Social Work* (*Scotland*) *Act 1968*) *outside the scope of this work.*)

4 Effect of rehabilitation

(1) Subject to sections 7 and 8 below, a person who has become a rehabilitated person for the purposes of this Act in respect of a conviction shall be treated for all purposes in law as a person who has not committed or been charged with or prosecuted for or convicted of or sentenced for the offence or offences which were the subject of that conviction; and, notwithstanding the provisions of any other enactment or rule of law to the contrary, but subject as aforesaid—

(a) no evidence shall be admissible in any proceedings before a judicial authority exercising its jurisdiction or functions in Great Britain to prove that any such person has committed or been charged with or prosecuted for or convicted of or sentenced for any offence which was the subject of a spent conviction; and

(b) a person shall not, in any such proceedings, be asked, and, if asked, shall not be required to answer, any question relating to his past which cannot be answered without acknowledging or referring to a spent conviction or spent convictions or any circumstances ancillary thereto.

(2) Subject to the provisions of any order made under subsection (4) below, where a question seeking information with respect to a person's previous convictions, offences, conduct or circumstances is put to him or to any other person otherwise than in proceedings before a judicial authority—

(a) the question shall be treated as not relating to spent convictions or to any circumstances ancillary to spent convictions, and the answer thereto may be framed accordingly; and

(b) the person questioned shall not be subjected to any liability or otherwise prejudiced in law by reason of any failure to acknowledge or disclose a spent conviction or any circumstances ancillary to a spent conviction in his answer to the question.

(3) Subject to the provisions of any order made under subsection (4) below,—

(a) any obligation imposed on any person by any rule of law or by the provisions of any agreement or arrangement to disclose any matters to any other person shall not extend to requiring him to disclose a spent conviction or any circumstances ancillary to a spent conviction (whether the conviction is his own or another's); and

(b) a conviction which has become spent or any circumstances ancillary thereto, or any failure to disclose a spent conviction or any such circumstances, shall not be a proper ground for dismissing or excluding a person from any office, profession, occupation or employment, or for prejudicing him in any way in any occupation or employment.

(4) The Secretary of State may by order—

(a) make such provision as seems to him appropriate for excluding or modifying the application of either or both of paragraphs (a) and (b) of subsection (2) above in relation to questions put in such circumstances as may be specified in the order;

(b) provide for such exceptions from the provisions of subsection (3) above as seem to him appropriate, in such cases or classes of case, and in relation to convictions of such a description, as may be specified in the order.

(5) For the purposes of this section and section 7 below any of the following are circumstances ancillary to a conviction, that is to say—

(a) the offence or offences which were the subject of that conviction;

(b) the conduct constituting that offence or those offences; and

(c) any process or proceedings preliminary to that conviction, any sentence imposed

PART 1

in respect of that conviction, any proceedings (whether by way of appeal or otherwise) for reviewing that conviction or any such sentence, and anything done in pursuance of or undergone in compliance with any such sentence.

(6) For the purposes of this section and section 7 below "proceedings before a judicial authority" includes, in addition to proceedings before any of the ordinary courts of law, proceedings before any tribunal, body or person having power—

(a) by virtue of any enactment, law, custom or practice;

(b) under the rules governing any association, institution, profession, occupation or employment; or

(c) under any provision of an agreement providing for arbitration with respect to questions arising thereunder;

to determine any question affecting the rights, privileges, obligations or liabilities of any person, or to receive evidence affecting the determination of any such question.

[92]

NOTES

Exceptions: for exceptions to this section, see ss 7, 8 and note sub-s (4) above. See also the Banking Act 1987, s 95 (repealed subject to savings), the National Lottery etc Act 1993, s 19 (repealed by the Police Act 1997, ss 133(d), 134(2), Sch 10, as from a day to be appointed), the Gambling Act 2005, s 125, the Rehabilitation of Offenders Act 1974 (Exceptions) Order 1975, SI 1975/1023 at **[2009]** et seq, and the Rehabilitation of Offenders Act 1974 (Exclusions and Exceptions) (Scotland) Order 2003, SSI 2003/231 at **[2881A]** et seq.

Secretary of State: the functions conferred by sub-s (4) are, in so far as exercisable in relation to Scotland, transferred to the Scottish Ministers, by the Scotland Act 1998 (Transfer of Functions to the Scottish Ministers etc) Order 2003, SI 2003/415, art 2.

Orders: the Rehabilitation of Offenders Act 1974 (Exceptions) Order 1975, SI 1975/1023 at **[2009]**; the Rehabilitation of Offenders Act 1974 (Exclusions and Exceptions) (Scotland) Order 2003, SSI 2003/231 at **[2881A]**.

5 Rehabilitation periods for particular sentences

(1) The sentences excluded from rehabilitation under this Act are—

(a) a sentence of imprisonment for life;

(b) a sentence of imprisonment[, youth custody] [detention in a young offender institution] or corrective training for a term exceeding thirty months;

(c) a sentence of preventive detention; …

(d) a sentence of detention during Her Majesty's pleasure or for life [under section 90 or 91 of the Powers of Criminal Courts (Sentencing) Act 2000], [or under section 209 or 218 of the Armed Forces Act 2006,] [or under section 205(2) or (3) of the Criminal Procedure (Scotland) Act 1975,] [or a sentence of detention for a term exceeding thirty months passed under section 91 of the said Act of 2000] [or section 209 of the said Act of 2006] [(young offenders convicted of grave crimes) or under section 206 of the said Act of 1975 (detention of children convicted on indictment)] [*or a corresponding court-martial punishment*];

[(e) a sentence of custody for life][; and

(f) a sentence of imprisonment for public protection under section 225 of the Criminal Justice Act 2003, a sentence of detention for public protection under section 226 of that Act or an extended sentence under section 227 or 228 of that Act [(including any sentence within this paragraph passed as a result of any of sections 219 to 222 of the Armed Forces Act 2006)]];

and any other sentence is a sentence subject to rehabilitation under this Act.

[(1A) In subsection (1)(d) above "corresponding court-martial punishment" means a punishment awarded under section 71A(3) or (4) of the Army Act 1955, section 71A(3) or (4) of the Air Force Act 1955 or section 43A(3) or (4) of the Naval Discipline Act 1957.]

(2) For the purposes of this Act—

(a) the rehabilitation period applicable to a sentence specified in the first column of Table A below is the period specified in the second column of that Table in relation to that sentence, or, where the sentence was imposed on a person who was under [eighteen years of age] at the date of his conviction, half that period; and

(b) the rehabilitation period applicable to a sentence specified in the first column of Table B below is the period specified in the second column of that Table in relation to that sentence;

reckoned in either case from the date of the conviction in respect of which the sentence was imposed.

Table A
Rehabilitation periods subject to reduction by half for persons [under 18]

Sentence	*Rehabilitation period*
A sentence of imprisonment [detention in a young offender institution] [or youth custody] or corrective training for a term exceeding six months but not exceeding thirty months.	Ten years
A sentence of cashiering, discharge with ignominy or dismissal with disgrace from Her Majesty's service.	Ten years
A sentence of imprisonment [detention in a young offender institution] [or youth custody] for a term not exceeding six months.	Seven years
A sentence of dismissal from Her Majesty's service.	Seven years
Any sentence of detention in respect of a conviction in service disciplinary proceedings.	Five years
A fine or any other sentence subject to rehabilitation under this Act, not being a sentence to which Table B below or any of subsections (3) [to (8)] below applies.	Five years

Table B
Rehabilitation periods for certain sentences confined to young offenders

Sentence	*Rehabilitation period*
A sentence of Borstal training.	Seven years
[A custodial order under Schedule 5A to the Army Act 1955 or the Air Force Act 1955, or under Schedule 4A to the Naval Discipline Act 1957, where the maximum period of detention specified in the order is more than six months.	Seven years]
[A custodial order under section 71AA of the Army Act 1955 or the Air Force Act 1955, or under section 43AA of the Naval Discipline Act 1957, where the maximum period of detention specified in the order is more than six months.	Seven years]
A sentence of detention for a term exceeding six months but not exceeding thirty months passed under [section 91 of the Powers of Criminal Courts (Sentencing) Act 2000] [or under section 209 of the Armed Forces Act 2006] or under section [206 of the Criminal Procedure (Scotland) Act 1975.]	Five years
A sentence of detention for a term not exceeding six months passed under *either of those provisions*.	Three years
An order for detention in a detention centre made under [section 4 of the Criminal Justice Act 1982,] section 4 of the Criminal Justice Act 1961 …	Three years
[A custodial order under any of the Schedules to the said Acts of 1955 and 1957 mentioned above, where the maximum period of detention specified in the order is six months or less.	Three years]

Sentence	Rehabilitation period
[A custodial order under section 71AA of the said Acts of 1955, or section 43AA of the said Act of 1957, where the maximum period of detention specified in the order is six months or less.	Three years]

[(2A) Table B applies in relation to a sentence under section 71A(4) of the Army Act 1955 or Air Force Act 1955 or section 43A(4) of the Naval Discipline Act 1957 as it applies in relation to one under section 209 of the Armed Forces Act 2006.]

(3) The rehabilitation period applicable—
(a) to an order discharging a person absolutely for an offence; and
(b) to the discharge by a children's hearing under section [69(1)(b) and (12) of the Children (Scotland) Act 1995] of the referral of a child's case;

shall be six months from the date of conviction.

(4) Where in respect of a conviction a person was conditionally discharged, bound over to keep the peace or be of good behaviour, ... the rehabilitation period applicable to the sentence shall be one year from the date of conviction or a period beginning with that date and ending when the order for conditional discharge ... or (as the case may be) the recognisance or bond of caution to keep the peace or be of good behaviour ceases or ceased to have effect, whichever is the longer.

[(4A) Where in respect of a conviction [a probation order [or a community order under section 177 of the Criminal Justice Act 2003] was made], the rehabilitation period applicable to the sentence shall be—
(a) in the case of a person aged eighteen years or over at the date of his conviction, five years from the date of conviction;
(b) in the case of a person aged under the age of eighteen years at the date of his conviction, two and a half years from the date of conviction or a period beginning with the date of conviction and ending when the [order in question] ceases or ceased to have effect, whichever is the longer.]

[(4B) Where in respect of a conviction a referral order (within the meaning of [the Powers of Criminal Courts (Sentencing) Act 2000]) is made in respect of the person convicted, the rehabilitation period applicable to the sentence shall be—
(a) if a youth offender contract takes effect under [section 23] of that Act between him and a youth offender panel, the period beginning with the date of conviction and ending on the date when (in accordance with [section 24] of that Act) the contract ceases to have effect;
(b) if no such contract so takes effect, the period beginning with the date of conviction and having the same length as the period for which such a contract would (ignoring any order under paragraph 11 or 12 of Schedule 1 to that Act) have had effect had one so taken effect.

(4C) Where in respect of a conviction an order is made in respect of the person convicted under paragraph 11 or 12 of Schedule 1 to [the Powers of Criminal Courts (Sentencing) Act 2000] (extension of period for which youth offender contract has effect), the rehabilitation period applicable to the sentence shall be—
(a) if a youth offender contract takes effect under [section 23] of that Act between the offender and a youth offender panel, the period beginning with the date of conviction and ending on the date when (in accordance with [section 24] of that Act) the contract ceases to have effect;
(b) if no such contract so takes effect, the period beginning with the date of conviction and having the same length as the period for which, in accordance with the order, such a contract would have had effect had one so taken effect.]

(5) Where in respect of a conviction any of the following sentences was imposed, that is to say—
(a) an order under section 57 of the Children and Young Persons Act 1933 or section 61 of the Children and Young Persons (Scotland) Act 1937 committing the person convicted to the care of a fit person;
(b) a supervision order under any provision of either of those Acts or of the Children and Young Persons Act 1963;

[(c) an order under section 413 of the Criminal Procedure (Scotland) Act 1975 committing a child for the purpose of his undergoing residential training;]
(d) an approved school order under section 61 of the said Act of 1937;
(e) ... a supervision order under [section 63(1) of the Powers of Criminal Courts (Sentencing) Act 2000]; or
(f) a supervision requirement under any provision of the [Children (Scotland) Act 1995];
[(g) a community supervision order under Schedule 5A to the Army Act 1955 or the Air Force Act 1955, or under Schedule 4A to the Naval Discipline Act 1957;
(h) ...]

the rehabilitation period applicable to the sentence shall be one year from the date of conviction or a period beginning with that date and ending when the order or requirement ceases or ceased to have effect, whichever is the longer.

(6) Where in respect of a conviction any of the following orders was made, that is to say—
(a) an order under section 54 of the said Act of 1933 committing the person convicted to custody in a remand home;
(b) an approved school order under section 57 of the said Act of 1933; or
(c) an attendance centre order under [section 60 of the Powers of Criminal Courts (Sentencing) Act 2000]; [or
(d) a secure training order under section 1 of the Criminal Justice and Public Order Act 1994;]

the rehabilitation period applicable to the sentence shall be a period beginning with the date of conviction and ending one year after the date on which the order ceases or ceased to have effect.

[(6A) Where in respect of a conviction a detention and training order was made under [section 100 of the Powers of Criminal Courts (Sentencing) Act 2000][, or an order under section 211 of the Armed Forces Act 2006 was made], the rehabilitation period applicable to the sentence shall be—
(a) in the case of a person aged fifteen years or over at the date of his conviction, five years if the order was, and three and a half years if the order was not, for a term exceeding six months;
(b) in the case of a person aged under fifteen years at the date of his conviction, a period beginning with that date and ending one year after the date on which the order ceases to have effect.]

(7) Where in respect of a conviction a hospital order under [Part III of the Mental Health Act 1983] or under [Part VI of the Criminal Procedure (Scotland) Act 1995] (with or without [a restriction order] was made, the rehabilitation period applicable to the sentence shall be the period of five years from the date of conviction or a period beginning with that date and ending two years after the date on which the hospital order ceases or ceased to have effect, whichever is the longer.

(8) Where in respect of a conviction an order was made imposing on the person convicted any disqualification, disability, prohibition or other penalty, the rehabilitation period applicable to the sentence shall be a period beginning with the date of conviction and ending on the date on which the disqualification, disability, prohibition or penalty (as the case may be) ceases or ceased to have effect.

(9) For the purposes of this section—
(a) "sentence of imprisonment" includes a sentence of detention [under section 207 or 415 of the Criminal Procedure (Scotland) Act 1975] and a sentence of penal servitude, and "term of imprisonment" shall be construed accordingly;
(b) consecutive terms of imprisonment or of detention under [section 91 of the Powers of Criminal Courts (Sentencing) Act 2000] or [section 206 of the said Act of 1975] and terms which are wholly or partly concurrent (being terms of imprisonment or detention imposed in respect of offences of which a person was convicted in the same proceedings) shall be treated as a single term;
(c) no account shall be taken of any subsequent variation, made by a court in dealing with a person in respect of a suspended sentence of imprisonment, of the term originally imposed; and
(d) a sentence imposed by a court outside Great Britain shall be treated as a sentence of that one of the descriptions mentioned in this section which most nearly corresponds to the sentence imposed.

(10) References in this section to the period during which a probation order, or a … supervision order under [the Powers of Criminal Courts (Sentencing) Act 2000], or a supervision requirement under the [Children (Scotland) Act 1995], is or was in force include references to any period during which any order or requirement to which this subsection applies, being an order or requirement made or imposed directly or indirectly in substitution for the first-mentioned order or requirement, is or was in force.

This subsection applies—

(a) to any such order or requirement as is mentioned above in this subsection;

(b) to any order having effect under section 25(2) of [the Children and Young Persons Act 1969] as if it were a training school order in Northern Ireland; and

(c) to any supervision order made under section 72(2) of the said Act of 1968 and having effect as a supervision order under the Children and Young Persons Act (Northern Ireland) 1950.

[(10A) The reference in subsection (5) above to the period during which a reception order has effect includes a reference to any subsequent period during which by virtue of the order having been made the Social Work (Scotland) Act 1968 or the Children and Young Persons Act (Northern Ireland) 1968 has effect in relation to the person in respect of whom the order was made and subsection (10) above shall accordingly have effect in relation to any such subsequent period.]

(11) The Secretary of State may by order—

(a) substitute different periods or terms for any of the periods or terms mentioned in subsections (1) to (8) above; and

(b) substitute a different age for the age mentioned in subsection (2)(a) above.

[93]

NOTES

Sub-s (1): words in first pair of square brackets in para (b) inserted by the Criminal Justice Act 1982, ss 77, 78, Sch 14, para 36; words in second pair of square brackets in para (b) inserted by the Criminal Justice Act 1988, s 123(6), Sch 8, para 9(a); word omitted from para (c) repealed, and para (e) added, by the Criminal Justice Act 1982, ss 77, 78, Sch 14, para 36, Sch 16; words in first pair of square brackets in para (d) inserted, and words in fourth pair of square brackets substituted, by the Powers of Criminal Courts (Sentencing) Act 2000, s 165(1), Sch 9, para 48(1), (2); words in second and fifth pairs of square brackets inserted by the Armed Forces Act 2006, s 378(1), Sch 16, para 65(1), (2)(a)(i), (ii), as from a day to be appointed; words in third pair of square brackets in para (d) inserted, and words in sixth pair of square brackets substituted, by the Criminal Justice (Scotland) Act 1980, s 83(2), Sch 7, para 24; words in final pair of square brackets in para (d) inserted by the Armed Forces Act 1976, s 22, Sch 9, para 20(4), and repealed by the Armed Forces Act 2006, s 378(1), Sch 16, para 65(1), (2)(a)(iii), Sch 17, as from a day to be appointed; para (f) and the word immediately preceding it added by the Criminal Justice Act 2003, s 304, Sch 32, Pt 1, para 18(1), (2)(b), as from 4 April 2005; words in square brackets in para (f) added by the Armed Forces Act 2006, s 378(1), Sch 16, para 65(1), (2)(b), as from a day to be appointed.

Sub-s (1A): inserted by the Armed Forces Act 1976, s 22, Sch 9, para 20(5), and substituted by the Armed Forces Act 2006, s 378(1), Sch 16, para 65(1), (3), as from a day to be appointed, as follows—

"(1A) In subsection (1)(d)—

(a) references to section 209 of the Armed Forces Act 2006 include references to section 71A(4) of the Army Act 1955 or Air Force Act 1955 or section 43A(4) of the Naval Discipline Act 1957;

(b) the reference to section 218 of the Armed Forces Act 2006 includes a reference to section 71A(3) of the Army Act 1955 or Air Force Act 1955 or section 43A(3) of the Naval Discipline Act 1957.".

Sub-s (2): words in square brackets in para (a) and in the heading to Table A substituted by the Criminal Justice Act 1991, ss 68, 101(1), Sch 8, para 5, Sch 12, para 22 (with additional effect in relation to any sentence imposed on any person who was convicted before 1 October 1992 and was aged 17 at the date of his conviction).

In Table A: words in first and third pairs of pairs of square brackets inserted by the Criminal Justice Act 1988, s 123(6), Sch 8, para 9(b); words in second and fourth pairs of square brackets inserted by the Criminal Justice Act 1982, s 77, Sch 14, para 37; word in fifth pair of square brackets inserted by the Criminal Justice and Public Order Act 1994, s 168(1), (3), Sch 9, para 11; for the words in italics there are substituted the words "Any sentence of service detention within the meaning of the Armed Forces Act 2006, or any sentence of detention corresponding to such a sentence," by the Armed Forces Act 2006, s 378(1), Sch 16, para 65(1), (4)(a), as from a day to be appointed; words in sixth pair of square brackets substituted by the Youth Justice and Criminal Evidence Act 1999, s 67, Sch 4, para 6(1), (2).

In Table B entry beginning with the words "A custodial order under Schedule 5A" inserted by the Armed Forces Act 1976, s 22, Sch 9, para 21(1); entry beginning with the words "A custodial order under section 71AA" inserted by the Armed Forces Act 1981, s 28, Sch 4, para 2; in entry beginning with the words "A sentence of detention for a term exceeding six months" words "section 91 of the Powers of Criminal Courts (Sentencing) Act 2000" in square brackets substituted by the Powers of Criminal Courts

(Sentencing) Act 2000, s 165(1), Sch 9, para 48(1), (3); in entry beginning with the words "A sentence of detention for a term exceeding six months" words "or under section 209 of the Armed Forces Act 2006" in square brackets inserted by the Armed Forces Act 2006, s 378(1), Sch 16, para 65(1), (4)(b)(i), as from a day to be appointed; in entry beginning with the words "A sentence of detention for a term exceeding six months" words "206 of the Criminal Procedure (Scotland) Act 1975." in square brackets substituted by the Criminal Justice (Scotland) Act 1980, s 83(2), Sch 7, para 24; for the words in italics in entry beginning with the words "A sentence of detention for a term not exceeding six months" there are substituted the words "any provision mentioned in the fourth entry in this Table" by the Armed Forces Act 2006, s 378(1), Sch 16, para 65(1), (4)(b)(ii), as from a day to be appointed; in entry beginning "An order for detention in a detention centre" words "section 4 of the Criminal Justice Act 1982" in square brackets inserted by the Criminal Justice Act 1982, s 77, Sch 14, para 37; words omitted from that entry repealed by the Criminal Justice (Scotland) Act 1980, s 83(2), Sch 7, para 24; penultimate entry in square brackets inserted by the Armed Forces Act 1976, s 22, Sch 9, para 21(1); final entry in square brackets inserted by the Armed Forces Act 1981, s 28, Sch 4, para 2.

Sub-s (2A): inserted by the Armed Forces Act 2006, s 378(1), Sch 16, para 65(1), (5), as from a day to be appointed.

Sub-s (3): words in square brackets substituted by the Children (Scotland) Act 1995, s 105(4), (5), Sch 4, para 23(1), (3).

Sub-s (4): words omitted repealed by the Criminal Justice and Public Order Act 1994, s 168(1), (3), Sch 9, para 11(1)(b), (2), Sch 11.

Sub-s (4A): inserted by the Criminal Justice and Public Order Act 1994, s 168(1), (3), Sch 9, para 11(1)(c), (2); words in first (outer) and fourth pairs of square brackets substituted by the Criminal Justice and Court Services Act 2000, s 74, Sch 7, Pt II, paras 48, 49; words in second (inner) pair of square brackets inserted by the Criminal Justice Act 2003, s 304, Sch 32, Pt 1, para 18(1), (3), as from 4 April 2005; words in third (inner) pair of square brackets inserted by the Armed Forces Act 2006, s 378(1), Sch 16, para 65(1), (6), as from a day to be appointed.

Sub-s (4B): inserted, together with sub-s (4C), by the Youth Justice and Criminal Evidence Act 1999, s 67, Sch 4, para 6(1), (3); words in square brackets substituted by the Powers of Criminal Courts (Sentencing) Act 2000, s 165(1), Sch 9, para 48(1), (4).

Sub-s (4C): inserted as noted above; words in square brackets substituted by the Powers of Criminal Courts (Sentencing) Act 2000, s 165(1), Sch 9, para 48(1), (5).

Sub-s (5): para (c) substituted by the Criminal Justice (Scotland) Act 1980, s 83(2), Sch 7, para 24; words omitted from para (e) repealed by the Children Act 1989, s 108(7), Sch 15; words in square brackets in para (e) substituted by the Powers of Criminal Courts (Sentencing) Act 2000, s 165(1), Sch 9, para 48(1), (6); words in square brackets in para (f) substituted by the Children (Scotland) Act 1995, s 105(4), (5), Sch 4, para 23(1), (3); paras (g), (h) added by the Armed Forces Act 1976, s 22, Sch 9, para 21(2); para (h) repealed by the Armed Forces Act 1991, s 26, Sch 3.

Sub-s (6): words in square brackets in para (c) substituted by the Powers of Criminal Courts (Sentencing) Act 2000, s 165(1), Sch 9, para 48(1), (7); para (d) and the word immediately preceding it added by the Criminal Justice and Public Order Act 1994, s 168(2), Sch 10, para 30.

Sub-s (6A): inserted by the Crime and Disorder Act 1998, s 119, Sch 8, para 35; words in first pair of square brackets substituted by the Powers of Criminal Courts (Sentencing) Act 2000, s 165(1), Sch 9, para 48(1), (8); words in second pair of square brackets inserted by the Armed Forces Act 2006, s 378(1), Sch 16, para 65(1), (7), as from a day to be appointed.

Sub-s (7): words in first pair of square brackets substituted by the Mental Health Act 1983, s 148, Sch 4, para 39; words in second pair of square brackets substituted by the Mental Health (Care and Treatment) (Scotland) Act 2003 (Modification of Enactments) Order 2005, SSI 2005/465, art 2, Sch 1, para 6, as from 27 September 2005; words in third pair of square brackets substituted by the Mental Health (Amendment) Act 1982, s 65(1), Sch 3, para 49.

Sub-s (9): words in first and fourth pairs of square brackets substituted by the Criminal Justice (Scotland) Act 1980, s 83(2), Sch 7, para 24; words in second pair of square brackets substituted by the Powers of Criminal Courts (Sentencing) Act 2000, s 165(1), Sch 9, para 48(1), (9); words in third pair of square brackets inserted by the Armed Forces Act 2006, s 378(1), Sch 16, para 65(1), (8), as from a day to be appointed.

Sub-s (10): words omitted repealed by the Children Act 1989, s 108(7), Sch 15; words in first and third pairs of square brackets substituted by the Powers of Criminal Courts (Sentencing) Act 2000, s 165(1), Sch 9, para 48(1), (10); words in second pair of square brackets substituted by the Children (Scotland) Act 1995, s 105(4), (5), Sch 4, para 23(1), (3), Sch 5.

Sub-s (10A): inserted by the Armed Forces Act 1976, s 22, Sch 9, para 21(3); repealed, in relation to Scotland only, by the Children (Scotland) Act 1995, s 105(4), (5), Sch 4, para 23(1), (3), Sch 5.

Youth custody; detention in a young offender institution: detention centre orders and youth custody sentences were amalgamated into a single custodial sentence of detention in a young offender institution by the Criminal Justice Act 1982, s 1A (repealed). As to detention in a young offender institution, see the Powers of Criminal Courts (Sentencing) Act 2000, ss 96–98 (repealed by the Criminal Justice and Court Services Act 2000, ss 74, 75, Sch 7, Pt II, paras 160, 182, Sch 8, as from a day to be appointed), and as to the abolition of this sentence, see s 61 of the 2000 Act.

Corrective training; preventive detention: these sentences were authorised in certain cases by the Criminal Justice Act 1948, s 21 (repealed) but were abolished by the Criminal Justice Act 1967, s 37(1) (repealed).

Custody for life: as to custody for life, see the Powers of Criminal Courts (Sentencing) Act 2000, ss 93–95 (repealed by the Criminal Justice and Court Services Act 2000, ss 74, 75, Sch 7, Pt II, paras 160, 182, Sch 8, as from a day to be appointed), and as to the abolition of this sentence, see s 61 of the 2000 Act.

Borstal training: borstal training was replaced by youth custody (as to which, see the note above).

Order for detention in a detention centre: see the note "Youth custody; detention in a young offender institution" above.

Probation orders: renamed community rehabilitation orders in accordance with the Criminal Justice and Court Services Act 2000, s 43. The power to make community rehabilitation orders was given by the Powers of Criminal Courts (Sentencing) Act 2000, ss 41–45 (repealed).

Penal Servitude: the courts no longer have the power to sentence a person to penal servitude (see the Criminal Justice Act 1948, s 1(1), (2)). That section also provides that every enactment conferring power on a court to pass such sentence is to be construed as conferring the power to pass a sentence of imprisonment for a similar term.

Children and Young Persons Act 1933: ss 54, 57 repealed by the Children and Young Persons Act 1969, ss 7(6), 72(4), Sch 6.

Criminal Justice Act 1961, s 4: repealed by the Criminal Justice Act 1982, s 78, Sch 16.

Criminal Justice Act 1982, s 4: repealed by the Criminal Justice Act 1988, s 170(2), Sch 16.

Criminal Justice and Public Order Act 1994, s 1: repealed by the Crime and Disorder Act 1998, ss 73(7)(b), 120(2), Sch 10.

Criminal Procedure (Scotland) Act 1975: repealed, subject to transitional provisions and savings, by the Criminal Procedure (Consequential Provisions) Act 1995, ss 4, 6, Schs 3, 5, 6.

Orders: as of 6 April 2008, no Orders had been made under this section.

6 The rehabilitation period applicable to a conviction

(1) Where only one sentence is imposed in respect of a conviction (not being a sentence excluded from rehabilitation under this Act) the rehabilitation period applicable to the conviction is, subject to the following provisions of this section, the period applicable to the sentence in accordance with section 5 above.

(2) Where more than one sentence is imposed in respect of a conviction (whether or not in the same proceedings) and none of the sentences imposed is excluded from rehabilitation under this Act, then, subject to the following provisions of this section, if the periods applicable to those sentences in accordance with section 5 above differ, the rehabilitation period applicable to the conviction shall be the longer or the longest (as the case may be) of those periods.

(3) Without prejudice to subsection (2) above, where in respect of a conviction a person was conditionally discharged or [a probation order was made] and after the end of the rehabilitation period applicable to the conviction in accordance with subsection (1) or (2) above he is dealt with, in consequence of a breach of conditional discharge [or a breach of the order], for the offence for which the order for conditional discharge or probation order was made, then, if the rehabilitation period applicable to the conviction in accordance with subsection (2) above (taking into account any sentence imposed when he is so dealt with) ends later than the rehabilitation period previously applicable to the conviction, he shall be treated for the purposes of this Act as not having become a rehabilitated person in respect of that conviction, and the conviction shall for those purposes be treated as not having become spent, in relation to any period falling before the end of the new rehabilitation period.

(4) Subject to subsection (5) below, where during the rehabilitation period applicable to a conviction—

(a) the person convicted is convicted of a further offence; and

(b) no sentence excluded from rehabilitation under this Act is imposed on him in respect of the later conviction;

if the rehabilitation period applicable in accordance with this section to either of the convictions would end earlier than the period so applicable in relation to the other, the rehabilitation period which would (apart from this subsection) end the earlier shall be extended so as to end at the same time as the other rehabilitation period.

(5) Where the rehabilitation period applicable to a conviction is the rehabilitation period applicable in accordance with section 5(8) above to an order imposing on a person any disqualification, disability, prohibition or other penalty, the rehabilitation period applicable to another conviction shall not by virtue of subsection (4) above be extended by reference to that period; but if any other sentence is imposed in respect of the first-mentioned conviction for which a rehabilitation period is prescribed by any other provision of section 5 above, the rehabilitation period applicable to another conviction shall, where appropriate, be extended under subsection (4) above by reference to the rehabilitation period applicable in accordance with that section to that sentence or, where more than one such sentence is imposed, by reference to the longer or longest of the periods so applicable to those sentences, as if the period in question were the rehabilitation period applicable to the first-mentioned conviction.

(6) …, for the purposes of subsection (4)(a) above there shall be disregarded—

(a) any conviction in England and Wales of [a summary offence or of a scheduled offence (within the meaning of [section 22 of the Magistrates' Courts Act 1980] tried summarily in pursuance of subsection (2) of that section (summary trial where value involved is small),] [or of an offence under section 17 of the Crime (Sentences) Act 1997 (breach of conditions of release supervision order);]

(b) any conviction in Scotland of an offence which is not excluded from the jurisdiction of inferior courts of summary jurisdiction by virtue of section 4 of the Summary Jurisdiction (Scotland) Act 1954 (certain crimes not to be tried in inferior courts of summary jurisdiction);

[(bb) any conviction in service disciplinary proceedings for an offence listed in the Schedule to this Act;] and

(c) any conviction by or before a court outside Great Britain of an offence in respect of conduct which, if it had taken place in any part of Great Britain, would not have constituted an offence under the law in force in that part of Great Britain.

(7) …

[94]

NOTES

Sub-s (3): words in square brackets substituted by the Criminal Justice and Court Services Act 2000, s 74, Sch 7, Pt II, paras 48, 50.

Sub-s (6): words omitted repealed, and para (bb) inserted, by the Armed Forces Act 1996, ss 13(1), (3)(a), (b), 35(2), Sch 7, Pt III; in para (a) words in first (outer) pair of square brackets substituted by the Criminal Law Act 1977, s 65(4), Sch 12, words in second (inner) square brackets substituted by the Magistrates' Courts Act 1980, s 154, Sch 7, para 134, words in final pair of square brackets inserted by the Crime (Sentences) Act 1997, s 55, Sch 4, para 9(2).

Sub-s (7): repealed by the Armed Forces Act 1996, s 35(2), Sch 7, Pt III.

Probation orders: see the note to s 5 at **[93]**.

Summary Jurisdiction (Scotland) Act 1954: repealed by the Criminal Procedure (Scotland) Act 1975, s 461(2), Sch 10, Pt I.

7 Limitations on rehabilitation under this Act, etc

(1) Nothing in section 4(1) above shall affect—

(a) any right of Her Majesty, by virtue of Her Royal prerogative or otherwise, to grant a free pardon, to quash any conviction or sentence, or to commute any sentence;

(b) the enforcement by any process or proceedings of any fine or other sum adjudged to be paid by or imposed on a spent conviction;

(c) the issue of any process for the purpose of proceedings in respect of any breach of a condition or requirement applicable to a sentence imposed in respect of a spent conviction; or

(d) the operation of any enactment by virtue of which, in consequence of any conviction, a person is subject, otherwise than by way of sentence, to any disqualification, disability, prohibition or other penalty the period of which extends beyond the rehabilitation period applicable in accordance with section 6 above to the conviction.

(2) Nothing in section 4(1) above shall affect the determination of any issue, or prevent the admission or requirement of any evidence, relating to a person's previous convictions or to circumstances ancillary thereto—

(a) in any criminal proceedings before a court in Great Britain (including any appeal or reference in a criminal matter);

(b) in any service disciplinary proceedings or in any proceedings on appeal from any service disciplinary proceedings;

[(bb) in any proceedings under Part 2 of the Sexual Offences Act 2003, or on appeal from any such proceedings;]

[(c) in any proceedings relating to adoption, the marriage of any minor, [or the formation of a civil partnership by any minor,] the exercise of the inherent jurisdiction of the High Court with respect to minors or the provision by any person of accommodation, care or schooling for minors;

(cc) in any proceedings brought under the Children Act 1989;

(d) in any proceedings relating to the variation or discharge of a supervision order under [the Powers of Criminal Courts (Sentencing) Act 2000], or on appeal from any such proceedings;]

(e) …

(f) in any proceedings in which he is a party or a witness, provided that, on the occasion when the issue or the admission or requirement of the evidence falls to be determined, he consents to the determination of the issue or, as the case may be, the admission or requirement of the evidence notwithstanding the provisions of section 4(1); […

(g) …]

…

(3) If at any stage in any proceedings before a judicial authority in Great Britain (not being proceedings to which, by virtue of any of paragraphs (a) to (e) of subsection (2) above or of any order for the time being in force under subsection (4) below, section 4(1) above has no application, or proceedings to which section 8 below applies) the authority is satisfied, in the light of any considerations which appear to it to be relevant (including any evidence which has been or may thereafter be put before it), that justice cannot be done in the case except by admitting or requiring evidence relating to a person's spent convictions or to circumstances ancillary thereto, that authority may admit or, as the case may be, require the evidence in question notwithstanding the provisions of subsection (1) of section 4 above, and may determine any issue to which the evidence relates in disregard, so far as necessary, of those provisions.

(4) The Secretary of State may by order exclude the application of section 4(1) above in relation to any proceedings specified in the order (other than proceedings to which section 8 below applies) to such extent and for such purposes as may be so specified.

(5) No order made by a court with respect to any person otherwise than on a conviction shall be included in any list or statement of that person's previous convictions given or made to any court which is considering how to deal with him in respect of any offence. **[95]**

NOTES

Sub-s (2) is amended as follows:

Para (bb) inserted by the Crime and Disorder Act 1998, s 119, Sch 8, para 36, and substituted by the Sexual Offences Act 2003, s 139, Sch 6, para 19, as from 1 May 2004.

Paras (c), (cc), (d) substituted, for original paras (c), (d), by the Children Act 1989, s 108(5), Sch 13, para 35, in relation to England and Wales only; words in square brackets in para (c) inserted by the Civil Partnership Act 2004, s 261(1), Sch 27, para 53, as from 5 December 2005.

Para (c) also substituted, in relation to Scotland only, by the Children (Scotland) Act 1995, s 105(4), Sch 4, para 23(1), (4)(a), as follows—

"(c) in any proceedings relating to parental responsibilities or parental rights (within the meaning of section 1(3) and section 2(4) respectively of the Children (Scotland) Act 1995), guardianship, adoption or the provision by any person of accommodation, care or schooling for children under the age of 18 years;

(cc) in any proceedings under Part II of the Children (Scotland) Act 1995;".

Words in square brackets in para (d) substituted by the Powers of Criminal Courts (Sentencing) Act 2000, s 165(1), Sch 9, para 49.

Para (e) and final words omitted repealed by the Children (Scotland) Act 1995, s 105(4), (5), Sch 4, para 23(1), (4)(b), (c), Sch 5.

Para (g) repealed by the Banking Act 1987, s 108(2), Sch 7, Pt I.

Secretary of State: the functions conferred by sub-s (4) are, in so far as exercisable in relation to Scotland, transferred to the Scottish Ministers, by the Scotland Act 1998 (Transfer of Functions to the Scottish Ministers etc) Order 2003, SI 2003/415, art 2.

Orders: the Rehabilitation of Offenders Act 1974 (Exceptions) Order 1975, SI 1975/1023 at **[2009]**; the Rehabilitation of Offenders Act 1974 (Exclusions and Exceptions) (Scotland) Order 2003, SSI 2003/231 at **[2881A]**.

8 ((*Defamation actions*) *outside the scope of this work.*)

9 Unauthorised disclosure of spent convictions

(1) In this section—

"official record" means a record kept for the purposes of its functions by any court, police force, Government department, local or other public authority in Great Britain, or a record kept, in Great Britain or elsewhere, for the purposes of any of Her Majesty's forces, being in either case a record containing information about persons convicted of offences; and

"specified information" means information imputing that a named or otherwise identifiable rehabilitated living person has committed or been charged with or prosecuted for or convicted of or sentenced for any offence which is the subject of a spent conviction.

(2) Subject to the provisions of any order made under subsection (5) below, any person who, in the course of his official duties, has or at any time has had custody of or access to any official record or the information contained therein, shall be guilty of an offence if, knowing or having reasonable cause to suspect that any specified information he has obtained in the course of those duties is specified information, he discloses it, otherwise than in the course of those duties, to another person.

(3) In any proceedings for an offence under subsection (2) above it shall be a defence for the defendant (or, in Scotland, the accused person) to show that the disclosure was made—

(a) to the rehabilitated person or to another person at the express request of the rehabilitated person; or

(b) to a person whom he reasonably believed to be the rehabilitated person or to another person at the express request of a person whom he reasonably believed to be the rehabilitated person.

(4) Any person who obtains any specified information from any official record by means of any fraud, dishonesty or bribe shall be guilty of an offence.

(5) The Secretary of State may by order make such provision as appears to him to be appropriate for excepting the disclosure of specified information derived from an official record from the provisions of subsection (2) above in such cases or classes of case as may be specified in the order.

(6) Any person guilty of an offence under subsection (2) above shall be liable on summary conviction to a fine not exceeding [level 4 on the standard scale].

(7) Any person guilty of an offence under subsection (4) above shall be liable on summary conviction to a fine not exceeding [level 5 on the standard scale] or to imprisonment for a term not exceeding six months, or to both.

(8) Proceedings for an offence under subsection (2) above shall not, in England and Wales, be instituted except by or on behalf of the Director of Public Prosecutions.

[96]

NOTES

Sub-ss (6), (7): maximum fines increased and converted to levels on the standard scale by the Criminal Justice Act 1982, ss 37, 38, 46.

10 Orders

(1) Any power of the Secretary of State to make an order under any provision of this Act shall be exercisable by statutory instrument, and an order made under any provision of this Act except section 11 below may be varied or revoked by a subsequent order made under that provision.

(2) No order shall be made by the Secretary of State under any provision of this Act other than section 11 below unless a draft of it has been laid before, and approved by resolution of, each House of Parliament.

[97]

11 Citation, commencement and extent

(1) This Act may be cited as the Rehabilitation of Offenders Act 1974.

(2) This Act shall come into force on 1st July 1975 or such earlier day as the Secretary of State may by order appoint.

(3) This Act shall not apply to Northern Ireland.

[98]

[SCHEDULE
SERVICE DISCIPLINARY CONVICTIONS

Section 6(4)

1. Any conviction for an offence mentioned in this Schedule is a conviction referred to in section 6(6)(bb) of this Act (convictions to be disregarded for the purposes of extending a period of rehabilitation following subsequent conviction).

Provisions of the Army Act 1955 and the Air Force Act 1955

2. Any offence under any of the provisions of the Army Act 1955 or the Air Force Act 1955 listed in the first column of the following table—

Provision	*Subject-matter*
Section 29	Offences by or in relation to sentries, persons on watch etc.
Section 29A	Failure to attend for duty, neglect of duty etc.
Section 33	Insubordinate behaviour.
Section 34	Disobedience to lawful commands.
Section 34A	Failure to provide a sample for drug testing.
Section 35	Obstruction of provost officers.
Section 36	Disobedience to standing orders.
Section 38	Absence without leave.
Section 39	Failure to report or apprehend deserters or absentees.
Section 42	Malingering.
Section 43	Drunkenness.
Section 43A	Fighting, threatening words etc.
Section 44	Damage to, and loss of, public or service property etc.
Section 44A	Damage to, and loss of, Her Majesty's aircraft or aircraft material.
Section 44B	Interference etc with equipment, messages or signals.
Section 45	Misapplication and waste of public or service property.
Section 46	Offences relating to issues and decorations.
Section 47	Billeting offences.
Section 48	Offences in relation to requisitioning of vehicles.
Section 50	Inaccurate certification.
Section 51	Low flying.
Section 52	Annoyance by flying.
Section 54	Permitting escape, and unlawful release of prisoners.
Section 55	Resistance to arrest.
Section 56	Escape from confinement.
Section 57	Offences in relation to courts-martial.
Section 61	Making of false statements on enlistment.
Section 62	Making of false documents.
Section 63	Offences against civilian population.
Section 69	Conduct to prejudice of military discipline or air-force discipline.

3. Any offence under section 68 (attempt to commit military offence) or 68A (aiding and abetting etc, and inciting, military offence) of the Army Act 1955 in relation to an offence under any of the provisions of that Act listed in paragraph 2.

4. Any offence under section 68 (attempt to commit air-force offence) or 68A (aiding and abetting etc, and inciting, air-force offence) of the Air Force Act 1955 in relation to an offence under any of the provisions of that Act listed in paragraph 2.

Provisions of the Naval Discipline Act 1957

5. Any offence under any of the provisions of the Naval Discipline Act 1957 listed in the first column of the following table:—

Provision	*Subject-matter*
Section 6	Offences by or in relation to sentries, persons on watch etc.
Section 7	Failure to attend for duty, neglect of duty etc.
Section 11	Insubordinate behaviour.
Section 12	Disobedience to lawful commands.
Section 12A	Failure to provide a sample for drug testing.
Section 13	Fighting, threatening words etc.
Section 14	Obstruction of provost officers.
Section 14A	Disobedience to standing orders.
Section 17	Absence without leave etc.
Section 18	Failure to report deserters and absentees.
Section 21	Low flying.
Section 22	Annoyance by flying.
Section 25	Inaccurate certification.
Section 27	Malingering.
Section 28	Drunkenness.
Section 29	Damage to, and loss of, public or service property etc.
Section 29A	Damage to, and loss of, Her Majesty's aircraft or aircraft material.
Section 29B	Interference etc with equipment, messages or signals.
Section 30	Misapplication and waste of public or service property.
Section 31	Offences relating to issues and decorations.
Section 32	Billeting offences.
Section 33	Offences in relation to the requisitioning of vehicles etc.
Section 33A	Permitting escape, and unlawful release of prisoners.
Section 33B	Resistance to arrest.
Section 33C	Escape from confinement.
Section 34A	False statements on entry.
Section 35	Falsification of documents.
Section 35A	Offences against civilian population.
Section 38	Offences in relation to courts-martial.
Section 39	Conduct to the prejudice of naval discipline.

6. Any offence under section 40 (attempt to commit naval offence) or 41 (aiding and abetting etc, and inciting, naval offence) of the Naval Discipline Act 1957 in relation to an offence under any of the provisions of that Act listed in paragraph 5.

[Provisions of the Armed Forces Act 2006

7. Any service offence within the meaning of the Armed Forces Act 2006 except one punishable in the case of an offender aged 18 or over with imprisonment for more than two years.]]

[99]

NOTES

Added by the Armed Forces Act 1996, s 13(1), (4), Sch 4.

Para 7: added by the Armed Forces Act 2006, s 378(1), Sch 16, para 66, as from a day to be appointed.

SEX DISCRIMINATION ACT 1975

(1975 c 65)

ARRANGEMENT OF SECTIONS

PART I
DISCRIMINATION TO WHICH ACT APPLIES

PART II
EMPLOYMENT FIELD

Discrimination by employers

Discrimination against office-holders etc

Discrimination by other bodies

Special cases

Relationships which have come to an end

PART III
DISCRIMINATION IN OTHER FIELDS

Education

Goods, facilities, services and premises

Barristers

Advocates

Relationships which have come to an end

Extent

PART IV
OTHER UNLAWFUL ACTS

PART V
GENERAL EXCEPTIONS FROM PARTS II TO IV

PART VII
ENFORCEMENT

General

Enforcement in employment field

Enforcement of Part III

Help for persons suffering discrimination

Period within which proceedings to be brought

PART VIII
SUPPLEMENTAL

SCHEDULES:

An Act to render unlawful certain kinds of sex discrimination and discrimination on the ground of marriage, and establish a Commission with the function of working towards the elimination of such discrimination and promoting equality of opportunity between men and women generally; and for related purposes

[12 November 1975]

NOTES

This Act is printed in full save for specific omissions noted in the text. Although Part III is mostly outside the scope of this work, it is included for ease of reference and because of its use as an aid to the interpretation of other Parts of the Act.

Exemptions: as to exemptions from certain provisions of Pts II–IV of this Act, see the Employment Act 1989, s 4 at **[404]** (exemption in connection with the protection of women at work), s 5 of the 1989 Act at **[405]** (exemption in connection with certain educational appointments), and s 6 of the 1989 Act at **[406]** (power of Secretary of State to order further exemptions).

Employment Appeal Tribunal: an appeal lies to the Employment Appeal Tribunal on any question of law arising from any decision of, or in any proceedings before, an employment tribunal under or by virtue of this Act; see the Employment Tribunals Act 1996, s 21(1)(b) at **[978]**.

Transfer of functions: as to the transfer of the functions of the Secretary of State for Trade and Industry under this Act to the Secretary of State for Communities and Local Government, see the Secretary of State for Communities and Local Government Order 2006, SI 2006/1926, arts 7(1), (2), (3)(b), 8. Note also that by the Transfer of Functions (Equality) Order 2007, SI 2007/2914, art 3(1), (2)(b), the functions of the Secretary of State under this Act (except ss 24, 25, 66(5), 78, 79, 85(9E), Sch 2) are transferred to the Lord Privy Seal (as from 12 October 2007).

See *Harvey* LI, Q.

PART I
DISCRIMINATION TO WHICH ACT APPLIES

[1 Direct and indirect discrimination against women

(1) In any circumstances relevant for the purposes of any provision of this Act, other than a provision to which subsection (2) applies, a person discriminates against a woman if—

(a) on the ground of her sex he treats her less favourably than he treats or would treat a man, or

(b) he applies to her a requirement or condition which he applies or would apply equally to a man but—

(i) which is such that the proportion of women who can comply with it is considerably smaller than the proportion of men who can comply with it, and

(ii) which he cannot show to be justifiable irrespective of the sex of the person to whom it is applied, and

(iii) which is to her detriment because she cannot comply with it.

(2) In any circumstances relevant for the purposes of a provision to which this subsection applies, a person discriminates against a woman if—

(a) on the ground of her sex, he treats her less favourably than he treats or would treat a man, or

[(b) he applies to her a provision, criterion or practice which he applies or would apply equally to a man, but—

(i) which puts or would put women at a particular disadvantage when compared with men,
(ii) which puts her at that disadvantage, and
(iii) which he cannot show to be a proportionate means of achieving a legitimate aim].

(3) Subsection (2) applies to—
(a) any provision of Part 2,
[(aa) sections 29 to 31, except in so far as they relate to an excluded matter,]
(b) sections 35A and 35B, and
(c) any other provision of Part 3, so far as it applies to vocational training.

(4) …]

[100]

NOTES

Substituted by the Sex Discrimination (Indirect Discrimination and Burden of Proof) Regulations 2001, SI 2001/2660, reg 3.

Sub-s (2): para (b) substituted by the Employment Equality (Sex Discrimination) Regulations 2005, SI 2005/2467, reg 3(1), as from 1 October 2005.

Sub-s (3): para (aa) inserted by the Sex Discrimination (Amendment of Legislation) Regulations 2008, SI 2008/963, reg 2(1), Sch 1, para 1, as from 6 April 2008.

Sub-s (4): repealed by the Civil Partnership Act 2004, ss 251(1), (3), 261(4), Sch 30, as from 5 December 2005.

2 Sex discrimination against men

(1) Section 1, and the provisions of Parts II and III relating to sex discrimination against women, are to be read as applying equally to the treatment of men, and for that purpose shall have effect with such modifications as are requisite.

(2) In the application of subsection (1) no account shall be taken of special treatment afforded to women in connection with pregnancy or childbirth.

[101]

[2A Discrimination on the grounds of gender reassignment

(1) A person ("A") discriminates against another person ("B") in any circumstances relevant for the purposes of—
(a) any provision of Part II,
[(aa) section 29, 30 or 31, except in so far as it relates to an excluded matter,]
(b) section 35A or 35B, or
(c) any other provision of Part III, so far as it applies to vocational training,

if he treats B less favourably than he treats or would treat other persons, and does so on the ground that B intends to undergo, is undergoing or has undergone gender reassignment.

(2) Subsection (3) applies to arrangements made by any person in relation to another's absence from work or from vocational training.

(3) For the purposes of subsection (1), B is treated less favourably than others under such arrangements if, in the application of the arrangements to any absence due to B undergoing gender reassignment—
(a) he is treated less favourably than he would be if the absence was due to sickness or injury, or
(b) he is treated less favourably than he would be if the absence was due to some other cause and, having regard to the circumstances of the case, it is reasonable for him to be treated no less favourably.

(4) In subsections (2) and (3) "arrangements" includes terms, conditions or arrangements on which employment, a pupillage or tenancy or vocational training is offered.

(5) For the purposes of subsection (1), a provision mentioned in that subsection framed with reference to discrimination against women shall be treated as applying equally to the treatment of men with such modifications as are requisite.]

[102]

NOTES

Inserted by the Sex Discrimination (Gender Reassignment) Regulations 1999, SI 1999/1102, reg 2(1).

Sub-s (1): para (aa) inserted by the Sex Discrimination (Amendment of Legislation) Regulations 2008, SI 2008/963, reg 2(1), Sch 1, para 2, as from 6 April 2008.

[3 Discrimination against married persons and civil partners in employment field

(1) In any circumstances relevant for the purposes of any provision of Part 2, a person discriminates against a person ("A") who fulfils the condition in subsection (2) if—

(a) on the ground of the fulfilment of the condition, he treats A less favourably than he treats or would treat a person who does not fulfil the condition, or

(b) he applies to A a provision, criterion or practice which he applies or would apply equally to a person who does not fulfil the condition, but—

(i) which puts or would put persons fulfilling the condition at a particular disadvantage when compared with persons not fulfilling the condition, and

(ii) which puts A at that disadvantage, and

(iii) which he cannot show to be a proportionate means of achieving a legitimate aim.

(2) The condition is that the person is—

(a) married, or

(b) a civil partner.

(3) For the purposes of subsection (1), a provision of Part 2 framed with reference to discrimination against women is to be treated as applying equally to the treatment of men, and for that purpose has effect with such modifications as are requisite.]

[103]

NOTES

Commencement: 5 December 2005.

Substituted by the Civil Partnership Act 2004, s 251(1), (2), as from 5 December 2005.

[3A Discrimination on the ground of pregnancy or maternity leave

(1) In any circumstances relevant for the purposes of a provision to which this subsection applies, a person discriminates against a woman if—

(a) at a time in a protected period, and on the ground of the woman's pregnancy, the person treats her less favourably … ; or

(b) on the ground that the woman is exercising or seeking to exercise, or has exercised or sought to exercise, a statutory right to maternity leave, the person treats her less favourably …

(2) In any circumstances relevant for the purposes of a provision to which this subsection applies, a person discriminates against a woman if, on the ground that section 72(1) of the Employment Rights Act 1996 (compulsory maternity leave) has to be complied with in respect of the woman, he treats her less favourably …

(3) For the purposes of subsection (1)—

(a) in relation to a woman, a protected period begins each time she becomes pregnant, and the protected period associated with any particular pregnancy of hers ends in accordance with the following rules—

(i) if she is entitled to ordinary but not additional maternity leave in connection with the pregnancy, the protected period ends at the end of her period of ordinary maternity leave connected with the pregnancy or, if earlier, when she returns to work after the end of her pregnancy;

(ii) if she is entitled to ordinary and additional maternity leave in connection with the pregnancy, the protected period ends at the end of her period of additional maternity leave connected with the pregnancy or, if earlier, when she returns to work after the end of her pregnancy;

(iii) if she is not entitled to ordinary maternity leave in respect of the pregnancy, the protected period ends at the end of the 2 weeks beginning with the end of the pregnancy;

(b) where a person's treatment of a woman is on grounds of illness suffered by the woman as a consequence of a pregnancy of hers, that treatment is to be taken to be on the ground of the pregnancy;

(c) a "statutory right to maternity leave" means a right conferred by section 71(1) or 73(1) of the Employment Rights Act 1996 (ordinary and additional maternity leave).

(4) In subsection (3) "ordinary maternity leave" and "additional maternity leave" shall be construed in accordance with sections 71 and 73 of the Employment Rights Act 1996.

(5) Subsections (1) and (2) apply to—
(a) any provision of Part 2,
(b) sections 35A and 35B, and
(c) any other provision of Part 3, so far as it applies to vocational training.]

[103A]

NOTES

Commencement: 1 October 2005.
Inserted by the Employment Equality (Sex Discrimination) Regulations 2005, SI 2005/2467, reg 4, as from 1 October 2005.
Sub-ss (1), (2): words omitted repealed by the Sex Discrimination Act 1975 (Amendment) Regulations 2008, SI 2008/656, reg 2, as from 6 April 2008.

[3B Discrimination on the ground of pregnancy or maternity: goods, facilities, services or premises

(1) In any circumstances relevant for the purposes of a provision to which this subsection applies, a person discriminates against a woman if he treats her less favourably—
(a) on the ground of her pregnancy, or
(b) within the period of 26 weeks beginning on the day on which she gives birth, on the ground that she has given birth.

(2) A person (P) is taken to discriminate against a woman on the ground of her pregnancy if—
(a) P refuses to provide her with goods, facilities or services because P thinks that providing them would, because of her pregnancy, create a risk to her health or safety, or
(b) P provides or offers to provide them on conditions intended to remove or reduce such a risk because P thinks that provision of them without the conditions would create such a risk.

(3) Subsection (2) does not apply if—
(a) it is reasonable for P to think as mentioned in paragraph (a) or (b), and
(b) P applies an equivalent policy.

(4) An equivalent policy is—
(a) for the purposes of subsection (2)(a), refusing to provide the goods, facilities or services to persons with other physical conditions because P thinks that to do so would, because of such physical conditions, create a risk to the health or safety of such persons;
(b) for the purposes of subsection (2)(b), imposing conditions on the provision of goods, facilities or services to such persons which are intended to remove or reduce the risk to their health or safety because P thinks that the provision without the conditions would create such a risk.

(5) Subsection (1) applies to sections 29 to 31, except in so far as they relate to an excluded matter.]

[103B]

NOTES

Commencement: 6 April 2008.
Inserted by the Sex Discrimination (Amendment of Legislation) Regulations 2008, SI 2008/963, reg 2(1), Sch 1, para 3(1), as from 6 April 2008.

4 Discrimination by way of victimisation

(1) A person ("the discriminator") discriminates against another person ("the person victimised") in any circumstances relevant for the purposes of any provision of this Act if he treats the person victimised less favourably than in those circumstances he treats or would treat other persons, and does so by reason that the person victimised has—
(a) brought proceedings against the discriminator or any other person under this Act or the Equal Pay Act 1970 [or sections 62 to 65 of the Pensions Act 1995], or
(b) given evidence or information in connection with proceedings brought by any

person against the discriminator or any other person under this Act or the Equal Pay Act 1970 [or sections 62 to 65 of the Pensions Act 1995], or

(c) otherwise done anything under or by reference to this Act or the Equal Pay Act 1970 [or sections 62 to 65 of the Pensions Act 1995] in relation to the discriminator or any other person, or

(d) alleged that the discriminator or any other person has committed an act which (whether or not the allegation so states) would amount to a contravention of this Act or give rise to a claim under the Equal Pay Act 1970 [or under sections 62 to 65 of the Pensions Act 1995],

or by reason that the discriminator knows the person victimised intends to do any of those things, or suspects the person victimised has done, or intends to do, any of them.

(2) Subsection (1) does not apply to treatment of a person by reason of any allegation made by him if the allegation was false and not made in good faith.

(3) For the purposes of subsection (1), a provision of Part II or III framed with reference to discrimination against women shall be treated as applying equally to the treatment of men and for that purpose shall have effect with such modifications as are requisite.

[104]

NOTES

Sub-s (1): words in square brackets in paras (a)–(d) inserted by the Pensions Act 1995, s 66(2).

[4A Harassment, including sexual harassment

(1) For the purposes of this Act, a person subjects a woman to harassment if—

(a) [he engages in unwanted conduct that is related to her sex or that of another person and] has the purpose or effect—

(i) of violating her dignity, or

(ii) of creating an intimidating, hostile, degrading, humiliating or offensive environment for her,

(b) he engages in any form of unwanted verbal, non-verbal or physical conduct of a sexual nature that has the purpose or effect—

(i) of violating her dignity, or

(ii) of creating an intimidating, hostile, degrading, humiliating or offensive environment for her, or

(c) on the ground of her rejection of or submission to unwanted conduct of a kind mentioned in paragraph (a) or (b), he treats her less favourably than he would treat her had she not rejected, or submitted to, the conduct.

(2) Conduct shall be regarded as having the effect mentioned in sub-paragraph (i) or (ii) of subsection (1)(a) or (b) only if, having regard to all the circumstances, including in particular the perception of the woman, it should reasonably be considered as having that effect.

(3) For the purposes of this Act, a person ("A") subjects another person ("B") to harassment if—

(a) A, on the ground that B intends to undergo, is undergoing or has undergone gender reassignment, engages in unwanted conduct that has the purpose or effect—

(i) of violating B's dignity, or

(ii) of creating an intimidating, hostile, degrading, humiliating or offensive environment for B, or

(b) A, on the ground of B's rejection of or submission to unwanted conduct of a kind mentioned in paragraph (a), treats B less favourably than A would treat B had B not rejected, or submitted to, the conduct.

(4) Conduct shall be regarded as having the effect mentioned in sub-paragraph (i) or (ii) of subsection (3)(a) only if, having regard to all the circumstances, including in particular the perception of B, it should reasonably be considered as having that effect.

(5) Subsection (1) is to be read as applying equally to the harassment of men, and for that purpose shall have effect with such modifications as are requisite.

(6) For the purposes of subsections (1) and (3), a provision of Part 2 or 3 framed with reference to harassment of women shall be treated as applying equally to the harassment of men, and for that purpose will have effect with such modifications as are requisite.]

[104A]

NOTES

Commencement: 1 October 2005.

Inserted by the Employment Equality (Sex Discrimination) Regulations 2005, SI 2005/2467, reg 5, as from 1 October 2005.

Sub-s (1): words in square brackets substituted by the Sex Discrimination Act 1975 (Amendment) Regulations 2008, SI 2008/656, reg 3, as from 6 April 2008.

5 Interpretation

(1) In this Act—

(a) references to discrimination refer to any discrimination falling within sections 1 to 4; and

(b) references to sex discrimination refer to any discrimination falling within [section 1, 2[, 3A or 3B]],

and related expressions shall be construed accordingly.

(2) In this Act—

"woman" includes a female of any age, and

"man" includes a male of any age.

[(3) Each of the following comparisons, that is—

(a) a comparison of the cases of persons of different sex under section 1(1) or (2),

(b) a comparison of the cases of persons required for the purposes of section 2A, and

(c) a comparison of the cases of persons who do and who do not fulfil the condition in section 3(2),

must be such that the relevant circumstances in the one case are the same, or not materially different, in the other.]

[(4) In this Act, references to an excluded matter must be construed in accordance with section 35ZA.]

[105]

NOTES

Sub-s (1): words in first (outer) pair of square brackets in para (b) substituted by the Employment Equality (Sex Discrimination) Regulations 2005, SI 2005/2467, reg 6, as from 1 October 2005; words in second (inner) pair of square brackets in that paragraph substituted by the Sex Discrimination (Amendment of Legislation) Regulations 2008, SI 2008/963, reg 2(1), Sch 1, para 3(2), as from 6 April 2008.

Sub-s (3): substituted by the Civil Partnership Act 2004, s 251(1), (3), as from 5 December 2005.

Sub-s (4): added by SI 2008/963, reg 2(1), Sch 1, para 9(2), as from 6 April 2008.

[PART II
EMPLOYMENT FIELD]

NOTES

Part heading substituted by the Employment Equality (Sex Discrimination) Regulations 2005, SI 2005/2467, reg 7(1), as from 1 October 2005.

Serious Organised Crime Agency: for the application of this Part to a constable or other person seconded to SOCA as a member of its staff, see the Serious Organised Crime and Police Act 2005, s 56(1), (2).

Discrimination by employers

6 … Applicants and employees

(1) It is unlawful for a person, in relation to employment by him at an establishment in Great Britain, to discriminate against a woman—

(a) in the arrangements he makes for the purpose of determining who should be offered that employment, or

(b) in the terms on which he offers her that employment, or

(c) by refusing or deliberately omitting to offer her that employment.

(2) It is unlawful for a person, in the case of a woman employed by him at an establishment in Great Britain, to discriminate against her—

(a) in the way he affords her access to opportunities for promotion, transfer or training, or to any other benefits, facilities or services, or by refusing or deliberately omitting to afford her access to them, or

(b) by dismissing her, or subjecting her to any other detriment.

[(2A) It is unlawful for an employer, in relation to employment by him at an establishment in Great Britain, to subject to harassment—

(a) a woman whom he employs, or

(b) a woman who has applied to him for employment.]

[(2B) For the purposes of subsection (2A), the circumstances in which an employer is to be treated as subjecting a woman to harassment shall include those where—

(a) a third party subjects the woman to harassment in the course of her employment, and

(b) the employer has failed to take such steps as would have been reasonably practicable to prevent the third party from doing so.

(2C) Subsection (2B) does not apply unless the employer knows that the woman has been subject to harassment in the course of her employment on at least two other occasions by a third party.

(2D) In subsections (2B) and (2C), "third party" means a person other than—

(a) the employer, or

(b) a person whom the employer employs,

and for the purposes of those subsections it is immaterial whether the third party is the same or a different person on each occasion.]

(3) …

[(4) Subsections (1)(b) and (2) do not render it unlawful for a person to discriminate against a woman in relation to her membership of, or rights under, an occupational pension scheme in such a way that, were any term of the scheme to provide for discrimination in that way, then, by reason only of any provision made by or under sections 62 to 64 of the Pensions Act 1995 (equal treatment), an equal treatment rule would not operate in relation to that term.

(4A) In subsection (4), "occupational pension scheme" has the same meaning as in the Pension Schemes Act 1993 and "equal treatment rule" has the same meaning given by section 62 of the Pensions Act 1995.]

(5) Subject to section 8(3), subsection (1)(b) does not apply to any provision for the payment of money which, if the woman in question were given the employment, would be included (directly … or otherwise) in the contract under which she was employed.

(6) Subsection (2) does not apply to benefits consisting of the payment of money when the provision of those benefits is regulated by the woman's contract of employment.

(7) Subsection (2) does not apply to benefits, facilities or services of any description if the employer is concerned with the provision (for payment or not) of benefits, facilities or services of that description to the public, or to a section of the public comprising the woman in question, unless—

(a) that provision differs in a material respect from the provision of the benefits, facilities or services by the employer to his employees, or

(b) the provision of the benefits, facilities or services to the woman in question is regulated by her contract of employment, or

(c) the benefits, facilities or services relate to training.

[(8) In its application to any discrimination falling within section 2A, this section shall have effect with the omission of subsections (4) to (6).]

[106]

NOTES

Section heading: words omitted repealed by SI 2005/2467, reg 7(2), (3), as from 1 October 2005.

Sub-s (2A): inserted by SI 2005/2467, reg 7(2), (4), as from 1 October 2005.

Sub-ss (2B)–(2D): inserted by the Sex Discrimination Act 1975 (Amendment) Regulations 2008, SI 2008/656, reg 4, as from 6 April 2008.

Sub-s (3): repealed by the Sex Discrimination Act 1986, ss 1(1), 9(2), Schedule, Pt II.

Sub-ss (4), (4A): substituted, for original sub-s (4), by the Pensions Act 1995, s 66(3).

Sub-s (5): words omitted repealed by the Sex Discrimination Act 1986, s 9, Schedule, Pt II.

Sub-s (8): added by the Sex Discrimination (Gender Reassignment) Regulations 1999, SI 1999/1102, reg 3(1).

Modified, in relation to governing bodies with delegated budgets, by the Education (Modification of Enactments Relating to Employment) (England) Order 2003, SI 2003/1964, art 3, Schedule at **[3035C]**, **[3035G]** and the Education (Modification of Enactments Relating to Employment) (Wales) Order 2006, SI 2006/1073, art 3, Schedule at **[3462B]**, **[3462F]**.

[6A Exception relating to terms and conditions during maternity leave

(1) Subject to subsections (2) and (5), section 6(1)(b) and (2) does not make it unlawful to deprive a woman who is on ordinary maternity leave of any benefit from the terms and conditions of her employment relating to remuneration.

(2) Subsection (1) does not apply to benefit by way of maternity-related remuneration.

(3) Subject to subsections (4) and (5), section 6(1)(b) and (2) does not make it unlawful to deprive a woman who is on additional maternity leave of any benefit from the terms and conditions of her employment.

(4) Subsection (3) does not apply to—

(a) benefit by way of maternity-related remuneration,

(b) the benefit of her employer's implied obligation to her of trust and confidence, or

(c) any benefit of terms and conditions in respect of—

(i) notice of the termination by her employer of her contract of employment,

(ii) compensation in the event of redundancy,

(iii) disciplinary or grievance procedures, or

(iv) membership of a pension scheme.

(5) Neither of subsections (1) and (3) applies to—

(a) benefit by way of remuneration in respect of times when the woman is neither on ordinary maternity leave nor on additional maternity leave, including increase-related remuneration in respect of such times; or

(b) benefit by way of maternity-related remuneration that is increase-related.

(6) For the purposes of subsection (5), remuneration is increase-related so far as it falls to be calculated by reference to increases in remuneration that the woman would have received had she not been on ordinary or additional maternity leave.

(7) In this section—

"maternity-related remuneration", in relation to a woman, means remuneration to which she is entitled as a result of being pregnant or being on ordinary or additional maternity leave;

"on additional maternity leave" means absent from work in exercise of the right conferred by section 73(1) of the Employment Rights Act 1996;

"on ordinary maternity leave" means absent from work in exercise of the right conferred by section 71(1) of that Act (ordinary maternity leave) or in consequence of the prohibition in section 72(1) of that Act (compulsory maternity leave);

"remuneration" means benefits—

(a) that consist of the payment of money to an employee by way of wages or salary, and

(b) that are not benefits whose provision is regulated by the employee's contract of employment.]

[106A]

NOTES

Commencement: 1 October 2005.

Inserted by the Employment Equality (Sex Discrimination) Regulations 2005, SI 2005/2467, reg 8, as from 1 October 2005.

Substituted by the Sex Discrimination Act 1975 (Amendment) Regulations 2008, SI 2008/656, regs 1(3), 5, in relation to a case where a woman's expected week of childbirth (as defined in the Maternity and Parental Leave etc Regulations 1999, SI 1999/3312, reg 2 (at **[2553]**)) begins on or after 5 October 2008, as follows—

"6A Exception relating to terms and conditions during maternity leave

(1) Subject to subsection (2), section 6(1)(b) and (2) does not make it unlawful to deprive a woman who is on maternity leave of any benefit from the terms and conditions of her employment relating to remuneration.

(2) The reference in subsection (1) to benefit from the terms and conditions of a woman's employment relating to remuneration does not include a reference to—

(a) maternity-related remuneration (including maternity-related remuneration that is increase-related),
(b) remuneration (including increase-related remuneration) in respect of times when the woman is not on maternity leave, or
(c) remuneration by way of bonus in respect of times when a woman is on compulsory maternity leave.

(3) For the purposes of subsection (2), remuneration is increase-related so far as it falls to be calculated by reference to increases in remuneration that the woman would have received had she not been on maternity leave.

(4) In this section—

"maternity-related remuneration", in relation to a woman, means remuneration to which she is entitled as a result of being pregnant or being on maternity leave;

"on compulsory maternity leave" means absent from work in consequence of the prohibition in section 72(1) of the Employment Rights Act 1996;

"on maternity leave" means—
(a) on compulsory maternity leave,
(b) absent from work in exercise of the right conferred by section 71(1) of the Employment Rights Act 1996 (ordinary maternity leave), or
(c) absent from work in exercise of the right conferred by section 73(1) of that Act (additional maternity leave); and

"remuneration" means benefits—
(a) that consist of the payment of money to an employee by way of wages or salary, and
(b) that are not benefits whose provision is regulated by the employee's contract of employment.".

---

7 Exception where sex is a genuine occupational qualification

(1) In relation to sex discrimination—
(a) section 6(1)(a) or (c) does not apply to any employment where being a man is a genuine occupational qualification for the job, and
(b) section 6(2)(a) does not apply to opportunities for promotion or transfer to, or training for, such employment.

(2) Being a man is a genuine occupational qualification for a job only where—
(a) the essential nature of the job calls for a man for reasons of physiology (excluding physical strength or stamina) or, in dramatic performances or other entertainment, for reasons of authenticity, so that the essential nature of the job would be materially different if carried out by a woman; or
(b) the job needs to be held by a man to preserve decency or privacy because—
(i) it is likely to involve physical contact with men in circumstances where they might reasonably object to its being carried out by a woman, or
(ii) the holder of the job is likely to do his work in circumstances where men might reasonably object to the presence of a woman because they are in a state of undress or are using sanitary facilities; or

[(ba) the job is likely to involve the holder of the job doing his work, or living, in a private home and needs to be held by a man because objection might reasonably be taken to allowing to a woman—
(i) the degree of physical or social contact with a person living in the home, or
(ii) the knowledge of intimate details of such a person's life,

which is likely, because of the nature or circumstances of the job or of the home, to be allowed to, or available to, the holder of the job; or]

(c) the nature or location of the establishment makes it impracticable for the holder of the job to live elsewhere than in premises provided by the employer, and—
(i) the only such premises which are available for persons holding that kind of job are lived in, or normally lived in, by men and are not equipped with separate sleeping accommodation for women and sanitary facilities which could be used by women in privacy from men, and
(ii) it is not reasonable to expect the employer either to equip those premises with such accommodation and facilities or to provide other premises for women; or
(d) the nature of the establishment, or of the part of it within which the work is done, requires the job to be held by a man because—
(i) it is, or is part of, a hospital, prison or other establishment for persons requiring special care, supervision or attention, and
(ii) those persons are all men (disregarding any woman whose presence is exceptional), and

(iii) it is reasonable, having regard to the essential character of the establishment or that part, that the job should not be held by a woman; or

(e) the holder of the job provides individuals with personal services promoting their welfare or education, or similar personal services, and those services can most effectively be provided by a man, or

(f) …

(g) the job needs to be held by a man because it is likely to involve the performance of duties outside the United Kingdom in a country whose laws or customs are such that the duties could not, or could not effectively, be performed by a woman, or

(h) the job is one of two to be held[—

(i) by a married couple,

(ii) by a couple who are civil partners of each other, or

(iii) by a married couple or a couple who are civil partners of each other].

(3) Subsection (2) applies where some only of the duties of the job fall within paragraphs (a) to (g) as well as where all of them do.

(4) Paragraph (a), (b), (c), (d), (e) … or (g) of subsection (2) does not apply in relation to the filling of a vacancy at a time when the employer already has male employees—

(a) who are capable of carrying out the duties falling within that paragraph, and

(b) whom it would be reasonable to employ on those duties, and

(c) whose numbers are sufficient to meet the employer's likely requirements in respect of those duties without undue inconvenience.

[107]

NOTES

Sub-s (2): para (ba) inserted by the Sex Discrimination Act 1986, s 1(2); para (f) repealed, with savings, by the Employment Act 1989, ss 3(1), (2), 29(4), (6), 53(2), Sch 7, Pt II, Sch 9, para 1; words in square brackets in para (h) substituted by the Civil Partnership Act 2004, s 251(1), (4), as from 5 December 2005.

Sub-s (4): paragraph reference omitted repealed, with savings, by the Employment Act 1989, s 29(4), Sch 7, Pt II, Sch 9.

Modified as noted to s 6 at **[106]**.

[7A Corresponding exception relating to gender reassignment

(1) In their application to discrimination falling within section 2A, subsections (1) and (2) of section 6 do not make unlawful an employer's treatment of another person if—

(a) in relation to the employment in question—

(i) being a man is a genuine occupational qualification for the job, or

(ii) being a woman is a genuine occupational qualification for the job, and

(b) the employer can show that the treatment is reasonable in view of the circumstances described in the relevant paragraph of section 7(2) and any other relevant circumstances.

(2) In subsection (1) the reference to the employment in question is a reference—

(a) in relation to any paragraph of section 6(1), to the employment mentioned in that paragraph;

(b) in relation to section 6(2)—

(i) in its application to opportunities for promotion or transfer to any employment or for training for any employment, to that employment;

(ii) otherwise, to the employment in which the person discriminated against is employed or from which that person is dismissed.

(3) In determining for the purposes of subsection (1) whether being a man or being a woman is a genuine occupational qualification for a job, section 7(4) applies in relation to dismissal from employment as it applies in relation to the filling of a vacancy.

[(4) Subsection (1) does not apply in relation to discrimination against a person whose gender has become the acquired gender under the Gender Recognition Act 2004.]]

[108]

NOTES

Inserted, together with s 7B, by the Sex Discrimination (Gender Reassignment) Regulations 1999, SI 1999/1102, reg 4(1).

Sub-s (4): added by the Gender Recognition Act 2004, s 14, Sch 6, Pt 1, paras 1, 2, as from 4 April 2005.

[7B Supplementary exceptions relating to gender reassignment

(1) In relation to discrimination falling within section 2A—

(a) section 6(1)(a) or (c) does not apply to any employment where there is a supplementary genuine occupational qualification for the job,

(b) section 6(2)(a) does not apply to a refusal or deliberate omission to afford access to opportunities for promotion or transfer to or training for such employment, and

(c) section 6(2)(b) does not apply to dismissing an employee from, or otherwise not allowing him to continue in, such employment.

(2) Subject to subsection (3), there is a supplementary genuine occupational qualification for a job only if—

(a) the job involves the holder of the job being liable to be called upon to perform intimate physical searches pursuant to statutory powers;

(b) the job is likely to involve the holder of the job doing his work, or living, in a private home and needs to be held otherwise than by a person who is undergoing or has undergone gender reassignment, because objection might reasonably be taken to allowing to such a person—

(i) the degree of physical or social contact with a person living in the home, or

(ii) the knowledge of intimate details of such a person's life,

which is likely, because of the nature or circumstances of the job or of the home, to be allowed to, or available to, the holder of the job;

(c) the nature or location of the establishment makes it impracticable for the holder of the job to live elsewhere than in premises provided by the employer, and—

(i) the only such premises which are available for persons holding that kind of job are such that reasonable objection could be taken, for the purpose of preserving decency and privacy, to the holder of the job sharing accommodation and facilities with either sex whilst undergoing gender reassignment, and

(ii) it is not reasonable to expect the employer either to equip those premises with suitable accommodation or to make alternative arrangements; or

(d) the holder of the job provides vulnerable individuals with personal services promoting their welfare, or similar personal services, and in the reasonable view of the employer those services cannot be effectively provided by a person whilst that person is undergoing gender reassignment.

[(3) Subsection (2) does not apply in relation to discrimination against a person whose gender has become the acquired gender under the Gender Recognition Act 2004.]

[(4) Paragraph (a) of subsection (2) does not apply in relation to the filling of a vacancy at a time when the employer already has employees falling within subsection (5)—

(a) who are capable of carrying out the duties falling within that paragraph, and

(b) whom it would be reasonable to employ on those duties, and

(c) whose numbers are sufficient to meet the employer's likely requirements in respect of those duties without undue inconvenience.

(5) An employee falls within this subsection if the employee does not intend to undergo and is not undergoing gender reassignment and either—

(a) the employee has not undergone gender reassignment; or

(b) the employee's gender has become the acquired gender under the Gender Recognition Act 2004.]]

[109]

NOTES

Inserted as noted to s 7A at **[108]**.

Sub-s (3): substituted by the Gender Recognition Act 2004, s 14, Sch 6, Pt 1, paras 1, 3, as from 4 April 2005.

Sub-ss (4), (5): added by the Employment Equality (Sex Discrimination) Regulations 2005, SI 2005/2467, reg 9, as from 1 October 2005.

8 Equal Pay Act 1970

(1) …

(2) Section 1(1) of the Equal Pay Act 1970 (as set out in subsection (1) above) does not apply in determining for the purposes of section 6(1)(b) of this Act the terms on which employment is offered.

(3) Where a person offers a woman employment on certain terms, and if she accepted the offer then, by virtue of an equality clause, any of those terms would fall to be modified, or any additional term would fall to be included, the offer shall be taken to contravene section 6(1)(b).

(4) Where a person offers a woman employment on certain terms, and subsection (3) would apply but for the fact that, on her acceptance of the offer, section 1(3) of the Equal Pay Act 1970 (as set out in subsection (1) above) would prevent the equality clause from operating, the offer shall be taken not to contravene section 6(1)(b).

(5) An act does not contravene section 6(2) if—

(a) it contravenes a term modified or included by virtue of an equality clause, or

(b) it would contravene such a term but for the fact that the equality clause is prevented from operating by section 1(3) of the Equal Pay Act 1970.

(6) The Equal Pay Act 1970 is further amended as specified in Part I of Schedule 1, and accordingly has effect as set out in Part II of Schedule 1.

[(7) In its application to any discrimination falling within section 2A, this section shall have effect with the omission of subsections (3), (4) and (5)(b).]

[110]

NOTES

Sub-s (1): amends the Equal Pay Act 1970, s 1 at **[5]**.

Sub-s (7): added by the Sex Discrimination (Gender Reassignment) Regulations 1999, SI 1999/1102, reg 3(2).

9 ... Contract workers

(1) This section applies to any work [at an establishment in Great Britain,] for a person ("the principal") which is available for doing by individuals ("contract workers") who are employed not by the principal himself but by another person, who supplies them under a contract made with the principal.

(2) It is unlawful for the principal, in relation to work to which this section applies, to discriminate against a woman who is a contract worker—

(a) in the terms on which he allows her to do that work, or

(b) by not allowing her to do it or continue to do it, or

(c) in the way he affords her access to any benefits, facilities or services or by refusing or deliberately omitting to afford her access to them, or

(d) by subjecting her to any other detriment.

[(2A) It is unlawful for a principal, in relation to contract work at an establishment in Great Britain, to subject a contract worker to harassment.]

(3) [Subject to subsection (3A),] the principal does not contravene subsection (2)(b) by doing any act in relation to a woman at a time when if the work were to be done by a person taken into his employment being a man would be a genuine occupational qualification for the job.

[(3A) Subsection (3) does not apply in relation to discrimination falling within section 2A.

(3B) In relation to discrimination falling within section 2A, the principal does not contravene subsection (2)(a), (b), (c) or (d) by doing any act in relation to a woman if—

(a) he does it at a time when, if the work were to be done by a person taken into his employment—

(i) being a man would be a genuine occupational qualification for the job, or

(ii) being a woman would be a genuine occupational qualification for the job, and

(b) he can show that the act is reasonable in view of the circumstances relevant for the purposes of paragraph (a) and any other relevant circumstances.

(3C) In relation to discrimination falling within section 2A, the principal does not contravene subsection (2)(b) by doing any act in relation to a woman at a time when, if the work were to be done by a person taken into his employment, there would be a supplementary genuine occupational qualification for the job.]

[(3D) Subsections (3B) and (3C) do not apply in relation to discrimination against a person whose gender has become the acquired gender under the Gender Recognition Act 2004.]

(4) Subsection (2)(c) does not apply to benefits, facilities or services of any description if the principal is concerned with the provision (for payment or not) of benefits, facilities or services of that description to the public, or to a section of the public to which the woman belongs, unless that provision differs in a material respect from the provision of the benefits, facilities or services by the principal to his contract workers.

[111]

NOTES

Section heading: words omitted repealed by the Employment Equality (Sex Discrimination) Regulations 2005, SI 2005/2467, reg 10(1), (2), as from 1 October 2005.

Sub-s (1): words in square brackets inserted by SI 2005/2467, reg 10(1), (3), as from 1 October 2005.

Sub-s (2A): inserted by SI 2005/2467, reg 10(1), (4), as from 1 October 2005.

Sub-s (3): words in square brackets inserted by the Sex Discrimination (Gender Reassignment) Regulations 1999, SI 1999/1102, reg 4(2).

Sub-ss (3A)–(3C): inserted by SI 1999/1102, reg 4(3).

Sub-s (3D): inserted by the Gender Recognition Act 2004, s 14, Sch 6, Pt 1, paras 1, 4, as from 4 April 2005.

Modified as noted to s 6 at **[106]**.

10 Meaning of employment at establishment in Great Britain

[(1) For the purposes of this Part and section 1 of the Equal Pay Act 1970 ("the relevant purposes"), employment is to be regarded as being at an establishment in Great Britain if—

(a) the employee does his work wholly or partly in Great Britain, or

(b) the employee does his work wholly outside Great Britain and subsection (1A) applies.

(1A) This subsection applies if—

(a) the employer has a place of business at an establishment in Great Britain,

(b) the work is for the purposes of the business carried on at that establishment, and

(c) the employee is ordinarily resident in Great Britain—

(i) at the time when he applies for or is offered the employment, or

(ii) at any time during the course of the employment.]

[(2) The reference to "employment" in subsection (1) includes—

(a) employment on board a ship[, only if the ship is] registered at a port of registry in Great Britain, and

(b) employment on aircraft or hovercraft[, only if the aircraft or hovercraft is] registered in the United Kingdom and operated by a person who has his principal place of business, or is ordinarily resident, in Great Britain.]

(3) In the case of employment on board a ship registered at a port of registry in Great Britain (except where the employee does his work wholly outside Great Britain [and subsection (1A) does not apply]) the ship shall for the relevant purposes be deemed to be the establishment.

(4) Where work is not done at an establishment it shall be treated for the relevant purposes as done at the establishment from which it is done or (where it is not done from any establishment) at the establishment with which it has the closest connection.

(5) In relation to employment concerned with *exploration of the sea bed or subsoil or the exploitation of their natural resources*, Her Majesty may by Order in Council [provide that subsections (1) and (3) shall have effect as if—

(a) the reference to Great Britain in each of paragraphs (a) and (b) of subsection (1), and

(b) each of the references to Great Britain in subsections (1A) to (3),

included] any area for the time being designated under section 1(7) of the Continental Shelf Act 1964 [or specified under section 10(8) of the Petroleum Act 1998], except an area or part of an area in which the law of Northern Ireland applies.

(6) An Order in Council under subsection (5) may provide that, in relation to employment to which the Order applies, this Part and section 1 of the Equal Pay Act 1970 are to have effect with such modifications as are specified in the Order.

(7) An Order in Council under subsection (5) shall be of no effect unless a draft of the Order was laid before and approved by each House of Parliament.

[(8) Subsections (1) to (4) or, where an Order in Council under subsection (5) is in force, those subsections as modified by the Order, apply for the purposes of determining whether contract work, within the meaning given by section 9, is at an establishment in Great Britain, but so apply with the following modifications—

(a) a reference to employment is to be read as a reference to work to which section 9 applies, and

(b) "employee" and "employer" shall be read (respectively) as "contract worker" and "principal", with "contract worker" and "principal" having the meaning given by section 9.]

[112]

NOTES

Sub-ss (1), (1A): substituted, for original sub-s (1), by the Employment Equality (Sex Discrimination) Regulations 2005, SI 2005/2467, reg 11(1), (2), as from 1 October 2005.

Sub-s (2): substituted by the Equal Opportunities (Employment Legislation) (Territorial Limits) Regulations 1999, SI 1999/3163, reg 2(1), (3); words in square brackets inserted by SI 2005/2467, reg 11(1), (3), (4), as from 1 October 2005.

Sub-s (3): words in square brackets substituted by SI 2005/2467, reg 11(1), (5), as from 1 October 2005.

Sub-s (5): for the words in italics there are substituted the words "any activity within section 11(2) of the Petroleum Act 1998", and the words in the second pair of square brackets are inserted, by the Petroleum Act 1998, s 50, Sch 4, para 8, as from a day to be appointed; words in first pair of square brackets substituted by SI 2005/2467, reg 11(1), (6), as from 1 October 2005.

Sub-s (8): added by SI 2005/2467, reg 11(1), (7), as from 1 October 2005.

Extension of Order making powers: see the Employment (Continental Shelf) Act 1978, which extends the power to make orders under sub-ss (5)–(7) above in relation to employment concerned with the exploration or exploitation of a cross-boundary petroleum field (but is prospectively repealed by the Petroleum Act 1998, s 51(1), Sch 5, Pt I, as from a day to be appointed).

Orders: the Sex Discrimination and Equal Pay (Offshore Employment) Order 1987, SI 1987/930.

[Discrimination against office-holders etc

10A Offices and posts to which section 10B applies

(1) Subject to subsections (2) and (3), section 10B applies to an office or post if—

(a) the office or post is one—

(i) to which persons are appointed to discharge functions personally under the direction of another person, and

(ii) in respect of which they are entitled to remuneration,

(b) the office or post is one to which appointments are made by a Minister of the Crown, a government department, the [Welsh Ministers, the First Minister for Wales, the Counsel General to the Welsh Assembly Government] or any part of the Scottish Administration, or

(c) the office or post is one to which appointments are made on the recommendation of, or subject to the approval of, a person referred to in paragraph (b).

(2) Section 10B does not apply to an office or post if section 6 (employment), section 9 (contract work), section 11 (partnerships), section 35A (barristers) or section 35B (advocates)—

(a) applies in relation to an appointment to the office or post, or

(b) would apply in relation to an appointment to the office or post but for the operation of any other provision of this Act.

(3) Section 10B does not apply to—

(a) any office of the House of Commons held by a member of it,

(b) a life peerage within the meaning of the Life Peerages Act 1958, or any office of the House of Lords held by a member of it,

(c) any office mentioned in Schedule 2 (Ministerial offices) to the House of Commons Disqualification Act 1975,

(d) the offices of Leader of the Opposition, Chief Opposition Whip or Assistant Opposition Whip within the meaning of the Ministerial and other Salaries Act 1975,

(e) any office of the Scottish Parliament held by a member of it,

(f) a member of the Scottish Executive within the meaning of section 44 of the Scotland Act 1998, or a junior Scottish Minister within the meaning of section 49 of that Act,
(g) any office of the National Assembly for Wales held by a member of it,
[(ga) a member of the Welsh Assembly Government,]
(h) in England, any office of a county council, a London borough council, a district council or a parish council held by a member of it,
(i) in Wales, any office of a county council, a county borough council or a community council held by a member of it,
(j) in relation to a council constituted under section 2 of the Local Government etc (Scotland) Act 1994, or a community council established under section 51 of the Local Government (Scotland) Act 1973, any office of such a council held by a member of it,
(k) any office of the Greater London Authority held by a member of it,
(l) any office of the Common Council of the City of London held by a member of it,
(m) any office of the Council of the Isles of Scilly held by a member of it, or
(n) any office of a political party.

(4) For the purposes of subsection (1)(a), the holder of an office or post—
(a) is to be regarded as discharging her functions under the direction of another person if that other person is entitled to direct her as to when and where she discharges those functions;
(b) is not to be regarded as entitled to remuneration merely because she is entitled to payments—
(i) in respect of expenses incurred by her in carrying out the functions of the office or post, or
(ii) by way of compensation for the loss of income or benefits she would or might have received from any person had she not been carrying out the functions of the office or post.

(5) In this section and section 10B, appointment to an office or post does not include election to an office or post.]

[112A]

NOTES

Commencement: 1 October 2005.

Inserted, together with the preceding heading and s 10B, by the Employment Equality (Sex Discrimination) Regulations 2005, SI 2005/2467, reg 13(1), as from 1 October 2005.

Sub-s (1): words in square brackets in para (b) substituted by the Government of Wales Act 2006 (Consequential Modifications and Transitional Provisions) Order 2007, SI 2007/1388, art 3, Sch 1, paras 2, 3(1), (2), as from 25 May 2007.

Sub-s (3): para (ga) inserted by SI 2007/1388, art 3, Sch 1, paras 2, 3(1), (3), as from 25 May 2007.

[10B Office-holders

(1) It is unlawful for a relevant person, in relation to an appointment to an office or post to which this section applies, to discriminate against a woman—
(a) in the arrangements which he makes for the purpose of determining to whom the appointment should be offered,
(b) in the terms on which he offers her the appointment, or
(c) by refusing to offer her the appointment.

(2) It is unlawful, in relation to an appointment to an office or post to which this section applies and which is an office or post referred to in section 10A(1)(c), for a relevant person on whose recommendation, or subject to whose approval, appointments to the office or post are made, to discriminate against a woman—
(a) in the arrangements which he makes for the purpose of determining who should be recommended or approved in relation to the appointment, or
(b) in making or refusing to make a recommendation, or giving or refusing to give an approval, in relation to the appointment.

(3) It is unlawful for a relevant person, in relation to a woman who has been appointed to an office or post to which this section applies, to discriminate against her—
(a) in the terms of the appointment,
(b) in the opportunities which he affords her for promotion, a transfer, training or receiving any other benefit, or by refusing to afford her any such opportunity,
(c) by terminating the appointment, or

(d) by subjecting her to any other detriment in relation to the appointment.

(4) It is unlawful for a relevant person, in relation to an office or post to which this section applies, to subject to harassment a woman—

(a) who has been appointed to the office or post,

(b) who is seeking or being considered for appointment to the office or post, or

(c) who, in relation to appointment to the office or post, is seeking or being considered for a recommendation or approval referred to in section 10A(1)(c).

(5) Subsections (1) and (3) do not apply to any act in relation to an office or post where, if holding the office or post constituted employment, that act would be lawful by virtue of section 7, 7A or 7B (exception where sex is a genuine occupational qualification etc) or section 19 (ministers of religion etc).

(6) Subsection (2) does not apply to any act in relation to an office or post where, if holding the office or post constituted employment, it would be lawful by virtue of section 7, 7A, 7B or 19 to refuse to offer the person such employment.

(7) Subsection (3) does not apply to benefits of any description if the relevant person is concerned with the provision (for payment or not) of benefits of that description to the public, or a section of the public to which the person appointed belongs, unless—

(a) that provision differs in a material respect from the provision of the benefits to persons appointed to offices or posts which are the same as, or not materially different from, that which the person appointed holds,

(b) the provision of the benefits to the person appointed is regulated by the terms and conditions of her appointment, or

(c) the benefits relate to training.

(8) In subsection (3)(c), the reference to the termination of the appointment includes a reference—

(a) to the termination of the appointment by the expiration of any period (including a period expiring by reference to an event or circumstance), not being a termination immediately after which the appointment is renewed on the same terms and conditions, and

(b) to the termination of the appointment by any act of the person appointed (including the giving of notice) in circumstances such that she is entitled to terminate the appointment without notice by reason of the conduct of the relevant person.

(9) In this section "relevant person", in relation to an office or post, means—

(a) in a case relating to an appointment to an office or post, the person with power to make that appointment;

(b) in a case relating to the making of a recommendation or the giving of an approval in relation to an appointment, a person or body referred to in section 10A(1)(b) with power to make that recommendation or (as the case may be) to give that approval;

(c) in a case relating to a term of an appointment, the person with power to determine that term;

(d) in a case relating to a working condition afforded in relation to an appointment—

(i) the person with power to determine that working condition, or

(ii) where there is no such person, the person with power to make the appointment;

(e) in a case relating to the termination of an appointment, the person with power to terminate the appointment;

(f) in a case relating to the subjection of a person to any other detriment or to harassment, any person or body falling within one or more of paragraphs (a) to (e) in relation to such cases as are there mentioned.

(10) In subsection (9)(d) "working condition" includes any opportunity for promotion, a transfer, training or receiving any other benefit.

(11) In this section—

(a) references to making a recommendation include references to making a negative recommendation;

(b) references to refusal include references to deliberate omission;

(c) "benefits" includes facilities and services.]

[112B]

NOTES

Commencement: 1 October 2005.

Inserted as noted to s 10A at **[112A]**.

Discrimination by other bodies

11 Partnerships

(1) It is unlawful for a firm … , in relation to a position as partner in the firm, to discriminate against a woman—

(a) in the arrangements they make for the purpose of determining who should be offered that position, or

(b) in the terms on which they offer her that position, or

(c) by refusing or deliberately omitting to offer her that position, or

(d) in a case where the woman already holds that position—

(i) in the way they afford her access to any benefits, facilities or services, or by refusing or deliberately omitting to afford her access to them, or

(ii) by expelling her from that position, or subjecting her to any other detriment.

(2) Subsection (1) shall apply in relation to persons proposing to form themselves into a partnership as it applies in relation to a firm.

[(2A) It is unlawful for a firm, in relation to a position as partner in the firm, to subject to harassment a woman who holds or has applied for that position.]

(3) [Subject to subsection (3A),] subsection (1)(a) and (c) do not apply to a position as partner where, if it were employment, being a man would be a genuine occupational qualification for the job.

[(3A) Subsection (3) does not apply in relation to discrimination falling within section 2A.

(3B) In relation to discrimination falling within section 2A, subsection (1) does not make unlawful a firm's treatment of a person in relation to a position as partner where—

(a) if it were employment—

(i) being a man would be a genuine occupational qualification for the job, or

(ii) being a woman would be a genuine occupational qualification for the job, and

(b) the firm can show that the treatment is reasonable in view of the circumstances relevant for the purposes of paragraph (a) and any other relevant circumstances.

(3C) In relation to discrimination falling within section 2A, subsection (1)(a), (c) and, so far as it relates to expulsion, (d)(ii) do not apply to a position as partner where, if it were employment, there would be a supplementary genuine occupational qualification for the job.]

[(3D) Subsections (3B) and (3C) do not apply in relation to discrimination against a person whose gender has become the acquired gender under the Gender Recognition Act 2004.]

(4) …

(5) In the case of a limited partnership references in subsection (1) to a partner shall be construed as references to a general partner as defined in section 3 of the Limited Partnerships Act 1907.

[(6) This section applies to a limited liability partnership as it applies to a firm; and, in its application to a limited liability partnership, references to a partner in a firm are references to a member of the limited liability partnership.]

[113]

NOTES

Sub-s (1): words omitted repealed by the Sex Discrimination Act 1986, ss 1(3), 9(2), Schedule, Pt II.

Sub-s (2A): inserted by the Employment Equality (Sex Discrimination) Regulations 2005, SI 2005/2467, reg 14(1), (2), as from 1 October 2005.

Sub-s (3): words in square brackets inserted by the Sex Discrimination (Gender Reassignment) Regulations 1999, SI 1999/1102, reg 4(4).

Sub-ss (3A)–(3C): inserted by SI 1999/1102, reg 4(5).
Sub-s (3D): inserted by the Gender Recognition Act 2004, s 14, Sch 6, Pt 1, paras 1, 5, as from 4 April 2005.
Sub-s (4): repealed by SI 2005/2467, reg 14(1), (3), as from 1 October 2005.
Sub-s (6): added by the Limited Liability Partnerships Regulations 2001, SI 2001/1090, reg 9(1), Sch 5, para 6.

12 Trade unions etc

(1) This section applies to an organisation of workers, an organisation of employers, or any other organisation whose members carry on a particular profession or trade for the purposes of which the organisation exists.

(2) It is unlawful for an organisation to which this section applies, in the case of a woman who is not a member of the organisation, to discriminate against her—
- (a) in the terms on which it is prepared to admit her to membership, or
- (b) by refusing, or deliberately omitting to accept, her application for membership.

(3) It is unlawful for an organisation to which this section applies, in the case of a woman who is a member of the organisation, to discriminate against her—
- (a) in the way it affords her access to any benefits, facilities or services, or by refusing or deliberately omitting to afford her access to them, or
- (b) by depriving her of membership, or varying the terms on which she is a member, or
- (c) by subjecting her to any other detriment.

[(3A) It is unlawful for an organisation to which this section applies, in relation to membership of that organisation, to subject to harassment a woman who—
- (a) is a member of the organisation, or
- (b) has applied for membership of the organisation.]

(4) …

[114]

NOTES

Sub-s (3A): inserted by the Employment Equality (Sex Discrimination) Regulations 2005, SI 2005/2467, reg 15(1), (2), as from 1 October 2005.
Sub-s (4): repealed by SI 2005/2467, reg 15(1), (3), as from 1 October 2005.

13 Qualifying bodies

(1) It is unlawful for an authority or body which can confer an authorisation or qualification which is needed for, or facilitates, engagement in a particular profession or trade to discriminate against a woman—
- (a) in the terms on which it is prepared to confer on her that authorisation or qualification, or
- (b) by refusing or deliberately omitting to grant her application for it, or
- (c) by withdrawing it from her or varying the terms on which she holds it.

[(1A) It is unlawful for a body to which this section applies, in relation to an authorisation or qualification of a kind mentioned in subsection (1), to subject to harassment a woman who holds or applies for such an authorisation or qualification.]

(2) Where an authority or body is required by law to satisfy itself as to his good character before conferring on a person an authorisation or qualification which is needed for, or facilitates, his engagement in any profession or trade then, without prejudice to any other duty to which it is subject, that requirement shall be taken to impose on the authority or body a duty to have regard to any evidence tending to show that he, or any of his employees, or agents (whether past or present), has practised unlawful discrimination in, or in connection with, the carrying on of any profession or trade.

(3) In this section—
- (a) "authorisation or qualification" includes recognition, registration, enrolment, approval and certification,
- (b) "confer" includes renew or extend.

(4) Subsection (1) does not apply to discrimination which is rendered unlawful by section 22 or 23.

[(5) Subsection (1A) does not apply to harassment which is rendered unlawful by section 22 or 23.]

[115]

NOTES

Sub-ss (1A), (5): inserted and added respectively by the Employment Equality (Sex Discrimination) Regulations 2005, SI 2005/2467, reg 16, as from 1 October 2005.

[14 Persons concerned with provision of vocational training

[(1) It is unlawful, in the case of a woman seeking or receiving vocational training, for any person who provides, or makes arrangements for the provision of, facilities for vocational training to discriminate against her—

(a) in the arrangements that person makes for the purpose of selecting people to receive vocational training,

(b) in the terms on which that person affords her access to any vocational training or facilities concerned with vocational training,

(c) by refusing or deliberately omitting to afford her such access,

(d) by terminating her vocational training, or

(e) by subjecting her to any detriment during the course of her vocational training.

(1A) It is unlawful for a provider of vocational training, in relation to such training, to subject to harassment a woman—

(a) to whom he is providing such training, or

(b) who has asked him to provide such training.

(1B) In this section "vocational training", in relation to a woman, includes (if it would not otherwise do so) any training which would help fit her for any employment.]

(2) Subsection (1) does not apply to—

(a) discrimination which is rendered unlawful by section 6(1) or (2) or section 22 or 23, or

(b) discrimination which would be rendered unlawful by any of those provisions but for the operation of any other provision of this Act.]

[116]

NOTES

Substituted by the Employment Act 1989, s 7(1).

Sub-ss (1), (1A), (1B): substituted, for original sub-s (1), by the Employment Equality (Sex Discrimination) Regulations 2005, SI 2005/2467, reg 17(1), as from 1 October 2005.

15 Employment agencies

(1) It is unlawful for an employment agency to discriminate against a woman—

(a) in the terms on which the agency offers to provide any of its services, or

(b) by refusing or deliberately omitting to provide any of its services, or

(c) in the way it provides any of its services.

[(1A) It is unlawful for an employment agency, in relation to the provision of its services, to subject to harassment a woman—

(a) to whom it provides such services, or

(b) who has requested the provision of such services.]

[(2) It is unlawful for a local education authority or education authority or any other person to do any act in providing services in pursuance of arrangements made, or a direction given, under section 10 of the Employment and Training Act 1973, which constitutes discrimination.]

(3) References in subsection (1) to the services of an employment agency include guidance on careers and any other services related to employment.

(4) This section does not apply if the discrimination only concerns employment which the employer could lawfully refuse to offer the woman.

(5) An employment agency or local education authority[, education authority or other person] shall not be subject to any liability under this section if it proves—

(a) that it acted in reliance on a statement made to it by the employer to the effect that, by reason of the operation of subsection (4), its action would not be unlawful, and

(b) that it was reasonable for it to rely on the statement.

(6) A person who knowingly or recklessly makes a statement such as is referred to in subsection (5)(a) which in a material respect is false or misleading commits an offence, and shall be liable on summary conviction to a fine not exceeding [level 5 on the standard scale].

[117]

NOTES

Sub-s (1A): inserted by the Employment Equality (Sex Discrimination) Regulations 2005, SI 2005/2467, reg 18, as from 1 October 2005.

Sub-s (2): substituted by the Trade Union Reform and Employment Rights Act 1993, s 49(2), Sch 8, para 8(a).

Sub-s (5): words in square brackets substituted by the Trade Union Reform and Employment Rights Act 1993, s 49(2), Sch 8, para 8(b).

Sub-s (6): maximum fine increased and converted to a level on the standard scale by the Criminal Justice Act 1982, ss 37, 38, 46.

16 [Training Commission] etc

[(1) It is unlawful for the [Secretary of State …] [or the Minister] to discriminate[, or subject a woman to harassment] in the provision of facilities or services under section 2 of the Employment and Training Act 1973.]

[(1A) It is unlawful for Scottish Enterprise or Highlands and Islands Enterprise to discriminate[, or subject a woman to harassment] in the provision of facilities or services under such arrangements as are mentioned in section 2(3) of the Enterprise and New Towns (Scotland) Act 1990 (arrangements analogous to arrangements in pursuance of section 2 of the said Act of 1973).]

(2) This section does not apply in a case where—

(a) section 14 applies, or

(b) the [Secretary of State] is acting as an employment agency.

[118]

NOTES

Section heading: words in square brackets substituted by the Employment Act 1988, s 24(3).

Sub-s (1): substituted by the Employment and Training Act 1981, s 9, Sch 2, Pt II, para 18; words in first pair of square brackets substituted by the Employment Act 1988, s 33(3), Sch 3, Pt II, para 11(2); words omitted repealed by the Employment Act 1989, s 29(4), Sch 7, Pt I; words in second pair of square brackets inserted by the Transfer of Functions (Equality) Order 2007, SI 2007/2914, art 8, Schedule, para 7, as from 12 October 2007; words in third pair of square brackets inserted by the Employment Equality (Sex Discrimination) Regulations 2005, SI 2005/2467, reg 19(1), (2), as from 1 October 2005.

Sub-s (1A): inserted by the Enterprise and New Towns (Scotland) Act 1990, s 18, in relation to Scotland only; words in square brackets inserted by SI 2005/2467, reg 19(1), (3), as from 1 October 2005.

Sub-s (2): words in square brackets substituted by the Employment Act 1989, s 29(3), Sch 6, para 12.

Special cases

17 Police

(1) For the purposes of this Part, the holding of the office of constable shall be treated as employment—

(a) by the chief officer of police as respects any act done by him in relation to a constable or that office;

(b) by the police authority as respects any act done by [it] in relation to a constable or that office.

[(1A) For the purposes of section 41—

(a) the holding of the office of constable shall be treated as employment by the chief officer of police (and as not being employment by any other person); and

(b) anything done by a person holding such an office in the performance, or purported performance, of his functions shall be treated as done in the course of that employment.]

(2) Regulations made under [section 50, 51 or 52 of the Police Act 1996] shall not treat men and women differently except—

(a) as to requirements relating to height, uniform or equipment, or allowances in lieu of uniform or equipment, or

(b) so far as special treatment is accorded to women in connection with pregnancy or childbirth, or

(c) in relation to pensions to or in respect of special constables or police cadets.

(3) Nothing in this Part renders unlawful any discrimination between male and female constables as to matters such as are mentioned in subsection (2)(a).

(4) There shall be paid out of the police fund—

(a) any compensation, costs or expenses awarded against a chief officer of police in any proceedings brought against him under this Act, and any costs or expenses incurred by him in any such proceedings so far as not recovered by him in the proceedings; and

(b) any sum required by a chief officer of police for the settlement of any claim made against him under this Act if the settlement is approved by the police authority.

(5) Any proceedings under this Act which, [by virtue of subsection (1) or (1A)], would lie against a chief officer of police shall be brought against the chief officer of police for the time being or, in the case of a vacancy in that office, against the person for the time being performing the functions of that office; and references in subsection (4) to the chief officer of police shall be construed accordingly.

[(5A) A police authority may, in such cases and to such extent as appear to it to be appropriate, pay out of the police fund—

(a) any compensation, costs or expenses awarded in proceedings under this Act against a person under the direction and control of the chief officer of police;

(b) any costs or expenses incurred and not recovered by such a person in such proceedings; and

(c) any sum required in connection with the settlement of a claim that has or might have given rise to such proceedings.]

(6) Subsections (1)[, (1A)] and (3) apply to a police cadet and appointment as a police cadet as they apply to a constable and the office of constable.

(7) [Subject to subsection (9),] in this section—

"chief officer of police"—

(a) in relation to a person appointed, or an appointment falling to be made, under a specified Act, has the same meaning as in [the Police Act 1996],

[(aa) …]

(b) in relation to any other person or appointment means the officer [or other person] who has the direction and control of the body of constables or cadets in question;

"police authority"—

(a) in relation to a person appointed, or an appointment falling to be made, under a specified Act, has the same meaning as in [the Police Act 1996],

[(aa) …]

(b) in relation to any other person or appointment, means the authority by whom the person in question is or on appointment would be paid;

"police cadet" means any person appointed to undergo training with a view to becoming a constable;

"police fund" in relation to a chief officer of police within paragraph (a) of the above definition of that term has the same meaning as in [the Police Act 1996][…], and in any other case means money provided by the police authority;

"specified Act" means the Metropolitan Police Act 1829, the City of London Police Act 1839 or [the Police Act 1996].

(8) In the application of this section to Scotland, in subsection (7) for any reference to [the Police Act 1996] there shall be substituted a reference to the Police (Scotland) Act 1967, and for the reference to [sections 50, 51 and 52] of the former Act in subsection (2) there shall be substituted a reference to sections 26 and 27 of the latter Act.

[(9) In relation to a constable of a force who is not under the direction and control of the chief officer of police for that force, references in this section to the chief officer of police are references to the chief officer for the force under whose direction and control he is, and references in this section to the police authority are references to the relevant police authority for that force.]

[119]

NOTES

Sub-s (1): word in square brackets in para (b) substituted by the Sex Discrimination Act 1975 (Amendment) Regulations 2003, SI 2003/1657, reg 2(1), (2), as from 19 July 2003.

Sub-ss (1A), (5A): inserted by SI 2003/1657, reg 2(1), (3), (4), as from 19 July 2003.

Sub-ss (2), (8): words in square brackets substituted by the Police Act 1996, s 103, Sch 7, para 27.

Sub-s (5): words in square brackets substituted by the Equality Act 2006, s 83(2), as from 6 April 2007.

Sub-s (7) is amended as follows:

Words in first pair of square brackets inserted by SI 2003/1657, reg 2(1), (6), as from 19 July 2003.

In definition "chief officer of police" words in square brackets in para (a) substituted by the Police Act 1996, s 103, Sch 7, para 27(2), (3); para (aa) inserted by the Police Act 1997, s 134, Sch 9, para 31(a), and repealed by the Serious Organised Crime and Police Act 2005, ss 59, 174(2), Sch 4, para 28(a), Sch 17, Pt 2, as from 1 April 2006; words in square brackets in para (b) inserted by SI 2003/1657, reg 2(1), (7), as from 19 July 2003.

In definition "police authority" words in square brackets in para (a) substituted by the Police Act 1996, s 103, Sch 7, para 27(2), (3); para (aa) inserted by SI 2003/1657, reg 2(1), (8), as from 19 July 2003, and repealed by the Serious Organised Crime and Police Act 2005, ss 59, 174(2), Sch 4, para 28(b), Sch 17, Pt 2, as from 1 April 2006.

In definition "police fund" words in first pair of square brackets substituted by the Police Act 1996, s 103, Sch 7, para 27(2), (3); words in second pair of square brackets inserted by the Police Act 1997, s 134, Sch 9, para 31(b), and repealed by the Serious Organised Crime and Police Act 2005, ss 59, 174(2), Sch 4, para 28(c), Sch 17, Pt 2, as from 1 April 2006.

Words in square brackets in definition "specified Act" substituted by the Police Act 1996, s 103, Sch 7, para 27(2), (3).

Sub-s (9): added by SI 2003/1657, reg 2(1), (9), as from 19 July 2003.

18 Prison officers

(1) Nothing in this Part renders unlawful any discrimination between male and female prison officers as to requirements relating to height.

(2) …

[120]

NOTES

Sub-s (2): amends the Prison Act 1952, s 7(2).

[19 Ministers of religion etc

(1) Nothing in this Part shall make it unlawful to apply a requirement in relation to employment where—

(a) the employment is for purposes of an organised religion,
(b) the requirement is one to which subsection (3) applies, and
(c) the requirement is applied—
  (i) so as to comply with the doctrines of the religion, or
  (ii) because of the nature of the employment and the context in which it is carried out, so as to avoid conflicting with the strongly-held religious convictions of a significant number of the religion's followers.

(2) Nothing in section 13 shall make it unlawful to apply a requirement in relation to an authorisation or qualification (as defined in that section) where—

(a) the authorisation or qualification is for purposes of an organised religion,
(b) the requirement is one to which subsection (3) applies, and
(c) the requirement is applied—
  (i) so as to comply with the doctrines of the religion, or
  (ii) by the authority or body concerned, or by the person by whom the authority or body acts in a particular case, so as to avoid conflicting with the strongly-held religious convictions of a significant number of the religion's followers.

(3) This subsection applies to—

(a) a requirement to be of a particular sex,
(b) a requirement not to be undergoing or to have undergone gender reassignment,
(c) a requirement relating to not being married or to not being a civil partner,

(d) a requirement, applied in relation to a person who is married, or is a civil partner, that relates—

(i) to the person, or the person's spouse or civil partner, not having a living former spouse or a living former civil partner, or

(ii) to how the person, or the person's spouse or civil partner, has at any time ceased to be married or ceased to be a civil partner.]

[121]

NOTES

Commencement: 1 October 2005.

Substituted by the Employment Equality (Sex Discrimination) Regulations 2005, SI 2005/2467, reg 20(1), as from 1 October 2005.

20 Midwives

(1) [Until 1st September 1983] section 6(1) does not apply to employment as a midwife.

(2) [Until 1st September 1983] section 6(2)(a) does not apply to promotion, transfer or training as a midwife.

(3) [Until 1st September 1983] section 14 does not apply to training as a midwife.

(4), (5) ...

[122]

NOTES

Sub-ss (1)–(3): words in square brackets inserted by the Sex Discrimination Act 1975 (Amendment of section 20) Order 1983, SI 1983/1202, art 2.

Sub-ss (4), (5): repealed by the Nurses, Midwives and Health Visitors Act 1979, s 23(5), Sch 8.

[Relationships which have come to an end

20A Relationships which have come to an end

(1) This section applies where—

(a) there has been a relevant relationship between a woman and another person ("the relevant person"), and

(b) the relationship has come to an end (whether before or after the commencement of this section).

(2) In this section, a "relevant relationship" is a relationship during the course of which an act of discrimination by one party to the relationship against the other party to it is unlawful under any preceding provision of this Part.

(3) It is unlawful for the relevant person to discriminate against the woman by subjecting her to a detriment where the discrimination arises out of and is closely connected to the relevant relationship.

[(4) It is unlawful for the relevant person to subject a woman to harassment where that treatment arises out of or is closely connected to the relevant relationship.]]

[123]

NOTES

Commencement: 19 July 2003.

Inserted, together with preceding heading, by the Sex Discrimination Act 1975 (Amendment) Regulations 2003, SI 2003/1657, reg 3, as from 19 July 2003.

Sub-s (4): added by the Employment Equality (Sex Discrimination) Regulations 2005, SI 2005/2467, reg 21, as from 1 October 2005.

21 *(Sub-s (1) repealed by the Employment Act 1989, s 29(4), Sch 7, Pt III; sub-s (2) repealed by the Coal Industry Act 1992, s 2, Schedule, Pt II.)*

PART III
DISCRIMINATION IN OTHER FIELDS

[21A Public authorities

(1) It is unlawful for a public authority exercising a function to do any act which constitutes—

(a) discrimination, or

(b) harassment within the meaning of section 4A(1) and (2), (5) and (6).

(2) In subsection (1)—

(a) "public authority" includes any person who has functions of a public nature (subject to subsections (3) and (4)), and

(b) "function" means function of a public nature.

(3) The prohibition in subsection (1) shall not apply to—

(a) the House of Commons,

(b) the House of Lords,

(c) the Security Service,

(d) the Secret Intelligence Service,

(e) the Government Communications Headquarters, or

(f) a part of the armed forces of the Crown which is, in accordance with a requirement of the Secretary of State, assisting the Government Communications Headquarters.

(4) The prohibition in subsection (1) shall not apply to the functions and actions listed in the Table of Exceptions in subsection (9) (but nothing in that Table permits anything which is prohibited by virtue of any Community law relating to discrimination).

(5) The [Minister] may by order amend the Table of Exceptions.

(6) In an action under section 66 in respect of a contravention of this section—

(a) the court shall not grant an injunction or interdict unless satisfied that it will not prejudice criminal proceedings or a criminal investigation, and

(b) the court shall grant any application to stay or sist the section 66 proceedings on the grounds of prejudice to criminal proceedings or to a criminal investigation, unless satisfied that the proceedings or investigation will not be prejudiced.

(7) Section 74(2)(b) shall not apply in relation to a respondent's reply, or a failure to reply, to a question in connection with an alleged contravention of this section—

(a) if the respondent reasonably asserts that to have replied differently or at all might have prejudiced criminal proceedings or a criminal investigation,

(b) if the respondent reasonably asserts that to have replied differently or at all would have revealed the reason for not instituting or not continuing criminal proceedings,

(c) where the reply is of a kind specified for the purposes of this paragraph by order of the [Minister],

(d) where the reply is given in circumstances specified for the purposes of this paragraph by order of the [Minister], or

(e) where the failure occurs in circumstances specified for the purposes of this paragraph by order of the [Minister].

(8) In this section "criminal investigation" means—

(a) an investigation into the commission of an alleged offence, and

(b) a decision whether to institute criminal proceedings.

(9) The following is the Table of Exceptions referred to in subsection (4).

Legislation
1. Preparing, making, or considering— (a) an Act of Parliament, (b) a Bill for an Act of Parliament, (c) an Act of the Scottish Parliament, … (d) a Bill for an Act of the Scottish Parliament.

[(e) a Measure of the National Assembly for Wales,

(f) a proposed Measure of the National Assembly for Wales,

(g) an Act of the National Assembly for Wales, or

(h) a Bill for an Act of the National Assembly for Wales].

2. Preparing, making, confirming, approving, or considering legislation made or to be made—

(a) by a Minister of the Crown,

(b) by Order in Council,

(c) by the Scottish Ministers or any member of the Scottish Executive,

(d) by the [Welsh Ministers, the First Minister for Wales or the Counsel General to the Welsh Assembly Government], or

(e) by or by virtue of a Measure of the General Synod of the Church of England.

3. Action which is necessary, or in so far as it is necessary, for the purpose of complying with—

(a) an Act of Parliament,

(b) an Act of the Scottish Parliament, …

[(ba) a Measure or Act of the National Assembly for Wales, or]

(c) legislation of a kind described in Item 2.

The courts, &c

4. A judicial function (whether in connection with a court or a tribunal).

5. Anything done on behalf of or on the instructions of a person exercising a judicial function (whether in connection with a court or a tribunal).

6. A decision not to institute or continue criminal proceedings.

7. Anything done for the purpose of reaching, or in pursuance of, a decision not to institute or continue criminal proceedings.

Separate services, &c

8. The provision of a service for one sex only where only persons of that sex require the service.

9. The provision of separate services for each sex where a joint service would or might be less effective.

10. The provision of a service for one sex only where—

(a) the service is also provided jointly for both sexes, and

(b) if the service were provided only jointly it would or might be insufficiently effective.

11. The provision of a service for one sex only where—

(a) if the service were provided for both sexes jointly it would or might be less effective, and

(b) the extent to which the service is required by the other sex makes it not reasonably practicable to provide separate services for that sex.

12. The provision of separate services for each sex in different ways or to different extents where—

(a) if the service were provided for both sexes jointly it would or might be less effective, and

(b) the extent to which the service is required by one sex makes it not reasonably practicable to provide the service for that sex in the same way or to the same extent as for the other sex.

13. Action taken for the purpose of assisting one sex to overcome—

(a) a disadvantage (as compared with the other sex), or

PART 1

(b) the effects of discrimination.
Miscellaneous
14. The exercise of a function of the [Charity Commission] for England and Wales or the holder of the Office of the Scottish Charity Regulator in relation to an instrument in relation to which section 43 applies. 15. Action which is unlawful by virtue of another provision of this Act. 16. Action which would be unlawful by virtue of another provision of this Act but for an express exception.]

[123A]

NOTES

Commencement: 6 April 2007.
Inserted by the Equality Act 2006, s 83(1), as from 6 April 2007.
Sub-ss (5), (7): words in square brackets substituted by the Transfer of Functions (Equality) Order 2007, SI 2007/2914, art 8, Schedule, para 6(a), as from 12 October 2007.
Sub-s (9): the Table in sub-s (9) is amended as follows:
Para 1: word omitted from sub-para (c) repealed, and sub-paras (e)–(h) added, by the Government of Wales Act 2006 (Consequential Modifications and Transitional Provisions) Order 2007, SI 2007/1388, art 3, Sch 1, paras 2, 4(a), (b), as from 25 May 2007.
Para 2: words in square brackets in sub-para (d) substituted by SI 2007/1388, art 3, Sch 1, paras 2, 4(c), as from 25 May 2007.
Para 3: word omitted from sub-para (b) repealed, and sub-para (ba) inserted, by SI 2007/1388, art 3, Sch 1, paras 2, 4(d), (e), as from 25 May 2007.
Para 14: words in square brackets substituted by the Charities Act 2006, s 75(1), Sch 8, para 57, as from 27 February 2007.
Orders: as of 6 April 2008, no Orders had been made under sub-s (5).

Education

22 … Bodies in charge of educational establishments

[(1)] It is unlawful, in relation to an educational establishment falling within column 1 of the following table, for a person indicated in relation to the establishment in column 2 (the "responsible body") to discriminate against a woman—

(a) in the terms on which it offers to admit her to the establishment as a pupil, or
(b) by refusing or deliberately omitting to accept an application for her admission to the establishment as a pupil, or
(c) where she is a pupil of the establishment—
  (i) in the way it affords her access to any benefits, facilities or services, or by refusing or deliberately omitting to afford her access to them, or
  (ii) by excluding her from the establishment or subjecting her to any other detriment.

TABLE

Establishment	*Responsible body*
ENGLAND AND WALES	
1. Educational establishment maintained by a local education authority.	Local education authority or … [governing body], according to which of them has the function in question.
2. Independent school not being a special school.	Proprietor.
3. Special school not maintained by a local education authority.	Proprietor.
[3A. …	…]
[3B. Institution within the further education sector (within the meaning of section 91(3) of the Further and Higher Education Act 1992).	Governing body.]

Establishment	***Responsible body***
4. University.	Governing body.
[4A. Institution, other than a university, within the higher education sector (within the meaning of section 91(5) of the Further and Higher Education Act 1992).	Governing body.]
5. Establishment (not falling within paragraphs 1 [to 4A]) providing full-time or part-time education, being an establishment designated under 24(1).	Governing body.
SCOTLAND	
6. Educational establishment managed by an education authority.	Education authority.
7. Educational establishment in respect of which the managers are for the time being receiving grants under section [73(c) or (d) of the Education (Scotland) Act 1980].	Managers of the educational establishment.
[7A. …	…]
[7B. College of further education within the meaning of section 36(1) of the Further and Higher Education (Scotland) Act 1992 under the management of a board of management.	Board of management.
7C. Designated institution within the meaning of Part II of the Further and Higher Education (Scotland) Act 1992.	Governing body.]
8. University.	Governing body.
9. Independent school.	Proprietor.
10. Any other educational establishment (not falling within paragraphs 6, 7 and 9) providing full or part-time school education or further education.	Managers of the educational establishment.

[(2) It is unlawful for the governing body of an institution of further or higher education to discriminate against a woman in the arrangements it makes for the purpose of selecting people for admission to the institution.

(3) It is unlawful for the governing body of an institution of further or higher education to subject a woman to harassment if that woman is a student at the institution or has applied for admission to the institution.

(4) In subsections (2) and (3) "institution of further or higher education" means—

(a) in England and Wales, an establishment falling within column 1 of paragraph 3B, 4 or 4A of the table in subsection (1);

(b) in Scotland—

(i) a college of further education within the meaning given by section 36(1) of the Further and Higher Education (Scotland) Act 1992 under the management of a board of management within the meaning of Part I of that Act,

(ii) a college of further education managed by an education authority in the exercise of its functions in providing courses of further education within the meaning of section 1(5)(b)(ii) of the Education (Scotland) Act 1980,

(iii) any other educational establishment (not being a school) which provides further education within the meaning of section 1 of the Further and Higher Education (Scotland) Act 1992,

(iv) an institution within the higher education sector (within the meaning of Part II of the Further and Higher Education (Scotland) Act 1992), or

(v) a central institution (within the meaning of section 135 of the Education (Scotland) Act 1980).]

[124]

NOTES

Section heading: words omitted repealed by the Employment Equality (Sex Discrimination) Regulations 2005, SI 2005/2467, reg 22(1), as from 1 October 2005.

Sub-s (1): numbered as such by SI 2005/2467, reg 22(2), as from 1 October 2005.

The Table in sub-s (1) is amended as follows:

Para 1: words omitted repealed by the Education Act 1980, s 1(3), Sch 1, para 27; words in square brackets substituted by the School Standards and Framework Act 1998, s 140(1), Sch 30, para 5.

Para 3A: inserted by the Education Reform Act 1988, s 237, Sch 12, Pt I, para 15; repealed by the School Standards and Framework Act 1998, s 140(3), Sch 31.

Para 3B: inserted by the Further and Higher Education Act 1992, s 93, Sch 8, Pt II, para 76.

Para 4A: inserted by the Education Reform Act 1988, s 237, Sch 12, Pt III, para 72; substituted by the Further and Higher Education Act 1992, s 93, Sch 8, Pt II, para 76.

Para 5: words in square brackets substituted by the Further and Higher Education Act 1992, s 93, Sch 8, Pt II, para 76.

Para 7: words in square brackets substituted by the Education (Scotland) Act 1980, s 136(2), Sch 4, para 6.

Para 7A: inserted by the Self-Governing Schools etc (Scotland) Act 1989, s 82(1), Sch 10, para 5(2); repealed by the Standards in Scotland's Schools etc Act 2000, s 60(2), Sch 3, as from 31 December 2004.

Paras 7B, 7C: inserted by the Further and Higher Education (Scotland) Act 1992, s 62, Sch 9, para 4(2).

Sub-ss (2)–(4): added by SI 2005/2467, reg 22(3), as from 1 October 2005.

[22A Meaning of pupil in section 22

For the purposes of section 22, "pupil" includes, in England and Wales, any person who receives education at a school or institution to which that section applies.]

[125]

NOTES

Inserted by the Further and Higher Education Act 1992, s 93, Sch 8, Pt II, para 77.

23 Other discrimination by local education authorities

(1) It is unlawful for a local education authority, in carrying out such of its functions under [the Education Acts] as do not fall under section 22, to do any act which constitutes sex discrimination.

(2) It is unlawful for an education authority, in carrying out such of its functions under the Education (Scotland) [Act 1980] as do not fall under section 22, to do any act which constitutes sex discrimination.

[126]

NOTES

Sub-s (1): words in square brackets substituted by the Education Act 1996, s 582(1), Sch 37, para 31.

Sub-s (2): words in square brackets substituted by the Education (Scotland) Act 1980, s 136(2), Sch 4, para 7.

[23A Discrimination by Further Education and Higher Education Funding Councils

It is unlawful for [the Learning and Skills Council for England, …] the Higher Education Funding Council for England or the Higher Education Funding Council for Wales in carrying out their functions under [the Education Acts] [and the Learning and Skills Act 2000] [and for the [Welsh Ministers in carrying out their functions] under Part 2 of the Learning and Skills Act 2000]], to do any act which constitutes sex discrimination.]

[127]

NOTES

Inserted by the Further and Higher Education Act 1992, s 93, Sch 8, Pt II, para 78.

Words in first pair of square brackets substituted, and words in third pair of square brackets inserted, by the Learning and Skills Act 2000, s 149, Sch 9, paras 1, 5; words omitted repealed, and words in fourth (outer) pair of square brackets inserted, by the National Council for Education and Training for Wales (Transfer of Functions to the National Assembly for Wales and Abolition) Order 2005, SI 2005/3238, art 9(1), Sch 1, paras 3, 4(b), as from 1 April 2006; words in second pair of square brackets substituted by the Education Act 1996, s 582(1), Sch 37, para 32; words in fifth (inner) pair of square brackets substituted by the Government of Wales Act 2006 (Consequential Modifications and Transitional Provisions) Order 2007, SI 2007/1388, art 3, Sch 1, paras 2, 5, as from 25 May 2007.

23B (*Inserted by the Further and Higher Education (Scotland) Act 1992, s 62(2), Sch 9, para 4(1), (3); repealed by the Further and Higher Education (Scotland) Act 2005, s 32, Sch 3, para 3, as from 3 October 2005.*)

[23BA Discrimination by Scottish Further and Higher Education Funding Council

It is unlawful for the Scottish Further and Higher Education Funding Council in carrying out any of its functions to do any act which constitutes sex discrimination.]

[128]

NOTES

Commencement: 3 October 2005.

Inserted by the Further and Higher Education (Scotland) Act 2005 (Consequential Modifications) Order 2005, SI 2005/2077, art 4, as from 3 October 2005.

23C (*Inserted by the Education Act 1993, s 307(1), Sch 19, para 57; repealed by the School Standards and Framework Act 1998, s 140(3), Sch 31.*)

[23D Discrimination by [Training and Development Agency for Schools]

It is unlawful for the [Training and Development Agency for Schools] in carrying out their functions under [any enactment] to do any act which constitutes sex discrimination.]

[129]

NOTES

Inserted by the Education Act 1994, s 24, Sch 2, para 5(3).

Words in square brackets substituted by the Education Act 2005, s 98, Sch 14, para 5, as from 1 September 2005.

24 Designated establishments

(1) The Secretary of State may by order designate for the purpose of paragraph 5 of the table in section 22 such establishments of the description mentioned in that paragraph as he thinks fit.

(2) An establishment shall not be designated under subsection (1) unless—

(a) …

(b) it is an establishment in respect of which grants are payable out of money provided by Parliament, or

(c) it is assisted by a local education authority [for the purposes] of [the Education Act 1996], or

(d) it provides full-time education for persons who have attained the upper limit of compulsory school age [construed in accordance with section 8 of the Education Act 1996)] but not the age of nineteen.

(3) A designation under subsection (1) shall remain in force until revoked notwithstanding that the establishment ceases to be within subsection (2).

[130]

NOTES

Sub-s (2): para (a) repealed, and words in first pair of square brackets in para (c) substituted, by the Education Reform Act 1988, s 237, Sch 12, Pt III, para 73, Sch 13, Pt II; words in second pair of square brackets in para (c) substituted, and words in square brackets in para (d) inserted, by the Education Act 1996 s 582(1), Sch 37, paras 34, 137.

Orders: the Sex Discrimination (Designated Educational Establishments) (Revocation) Order 1995, SI 1995/2019 (which revokes SI 1975/1902, SI 1980/1860 and SI 1993/560).

25 General duty in public sector of education

(1) Without prejudice to its obligation to comply with any other provision of this Act, a body to which this subsection applies shall be under a general duty to secure that facilities for education provided by it, and any ancillary benefits or services, are provided without sex discrimination.

(2) The following provisions of [the Education Act 1996], namely—

(a) [section 496] (power of Secretary of State to require duties under that Act to be exercised reasonably), and

(b) [section 497] (powers of Secretary of State where local education authorities etc are in default),

shall apply to the performance by a body to which subsection (1) applies of the duties imposed by sections 22 [23, 23A[… and 23D]] and shall also apply to the performance of the general duty imposed by subsection (1), as they apply to the performance by a local education authority of a duty imposed by that Act.

(3) Section [70 of the Education (Scotland) Act 1980] (powers of the Secretary of State to require duties in that Act to be exercised) shall apply to the performance by a body to which subsection (1) applies of the duties imposed by sections 22 and 23 and shall also apply to the performance of the general duty imposed by subsection (1), as the [said section 70] applies to the performance by an education authority of a duty imposed by that Act.

(4) The sanctions in subsections (2) and (3) shall be the only sanctions for breach of the general duty in subsection (1), but without prejudice to the enforcement of sections 22 [23, 23A[… and 23D]] under section 66 or otherwise (where the breach is also a contravention of [any] of those sections).

(5) The Secretary of State shall have the power to cause a local inquiry to be held into any matter arising from subsection (3) under section [67 of the Education (Scotland) Act 1980].

(6) Subsection (1) applies to—

(a) local education authorities in England and Wales;

(b) education authorities in Scotland;

(c) any other body which is a responsible body in relation to—

(i) an establishment falling within paragraph 1, 3 […] [3B] [[or 7], 7B or 7C] of the table in section 22;

(ii) an establishment designated under section 24(1) as falling within paragraph … (c) or section 24(2);

(iii) an establishment designated under section 24(1) as falling within paragraph (b) of section 24(2) where the grants in question are payable under [section 485 of the Education Act 1996];

[(d), (e) …]

[(f) the Training and Development Agency for Schools].

[131]

NOTES

Sub-s (2): words in first, second and third pairs of square brackets substituted by the Education Act 1996, s 582(1), Sch 37, para 35(2); words in fourth (outer) pair of square brackets substituted by the Education Act 1993, s 307(1), Sch 19, para 59(a); words in fifth (inner) pair of square brackets substituted by the Education Act 1994, s 24, Sch 2, para 5(4)(a), and words omitted therefrom repealed by the School Standards and Framework Act 1998, s 140(3), Sch 31.

Sub-ss (3), (5): words in square brackets substituted by the Education (Scotland) Act 1980, s 136(2), Sch 4, para 8(a), (b).

Sub-s (4): words in first (outer) pair of square brackets substituted by the Education Act 1993, s 307(1), Sch 19, para 59(a); words in second (inner) pair of square brackets substituted by the Education Act 1994, s 24, Sch 2, para 5(4)(a), and words omitted therefrom repealed by the School Standards and Framework Act 1998, s 140(3), Sch 31; word in final pair of square brackets substituted by the Education Act 1996, s 582(1), Sch 37, para 35(1)(a), (3)(b).

Sub-s (6): word omitted from para (c)(i) originally inserted by the Education Reform Act 1988, s 237, Sch 12, para 6, and repealed by the School Standards and Framework Act 1998, s 140(3), Sch 31; figure "3B" in para (c)(i) substituted (for figure "4A" as inserted by the Education Reform Act 1988, s 237, Sch 12, para 74) by the Further and Higher Education Act 1992, s 93, Sch 8, para 79(1); words in third (outer) pair of square brackets in para (c)(i) substituted by the Further and Higher Education (Scotland) Act 1992, s 62, Sch 9, para 4(4), and words in fourth (inner) pair of square brackets substituted by the Standards in Scotland's Schools etc Act 2000, s 60(1), Sch 2, para 2(1), (2), as from 31 December 2004; words omitted from para (c)(ii) repealed by the Education Reform Act 1988, s 237, Sch 12, para 74, Sch 13, Pt II; words in square brackets in para (c)(iii) substituted by the Education Act 1996, s 582(1), Sch 37, para 35(1)(a), (4)(a); para (d) added by the Further and Higher Education Act 1992, s 93, Sch 8, para 79(1), and repealed by the Learning and Skills Act 2000, s 153, Sch 11; para (e) added by the Education Act 1993, s 307(1), Sch 19, para 59(b), and repealed by the School Standards and Framework Act 1998, s 140(3), Sch 31; para (f) added by the Education Act 1994, s 24, Sch 2, para 5(4)(b), and substituted by the Education Act 2005, s 98, Sch 14, para 6, as from 1 September 2005.

Transfer of functions in relation to Wales: as to the transfer of functions under this section from Ministers of the Crown to the National Assembly for Wales, see the National Assembly for Wales (Transfer of Functions) Order 1999, SI 1999/672.

[25A General duty: post-16 education and training etc

[(1) The Learning and Skills Council for England [and the [Welsh Ministers]] shall be under a general duty to secure that the facilities falling within subsection (2) and any ancillary benefits or services are provided without sex discrimination.

(2) Facilities falling within this subsection are facilities for—

(a) education,

(b) training, and

(c) organised leisure-time occupation connected with such education or training,

the provision of which is secured by the Learning and Skills Council for England [or the [Welsh Ministers by virtue of their functions] under Part 2 of the Learning and Skills Act 2000].

[(3) The provisions of section 25 of the Learning and Skills Act 2000 shall be the only sanction for breach of the general duty in subsection (1) by the Learning and Skills Council for England.

(4) There shall be no sanction for breach of the general duty in subsection (1) by the [Welsh Ministers].

(5) Subsections (3) and (4) are without prejudice to the enforcement of section 23A under section 66 or otherwise (where the breach is also a contravention of that section).]]

[132]

NOTES

Inserted by the Learning and Skills Act 2000, s 149, Sch 9, paras 1, 6.

Sub-ss (1), (2): words in first (outer) pair of square brackets substituted by the National Council for Education and Training for Wales (Transfer of Functions to the National Assembly for Wales and Abolition) Order 2005, SI 2005/3238, art 9(1), Sch 1, paras 3, 5(a), (b), as from 1 April 2006; words in second (inner) pair of square brackets substituted by the Government of Wales Act 2006 (Consequential Modifications and Transitional Provisions) Order 2007, SI 2007/1388, art 3, Sch 1, paras 2, 6(1)–(3), as from 25 May 2007.

Sub-ss (3), (5): substituted, together with sub-s (4) for original sub-s (3), by SI 2005/3238, art 9(1), Sch 1, paras 3, 5(c), as from 1 April 2006.

Sub-s (4): substituted as noted above; words in square brackets substituted by SI 2007/1388, art 3, Sch 1, paras 2, 6(1), (4), as from 25 May 2007.

26 Exception for single-sex establishments

(1) [Section 22(1)(a) and (b)][, 25 and 25A] do not apply to the admission of pupils to any establishment (a "single-sex establishment") which admits pupils of one sex only, or which would be taken to admit pupils of one sex only if there were disregarded pupils of the opposite sex—

(a) whose admission is exceptional, or

(b) whose numbers are comparatively small and whose admission is confined to particular courses of instruction or teaching classes.

(2) Where a school which is not a single-sex establishment has some pupils as boarders and others as non-boarders, and admits as boarders pupils of one sex only (or would be taken to admit as boarders pupils of one sex only if there were disregarded boarders of the opposite sex whose numbers are comparatively small), and [sections 22(1)(a) and (b)][, 25 and 25A] do not apply to the admission of boarders and [sections 22(1)(c)(i)][, 25 and 25A] do not apply to boarding facilities.

(3) Where an establishment is a single-sex establishment by reason of its inclusion in subsection (1)(b), the fact that pupils of one sex are confined to particular courses of instruction or teaching classes shall not be taken to contravene section 22(c)(i) or the duty in section 25 [or 25A].

[(4) In this section, as it applies to an establishment in England and Wales, "pupil" includes any person who receives education at that establishment.]

[133]

NOTES

Sub-s (1): words in first pair of square brackets substituted by the Employment Equality (Sex Discrimination) Regulations 2005, SI 2005/2467, reg 22(4)(a), as from 1 October 2005; words in second pair of square brackets substituted by the Learning and Skills Act 2000, s 149, Sch 9, paras 1, 7(1), (2).

Sub-s (2): words in first and third pairs of square brackets substituted by SI 2005/2467, reg 22(4)(b), as from 1 October 2005; words in second and fourth pairs of square brackets substituted by the Learning and Skills Act 2000, s 149, Sch 9, paras 1, 7(1), (2).

Sub-s (3): words in square brackets inserted by the Learning and Skills Act 2000, s 149, Sch 9, paras 1, 7(1), (3).

Sub-s (4): added by the Further and Higher Education Act 1992, s 93, Sch 8, Pt II, para 80.

27 Exception for single-sex establishments turning co-educational

(1) Where at any time—

(a) the responsible body for a single-sex establishment falling within column 1 of the table in [section 22(1)] determines to alter its admissions arrangements so that the establishment will cease to be a single-sex establishment, or

(b) section 26(2) applies to the admission of boarders to a school falling within column 1 of that table but the responsible body determines to alter its admissions arrangements so that section 26(2) will cease so to apply,

the responsible body may apply in accordance with Schedule 2 for an order (a "transitional exemption order") authorising discriminatory admissions during the transitional period specified in the order.

[(1A) Without prejudice to subsection (1), a transitional exemption order may be made—

(a) in accordance with regulations made by virtue of section 21(5) of the Education and Inspections Act 2006 (which relates to the alteration of maintained schools in England), or

(b) in accordance with paragraph 21 or 22 of Schedule 6 or paragraph 16 or 17 of Schedule 7 to the School Standards and Framework Act 1998 (which relate to the alteration of maintained schools and the rationalisation of school places in Wales).]

(2) Where during the transitional period specified in a transitional exemption order applying to an establishment the responsible body refuses or deliberately omits to accept an application for the admission of a person to the establishment as a pupil the refusal or omission shall not be taken to contravene any provision of this Act.

(3) Subsection (2) does not apply if the refusal or omission contravenes any condition of the transitional exemption order.

(4) Except as mentioned in subsection (2), a transitional exemption order shall not afford any exemption from liability under this Act.

(5) Where, during the period between the making of an application for a transitional exemption order in relation to an establishment and the determination of the application, the responsible body refuses or deliberately omits to accept an application for the admission of a person to the establishment as a pupil the refusal or omission shall not be taken to contravene any provision of this Act.

[(6) In this section, as it applies to an establishment in England and Wales, "pupil" includes any person who receives education at that establishment.]

[134]–[135]

NOTES

Sub-s (1): words in square brackets in para (a) substituted by the Employment Equality (Sex Discrimination) Regulations 2005, SI 2005/2467, reg 22(5), as from 1 October 2005.

Sub-s (1A): inserted by the School Standards and Framework Act 1998, s 140(1), Sch 30, para 6, and substituted by the Education and Inspections Act 2006, s 30, Sch 3, para 3, as from 25 May 2007.

Sub-s (6): added by the Further and Higher Education Act 1992, s 93, Sch 8, Pt II, para 81.

28 *(Repealed by the Employment Equality (Sex Discrimination) Regulations 2005, SI 2005/2467, reg 23(1)(a), as from 1 October 2005.)*

Goods, facilities, services and premises

29 Discrimination in provision of goods, facilities or services

(1) It is unlawful for any person concerned with the provision (for payment or not) of goods, facilities or services to the public or a section of the public to discriminate against a woman who seeks to obtain or use those goods, facilities or services—

(a) by refusing or deliberately omitting to provide her with any of them, or

(b) by refusing or deliberately omitting to provide her with goods, facilities or services of the like quality, in the like manner and on the like terms as are normal in his case in relation to male members of the public or (where she belongs to a section of the public) to male members of that section.

(2) The following are examples of the facilities and services mentioned in subsection (1)—

(a) access to and use of any place which members of the public or a section of the public are permitted to enter;

(b) accommodation in a hotel, boarding house or other similar establishment;

(c) facilities by way of banking or insurance or for grants, loans, credit or finance;

(d) facilities for education;

(e) facilities for entertainment, recreation or refreshment;

(f) facilities for transport or travel;

(g) the services of any profession or trade, or any local or other public authority.

[(2A) It is unlawful in connection with the provision of goods, facilities or services to the public or a section of the public (except in so far as they relate to an excluded matter) for any person to subject to harassment—

(a) a woman who seeks to obtain or use those goods, facilities or services, or

(b) a woman to whom he provides those goods, facilities or services.]

(3) For the avoidance of doubt it is hereby declared that where a particular skill is commonly exercised in a different way for men and for women it does not contravene subsection (1) for a person who does not normally exercise it for women to insist on exercising it for a woman only in accordance with his normal practice or, if he reasonably considers it impracticable to do that in her case, to refuse or deliberately omit to exercise it.

[(4) In its application in relation … to discrimination falling within section 2A, subsection (1)(b) shall have effect as if references to male members of the public, or of a section of the public, were references to members of the public, or of a section of the public, who do not intend to undergo, are not undergoing and have not undergone gender reassignment.]

[136]

NOTES

Sub-s (2A): inserted by the Sex Discrimination (Amendment of Legislation) Regulations 2008, SI 2008/963, reg 2(1), Sch 1, para 4(a), as from 6 April 2008.

Sub-s (4): added by the Sex Discrimination (Gender Reassignment) Regulations 1999, SI 1999/1102, reg 6; words omitted repealed by SI 2008/963, reg 2(1), Sch 1, para 4(b), as from 6 April 2008.

30 Discrimination in disposal or management of premises

(1) It is unlawful for a person, in relation to premises in Great Britain of which he has power to dispose, to discriminate against a women—

(a) in the terms on which he offers her those premises, or

(b) by refusing her application for those premises, or

(c) in his treatment of her in relation to any list of persons in need of premises of that description.

[(1A) It is unlawful for such a person to subject to harassment a woman who applies for the premises.]

(2) It is unlawful for a person, in relation to premises managed by him, to discriminate against a woman occupying the premises—

(a) in the way he affords her access to any benefits or facilities, or by refusing or deliberately omitting to afford her access to them, or

(b) by evicting her, or subjecting her to any other detriment.

[(2A) It is unlawful for such a person to subject to harassment a woman who occupies the premises.]

(3) Subsection (1) does not apply to a person who owns an estate or interest in the premises and wholly occupies them unless he uses the services of an estate agent for the purposes of the disposal of the premises, or publishes or causes to be published an advertisement in connection with the disposal.

[(4) Subsections (1A) and (2A) apply in relation to an application for or occupation of premises except in so far as they relate to an excluded matter.]

[137]

NOTES

Sub-ss (1A), (2A), (4): inserted and added respectively by the Sex Discrimination (Amendment of Legislation) Regulations 2008, SI 2008/963, reg 2(1), Sch 1, para 5, as from 6 April 2008.

31 Discrimination: consent for assignment or sub-letting

(1) Where the licence or consent of the landlord or of any other person is required for the disposal to any person of premises in Great Britain comprised in a tenancy, it is unlawful for the landlord or other person—

[(a) to discriminate against a woman by withholding the licence or consent for disposal of the premises to her, or

(b) in relation to such a licence or consent, to subject to harassment a woman to whom the disposal would be made if the licence or consent were given.]

(2) Subsection (1) does not apply if—

(a) the person withholding a licence or consent, or a near relative of his ("the relevant occupier") resides, and intends to continue to reside, on the premises, and

(b) there is on the premises, in addition to the accommodation occupied by the relevant occupier, accommodation (not being storage accommodation or means of access) shared by the relevant occupier with other persons residing on the premises who are not members of his household, and

(c) the premises are small premises as defined in section 32(2).

(3) In this section "tenancy" means a tenancy created by a lease or sub- lease, by an agreement for a lease or sub-lease or by a tenancy agreement or in pursuance of any enactment; and "disposal", in relation to premises comprised in a tenancy, includes assignment or assignation of the tenancy and sub-letting or parting with possession of the premises or any part of the premises.

(4) This section applies to tenancies created before the passing of this Act, as well as to others.

[138]

NOTES

Sub-s (1): words in square brackets substituted by the Sex Discrimination (Amendment of Legislation) Regulations 2008, SI 2008/963, reg 2(1), Sch 1, para 6, as from 6 April 2008.

32 Exception for small dwellings

(1) Sections 29(1) and 30 do not apply to the provision by a person of accommodation in any premises, or the disposal of premises by him, if—

(a) that person or a near relative of his ("the relevant occupier") resides, and intends to continue to reside, on the premises, and

(b) there is on the premises, in addition to the accommodation occupied by the relevant occupier, accommodation (not being storage accommodation or means of access) shared by the relevant occupier with other persons residing on the premises who are not members of his household, and

(c) the premises are small premises.

(2) Premises shall be treated for the purposes of subsection (1) as small premises if—

(a) in the case of premises comprising residential accommodation for one or more households (under separate letting or similar agreements) in addition to the accommodation occupied by the relevant occupier, there is not normally residential accommodation for more than two such households and only the relevant occupier and any member of his household reside in the accommodation occupied by him;

(b) in the case of premises not falling within paragraph (a), there is not normally residential accommodation on the premises for more than six persons in addition to the relevant occupier and any members of his household.

[139]

33 Exception for political parties

(1) This section applies to a political party if—

(a) it has as its main object, or one of its main objects, the promotion of parliamentary candidatures for the Parliament of the United Kingdom, or

(b) it is an affiliate of, or has as an affiliate, or has similar formal links with, a political party within paragraph (a).

(2) Nothing in section 29(1) shall be construed as affecting any special provision for persons of one sex only in the constitution, organisation or administration of the political party.

(3) Nothing in section 29(1) shall render unlawful an act done in order to give effect to such a special provision.

[140]

34 Exception for voluntary bodies

(1) This section applies to a body—

(a) the activities of which are carried on otherwise than for profit, and

(b) which was not set up by any enactment.

(2) Sections 29(1) and 30 shall not be construed as rendering unlawful—

(a) the restriction of membership of any such body to persons of one sex (disregarding any minor exceptions), or

(b) the provision of benefits, facilities or services to members of any such body where the membership is so restricted,

even though membership of the body is open to the public, or to a section of the public.

(3) Nothing in section 29 or 30 shall—

(a) be construed as affecting a provision to which this subsection applies, or

(b) render unlawful an act which is done in order to give effect to such a provision.

(4) Subsection (3) applies to a provision for conferring benefits on persons of one sex only (disregarding any benefits to persons to the opposite sex which are exceptional or are relatively insignificant), being a provision which constitutes the main object of a body within subsection (1).

[(5) Subsections (2) to (4) do not apply to discrimination under section 1 or 2A in its application to sections 29 to 31 unless the treatment mentioned in those subsections is—

(a) a proportionate means of achieving a legitimate aim, or

(b) for the purpose of preventing or compensating for a disadvantage linked to sex.]

[141]

NOTES

Sub-s (5): added by the Sex Discrimination (Amendment of Legislation) Regulations 2008, SI 2008/963, reg 2(1), Sch 1, para 7, as from 6 April 2008.

35 Further exceptions from ss 29(1) and 30

(1) A person who provides at any place facilities or services restricted to men does not for that reason contravene section 29(1) if [any of the conditions in subsections (1A) to (1C) is satisfied.]

[(1A) The condition is that the place is, or is part of—

(a) a hospital, or

(b) any other establishment for persons requiring special care, supervision or attention.

(1B) The condition is that the place is (permanently or for the time being) occupied or used for the purposes of an organised religion, and the facilities or services are restricted to men so as to comply with the doctrines of that religion or avoid offending the religious susceptibilities of a significant number of its followers.

(1C) The condition is that the facilities or services are provided for, or are likely to be used by, two or more persons at the same time, and—

(a) the facilities or services are such, or those persons are such, that male users are likely to suffer serious embarrassment at the presence of a woman, or

(b) the facilities or services are such that a user is likely to be in a state of undress and a male user might reasonably object to the presence of a female user.]

(2) A person who provides facilities or services restricted to men does not for that reason contravene section 29(1) if the services or facilities are such that physical contact between the user and any other person is likely, and that other person might reasonably object if the user were a woman.

[(2A) In their application to discrimination falling within section 2A, subsections (1A), (1C) and (2) shall apply to the extent that any such discrimination is a proportionate means of achieving a legitimate aim.]

(3) Sections 29(1) and 30 do not apply—

(a) to discrimination [or harassment] which is rendered unlawful by any provision in column 1 of the table below, or

(b) to discrimination [or harassment] which would be so unlawful but for any provision in column 2 of that table, or

(c) to discrimination [or harassment] which contravenes a term modified or included by virtue of an equality clause.

Table

Provision creating illegality	*Exception*
Part II	Sections 6(3), 7(1)(b), 15(4), 19 and 20.
	Schedule 4 paragraphs 1 and 2.
Section 22 or 23	[Sections 26 and 27].
	Schedule 4 paragraph 4.

[142]

NOTES

Sub-s (1): words in square brackets substituted by the Sex Discrimination (Amendment of Legislation) Regulations 2008, SI 2008/963, reg 2(1), Sch 1, para 8(a), as from 6 April 2008.

Sub-ss (1A)–(1C), (2A): inserted by SI 2008/963, reg 2(1), Sch 1, para 8(b), (c), as from 6 April 2008.

Sub-s (3): words "or harassment" in square brackets (in each place they occur) inserted by SI 2008/963, reg 2(1), Sch 1, para 8(d), as from 6 April 2008; words in square brackets in the table substituted by the Employment Equality (Sex Discrimination) Regulations 2005, SI 2005/2467, reg 23(1)(b), as from 1 October 2005.

Supplementary Benefits Act 1976, Sch 5: repealed by the Jobseekers Act 1995, ss 30(4), 41(5), Sch 3.

[35ZA Excluded matters

Each of the following is an excluded matter for the purposes of sections 29 to 31—

(a) education (including vocational training);

(b) the content of media and advertisements;

(c) the provision of goods, facilities or services (not normally provided on a commercial basis) at a place (permanently or for the time being) occupied or used for the purposes of an organised religion.]

[142A]

NOTES

Commencement: 6 April 2008.

Inserted by the Sex Discrimination (Amendment of Legislation) Regulations 2008, SI 2008/963, reg 2(1), Sch 1, para 9(1), as from 6 April 2008.

Barristers

35A ... Barristers

(1) It is unlawful for a barrister or barrister's clerk, in relation to any offer of a pupillage or tenancy, to discriminate against a woman—

(a) in the arrangements which are made for the purpose of determining to whom it should be offered;
(b) in respect of any terms on which it is offered; or
(c) by refusing, or deliberately omitting, to offer it to her.

(2) It is unlawful for a barrister or barrister's clerk, in relation to a woman who is a pupil or tenant in the chambers in question, to discriminate against her—

(a) in respect of any terms applicable to her as a pupil or tenant;
(b) in the opportunities for training, or gaining experience, which are afforded or denied to her;
(c) in the benefits, facilities or services which are afforded or denied to her; or
(d) by terminating her pupillage or by subjecting her to any pressure to leave the chambers or other detriment.

[(2A) It is unlawful for a barrister or barrister's clerk, in relation to a pupillage or tenancy, to subject to harassment a person who is, or who has applied to be, a pupil or tenant in the set of chambers concerned.]

(3) It is unlawful for any person, in relation to the giving, withholding or acceptance of instructions to a barrister, [to—

(a) discriminate against a woman by subjecting her to a detriment, or
(b) subject a woman to harassment].

(4) In this section—

"barrister's clerk" includes any person carrying out any of the functions of a barrister's clerk; and

"pupil", "pupillage", "tenancy" and "tenant" have the meanings commonly associated with their use in the context of a of a set of barristers' chambers[, but "tenant" shall also include any barrister permitted to work in a set of chambers who is not a tenant (and "tenancy" shall be construed accordingly)].

(5) This section does not apply to Scotland.]

[143]

NOTES

Inserted, together with preceding heading, by the Courts and Legal Services Act 1990, s 64(1), subject to savings contained in Sch 19, para 1 thereto, in relation to a pupillage or tenancy which began before 1 January 1991.

Section heading: words omitted repealed by the Employment Equality (Sex Discrimination) Regulations 2005, SI 2005/2467, reg 24(1), (2), as from 1 October 2005.

Sub-s (2A): inserted by SI 2005/2467, reg 24(1), (3), as from 1 October 2005.

Sub-s (3): words in square brackets substituted by SI 2005/2467, reg 24(1), (4), as from 1 October 2005.

Sub-s (4): words in square brackets inserted by SI 2005/2467, reg 24(1), (5), as from 1 October 2005.

[Advocates

35B ... Advocates

(1) It is unlawful for an advocate, in relation to taking any person as his pupil, to discriminate against a woman—

(a) in the arrangements which are made for the purpose of determining whom he will take as his pupil;
(b) in respect of any terms on which he offers to take her as his pupil; or
(c) by refusing, or deliberately omitting, to take her as his pupil.

(2) It is unlawful for an advocate, in relation to a woman who is a pupil, to discriminate against her—

(a) in respect of any terms applicable to her as a pupil;
(b) in the opportunities for training, or gaining experience, which are afforded or denied to her;

(c) in the benefits, facilities or services which are afforded or denied to her; or

(d) by terminating her the relationship or by subjecting her to any pressure to terminate the relationship or other detriment.

[(2A) It is unlawful for an advocate, in relation to taking any person as that advocate's pupil, to subject to harassment a person who is, or who has applied to be taken as, his pupil.]

(3) It is unlawful for any person, in relation to the giving, withholding or acceptance of instructions to an advocate, to discriminate against a woman [by subjecting her to a detriment or to subject her to harassment].

(4) In this section—

"advocate" means a member of the Faculty of Advocates practising as such; and

"pupil" has the meaning commonly associated its use in the context of a person training to be an advocate.

(5) Section 3 applies for the purposes of this section as it applies for the purposes of any provision of Part II.

(6) This section does not apply to England and Wales.]

[144]

NOTES

Inserted, together with preceding heading, by the Courts and Legal Services Act 1990, s 65(1).
Section heading: words omitted repealed by the Employment Equality (Sex Discrimination) Regulations 2005, SI 2005/2467, reg 25(1), (2), as from 1 October 2005.
Sub-s (2A): inserted by SI 2005/2467, reg 25(1), (3), as from 1 October 2005.
Sub-s (3): words in square brackets inserted by SI 2005/2467, reg 25(1), (4), as from 1 October 2005.

[Relationships which have come to an end

35C Relationships which have come to an end

(1) This section applies where—

(a) there has been a relevant relationship between a woman and another person ("the relevant person"), and

(b) the relationship has come to an end (whether before or after the commencement of this section).

(2) In this section, a "relevant relationship" is a relationship during the course of which an act of discrimination by one party to the relationship against the other party to it is unlawful under—

[(za) sections 29 to 31, except in so far as they relate to an excluded matter,]

(a) section 35A or 35B, or

(b) any other provision of this Part, so far as the provision applies to vocational training.

(3) It is unlawful for the relevant person to discriminate against the woman by subjecting her to a detriment where the discrimination arises out of and is closely connected to the relevant relationship.

[(4) It is unlawful for the relevant person to subject a woman to harassment where that treatment arises out of or is closely connected to the relevant relationship.]]

[145]

NOTES

Commencement: 19 July 2003.
Inserted, together with preceding heading, by the Sex Discrimination Act 1975 (Amendment) Regulations 2003, SI 2003/1657, reg 4, as from 19 July 2003.
Sub-s (2): para (za) inserted by the Sex Discrimination (Amendment of Legislation) Regulations 2008, SI 2008/963, reg 2(1), Sch 1, para 10, as from 6 April 2008.
Sub-s (4): added by the Employment Equality (Sex Discrimination) Regulations 2005, SI 2005/2467, reg 26, as from 1 October 2005.

Extent

36 Extent of Part III

(1) Section 29(1)—

(a) does not apply to goods, facilities or services outside Great Britain except as provided in subsections (2) and (3), and

(b) does not apply to facilities by way of banking or insurance or for grants, loans, credit or finance, where the facilities are for a purpose to be carried out, or in connection with risks wholly or mainly arising, outside Great Britain.

(2) Section 29(1) applies to the provision of facilities for travel outside Great Britain where the refusal or omission occurs in Great Britain or on a ship, aircraft or hovercraft within subsection (3).

(3) Section 29(1) applies on and in relation to—

(a) any ship registered at a port of registry in Great Britain, and

(b) any aircraft or hovercraft registered in the United Kingdom and operated by a person who has his principal place of business, or is ordinarily resident, in Great Britain,

(c) any ship, aircraft or hovercraft belonging to or possessed by Her Majesty in right of the Government of the United Kingdom,

even if the ship, aircraft or hovercraft is outside Great Britain.

(4) This section shall not render unlawful an act done in or over a country outside the United Kingdom, or in or over that country's territorial waters, for the purpose of complying with the laws of that country.

(5) Sections 22, 23 and 25 do not apply to benefits, facilities or services outside Great Britain except—

(a) travel on a ship registered at a port of registry in Great Britain, and

(b) benefits, facilities or services provided on a ship so registered.

[146]

PART IV
OTHER UNLAWFUL ACTS

37 Discriminatory practices

[(1) In this section "discriminatory practice" means—

(a) the application of a provision, criterion or practice which results in an act of discrimination which is unlawful by virtue of any provision of Part 2 or 3 taken with section 1(2)(b) or 3(1)(b) or which would be likely to result in such an act of discrimination if the persons to whom it is applied were not all of one sex, or

(b) the application of a requirement or condition which results in an act of discrimination which is unlawful by virtue of any provision of Part 3 taken with section 1(1)(b) or which would be likely to result in such an act of discrimination if the persons to whom it is applied were not all of one sex.]

(2) A person acts in contravention of this section if and so long as—

(a) he applies a discriminatory practice, or

(b) he operates practices or other arrangements which in any circumstances would call for the application by him of a discriminatory practice.

(3) Proceedings in respect of a contravention of this section shall be brought only by the Commission in accordance with [sections 20 to 24 of the Equality Act 2006].

[147]

NOTES

Sub-s (1): substituted by the Sex Discrimination (Indirect Discrimination and Burden of Proof) Regulations 2001, SI 2001/2660, reg 8(2), as from 12 October 2001.

Sub-s (3): words in square brackets substituted by the Equality Act 2006, s 40, Sch 3, paras, 6, 7, as from a day to be appointed.

38 Discriminatory advertisements

(1) It is unlawful to publish or cause to be published an advertisement which indicates, or might reasonably be understood as indicating, an intention by a person to do any act which is or might be unlawful by virtue of Part II or III.

(2) Subsection (1) does not apply to an advertisement if the intended act would not in fact be unlawful.

(3) For the purposes of subsection (1), use of a job description with a sexual connotation (such as "waiter", "salesgirl", "postman" or "stewardess") shall be taken to indicate an intention to discriminate, unless the advertisement contains an indication to the contrary.

(4) The publisher of an advertisement made unlawful by subsection (1) shall not be subject to any liability under that subsection in respect of the publication of the advertisement if he proves—

(a) that the advertisement was published in reliance on a statement made to him by the person who caused it to be published to the effect that, by reason of the operation of subsection (2), the publication would not be unlawful, and

(b) that it was reasonable for him to rely on the statement.

(5) A person who knowingly or recklessly makes a statement such as is referred to in subsection (4) which in a material respect is false or misleading commits an offence, and shall be liable on summary conviction to a fine not exceeding [level 5 on the standard scale].

[(6) Proceedings in respect of a contravention of subsection (1) may be brought only—

(a) by the Commission, and

(b) in accordance with section 25 of the Equality Act 2006.]

[148]

NOTES

Sub-s (5): maximum fine increased and converted to a level on the standard scale by the Criminal Justice Act 1982, ss 37, 38, 46.

Sub-s (6): added by the Equality Act 2006, s 40, Sch 3, paras, 6, 8, as from 1 October 2007.

Proceedings in respect of a contravention of subsection (1): see further the Equality Act 2006, ss 25, 26 at **[1668]**, **[1669]**.

39 Instructions to discriminate

[(1)] It is unlawful for a person—

(a) who has authority over another person, or

(b) in accordance with whose wishes that other person is accustomed to act,

to instruct him to do any act which is unlawful by virtue of Part II or III, or procure or attempt to procure the doing by him of any such act.

[(2) Proceedings in respect of a contravention of subsection (1) may be brought only—

(a) by the Commission, and

(b) in accordance with section 25 of the Equality Act 2006.]

[149]

NOTES

Sub-s (1) numbered as such, and sub-s (2) added, by the Equality Act 2006, s 40, Sch 3, paras, 6, 9, as from 1 October 2007.

Proceedings in respect of a contravention of subsection (1): see further the Equality Act 2006, ss 25, 26 at **[1668]**, **[1669]**.

40 Pressure to discriminate

(1) It is unlawful to induce, or attempt to induce, a person to do any act which contravenes Part II or III by—

(a) providing or offering to provide him with any benefit, or

(b) subjecting or threatening to subject him to any detriment.

(2) An offer or threat is not prevented from falling within subsection (1) because it is not made directly to the person in question, if it is made in such a way that he is likely to hear of it.

[(3) Proceedings in respect of a contravention of subsection (1) may be brought only—

(a) by the Commission, and
(b) in accordance with section 25 of the Equality Act 2006.]

[150]

NOTES

Sub-s (3): added by the Equality Act 2006, s 40, Sch 3, paras, 6, 10, as from 1 October 2007.

Proceedings in respect of a contravention of subsection (1): see further the Equality Act 2006, ss 25, 26 at **[1668]**, **[1669]**.

41 Liability of employers and principals

(1) Anything done by a person in the course of his employment shall be treated for the purposes of this Act as done by his employer as well as by him, whether or not it was done with the employer's knowledge or approval.

(2) Anything done by a person as agent for another person with the authority (whether express or implied, and whether precedent or subsequent) of that other person shall be treated for the purposes of this Act as done by that other person as well as by him.

(3) In proceedings brought under this Act against any person in respect of an act alleged to have been done by an employee of his it shall be a defence for that person to prove that he took such steps as were reasonably practicable to prevent the employee from doing that act, or from doing in the course of his employment acts of that description.

[151]

NOTES

Modified as noted to s 6 at **[106]**.

Serious Organised Crime Agency: for the application of this section to any constable or other person who has been seconded to SOCA to serve as a member of its staff, see the Serious Organised Crime and Police Act 2005, s 56(3), (4).

42 Aiding unlawful acts

(1) A person who knowingly aids another person to do an act made unlawful by this Act shall be treated for the purposes of this Act as himself doing an unlawful act of the like description.

(2) For the purposes of subsection (1) an employee or agent for whose act the employer or principal is liable under section 41 (or would be so liable but for section 41(3)) shall be deemed to aid the doing of the act by the employer or principal.

(3) A person does not under this section knowingly aid another to do an unlawful act if—
(a) he acts in reliance on a statement made to him by that other person that, by reason of any provision of this Act, the act which he aids would not be unlawful, and
(b) it is reasonable for him to rely on the statement.

(4) A person who knowingly or recklessly makes a statement such as is referred to in subsection (3)(a) which in a material respect is false or misleading commits an offence, and shall be liable on summary conviction to a fine not exceeding [level 5 on the standard scale].

[152]

NOTES

Sub-s (4): maximum fine increased and converted to a level on the standard scale by the Criminal Justice Act 1982, ss 37, 38, 46.

PART V
GENERAL EXCEPTIONS FROM PARTS II TO IV

[42A Selection of candidates

(1) Nothing in Parts 2 to 4 shall—
(a) be construed as affecting arrangements to which this section applies, or
(b) render unlawful anything done in accordance with such arrangements.

(2) This section applies to arrangements made by a registered political party which—
(a) regulate the selection of the party's candidates in a relevant election, and

(b) are adopted for the purpose of reducing inequality in the numbers of men and women elected, as candidates of the party, to be members of the body concerned.

(3) The following elections are relevant elections for the purposes of this section—

(a) parliamentary elections;
(b) elections to the European Parliament;
(c) elections to the Scottish Parliament;
(d) elections to the National Assembly for Wales;
(e) local government elections within the meaning of section 191, 203 or 204 of the Representation of the People Act 1983 (c 2) (excluding any election of the Mayor of London).

(4) In this section "registered political party" means a party registered in the Great Britain register under Part 2 of the Political Parties, Elections and Referendums Act 2000 (c 41).]

[153]

NOTES

Inserted by the Sex Discrimination (Election Candidates) Act 2002, s 1.

Expiry: by virtue of the Sex Discrimination (Election Candidates) Act 2002, s 3, the 2002 Act, and therefore this section, will expire at the end of 2015 unless an order is made under that section.

43 Charities

(1) Nothing in Parts II to IV shall—

(a) be construed as affecting a provision to which this subsection applies, or
(b) render unlawful an act which is done in order to give effect to such a provision.

(2) Subsection (1) applies to a provision for conferring benefits on persons of one sex only (disregarding any benefits to persons of the opposite sex which are exceptional or are relatively insignificant), being a provision which is contained in a charitable instrument.

[(2A) But subsection (1) does not apply to discrimination under section 1 or 2A in its application to sections 29 to 31 unless the conferral of benefits is—

(a) a proportionate means of achieving a legitimate aim, or
(b) for the purpose of preventing or compensating for a disadvantage linked to sex.]

[(3) In this section "charitable instrument" means an enactment or other instrument passed or made for charitable purposes, or an enactment or other instrument so far as it relates to charitable purposes, and in Scotland includes the governing instrument of an endowment or of an educational endowment as those expressions are defined in section 135(1) of the Education (Scotland) Act 1962.

In the application of this section to England and Wales, "charitable purposes" means purposes which are exclusively charitable according to the law of England and Wales.]

[154]

NOTES

Sub-s (2A): inserted by the Sex Discrimination (Amendment of Legislation) Regulations 2008, SI 2008/963, reg 2(1), Sch 1, para 11, as from 6 April 2008.

Sub-s (3): substituted, for original sub-ss (3), (4), by the Sex Discrimination Act 1975 (Amendment of section 43) Order 1977, SI 1977/528, art 2.

44 Sport etc

[(1)] Nothing in Parts II to IV shall, in relation to any sport, game or other activity of a competitive nature where the physical strength, stamina or physique of the average woman puts her at a disadvantage to the average man, render unlawful any act related to the participation of a person as a competitor in events involving that activity which are confined to competitors of one sex.

[(2) Subsection (1) applies to discrimination under sections 29 to 31 which falls within section 2A, only if the discrimination is necessary to secure—

(a) fair competition, or
(b) the safety of competitors,

at such events.]

[155]

NOTES

Sub-s (1) numbered as such, and sub-s (2) added, by the Sex Discrimination (Amendment of Legislation) Regulations 2008, SI 2008/963, reg 2(1), Sch 1, para 12, as from 6 April 2008.

45 Insurance

[(1)] Nothing in Parts II to IV shall render unlawful the treatment of a person in relation to an annuity, life assurance policy, accident insurance policy, or similar matter involving the assessment of risk, where the treatment—

(a) was effected by reference to actuarial or other data from a source on which it was reasonable to rely, and

(b) was reasonable having regard to the data and any other relevant factors.

[(2) In the case of discrimination under section 29, 30 or 31, subsection (1) applies only in so far as that section relates to—

(a) an excluded matter; or

(b) differences in premiums and benefits applicable to a person under a contract of insurance or related financial services entered into before the appropriate date.

(3) Despite subsection (2), the treatment is not unlawful under section 29(1) if—

(a) in the case of discrimination under a contract entered into on or after the appropriate date which relates to differences in premiums and benefits, each of the following conditions is satisfied—

(i) the use of sex as a factor in the assessment of risk is based on relevant and accurate actuarial and statistical data;

(ii) the data referred to in subparagraph (i) are compiled, published (whether in full or in summary form) and regularly updated in accordance with guidance issued by the Treasury;

(iii) the differences in treatment are proportionate having regard to the data mentioned in subparagraph (i);

(iv) the differences do not result from costs related to pregnancy or to the fact that a woman has given birth at any time in the period of 26 weeks ending on the day the treatment occurs or begins; or

(b) insurance or related financial services are provided only to members of one sex in relation to risks which only affect that sex.

(4) Subsection (3)(a) applies to discrimination under section 2A as if, in subsection (1) of that section, after "other persons" there were inserted "of B's sex".

(5) For the purposes of this section, "the appropriate date" means the date on which the Sex Discrimination (Amendment of Legislation) Regulations 2008 came into force.]

[156]

NOTES

Sub-s (1) numbered as such, and sub-ss (2)–(5) added, by the Sex Discrimination (Amendment of Legislation) Regulations 2008, SI 2008/963, reg 2(1), Sch 1, para 13, as from 6 April 2008. For transitional provisions see reg 4(3) of the 2008 Regulations (at **[3474R]**) which provides that sub-s (3)(a)(iv) shall not apply to contracts entered into before 22 December 2008.

46 Communal accommodation

(1) In this section "communal accommodation" means residential accommodation which includes dormitories or other shared sleeping accommodation which for reasons of privacy or decency should be used by men only, or by women only (but which may include some shared sleeping accommodation for men, and some for women, or some ordinary sleeping accommodation).

(2) In this section "communal accommodation" also includes residential accommodation all or part of which should be used by men only, or by women only, because of the nature of the sanitary facilities serving the accommodation.

(3) Nothing in Part II or III shall render unlawful sex discrimination in the admission of persons to communal accommodation if the accommodation is managed in a way which, given the exigencies of the situation, comes as near as may be to fair and equitable treatment of men and women.

(4) In applying subsection (3) account shall be taken of—

(a) whether and how far it is reasonable to expect that the accommodation should be altered or extended, or that further alternative accommodation should be provided; and

(b) the frequency of the demand or need for use of the accommodation by men as compared with women[; and]

[(c) in respect of discrimination falling within section 2A, whether and how far such discrimination is a proportionate means of achieving a legitimate aim.]

(5) Nothing in Part II or III shall render unlawful sex discrimination against a woman, or against a man, as respects the provision of any benefit, facility or service if—

(a) the benefit, facility or service cannot properly and effectively be provided except for those using communal accommodation, and

(b) in the relevant circumstances the woman or, as the case may be, the man could lawfully be refused the use of the accommodation by virtue of subsection (3).

(6) Neither subsection (3) nor subsection (5) is a defence to an act of sex discrimination under Part II unless such arrangements as are reasonably practicable are made to compensate for the detriment caused by the discrimination; but in considering under subsection (5)(b) whether the use of communal accommodation could lawfully be refused (in a case based on Part II), it shall be assumed that the requirements of this subsection have been complied with as respects subsection (3).

(7) Section 25 shall not apply to sex discrimination within subsection (3) or (5).

(8) This section is without prejudice to the generality of [section 35(1) and (1C)].

[157]

NOTES

Sub-s (4): para (c) (and the word immediately preceding it) inserted by the Sex Discrimination (Amendment of Legislation) Regulations 2008, SI 2008/963, reg 2(1), Sch 1, para 14(a), as from 6 April 2008.

Sub-s (8): words in square brackets substituted by SI 2008/963, reg 2(1), Sch 1, para 14(b), as from 6 April 2008.

47 Discriminatory training by certain bodies

(1) Nothing in Parts II to IV shall render unlawful any act done in relation to particular work by [any person] in, or in connection with—

(a) affording women only, or men only, access to facilities for training which would help to fit them for that work, or

(b) encouraging women only, or men only, to take advantage of opportunities for doing that work,

where [it reasonably appears to that person] that at any time within the 12 months immediately preceding the doing of the act there were no persons of the sex in question doing that work in Great Britain, or the number of persons of that sex doing the work in Great Britain was comparatively small.

(2) Where in relation to particular work [it reasonably appears to any person] that although the condition for the operation of subsection (1) is not met for the whole of Great Britain it is met for an area within Great Britain, nothing in Parts II to IV shall render unlawful any act done by [that person] in, or in connection with—

(a) affording persons who are of the sex in question, and who appear likely to take up that work in that area, access to facilities for training which would help to fit them for that work, or

(b) encouraging persons of that sex to take advantage of opportunities in the area for doing that work.

(3) Nothing in Parts II to IV shall render unlawful any act done by [any person] in, or in connection with, affording persons access to facilities for training which would help to fit them for employment, where [it reasonably appears to that person] that those persons are in special need of training by reason of the period for which they have been discharging domestic or family responsibilities to the exclusion of regular full time employment.

The discrimination in relation to which this subsection applies may result from confining the training to persons who have been discharging domestic or family responsibilities, or from the way persons are selected for training, or both.

[(4) The preceding provisions of this section shall not apply in relation to any discrimination which is rendered unlawful by section 6.]

[158]

NOTES

Sub-ss (1)–(3): words in square brackets substituted by the Sex Discrimination Act 1986, s 4(1)–(3).
Sub-s (4): substituted by the Sex Discrimination Act 1986, s 4(1), (4).

48 Other discriminatory training etc

(1) Nothing in Parts II to IV shall render unlawful any act done by an employer in relation to particular work in his employment, being an act done in, or in connection with,—

(a) affording his female employees only, or his male employees only, access to facilities for training which would help to fit them for that work, or

(b) encouraging women only, or men only, to take advantage of opportunities for doing that work,

where at any time within the twelve months immediately preceding the doing of the act there were no persons of the sex in question among those doing that work or the number of persons of that sex doing the work was comparatively small.

(2) Nothing in section 12 shall render unlawful any act done by an organisation to which that section applies in, or in connection with,—

(a) affording female members of the organisation only, or male members of the organisation only, access to facilities for training which would help to fit them for holding a post of any kind in the organisation, or

(b) encouraging female members only, or male members only, to take advantage of opportunities for holding such posts in the organisation,

where at any time within the twelve months immediately preceding the doing of the act there were no persons of the sex in question among persons holding such posts in the organisation or the number of persons of that sex holding such posts was comparatively small.

(3) Nothing in Parts II to IV shall render unlawful any act done by an organisation to which section 12 applies in, or in connection with, encouraging women only, or men only, to become members of the organisation where at any time within the twelve months immediately preceding the doing of the act there were no persons of the sex in question among those members or the number of persons of that sex among the members was comparatively small.

[159]

49 Trade unions etc: elective bodies

(1) If an organisation to which section 12 applies comprises a body the membership of which is wholly or mainly elected, nothing in section 12 shall render unlawful provision which ensures that a minimum number of persons of one sex are members of the body—

(a) by reserving seats on the body for persons of that sex, or

(b) by making extra seats on the body available (by election or co-option or otherwise) for persons of that sex on occasions when the number of persons of that sex in the other seats is below the minimum,

where in the opinion of the organisation the provision is in the circumstances needed to secure a reasonable lower limit to the number of members of that sex serving on the body; and nothing in Parts II to IV shall render unlawful any act done in order to give effect to such a provision.

(2) This section shall not be taken as making lawful—

(a) discrimination in the arrangements for determining the persons entitled to vote in an election of members of the body, or otherwise to choose the persons to serve on the body, or

(b) discrimination in any arrangements concerning membership of the organisation itself.

[160]

50 Indirect access to benefits etc

(1) References in this Act to the affording by any person of access to benefits, facilities or services are not limited to benefits, facilities or services provided by that person himself,

but include any means by which it is in that person's power to facilitate access to benefits, facilities or services provided by any other person (the "actual provider").

(2) Where by any provision of this Act the affording by any person of access to benefits, facilities or services in a discriminatory way is in certain circumstances prevented from being unlawful, the effect of the provision shall extend also to the liability under this Act of any actual provider.

[161]

[51 Acts done for purposes of protection of women

(1) Nothing in the following provisions, namely—

(a) Part II,

[(aa) sections 35A and 35B,]

(b) [the remainder of] Part III so far as it applies to vocational training, or

(c) Part IV so far as it has effect in relation to the provisions mentioned in paragraphs (a) and (b),

shall render unlawful any act done by a person in relation to a woman if—

(i) it was necessary for that person to do it in order to comply with a requirement of an existing statutory provision concerning the protection of women, or

(ii) it was necessary for that person to do it in order to comply with a requirement of a relevant statutory provision (within the meaning of Part I of the Health and Safety at Work etc Act 1974) and it was done by that person for the purpose of the protection of the woman in question (or of any class of women that included that woman).

(2) In subsection (1)—

(a) the reference in paragraph (i) of that subsection to an existing statutory provision concerning the protection of women is a reference to any such provision having effect for the purpose of protecting women as regards—

(i) pregnancy or maternity, or

(ii) other circumstances giving rise to risks specifically affecting women,

whether the provision relates only to such protection or to the protection of any other class of persons as well; and

(b) the reference in paragraph (ii) of that subsection to the protection of a particular woman or class of women is a reference to the protection of that woman or those women as regards any circumstances falling within paragraph (a)(i) or (ii) above.

(3) In this section "existing statutory provision" means (subject to subsection (4)) any provision of—

(a) an Act passed before this Act, or

(b) an instrument approved or made by or under such an Act (including one approved or made after the passing of this Act).

(4) Where an Act passed after this Act re-enacts (with or without modification) a provision of an Act passed before this Act, that provision as re-enacted shall be treated for the purposes of subsection (3) as if it continued to be contained in an Act passed before this Act.]

[162]

NOTES

Substituted, together with s 51A for original s 51, by the Employment Act 1989, ss 3(1), (3), 29(6), Sch 9, para 1.

Sub-s (1): para (aa) inserted, and words in square brackets in para (b) inserted, by the Sex Discrimination (Amendment of Legislation) Regulations 2008, SI 2008/963, reg 2(1), Sch 1, para 15, as from 6 April 2008.

[51A Acts done under statutory authority to be exempt from certain provisions of Part III

(1) Nothing in—

[(za) sections 21A to 27, 32 and 33,]

(a) the relevant provisions of Part III, or

(b) Part IV so far as it has effect in relation to those provisions,

shall render unlawful any act done by a person if it was necessary for that person to do it in order to comply with a requirement of an existing statutory provision within the meaning of section 51.

(2) In subsection (1) "the relevant provisions of Part III" means the provisions of that Part [(except sections 21A to 27, 32 and 33) in so far as they relate to an excluded matter].]

[163]

NOTES

Substituted as noted to s 51 at **[162]**.

Sub-s (1): para (za) inserted by the Sex Discrimination (Amendment of Legislation) Regulations 2008, SI 2008/963, reg 2(1), Sch 1, para 16(a), as from 6 April 2008.

Sub-s (2): words in square brackets substituted by SI 2008/963, reg 2(1), Sch 1, para 16(b), as from 6 April 2008.

PART 1

52 Acts safeguarding national security

(1) Nothing in Parts II to IV shall render unlawful an act done for the purpose of safeguarding national security.

(2) *A certificate purporting to be signed by or on behalf of a Minister of the Crown and certifying that an act specified in the certificate was done for the purpose of safeguarding national security shall be conclusive evidence that it was done for that purpose.*

(3) *A document purporting to be a certificate such as is mentioned in subsection (2) shall be received in evidence and, unless the contrary is proved, shall be deemed to be such a certificate.*

[164]

NOTES

Partial repeal: the Sex Discrimination (Amendment) Order 1988, SI 1988/249, art 2, provides that sub-ss (2), (3) shall "cease to have effect in relation to the determination of the question whether any act is rendered unlawful by virtue of Part II of [this] Act, or by Part III of [this] Act as it applies to vocational training, or by Part IV of [this] Act taken with Part II, or with Part III as it so applies".

[52A Construction of references to vocational training

In the following provisions, namely—

(a) …

(b) the provisions of any Order in Council modifying the effect of section 52,

"vocational training" includes advanced vocational training and retraining; and any reference to vocational training in those provisions shall be construed as including a reference to vocational guidance.]

[165]–[175]

NOTES

Inserted by the Employment Act 1989, ss 3(1), (4), 29(6), Sch 9, para 1.

Para (a) repealed by the Employment Equality (Sex Discrimination) Regulations 2005, SI 2005/2467, reg 17(2), as from 1 October 2005.

53–61 (*Ss 53–61* (*Pt VI: Equal Opportunities Commission*) *repealed by the Equality Act 2006, ss 40, 91, Sch 3, paras, 6, 11, Sch 4, as from 1 October 2007. For savings see the Equality Act 2006* (*Commencement No 3 and Savings*) *Order 2007, SI 2007/2603, art 3 at* **[3473R]**. *For transitional provisions relating to the discharge by the Commission for Equality and Human Rights of the former functions of the Equal Opportunities Commission, see the Equality Act 2006* (*Dissolution of Commissions and Consequential and Transitional Provisions*) *Order 2007, SI 2007/2602, art 5 at* **[3473O]**).

PART VII
ENFORCEMENT

General

[62 Restriction of proceedings for breach of Act

(1) Except as provided by this Act no proceedings, whether civil or criminal, shall lie against any person in respect of an act by reason that the act is unlawful by virtue of a provision of this Act.

(2) Subsection (1) does not preclude the making of an order of certiorari, mandamus or prohibition.

(3) In Scotland, subsection (1) does not preclude the exercise of the jurisdiction of the Court of Session to entertain an application for reduction or suspension of any order or determination, or otherwise to consider the validity of any order or determination, or to require reasons for any order or determination to be stated.]

[176]

NOTES

Substituted by the Race Relations Act 1976, s 79(4), Sch 4, para 3.

Enforcement in employment field

63 Jurisdiction of [employment tribunals]

(1) A complaint by any person ("the complainant") that another person ("the respondent")—

(a) has committed an act of discrimination [or harassment] against the complainant which is unlawful by virtue of Part II [or section 35A or 35B], or

(b) is by virtue of section 41 or 42 to be treated as having committed such an act of discrimination [or harassment] against the complainant,

may be presented to an [employment tribunal].

(2) Subsection (1) does not apply to a complaint under section 13(1) of an act in respect of which an appeal, or proceedings in the nature of an appeal, may be brought under any enactment.

[177]

NOTES

Section heading: words in square brackets substituted by the Employment Rights (Dispute Resolution) Act 1998, s 1(2)(b).

Sub-s (1): words in first and third pairs of square brackets inserted by the Employment Equality (Sex Discrimination) Regulations 2005, SI 2005/2467, reg 28(1), (2), as from 1 October 2005; words in second pair of square brackets inserted by reg 28(1), (3) of the 2005 Regulations, as from 1 October 2005, except in relation to proceedings where the act complained of took place before that date; final words in square brackets substituted by the Employment Rights (Dispute Resolution) Act 1998, s 1(2)(a).

Conciliation: employment tribunal proceedings and claims which could be the subject of employment tribunal proceedings under this section are proceedings to which the Employment Tribunals Act 1996, s 18 applies; see s 18(1)(a)(ii) of that Act at **[975]**.

For rules of procedure relating to employment tribunal proceedings, see the Employment Tribunals (Constitution and Rules of Procedure) Regulations 2004, SI 2004/1861 at **[3151]**.

Tribunal jurisdiction: the Employment Act 2002, ss 31, 32, 38 at **[1493]**, **[1494]**, **[1496]** apply to proceedings before the employment tribunal relating to a claim under this section; see ss 31(1), 32(1), 38(1) of, and Schs 3–5 to, the 2002 Act at **[1508]**–**[1510]**.

For the circumstances in which the normal time limit for presenting a complaint under this section is extended for a period of three months, see the Employment Act 2002 (Dispute Resolution) Regulations 2004, SI 2004/752, regs 15 and 18 at **[3096]** and **[3098]**.

[63A Burden of proof: employment tribunals

(1) This section applies to any complaint presented under section 63 to an employment tribunal.

(2) Where, on the hearing of the complaint, the complainant proves facts from which the tribunal could, apart from this section, conclude in the absence of an adequate explanation that the respondent—

(a) has committed an act of discrimination [or harassment] against the complainant which is unlawful by virtue of Part 2 [or section 35A or 35B], or

(b) is by virtue of section 41 or 42 to be treated as having committed such an act of discrimination [or harassment] against the complainant,

the tribunal shall uphold the complaint unless the respondent proves that he did not commit, or, as the case may be, is not to be treated as having committed, that act.]

[178]

PART 1

NOTES

Inserted by the Sex Discrimination (Indirect Discrimination and Burden of Proof) Regulations 2001, SI 2001/2660, regs 2(2), 5, in relation to any proceedings under s 63 in an employment tribunal whenever instituted, except proceedings which were determined before 12 October 2001.

Sub-s (2): words in first and third pairs of square brackets inserted by the Employment Equality (Sex Discrimination) Regulations 2005, SI 2005/2467, reg 29(1), (2), as from 1 October 2005; words in second pair of square brackets inserted by reg 29(1), (3) of the 2005 Regulations, as from 1 October 2005, except in relation to proceedings where the act complained of took place before that date.

64 *(Repealed by the Employment Tribunals Act 1996, s 45, Sch 3, Pt I; the 1996 Act re-enacts these provisions in s 18(2), (3), (6) and (7).)*

65 Remedies on complaint under section 63

(1) Where an [employment tribunal] finds that a complaint presented to it under section 63 is well-founded the tribunal shall make such of the following as it considers just and equitable—

(a) an order declaring the rights of the complainant and the respondent in relation to the act to which the complaint relates;

(b) an order requiring the respondent to pay to the complainant compensation of an amount corresponding to any damages he could have been ordered by a county court or by a sheriff court to pay to the complainant if the complaint had fallen to be dealt with under section 66;

(c) a recommendation that the respondent take within a specified period action appearing to the tribunal to be practicable for the purpose of obviating or reducing the adverse effect on the complainant of any act of discrimination to which the complaint relates.

[(1A) In applying section 66 for the purposes of subsection (1)(b), no account shall be taken of subsection (3) of that section.

(1B) As respects an unlawful act of discrimination falling within [section 1(2)(b)] or section 3(1)(b), if the respondent proves that the [provision, criterion or practice] in question was not applied with the intention of treating the complainant unfavourably on the ground of his sex [or (as the case may be) fulfilment of the condition in section 3(2)], an order may be made under subsection (1)(b) only if the [employment tribunal]—

(a) makes such order under subsection (1)(a) and such recommendation under subsection (1)(c) (if any) as it would have made if it had no power to make an order under subsection (1)(b); and

(b) (where it makes an order under subsection (1)(a) or a recommendation under subsection (1)(c) or both) considers that it is just and equitable to make an order under subsection (1)(b) as well.]

(2) …

(3) If without reasonable justification the respondent to a complaint fails to comply with a recommendation made by an [employment tribunal] under subsection (1)(c), then, if they think it just and equitable to do so—

(a) the tribunal may […] increase the amount of compensation required to be paid to the complainant in respect of the complaint by an order made under subsection (1)(b), or

(b) if an order under subsection (1)(b) [was not made], the tribunal may make such an order.

[179]

NOTES

Sub-s (1): words in square brackets substituted by the Employment Rights (Dispute Resolution) Act 1998, s 1(2)(a).

Sub-s (1A): inserted, together with sub-s (1B), by the Sex Discrimination and Equal Pay (Miscellaneous Amendments) Regulations 1996, SI 1996/438, reg 2(2).

Sub-s (1B): inserted as noted above; words in first and second pairs of square brackets substituted by the Sex Discrimination (Indirect Discrimination and Burden of Proof) Regulations 2001, SI 2001/2660, reg 8(3); words in third pair of square brackets substituted by the Civil Partnership Act 2004, s 251(1), (5), as from 5 December 2005; words in final pair of square brackets substituted by the Employment Rights (Dispute Resolution) Act 1998, s 1(2)(a).

Sub-s (2): repealed by the Sex Discrimination and Equal Pay (Remedies) Regulations 1993, SI 1993/2798, regs 1(3), 2.

Sub-s (3): words in first pair of square brackets substituted by the Employment Rights (Dispute Resolution) Act 1998, s 1(2)(a); words omitted from para (a) originally inserted by the Race Relations Act 1976, s 79(4), Sch 4, para 4, and repealed by the Sex Discrimination and Equal Pay (Remedies) Regulations 1993, SI 1993/2798, reg 1(3), Schedule, para 1; words in final pair of square brackets substituted by the Sex Discrimination and Equal Pay (Miscellaneous Amendments) Regulations 1996, SI 1996/438, reg 2(3).

Compensation for dismissal: as to the powers of an employment tribunal to award compensation where any act constitutes both unfair dismissal under the Employment Rights Act 1996, and discrimination under any one or more of the Sex Discrimination Act 1975, the Race Relations Act 1976, the Disability Discrimination Act 1995, the Employment Equality (Sexual Orientation) Regulations 2003, the Employment Equality (Religion or Belief) Regulations 2003, or the Employment Equality (Age) Regulations 2006, see s 126 of the 1996 Act at **[1170]**.

Enforcement of Part III

66 Claims under Part III

(1) A claim by any person ("the claimant") that another person ("the respondent")—

(a) has committed an act of discrimination [or harassment] against the claimant which is unlawful by virtue of Part III, [other than section 35A or 35B,] or

(b) is by virtue of section 41 or 42 to be treated as having committed such an act of discrimination [or harassment] against the claimant,

may be made the subject of civil proceedings in like manner as any other claim in tort or (in Scotland) in reparation for breach of statutory duty.

(2) Proceedings under subsection (1)—

(a) shall be brought in England and Wales only in a county court, and

(b) shall be brought in Scotland only in a sheriff court.

but all such remedies shall be obtainable in such proceedings as, apart from this subsection [and section 62(1)], would be obtainable in the High Court or the Court of Session, as the case may be.

(3) As respects an unlawful act of discrimination falling within section 1(1)(b) … no award of damages shall be made if the respondent proves that the requirement or condition in question was not applied with the intention of treating the claimant unfavourably on the ground of his sex …

[(3A) Subsection (3) does not affect the award of damages in respect of an unlawful act of discrimination falling within section 1(2)(b).]

(4) For the avoidance of doubt it is hereby declared that damages in respect of an unlawful act of discrimination [or harassment] may include compensation for injury to feelings whether or not they include compensation under any other head.

(5) Civil proceedings in respect of a claim by any person that he has been discriminated against[, or subjected to harassment,] in contravention of section 22 or 23 by a body to which section 25(1) applies shall not be instituted unless the claimant has given notice of the claim to the Secretary of State and either the Secretary of State has by notice informed the claimant that the Secretary of State does not require further time to consider the matter, or the period of two months has elapsed since the claimant gave notice to the Secretary of State; but nothing in this subsection applies to a counterclaim.

[(5A) In Scotland, when any proceedings are brought under this section, in addition to the service on the defender of a copy of the summons or initial writ initiating the action a copy thereof shall be sent as soon as practicable to the Commission in a manner to be prescribed by Act of Sederunt.]

(6) For the purposes of proceedings under subsection (1)—

(a) [section 63(1) (assessors) of the County Courts Act 1984] shall apply with the omission of the words "on the application of any party", and

(b) the remuneration of assessors appointed under the said section [63(1)] shall be at such rate as may be determined by the Lord Chancellor with the approval of the Minister for the Civil Service.

(7) For the purposes of proceedings before the sheriff, provision may be made by Act of Sederunt for the appointment of assessors by him, and the remuneration of any assessors so appointed shall be at such rates as the Lord President of the Court of Session with the approval of the Minister for the Civil Service may determine.

(8) A county court or sheriff court shall have jurisdiction to entertain proceedings under subsection (1) with respect to an act done on a ship, aircraft or hovercraft outside its district, including such an act done outside Great Britain.

[180]

NOTES

Sub-s (1): words in first and third pairs of square brackets inserted by the Employment Equality (Sex Discrimination) Regulations 2005, SI 2005/2467, reg 30(1), (2), as from 1 October 2005; words in second pair of square brackets inserted by reg 30(1), (3) of the 2005 Regulations, as from 1 October 2005, except in relation to proceedings where the act complained of took place before that date.

Sub-s (2): words in square brackets inserted by the Race Relations Act 1976, s 79(4), Sch 4, para 5.

Sub-s (3): words omitted repealed by the Sex Discrimination and Equal Pay (Miscellaneous Amendments) Regulations 1996, SI 1996/438, reg 2(4).

Sub-s (3A): inserted by the Sex Discrimination (Indirect Discrimination and Burden of Proof) Regulations 2001, SI 2001/2660, reg 7.

Sub-ss (4), (5): words in square brackets inserted by SI 2005/2467, reg 30(1), (4), (5), as from 1 October 2005.

Sub-s (5A): inserted by the Race Relations Act 1976, s 79(4), Sch 4, para 5.

Sub-s (6): words in square brackets inserted by the County Courts Act 1984, s 148(1), Sch 2, para 55.

Conciliation: for the powers of the Commission for Equality and Human Rights to make arrangements for the provision of conciliation services for disputes in respect of which proceedings have been, or could be, brought under this section, see the Equality Act 2006, s 27 at **[1670]**.

Transfer of functions: functions of the Secretary of State under sub-s (5), so far as exercisable in relation to Wales, are transferred to the National Assembly for Wales by the National Assembly for Wales (Transfer of Functions) Order 1999, SI 1999/672, art 2, Sch 1.

[66A Burden of proof: county and sheriff courts

(1) This section applies to any claim brought under section 66(1) in a county court in England and Wales or a sheriff court in Scotland.

(2) Where, on the hearing of the claim, the claimant proves facts from which the court could, apart from this section, conclude in the absence of an adequate explanation that the respondent—

[(a) has committed an act of discrimination or harassment against the claimant which is unlawful by virtue of—
  (i) section 29, 30 or 31, or
  (ii) any other provision of Part 3 so far as it applies to vocational training, or]

(b) is by virtue of section 41 or 42 to be treated as having committed such an act of discrimination [or harassment] against the claimant,

the court shall uphold the claim unless the respondent proves that he did not commit, or, as the case may be, is not to be treated as having committed, that act.]

[180A]

NOTES

Inserted by the Sex Discrimination (Indirect Discrimination and Burden of Proof) Regulations 2001, SI 2001/2660, regs 2(2), 6, in relation to any claim under s 66(1) in a county court or sheriff court whenever instituted, except proceedings which were determined before 12 October 2001.

Sub-s (2) is amended as follows:

Para (a) substituted by the Sex Discrimination (Amendment of Legislation) Regulations 2008, SI 2008/963, reg 2(1), Sch 1, para 17, as from 6 April 2008, except in relation to proceedings where the act complained of took place before that date (see reg 4(1) of the 2008 Regulations at **[3474R]**). Para (a) (as previously substituted by the Employment Equality (Sex Discrimination) Regulations 2005, SI 2005/2467, reg 31(1), (2), as from 1 October 2005, except in relation to proceedings where the act complained of took place before that date) read as follows—

"[(a) has committed an act of discrimination or harassment against the claimant which is unlawful by virtue of any provision of Part 3 so far as it applies to vocational training, or]".

Words in square brackets in para (b) inserted by SI 2005/2467, reg 31(1), (3), as from 1 October 2005.

[66B National security

(1) Rules of court may make provision for enabling a county court or sheriff court in which a claim is brought under section 66(1), where the court considers it expedient in the interests of national security—

(a) to exclude from all or part of the proceedings—
  (i) the claimant;
  (ii) the claimant's representatives;

(iii) any assessors;

(b) to permit a claimant or representative who has been excluded to make a statement to the court before the commencement of the proceedings, or the part of the proceedings, from which he is excluded;

(c) to take steps to keep secret all or part of the reasons for the court's decision in the proceedings.

(2) The Attorney General or, in Scotland, the Advocate General for Scotland, may appoint a person to represent the interests of a claimant in, or in any part of, proceedings from which the claimant or his representatives are excluded by virtue of subsection (1).

(3) A person may be appointed under subsection (2) only—

(a) in relation to proceedings in England and Wales, if he has a general qualification (within the meaning of section 71 of the Courts and Legal Services Act 1990 (c 41)), or

(b) in relation to proceedings in Scotland, if he is—

(i) an advocate, or

(ii) qualified to practice as a solicitor in Scotland.

(4) A person appointed under subsection (2) shall not be responsible to the person whose interests he is appointed to represent.]

[180B]–[187]

NOTES

Commencement: 18 April 2006.

Inserted by the Equality Act 2006, s 87, as from 18 April 2006.

67–73 *(Repealed by the Equality Act 2006, ss 40, 91, Sch 3, paras, 6, 12, Sch 4, as from 1 October 2007. For savings see the Equality Act 2006 (Commencement No 3 and Savings) Order 2007, SI 2007/2603, art 3 at* **[3473R]**. *For transitional provisions relating to the discharge by the Commission for Equality and Human Rights of the former functions of the Equal Opportunities Commission, see the Equality Act 2006 (Dissolution of Commissions and Consequential and Transitional Provisions) Order 2007, SI 2007/2602, art 5 at* **[3473O]**).

Help for persons suffering discrimination

74 Help for aggrieved persons in obtaining information etc

(1) With a view to helping a person ("the person aggrieved") who considers he may have been discriminated against [or subjected to harassment] in contravention of this Act to decide whether to institute proceedings and, if he does so, to formulate and present his case in the most effective manner, the [Minister] shall by order prescribe—

(a) forms by which the person aggrieved may question the respondent on his reasons for doing any relevant act, or on any other matter which is or may be relevant;

(b) forms by which the respondent may if he so wishes reply to any questions.

(2) Where the person aggrieved questions the respondent (whether in accordance with an order under subsection (1) or not)—

(a) the question, and any reply by the respondent (whether in accordance with such an order or not) shall, subject to the following provisions of this section, be admissible as evidence in the proceedings;

(b) if it appears to the court or tribunal that the respondent deliberately, and without reasonable excuse omitted to reply within [the period applicable under subsection (2A)] or that his reply is evasive or equivocal, the court or tribunal may draw any inference from that fact that it considers it just and equitable to draw, including an inference that he committed an unlawful act.

[(2A) The period applicable for the purposes of subsection (2)(b) is—

(a) eight weeks beginning with the day when the question was served on the respondent, if the question relates to discrimination under—

(i) any provision of Part 2,

[(ia) section 29, 30 or 31, except in so far as it relates to an excluded matter,]

(ii) section 35A or 35B, or

(iii) any other provision of Part 3, so far as it applies to vocational training;

(b) a reasonable period, as regards any other question.]

(3) The [Minister] may by order—

(a) prescribe the period within which questions must be duly served in order to be admissible under subsection (2)(a), and

(b) prescribe the manner in which a question, and any reply by the respondent, may be duly served.

(4) Rules may enable the court entertaining a claim under section 66 to determine, before the date fixed for the hearing of the claim, whether a question or reply is admissible under this section or not.

(5) This section is without prejudice to any other enactment or rule of law regulating interlocutory and preliminary matters in proceedings before a county court, sheriff court or [employment tribunal], and has effect subject to any enactment or rule of law regulating the admissibility of evidence in such proceedings.

(6) In this section "respondent" includes a prospective respondent and "rules"—

(a) in relation to county court proceedings, means county court rules;

(b) in relation to sheriff court proceedings, means sheriff court rules.

[188]–[189]

NOTES

Sub-s (1): words in first pair of square brackets inserted by the Employment Equality (Sex Discrimination) Regulations 2005, SI 2005/2467, reg 32(1), (2), as from 1 October 2005, except in the case of a question served on a respondent before that date; word in second pair of square brackets substituted by the Transfer of Functions (Equality) Order 2007, SI 2007/2914 art 8, Schedule, para 6(b), as from 12 October 2007.

Sub-s (2): words in square brackets in para (b) substituted by SI 2005/2467, reg 32(1), (3), as from 1 October 2005, except in the case of a question served on a respondent before that date.

Sub-s (2A): inserted by SI 2005/2467, reg 32(1), (4), as from 1 October 2005, except in the case of a question served on a respondent before that date; para (a)(ia) inserted by the Sex Discrimination (Amendment of Legislation) Regulations 2008, SI 2008/963, reg 2(1), Sch 1, para 18, as from 6 April 2008, except in the case of a question served on a respondent before that date (see reg 4(2) of the 2008 Regulations at **[3474R]**).

Sub-s (3): word in square brackets substituted by SI 2007/2914 art 8, Schedule, para 6(b), as from 12 October 2007.

Sub-s (5): words in square brackets substituted by the Employment Rights (Dispute Resolution) Act 1998, s 1(2)(a).

Orders: the Sex Discrimination (Questions and Replies) Order 1975, SI 1975/2048 at **[2026]**.

75 *(Repealed by the Equality Act 2006, ss 40, 91, Sch 3, paras, 6, 13, Sch 4, as from 1 October 2007.)*

Period within which proceedings to be brought

76 Period within which proceedings to be brought

(1) An [employment tribunal] shall not consider a complaint under section 63 unless it is presented to the tribunal before the end of[—

(a) the period of three months beginning when the act complained of was done; or

(b) in a case to which section 85(9A) applies, the period of six months so beginning.]

(2) A county court or a sheriff court shall not consider a claim under section 66 unless proceedings in respect of the claim are instituted before the end of—

[(a) the period of six months beginning when the act complained of was done; or

(b) in a case to which section 66(5) applies, the period of eight months so beginning.]

[(2A) Where in England and Wales—

(a) proceedings or prospective proceedings under section 66 relate to the act or omission of a qualifying institution, and

(b) the dispute concerned is referred as a complaint under the student complaints scheme before the end of the period of six months mentioned in subsection (2)(a),

the period allowed by subsection (2)(a) shall be extended by [three months].

(2B) In subsection (2A)—

"qualifying institution" has the meaning given by section 11 of the Higher Education Act 2004;

"the student complaints scheme" means a scheme for the review of qualifying complaints, as defined by section 12 of that Act, that is provided by the designated operator, as defined by section 13(5)(b) of that Act.]

[(2C) The period allowed by subsection (2)(a) or (b) shall be extended by three months in the case of a dispute which is referred for conciliation in pursuance of arrangements under section 27 of the Equality Act 2006 (unless the period is extended under subsection (2A)).]

(3), (4) …

(5) A court or tribunal may nevertheless consider any such [complaint or claim] which is out of time if, in all the circumstances of the case, it considers that it is just and equitable to do so.

(6) For the purposes of this section—

(a) where the inclusion of any term in a contract renders the making of the contract an unlawful act that act shall be treated as extending throughout the duration of the contract, and

(b) any act extending over a period shall be treated as done at the end of that period, and

(c) a deliberate omission shall be treated as done when the person in question decided upon it,

and in the absence of evidence establishing the contrary a person shall be taken for the purposes of this section to decide upon an omission when he does an act inconsistent with doing the omitted act or, if he has done no such inconsistent act, when the period expires within which he might reasonably have been expected to do the omitted act if it was to be done.

[190]

NOTES

Sub-s (1): words in first pair of square brackets substituted by the Employment Rights (Dispute Resolution) Act 1998, s 1(2)(a); words in second pair of square brackets substituted by the Armed Forces Act 1996, s 21(6).

Sub-s (2): words in square brackets substituted by the Race Relations Act 1976, s 79(4), Sch 4, para 8(a).

Sub-s (2A): inserted, together with sub-s (2B), by the Higher Education Act 2004, s 19(1), as from 1 November 2004; words in square brackets substituted by the Equality Act 2006, s 40, Sch 3, paras, 6, 14(1), (2), as from 1 October 2007.

Sub-s (2B): inserted as noted above.

Sub-s (2C): inserted by the Equality Act 2006, s 40, Sch 3, paras, 6, 14(1), (3), as from 1 October 2007.

Sub-ss (3), (4): repealed by the Equality Act 2006, ss 40, 91, Sch 3, paras 6, 14(1), (4), Sch 4, as from 1 October 2007.

Sub-s (5): words in square brackets substituted by the Equality Act 2006, s 40, Sch 3, paras, 6, 14(1), (5), as from 1 October 2007.

For the circumstances in which the normal time limit for presenting a complaint under s 63 is extended for a period of three months, see the Employment Act 2002 (Dispute Resolution) Regulations 2004, SI 2004/752, regs 15 and 18 at **[3096]** and **[3098]**.

PART VIII
SUPPLEMENTAL

[76A Public authorities: general statutory duty

(1) A public authority shall in carrying out its functions have due regard to the need—

(a) to eliminate unlawful discrimination and harassment, and

(b) to promote equality of opportunity between men and women.

(2) In subsection (1)—

(a) "public authority" includes any person who has functions of a public nature (subject to subsections (3) and (4)),

(b) "functions" means functions of a public nature, and

(c) the reference to unlawful discrimination shall be treated as including a reference to contravention of terms of contracts having effect in accordance with an equality clause within the meaning of section 1 of the Equal Pay Act 1970 (c 41).

(3) The duty in subsection (1) shall not apply to—

(a) the House of Commons,

(b) the House of Lords,

(c) the Scottish Parliament,

[(ca) the National Assembly for Wales,]

(d) the General Synod of the Church of England,

(e) the Security Service,

(f) the Secret Intelligence Service,

(g) the Government Communications Headquarters,

(h) a part of the armed forces of the Crown which is, in accordance with a requirement of the Secretary of State, assisting the Government Communications Headquarters, or

(i) a person specified for the purpose of this paragraph by order of the [Minister] (and a person may be specified generally or only in respect of specified functions).

(4) The duty in subsection (1) shall not apply to the exercise of—

(a) a function in connection with proceedings in the House of Commons or the House of Lords,

(b) a function in connection with proceedings in the Scottish Parliament (other than a function of the Scottish Parliamentary Corporate Body),

[(ba) a function in connection with proceedings in the National Assembly for Wales (other than a function of the National Assembly for Wales Commission),]

(c) a judicial function (whether in connection with a court or a tribunal),

(d) a function exercised on behalf of or on the instructions of a person exercising a judicial function (whether in connection with a court or a tribunal), or

(e) a function specified for the purpose of this paragraph by order of the [Minister].

(5) Subsection (1)(b) is without prejudice to the effect of any exception to or limitation of the law about sex discrimination.

(6) A failure in respect of performance of the duty under subsection (1) does not confer a cause of action at private law.]

[190A]

NOTES

Commencement: 18 April 2006 (for the purpose only of exercising any power to make orders under ss 76B and 76C); 6 April 2007 (otherwise).

Inserted by the Equality Act 2006, s 84(1), as from 18 April 2006 (for the purpose only of exercising any power to make orders under ss 76B and 76C), and as from 6 April 2007 (otherwise).

Sub-s (3): para (ca) inserted by the Government of Wales Act 2006 (Consequential Modifications and Transitional Provisions) Order 2007, SI 2007/1388, art 3, Sch 1, paras 2, 7(1), (2), as from 25 May 2007; word in square brackets in para (i) substituted by the Transfer of Functions (Equality) Order 2007, SI 2007/2914, art 8, Schedule, para 6(c), as from 12 October 2007.

Sub-s (4): para (ba) inserted by SI 2007/1388, art 3, Sch 1, paras 2, 7(1), (3), as from 25 May 2007; word in square brackets in para (e) substituted by SI 2007/2914, art 8, Schedule, para 6(c), as from 12 October 2007.

Assessment and compliance: for the powers of the Commission for Equality and Human Rights to assess the extent to which, or the manner in which, a person has complied with a duty under this section and ss 76B, 76C and, where it thinks that a person has failed to comply with such duty, to give the person a notice requiring him to: (i) comply with the duty, and (ii) to give the Commission (within the period of 28 days beginning with the date on which he receives the notice) written information of steps taken, or proposed, for the purpose of complying with the duty, see the Equality Act 2006, ss 31, 32 at **[1674]**, **[1675]**.

[76B Specific duties

[(1) The [Minister] may by order impose on a person to whom the duty in section 76A(1) applies, or in so far as that duty applies to a person, a duty which the [Minister] thinks will ensure better performance of the duty under section 76A(1).

(2) Before making an order under subsection (1) the [Minister] shall consult the Commission.

(3) The [Minister]—

(a) must consult the [Welsh Ministers] before making an order under subsection (1) in respect of a person exercising functions in relation to Wales, and

(b) may not, without the consent of the [Welsh Ministers], make an order under subsection (1) in respect of a person all of whose functions are public functions in relation to Wales.

(4) A failure in respect of performance of a duty imposed under subsection (1) does not confer a cause of action at private law.]

[190B]

NOTES

Commencement: 18 April 2006 (for the purpose only of exercising any power to make orders); 6 April 2007 (otherwise).

Inserted by the Equality Act 2006, s 85(1), as from 18 April 2006 (for the purpose only of exercising any power to make orders), and as from 6 April 2007 (otherwise).

The word "Minister" in square brackets in each place it occurs was substituted by the Transfer of Functions (Equality) Order 2007, SI 2007/2914, art 8, Schedule, para 6(d), as from 12 October 2007; the words "Welsh Ministers" in sub-s (3) were substituted by the Government of Wales Act 2006 (Consequential Modifications and Transitional Provisions) Order 2007, SI 2007/1388, art 3, Sch 1, paras 1, 8, as from 25 May 2007.

Assessment and compliance: see the note to s 76A at **[190A]**.

Orders: the Sex Discrimination Act 1975 (Public Authorities) (Statutory Duties) Order 2006, SI 2006/2930 at **[3467]**.

[76C Specific duties: Scotland

(1) Section 76B(1) shall not apply in relation to a person who is a relevant Scottish authority or a cross-border authority.

(2) The [Minister] may by order impose on a cross-border authority to whom the duty under section 76A(1) applies, or in so far as that duty applies to the cross-border authority, a duty which the [Minister] thinks will ensure better performance of the duty under section 76A(1), to the extent that the cross-border authority's functions are not Scottish functions.

(3) The Scottish Ministers may by order impose on a relevant Scottish authority to whom the duty under section 76A(1) applies, or in so far as that duty applies to the relevant Scottish authority, a duty which the Scottish Ministers think will ensure better performance of the duty under section 76A(1).

(4) The Scottish Ministers may by order impose on a cross-border authority to whom the duty under section 76A(1) applies, or in so far as that duty applies to the cross-border authority, a duty which the Scottish Ministers think will ensure better performance of the duty under section 76A(1), to the extent that the cross-border authority's functions are Scottish functions.

(5) Before making an order under any of subsections (2) to (4) the person making the order shall consult the Commission.

(6) Before making an order under subsection (2) the [Minister] shall consult the Scottish Ministers.

(7) Before making an order under subsection (4) the Scottish Ministers shall consult the [Minister].

(8) A failure in respect of performance of a duty imposed under this section does not confer a cause of action at private law.

(9) In this section—

"relevant Scottish authority" means—

- (a) a member of the Scottish Executive or a junior Scottish Minister,
- (b) the Registrar General of Births, Deaths and Marriages for Scotland, the Keeper of the Registers of Scotland or the Keeper of the Records of Scotland,
- (c) an office of a description specified in an Order in Council under section 126(8)(b) of the Scotland Act 1998 (c 46) (other non-ministerial offices in the Scottish Administration), or
- (d) a public body, public office or holder of a public office—
  - (i) which is not a cross-border authority or the Scottish Parliamentary Corporate Body,
  - (ii) whose functions are exercisable only in or as regards Scotland, and
  - (iii) some at least of whose functions do not relate to reserved matters (within the meaning of the Scotland Act 1998),

"cross-border authority" means a cross-border public authority within the meaning given by section 88(5) of the Scotland Act 1998, and

"Scottish functions" means functions which are exercisable in or as regards Scotland and which do not relate to reserved matters (within the meaning of the Scotland Act 1998).]

[190C]

NOTES

Commencement: 18 April 2006 (for the purpose only of exercising any power to make orders); 6 April 2007 (otherwise).

Inserted by the Equality Act 2006, s 85(1), as from 18 April 2006 (for the purpose only of exercising any power to make orders), and as from 6 April 2007 (otherwise).

Sub-ss (2), (6), (7): words in square brackets substituted by the Transfer of Functions (Equality) Order 2007, SI 2007/2914, art 8, Schedule, para 6(e), as from 12 October 2007.

Assessment and compliance: see the note to s 76A at **[190A]**.

Orders: the Sex Discrimination Act 1975 (Public Authorities) (Statutory Duties) Order 2006, SI 2006/2930 at **[3467]**; the Sex Discrimination (Public Authorities) (Statutory Duties) (Scotland) Order 2007, SSI 2007/32 at **[3472]**.

76D, 76E *(S 76D inserted by the Equality Act 2006, s 85(1), as from 6 April 2007, and repealed by ss 40, 91 of, and Sch 3, paras, 6, 15, Sch 4 to, that Act as from 1 October 2007; s 76E inserted by the Equality Act 2006, s 86, as from 16 February 2006, and repealed by ss 40, 91 of, and Sch 3, paras, 6, 15, Sch 4 to, that Act as from 1 October 2007.)*

77 Validity and revision of contracts

(1) A term of a contract is void where—

(a) its inclusion renders the making of the contract unlawful by virtue of this Act, or

(b) it is included in furtherance of an act rendered unlawful by this Act, or

(c) it provides for the doing of an act which would be rendered unlawful by this Act.

(2) Subsection (1) does not apply to a term the inclusion of which constitutes, or is in furtherance of, or provides for, unlawful discrimination against a party to the contract, but the term shall be unenforceable against that party.

(3) A term in a contract which purports to exclude or limit any provision of this Act or the Equal Pay Act 1970 is unenforceable by any person in whose favour the term would operate apart from this subsection.

(4) Subsection (3) does not apply—

(a) to a contract settling a complaint to which section 63(1) of this Act or section 2 of the Equal Pay Act 1970 applies where the contract is made with the assistance of a conciliation officer;

[(aa) to a contract settling a complaint to which section 63(1) of this Act or section 2 of the Equal Pay Act 1970 applies if the conditions regulating compromise contracts under this Act are satisfied in relation to the contract;]

(b) to a contract settling a claim to which section 66 applies.

[(4A) The conditions regulating compromise contracts under this Act are that—

(a) the contract must be in writing;

(b) the contract must relate to the particular complaint;

(c) the complainant must have received [advice from a relevant independent adviser] as to the terms and effect of the proposed contract and in particular its effect on his ability to pursue his complaint before an [employment tribunal];

(d) there must be in force, when the adviser gives the advice, a [contract of insurance, or an indemnity provided for members of a professional body,] covering the risk of a claim by the complainant in respect of loss arising in consequence of the advice;

(e) the contract must identify the adviser; and

(f) the contract must state that the conditions regulating compromise contracts under this Act are satisfied.

[(4B) A person is a relevant independent adviser for the purposes of subsection (4A)(c)—

(a) if he is a qualified lawyer,

(b) if he is an officer, official, employee or member of an independent trade union who has been certified in writing by the trade union as competent to give advice and as authorised to do so on behalf of the trade union,

(c) if he works at an advice centre (whether as an employee or a volunteer) and has been certified in writing by the centre as competent to give advice and as authorised to do so on behalf of the centre, or

(d) if he is a person of a description specified in an order made by the [Minister].

(4BA) But a person is not a relevant independent adviser for the purposes of subsection (4A)(c) in relation to the complainant—

(a) if he is, is employed by or is acting in the matter for the other party or a person who is connected with the other party,

(b) in the case of a person within subsection (4B)(b) or (c), if the trade union or advice centre is the other party or a person who is connected with the other party,

(c) in the case of a person within subsection (4B)(c), if the complainant makes a payment for the advice received from him, or

(d) in the case of a person of a description specified in an order under subsection (4B)(d), if any condition specified in the order in relation to the giving of advice by persons of that description is not satisfied.

(4BB) In subsection (4B)(a) "qualified lawyer" means—

(a) as respects England and Wales, *a barrister (whether in practice as such or employed to give legal advice), a solicitor who holds a practising certificate, or a person other than a barrister or solicitor who is an authorised advocate or authorised litigator (within the meaning of the Courts and Legal Services Act 1990), and*

(b) as respects Scotland, an advocate (whether in practice as such or employed to give legal advice), or a solicitor who holds a practising certificate.

(4BC) In subsection (4B)(b) "independent trade union" has the same meaning as in the Trade Union and Labour Relations (Consolidation) Act 1992.

(4C) For the purposes of subsection (4BA) any two persons are to be treated as connected—

(a) if one is a company of which the other (directly or indirectly) has control, or

(b) if both are companies of which a third person (directly or indirectly) has control.]]

[(4D) An agreement under which the parties agree to submit a dispute to arbitration—

(a) shall be regarded for the purposes of subsection (4)(a) and (aa) as being a contract settling a complaint if—

(i) the dispute is covered by a scheme having effect by virtue of an order under section 212A of the Trade Union and Labour Relations (Consolidation) Act 1992, and

(ii) the agreement is to submit it to arbitration in accordance with the scheme, but

(b) shall be regarded for those purposes as neither being nor including such a contract in any other case.]

(5) On the application of any person interested in a contract to which subsection (2) applies, a county court or sheriff court may make such order as it thinks just for removing or modifying any term made unenforceable by that subsection; but such an order shall not be made unless all persons affected have been given notice of the application (except where under rules of court notice may be dispensed with) and have been afforded an opportunity to make representations to the court.

(6) An order under subsection (5) may include provision as respects any period before the making of the order.

[191]

NOTES

Sub-s (4): para (aa) inserted by the Trade Union Reform and Employment Rights Act 1993, s 39(2), Sch 6, para 1(a).

Sub-s (4A): inserted by the Trade Union Reform and Employment Rights Act 1993, s 39(2), Sch 6, para 1(b); words in square brackets substituted by the Employment Rights (Dispute Resolution) Act 1998, ss 1(2)(a), 9(1), (2)(a), 10(1), (2)(a).

Sub-ss (4B), (4BA), (4BB), (4BC), (4C): substituted (for subs-ss (4B), (4C) as inserted by the Trade Union Reform and Employment Rights Act 1993, s 39(2), Sch 6, para 1(b)) by the Employment Rights (Dispute Resolution) Act 1998, s 15, Sch 1, para 2.

Word in square brackets in sub-s (4B)(d) substituted by the Transfer of Functions (Equality) Order 2007, SI 2007/2914, art 8, Schedule, para 6(f), as from 12 October 2007.

For the words in italics in sub-s (4BB)(a) there are substituted the words "a person who, for the purposes of the Legal Services Act 2007, is an authorised person in relation to an activity which constitutes the exercise of a right of audience or the conduct of litigation (within the meaning of that Act), and" by the Legal Services Act 2007, s 208(1), Sch 21, para 32, as from a day to be appointed.

Sub-s (4D): inserted by the Employment Rights (Dispute Resolution) Act 1998, s 8(1).

Term of a contract: this section, as it applies to a term of a contract, is applied by the Sex Discrimination Act 1986, s 6 at **[378]**, to a term of a collective agreement (whether or not legally enforceable), a rule made by an employer in relation to his employees or prospective employees, and a rule made by certain organisations for application to any of its members or prospective members or to persons on whom it has conferred or could confer an authorisation or qualification.

Orders: the Compromise Agreements (Description of Person) Order 2004, SI 2004/754 at **[3138]**.

78 Educational charities in England and Wales

(1) This section applies to any trust deed or other instrument—

(a) which concerns property applicable for or in connection with the provision of education in any establishment in paragraphs 1 to 5 of the Table in section 22, and

(b) which in any way restricts the benefits available under the instrument to persons of one sex.

(2) If on the application of the trustees, or of the responsible body (as defined in section 22), the Secretary of State is satisfied that the removal or modification of the restriction would conduce to the advancement of education without sex discrimination, he may by order make such modifications of the instrument as appear to him expedient for removing or modifying the restriction, and for any supplemental or incidental purposes.

(3) If the trust was created by gift or bequest, no order shall be made until 25 years after the date on which the gift or bequest took effect, unless the donor or his personal representatives, or the personal representatives of the testator, have consented in writing to the making of the application for the order.

(4) The Secretary of State shall require the applicant to publish notice—

(a) containing particulars of the proposed order, and

(b) stating that representations may be made to the Secretary of State within a period specified in the notice.

(5) The period specified in the notice shall not be less than one month from the date of the notice.

(6) The applicants shall publish the notice in such manner as may be specified by the Secretary of State, and the cost of any publication of the notice may be defrayed out of the property of the trust.

(7) Before making the order the Secretary of State shall take into account any representations duly made in accordance with the notice.

(8) This section does not apply in Scotland.

[192]

NOTES

Transfer of functions in relation to Wales: as to the transfer of functions under this section from Ministers of the Crown to the National Assembly for Wales, see the National Assembly for Wales (Transfer of Functions) Order 1999, SI 1999/672.

79 Educational endowments etc to which [Part VI of the Education (Scotland) Act 1980] applies

(1) This section applies to any educational endowment to which [[section 104] of the Education (Scotland) Act 1980] applies and which in any way restricts the benefit of the endowment to persons of one sex, and any reference to an educational endowment in this section includes a reference to—

(a) a scheme made or approved for that endowment under [Part VI] of the [Education (Scotland) Act 1980];

[(aa) in the case of an endowment the governing body of which is entered in the Scottish Charity Register, a scheme approved for that endowment under section 39 or 40 of the Charities and Trustee Investment (Scotland) Act 2005 (asp 10);]

(b) any endowment which is, by virtue of [section 108(1)] of [the Education (Scotland) Act 1980], dealt with as if it were an educational endowment [(or which would, but for the disapplication of that section by section 122(4) of that Act, be so dealt with)]; and

(c) a university endowment, the Carnegie Trust, a theological endowment and a new endowment.

(2) If, on the application of the governing body of an educational endowment, the Secretary of State is satisfied that the removal or modification of the provision which restricts the benefit of the endowment to persons of one sex would conduce to the advancement of education without sex discrimination, he may, by order, make such modifications to the endowment as appear to him expedient for removing or modifying the restriction and for any supplemental or incidental purposes.

(3) Where the Secretary of State proposes to make an order under this section, he shall publish a notice, in such manner as he thinks sufficient for giving information to persons whom he considers may be interested in the endowment—

(a) containing particulars of the proposed order; and

(b) stating that representations may be made with respect thereto within such period as may be specified in the notice, not being less than one month from the date of publication of the notice,

and the cost of publication of any such notice shall be paid out of the funds of the endowment to which the notice relates.

(4) Before making any order under this section, the Secretary of State shall consider any representations duly made in accordance with the said notice and he may cause a local inquiry to be held into such representations under [section 67 of the Education (Scotland) Act 1980].

(5) Without prejudice to section 81(5) of this Act, any order made under this section may be varied or revoked in a scheme made or approved under [Part VI of the Education (Scotland) Act 1980] [or, in the case of an endowment the governing body of which is entered in the Scottish Charity Register, a scheme approved for that endowment under section 39 or 40 of the Charities and Trustee Investment (Scotland) Act 2005 (asp 10)].

(6) …

(7) This section shall be construed as one with [Part VI of the Education (Scotland) Act 1980].

[193]

NOTES

Section heading, sub-ss (4), (7): words in square brackets substituted by virtue of the Education (Scotland) Act 1980, s 136(2), Sch 4, para 9.

Sub-s (1): words in first (outer), fourth and sixth pairs of square brackets substituted by virtue of the Education (Scotland) Act 1980, s 136(2), Sch 4, para 9(a); other words in square brackets substituted or inserted by the Charities and Trustee Investment (Scotland) Act 2005, s 104, Sch 4, Pt 1, para 3(1), as from 1 April 2006.

Sub-s (5): words in first pair of square brackets substituted by virtue of the Education (Scotland) Act 1980, s 136(2), Sch 4, para 9; words in second pair of square brackets inserted by the Charities and Trustee Investment (Scotland) Act 2005, s 104, Sch 4, Pt 1, para 3(2), as from 1 April 2006.

Sub-s (6): repealed by the Education (Scotland) Act 1980, s 136(3), Sch 5.

80 Power to amend certain provisions of Act

(1) The [Minister] may by an order the draft of which has been approved by each House of Parliament—

(a) amend any of the following provisions, namely, sections 6(3), 7, 19, 20(1), (2) and (3), 31(2), 32, 34, 35 and 43 to 48 (including any such provision as amended by a previous order under this subsection);

(b) amend or repeal any of the following provisions, namely, sections 11(4), 12(4), 33 and 49 (including any such provision as amended by a previous order under this subsection);

(c) amend Part II, III or IV so as to render lawful an act which, apart from the amendment, would be unlawful by reason of section 6(1) or (2), 29(1), 30 or 31;

(d) …

(2) The [Minister] shall not lay before Parliament the draft of an order under subsection (1) unless he has consulted the Commission about the contents of the draft.

(3) An order under subsection (1)(*c*) may make such amendments to the list of provisions given in subsection (1)(*a*) as in the opinion of the [Minister] are expedient having regard to the contents of the order.

[194]

NOTES

Sub-s (1): word in square brackets substituted by the Transfer of Functions (Equality) Order 2007, SI 2007/2914, art 8, Schedule, para 6(g), as from 12 October 2007; para (d) repealed by the Sex Discrimination Act 1986, s 9(2), Schedule, Pt II.

Sub-ss (2), (3): words in square brackets substituted by SI 2007/2914, art 8, Schedule, para 6(g), as from 12 October 2007.

Orders: the Sex Discrimination Act 1975 (Amendment of Section 43) Order 1977, SI 1977/528; the Sex Discrimination Act 1975 (Amendment of Section 20) Order 1983, SI 1983/1202.

81 Orders

(1) Any power of the [Minister or the Secretary of State] to make orders under the provisions of this Act (except sections … 27 …) shall be exercisable by statutory instrument.

(2) An order made by the [Minister or the Secretary of State] under the preceding provisions of this Act (except sections [21A,] … 27, … and 80(1)) shall be subject to annulment in pursuance of a resolution of either House of Parliament.

[(2A) An order under section 21A(5) may not be made unless—

(a) the [Minister] has consulted the Commission, and

(b) a draft has been laid before and approved by resolution of each House of Parliament.]

[(2B) An order under section 76A(3)(i) or (4)(e) may not be made unless the [Minister] has consulted the Commission.]

[(2C) An order under section 76C(3) or (4) is subject to annulment in pursuance of a resolution of the Scottish Parliament.]

(3) Subsections (1) and (2) do not apply to an order under section 78 or 79, but—

(a) an order under section 78 which modifies an enactment, and

(b) any order under section 79 other than one which relates to an endowment to which [section 115 of the Education (Scotland) Act 1980] (small endowments) applies,

shall be made by statutory instrument subject to annulment in pursuance of a resolution of either House of Parliament.

(4) An order under this Act may make different provision in relation to different cases or classes of case, may exclude certain cases or classes of case, and may contain transitional provisions and savings.

(5) Any power conferred by this Act to make orders includes power (exercisable in the like manner and subject to the like conditions) to vary or revoke any order so made.

[195]

NOTES

Sub-s (1): words in square brackets substituted by the Transfer of Functions (Equality) Order 2007, SI 2007/2914, art 8, Schedule, para 8, as from 12 October 2007; first words omitted repealed by the Employment Act 1989, s 29(4), Sch 7, Pt II; second words omitted repealed by a combination of the Sex Discrimination Act 1986, s 9(2), Schedule, Pt I, and the Equality Act 2006, ss 40, 91, Sch 3, paras, 6, 17(a), Sch 4, as from 1 October 2007.

Sub-s (2): words "Minister or the Secretary of State" in square brackets substituted by SI 2007/2914, art 8, Schedule, para 8, as from 12 October 2007; figure "21A," in square brackets inserted by the Equality Act 2006, s 83(3)(a), as from 6 April 2007; first words omitted repealed by the Employment Act 1989, s 29(4), Sch 7, Pt II; second words omitted repealed by a combination of the Sex Discrimination Act 1986, s 9, Schedule, Pt I, and the Equality Act 2006, ss 40, 91, Sch 3, paras 6, 17(b), Sch 4, as from 1 October 2007.

Sub-ss (2A)–(2C): inserted by the Equality Act 2006, ss 83(3)(b), 84(2), 85(2), as from 6 April 2007; words in square brackets in sub-ss (2A), (2B) substituted by SI 2007/2914, art 8, Schedule, para 6(h), as from 12 October 2007.

Sub-s (3): words in square brackets substituted by the Education (Scotland) Act 1980, s 136(2), Sch 4, para 10.

82 General interpretation provisions

(1) In this Act, unless the context otherwise requires—

"access" shall be construed in accordance with section 50;

"act" includes a deliberate omission;

"advertisement" includes every form of advertisement, whether to the public or not, and whether in a newspaper or other publication, by television or radio, by display of notices, signs, labels, showcards or goods, by distribution of samples, circulars, catalogues, price lists or other material by exhibition of pictures, models or films, or in any other way, and references to the publishing of advertisements shall be construed accordingly;

"associated employer" shall be construed in accordance with subsection (2);

[. . .]

["Board of management" in relation to a college of further education within the meaning of Part I of the Further and Higher Education (Scotland) Act 1992, has the same meaning as in that Part;]

"the Commission" means the [Commission for Equality and Human Rights];

"Commissioner" means a member of the Commission;

. . .

"designate" shall be construed in accordance with subsection (3); [references in Parts 2 and 3 to subjecting a person to a detriment do not include subjecting a person to harassment;]

"discrimination" and related terms shall be construed in accordance with section 5(1);

"dispose", in relation to premises, includes granting a right to occupy the premises, and any reference to acquiring premises shall be construed accordingly;

"education" includes any form of training or instruction;

["the Education Acts" has the meaning given by section 578 of the Education Act 1996;]

"education authority" and "educational establishment" in relation to Scotland have the same meaning as they have respectively in section [135(1) of the Education (Scotland) Act 1980];

"employment" means employment under a contract of service or of apprenticeship or a contract personally to execute any work or labour, and related expressions shall be construed accordingly;

"employment agency" means a person who, for profit or not, provides services for the purpose of finding employment for workers or supplying employers with workers;

["enactment" includes an enactment comprised in, or in an instrument made under, an Act of the Scottish Parliament;]

"equality clause" has the meaning given in section 1(2) of the Equal Pay Act 1970 (as set out in section 8(1) of this Act);

"estate agent" means a person who, by way of profession or trade, provides services for the purpose of finding premises for persons seeking to acquire them or assisting in the disposal of premises;

["excluded matter" shall be construed in accordance with section 5(4);]

"final" shall be construed in accordance with subsection (4);

"firm" has the meaning given by section 4 of the Partnership Act 1890;

. . .

"further education" has the meaning given by [section 2 of the Education Act 1996] and in Scotland has the meaning given by section [135(1) of the Education (Scotland) Act 1980];

["gender reassignment" means a process which is undertaken under medical supervision for the purpose of reassigning a person's sex by changing physiological or other characteristics of sex, and includes any part of such a process;]

"general notice", in relation to any person, means a notice published by him at a time and a manner appearing to him suitable for securing that the notice is seen within a reasonable time by persons likely to be affected by it;

"genuine occupational qualification" shall be construed in accordance with section 7(2)[, except in the expression "supplementary genuine occupational qualification", which shall be construed in accordance with section 7B(2);]

"Great Britain" includes such of the territorial waters of the United Kingdom as are adjacent to Great Britain; [references to subjecting a person to harassment, and to acts of harassment, shall be construed in accordance with section 4A;]

"independent school" has the meaning given by [section 463 of the Education Act 1996] and in Scotland has the meaning given by section [135(1) of the Education (Scotland) Act 1980];

. . .

"man" includes a male of any age;

"managers" has the same meaning for Scotland as in section [135(1) of the Education (Scotland) Act 1980];

["the Minister" means the Lord Privy Seal;]

"near relative" shall be construed in accordance with subsection (5);

. . .

"notice" means a notice in writing;

"prescribed" means prescribed by regulations made by the [Minister or the Secretary of State] by statutory instrument;

"profession" includes any vocation or occupation;

"proprietor", in relation to any school, has the meaning given by [section 579 of the Education Act 1996] and in Scotland has the meaning given by section [135(1) of the Education (Scotland) Act 1980];

["provision, criterion or practice" includes "requirement or condition"];

"pupil", in Scotland, includes a student of any age;

"retirement" includes retirement (whether voluntary or not) on grounds of age, length of service or incapacity;

"school" has the meaning given by [section 4 of the Education Act 1996], and in Scotland has the meaning given by section [135(1) of the Education (Scotland) Act 1980];

"school education" has the same meaning given by section [135(1) of the Education (Scotland) Act 1980];

[…]

"trade" includes any business;

"training" includes any form of education or instruction;

"university" includes a university college and the college, school or hall of a university;

…

["vocational training"—

(a) means all types, and all levels, of—

(i) vocational training, advanced vocational training and retraining, and

(ii) vocational guidance, and

(b) includes practical work experience undertaken for a limited period for the purposes of a person's vocational training (as defined by paragraph (a));]

"woman" includes a female of any age.

[(1A) References in this Act to the dismissal of a person from employment or to the expulsion of a person from a position as partner include references—

(a) to the termination of that person's employment or partnership by the expiration of any period (including a period expiring by reference to an event or circumstance), not being a termination immediately after which the employment or partnership is renewed on the same terms; and

(b) to the termination of that person's employment or partnership by any act of his (including the giving of notice) in circumstances such that he is entitled to terminate it without notice by reason of the conduct of the employer or, as the case may be, the conduct of the other partners.]

(2) For the purposes of this Act two employers are to be treated as associated if one is a company of which the other (directly or indirectly) has control or if both are companies of which a third person (directly or indirectly) has control.

(3) Any power conferred by this Act to designate establishments or persons may be exercised either by naming them or by identifying them by reference to a class or other description.

(4) For the purposes of this Act … a finding by a court or tribunal becomes final when an appeal against the … finding is dismissed, withdrawn or abandoned or when the time for appealing expires without an appeal having been brought; …

(5) For the purposes of this Act a person is a near relative of another if that person is the wife or husband [or civil partner], or parent or child, a grandparent or grandchild, or a brother or sister of the other (whether of full blood or half-blood or [by marriage or civil partnership]), and "child" includes an illegitimate child and the wife or husband [or civil partner] of an illegitimate child.

(6) Except so far as the context otherwise requires, any reference in this Act to an enactment shall be construed as a reference to that enactment as amended by or under any other enactment including this Act.

(7) In this Act, except where otherwise indicated—

(a) a reference to a numbered Part, section or Schedule is a reference to the Part or section of, or the Schedule to, this Act so numbered, and

(b) a reference in a section to a numbered subsection is a reference to the subsection of that section so numbered, and

(c) a reference in a section, subsection or Schedule to a numbered paragraph is a reference to the paragraph of that section, subsection or Schedule so numbered, and

(d) a reference to any provision of an Act (including this Act) includes a Schedule incorporated in the Act by that provision.

[196]

NOTES

Sub-s (1) is amended as follows:

Definition "board of management" (in relation to a self-governing school) (omitted) originally inserted by the Self-Governing Schools etc (Scotland) Act 1989, s 82(1), Sch 10, para 5(1), (4), and repealed by the Standards in Scotland's Schools etc Act 2000, s 60(2), Sch 3, as from 31 December 2004.

Definition "Board of management" (in relation to a college of further education) inserted by the Further and Higher Education (Scotland) Act 1992, s 62, Sch 9, para 4(1), (5).

In definition "the Commission" words in square brackets substituted by the Equality Act 2006, s 40, Sch 3, paras, 6, 18(a)(i), as from 1 October 2007.

Definition "conciliation officer" (omitted) repealed by the Employment Protection Act 1975, s 125(3), Sch 18.

In definition "designate" words in square brackets inserted by the Employment Equality (Sex Discrimination) Regulations 2005, SI 2005/2467, reg 33(1), (2), as from 1 October 2005.

Definition "the Education Acts" inserted by the Education Act 1996, s 582(1), Sch 37, Pt I, para 36(a).

Definition "enactment" inserted by the Scotland Act 1998 (Consequential Modifications) Order 2000, SI 2000/2040, arts 1(1), 2(1), Schedule, Pt I, para 8.

Definition "excluded matter" inserted by the Sex Discrimination (Amendment of Legislation) Regulations 2008, SI 2008/963, reg 2(1), Sch 1, para 9(3), as from 6 April 2008.

Definition "formal investigation" (omitted) repealed by the Equality Act 2006, ss 40, 91, Sch 3, paras, 6, 18(a)(ii), Sch 4, as from 1 October 2007.

In definition "further education" words in first pair of square brackets substituted by the Education Act 1996, s 582(1), Sch 37, Pt I, para 36(b).

Definition "gender reassignment" inserted by the Sex Discrimination (Gender Reassignment) Regulations 1999, SI 1999/1102, reg 2(3).

In definition "genuine occupational qualification" words in square brackets added by SI 1999/1102, reg 4(6).

In definition "Great Britain" words in square brackets inserted by SI 2005/2467, reg 33(1), (3), as from 1 October 2005.

In definition "independent school" words in first pair of square brackets substituted by the Education Act 1996, s 582(1), Sch 37, Pt I, para 36(c).

Definition "industrial tribunal" (omitted) repealed by the Industrial Training Act 1982, s 20, Sch 3, para 5(b), Sch 4.

Definition "the Minister" inserted by the Transfer of Functions (Equality) Order 2007, SI 2007/2914, art 8, Schedule, para 5, as from 12 October 2007.

Definition "non-discrimination notice" (omitted) repealed by the Equality Act 2006, ss 40, 91, Sch 3, paras, 6, 18(a)(ii), Sch 4, as from 1 October 2007.

In definition "prescribed" words in square brackets substituted by SI 2007/2914, art 8, Schedule, para 8, as from 12 October 2007.

In definition "proprietor" words in first pair of square brackets substituted by the Education Act 1996, s 582(1), Sch 37, Pt I, para 36(d).

Definition "provision, criterion or practice" inserted by the Sex Discrimination (Indirect Discrimination and Burden of Proof) Regulations 2001, SI 2001/2660, reg 8(4).

In definition "school" words in first pair of square brackets substituted by the Education Act 1996, s 582(1), Sch 37, Pt I, para 36(e).

Definition "self-governing school" (omitted) inserted by the Self-Governing Schools etc (Scotland) Act 1989, s 82(1), Sch 10, para 5(4), and repealed by the Standards in Scotland's Schools etc Act 2000, s 60(2), Sch 3, as from 31 December 2004.

Definition "upper limit of compulsory school age" (omitted) repealed by the Education Act 1996, s 582(2), Sch 38, Pt II.

Definition "vocational training" inserted by SI 2005/2467, reg 33(1), (4), as from 1 October 2005.

All other amendments to sub-s (1) made by the Education (Scotland) Act 1980, s 136(2), Sch 4, para 11.

Sub-s (1A): inserted by the Sex Discrimination Act 1986, s 2(3).

Sub-s (4): words omitted repealed by the Equality Act 2006, ss 40, 91, Sch 3, paras, 6, 18(b), Sch 4, as from 1 October 2007.

Sub-s (5): words in first and third pairs of square brackets inserted, and words in second pair of square brackets substituted, by the Civil Partnership Act 2004, s 261(1), Sch 27, para 54, as 5 December 2005.

Modified as noted to s 6 at **[106]**.

83 Transitional and commencement provisions, amendments and repeals

(1) The provisions of Schedule 4 shall have effect for making transitional provision for the purposes of this Act.

(2) Parts II to VII shall come into operation on such day as the Secretary of State may by order appoint, and different days may be so appointed for different provisions and for different purposes.

(3) Subject to subsection (4)—

(a) the enactments specified in Schedule 5 shall have effect subject to the amendments specified in that Schedule (being minor amendments or amendments consequential on the preceding provisions of this Act), and

(b) the enactments specified in Schedule 6 are hereby repealed to the extent shown in column 3 of that Schedule.

(4) The Secretary of State shall by order provide for the coming into operation of the amendments contained in Schedule 5 and the repeals contained in Schedule 6, and those amendments and repeals shall have effect only as provided by an order so made.

(5) An order under this section may make such transitional provision as appears to the Secretary of State to be necessary or expedient in connection with the provisions thereby brought into operation, including such adaptations of those provisions, or of any provisions of this Act then in operation, as appear to the Secretary of State necessary or expedient in consequence of the partial operation of this Act.

[197]

NOTES

Orders: the Sex Discrimination Act 1975 (Commencement) Order 1975, SI 1975/1845' the Sex Discrimination Act 1975 (Commencement) (Amendment) Order 1975, SI 1975/2112.

84 Financial provisions

There shall be defrayed out of money provided by Parliament—

(a) sums required by the Secretary of State for making payments under paragraph 5 or 14 of Schedule 3, and for defraying any other expenditure falling to be made by him under or by virtue of this Act;

(b) payments falling to be made under section 66(6)(b) or (7) in respect of the remuneration of assessors; and

(c) any increase attributable to the provisions of this Act in the sums payable out of money provided by Parliament under any other Act.

[198]

85 Application to Crown

(1) This Act applies—

(a) to an act done by or for purposes of a Minister of the Crown or government department, or

(b) to an act done on behalf of the Crown by a statutory body, or a person holding a statutory office,

as it applies to an act done by a private person.

(2) Parts II and IV apply to—

(a) service for purposes of a Minister of the Crown or government department, other than service of a person holding a statutory office, or

(b) service on behalf of the Crown for purposes of a person holding a statutory office or purposes of a statutory body, [or

(c) service in the armed forces,]

as they apply to employment by a private person, and shall so apply as if references to a contract of employment included references to the terms of service.

(3) Subsections (1) and (2) have effect subject to section 17.

[(3A) Section 21A binds the Crown.]

[(3B) Section 76A binds the Crown.]

[(4) Nothing in this Act shall render unlawful an act done for the purpose of ensuring the combat effectiveness of the [armed forces.]]

(5), (6) …

(7) Subsection (2) of section 10 shall have effect in relation to any ship, aircraft or hovercraft belonging to or possessed by Her Majesty in right of the Government of the United

Kingdom as it has effect in relation to a ship, aircraft or hovercraft mentioned in paragraph (a) or (b) of that subsection, and section 10(5) shall apply accordingly.

(8) The provisions of Parts II to IV of the Crown Proceedings Act 1947 shall apply to proceedings against the Crown under this Act as they apply to proceedings in England and Wales which by virtue of section 23 of that Act are treated for the purposes of Part II of that Act as civil proceedings by or against the Crown …

(9) The provisions of Part V of the Crown Proceedings Act 1947 shall apply to proceedings against the Crown under this Act as they apply to proceedings in Scotland which by virtue of the said Part are treated as civil proceedings by or against the Crown, except that in their application to proceedings under this Act the proviso to section 44 of that Act (removal of proceedings from the sheriff court to the Court of Session) shall not apply.

[(9A) This subsection applies to any complaint by a person ("the complainant") that another person—

(a) has committed an act of discrimination against the complainant which is unlawful by virtue of section 6; or

(b) is by virtue of section 41 or 42 to be treated as having committed such an act of discrimination against the complainant,

if at the time when the act complained of was done the complainant was serving in the armed forces and the discrimination in question relates to his service in those forces.

(9B) No complaint to which subsection (9A) applies shall be presented to an [employment tribunal] under section 63 unless—

(a) the complainant has made [a service complaint in respect of the act complained of]; and

(b) the Defence Council have made a determination with respect to the [service complaint].

(9C) Regulations may make provision enabling a complaint to which subsection (9A) applies to be presented to an [employment tribunal] under section 63 in such circumstances as may be specified by the regulations, notwithstanding that subsection (9B) would otherwise preclude the presentation of the complaint to an [employment tribunal].

(9D) Where a complaint is presented to an [employment tribunal] under section 63 by virtue of regulations under subsection (9C), [the service complaint procedures] may continue after the complaint is so presented.

(9E) Regulations under subsection (9C) shall be made by the Secretary of State by statutory instrument and shall be subject to annulment in pursuance of a resolution of either House of Parliament.]

[(10) In this section—

"armed forces" means any of the naval, military or air forces of the Crown;

"service for purposes of a Minister of the Crown or government department" does not include service in any office for the time being mentioned in Schedule 2 (Ministerial offices) to the House of Commons Disqualification Act 1975;

["service complaint" means a complaint under section 334 of the Armed Forces Act 2006;

"the service complaint procedures" means the procedures prescribed by regulations under that section;] and

"statutory body" means a body set up by or in pursuance of an enactment and "statutory office" means an office so set up.]

[199]

NOTES

Sub-s (2): para (c) and word immediately preceding it inserted by the Armed Forces Act 1996, s 21(1), (2).

Sub-ss (3A), (3B): inserted by the Equality Act 2006, ss 83(4), 84(3), as from 6 April 2007.

Sub-s (4): substituted by the Sex Discrimination Act 1975 (Application to Armed Forces etc) Regulations 1994, SI 1994/3276, reg 2(a); words in square brackets substituted by the Armed Forces Act 1996, s 21(1), (3).

Sub-s (5): repealed by the Employment Equality (Sex Discrimination) Regulations 2005, SI 2005/2467, reg 34, as from 1 October 2005.

Sub-s (6): repealed by SI 1994/3276, reg 2(b).

Sub-s (8): words omitted repealed by the Civil Procedure (Modification of Crown Proceedings Act 1947) Order 2005, SI 2005/2712, art 3, Sch 2, para 1, as from 1 October 2005.

Sub-ss (9A), (9E): inserted, together with sub-ss (9B)–(9D), by the Armed Forces Act 1996, s 21(1), (4).

Sub-s (9B): inserted as noted above; words in first pair of square brackets substituted by the Employment Rights (Dispute Resolution) Act 1998, s 1(2)(a); words in second and third pairs of square brackets substituted by the Armed Forces Act 2006, s 378(1), Sch 16, para 71(1), (2), as from 1 January 2008.

Sub-s (9C): inserted as noted above; words in square brackets substituted by the Employment Rights (Dispute Resolution) Act 1998, s 1(2)(a).

Sub-s (9D): inserted as noted above; words in first pair of square brackets substituted by the Employment Rights (Dispute Resolution) Act 1998, s 1(2)(a); words in second pair of square brackets substituted by the Armed Forces Act 2006, s 378(1), Sch 16, para 71(1), (3), as from 1 January 2008.

Sub-s (10): substituted by the Armed Forces Act 1996, s 21(1), (5); definitions "service complaint" and "the service complaint procedures" substituted (for original definition "the service redress procedures") by the Armed Forces Act 2006, s 378(1), Sch 16, para 71(1), (4), as from 1 January 2008.

Regulations: the Sex Discrimination (Complaints to Employment Tribunals) (Armed Forces) Regulations 1997, SI 1997/2163 at **[2406]**.

[85A Application to House of Commons staff

(1) Parts II and IV apply to an act done by an employer of a relevant member of the House of Commons staff, and to service as such a member, as they apply to an act done by and to service for the purposes of a Minister of the Crown or government department, and accordingly apply as if references to a contract of employment included references to the terms of service of such a member.

(2) In this section "relevant member of the House of Commons staff" has the same meaning as in [section 195 of the Employment Rights Act 1996]; and [subsections (6) to (12)] of that section (person to be treated as employer of House of Commons staff) apply, with any necessary modifications, for the purposes of Parts II and IV as they apply by virtue of this section.]

[200]

NOTES

Inserted by the Trade Union and Labour Relations (Consolidation) Act 1992, s 300(2), Sch 2, para 6.

Sub-s (2): words in square brackets substituted by the Employment Rights Act 1996, s 240, Sch 1, para 6.

[85B Application to House of Lords staff

(1) Parts II and IV apply in relation to employment as a relevant member of the House of Lords staff as they apply in relation to other employment.

(2) In this section "relevant member of the House of Lords staff" has the same meaning as in [section 194 of the Employment Rights Act 1996]; and [subsection (7)] of that section applies for the purposes of this section.]

[201]–[202]

NOTES

Inserted by the Trade Union Reform and Employment Rights Act 1993, s 49(1), Sch 7, para 9.

Sub-s (2): words in square brackets substituted by the Employment Rights Act 1996, s 240, Sch 1.

86 *(Repealed by the Employment Equality (Sex Discrimination) Regulations 2005, SI 2005/2467, reg 13(2), as from 1 October 2005.)*

87 Short title and extent

(1) This Act may be cited as the Sex Discrimination Act 1975.

(2) This Act (except paragraph 16 of Schedule 3) does not extend to Northern Ireland.

[203]

SCHEDULES

(*Sch 1 amends the Equal Pay Act 1970 at* **[5]** *et seq.*)

SCHEDULE 2
TRANSITIONAL EXEMPTION ORDERS FOR EDUCATIONAL ADMISSIONS

Section 27

Public sector (*England and Wales*)

1. Where [under section 35, 41 or 259 of the Education Act 1996 a responsible body submits to the Secretary of State] proposals for an alteration in its admissions arrangements such as is mentioned in section 27(1) of this Act the submission of those proposals shall be treated as an application for the making by the Secretary of State of a transitional exemption order, and if he thinks fit the Secretary of State may make the order accordingly.

2. …

3. Regulations under [section 485 of the Education Act 1996] may provide for the submission to the Secretary of State of an application for the making by him of a transitional exemption order in relation to an establishment—

(a) which is designated under section 24(1), and

(b) in respect of which grants are payable under [the said section 485],

and for the making by him of the order.

[4. …]

[4A. Where, under section 113A of the Learning and Skills Act 2000, the Learning and Skills Council for England submit proposals to the Secretary of State for an alteration in the admission arrangements of a school such as is mentioned in section 27(1) of this Act, the submission of the proposals shall be treated as an application for the making by the Secretary of State of a transitional exemption order, and if he thinks fit the Secretary of State may make the order accordingly.]

Private sector (*England and Wales*)

5.—(1) In the case of an establishment in England or Wales not falling within paragraphs 1 to 4 the responsible body may submit to [the Commission] an application for the making by the Commission of a transitional exemption order in relation to the establishment, and if they think fit the Commission may make the order accordingly.

(2) An application under this paragraph shall specify the transitional period proposed by the responsible body to be provided for in the order, the stages by which within that period the body proposes to move to the position where section 22(*b*) is complied with, and any other matters relevant to the terms and operation of the order applied for.

(3) The Commission shall not make an order on an application under this paragraph unless they are satisfied that the terms of the application are reasonable having regard to the nature of the premises at which the establishment is carried on, the accommodation, equipment and facilities available, and the financial resources of the responsible body.

Public and private sectors (*Scotland*)

6. Any application for a transitional exemption order made by the responsible body in relation to an establishment falling within paragraph 6 [[or 7], 7B or 7C] of the Table in section 22 shall be made to the Secretary of State, and in relation to an establishment falling within paragraphs 8, 9 and 10 of that Table shall be made to [the Commission].

7. An application under paragraph 6 shall specify the transitional period proposed by the responsible body to be provided for in the order, the stages by which within that period the body proposes to move to the position where section 22(b) is complied with, and any other matters relevant to the terms and operation of the order applied for.

8. The Secretary of State on any application under paragraph 6 may make a transitional exemption order on such terms and conditions as he may think fit.

9. The Commission on any application under paragraph 6 may if they think fit make a transitional exemption order, but shall not make such an order unless they are satisfied that the terms of the application are reasonable having regard to the nature of the premises at which the establishment is carried on, the accommodation, equipment and facilities available, and the financial resources of the responsible body.

[204]–[205]

NOTES

Para 1: repealed by the School Standards and Framework Act 1998, s 140(3), Sch 31, as from a day to be appointed; words in square brackets substituted by the Education Act 1996, s 582(1), Sch 37, para 37.

Para 2: repealed by the Education Act 1980, ss 33(3), 38(6), Sch 7.

Para 3: words in square brackets substituted by the Education Act 1996, s 582(1), Sch 37, para 37.

Para 4: substituted by the Further and Higher Education Act 1992, s 93, Sch 8, para 83; repealed by the Education Act 2002, s 215, Sch 21, para 3(a), Sch 22, Pt 3, as from 6 November 2006 (in relation to England), and as from 2 January 2008 (in relation to Wales).

Para 4A: inserted by the Education Act 2002, s 215(1), Sch 21, para 3(b), as from 1 April 2003.

Para 5: words in square brackets substituted by the Equality Act 2006, s 40, Sch 3, paras, 6, 19(a), as from 1 October 2007.

Para 6: words in first (outer) pair of square brackets substituted by the Further and Higher Education (Scotland) Act 1992, s 62(2), Sch 9, para 5(1), (5); words in second (inner) pair of square brackets substituted by the Standards in Scotland's Schools etc Act 2000, s 60(1), Sch 2, para 2(1), (3), as from 31 December 2004; words in third pair of square brackets substituted by the Equality Act 2006, s 40, Sch 3, paras, 6, 19(b), as from 1 October 2007.

Transfer of functions in relation to Wales: as to the transfer of functions under this Schedule from Ministers of the Crown to the National Assembly for Wales, see the National Assembly for Wales (Transfer of Functions) Order 1999, SI 1999/672.

Education Act 1996, ss 35, 41, 259: repealed by the School Standards and Framework Act 1998, s 140(3), Sch 31.

(Sch 3 repealed by the Equality Act 2006, ss 40, 91, Sch 3, paras, 6, 20, Sch 4, as from 1 October 2007. For savings see the Equality Act 2006 (Commencement No 3 and Savings) Order 2007, SI 2007/2603, art 3 at **[3473R]**. *For transitional provisions relating to the discharge by the Commission for Equality and Human Rights of the former functions of the Equal Opportunities Commission, see the Equality Act 2006 (Dissolution of Commissions and Consequential and Transitional Provisions) Order 2007, SI 2007/2602, art 5 at* **[3473O]**).

SCHEDULE 4
TRANSITIONAL PROVISIONS

Section 83

1, 2. *(Spent.)*

3.—(1) Until a date specified by order made by the Secretary of State the courses of training to be undergone by men as a condition of [registration as midwives under the Nurses, Midwives and Health Visitors Act 1979] must be courses approved in writing by or on behalf of the Secretary of State for the purposes of this paragraph.

(2), (3) …

(4) An order under this paragraph shall be laid in draft before each House of Parliament, and section 6(1) of the Statutory Instruments Act 1946 (Parliamentary control by negative resolution of draft instruments) shall apply accordingly.

4. *(Spent.)*

5.—(1) Section 6 of the Equal Pay Act 1970 (as amended by paragraph 3 of Schedule 1 to this Act) shall apply as if the references to death or retirement in subsection (1A)(b) of the said section 6 included references to sums payable on marriage in pursuance of a contract of employment made before the passing of this Act, or the commutation, at any time, of the right to such sums.

(2) In relation to service within section 1(8) of the said Act of 1970 (service of the Crown) for the reference in this paragraph to a contract of employment made before the passing of this Act there shall be substituted a reference to terms of service entered into before the passing of this Act.

[206]

NOTES

Para 3: words in square brackets in sub-para (1) substituted, and sub-paras (2), (3) repealed, by the Nurses, Midwives and Health Visitors Act 1979, s 23(4), (5), Sch 7, para 26, Sch 8.

Orders: the Sex Discrimination (Midwives) (Specified Date) Order 1983, SI 1983/1841 (specifying 1 January 1984 as the specified date).

(*Schs 5 and 6 (minor amendments and repeals) outside the scope of this work.*)

RACE RELATIONS ACT 1976

(1976 c 74)

ARRANGEMENT OF SECTIONS

PART I
DISCRIMINATION TO WHICH ACT APPLIES

PART II
DISCRIMINATION IN THE EMPLOYMENT FIELD

Discrimination by employers

Discrimination by other bodies

PART III
DISCRIMINATION IN OTHER FIELDS

Education

Planning

Public authorities

Goods, facilities, services and premises

Barristers

Advocates

Extent

PART IV
OTHER UNLAWFUL ACTS

PART V
CHARITIES

PART VI
GENERAL EXCEPTIONS FROM PARTS II TO IV

PART VIII
ENFORCEMENT

General

Enforcement in employment field

Enforcement of Part III

Help for persons suffering discrimination

Sheriff courts and designated county courts

Period within which proceedings to be brought

Evidence

PART X
SUPPLEMENTAL

SCHEDULES:

An Act to make fresh provision with respect to discrimination on racial grounds and relations between people of different racial groups; and to make in the Sex Discrimination Act 1975 amendments for bringing provisions in that Act relating to its administration and enforcement into conformity with the corresponding provisions in this Act

[22 November 1976]

NOTES

This Act is printed in full save for specific omissions noted in the text. Although Part III is mostly outside the scope of this work, it is included for ease of reference and because of its use as an aid to the interpretation of other parts of the Act.

Employment Appeal Tribunal: an appeal lies to the Employment Appeal Tribunal on any question of law arising from any decision of, or in any proceedings before, an employment tribunal under or by virtue of this Act; see the Employment Tribunals Act 1996, s 21(1)(c) at **[978]**.

Transfer of functions: as to the transfer of the functions of the Secretary of State under this Act (except ss 19E, 57(5) and 75(10)(aa)) to the Lord Privy Seal, see the Transfer of Functions (Equality) Order 2007, SI 2007/2914, art 3(1), (2)(c).

See *Harvey* L2, Q.

PART I
DISCRIMINATION TO WHICH ACT APPLIES

1 Racial discrimination

(1) A person discriminates against another in any circumstances relevant for the purposes of any provision of this Act if—

(a) on racial grounds he treats that other less favourably than he treats or would treat other persons; or

(b) he applies to that other a requirement or condition which he applies or would apply equally to persons not of the same racial group as that other but—

(i) which is such that the proportion of persons of the same racial group as that other who can comply with it is considerably smaller than the proportion of persons not of that racial group who can comply with it; and

(ii) which he cannot show to be justifiable irrespective of the colour, race, nationality or ethnic or national origins of the person to whom it is applied; and

(iii) which is to the detriment of that other because he cannot comply with it.

[(1A) A person also discriminates against another if, in any circumstances relevant for the purposes of any provision referred to in subsection (1B), he applies to that other a provision, criterion or practice which he applies or would apply equally to persons not of the same race or ethnic or national origins as that other, but—

(a) which puts or would put persons of the same race or ethnic or national origins as that other at a particular disadvantage when compared with other persons,

(b) which puts that other at that disadvantage, and

(c) which he cannot show to be a proportionate means of achieving a legitimate aim.

(1B) The provisions mentioned in subsection (1A) are—

(a) Part II;
(b) sections 17 to 18D;
(c) section 19B, so far as relating to—
 (i) any form of social security;
 (ii) health care;
 (iii) any other form of social protection; and
 (iv) any form of social advantage;

which does not fall within section 20;
(d) sections 20 to 24;
(e) sections 26A and 26B;
(f) sections 76 and 76ZA; and
(g) Part IV, in its application to the provisions referred to in paragraphs (a) to (f).

(1C) Where, by virtue of subsection (1A), a person discriminates against another, subsection (1)(b) does not apply to him.]

(2) It is hereby declared that, for the purposes of this Act, segregating a person from other persons on racial grounds is treating him less favourably than they are treated. **[207]**

NOTES

Sub-ss (1A)–(1C): inserted by the Race Relations Act 1976 (Amendment) Regulations 2003, SI 2003/1626, reg 3, as from 19 July 2003.

2 Discrimination by way of victimisation

(1) A person ("the discriminator") discriminates against another person ("the person victimised") in any circumstances relevant for the purposes of any provision of this Act if he treats the person victimised less favourably than in those circumstances he treats or would treat other persons, and does so by reason that the person victimised has—

(a) brought proceedings against the discriminator or any other person under this Act; or
(b) given evidence or information in connection with proceedings brought by any person against the discriminator or any other person under this Act; or
(c) otherwise done anything under or by reference to this Act in relation to the discriminator or any other person; or
(d) alleged that the discriminator or any other person has committed an act which (whether or not the allegation so states) would amount to a contravention of this Act,

or by reason that the discriminator knows that the person victimised intends to do any of those things, or suspects that the person victimised has done, or intends to do, any of them.

(2) Subsection (1) does not apply to treatment of a person by reason of any allegation made by him if the allegation was false and not made in good faith. **[208]**

3 Meaning of "racial grounds", "racial group" etc

(1) In this Act, unless the context otherwise requires—

"racial grounds" means any of the following grounds, namely colour, race nationality or ethnic or national origins;

"racial group" means a group of persons defined by reference to colour, race, nationality or ethnic or national origins, and references to a person's racial group refer to any racial group into which he falls.

(2) The fact that a racial group comprises two or more distinct racial groups does not prevent it from constituting a particular racial group for the purposes of this Act.

(3) In this Act—

(a) references to discrimination refer to any discrimination falling within section 1 or 2; and
(b) references to racial discrimination refer to any discrimination falling within section 1,

and related expressions shall be construed accordingly.

(4) A comparison of the case of a person of a particular racial group with that of a person not of that group under section 1(1) [or (1A)] must be such that the relevant circumstances in the one case are the same, or not materially different, in the other.

[209]

NOTES

Sub-s (4): words in square brackets inserted by the Race Relations Act 1976 (Amendment) Regulations 2003, SI 2003/1626, reg 4, as from 19 July 2003.

[3A Harassment

(1) A person subjects another to harassment in any circumstances relevant for the purposes of any provision referred to in section 1(1B) where, on grounds of race or ethnic or national origins, he engages in unwanted conduct which has the purpose or effect of—

(a) violating that other person's dignity, or

(b) creating an intimidating, hostile, degrading, humiliating or offensive environment for him.

(2) Conduct shall be regarded as having the effect specified in paragraph (a) or (b) of subsection (1) only if, having regard to all the circumstances, including in particular the perception of that other person, it should reasonably be considered as having that effect.]

[210]

NOTES

Commencement: 19 July 2003.

Inserted by the Race Relations Act 1976 (Amendment) Regulations 2003, SI 2003/1626, reg 5, as from 19 July 2003.

PART II
DISCRIMINATION IN THE EMPLOYMENT FIELD

NOTES

Serious Organised Crime Agency: for the application of this Part to a constable or other person seconded to SOCA as a member of its staff, see the Serious Organised Crime and Police Act 2005, s 56(1), (2).

Discrimination by employers

4 … Applicants and employees

(1) It is unlawful for a person, in relation to employment by him at an establishment in Great Britain, to discriminate against another—

(a) in the arrangements he makes for the purpose of determining who should be offered that employment; or

(b) in the terms on which he offers him that employment; or

(c) by refusing or deliberately omitting to offer him that employment.

(2) It is unlawful for a person, in the case of a person employed by him at an establishment in Great Britain, to discriminate against that employee—

(a) in the terms of employment which he affords him; or

(b) in the way he affords him access to opportunities for promotion, transfer or training, or to any other benefits, facilities or services, or by refusing or deliberately omitting to afford him access to them; or

(c) by dismissing him, or subjecting him to any other detriment.

[(2A) It is unlawful for an employer, in relation to employment by him at an establishment in Great Britain, to subject to harassment a person whom he employs or who has applied to him for employment.]

(3) Except in relation to discrimination falling within section 2 [or discrimination on grounds of race or ethnic or national origins], subsections (1) and (2) do not apply to employment for the purposes of a private household.

(4) Subsection (2) does not apply to benefits, facilities or services of any description if the employer is concerned with the provision (for payment or not) of benefits, facilities or services of that description to the public, or to a section of the public comprising the employee in question, unless—

(a) that provision differs in a material respect from the provision of the benefits, facilities or services by the employer to his employees; or

(b) the provision of the benefits, facilities or services to the employee in question is regulated by his contract of employment; or

(c) the benefits, facilities or services relate to training.

[(4A) In subsection (2)(c) reference to the dismissal of a person from employment includes, where the discrimination is on grounds of race or ethnic or national origins, reference—

(a) to the termination of that person's employment by the expiration of any period (including a period expiring by reference to an event or circumstance), not being a termination immediately after which the employment is renewed on the same terms; and

(b) to the termination of that person's employment by any act of his (including the giving of notice) in circumstances such that he is entitled to terminate it without notice by reason of the conduct of the employer.]

[211]

NOTES

Section heading: words omitted repealed by the Race Relations Act 1976 (Amendment) Regulations 2003, SI 2003/1626, reg 6(1), as from 19 July 2003.

Sub-ss (2A), (4A): inserted by SI 2003/1626, reg 6(2)(a), (c), as from 19 July 2003.

Sub-s (3): words in square brackets inserted by SI 2003/1626, reg 6(2)(b), as from 19 July 2003.

Modified, in relation to governing bodies with delegated budgets, by the Education (Modification of Enactments Relating to Employment) (England) Order 2003, SI 2003/1964, art 3, Schedule at **[3035C]**, **[3035G]** and the Education (Modification of Enactments Relating to Employment) (Wales) Order 2006, SI 2006/1073, art 3, Schedule at **[3462B]**, **[3462F]**.

[4A Exception for genuine occupational requirement

(1) In relation to discrimination on grounds of race or ethnic or national origins—

(a) section 4(1)(a) or (c) does not apply to any employment; and

(b) section 4(2)(b) does not apply to promotion or transfer to, or training for, any employment; and

(c) section 4(2)(c) does not apply to dismissal from any employment;

where subsection (2) applies.

(2) This subsection applies where, having regard to the nature of the employment or the context in which it is carried out—

(a) being of a particular race or of particular ethnic or national origins is a genuine and determining occupational requirement;

(b) it is proportionate to apply that requirement in the particular case; and

(c) either—

(i) the person to whom that requirement is applied does not meet it, or

(ii) the employer is not satisfied, and in all the circumstances it is reasonable for him not to be satisfied, that that person meets it.]

[212]

NOTES

Commencement: 19 July 2003.

Inserted by the Race Relations Act 1976 (Amendment) Regulations 2003, SI 2003/1626, reg 7, as from 19 July 2003.

Modification: see the note to s 5 at **[213]**.

5 Exceptions for genuine occupational qualifications

(1) In relation to racial discrimination [in cases where section 4A does not apply]—

(a) section 4(1)(a) or (c) does not apply to any employment where being of a particular racial group is a genuine occupational qualification for the job; and

(b) section 4(2)(b) does not apply to opportunities for promotion or transfer to, or training for, such employment.

(2) Being of a particular racial group is a genuine occupational qualification for a job only where—

(a) the job involves participation in a dramatic performance or other entertainment in a capacity for which a person of that racial group is required for reasons of authenticity; or

(b) the job involves participation as an artist's or photographic model in the production of a work of art, visual image or sequence of visual images for which a person of that racial group is required for reasons of authenticity; or

(c) the job involves working in a place where food or drink is (for payment or not) provided to and consumed by members of the public or a section of the public in a particular setting for which, in that job, a person of that racial group is required for reasons of authenticity; or

(d) the holder of the job provides persons of that racial group with personal services promoting their welfare, and those services can most effectively be provided by a person of that racial group.

(3) Subsection (2) applies where some only of the duties of the job fall within paragraph (a), (b), (c) or (d) as well as where all of them do.

(4) Paragraph (a), (b), (c) or (d) of subsection (2) does not apply in relation to the filling of a vacancy at a time when the employer already has employees of the racial group in question—

(a) who are capable of carrying out the duties falling within that paragraph; and

(b) whom it would be reasonable to employ on those duties; and

(c) whose numbers are sufficient to meet the employer's likely requirements in respect of those duties without undue inconvenience.

[213]

NOTES

Sub-s (1): words in square brackets inserted by the Race Relations Act 1976 (Amendment) Regulations 2003, SI 2003/1626, reg 8, as from 19 July 2003.

Modified as noted to s 4 at **[211]**. Note that s 4A has not been added to the list of provisions so modified.

6 Exception for employment intended to provide training in skills to be exercised outside Great Britain

Nothing in section 4 shall render unlawful any act done by an employer[, on grounds other than those of race or ethnic or national origins,] for the benefit of a person not ordinarily resident in Great Britain in or in connection with employing him at an establishment in Great Britain, where the purpose of that employment is to provide him with training in skills which he appears to the employer to intend to exercise wholly outside Great Britain.

[214]

NOTES

Words in square brackets inserted by the Race Relations Act 1976 (Amendment) Regulations 2003, SI 2003/1626, reg 9, as from 19 July 2003.

7 ... Contract workers

(1) This section applies to any work for a person ("the principal") which is available for doing by individuals ("contract workers") who are employed not by the principal himself but by another person, who supplies them under a contract made with the principal.

(2) It is unlawful for the principal, in relation to work to which this section applies, to discriminate against a contract worker—

(a) in the terms on which he allows him to do that work; or

(b) by not allowing him to do it or continue to do it; or

(c) in the way he affords him access to any benefits, facilities or services or by refusing or deliberately omitting to afford him access to them; or

(d) by subjecting him to any other detriment.

(3) The principal does not contravene subsection (2)(b) by doing any act in relation to a person not of a particular racial group[, or not of a particular race or particular ethnic or national origins,] at a time when, if the work were to be done by a person taken into the

principal's employment, being of that racial group [or of that race or those origins] would be a genuine occupational qualification [or, as the case may be, that act would be lawful by virtue of section 4A] for the job.

[(3A) It is unlawful for the principal, in relation to work to which this section applies, to subject a contract worker to harassment.]

(4) Nothing in this section shall render unlawful any act done by the principal [on grounds other than those of race or ethnic or national origins,] for the benefit of a contract worker not ordinarily resident in Great Britain in or in connection with allowing him to do work to which this section applies, where the purpose of his being allowed to do that work is to provide him with training skills which he appears to the principal to intend to exercise wholly outside Great Britain.

(5) Subsection (2)(c) does not apply to benefits, facilities or services of any description if the principal is concerned with the provision (for payment or not) of benefits, facilities or services of that description to the public, or to a section of the public to which the contract worker in question belongs, unless that provision differs in a material respect from the provision of the benefits, facilities or services by the principal to his contract workers.
[215]

NOTES

Section heading: words omitted repealed by the Race Relations Act 1976 (Amendment) Regulations 2003, SI 2003/1626, reg 10(1), as from 19 July 2003.

Sub-ss (3), (4): words in square brackets inserted by SI 2003/1626, reg 10(2)(a), (c), as from 19 July 2003.

Sub-s (3A): inserted by SI 2003/1626, reg 10(2)(b), as from 19 July 2003.

Modified as noted to s 4 at **[211]**.

8 Meaning of employment at establishment in Great Britain

(1) For the purposes of this Part ("the relevant purposes"), employment is to be regarded as being at an establishment in Great Britain [if the employee—

(a) does his work wholly or partly in Great Britain; or

(b) does his work wholly outside Great Britain and subsection (1A) applies].

[(1A) This subsection applies if, in a case involving discrimination on grounds of race or ethnic or national origins, or harassment—

(a) the employer has a place of business at an establishment in Great Britain;

(b) the work is for the purposes of the business carried on at that establishment; and

(c) the employee is ordinarily resident in Great Britain—

(i) at the time when he applies for or is offered the employment, or

(ii) at any time during the course of the employment.]

(2) …

(3) In the case of employment on board a ship registered at a port of registry in Great Britain (except where the employee does his work wholly outside Great Britain) the ship shall for the relevant purposes be deemed to be the establishment.

(4) Where work is not done at an establishment it shall be treated for the relevant purposes as done at the establishment from which it is done or (where it is not done from any establishment) at the establishment with which it has the closest connection.

(5) In relation to employment concerned with *exploration of the sea bed or subsoil or the exploitation of their natural resources*, Her Majesty may by Order in Council provide that subsections (1) to (3) shall have effect as if in both subsection (1) and subsection (3) the last reference to Great Britain included any area for the time being designated under section 1(7) of the Continental Shelf Act 1964 [or specified under section 10(8) of the Petroleum Act 1998], except an area or part of an area in which the law of Northern Ireland applies.

(6) An Order in Council under subsection (5) may provide that, in relation to the employment to which the Order applies, this Part is to have effect with such modifications as are specified in the Order.

(7) An Order in Council under subsection (5) shall be of no effect unless a draft of the Order has been laid before and approved by resolution of each House of Parliament.
[216]

NOTES

Sub-s (1): words in square brackets substituted by the Race Relations Act 1976 (Amendment) Regulations 2003, SI 2003/1626, reg 11(1), as from 19 July 2003.

Sub-s (1A): inserted by SI 2003/1626, reg 11(2), as from 19 July 2003.

Sub-s (2): repealed by the Equal Opportunities (Employment Legislation) (Territorial Limits) Regulations 1999, SI 1999/3163, reg 3(1), (3).

Sub-s (5): for the words in italics there are substituted the words "any activity within section 11(2) of the Petroleum Act 1998", and the words in square brackets are inserted, by the Petroleum Act 1998, s 50, Sch 4, para 11, as from a day to be appointed.

Orders: the Race Relations (Offshore Employment) Order 1987, SI 1987/929.

See further, the Employment (Continental Shelf) Act 1978, which extends the power to make orders under sub-s (5) above (but is prospectively repealed by the Petroleum Act 1998, s 51(1), Sch 5, Pt I, as from a day to be appointed).

9 Exception for seamen recruited abroad

(1) Nothing in section 4 shall render unlawful any act done by an employer in or in connection with employment by him on any ship in the case of a person who applied or was engaged for that employment outside Great Britain [to the extent that the act—

(a) relates to the pay the person receives in respect of his employment, and

(b) amounts to discrimination against the person on the basis of his nationality].

(2) Nothing in section 7 shall, as regards work to which that section applies, render unlawful any act done by the principal in or in connection with such work on any ship in the case of a contract worker who was engaged outside Great Britain by the person by whom he is supplied [to the extent that the act—

(a) relates to the pay the person receives in respect of the work, and

(b) amounts to discrimination against the person on the basis of his nationality].

(3) Subsections (1) and (2) do not apply to employment or work concerned with *exploration of the sea bed or subsoil or the exploitation of their natural resources* in any area for the time being designated under section 1(7) of the Continental Shelf Act 1964 [or specified under section 10(8) of the Petroleum Act 1998], not being an area or part of an area in which the law of Northern Ireland applies.

(4) For the purposes of subsection (1) a person brought to Great Britain with a view to his entering into an agreement in Great Britain to be employed on any ship shall be treated as having applied for the employment outside Great Britain.

[(5) In this section—

"pay" includes retirement or death benefit;

"retirement or death benefit" means a pension, annuity, lump sum, gratuity or other similar benefit which will be paid or given to the employee or contract worker or a member of his family or household in the event of his retirement or death.]

[217]

NOTES

Sub-ss (1), (2): words in square brackets added by the Race Relations Act 1976 (Seamen Recruited Abroad) Order 2003, SI 2003/1651, art 2(1)–(3), as from 19 July 2003.

Sub-s (3): for the words in italics there are substituted the words "any activity within section 11(2) of the Petroleum Act 1998", and the words in square brackets are inserted, by the Petroleum Act 1998, s 50, Sch 4, para 11, as from a day to be appointed.

Sub-s (5): added by SI 2003/1651, art 2(1), (4), as from 19 July 2003.

Discrimination by other bodies

10 Partnerships

(1) It is unlawful for a firm consisting of six or more partners, in relation to a position as partner in the firm, to discriminate against a person—

(a) in the arrangements they make for the purpose of determining who should be offered that position; or

(b) in the terms on which they offer him that position; or

(c) by refusing or deliberately omitting to offer him that position; or

(d) in a case where the person already holds that position—

(i) in the way they afford him access to any benefits, facilities or services, or by refusing or deliberately omitting to afford him access to them; or

(ii) by expelling him from that position, or subjecting him to any other detriment.

[(1A) The limitation of subsection (1) to six or more partners does not apply in relation to discrimination on grounds of race or ethnic or national origins.

(1B) It is unlawful for a firm, in relation to a position as a partner in the firm, to subject to harassment a person who holds or has applied for that position.]

(2) [Subsections (1), (1A) and (1B)] shall apply in relation to persons proposing to form themselves into a partnership as it applies in relation to a firm.

(3) Subsection (1)(a) and (c) do not apply to a position as partner where, if it were employment, [section 4A or 5 would apply to such employment].

(4) In the case of a limited partnership references in this section to a partner shall be construed as references to a general partner as defined in section 3 of the Limited Partnerships Act 1907.

[(5) This section applies to a limited liability partnership as it applies to a firm; and, in its application to a limited liability partnership, references to a partner in a firm are references to a member of the limited liability partnership.]

[(6) In subsection (1)(d)(ii) reference to the expulsion of a person from a position as partner includes, where the discrimination is on grounds of race or ethnic or national origins, reference—

(a) to the termination of that person's partnership by the expiration of any period (including a period expiring by reference to an event or circumstance), not being a termination immediately after which the partnership is renewed on the same terms; and

(b) to the termination of that person's partnership by any act of his (including the giving of notice) in circumstances such that he is entitled to terminate it without notice by reason of the conduct of the other partners.]

[218]

NOTES

Sub-ss (1A), (1B): inserted by the Race Relations Act 1976 (Amendment) Regulations 2003, SI 2003/1626, reg 12(a), as from 19 July 2003.

Sub-ss (2), (3): words in square brackets substituted by SI 2003/1626, reg 12(b), (c), as from 19 July 2003.

Sub-s (5): added by the Limited Liability Partnerships Regulations 2001, SI 2001/1090, reg 9(1), Sch 5, para 7.

Sub-s (6): added by SI 2003/1626, reg 12(d), as from 19 July 2003.

11 Trade unions etc

(1) This section applies to an organisation of workers, an organisation of employers, or any other organisation whose members carry on a particular profession or trade for the purposes of which the organisation exists.

(2) It is unlawful for an organisation to which this section applies, in the case of a person who is not a member of the organisation, to discriminate against him—

(a) in the terms on which it is prepared to admit him to membership; or

(b) by refusing, or deliberately omitting to accept, his application for membership.

(3) It is unlawful for an organisation to which this section applies, in the case of a person who is a member of the organisation, to discriminate against him—

(a) in the way it affords him access to any benefits, facilities or services, or by refusing or deliberately omitting to afford him access to them; or

(b) by depriving him of membership, or varying the terms on which he is a member; or

(c) by subjecting him to any other detriment.

[(4) It is unlawful for an organisation to which this section applies, in relation to a person's membership or application for membership of that organisation, to subject him to harassment.]

[219]

NOTES

Sub-s (4): added by the Race Relations Act 1976 (Amendment) Regulations 2003, SI 2003/1626, reg 13, as from 19 July 2003.

12 Qualifying bodies

(1) It is unlawful for an authority or body which can confer an authorisation or qualification which is needed for, or facilitates, engagement in a particular profession or trade to discriminate against a person—

(a) in the terms on which it is prepared to confer on him that authorisation or qualification; or

(b) by refusing, or deliberately omitting to grant, his application for it; or

(c) by withdrawing it from him or varying the terms on which he holds it.

[(1A) It is unlawful for an authority or body to which subsection (1) applies, in relation to an authorisation or qualification conferred by it, to subject to harassment a person who holds or applies for such an authorisation or qualification.]

(2) In this section—

(a) "authorisation or qualification" includes recognition, registration, enrolment, approval and certification;

(b) "confer" includes renew or extend.

[(3) Subsections (1) and (1A) do not apply to discrimination or harassment which is rendered unlawful by section 17 or 18.]

[220]

NOTES

Sub-s (1A): inserted by the Race Relations Act 1976 (Amendment) Regulations 2003, SI 2003/1626, reg 14(a), as from 19 July 2003.

Sub-s (3): substituted by SI 2003/1626, reg 14(b), as from 19 July 2003.

[13 Persons concerned with provision of vocational training

(1) It is unlawful, in the case of an individual seeking or undergoing training which would help fit him for any employment, for any person who provides, or makes arrangements for the provision of, facilities for such training to discriminate against him—

(a) in the terms on which that person affords him access to any training course or other facilities concerned with such training; or

(b) by refusing or deliberately omitting to afford him such access; or

(c) by terminating his training; or

(d) by subjecting him to any detriment during the course of his training.

(2) Subsection (1) does not apply to—

(a) discrimination which is rendered unlawful by section 4(1) or (2) or section 17 or 18; or

(b) discrimination which would be rendered unlawful by any of those provisions but for the operation of any other provision of this Act.

[(3) It is unlawful for any person who provides, or makes arrangements for the provision of, facilities for training to which subsection (1) applies, in relation to such facilities or training, to subject to harassment a person to whom he provides such training or who is seeking to undergo such training.

(4) Subsection (3) does not apply to harassment which is rendered unlawful by section 4(2A) or by section 17 or 18.]]

[221]

NOTES

Substituted by the Employment Act 1989, s 7(2).

Sub-ss (3), (4): added by the Race Relations Act 1976 (Amendment) Regulations 2003, SI 2003/1626, reg 15, as from 19 July 2003.

14 Employment agencies

(1) It is unlawful for an employment agency to discriminate against a person—

(a) in the terms on which the agency offers to provide any of its services; or
(b) by refusing or deliberately omitting to provide any of its services; or
(c) in the way it provides any of its services.

[(1A) It is unlawful for an employment agency, in relation to the provision of its services, to subject to harassment a person to whom it provides such services or who requests the provision of such services.]

[(2) It is unlawful for a local education authority or education authority or any other person to do any act in providing services in pursuance of arrangements made, or a direction given, under section 10 of the Employment and Training Act 1973 which constitutes discrimination [or harassment].]

(3) References in [subsections (1) and (1A)] to the services of an employment agency include guidance on careers and any other services related to employment.

(4) This section does not apply if the discrimination only concerns employment which the employer could lawfully refuse to offer the person in question.

(5) An employment agency or local education authority[, education authority or other person] shall not be subject to any liability under this section if it proves—

(a) that it acted in reliance on a statement made to it by the employer to the effect that, by reason of the operation of subsection (4), its action would not be unlawful; and
(b) that it was reasonable for it to rely on the statement.

(6) A person who knowingly or recklessly makes a statement such as is referred to in subsection (5)(a) which in a material respect is false or misleading commits an offence, and shall be liable on summary conviction to a fine not exceeding [level 5 on the standard scale].

[222]

NOTES

Sub-s (1A): inserted by the Race Relations Act 1976 (Amendment) Regulations 2003, SI 2003/1626, reg 16(a), as from 19 July 2003.

Sub-s (2): substituted by the Trade Union Reform and Employment Rights Act 1993, s 49(2), Sch 8, para 9(a); words in square brackets added by SI 2003/1626, reg 16(b), as from 19 July 2003.

Sub-s (3): words in square brackets substituted by SI 2003/1626, reg 16(c), as from 19 July 2003.

Sub-s (5): words in square brackets substituted by the Trade Union Reform and Employment Rights Act 1993, s 49(2), Sch 8, para 9(b).

Sub-s (6): maximum fine increased and converted to a level on the standard scale by the Criminal Justice Act 1982, ss 37, 38, 46.

15 [Training Commission] etc

[(1) It is unlawful for the [Secretary of State …][or the Minister] to discriminate [or to subject a person to harassment] in the provision of facilities or services under section 2 of the Employment and Training Act 1973.]

[(1A) It is unlawful for Scottish Enterprise or Highlands and Islands Enterprise to discriminate in the provision of facilities or services under such arrangements as are mentioned in section 2(3) of the Enterprise and New Towns (Scotland) Act 1990 (arrangements analogous to arrangements in pursuance of section 2 of the said Act of 1973).]

(2) This section does not apply in a case where—

(a) section 13 applies; or
(b) the [Secretary of State] is acting as an employment agency.

[223]

NOTES

Section heading: words in square brackets substituted by the Employment Act 1988, s 24(3).

Sub-s (1): substituted by the Employment and Training Act 1981, s 9, Sch 2, Pt II, para 20; words in first pair of square brackets substituted by the Employment Act 1988, s 33, Sch 3, Pt II, para 12(2), and words omitted therefrom repealed by the Employment Act 1989, s 29(4), Sch 7, Pt I; words in second pair of square brackets inserted by the Transfer of Functions (Equality) Order 2007, SI 2007/2914, art 8, Schedule, para 11, as from 12 October 2007; words in final pair of square brackets inserted by the Race Relations Act 1976 (Amendment) Regulations 2003, SI 2003/1626, reg 17, as from 19 July 2003.

Sub-s (1A): inserted by the Enterprise and New Towns (Scotland) Act 1990, s 18.

Sub-s (2): words in square brackets substituted by the Employment Act 1989, s 29(3), Sch 6, para 15.

16 (*Repealed by the Race Relations* (*Amendment*) *Act 2000, s 9*(*2*), *Sch 3.*)

PART III
DISCRIMINATION IN OTHER FIELDS

Education

17 … Bodies in charge of educational establishments

[(1)] It is unlawful, in relation to an educational establishment falling within column 1 of the following table, for a person indicated in relation to the establishment in column 2 (the "responsible body") to discriminate against a person—

(a) in the terms on which it offers to admit him to the establishment as a pupil; or

(b) by refusing or deliberately omitting to accept an application for his admission to the establishment as a pupil; or

(c) where he is a pupil of the establishment—

(i) in the way it affords him access to any benefits, facilities or services, or by refusing or deliberately omitting to afford him access to them; or

(ii) by excluding him from the establishment or subjecting him to any other detriment.

Table

Establishment	***Responsible body***
ENGLAND AND WALES	
1. Educational establishment maintained by a local education authority.	Local education authority or … [governing body], according to which of them has the function in question.
2. Independent school not being a special school.	Proprietor.
3. Special school not maintained by a local education authority.	Proprietor.
[3A. …	…]
[3B. Institution within the further education sector (within the meaning of section 91(3) of the Further and Higher Education Act 1992).	Governing body.]
4. University.	Governing body.
[4A. Institution, other than a university, within the higher education sector (within the meaning of section 91(5) of the Further and Higher Education Act 1992).	Governing body.]
5. Establishment (not falling within paragraphs 1 [to 4A]) providing full- time or part-time education, being an establishment designated under section 24(1) of the Sex Discrimination Act 1975 for the purposes of paragraph 5 of the corresponding table in section 22 of that Act.	Governing body.

Establishment	*Responsible body*
SCOTLAND	
6. Educational establishment managed by an education authority.	Education authority.
7. Educational establishment in respect of which the managers are for the time being receiving grants under section [[73(d)] of the Education (Scotland) Act 1980].	Managers of the educational establishment.
[7AA. A grant-aided school, within the meaning of section 135 of the Education (Scotland) Act 1980.	The managers of the school.]
[7A. …	…]
[7B. College of further education within the meaning of section 36(1) of the Further and Higher Education (Scotland) Act 1992 under the management of a board of management.	Board of management.
7C. Designated institution within the meaning of Part II of the Further and Higher Education (Scotland) Act 1992.	Governing body.]
8. University.	Governing body.
9. Independent school	Proprietor.
10. Any other educational establishment (not falling within paragraphs 6, 7 and 9) providing full or part-time education or further education.	Managers of the educational establishment.

[(2) It is unlawful for a responsible body, in relation to an establishment falling within column 1 of the table in subsection (1), to subject to harassment—

(a) a person who applies for admission to the establishment as a pupil; or

(b) a pupil at the establishment.]

[224]

NOTES

Section heading: words omitted repealed by the Race Relations Act 1976 (Amendment) Regulations 2003, SI 2003/1626, reg 18(1), as from 19 July 2003.

Sub-s (1): numbered as such by SI 2003/1626, reg 18(2), as from 19 July 2003. The Table in sub-s (1) is amended as follows—

Para 1: words omitted repealed by the Education Act 1980, s 1(3), Sch 1, para 28; words in square brackets substituted by the School Standards and Framework Act 1998, s 140(1), Sch 30, para 7.

Para 3A: inserted by the Education Reform Act 1988, s 237, Sch 12, Pt I, para 18; repealed by the School Standards and Framework Act 1998, s 140(3), Sch 31.

Para 3B: inserted by the Further and Higher Education Act 1992, s 93, Sch 8, Pt II, para 85.

Para 4A: inserted by the Education Reform Act 1988, s 237, Sch 12, Pt III, para 78; substituted by the Further and Higher Education Act 1992, s 93, Sch 8, para 85.

Para 5: words in square brackets substituted by the Further and Higher Education Act 1992, s 93, Sch 8, Pt II, para 85.

Para 7: words in first (outer) pair of square brackets substituted by the Education (Scotland) Act 1980, s 136(2), Sch 4, para 6; number in second (inner) pair of square brackets substituted by the Race Relations (Amendment) Act 2000, s 9(1), Sch 2, para 1(a).

Para 7AA: inserted by the Race Relations (Amendment) Act 2000, s 9(1), Sch 2, para 1(b).

Para 7A: inserted by the Self-Governing Schools etc (Scotland) Act 1989, s 82(1), Sch 10, para 6(2); repealed by the Standards in Scotland's Schools etc Act 2000, s 60(2), Sch 3, as from 31 December 2004.

Paras 7B, 7C: inserted by the Further and Higher Education (Scotland) Act 1992, s 62, Sch 9, para 5(2).

Sub-s (2): added by SI 2003/1626, reg 18(2), as from 19 July 2003.

[17A Meaning of pupil in section 17

For the purposes of section 17, "pupil" includes, in England and Wales, any person who receives education at a school or institution to which that section applies.]

[225]

NOTES
Inserted by the Further and Higher Education Act 1992, s 93, Sch 8, Pt II, para 86.

18 Other discrimination [etc] by local education authorities

(1) It is unlawful for a local education authority, in carrying out such of its functions under [the Education Acts] as do not fall under section 17, to do any act which constitutes racial discrimination [or harassment].

(2) It is unlawful for an education authority, in carrying out such of its functions under the Education (Scotland) [Act 1980] as do not fall under section 17, to do any act which constitutes racial discrimination [or harassment].

[226]

NOTES
Section heading: word in square brackets inserted by the Race Relations Act 1976 (Amendment) Regulations 2003, SI 2003/1626, reg 19(1), as from 19 July 2003.
Sub-s (1): words in first pair of square brackets substituted by the Education Act 1996, s 582(1), Sch 37, para 39; words in second pair of square brackets added by SI 2003/1626, reg 19(3), as from 19 July 2003.
Sub-s (2): words in first pair of square brackets substituted by the Education (Scotland) Act 1980, s 136(2), Sch 4, para 13; words in second pair of square brackets added by SI 2003/1626, reg 19(3), as from 19 July 2003.

[18A … Further Education and Higher Education Funding Councils

It is unlawful for [the Learning and Skills Council for England, …] the Higher Education Funding Council for England or the Higher Education Funding Council for Wales in carrying out their functions under [the Education Acts] [and the Learning and Skills Act 2000], to do any act which constitutes racial discrimination [or harassment].]

[227]

NOTES
Inserted by the Further and Higher Education Act 1992, s 93, Sch 8, Pt II, para 87.
Section heading: words omitted repealed by the Race Relations Act 1976 (Amendment) Regulations 2003, SI 2003/1626, reg 19(2), as from 19 July 2003.
Words in first pair of square brackets substituted, and words in third pair of square brackets inserted, by the Learning and Skills Act 2000, s 149, Sch 9, paras 1, 9; words omitted repealed by the National Council for Education and Training for Wales (Transfer of Functions to the National Assembly for Wales and Abolition) Order 2005, SI 2005/3238, art 9(1), Sch 1, paras 3, 4(a), as from 1 April 2006; words in second pair of square brackets substituted by the Education Act 1996, s 582(1), Sch 37, para 40; words in fourth pair of square brackets added by SI 2003/1626, reg 19(3), as from 19 July 2003.

18B *(Inserted by the Further and Higher Education (Scotland) Act 1992, s 62(2), Sch 9, para 5(1), (3); repealed by the Further and Higher Education (Scotland) Act 2005, s 32, Sch 3, para 4(a), as from 3 October 2005.)*

[18BA Scottish Further and Higher Education Funding Council

It is unlawful for the Scottish Further and Higher Education Funding Council in carrying out any of its functions to do any act which constitutes racial discrimination or harassment.]

[228]

NOTES
Commencement: 3 October 2005.
Inserted by the Further and Higher Education (Scotland) Act 2005 (Consequential Modifications) Order 2005, SI 2005/2077, art 5(a), as from 3 October 2005.

18C *(Inserted by the Education Act 1993, s 307(1), Sch 19, para 65; repealed by the School Standards and Framework Act 1998, s 140(3), Sch 31.)*

[18D … [Training and Development Agency for Schools]

It is unlawful for the [Training and Development Agency for Schools] in carrying out their functions under [any enactment] to do any act which constitutes racial discrimination [or harassment].]

[229]

NOTES

Inserted by the Education Act 1994, s 24, Sch 2, para 6(3).

Section heading: words omitted repealed by the Race Relations Act 1976 (Amendment) Regulations 2003, SI 2003/1626, reg 19(2), as from 19 July 2003; words in square brackets substituted by the Education Act 2005, s 98, Sch 14, para 7(a), as from 1 September 2005.

Words in first and second pairs of square brackets substituted by the Education Act 2005, s 98, Sch 14, para 7(a), (b), as from 1 September 2005; words in third pair of square brackets added by SI 2003/1626, reg 19(3), as from 19 July 2003.

19, 19ZA *(S 19 repealed by the Race Relations (Amendment) Act 2000, s 9(2), Sch 3; s 19ZA inserted by the Learning and Skills Act 2000, s 149, Sch 9, paras 1, 10, and repealed by the Race Relations (Amendment) Act 2000, s 9(2), Sch 3.)*

[Planning

19A Discrimination by planning authorities

(1) It is unlawful for a planning authority to discriminate against a person carrying out their planning functions.

(2) In this section "planning authority" means—

(a) in England and Wales, a county, [county borough,] district or London borough council, [the Broads Authority] [a National Park authority or] a joint planning board, … , and

(b) in Scotland, a planning authority or regional planning authority,

and includes an urban development corporation and a body having functions (whether as an enterprise zone authority or a body invited to prepare a scheme) under Schedule 32 to the Local Government, Planning and Land Act 1980.

(3) In this section "planning functions" means—

(a) in England and Wales, functions under [the Town and Country Planning Act 1990, the Planning (Listed Buildings and Conservation Areas) Act 1990 and the Planning (Hazardous Substances) Act 1990], and such other functions as may be prescribed, and

(b) in Scotland, functions under [the Town and Country Planning (Scotland) Act 1997, the Planning (Listed Buildings and Conservation Areas) (Scotland) Act 1997 and the Planning (Hazardous Substances) (Scotland) Act 1997] or Part IX of the Local Government (Scotland) Act 1973, and such other functions as may be prescribed,

and includes, in relation to an urban development corporation, planning functions under Part XVI of the Local Government, Planning and Land Act 1980 and, in relation to an enterprise zone authority or body invited to prepare an enterprise zone scheme, functions under Part XVIII of that Act.]

[230]

NOTES

Inserted, together with preceding heading, by the Housing and Planning Act 1986, s 55.

Sub-s (2): words in first pair of square brackets inserted by the Local Government (Wales) Act 1994, s 66(6), Sch 16, para 52; words in second pair of square brackets inserted by the Norfolk and Suffolk Broads Act 1988, s 2(5), (6), Sch 3, Pt I; words in third pair of square brackets inserted, and words omitted repealed, by the Environment Act 1995, ss 78, 120, Sch 10, para 15(1), Sch 24.

Sub-s (3): words in square brackets in para (a) substituted by the Planning (Consequential Provisions) Act 1990, s 4, Sch 2, para 36; words in square brackets in para (b) substituted by the Planning (Consequential Provisions) (Scotland) Act 1997, s 4, Sch 2, para 26.

Transfer of functions in relation to Wales: as to the transfer of functions under sub-s (3) from Ministers of the Crown to the National Assembly for Wales, see the National Assembly for Wales (Transfer of Functions) Order 1999, SI 1999/672.

[Public authorities

19B ... Public authorities

(1) It is unlawful for a public authority in carrying out any functions of the authority to do any act which constitutes discrimination.

[(1A) It is unlawful for a public authority to subject a person to harassment in the course of carrying out any functions of the authority which consist of the provision of—
(a) any form of social security;
(b) healthcare;
(c) any other form of social protection; or
(d) any form of social advantage,
which does not fall within section 20.]

(2) In this section "public authority"—
(a) includes any person certain of whose functions are functions of a public nature; but
(b) does not include any person mentioned in subsection (3).

(3) The persons mentioned in this subsection are—
(a) either House of Parliament;
(b) a person exercising functions in connection with proceedings in Parliament;
(c) the Security Service;
(d) the Secret Intelligence Service;
(e) the Government Communications Headquarters; and
(f) any unit or part of a unit of any of the naval, military or air forces of the Crown which is for the time being required by the Secretary of State to assist the Government Communications Headquarters in carrying out its functions.

(4) In relation to a particular act, a person is not a public authority by virtue only of subsection (2)(a) if the nature of the act is private.

(5) This section is subject to sections 19C to 19F.

(6) Nothing in this section makes unlawful any act of discrimination [or harassment] which—
(a) is made unlawful by virtue of any other provision of this Act; or
(b) would be so made but for any provision made by or under this Act.]

[231]

NOTES

Inserted, together with preceding heading and ss 19C–19F, by the Race Relations (Amendment) Act 2000, s 1.

Section heading: words omitted repealed by the Race Relations Act 1976 (Amendment) Regulations 2003, SI 2003/1626, reg 20(1), as from 19 July 2003.

Sub-s (1A): inserted by SI 2003/1626, reg 20(2)(a), as from 19 July 2003.

Sub-s (6): words in square brackets inserted by SI 2003/1626, reg 20(2)(b), as from 19 July 2003.

[19C Exceptions or further exceptions from section 19B for judicial and legislative acts etc

(1) Section 19B does not apply to—
(a) any judicial act (whether done by a court, tribunal or other person); or
(b) any act done on the instructions, or on behalf, of a person acting in a judicial capacity.

(2) Section 19B does not apply to any act of, or relating to, making, confirming or approving any enactment or Order in Council or any instrument made by a Minister of the Crown under an enactment.

(3) Section 19B does not apply to any act of, or relating to, making or approving arrangements, or imposing requirements or conditions, of a kind [excepted by] section 41.

(4) Section 19B does not apply to any act of, or relating to, imposing a requirement, or giving an express authorisation, of a kind mentioned in section 19D(3) in relation to the carrying out of [immigration functions].

(5) In this section—

"[immigration functions]" has the meaning given in section 19D; and

"Minister of the Crown" includes the [Welsh Ministers, the First Minister for Wales, the Counsel General to the Welsh Assembly Government] and a member of the Scottish Executive.]

[232]

NOTES

Inserted as noted to s 19B at **[231]**.

Sub-s (3): words in square brackets substituted by the Race Relations Act 1976 (Amendment) Regulations 2003, SI 2003/1626, reg 21, as from 19 July 2003.

Sub-s (4): words in square brackets substituted by the Nationality, Immigration and Asylum Act 2002 (Consequential and Incidental Provisions) Order 2003, SI 2003/1016, art 3, Schedule, para 2.

Sub-s (5): words in first pair of square brackets substituted by SI 2003/1016, art 3, Schedule, para 2; words in square brackets in the definition "Minister of the Crown" substituted by the Government of Wales Act 2006 (Consequential Modifications and Transitional Provisions) Order 2007, SI 2007/1388, art 3, Sch 1, paras 10, 11, as from 25 May 2007.

[19D Exception from section 19B for certain acts in immigration and nationality cases

(1) Section 19B does not make it unlawful for a relevant person to discriminate against another person on grounds of nationality or ethnic or national origins in carrying out [immigration functions].

(2) For the purposes of subsection (1), "relevant person" means—

(a) a Minister of the Crown acting personally; or

(b) any other person acting in accordance with a relevant authorisation.

(3) In subsection (2), "relevant authorisation" means a requirement imposed or express authorisation given—

(a) with respect to a particular case or class of case, by a Minister of the Crown acting personally;

(b) with respect to a particular class of case—

(i) by any of the enactments mentioned in subsection (5); or

(ii) by any instrument made under or by virtue of any of those enactments.

[(4) In subsection (1) "immigration functions" means functions exercisable by virtue of any of the enactments mentioned in subsection (5).

(5) Those enactments are—

(a) the Immigration Acts [(within the meaning of section 44 of the Asylum and Immigration (Treatment of Claimants, etc) Act 2004)] excluding sections 28A to 28K of the Immigration Act 1971 (c 77) so far as they relate to offences under Part III of that Act [and excluding section 14 of the Asylum and Immigration (Treatment of Claimants, etc) Act 2004];

(b) the Special Immigration Appeals Commission Act 1997 (c 68);

(c) provision made under section 2(2) of the European Communities Act 1972 (c 68) which relates to immigration or asylum; and

(d) any provision of Community law which relates to immigration or asylum.]]

[233]–[234]

NOTES

Inserted by the Race Relations (Amendment) Act 2000, s 1.

Sub-s (1): words in square brackets substituted by the Nationality, Immigration and Asylum Act 2002, s 6(1), (2).

Sub-s (4): substituted by the Nationality, Immigration and Asylum Act 2002, s 6(1), (3).

Sub-s (5): substituted by the Nationality, Immigration and Asylum Act 2002, s 6(1), (3); words in first pair of square brackets substituted, and words in second pair of square brackets inserted, by the Asylum and Immigration (Treatment of Claimants, etc) Act 2004, s 14(4), as from 1 December 2004.

19E (*Inserted by the Race Relations (Amendment) Act 2000, s 1; repealed by the UK Borders Act 2007, ss 54(a), 58, Schedule, as from 1 April 2008.*)

[19F Exceptions from section 19B for decisions not to prosecute etc

Section 19B does not apply to—

(a) a decision not to institute criminal proceedings and, where such a decision has been made, any act done for the purpose of enabling the decision whether to institute criminal proceedings to be made;

(b) where criminal proceedings are not continued as a result of a decision not to continue them, the decision and, where such a decision has been made—

(i) any act done for the purpose of enabling the decision whether to continue the proceedings to be made; and

(ii) any act done for the purpose of securing that the proceedings are not continued.]

[235]

NOTES

Inserted as noted to s 19B at **[231]**.

Goods, facilities, services and premises

20 … Provision of goods, facilities or services

(1) It is unlawful for any person concerned with the provision (for payment or not) of goods, facilities or services to the public or a section of the public to discriminate against a person who seeks to obtain or use those goods, facilities or services—

(a) by refusing or deliberately omitting to provide him with any of them; or

(b) by refusing or deliberately omitting to provide him with goods, facilities or services of the like quality, in the like manner and on the like terms as are normal in the first-mentioned person's case in relation to other members of the public or (where the person so seeking belongs to a section of the public) to other members of that section.

(2) The following are examples of the facilities and services mentioned in subsection (1)—

(a) access to and use of any place which members of the public are permitted to enter;

(b) accommodation in a hotel, boarding house or other similar establishment;

(c) facilities by way of banking or insurance or for grants, loans, credit or finance;

(d) facilities for education;

(e) facilities for entertainment, recreation or refreshment;

(f) facilities for transport or travel;

(g) the services of any profession or trade, or any local or other public authority.

[(3) It is unlawful for any person concerned with the provision of goods, facilities or services as mentioned in subsection (1), in relation to such provision, to subject to harassment—

(a) a person who seeks to obtain or use those goods, facilities or services, or

(b) a person to whom he provides those goods, facilities or services.]

[236]

NOTES

Section heading: words omitted repealed by the Race Relations Act 1976 (Amendment) Regulations 2003, SI 2003/1626, reg 22(1), as from 19 July 2003.

Sub-s (3): added by SI 2003/1626, reg 22(2), as from 19 July 2003.

21 … Disposal or management of premises

(1) It is unlawful for a person, in relation to premises in Great Britain of which he has power to dispose, to discriminate against another—

(a) in the terms on which he offers him those premises; or

(b) by refusing his application for those premises; or

(c) in his treatment of him in relation to any list of persons in need of premises of that description.

(2) It is unlawful for a person, in relation to premises managed by him, to discriminate against a person occupying the premises—

(a) in the way he affords him access to any benefits or facilities, or by refusing or deliberately omitting to afford him access to them; or

(b) by evicting him, or subjecting him to any other detriment.

[(2A) It is unlawful for a person, in relation to such premises as are referred to in subsection (1) or (2), to subject to harassment a person who applies for or, as the case may be, occupies such premises.]

(3) Subsection (1) does not apply to [discrimination, on grounds other than those of race or ethnic or national origins, by] a person who owns an estate or interest in the premises and wholly occupies them unless he uses the services of an estate agent for the purposes of the disposal of the premises, or publishes or causes to be published an advertisement in connection with the disposal.

[237]

NOTES

Section heading: words omitted repealed by the Race Relations Act 1976 (Amendment) Regulations 2003, SI 2003/1626, reg 23(1), as from 19 July 2003.

Sub-s (2A): inserted by SI 2003/1626, reg 23(2)(a), as from 19 July 2003.

Sub-s (3): words in square brackets inserted by SI 2003/1626, reg 23(2)(b), as from 19 July 2003.

22 Exception from ss 20(1) and 21: small dwellings

(1) Sections 20(1) and 21 do not apply to [discrimination on grounds other than those of race or ethnic or national origins in either] the provision by a person of accommodation in any premises, or the disposal of premises by him, if—

(a) that person or a near relative of his ("the relevant occupier") resides, and intends to continue to reside, on the premises; and

(b) there is on the premises, in addition to the accommodation occupied by the relevant occupier, accommodation (not being storage accommodation or means of access) shared by the relevant occupier with other persons residing on the premises who are not members of his household; and

(c) the premises are small premises.

(2) Premises shall be treated for the purposes of this section as small premises if—

(a) in the case of premises comprising residential accommodation for one or more households (under separate letting or similar agreements) in addition to the accommodation occupied by the relevant occupier, there is not normally residential accommodation for more than two such households and only the relevant occupier and any member of his household reside in the accommodation occupied by him;

(b) in the case of premises not falling within paragraph (a), there is not normally residential accommodation on the premises for more than six persons in addition to the relevant occupier and any members of his household.

[238]

NOTES

Sub-s (1): words in square brackets inserted by the Race Relations Act 1976 (Amendment) Regulations 2003, SI 2003/1626, reg 24, as from 19 July 2003.

23 Further exceptions from [ss 20] and 21

(1) Sections [20] and 21 do not apply—

(a) to discrimination [or harassment] which is rendered unlawful by any provision of Part II or section 17 or 18; or

(b) to discrimination which would be rendered unlawful by any provision of Part II but for any of the following provisions, namely sections 4(3)[, 4A(1)(b)], 5(1)(b), 6, 7(4), 9 and 14(4).

(2) Section 20(1) does not apply to anything done by a person as a participant in arrangements under which he (for reward or not) takes into his home, and treats as if they were members of his family, children, elderly persons, or persons requiring a special degree of care and attention.

[239]

NOTES

Section heading: words in square brackets substituted by the Race Relations Act 1976 (Amendment) Regulations 2003, SI 2003/1626, reg 25(1), as from 19 July 2003.

Sub-s (1): first number in square brackets substituted, and other words in square brackets inserted, by SI 2003/1626, reg 25(2), as from 19 July 2003.

24 … Consent for assignment or sub-letting

(1) Where the licence or consent of the landlord or of any other person is required for the disposal to any person of premises in Great Britain comprised in a tenancy, it is unlawful for the landlord or other person—

[(a) to discriminate against a person by withholding the licence or consent for disposal of the premises to him, or

(b) in relation to such a licence or consent, to subject to harassment a person who applies for the licence or consent, or from whom the licence or consent is withheld].

(2) Subsection (1) does not apply [to discrimination on grounds other than those of race or ethnic or national origins] if—

(a) the person withholding a licence or consent, or a near relative of his ("the relevant occupier") resides, and intends to continue to reside, on the premises; and

(b) there is on the premises, in addition to the accommodation occupied by the relevant occupier, accommodation (not being storage accommodation or means of access) shared by the relevant occupier with other persons residing on the premises who are not members of his household; and

(c) the premises are small premises.

(3) Section 22(2) (meaning of "small premises") shall apply for the purposes of this as well as of that section.

(4) In this section "tenancy" means a tenancy created by a lease or sub-lease, by an agreement for a lease or sub-lease or by a tenancy agreement or in pursuance of any enactment; and "disposal", in relation to premises comprised in a tenancy, includes assignment or assignation of the tenancy and sub-letting or parting with possession of the premises or any part of the premises.

(5) This section applies to tenancies created before the passing of this Act, as well as to others.

[240]

NOTES

Section heading: word omitted repealed by the Race Relations Act 1976 (Amendment) Regulations 2003, SI 2003/1626, reg 26(1), as from 19 July 2003.

Sub-s (1): paras (a), (b) substituted by SI 2003/1626, reg 26(2)(a), as from 19 July 2003.

Sub-s (2): words in square brackets inserted by SI 2003/1626, reg 26(2)(b), as from 19 July 2003.

25 Discrimination: associations not within s 11

(1) This section applies to any association of persons (however described, whether corporate or unincorporate, and whether or not its activities are carried on for profit) if—

(a) it has twenty-five or more members; and

(b) admission to membership is regulated by its constitution and is so conducted that the members do not constitute a section of the public within the meaning of section 20(1); and

(c) it is not an organisation to which section 11 applies.

(2) It is unlawful for an association to which this section applies, in the case of a person who is not a member of the association, to discriminate against him—

(a) in the terms on which it is prepared to admit him to membership; or

(b) by refusing or deliberately omitting to accept his application for membership.

(3) It is unlawful for an association to which this section applies, in the case of a person who is a member or associate of the association, to discriminate against him—

(a) in the way it affords him access to any benefits, facilities or services, or by refusing or deliberately omitting to afford him access to them; or

(b) in the case of a member, by depriving him of membership, or varying the terms on which he is a member; or

(c) in the case of an associate, by depriving him of his rights as an associate, or varying those rights; or

(d) in either case, by subjecting him to any other detriment.

(4) For the purposes of this section—

(a) a person is a member of an association if he belongs to it by virtue of his admission to any sort of membership provided for by its constitution (and is not merely a person with certain rights under its constitution by virtue of his membership of some other association), and references to membership of an association shall be construed accordingly;

(b) a person is an associate of an association to which this section applies if, not being a member of it, he has under its constitution some or all of the rights enjoyed by members (or would have apart from any provision in its constitution authorising the refusal of those rights in particular cases).

[241]

26 Exception from s 25 for certain associations

(1) An association to which section 25 applies is within this subsection if the main object of the association is to enable the benefits of membership (whatever they may be) to be enjoyed by persons of a particular racial group defined otherwise than by reference to colour; and in determining whether that is the main object of an association regard shall be had to the essential character of the association and to all relevant circumstances including, in particular, the extent to which the affairs of the association are so conducted that the persons primarily enjoying the benefits of membership are of the racial group in question.

(2) In the case of an association within subsection (1), nothing in section 25 shall render unlawful any act not involving discrimination on the ground of colour.

[242]

[Barristers

26A … Barristers

(1) It is unlawful for a barrister or barrister's clerk, in relation to any offer of a pupillage or tenancy, to discriminate against a person—

(a) in the arrangements which are made for the purpose of determining to whom it should be offered;

(b) in respect of any terms on which it is offered; or

(c) by refusing, or deliberately omitting, to offer it to him.

(2) It is unlawful for a barrister or barrister's clerk, in relation to a pupil or tenant in the chambers in question, to discriminate against him—

(a) in respect of any terms applicable to him as a pupil or tenant;

(b) in the opportunities for training, or gaining experience, which are afforded or denied to him;

(c) in the benefits, facilities or services which are afforded or denied to him; or

(d) by terminating his pupillage or by subjecting him to any pressure to leave the chambers or other detriment.

(3) It is unlawful for any person, in relation to the giving, withholding or acceptance of instructions to a barrister, to discriminate against any person [or to subject any person to harassment].

[(3A) It is unlawful for a barrister or barrister's clerk, in relation to a pupillage or tenancy in the set of chambers in question, to subject to harassment a person who is, or has applied to be, a pupil or tenant.]

(4) In this section—

"barrister's clerk" includes any person carrying out any of the functions of a barrister's clerk; and

"pupil", "pupillage", "tenancy" and "tenant" have the meaning commonly associated with their use in the context of a set of barristers' chambers.

(5) This section does not apply to Scotland.]

[243]

NOTES

Inserted, together with preceding heading, by the Courts and Legal Services Act 1990, s 64(2), subject to savings contained in Sch 19, para 1 thereto, in relation to a pupillage or tenancy which began before 1 January 1991.

Section heading: words omitted repealed by the Race Relations Act 1976 (Amendment) Regulations 2003, SI 2003/1626, reg 27(1), as from 19 July 2003.
Sub-s (3): words in square brackets inserted by SI 2003/1626, reg 27(2)(a), as from 19 July 2003.
Sub-s (3A): inserted by SI 2003/1626, reg 27(2)(b), as from 19 July 2003.

[Advocates

26B … Advocates

(1) It is unlawful for an advocate, in relation to taking any person as his pupil, to discriminate against a person—

(a) in the arrangements which he makes for the purpose of determining whom he will take as his pupil;
(b) in respect of any terms on which he offers to take any person as his pupil; or
(c) by refusing, or deliberately omitting, to take a person as his pupil.

(2) It is unlawful for an advocate, in relation to a person who is a pupil, to discriminate against him—

(a) in respect of any terms applicable to him as a pupil;
(b) in the opportunities for training, or gaining experience, which are afforded or denied to him;
(c) in the benefits, facilities or services which are afforded or denied to him; or
(d) by terminating her the relationship or by subjecting him to any pressure to terminate the relationship or other detriment.

(3) It is unlawful for any person, in relation to the giving, withholding or acceptance of instructions to an advocate, to discriminate against any person [or to subject any person to harassment].

[(3A) It is unlawful for an advocate, in relation to taking any person as his pupil, to subject to harassment a person who has applied to be, or is, a pupil.]

(4) In this section—

"advocate" means a member of the Faculty of Advocates practising as such; and
"pupil" has the meaning commonly associated with its use in the context of a person training to be an advocate.

(5) Section 3 applies for the purposes of this section as it applies for the purposes of any provision of Part II.

(6) This section does not apply to England and Wales.]

[244]

NOTES

Inserted, together with preceding heading, by the Courts and Legal Services Act 1990, s 65(2).
Section heading: words omitted repealed by the Race Relations Act 1976 (Amendment) Regulations 2003, SI 2003/1626, reg 28(1), as from 19 July 2003.
Sub-s (3): words in square brackets inserted by SI 2003/1626, reg 28(2)(a), as from 19 July 2003.
Sub-s (3A): inserted by SI 2003/1626, reg 28(2)(b), as from 19 July 2003.

Extent

27 Extent of Part III

(1) Sections 17 to [18D] do not apply to benefits, facilities or services outside Great Britain except—

(a) travel on a ship registered at a port of registry in Great Britain; and
(b) benefits, facilities or services provided on a ship so registered.

[(1A) In its application in relation to granting entry clearance (within the meaning of the Immigration Act 1971) section 19B applies in relation to acts done outside the United Kingdom, as well as those done within Great Britain.]

(2) Section 20(1)—

(a) does not apply to goods, facilities or services outside Great Britain except as provided in subsections (3) and (4); and
(b) does not apply to facilities by way of banking or insurance or for grants, loans,

credit or finance, where the facilities are for a purpose to be carried out, or in connection with risks wholly or mainly arising, outside Great Britain.

(3) Section 20(1) applies to the provision of facilities for travel outside Great Britain where the refusal or omission occurs in Great Britain or on a ship, aircraft or hovercraft within subsection (4).

(4) Section 20(1) applies on and in relation to—

(a) any ship registered at a port of registry in Great Britain; and

(b) any aircraft or hovercraft registered in the United Kingdom and operated by a person who has his principal place of business, or is ordinarily resident, in Great Britain,

even if the ship, aircraft or hovercraft is outside Great Britain.

(5) This section shall not render unlawful an act done in or over a country outside the United Kingdom, or in or over that country's territorial waters, for the purpose of complying with the laws of that country.

[245]

NOTES

Sub-s (1): number in square brackets substituted by the Race Relations (Amendment) Act 2000, s 9(1), Sch 2, para 2.

Sub-s (1A): inserted by the Race Relations (Amendment) Act 2000, s 9(1), Sch 2, para 3.

PART IV
OTHER UNLAWFUL ACTS

[27A Relationships which have come to an end

(1) In this section a "relevant relationship" is a relationship during the course of which, by virtue of any provision referred to in section 1(1B), taken with section 1(1) or (1A), or (as the case may be) by virtue of section 3A—

(a) an act of discrimination by one party to the relationship ("the relevant party") against another party to the relationship, on grounds of race or ethnic or national origins, or

(b) harassment of another party to the relationship by the relevant party,

is unlawful.

(2) Where a relevant relationship has come to an end it is unlawful for the relevant party—

(a) to discriminate against another party, on grounds of race or ethnic or national origins, by subjecting him to a detriment, or

(b) to subject another party to harassment,

where the discrimination or harassment arises out of and is closely connected to that relationship.

(3) In subsection (1) reference to an act of discrimination or harassment which is unlawful includes, in the case of a relationship which has come to an end before 19th July 2003, reference to such an act which would, after that date, be unlawful.

(4) For the purposes of any proceedings in respect of an unlawful act under subsection (2), that act shall be treated as falling within circumstances relevant for the purposes of such of the provisions, or Parts, referred to in subsection (1) as determine most closely the nature of the relevant relationship.]

[246]

NOTES

Commencement: 19 July 2003.

Inserted by the Race Relations Act 1976 (Amendment) Regulations 2003, SI 2003/1626, reg 29, as from 19 July 2003.

28 Discriminatory practices

(1) In this section "discriminatory practice" means—

[(a)] the application of a requirement or condition which results in an act of discrimination which is unlawful by virtue of any provision of Part II or III taken with section 1(1)(b), or which would be likely to result in such an act of discrimination if the persons to whom it is applied included persons of any particular racial group as regards which there has been no occasion for applying it; [or

(b) the application of a provision, criterion or practice which results in an act of discrimination which is unlawful by virtue of any provision referred to in section 1(1B), taken with section 1(1A), or which would be likely to result in such an act of discrimination, if the persons to whom it is applied included persons of any particular race or of any particular ethnic or national origins, as regards which there has been no occasion for applying it].

(2) A person acts in contravention of this section if and so long as—

(a) he applies a discriminatory practice; or

(b) he operates practices or other arrangements which in any circumstances would call for the application by him of a discriminatory practice.

(3) Proceedings in respect of a contravention of this section shall be brought only by the Commission in accordance with [sections 20 to 24 of the Equality Act 2006].

[247]

NOTES

Sub-s (1): para (a) designated as such, and para (b) and the word immediately preceding it added, by the Race Relations Act 1976 (Amendment) Regulations 2003, SI 2003/1626, reg 30, as from 19 July 2003.

Sub-s (3): words in square brackets substituted by the Equality Act 2006, s 40, Sch 3, paras, 21, 22, as from 1 October 2007.

29 Discriminatory advertisements

(1) It is unlawful to publish or to cause to be published an advertisement which indicates, or might reasonably be understood as indicating, an intention by a person to do an act of discrimination, whether the doing of that act by him would be lawful or, by virtue of Part II or III, unlawful.

(2) Subsection (1) does not apply to an advertisement—

(a) if the intended act would be lawful by virtue of any of sections 5, 6, 7(3) and (4), 10(3), 26, 34(2)(b), 35 to 39 and 41; or

(b) if the advertisement relates to the services of an employment agency (within the meaning of section 14(1)) and the intended act only concerns employment which the employer could by virtue of section 5, 6 or 7(3) or (4) lawfully refuse to offer to persons against whom the advertisement indicates an intention to discriminate.

(3) Subsection (1) does not apply to an advertisement which indicates that persons of any class defined otherwise than by reference to colour, race or ethnic or national origins are required for employment outside Great Britain.

(4) The publisher of an advertisement made unlawful by subsection (1) shall not be subject to any liability under that subsection in respect of the publication of the advertisement if he proves—

(a) that the advertisement was published in reliance on a statement made to him by the person who caused it to be published to the effect that, by reason of the operation of subsection (2) or (3), the publication would not be unlawful; and

(b) that it was reasonable for him to rely on the statement.

(5) A person who knowingly or recklessly makes a statement such as is mentioned in subsection (4)(a) which in a material respect is false or misleading commits an offence, and shall be liable on summary conviction to a fine not exceeding [level 5 on the standard scale].

[(6) Proceedings in respect of a contravention of subsection (1) may be brought only—

(a) by the Commission, and

(b) in accordance with section 25 of the Equality Act 2006.]

[248]

NOTES

Sub-s (5): maximum fine increased and converted to a level on the standard scale by the Criminal Justice Act 1982, ss 37, 38, 46.

Sub-s (6): added by the Equality Act 2006, s 40, Sch 3, paras, 21, 23, as from 1 October 2007.

Proceedings in respect of a contravention of subsection (1): see further, the Equality Act 2006, ss 25, 26 at **[1668]**, **[1669]**.

30 Instructions to [commit unlawful acts]

[(1)] It is unlawful for a person—

(a) who has authority over another person; or

(b) in accordance with whose wishes that other person is accustomed to act,

to instruct him to do any act which is unlawful by virtue of Part II or III, [section 76ZA or, where it renders an act unlawful on grounds of race or ethnic or national origins, section 76,] or procure or attempt to procure the doing by him of any such act.

[(2) Proceedings in respect of a contravention of subsection (1) may be brought only—

(a) by the Commission, and

(b) in accordance with section 25 of the Equality Act 2006.]

[249]

NOTES

Section heading: words in square brackets substituted by the Race Relations Act 1976 (Amendment) Regulations 2003, SI 2003/1626, reg 31(1), as from 19 July 2003.

Sub-s (1): numbered as such by the Equality Act 2006, s 40, Sch 3, paras, 21, 24, as from 1 October 2007; words in square brackets inserted by SI 2003/1626, reg 31(2), as from 19 July 2003.

Sub-s (2): added by the Equality Act 2006, s 40, Sch 3, paras, 21, 24, as from 1 October 2007.

Proceedings in respect of a contravention of subsection (1): see further, the Equality Act 2006, ss 25, 26 at **[1668]**, **[1669]**.

31 Pressure to [commit unlawful acts]

(1) It is unlawful to induce, or attempt to induce, a person to do any act which contravenes Part II or III[, section 76ZA or, where it renders an act unlawful on grounds of race or ethnic or national origins, section 76].

(2) An attempted inducement is not prevented from falling within subsection (1) because it is not made directly to the person in question, if it is made in such a way that he is likely to hear of it.

[(3) Proceedings in respect of a contravention of subsection (1) may be brought only—

(a) by the Commission, and

(b) in accordance with section 25 of the Equality Act 2006.]

[250]

NOTES

Section heading: words in square brackets substituted by the Race Relations Act 1976 (Amendment) Regulations 2003, SI 2003/1626, reg 32(1), as from 19 July 2003.

Sub-s (1): words in square brackets inserted by SI 2003/1626, reg 32(2), as from 19 July 2003.

Sub-s (3): added by the Equality Act 2006, s 40, Sch 3, paras, 21, 25, as from 1 October 2007.

Proceedings in respect of a contravention of subsection (1): see further, the Equality Act 2006, ss 25, 26 at **[1668]**, **[1669]**.

32 Liability of employers and principals

(1) Anything done by a person in the course of his employment shall be treated for the purposes of this Act (except as regards offences thereunder) as done by his employer as well as by him, whether or not it was done with the employer's knowledge or approval.

(2) Anything done by a person as agent for another person with the authority (whether express or implied, and whether precedent or subsequent) of that other person shall be treated for the purposes of this Act (except as regards offences thereunder) as done by that other person as well as by him.

(3) In proceedings brought under this Act against any person in respect of an act alleged to have been done by an employee of his it shall be a defence for that person to prove that he took such steps as were reasonably practicable to prevent the employee from doing that act, or from doing in the course of his employment acts of that description.

[251]

NOTES

Modified as noted to s 4 at **[211]**.

Serious Organised Crime Agency: for the application of this section to any constable or other person who has been seconded to SOCA to serve as a member of its staff, see the Serious Organised Crime and Police Act 2005, s 56(3), (4).

33 Aiding unlawful acts

(1) A person who knowingly aids another person to do an act made unlawful by this Act shall be treated for the purposes of this Act as himself doing an unlawful act of the like description.

(2) For the purposes of subsection (1) an employee or agent for whose act the employer or principal is liable under section 32 (or would be so liable but for section 32(3)) shall be deemed to aid the doing of the act by the employer or principal.

(3) A person does not under this section knowingly aid another to do an unlawful act if—

(a) he acts in reliance on a statement made to him by that other person that, by reason of any provision of this Act, the act which he aids would not be unlawful; and

(b) it is reasonable for him to rely on the statement.

(4) A person who knowingly or recklessly makes a statement such as is mentioned in subsection (3)(a) which in a material respect is false or misleading commits an offence, and shall be liable on summary conviction to a fine not exceeding [level 5 on the standard scale].

[252]

NOTES

Sub-s (4): maximum fine increased and converted to a level on the standard scale by the Criminal Justice Act 1982, ss 37, 38, 46.

PART V
CHARITIES

34 Charities

(1) A provision which is contained in a charitable instrument (whenever that instrument took or takes effect) and which provides for conferring benefits on persons of a class defined by reference to colour shall have effect for all purposes as if it provided for conferring the like benefits—

(a) on persons of the class which results if the restriction by reference to colour is disregarded; or

(b) where the original class is defined by reference to colour only, on persons generally;

but nothing in this subsection shall be taken to alter the effect of any provision as regards any time before the coming into operation of this subsection.

(2) Nothing in Parts II to IV shall—

(a) be construed as affecting a provision to which this subsection applies; or

(b) render unlawful an act which is done in order to give effect to such a provision.

(3) Subsection (2) applies to any provision which is contained in a charitable instrument (whenever that instrument took or takes effect) and which provides for conferring benefits on persons of a class defined otherwise than by reference to colour (including a class resulting from the operation of subsection (1)).

[(3A) Subsection (2)(b) does not apply to an act which is unlawful, on grounds of race or ethnic or national origins, by virtue of section 4 or 7.]

(4) In this section "charitable instrument" means an enactment or other instrument passed or made for charitable purposes, or an enactment or other instrument so far as it relates to charitable purposes, and in Scotland includes the governing instrument of an endowment or of an educational endowment as those expressions are defined in section 135(1) of the Education (Scotland) Act 1962.

In the application of this section to England and Wales, "charitable purposes" means purposes which are exclusively charitable according to the law of England and Wales.

[253]

NOTES

Sub-s (3A): inserted by the Race Relations Act 1976 (Amendment) Regulations 2003, SI 2003/1626, reg 33, as from 19 July 2003.

The definitions referred to in sub-s (4) as being in the Education (Scotland) Act 1962, s 135 have been repealed and re-enacted in the Education (Scotland) Act 1980, s 122(1), but no consequential amendment to sub-s (4) has been made.

PART VI
GENERAL EXCEPTIONS FROM PARTS II TO IV

35 Special needs of racial groups in regard to education, training or welfare

Nothing in Parts II to IV shall render unlawful any act done in affording persons of a particular racial group access to facilities or services to meet the special needs of persons of that group in regard to their education, training or welfare, or any ancillary benefits.

[254]

36 Provision of education or training for persons not ordinarily resident in Great Britain

Nothing in Parts II to IV shall render unlawful any act done by a person[, on grounds other than race or ethnic or national origins,] for the benefit of persons not ordinarily resident in Great Britain in affording them access to facilities for education or training or any ancillary benefits, where it appears to him that the persons in question do not intend to remain in Great Britain after their period of education or training there.

[255]

NOTES

Words in square brackets inserted by the Race Relations Act 1976 (Amendment) Regulations 2003, SI 2003/1626, reg 34, as from 19 July 2003.

37 Discriminatory training by certain bodies

(1) Nothing in Parts II to IV shall render unlawful any act done in relation to particular work by [any person] in or in connection with—

(a) affording only persons of a particular racial group access to facilities for training which would help to fit them for that work; or

(b) encouraging only persons of a particular racial group to take advantage of opportunities for doing that work,

where [it reasonably appears to that person] that at any time within the twelve months immediately preceding the doing of the act—

(i) there were no persons of that group among those doing that work in Great Britain; or

(ii) the proportion of persons of that group among those doing that work in Great Britain was small in comparison with the proportion of persons of that group among the population of Great Britain.

(2) Where in relation to particular work [it reasonably appears to any person] that although the condition for the operation of subsection (1) is not met for the whole of Great Britain it is met for an area within Great Britain, nothing in Parts II to IV shall render unlawful any act done by [that person] in or in connection with—

(a) affording persons who are of the racial group in question, and who appear likely to take up that work in that area, access to facilities for training which would help to fit them for that work; or

(b) encouraging persons of that group to take advantage of opportunities in the area for doing that work.

[(3) The preceding provisions of this section shall not apply to any discrimination which is rendered unlawful by section 4(1) or (2).]

[256]

NOTES

Sub-ss (1), (2): words in square brackets substituted by the Employment Act 1989, s 7(3)(a), (b).

Sub-s (3): substituted by the Employment Act 1989, s 7(3)(c).

38 Other discriminatory training etc

(1) Nothing in Parts II to IV shall render unlawful any act done by an employer in relation to particular work in his employment at a particular establishment in Great Britain, being an act done in or in connection with—

(a) affording only those of his employees working at that establishment who are of a particular racial group access to facilities for training which would help to fit them for that work; or

(b) encouraging only persons of a particular racial group to take advantage of opportunities for doing that work at that establishment,

where any of the conditions in subsection (2) was satisfied at any time within the twelve months immediately preceding the doing of the act.

(2) Those conditions are—

(a) that there are no persons of the racial group in question among those doing that work at that establishment; or

(b) that the proportion of persons of that group among those doing that work at that establishment is small in comparison with the proportion of persons of that group—

(i) among all those employed by that employer there; or

(ii) among the population of the area from which that employer normally recruits persons for work in his employment at that establishment.

(3) Nothing in section 11 shall render unlawful any act done by an organisation to which that section applies in or in connection with—

(a) affording only members of the organisation who are of a particular racial group access to facilities for training which would help to fit them for holding a post of any kind in the organisation; or

(b) encouraging only members of the organisation who are of a particular racial group to take advantage of opportunities for holding such posts in the organisation,

where either of the conditions in subsection (4) was satisfied at any time within the twelve months immediately preceding the doing of the act.

(4) Those conditions are—

(a) that there are no persons of the racial group in question among persons holding such posts in that organisation; or

(b) that the proportion of persons of that group among those holding such posts in that organisation is small in comparison with the proportion of persons of that group among the members of the organisation.

(5) Nothing in Parts II to IV shall render unlawful any act done by an organisation to which section 11 applies in or in connection with encouraging only persons of a particular racial group to become members of the organisation where at any time within the twelve months immediately preceding the doing of the act—

(a) no persons of that group were members of the organisation; or

(b) the proportion of persons of that group among members of the organisation was small in comparison with the proportion of persons of that group among those eligible for membership of the organisation.

(6) Section 8 (meaning of employment at establishment in Great Britain) shall apply for the purposes of this section as if this section were contained in Part II.

[257]

39 Sports and competitions

Nothing in Parts II to IV shall render unlawful any act whereby a person discriminates against another on the basis of that other's nationality or place of birth or the length of time for which he has been resident in a particular area or place, if the act is done—

(a) in selecting one or more persons to represent a country, place or area, or any related association, in any sport or game; or

(b) in pursuance of the rules of any competition so far as they relate to eligibility to compete in any sport or game.

[258]

40 Indirect access to benefits etc

(1) References in this Act to the affording by any person of access to benefits, facilities or services are not limited to benefits, facilities or services provided by that person himself,

but include any means by which it is in that person's power to facilitate access to benefits, facilities or services provided by any other person (the "actual provider").

(2) Where by any provision of this Act the affording by any person of access to benefits, facilities or services in a discriminatory way is in certain circumstances prevented from being unlawful, the effect of the provision shall extend also to the liability under this Act of any actual provider.

[259]

41 Acts done under statutory authority etc

(1) Nothing in Parts II to IV shall render unlawful any act of discrimination done—
- (a) in pursuance of any enactment or Order in Council; or
- (b) in pursuance of any instrument made under any enactment by a Minister of the Crown; or
- (c) in order to comply with any condition or requirement imposed by a Minister of the Crown (whether before or after the passing of this Act) by virtue of any enactment.

References in this [section] to an enactment, Order in Council or instrument include an enactment, Order in Council or instrument passed or made after the passing of this Act.

[(1A) Subsection (1) does not apply to an act which is unlawful, on grounds of race or ethnic or national origins, by virtue of a provision referred to in section 1(1B).]

(2) Nothing in Parts II to IV shall render unlawful any act whereby a person discriminates against another on the basis of that other's nationality or place of ordinary residence or the length of time for which he has been present or resident in or outside the United Kingdom or an area within the United Kingdom, if that Act is done—
- [(a) in pursuance of any enactment or Order in Council; or
- (b) in pursuance of any instrument made under any enactment by a Minister of the Crown; or
- (c) in order to comply with any requirement imposed by a Minister of the Crown (whether before or after the passing of this Act) by virtue of any enactment; or
- (d) in pursuance of any arrangements made (whether before or after the passing of this Act) by or with the approval of, or for the time being approved by, a Minister of the Crown; or
- (e) in order to comply with any condition imposed (whether before or after the passing of this Act) by a Minister of the Crown].

[260]

NOTES

Sub-s (1): word in square brackets substituted by the Race Relations Act 1976 (Amendment) Regulations 2003, SI 2003/1626, reg 35(a), as from 19 July 2003.

Sub-s (1A): inserted by SI 2003/1626, reg 35(b), as from 19 July 2003.

Sub-s (2): paras (a)–(e) substituted, for original paras (a), (b), by SI 2003/1626, reg 35(c), as from 19 July 2003.

Minister of the Crown: by virtue of the National Assembly for Wales (Transfer of Functions) Order 1999, SI 1999/672, references to a Minister of the Crown in this section are to be construed as including references to the Assembly.

42 Acts safeguarding national security

Nothing in Parts II to IV shall render unlawful an act done for the purpose of safeguarding national security [if the doing of the act was justified by that purpose].

[261]–[271]

NOTES

Words in square brackets added by the Race Relations (Amendment) Act 2000, s 7(1).

43–52 *(SS 43–52 (Pt VII: the Commission for Racial Equality) repealed by the Equality Act 2006, ss 40, 91, Sch 3, paras, 21, 26, Sch 4, as from 1 October 2007. For savings see the Equality Act 2006 (Commencement No 3 and Savings) Order 2007, SI 2007/2603, art 3 at* **[3473R]**. *For transitional provisions relating to the discharge by the Commission for Equality and Human Rights of the former functions of the CRE, see the Equality Act 2006 (Dissolution of Commissions and Consequential and Transitional Provisions) Order 2007, SI 2007/2602, art 5 at* **[3473O]**).)

PART VIII
ENFORCEMENT

General

53 Restriction of proceedings for breach of Act

(1) Except as provided by this Act [or the Special Immigration Appeals Commission Act 1997 or [Part 5 of the Nationality, Immigration and Asylum Act 2002]] no proceedings, whether civil or criminal, shall lie against any person in respect of an act by reason that the act is unlawful by virtue of a provision of this Act.

(2) Subsection (1) does not preclude the making of an order of certiorari, mandamus or prohibition.

(3) In Scotland, subsection (1) does not preclude the exercise of the jurisdiction of the Court of Session to entertain an application for reduction or suspension of any order or determination or otherwise to consider the validity of any order or determination, or to require reasons for any order or determination to be stated.

[(4) Subsections (2) and (3) do not, except so far as provided by section 76, apply to any act which is unlawful by virtue of section 76(5) or (9) or by virtue of section 76(10)(b)[, (11) and (11B)].]

[272]

NOTES

Sub-s (1): words in first (outer) pair of square brackets inserted by the Race Relations (Amendment) Act 2000, s 9(1), Sch 2, para 4; words in second (inner) pair of square brackets substituted by the Nationality, Immigration and Asylum Act 2002, s 114(3), Sch 7, para 11, except in relation to events which took place before 1 April 2003.

Sub-s (4): added by the Race Relations (Amendment) Act 2000, s 9(1), Sch 2, para 5; words in square brackets substituted by the Race Relations Act 1976 (Amendment) Regulations 2003, SI 2003/1626, reg 39, as from 19 July 2003.

Enforcement in employment field

54 Jurisdiction of [employment tribunals]

(1) A complaint by any person ("the complainant") that another person ("the respondent")—

(a) has committed an act … against the complainant which is unlawful by virtue of Part II[, section 76ZA or, in relation to discrimination on grounds of race or ethnic or national origins, or harassment, section 26A, 26B or 76]; or

(b) is by virtue of section 32 or 33 to be treated as having committed such an act … against the complainant,

may be presented to an [employment tribunal].

(2) Subsection (1) does not apply to a complaint under section 12(1) of an act in respect of which an appeal, or proceedings in the nature of an appeal, may be brought under any enactment …

[273]

NOTES

Section heading: words in square brackets substituted by the Employment Rights (Dispute Resolution) Act 1998, s 1(2)(b).

Sub-s (1): words omitted from paras (a), (b) repealed, and words in square brackets in para (a) inserted, by the Race Relations Act 1976 (Amendment) Regulations 2003, SI 2003/1626, reg 40, as from 19 July 2003, except in relation to proceedings commenced before that date (see **[2938]**); words in final pair of square brackets substituted by the Employment Rights (Dispute Resolution) Act 1998, s 1(2)(a).

Sub-s (2): words omitted repealed by the Armed Forces Act 1996, s 35(2), Sch 7, Pt III.

Conciliation: employment tribunal proceedings and claims which could be the subject of employment tribunal proceedings under this section are proceedings to which the Employment Tribunals Act 1996, s 18 applies; see s 18(1)(a)(iii) of that Act at **[975]**.

Tribunal jurisdiction: the Employment Act 2002, ss 31, 32, 38 at **[1493]**, **[1494]**, **[1496]** apply to proceedings before the employment tribunal relating to a claim under this section; see ss 31(1), 32(1), 38(1) of, and Schs 3–5 to, the 2002 Act at **[1508]**–**[1510]**.

For the circumstances in which the normal time limit for presenting a complaint under this section is extended for a period of three months, see the Employment Act 2002 (Dispute Resolution) Regulations 2004, SI 2004/752, regs 15 and 18 at **[3096]** and **[3098]**.

[54A Burden of proof: employment tribunals

(1) This section applies where a complaint is presented under section 54 and the complaint is that the respondent—

(a) has committed an act of discrimination, on grounds of race or ethnic or national origins, which is unlawful by virtue of any provision referred to in section 1(1B)(a), (e) or (f), or Part IV in its application to those provisions, or

(b) has committed an act of harassment.

(2) Where, on the hearing of the complaint, the complainant proves facts from which the tribunal could, apart from this section, conclude in the absence of an adequate explanation that the respondent—

(a) has committed such an act of discrimination or harassment against the complainant, or

(b) is by virtue of section 32 or 33 to be treated as having committed such an act of discrimination or harassment against the complainant,

the tribunal shall uphold the complaint unless the respondent proves that he did not commit or, as the case may be, is not to be treated as having committed, that act.]

[274]

NOTES

Commencement: 19 July 2003.

Inserted by the Race Relations Act 1976 (Amendment) Regulations 2003, SI 2003/1626, reg 41, as from 19 July 2003.

Note: by virtue of SI 2003/1626, reg 2(2), this section applies to proceedings commenced before 19 July 2003, as well as proceedings instituted on or after that date, but does not affect any case in which proceedings were determined before that date (see **[2938]**).

55 *(Repealed by the Employment Tribunals Act 1996, s 45, Sch 3, Pt I. The equivalent provisions as re-enacted are in s 18(1)–(3), (6) and (7) of the 1996 Act.)*

56 Remedies on complaint under s 54

(1) Where an [employment tribunal] finds that a complaint presented to it under section 54 is well-founded, the tribunal shall make such of the following as it considers just and equitable—

(a) an order declaring the rights of the complainant and the respondent in relation to the act to which the complaint relates;

(b) an order requiring the respondent to pay to the complainant compensation of an amount corresponding to any damages he could have been ordered by a county court or by a sheriff court to pay to the complainant if the complaint had fallen to be dealt with under section 57;

(c) a recommendation that the respondent take within a specified period action appearing to the tribunal to be practicable for the purpose of obviating or reducing the adverse effect on the complainant of any act of discrimination to which the complaint relates.

(2), (3) …

(4) If without reasonable justification the respondent to a complaint fails to comply with a recommendation made by an [employment tribunal] under subsection (1)(c), then, if it thinks it just and equitable to do so—

(a) the tribunal may … increase the amount of compensation required to be paid to the complainant in respect of the complaint by an order made under subsection (1)(b); or

(b) if an order under subsection (1)(b) could have been made but was not, the tribunal may make such an order.

[(5) The [Minister] may by regulations make provision—

(a) for enabling a tribunal, where an amount of compensation falls to be awarded under subsection (1)(b), to include in the award interest on that amount; and

(b) specifying, for cases where a tribunal decides that an award is to include an amount in respect of interest, the manner in which and the periods and rate by reference to which the interest is to be determined;

and the regulations may contain such incidental and supplementary provisions as the [Minister] considers appropriate.

(6) The [Minister] may by regulations modify the operation of any order made under [section 14 of [the Employment Tribunals Act 1996]] (power to make provision as to interest on sums payable in pursuance of [employment tribunal] decisions) to the extent that it relates to an award of compensation under subsection (1)(b).]

[275]

NOTES

Sub-s (1): words in square brackets substituted by the Employment Rights (Dispute Resolution) Act 1998, s 1(2)(a).

Sub-s (2): repealed by the Race Relations (Remedies) Act 1994, ss 1(1), 3(2), Schedule.

Sub-s (3): repealed by the Sex Discrimination and Equal Pay (Remedies) Regulations 1993, SI 1993/2798, reg 1(3), Schedule, para 1.

Sub-s (4): words in square brackets substituted by the Employment Rights (Dispute Resolution) Act 1998, s 1(2)(a); words omitted repealed by the Race Relations (Remedies) Act 1994, s 3(2), Schedule.

Sub-s (5): added, together with sub-s (6), by the Race Relations (Remedies) Act 1994, s 2(1); words in square brackets substituted by the Transfer of Functions (Equality) Order 2007, SI 2007/2914, art 8, Schedule, para 10(a), as from 12 October 2007.

Sub-s (6): added as noted above; word in first pair of square brackets substituted by SI 2007/2914, art 8, Schedule, para 10(a), as from 12 October 2007; words in second (outer) pair of square brackets substituted by the Employment Tribunals Act 1996, s 43, Sch 1, para 4; words in third (inner) pair and final pair of square brackets substituted by the Employment Rights (Dispute Resolution) Act 1998, s 1(2)(a), (c).

Compensation for dismissal: as to the powers of an employment tribunal to award compensation where any act constitutes both unfair dismissal under the Employment Rights Act 1996, and discrimination under any one or more of the Sex Discrimination Act 1975, the Race Relations Act 1976, the Disability Discrimination Act 1995, the Employment Equality (Sexual Orientation) Regulations 2003, the Employment Equality (Religion or Belief) Regulations 2003, or the Employment Equality (Age) Regulations 2006, see s 126 of the 1996 Act at **[1170]**.

Regulations: the Employment Tribunals (Interest on Awards in Discrimination Cases) Regulations 1996, SI 1996/2803 at **[2390]**.

Enforcement of Part III

57 Claims under Part III [etc]

(1) A claim by any person ("the claimant") that another person ("the respondent")—

(a) has committed an act … against the claimant which is unlawful by virtue of Part III [other than, in relation to discrimination on grounds of race or ethnic or national origins, or harassment, section 26A or 26B]; or

(b) is by virtue of section 32 or 33 to be treated as having committed such an act … against the claimant, may be made the subject of civil proceedings in like manner as any other claim in tort or (in Scotland) in reparation for breach of statutory duty.

(2) Proceedings under subsection (1)—

(a) shall, in England and Wales, be brought only in a designated county court; and

(b) shall, in Scotland, be brought only in a sheriff court.

(3) As respects an unlawful act of discrimination falling within section 1(1)(b), no award of damages shall be made if the respondent proves that the requirement or condition in question was not applied with the intention of treating the claimant unfavourably on racial grounds.

(4) For the avoidance of doubt it is hereby declared that damages in respect of an unlawful act of discrimination may include compensation for injury to feelings whether or not they include compensation under any other head.

[(4A) As respects an act which is done, or by virtue of section 32 or 33 is treated as done, by a person in carrying out public investigator functions or functions as a public prosecutor and which is unlawful by virtue of section 19B, no remedy other than—

(a) damages; or

(b) a declaration or, in Scotland, a declarator;

PART 1

shall be obtainable unless the court is satisfied that the remedy concerned would not prejudice a criminal investigation, a decision to institute criminal proceedings or any criminal proceedings.

(4B) In this section—

"criminal investigation" means—

(a) any investigation which a person in carrying out functions to which section 19B applies has a duty to conduct with a view to it being ascertained whether a person should be charged with, or in Scotland prosecuted for, an offence, or whether a person charged with or prosecuted for an offence is guilty of it;

(b) any investigation which is conducted by a person in carrying out functions to which section 19B applies and which in the circumstances may lead to a decision by that person to institute criminal proceedings which the person has power to conduct; or

(c) any investigation which is conducted by a person in carrying out functions to which section 19B applies and which in the circumstances may lead to a decision by that person to make a report to the procurator fiscal for the purpose of enabling him to determine whether criminal proceedings should be instituted; and

"public investigator functions" means functions of conducting criminal investigations or charging offenders;

and in this subsection "offence" includes *any offence under the Army Act 1955, the Air Force Act 1955 or the Naval Discipline Act 1957* (and "offender" shall be construed accordingly).

(4C) Subsection (4D) applies where a party to proceedings under subsection (1) which have arisen by virtue of section 19B has applied for a stay or sist of those proceedings on the grounds of prejudice to—

(a) particular criminal proceedings;

(b) a criminal investigation; or

(c) a decision to institute criminal proceedings.

(4D) The court shall grant the stay or sist unless it is satisfied that the continuance of the proceedings under subsection (1) would not result in the prejudice alleged.]

(5) Civil proceedings in respect of a claim by any person that he has been discriminated against in contravention of section 17 or 18 by a body to which [subsection (5A)] applies shall not be instituted unless the claimant has given notice of the claim to the Secretary of State …

[(5A) This subsection applies to—

(a) local education authorities in England and Wales;

(b) education authorities in Scotland; and

(c) any body which is a responsible body in relation to an establishment falling within paragraph 3, 3B or 7B of the table in section 17.]

(6) In Scotland, when any proceedings are brought under this section, in addition to the service on the defender of a copy of the summons or initial writ initiating the action a copy thereof shall be sent as soon as practicable to the Commission in a manner to be prescribed by Act of Sederunt.

[(7) This section has effect subject to section 57A].

[276]

NOTES

Section heading: word in square brackets added by the Race Relations Act 1976 (Amendment) Regulations 2003, SI 2003/1626, reg 42(1), as from 19 July 2003, except in relation to proceedings commenced before that date (see **[2938]**).

Sub-s (1): words omitted from paras (a), (b) repealed, and words in square brackets in para (a) inserted, by SI 2003/1626, reg 42(2), as from 19 July 2003, except in relation to proceedings commenced before that date (see **[2938]**).

Sub-ss (4A), (4C), (4D), (5A): inserted, together with sub-s (4B), by the Race Relations (Amendment) Act 2000, ss 5(1), 9(1), Sch 2, para 7.

Sub-s (4B): inserted as noted above; for the words in italics there are substituted the words "any service offence within the meaning of the Armed Forces Act 2006" by the Armed Forces Act 2006, s 378(1), Sch 16, para 79, as from a day to be appointed.

Sub-s (5): words in square brackets substituted, and words omitted repealed, by the Race Relations (Amendment) Act 2000, s 9, Sch 2, para 6, Sch 3;

Sub-s (7): added by the Race Relations (Amendment) Act 2000, s 6(1).

Conciliation: for the powers of the Commission for Equality and Human Rights to make arrangements for the provision of conciliation services for disputes in respect of which proceedings have been, or could be, brought under this section, see the Equality Act 2006, s 27 at **[1670]**.

Transfer of functions: functions of the Secretary of State, so far as exercisable in relation to Wales, are transferred to the National Assembly for Wales by the National Assembly for Wales (Transfer of Functions) Order 1999, SI 1999/672, art 2, Sch 1. Functions under sub-s (5) are transferred, in so far as they are exercisable in or as regards Scotland, to the Scottish Ministers, by the Scotland Act 1998 (Transfer of Functions to the Scottish Ministers etc) Order 1999, SI 1999/1750, art 2, Sch 1.

[57ZA Burden of proof: County and Sheriff Courts

(1) This section applies where a claim is brought under section 57 and the claim is that the respondent—

(a) has committed an act of discrimination, on grounds of race or ethnic or national origins, which is unlawful by virtue of any provision referred to in section 1(1B)(b) to (d), or Part IV in its application to those provisions, or

(b) has committed an act of harassment.

(2) Where, on the hearing of the claim, the claimant proves facts from which the court could, apart from this section, conclude in the absence of an adequate explanation that the respondent—

(a) has committed such an act of discrimination or harassment against the claimant, or

(b) is by virtue of section 32 or 33 to be treated as having committed such an act of discrimination or harassment against the claimant,

the court shall uphold the claim unless the respondent proves that he did not commit or, as the case may be, is not to be treated as having committed, that act.]

[277]

NOTES

Commencement: 19 July 2003.

Inserted by the Race Relations Act 1976 (Amendment) Regulations 2003, SI 2003/1626, reg 43, as from 19 July 2003.

Note: by virtue of SI 2003/1626, reg 2(2), this section applies to proceedings commenced before 19 July 2003, as well as proceedings instituted on or after that date, but does not affect any case in which proceedings were determined before that date (see **[2938]**).

[57A Claims under section 19B in immigration cases

(1) No proceedings may be brought by a claimant under section 57(1) in respect of an immigration claim if—

(a) the act to which the claim relates was done in the taking by an immigration authority of a relevant decision and the question whether that act was unlawful by virtue of section 19B has been or could be raised in proceedings on an appeal which is pending, or could be brought, under the 1997 Act or [Part 5 of the 2002 Act]; or

(b) it has been decided in relevant immigration proceedings that that act was not unlawful by virtue of that section.

(2) For the purposes of this section an immigration claim is a claim that a person—

(a) has committed a relevant act of discrimination against the claimant which is unlawful by virtue of section 19B; or

(b) is by virtue of section 32 or 33 to be treated as having committed such an act of discrimination against the claimant.

(3) Where it has been decided in relevant immigration proceedings that an act to which an immigration claim relates was unlawful by virtue of section 19B, any court hearing that claim under section 57 shall treat that act as an act which is unlawful by virtue of section 19B for the purposes of the proceedings before it.

(4) No relevant decision of an immigration authority involving an act to which an immigration claim relates and no relevant decision of an immigration appellate body in relation to such a decision shall be subject to challenge or otherwise affected by virtue of a decision of a court hearing the immigration claim under section 57.

(5) In this section—

["the Immigration Acts" has the meaning given by section 158 of the 2002 Act;]

"immigration appellate body" means [the Asylum and Immigration Tribunal,] the Special Immigration Appeals Commission, the Court of Appeal, the Court of Session or the *House of Lords*;

["immigration authority" means the Secretary of State, an immigration officer or a person responsible for the grant or refusal of entry clearance (within the meaning of section 33(1) of the Immigration Act 1971 (c 77));]

"immigration claim" has the meaning given by subsection (2) above;

"pending" has the same meaning as in the 1997 Act or, as the case may be, [Part 5 of the 2002 Act];

"relevant act of discrimination" means an act of discrimination done by an immigration authority in taking any relevant decision;

"relevant decision" means—

(a) in relation to an immigration authority, any decision under the Immigration Acts relating to the entitlement of the claimant to enter or remain in the United Kingdom; and

(b) in relation to an immigration appellate body, any decision on an appeal under the 1997 Act or [Part 5 of the 2002 Act] in relation to a decision falling within paragraph (a);

"relevant immigration proceedings" means proceedings on an appeal under the 1997 Act or [Part 5 of the 2002 Act];

"the 1997 Act" means the Special Immigration Appeals Commission Act 1997;

["the 2002 Act" means the Nationality, Immigration and Asylum Act 2002;]

and, for the purposes of subsection (1)(a), any power to grant leave to appeal out of time shall be disregarded.]

[278]–[285]

NOTES

Inserted by the Race Relations (Amendment) Act 2000, s 6(2).

Sub-s (1): words in square brackets substituted by the Nationality, Immigration and Asylum Act 2002, s 114(3), Sch 7, para 12, except in relation to events which took place before 1 April 2003.

Sub-s (5): words in square brackets in definition "immigration appellate body" substituted by the Immigration, Asylum and Nationality Act 2006, s 14, Sch 1, para 12, as from 31 August 2006; for the words in italics in that definition there are substituted the words "Supreme Court" by the Constitutional Reform Act 2005, s 40, Sch 9, Pt 1, para 28, as from a day to be appointed; other words in square brackets substituted by the Nationality, Immigration and Asylum Act 2002, s 114(3), Sch 7, para 12, except in relation to events which took place before 1 April 2003.

58–64 (*Repealed by the Equality Act 2006, ss 40, 91, Sch 3, paras, 21, 27, Sch 4, as from 1 October 2007. For savings see the Equality Act 2006 (Commencement No 3 and Savings) Order 2007, SI 2007/2603, art 3 at* **[3473R]**. *For transitional provisions relating to the discharge by the Commission for Equality and Human Rights of the former functions of the CRE, see the Equality Act 2006 (Dissolution of Commissions and Consequential and Transitional Provisions) Order 2007, SI 2007/2602, art 5 at* **[3473O]**).)

Help for persons suffering discrimination

65 Help for aggrieved persons in obtaining information etc

(1) With a view to helping a person ("the person aggrieved") who considers he may have been discriminated against [or subjected to harassment] in contravention of this Act to decide whether to institute proceedings and, if he does so, to formulate and present his case in the most effective manner, the [Minister] shall by order prescribe—

(a) forms by which the person aggrieved may question the respondent on his reasons for doing any relevant act, or on any other matter which is or may be relevant; and

(b) forms by which the respondent may if he so wishes reply to any questions.

(2) Where the person aggrieved questions the respondent (whether in accordance with an order under subsection (1) or not)—

(a) the question, and any reply by the respondent (whether in accordance with such an order or not) shall, subject to the following provisions of this section, be admissible as evidence in the proceedings;

(b) if it appears to the court or tribunal that the respondent deliberately, and without reasonable excuse, omitted to reply within a reasonable period [or, where the question relates to discrimination on grounds of race or ethnic or national origins, or to harassment, the period of eight weeks beginning with the day on which the question was served on him] or that his reply is evasive or equivocal, the court or tribunal may draw any inference from that fact that it considers it just and equitable to draw, including an inference that he committed an unlawful act.

(3) The [Minister] may by order—

(a) prescribe the period within which questions must be duly served in order to be admissible under subsection (2)(a); and

(b) prescribe the manner in which a question, and any reply by the respondent, may be duly served.

(4) Rules may enable the court entertaining a claim under section 57 to determine, before the date fixed for the hearing of the claim, whether a question or reply is admissible under this section or not.

[(4A) In section 19B proceedings, subsection (2)(b) does not apply in relation to a failure to reply, or a particular reply, if the conditions specified in subsection (4B) are satisfied.

(4B) Those conditions are that—

(a) at the time of doing any relevant act, the respondent was carrying out public investigator functions or was a public prosecutor; and

(b) he reasonably believes that a reply or (as the case may be) a different reply would be likely to prejudice any criminal investigation, any decision to institute criminal proceedings or any criminal proceedings or would reveal the reasons behind a decision not to institute, or a decision not to continue, criminal proceedings.

(4C) For the purposes of subsections (4A) and (4B)—

"public investigator functions" has the same meaning as in section 57;

"section 19B proceedings" means proceedings in respect of a claim under section 57 which has arisen by virtue of section 19B.]

(5) This section is without prejudice to any other enactment or rule of law regulating interlocutory and preliminary matters in proceedings before a county court, sheriff court or [employment tribunal], and has effect subject to any enactment or rule of law regulating the admissibility of evidence in such proceedings.

(6) In this section "respondent" includes a prospective respondent and "rules"—

(a) in relation to county court proceedings, means county court rules;

(b) in relation to sheriff court proceedings, means sheriff court rules.

[(7) This section does not apply in relation to any proceedings under—

(a) the Special Immigration Appeals Commission Act 1997; or

(b) [Part 5 of the Nationality, Immigration and Asylum Act 2002].]

[286]–[287]

NOTES

Sub-s (1): words in first pair of square brackets inserted by the Race Relations Act 1976 (Amendment) Regulations 2003, SI 2003/1626, reg 47(a), as from 19 July 2003; word in second pair of square brackets substituted by the Transfer of Functions (Equality) Order 2007, SI 2007/2914, art 8, Schedule, para 10(b), as from 12 October 2007.

Sub-s (2): words in square brackets in para (b) inserted by SI 2003/1626, reg 47(b), as from 19 July 2003, except in relation to a question served on a respondent before that date.

Sub-s (3): word in square brackets substituted SI 2007/2914, art 8, Schedule, para 10(b), as from 12 October 2007.

Sub-ss (4A)–(4C): inserted by the Race Relations (Amendment) Act 2000, s 5(2).

Sub-s (5): words in square brackets substituted by the Employment Rights (Dispute Resolution) Act 1998, s 1(2)(a).

Sub-s (7): added by the Race Relations (Amendment) Act 2000, s 9(1), Sch 2, para 10; words in square brackets in para (b) substituted by the Nationality, Immigration and Asylum Act 2002, s 114(3), Sch 7, para 14, as from 1 April 2003, except in relation to events which took place before that date.

Orders: the Race Relations (Questions and Replies) Order 1977, SI 1977/842 at **[2057]**.

66 *(Repealed by the Equality Act 2006, ss 40, 91, Sch 3, paras, 21, 28, Sch 4, as from 1 October 2007.)*

Sheriff courts and designated county courts

67 Sheriff courts and designated county courts

(1) For the purposes of this Act a "designated" county court is one designated for the time being for those purposes by an order made by the Lord Chancellor [with the concurrence of the Lord Chief Justice].

(2) An order under subsection (1) designating any county court for the purposes of this Act shall assign to that court as its district for those purposes any county court district or two or more county court districts.

(3) A designated county court or a sheriff court shall have jurisdiction to entertain proceedings under this Act with respect to an act done on a ship, aircraft or hovercraft outside its district, including such an act done outside Great Britain.

[(3A) A designated county court or a sheriff court shall have jurisdiction to entertain proceedings under this Act with respect to an act done outside the United Kingdom where section 19B applies in relation to such an act by virtue of section 27(1A).]

(4) In any proceedings under this Act in a designated county court or a sheriff court the judge or sheriff shall, unless with the consent of the parties he sits without assessors, be assisted by two assessors appointed from a list of persons prepared and maintained by the [Minister], being persons appearing to the [Minister] to have special knowledge and experience of problems connected with relations between persons of different racial groups.

(5) The remuneration of assessors appointed under subsection (4) shall be at such rate as may, with the approval of the Minister for the Civil Service, be determined by the Lord Chancellor (for proceedings in England and Wales) or the Lord President of the Court of Session (for proceedings in Scotland).

(6) Without prejudice to section 74(3), an order for the discontinuance of the jurisdiction of any county court under this Act, whether wholly or within a part of the district assigned to it for the purposes of this Act, may include provision with respect to any proceedings under this Act commenced in that court before the order comes into operation.

[(6) The Lord Chief Justice may nominate a judicial office holder (as defined in section 109(4) of the Constitutional Reform Act 2005) to exercise his functions under this section.]

[288]

NOTES

Sub-s (1): words in square brackets added by the Constitutional Reform Act 2005, s 15, Sch 4, Pt 1, para 87(1), (2), as from 3 April 2006.

Sub-s (3A): inserted by the Race Relations (Amendment) Act 2000, s 9(1), Sch 2, para 12.

Sub-s (4): words in square brackets substituted by the Transfer of Functions (Equality) Order 2007, SI 2007/2914, art 8, Schedule, para 10(c), as from 12 October 2007.

Second sub-s (6): added by the Constitutional Reform Act 2005, s 15, Sch 4, Pt 1, para 87(1), (3), as from 3 April 2006.

Orders: the Civil Courts Order 1983, SI 1983/713.

[67A National security: procedure

(1) Rules may make provision for enabling a court in which relevant proceedings have been brought, where it considers it expedient in the interests of national security—

(a) to exclude from all or part of the proceedings—
  (i) the claimant;
  (ii) the claimant's representatives; or
  (iii) the assessors (if any) appointed by virtue of section 67(4);

(b) to permit a claimant or representative who has been excluded to make a statement to the court before the commencement of the proceedings, or the part of the proceedings, from which he is excluded;

(c) to take steps to keep secret all or part of the reasons for its decision in the proceedings.

(2) The Attorney General or, in Scotland, the Advocate General for Scotland, may appoint a person to represent the interests of a claimant in, or in any part of, any proceedings from which [the claimant or his representatives] are excluded by virtue of subsection (1).

(3) A person appointed under subsection (2)—

(a) if appointed for the purposes of proceedings in England and Wales, must *have a general qualification (within the meaning of section 71 of the Courts and Legal Services Act 1990); and*

(b) if appointed for the purposes of proceedings in Scotland, must be—

(i) an advocate; or

[(ii) qualified to practise as a solicitor in Scotland.]

(4) A person appointed under subsection (2) shall not be responsible to the person whose interests he is appointed to represent.

(5) In this section—

"relevant proceedings" means proceedings brought under this Act—

(a) in England and Wales, in a designated county court; or

(b) in Scotland, in a sheriff court; and

"rules" has the same meaning as in section 65.]

[288A]

NOTES

Inserted by the Race Relations (Amendment) Act 2000, s 8.

Sub-s (2): words in square brackets substituted by the Equality Act 2006, s 90(a), as from 18 April 2006.

Sub-s (3): for the words in italics in para (a) there are substituted the words "be a person who, for the purposes of the Legal Services Act 2007, is an authorised person in relation to an activity which constitutes the exercise of a right of audience or the conduct of litigation (within the meaning of that Act), and" by the Legal Services Act 2007, s 208(1), Sch 21, paras 36, 37, as from a day to be appointed; sub-para (b)(ii) substituted by the Equality Act 2006, s 90(b), as from 18 April 2006.

Period within which proceedings to be brought

68 Period within which proceedings to be brought

(1) An [employment tribunal] shall not consider a complaint under section 54 unless it is presented to the tribunal before the end of[—

(a) the period of three months beginning when the act complained of was done; or

(b) in a case to which section 75(8) applies, the period of six months so beginning.]

(2) [Subject to subsection (2A)] a county court or a sheriff court shall not consider a claim under section 57 unless proceedings in respect of the claim are instituted before the end of—

(a) the period of six months beginning when the act complained of was done; …

(b) …

[(2A) In relation to an immigration claim within the meaning of section 57A, the period of six months mentioned in subsection (2)(a) begins on the expiry of the period during which, by virtue of section 57A(1)(a), no proceedings may be brought under section 57(1) in respect of the claim.]

(3) …

[(3A) Where in England and Wales—

(a) proceedings or prospective proceedings by way of a claim under section 57 relate to the act or omission of a qualifying institution,

(b) the dispute concerned is referred as a complaint under the student complaints scheme before the end of the period of six months mentioned in subsection (2), and

(c) …

the period allowed by subsection (2) for instituting proceedings in respect of the claim shall be extended by [three months].

(3B) In subsection (3A)—

"qualifying institution" has the meaning given by section 11 of the Higher Education Act 2004;

"the student complaints scheme" means a scheme for the review of qualifying complaints, as defined by section 12 of that Act, that is provided by the designated operator, as defined by section 13(5)(b) of that Act.]

[(3C) The period allowed by subsection (2)(a) shall be extended by three months in the case of a dispute which is referred for conciliation in pursuance of arrangements under section 27 of the Equality Act 2006 (unless it is extended under subsection (3A)).]

(4), (5) …

(6) A court or tribunal may nevertheless consider any such [complaint or claim] which is out of time if, in all the circumstances of the case, it considers that it is just and equitable to do so.

(7) For the purposes of this section—

(a) when the inclusion of any term in a contract renders the making of the contract an unlawful act, that act shall be treated as extending throughout the duration of the contract; and

(b) any act extending over a period shall be treated as done at the end of that period; and

(c) a deliberate omission shall be treated as done when the person in question decided upon it;

and in the absence of evidence establishing the contrary a person shall be taken for the purposes of this section to decide upon an omission when he does an act inconsistent with doing the omitted act or, if he has done no such inconsistent act, when the period expires within which he might reasonably have been expected to do the omitted act if it was to be done.

[289]

NOTES

Sub-s (1): words in first pair of square brackets substituted by the Employment Rights (Dispute Resolution) Act 1998, s 1(2)(a); words in second pair of square brackets substituted by the Armed Forces Act 1996, s 23(4).

Sub-s (2): words in square brackets inserted, and para (b) and word immediately preceding it repealed, by the Race Relations (Amendment) Act 2000, s 9, Sch 2, para 13, Sch 3.

Sub-s (2A): inserted by the Race Relations (Amendment) Act 2000, s 9(1), Sch 2, para 14.

Sub-s (3): repealed by the Equality Act 2006, ss 40, 91, Sch 3, paras, 21, 29(1), (2), Sch 4, as from 1 October 2007.

Sub-s (3A): inserted, together with sub-s (3B), by the Higher Education Act 2004, s 19(2), as from 1 November 2004; para (c) repealed, and words in square brackets substituted, by the Equality Act 2006, ss 40, 91, Sch 3, paras, 21, 29(1), (3), Sch 4, as from 1 October 2007.

Sub-s (3B): inserted as noted above.

Sub-s (3C): inserted by the Equality Act 2006, s 40, Sch 3, paras, 21, 29(1), (4), as from 1 October 2007.

Sub-ss (4), (5): repealed by the Equality Act 2006, ss 40, 91, Sch 3, paras, 21, 29(1), (5), Sch 4, as from 1 October 2007.

Sub-s (6): words in square brackets substituted by the Equality Act 2006, s 40, Sch 3, paras, 21, 29(1), (6), as from 1 October 2007.

For the circumstances in which the normal time limit for presenting a complaint under s 54 is extended for a period of three months, see the Employment Act 2002 (Dispute Resolution) Regulations 2004, SI 2004/752, regs 15 and 18 at **[3096]** and **[3098]**.

Evidence

69 Evidence

(1) Any finding by a court under section 19 or 20 of the Race Relations Act 1968, or by a court or [employment tribunal] under this Act, in respect of any act shall, if it has become final, be treated as conclusive in any proceedings under this Act.

(2) In any proceedings under this Act [or any enactment mentioned in section 19D(5)] a certificate signed by or on behalf of a Minister of the Crown and certifying—

(a) that any arrangements or conditions specified in the certificate were made, approved or imposed by a Minister of the Crown and were in operation at a time or throughout a period so specified; …

(b) …

shall be conclusive evidence of the matters certified.

[(2A) …]

(3) A document purporting to be a certificate such as is mentioned in subsection (2) shall be received in evidence and, unless the contrary is proved, shall be deemed to be such a certificate.

[290]

NOTES

Sub-s (1): words in square brackets substituted by the Employment Rights (Dispute Resolution) Act 1998, s 1(2)(a).

Sub-s (2): words in square brackets inserted, and para (b) and word immediately preceding it repealed, by the Race Relations (Amendment) Act 2000, ss 7(2), 9, Sch 2, para 15, Sch 3.

Sub-s (2A): inserted by the Employment Relations Act 1999, s 41, Sch 8, para 6; repealed prior to coming into effect by the Race Relations (Amendment) Act 2000, s 9(2), Sch 3.

Transfer of functions: as to the exercise of the functions of a Minister of the Crown under this section concurrently with the National Assembly for Wales, see the National Assembly for Wales (Transfer of Functions) Order 1999, SI 1999/672, art 2, Sch 1.

Race Relations Act 1968: repealed by s 79(5) of, and Sch 5 to, this Act.

70 ((*Pt IX*) *Repealed by the Public Order Act 1986, s 40(3), Sch 3.*)

PART X
SUPPLEMENTAL

[71 Specified authorities: general statutory duty

(1) Every body or other person specified in Schedule 1A or of a description falling within that Schedule shall, in carrying out its functions, have due regard to the need—

(a) to eliminate unlawful racial discrimination; and

(b) to promote equality of opportunity and good relations between persons of different racial groups.

(2) The [Minister] may by order impose, on such persons falling within Schedule 1A as he considers appropriate, such duties as he considers appropriate for the purpose of ensuring the better performance by those persons of their duties under subsection (1).

(3) An order under subsection (2)—

(a) may be made in relation to a particular person falling within Schedule 1A, any description of persons falling within that Schedule or every person falling within that Schedule;

(b) may make different provision for different purposes.

(4) Before making an order under subsection (2), the [Minister] shall consult the Commission.

(5) The [Minister] may by order amend Schedule 1A; but no such order may extend the application of this section unless the [Minister] considers that the extension relates to a person who exercises functions of a public nature.

(6) An order under subsection (2) or (5) may contain such incidental, supplementary or consequential provision as the [Minister] considers appropriate (including provision amending or repealing provision made by or under this Act or any other enactment).

(7) This section is subject to section 71A and 71B and is without prejudice to the obligation of any person to comply with any other provision of this Act.]

[291]

NOTES

Substituted, together with ss 71A–71E, for original s 71, by the Race Relations (Amendment) Act 2000, s 2(1).

Sub-ss (2), (4)–(6): words in square brackets substituted by the Transfer of Functions (Equality) Order 2007, SI 2007/2914, art 8, Schedule, para 10(d), as from 12 October 2007.

Assessment and compliance: for the powers of the Commission for Equality and Human Rights to assess the extent to which, or the manner in which, a person has complied with a duty under this section and, where it thinks that a person has failed to comply with such duty, to give the person a notice requiring him to: (i) comply with the duty, and (ii) to give the Commission (within the period of 28 days beginning with the date on which he receives the notice) written information of steps taken, or proposed, for the purpose of complying with the duty, see the Equality Act 2006, ss 31, 32 at **[1674]**, **[1675]**.

Orders: the Race Relations Act 1976 (General Statutory Duty) Order 2001, SI 2001/3457; the Race Relations (Statutory Duties) Order 2001, SI 2001/3458 at **[2706]**; the Race Relations Act 1976 (Statutory Duties) (Scotland) Order 2002, SSI 2002/62 at **[2718]**; the Race Relations Act 1976 (Statutory Duties)

Order 2003, SI 2003/3006 at **[3037]**; the Race Relations Act 1976 (General Statutory Duty) Order 2003, SI 2003/3007; the Race Relations Act 1976 (Statutory Duties) Order 2004, SI 2004/3125; the Race Relations Act 1976 (General Statutory Duty) Order 2004, SI 2004/3127; the Race Relations Act 1976 (General Statutory Duty) Order 2006, SI 2006/2470; the Race Relations Act 1976 (Statutory Duties) Order 2006, SI 2006/2471 at **[3465]**.

[71A General statutory duty: special cases

(1) In relation to the carrying out of immigration and nationality functions… , section 71(1)(b) has effect with the omission of the words "equality of opportunity and".

[(1A) In subsection (1) "immigration and nationality functions" means functions exercisable by virtue of—

- (a) the Immigration Acts (within the meaning of section 158 of the Nationality, Immigration and Asylum Act 2002) excluding sections 28A to 28K of the Immigration Act 1971 so far as they relate to offences under Part III of that Act;
- (b) the British Nationality Act 1981;
- (c) the British Nationality (Falkland Islands) Act 1983 (c 6);
- (d) the British Nationality (Hong Kong) Act 1990 (c 34);
- (e) the Hong Kong (War Wives and Widows) Act 1996 (c 41);
- (f) the British Nationality (Hong Kong) Act 1997 (c 20);
- (g) the Special Immigration Appeals Commission Act 1997 (c 68);
- (h) provision made under section 2(2) of the European Communities Act 1972 (c 68) which relates to the subject matter of an enactment within any of paragraphs (a) to (g); or
- (i) any provision of Community law which relates to the subject matter of an enactment within any of those paragraphs.]

(2) Where an entry in Schedule 1A is limited to a person in a particular capacity, section 71(1) does not apply to that person in any other capacity.

(3) Where an entry in Schedule 1A is limited to particular functions of a person, section 71(1) does not apply to that person in relation to any other functions.]

[292]

NOTES

Substituted as noted to s 71 at **[291]**.

Sub-s (1): words omitted repealed by the Nationality, Immigration and Asylum Act 2002, ss 6(1), (5)(a), 161, Sch 9.

Sub-s (1A): inserted by the Nationality, Immigration and Asylum Act 2002, s 6(1), (5)(b).

[71B General statutory duty: Scotland and Wales

[(1) For the purposes of the Scotland Act 1998, subsections (2) to (4) of section 71 (and sections 71(6) and 74 so far as they apply to the power conferred by subsection (2) of section 71) shall be taken to be pre-commencement enactments within the meaning of that Act.

(2) Before making an order under section 71(2) in relation to functions exercisable in relation to Wales by a person who is not a Welsh public authority, the [Minister] shall consult the [Welsh Ministers].

(3) The [Minister] shall not make an order under section 71(2) in relation to functions of a Welsh public authority except with the consent of the [Welsh Ministers].

(4) In this section "Welsh public authority" means any person whose functions are exercisable only in relation to Wales and [includes—

- (a) the National Assembly for Wales Commission;
- (b) the Welsh Ministers, the First Minister for Wales and the Counsel General to the Welsh Assembly Government].]

[293]–[296]

NOTES

Substituted as noted to s 71 at **[291]**.

Sub-ss (2), (3): words in first pair of square brackets substituted by the Transfer of Functions (Equality) Order 2007, SI 2007/2914, art 8, Schedule, para 10(e), as from 12 October 2007; words in second pair of square brackets substituted by the Government of Wales Act 2006 (Consequential Modifications and Transitional Provisions) Order 2007, SI 2007/1388, art 3, Sch 1, paras 10, 12(1)–(3), as from 25 May 2007.

Sub-s (4): words in square brackets substituted by SI 2007/1388, art 3, Sch 1, paras 10, 12(1), (4), as from 25 May 2007.

71C–71E (*Substituted as noted to s 71 at* **[291]**; *repealed by the Equality Act 2006, ss 40, 91, Sch 3, paras, 21, 30, Sch 4, as from 1 October 2007.*)

72 Validity and revision of contracts

(1) A term of a contract is void where—

(a) its inclusion renders the making of the contract unlawful by virtue of this Act; or

(b) it is included in furtherance of an act rendered unlawful by this Act; or

(c) it provides for the doing of an act which would be rendered unlawful by this Act.

(2) Subsection (1) does not apply to a term the inclusion of which constitutes, or is in furtherance of, or provides for, unlawful discrimination against [or harassment of,] a party to the contract, but the term shall be unenforceable against that party.

(3) A term in a contract which purports to exclude or limit any provision of this Act is unenforceable by any person in whose favour the term would operate apart from this subsection.

(4) Subsection (3) does not apply—

(a) to a contract settling a complaint to which section 54(1) applies where the contract is made with the assistance of a conciliation officer; or

[(aa) to a contract settling a complaint to which section 54(1) applies if the conditions regulating compromise contracts under this Act are satisfied in relation to the contract;]

(b) to a contract settling a claim to which section 57 applies.

[(4A) The conditions regulating compromise contracts under this Act are that—

(a) the contract must be in writing;

(b) the contract must relate to the particular complaint;

(c) the complainant must have received [advice from a relevant independent adviser] as to the terms and effect of the proposed contract and in particular its effect on his ability to pursue his complaint before an [employment tribunal];

(d) there must be in force, when the adviser gives the advice, a [contract of insurance, or an indemnity provided for members of a profession or professional body,] covering the risk of a claim by the complainant in respect of loss arising in consequence of the advice;

(e) the contract must identify the adviser; and

(f) the contract must state that the conditions regulating compromise contracts under this Act are satisfied.

[(4B) A person is a relevant independent adviser for the purposes of subsection (4A)(c)—

(a) if he is a qualified lawyer,

(b) if he is an officer, official, employee or member of an independent trade union who has been certified in writing by the trade union as competent to give advice and as authorised to do so on behalf of the trade union,

(c) if he works at an advice centre (whether as an employee or a volunteer) and has been certified in writing by the centre as competent to give advice and as authorised to do so on behalf of the centre, or

(d) if he is a person of a description specified in an order made by the [Minister].

(4BA) But a person is not a relevant independent adviser for the purposes of subsection (4A)(c) in relation to the complainant—

(a) if he is, is employed by or is acting in the matter for the other party or a person who is connected with the other party,

(b) in the case of a person within subsection (4B)(b) or (c), if the trade union or advice centre is the other party or a person who is connected with the other party,

(c) in the case of a person within subsection (4B)(c), if the complainant makes a payment for the advice received from him, or

(d) in the case of a person of a description specified in an order under subsection (4B)(d), if any condition specified in the order in relation to the giving of advice by persons of that description is not satisfied.

(4BB) In subsection (4B)(a) "qualified lawyer" means—
(a) as respects England and Wales, *a barrister (whether in practice as such or employed to give legal advice), a solicitor who holds a practising certificate, or a person other than a barrister or solicitor who is an authorised advocate or authorised litigator (within the meaning of the Courts and Legal Services Act 1990), and*
(b) as respects Scotland, an advocate (whether in practice as such or employed to give legal advice), or a solicitor who holds a practising certificate.

(4BC) In subsection (4B)(b) "independent trade union" has the same meaning as in the Trade Union and Labour Relations (Consolidation) Act 1992.

(4C) For the purposes of subsection (4BA) any two persons are to be treated as connected—
(a) if one is a company of which the other (directly or indirectly) has control, or
(b) if both are companies of which a third person (directly or indirectly) has control.]]

[(4D) An agreement under which the parties agree to submit a dispute to arbitration—
(a) shall be regarded for the purposes of subsection (4)(a) and (aa) as being a contract settling a complaint if—
(i) the dispute is covered by a scheme having effect by virtue of an order under section 212A of the Trade Union and Labour Relations (Consolidation) Act 1992, and
(ii) the agreement is to submit it to arbitration in accordance with the scheme, but
(b) shall be regarded for those purposes as neither being nor including such a contract in any other case.]

(5) On the application of any person interested in a contract to which subsection (2) applies, a designated county court or a sheriff court may make such order as it thinks just for removing or modifying any term made unenforceable by that subsection; but such an order shall not be made unless all persons affected have been given notice of the application (except where under rules of court notice may be dispensed with) and have been afforded an opportunity to make representations to the court.

(6) An order under subsection (5) may include provision as respects any period before the making of the order.

[297]

NOTES

Sub-s (2): words in square brackets inserted by the Race Relations Act 1976 (Amendment) Regulations 2003, SI 2003/1626, reg 48, as from 19 July 2003.

Sub-s (4): para (aa) inserted by the Trade Union Reform and Employment Rights Act 1993, s 39(2), Sch 6, para 2(a).

Sub-s (4A): inserted by the Trade Union Reform and Employment Rights Act 1993, s 39(2), Sch 6, para 2(b); words in square brackets substituted by the Employment Rights (Dispute Resolution) Act 1998, ss 1(2)(a), 9(1), (2)(b), 10(1), (2)(b).

Sub-ss (4B), (4BA), (4BB), (4BC), (4C): substituted, for original sub-ss (4B), (4C) (as inserted by the Trade Union Reform and Employment Rights Act 1993, s 39(2), Sch 6, para 2(b)), by the Employment Rights (Dispute Resolution) Act 1998, s 15, Sch 1, para 3.

Word in square brackets in sub-s (4B)(d) substituted by the Transfer of Functions (Equality) Order 2007, SI 2007/2914, art 8, Schedule, para 10(f), as from 12 October 2007.

For the words in italics in sub-s (4BB)(a) there are substituted the words "a person who, for the purposes of the Legal Services Act 2007, is an authorised person in relation to an activity which constitutes the exercise of a right of audience or the conduct of litigation (within the meaning of that Act), and" by the Legal Services Act 2007, s 208(1), Sch 21, paras 36, 38, as from a day to be appointed.

Sub-s (4D): inserted by the Employment Rights (Dispute Resolution) Act 1998, s 8(2).

Orders: the Compromise Agreements (Description of Person) Order 2004, SI 2004/754 at **[3138]**.

[72A Collective agreements and rules of undertakings

(1) This section applies to—
(a) any term of a collective agreement, including an agreement which was not intended, or is presumed not to have been intended, to be a legally enforceable contract;
(b) any rule made by an employer for application to all or any of the persons who are employed by him or who apply to be, or are, considered by him for employment;

(c) any rule made by an organisation to which section 11 (trade organisations) applies, or by a body to which section 12 (qualifying bodies) applies, for application to—
   (i) all or any of its members or prospective members; or
   (ii) all or any of the persons on whom it has conferred authorisations or qualifications or who are seeking the authorisations or qualifications which it has power to confer.

(2) Any term or rule to which this section applies is void where—
(a) the making of the collective agreement is, by reason of the inclusion of the term, unlawful on grounds of race or ethnic or national origins, by virtue of a provision referred to in section 1(1B);
(b) the term or rule is included or made in furtherance of an act which is unlawful on such grounds by virtue of such a provision; or
(c) the term or rule provides for the doing of such an act.

(3) Subsection (2) applies whether the agreement was entered into, or the rule made, before, on or after 19th July 2003; but in the case of an agreement entered into, or a rule made, before that date, that subsection does not apply in relation to any period before that date.

(4) In this section, and in section 72B, "collective agreement" means any agreement relating to one or more of the matters mentioned in section 178(2) of the Trade Union and Labour Relations (Consolidation) Act 1992 (meaning of trade dispute), being an agreement made by or on behalf of one or more employers or one or more organisations of employers or associations of such organisations with one or more organisations of workers or associations of such organisations.]

[298]

NOTES

Commencement: 19 July 2003.
Inserted, together with s 72B, by the Race Relations Act 1976 (Amendment) Regulations 2003, SI 2003/1626, reg 49, as from 19 July 2003.

[72B—(1) A person to whom this subsection applies may present a complaint to an employment tribunal that a term or rule is void by virtue of section 72A if he has reason to believe—
(a) that the term or rule may at some future time have effect in relation to him; and
(b) where he alleges that it is void by virtue of section 72A(2)(c), that—
   (i) an act for the doing of which it provides may at some such time be done in relation to him, and
   (ii) the act would be rendered unlawful on grounds of race or ethnic or national origins by a provision referred to in section 1(1B) if done in relation to him in present circumstances.

(2) In the case of a complaint about—
(a) a term of a collective agreement made by or on behalf of—
   (i) an employer;
   (ii) an organisation of employers of which an employer is a member; or
   (iii) an association of such organisations of one of which an employer is a member; or
(b) a rule made by an employer, within the meaning of section 72A(1)(b);

subsection (1) applies to any person who is, or is genuinely and actively seeking to become, one of his employees.

(3) In the case of a complaint about a rule made by an organisation or body to which section 72A(1)(c) applies, subsection (1) applies to any person—
(a) who is, or is genuinely and actively seeking to become, a member of the organisation or body;
(b) on whom the organisation or body has conferred an authorisation or qualification; or
(c) who is genuinely and actively seeking an authorisation or qualification which the organisation or body has power to confer.

(4) When an employment tribunal finds that a complaint presented to it under subsection (1) is well-founded the tribunal shall make an order declaring that the term or rule is void.

(5) An order under subsection (4) may include provision as respects any period before the making of the order (but after 19th July 2003).

(6) The avoidance by virtue of section 72 A(2) of any term or rule which provides for any person to be discriminated against shall be without prejudice to the following rights (except in so far as they enable any person to require another person to be treated less favourably than himself) namely—

(a) such of the rights of the person to be discriminated against, and

(b) such of the rights of any person who will be treated more favourably in direct or indirect consequence of the discrimination,

as are conferred by or in respect of a contract made or modified wholly or partly in pursuance of, or by reference to, that term or rule.]

[299]

NOTES

Commencement: 19 July 2003.

Inserted as noted to s 72A at **[298]**.

73 Power to amend certain provisions of Act

(1) The [Minister] may by an order the draft of which has been approved by each House of Parliament—

(a) amend or repeal section 9 (including that section as amended by a previous order under this subsection);

(b) amend Part II, III or IV so as to render lawful an act which, apart from the amendment, would be unlawful by reason of section 4(1) or (2), [19B,] 20(1), 21, 24 or 25;

(c) amend section 10(1) or 25(1)(a) so as to alter the number of partners or members specified in that provision.

(2) The [Minister] shall not lay before Parliament the draft of an order under subsection (1) unless he has consulted the Commission about the contents of the draft.

[300]

NOTES

Sub-s (1): word in first pair of square brackets substituted by the Transfer of Functions (Equality) Order 2007, SI 2007/2914, art 8, Schedule, para 10(g), as from 12 October 2007; number in square brackets in para (b) inserted by the Race Relations (Amendment) Act 2000, s 9(1), Sch 2, para 16.

Sub-s (2): word in square brackets substituted by SI 2007/2914, art 8, Schedule, para 10(g), as from 12 October 2007.

Orders: the Race Relations Act 1976 (Seamen Recruited Abroad) Order 2003, SI 2003/1651.

74 Orders and regulations

(1) Any power of a Minister of the Crown to make orders or regulations under the provisions of this Act … shall be exercisable by statutory instrument.

(2) An order made by a Minister of the Crown under the preceding provisions of this Act [(except section 73(1))], and any regulations made under section [56(5), (6) or] 75(5)(a) [or (9A)], shall be subject to annulment in pursuance of a resolution of either House of Parliament.

(3) An order under this Act may make different provision in relation to different cases or classes of case, may exclude certain cases or classes of case, and may contain transitional provisions and savings.

(4) Any power conferred by this Act to make orders includes power (exercisable in the like manner and subject to the like conditions) to vary or revoke any order so made.

(5) …

[301]

NOTES

Sub-s (1): words omitted repealed by the Equality Act 2006, ss 40, 91, Sch 3, paras, 21, 32(a), Sch 4, as from 1 October 2007.

Sub-s (2): words in first pair of square brackets substituted by the Equality Act 2006, s 40, Sch 3, paras, 21, 32(b), as from 1 October 2007; words in second pair of square brackets inserted by the Race Relations (Remedies) Act 1994, s 2(2); words in third pair of square brackets inserted by the Armed Forces Act 1996, s 23(5).

Sub-s (5): repealed the Equality Act 2006, ss 40, 91, Sch 3, paras, 21, 32(c), Sch 4, as from 1 October 2007.

75 Application to Crown etc

(1) This Act applies—

(a) to an act done by or for purposes of a Minister of the Crown or government department; or

(b) to an act done on behalf of the Crown by a statutory body, or a person holding a statutory office,

as it applies to an act done by a private person.

(2) Parts II and IV apply to—

(a) service for purposes of a Minister of the Crown or government department, other than service of a person holding a statutory office; or

(b) service on behalf of the Crown for purposes of a person holding a statutory office or purposes of a statutory body; or

(c) service in the armed forces,

as they apply to employment by a private person, and shall so apply as if references to a contract of employment included references to the terms of service.

[(2A) Subsections (1) and (2) do not apply in relation to the provisions mentioned in subsection (2B).

(2B) Sections 19B to 19F, sections 71 to 71E (including Schedule 1A) and section 76 bind the Crown; and the other provisions of this Act so far as they relate to those provisions shall be construed accordingly (including, in particular, references to employment in Part IV).]

(3) Subsections (1) [to (2B)] have effect subject to [sections 76A and 76B].

(4) Subsection (2) of section 8 and subsection (4) of section 27 shall have effect in relation to any ship, aircraft or hovercraft belonging to or possessed by Her Majesty in right of the Government of the United Kingdom as it has effect in relation to a ship, aircraft or hovercraft such as is mentioned in paragraph (a) or (b) of the subsection in question; and section 8(3) shall apply accordingly.

(5) Nothing in this Act shall—

(a) invalidate any rules (whether made before or after the passing of this Act) restricting employment in the service of the Crown or by any public body prescribed for the purposes of this subsection by regulations made by the Minister for the Civil Service to persons of particular birth, nationality, descent or residence; or

(b) render unlawful the publication, display or implementation of any such rules, or the publication of advertisements stating the gist of any such rules.

In this subsection "employment" includes service of any kind, and "public body" means a body of persons, whether corporate or unincorporate, carrying on a service or undertaking of a public nature.

(6) The provisions of Parts II to IV of the Crown Proceedings Act 1947 shall apply to proceedings against the Crown under this Act as they apply to proceedings in England and Wales which by virtue of section 23 of that Act are treated for the purposes of Part II of that Act as civil proceedings by or against the Crown …

(7) The provisions of Part V of the Crown Proceedings Act 1947 shall apply to proceedings against the Crown under this Act as they apply to proceedings in Scotland which by virtue of the said Part are treated as civil proceedings by or against the Crown …

(8) This subsection applies to any complaint by a person ("the complainant") that another person—

(a) has committed an act of discrimination against the complainant which is unlawful by virtue of section 4; or

(b) is by virtue of section 32 or 33 to be treated as having committed such an act of discrimination against the complainant,

if at the time when the act complained of was done the complainant was serving in the armed forces and the discrimination in question relates to his service in those forces.

[(9) No complaint to which subsection (8) applies shall be presented to an [employment tribunal] under section 54 unless–

(a) the complainant has made [a service complaint in respect of the act complained of]; and

(b) the Defence Council have made a determination with respect to the [service complaint].

(9A) Regulations may make provision enabling a complaint to which subsection (8) applies to be presented to an [employment tribunal] under section 54 in such circumstances as may be specified by the regulations, notwithstanding that subsection (9) would otherwise preclude the presentation of the complaint to an [employment tribunal].

(9B) Where a complaint is presented to an [employment tribunal] under section 54 by virtue of regulations under subsection (9A), [the service complaint procedures] may continue after the complaint is so presented.]

(10) In this section—

(a) "the armed forces" means any of the naval, military or air forces of the Crown … ;

[(aa) "regulations" means regulations made by the Secretary of State;

[(ac) "service complaint" means a complaint under section 334 of the Armed Forces Act 2006;

(ad) "the service complaint procedures" means the procedures prescribed by regulations under that section;]]

(b) "statutory body" means a body set up by or in pursuance of an enactment, and "statutory office" means an office so set up; and

(c) service "for purposes of" a Minister of the Crown or government department does not include service in any office in Schedule 2 (Ministerial offices) to the House of Commons Disqualification Act 1975 as for the time being in force.

[302]

NOTES

Sub-ss (2A), (2B): inserted by the Race Relations (Amendment) Act 2000, s 9(1), Sch 2, para 17.

Sub-s (3): words in square brackets substituted by the Race Relations (Amendment) Act 2000, s 9(1), Sch 2, para 18.

Sub-s (6): words omitted repealed by the Civil Procedure (Modification of Crown Proceedings Act 1947) Order 2005, SI 2005/2712, art 3, Sch 2, para 2, as from 1 October 2005.

Sub-s (9): substituted, together with sub-ss (9A), (9B), by the Armed Forces Act 1996, s 23(1), (2); words in first pair of square brackets substituted by the Employment Rights (Dispute Resolution) Act 1998, s 1(2)(a); other words in square brackets substituted by the Armed Forces Act 2006, s 378(1), Sch 16, para 80(1), (2), as from 1 January 2008.

Sub-s (9A): substituted as noted above; words in square brackets substituted by the Employment Rights (Dispute Resolution) Act 1998, s 1(2)(a).

Sub-s (9B): substituted as noted above; words in first pair of square brackets substituted by the Employment Rights (Dispute Resolution) Act 1998, s 1(2)(a); words in second pair of square brackets substituted by the Armed Forces Act 2006, s 378(1), Sch 16, para 80(1), (3), as from 1 January 2008.

Sub-s (10): words omitted from para (a) repealed by the Armed Forces Act 1981, s 28(2), Sch 5, Pt I; para (aa) and original para (ab) inserted by the Armed Forces Act 1996, s 23(1), (3); paras (ac), (ad) substituted, for para (ab) (as inserted as noted ante), by the Armed Forces Act 2006, s 378(1), Sch 16, para 80(1), (4), as from 1 January 2008.

Regulations: the Race Relations (Complaints to Employment Tribunals) (Armed Forces) Regulations 1997, SI 1997/2161 at **[2402]**. The current regulations prescribed for the purposes of sub-s (5) are the Race Relations (Prescribed Public Bodies) (No 2) Regulations 1994, SI 1994/1986, which revoke previous Regulations and prescribe the following public bodies for the purposes of sub-s (5)—

Bank of England
Board of Trustees of the Armouries
British Council
House of Commons
House of Lords
Metropolitan Police Office
National Army Museum
National Audit Office
Natural Environment Research Council
United Kingdom Atomic Energy Authority.

[75A Application to House of Commons Staff

(1) Parts II and IV apply to an act done by an employer of a relevant member of the House of Commons staff, and to service as such a member, as they apply to an act done by

and to service for the purposes of a Minister of the Crown or government department, and accordingly apply as if references to a contract of employment included references to the terms of service of such a member.

(2) In this section "relevant member of the House of Commons staff" has the same meaning as in [section 195 of the Employment Rights Act 1996]; and [subsections (6) to (12)] of that section (person to be treated as employer of House of Commons staff) apply, with any necessary modifications, for the purposes of Parts II and IV as they apply by virtue of this section.]

[303]

NOTES

Inserted by the Trade Union and Labour Relations (Consolidation) Act 1992, s 300(2), Sch 2, para 7.

Sub-s (2): words in square brackets substituted by the Employment Rights Act 1996, s 240, Sch 1, para 10(1), (2).

[75B Application to House of Lords Staff

(1) Parts II and IV apply in relation to employment as a relevant member of the House of Lords staff as they apply in relation to other employment.

(2) In this section "relevant member of the House of Lords staff" has the same meaning as in [section 194 of the Employment Rights Act 1996]; and [subsection (7)] of that section applies for the purposes of this section.]

[304]

NOTES

Inserted by the Trade Union Reform and Employment Rights Act 1993, s 49(1), Sch 7, para 10.

Sub-s (2): words in square brackets substituted by the Employment Rights Act 1996, s 240, Sch 1, para 10(1), (3).

76 Government appointments outside s 4

(1) [Subsection (2)] applies to any appointment by a Minister of the Crown or government department to an office or post where section 4 does not apply in relation to the appointment.

(2) In making the appointment, and in making the arrangements for determining who should be offered the office or post, the Minister of the Crown or government department shall not do an act which would be unlawful under section 4 if the Crown were the employer for the purposes of this Act.

[(3) Subsection (5) applies to—

(a) any recommendation made by a Minister of the Crown or government department in relation to an appointment to an office or post where section 4 does not apply in relation to the appointment; and

(b) any approval given by such a Minister or department in relation to any such appointment.

(4) Subsection (5) also applies to—

(a) any recommendation made by a Minister of the Crown or government department in relation to a conferment by the Crown of a dignity or honour; and

(b) any approval given by such a Minister or department in relation to any such conferment.

(5) In making the recommendation, or giving the approval, and in making the arrangements for determining who should be recommended or approved, the Minister of the Crown or government department shall not do an act which would be unlawful under section 4 if the recommendation or approval were an offer of employment and the Crown were the employer for the purposes of this Act.

(6) Subsections (3) to (5) do not apply in relation to the making of negative recommendations.

(7) Subsection (9) applies to—

(a) any negative recommendation made by a Minister of the Crown or government department, or any refusal to make a recommendation by such a Minister or department, in relation to an appointment to an office or post where section 4 does not apply in relation to the appointment; and

(b) any approval refused by such a Minister or department in relation to any such appointment.

(8) Subsection (9) also applies to—

(a) any negative recommendation made by a Minister of the Crown or government department, or any refusal to make a recommendation by such a Minister or department, in relation to a conferment by the Crown of a dignity or honour; and

(b) any approval refused by such a Minister or department in relation to any such conferment.

(9) In making a negative recommendation or in refusing to make a recommendation or give an approval, and in making the arrangements for determining whether to make such a recommendation or refusal, the Minister of the Crown or government department shall not do an act which would be unlawful under section 4 if the recommendation or refusal were a refusal to offer the person concerned employment and the Crown were the employer for the purposes of this Act.

(10) [Subsections (11) and (11B) apply] in relation to any appointment to an office or post where section 4 does not apply and—

(a) the appointment is made by a Minister of the Crown or government department; or

(b) the office or post is an office or post in relation to which a Minister of the Crown or government department has made a recommendation (other than a negative recommendation) or given an approval.

(11) A Minister of the Crown or government department shall not do an act in connection with—

(a) the terms of the appointment;

(b) access for the person appointed to opportunities for promotion, transfer or training, or to any other benefits, facilities or services; or

(c) the termination of the appointment, or subjecting the person appointed to any other detriment;

which would be unlawful under section 4 if the Crown were the employer for the purposes of this Act.

[(11A) In subsection (11)(c) reference to the termination of the appointment includes, where the act is committed on the grounds of race or ethnic or national origins, reference—

(a) to the termination of the appointment by the expiration of any period (including a period expiring by reference to an event or circumstance), not being a termination immediately after which the appointment is renewed on the same terms and conditions; and

(b) to the termination of the appointment by any act of the person appointed (including the giving of notice) in circumstances such that he is entitled to terminate the appointment by reason of the conduct of the Minister or the department, as the case may be.

(11B) It is unlawful for a Minister of the Crown or government department to subject to harassment a person who has been appointed, or who is seeking or being considered for, the appointment.]

(12) The High Court may, on an application for judicial review, make a declaration to the effect that a Minister of the Crown or government department has [contravened—

(a) subsection (5);

(b) subsection (9);

(c) in relation to an appointment falling within subsection (10)(b), subsection (11); or

(d) subsection (11B),

and may award damages in respect of the contravention].

(13) In Scotland, the Court of Session may, in a petition for judicial review, grant declarator to the like effect and may award damages in respect of the contravention.

[(14) The provision made by subsection (12) in respect of judicial review does not affect the ability, where an act on grounds of race or ethnic or national origins, or harassment, is alleged, to present a complaint to an employment tribunal under section 54A(1).]

(15) In this section—

(a) references to refusal include references to deliberate omission;

(b) references to Ministers of the Crown and government departments include references to the [Welsh Ministers, the First Minister for Wales, the Counsel General to the Welsh Assembly Government] and any part of the Scottish Administration; and

(c) references to Ministers of the Crown and government departments so far as they relate to the making of a recommendation or a refusal to make a recommendation, or the giving or refusal of an approval, in relation to a conferment of a peerage for life under section 1 of the Life Peerages Act 1958 include references to any body established by a Minister of the Crown to make such a recommendation to the Prime Minister or to determine whether to give such an approval.]

[305]

NOTES

Sub-s (1): words in square brackets substituted by the Race Relations (Amendment) Act 2000, s 3(1), (2).

Sub-ss (3)–(9), (11), (13), (15): added, together with sub-ss (10), (12), (14), by the Race Relations (Amendment) Act 2000, s 3(1), (3).

Sub-ss (10), (12): added as noted above; words in square brackets substituted by the Race Relations Act 1976 (Amendment) Regulations 2003, SI 2003/1626, reg 50(a), (c), as from 19 July 2003.

Sub-ss (11A), (11B): inserted by SI 2003/1626, reg 50(b), as from 19 July 2003.

Sub-s (14): added as noted above; substituted by SI 2003/1626, reg 50(d), as from 19 July 2003.

Sub-s (15): words in square brackets in para (b) substituted by the Government of Wales Act 2006 (Consequential Modifications and Transitional Provisions) Order 2007, SI 2007/1388, art 3, Sch 1, paras 10, 14, as from 25 May 2007.

[76ZA Other office holders

(1) It is unlawful for a relevant person, in relation to an appointment to an office or post to which this section applies, to discriminate against a person on the grounds of race or ethnic or national origins—

(a) in the arrangements which he makes for the purpose of determining to whom the appointment should be offered;

(b) in the terms on which he offers him the appointment; or

(c) by refusing or deliberately omitting to offer him the appointment.

(2) It is unlawful for a relevant person, in relation to a person who has been appointed to an office or post to which this section applies, to discriminate against him on grounds of race or ethnic or national origins—

(a) in the terms of the appointment;

(b) in the way he affords him access to opportunities for promotion, transfer, training or to any other benefits, facilities or services, or by refusing or deliberately omitting to afford him access to them;

(c) by terminating the appointment; or

(d) by subjecting him to any other detriment in relation to the appointment.

(3) It is unlawful for a relevant person, in relation to an office or post to which this section applies, to subject to harassment a person who has been appointed to, or is seeking or being considered for appointment to, such an office or post.

(4) Subsections (1) and (2) do not apply to any act in relation to an office or post where, if the office or post constituted employment, the act would be lawful by virtue of section 4A (exception for genuine occupational requirement).

(5) Subsection (2) does not apply to benefits, facilities or services of any description if the relevant person is concerned with the provision (for payment or not) of benefits, facilities or services of that description to the public, or a section of the public to which the person belongs, unless—

(a) that provision differs in a material respect from the provision of the benefits, facilities or services to persons appointed to offices or posts which are the same as, or not materially different from, that to which the person has been appointed;

(b) the provision of the benefits, facilities or services to the person appointed is regulated by the terms and conditions of his appointment; or

(c) the benefits, facilities or services relate to training.

(6) In subsection (2)(c) reference to the termination of the appointment includes reference—

(a) to the termination of the appointment by the expiration of any period (including a period expiring by reference to an event or circumstance), not being a termination immediately after which the appointment is renewed on the same terms and conditions; and

(b) to the termination of the appointment by any act of the person appointed (including the giving of notice) in circumstances such that he is entitled to terminate the appointment by reason of the conduct of the relevant person.

(7) This section applies to any office or post, other than a political office or post, where—

(a) sections 4, 7, 10, 26A, 26B and 76 do not apply in relation to appointment to that office or post;

(b) it is an office or post to which persons are appointed to discharge functions personally under the direction of another person; and

(c) it is an office or post in respect of which they are entitled to remuneration.

(8) For the purposes of subsection (7) the holder of an office or post—

(a) is to be regarded as discharging his functions under the direction of another person if that other person is entitled to direct him as to when and where he discharges those functions; and

(b) is not to be regarded as entitled to remuneration merely because he is entitled to payments—

(i) in respect of expenses incurred by him in carrying out the functions of the office or post, or

(ii) by way of compensation for the loss of income or benefits he would or might have received from any person had he not been carrying out the functions of the office or post.

(9) In this section—

(a) appointment to an office or post does not include election to an office or post;

(b) "political office or post" means—

(i) any office of the House of Commons held by a member of it;

(ii) a life peerage within the meaning of the Life Peerages Act 1958 , or any office held in the House of Lords by a member of it;

(iii) any office mentioned in Schedule 2 (Ministerial offices) to the House of Commons Disqualification Act 1975;

(iv) the offices of Leader of the Opposition, Chief Opposition Whip or Assistant Opposition Whip within the meaning of the Ministerial and other Salaries Act 1975;

(v) any office of the Scottish Parliament held by a member of it;

(vi) a member of the Scottish Executive within the meaning of section 44 of the Scotland Act 1998, or a junior Scottish Minister within the meaning of section 49 of that Act;

(vii) any office of the National Assembly for Wales held by a member of it;

[(viia) a member of the Welsh Assembly Government;]

(viii) in England, any office of a county council, a London borough council, a district council or a parish council held by a member of it;

(ix) in Wales, any office of a county council, a county borough council or a community council held by a member of it;

(x) in relation to a council constituted under section 2 of the Local Government etc (Scotland) Act 1994 or a community council established under section 51 of the Local Government (Scotland) Act 1973, which is held by a member of it;

(xi) any office of the Greater London Authority held by a member of it;

(xii) any office of the Common Council of the City of London held by a member of it;

(xiii) any office of the Council of the Isles of Scilly held by a member of it; or

(xiv) any office of a political party; and

(c) "relevant person", in relation to an office or post, means—

(i) any person with power to make or terminate appointments to the office or post, or to determine the terms of appointment; and

(ii) any person with power to determine the working conditions of a person appointed to the office or post in relation to opportunities for promotion, a transfer, training or for receiving any other benefit.]

[306]

NOTES

Commencement: 19 July 2003.

Inserted by the Race Relations Act 1976 (Amendment) Regulations 2003, SI 2003/1626, reg 51, as from 19 July 2003.

Sub-s (9): para (b)(viia) inserted by the Government of Wales Act 2006 (Consequential Modifications and Transitional Provisions) Order 2007, SI 2007/1388, art 3, Sch 1, paras 10, 15, as from 25 May 2007.

[Police

76A Police forces

(1) In this section, "relevant police office" means—

(a) the office of constable held—

(i) as a member of a police force; or

(ii) on appointment as a special constable for a police area; or

(b) an appointment as police cadet to undergo training with a view to becoming a member of a police force.

(2) For the purposes of Part II, the holding of a relevant police office shall be treated as employment—

(a) by the chief officer of police as respects any act done by him in relation to that office or a holder of it;

(b) by the police authority as respects any act done by it in relation to that office or a holder of it.

(3) For the purposes of section 32—

(a) the holding of a relevant police office shall be treated as employment by the chief officer of police (and as not being employment by any other person); and

(b) anything done by a person holding such an office in the performance, or purported performance, of his functions shall be treated as done in the course of that employment.

(4) There shall be paid out of the police fund—

(a) any compensation, costs or expenses awarded against a chief officer of police in any proceedings brought against him under this Act, and any costs or expenses incurred by him in any such proceedings so far as not recovered by him in the proceedings; and

(b) any sum required by a chief officer of police for the settlement of any claim made against him under this Act if the settlement is approved by the police authority.

(5) Any proceedings under this Act which, by virtue of this section, would lie against a chief officer of police shall be brought against—

(a) the chief officer of police for the time being; or

(b) in the case of a vacancy in that office, against the person for the time being performing the functions of that office;

and references in subsection (4) to the chief officer of police shall be construed accordingly.

(6) A police authority may, in such cases and to such extent as appear to it to be appropriate, pay out of the police fund—

(a) any damages or costs awarded in proceedings under this Act against a person under the direction and control of the chief officer of police;

(b) any costs incurred and not recovered by such a person in such proceedings; and

(c) any sum required in connection with the settlement of a claim that has or might have given rise to such proceedings.]

[307]

NOTES

Inserted, together with the preceding heading and s 76B, by the Race Relations (Amendment) Act 2000, s 4.

[76B Other police bodies etc

(1) …

(2) Section 76A … applies in relation to any other body of constables or cadets as it applies in relation to a police force, but as if any reference—

(a) to the chief officer of police were to the officer or other person who has the direction and control of the body in question;

(b) to the police authority were to the authority by whom the members of the body are paid;

(c) to the police fund were to money provided by that authority.

[(2A) Constables serving with the Serious Organised Crime Agency do not constitute a body of constables for the purposes of subsection (2).]

(3) In relation to a member of a police force or a special constable who is not under the direction and control of the chief officer of police for that police force or, as the case may be, for the police area to which he is appointed, references in section 76A to the chief officer of police are references to the chief officer under whose direction and control he is.]

[308]

NOTES

Inserted as noted to s 76A at **[307]**.

Sub-s (1): repealed by the Serious Organised Crime and Police Act 2005, ss 59, 174(2), Sch 4, paras 33, 34(1), (2), Sch 17, Pt 2, as from 1 April 2006.

Sub-s (2): word omitted repealed by the Serious Organised Crime and Police Act 2005, ss 59, 174(2), Sch 4, paras 33, 34(1), (3), Sch 17, Pt 2, as from 1 April 2006.

Sub-s (2A): inserted by the Serious Organised Crime and Police Act 2005, s 59, Sch 4, paras 33, 34(1), (4), as from 1 April 2006.

77 Financial provisions

There shall be defrayed out of money provided by Parliament—

(a) sums required by the Secretary of State for making payments under paragraph 5 or 16 of Schedule 1 or paragraph 12 of Schedule 2, and for defraying any other expenditure falling to be made by him under or by virtue of this Act;

(b) any expenses incurred by the Secretary of State with the consent of the Treasury in undertaking, or financially assisting the undertaking by other persons of, research into any matter connected with relations between persons of different racial groups;

(c) payments falling to be made under section 67(5) in respect of the remuneration of assessors; and

(d) any increase attributable to the provisions of this Act in the sums payable out of money provided by Parliament under any other Act.

[309]

78 General interpretation provisions

(1) In this Act, unless the context otherwise requires—

"access" shall be construed in accordance with section 40;

"act" includes a deliberate omission;

"advertisement" includes every form of advertisement or notice, whether to the public or not, and whether in a newspaper or other publication, by television or radio, by display of notices, signs, labels, showcards or goods, by distribution of samples, circulars, catalogues, price lists or other material, by exhibition of pictures, models or films, or in any other way, and references to the publishing of advertisements shall be construed accordingly;

[…]

["board of management" in relation to a college of further education within the meaning of Part I of the Further and Higher Education (Scotland) Act 1992, has the same meaning as in that Part;]

["body" includes an unincorporated association;]

"the Commission" means the [Commission for Equality and Human Rights];

"Commissioner" means a member of the Commission;

["criminal investigation" has the meaning given by section 57(4B);

"criminal proceedings" includes—

(*a*) *proceedings on dealing summarily with a charge under the Army Act 1955 or the Air Force Act 1955 or on summary trial under the Naval Discipline Act 1957;*

(*b*) *proceedings before a summary appeal court constituted under any of those Acts;*

(*c*) *proceedings before a court-martial constituted under any of those Acts or a disciplinary court constituted under section 52G of the Act of 1957;*
(*d*) *proceedings before the Courts-Martial Appeal Court; and*
(*e*) *proceedings before a Standing Civilian Court;]*

"designated county court" has the meaning given by section 67(1);

["detriment" does not include conduct of a nature such as to constitute harassment under section 3A;]

"discrimination" and related terms shall be construed in accordance with section 3(3);

"dispose", in relation to premises, includes granting a right to occupy the premises, and any reference to acquiring premises shall be construed accordingly;

"education" includes any form of training or instruction;

["the Education Acts" has the meaning given by section 578 of the Education Act 1996;]

"education authority" and "educational establishment" have for Scotland the same meaning as they have respectively in section [135(1) of the Education (Scotland) Act 1980];

"employment" means employment under a contract of service or of apprenticeship or a contract personally to execute any work or labour, and related expressions shall be construed accordingly;

"employment agency" means a person who, for profit or not, provides services for the purpose of finding employment for workers or supplying employers with workers;

["enactment" includes an enactment comprised in, or in an instrument made under, an Act of the Scottish Parliament;]

"estate agent" means a person who, by way of profession or trade, provides services for the purpose of finding premises for persons seeking to acquire them or assisting in the disposal of premises;

"final" shall be construed in accordance with subsection (4);

"firm" has the meaning given by section 4 of the Partnership Act 1890;

…

"further education" has … for Scotland the meaning given by [section 135(1) of the Education (Scotland) Act 1980];

"general notice", in relation to any person, means a notice published by him at a time and in a manner appearing to him suitable for securing that the notice is seen within a reasonable time by persons likely to be affected by it;

"genuine occupational qualification" shall be construed in accordance with section 5;

"Great Britain" includes such of the territorial waters of the United Kingdom as are adjacent to Great Britain;

"independent school" has for England and Wales the meaning given by [section 463 of the Education Act 1996], and for Scotland the meaning given by section [135(1) of the Education (Scotland) Act 1980];

…

"managers" has for Scotland the same meaning as in section [135(1) of the Education (Scotland) Act 1980];

["the Minister" means the Lord Privy Seal;]

"Minister of the Crown" includes the Treasury and the Defence Council;

"nationality" includes citizenship;

"near relative" shall be construed in accordance with subsection (5);

…

"notice" means a notice in writing;

"prescribed" means prescribed by regulations made by the [Minister or the Secretary of State];

"profession" includes any vocation or occupation;

"proprietor", in relation to a school, has for England and Wales the meaning given by [section 579 of the Education Act 1996], and for Scotland the meaning given by section [135(1) of the Education (Scotland) Act 1980];

"pupil" in Scotland includes a student of any age;

"racial grounds" and "racial group" have the meaning given by section 3(1);

"school" has for England and Wales the meaning given by [section 4 of the Education Act 1996], and for Scotland the meaning given by section [135(1) of the Education (Scotland) Act 1980];

"school education" has for Scotland the meaning given by section [135(1) of the Education (Scotland) Act 1980];

[…]

["social protection" and "social advantage" have the same meaning as in Article 3 of Council Directive 2000/43/EC;]

"trade" includes any business;

"training" includes any form of education or instruction;
"university" includes a university college and the college, school or hall of a university;
...

(2) It is hereby declared that in this Act "premises", unless the context otherwise requires, includes land of any description.

(3) Any power conferred by this Act to designate establishments or persons may be exercised either by naming them or by identifying them by reference to a class or other description.

(4) For the purposes of this Act ... a finding by a court or tribunal becomes final when an appeal against the ... finding is dismissed, withdrawn or abandoned or when the time for appealing expires without an appeal having been brought; ...

(5) For the purposes of this Act a person is a near relative of another if that person is the wife or husband [or civil partner], a parent or child, a grandparent or grandchild, or a brother or sister of the other (whether of full blood or half-blood or [by marriage or civil partnership]), and "child" includes an illegitimate child and the wife or husband [or civil partner] of an illegitimate child.

(6) Except so far as the context otherwise requires, any reference in this Act to an enactment shall be construed as a reference to that enactment as amended by or under any other enactment, including this Act.

(7) In this Act, except where otherwise indicated—
- (a) a reference to a numbered Part, section or Schedule is a reference to the Part or section of, or the Schedule to, this Act so numbered; and
- (b) a reference in a section to a numbered subsection is a reference to the subsection of that section so numbered; and
- (c) a reference in a section, subsection or Schedule to a numbered paragraph is a reference to the paragraph of that section, subsection or Schedule so numbered; and
- (d) a reference to any provision of an Act (including this Act) includes a Schedule incorporated in the Act by that provision.

[310]

NOTES

Sub-s (1) is amended as follows:

Definition "board of management" (in relation to a self-governing school) (omitted) inserted by the Self-Governing Schools etc (Scotland) Act 1989, s 82(1), Sch 10, para 6(4), and repealed by the Standards in Scotland's Schools etc Act 2000, s 60(2), Sch 3, as from 31 December 2004.

Definition "board of management" (in relation to a college of further education) inserted by the Further and Higher Education (Scotland) Act 1992, s 93, Sch 9, para 5(5).

Definitions "body", "criminal investigation" and "criminal proceedings" inserted by the Race Relations (Amendment) Act 2000, s 9(1), Sch 2, para 19.

Words in square brackets in definition "the Commission" substituted by the Equality Act 2006, s 40, Sch 3, paras, 21, 33(a)(i), as from 1 October 2007.

Definition "criminal proceedings" inserted as noted above and substituted by the Armed Forces Act 2006, s 378(1), Sch 16, para 81, as from a day to be appointed, as follows—

""criminal proceedings" includes service law proceedings (as defined by section 324(5) of the Armed Forces Act 2006);".

Definitions "detriment", "social protection" and "social advantage" inserted by the Race Relations Act 1976 (Amendment) Regulations 2003, SI 2003/1626, reg 52, as from 19 July 2003.

Definition "the Education Acts" inserted by the Education Act 1996, s 582(1), Sch 37, para 43.

In definitions "education authority" and "educational establishment" words in square brackets substituted by the Education (Scotland) Act 1980, s 136(2), Sch 4, para 15.

Definition "enactment" inserted by the Scotland Act 1998 (Consequential Modifications) Order 2000, SI 2000/2040, art 2(1), Schedule, Pt I, para 9.

Definition "formal investigation" (omitted) repealed by the Equality Act 2006, ss 40, 91, Sch 3, paras 21, 33(a)(ii), Sch 4, as from 1 October 2007.

In definition "further education" words omitted repealed by the Education Reform Act 1988, s 237, Sch 13, Pt II, and words in square brackets substituted by the Education (Scotland) Act 1980, s 136(2), Sch 4, para 15.

In definition "independent school" words in first pair of square brackets substituted by the Education Act 1996, s 582(1), Sch 37, para 43, and words in second pair of square brackets substituted by the Education (Scotland) Act 1980, s 136(2), Sch 4, para 15.

Definition "industrial tribunal" (omitted) repealed by the Industrial Training Act 1982, s 20, Sch 3, para 7(b), Sch 4.

In definition "managers" words in square brackets substituted by the Education (Scotland) Act 1980, s 136(2), Sch 4, para 15.

Definition "the Minister" inserted by the Transfer of Functions (Equality) Order 2007, SI 2007/2914, art 8, Schedule, para 9, as from 12 October 2007.

Definition "non-discrimination notice" (omitted) repealed by the Equality Act 2006, ss 40, 91, Sch 3, paras 21, 33(a)(ii), Sch 4, as from 1 October 2007.

In definition "prescribed" words in square brackets substituted by SI 2007/2914, art 8, Schedule, para 12, as from 12 October 2007.

In definition "proprietor" words in first pair of square brackets substituted by the Education Act 1996, s 582(1), Sch 37, para 43, and words in second pair of square brackets substituted by the Education (Scotland) Act 1980, s 136(2), Sch 4, para 15.

In definition "school" words in first pair of square brackets substituted by the Education Act 1996, s 582(1), Sch 37, para 43, and words in second pair of square brackets substituted by the Education (Scotland) Act 1980, s 136(2), Sch 4, para 15.

In definition "school education" words in square brackets substituted by the Education (Scotland) Act 1980, s 136(2), Sch 4, para 15.

Definition "self-governing school" (omitted) inserted by the Self-Governing Schools etc (Scotland) Act 1989, s 82(1), Sch 10, para 6(4), and repealed by the Standards in Scotland's Schools etc Act 2000, s 60(2), Sch 3, as from 31 December 2004.

Definition "upper limit of compulsory school age" (omitted) repealed by the Education Act 1996, s 582(2), Sch 38, Pt II.

Sub-s (4): words omitted repealed by the Equality Act 2006, ss 40, 91, Sch 3, paras, 21, 33(b), Sch 4, as from 1 October 2007.

Sub-s (5): words in first and third pairs of square brackets inserted, and words in second pair of square brackets substituted, by the Civil Partnership Act 2004, s 261(1), Sch 27, para 55, as from 5 December 2005.

---

79 Transitional and commencement provisions, amendments and repeals

(1) The provisions of Schedule 2 shall have effect for making transitional provision for the purposes of this Act.

(2) This Act shall come into operation on such day as the Secretary of State may by order appoint, and different days may be so appointed for different provisions and for different purposes.

(3) The enactments specified in Schedule 3 shall have effect subject to the amendments specified in that Schedule (being minor amendments or amendments consequential on the preceding provisions of this Act).

(4) The Sex Discrimination Act 1975 shall have effect subject to the amendments specified in Schedule 4, being amendments for bringing provisions in that Act relating to its administration and enforcement into conformity with the corresponding provisions in this Act.

(5) Subject to the provisions of Schedule 2, the enactments specified in Schedule 5 are hereby repealed to the extent shown in column 3 of that Schedule.

(6) …

(7) An order under this section may make such transitional provision as appears to the Secretary of State to be necessary or expedient in connection with the provisions thereby brought into operation, including such adaptations of those provisions, or of any provisions of this Act then in operation, as appear to the Secretary of State necessary or expedient in consequence of the partial operation of this Act.

[311]

NOTES

Sub-s (6): repealed by the Public Order Act 1986, s 40(3), Sch 3.

Orders: the Race Relations Act 1976 (Commencement No 1) Order 1977, SI 1977/680; the Race Relations Act 1976 (Commencement No 2) Order 1977, SI 1977/840.

---

80 Short title and extent

(1) This Act may be cited as the Race Relations Act 1976.

(2) This Act, except so far as it amends or repeals any provision of the House of Commons Disqualification Act 1975 or the Northern Ireland Assembly Disqualification Act 1975, does not extend to Northern Ireland.

[312]–[313]

NOTES

Extent: as to the application of this Act in a control zone or supplementary control zone accorded to the United Kingdom in France, see the Channel Tunnel (International Arrangements) Order 1993, SI 1993/1813, art 4.

SCHEDULES

(*Sch 1 repealed by the Equality Act 2006, ss 40, 91, Sch 3, paras, 21, 34, Sch 4, as from 1 October 2007. For savings see the Equality Act 2006 (Commencement No 3 and Savings) Order 2007, SI 2007/2603, art 3 at* **[3473R]**. *For transitional provisions relating to the discharge by the Commission for Equality and Human Rights of the former functions of the CRE, see the Equality Act 2006 (Dissolution of Commissions and Consequential and Transitional Provisions) Order 2007, SI 2007/2602, art 5 at* **[3473O]**).)

[SCHEDULE 1A
BODIES AND OTHER PERSONS SUBJECT TO GENERAL STATUTORY DUTY

Sections 71, 71A, 71E

[PART I
ORIGINAL CATEGORIES OF BODIES AND OTHER PERSONS]

Ministers of the Crown and government departments

1.—(1) A Minister of the Crown or government department.

(2) Sub-paragraph (1) does not include the Security Service, the Intelligence Service or the Government Communications Headquarters.

Scottish Administration

2.—(1) An office-holder in the Scottish Administration within the meaning given by section 126(7)(a) of the Scotland Act 1998.

(2) Members of the staff of the Scottish Administration within the meaning given by section 126(7)(b) of that Act.

[National Assembly for Wales Commission

3A. The National Assembly for Wales Commission.

Welsh Assembly Government

3B.—(1) The Welsh Ministers, the First Minister for Wales or the Counsel General to the Welsh Assembly Government.

(2) A subsidiary of the Welsh Ministers (as defined by section 134(4) of the Government of Wales Act 2006).]

Armed forces

4. Any of the naval, military or air forces of the Crown.

National Health Service: England and Wales

5. A [Strategic Health Authority [established under section 13 of the National Health Service Act 2006]] …

[5A. A Local Health Board established under section 11 of the National Health Service (Wales) Act 2006.]

6. A special health authority established under [section 28 of that Act or section 22 of the National Health Service (Wales) Act 2006].

7. A primary care trust established under [section 18 of the National Health Service Act 2006].

8. A National Health Service trust established under [section 25 of that Act, or section 18 of the National Health Service (Wales) Act 2006].

[8A. An NHS foundation trust.]

National Health Service: Scotland

9. A Health Board constituted under section 2 of the National Health Service (Scotland) Act 1978.

10. A Special Health Board constituted under section 2 of that Act.

11. A National Health Service Trust established under section 12A of that Act.

Local government

12. A local authority within the meaning of the Local Government Act 1972, namely—

(a) in England, a county council, a London borough council, a district council or a parish council;

(b) in Wales, a county council, a county borough council or a community council.

13. A council constituted under section 2 of the Local Government etc (Scotland) Act 1994.

14. A community council established under section 51 of the Local Government (Scotland) Act 1973.

15. The Greater London Authority.

16. The Common Council of the City of London in its capacity as a local authority or port health authority.

17. The Sub-Treasurer of the Inner Temple or the Under-Treasurer of the Middle Temple, in his capacity as a local authority.

18. The Council of the Isles of Scilly.

19. A parish meeting constituted under section 13 of the Local Government Act 1972.

20. Any charter trustees constituted under section 246 of that Act.

[21. A fire and rescue authority constituted by a scheme under section 2 of the Fire and Rescue Services Act 2004 or a scheme to which section 4 of that Act applies.]

22. A waste disposal authority established by virtue of an order under section 10(1) of the Local Government Act 1985.

23. …

24. A port health authority constituted by an order under section 2 of the Public Health (Control of Disease) Act 1984.

25. …

26. A licensing board constituted under section 1 of the Licensing (Scotland) Act 1976.

27. An internal drainage board which is continued in being by virtue of section 1 of the Land Drainage Act 1991.

[28. A local probation board established under section 4 of the Criminal Justice and Court Services Act 2000.]

29. A joint authority established under Part IV of the Local Government Act 1985 [(fire and rescue services and transport)].

30. A joint board within the meaning of section 235(1) of the Local Government (Scotland) Act 1973.

31. The London Fire and Emergency Planning Authority.

32. A body corporate established pursuant to an order under section 67 of the Local Government Act 1985 (transfer of functions to successors of residuary bodies, etc).

33. …

34. The Broads Authority established by section 1 of the Norfolk and Suffolk Broads Act 1988.

35. A joint committee constituted in accordance with section 102(1)(b) of the Local Government Act 1972.

36. A joint board which is continued in being by virtue of section 263(1) of that Act.

37. A joint authority established under section 21 of the Local Government Act 1992.

38. A Passenger Transport Executive for a passenger transport area within the meaning of Part II of the Transport Act 1968.

39. Transport for London.

40. The London Development Agency.

41. A regional development agency established under the Regional Development Agencies Act 1998 (other than the London Development Agency).

42. Scottish Enterprise and Highland and Islands Enterprise, established under the Enterprise and New Towns (Scotland) Act 1990.

43. A National Park authority established by an order under section 63 of the Environment Act 1995.

44. A joint planning board constituted for an area in Wales outside a National Park by an order under section 2(1B) of the Town and Country Planning Act 1990.

45. …

Other educational bodies

46. Governing bodies of—

(a) educational establishments maintained by local education authorities;

(b) institutions within the further education sector (within the meaning of section 91(3) of the Further and Higher Education Act 1992); or

(c) institutions within the higher education sector (within the meaning of section 91(5) of the Act of 1992).

47. The managers of a grant-aided school (within the meaning of section 135 of the Education (Scotland) Act 1980).

48. The managers of a central institution (within the meaning of section 135 of the Act of 1980).

49. The board of management of a self-governing school (within the meaning of the Self-Governing Schools etc (Scotland) Act 1989).

50. The board of management of a college of further education (within the meaning of section 36(1) of the Further and Higher Education (Scotland) Act 1992).

51. The governing body of an institution within the higher education sector (within the meaning of Part II of the Further and Higher Education (Scotland) Act 1992).

Other housing bodies

52. The Housing Corporation.

53. …

54. A housing action trust established under Part III of the Housing Act 1988.

Police

55. A police authority established under section 3 of the Police Act 1996.

56. A police authority established under section 2 of the Police (Scotland) Act 1967.

57. The Metropolitan Police Authority established under section 5B of the Police Act 1996.

58. The Common Council of the City of London in its capacity as a police authority.

59, 60. …

[314]

NOTES

Inserted by the Race Relations (Amendment) Act 2000, s 2(2), Sch 1.

Part I heading inserted by the Race Relations Act 1976 (General Statutory Duty) Order 2001, SI 2001/3457, art 2(a).

Paras 3A, 3B: substituted, for original para 3, by the Government of Wales Act 2006 (Consequential Modifications and Transitional Provisions) Order 2007, SI 2007/1388, art 3, Sch 1, paras 10, 16, as from 25 May 2007.

Para 5: words in first (outer) pair of square brackets inserted by the National Health Service Reform and Health Care Professions Act 2002 (Supplementary, Consequential etc Provisions) Regulations 2002, SI 2002/2469, reg 4, Sch 1, para 9; words in second (inner) pair of square brackets inserted by the National Health Service (Consequential Provisions) Act 2006, s 2, Sch 1, paras 55, 56(a), as from 1 March 2007; words omitted repealed by a combination of the National Health Service (Consequential Provisions) Act 2006, s 2, Sch 1, paras 55, 56(a), as from 1 March 2007, and the References to Health Authorities Order 2007, SI 2007/961, art 3, Schedule, para 12(1), (2)(a), as from 1 April 2007.

Para 5A: inserted by SI 2007/961, art 3, Schedule, para 12(1), (2)(b), as from 1 April 2007.

Paras 6–8: words in square brackets substituted by the National Health Service (Consequential Provisions) Act 2006, s 2, Sch 1, paras 55, 56(b)–(d), as from 1 March 2007.

Para 8A: inserted by the Health and Social Care (Community Health and Standards) Act 2003, s 34, Sch 4, paras 21, 22, as from 1 April 2004.

Para 21: substituted by the Fire and Rescue Services Act 2004, s 53(1), Sch 1, para 48, as from 1 October 2004 (in relation to England only), and as from 1 November 2004 (in relation to Wales only). The original paragraph, as it applies in Scotland, reads as follows—

"21. A fire authority constituted by a combination scheme under section 5 or 6 of the Fire Services Act 1947.".

Para 23: repealed by the Water Industry (Scotland) Act 2002, s 71(2), Sch 7, para 9.

Para 25: repealed by SI 2001/3457, art 2(b).

Para 28: substituted by SI 2001/3457, art 2(c).

Para 29: words in square brackets substituted by the Civil Contingencies Act 2004, s 32(1), Sch 2, Pt 1, para 10(3)(a), as from 1 April 2005.

Para 33: repealed by the Local Government and Public Involvement in Health Act 2007, ss 22, 241, Sch 1, Pt 2, para 12, Sch 18, Pt 1, as from 1 November 2007.

Para 45: repealed by the Courts Act 2003, s 109(1), (3), Sch 8, para 187(1), (2), Sch 10, as from 1 April 2005.

Para 53: repealed by the Race Relations Act 1976 (General Statutory Duty) Order 2006, SI 2006/2470, art 2(a), as from 3 October 2006.

Paras 59, 60: repealed by the Serious Organised Crime and Police Act 2005, ss 59, 174(2), Sch 4, paras 33, 35(a), Sch 17, Pt 2, as from 1 April 2006.

Note: see also the Race Relations Act 1976 (General Statutory Duty) Order 2003, SI 2003/3007, art 2(a) which purports to make the following amendment to para 5 above (as from 31 December 2003)—

(a) in Part I (original categories of bodies and other persons), under the sub-heading "National Health Service: England and Wales", for the words "A Health Authority established under section 8 of the National Health Service Act 1977" substitute "A Strategic Health Authority";

[PART II
BODIES AND OTHER PERSONS ADDED AFTER COMMENCEMENT OF GENERAL STATUTORY DUTY

Health

The Administration of Radioactive Substances Advisory Committee.

…

[Commission for Healthcare Audit and Inspection.]

[Commission for Social Care Inspection.]

The Commons Services Agency for the NHS in Scotland.

…

…

…

[The Health Protection Agency.]

The Human Fertilisation and Embryology Authority.

…

The Joint Committee on Vaccination and Immunisation.

The Mental Welfare Commission for Scotland.

The National Biological Standards Board.

[The Postgraduate Medical Education and Training Board.]

…

The Royal College of Anaesthetists, in respect of its public functions.

The Royal College of General Practitioners, in respect of its public functions.

The Royal College of Midwives, in respect of its public functions.

The Royal College of Nursing, in respect of its public functions.

The Royal College of Obstetricians and Gynaecologists, in respect of its public functions.

The Royal College of Ophthalmologists, in respect of its public functions.

The Royal College of Paediatrics and Child Health, in respect of its public functions.

The Royal College of Pathologists, in respect of its public functions.

The Royal College of Physicians, in respect of its public functions.

The Royal College of Psychiatrists, in respect of its public functions.

The Royal College of Radiologists, in respect of its public functions.

The Royal College of Speech and Language Therapists, in respect of its public functions.

The Royal College of Surgeons of England, in respect of its public functions.

The Scottish Dental Practice Board.

The Scottish Hospital Endowments Research Trust.

…

…

…

The Standing Dental Advisory Committee.

The Standing Medical Advisory Committee.

The Standing Nursing and Midwifery Advisory Committee.

The Standing Pharmaceutical Advisory Committee.

The Unrelated Live Transplant Regulatory Authority.

The Welsh Committee for Professional Development of Pharmacy.

The Welsh Dental Committee.

The Welsh Medical Committee.

…

The Welsh Nursing and Midwifery Committee.

The Welsh Optometric Committee.

The Welsh Pharmaceutical Committee.

Education

…

The British Educational [Communications] and Technology Agency.

A City Academy established by an agreement under section 482 of the Education Act 1996.

A City College for the Technology of the Arts established by an agreement under section 482 of the Education Act 1996.

A City Technology College established by an agreement under section 482 of the Education Act 1996.

A college of further education maintained by an education authority, in the exercise of its further education functions in providing courses of further education within the meaning of section 1(5)(b)(ii) of the Education (Scotland) Act 1980.

…

The Construction Industry Training Board.

The Engineering Construction Industry Training Board.

The General Teaching Council for England.

The General Teaching Council for Scotland.

The General Teaching Council for Wales.

The Higher Education Funding Council for England.

The Higher Education Funding Council for Wales.

The Learning and Skills Council for England.

Learning and Teaching Scotland.

…

Newbattle Abbey College.

The Qualifications and Curriculum Authority.

…

The Quality Assurance Agency for Higher Education.

Sabhal Mòr Ostaig College.

The School Teachers' Review Body.

[The Scottish Further and Higher Education Funding Council.]

...

The Scottish Further Education Unit, in respect of its public functions.

...

The Scottish Qualifications Authority.

The Students Loans Company.

The Teacher Training Agency.

[The Training and Development Agency for Schools.]

Police

The British Transport Police.

The Chief Constable for the Ministry of Defence Police appointed by the Secretary of State under section 1(3) of the Ministry of Defence Police Act 1987.

[The Civil Nuclear Police Authority.]

[The chief constable of the Civil Nuclear Constabulary.]

A chief constable of a police force maintained under section 2 of the Police Act 1996.

A chief constable of a police force maintained under section 1 of the Police (Scotland) Act 1967.

The Commissioner of Police for the City of London.

The Commissioner of Police of the Metropolis.

[The National Policing Improvement Agency.]

...

...

The Police Negotiating Board.

A Selection Panel for Independent Members of Police Authorities.

Libraries, museums and arts

The Advisory Committee on Sites of Special Scientific Interest.

The Advisory Council on Public Records.

...

...

The Arts Council of England.

The Arts Council of Wales.

The British Library.

The British Museum.

The British Tourist Authority.

The Commission for Architecture and the Built Environment.

The Countryside Council for Wales.

The Design Council.

...

The English Tourist Board.

The Film Council.

The Geffrye Museum.

The Historic Buildings and Monuments Commission for England [(known as English Heritage)].

…

…

The Historic Royal Palaces Trust.

The Horniman Museum.

The Imperial War Museum.

…

…

[The Museum, Archives and Libraries Council.]

The Museum of London.

The Museum of Science and Industry in Manchester.

The National Endowment for Science, Technology and the Arts.

The National Galleries of Scotland.

The National Gallery.

The National Heritage Memorial Fund.

The National Library of Scotland.

The National Library of Wales.

…

The National Maritime Museum.

National Museums and Galleries on Merseyside.

National Museums and Galleries of Wales.

National Museums of Scotland.

The National Portrait Gallery.

The Natural History Museum.

The Registrar of Public Lending Right.

…

The Royal Armouries.

The Royal Botanic Garden, Edinburgh.

The Royal Botanic Gardens, Kew.

The Royal Commission on Ancient and Historical Monuments of Scotland.

The Royal Commission on Ancient and Historical Monuments of Wales.

The Royal Commission on Historical Manuscripts.

…

…

The Scottish Arts Council.

Scottish Natural Heritage.

Scottish Screen.

Scottish Sports Council.

…

Sir John Soane's Museum.

Sport England.

The Sports Council for Wales.

The Tate Gallery.

The Theatres Trust.

The Treasure Valuation Committee.

The UK Sports Council.

The Victoria and Albert Museum.

[VisitScotland.]

…

The Wallace Collection.

Public corporations and nationalised industries

The Bank of England, in respect of its public functions.

The British Broadcasting Corporation, in respect of its public functions.

…

The Channel Four Television Corporation, in respect of its public functions.

The Civil Aviation Authority.

The Coal Authority.

The Covent Garden Market Authority.

[The Consumer Council for Water.]

…

…

Sianel Pedwar Cymru (Welsh Fourth Channel Authority), in respect of its public functions.

The United Kingdom Atomic Energy Authority, in respect of its public functions.

Regulatory, audit and inspection

The Accounts Commission for Scotland.

The Advisory, Conciliation and Arbitration Service (ACAS).

The Association of Authorised Public Accountants.

The Association of Certified Chartered Accountants.

The Association of Child Psychotherapy.

The Audit Commission for Local Authorities and the National Health Service in England *and Wales*.

Audit Scotland.

The British Hallmarking Council.

The British Standards Institute.

The Chartered Institute of Patent *Agents*, in respect of its public functions.

The Council for Licensed Conveyancers, in respect of its public functions.

The Engineering Council [(UK)].

The Financial Services Authority.

The General Chiropractic Council.

The General Council of the Bar of England and Wales, in respect of its public functions.

The General Dental Council.

The General Medical Council.

The General Optical Council.

The General Osteopathic Council.

The General Social Care Council.

[The Health Professions Council.]

The Insolvency Practitioners Association.

The Institute of Chartered Accountants in England and Wales.

The Institute of Chartered Accountants of Scotland.

The Institute of Legal Executives, in respect of its public functions.

The Institute of Trade Mark Attorneys.

The Law Society of England and Wales, in respect of its public functions.

The Law Society of Scotland, in respect of its public functions.

[Her Majesty's Inspectorate of Court Administration.]

…

The Master of the Court of the Faculties of the Archbishop of Canterbury, in respect of its public functions.

The National Audit Office.

The Royal Pharmaceutical Society of Great Britain, in respect of its statutory functions and the regulation of the pharmacy profession.

…

Research

The Alcohol Education and Research Council.

…

The Biotechnology and Biological Sciences Research Council.

The Council for the Central Laboratory of the Research Councils.

The Economic and Social Research Council.

The Engineering and Physical Sciences Research Council.

The Fire Service Research and Training Trust.

The Horticultural Development Council.

The Medical Research Council.

The Natural Environment Research Council.

The Particle Physics and Astronomy Research Council.

Other Bodies, Etc

[The Administrative Justice and Tribunals Council.]

The Advisory Committee on Hazardous Substances.

The Advisory Committee on Pesticides.

The Advisory Committee on Releases to the Environment.

The Advisory Council on the Misuse of Drugs.

[The Agriculture and Horticulture Development Board.]

An Agricultural Dwelling House Advisory Committee established under the Rent (Agriculture) Act 1976.

The Agricultural Wages Board for England and Wales.

An Agricultural Wages Committee.

The Animal Procedures Committee.

…

The Britain-Russia Centre.

The British Association for Central and Eastern Europe.

The British Council.

…

The British Waterways Board.

The British Wool Marketing Board.

The Building Regulations Advisory Committee.

The Building Standards Advisory Committee.

The Central Advisory Committee on War Pensions.

The Children and Family Court Advisory and Support Service.

The Civil Justice Council.

The Civil Procedure Rule Committee.

[Commission for Equality and Human Rights.]

…

[Commission for Rural Communities.]

…

The Commonwealth Scholarship Commission in the United Kingdom.

The Community Development Foundation.

The Consumer Council for Postal Services [(Postwatch)].

…

The Criminal Injuries Compensation Authority.

The Crofters' Commission.

The Crown Court Rule Committee.

The Deer Commission for Scotland.

The Disability Living Allowance Advisory Board.

…

The Disabled Persons Transport Advisory Committee.

The Electoral Commission.

English Partnerships.

The Environment Agency.

The Environment Agency Advisory Committee for Wales.

…

The Family Proceedings Rule Committee.

The Firearms Consultative Committee.

The Fisheries (Electricity) Committee.

Food From Britain.

[The Gambling Commission.]

The Gas and Electricity Consumer Council [(Energywatch)].

The Government Hospitality Advisory Committee for the Purchase of Wine.

The Great Britain-China Centre.

…

The Health and Safety Executive.

…

…

…

The Honours Scrutiny Committee.

…

…

[An Independent Monitoring Board appointed under section 6(2) of the Prison Act 1952.]

The Industrial Injuries Advisory Council.

The Information Commissioner.

The [Inland Waterways Advisory Council].

The Insolvency Rules Committee.

Investors in People UK.

The Joint Nature Conservation Committee.

The Land Registration Rule Committee.

The Law Commission.

The Legal Services Commission.

The Legal Services Consultative Panel.

The Local Government Boundary Commission for Scotland.

The Local Government Boundary Commission for Wales.

…

The Low Pay Commission.

The Magistrates' Courts Rule Committee.

The Marshall Aid Commemoration Commission.

…

…

The National Consumer Council.

The National Forest Company.

…

[Natural England.]

…

The Northern Lighthouse Board.

The Oil and Pipelines Agency.

[The Olympic Delivery Authority.]

The Overseas Service Pensions Scheme Advisory Board.

[A probation trust.

A provider of probation services (other than the Secretary of State or a probation trust), in respect of its statutory functions and the carrying out by it of activities of a public nature in pursuance of arrangements made with it under section 3(2) of the Offender Management Act 2007.]

A Regional Flood Defence Committee established under section 14 of the Environment Act 1995.

The Scottish Agricultural Wages Board.

[The Scottish Committee of the Administrative Justice and Tribunals Council.]

…

The Scottish Environment Protection Agency.

The Scottish Industrial Development Advisory Board.

The Scottish Law Commission.

The Scottish Legal Aid Board.

The Scottish Parliamentary Corporate Body.

The Scottish Records Advisory Council.

The Sea Fish Industry Authority.

The Sentencing Advisory Panel.

[The Serious Organised Crime Agency.]

The Social Security Advisory Committee.

…

The Trinity House Lighthouse Service.

A Visiting Committee appointed under section 152 of the Immigration and Asylum Act 1999 for an immigration detention centre.

The Wales New Deal Advisory Task Force.

A War Pensions Committee.

[The Water Industry Commission for Scotland.]

…

[The Welsh Committee of the Administrative Justice and Tribunals Council.]

…

The Welsh Industrial Development Advisory Board.

The Welsh Language Board.

The Welsh Scientific Advisory Committee.

The Westminster Foundation for Democracy.

The Wilton Park Academic Council.

The Wine Standards Board of the Vintners' Company.

The Youth Justice Board for England and Wales.]

[315]

NOTES

Added by the Race Relations Act 1976 (General Statutory Duty) Order 2001, SI 2001/3457, art 2(d), Schedule.

Health: entry "The Commission for Health Improvement" (omitted) repealed by the Health and Social Care (Community Health and Standards) Act 2003 (Commission for Healthcare Audit and Inspection and Commission for Social Care Inspection) (Consequential Provisions) Order 2004, SI 2004/2987, art 2(2)(a), as from 11 November 2004.

Health: entry "Commission for Healthcare Audit and Inspection" inserted by SI 2004/2987, art 2(1)(e), as from 11 November 2004.

Health: entry "Commission for Social Care Inspection" inserted by SI 2004/2987, art 2(1)(e), as from 11 November 2004.

Health: entry "The Council for Professions Supplementary to Medicine, in respect of its public functions" (omitted) repealed by Health Professions Order 2001 (Consequential Amendments) Order 2003, SI 2003/1590, art 3, Schedule, Pt 1, para 4(a), as from 9 July 2003 (see further the miscellaneous note below).

Health: entry "The Dental Practice Board" (omitted) repealed by the Health and Social Care (Community Health and Standards) Act 2003, s 196, Sch 14, Pt 4, as from 1 April 2006.

Health: entry "The English National Board for Nursing, Midwifery and Health Visiting" (omitted) repealed by the Health Act 1999 (Consequential Amendments) (Nursing and Midwifery) Order 2004, SI 2004/1771, art 3, Schedule, Pt 1, para 9, as from 1 August 2004.

Health: entry "The Health Protection Agency" inserted by the Health Protection Agency Act 2004, s 11(1), Sch 3, para 8, as from 1 April 2005.

Health: entry "The Joint Committee on Postgraduate Training for General Practice" (omitted) repealed by the General and Specialist Medical Practice (Education, Training and Qualifications) Order 2003, SI 2003/1250, art 31(5), Sch 9, para 1(a), as from 30 September 2005.

Health: entry "The Postgraduate Medical Education and Training Board" inserted by SI 2003/1250, art 31(5), Sch 9, para 1(b), as from 30 September 2005.

Health: entry "The Public Health Laboratory Service Board" (omitted) repealed by the Health and Social Care (Community Health and Standards) Act 2003, ss 190(2), 196, Sch 13, para 3, Sch 14, Pt 7, as from 1 April 2005.

Health: entry "The Scottish Hospital Trust" (omitted) repealed by the Public Appointments and Public Bodies etc (Scotland) Act 2003, s 17, Sch 4, para 4(c), as from 6 February 2004.

Health: entry "The Scottish Medical Practices Committee" (omitted) repealed by the Public Appointments and Public Bodies etc (Scotland) Act 2003, s 17, Sch 4, para 4(d), as from 1 April 2004.

Health: entry "The Specialist Training Authority of the Medical Royal Colleges" (omitted) repealed by SI 2003/1250, art 31(5), Sch 9, para 1(a), as from 30 September 2005.

Health: entry "The Welsh National Board for Nursing, Midwifery and Health Visiting" (omitted) repealed by the Health Act 1999 (Consequential Amendments) (Nursing and Midwifery) Order 2004, SI 2004/1771, art 3, Schedule, Pt 1, para 9, as from 1 August 2004.

Education: entry "The Adult Learning Inspectorate" (omitted) repealed by the Education and Inspections Act 2006, ss 157, 184, Sch 14, para 7, Sch 18, Pt 5, as from 1 April 2007.

Education: in entry "The British Educational Communications and Technology Agency" word in square brackets substituted by the Race Relations Act 1976 (General Statutory Duty) Order 2003, SI 2003/3007, art 2(b)(ii), as from 31 December 2003.

Education: entry "Community Learning Scotland" (omitted) repealed by SI 2003/3007, art 2(b)(ii), as from 31 December 2003.

Education: entry "The National Council for Education and Training for Wales" (omitted) repealed by the National Council for Education and Training for Wales (Transfer of Functions to the National Assembly for Wales and Abolition) Order 2005, SI 2005/3238, art 9(1), Sch 1, paras 6, 8, as from 1 April 2006.

Education: entry "The Qualifications, Curriculum and Assessment Authority for Wales" (omitted) repealed by the Qualifications, Curriculum and Assessment Authority for Wales (Transfer of Functions to the National Assembly for Wales and Abolition) Order 2005, SI 2005/3239, art 9(1), Sch 1, para 3, as from 1 April 2006.

Education: entry "The Scottish Further and Higher Education Funding Council" inserted by the Further and Higher Education (Scotland) Act 2005 (Consequential Modifications) Order 2005, SI 2005/2077, art 5(b), as from 3 October 2005.

Education: entry "The Scottish Further Education Funding Council" (omitted) repealed by the Further and Higher Education (Scotland) Act 2005, s 32, Sch 3, para 4(b)(i), as from 3 October 2005.

Education: entry "The Scottish Higher Education Funding Council" (omitted) repealed by the Further and Higher Education (Scotland) Act 2005, s 32, Sch 3, para 4(b)(ii), as from 3 October 2005.

Education: entry "The Training and Development Agency for Schools" inserted by the Education Act 2005, s 98, Sch 14, para 8, as from 1 September 2005.

Police: entry "The Civil Nuclear Police Authority" inserted by the Energy Act 2004, s 69(1), Sch 14, para 4, as from 1 March 2005.

Police: entry "The chief constable of the Civil Nuclear Constabulary" inserted by the Energy Act 2004, s 69(1), Sch 14, para 4, as from 1 March 2005.

Police: entry "The National Policing Improvement Agency" inserted by the Police and Justice Act 2006, s 1(3), Sch 1, Pt 7, para 60, as from 1 April 2007.

Police: entry "The Police Complaints Authority" (omitted) repealed by SI 2003/3007, art 2(b)(iii), as from 31 December 2003.

Police: entry "The Police Information Technology Organisation" (omitted) repealed by the Police and Justice Act 2006, s 52, Sch 15, Pt 1, as from 1 April 2007.

Libraries, museums and arts: entry "The Ancient Monuments Board for Scotland" (omitted) repealed by the Public Appointments and Public Bodies etc (Scotland) Act 2003, s 17, Sch 4, para 4(a), as from 31 May 2003 (see further the miscellaneous note below).

Libraries, museums and arts: entry "The Ancient Monuments Board for Wales" (omitted) repealed by the Ancient Monuments Board for Wales (Abolition) Order 2006, SI 2006/64, art 3(1)(b)(i), as from 1 April 2006.

Libraries, museums and arts: entry "English Nature" (omitted) repealed by the Natural Environment and Rural Communities Act 2006, s 105, Sch 11, Pt 1, para 61(1), (4), Sch 12, as from 1 October 2006.

Libraries, museums and arts: in entry "The Historic Buildings and Monuments Commission for England" words in square brackets added by the Race Relations Act 1976 (General Statutory Duty) Order 2004, SI 2004/3127, art 2(a)(i), as from 31 December 2004.

Libraries, museums and arts: entry "The Historic Buildings Council for Scotland" (omitted) repealed by the Public Appointments and Public Bodies etc (Scotland) Act 2003, s 17, Sch 4, para 4(b), as from 31 May 2003 (see further the miscellaneous note below).

Libraries, museums and Arts: entry "The Historic Buildings Council for Wales" (omitted) repealed by the Historic Buildings Council for Wales (Abolition) Order 2006, SI 2006/63, art 3(1)(c)(i), as from 1 April 2006.

Libraries, museums and arts: entry "The Library and Information Services Council (Wales)" (omitted) repealed by the Library Advisory Council for Wales Abolition and Consequential Amendments Order 2004, SI 2004/803, art 3(2), as from 1 April 2004.

Libraries, museums and arts: entry "The Millennium Commission" (omitted) repealed by the National Lottery Act 2006, s 21, Sch 3, as from 1 December 2006.

Libraries, museums and arts: entry "The Museum, Archives and Libraries Council" inserted by SI 2004/3127, art 2(a)(i), as from 31 December 2004.

Libraries, museums and arts: entry "The National Lottery Charities Board" (omitted) repealed by the National Lottery Act 2006, s 21, Sch 3, as from 1 December 2006.

Libraries, museums and arts: entry "Resource: The Council for Museums, Archives and Libraries" (omitted) repealed by SI 2004/3127, art 2(a)(i), as from 31 December 2004.

Libraries, museums and arts: entry "The Royal Fine Art Commission for Scotland" (omitted) repealed by the Race Relations Act 1976 (General Statutory Duty) Order 2006, SI 2006/2470, art 2(b), as from 3 October 2006.

Libraries, museums and arts: entry "The Science Museum" (omitted) repealed by SI 2004/3127, art 2(a)(i), as from 31 December 2004.

Libraries, museums and arts: entry "The Scottish Tourist Board" (omitted) repealed by the Tourist Boards (Scotland) Act 2006, s 4, Sch 2, Pt 1, para 3(a), as from 1 April 2007 (in relation to Scotland), and by the Tourist Boards (Scotland) Act 2006 (Consequential Modifications) Order 2007, SI 2007/1103, art 2, Schedule, Pt 1, para 3(a), as from 29 March 2007 (in relation to England and Wales).

Libraries, museums and arts: entry "VisitScotland" inserted by the Tourist Boards (Scotland) Act 2006, s 4, Sch 2, Pt 1, para 3(b), as from 1 April 2007 (in relation to Scotland), and by SI 2007/1103, art 2, Schedule, Pt 1, para 3(b), as from 29 March 2007 (in relation to England and Wales).

Libraries, museums and arts: entry "The Wales Tourist Board" (omitted) repealed by the Wales Tourist Board (Transfer of Functions to the National Assembly for Wales and Abolition) Order 2005, SI 2005/3225, art 6(2), Sch 2, Pt 1, para 2, as from 1 April 2006.

Public corporations and nationalised industries: entry "The Broadcasting Standards Commission, in respect of its public functions" repealed (omitted) by SI 2003/3007, art 2(b)(v), as from 31 December 2003.

Public corporations and nationalised industries: entry "The Consumer Council for Water" substituted, for original entry "A Customer Service Committee maintained under section 28 of the Water Industry Act 1991", by the Water Act 2003, s 101(2), Sch 7, Pt 2, para 22, as from 1 October 2005.

Public corporations and nationalised industries: entry "The Independent Television Commission, in respect of its public functions" (omitted) repealed by SI 2003/3007, art 2(b)(v), as from 31 December 2003.

Public corporations and nationalised industries: entry "The Radio Authority, in respect of its public functions" (omitted) repealed by SI 2003/3007, art 2(b)(v), as from 31 December 2003.

Regulatory, audit and inspection: words in italics in entry "The Audit Commission for Local Authorities and the National Health Service in England and Wales" repealed by the Local Government and Public Involvement in Health Act 2007, ss 146(3), 241, Sch 9, para 1(1), (2)(c), Sch 18, Pt 9, as from a day to be appointed.

Regulatory, audit and inspection: for the word in italics in entry "The Chartered Institute of Patent Agents, in respect of its public functions" there is substituted the word "Attorneys" by the Legal Services Act 2007, s 208(1), Sch 21, paras 36, 39, as from a day to be appointed.

Regulatory, audit and inspection: in entry "The Engineering Council (UK)" reference to "(UK)" in square brackets inserted by SI 2004/3127, art 2(a)(ii), as from 31 December 2004.

Regulatory, audit and inspection: entry "The Health Professions Council" inserted by SI 2003/1590, art 3, Schedule, Pt 1, para 4(b), as from 9 July 2003.

Regulatory, audit and inspection: entry "Her Majesty's Inspectorate of Court Administration" inserted by the Courts Act 2003, s 109(1), Sch 8, para 187(1), (3)(a), as from 1 April 2005.

Regulatory, audit and inspection: entry "Her Majesty's Magistrates' Courts Service Inspectorate" (omitted) repealed by the Courts Act 2003, s 109(1), (3), Sch 8, para 187(1), (3)(b), Sch 10, as from 1 April 2005.

Regulatory, audit and inspection: entry "The United Kingdom Central Council for Nursing, Midwifery and Health Visiting, in respect of its public functions" (omitted) repealed by SI 2003/3007, art 2(b)(vi), as from 31 December 2003.

Research: entry "The Apple and Pear Research Council" (omitted) repealed by SI 2003/3007, art 2(b)(vii), as from 31 December 2003.

Other Bodies, Etc: entry "The Administrative Justice and Tribunals Council" inserted by the Tribunals, Courts and Enforcement Act 2007, s 48(1), Sch 8, para 7, as from 1 November 2007.

Other Bodies, Etc: entry "The Agriculture and Horticulture Development Board" inserted by the Agriculture and Horticulture Development Board Order 2008, SI 2008/576, art 18, Sch 5, para 4, as from 29 February 2008.

Other Bodies, Etc: entry "A Board of Visitors established under section 6(2) of the Prison Act 1952" (omitted) repealed by the Offender Management Act 2007, s 39, Sch 5, Pt 2, as from 1 November 2007.

Other Bodies, Etc: entries "The British Potato Council", "The Home-Grown Cereals Authority", "The Meat and Livestock Commission", and "The Milk Development Council" (omitted) repealed by SI 2008/576, art 18, Sch 5, para 7, as from 1 April 2008.

Other Bodies, Etc: entry "Commission for Equality and Human Rights" inserted by the Equality Act 2006, s 40, Sch 3, paras, 21, 35(b), as from 18 April 2006.

Other Bodies, Etc: entries "The Commission for Racial Equality", "The Disability Rights Commission", and "The Equal Opportunities Commission" (all omitted) repealed by the Equality Act 2006, ss 40, 91, Sch 3, paras, 21, 35(a), Sch 4, as from 1 October 2007.

Other Bodies, Etc: entry "Commission for Rural Communities" inserted by the Natural Environment and Rural Communities Act 2006, s 105(1), Sch 11, Pt 1, para 61(1), (2), as from 1 October 2006.

Other Bodies, Etc: entry "The Commissioner for Local Administration in Scotland" (omitted) repealed by SI 2003/3007, art 2(b)(viii), as from 31 December 2003.

Other Bodies etc: entry "The Consumer Council for Postal Services ("Postwatch")" repealed by the Consumers, Estate Agents and Redress Act 2007, s 64, Sch 8, as from a day to be appointed; word in square brackets in this entry added by SI 2003/3007, art 2(b)(viii), as from 31 December 2003.

Other Bodies, Etc: entry "The Council on Tribunals" (omitted) repealed by the Tribunals, Courts and Enforcement Act 2007, s 146, Sch 23, Pt 1, as from 1 November 2007.

Other Bodies, Etc: entry "The Gambling Commission" substituted, for original entry "The Gaming Board", by the Gambling Act 2005, s 356(1), Sch 16, Pt 2, para 9, as from 1 October 2005.

Other Bodies, Etc: entry "The Health and Safety Commission" (omitted) repealed by the Legislative Reform (Health and Safety Executive) Order 2008, SI 2008/960, art 22, Sch 3, as from 1 April 2008. As to the abolition of the Health and Safety Commission and the Health and Safety Executive (with effect from 1 April 2008) and their replacement with a single Health and Safety Executive exercising the combined functions of those bodies, see the Legislative Reform (Health and Safety Executive) Order 2008, SI 2008/960 (at **[3474L]**), and the amendments made by that Order to the Health and Safety at Work etc Act 1974 (at **[30]** et seq). For transitional provisions in relation to the abolition of the former bodies and the establishment of the new Health and Safety Executive, see art 21 of, and Sch 2 to, the 2008 Order at **[3474N]**, **[3474O]**.

Other Bodies, Etc: entry "The Gas and Electricity Consumer Council (Energywatch)" repealed by the Consumers, Estate Agents and Redress Act 2007, s 64, Sch 8, as from a day to be appointed; word in square brackets in this entry inserted by SI 2004/3127, art 2(a)(iii), as from 31 December 2004.

Other Bodies, Etc: entries "The Hill Farming Advisory Committee for Scotland" and "The Hill Farming Advisory Sub-Committee for Wales" (both omitted) repealed by the Natural Environment and Rural Communities Act 2006, s 105, Sch 11, Pt 1, para 61(1), (4), Sch 12, as from 1 October 2006.

Other Bodies, Etc: entry "The Horserace Betting Levy Board" (omitted) repealed by SI 2003/3007, art 2(b)(viii), as from 31 December 2003 (see further the miscellaneous note below).

Other Bodies, Etc: entry "The Horserace Totalisator Board" (omitted) repealed by SI 2003/3007, art 2(b)(viii), as from 31 December 2003 (see further the miscellaneous note below).

Other Bodies, Etc: entry "An Independent Monitoring Board" inserted by the Offender Management Act 2007, s 39, Sch 3, Pt 2, para 7, as from 1 November 2007.

Other Bodies, Etc: words in square brackets in entry "The Inland Waterways Advisory Council" substituted (for the original words "Inland Waterways Amenity Advisory Council") by the Natural Environment and Rural Communities Act 2006, s 105(1), Sch 11, Pt 2, para 175, as from 1 April 2007.

Other Bodies, Etc: entry "The Legal Services Consultative Panel" repealed by the Legal Services Act 2007, s 210, Sch 23, as from a day to be appointed.

Other Bodies, Etc: entry "The Local Government Commission for England" (omitted) repealed by SI 2003/3007, art 2(b)(viii), as from 31 December 2003.

Other Bodies etc: entry "The National Consumer Council" (omitted) repealed by the Consumers, Estate Agents and Redress Act 2007, s 64, Sch 8, as from a day to be appointed.

Other Bodies, Etc: entry "The National Radiological Protection Board" (omitted) repealed by the Health Protection Agency Act 2004, s 11(2), Sch 4, as from 1 April 2005.

Other Bodies, Etc: entry "Natural England" inserted by the Natural Environment and Rural Communities Act 2006, s 105(1), Sch 11, Pt 1, para 61(1), (3), as from 2 May 2006.

Other Bodies, Etc: entry "The New Opportunities Fund" (omitted) repealed by the National Lottery Act 2006, s 21, Sch 3, as from 1 December 2006.

Other Bodies, Etc: entry "The Olympic Delivery Authority" inserted by the London Olympic Games and Paralympic Games Act 2006, s 3, Sch 1, Pt 2, para 21, as from 30 March 2006.

Other Bodies, Etc: entry "A probation trust" and entry beginning "A provider of probation services" inserted by the Offender Management Act 2007, s 39, Sch 3, Pt 1, para 1, as from 1 April 2008.

Other Bodies, Etc: entry "The Scottish Committee of the Administrative Justice and Tribunals Council" inserted by the Tribunals, Courts and Enforcement Act 2007, s 48(1), Sch 8, para 7, as from 1 November 2007.

Other Bodies, Etc: entry "The Scottish Conveyancing and Executry Services Board" (omitted) repealed by the Public Appointments and Public Bodies etc (Scotland) Act 2003, s 17, Sch 4, para 4(e), as from 15 August 2003 (see further the miscellaneous note below).

Other Bodies, Etc: entry "The Serious Organised Crime Agency" inserted by the Serious Organised Crime and Police Act 2005, s 59, Sch 4, paras 33, 35(b), as from 1 April 2006.

Other Bodies, Etc: entry "The Strategic Rail Authority" (omitted) repealed by the Railways Act 2005, s 59(6), Sch 13, Pt 1, as from 1 December 2006.

Other Bodies, Etc: entry "The Water Industry Commission for Scotland" inserted by the Water Services etc (Scotland) Act 2005 (Consequential Provisions and Modifications) Order 2005, SI 2005/3172, art 11, Schedule, Pt 1, para 2, as from 11 November 2005.

Other Bodies, Etc: entry "The Water Industry Commissioner for Scotland" (omitted) repealed by the Water Services etc (Scotland) Act 2005, s 32, Sch 4, para 3, as from 1 July 2005.

Other Bodies, Etc: entry "The Welsh Committee of the Administrative Justice and Tribunals Council" inserted by the Tribunals, Courts and Enforcement Act 2007, s 48(1), Sch 8, para 7, as from 1 June 2008.

Other Bodies, Etc: entry "The Welsh Development Agency" (omitted) repealed by the Welsh Development Agency (Transfer of Functions to the National Assembly for Wales and Abolition) Order 2005, SI 2005/3226, art 7(1)(b), Sch 2, Pt 1, para 7, as from 1 April 2006.

Miscellaneous: (i) The Race Relations Act 1976 (General Statutory Duty) Order 2003, SI 2003/3007, art 2 provides that the entries "The Council for Professions Supplementary to Medicine, in respect of its public functions", "The Ancient Monuments Board for Scotland", "The Historic Buildings Council for Scotland", and "The Scottish Conveyancing and Executry Services Board" should be repealed, as from 31 December 2003; however, all of these entries have already been repealed as noted above. (ii) The Horserace Betting and Olympic Lottery Act 2004, ss 13, 17(2), 38, Sch 2, para 20, Sch 4, para 8, Sch 6 provides that the entries "The Horserace Betting Levy Board" and "The Horserace Totalisator Board" should be repealed, as from a day to be appointed; however, these entries have already been repealed as noted above.

[PART III
BODIES AND OTHER PERSONS ADDED ON 31ST DECEMBER 2003

Local Government

A National Park authority established by a designation order made under section 6 of the National Parks (Scotland) Act 2000.

Health

The Commission for Patient and Public Involvement in Health.

The Council for the Regulation of Health Care Professionals.

The Health Professions Council.

The Nursing and Midwifery Council.

The Royal College of Physicians and Surgeons of Glasgow, in respect of its public functions.

The Royal College of Physicians of Edinburgh, in respect of its public functions.

The Royal College of Surgeons of Edinburgh, in respect of its public functions.

Education

[The National College for School Leadership.]

Police

…

…

The Independent Police Complaints Commission.

A Port Police Force established under an order made under section 14 of the Harbours Act 1964.

The Port Police Force established under Part X of the Port of London Act 1968.

A Port Police Force established under section 79 of the Harbours, Docks and Piers Clauses Act 1847.

Regulatory, Audit and Inspection

The Association of International Accountants, in respect of its public functions.

The Financial Reporting Review Panel.

The National Lottery Commission.

The Scottish Information Commissioner.

The Scottish Commission for the Regulation of Care.

The Scottish Social Services Council.

The Security Industry Authority.

The Standards Board for England.

Other Bodies etc

…

The Historic Environment Advisory Council for Scotland.

The League for the Exchange of Commonwealth Teachers.

…

The Royal College of Veterinary Surgeons, in respect of its public functions.

The Royal Commission on Environmental Pollution.

Scottish Water.

The Sector Skills Development Agency.

SITPRO Ltd, in respect of its public functions.

A Water Customer Consultation Panel established by an order pursuant to section 2(1) of the Water Industry (Scotland) Act 2002.]

[315A]

NOTES

Commencement: 31 December 2003.

Inserted by the Race Relations Act 1976 (General Statutory Duty) Order 2003, SI 2003/3007, art 2(c), Schedule, as from 31 December 2003.

Health: entry "The Commission for Patient and Public Involvement in Health." repealed by the Local Government and Public Involvement in Health Act 2007, s 241, Sch 18, Pt 18, as from 30 June 2008.

Education: entry "The National College for School Leadership" substituted, for original entry "The National College of School Leadership", by the Race Relations Act 1976 (General Statutory Duty) Order 2004, SI 2004/3127, art 2(b), as from 31 December 2004.

Police: entry "The Central Police Training and Development Authority ("CENTREX")" (omitted) repealed by the Police and Justice Act 2006, s 52, Sch 15, Pt 1, as from 1 April 2007.

Police: entry "The Director-General of the National Crime Squad" (omitted) repealed by the Serious Organised Crime and Police Act 2005, ss 59, 174(2), Sch 4, paras 33, 35(c), Sch 17, Pt 2, as from 1 April 2006.

Other Bodies, Etc: entry "The Countryside Agency" (omitted) repealed by the Natural Environment and Rural Communities Act 2006, s 105, Sch 11, Pt 1, para 61(1), (5), Sch 12, as from 1 October 2006.

Other Bodies etc: entry "The Pensions Compensation Board" (omitted) repealed by the Race Relations Act 1976 (General Statutory Duty) Order 2006, SI 2006/2470, art 2(c), as from 3 October 2006.

[PART IV
BODIES AND OTHER PERSONS ADDED ON 31ST DECEMBER 2004

Health

The Commission for Healthcare Audit and Inspection

Independent Regulator of NHS Foundation Trusts

Regulatory, Audit and Inspection

The Commission for Social Care Inspection

The Office of Communications (Ofcom)

The Social Fund Commissioner of the Independent Review Service

Other Bodies etc

…

National Museum for Science and Industry

Remploy Limited

Royal Parks in England

UK Sport

Women's National Commission]

[315B]

NOTES

Commencement: 31 December 2004.

Inserted by the Race Relations Act 1976 (General Statutory Duty) Order 2004, SI 2004/3127, art 2(c), Schedule, as from 31 December 2004.

Other Bodies etc: entry "Bòrd na Gàidhlig (Alba)" (omitted) repealed by the Race Relations Act 1976 (General Statutory Duty) Order 2006, SI 2006/2470, art 2(d), as from 3 October 2006.

[PART V
BODIES AND OTHER PERSONS ADDED ON 3RD OCTOBER 2006

Libraries, museums and arts

Architecture and Design Scotland.

The Arts and Humanities Research Council.

The Scottish Library and Information Council.

The Scottish Museums Council.

Regulatory, audit and inspection

The Football Licensing Authority.

The Gas and Electricity Markets Authority.

The Pensions Regulator.

Other bodies etc

Bòrd na Gàidhlig.

The Board of the Pension Protection Fund.

The British Transport Police Authority.

A chief officer of a community justice authority appointed under section 4 of the Management of Offenders etc (Scotland) Act 2005.

A Chief Officer of a relevant authority appointed under section 7 of the Fire (Scotland) Act 2005.

The Commissioner for Children and Young People in Scotland.

A community justice authority established under section 3 of the Management of Offenders etc (Scotland) Act 2005.

A joint fire and rescue board constituted by a scheme under section 2(1) of the Fire (Scotland) Act 2005.

The Mobility and Access Committee for Scotland.

The Office for Fair Access.

The panel constituted under Schedule 4 to the Rent (Scotland) Act 1984.

The Risk Management Authority.

Scottish UfI Ltd.

Scottish UfI Trust Ltd.

Transport Partnerships created under the Transport (Scotland) Act 2005.]

[315C]

NOTES

Commencement: 3 October 2006.

Inserted by the Race Relations Act 1976 (General Statutory Duty) Order 2006, SI 2006/2470, art 2(e), Schedule, as from 3 October 2006.

(*Sch 2* (*Transitional provisions: effectively spent and largely repealed by the Statute Law* (*Repeals*) *Act 2004, as from 22 July 2004*)*; Sch 3 repealed by the Trade Union and Labour Relations* (*Consolidation*) *Act 1992, s 300*(*1*)*, Sch 1; Sch 4 amends the Sex Discrimination Act 1975 at* **[100]** *et seq; Sch 5 contains repeals only.*)

PATENTS ACT 1977

(1977 c 37)

ARRANGEMENT OF SECTIONS

PART I
NEW DOMESTIC LAW

Employees' inventions

PART III
MISCELLANEOUS AND GENERAL

Supplemental

An Act to establish a new law of patents applicable to future patents and applications for patents; to amend the law of patents applicable to existing patents and applications for patents; to give effect to certain international conventions on patents; and for connected purposes

[29 July 1977]

NOTES

Only those sections of this Act concerned with inventions made by employees are reproduced here, i e ss 39–43 (and s 132 which makes provision as to the extent, etc of the Act). For definitions within the Act see s 130 (not reproduced). For reasons of space, the subject matter of sections, etc, not printed is not annotated.

PART I
NEW DOMESTIC LAW

Employees' inventions

39 Right to employees' inventions

(1) Notwithstanding anything in any rule of law, an invention made by an employee shall, as between him and his employer, be taken to belong to his employer for the purposes of this Act and all other purposes if—

(a) it was made in the course of the normal duties of the employee or in the course of duties falling outside his normal duties, but specifically assigned to him, and the circumstances in either case were such that an invention might reasonably be expected to result from the carrying out of his duties; or

(b) the invention was made in the course of the duties of the employee and, at the time of making the invention, because of the nature of his duties and the particular responsibilities arising from the nature of his duties he had a special obligation to further the interests of the employer's undertaking.

(2) Any other invention made by an employee shall, as between him and his employer, be taken for those purposes to belong to the employee.

[(3) Where by virtue of this section an invention belongs, as between him and his employer, to an employee, nothing done—

(a) by or on behalf of the employee or any person claiming under him for the purposes of pursuing an application for a patent, or

(b) by any person for the purpose of performing or working the invention,

shall be taken to infringe any copyright or design right to which, as between him and his employer, his employer is entitled in any model or document relating to the invention.]

[316]

NOTES

Sub-s (3): added by the Copyright, Designs and Patents Act 1988, s 295, Sch 5, para 11(1).

40 Compensation of employees for certain inventions

[(1) Where it appears to the court or the comptroller on an application made by an employee within the prescribed period that—

(a) the employee has made an invention belonging to the employer for which a patent has been granted,

(b) having regard among other things to the size and nature of the employer's undertaking, the invention or the patent for it (or the combination of both) is of outstanding benefit to the employer, and

(c) by reason of those facts it is just that the employee should be awarded compensation to be paid by the employer,

the court or the comptroller may award him such compensation of an amount determined under section 41 below.]

(2) Where it appears to the court or the comptroller on an application made by an employee within the prescribed period that—

(a) a patent has been granted for an invention made by and belonging to the employee;

(b) his rights in the invention, or in any patent or application for a patent for the invention, have since the appointed day been assigned to the employer or an exclusive licence under the patent or application has since the appointed day been granted to the employer;

(c) the benefit derived by the employee from the contract of assignment, assignation or grant or any ancillary contract ("the relevant contract") is inadequate in relation to the benefit derived by the employer from [the invention or the patent for it (or both)]; and

(d) by reason of those facts it is just that the employee should be awarded compensation to be paid by the employer in addition to the benefit derived from the relevant contract;

the court or the comptroller may award him such compensation of an amount determined under section 41 below.

(3) Subsections (1) and (2) above shall not apply to the invention of an employee where a relevant collective agreement provides for the payment of compensation in respect of inventions of the same description as that invention to employees of the same description as that employee.

(4) Subsection (2) above shall have effect notwithstanding anything in the relevant contract or any agreement applicable to the invention (other than any such collective agreement).

(5) If it appears to the comptroller on an application under this section that the application involves matters which would more properly be determined by the court, he may decline to deal with it.

(6) In this section—

"the prescribed period", in relation to proceedings before the court, means the period prescribed by rules of court, and

"relevant collective agreement" means a collective agreement within the meaning of [the Trade Union and Labour Relations (Consolidation) Act 1992], made by or on behalf of a trade union to which the employee belongs, and by the employer or an employers' association to which the employer belongs which is in force at the time of the making of the invention.

(7) References in this section to an invention belonging to an employer or employee are references to it so belonging as between the employer and the employee.

[317]

NOTES

Sub-s (1): substituted by the Patents Act 2004, s 10(1), as from 1 January 2005, in relation to an invention the patent for which is applied for on or after that date.

Sub-s (2): words in square brackets in para (c) substituted by the Patents Act 2004, s 10(2), as from 1 January 2005, in relation to an invention the patent for which is applied for on or after that date.

Sub-s (6): words in square brackets substituted by the Trade Union and Labour Relations (Consolidation) Act 1992, s 300(2), Sch 2, para 9.

Rules: the Patents Rules 2007, SI 2007/3291 replacing, as from 17 December 2007, the Patent Rules 1995, SI 1995/2093 (revoked). See r 91 of the 2007 Rules (period prescribed for applications by employee for compensation for the purposes of sub-ss (1), (2)). See also r 73 of, and Sch 3 to, the 2007 Rules in relation to applications under this section and s 41(8) post.

41 Amount of compensation

[(1) An award of compensation to an employee under section 40(1) or (2) above shall be such as will secure for the employee a fair share (having regard to all the circumstances) of the benefit which the employer has derived, or may reasonably be expected to derive, from any of the following—

(a) the invention in question;
(b) the patent for the invention;
(c) the assignment, assignation or grant of—
  (i) the property or any right in the invention, or
  (ii) the property in, or any right in or under, an application for the patent,

to a person connected with the employer.]

(2) For the purposes of subsection (1) above the amount of any benefit derived or expected to be derived by an employer from the assignment, assignation or grant of—

(a) the property in, or any right in or under, a patent for the invention or an application for such a patent; or
(b) the property or any right in the invention;

to a person connected with him shall be taken to be the amount which could reasonably be expected to be so derived by the employer if that person had not been connected with him.

(3) Where the Crown or a Research Council in its capacity as employer assigns or grants the property in, or any right in or under, an invention, patent or application for a patent to a body having among its functions that of developing or exploiting inventions resulting from public research and does so for no consideration or only a nominal consideration, any benefit derived from the invention, patent or application by that body shall be treated for the purposes of the foregoing provisions of this section as so derived by the Crown or, as the case may be, Research Council.

In this subsection "Research Council" means a body which is a Research Council for the purposes of the Science and Technology Act 1965 [or the Arts and Humanities Research Council (as defined by section 1 of the Higher Education Act 2004)].

(4) In determining the fair share of the benefit to be secured for an employee in respect of … an invention which has always belonged to an employer, the court or the comptroller shall, among other things, take the following matters into account, that is to say—

(a) the nature of the employee's duties, his remuneration and the other advantages he derives or has derived from his employment or has derived in relation to the invention under this Act;
(b) the effort and skill which the employee has devoted to making the invention;
(c) the effort and skill which any other person has devoted to making the invention jointly with the employee concerned, and the advice and other assistance contributed by any other employee who is not a joint inventor of the invention; and
(d) the contribution made by the employer to the making, developing and working of the invention by the provision of advice, facilities and other assistance, by the provision of opportunities and by his managerial and commercial skill and activities.

(5) In determining the fair share of the benefit to be secured for an employee in respect of ... an invention which originally belonged to him, the court or the comptroller shall, among other things, take the following matters into account, that is to say—

(a) any conditions in a licence or licences granted under this Act or otherwise in respect of the invention or the patent [for it];

(b) the extent to which the invention was made jointly by the employee with any other person; and

(c) the contribution made by the employer to the making, developing and working of the invention as mentioned in subsection (4)(d) above.

(6) Any order for the payment of compensation under section 40 above may be an order for the payment of a lump sum or for periodical payment, or both.

(7) Without prejudice to section 32 of the Interpretation Act 1889 (which provides that a statutory power may in general be exercised from time to time), the refusal of the court or the comptroller to make any such order on an application made by an employee under section 40 above shall not prevent a further application being made under that section by him or any successor in title of his.

(8) Where the court or the comptroller has made any such order, the court or he may on the application of either the employer or the employee vary or discharge it or suspend any provision of the order and revive any provision so suspended, and section 40(5) above shall apply to the application as it applies to an application under that section.

(9) In England and Wales any sums awarded by the comptroller under section 40 above shall, if a county court so orders, be recoverable *by execution issued from the county court* or otherwise as if they were payable under an order of that court.

(10) In Scotland an order made under section 40 above by the comptroller for the payment of any sums may be enforced in like manner as [an extract registered decree arbitral bearing a warrant for execution issued by the sheriff court of any sheriffdom in Scotland].

(11) In Northern Ireland an order made under section 40 above by the comptroller for the payment of any sums may be enforced as if it were a money judgment.

[318]

NOTES

Sub-s (1): substituted by the Patents Act 2004, s 10(3), as from 1 January 2005, in relation to an invention the patent for which is applied for on or after that date.

Sub-s (3): words in square brackets inserted by the Higher Education Act 2004, s 49, Sch 6, para 5, as from 16 December 2004.

Sub-s (4): words omitted repealed by the Patents Act 2004, ss 10(4), 16(2), Sch 3, as from 1 January 2005, in relation to an invention the patent for which is applied for on or after that date.

Sub-s (5): words omitted repealed, and words in square brackets inserted, by the Patents Act 2004, ss 10(4), (5), 16(2), Sch 3, as from 1 January 2005, in relation to an invention the patent for which is applied for on or after that date.

Sub-s (9): for the words in italics there are substituted the words "under section 85 of the County Courts Act 1984" by the Tribunals, Courts and Enforcement Act 2007, s 62(3), Sch 13, paras 39, 40, as from a day to be appointed.

Sub-s (10): words in square brackets substituted by the Patents Act 2004, s 16(1), Sch 2, paras 1(1), 11, as from 1 January 2005.

Applications under sub-s (8): see the note "Rules" to s 40 at **[317]**.

Interpretation Act 1889, s 32: repealed and replaced by the Interpretation Act 1978.

42 Enforceability of contracts relating to employees' inventions

(1) This section applies to any contract (whenever made) relating to inventions made by an employee, being a contract entered into by him—

(a) with the employer (alone or with another); or

(b) with some other person at the request of the employer or in pursuance of the employee's contract of employment.

(2) Any term in a contract to which this section applies which diminishes the employee's rights in inventions of any description made by him after the appointed day and the date of the contract, or in or under patents for those inventions or applications for such patents, shall be unenforceable against him to the extent that it diminishes his rights in an invention of that description so made, or in or under a patent for such an invention or an application for any such patent.

(3) Subsection (2) above shall not be construed as derogating from any duty of confidentiality owed to his employer by an employee by virtue of any rule of law or otherwise.

(4) This section applies to any arrangement made with a Crown employee by or on behalf of the Crown as his employer as it applies to any contract made between an employee and an employer other than the Crown, and for the purposes of this section "Crown employee" means a person employed under or for the purposes of a government department or any officer or body exercising on behalf of the Crown functions conferred by any enactment [or a person serving in the naval, military or air forces of the Crown].

[319]

NOTES

Words in square brackets added with retrospective effect by the Armed Forces Act 1981, s 22(1), (2).

43 Supplementary

(1) Sections 39 to 42 above shall not apply to an invention made before the appointed day.

(2) Sections 39 to 42 above shall not apply to an invention made by an employee unless at the time he made the invention one of the following conditions was satisfied in his case, that is to say—

(a) he was mainly employed in the United Kingdom; or

(b) he was not mainly employed anywhere or his place of employment could not be determined, but his employer had a place of business in the United Kingdom to which the employee was attached, whether or not he was also attached elsewhere.

(3) In section 39 to 42 above and this section, except so far as the context otherwise requires, references to the making of an invention by an employee are references to his making it alone or jointly with any other person, but do not include references to his merely contributing advice or other assistance in the making of an invention by another employee.

(4) Any references [in sections 39 to 42] above to a patent and to a patent being granted are respectively references to a patent or other protection and to its being granted whether under the law of the United Kingdom or the law in force in any other country or under any treaty or international convention.

(5) For the purposes of sections 40 and 41 above the benefit derived or expected to be derived by an employer from [an invention or patent] shall, where he dies before any award is made under section 40 above in respect of [it], include any benefit derived or expected to be derived from [it] by his personal representatives or by any person in whom it was vested by their assent.

[(5A) For the purposes of sections 40 and 41 above the benefit derived or expected to be derived by an employer from an invention shall not include any benefit derived or expected to be derived from the invention after the patent for it has expired or has been surrendered or revoked.]

(6) Where an employee dies before an award is made under section 40 above in respect of a patented invention made by him, his personal representatives or their successors in title may exercise his right to make or proceed with an application for compensation under subsection (1) or (2) of that section.

(7) In sections 40 and 41 above and this section "benefit" means benefit in money or money's worth.

(8) Section 533 of the Income and Corporation Taxes Act 1970 (definition of connected persons) shall apply for determining for the purposes of section 41(2) above whether one person is connected with another as it applies for determining that question for the purposes of the Tax Acts.

[320]

NOTES

Sub-s (4): words in square brackets substituted by the Copyright, Designs and Patents Act 1988, s 295, Sch 5, para 11(2).

Sub-s (5): words in square brackets substituted by the Patents Act 2004, s 10(6), as from 1 January 2005, in relation to an invention the patent for which is applied for on or after that date.

Sub-s (5A): inserted by the Patents Act 2004, s 10(7), in relation to an invention the patent for which is applied for on or after that date.

Income and Corporation Taxes Act 1970: repealed and replaced by the Income and Corporation Taxes Act 1988. The relevant section of the 1988 Act is s 839. There has been no amendment to this section to reflect the change.

PART III
MISCELLANEOUS AND GENERAL

Supplemental

132 Short title, extent, commencement, consequential amendments and repeals

(1) This Act may be cited as the Patents Act 1977.

(2) This Act shall extend to the Isle of Man, subject to any modifications contained in an Order made by Her Majesty in Council, and accordingly, subject to any such order, references in this Act to the United Kingdom shall be construed as including references to the Isle of Man.

(3) For the purposes of this Act the territorial waters of the United Kingdom shall be treated as part of the United Kingdom.

(4) This Act applies to acts done in an area designated by order under section 1(7) of the Continental Shelf Act 1964, [or specified by Order under [section 10(8) of the Petroleum Act 1998] in connection with any activity falling within [section 11(2)] of that Act], as it applies to acts done in the United Kingdom.

(5) This Act (except sections 77(6), (7) and (9), 78(7) and (8), this subsection and the repeal of section 41 of the 1949 Act) shall come into operation on such day as may be appointed by the Secretary of State by order, and different days may be appointed under this subsection for different purposes.

(6), (7) (*Outside the scope of this work.*)

[321]

NOTES

Sub-s (4): words in first (outer) pair of square brackets substituted by the Oil and Gas (Enterprise) Act 1982, s 37(1), Sch 3, para 39; words in second and third (inner) pairs of square brackets substituted by the Petroleum Act 1998, s 50, Sch 4, para 14.

Orders: the Patents Act 1977 (Commencement No 1) Order 1977, SI 1977/2090; the Patents Act 1977 (Commencement No 2) Order 1978, SI 1978/586; the Patents Act 1977 (Isle of Man) Order 2003, SI 2003/1249.

UNFAIR CONTRACT TERMS ACT 1977 (NOTE)

(1977 c 50)

NOTES

This Act was included in previous editions of this work but has been omitted from this edition in the light of the decision of the Court of Appeal in *Commerzbank AG v Keen* [2006] EWCA Civ 1536, [2007] IRLR132 as to its application to contracts of employment.

See *Harvey* A.

[322]–[344]

STATE IMMUNITY ACT 1978

(1978 c 33)

ARRANGEMENT OF SECTIONS

PART I
PROCEEDINGS IN UNITED KINGDOM BY OR AGAINST OTHER STATES

Immunity from jurisdiction

Exceptions from immunity

Supplementary provisions

PART III
MISCELLANEOUS AND SUPPLEMENTARY

An Act to make new provision with respect to proceedings in the United Kingdom by or against other States; to provide for the effect of judgments given against the United Kingdom in the courts of States parties to the European Convention on State Immunity; to make new provision with respect to the immunities and privileges of heads of State; and for connected purposes

[20 July 1978]

NOTES

Only sections of this Act relevant to employment law are reproduced here. For reasons of space, the subject matter of sections not printed is not annotated.

See *Harvey* DI, T.

PART I
PROCEEDINGS IN UNITED KINGDOM BY OR AGAINST OTHER STATES

Immunity from jurisdiction

1 General immunity from jurisdiction

(1) A State is immune from the jurisdiction of the courts of the United Kingdom except as provided in the following provisions of this Part of this Act.

(2) A court shall give effect to the immunity conferred by this section even though the State does not appear in the proceedings in question.

[345]

Exceptions from immunity

2 Submission to jurisdiction

(1) A State is not immune as respects proceedings in respect of which it has submitted to the jurisdiction of the courts of the United Kingdom.

(2) A State may submit after the dispute giving rise to the proceedings has arisen or by a prior written agreement; but a provision in any agreement that it is to be governed by the law of the United Kingdom is not to be regarded as a submission.

(3) A State is deemed to have submitted—
- (a) if it has instituted the proceedings; or
- (b) subject to subsections (4) and (5) below, if it has intervened or taken any step in the proceedings.

(4) Subsection (3)(b) above does not apply to intervention or any step taken for the purpose only of—
- (a) claiming immunity; or
- (b) asserting an interest in property in circumstances such that the State would have been entitled to immunity if the proceedings had been brought against it.

(5) Subsection (3)(b) above does not apply to any step taken by the State in ignorance of facts entitling it to immunity if those facts could not reasonably have been ascertained and immunity is claimed as soon as reasonably practicable.

(6) A submission in respect of any proceedings extends to any appeal but not to any counter-claim unless it arises out of the same legal relationship or facts as the claim.

(7) The head of a State's diplomatic mission in the United Kingdom, or the person for the time being performing his functions, shall be deemed to have authority to submit on behalf of the State in respect of any proceedings; and any person who has entered into a contract on behalf of and with the authority of a State shall be deemed to have authority to submit on its behalf in respect of proceedings arising out of the contract.

[346]

4 Contracts of employment

(1) A State is not immune as respects proceedings relating to a contract of employment between the State and an individual where the contract was made in the United Kingdom or the work is to be wholly or partly performed there.

(2) Subject to subsections (3) and (4) below, this section does not apply if—
- (a) at the time when the proceedings are brought the individual is a national of the State concerned; or
- (b) at the time when the contract was made the individual was neither a national of the United Kingdom nor habitually resident there; or
- (c) the parties to the contract have otherwise agreed in writing.

(3) Where the work is for an office, agency or establishment maintained by the State in the United Kingdom for commercial purposes, subsection (2) (a) and (b) above do not exclude the application of this section unless the individual was, at the time when the contract was made, habitually resident in that State.

(4) Subsection (2)(c) above does not exclude the application of this section where the law of the United Kingdom requires the proceedings to be brought before a court of the United Kingdom.

(5) In subsection (2)(b) above "national of the United Kingdom" [means—
- (a) a British citizen, a [British overseas territories citizen][, a British National (Overseas)] or a British Overseas citizen; or
- (b) a person who under the British Nationality Act 1981 is a British subject; or
- (c) a British protected person (within the meaning of that Act)].

(6) In this section "proceedings relating to a contract of employment" includes proceedings between the parties to such a contract in respect of any statutory rights or duties to which they are entitled or subject as employer or employee.

[347]

NOTES

Sub-s (5): words in first (outer) pair of square brackets substituted by the British Nationality Act 1981, s 52(6), Sch 7; words in second (inner) pair of square brackets substituted by virtue of the British Overseas Territories Act 2002, s 2(3); words in third (inner) pair of square brackets inserted by the Hong Kong (British Nationality) Order 1986, SI 1986/948, art 8, Schedule.

Supplementary provisions

16 Excluded matters

(1) This Part of this Act does not affect any immunity or privilege conferred by the Diplomatic Privileges Act 1964 or the Consular Relations Act 1968; and—

- (a) section 4 above does not apply to proceedings concerning the employment of the members of a mission within the meaning of the Convention scheduled to the said Act of 1964 or of the members of a consular post within the meaning of the Convention scheduled to the said Act of 1968;
- (b) section 6(1) above does not apply to proceedings concerning a State's title to or its possession of property used for the purposes of a diplomatic mission.

(2) This Part of this Act does not apply to proceedings relating to anything done by or in relation to the armed forces of a State while present in the United Kingdom and, in particular, has effect subject to the Visiting Forces Act 1952.

(3) This Part of this Act does not apply to proceedings to which section 17(6) of the Nuclear Installations Act 1965 applies.

(4) This Part of this Act does not apply to criminal proceedings.

(5) This Part of this Act does not apply to any proceedings relating to taxation other than those mentioned in section 11 above.

[348]

17 Interpretation of Part I

(1) In this Part of this Act—

"the Brussels Convention" means the International Convention for the Unification of Certain Rules Concerning the Immunity of State-owned Ships signed in Brussels on 10th April 1926;

"commercial purposes" means purposes of such transactions or activities as are mentioned in section 3(3) above;

"ship" includes hovercraft.

(2) In sections 2(2) and 13(3) above references to an agreement include references to a treaty, convention or other international agreement.

(3) For the purposes of sections 3 to 8 above the territory of the United Kingdom shall be deemed to include any [British overseas territory] in respect of which the United Kingdom is a party to the European Convention on State Immunity.

(4) In sections 3(1), 4(1), 5 and 16(2) above references to the United Kingdom include references to its territorial waters and any area designated under section 1(7) of the Continental Shelf Act 1964.

(5) In relation to Scotland in this Part of this Act "action in rem" means such an action only in relation to Admiralty proceedings.

[349]

NOTES

Sub-s (3): words in square brackets substituted by virtue of the British Overseas Territories Act 2002, s 1(2).

Brussels Convention: the text of the Brussels Convention is set out in Cmd 5672.

PART III
MISCELLANEOUS AND SUPPLEMENTARY

23 Short title, repeals commencement and extent

(1) This Act may be cited as the State Immunity Act 1978.

(2) …

(3) Subject to subsection (4) below, Parts I and II of this Act do not apply to proceedings in respect of matters that occurred before the date of the coming into force of this Act and, in particular—

- (a) sections 2(2) and 13(3) do not apply to any prior agreement, and

(b) sections 3, 4 and 9 do not apply to any transaction, contract or arbitration agreement,

entered into before that date.

(4) Section 12 above applies to any proceedings instituted after the coming into force of this Act.

(5) This Act shall come into force on such date as may be specified by an order made by the Lord Chancellor by statutory instrument.

(6) This Act extends to Northern Ireland.

(7) Her Majesty may by Order in Council extend any of the provisions of this Act, with or without modification, to any [British overseas territory].

[350]

NOTES

Sub-s (2): repeals the Administration of Justice (Miscellaneous Provisions) Act 1938, s 13, and the Law Reform (Miscellaneous Provisions) (Scotland) Act 1940, s 7.

Sub-s (7): words in square brackets substituted by virtue of the British Overseas Territories Act 2002, s 1(2).

Orders: the State Immunity Act 1978 (Commencement) Order 1978, SI 1978/1572 (bringing this Act into force on 22 November 1978); the State Immunity (Overseas Territories) Order 1979, SI 1979/458 (extending the provisions of this Act, with modifications, to the following dependent territories: Belize, British Antarctic Territory, British Virgin Islands, Cayman Islands, Falkland Islands and Dependencies, Gilbert Islands, Hong Kong, Montserrat, Pitcairn, Henderson, Ducie and Oeno Islands, Sovereign Base Areas of Akrotiri and Dhekelia, Turks and Caicos Islands); the State Immunity (Guernsey) Order 1980, SI 1980/871 (extending the provisions of this Act, with exceptions, adaptations and modifications, to the Bailiwick of Guernsey); the State Immunity (Isle of Man) Order 1981, SI 1981/1112 (extending the provisions of this Act, with modifications, to the Isle of Man); the State Immunity (Jersey) Order 1985, SI 1985/1642 (extending the provisions of this Act, with modifications, to the Bailiwick of Jersey).

EMPLOYMENT PROTECTION (CONSOLIDATION) ACT 1978 (NOTE)

(1978 c 44)

NOTES

This Act originally consolidated the major employment protection legislation within the jurisdiction of what were then industrial tribunals. It was then subjected to numerous amendments, and those parts relating to collective labour relations were repealed and re-consolidated by the Trade Union and Labour Relations (Consolidation) Act 1992. Substantial further amendments and substitutions were made by the Trade Union Reform and Employment Rights Act 1993. The Act was repealed in its entirety by the combined effect of the Employment Tribunals Act 1996 and the Employment Rights Act 1996, as from 22 August 1996. The provisions of this Act, together with other employment protection legislation (principally the Wages Act 1986) are consolidated and re-enacted by the two 1996 Acts at **[954]** and **[1006]**. Tables of destinations for the provisions consolidated are at **[1005]**, **[1285]**.

[351]

EMPLOYMENT ACT 1980 (NOTE)

(1980 c 42)

NOTES

The whole of this Act has been repealed by a combination of the following enactments: the Contempt of Court Act 1981, the Employment Act 1982, the Insolvency Act 1985, the Employment Act 1989, the Employment Act 1990, the Trade Union and Labour Relations (Consolidation) Act 1992, the Trade Union Reform and Employment Rights Act 1993, the Employment Tribunals Act 1996, and the Employment Rights Act 1996.

Ss 1–5, 16 and 19 are consolidated in the Trade Union and Labour Relations (Consolidation) Act 1992. Ss 6, 8(2), 9, 12–14, 20, 21, and part of Sch 1 are consolidated in the Employment Rights Act 1996: see Destination Table below at **[1285]** for details.

[352]

LIMITATION ACT 1980

(1980 c 58)

ARRANGEMENT OF SECTIONS

PART I
ORDINARY TIME LIMITS FOR DIFFERENT CLASSES OF ACTION

Time limits under Part I subject to extension or exclusion under Part II

Actions founded on tort

Actions founded on simple contract

Actions for sums recoverable by statute

Actions in respect of wrongs causing personal injuries or death

Actions in respect of latent damage not involving personal injuries

PART II
EXTENSION OR EXCLUSION OF ORDINARY TIME LIMITS

Disability

Fraud, concealment and mistake

Discretionary exclusion of time limit for actions for defamation or malicious falsehood

Discretionary exclusion of time limit for actions in respect of personal injuries or death

PART III
MISCELLANEOUS AND GENERAL

An Act to consolidate the Limitation Acts 1939 to 1980

[13 November 1980]

NOTES

Only certain sections of this Act are relevant to employment law, and accordingly, only those sections of most relevance have been included in this work. For reasons of space, the subject matter of the sections and Schedules omitted is not annotated.

Application to arbitral proceedings: this Act applies to arbitral proceedings as it applies to legal proceedings; see the Arbitration Act 1996, s 13(1). As to the commencement of arbitral proceedings for the purposes of this Act, see ss 12 (in particular sub-s (5)), 13(2), (4), 14 of the 1996 Act, and as to when a cause of action accrued, see s 13(3), (4) of the 1996 Act.

PART I
ORDINARY TIME LIMITS FOR DIFFERENT CLASSES OF ACTION

Time limits under Part I subject to extension or exclusion under Part II

1 Time limits under Part I subject to extension or exclusion under Part II

(1) This Part of this Act gives the ordinary time limits for bringing actions of the various classes mentioned in the following provisions of this Part.

(2) The ordinary time limits given in this Part of this Act are subject to extension or exclusion in accordance with the provisions of Part II of this Act.

[352A]

Actions founded on tort

2 Time limit for actions founded on tort

An action founded on tort shall not be brought after the expiration of six years from the date on which the cause of action accrued.

[352B]

[4A Time limit for actions for defamation or malicious falsehood

The time limit under section 2 of this Act shall not apply to an action for—

(a) libel or slander, or malicious falsehood.
(b) slander of title, slander of goods or other malicious falsehood,

but no such action shall be brought after the expiration of one year from the date on which the cause of action accrued.]

[352C]

NOTES

Inserted by the Administration of Justice Act 1985, s 57(2).
Substituted by the Defamation Act 1996, s 5(2), (6).

Actions founded on simple contract

5 Time limit for actions founded on simple contract

An action founded on simple contract shall not be brought after the expiration of six years from the date on which the cause of action accrued.

[352D]

Actions for sums recoverable by statute

9 Time limit for actions for sums recoverable by statute

(1) An action to recover any sum recoverable by virtue of any enactment shall not be brought after the expiration of six years from the date on which the cause of action accrued.

(2) Subsection (1) above shall not affect any action to which section 10 of this Act applies.

[352E]

10 Special time limit for claiming contribution

(1) Where under section 1 of the Civil Liability (Contribution) Act 1978 any person becomes entitled to a right to recover contribution in respect of any damage from any other person, no action to recover contribution by virtue of that right shall be brought after the expiration of two years from the date on which that right accrued.

(2) For the purposes of this section the date on which a right to recover contribution in respect of any damage accrues to any person (referred to below in this section as "the relevant date") shall be ascertained as provided in subsections (3) and (4) below.

(3) If the person in question is held liable in respect of that damage—

(a) by a judgment given in any civil proceedings; or

(b) by an award made on any arbitration;

the relevant date shall be the date on which the judgment is given, or the date of the award (as the case may be).

For the purposes of this subsection no account shall be taken of any judgment or award given or made on appeal in so far as it varies the amount of damages awarded against the person in question.

(4) If, in any case not within subsection (3) above, the person in question makes or agrees to make any payment to one or more persons in compensation for that damage (whether he admits any liability in respect of the damage or not), the relevant date shall be the earliest date on which the amount to be paid by him is agreed between him (or his representative) and the person (or each of the persons, as the case may be) to whom the payment is to be made.

(5) An action to recover contribution shall be one to which sections 28, 32 and 35 of this Act apply, but otherwise Parts II and III of this Act (except sections 34, 37 and 38) shall not apply for the purposes of this section.

[352F]

Actions in respect of wrongs causing personal injuries or death

11 Special time limit for actions in respect of personal injuries

(1) This section applies to any action for damages for negligence, nuisance or breach of duty (whether the duty exists by virtue of a contract or of provision made by or under a statute or independently of any contract or any such provision) where the damages claimed by the plaintiff for the negligence, nuisance or breach of duty consist of or include damages in respect of personal injuries to the plaintiff or any other person.

[(1A) This section does not apply to any action brought for damages under section 3 of the Protection from Harassment Act 1997.]

(2) None of the time limits given in the preceding provisions of this Act shall apply to an action to which this section applies.

(3) An action to which this section applies shall not be brought after the expiration of the period applicable in accordance with subsection (4) or (5) below.

(4) Except where subsection (5) below applies, the period applicable is three years from—

(a) the date on which the cause of action accrued; or

(b) the date of knowledge (if later) of the person injured.

(5) If the person injured dies before the expiration of the period mentioned in subsection (4) above, the period applicable as respects the cause of action surviving for the benefit of his estate by virtue of section 1 of the Law Reform (Miscellaneous Provisions) Act 1934 shall be three years from—

(a) the date of death; or

(b) the date of the personal representative's knowledge;

whichever is the later.

(6) For the purposes of this section "personal representative" includes any person who is or has been a personal representative of the deceased, including an executor who has not proved the will (whether or not he has renounced probate) but not anyone appointed only as a special personal representative in relation to settled land; and regard shall be had to any knowledge acquired by any such person while a personal representative or previously.

(7) If there is more than one personal representative, and their dates of knowledge are different, subsection (5)(b) above shall be read as referring to the earliest of those dates.

[352G]

NOTES

Sub-s (1A): inserted by the Protection from Harassment Act 1997, s 6.

14 Definition of date of knowledge for purposes of sections 11 and 12

(1) [Subject to subsection (1A) below,] In sections 11 and 12 of this Act references to a person's date of knowledge are references to the date on which he first had knowledge of the following facts—

(a) that the injury in question was significant; and

(b) that the injury was attributable in whole or in part to the act or omission which is alleged to constitute negligence, nuisance or breach of duty; and

(c) the identity of the defendant; and

(d) if it is alleged that the act or omission was that of a person other than the defendant, the identity of that person and the additional facts supporting the bringing of an action against the defendant;

and knowledge that any acts or omissions did or did not, as a matter of law, involve negligence, nuisance or breach of duty is irrelevant.

[(1A) In section 11A of this Act and in section 12 of this Act so far as that section applies to an action by virtue of section 6(1)(a) of the Consumer Protection Act 1987 (death caused by defective product) references to a person's date of knowledge are references to the date on which he first had knowledge of the following facts—

(a) such facts about the damage caused by the defect as would lead a reasonable person who had suffered such damage to consider it sufficiently serious to justify his instituting proceedings for damages against a defendant who did not dispute liability and was able to satisfy a judgment; and

(b) that the damage was wholly or partly attributable to the facts and circumstances alleged to constitute the defect; and

(c) the identity of the defendant;

but, in determining the date on which a person first had such knowledge there shall be disregarded both the extent (if any) of that person's knowledge on any date of whether particular facts or circumstances would or would not, as a matter of law, constitute a defect and, in a case relating to loss of or damage to property, any knowledge which that person had on a date on which he had no right of action by virtue of Part I of that Act in respect of the loss or damage.]

(2) For the purposes of this section an injury is significant if the person whose date of knowledge is in question would reasonably have considered it sufficiently serious to justify his instituting proceedings for damages against a defendant who did not dispute liability and was able to satisfy a judgment.

(3) For the purposes of this section a person's knowledge includes knowledge which he might reasonably have been expected to acquire—

(a) from facts observable or ascertainable by him; or

(b) from facts ascertainable by him with the help of medical or other appropriate expert advice which it is reasonable for him to seek;

but a person shall not be fixed under this subsection with knowledge of a fact ascertainable only with the help of expert advice so long as he has taken all reasonable steps to obtain (and, where appropriate, to act on) that advice.

[352H]

NOTES

Sub-s (1): words in square brackets inserted by the Consumer Protection Act 1987, s 6, Sch 1, Pt I, para 3.

Sub-s (1A): inserted by the Consumer Protection Act 1987, s 6, Sch 1, Pt I, para 3.

[Actions in respect of latent damage not involving personal injuries

14A Special time limit for negligence actions where facts relevant to cause of action are not known at date of accrual

(1) This section applies to any action for damages for negligence, other than one to which section 11 of this Act applies, where the starting date for reckoning the period of limitation under subsection (4)(b) below falls after the date on which the cause of action accrued.

(2) Section 2 of this Act shall not apply to an action to which this section applies.

(3) An action to which this section applies shall not be brought after the expiration of the period applicable in accordance with subsection (4) below.

(4) That period is either—

(a) six years from the date on which the cause of action accrued; or

(b) three years from the starting date as defined by subsection (5) below, if that period expires later than the period mentioned in paragraph (a) above.

(5) For the purposes of this section, the starting date for reckoning the period of limitation under subsection (4)(b) above is the earliest date on which the plaintiff or any person in whom the cause of action was vested before him first had both the knowledge required for bringing an action for damages in respect of the relevant damage and a right to bring such an action.

(6) In subsection (5) above "the knowledge required for bringing an action for damages in respect of the relevant damage" means knowledge both—

(a) of the material facts about the damage in respect of which damages are claimed; and

(b) of the other facts relevant to the current action mentioned in subsection (8) below.

(7) For the purposes of subsection (6)(a) above, the material facts about the damage are such facts about the damage as would lead a reasonable person who had suffered such damage to consider it sufficiently serious to justify his instituting proceedings for damages against a defendant who did not dispute liability and was able to satisfy a judgment.

(8) The other facts referred to in subsection (6)(b) above are—

(a) that the damage was attributable in whole or in part to the act or omission which is alleged to constitute negligence; and

(b) the identity of the defendant; and

(c) if it is alleged that the act or omission was that of a person other than the defendant, the identity of that person and the additional facts supporting the bringing of an action against the defendant.

(9) Knowledge that any acts or omissions did or did not, as a matter of law, involve negligence is irrelevant for the purposes of subsection (5) above.

(10) For the purposes of this section a person's knowledge includes knowledge which he might reasonably have been expected to acquire—

(a) from facts observable or ascertainable by him; or

(b) from facts ascertainable by him with the help of appropriate expert advice which it is reasonable for him to seek;

but a person shall not be taken by virtue of this subsection to have knowledge of a fact ascertainable only with the help of expert advice so long as he has taken all reasonable steps to obtain (and, where appropriate, to act on) that advice.]

[352I]

NOTES

Inserted, together with the preceding heading and s 14B, by the Latent Damage Act 1986, s 1.

[14B Overriding time limit for negligence actions not involving personal injuries

(1) An action for damages for negligence, other than one to which section 11 of this Act applies, shall not be brought after the expiration of fifteen years from the date (or, if more than one, from the last of the dates) on which there occurred any act or omission—

(a) which is alleged to constitute negligence; and

(b) to which the damage in respect of which damages are claimed is alleged to be attributable (in whole or in part).

(2) This section bars the right of action in a case to which subsection (1) above applies notwithstanding that—

(a) the cause of action has not yet accrued; or

(b) where section 14A of this Act applies to the action, the date which is for the purposes of that section the starting date for reckoning the period mentioned in subsection (4)(b) of that section has not yet occurred;

before the end of the period of limitation prescribed by this section.]

[352J]

NOTES

Inserted as noted to s 14A at **[352I]**.

PART II
EXTENSION OR EXCLUSION OF ORDINARY TIME LIMITS

Disability

28 Extension of limitation period in case of disability

(1) Subject to the following provisions of this section, if on the date when any right of action accrued for which a period of limitation is prescribed by this Act, the person to whom it accrued was under a disability, the action may be brought at any time before the expiration of six years from the date when he ceased to be under a disability or died (whichever first occurred) notwithstanding that the period of limitation has expired.

(2) This section shall not affect any case where the right of action first accrued to some person (not under a disability) through whom the person under a disability claims.

(3) When a right of action which has accrued to a person under a disability accrues, on the death of that person while still under a disability, to another person under a disability, no further extension of time shall be allowed by reason of the disability of the second person.

(4) No action to recover land or money charged on land shall be brought by virtue of this section by any person after the expiration of thirty years from the date on which the right of action accrued to that person or some person through whom he claims.

[(4A) If the action is one to which section 4A of this Act applies, subsection (1) above shall have effect—

(a) in the case of an action for libel or slander, as if for the words from "at any time" to "occurred)" there were substituted the words "by him at any time before the expiration of one year from the date on which he ceased to be under a disability"; and

(b) in the case of an action for slander of title, slander of goods or other malicious falsehood, as if for the words "six years" there were substituted the words "one year".]

(5) If the action is one to which section 10 of this Act applies, subsection (1) above shall have effect as if for the words "six years" there were substituted the words "two years".

(6) If the action is one to which section 11 or 12(2) of this Act applies, subsection (1) above shall have effect as if for the words "six years" there were substituted the words "three years".

[(7) If the action is one to which section 11A of this Act applies or one by virtue of section 6(1)(a) of the Consumer Protection Act 1987 (death caused by defective product), subsection (1) above—

(a) shall not apply to the time limit prescribed by subsection (3) of the said section 11A or to that time limit as applied by virtue of section 12(1) of this Act; and

(b) in relation to any other time limit prescribed by this Act shall have effect as if for the word "six years" there were substituted the words "three years".]

[352K]

NOTES

Sub-s (4A): inserted by the Administration of Justice Act 1985, ss 57(3), 69(5), Sch 9, para 14; substituted by the Defamation Act 1996, s 5(3), (6), in relation to causes of action arising on or after 4 September 1996.

Sub-s (7): added by the Consumer Protection Act 1987, s 6, Sch 1, Pt I, para 4.

[28A Extension for cases where the limitation period is the period under section 14A(4)(b)

(1) Subject to subsection (2) below, if in the case of any action for which a period of limitation is prescribed by section 14A of this Act—

(a) the period applicable in accordance with subsection (4) of that section is the period mentioned in paragraph (b) of that subsection;

(b) on the date which is for the purposes of that section the starting date for reckoning that period the person by reference to whose knowledge that date fell to be determined under subsection (5) of that section was under a disability; and

(c) section 28 of this Act does not apply to the action;

the action may be brought at any time before the expiration of three years from the date when he ceased to be under a disability or died (whichever first occurred) notwithstanding that the period mentioned above has expired.

(2) An action may not be brought by virtue of subsection (1) above after the end of the period of limitation prescribed by section 14B of this Act.]

[352L]

NOTES

Inserted by the Latent Damage Act 1986, s 2(1).

Fraud, concealment and mistake

32 Postponement of limitation period in case of fraud, concealment or mistake

(1) Subject to [subsections (3) and (4A)] below, where in the case of any action for which a period of limitation is prescribed by this Act, either—

(a) the action is based upon the fraud of the defendant; or

(b) any fact relevant to the plaintiff's right of action has been deliberately concealed from him by the defendant; or

(c) the action is for relief from the consequences of a mistake;

the period of limitation shall not begin to run until the plaintiff has discovered the fraud, concealment or mistake (as the case may be) or could with reasonable diligence have discovered it.

References in this subsection to the defendant include references to the defendant's agent and to any person through whom the defendant claims and his agent.

(2) For the purposes of subsection (1) above, deliberate commission of a breach of duty in circumstances in which it is unlikely to be discovered for some time amounts to deliberate concealment of the facts involved in that breach of duty.

(3) Nothing in this section shall enable any action—

(a) to recover, or recover the value of, any property; or

(b) to enforce any charge against, or set aside any transaction affecting, any property;

to be brought against the purchaser of the property or any person claiming through him in any case where the property has been purchased for valuable consideration by an innocent third party since the fraud or concealment or (as the case may be) the transaction in which the mistake was made took place.

(4) A purchaser is an innocent third party for the purposes of this section—

(a) in the case of fraud or concealment of any fact relevant to the plaintiff's right of action, if he was not a party to the fraud or (as the case may be) to the concealment of that fact and did not at the time of the purchase know or have reason to believe that the fraud or concealment had taken place; and

(b) in the case of mistake, if he did not at the time of the purchase know or have reason to believe that the mistake had been made.

[(4A) Subsection (1) above shall not apply in relation to the time limit prescribed by section 11A(3) of this Act or in relation to that time limit as applied by virtue of section 12(1) of this Act].

[(5) Sections 14A and 14B of this Act shall not apply to any action to which subsection (1)(b) above applies (and accordingly the period of limitation referred to in that subsection, in any case to which either of those sections would otherwise apply, is the period applicable under section 2 of this Act).]

[352M]

NOTES

Sub-s (1): words in square brackets substituted by the Consumer Protection Act 1987, s 6, Sch 1, Pt I, para 5(a).

Sub-s (4A): inserted by the Consumer Protection Act 1987, s 6, Sch 1, Pt I, para 5(b).

Sub-s (5): added by the Latent Damage Act 1986, s 2(2).

Disapplication of sub-s (1)(c): sub-s (1)(c) is disapplied with respect to certain actions for mistake of law relating to tax brought before 8 September 2003; see the Finance Act 2007, s 107.

[Discretionary exclusion of time limit for actions for defamation or malicious falsehood

32A Discretionary exclusion of time limit for actions for defamation or malicious falsehood

(1) If it appears to the court that it would be exclusion of time equitable to allow an action to proceed having regard to limit for actions the degree to which—

(a) the operation of section 4A of this Act prejudices the plaintiff or any person whom he represents, and

(b) any decision of the court under this subsection would prejudice the defendant or any person whom he represents,

the court may direct that that section shall not apply to the action or shall not apply to any specified cause of action to which the action relates.

(2) In acting under this section the court shall have regard to all the circumstances of the case and in particular to—

(a) the length of, and the reasons for, the delay on the part of the plaintiff;

(b) where the reason or one of the reasons for the delay was that all or any of the facts relevant to the cause of action did not become known to the plaintiff until after the end of the period mentioned in section 4A—

(i) the date on which any such facts did become known to him, and

(ii) the extent to which he acted promptly and reasonably once he knew whether or not the facts in question might be capable of giving rise to an action; and

(c) the extent to which, having regard to the delay, relevant evidence is likely—

(i) to be unavailable, or

(ii) to be less cogent than if the action had been brought within the period mentioned in section 4A.

(3) In the case of an action for slander of title, slander of goods or other malicious falsehood brought by a personal representative—

(a) the references in subsection (2) above to the plaintiff shall be construed as including the deceased person to whom the cause of action accrued and any previous personal representative of that person; and

(b) nothing in section 28(3) of this Act shall be construed as affecting the court's discretion under this section.

(4) In this section "the court" means the court in which the action has been brought.]

[352N]

NOTES

Inserted, together with the preceding heading, by the Administration of Justice Act 1985, s 57(4). Substituted by the Defamation Act 1996, s 5(4), (6).

Discretionary exclusion of time limit for actions in respect of personal injuries or death

33 Discretionary exclusion of time limit for actions in respect of personal injuries or death

(1) If it appears to the court that it would be equitable to allow an action to proceed having regard to the degree to which—

(a) the provisions of section 11 [or 11A] or 12 of this Act prejudice the plaintiff or any person whom he represents; and

(b) any decision of the court under this subsection would prejudice the defendant or any person whom he represents;

the court may direct that those provisions shall not apply to the action, or shall not apply to any specified cause of action to which the action relates.

[(1A) The court shall not under this section disapply—

(a) subsection (3) of section 11A; or

(b) where the damages claimed by the plaintiff are confined to damages for loss of or damage to any property, any other provision in its application to an action by virtue of Part I of the Consumer Protection Act 1987.]

(2) The court shall not under this section disapply section 12(1) except where the reason why the person injured could no longer maintain an action was because of the time limit in section 11 [or subsection (4) of section 11A].

If, for example, the person injured could at his death no longer maintain an action under the Fatal Accidents Act 1976 because of the time limit in Article 29 in Schedule 1 to the Carriage by Air Act 1961, the court has no power to direct that section 12(1) shall not apply.

(3) In acting under this section the court shall have regard to all the circumstances of the case and in particular to—

(a) the length of, and the reasons for, the delay on the part of the plaintiff;

(b) the extent to which, having regard to the delay, the evidence adduced or likely to be adduced by the plaintiff or the defendant is or is likely to be less cogent than if the action had been brought within the time allowed by section 11 [, by section 11A] or (as the case may be) by section 12;

(c) the conduct of the defendant after the cause of action arose, including the extent (if any) to which he responded to requests reasonably made by the plaintiff for information or inspection for the purpose of ascertaining facts which were or might be relevant to the plaintiff's cause of action against the defendant;

(d) the duration of any disability of the plaintiff arising after the date of the accrual of the cause of action;

(e) the extent to which the plaintiff acted promptly and reasonably once he knew whether or not the act or omission of the defendant, to which the injury was attributable, might be capable at that time of giving rise to an action for damages;

(f) the steps, if any, taken by the plaintiff to obtain medical, legal or other expert advice and the nature of any such advice he may have received.

(4) In a case where the person injured died when, because of section 11 [or subsection (4) of section 11A], he could no longer maintain an action and recover damages in respect of the injury, the court shall have regard in particular to the length of, and the reasons for, the delay on the part of the deceased.

(5) In a case under subsection (4) above, or any other case where the time limit, or one of the time limits, depends on the date of knowledge of a person other than the plaintiff, subsection (3) above shall have effect with appropriate modifications, and shall have effect in particular as if references to the plaintiff included references to any person whose date of knowledge is or was relevant in determining a time limit.

(6) A direction by the court disapplying the provisions of section 12(1) shall operate to disapply the provisions to the same effect in section 1(1) of the Fatal Accidents Act 1976.

(7) In this section "the court" means the court in which the action has been brought.

(8) References in this section to section 11 [or 11A] include references to that section as extended by any of the preceding provisions of this Part of this Act or by any provision of Part III of this Act.

[352O]

NOTES

Sub-ss (1), (3), (4), (8): words in square brackets inserted by the Consumer Protection Act 1987, s 6, Sch 1, Pt I, para 6(a), (c)–(e).

Sub-s (1A): inserted by the Consumer Protection Act 1987, s 6, Sch 1, Pt I, para 6(b).

PART III
MISCELLANEOUS AND GENERAL

41 Short title, commencement and extent

(1) This Act may be cited as the Limitation Act 1980.

(2) This Act, except section 35, shall come into force on 1st May 1981.

(3) (*Relates to the commencement of s 35* (*outside the scope of this work*).)

(4) The repeal by this Act of section 14(1) of the Limitation Act 1963 and the corresponding saving in paragraph 2 of Schedule 2 to this Act shall extend to Northern Ireland, but otherwise this Act does not extend to Scotland or to Northern Ireland.

[352P]

NOTES

Orders: the Limitation Act 1980 (Commencement) Order 1981, SI 1981/588.

Limitation Act 1939: repealed by this Act.

SOCIAL SECURITY AND HOUSING BENEFITS ACT 1982 (NOTE)

(1982 c 24)

NOTES

Relevant parts of this Act (ie, those dealing with Statutory Sick Pay) were repealed and re-enacted in the Social Security Contributions and Benefits Act 1992, Pt XI (at **[421]** et seq).

[353]

EMPLOYMENT ACT 1982 (NOTE)

(1982 c 46)

NOTES

The main parts of this Act were repealed and consolidated in either the Trade Union and Labour Relations (Consolidation) Act 1992 (ss 2–19, Sch 1) or the Employment Rights Act 1996 (s 20, parts of s 21, Schs 2, 3 and 4). Section 1 was repealed by the Companies Consolidation (Consequential Provisions) Act 1985, Sch 2. The remaining provisions were repealed by the Statute Law (Repeals) Act 2004, as from 22 July 2004.

[354]

DATA PROTECTION ACT 1984 (NOTE)

(1984 c 35)

NOTES

The whole of this Act was repealed by the Data Protection Act 1998 at **[1311]**.

[355]–[360]

COMPANIES ACT 1985

(1985 c 6)

An Act to consolidate the greater part of the Companies Acts

[11 March 1985]

NOTES

Only a small part of this Act is directly relevant to employment law, and accordingly, only those sections of most relevance have been included in this work. Of the provisions of this Act printed in the fifteenth (2007) edition of this work, only ss 317, 719, 746, 747 remain in force on 6 April 2008. The other provisions were repealed as follows:

Ss 282, 292, 303, 309 repealed by the Companies Act 2006, s 1295, Sch 16, as from 1 October 2007.

Ss 283–284 repealed by the Companies Act 2006, s 1295, Sch 16, as from 6 April 2008.

S 285 (Validity of acts of directors) repealed by the Companies Act 2006, s 1295, Sch 16, as from 1 October 2007, subject to savings in relation to acts done before that date (see the Companies Act 2006 (Commencement No 3, Consequential Amendments, Transitional Provisions and Savings) Order 2007, SI 2007/2194, Sch 3, para 4).

S 286 (Qualifications of company secretaries) repealed by the Companies Act 2006, s 1295, Sch 16, as from 6 April 2008, subject to savings in relation to company secretaries appointed before that date (see the Companies Act 2006 (Commencement No 5, Transitional Provisions and Savings) Order 2007, SI 2007/3495, Sch 4, Pt 1, para 5).

S 304 (Director's right to protest removal) repealed by the Companies Act 2006, s 1295, Sch 16, as from 1 October 2007 (note, however, that SI 2007/2194, Sch 3, para 5 provides that sub-s (4) continues to apply where, in the case of an intended resolution to remove a director under s 303, the written representations made by the director concerned were received by the company before that date).

Ss 309A (Provisions protecting directors from liability), 309B (Qualifying third party indemnity provisions), and 309C (Disclosure of qualifying third party indemnity provisions) repealed by the Companies Act 2006, s 1295, Sch 16, as from 1 October 2007, except in relation to any provision to which they applied immediately before that date (see SI 2007/2194, Sch 3, paras 15–17).

Ss 312 (Payment to director for loss of office, etc), 313 (Company approval for property transfer), 316 (Provisions supplementing ss 312 to 315), repealed by the Companies Act 2006, s 1295, Sch 16, as from 1 October 2007, except in relation to loss of office or retirement occurring before that date (see SI 2007/2194, Sch 3, para 12).

S 318 (Directors' service contracts to be open to inspection) repealed by the Companies Act 2006, s 1295, Sch 16, as from 1 October 2007, except in relation to (a) any default before 1 October 2007 in complying with s 318(1) or (5); (b) any request for inspection under s 318(7) made before that date; and (c) any duty to give notice under s 318(4) arising before that date (see SI 2007/2194, Sch 3, para 13(4)).

S 319 (Director's contract of employment for more than 5 years) repealed by the Companies Act 2006, s 1295, Sch 16, as from 1 October 2007, except in relation to apply to agreements made before that date (see SI 2007/2194, Sch 3, para 6).

Sch 7, Pts III, V repealed by the Companies Act 2006, s 1295, Sch 16, as from 6 April 2008. For general savings and transitional provisions in connection with the repeal of Pt VII of the Companies Act 1985 (Accounts and Audit) and the commencement of the equivalent provisions of the 2006 Act, see SI 2007/3495, Sch 4, Pt 1, paras 6–9, 12.

For the Companies Act 2006, see **[1745]** et seq.

See *Harvey* A, N, M, U.

PART X
ENFORCEMENT OF FAIR DEALING BY DIRECTORS

Restrictions on directors taking financial advantage

317 Directors to disclose interest in contracts

(1) *It is the duty of a director of a company who is in any way, whether directly or indirectly, interested in a contract or proposed contract with the company to declare the nature of his interest at a meeting of the directors of the company.*

(2) *In the case of a proposed contract, the declaration shall be made—*

(*a*) *at the meeting of the directors at which the question of entering into the contract is first taken into consideration; or*

(*b*) *if the director was not at the date of that meeting interested in the proposed contract, at the next meeting of the directors held after he became so interested;*

and, in a case where the director becomes interested in a contract after it is made, the declaration shall be made at the first meeting of the directors held after he becomes so interested.

(3) For purposes of this section, a general notice given to the directors of a company by a director to the effect that—

(a) he is a member of a specified company or firm and is to be regarded as interested in any contract which may, after the date of the notice, be made with that company or firm; or

(b) he is to be regarded as interested in any contract which may after the date of the notice be made with a specified person who is connected with him (within the meaning of section 346 below),

is deemed a sufficient declaration of interest in relation to any such contract.

(4) However, no such notice is of effect unless either it is given at a meeting of the directors or the director takes reasonable steps to secure that it is brought up and read at the next meeting of the directors after it is given.

(5) A reference in this section to a contract includes any transaction or arrangement (whether or not constituting a contract) made or entered into on or after 22nd December 1980.

(6) For purposes of this section, a transaction or arrangement of a kind described in [section 197, 198, 200, 201 or 203 of the Companies Act 2006] (prohibition of loans, quasi-loans etc to directors) made by a company for a director of the company or a person connected with such a director is treated (if it would not otherwise be so treated, and whether or not it is prohibited by that section) as a transaction or arrangement in which that director is interested.

(7) A director who fails to comply with this section is liable to a fine.

(8) This section applies to a shadow director as it applies to a director, except that a shadow director shall declare his interest, not at a meeting of the directors, but by a notice in writing to the directors which is either—

(a) a specific notice given before the date of the meeting at which, if he had been a director, the declaration would be required by subsection (2) to be made; or

(b) a notice which under subsection (3) falls to be treated as a sufficient declaration of that interest (or would fall to be so treated apart from subsection (4)).

(9) Nothing in this section prejudices the operation of any rule of law restricting directors of a company from having an interest in contracts with the company.

[360A]–[362]

NOTES

Repealed by the Companies Act 2006, s 1295, Sch 16, as from 1 October 2008, except in relation to (i) a duty arising before that date, and (ii) transactions or arrangements entered into before that date (see the Companies Act 2006 (Commencement No 5, Transitional Provisions and Savings) Order 2007, SI 2007/3495, Sch 4, Pt 3, paras 48, 50).

Sub-s (6): words in square brackets substituted by the Companies Act 2006 (Commencement No 3, Consequential Amendments, Transitional Provisions and Savings) Order 2007, SI 2007/2194, art 10(1), Sch 4, Pt 1, para 5, as from 1 October 2007.

Note also that the repeal of s 346 of this Act does not affect sub-s (3)(b) above; see the Companies Act 2006 (Commencement No 3, Consequential Amendments, Transitional Provisions and Savings) Order 2007, SI 2007/2194, Sch 3 para 50(a).

PART XXV
MISCELLANEOUS AND SUPPLEMENTARY PROVISIONS

719 Power of company to provide for employees on cessation or transfer of business

(1) The powers of a company include (if they would not otherwise do so apart from this section) power to make the following provision for the benefit of persons employed or formerly employed by the company or any of its subsidiaries, that is to say, provision in connection with the cessation or the transfer to any person of the whole or part of the undertaking of the company or that subsidiary.

(2) The power conferred by subsection (1) is exercisable notwithstanding that its exercise is not in the best interests of the company.

(3) The power which a company may exercise by virtue only of subsection (1) shall only be exercised by the company if sanctioned—

(*a*) *in a case not falling within paragraph (b) or (c) below, by an ordinary resolution of the company, or*

(*b*) *if so authorised by the memorandum or articles, a resolution of the directors, or*

(*c*) *if the memorandum or articles require the exercise of the power to be sanctioned by a resolution of the company of some other description for which more than a simple majority of the members voting is necessary, with the sanction of a resolution of that description;*

and in any case after compliance with any other requirements of the memorandum or articles applicable to its exercise.

(4) *Any payment which may be made by a company under this section may, if made before the commencement of any winding up of the company, be made out of profits of the company which are available for dividend.*

[363]

NOTES

Repealed by the Companies Act 2006, s 1295, Sch 16, as from a day to be appointed.

On the winding up of a company the liquidator may make any payment which the company has, before the commencement of the winding up, decided to make under this section, and the powers which a company may exercise by virtue only of this section may be exercised, in certain circumstances, by the liquidator himself; see the Insolvency Act 1986, s 187.

Note: the Companies Act 2006 (Commencement No 3, Consequential Amendments, Transitional Provisions and Savings) Order 2007, SI 2007/2194, Sch 2, Pt 1 originally provided that this section would be repealed as from 1 October 2007. That Schedule was amended by the Companies Act 2006 (Commencement No 4 and Commencement No 3 (Amendment)) Order 2007, SI 2007/2607, as from 30 September 2007, so that the reference to this section was removed from the provisions scheduled to be repealed as from 1 October 2007.

PART XXVII
FINAL PROVISIONS

746 Commencement

... *this Act comes into force on 1st July 1985.*

[364]

NOTES

Repealed by the Companies Act 2006, s 1295, Sch 16, as from a day to be appointed.
Words omitted repealed by the Companies Act 1989, s 212, Sch 24.

747 Citation

This Act may be cited as the Companies Act 1985.

[365]–[367]

INSOLVENCY ACT 1986

(1986 c 45)

ARRANGEMENT OF SECTIONS

THE FIRST GROUP OF PARTS
COMPANY INSOLVENCY; COMPANIES WINDING UP

PART II
ADMINISTRATION

PART III
RECEIVERSHIP

CHAPTER I
RECEIVERS AND MANAGERS (ENGLAND AND WALES)

Receivers and managers appointed out of court

Administrative receivers: general

CHAPTER II
RECEIVERS (SCOTLAND)

PART IV
WINDING UP OF COMPANIES REGISTERED UNDER THE COMPANIES ACTS

CHAPTER VI
WINDING UP BY THE COURT

Commencement of winding up

THE SECOND GROUP OF PARTS
INSOLVENCY OF INDIVIDUALS; BANKRUPTCY

PART VIII
INDIVIDUAL VOLUNTARY ARRANGEMENTS

Moratorium for insolvent debtor

Consideration and implementation of debtor's proposal

PART IX
BANKRUPTCY

CHAPTER II
PROTECTION OF BANKRUPT'S ESTATE AND INVESTIGATION OF HIS AFFAIRS

THE THIRD GROUP OF PARTS
MISCELLANEOUS MATTERS BEARING ON BOTH COMPANY AND INDIVIDUAL INSOLVENCY; GENERAL INTERPRETATION; FINAL PROVISIONS

PART XII
PREFERENTIAL DEBTS IN COMPANY AND INDIVIDUAL INSOLVENCY

PART XIX
FINAL PROVISIONS

SCHEDULES:

An Act to consolidate the enactments relating to company insolvency and winding up (including the winding up of companies that are not insolvent, and of unregistered companies); enactments relating to the insolvency and bankruptcy of individuals; and other enactments bearing on those two subject matters, including the functions and qualification of insolvency practitioners, the public administration of insolvency, the penalisation and redress of malpractice and wrongdoing, and the avoidance of certain transactions at an undervalue

[25 July 1986]

NOTES

Most of this Act covers matters outside the scope of this work, and only those provisions most directly relevant to employment law are printed. For reasons of space, the subject matter of sections, etc, not printed is not annotated. All provisions of the Act printed here except ss 37, 44, 57, and the provisions in the Second Group of Parts (ss 252, 254, 260, 285) apply to England, Wales and Scotland. Sections 37 and 44 apply only to England and Wales (by virtue of s 28) and s 57 applies only to Scotland (by virtue of s 50). None of the provisions in the Second Group of Parts (insolvency of individuals) apply to Scotland (by virtue of s 440). For provisions relating to individual insolvency in Scotland, see the Bankruptcy (Scotland) Act 1985 (outside the scope of this work).

For the application of this Act to limited liability partnerships, see the Limited Liability Partnerships Act 2000, the Limited Liability Partnerships Regulations 2001, SI 2001/1090 and the Limited Liability Partnerships (Scotland) Regulations 2001, SSI 2001/128.

See *Harvey* G, Q.

THE FIRST GROUP OF PARTS
COMPANY INSOLVENCY; COMPANIES WINDING UP

[PART II
ADMINISTRATION

8 Administration

Schedule B1 to this Act (which makes provision about the administration of companies) shall have effect.]

[367A]

NOTES

Commencement: 15 September 2003.

This section was substituted for Pt II of this Act (ss 8–27) by the Enterprise Act 2002, s 248(1), as from 15 September 2003, except in relation to cases where a petition for an administration order was presented before that date, and subject to savings in relation to special administration regimes (as to which see below).

Special administration regimes: the Enterprise Act 2002, s 249(1) provides that s 248 shall have no effect in relation to the following: (a) a company holding an appointment under Chapter I of Part II of the Water Industry Act 1991 (water and sewerage undertakers); (aa) a qualifying licensed water supplier within the meaning of the Water Industry Act 1991, s 23(6) (meaning and effect of special administration order); (b) a protected railway company within the meaning of the Railways Act 1993, s 59 (railway administration order) (including that section as it has effect by virtue of the Channel Tunnel Rail Link Act 1996, s 19 (administration)); (c) a licence company within the meaning of the Transport Act 2000, s 26 (air traffic services); (d) a public-private partnership company within the meaning of the Greater London Authority Act 1999, s 210 (public-private partnership agreement); (e) a building society within the meaning of the Building Societies Act 1986, s 119. Accordingly, Pt II of this Act as it had effect prior to its substitution as noted above, continues to apply to such companies

For amendments to the original Part II (ie, as it applies without the amendments made by the Enterprise Act 2002), see the Companies Act 2006 (Consequential Amendments etc) Order 2008, SI 2008/948, art 3(1), Sch 1, Pt 2, para 101.

PART III
RECEIVERSHIP

CHAPTER I
RECEIVERS AND MANAGERS (ENGLAND AND WALES)

Receivers and managers appointed out of court

37 Liability for contracts, etc

(1) A receiver or manager appointed under powers conferred in an instrument (other than an administrative receiver) is, to the same extent as if he had been appointed by order of the court—

(a) personally liable on any contract entered into by him in the performance of his functions (except in so far as the contract otherwise provides) and on any contract of employment adopted by him in the performance of those functions, and

(b) entitled in respect of that liability to indemnity out of the assets.

(2) For the purposes of subsection (1)(a), the receiver or manager is not to be taken to have adopted a contract of employment by reason of anything done or omitted to be done within 14 days after his appointment.

(3) Subsection (1) does not limit any right to indemnity which the receiver or manager would have apart from it, nor limit his liability on contracts entered into without authority, nor confer any right to indemnity in respect of that liability.

(4) Where at any time the receiver or manager so appointed vacates office—

(a) his remuneration and any expenses properly incurred by him, and

(b) any indemnity to which he is entitled out of the assets of the company,

shall be charged on and paid out of any property of the company which is in his custody or under his control at that time in priority to any charge or other security held by the person by or on whose behalf he was appointed.

[368]

Administrative receivers: general

44 Agency and liability for contracts

(1) The administrative receiver of a company—

(a) is deemed to be the company's agent, unless and until the company goes into liquidation;

(b) is personally liable on any contract entered into by him in the carrying out of his functions (except in so far as the contract otherwise provides) and[, to the extent of any qualifying liability,] on any contract of employment adopted by him in the carrying out of those functions; and

(c) is entitled in respect of that liability to an indemnity out of the assets of the company.

(2) For the purposes of subsection (1)(b) the administrative receiver is not to be taken to have adopted a contract of employment by reason of anything done or omitted to be done within 14 days after his appointment.

[(2A) For the purposes of subsection (1)(b), a liability under a contract of employment is a qualifying liability if—

(a) it is a liability to pay a sum by way of wages or salary or contribution to an occupational pension scheme,

(b) it is incurred while the administrative receiver is in office, and

(c) it is in respect of services rendered wholly or partly after the adoption of the contract.

(2B) Where a sum payable in respect of a liability which is a qualifying liability for the purposes of subsection (1)(b) is payable in respect of services rendered partly before and partly after the adoption of the contract, liability under subsection (1)(b) shall only extend to so much of the sum as is payable in respect of services rendered after the adoption of the contract.

(2C) For the purposes of subsections (2A) and (2B)—

(a) wages or salary payable in respect of a period of holiday or absence from work through sickness or other good cause are deemed to be wages or (as the case may be) salary in respect of services rendered in that period, and

(b) a sum payable in lieu of holiday is deemed to be wages or (as the case may be) salary in respect of services rendered in the period by reference to which the holiday entitlement arose.

(2D) In subsection (2C)(a), the reference to wages or salary payable in respect of a period of holiday includes any sums which, if they had been paid, would have been treated for the purposes of the enactments relating to social security as earnings in respect of that period.]

(3) This section does not limit any right to indemnity which the administrative receiver would have apart from it, nor limit his liability on contracts entered into or adopted without authority, nor confer any right to indemnity in respect of that liability.

[369]

NOTES

Sub-s (1): words in square brackets in para (b) inserted by the Insolvency Act 1994, s 2(1), (2), (4), in relation to contracts of employment adopted on or after 15 March 1994.

Sub-ss (2A)–(2D): inserted by the Insolvency Act 1994, s 2(1), (3), (4), in relation to contracts of employment adopted on or after 15 March 1994.

CHAPTER II
RECEIVERS (SCOTLAND)

57 Agency and liability of receiver for contracts

(1) A receiver is deemed to be the agent of the company in relation to such property of the company as is attached by the floating charge by virtue of which he was appointed.

[(1A) Without prejudice to subsection (1), a receiver is deemed to be the agent of the company in relation to any contract of employment adopted by him in the carrying out of his functions.]

(2) A receiver (including a receiver whose powers are subsequently suspended under section 56) is personally liable on any contract entered into by him in the performance of his functions, except in so far as the contract otherwise provides, and[, to the extent of any qualifying liability,] on any contract of employment adopted by him in the carrying out of those functions.

[(2A) For the purposes of subsection (2), a liability under a contract of employment is a qualifying liability if—

(a) it is a liability to pay a sum by way of wages or salary or contribution to an occupational pension scheme,

(b) it is incurred while the receiver is in office, and

(c) it is in respect of services rendered wholly or partly after the adoption of the contract.

(2B) Where a sum payable in respect of a liability which is a qualifying liability for the purposes of subsection (2) is payable in respect of services rendered partly before and partly after the adoption of the contract, liability under that subsection shall only extend to so much of the sum as is payable in respect of services rendered after the adoption of the contract.

(2C) For the purposes of subsections (2A) and (2B)—

(a) wages or salary payable in respect of a period of holiday or absence from work through sickness or other good cause are deemed to be wages or (as the case may be) salary in respect of services rendered in that period, and

(b) a sum payable in lieu of holiday is deemed to be wages or (as the case may be) salary in respect of services rendered in the period by reference to which the holiday entitlement arose.

(2D) In subsection (2C)(a), the reference to wages or salary payable in respect of a period of holiday includes any sums which, if they had been paid, would have been treated for the purposes of the enactments relating to social security as earnings in respect of that period.]

(3) A receiver who is personally liable by virtue of subsection (2) is entitled to be indemnified out of the property in respect of which he was appointed.

(4) Any contract entered into by or on behalf of the company prior to the appointment of a receiver continues in force (subject to its terms) notwithstanding that appointment, but the receiver does not by virtue only of his appointment incur any personal liability on any such contract.

(5) For the purposes of subsection (2), a receiver is not to be taken to have adopted a contract of employment by reason of anything done or omitted to be done within 14 days after his appointment.

(6) This section does not limit any right to indemnity which the receiver would have apart from it, nor limit his liability on contracts entered into or adopted without authority, nor confer any right to indemnity in respect of that liability.

(7) Any contract entered into by a receiver in the performance of his functions continues in force (subject to its terms) although the powers of the receiver are subsequently suspended under section 56.

[370]

NOTES

Sub-ss (1A), (2A)–(2D): inserted by the Insolvency Act 1994, s 3(1), (2), (4), (5), in relation to contracts of employment adopted on or after 15 March 1994.

Sub-s (2): words in square brackets inserted by the Insolvency Act 1994, s 3(1), (3), (5), in relation to contracts of employment adopted on or after 15 March 1994.

PART IV
WINDING UP OF COMPANIES REGISTERED UNDER THE COMPANIES ACTS

CHAPTER VI
WINDING UP BY THE COURT

Commencement of winding up

130 Consequences of winding-up order

(1) On the making of a winding-up order, a copy of the order must forthwith be forwarded by the company (or otherwise as may be prescribed) to the registrar of companies, who shall enter it in his records relating to the company.

(2) When a winding-up order has been made or a provisional liquidator has been appointed, no action or proceeding shall be proceeded with or commenced against the company or its property, except by leave of the court and subject to such terms as the court may impose.

(3) When an order has been made for winding up a company registered under section 680 of the Companies Act, no action or proceeding shall be commenced or proceeded with against the company or its property or any contributory of the company, in respect of any debt of the company, except by leave of the court, and subject to such terms as the court may impose.

(4) An order for winding up a company operates in favour of all the creditors and of all contributories of the company as if made on the joint petition of a creditor and of a contributory.

[370A]

THE SECOND GROUP OF PARTS
INSOLVENCY OF INDIVIDUALS; BANKRUPTCY

PART VIII
INDIVIDUAL VOLUNTARY ARRANGEMENTS

Moratorium for insolvent debtor

252 Interim order of court

(1) In the circumstances specified below, the court may in the case of a debtor (being an individual) make an interim order under this section.

(2) An interim order has the effect that, during the period for which it is in force—

(a) no bankruptcy petition relating to the debtor may be presented or proceeded with,

[(aa) no landlord or other person to whom rent is payable may exercise any right of forfeiture by peaceable re-entry in relation to premises let to the debtor in respect of a failure by the debtor to comply with any term or condition of his tenancy of such premises, except with the leave of the court] and

(b) no other proceedings, and no execution or other legal process, may be commenced or continued [and no distress may be levied] against the debtor or his property except with the leave of the court.

[370B]

NOTES

Sub-s (2): para (aa), and words in square brackets in para (b), inserted by the Insolvency Act 2000, s 3, Sch 3, paras 1, 2, subject to transitional provisions in cases where a proposal (within the meaning of s 253 of this Act) is made before 1 January 2003.

254 Effect of application

(1) At any time when an application under section 253 for an interim order is pending,

[(a) no landlord or other person to whom rent is payable may exercise any right of forfeiture by peaceable re-entry in relation to premises let to the debtor in respect of a failure by the debtor to comply with any term or condition of his tenancy of such premises, except with the leave of the court, and

(b)] the court may [forbid the levying of any distress on the debtor's property or its subsequent sale, or both, and] stay any action, execution or other legal process against the property or person of the debtor.

(2) Any court in which proceedings are pending against an individual may, on proof that an application under that section has been made in respect of that individual, either stay the proceedings or allow them to continue on such terms as it thinks fit.

[370C]

NOTES

Sub-s (1): words in square brackets inserted by the Insolvency Act 2000, s 3, Sch 3, paras 1, 4, subject to transitional provisions in cases where a proposal (within the meaning of s 253 of this Act) is made before 1 January 2003.

Consideration and implementation of debtor's proposal

260 Effect of approval

(1) This section has effect where the meeting summoned under section 257 approves the proposed voluntary arrangement (with or without modifications).

(2) The approved arrangement—

(a) takes effect as if made by the debtor at the meeting, and

[(b) binds every person who in accordance with the rules—

(i) was entitled to vote at the meeting (whether or not he was present or represented at it), or

(ii) would have been so entitled if he had had notice of it,

as if he were a party to the arrangement.

(2A) If—

(a) when the arrangement ceases to have effect any amount payable under the arrangement to a person bound by virtue of subsection (2)(b)(ii) has not been paid, and

(b) the arrangement did not come to an end prematurely,

the debtor shall at that time become liable to pay to that person the amount payable under the arrangement.]

(3) The Deeds of Arrangement Act 1914 does not apply to the approved voluntary arrangement.

(4) Any interim order in force in relation to the debtor immediately before the end of the period of 28 days beginning with the day on which the report with respect to the creditors' meeting was made to the court under section 259 ceases to have effect at the end of that period.

This subsection applies except to such extent as the court may direct for the purposes of any application under section 262 below.

(5) Where proceedings on a bankruptcy petition have been stayed by an interim order which ceases to have effect under subsection (4), the petition is deemed, unless the court otherwise orders, to have been dismissed.

[370D]

NOTES

Sub-s (2): para (b) of subsection (2) and sub-s (2A) were substituted for the original para (b) by the Insolvency Act 2000, s 3, Sch 3, paras 1, 10, subject to transitional provisions in cases where a proposal (within the meaning of s 253 of this Act) is made before 1 January 2003.

Sub-s (2A): substituted as noted above.

PART IX
BANKRUPTCY

CHAPTER II
PROTECTION OF BANKRUPT'S ESTATE AND INVESTIGATION OF HIS AFFAIRS

285 Restriction on proceedings and remedies

(1) At any time when proceedings on a bankruptcy petition are pending or an individual has been adjudged bankrupt the court may stay any action, execution or other legal process against the property or person of the debtor or, as the case may be, of the bankrupt.

(2) Any court in which proceedings are pending against any individual may, on proof that a bankruptcy petition has been presented in respect of that individual or that he is an undischarged bankrupt, either stay the proceedings or allow them to continue on such terms as it thinks fit.

(3) After the making of a bankruptcy order no person who is a creditor of the bankrupt in respect of a debt provable in the bankruptcy shall—

(a) have any remedy against the property or person of the bankrupt in respect of that debt, or

(b) before the discharge of the bankrupt, commence any action or other legal proceedings against the bankrupt except with the leave of the court and on such terms as the court may impose.

This is subject to sections 346 (enforcement procedures) and 347 (limited right to distress).

(4) Subject as follows, subsection (3) does not affect the right of a secured creditor of the bankrupt to enforce his security.

(5) Where any goods of an undischarged bankrupt are held by any person by way of pledge, pawn or other security, the official receiver may, after giving notice in writing of his intention to do so, inspect the goods.

Where such a notice has been given to any person, that person is not entitled, without leave of the court, to realise his security unless he has given the trustee of the bankrupt's estate a reasonable opportunity of inspecting the goods and of exercising the bankrupt's right of redemption.

(6) References in this section to the property or goods of the bankrupt are to any of his property or goods, whether or not comprised in his estate.

[370E]

THE THIRD GROUP OF PARTS
MISCELLANEOUS MATTERS BEARING ON BOTH COMPANY AND INDIVIDUAL INSOLVENCY; GENERAL INTERPRETATION; FINAL PROVISIONS

PART XII
PREFERENTIAL DEBTS IN COMPANY AND INDIVIDUAL INSOLVENCY

386 Categories of preferential debts

(1) A reference in this Act to the preferential debts of a company or an individual is to the debts listed in Schedule 6 to this Act [(contributions to occupational pension schemes; remuneration, &c of employees; levies on coal and steel production)]; and references to preferential creditors are to be read accordingly.

(2) In that Schedule "the debtor" means the company or the individual concerned.

(3) Schedule 6 is to be read with [Schedule 4 to the Pension Schemes Act 1993] (occupational pension scheme contributions).

[371]

NOTES

Sub-s (1): words in square brackets substituted by the Enterprise Act 2002, s 251(3), as from 15 September 2003, subject to transitional provisions in relation to the abolition of preferential status for Crown debts in cases which were started before that date.

Sub-s (3): words in square brackets substituted by the Pension Schemes Act 1993, s 190, Sch 8, para 18.

PART XIX
FINAL PROVISIONS

443 Commencement

This Act comes into force on the day appointed under section 236(2) of the Insolvency Act 1985 for the coming into force of Part III of that Act (individual insolvency and bankruptcy), immediately after that Part of that Act comes into force for England and Wales.

[372]

444 Citation

This Act may be cited as the Insolvency Act 1986.

[373]

SCHEDULES

[SCHEDULE B1
ADMINISTRATION

Section 8

NOTES

Only the provisions of this Schedule most directly relevant to employment law are printed; omitted paragraphs are not annotated.

NATURE OF ADMINISTRATION

Administration

1.—(1) For the purposes of this Act "administrator" of a company means a person appointed under this Schedule to manage the company's affairs, business and property.

(2) For the purposes of this Act—

(a) a company is "in administration" while the appointment of an administrator of the company has effect,

(b) a company "enters administration" when the appointment of an administrator takes effect,

(c) a company ceases to be in administration when the appointment of an administrator of the company ceases to have effect in accordance with this Schedule, and

(d) a company does not cease to be in administration merely because an administrator vacates office (by reason of resignation, death or otherwise) or is removed from office.

2. A person may be appointed as administrator of a company—

(a) by administration order of the court under paragraph 10,

(b) by the holder of a floating charge under paragraph 14, or

(c) by the company or its directors under paragraph 22.

Purpose of administration

3.—(1) The administrator of a company must perform his functions with the objective of—

(a) rescuing the company as a going concern, or

(b) achieving a better result for the company's creditors as a whole than would be likely if the company were wound up (without first being in administration), or

(c) realising property in order to make a distribution to one or more secured or preferential creditors.

(2) Subject to sub-paragraph (4), the administrator of a company must perform his functions in the interests of the company's creditors as a whole.

(3) The administrator must perform his functions with the objective specified in sub-paragraph (1)(a) unless he thinks either—

(a) that it is not reasonably practicable to achieve that objective, or

(b) that the objective specified in sub-paragraph (1)(b) would achieve a better result for the company's creditors as a whole.

(4) The administrator may perform his functions with the objective specified in sub-paragraph (1)(c) only if—

(a) he thinks that it is not reasonably practicable to achieve either of the objectives specified in sub-paragraph (1)(a) and (b), and

(b) he does not unnecessarily harm the interests of the creditors of the company as a whole.

4. The administrator of a company must perform his functions as quickly and efficiently as is reasonably practicable.

Status of administrator

5. An administrator is an officer of the court (whether or not he is appointed by the court).

EFFECT OF ADMINISTRATION

Moratorium on other legal process

43.—(1) This paragraph applies to a company in administration.

(2) No step may be taken to enforce security over the company's property except—

(a) with the consent of the administrator, or

(b) with the permission of the court.

(3) No step may be taken to repossess goods in the company's possession under a hire-purchase agreement except—

(a) with the consent of the administrator, or

(b) with the permission of the court.

(4) A landlord may not exercise a right of forfeiture by peaceable re-entry in relation to premises let to the company except—

(a) with the consent of the administrator, or

(b) with the permission of the court.

(5) In Scotland, a landlord may not exercise a right of irritancy in relation to premises let to the company except—

(a) with the consent of the administrator, or
(b) with the permission of the court.

(6) No legal process (including legal proceedings, execution, distress and diligence) may be instituted or continued against the company or property of the company except—

(a) with the consent of the administrator, or
(b) with the permission of the court.

[(6A) An administrative receiver of the company may not be appointed.]

(7) Where the court gives permission for a transaction under this paragraph it may impose a condition on or a requirement in connection with the transaction.

(8) In this paragraph "landlord" includes a person to whom rent is payable.

Interim moratorium

44.—(1) This paragraph applies where an administration application in respect of a company has been made and—

(a) the application has not yet been granted or dismissed, or
(b) the application has been granted but the administration order has not yet taken effect.

(2) This paragraph also applies from the time when a copy of notice of intention to appoint an administrator under paragraph 14 is filed with the court until—

(a) the appointment of the administrator takes effect, or
(b) the period of five business days beginning with the date of filing expires without an administrator having been appointed.

(3) Sub-paragraph (2) has effect in relation to a notice of intention to appoint only if it is in the prescribed form.

(4) This paragraph also applies from the time when a copy of notice of intention to appoint an administrator is filed with the court under paragraph 27(1) until—

(a) the appointment of the administrator takes effect, or
(b) the period specified in paragraph 28(2) expires without an administrator having been appointed.

(5) The provisions of paragraphs 42 and 43 shall apply (ignoring any reference to the consent of the administrator).

(6) If there is an administrative receiver of the company when the administration application is made, the provisions of paragraphs 42 and 43 shall not begin to apply by virtue of this paragraph until the person by or on behalf of whom the receiver was appointed consents to the making of the administration order.

(7) This paragraph does not prevent or require the permission of the court for—

(a) the presentation of a petition for the winding up of the company under a provision mentioned in paragraph 42(4),
(b) the appointment of an administrator under paragraph 14,
(c) the appointment of an administrative receiver of the company, or
(d) the carrying out by an administrative receiver (whenever appointed) of his functions.

REPLACING ADMINISTRATOR

Vacation of office: charges and liabilities

99.—(1) This paragraph applies where a person ceases to be the administrator of a company (whether because he vacates office by reason of resignation, death or otherwise, because he is removed from office or because his appointment ceases to have effect).

(2) In this paragraph—

"the former administrator" means the person referred to in sub-paragraph (1), and
"cessation" means the time when he ceases to be the company's administrator.

(3) The former administrator's remuneration and expenses shall be—

(a) charged on and payable out of property of which he had custody or control immediately before cessation, and
(b) payable in priority to any security to which paragraph 70 applies.

(4) A sum payable in respect of a debt or liability arising out of a contract entered into by the former administrator or a predecessor before cessation shall be—
(a) charged on and payable out of property of which the former administrator had custody or control immediately before cessation, and
(b) payable in priority to any charge arising under sub-paragraph (3).

(5) Sub-paragraph (4) shall apply to a liability arising under a contract of employment which was adopted by the former administrator or a predecessor before cessation; and for that purpose—
(a) action taken within the period of 14 days after an administrator's appointment shall not be taken to amount or contribute to the adoption of a contract,
(b) no account shall be taken of a liability which arises, or in so far as it arises, by reference to anything which is done or which occurs before the adoption of the contract of employment, and
(c) no account shall be taken of a liability to make a payment other than wages or salary.

(6) In sub-paragraph (5)(c) "wages or salary" includes—
(a) a sum payable in respect of a period of holiday (for which purpose the sum shall be treated as relating to the period by reference to which the entitlement to holiday accrued),
(b) a sum payable in respect of a period of absence through illness or other good cause,
(c) a sum payable in lieu of holiday,
(d) in respect of a period, a sum which would be treated as earnings for that period for the purposes of an enactment about social security, and
(e) a contribution to an occupational pension scheme.]

[374]

NOTES

Commencement: 15 September 2003.

Inserted by the Enterprise Act 2002, s 248(2), Sch 16, as from 15 September 2003, except in relation to cases where a petition for an administration order was presented before that date, and subject to savings in relation to special administration regimes (within the meaning of s 249 of the 2002 Act). Note that para 43(6A) was inserted into Sch 16 to the 2002 Act by the Enterprise Act 2002 (Insolvency) Order 2003, SI 2003/2096, art 2(1), (3), as from the same date.

SCHEDULE 6
THE CATEGORIES OF PREFERENTIAL DEBTS

Section 386

1–7. …

Category 4: Contributions to occupational pension schemes, etc

8. Any sum which is owed by the debtor and is a sum to which [Schedule 4 to the Pension Schemes Act 1993] applies (contributions to occupational pension schemes and state scheme premiums).

Category 5: Remuneration, etc, of employees

9. So much of any amount which—
(a) is owed by the debtor to a person who is or has been an employee of the debtor, and
(b) is payable by way of remuneration in respect of the whole or any part of the period of 4 months next before the relevant date,

as does not exceed so much as may be prescribed by order made by the Secretary of State.

10. An amount owed by way of accrued holiday remuneration, in respect of any period of employment before the relevant date, to a person whose employment by the debtor has been terminated, whether before, on or after that date.

11. So much of any sum owed in respect of money advanced for the purpose as has been applied for the payment of a debt which, if it had not been paid, would have been a debt falling within paragraph 9 or 10.

12. So much of any amount which—
   (a) is ordered (whether before or after the relevant date) to be paid by the debtor under the Reserve Forces (Safeguard of Employment) Act 1985, and
   (b) is so ordered in respect of a default made by the debtor before that date in the discharge of his obligations under that Act,

as does not exceed such amount as may be prescribed by order made by the Secretary of State.

Interpretation for Category 5

13.—(1) For the purposes of paragraphs 9 to 12, a sum is payable by the debtor to a person by way of remuneration in respect of any period if—
   (a) it is paid as wages or salary (whether payable for time or for piece work or earned wholly or partly by way of commission) in respect of services rendered to the debtor in that period, or
   (b) it is an amount falling within the following sub-paragraph and is payable by the debtor in respect of that period.

[(2) An amount falls within this sub-paragraph if it is—
   (a) a guarantee payment under Part III of the Employment Rights Act 1996 (employee without work to do);
   (b) any payment for time off under section 53 (time off to look for work or arrange training) or section 56 (time off for ante-natal care) of that Act or under section 169 of the Trade Union and Labour Relations (Consolidation) Act 1992 (time off for carrying out trade union duties etc);
   (c) remuneration on suspension on medical grounds, or on maternity grounds, under Part VII of the Employment Rights Act 1996; or
   (d) remuneration under a protective award under section 189 of the Trade Union and Labour Relations (Consolidation) Act 1992 (redundancy dismissal with compensation).]

14.—(1) This paragraph relates to a case in which a person's employment has been terminated by or in consequence of his employer going into liquidation or being adjudged bankrupt or (his employer being a company not in liquidation) by or in consequence of—
   (a) a receiver being appointed as mentioned in section 40 of this Act (debenture-holders secured by floating charge), or
   (b) the appointment of a receiver under section 53(6) or 54(5) of this Act (Scottish company with property subject to floating charge), or
   (c) the taking of possession by debenture-holders (so secured), as mentioned in [section 754 of the Companies Act 2006].

(2) For the purposes of paragraphs 9 to 12, holiday remuneration is deemed to have accrued to that person in respect of any period of employment if, by virtue of his contract of employment or of any enactment that remuneration would have accrued in respect of that period if his employment had continued until he became entitled to be allowed the holiday.

(3) The reference in sub-paragraph (2) to any enactment includes an order or direction made under an enactment.

15. Without prejudice to paragraphs 13 and 14—
   (a) any remuneration payable by the debtor to a person in respect of a period of holiday or of absence from work through sickness or other good cause is deemed to be wages or (as the case may be) salary in respect of services rendered to the debtor in that period, and
   (b) references here and in those paragraphs to remuneration in respect of a period of holiday include any sums which, if they had been paid, would have been treated for the purposes of the enactments to social security as earnings in respect of that period.

[Category 6: Levies on coal and steel production

15A. (Outside the scope of this work.)]

Orders

16. An order under paragraph 9 or 12—
   (a) may contain such transitional provisions as may appear to the Secretary of State necessary or expedient;
   (b) shall be made by statutory instrument subject to annulment in pursuance of a resolution of either House of Parliament.

[375]

NOTES

Paras 1–7: repealed by the Enterprise Act 2002, ss 251(1), 278(2), Sch 26, as from 15 September 2003, subject to transitional provisions in relation to the abolition of preferential status for Crown debts in cases which were started before that date.

Para 8: words in square brackets substituted by the Pension Schemes Act 1993, s 190, Sch 8, para 18.

Para 13: sub-para (2) substituted by the Employment Rights Act 1996, s 240, Sch 1, para 29.

Para 14: words in square brackets in sub-para (1)(c) substituted by the Companies Act 2006 (Consequential Amendments etc) Order 2008, SI 2008/948, arts 3(1)(b), 6, Sch 1, Pt 2, para 104, as from 6 April 2008.

Orders: the Insolvency Proceedings (Monetary Limits) Order 1986, SI 1986/1996 (art 4 of which prescribes £800 for the purposes of paras 9, 12 above).

WAGES ACT 1986 (NOTE)

(1986 c 48)

NOTES

The whole of this Act has been repealed. Ss 12–26 (Pt II) and Schs 2, 3 were repealed by the Trade Union Reform and Employment Rights Act 1993, ss 35, 51, Sch 10 (see Sch 9 to the 1993 Act for transitional provisions and savings); s 27 was repealed by the Employment Act 1989, s 29(4), Sch 7, Pt II; ss 1–11 (Pt I), 28–33, and Schs 1, 5, were repealed and re-enacted by the Employment Rights Act 1996, s 242, Sch 3 (for the corresponding provisions in the 1996 Act see Destination Table at **[1285]**). The remaining provisions of the Act were repealed by a combination of the Coal Industry Act 1992 and the Employment Tribunals Act 1996.

[376]–[377]

SEX DISCRIMINATION ACT 1986

(1986 c 59)

An Act to amend the Sex Discrimination Act 1975 and sections 64 and 73 of the Employment Protection (Consolidation) Act 1978; to make provision with respect to requirements to discriminate in relation to employment which are contained in public entertainment licences; to provide for the removal of certain restrictions applying to the working hours and other working conditions of women; and to repeal the Baking Industry (Hours of Work) Act 1954

[7 November 1986]

NOTES

See *Harvey* L1.

1–5 (*S 1 repeals the Sex Discrimination Act 1975, s 6(3) at* **[106]**, *and amends ss 7(2), 11(1) of that Act at* **[107]**, **[113]**; *s 2 amends ss 6, 11, 82 of the 1975 Act at* **[106]**, **[113]**, **[196]**, *and the Equal Pay Act 1970, s 6 at* **[8]** (*and was repealed in part by the Employment Equality (Sex Discrimination) Regulations 2005, SI 2005/2467, reg 14, as from 1 October 2005*); *s 3* *repealed by the Employment Rights Act 1996; s 4 amends the Sex Discrimination Act 1975, s 47 at* **[158]***; s 5 repealed by the Licensing Act 2003, ss 198(1), 199, Sch 6, para 105, Sch 7, as from 24 November 2005.)*

6 Collective agreements and rules of undertakings

(1) Without prejudice to the generality of section 77 of the 1975 Act (which makes provision with respect to the validity and revision of contracts), that section shall apply, as it applies in relation to the term of a contract, to the following, namely—

(a) any term of a collective agreement, including an agreement which was not intended, or is presumed not to have been intended, to be a legally enforceable contract;

(b) any rule made by an employer for application to all or any of the persons who are employed by him or who apply to be, or are, considered by him for employment;

(c) any rule made by an organisation, authority or body to which subsection (2) below applies for application to all or any of its members or prospective members or to all or any of the persons on whom it has conferred authorisations or qualifications or who are seeking the authorisations or qualifications which it has power to confer;

and that section shall so apply whether the agreement was entered into, or the rule made, before or after the coming into force of this section.

(2) This subsection applies to—

(a) any organisation of workers;

(b) any organisation of employers;

(c) any organisation whose members carry on a particular profession or trade for the purposes of which the organisation exists;

(d) any authority or body which can confer an authorisation or qualification which is needed for, or facilitates, engagement in a particular profession or trade.

(3) For the purposes of the said section 77 a term or rule shall be deemed to provide for the doing of an act which would be rendered unlawful by the 1975 Act if—

(a) it provides for the inclusion in any contract of employment of any term which by virtue of an equality clause would fall either to be modified or to be supplemented by an additional term; and

(b) that clause would not be prevented from operating in relation to that contract by section 1(3) of the Equal Pay Act 1970 (material factors justifying discrimination).

(4) Nothing in the said section 77 shall affect the operation of any term or rule in so far as it provides for the doing of a particular act in circumstances where the doing of that act would not be, or be deemed by virtue of subsection (3) above to be, rendered unlawful by the 1975 Act.

[(4A) A person to whom this subsection applies may present a complaint to an [employment tribunal] that a term or rule is void by virtue of subsection (1) of the said section 77 if he has reason to believe—

(a) that the term or rule may at some future time have effect in relation to him, and

(b) where he alleges that it is void by virtue of paragraph (c) of that subsection, that—

(i) an act for the doing of which it provides may at some such time be done in relation to him, and

(ii) the act would be, or be deemed by virtue of subsection (3) above to be, rendered unlawful by the 1975 Act if done in relation to him in present circumstances.

(4B) In the case of a complaint about—

(a) a term of a collective agreement made by or on behalf of—

(i) an employer,

(ii) an organisation of employers of which an employer is a member, or

(iii) an association of such organisations of one of which an employer is a member, or

(b) a rule made by an employer,

subsection (4A) applies to any person who is, or is genuinely and actively seeking to become, one of his employees.

(4C) In the case of a complaint about a rule made by an organisation, authority or body to which subsection (2) above applies, subsection (4A) applies to any person—

(a) who is, or is genuinely and actively seeking to become, a member of the organisation, authority or body,

(b) on whom the organisation, authority or body has conferred an authorisation or qualification, or

(c) who is genuinely and actively seeking an authorisation or qualification which the organisation, authority or body has power to confer.

(4D) When an [employment tribunal] finds that a complaint presented to it under subsection (4A) above is well-founded the tribunal shall make an order declaring that the term or rule is void.]

(5) The avoidance by virtue of the said section 77 of any term or rule which provides for any person to be discriminated against shall be without prejudice to the following rights except in so far as they enable any person to require another person to be treated less favourably than himself, namely—

(a) such of the rights of the person to be discriminated against; and

(b) such of the rights of any person who will be treated more favourably in direct or indirect consequence of the discrimination,

as are conferred by or in respect of a contract made or modified wholly or partly in pursuance of, or by reference to, that term or rule.

(6) In this section "collective agreement" means any agreement relating to one or more of the matters mentioned in [section 178(2) of the Trade Union and Labour Relations (Consolidation) Act 1992] (meaning of trade dispute), being an agreement made by or on behalf of one or more employers or one or more organisations of employers or associations of such organisations with one or more organisations of workers or associations of such organisations.

(7) Any expression used in this section and in the 1975 Act has the same meaning in this section as in that Act, and this section shall have effect as if the terms of any service to which Parts II and IV of that Act apply by virtue of subsection (2) of section 85 of that Act (Crown application) were terms of a contract of employment and, in relation to the terms of any such service, as if service for the purposes of any person mentioned in that subsection were employment by that person.

[378]

NOTES

Sub-ss (4A), (4D): inserted, together with sub-ss (4B), (4C), by the Trade Union Reform and Employment Rights Act 1993, s 32; words in square brackets substituted by the Employment Rights (Dispute Resolution) Act 1998, s 1(2)(a).

Sub-ss (4B), (4C): inserted as noted above.

Sub-s (6): words in square brackets substituted by the Trade Union and Labour Relations (Consolidation) Act 1992, s 300(2), Sch 2, para 36.

1975 Act: Sex Discrimination Act 1975.

7, 8 *(S 7 repealed by the Employment Act 1989, s 29(4), Sch 7, Pt II; s 8 repeals the Baking Industry (Hours of Work) Act 1954.)*

9 Consequential amendment, repeals and saving

(1) …

(2) The enactments mentioned in the Schedule to this Act (which include enactments that are no longer of practical effect) are hereby repealed to the extent specified in the third column of that Schedule.

(3) Neither the repeal by this Act of section 3 of the Equal Pay Act 1970 (collective agreements and pay structures) nor the amendment made by subsection (1) above shall affect—

(a) the continuing effect, after the coming into force of that repeal, of any declaration made under that section before the coming into force of that repeal; or

(b) the operation, at any time after the coming into force of that repeal, of section 5(1) of that Act in so far as it refers to the rules which apply under subsection (4) of the said section 3.

[379]

NOTES

Sub-s (1): amends the Equal Pay Act 1970, s 6 at [11].

10 Short title, commencement and extent

(1) This Act may be cited as the Sex Discrimination Act 1986.

(2) Sections 1, 6 and 9(1) and (3) above and Part II of the Schedule to this Act shall come into force at the end of the period of three months beginning with the day on which this Act is passed.

(3) Subject to subsection (4) below, sections 2, 3 … and 8 above and Part III of the Schedule to this Act shall come into force on such day as the Secretary of State may by order made by statutory instrument appoint, and different days may be so appointed for different provisions or for different purposes.

(4) Except in so far as they come into force at an earlier time under subsection (3) above, sections 2 and 3 above shall come into force at the end of the period of twelve months beginning with the day on which this Act is passed.

(5) This Act does not extend to Northern Ireland …

[380]

NOTES

Sub-ss (3), (5): words omitted repealed by the Employment Act 1989, s 29(4), Sch 7, Pt II.

Orders: the Sex Discrimination Act 1986 (Commencement) Order 1986, SI 1986/2313; the Sex Discrimination Act 1986 (Commencement No 2) Order 1988, SI 1988/99.

(Schedule (Repeals) in so far as relevant these have been incorporated at the appropriate place.)

INCOME AND CORPORATION TAXES ACT 1988 (NOTE)

(1988 c 1)

NOTES

The provisions of this Act within the scope of this work have been repealed and re-enacted in the Income Tax (Earnings and Pensions) Act 2003 at [1511] et seq.

[381]

EMPLOYMENT ACT 1988

(1988 c 19)

An Act to make provision with respect to trade unions, their members and their property, to things done for the purpose of enforcing membership of a trade union, to trade union ballots and elections and to proceedings involving trade unions; to provide for the Manpower Services Commission to be known as the Training Commission; to amend the law with respect to the constitution and functions of that Commission and with respect to persons to whom facilities for work-experience and training for employment are made available; to enable additional members to be appointed to industrial training boards and to the Agricultural Training Board; and to provide that the terms on which certain persons hold office or employment under the Crown are to be treated for certain purposes as contained in contracts of employment

[26 May 1988]

NOTES

Most of this Act has been repealed by, and re-enacted in, the Trade Union and Labour Relations (Consolidation) Act 1992 at **[469]** et seq. The provisions so affected are ss 1–23, 30, Sch 1 and parts of Sch 3. Various other provisions have also been repealed, as noted below. Remaining provisions of the Act are printed in full except as noted below.

1–23 *((Pt I) repealed by the Trade Union and Labour Relations (Consolidation) Act 1992, s 300(1), Sch 1.)*

PART II
EMPLOYMENT AND TRAINING

24, 25 *(S 24 repealed by the Employment Act 1989, s 29(4), Sch 7, Pt I; s 25 substitutes the Employment and Training Act 1973, ss 2, 3 and introduces Sch 2 (further amendments, etc, to the 1973 Act).)*

26 Status of trainees etc

(1) Where it appears to the Secretary of State that provision has been made under section 2 of the 1973 Act[, or under section 2(3) [or section 14A] of the Enterprise and New Towns (Scotland) Act 1990,] for persons using facilities provided in pursuance of arrangements under [any of those three sections] to receive payments from any person in connection with their use of those facilities, the Secretary of State may by order provide—

(a) that those persons are, for the purposes and in the cases specified or described in or determined under the order, to be treated in respect of their use of those facilities as being or as not being employed;

(b) that where those persons are treated as being employed they are to be treated as being the employees of the persons so specified, described or determined and of no others;

(c) that where those persons are treated as not being employed they are to be treated as being trained, or are to be treated in such other manner as may be so specified, described or determined; and

(d) that those payments are to be treated for the purposes of such enactments and subordinate legislation as may be so specified, described or determined in such manner as may be so specified, described or determined.

[(1A) Where it appears to the Secretary of State that provision has been made under section 5(1)(c) or 34(1)(c) of the Learning and Skills Act 2000 for trainees to receive payments from the Learning and Skills Council for England or the [National Assembly for Wales], the Secretary of State may by order provide—

(a) that those trainees are, for the purposes and in the cases specified or described in or determined under the order, to be treated in respect of the training as being or as not being employed;

(b) that where those trainees are treated as being employed they are to be treated as being the employees of the persons so specified, described or determined and of no others;

(c) that where those trainees are treated as not being employed they are to be treated in such other manner as may be so specified, described or determined; and

(d) that those payments are to be treated for the purposes of such enactments and subordinate legislation as may be so specified, described or determined in such manner as may be so specified, described or determined;

and for the purposes of this subsection trainees are persons receiving or proposing to receive training.]

(2) The power to make an order under this section shall be exercisable by statutory instrument subject to annulment in pursuance of a resolution of either House of Parliament; and such an order may—

(a) modify any enactment or subordinate legislation;

(b) make different provision for different purposes and for different cases; and

(c) contain such incidental, consequential and transitional provision as appears to the Secretary of State to be appropriate.

(3) The consent of the Treasury shall be required for the making of any order under this section which contains provision for the manner in which any payment is to be treated for the purposes of the Income Tax Acts.

(4) In this section—

"enactment" includes an enactment contained in this Act or in any Act passed after this Act; and

"subordinate legislation" has the same meaning as in the Interpretation Act 1978.

[382]

NOTES

Sub-s (1): words in first (outer) pair of square brackets inserted by the Enterprise and New Towns (Scotland) Act 1990, s 38(1), Sch 4, para 16; words in second (inner) pair of square brackets inserted, and words in third pair of square brackets substituted, by the Trade Union Reform and Employment Rights Act 1993, s 49(2), Sch 8, para 38.

Sub-s (1A): inserted by the Learning and Skills Act 2000, s 149, Sch 9, paras 1, 14; words in square brackets substituted by the National Council for Education and Training for Wales (Transfer of Functions to the National Assembly for Wales and Abolition) Order 2005, SI 2005/3238, art 9(1), Sch 1, para 11. as from 1 April 2006.

Orders: the Social Security (Employment Training: Payments) Order 1988, SI 1988/1409; the Employment Action (Miscellaneous Provisions) Order 1991, SI 1991/1995; the Training for Work (Scottish Enterprise and Highlands and Islands Enterprise Programmes) Order 1993, SI 1993/498; the North Norfolk Action (Miscellaneous Provisions) Order 1993, SI 1993/1065; the Community Action (Miscellaneous Provisions) Order 1993, SI 1993/1621; the Learning for Work (Miscellaneous Provisions) Order 1993, SI 1993/1949; the Training for Work (Miscellaneous Provisions) Order 1995, SI 1995/1780; the Project Work (Miscellaneous Provisions) Order 1996, SI 1996/1623; the New Deal (Miscellaneous Provisions) Order 1998, SI 1998/217; the New Deal (25 plus) (Miscellaneous Provisions) Order 1999, SI 1999/779; the New Deal (Miscellaneous Provisions) Order 2001, SI 2001/970; the New Deal (Lone Parents) (Miscellaneous Provisions) Order 2001, SI 2001/2915.

27–29 (*S 27 repealed by the Social Security* (*Consequential Provisions*) *Act 1992, s 3*(*1*)*, Sch 1; s 28 amends the Employment and Training Act 1973, s 4*(*3*)*,* (*5*)*; s 29* (*membership of training boards*) *outside the scope of this work.*)

PART III
MISCELLANEOUS AND SUPPLEMENTAL

30 (*Repealed by the Trade Union and Labour Relations* (*Consolidation*) *Act 1992, s 300*(*1*)*, Sch 1.*)

Supplemental

31 Financial provisions

There shall be paid out of money provided by Parliament any increases attributable to this Act in the sums payable under any other Act out of money so provided.

[383]

32 Interpretation

(1) In this Act, except in so far as the context otherwise requires—

…

"the 1973 Act" means the Employment and Training Act 1973;

…

"modifications" includes additions, alterations and omissions, and cognate expressions shall be construed accordingly;

…

(2) …

[384]

NOTES

Sub-s (1): definitions omitted repealed by the Trade Union and Labour Relations (Consolidation) Act 1992, s 300(1), Sch 1.

Sub-s (2): repealed by the Trade Union and Labour Relations (Consolidation) Act 1992, s 300(1), Sch 1.

33 (*Introduces Schs 3 and 4 (minor and consequential amendments, and repeals) outside the scope of this work.*)

34 Short title, commencement and extent

(1) This Act may be cited as the Employment Act 1988.

(2), (3) …

(4)–(6) (*Outside the scope of this work.*)

[385]

NOTES

Sub-ss (2), (3): repealed by the Trade Union and Labour Relations (Consolidation) Act 1992, s 300(1), Sch 1.

(*Sch 1, Sch 3, Pt I repealed by the Trade Union and Labour Relations (Consolidation) Act 1992, s 300(1), Sch 1; Sch 2 repealed in part by the Employment Act 1989, s 29(4), Sch 7, Pt I, remainder amends the Employment and Training Act 1973, ss 11(3), 12; Sch 3, Pt II (minor and consequential amendments), Sch 4 (repeals) outside the scope of this work.*)

ACCESS TO MEDICAL REPORTS ACT 1988

(1988 c 28)

ARRANGEMENT OF SECTIONS

An Act to establish a right of access by individuals to reports relating to themselves provided by medical practitioners for employment or insurance purposes and to make provision for related matters

[29 July 1988]

NOTES

See *Harvey* DI(8)(d).

1 Right of access

It shall be the right of an individual to have access, in accordance with the provisions of this Act, to any medical report relating to the individual which is to be, or has been, supplied by a medical practitioner for employment purposes or insurance purposes.

[386]

2 Interpretation

(1) In this Act—

"the applicant" means the person referred to in section 3(1) below;

"care" includes examination, investigation or diagnosis for the purposes of, or in connection with, any form of medical treatment;

"employment purposes", in the case of any individual, means the purposes in relation to the individual of any person by whom he is or has been, or is seeking to be, employed (whether under a contract of service or otherwise);

"health professional" has the same meaning as in [the Data Protection Act 1998];

["insurance purposes", in a case of any individual who has entered into, or is seeking to enter into, a contract of insurance with an insurer, means the purposes of that insurer in relation to that individual;

"insurer" means—

(a) a person who has permission under Part 4 of the Financial Services and Markets Act 2000 to effect or carry out contracts of insurance;

(b) an EEA firm of the kind mentioned in paragraph 5(d) of Schedule 3 to that Act, which has permission under paragraph 15 of that Schedule (as a result of qualifying for authorisation under paragraph 12 of that Schedule) to effect or carry out relevant contracts of insurance.]

"medical practitioner" means a person registered under the Medical Act 1983;

"medical report", in the case of an individual, means a report relating to the physical or mental health of the individual prepared by a medical practitioner who is or has been responsible for the clinical care of the individual.

[(1A) The definitions of "insurance purposes" and "insurer" in subsection (1) must be read with—

(a) section 22 of the Financial Services and Markets Act 2000;

(b) any relevant order under that section; and

(c) Schedule 2 to that Act.]

(2) Any reference in this Act to the supply of a medical report for employment or insurance purposes shall be construed—

(a) as a reference to the supply of such a report for employment or insurance purposes which are purposes of the person who is seeking to be supplied with it; or

(b) (in the case of a report that has already been supplied) as a reference to the supply of such a report for employment or insurance purposes which, at the time of its being supplied, were purposes of the person to whom it was supplied.

[387]

NOTES

Sub-s (1): in definition "health professional" words in square brackets substituted by the Data Protection Act 1998, s 74(1), Sch 15, para 8; definitions "insurance purposes" and "insurer" substituted for original definition "insurance purposes" by the Financial Services and Markets Act 2000 (Consequential Amendments and Repeals) Order 2001, SI 2001/3649, art 311(1), (2).

Sub-s (1A): inserted by SI 2001/3649, art 311(1), (3).

3 Consent to applications for medical reports for employment or insurance purposes

(1) A person shall not apply to a medical practitioner for a medical report relating to any individual to be supplied to him for employment or insurance purposes unless—

(a) that person ("the applicant") has notified the individual that he proposes to make the application; and

(b) the individual has notified the applicant that he consents to the making of the application.

(2) Any notification given under subsection (1)(a) above must inform the individual of his right to withhold his consent to the making of the application, and of the following rights under this Act, namely—

(a) the rights arising under sections 4(1) to (3) and 6(2) below with respect to access to the report before or after it is supplied,

(b) the right to withhold consent under subsection (1) of section 5 below, and

(c) the right to request the amendment of the report under subsection (2) of that section,

as well as of the effect of section 7 below.

[388]

4 Access to reports before they are supplied

(1) An individual who gives his consent under section 3 above to the making of an application shall be entitled, when giving his consent, to state that he wishes to have access to the report to be supplied in response to the application before it is so supplied; and, if he does so, the applicant shall—

(a) notify the medical practitioner of that fact at the time when the application is made, and

(b) at the same time notify the individual of the making of the application;

and each such notification shall contain a statement of the effect of subsection (2) below.

(2) Where a medical practitioner is notified by the applicant under subsection (1) above that the individual in question wishes to have access to the report before it is supplied, the practitioner shall not supply the report unless—

(a) he has given the individual access to it and any requirements of section 5 below have been complied with, or

(b) the period of 21 days beginning with the date of the making of the application has elapsed without his having received any communication from the individual concerning arrangements for the individual to have access to it.

(3) Where a medical practitioner—

(a) receives an application for a medical report to be supplied for employment or insurance purposes without being notified by the applicant as mentioned in subsection (1) above, but

(b) before supplying the report receives a notification from the individual that he wishes to have access to the report before it is supplied,

the practitioner shall not supply the report unless—

(i) he has given the individual access to it and any requirements of section 5 below have been complied with, or

(ii) the period of 21 days beginning with the date of that notification has elapsed without his having received (either with that notification or otherwise) any communication from the individual concerning arrangements for the individual to have access to it.

(4) References in this section and section 5 below to giving an individual access to a medical report are references to—

(a) making the report or a copy of it available for his inspection; or

(b) supplying him with a copy of it;

and where a copy is supplied at the request, or otherwise with the consent, of the individual the practitioner may charge a reasonable fee to cover the costs of supplying it.

[389]

5 Consent to supplying of report and correction of errors

(1) Where an individual has been given access to a report under section 4 above the report shall not be supplied in response to the application in question unless the individual has notified the medical practitioner that he consents to its being so supplied.

(2) The individual shall be entitled, before giving his consent under subsection (1) above, to request the medical practitioner to amend any part of the report which the individual considers to be incorrect or misleading; and, if the individual does so, the practitioner—

(a) if he is to any extent prepared to accede to the individual's request, shall amend the report accordingly;

(b) if he is to any extent not prepared to accede to it but the individual requests him to attach to the report a statement of the individual's views in respect of any part of the report which he is declining to amend, shall attach such a statement to the report.

(3) Any request made by an individual under subsection (2) above shall be made in writing.

[390]

6 Retention of reports

(1) A copy of any medical report which a medical practitioner has supplied for employment or insurance purposes shall be retained by him for at least six months from the date on which it was supplied.

(2) A medical practitioner shall, if so requested by an individual, give the individual access to any medical report relating to him which the practitioner has supplied for employment or insurance purposes in the previous six months.

(3) The reference in subsection (2) above to giving an individual access to a medical report is a reference to—

(a) making a copy of the report available for his inspection; or

(b) supplying him with a copy of it;

and where a copy is supplied at the request, or otherwise with the consent, of the individual the practitioner may charge a reasonable fee to cover the costs of supplying it.

[391]

7 Exemptions

(1) A medical practitioner shall not be obliged to give an individual access, in accordance with the provisions of section 4(4) or 6(3) above, to any part of a medical report whose disclosure would in the opinion of the practitioner be likely to cause serious harm to the physical or mental health of the individual or others or would indicate the intentions of the practitioner in respect of the individual.

(2) A medical practitioner shall not be obliged to give an individual access, in accordance with those provisions, to any part of a medical report whose disclosure would be likely to reveal information about another person, or to reveal the identity of another person who has supplied information to the practitioner about the individual, unless—

(a) that person has consented; or

(b) that person is a health professional who has been involved in the care of the individual and the information relates to or has been provided by the professional in that capacity.

(3) Where it appears to a medical practitioner that subsection (1) or (2) above is applicable to any part (but not the whole) of a medical report—

(a) he shall notify the individual of that fact; and

(b) references in the preceding sections of this Act to the individual being given access to the report shall be construed as references to his being given access to the remainder of it;

and other references to the report in sections 4(4), 5(2) and 6(3) above shall similarly be construed as references to the remainder of the report.

(4) Where it appears to a medical practitioner that subsection (1) or (2) above is applicable to the whole of a medical report—

(a) he shall notify the individual of that fact; but

(b) he shall not supply the report unless he is notified by the individual that the individual consents to its being supplied;

and accordingly, if he is so notified by the individual, the restrictions imposed by section 4(2) and (3) above on the supply of the report shall not have effect in relation to it.

[392]

8 Application to the court

(1) If a court is satisfied on the application of an individual that any person, in connection with a medical report relating to that individual, has failed or is likely to fail to comply with any requirement of this Act, the court may order that person to comply with that requirement.

(2) The jurisdiction conferred by this section shall be exercisable by a county court or, in Scotland, by the sheriff.

[393]

9 Notifications under this Act

Any notification required or authorised to be given under this Act—

(a) shall be given in writing; and

(b) may be given by post.

[394]

10 Short title, commencement and extent

(1) This Act may be cited as the Access to Medical Reports Act 1988.

(2) This Act shall come into force on 1st January 1989.

(3) Nothing in this Act applies to a medical report prepared before the coming into force of this Act.

(4) This Act does not extend to Northern Ireland.

[395]

EDUCATION REFORM ACT 1988

(1988 c 40)

An Act to amend the law relating to education

[29 July 1988]

NOTES

Most of the provisions of this Act that were within the scope of this work were repealed and re-enacted by the Education Act 1996. Those provisions have in turn been repealed and re-enacted with (relatively minor) amendments by the School Standards and Framework Act 1998: see **[1307]** et seq for the 1998 Act. For reasons of space, the subject matter of sections, etc, not printed is not annotated.

PART IV
MISCELLANEOUS AND GENERAL

Miscellaneous provisions

221 Avoidance of certain contractual terms

(1) This section applies to any contract made after 20th November 1987 between—

(a) a local education authority in their capacity as such an authority;

(b) the governing body of [a foundation, voluntary aided or foundation special school;] or

(c) …

and any person employed by them, not being a contract made in contemplation of the employee's pending dismissal by reason of redundancy.

(2) In so far as a contract to which this section applies provides that the employee—

(a) shall not be dismissed by reason of redundancy; or

(b) if he is so dismissed, shall be paid a sum in excess of the sum which the employer is liable to pay him under [section 135 of the Employment Rights Act 1996],

the contract shall be void and of no effect.

(3) In this section—

"governing body, in relation to an institution, includes a body corporate established for the purpose of conducting that institution;

…

[396]–[397]

NOTES

Sub-s (1): words in square brackets in para (b) substituted by the School Standards and Framework Act 1998, s 140(1), Sch 30, paras 16, 18; para (c) repealed by the Further and Higher Education Act 1992, s 93, Sch 8, Pt I, paras 27, 52, Sch 9.

Sub-s (2): words in square brackets substituted by the Employment Rights Act 1996, s 240, Sch 1, paras 37(1), (4).

Sub-s (3): definition omitted repealed by the Further and Higher Education Act 1992, s 93, Sch 8, Pt I, paras 27, 52, Sch 9.

238 Citation, extent etc

(1) This Act may be cited as the Education Reform Act 1988.

(2) …

(3) Subject to subsections (4) to (6) below, this Act does not extend to Scotland or Northern Ireland.

(4)–(6) (*Outside the scope of this work.*)

[398]

NOTES

Sub-s (2): repealed by the Education Act 1996, s 582(2), Sch 38, Pt I.

SOCIAL SECURITY ACT 1989

(1989 c 24)

An Act to amend the law relating to social security and occupational and personal pension schemes; to make provision with respect to certain employment-related benefit schemes; to provide for the recovery, out of certain compensation payments, of amounts determined by reference to payments of benefit; to make fresh provision with respect to the constitution and functions of war pensions committees; and for connected purposes

[21 July 1989]

NOTES

Only s 23 and Sch 5, which implement Council Directive 86/378/EEC at **[3758]**, and s 33 (short title, etc) are printed here. The Directive itself required implementation by 1 January 1993, but as at 6 April 2008 only those parts of Sch 5 relating to (i) unfair maternity and parental leave provisions, (ii) unfair paternity leave provisions, and (iii) non-compliance – compulsory levelling up (in respect of unfair paternity leave provisions and unfair adoption leave provisions) have been brought into force (as from 23 June 1994, 6 April 2005, and 24 August 2007, respectively); see the first note to Sch 5 for details. No provisions of Sch 5, Pt II have been brought into effect, and all have been repealed. Additional provisions relating to paternity and adoption leave were inserted into Sch 5 by the Pensions Act 2004, s 265(1).

Occupational and personal pensions etc

23 Equal treatment for men and women

Schedule 5 to this Act shall have effect for the purpose of implementing the directive of the Council of the European Communities, dated 24th July 1986, relating to the principle of equal treatment for men and women in occupational social security schemes, and of making additional, supplemental and consequential provision.

[399]

NOTES

Commencement: 23 June 1994, 6 April 2005, and 24 August 2007, in so far as relating to those provisions of Sch 5 which came into force on those dates (see the note to Sch 5 at **[401]** for details); to be appointed (otherwise).

Council Directive: 86/378/EEC at **[3758]**.

33 Short title, commencement and extent

(1) This Act may be cited as the Social Security Act 1989; and this Act, other than section 25, and the Social Security Acts 1975 to 1988 may be cited together as the Social Security Acts 1975 to 1989.

(2) Apart from the provisions specified in subsection (3) below, this Act shall come into force on such day as the Secretary of State may by order appoint; and different days may be so appointed for different provisions or different purposes of the same provision.

(3)–(7) (*Outside the scope of this work.*)

[400]

NOTES

Orders: the commencement orders relevant to the provisions printed here are the Social Security Act 1989 (Commencement No 5) Order 1994, SI 1994/1661 and the Social Security Act 1989 (Commencement No 6) Order 2007, SI 2007/2445.

SCHEDULES

SCHEDULE 5
EMPLOYMENT-RELATED SCHEMES FOR PENSIONS OR OTHER BENEFITS: EQUAL TREATMENT FOR MEN AND WOMEN

Section 23

PART I
COMPLIANCE BY SCHEMES

Schemes to comply with the principle of equal treatment

1. Every employment-related benefit scheme shall comply with the principle of equal treatment.

The principle

2.—(1) The principle of equal treatment is that persons of the one sex shall not, on the basis of sex, be treated less favourably than persons of the other sex in any respect relating to an employment-related benefit scheme.

(2) Sub-paragraphs (3) to (6) below have effect, where applicable, for the purpose of determining whether a scheme complies with the principle of equal treatment.

(3) Where any provision of the scheme imposes on both male and female members a requirement or condition—

(a) which is such that the proportion of persons of the one sex ("the sex affected") who can comply with it is considerably smaller than the proportion of persons of the other sex who can do so, and

(b) which is not justifiable irrespective of the sex of the members,

the imposition of that requirement or condition shall be regarded as less favourable treatment of persons of the sex affected.

(4) No account shall be taken of—

(a) any difference, on the basis of the sex of members, in the levels of contributions—

(i) …

(ii) which the employer makes, to the extent that the difference is for the purpose of removing or limiting differences, as between men and women, in the amount or value of money purchase benefits;

(b) any difference, on the basis of sex, in the amount or value of money purchase benefits, to the extent that the difference is justifiable on actuarial grounds;

(c) any special treatment for the benefit of women in connection with pregnancy or childbirth;

(d) any permitted age-related differences;

(e) any difference of treatment in relation to benefits for a deceased member's surviving husband, wife or other dependants;

(f) any difference of treatment in relation to any optional provisions available; or

(g) any provisions of a scheme to the extent that they have been specially arranged for the benefit of one particular member of the scheme;

but where the scheme includes any unfair maternity provisions, it shall to that extent be regarded as according less favourable treatment to women on the basis of sex.

(5) Where the scheme treats persons of the one sex differently according to their marital or family status, that treatment is to be compared with the scheme's treatment of persons of the other sex who have the same status.

(6) The principle of equal treatment applies in relation to members' dependants as it applies in relation to members.

(7) If any question arises whether a condition or requirement falling within sub-paragraph (3)(a) above is or is not justifiable irrespective of the sex of the members, it shall be for those who assert that it is so justifiable to prove that fact.

(8) In this paragraph—

"money purchase benefits" has the meaning given by *section 84(1) of the 1986 Act*, but with the substitution for references to a personal or occupational pension scheme of references to an employment-related benefit scheme;

"optional provisions available" means those provisions of a scheme—

(a) which apply only in the case of members who elect for them to do so; and

(b) whose purpose is to secure for those members—

(i) benefits in addition to those otherwise provided under the scheme; or

(ii) a choice with respect to the date on which benefits under the scheme are to commence; or

(iii) a choice between any two or more benefits;

"permitted age-related difference" means any difference, on the basis of sex, in the age—

(a) at which a service-related benefit in respect of old age or retirement commences; or

(b) at which, in consequence of the commencement of such a benefit, any other service-related benefit either ceases to be payable or becomes payable at a reduced rate calculated by reference to the amount of the benefit so commencing.

(9) For the purposes of this paragraph—

(a) any reference to a person's family status is a reference to his having an unmarried partner or any dependants; and

(b) a person "has an unmarried partner" if that person and some other person to whom he is not married live together as husband and wife.

Non-compliance: compulsory levelling up

3.—(1) To the extent that any provision of an employment-related benefit scheme does not comply with the principle of equal treatment, it shall be overridden by this Schedule and the more favourable treatment accorded to persons of the one sex shall also be accorded to persons of the other sex.

(2) Where more favourable treatment is accorded to any persons by virtue of sub-paragraph (1) above, that sub-paragraph requires them, in accordance with the principle of equal treatment—

(a) to pay contributions at a level appropriate to the treatment so accorded; and

(b) to bear any other burden which is an incident of that treatment;

but persons of either sex may instead elect to receive the less favourable treatment and, in accordance with the principle of equal treatment, pay contributions at the level appropriate to that treatment and bear the other burdens incidental to it.

(3) Where any provision of a scheme is overridden by sub-paragraph (1) above, nothing in this Schedule shall affect any rights accrued or obligations incurred during the period before the date on which that provision is so overridden.

(4) Sub-paragraph (1) above is without prejudice to the exercise, in compliance with the principle of equal treatment, of any power to amend the scheme.

4. …

Unfair maternity provisions

5.—(1) In this Schedule "unfair maternity provisions", in relation to an employment-related benefit scheme, means any provision—

(a) which relates to continuing membership of, or the accrual of rights under, the scheme during any period of paid maternity absence in the case of any woman who is (or who, immediately before the commencement of such a period, was) an employed earner and which treats such a woman otherwise than in accordance with the normal employment requirement; or

(b) which requires the amount of any benefit payable under the scheme to or in respect of any such woman, to the extent that it falls to be determined by reference to her earnings during a period which included a period of paid maternity absence, to be determined otherwise than in accordance with the normal employment requirement.

(2) In the case of any unfair maternity provision—

(a) the more favourable treatment required by paragraph 3(1) above is treatment no less favourable than would be accorded to the women [members] in accordance with the normal employment requirement;
(b) paragraph 3(2) above does not authorise the making of any such election as is there mentioned; and
(c) paragraph 4(1)(a) above does not authorise the making of any modification which does not satisfy the requirements of paragraph (a) above;

but, in respect of a period of paid maternity absence, a woman shall only be required to pay contributions on the amount of contractual remuneration or statutory maternity pay actually paid to or for her in respect of that period.

(3) In this paragraph—
(a) "period of paid maternity absence" means any period—
(i) throughout which a woman is absent from work due to pregnancy or confinement; and
(ii) for which her employer (or, if she is no longer in his employment, her former employer) pays her any contractual remuneration or statutory maternity pay;
(b) "the normal employment requirement" is the requirement that any period of paid maternity absence shall be treated as if it were a period throughout which the woman in question works normally and receives the remuneration likely to be paid for doing so.

[Unfair paternity leave provisions

5A.—(1) Where an employment-related benefit scheme includes any unfair paternity leave provisions (irrespective of any differences on the basis of sex in the treatment accorded to members under those provisions), then—
(a) the scheme shall be regarded to that extent as not complying with the principle of equal treatment; and
(b) subject to sub-paragraph (3), this Schedule shall apply accordingly.

(2) In this paragraph "unfair paternity leave provisions", in relation to an employment-related benefit scheme, means any provision—
(a) which relates to continuing membership of, or the accrual of rights under, the scheme during any period of paid paternity leave in the case of any member who is (or who, immediately before the commencement of such a period, was) an employed earner and which treats such a member otherwise than in accordance with the normal employment requirement; or
(b) which requires the amount of any benefit payable under the scheme to or in respect of any such member, to the extent that it falls to be determined by reference to earnings during a period which included a period of paid paternity leave, to be determined otherwise than in accordance with the normal employment requirement.

(3) In the case of any unfair paternity leave provision—
(a) the more favourable treatment required by paragraph 3(1) is treatment no less favourable than would be accorded to the member in accordance with the normal employment requirement; and
(b) paragraph 3(2) does not authorise the making of any such election as is there mentioned;

but, in respect of any period of paid paternity leave, a member shall only be required to pay contributions on the amount of contractual remuneration *or statutory paternity pay* actually paid to or for him in respect of that period.

(4) In this paragraph—
"period of paid paternity leave", in the case of a member, means a period—
(a) throughout which the member is absent from work in circumstances where sub-paragraph (5), (6) *or (7)* applies, and
(b) for which the employer (or if he is no longer in his employment, his former employer) pays him any contractual remuneration *or statutory paternity pay*; and

"the normal employment requirement" is the requirement that any period of paid paternity leave shall be treated as if it were a period throughout which the member in question works normally and receives the remuneration likely to be paid for doing so.

(5) This sub-paragraph applies if—

(a) the member's absence from work is due to the birth or expected birth of a child, and

(b) the member satisfies the conditions prescribed under section 171ZA(2)(a)(i) and (ii) of the Social Security Contributions and Benefits Act 1992 in relation to that child.

(6) This sub-paragraph applies if—

(a) the member's absence from work is due to the placement or expected placement of a child for adoption under the law of any part of the United Kingdom, and

(b) the member satisfies the conditions prescribed under section 171ZB(2)(a)(i) and (ii) of that Act in relation to that child.

(7) This sub-paragraph applies if—

(a) the member's absence from work is due to the adoption or expected adoption of a child who has entered the United Kingdom in connection with or for the purposes of adoption which does not involve the placement of the child for adoption under the law of any part of the United Kingdom, and

(b) the member satisfies the conditions prescribed under section 171ZB(2)(a)(i) and (ii) of that Act (as applied by virtue of section 171ZK of that Act (adoption cases not involving placement under the law of the United Kingdom)) in relation to that child.

[(8) This sub-paragraph applies if—

(a) the member's absence from work is due to the fact that he is caring for a child, and

(b) in relation to that child, the member satisfies the conditions prescribed—

(i) under section 171ZEA(2)(a)(i) and (ii) of that Act,

(ii) under section 171ZEB(2)(a)(i) and (ii) of that Act, or

(iii) under section 171ZEB(2)(a)(i) and (ii) of that Act as applied by virtue of section 171ZK of that Act (adoption cases not involving placement under the law of the United Kingdom).]

Unfair adoption leave provisions

5B.—(1) Where an employment-related benefit scheme includes any unfair adoption leave provisions (irrespective of any differences on the basis of sex in the treatment accorded to members under those provisions), then—

(a) the scheme shall be regarded to that extent as not complying with the principle of equal treatment; and

(b) subject to sub-paragraph (3), this Schedule shall apply accordingly.

(2) In this paragraph "unfair adoption leave provisions", in relation to an employment-related benefit scheme, means any provision—

(a) which relates to continuing membership of, or the accrual of rights under, the scheme during any period of paid adoption leave in the case of any member who is (or who, immediately before the commencement of such a period, was) an employed earner and which treats such a member otherwise than in accordance with the normal employment requirement; or

(b) which requires the amount of any benefit payable under the scheme to or in respect of any such member, to the extent that it falls to be determined by reference to earnings during a period which included a period of paid adoption leave, to be determined otherwise than in accordance with the normal employment requirement.

(3) In the case of any unfair adoption leave provision—

(a) the more favourable treatment required by paragraph 3(1) is treatment no less favourable than would be accorded to the member in accordance with the normal employment requirement; and

(b) paragraph 3(2) does not authorise the making of any such election as is there mentioned;

but, in respect of any period of paid adoption leave, a member shall only be required to pay contributions on the amount of contractual remuneration or statutory adoption pay actually paid to or for him in respect of that period.

(4) In this paragraph—

"period of paid adoption leave", in the case of a member, means a period—

(a) throughout which the member is absent from work in circumstances where sub-paragraph (5) or (6) applies, and

(b) for which the employer (or, if he is no longer in his employment, his former employer) pays him any contractual remuneration or statutory adoption pay; and

"the normal employment requirement" is the requirement that any period of paid adoption leave shall be treated as if it were a period throughout which the member in question works normally and receives the remuneration likely to be paid for doing so.

(5) This sub-paragraph applies if—

(a) the member's absence from work is due to the placement, or expected placement, of a child for adoption under the law of any part of the United Kingdom, and

(b) the member is a person with whom the child is, or is expected to be, placed for such adoption.

(6) This sub-paragraph applies if—

(a) the member's absence from work is due to the adoption or expected adoption of a child who has entered the United Kingdom in connection with or for the purposes of adoption which does not involve the placement of the child for adoption under the law of any part of the United Kingdom, and

(b) the member is a person by whom the child has been or is expected to be adopted.]

Unfair family leave provisions

6.—(1) Where an employment-related benefit scheme includes any unfair family leave provisions (irrespective of any differences on the basis of sex in the treatment accorded to members under those provisions), then—

(a) the scheme shall be regarded to that extent as not complying with the principle of equal treatment; and

(b) subject to sub-paragraph (3) below, this Schedule shall apply accordingly.

(2) In this Schedule "unfair family leave provisions" means any provision—

(a) which relates to continuing membership of, or the accrual of rights under, the scheme during any period of paid family leave in the case of any member who is an employed earner and which treats such a member otherwise than in accordance with the normal leave requirement; or

(b) which requires the amount of any benefit payable under the scheme to or in respect of any such member to the extent that it falls to be determined by reference to earnings during a period which included a period of paid family leave, to be determined otherwise than in accordance with the normal leave requirement.

(3) In the case of any unfair family leave provision—

(a) the more favourable treatment required by paragraph 3(1) above is treatment no less favourable than would be accorded to the members in accordance with the normal leave requirement;

(b) paragraph 3(2) above does not authorise the making of any such election as is there mentioned; and

(c) paragraph 4(1)(a) above does not authorise the making of any modification which does not satisfy the requirements of paragraph (a) above;

but, in respect of a period of paid family leave, a member shall only be required to pay contributions on the amount of contractual remuneration actually paid to or for him in respect of that period.

(4) In this paragraph—

(a) "period of paid family leave" means any period—

(i) throughout which a member is absent from work for family reasons; and

(ii) for which the employer pays him any contractual remuneration;

(b) "the normal leave requirement" is the requirement that any period of paid family leave shall be treated as if it were a period throughout which the member in question works normally but only receives the remuneration in fact paid to him for that period.

Meaning of "employment-related benefit scheme" etc

7. In this Schedule—

(a) "employment-related benefit scheme" means any scheme or arrangement which is comprised in one or more instruments or agreements and which has, or is capable

of having, effect in relation to one or more descriptions or categories of employments so as to provide service-related benefits to or in respect of employed or self-employed earners—
- (i) who have qualifying service in an employment of any such description or category, or
- (ii) who have made arrangements with the trustees or managers of the scheme to enable them to become members of the scheme,

but does not include a limited scheme;

(b) "limited scheme" means—
- (i) any personal scheme for employed earners to which the employer does not contribute;
- (ii) any scheme which has only one member, other than a personal scheme for an employed earner to which his employer contributes;
- (iii) any contract of insurance which is made for the benefit of employed earners only and to which the employer is not a party;

(c) "personal scheme" means any scheme or arrangement which falls within paragraph (a) above by virtue of sub-paragraph (ii) of that paragraph (or which would so fall apart from paragraph (b) above);

(d) "public service scheme" has *the meaning given by section 51(3)(b) of the 1973 Act*;

(e) "service-related benefits" means benefits, in the form of pensions or otherwise, payable in money or money's worth in respect of—
- (i) termination of service;
- (ii) retirement, old age or death;
- (iii) interruptions of service by reason of sickness or invalidity;
- (iv) accidents, injuries or diseases connected with employment;
- (v) unemployment; or
- (vi) expenses incurred in connection with children or other dependants;

and includes, in the case of a member who is an employed earner, any other benefit so payable to or in respect of the member in consequence of his employment.

Extension of ban on compulsory membership

8. *Section 15(1) of the 1986 Act* (which renders void any provision making membership of a pension scheme compulsory for an employed earner) shall apply in relation to a self-employed earner as it applies in relation to an employed earner, but with the substitution for references to a personal pension scheme of references to an employment-related benefit scheme which would be such a pension scheme if self-employed earners were regarded as employed earners.

Jurisdiction

9.—(1) The court, on the application of any person interested, shall have jurisdiction to determine any question arising as to—

(a) whether any provision of an employment-related benefit scheme does or does not comply with the principle of equal treatment; or

(b) whether, and with what effect, any such provision is overridden by paragraph 3 above.

(2) In sub-paragraph (1) above "the court" means—

(a) in England and Wales, the High Court or a county court; and

(b) in Scotland, the Court of Session or the sheriff court.

(3) An application under sub-paragraph (1) above may be commenced in a county court notwithstanding—

(a) any financial limit otherwise imposed on the jurisdiction of such a court; or

(b) that the only relief claimed is a declaration or an injunction.

Interpretation

10. Expressions other than "benefit" which are used in this Part of this Schedule and in the principal Act have the same meaning in this Part of this Schedule as they have in that Act.

Supplemental

11. …

Future repeal of actuarial provisions

12. The Secretary of State may by order repeal paragraph 2(4)(a)(i) above; and if and to the extent that he has not done so before 30th July 1999 it shall cease to have effect on that date. **[401]**

NOTES

Commencement: this Schedule has been brought into force as follows (and is to be appointed otherwise)—

(i) on 23 June 1994 in so far as relating to paras 5 (except sub-para (2)(b) and (c)) and 6 (except sub-para (3)(b) and (c)); also paras 1, 2(1), (2), (4)(c), (5), (9), 3 (except sub-para (2)), 7 (except sub-para (d)), 9 and 10, but for the purposes only of giving effect to the provisions of paras 5 and 6 brought into force from that date: see SI 1994/1661, art 2(a), (b), Schedule, Pts I, II.

(ii) on 24 August 2007 in so far as relating to para 3 (except sub-paragraph (2)) for the purposes of paras 5A, 5B: see SI 2007/2445, art 2.

Note that paras 5A, 5B came into force on 6 April 2005 (see below).

Para 2: sub-para (4)(a)(i) repealed as from 30 July 1999 by para 12 (qv; no order was made under para 12 prior to the date there stated), for the words in italics in sub-para (8) there are substituted the words "section 181(1) of the Pension Schemes Act 1993" by the Pension Schemes Act 1993, s 190, Sch 7, para 2(a), as from a day to be appointed.

Para 4: repealed by the Pensions Act 1995, ss 151, 177, Sch 5, para 13(2), Sch 7, Pt III.

Para 5: word in square brackets in sub-para (2)(a) inserted by the Social Security Act 1990, s 21(1), Sch 6, para 29, as from a day to be appointed.

Para 5A: inserted, together with para 5B, by the Pensions Act 2004, s 265(1), as from 6 April 2005, except in relation to any period of paternity leave or adoption leave which began before that date (see SI 2005/275); for the words in italics in sub-para (3) there are substituted the words ", ordinary statutory paternity pay or additional statutory paternity pay", for the first words in italics in the definition "period of paid paternity leave" in sub-para (4) there are substituted the words ", (7) or (8)", and for the second words in italics in that definition there are substituted the words ", ordinary statutory paternity pay or additional statutory paternity pay", and sub-para (8) is added, by the Work and Families Act 2006, s 11(1), Sch 1, para 1, as from a day to be appointed.

Para 5B: inserted as noted above.

Para 7: for the words in italics in sub-para (d) there are substituted the words "the same meaning as "public service pension scheme" in section 1 of the Pension Schemes Act 1993" by the Pension Schemes Act 1993, s 190, Sch 7, para 2(b), as from a day to be appointed.

Para 8: for the words in italics there are substituted the words "section 160(1) of the Pension Schemes Act 1993" by the Pension Schemes Act 1993, s 190, Sch 7, para 2(c), as from a day to be appointed.

Para 11: repealed by the Pension Schemes Act 1993, s 188(1), Sch 5, Pt I.

1986 Act: ie, the Social Security Act 1986. Section 15(1) and the definition "money purchase benefits" in s 84(1) were repealed and replaced by the Pension Schemes Act 1993 (see now s 160(1) and s 181(1) of that Act respectively).

1973 Act: ie, the Social Security Act 1973. Section 51(3)(b) was repealed by the Pension Schemes Act 1993. The definition "public service scheme" is now replaced by the definition "public service pension scheme" in s 1 of that Act.

Principal Act: ie, the Social Security Act 1975. Repealed by the Social Security (Consequential Provisions) Act 1992 and replaced by the Social Security Administration Act 1992 and the Social Security Contributions and Benefits Act 1992.

(Sch 5, Pt II: para 13 repealed by the Pension Schemes Act 1993, s 188(1), Sch 5, Pt I; para 14 repealed by the Pensions Act 1995, s 177, Sch 7, Pt I; para 15 repealed by the Trade Union Reform and Employment Rights Act 1993, s 51, Sch 10.)

EMPLOYMENT ACT 1989

(1989 c 38)

ARRANGEMENT OF SECTIONS

Overriding of provisions requiring discrimination as respects employment or training

An Act to amend the Sex Discrimination Act 1975 in pursuance of the Directive of the Council of the European Communities, dated 9th February 1976, (No 76/207/EEC) on the implementation of the principle of equal treatment for men and women as regards access to employment, vocational training and promotion, and working conditions; to repeal or amend prohibitions or requirements relating to the employment of young persons and other categories of employees; to make other amendments of the law relating to employment and training; to repeal section 1(1)(a) of the Celluloid and Cinematograph Film Act 1922; to dissolve the Training Commission; to make further provision with respect to industrial training boards; to make provision with respect to the transfer of staff employed in the Skills Training Agency; and for connected purposes

[16 November 1989]

NOTES

Various provisions of this Act are omitted as outside the scope of this work or amending other legislation, as individually noted in respect of each section or Schedule omitted.

Transfer of functions in relation to Wales: as to the transfer of functions under this Act from Ministers of the Crown to the National Assembly for Wales, see the National Assembly for Wales (Transfer of Functions) Order 1999, SI 1999/672.

See *Harvey* L2(B).

Overriding of provisions requiring discrimination as respects employment or training

1 Overriding of statutory requirements which conflict with certain provisions of 1975 Act

(1) Any provision of—

(a) an Act passed before the Sex Discrimination Act 1975, or

(b) an instrument approved or made by or under such an Act (including one approved or made after the passing of the 1975 Act),

shall be of no effect in so far as it imposes a requirement to do an act which would be rendered unlawful by any of the provisions of that Act referred to in subsection (2).

(2) Those provisions are—

(a) Part II (discrimination as respects employment);

(b) Part III (discrimination as respects education etc) so far as it applies to vocational training; and

(c) Part IV (other unlawful acts) so far as it has effect in relation to the provisions mentioned in paragraphs (a) and (b) above.

(3) Where in any legal proceedings (of whatever nature) there falls to be determined the question whether subsection (1) operates to negative the effect of any provision in so far as it requires the application by any person of a [provision, criterion or practice] falling within [section 1(2)(b)(i) or 3(1)(b)(i)] of the 1975 Act (indirect discrimination on grounds of sex or marital status)—

(a) it shall be for any party to the proceedings who claims that subsection (1) does not so operate in relation to that provision to show the [provision, criterion or practice] in question to be justifiable as mentioned in [section 1(2)(b)(ii) or 3(1)(b)(ii) of that Act]; and

(b) the said [section 1(2)(b)(ii) or 3(1)(b)(ii)] shall accordingly have effect in relation to the [provision, criterion or practice] as if the reference to the person applying it were a reference to any such party to the proceedings.

(4) Where an Act passed after the 1975 Act, whether before or after the passing of this Act, re-enacts (with or without modification) a provision of an Act passed before the 1975 Act, that provision as re-enacted shall be treated for the purposes of subsection (1) as if it continued to be contained in an Act passed before the 1975 Act.

[402]

NOTES

Sub-s (3): words in square brackets substituted by the Sex Discrimination (Indirect Discrimination and Burden of Proof) Regulations 2001, SI 2001/2660, reg 9.

2 Power of Secretary of State to repeal statutory provisions requiring discrimination as respects employment or training

(1) Where it appears to the Secretary of State that a relevant provision, namely any provision of—

(a) an Act passed before this Act, or

(b) an instrument approved or made by or under such an Act (including one approved or made after the passing of this Act),

requires the doing of an act which would (within the meaning of the 1975 Act) constitute an act of discrimination in circumstances relevant for the purposes of any of the provisions of that Act falling within section 1(2) above, he may by order make such provision (whether by amending, repealing or revoking the relevant provision or otherwise) as he considers appropriate for removing any such requirement.

(2) Subsection (1) shall have effect in relation to a provision to which section 1(1) above applies as if the reference to a relevant provision requiring the doing of an act were a reference to its so requiring but for the operation of section 1(1).

(3) Any order under this section which makes any amendment, repeal or revocation of a relevant provision within the meaning of subsection (1) may (without prejudice to the generality of section 28(5) below) amend or repeal any provision of this Act by virtue of which acts done in pursuance of the relevant provision are not to be unlawful for the purposes of provisions of the 1975 Act.

(4) Where an Act passed after this Act re-enacts (with or without modification) a provision of an Act passed before this Act, that provision as re-enacted shall be treated for the purposes of subsection (1) as if it continued to be contained in an Act passed before this Act.

[403]

NOTES

Orders: as of 6 April 2008, no Orders had been made under this section.

Circumstances where discrimination as respects employment or training is permissible

3 (*Amends the Sex Discrimination Act 1975, s 7 at* **[107]**, *substitutes ss 51, 51A for the original s 51 thereof at* **[162]**, **[163]**, *and inserts s 52A thereof at* **[165]**, *and is repealed in part by the Statute Law* (*Repeals*) *Act 2004, as from 22 July 2004.*)

4 Exemption for discrimination under certain provisions concerned with the protection of women at work

(1) Without prejudice to the operation of section 51 of the 1975 Act (as substituted by section 3(3) above), nothing in—

(a) Part II of that Act,

(b) Part III of that Act so far as it applies to vocational training, or

(c) Part IV of that Act so far as it has effect in relation to the provisions mentioned in paragraphs (a) and (b) above,

shall render unlawful any act done by a person in relation to a woman if it was necessary for that person to do that act in order to comply with any requirement of any of the provisions specified in Schedule 1 to this Act (which are concerned with the protection of women at work).

(2) Each of the last two entries in that Schedule shall be construed as including a reference to any provision or provisions for the time being having effect in place of the provision or provisions specified in that entry.

(3) In this section "woman" means a female person of any age.

[404]

5 Exemption for discrimination in connection with certain educational appointments

(1) Nothing in Parts II to IV of the 1975 Act shall render unlawful any act done by a person in connection with the employment of another person as the head teacher or principal of any educational establishment if it was necessary for that person to do that act in order to comply with any requirement of any instrument relating to the establishment that its head teacher or principal should be a member of a particular religious order.

(2) Nothing in—

(a) Part II of the 1975 Act, or

(b) Part IV of that Act so far as it has effect in relation to Part II,

shall render unlawful any act done by a person in connection with the employment of another person as a professor in any university if the professorship in question is, in accordance with any Act or instrument relating to the university, either a canon professorship or one to which a canonry is annexed.

(3) Nothing in the provisions of the 1975 Act referred to in subsection (2)(a) or (b) shall render unlawful any act done by a person in connection with the employment of another person as the head, a fellow or any other member of the academic staff of any college, or institution in the nature of a college, in a university if it was necessary for that person to do that act in order to comply with any requirement of any instrument relating to the college or institution that the holder of the position in question should be a woman.

(4) Subsection (3) shall not apply in relation to instruments taking effect after the commencement of that subsection; and section 6(b) of the Interpretation Act 1978 (words importing the feminine gender to include the masculine) shall not apply to that subsection.

(5) The Secretary of State may by order provide that any provision of subsections (1) to (3) shall not have effect in relation to—

(a) any educational establishment or university specified in the order; or

(b) any class or description of educational establishments so specified.

(6) In this section "educational establishment" means—

(a) any school within the meaning of the Education Act 1944 or the Education (Scotland) Act 1980;

(b) any college, or institution in the nature of a college, in a university; or

[(ba) any institution designated by order under section 28 of the Further and Higher Education Act 1992]

[(c) any institution designated by order made or having effect as if made under section 129 of the Education Reform Act 1988.]

(7) Nothing in this section shall be construed as prejudicing the operation of section 19 of the 1975 Act (exemption for discrimination in relation to employment of ministers of religion).

[405]

NOTES

Sub-s (6): para (ba) inserted, and para (c) substituted, by the Further and Higher Education Act 1992, s 93(1), Sch 8, Pt II, para 93.

The reference to the Education Act 1944 has not been amended although that Act was repealed by the Education Act 1996. For the meaning of "school" see s 4 of that Act.

---

6 Power of Secretary of State to exempt particular acts of discrimination required by or under statute

(1) The Secretary of State may by order make such provision as he considers appropriate—

(a) for disapplying subsection (1) of section 1 above in the case of any provision to which it appears to him that that subsection would otherwise apply;

(b) for rendering lawful under any of the provisions of the 1975 Act falling within section 1(2) above acts done in order to comply with any requirement—

(i) of a provision whose effect is preserved by virtue of paragraph (a) above, or

(ii) of an instrument approved or made by or under an Act passed after the 1975 Act but before this Act (including one approved or made after the passing of this Act).

(2) Where an Act passed after this Act re-enacts (with or without modification) a provision of an Act passed as mentioned in sub-paragraph (ii) of subsection (1)(b), that provision as re-enacted shall be treated for the purposes of that sub-paragraph as if it continued to be contained in an Act passed as mentioned in that sub-paragraph.

[406]

NOTES

Orders: the Sex Discrimination Act 1975 (Exemption of Police Federation Constitutional and Electoral Arrangements) Order 1989, SI 1989/2420.

Discrimination as respects training

7 (*Substitutes the Sex Discrimination Act 1975, s 14 at* **[116]**, *substitutes the Race Relations Act 1976, s 13 at* **[221]**, *and amends s 37 of the 1976 Act at* **[256]**.)

8 Power to exempt discrimination in favour of lone parents in connection with training

(1) The Secretary of State may by order provide with respect to—

(a) any specified arrangements made under section 2 of the Employment and Training Act 1973 (functions of the Secretary of State as respects employment and training) [or under section 2(3) of the Enterprise and New Towns (Scotland) Act 1990 (arrangements by Scottish Enterprise and Highlands and Islands Enterprise in connection with training etc)], or

(b) any specified class or description of training for employment provided otherwise than in pursuance of [either of those sections], …

(c) …

that this section shall apply to such special treatment afforded to or in respect of lone parents in connection with their participation in those arrangements, or in that training or scheme, as is specified or referred to in the order.

(2) Where this section applies to any treatment afforded to or in respect of lone parents, neither the treatment so afforded nor any act done in the implementation of any such treatment shall be regarded for the purposes of the 1975 Act as giving rise to any discrimination falling within section 3 of that Act (discrimination against married persons for purposes of Part II of that Act).

(3) An order under subsection (1) above may specify or refer to special treatment afforded as mentioned in that subsection—

(a) whether it is afforded by the making of any payment or by the fixing of special conditions for participation in the arrangements, training or scheme in question, or otherwise, and

(b) whether it is afforded by the Secretary of State or by some other person;

and, without prejudice to the generality of paragraph (b) of that subsection, any class or description of training for employment specified in such an order by virtue of that paragraph may be framed by reference to the person, or the class or description of persons, by whom the training is provided.

(4) In this section—

(a) "employment" and "training" have the same meaning as in the Employment and Training Act 1973; and

(b) "lone parent" has the same meaning as it has for the purposes of any regulations made in pursuance of section 20(1)(a) of the Social Security Act 1986 (income support).

[407]

NOTES

Sub-s (1): words in square brackets in para (a) inserted, and words in square brackets in para (b) substituted, by the Enterprise and New Towns (Scotland) Act 1990, s 38(1), Sch 4, para 18; para (c) and word omitted immediately preceding it repealed by the Statute Law (Repeals) Act 2004, as from 22 July 2004.

Social Security Act 1986, s 20(1)(a): repealed by the Social Security (Consequential Provisions) Act 1992; see now the Social Security Contributions and Benefits Act 1992.

Orders: the Sex Discrimination Act (Exemption of Special Treatment for Lone Parents) Order 1989, SI 1989/2140 at **[2161]**; the Sex Discrimination Act (Exemption of Special Treatment for Lone Parents) Order 1991, SI 1991/2813 at **[2176]**.

Removal of restrictions and other requirements relating to employment

9, 10 ((*Repeal or modification of provisions requiring different treatment of different categories of employees and removal of restrictions relating to employment of young persons*) *partly repealed by the Statute Law* (*Repeals*) *Act 2004, as from 22 July 2004; remainder outside the scope of this work.*)

11 Exemption of Sikhs from requirements as to wearing of safety helmets on construction sites

(1) Any requirement to wear a safety helmet which (apart from this section) would, by virtue of any statutory provision or rule of law, be imposed on a Sikh who is on a construction site shall not apply to him at any time when he is wearing a turban.

(2) Accordingly, where—

(a) a Sikh who is on a construction site is for the time being wearing a turban, and

(b) (apart from this section) any associated requirement would, by virtue of any statutory provision or rule of law, be imposed—

(i) on the Sikh, or

(ii) on any other person,

in connection with the wearing by the Sikh of a safety helmet, that requirement shall not apply to the Sikh or (as the case may be) to that other person.

(3) In subsection (2) "associated requirement" means any requirement (other than one falling within subsection (1)) which is related to or connected with the wearing, provision or maintenance of safety helmets.

(4) It is hereby declared that, where a person does not comply with any requirement, being a requirement which for the time being does not apply to him by virtue of subsection (1) or (2)—

(a) he shall not be liable in tort to any person in respect of any injury, loss or damage caused by his failure to comply with that requirement; and
(b) in Scotland no action for reparation shall be brought against him by any person in respect of any such injury, loss or damage.

(5) If a Sikh who is on a construction site—
(a) does not comply with any requirement to wear a safety helmet, being a requirement which for the time being does not apply to him by virtue of subsection (1), and
(b) in consequence of any act or omission of some other person sustains any injury, loss or damage which is to any extent attributable to the fact that he is not wearing a safety helmet in compliance with the requirement,

that other person shall, if liable to the Sikh in tort (or, in Scotland, in an action for reparation), be so liable only to the extent that injury, loss or damage would have been sustained by the Sikh even if he had been wearing a safety helmet in compliance with the requirement.

(6) Where—
(a) the act or omission referred to in subsection (5) causes the death of the Sikh, and
(b) the Sikh would have sustained some injury (other than loss of life) in consequence of the act or omission even if he had been wearing a safety helmet in compliance with the requirement in question,

the amount of any damages which, by virtue of that subsection, are recoverable in tort (or, in Scotland, in an action for reparation) in respect of that injury shall not exceed the amount of any damages which would (apart from that subsection) be so recoverable in respect of the Sikh's death.

(7) In this section—
"building operations" and "works of engineering construction" have the same meaning as in the Factories Act 1961;
"construction site" means any place where any building operations or works of engineering construction are being undertaken;
"injury" includes loss of life, any impairment of a person's physical or mental condition and any disease;
"safety helmet" means any form of protective headgear; and
"statutory provision" means a provision of an Act or of subordinate legislation.

(8) In this section—
(a) any reference to a Sikh is a reference to a follower of the Sikh religion; and
(b) any reference to a Sikh being on a construction site is a reference to his being there whether while at work or otherwise.

(9) This section shall have effect in relation to any relevant construction site within the territorial sea adjacent to Great Britain as it has effect in relation to any construction site within Great Britain.

(10) In subsection (9) "relevant construction site" means any construction site where there are being undertaken any building operations or works of engineering construction which are activities falling within Article 7(a) of the Health and Safety at Work etc Act 1974 (Application outside Great Britain) Order 1989.

[408]

NOTES

Health and Safety at Work etc Act 1974 (Application outside Great Britain) Order 1989: revoked; see now the Health and Safety at Work etc Act 1974 (Application outside Great Britain) Order 2001, SI 2001/2127.

12 Protection of Sikhs from racial discrimination in connection with requirements as to wearing of safety helmets

(1) Where—
(a) any person applies to a Sikh any requirement or condition relating to the wearing by him of a safety helmet while he is on a construction site, and
(b) at the time when he so applies the requirement or condition that person has no reasonable grounds for believing that the Sikh would not wear a turban at all times when on such a site,

then, for the purpose of determining whether the application of the requirement or condition to the Sikh constitutes an act of discrimination falling within section 1(1)(b) of the Race

Relations Act 1976 (indirect racial discrimination), the requirement or condition shall be taken to be one which cannot be shown to be justifiable as mentioned in sub-paragraph (ii) of that provision.

(2) Any special treatment afforded to a Sikh in consequence of section 11(1) or (2) above shall not be regarded for the purposes of the Race Relations Act 1976 as giving rise, in relation to any other person, to any discrimination falling within section 1 of that Act.

(3) Subsections (7) to (10) of section 11 above shall apply for the purposes of this section as they apply for the purposes of that section.

[409]

13–26 (*Ss 13–20 amended the Employment Protection (Consolidation) Act 1978, and are repealed as follows: s 13 repealed by the Trade Union Reform and Employment Rights Act 1993, s 51, Sch 10; s 14 repealed by the Trade Union and Labour Relations (Consolidation) Act 1992, s 300(1), Sch 1; ss 15–18 repealed by the Employment Rights Act 1996, s 242, Sch 3, Pt I; s 19 repealed by the Pension Schemes Act 1993, s 188(1), Sch 5, Pt I and the Employment Rights Act 1996, s 242, Sch 3, Pt I; s 20 repealed by the Employment Tribunals Act 1996, s 45, Sch 3, Pt I; s 21 repealed by the Statute Law (Repeals) Act 2004, as from 22 July 2004; ss 22 (dissolution of Training Commission), 23–25 (Industrial Training Boards) outside the scope of this work; s 26 repealed by the Education and Inspections Act 2006, s 184, Sch 18, Pt 2, as from 8 January 2007.*)

General

27 ((*Power to legislate for Northern Ireland*) *outside the scope of this work.*)

28 Orders

(1) Any power to make an order under this Act shall be exercisable by statutory instrument.

(2) The Secretary of State shall consult the [Commission for Equality and Human Rights] before making—
- (a) an order under section 2 which makes any amendment or repeal of any provision of an Act, or
- (b) an order under section 6.

(3) An order of one of the following descriptions, namely—
- (a) such an order under section 2 as is mentioned in subsection (2)(a), or
- (b) an order under section 6(1)(a) which preserves the effect of any provision of an Act,

shall not be made unless a draft of it has been laid before and approved by resolution of each House of Parliament.

(4) Any statutory instrument containing an order under this Act other than—
- (a) an order to which subsection (3) applies,
- (b) …
- (c) an order under section 30,

shall be subject to annulment in pursuance of a resolution of either House of Parliament.

(5) An order under this Act may contain such consequential or transitional provisions or savings as appear to the Secretary of State to be necessary or expedient.

[410]

NOTES

Sub-s (2): words in square brackets substituted by the Equality Act 2006, s 40, Sch 3, paras, 21, 40, as from 1 October 2007.

Sub-s (4): para (b) repealed by the Education and Inspections Act 2006, s 184, Sch 18, Pt 2, as from 8 January 2007.

29 Interpretation, minor and consequential amendments, repeals, etc

(1) In this Act—

"the 1975 Act" means the Sex Discrimination Act 1975;

…

"act" includes a deliberate omission;
"subordinate legislation" has the same meaning as in the Interpretation Act 1978;
"vocational training" includes advanced vocational training and retraining.

(2) Any reference in this Act to vocational training shall be construed as including a reference to vocational guidance.

(3)–(6) (*Outside the scope of this work.*)

[411]

NOTES

Sub-s (1): definition omitted repealed by the Employment Rights Act 1996, s 242, Sch 3, Pt I.

30 Short title, commencement and extent

(1) This Act may be cited as the Employment Act 1989.

(2)–(4) ...

(5), (6) (*Outside the scope of this work.*)

[412]

NOTES

Sub-ss (2)–(4): repealed by the Statute Law (Repeals) Act 2004, as from 22 July 2004.

SCHEDULES

SCHEDULE 1
PROVISIONS CONCERNED WITH PROTECTION OF WOMEN AT WORK
Section 4

Enactments

Section 61 of the Factory and Workshop Act 1901, as set out in Schedule 5 to the Factories Act 1961.

Section 205 of the Public Health Act 1936.

Sections 74, 128 and 131 of the Factories Act 1961.

Statutory instruments

Regulation 3 of the Regulations dated 21st January 1907 (Manufacture of paints and colours).

Regulation 10 of the Regulations dated 12th August 1911 (Smelting of materials containing lead, the manufacture of red or orange lead, and the manufacture of flaked litharge).

Regulation 1 of the Indiarubber Regulations 1922.

Regulation 1(ii) of the Electric Accumulator Regulations 1925.

Regulation 6(1)(i) to (vi) of the Pottery (Health and Welfare) Special Regulations 1950.

[Paragraphs 5 and 11 of Schedule 4 to the Ionising Radiations Regulations 1999 (SI 1999/3232).]

Article 20(8) of the Air Navigation Order 1985 so far as relating to pregnancy.

Other instruments

Paragraph 118 of the Approved Code of Practice relating to the Control of Lead at Work Regulations 1980 (approved under section 16 of the Health and Safety at Work etc Act 1974).

The following provisions of the medical standards contained in Merchant Shipping Notice No M1331 (issued for the purposes of Regulation 7 of the Merchant Shipping (Medical Examination) Regulations 1983), namely—

(a) Part X so far as relating to gynaecological conditions, and
(b) Part XI.

[413]

NOTES

Words in square brackets substituted by the Ionising Radiations Regulations 1999, SI 1999/3232, reg 41(1), Sch 9, para 1.

Factories Act 1961, Sch 5: repealed by the London Government Act 1963, s 93(1), Sch 18, Pt II.

Factories Act 1961, ss 74, 128, 131: repealed by the Control of Lead at Work Regulations 1998, SI 1998/543, reg 14(1).

Air Navigation Order 1985, SI 1985/1643: revoked; see now the Air Navigation Order 2005, SI 2005/1970.

Control of Lead at Work Regulations 1980; Electric Accumulator Regulations 1925; Indiarubber Regulations 1922; Regulations dated 21st January 1907 (Manufacture of paints and colours); Pottery (Health and Welfare) Special Regulations 1950; Regulations dated 12th August 1911 (Smelting of materials containing lead, the manufacture of red or orange lead, and the manufacture of flaked litharge): ie, SR & O 1907/17; SR & O 1911/752; SR & O 1922/329; SR & O 1925/28; SI 1950/65; SI 1980/1248: all revoked and replaced by the Control of Lead at Work Regulations 1998, SI 1998/543 (see the note below).

Control of Lead at Work Regulations 1998, SI 1998/543: revoked and replaced by the Control of Lead at Work Regulations 2002, SI 2002/2676.

Merchant Shipping (Medical Examination) Regulations 1983, SI 1983/808: revoked and replaced by the Merchant Shipping (Medical Examination) Regulations 2002, SI 2002/2055.

(*Sch 2* (*Revocation etc of subordinate legislation requiring different treatment of certain employees*)*; Sch 3* (*Removal of restrictions relating to employment of young persons*)*; Schs 4, 5* (*dissolution of Training Commission*)*, 6–8* (*minor and consequential amendments, repeals and revocations*)*; Sch 9* (*transitional provisions and savings*)*: in so far as these provisions are still in force, they are outside the scope of this work.*)

CONTRACTS (APPLICABLE LAW) ACT 1990

(1990 c 36)

ARRANGEMENT OF SECTIONS

SCHEDULES:

An Act to make provision as to the law applicable to contractual obligations in the case of conflict of laws

[26 July 1990]

NOTES

This Act is included for its provisions as to the applicable law of contracts of employment only, and other provisions of the Act and of the Rome Convention are omitted. So far as relevant and except as indicated in the notes below, the Act came into force on 1 April 1991.

See *Harvey* C1(3)(B).

1 Meaning of "the Conventions"

In this Act—

(a) "the Rome Convention" means the Convention on the law applicable to contractual obligations opened for signature in Rome on 19th June 1980 and signed by the United Kingdom on 7th December 1981;

(b) "the Luxembourg Convention" means the Convention on the accession of the Hellenic Republic to the Rome Convention signed by the United Kingdom in Luxembourg on 10th April 1984; and

(c) "the Brussels Protocol" means the first Protocol on the interpretation of the Rome Convention by the European Court signed by the United Kingdom in Brussels on 19th December 1988;

[(d) "the Funchal Convention" means the Convention on the accession of the Kingdom of Spain and the Portuguese Republic to the Rome Convention and the Brussels Protocol, with adjustments made to the Rome Convention by the Luxembourg Convention, signed by the United Kingdom in Funchal on 18th May 1992;]

[(e) "the 1996 Accession Convention" means the Convention on the accession of the Republic of Austria, the Republic of Finland and the Kingdom of Sweden to the Rome Convention and the Brussels Protocol, with the adjustments made to the Rome Convention by the Luxembourg Convention and the Funchal Convention, signed by the United Kingdom in Brussels on 29th November 1996;]

and [these Conventions and this Protocol] are together referred to as "the Conventions".

[414]

NOTES

Para (d) added, and words in final pair of square brackets substituted, by the Contracts (Applicable Law) Act 1990 (Amendment) Order 1994, SI 1994/1900, arts 3, 4, with effect from 1 December 1997 (ie, the date on which the Funchal Convention came into force in respect of the UK); para (e) added by the Contracts (Applicable Law) Act 1990 (Amendment) Order 2000, SI 2000/1825, art 3, with effect from 1 January 2001 (ie, the date on which the Convention on the accession of the Republic of Austria, the Republic of Finland and the Kingdom of Sweden came into force in respect of the UK).

2 Conventions to have force of law

(1) Subject to subsections (2) and (3) below, the Conventions shall have the force of law in the United Kingdom.

[(1A) The internal law for the purposes of Article 1(3) of the Rome Convention is the provisions of the regulations for the time being in force under section 424(3) of the Financial Services and Markets Act 2000.]

(2) Articles 7(1) and 10(1)(e) of the Rome Convention shall not have the force of law in the United Kingdom.

(3) Notwithstanding Article 19(2) of the Rome Convention, the Conventions shall apply in the case of conflicts between the laws of different parts of the United Kingdom.

(4) For ease of reference there are set out in [Schedules 1, 2, 3[, 3A and 3B]] to this Act respectively the English texts of—

(a) the Rome Convention;

(b) the Luxembourg Convention; …

(c) the Brussels Protocol[, and

[(d) the Funchal Convention; and

(e) the 1996 Accession Convention.]]

[415]

NOTES

Commencement: 1 April 1991 (sub-s (1) in so far as relating to the Rome Convention and Luxembourg Convention, and sub-ss (2)–(4)); 1 March 2005 (sub-s (1) in so far as relating to the Brussels Protocol); to be appointed (sub-s (1) otherwise).

Sub-s (1A): inserted by the Insurance Companies (Amendment) Regulations 1993, SI 1993/174, reg 9; substituted by the Financial Services and Markets Act 2000 (Consequential Amendments and Repeals) Order 2001, SI 2001/3649, art 320.

Sub-s (4): words in first (outer) pair of square brackets substituted, word omitted repealed, and original para (d) and the word immediately preceding it added, by the Contracts (Applicable Law) Act 1990 (Amendment) Order 1994, SI 1994/1900, arts 5, 6 with effect from 1 September 1994 (in accordance with art 1 thereof); words in second (inner) pair of square brackets substituted, and paras (d), (e) substituted for para (d) (as added as noted above), by the Contracts (Applicable Law) Act 1990 (Amendment) Order 2000, SI 2000/1825, art 4, with effect from 1 January 2001 (ie, the date on which the Convention on the accession of the Republic of Austria, the Republic of Finland and the Kingdom of Sweden came into force in respect of the UK).

3 Interpretation of Conventions

(1) Any question as to the meaning or effect of any provision of the Conventions shall, if not referred to the European Court in accordance with the Brussels Protocol, be determined in accordance with the principles laid down by, and any relevant decision of, the European Court.

(2) Judicial notice shall be taken of any decision of, or expression of opinion by, the European Court on any such question.

(3) Without prejudice to any practice of the courts as to the matters which may be considered apart from this subsection—

(a) the report on the Rome Convention by Professor Mario Giuliano and Professor Paul Lagarde which is reproduced in the Official Journal of the Communities of 31st October 1980 may be considered in ascertaining the meaning or effect of any provision of that Convention; and

(b) any report on the Brussels Protocol which is reproduced in the Official Journal of the Communities may be considered in ascertaining the meaning or effect of any provision of that Protocol.

[416]

NOTES

Commencement: 1 April 1991 (sub-s (3)(a)); 1 March 2005 (otherwise).

4–6 (*Ss 4, 5 outside the scope of this work; s 6 provides that this Act binds the Crown.*)

7 Commencement

This Act shall come into force on such day as the Lord Chancellor and the Lord Advocate may by order made by statutory instrument appoint; and different days may be appointed for different provisions or different purposes.

[417]

NOTES

Orders: the Contracts (Applicable Law) Act 1990 (Commencement No 1) Order 1991, SI 1991/707; the Contracts (Applicable Law) Act 1990 (Commencement No 2) Order 2004, SI 2004/3448.

8 (*Outside the scope of this work.*)

9 Short title

This Act may be cited as the Contracts (Applicable Law) Act 1990.

[418]

SCHEDULES

SCHEDULE 1
THE ROME CONVENTION

Section 2

NOTES

Only provisions relevant to employment law are reproduced. Provisions omitted are outside the scope of this work. Article 27 of the Convention has been rescinded and, as included in this Schedule, was repealed by the Contracts (Applicable Law) Act 1990 (Amendment) Order 1994, SI 1994/1900. The Protocol to the Convention (not reproduced) was substituted by the Contracts (Applicable Law) Act 1990 (Amendment) Order 2000, SI 2000/1825, art 5. The Convention has not otherwise been amended.

The High Contracting Parties to the Treaty establishing the European Economic Community,

Anxious to continue in the field of private international law the work of unification of law which has already been done within the Community, in particular in the field of jurisdiction and enforcement of judgments,

Wishing to establish uniform rules concerning the law applicable to contractual obligations,

Have agreed as follows:

TITLE I
SCOPE OF THE CONVENTION

Article 1
Scope of the Convention

1. The rules of this Convention shall apply to contractual obligations in any situation involving a choice between the laws of different countries.

2–4. …

Article 2
Application of law of non-contracting States

Any law specified by this Convention shall be applied whether or not it is the law of a Contracting State.

TITLE II
UNIFORM RULES

Article 3
Freedom of choice

1. A contract shall be governed by the law chosen by the parties. The choice must be express or demonstrated with reasonable certainty by the terms of the contract or the circumstances of the case. By their choice the parties can select the law applicable to the whole or a part only of the contract.

2. The parties may at any time agree to subject the contract to a law other than that which previously governed it, whether as a result of an earlier choice under this Article or of other provisions of this Convention. Any variation by the parties of the law to be applied made after the conclusion of the contract shall not prejudice its formal validity under Article 9 or adversely affect the rights of third parties.

3. The fact that the parties have chosen a foreign law, whether or not accompanied by the choice of a foreign tribunal, shall not, where all the other elements relevant to the situation at the time of the choice are connected with one country only, prejudice the application of rules of the law of that country which cannot be derogated from by contract, hereinafter called "mandatory rules".

4. The existence and validity of the consent of the parties as to the choice of the applicable law shall be determined in accordance with the provisions of Articles 8, 9 and 11.

Article 4
Applicable law in the absence of choice

1. To the extent that the law applicable to the contract has not been chosen in accordance with Article 3, the contract shall be governed by the law of the country with which it is most closely connected. Nevertheless, a severable part of the contract which has a closer connection with another country may by way of exception be governed by the law of that other country.

2. Subject to the provisions of paragraph 5 of this Article, it shall be presumed that the contract is most closely connected with the country where the party who is to effect the performance which is characteristic of the contract has, at the time of conclusion of the contract, his habitual residence, or, in the case of a body corporate or unincorporate, its central administration. However, if the contract is entered into in the course of that party's trade or profession, that country shall be the country in which the principal place of business is situated or, where under the terms of the contract the performance is to be effected through a place of business other than the principal place of business, the country in which that other place of business is situated.

3, 4. …

5. Paragraph 2 shall not apply if the characteristic performance cannot be determined, and the presumptions in paragraphs 2, 3 and 4 shall be disregarded if it appears from the circumstances as a whole that the contract is more closely connected with another country.

Article 6
Individual employment contracts

1. Notwithstanding the provisions of Article 3, in a contract of employment a choice of law made by the parties shall not have the result of depriving the employee of the protection afforded to him by the mandatory rules of the law which would be applicable under paragraph 2 in the absence of choice.

2. Notwithstanding the provisions of Article 4, a contract of employment shall, in the absence of choice in accordance with Article 3, be governed:
  (a) by the law of the country in which the employee habitually carries out his work in performance of the contract, even if he is temporarily employed in another country; or
  (b) if the employee does not habitually carry out his work in any one country, by the law of the country in which the place of business through which he was engaged is situated;

unless it appears from the circumstances as a whole that the contract is more closely connected with another country, in which case the contract shall be governed by the law of that country.

Article 7
Mandatory rules

1. When applying under this Convention the law of a country, effect may be given to the mandatory rules of the law of another country with which the situation has a close connection, if and in so far as, under the law of the latter country, those rules must be applied whatever the law applicable to the contract. In considering whether to give effect to these mandatory rules, regard shall be had to their nature and purpose and to the consequences of their application or non-application.

2. Nothing in this Convention shall restrict the application of the rules of the law of the forum in a situation where they are mandatory irrespective of the law otherwise applicable to the contract.

Article 9
Formal validity

1. A contract concluded between persons who are in the same country is formally valid if it satisfies the formal requirements of the law which governs it under this Convention or of the law of the country where it is concluded.

2. A contract concluded between persons who are in different countries is formally valid if it satisfies the formal requirements of the law which governs it under this Convention or of the law of one of those countries.

3–6. …

Article 10
Scope of the applicable law

1. The law applicable to a contract by virtue of Articles 3 to 6 and 12 of this Convention shall govern in particular:
  (a) interpretation;
  (b) performance;

(c) within the limits of the powers conferred on the court by its procedural law, the consequences of breach, including the assessment of damages in so far as it is governed by rules of law;
(d) the various ways of extinguishing obligations, and prescription and limitation of actions;
(e) the consequences of nullity of the contract.

2. In relation to the manner of performance and the steps to be taken in the event of defective performance regard shall be had to the law of the country in which performance takes place.

Article 14
Burden of proof, etc

1. The law governing the contract under this Convention applies to the extent that it contains, in the law of contract, rules which raise presumptions of law or determine the burden of proof.

2. A contract or an act intended to have legal effect may be proved by any mode of proof recognised by the law of the forum or by any of the laws referred to in Article 9 under which that contract or act is formally valid, provided that such mode of proof can be administered by the forum.

Article 17
No retrospective effect

This Convention shall apply in a Contracting State to contracts made after the date on which this Convention has entered into force with respect to that State.

Article 18
Uniform interpretation

In the interpretation and application of the preceding uniform rules, regard shall be had to their international character and to the desirability of achieving uniformity in their interpretation and application.

Article 19
States with more than one legal system

1. Where a State comprises several territorial units each of which has its own rules of law in respect of contractual obligations, each territorial unit shall be considered as a country for the purposes of identifying the law applicable under this Convention.

2. A State within which different territorial units have their own rules of law in respect of contractual obligations shall not be bound to apply this Convention to conflicts solely between the laws of such units.

[419]

(*Schs 2–4 outside the scope of this work.*)

EMPLOYMENT ACT 1990 (NOTE)

(1990 c 38)

NOTES

Substantially the whole of this Act has been repealed and consolidated into the Trade Union and Labour Relations (Consolidation) Act 1992 and the Employment Rights Act 1996. The remaining provisions, ie, s 13 (Merger of Redundancy Fund with National Insurance Fund, &c), s 15 (Financial provision), s 17 (Northern Ireland), and s 18 (Short title and commencement) are outside the scope of this work.

[420]

SOCIAL SECURITY CONTRIBUTIONS AND BENEFITS ACT 1992

(1992 c 4)

ARRANGEMENT OF SECTIONS

PART XI
STATUTORY SICK PAY

Employer's liability

The qualifying conditions

Limitations on entitlement etc

Rates of payment, etc

Miscellaneous

PART XII
STATUTORY MATERNITY PAY

PART XIIZA
STATUTORY PATERNITY PAY

Ordinary statutory paternity pay

Additional statutory paternity pay

Ordinary and additional statutory paternity pay: supplementary provisions

PART XIIZB
STATUTORY ADOPTION PAY

PART XIII
GENERAL

Short title, commencement and extent

SCHEDULES:

An Act to consolidate certain enactments relating to social security contributions and benefits with amendments to give effect to recommendations of the Law Commission and the Scottish Law Commission

[13 February 1992]

NOTES

This consolidating Act re-enacts the statutory provisions as to statutory sick pay (Pt XI) and statutory maternity pay (Pt XII) previously in the Social Security and Housing Benefits Act 1982 and the Social Security Act 1986 respectively. By virtue of the Social Security (Consequential Provisions) Act 1992, s 2 (Continuity of the law), Regulations made under the repealed Acts continue to have effect as if made under the corresponding provision of the consolidating Acts (ie, this Act, the Social Security Administration Act 1992, and the Social Security (Consequential Provisions) Act 1992). Pre-1992 Regulations that continue to have effect (and which are amended by Regulations made under this Act) are noted to the appropriate section/Schedule below. Parts XIIZA and XIIZB, providing respectively for statutory paternity pay and statutory adoption pay, were inserted by the Employment Act 2002, ss 2 and 4 respectively, and ss 171ZEA–171ZEE inserted therein by the Work and families Act 2006, ss 6–10, as from a day to be appointed. These are reproduced here, together with the associated Schedules. Other provisions not printed here are not annotated.

See *Harvey* B8, HI, J.

PART XI
STATUTORY SICK PAY

Employer's liability

151 Employer's liability

(1) Where an employee has a day of incapacity for work in relation to his contract of service with an employer, that employer shall, if the conditions set out in sections 152 to 154 below are satisfied, be liable to make him, in accordance with the following provisions of this Part of this Act, a payment (to be known as "statutory sick pay") in respect of that day.

(2) Any agreement shall be void to the extent that it purports—

(a) to exclude, limit or otherwise modify any provision of this Part of this Act, or

(b) to require an employee to contribute (whether directly or indirectly) towards any costs incurred by his employer under this Part of this Act.

(3) For the avoidance of doubt, any agreement between an employer and an employee authorising any deductions from statutory sick pay which the employer is liable to pay to the employee in respect of any period shall not be void by virtue of subsection (2)(a) above if the employer—

(a) is authorised by that or another agreement to make the same deductions from any contractual remuneration which he is liable to pay in respect of the same period, or

(b) would be so authorised if he were liable to pay contractual remuneration in respect of that period.

(4) For the purposes of this Part of this Act [a day of incapacity for work in relation to a contract of service means a day on which] the employee concerned is, or is deemed in accordance with regulations to be, incapable by reason of some specific disease or bodily or mental disablement of doing work which he can reasonably be expected to do under that contract.

(5) In any case where an employee has more than one contract of service with the same employer the provisions of this Part of this Act shall, except in such cases as may be prescribed and subject to the following provisions of this Part of this Act, have effect as if the employer were a different employer in relation to each contract of service.

(6) Circumstances may be prescribed in which, notwithstanding the provisions of subsections (1) to (5) above, the liability to make payments of statutory sick pay is to be a liability of the [Commissioners of Inland Revenue].

[(7) Regulations under subsection (6) above must be made with the concurrence of the Commissioners of Inland Revenue.]

[421]

NOTES

Sub-s (4): words in square brackets substituted by the Social Security (Incapacity for Work) Act 1994, s 11(1), Sch 1, Pt I, para 34.

Sub-s (6): words in square brackets substituted by the Social Security Contributions (Transfer of Functions, etc) Act 1999, s 1(1), Sch 1, para 9.

Sub-s (7): added by the Social Security Contributions (Transfer of Functions, etc) Act 1999, s 1(1), Sch 1, para 9.

Commissioners of Inland Revenue: a reference to the Commissioners of Inland Revenue is now to be taken as a reference to the Commissioners for Her Majesty's Revenue and Customs; see the Commissioners for Revenue and Customs Act 2005, s 50(1), (7).

Regulations: the Statutory Sick Pay (General) Regulations 1982, SI 1982/894 (as amended) at **[2080]**, have effect as if made under this section by virtue of the Social Security (Consequential Provisions) Act 1992, s 2(2).

The qualifying conditions

152 Period of incapacity for work

(1) The first condition is that the day in question forms part of a period of incapacity for work.

(2) In this Part of this Act "period of incapacity for work" means any period of four or more consecutive days, each of which is a day of incapacity for work in relation to the contract of service in question.

(3) Any two periods of incapacity for work which are separated by a period of not more than 8 weeks shall be treated as a single period of incapacity for work.

(4) The Secretary of State may by regulations direct that a larger number of weeks specified in the regulations shall be substituted for the number of weeks for the time being specified in subsection (3) above.

(5) No day of the week shall be disregarded in calculating any period of consecutive days for the purposes of this section.

(6) A day may be a day of incapacity for work in relation to a contract of service, and so form part of a period of incapacity for work, notwithstanding that—

(a) it falls before the making of the contract or after the contract expires or is brought to an end; or

(b) it is not a day on which the employee concerned would be required by that contract to be available for work.

[422]

NOTES

Regulations: as of 6 April 2008, no Regulations had been made under sub-s (4).

153 Period of entitlement

(1) The second condition is that the day in question falls within a period which is, as between the employee and his employer, a period of entitlement.

(2) For the purposes of this Part of this Act a period of entitlement, as between an employee and his employer, is a period beginning with the commencement of a period of incapacity for work and ending with whichever of the following first occurs—

(a) the termination of that period of incapacity for work;

(b) the day on which the employee reaches, as against the employer concerned, his maximum entitlement to statutory sick pay (determined in accordance with section 155 below);

(c) the day on which the employee's contract of service with the employer concerned expires or is brought to an end;

(d) in the case of an employee who is, or has been, pregnant, the day immediately preceding the beginning of the disqualifying period.

(3) Schedule 11 to this Act has effect for the purpose of specifying circumstances in which a period of entitlement does not arise in relation to a particular period of incapacity for work.

(4) A period of entitlement as between an employee and an employer of his may also be, or form part of, a period of entitlement as between him and another employer of his.

(5) The Secretary of State may by regulations—

(a) specify circumstances in which, for the purpose of determining whether an employee's maximum entitlement to statutory sick pay has been reached in a period of entitlement as between him and an employer of his, days falling within a previous period of entitlement as between the employee and any person who is or has in the past been an employer of his are to be counted; and

(b) direct that in prescribed circumstances an employer shall provide a person who is about to leave his employment, or who has been employed by him in the past, with a statement in the prescribed form containing such information as may be prescribed in relation to any entitlement of the employee to statutory sick pay.

(6) Regulations may provide, in relation to prescribed cases, for a period of entitlement to end otherwise than in accordance with subsection (2) above.

(7) In a case where the employee's contract of service first takes effect on a day which falls within a period of incapacity for work, the period of entitlement begins with that day.

(8) In a case where the employee's contract of service first takes effect between two periods of incapacity for work which by virtue of section 152(3) above are treated as one, the period of entitlement begins with the first day of the second of those periods.

(9) In any case where, otherwise than by virtue of section 6(1)(b) above, an employee's earnings under a contract of service in respect of the day on which the contract takes effect do not attract a liability to pay secondary Class 1 contributions, subsections (7) and (8) above shall have effect as if for any reference to the contract first taking effect there were substituted a reference to the first day in respect of which the employee's earnings attract such a liability.

(10) Regulations shall make provision as to an employer's liability under this Part of this Act to pay statutory sick pay to an employee in any case where the employer's contract of service with that employee has been brought to an end by the employer solely, or mainly, for the purpose of avoiding liability for statutory sick pay.

(11) Subsection (2)(d) above does not apply in relation to an employee who has been pregnant if her pregnancy terminated, before the beginning of the disqualifying period, otherwise than by confinement.

(12) In this section—

"confinement" is to be construed in accordance with section 171(1) below;

"disqualifying period" means—

- (a) in relation to a woman entitled to statutory maternity pay, the maternity pay period; and
- (b) in relation to a woman entitled to maternity allowance, the maternity allowance period;

"maternity allowance period" has the meaning assigned to it by section 35(2) above, and "maternity pay period" has the meaning assigned to it by section 165(1) below.

[423]

NOTES

Regulations: the Statutory Sick Pay (General) Regulations 1982, SI 1982/894 (as amended) at **[2080]**, and the Statutory Sick Pay (Mariners, Airmen and Persons Abroad) Regulations 1982, SI 1982/1349, have effect as if made under this section by virtue of the Social Security (Consequential Provisions) Act 1992, s 2(2).

154 Qualifying days

(1) The third condition is that the day in question is a qualifying day.

(2) The days which are for the purposes of this Part of this Act to be qualifying days as between an employee and an employer of his (that is to say, those days of the week on which he is required by his contract of service with that employer to be available for work or which are chosen to reflect the terms of that contract) shall be such day or days as may, subject to regulations, be agreed between the employee and his employer or, failing such agreement, determined in accordance with regulations.

(3) In any case where qualifying days are determined by agreement between an employee and his employer there shall, in each week (beginning with Sunday), be at least one qualifying day.

(4) A day which is a qualifying day as between an employee and an employer of his may also be a qualifying day as between him and another employer of his.

[424]

NOTES

Regulations: the Statutory Sick Pay (General) Regulations 1982, SI 1982/894 (as amended) at **[2080]**, have effect as if made under this section by virtue of the Social Security (Consequential Provisions) Act 1992, s 2(2).

Limitations on entitlement, etc

155 Limitations on entitlement

(1) Statutory sick pay shall not be payable for the first three qualifying days in any period of entitlement.

(2) An employee shall not be entitled, as against any one employer, to an aggregate amount of statutory sick pay in respect of any one period of entitlement which exceeds his maximum entitlement.

(3) The maximum entitlement as against any one employer is reached on the day on which the amount to which the employee has become entitled by way of statutory sick pay during the period of entitlement in question first reaches or passes the entitlement limit.

(4) The entitlement limit is an amount equal to 28 times [the weekly rate applicable in accordance with] section 157 below.

(5) Regulations may make provision for calculating the entitlement limit in any case where an employee's entitlement to statutory sick pay is calculated by reference to different weekly rates in the same period of entitlement.

[425]

NOTES

Sub-s (4): words in square brackets substituted by the Social Security (Incapacity for Work) Act 1994, s 8(4).

Regulations: the Statutory Sick Pay (General) Regulations 1982, SI 1982/894 (as amended) at **[2080]**, have effect as if made under this section by virtue of the Social Security (Consequential Provisions) Act 1992, s 2(2).

156 Notification of incapacity for work

(1) Regulations shall prescribe the manner in which, and the time within which, notice of any day of incapacity for work is to be given by or on behalf of an employee to his employer.

(2) An employer who would, apart from this section, be liable to pay an amount of statutory sick pay to an employee in respect of a qualifying day (the "day in question") shall be entitled to withhold payment of that amount if—

- (a) the day in question is one in respect of which he has not been duly notified in accordance with regulations under subsection (1) above; or
- (b) he has not been so notified in respect of any of the first three qualifying days in a period of entitlement (a "waiting day") and the day in question is the first qualifying day in that period of entitlement in respect of which the employer is not entitled to withhold payment—
  - (i) by virtue of paragraph (a) above; or
  - (ii) in respect of an earlier waiting day by virtue of this paragraph.

(3) Where an employer withholds any amount of statutory sick pay under this section—

- (a) the period of entitlement in question shall not be affected; and
- (b) for the purposes of calculating his maximum entitlement in accordance with section 155 above the employee shall not be taken to have become entitled to the amount so withheld.

[426]

NOTES

Regulations: the Statutory Sick Pay (General) Regulations 1982, SI 1982/894 (as amended) at **[2080]**, have effect as if made under this section by virtue of the Social Security (Consequential Provisions) Act 1992, s 2(2).

Rates of payment, etc

157 Rates of payment

(1) Statutory sick pay shall be payable by an employer at the weekly rate of [£75.40].

(2) The Secretary of State may by order—

[(a) amend subsection (1) above so as to substitute different provision as to weekly rate or rates of statutory sick pay; and]

(b) make such consequential amendments as appear to him to be required of any provision contained in this Part of this Act.

(3) The amount of statutory sick pay payable by any one employer in respect of any day shall be the weekly rate applicable on that day divided by the number of days which are, in the week (beginning with Sunday) in which that day falls, qualifying days as between that employer and the employee concerned.

[427]

NOTES

Sub-s (1): sum in square brackets substituted by the Social Security Benefits Up-rating Order 2008, SI 2008/632, art 9, as from 6 April 2008. Previous amounts were: £72.55 (as from 6 April 2007, see the Social Security Benefits Up-rating Order 2007, SI 2007/688, art 9); £70.05 (as from 6 April 2006, see the Social Security Benefits Up-rating Order 2006, SI 2006/645, art 9); £68.20 (as from 6 April 2005, see the Social Security Benefits Up-rating Order 2005, SI 2005/522, art 9); £66.15 (as from 6 April 2004, see the Social Security Benefits Up-rating Order 2004, SI 2004/552, art 9).

Sub-s (2): para (a) substituted by the Social Security (Incapacity for Work) Act 1994, s 8(3).

Orders: as of 6 April 2008, no Order had been made under sub-s (2). Note that annual increases in statutory sick pay are effected by Orders made under the Social Security Administration Act 1992, s 150.

158, 159 (*Repealed by the Statutory Sick Pay Percentage Threshold Order 1995, SI 1995/512, art 5(a).*)

[159A Power to provide for recovery by employers of sums paid by way of statutory sick pay

(1) The Secretary of State may by order provide for the recovery by employers, in accordance with the order, of the amount (if any) by which their payments of, or liability incurred for, statutory sick pay in any period exceeds the specified percentage of the amount of their liability for contributions payments in respect of the corresponding period.

(2) An order under subsection (1) above may include provision—

(a) as to the periods by reference to which the calculation referred to above is to be made,

(b) for amounts which would otherwise be recoverable but which do not exceed the specified minimum for recovery not to be recoverable,

(c) for the rounding up or down of any fraction of a pound which would otherwise result from a calculation made in accordance with the order, and

(d) for any deduction from contributions payments made in accordance with the order to be disregarded for such purposes as may be specified,

and may repeal sections 158 and 159 above and make any amendments of other enactments which are consequential on the repeal of those sections.

(3) In this section—

"contributions payments" means payments which a person is required by or under any enactment to make in discharge of any liability of his as an employer in respect of primary or secondary Class 1 contributions; and

"specified" means specified in or determined in accordance with an order under subsection (1).

(4) The Secretary of State may by regulations make such transitional and consequential provision, and such savings, as he considers necessary or expedient for or in connection with the coming into force of any order under subsection (1) above.]

[428]

NOTES

Inserted by the Statutory Sick Pay Act 1994, s 3(1).

Orders: the Statutory Sick Pay Percentage Threshold Order 1995, SI 1995/512.

Regulations: the Statutory Sick Pay Percentage Threshold Order 1995 (Consequential) Regulations 1995, SI 1995/513.

Miscellaneous

160 Relationship with benefits and other payments, etc

Schedule 12 to this Act has effect with respect to the relationship between statutory sick pay and certain benefits and payments.

[429]

161 Crown employment—Part XI

(1) Subject to subsection (2) below, the provisions of this Part of this Act apply in relation to persons employed by or under the Crown as they apply in relation to persons employed otherwise than by or under the Crown.

(2) The provisions of this Part of this Act do not apply in relation to persons serving as members of Her Majesty's forces, in their capacity as such.

(3) For the purposes of this section Her Majesty's forces shall be taken to consist of such establishments and organisations as may be prescribed [by regulations made by the Secretary of State with the concurrence of the Treasury], being establishments and organisations in which persons serve under the control of the Defence Council.

[430]

NOTES

Sub-s (3): words in square brackets inserted by the Social Security Contributions (Transfer of Functions, etc) Act 1999, s 1(1), Sch 1, para 10.

Regulations: as of 6 April 2008, no Regulations had been made under this section.

162 Special classes of persons

(1) The Secretary of State may [with the concurrence of the Treasury] make regulations modifying this Part of this Act in such manner as he thinks proper in their application to any person who is, has been or is to be—

(a) employed on board any ship, vessel, hovercraft or aircraft;
(b) outside Great Britain at any prescribed time or in any prescribed circumstances; or
(c) in prescribed employment in connection with continental shelf operations, as defined in section 120(2) above.

(2) Regulations under subsection (1) above may in particular provide—

(a) for any provision of this Part of this Act to apply to any such person, notwithstanding that it would not otherwise apply;
(b) for any such provision not to apply to any such person, notwithstanding that it would otherwise apply;
(c) for excepting any such person from the application of any such provision where he neither is domiciled nor has a place of residence in any part of Great Britain;
(d) for the taking of evidence, for the purposes of the determination of any question arising under any such provision, in a country or territory outside Great Britain, by a British consular official or such other person as may be determined in accordance with the regulations.

[431]

NOTES

Sub-s (1): words in square brackets inserted by the Social Security Contributions (Transfer of Functions, etc) Act 1999, s 1(1), Sch 1, para 11.

Regulations: the Statutory Sick Pay (Mariners, Airmen and Persons Abroad) Regulations 1982, SI 1982/1349, have effect as if made under this section by virtue of the Social Security (Consequential Provisions) Act 1992, s 2(2).

163 Interpretation of Part XI and supplementary provisions

(1) In this Part of this Act—

"contract of service" (except in paragraph (a) of the definition below of "employee") includes any arrangement providing for the terms of appointment of an employee;

"employee" means a person who is—

(a) gainfully employed in Great Britain either under a contract of service or in an office (including elective office) with [general earnings (as defined by section 7 of the Income Tax (Earnings and Pensions) Act 2003)]; …

(b) …

but subject to regulations, which may provide for cases where any such person is not to be treated as an employee for the purposes of this Part of this Act and for cases where any person who would not otherwise be an employee for those purposes is to be treated as an employee for those purposes;

["employer", in relation to an employee and a contract of service of his, means a person who—

(a) under section 6 above is liable to pay secondary Class 1 contributions in relation to any earnings of the employee under the contract, or

(b) would be liable to pay such contributions but for—

(i) the condition in section 6(1)(b), or

(ii) the employee being under the age of 16;]

"period of entitlement" has the meaning given by section 153 above;

"period of incapacity for work" has the meaning given by section 152 above;

…

"prescribed" means prescribed by regulations;

"qualifying day" has the meaning given by section 154 above;

"week" means any period of 7 days.

(2) For the purposes of this Part of this Act an employee's normal weekly earnings shall, subject to subsection (4) below, be taken to be the average weekly earnings which in the relevant period have been paid to him or paid for his benefit under his contract of service with the employer in question.

(3) For the purposes of subsection (2) above, the expressions "earnings" and "relevant period" shall have the meaning given to them by regulations.

(4) In such cases as may be prescribed an employee's normal weekly earnings shall be calculated in accordance with regulations.

(5) Without prejudice to any other power to make regulations under this Part of this Act, regulations may specify cases in which, for the purposes of this Part of this Act or such of its provisions as may be prescribed—

(a) two or more employers are to be treated as one;

(b) two or more contracts of service in respect of which the same person is an employee are to be treated as one.

(6) Where, in consequence of the establishment of one or more National Health Service trusts under [the National Health Service Act 2006, the National Health Service (Wales) Act 2006] or the National Health Service (Scotland) Act 1978, a person's contract of employment is treated by a scheme under [any of those Acts] as divided so as to constitute two or more contracts, [or where an order under [paragraph 26(1) of Schedule 3 to the National Health Service Act 2006] provides that a person's contract of employment is so divided,] regulations may make provision enabling him to elect for all of those contracts to be treated as one contract for the purposes of this Part of this Act or of such provisions of this Part of this Act as may be prescribed; and any such regulations may prescribe—

(a) the conditions that must be satisfied if a person is to be entitled to make such an election;

(b) the manner in which, and the time within which, such an election is to be made;

(c) the persons to whom, and the manner in which, notice of such an election is to be given;

(d) the information which a person who makes such an election is to provide, and the persons to whom, and the time within which, he is to provide it;

(e) the time for which such an election is to have effect;

(f) which one of the person's employers under the two or more contracts is to be regarded for the purposes of statutory sick pay as his employer under the one contract;

and the powers conferred by this subsection are without prejudice to any other power to make regulations under this Part of this Act.

(7) Regulations may provide for periods of work which begin on one day and finish on the following day to be treated, for the purposes of this Part of this Act, as falling solely within one or other of those days.

[432]

NOTES

Sub-s (1) is amended as follows:

Words in square brackets in definition "employee" substituted by the Income Tax (Earnings and Pensions) Act 2003, s 722, Sch 6, Pt 2, paras 169, 181, for the purposes of income tax for the year 2003–04 and subsequent years of assessment, and for the purposes of corporation tax for accounting periods ending after 5 April 2003.

Para (b) of definition "employee" (and the word immediately preceding it) repealed by the Employment Equality (Age) Regulations 2006, SI 2006/1031, reg 49(1), Sch 8, Pt 1, paras 8, 9(1), (2), as from 1 October 2006.

Definition "employer" substituted by SI 2006/1031, reg 49(1), Sch 8, Pt 1, paras 8, 9(1), (3), as from 1 October 2006.

Definition omitted repealed by the Jobseekers Act 1995, s 41(5), Sch 3.

Sub-s (6): words in first, second and fourth (inner) pairs of square brackets substituted by the National Health Service (Consequential Provisions) Act 2006, s 2, Sch 1, paras 142, 147, as from 1 March 2007; words in third (outer) pair of square brackets inserted by the Health Act 1999 (Supplementary, Consequential etc Provisions) Order 2000, SI 2000/90, art 3(1), Sch 1, para 27(1), (2).

Regulations: the Statutory Sick Pay Percentage Threshold Order 1995 (Consequential) Regulations 1995, SI 1995/513 (made under sub-s (5)). Also, by virtue of the Social Security (Consequential Provisions) Act 1992, s 2(2), the Statutory Sick Pay (General) Regulations 1982, SI 1982/894 (as amended) at **[2080]**, the Statutory Sick Pay (Mariners, Airmen and Persons Abroad) Regulations 1982, SI 1982/1349, and the Statutory Sick Pay (National Health Service Employees) Regulations 1991, SI 1991/589, have effect as if made under this section. As of 6 April 2008, no Regulations had been made under sub-s (7).

PART XII
STATUTORY MATERNITY PAY

164 Statutory maternity pay—entitlement and liability to pay

(1) Where a woman who is or has been an employee satisfies the conditions set out in this section, she shall be entitled, in accordance with the following provisions of this Part of this Act, to payments to be known as "statutory maternity pay".

(2) The conditions mentioned in subsection (1) above are—

(a) that she has been in employed earner's employment with an employer for a continuous period of at least 26 weeks ending with the week immediately preceding the 14th week before the expected week of confinement but has ceased to work for him … ;

(b) that her normal weekly earnings for the period of 8 weeks ending with the week immediately preceding the 14th week before the expected week of confinement are not less than the lower earnings limit in force under section 5(1)(a) above immediately before the commencement of the 14th week before the expected week of confinement; and

(c) that she has become pregnant and has reached, or been confined before reaching, the commencement of the 11th week before the expected week of confinement.

(3) The liability to make payments of statutory maternity pay to a woman is a liability of any person of whom she has been an employee as mentioned in subsection (2)(a) above.

[(4) A woman shall be entitled to payments of statutory maternity pay only if—

(a) she gives the person who will be liable to pay it notice of the date from which she expects his liability to pay her statutory maternity pay to begin; and

(b) the notice is given at least 28 days before that date or, if that is not reasonably practicable, as soon as is reasonably practicable.]

(5) The notice shall be in writing if the person who is liable to pay the woman statutory maternity pay so requests.

(6) Any agreement shall be void to the extent that it purports—

(a) to exclude, limit or otherwise modify any provision of this Part of this Act; or

(b) to require an employee or former employee to contribute (whether directly or indirectly) towards any costs incurred by her employer or former employer under this Part of this Act.

(7) For the avoidance of doubt, any agreement between an employer and an employee authorising any deductions from statutory maternity pay which the employer is liable to pay to the employee in respect of any period shall not be void by virtue of subsection (6)(a) above if the employer—

(a) is authorised by that or another agreement to make the same deductions from any contractual remuneration which he is liable to pay in respect of the same period, or

(b) would be so authorised if he were liable to pay contractual remuneration in respect of that period.

(8) Regulations shall make provision as to a former employer's liability to pay statutory maternity pay to a woman in any case where the former employer's contract of service with her has been brought to an end by the former employer solely, or mainly, for the purpose of avoiding liability for statutory maternity pay.

(9) The Secretary of State may by regulations—

(a) specify circumstances in which, notwithstanding subsections (1) to (8) above, there is to be no liability to pay statutory maternity pay in respect of a week;

(b) specify circumstances in which, notwithstanding subsections (1) to (8) above, the liability to make payments of statutory maternity pay is to be a liability [of the Commissioners of Inland Revenue];

(c) specify in what circumstances employment is to be treated as continuous for the purposes of this Part of this Act;

(d) provide that a woman is to be treated as being employed for a continuous period of at least 26 weeks where—

  (i) she has been employed by the same employer for at least 26 weeks under two or more separate contracts of service; and

  (ii) those contracts were not continuous;

(e) provide that any of the provisions specified in subsection (10) below shall have effect subject to prescribed modifications [in such cases as may be prescribed]—

[(ea) provide that subsection (4) above shall not have effect, or shall have effect subject to prescribed modifications, in such cases as may be prescribed;]

(f) provide for amounts earned by a woman under separate contracts of service with the same employer to be aggregated for the purposes of this Part of this Act; and

(g) provide that—

  (i) the amount of a woman's earnings for any period, or

  (ii) the amount of her earnings to be treated as comprised in any payment made to her or for her benefit,

shall be calculated or estimated in such manner and on such basis as may be prescribed and that for that purpose payments of a particular class or description made or falling to be made to or by a woman shall, to such extent as may be prescribed, be disregarded or, as the case may be, be deducted from the amount of her earnings.

(10) The provisions mentioned in subsection (9)(e) above are—

(a) subsection (2)(a) and (b) above; and

(b) [section 166(1) and (2)], … below.

[(11) Any regulations under subsection (9) above which are made by virtue of paragraph (b) of that subsection must be made with the concurrence of the Commissioners of Inland Revenue.]

[433]

NOTES

Sub-s (2): words omitted repealed by the Employment Act 2002, ss 20(a), 54, Sch 8 (with effect in relation to those women whose expected week of confinement commences on or after 6 April 2003).

Sub-s (4): substituted by the Employment Act 2002, s 20(b) (with effect in relation to those women whose expected week of confinement commences on or after 6 April 2003).

Sub-s (9): words in square brackets in para (b) substituted by the Social Security Contributions (Transfer of Functions, etc) Act 1999, s 1(1), Sch 1, para 12(1), (2); words in square brackets in para (e) substituted, and para (ea) added, by the Employment Act 2002, s 20(c), (d) (with effect in relation to those women whose expected week of confinement commences on or after 6 April 2003).

Sub-s (10): words in square brackets substituted by the Employment Act 2002, s 53, Sch 7, paras 2, 6; words omitted repealed by the Maternity Allowance and Statutory Maternity Pay Regulations 1994, SI 1994/1230, regs 1(2), 6(1).

Sub-s (11): added by the Social Security Contributions (Transfer of Functions, etc) Act 1999, s 1(1), Sch 1, para 12(1), (3).

Commissioners of Inland Revenue: a reference to the Commissioners of Inland Revenue is now to be taken as a reference to the Commissioners for Her Majesty's Revenue and Customs; see the Commissioners for Revenue and Customs Act 2005, s 50(1), (7).

Regulations: the Statutory Maternity Pay (General) Regulations 1986, SI 1986/1960 (as amended) at **[2115]**, have effect as if made under this section by virtue of the Social Security (Consequential Provisions) Act 1992, s 2(2). See, in particular, the Social Security, Statutory Maternity Pay and Statutory Sick Pay (Miscellaneous Amendments) Regulations 2002, SI 2002/2690, which make significant amendments to the 1986 Regulations.

165 The maternity pay period

(1) Statutory maternity pay shall be payable, subject to the provisions of this Part of this Act, in respect of each week during a prescribed period ("the maternity pay period") of a duration not exceeding [52 weeks].

[(2) Subject to subsections (3) and (7), the maternity pay period shall begin with the 11th week before the expected week of confinement.

(3) Cases may be prescribed in which the first day of the period is to be a prescribed day after the beginning of the 11th week before the expected week of confinement, but not later than the day immediately following the day on which she is confined.]

(4) [Except in such cases as may be prescribed,] statutory maternity pay shall not be payable to a woman by a person in respect of any week during any part of which she works under a contract of service with him.

(5) It is immaterial for the purposes of subsection (4) above whether the work referred to in that subsection is work under a contract of service which existed immediately before the maternity pay period or a contract of service which did not so exist.

(6) Except in such cases as may be prescribed, statutory maternity pay shall not be payable to a woman in respect of any week after she has been confined and during any part of which she works for any employer who is not liable to pay her statutory maternity pay.

(7) Regulations may provide that this section shall have effect subject to prescribed modifications in relation—

(a) to cases in which a woman has been confined before the 11th week before the expected week of confinement; and

(b) to cases in which—

(i) a woman is confined [at any time after the end of the week immediately preceding the 11th week] before the expected week of confinement; and

(ii) the maternity pay period has not then commenced for her.

[(8) In subsections (1), (4) and (6) "week" means a period of seven days beginning with the day of the week on which the maternity pay period begins.]

[434]

NOTES

Sub-s (1): words in square brackets substituted by the Work and Families Act 2006, s 1, as from 27 June 2006 (for the purpose of the power to prescribe the maternity pay period), and as from 1 October 2006 (otherwise).

Sub-ss (2), (3): substituted by the Work and Families Act 2006, s 11(1), Sch 1, para 7(1), (2), as from 27 June 2006 (for the purpose of the powers to prescribe matters by regulations), and as from 1 October 2006 (otherwise).

Sub-s (4): words in square brackets inserted by the Work and Families Act 2006, s 11(1), Sch 1, para 7(1), (3), as from 27 June 2006 (for the purpose of the powers to prescribe matters by regulations), and as from 1 October 2006 (otherwise).

Sub-s (7): words in square brackets substituted by the Maternity Allowance and Statutory Maternity Pay Regulations 1994, SI 1994/1230, regs 1(2), 3.

Sub-s (8): inserted by the Work and Families Act 2006, s 11(1), Sch 1, para 7(1), (4), as from 27 June 2006 (for the purpose of the powers to prescribe matters by regulations), and as from 1 October 2006 (otherwise).

Regulations: the Statutory Maternity Pay (General) Regulations 1986, SI 1986/1960 (as amended) at **[2115]**, have effect as if made under this section by virtue of the Social Security (Consequential Provisions) Act 1992, s 2(2).

[166 Rate of statutory maternity pay

(1) Statutory maternity pay shall be payable to a woman—

(a) at the earnings-related rate, in respect of the first 6 weeks in respect of which it is payable; and

(b) at whichever is the lower of the earnings-related rate and such weekly rate as may be prescribed, in respect of the remaining portion of the maternity pay period.

[(1A) In subsection (1) "week" means any period of seven days.]

(2) The earnings-related rate is a weekly rate equivalent to 90 per cent of a woman's normal weekly earnings for the period of 8 weeks immediately preceding the 14th week before the expected week of confinement.

(3) The weekly rate prescribed under subsection (1)(b) above must not be less than the weekly rate of statutory sick pay for the time being specified in section 157(1) above or, if two or more such rates are for the time being so specified, the higher or highest of those rates.

[(4) Where for any purpose of this Part of this Act or of regulations it is necessary to calculate the daily rate of statutory maternity pay, the amount payable by way of statutory maternity pay for any day shall be taken as one seventh of the weekly rate.]]

[435]

NOTES

Substituted by the Employment Act 2002, s 19 (for savings see SI 2002/2866, Sch 3, para 5).

Sub-ss (1A), (4): inserted and added respectively by the Work and Families Act 2006, s 11(1), Sch 1, para 8, as from 1 October 2006.

The rate prescribed under sub-s (1)(b) is £117.18 (see the Statutory Maternity Pay (General) Regulations 1986, SI 1986/1960, reg 6, as amended by the Social Security Benefits Up-rating Order 2008, SI 2008/632, art 10, and note that this has effect as from 6 April 2008, except for the purpose of determining the rate of maternity allowance in accordance with s 35A(1) of this Act, for which purpose it comes into force on 7 April 2008). Previous prescribed rates were: £112.75 (as from 1 and 9 April 2007, see SI 2007/688, art 10); £108.85 (as from 2 and 10 April 2006, see SI 2006/645, art 10); £106 (as from 3 and 10 April 2005, see SI 2005/522, art 10); and £102.80 (as from 4 April 2004, see SI 2004/552, art 10).

Regulations: the Statutory Maternity Pay (General) Regulations 1986, SI 1986/1960 at **[2115]**, have effect as if made under this section by virtue of the Social Security (Consequential Provisions) Act 1992, s 2(2).

[167 Funding of employers' liabilities in respect of statutory maternity pay

(1) Regulations shall make provision for the payment by employers of statutory maternity pay to be funded by the Commissioners of Inland Revenue to such extent as may be prescribed.

(2) Regulations under subsection (1) shall—

(a) make provision for a person who has made a payment of statutory maternity pay to be entitled, except in prescribed circumstances, to recover an amount equal to the sum of—
   - (i) the aggregate of such of those payments as qualify for small employers' relief; and
   - (ii) an amount equal to 92 per cent of the aggregate of such of those payments as do not so qualify; and

(b) include provision for a person who has made a payment of statutory maternity pay qualifying for small employers' relief to be entitled, except in prescribed circumstances, to recover an additional amount, determined in such manner as may be prescribed—
   - (i) by reference to secondary Class 1 contributions paid in respect of statutory maternity pay;
   - (ii) by reference to secondary Class 1 contributions paid in respect of statutory sick pay; or
   - (iii) by reference to the aggregate of secondary Class 1 contributions paid in respect of statutory maternity pay and secondary Class 1 contributions paid in respect of statutory sick pay.

(3) For the purposes of this section a payment of statutory maternity pay which a person is liable to make to a woman qualifies for small employers' relief if, in relation to that woman's maternity pay period, the person liable to make the payment is a small employer.

(4) For the purposes of this section "small employer", in relation to a woman's maternity pay period, shall have the meaning assigned to it by regulations, and, without prejudice to the generality of the foregoing, any such regulations—

(a) may define that expression by reference to the amount of a person's contributions payments for any prescribed period; and

(b) if they do so, may in that connection make provision for the amount of those payments for that prescribed period—
   (i) to be determined without regard to any deductions that may be made from them under this section or under any other enactment or instrument; and
   (ii) in prescribed circumstances, to be adjusted, estimated or otherwise attributed to him by reference to their amount in any other prescribed period.

(5) Regulations under subsection (1) may, in particular, make provision—
   (a) for funding in advance as well as in arrear;
   (b) for funding, or the recovery of amounts due under provision made by virtue of subsection (2)(b), by means of deductions from such amounts for which employers are accountable to the Commissioners of Inland Revenue as may be prescribed, or otherwise;
   (c) for the recovery by the Commissioners of Inland Revenue of any sums overpaid to employers under the regulations.

(6) Where in accordance with any provision of regulations under subsection (1) an amount has been deducted from an employer's contributions payments, the amount so deducted shall (except in such cases as may be prescribed) be treated for the purposes of any provision made by or under any enactment in relation to primary or secondary Class 1 contributions—
   (a) as having been paid (on such date as may be determined in accordance with the regulations), and
   (b) as having been received by the Commissioners of Inland Revenue,

towards discharging the employer's liability in respect of such contributions.

(7) Regulations under this section must be made with the concurrence of the Commissioners of Inland Revenue.

(8) In this section "contributions payments", in relation to an employer, means any payments which the employer is required, by or under any enactment, to make in discharge of any liability in respect of primary or secondary Class 1 contributions.]

[436]

NOTES

Substituted by the Employment Act 2002, s 21(1).

Commissioners of Inland Revenue: a reference to the Commissioners of Inland Revenue is now to be taken as a reference to the Commissioners for Her Majesty's Revenue and Customs; see the Commissioners for Revenue and Customs Act 2005, s 50(1), (7).

Regulations: the Statutory Maternity Pay (Compensation of Employers) and Miscellaneous Amendment Regulations 1994, SI 1994/1882.

168 Relationship with benefits and other payments etc

Schedule 13 to this Act has effect with respect to the relationship between statutory maternity pay and certain benefits and payments.

[437]

169 Crown employment—Part XII

The provisions of this Part of this Act apply in relation to women employed by or under the Crown as they apply in relation to women employed otherwise than by or under the Crown.

[438]

170 Special classes of person

(1) The Secretary of State may [with the concurrence of the Treasury] make regulations modifying this Part of this Act in such manner as he thinks proper in their application to any person who is, has been or is to be—
   (a) employed on board any ship, vessel, hovercraft or aircraft;
   (b) outside Great Britain at any prescribed time or in any prescribed circumstances; or
   (c) in prescribed employment in connection with continental shelf operations, as defined in section 120(2) above.

(2) Regulations under subsection (1) above may in particular provide—
   (a) for any provision of this Part of this Act to apply to any such person, notwithstanding that it would not otherwise apply;

(b) for any such provision not to apply to any such person, notwithstanding that it would otherwise apply;
(c) for excepting any such person from the application of any such provision where he neither is domiciled nor has a place of residence in any part of Great Britain;
(d) for the taking of evidence, for the purposes of the determination of any question arising under any such provision, in a country or territory outside Great Britain, by a British consular official or such other person as may be determined in accordance with the regulations.

[439]

NOTES

Sub-s (1): words in square brackets inserted by the Social Security Contributions (Transfer of Functions, etc) Act 1999, s 1(1), Sch 1, para 14.

Regulations: the Statutory Maternity Pay (Persons Abroad and Mariners) Regulations 1987, SI 1987/418, have effect as if made under this section by virtue of the Social Security (Consequential Provisions) Act 1992, s 2(2).

171 Interpretation of Part XII and supplementary provisions

(1) In this Part of this Act—

"confinement" means—
(a) labour resulting in the issue of a living child, or
(b) labour after [24 weeks] of pregnancy resulting in the issue of a child whether alive or dead,

and "confined" shall be construed accordingly; and where a woman's labour begun on one day results in the issue of a child on another day she shall be taken to be confined on the day of the issue of the child or, if labour results in the issue of twins or a greater number of children, she shall be taken to be confined on the day of the issue of the last of them;

"dismissed" is to be construed in accordance with [Part X of the Employment Rights Act 1996];

"employee" means a woman who is—
(a) gainfully employed in Great Britain either under a contract of service or in an office (including elective office) with [general earnings (as defined by section 7 of the Income Tax (Earnings and Pensions) Act 2003)]; …
(b) …

but subject to regulations [made with the concurrence of [Her Majesty's Revenue and Customs]] which may provide for cases where any such woman is not to be treated as an employee for the purposes of this Part of this Act and for cases where a woman who would not otherwise be an employee for those purposes is to be treated as an employee for those purposes;

["employer", in relation to a woman who is an employee, means a person who—
(a) under section 6 above is liable to pay secondary Class 1 contributions in relation to any of her earnings; or
(b) would be liable to pay such contributions but for—
(i) the condition in section 6(1)(b), or
(ii) the employee being under the age of 16;]

"maternity pay period" has the meaning assigned to it by section 165(1) above;

"modifications" includes additions, omissions and amendments, and related expressions shall be construed accordingly;

"prescribed" means specified in or determined in accordance with regulations;

…

[(1A) In this Part, except section 165(1), (4) and (6), section 166(1) and paragraph 3(2) of Schedule 13, "week" means a period of 7 days beginning with Sunday or such other period as may be prescribed in relation to any particular case or class of case.]

(2) Without prejudice to any other power to make regulations under this Part of this Act, regulations may specify cases in which, for the purposes of this Part of this Act or of such provisions of this Part of this Act as may be prescribed—
(a) two or more employers are to be treated as one;
(b) two or more contracts of service in respect of which the same woman is an employee are to be treated as one.

(3) Where, in consequence of the establishment of one or more National Health Service trusts under [the National Health Service Act 2006, the National Health Service (Wales)

Act 2006] or the National Health Service (Scotland) Act 1978, a woman's contract of employment is treated by a scheme under [any of those Acts] as divided so as to constitute two or more contracts, [or where an order under [paragraph 26(1) of Schedule 3 to the National Health Service Act 2006] provides that a woman's contract of employment is so divided,] regulations may make provision enabling her to elect for all of those contracts to be treated as one contract for the purposes of this Part of this Act or of such provisions of this Part of this Act as may be prescribed; and any such regulations may prescribe—

(a) the conditions that must be satisfied if a woman is to be entitled to make such an election;

(b) the manner in which, and the time within which, such an election is to be made;

(c) the persons to whom, and the manner in which, notice of such an election is to be given;

(d) the information which a woman who makes such an election is to provide, and the persons to whom, and the time within which, she is to provide it;

(e) the time for which such an election is to have effect;

(f) which one of the woman's employers under the two or more contracts is to be regarded for the purposes of statutory maternity pay as her employer under the one contract;

and the powers conferred by this subsection are without prejudice to any other power to make regulations under this Part of this Act.

(4) For the purposes of this Part of this Act a woman's normal weekly earnings shall, subject to subsection (6) below, be taken to be the average weekly earnings which in the relevant period have been paid to her or paid for her benefit under the contract of service with the employer in question.

(5) For the purposes of subsection (4) above "earnings" and "relevant period" shall have the meanings given to them by regulations.

(6) In such cases as may be prescribed a woman's normal weekly earnings shall be calculated in accordance with regulations.

[(7) Regulations under any of subsections (2) to (6) above must be made with the concurrence of the Commissioners of Inland Revenue.]

[440]

NOTES

Sub-s (1) is amended as follows:

Words in square brackets in definition "confinement" substituted by the Still-Birth (Definition) Act 1992, ss 2(1), 4(2).

Words in square brackets in definition "dismissed" substituted by the Employment Rights Act 1996, s 240, Sch 1, para 51.

Words in first pair of square brackets in definition "employee" substituted by the Income Tax (Earnings and Pensions) Act 2003, s 722, Sch 6, Pt 2, paras 169, 182, for the purposes of income tax for the year 2003–04 and subsequent years of assessment, and for the purposes of corporation tax for accounting periods ending after 5 April 2003.

Para (b) of the definition "employee" (and the word omitted immediately preceding it) repealed by the Employment Equality (Age) Regulations 2006, SI 2006/1031, reg 49(1), Sch 8, Pt 1, paras 8, 10(1), (2), as from 1 October 2006 (in relation to any case where the expected week of confinement begins on or after 14 January 2007).

Words in second (outer) pair of square brackets in definition "employee" inserted by the Social Security Contributions (Transfer of Functions, etc) Act 1999, s 1(1), Sch 1, para 15(1), (2).

Words in third (inner) pair of square brackets in definition "employee" substituted by the Commissioners for Revenue and Customs Act 2005, s 50(6), Sch 4, para 43, as from 18 April 2005.

Definition "employer" substituted by SI 2006/1031, reg 49(1), Sch 8, Pt 1, paras 8, 10(1), (3), as from 1 October 2006 (in relation to any case where the expected week of confinement begins on or after 14 January 2007).

Definition "week" (omitted) repealed by the Work and Families Act 2006, ss 11(1), 15, Sch 1, para 9(1), (2), Sch 2, as from 27 June 2006 (for the purpose of the power to prescribe matters by regulations), and as from 1 October 2006 (otherwise).

Sub-s (1A): inserted by the Work and Families Act 2006, s 11(1), Sch 1, para 9(1), (3), as from 27 June 2006 (for the purpose of the power to prescribe matters by regulations), and as from 1 October 2006 (otherwise).

Sub-s (3): words in first, second and fourth (inner) pairs of square brackets substituted by the National Health Service (Consequential Provisions) Act 2006, s 2, Sch 1, paras 142, 148, as from 1 March 2007; words in third (outer) pair of square brackets inserted by the Health Act 1999 (Supplementary, Consequential etc Provisions) Order 2000, SI 2000/90, art 3(1), Sch 1, para 27(1), (3).

Sub-s (7): added by the Social Security Contributions (Transfer of Functions, etc) Act 1999, s 1(1), Sch 1, para 15(1), (3).

Commissioners of Inland Revenue: a reference to the Commissioners of Inland Revenue is now to be taken as a reference to the Commissioners for Her Majesty's Revenue and Customs; see the Commissioners for Revenue and Customs Act 2005, s 50(1), (7).

Regulations: the Statutory Maternity Pay (Compensation of Employers) and Miscellaneous Amendment Regulations 1994, SI 1994/1882. In addition, the Statutory Maternity Pay (General) Regulations 1986, SI 1986/1960 (as amended) at **[2115]**, the Statutory Maternity Pay (Persons Abroad and Mariners) Regulations 1987, SI 1987/418, and the Statutory Maternity Pay (National Health Service Employees) Regulations 1991, SI 1991/590 have effect as if made under this section by virtue of the Social Security (Consequential Provisions) Act 1992, s 2(2).

[PART XIIZA
STATUTORY PATERNITY PAY

NOTES

Pt XIIZA inserted by the Employment Act 2002, s 2, in relation to a person who satisfies the prescribed conditions of entitlement in respect of a child (a) born on or after 6 April 2003, or whose expected week of birth begins on or after that date; or (b) matched for the purposes of adoption with a person who is notified of having been matched on or after 6 April 2003, or placed for adoption on or after that date. Sections 171ZEA–171ZEE are inserted in this Part by the Work and Families Act 2006, ss 6–10, as from a day to be appointed.

For the words in italics in the Part heading (above) there are substituted the words "Ordinary and Additional Statutory Paternity Pay", and the cross-heading "Ordinary statutory paternity pay" (below) is inserted, by the Work and Families Act 2006, s 11(1), Sch 1, paras 10, 11, as from a day to be appointed.

Adoptions from overseas: this Part is modified in relation to adoptions from overseas as noted to the sections affected. See the Social Security Contributions and Benefits Act 1992 (Application of Parts 12ZA and 12ZB to Adoptions from Overseas) Regulations 2003, SI 2003/499.

[Ordinary statutory paternity pay]

171ZA Entitlement: birth

(1) Where a person satisfies the conditions in subsection (2) below, he shall be entitled in accordance with the following provisions of this Part to payments to be known as "*statutory paternity pay*".

(2) The conditions are—

(a) that he satisfies prescribed conditions—

(i) as to relationship with a newborn child, and

(ii) as to relationship with the child's mother;

(b) that he has been in employed earner's employment with an employer for a continuous period of at least 26 weeks ending with the relevant week;

(c) that his normal weekly earnings for the period of 8 weeks ending with the relevant week are not less than the lower earnings limit in force under section 5(1)(a) above at the end of the relevant week; and

(d) that he has been in employed earner's employment with the employer by reference to whom the condition in paragraph (b) above is satisfied for a continuous period beginning with the end of the relevant week and ending with the day on which the child is born.

(3) The references in subsection (2) above to the relevant week are to the week immediately preceding the 14th week before the expected week of the child's birth.

(4) A person's entitlement to *statutory paternity pay* under this section shall not be affected by the birth, or expected birth, of more than one child as a result of the same pregnancy.

(5) In this section, "newborn child" includes a child stillborn after twenty-four weeks of pregnancy.]

[441]

NOTES

Inserted as noted at the beginning of this Part.

Sub-ss (1), (4): for the words in italics there are substituted the words "ordinary statutory paternity pay" by the Work and Families Act 2006, s 11(1), Sch 1, para 12, as from a day to be appointed.

Regulations: the Statutory Paternity Pay and Statutory Adoption Pay (General) Regulations 2002, SI 2002/2822 at **[2801]**.

[171ZB Entitlement: adoption

(1) Where a person satisfies the conditions in subsection (2) below, he shall be entitled in accordance with the following provisions of this Part to payments to be known as "*statutory paternity pay*".

(2) The conditions are—

(a) that he satisfies prescribed conditions—

(i) as to relationship with a child who is placed for adoption under the law of any part of the United Kingdom, and

(ii) as to relationship with a person with whom the child is so placed for adoption;

(b) that he has been in employed earner's employment with an employer for a continuous period of at least 26 weeks ending with the relevant week;

(c) that his normal weekly earnings for the period of 8 weeks ending with the relevant week are not less than the lower earnings limit in force under section 5(1)(a) at the end of the relevant week;

(d) that he has been in employed earner's employment with the employer by reference to whom the condition in paragraph (b) above is satisfied for a continuous period beginning with the end of the relevant week and ending with the day on which the child is placed for adoption; and

(e) where he is a person with whom the child is placed for adoption, that he has elected to receive statutory paternity pay.

(3) The references in subsection (2) to the relevant week are to the week in which the adopter is notified of being matched with the child for the purposes of adoption.

(4) A person may not elect to receive *statutory paternity pay* if he has elected in accordance with section 171ZL below to receive statutory adoption pay.

(5) Regulations may make provision about elections for the purposes of subsection (2)(e) above.

(6) A person's entitlement to *statutory paternity pay* under this section shall not be affected by the placement for adoption of more than one child as part of the same arrangement.

(7) In this section, "adopter", in relation to a person who satisfies the condition under subsection (2)(a)(ii) above, means the person by reference to whom he satisfies that condition.]

[442]

NOTES

Inserted as noted at the beginning of this Part.

Sub-ss (1), (4), (6): for the words in italics there are substituted the words "ordinary statutory paternity pay" by the Work and Families Act 2006, s 11(1), Sch 1, para 13, as from a day to be appointed.

Adoptions from overseas: this section is modified in relation to adoptions from overseas which are adoptions of children who enter Great Britain from outside the United Kingdom in connection with, or for the purposes of, adoption which does not involve the placement of a child for adoption under the law of any part of the United Kingdom; see the Social Security Contributions and Benefits Act 1992 (Application of Parts 12ZA and 12ZB to Adoptions from Overseas) Regulations 2003, SI 2003/499, reg 2, Sch 1.

Regulations: the Statutory Paternity Pay and Statutory Adoption Pay (General) Regulations 2002, SI 2002/2822 at **[2801]**; the Statutory Paternity Pay (Adoption) and Statutory Adoption Pay (Adoptions from Overseas) (No 2) Regulations 2003, SI 2003/1194.

[171ZC Entitlement: general

(1) A person shall be entitled to payments of *statutory paternity pay* in respect of any period only if—

(a) he gives the person who will be liable to pay it notice of the date from which he expects the liability to pay him *statutory paternity pay* to begin; and

(b) the notice is given at least 28 days before that date or, if that is not reasonably practicable, as soon as is reasonably practicable.

(2) The notice shall be in writing if the person who is liable to pay the *statutory paternity pay* so requests.

(3) The Secretary of State may by regulations—

(a) provide that subsection (2)(b), (c) or (d) of section 171ZA or 171ZB above shall have effect subject to prescribed modifications in such cases as may be prescribed;
(b) provide that subsection (1) above shall not have effect, or shall have effect subject to prescribed modifications, in such cases as may be prescribed;
(c) impose requirements about evidence of entitlement;
(d) specify in what circumstances employment is to be treated as continuous for the purposes of section 171ZA or 171ZB above;
(e) provide that a person is to be treated for the purposes of section 171ZA or 171ZB above as being employed for a continuous period of at least 26 weeks where—
 (i) he has been employed by the same employer for at least 26 weeks under two or more separate contracts of service; and
 (ii) those contracts were not continuous;
(f) provide for amounts earned by a person under separate contracts of service with the same employer to be aggregated for the purposes of section 171ZA or 171ZB above;
(g) provide that—
 (i) the amount of a person's earnings for any period, or
 (ii) the amount of his earnings to be treated as comprised in any payment made to him or for his benefit,

shall be calculated or estimated for the purposes of section 171ZA or 171ZB above in such manner and on such basis as may be prescribed and that for that purpose payments of a particular class or description made or falling to be made to or by a person shall, to such extent as may be prescribed, be disregarded or, as the case may be, be deducted from the amount of his earnings.]

[443]

NOTES

Inserted as noted at the beginning of this Part.

Sub-ss (1), (2): for the words in italics there are substituted the words "ordinary statutory paternity pay" by the Work and Families Act 2006, s 11(1), Sch 1, para 14, as from a day to be appointed.

Regulations: the Statutory Paternity Pay and Statutory Adoption Pay (General) Regulations 2002, SI 2002/2822 at **[2801]**; the Statutory Paternity Pay (Adoption) and Statutory Adoption Pay (Adoptions from Overseas) (No 2) Regulations 2003, SI 2003/1194.

[171ZD Liability to make payments

(1) The liability to make payments of [ordinary] statutory paternity pay under section 171ZA or 171ZB above is a liability of any person of whom the person entitled to the payments has been an employee as mentioned in subsection (2)(b) and (d) of that section.

(2) Regulations shall make provision as to a former employer's liability to pay *statutory paternity pay* to a person in any case where the former employee's contract of service with him has been brought to an end by the former employer solely, or mainly, for the purpose of avoiding *liability for statutory paternity pay*.

(3) The Secretary of State may, with the concurrence of the Board, by regulations specify circumstances in which, notwithstanding this section, liability to make payments of statutory paternity pay is to be a liability of the Board.]

[444]

NOTES

Inserted as noted at the beginning of this Part.

Sub-s (1): word in square brackets inserted by the Work and Families Act 2006, s 11(1), Sch 1, para 15(1), (2), as from a day to be appointed.

Sub-s (2): for the first words in italics there are substituted the words "ordinary statutory paternity pay", and for the second words in italics there are substituted the words "liability for ordinary statutory paternity pay or additional statutory paternity pay (or both)", by the Work and Families Act 2006, s 11(1), Sch 1, para 15(1), (3), as from a day to be appointed.

Regulations: the Statutory Paternity Pay and Statutory Adoption Pay (General) Regulations 2002, SI 2002/2822 at **[2801]**; the Statutory Paternity Pay (Adoption) and Statutory Adoption Pay (Adoptions from Overseas) (No 2) Regulations 2003, SI 2003/1194.

[171ZE Rate and period of pay

(1) *Statutory paternity pay* shall be payable at such fixed or earnings-related weekly rate as may be prescribed by regulations, which may prescribe different kinds of rate for different cases.

(2) *Statutory paternity pay* shall be payable in respect of—

(a) a period of two consecutive weeks within the qualifying period beginning on such date within that period as the person entitled may choose in accordance with regulations, or

(b) if regulations permit the person entitled to choose to receive *statutory paternity pay* in respect of—

(i) a period of a week, or

(ii) two non-consecutive periods of a week,

such week or weeks within the qualifying period as he may choose in accordance with regulations.

(3) For the purposes of subsection (2) above, the qualifying period shall be determined in accordance with regulations, which shall secure that it is a period of at least 56 days beginning—

(a) in the case of a person to whom the conditions in section 171ZA(2) above apply, with the date of the child's birth, and

(b) in the case of a person to whom the conditions in section 171ZB(2) above apply, with the date of the child's placement for adoption.

(4) *Statutory paternity pay* shall not be payable to a person in respect of a statutory pay week if it is not his purpose at the beginning of the week—

(a) to care for the child by reference to whom he satisfies the condition in sub-paragraph (i) of section 171ZA(2)(a) or 171ZB(2)(a) above, or

(b) to support the person by reference to whom he satisfies the condition in sub-paragraph (ii) of that provision.

(5) A person shall not be liable to pay *statutory paternity pay* to another in respect of a statutory pay week during any part of which the other works under a contract of service with him.

(6) It is immaterial for the purposes of subsection (5) above whether the work referred to in that subsection is work under a contract of service which existed immediately before the statutory pay week or a contract of service which did not so exist.

(7) Except in such cases as may be prescribed, *statutory paternity pay* shall not be payable to a person in respect of a statutory pay week during any part of which he works for any employer who is not liable to pay him *statutory paternity pay*.

(8) The Secretary of State may by regulations specify circumstances in which there is to be no liability to pay *statutory paternity pay* in respect of a statutory pay week.

(9) Where more than one child is born as a result of the same pregnancy, the reference in subsection (3)(a) to the date of the child's birth shall be read as a reference to the date of birth of the first child born as a result of the pregnancy.

(10) Where more than one child is placed for adoption as part of the same arrangement, the reference in subsection (3)(b) to the date of the child's placement shall be read as a reference to the date of placement of the first child to be placed as part of the arrangement.

[(10A) Where for any purpose of this Part of this Act or of regulations it is necessary to calculate the daily rate of ordinary statutory paternity pay, the amount payable by way of ordinary statutory paternity pay for any day shall be taken as one seventh of the weekly rate.]

(11) In this section—

"statutory pay week", in relation to a person entitled to *statutory paternity pay*, means a week chosen by him as a week in respect of which *statutory paternity pay* shall be payable;

"week" means any period of seven days.]

[445]

NOTES

Inserted as noted at the beginning of this Part.

Sub-ss (1), (2), (4), (5), (7), (8), (11): for the words in italics there are substituted the words "Ordinary statutory paternity pay" (or "ordinary statutory paternity pay" as appropriate) by the Work and Families Act 2006, s 11(1), Sch 1, para 16(1), (2), as from a day to be appointed.

Sub-s (10A): inserted by the Work and Families Act 2006, s 11(1), Sch 1, para 16(1), (3), as from 1 October 2006.

Adoptions from overseas: this section is modified as noted to s 171ZB at **[442]**.

The fixed rate, as from 6 April 2008, is £117.18 per week (see the Statutory Paternity Pay and Statutory Adoption Pay (Weekly Rates) Regulations, SI 2002/2818, reg 2 at **[2784]**, as amended by the Social

Security Benefits Up-rating Order 2008, SI 2008/632, art 11(a)). Previous rates were: £112.75 (as from 1 April 2007, see SI 2007/688); £108.85 (as from 2 April 2006, see SI 2006/645); £106.00 (as from 3 April 2005, see SI 2005/522); and £102.80 (as from 4 April 2004, see SI 2004/925).

Regulations: the Statutory Paternity Pay and Statutory Adoption Pay (Weekly Rates) Regulations 2002, SI 2002/2818 at **[2783]**; the Statutory Paternity Pay and Statutory Adoption Pay (General) Regulations 2002, SI 2002/2822 at **[2801]**; the Statutory Paternity Pay (Adoption) and Statutory Adoption Pay (Adoptions from Overseas) (No 2) Regulations 2003, SI 2003/1194.

[Additional statutory paternity pay

171ZEA Entitlement to additional statutory paternity pay: birth

(1) The Secretary of State may by regulations provide that, where all the conditions in subsection (2) are satisfied in relation to a person ("the claimant"), the claimant shall be entitled in accordance with the following provisions of this Part to payments to be known as "additional statutory paternity pay".

(2) Those conditions are—

(a) that the claimant satisfies prescribed conditions—

(i) as to relationship with a child, and

(ii) as to relationship with the child's mother;

(b) that the claimant has been in employed earner's employment with an employer for a continuous period of at least the prescribed length ending with a prescribed week;

(c) that the claimant's normal weekly earnings for a prescribed period ending with a prescribed week are not less than the lower earnings limit in force under section 5(1)(a) at the end of that week;

(d) if regulations so provide, that the claimant continues in employed earner's employment (whether or not with that employer) until a prescribed time;

(e) that the mother of the child by reference to whom the condition in paragraph (a) is satisfied became entitled, by reference to the birth of the child—

(i) to a maternity allowance, or

(ii) to statutory maternity pay;

(f) that the mother has, in relation to employment as an employed or self-employed earner, taken action that is treated by regulations as constituting for the purposes of this section her return to work;

(g) that the day on which the mother is treated as returning to work falls—

(i) after the end of a prescribed period beginning with the birth of the child, but

(ii) at a time when at least a prescribed part of her maternity allowance period or maternity pay period remains unexpired;

(h) that it is the claimant's intention to care for the child during a period beginning not later than a prescribed time.

(3) The regulations may—

(a) exclude the application of the conditions mentioned in paragraphs (f) and (g) of subsection (2) in cases where the child's mother has died, and

(b) provide that the condition mentioned in paragraph (e) of that subsection shall have effect with prescribed modifications in such cases.

(4) A person's entitlement to additional statutory paternity pay under this section shall not be affected by the birth of more than one child as a result of the same pregnancy.]

[445A]

NOTES

Commencement: to be appointed.

Inserted, together with the preceding heading, by the Work and Families Act 2006, s 6, as from a day to be appointed.

[171ZEB Entitlement to additional statutory paternity pay: adoption

(1) The Secretary of State may by regulations provide that, where all the conditions in subsection (2) are satisfied in relation to a person ("the claimant"), the claimant shall be entitled in accordance with the following provisions of this Part to payments to be known as "additional statutory paternity pay".

(2) Those conditions are—

(a) that the claimant satisfies prescribed conditions—

(i) as to relationship with a child who has been placed for adoption under the law of any part of the United Kingdom, and

(ii) as to relationship with a person with whom the child is so placed for adoption ("the adopter");

(b) that the claimant has been in employed earner's employment with an employer for a continuous period of at least the prescribed length ending with a prescribed week;

(c) that the claimant's normal weekly earnings for a prescribed period ending with a prescribed week are not less than the lower earnings limit in force under section 5(1)(a) at the end of that week;

(d) if regulations so provide, that the claimant continues to work in employed earner's employment (whether or not with that employer) until a prescribed time;

(e) that the adopter became entitled to statutory adoption pay by reference to the placement of the child for adoption;

(f) that the adopter has, in relation to employment as an employed or self-employed earner, taken action that is treated by regulations as constituting for the purposes of this section the adopter's return to work;

(g) that the day on which the adopter is treated as returning to work falls—

(i) after the end of a prescribed period beginning with the placement of the child for adoption, but

(ii) at a time when at least a prescribed part of the adopter's adoption pay period remains unexpired;

(h) that it is the claimant's intention to care for the child during a period beginning not later than a prescribed time.

(3) The regulations may—

(a) exclude the application of the conditions mentioned in paragraphs (f) and (g) of subsection (2) in cases where the adopter has died, and

(b) provide that the condition mentioned in paragraph (e) of that subsection shall have effect with prescribed modifications in such cases.

(4) A person may not elect to receive additional statutory paternity pay if he has elected in accordance with section 171ZL to receive statutory adoption pay.

(5) A person's entitlement to additional statutory paternity pay under this section shall not be affected by the placement for adoption of more than one child as part of the same arrangement.]

[445B]

NOTES

Commencement: to be appointed.
Inserted by the Work and Families Act 2006, s 7, as from a day to be appointed.

[171ZEC Entitlement to additional statutory paternity pay: general

(1) A person shall not be entitled to payments of additional statutory paternity pay in respect of any period unless—

(a) he gives the person who will be liable to pay it notice of the date from which he expects the liability to pay him additional statutory paternity pay to begin and the date on which he expects that liability to end, and

(b) the notice is given by such time as may be prescribed.

(2) The notice shall be in writing if the person who is liable to pay the additional statutory paternity pay so requests.

(3) The Secretary of State may by regulations—

(a) provide that the conditions mentioned in subsection (2)(b) or (c) of section 171ZEA or 171ZEB shall have effect subject to prescribed modifications in such cases as may be prescribed;

(b) provide that subsection (1) of this section shall not have effect, or shall have effect subject to prescribed modifications, in such cases as may be prescribed;

(c) impose requirements about evidence of entitlement;

(d) specify in what circumstances employment is to be treated as continuous for the purposes of section 171ZEA or 171ZEB;

(e) provide that a person is to be treated for the purposes of section 171ZEA or 171ZEB as being employed for a continuous period of the length prescribed under that section where—
  (i) he has been employed by the same employer for a period of at least that length under two or more contracts of service, and
  (ii) those contracts were not continuous;

(f) provide for amounts earned by a person under separate contracts of service with the same employer to be aggregated for the purposes of section 171ZEA or 171ZEB;

(g) provide that—
  (i) the amount of a person's earnings for any period, or
  (ii) the amount of his earnings to be treated as comprised in any payment made to him or for his benefit,

shall be calculated or estimated for the purposes of section 171ZEA or 171ZEB in such manner and on such basis as may be prescribed and that for that purpose payments of a particular class or description made or falling to be made to or by a person shall, to such extent as may be prescribed, be disregarded or, as the case may be, be deducted from the amount of his earnings.]

[445C]

NOTES

Commencement: to be appointed.
Inserted by the Work and Families Act 2006, s 8, as from a day to be appointed.

[171ZED Liability to make payments of additional statutory paternity pay

(1) The liability to make payments of additional statutory paternity pay under section 171ZEA or 171ZEB is a liability of any person of whom the person entitled to the payments has been an employee as mentioned in subsection (2)(b) of that section.

(2) Regulations shall make provision as to a former employer's liability to pay additional statutory paternity pay to a person in any case where the former employee's contract of service with him has been brought to an end solely, or mainly, for the purpose of avoiding liability for additional statutory paternity pay or ordinary statutory paternity pay, or both.

(3) The Secretary of State may, with the concurrence of the Commissioners for Her Majesty's Revenue and Customs, by regulations specify circumstances in which, notwithstanding this section, liability to make payments of additional statutory paternity pay is to be a liability of the Commissioners.]

[445D]

NOTES

Commencement: to be appointed.
Inserted by the Work and Families Act 2006, s 9, as from a day to be appointed.

[171ZEE Rate and period of pay: additional statutory paternity pay

(1) Additional statutory paternity pay shall be payable at such fixed or earnings-related weekly rate as may be prescribed by regulations, which may prescribe different kinds of rate for different cases.

(2) Subject to the following provisions of this section, additional statutory paternity pay shall be payable in respect of a period ("the additional paternity pay period")—

(a) beginning with such day as may (subject to subsection (3)) be determined in accordance with regulations, and

(b) ending with—
  (i) the day on which the additional statutory pay period is ended by virtue of subsection (4) or (8), or
  (ii) such earlier day as the employee may choose in accordance with regulations.

(3) The first day of the additional paternity pay period must not be earlier than the day on which the child's mother or the person with whom the child is placed for adoption ("the mother or adopter") is treated for the purpose of section 171ZEA or 171ZEB as returning to work; but this subsection does not apply in a case where the mother or adopter has died.

(4) The additional paternity pay period—
  (a) shall not last longer than any prescribed number of weeks,
  (b) shall not continue after the end of the period of 12 months beginning with the relevant date, and
  (c) shall not continue after the end—
    (i) in a case falling within section 171ZEA, of the mother's maternity allowance period or maternity pay period, or
    (ii) in a case falling within section 171ZEB, of the adoption pay period of the person with whom the child is placed for adoption.

(5) In subsection (4)(b), "the relevant date" means—
  (a) in the case of a person to whom the conditions in section 171ZEA(2) apply, the date of the child's birth (or, where more than one child is born as a result of the same pregnancy, the date of birth of the first child born as a result of the pregnancy), and
  (b) in the case of a person to whom the conditions in section 171ZEB(2) apply, the date of the child's placement for adoption (or, where more than one child is placed for adoption as part of the same arrangement, the date of placement of the first child to be placed as part of the arrangement).

(6) Additional statutory paternity pay shall not be payable to a person in respect of a week if it is not his purpose at the beginning of the week to care for the child by reference to whom he satisfies the condition in sub-paragraph (i) of section 171ZEA(2)(a) or 171ZEB(2)(a).

(7) Except in such cases as may be prescribed, additional statutory paternity pay shall not be payable to a person in respect of a week during any part of which he works for any employer.

(8) Where subsection (6) or (7) prevents additional statutory paternity pay being payable to a person in respect of any week, the person's additional paternity pay period shall be taken to have ended at the end of the previous week.

(9) Where for any purpose of this Part of this Act or of regulations it is necessary to calculate the daily rate of additional statutory paternity pay, the amount payable by way of additional statutory paternity pay for that day shall be taken to be one seventh of the weekly rate.

(10) In this section "week" means a period of seven days beginning with the day of the week on which the additional paternity pay period began.]

[445E]

NOTES

Commencement: to be appointed.
Inserted by the Work and Families Act 2006, s 10, as from a day to be appointed.

[Ordinary and additional statutory paternity pay: supplementary provisions]

[171ZF Restrictions on contracting out

(1) Any agreement shall be void to the extent that it purports—
  (a) to exclude, limit or otherwise modify any provision of this Part of this Act, or
  (b) to require an employee or former employee to contribute (whether directly or indirectly) towards any costs incurred by his employer or former employer under this Part of this Act.

(2) For the avoidance of doubt, any agreement between an employer and an employee authorising any deductions from *statutory paternity pay* which the employer is liable to pay to the employee in respect of any period shall not be void by virtue of subsection (1)(a) above if the employer—
  (a) is authorised by that or another agreement to make the same deductions from any contractual remuneration which he is liable to pay in respect of the same period, or
  (b) would be so authorised if he were liable to pay contractual remuneration in respect of that period.]

[446]

NOTES

Inserted as noted at the beginning of this Part.

The heading preceding this section was inserted by the Work and Families Act 2006, s 11(1), Sch 1, para 17, as from a day to be appointed.

Sub-s (2): for the words in italics there are substituted the words "ordinary statutory paternity pay or additional statutory paternity pay" by the Work and Families Act 2006, s 11(1), Sch 1, para 18, as from a day to be appointed.

[171ZG Relationship with contractual remuneration

(1) Subject to subsections (2) and (3) below, any entitlement to statutory paternity pay shall not affect any right of a person in relation to remuneration under any contract of service ("contractual remuneration").

(2) Subject to subsection (3) below—

(a) any contractual remuneration paid to a person by an employer of his in respect of any period shall go towards discharging any liability of that employer to pay statutory paternity pay to him in respect of that period; and

(b) any statutory paternity pay paid by an employer to a person who is an employee of his in respect of any period shall go towards discharging any liability of that employer to pay contractual remuneration to him in respect of that period.

(3) Regulations may make provision as to payments which are, and those which are not, to be treated as contractual remuneration for the purposes of subsections (1) and (2) above.

[(4) In this section "statutory paternity pay" means ordinary statutory paternity pay or additional statutory paternity pay.]]

[447]

NOTES

Inserted as noted at the beginning of this Part.

Sub-s (4): added by the Work and Families Act 2006, s 11(1), Sch 1, para 19, as from a day to be appointed.

Regulations: the Statutory Paternity Pay and Statutory Adoption Pay (General) Regulations 2002, SI 2002/2822 at **[2801]**; the Statutory Paternity Pay (Adoption) and Statutory Adoption Pay (Adoptions from Overseas) (No 2) Regulations 2003, SI 2003/1194.

[171ZH Crown employment—Part 12ZA

The provisions of this Part of this Act apply in relation to persons employed by or under the Crown as they apply in relation to persons employed otherwise than by or under the Crown.]

[448]

NOTES

Inserted as noted at the beginning of this Part.

[171ZI Special classes of person

(1) The Secretary of State may with the concurrence of the Treasury make regulations modifying any provision of this Part of this Act in such manner as he thinks proper in its application to any person who is, has been or is to be—

(a) employed on board any ship, vessel, hovercraft or aircraft;

(b) outside Great Britain at any prescribed time or in any prescribed circumstances; or

(c) in prescribed employment in connection with continental shelf operations, as defined in section 120(2) above.

(2) Regulations under subsection (1) above may, in particular, provide—

(a) for any provision of this Part of this Act to apply to any such person, notwithstanding that it would not otherwise apply;

(b) for any such provision not to apply to any such person, notwithstanding that it would otherwise apply;

(c) for excepting any such person from the application of any such provision where he neither is domiciled nor has a place of residence in any part of Great Britain;

(d) for the taking of evidence, for the purposes of the determination of any question arising under any such provision, in a country or territory outside Great Britain, by a British consular official or such other person as may be determined in accordance with the regulations.]

[449]

NOTES

Inserted as noted at the beginning of this Part.

Regulations: the Statutory Paternity Pay and Statutory Adoption Pay (Persons Abroad and Mariners) Regulations 2002, SI 2002/2821; the Statutory Paternity Pay (Adoption) and Statutory Adoption Pay (Adoptions from Overseas) (Persons Abroad and Mariners) Regulations 2003, SI 2003/1193.

[171ZJ Part 12ZA: supplementary

(1) In this Part of this Act—

"the Board" means the Commissioners of Inland Revenue;

["employer", in relation to a person who is an employee, means a person who—

(a) under section 6 above is, liable to pay secondary Class 1 contributions in relation to any of the earnings of the person who is an employee; or

(b) would be liable to pay such contributions but for—

(i) the condition in section 6(1)(b), or

(ii) the employee being under the age of 16;]

"modifications" includes additions, omissions and amendments, and related expressions are to be read accordingly;

"prescribed" means prescribed by regulations.

(2) In this Part of this Act, "employee" means a person who is—

(a) gainfully employed in Great Britain either under a contract of service or in an office (including elective office) with [general earnings (as defined by section 7 of the Income Tax (Earnings and Pensions) Act 2003)]; …

(b) …

(3) Regulations may provide—

(a) for cases where a person who falls within the definition in subsection (2) above is not to be treated as an employee for the purposes of this Part of this Act, and

(b) for cases where a person who would not otherwise be an employee for the purposes of this Part of this Act is to be treated as an employee for those purposes.

(4) Without prejudice to any other power to make regulations under this Part of this Act, regulations may specify cases in which, for the purposes of this Part of this Act or of such provisions of this Part of this Act as may be prescribed—

(a) two or more employers are to be treated as one;

(b) two or more contracts of service in respect of which the same person is an employee are to be treated as one.

(5) In this Part, except *section 171ZE*, "week" means a period of 7 days beginning with Sunday or such other period as may be prescribed in relation to any particular case or class of cases.

(6) For the purposes of this Part of this Act, a person's normal weekly earnings shall, subject to subsection (8) below, be taken to be the average weekly earnings which in the relevant period have been paid to him or paid for his benefit under the contract of service with the employer in question.

(7) For the purposes of subsection (6) above, "earnings" and "relevant period" shall have the meanings given to them by regulations.

(8) In such cases as may be prescribed, a person's normal weekly earnings shall be calculated in accordance with regulations.

(9) Where—

(a) in consequence of the establishment of one or more National Health Service trusts under [the National Health Service Act 2006, the National Health Service (Wales) Act 2006] or the National Health Service (Scotland) Act 1978 (c 29), a person's contract of employment is treated by a scheme under [any of those Acts] as divided so as to constitute two or more contracts, or

(b) an order under [paragraph 26(1) of Schedule 3 to the National Health Service Act 2006] provides that a person's contract of employment is so divided, regulations may make provision enabling the person to elect for all of those contracts to be treated as one contract for the purposes of this Part of this Act or such provisions of this Part of this Act as may be prescribed.

(10) Regulations under subsection (9) above may prescribe—

(a) the conditions that must be satisfied if a person is to be entitled to make such an election;

(b) the manner in which, and the time within which, such an election is to be made;

(c) the persons to whom, and the manner in which, notice of such an election is to be given;

(d) the information which a person who makes such an election is to provide, and the persons to whom, and the time within which, he is to provide it;

(e) the time for which such an election is to have effect;

(f) which one of the person's employers under two or more contracts is to be regarded for the purposes of *statutory paternity pay* as his employer under the contract.

(11) The powers under subsections (9) and (10) are without prejudice to any other power to make regulations under this Part of this Act.

(12) Regulations under any of subsections (4) to (10) above must be made with the concurrence of the Board.]

[450]

NOTES

Inserted as noted at the beginning of this Part.

Sub-s (1): definition "employer" substituted by the Employment Equality (Age) Regulations 2006, SI 2006/1031, reg 49(1), Sch 8, Pt 1, paras 8, 11(1), (2), (4), as from 1 October 2006 (note that this amendment applies in relation to an entitlement to (a) statutory paternity pay (birth) in respect of children whose expected week of birth begins on or after 14 January 2007; (b) statutory paternity pay (adoption) in respect of children (i) matched with a person who is notified of having been matched on or after 1 October 2006; or (ii) placed for adoption on or after that date).

Sub-s (2): words in square brackets in para (a) substituted by the Income Tax (Earnings and Pensions) Act 2003, s 722, Sch 6, Pt 2, paras 169, 183, for the purposes of income tax for the year 2003–04 and subsequent years of assessment, and for the purposes of corporation tax for accounting periods ending after 5 April 2003; para (b) (and the word omitted immediately preceding it) repealed by SI 2006/1031, reg 49(1), Sch 8, Pt 1, paras 8, 11(1), (3), (4), as from 1 October 2006 (as to the effect of this amendment, see the note above).

Sub-s (5): for the words in italics there are substituted the words "sections 171ZE and 171ZEE" by the Work and Families Act 2006, s 11(1), Sch 1, para 20(1), (2), as from a day to be appointed.

Sub-s (9): words in square brackets substituted by the National Health Service (Consequential Provisions) Act 2006, s 2, Sch 1, paras 142, 149, as from 1 March 2007.

Sub-s (10): for the words in italics in para (f) there are substituted the words "ordinary statutory paternity pay or additional statutory paternity pay" by the Work and Families Act 2006, s 11(1), Sch 1, para 20(1), (3), as from a day to be appointed.

Adoptions from overseas: this section is modified as noted to s 171ZB at **[442]**.

Commissioners of Inland Revenue: a reference to the Commissioners of Inland Revenue is now to be taken as a reference to the Commissioners for Her Majesty's Revenue and Customs; see the Commissioners for Revenue and Customs Act 2005, s 50(1), (7).

Regulations: the Statutory Paternity Pay and Statutory Adoption Pay (National Health Service Employees) Regulations 2002, SI 2002/2819; the Statutory Paternity Pay and Statutory Adoption Pay (General) Regulations 2002, SI 2002/2822 at **[2801]**; the Statutory Paternity Pay (Adoption) and Statutory Adoption Pay (Adoptions from Overseas) (No 2) Regulations 2003, SI 2003/1194.

[171ZK Power to apply Part 12ZA to adoption cases not involving placement

The Secretary of State may by regulations provide for this Part to have effect in relation to cases which involve adoption, but not the placement of a child for adoption under the law of any part of the United Kingdom, with such modifications as the regulations may prescribe.]

[451]

NOTES

Inserted as noted at the beginning of this Part.

Regulations: the Social Security Contributions and Benefits Act 1992 (Application of Parts 12ZA and 12ZB to Adoptions from Overseas) Regulations 2003, SI 2003/499.

[PART XIIZB
STATUTORY ADOPTION PAY

NOTES

Pt XIIZB inserted by the Employment Act 2002, s 4, in relation to a person with whom a child is, or is expected to be placed for adoption on or after 6 April 2003.

Adoptions from overseas: this Part is modified in relation to adoptions from overseas as noted to the sections affected. See the Social Security Contributions and Benefits Act 1992 (Application of Parts 12ZA and 12ZB to Adoptions from Overseas) Regulations 2003, SI 2003/499.

171ZL Entitlement

(1) Where a person who is, or has been, an employee satisfies the conditions in subsection (2) below, he shall be entitled in accordance with the following provisions of this Part to payments to be known as "statutory adoption pay".

(2) The conditions are—

(a) that he is a person with whom a child is, or is expected to be, placed for adoption under the law of any part of the United Kingdom;

(b) that he has been in employed earner's employment with an employer for a continuous period of at least 26 weeks ending with the relevant week;

(c) that he has ceased to work for the employer;

(d) that his normal weekly earnings for the period of 8 weeks ending with the relevant week are not less than the lower earnings limit in force under section 5(1)(a) at the end of the relevant week; and

(e) that he has elected to receive statutory adoption pay.

(3) The references in subsection (2)(b) and (d) above to the relevant week are to the week in which the person is notified that he has been matched with the child for the purposes of adoption.

(4) A person may not elect to receive statutory adoption pay if—

(a) he has elected in accordance with section 171ZB above to receive statutory paternity pay, or

[(b) he falls within subsection (4A)].

[(4A) A person falls within this subsection if—

(a) the child is, or is expected to be, placed for adoption with him as a member of a couple;

(b) the other member of the couple is a person to whom the conditions in subsection (2) above apply; and

(c) the other member of the couple has elected to receive statutory adoption pay.

(4B) For the purposes of subsection (4A), a person is a member of a couple if—

(a) in the case of an adoption or expected adoption under the law of England and Wales, he is a member of a couple within the meaning of section 144(4) of the Adoption and Children Act 2002;

(b) in the case of an adoption or an expected adoption under the law of Scotland or of Northern Ireland, he is a member of a married couple.]

(5) A person's entitlement to statutory adoption pay shall not be affected by the placement, or expected placement, for adoption of more than one child as part of the same arrangement.

(6) A person shall be entitled to payments of statutory adoption pay only if—

(a) he gives the person who will be liable to pay it notice of the date from which he expects the liability to pay him statutory adoption pay to begin; and

(b) the notice is given at least 28 days before that date or, if that is not reasonably practicable, as soon as is reasonably practicable.

(7) The notice shall be in writing if the person who is liable to pay the statutory adoption pay so requests.

(8) The Secretary of State may by regulations—

(a) provide that subsection (2)(b), (c) or (d) above shall have effect subject to prescribed modifications in such cases as may be prescribed;

(b) provide that subsection (6) above shall not have effect, or shall have effect subject to prescribed modifications, in such cases as may be prescribed;

(c) impose requirements about evidence of entitlement;

(d) specify in what circumstances employment is to be treated as continuous for the purposes of this section;

(e) provide that a person is to be treated for the purposes of this section as being employed for a continuous period of at least 26 weeks where—

(i) he has been employed by the same employer for at least 26 weeks under two or more separate contracts of service; and

(ii) those contracts were not continuous;

(f) provide for amounts earned by a person under separate contracts of service with the same employer to be aggregated for the purposes of this section;

(g) provide that—

(i) the amount of a person's earnings for any period, or

(ii) the amount of his earnings to be treated as comprised in any payment made to him or for his benefit,

shall be calculated or estimated for the purposes of this section in such manner and on such basis as may be prescribed and that for that purpose payments of a particular class or description made or falling to be made to or by a person shall, to such extent as may be prescribed, be disregarded or, as the case may be, be deducted from the amount of his earnings;

(h) make provision about elections for statutory adoption pay.]

[452]

NOTES

Inserted as noted at the beginning of this Part.

Sub-s (4): para (b) substituted by the Adoption and Children Act 2002 (Consequential Amendment to Statutory Adoption Pay) Order 2006, SI 2006/2012, art 3(a), as from 1 October 2006 (with effect in relation to a person with whom a child is expected to be placed for adoption, where the placement is expected to occur on or after that date (note that the date on which the child is actually placed for adoption is immaterial)).

Sub-ss (4A), (4B): inserted by SI 2006/2012, art 3(b), as from 1 October 2006 (as to the commencement and application of this amendment, see the note above).

Adoptions from overseas: this section is modified in relation to adoptions from overseas which are adoptions of children who enter Great Britain from outside the United Kingdom in connection with, or for the purposes of, adoption which does not involve the placement of a child for adoption under the law of any part of the United Kingdom; see the Social Security Contributions and Benefits Act 1992 (Application of Parts 12ZA and 12ZB to Adoptions from Overseas) Regulations 2003, SI 2003/499, reg 3, Sch 2.

Regulations: the Statutory Paternity Pay and Statutory Adoption Pay (General) Regulations 2002, SI 2002/2822 at **[2801]**; the Statutory Paternity Pay (Adoption) and Statutory Adoption Pay (Adoptions from Overseas) (No 2) Regulations 2003, SI 2003/1194.

[171ZM Liability to make payments

(1) The liability to make payments of statutory adoption pay is a liability of any person of whom the person entitled to the payments has been an employee as mentioned in section 171ZL(2)(b) above.

(2) Regulations shall make provision as to a former employer's liability to pay statutory adoption pay to a person in any case where the former employee's contract of service with him has been brought to an end by the former employer solely, or mainly, for the purpose of avoiding liability for statutory adoption pay.

(3) The Secretary of State may, with the concurrence of the Board, by regulations specify circumstances in which, notwithstanding this section, liability to make payments of statutory adoption pay is to be a liability of the Board.]

[453]

NOTES

Inserted as noted at the beginning of this Part.

Regulations: the Statutory Paternity Pay and Statutory Adoption Pay (General) Regulations 2002, SI 2002/2822 at **[2801]**; the Statutory Paternity Pay (Adoption) and Statutory Adoption Pay (Adoptions from Overseas) (No 2) Regulations 2003, SI 2003/1194.

[171ZN Rate and period of pay

(1) Statutory adoption pay shall be payable at such fixed or earnings-related weekly rate as the Secretary of State may prescribe by regulations, which may prescribe different kinds of rate for different cases.

(2) Statutory adoption pay shall be payable, subject to the provisions of this Part of this Act, in respect of each week during a prescribed period ("the adoption pay period") of a duration not exceeding [52 weeks].

(3) [Except in such cases as may be prescribed,] a person shall not be liable to pay statutory adoption pay to another in respect of any week during any part of which the other works under a contract of service with him.

(4) It is immaterial for the purposes of subsection (3) above whether the work referred to in that subsection is work under a contract of service which existed immediately before the adoption pay period or a contract of service which did not so exist.

(5) Except in such cases as may be prescribed, statutory adoption pay shall not be payable to a person in respect of any week during any part of which he works for any employer who is not liable to pay him statutory adoption pay.

(6) The Secretary of State may by regulations specify circumstances in which there is to be no liability to pay statutory adoption pay in respect of a week.

[(6A) Where for any purpose of this Part of this Act or of regulations it is necessary to calculate the daily rate of statutory adoption pay, the amount payable by way of statutory adoption pay for any day shall be taken as one seventh of the weekly rate.]

(7) In subsection (2) above, "week" means any period of seven days.

(8) In subsections (3), (5) and (6) above, "week" means a period of seven days beginning with the day of the week on which the adoption pay period begins.]

[454]

NOTES

Inserted as noted at the beginning of this Part.

Sub-s (2): words in square brackets substituted by the Work and Families Act 2006, s 2, as from 27 June 2006 (for the purpose of the power to prescribe the adoption pay period), and as from 1 October 2006 (otherwise).

Sub-s (3): words in square brackets inserted by the Work and Families Act 2006, s 11(1), Sch 1, para 21(1), (2), as from 27 June 2006 (for the purpose of the power to prescribe matters by regulations), and as from 1 October 2006 (otherwise).

Sub-s (6A): inserted by the Work and Families Act 2006, s 11(1), Sch 1, para 21(1), (3), as from 27 June 2006 (for the purpose of the power to prescribe matters by regulations), and as from 1 October 2006 (otherwise).

The fixed rate, as from 6 April 2008, is £117.18 per week (see the Statutory Paternity Pay and Statutory Adoption Pay (Weekly Rates) Regulations, SI 2002/2818, reg 3 at **[2785]**, as amended by the Social Security Benefits Up-rating Order 2008, SI 2008/632, art 11(b)). Previous rates were: £112.75 (as from 1 April 2007, see SI 2007/688); £108.85 (as from 2 April 2006, see SI 2006/645); £106.00 (as from 3 April 2005, see SI 2005/522); and £102.80 (as from 4 April 2004, see SI 2004/925).

Regulations: the Statutory Paternity Pay and Statutory Adoption Pay (Weekly Rates) Regulations 2002, SI 2002/2818 at **[2783]**; the Statutory Paternity Pay and Statutory Adoption Pay (General) Regulations 2002, SI 2002/2822 at **[2801]**; the Statutory Paternity Pay (Adoption) and Statutory Adoption Pay (Adoptions from Overseas) (No 2) Regulations 2003, SI 2003/1194.

[171ZO Restrictions on contracting out

(1) Any agreement shall be void to the extent that it purports—

(a) to exclude, limit or otherwise modify any provision of this Part of this Act, or

(b) to require an employee or former employee to contribute (whether directly or indirectly) towards any costs incurred by his employer or former employer under this Part of this Act.

(2) For the avoidance of doubt, any agreement between an employer and an employee authorising any deductions from statutory adoption pay which the employer is liable to pay to the employee in respect of any period shall not be void by virtue of subsection (1)(a) above if the employer—

(a) is authorised by that or another agreement to make the same deductions from any contractual remuneration which he is liable to pay in respect of the same period, or

(b) would be so authorised if he were liable to pay contractual remuneration in respect of that period.]

[455]

NOTES

Inserted as noted at the beginning of this Part.

[171ZP Relationship with benefits and other payments etc

(1) Except as may be prescribed, a day which falls within the adoption pay period shall not be treated as a day of incapacity for work for the purposes of determining, for this Act, whether it forms part of a period of incapacity for work for the purposes of incapacity benefit.

(2) Regulations may provide that in prescribed circumstances a day which falls within the adoption pay period shall be treated as a day of incapacity for work for the purposes of determining entitlement to the higher rate of short-term incapacity benefit or to long-term incapacity benefit.

(3) Regulations may provide that an amount equal to a person's statutory adoption pay for a period shall be deducted from any such benefit in respect of the same period and a person shall be entitled to such benefit only if there is a balance after the deduction and, if there is such a balance, at a weekly rate equal to it.

(4) Subject to subsections (5) and (6) below, any entitlement to statutory adoption pay shall not affect any right of a person in relation to remuneration under any contract of service ("contractual remuneration").

(5) Subject to subsection (6) below—

(a) any contractual remuneration paid to a person by an employer of his in respect of a week in the adoption pay period shall go towards discharging any liability of that employer to pay statutory adoption pay to him in respect of that week; and

(b) any statutory adoption pay paid by an employer to a person who is an employee of his in respect of a week in the adoption pay period shall go towards discharging any liability of that employer to pay contractual remuneration to him in respect of that week.

(6) Regulations may make provision as to payments which are, and those which are not, to be treated as contractual remuneration for the purposes of subsections (4) and (5) above.

(7) In subsection (5) above, "week" means a period of seven days beginning with the day of the week on which the adoption pay period begins.]

[456]

NOTES

Inserted as noted at the beginning of this Part.

Sub-ss (1)–(3): repealed by the Welfare Reform Act 2007, s 67, Sch 8, as from a day to be appointed.

Regulations: the Social Security, Statutory Maternity Pay and Statutory Sick Pay (Miscellaneous Amendments) Regulations 2002, SI 2002/2690; the Statutory Paternity Pay and Statutory Adoption Pay (General) Regulations 2002, SI 2002/2822 at **[2801]**; the Statutory Paternity Pay (Adoption) and Statutory Adoption Pay (Adoptions from Overseas) (No 2) Regulations 2003, SI 2003/1194.

[171ZQ Crown employment—Part 12ZB

The provisions of this Part of this Act apply in relation to persons employed by or under the Crown as they apply in relation to persons employed otherwise than by or under the Crown.]

[457]

NOTES

Inserted as noted at the beginning of this Part.

[171ZR Special classes of person

(1) The Secretary of State may with the concurrence of the Treasury make regulations modifying any provision of this Part of this Act in such manner as he thinks proper in its application to any person who is, has been or is to be—

(a) employed on board any ship, vessel, hovercraft or aircraft;

(b) outside Great Britain at any prescribed time or in any prescribed circumstances; or

(c) in prescribed employment in connection with continental shelf operations, as defined in section 120(2) above.

(2) Regulations under subsection (1) above may, in particular, provide—

(a) for any provision of this Part of this Act to apply to any such person, notwithstanding that it would not otherwise apply;

(b) for any such provision not to apply to any such person, notwithstanding that it would otherwise apply;

(c) for excepting any such person from the application of any such provision where he neither is domiciled nor has a place of residence in any part of Great Britain;

(d) for the taking of evidence, for the purposes of the determination of any question arising under any such provision, in a country or territory outside Great Britain, by a British consular official or such other person as may be determined in accordance with the regulations.]

[458]

NOTES

Inserted as noted at the beginning of this Part.

Regulations: the Statutory Paternity Pay and Statutory Adoption Pay (Persons Abroad and Mariners) Regulations 2002, SI 2002/2821; the Statutory Paternity Pay (Adoption) and Statutory Adoption Pay (Adoptions from Overseas) (Persons Abroad and Mariners) Regulations 2003, SI 2003/1193.

[171ZS Part 12ZB: supplementary

(1) In this Part of this Act—

"adoption pay period" has the meaning given by section 171ZN(2) above;

"the Board" means the Commissioners of Inland Revenue;

["employer", in relation to a person who is an employee, means a person who—

(a) under section 6 above is liable to pay secondary Class 1 contributions in relation to any of the earnings of the person who is an employee; or

(b) would be liable to pay such contributions but for—

(ii) the condition in section 6(1)(b), or

(ii) the employee being under the age of 16;]

"modifications" includes additions, omissions and amendments, and related expressions are to be read accordingly;

"prescribed" means prescribed by regulations.

(2) In this Part of this Act, "employee" means a person who is—

(a) gainfully employed in Great Britain either under a contract of service or in an office (including elective office) with [general earnings (as defined by section 7 of the Income Tax (Earnings and Pensions) Act 2003)]; …

(b) …

(3) Regulations may provide—

(a) for cases where a person who falls within the definition in subsection (2) above is not to be treated as an employee for the purposes of this Part of this Act, and

(b) for cases where a person who would not otherwise be an employee for the purposes of this Part of this Act is to be treated as an employee for those purposes.

(4) Without prejudice to any other power to make regulations under this Part of this Act, regulations may specify cases in which, for the purposes of this Part of this Act or of such provisions of this Part of this Act as may be prescribed—

(a) two or more employers are to be treated as one;

(b) two or more contracts of service in respect of which the same person is an employee are to be treated as one.

(5) In this Part, except sections 171ZN and 171ZP, "week" means a period of 7 days beginning with Sunday or such other period as may be prescribed in relation to any particular case or class of cases.

(6) For the purposes of this Part of this Act, a person's normal weekly earnings shall, subject to subsection (8) below, be taken to be the average weekly earnings which in the relevant period have been paid to him or paid for his benefit under the contract of service with the employer in question.

(7) For the purposes of subsection (6) above, "earnings" and "relevant period" shall have the meanings given to them by regulations.

(8) In such cases as may be prescribed, a person's normal weekly earnings shall be calculated in accordance with regulations.

(9) Where—

(a) in consequence of the establishment of one or more National Health Service trusts under [the National Health Service Act 2006, the National Health Service (Wales) Act 2006] or the National Health Service (Scotland) Act 1978 (c 29), a person's contract of employment is treated by a scheme under [any of those Acts] as divided so as to constitute two or more contracts, or

(b) an order under [paragraph 26(1) of Schedule 3 to the National Health Service Act 2006] provides that a person's contract of employment is so divided,

regulations may make provision enabling the person to elect for all of those contracts to be treated as one contract for the purposes of this Part of this Act or such provisions of this Part of this Act as may be prescribed.

(10) Regulations under subsection (9) above may prescribe—

(a) the conditions that must be satisfied if a person is to be entitled to make such an election;

(b) the manner in which, and the time within which, such an election is to be made;

(c) the persons to whom, and the manner in which, notice of such an election is to be given;

(d) the information which a person who makes such an election is to provide, and the persons to whom, and the time within which, he is to provide it;

(e) the time for which such an election is to have effect;

(f) which one of the person's employers under two or more contracts is to be regarded for the purposes of statutory adoption pay as his employer under the contract.

(11) The powers under subsections (9) and (10) are without prejudice to any other power to make regulations under this Part of this Act.

(12) Regulations under any of subsections (4) to (10) above must be made with the concurrence of the Board.]

[459]

NOTES

Inserted as noted at the beginning of this Part.

Sub-s (1): definition "employer" substituted by the Employment Equality (Age) Regulations 2006, SI 2006/1031, reg 49(1), Sch 8, Pt 1, paras 8, 12(1), (2), as from 1 October 2006 (note that this amendment applies in relation to an entitlement to statutory adoption pay in respect of children (a) matched with a person who is notified of having been matched on or after the commencement date; or (b) placed for adoption on or after that commencement).

Sub-s (2): words in square brackets in para (a) substituted by the Income Tax (Earnings and Pensions) Act 2003, s 722, Sch 6, Pt 2, paras 169, 184, for the purposes of income tax for the year 2003–04 and subsequent years of assessment, and for the purposes of corporation tax for accounting periods ending after 5 April 2003; para (b) (and the word omitted immediately preceding it) repealed by SI 2006/1031, reg 49(1), Sch 8, Pt 1, paras 8, 12(1), (3), (4), as from 1 October 2006 (as to the commencement and application of this amendment, see the note above).

Sub-s (9): words in square brackets substituted by the National Health Service (Consequential Provisions) Act 2006, s 2, Sch 1, paras 142, 150, as from 1 March 2007.

Adoptions from overseas: this section is modified as noted to s 171ZL at **[452]**.

Commissioners of Inland Revenue: a reference to the Commissioners of Inland Revenue is now to be taken as a reference to the Commissioners for Her Majesty's Revenue and Customs; see the Commissioners for Revenue and Customs Act 2005, s 50(1), (7).

Regulations: the Statutory Paternity Pay and Statutory Adoption Pay (National Health Service Employees) Regulations 2002, SI 2002/2819; the Statutory Paternity Pay and Statutory Adoption Pay (General) Regulations 2002, SI 2002/2822 at **[2801]**; the Statutory Paternity Pay (Adoption) and Statutory Adoption Pay (Adoptions from Overseas) (No 2) Regulations 2003, SI 2003/1194.

[171ZT Power to apply Part 12ZB to adoption cases not involving placement

The Secretary of State may by regulations provide for this Part to have effect in relation to cases which involve adoption, but not the placement of a child for adoption under the law of any part of the United Kingdom, with such modifications as the regulations may prescribe.]

[460]

NOTES

Inserted as noted at the beginning of this Part.

Regulations: the Social Security Contributions and Benefits Act 1992 (Application of Parts 12ZA and 12ZB to Adoptions from Overseas) Regulations 2003, SI 2003/499.

PART XIII
GENERAL

Short title, commencement and extent

177 Short title, commencement and extent

(1) This Act may be cited as the Social Security Contributions and Benefits Act 1992.

(2) (*Outside the scope of this work.*)

(3) The enactments consolidated by this Act are repealed, in consequence of the consolidation, by the Consequential Provisions Act.

(4) Except as provided in Schedule 4 to the Consequential Provisions Act, this Act shall come into force on 1st July 1992.

(5), (6) (*Outside the scope of this work.*)

[461]

SCHEDULES

SCHEDULE 11
CIRCUMSTANCES IN WHICH PERIODS OF ENTITLEMENT TO STATUTORY SICK PAY DO NOT ARISE

Section 153(3)

1. A period of entitlement does not arise in relation to a particular period of incapacity for work in any of the circumstances set out in paragraph 2 below or in such other circumstances as may be prescribed.

[1A. Regulations under paragraph 1 above must be made with the concurrence of the Treasury.]

2. The circumstances are that—

(a), (b) …

(c) at the relevant date the employee's normal weekly earnings are less than the lower earnings limit then in force under section 5(1)(a) above;

[(d) in the period of 57 days ending immediately before the relevant date the employee had at least one day on which—

(i) *he was entitled to incapacity benefit* (*or would have been so entitled had he satisfied the contribution conditions mentioned in section 30A*(2)(*a*) *above*), …

(ii), (iii) …]

(f) the employee has done no work for his employer under his contract of service;

(g) on the relevant date there is … a stoppage of work due to a trade dispute at the employee's place of employment;

(h) the employee is, or has been, pregnant and the relevant date falls within the disqualifying period (within the meaning of section 153(12) above).

3. In this Schedule "relevant date" means the date on which a period of entitlement would begin in accordance with section 153 above if this Schedule did not prevent it arising.

4, 5. …

[5A.—(1) Paragraph 2(d)(i) above does not apply if, at the relevant date, the employee is over pensionable age and is not entitled to incapacity benefit.

(2) Paragraph 2(d)(i) above ceases to apply if, at any time after the relevant date, the employee is over pensionable age and is not entitled to incapacity benefit.

(3) In this paragraph "pensionable age" has the meaning given by the rules in paragraph 1 of Schedule 4 to the Pensions Act 1995.]

6. For the purposes of paragraph 2(f) above, if an employee enters into a contract of service which is to take effect not more than 8 weeks after the date on which a previous contract of service entered into by him with the same employer ceased to have effect, the two contracts shall be treated as one.

7. Paragraph 2(g) above does not apply in the case of an employee who proves that at no time on or before the relevant date did he have a direct interest in the trade dispute in question.

8. Paragraph 2(h) above does not apply in relation to an employee who has been pregnant if her pregnancy terminated, before the beginning of the disqualifying period, otherwise than by confinement (as defined for the purposes of statutory maternity pay in section 171(1) above). **[462]**

NOTES

Para 1A: inserted by the Social Security Contributions (Transfer of Functions, etc) Act 1999, s 1(1), Sch 1, para 20.

Para 2: sub-para (a) repealed by the Employment Equality (Age) Regulations 2006, SI 2006/1031, reg 49(1), Sch 8, Pt 1, paras 8, 13(1), as from 1 October 2006 (for transitional provisions, see the note below); sub-para (b) repealed by the Fixed-term Employees (Prevention of Less Favourable Treatment) Regulations 2002, SI 2002/2034, reg 11, Sch 2, Pt 1, para 1(a); sub-para (d) substituted, for original sub-paras (d), (e), by the Social Security (Incapacity for Work) Act 1994, s 11, Sch 1, Pt I, para 43, Sch 2; sub-para (d)(i) repealed by the Welfare Reform Act 2007, s 67, Sch 8, as from a day to be appointed; word omitted from sub-para (d)(i), and sub-para (d)(iii), repealed by the Welfare Reform and Pensions Act 1999, s 88, Sch 13, Pt IV; sub-para (d)(ii) repealed by the Social Security Act 1998, ss 73, 86(2), Sch 8; words omitted from para (g) repealed by the Jobseekers Act 1995, s 41(5), Sch 3.

Para 4: repealed by SI 2002/2034, reg 11, Sch 2, Pt 1, para 1(b).

Para 5: repealed by the Social Security (Incapacity for Work) Act 1994, s 11, Sch 1, Pt I, para 43, Sch 2.

Para 5A: inserted by the Employment Equality (Age) (Consequential Amendments) Regulations 2007, SI 2007/825, reg 2, as from 6 April 2007.

Transitional provisions: the Employment Equality (Age) Regulations 2006, SI 2006/1031, Sch 8, Pt 1, para 13(2), (3) provide as follows (note that by virtue of art 2 "commencement date" means 1 October 2006)—

"(2) Sub-paragraph (1) applies in relation to a period of incapacity for work which—

(a) begins on or after the commencement date, or

(b) begins before and continues on or after the commencement date.

(3) But in a case falling within sub-paragraph (2)(b), sub-paragraph (1) does not affect the application of paragraph 1 of Schedule 11 to the 1992 Act in relation to the part of the period of incapacity for work that falls before the commencement date.".

Regulations: the Social Security (Welfare to Work) Regulations 1998, SI 1998/2231. Also, the Statutory Sick Pay (General) Regulations 1982, SI 1982/894 (as amended) at **[2080]**, and the Statutory Sick Pay (Mariners, Airmen and Persons Abroad) Regulations 1982, SI 1982/1349, have effect as if made under this Schedule by virtue of the Social Security (Consequential Provisions) Act 1992, s 2(2).

SCHEDULE 12
RELATIONSHIP OF STATUTORY SICK PAY WITH BENEFITS AND OTHER PAYMENTS, ETC

Section 160

The general principle

1. Any day which—

(a) is a day of incapacity for work in relation to any contract of service; and

(b) falls within a period of entitlement (whether or not it is also a qualifying day),

shall not be treated for the purposes of this Act as a day of incapacity for work for the purposes of determining whether a period is ... a period of incapacity for work for the purposes of incapacity benefit].

Contractual remuneration

2.—(1) Subject to sub-paragraphs (2) and (3) below, any entitlement to statutory sick pay shall not affect any right of an employee in relation to remuneration under any contract of service ("contractual remuneration").

(2) Subject to sub-paragraph (3) below—

(a) any contractual remuneration paid to an employee by an employer of his in respect of a day of incapacity for work shall go towards discharging any liability of that employer to pay statutory sick pay to that employee in respect of that day; and

(b) any statutory sick pay paid by an employer to an employee of his in respect of a day of incapacity for work shall go towards discharging any liability of that employer to pay contractual remuneration to that employee in respect of that day.

(3) Regulations may make provision as to payments which are, and those which are not, to be treated as contractual remuneration for the purposes of sub-paragraph (1) or (2) above.

[Incapacity benefit

3.—(1) This paragraph and paragraph 4 below have effect to exclude, where a period of entitlement as between an employee and an employer of his comes to an end, the provisions by virtue of which short-term incapacity benefit is not paid for the first three days.

(2) If the first day immediately following the day on which the period of entitlement came to an end—

(a) is the day of incapacity for work in relation to that employee, and

(b) is not a day in relation to which paragraph 1 above applies by reason of any entitlement as between the employee and another employer,

that day shall, except in prescribed cases, be or form part of a period of incapacity for work notwithstanding section 30C(1)(b) above (by virtue of which a period of incapacity for work must be at least 4 days long).

(3) Where each of the first two consecutive days, or the first three consecutive days, following the day on which the period of entitlement came to an end is a day to which paragraphs (a) and (b) of sub-paragraph (2) above apply, that sub-paragraph has effect in relation to the second day or, as the case may be, in relation to the second and third days, as it has effect in relation to the first.

4.—(1) Where a period of entitlement as between an employee and an employer of his comes to an end, section 30A(3) above (exclusion of benefit for first 3 days of period) does not apply in relation to any day which—

(a) is or forms part of a period of incapacity for work (whether by virtue of paragraph 3 above or otherwise), and

(b) falls within the period of 57 days immediately following the day on which the period of entitlement came to an end.

(2) Where sub-paragraph (1) above applies in relation to a day, section 30A(3) above does not apply in relation to any later day in the same period of incapacity for work.

Incapacity benefit for widows and widowers

5. Paragraph 1 above does not apply for the purpose of determining whether the conditions specified in section 40(3) or (4) or 41(2) or (3) above are satisfied.]

Unemployability supplement

6. Paragraph 1 above does not apply in relation to paragraph 3 of Schedule 7 to this Act and accordingly the references in paragraph 3 of that Schedule to a period of interruption of employment shall be construed as if the provisions re-enacted in this Part of this Act had not been enacted.

[463]

NOTES

Para 1: repealed by the Welfare Reform Act 2007, s 67, Sch 8, as from a day to be appointed; words in square brackets inserted by the Social Security (Incapacity for Work) Act 1994, s 11, Sch 1, Pt I, para 44; words omitted repealed by the Jobseekers Act 1995, s 41(5), Sch 3.

Paras 3–5: substituted by the Social Security (Incapacity for Work) Act 1994, s 11, Sch 1, Pt I, para 44; repealed by the Welfare Reform Act 2007, s 67, Sch 8, as from a day to be appointed.

Para 6: repealed by the Welfare Reform Act 2007, s 67, Sch 8, as from a day to be appointed.

Regulations: the Statutory Sick Pay (General) Regulations 1982, SI 1982/894 at **[2080]** have effect as if made under this Schedule by virtue of the Social Security (Consequential Provisions) Act 1992, s 2(2).

SCHEDULE 13
RELATIONSHIP OF STATUTORY MATERNITY PAY WITH BENEFITS AND OTHER PAYMENTS, ETC

Section 168

The general principle

[1. Except as may be prescribed, a day which falls within the maternity pay period shall not be treated as a day of incapacity for work for the purposes of determining, for this Act, whether it forms part of a period of incapacity for work for the purposes of incapacity benefit.]

[Incapacity benefit

2.—(1) Regulations may provide that in prescribed circumstances a day which falls within the maternity pay period shall be treated as a day of incapacity for work for the purpose of determining entitlement to the higher rate of short-term incapacity benefit or to long-term incapacity benefit.

(2) Regulations may provide that an amount equal to a woman's statutory maternity pay for a period shall be deducted from any such benefit in respect of the same period and a woman shall be entitled to such benefit only if there is a balance after the deduction and, if there is such a balance, at a weekly rate equal to it.]

Contractual remuneration

3.—(1) Subject to sub-paragraphs (2) and (3) below, any entitlement to statutory maternity pay shall not affect any right of a woman in relation to remuneration under any contract of service ("contractual remuneration").

(2) Subject to sub-paragraph (3) below—

(a) any contractual remuneration paid to a woman by an employer of hers in respect of a week in the maternity pay period shall go towards discharging any liability of that employer to pay statutory maternity pay to her in respect of that week; and

(b) any statutory maternity pay paid by an employer to a woman who is an employee of his in respect of a week in the maternity pay period shall go towards discharging any liability of that employer to pay contractual remuneration to her in respect of that week.

[(2A) In sub-paragraph (2) "week" means a period of seven days beginning with the day of the week on which the maternity pay period begins.]

(3) Regulations may make provision as to payments which are, and those which are not, to be treated as contractual remuneration for the purposes of sub-paragraphs (1) and (2) above.

[464]

NOTES

Para 1: substituted by the Jobseekers Act 1995, s 41(4), Sch 2, para 37; repealed by the Welfare Reform Act 2007, s 67, Sch 8, as from a day to be appointed.

Para 2: substituted by the Social Security (Incapacity for Work) Act 1994, s 11(1), Sch 1, Pt I, para 45(1), (3); repealed by the Welfare Reform Act 2007, s 67, Sch 8, as from a day to be appointed.

Para 3: sub-para (2A) inserted by the Work and Families Act 2006, s 11(1), Sch 1, para 23, as from 1 October 2006.

Regulations: the Statutory Maternity Pay (General) Regulations 1986, SI 1986/1960 (as amended) at **[2115]** have effect as if made under this Schedule by virtue of the Social Security (Consequential Provisions) Act 1992, s 2(2).

OFFSHORE SAFETY ACT 1992

(1992 c 15)

An Act to extend the application of Part I of the Health and Safety at Work etc Act 1974; to increase the penalties for certain offences under that Part; to confer powers for preserving the security of supplies of petroleum and petroleum products; and for connected purposes

[6 March 1992]

NOTES

Regulatory functions: the regulatory functions conferred by, or under, this Act are subject to the Legislative and Regulatory Reform Act 2006, ss 21, 22 at **[1783]**, **[1784]**; see the Legislative and Regulatory Reform (Regulatory Functions) Order 2007, SI 2007/3544 (made under s 24(2) of the 2006 Act) for details.

1 Application of Part I of 1974 Act for offshore purposes

(1) The general purposes of Part I of the Health and Safety at Work etc Act 1974 ("the 1974 Act") shall include—

(a) securing the safety, health and welfare of persons on offshore installations or engaged on pipe-line works;

(b) securing the safety of such installations and preventing accidents on or near them;

(c) securing the proper construction and safe operation of pipe-lines and preventing damage to them; and

(d) securing the safe dismantling, removal and disposal of offshore installations and pipe-lines;

and that Part shall have effect as if the provisions mentioned in subsection (3) below were existing statutory provisions within the meaning of that Part and, in the case of the enactments there mentioned, were specified in the third column of Schedule 1 to that Act.

(2) Without prejudice to the generality of subsection (1) of section 15 of the 1974 Act (health and safety regulations), regulations under that section may—

(a) repeal or modify any of the provisions mentioned in subsection (3) below; and

(b) make any provision which, but for any such repeal or modification, could be made by regulations or orders made under any enactment there mentioned.

(3) The provisions referred to in subsections (1) and (2) above are—

(a) the Mineral Workings (Offshore Installations) Act 1971;

[(b) sections 20 and 25 of the Petroleum Act 1998;]

(c) in the Petroleum Act 1987, … sections 21 to 24 (safety zones); and

(d) the provisions of any regulations or orders made or having effect under any enactment mentioned in the foregoing paragraphs.

(4) In this section—

"offshore installation" means any installation which is an offshore installation within the meaning of the Mineral Workings (Offshore Installations) Act 1971, or is to be taken to be an installation for the purposes of sections 21 to 23 of the Petroleum Act 1987;

["pipe-line" means, subject to subsection (4A), a controlled pipeline within the meaning of Part III of the Petroleum Act 1998; and

"pipe-line works" means works of any of the following kinds, namely—

(a) assembling or placing a pipe-line or length of pipe-line;

(b) inspecting, testing, maintaining, adjusting, repairing, altering or renewing a pipe-line or length of pipe-line;

(c) changing the position of or dismantling or removing a pipe-line or length of pipe-line;

(d) opening the bed of the sea for the purposes of works mentioned in paragraphs (a) to (c), tunnelling or boring for those purposes and other works needed for or incidental to those purposes;

(e) works for the purpose of determining whether a place is suitable as part of the site of a proposed pipe-line and the carrying out of surveying operations for the purpose of settling the route of a proposed pipe-line.]

[(4A) In this section "pipe-line" does not include—

(a) any pipe-line so far as it forms part of the equipment of a vessel or vehicle; or

(b) any apparatus and works associated with a pipe or system of pipes and prescribed for the purpose of this paragraph by regulations made by the Secretary of State.

(4B) A statutory instrument containing regulations made by virtue of subsection (4A) shall be subject to annulment in pursuance of a resolution of either House of Parliament; and section 25 of the Petroleum Act 1998 shall apply in relation to any such regulations as it applies in relation to regulations under section 20 of that Act.]

(5) The provisions mentioned in subsection (3) above and the definitions in subsection (4) above shall have effect as if any reference in—

(a) section 1(4) of the Mineral Workings (Offshore Installations) Act 1971;

(b) …
(c) section … 21(7) of the Petroleum Act 1987[; or
(d) section 14(2) or 45 of the Petroleum Act 1998,]

to tidal waters and parts of the sea in or adjacent to the United Kingdom, or to the territorial sea adjacent to the United Kingdom, were a reference to tidal waters and parts of the sea in or adjacent to Great Britain, or to the territorial sea adjacent to Great Britain.

[465]

NOTES

Sub-s (3): para (b) substituted, and words omitted from para (c) repealed, by the Petroleum Act 1998, ss 50, 51(1), Sch 4, para 33(1), (2)(a), Sch 5, Pt I.

Sub-s (4): definitions "pipe-line" and "pipe-line works" substituted by the Petroleum Act 1998, s 50, Sch 4, para 33(1), (2)(b).

Sub-ss (4A), (4B): inserted by the Petroleum Act 1998, s 50, Sch 4, para 33(1), (2)(c).

Sub-s (5): para (b) and words omitted from para (c) repealed, and para (d) and word immediately preceding it inserted, by the Petroleum Act 1998, ss 50, 51(1), Sch 4, para 33(1), (2)(d), Sch 5, Pt I.

Regulations: the Offshore Safety (Repeals and Modifications) Regulations 1993, SI 1993/1823; the Reporting of Injuries, Diseases and Dangerous Occurrences Regulations 1995, SI 1995/3163; the Offshore Safety (Miscellaneous Amendments) Regulations 2002, SI 2002/2175; the Offshore Installations (Safety Case) Regulations 2005, SI 2005/3117.

2 Application of Part I for other purposes

(1) The general purposes of Part I of the 1974 Act shall include—
(a) securing the proper construction and safe operation of pipe-lines and preventing damage to them;
(b) securing that, in the event of the accidental escape or ignition of anything in a pipe-line, immediate notice of the event is given to persons who will or may have to discharge duties or take steps in consequence of the happening of the event; and
(c) protecting the public from personal injury, fire, explosions and other dangers arising from the transmission, distribution, supply or use of gas;

and that Part shall have effect as if the provisions mentioned in subsection (3) below were existing statutory provisions within the meaning of that Part and, in the case of the enactments there mentioned, were specified in the third column of Schedule 1 to that Act.

(2) Without prejudice to the generality of subsection (1) of section 15 of the 1974 Act (health and safety regulations), regulations under that section may—
(a) repeal or modify any of the provisions mentioned in subsection (3) below; and
(b) make any provision which, but for any such repeal or modification, could be made by regulations made under any enactment mentioned in paragraph (b) of that subsection.

(3) The provisions referred to in subsections (1) and (2) above are—
(a) sections 27 to 32 and 37 (avoidance of damage to pipe-lines and notification of accidents etc) of the Pipe-lines Act 1962;
(b) …
(c) the provisions of any regulations made or having effect under any enactment mentioned in paragraph (b) above.

(4) In this section—
"gas" means any substance which is or (if it were in a gaseous state) would be gas within the meaning of Part I of the Gas Act 1986;
"pipe-line" has the same meaning as in the Pipe-lines Act 1962.

[466]

NOTES

Sub-s (3): para (b) repealed by the Utilities Act 2000, s 108, Sch 8.

3 ((*Provisions consequential on ss 1, 2) outside the scope of this work.*)

4 Increased penalties under Part I

(1)–(5) …

(6) This section does not affect the punishment for any offence committed before the commencement of this section.

[467]

NOTES

Sub-ss (1)–(5): amend the Health and Safety at Work etc Act 1974, ss 15, 33 at **[43]**, **[59]**.

5, 6 *(S 5 (directions by the Secretary of State for preserving the security of petroleum and petroleum products), s 6 (corresponding provisions for Northern Ireland) outside the scope of this work.)*

7 Short title, repeals, commencement and extent

(1) This Act may be cited as the Offshore Safety Act 1992.

(2) The enactments mentioned in Schedule 2 to this Act are hereby repealed to the extent specified in the third column of that Schedule.

(3) The following provisions of this Act, namely—

(a) section 2(3)(b) and (c);
(b) section 3(1)(a) and (e), (2) and (3)(b); and
(c) subsection (2) above so far as relating to the repeal in the Continental Shelf Act 1964 and the second repeal in the Gas Act 1986,

shall not come into force until such day as the Secretary of State may by order made by statutory instrument appoint, and different days may be appointed for different provisions or for different purposes.

(4) This Act, except section 6 above, does not extend to Northern Ireland.

[468]

NOTES

Orders: the Offshore Safety Act 1992 (Commencement No 1) Order 1993, SI 1993/2406; the Offshore Safety Act 1992 (Commencement No 2) Order 1996, SI 1996/487.

(Sch 1 (model clauses), Sch 2 (repeals) outside the scope of this work.)

TRADE UNION AND LABOUR RELATIONS (CONSOLIDATION) ACT 1992

(1992 c 52)

ARRANGEMENT OF SECTIONS

PART I
TRADE UNIONS

CHAPTER I
INTRODUCTORY

Meaning of "trade union"

The list of trade unions

Certification as independent trade union

Annual return, accounts and audit

Investigation of financial affairs

Members' superannuation schemes

Supplementary

CHAPTER IV
ELECTIONS FOR CERTAIN POSITIONS

Duty to hold elections

Requirements to be satisfied with respect to elections

Remedy for failure to comply with requirements

Supplementary

CHAPTER V
RIGHTS OF TRADE UNION MEMBERS

Right to a ballot before industrial action

Right not to be denied access to the courts

Right not to be unjustifiably disciplined

Right not to suffer deduction of unauthorised or excessive union subscriptions

Right to terminate membership of union

Supplementary

CHAPTER VA
COLLECTIVE BARGAINING: RECOGNITION

CHAPTER VI
APPLICATION OF FUNDS FOR POLITICAL OBJECTS

Restriction on use of funds for certain political objects

Administration of employers' associations

Application of funds for political objects

Amalgamations and similar matters

General

PART III
RIGHTS IN RELATION TO UNION MEMBERSHIP AND ACTIVITIES

Access to employment

Contracts for supply of goods or services

Inducements

Detriment

Dismissal of employee

Time off for trade union duties and activities

Right to membership of trade union

PART IV
INDUSTRIAL RELATIONS

CHAPTER I
COLLECTIVE BARGAINING

Introductory

Enforceability of collective agreements

Disclosure of information for purposes of collective bargaining

Prohibition of union recognition requirements

CHAPTER II
PROCEDURE FOR HANDLING REDUNDANCIES

Duty of employer to consult representatives

Duty of employer to notify secretary of state

Supplementary provisions

CHAPTER III
CODES OF PRACTICE

Codes of Practice issued by ACAS

Codes of Practice issued by the Secretary of State

Supplementary provisions

CHAPTER IV
GENERAL

Functions of ACAS

Courts of inquiry

Supplementary provisions

PART V
INDUSTRIAL ACTION

Protection of acts in contemplation or furtherance of trade dispute

Action excluded from protection

Requirement of ballot before action by trade union

Requirement on trade union to give notice of industrial action

Industrial action affecting supply of goods or services to an individual

No compulsion to work

Loss of unfair dismissal protection

Criminal offences

Supplementary

PART VI
ADMINISTRATIVE PROVISIONS

ACAS

The certification officer

Central arbitration committee

Supplementary

PART VII
MISCELLANEOUS AND GENERAL

Crown employment, etc

House of lords and house of commons staff

Health service practitioners

Police service

Excluded classes of employment

Offshore employment

Contracting out, &c

Other supplementary provisions

Interpretation

PART 1

An Act to consolidate the enactments relating to collective labour relations, that is to say, to trade unions, employers' associations, industrial relations and industrial action

[16 July 1992]

NOTES

This Act consolidates the legislation relating to trade unions and industrial relations. It came into force on 16 October 1992.

The Act is printed in full except for provisions relating to Northern Ireland (ss 294, 301(2), (3), Sch 3, para 12) and repealing and amending provisions (s 300(1), (2), Schs 1, 2), and provisions subsequently repealed. The Act was further and substantially amended by, inter alia, the Trade Union Reform and Employment Rights Act 1993, the Employment Relations Act 1999, the Employment Act 2002, and the Employment Relations Act 2004 (details are given in notes to each section affected). As to the further power to amend this Act, see the Employment Relations Act 2004, s 42(1), (4)(d) at **[1616]**.

Employment Appeal Tribunal: an appeal lies to the Employment Appeal Tribunal on any question of law arising from any decision of, or in any proceedings before, an employment tribunal under or by virtue of this Act; see the Employment Tribunals Act 1996, s 21(1)(d) at **[978]**.

Ballots or elections under this Act: as to the power of the Secretary of State to provide that any ballot or election authorised or required by this Act should be conducted in a specified permissible manner, see the Employment Relations Act 2004, s 54 at **[1617]**.

See *Harvey* M, N, H2.

PART I
TRADE UNIONS

CHAPTER I
INTRODUCTORY

Meaning of "trade union"

1 Meaning of "trade union"

In this Act a "trade union" means an organisation (whether temporary or permanent)—

(a) which consists wholly or mainly of workers of one or more descriptions and whose principal purposes include the regulation of relations between workers of that description or those descriptions and employers or employers' associations; or

(b) which consists wholly or mainly of—

(i) constituent or affiliated organisations which fulfil the conditions in paragraph (a) (or themselves consist wholly or mainly of constituent or affiliated organisations which fulfil those conditions), or

(ii) representatives of such constituent or affiliated organisations,

and whose principal purposes include the regulation of relations between workers and employers or between workers and employers' associations, or the regulation of relations between its constituent or affiliated organisations.

[469]

The list of trade unions

2 The list of trade unions

(1) The Certification Officer shall keep a list of trade unions containing the names of—

(a) the organisations whose names were, immediately before the commencement of this Act, duly entered in the list of trade unions kept by him under section 8 of the Trade Union and Labour Relations Act 1974, and

(b) the names of the organisations entitled to have their names entered in the list in accordance with this Part.

(2) The Certification Officer shall keep copies of the list of trade unions, as for the time being in force, available for public inspection at all reasonable hours free of charge.

(3) A copy of the list shall be included in his annual report.

(4) The fact that the name of an organisation is included in the list of trade unions is evidence (in Scotland, sufficient evidence) that the organisation is a trade union.

(5) On the application of an organisation whose name is included in the list, the Certification Officer shall issue it with a certificate to that effect.

(6) A document purporting to be such a certificate is evidence (in Scotland, sufficient evidence) that the name of the organisation is entered in the list.

[470]

NOTES

Trade Union and Labour Relations Act 1974, s 8: repealed by this Act.

3 Application to have name entered on list

(1) An organisation of workers, whenever formed, whose name is not entered in the list of trade unions may apply to the Certification Officer to have its name entered in the list.

(2) The application shall be made in such form and manner as the Certification Officer may require and shall be accompanied by—

(a) a copy of the rules of the organisation,

(b) a list of its officers,

(c) the address of its head or main office, and

(d) the name under which it is or is to be known,

and by the prescribed fee.

(3) If the Certification Officer is satisfied—

(a) that the organisation is a trade union,

(b) that subsection (2) has been complied with, and

(c) that entry of the name in the list is not prohibited by subsection (4),

he shall enter the name of the organisation in the list of trade unions.

(4) The Certification Officer shall not enter the name of an organisation in the list of trade unions if the name is the same as that under which another organisation—

(a) was on 30th September 1971 registered as a trade union under the Trade Union Acts 1871 to 1964,

(b) was at any time registered as a trade union or employers' association under the Industrial Relations Act 1971, or

(c) is for the time being entered in the list of trade unions or in the list of employers' associations kept under Part II of this Act,

or if the name is one so nearly resembling any such name as to be likely to deceive the public.

[471]

NOTES

Trade Union Acts 1871 to 1964: the Acts which were cited together under this collective title were: the Trade Union Act 1871 (repealed); the Trade Union Act Amendment Act 1876 (repealed); the Trade Disputes Act 1906 (repealed); the Trade Union Act 1913 (repealed, with a saving, by this Act); the Trade Union (Amalgamation) Act 1917 (repealed); the Trade Disputes and Trade Unions Act 1927 (repealed); the Societies (Miscellaneous Provisions) Act 1940, s 6 (repealed); and the Trade Union (Amalgamations, etc) Act 1964 (repealed by this Act).

Industrial Relations Act 1971: repealed by the Trade Union and Labour Relations Act 1974, ss 1, 25(3), Sch 5.

Prescribed fee: the current fee is £150 (see the Certification Officer (Amendment of Fees) Regulations 2005, SI 2005/713, reg 5).

4 Removal of name from the list

(1) If it appears to the Certification Officer, on application made to him or otherwise, that an organisation whose name is entered in the list of trade unions is not a trade union, he may remove its name from the list.

(2) He shall not do so without giving the organisation notice of his intention and considering any representations made to him by the organisation within such period (of not less than 28 days beginning with the date of the notice) as may be specified in the notice.

(3) The Certification Officer shall remove the name of an organisation from the list of trade unions if—

(a) he is requested by the organisation to do so, or
(b) he is satisfied that the organisation has ceased to exist.

[472]

Certification as independent trade union

5 Meaning of "independent trade union"

In this Act an "independent trade union" means a trade union which—

(a) is not under the domination or control of an employer or group of employers or of one or more employers' associations, and
(b) is not liable to interference by an employer or any such group or association (arising out of the provision of financial or material support or by any other means whatsoever) tending towards such control;

and references to "independence", in relation to a trade union, shall be construed accordingly.

[473]

6 Application for certificate of independence

(1) A trade union whose name is entered on the list of trade unions may apply to the Certification Officer for a certificate that it is independent.

The application shall be made in such form and manner as the Certification Officer may require and shall be accompanied by the prescribed fee.

(2) The Certification Officer shall maintain a record showing details of all applications made to him under this section and shall keep it available for public inspection (free of charge) at all reasonable hours.

(3) If an application is made by a trade union whose name is not entered on the list of trade unions, the Certification Officer shall refuse a certificate of independence and shall enter that refusal on the record.

(4) In any other case, he shall not come to a decision on the application before the end of the period of one month after it has been entered on the record; and before coming to his decision he shall make such enquiries as he thinks fit and shall take into account any relevant information submitted to him by any person.

(5) He shall then decide whether the applicant trade union is independent and shall enter his decision and the date of his decision on the record.

(6) If he decides that the trade union is independent he shall issue a certificate accordingly; and if he decides that it is not, he shall give reasons for his decision.

[474]

NOTES

Prescribed fee: the current fee is £4,066 (see the Certification Officer (Amendment of Fees) Regulations 2005, SI 2005/713, reg 7).

7 Withdrawal or cancellation of certificate

(1) The Certification Officer may withdraw a trade union's certificate of independence if he is of the opinion that the union is no longer independent.

(2) Where he proposes to do so he shall notify the trade union and enter notice of the proposal in the record.

(3) He shall not come to a decision on the proposal before the end of the period of one month after notice of it was entered on the record; and before coming to his decision he shall make such enquiries as he thinks fit and shall take into account any relevant information submitted to him by any person.

(4) He shall then decide whether the trade union is independent and shall enter his decision and the date of his decision on the record.

(5) He shall confirm or withdraw the certificate accordingly; and if he decides to withdraw it, he shall give reasons for his decision.

(6) Where the name of an organisation is removed from the list of trade unions, the Certification Officer shall cancel any certificate of independence in force in respect of that organisation by entering on the record the fact that the organisation's name has been removed from that list and that the certificate is accordingly cancelled.

[475]

8 Conclusive effect of Certification Officer's decision

(1) A certificate of independence which is in force is conclusive evidence for all purposes that a trade union is independent; and a refusal, withdrawal or cancellation of a certificate of independence, entered on the record, is conclusive evidence for all purposes that a trade union is not independent.

(2) A document purporting to be a certificate of independence and to be signed by the Certification Officer, or by a person authorised to act on his behalf, shall be taken to be such a certificate unless the contrary is proved.

(3) A document purporting to be a certified copy of an entry on the record and to be signed by the Certification Officer, or by a person authorised to act on his behalf, shall be taken to be a true copy of such an entry unless the contrary is proved.

(4) If in any proceedings before a court, the Employment Appeal Tribunal, the Central Arbitration Committee, ACAS or an [employment tribunal] a question arises whether a trade union is independent and there is no certificate of independence in force and no refusal, withdrawal or cancellation of a certificate recorded in relation to that trade union—

(a) that question shall not be decided in those proceedings, and

(b) the proceedings shall instead be stayed or sisted until a certificate of independence has been issued or refused by the Certification Officer.

(5) The body before whom the proceedings are stayed or sisted may refer the question of the independence of the trade union to the Certificate Officer who shall proceed in accordance with section 6 as on an application by that trade union.

[476]

NOTES

Sub-s (4): words in square brackets substituted by the Employment Rights (Dispute Resolution) Act 1998, s 1(2)(a).

Supplementary

9 Appeal against decision of Certification Officer

(1) An organisation aggrieved by the refusal of the Certification Officer to enter its name in the list of trade unions, or by a decision of his to remove its name from the list, may appeal to the Employment Appeal Tribunal [on any appealable question].

(2) A trade union aggrieved by the refusal of the Certification Officer to issue it with a certificate of independence, or by a decision of his to withdraw its certificate, may appeal to the Employment Appeal Tribunal [on any appealable question].

(3) …

(4) [For the purposes of this section, an appealable question is any question of law] arising in the proceedings before, or arising from the decision of, the Certification Officer.

[477]

NOTES

Sub-ss (1), (2): words in square brackets added by the Employment Relations Act 2004, s 51(1)(a), as from 6 April 2005, except in relation to any refusal or decision of the Certification Officer made before that date (see SI 2005/872, art 19).

Sub-s (3): repealed by the Employment Relations Act 2004, ss 51(1)(b), 57(2), Sch 2, as from 6 April 2005 (subject to the same exception in SI 2005/872, art 19 as noted above).

Sub-s (4): words in square brackets substituted by the Employment Relations Act 2004, s 51(1)(c), as from 6 April 2005 (subject to the same exception in SI 2005/872, art 19 as noted above).

CHAPTER II
STATUS AND PROPERTY OF TRADE UNIONS

General

10 Quasi-corporate status of trade unions

(1) A trade union is not a body corporate but—

(a) it is capable of making contracts;

(b) it is capable of suing and being sued in its own name, whether in proceedings relating to property or founded on contract or tort or any other cause of action; and

(c) proceedings for an offence alleged to have been committed by it or on its behalf may be brought against it in its own name.

(2) A trade union shall not be treated as if it were a body corporate except to the extent authorised by the provisions of this Part.

(3) A trade union shall not be registered—

(a) as a company under the Companies Act 1985, or

(b) under the Friendly Societies Act 1974 or the Industrial and Provident Societies Act 1965;

and any such registration of a trade union (whenever effected) is void.

[478]

11 Exclusion of common law rules as to restraint of trade

(1) The purposes of a trade union are not, by reason only that they are in restraint of trade, unlawful so as—

(a) to make any member of the trade union liable to criminal proceedings for conspiracy or otherwise, or

(b) to make any agreement or trust void or voidable.

(2) No rule of a trade union is unlawful or unenforceable by reason only that it is in restraint of trade.

[479]

Property of trade union

12 Property to be vested in trustees

(1) All property belonging to a trade union shall be vested in trustees in trust for it.

(2) A judgment, order or award made in proceedings of any description brought against a trade union is enforceable, by way of execution, diligence, punishment for contempt or otherwise, against any property held in trust for it to the same extent and in the same manner as if it were a body corporate.

(3) Subsection (2) has effect subject to section 23 (restriction on enforcement of awards against certain property).

[480]

13 Vesting of property in new trustees

(1) The provisions of this section apply in relation to the appointment or discharge of trustees in whom any property is vested in trust for a trade union whose name is entered in the list of trade unions.

(2) In the following sections as they apply to such trustees references to a deed shall be construed as references to an instrument in writing—

(a) section 39 of the Trustee Act 1925 and section 38 of the Trustee Act (Northern Ireland) 1958 (retirement of trustee without a new appointment), and

(b) section 40 of the Trustee Act 1925 and section 39 of the Trustee Act (Northern Ireland) 1958 (vesting of trust property in new or continuing trustees).

(3) Where such a trustee is appointed or discharged by a resolution taken by or on behalf of the union, the written record of the resolution shall be treated for the purposes of those sections as an instrument in writing appointing or discharging the trustee.

(4) In section 40 of the Trustee Act 1925 and section 39 of the Trustee Act (Northern Ireland) 1958 as they apply to such trustees, paragraphs (a) and (c) of subsection (4) (which exclude certain property from the section) shall be omitted.

[481]

14 Transfer of securities held in trust for trade union

(1) In this section—

"instrument of appointment" means an instrument in writing appointing a new trustee of a trade union whose name is entered in the list of trade unions, and

"instrument of discharge" means an instrument in writing discharging a trustee of such a trade union;

and for the purposes of this section where a trustee is appointed or discharged by a resolution taken by or on behalf of such a trade union, the written record of the resolution shall be treated as an instrument in writing appointing or discharging the trustee.

(2) Where by any enactment or instrument the transfer of securities of any description is required to be effected or recorded by means of entries in a register, then if—

(a) there is produced to the person authorised or required to keep the register a copy of an instrument of appointment or discharge which contains or has attached to it a list identifying the securities of that description held in trust for the union at the date of the appointment or discharge, and

(b) it appears to that person that any of the securities so identified are included in the register kept by him,

he shall make such entries as may be necessary to give effect to the instrument of appointment or discharge.

This subsection has effect notwithstanding anything in any enactment or instrument regulating the keeping of the register.

(3) A document which purports to be a copy of an instrument of appointment or discharge containing or having attached to it such a list, and to be certified in accordance with the following subsection to be a copy of such an instrument, shall be taken to be a copy of such an instrument unless the contrary is proved.

(4) The certificate shall be given by the president and general secretary of the union and, in the case of an instrument to which a list of securities is attached, shall appear both on the instrument and on the list.

(5) Nothing done for the purposes of or in pursuance of this section shall be taken to affect any person with notice of any trust or to impose on any person a duty to inquire into any matter.

(6) In relation to a Scottish trust, references in this section to the appointment and discharge of a trustee shall be construed as including references to, respectively, the assumption and resignation of a trustee; and references to an instrument appointing or discharging a trustee shall be construed accordingly.

[482]

15 Prohibition on use of funds to indemnify unlawful conduct

(1) It is unlawful for property of a trade union to be applied in or towards—

(a) the payment for an individual of a penalty which has been or may be imposed on him for an offence or for contempt of court,

(b) the securing of any such payment, or

(c) the provision of anything for indemnifying an individual in respect of such a penalty.

(2) Where any property of a trade union is so applied for the benefit of an individual on whom a penalty has been or may be imposed, then—

(a) in the case of a payment, an amount equal to the payment is recoverable by the union from him, and

(b) in any other case, he is liable to account to the union for the value of the property applied.

(3) If a trade union fails to bring or continue proceedings which it is entitled to bring by virtue of subsection (2), a member of the union who claims that the failure is unreasonable may apply to the court on that ground for an order authorising him to bring or continue the proceedings on the union's behalf and at the union's expense.

(4) In this section "penalty", in relation to an offence, includes an order to pay compensation and an order for the forfeiture of any property; and references to the imposition of a penalty for an offence shall be construed accordingly.

(5) The Secretary of State may by order designate offences in relation to which the provisions of this section do not apply.

Any such order shall be made by statutory instrument which shall be subject to annulment in pursuance of a resolution of either House of Parliament.

(6) This section does not affect—

(a) any other enactment, any rule of law or any provision of the rules of a trade union which makes it unlawful for the property of a trade union to be applied in a particular way; or

(b) any other remedy available to a trade union, the trustees of its property or any of its members in respect of an unlawful application of the union's property.

(7) In this section "member", in relation to a trade union consisting wholly or partly of, or of representatives of, constituent or affiliated organisations, includes a member of any of the constituent or affiliated organisations.

[483]

NOTES

Orders: as of 6 April 2008 no Orders had been made under this section.

16 Remedy against trustees for unlawful use of union property

(1) A member of a trade union who claims that the trustees of the union's property—

(a) have so carried out their functions, or are proposing so to carry out their functions, as to cause or permit an unlawful application of the union's property, or

(b) have complied, or are proposing to comply, with an unlawful direction which has been or may be given, or purportedly given, to them under the rules of the union,

may apply to the court for an order under this section.

(2) In a case relating to property which has already been unlawfully applied, or to an unlawful direction that has already been complied with, an application under this section may be made only by a person who was a member of the union at the time when the property was applied or, as the case may be, the direction complied with.

(3) Where the court is satisfied that the claim is well-founded, it shall make such order as it considers appropriate.

The court may in particular—

(a) require the trustees (if necessary, on behalf of the union) to take all such steps as may be specified in the order for protecting or recovering the property of the union;

(b) appoint a receiver of, or in Scotland a judicial factor on, the property of the union;

(c) remove one or more of the trustees.

(4) Where the court makes an order under this section in a case in which—

(a) property of the union has been applied in contravention of an order of any court, or in compliance with a direction given in contravention of such an order, or

(b) the trustees were proposing to apply property in contravention of such an order or to comply with any such direction,

the court shall by its order remove all the trustees except any trustee who satisfies the court that there is a good reason for allowing him to remain a trustee.

(5) Without prejudice to any other power of the court, the court may on an application for an order under this section grant such interlocutory relief (in Scotland, such interim order) as it considers appropriate.

(6) This section does not affect any other remedy available in respect of a breach of trust by the trustees of a trade union's property.

(7) In this section "member", in relation to a trade union consisting wholly or partly of, or of representatives of, constituent or affiliated organisations, includes a member of any of the constituent or affiliated organisations.

[484]

17 Nomination by members of trade unions

(1) The Secretary of State may make provision by regulations for enabling members of trade unions who are not under 16 years of age to nominate a person or persons to become entitled, on the death of the person making the nomination, to the whole or part of any money payable on his death out of the funds of the trade union.

(2) The regulations may include provision as to the manner in which nominations may be made and as to the manner in which nominations may be varied or revoked.

(3) The regulations may provide that, subject to such exceptions as may be prescribed, no nomination made by a member of a trade union shall be valid if at the date of the nomination the person nominated is an officer or employee of the trade union or is otherwise connected with the trade union in such manner as may be prescribed by the regulations.

(4) The regulations may include such incidental, transitional or supplementary provisions as the Secretary of State may consider appropriate.

(5) They may, in particular, include provision for securing, to such extent and subject to such conditions as may be prescribed in the regulations, that nominations made under the Trade Union Act 1871 Amendment Act 1876 have effect as if made under the regulations and may be varied or revoked accordingly.

(6) Regulations under this section shall be made by statutory instrument which shall be subject to annulment in pursuance of a resolution of either House of Parliament.

[485]

NOTES

Regulations: the Trade Union (Nominations) Regulations 1977, SI 1977/789, have effect as if made under this section by virtue of s 300(3) of, and Sch 3, para 1(2) to, this Act, and the Interpretation Act 1978, s 17(2)(b).

18 Payments out of union funds on death of member

(1) The Secretary of State may make provision by regulations for enabling money payable out of the funds of a trade union on the death of a member, to an amount not exceeding £5,000, to be paid or distributed on his death without letters of administration, probate of any will or confirmation.

(2) The regulations may include such incidental, transitional and supplementary provisions as the Secretary of State may consider appropriate.

(3) Regulations under this section shall be made by statutory instrument which shall be subject to annulment in pursuance of a resolution of either House of Parliament.

(4) The Treasury may by order under section 6(1) of the Administration of Estates (Small Payments) Act 1965 direct that subsection (1) above shall have effect with the substitution for the reference to £5,000 of a reference to such higher amount as may be specified in the order.

[486]

NOTES

Regulations: the Trade Union (Nominations) Regulations 1977, SI 1977/789, have effect as if made under this section by virtue of s 300(3) of, and Sch 3, para 1(2) to, this Act, and the Interpretation Act 1978, s 17(2)(b).

19 Application of certain provisions relating to industrial assurance or friendly societies

[(1) Section 99 of the Friendly Societies Act 1992 (insurance of lives of children under 10) applies to a trade union as to [a friendly society].]

(2) …

(3) Section 52 of the Friendly Societies Act 1974 (charitable subscriptions and contributions to other registered societies) extends to a trade union, or branch of a trade union, as regards contributing to the funds and taking part in the government of a medical society, that is, a society for the purpose of relief in sickness by providing medical attendance and medicine.

A trade union, or branch of a trade union, shall not withdraw from contributing to the funds of such a society except on three months' notice to the society and on payment of all contributions accrued or accruing due to the date of the expiry of the notice.

[(4) …]

[487]

NOTES

Sub-s (1): substituted by the Friendly Societies Act 1992 (Transitional and Consequential Provisions) Regulations 1993, SI 1993/3084, reg 7; words in square brackets substituted by the Financial Services and Markets Act 2000 (Consequential Amendments and Repeals) Order 2001, SI 2001/3649, art 332.

Sub-s (2): repealed by SI 1993/3084, reg 8.

Sub-s (4): added by the Financial Services and Markets Act 2000 (Consequential Amendments and Savings) (Industrial Assurance) Order 2001, SI 2001/3647, art 5, Sch 3, Pt I, para 14; repealed by the Employment Relations Act 2004, s 57, Sch 1, para 3, Sch 2, as from 6 April 2005.

Liability of trade unions in proceedings in tort

20 Liability of trade union in certain proceedings in tort

(1) Where proceedings in tort are brought against a trade union—

(a) on the ground that an act—

(i) induces another person to break a contract or interferes or induces another person to interfere with its performance, or

(ii) consists in threatening that a contract (whether one to which the union is a party or not) will be broken or its performance interfered with, or that the union will induce another person to break a contract or interfere with its performance, or

(b) in respect of an agreement or combination by two or more persons to do or to procure the doing of an act which, if it were done without any such agreement or combination, would be actionable in tort on such a ground,

then, for the purpose of determining in those proceedings whether the union is liable in respect of the act in question, that act shall be taken to have been done by the union if, but only if, it is to be taken to have been authorised or endorsed by the trade union in accordance with the following provisions.

(2) An act shall be taken to have been authorised or endorsed by a trade union if it was done, or was authorised or endorsed—

(a) by any person empowered by the rules to do, authorise or endorse acts of the kind in question, or

(b) by the principal executive committee or the president or general secretary, or

(c) by any other committee of the union or any other official of the union (whether employed by it or not).

(3) For the purposes of paragraph (c) of subsection (2)—

(a) any group of persons constituted in accordance with the rules of the union is a committee of the union; and

(b) an act shall be taken to have been done, authorised or endorsed by an official if it was done, authorised or endorsed by, or by any member of, any group of persons of which he was at the material time a member, the purposes of which included organising or co-ordinating industrial action.

(4) The provisions of paragraphs (b) and (c) of subsection (2) apply notwithstanding anything in the rules of the union, or in any contract or rule of law, but subject to the provisions of section 21 (repudiation by union of certain acts).

(5) Where for the purposes of any proceedings an act is by virtue of this section taken to have been done by a trade union, nothing in this section shall affect the liability of any other person, in those or any other proceedings, in respect of that act.

(6) In proceedings arising out of an act which is by virtue of this section taken to have been done by a trade union, the power of the court to grant an injunction or interdict includes power to require the union to take such steps as the court considers appropriate for ensuring—

(a) that there is no, or no further, inducement of persons to take part or to continue to take part in industrial action, and

(b) that no person engages in any conduct after the granting of the injunction or interdict by virtue of having been induced before it was granted to take part or to continue to take part in industrial action.

The provisions of subsections (2) to (4) above apply in relation to proceedings for failure to comply with any such injunction or interdict as they apply in relation to the original proceedings.

(7) In this section "rules", in relation to a trade union, means the written rules of the union and any other written provision forming part of the contract between a member and the other members.

[488]

21 Repudiation by union of certain acts

(1) An act shall not be taken to have been authorised or endorsed by a trade union by virtue only of paragraph (c) of section 20(2) if it was repudiated by the executive, president or general secretary as soon as reasonably practicable after coming to the knowledge of any of them.

(2) Where an act is repudiated—

(a) written notice of the repudiation must be given to the committee or official in question, without delay, and

(b) the union must do its best to give individual written notice of the fact and date of repudiation, without delay—

 (i) to every member of the union who the union has reason to believe is taking part, or might otherwise take part, in industrial action as a result of the act, and

 (ii) to the employer of every such member.

(3) The notice given to members in accordance with paragraph (b)(i) of subsection (2) must contain the following statement—

"Your union has repudiated the call (or calls) for industrial action to which this notice relates and will give no support to unofficial industrial action taken in response to it (or them). If you are dismissed while taking unofficial industrial action, you will have no right to complain of unfair dismissal."

(4) If subsection (2) or (3) is not complied with, the repudiation shall be treated as ineffective.

(5) An act shall not be treated as repudiated if at any time after the union concerned purported to repudiate it the executive, president or general secretary has behaved in a manner which is inconsistent with the purported repudiation.

(6) The executive, president or general secretary shall be treated as so behaving if, on a request made to any of them within [three months] of the purported repudiation by a person who—

(a) is a party to a commercial contract whose performance has been or may be interfered with as a result of the act in question, and

(b) has not been given written notice by the union of the repudiation,

it is not forthwith confirmed in writing that the act has been repudiated.

(7) In this section "commercial contract" means any contract other than—
(a) a contract of employment, or
(b) any other contract under which a person agrees personally to do work or perform services for another.

[489]

NOTES

Sub-s (6): words in square brackets substituted by the Trade Union Reform and Employment Rights Act 1993, s 49(1), Sch 7, para 17.

22 Limit on damages awarded against trade unions in actions in tort

(1) This section applies to any proceedings in tort brought against a trade union, except—
(a) proceedings for personal injury as a result of negligence, nuisance or breach of duty;
(b) proceedings for breach of duty in connection with the ownership, occupation, possession, control or use of property;
(c) proceedings brought by virtue of Part I of the Consumer Protection Act 1987 (product liability).

(2) In any proceedings in tort to which this section applies the amount which may be awarded against the union by way of damages shall not exceed the following limit—

Number of members of union	*Maximum award of damages*
Less than 5,000	£10,000
5,000 or more but less than 25,000	£50,000
25,000 or more but less than 100,000	£125,000
100,000 or more	£250,000

(3) The Secretary of State may by order amend subsection (2) so as to vary any of the sums specified; and the order may make such transitional provision as the Secretary of State considers appropriate.

(4) Any such order shall be made by statutory instrument which shall be subject to annulment in pursuance of a resolution of either House of Parliament.

(5) In this section—
"breach of duty" means breach of a duty imposed by any rule of law or by or under any enactment;
"personal injury" includes any disease and any impairment of a person's physical or mental condition; and
"property" means any property, whether real or personal (or in Scotland, heritable or moveable).

[490]

NOTES

Orders: as of 6 April 2008 no Orders had been made under this section.

Restriction on enforcement against certain property

23 Restriction on enforcement of awards against certain property

(1) Where in any proceedings an amount is awarded by way of damages, costs or expenses—
(a) against a trade union,
(b) against trustees in whom property is vested in trust for a trade union, in their capacity as such (and otherwise than in respect of a breach of trust on their part), or

(c) against members or officials of a trade union on behalf of themselves and all of the members of the union,

no part of that amount is recoverable by enforcement against any protected property.

(2) The following is protected property—

(a) property belonging to the trustees otherwise than in their capacity as such;

(b) property belonging to any member of the union otherwise than jointly or in common with the other members;

(c) property belonging to an official of the union who is neither a member nor a trustee;

(d) property comprised in the union's political fund where that fund—

(i) is subject to rules of the union which prevent property which is or has been comprised in the fund from being used for financing strikes or other industrial action, and

(ii) was so subject at the time when the act in respect of which the proceedings are brought was done;

(e) property comprised in a separate fund maintained in accordance with the rules of the union for the purpose only of providing provident benefits.

(3) For this purpose "provident benefits" includes—

(a) any payment expressly authorised by the rules of the union which is made—

(i) to a member during sickness or incapacity from personal injury or while out of work, or

(ii) to an aged member by way of superannuation, or

(iii) to a member who has met with an accident or has lost his tools by fire or theft;

(b) a payment in discharge or aid of funeral expenses on the death of a member or [the spouse or civil partner] of a member or as provision for the children of a deceased member.

[491]

NOTES

Sub-s (3): words in square brackets in para (b) substituted by the Civil Partnership Act 2004, s 261(1), Sch 27, para 144, as from 5 December 2005.

CHAPTER III
TRADE UNION ADMINISTRATION

Register of members' names and addresses

24 Duty to maintain register of members' names and addresses

(1) A trade union shall compile and maintain a register of the names and addresses of its members, and shall secure, so far as is reasonably practicable, that the entries in the register are accurate and are kept up-to-date.

(2) The register may be kept by means of a computer.

(3) A trade union shall—

(a) allow any member, upon reasonable notice, to ascertain from the register, free of charge and at any reasonable time, whether there is an entry on it relating to him; and

(b) if requested to do so by any member, supply him as soon as reasonably practicable, either free of charge or on payment of a reasonable fee, with a copy of any entry on the register relating to him.

(4) …

(5) For the purposes of this section a member's address means either his home address or another address which he has requested the union in writing to treat as his postal address.

(6) The remedy for failure to comply with the requirements of this section is by way of application under section 25 (to the Certification Officer) or section 26 (to the court).

…

[492]

NOTES

Sub-s (4): repealed by the Trade Union Reform and Employment Rights Act 1993, s 51, Sch 10.

Sub-s (6): words omitted repealed by the Employment Relations Act 1999, ss 29, 44, Sch 6, paras 1, 2, Sch 9(7).

[24A Securing confidentiality of register during ballots

(1) This section applies in relation to a ballot of the members of a trade union on—

(a) an election under Chapter IV for a position to which that Chapter applies,

(b) a political resolution under Chapter VI, and

(c) a resolution to approve an instrument of amalgamation or transfer under Chapter VII.

(2) Where this section applies in relation to a ballot the trade union shall impose the duty of confidentiality in relation to the register of members' names and addresses on the scrutineer appointed by the union for the purposes of the ballot and on any person appointed by the union as the independent person for the purposes of the ballot.

(3) The duty of confidentiality in relation to the register of members' names and addresses is, when imposed on a scrutineer or on an independent person, a duty—

(a) not to disclose any name or address in the register except in permitted circumstances; and

(b) to take all reasonable steps to secure that there is no disclosure of any such name or address by any other person except in permitted circumstances;

and any reference in this Act to "the duty of confidentiality" is a reference to the duty prescribed in this subsection.

(4) The circumstances in which disclosure of a member's name and address is permitted are—

(a) where the member consents;

(b) where it is requested by the Certification Officer for the purposes of the discharge of any of his functions or it is required for the purposes of the discharge of any of the functions of an inspector appointed by him;

(c) where it is required for the purposes of the discharge of any of the functions of the scrutineer or independent person, as the case may be, under the terms of his appointment;

(d) where it is required for the purposes of the investigation of crime or of criminal proceedings.

(5) Any provision of this Part which incorporates the duty of confidentiality as respects the register into the appointment of a scrutineer or an independent person has the effect of imposing that duty on the scrutineer or independent person as a duty owed by him to the trade union.

(6) The remedy for failure to comply with the requirements of this section is by way of application under section 25 (to the Certification Officer) or section 26 (to the court).

...

[493]

NOTES

Inserted by the Trade Union Reform and Employment Rights Act 1993, s 6.

Sub-s (6): words omitted repealed by the Employment Relations Act 1999, ss 29, 44, Sch 6, paras 1, 3, Sch 9(7).

25 Remedy for failure: application to Certification Officer

(1) A member of a trade union who claims that the union has failed to comply with any of the requirements of section 24 [or 24A] (duties with respect to register of members' names and addresses) may apply to the Certification Officer for a declaration to that effect.

(2) On an application being made to him, the Certification Officer shall—

(a) make such enquiries as he thinks fit, and

(b) ... give the applicant and the trade union an opportunity to be heard,

and may make or refuse the declaration asked for.

(3) If he makes a declaration he shall specify in it the provisions with which the trade union has failed to comply.

(4) Where he makes a declaration and is satisfied that steps have been taken by the union with a view to remedying the declared failure, or securing that a failure of the same or any similar kind does not occur in future, or that the union has agreed to take such steps, he shall specify those steps in the declaration.

(5) Whether he makes or refuses a declaration, he shall give reasons for his decision in writing; and the reasons may be accompanied by written observations on any matter arising from, or connected with, the proceedings.

[(5A) Where the Certification Officer makes a declaration he shall also, unless he considers that to do so would be inappropriate, make an enforcement order, that is, an order imposing on the union one or both of the following requirements—

(a) to take such steps to remedy the declared failure, within such period, as may be specified in the order;

(b) to abstain from such acts as may be so specified with a view to securing that a failure of the same or a similar kind does not occur in future.

(5B) Where an enforcement order has been made, any person who is a member of the union and was a member at the time it was made is entitled to enforce obedience to the order as if he had made the application on which the order was made.]

(6) In exercising his functions under this section the Certification Officer shall ensure that, so far as is reasonably practicable, an application made to him is determined within six months of being made.

(7) Where he requests a person to furnish information to him in connection with enquiries made by him under this section, he shall specify the date by which that information is to be furnished and, unless he considers that it would be inappropriate to do so, shall proceed with his determination of the application notwithstanding that the information has not been furnished to him by the specified date.

[(8) The Certification Officer shall not entertain an application for a declaration as respects an alleged failure to comply with the requirements of section 24A in relation to a ballot to which that section applies unless the application is made before the end of the period of one year beginning with the last day on which votes could be cast in the ballot.]

[(9) A declaration made by the Certification Officer under this section may be relied on as if it were a declaration made by the court.

(10) An enforcement order made by the Certification Officer under this section may be enforced in the same way as an order of the court.

(11) The following paragraphs have effect if a person applies under section 26 in relation to an alleged failure—

(a) that person may not apply under this section in relation to that failure;

(b) on an application by a different person under this section in relation to that failure, the Certification Officer shall have due regard to any declaration, order, observations or reasons made or given by the court regarding that failure and brought to the Certification Officer's notice.]

[494]

NOTES

Sub-s (1): words in square brackets inserted by the Trade Union Reform and Employment Rights Act 1993, s 49(2), Sch 8, para 40(a).

Sub-s (2): words omitted repealed by the Employment Relations Act 1999, ss 29, 44, Sch 6, paras 1, 4(1), (2), Sch 9(7).

Sub-ss (5A), (5B), (9)–(11): inserted and added respectively by the Employment Relations Act 1999, s 29, Sch 6, paras 1, 4(1), (3), (4).

Sub-s (8): added by the Trade Union Reform and Employment Rights Act 1993, s 49(2), Sch 8, para 40(b).

26 Remedy for failure: application to court

(1) A member of a trade union who claims that the union has failed to comply with any of the requirements of section 24 [or 24A] (duties with respect to register of members' names and addresses) may apply to the court for a declaration to that effect.

(2) …

(3) If the court makes a declaration it shall specify in it the provisions with which the trade union has failed to comply.

(4) Where the court makes a declaration it shall also, unless it considers that to do so would be inappropriate, make an enforcement order, that is, an order imposing on the union one or both of the following requirements—

(a) to take such steps to remedy the declared failure, within such period, as may be specified in the order;

(b) to abstain from such acts as may be so specified with a view to securing that a failure of the same or a similar kind does not occur in future.

(5) Where an enforcement order has been made, any person who is a member of the union and was a member at the time it was made, is entitled to enforce obedience to the order as if he had made the application on which the order was made.

(6) Without prejudice to any other power of the court, the court may on an application under this section grant such interlocutory relief (in Scotland, such interim order) as it considers appropriate.

[(7) The court shall not entertain an application for a declaration as respects an alleged failure to comply with the requirements of section 24A in relation to a ballot to which that section applies unless the application is made before the end of the period of one year beginning with the last day on which votes could be cast in the ballot.]

[(8) The following paragraphs have effect if a person applies under section 25 in relation to an alleged failure—

(a) that person may not apply under this section in relation to that failure;

(b) on an application by a different person under this section in relation to that failure, the court shall have due regard to any declaration, order, observations or reasons made or given by the Certification Officer regarding that failure and brought to the court's notice.]

[495]

NOTES

Sub-s (1): words in square brackets inserted by the Trade Union Reform and Employment Rights Act 1993, s 49(2), Sch 8, para 41(a).

Sub-s (2): repealed by the Employment Relations Act 1999, ss 29, 44, Sch 6, paras 1, 5(1), (2), Sch 9(7).

Sub-s (7): added by the Trade Union Reform and Employment Rights Act 1993, s 49(2), Sch 8, para 41(b).

Sub-s (8): added by the Employment Relations Act 1999, s 29, Sch 6, paras 1, 5(1), (3).

Duty to supply copy of rules

27 Duty to supply copy of rules

A trade union shall at the request of any person supply him with a copy of its rules either free of charge or on payment of a reasonable charge.

[496]

Accounting records

28 Duty to keep accounting records

(1) A trade union shall—

(a) cause to be kept proper accounting records with respect to its transactions and its assets and liabilities, and

(b) establish and maintain a satisfactory system of control of its accounting records, its cash holdings and all its receipts and remittances.

(2) Proper accounting records shall not be taken to be kept with respect to the matters mentioned in subsection (1)(a) unless there are kept such records as are necessary to give a true and fair view of the state of the affairs of the trade union and to explain its transactions.

[497]

PART 1

29 Duty to keep records available for inspection

(1) A trade union shall keep available for inspection from their creation until the end of the period of six years beginning with the 1st January following the end of the period to which they relate such of the records of the union, or of any branch or section of the union, as are, or purport to be, records required to be kept by the union under section 28.

This does not apply to records relating to periods before 1st January 1988.

(2) In section 30 (right of member to access to accounting records)—

(a) references to a union's accounting records are to any such records as are mentioned in subsection (1) above, and

(b) references to records available for inspection are to records which the union is required by that subsection to keep available for inspection.

(3) The expiry of the period mentioned in subsection (1) above does not affect the duty of a trade union to comply with a request for access made under section 30 before the end of that period.

[498]

30 Right of access to accounting records

(1) A member of a trade union has a right to request access to any accounting records of the union which are available for inspection and relate to periods including a time when he was a member of the union.

In the case of records relating to a branch or section of the union, it is immaterial whether he was a member of that branch or section.

(2) Where such access is requested the union shall—

(a) make arrangements with the member for him to be allowed to inspect the records requested before the end of the period of twenty-eight days beginning with the day the request was made,

(b) allow him and any accountant accompanying him for the purpose to inspect the records at the time and place arranged, and

(c) secure that at the time of the inspection he is allowed to take, or is supplied with, any copies of, or of extracts from, records inspected by him which he requires.

(3) The inspection shall be at a reasonable hour and at the place where the records are normally kept, unless the parties to the arrangements agree otherwise.

(4) An "accountant" means a person who is eligible for appointment as a [statutory auditor under Part 42 of the Companies Act 2006].

(5) The union need not allow the member to be accompanied by an accountant if the accountant fails to enter into such agreement as the union may reasonably require for protecting the confidentiality of the records.

(6) Where a member who makes a request for access to a union's accounting records is informed by the union, before any arrangements are made in pursuance of the request—

(a) of the union's intention to charge for allowing him to inspect the records to which the request relates, for allowing him to take copies of, or extracts from, those records or for supplying any such copies, and

(b) of the principles in accordance with which its charges will be determined,

then, where the union complies with the request, he is liable to pay the union on demand such amount, not exceeding the reasonable administrative expenses incurred by the union in complying with the request, as is determined in accordance with those principles.

(7) In this section "member", in relation to a trade union consisting wholly or partly of, or of representatives of, constituent or affiliated organisations, includes a member of any of the constituent or affiliated organisations.

[499]

NOTES

Sub-s (4): words in square brackets substituted (for the original words "company auditor under section 25 of the Companies Act 1989") by the Companies Act 2006 (Consequential Amendments etc) Order 2008, SI 2008/948, art 3(1)(a), Sch 1, Pt 1, para 1(qq)(i), as from 6 April 2008; for transitional provisions see the note below.

Transitional provisions: the Companies Act 2006 (Consequential Amendments etc) Order 2008, SI 2008/948, art 6(4) provides that where by virtue of any transitional provision a provision of the

Companies Act 2006 has effect only (a) on or after a specified date, or (b) in relation to matters occurring or arising on or after a specified date, then any amendment substituting or inserting a reference to that provision has effect correspondingly. By virtue of transitional provisions contained in Sch 4, Pt 1 to the Companies Act 2006 (Commencement No 5, Transitional Provisions and Savings) Order 2007, SI 2007/3495, Part 42, Chapter 2 of the Companies Act 2006 applies in relation to financial years beginning on or after 6 April 2008. The original reference to the equivalent provision of the Companies Act 1985 therefore has effect in relation to financial years beginning before that date.

---

31 Remedy for failure to comply with request for access

(1) A person who claims that a trade union has failed in any respect to comply with a request made by him under section 30 may apply to the court [or to the Certification Officer].

(2) Where [on an application to it] the court is satisfied that the claim is well-founded, it shall make such order as it considers appropriate for ensuring that [the applicant]—

(a) is allowed to inspect the records requested,

(b) is allowed to be accompanied by an accountant when making the inspection of those records, and

(c) is allowed to take, or is supplied with, such copies of, or of extracts from, the records as he may require.

[(2A) On an application to him the Certification Officer shall—

(a) make such enquiries as he thinks fit, and

(b) give the applicant and the trade union an opportunity to be heard.

(2B) Where the Certification Officer is satisfied that the claim is well-founded he shall make such order as he considers appropriate for ensuring that the applicant—

(a) is allowed to inspect the records requested,

(b) is allowed to be accompanied by an accountant when making the inspection of those records, and

(c) is allowed to take, or is supplied with, such copies of, or of extracts from, the records as he may require.

(2C) In exercising his functions under this section the Certification Officer shall ensure that, so far as is reasonably practicable, an application made to him is determined within six months of being made.]

(3) Without prejudice to any other power of the court, the court may on an application [to it] under this section grant such interlocutory relief (in Scotland, such interim order) as it considers appropriate.

[(4) Where the Certification Officer requests a person to furnish information to him in connection with enquiries made by him under this section, he shall specify the date by which that information is to be furnished and, unless he considers that it would be inappropriate to do so, shall proceed with his determination of the application notwithstanding that the information has not been furnished to him by the specified date.

(5) An order made by the Certification Officer under this section may be enforced in the same way as an order of the court.

(6) If a person applies to the court under this section in relation to an alleged failure he may not apply to the Certification Officer under this section in relation to that failure.

(7) If a person applies to the Certification Officer under this section in relation to an alleged failure he may not apply to the court under this section in relation to that failure.]

[500]

NOTES

Sub-ss (1), (3): words in square brackets inserted by the Employment Relations Act 1999, s 29, Sch 6, paras 1, 6(1), (2), (5).

Sub-s (2): words in first pair of square brackets inserted, and words in second pair of square brackets substituted, by the Employment Relations Act 1999, s 29, Sch 6, paras 1, 6(1), (3).

Sub-ss (2A)–(2C), (4)–(7): inserted and added respectively by the Employment Relations Act 1999, s 29, Sch 6, paras 1, 6(1), (4), (6).

Annual return, accounts and audit

32 Annual return

(1) A trade union shall send to the Certification Officer as respects each calendar year a return relating to its affairs.

(2) The annual return shall be in such form and be signed by such persons as the Certification Officer may require and shall be sent to him before 1st June in the calendar year following that to which it relates.

(3) The annual return shall contain—

(a) the following accounts—

(i) revenue accounts indicating the income and expenditure of the trade union for the period to which the return relates,

(ii) a balance sheet as at the end of that period, and

(iii) such other accounts as the Certification Officer may require,

each of which must give a true and fair view of the matters to which it relates,

[(aa) details of the salary paid to and other benefits provided to or in respect of—

(i) each member of the executive,

(ii) the president, and

(iii) the general secretary,

by the trade union during the period to which the return relates,]

(b) a copy of the report made by the auditor or auditors of the trade union on those accounts and such other documents relating to those accounts and such further particulars as the Certification Officer may require, …

(c) a copy of the rules of the trade union as in force at the end of the period to which the return relates[, and

(d) in the case of a trade union required to maintain a register by section 24, a statement of the number of names on the register as at the end of the period to which the return relates and the number of those names which were not accompanied by an address which is a member's address for the purposes of that section;]

and shall have attached to it a note of all the changes in the officers of the union and of any change in the address of the head or main office of the union during the period to which the return relates.

(4) The Certification Officer may, if in any particular case he considers it appropriate to do so—

(a) direct that the period for which a return is to be sent to him shall be a period other than the calendar year last preceding the date on which the return is sent;

(b) direct that the date before which a return is to be sent to him shall be such date (whether before or after 1st June) as may be specified in the direction.

(5) A trade union shall at the request of any person supply him with a copy of its most recent return either free of charge or on payment of a reasonable charge.

(6) The Certification Officer shall at all reasonable hours keep available for public inspection either free of charge or on payment of a reasonable charge, copies of all annual returns sent to him under this section.

[(7) For the purposes of this section and section 32A "member of the executive" includes any person who, under the rules or practice of the union, may attend and speak at some or all of the meetings of the executive, otherwise than for the purpose of providing the committee with factual information or with technical or professional advice with respect to matters taken into account by the executive in carrying out its functions.]

[501]

NOTES

Sub-s (3): para (aa) inserted, word omitted from para (b) repealed, and para (d) and the word immediately preceding it inserted, by the Trade Union Reform and Employment Rights Act 1993, ss 8, 51, Sch 10.

Sub-s (7): added by the Trade Union Reform and Employment Rights Act 1993, s 49(2), Sch 8, para 42.

[32A Statement to members following annual return

(1) A trade union shall take all reasonable steps to secure that, not later than the end of the period of eight weeks beginning with the day on which the annual return of the union is

sent to the Certification Officer, all the members of the union are provided with the statement required by this section by any of the methods allowed by subsection (2).

(2) Those methods are—

(a) the sending of individual copies of the statement to members; or

(b) any other means (whether by including the statement in a publication of the union or otherwise) which it is the practice of the union to use when information of general interest to all its members needs to be provided to them.

(3) The statement required by this section shall specify—

(a) the total income and expenditure of the trade union for the period to which the return relates,

(b) how much of the income of the union for that period consisted of payments in respect of membership,

(c) the total income and expenditure for that period of any political fund of the union, and

(d) the salary paid to and other benefits provided to or in respect of—

(i) each member of the executive,

(ii) the president, and

(iii) the general secretary,

by the trade union during that period.

(4) The requirement imposed by this section is not satisfied if the statement specifies anything inconsistent with the contents of the return.

(5) The statement—

(a) shall also set out in full the report made by the auditor or auditors of the union on the accounts contained in the return and state the name and address of that auditor or of each of those auditors, and

(b) may include any other matter which the union considers may give a member significant assistance in making an informed judgment about the financial activities of the union in the period to which the return relates.

(6) The statement—

(a) shall also include the following statement—

"A member who is concerned that some irregularity may be occurring, or have occurred, in the conduct of the financial affairs of the union may take steps with a view to investigating further, obtaining clarification and, if necessary, securing regularisation of that conduct.

The member may raise any such concern with such one or more of the following as it seems appropriate to raise it with: the officials of the union, the trustees of the property of the union, the auditor or auditors of the union, the Certification Officer (who is an independent officer appointed by the Secretary of State) and the police.

Where a member believes that the financial affairs of the union have been or are being conducted in breach of the law or in breach of rules of the union and contemplates bringing civil proceedings against the union or responsible officials or trustees, he [should] consider obtaining independent legal advice."; and

(b) may include such other details of the steps which a member may take for the purpose mentioned in the statement set out above as the trade union considers appropriate.

(7) A trade union shall send to the Certification Officer a copy of the statement which is provided to its members in pursuance of this section as soon as is reasonably practicable after it is so provided.

(8) Where the same form of statement is not provided to all the members of a trade union, the union shall send to the Certification Officer in accordance with subsection (7) a copy of each form of statement provided to any of them.

(9) If at any time during the period of two years beginning with the day referred to in subsection (1) any member of the trade union requests a copy of the statement required by this section, the union shall, as soon as practicable, furnish him with such a copy free of charge.]
[502]

NOTES

Inserted by the Trade Union Reform and Employment Rights Act 1993, s 9.

Sub-s (6): word in square brackets substituted by the Employment Relations Act 1999, s 28(3).

33 Duty to appoint auditors

(1) A trade union shall in respect of each accounting period appoint an auditor or auditors to audit the accounts contained in its annual return.

(2) An "accounting period" means any period in relation to which it is required to send a return to the Certification Officer.

[503]

34 Eligibility for appointment as auditor

(1) A person is not qualified to be the auditor or one of the auditors of a trade union unless he is eligible for appointment as a [statutory auditor under Part 42 of the Companies Act 2006].

(2) Two or more persons who are not so qualified may act as auditors of a trade union in respect of an accounting period if—

- (a) the receipts and payments in respect of the union's last preceding accounting period did not in the aggregate exceed £5,000,
- (b) the number of its members at the end of that period did not exceed 500, and
- (c) the value of its assets at the end of that period did not in the aggregate exceed £5,000.

(3) Where by virtue of subsection (2) persons who are not qualified as mentioned in subsection (1) act as auditors of a trade union in respect of an accounting period, the Certification Officer may (during that period or after it comes to an end) direct the union to appoint a person who is so qualified to audit its accounts for that period.

(4) The Secretary of State may by regulations—

- (a) substitute for any sum or number specified in subsection (2) such sum or number as may be specified in the regulations; and
- (b) prescribe what receipts and payments are to be taken into account for the purposes of that subsection.

Any such regulations shall be made by statutory instrument which shall be subject to annulment in pursuance of a resolution of either House of Parliament.

(5) None of the following shall act as auditor of a trade union—

- (a) an officer or employee of the trade union or of any of its branches or sections;
- (b) a person who is a partner of, or in the employment of, or who employs, such an officer or employee;
- (c) …

…

[504]

NOTES

Sub-s (1): words in square brackets substituted (for the original words "company auditor under section 25 of the Companies Act 1989") by the Companies Act 2006 (Consequential Amendments etc) Order 2008, SI 2008/948, art 3(1)(a), Sch 1, Pt 1, para 1(qq)(ii), as from 6 April 2008 (for transitional provisions see the note to s 30 at **[499]**).

Sub-s (5): para (c) repealed by the Employment Relations Act 2004, s 53(1), 57(2), Sch 2, as from 6 April 2005; final words omitted repealed by the Trade Union Reform and Employment Rights Act 1993, ss 49(1), 51, Sch 7, para 18, Sch 10.

Regulations: as of 6 April 2008 no Regulations had been made under sub-s (4).

35 Appointment and removal of auditors

(1) The rules of every trade union shall contain provision for the appointment and removal of auditors.

But the following provisions have effect notwithstanding anything in the rules.

(2) An auditor of a trade union shall not be removed from office except by resolution passed at a general meeting of its members or of delegates of its members.

(3) An auditor duly appointed to audit the accounts of a trade union shall be re-appointed as auditor for the following accounting period, unless—

(a) a resolution has been passed at a general meeting of the trade union appointing somebody instead of him or providing expressly that he shall not be re-appointed, or
(b) he has given notice to the trade union in writing of his unwillingness to be re-appointed, or
(c) he is ineligible for re-appointment, or
(d) he has ceased to act as auditor by reason of incapacity.

(4) Where notice has been given of an intended resolution to appoint somebody in place of a retiring auditor but the resolution cannot be proceeded with at the meeting because of the death or incapacity of that person, or because he is ineligible for the appointment, the retiring auditor need not automatically be re-appointed.

(5) The references above to a person being ineligible for appointment as auditor of a trade union are to his not being qualified for the appointment in accordance with [subsections (1) to (4)] of section 34 or being precluded by [subsection (5)] of that section from acting as its auditor.

(6) The Secretary of State may make provision by regulations as to the procedure to be followed when it is intended to move a resolution—

(a) appointing another auditor in place of a retiring auditor, or
(b) providing expressly that a retiring auditor shall not be reappointed,

and as to the rights of auditors and members of the trade union in relation to such a motion.

Any such regulations shall be made by statutory instrument which shall be subject to annulment in pursuance of a resolution of either House of Parliament.

(7) Where regulations under subsection (6)—

(a) require copies of any representations made by a retiring auditor to be sent out, or
(b) require any such representations to be read out at a meeting,

the court, on the application of the trade union or of any other person, may dispense with the requirement if satisfied that the rights conferred on the retiring auditor by the regulations are being abused to secure needless publicity for defamatory matter.

(8) On such an application the court may order the costs or expenses of the trade union to be paid, in whole or in part, by the retiring auditor, whether he is a party to the application or not.

[505]

NOTES

Sub-s (5): words in square brackets substituted by the Trade Union Reform and Employment Rights Act 1993, s 49(1), Sch 7, para 19.

Regulations: as of 6 April 2008 no Regulations had been made under this section.

36 Auditor's report

(1) The auditor or auditors of a trade union shall make a report to it on the accounts audited by him or them and contained in its annual return.

[(1A) The report shall state the names of, and be signed by, the auditor or auditors.]

(2) The report shall state whether, in the opinion of the auditor or auditors, the accounts give a true and fair view of the matters to which they relate.

(3) It is the duty of the auditor or auditors in preparing their report to carry out such investigations as will enable them to form an opinion as to—

(a) whether the trade union has kept proper accounting records in accordance with the requirements of section 28,

(b) whether it has maintained a satisfactory system of control over its transactions in accordance with the requirements of that section, and

(c) whether the accounts to which the report relates agree with the accounting records.

(4) If in the opinion of the auditor or auditors the trade union has failed to comply with section 28, or if the accounts do not agree with the accounting records, the auditor or auditors shall state that fact in the report.

[(5) Any reference in this section to signature by an auditor is, where the office of auditor is held by a body corporate or partnership, to signature in the name of the body corporate or partnership by an individual authorised to sign on its behalf.]

[506]

NOTES

Sub-ss (1A), (5): inserted and added respectively by the Employment Relations Act 2004, s 53(2), (3), as from 6 April 2005.

37 Rights of auditors

(1) Every auditor of a trade union—

(a) has a right of access at all times to its accounting records and to all other documents relating to its affairs, and

(b) is entitled to require from its officers, or the officers of any of its branches or sections, such information and explanations as he thinks necessary for the performance of his duties as auditor.

(2) If an auditor fails to obtain all the information and explanations which, to the best of his knowledge and belief, are necessary for the purposes of an audit, he shall state that fact in his report.

(3) Every auditor of a trade union is entitled—

(a) to attend any general meeting of its members, or of delegates of its members, and to receive all notices of and other communications relating to any general meeting which any such member or delegate is entitled to receive, and

(b) to be heard at any meeting which he attends on any part of the business of the meeting which concerns him as auditor.

[(4) In the case of an auditor which is a body corporate or partnership, its right to attend or be heard at a meeting is exercisable by an individual authorised by it to act as its representative at the meeting.]

[507]

NOTES

Sub-s (4): added by the Employment Relations Act 2004, s 53(4), as from 6 April 2005.

[Investigation of financial affairs

37A Power of Certification Officer to require production of documents etc

(1) The Certification Officer may at any time, if he thinks there is good reason to do so, give directions to a trade union, or a branch or section of a trade union, requiring it to produce such relevant documents as may be specified in the directions; and the documents shall be produced at such time and place as may be so specified.

(2) The Certification Officer may at any time, if he thinks there is good reason to do so, authorise a member of his staff or any other person, on producing (if so required) evidence of his authority, to require a trade union, or a branch or section of a trade union, to produce forthwith to the member of staff or other person such relevant documents as the member of staff or other person may specify.

(3) Where the Certification Officer, or a member of his staff or any other person, has power to require the production of documents by virtue of subsection (1) or (2), the Certification Officer, member of staff or other person has the like power to require production of those documents from any person who appears to the Certification Officer, member of staff or other person to be in possession of them.

(4) Where such a person claims a lien on documents produced by him, the production is without prejudice to the lien.

(5) The power under this section to require the production of documents includes power—

(a) if the documents are produced—
  (i) to take copies of them or extracts from them, and
  (ii) to require the person by whom they are produced, or any person who is or has been an official or agent of the trade union, to provide an explanation of any of them; and
(b) if the documents are not produced, to require the person who was required to produce them to state, to the best of his knowledge and belief, where they are.

(6) In subsections (1) and (2) "relevant documents", in relation to a trade union or a branch or section of a trade union, means accounting documents, and documents of any other description, which may be relevant in considering the financial affairs of the trade union.

(7) A person shall not be excused from providing an explanation or making a statement in compliance with a requirement imposed under subsection (5) on the ground that to do so would tend to expose him to proceedings for an offence; but an explanation so provided or statement so made may only be used in evidence against the person by whom it is made or provided—
(a) on a prosecution for an offence under section 45(9) (false explanations and statements), or
(b) on a prosecution for some other offence where in giving evidence the person makes a statement inconsistent with it.]

[508]

NOTES

Inserted, together with the preceding heading, and ss 37B–37E, by the Trade Union Reform and Employment Rights Act 1993, s 10.

[37B Investigations by inspectors

(1) The Certification Officer may appoint one or more members of his staff or other persons as an inspector or inspectors to investigate the financial affairs of a trade union and to report on them in such manner as he may direct.

(2) The Certification Officer may only make such an appointment if it appears to him that there are circumstances suggesting—
(a) that the financial affairs of the trade union are being or have been conducted for a fraudulent or unlawful purpose,
(b) that persons concerned with the management of those financial affairs have, in connection with that management, been guilty of fraud, misfeasance or other misconduct,
(c) that the trade union has failed to comply with any duty imposed on it by this Act in relation to its financial affairs, or
(d) that a rule of the union relating to its financial affairs has not been complied with.

(3) Where an inspector is, or inspectors are, appointed under this section it is the duty of all persons who are or have been officials or agents of the trade union—
(a) to produce to the inspector or inspectors all relevant documents which are in their possession,
(b) to attend before the inspector or inspectors when required to do so, and
(c) otherwise to give the inspector or inspectors all assistance in connection with the investigation which they are reasonably able to give.

(4) Where any person (whether or not within subsection (3)) appears to the inspector or inspectors to be in possession of information relating to a matter which he considers, or they consider, to be relevant to the investigation, the inspector or inspectors may require him—
(a) to produce to the inspector or inspectors any relevant documents relating to that matter,
(b) to attend before the inspector or inspectors, and
(c) otherwise to give the inspector or inspectors all assistance in connection with the investigation which he is reasonably able to give;

and it is the duty of the person to comply with the requirement.

(5) In subsections (3) and (4) "relevant documents", in relation to an investigation of the financial affairs of a trade union, means accounting documents, and documents of any other description, which may be relevant to the investigation.

(6) A person shall not be excused from providing an explanation or making a statement in compliance with subsection (3) or a requirement imposed under subsection (4) on the ground that to do so would tend to expose him to proceedings for an offence; but an explanation so provided or statement so made may only be used in evidence against the person by whom it is provided or made—

(a) on a prosecution for an offence under section 45(9) (false explanations and statements), or

(b) on a prosecution for some other offence where in giving evidence the person makes a statement inconsistent with it.]

[509]

NOTES

Inserted as noted to s 37A at **[508]**.

[37C Inspectors' reports etc

(1) An inspector or inspectors appointed under section 37B—

(a) may, and if so directed by the Certification Officer shall, make interim reports, and

(b) on the conclusion of their investigation shall make a final report,

to the Certification Officer.

(2) Any report under subsection (1) shall be written or printed, as the Certification Officer directs.

(3) An inspector or inspectors appointed under section 37B may at any time, and if so directed by the Certification Officer shall, inform the Certification Officer of any matters coming to his or their knowledge as a result of the investigation.

(4) The Certification Officer may direct an inspector or inspectors appointed under section 37B to take no further steps in the investigation, or to take only such further steps as are specified in the direction, if—

(a) it appears to the Certification Officer that matters have come to light in the course of the investigation which suggest that a criminal offence has been committed and those matters have been referred to the appropriate prosecuting authority, or

(b) it appears to the Certification Officer appropriate to do so in any other circumstances.

(5) Where an investigation is the subject of a direction under subsection (4), the inspector or inspectors shall make a final report to the Certification Officer only where the Certification Officer directs him or them to do so at the time of the direction under that subsection or subsequently.

(6) The Certification Officer shall publish a final report made to him under this section.

(7) The Certification Officer shall furnish a copy of such a report free of charge—

(a) to the trade union which is the subject of the report,

(b) to any auditor of that trade union or of any branch or section of the union, if he requests a copy before the end of the period of three years beginning with the day on which the report is published, and

(c) to any member of the trade union if—

(i) he has complained to the Certification Officer that there are circumstances suggesting any of the states of affairs specified in section 37B(2)(a) to (d),

(ii) the Certification Officer considers that the report contains findings which are relevant to the complaint, and

(iii) the member requests a copy before the end of the period of three years beginning with the day on which the report is published.

(8) A copy of any report under this section, certified by the Certification Officer to be a true copy, is admissible in any legal proceedings as evidence of the opinion of the inspector or inspectors in relation to any matter contained in the report; and a document purporting to be a certificate of the Certification Officer under this subsection shall be received in evidence and be deemed to be such a certificate unless the contrary is proved.]

[510]

NOTES

Inserted as noted to s 37A at **[508]**.

[37D Expenses of investigations

(1) The expenses of an investigation under section 37B shall be defrayed in the first instance by the Certification Officer.

(2) For the purposes of this section there shall be treated as expenses of an investigation, in particular, such reasonable sums as the Certification Officer may determine in respect of general staff costs and overheads.

(3) A person who is convicted on a prosecution instituted as a result of the investigation may in the same proceedings be ordered to pay the expenses of the investigation to such extent as may be specified in the order.]

[511]

NOTES

Inserted as noted to s 37A at **[508]**.

[37E Sections 37A and 37B: supplementary

(1) Where—

(a) a report of the auditor or auditors of a trade union, or a branch or section of a trade union, on the accounts audited by him or them and contained in the annual return of the union, or branch or section—

(i) does not state without qualification that the accounts give a true and fair view of the matters to which they relate, or

(ii) includes a statement in compliance with section 36(4), or

(b) a member of a trade union has complained to the Certification Officer that there are circumstances suggesting any of the states of affairs specified in section 37B(2)(a) to (d),

the Certification Officer shall consider whether it is appropriate for him to exercise any of the powers conferred on him by sections 37A and 37B.

(2) If in a case where a member of a trade union has complained as mentioned in subsection (1)(b) the Certification Officer decides not to exercise any of the powers conferred by those sections he shall, as soon as reasonably practicable after making a decision not to do so, notify the member of his decision and, if he thinks fit, of the reasons for it.

(3) Nothing in section 37A or 37B—

(a) requires or authorises anyone to require the disclosure by a person of information which he would in an action in the High Court or the Court of Session be entitled to refuse to disclose on grounds of legal professional privilege except, if he is a lawyer, the name and address of his client, or

(b) requires or authorises anyone to require the production by a person of a document which he would in such an action be entitled to refuse to produce on such grounds.

(4) Nothing in section 37A or 37B requires or authorises anyone to require the disclosure of information or the production of documents in respect of which the person to whom the requirement would relate owes an obligation of confidence by virtue of carrying on the business of banking unless—

(a) the person to whom the obligation is owed is the trade union, or any branch or section of the union, concerned or a trustee of any fund concerned, or

(b) the person to whom the obligation of confidence is owed consents to the disclosure or production.

(5) In sections 37A and 37B and this section—

(a) references to documents include information recorded in any form, and

(b) in relation to information recorded otherwise than in legible form, references to its production are to the production of a copy of the information in legible form.]

[512]

NOTES

Inserted as noted to s 37A at **[508]**.

Members' superannuation schemes

38 Members' superannuation schemes: separate fund to be maintained

(1) In the following provisions a "members' superannuation scheme" means any scheme or arrangement made by or on behalf of a trade union (including a scheme or arrangement shown in the rules of the union) in so far as it provides—

(a) for benefits to be paid by way of pension (including any widows' or children's pensions or dependants' pensions) to or in respect of members or former members of the trade union, and

(b) for those benefits to be so paid either out of the funds of the union or under an insurance scheme maintained out of those funds.

(2) A trade union shall not maintain a members' superannuation scheme unless it maintains a separate fund for the payment of benefits in accordance with the scheme.

A "separate fund" means a fund separate from the general funds of the trade union.

[513]

39 Examination of proposals for new scheme

(1) A trade union shall not begin to maintain a members' superannuation scheme unless, before the date on which the scheme begins to be maintained—

(a) the proposals for the scheme have been examined by an appropriately qualified actuary, and

(b) a copy of a report made to the trade union by the actuary on the results of his examination of the proposals, signed by the actuary, has been sent to the Certification Officer.

(2) The actuary's report shall state—

(a) whether in his opinion the premium or contribution rates will be adequate,

(b) whether the accounting or funding arrangements are suitable, and

(c) whether in his opinion the fund for the payment of benefits will be adequate.

(3) A copy of the actuary's report shall, on the application of any of the union's members, be supplied to him free of charge.

[514]

40 Periodical re-examination of existing schemes

(1) Where a trade union maintains a members' superannuation scheme, it shall arrange for the scheme to be examined periodically by an appropriately qualified actuary and for a report to be made to it by the actuary on the result of his examination.

(2) The examination shall be of the scheme as it has effect at such date as the trade union may determine, not being more than five years after the date by reference to which the last examination or, as the case may be, the examination of the proposals for the scheme was carried out.

(3) The examination shall include a valuation (as at the date by reference to which the examination is carried out) of the assets comprised in the fund maintained for the payment of benefits and of the liabilities falling to be discharged out of it.

(4) The actuary's report shall state—

(a) whether in his opinion the premium or contribution rates are adequate,

(b) whether the accounting or funding arrangements are suitable, and

(c) whether in his opinion the fund for the payment of benefits is adequate.

(5) A copy of the report, signed by the actuary, shall be sent to the Certification Officer.

(6) The trade union shall make such arrangements as will enable the report to be sent to the Certification Officer within a year of the date by reference to which the examination was carried out.

(7) A copy of the actuary's report shall, on the application of any of the union's members, be supplied to him free of charge.

[515]

41 Powers of the Certification Officer

(1) The Certification Officer may, on the application of a trade union—

(a) exempt a members' superannuation scheme which the union proposes to maintain from the requirements of section 39 (examination of proposals for new scheme), or

(b) exempt a members' superannuation scheme which the union maintains from the requirements of section 40 (periodical re–examination of scheme),

if he is satisfied that, by reason of the small number of members to which the scheme is applicable or for any other special reasons, it is unnecessary for the scheme to be examined in accordance with those provisions.

(2) An exemption may be revoked if it appears to the Certification Officer that the circumstances by reason of which it was granted have ceased to exist.

(3) Where an exemption is revoked under subsection [(2)], the date as at which the next periodical examination is to be carried out under section 40 shall be such as the Certification Officer may direct.

(4) The Certification Officer may in any case direct that section 40 (periodical re-examination of schemes) shall apply to a trade union with the substitution for the reference to five years of a reference to such shorter period as may be specified in the direction.

[516]

NOTES

Sub-s (3): number in square brackets substituted by the Employment Relations Act 2004, s 57(1), Sch 1, para 4, as from 6 April 2005.

42 Meaning of "appropriately qualified actuary"

In sections 39 and 40 an "appropriately qualified actuary" means a person who is either—

(a) a Fellow of the Institute of Actuaries, or

(b) a Fellow of the Faculty of Actuaries,

or is approved by the Certification Officer on the application of the trade union as a person having actuarial knowledge.

[517]

Supplementary

43 Newly-formed trade unions

(1) The following provisions of this Chapter do not apply to a trade union which has been in existence for less than twelve months—

(a) section 27 (duty to supply copy of rules),

(b) sections 32 to 37 (annual return, [statement for members,] accounts and audit), …

[(ba) sections 37A to 37E (investigation of financial affairs), and]

(c) sections 38 to 42 (members' superannuation schemes).

(2) Sections 24 to 26 (register of members' names and addresses) do not apply to a trade union until more than one year has elapsed since its formation (by amalgamation or otherwise).

For this purpose the date of formation of a trade union formed otherwise than by amalgamation shall be taken to be the date on which the first members of the executive of the union are first appointed or elected.

[518]

NOTES

Sub-s (1): words in square brackets in para (b) inserted, word omitted repealed, and para (ba) inserted, by the Trade Union Reform and Employment Rights Act 1993, ss 49(2), 51, Sch 8, para 43, Sch 10.

44 Discharge of duties in case of union having branches or sections

(1) The following provisions apply where a trade union consists of or includes branches or sections.

(2) Any duty falling upon the union in relation to a branch or section under the provisions of—

section 28 (duty to keep accounting records),

[sections 32 and 33 to 37] (annual return, accounts and audit), or
sections 38 to 42 (members' superannuation schemes),

shall be treated as discharged to the extent to which a branch or section discharges it instead of the union.

(3) In sections 29 to 31 (right of member to access to accounting records) references to a branch or section do not include a branch or section which is itself a trade union.

(4) Any duty falling upon a branch or section by reason of its being a trade union under—

section 24 (register of members' names and addresses),
section 28 (duty to keep accounting records),
[sections 32 and 33 to 37] (annual return, accounts and audit), or
sections 38 to 42 (members' superannuation schemes),

shall be treated as discharged to the extent to which the union of which it is a branch or section discharges the duty instead of it.

[(5) Where the duty falling on a trade union under section 32 to send to the Certification Officer a return relating to its affairs is treated as discharged by the union by virtue of subsection (2) or (4) of this section, the duties imposed by section 32A in relation to the return shall be treated as duties of the branch or section of the union, or the trade union of which it is a branch or section, by which that duty is in fact discharged.]

[519]

NOTES

Sub-ss (2), (4): words in square brackets substituted by the Trade Union Reform and Employment Rights Act 1993, s 49(2), Sch 8, para 44(a).

Sub-s (5): added by the Trade Union Reform and Employment Rights Act 1993, s 49(2), Sch 8, para 44(b).

45 Offences

(1) If a trade union refuses or wilfully neglects to perform a duty imposed on it by or under any of the provisions of—

section 27 (duty to supply copy of rules),
sections 28 to 30 (accounting records),
sections 32 to 37 (annual return, [statement for members,] accounts and audit), or
sections 38 to 42 (members' superannuation schemes),

it commits an offence.

(2) The offence shall be deemed to have been also committed by—

(a) every officer of the trade union who is bound by the rules of the union to discharge on its behalf the duty breach of which constitutes the offence, or
(b) if there is no such officer, every member of the general committee of management of the union.

(3) In any proceedings brought against an officer or member by virtue of subsection (2) in respect of a breach of duty, it is a defence for him to prove that he had reasonable cause to believe, and did believe, that some other person who was competent to discharge that duty was authorised to discharge it instead of him and had discharged it or would do so.

(4) A person who wilfully alters or causes to be altered a document which is required for the purposes of any of the provisions mentioned in subsection (1), with intent to falsify the document or to enable a trade union to evade any of those provisions, commits an offence.

[(5) If a person contravenes any duty, or requirement imposed, under section 37A (power of Certification officer to require production of documents etc) or 37B (investigations by inspectors) he commits an offence.

(6) In any proceedings brought against a person in respect of a contravention of a requirement imposed under section 37A(3) or 37B(4) to produce documents it is a defence for him to prove—

(a) that the documents were not in his possession, and
(b) that it was not reasonably practicable for him to comply with the requirement.

(7) If an official or agent of a trade union—

(a) destroys, mutilates or falsifies, or is privy to the destruction, mutilation or falsification of, a document relating to the financial affairs of the trade union, or

(b) makes, or is privy to the making of, a false entry in any such document,

he commits an offence unless he proves that he had no intention to conceal the financial affairs of the trade union or to defeat the law.

(8) If such a person fraudulently—

(a) parts with, alters or deletes anything in any such document, or

(b) is privy to the fraudulent parting with, fraudulent alteration of or fraudulent deletion in, any such document,

he commits an offence.

(9) If a person in purported compliance with a duty, or requirement imposed, under section 37A or 37B to provide an explanation or make a statement—

(a) provides or makes an explanation or statement which he knows to be false in a material particular, or

(b) recklessly provides or makes an explanation or statement which is false in a material particular,

he commits an offence.]

[520]

NOTES

Sub-s (1): words in square brackets inserted by the Trade Union Reform and Employment Rights Act 1993, s 49(2), Sch 8, para 45.

Sub-ss (5)–(9): substituted, for original sub-s (5), by the Trade Union Reform and Employment Rights Act 1993, s 11(1).

[45A Penalties and prosecution time limits

(1) A person guilty of an offence under section 45 is liable on summary conviction—

(a) in the case of an offence under subsection (1) or (5), to a fine not exceeding level 5 on the standard scale;

(b) in the case of an offence under subsection (4), (7), (8) or (9), to imprisonment for a term not exceeding six months or to a fine not exceeding level 5 on the standard scale or to both.

(2) Proceedings for an offence under section 45(1) relating to the duty imposed by section 32 (duty to send annual return to Certification Officer) may be commenced at any time before the end of the period of three years beginning with the date when the offence was committed.

(3) Proceedings for any other offence under section 45(1) may be commenced—

(a) at any time before the end of the period of six months beginning with the date when the offence was committed, or

(b) at any time after the end of that period but before the end of the period of twelve months beginning with the date when evidence sufficient in the opinion of the Certification Officer or, in Scotland, the procurator fiscal, to justify the proceedings came to his knowledge;

but no proceedings may be commenced by virtue of paragraph (b) after the end of the period of three years beginning with the date when the offence was committed.

(4) For the purposes of subsection (3)(b), a certificate signed by or on behalf of the Certification Officer or the procurator fiscal which states the date on which evidence sufficient in his opinion to justify the proceedings came to his knowledge shall be conclusive evidence of that fact.

(5) A certificate stating that matter and purporting to be so signed shall be deemed to be so signed unless the contrary is proved.

(6) For the purposes of this section—

(a) in England and Wales, proceedings are commenced when an information is laid, and

(b) in Scotland, subsection (3) of [section 136 of the Criminal Procedure (Scotland) Act 1995] (date of commencement of proceedings) applies as it applies for the purposes of that section.]

[521]

NOTES

Inserted by the Trade Union Reform and Employment Rights Act 1993, s 11(2).

Sub-s (6): words in square brackets substituted by the Criminal Procedure (Consequential Provisions) (Scotland) Act 1995, s 5, Sch 4, para 85.

PART 1

[45B Duty to secure positions not held by certain offenders

(1) A trade union shall secure that a person does not at any time hold a position in the union to which this section applies if—

(a) within the period of five years immediately preceding that time he has been convicted of an offence under subsection (1) or (5) of section 45, or

(b) within the period of ten years immediately preceding that time he has been convicted of an offence under subsection (4), (7), (8) or (9) of that section.

(2) Subject to subsection (4), the positions to which this section applies are—

(a) member of the executive,

(b) any position by virtue of which a person is a member of the executive,

(c) president, and

(d) general secretary.

(3) For the purposes of subsection (2)(a) "member of the executive" includes any person who, under the rules or practice of the union, may attend and speak at some or all of the meetings of the executive, otherwise than for the purpose of providing the committee with factual information or with technical or professional advice with respect to matters taken into account by the executive in carrying out its functions.

(4) This section does not apply to the position of president or general secretary if the holder of that position—

(a) is not, in respect of that position, either a voting member of the executive or an employee of the union,

(b) holds that position for a period which under the rules of the union cannot end more than thirteen months after he took it up, and

(c) has not held either position at any time in the period of twelve months ending with the day before he took up that position.

(5) In subsection (4)(a) "a voting member of the executive" means a person entitled in his own right to attend meetings of the executive and to vote on matters on which votes are taken by the executive (whether or not he is entitled to attend all such meetings or to vote on all such matters or in all circumstances).]

[522]

NOTES

Inserted, together with s 45C, by the Trade Union Reform and Employment Rights Act 1993, s 12.

[45C Remedies and enforcement

(1) A member of a trade union who claims that the union has failed to comply with the requirement of section 45B may apply to the Certification Officer or to the court for a declaration to that effect.

(2) On an application being made to him, the Certification Officer—

[(aa) shall make such enquiries as he thinks fit,]

(a) shall … give the applicant and the trade union an opportunity to be heard,

(b) shall ensure that, so far as is reasonably practicable, the application is determined within six months of being made,

(c) may make or refuse the declaration asked for, and

(d) shall, whether he makes or refuses the declaration, give reasons for his decision in writing.

(3), (4) …

(5) Where the court makes a declaration it shall also, unless it considers that it would be inappropriate, make an order imposing on the trade union a requirement to take within such period as may be specified in the order such steps to remedy the declared failure as may be so specified.

[(5A) Where the Certification Officer makes a declaration he shall also, unless he considers that it would be inappropriate, make an order imposing on the trade union a requirement to take within such period as may be specified in the order such steps to remedy the declared failure as may be so specified.

(5B) The following paragraphs have effect if a person applies to the Certification Officer under this section in relation to an alleged failure—
- (a) that person may not apply to the court under this section in relation to that failure;
- (b) on an application by a different person to the court under this section in relation to that failure, the court shall have due regard to any declaration, order, observations or reasons made or given by the Certification Officer regarding that failure and brought to the court's notice.

(5C) The following paragraphs have effect if a person applies to the court under this section in relation to an alleged failure—
- (a) that person may not apply to the Certification Officer under this section in relation to that failure;
- (b) on an application by a different person to the Certification Officer under this section in relation to that failure, the Certification Officer shall have regard to any declaration, order, observations or reasons made or given by the court regarding that failure and brought to the Certification Officer's notice.]

(6) Where an order has been made [under subsection (5) or (5A)], any person who is a member of the trade union and was a member at the time the order was made is entitled to enforce the order as if he had made the application on which the order was made.

[(7) Where the Certification Officer requests a person to furnish information to him in connection with enquiries made by him under this section, he shall specify the date by which that information is to be furnished and, unless he considers that it would be inappropriate to do so, shall proceed with his determination of the application notwithstanding that the information has not been furnished to him by the specified date.

(8) A declaration made by the Certification Officer under this section may be relied on as if it were a declaration made by the court.

(9) An order made by the Certification Officer under this section may be enforced in the same way as an order of the court.]]

[523]

NOTES

Inserted as noted to s 45B at **[522]**.

Sub-s (2): para (aa) inserted, and words omitted from para (a) repealed, by the Employment Relations Act 1999, ss 29, 44, Sch 6, paras 1, 7(1)–(3), Sch 9(7).

Sub-ss (3), (4): repealed by the Employment Relations Act 1999, ss 29, 44, Sch 6, paras 1, 7(1), (4), Sch 9(7).

Sub-ss (5A)–(5C), (7)–(9): inserted and added respectively by the Employment Relations Act 1999, s 29, Sch 6, paras 1, 7(1), (5), (7).

Sub-s (6): words in square brackets inserted by the Employment Relations Act 1999, s 29, Sch 6, paras 1, 7(1), (6).

[45D Appeals from Certification Officer

An appeal lies to the Employment Appeal Tribunal on any question of law arising in proceedings before or arising from any decision of the Certification Officer under section 25, 31 or 45C.]

[524]

NOTES

Inserted by the Employment Relations Act 1999, s 29, Sch 6, paras 1, 8.

CHAPTER IV
ELECTIONS FOR CERTAIN POSITIONS

Duty to hold elections

46 Duty to hold elections for certain positions

(1) A trade union shall secure—
- (a) that every person who holds a position in the union to which this Chapter applies does so by virtue of having been elected to it at an election satisfying the requirements of this Chapter, and

(b) that no person continues to hold such a position for more than five years without being re-elected at such an election.

(2) The positions to which this Chapter applies (subject as mentioned below) are—

(a) member of the executive,

(b) any position by virtue of which a person is a member of the executive,

(c) president, and

(d) general secretary;

...

(3) In this Chapter "member of the executive" includes any person who, under the rules or practice of the union, may attend and speak at some or all of the meetings of the executive, otherwise than for the purpose of providing the committee with factual information or with technical or professional advice with respect to matters taken into account by the executive in carrying out its functions.

(4) This Chapter does not apply to the position of president or general secretary if the holder of that position—

(a) is not, in respect of that position, either a voting member of the executive or an employee of the union,

(b) holds that position for a period which under the rules of the union cannot end more than 13 months after he took it up, and

(c) has not held either position at any time in the period of twelve months ending with the day before he took up that position.

[(4A) This Chapter also does not apply to the position of president if—

(a) the holder of that position was elected or appointed to it in accordance with the rules of the union,

(b) at the time of his election or appointment as president he held a position mentioned in paragraph (a), (b) or (d) of subsection (2) by virtue of having been elected to it at a qualifying election,

(c) it is no more than five years since—

(i) he was elected, or re-elected, to the position mentioned in paragraph (b) which he held at the time of his election or appointment as president, or

(ii) he was elected to another position of a kind mentioned in that paragraph at a qualifying election held after his election or appointment as president of the union, and

(d) he has, at all times since his election or appointment as president, held a position mentioned in paragraph (a), (b) or (d) of subsection (2) by virtue of having been elected to it at a qualifying election.]

(5) [In subsection (4)] a "voting member of the executive" means a person entitled in his own right to attend meetings of the executive and to vote on matters on which votes are taken by the executive (whether or not he is entitled to attend all such meetings or to vote on all such matters or in all circumstances).

[(5A) In subsection (4A) "qualifying election" means an election satisfying the requirements of this Chapter.

(5B) The "requirements of this Chapter" referred to in subsections (1) and (5A) are those set out in sections 47 to 52 below.]

(6) The provisions of this Chapter apply notwithstanding anything in the rules or practice of the union; and the terms and conditions on which a person is employed by the union shall be disregarded in so far as they would prevent the union from complying with the provisions of this Chapter.

[525]

NOTES

Sub-s (2): words omitted repealed by the Employment Relations Act 2004, ss 52(1), (2), 57(2), Sch 2, as from 6 April 2005.

Sub-ss (4A), (5A), (5B): inserted by the Employment Relations Act 2004, s 52(1), (3), (5), as from 6 April 2005.

Sub-s (5): words in square brackets inserted by the Employment Relations Act 2004, s 52(1), (4), as from 6 April 2005.

Requirements to be satisfied with respect to elections

47 Candidates

(1) No member of the trade union shall be unreasonably excluded from standing as a candidate.

(2) No candidate shall be required, directly or indirectly, to be a member of a political party.

(3) A member of a trade union shall not be taken to be unreasonably excluded from standing as a candidate if he is excluded on the ground that he belongs to a class of which all the members are excluded by the rules of the union.

But a rule which provides for such a class to be determined by reference to whom the union chooses to exclude shall be disregarded.

[526]

48 Election addresses

(1) The trade union shall—

(a) provide every candidate with an opportunity of preparing an election address in his own words and of submitting it to the union to be distributed to the persons accorded entitlement to vote in the election; and

(b) secure that, so far as reasonably practicable, copies of every election address submitted to it in time are distributed to each of those persons by post along with the voting papers for the election.

(2) The trade union may determine the time by which an election address must be submitted to it for distribution; but the time so determined must not be earlier than the latest time at which a person may become a candidate in the election.

(3) The trade union may provide that election addresses submitted to it for distribution—

(a) must not exceed such length, not being less than one hundred words, as may be determined by the union, and

(b) may, as regards photographs and other matter not in words, incorporate only such matter as the union may determine.

(4) The trade union shall secure that no modification of an election address submitted to it is made by any person in any copy of the address to be distributed except—

(a) at the request or with the consent of the candidate, or

(b) where the modification is necessarily incidental to the method adopted for producing that copy.

(5) The trade union shall secure that the same method of producing copies is applied in the same way to every election address submitted and, so far as reasonably practicable, that no such facility or information as would enable a candidate to gain any benefit from—

(a) the method by which copies of the election addresses are produced, or

(b) the modifications which are necessarily incidental to that method,

is provided to any candidate without being provided equally to all the others.

(6) The trade union shall, so far as reasonably practicable, secure that the same facilities and restrictions with respect to the preparation, submission, length or modification of an election address, and with respect to the incorporation of photographs or other matter not in words, are provided or applied equally to each of the candidates.

(7) The arrangements made by the trade union for the production of the copies to be so distributed must be such as to secure that none of the candidates is required to bear any of the expense of producing the copies.

(8) No-one other than the candidate himself shall incur any civil or criminal liability in respect of the publication of a candidate's election address or of any copy required to be made for the purposes of this section.

[527]

49 Appointment of independent scrutineer

(1) The trade union shall, before the election is held, appoint a qualified independent person ("the scrutineer") to carry out—

(a) the functions in relation to the election which are required under this section to be contained in his appointment; and
(b) such additional functions in relation to the election as may be specified in his appointment.

(2) A person is a qualified independent person in relation to an election if—
(a) he satisfies such conditions as may be specified for the purposes of this section by order of the Secretary of State or is himself so specified; and
(b) the trade union has no grounds for believing either that he will carry out any functions conferred on him in relation to the election otherwise than competently or that his independence in relation to the union, or in relation to the election, might reasonably be called into question.

An order under paragraph (a) shall be made by statutory instrument which shall be subject to annulment in pursuance of a resolution of either House of Parliament.

(3) The scrutineer's appointment shall require him—
(a) to be the person who supervises the production [of the voting papers and (unless he is appointed under section 51A to undertake the distribution of the voting papers) their distribution] and to whom the voting papers are returned by those voting;
[(aa) to—
(i) inspect the register of names and addresses of the members of the trade union, or
(ii) examine the copy of the register as at the relevant date which is supplied to him in accordance with subsection (5A)(a),

whenever it appears to him appropriate to do so and, in particular, when the conditions specified in subsection (3A) are satisfied;]
(b) to take such steps as appear to him to be appropriate for the purpose of enabling him to make his report (see section 52);
(c) to make his report to the trade union as soon as reasonably practicable after the last date for the return of voting papers; and
(d) to retain custody of all voting papers returned for the purposes of the election [and the copy of the register supplied to him in accordance with subsection (5A)(a)]—
(i) until the end of the period of one year beginning with the announcement by the union of the result of the election; and
(ii) if within that period an application is made under section 54 (complaint of failure to comply with election requirements), until the Certification Officer or the court authorises him to dispose of the papers [or copy].

[(3A) The conditions referred to in subsection (3)(aa) are—
(a) that a request that the scrutineer inspect the register or examine the copy is made to him during the appropriate period by a member of the trade union or candidate who suspects that the register is not, or at the relevant date was not, accurate and up-to-date, and
(b) that the scrutineer does not consider that the suspicion of the member or candidate is ill-founded.

(3B) In subsection (3A) "the appropriate period" means the period—
(a) beginning with the first day on which a person may become a candidate in the election or, if later, the day on which the scrutineer is appointed, and
(b) ending with the day before the day on which the scrutineer makes his report to the trade union.

(3C) The duty of confidentiality as respects the register is incorporated in the scrutineer's appointment.]

(4) The trade union shall ensure that nothing in the terms of the scrutineer's appointment (including any additional functions specified in the appointment) is such as to make it reasonable for any person to call the scrutineer's independence in relation to the union into question.

(5) The trade union shall, before the scrutineer begins to carry out his functions, either—
(a) send a notice stating the name of the scrutineer to every member of the union to whom it is reasonably practicable to send such a notice, or
(b) take all such other steps for notifying members of the name of the scrutineer as it is the practice of the union to take when matters of general interest to all its members need to be brought to their attention.

[(5A) The trade union shall—

(a) supply to the scrutineer as soon as is reasonably practicable after the relevant date a copy of the register of names and addresses of its members as at that date, and

(b) comply with any request made by the scrutineer to inspect the register.

(5B) Where the register is kept by means of a computer the duty imposed on the trade union by subsection (5A)(a) is either to supply a legible printed copy or (if the scrutineer prefers) to supply a copy of the computer data and allow the scrutineer use of the computer to read it at any time during the period when he is required to retain custody of the copy.]

(6) The trade union shall ensure that the scrutineer duly carries out his functions and that there is no interference with his carrying out of those functions which would make it reasonable for any person to call the scrutineer's independence in relation to the union into question.

(7) The trade union shall comply with all reasonable requests made by the scrutineer for the purposes of, or in connection with, the carrying out of his functions.

[(8) In this section "the relevant date" means—

(a) where the trade union has rules determining who is entitled to vote in the election by reference to membership on a particular date, that date, and

(b) otherwise, the date, or the last date, on which voting papers are distributed for the purposes of the election.]

[528]

NOTES

Sub-s (3): words in square brackets in para (a) substituted, and para (aa) and the words in square brackets in para (d) inserted, by the Trade Union Reform and Employment Rights Act 1993, ss 1(1)(a), (b), 49(2), Sch 8, para 46.

Sub-ss (3A)–(3C), (5A), (5B), (8): inserted and added respectively by the Trade Union Reform and Employment Rights Act 1993, s 1(1)(c)–(e).

Orders: the Trade Union Ballots and Elections (Independent Scrutineer Qualifications) Order 1993, SI 1993/1909 at **[2179]**.

---

50 Entitlement to vote

(1) Subject to the provisions of this section, entitlement to vote shall be accorded equally to all members of the trade union.

(2) The rules of the union may exclude entitlement to vote in the case of all members belonging to one of the following classes, or to a class falling within one of the following—

(a) members who are not in employment;

(b) members who are in arrears in respect of any subscription or contribution due to the union;

(c) members who are apprentices, trainees or students or new members of the union.

(3) The rules of the union may restrict entitlement to vote to members who fall within—

(a) a class determined by reference to a trade or occupation,

(b) a class determined by reference to a geographical area, or

(c) a class which is by virtue of the rules of the union treated as a separate section within the union,

or to members who fall within a class determined by reference to any combination of the factors mentioned in paragraphs (a), (b) and (c).

The reference in paragraph (c) to a section of a trade union includes a part of the union which is itself a trade union.

(4) Entitlement may not be restricted in accordance with subsection (3) if the effect is that any member of the union is denied entitlement to vote at all elections held for the purposes of this Chapter otherwise than by virtue of belonging to a class excluded in accordance with subsection (2).

[529]

51 Voting

(1) The method of voting must be by the marking of a voting paper by the person voting.

(2) Each voting paper must—

(a) state the name of the independent scrutineer and clearly specify the address to which, and the date by which, it is to be returned,
(b) be given one of a series of consecutive whole numbers every one of which is used in giving a different number in that series to each voting paper printed or otherwise produced for the purposes of the election, and
(c) be marked with its number.

(3) Every person who is entitled to vote at the election must—
(a) be allowed to vote without interference from, or constraint imposed by, the union or any of its members, officials or employees, and
(b) so far as is reasonably practicable, be enabled to do so without incurring any direct cost to himself.

(4) So far as is reasonably practicable, every person who is entitled to vote at the election must—
(a) have sent to him by post, at his home address or another address which he has requested the trade union in writing to treat as his postal address, a voting paper which either lists the candidates at the election or is accompanied by a separate list of those candidates; and
(b) be given a convenient opportunity to vote by post.

(5) The ballot shall be conducted so as to secure that—
(a) so far as is reasonably practicable, those voting do so in secret, and
(b) the votes given at the election are fairly and accurately counted.

For the purposes of paragraph (b) an inaccuracy in counting shall be disregarded if it is accidental and on a scale which could not affect the result of the election.

(6) The ballot shall be so conducted as to secure that the result of the election is determined solely by counting the number of votes cast directly for each candidate.

(7) Nothing in subsection (6) shall be taken to prevent the system of voting used for the election being the single transferable vote, that is, a vote capable of being given so as to indicate the voter's order of preference for the candidates and of being transferred to the next choice—
(a) when it is not required to give a prior choice the necessary quota of votes, or
(b) when, owing to the deficiency in the number of votes given for a prior choice, that choice is eliminated from the list of candidates.

[530]

[51A Counting of votes etc by independent person

(1) The trade union shall ensure that—
(a) the storage and distribution of the voting papers for the purposes of the election, and
(b) the counting of the votes cast in the election,

are undertaken by one or more independent persons appointed by the union.

(2) A person is an independent person in relation to an election if—
(a) he is the scrutineer, or
(b) he is a person other than the scrutineer and the trade union has no grounds for believing either that he will carry out any functions conferred on him in relation to the election otherwise than competently or that his independence in relation to the union, or in relation to the election, might reasonably be called into question.

(3) An appointment under this section shall require the person appointed to carry out his functions so as to minimise the risk of any contravention of requirements imposed by or under any enactment or the occurrence of any unfairness or malpractice.

(4) The duty of confidentiality as respects the register is incorporated in an appointment under this section.

(5) Where the person appointed to undertake the counting of votes is not the scrutineer, his appointment shall require him to send the voting papers back to the scrutineer as soon as reasonably practicable after the counting has been completed.

(6) The trade union—
(a) shall ensure that nothing in the terms of an appointment under this section is such as to make it reasonable for any person to call into question the independence of the person appointed in relation to the union,

(b) shall ensure that a person appointed under this section duly carries out his functions and that there is no interference with his carrying out of those functions which would make it reasonable for any person to call into question the independence of the person appointed in relation to the union, and

(c) shall comply with all reasonable requests made by a person appointed under this section for the purposes of, or in connection with, the carrying out of his functions.]

[531]

NOTES

Inserted by the Trade Union Reform and Employment Rights Act 1993, s 2(1).

52 Scrutineer's report

(1) The scrutineer's report on the election shall state—

(a) the number of voting papers distributed for the purposes of the election,

(b) the number of voting papers returned to the scrutineer,

(c) the number of valid votes cast in the election for each candidate, …

(d) the number of spoiled or otherwise invalid voting papers returned[, and

(e) the name of the person (or of each of the persons) appointed under section 51A or, if no person was so appointed, that fact.]

(2) The report shall also state whether the scrutineer is satisfied—

(a) that there are no reasonable grounds for believing that there was any contravention of a requirement imposed by or under any enactment in relation to the election,

(b) that the arrangements made [(whether by him or any other person)] with respect to the production, storage, distribution, return or other handling of the voting papers used in the election, and the arrangements for the counting of the votes, included all such security arrangements as were reasonably practicable for the purpose of minimising the risk that any unfairness or malpractice might occur, and

(c) that he has been able to carry out his functions without such interference as would make it reasonable for any person to call his independence in relation to the union into question;

and if he is not satisfied as to any of those matters, the report shall give particulars of his reasons for not being satisfied as to that matter.

[(2A) The report shall also state—

(a) whether the scrutineer—

(i) has inspected the register of names and addresses of the members of the trade union, or

(ii) has examined the copy of the register as at the relevant date which is supplied to him in accordance with section 49(5A)(a),

(b) if he has, whether in the case of each inspection or examination he was acting on a request by a member of the trade union or candidate or at his own instance,

(c) whether he declined to act on any such request, and

(d) whether any inspection of the register, or any examination of the copy of the register, has revealed any matter which he considers should be drawn to the attention of the trade union in order to assist it in securing that the register is accurate and up-to-date,

but shall not state the name of any member or candidate who has requested such an inspection or examination.]

[(2B) Where one or more persons other than the scrutineer are appointed under section 51A, the statement included in the scrutineer's report in accordance with subsection (2)(b) shall also indicate—

(a) whether he is satisfied with the performance of the person, or each of the persons, so appointed, and

(b) if he is not satisfied with the performance of the person, or any of them, particulars of his reasons for not being so satisfied.]

(3) The trade union shall not publish the result of the election until it has received the scrutineer's report.

(4) The trade union shall within the period of three months after it receives the report either—

(a) send a copy of the report to every member of the union to whom it is reasonably practicable to send such a copy; or

(b) take all such other steps for notifying the contents of the report to the members of the union (whether by publishing the report or otherwise) as it is the practice of the union to take when matters of general interest to all its members need to be brought to their attention.

(5) Any such copy or notification shall be accompanied by a statement that the union will, on request, supply any member of the union with a copy of the report, either free of charge or on payment of such reasonable fee as may be specified in the notification.

(6) The trade union shall so supply any member of the union who makes such a request and pays the fee (if any) notified to him.

[532]

NOTES

Sub-s (1): word omitted from para (c) repealed, and para (e) and the word immediately preceding it added, by the Trade Union Reform and Employment Rights Act 1993, ss 2(2)(a), 51, Sch 10.

Sub-s (2): words in square brackets in para (b) inserted by the Trade Union Reform and Employment Rights Act 1993, s 2(2)(b).

Sub-ss (2A), (2B): inserted by the Trade Union Reform and Employment Rights Act 1993, ss 1(2), 2(2)(c).

53 Uncontested elections

Nothing in this Chapter shall be taken to require a ballot to be held at an uncontested election.

[533]

Remedy for failure to comply with requirements

54 Remedy for failure to comply with requirements: general

(1) The remedy for a failure on the part of a trade union to comply with the requirements of this Chapter is by way of application under section 55 (to the Certification Officer) or section 56 (to the court).

…

(2) An application under those sections may be made—

(a) by a person who is a member of the trade union (provided, where the election has been held, he was also a member at the time when it was held), or

(b) by a person who is or was a candidate at the election;

and the references in those sections to a person having a sufficient interest are to such a person.

(3) [Where an election has been held, no application under those sections with respect to that election] may be made after the end of the period of one year beginning with the day on which the union announced the result of the election.

[534]

NOTES

Sub-s (1): words omitted repealed by the Employment Relations Act 1999, ss 29, 44, Sch 6, paras 1, 9, Sch 9(7).

Sub-s (3): words in square brackets substituted by the Employment Relations Act 2004, s 57(1), Sch 1, para 5, as from 6 April 2005.

55 Application to Certification Officer

(1) A person having a sufficient interest (see section 54(2)) who claims that a trade union has failed to comply with any of the requirements of this Chapter may apply to the Certification Officer for a declaration to that effect.

(2) On an application being made to him, the Certification Officer shall—

(a) make such enquiries as he thinks fit, and

(b) … give the applicant and the trade union an opportunity to be heard,

and may make or refuse the declaration asked for.

(3) If he makes a declaration he shall specify in it the provisions with which the trade union has failed to comply.

(4) Where he makes a declaration and is satisfied that steps have been taken by the union with a view to remedying the declared failure, or securing that a failure of the same or any similar kind does not occur in future, or that the union has agreed to take such steps, he shall specify those steps in the declaration.

(5) Whether he makes or refuses a declaration, he shall give reasons for his decision in writing; and the reasons may be accompanied by written observations on any matter arising from, or connected with, the proceedings.

[(5A) Where the Certification Officer makes a declaration he shall also, unless he considers that to do so would be inappropriate, make an enforcement order, that is, an order imposing on the union one or more of the following requirements—

(a) to secure the holding of an election in accordance with the order;

(b) to take such other steps to remedy the declared failure as may be specified in the order;

(c) to abstain from such acts as may be so specified with a view to securing that a failure of the same or a similar kind does not occur in future.

The Certification Officer shall in an order imposing any such requirement as is mentioned in paragraph (a) or (b) specify the period within which the union is to comply with the requirements of the order.

(5B) Where the Certification Officer makes an order requiring the union to hold a fresh election, he shall (unless he considers that it would be inappropriate to do so in the particular circumstances of the case) require the election to be conducted in accordance with the requirements of this Chapter and such other provisions as may be made by the order.

(5C) Where an enforcement order has been made—

(a) any person who is a member of the union and was a member at the time the order was made, or

(b) any person who is or was a candidate in the election in question,

is entitled to enforce obedience to the order as if he had made the application on which the order was made.]

(6) In exercising his functions under this section the Certification Officer shall ensure that, so far as is reasonably practicable, an application made to him is determined within six months of being made.

(7) Where he requests a person to furnish information to him in connection with enquiries made by him under this section, he shall specify the date by which that information is to be furnished and, unless he considers that it would be inappropriate to do so, shall proceed with his determination of the application notwithstanding that the information has not been furnished to him by the specified date.

[(8) A declaration made by the Certification Officer under this section may be relied on as if it were a declaration made by the court.

(9) An enforcement order made by the Certification Officer under this section may be enforced in the same way as an order of the court.

(10) The following paragraphs have effect if a person applies under section 56 in relation to an alleged failure—

(a) that person may not apply under this section in relation to that failure;

(b) on an application by a different person under this section in relation to that failure, the Certification Officer shall have due regard to any declaration, order, observations or reasons made or given by the court regarding that failure and brought to the Certification Officer's notice.]

[535]

NOTES

Sub-s (2): words omitted from para (b) repealed by the Employment Relations Act 1999, ss 29, 44, Sch 6, paras 1, 10(1), (2), Sch 9(7).

Sub-ss (5A)–(5C), (8)–(10): inserted and added respectively by the Employment Relations Act 1999, s 29, Sch 6, paras 1, 10(1), (3), (4).

56 Application to court

(1) A person having a sufficient interest (see section 54(2)) who claims that a trade union has failed to comply with any of the requirements of this Chapter may apply to the court for a declaration to that effect.

(2) …

(3) If the court makes the declaration asked for, it shall specify in the declaration the provisions with which the trade union has failed to comply.

(4) Where the court makes a declaration it shall also, unless it considers that to do so would be inappropriate, make an enforcement order, that is, an order imposing on the union one or more of the following requirements—

(a) to secure the holding of an election in accordance with the order;

(b) to take such other steps to remedy the declared failure as may be specified in the order;

(c) to abstain from such acts as may be so specified with a view to securing that a failure of the same or a similar kind does not occur in future.

The court shall in an order imposing any such requirement as is mentioned in paragraph (a) or (b) specify the period within which the union is to comply with the requirements of the order.

(5) Where the court makes an order requiring the union to hold a fresh election, the court shall (unless it considers that it would be inappropriate to do so in the particular circumstances of the case) require the election to be conducted in accordance with the requirements of this Chapter and such other provisions as may be made by the order.

(6) Where an enforcement order has been made—

(a) any person who is a member of the union and was a member at the time the order was made, or

(b) any person who is or was a candidate in the election in question,

is entitled to enforce obedience to the order as if he had made the application on which the order was made.

(7) Without prejudice to any other power of the court, the court may on an application under this section grant such interlocutory relief (in Scotland, such interim order) as it considers appropriate.

[(8) The following paragraphs have effect if a person applies under section 55 in relation to an alleged failure—

(a) that person may not apply under this section in relation to that failure;

(b) on an application by a different person under this section in relation to that failure, the court shall have due regard to any declaration, order, observations or reasons made or given by the Certification Officer regarding that failure and brought to the court's notice.]

[536]

NOTES

Sub-s (2): repealed by the Employment Relations Act 1999, ss 29, 44, Sch 6, paras 1, 11(1), (2), Sch 9(7).

Sub-s (8): added by the Employment Relations Act 1999, s 29, Sch 6, paras 1, 11(1), (3).

[56A Appeals from Certification Officer

An appeal lies to the Employment Appeal Tribunal on any question of law arising in proceedings before or arising from any decision of the Certification Officer under section 55.]

[537]

NOTES

Inserted by the Employment Relations Act 1999, s 29, Sch 6, paras 1, 12.

Supplementary

57 Exemption of newly-formed trade unions, &c

(1) The provisions of this Chapter do not apply to a trade union until more than one year has elapsed since its formation (by amalgamation or otherwise).

For this purpose the date of formation of a trade union formed otherwise than by amalgamation shall be taken to be the date on which the first members of the executive of the union are first appointed or elected.

(2) Where a trade union is formed by amalgamation, the provisions of this Chapter do not apply in relation to a person who—

(a) by virtue of an election held a position to which this Chapter applies in one of the amalgamating unions immediately before the amalgamation, and

(b) becomes the holder of a position to which this Chapter applies in the amalgamated union in accordance with the instrument of transfer,

until after the end of the period for which he would have been entitled in accordance with this Chapter to continue to hold the first-mentioned position without being re-elected.

(3) Where a trade union transfers its engagements to another trade union, the provisions of this Chapter do not apply in relation to a person who—

(a) held a position to which this Chapter applies in the transferring union immediately before the transfer, and

(b) becomes the holder of a position to which this Chapter applies in the transferee union in accordance with the instrument of transfer,

until after the end of the period of one year beginning with the date of the transfer or, if he held the first-mentioned position by virtue of an election, any longer period for which he would have been entitled in accordance with this Chapter to continue to hold that position without being re-elected.

[538]

58 Exemption of certain persons nearing retirement

(1) Section 46(1)(b) (requirement of re-election) does not apply to a person holding a position to which this Chapter applies if the following conditions are satisfied.

(2) The conditions are that—

(a) he holds the position by virtue of having been elected at an election in relation to which the requirements of this Chapter were satisfied,

(b) he is a full-time employee of the union by virtue of the position,

(c) he will reach retirement age within five years,

(d) he is entitled under the rules of the union to continue as the holder of the position until retirement age without standing for re-election,

(e) he has been a full-time employee of the union for a period (which need not be continuous) of at least ten years, and

(f) the period between the day on which the election referred to in paragraph (a) took place and the day immediately preceding that on which paragraph (c) is first satisfied does not exceed five years.

(3) For the purposes of this section "retirement age", in relation to any person, means the earlier of—

(a) the age fixed by, or in accordance with, the rules of the union for him to retire from the position in question, or

(b) the age which is for the time being pensionable age [within the meaning given by the rules in paragraph 1 of Schedule 4 to the Pensions Act 1995].

[539]

NOTES

Sub-s (3): words in square brackets substituted by the Pensions Act 1995, s 126(c), Sch 4, Pt III, para 15.

59 Period for giving effect to election

Where a person holds a position to which this Chapter applies immediately before an election at which he is not re-elected to that position, nothing in this Chapter shall be taken to require the union to prevent him from continuing to hold that position for such period (not exceeding six months) as may reasonably be required for effect to be given to the result of the election.

[540]

60 Overseas members

(1) A trade union which has overseas members may choose whether or not to accord any of those members entitlement to vote at an election for a position to which this Chapter applies.

(2) An "overseas member" means a member of the union (other than a merchant seaman or offshore worker) who is outside Great Britain throughout the period during which votes may be cast.

For this purpose—

"merchant seaman" means a person whose employment, or the greater part of it, is carried out on board sea-going ships; and

"offshore worker" means a person in offshore employment, other than one who is in such employment in an area where the law of Northern Ireland applies.

(3) Where the union chooses to accord an overseas member entitlement to vote, section 51 (requirements as to voting) applies in relation to him; but nothing in section 47 (candidates) or section 50 (entitlement to vote) applies in relation to an overseas member or in relation to a vote cast by such a member.

[541]

61 Other supplementary provisions

(1) For the purposes of this Chapter the date on which a contested election is held shall be taken, in the case of an election in which votes may be cast on more than one day, to be the last of those days.

(2) Nothing in this Chapter affects the validity of anything done by a person holding a position to which this Chapter applies.

[542]

CHAPTER V
RIGHTS OF TRADE UNION MEMBERS

Right to a ballot before industrial action

62 Right to ballot before industrial action

(1) A member of a trade union who claims that members of the union, including himself, are likely to be or have been induced by the union to take part or to continue to take part in industrial action which does not have the support of a ballot may apply to the court for an order under this section.

[In this section "the relevant time" means the time when the application is made.]

(2) For this purpose industrial action shall be regarded as having the support of a ballot only if—

[(a) the union has held a ballot in respect of the action—
- (i) in relation to which the requirements of section 226B so far as applicable before and during the holding of the ballot were satisfied,
- (ii) in relation to which the requirements of sections 227 to 231 were satisfied, and
- (iii) in which the majority voting in the ballot answered "Yes" to the question applicable in accordance with section 229(2) to industrial action of the kind which the applicant has been or is likely to be induced to take part in;

(b) such of the requirements of the following sections as have fallen to be satisfied at the relevant time have been satisfied, namely—
- (i) section 226B so far as applicable after the holding of the ballot, and
- (ii) section 231B; …

[(bb) section 232A does not prevent the industrial action from being regarded as having the support of the ballot; and]

(c) the requirements of section 233 (calling of industrial action with support of ballot) are satisfied.

Any reference in this subsection to a requirement of a provision which is disapplied or modified by section 232 has effect subject to that section.]

(3) Where on an application under this section the court is satisfied that the claim is well-founded, it shall make such order as it considers appropriate for requiring the union to take steps for ensuring—

- (a) that there is no, or no further, inducement of members of the union to take part or to continue to take part in the industrial action to which the application relates, and
- (b) that no member engages in conduct after the making of the order by virtue of having been induced before the making of the order to take part or continue to take part in the action.

(4) Without prejudice to any other power of the court, the court may on an application under this section grant such interlocutory relief (in Scotland, such interim order) as it considers appropriate.

(5) For the purposes of this section an act shall be taken to be done by a trade union if it is authorised or endorsed by the union; and the provisions of section 20(2) to (4) apply for the purpose of determining whether an act is to be taken to be so authorised or endorsed.

Those provisions also apply in relation to proceedings for failure to comply with an order under this section as they apply in relation to the original proceedings.

(6) In this section—

"inducement" includes an inducement which is or would be ineffective, whether because of the member's unwillingness to be influenced by it or for any other reason; and

"industrial action" means a strike or other industrial action by persons employed under contracts of employment.

(7) Where a person holds any office or employment under the Crown on terms which do not constitute a contract of employment between that person and the Crown, those terms shall nevertheless be deemed to constitute such a contract for the purposes of this section.

(8) References in this section to a contract of employment include any contract under which one person personally does work or performs services for another; and related expressions shall be construed accordingly.

(9) Nothing in this section shall be construed as requiring a trade union to hold separate ballots for the purposes of this section and sections 226 to 234 (requirement of ballot before action by trade union).

[543]

NOTES

Sub-s (1): words in square brackets added by the Trade Union Reform and Employment Rights Act 1993, s 49(2), Sch 8, para 47(a).

Sub-s (2): paras (a)–(c) substituted by the Trade Union Reform and Employment Rights Act 1993, s 49(2), Sch 8, para 47(b); word omitted from para (b) repealed, and para (bb) inserted, by the Employment Relations Act 2004, ss 24(2), 57(2), Sch 2, as from 6 April 2005.

Right not to be denied access to the courts

63 Right not to be denied access to the courts

(1) This section applies where a matter is under the rules of a trade union required or allowed to be submitted for determination or conciliation in accordance with the rules of the union, but a provision of the rules purporting to provide for that to be a person's only remedy has no effect (or would have no effect if there were one).

(2) Notwithstanding anything in the rules of the union or in the practice of any court, if a member or former member of the union begins proceedings in a court with respect to a matter to which this section applies, then if—

- (a) he has previously made a valid application to the union for the matter to be submitted for determination or conciliation in accordance with the union's rules, and
- (b) the court proceedings are begun after the end of the period of six months beginning with the day on which the union received the application,

the rules requiring or allowing the matter to be so submitted, and the fact that any relevant steps remain to be taken under the rules, shall be regarded for all purposes as irrelevant to any question whether the court proceedings should be dismissed, stayed or sisted, or adjourned.

(3) An application shall be deemed to be valid for the purposes of subsection (2)(a) unless the union informed the applicant, before the end of the period of 28 days beginning with the date on which the union received the application, of the respects in which the application contravened the requirements of the rules.

(4) If the court is satisfied that any delay in the taking of relevant steps under the rules is attributable to unreasonable conduct of the person who commenced the proceedings, it may treat the period specified in subsection (2)(b) as extended by such further period as it considers appropriate.

(5) In this section—

(a) references to the rules of a trade union include any arbitration or other agreement entered into in pursuance of a requirement imposed by or under the rules; and

(b) references to the relevant steps under the rules, in relation to any matter, include any steps falling to be taken in accordance with the rules for the purposes of or in connection with the determination or conciliation of the matter, or any appeal, review or reconsideration of any determination or award.

(6) This section does not affect any enactment or rule of law by virtue of which a court would apart from this section disregard any such rules of a trade union or any such fact as is mentioned in subsection (2).

[544]

Right not to be unjustifiably disciplined

64 Right not to be unjustifiably disciplined

(1) An individual who is or has been a member of a trade union has the right not to be unjustifiably disciplined by the union.

(2) For this purpose an individual is "disciplined" by a trade union if a determination is made, or purportedly made, under the rules of the union or by an official of the union or a number of persons including an official that—

(a) he should be expelled from the union or a branch or section of the union,

(b) he should pay a sum to the union, to a branch or section of the union or to any other person;

(c) sums tendered by him in respect of an obligation to pay subscriptions or other sums to the union, or to a branch or section of the union, should be treated as unpaid or paid for a different purpose,

(d) he should be deprived to any extent of, or of access to, any benefits, services or facilities which would otherwise be provided or made available to him by virtue of his membership of the union, or a branch or section of the union,

(e) another trade union, or a branch or section of it, should be encouraged or advised not to accept him as a member, or

(f) he should be subjected to some other detriment;

and whether an individual is "unjustifiably disciplined" shall be determined in accordance with section 65.

(3) Where a determination made in infringement of an individual's right under this section requires the payment of a sum or the performance of an obligation, no person is entitled in any proceedings to rely on that determination for the purpose of recovering the sum or enforcing the obligation.

(4) Subject to that, the remedies for infringement of the right conferred by this section are as provided by sections 66 and 67, and not otherwise.

(5) The right not to be unjustifiably disciplined is in addition to (and not in substitution for) any right which exists apart from this section; [and, subject to section 66(4), nothing] in this section or sections 65 to 67 affects any remedy for infringement of any such right.

[545]

NOTES

Sub-s (5): words in square brackets substituted by the Trade Union Reform and Employment Rights Act 1993, s 49(2), Sch 8, para 48.

Conciliation: employment tribunal proceedings and claims which could be the subject of employment tribunal proceedings arising out of a contravention, or alleged contravention, of this section are proceedings to which the Employment Tribunals Act 1996, s 18 applies; see s 18(1)(b) of that Act at **[975]**. The standard conciliation period applies to such claims by virtue of the Employment Tribunals (Constitution and Rules of Procedure) Regulations 2004, SI 2004/1861, Sch 1, rule 22(1), (6).

65 Meaning of "unjustifiably disciplined"

(1) An individual is unjustifiably disciplined by a trade union if the actual or supposed conduct which constitutes the reason, or one of the reasons, for disciplining him is—

(a) conduct to which this section applies, or

(b) something which is believed by the union to amount to such conduct;

but subject to subsection (6) (cases of bad faith in relation to assertion of wrongdoing).

(2) This section applies to conduct which consists in—

(a) failing to participate in or support a strike or other industrial action (whether by members of the union or by others), or indicating opposition to or a lack of support for such action;

(b) failing to contravene, for a purpose connected with such a strike or other industrial action, a requirement imposed on him by or under a contract of employment;

(c) asserting (whether by bringing proceedings or otherwise) that the union, any official or representative of it or a trustee of its property has contravened, or is proposing to contravene, a requirement which is, or is thought to be, imposed by or under the rules of the union or any other agreement or by or under any enactment (whenever passed) or any rule of law;

(d) encouraging or assisting a person

(i) to perform an obligation imposed on him by a contract of employment, …

(ii) to make or attempt to vindicate any such assertion as is mentioned in paragraph (c); …

(e) contravening a requirement imposed by or in consequence of a determination which infringes the individual's or another individual's right not to be unjustifiably disciplined,

[(f) failing to agree, or withdrawing agreement, to the making from his wages (in accordance with arrangements between his employer and the union) of deductions representing payments to the union in respect of his membership,

(g) resigning or proposing to resign from the union or from another union, becoming or proposing to become a member of another union, refusing to become a member of another union, or being a member of another union,

(h) working with, or proposing to work with, individuals who are not members of the union or who are or are not members of another union,

(i) working for, or proposing to work for, an employer who employs or who has employed individuals who are not members of the union or who are or are not members of another union, or

(j) requiring the union to do an act which the union is, by any provision of this Act, required to do on the requisition of a member].

(3) This section applies to conduct which involves … the Certification Officer being consulted or asked to provide advice or assistance with respect to any matter whatever, or which involves any person being consulted or asked to provide advice or assistance with respect to a matter which forms, or might form, the subject-matter of any such assertion as is mentioned in subsection (2)(c) above.

(4) This section also applies to conduct which consists in proposing to engage in, or doing anything preparatory or incidental to, conduct falling within subsection (2) or (3).

(5) This section does not apply to an act, omission or statement comprised in conduct falling within subsection (2), (3) or (4) above if it is shown that the act, omission or statement is one in respect of which individuals would be disciplined by the union irrespective of whether their acts, omissions or statements were in connection with conduct within subsection (2) or (3) above.

(6) An individual is not unjustifiably disciplined if it is shown—

(a) that the reason for disciplining him, or one of them, is that he made such an assertion as is mentioned in subsection (2)(c), or encouraged or assisted another person to make or attempt to vindicate such an assertion,

(b) that the assertion was false, and

(c) that he made the assertion, or encouraged or assisted another person to make or attempt to vindicate it, in the belief that it was false or otherwise in bad faith,

and that there was no other reason for disciplining him or that the only other reasons were reasons in respect of which he does not fall to be treated as unjustifiably disciplined.

(7) In this section—

"conduct" includes statements, acts and omissions;

"contract of employment", in relation to an individual, includes any agreement between that individual and a person for whom he works or normally works[, "employer" includes such a person and related expressions shall be construed accordingly;] …

"representative", in relation to a union, means a person acting or purporting to act—

(a) in his capacity as a member of the union, or

(b) on the instructions or advice of a person acting or purporting to act in that capacity or in the capacity of an official of the union;

["require" (on the part of an individual) includes request or apply for, and "requisition" shall be construed accordingly; and

"wages" shall be construed in accordance with the definitions of "contract of employment", "employer" and related expressions.]

(8) Where a person holds any office or employment under the Crown on terms which do not constitute a contract of employment between him and the Crown, those terms shall nevertheless be deemed to constitute such a contract for the purposes of this section.

[546]

NOTES

Sub-s (2): word omitted from para (d) repealed, and paras (f)–(j) added, by the Trade Union Reform and Employment Rights Act 1993, ss 16(1), 51, Sch 10.

Sub-s (3): words omitted repealed by the Employment Relations Act 1999, s 44, Sch 9(6).

Sub-s (7): in definition "contract of employment", words in square brackets added, and word omitted repealed, and definitions "require" and "wages" added, by the Trade Union Reform and Employment Rights Act 1993, ss 16(2), 49(2), 51, Sch 8, para 49, Sch 10.

66 Complaint of infringement of right

(1) An individual who claims that he has been unjustifiably disciplined by a trade union may present a complaint against the union to an [employment tribunal].

(2) The tribunal shall not entertain such a complaint unless it is presented—

(a) before the end of the period of three months beginning with the date of the making of the determination claimed to infringe the right, or

(b) where the tribunal is satisfied—

(i) that it was not reasonably practicable for the complaint to be presented before the end of that period, or

(ii) that any delay in making the complaint is wholly or partly attributable to a reasonable attempt to appeal against the determination or to have it reconsidered or reviewed,

within such further period as the tribunal considers reasonable.

(3) Where the tribunal finds the complaint well-founded, it shall make a declaration to that effect.

[(4) Where a complaint relating to an expulsion which is presented under this section is declared to be well-founded, no complaint in respect of the expulsion shall be presented or proceeded with under section 174 (right not to be excluded or expelled from trade union).]

[547]

NOTES

Sub-s (1): words in square brackets substituted by the Employment Rights (Dispute Resolution) Act 1998, s 1(2)(a).

Sub-s (4): substituted by the Trade Union Reform and Employment Rights Act 1993, s 49(2), Sch 8, para 50.

Conciliation: see the note to s 64 at **[545]**.

67 Further remedies for infringement of right

(1) An individual whose complaint under section 66 has been declared to be well-founded may make an application [to an employment tribunal] for one or both of the following—

(a) an award of compensation to be paid to him by the union;
(b) an order that the union pay him an amount equal to any sum which he has paid in pursuance of any such determination as is mentioned in section 64(2)(b).

(2) …

(3) An application under this section shall not be entertained if made before the end of the period of four weeks beginning with the date of the declaration or after the end of the period of six months beginning with that date.

(4) …

(5) The amount of compensation awarded shall, subject to the following provisions, be such as the … [employment tribunal] considers just and equitable in all the circumstances.

(6) In determining the amount of compensation to be awarded, the same rule shall be applied concerning the duty of a person to mitigate his loss as applies to damages recoverable under the common law in England and Wales or Scotland.

(7) Where the … [employment tribunal] finds that the infringement complained of was to any extent caused or contributed to by the action of the applicant, it shall reduce the amount of the compensation by such proportion as it considers just and equitable having regard to that finding.

(8) The amount of compensation [calculated in accordance with subsections (5) to (7)] shall not exceed the aggregate of—
(a) an amount equal to 30 times the limit for the time being imposed by [section 227(1)(a) of the Employment Rights Act 1996] (maximum amount of a week's pay for basic award in unfair dismissal cases), and
(b) an amount equal to the limit for the time being imposed by [section 124(1)] of that Act (maximum compensatory award in such cases);

…

[(8A) If on the date on which the application was made—
(a) the determination infringing the applicant's right not to be unjustifiably disciplined has not been revoked, or
(b) the union has failed to take all the steps necessary for securing the reversal of anything done for the purpose of giving effect to the determination,

the amount of compensation shall be not less than the amount for the time being specified in section 176(6A).]

(9) …

[548]

NOTES

Sub-s (1): words in square brackets inserted by the Employment Relations Act 2004, s 34(1), (2), as from 31 December 2004, except in relation to any complaint presented by an individual under s 66 of this Act which relates to a decision to discipline the individual which was taken by the union before that date (see SI 2004/3342, art 8).

Sub-ss (2), (4): repealed by the Employment Relations Act 2004, ss 34(1), (3), 57(2), Sch 2, as from 31 December 2004 (subject to the same exception in SI 2004/3342, art 8 as noted above).

Sub-ss (5), (7): words omitted repealed by the Employment Relations Act 2004, ss 34(1), (4), 57(2), Sch 2, as from 31 December 2004 (subject to the same exception in SI 2004/3342, art 8 as noted above); words in square brackets substituted by the Employment Rights (Dispute Resolution) Act 1998, s 1(2)(a).

Sub-s (8): words in first pair of square brackets substituted by the Trade Union Reform and Employment Rights Act 1993, s 49(2), Sch 8, para 51(a); words in second and third pairs of square brackets substituted by the Employment Rights Act 1996, s 240, Sch 1, para 56(1), (2); words omitted repealed by the Employment Relations Act 2004, ss 34(1), (5), 57(2), Sch 2, as from 31 December 2004 (subject to the same exception in SI 2004/3342, art 8 as noted above).

Sub-s (8A): inserted by the Employment Relations Act 2004, s 34(1), (6), as from 31 December 2004 (subject to the same exception in SI 2004/3342, art 8 as noted above).

Sub-s (9): repealed by the Trade Union Reform and Employment Rights Act 1993, ss 49(2), 51, Sch 8, para 51(b), Sch 10.

[Right not to suffer deduction of unauthorised or excessive union subscriptions

[68 Right not to suffer deduction of unauthorised subscriptions

(1) Where arrangements ("subscription deduction arrangements") exist between the employer of a worker and a trade union relating to the making from workers' wages of

deductions representing payments to the union in respect of the workers' membership of the union ("subscription deductions"), the employer shall ensure that no subscription deduction is made from wages payable to the worker on any day unless—

(a) the worker has authorised in writing the making from his wages of subscription deductions; and

(b) the worker has not withdrawn the authorisation.

(2) A worker withdraws an authorisation given for the purposes of subsection (1), in relation to a subscription deduction which falls to be made from wages payable to him on any day, if a written notice withdrawing the authorisation has been received by the employer in time for it to be reasonably practicable for the employer to secure that no such deduction is made.

(3) A worker's authorisation of the making of subscription deductions from his wages shall not give rise to any obligation on the part of the employer to the worker to maintain or continue to maintain subscription deduction arrangements.

(4) In this section and section 68A, "employer", "wages" and "worker" have the same meanings as in the Employment Rights Act 1996.]]

[549]

NOTES

Substituted, together with the preceding heading and s 68A, for original s 68, by the Trade Union Reform and Employment Rights Act 1993, s 15; this section was further substituted by the Deregulation (Deduction from Pay of Union Subscriptions) Order 1998, SI 1998/1529, art 2(1).

Conciliation: employment tribunal proceedings and claims which could be the subject of employment tribunal proceedings arising out of a contravention, or alleged contravention, of this section are proceedings to which the Employment Tribunals Act 1996, s 18 applies; see s 18(1)(b) of that Act at **[975]**. The short conciliation period applies to such claims by virtue of the Employment Tribunals (Constitution and Rules of Procedure) Regulations 2004, SI 2004/1861, Sch 1, rule 22(5).

[68A Complaint of infringement of rights

(1) A worker may present a complaint to an [employment tribunal] that his employer has made a deduction from his wages in contravention of section 68—

(a) within the period of three months beginning with the date of the payment of the wages from which the deduction, or (if the complaint relates to more than one deduction) the last of the deductions, was made, or

(b) where the tribunal is satisfied that it was not reasonably practicable for the complaint to be presented within that period, within such further period as the tribunal considers reasonable.

[(2) Where a tribunal finds that a complaint under this section is well founded, it shall make a declaration to that effect and shall order the employer to pay to the worker the whole amount of the deduction, less any such part of the amount as has already been paid to the worker by the employer.]

(3) Where the making of a deduction from the wages of a worker both contravenes section 68(1) and involves one or more of the contraventions specified in subsection (4) of this section, the aggregate amount which may be ordered by an [employment tribunal] or court (whether on the same occasion or on different occasions) to be paid in respect of the contraventions shall not exceed the amount, or (where different amounts may be ordered to be paid in respect of different contraventions) the greatest amount, which may be ordered to be paid in respect of any one of them.

(4) The contraventions referred to in subsection (3) are—

(a) a contravention of the requirement not to make a deduction without having given the particulars required by section 8 (itemised pay statements) or 9(1) (standing statements of fixed deductions) of [the Employment Rights Act 1996],

(b) a contravention of [section 13 of that Act] (requirement not to make unauthorised deductions), and

(c) a contravention of section 86(1) or 90(1) of this Act (requirements not to make deductions of political fund contributions in certain circumstances).]

[550]

NOTES

Substituted as noted to s 68 at **[549]**.

Sub-ss (1), (3): words in square brackets substituted by the Employment Rights (Dispute Resolution) Act 1998, s 1(2)(a).

Sub-s (2): substituted by the Deregulation (Deduction from Pay of Union Subscriptions) Order 1998, SI 1998/1529, art 2(2).

Sub-s (4): words in square brackets substituted by the Employment Rights Act 1996, s 240, Sch 1, para 56(1), (4).

Conciliation: see the note to s 68 at **[549]**.

Right to terminate membership of union

69 Right to terminate membership of union

In every contract of membership of a trade union, whether made before or after the passing of this Act, a term conferring a right on the member, on giving reasonable notice and complying with any reasonable conditions, to terminate his membership of the union shall be implied.

[551]

Supplementary

70 Membership of constituent or affiliated organisation

In this Chapter "member", in relation to a trade union consisting wholly or partly of, or of representatives of, constituent or affiliated organisations, includes a member of any of the constituent or affiliated organisations.

[552]

[CHAPTER VA
COLLECTIVE BARGAINING: RECOGNITION

70A Recognition of trade unions

Schedule A1 shall have effect.]

[553]

NOTES

Inserted, together with the preceding heading, by the Employment Relations Act 1999, s 1(1), (2).

[70B Training

(1) This section applies where—

(a) a trade union is recognised, in accordance with Schedule A1, as entitled to conduct collective bargaining on behalf of a bargaining unit (within the meaning of Part I of that Schedule), and

(b) a method for the conduct of collective bargaining is specified by the Central Arbitration Committee under paragraph 31(3) of that Schedule (and is not the subject of an agreement under paragraph 31(5)(a) or (b)).

(2) The employer must from time to time invite the trade union to send representatives to a meeting for the purpose of—

(a) consulting about the employer's policy on training for workers within the bargaining unit,

(b) consulting about his plans for training for those workers during the period of six months starting with the day of the meeting, and

(c) reporting about training provided for those workers since the previous meeting.

(3) The date set for a meeting under subsection (2) must not be later than—

(a) in the case of a first meeting, the end of the period of six months starting with the day on which this section first applies in relation to a bargaining unit, and

(b) in the case of each subsequent meeting, the end of the period of six months starting with the day of the previous meeting.

(4) The employer shall, before the period of two weeks ending with the date of a meeting, provide to the trade union any information—

(a) without which the union's representatives would be to a material extent impeded in participating in the meeting, and

(b) which it would be in accordance with good industrial relations practice to disclose for the purposes of the meeting.

(5) Section 182(1) shall apply in relation to the provision of information under subsection (4) as it applies in relation to the disclosure of information under section 181.

(6) The employer shall take account of any written representations about matters raised at a meeting which he receives from the trade union within the period of four weeks starting with the date of the meeting.

(7) Where more than one trade union is recognised as entitled to conduct collective bargaining on behalf of a bargaining unit, a reference in this section to "the trade union" is a reference to each trade union.

(8) Where at a meeting under this section (Meeting 1) an employer indicates his intention to convene a subsequent meeting (Meeting 2) before the expiry of the period of six months beginning with the date of Meeting 1, for the reference to a period of six months in subsection (2)(b) there shall be substituted a reference to the expected period between Meeting 1 and Meeting 2.

(9) The Secretary of State may by order made by statutory instrument amend any of subsections (2) to (6).

(10) No order shall be made under subsection (9) unless a draft has been laid before, and approved by resolution of, each House of Parliament.]

[554]

NOTES

Inserted, together with s 70C, by the Employment Relations Act 1999, s 5.

Conciliation: employment tribunal proceedings and claims which could be the subject of employment tribunal proceedings under or arising out of a contravention, or alleged contravention, of this section are proceedings to which the Employment Tribunals Act 1996, s 18 applies; see s 18(1)(f) of that Act at **[975]**, and the Employment Tribunals Act 1996 (Application of Conciliation Provisions) Order 2000, SI 2000/1337 (made under s 18(8)(a), (b)). The standard conciliation period applies to such claims by virtue of the Employment Tribunals (Constitution and Rules of Procedure) Regulations 2004, SI 2004/1861, Sch 1, rule 22(1), (6).

Orders: as of 6 April 2008 no Orders had been made under this section.

[70C Section 70B: complaint to employment tribunal

(1) A trade union may present a complaint to an employment tribunal that an employer has failed to comply with his obligations under section 70B in relation to a bargaining unit.

(2) An employment tribunal shall not consider a complaint under this section unless it is presented—

(a) before the end of the period of three months beginning with the date of the alleged failure, or

(b) within such further period as the tribunal considers reasonable in a case where it is satisfied that it was not reasonably practicable for the complaint to be presented before the end of that period of three months.

(3) Where an employment tribunal finds a complaint under this section well-founded it—

(a) shall make a declaration to that effect, and

(b) may make an award of compensation to be paid by the employer to each person who was, at the time when the failure occurred, a member of the bargaining unit.

(4) The amount of the award shall not, in relation to each person, exceed two weeks' pay.

(5) For the purpose of subsection (4) a week's pay—

(a) shall be calculated in accordance with Chapter II of Part XIV of the Employment Rights Act 1996 (taking the date of the employer's failure as the calculation date), and

(b) shall be subject to the limit in section 227(1) of that Act.

(6) Proceedings for enforcement of an award of compensation under this section—

(a) may, in relation to each person to whom compensation is payable, be commenced by that person, and

(b) may not be commenced by a trade union.]

[555]

NOTES

Inserted as noted to s 70B at **[554]**.

CHAPTER VI
APPLICATION OF FUNDS FOR POLITICAL OBJECTS

Restriction on use of funds for certain political objects

71 Restriction on use of funds for certain political objects

(1) The funds of a trade union shall not be applied in the furtherance of the political objects to which this Chapter applies unless—

(a) there is in force in accordance with this Chapter a resolution (a "political resolution") approving the furtherance of those objects as an object of the union (see sections 73 to 81), and

(b) there are in force rules of the union as to—

(i) the making of payments in furtherance of those objects out of a separate fund, and

(ii) the exemption of any member of the union objecting to contribute to that fund,

which comply with this Chapter (see sections 82, 84 and 85) and have been approved by the Certification Officer.

(2) This applies whether the funds are so applied directly, or in conjunction with another trade union, association or body, or otherwise indirectly.

[556]

72 Political objects to which restriction applies

(1) The political objects to which this Chapter applies are the expenditure of money—

(a) on any contribution to the funds of, or on the payment of expenses incurred directly or indirectly by, a political party;

(b) on the provision of any service or property for use by or on behalf of any political party;

(c) in connection with the registration of electors, the candidature of any person, the selection of any candidate or the holding of any ballot by the union in connection with any election to a political office;

(d) on the maintenance of any holder of a political office;

(e) on the holding of any conference or meeting by or on behalf of a political party or of any other meeting the main purpose of which is the transaction of business in connection with a political party;

(f) on the production, publication or distribution of any literature, document, film, sound recording or advertisement the main purpose of which is to persuade people to vote for a political party or candidate or to persuade them not to vote for a political party or candidate.

(2) Where a person attends a conference or meeting as a delegate or otherwise as a participator in the proceedings, any expenditure incurred in connection with his attendance as such shall, for the purposes of subsection (1)(e), be taken to be expenditure incurred on the holding of the conference or meeting.

(3) In determining for the purposes of subsection (1) whether a trade union has incurred expenditure of a kind mentioned in that subsection, no account shall be taken of the ordinary administrative expenses of the union.

(4) In this section—

"candidate" means a candidate for election to a political office and includes a prospective candidate;

"contribution", in relation to the funds of a political party, includes any fee payable for affiliation to, or membership of, the party and any loan made to the party;

"electors" means electors at an election to a political office;

"film" includes any record, however made, of a sequence of visual images, which is capable of being used as a means of showing that sequence as a moving picture;

"local authority" means a local authority within the meaning of section 270 of the Local Government Act 1972 or section 235 of the Local Government (Scotland) Act 1973; and

"political office" means the office of member of Parliament, member of the European Parliament or member of a local authority or any position within a political party.

[557]

[72A Application of funds in breach of section 71

(1) A person who is a member of a trade union and who claims that it has applied its funds in breach of section 71 may apply to the Certification Officer for a declaration that it has done so.

(2) On an application under this section the Certification Officer—

(a) shall make such enquiries as he thinks fit,

(b) shall give the applicant and the union an opportunity to be heard,

(c) shall ensure that, so far as is reasonably practicable, the application is determined within six months of being made,

(d) may make or refuse the declaration asked for,

(e) shall, whether he makes or refuses the declaration, give reasons for his decision in writing, and

(f) may make written observations on any matter arising from, or connected with, the proceedings.

(3) If he makes a declaration he shall specify in it—

(a) the provisions of section 71 breached, and

(b) the amount of the funds applied in breach.

(4) If he makes a declaration and is satisfied that the union has taken or agreed to take steps with a view to—

(a) remedying the declared breach, or

(b) securing that a breach of the same or any similar kind does not occur in future,

he shall specify those steps in making the declaration.

(5) If he makes a declaration he may make such order for remedying the breach as he thinks just under the circumstances.

(6) Where the Certification Officer requests a person to furnish information to him in connection with enquiries made by him under this section, he shall specify the date by which that information is to be furnished and, unless he considers that it would be inappropriate to do so, shall proceed with his determination of the application notwithstanding that the information has not been furnished to him by the specified date.

(7) A declaration made by the Certification Officer under this section may be relied on as if it were a declaration made by the court.

(8) Where an order has been made under this section, any person who is a member of the union and was a member at the time it was made is entitled to enforce obedience to the order as if he had made the application on which the order was made.

(9) An order made by the Certification Officer under this section may be enforced in the same way as an order of the court.

(10) If a person applies to the Certification Officer under this section in relation to an alleged breach he may not apply to the court in relation to the breach; but nothing in this subsection shall prevent such a person from exercising any right to appeal against or challenge the Certification Officer's decision on the application to him.

(11) If—

(a) a person applies to the court in relation to an alleged breach, and

(b) the breach is one in relation to which he could have made an application to the Certification Officer under this section,

he may not apply to the Certification Officer under this section in relation to the breach.]

[558]

NOTES

Inserted by the Employment Relations Act 1999, s 29, Sch 6, paras 1, 13.

Political resolution

73 Passing and effect of political resolution

(1) A political resolution must be passed by a majority of those voting on a ballot of the members of the trade union held in accordance with this Chapter.

(2) A political resolution so passed shall take effect as if it were a rule of the union and may be rescinded in the same manner and subject to the same provisions as such a rule.

(3) If not previously rescinded, a political resolution shall cease to have effect at the end of the period of ten years beginning with the date of the ballot on which it was passed.

(4) Where before the end of that period a ballot is held on a new political resolution, then—

(a) if the new resolution is passed, the old resolution shall be treated as rescinded, and
(b) if it is not passed, the old resolution shall cease to have effect at the end of the period of two weeks beginning with the date of the ballot.

[559]

74 Approval of political ballot rules

(1) A ballot on a political resolution must be held in accordance with rules of the trade union (its "political ballot rules") approved by the Certification Officer.

(2) Fresh approval is required for the purposes of each ballot which it is proposed to hold, notwithstanding that the rules have been approved for the purposes of an earlier ballot.

(3) The Certification Officer shall not approve a union's political ballot rules unless he is satisfied that the requirements set out in—

section 75 (appointment of independent scrutineer),
section 76 (entitlement to vote),
section 77 (voting), …
[section 77A (counting of votes etc. by independent person), and]
section 78 (scrutineer's report),

would be satisfied in relation to a ballot held by the union in accordance with the rules.

[560]

NOTES

Sub-s (3): word omitted repealed, and words in square brackets inserted, by the Trade Union Reform and Employment Rights Act 1993, ss 3, 51, Sch 1, para 1, Sch 10.

75 Appointment of independent scrutineer

(1) The trade union shall, before the ballot is held, appoint a qualified independent person ("the scrutineer") to carry out—

(a) the functions in relation to the ballot which are required under this section to be contained in his appointment; and
(b) such additional functions in relation to the ballot as may be specified in his appointment.

(2) A person is a qualified independent person in relation to a ballot if—

(a) he satisfies such conditions as may be specified for the purposes of this section by order of the Secretary of State or is himself so specified; and
(b) the trade union has no grounds for believing either that he will carry out any functions conferred on him in relation to the ballot otherwise than competently or that his independence in relation to the union, or in relation to the ballot, might reasonably be called into question.

An order under paragraph (a) shall be made by statutory instrument which shall be subject to annulment in pursuance of a resolution of either House of Parliament.

(3) The scrutineer's appointment shall require him—

(a) to be the person who supervises the production [of the voting papers and (unless he is appointed under section 77A to undertake the distribution of the voting papers) their distribution] and to whom the voting papers are returned by those voting;
[(aa) to—

(i) inspect the register of names and addresses of the members of the trade union, or

(ii) examine the copy of the register as at the relevant date which is supplied to him in accordance with subsection (5A)(a),

whenever it appears to him appropriate to do so and, in particular, when the conditions specified in subsection (3A) are satisfied;]

(b) to take such steps as appear to him to be appropriate for the purpose of enabling him to make his report (see section 78);

(c) to make his report to the trade union as soon as reasonably practicable after the last date for the return of voting papers; and

(d) to retain custody of all voting papers returned for the purposes of the ballot [and the copy of the register supplied to him in accordance with subsection (5A)(a)]—

(i) until the end of the period of one year beginning with the announcement by the union of the result of the ballot; and

(ii) if within that period an application is made under section 79 (complaint of failure to comply with ballot rules), until the Certification Officer or the court authorises him to dispose of the papers [or copy].

[(3A) The conditions referred to in subsection (3)(aa) are—

(a) that a request that the scrutineer inspect the register or examine the copy is made to him during the appropriate period by a member of the trade union who suspects that the register is not, or at the relevant date was not, accurate and up-to-date, and

(b) that the scrutineer does not consider that the member's suspicion is ill-founded.

(3B) In subsection (3A) "the appropriate period" means the period—

(a) beginning with the day on which the scrutineer is appointed, and

(b) ending with the day before the day on which the scrutineer makes his report to the trade union.

(3C) The duty of confidentiality as respects the register is incorporated in the scrutineer's appointment.]

(4) The trade union shall ensure that nothing in the terms of the scrutineer's appointment (including any additional functions specified in the appointment) is such as to make it reasonable for any person to call the scrutineer's independence in relation to the union into question.

(5) The trade union shall, before the scrutineer begins to carry out his functions, either—

(a) send a notice stating the name of the scrutineer to every member of the union to whom it is reasonably practicable to send such a notice, or

(b) take all such other steps for notifying members of the name of the scrutineer as it is the practice of the union to take when matters of general interest to all its members need to be brought to their attention.

[(5A) The trade union shall—

(a) supply to the scrutineer as soon as is reasonably practicable after the relevant date a copy of the register of names and addresses of its members as at that date, and

(b) comply with any request made by the scrutineer to inspect the register.

(5B) Where the register is kept by means of a computer the duty imposed on the trade union by subsection (5A)(a) is either to supply a legible printed copy or (if the scrutineer prefers) to supply a copy of the computer data and allow the scrutineer use of the computer to read it at any time during the period when he is required to retain custody of the copy.]

(6) The trade union shall ensure that the scrutineer duly carries out his functions and that there is no interference with his carrying out of those functions which would make it reasonable for any person to call the scrutineer's independence in relation to the union into question.

(7) The trade union shall comply with all reasonable requests made by the scrutineer for the purposes of, or in connection with, the carrying out of his functions.

[(8) In this section "the relevant date" means—

(a) where the trade union has rules determining who is entitled to vote in the ballot by reference to membership on a particular date, that date, and

(b) otherwise, the date, or the last date, on which voting papers are distributed for the purposes of the ballot.]

[561]

NOTES

Sub-s (3): words in square brackets in para (a) substituted, para (aa) inserted, and words in square brackets in para (d) inserted, by the Trade Union Reform and Employment Rights Act 1993, s 3, Sch 1, para 2(a)–(c).

Sub-ss (3A)–(3C), (5A), (5B), (8): inserted and added respectively by the Trade Union Reform and Employment Rights Act 1993, s 3, Sch 1, para 2(d)–(f).

Orders: the Trade Union Ballots and Elections (Independent Scrutineer Qualifications) Order 1993, SI 1993/1909 at **[2179]**.

76 Entitlement to vote

Entitlement to vote in the ballot shall be accorded equally to all members of the trade union.

[562]

77 Voting

(1) The method of voting must be by the marking of a voting paper by the person voting.

(2) Each voting paper must—

(a) state the name of the independent scrutineer and clearly specify the address to which, and the date by which, it is to be returned, and

(b) be given one of a series of consecutive whole numbers every one of which is used in giving a different number in that series to each voting paper printed or otherwise produced for the purposes of the ballot, and

(c) be marked with its number.

(3) Every person who is entitled to vote in the ballot must—

(a) be allowed to vote without interference from, or constraint imposed by, the union or any of its members, officials or employees, and

(b) so far as is reasonably practicable, be enabled to do so without incurring any direct cost to himself.

(4) So far as is reasonably practicable, every person who is entitled to vote in the ballot must—

(a) have a voting paper sent to him by post at his home address or another address which he has requested the trade union in writing to treat as his postal address, and

(b) be given a convenient opportunity to vote by post.

(5) The ballot shall be conducted so as to secure that—

(a) so far as is reasonably practicable, those voting do so in secret, and

(b) the votes given in the ballot are fairly and accurately counted.

For the purposes of paragraph (b) an inaccuracy in counting shall be disregarded if it is accidental and on a scale which could not affect the result of the ballot.

[563]

[77A Counting of votes etc by independent person

(1) The trade union shall ensure that—

(a) the storage and distribution of the voting papers for the purposes of the ballot, and

(b) the counting of the votes cast in the ballot,

are undertaken by one or more independent persons appointed by the union.

(2) A person is an independent person in relation to a ballot if—

(a) he is the scrutineer, or

(b) he is a person other than the scrutineer and the trade union has no grounds for believing either that he will carry out any functions conferred on him in relation to the ballot otherwise than competently or that his independence in relation to the union, or in relation to the ballot, might reasonably be called into question.

(3) An appointment under this section shall require the person appointed to carry out his functions so as to minimise the risk of any contravention of requirements imposed by or under any enactment or the occurrence of any unfairness or malpractice.

(4) The duty of confidentiality as respects the register is incorporated in an appointment under this section.

(5) Where the person appointed to undertake the counting of votes is not the scrutineer, his appointment shall require him to send the voting papers back to the scrutineer as soon as reasonably practicable after the counting has been completed.

(6) The trade union—

(a) shall ensure that nothing in the terms of an appointment under this section is such as to make it reasonable for any person to call into question the independence of the person appointed in relation to the union,

(b) shall ensure that a person appointed under this section duly carries out his functions and that there is no interference with his carrying out of those functions which would make it reasonable for any person to call into question the independence of the person appointed in relation to the union, and

(c) shall comply with all reasonable requests made by a person appointed under this section for the purposes of, or in connection with, the carrying out of his functions.]

[564]

NOTES

Inserted by the Trade Union Reform and Employment Rights Act 1993, s 3, Sch 1, para 3.

78 Scrutineer's report

(1) The scrutineer's report on the ballot shall state—

(a) the number of voting papers distributed for the purposes of the ballot,

(b) the number of voting papers returned to the scrutineer,

(c) the number of valid votes cast in the ballot for and against the resolution, …

(d) the number of spoiled or otherwise invalid voting papers returned[; and

(e) the name of the person (or of each of the persons) appointed under section 77A or, if no person was so appointed, that fact.]

(2) The report shall also state whether the scrutineer is satisfied—

(a) that there are no reasonable grounds for believing that there was any contravention of a requirement imposed by or under any enactment in relation to the ballot,

(b) that the arrangements made [(whether by him or any other person)] with respect to the production, storage, distribution, return or other handling of the voting papers used in the ballot, and the arrangements for the counting of the votes, included all such security arrangements as were reasonably practicable for the purpose of minimising the risk that any unfairness or malpractice might occur, and

(c) that he has been able to carry out his functions without such interference as would make it reasonable for any person to call his independence in relation to the union into question;

and if he is not satisfied as to any of those matters, the report shall give particulars of his reasons for not being satisfied as to that matter.

[(2A) The report shall also state—

(a) whether the scrutineer—

(i) has inspected the register of names and addresses of the members of the trade union, or

(ii) has examined the copy of the register as at the relevant date which is supplied to him in accordance with section 75(5A)(a),

(b) if he has, whether in the case of each inspection or examination he was acting on a request by a member of the trade union or at his own instance,

(c) whether he declined to act on any such request, and

(d) whether any inspection of the register, or any examination of the copy of the register, has revealed any matter which he considers should be drawn to the attention of the trade union in order to assist it in securing that the register is accurate and up-to-date,

but shall not state the name of any member who has requested such an inspection or examination.

(2B) Where one or more persons other than the scrutineer are appointed under section 77A, the statement included in the scrutineer's report in accordance with subsection (2)(b) shall also indicate—

(a) whether he is satisfied with the performance of the person, or each of the persons, so appointed, and

(b) if he is not satisfied with the performance of the person, or any of them, particulars of his reasons for not being so satisfied.]

(3) The trade union shall not publish the result of the ballot until it has received the scrutineer's report.

(4) The trade union shall within the period of three months after it receives the report—

(a) send a copy of the report to every member of the union to whom it is reasonably practicable to send such a copy; or

(b) take all such other steps for notifying the contents of the report to the members of the union (whether by publishing the report or otherwise) as it is the practice of the union to take when matters of general interest to all its members need to be brought to their attention.

(5) Any such copy or notification shall be accompanied by a statement that the union will, on request, supply any member of the union with a copy of the report, either free of charge or on payment of such reasonable fee as may be specified in the notification.

(6) The trade union shall so supply any member of the union who makes such a request and pays the fee (if any) notified to him.

[565]

NOTES

Sub-s (1): word omitted from para (c) repealed, and para (e) and the word immediately preceding it added, by the Trade Union Reform and Employment Rights Act 1993, ss 3, 51, Sch 1, para 4(a), Sch 10.

Sub-s (2): words in square brackets inserted by the Trade Union Reform and Employment Rights Act 1993, s 3, Sch 1, para 4(b).

Sub-ss (2A), (2B): inserted by the Trade Union Reform and Employment Rights Act 1993, s 3, Sch 1, para 4(c).

79 Remedy for failure to comply with ballot rules: general

(1) The remedy for—

(a) the taking by a trade union of a ballot on a political resolution otherwise than in accordance with political ballot rules approved by the Certification Officer, or

(b) the failure of a trade union, in relation to a proposed ballot on a political resolution, to comply with the political ballot rules so approved,

is by way of application under section 80 (to the Certification Officer) or 81 (to the court).

…

(2) An application under those sections may be made only by a person who is a member of the trade union and, where the ballot has been held, was a member at the time when it was held.

References in those sections to a person having a sufficient interest are to such a person.

(3) No such application may be made after the end of the period of one year beginning with the day on which the union announced the result of the ballot.

[566]

NOTES

Sub-s (1): words omitted repealed by the Employment Relations Act 1999, ss 29, 44, Sch 6, paras 1, 14, Sch 9(7).

80 Application to Certification Officer

(1) A person having a sufficient interest (see section 79(2)) who claims that a trade union—

(a) has held a ballot on a political resolution otherwise than in accordance with political ballot rules approved by the Certification Officer, or

(b) has failed in relation to a proposed ballot on a political resolution to comply with political ballot rules so approved,

may apply to the Certification Officer for a declaration to that effect.

(2) On an application being made to him, the Certification Officer shall—

(a) make such enquiries as he thinks fit, and

(b) … give the applicant and the trade union an opportunity to be heard,

and may make or refuse the declaration asked for.

(3) If he makes a declaration he shall specify in it the provisions with which the trade union has failed to comply.

(4) Where he makes a declaration and is satisfied that steps have been taken by the union with a view to remedying the declared failure, or securing that a failure of the same or any similar kind does not occur in future, or that the union has agreed to take such steps, he shall in making the declaration specify those steps.

(5) Whether he makes or refuses a declaration, he shall give reasons for his decision in writing; and the reasons may be accompanied by written observations on any matter arising from, or connected with, the proceedings.

[(5A) Where the Certification Officer makes a declaration he shall also, unless he considers that to do so would be inappropriate, make an enforcement order, that is, an order imposing on the union one or more of the following requirements—

(a) to secure the holding of a ballot in accordance with the order;
(b) to take such other steps to remedy the declared failure as may be specified in the order;
(c) to abstain from such acts as may be so specified with a view to securing that a failure of the same or a similar kind does not occur in future.

The Certification Officer shall in an order imposing any such requirement as is mentioned in paragraph (a) or (b) specify the period within which the union must comply with the requirements of the order.

(5B) Where the Certification Officer makes an order requiring the union to hold a fresh ballot, he shall (unless he considers that it would be inappropriate to do so in the particular circumstances of the case) require the ballot to be conducted in accordance with the union's political ballot rules and such other provisions as may be made by the order.

(5C) Where an enforcement order has been made, any person who is a member of the union and was a member at the time the order was made is entitled to enforce obedience to the order as if he had made the application on which the order was made.]

(6) In exercising his functions under this section the Certification Officer shall ensure that, so far as is reasonably practicable, an application made to him is determined within six months of being made.

(7) Where he requests a person to furnish information to him in connection with enquiries made by him under this section, he shall specify the date by which that information is to be furnished and shall, unless he considers that it would be inappropriate to do so, proceed with his determination of the application notwithstanding that the information has not been furnished to him by the specified date.

[(8) A declaration made by the Certification Officer under this section may be relied on as if it were a declaration made by the court.

(9) An enforcement order made by the Certification Officer under this section may be enforced in the same way as an order of the court.

(10) The following paragraphs have effect if a person applies under section 81 in relation to a matter—

(a) that person may not apply under this section in relation to that matter;
(b) on an application by a different person under this section in relation to that matter, the Certification Officer shall have due regard to any declaration, order, observations, or reasons made or given by the court regarding that matter and brought to the Certification Officer's notice.]

[567]

NOTES

Sub-s (2): words omitted from para (b) repealed by the Employment Relations Act 1999, ss 29, 44, Sch 6, paras 1, 15(1), (2), Sch 9(7).

Sub-ss (5A)–(5C), (8)–(10): inserted and added respectively by the Employment Relations Act 1999, s 29, Sch 6, paras 1, 15(1), (3), (4).

81 Application to court

(1) A person having a sufficient interest (see section 79(2)) who claims that a trade union—

(a) has held a ballot on a political resolution otherwise than in accordance with political ballot rules approved by the Certification Officer, or
(b) has failed in relation to a proposed ballot on a political resolution to comply with political ballot rules so approved,

may apply to the court for a declaration to that effect.

(2) …

(3) If the court makes the declaration asked for, it shall specify in the declaration the provisions with which the trade union has failed to comply.

(4) Where the court makes a declaration it shall also, unless it considers that to do so would be inappropriate, make an enforcement order, that is, an order imposing on the union one or more of the following requirements—
(a) to secure the holding of a ballot in accordance with the order;
(b) to take such other steps to remedy the declared failure as may be specified in the order;
(c) to abstain from such acts as may be so specified with a view to securing that a failure of the same or a similar kind does not occur in future.

The court shall in an order imposing any such requirement as is mentioned in paragraph (a) or (b) specify the period within which the union must comply with the requirements of the order.

(5) Where the court makes an order requiring the union to hold a fresh ballot, the court shall (unless it considers that it would be inappropriate to do so in the particular circumstances of the case) require the ballot to be conducted in accordance with the union's political ballot rules and such other provisions as may be made by the order.

(6) Where an enforcement order has been made, any person who is a member of the union and was a member at the time the order was made is entitled to enforce obedience to the order as if he had made the application on which the order was made.

(7) Without prejudice to any other power of the court, the court may on an application under this section grant such interlocutory relief (in Scotland, such interim order) as it considers appropriate.

[(8) The following paragraphs have effect if a person applies under section 80 in relation to a matter—
(a) that person may not apply under this section in relation to that matter;
(b) on an application by a different person under this section in relation to that matter, the court shall have due regard to any declaration, order, observations or reasons made or given by the Certification Officer regarding that matter and brought to the court's notice.]

[568]

NOTES

Sub-s (2): repealed by the Employment Relations Act 1999, ss 29, 44, Sch 6, paras 1, 16(1), (2), Sch 9(7).

Sub-s (8): added by the Employment Relations Act 1999, s 29, Sch 6, paras 1, 16(1), (3).

The political fund

82 Rules as to political fund

(1) The trade union's rules must provide—
(a) that payments in the furtherance of the political objects to which this Chapter applies shall be made out of a separate fund (the "political fund" of the union);
(b) that a member of the union who gives notice in accordance with section 84 that he objects to contributing to the political fund shall be exempt from any obligation to contribute to it;
(c) that a member shall not by reason of being so exempt—
  (i) be excluded from any benefits of the union, or
  (ii) be placed in any respect either directly or indirectly under a disability or at a disadvantage as compared with other members of the union (except in relation to the control or management of the political fund); and

(d) that contribution to the political fund shall not be made a condition for admission to the union.

(2) A member of a trade union who claims that he is aggrieved by a breach of any rule made in pursuance of this section may complain to the Certification Officer.

[(2A) On a complaint being made to him the Certification Officer shall make such enquiries as he thinks fit.]

(3) Where, after giving the member and a representative of the union an opportunity of being heard, the Certification Officer considers that a breach has been committed, he may make such order for remedying the breach as he thinks just under the circumstances.

[(3A) Where the Certification Officer requests a person to furnish information to him in connection with enquiries made by him under this section, he shall specify the date by which that information is to be furnished and, unless he considers that it would be inappropriate to do so, shall proceed with his determination of the application notwithstanding that the information has not been furnished to him by the specified date.]

[(4A) Where an order has been made under this section, any person who is a member of the union and was a member at the time it was made is entitled to enforce obedience to the order as if he had made the complaint on which it was made.

(4B) An order made by the Certification Officer under this section may be enforced—

(a) in England and Wales, in the same way as an order of the county court;
(b) in Scotland, in the same way as an order of the sheriff.]

[569]

NOTES

Sub-ss (2A), (3A): inserted by the Employment Relations Act 1999, s 29, Sch 6, paras 1, 17.

Sub-ss (4A), (4B): substituted, for original sub-s (4), by the Employment Relations Act 2004, s 57(1), Sch 1, para 6, as from 6 April 2005, except in relation to any order made under sub-s (3) above before that date (see SI 2005/872, art 20).

83 Assets and liabilities of political fund

(1) There may be added to a union's political fund only—

(a) sums representing contributions made to the fund by members of the union or by any person other than the union itself, and
(b) property which accrues to the fund in the course of administering the assets of the fund.

(2) The rules of the union shall not be taken to require any member to contribute to the political fund at a time when there is no political resolution in force in relation to the union.

(3) No liability of a union's political fund shall be discharged out of any other fund of the union.

This subsection applies notwithstanding any term or condition on which the liability was incurred or that an asset of the other fund has been charged in connection with the liability.

[570]

84 Notice of objection to contributing to political fund

(1) A member of a trade union may give notice in the following form, or in a form to the like effect, that he objects to contribute to the political fund—

Name of Trade Union

POLITICAL FUND (EXEMPTION NOTICE)

I give notice that I object to contributing to the Political Fund of the Union, and am in consequence exempt, in manner provided by Chapter VI of Part I of the Trade Union and Labour Relations (Consolidation) Act 1992, from contributing to that fund.

A.B.

Address..

day of.. 19...

---

(2) On the adoption of a political resolution, notice shall be given to members of the union acquainting them—

(a) that each member has a right to be exempted from contributing to the union's political fund, and

(b) that a form of exemption notice can be obtained by or on behalf of a member either by application at or by post from—

(i) the head office or any branch office of the union, or

(ii) the office of the Certification Officer.

(3) The notice to members shall be given in accordance with rules of the union approved for the purpose by the Certification Officer, who shall have regard in each case to the existing practice and character of the union.

(4) On giving an exemption notice in accordance with this section, a member shall be exempt from contributing to the union's political fund—

(a) where the notice is given within one month of the giving of notice to members under subsection (2) following the passing of a political resolution on a ballot held at a time when no such resolution is in force, as from the date on which the exemption notice is given;

(b) in any other case, as from the 1st January next after the exemption notice is given.

(5) An exemption notice continues to have effect until it is withdrawn.

[571]

85 Manner of giving effect to exemptions

(1) Effect may be given to the exemption of members from contributing to the political fund of a union either—

(a) by a separate levy of contributions to that fund from the members who are not exempt, or

(b) by relieving members who are exempt from the payment of the whole or part of any periodical contribution required from members towards the expenses of the union.

(2) In the latter case, the rules shall provide—

(a) that relief shall be given as far as possible to all members who are exempt on the occasion of the same periodical payment, and

(b) for enabling each member of the union to know what portion (if any) of any periodical contribution payable by him is a contribution to the political fund.

[572]

Duties of employer who deducts union contributions

86 Certificate of exemption or objection to contributing to political fund

(1) If a member of a trade union which has a political fund certifies in writing to his employer that, or to the effect that—

(a) he is exempt from the obligation to contribute to the fund, or

(b) he has, in accordance with section 84, notified the union in writing of his objection to contributing to the fund,

the employer shall ensure that no amount representing a contribution to the political fund is deducted by him from emoluments payable to the member.

(2) The employer's duty under subsection (1) applies from the first day, following the giving of the certificate, on which it is reasonably practicable for him to comply with that subsection, until the certificate is withdrawn.

(3) An employer may not refuse to deduct any union dues from emoluments payable to a person who has given a certificate under this section if he continues to deduct union dues from emoluments payable to other members of the union, unless his refusal is not attributable to the giving of the certificate or otherwise connected with the duty imposed by subsection (1).

[573]

NOTES

Conciliation: employment tribunal proceedings and claims which could be the subject of employment tribunal proceedings arising out of a contravention, or alleged contravention, of this section are proceedings to which the Employment Tribunals Act 1996, s 18 applies; see s 18(1)(b) of that Act at

[975]. The standard conciliation period applies to such claims by virtue of the Employment Tribunals (Constitution and Rules of Procedure) Regulations 2004, SI 2004/1861, Sch 1, rule 22(1), (6).

[87 Complaint in respect of employer's failure

(1) A person who claims his employer has failed to comply with section 86 in deducting or refusing to deduct any amount from emoluments payable to him may present a complaint to an employment tribunal.

(2) A tribunal shall not consider a complaint under subsection (1) unless it is presented—

(a) within the period of three months beginning with the date of the payment of the emoluments or (if the complaint relates to more than one payment) the last of the payments, or

(b) where the tribunal is satisfied that it was not reasonably practicable for the complaint to be presented within that period, within such further period as the tribunal considers reasonable.

(3) Where on a complaint under subsection (1) arising out of subsection (3) (refusal to deduct union dues) of section 86 the question arises whether the employer's refusal to deduct an amount was attributable to the giving of the certificate or was otherwise connected with the duty imposed by subsection (1) of that section, it is for the employer to satisfy the tribunal that it was not.

(4) Where a tribunal finds that a complaint under subsection (1) is well-founded—

(a) it shall make a declaration to that effect and, where the complaint arises out of subsection (1) of section 86, order the employer to pay to the complainant the amount deducted in contravention of that subsection less any part of that amount already paid to him by the employer, and

(b) it may, if it considers it appropriate to do so in order to prevent a repetition of the failure, make an order requiring the employer to take, within a specified time, the steps specified in the order in relation to emoluments payable by him to the complainant.

(5) A person who claims his employer has failed to comply with an order made under subsection (4)(b) on a complaint presented by him may present a further complaint to an employment tribunal; but only one complaint may be presented under this subsection in relation to any order.

(6) A tribunal shall not consider a complaint under subsection (5) unless it is presented—

(a) after the end of the period of four weeks beginning with the date of the order, but

(b) before the end of the period of six months beginning with that date.

(7) Where on a complaint under subsection (5) a tribunal finds that an employer has, without reasonable excuse, failed to comply with an order made under subsection (4)(b), it shall order the employer to pay to the complainant an amount equal to two weeks' pay.

(8) Chapter II of Part XIV of the Employment Rights Act 1996 (calculation of a week's pay) applies for the purposes of subsection (7) with the substitution for section 225 of the following—

> "For the purposes of this Chapter in its application to subsection (7) of section 87 of the Trade Union and Labour Relations (Consolidation) Act 1992, the calculation date is the date of the payment, or (if more than one) the last of the payments, to which the complaint related."]

[574]

NOTES

Substituted by the Employment Rights (Dispute Resolution) Act 1998, s 6.
Conciliation: see the note to s 86 at **[573]**.

88 ((*Application of provisions of Wages Act 1986*) *repealed by the Employment Rights* (*Dispute Resolution*) *Act 1998, s 15, Sch 2.*)

Position where political resolution ceases to have effect

89 Administration of political fund where no resolution in force

(1) The following provisions have effect with respect to the political fund of a trade union where there ceases to be any political resolution in force in relation to the union.

(2) If the resolution ceases to have effect by reason of a ballot being held on which a new political resolution is not passed, the union may continue to make payments out of the fund as if the resolution had continued in force for six months beginning with the date of the ballot.

But no payment shall be made which causes the fund to be in deficit or increases a deficit in it.

(3) There may be added to the fund only—

(a) contributions to the fund paid to the union (or to a person on its behalf) before the resolution ceased to have effect, and

(b) property which accrues to the fund in the course of administering the assets of the fund.

(4) The union may, notwithstanding any of its rules or any trusts on which the fund is held, transfer the whole or part of the fund to such other fund of the union as it thinks fit.

(5) If a new political resolution is subsequently passed, no property held immediately before the date of the ballot by or on behalf of the union otherwise than in its political fund, and no sums representing such property, may be added to the fund.

[575]

90 Discontinuance of contributions to political fund

(1) Where there ceases to be any political resolution in force in relation to a trade union, the union shall take such steps as are necessary to ensure that the collection of contributions to its political fund is discontinued as soon as is reasonably practicable.

(2) The union may, notwithstanding any of its rules, pay into any of its other funds any such contribution which is received by it after the resolution ceases to have effect.

(3) If the union continues to collect contributions, it shall refund to a member who applies for a refund the contributions made by him collected after the resolution ceased to have effect.

(4) A member of a trade union who claims that the union has failed to comply with subsection (1) may apply to the court for a declaration to that effect.

(5) Where the court is satisfied that the complaint is well-founded, it may, if it considers it appropriate to do so in order to secure that the collection of contributions to the political fund is discontinued, make an order requiring the union to take, within such time as may be specified in the order, such steps as may be so specified.

Such an order may be enforced by a person who is a member of the union and was a member at the time the order was made as if he had made the application.

(6) The remedy for failure to comply with subsection (1) is in accordance with subsections (4) and (5), and not otherwise; but this does not affect any right to recover sums payable to a person under subsection (3).

[576]

91 Rules to cease to have effect

(1) If there ceases to be any political resolution in force in relation to a trade union, the rules of the union made for the purpose of complying with this Chapter also cease to have effect, except so far as they are required to enable the political fund to be administered at a time when there is no such resolution in force.

(2) If the resolution ceases to have effect by reason of a ballot being held on which a new political resolution is not passed, the rules cease to have effect at the end of the period of six months beginning with the date of the ballot.

In any other case the rules cease to have effect when the resolution ceases to have effect.

(3) Nothing in this section affects the operation of section 82(2) (complaint to Certification Officer in respect of breach of rules) in relation to a breach of a rule occurring before the rule in question ceased to have effect.

(4) No member of a trade union who has at any time been exempt from the obligation to contribute to its political fund shall by reason of his having been exempt—

(a) be excluded from any benefits of the union, or

(b) be placed in any respect either directly or indirectly under a disability or at a disadvantage as compared with other members (except in relation to the control or management of the political fund).

[577]

Supplementary

92 Manner of making union rules

If the Certification Officer is satisfied, and certifies, that rules of a trade union made for any of the purposes of this Chapter and requiring approval by him have been approved—

(a) by a majority of the members of the union voting for the purpose, or

(b) by a majority of delegates of the union at a meeting called for the purpose,

the rules shall have effect as rules of the union notwithstanding that the rules of the union as to the alteration of rules or the making of new rules have not been complied with.

[578]

93 Effect of amalgamation

(1) Where on an amalgamation of two or more trade unions—

(a) there is in force in relation to each of the amalgamating unions a political resolution and such rules as are required by this Chapter, and

(b) the rules of the amalgamated union in force immediately after the amalgamation include such rules as are required by this Chapter,

the amalgamated union shall be treated for the purposes of this Chapter as having passed a political resolution.

(2) That resolution shall be treated as having been passed on the date of the earliest of the ballots on which the resolutions in force immediately before the amalgamation with respect to the amalgamating unions were passed.

(3) Where one of the amalgamating unions is a Northern Ireland union, the references above to the requirements of this Chapter shall be construed as references to the requirements of the corresponding provisions of the law of Northern Ireland.

[579]

94 Overseas members of trade unions

(1) Where a political resolution is in force in relation to the union—

(a) rules made by the union for the purpose of complying with section 74 (political ballot rules) in relation to a proposed ballot may provide for overseas members of the union not to be accorded entitlement to vote in the ballot, and

(b) rules made by the union for the purpose of complying with section 84 (notice of right to object to contribute to political fund to be given where resolution passed) may provide for notice not to be given by the union to its overseas members.

(2) Accordingly, where provision is made in accordance with subsection (1)(a), the Certification Officer shall not on that ground withhold his approval of the rules; and where provision is made in accordance with subsection (1)(b), section 84(2) (duty to give notice) shall not be taken to require notice to be given to overseas members.

(3) An "overseas member" means a member of the trade union (other than a merchant seaman or offshore worker) who is outside Great Britain throughout the period during which votes may be cast.

For this purpose—

"merchant seaman" means a person whose employment, or the greater part of it, is carried out on board sea-going ships; and

"offshore worker" means a person in offshore employment, other than one who is in such employment in an area where the law of Northern Ireland applies.

[580]

95 Appeals from Certification Officer

An appeal lies to the Employment Appeal Tribunal on any question of law arising in proceedings before or arising from any decision of the Certification Officer under this Chapter.

[581]

96 Meaning of "date of the ballot"

In this Chapter the "date of the ballot" means, in the case of a ballot in which votes may be cast on more than one day, the last of those days.

[582]

CHAPTER VII
AMALGAMATIONS AND SIMILAR MATTERS

NOTES

Regulations: for Regulations supplementing the provisions of this Chapter, see the Trade Unions and Employers' Associations (Amalgamations etc) Regulations 1975, SI 1975/536 at **[2008A]**.

Amalgamation or transfer of engagements

97 Amalgamation or transfer of engagements

(1) Two or more trade unions may amalgamate and become one trade union, with or without a division or dissolution of the funds of any one or more of the amalgamating unions, but shall not do so unless—

(a) the instrument of amalgamation is approved in accordance with section 98, and

(b) the requirements of [section 99 (notice to members) and section 100 (resolution to be passed by required majority in ballot held in accordance with sections 100A to 100E)] are complied with in respect of each of the amalgamating unions.

(2) A trade union may transfer its engagements to another trade union which undertakes to fulfil those engagements, but shall not do so unless—

(a) the instrument of transfer is approved in accordance with section 98, and

(b) the requirements of [section 99 (notice to members) and section 100 (resolution to be passed by required majority in ballot held in accordance with sections 100A to 100E)] are complied with in respect of the transferor union.

(3) An amalgamation or transfer of engagements does not prejudice any right of any creditor of any trade union party to the amalgamation or transfer.

(4) The above provisions apply to every amalgamation or transfer of engagements notwithstanding anything in the rules of any of the trade unions concerned.

[583]

NOTES

Sub-ss (1), (2): words in square brackets substituted by the Trade Union Reform and Employment Rights Act 1993, s 49(2), Sch 8, para 52.

98 Approval of instrument of amalgamation or transfer

(1) The instrument of amalgamation or transfer must be approved by the Certification Officer and shall be submitted to him for approval before [a ballot of the members of any amalgamating union, or (as the case may be) of the transferor union, is held on the resolution to approve the instrument].

[(2) If the Certification Officer is satisfied—

(a) that an instrument of amalgamation complies with the requirements of any regulations in force under this Chapter, and

(b) that he is not prevented from approving the instrument of amalgamation by subsection (3),

he shall approve the instrument.

(3) The Certification Officer shall not approve an instrument of amalgamation if it appears to him that the proposed name of the amalgamated union is the same as the name under which another organisation—

(a) was on 30th September 1971 registered as a trade union under the Trade Union Acts 1871 to 1964,
(b) was at any time registered as a trade union or employers' association under the Industrial Relations Act 1971, or
(c) is for the time being entered in the list of trade unions or in the list of employers' associations,

or if the proposed name is one so nearly resembling any such name as to be likely to deceive the public.

(4) Subsection (3) does not apply if the proposed name is the name of one of the amalgamating unions.

(5) If the Certification Officer is satisfied that an instrument of transfer complies with the requirements of any regulations in force under this Chapter, he shall approve the instrument.]

[584]

NOTES

Sub-s (1): words in square brackets substituted by the Trade Union Reform and Employment Rights Act 1993, s 49(2), Sch 8, para 53.

Sub-ss (2)–(5): substituted, for original sub-s (2), by the Employment Relations Act 2004, s 50(1), as from 6 April 2005, except in relation to any instrument submitted to the Certification Officer for approval before that date (see SI 2005/872, art 17).

99 Notice to be given to members

(1) The trade union shall take all reasonable steps to secure [that every voting paper which is supplied for voting in the ballot on the resolution to approve the instrument of amalgamation or transfer is accompanied by] a notice in writing approved for the purpose by the Certification Officer.

(2) The notice shall be in writing and shall either—
(a) set out in full the instrument of amalgamation or transfer to which the resolution relates, or
(b) give an account of it sufficient to enable those receiving the notice to form a reasonable judgment of the main effects of the proposed amalgamation or transfer.

(3) If the notice does not set out the instrument in full it shall state where copies of the instrument may be inspected by those receiving the notice.

[(3A) The notice shall not contain any statement making a recommendation or expressing an opinion about the proposed amalgamation or transfer.]

(4) The notice shall also comply with the requirements of any regulations in force under this Chapter.

(5) The notice proposed to be supplied to members of the union under this section shall be submitted to the Certification Officer for approval; and he shall approve it if he is satisfied that it meets the requirements of this section.

[585]

NOTES

Sub-s (1): words in square brackets substituted by the Trade Union Reform and Employment Rights Act 1993, s 49(2), Sch 8, para 54.

Sub-s (3A): inserted by the Trade Union Reform and Employment Rights Act 1993, s 5.

[100 Requirement of ballot on resolution

(1) A resolution approving the instrument of amalgamation or transfer must be passed on a ballot of the members of the trade union held in accordance with sections 100A to 100E.

(2) A simple majority of those voting is sufficient to pass such a resolution unless the rules of the trade union expressly require it to be approved by a greater majority or by a specified proportion of the members of the union.]

[586]

NOTES

Substituted, together with ss 100A–100E for original s 100, by the Trade Union Reform and Employment Rights Act 1993, s 4.

[100A Appointment of independent scrutineer

(1) The trade union shall, before the ballot is held, appoint a qualified independent person ("the scrutineer") to carry out—

(a) the functions in relation to the ballot which are required under this section to be contained in his appointment; and

(b) such additional functions in relation to the ballot as may be specified in his appointment.

(2) A person is a qualified independent person in relation to a ballot if—

(a) he satisfies such conditions as may be specified for the purposes of this section by order of the Secretary of State or is himself so specified; and

(b) the trade union has no grounds for believing either that he will carry out any functions conferred on him in relation to the ballot otherwise than competently or that his independence in relation to the union, or in relation to the ballot, might reasonably be called into question.

An order under paragraph (a) shall be made by statutory instrument which shall be subject to annulment in pursuance of a resolution of either House of Parliament.

(3) The scrutineer's appointment shall require him—

(a) to be the person who supervises the production of the voting papers and (unless he is appointed under section 100D to undertake the distribution of the voting papers) their distribution and to whom the voting papers are returned by those voting;

(b) to—

(i) inspect the register of names and addresses of the members of the trade union, or

(ii) examine the copy of the register as at the relevant date which is supplied to him in accordance with subsection (9)(a),

whenever it appears to him appropriate to do so and, in particular, when the conditions specified in subsection (4) are satisfied;

(c) to take such steps as appear to him to be appropriate for the purpose of enabling him to make his report (see section 100E);

(d) to make his report to the trade union as soon as reasonably practicable after the last date for the return of voting papers; and

(e) to retain custody of all voting papers returned for the purposes of the ballot and the copy of the register supplied to him in accordance with subsection (9)(a)—

(i) until the end of the period of one year beginning with the announcement by the union of the result of the ballot; and

(ii) if within that period a complaint is made under section 103 (complaint as regards passing of resolution), until the Certification Officer or Employment Appeal Tribunal authorises him to dispose of the papers or copy.

(4) The conditions referred to in subsection (3)(b) are—

(a) that a request that the scrutineer inspect the register or examine the copy is made to him during the appropriate period by a member of the trade union who suspects that the register is not, or at the relevant date was not, accurate and up-to-date, and

(b) that the scrutineer does not consider that the member's suspicion is ill-founded.

(5) In subsection (4) "the appropriate period" means the period—

(a) beginning with the day on which the scrutineer is appointed, and

(b) ending with the day before the day on which the scrutineer makes his report to the trade union.

(6) The duty of confidentiality as respects the register is incorporated in the scrutineer's appointment.

(7) The trade union shall ensure that nothing in the terms of the scrutineer's appointment (including any additional functions specified in the appointment) is such as to make it reasonable for any person to call the scrutineer's independence in relation to the union into question.

(8) The trade union shall, before the scrutineer begins to carry out his functions, either—

(a) send a notice stating the name of the scrutineer to every member of the union to whom it is reasonably practicable to send such a notice, or

(b) take all such other steps for notifying members of the name of the scrutineer as it is the practice of the union to take when matters of general interest to all its members need to be brought to their attention.

(9) The trade union shall—

(a) supply to the scrutineer as soon as is reasonably practicable after the relevant date a copy of the register of names and addresses of its members as at that date, and

(b) comply with any request made by the scrutineer to inspect the register.

(10) Where the register is kept by means of a computer the duty imposed on the trade union by subsection (9)(a) is either to supply a legible printed copy or (if the scrutineer prefers) to supply a copy of the computer data and allow the scrutineer use of the computer to read it at any time during the period when he is required to retain custody of the copy.

(11) The trade union shall ensure that the scrutineer duly carries out his functions and that there is no interference with his carrying out of those functions which would make it reasonable for any person to call the scrutineer's independence in relation to the union into question.

(12) The trade union shall comply with all reasonable requests made by the scrutineer for the purposes of, or in connection with, the carrying out of his functions.

(13) In this section "the relevant date" means—

(a) where the trade union has rules determining who is entitled to vote in the ballot by reference to membership on a particular date, that date, and

(b) otherwise, the date, or the last date, on which voting papers are distributed for the purposes of the ballot.]

[587]

NOTES

Substituted as noted to s 100 at **[586]**.

Orders: the Trade Union Ballots and Elections (Independent Scrutineer Qualifications) Order 1993, SI 1993/1909 at **[2179]**.

[100B Entitlement to vote

Entitlement to vote in the ballot shall be accorded equally to all members of the trade union.]

[588]

NOTES

Substituted as noted to s 100 at **[586]**.

[100C Voting

(1) The method of voting must be by the marking of a voting paper by the person voting.

(2) Each voting paper must—

(a) state the name of the independent scrutineer and clearly specify the address to which, and the date by which, it is to be returned, and

(b) be given one of a series of consecutive whole numbers every one of which is used in giving a different number in that series to each voting paper printed or otherwise produced for the purposes of the ballot, and

(c) be marked with its number.

(3) Every person who is entitled to vote in the ballot must—

(a) be allowed to vote without interference or constraint, and

(b) so far as is reasonably practicable, be enabled to do so without incurring any direct cost to himself.

(4) So far as is reasonably practicable, every person who is entitled to vote in the ballot must—

(a) have a voting paper sent to him by post at his home address or another address which he has requested the trade union in writing to treat as his postal address, and

(b) be given a convenient opportunity to vote by post.

(5) No voting paper which is sent to a person for voting shall have enclosed with it any other document except—

(a) the notice which, under section 99(1), is to accompany the voting paper,

(b) an addressed envelope, and

(c) a document containing instructions for the return of the voting paper, without any other statement.

(6) The ballot shall be conducted so as to secure that—

(a) so far as is reasonably practicable, those voting do so in secret, and

(b) the votes given in the ballot are fairly and accurately counted.

For the purposes of paragraph (b) an inaccuracy in counting shall be disregarded if it is accidental and on a scale which could not affect the result of the ballot.]

[589]

NOTES

Substituted as noted to s 100 at **[586]**.

[100D Counting of votes etc by independent person

(1) The trade union shall ensure that—

(a) the storage and distribution of the voting papers for the purposes of the ballot, and

(b) the counting of the votes cast in the ballot,

are undertaken by one or more independent persons appointed by the trade union.

(2) A person is an independent person in relation to a ballot if—

(a) he is the scrutineer, or

(b) he is a person other than the scrutineer and the trade union has no grounds for believing either that he will carry out any functions conferred on him in relation to the ballot otherwise than competently or that his independence in relation to the union, or in relation to the ballot, might reasonably be called into question.

(3) An appointment under this section shall require the person appointed to carry out his functions so as to minimise the risk of any contravention of requirements imposed by or under any enactment or the occurrence of any unfairness or malpractice.

(4) The duty of confidentiality as respects the register is incorporated in the scrutineer's appointment.

(5) Where the person appointed to undertake the counting of votes is not the scrutineer, his appointment shall require him to send the voting papers back to the scrutineer as soon as reasonably practicable after the counting has been completed.

(6) The trade union—

(a) shall ensure that nothing in the terms of an appointment under this section is such as to make it reasonable for any person to call into question the independence of the person appointed in relation to the union,

(b) shall ensure that a person appointed under this section duly carries out his functions and that there is no interference with his carrying out of those functions which would make it reasonable for any person to call into question the independence of the person appointed in relation to the union, and

(c) shall comply with all reasonable requests made by a person appointed under this section for the purposes of, or in connection with, the carrying out of his functions.]

[590]

NOTES

Substituted as noted to s 100 at **[586]**.

[100E Scrutineer's report

(1) The scrutineer's report on the ballot shall state—

(a) the number of voting papers distributed for the purposes of the ballot,

(b) the number of voting papers returned to the scrutineer,

(c) the number of valid votes cast in the ballot for and against the resolution,

(d) the number of spoiled or otherwise invalid voting papers returned, and

(e) the name of the person (or of each of the persons) appointed under section 100D or, if no person was so appointed, that fact.

(2) The report shall also state whether the scrutineer is satisfied—

(a) that there are no reasonable grounds for believing that there was any contravention of a requirement imposed by or under any enactment in relation to the ballot,

(b) that the arrangements made (whether by him or any other person) with respect to the production, storage, distribution, return or other handling of the voting papers used in the ballot, and the arrangements for the counting of the votes, included all such security arrangements as were reasonably practicable for the purpose of minimising the risk that any unfairness or malpractice might occur, and

(c) that he has been able to carry out his functions without any such interference as would make it reasonable for any person to call his independence in relation to the union into question;

and if he is not satisfied as to any of those matters, the report shall give particulars of his reasons for not being satisfied as to that matter.

(3) The report shall also state—

(a) whether the scrutineer—

(i) has inspected the register of names and addresses of the members of the trade union, or

(ii) has examined the copy of the register as at the relevant date which is supplied to him in accordance with section 100A(9)(a),

(b) if he has, whether in the case of each inspection or examination he was acting on a request by a member of the trade union or at his own instance,

(c) whether he declined to act on any such request, and

(d) whether any inspection of the register, or any examination of the copy of the register, has revealed any matter which he considers should be drawn to the attention of the trade union in order to assist it in securing that the register is accurate and up-to-date,

but shall not state the name of any member who has requested such an inspection or examination.

(4) Where one or more persons other than the scrutineer are appointed under section 100D, the statement included in the scrutineer's report in accordance with subsection (2)(b) shall also indicate—

(a) whether he is satisfied with the performance of the person, or each of the persons, so appointed, and

(b) if he is not satisfied with the performance of the person, or any of them, particulars of his reasons for not being so satisfied.

(5) The trade union shall not publish the result of the ballot until it has received the scrutineer's report.

(6) The trade union shall within the period of three months after it receives the report—

(a) send a copy of the report to every member of the union to whom it is reasonably practicable to send such a copy; or

(b) take all such other steps for notifying the contents of the report to the members of the union (whether by publishing the report or otherwise) as it is the practice of the union to take when matters of general interest to all its members need to be brought to their attention.

(7) Any such copy or notification shall be accompanied by a statement that the union will, on request, supply any member of the trade union with a copy of the report, either free of charge or on payment of such reasonable fee as may be specified in the notification.

(8) The trade union shall so supply any member of the union who makes such a request and pays the fee (if any) notified to him.]

[591]

NOTES

Substituted as noted to s 100 at **[586]**.

101 Registration of instrument of amalgamation or transfer

(1) An instrument of amalgamation or transfer shall not take effect before it has been registered by the Certification Officer under this Chapter.

(2) It shall not be so registered before the end of the period of six weeks beginning with the date on which an application for its registration is sent to the Certification Officer.

[(3) An application for registration of an instrument of amalgamation or transfer shall not be sent to the Certification Officer until section 100E(6) has been complied with in relation to the scrutineer's report on the ballot held on the resolution to approve the instrument.]

[592]

NOTES

Sub-s (3): added by the Trade Union Reform and Employment Rights Act 1993, s 49(2), Sch 8, para 55.

[101A Listing and certification after amalgamation

(1) Subsection (2) applies if when an instrument of amalgamation is registered by the Certification Officer under this Chapter each of the amalgamating unions is entered in the list of trade unions.

(2) The Certification Officer shall—

(a) enter, with effect from the amalgamation date, the name of the amalgamated union in the list of trade unions, and

(b) remove, with effect from that date, the names of the amalgamating unions from that list.

(3) Subsection (4) applies if when an instrument of amalgamation is registered by the Certification Officer under this Chapter each of the amalgamating unions has a certificate of independence which is in force.

(4) The Certification Officer shall issue to the amalgamated trade union, with effect from the amalgamation date, a certificate that the union is independent.

(5) In this section "the amalgamation date" means the date on which the instrument of amalgamation takes effect.]

[592A]

NOTES

Commencement: 6 April 2005.

Inserted, together with s 101B, by the Employment Relations Act 2004, s 50(2), as from 6 April 2005, except in relation to any application for registration of an instrument of amalgamation or transfer which was sent to the Certification Officer before that date (see SI 2005/872, art 18).

[101B Supply of information by amalgamated union

(1) If an instrument of amalgamation is registered under this Chapter by the Certification Officer and the amalgamated union is entered in the list of trade unions in accordance with section 101A, that union shall send to him, in such manner and form as he may require—

(a) a copy of the rules of the union,

(b) a list of its officers, and

(c) the address of its head or main office.

(2) The information required to be sent under subsection (1) must be accompanied by any fee prescribed for the purpose under section 108.

(3) The information must be sent—

(a) before the end of the period of six weeks beginning with the date on which the instrument of amalgamation takes effect, or

(b) if the Certification Officer considers that it is not reasonably practicable for the amalgamated union to send it in that period, before the end of such longer period, beginning with that date, as he may specify to the amalgamated union.

(4) If any of subsections (1) to (3) are not complied with by the amalgamated union, the Certification Officer shall remove its name from the list of trade unions.]

[592B]

NOTES

Commencement: 6 April 2005.

Inserted as noted to s 101A at **[592A]**.

Prescribed fee: the fee of £41 is prescribed for the purposes of sub-s (2) above in circumstances where, at the time the instrument of amalgamation was registered by the Certification Officer, the condition in s 101A(3) was satisfied and the Certification Officer was, accordingly, under the duty in sub-s (4) of that section to issue a certificate of independence to the amalgamated union (see the Certification Officer (Amendment of Fees) Regulations 2005, SI 2005/713, reg 8).

102 Power to alter rules of transferee union for purposes of transfer

(1) Where a trade union proposes to transfer its engagements to another trade union and an alteration of the rules of the transferee union is necessary to give effect to provisions in the instrument of transfer, the committee of management or other governing body of that union may by memorandum in writing alter the rules of that union so far as is necessary to give effect to those provisions.

This subsection does not apply if the rules of the trade union expressly provide that this section is not to apply to that union.

(2) An alteration of the rules of a trade union under subsection (1) shall not take effect unless or until the instrument of transfer takes effect.

(3) The provisions of subsection (1) have effect, where they apply, notwithstanding anything in the rules of the union.

[593]

103 Complaints as regards passing of resolution

[(1) A member of a trade union who claims that the union—

(a) has failed to comply with any of the requirements of sections 99 to 100E, or

(b) has, in connection with a resolution approving an instrument of amalgamation or transfer, failed to comply with any rule of the union relating to the passing of the resolution,

may complain to the Certification Officer.]

(2) Any complaint must be made before the end of the period of six weeks beginning with the date on which an application for registration of the instrument of amalgamation or transfer is sent to the Certification Officer.

Where a complaint is made, the Certification Officer shall not register the instrument before the complaint is finally determined or is withdrawn.

[(2A) On a complaint being made to him the Certification Officer shall make such enquiries as he thinks fit].

(3) If the Certification Officer, after giving the complainant and the trade union an opportunity of being heard, finds the complaint to be justified—

(a) he shall make a declaration to that effect, and

(b) he may make an order specifying the steps which must be taken before he will entertain any application to register the instrument of amalgamation or transfer;

and where he makes such an order, he shall not entertain any application to register the instrument unless he is satisfied that the steps specified in the order have been taken.

An order under this subsection may be varied by the Certification Officer by a further order.

(4) The Certification Officer shall furnish a statement, orally or in writing, of the reasons for his decision on a complaint under this section.

(5) The validity of a resolution approving an instrument of amalgamation or transfer shall not be questioned in any legal proceedings whatsoever (except proceedings before the Certification Officer under this section or proceedings arising out of such proceedings) on any ground on which a complaint could be, or could have been, made to the Certification Officer under this section.

[(6) Where the Certification Officer requests a person to furnish information to him in connection with enquiries made by him under this section, he shall specify the date by which that information is to be furnished and, unless he considers that it would be inappropriate to do so, shall proceed with his determination of the application notwithstanding that the information has not been furnished to him by the specified date.

(7) A declaration made by the Certification Officer under this section may be relied on as if it were a declaration made by the court.

(8) Where an order has been made under this section, any person who is a member of the union and was a member at the time it was made is entitled to enforce obedience to the order as if he had made the [complaint] on which the order was made.

(9) An order made by the Certification Officer under this section may be enforced in the same way as an order of the court].

[594]

NOTES

Sub-s (1): substituted by the Trade Union Reform and Employment Rights Act 1993, s 49(2), Sch 8, para 56.

Sub-ss (2A), (6), (7), (9): inserted and added respectively by the Employment Relations Act 1999, s 29, Sch 6, paras 1, 18.

Sub-s (8): added by the Employment Relations Act 1999, s 29, Sch 6, paras 1, 18; word in square brackets substituted by the Employment Relations Act 2004, s 57(1), Sch 1, para 7, as from 6 April 2005.

104 Appeal from decision of Certification Officer

An appeal lies to the Employment Appeal Tribunal, at the instance of the complainant or the trade union, on any question of law arising in any proceedings before, or arising from any decision of, the Certification Officer under section 103.

[595]

105 Transfer of property on amalgamation or transfer

(1) Where an instrument of amalgamation or transfer takes effect, the property held—

(a) for the benefit of any of the amalgamating unions, or for the benefit of a branch of any of those unions, by the trustees of the union or branch, or

(b) for the benefit of the transferor trade union, or for the benefit of a branch of the transferor trade union, by the trustees of the union or branch,

shall without any conveyance, assignment or assignation vest, on the instrument taking effect, or on the appointment of the appropriate trustees, whichever is the later, in the appropriate trustees.

(2) In the case of property to be held for the benefit of a branch of the amalgamated union, or of the transferee union, "the appropriate trustees" means the trustees of that branch, unless the rules of the amalgamated or transferee union provide that the property to be so held is to be held by the trustees of the union.

(3) In any other case "the appropriate trustees" means the trustees of the amalgamated or transferee union.

(4) This section does not apply—

(a) to property excepted from the operation of this section by the instrument of amalgamation or transfer, or

(b) to stocks and securities in the public funds of the United Kingdom or Northern Ireland.

[596]

106 Amalgamation or transfer involving Northern Ireland

(1) This Chapter has effect subject to the following modifications in the case of an amalgamation or transfer of engagements to which a trade union and a Northern Ireland union are party.

(2) The requirements of sections [98 to 100E and 101(3) (approval of instrument, notice to members and ballot on resolution)] do not apply in relation to the Northern Ireland union; but the Certification Officer shall not register the instrument under section 101 unless he is satisfied that it will be effective under the law of Northern Ireland.

(3) The instrument of amalgamation or transfer submitted to the Certification Officer for his approval under section 98 shall state which of the bodies concerned is a Northern Ireland union and, in the case of an amalgamation, whether the amalgamated body is to be a Northern Ireland union; and the Certification Officer shall withhold his approval if the instrument does not contain that information.

(4) Nothing in section 102 (alteration of rules) or [sections 103 and 104] (complaint as to passing of resolution) applies in relation to the Northern Ireland union.

(5) Subject to the exceptions specified above, the provisions of this Chapter as to amalgamations or transfers of engagements apply in relation to the Northern Ireland union.

[597]

NOTES

Sub-ss (2), (4): words in square brackets substituted by the Trade Union Reform and Employment Rights Act 1993, s 49(2), Sch 8, para 57(a), (b).

Change of name

107 Change of name of trade union

(1) A trade union may change its name by any method expressly provided for by its rules or, if its rules do not expressly provide for a method of doing so, by adopting in accordance with its rules an alteration of the provision in them which gives the union its name.

(2) If the name of the trade union is entered in the list of trade unions a change of name shall not take effect until approved by the Certification Officer.

(3) The Certification Officer shall not approve a change of name if it appears to him that the proposed new name—

(a) is the same as one entered in the list as the name of another trade union, or

(b) is the same as one entered in the list of employers' associations kept under Part II of this Act,

or is a name so nearly resembling such a name as to be likely to deceive the public.

(4) A change of name by a trade union does not affect any right or obligation of the union or any of its members; and any pending legal proceedings may be continued by or against the union, the trustees of the union or any other officer of the union who can sue or be sued on its behalf notwithstanding its change of name.

[598]

Supplementary

108 General powers to make regulations

(1) The Secretary of State may make regulations as respects—

(a) applications to the Certification Officer under this Chapter,

(b) the registration under this Chapter of any document or matter,

(c) the inspection of documents kept by the Certification Officer under this Chapter,

(d) the charging of fees in respect of such matters, and of such amounts, as may with the approval of the Treasury be prescribed by the regulations,

and generally for carrying this Chapter into effect.

(2) Provision may in particular be made—

(a) requiring an application for the registration of an instrument of amalgamation or transfer, or of a change of name, to be accompanied by such statutory declarations or other documents as may be specified in the regulations;

(b) as to the form or content of any document required by this Chapter, or by the regulations, to be sent or submitted to the Certification Officer and as to the manner in which any such document is to be signed or authenticated;

(c) authorising the Certification Officer to require notice to be given or published in such manner as he may direct of the fact that an application for registration of an instrument of amalgamation or transfer has been or is to be made to him.

(3) Regulations under this section may make different provision for different circumstances.

(4) Regulations under this section shall be made by statutory instrument which shall be subject to annulment in pursuance of a resolution of either House of Parliament.

[599]

NOTES

Regulations: the Certification Officer (Amendment of Fees) Regulations 2005, SI 2005/713. Also, by virtue of s 300(3) of, and Sch 3, para 1(2) to, this Act, and the Interpretation Act 1978, s 17(2)(b), the Trade Union and Employers' Associations (Amalgamations, etc) Regulations 1975, SI 1975/536 (at **[2008A]**), have effect as if made under this section.

[CHAPTER VIIA
BREACH OF RULES

108A Right to apply to Certification Officer

(1) A person who claims that there has been a breach or threatened breach of the rules of a trade union relating to any of the matters mentioned in subsection (2) may apply to the Certification Officer for a declaration to that effect, subject to subsections (3) to (7).

(2) The matters are—
(a) the appointment or election of a person to, or the removal of a person from, any office;
(b) disciplinary proceedings by the union (including expulsion);
(c) the balloting of members on any issue other than industrial action;
(d) the constitution or proceedings of any executive committee or of any decision-making meeting;
(e) such other matters as may be specified in an order made by the Secretary of State.

(3) The applicant must be a member of the union, or have been one at the time of the alleged breach or threatened breach.

(4) A person may not apply under subsection (1) in relation to a claim if he is entitled to apply under section 80 in relation to the claim.

(5) No application may be made regarding—
(a) the dismissal of an employee of the union;
(b) disciplinary proceedings against an employee of the union.

(6) An application must be made—
(a) within the period of six months starting with the day on which the breach or threatened breach is alleged to have taken place, or
(b) if within that period any internal complaints procedure of the union is invoked to resolve the claim, within the period of six months starting with the earlier of the days specified in subsection (7).

(7) Those days are—
(a) the day on which the procedure is concluded, and
(b) the last day of the period of one year beginning with the day on which the procedure is invoked.

(8) The reference in subsection (1) to the rules of a union includes references to the rules of any branch or section of the union.

(9) In subsection (2)(c) "industrial action" means a strike or other industrial action by persons employed under contracts of employment.

(10) For the purposes of subsection (2)(d) a committee is an executive committee if—
(a) it is a committee of the union concerned and has power to make executive decisions on behalf of the union or on behalf of a constituent body,
(b) it is a committee of a major constituent body and has power to make executive decisions on behalf of that body, or
(c) it is a sub-committee of a committee falling within paragraph (a) or (b).

(11) For the purposes of subsection (2)(d) a decision-making meeting is—
(a) a meeting of members of the union concerned (or the representatives of such members) which has power to make a decision on any matter which, under the rules of the union, is final as regards the union or which, under the rules of the union or a constituent body, is final as regards that body, or
(b) a meeting of members of a major constituent body (or the representatives of such members) which has power to make a decision on any matter which, under the rules of the union or the body, is final as regards that body.

(12) For the purposes of subsections (10) and (11), in relation to the trade union concerned—
(a) a constituent body is any body which forms part of the union, including a branch, group, section or region;
(b) a major constituent body is such a body which has more than 1,000 members.

(13) Any order under subsection (2)(e) shall be made by statutory instrument; and no such order shall be made unless a draft of it has been laid before and approved by resolution of each House of Parliament.

(14) If a person applies to the Certification Officer under this section in relation to an alleged breach or threatened breach he may not apply to the court in relation to the breach or threatened breach; but nothing in this subsection shall prevent such a person from exercising any right to appeal against or challenge the Certification Officer's decision on the application to him.

(15) If—

(a) a person applies to the court in relation to an alleged breach or threatened breach, and

(b) the breach or threatened breach is one in relation to which he could have made an application to the Certification Officer under this section,

he may not apply to the Certification Officer under this section in relation to the breach or threatened breach.]

[600]

NOTES

Inserted, together with the preceding heading and ss 108B, 108C, by the Employment Relations Act 1999, s 29, Sch 6, paras 1, 19.

Orders: as of 6 April 2008 no Orders had been made under this section.

[108B Declarations and orders

(1) The Certification Officer may refuse to accept an application under section 108A unless he is satisfied that the applicant has taken all reasonable steps to resolve the claim by the use of any internal complaints procedure of the union.

(2) If he accepts an application under section 108A the Certification Officer—

(a) shall make such enquiries as he thinks fit,

(b) shall give the applicant and the union an opportunity to be heard,

(c) shall ensure that, so far as is reasonably practicable, the application is determined within six months of being made,

(d) may make or refuse the declaration asked for, and

(e) shall, whether he makes or refuses the declaration, give reasons for his decision in writing.

(3) Where the Certification Officer makes a declaration he shall also, unless he considers that to do so would be inappropriate, make an enforcement order, that is, an order imposing on the union one or both of the following requirements—

(a) to take such steps to remedy the breach, or withdraw the threat of a breach, as may be specified in the order;

(b) to abstain from such acts as may be so specified with a view to securing that a breach or threat of the same or a similar kind does not occur in future.

(4) The Certification Officer shall in an order imposing any such requirement as is mentioned in subsection (3)(a) specify the period within which the union is to comply with the requirement.

(5) Where the Certification Officer requests a person to furnish information to him in connection with enquiries made by him under this section, he shall specify the date by which that information is to be furnished and, unless he considers that it would be inappropriate to do so, shall proceed with his determination of the application notwithstanding that the information has not been furnished to him by the specified date.

(6) A declaration made by the Certification Officer under this section may be relied on as if it were a declaration made by the court.

(7) Where an enforcement order has been made, any person who is a member of the union and was a member at the time it was made is entitled to enforce obedience to the order as if he had made the application on which the order was made.

(8) An enforcement order made by the Certification Officer under this section may be enforced in the same way as an order of the court.

(9) An order under section 108A(2)(e) may provide that, in relation to an application under section 108A with regard to a prescribed matter, the preceding provisions of this section shall apply with such omissions or modifications as may be specified in the order; and a prescribed matter is such matter specified under section 108A(2)(e) as is prescribed under this subsection].

[601]

NOTES

Inserted as noted to s 108A at **[600]**.

Regulations: as of 6 April 2008 no Regulations had been made under this section.

[108C Appeals from Certification Officer

An appeal lies to the Employment Appeal Tribunal on any question of law arising in proceedings before or arising from any decision of the Certification Officer under this Chapter.]

[602]

NOTES

Inserted as noted to s 108A at **[600]**.

109–114 *((Chapter VIII) repealed by the Employment Relations Act 1999, ss 28(2)(a), 44, Sch 9(6).)*

CHAPTER IX
MISCELLANEOUS AND GENERAL PROVISIONS

115, 116 (*Repealed by the Trade Union Reform and Employment Rights Act 1993, ss 7(1), (4), 51, Sch 10.)*

[Union modernisation

116A Provision of money for union modernisation

(1) The Secretary of State may provide money to a trade union to enable or assist it to do any or all of the following—

(a) improve the carrying out of any of its existing functions;
(b) prepare to carry out any new function;
(c) increase the range of services it offers to persons who are or may become members of it;
(d) prepare for an amalgamation or the transfer of any or all of its engagements;
(e) ballot its members (whether as a result of a requirement imposed by this Act or otherwise).

(2) No money shall be provided to a trade union under this section unless at the time when the money is provided the union has a certificate of independence.

(3) Money may be provided in such a way as the Secretary of State thinks fit (whether as grants or otherwise) and on such terms as he thinks fit (whether as to repayment or otherwise).

(4) If money is provided to a trade union under this section, the terms on which it is so provided shall be deemed to include a prohibition ("a political fund prohibition") on any of it being added to the political fund of the union.

(5) If a political fund prohibition is contravened, the Secretary of State—

(a) is entitled to recover from the trade union as a debt due to him an amount equal to the amount of money added to the union's political fund in contravention of the prohibition (whether or not that money continues to form part of the political fund); and
(b) must take such steps as are reasonably practicable to recover that amount.

(6) An amount recoverable under subsection (5) is a liability of the trade union's political fund.

(7) Subsection (5) does not prevent money provided to a trade union under this section from being provided on terms containing further sanctions for a contravention of the political fund prohibition.]

[602A]

NOTES

Commencement: 6 April 2005.

Inserted, together with the preceding heading, by the Employment Relations Act 2004, s 55(1), as from 6 April 2005.

Exceptions and adaptations for certain bodies

117 Special register bodies

(1) In this section a "special register body" means an organisation whose name appeared in the special register maintained under section 84 of the Industrial Relations Act 1971 immediately before 16 September 1974, and which is a company registered under the Companies Act 1985 or is incorporated by charter or letters patent.

(2) The provisions of this Part apply to special register bodies as to other trade unions, subject to the following exceptions and adaptations.

(3) In Chapter II (status and property of trade unions)—

(a) in section 10 (quasi-corporate status of trade unions)—

(i) subsections (1) and (2) (prohibition on trade union being incorporated) do not apply, and

(ii) subsection (3) (prohibition on registration under certain Acts) does not apply so far as it relates to registration as a company under the Companies Act 1985;

(b) section 11 (exclusion of common law rules as to restraint of trade) applies to the purposes or rules of a special register body only so far as they relate to the regulation of relations between employers or employers' associations and workers;

(c) sections 12 to 14 (vesting of property in trustees; transfer of securities) do not apply; and

(d) in section 20 (liability of trade union in certain proceedings in tort) in subsection (7) the reference to the contract between a member and the other members shall be construed as a reference to the contract between a member and the body.

(4) Sections 33 to 35 (appointment and removal of auditors) do not apply to a special register body which is registered as a company under the Companies Act 1985; and sections 36 and 37 (rights and duties of auditors) apply to the auditors appointed by such a body under Chapter V of Part XI of that Act [or Chapter 2 of Part 16 of the Companies Act 2006].

(5) [Sections 45B and 45C (disqualification) and Chapter IV (elections) apply only] to—

(a) the position of voting member of the executive, and

(b) any position by virtue of which a person is a voting member of the executive.

In this subsection "voting member of the executive" has the meaning given by section 46(5).

[603]

NOTES

Sub-s (4): words in square brackets added by the Companies Act 2006 (Commencement No 3, Consequential Amendments, Transitional Provisions and Savings) Order 2007, SI 2007/2194, art 10(1), (2), Sch 4, Pt 3, para 73, as from 1 October 2007.

Sub-s (5): words in square brackets substituted by the Trade Union Reform and Employment Rights Act 1993, s 49(3), Sch 8, para 61.

Industrial Relations Act 1971: repealed by the Trade Union and Labour Relations Act 1974, ss 1, 25(3), Sch 5.

118 Federated trade unions

(1) In this section a "federated trade union" means a trade union which consists wholly or mainly of constituent or affiliated organisations, or representatives or such organisations, as described in paragraph (b) of the definition of "trade union" in section 1.

(2) The provisions of this Part apply to federated trade unions subject to the following exceptions and adaptations.

(3) For the purposes of section 22 (limit on amount of damages) as it applies to a federated trade union, the members of such of its constituent or affiliated organisations as have their head or main office in Great Britain shall be treated as members of the union.

(4) The following provisions of Chapter III (trade union administration) do not apply to a federated trade union which consists wholly or mainly of representatives of constituent or affiliated organisations—

(a) section 27 (duty to supply copy of rules),
(b) section 28 (duty to keep accounting records),
(c) sections 32 to 37 (annual return, [statement for members,] accounts and audit), …
[(ca) sections 37A to 37E (investigation of financial affairs), and]
(d) sections 38 to 42 (members' superannuation schemes).

(5) Sections 29 to 31 (right of member to access to accounting records) do not apply to a federated trade union which has no members other than constituent or affiliated organisations or representatives of such organisations.

(6) Sections 24 to 26 (register of members' names and addresses) and Chapter IV (elections for certain trade union positions) do not apply to a federated trade union—

(a) if it has no individual members other than representatives of constituent or affiliated organisations, or
(b) if its individual members (other than such representatives) are all merchant seamen and a majority of them are ordinarily resident outside the United Kingdom.

For this purpose "merchant seaman" means a person whose employment, or the greater part of it, is carried out on board sea-going ships.

(7) The provisions of Chapter VI (application of funds for political objects) apply to a trade union which is in whole or part an association or combination of other unions as if the individual members of the component unions were members of that union and not of the component unions.

But nothing in that Chapter prevents a component union from collecting contributions on behalf of the association or combination from such of its members as are not exempt from the obligation to contribute to the political fund of the association or combination.

[(8) In the application of section 116A to a federated trade union, subsection (2) of that section shall be omitted.]

[604]

NOTES

Sub-s (4): words in square brackets in para (c) inserted, word omitted from that paragraph repealed, and para (ca) inserted, by the Trade Union Reform and Employment Rights Act 1993, ss 49(3), 51, Sch 8, para 62, Sch 10.

Sub-s (8): added by the Employment Relations Act 2004, s 55(2), as from 6 April 2005.

Interpretation

119 Expressions relating to trade unions

In this Act, in relation to a trade union—

["agent" means a banker or solicitor of, or any person employed as an auditor by, the union or any branch or section of the union;]

"branch or section", except where the context otherwise requires, includes a branch or section which is itself a trade union;

"executive" means the principal committee of the union exercising executive functions, by whatever name it is called;

["financial affairs" means affairs of the union relating to any fund which is applicable for the purposes of the union (including any fund of a branch or section of the union which is so applicable);]

"general secretary" means the official of the union who holds the office of general secretary or, where there is no such office, holds an office which is equivalent, or (except in section 14(4)) the nearest equivalent, to that of general secretary;

"officer" includes—

(a) any member of the governing body of the union, and
(b) any trustee of any fund applicable for the purposes of the union;

"official" means—

(a) an officer of the union or of a branch or section of the union, or

(b) a person elected or appointed in accordance with the rules of the union to be a representative of its members or of some of them,

and includes a person so elected or appointed who is an employee of the same employer as the members or one or more of the members whom he is to represent;

"president" means the official of the union who holds the office of president or, where there is no such office, who holds an office which is equivalent, or (except in section 14(4) or Chapter IV) the nearest equivalent, to that of president; and

"rules", except where the context otherwise requires, includes the rules of any branch or section of the union.

[605]

NOTES

Definitions "agent" and "financial affairs" inserted by the Trade Union Reform and Employment Rights Act 1993, s 49(2), Sch 8, para 63.

120 Northern Ireland unions

In this Part a "Northern Ireland union" means a trade union whose principal office is situated in Northern Ireland.

[606]

121 Meaning of "the court"

In this Part "the court" (except where the reference is expressed to be to the county court or sheriff court) means the High Court or the Court of Session.

[607]

PART II
EMPLOYERS' ASSOCIATIONS

Introductory

122 Meaning of "employers' association"

(1) In this Act an "employers' association" means an organisation (whether temporary or permanent)—

(a) which consists wholly or mainly of employers or individual owners of undertakings of one or more descriptions and whose principal purposes include the regulation of relations between employers of that description or those descriptions and workers or trade unions; or

(b) which consists wholly or mainly of—

(i) constituent or affiliated organisations which fulfil the conditions in paragraph (a) (or themselves consist wholly or mainly of constituent or affiliated organisations which fulfil those conditions), or

(ii) representatives of such constituent or affiliated organisations,

and whose principal purposes include the regulation of relations between employers and workers or between employers and trade unions, or the regulation of relations between its constituent or affiliated organisations.

(2) References in this Act to employers' associations include combinations of employers and employers' associations.

[608]

The list of employers' associations

123 The list of employers' associations

(1) The Certification Officer shall keep a list of employers' associations containing the names of—

(a) the organisations whose names were, immediately before the commencement of this Act, duly entered in the list of employers' associations kept by him under section 8 of the Trade Union and Labour Relations Act 1974, and

(b) the names of the organisations entitled to have their names entered in the list in accordance with this Part.

(2) The Certification Officer shall keep copies of the list of employers' associations, as for the time being in force, available for public inspection at all reasonable hours free of charge.

(3) A copy of the list shall be included in his annual report.

(4) The fact that the name of an organisation is included in the list of employers' associations is evidence (in Scotland, sufficient evidence) that the organisation is an employers' association.

(5) On the application of an organisation whose name is included in the list, the Certification Officer shall issue it with a certificate to that effect.

(6) A document purporting to be such a certificate is evidence (in Scotland, sufficient evidence) that the name of the organisation is entered in the list.
[609]

NOTES

Trade Union and Labour Relations Act 1974, s 8: repealed by this Act.

124 Application to have name entered in the list

(1) An organisation of employers, whenever formed, whose name is not entered in the list of employers' associations may apply to the Certification Officer to have its name entered in the list.

(2) The application shall be made in such form and manner as the Certification Officer may require and shall be accompanied by—

(a) a copy of the rules of the organisation,
(b) a list of its officers,
(c) the address of its head or main office, and
(d) the name under which it is or is to be known,

and by the prescribed fee.

(3) If the Certification Officer is satisfied—

(a) that the organisation is an employers' association,
(b) that subsection (2) has been complied with, and
(c) that entry of the name in the list is not prohibited by subsection (4),

he shall enter the name of the organisation in the list of employers' associations.

(4) The Certification Officer shall not enter the name of an organisation in the list of employers' associations if the name is the same as that under which another organisation—

(a) was on 30th September 1971 registered as a trade union under the Trade Union Acts 1871 to 1964,
(b) was at any time registered as an employers' association or trade union under the Industrial Relations Act 1971, or
(c) is for the time being entered in the list of employers' associations or in the list of trade unions kept under Chapter I of Part I of this Act,

or if the name is one so nearly resembling any such name as to be likely to deceive the public.
[610]

NOTES

Trade Union Acts 1871 to 1964: the Acts which were cited together under this collective title were: the Trade Union Act 1871 (repealed); the Trade Union Act Amendment Act 1876 (repealed); the Trade Disputes Act 1906 (repealed); the Trade Union Act 1913 (repealed, with a saving, by this Act); the Trade Union (Amalgamation) Act 1917 (repealed); the Trade Disputes and Trade Unions Act 1927 (repealed); the Societies (Miscellaneous Provisions) Act 1940, s 6 (repealed); and the Trade Union (Amalgamations, etc) Act 1964 (repealed by this Act).

Industrial Relations Act 1971: repealed by the Trade Union and Labour Relations Act 1974, ss 1, 25(3), Sch 5.

Prescribed fee: the current fee is £150 (see the Certification Officer (Amendment of Fees) Regulations 2005, SI 2005/713, reg 6).

125 Removal of name from the list

(1) If it appears to the Certification Officer, on application made to him or otherwise, that an organisation whose name is entered in the list of employers' associations is not an employers' association, he may remove its name from the list.

(2) He shall not do so without giving the organisation notice of his intention and considering any representations made to him by the organisation within such period (of not less than 28 days beginning with the date of the notice) as may be specified in the notice.

(3) The Certification Officer shall remove the name of an organisation from the list of employers' associations if—

(a) he is requested by the organisation to do so, or

(b) he is satisfied that the organisation has ceased to exist.

[611]

126 Appeal against decision of Certification Officer

(1) An organisation aggrieved by the refusal of the Certification Officer to enter its name in the list of employers' associations, or by a decision of his to remove its name from the list, may appeal to the Employment Appeal Tribunal [on any appealable question].

(2) …

(3) [For the purposes of this section, an appealable question is any question of law] arising in the proceedings before, or arising from the decision of, the Certification Officer.

[612]

NOTES

Sub-s (1): words in square brackets added by the Employment Relations Act 2004, s 51(2)(a), as from 6 April 2005, except in relation to any refusal or decision of the Certification Officer made before that date (see SI 2005/872, art 19).

Sub-s (2): repealed by the Employment Relations Act 2004, ss 51(2)(b), 57(2), Sch 2, as from 6 April 2005 (subject to the same exception in SI 2005/872, art 19 as noted above).

Sub-s (3): words in square brackets substituted by the Employment Relations Act 2004, s 51(2)(c), as from 6 April 2005 (subject to the same exception in SI 2005/872, art 19 as noted above).

Status and property of employers' associations

127 Corporate or quasi-corporate status of employers' associations

(1) An employers' association may be either a body corporate or an unincorporated association.

(2) Where an employers' association is unincorporated—

(a) it is capable of making contracts;

(b) it is capable of suing and being sued in its own name, whether in proceedings relating to property or founded on contract or tort or any other cause of action; and

(c) proceedings for an offence alleged to have been committed by it or on its behalf may be brought against it in its own name.

(3) …

[613]

NOTES

Sub-s (3): repealed by the Regulatory Reform (Removal of 20 Member Limit in Partnerships etc) Order 2002, SI 2002/3203, art 4.

128 Exclusion of common law rules as to restraint of trade

(1) The purposes of an unincorporated employers' association and, so far as they relate to the regulation of relations between employers and workers or trade unions, the purposes of an employers' association which is a body corporate are not, by reason only that they are in restraint of trade, unlawful so as—

(a) to make any member of the association liable to criminal proceedings for conspiracy or otherwise, or

(b) to make any agreement or trust void or voidable.

(2) No rule of an unincorporated employers' association or, so far as it relates to the regulation of relations between employers and workers or trade unions, of an employers' association which is a body corporate, is unlawful or unenforceable by reason only that it is in restraint of trade.

[614]

129 Property of unincorporated employers' associations, &c

(1) The following provisions of Chapter II of Part I of this Act apply to an unincorporated employers' association as in relation to a trade union—

(a) section 12(1) and (2) (property to be vested in trustees),
(b) section 13 (vesting of property in new trustees), and
(c) section 14 (transfer of securities held in trust for trade union).

(2) In sections 13 and 14 as they apply by virtue of subsection (1) the reference to entry in the list of trade unions shall be construed as a reference to entry in the list of employers' associations.

(3) Section 19 (application of certain provisions relating to … friendly societies) applies to any employers' association as in relation to a trade union.

[615]

NOTES

Sub-s (3): words omitted repealed by the Financial Services and Markets Act 2000 (Consequential Amendments and Repeals) Order 2001, SI 2001/3649, art 333.

130 Restriction on enforcement of awards against certain property

(1) Where in any proceedings an amount is awarded by way of damages, costs or expenses—

(a) against an employers' association,
(b) against trustees in whom property is vested in trust for an employers' association, in their capacity as such (and otherwise than in respect of a breach of trust on their part), or
(c) against members or officials of an employers' association on behalf of themselves and all of the members of the association,

no part of that amount is recoverable by enforcement against any protected property.

(2) The following is protected property—

(a) property belonging to the trustees otherwise than in their capacity as such;
(b) property belonging to any member of the association otherwise than jointly or in common with the other members;
(c) property belonging to an official of the association who is neither a member nor a trustee.

[616]

Administration of employers' associations

131 Administrative provisions applying to employers' associations

(1) The following provisions of Chapter III of Part I of this Act apply to an employers' association as in relation to a trade union—

section 27 (duty to supply copy of rules),
section 28 (duty to keep accounting records),
[section 32(1), (2), (3)(a), (b) and (c) and (4) to (6) and sections 33 to 37] (annual return, accounts and audit),
[sections 37A to 37E (investigation of financial affairs),]
sections 38 to 42 (members' superannuation schemes),
section 43(1) (exemption for newly-formed organisations),
section 44(1), (2) and (4) (discharge of duties in case of organisation having branches or sections), and
[sections 45 and 45A] (offences).

(2) Sections 33 to 35 (appointment and removal of auditors) do not apply to an employers' association which is registered as a company under the Companies Act 1985; and sections 36 and 37 (rights and duties of auditors) apply to the auditors appointed by such an association under … [… Chapter 2 of Part 16 of the Companies Act 2006].

[617]

NOTES

Sub-s (1): words in first and third pairs of square brackets substituted, and words in second pair of square brackets inserted, by the Trade Union Reform and Employment Rights Act 1993, s 49(2), Sch 8, para 64.

Sub-s (2): words omitted repealed by the Companies Act 2006 (Consequential Amendments etc) Order 2008, SI 2008/948, art 3(1)(b), (2), Sch 1, Pt 2, para 188, Sch 2, as from 6 April 2008; words in square brackets added by the Companies Act 2006 (Commencement No 3, Consequential Amendments, Transitional Provisions and Savings) Order 2007, SI 2007/2194, art 10(1), (2), Sch 4, Pt 3, para 74, as from 1 October 2007.

Application of funds for political objects

132 Application of funds for political objects

[(1)] [Subject to subsections (2) to (5), the] provisions of Chapter VI of Part I of this Act (application of funds for political objects) apply to an unincorporated employers' association as in relation to a trade union.

[(2) Subsection (1) does not apply to these provisions—

(a) section 72A;

(b) in section 80, subsections (5A) to (5C) and (8) to (10);

(c) in section 81, subsection (8).

(3) In its application to an unincorporated employers' association, section 79 shall have effect as if at the end of subsection (1) there were inserted—

"The making of an application to the Certification Officer does not prevent the applicant, or any other person, from making an application to the court in respect of the same matter."

(4) In its application to an unincorporated employers' association, section 80(2)(b) shall have effect as if the words "where he considers it appropriate," were inserted at the beginning.

(5) In its application to an unincorporated employers' association, section 81 shall have effect as if after subsection (1) there were inserted—

"(2) If an application in respect of the same matter has been made to the Certification Officer, the court shall have due regard to any declaration, reasons or observations of his which are brought to its notice."]

[618]

NOTES

Original text of this section numbered sub-s (1), words in square brackets therein substituted, and sub-ss (2)–(5) added by the Employment Relations Act 1999, s 29, Sch 6, paras 1, 20.

Amalgamations and similar matters

[133 Amalgamations and transfers of engagements

(1) Subject to subsection (2), the provisions of Chapter VII of Part I of this Act (amalgamations and similar matters) apply to unincorporated employers' associations as in relation to trade unions.

(2) In its application to such associations that Chapter shall have effect—

(a) as if in section 99(1) for the words from "that every" to "accompanied by" there were substituted the words "that, not less than seven days before the ballot on the resolution to approve the instrument of amalgamation or transfer is held, every member is supplied with",

(b) as if the requirements imposed by sections 100A to 100E consisted only of those specified in sections 100B and 100C(1) and (3)(a) together with the requirement that every member must, so far as is reasonably possible, be given a fair opportunity of voting, …

[(ba) as if the references in sections 101A and 101B to the list of trade unions were to the list of employers' associations, and]

(c) with the omission of sections 101(3)[, 101A(3) and (4)][, 103(2A) and (6) to (9)] and 107.]

[619]

NOTES

Substituted by the Trade Union Reform and Employment Rights Act 1993, s 49(2), Sch 8, para 65.

Sub-s (2): word omitted from para (b) repealed, para (ba) inserted, and words in first pair of square brackets in para (c) inserted, by the Employment Relations Act 2004, ss 50(3), 57(2), Sch 2, as from 6 April 2005, except in relation to any application for registration of an instrument of amalgamation or transfer which is sent to the Certification Officer before that date (see SI 2005/872, art 18); words in second pair of square brackets in para (c) inserted by the Employment Relations Act 1999, s 29, Sch 6, paras 1, 21.

134 Change of name of employers' association

(1) An unincorporated employers' association may change its name by any method expressly provided for by its rules or, if its rules do not expressly provide for a method of doing so, by adopting in accordance with its rules an alteration of the provision in them which gives the association its name.

(2) If the name of an employers' association, whether incorporated or unincorporated, is entered in the list of employers' associations a change of name shall not take effect until approved by the Certification Officer.

(3) The Certification Officer shall not approve a change of name if it appears to him that the proposed new name—

(a) is the same as one entered in the list as the name of another employers' association, or

(b) is the same as one entered in the list of trade unions kept under Part I of this Act,

or is a name so nearly resembling such a name as to be likely to deceive the public.

(4) A change of name by an unincorporated employers' association does not affect any right or obligation of the association or any of its members; and any pending legal proceedings may be continued by or against the association, the trustees of the association or any other officer of the association who can sue or be sued on its behalf notwithstanding its change of name.

(5) The power conferred by section 108 (power to make regulations for carrying provisions into effect) applies in relation to this section as in relation to a provision of Chapter VII of Part I.

[620]

General

135 Federated employers' associations

(1) In this section a "federated employers' association" means an employers' association which consists wholly or mainly of constituent or affiliated organisations, or representatives or such organisations, as described in paragraph (b) of the definition of "employers' association" in section 122.

(2) The provisions of Part I applied by this Part to employers' associations apply to federated employers' associations subject to the following exceptions and adaptations.

(3) The following provisions of Chapter III of Part I (administration) do not apply to a federated employers' association which consists wholly or mainly of representatives of constituent or affiliated organisations—

(a) section 27 (duty to supply copy of rules),

(b) section 28 (duty to keep accounting records),

(c) [section 32(1), (2), (3)(a), (b) and (c) and (4) to (6) and sections 33 to 37] (annual return, accounts and audit), …

[(ca) sections 37A to 37E (investigation of financial affairs), and]

(d) sections 38 to 42 (members' superannuation schemes).

(4) The provisions of Chapter VI of Part I (application of funds for political objects) apply to a employers' association which is in whole or part an association or combination of other associations as if the individual members of the component associations were members of that association and not of the component associations.

But nothing in that Chapter prevents a component association from collecting contributions on behalf of the association or combination from such of its members as are not exempt from the obligation to contribute to the political fund of the association or combination.

[621]

NOTES

Sub-s (3): words in square brackets in para (c) substituted, word omitted from that paragraph repealed, and para (ca) inserted, by the Trade Union Reform and Employment Rights Act 1993, ss 49(2), 51, Sch 8, para 66, Sch 10.

136 Meaning of "officer" of employers' association

In this Act "officer", in relation to an employers' association, includes—

(a) any member of the governing body of the association, and

(b) any trustee of any fund applicable for the purposes of the association.

[622]

PART III
RIGHTS IN RELATION TO UNION MEMBERSHIP AND ACTIVITIES

Access to employment

137 Refusal of employment on grounds related to union membership

(1) It is unlawful to refuse a person employment—

(a) because he is, or is not, a member of a trade union, or

(b) because he is unwilling to accept a requirement—

(i) to take steps to become or cease to be, or to remain or not to become, a member of a trade union, or

(ii) to make payments or suffer deductions in the event of his not being a member of a trade union.

(2) A person who is thus unlawfully refused employment has a right of complaint to an [employment tribunal].

(3) Where an advertisement is published which indicates, or might reasonably be understood as indicating—

(a) that employment to which the advertisement relates is open only to a person who is, or is not, a member of a trade union, or

(b) that any such requirement as is mentioned in subsection (1)(b) will be imposed in relation to employment to which the advertisement relates,

a person who does not satisfy that condition or, as the case may be, is unwilling to accept that requirement, and who seeks and is refused employment to which the advertisement relates, shall be conclusively presumed to have been refused employment for that reason.

(4) Where there is an arrangement or practice under which employment is offered only to persons put forward or approved by a trade union, and the trade union puts forward or approves only persons who are members of the union, a person who is not a member of the union and who is refused employment in pursuance of the arrangement or practice shall be taken to have been refused employment because he is not a member of the trade union.

(5) A person shall be taken to be refused employment if he seeks employment of any description with a person and that person—

(a) refuses or deliberately omits to entertain and process his application or enquiry, or

(b) causes him to withdraw or cease to pursue his application or enquiry, or

(c) refuses or deliberately omits to offer him employment of that description, or

(d) makes him an offer of such employment the terms of which are such as no reasonable employer who wished to fill the post would offer and which is not accepted, or

(e) makes him an offer of such employment but withdraws it or causes him not to accept it.

(6) Where a person is offered employment on terms which include a requirement that he is, or is not, a member of a trade union, or any such requirement as is mentioned in subsection (1)(b), and he does not accept the offer because he does not satisfy or, as the case may be, is unwilling to accept that requirement, he shall be treated as having been refused employment for that reason.

(7) Where a person may not be considered for appointment or election to an office in a trade union unless he is a member of the union, or of a particular branch or section of the

union or of one of a number of particular branches or sections of the union, nothing in this section applies to anything done for the purpose of securing compliance with that condition although as holder of the office he would be employed by the union.

For this purpose an "office" means any position—

(a) by virtue of which the holder is an official of the union, or

(b) to which Chapter IV of Part I applies (duty to hold elections).

(8) The provisions of this section apply in relation to an employment agency acting, or purporting to act, on behalf of an employer as in relation to an employer.

[623]

NOTES

Sub-s (2): words in square brackets substituted by the Employment Rights (Dispute Resolution) Act 1998, s 1(2)(a).

Conciliation: employment tribunal proceedings and claims which could be the subject of employment tribunal proceedings arising out of a contravention, or alleged contravention, of this section are proceedings to which the Employment Tribunals Act 1996, s 18 applies; see s 18(1)(b) of that Act at **[975]**. The standard conciliation period applies to such claims by virtue of the Employment Tribunals (Constitution and Rules of Procedure) Regulations 2004, SI 2004/1861, Sch 1, rule 22(1), (6).

138 Refusal of service of employment agency on grounds related to union membership

(1) It is unlawful for an employment agency to refuse a person any of its services—

(a) because he is, or is not, a member of a trade union, or

(b) because he is unwilling to accept a requirement to take steps to become or cease to be, or to remain or not to become, a member of a trade union.

(2) A person who is thus unlawfully refused any service of an employment agency has a right of complaint to an [employment tribunal].

(3) Where an advertisement is published which indicates, or might reasonably be understood as indicating—

(a) that any service of an employment agency is available only to a person who is, or is not, a member of a trade union, or

(b) that any such requirement as is mentioned in subsection (1)(b) will be imposed in relation to a service to which the advertisement relates,

a person who does not satisfy that condition or, as the case may be, is unwilling to accept that requirement, and who seeks to avail himself of and is refused that service, shall be conclusively presumed to have been refused it for that reason.

(4) A person shall be taken to be refused a service if he seeks to avail himself of it and the agency—

(a) refuses or deliberately omits to make the service available to him, or

(b) causes him not to avail himself of the service or to cease to avail himself of it, or

(c) does not provide the same service, on the same terms, as is provided to others.

(5) Where a person is offered a service on terms which include a requirement that he is, or is not, a member of a trade union, or any such requirement as is mentioned in subsection (1)(b), and he does not accept the offer because he does not satisfy or, as the case may be, is unwilling to accept that requirement, he shall be treated as having been refused the service for that reason.

[624]

NOTES

Sub-s (2): words in square brackets substituted by the Employment Rights (Dispute Resolution) Act 1998, s 1(2)(a).

Conciliation: employment tribunal proceedings and claims which could be the subject of employment tribunal proceedings arising out of a contravention, or alleged contravention, of this section are proceedings to which the Employment Tribunals Act 1996, s 18 applies; see s 18(1)(b) of that Act at **[975]**. The standard conciliation period applies to such claims by virtue of the Employment Tribunals (Constitution and Rules of Procedure) Regulations 2004, SI 2004/1861, Sch 1, rule 22(1), (6).

139 Time limit for proceedings

(1) An [employment tribunal] shall not consider a complaint under section 137 or 138 unless it is presented to the tribunal—

(a) before the end of the period of three months beginning with the date of the conduct to which the complaint relates, or
(b) where the tribunal is satisfied that it was not reasonably practicable for the complaint to be presented before the end of that period, within such further period as the tribunal considers reasonable.

(2) The date of the conduct to which a complaint under section 137 relates shall be taken to be—
(a) in the case of an actual refusal, the date of the refusal;
(b) in the case of a deliberate omission—
(i) to entertain and process the complainant's application or enquiry, or
(ii) to offer employment,
the end of the period within which it was reasonable to expect the employer to act;
(c) in the case of conduct causing the complainant to withdraw or cease to pursue his application or enquiry, the date of that conduct;
(d) in a case where an offer was made but withdrawn, the date when it was withdrawn;
(e) in any other case where an offer was made but not accepted, the date on which it was made.

(3) The date of the conduct to which a complaint under section 138 relates shall be taken to be—
(a) in the case of an actual refusal, the date of the refusal;
(b) in the case of a deliberate omission to make a service available, the end of the period within which it was reasonable to expect the employment agency to act;
(c) in the case of conduct causing the complainant not to avail himself of a service or to cease to avail himself of it, the date of that conduct;
(d) in the case of failure to provide the same service, on the same terms, as is provided to others, the date or last date on which the service in fact provided was provided.

[625]

NOTES

Sub-s (1): words in square brackets substituted by the Employment Rights (Dispute Resolution) Act 1998, s 1(2)(a).

140 Remedies

(1) Where the [employment tribunal] finds that a complaint under section 137 or 138 is well-founded, it shall make a declaration to that effect and may make such of the following as it considers just and equitable—
(a) an order requiring the respondent to pay compensation to the complainant of such amount as the tribunal may determine;
(b) a recommendation that the respondent take within a specified period action appearing to the tribunal to be practicable for the purpose of obviating or reducing the adverse effect on the complainant of any conduct to which the complaint relates.

(2) Compensation shall be assessed on the same basis as damages for breach of statutory duty and may include compensation for injury to feelings.

(3) If the respondent fails without reasonable justification to comply with a recommendation to take action, the tribunal may increase its award of compensation or, if it has not made such an award, make one.

(4) The total amount of compensation shall not exceed the limit for the time being imposed by [section 124(1) of the Employment Rights Act 1996] (limit on compensation for unfair dismissal).

[626]

NOTES

Sub-s (1): words in square brackets substituted by the Employment Rights (Dispute Resolution) Act 1998, s 1(2)(a).

Sub-s (4): words in square brackets substituted by the Employment Rights Act 1996, s 240, Sch 1, para 56(1), (6).

141 Complaint against employer and employment agency

(1) Where a person has a right of complaint against a prospective employer and against an employment agency arising out of the same facts, he may present a complaint against either of them or against them jointly.

(2) If a complaint is brought against one only, he or the complainant may request the tribunal to join or sist the other as a party to the proceedings.

The request shall be granted if it is made before the hearing of the complaint begins, but may be refused if it is made after that time; and no such request may be made after the tribunal has made its decision as to whether the complaint is well-founded.

(3) Where a complaint is brought against an employer and an employment agency jointly, or where it is brought against one and the other is joined or sisted as a party to the proceedings, and the tribunal—

(a) finds that the complaint is well-founded as against the employer and the agency, and

(b) makes an award of compensation,

it may order that the compensation shall be paid by the one or the other, or partly by one and partly by the other, as the tribunal may consider just and equitable in the circumstances.

[627]

142 Awards against third parties

(1) If in proceedings on a complaint under section 137 or 138 either the complainant or the respondent claims that the respondent was induced to act in the manner complained of by pressure which a trade union or other person exercised on him by calling, organising, procuring or financing a strike or other industrial action, or by threatening to do so, the complainant or the respondent may request the [employment tribunal] to direct that the person who he claims exercised the pressure be joined or sisted as a party to the proceedings.

(2) The request shall be granted if it is made before the hearing of the complaint begins, but may be refused if it is made after that time; and no such request may be made after the tribunal has made its decision as to whether the complaint is well-founded.

(3) Where a person has been so joined or sisted as a party to the proceedings and the tribunal—

(a) finds that the complaint is well-founded,

(b) makes an award of compensation, and

(c) also finds that the claim in subsection (1) above is well-founded,

it may order that the compensation shall be paid by the person joined instead of by the respondent, or partly by that person and partly by the respondent, as the tribunal may consider just and equitable in the circumstances.

(4) Where by virtue of section 141 (complaint against employer and employment agency) there is more than one respondent, the above provisions apply to either or both of them.

[628]

NOTES

Sub-s (1): words in square brackets substituted by the Employment Rights (Dispute Resolution) Act 1998, s 1(2)(a).

143 Interpretation and other supplementary provisions

(1) In sections 137 to 143—

"advertisement" includes every form of advertisement or notice, whether to the public or not, and references to publishing an advertisement shall be construed accordingly;

"employment" means employment under a contract of employment, and related expressions shall be construed accordingly; and

"employment agency" means a person who, for profit or not, provides services for the purpose of finding employment for workers or supplying employers with workers, but subject to subsection (2) below.

(2) For the purposes of sections 137 to 143 as they apply to employment agencies—

(a) services other than those mentioned in the definition of "employment agency" above shall be disregarded, and

(b) a trade union shall not be regarded as an employment agency by reason of services provided by it only for, or in relation to, its members.

(3) References in sections 137 to 143 to being or not being a member of a trade union are to being or not being a member of any trade union, of a particular trade union or of one of a number of particular trade unions.

Any such reference includes a reference to being or not being a member of a particular branch or section of a trade union or of one of a number of particular branches or sections of a trade union.

(4) The remedy of a person for conduct which is unlawful by virtue of section 137 or 138 is by way of a complaint to an [employment tribunal] in accordance with this Part, and not otherwise.

No other legal liability arises by reason that conduct is unlawful by virtue of either of those sections.

[629]

NOTES

Sub-s (4): words in square brackets substituted by the Employment Rights (Dispute Resolution) Act 1998, s 1(2)(a).

Contracts for supply of goods or services

144 Union membership requirement in contract for goods or services void

A term or condition of a contract for the supply of goods or services is void in so far as it purports to require that the whole, or some part, of the work done for the purposes of the contract is done only by persons who are, or are not, members of trade unions or of a particular trade union.

[630]

145 Refusal to deal on union membership grounds prohibited

(1) A person shall not refuse to deal with a supplier or prospective supplier of goods or services on union membership grounds.

"Refuse to deal" and "union membership grounds" shall be construed as follows.

(2) A person refuses to deal with a person if, where he maintains (in whatever form) a list of approved suppliers of goods or services, or of persons from whom tenders for the supply of goods or services may be invited, he fails to include the name of that person in that list.

He does so on union membership grounds if the ground, or one of the grounds, for failing to include his name is that if that person were to enter into a contract with him for the supply of goods or services, work to be done for the purposes of the contract would, or would be likely to, be done by persons who were, or who were not, members of trade unions or of a particular trade union.

(3) A person refuses to deal with a person if, in relation to a proposed contract for the supply of goods or services—

(a) he excludes that person from the group of persons from whom tenders for the supply of the goods or services are invited, or

(b) he fails to permit that person to submit such a tender, or

(c) he otherwise determines not to enter into a contract with that person for the supply of the goods or services.

He does so on union membership grounds if the ground, or one of the grounds, on which he does so is that if the proposed contract were entered into with that person, work to be done for the purposes of the contract would, or would be likely to, be done by persons who were, or who were not, members of trade unions or of a particular trade union.

(4) A person refuses to deal with a person if he terminates a contract with him for the supply of goods or services.

He does so on union membership grounds if the ground, or one of the grounds, on which he does so is that work done, or to be done, for the purposes of the contract has been, or is likely to be, done by persons who are or are not members of trade unions or of a particular trade union.

(5) The obligation to comply with this section is a duty owed to the person with whom there is a refusal to deal and to any other person who may be adversely affected by its contravention; and a breach of the duty is actionable accordingly (subject to the defences and other incidents applying to actions for breach of statutory duty).

[631]

[Inducements

145A Inducements relating to union membership or activities

(1) A worker has the right not to have an offer made to him by his employer for the sole or main purpose of inducing the worker—

(a) not to be or seek to become a member of an independent trade union,

(b) not to take part, at an appropriate time, in the activities of an independent trade union,

(c) not to make use, at an appropriate time, of trade union services, or

(d) to be or become a member of any trade union or of a particular trade union or of one of a number of particular trade unions.

(2) In subsection (1) "an appropriate time" means—

(a) a time outside the worker's working hours, or

(b) a time within his working hours at which, in accordance with arrangements agreed with or consent given by his employer, it is permissible for him to take part in the activities of a trade union or (as the case may be) make use of trade union services.

(3) In subsection (2) "working hours", in relation to a worker, means any time when, in accordance with his contract of employment (or other contract personally to do work or perform services), he is required to be at work.

(4) In subsections (1) and (2)—

(a) "trade union services" means services made available to the worker by an independent trade union by virtue of his membership of the union, and

(b) references to a worker's "making use" of trade union services include his consenting to the raising of a matter on his behalf by an independent trade union of which he is a member.

(5) A worker or former worker may present a complaint to an employment tribunal on the ground that his employer has made him an offer in contravention of this section.]

[631A]

NOTES

Commencement: 1 October 2004.

Inserted, together with the preceding heading and ss 145B–145F, by the Employment Relations Act 2004, s 29, as from 1 October 2004, except in relation to an offer made to a complainant before that date or to an offer that is part of a series of similar offers made to a complainant where the first offer in the series was made to him before that date (see SI 2004/2566, art 5).

Conciliation: employment tribunal proceedings and claims which could be the subject of employment tribunal proceedings arising out of a contravention, or alleged contravention, of this section are proceedings to which the Employment Tribunals Act 1996, s 18 applies; see s 18(1)(b) of that Act at **[975]**. The standard conciliation period applies to such claims by virtue of the Employment Tribunals (Constitution and Rules of Procedure) Regulations 2004, SI 2004/1861, Sch 1, rule 22(1), (6).

Tribunal jurisdiction: the Employment Act 2002, ss 31, 32, 38 at **[1493]**, **[1494]**, **[1496]** apply to proceedings before the employment tribunal relating to a claim under this section; see ss 31(1), 32(1), 38(1) of, and Schs 3–5 to, the 2002 Act at **[1508]–[1510]**.

For the circumstances in which the normal time limit for presenting a complaint under this section is extended for a period of three months, see the Employment Act 2002 (Dispute Resolution) Regulations 2004, SI 2004/752, regs 15 and 18 at **[3096]** and **[3098]**.

[145B Inducements relating to collective bargaining

(1) A worker who is a member of an independent trade union which is recognised, or seeking to be recognised, by his employer has the right not to have an offer made to him by his employer if—

(a) acceptance of the offer, together with other workers' acceptance of offers which the employer also makes to them, would have the prohibited result, and

(b) the employer's sole or main purpose in making the offers is to achieve that result.

(2) The prohibited result is that the workers' terms of employment, or any of those terms, will not (or will no longer) be determined by collective agreement negotiated by or on behalf of the union.

(3) It is immaterial for the purposes of subsection (1) whether the offers are made to the workers simultaneously.

(4) Having terms of employment determined by collective agreement shall not be regarded for the purposes of section 145A (or section 146 or 152) as making use of a trade union service.

(5) A worker or former worker may present a complaint to an employment tribunal on the ground that his employer has made him an offer in contravention of this section.]

[631B]

NOTES

Commencement: 1 October 2004.

Inserted as noted to s 145A at **[631A]**.

Conciliation: employment tribunal proceedings and claims which could be the subject of employment tribunal proceedings arising out of a contravention, or alleged contravention, of this section are proceedings to which the Employment Tribunals Act 1996, s 18 applies; see s 18(1)(b) of that Act at **[975]**. The standard conciliation period applies to such claims by virtue of the Employment Tribunals (Constitution and Rules of Procedure) Regulations 2004, SI 2004/1861, Sch 1, rule 22(1), (6).

Tribunal jurisdiction: the Employment Act 2002, ss 31, 32, 38 at **[1493]**, **[1494]**, **[1496]** apply to proceedings before the employment tribunal relating to a claim under this section; see ss 31(1), 32(1), 38(1) of, and Schs 3–5 to, the 2002 Act at **[1508]**–**[1510]**.

For the circumstances in which the normal time limit for presenting a complaint under this section is extended for a period of three months, see the Employment Act 2002 (Dispute Resolution) Regulations 2004, SI 2004/752, regs 15 and 18 at **[3096]** and **[3098]**.

[145C Time limit for proceedings

An employment tribunal shall not consider a complaint under section 145A or 145B unless it is presented—

(a) before the end of the period of three months beginning with the date when the offer was made or, where the offer is part of a series of similar offers to the complainant, the date when the last of them was made, or

(b) where the tribunal is satisfied that it was not reasonably practicable for the complaint to be presented before the end of that period, within such further period as it considers reasonable.]

[631C]

NOTES

Commencement: 1 October 2004.

Inserted as noted to s 145A at **[631A]**.

Tribunal jurisdiction: see the note to s 145B at **[631B]**.

For the circumstances in which the time limit laid down by para (a) is extended for a period of three months, see the Employment Act 2002 (Dispute Resolution) Regulations 2004, SI 2004/752, regs 15 and 18 at **[3096]** and **[3098]**.

[145D Consideration of complaint

(1) On a complaint under section 145A it shall be for the employer to show what was his sole or main purpose in making the offer.

(2) On a complaint under section 145B it shall be for the employer to show what was his sole or main purpose in making the offers.

(3) On a complaint under section 145A or 145B, in determining any question whether the employer made the offer (or offers) or the purpose for which he did so, no account shall be taken of any pressure which was exercised on him by calling, organising, procuring or financing a strike or other industrial action, or by threatening to do so; and that question shall be determined as if no such pressure had been exercised.

(4) In determining whether an employer's sole or main purpose in making offers was the purpose mentioned in section 145B(1), the matters taken into account must include any evidence—

(a) that when the offers were made the employer had recently changed or sought to change, or did not wish to use, arrangements agreed with the union for collective bargaining,

(b) that when the offers were made the employer did not wish to enter into arrangements proposed by the union for collective bargaining, or
(c) that the offers were made only to particular workers, and were made with the sole or main purpose of rewarding those particular workers for their high level of performance or of retaining them because of their special value to the employer.]

[631D]

NOTES

Commencement: 1 October 2004.
Inserted as noted to s 145A at **[631A]**.

[145E Remedies

(1) Subsections (2) and (3) apply where the employment tribunal finds that a complaint under section 145A or 145B is well-founded.

(2) The tribunal—
(a) shall make a declaration to that effect, and
(b) shall make an award to be paid by the employer to the complainant in respect of the offer complained of.

(3) The amount of the award shall be [£2,900] (subject to any adjustment of the award that may fall to be made under Part 3 of the Employment Act 2002).

(4) Where an offer made in contravention of section 145A or 145B is accepted—
(a) if the acceptance results in the worker's agreeing to vary his terms of employment, the employer cannot enforce the agreement to vary, or recover any sum paid or other asset transferred by him under the agreement to vary;
(b) if as a result of the acceptance the worker's terms of employment are varied, nothing in section 145A or 145B makes the variation unenforceable by either party.

(5) Nothing in this section or sections 145A and 145B prejudices any right conferred by section 146 or 149.

(6) In ascertaining any amount of compensation under section 149, no reduction shall be made on the ground—
(a) that the complainant caused or contributed to his loss, or to the act or failure complained of, by accepting or not accepting an offer made in contravention of section 145A or 145B, or
(b) that the complainant has received or is entitled to an award under this section.]

[631E]

NOTES

Commencement: 1 October 2004.
Inserted as noted to s 145A at **[631A]**.
Sub-s (3): sum in square brackets substituted by the Employment Rights (Increase of Limits) Order 2007, SI 2007/3570, art 3, Schedule, as from 1 February 2008, in relation to any case where the appropriate date falls on or after that date (see SI 2007/3570, art 4 at **[3474H]**). The previous sum was £2,700. This sum may be further varied by the Secretary of State, see the Employment Relations Act 1999, s 34(1)(ea), (3)(b) at **[1445]**.

[145F Interpretation and other supplementary provisions

(1) References in sections 145A to 145E to being or becoming a member of a trade union include references—
(a) to being or becoming a member of a particular branch or section of that union, and
(b) to being or becoming a member of one of a number of particular branches or sections of that union.

(2) References in those sections—
(a) to taking part in the activities of a trade union, and
(b) to services made available by a trade union by virtue of membership of the union,
shall be construed in accordance with subsection (1).

(3) In sections 145A to 145E—
"worker" means an individual who works, or normally works, as mentioned in paragraphs (a) to (c) of section 296(1), and

"employer" means—
(a) in relation to a worker, the person for whom he works;
(b) in relation to a former worker, the person for whom he worked.

(4) The remedy of a person for infringement of the right conferred on him by section 145A or 145B is by way of a complaint to an employment tribunal in accordance with this Part, and not otherwise.]

[631F]

NOTES

Commencement: 1 October 2004.
Inserted as noted to s 145A at **[631A]**.

[Detriment]

146 [Detriment] on grounds related to union membership or activities

(1) [A worker] has the right not to [be subjected to any detriment as an individual by any act, or any deliberate failure to act, by his employer if the act or failure takes place] for [the sole or main purpose] of—
(a) preventing or deterring him from being or seeking to become a member of an independent trade union, or penalising him for doing so,
(b) preventing or deterring him from taking part in the activities of an independent trade union at an appropriate time, or penalising him for doing so, ...
[(ba) preventing or deterring him from making use of trade union services at an appropriate time, or penalising him for doing so, or]
(c) compelling him to be or become a member of any trade union or of a particular trade union or of one of a number of particular trade unions.

(2) In subsection [(1)] "an appropriate time" means—
(a) a time outside the [worker's] working hours, or
(b) a time within his working hours at which, in accordance with arrangements agreed with or consent given by his employer, it is permissible for him to take part in the activities of a trade union [or (as the case may be) make use of trade union services];

and for this purpose "working hours", in relation to [a worker], means any time when, in accordance with his contract of employment [(or other contract personally to do work or perform services)], he is required to be at work.

[(2A) In this section—
(a) "trade union services" means services made available to the worker by an independent trade union by virtue of his membership of the union, and
(b) references to a worker's "making use" of trade union services include his consenting to the raising of a matter on his behalf by an independent trade union of which he is a member.

(2B) If an independent trade union of which a worker is a member raises a matter on his behalf (with or without his consent), penalising the worker for that is to be treated as penalising him as mentioned in subsection (1)(ba).

(2C) A worker also has the right not to be subjected to any detriment as an individual by any act, or any deliberate failure to act, by his employer if the act or failure takes place because of the worker's failure to accept an offer made in contravention of section 145A or 145B.

(2D) For the purposes of subsection (2C), not conferring a benefit that, if the offer had been accepted by the worker, would have been conferred on him under the resulting agreement shall be taken to be subjecting him to a detriment as an individual (and to be a deliberate failure to act).]

(3) [A worker] also has the right not to [be subjected to any detriment as an individual by any act, or any deliberate failure to act, by his employer if the act or failure takes place] for [the sole or main purpose] of enforcing a requirement (whether or not imposed by [a contract of employment] or in writing) that, in the event of his not being a member of any trade union or of a particular trade union or of one of a number of particular trade unions, he must make one or more payments.

(4) For the purposes of subsection (3) any deduction made by an employer from the remuneration payable to [a worker] in respect of his employment shall, if it is attributable to his not being a member of any trade union or of a particular trade union or of one of a number of particular trade unions, be treated as [a detriment to which he has been subjected as an individual by an act of his employer taking place] for [the sole or main purpose] of enforcing a requirement of a kind mentioned in that subsection.

(5) [A worker or former worker] may present a complaint to an [employment tribunal] on the ground that [he has been subjected to a detriment] by his employer in contravention of this section.

[(5A) This section does not apply where—

(a) the worker is an employee; and

(b) the detriment in question amounts to dismissal.]

[632]

NOTES

The heading preceding this section and the words in square brackets in the section heading were substituted by the Employment Relations Act 2004, s 30(7), as from 1 October 2004, except in relation to cases where the act or failure to act to which the complaint relates was done before that date, or where the act or failure to act to which the complaint relates is part of a series and the first act or failure in the series was done before that date (see SI 2004/2566, art 6).

Sub-s (1): words in first and third pairs of square brackets substituted, word omitted from para (b) repealed, and para (ba) inserted, by the Employment Relations Act 2004, ss 30(1), (2), 31(1), (2), 57, Sch 1, para 8, Sch 2, as from 1 October 2004 (subject to the same exception in SI 2004/2566, art 6 as noted above); words in second pair of square brackets substituted by the Employment Relations Act 1999, s 2, Sch 2, paras 1, 2(1), (2).

Sub-s (2): words in first, second and fourth pairs of square brackets substituted, and words in third and fifth pairs of square brackets inserted, by the Employment Relations Act 2004, ss 30(1)–(3), 31(1), (3), as from 1 October 2004 (subject to the same exception in SI 2004/2566, art 6 as noted above).

Sub-ss (2A)–(2D): inserted by the Employment Relations Act 2004, s 31(1), (4), as from 1 October 2004 (subject to the same exception in SI 2004/2566, art 6 as noted above).

Sub-s (3): words in first, third and fourth pairs of square brackets substituted by the Employment Relations Act 2004, ss 30(1), (2), (4), 57(1), Sch 1, para 8, as from 1 October 2004 (subject to the same exception in SI 2004/2566, art 6 as noted above); words in second pair of square brackets substituted by the Employment Relations Act 1999, s 2, Sch 2, paras 1, 2(1), (3).

Sub-s (4): words in first and third pairs of square brackets substituted by the Employment Relations Act 2004, ss 30(1), (2), 57(1), Sch 1, para 8, as from 1 October 2004 (subject to the same exception in SI 2004/2566, art 6 as noted above); words in second pair of square brackets substituted by the Employment Relations Act 1999, s 2, Sch 2, paras 1, 2(1), (4).

Sub-s (5): words in first pair of square brackets substituted by the Employment Relations Act 2004, s 30(1), (5), as from 1 October 2004 (subject to the same exception in SI 2004/2566, art 6 as noted above); words in second pair of square brackets substituted by the Employment Rights (Dispute Resolution) Act 1998, s 1(2)(a); words in third pair of square brackets substituted by the Employment Relations Act 1999, s 2, Sch 2, paras 1, 2(1), (5).

Sub-s (5A): added (as sub-s (6)) by the Employment Relations Act 1999, s 2, Sch 2, paras 1, 2(1), (6); substituted (and renumbered) by the Employment Relations Act 2004, s 30(1), (6), as from 1 October 2004 (subject to the same exception in SI 2004/2566, art 6 as noted above).

Modified, in relation to governing bodies with delegated budgets, by the Education (Modification of Enactments Relating to Employment) (England) Order 2003, SI 2003/1964, art 3, Schedule at **[3035C]**, **[3035G]** and the Education (Modification of Enactments Relating to Employment) (Wales) Order 2006, SI 2006/1073, art 3, Schedule at **[3462B]**, **[3462F]**.

Conciliation: employment tribunal proceedings and claims which could be the subject of employment tribunal proceedings arising out of a contravention, or alleged contravention, of this section are proceedings to which the Employment Tribunals Act 1996, s 18 applies; see s 18(1)(b) of that Act at **[975]**. The standard conciliation period applies to such claims by virtue of the Employment Tribunals (Constitution and Rules of Procedure) Regulations 2004, SI 2004/1861, Sch 1, rule 22(1), (6).

Tribunal jurisdiction: the Employment Act 2002, ss 31, 32, 38 at **[1493]**, **[1494]**, **[1496]** apply to proceedings before the employment tribunal relating to a claim under this section; see ss 31(1), 32(1), 38(1) of, and Schs 3–5 to, the 2002 Act at **[1508]**–**[1510]**.

For the circumstances in which the normal time limit for presenting a complaint under this section is extended for a period of three months, see the Employment Act 2002 (Dispute Resolution) Regulations 2004, SI 2004/752, regs 15 and 18 at **[3096]** and **[3098]**.

147 Time limit for proceedings

[(1)] An [employment tribunal] shall not consider a complaint under section 146 unless it is presented—

(a) before the end of the period of three months beginning with the date of the [act or failure to which the complaint relates or, where that act or failure is part of a series of similar acts or failures (or both) the last of them], or

(b) where the tribunal is satisfied that it was not reasonably practicable for the complaint to be presented before the end of that period, within such further period as it considers reasonable.

[(2) For the purposes of subsection (1)—

(a) where an act extends over a period, the reference to the date of the act is a reference to the last day of that period;

(b) a failure to act shall be treated as done when it was decided on.

(3) For the purposes of subsection (2), in the absence of evidence establishing the contrary an employer shall be taken to decide on a failure to act—

(a) when he does an act inconsistent with doing the failed act, or

(b) if he has done no such inconsistent act, when the period expires within which he might reasonably have been expected to do the failed act if it was to be done.]

[633]

NOTES

Sub-s (1): original text renumbered as sub-s (1) and words in second pair of square brackets substituted by the Employment Relations Act 1999, s 2, Sch 2, paras 1, 3(1)–(3); words in first pair of square brackets substituted by the Employment Rights (Dispute Resolution) Act 1998, s 1(2)(a).

Sub-ss (2), (3): added by the Employment Relations Act 1999, s 2, Sch 2, paras 1, 3(1), (4).

Modified as noted to s 146 at **[632]**.

Conciliation: see note to s 146 at **[632]**.

Tribunal jurisdiction: see the note to s 146 at **[632]**.

For the circumstances in which the time limit laid down by sub-s (1)(a) is extended for a period of three months, see the Employment Act 2002 (Dispute Resolution) Regulations 2004, SI 2004/752, regs 15 and 18 at **[3096]** and **[3098]**.

148 Consideration of complaint

(1) On a complaint under section 146 it shall be for the employer to show [what was the sole or main purpose] for which [he acted or failed to act].

(2) In determining any question whether [the employer acted or failed to act, or the purpose for which he did so], no account shall be taken of any pressure which was exercised on him by calling, organising, procuring or financing a strike or other industrial action, or by threatening to do so; and that question shall be determined as if no such pressure had been exercised.

[(3)–(5) …]

[634]

NOTES

Sub-s (1): words in first pair of square brackets substituted by the Employment Relations Act 2004, s 57(1), Sch 1, para 9, as from 1 October 2004, except in relation to cases where the act or failure to act to which the complaint relates was done before that date, or where the act or failure to act to which the complaint relates is part of a series and the first act or failure in the series was done before that date (see SI 2004/2566, art 6); words in second pair of square brackets substituted by the Employment Relations Act 1999, s 2, Sch 2, paras 1, 4(1), (2).

Sub-s (2): words in square brackets substituted by the Employment Relations Act 1999, s 2, Sch 2, paras 1, 4(1), (3).

Sub-ss (3)–(5): added by the Trade Union Reform and Employment Rights Act 1993, s 13; repealed by the Employment Relations Act 2004, ss 31, 57(2), Sch 2, as from 1 October 2004 (subject to the same exception in SI 2004/2566, art 6 as noted above).

149 Remedies

(1) Where the [employment tribunal] finds that a complaint under section 146 is well-founded, it shall make a declaration to that effect and may make an award of compensation to be paid by the employer to the complainant in respect of the [act or failure] complained of.

(2) The amount of the compensation awarded shall be such as the tribunal considers just and equitable in all the circumstances having regard to the infringement complained of and to any loss sustained by the complainant which is attributable to the [act or failure] which infringed his right.

(3) The loss shall be taken to include—

(a) any expenses reasonably incurred by the complainant in consequence of the [act or failure] complained of, and

(b) loss of any benefit which he might reasonably be expected to have had but for that [act or failure].

(4) In ascertaining the loss, the tribunal shall apply the same rule concerning the duty of a person to mitigate his loss as applies to damages recoverable under the common law of England and Wales or Scotland.

(5) In determining the amount of compensation to be awarded no account shall be taken of any pressure which was exercised on the employer by calling, organising, procuring or financing a strike or other industrial action, or by threatening to do so; and that question shall be determined as if no such pressure had been exercised.

(6) Where the tribunal finds that the [act or failure] complained of was to any extent caused or contributed to by action of the complainant, it shall reduce the amount of the compensation by such proportion as it considers just and equitable having regard to that finding.

[635]

NOTES

Sub-s (1): words in first pair of square brackets substituted by the Employment Rights (Dispute Resolution) Act 1998, s 1(2)(a); words in second pair of square brackets substituted by the Employment Relations Act 1999, s 2, Sch 2, paras 1, 5(a).

Sub-ss (2), (3), (6): words in square brackets substituted by the Employment Relations Act 1999, s 2, Sch 2, paras 1, 5(a), (b).

150 Awards against third parties

(1) If in proceedings on a complaint under section 146—

(a) the complaint is made on the ground that [the complainant has been subjected to detriment by an act or failure by his employer taking place] for [the sole or main purpose] of compelling him to be or become a member of any trade union or of a particular trade union or of one of a number of particular trade unions, and

(b) either the complainant or the employer claims in proceedings before the tribunal that the employer was induced to [act or fail to act in the way] complained of by pressure which a trade union or other person exercised on him by calling, organising, procuring or financing a strike or other industrial action, or by threatening to do so,

the complainant or the employer may request the tribunal to direct that the person who he claims exercised the pressure be joined or sisted as a party to the proceedings.

(2) The request shall be granted if it is made before the hearing of the complaint begins, but may be refused if it is made after that time; and no such request may be made after the tribunal has made a declaration that the complaint is well-founded.

(3) Where a person has been so joined or sisted as a party to proceedings and the tribunal—

(a) makes an award of compensation, and

(b) finds that the claim mentioned in subsection (1)(b) is well-founded,

it may order that the compensation shall be paid by the person joined instead of by the employer, or partly by that person and partly by the employer, as the tribunal may consider just and equitable in the circumstances.

[636]

NOTES

Sub-s (1): words in first pair of square brackets in para (a) and words in square brackets in para (b) substituted by the Employment Relations Act 1999, s 2, Sch 2, paras 1, 6; words in second pair of square brackets in para (a) substituted by the Employment Relations Act 2004, s 57(1), Sch 1, para 10, as from 1 October 2004, except in relation to cases where the act or failure to act to which the complaint relates was done before that date, or where the act or failure to act to which the complaint relates is part of a series and the first act or failure in the series was done before that date (see SI 2004/2566, art 6).

151 Interpretation and other supplementary provisions

(1) References in sections 146 to 150 to being, becoming or ceasing to remain a member of a trade union include references to being, becoming or ceasing to remain a member of a

particular branch or section of that union and to being, becoming or ceasing to remain a member of one of a number of particular branches or sections of that union …

[(1A) References in those sections—

(a) to taking part in the activities of a trade union, and

(b) to services made available by a trade union by virtue of membership of the union,

shall be construed in accordance with subsection (1).]

[(1B) In sections 146 to 150—

"worker" means an individual who works, or normally works, as mentioned in paragraphs (a) to (c) of section 296(1), and

"employer" means—

(a) in relation to a worker, the person for whom he works;

(b) in relation to a former worker, the person for whom he worked.]

(2) The remedy of [a person] for infringement of the right conferred on him by section 146 is by way of a complaint to an [employment tribunal] in accordance with this Part, and not otherwise.

[637]

NOTES

Sub-s (1): words omitted repealed by the Employment Relations Act 2004, ss 31(6), 57(2), Sch 2, as from 1 October 2004, except in relation to cases where the act or failure to act to which the complaint relates was done before that date, or where the act or failure to act to which the complaint relates is part of a series and the first act or failure in the series was done before that date (see SI 2004/2566, art 6).

Sub-ss (1A), (1B): inserted by the Employment Relations Act 2004, s 31(7), (8), as from 1 October 2004 (subject to the same exception in SI 2004/2566, art 6 as noted above).

Sub-s (2): words in first pair of square brackets substituted by the Employment Relations Act 2004, s 30(9), as from 1 October 2004 (subject to the same exception in SI 2004/2566, art 6 as noted above); words in second pair of square brackets substituted by the Employment Rights (Dispute Resolution) Act 1998, s 1(2)(a).

Dismissal [of employee]

152 Dismissal [of employee] on grounds related to union membership or activities

(1) For purposes of [Part X of the Employment Rights Act 1996] (unfair dismissal) the dismissal of an employee shall be regarded as unfair if the reason for it (or, if more than one, the principal reason) was that the employee—

(a) was, or proposed to become, a member of an independent trade union, …

(b) had taken part, or proposed to take part, in the activities of an independent trade union at an appropriate time, …

[(ba) had made use, or proposed to make use, of trade union services at an appropriate time,

(bb) had failed to accept an offer made in contravention of section 145A or 145B, or]

(c) was not a member of any trade union, or of a particular trade union, or of one of a number of particular trade unions, or had refused, or proposed to refuse, to become or remain a member.

(2) In subsection [(1)] "an appropriate time" means—

(a) a time outside the employee's working hours, or

(b) a time within his working hours at which, in accordance with arrangements agreed with or consent given by his employer, it is permissible for him to take part in the activities of a trade union [or (as the case may be) make use of trade union services];

and for this purpose "working hours", in relation to an employee, means any time when, in accordance with his contract of employment, he is required to be at work.

[(2A) In this section—

(a) "trade union services" means services made available to the employee by an independent trade union by virtue of his membership of the union, and

(b) references to an employee's "making use" of trade union services include his consenting to the raising of a matter on his behalf by an independent trade union of which he is a member.

(2B) Where the reason or one of the reasons for the dismissal was that an independent trade union (with or without the employee's consent) raised a matter on behalf of the employee as one of its members, the reason shall be treated as falling within subsection (1)(ba).]

(3) Where the reason, or one of the reasons, for the dismissal was—

(a) the employee's refusal, or proposed refusal, to comply with a requirement (whether or not imposed by his contract of employment or in writing) that, in the event of his not being a member of any trade union, or of a particular trade union, or of one of a number of particular trade unions, he must make one or more payments, or

(b) his objection, or proposed objection, (however expressed) to the operation of a provision (whether or not forming part of his contract of employment or in writing) under which, in the event mentioned in paragraph (a), his employer is entitled to deduct one or more sums from the remuneration payable to him in respect of his employment,

the reason shall be treated as falling within subsection (1)(c).

(4) References in this section to being, becoming or ceasing to remain a member of a trade union include references to being, becoming or ceasing to remain a member of a particular branch or section of that union or of one of a number of particular branches or sections of that trade union …

[(5) References in this section—

(a) to taking part in the activities of a trade union, and

(b) to services made available by a trade union by virtue of membership of the union,

shall be construed in accordance with subsection (4).]

[638]

NOTES

Words in square brackets in the heading preceding this section and in the section heading were substituted by the Employment Relations Act 2004, s 30(10), as from 1 October 2004, except in relation to cases where the act or failure to act to which the complaint relates was done before that date, or where the act or failure to act to which the complaint relates is part of a series and the first act or failure in the series was done before that date (see SI 2004/2566, art 6).

Sub-s (1): words in first pair of square brackets substituted by the Employment Rights Act 1996, s 240, Sch 1, para 56(1), (7); words omitted from paras (a), (b) repealed, and paras (ba), (bb) inserted, by the Employment Relations Act 2004, ss 32(1), (2), 57(2), Sch 2, as from 1 October 2004, except in relation to a dismissal where the effective date of termination (as defined in the Employment Rights Act 1996, s 97) occurred before that date (see SI 2004/2566, art 7).

Sub-s (2): number in square brackets substituted, and words in square brackets inserted, by the Employment Relations Act 2004, s 32(1), (3), as from 1 October 2004 (subject to the same exception in SI 2004/2566, art 7 as noted above).

Sub-ss (2A), (2B), (5): inserted and added respectively by the Employment Relations Act 2004, s 32(1), (4), (6), as from 1 October 2004 (subject to the same exception in SI 2004/2566, art 7 as noted above).

Sub-s (4): words omitted repealed by the Employment Relations Act 2004, ss 32(1), (5), 57(2), Sch 2, as from 1 October 2004 (subject to the same exception in SI 2004/2566, art 7 as noted above).

Modified as noted to s 146 at **[632]**.

153 Selection for redundancy on grounds related to union membership or activities

Where the reason or principal reason for the dismissal of an employee was that he was redundant, but it is shown—

(a) that the circumstances constituting the redundancy applied equally to one or more other employees in the same undertaking who held positions similar to that held by him and who have not been dismissed by the employer, and

(b) that the reason (or, if more than one, the principal reason) why he was selected for dismissal was one of those specified in section 152(1),

the dismissal shall be regarded as unfair for the purposes of [Part X of the Employment Rights Act 1996] (unfair dismissal).

[639]

NOTES

Words in square brackets substituted by the Employment Rights Act 1996, s 240, Sch 1, para 56(1), (7).

Modified as noted to s 146 at **[632]**.

[154 Disapplication of qualifying period and upper age limit for unfair dismissal

Sections 108(1) and 109(1) of the Employment Rights Act 1996 (qualifying period and upper age limit for unfair dismissal protection) do not apply to a dismissal which by virtue of section 152 or 153 is regarded as unfair for the purposes of Part 10 of that Act.]

[640]

NOTES

Commencement: 6 April 2005.

Substituted by the Employment Relations Act 2004, s 35, as from 6 April 2005, except in relation to a dismissal where the effective date of termination (as defined in the Employment Rights Act 1996, s 97) occurred before that date (see SI 2005/872, art 12).

Modified as noted to s 146 at **[632]**.

Section 109 of the Employment Rights Act 1996 was repealed by the Employment Equality (Age) Regulations 2006, SI 2006/1031, reg 49(1), Sch 8, Pt 1, paras 21, 25, as from 1 October 2006, but there has been no corresponding amendment to this section.

155 Matters to be disregarded in assessing contributory fault

(1) Where an [employment tribunal] makes an award of compensation for unfair dismissal in a case where the dismissal is unfair by virtue of section 152 or 153, the tribunal shall disregard, in considering whether it would be just and equitable to reduce, or further reduce, the amount of any part of the award, any such conduct or action of the complainant as is specified below.

(2) Conduct or action of the complainant shall be disregarded in so far as it constitutes a breach or proposed breach of a requirement—

- (a) to be or become a member of any trade union or of a particular trade union or of one of a number of particular trade unions,
- (b) to cease to be, or refrain from becoming, a member of any trade union or of a particular trade union or of one of a number of particular trade unions, ...
- (c) not to take part in the activities of any trade union or of a particular trade union or of one of a number of particular trade unions[, or
- (d) not to make use of services made available by any trade union or by a particular trade union or by one of a number of particular trade unions].

For the purposes of this subsection a requirement means a requirement imposed on the complainant by or under an arrangement or contract of employment or other agreement.

[(2A) Conduct or action of the complainant shall be disregarded in so far as it constitutes acceptance of or failure to accept an offer made in contravention of section 145A or 145B.]

(3) Conduct or action of the complainant shall be disregarded in so far as it constitutes a refusal, or proposed refusal, to comply with a requirement of a kind mentioned in section 152(3)(a) (payments in lieu of membership) or an objection, or proposed, objection, (however expressed) to the operation of a provision of a kind mentioned in section 152(3)(b) (deductions in lieu of membership).

[641]

NOTES

Sub-s (1): words in square brackets substituted by the Employment Rights (Dispute Resolution) Act 1998, s 1(2)(a).

Sub-s (2): word omitted from para (b) repealed, and para (d) and the word immediately preceding it inserted, by the Employment Relations Act 2004, s 57, Sch 1, para 11(1), (2), Sch 2, as from 1 October 2004, except in relation to cases where the act or failure to act to which the complaint relates was done before that date, or where the act or failure to act to which the complaint relates is part of a series and the first act or failure in the series was done before that date (see SI 2004/2566, art 6).

Sub-s (2A): inserted by the Employment Relations Act 2004, s 57(1), Sch 1, para 11(1), (3), as from 1 October 2004 (subject to the same exception in SI 2004/2566, art 6 as noted above).

156 Minimum basic award

(1) Where a dismissal is unfair by virtue of section 152(1) or 153, the amount of the basic award of compensation, before any reduction is made under [section 122 of the Employment Rights Act 1996], shall be not less than [£4,400].

(2) But where the dismissal is unfair by virtue of section 153, [subsection (2)] of that section (reduction for contributory fault) applies in relation to so much of the basic award as is payable because of subsection (1) above.

[642]

NOTES

Sub-s (1): words in first pair of square brackets substituted by the Employment Rights Act 1996, s 240, Sch 1, para 56(1), (9); sum in second pair of square brackets substituted by the Employment Rights (Increase of Limits) Order 2007, SI 2007/3570, art 3, Schedule, as from 1 February 2008, in relation to any case where the appropriate date falls on or after that date (see SI 2007/3570, art 4 at **[3474H]**). The previous sum was £4,200. This sum may be further varied by the Secretary of State, see the Employment Relations Act 1999, s 34(1)(f), (3)(b) at **[1445]**.

Sub-s (2): words in square brackets substituted by the Employment Rights Act 1996, s 240, Sch 1, para 56(1), (9).

157–159 *(Ss 157, 158 repealed by the Employment Relations Act 1999, ss 33(1)(b), 36(1)(b), 44, Sch 9(10); s 159 repealed by the Employment Relations Act 1999, ss 36(1)(b), (3), 44, Sch 9(10).)*

160 Awards against third parties

(1) If in proceedings before an [employment tribunal] on a complaint of unfair dismissal either the employer or the complainant claims—

(a) that the employer was induced to dismiss the complainant by pressure which a trade union or other person exercised on the employer by calling, organising, procuring or financing a strike or other industrial action, or by threatening to do so, and

(b) that the pressure was exercised because the complainant was not a member of any trade union or of a particular trade union or of one of a number of particular trade unions,

the employer or the complainant may request the tribunal to direct that the person who he claims exercised the pressure be joined or sisted as a party to the proceedings.

(2) The request shall be granted if it is made before the hearing of the complaint begins, but may be refused after that time; and no such request may be made after the tribunal has made an award of compensation for unfair dismissal or an order for reinstatement or re-engagement.

(3) Where a person has been so joined or sisted as a party to the proceedings and the tribunal—

(a) makes an award of compensation for unfair dismissal, and

(b) finds that the claim mentioned in subsection (1) is well-founded,

the tribunal may order that the compensation shall be paid by that person instead of the employer, or partly by that person and partly by the employer, as the tribunal may consider just and equitable.

[643]

NOTES

Sub-s (1): words in square brackets substituted by the Employment Rights (Dispute Resolution) Act 1998, s 1(2)(a).

161 Application for interim relief

(1) An employee who presents a complaint of unfair dismissal alleging that the dismissal is unfair by virtue of section 152 may apply to the tribunal for interim relief.

(2) The tribunal shall not entertain an application for interim relief unless it is presented to the tribunal before the end of the period of seven days immediately following the effective date of termination (whether before, on or after that date).

(3) In a case where the employee relies on [section 152(1)(a), (b) or (ba), or on section 152(1)(bb) otherwise than in relation to an offer made in contravention of section 145A(1)(d),] the tribunal shall not entertain an application for interim relief unless before the end of that period there is also so presented a certificate in writing signed by an authorised official of the independent trade union of which the employee was or proposed to become a member stating—

(a) that on the date of the dismissal the employee was or proposed to become a member of the union, and

(b) that there appear to be reasonable grounds for supposing that the reason for his dismissal (or, if more than one, the principal reason) was one alleged in the complaint.

(4) An "authorised official" means an official of the trade union authorised by it to act for the purposes of this section.

(5) A document purporting to be an authorisation of an official by a trade union to act for the purposes of this section and to be signed on behalf of the union shall be taken to be such an authorisation unless the contrary is proved; and a document purporting to be a certificate signed by such an official shall be taken to be signed by him unless the contrary is proved.

(6) For the purposes of subsection (3) the date of dismissal shall be taken to be—

(a) where the employee's contract of employment was terminated by notice (whether given by his employer or by him), the date on which the employer's notice was given, and

(b) in any other case, the effective date of termination.

[644]

NOTES

Sub-s (3): words in square brackets substituted by the Employment Relations Act 2004, s 57(1), Sch 1, para 12, as from 1 October 2004, except in relation to cases where the act or failure to act to which the complaint relates was done before that date, or where the act or failure to act to which the complaint relates is part of a series and the first act or failure in the series was done before that date (see SI 2004/2566, art 6).

162 Application to be promptly determined

(1) An [employment tribunal] shall determine an application for interim relief as soon as practicable after receiving the application and, where appropriate, the requisite certificate.

(2) The tribunal shall give to the employer, not later than seven days before the hearing, a copy of the application and of any certificate, together with notice of the date, time and place of the hearing.

(3) If a request under section 160 (awards against third parties) is made three days or more before the date of the hearing, the tribunal shall also give to the person to whom the request relates, as soon as reasonably practicable, a copy of the application and of any certificate, together with notice of the date, time and place of the hearing.

(4) The tribunal shall not exercise any power it has of postponing the hearing of an application for interim relief except where it is satisfied that special circumstances exist which justify it in doing so.

[645]

NOTES

Sub-s (1): words in square brackets substituted by the Employment Rights (Dispute Resolution) Act 1998, s 1(2)(a).

163 Procedure on hearing of application and making of order

(1) If on hearing an application for interim relief it appears to the tribunal that it is likely that on determining the complaint to which the application relates that it will find that, by virtue of section 152, the complainant has been unfairly dismissed, the following provisions apply.

(2) The tribunal shall announce its findings and explain to both parties (if present) what powers the tribunal may exercise on the application and in what circumstances it will exercise them, and shall ask the employer (if present) whether he is willing, pending the determination or settlement of the complaint—

(a) to reinstate the employee, that is to say, to treat him in all respects as if he had not been dismissed, or

(b) if not, to re-engage him in another job on terms and conditions not less favourable than those which would have been applicable to him if he had not been dismissed.

(3) For this purpose "terms and conditions not less favourable than those which would have been applicable to him if he had not been dismissed" means as regards seniority, pension rights and other similar rights that the period prior to the dismissal shall be regarded as continuous with his employment following the dismissal.

(4) If the employer states that he is willing to reinstate the employee, the tribunal shall make an order to that effect.

(5) If the employer states that he is willing to re-engage the employee in another job, and specifies the terms and conditions on which he is willing to do so, the tribunal shall ask the employee whether he is willing to accept the job on those terms and conditions; and—

(a) if the employee is willing to accept the job on those terms and conditions, the tribunal shall make an order to that effect, and

(b) if he is not, then, if the tribunal is of the opinion that the refusal is reasonable, the tribunal shall make an order for the continuation of his contract of employment, and otherwise the tribunal shall make no order.

(6) If on the hearing of an application for interim relief the employer fails to attend before the tribunal, or states that he is unwilling either to reinstate the employee or re-engage him as mentioned in subsection (2), the tribunal shall make an order for the continuation of the employee's contract of employment.

[646]

164 Order for continuation of contract of employment

(1) An order under section 163 for the continuation of a contract of employment is an order that the contract of employment continue in force—

(a) for the purposes of pay or [any other benefit] derived from the employment, seniority, pension rights and other similar matters, and

(b) for the purpose of determining for any purpose the period for which the employee has been continuously employed,

from the date of its termination (whether before or after the making of the order) until the determination or settlement of the complaint.

(2) Where the tribunal makes such an order it shall specify in the order the amount which is to be paid by the employer to the employee by way of pay in respect of each normal pay period, or part of any such period, falling between the date of dismissal and the determination or settlement of the complaint.

(3) Subject as follows, the amount so specified shall be that which the employee could reasonably have been expected to earn during that period, or part, and shall be paid—

(a) in the case of payment for any such period falling wholly or partly after the making of the order, on the normal pay day for that period, and

(b) in the case of a payment for any past period, within such time as may be specified in the order.

(4) If an amount is payable in respect only of part of a normal pay period, the amount shall be calculated by reference to the whole period and reduced proportionately.

(5) Any payment made to an employee by an employer under his contract of employment, or by way of damages for breach of that contract, in respect of a normal pay period or part of any such period shall go towards discharging the employer's liability in respect of that period under subsection (2); and conversely any payment under that subsection in respect of a period shall go towards discharging any liability of the employer under, or in respect of the breach of, the contract of employment in respect of that period.

(6) If an employee, on or after being dismissed by his employer, receives a lump sum which, or part of which, is in lieu of wages but is not referable to any normal pay period, the tribunal shall take the payment into account in determining the amount of pay to be payable in pursuance of any such order.

(7) For the purposes of this section the amount which an employee could reasonably have been expected to earn, his normal pay period and the normal pay day for each such period shall be determined as if he had not been dismissed.

[647]

NOTES

Sub-s (1): words in square brackets substituted by the Trade Union Reform and Employment Rights Act 1993, s 49(2), Sch 8, para 69.

165 Application for variation or revocation of order

(1) At any time between the making of an order under section 163 and the determination or settlement of the complaint, the employer or the employee may apply to an [employment tribunal] for the revocation or variation of the order on the ground of a relevant change of circumstances since the making of the order.

(2) Sections 161 to 163 apply in relation to such an application as in relation to an original application for interim relief, except that—

(a) no certificate need be presented to the tribunal under section 161(3), and

(b) in the case of an application by the employer, section 162(2) (service of copy of application and notice of hearing) has effect with the substitution of a reference to the employee for the reference to the employer.

[648]

NOTES

Sub-s (1): words in square brackets substituted by the Employment Rights (Dispute Resolution) Act 1998, s 1(2)(a).

166 Consequences of failure to comply with order

(1) If on the application of an employee an [employment tribunal] is satisfied that the employer has not complied with the terms of an order for the reinstatement or re-engagement of the employee under section 163(4) or [(5)], the tribunal shall—

(a) make an order for the continuation of the employee's contract of employment, and

(b) order the employer to pay the employee such compensation as the tribunal considers just and equitable in all the circumstances having regard—

(i) to the infringement of the employee's right to be reinstated or re-engaged in pursuance of the order, and

(ii) to any loss suffered by the employee in consequence of the non-compliance.

(2) Section 164 applies to an order under subsection (1)(a) as in relation to an order under section 163.

(3) If on the application of an employee an [employment tribunal] is satisfied that the employer has not complied with the terms of an order for the continuation of a contract of employment, the following provisions apply.

(4) If the non-compliance consists of a failure to pay an amount by way of pay specified in the order, the tribunal shall determine the amount owed by the employer on the date of the determination.

If on that date the tribunal also determines the employee's complaint that he has been unfairly dismissed, it shall specify that amount separately from any other sum awarded to the employee.

(5) In any other case, the tribunal shall order the employer to pay the employee such compensation as the tribunal considers just and equitable in all the circumstances having regard to any loss suffered by the employee in consequence of the non-compliance.

[649]

NOTES

Sub-s (1): words in first pair of square brackets substituted by the Employment Rights (Dispute Resolution) Act 1998, s 1(2)(a); number in second pair of square brackets substituted by the Trade Union Reform and Employment Rights Act 1993, s 49(1), Sch 7, para 22.

Sub-s (3): words in square brackets substituted by the Employment Rights (Dispute Resolution) Act 1998, s 1(2)(a).

167 Interpretation and other supplementary provisions

(1) [Part X of the Employment Rights Act 1996] (unfair dismissal) has effect subject to the provisions of sections 152 to 166 above.

(2) Those sections shall be construed as one with that Part; and in those sections—

"complaint of unfair dismissal" means a complaint under [section 111 of the Employment Rights Act 1996];

"award of compensation for unfair dismissal" means an award of compensation for unfair dismissal under [section 112(4) or 117(3)(a)] of that Act; and

"order for reinstatement or re-engagement" means an order for reinstatement or re-engagement under [section 113] of that Act.

(3) Nothing in those sections shall be construed as conferring a right to complain of unfair dismissal from employment of a description to which that Part does not otherwise apply.

[650]

NOTES
Sub-ss (1), (2): words in square brackets substituted by the Employment Rights Act 1996, s 240, Sch 1, para 56(1), (12).

Time off for trade union duties and activities

168 Time off for carrying out trade union duties

(1) An employer shall permit an employee of his who is an official of an independent trade union recognised by the employer to take time off during his working hours for the purpose of carrying out any duties of his, as such an official, concerned with—

(a) negotiations with the employer related to or connected with matters falling within section 178(2) (collective bargaining) in relation to which the trade union is recognised by the employer, or

(b) the performance on behalf of employees of the employer of functions related to or connected with matters falling within that provision which the employer has agreed may be so performed by the trade union[, or

(c) receipt of information from the employer and consultation by the employer under section 188 (redundancies) or under the [Transfer of Undertakings (Protection of Employment) Regulations 2006]][, or

(d) negotiations with a view to entering into an agreement under regulation 9 of the Transfer of Undertakings (Protection of Employment) Regulations 2006 that applies to employees of the employer, or

(e) the performance on behalf of employees of the employer of functions related to or connected with the making of an agreement under that regulation.]

(2) He shall also permit such an employee to take time off during his working hours for the purpose of undergoing training in aspects of industrial relations—

(a) relevant to the carrying out of such duties as are mentioned in subsection (1), and

(b) approved by the Trades Union Congress or by the independent trade union of which he is an official.

(3) The amount of time off which an employee is to be permitted to take under this section and the purposes for which, the occasions on which and any conditions subject to which time off may be so taken are those that are reasonable in all the circumstances having regard to any relevant provisions of a Code of Practice issued by ACAS.

(4) An employee may present a complaint to an [employment tribunal] that his employer has failed to permit him to take time off as required by this section.

[651]

NOTES
Sub-s (1): para (c) and the word immediately preceding it added by the Collective Redundancies and Transfer of Undertakings (Protection of Employment) (Amendment) Regulations 1999, SI 1999/1925, reg 14; words in square brackets in para (c) substituted, and paras (d), (e) and the word immediately preceding them added, by the Transfer of Undertakings (Protection of Employment) Regulations 2006, SI 2006/246, regs 9(4), 20, Sch 2, para 1(e), as from 6 April 2006 (for transitional provisions in relation to a relevant transfer, etc, that took place before that date, see reg 21 of the 2006 Regulations at **[3395]**).

Sub-s (4): words in square brackets substituted by the Employment Rights (Dispute Resolution) Act 1998, s 1(2)(a).

Conciliation: employment tribunal proceedings and claims which could be the subject of employment tribunal proceedings arising out of a contravention, or alleged contravention, of this section are proceedings to which the Employment Tribunals Act 1996, s 18 applies; see s 18(1)(b) of that Act at **[975]**. The short conciliation period applies to such claims by virtue of the Employment Tribunals (Constitution and Rules of Procedure) Regulations 2004, SI 2004/1861, Sch 1, rule 22(5).

The relevant code is ACAS Code of Practice 3: Time off for Trade Union Duties and Activities (2003) at **[4640]**.

[168A Time off for union learning representatives

(1) An employer shall permit an employee of his who is—

(a) a member of an independent trade union recognised by the employer, and

(b) a learning representative of the trade union,

to take time off during his working hours for any of the following purposes.

(2) The purposes are—

(a) carrying on any of the following activities in relation to qualifying members of the trade union—

(i) analysing learning or training needs,

(ii) providing information and advice about learning or training matters,

(iii) arranging learning or training, and

(iv) promoting the value of learning or training,

(b) consulting the employer about carrying on any such activities in relation to such members of the trade union,

(c) preparing for any of the things mentioned in paragraphs (a) and (b).

(3) Subsection (1) only applies if—

(a) the trade union has given the employer notice in writing that the employee is a learning representative of the trade union, and

(b) the training condition is met in relation to him.

(4) The training condition is met if—

(a) the employee has undergone sufficient training to enable him to carry on the activities mentioned in subsection (2), and the trade union has given the employer notice in writing of that fact,

(b) the trade union has in the last six months given the employer notice in writing that the employee will be undergoing such training, or

(c) within six months of the trade union giving the employer notice in writing that the employee will be undergoing such training, the employee has done so, and the trade union has given the employer notice of that fact.

(5) Only one notice under subsection (4)(b) may be given in respect of any one employee.

(6) References in subsection (4) to sufficient training to carry out the activities mentioned in subsection (2) are to training that is sufficient for those purposes having regard to any relevant provision of a Code of Practice issued by ACAS or the Secretary of State.

(7) If an employer is required to permit an employee to take time off under subsection (1), he shall also permit the employee to take time off during his working hours for the following purposes—

(a) undergoing training which is relevant to his functions as a learning representative, and

(b) where the trade union has in the last six months given the employer notice under subsection (4)(b) in relation to the employee, undergoing such training as is mentioned in subsection (4)(a).

(8) The amount of time off which an employee is to be permitted to take under this section and the purposes for which, the occasions on which and any conditions subject to which time off may be so taken are those that are reasonable in all the circumstances having regard to any relevant provision of a Code of Practice issued by ACAS or the Secretary of State.

(9) An employee may present a complaint to an employment tribunal that his employer has failed to permit him to take time off as required by this section.

(10) In subsection (2)(a), the reference to qualifying members of the trade union is to members of the trade union—

(a) who are employees of the employer of a description in respect of which the union is recognised by the employer, and

(b) in relation to whom it is the function of the union learning representative to act as such.

(11) For the purposes of this section, a person is a learning representative of a trade union if he is appointed or elected as such in accordance with its rules.]

[652]

NOTES

Commencement: 27 April 2003.

Inserted by the Employment Act 2002, s 43(1), (2), as from 27 April 2003.

Conciliation: employment tribunal proceedings and claims which could be the subject of employment tribunal proceedings arising out of a contravention, or alleged contravention, of this section are proceedings to which the Employment Tribunals Act 1996, s 18 applies; see s 18(1)(b) of that Act at

[975]. The standard conciliation period applies to such claims by virtue of the Employment Tribunals (Constitution and Rules of Procedure) Regulations 2004, SI 2004/1861, Sch 1, rule 22(5).

The relevant code is ACAS Code of Practice 3: Time off for Trade Union Duties and Activities (2003) at [4640].

Note: the Employment Act 2002 (Commencement No 4 and Transitional Provisions) Order 2003, SI 2003/1190, art 3 provides that the requirements of sub-s (3) above shall be treated as being satisfied in relation to an employee if (a) immediately before 27 April 2003 he has the function of carrying on any or all of the activities mentioned in sub-s (2) above in relation to qualifying members of the union and has had that function for a continuous period of six months or more, and (b) he acquired that function by reason of being appointed or elected, in accordance with the rules of the union, to carry it on.

169 Payment for time off under section 168

(1) An employer who permits an employee to take time off under section 168 [or 168A] shall pay him for the time taken off pursuant to the permission.

(2) Where the employee's remuneration for the work he would ordinarily have been doing during that time does not vary with the amount of work done, he shall be paid as if he had worked at that work for the whole of that time.

(3) Where the employee's remuneration for the work he would ordinarily have been doing during that time varies with the amount of work done, he shall be paid an amount calculated by reference to the average hourly earnings for that work.

The average hourly earnings shall be those of the employee concerned or, if no fair estimate can be made of those earnings, the average hourly earnings for work of that description of persons in comparable employment with the same employer or, if there are no such persons, a figure of average hourly earnings which is reasonable in the circumstances.

(4) A right to be paid an amount under this section does not affect any right of an employee in relation to remuneration under his contract of employment, but—

- (a) any contractual remuneration paid to an employee in respect of a period of time off to which this section applies shall go towards discharging any liability of the employer under this section in respect of that period, and
- (b) any payment under this section in respect of a period shall go towards discharging any liability of the employer to pay contractual remuneration in respect of that period.

(5) An employee may present a complaint to an [employment tribunal] that his employer has failed to pay him in accordance with this section.

[653]

NOTES

Sub-s (1): words in square brackets inserted by the Employment Act 2002, s 43(1), (3), as from 27 April 2003.

Sub-s (5): words in square brackets substituted by the Employment Rights (Dispute Resolution) Act 1998, s 1(2)(a).

Conciliation: employment tribunal proceedings and claims which could be the subject of employment tribunal proceedings arising out of a contravention, or alleged contravention, of this section are proceedings to which the Employment Tribunals Act 1996, s 18 applies; see s 18(1)(b) of that Act at [975]. The short conciliation period applies to claims in relation to s 168, and the standard conciliation period applies to claims in relation to s 168A, by virtue of the Employment Tribunals (Constitution and Rules of Procedure) Regulations 2004, SI 2004/1861, Sch 1, rule 22(5) and Rule 22(1), (6) respectively.

170 Time off for trade union activities

(1) An employer shall permit an employee of his who is a member of an independent trade union recognised by the employer in respect of that description of employee to take time off during his working hours for the purpose of taking part in—

- (a) any activities of the union, and
- (b) any activities in relation to which the employee is acting as a representative of the union.

(2) The right conferred by subsection (1) does not extent to activities which themselves consist of industrial action, whether or not in contemplation or furtherance of a trade dispute.

[(2A) The right conferred by subsection (1) does not extend to time off for the purpose of acting as, or having access to services provided by, a learning representative of a trade union.

(2B) An employer shall permit an employee of his who is a member of an independent trade union recognised by the employer in respect of that description of employee to take time off during his working hours for the purpose of having access to services provided by a person in his capacity as a learning representative of the trade union.

(2C) Subsection (2B) only applies if the learning representative would be entitled to time off under subsection (1) of section 168A for the purpose of carrying on in relation to the employee activities of the kind mentioned in subsection (2) of that section.]

(3) The amount of time off which an employee is to be permitted to take under this section and the purposes for which, the occasions on which and any conditions subject to which time off may be so taken are those that are reasonable in all the circumstances having regard to any relevant provisions of a Code of Practice issued by ACAS.

(4) An employee may present a complaint to an [employment tribunal] that his employer has failed to permit him to take time off as required by this section.

[(5) For the purposes of this section—

(a) a person is a learning representative of a trade union if he is appointed or elected as such in accordance with its rules, and

(b) a person who is a learning representative of a trade union acts as such if he carries on the activities mentioned in section 168A(2) in that capacity.]

[654]

NOTES

Sub-ss (2A)–(2C), (5): inserted and added respectively by the Employment Act 2002, s 43(1), (4), (5), as from 27 April 2003.

Sub-s (4): words in square brackets substituted by the Employment Rights (Dispute Resolution) Act 1998, s 1(2)(a).

Code of Practice under sub-s (3): the code under the provisions contained in this subsection is ACAS Code of Practice 3: Time off for Trade Union Duties and Activities (2003) at **[4640]**.

Conciliation: employment tribunal proceedings and claims which could be the subject of employment tribunal proceedings arising out of a contravention, or alleged contravention, of this section are proceedings to which the Employment Tribunals Act 1996, s 18 applies; see s 18(1)(b) of that Act at **[975]**. The short conciliation period applies to such claims by virtue of the Employment Tribunals (Constitution and Rules of Procedure) Regulations 2004, SI 2004/1861, Sch 1, rule 22(5).

171 Time limit for proceedings

An [employment tribunal] shall not consider a complaint under section 168, [168A,] 169 or 170 unless it is presented to the tribunal—

(a) within three months of the date when the failure occurred, or

(b) where the tribunal is satisfied that it was not reasonably practicable for the complaint to be presented within that period, within such further period as the tribunal considers reasonable.

[655]

NOTES

Words in first pair of square brackets substituted by the Employment Rights (Dispute Resolution) Act 1998, s 1(2)(a); number in second pair of square brackets inserted by the Employment Act 2002, s 53, Sch 7, paras 18, 19, as from 27 April 2003.

172 Remedies

(1) Where the tribunal finds a complaint under section 168[, 168A] or 170 is well-founded, it shall make a declaration to that effect and may make an award of compensation to be paid by the employer to the employee.

(2) The amount of the compensation shall be such as the tribunal considers just and equitable in all the circumstances having regard to the employer's default in failing to permit time off to be taken by the employee and to any loss sustained by the employee which is attributable to the matters complained of.

(3) Where on a complaint under section 169 the tribunal finds that the employer has failed to pay the employee in accordance with that section, it shall order him to pay the amount which it finds to be due.

[656]

NOTES

Sub-s (1): number in square brackets inserted by the Employment Act 2002, s 53, Sch 7, paras 18, 20, as from 27 April 2003.

173 Interpretation and other supplementary provisions

(1) For the purposes of sections 168[, 168A] and 170 the working hours of an employee shall be taken to be any time when in accordance with his contract of employment he is required to be at work.

(2) The remedy of an employee for infringement of the rights conferred on him by section 168, [168A,] 169 or 170 is by way of complaint to an [employment tribunal] in accordance with this Part, and not otherwise.

[(3) The Secretary of State may by order made by statutory instrument amend section 168A for the purpose of changing the purposes for which an employee may take time off under that section.

(4) No order may be made under subsection (3) unless a draft of the order has been laid before and approved by resolution of each House of Parliament.]

[657]

NOTES

Sub-s (1): number in square brackets inserted by the Employment Act 2002, s 53, Sch 7, paras 18, 21(a), as from 27 April 2003.

Sub-s (2): number in first pair of square brackets inserted by the Employment Act 2002, s 53, Sch 7, paras 18, 21(b), as from 27 April 2003; words in second pair of square brackets substituted by the Employment Rights (Dispute Resolution) Act 1998, s 1(2)(a).

Sub-ss (3), (4): added by the Employment Act 2002, s 43(1), (6), as from 27 April 2003.

Orders: as of 6 April 2008, no Orders had been made under this section.

[Right to membership of trade union

174 Right not to be excluded or expelled from union

(1) An individual shall not be excluded or expelled from a trade union unless the exclusion or expulsion is permitted by this section.

(2) The exclusion or expulsion of an individual from a trade union is permitted by this section if (and only if)—

(a) he does not satisfy, or no longer satisfies, an enforceable membership requirement contained in the rules of the union,

(b) he does not qualify, or no longer qualifies, for membership of the union by reason of the union operating only in a particular part or particular parts of Great Britain,

(c) in the case of a union whose purpose is the regulation of relations between its members and one particular employer or a number of particular employers who are associated, he is not, or is no longer, employed by that employer or one of those employers, or

(d) the exclusion or expulsion is entirely attributable to [conduct of his (other than excluded conduct) and the conduct to which it is wholly or mainly attributable is not protected conduct].

(3) A requirement in relation to membership of a union is "enforceable" for the purposes of subsection (2)(a) if it restricts membership solely by reference to one or more of the following criteria—

(a) employment in a specified trade, industry or profession,

(b) occupational description (including grade, level or category of appointment), and

(c) possession of specified trade, industrial or professional qualifications or work experience.

[(4) For the purposes of subsection (2)(d) "excluded conduct", in relation to an individual, means—

(a) conduct which consists in his being or ceasing to be, or having been or ceased to be, a member of another trade union,

(b) conduct which consists in his being or ceasing to be, or having been or ceased to be, employed by a particular employer or at a particular place, or

(c) conduct to which section 65 (conduct for which an individual may not be disciplined by a union) applies or would apply if the references in that section to the trade union which is relevant for the purposes of that section were references to any trade union.

(4A) For the purposes of subsection (2)(d) "protected conduct" is conduct which consists in the individual's being or ceasing to be, or having been or ceased to be, a member of a political party.

(4B) Conduct which consists of activities undertaken by an individual as a member of a political party is not conduct falling within subsection (4A).]

(5) An individual who claims that he has been excluded or expelled from a trade union in contravention of this section may present a complaint to an [employment tribunal].]

[658]

NOTES

Substituted, together with the preceding heading, by the Trade Union Reform and Employment Rights Act 1993, s 14.

Sub-s (2): words in square brackets in para (d) substituted by the Employment Relations Act 2004, s 33(1), (2), (7), as from 31 December 2004, except in relation to any decision by a union to exclude or expel an individual which is taken before that date (see SI 2004/3342, art 7).

Sub-ss (4), (4A), (4B): substituted, for original sub-s (4), by the Employment Relations Act 2004, s 33(1), (3), (7), as from 31 December 2004 (subject to the same exception in SI 2004/3342, art 7 as noted above).

Sub-s (5): words in square brackets substituted by the Employment Rights (Dispute Resolution) Act 1998, s 1(2)(a).

Conciliation: employment tribunal proceedings and claims which could be the subject of employment tribunal proceedings arising out of a contravention, or alleged contravention, of this section are proceedings to which the Employment Tribunals Act 1996, s 18 applies; see s 18(1)(b) of that Act at **[975]**. The standard conciliation period applies to such claims by virtue of the Employment Tribunals (Constitution and Rules of Procedure) Regulations 2004, SI 2004/1861, Sch 1, rule 22(1), (6).

[175 Time limit for proceedings

An [employment tribunal] shall not entertain a complaint under section 174 unless it is presented—

(a) before the end of the period of six months beginning with the date of the exclusion or expulsion, or

(b) where the tribunal is satisfied that it was not reasonably practicable for the complaint to be presented before the end of that period, within such further period as the tribunal considers reasonable.]

[659]

NOTES

Substituted by the Trade Union Reform and Employment Rights Act 1993, s 14.

Words in square brackets substituted by the Employment Rights (Dispute Resolution) Act 1998, s 1(2)(a).

[176 Remedies

(1) Where the [employment tribunal] finds a complaint under section 174 is well-founded, it shall make a declaration to that effect.

[(1A) If a tribunal makes a declaration under subsection (1) and it appears to the tribunal that the exclusion or expulsion was mainly attributable to conduct falling within section 174(4A) it shall make a declaration to that effect.

(1B) If a tribunal makes a declaration under subsection (1A) and it appears to the tribunal that the other conduct to which the exclusion or expulsion was attributable consisted wholly or mainly of conduct of the complainant which was contrary to—

(a) a rule of the union, or

(b) an objective of the union,

it shall make a declaration to that effect.

(1C) For the purposes of subsection (1B), it is immaterial whether the complainant was a member of the union at the time of the conduct contrary to the rule or objective.

(1D) A declaration by virtue of subsection (1B)(b) shall not be made unless the union shows that, at the time of the conduct of the complainant which was contrary to the objective in question, it was reasonably practicable for that objective to be ascertained—

(a) if the complainant was not at that time a member of the union, by a member of the general public, and

(b) if he was at that time a member of the union, by a member of the union.]

(2) An individual whose complaint has been declared to be well-founded may make an application [to an employment tribunal] for an award of compensation to be paid to him by the union.

…

(3) The application shall not be entertained if made—

(a) before the end of the period of four weeks beginning with the date of the declaration [under subsection (1)], or

(b) after the end of the period of six months beginning with that date.

(4) The amount of compensation awarded shall, subject to the following provisions, be such as the [employment tribunal] … considers just and equitable in all the circumstances.

(5) Where the [employment tribunal] … finds that the exclusion or expulsion complained of was to any extent caused or contributed to by the action of the applicant, it shall reduce the amount of the compensation by such proportion as it considers just and equitable having regard to that finding.

(6) The amount of compensation calculated in accordance with subsections (4) and (5) shall not exceed the aggregate of—

(a) an amount equal to thirty times the limit for the time being imposed by [section 227(1)(a) of the Employment Rights Act 1996] (maximum amount of a week's pay for basic award in unfair dismissal cases), and

(b) an amount equal to the limit for the time being imposed by [section 113] of that Act (maximum compensatory award in such cases);

…

[(6A) If on the date on which the application was made the applicant had not been admitted or re-admitted to the union, the award shall not be less than [£6,900].

(6B) Subsection (6A) does not apply in a case where the tribunal which made the declaration under subsection (1) also made declarations under subsections (1A) and (1B).]

(7), (8) …] **[660]**

NOTES

Substituted by the Trade Union Reform and Employment Rights Act 1993, s 14.

Sub-s (1): words in square brackets substituted by the Employment Rights (Dispute Resolution) Act 1998, s 1(2)(a).

Sub-ss (1A)–(1D): inserted by the Employment Relations Act 2004, s 33(1), (4), (7), as from 31 December 2004, except in relation to any decision by a union to exclude or expel an individual which is taken before that date (see SI 2004/3342, art 7).

Sub-s (2): words in square brackets inserted, and words omitted repealed, by the Employment Relations Act 2004, ss 34(7), (8)(b), 57(2), Sch 2, as from 31 December 2004, except in relation to any complaint presented by an individual which relates to a decision to exclude or expel the individual under s 174 of this Act which was taken by the union before that date (see SI 2004/3342, art 9).

Sub-s (3): words in square brackets in para (a) inserted by the Employment Relations Act 2004, s 33(1), (5), (7), as from 31 December 2004 (subject to the same exception in SI 2004/3342, art 7 as noted above).

Sub-ss (4), (5): words in square brackets substituted by the Employment Rights (Dispute Resolution) Act 1998, s 1(2)(a); words omitted repealed by the Employment Relations Act 2004, ss 34(7), (9), (10), 57(2), Sch 2, as from 31 December 2004 (subject to the same exception in SI 2004/3342, art 9 as noted above).

Sub-s (6): words in square brackets substituted by the Employment Rights Act 1996, s 240, Sch 1, para 56(1), (13); words omitted repealed by the Employment Relations Act 2004, ss 34(7), (11), 57(2), Sch 2, as from 31 December 2004 (subject to the same exception in SI 2004/3342, art 9 as noted above).

Sub-s (6A): inserted, together with sub-s (6B), by the Employment Relations Act 2004, s 33(1), (6), (7), as from 31 December 2004 (subject to the same exception in SI 2004/3342, art 7 as noted above); sum in square brackets substituted by the Employment Rights (Increase of Limits) Order 2007, SI 2007/3570, art 3, Schedule, as from 1 February 2008, in relation to any case where the appropriate date falls on or after that date (see SI 2007/3570, art 4 at **[3474H]**). The previous sum was £6,600. This sum may be further varied by the Secretary of State, see the Employment Relations Act 1999, s 34(1)(g), (3)(b) at **[1445]**.

Sub-s (6B): inserted as noted above.
Sub-ss (7), (8): repealed by the Employment Relations Act 1999, ss 36(1)(b), 44, Sch 9(10).

[177 Interpretation and other supplementary provisions

(1) For the purposes of section 174—

(a) "trade union" does not include an organisation falling within paragraph (b) of section 1,

(b) "conduct" includes statements, acts and omissions, and

(c) "employment" includes any relationship whereby an individual personally does work or performs services for another person (related expressions being construed accordingly).

(2) For the purposes of sections 174 to 176—

(a) if an individual's application for membership of a trade union is neither granted nor rejected before the end of the period within which it might reasonably have been expected to be granted if it was to be granted, he shall be treated as having been excluded from the union on the last day of that period, and

(b) an individual who under the rules of a trade union ceases to be a member of the union on the happening of an event specified in the rules shall be treated as having been expelled from the union.

(3) The remedy of an individual for infringement of the rights conferred by section 174 is by way of a complaint to an [employment tribunal] in accordance with that section, sections 175 and 176 and this section, and not otherwise.

(4) Where a complaint relating to an expulsion which is presented under section 174 is declared to be well-founded, no complaint in respect of the expulsion shall be presented or proceeded with under section 66 (complaint of infringement of right not to be unjustifiably disciplined).

(5) The rights conferred by section 174 are in addition to, and not in substitution for, any right which exists apart from that section; and, subject to subsection (4), nothing in that section, section 175 or 176 or this section affects any remedy for infringement of any such right.]

[661]

NOTES

Substituted by the Trade Union Reform and Employment Rights Act 1993, s 14.
Sub-s (3): words in square brackets substituted by the Employment Rights (Dispute Resolution) Act 1998, s 1(2)(a).

PART IV
INDUSTRIAL RELATIONS

CHAPTER I
COLLECTIVE BARGAINING

Introductory

178 Collective agreements and collective bargaining

(1) In this Act "collective agreement" means any agreement or arrangement made by or on behalf of one or more trade unions and one or more employers or employers' associations and relating to one or more of the matters specified below; and "collective bargaining" means negotiations relating to or connected with one or more of those matters.

(2) The matters referred to above are—

(a) terms and conditions of employment, or the physical conditions in which any workers are required to work;

(b) engagement or non-engagement, or termination or suspension of employment or the duties of employment, of one or more workers;

(c) allocation of work or the duties of employment between workers or groups of workers;

(d) matters of discipline;

(e) a worker's membership or non-membership of a trade union;

(f) facilities for officials of trade unions; and

(g) machinery for negotiation or consultation, and other procedures, relating to any of the above matters, including the recognition by employers or employers' associations of the right of a trade union to represent workers in such negotiation or consultation or in the carrying out of such procedures.

(3) In this Act "recognition", in relation to a trade union, means the recognition of the union by an employer, or two or more associated employers, to any extent, for the purpose of collective bargaining; and "recognised" and other related expressions shall be construed accordingly.

[662]

Enforceability of collective agreements

179 Whether agreement intended to be a legally enforceable contract

(1) A collective agreement shall be conclusively presumed not to have been intended by the parties to be a legally enforceable contract unless the agreement—

(a) is in writing, and

(b) contains a provision which (however expressed) states that the parties intend that the agreement shall be a legally enforceable contract.

(2) A collective agreement which does satisfy those conditions shall be conclusively presumed to have been intended by the parties to be a legally enforceable contract.

(3) If a collective agreement is in writing and contains a provision which (however expressed) states that the parties intend that one or more parts of the agreement specified in that provision, but not the whole of the agreement, shall be a legally enforceable contract, then—

(a) the specified part or parts shall be conclusively presumed to have been intended by the parties to be a legally enforceable contract, and

(b) the remainder of the agreement shall be conclusively presumed not to have been intended by the parties to be such a contract.

(4) A part of a collective agreement which by virtue of subsection (3)(b) is not a legally enforceable contract may be referred to for the purpose of interpreting a party of the agreement which is such a contract.

[663]

180 Effect of provisions restricting right to take industrial action

(1) Any terms of a collective agreement which prohibit or restrict the right of workers to engage in a strike or other industrial action, or have the effect of prohibiting or restricting that right, shall not form part of any contract between a worker and the person for whom he works unless the following conditions are met.

(2) The conditions are that the collective agreement—

(a) is in writing,

(b) contains a provision expressly stating that those terms shall or may be incorporated in such a contract,

(c) is reasonably accessible at his place of work to the worker to whom it applies and is available for him to consult during working hours, and

(d) is one where each trade union which is a party to the agreement is an independent trade union;

and that the contract with the worker expressly or impliedly incorporates those terms in the contract.

(3) The above provisions have effect notwithstanding anything in section 179 and notwithstanding any provision to the contrary in any agreement (including a collective agreement or a contract with any worker).

[664]

Disclosure of information for purposes of collective bargaining

181 General duty of employers to disclose information

(1) An employer who recognises an independent trade union shall, for the purposes of all stages of collective bargaining about matters, and in relation to descriptions of workers, in respect of which the union is recognised by him, disclose to representatives of the union, on request, the information required by this section.

In this section and sections 182 to 185 "representative", in relation to a trade union, means an official or other person authorised by the union to carry on such collective bargaining.

(2) The information to be disclosed is all information relating to the employer's undertaking which is in his possession, or that of an associated employer, and is information—

(a) without which the trade union representatives would be to a material extent impeded in carrying on collective bargaining with him, and

(b) which it would be in accordance with good industrial relations practice that he should disclose to them for the purposes of collective bargaining.

(3) A request by trade union representatives for information under this section shall, if the employer so requests, be in writing or be confirmed in writing.

(4) In determining what would be in accordance with good industrial relations practice, regard shall be had to the relevant provisions of any Code of Practice issued by ACAS, but not so as to exclude any other evidence of what that practice is.

(5) Information which an employer is required by virtue of this section to disclose to trade union representatives shall, if they so request, be disclosed or confirmed in writing.

[665]

NOTES

Code of Practice for the purposes of sub-s (4): see ACAS Code of Practice 2: Disclosure of Information to Trade Unions for Collective Bargaining Purposes (1998) at **[4529]**.

Modified as noted to s 146 at **[632]**.

182 Restrictions on general duty

(1) An employer is not required by section 181 to disclose information—

(a) the disclosure of which would be against the interests of national security, or

(b) which he could not disclose without contravening a prohibition imposed by or under an enactment, or

(c) which has been communicated to him in confidence, or which he has otherwise obtained in consequence of the confidence reposed in him by another person, or

(d) which relates specifically to an individual (unless that individual has consented to its being disclosed), or

(e) the disclosure of which would cause substantial injury to his undertaking for reasons other than its effect on collective bargaining, or

(f) obtained by him for the purpose of bringing, prosecuting or defending any legal proceedings.

In formulating the provisions of any Code of Practice relating to the disclosure of information, ACAS shall have regard to the provisions of this subsection.

(2) In the performance of his duty under section 181 an employer is not required—

(a) to produce, or allow inspection of, any document (other than a document prepared for the purpose of conveying or confirming the information) or to make a copy of or extracts from any document, or

(b) to compile or assemble any information where the compilation or assembly would involve an amount of work or expenditure out of reasonable proportion to the value of the information in the conduct of collective bargaining.

[666]

NOTES

Modified as noted to s 146 at **[632]**.

183 Complaint of failure to disclose information

(1) A trade union may present a complaint to the Central Arbitration Committee that an employer has failed—

(a) to disclose to representatives of the union information which he was required to disclose to them by section 181, or

(b) to confirm such information in writing in accordance with that section.

The complaint must be in writing and in such form as the Committee may require.

(2) If on receipt of a complaint the Committee is of the opinion that it is reasonably likely to be settled by conciliation, it shall refer the complaint to ACAS and shall notify the trade union and employer accordingly, whereupon ACAS shall seek to promote a settlement of the matter.

If a complaint so referred is not settled or withdrawn and ACAS is of the opinion that further attempts at conciliation are unlikely to result in a settlement, it shall inform the Committee of its opinion.

(3) If the complaint is not referred to ACAS or, if it is so referred, on ACAS informing the Committee of its opinion that further attempts at conciliation are unlikely to result in a settlement, the Committee shall proceed to hear and determine the complaint and shall make a declaration stating whether it finds the complaint well-founded, wholly or in part, and stating the reasons for its findings.

(4) On the hearing of a complaint any person who the Committee considers has a proper interest in the complaint is entitled to be heard by the Committee, but a failure to accord a hearing to a person other than the trade union and employer directly concerned does not affect the validity of any decision of the Committee in those proceedings.

(5) If the Committee finds the complaint wholly or partly well founded, the declaration shall specify—

(a) the information in respect of which the Committee finds that the complaint is well founded,

(b) the date (or, if more than one, the earliest date) on which the employer refused or failed to disclose or, as the case may be, to confirm in writing, any of the information in question, and

(c) a period (not being less than one week from the date of the declaration) within which the employer ought to disclose that information, or, as the case may be, to confirm it in writing.

(6) On a hearing of a complaint under this section a certificate signed by or on behalf of a Minister of the Crown and certifying that a particular request for information could not be complied with except by disclosing information the disclosure of which would have been against the interests of national security shall be conclusive evidence of that fact.

A document which purports to be such a certificate shall be taken to be such a certificate unless the contrary is proved.

[667]

NOTES

Modified as noted to s 146 at **[632]**.

184 Further complaint of failure to comply with declaration

(1) After the expiration of the period specified in a declaration under section 183(5)(c) the trade union may present a further complaint to the Central Arbitration Committee that the employer has failed to disclose or, as the case may be, to confirm in writing to representatives of the union information specified in the declaration.

The complaint must be in writing and in such form as the Committee may require.

(2) On receipt of a further complaint the Committee shall proceed to hear and determine the complaint and shall make a declaration stating whether they find the complaint well-founded, wholly or in part, and stating the reasons for their finding.

(3) On the hearing of a further complaint any person who the Committee consider has a proper interest in that complaint shall be entitled to be heard by the Committee, but a failure to accord a hearing to a person other than the trade union and employer directly concerned shall not affect the validity of any decision of the Committee in those proceedings.

(4) If the Committee find the further complaint wholly or partly well-founded the declaration shall specify the information in respect of which the Committee find that that complaint is well-founded.

[668]

NOTES

Modified as noted to s 146 at **[632]**.

185 Determination of claim and award

(1) On or after presenting a further complaint under section 184 the trade union may present to the Central Arbitration Committee a claim, in writing, in respect of one or more descriptions of employees (but not workers who are not employees) specified in the claim that their contracts should include the terms and conditions specified in the claim.

(2) The right to present a claim expires if the employer discloses or, as the case may be, confirms in writing, to representatives of the trade union the information specified in the declaration under section 183(5) or 184(4); and a claim presented shall be treated as withdrawn if the employer does so before the Committee make an award on the claim.

(3) If the Committee find, or have found, the further complaint wholly or partly well-founded, they may, after hearing the parties, make an award that in respect of any description of employees specified in the claim the employer shall, from a specified date, observe either—

(a) the terms and conditions specified in the claim; or

(b) other terms and conditions which the Committee consider appropriate.

The date specified may be earlier than that on which the award is made but not earlier than the date specified in accordance with section 183(5)(b) in the declaration made by the Committee on the original complaint.

(4) An award shall be made only in respect of a description of employees, and shall comprise only terms and conditions relating to matters in respect of which the trade union making the claim is recognised by the employer.

(5) Terms and conditions which by an award under this section an employer is required to observe in respect of an employee have effect as part of the employee's contract of employment as from the date specified in the award, except in so far as they are superseded or varied—

(a) by a subsequent award under this section,

(b) by a collective agreement between the employer and the union for the time being representing that employee, or

(c) by express or implied agreement between the employee and the employer so far as that agreement effects an improvement in terms and conditions having effect by virtue of the award.

(6) Where—

(a) by virtue of any enactment, other than one contained in this section, providing for minimum remuneration or terms and conditions, a contract of employment is to have effect as modified by an award, order or other instrument under that enactment, and

(b) by virtue of an award under this section any terms and conditions are to have effect as part of that contract,

that contract shall have effect in accordance with that award, order or other instrument or in accordance with the award under this section, whichever is the more favourable, in respect of any terms and conditions of that contract, to the employee.

(7) No award may be made under this section in respect of terms and conditions of employment which are fixed by virtue of any enactment.

[669]

NOTES

Modified as noted to s 146 at **[632]**.

Prohibition of union recognition requirements

186 Recognition requirement in contract for goods or services void

A term or condition of a contract for the supply of goods or services is void in so far as it purports to require a party to the contract—

(a) to recognise one or more trade unions (whether or not named in the contract) for the purpose of negotiating on behalf of workers, or any class of worker, employed by him, or

(b) to negotiate or consult with, or with an official of, one or more trade unions (whether or not so named).

[670]

187 Refusal to deal on grounds of union exclusion prohibited

(1) A person shall not refuse to deal with a supplier or prospective supplier of goods or services if the ground or one of the grounds for his action is that the person against whom it is taken does not, or is not likely to—

(a) recognise one or more trade unions for the purpose of negotiating on behalf of workers, or any class of worker, employed by him, or

(b) negotiate or consult with, or with an official of, one or more trade unions.

(2) A person refuses to deal with a person if—

(a) where he maintains (in whatever form) a list of approved suppliers of goods or services, or of persons from whom tenders for the supply of goods or services may be invited, he fails to include the name of that person in that list; or

(b) in relation to a proposed contract for the supply of goods or services—

(i) he excludes that person from the group of persons from whom tenders for the supply of the goods or services are invited, or

(ii) he fails to permit that person to submit such a tender; or

[(iii)] he otherwise determines not to enter into a contract with that person for the supply of the goods or services [or

(c) he terminates a contract with that person for the supply of goods or services.]

(3) The obligation to comply with this section is a duty owed to the person with whom there is a refusal to deal and to any other person who may be adversely affected by its contravention; and a breach of the duty is actionable accordingly (subject to the defences and other incidents applying to actions for breach of statutory duty).

[671]

NOTES

Sub-s (2): original para (c) renumbered as sub-para (iii) of para (b), and new para (c) and the word immediately preceding it added, by the Trade Union Reform and Employment Rights Act 1993, s 49(1), Sch 7, para 23.

CHAPTER II
PROCEDURE FOR HANDLING REDUNDANCIES

Duty of employer to consult ... representatives

188 Duty of employer to consult ... representatives

[(1) Where an employer is proposing to dismiss as redundant 20 or more employees at one establishment within a period of 90 days or less, the employer shall consult about the dismissals all the persons who are appropriate representatives of any of the employees who may be [affected by the proposed dismissals or may be affected by measures taken in connection with those dismissals.]

(1A) The consultation shall begin in good time and in any event—

(a) where the employer is proposing to dismiss 100 or more employees as mentioned in subsection (1), at least 90 days, and

(b) otherwise, at least 30 days,

before the first of the dismissals takes effect.

[(1B) For the purposes of this section the appropriate representatives of any affected employees are—

(a) if the employees are of a description in respect of which an independent trade union is recognised by their employer, representatives of the trade union, or

(b) in any other case, whichever of the following employee representatives the employer chooses:—

(i) employee representatives appointed or elected by the affected employees otherwise than for the purposes of this section, who (having regard to the purposes for and the method by which they were appointed or elected) have authority from those employees to receive information and to be consulted about the proposed dismissals on their behalf;

(ii) employee representatives elected by the affected employees, for the purposes of this section, in an election satisfying the requirements of section 188A(1).]

(2) The consultation shall include consultation about ways of—

(a) avoiding the dismissals,

(b) reducing the numbers of employees to be dismissed, and

(c) mitigating the consequences of the dismissals,

and shall be undertaken by the employer with a view to reaching agreement with the appropriate representatives.]

(3) In determining how many employees an employer is proposing to dismiss as redundant no account shall be taken of employees in respect of whose proposed dismissals consultation has already begun.

(4) For the purposes of the consultation the employer shall disclose in writing to the [appropriate] representatives—

(a) the reasons for his proposals,

(b) the numbers and descriptions of employees whom it is proposed to dismiss as redundant,

(c) the total number of employees of any such description employed by the employer at the establishment in question,

(d) the proposed method of selecting the employees who may be dismissed, …

(e) the proposed method of carrying out the dismissals, with due regard to any agreed procedure, including the period over which the dismissals are to take effect [and

(f) the proposed method of calculating the amount of any redundancy payments to be made (otherwise than in compliance with an obligation imposed by or by virtue of any enactment) to employees who may be dismissed].

(5) That information shall be [given to each of the appropriate representatives by being delivered to them], or sent by post to an address notified by them to the employer, or [in the case of representatives of a trade union)] sent by post to the union at the address of its head or main office.

[(5A) The employer shall allow the appropriate representatives access to [the affected employees] and shall afford to those representatives such accommodation and other facilities as may be appropriate.]

(6) …

(7) If in any case there are special circumstances which render it not reasonably practicable for the employer to comply with a requirement of subsection [(1A), (2) or (4)], the employer shall take all such steps towards compliance with that requirement as are reasonably practicable in those circumstances.

[Where the decision leading to the proposed dismissals is that of a person controlling the employer (directly or indirectly), a failure on the part of that person to provide information to the employer shall not constitute special circumstances rendering it not reasonably practicable for the employer to comply with such a requirement.]

[(7A) Where—

[(a) the employer has invited any of the affected employees to elect employee representatives, and]

(b) the invitation was issued long enough before the time when the consultation is required by subsection (1A)(a) or (b) to begin to allow them to elect representatives by that time,

the employer shall be treated as complying with the requirements of this section in relation to those employees if he complies with those requirements as soon as is reasonably practicable after the election of the representatives.]

[(7B) If, after the employer has invited affected employees to elect representatives, the affected employees fail to do so within a reasonable time, he shall give to each affected employee the information set out in subsection (4).]

(8) This section does not confer any rights on a trade union[, a representative] or an employee except as provided by sections 189 to 192 below.

[672]

NOTES

In the section-heading and the heading preceding this section, words omitted repealed by the Collective Redundancies and Transfer of Undertakings (Protection of Employment) (Amendment) Regulations 1995, SI 1995/2587, reg 3(1), (10).

Sub-s (1): substituted, together with sub-ss (1A), (1B), (2), for original sub-ss (1), (2), by SI 1995/2587, reg 3(1), (2); words in square brackets substituted by the Collective Redundancies and Transfer of Undertakings (Protection of Employment) (Amendment) Regulations 1999, SI 1999/1925, regs 2(1), (2), 3(1), (2).

Sub-ss (1A), (2): substituted as noted above.

Sub-s (1B): substituted as noted above; further substituted by SI 1999/1925, regs 2(1), (2), 3(1), (3).

Sub-s (4): words in first pair of square brackets substituted by SI 1995/2587, reg 3(1), (3); word omitted from para (d) repealed, and para (f) and the word immediately preceding it added, by the Trade Union Reform and Employment Rights Act 1993, ss 34(1), (2)(a), 51, Sch 10.

Sub-s (5): words in square brackets substituted or inserted by SI 1995/2587, reg 3(1), (4).

Sub-s (5A): inserted by SI 1995/2587, reg 3(1), (5); words in square brackets substituted by SI 1999/1925, regs 2(1), (2), 3(1), (4).

Sub-s (6): repealed by SI 1995/2587, reg 3(1), (6).

Sub-s (7): words in first pair of square brackets substituted by SI 1995/2587, reg 3(1), (7); words in second pair of square brackets added by the Trade Union Reform and Employment Rights Act 1993, s 34(1), (2)(c).

Sub-s (7A): inserted by SI 1995/2587, reg 3(1), (8); para (a) substituted by SI 1999/1925, regs 2(1), (2), 3(1), (5).

Sub-s (7B): inserted by SI 1999/1925, regs 2(1), (2), 3(1), (6).

Sub-s (8): words in square brackets inserted by SI 1995/2587, reg 3(1), (9).

Conciliation: employment tribunal proceedings and claims which could be the subject of employment tribunal proceedings arising out of a contravention, or alleged contravention, of this section are proceedings to which the Employment Tribunals Act 1996, s 18 applies; see s 18(1)(b) of that Act at **[975]**. The standard conciliation period applies to such claims by virtue of the Employment Tribunals (Constitution and Rules of Procedure) Regulations 2004, SI 2004/1861, Sch 1, rule 22(1), (6).

[188A—(1) The requirements for the election of employee representatives under section 188(1B)(b)(ii) are that—

(a) the employer shall make such arrangements as are reasonably practical to ensure that the election is fair;

(b) the employer shall determine the number of representatives to be elected so that there are sufficient representatives to represent the interests of all the affected employees having regard to the number and classes of those employees;

(c) the employer shall determine whether the affected employees should be represented either by representatives of all the affected employees or by representatives of particular classes of those employees;

(d) before the election the employer shall determine the term of office as employee representatives so that it is of sufficient length to enable information to be given and consultations under section 188 to be completed;

(e) the candidates for election as employee representatives are affected employees on the date of the election;

(f) no affected employee is unreasonably excluded from standing for election;

(g) all affected employees on the date of the election are entitled to vote for employee representatives;

(h) the employees entitled to vote may vote for as many candidates as there are representatives to be elected to represent them or, if there are to be representatives for particular classes of employees, may vote for as many candidates as there are representatives to be elected to represent their particular class of employee;

(i) the election is conducted so as to secure that—

(i) so far as is reasonably practicable, those voting do so in secret, and

(ii) the votes given at the election are accurately counted.

(2) Where, after an election of employee representatives satisfying the requirements of subsection (1) has been held, one of those elected ceases to act as an employee representative

and any of those employees are no longer represented, they shall elect another representative by an election satisfying the requirements of subsection (1)(a), (e), (f) and (i).]

[673]

NOTES

Inserted by the Collective Redundancies and Transfer of Undertakings (Protection of Employment) (Amendment) Regulations 1999, SI 1999/1925, regs 2(1), (2), 4.

189 Complaint … and protective award

[(1) Where an employer has failed to comply with a requirement of section 188 or section 188A, a complaint may be presented to an employment tribunal on that ground—

(a) in the case of a failure relating to the election of employee representatives, by any of the affected employees or by any of the employees who have been dismissed as redundant;

(b) in the case of any other failure relating to employee representatives, by any of the employee representatives to whom the failure related,

(c) in the case of failure relating to representatives of a trade union, by the trade union, and

(d) in any other case, by any of the affected employees or by any of the employees who have been dismissed as redundant.]

[(1A) If on a complaint under subsection (1) a question arises as to whether or not any employee representative was an appropriate representative for the purposes of section 188, it shall be for the employer to show that the employee representative had the authority to represent the affected employees.

(1B) On a complaint under subsection (1)(a) it shall be for the employer to show that the requirements in section 188A have been satisfied.]

(2) If the tribunal finds the complaint well-founded it shall make a declaration to that effect and may also make a protective award.

(3) A protective award is an award in respect of one or more descriptions of employees—

(a) who have been dismissed as redundant, or whom it is proposed to dismiss as redundant, and

(b) in respect of whose dismissal or proposed dismissal the employer has failed to comply with a requirement of section 188,

ordering the employer to pay remuneration for the protected period.

(4) The protected period—

(a) begins with the date on which the first of the dismissals to which the complaint relates takes effect, or the date of the award, whichever is the earlier, and

(b) is of such length as the tribunal determines to be just and equitable in all the circumstances having regard to the seriousness of the employer's default in complying with any requirement of section 188;

but shall not exceed 90 days …

(5) An [employment tribunal] shall not consider a complaint under this section unless it is presented to the tribunal—

(a) before the [date on which the last of the dismissals to which the complaint relates] takes effect, or

(b) [during] the period of three months beginning with [that date], or

(c) where the tribunal is satisfied that it was not reasonably practicable for the complaint to be presented [during the] period of three months, within such further period as it considers reasonable.

(6) If on a complaint under this section a question arises—

(a) whether there were special circumstances which rendered it not reasonably practicable for the employer to comply with any requirement of section 188, or

(b) whether he took all such steps towards compliance with that requirement as were reasonably practicable in those circumstances,

it is for the employer to show that there were and that he did.

[674]

NOTES

Section heading: words omitted repealed by the Collective Redundancies and Transfer of Undertakings (Protection of Employment) (Amendment) Regulations 1995, SI 1995/2587, reg 4(1), (5).

Sub-s (1): substituted by the Collective Redundancies and Transfer of Undertakings (Protection of Employment) (Amendment) Regulations 1999, SI 1999/1925, regs 2(1), (2), 5(1), (2).

Sub-ss (1A), (1B): inserted by SI 1999/1925, regs 2(1), (2), 5(1), (3).

Sub-s (4): words omitted repealed by SI 1999/1925, regs 2(1), (2), 5(1), (4).

Sub-s (5): words in first pair of square brackets substituted by the Employment Rights (Dispute Resolution) Act 1998, s 1(2)(a); other words in square brackets substituted by SI 1995/2587, reg 4(1), (4).

Conciliation: see the note to s 188 at **[672]**.

190 Entitlement under protective award

(1) Where an [employment tribunal] has made a protective award, every employee of a description to which the award relates is entitled, subject to the following provisions and to section 191, to be paid remuneration by his employer for the protected period.

(2) The rate of remuneration payable is a week's pay for each week of the period; and remuneration in respect of a period less than one week shall be calculated by reducing proportionately the amount of a week's pay.

(3) …

(4) An employee is not entitled to remuneration under a protective award in respect of a period during which he is employed by the employer unless he would be entitled to be paid by the employer in respect of that period—

(a) by virtue of his contract of employment, or

(b) by virtue of [sections 87 to 91 of the Employment Rights Act 1996] (rights of employee in period of notice),

if that period fell within the period of notice required to be given by [section 86(1)] of that Act.

(5) [Chapter II of Part XIV of the Employment Rights Act 1996] applies with respect to the calculation of a week's pay for the purposes of this section.

The calculation date for the purposes of [that Chapter] is the date on which the protective award was made or, in the case of an employee who was dismissed before the date on which the protective award was made, the date which by virtue of [section 226(5)] is the calculation date for the purpose of computing the amount of a redundancy payment in relation to that dismissal (whether or not the employee concerned is entitled to any such payment).

(6) If an employee of a description to which a protective award relates dies during the protected period, the award has effect in his case as if the protected period ended on his death.
[675]

NOTES

Sub-s (1): words in square brackets substituted by the Employment Rights (Dispute Resolution) Act 1998, s 1(2)(a).

Sub-s (3): repealed by the Trade Union Reform and Employment Rights Act 1993, ss 34(1), (3), 51, Sch 10.

Sub-ss (4), (5): words in square brackets substituted by the Employment Rights Act 1996, s 240, Sch 1, para 56(1), (14).

Conciliation: employment tribunal proceedings and claims which could be the subject of employment tribunal proceedings arising out of a contravention, or alleged contravention, of this section are proceedings to which the Employment Tribunals Act 1996, s 18 applies; see s 18(1)(b) of that Act at **[975]**. The short conciliation period applies to such claims by virtue of the Employment Tribunals (Constitution and Rules of Procedure) Regulations 2004, SI 2004/1861, Sch 1, rule 22(5).

191 Termination of employment during protected period

(1) Where the employee is employed by the employer during the protected period and—

(a) he is fairly dismissed by his employer [otherwise than as redundant], or

(b) he unreasonably terminates the contract of employment,

then, subject to the following provisions, he is not entitled to remuneration under the protective award in respect of any period during which but for that dismissal or termination he would have been employed.

(2) If an employer makes an employee an offer (whether in writing or not and whether before or after the ending of his employment under the previous contract) to renew his

contract of employment, or to re-engage him under a new contract, so that the renewal or re-engagement would take effect before or during the protected period, and either—

(a) the provisions of the contract as renewed, or of the new contract, as to the capacity and place in which he would be employed, and as to the other terms and conditions of his employment, would not differ from the corresponding provisions of the previous contract, or

(b) the offer constitutes an offer of suitable employment in relation to the employee,

the following subsections have effect.

(3) If the employee unreasonably refuses the offer, he is not entitled to remuneration under the protective award in respect of a period during which but for that refusal he would have been employed.

(4) If the employee's contract of employment is renewed, or he is re-engaged under a new contract of employment, in pursuance of such an offer as is referred to in subsection (2)(b), there shall be a trial period in relation to the contract as renewed, or the new contract (whether or not there has been a previous trial period under this section).

(5) The trial period begins with the ending of his employment under the previous contract and ends with the expiration of the period of four weeks beginning with the date on which he starts work under the contract as renewed, or the new contract, or such longer period as may be agreed in accordance with subsection (6) for the purpose of retraining the employee for employment under that contract.

(6) Any such agreement—

(a) shall be made between the employer and the employee or his representative before the employee starts work under the contract as renewed or, as the case may be, the new contract,

(b) shall be in writing,

(c) shall specify the date of the end of the trial period, and

(d) shall specify the terms and conditions of employment which will apply in the employee's case after the end of that period.

(7) If during the trial period—

(a) the employee, for whatever reason, terminates the contract, or gives notice to terminate it and the contract is thereafter, in consequence, terminated, or

(b) the employer, for a reason connected with or arising out of the change to the renewed, or new, employment, terminates the contract, or gives notice to terminate it and the contract is thereafter, in consequence, terminated,

the employee remains entitled under the protective award unless, in a case falling within paragraph (a), he acted unreasonably in terminating or giving notice to terminate the contract.

[676]

NOTES

Sub-s (1): words in square brackets substituted by the Trade Union Reform and Employment Rights Act 1993, s 49(2), Sch 8, para 70.

192 Complaint by employee to [employment tribunal]

(1) An employee may present a complaint to an [employment tribunal] on the ground that he is an employee of a description to which a protective award relates and that his employer has failed, wholly or in part, to pay him remuneration under the award.

(2) An [employment tribunal] shall not entertain a complaint under this section unless it is presented to the tribunal—

(a) before the end of the period of three months beginning with the day (or, if the complaint relates to more than one day, the last of the days) in respect of which the complaint is made of failure to pay remuneration, or

(b) where the tribunal is satisfied that it was not reasonably practicable for the complaint to be presented within the period of three months, within such further period as it may consider reasonable.

(3) Where the tribunal finds a complaint under this section well founded it shall order the employer to pay the complainant the amount of remuneration which it finds is due to him.

(4) The remedy of an employee for infringement of his right to remuneration under a protective award is by way of complaint under this section, and not otherwise.

[677]

NOTES

Section heading, sub-ss (1), (2): words in square brackets substituted by the Employment Rights (Dispute Resolution) Act 1998, s 1(2)(a).

Conciliation: see the note to s 190 at **[675]**.

Duty of employer to notify Secretary of State

193 Duty of employer to notify Secretary of State of certain redundancies

(1) An employer proposing to dismiss as redundant 100 or more employees at one establishment within a period of 90 days or less shall notify the Secretary of State, in writing, of his proposal[—

(a) before giving notice to terminate an employee's contract of employment in respect of any of those dismissals, and

(b)] at least 90 days before the first of those dismissals takes effect.

(2) An employer proposing to dismiss as redundant [20] or more employees at one establishment within [such a period] shall notify the Secretary of State, in writing, of his proposal[—

(a) before giving notice to terminate an employee's contract of employment in respect of any of those dismissals, and

(b)] at least 30 days before the first of those dismissals takes effect.

(3) In determining how many employees an employer is proposing to dismiss as redundant within the period mentioned in subsection (1) or (2), no account shall be taken of employees in respect of whose proposed dismissal notice has already been given to the Secretary of State.

(4) A notice under this section shall—

(a) be given to the Secretary of State by delivery to him or by sending it by post to him, at such address as the Secretary of State may direct in relation to the establishment where the employees proposed to be dismissed are employed,

[(b) where there are representatives to be consulted under section 188, identify them and state the date when consultation with them under that section began,] and

(c) be in such form and contain such particulars, in addition to those required by paragraph (b), as the Secretary of State may direct.

(5) After receiving a notice under this section from an employer the Secretary of State may by written notice require the employer to give him such further information as may be specified in the notice.

(6) [Where there are representatives to be consulted under section 188 the employer shall give to each of them a copy of any notice given under section (1) or (2).]

The copy shall be delivered to them or sent by post to an address notified by them to the employer, or [(in the case of representatives of a trade union)] sent by post to the union at the address of its head or main office.

(7) If in any case there are special circumstances rendering it not reasonably practicable for the employer to comply with any of the requirements of subsections (1) to (6), he shall take all such steps towards compliance with that requirement as are reasonably practicable in the circumstances.

[Where the decision leading to the proposed dismissals is that of a person controlling the employer (directly or indirectly), a failure on the part of that person to provide information to the employer shall not constitute special circumstances rendering it not reasonably practicable for the employer to comply with any of those requirements.]

[678]

NOTES

Sub-s (1): words in square brackets inserted by the Collective Redundancies (Amendment) Regulations 2006, SI 2006/2387, reg 3, as from 1 October 2006.

Sub-s (2): number and words in first and second pairs of square brackets substituted by the Collective Redundancies and Transfer of Undertakings (Protection of Employment) (Amendment) Regulations 1995, SI 1995/2587, reg 5(1), (2); final words in square brackets inserted by SI 2006/2387, reg 3, as from 1 October 2006.

Sub-s (4): para (b) substituted by SI 1995/2587, regs 2(2), 5(1), (3).

Sub-s (6): words in first pair of square brackets substituted, and words in second pair of square brackets added, by SI 1995/2587, reg 5(1), (4).

Sub-s (7): words in square brackets added by the Trade Union Reform and Employment Rights Act 1993, s 34(1), (4).

194 Offence of failure to notify

(1) An employer who fails to give notice to the Secretary of State in accordance with section 193 commits an offence and is liable on summary conviction to a fine not exceeding level 5 on the standard scale.

(2) Proceedings in England or Wales for such an offence shall be instituted only by or with the consent of the Secretary of State or by an officer authorised for that purpose by special or general directions of the Secretary of State.

An officer so authorised may, *although not of counsel or a solicitor,* prosecute or conduct proceedings for such an offence before a magistrates' court.

(3) Where an offence under this section committed by a body corporate is proved to have been committed with the consent or connivance of, or to be attributable to neglect on the part of, any director, manager, secretary or other similar officer of the body corporate, or any person purporting to act in any such capacity, he as well as the body corporate is guilty of the offence and liable to be proceeded against and punished accordingly.

(4) Where the affairs of a body corporate are managed by its members, subsection (3) applies in relation to the acts and defaults of a member in connection with his functions of management as if he were a director of the body corporate.

[679]

NOTES

Sub-s (2): words in italics repealed by the Legal Services Act 2007, ss 208(1), 210, Sch 21, paras 104, 105, Sch 23, as from a day to be appointed.

Supplementary provisions

[195 Construction of references to dismissal as redundant etc

(1) In this Chapter references to dismissal as redundant are references to dismissal for a reason not related to the individual concerned or for a number of reasons all of which are not so related.

(2) For the purposes of any proceedings under this Chapter, where an employee is or is proposed to be dismissed it shall be presumed, unless the contrary is proved, that he is or is proposed to be dismissed as redundant.]

[680]

NOTES

Substituted by the Trade Union Reform and Employment Rights Act 1993, s 34(1), (5).

[196 Construction of references to representatives

(1) For the purposes of this Chapter persons are employee representatives if—

(a) they have been elected by employees for the specific purpose of being consulted by their employer about dismissals proposed by him, or

(b) having been elected [or appointed] by employees (whether before or after dismissals have been proposed by their employer) otherwise than for that specific purpose, it is appropriate (having regard to the purposes for which they were elected) for the employer to consult them about dismissals proposed by him,

and (in either case) they are employed by the employer at the time when they are elected [or appointed].

(2) References in this Chapter to representatives of a trade union, in relation to an employer, are to officials or other persons authorised by the trade union to carry on collective bargaining with the employer.]

[(3) References in this Chapter to affected employees are to employees who may be affected by the proposed dismissals or who may be affected by measures taken in connection with such dismissals.]

[681]

NOTES

Substituted by the Collective Redundancies and Transfer of Undertakings (Protection of Employment) (Amendment) Regulations 1995, SI 1995/2587, reg 6.

Sub-s (1): words in square brackets inserted by the Collective Redundancies and Transfer of Undertakings (Protection of Employment) (Amendment) Regulations 1999, SI 1999/1925, regs 2(1), (2), 6(1)–(3).

Sub-s (3): added by SI 1999/1925, regs 2(1), (2), 6(1), (4).

197 Power to vary provisions

(1) The Secretary of State may by order made by statutory instrument vary—

(a) the provisions of sections 188(2) and 193(1) (requirements as to consultation and notification), and

(b) the periods referred to at the end of section 189(4) (maximum protected period);

but no such order shall be made which has the effect of reducing to less than 30 days the periods referred to in sections 188(2) and 193(1) as the periods which must elapse before the first of the dismissals takes effect.

(2) No such order shall be made unless a draft of the order has been laid before Parliament and approved by a resolution of each House of Parliament.

[682]

NOTES

Orders: as of 6 April 2008 no Orders had been made under this section.

198 Power to adapt provisions in case of collective agreement

(1) This section applies where there is in force a collective agreement which establishes—

(a) arrangements for providing alternative employment for employees to whom the agreement relates if they are dismissed as redundant by an employer to whom it relates, or

(b) arrangements for [handling the dismissal of employees as redundant].

(2) On the application of all the parties to the agreement the Secretary of State may, if he is satisfied having regard to the provisions of the agreement that the arrangements are on the whole at least as favourable to those employees as the foregoing provisions of this Chapter, by order made by statutory instrument adapt, modify or exclude any of those provisions both in their application to all or any of those employees and in their application to any other employees of any such employer.

(3) The Secretary of State shall not make such an order unless the agreement—

(a) provides for procedures to be followed (whether by arbitration or otherwise) in cases where an employee to whom the agreement relates claims that any employer or other person to whom it relates has not complied with the provisions of the agreement, and

(b) provides that those procedures include a right to arbitration or adjudication by an independent referee or body in cases where (by reason of an equality of votes or otherwise) a decision cannot otherwise be reached,

or indicates that any such employee may present a complaint to an [employment tribunal] that any such employer or other person has not complied with those provisions.

(4) An order under this section may confer on an [employment tribunal] to whom a complaint is presented as mentioned in subsection (3) such powers and duties as the Secretary of State considers appropriate.

(5) An order under this section may be varied or revoked by a subsequent order thereunder either in pursuance of an application made by all or any of the parties to the agreement in question or without any such application.

[683]

NOTES

Sub-s (1): words in square brackets in para (b) substituted by the Trade Union Reform and Employment Rights Act 1993, s 49(2), Sch 8, para 71.

Sub-ss (3), (4): words in square brackets substituted by the Employment Rights (Dispute Resolution) Act 1998, s 1(2)(a).

Orders: as of 6 April 2008, no Orders had been made under this section.

CHAPTER III
CODES OF PRACTICE

Codes of Practice issued by ACAS

199 Issue of Codes of Practice by ACAS

(1) ACAS may issue Codes of Practice containing such practical guidance as it thinks fit for the purpose of promoting the improvement of industrial relations [or for purposes connected with trade union learning representatives].

(2) In particular, ACAS shall in one or more Codes of Practice provide practical guidance on the following matters—

(a) the time off to be permitted by an employer to a trade union official in accordance with section 168 (time off for carrying out trade union duties);

(b) the time off to be permitted by an employer to a trade union member in accordance with section 170 (time off for trade union activities); and

(c) the information to be disclosed by employers to trade union representatives in accordance with sections 181 and 182 (disclosure of information for purposes of collective bargaining).

(3) The guidance mentioned in subsection (2)(a) shall include guidance on the circumstances in which a trade union official is to be permitted to take time off under section 168 in respect of duties connected with industrial action; and the guidance mentioned in subsection (2)(b) shall include guidance on the question whether, and the circumstances in which, a trade union member is to be permitted to take time off under section 170 for trade union activities connected with industrial action.

(4) ACAS may from time to time revise the whole or any part of a Code of Practice issued by it and issue that revised Code.

[684]

NOTES

Sub-s (1): words in square brackets added by the Employment Act 2002, s 43(1), (7), as from 27 April 2003.

Codes made under this section: the current codes are: ACAS Code of Practice 1–Disciplinary and Grievance Procedures (2004) at **[4653]**; ACAS Code of Practice 2–Disclosure of information to trade unions for collective bargaining purposes (1998) at **[4529]**; ACAS Code of Practice 3–Time off for trade union duties and activities (2003) at **[4640]**.

200 Procedure for issue of Code by ACAS

(1) Where ACAS proposes to issue a Code of Practice, or a revised Code, it shall prepare and publish a draft of the Code, shall consider any representations made to it about the draft and may modify the draft accordingly.

(2) If ACAS determines to proceed with the draft, it shall transmit the draft to the Secretary of State who—

(a) if he approves of it, shall lay it before both Houses of Parliament, and

(b) if he does not approve of it, shall publish details of his reasons for withholding approval.

[(3) A Code containing practical guidance—

(a) on the time off to be permitted to a trade union learning representative in accordance with section 168A (time off for training and carrying out functions as a learning representative),

(b) on the training that is sufficient to enable a trade union learning representative to carry on the activities mentioned in section 168A(2) (activities for which time off is to be permitted), or

(c) on any of the matters referred to in section 199(2),

shall not be issued unless the draft has been approved by a resolution of each House of Parliament; and if it is so approved, ACAS shall issue the Code in the form of the draft.]

(4) In any other case the following procedure applies—

(a) if, within the period of 40 days beginning with the day on which the draft is laid before Parliament, (or, if copies are laid before the two Houses on different days, with the later of the two days) either House so resolves, no further proceedings shall be taken thereon, but without prejudice to the laying before Parliament of a new draft;

(b) if no such resolution is passed, ACAS shall issue the Code in the form of the draft.

In reckoning the period of 40 days no account shall be taken of any period during which Parliament is dissolved or prorogued or during which both Houses are adjourned for more than four days.

(5) A Code issued in accordance with this section shall come into effect on such day as the Secretary of State may appoint by order made by statutory instrument.

The order may contain such transitional provisions or savings as appear to him to be necessary or expedient.

[685]

NOTES

Sub-s (3): substituted by the Employment Act 2002, s 43(1), (8), as from 27 April 2003.

The current codes are as noted to s 199 at **[684]**.

Orders: the Employment Code of Practice (Disciplinary and Grievance Procedures) Order 2000, SI 2000/2247 (effectively superseded by SI 2004/2356 below); the Employment Protection Code of Practice (Time Off) Order 2003, SI 2003/1191; the Employment Code of Practice (Disciplinary and Grievance Procedures) Order 2004, SI 2004/2356.

201 Consequential revision of Code issued by ACAS

(1) A Code of Practice issued by ACAS may be revised by it in accordance with this section for the purpose of bringing it into conformity with subsequent statutory provisions by the making of consequential amendments and the omission of obsolete passages.

"Subsequent statutory provisions" means provisions made by or under an Act of Parliament and coming into force after the Code was issued (whether before or after the commencement of this Act).

(2) Where ACAS proposes to revise a Code under this section, it shall transmit a draft of the revised Code to the Secretary of State who—

(a) if he approves of it, shall lay the draft before each House of Parliament, and

(b) if he does not approve of it, shall publish details of his reasons for withholding approval.

(3) If within the period of 40 days beginning with the day on which the draft is laid before Parliament, (or, if copies are laid before the two Houses on different days, with the later of the two days) either House so resolves, no further proceedings shall be taken thereon, but without prejudice to the laying before Parliament of a new draft.

In reckoning the period of 40 days no account shall be taken of any period during which Parliament is dissolved or prorogued or during which both Houses are adjourned for more than four days.

(4) If no such resolution is passed ACAS shall issue the Code in the form of the draft and it shall come into effect on such day as the Secretary of State may appoint by order made by statutory instrument.

The order may contain such transitional provisions or savings as appear to the Secretary of State to be necessary or expedient.

[686]

NOTES

Orders: the Employment Protection Code of Practice (Disclosure of Information) Order 1998, SI 1998/45.

202 Revocation of Code issued by ACAS

(1) A Code of Practice issued by ACAS may, at the request of ACAS, be revoked by the Secretary of State by order made by statutory instrument.

The order may contain such transitional provisions and savings as appear to him to be appropriate.

(2) If ACAS requests the Secretary of State to revoke a Code and he decides not to do so, he shall publish details of his reasons for his decision.

(3) An order shall not be made under this section unless a draft of it has been laid before and approved by resolution of each House of Parliament.

[687]

NOTES

Orders: as of 6 April 2008 no Orders had been made under this section, but by virtue of s 300(3) of, and Sch 3, para 1(2) to, this Act, and the Interpretation Act 1978, s 17(2)(b), the Employment Codes of Practice (Revocation) Order 1991, SI 1991/1264 has effect as if made under this section.

Codes of Practice issued by the Secretary of State

203 Issue of Codes of Practice by the Secretary of State

(1) The Secretary of State may issue Codes of Practice containing such practical guidance as he thinks fit for the purpose—

(a) of promoting the improvement of industrial relations, or

(b) of promoting what appear to him to be to be desirable practices in relation to the conduct by trade unions of ballots and elections [or for purposes connected with trade union learning representatives].

(2) The Secretary of State may from time to time revise the whole or any part of a Code of Practice issued by him and issue that revised Code.

[688]

NOTES

Sub-s (1): words in square brackets in para (b) added by the Employment Act 2002, s 43(1), (7), as from 27 April 2003.

Codes issued under this section: Picketing (1992) at **[4511]**; Access and unfair practices during recognition and derecognition ballots (2005) at **[4690]**; Industrial Action Ballots and Notice to Employers (2005) at **[4697]**.

204 Procedure for issue of Code by Secretary of State

(1) When the Secretary of State proposes to issue a Code of Practice, or a revised Code, he shall after consultation with ACAS prepare and publish a draft of the Code, shall consider any representations made to him about the draft and may modify the draft accordingly.

(2) If he determines to proceed with the draft, he shall lay it before both Houses of Parliament and, if it is approved by resolution of each House, shall issue the Code in the form of the draft.

(3) A Code issued under this section shall come into effect on such day as the Secretary of State may by order appoint.

The order may contain such transitional provisions or savings as appear to him to be necessary or expedient.

(4) An order under subsection (3) shall be made by statutory instrument, which shall be subject to annulment in pursuance of a resolution of either House of Parliament.

[689]

NOTES

Orders: the Employment Code of Practice (Access to Workers during Recognition and Derecognition Ballots) Order 2000, SI 2000/1443 (effectively superseded by SI 2005/2421 below); the Employment Code of Practice (Industrial Action Ballots and Notice to Employers) Order 2000, SI 2000/2241 (effectively superseded by SI 2005/2420 below); the Employment Code of Practice (Industrial Action Ballots and Notice to Employers) Order 2005, SI 2005/2420; the Employment Code of Practice (Access and Unfair Practices during Recognition and Derecognition Ballots) Order 2005, SI 2005/2421. Also, by virtue of s 300(3) of, and Sch 3, para 1(2) to, this Act, and the Interpretation Act 1978, s 17(2)(b), the Employment Code of Practice (Picketing) Order 1992, SI 1992/476, has effect as if made under this section.

205 Consequential revision of Code issued by Secretary of State

(1) A Code of Practice issued by the Secretary of State may be revised by him in accordance with this section for the purpose of bringing it into conformity with subsequent statutory provisions by the making of consequential amendments and the omission of obsolete passages.

"Subsequent statutory provisions" means provisions made by or under an Act of Parliament and coming into force after the Code was issued (whether before or after the commencement of this Act).

(2) Where the Secretary of State proposes to revise a Code under this section, he shall lay a draft of the revised Code before each House of Parliament.

(3) If within the period of 40 days beginning with the day on which the draft is laid before Parliament, or, if copies are laid before the two Houses on different days, with the later of the two days, either House so resolves, no further proceedings shall be taken thereon, but without prejudice to the laying before Parliament of a new draft.

In reckoning the period of 40 days no account shall be taken of any period during which Parliament is dissolved or prorogued or during which both Houses are adjourned for more than four days.

(4) If no such resolution is passed the Secretary of State shall issue the Code in the form of the draft and it shall come into effect on such day as he may appoint by order made by statutory instrument.

The order may contain such transitional provisions and savings as appear to him to be appropriate.

[690]

206 Revocation of Code issued by Secretary of State

(1) A Code of Practice issued by the Secretary of State may be revoked by him by order made by statutory instrument.

The order may contain such transitional provisions and savings as appear to him to be appropriate.

(2) An order shall not be made under this section unless a draft of it has been laid before and approved by resolution of each House of Parliament.

[691]

Supplementary provisions

207 Effect of failure to comply with Code

(1) A failure on the part of any person to observe any provision of a Code of Practice issued under this Chapter shall not of itself render him liable to any proceedings.

(2) In any proceedings before an [employment tribunal] or the Central Arbitration Committee any Code of Practice issued under this Chapter by ACAS shall be admissible in evidence, and any provision of the Code which appears to the tribunal or Committee to be relevant to any question arising in the proceedings shall be taken into account in determining that question.

(3) In any proceedings before a court or [employment tribunal] or the Central Arbitration Committee any Code of Practice issued under this Chapter by the Secretary of State shall be admissible in evidence, and any provision of the Code which appears to the court, tribunal or Committee to be relevant to any question arising in the proceedings shall be taken into account in determining that question.

[692]

NOTES

Sub-ss (2), (3): words in square brackets substituted by the Employment Rights (Dispute Resolution) Act 1998, s 1(2)(a).

208 Provisions of earlier Code superseded by later

(1) If ACAS is of the opinion that the provisions of a Code of Practice to be issued by it under this Chapter will supersede the whole or part of a Code previously issued under this Chapter, by it or by the Secretary of State, it shall in the new Code state that on the day on which the new Code comes into effect the old Code or a specified part of it shall cease to have effect.

(2) If the Secretary of State is of the opinion that the provisions of a Code of Practice to be issued by him under this Chapter will supersede the whole or part of a Code previously issued under this Chapter by him or by ACAS, he shall in the new Code state that on the day on which the new Code comes into effect the old Code or a specified part of it shall cease to have effect.

(3) The above provisions do not affect any transitional provisions or savings made by the order bringing the new Code into effect.

[693]

CHAPTER IV
GENERAL

Functions of ACAS

209 General duty to promote improvement of industrial relations

It is the general duty of ACAS to promote the improvement of industrial relations …

[694]

NOTES

Words omitted repealed by the Employment Relations Act 1999, ss 26, 44, Sch 9(5).

210 Conciliation

(1) Where a trade dispute exists or is apprehended ACAS may, at the request of one or more parties to the dispute or otherwise, offer the parties to the dispute its assistance with a view to bringing about a settlement.

(2) The assistance may be by way of conciliation or by other means, and may include the appointment of a person other than an officer or servant of ACAS to offer assistance to the parties to the dispute with a view to bringing about a settlement.

(3) In exercising its functions under this section ACAS shall have regard to the desirability of encouraging the parties to a dispute to use any appropriate agreed procedures for negotiation or the settlement of disputes.

[695]

[210A Information required by ACAS for purpose of settling recognition disputes

(1) This section applies where ACAS is exercising its functions under section 210 with a view to bringing about a settlement of a recognition dispute.

(2) The parties to the recognition dispute may jointly request ACAS or a person nominated by ACAS to do either or both of the following—

(a) hold a ballot of the workers involved in the dispute;

(b) ascertain the union membership of the workers involved in the dispute.

(3) In the following provisions of this section references to ACAS include references to a person nominated by ACAS; and anything done by such a person under this section shall be regarded as done in the exercise of the functions of ACAS mentioned in subsection (1).

(4) At any time after ACAS has received a request under subsection (2), it may require any party to the recognition dispute—

(a) to supply ACAS with specified information concerning the workers involved in the dispute, and

(b) to do so within such period as it may specify.

(5) ACAS may impose a requirement under subsection (4) only if it considers that it is necessary to do so—

(a) for the exercise of the functions mentioned in subsection (1); and
(b) in order to enable or assist it to comply with the request.

(6) The recipient of a requirement under this section must, within the specified period, supply ACAS with such of the specified information as is in the recipient's possession.

(7) A request under subsection (2) may be withdrawn by any party to the recognition dispute at any time and, if it is withdrawn, ACAS shall take no further steps to hold the ballot or to ascertain the union membership of the workers involved in the dispute.

(8) If a party to a recognition dispute fails to comply with subsection (6), ACAS shall take no further steps to hold the ballot or to ascertain the union membership of the workers involved in the dispute.

(9) Nothing in this section requires ACAS to comply with a request under subsection (2).

(10) In this section—

"party", in relation to a recognition dispute, means each of the employers, employers' associations and trade unions involved in the dispute;

"a recognition dispute" means a trade dispute between employers and workers which is connected wholly or partly with the recognition by employers or employers' associations of the right of a trade union to represent workers in negotiations, consultations or other procedures relating to any of the matters mentioned in paragraphs (a) to (f) of section 218(1);

"specified" means specified in a requirement under this section; and

"workers" has the meaning given in section 218(5).]

[695A]

NOTES

Commencement: 6 April 2005.
Inserted by the Employment Relations Act 2004, s 21, as from 6 April 2005.

211 Conciliation officers

(1) ACAS shall designate some of its officers to perform the functions of conciliation officers under any enactment (whenever passed) relating to matters which are or could be the subject of proceedings before an [employment tribunal].

(2) References in any such enactment to a conciliation officer are to an officer designated under this section.

[696]

NOTES

Sub-s (1): words in square brackets substituted by the Employment Rights (Dispute Resolution) Act 1998, s 1(2)(a).

212 Arbitration

(1) Where a trade dispute exists or is apprehended ACAS may, at the request of one or more of the parties to the dispute and with the consent of all the parties to the dispute, refer all or any of the matters to which the dispute relates for settlement to the arbitration of—
(a) one or more persons appointed by ACAS for that purpose (not being officers or employees of ACAS), or
(b) the Central Arbitration Committee.

(2) In exercising its functions under this section ACAS shall consider the likelihood of the dispute being settled by conciliation.

(3) Where there exist appropriate agreed procedures for negotiation or the settlement of disputes, ACAS shall not refer a matter for settlement to arbitration under this section unless—
(a) those procedures have been used and have failed to result in a settlement, or
(b) there is, in ACAS's opinion, a special reason which justifies arbitration under this section as an alternative to those procedures.

(4) Where a matter is referred to arbitration under subsection (1)(a)—
(a) if more than one arbitrator or arbiter is appointed, ACAS shall appoint one of them to act as chairman; and

(b) the award may be published if ACAS so decides and all the parties consent.

(5) [Part I of the Arbitration Act 1996] (general provisions as to arbitration) does not apply to an arbitration under this section.

[697]

NOTES

Sub-s (5): words in square brackets substituted by the Arbitration Act 1996, s 107(1), Sch 3, para 56.

[212A Arbitration scheme for unfair dismissal cases etc

(1) ACAS may prepare a scheme providing for arbitration in the case of disputes involving proceedings, or claims which could be the subject of proceedings, before an employment tribunal [under, or] arising out of a contravention or alleged contravention of—

[(za) section 80G(1) or 80H(1)(b) of the Employment Rights Act 1996 (flexible working),]

(a) Part X of [that Act] (unfair dismissal), or

(b) any enactment specified in an order made by the Secretary of State.

(2) When ACAS has prepared such a scheme it shall submit a draft of the scheme to the Secretary of State who, if he approves it, shall make an order—

(a) setting out the scheme, and

(b) making provision for it to come into effect.

(3) ACAS may from time to time prepare a revised version of such a scheme and, when it has done so, shall submit a draft of the revised scheme to the Secretary of State who, if he approves it, shall make an order—

(a) setting out the revised scheme, and

(b) making provision for it to come into effect.

(4) ACAS may take any steps appropriate for promoting awareness of a scheme prepared under this section.

(5) Where the parties to any dispute within subsection (1) agree in writing to submit the dispute to arbitration in accordance with a scheme having effect by virtue of an order under this section, ACAS shall refer the dispute to the arbitration of a person appointed by ACAS for the purpose (not being an officer or employee of ACAS).

(6) Nothing in the Arbitration Act 1996 shall apply to an arbitration conducted in accordance with a scheme having effect by virtue of an order under this section except to the extent that the order provides for any provision of Part I of that Act so to apply; and the order may provide for any such provision so to apply subject to modifications.

(7) A scheme set out in an order under this section may, in relation to an arbitration conducted in accordance with the law of Scotland, make provision—

(a) that a reference on a preliminary point may be made, or

(b) conferring a right of appeal which shall lie,

to the relevant court on such grounds and in respect of such matters as may be specified in the scheme; and in this subsection "relevant court" means such court, being the Court of Session or the Employment Appeal Tribunal, as may be specified in the scheme, and a different court may be specified as regards different grounds or matters.

(8) Where a scheme set out in an order under this section includes provision for the making of re-employment orders in arbitrations conducted in accordance with the scheme, the order setting out the scheme may require employment tribunals to enforce such orders—

(a) in accordance with section 117 of the Employment Rights Act 1996 (enforcement by award of compensation), or

(b) in accordance with that section as modified by the order.

For this purpose "re-employment orders" means orders requiring that persons found to have been unfairly dismissed be reinstated, re-engaged or otherwise re-employed.

(9) An order under this section setting out a scheme may provide that, in the case of disputes within subsection (1)(a), such part of an award made in accordance with the scheme as is specified by the order shall be treated as a basic award of compensation for unfair dismissal for the purposes of section 184(1)(d) of the Employment Rights Act 1996 (which specifies such an award as a debt which the Secretary of State must satisfy if the employer has become insolvent).

(10) An order under this section shall be made by statutory instrument.

(11) No order shall be made under subsection (1)(b) unless a draft of the statutory instrument containing it has been laid before Parliament and approved by a resolution of each House.

(12) A statutory instrument containing an order under this section (other than one of which a draft has been approved by resolution of each House of Parliament) shall be subject to annulment in pursuance of a resolution of either House of Parliament.]

[698]

NOTES

Inserted by the Employment Rights (Dispute Resolution) Act 1998, s 7.

Sub-s (1): words in first pair of square brackets, and whole of para (za) inserted, and words in square brackets in para (a) substituted, by the Employment Act 2002, s 53, Sch 7, paras 18, 22.

Orders: the ACAS Arbitration Scheme (Great Britain) Order 2004, SI 2004/753 at **[3099]**; the ACAS (Flexible Working) Arbitration Scheme (Great Britain) Order 2004, SI 2004/2333 at **[3218]**.

[212B Dismissal procedures agreements

ACAS may, in accordance with any dismissal procedures agreement (within the meaning of the Employment Rights Act 1996), refer any matter to the arbitration of a person appointed by ACAS for the purpose (not being an officer or employee of ACAS).]

[699]

NOTES

Inserted by the Employment Rights (Dispute Resolution) Act 1998, s 15, Sch 1, para 7.

[213 Advice

(1) ACAS may, on request or otherwise, give employers, employers' associations, workers and trade unions such advice as it thinks appropriate on matters concerned with or affecting or likely to affect industrial relations.

(2) ACAS may also publish general advice on matters concerned with or affecting or likely to affect industrial relations.]

[700]

NOTES

Substituted by the Trade Union Reform and Employment Rights Act 1993, s 43(2).

214 Inquiry

(1) ACAS may, if it thinks fit, inquire into any question relating to industrial relations generally or to industrial relations in any particular industry or in any particular undertaking or part of an undertaking.

(2) The findings of an inquiry under this section, together with any advice given by ACAS in connection with those findings, may be published by ACAS if—

(a) it appears to ACAS that publication is desirable for the improvement of industrial relations, either generally or in relation to the specific question inquired into, and

(b) after sending a draft of the findings to all parties appearing to be concerned and taking account of their views, it thinks fit.

[701]

Courts of inquiry

215 Inquiry and report by court of inquiry

(1) Where a trade dispute exists or is apprehended, the Secretary of State may inquire into the causes and circumstances of the dispute, and, if he thinks fit, appoint a court of inquiry and refer to it any matters appearing to him to be connected with or relevant to the dispute.

(2) The court shall inquire into the matters referred to it and report on them to the Secretary of State; and it may make interim reports if it thinks fit.

(3) Any report of the court, and any minority report, shall be laid before both Houses of Parliament as soon as possible.

(4) The Secretary of State may, before or after the report has been laid before Parliament, publish or cause to be published from time to time, in such manner as he thinks fit, any information obtained or conclusions arrived at by the court as the result or in the course of its inquiry.

(5) No report or publication made or authorised by the court or the Secretary of State shall include any information obtained by the court of inquiry in the course of its inquiry—

(a) as to any trade union, or

(b) as to any individual business (whether carried on by a person, firm, or company),

which is not available otherwise than through evidence given at the inquiry, except with the consent of the secretary of the trade union or of the person, firm, or company in question.

Nor shall any individual member of the court or any person concerned in the inquiry disclose such information without such consent.

(6) The Secretary of State shall from time to time present to Parliament a report of his proceedings under this section.

[702]

216 Constitution and proceedings of court of inquiry

(1) A court of inquiry shall consist of—

(a) a chairman and such other persons as the Secretary of State thinks fit to appoint, or

(b) one person appointed by the Secretary of State,

as the Secretary of State thinks fit.

(2) A court may act notwithstanding any vacancy in its number.

(3) A court may conduct its inquiry in public or. in private, at its discretion.

(4) The Secretary of State may make rules regulating the procedure of a court of inquiry, including rules as to summoning of witnesses, quorum, and the appointment of committees and enabling the court to call for such documents as the court may determine to be relevant to the subject matter of the inquiry.

(5) A court of inquiry may, if and to such extent as may be authorised by rules under this section, by order require any person who appears to the court to have knowledge of the subject-matter of the inquiry—

(a) to supply (in writing or otherwise) such particulars in relation thereto as the court may require, and

(b) where necessary, to attend before the court and give evidence on oath;

and the court may administer or authorise any person to administer an oath for that purpose.

(6) Provision shall be made by rules under this section with respect to the cases in which persons may appear by *counsel or solicitor* in proceedings before a court of inquiry, and except as provided by those rules no person shall be entitled to appear in any such proceedings by *counsel or solicitor*.

[(7) In subsection (6) "relevant lawyer" means—

(a) a person who, for the purposes of the Legal Services Act 2007, is an authorised person in relation to an activity which constitutes the exercise of a right of audience or the conduct of litigation within the meaning of that Act, or

(b) an advocate or solicitor in Scotland.]

[703]

NOTES

Sub-s (6): for the words in italics there are substituted the words "a relevant lawyer" by the Legal Services Act 2007, s 208(1), Sch 21, paras 104, 106(a), as from a day to be appointed.

Sub-s (7): added by the Legal Services Act 2007, s 208(1), Sch 21, paras 104, 106(b), as from a day to be appointed.

Rules: as of 6 April 2008 no Rules had been made under this section.

Supplementary provisions

217 Exclusion of power of arbiter to state case to Court of Session

Section 3 of the Administration of Justice (Scotland) Act 1972 (power of arbiter to state case for opinion of Court of Session) does not apply to—
(a) any form of arbitration relating to a trade dispute, or
(b) any other arbitration arising from a collective agreement.

[704]

218 Meaning of "trade dispute" in Part IV

(1) In this Part "trade dispute" means a dispute between employers and workers, or between workers and workers, which is connected with one or more of the following matters—
(a) terms and conditions of employment, or the physical conditions in which any workers are required to work;
(b) engagement or non-engagement, or termination or suspension of employment or the duties of employment, of one or more workers;
(c) allocation of work or the duties of employment as between workers or groups of workers;
(d) matters of discipline;
(e) the membership or non-membership of a trade union on the part of a worker;
(f) facilities for officials of trade unions; and
(g) machinery for negotiation or consultation, and other procedures, relating to any of the foregoing matters, including the recognition by employers or employers' associations of the right of a trade union to represent workers in any such negotiation or consultation or in the carrying out of such procedures.

(2) A dispute between a Minister of the Crown and any workers shall, notwithstanding that he is not the employer of those workers, be treated for the purposes of this Part as a dispute between an employer and those workers if the dispute relates—
(a) to matters which have been referred for consideration by a joint body on which, by virtue of any provision made by or under any enactment, that Minister is represented, or
(b) to matters which cannot be settled without that Minister exercising a power conferred on him by or under an enactment.

(3) There is a trade dispute for the purpose of this Part even though it relates to matters occurring outside Great Britain.

(4) A dispute to which a trade union or employer's association is a party shall be treated for the purposes of this Part as a dispute to which workers or, as the case may be, employers are parties.

(5) In this section—
"employment" includes any relationship whereby one person personally does work or performs services for another; and
"worker", in relation to a dispute to which an employer is a party, includes any worker even if not employed by that employer.

[705]

PART V
INDUSTRIAL ACTION

Protection of acts in contemplation or furtherance of trade dispute

219 Protection from certain tort liabilities

(1) An act done by a person in contemplation or furtherance of a trade dispute is not actionable in tort on the ground only—
(a) that it induces another person to break a contract or interferes or induces another person to interfere with its performance, or
(b) that it consists in his threatening that a contract (whether one to which he is a party or not) will be broken or its performance interfered with, or that he will induce another person to break a contract or interfere with its performance.

(2) An agreement or combination by two or more persons to do or procure the doing of an act in contemplation or furtherance of a trade dispute is not actionable in tort if the act is one which if done without any such agreement or combination would not be actionable in tort.

(3) Nothing in subsections (1) and (2) prevents an act done in the course of picketing from being actionable in tort unless it is done in the course of attendance declared lawful by section 220 (peaceful picketing).

(4) Subsections (1) and (2) have effect subject to sections 222 to 225 (action excluded from protection) and [to sections 226 (requirement of ballot before action by trade union) and 234A (requirement of notice to employer of industrial action); and in those sections "not protected" means excluded from the protection afforded by this section or, where the expression is used with reference to a particular person, excluded from that protection as respects that person.]

[706]

NOTES

Sub-s (4): words in square brackets substituted by the Trade Union Reform and Employment Rights Act 1993, s 49(2), Sch 8, para 72.

220 Peaceful picketing

(1) It is lawful for a person in contemplation or furtherance of a trade dispute to attend—

(a) at or near his own place of work, or

(b) if he is an official of a trade union, at or near the place of work of a member of the union whom he is accompanying and whom he represents,

for the purpose only of peacefully obtaining or communicating information, or peacefully persuading any person to work or abstain from working.

(2) If a person works or normally works—

(a) otherwise than at any one place, or

(b) at a place the location of which is such that attendance there for a purpose mentioned in subsection (1) is impracticable,

his place of work for the purposes of that subsection shall be any premises of his employer from which he works or from which his work is administered.

(3) In the case of a worker not in employment where—

(a) his last employment was terminated in connection with a trade dispute, or

(b) the termination of his employment was one of the circumstances giving rise to a trade dispute,

in relation to that dispute his former place of work shall be treated for the purposes of subsection (1) as being his place of work.

(4) A person who is an official of a trade union by virtue only of having been elected or appointed to be a representative of some of the members of the union shall be regarded for the purposes of subsection (1) as representing only those members; but otherwise an official of a union shall be regarded for those purposes as representing all its members.

[707]

221 Restrictions on grant of injunctions and interdicts

(1) Where—

(a) an application for an injunction or interdict is made to a court in the absence of the party against whom it is sought or any in representative of his, and

(b) he claims, or in the opinion of the court would be likely to claim, that he acted in contemplation or furtherance of a trade dispute,

the court shall not grant the injunction or interdict unless satisfied that all steps which in the circumstances were reasonable have been taken with a view to securing that notice of the application and an opportunity of being heard with respect to the application have been given to him.

(2) Where—

(a) an application for an interlocutory injunction is made to a court pending the trial of an action, and

(b) the party against whom it is sought claims that he acted in contemplation or furtherance of a trade dispute, the court shall, in exercising its discretion whether or not to grant the injunction, have regard to the likelihood of that party's succeeding at the trial of the action in establishing any matter which would afford a defence to the action under section 219 (protection from certain tort liabilities) or section 220 (peaceful picketing).

This subsection does not extend to Scotland.

[708]

Action excluded from protection

222 Action to enforce trade union membership

(1) An act is not protected if the reason, or one of the reasons, for which it is done is the fact or belief that a particular employer—

- (a) is employing, has employed or might employ a person who is not a member of a trade union, or
- (b) is failing, has failed or might fail to discriminate against such a person.

(2) For the purposes of subsection (1)(b) an employer discriminates against a person if, but only if, he ensures that his conduct in relation to—

- (a) persons, or persons of any description, employed by him, or who apply to be, or are, considered by him for employment, or
- (b) the provision of employment for such persons,

is different, in some or all cases, according to whether or not they are members of a trade union, and is more favourable to those who are.

(3) An act is not protected if it constitutes, or is one of a number of acts which together constitute, an inducement or attempted inducement of a person—

- (a) to incorporate in a contract to which that person is a party, or a proposed contract to which he intends to be a party, a term or condition which is or would be void by virtue of section 144 (union membership requirement in contract for goods or services), or
- (b) to contravene section 145 (refusal to deal with person on grounds relating to union membership).

(4) References in this section to an employer employing a person are to a person acting in the capacity of the person for whom a worker works or normally works.

(5) References in this section to not being a member of a trade union are to not being a member of any trade union, of a particular trade union or of one of a number of particular trade unions.

Any such reference includes a reference to not being a member of a particular branch or section of a trade union or of one of a number of particular branches or sections of a trade union.

[709]

223 Action taken because of dismissal for taking unofficial action

An act is not protected if the reason, or one of the reasons, for doing it is the fact or belief that an employer has dismissed one or more employees in circumstances such that by virtue of section 237 (dismissal in connection with unofficial action) they have no right to complain of unfair dismissal.

[710]

224 Secondary action

(1) An act is not protected if one of the facts relied on for the purpose of establishing liability is that there has been secondary action which is not lawful picketing.

(2) There is secondary action in relation to a trade dispute when, and only when, a person—

- (a) induces another to break a contract of employment or interferes or induces another to interfere with its performance, or
- (b) threatens that a contract of employment under which he or another is employed will be broken or its performance interfered with, or that he will induce another to break a contract of employment or to interfere with its performance,

and the employer under the contract of employment is not the employer party to the dispute.

(3) Lawful picketing means acts done in the course of such attendance as is declared lawful by section 220 (peaceful picketing)—

(a) by a worker employed (or, in the case of a worker not in employment, last employed) by the employer party to the dispute, or

(b) by a trade union official whose attendance is lawful by virtue of subsection (1)(b) of that section.

(4) For the purposes of this section an employer shall not be treated as party to a dispute between another employer and workers of that employer; and where more than one employer is in dispute with his workers, the dispute between each employer and his workers shall be treated as a separate dispute.

In this subsection "worker" has the same meaning as in section 244 (meaning of "trade dispute").

(5) An act in contemplation or furtherance of a trade dispute which is primary action in relation to that dispute may not be relied on as secondary action in relation to another trade dispute.

Primary action means such action as is mentioned in paragraph (a) or (b) of subsection (2) where the employer under the contract of employment is the employer party to the dispute.

(6) In this section "contract of employment" includes any contract under which one person personally does work or performs services for another, and related expressions shall be construed accordingly.

[711]

225 Pressure to impose union recognition requirement

(1) An act is not protected if it constitutes, or is one of a number of acts which together constitute, an inducement or attempted inducement of a person—

(a) to incorporate in a contract to which that person is a party, or a proposed contract to which he intends to be a party, a term or condition which is or would be void by virtue of section 186 (recognition requirement in contract for goods or services), or

(b) to contravene section 187 (refusal to deal with person on grounds of union exclusion).

(2) An act is not protected if—

(a) it interferes with the supply (whether or not under a contract) of goods or services, or can reasonably be expected to have that effect, and

(b) one of the facts relied upon for the purpose of establishing liability is that a person has—

(i) induced another to break a contract of employment or interfered or induced another to interfere with its performance, or

(ii) threatened that a contract of employment under which he or another is employed will be broken or its performance interfered with, or that he will induce another to break a contract of employment or to interfere with its performance, and

(c) the reason, or one of the reasons, for doing the act is the fact or belief that the supplier (not being the employer under the contract of employment mentioned in paragraph (b)) does not, or might not—

(i) recognise one or more trade unions for the purpose of negotiating on behalf of workers, or any class of worker, employed by him, or

(ii) negotiate or consult with, or with an official of, one or more trade unions.

[712]

Requirement of ballot before action by trade union

226 Requirement of ballot before action by trade union

(1) An act done by a trade union to induce a person to take part, or continue to take part, in industrial action—

[(a) is not protected unless the industrial action has the support of a ballot, and

(b) where section 226A falls to be complied with in relation to the person's employer, is not protected as respects the employer unless the trade union has complied with section 226A in relation to him.]

[In this section "the relevant time", in relation to an act by a trade union to induce a person to take part, or continue to take part, in industrial action, means the time at which proceedings are commenced in respect of the act.]

(2) Industrial action shall be regarded as having the support of a ballot only if—

[(a) the union has held a ballot in respect of the action—

(i) in relation to which the requirements of section 226B so far as applicable before and during the holding of the ballot were satisfied,

(ii) in relation to which the requirements of sections 227 to [231] were satisfied, and

(iii) in which the majority voting in the ballot answered "Yes" to the question applicable in accordance with section 229(2) to industrial action of the kind to which the act of inducement relates;

(b) such of the requirements of the following sections as have fallen to be satisfied at the relevant time have been satisfied, namely—

(i) section 226B so far as applicable after the holding of the ballot, and

(ii) section 231B; ...

[(bb) section 232A does not prevent the industrial action from being regarded as having the support of the ballot; and]

(c) the requirements of section 233 (calling of industrial action with support of ballot) are satisfied.

Any reference in this subsection to a requirement of a provision which is disapplied or modified by section 232 has effect subject to that section.]

(3) Where separate workplace ballots are held by virtue of [section 228(1)—

(a) industrial action shall be regarded as having the support of a ballot if the conditions specified in subsection (2) are satisfied, and

(b) the trade union shall be taken to have complied with the requirements relating to a ballot imposed by section 226A if those requirements are complied with,

in relation] to the ballot for the place of work of the person induced to take part, or continue to take part, in the industrial action.

[(3A) If the requirements of section 231A fall to be satisfied in relation to an employer, as respects that employer industrial action shall not be regarded as having the support of a ballot unless those requirements are satisfied in relation to that employer.]

(4) For the purposes of this section an inducement, in relation to a person, includes an inducement which is or would be ineffective, whether because of his unwillingness to be influenced by it or for any other reason.

[713]

NOTES

Sub-s (1): words in first pair of square brackets substituted, and words in second pair of square brackets added, by the Trade Union Reform and Employment Rights Act 1993, ss 18(1), 49(2), Sch 8, para 73(a).

Sub-s (2): paras (a)–(c) substituted by the Trade Union Reform and Employment Rights Act 1993, s 49(2), Sch 8, para 73(b); number in square brackets in para (a)(ii) substituted, word omitted from para (b) repealed, and para (bb) inserted, by the Employment Relations Act 1999, ss 4, 44, Sch 3, paras 1, 2(1), (2), Sch 9(1).

Sub-s (3): words in square brackets substituted by the Trade Union Reform and Employment Rights Act 1993, s 49(2), Sch 8, para 73(c).

Sub-s (3A): inserted by the Employment Relations Act 1999, s 4, Sch 3, paras 1, 2(1), (3).

[226A Notice of ballot and sample voting paper for employers

[(1) The trade union must take such steps as are reasonably necessary to ensure that—

(a) not later than the seventh day before the opening day of the ballot, the notice specified in subsection (2), and

(b) not later than the third day before the opening day of the ballot, the sample voting paper specified in [subsection (2F)],

is received by every person who it is reasonable for the union to believe (at the latest time when steps could be taken to comply with paragraph (a)) will be the employer of persons who will be entitled to vote in the ballot.

(2) The notice referred to in paragraph (a) of subsection (1) is a notice in writing—

(a) stating that the union intends to hold the ballot,

(b) specifying the date which the union reasonably believes will be the opening day of the ballot, and

[(c) containing—

(i) the lists mentioned in subsection (2A) and the figures mentioned in subsection (2B), together with an explanation of how those figures were arrived at, or

(ii) where some or all of the employees concerned are employees from whose wages the employer makes deductions representing payments to the union, either those lists and figures and that explanation or the information mentioned in subsection (2C)].

[(2A) The lists are—

(a) a list of the categories of employee to which the employees concerned belong, and

(b) a list of the workplaces at which the employees concerned work.

(2B) The figures are—

(a) the total number of employees concerned,

(b) the number of the employees concerned in each of the categories in the list mentioned in subsection (2A)(a), and

(c) the number of the employees concerned who work at each workplace in the list mentioned in subsection (2A)(b).

(2C) The information referred to in subsection (2)(c)(ii) is such information as will enable the employer readily to deduce—

(a) the total number of employees concerned,

(b) the categories of employee to which the employees concerned belong and the number of the employees concerned in each of those categories, and

(c) the workplaces at which the employees concerned work and the number of them who work at each of those workplaces.

(2D) The lists and figures supplied under this section, or the information mentioned in subsection (2C) that is so supplied, must be as accurate as is reasonably practicable in the light of the information in the possession of the union at the time when it complies with subsection (1)(a).

(2E) For the purposes of subsection (2D) information is in the possession of the union if it is held, for union purposes—

(a) in a document, whether in electronic form or any other form, and

(b) in the possession or under the control of an officer or employee of the union.

(2F) The sample voting paper referred to in paragraph (b) of subsection (1) is—

(a) a sample of the form of voting paper which is to be sent to the employees concerned, or

(b) where the employees concerned are not all to be sent the same form of voting paper, a sample of each form of voting paper which is to be sent to any of them.

(2G) Nothing in this section requires a union to supply an employer with the names of the employees concerned.

(2H) In this section references to the "employees concerned" are references to those employees of the employer in question who the union reasonably believes will be entitled to vote in the ballot.

(2I) For the purposes of this section, the workplace at which an employee works is—

(a) in relation to an employee who works at or from a single set of premises, those premises, and

(b) in relation to any other employee, the premises with which his employment has the closest connection.]

(3), [(3A), (3B)] …

(4) In this section references to the opening day of the ballot are references to the first day when a voting paper is sent to any person entitled to vote in the ballot.

(5) This section, in its application to a ballot in which merchant seamen to whom section 230(2A) applies are entitled to vote, shall have effect with the substitution in

[subsection (2F)], for references to the voting paper which is to be sent to the employees, of references to the voting paper which is to be sent or otherwise provided to them.] **[714]**

NOTES

Inserted by the Trade Union Reform and Employment Rights Act 1993, s 18(2).

Sub-ss (1), (5): words in square brackets substituted by the Employment Relations Act 2004, s 22(1), (2), (6), as from 1 October 2005, except where a trade union took the steps in relation to the notice mentioned in sub-s (1)(a) above before that date (see SI 2005/2419, art 6).

Sub-s (2): para (c) substituted by the Employment Relations Act 2004, s 22(1), (3), as from 1 October 2005 (subject to the same exception in SI 2005/2419, art 6 as noted above).

Sub-ss (2A)–(2I): inserted by the Employment Relations Act 2004, s 22(1), (4), as from 1 October 2005 (subject to the same exception in SI 2005/2419, art 6 as noted above).

Sub-s (3): repealed by the Employment Relations Act 2004, ss 22(1), (5), 57(2), Sch 2, as from 1 October 2005 (subject to the same exception in SI 2005/2419, art 6 as noted above).

Sub-ss (3A), (3B): inserted by the Employment Relations Act 1999, s 4, Sch 3, paras 1, 3(1), (3), and repealed by the Employment Relations Act 2004, ss 22(1), (5), 57(2), Sch 2, as from 1 October 2005 (subject to the same exception in SI 2005/2419, art 6 as noted above).

[226B Appointment of scrutineer

(1) The trade union shall, before the ballot in respect of the industrial action is held, appoint a qualified person ("the scrutineer") whose terms of appointment shall require him to carry out in relation to the ballot the functions of—

- (a) taking such steps as appear to him to be appropriate for the purpose of enabling him to make a report to the trade union (see section 231B); and
- (b) making the report as soon as reasonably practicable after the date of the ballot and, in any event, not later than the end of the period of four weeks beginning with that date.

(2) A person is a qualified person in relation to a ballot if—

- (a) he satisfies such conditions as may be specified for the purposes of this section by order of the Secretary of State or is himself so specified; and
- (b) the trade union has no grounds for believing either that he will carry out the functions conferred on him under subsection (1) otherwise than competently or that his independence in relation to the union, or in relation to the ballot, might reasonably be called into question.

An order under paragraph (a) shall be made by statutory instrument which shall be subject to annulment in pursuance of a resolution of either House of Parliament.

(3) The trade union shall ensure that the scrutineer duly carries out the functions conferred on him under subsection (1) and that there is no interference with the carrying out of those functions from the union or any of its members, officials or employees.

(4) The trade union shall comply with all reasonable requests made by the scrutineer for the purposes of, or in connection with, the carrying out of those functions.] **[715]**

NOTES

Inserted by the Trade Union Reform and Employment Rights Act 1993, s 20(1).

Orders: the Trade Union Ballots and Elections (Independent Scrutineer Qualifications) Order 1993, SI 1993/1909 at **[2179]**.

[226C Exclusion for small ballots

Nothing in section 226B, section 229(1A)(a) or section 231B shall impose a requirement on a trade union unless—

- (a) the number of members entitled to vote in the ballot, or
- (b) where separate workplace ballots are held in accordance with section 228(1), the aggregate of the number of members entitled to vote in each of them,

exceeds 50.] **[716]**

NOTES

Inserted by the Trade Union Reform and Employment Rights Act 1993, s 20(4).

227 Entitlement to vote in ballot

(1) Entitlement to vote in the ballot must be accorded equally to all the members of the trade union who it is reasonable at the time of the ballot for the union to believe will be induced [by the union] to take part or, as the case may be, to continue to take part in the industrial action in question, and to no others.

(2) …

[717]

NOTES

Sub-s (1): words in square brackets inserted by the Employment Relations Act 2004, s 23, as from 6 April 2005.

Sub-s (2): repealed by the Employment Relations Act 1999, ss 4, 44, Sch 3, paras 1, 4, Sch 9(1).

[228 Separate workplace ballots

(1) Subject to subsection (2), this section applies if the members entitled to vote in a ballot by virtue of section 227 do not all have the same workplace.

(2) This section does not apply if the union reasonably believes that all those members have the same workplace.

(3) Subject to section 228A, a separate ballot shall be held for each workplace; and entitlement to vote in each ballot shall be accorded equally to, and restricted to, members of the union who—

(a) are entitled to vote by virtue of section 227, and
(b) have that workplace.

(4) In this section and section 228A "workplace" in relation to a person who is employed means—

(a) if the person works at or from a single set of premises, those premises, and
(b) in any other case, the premises with which the person's employment has the closest connection.]

[718]

NOTES

Substituted, together with s 228A for original s 228, by the Employment Relations Act 1999, s 4, Sch 3, paras 1, 5.

[228A Separate workplaces: single and aggregate ballots

(1) Where section 228(3) would require separate ballots to be held for each workplace, a ballot may be held in place of some or all of the separate ballots if one of subsections (2) to (4) is satisfied in relation to it.

(2) This subsection is satisfied in relation to a ballot if the workplace of each member entitled to vote in the ballot is the workplace of at least one member of the union who is affected by the dispute.

(3) This subsection is satisfied in relation to a ballot if entitlement to vote is accorded to, and limited to, all the members of the union who—

(a) according to the union's reasonable belief have an occupation of a particular kind or have any of a number of particular kinds of occupation, and
(b) are employed by a particular employer, or by any of a number of particular employers, with whom the union is in dispute.

(4) This subsection is satisfied in relation to a ballot if entitlement to vote is accorded to, and limited to, all the members of the union who are employed by a particular employer, or by any of a number of particular employers, with whom the union is in dispute.

(5) For the purposes of subsection (2) the following are members of the union affected by a dispute—

(a) if the dispute relates (wholly or partly) to a decision which the union reasonably believes the employer has made or will make concerning a matter specified in subsection (1)(a), (b) or (c) of section 244 (meaning of "trade dispute"), members whom the decision directly affects,

(b) if the dispute relates (wholly or partly) to a matter specified in subsection (1)(d) of that section, members whom the matter directly affects,
(c) if the dispute relates (wholly or partly) to a matter specified in subsection (1)(e) of that section, persons whose membership or non-membership is in dispute,
(d) if the dispute relates (wholly or partly) to a matter specified in subsection (1)(f) of that section, officials of the union who have used or would use the facilities concerned in the dispute.]

[719]

NOTES

Substituted as noted to s 228 at **[718]**.

229 Voting paper

(1) The method of voting in a ballot must be by the marking of a voting paper by the person voting.

[(1A) Each voting paper must—
(a) state the name of the independent scrutineer,
(b) clearly specify the address to which, and the date by which, it is to be returned,
(c) be given one of a series of consecutive whole numbers every one of which is used in giving a different number in that series to each voting paper printed or otherwise produced for the purposes of the ballot, and
(d) be marked with its number.

This subsection, in its application to a ballot in which merchant seamen to whom section 230(2A) applies are entitled to vote, shall have effect with the substitution, for the reference to the address to which the voting paper is to be returned, of a reference to the ship to which the seamen belong.]

(2) The voting paper must contain at least one of the following questions—
(a) a question (however framed) which requires the person answering it to say, by answering "Yes" or "No", whether he is prepared to take part or, as the case may be, to continue to take part in a strike;
(b) a question (however framed) which requires the person answering it to say, by answering "Yes" or "No", whether he is prepared to take part or, as the case may be, to continue to take part in industrial action short of a strike.

[(2A) For the purposes of subsection (2) an overtime ban and a call-out ban constitute industrial action short of a strike.]

(3) The voting paper must specify who, in the event of a vote in favour of industrial action, is authorised for the purposes of section 233 to call upon members to take part or continue to take part in the industrial action.

The person or description of persons so specified need not be authorised under the rules of the union but must be within section [20(2)] (persons for whose acts the union is taken to be responsible).

(4) The following statement must (without being qualified or commented upon by anything else on the voting paper) appear on every voting paper—

"If you take part in a strike or other industrial action, you may be in breach of your contract of employment.

[However, if you are dismissed for taking part in strike or other industrial action which is called officially and is otherwise lawful, the dismissal will be unfair if it takes place fewer than [twelve] weeks after you started taking part in the action, and depending on the circumstances may be unfair if it takes place later.]".

[720]

NOTES

Sub-s (1A): inserted by the Trade Union Reform and Employment Rights Act 1993, s 20(2).
Sub-s (2A): inserted by the Employment Relations Act 1999, s 4, Sch 3, paras 1, 6(1), (2).
Sub-s (3): number in square brackets substituted by the Trade Union Reform and Employment Rights Act 1993, s 49(1), Sch 7, para 25.
Sub-s (4): words in first (outer) pair of square brackets added by the Employment Relations Act 1999, s 4, Sch 3, paras 1, 6(1), (3); word in second (inner) pair of square brackets substituted by the Employment Relations Act 2004, s 57(1), Sch 1, para 13, as from 6 April 2005.

230 Conduct of ballot

(1) Every person who is entitled to vote in the ballot must—

(a) be allowed to vote without interference from, or constraint imposed by, the union or any of its members, officials or employees, and

(b) so far as is reasonably practicable, be enabled to do so without incurring any direct cost to himself.

[(2) Except as regards persons falling within subsection (2A), so far as is reasonably practicable, every person who is entitled to vote in the ballot must—

(a) have a voting paper sent to him by post at his home address or any other address which he has requested the trade union in writing to treat as his postal address; and

(b) be given a convenient opportunity to vote by post.]

[(2A) Subsection (2B) applies to a merchant seaman if the trade union reasonably believes that—

(a) he will be employed in a ship either at sea or at a place outside Great Britain at some time in the period during which votes may be cast, and

(b) it will be convenient for him to receive a voting paper and to vote while on the ship or while at a place where the ship is rather than in accordance with subsection (2).

(2B) Where this subsection applies to a merchant seaman he shall, if it is reasonably practicable—

(a) have a voting paper made available to him while on the ship or while at a place where the ship is, and

(b) be given an opportunity to vote while on the ship or while at a place where the ship is.]

[(2C) In subsections (2A) and (2B) "merchant seaman" means a person whose employment, or the greater part of it, is carried out on board sea going ships.]

(4) A ballot shall be conducted so as to secure that—

(a) so far as is reasonably practicable, those voting do so in secret, and

(b) the votes given in the ballot are fairly and accurately counted.

For the purposes of paragraph (b) an inaccuracy in counting shall be disregarded if it is accidental and on a scale which could not affect the result of the ballot.

[721]

NOTES

Sub-ss (2)–(2C): substituted, for original sub-ss (2), (3), by the Trade Union Reform and Employment Rights Act 1993, s 17; sub-ss (2A), (2B) further substituted by the Employment Relations Act 1999, s 4, Sch 3, paras 1, 7.

231 Information as to result of ballot

As soon as is reasonably practicable after the holding of the ballot, the trade union shall take such steps as are reasonably necessary to ensure that all persons entitled to vote in the ballot are informed of the number of—

(a) votes cast in the ballot,

(b) individuals answering "Yes" to the question, or as the case may be, to each question,

(c) individuals answering "No" to the question, or, as the case may be, to each question, and

(d) spoiled voting papers.

[722]

[231A Employers to be informed of ballot result

(1) As soon as reasonably practicable after the holding of the ballot, the trade union shall take such steps as are reasonably necessary to ensure that every relevant employer is informed of the matters mentioned in section 231.

(2) In subsection (1) "relevant employer" means a person who it is reasonable for the trade union to believe (at the time when the steps are taken) was at the time of the ballot the employer of any persons entitled to vote.]

[723]

NOTES

Inserted by the Trade Union Reform and Employment Rights Act 1993, s 19.

[231B Scrutineer's report

(1) The scrutineer's report on the ballot shall state whether the scrutineer is satisfied—

(a) that there are no reasonable grounds for believing that there was any contravention of a requirement imposed by or under any enactment in relation to the ballot,

(b) that the arrangements made with respect to the production, storage, distribution, return or other handling of the voting papers used in the ballot, and the arrangements for the counting of the votes, included all such security arrangements as were reasonably practicable for the purpose of minimising the risk that any unfairness or malpractice might occur, and

(c) that he has been able to carry out the functions conferred on him under section 226B(1) without any interference from the trade union or any of its members, officials or employees;

and if he is not satisfied as to any of those matters, the report shall give particulars of his reason for not being satisfied as to that matter.

(2) If at any time within six months from the date of the ballot—

(a) any person entitled to vote in the ballot, or

(b) the employer of any such person,

requests a copy of the scrutineer's report, the trade union must, as soon as practicable, provide him with one either free of charge or on payment of such reasonable fee as may be specified by the trade union.]

[724]

NOTES

Inserted by the Trade Union Reform and Employment Rights Act 1993, s 20(3).

232 Balloting of overseas members

(1) A trade union which has overseas members may choose whether or not to accord any of those members entitlement to vote in a ballot; and nothing in section [226B to 230 and 231B] applies in relation to an overseas member or a vote cast by such a member.

[(2) Where overseas members have voted in the ballot—

(a) the references in sections 231 and 231A to persons entitled to vote in the ballot do not include overseas members, and

(b) those sections shall be read as requiring the information mentioned in section 231 to distinguish between overseas members and other members.]

(3) An "overseas member" of a trade union means a member (other than a merchant seaman or offshore worker) who is outside Great Britain throughout the period during which votes may be cast.

For this purpose—

"merchant seaman" means a person whose employment, or the greater part of it, is carried out on board sea-going ships; and

"offshore worker" means a person in offshore employment, other than one who is in such employment in an area where the law of Northern Ireland applies.

(4) A member who throughout the period during which votes may be cast is in Northern Ireland shall not be treated as an overseas member—

(a) where the ballot is one to which section 228(1) or (2) applies (workplace ballots) and his place of work is in Great Britain, or

(b) where the ballot is one to which section 228(3) applies (general ballots) and relates to industrial action involving members both in Great Britain and in Northern Ireland.

(5) In relation to offshore employment the references in subsection (4) to Northern Ireland include any area where the law of Northern Ireland applies and the references to Great Britain include any area where the law of England and Wales or Scotland applies.

[725]

NOTES

Sub-s (1): words in square brackets substituted by the Trade Union Reform and Employment Rights Act 1993, s 49(2), Sch 8, para 74(a).

Sub-s (2): substituted by the Trade Union Reform and Employment Rights Act 1993, s 49(2), Sch 8, para 74(b).

[232A Inducement of member denied entitlement to vote

Industrial action shall not be regarded as having the support of a ballot if the following conditions apply in the case of any person—

(a) he was a member of the trade union at the time when the ballot was held,
(b) it was reasonable at that time for the trade union to believe he would be induced to take part or, as the case may be, to continue to take part in the industrial action,
(c) he was not accorded entitlement to vote in the ballot, and
(d) he was induced by the trade union to take part or, as the case may be, to continue to take part in the industrial action.]

[726]

NOTES

Inserted by the Employment Relations Act 1999, s 4, Sch 3, paras 1, 8.

[232B Small accidental failures to be disregarded

(1) If—

(a) in relation to a ballot there is a failure (or there are failures) to comply with a provision mentioned in subsection (2) or with more than one of those provisions, and
(b) the failure is accidental and on a scale which is unlikely to affect the result of the ballot or, as the case may be, the failures are accidental and taken together are on a scale which is unlikely to affect the result of the ballot,

the failure (or failures) shall be disregarded [for all purposes (including, in particular, those of section 232A(c))].

(2) The provisions are section 227(1), section 230(2) and section [230(2B)].]

[727]

NOTES

Inserted by the Employment Relations Act 1999, s 4, Sch 3, paras 1, 9.

Sub-s (1): words in square brackets inserted by the Employment Relations Act 2004, s 24(1)(a), as from 6 April 2005.

Sub-s (2): number in square brackets substituted by the Employment Relations Act 2004, s 24(1)(b), as from 6 April 2005.

233 Calling of industrial action with support of ballot

(1) Industrial action shall not be regarded as having the support of a ballot unless it is called by a specified person and the conditions specified below are satisfied.

(2) A "specified person" means a person specified or of a description specified in the voting paper for the ballot in accordance with section 229(3).

(3) The conditions are that—

(a) there must have been no call by the trade union to take part or continue to take part in industrial action to which the ballot relates, or any authorisation or endorsement by the union of any such industrial action, before the date of the ballot;
(b) there must be a call for industrial action by a specified person, and industrial action to which it relates must [begin], before the ballot ceases to be effective in accordance with section 234.

(4) For the purposes of this section a call shall be taken to have been made by a trade union if it was authorised or endorsed by the union; and the provisions of section 20(2) to (4) apply for the purpose of determining whether a call, or industrial action, is to be taken to have been so authorised or endorsed.

[728]

NOTES

Sub-s (3): word in square brackets substituted by the Employment Relations Act 2004, s 57(1), Sch 1, para 14, as from 6 April 2005.

234 Period after which ballot ceases to be effective

[(1) Subject to the following provisions, a ballot ceases to be effective for the purposes of section 233(3)(b) in relation to industrial action by members of a trade union at the end of the period, beginning with the date of the ballot—

(a) of four weeks, or

(b) of such longer duration not exceeding eight weeks as is agreed between the union and the members' employer.]

(2) Where for the whole or part of that period the calling or organising of industrial action is prohibited—

(a) by virtue of a court order which subsequently lapses or is discharged, recalled or set aside, or

(b) by virtue of an undertaking given to a court by any person from which he is subsequently released or by which he ceases to be bound,

the trade union may apply to the court for an order that the period during which the prohibition had effect shall not count towards the period referred to in subsection (1).

(3) The application must be made forthwith upon the prohibition ceasing to have effect—

(a) to the court by virtue of whose decision it ceases to have effect, or

(b) where an order lapses or an undertaking ceases to bind without any such decision, to the court by which the order was made or to which the undertaking was given;

and no application may be made after the end of the period of eight weeks beginning with the date of the ballot.

(4) The court shall not make an order if it appears to the court—

(a) that the result of the ballot no longer represents the views of the union members concerned, or

(b) that an event is likely to occur as a result of which those members would vote against industrial action if another ballot were to be held.

(5) No appeal lies from the decision of the court to make or refuse an order under this section.

(6) The period between the making of an application under this section and its determination does not count towards the period referred to in subsection (1).

But a ballot shall not by virtue of this subsection (together with any order of the court) be regarded as effective for the purposes of section 233(3)(b) after the end of the period of twelve weeks beginning with the date of the ballot.

[729]

NOTES

Sub-s (1): substituted by the Employment Relations Act 1999, s 4, Sch 3, paras 1, 10.

[Requirement on trade union to give notice of industrial action

234A Notice to employers of industrial action

(1) An act done by a trade union to induce a person to take part, or continue to take part, in industrial action is not protected as respects his employer unless the union has taken or takes such steps as are reasonably necessary to ensure that the employer receives within the appropriate period a relevant notice covering the act.

(2) Subsection (1) imposes a requirement in the case of an employer only if it is reasonable for the union to believe, at the latest time when steps could be taken to ensure that he receives such a notice, that he is the employer of persons who will be or have been induced to take part, or continue to take part, in the industrial action.

(3) For the purposes of this section a relevant notice is a notice in writing which—

[(a) contains—

(i) the lists mentioned in subsection (3A) and the figures mentioned in subsection (3B), together with an explanation of how those figures were arrived at, or

(ii) where some or all of the affected employees are employees from whose wages the employer makes deductions representing payments to the union, either those lists and figures and that explanation or the information mentioned in subsection (3C), and]

(b) states whether industrial action is intended to be continuous or discontinuous and specifies—

(i) where it is to be continuous, the intended date for any of the affected employees to begin to take part in the action,

(ii) where it is to be discontinuous, the intended dates for any of the affected employees to take part in the action, …

(c) …

[(3A) The lists referred to in subsection (3)(a) are—

(a) a list of the categories of employee to which the affected employees belong, and

(b) a list of the workplaces at which the affected employees work.

(3B) The figures referred to in subsection (3)(a) are—

(a) the total number of the affected employees,

(b) the number of the affected employees in each of the categories in the list mentioned in subsection (3A)(a), and

(c) the number of the affected employees who work at each workplace in the list mentioned in subsection (3A)(b).

(3C) The information referred to in subsection (3)(a)(ii) is such information as will enable the employer readily to deduce—

(a) the total number of the affected employees,

(b) the categories of employee to which the affected employees belong and the number of the affected employees in each of those categories, and

(c) the workplaces at which the affected employees work and the number of them who work at each of those workplaces.

(3D) The lists and figures supplied under this section, or the information mentioned in subsection (3C) that is so supplied, must be as accurate as is reasonably practicable in the light of the information in the possession of the union at the time when it complies with subsection (1).

(3E) For the purposes of subsection (3D) information is in the possession of the union if it is held, for union purposes—

(a) in a document, whether in electronic form or any other form, and

(b) in the possession or under the control of an officer or employee of the union.

(3F) Nothing in this section requires a union to supply an employer with the names of the affected employees.]

(4) For the purposes of subsection (1) the appropriate period is the period—

(a) beginning with the day when the union satisfies the requirement of section 231A in relation to the ballot in respect of the industrial action, and

(b) ending with the seventh day before the day, or before the first of the days, specified in the relevant notice.

(5) For the purposes of subsection (1) a relevant notice covers an act done by the union if the person induced [falls within a notified category of employee and the workplace at which he works is a notified workplace] and—

(a) where he is induced to take part or continue to take part in industrial action which the union intends to be continuous, if—

(i) the notice states that the union intends the industrial action to be continuous, and

(ii) there is no participation by him in the industrial action before the date specified in the notice in consequence of any inducement by the union not covered by a relevant notice; and

(b) where he is induced to take part or continue to take part in industrial action which the union intends to be discontinuous, if there is no participation by him in the industrial action on a day not so specified in consequence of any inducement by the union not covered by a relevant notice.

[(5B) In subsection (5)—

(a) a "notified category of employee" means—
(i) a category of employee that is listed in the notice, or
(ii) where the notice contains the information mentioned in subsection (3C), a category of employee that the employer (at the time he receives the notice) can readily deduce from the notice is a category of employee to which some or all of the affected employees belong, and

(b) a "notified workplace" means—
(i) a workplace that is listed in the notice, or
(ii) where the notice contains the information mentioned in subsection (3C), a workplace that the employer (at the time he receives the notice) can readily deduce from the notice is the workplace at which some or all of the affected employees work.

(5C) In this section references to the "affected employees" are references to those employees of the employer who the union reasonably believes will be induced by the union, or have been so induced, to take part or continue to take part in the industrial action.

(5D) For the purposes of this section, the workplace at which an employee works is—
(a) in relation to an employee who works at or from a single set of premises, those premises, and
(b) in relation to any other employee, the premises with which his employment has the closest connection.]

(6) For the purposes of this section—
(a) a union intends industrial action to be discontinuous if it intends it to take place only on some days on which there is an opportunity to take the action, and
(b) a union intends industrial action to be continuous if it intends it to be not so restricted.

(7) [Subject to subsections (7A) and (7B),] where—
(a) continuous industrial action which has been authorised or endorsed by a union ceases to be so authorised or endorsed …, and
(b) the industrial action has at a later date again been authorised or endorsed by the union (whether as continuous or discontinuous action),

no relevant notice covering acts done to induce persons to take part in the earlier action shall operate to cover acts done to induce persons to take part in the action authorised or endorsed at the later date and this section shall apply in relation to an act to induce a person to take part, or continue to take part, in the industrial action after that date as if the references in subsection (3)(b)(i) to the industrial action were to the industrial action taking place after that date.

[(7A) Subsection (7) shall not apply where industrial action ceases to be authorised or endorsed in order to enable the union to comply with a court order or an undertaking given to a court.

(7B) Subsection (7) shall not apply where—
(a) a union agrees with an employer, before industrial action ceases to be authorised or endorsed, that it will cease to be authorised or endorsed with effect from a date specified in the agreement ("the suspension date") and that it may again be authorised or endorsed with effect from a date not earlier than a date specified in the agreement ("the resumption date"),
(b) the action ceases to be authorised or endorsed with effect from the suspension date, and
(c) the action is again authorised or endorsed with effect from a date which is not earlier than the resumption date or such later date as may be agreed between the union and the employer.]

(8) The requirement imposed on a trade union by subsection (1) shall be treated as having been complied with if the steps were taken by other relevant persons or committees whose acts were authorised or endorsed by the union and references to the belief or intention of the union in subsection (2) or, as the case may be, subsections (3), (5)[, (5C)] and (6) shall be construed as references to the belief or the intention of the person or committee taking the steps.

(9) The provisions of section 20(2) to (4) apply for the purpose of determining for the purposes of subsection (1) who are relevant persons or committees and whether the trade

union is to be taken to have authorised or endorsed the steps the person or committee took and for the purposes of [subsections (7) to (7B)] whether the trade union is to be taken to have authorised or endorsed the industrial action.]

[730]

NOTES

Inserted, together with the preceding heading, by the Trade Union Reform and Employment Rights Act 1993, s 21.

Sub-s (3): para (a) substituted, and para (c) and the word immediately preceding it repealed, by the Employment Relations Act 2004, ss 25(1), (2). 57(2), Sch 2, as from 1 October 2005, except where a trade union took the steps in relation to the notice mentioned in sub-s (1) above before that date (see SI 2005/2419, art 7).

Sub-ss (3A)–(3F): inserted by the Employment Relations Act 2004, s 25(1), (3), as from 1 October 2005 (subject to the same exception in SI 2005/2419, art 7 as noted above).

Sub-s (5): words in square brackets substituted by the Employment Relations Act 2004, s 25(1), (4), as from 1 October 2005 (subject to the same exception in SI 2005/2419, art 7 as noted above).

Sub-ss (5B)–(5D): substituted (for original sub-s (5A) as inserted by the Employment Relations Act 1999, s 4, Sch 3, paras 1, 11(1), (3)) by the Employment Relations Act 2004, s 25(1), (5), as from 1 October 2005 (subject to the same exception in SI 2005/2419, art 7 as noted above).

Sub-s (7): words in square brackets inserted, and words omitted repealed, by the Employment Relations Act 1999, ss 4, 44, Sch 3, paras 1, 11(1), (4), Sch 9(1).

Sub-ss (7A), (7B): inserted by the Employment Relations Act 1999, s 4, Sch 3, paras 1, 11(1), (5).

Sub-s (8): number in square brackets inserted by the Employment Relations Act 2004, s 25(1), (6), as from 1 October 2005 (subject to the same exception in SI 2005/2419, art 7 as noted above).

Sub-s (9): words in square brackets substituted by the Employment Relations Act 1999, s 4, Sch 3, paras 1, 11(1), (6).

235 Construction of references to contract of employment

In sections 226 to [234A] (requirement of ballot before action by trade union) references to a contract of employment include any contract under which one person personally does work or performs services for another; [and "employer" and other related expressions] shall be construed accordingly.

[731]

NOTES

Number and words in square brackets substituted by the Trade Union Reform and Employment Rights Act 1993, s 49(2), Sch 8, para 75.

[Industrial action affecting supply of goods or services to an individual

235A Industrial action affecting supply of goods or services to an individual

(1) Where an individual claims that—

(a) any trade union or other person has done, or is likely to do, an unlawful act to induce any person to take part, or to continue to take part, in industrial action, and

(b) an effect, or a likely effect, of the industrial action is or will be to—

(i) prevent or delay the supply of goods or services, or

(ii) reduce the quality of goods or services supplied,

to the individual making the claim,

he may apply to the High Court or the Court of Session for an order under this section.

(2) For the purposes of this section an act to induce any person to take part, or to continue to take part, in industrial action is unlawful—

(a) if it is actionable in tort by any one or more persons, or

(b) (where it is or would be the act of a trade union) if it could form the basis of an application by a member under section 62.

(3) In determining whether an individual may make an application under this section it is immaterial whether or not the individual is entitled to be supplied with the goods or services in question.

(4) Where on an application under this section the court is satisfied that the claim is well-founded, it shall make such order as it considers appropriate for requiring the person by whom the act of inducement has been, or is likely to be, done to take steps for ensuring—

(a) that no, or no further, act is done by him to induce any persons to take part or to continue to take part in the industrial action, and

(b) that no person engages in conduct after the making of the order by virtue of having been induced by him before the making of the order to take part or continue to take part in the industrial action.

(5) Without prejudice to any other power of the court, the court may on an application under this section grant such interlocutory relief (in Scotland, such interim order) as it considers appropriate.

(6) For the purposes of this section an act of inducement shall be taken to be done by a trade union if it is authorised or endorsed by the union; and the provisions of section 20(2) to (4) apply for the purposes of determining whether such an act is to be taken to be so authorised or endorsed.

Those provisions also apply in relation to proceedings for failure to comply with an order under this section as they apply in relation to the original proceedings.]

[732]

NOTES

Inserted, together with the preceding heading and ss 235B, 235C, by the Trade Union Reform and Employment Rights Act 1993, s 22.

235B, 235C (*Inserted by the Trade Union Reform and Employment Rights Act 1993, s 22; repealed by the Employment Relations Act 1999, ss 28(2)(b), 44, Sch 9(6).*)

No compulsion to work

236 No compulsion to work

No court shall, whether by way of—

(a) an order for specific performance or specific implement of a contract of employment, or

(b) an injunction or interdict restraining a breach or threatened breach of such a contract,

compel an employee to do any work or attend at any place for the doing of any work.

[733]

Loss of unfair dismissal protection

237 Dismissal of those taking part in unofficial industrial action

(1) An employee has no right to complain of unfair dismissal if at the time of dismissal he was taking part in an unofficial strike or other unofficial industrial action.

[(1A) Subsection (1) does not apply to the dismissal of the employee if it is shown that the reason (or, if more than one, the principal reason) for the dismissal or, in a redundancy case, for selecting the employee for dismissal was one of those specified in [or under—

(a) section [98B,] 99, 100, 101A(d), 103[, 103A or 104C] of the Employment Rights Act 1996 (dismissal in [jury service,] family, health and safety, working time, employee representative[, protected disclosure and flexible working] cases),

(b) section 104 of that Act in its application in relation to time off under section 57A of that Act (dependants)].]

In this subsection "redundancy case" has the meaning given in [section 105(9)] of that Act[; and a reference to a specified reason for dismissal includes a reference to specified circumstances of dismissal].]

(2) A strike or other industrial action is unofficial in relation to an employee unless—

(a) he is a member of a trade union and the action is authorised or endorsed by that union, or

(b) he is not a member of a trade union but there are among those taking part in the industrial action members of a trade union by which the action has been authorised or endorsed.

Provided that, a strike or other industrial action shall not be regarded as unofficial if none of those taking part in it are members of a trade union.

(3) The provisions of section 20(2) apply for the purpose of determining whether industrial action is to be taken to have been authorised or endorsed by a trade union.

(4) The question whether industrial action is to be so taken in any case shall be determined by reference to the facts as at the time of dismissal.

Provided that, where an act is repudiated as mentioned in section 21, industrial action shall not thereby be treated as unofficial before the end of the next working day after the day on which the repudiation takes place.

(5) In this section the "time of dismissal" means—

(a) where the employee's contract of employment is terminated by notice, when the notice is given,

(b) where the employee's contract of employment is terminated without notice, when the termination takes effect, and

(c) where the employee is employed under a contract for a fixed term which expires without being renewed under the same contract, when that term expires;

and a "working day" means any day which is not a Saturday or Sunday, Christmas Day, Good Friday or a bank holiday under the Banking and Financial Dealings Act 1971.

(6) For the purposes of this section membership of a trade union for purposes unconnected with the employment in question shall be disregarded; but an employee who was a member of a trade union when he began to take part in industrial action shall continue to be treated as a member for the purpose of determining whether that action is unofficial in relation to him or another notwithstanding that he may in fact have ceased to be a member.

[734]

NOTES

Sub-s (1A): inserted by the Trade Union Reform and Employment Rights Act 1993, s 49(2), Sch 8, para 76, and subsequently amended as follows—

Words in first (outer) pair of square brackets substituted by the Employment Relations Act 1999, s 9, Sch 4, Pt III, paras 1, 2(a).

Number "98B," in square brackets inserted by the Employment Relations Act 2004, s 40(8)(a), as from 6 April 2005, except in relation to any dismissal where the effective date of termination (within the meaning of the Employment Rights Act 1996, s 97) was before that date (see SI 2005/872, art 13).

Words ", 103A or 104C" in square brackets substituted by the Employment Relations Act 2004, s 41(1)(a), as from 6 April 2005 (subject to the same exception in SI 2005/872, art 13 as noted above).

Words "jury service," in square brackets inserted by the Employment Relations Act 2004, s 40(8)(b), as from 6 April 2005 (subject to the same exception in SI 2005/872, art 13 as noted above).

Words ", protected disclosure and flexible working" in square brackets substituted by the Employment Relations Act 2004, s 41(1)(b), as from 6 April 2005, (subject to the same exception in SI 2005/872, art 13 as noted above).

Words "section 105(9)" in square brackets substituted by the Employment Rights Act 1996, s 240, Sch 1, para 56(1), (15).

Words "; and a reference to a specified reason for dismissal includes a reference to specified circumstances of dismissal" in square brackets inserted by the Employment Relations Act 1999, s 9, Sch 4, Pt III, paras 1, 2(b).

238 Dismissals in connection with other industrial action

(1) This section applies in relation to an employee who has a right to complain of unfair dismissal (the "complainant") and who claims to have been unfairly dismissed, where at the date of the dismissal—

(a) the employer was conducting or instituting a lock-out, or

(b) the complainant was taking part in a strike or other industrial action.

(2) In such a case an [employment tribunal] shall not determine whether the dismissal was fair or unfair unless it is shown—

(a) that one or more relevant employees of the same employer have not been dismissed, or

(b) that a relevant employee has before the expiry of the period of three months beginning with the date of his dismissal been offered re-engagement and that the complainant has not been offered re-engagement.

[(2A) Subsection (2) does not apply to the dismissal of the employee if it is shown that the reason (or, if more than one, the principal reason) for the dismissal or, in a redundancy case, for selecting the employee for dismissal was one of those specified in [or under—

(a) section [98B,] 99, 100, 101A(d)[, 103A or 104C] of the Employment Rights Act 1996 (dismissal in [jury service,] family, health and safety, working time[, employee representative and flexible working] cases),

(b) section 104 of that Act in its application in relation to time off under section 57A of that Act (dependants);]

In this subsection "redundancy case" has the meaning given in [section 105(9)] of that Act[; and a reference to a specified reason for dismissal includes a reference to specified circumstances of dismissal].]

[(2B) Subsection (2) does not apply in relation to an employee who is regarded as unfairly dismissed by virtue of section 238A below.]

(3) For this purpose "relevant employees" means—

(a) in relation to a lock-out, employees who were directly interested in the dispute in contemplation or furtherance of which the lock-out occurred, and

(b) in relation to a strike or other industrial action, those employees at the establishment of the employer at or from which the complainant works who at the date of his dismissal were taking part in the action.

Nothing in section 237 (dismissal of those taking part in unofficial industrial action) affects the question who are relevant employees for the purposes of this section.

(4) An offer of re-engagement means an offer (made either by the original employer or by a successor of that employer or an associated employer) to re-engage an employee, either in the job which he held immediately before the date of dismissal or in a different job which would be reasonably suitable in his case.

(5) In this section "date of dismissal" means—

(a) where the employee's contract of employment was terminated by notice, the date on which the employer's notice was given, and

(b) in any other case, the effective date of termination.

[735]

NOTES

Sub-s (2): words in square brackets substituted by the Employment Rights (Dispute Resolution) Act 1998, s 1(2)(a).

Sub-s (2A): inserted by the Trade Union Reform and Employment Rights Act 1993, s 49(2), Sch 8, para 77, and subsequently amended as follows—

Words in first (outer) pair of square brackets substituted by the Employment Relations Act 1999, s 9, Sch 4, Pt III, paras 1, 3(a).

Number "98B," in square brackets inserted by the Employment Relations Act 2004, s 40(9)(a), as from 6 April 2005, except in relation to any dismissal where the effective date of termination (within the meaning of the Employment Rights Act 1996, s 97) is before that date (see SI 2005/872, art 13).

Words ", 103A or 104C" in square brackets substituted by the Employment Relations Act 2004, s 41(2)(a), as from 6 April 2005 (subject to the same exception in SI 2005/872, art 13 as noted above).

Words "jury service," in square brackets inserted by the Employment Relations Act 2004, s 40(9)(b), as from 6 April 2005 (subject to the same exception in SI 2005/872, art 13 as noted above).

Words ", employee representative and flexible working" in square brackets substituted by the Employment Relations Act 2004, s 41(2)(b), as from 6 April 2005 (subject to the same exception in SI 2005/872, art 13 as noted above).

Words "section 105(9)" in square brackets substituted by the Employment Rights Act 1996, s 240, Sch 1, para 56(1), (15).

Words "; and a reference to a specified reason for dismissal includes a reference to specified circumstances of dismissal" in square brackets inserted by the Employment Relations Act 1999, s 9, Sch 4, Pt III, paras 1, 3(b).

Sub-s (2B): inserted by the Employment Relations Act 1999, s 16, Sch 5, paras 1, 2.

[238A Participation in official industrial action

(1) For the purposes of this section an employee takes protected industrial action if he commits an act which, or a series of acts each of which, he is induced to commit by an act which by virtue of section 219 is not actionable in tort.

(2) An employee who is dismissed shall be regarded for the purposes of Part X of the Employment Rights Act 1996 (unfair dismissal) as unfairly dismissed if—

(a) the reason (or, if more than one, the principal reason) for the dismissal is that the employee took protected industrial action, and

(b) subsection (3), (4) or (5) applies to the dismissal.

(3) This subsection applies to a dismissal if [the date of the dismissal is] [within the protected period].

(4) This subsection applies to a dismissal if—

(a) [the date of the dismissal is] after the end of that period, and
(b) the employee had stopped taking protected industrial action before the end of that period.

(5) This subsection applies to a dismissal if—
(a) [the date of the dismissal is] after the end of that period,
(b) the employee had not stopped taking protected industrial action before the end of that period, and
(c) the employer had not taken such procedural steps as would have been reasonable for the purposes of resolving the dispute to which the protected industrial action relates.

(6) In determining whether an employer has taken those steps regard shall be had, in particular, to—
(a) whether the employer or a union had complied with procedures established by any applicable collective or other agreement;
(b) whether the employer or a union offered or agreed to commence or resume negotiations after the start of the protected industrial action;
(c) whether the employer or a union unreasonably refused, after the start of the protected industrial action, a request that conciliation services be used;
(d) whether the employer or a union unreasonably refused, after the start of the protected industrial action, a request that mediation services be used in relation to procedures to be adopted for the purposes of resolving the dispute;
[(e) where there was agreement to use either of the services mentioned in paragraphs (c) and (d), the matters specified in section 238B].

(7) In determining whether an employer has taken those steps no regard shall be had to the merits of the dispute.

[(7A) For the purposes of this section "the protected period", in relation to the dismissal of an employee, is the sum of the basic period and any extension period in relation to that employee.

(7B) The basic period is twelve weeks beginning with the first day of protected industrial action.

(7C) An extension period in relation to an employee is a period equal to the number of days falling on or after the first day of protected industrial action (but before the protected period ends) during the whole or any part of which the employee is locked out by his employer.

(7D) In subsections (7B) and (7C), the "first day of protected industrial action" means the day on which the employee starts to take protected industrial action (even if on that day he is locked out by his employer).]

(8) For the purposes of this section no account shall be taken of the repudiation of any act by a trade union as mentioned in section 21 in relation to anything which occurs before the end of the next working day (within the meaning of section 237) after the day on which the repudiation takes place.

[(9) In this section "date of dismissal" has the meaning given by section 238(5).]]

[736]

NOTES

Inserted by the Employment Relations Act 1999, s 16, Sch 5, paras 1, 3.

Sub-ss (3)–(5): words in square brackets substituted by the Employment Relations Act 2004, ss 26(1), (2), 27(1)–(4), as from 6 April 2005, except in relation to protected industrial action taken by an employee where the employee started to take the action before that date (see SI 2005/872, art 11).

Sub-s (6): para (e) inserted by the Employment Relations Act 2004, s 28(1), as from 6 April 2005 (subject to the same exception in SI 2005/872, art 11 as noted above).

Sub-ss (7A)–(7D), (9): inserted and added respectively by the Employment Relations Act 2004, ss 26(1), (3), 27(1), (5), as from 6 April 2005 (subject to the same exception in SI 2005/872, art 11 as noted above).

[238B Conciliation and mediation: supplementary provisions

(1) The matters referred to in subsection (6)(e) of section 238A are those specified in subsections (2) to (5); and references in this section to "the service provider" are to any person who provided a service mentioned in subsection (6)(c) or (d) of that section.

(2) The first matter is: whether, at meetings arranged by the service provider, the employer or, as the case may be, a union was represented by an appropriate person.

(3) The second matter is: whether the employer or a union, so far as requested to do so, co-operated in the making of arrangements for meetings to be held with the service provider.

(4) The third matter is: whether the employer or a union fulfilled any commitment given by it during the provision of the service to take particular action.

(5) The fourth matter is: whether, at meetings arranged by the service provider between the parties making use of the service, the representatives of the employer or a union answered any reasonable question put to them concerning the matter subject to conciliation or mediation.

(6) For the purposes of subsection (2) an "appropriate person" is—

(a) in relation to the employer—

(i) a person with the authority to settle the matter subject to conciliation or mediation on behalf of the employer, or

(ii) a person authorised by a person of that type to make recommendations to him with regard to the settlement of that matter, and

(b) in relation to a union, a person who is responsible for handling on the union's behalf the matter subject to conciliation or mediation.

(7) For the purposes of subsection (4) regard may be had to any timetable which was agreed for the taking of the action in question or, if no timetable was agreed, to how long it was before the action was taken.

(8) In any proceedings in which regard must be had to the matters referred to in section 238A(6)(e)—

(a) notes taken by or on behalf of the service provider shall not be admissible in evidence;

(b) the service provider must refuse to give evidence as to anything communicated to him in connection with the performance of his functions as a conciliator or mediator if, in his opinion, to give the evidence would involve his making a damaging disclosure; and

(c) the service provider may refuse to give evidence as to whether, for the purposes of subsection (5), a particular question was or was not a reasonable one.

(9) For the purposes of subsection (8)(b) a "damaging disclosure" is—

(a) a disclosure of information which is commercially sensitive, or

(b) a disclosure of information that has not previously been disclosed which relates to a position taken by a party using the conciliation or mediation service on the settlement of the matter subject to conciliation or mediation,

to which the person who communicated the information to the service provider has not consented.]

[736A]

NOTES

Commencement: 6 April 2005.

Inserted by the Employment Relations Act 2004, s 28(2), as from 6 April 2005, except in relation to protected industrial action taken by an employee where the employee started to take the action before that date (see SI 2005/872, art 11).

239 Supplementary provisions relating to unfair dismissal

(1) [Sections 237 to 238A] (loss of unfair dismissal protection in connection with industrial action) shall be construed as one with [Part X of the Employment Rights Act 1996][; but sections 108 and 109 of that Act (qualifying period and age limit) shall not apply in relation to section 238A of this Act].

(2) In relation to a complaint to which section 238 [or 238A] applies, [section 111(2)] of that Act (time limit for complaint) does not apply, but an [employment tribunal] shall not consider the complaint unless it is presented to the tribunal—

(a) before the end of the period of six months beginning with the date of the complainant's dismissal (as defined by section 238(5)), or

(b) where the tribunal is satisfied that it was not reasonably practicable for the complaint to be presented before the end of that period, within such further period as the tribunal considers reasonable.

(3) Where it is shown that the condition referred to in section 238(2)(b) is fulfilled (discriminatory re-engagement), the references in—

(a) [sections 98 to 106 of the Employment Rights Act 1996], and

(b) sections 152 and 153 of this Act,

to the reason or principal reason for which the complainant was dismissed shall be read as references to the reason or principal reason he has not been offered re-engagement.

[(4) In relation to a complaint under section 111 of the 1996 Act (unfair dismissal: complaint to employment tribunal) that a dismissal was unfair by virtue of section 238A of this Act—

(a) no order shall be made under section 113 of the 1996 Act (reinstatement or re-engagement) until after the conclusion of protected industrial action by any employee in relation to the relevant dispute,

(b) regulations under section 7 of the Employment Tribunals Act 1996 may make provision about the adjournment and renewal of applications (including provision requiring adjournment in specified circumstances), and

(c) regulations under section 9 of that Act may require a pre-hearing review to be carried out in specified circumstances.]

[737]

NOTES

Sub-s (1): words in first pair of square brackets substituted, and words in third pair of square brackets added, by the Employment Relations Act 1999, s 16, Sch 5, paras 1, 4(1)–(3); words in second pair of square brackets substituted by the Employment Rights Act 1996, s 240, Sch 1, para 56(1), (16).

Sub-s (2): words in first pair of square brackets inserted by the Employment Relations Act 1999, s 16, Sch 5, paras 1, 4(1), (4); words in second pair of square brackets substituted by the Employment Rights Act 1996, s 240, Sch 1, para 56(1), (16); words in final pair of square brackets substituted by the Employment Rights (Dispute Resolution) Act 1998, s 1(2)(a).

Sub-s (3): words in square brackets substituted by the Employment Rights Act 1996, s 240, Sch 1, para 56(1), (16).

Sub-s (4): added by the Employment Relations Act 1999, s 16, Sch 5, paras 1, 4(1), (5).

Criminal offences

240 Breach of contract involving injury to persons or property

(1) A person commits an offence who wilfully and maliciously breaks a contract of service or hiring, knowing or having reasonable cause to believe that the probable consequences of his so doing, either alone or in combination with others, will be—

(a) to endanger human life or cause serious bodily injury, or

(b) to expose valuable property, whether real or personal, to destruction or serious injury.

(2) Subsection (1) applies equally whether the offence is committed from malice conceived against the person endangered or injured or, as the case may be, the owner of the property destroyed or injured, or otherwise.

(3) A person guilty of an offence under this section is liable on summary conviction *to imprisonment for a term not exceeding three months or* to a fine not exceeding level 2 on the standard scale *or both.*

(4) This section does not apply to seamen.

[738]

NOTES

Sub-s (3): words in italics repealed by the Criminal Justice Act 2003, s 332, Sch 37, Pt 9, in relation to England and Wales, as from a day to be appointed.

By virtue of the Criminal Justice Act 2003, s 280(1), Sch 25, para 95, a summary offence under this section is not punishable with imprisonment.

241 Intimidation or annoyance by violence or otherwise

(1) A person commits an offence who, with a view to compelling another person to abstain from doing or to do any act which that person has a legal right to do or abstain from doing, wrongfully and without legal authority—

(a) uses violence to or intimidates that person or his [spouse or civil partner] or children, or injures his property,

(b) persistently follows that person about from place to place,
(c) hides any tools, clothes or other property owned or used by that person, or deprives him of or hinders him in the use thereof,
(d) watches or besets the house or other place where that person resides, works, carries on business or happens to be, or the approach to any such house or place, or
(e) follows that person with two or more other persons in a disorderly manner in or through any street or road.

(2) A person guilty of an offence under this section is liable on summary conviction to imprisonment for a term not exceeding six months or a fine not exceeding level 5 on the standard scale, or both.

(3) …

[739]

NOTES

Sub-s (1): words in square brackets substituted by the Civil Partnership Act 2004, s 261(1), Sch 27, para 145, as from 5 December 2005.

Sub-s (3): repealed by the Serious Organised Crime and Police Act 2005, ss 111, 174(2), Sch 7, Pt 1, para 30, Sch 17, Pt 2, as from 1 January 2006.

242 Restriction of offence of conspiracy: England and Wales

(1) Where in pursuance of any such agreement as is mentioned in section 1(1) of the Criminal Law Act 1977 (which provides for the offence of conspiracy) the acts in question in relation to an offence are to be done in contemplation or furtherance of a trade dispute, the offence shall be disregarded for the purposes of that subsection if it is a summary offence which is not punishable with imprisonment.

(2) This section extends to England and Wales only.

[740]

243 Restriction of offence of conspiracy: Scotland

(1) An agreement or combination by two or more persons to do or procure to be done an act in contemplation or furtherance of a trade dispute is not indictable as a conspiracy if that act committed by one person would not be punishable as a crime.

(2) A crime for this purpose means an offence punishable on indictment, or an offence punishable on summary conviction, and for the commission of which the offender is liable under the statute making the offence punishable to be imprisoned either absolutely or at the discretion of the court as an alternative for some other punishment.

(3) Where a person is convicted of any such agreement or combination as is mentioned above to do or procure to be done an act which is punishable only on summary conviction, and is sentenced to imprisonment, the imprisonment shall not exceed three months or such longer time as may be prescribed by the statute for the punishment of the act when committed by one person.

(4) Nothing in this section—
(a) exempts from punishment a person guilty of a conspiracy for which a punishment is awarded by an Act of Parliament, or
(b) affects the law relating to riot, unlawful assembly, breach of the peace, or sedition or any offence against the State or the Sovereign.

(5) This section extends to Scotland only.

[741]

Supplementary

244 Meaning of "trade dispute" in Part V

(1) In this Part a "trade dispute" means a dispute between workers and their employer which relates wholly or mainly to one or more of the following—
(a) terms and conditions of employment, or the physical conditions in which any workers are required to work;

(b) engagement or non-engagement, or termination or suspension of employment or the duties of employment, of one or more workers;
(c) allocation of work or the duties of employment between workers or groups of workers;
(d) matters of discipline;
(e) a worker's membership or non-membership of a trade union;
(f) facilities for officials of trade unions; and
(g) machinery for negotiation or consultation, and other procedures, relating to any of the above matters, including the recognition by employers or employers' associations of the right of a trade union to represent workers in such negotiation or consultation or in the carrying out of such procedures.

(2) A dispute between a Minister of the Crown and any workers shall, notwithstanding that he is not the employer of those workers, be treated as a dispute between those workers and their employer if the dispute relates to matters which—
(a) have been referred for consideration by a joint body on which, by virtue of provision made by or under any enactment, he is represented, or
(b) cannot be settled without him exercising a power conferred on him by or under an enactment.

(3) There is a trade dispute even though it relates to matters occurring outside the United Kingdom, so long as the person or persons whose actions in the United Kingdom are said to be in contemplation or furtherance of a trade dispute relating to matters occurring outside the United Kingdom are likely to be affected in respect of one or more of the matters specified in subsection (1) by the outcome of the dispute.

(4) An act, threat or demand done or made by one person or organisation against another which, if resisted, would have led to a trade dispute with that other, shall be treated as being done or made in contemplation of a trade dispute with that other, notwithstanding that because that other submits to the act or threat or accedes to the demand no dispute arises.

(5) In this section—
"employment" includes any relationship whereby one person personally does work or performs services for another; and
"worker", in relation to a dispute with an employer, means—
(a) a worker employed by that employer; or
(b) a person who has ceased to be so employed if his employment was terminated in connection with the dispute or if the termination of his employment was one of the circumstances giving rise to the dispute.

[742]

245 Crown employees and contracts

Where a person holds any office or employment under the Crown on terms which do not constitute a contract of employment between that person and the Crown, those terms shall nevertheless be deemed to constitute such a contract for the purposes of—
(a) the law relating to liability in tort of a person who commits an act which—
(i) induces another person to break a contract, interferes with the performance of a contract or induces another person to interfere with its performance, or
(ii) consists in a threat that a contract will be broken or its performance interfered with, or that any person will be induced to break a contract or interfere with its performance, and
(b) the provisions of this or any other Act which refer (whether in relation to contracts generally or only in relation to contracts of employment) to such an act.

[743]

246 Minor definitions

In this Part—
"date of the ballot" means, in the case of a ballot in which votes may be cast on more than one day, the last of those days;
…
"strike" means [(except for the purposes of section 229(2))] any concerted stoppage of work;
"working hours", in relation to a person, means any time when under his contract of employment, or other contract personally to do work or perform services, he is required to be at work.

[744]

NOTES

Definition "place of work" repealed by the Trade Union Reform and Employment Rights Act 1993, ss 49(1), 51, Sch 7, para 26, Sch 10; words in square brackets in definition "strike" inserted by the Employment Relations Act 1999, s 4, Sch 3, paras 1, 6(4).

PART VI
ADMINISTRATIVE PROVISIONS
ACAS

247 ACAS

(1) There shall continue to be a body called the Advisory, Conciliation and Arbitration Service (referred to in this Act as "ACAS").

(2) ACAS is a body corporate of which the corporators are the members of its Council.

(3) Its functions, and those of its officers and servants, shall be performed on behalf of the Crown, but not so as to make it subject to directions of any kind from any Minister of the Crown as to the manner in which it is to exercise its functions under any enactment.

(4) For the purposes of civil proceedings arising out of those functions the Crown Proceedings Act 1947 applies to ACAS as if it were a government department and the Crown Suits (Scotland) Act 1857 applies to it as if it were a public department.

(5) Nothing in section 9 of the Statistics of Trade Act 1947 (restriction on disclosure of information obtained under that Act) shall prevent or penalise the disclosure to ACAS, for the purposes of the exercise of any of its functions, of information obtained under that Act by a government department.

(6) ACAS shall maintain offices in such of the major centres of employment in Great Britain as it thinks fit for the purposes of discharging its functions under any enactment.

[745]

248 The Council of ACAS

(1) ACAS shall be directed by a Council which, subject to the following provisions, shall consist of a chairman and nine ordinary members appointed by the Secretary of State.

(2) Before appointing those ordinary members of the Council, the Secretary of State shall—

(a) as to three of them, consult such organisations representing employers as he considers appropriate, and

(b) as to three of them, consult such organisations representing workers as he considers appropriate.

(3) The Secretary of State may, if he thinks fit, appoint a further two ordinary members of the Council (who shall be appointed so as to take office at the same time); and before making those appointments he shall—

(a) as to one of them, consult such organisations representing employers as he considers appropriate, and

(b) as to one of them, consult such organisations representing workers as he considers appropriate.

(4) The Secretary of State may appoint up to three deputy chairman who may be appointed from the ordinary members, or in addition to those members.

(5) The Council shall determine its own procedure, including the quorum necessary for its meetings.

(6) If the Secretary of State has not appointed a deputy chairman, the Council may choose a member to act as chairman in the absence or incapacity of the chairman.

(7) The validity of proceedings of the Council is not affected by any vacancy among the members of the Council or by any defect in the appointment of any of them.

[746]

249 Terms of appointment of members of Council

(1) The members of the Council shall hold and vacate office in accordance with their terms of appointment, subject to the following provisions.

(2) …

Appointment as [chairman, or as] deputy chairman, or as an ordinary member of the Council, may be a full-time or part-time appointment; and the Secretary of State may, with the consent of the member concerned, vary the terms of his appointment as to whether his appointment is full-time or part-time.

(3) A person shall not be appointed to the Council for a term exceeding five years, but previous membership does not affect eligibility for re-appointment.

(4) A member may at any time resign his membership, and the chairman or a deputy chairman may at any time resign his office as such, by notice in writing to the Secretary of State.

A deputy chairman appointed in addition to the ordinary members of the Council shall on resigning his office as deputy chairman cease to be a member of the Council.

(5) If the Secretary of State is satisfied that a member—
- (a) has been absent from meetings of the Council for a period longer than six consecutive months without the permission of the Council, or
- (b) has become bankrupt or made an arrangement with his creditors (or, in Scotland, has had his estate sequestrated or has made a trust deed for his creditors or has made and had accepted a composition contract), or
- (c) is incapacitated by physical or mental illness, or
- (d) is otherwise unable or unfit to discharge the functions of a member,

the Secretary of State may declare his office as a member to be vacant and shall notify the declaration in such manner as he thinks fit, whereupon the office shall become vacant.

If the chairman or a deputy chairman ceases to be a member of the Council, he shall also cease to be chairman or, as the case may be, a deputy chairman.

[747]

NOTES

Sub-s (2): words omitted repealed, and words in square brackets inserted, by the Trade Union Reform and Employment Rights Act 1993, ss 43(3), 51, Sch 10.

---

250 Remuneration, &c of members of Council

(1) ACAS shall pay to the members of its Council such remuneration and travelling and other allowances as may be determined by the Secretary of State.

(2) The Secretary of State may pay, or make provision for payment, to or in respect of a member of the Council such pension, allowance or gratuity on death or retirement as he may determine.

(3) Where a person ceases to be the holder of the Council otherwise than on the expiry of his term of office and it appears to the Secretary of State that there are special circumstances which make it right for him to receive compensation, he may make him a payment of such amount he may determine.

(4) The approval of the Treasury is required for any determination by the Secretary of State under this section.

[748]

NOTES

Transfer of Functions: by the Transfer of Functions (Treasury and Minister for the Civil Service) Order 1995, SI 1995/269, arts 3, 5(2), Schedule, para 21, the function of the Treasury under this section was transferred to the Minister for the Civil Service, and accordingly the reference to the Treasury in sub-s (4) above is to be read as if it were a reference to the Minister for the Civil Service.

---

251 Secretary, officers and staff of ACAS

(1) ACAS may, with the approval of the Secretary of State, appoint a secretary.

The consent of the Secretary of State is required as to his terms and conditions of service.

(2) ACAS may appoint such other officers and staff as it may determine.

The consent of the Secretary of State is required as to their numbers, manner of appointment and terms and conditions of service.

(3) The Secretary of State shall not give his consent under subsection (1) or (2) without the approval of the Treasury.

(4) ACAS shall pay to the Treasury, at such times in each accounting year as may be determined by the Treasury, sums of such amounts as may be so determined as being equivalent to the increase in that year of such liabilities of his as are attributable to the provision of pensions, allowances or gratuities to or in respect of persons who are or have been in the service of ACAS in so far as that increase results from the service of those persons during that accounting year and to the expense to be incurred in administering those pensions, allowances or gratuities.

(5) The fixing of the common seal of ACAS shall be authenticated by the signature of the secretary of ACAS or some other person authorised by ACAS to act for that purpose.

A document purporting to be duly executed under the seal of ACAS shall be received in evidence and shall, unless the contrary is proved, be deemed to be so executed.

[749]

[251A Fees for exercise of functions by ACAS

(1) ACAS may, in any case in which it thinks it appropriate to do so, but subject to any directions under subsection (2) below, charge a fee for exercising a function in relation to any person.

(2) The Secretary of State may direct ACAS to charge fees, in accordance with the direction, for exercising any function specified in the direction, but the Secretary of State shall not give a direction under this subsection without consulting ACAS.

(3) A direction under subsection (2) above may require ACAS to charge fees in respect of the exercise of a function only in specified descriptions of case.

(4) A direction under subsection (2) above shall specify whether fees are to be charged in respect of the exercise of any specified function—

(a) at the full economic cost level, or
(b) at a level less than the full economic cost but not less than a specified proportion or percentage of the full economic cost.

(5) Where a direction requires fees to be charged at the full economic cost level ACAS shall fix the fee for the case at an amount estimated to be sufficient to cover the administrative costs of ACAS of exercising the function including an appropriate sum in respect of general staff costs and overheads.

(6) Where a direction requires fees to be charged at a level less than the full economic cost ACAS shall fix the fee for the case at such amount, not being less than the proportion or percentage of the full economic cost specified under subsection (4)(b) above, as it thinks appropriate (computing that cost in the same way as under subsection (5) above).

(7) No liability to pay a fee charged under this section shall arise on the part of any person unless ACAS has notified that person that a fee may or will be charged.

(8) For the purposes of this section—

(a) a function is exercised "in relation to" a person who avails himself of the benefit of its exercise, whether or not he requested its exercise and whether the function is such as to be exercisable in relation to particular persons only or in relation to persons generally; and
(b) where a function is exercised in relation to two or more persons the fee chargeable for its exercise shall be apportioned among them as ACAS thinks appropriate.]

[750]

NOTES

Inserted by the Trade Union Reform and Employment Rights Act 1993, s 44.

252 General financial provisions

(1) The Secretary of State shall pay to ACAS such sums as are approved by the Treasury and as he considers appropriate for the purpose of enabling ACAS to perform its functions.

(2) ACAS may pay to—

(a) persons appointed under section 210(2) (conciliation) who are not officers or servants of ACAS, and

(b) arbitrators or arbiters appointed by ACAS under any enactment,

such fees and travelling and other allowances as may be determined by the Secretary of State with the approval of the Treasury.

[751]

253 Annual report and accounts

(1) ACAS shall as soon as practicable after the end of each [financial year] make a report to the Secretary of State on its activities during that year.

The Secretary of State shall lay a copy of the report before each House of Parliament and arrange for it to be published.

(2) ACAS shall keep proper accounts and proper records in relation to the accounts and shall prepare in respect of each financial year a statement of accounts, in such form as the Secretary of State may, with the approval of the Treasury, direct.

(3) ACAS shall not later than 30th November following the end of the financial year to which the statement relates, send copies of the statement to the Secretary of State and to the Comptroller and Auditor General.

(4) The Comptroller and Auditor General shall examine, certify and report on each such statement and shall lay a copy of the statement and of his report before each House of Parliament.

[752]

NOTES

Sub-s (1): words in square brackets substituted by the Employment Relations Act 1999, s 27(1).

The Certification Officer

254 The Certification Officer

(1) There shall continue to be an officer called the Certification Officer.

(2) The Certification Officer shall be appointed by the Secretary of State after consultation with ACAS.

(3) The Certification Officer may appoint one or more assistant certification officers and shall appoint an assistant certification officer for Scotland.

(4) The Certification Officer may delegate to an assistant certification officer such functions as he thinks appropriate, and in particular may delegate to the assistant certification officer for Scotland such functions as he thinks appropriate in relation to organisations whose principal office is in Scotland.

References to the Certification Officer in enactments relating to his functions shall be construed accordingly.

(5) ACAS shall provide for the Certification Officer the requisite staff (from among the officers and servants of ACAS) and the requisite accommodation, equipment and other facilities.

[(5A) Subject to subsection (6), ACAS shall pay to the Certification Officer such sums as he may require for the performance of any of his functions.]

(6) The Secretary of State shall pay to the Certification Officer such sums as he may require for making payments under the scheme under section 115 (payments towards expenditure in connection with secret ballots).

[753]

NOTES

Sub-s (5A): inserted by the Trade Union Reform and Employment Rights Act 1993, s 49(2), Sch 8, para 78.

255 Remuneration, &c of Certification Officer and assistants

(1) ACAS shall pay to the Certification Officer and any assistant certification officer such remuneration and travelling and other allowances as may be determined by the Secretary of State.

(2) The Secretary of State may pay, or make provision for payment, to or in respect of the Certification Officer and any assistant certification officer such pension, allowance or gratuity on death or retirement as he may determine.

(3) Where a person ceases to be the Certification Officer or an assistant certification officer otherwise than on the expiry of his term of office and it appears to the Secretary of State that there are special circumstances which make it right for him to receive compensation, he may make him a payment of such amount as he may determine.

(4) The approval of the Treasury is required for any determination by the Secretary of State under this section.

[754]

256 Procedure before the Certification Officer

(1) Except in relation to matters as to which express provision is made by or under an enactment, the Certification Officer may regulate the procedure to be followed—

(a) on any application or complaint made to him, or

(b) where his approval is sought with respect to any matter.

[(2) He shall in particular make provision about the disclosure, and restriction of the disclosure, of the identity of an individual who has made or is proposing to make any such application or complaint.

(2A) Provision under subsection (2) shall be such that if the application or complaint relates to a trade union—

(a) the individual's identity is disclosed to the union unless the Certification Officer thinks the circumstances are such that it should not be so disclosed;

(b) the individual's identity is disclosed to such other persons (if any) as the Certification Officer thinks fit.]

(3) The Secretary of State may, with the consent of the Treasury, make a scheme providing for the payment by the Certification Officer to persons of such sums as may be specified in or determined under the scheme in respect of expenses incurred by them for the purposes of, or in connection with, their attendance at hearings held by him in the course of carrying out his functions.

(4) …

[755]

NOTES

Sub-ss (2), (2A): substituted, for original sub-s (2), by the Employment Relations Act 1999, s 29, Sch 6, paras 1, 22.

Sub-s (4): repealed by the Trade Union Reform and Employment Rights Act 1993, s 51, Sch 10.

[256ZA Striking out

(1) At any stage of proceedings on an application or complaint made to the Certification Officer, he may—

(a) order the application or complaint, or any response, to be struck out on the grounds that it is scandalous, vexatious, has no reasonable prospect of success or is otherwise misconceived,

(b) order anything in the application or complaint, or in any response, to be amended or struck out on those grounds, or

(c) order the application or complaint, or any response, to be struck out on the grounds that the manner in which the proceedings have been conducted by or on behalf of the applicant or complainant or (as the case may be) respondent has been scandalous, vexatious, or unreasonable.

(2) The Certification Officer may order an application or complaint made to him to be struck out for excessive delay in proceeding with it.

(3) An order under this section may be made on the Certification Officer's own initiative and may also be made—

(a) if the order sought is to strike out an application or complaint, or to amend or strike out anything in an application or complaint, on an application by the respondent, or

(b) if the order sought is to strike out any response, or to amend or strike out anything in any response, on an application by the person who made the application or complaint mentioned in subsection (1).

(4) Before making an order under this section, the Certification Officer shall send notice to the party against whom it is proposed that the order should be made giving him an opportunity to show cause why the order should not be made.

(5) Subsection (4) shall not be taken to require the Certification Officer to send a notice under that subsection if the party against whom it is proposed that the order under this section should be made has been given an opportunity to show cause orally why the order should not be made.

(6) Nothing in this section prevents the Certification Officer from making further provision under section 256(1) about the striking out of proceedings on any application or complaint made to him.

(7) An appeal lies to the Employment Appeal Tribunal on any question of law arising from a decision of the Certification Officer under this section.

(8) In this section—

"response" means any response made by a trade union or other body in the exercise of a right to be heard, or to make representations, in response to the application or complaint;

"respondent" means any trade union, or other body, that has such a right.]

[755A]

NOTES

Commencement: 6 April 2005.

Inserted by the Employment Relations Act 2004, s 48, as from 6 April 2005, except in relation to any application or complaint which was made to the Certification Officer before that date (see SI 2005/872, art 16).

[256A Vexatious litigants

(1) The Certification Officer may refuse to entertain any application or complaint made to him under a provision of Chapters III to VIIA of Part I by a vexatious litigant.

(2) The Certification Officer must give reasons for such a refusal.

(3) Subsection (1) does not apply to a complaint under section 37E(1)(b) or to an application under section 41.

(4) For the purposes of subsection (1) a vexatious litigant is a person who is the subject of—

(a) …

(b) a civil proceedings order or an all proceedings order which is made under section 42(1) of the *Supreme Court Act 1981* and which remains in force,

(c) an order which is made under section 1 of the Vexatious Actions (Scotland) Act 1898, or

(d) an order which is made under section 32 of the Judicature (Northern Ireland) Act 1978.]

[756]

NOTES

Inserted by the Employment Relations Act 1999, s 29, Sch 6, paras 1, 23.

Sub-s (4): para (a) repealed by the Employment Relations Act 2004, ss 49(1), (9), 57(2), Sch 2, as from 6 April 2005; for the words in italics in para (b) there are substituted the words "Senior Courts Act 1981" by the Constitutional Reform Act 2005, s 59(5), Sch 11, Pt 1, para 1(2), as from a day to be appointed.

[256B Vexatious litigants: applications disregarded

(1) For the purposes of a relevant enactment an application to the Certification Officer shall be disregarded if—

(a) it was made under a provision mentioned in the relevant enactment, and

(b) it was refused by the Certification Officer under section 256A(1).

(2) The relevant enactments are sections 26(8), 31(7), 45C(5B), 56(8), 72A(10), 81(8) and 108A(13).]

[757]

NOTES

Inserted by the Employment Relations Act 1999, s 29, Sch 6, paras 1, 23.

257 Custody of documents submitted under earlier legislation

(1) The Certification Officer shall continue to have custody of the annual returns, accounts, copies of rules and other documents submitted for the purposes of—

(a) the Trade Union Acts 1871 to 1964,

(b) the Industrial Relations Act 1971, or

(c) the Trade Union and Labour Relations Act 1974,

of which he took custody under section 9 of the Employment Protection Act 1975.

(2) He shall keep available for public inspection (either free of charge or on payment of a reasonable charge) at all reasonable hours such of those documents as were available for public inspection in pursuance of any of those Acts.

[758]

NOTES

Trade Union Acts 1871 to 1964: the Acts which were cited together under this collective title were: the Trade Union Act 1871 (repealed); the Trade Union Act Amendment Act 1876 (repealed); the Trade Disputes Act 1906 (repealed); the Trade Union Act 1913 (repealed, with a saving, by this Act); the Trade Union (Amalgamation) Act 1917 (repealed); the Trade Disputes and Trade Unions Act 1927 (repealed); the Societies (Miscellaneous Provisions) Act 1940, s 6 (repealed); and the Trade Union (Amalgamations, etc) Act 1964 (repealed by this Act).

Industrial Relations Act 1971: repealed by the Trade Union and Labour Relations Act 1974, ss 1, 25(3), Sch 5.

Trade Union and Labour Relations Act 1974; Employment Protection Act 1975, s 9: repealed by this Act.

258 Annual report and accounts

(1) The Certification Officer shall, as soon as practicable after the end of each [financial year], make a report of his activities during that year to ACAS and to the Secretary of State.

The Secretary of State shall lay a copy of the report before each House of Parliament and arrange for it to be published.

(2) The accounts prepared by ACAS in respect of any financial year shall show separately any sums disbursed to or on behalf of the Certification Officer in consequence of the provisions of this Part.

[759]

NOTES

Sub-s (1): words in square brackets substituted by the Employment Relations Act 1999, s 29, Sch 6, paras 1, 24.

Central Arbitration Committee

259 The Central Arbitration Committee

(1) There shall continue to be a body called the Central Arbitration Committee.

(2) The functions of the Committee shall be performed on behalf of the Crown, but not so as to make it subject to directions of any kind from any Minister of the Crown as to the manner in which it is to exercise its functions.

(3) ACAS shall provide for the Committee the requisite staff (from among the officers and servants of ACAS) and the requisite accommodation, equipment and other facilities.

[760]

260 The members of the Committee

[(1) The Central Arbitration Committee shall consist of members appointed by the Secretary of State.

(2) The Secretary of State shall appoint a member as chairman, and may appoint a member as deputy chairman or members as deputy chairmen.

(3) The Secretary of State may appoint as members only persons experienced in industrial relations, and they shall include some persons whose experience is as representatives of employers and some whose experience is as representatives of workers.

(3A) Before making an appointment under subsection (1) or (2) the Secretary of State shall consult ACAS and may consult other persons.]

(4) At any time when the chairman of the Committee is absent or otherwise incapable of acting, or there is a vacancy in the office of chairman, and the Committee has a deputy chairman or deputy chairmen—

(a) the deputy chairman, if there is only one, or

(b) if there is more than one, such of the deputy chairmen as they may agree or in default of agreement as the Secretary of State may direct,

may perform any of the functions of chairman of the Committee.

(5) At any time when every person who is chairman or deputy chairman is absent or otherwise incapable of acting, or there is no such person, such member of the Committee as the Secretary of State may direct may perform any of the functions of the chairman of the Committee.

(6) The validity of any proceedings of the Committee shall not be affected by any vacancy among the members of the Committee or by any defect in the appointment of a member of the Committee.

[761]

NOTES

Sub-ss (1)–(3A): substituted, for original sub-ss (1)–(3), by the Employment Relations Act 1999, s 24.

261 Terms of appointment of members of Committee

(1) The members of the Central Arbitration Committee shall hold and vacate office in accordance with their terms of appointment, subject to the following provisions.

(2) A person shall not be appointed to the Committee for a term exceeding five years, but previous membership does not affect eligibility for re-appointment.

(3) The Secretary of State may, with the consent of the member concerned, vary the terms of his appointment as to whether he is a full-time or part-time member.

(4) A member may at any time resign his membership, and the chairman or a deputy chairman may at any time resign his office as such, by notice in writing to the Secretary of State.

(5) If the Secretary of State is satisfied that a member—

(a) has become bankrupt or made an arrangement with his creditors (or, in Scotland, has had his estate sequestrated or has made a trust deed for his creditors or has made and had accepted a composition contract), or

(b) is incapacitated by physical or mental illness, or

(c) is otherwise unable or unfit to discharge the functions of a member,

the Secretary of State may declare his office as a member to be vacant and shall notify the declaration in such manner as he thinks fit, whereupon the office shall become vacant.

(6) If the chairman or a deputy chairman ceases to be a member of the Committee, he shall also cease to be chairman or, as the case may be, a deputy chairman.

[762]

262 Remuneration, &c of members of Committee

(1) ACAS shall pay to the members of the Central Arbitration Committee such remuneration and travelling and other allowances as may be determined by the Secretary of State.

(2) The Secretary of State may pay, or make provision for payment, to or in respect of a member of the Committee such pension, allowance or gratuity on death or retirement as he may determine.

(3) Where a person ceases to be the holder of the Committee otherwise than on the expiry of his term of office and it appears to the Secretary of State that there are special circumstances which make it right for him to receive compensation, he may make him a payment of such amount he may determine.

(4) The approval of the Treasury is required for any determination by the Secretary of State under this section.

[763]

263 Proceedings of the Committee

(1) For the purpose of discharging its functions in any particular case the Central Arbitration Committee shall consist of the chairman and such other members as the chairman may direct:

Provided that, it may sit in two or more divisions constituted of such members as the chairman may direct, and in a division in which the chairman does not sit the functions of the chairman shall be performed by a deputy chairman.

(2) The Committee may, at the discretion of the chairman, where it appears expedient to do so, call in the aid of one or more assessors, and may settle the matter wholly or partly with their assistance.

(3) The Committee may at the discretion of the chairman sit in private where it appears expedient to do so.

(4) If in any case the Committee cannot reach a unanimous decision on its award, the chairman shall decide the matter acting with the full powers of an umpire or, in Scotland, an oversman.

(5) Subject to the above provisions, the Committee shall determine its own procedure.

(6) [Part I of the Arbitration Act 1996] (general provisions as to arbitration) and section 3 of the Administration of Justice (Scotland) Act 1972 (power of arbiter to state case to Court of Session) do not apply to proceedings before the Committee.

[(7) In relation to the discharge of the Committee's functions under Schedule A1—

(a) section 263A and subsection (6) above shall apply, and

(b) subsections (1) to (5) above shall not apply.]

[764]

NOTES

Sub-s (6): words in square brackets substituted by the Arbitration Act 1996, s 107(1), Sch 3, para 6.
Sub-s (7): added by the Employment Relations Act 1999, s 25(1), (2).

[263A Proceedings of the Committee under Schedule A1

(1) For the purpose of discharging its functions under Schedule A1 in any particular case, the Central Arbitration Committee shall consist of a panel established under this section.

(2) The chairman of the Committee shall establish a panel or panels, and a panel shall consist of these three persons appointed by him—

(a) the chairman or a deputy chairman of the Committee, who shall be chairman of the panel;

(b) a member of the Committee whose experience is as a representative of employers;

(c) a member of the Committee whose experience is as a representative of workers.

(3) The chairman of the Committee shall decide which panel is to deal with a particular case.

(4) A panel may at the discretion of its chairman sit in private where it appears expedient to do so.

(5) If—

(a) a panel cannot reach a unanimous decision on a question arising before it, and

(b) a majority of the panel have the same opinion,

the question shall be decided according to that opinion.

(6) If—

(a) a panel cannot reach a unanimous decision on a question arising before it, and

(b) a majority of the panel do not have the same opinion,

the chairman of the panel shall decide the question acting with the full powers of an umpire or, in Scotland, an oversman.

(7) Subject to the above provisions, a panel shall determine its own procedure.

[(8) The reference in subsection (1) to the Committee's functions under Schedule A1 does not include a reference to its functions under paragraph 166 of that Schedule.]]

[765]

NOTES

Inserted by the Employment Relations Act 1999, s 25(1), (3).

Sub-s (8): added by the Employment Relations Act 2004, s 57(1), Sch 1, para 15, as from 6 April 2005.

264 Awards of the Committee

(1) The Central Arbitration Committee may correct in any award[, or in any decision or declaration of the Committee under Schedule A1] any clerical mistake or error arising from an accidental slip or omission.

(2) If a question arises as to the interpretation of an award of the Committee, [or of a decision or declaration of the Committee under Schedule A1] any party may apply to the Committee for a decision; and the Committee shall decide the question after hearing the parties or, if the parties consent, without a hearing, and shall notify the parties.

(3) Decisions of the Committee in the exercise of any of its functions shall be published.

[766]

NOTES

Sub-ss (1), (2): words in square brackets inserted by the Employment Relations Act 1999, s 25(1), (4).

265 Annual report and accounts

(1) ACAS shall, as soon as practicable after the end of each [financial year], make a report to the Secretary of State on the activities of the Central Arbitration Committee during that year.

For that purpose the Committee shall, as soon as practicable after the end of each [financial year], transmit to ACAS an account of its activities during that year.

(2) The accounts prepared by ACAS in respect of any financial year shall show separately any sums disbursed to or on behalf of the Committee in consequence of the provisions of this Part.

[767]

NOTES

Sub-s (1): words in square brackets substituted by the Employment Relations Act 1999, s 27(2).

266–271 (*Repealed by the Employment Relations Act 1999, ss 28(2)(c), 44, Sch 9(6).*)

Supplementary

272 Meaning of "financial year"

In this Part "financial year" means the twelve months ending with 31st March.

[768]

PART VII
MISCELLANEOUS AND GENERAL

Crown employment, etc

273 Crown employment

(1) The provisions of this Act have effect (except as mentioned below) in relation to Crown employment and persons in Crown employment as in relation to other employment and other workers or employees.

(2) The following provisions are excepted from subsection (1)—

[section 87(4)(b) (power of tribunal] to make order in respect of employer's failure to comply with duties as to union contributions);

sections 184 and 185 (remedy for failure to comply with declaration as to disclosure of information);

Chapter II of Part IV (procedure for handling redundancies).

(3) In this section "Crown employment" means employment under or for the purposes of a government department or any officer or body exercising on behalf of the Crown functions conferred by an enactment.

(4) For the purposes of the provisions of this Act as they apply in relation to Crown employment or persons in Crown employment—

(a) "employee" and "contract of employment" mean a person in Crown employment and the terms of employment of such a person (but subject to subsection (5) below);

(b) "dismissal" means the termination of Crown employment;

(c) …

(d) the reference in 182(1)(e) (disclosure of information for collective bargaining: restrictions on general duty) to the employer's undertaking shall be construed as a reference to the national interest; and

(e) any other reference to an undertaking shall be construed, in relation to a Minister of the Crown, as a reference to his functions or (as the context may require) to the department of which he is in charge, and in relation to a government department, officer or body shall be construed as a reference to the functions of the department, officer or body or (as the context may require) to the department, officer or body.

(5) Sections 137 to 143 (rights in relation to trade union membership: access to employment) apply in relation to Crown employment otherwise than under a contract only where the terms of employment correspond to those of a contract of employment.

(6) This section has effect subject to section 274 (armed forces) and section 275 (exemption on grounds of national security).

[769]

NOTES

Sub-s (2): words in square brackets substituted by the Employment Rights (Dispute Resolution) Act 1998, s 15, Sch 1, para 8.

Sub-s (4): para (c) repealed by the Trade Union Reform and Employment Rights Act 1993, s 51, Sch 10.

274 Armed forces

(1) Section 273 (application of Act to Crown employment) does not apply to service as a member of the naval, military or air forces of the Crown.

(2) But that section applies to employment by an association established for the purposes of [Part XI of the Reserve Forces Act 1996] (territorial, auxiliary and reserve forces associations) as it applies to employment for the purposes of a government department.

[770]

NOTES

Sub-s (2): words in square brackets substituted by the Reserve Forces Act 1996, s 131(1), Sch 10, para 24.

275 Exemption on grounds of national security

(1) Section 273 (application of Act to Crown employment) does not apply to employment in respect of which there is in force a certificate issued by or on behalf of a Minister of the Crown certifying that employment of a description specified in the certificate, or the employment of a particular person so specified, is (or, at a time specified in the certificate, was) required to be excepted from that section for the purpose of safeguarding national security.

(2) A document purporting to be such a certificate shall, unless the contrary is proved, be deemed to be such a certificate.

[771]

276 Further provision as to Crown application

(1) Section 138 (refusal of service of employment agency on grounds related to union membership), and the other provisions of Part III applying in relation to that section, bind the Crown so far as they relate to the activities of an employment agency in relation to employment to which those provisions apply.

This does not affect the operation of those provisions in relation to Crown employment by virtue of section 273.

(2) Sections 144 and 145 (prohibition of union membership requirements) and sections 186 and 187 (prohibition of union recognition requirements) bind the Crown.

[772]

House of Lords and House of Commons staff

277 House of Lords staff

(1) [The provisions of this Act (except those specified below)] apply in relation to employment as a relevant member of the House of Lords staff as in relation to other employment.

[(1A) The following provisions are excepted from subsection (1)—

sections 184 and 185 (remedy for failure to comply with declaration as to disclosure of information),

Chapter II of Part IV (procedure for handling redundancies).]

(2) Nothing in any rule of law or the law or practice of Parliament prevents a person from bringing [a civil employment claim before the court or from bringing] before an [employment tribunal] proceedings of any description … which could be brought before such a tribunal in relation to other employment.

[(2A) For the purposes of the application of the other provisions of this Act as they apply by virtue of this section—

(a) the reference in section 182(1)(e) (disclosure of information for collective bargaining: restrictions) to a person's undertaking shall be construed as a reference to the national interest or, if the case so requires, the interests of the House of Lords; and

(b) any other reference to an undertaking shall be construed as a reference to the House of Lords.]

[(3) In this section—

"relevant member of the House of Lords staff" means any person who is employed under a contract of employment with the Corporate Officer of the House of Lords;

"civil employment claim" means a claim arising out of or relating to a contract of employment or any other contract connected with employment, or a claim in tort arising in connection with a person's employment; and

"the court" means the High Court or a county court.]

[773]

NOTES

Sub-s (1): words in square brackets substituted by the Trade Union Reform and Employment Rights Act 1993, s 49(1), Sch 7, para 12(a).

Sub-s (1A): inserted by the Trade Union Reform and Employment Rights Act 1993, s 49(1), Sch 7, para 12(b).

Sub-s (2): words in first pair of square brackets inserted, and words omitted repealed, by the Trade Union Reform and Employment Rights Act 1993, ss 49(1), 51, Sch 7, para 12(c), Sch 10; words in second pair of square brackets substituted by the Employment Rights (Dispute Resolution) Act 1998, s 1(2)(a).

Sub-s (2A): inserted by the Trade Union Reform and Employment Rights Act 1993, s 49(1), Sch 7, para 12(d).

Sub-s (3): substituted, for original sub-ss (3)–(6), by the Trade Union Reform and Employment Rights Act 1993, s 49(1), Sch 7, para 12(e).

278 House of Commons staff

(1) The provisions of this Act (except those specified below) apply in relation to employment as a relevant member of the House of Commons staff as in relation to other employment.

(2) The following provisions are excepted from subsection (1)—

sections 184 and 185 (remedy for failure to comply with declaration as to disclosure of information),

Chapter II of Part IV (procedure for handling redundancies).

[(2A) Nothing in any rule of law or the law or practice of Parliament prevents a relevant member of the House of Commons staff from bringing a civil employment claim before the court or from bringing before an [employment tribunal] proceedings of any description which could be brought before such a tribunal by any person who is not such a member.]

(3) In this section "relevant member of the House of Commons staff" has the same meaning as in section 139 of the Employment Protection (Consolidation) Act 1978.

["civil employment claim" means a claim arising out of or relating to a contract of employment or any other contract connected with employment, or a claim in tort arising in connection with a person's employment; and

"the court" means the High Court or the county court.]

(4) For the purposes of the other provisions of this Act as they apply by virtue of this section—

(a) "employee" and "contract of employment" include a relevant member of the House of Commons staff and the terms of employment of any such member (but subject to subsection (5) below);

(b) "dismissal" includes the termination of any such member's employment;

(c) the reference in [section] 182(1)(e) (disclosure of information for collective bargaining: restrictions on general duty) to the employer's undertaking shall be construed as a reference to the national interest or, if the case so requires, the interests of the House of Commons; and

(d) any other reference to an undertaking shall be construed as a reference to the House of Commons.

(5) Sections 137 to 143 (access to employment) apply by virtue of this section in relation to employment otherwise than under a contract only where the terms of employment correspond to those of a contract of employment.

(6) [Subsections (6) to (12) of section 195 of the Employment Rights Act 1996] (person to be treated as employer of House of Commons staff) apply, with any necessary modifications, for the purposes of this section.

[774]

NOTES

Sub-s (2A): inserted by the Trade Union Reform and Employment Rights Act 1993, s 49(2), Sch 8, para 85(a); words in square brackets substituted by the Employment Rights (Dispute Resolution) Act 1998, s 1(2)(a).

Sub-s (3): definitions "civil employment claim" and "the court" inserted by the Trade Union Reform and Employment Rights Act 1993, s 49(2), Sch 8, para 85(b). See further note to sub-s (6) below.

Sub-s (4): word in square brackets in para (c) inserted by the Trade Union Reform and Employment Rights Act 1993, s 49(1), Sch 7, para 27.

Sub-s (6): words in square brackets substituted by the Employment Rights Act 1996, s 240, Sch 1, para 56(1), (17). The 1996 Act does not provide for the equivalent substitution of s 195 for the reference to s 139 of the 1978 Act in sub-s (3) of this section; this is presumably a drafting error.

Employment Protection (Consolidation) Act 1978, s 139: repealed so far as relevant by the Employment Rights Act 1996, s 242, Sch 3, Pt I; for the meaning of "relevant member of the House of Commons staff", see now s 195(5) of the 1996 Act at **[1239]**.

Health service practitioners

279 Health service practitioners

[(1)] In this Act "worker" includes an individual regarded in his capacity as one who works or normally works or seeks to work as a person [performing … personal dental services or] providing … general dental services, general ophthalmic services or pharmaceutical services in accordance with arrangements made—

(a) by a […] [Primary Care Trust [under section 126 of the National Health Service Act 2006] or] [Local Health Board] under section […] … , [71 or 80 of the National Health Service (Wales) Act 2006] of the National Health Service Act 1977, or

(b) by a Health Board under section [17C,] … , 25, *26, or 27* of the National Health Service (Scotland) Act 1978 [or as a person providing local pharmaceutical services under a pilot scheme [established under section 134 of the National Health Service Act 2006 or section 92 of the National Health Service (Wales) Act 2006, or under an LPS scheme established under Schedule 12 to the National Health Service Act 2006 or Schedule 7 to the National Health Service (Wales) Act 2006]];

and "employer", in relation to such an individual, regarded in that capacity, means that authority or board.

[(2) In this Act "worker" also includes an individual regarded in his capacity as one who works or normally works or seeks to work as a person performing primary medical services *or primary dental services*—

(a) in accordance with arrangements made by a Primary Care Trust, Strategic Health Authority or Local Health Board under [section 92 or 107 of the National Health Service Act 2006, or section 50 or 64 of the National Health Service (Wales) Act 2006]; or

(b) under a contract under [section 84 or 100 of the National Health Service Act 2006 or section 42 or 57 of the National Health Service (Wales) Act 2006] entered into by him with a Primary Care Trust or Local Health Board, [or under a contract under section 117 of the National Health Service Act 2006 entered into by him with a Primary Care Trust,]

and "employer" in relation to such an individual, regarded in that capacity, means that Trust, Authority or Board.]

[(3) In this Act "worker" also includes an individual regarded in his capacity as one who works or normally works or seeks to work as a person performing primary medical services—

(a) in accordance with arrangements made by a Health Board under section 17C of the National Health Service (Scotland) Act 1978; or

(b) under a contract under section 17J of that Act entered into by him with a Health Board,

and "employer" in relation to such an individual, regarded in that capacity, means that Health Board.]

[(4) In this Act—

(a) "worker" also includes an individual regarded in his capacity as one who works or normally works or seeks to work as a person performing pharmaceutical care services under a contract entered into by him with a Health Board under section 17Q of the National Health Service (Scotland) Act 1978; and

(b) "employer" in relation to such a person, regarded in that capacity, means that Health Board.]

[775]

NOTES

This section has been amended as follows:

Sub-s (1): numbered as such by the Health and Social Care (Community Health and Standards) Act 2003, s 184, Sch 11, para 59(1), (3), as from 1 April 2004.

Sub-s (1) (opening paragraph): words in square brackets inserted by the National Health Service (Primary Care) Act 1997, s 41(10), Sch 2, Pt I, para 67(a); words omitted repealed by the Primary Medical Services (Scotland) Act 2004 (Consequential Modifications) Order 2004, SI 2004/957, art 2, Schedule, para 7(a)(i), as from 1 April 2004.

Sub-s (1)(a): words in first pair of square brackets inserted by the National Health Service Reform and Health Care Professions Act 2002, s 4(3), Sch 3, Pt 2, para 13, and repealed by the National Health Service (Consequential Provisions) Act 2006, s 2, Sch 1, paras 153, 154(a)(i), as from 1 March 2007; words in second (outer) pair of square brackets inserted by the National Health Service Reform and

Health Care Professions Act 2002, s 2(5), Sch 2, Pt 2, para 60; words in third (inner) pair of square brackets inserted by the National Health Service (Consequential Provisions) Act 2006, s 2, Sch 1, paras 153, 154(a)(ii), as from 1 March 2007; words in fourth pair of square brackets substituted by the References to Health Authorities Order 2007, SI 2007/961, art 3, Schedule, para 22, as from 1 April 2007; reference in fifth pair of square brackets inserted by the National Health Service (Primary Care) Act 1997, s 41(10), Sch 2, Pt I, para 67(b), and repealed by the Health and Social Care (Community Health and Standards) Act 2003, ss 184, 196, Sch 11, para 59(1), (2), Sch 14, Pt 4, as from 1 April 2004; second reference omitted repealed by the Health and Social Care (Community Health and Standards) Act 2003, ss 184, 196, Sch 11, para 59(1), (2), Sch 14, Pt 4, as from 1 April 2004; final words in square brackets substituted by the National Health Service (Consequential Provisions) Act 2006, s 2, Sch 1, paras 153, 154(a)(iii), as from 1 March 2007 (it is assumed that a drafting error has occurred in this paragraph).

Sub-s (1)(b): reference in first pair of square brackets inserted by the National Health Service (Primary Care) Act 1997, s 41(10), Sch 2, Pt I, para 67(c); reference omitted repealed by the Primary Medical Services (Scotland) Act 2004 (Consequential Modifications) Order 2004, SI 2004/957, art 2, Schedule, para 7(a)(ii), as from 1 April 2004; for the words in italics there are substituted the words "or 26" by the Smoking, Health and Social Care (Scotland) Act 2005 (Consequential Modifications) (England, Wales and Northern Ireland) Order 2006, SI 2006/1056, art 2, Schedule, Pt 1, para 6(a), as from a day to be appointed; words in second (outer) pair of square brackets inserted by the Health and Social Care Act 2001, s 67(1), Sch 5, Pt I, para 9; words in third (inner) pair of square brackets substituted by the National Health Service (Consequential Provisions) Act 2006, s 2, Sch 1, paras 153, 154(b), as from 1 March 2007.

Sub-s (2): added by the Health and Social Care (Community Health and Standards) Act 2003, s 184, Sch 11, para 59(1), (4), as from 1 April 2004; for the words in italics there are substituted the words ", primary dental services or primary ophthalmic services" by the Health Act 2006, s 80(1), Sch 8, para 30(a), as from a day to be appointed; words in square brackets in para (a) and words in first pair of square brackets in para (b) substituted by the National Health Service (Consequential Provisions) Act 2006, s 2, Sch 1, paras 153, 155, as from 1 March 2007; words in second pair of square brackets in para (b) inserted by the Health Act 2006, s 80(1), Sch 8, para 30(b) (as amended by the National Health Service (Consequential Provisions) Act 2006, s 2, Sch 1, paras 281, 291), as from a day to be appointed.

Sub-s (3): added by the Primary Medical Services (Scotland) Act 2004 (Consequential Modifications) Order 2004, SI 2004/957, art 2, Schedule, para 7(b), as from 1 April 2004.

Sub-s (4): added by SI 2006/1056, art 2, Schedule, Pt 1, para 6(b), as from a day to be appointed.

Transitional provisions and miscellaneous:

Note that notwithstanding the coming into force of the amendments to the definition of worker in this section made by the Health and Social Care (Community Health and Standards) Act 2003, Sch 11, para 59, in relation to any complaint arising in respect of a matter which occurred before 1 April 2004, this section has effect as if those amendments had not been brought into force; see the General Medical Services and Personal Medical Services Transitional and Consequential Provisions Order 2004, SI 2004/865, art 112, and the General Medical Services Transitional and Consequential Provisions (Wales) (No 2) Order 2004, SI 2004/1016, art 88.

The General Medical Services and Personal Medical Services Transitional and Consequential Provisions Order 2004, SI 2004/865, art 109(1), (2)(d), and the General Medical Services Transitional and Consequential Provisions (Wales) (No 2) Order 2004, SI 2004/1016, art 85(1), (2)(d) (both made under the Health and Social Care (Community Health and Standards) Act 2003, ss 176, 195(1), 200, 201) provide that until such time as default contracts entered into pursuant s 176(3) of the 2003 Act cease to exist, any reference to a general medical services contract or to a contract under the National Health Service Act 1977, s 28Q includes a reference to a default contract.

Transitional amendments having effect until the commencement of the Health and Social Care (Community Health and Standards) Act 2003, s 172(1), in relation to general dental services contracts, are made by Orders made under ss 195(1), 199(1) of the 2003 Act. Note that s 172(1) came into force on 1 December 2005 (for certain purposes) and 1 April 2006 (for remaining purposes) in relation to England only.

Health Authorities: as to the establishment of Health Authorities in Wales, see the National Health Service Act 1977, s 8, Sch 5, Pt I. The functions of Health Authorities in Wales have been transferred to the National Assembly for Wales by Order made under the Government of Wales Act 1998, s 27, and have subsequently been transferred to Local Health Boards established by the National Health Service Act 1977, s 16BA, Sch 5B, by Order made under s 16BA(1)–(3) of that Act. As to the repeal of the 1977 Act, see the National Health Service (Consequential Provisions) Act 2006, s 6, Sch 4.

Police service

280 Police service

(1) In this Act "employee" or "worker" does not include a person in police service; and the provisions of sections 137 and 138 (rights in relation to trade union membership: access to employment) do not apply in relation to police service.

(2) "Police service" means service as a member of any constabulary maintained by virtue of an enactment, or in any other capacity by virtue of which a person has the powers or privileges of a constable.

[776]

Excluded classes of employment

281 (*Repealed by the Employment Protection (Part-time Employees) Regulations 1995, SI 1995/31, regs 5, 6, Schedule.*)

282 Short-term employment

(1) The provisions of Chapter II of Part IV (procedure for handling redundancies) do not apply to employment—

(a) under a contract for a fixed term of three months or less, or

(b) under a contract made in contemplation of the performance of a specific task which is not expected to last for more than three months,

where the employee has not been continuously employed for a period of more than three months.

[(2) Chapter I of Part XIV of the Employment Rights Act 1996 (computation of period of continuous employment), and any provision modifying or supplementing that Chapter for the purposes of that Act, apply for the purposes of this section.]

[777]

NOTES

Sub-s (2): substituted by the Employment Rights Act 1996, s 240, Sch 1, para 56(1), (18).

283 (*Repealed by the Trade Union Reform and Employment Rights Act 1993, ss 34(1), (6), 51, Sch 10.*)

284 Share fishermen

The following provisions of this Act do not apply to employment as master or as member of the crew of a fishing vessel where the employee [(or, in the case of sections 145A to 151, the worker)] is remunerated only by a share in the profits or gross earnings of the vessel—

In Part III (rights in relation to trade union membership and activities)—

sections 137 to 143 (access to employment),

[sections 145A to 151 (inducements and detriment)], and

sections 168 to 173 (time off for trade union duties and activities);

In Part IV, Chapter II (procedure for handling redundancies).

[778]

NOTES

Words in first pair of square brackets inserted, and words in second pair of square brackets substituted, by the Employment Relations Act 2004, s 57(1), Sch 1, para 16, as from 1 October 2004, except in relation to cases where the act or failure to act to which the complaint relates was done before that date, or where the act or failure to act to which the complaint relates is part of a series and the first act or failure in the series was done before that date (see SI 2004/2566, art 6).

285 Employment outside Great Britain

(1) The following provisions of this Act do not apply to employment where under his contract of employment an employee works, or in the case of a prospective employee would ordinarily work, outside Great Britain—

In Part III (rights in relation to trade union membership and activities)—

sections 137 to 143 (access to employment),

[sections 145A to 151 (inducements and detriment)], and

sections 168 to 173 (time off for trade union duties and activities);

In Part IV, [sections 193 and 194 (duty to notify Secretary of State of certain redundancies)].

[(1A) Sections 145A to 151 do not apply to employment where under his contract personally to do work or perform services a worker who is not an employee works outside Great Britain.]

(2) For the purposes of [subsections (1) and (1A)] employment on board a ship registered in the United Kingdom shall be treated as employment where under his contract a person ordinarily works in Great Britain unless—

(a) the ship is registered at a port outside Great Britain, or

(b) the employment is wholly outside Great Britain, or
(c) the employee or, as the case may be, [the worker or] the person seeking employment or seeking to avail himself of a service of an employment agency, is not ordinarily resident in Great Britain.

[779]

NOTES

Sub-s (1): words in first pair of square brackets substituted by the Employment Relations Act 2004, s 57(1), Sch 1, para 17(1), (2), as from 1 October 2004, except in relation to cases where the act or failure to act to which the complaint relates was done before that date, or where the act or failure to act to which the complaint relates is part of a series and the first act or failure in the series was done before that date (see SI 2004/2566, art 6); words in second pair of square brackets substituted by the Employment Relations Act 1999, s 32(1).

Sub-s (1A): inserted by the Employment Relations Act 2004, s 57(1), Sch 1, para 17(1), (3), as from 1 October 2004 (subject to the same exception in SI 2004/2566, art 6 as noted above).

Sub-s (2): words in first pair of square brackets substituted, and words in square brackets in para (c) inserted, by the Employment Relations Act 2004, s 57(1), Sch 1, para 17(1), (4), as from 1 October 2004 (subject to the same exception in SI 2004/2566, art 6 as noted above).

286 Power to make further provision as to excluded classes of employment

(1) This section applies in relation to the following provisions—

In Part III (rights in relation to trade union membership and activities), [sections 145A to 151 (inducements and detriment)],

In Part IV, Chapter II (procedure for handling redundancies), and

In Part V (industrial action), section 237 (dismissal of those taking part in unofficial industrial action).

(2) The Secretary of State may by order made by statutory instrument provide that any of those provisions—

(a) shall not apply to persons or to employment of such classes as may be prescribed by the order, or
(b) shall apply to persons or employments of such classes as may be prescribed by the order subject to such exceptions and modifications as may be so prescribed,

and may vary or revoke any of the provisions of sections 281 to 285 above (excluded classes of employment) so far as they relate to any such provision.

(3) Any such order shall be made by statutory instrument and may contains such incidental, supplementary or transitional provisions as appear to the Secretary of State to be necessary or expedient.

(4) No such order shall be made unless a draft of the order has been laid before Parliament and approved by a resolution of each House of Parliament.

[780]

NOTES

Sub-s (1): words in square brackets substituted by the Employment Relations Act 2004, s 57(1), Sch 1, para 18, as from 1 October 2004, except in relation to cases where the act or failure to act to which the complaint relates was done before that date, or where the act or failure to act to which the complaint relates is part of a series and the first act or failure in the series was done before that date (see SI 2004/2566, art 6).

Orders: as of 6 April 2008 no Orders had been made under this section.

Offshore employment

287 Offshore employment

(1) In this Act "offshore employment" means employment for the purposes of activities—

(a) in the territorial waters of the United Kingdom, or
(b) connected with the exploration of the sea-bed or subsoil, or the exploitation of their natural resources, in the United Kingdom sector of the continental shelf, or
(c) connected with the exploration or exploitation, in a foreign sector of the continental shelf, of a cross-boundary petroleum field.

(2) Her Majesty may by Order in Council provide that—

(a) the provisions of this Act, and

(b) any Northern Ireland legislation making provision for purposes corresponding to any of the purposes of this Act,

apply, to such extent and for such purposes as may be specified in the Order and with or without modification, to or in relation to a person in offshore employment or, in relation to sections 137 to 143 (access to employment), a person seeking such employment.

(3) An Order in Council under this section—

(a) may make different provision for different cases;

(b) may provide that the enactments to which this section applies, as applied, apply—

(i) to individuals whether or not they are British subjects, and

(ii) to bodies corporate whether or not they are incorporated under the law of a part of the United Kingdom,

and apply notwithstanding that the application may affect the activities of such an individual or body outside the United Kingdom;

(c) may make provision for conferring jurisdiction on any court or class of court specified in the Order, or on [employment tribunal]s, in respect of offences, causes of action or other matters arising in connection with offshore employment;

(d) may provide that the enactments to which this section applies apply in relation to a person in offshore employment in a part of the areas referred to in subsection (1)(a) and (b);

(e) may exclude from the operation of section 3 of the Territorial Waters Jurisdiction Act 1878 (consents required for prosecutions) proceedings for offences under the enactments to which this section applies in connection with offshore employment;

(f) may provide that such proceedings shall not be brought without such consent as may be required by the Order;

(g) may modify or exclude any of sections 281 to 285 (excluded classes of employment) or any corresponding provision of Northern Ireland legislation.

[(3A) An Order in Council under this section shall be subject to annulment in pursuance of a resolution of either House of Parliament.]

(4) Any jurisdiction conferred on a court or tribunal under this section is without prejudice to jurisdiction exercisable apart from this section, by that or any other court or tribunal.

(5) In this section—

"cross-boundary petroleum field" means a petroleum field that extends across the boundary between the United Kingdom sector of the continental shelf and a foreign sector;

"foreign sector of the continental shelf" means an area outside the territorial waters of any state, within which rights with respect to the sea-bed and subsoil and their natural resources are exercisable by a state other than the United Kingdom;

"petroleum field" means a geological structure identified as an oil or gas field by the Order in Council concerned; and

"United Kingdom sector of the continental shelf" means the areas designated under section 1(7) of the Continental Shelf Act 1964.

[781]

NOTES

Sub-s (1): substituted by the Petroleum Act 1998, s 50, Sch 4, para 34(2), as from a day to be appointed, as follows—

"(1) In this Act "offshore employment" means employment for the purposes of—

(a) any activities in the territorial sea adjacent to the United Kingdom, and

(b) any such activities as are mentioned in section 11(2) of the Petroleum Act 1998 in waters within subsection (8)(b) or (c) of that section.".

Sub-s (3): words in square brackets in para (c) substituted by the Employment Rights (Dispute Resolution) Act 1998, s 1(2)(a).

Sub-s (3A): inserted by the Employment Relations Act 1999, s 32(2).

Sub-s (5): repealed by the Petroleum Act 1998, ss 50, 51, Sch 4, para 34(3), Sch 5, Pt I, as from a day to be appointed.

Orders: the Employment Relations (Offshore Employment) Order 2000, SI 2000/1828. Also, by virtue of s 300(3) of, and Sch 3, para 1(2) to, this Act, and the Interpretation Act 1978, s 17(2)(b), the Employment Protection (Offshore Employment) Order 1976, SI 1976/766, has effect as if made under this section.

Contracting out, &c

288 Restriction on contracting out

(1) Any provision in an agreement (whether a contract of employment or not) is void in so far as it purports—

(a) to exclude or limit the operation of any provision of this Act, or

(b) to preclude a person from bringing—

(i) proceedings before an [employment tribunal] or the Central Arbitration Committee under any provision of this Act, …

(ii) …

(2) Subsection (1) does not apply to an agreement to refrain from instituting or continuing proceedings where a conciliation officer has taken action under [section 18 of [the Employment Tribunals Act 1996] (conciliation).]

[(2A) Subsection (1) does not apply to an agreement to refrain from instituting or continuing any proceedings, other than excepted proceedings, specified in [subsection (1)(b) of that section] before an [employment tribunal] if the conditions regulating compromise agreements under this Act are satisfied in relation to the agreement.

(2B) The conditions regulating compromise agreements under this Act are that—

(a) the agreement must be in writing;

(b) the agreement must relate to the particular [proceedings];

(c) the complainant must have received [advice from a relevant independent adviser] as to the terms and effect of the proposed agreement and in particular its effect on his ability to pursue his rights before an [employment tribunal];

(d) there must be in force, when the adviser gives the advice, a [contract of insurance, or an indemnity provided for members of a professional body] covering the risk of a claim by the complainant in respect of loss arising in consequence of the advice;

(e) the agreement must identify the adviser; and

(f) the agreement must state that the conditions regulating compromise agreements under this Act are satisfied.

(2C) The proceedings excepted from subsection (2A) are proceedings on a complaint of non-compliance with section 188.]

(3) Subsection (1) does not apply—

(a) to such an agreement as is referred to in section 185(5)(b) or (c) to the extent that it varies or supersedes an award under that section;

(b) to any provision in a collective agreement excluding rights under Chapter II of Part IV (procedure for handling redundancies), if an order under section 198 is in force in respect of it.

[(4) A person is a relevant independent adviser for the purposes of subsection (2B)(c)—

(a) if he is a qualified lawyer,

(b) if he is an officer, official, employee or member of an independent trade union who has been certified in writing by the trade union as competent to give advice and as authorised to do so on behalf of the trade union,

(c) if he works at an advice centre (whether as an employee or a volunteer) and has been certified in writing by the centre as competent to give advice and as authorised to do so on behalf of the centre, or

(d) if he is a person of a description specified in an order made by the Secretary of State.

(4A) But a person is not a relevant independent adviser for the purposes of subsection (2B)(c) in relation to the complainant—

(a) if he is, is employed by or is acting in the matter for the other party or a person who is connected with the other party,

(b) in the case of a person within subsection (4)(b) or (c), if the trade union or advice centre is the other party or a person who is connected with the other party,

(c) in the case of a person within subsection (4)(c), if the complainant makes a payment for the advice received from him, or

(d) in the case of a person of a description specified in an order under subsection (4)(d), if any condition specified in the order in relation to the giving of advice by persons of that description is not satisfied.

(4B) In subsection (4)(a) "qualified lawyer" means—

(a) as respects England and Wales, a *barrister (whether in practice as such or employed to give legal advice), a solicitor who holds a practising certificate, or a person other than a barrister or solicitor who is an authorised advocate or authorised litigator (within the meaning of the Courts and Legal Services Act 1990), and*

(b) as respects Scotland, an advocate (whether in practice as such or employed to give legal advice), or a solicitor who holds a practising certificate.

(4C) An order under subsection (4)(d) shall be made by statutory instrument which shall be subject to annulment in pursuance of a resolution of either House of Parliament.

(5) For the purposes of subsection (4A) any two persons are to be treated as connected—

(a) if one is a company of which the other (directly or indirectly) has control, or

(b) if both are companies of which a third person (directly or indirectly) has control.]

[(6) An agreement under which the parties agree to submit a dispute to arbitration—

(a) shall be regarded for the purposes of subsections (2) and (2A) as being an agreement to refrain from instituting or continuing proceedings if—

(i) the dispute is covered by a scheme having effect by virtue of an order under section 212A, and

(ii) the agreement is to submit it to arbitration in accordance with the scheme, but

(b) shall be regarded for those purposes as neither being nor including such an agreement in any other case.]

[782]

NOTES

Sub-s (1): words in square brackets in para (b)(i) substituted by the Employment Rights (Dispute Resolution) Act 1998, s 1(2)(a); para (b)(ii) and the word immediately preceding it repealed by the Employment Relations Act 2004, s 57, Sch 1, para 19, Sch 2, as from 6 April 2005.

Sub-s (2): words in first (outer) pair of square brackets substituted by the Employment Tribunals Act 1996, s 43, Sch 1, para 8(a); words in second (inner) pair of square brackets substituted by the Employment Rights (Dispute Resolution) Act 1998, s 1(2)(c).

Sub-s (2A): inserted, together with sub-ss (2B), (2C), by the Trade Union Reform and Employment Rights Act 1993, s 39(2), Sch 6, para 4(a); words in first pair of square brackets substituted by the Employment Tribunals Act 1996, s 43, Sch 1, para 8(b); words in second pair of square brackets substituted by the Employment Rights (Dispute Resolution) Act 1998, s 1(2)(a).

Sub-s (2B): inserted as noted above; words in square brackets substituted by the Employment Rights (Dispute Resolution) Act 1998, ss 1(2)(a), 9(1), (2)(c), 10(1), (2)(c), 15, Sch 1, para 9(1), (2).

Sub-s (2C): inserted as noted above.

Sub-ss (4), (4A)–(4C), (5): substituted, for original sub-ss (4), (5) (as added by the Trade Union Reform and Employment Rights Act 1993, s 39(2), Sch 6, para 4(b)), by the Employment Rights (Dispute Resolution) Act 1998, s 15, Sch 1, para 9(1), (3).

Sub-s (4B): substituted as noted above; for the words in italics there are substituted the words "a person who, for the purposes of the Legal Services Act 2007, is an authorised person in relation to an activity which constitutes the exercise of a right of audience or the conduct of litigation (within the meaning of that Act), and" by the Legal Services Act 2007, s 208(1), Sch 21, paras 104, 107, as from a day to be appointed.

Sub-s (6): added by the Employment Rights (Dispute Resolution) Act 1998, s 8(3).

Orders: the Compromise Agreements (Description of Person) Order 2004, SI 2004/754 at **[3138]**.

289 Employment governed by foreign law

For the purposes of this Act it is immaterial whether the law which (apart from this Act) governs any person's employment is the law of the United Kingdom, or of a part of the United Kingdom, or not.

[783]

290, 291 (*Repealed by the Employment Tribunals Act 1996, s 45, Sch 3, Pt I. S 291(1) had been repealed by the Trade Union Reform and Employment Rights Act 1993. S 290 and s 291(2) and (3) are re-enacted respectively as ss 18(1) and 21(1) and (2) of the 1996 Act, at* **[975]**, **[978]**.)

Other supplementary provisions

292 Death of employee or employer

(1) This section has effect in relation to the following provisions so far as they confer rights on employees or make provision in connection therewith—

(a) …
(b) sections 168 to 173 (time off for trade union duties and activities);
(c) sections 188 to 198 (procedure for handling redundancies).

[(1A) This section also has effect in relation to sections 145A to 151 so far as those sections confer rights on workers or make provision in connection therewith.]

(2) Where the employee [or worker] or employer dies, tribunal proceedings may be instituted or continued by a personal representative of the deceased employee [or worker] or, as the case may be, defended by a personal representative of the deceased employer.

(3) If there is no personal representative of a deceased employee [or worker], tribunal proceedings or proceedings to enforce a tribunal award may be instituted or continued on behalf of his estate by such other person as the [employment tribunal] may appoint, being either—

(a) a person authorised by the employee [or worker] to act in connection with the proceedings before his death, or
(b) the widower, widow, [surviving civil partner,] child, father, mother, brother or sister of the employee [or worker].

In such a case any award made by the [employment tribunal] shall be in such terms and shall be enforceable in such manner as may be prescribed.

(4) Any right arising under any of the provisions mentioned in subsection (1) [or (1A)] which by virtue of this section accrues after the death of the employee [or worker] in question shall devolve as if it had accrued before his death.

(5) Any liability arising under any of those provisions which by virtue of this section accrues after the death of the employer in question shall be treated for all purposes as if it had accrued immediately before his death.

[784]

NOTES

Sub-s (1): para (a) repealed by the Employment Relations Act 2004, s 57, Sch 1, para 20(1), (2), Sch 2, as from 1 October 2004, except in relation to cases where the act or failure to act to which the complaint relates was done before that date, or where the act or failure to act to which the complaint relates is part of a series and the first act or failure in the series was done before that date (see SI 2004/2566, art 6).

Sub-s (1A): inserted by the Employment Relations Act 2004, s 57(1), Sch 1, para 20(1), (3), as from 1 October 2004 (subject to the same exception in SI 2004/2566, art 6 as noted above).

Sub-ss (2), (4): words in square brackets inserted by the Employment Relations Act 2004, s 57(1), Sch 1, para 20(1), (4), (5), as from 1 October 2004 (subject to the same exception in SI 2004/2566, art 6 as noted above).

Sub-s (3): words in first, third and fifth pairs of square brackets inserted by the Employment Relations Act 2004, s 57(1), Sch 1, para 20(1), (4), as from 1 October 2004 (subject to the same exception in SI 2004/2566, art 6 as noted above); words in second and final pairs of square brackets substituted by the Employment Rights (Dispute Resolution) Act 1998, s 1(1), (2)(a); words in fourth pair of square brackets inserted by the Civil Partnership Act 2004, s 261(1), Sch 27, para 146, as from 5 December 2005.

Regulations: by virtue of s 300(3) of, and Sch 3, para 1(2) to, this Act, and the Interpretation Act 1978, s 17(2)(b), the Employment Tribunal Awards (Enforcement in case of death) Regulations 1976, SI 1976/663, have effect as if made under this section.

293 Regulations

(1) The Secretary of State may by regulations prescribe anything authorised or required to be prescribed for the purposes of this Act.

(2) The regulations may contain such incidental, supplementary or transitional provisions as appear to the Secretary of State to be necessary or expedient.

(3) Regulations under this section shall be made by statutory instrument which shall be subject to annulment in pursuance of a resolution of either House of Parliament.

[785]

294 (*Reciprocal arrangements with Northern Ireland: outside the scope of this work.*)

Interpretation

295 Meaning of "employee" and related expressions

(1) In this Act—

"contract of employment" means a contract of service or of apprenticeship, "employee" means an individual who has entered into or works under (or, where the employment has ceased, worked under) a contract of employment, and

"employer", in relation to an employee, means the person by whom the employee is (or, where the employment has ceased, was) employed.

(2) Subsection (1) has effect subject to section 235 and other provisions conferring a wider meaning on "contract of employment" or related expressions.

[786]

296 Meaning of "worker" and related expressions

(1) In this Act "worker" means an individual who works, or normally works or seeks to work—

(a) under a contract of employment, or

(b) under any other contract whereby he undertakes to do or perform personally any work or services for another party to the contract who is not a professional client of his, or

(c) in employment under or for the purposes of a government department (otherwise than as a member of the naval, military or air forces of the Crown) in so far as such employment does not fall within paragraph (a) or (b) above.

(2) In this Act "employer", in relation to a worker, means a person for whom one or more workers work, or have worked or normally work or seek to work.

[(3) This section has effect subject to [sections 68(4), 145F(3) and 151(1B)].]

[787]

NOTES

Sub-s (3): added by the Trade Union Reform and Employment Rights Act 1993, s 49(2), Sch 8, para 88; words in square brackets substituted by the Employment Relations Act 2004, s 57(1), Sch 1, para 21, as from 1 October 2004, except in relation to cases where the act or failure to act to which the complaint relates was done before that date, or where the act or failure to act to which the complaint relates is part of a series and the first act or failure in the series was done before that date (see SI 2004/2566, art 6).

297 Associated employers

For the purposes of this Act any two employers shall be treated as associated if—

(a) one is a company of which the other (directly or indirectly) has control, or

(b) both are companies of which a third person (directly or indirectly) has control;

and "associated employer" shall be construed accordingly.

[788]

298 Minor definitions: general

In this Act, unless the context otherwise requires—

"act" and "action" each includes omission, and references to doing an act or taking action shall be construed accordingly;

["certificate of independence" means a certificate issued under—

(a) section 6(6), or

(b) section 101A(4);]

"contravention" includes a failure to comply, and cognate expressions shall be construed accordingly;

"dismiss", "dismissal" and "effective date of termination", in relation to an employee, shall be construed in accordance with [Part X of the Employment Rights Act 1996];

. . .

"tort", as respects Scotland, means delict, and cognate expressions shall be construed accordingly.

[789]

NOTES

Definition "certificate of independence" inserted by the Employment Relations Act 2004, s 50(4), as from 6 April 2005; words in square brackets in definitions "dismiss, "dismissal", and "effective date of termination" substituted by the Employment Rights Act 1996, s 240, Sch 1, para 56(1), (19); definition "post" repealed by the Postal Services Act 2000 (Consequential Modifications No 1) Order 2001, SI 2001/1149, art 3(2), Sch 2.

299 Index of defined expressions

In this Act the expressions listed below are defined by or otherwise fall to be construed in accordance with the provisions indicated—

ACAS	section 247(1)
act and action	section 298
advertisement (in sections 137 to 143)	section 143(1)
[affected employees (in Part IV, Chapter II)	section 196(3)]
[agent (of trade union)	section 119]
appropriately qualified actuary (in sections 38 to 41)	section 42
associated employer	section 297
branch or section (of trade union)	section 119
[certificate of independence	section 298]
collective agreement and collective bargaining	section 178(1)
…	…
contract of employment —generally —in sections 226 to 234 —in relation to Crown employment —in relation to House of Lords or House of Commons staff	 section 295(1) section 235 section 273(4)(a) section 277(4) and 278(4)(a)
contravention	section 298
the court (in Part I)	section 121
date of the ballot (in Part V)	section 246
dismiss and dismissal —generally —in relation to Crown employment —in relation to House of Commons staff	 section 298 section 273(4)(c) section 278(4)(b)
[the duty of confidentiality	section 24A(3)]
effective date of termination	section 298
employee —generally —in relation to Crown employment —in relation to House of Commons staff —excludes police service	 section 295(1) section 273(4)(a) section 278(4)(a) section 280
[employee representatives (in Part IV, Chapter II)	section 196(1)]
employer —in relation to an employee —in relation to a worker —in relation to health service practitioners	 section 295(1) section 296(2) section 279
employment and employment agency (in sections 137 to 143)	section 143(1)
executive (of trade union)	section 119
[financial affairs (of trade union)	section 119]
financial year (in Part VI)	section 72

general secretary	section 119
independent trade union (and related expressions)	section 5
list —of trade unions —of employers' associations	 section 2 section 123
Northern Ireland union (in Part I)	section 120
not protected (in sections 222 to 226)	section 219(4)
officer —of trade union —of employers' association	 section 119 section 136
official (of trade union)	section 119
offshore employment	section 287
…	…
political fund political resolution	section 82(1)(a) section 82(1)(a)
…	
prescribed	section 293(1)
president	section 119
recognised, recognition and related expressions	section 178(3)
…	…
[representatives of a trade union (in Part IV, Chapter II)	section 196(2)]
rules (of trade union)	section 119
strike (in Part V)	section 246
tort (as respects Scotland)	section 298
trade dispute —in Part IV —in Part V	 section 218 section 244
trade union	section 1
undertaking (of employer) —in relation to Crown employment —in relation to House of Commons staff	 section 273(4)(e) and (f) section 278(4)(c) and (d)
worker —generally —includes health service practitioners —excludes police service	 section 296(1) section 279 section 280
working hours (in Part V)	section 246

[790]

NOTES

Definition "affected employees" inserted by the Collective Redundancies and Transfer of Undertakings (Protection of Employment) (Amendment) Regulations 1999, SI 1999/1925, regs 2(1), (2), 7.

Definitions "agent (of trade union)", "the duty of confidentiality" and "financial affairs (of trade union)" inserted by the Trade Union Reform and Employment Rights Act 1993, s 49(2), Sch 8, para 89.

Entry "certificate of independence" inserted by the Employment Relations Act 2004, s 50(5), as from 6 April 2005.

Definitions "the Commissioner" and "redundancy" repealed by the Trade Union Reform and Employment Rights Act 1993, s 51, Sch 10.

Definition "employee representatives" inserted, and definition "representatives of a trade union" substituted, by the Collective Redundancies and Transfer of Undertakings (Protection of Employment) (Amendment) Regulations 1995, SI 1995/2587, reg 7.
Entry relating to "place of work (in Part V)" repealed by the Employment Relations Act 2004, s 57, Sch 1, para 22, Sch 2, as from 6 April 2005.
Definition "post" repealed by the Postal Services Act 2000 (Consequential Modifications No 1) 2001, SI 2001/1149, art 3(2), Sch 2.

Final provisions

300 Repeals, consequential amendments, transitional provisions and savings

(1), (2) *(Introduce Sch 1 (repeals), and Sch 2 (amendments) respectively (outside the scope of this work).)*

(3) Schedule 3 contains transitional provisions and savings.

[791]

301 Extent

(1) This Act extends to England and Wales and [(apart from section 212A(6)) to] Scotland.

(2), (3) *(Application to Northern Ireland (outside the scope of this work).)*

[792]

NOTES

Sub-s (1): words in square brackets inserted by the Employment Rights (Dispute Resolution) Act 1998, s 15, Sch 1, para 10.

302 Commencement

This Act comes into force at the end of the period of three months beginning with the day on which it is passed.

[793]

303 Short title

This Act may be cited as the Trade Union and Labour Relations (Consolidation) Act 1992.

[794]

SCHEDULES

[SCHEDULE A1
COLLECTIVE BARGAINING: RECOGNITION

Section 70A

NOTES

This Schedule was inserted by the Employment Relations Act 1999, s 1(1), (3), Sch 1.

PART I
RECOGNITION

Introduction

1. A trade union (or trade unions) seeking recognition to be entitled to conduct collective bargaining on behalf of a group or groups of workers may make a request in accordance with this Part of this Schedule.

2.—(1) This paragraph applies for the purposes of this Part of this Schedule.

(2) References to the bargaining unit are to the group of workers concerned (or the groups taken together).

(3) References to the proposed bargaining unit are to the bargaining unit proposed in the request for recognition.

[(3A) References to an appropriate bargaining unit's being decided by the CAC are to a bargaining unit's being decided by the CAC to be appropriate under paragraph 19(2) or (3) or 19A(2) or (3).]

(4) References to the employer are to the employer of the workers constituting the bargaining unit concerned.

(5) References to the parties are to the union (or unions) and the employer.

3.—(1) This paragraph applies for the purposes of this Part of this Schedule.

(2) The meaning of collective bargaining given by section 178(1) shall not apply.

(3) References to collective bargaining are to negotiations relating to pay, hours and holidays; but this has effect subject to sub-paragraph (4).

(4) If the parties agree matters as the subject of collective bargaining, references to collective bargaining are to negotiations relating to the agreed matters; and this is the case whether the agreement is made before or after the time when the CAC issues a declaration, or the parties agree, that the union is (or unions are) entitled to conduct collective bargaining on behalf of a bargaining unit.

(5) Sub-paragraph (4) does not apply in construing paragraph 31(3).

(6) Sub-paragraphs (2) to (5) do not apply in construing paragraph 35 or 44.

[795]

NOTES

Inserted as noted at the beginning of this Schedule.

Para 2: sub-para (3A) inserted by the Employment Relations Act 2004, s 57(1), Sch 1, para 23(1), (2), as from 6 April 2005.

Request for recognition

4.—(1) The union or unions seeking recognition must make a request for recognition to the employer.

(2) Paragraphs 5 to 9 apply to the request.

5. The request is not valid unless it is received by the employer.

6. The request is not valid unless the union (or each of the unions) has a certificate [of independence].

7.—(1) The request is not valid unless the employer, taken with any associated employer or employers, employs—

(a) at least 21 workers on the day the employer receives the request, or
(b) an average of at least 21 workers in the 13 weeks ending with that day.

(2) To find the average under sub-paragraph (1)(b)—

(a) take the number of workers employed in each of the 13 weeks (including workers not employed for the whole of the week);
(b) aggregate the 13 numbers;
(c) divide the aggregate by 13.

(3) For the purposes of sub-paragraph (1)(a) any worker employed by an associated company incorporated outside Great Britain must be ignored unless the day the request was made fell within a period during which he ordinarily worked in Great Britain.

(4) For the purposes of sub-paragraph (1)(b) any worker employed by an associated company incorporated outside Great Britain must be ignored in relation to a week unless the whole or any part of that week fell within a period during which he ordinarily worked in Great Britain.

(5) For the purposes of sub-paragraphs (3) and (4) a worker who is employed on board a ship registered in the register maintained under section 8 of the Merchant Shipping Act 1995 shall be treated as ordinarily working in Great Britain unless—

(a) the ship's entry in the register specifies a port outside Great Britain as the port to which the vessel is to be treated as belonging,

(b) the employment is wholly outside Great Britain, or

(c) the worker is not ordinarily resident in Great Britain.

(6) The Secretary of State may by order—

(a) provide that sub-paragraphs (1) to (5) are not to apply, or are not to apply in specified circumstances, or

(b) vary the number of workers for the time being specified in sub-paragraph (1);

and different provision may be made for different circumstances.

(7) An order under sub-paragraph (6)—

(a) shall be made by statutory instrument, and

(b) may include supplementary, incidental, saving or transitional provisions.

(8) No such order shall be made unless a draft of it has been laid before Parliament and approved by a resolution of each House of Parliament.

8. The request is not valid unless it—

(a) is in writing,

(b) identifies the union or unions and the bargaining unit, and

(c) states that it is made under this Schedule.

9. The Secretary of State may by order made by statutory instrument prescribe the form of requests and the procedure for making them; and if he does so the request is not valid unless it complies with the order.

[796]

NOTES

Inserted as noted at the beginning of this Schedule.

Para 6: words in square brackets substituted by the Employment Relations Act 2004, s 50(6), as from 6 April 2005.

Orders: as of 6 April 2008 no Orders had been made under para 7 or 9.

Parties agree

10.—(1) If before the end of the first period the parties agree a bargaining unit and that the union is (or unions are) to be recognised as entitled to conduct collective bargaining on behalf of the unit, no further steps are to be taken under this Part of this Schedule.

(2) If before the end of the first period the employer informs the union (or unions) that the employer does not accept the request but is willing to negotiate, sub-paragraph (3) applies.

(3) The parties may conduct negotiations with a view to agreeing a bargaining unit and that the union is (or unions are) to be recognised as entitled to conduct collective bargaining on behalf of the unit.

(4) If such an agreement is made before the end of the second period no further steps are to be taken under this Part of this Schedule.

(5) The employer and the union (or unions) may request ACAS to assist in conducting the negotiations.

(6) The first period is the period of 10 working days starting with the day after that on which the employer receives the request for recognition.

(7) The second period is—

(a) the period of 20 working days starting with the day after that on which the first period ends, or

(b) such longer period (so starting) as the parties may from time to time agree.

[797]

NOTES

Inserted as noted at the beginning of this Schedule.

Employer rejects request

11.—(1) This paragraph applies if—
(a) before the end of the first period the employer fails to respond to the request, or
(b) before the end of the first period the employer informs the union (or unions) that the employer does not accept the request (without indicating a willingness to negotiate).

(2) The union (or unions) may apply to the CAC to decide both these questions—
[(a) whether the proposed bargaining unit is appropriate;]
(b) whether the union has (or unions have) the support of a majority of the workers constituting the appropriate bargaining unit.

[798]

NOTES

Inserted as noted at the beginning of this Schedule.

Para 11: sub-para (2)(a) substituted by the Employment Relations Act 2004, s 1(1), as from 6 April 2005, except in relation to any application for recognition which was accepted by the CAC under para 15(5) of this Schedule before that date (see SI 2005/872, art 6).

Negotiations fail

12.—(1) Sub-paragraph (2) applies if—
(a) the employer informs the union (or unions) under paragraph 10(2), and
(b) no agreement is made before the end of the second period.

(2) The union (or unions) may apply to the CAC to decide both these questions—
[(a) whether the proposed bargaining unit is appropriate;]
(b) whether the union has (or unions have) the support of a majority of the workers constituting the appropriate bargaining unit.

(3) Sub-paragraph (4) applies if—
(a) the employer informs the union (or unions) under paragraph 10(2), and
(b) before the end of the second period the parties agree a bargaining unit but not that the union is (or unions are) to be recognised as entitled to conduct collective bargaining on behalf of the unit.

(4) The union (or unions) may apply to the CAC to decide the question whether the union has (or unions have) the support of a majority of the workers constituting the bargaining unit.

(5) But no application may be made under this paragraph if within the period of 10 working days starting with the day after that on which the employer informs the union (or unions) under paragraph 10(2) the employer proposes that ACAS be requested to assist in conducting the negotiations and—
(a) the union rejects (or unions reject) the proposal, or
(b) the union fails (or unions fail) to accept the proposal within the period of 10 working days starting with the day after that on which the employer makes the proposal.

[799]

NOTES

Inserted as noted at the beginning of this Schedule.

Para 12: sub-para (2)(a) substituted by the Employment Relations Act 2004, s 1(2), as from 6 April 2005, except in relation to any application for recognition which was accepted by the CAC under para 15(5) of this Schedule before that date (see SI 2005/872, art 6).

Acceptance of applications

13. The CAC must give notice to the parties of receipt of an application under paragraph 11 or 12.

14.—(1) This paragraph applies if—
(a) two or more relevant applications are made,

(b) at least one worker falling within one of the relevant bargaining units also falls within the other relevant bargaining unit (or units), and
(c) the CAC has not accepted any of the applications.

(2) A relevant application is an application under paragraph 11 or 12.

(3) In relation to a relevant application, the relevant bargaining unit is—
(a) the proposed bargaining unit, where the application is under paragraph 11(2) or 12(2);
(b) the agreed bargaining unit, where the application is under paragraph 12(4).

(4) Within the acceptance period the CAC must decide, with regard to each relevant application, whether the 10 per cent test is satisfied.

(5) The 10 per cent test is satisfied if members of the union (or unions) constitute at least 10 per cent of the workers constituting the relevant bargaining unit.

(6) The acceptance period is—
(a) the period of 10 working days starting with the day after that on which the CAC receives the last relevant application, or
(b) such longer period (so starting) as the CAC may specify to the parties by notice containing reasons for the extension.

(7) If the CAC decides that—
(a) the 10 per cent test is satisfied with regard to more than one of the relevant applications, or
(b) the 10 per cent test is satisfied with regard to none of the relevant applications,

the CAC must not accept any of the relevant applications.

(8) If the CAC decides that the 10 per cent test is satisfied with regard to one only of the relevant applications the CAC—
(a) must proceed under paragraph 15 with regard to that application, and
(b) must not accept any of the other relevant applications.

(9) The CAC must give notice of its decision to the parties.

(10) If by virtue of this paragraph the CAC does not accept an application, no further steps are to be taken under this Part of this Schedule in relation to that application.

15.—(1) This paragraph applies to these applications—
(a) any application with regard to which no decision has to be made under paragraph 14;
(b) any application with regard to which the CAC must proceed under this paragraph by virtue of paragraph 14.

(2) Within the acceptance period the CAC must decide whether—
(a) the request for recognition to which the application relates is valid within the terms of paragraphs 5 to 9, and
(b) the application is made in accordance with paragraph 11 or 12 and admissible within the terms of paragraphs 33 to 42.

(3) In deciding those questions the CAC must consider any evidence which it has been given by the employer or the union (or unions).

(4) If the CAC decides that the request is not valid or the application is not made in accordance with paragraph 11 or 12 or is not admissible—
(a) the CAC must give notice of its decision to the parties,
(b) the CAC must not accept the application, and
(c) no further steps are to be taken under this Part of this Schedule.

(5) If the CAC decides that the request is valid and the application is made in accordance with paragraph 11 or 12 and is admissible it must—
(a) accept the application, and
(b) give notice of the acceptance to the parties.

(6) The acceptance period is—
(a) the period of 10 working days starting with the day after that on which the CAC receives the application, or
(b) such longer period (so starting) as the CAC may specify to the parties by notice containing reasons for the extension.

[800]

NOTES

Inserted as noted at the beginning of this Schedule.

Withdrawal of application

16.—(1) If an application under paragraph 11 or 12 is accepted by the CAC, the union (or unions) may not withdraw the application—

(a) after the CAC issues a declaration under paragraph [19F(5) or] 22(2), or

(b) after the union (or the last of the unions) receives notice under paragraph 22(3) or 23(2).

(2) If an application is withdrawn by the union (or unions)—

(a) the CAC must give notice of the withdrawal to the employer, and

(b) no further steps are to be taken under this Part of this Schedule.

[801]

NOTES

Inserted as noted at the beginning of this Schedule.

Para 16: words in square brackets in sub-para (1) inserted by the Employment Relations Act 2004, s 57(1), Sch 1, para 23(1), (3), as from 6 April 2005.

Notice to cease consideration of application

17.—(1) This paragraph applies if the CAC has received an application under paragraph 11 or 12 and—

(a) it has not decided whether the application is admissible, or

(b) it has decided that the application is admissible.

(2) No further steps are to be taken under this Part of this Schedule if, before the final event occurs, the parties give notice to the CAC that they want no further steps to be taken.

(3) The final event occurs when the first of the following occurs—

(a) the CAC issues a declaration under paragraph [19F(5) or] 22(2) in consequence of the application;

(b) the last day of the notification period ends;

and the notification period is that defined by paragraph [24(6)] and arising from the application.

[802]

NOTES

Inserted as noted at the beginning of this Schedule.

Para 17: words in square brackets in sub-para (3) inserted, and number in square brackets in that subparagraph substituted, by the Employment Relations Act 2004, s 57(1), Sch 1, para 23(1), (4), as from 6 April 2005.

Appropriate bargaining unit

18.—(1) If the CAC accepts an application under paragraph 11(2) or 12(2) it must try to help the parties to reach within the appropriate period an agreement as to what the appropriate bargaining unit is.

(2) The appropriate period is [(subject to any notice under sub-paragraph (3), (4) or (5))]—

(a) the period of 20 working days starting with the day after that on which the CAC gives notice of acceptance of the application, or

(b) such longer period (so starting) as the CAC may specify to the parties by notice containing reasons for the extension.

[(3) If, during the appropriate period, the CAC concludes that there is no reasonable prospect of the parties' agreeing an appropriate bargaining unit before the time when (apart from this sub-paragraph) the appropriate period would end, the CAC may, by a notice given to the parties, declare that the appropriate period ends with the date of the notice.

(4) If, during the appropriate period, the parties apply to the CAC for a declaration that the appropriate period is to end with a date (specified in the application) which is earlier than the date with which it would otherwise end, the CAC may, by a notice given to the parties, declare that the appropriate period ends with the specified date.

(5) If the CAC has declared under sub-paragraph (4) that the appropriate period ends with a specified date, it may before that date by a notice given to the parties specify a later date with which the appropriate period ends.

(6) A notice under sub-paragraph (3) must contain reasons for reaching the conclusion mentioned in that sub-paragraph.

(7) A notice under sub-paragraph (5) must contain reasons for the extension of the appropriate period.]

[18A.—(1) This paragraph applies if the CAC accepts an application under paragraph 11(2) or 12(2).

(2) Within 5 working days starting with the day after that on which the CAC gives the employer notice of acceptance of the application, the employer must supply the following information to the union (or unions) and the CAC—

(a) a list of the categories of worker in the proposed bargaining unit,
(b) a list of the workplaces at which the workers in the proposed bargaining unit work, and
(c) the number of workers the employer reasonably believes to be in each category at each workplace.

(3) The lists and numbers supplied under this paragraph must be as accurate as is reasonably practicable in the light of the information in the possession of the employer at the time when he complies with sub-paragraph (2).

(4) The lists and numbers supplied to the union (or unions) and to the CAC must be the same.

(5) For the purposes of this paragraph, the workplace at which a worker works is—

(a) if the person works at or from a single set of premises, those premises, and
(b) in any other case, the premises with which the worker's employment has the closest connection.]

[19.—(1) This paragraph applies if—

(a) the CAC accepts an application under paragraph 11(2) or 12(2),
(b) the parties have not agreed an appropriate bargaining unit at the end of the appropriate period (defined by paragraph 18), and
(c) at the end of that period either no request under paragraph 19A(1)(b) has been made or such a request has been made but the condition in paragraph 19A(1)(c) has not been met.

(2) Within the decision period, the CAC must decide whether the proposed bargaining unit is appropriate.

(3) If the CAC decides that the proposed bargaining unit is not appropriate, it must also decide within the decision period a bargaining unit which is appropriate.

(4) The decision period is—

(a) the period of 10 working days starting with the day after that with which the appropriate period ends, or
(b) such longer period (so starting) as the CAC may specify to the parties by notice containing reasons for the extension.

19A.—(1) This paragraph applies if—

(a) the CAC accepts an application under paragraph 11(2) or 12(2),
(b) during the appropriate period (defined by paragraph 18), the CAC is requested by the union (or unions) to make a decision under this paragraph, and
(c) the CAC is, either at the time the request is made or at a later time during the appropriate period, of the opinion that the employer has failed to comply with the duty imposed by paragraph 18A.

(2) Within the decision period, the CAC must decide whether the proposed bargaining unit is appropriate.

(3) If the CAC decides that the proposed bargaining unit is not appropriate, it must also decide within the decision period a bargaining unit which is appropriate.

(4) The decision period is—

(a) the period of 10 working days starting with the day after the day on which the request is made, or

(b) such longer period (so starting) as the CAC may specify to the parties by notice containing reasons for the extension.

19B.—(1) This paragraph applies if the CAC has to decide whether a bargaining unit is appropriate for the purposes of paragraph 19(2) or (3) or 19A(2) or (3).

(2) The CAC must take these matters into account—

(a) the need for the unit to be compatible with effective management;

(b) the matters listed in sub-paragraph (3), so far as they do not conflict with that need.

(3) The matters are—

(a) the views of the employer and of the union (or unions);

(b) existing national and local bargaining arrangements;

(c) the desirability of avoiding small fragmented bargaining units within an undertaking;

(d) the characteristics of workers falling within the bargaining unit under consideration and of any other employees of the employer whom the CAC considers relevant;

(e) the location of workers.

(4) In taking an employer's views into account for the purpose of deciding whether the proposed bargaining unit is appropriate, the CAC must take into account any view the employer has about any other bargaining unit that he considers would be appropriate.

(5) The CAC must give notice of its decision to the parties.]

[803]

NOTES

Inserted as noted at the beginning of this Schedule.

Para 18: words in square brackets in sub-para (2) inserted, and sub-paras (3)–(7) added, by the Employment Relations Act 2004, s 2(1), (2), as from 6 April 2005, except in relation to any application for recognition which was accepted by the CAC under para 15(5) of this Schedule before that date (see SI 2005/872, art 6).

Para 18A: inserted by the Employment Relations Act 2004, s 3, as from 6 April 2005 (subject to the same exception in SI 2005/872, art 6 as noted above).

Paras 19, 19A, 19B: substituted, for original para 19, by the Employment Relations Act 2004, s 4, as from 6 April 2005 (subject to the same exception in SI 2005/872, art 6 as noted above).

[Union communications with workers after acceptance of application

19C.—(1) This paragraph applies if the CAC accepts an application under paragraph 11(2) or 12(2) or (4).

(2) The union (or unions) may apply to the CAC for the appointment of a suitable independent person to handle communications during the initial period between the union (or unions) and the relevant workers.

(3) In the case of an application under paragraph 11(2) or 12(2), the relevant workers are—

(a) in relation to any time before an appropriate bargaining unit is agreed by the parties or decided by the CAC, those falling within the proposed bargaining unit, and

(b) in relation to any time after an appropriate bargaining unit is so agreed or decided, those falling within the bargaining unit agreed or decided upon.

(4) In the case of an application under paragraph 12(4), the relevant workers are those falling within the bargaining unit agreed by the parties.

(5) The initial period is the period starting with the day on which the CAC informs the parties under sub-paragraph (7)(b) and ending with the first day on which any of the following occurs—

(a) the application under paragraph 11 or 12 is withdrawn;
(b) the CAC gives notice to the union (or unions) of a decision under paragraph 20 that the application is invalid;
(c) the CAC notifies the union (or unions) of a declaration issued under paragraph 19F(5) or 22(2);
(d) the CAC informs the union (or unions) under paragraph 25(9) of the name of the person appointed to conduct a ballot.

(6) A person is a suitable independent person if—

(a) he satisfies such conditions as may be specified for the purposes of paragraph 25(7)(a) by an order under that provision, or is himself specified for those purposes by such an order, and
(b) there are no grounds for believing either that he will carry out any functions arising from his appointment otherwise than competently or that his independence in relation to those functions might reasonably be called into question.

(7) On an application under sub-paragraph (2) the CAC must as soon as reasonably practicable—

(a) make such an appointment as is mentioned in that sub-paragraph, and
(b) inform the parties of the name of the person appointed and the date of his appointment.

(8) The person appointed by the CAC is referred to in paragraphs 19D and 19E as "the appointed person".

19D.—(1) An employer who is informed by the CAC under paragraph 19C(7)(b) must comply with the following duties (so far as it is reasonable to expect him to do so).

(2) The duties are—

(a) to give to the CAC, within the period of 10 working days starting with the day after that on which the employer is informed under paragraph 19C(7)(b), the names and home addresses of the relevant workers;
(b) if the relevant workers change as a result of an appropriate bargaining unit being agreed by the parties or decided by the CAC, to give to the CAC, within the period of 10 working days starting with the day after that on which the bargaining unit is agreed or the CAC's decision is notified to the employer, the names and home addresses of those who are now the relevant workers;
(c) to give to the CAC, as soon as reasonably practicable, the name and home address of any worker who joins the bargaining unit after the employer has complied with paragraph (a) or (b);
(d) to inform the CAC, as soon as reasonably practicable, of any worker whose name has been given to the CAC under paragraph (a), (b) or (c) and who ceases to be a relevant worker (otherwise than by reason of a change mentioned in paragraph (b)).

(3) Nothing in sub-paragraph (2) requires the employer to give information to the CAC after the end of the initial period.

(4) As soon as reasonably practicable after the CAC receives any information under sub-paragraph (2), it must pass it on to the appointed person.

19E.—(1) During the initial period, the appointed person must if asked to do so by the union (or unions) send to any worker—

(a) whose name and home address have been passed on to him under paragraph 19D(4), and
(b) who is (so far as the appointed person is aware) still a relevant worker,

any information supplied by the union (or unions) to the appointed person.

(2) The costs of the appointed person shall be borne—

(a) if the application under paragraph 19C was made by one union, by the union, and
(b) if that application was made by more than one union, by the unions in such proportions as they jointly indicate to the appointed person or, in the absence of such an indication, in equal shares.

(3) The appointed person may send to the union (or each of the unions) a demand stating his costs and the amount of those costs to be borne by the recipient.

(4) In such a case the recipient must pay the amount stated to the person sending the demand and must do so within the period of 15 working days starting with the day after that on which the demand is received.

(5) In England and Wales, if the amount stated is not paid in accordance with sub-paragraph (4) it shall, if a county court so orders, be recoverable *by execution issued from that court* or otherwise as if it were payable under an order of that court.

(6) *Where an amount is recoverable under sub-paragraph (5) execution may be carried out*, to the same extent and in the same manner as if the union were a body corporate, against any property held in trust for the union other than protected property as defined in section 23(2).

(7) References to the costs of the appointed person are to—

(a) the costs wholly, exclusively and necessarily incurred by the appointed person in connection with handling during the initial period communications between the union (or unions) and the relevant workers,

(b) such reasonable amount as the appointed person charges for his services, and

(c) such other costs as the union (or unions) agree.

19F.—(1) If the CAC is satisfied that the employer has failed to fulfil a duty mentioned in paragraph 19D(2), and the initial period has not yet ended, the CAC may order the employer—

(a) to take such steps to remedy the failure as the CAC considers reasonable and specifies in the order, and

(b) to do so within such period as the CAC considers reasonable and specifies in the order;

and in this paragraph a "remedial order" means an order under this sub-paragraph.

(2) If the CAC is satisfied that the employer has failed to comply with a remedial order and the initial period has not yet ended, the CAC must as soon as reasonably practicable notify the employer and the union (or unions) that it is satisfied that the employer has failed to comply.

(3) A remedial order and a notice under sub-paragraph (2) must draw the recipient's attention to the effect of sub-paragraphs (4) and (5).

(4) Sub-paragraph (5) applies if—

(a) the CAC is satisfied that the employer has failed to comply with a remedial order,

(b) the parties have agreed an appropriate bargaining unit or the CAC has decided an appropriate bargaining unit,

(c) in the case of an application under paragraph 11(2) or 12(2), the CAC, if required to do so, has decided under paragraph 20 that the application is not invalid, and

(d) the initial period has not yet ended.

(5) The CAC may issue a declaration that the union is (or unions are) recognised as entitled to conduct collective bargaining on behalf of the workers constituting the bargaining unit.]

[803A]

NOTES

This Schedule was inserted as noted at the beginning of this Schedule.

Paras 19C–19F: inserted by the Employment Relations Act 2004, s 5(1), as from 6 April 2005, except in relation to any application for recognition which was accepted by the CAC under para 15(5) of this Schedule before that date (see SI 2005/872, art 6).

Para 19E: inserted as noted above; for the words in italics in sub-para (5) there are substituted the words "under section 85 of the County Courts Act 1984" and for the words in italics in sub-para (6) there are substituted the words "Where a warrant of control is issued under section 85 of the 1984 Act to recover an amount in accordance with sub-paragraph (5), the power conferred by the warrant is exercisable" by the Tribunals, Courts and Enforcement Act 2007, s 62(3), Sch 13, paras 108, 109, as from a day to be appointed.

Union recognition

20.—(1) This paragraph applies if—

(a) the CAC accepts an application under paragraph 11(2) or 12(2),

(b) the parties have agreed an appropriate bargaining unit at the end of the appropriate period [(defined by paragraph 18)], or the CAC has decided an appropriate bargaining unit, and

(c) that bargaining unit differs from the proposed bargaining unit.

(2) Within the decision period the CAC must decide whether the application is invalid within the terms of paragraphs 43 to 50.

(3) In deciding whether the application is invalid, the CAC must consider any evidence which it has been given by the employer or the union (or unions).

(4) If the CAC decides that the application is invalid—

(a) the CAC must give notice of its decision to the parties,

(b) the CAC must not proceed with the application, and

(c) no further steps are to be taken under this Part of this Schedule.

(5) If the CAC decides that the application is not invalid it must—

(a) proceed with the application, and

(b) give notice to the parties that it is so proceeding.

(6) The decision period is—

(a) the period of 10 working days starting with the day after that on which the parties agree an appropriate bargaining unit or the CAC decides an appropriate bargaining unit, or

(b) such longer period (so starting) as the CAC may specify to the parties by notice containing reasons for the extension.

21.—(1) This paragraph applies if—

(a) the CAC accepts an application under paragraph 11(2) or 12(2),

(b) the parties have agreed an appropriate bargaining unit at the end of the appropriate period [(defined by paragraph 18)], or the CAC has decided an appropriate bargaining unit, and

(c) that bargaining unit is the same as the proposed bargaining unit.

(2) This paragraph also applies if the CAC accepts an application under paragraph 12(4).

(3) The CAC must proceed with the application.

22.—(1) This paragraph applies if—

(a) the CAC proceeds with an application in accordance with paragraph 20 or 21 [(and makes no declaration under paragraph 19F(5))], and

(b) the CAC is satisfied that a majority of the workers constituting the bargaining unit are members of the union (or unions).

(2) The CAC must issue a declaration that the union is (or unions are) recognised as entitled to conduct collective bargaining on behalf of the workers constituting the bargaining unit.

(3) But if any of the three qualifying conditions is fulfilled, instead of issuing a declaration under sub-paragraph (2) the CAC must give notice to the parties that it intends to arrange for the holding of a secret ballot in which the workers constituting the bargaining unit are asked whether they want the union (or unions) to conduct collective bargaining on their behalf.

(4) These are the three qualifying conditions—

(a) the CAC is satisfied that a ballot should be held in the interests of good industrial relations;

[(b) the CAC has evidence, which it considers to be credible, from a significant number of the union members within the bargaining unit that they do not want the union (or unions) to conduct collective bargaining on their behalf;]

(c) membership evidence is produced which leads the CAC to conclude that there are doubts whether a significant number of the union members within the bargaining unit want the union (or unions) to conduct collective bargaining on their behalf.

(5) For the purposes of sub-paragraph (4)(c) membership evidence is—

(a) evidence about the circumstances in which union members became members;

(b) evidence about the length of time for which union members have been members, in a case where the CAC is satisfied that such evidence should be taken into account.

23.—(1) This paragraph applies if—
(a) the CAC proceeds with an application in accordance with paragraph 20 or 21 [(and makes no declaration under paragraph 19F(5))], and
(b) the CAC is not satisfied that a majority of the workers constituting the bargaining unit are members of the union (or unions).

(2) The CAC must give notice to the parties that it intends to arrange for the holding of a secret ballot in which the workers constituting the bargaining unit are asked whether they want the union (or unions) to conduct collective bargaining on their behalf.

24.—(1) This paragraph applies if the CAC gives notice under paragraph 22(3) or 23(2).

(2) Within the notification period—
(a) the union (or unions), or
(b) the union (or unions) and the employer,

may notify the CAC that the party making the notification does not (or the parties making the notification do not) want the CAC to arrange for the holding of the ballot.

(3) If the CAC is so notified—
(a) it must not arrange for the holding of the ballot,
(b) it must inform the parties that it will not arrange for the holding of the ballot, and why, and
(c) no further steps are to be taken under this Part of this Schedule.

(4) If the CAC is not so notified it must arrange for the holding of the ballot.

[(5) The notification period is, in relation to notification by the union (or unions)—
(a) the period of 10 working days starting with the day on which the union (or last of the unions) receives the CAC's notice under paragraph 22(3) or 23(2), or
(b) such longer period so starting as the CAC may specify to the parties by notice.

(6) The notification period is, in relation to notification by the union (or unions) and the employer—
(a) the period of 10 working days starting with the day on which the last of the parties receives the CAC's notice under paragraph 22(3) or 23(2), or
(b) such longer period so starting as the CAC may specify to the parties by notice.

(7) The CAC may give a notice under sub-paragraph (5)(b) or (6)(b) only if the parties have applied jointly to it for the giving of such a notice.]

25.—(1) This paragraph applies if the CAC arranges under paragraph 24 for the holding of a ballot.

(2) The ballot must be conducted by a qualified independent person appointed by the CAC.

(3) The ballot must be conducted within—
(a) the period of 20 working days starting with the day after that on which the qualified independent person is appointed, or
(b) such longer period (so starting) as the CAC may decide.

(4) The ballot must be conducted—
(a) at a workplace or workplaces decided by the CAC,
(b) by post, or
(c) by a combination of the methods described in sub-paragraphs (a) and (b),

depending on the CAC's preference.

(5) In deciding how the ballot is to be conducted the CAC must take into account—
(a) the likelihood of the ballot being affected by unfairness or malpractice if it were conducted at a workplace or workplaces;
(b) costs and practicality;
(c) such other matters as the CAC considers appropriate.

(6) The CAC may not decide that the ballot is to be conducted as mentioned in sub-paragraph (4)(c) unless there are special factors making such a decision appropriate; and special factors include—
(a) factors arising from the location of workers or the nature of their employment;
(b) factors put to the CAC by the employer or the union (or unions).

[(6A) If the CAC decides that the ballot must (in whole or in part) be conducted at a workplace (or workplaces), it may require arrangements to be made for workers—

(a) who (but for the arrangements) would be prevented by the CAC's decision from voting by post, and
(b) who are unable, for reasons relating to those workers as individuals, to cast their votes in the ballot at the workplace (or at any of them),

to be given the opportunity (if they request it far enough in advance of the ballot for this to be practicable) to vote by post; and the CAC's imposing such a requirement is not to be treated for the purposes of sub-paragraph (6) as a decision that the ballot be conducted as mentioned in sub-paragraph (4)(c).]

(7) A person is a qualified independent person if—
(a) he satisfies such conditions as may be specified for the purposes of this paragraph by order of the Secretary of State or is himself so specified, and
(b) there are no grounds for believing either that he will carry out any functions conferred on him in relation to the ballot otherwise than competently or that his independence in relation to the ballot might reasonably be called into question.

(8) An order under sub-paragraph (7)(a) shall be made by statutory instrument subject to annulment in pursuance of a resolution of either House of Parliament.

(9) As soon as is reasonably practicable after the CAC is required under paragraph 24 to arrange for the holding of a ballot it must inform the parties—
(a) that it is so required;
(b) of the name of the person appointed to conduct the ballot and the date of his appointment;
(c) of the period within which the ballot must be conducted;
(d) whether the ballot is to be conducted by post or at a workplace or workplaces;
(e) of the workplace or workplaces concerned (if the ballot is to be conducted at a workplace or workplaces).

26.—(1) An employer who is informed by the CAC under paragraph 25(9) must comply with the following [five] duties.

(2) The first duty is to co-operate generally, in connection with the ballot, with the union (or unions) and the person appointed to conduct the ballot; and the second and third duties are not to prejudice the generality of this.

(3) The second duty is to give to the union (or unions) such access to the workers constituting the bargaining unit as is reasonable to enable the union (or unions) to inform the workers of the object of the ballot and to seek their support and their opinions on the issues involved.

(4) The third duty is to do the following (so far as it is reasonable to expect the employer to do so)—
(a) to give to the CAC, within the period of 10 working days starting with the day after that on which the employer is informed under paragraph 25(9), the names and home addresses of the workers constituting the bargaining unit;
(b) to give to the CAC, as soon as is reasonably practicable, the name and home address of any worker who joins the unit after the employer has complied with paragraph (a);
(c) to inform the CAC, as soon as is reasonably practicable, of any worker whose name has been given to the CAC under paragraph [19D or paragraph (a) or (b) of this sub-paragraph and] who ceases to be within the unit.

[(4A) The fourth duty is to refrain from making any offer to any or all of the workers constituting the bargaining unit which—
(a) has or is likely to have the effect of inducing any or all of them not to attend any relevant meeting between the union (or unions) and the workers constituting the bargaining unit, and
(b) is not reasonable in the circumstances.

(4B) The fifth duty is to refrain from taking or threatening to take any action against a worker solely or mainly on the grounds that he—
(a) attended or took part in any relevant meeting between the union (or unions) and the workers constituting the bargaining unit, or
(b) indicated his intention to attend or take part in such a meeting.

(4C) A meeting is a relevant meeting in relation to a worker for the purposes of sub-paragraphs (4A) and (4B) if—

(a) it is organised in accordance with any agreement reached concerning the second duty or as a result of a step ordered to be taken under paragraph 27 to remedy a failure to comply with that duty, and
(b) it is one which the employer is, by such an agreement or order as is mentioned in paragraph (a), required to permit the worker to attend.

(4D) Without prejudice to the generality of the second duty imposed by this paragraph, an employer is to be taken to have failed to comply with that duty if—
(a) he refuses a request for a meeting between the union (or unions) and any or all of the workers constituting the bargaining unit to be held in the absence of the employer or any representative of his (other than one who has been invited to attend the meeting) and it is not reasonable in the circumstances for him to do so,
(b) he or a representative of his attends such a meeting without having been invited to do so,
(c) he seeks to record or otherwise be informed of the proceedings at any such meeting and it is not reasonable in the circumstances for him to do so, or
(d) he refuses to give an undertaking that he will not seek to record or otherwise be informed of the proceedings at any such meeting unless it is reasonable in the circumstances for him to do either of those things.

(4E) The fourth and fifth duties do not confer any rights on a worker; but that does not affect any other right which a worker may have.]

[(4F) Sub-paragraph (4)(a) does not apply to names and addresses that the employer has already given to the CAC under paragraph 19D.

(4G) Where (because of sub-paragraph (4F)) the employer does not have to comply with sub-paragraph (4)(a), the reference in sub-paragraph (4)(b) to the time when the employer complied with sub-paragraph (4)(a) is to be read as a reference to the time when the employer is informed under paragraph 25(9).

(4H) If—
(a) a person was appointed on an application under paragraph 19C, and
(b) the person appointed to conduct the ballot is not that person,
the CAC must, as soon as is reasonably practicable, pass on to the person appointed to conduct the ballot the names and addresses given to it under paragraph 19D.]

(5) As soon as is reasonably practicable after the CAC receives any information under sub-paragraph (4) it must pass it on to the person appointed to conduct the ballot.

(6) If asked to do so by the union (or unions) the person appointed to conduct the ballot must send to any worker—
(a) whose name and home address have been [passed on to him under paragraph 19D or this paragraph], and
(b) who is still within the unit (so far as the person so appointed is aware),
any information supplied by the union (or unions) to the person so appointed.

(7) The duty under sub-paragraph (6) does not apply unless the union bears (or unions bear) the cost of sending the information.

[(8) Each of the powers specified in sub-paragraph (9) shall be taken to include power to issue Codes of Practice—
(a) about reasonable access for the purposes of sub-paragraph (3), and
(b) about the fourth duty imposed by this paragraph.

(9) The powers are—
(a) the power of ACAS under section 199(1);
(b) the power of the Secretary of State under section 203(1)(a).]

27.—(1) If the CAC is satisfied that the employer has failed to fulfil any of the [duties imposed on him] by paragraph 26, and the ballot has not been held, the CAC may order the employer—
(a) to take such steps to remedy the failure as the CAC considers reasonable and specifies in the order, and
(b) to do so within such period as the CAC considers reasonable and specifies in the order.

(2) If the CAC is satisfied that the employer has failed to comply with an order under sub-paragraph (1), and the ballot has not been held, the CAC may issue a declaration that the union is (or unions are) recognised as entitled to conduct collective bargaining on behalf of the bargaining unit.

(3) If the CAC issues a declaration under sub-paragraph (2) it shall take steps to cancel the holding of the ballot; and if the ballot is held it shall have no effect.

[27A.—(1) Each of the parties informed by the CAC under paragraph 25(9) must refrain from using any unfair practice.

(2) A party uses an unfair practice if, with a view to influencing the result of the ballot, the party—
(a) offers to pay money or give money's worth to a worker entitled to vote in the ballot in return for the worker's agreement to vote in a particular way or to abstain from voting,
(b) makes an outcome-specific offer to a worker entitled to vote in the ballot,
(c) coerces or attempts to coerce a worker entitled to vote in the ballot to disclose—
(i) whether he intends to vote or to abstain from voting in the ballot, or
(ii) how he intends to vote, or how he has voted, in the ballot,
(d) dismisses or threatens to dismiss a worker,
(e) takes or threatens to take disciplinary action against a worker,
(f) subjects or threatens to subject a worker to any other detriment, or
(g) uses or attempts to use undue influence on a worker entitled to vote in the ballot.

(3) For the purposes of sub-paragraph (2)(b) an "outcome-specific offer" is an offer to pay money or give money's worth which—
(a) is conditional on the issuing by the CAC of a declaration that—
(i) the union is (or unions are) recognised as entitled to conduct collective bargaining on behalf of the bargaining unit, or
(ii) the union is (or unions are) not entitled to be so recognised, and
(b) is not conditional on anything which is done or occurs as a result of the declaration in question.

(4) The duty imposed by this paragraph does not confer any rights on a worker; but that does not affect any other right which a worker may have.

(5) Each of the following powers shall be taken to include power to issue Codes of Practice about unfair practices for the purposes of this paragraph—
(a) the power of ACAS under section 199(1);
(b) the power of the Secretary of State under section 203(1)(a).

27B.—(1) A party may complain to the CAC that another party has failed to comply with paragraph 27A.

(2) A complaint under sub-paragraph (1) must be made on or before the first working day after—
(a) the date of the ballot, or
(b) if votes may be cast in the ballot on more than one day, the last of those days.

(3) Within the decision period the CAC must decide whether the complaint is well-founded.

(4) A complaint is well-founded if—
(a) the CAC finds that the party complained against used an unfair practice, and
(b) the CAC is satisfied that the use of that practice changed or was likely to change, in the case of a worker entitled to vote in the ballot—
(i) his intention to vote or to abstain from voting,
(ii) his intention to vote in a particular way, or
(iii) how he voted.

(5) The decision period is—
(a) the period of 10 working days starting with the day after that on which the complaint under sub-paragraph (1) was received by the CAC, or
(b) such longer period (so starting) as the CAC may specify to the parties by a notice containing reasons for the extension.

(6) If, at the beginning of the decision period, the ballot has not begun, the CAC may by notice to the parties and the qualified independent person postpone the date on which it is to begin until a date which falls after the end of the decision period.

27C.—(1) This paragraph applies if the CAC decides that a complaint under paragraph 27B is well-founded.

(2) The CAC must, as soon as is reasonably practicable, issue a declaration to that effect.

(3) The CAC may do either or both of the following—
(a) order the party concerned to take any action specified in the order within such period as may be so specified, or
(b) give notice to the employer and to the union (or unions) that it intends to arrange for the holding of a secret ballot in which the workers constituting the bargaining unit are asked whether they want the union (or unions) to conduct collective bargaining on their behalf.

(4) The CAC may give an order or a notice under sub-paragraph (3) either at the same time as it issues the declaration under sub-paragraph (2) or at any other time before it acts under paragraph 29.

(5) The action specified in an order under sub-paragraph (3)(a) shall be such as the CAC considers reasonable in order to mitigate the effect of the failure of the party concerned to comply with the duty imposed by paragraph 27A.

(6) The CAC may give more than one order under sub-paragraph (3)(a).

27D.—(1) This paragraph applies if the CAC issues a declaration under paragraph 27C(2) and the declaration states that the unfair practice used consisted of or included—
(a) the use of violence, or
(b) the dismissal of a union official.

(2) This paragraph also applies if the CAC has made an order under paragraph 27C(3)(a) and—
(a) it is satisfied that the party subject to the order has failed to comply with it, or
(b) it makes another declaration under paragraph 27C(2) in relation to a complaint against that party.

(3) If the party concerned is the employer, the CAC may issue a declaration that the union is (or unions are) recognised as entitled to conduct collective bargaining on behalf of the bargaining unit.

(4) If the party concerned is a union, the CAC may issue a declaration that the union is (or unions are) not entitled to be so recognised.

(5) The powers conferred by this paragraph are in addition to those conferred by paragraph 27C(3).

27E.—(1) This paragraph applies if the CAC issues a declaration that a complaint under paragraph 27B is well-founded and—
(a) gives a notice under paragraph 27C(3)(b), or
(b) issues a declaration under paragraph 27D.

(2) If the ballot in connection with which the complaint was made has not been held, the CAC shall take steps to cancel it.

(3) If that ballot is held, it shall have no effect.

27F.—(1) This paragraph applies if the CAC gives a notice under paragraph 27C(3)(b).

(2) Paragraphs 24 to 29 apply in relation to that notice as they apply in relation to a notice given under paragraph 22(3) or 23(2) but with the modifications specified in sub-paragraphs (3) to (6).

(3) In each of sub-paragraphs (5)(a) and (6)(a) of paragraph 24 for "10 working days" substitute "5 working days".

(4) An employer's duty under paragraph (a) of paragraph 26(4) is limited to—
(a) giving the CAC the names and home addresses of any workers in the bargaining unit which have not previously been given to it in accordance with that duty;
(b) giving the CAC the names and home addresses of those workers who have joined the bargaining unit since he last gave the CAC information in accordance with that duty;
(c) informing the CAC of any change to the name or home address of a worker whose name and home address have previously been given to the CAC in accordance with that duty; and
(d) informing the CAC of any worker whose name had previously been given to it in accordance with that duty who has ceased to be within the bargaining unit.

(5) Any order given under paragraph 27(1) or 27C(3)(a) for the purposes of the cancelled or ineffectual ballot shall have effect (to the extent that the CAC specifies in a notice to the parties) as if it were made for the purposes of the ballot to which the notice under paragraph 27C(3)(b) relates.

(6) The gross costs of the ballot shall be borne by such of the parties and in such proportions as the CAC may determine and, accordingly, sub-paragraphs (2) and (3) of paragraph 28 shall be omitted and the reference in sub-paragraph (4) of that paragraph to the employer and the union (or each of the unions) shall be construed as a reference to the party or parties which bear the costs in accordance with the CAC's determination.]

28.—(1) This paragraph applies if the holding of a ballot has been arranged under paragraph 24 whether or not it has been cancelled.

(2) The gross costs of the ballot shall be borne—
- (a) as to half, by the employer, and
- (b) as to half, by the union (or unions).

(3) If there is more than one union they shall bear their half of the gross costs—
- (a) in such proportions as they jointly indicate to the person appointed to conduct the ballot, or
- (b) in the absence of such an indication, in equal shares.

(4) The person appointed to conduct the ballot may send to the employer and the union (or each of the unions) a demand stating—
- (a) the gross costs of the ballot, and
- (b) the amount of the gross costs to be borne by the recipient.

(5) In such a case the recipient must pay the amount stated to the person sending the demand, and must do so within the period of 15 working days starting with the day after that on which the demand is received.

(6) In England and Wales, if the amount stated is not paid in accordance with sub-paragraph (5) it shall, if a county court so orders, be recoverable *by execution issued from that court* or otherwise as if it were payable under an order of that court.

[(6A) *Where an amount is recoverable from a union under sub-paragraph (6) execution may be carried out*, to the same extent and in the same manner as if the union were a body corporate, against any property held in trust for the union other than protected property as defined in section 23(2).]

(7) References to the costs of the ballot are to—
- (a) the costs wholly, exclusively and necessarily incurred in connection with the ballot by the person appointed to conduct it,
- (b) such reasonable amount as the person appointed to conduct the ballot charges for his services, and
- (c) such other costs as the employer and the union (or unions) agree.

29.—(1) As soon as is reasonably practicable after the CAC is informed of the result of a ballot by the person conducting it, the CAC must act under this paragraph.

[(1A) The duty in sub-paragraph (1) does not apply if the CAC gives a notice under paragraph 27C(3)(b).]

(2) The CAC must inform the employer and the union (or unions) of the result of the ballot.

(3) If the result is that the union is (or unions are) supported by—
- (a) a majority of the workers voting, and
- (b) at least 40 per cent of the workers constituting the bargaining unit,

the CAC must issue a declaration that the union is (or unions are) recognised as entitled to conduct collective bargaining on behalf of the bargaining unit.

(4) If the result is otherwise the CAC must issue a declaration that the union is (or unions are) not entitled to be so recognised.

(5) The Secretary of State may by order amend sub-paragraph (3) so as to specify a different degree of support; and different provision may be made for different circumstances.

(6) An order under sub-paragraph (5) shall be made by statutory instrument.

(7) No such order shall be made unless a draft of it has been laid before Parliament and approved by a resolution of each House of Parliament.

[804]

NOTES

Inserted as noted at the beginning of this Schedule.

Paras 20, 21: words in square brackets inserted by the Employment Relations Act 2004, s 57(1), Sch 1, para 23(1), (5), as from 6 April 2005.

Para 22: words in square brackets in sub-para (1)(a) inserted, and sub-para (4)(b) substituted, by the Employment Relations Act 2004, ss 5(2), 6(1), as from 6 April 2005, except in relation to any application for recognition which was accepted by the CAC under para 15(5) of this Schedule before that date (see SI 2005/872, art 6).

Para 23: words in square brackets in sub-para (1)(a) inserted by the Employment Relations Act 2004, s 5(2), as from 6 April 2005 (subject to the same exception in SI 2005/872, art 6 as noted above).

Para 24: sub-paras (5)–(7) substituted, for original sub-para (5), by the Employment Relations Act 2004, s 7, as from 6 April 2005 (subject to the same exception in SI 2005/872, art 6 as noted above).

Para 25: sub-para (6A) inserted by the Employment Relations Act 2004, s 8(1), as from 6 April 2005, except where, before that date, the CAC had informed the parties, in accordance with paras 25(9) or 117(11) of this Schedule (see SI 2005/872, art 7).

Para 26: word in square brackets in sub-para (1) substituted, sub-paras (4A)–(4E) inserted, and sub-paras (8), (9) substituted (for original sub-para (8)), by the Employment Relations Act 2004, s 9(1)–(4), as from 1 October 2005, except where, before that date, the CAC had informed the parties, in accordance with paras 25(9) or 117(11) of this Schedule (see SI 2005/2419, art 5); words in square brackets in sub-paras (4)(c), (6)(a) substituted, and sub-paras (4F)–(4H) inserted, by s 5(3)–(5) of the 2004 Act, as from 6 April 2005 (subject to the same exception in SI 2005/872, art 6 as noted above).

Para 27: words in square brackets substituted by the Employment Relations Act 2004, s 9(5), as from 1 October 2005 (subject to the same exception in SI 2005/2419, art 5 as noted above).

Paras 27A–27F: inserted by the Employment Relations Act 2004, s 10(1), as from 1 October 2005 (subject to the same exception in SI 2005/2419, art 5 as noted above).

Para 28: for the words in italics in sub-para (6) there are substituted the words "under section 85 of the County Courts Act 1984" by the Tribunals, Courts and Enforcement Act 2007, s 62(3), Sch 13, paras 108, 110(1), (2), as from a day to be appointed; sub-para (6A) inserted by the Employment Relations Act 2004, s 57(1), Sch 1, para 23(1), (6), as from 6 April 2005, except in relation to any demand which the person appointed to conduct the ballot had sent, under paras 28(4) or 120(4) of this Schedule, to the employer and the union (or each of the unions) before that date (see SI 2005/872, art 10); for the words in italics in sub-para (6A) there are substituted the words "Where a warrant of control is issued under section 85 of the 1984 Act to recover an amount in accordance with sub-paragraph (6), the power conferred by the warrant is exercisable" by the Tribunals, Courts and Enforcement Act 2007, s 62(3), Sch 13, paras 108, 110(1), (3), as from a day to be appointed.

Para 29: sub-para (1A) inserted by the Employment Relations Act 2004, s 10(2), as from 1 October 2005 (subject to the same exception in SI 2005/2419, art 5 as noted above).

Orders: the Recognition and Derecognition Ballots (Qualified Persons) Order 2000, SI 2000/1306 at **[2631]** (made under para 25). As of 6 April 2008 no Orders had been made under para 29.

Consequences of recognition

30.—(1) This paragraph applies if the CAC issues a declaration under this Part of this Schedule that the union is (or unions are) recognised as entitled to conduct collective bargaining on behalf of a bargaining unit.

(2) The parties may in the negotiation period conduct negotiations with a view to agreeing a method by which they will conduct collective bargaining.

(3) If no agreement is made in the negotiation period the employer or the union (or unions) may apply to the CAC for assistance.

(4) The negotiation period is—

(a) the period of 30 working days starting with the start day, or
(b) such longer period (so starting) as the parties may from time to time agree.

(5) The start day is the day after that on which the parties are notified of the declaration.

31.—(1) This paragraph applies if an application for assistance is made to the CAC under paragraph 30.

(2) The CAC must try to help the parties to reach in the agreement period an agreement on a method by which they will conduct collective bargaining.

(3) If at the end of the agreement period the parties have not made such an agreement the CAC must specify to the parties the method by which they are to conduct collective bargaining.

(4) Any method specified under sub-paragraph (3) is to have effect as if it were contained in a legally enforceable contract made by the parties.

(5) But if the parties agree in writing—

(a) that sub-paragraph (4) shall not apply, or shall not apply to particular parts of the method specified by the CAC, or

(b) to vary or replace the method specified by the CAC,

the written agreement shall have effect as a legally enforceable contract made by the parties.

(6) Specific performance shall be the only remedy available for breach of anything which is a legally enforceable contract by virtue of this paragraph.

(7) If at any time before a specification is made under sub-paragraph (3) the parties jointly apply to the CAC requesting it to stop taking steps under this paragraph, the CAC must comply with the request.

(8) The agreement period is—

(a) the period of 20 working days starting with the day after that on which the CAC receives the application under paragraph 30, or

(b) such longer period (so starting) as the CAC may decide with the consent of the parties.

[805]

NOTES

Inserted as noted at the beginning of this Schedule.

Method not carried out

32.—(1) This paragraph applies if—

(a) the CAC issues a declaration under this Part of this Schedule that the union is (or unions are) recognised as entitled to conduct collective bargaining on behalf of a bargaining unit,

(b) the parties agree a method by which they will conduct collective bargaining, and

(c) one or more of the parties fails to carry out the agreement.

(2) The [employer or the union (or unions)] may apply to the CAC for assistance.

(3) Paragraph 31 applies as if "paragraph 30" (in each place) read "paragraph 30 or paragraph 32".

[806]

NOTES

Inserted as noted at the beginning of this Schedule.

Para 32: words in square brackets in sub-para (2) substituted by the Employment Relations Act 2004, s 57(1), Sch 1, para 23(1), (7), as from 6 April 2005.

General provisions about admissibility

33. An application under paragraph 11 or 12 is not admissible unless—

(a) it is made in such form as the CAC specifies, and

(b) it is supported by such documents as the CAC specifies.

34. An application under paragraph 11 or 12 is not admissible unless the union gives (or unions give) to the employer—

(a) notice of the application, and

(b) a copy of the application and any documents supporting it.

35.—(1) An application under paragraph 11 or 12 is not admissible if the CAC is satisfied that there is already in force a collective agreement under which a union is (or unions are) recognised as entitled to conduct collective bargaining on behalf of any workers falling within the relevant bargaining unit.

(2) But sub-paragraph (1) does not apply to an application under paragraph 11 or 12 if—

(a) the union (or unions) recognised under the collective agreement and the union (or unions) making the application under paragraph 11 or 12 are the same, and
(b) the matters in respect of which the union is (or unions are) entitled to conduct collective bargaining do not include [all of the following: pay, hours and holidays ("the core topics")].

(3) A declaration of recognition which is the subject of a declaration under paragraph 83(2) must for the purposes of sub-paragraph (1) be treated as ceasing to have effect to the extent specified in paragraph 83(2) on the making of the declaration under paragraph 83(2).

(4) In applying sub-paragraph (1) an agreement for recognition (the agreement in question) must be ignored if—
(a) the union does not have (or none of the unions has) a certificate [of independence],
(b) at some time there was an agreement (the old agreement) between the employer and the union under which the union (whether alone or with other unions) was recognised as entitled to conduct collective bargaining on behalf of a group of workers which was the same or substantially the same as the group covered by the agreement in question, and
(c) the old agreement ceased to have effect in the period of three years ending with the date of the agreement in question.

(5) It is for the CAC to decide whether one group of workers is the same or substantially the same as another, but in deciding the CAC may take account of the views of any person it believes has an interest in the matter.

(6) The relevant bargaining unit is—
(a) the proposed bargaining unit, where the application is under paragraph 11(2) or 12(2);
(b) the agreed bargaining unit, where the application is under paragraph 12(4).

36.—(1) An application under paragraph 11 or 12 is not admissible unless the CAC decides that—
(a) members of the union (or unions) constitute at least 10 per cent of the workers constituting the relevant bargaining unit, and
(b) a majority of the workers constituting the relevant bargaining unit would be likely to favour recognition of the union (or unions) as entitled to conduct collective bargaining on behalf of the bargaining unit.

(2) The relevant bargaining unit is—
(a) the proposed bargaining unit, where the application is under paragraph 11(2) or 12(2);
(b) the agreed bargaining unit, where the application is under paragraph 12(4).

(3) The CAC must give reasons for the decision.

37.—(1) This paragraph applies to an application made by more than one union under paragraph 11 or 12.

(2) The application is not admissible unless—
(a) the unions show that they will co-operate with each other in a manner likely to secure and maintain stable and effective collective bargaining arrangements, and
(b) the unions show that, if the employer wishes, they will enter into arrangements under which collective bargaining is conducted by the unions acting together on behalf of the workers constituting the relevant bargaining unit.

(3) The relevant bargaining unit is—
(a) the proposed bargaining unit, where the application is under paragraph 11(2) or 12(2);
(b) the agreed bargaining unit, where the application is under paragraph [12(4)].

38.—(1) This paragraph applies if—
(a) the CAC accepts a relevant application relating to a bargaining unit or proceeds under paragraph 20 with an application relating to a bargaining unit,
(b) the application has not been withdrawn,
(c) no notice has been given under paragraph 17(2),
(d) the CAC has not issued a declaration under paragraph [19F(5), 22(2), 27(2), 27D(3), 27D(4),] 29(3) or 29(4) in relation to that bargaining unit, and

(e) no notification has been made under paragraph 24(2).

(2) Another relevant application is not admissible if—

(a) at least one worker falling within the relevant bargaining unit also falls within the bargaining unit referred to in sub-paragraph (1), and

(b) the application is made by a union (or unions) other than the union (or unions) which made the application referred to in sub-paragraph (1).

(3) A relevant application is an application under paragraph 11 or 12.

(4) The relevant bargaining unit is—

(a) the proposed bargaining unit, where the application is under paragraph 11(2) or 12(2);

(b) the agreed bargaining unit, where the application is under paragraph 12(4).

39.—(1) This paragraph applies if the CAC accepts a relevant application relating to a bargaining unit or proceeds under paragraph 20 with an application relating to a bargaining unit.

(2) Another relevant application is not admissible if—

(a) the application is made within the period of 3 years starting with the day after that on which the CAC gave notice of acceptance of the application mentioned in sub-paragraph (1),

(b) the relevant bargaining unit is the same or substantially the same as the bargaining unit mentioned in sub-paragraph (1), and

(c) the application is made by the union (or unions) which made the application mentioned in sub-paragraph (1).

(3) A relevant application is an application under paragraph 11 or 12.

(4) The relevant bargaining unit is—

(a) the proposed bargaining unit, where the application is under paragraph 11(2) or 12(2);

(b) the agreed bargaining unit, where the application is under paragraph 12(4).

(5) This paragraph does not apply if paragraph 40 or 41 applies.

40.—(1) This paragraph applies if the CAC issues a declaration under paragraph [27D(4) or] 29(4) that a union is (or unions are) not entitled to be recognised as entitled to conduct collective bargaining on behalf of a bargaining unit; and this is so whether the ballot concerned is [arranged] under this Part or Part III of this Schedule.

(2) An application under paragraph 11 or 12 is not admissible if—

(a) the application is made within the period of 3 years starting with the day after that on which the declaration was issued,

(b) the relevant bargaining unit is the same or substantially the same as the bargaining unit mentioned in sub-paragraph (1), and

(c) the application is made by the union (or unions) which made the application leading to the declaration.

(3) The relevant bargaining unit is—

(a) the proposed bargaining unit, where the application is under paragraph 11(2) or 12(2);

(b) the agreed bargaining unit, where the application is under paragraph 12(4).

41.—(1) This paragraph applies if the CAC issues a declaration under paragraph [119D(4), 119H(5) or] 121(3) that bargaining arrangements are to cease to have effect; and this is so whether the ballot concerned is [arranged] under Part IV or Part V of this Schedule.

(2) An application under paragraph 11 or 12 is not admissible if—

(a) the application is made within the period of 3 years starting with the day after that on which the declaration was issued,

(b) the relevant bargaining unit is the same or substantially the same as the bargaining unit to which the bargaining arrangements mentioned in sub-paragraph (1) relate, and

(c) the application is made by the union which was a party (or unions which were parties) to the proceedings leading to the declaration.

(3) The relevant bargaining unit is—

(a) the proposed bargaining unit, where the application is under paragraph 11(2) or 12(2);
(b) the agreed bargaining unit, where the application is under paragraph 12(4).

42.—(1) This paragraph applies for the purposes of paragraphs 39 to 41.

(2) It is for the CAC to decide whether one bargaining unit is the same or substantially the same as another, but in deciding the CAC may take account of the views of any person it believes has an interest in the matter.

[807]

NOTES

Inserted as noted at the beginning of this Schedule.

Para 35: words in square brackets in sub-para (2)(b) substituted by the Employment Relations Act 2004, s 11, as from 6 April 2005, except in relation to any application which was made to the CAC under paras 11 or 12 of this Schedule before that date (see SI 2005/872, art 8); words in square brackets in sub-para (4)(a) substituted by s 50(6) of the 2004 Act, as from 6 April 2005.

Paras 37, 38: numbers in square brackets substituted by the Employment Relations Act 2004, s 57(1), Sch 1, para 23(1), (8), (9), as from 6 April 2005.

Paras 40, 41: words in first pair of square brackets in sub-para (1) inserted, and word in second pair of square brackets in that sub-paragraph substituted, by the Employment Relations Act 2004, s 57(1), Sch 1, para 23(1), (10), (11), as from 6 April 2005.

General provisions about validity

43.—(1) Paragraphs 44 to 50 apply if the CAC has to decide under paragraph 20 whether an application is valid.

(2) In those paragraphs—
(a) references to the application in question are to that application, and
(b) references to the relevant bargaining unit are to the bargaining unit agreed by the parties or decided by the CAC.

44.—(1) The application in question is invalid if the CAC is satisfied that there is already in force a collective agreement under which a union is (or unions are) recognised as entitled to conduct collective bargaining on behalf of any workers falling within the relevant bargaining unit.

(2) But sub-paragraph (1) does not apply to the application in question if—
(a) the union (or unions) recognised under the collective agreement and the union (or unions) making the application in question are the same, and
(b) the matters in respect of which the union is (or unions are) entitled to conduct collective bargaining do not include [all of the following: pay, hours and holidays ("the core topics")].

(3) A declaration of recognition which is the subject of a declaration under paragraph 83(2) must for the purposes of sub-paragraph (1) be treated as ceasing to have effect to the extent specified in paragraph 83(2) on the making of the declaration under paragraph 83(2).

(4) In applying sub-paragraph (1) an agreement for recognition (the agreement in question) must be ignored if—
(a) the union does not have (or none of the unions has) a certificate [of independence],
(b) at some time there was an agreement (the old agreement) between the employer and the union under which the union (whether alone or with other unions) was recognised as entitled to conduct collective bargaining on behalf of a group of workers which was the same or substantially the same as the group covered by the agreement in question, and
(c) the old agreement ceased to have effect in the period of three years ending with the date of the agreement in question.

(5) It is for the CAC to decide whether one group of workers is the same or substantially the same as another, but in deciding the CAC may take account of the views of any person it believes has an interest in the matter.

45. The application in question is invalid unless the CAC decides that—

(a) members of the union (or unions) constitute at least 10 per cent of the workers constituting the relevant bargaining unit, and

(b) a majority of the workers constituting the relevant bargaining unit would be likely to favour recognition of the union (or unions) as entitled to conduct collective bargaining on behalf of the bargaining unit.

46.—(1) This paragraph applies if—

(a) the CAC accepts an application under paragraph 11 or 12 relating to a bargaining unit or proceeds under paragraph 20 with an application relating to a bargaining unit,

(b) the application has not been withdrawn,

(c) no notice has been given under paragraph 17(2),

(d) the CAC has not issued a declaration under paragraph [19F(5), 22(2), 27(2), 27D(3), 27D(4),] 29(3) or 29(4) in relation to that bargaining unit, and

(e) no notification has been made under paragraph 24(2).

(2) The application in question is invalid if—

(a) at least one worker falling within the relevant bargaining unit also falls within the bargaining unit referred to in sub-paragraph (1), and

(b) the application in question is made by a union (or unions) other than the union (or unions) which made the application referred to in sub-paragraph (1).

47.—(1) This paragraph applies if the CAC accepts an application under paragraph 11 or 12 relating to a bargaining unit or proceeds under paragraph 20 with an application relating to a bargaining unit.

(2) The application in question is invalid if—

(a) the application is made within the period of 3 years starting with the day after that on which the CAC gave notice of acceptance of the application mentioned in sub-paragraph (1),

(b) the relevant bargaining unit is the same or substantially the same as the bargaining unit mentioned in sub-paragraph (1), and

(c) the application is made by the union (or unions) which made the application mentioned in sub-paragraph (1).

(3) This paragraph does not apply if paragraph 48 or 49 applies.

48.—(1) This paragraph applies if the CAC issues a declaration under paragraph [27D(4) or] 29(4) that a union is (or unions are) not entitled to be recognised as entitled to conduct collective bargaining on behalf of a bargaining unit; and this is so whether the ballot concerned is [arranged] under this Part or Part III of this Schedule.

(2) The application in question is invalid if—

(a) the application is made within the period of 3 years starting with the date of the declaration,

(b) the relevant bargaining unit is the same or substantially the same as the bargaining unit mentioned in sub-paragraph (1), and

(c) the application is made by the union (or unions) which made the application leading to the declaration.

49.—(1) This paragraph applies if the CAC issues a declaration under paragraph [119D(4), 119H(5) or] 121(3) that bargaining arrangements are to cease to have effect; and this is so whether the ballot concerned is [arranged] under Part IV or Part V of this Schedule.

(2) The application in question is invalid if—

(a) the application is made within the period of 3 years starting with the day after that on which the declaration was issued,

(b) the relevant bargaining unit is the same or substantially the same as the bargaining unit to which the bargaining arrangements mentioned in sub-paragraph (1) relate, and

(c) the application is made by the union which was a party (or unions which were parties) to the proceedings leading to the declaration.

50.—(1) This paragraph applies for the purposes of paragraphs 47 to 49.

(2) It is for the CAC to decide whether one bargaining unit is the same or substantially the same as another, but in deciding the CAC may take account of the views of any person it believes has an interest in the matter.

[808]

NOTES

Inserted as noted at the beginning of this Schedule.

Para 44: words in square brackets in sub-para (2)(b) substituted by the Employment Relations Act 2004, s 11, as from 6 April 2005, except in relation to any application which was made to the CAC under paras 11 or 12 of this Schedule before that date (see SI 2005/872, art 8); words in square brackets in sub-para (4)(a) substituted by s 50(6) of the 2004 Act, as from 6 April 2005.

Para 46: numbers in square brackets substituted by the Employment Relations Act 2004, s 57(1), Sch 1, para 23(1), (12), as from 6 April 2005.

Paras 48, 49: words in first pair of square brackets in sub-para (1) inserted, and word in second pair of square brackets in that sub-paragraph substituted, by the Employment Relations Act 2004, s 57(1), Sch 1, para 23(1), (13), (14), as from 6 April 2005.

Competing applications

51.—(1) For the purposes of this paragraph—

(a) the original application is the application referred to in paragraph 38(1) or 46(1), and

(b) the competing application is the other application referred to in paragraph 38(2) or the application in question referred to in paragraph 46(2);

but an application cannot be an original application unless it was made under paragraph 11(2) or 12(2).

(2) This paragraph applies if—

(a) the CAC decides that the competing application is not admissible by reason of paragraph 38 or is invalid by reason of paragraph 46,

(b) at the time the decision is made the parties to the original application have not agreed the appropriate bargaining unit under paragraph 18, and the CAC has not decided the appropriate bargaining unit under paragraph 19 [or 19A], in relation to the application, and

(c) the 10 per cent test (within the meaning given by paragraph 14) is satisfied with regard to the competing application.

(3) In such a case—

(a) the CAC must cancel the original application,

(b) the CAC must give notice to the parties to the application that it has been cancelled,

(c) no further steps are to be taken under this Part of this Schedule in relation to the application, and

(d) the application shall be treated as if it had never been admissible.

[809]

NOTES

Inserted as noted at the beginning of this Schedule.

Para 51: words in square brackets in sub-para (2)(b) inserted by the Employment Relations Act 2004, s 57(1), Sch 1, para 23(1), (15), as from 6 April 2005.

PART II
VOLUNTARY RECOGNITION

Agreements for recognition

52.—(1) This paragraph applies for the purposes of this Part of this Schedule.

(2) An agreement is an agreement for recognition if the following conditions are fulfilled in relation to it—

(a) the agreement is made in the permitted period between a union (or unions) and an employer in consequence of a request made under paragraph 4 and valid within the terms of paragraphs 5 to 9;

(b) under the agreement the union is (or unions are) recognised as entitled to conduct collective bargaining on behalf of a group or groups of workers employed by the employer;

(c) if sub-paragraph (5) applies to the agreement, it is satisfied.

(3) The permitted period is the period which begins with the day on which the employer receives the request and ends when the first of the following occurs—

(a) the union withdraws (or unions withdraw) the request;

(b) the union withdraws (or unions withdraw) any application under paragraph 11 or 12 made in consequence of the request;

(c) the CAC gives notice of a decision under paragraph 14(7) which precludes it from accepting such an application under paragraph 11 or 12;

(d) the CAC gives notice under paragraph 15(4)(a) or 20(4)(a) in relation to such an application under paragraph 11 or 12;

(e) the parties give notice to the CAC under paragraph 17(2) in relation to such an application under paragraph 11 or 12;

(f) the CAC issues a declaration under paragraph [19F(5) or] 22(2) in consequence of such an application under paragraph 11 or 12;

(g) the CAC is notified under paragraph 24(2) in relation to such an application under paragraph 11 or 12;

(h) the last day of the notification period ends (the notification period being that defined by paragraph [24(6)]) and arising from such an application under paragraph 11 or 12);

(i) the CAC is required under paragraph 51(3) to cancel such an application under paragraph 11 or 12.

(4) Sub-paragraph (5) applies to an agreement if—

(a) at the time it is made the CAC has received an application under paragraph 11 or 12 in consequence of the request mentioned in sub-paragraph (2), and

(b) the CAC has not decided whether the application is admissible or it has decided that it is admissible.

(5) This sub-paragraph is satisfied if, in relation to the application under paragraph 11 or 12, the parties give notice to the CAC under paragraph 17 before the final event (as defined in paragraph 17) occurs.

[810]

NOTES

Inserted as noted at the beginning of this Schedule.

Para 52: words in square brackets in sub-para (3)(f) inserted, and number in square brackets in sub-para (3)(h) substituted, by the Employment Relations Act 2004, s 57(1), Sch 1, para 23(1), (16), as from 6 April 2005.

Other interpretation

53.—(1) This paragraph applies for the purposes of this Part of this Schedule.

(2) In relation to an agreement for recognition, references to the bargaining unit are to the group of workers (or the groups taken together) to which the agreement for recognition relates.

(3) In relation to an agreement for recognition, references to the parties are to the union (or unions) and the employer who are parties to the agreement.

54.—(1) This paragraph applies for the purposes of this Part of this Schedule.

(2) The meaning of collective bargaining given by section 178(1) shall not apply.

(3) Except in paragraph 63(2), in relation to an agreement for recognition references to collective bargaining are to negotiations relating to the matters in respect of which the union is (or unions are) recognised as entitled to conduct negotiations under the agreement for recognition.

(4) In paragraph 63(2) the reference to collective bargaining is to negotiations relating to pay, hours and holidays.

[811]

NOTES

Inserted as noted at the beginning of this Schedule.

Determination of type of agreement

55.—(1) This paragraph applies if one or more of the parties to an agreement applies to the CAC for a decision whether or not the agreement is an agreement for recognition.

(2) The CAC must give notice of receipt of an application under sub-paragraph (1) to any parties to the agreement who are not parties to the application.

(3) The CAC must within the decision period decide whether the agreement is an agreement for recognition.

(4) If the CAC decides that the agreement is an agreement for recognition it must issue a declaration to that effect.

(5) If the CAC decides that the agreement is not an agreement for recognition it must issue a declaration to that effect.

(6) The decision period is—

(a) the period of 10 working days starting with the day after that on which the CAC receives the application under sub-paragraph (1), or

(b) such longer period (so starting) as the CAC may specify to the parties to the agreement by notice containing reasons for the extension.

[812]

NOTES

Inserted as noted at the beginning of this Schedule.

Termination of agreement for recognition

56.—(1) The employer may not terminate an agreement for recognition before the relevant period ends.

(2) After that period ends the employer may terminate the agreement, with or without the consent of the union (or unions).

(3) The union (or unions) may terminate an agreement for recognition at any time, with or without the consent of the employer.

(4) Sub-paragraphs (1) to (3) have effect subject to the terms of the agreement or any other agreement of the parties.

(5) The relevant period is the period of three years starting with the day after the date of the agreement.

57.—(1) If an agreement for recognition is terminated, as from the termination the agreement and any provisions relating to the collective bargaining method shall cease to have effect.

(2) For this purpose provisions relating to the collective bargaining method are—

(a) any agreement between the parties as to the method by which collective bargaining is to be conducted with regard to the bargaining unit, or

(b) anything effective as, or as if contained in, a legally enforceable contract and relating to the method by which collective bargaining is to be conducted with regard to the bargaining unit.

[813]

NOTES

Inserted as noted at the beginning of this Schedule.

Application to CAC to specify method

58.—(1) This paragraph applies if the parties make an agreement for recognition.

(2) The parties may in the negotiation period conduct negotiations with a view to agreeing a method by which they will conduct collective bargaining.

(3) If no agreement is made in the negotiation period the employer or the union (or unions) may apply to the CAC for assistance.

(4) The negotiation period is—
(a) the period of 30 working days starting with the start day, or
(b) such longer period (so starting) as the parties may from time to time agree.

(5) The start day is the day after that on which the agreement is made.

59.—(1) This paragraph applies if—
(a) the parties to an agreement for recognition agree a method by which they will conduct collective bargaining, and
(b) one or more of the parties fails to carry out the agreement as to a method.

(2) The employer or the union (or unions) may apply to the CAC for assistance.

60.—(1) This paragraph applies if an application for assistance is made to the CAC under paragraph 58 or 59.

(2) The application is not admissible unless the conditions in sub-paragraphs (3) and (4) are satisfied.

(3) The condition is that the employer, taken with any associated employer or employers, must—
(a) employ at least 21 workers on the day the application is made, or
(b) employ an average of at least 21 workers in the 13 weeks ending with that day.

(4) The condition is that the union (or every union) has a certificate [of independence].

(5) To find the average under sub-paragraph (3)(b)—
(a) take the number of workers employed in each of the 13 weeks (including workers not employed for the whole of the week);
(b) aggregate the 13 numbers;
(c) divide the aggregate by 13.

(6) For the purposes of sub-paragraph (3)(a) any worker employed by an associated company incorporated outside Great Britain must be ignored unless the day the application was made fell within a period during which he ordinarily worked in Great Britain.

(7) For the purposes of sub-paragraph (3)(b) any worker employed by an associated company incorporated outside Great Britain must be ignored in relation to a week unless the whole or any part of that week fell within a period during which he ordinarily worked in Great Britain.

(8) For the purposes of sub-paragraphs (6) and (7) a worker who is employed on board a ship registered in the register maintained under section 8 of the Merchant Shipping Act 1995 shall be treated as ordinarily working in Great Britain unless—
(a) the ship's entry in the register specifies a port outside Great Britain as the port to which the vessel is to be treated as belonging,
(b) the employment is wholly outside Great Britain, or
(c) the worker is not ordinarily resident in Great Britain.

(9) An order made under paragraph 7(6) may also—
(a) provide that sub-paragraphs (2), (3) and (5) to (8) of this paragraph are not to apply, or are not to apply in specified circumstances, or
(b) vary the number of workers for the time being specified in sub-paragraph (3).

61.—(1) An application to the CAC is not admissible unless—
(a) it is made in such form as the CAC specifies, and
(b) it is supported by such documents as the CAC specifies.

(2) An application which is made by a union (or unions) to the CAC is not admissible unless the union gives (or unions give) to the employer—
(a) notice of the application, and
(b) a copy of the application and any documents supporting it.

(3) An application which is made by an employer to the CAC is not admissible unless the employer gives to the union (or each of the unions)—

(a) notice of the application, and
(b) a copy of the application and any documents supporting it.

[814]

NOTES

Inserted as noted at the beginning of this Schedule.

Para 60: words in square brackets in sub-para (4) substituted by the Employment Relations Act 2004, s 50(6), as from 6 April 2005.

CAC's response to application

62.—(1) The CAC must give notice to the parties of receipt of an application under paragraph 58 or 59.

(2) Within the acceptance period the CAC must decide whether the application is admissible within the terms of paragraphs 60 and 61.

(3) In deciding whether an application is admissible the CAC must consider any evidence which it has been given by the employer or the union (or unions).

(4) If the CAC decides that the application is not admissible—
(a) the CAC must give notice of its decision to the parties,
(b) the CAC must not accept the application, and
(c) no further steps are to be taken under this Part of this Schedule.

(5) If the CAC decides that the application is admissible it must—
(a) accept the application, and
(b) give notice of the acceptance to the parties.

(6) The acceptance period is—
(a) the period of 10 working days starting with the day after that on which the CAC receives the application, or
(b) such longer period (so starting) as the CAC may specify to the parties by notice containing reasons for the extension.

63.—(1) If the CAC accepts an application it must try to help the parties to reach in the agreement period an agreement on a method by which they will conduct collective bargaining.

(2) If at the end of the agreement period the parties have not made such an agreement the CAC must specify to the parties the method by which they are to conduct collective bargaining.

(3) Any method specified under sub-paragraph (2) is to have effect as if it were contained in a legally enforceable contract made by the parties.

(4) But if the parties agree in writing—
(a) that sub-paragraph (3) shall not apply, or shall not apply to particular parts of the method specified by the CAC, or
(b) to vary or replace the method specified by the CAC,

the written agreement shall have effect as a legally enforceable contract made by the parties.

(5) Specific performance shall be the only remedy available for breach of anything which is a legally enforceable contract by virtue of this paragraph.

(6) If the CAC accepts an application, the applicant may not withdraw it after the end of the agreement period.

(7) If at any time before a specification is made under sub-paragraph (2) the parties jointly apply to the CAC requesting it to stop taking steps under this paragraph, the CAC must comply with the request.

(8) The agreement period is—
(a) the period of 20 working days starting with the day after that on which the CAC gives notice of acceptance of the application, or
(b) such longer period (so starting) as the parties may from time to time agree.

[815]

NOTES

Inserted as noted at the beginning of this Schedule.

PART III
CHANGES AFFECTING BARGAINING UNIT

Introduction

64.—(1) This Part of this Schedule applies if—

(a) the CAC has issued a declaration that a union is (or unions are) recognised as entitled to conduct collective bargaining on behalf of a bargaining unit, and

(b) provisions relating to the collective bargaining method apply in relation to the unit.

(2) In such a case, in this Part of this Schedule—

(a) references to the original unit are to the bargaining unit on whose behalf the union is (or unions are) recognised as entitled to conduct collective bargaining, and

(b) references to the bargaining arrangements are to the declaration and to the provisions relating to the collective bargaining method which apply in relation to the original unit.

(3) For this purpose provisions relating to the collective bargaining method are—

(a) the parties' agreement as to the method by which collective bargaining is to be conducted with regard to the original unit,

(b) anything effective as, or as if contained in, a legally enforceable contract and relating to the method by which collective bargaining is to be conducted with regard to the original unit, or

(c) any provision of this Part of this Schedule that a method of collective bargaining is to have effect with regard to the original unit.

65. References in this Part of this Schedule to the parties are to the employer and the union (or unions) concerned.

[816]

NOTES

Inserted as noted at the beginning of this Schedule.

Either party believes unit no longer appropriate

66.—(1) This paragraph applies if the employer believes or the union believes (or unions believe) that the original unit is no longer an appropriate bargaining unit.

(2) The employer or union (or unions) may apply to the CAC to make a decision as to what is an appropriate bargaining unit.

67.—(1) An application under paragraph 66 is not admissible unless the CAC decides that it is likely that the original unit is no longer appropriate by reason of any of the matters specified in sub-paragraph (2).

(2) The matters are—

(a) a change in the organisation or structure of the business carried on by the employer;

(b) a change in the activities pursued by the employer in the course of the business carried on by him;

(c) a substantial change in the number of workers employed in the original unit.

68.—(1) The CAC must give notice to the parties of receipt of an application under paragraph 66.

(2) Within the acceptance period the CAC must decide whether the application is admissible within the terms of paragraphs 67 and 92.

(3) In deciding whether the application is admissible the CAC must consider any evidence which it has been given by the employer or the union (or unions).

(4) If the CAC decides that the application is not admissible—
(a) the CAC must give notice of its decision to the parties,
(b) the CAC must not accept the application, and
(c) no further steps are to be taken under this Part of this Schedule.

(5) If the CAC decides that the application is admissible it must—
(a) accept the application, and
(b) give notice of the acceptance to the parties.

(6) The acceptance period is—
(a) the period of 10 working days starting with the day after that on which the CAC receives the application, or
(b) such longer period (so starting) as the CAC may specify to the parties by notice containing reasons for the extension.

69.—(1) This paragraph applies if—
(a) the CAC gives notice of acceptance of the application, and
(b) before the end of the first period the parties agree a bargaining unit or units (the new unit or units) differing from the original unit and inform the CAC of their agreement.

(2) If in the CAC's opinion the new unit (or any of the new units) contains at least one worker falling within an outside bargaining unit no further steps are to be taken under this Part of this Schedule.

(3) If sub-paragraph (2) does not apply—
(a) the CAC must issue a declaration that the union is (or unions are) recognised as entitled to conduct collective bargaining on behalf of the new unit or units;
(b) so far as it affects workers in the new unit (or units) who fall within the original unit, the declaration shall have effect in place of any declaration that the union is (or unions are) recognised as entitled to conduct collective bargaining on behalf of the original unit;
(c) the method of collective bargaining relating to the original unit shall have effect in relation to the new unit or units, with any modifications which the CAC considers necessary to take account of the change of bargaining unit and specifies in the declaration.

(4) The first period is—
(a) the period of 10 working days starting with the day after that on which the CAC gives notice of acceptance of the application, or
(b) such longer period (so starting) as the parties may from time to time agree and notify to the CAC.

(5) An outside bargaining unit is a bargaining unit which fulfils these conditions—
(a) it is not the original unit;
(b) a union is (or unions are) recognised as entitled to conduct collective bargaining on its behalf;
(c) the union (or at least one of the unions) is not a party referred to in paragraph 64.

70.—(1) This paragraph applies if—
(a) the CAC gives notice of acceptance of the application, and
(b) the parties do not inform the CAC before the end of the first period that they have agreed a bargaining unit or units differing from the original unit.

(2) During the second period—
(a) the CAC must decide whether or not the original unit continues to be an appropriate bargaining unit;
(b) if the CAC decides that the original unit does not so continue, it must decide what other bargaining unit is or units are appropriate;
(c) the CAC must give notice to the parties of its decision or decisions under paragraphs (a) and (b).

(3) In deciding whether or not the original unit continues to be an appropriate bargaining unit the CAC must take into account only these matters—
(a) any change in the organisation or structure of the business carried on by the employer;

(b) any change in the activities pursued by the employer in the course of the business carried on by him;
(c) any substantial change in the number of workers employed in the original unit.

(4) In deciding what other bargaining unit is or units are appropriate the CAC must take these matters into account—
(a) the need for the unit or units to be compatible with effective management;
(b) the matters listed in sub-paragraph (5), so far as they do not conflict with that need.

(5) The matters are—
(a) the views of the employer and of the union (or unions);
(b) existing national and local bargaining arrangements;
(c) the desirability of avoiding small fragmented bargaining units within an undertaking;
(d) the characteristics of workers falling within the original unit and of any other employees of the employer whom the CAC considers relevant;
(e) the location of workers.

(6) If the CAC decides that two or more bargaining units are appropriate its decision must be such that no worker falls within more than one of them.

(7) The second period is—
(a) the period of 10 working days starting with the day after that on which the first period ends, or
(b) such longer period (so starting) as the CAC may specify to the parties by notice containing reasons for the extension.

71. If the CAC gives notice under paragraph 70 of a decision that the original unit continues to be an appropriate bargaining unit no further steps are to be taken under this Part of this Schedule.

72. Paragraph 82 applies if the CAC gives notice under paragraph 70 of—
(a) a decision that the original unit is no longer an appropriate bargaining unit, and
(b) a decision as to the bargaining unit which is (or units which are) appropriate.

73.—(1) This paragraph applies if—
(a) the parties agree under paragraph 69 a bargaining unit or units differing from the original unit,
(b) paragraph 69(2) does not apply, and
(c) at least one worker falling within the original unit does not fall within the new unit (or any of the new units).

(2) In such a case—
(a) the CAC must issue a declaration that the bargaining arrangements, so far as relating to the worker or workers mentioned in sub-paragraph (1)(c), are to cease to have effect on a date specified by the CAC in the declaration, and
(b) the bargaining arrangements shall cease to have effect accordingly.

[817]

NOTES

Inserted as noted at the beginning of this Schedule.

Employer believes unit has ceased to exist

74.—(1) If the employer—
(a) believes that the original unit has ceased to exist, and
(b) wishes the bargaining arrangements to cease to have effect,

he must give the union (or each of the unions) a notice complying with sub-paragraph (2) and must give a copy of the notice to the CAC.

(2) A notice complies with this sub-paragraph if it—
(a) identifies the unit and the bargaining arrangements,
(b) states the date on which the notice is given,
(c) states that the unit has ceased to exist, and
(d) states that the bargaining arrangements are to cease to have effect on a date which

is specified in the notice and which falls after the end of the period of 35 working days starting with the day after that on which the notice is given.

(3) Within the validation period the CAC must decide whether the notice complies with sub-paragraph (2).

(4) If the CAC decides that the notice does not comply with sub-paragraph (2)—
(a) the CAC must give the parties notice of its decision, and
(b) the employer's notice shall be treated as not having been given.

(5) If the CAC decides that the notice complies with sub-paragraph (2) it must give the parties notice of the decision.

(6) The bargaining arrangements shall cease to have effect on the date specified under sub-paragraph (2)(d) if—
(a) the CAC gives notice under sub-paragraph (5), and
(b) the union does not (or unions do not) apply to the CAC under paragraph 75.

(7) The validation period is—
(a) the period of 10 working days starting with the day after that on which the CAC receives the copy of the notice, or
(b) such longer period (so starting) as the CAC may specify to the parties by notice containing reasons for the extension.

75.—(1) Paragraph 76 applies if—
(a) the CAC gives notice under paragraph 74(5), and
(b) within the period of 10 working days starting with the day after that on which the notice is given the union makes (or unions make) an application to the CAC for a decision on the questions specified in sub-paragraph (2).

(2) The questions are—
(a) whether the original unit has ceased to exist;
(b) whether the original unit is no longer appropriate by reason of any of the matters specified in sub-paragraph (3).

(3) The matters are—
(a) a change in the organisation or structure of the business carried on by the employer;
(b) a change in the activities pursued by the employer in the course of the business carried on by him;
(c) a substantial change in the number of workers employed in the original unit.

76.—(1) The CAC must give notice to the parties of receipt of an application under paragraph 75.

(2) Within the acceptance period the CAC must decide whether the application is admissible within the terms of paragraph 92.

(3) In deciding whether the application is admissible the CAC must consider any evidence which it has been given by the employer or the union (or unions).

(4) If the CAC decides that the application is not admissible—
(a) the CAC must give notice of its decision to the parties,
(b) the CAC must not accept the application, and
(c) no further steps are to be taken under this Part of this Schedule.

(5) If the CAC decides that the application is admissible it must—
(a) accept the application, and
(b) give notice of the acceptance to the parties.

(6) The acceptance period is—
(a) the period of 10 working days starting with the day after that on which the CAC receives the application, or
(b) such longer period (so starting) as the CAC may specify to the parties by notice containing reasons for the extension.

77.—(1) If the CAC accepts an application it—
(a) must give the employer and the union (or unions) an opportunity to put their views on the questions in relation to which the application was made;
(b) must decide the questions before the end of the decision period.

(2) If the CAC decides that the original unit has ceased to exist—
(a) the CAC must give the parties notice of its decision, and
(b) the bargaining arrangements shall cease to have effect on the termination date.

(3) If the CAC decides that the original unit has not ceased to exist, and that it is not the case that the original unit is no longer appropriate by reason of any of the matters specified in paragraph 75(3)—
(a) the CAC must give the parties notice of its decision, and
(b) the employer's notice shall be treated as not having been given.

(4) If the CAC decides that the original unit has not ceased to exist, and that the original unit is no longer appropriate by reason of any of the matters specified in paragraph 75(3), the CAC must give the parties notice of its decision.

(5) The decision period is—
(a) the period of 10 working days starting with the day after that on which the CAC gives notice of acceptance of the application, or
(b) such longer period (so starting) as the CAC may specify to the parties by notice containing reasons for the extension.

(6) The termination date is the later of—
(a) the date specified under paragraph 74(2)(d), and
(b) the day after the last day of the decision period.

78.—(1) This paragraph applies if—
(a) the CAC gives notice under paragraph 77(4), and
(b) before the end of the first period the parties agree a bargaining unit or units (the new unit or units) differing from the original unit and inform the CAC of their agreement.

(2) If in the CAC's opinion the new unit (or any of the new units) contains at least one worker falling within an outside bargaining unit no further steps are to be taken under this Part of this Schedule.

(3) If sub-paragraph (2) does not apply—
(a) the CAC must issue a declaration that the union is (or unions are) recognised as entitled to conduct collective bargaining on behalf of the new unit or units;
(b) so far as it affects workers in the new unit (or units) who fall within the original unit, the declaration shall have effect in place of any declaration that the union is (or unions are) recognised as entitled to conduct collective bargaining on behalf of the original unit;
(c) the method of collective bargaining relating to the original unit shall have effect in relation to the new unit or units, with any modifications which the CAC considers necessary to take account of the change of bargaining unit and specifies in the declaration.

(4) The first period is—
(a) the period of 10 working days starting with the day after that on which the CAC gives notice under paragraph 77(4), or
(b) such longer period (so starting) as the parties may from time to time agree and notify to the CAC.

(5) An outside bargaining unit is a bargaining unit which fulfils these conditions—
(a) it is not the original unit;
(b) a union is (or unions are) recognised as entitled to conduct collective bargaining on its behalf;
(c) the union (or at least one of the unions) is not a party referred to in paragraph 64.

79.—(1) This paragraph applies if—
(a) the CAC gives notice under paragraph 77(4), and
(b) the parties do not inform the CAC before the end of the first period that they have agreed a bargaining unit or units differing from the original unit.

(2) During the second period the CAC—
(a) must decide what other bargaining unit is or units are appropriate;
(b) must give notice of its decision to the parties.

(3) In deciding what other bargaining unit is or units are appropriate, the CAC must take these matters into account—
(a) the need for the unit or units to be compatible with effective management;

(b) the matters listed in sub-paragraph (4), so far as they do not conflict with that need.

(4) The matters are—

(a) the views of the employer and of the union (or unions);
(b) existing national and local bargaining arrangements;
(c) the desirability of avoiding small fragmented bargaining units within an undertaking;
(d) the characteristics of workers falling within the original unit and of any other employees of the employer whom the CAC considers relevant;
(e) the location of workers.

(5) If the CAC decides that two or more bargaining units are appropriate its decision must be such that no worker falls within more than one of them.

(6) The second period is—

(a) the period of 10 working days starting with the day after that on which the first period ends, or
(b) such longer period (so starting) as the CAC may specify to the parties by notice containing reasons for the extension.

80. Paragraph 82 applies if the CAC gives notice under paragraph 79 of a decision as to the bargaining unit which is (or units which are) appropriate.

81.—(1) This paragraph applies if—

(a) the parties agree under paragraph 78 a bargaining unit or units differing from the original unit,
(b) paragraph 78(2) does not apply, and
(c) at least one worker falling within the original unit does not fall within the new unit (or any of the new units).

(2) In such a case—

(a) the CAC must issue a declaration that the bargaining arrangements, so far as relating to the worker or workers mentioned in sub-paragraph (1)(c), are to cease to have effect on a date specified by the CAC in the declaration, and
(b) the bargaining arrangements shall cease to have effect accordingly.

[818]

NOTES

Inserted as noted at the beginning of this Schedule.

Position where CAC decides new unit

82.—(1) This paragraph applies if the CAC gives notice under paragraph 70 of—

(a) a decision that the original unit is no longer an appropriate bargaining unit, and
(b) a decision as to the bargaining unit which is (or units which are) appropriate.

(2) This paragraph also applies if the CAC gives notice under paragraph 79 of a decision as to the bargaining unit which is (or units which are) appropriate.

(3) The CAC—

(a) must proceed as stated in paragraphs 83 to 89 with regard to the appropriate unit (if there is one only), or
(b) must proceed as stated in paragraphs 83 to 89 with regard to each appropriate unit separately (if there are two or more).

(4) References in those paragraphs to the new unit are to the appropriate unit under consideration.

83.—(1) This paragraph applies if in the CAC's opinion the new unit contains at least one worker falling within a statutory outside bargaining unit.

(2) In such a case—

(a) the CAC must issue a declaration that the relevant bargaining arrangements, so far as relating to workers falling within the new unit, are to cease to have effect on a date specified by the CAC in the declaration, and
(b) the relevant bargaining arrangements shall cease to have effect accordingly.

(3) The relevant bargaining arrangements are—
(a) the bargaining arrangements relating to the original unit, and
(b) the bargaining arrangements relating to each statutory outside bargaining unit containing workers who fall within the new unit.

(4) The bargaining arrangements relating to the original unit are the bargaining arrangements as defined in paragraph 64.

(5) The bargaining arrangements relating to an outside unit are—
(a) the declaration recognising a union (or unions) as entitled to conduct collective bargaining on behalf of the workers constituting the outside unit, and
(b) the provisions relating to the collective bargaining method.

(6) For this purpose the provisions relating to the collective bargaining method are—
(a) any agreement by the employer and the union (or unions) as to the method by which collective bargaining is to be conducted with regard to the outside unit,
(b) anything effective as, or as if contained in, a legally enforceable contract and relating to the method by which collective bargaining is to be conducted with regard to the outside unit, or
(c) any provision of this Part of this Schedule that a method of collective bargaining is to have effect with regard to the outside unit.

(7) A statutory outside bargaining unit is a bargaining unit which fulfils these conditions—
(a) it is not the original unit;
(b) a union is (or unions are) recognised as entitled to conduct collective bargaining on its behalf by virtue of a declaration of the CAC;
(c) the union (or at least one of the unions) is not a party referred to in paragraph 64.

(8) The date specified under sub-paragraph [(2)(a)] must be—
(a) the date on which the relevant period expires, or
(b) if the CAC believes that to maintain the relevant bargaining arrangements would be impracticable or contrary to the interests of good industrial relations, the date after the date on which the declaration is issued;

and the relevant period is the period of 65 working days starting with the day after that on which the declaration is issued.

84.—(1) This paragraph applies if in the CAC's opinion the new unit contains—
(a) at least one worker falling within a voluntary outside bargaining unit, but
(b) no worker falling within a statutory outside bargaining unit.

(2) In such a case—
(a) the CAC must issue a declaration that the original bargaining arrangements, so far as relating to workers falling within the new unit, are to cease to have effect on a date specified by the CAC in the declaration, and
(b) the original bargaining arrangements shall cease to have effect accordingly.

(3) The original bargaining arrangements are the bargaining arrangements as defined in paragraph 64.

(4) A voluntary outside bargaining unit is a bargaining unit which fulfils these conditions—
(a) it is not the original unit;
(b) a union is (or unions are) recognised as entitled to conduct collective bargaining on its behalf by virtue of an agreement with the employer;
(c) the union (or at least one of the unions) is not a party referred to in paragraph 64.

(5) The date specified under sub-paragraph (2)(a) must be—
(a) the date on which the relevant period expires, or
(b) if the CAC believes that to maintain the original bargaining arrangements would be impracticable or contrary to the interests of good industrial relations, the date after the date on which the declaration is issued;

and the relevant period is the period of 65 working days starting with the day after that on which the declaration is issued.

85.—(1) If the CAC's opinion is not that mentioned in paragraph 83(1) or 84(1) it must—
(a) decide whether the difference between the original unit and the new unit is such that the support of the union (or unions) within the new unit needs to be assessed, and

(b) inform the parties of its decision.

(2) If the CAC's decision is that such support does not need to be assessed—

(a) the CAC must issue a declaration that the union is (or unions are) recognised as entitled to conduct collective bargaining on behalf of the new unit;

(b) so far as it affects workers in the new unit who fall within the original unit, the declaration shall have effect in place of any declaration that the union is (or unions are) recognised as entitled to conduct collective bargaining on behalf of the original unit;

(c) the method of collective bargaining relating to the original unit shall have effect in relation to the new unit, with any modifications which the CAC considers necessary to take account of the change of bargaining unit and specifies in the declaration.

86.—(1) This paragraph applies if the CAC decides under paragraph 85(1) that the support of the union (or unions) within the new unit needs to be assessed.

(2) The CAC must decide these questions—

(a) whether members of the union (or unions) constitute at least 10 per cent of the workers constituting the new unit;

(b) whether a majority of the workers constituting the new unit would be likely to favour recognition of the union (or unions) as entitled to conduct collective bargaining on behalf of the new unit.

(3) If the CAC decides one or both of the questions in the negative—

(a) the CAC must issue a declaration that the bargaining arrangements, so far as relating to workers falling within the new unit, are to cease to have effect on a date specified by the CAC in the declaration, and

(b) the bargaining arrangements shall cease to have effect accordingly.

87.—(1) This paragraph applies if—

(a) the CAC decides both the questions in paragraph 86(2) in the affirmative, and

(b) the CAC is satisfied that a majority of the workers constituting the new unit are members of the union (or unions).

(2) The CAC must issue a declaration that the union is (or unions are) recognised as entitled to conduct collective bargaining on behalf of the workers constituting the new unit.

(3) But if any of the three qualifying conditions is fulfilled, instead of issuing a declaration under sub-paragraph (2) the CAC must give notice to the parties that it intends to arrange for the holding of a secret ballot in which the workers constituting the new unit are asked whether they want the union (or unions) to conduct collective bargaining on their behalf.

(4) These are the three qualifying conditions—

(a) the CAC is satisfied that a ballot should be held in the interests of good industrial relations;

[(b) the CAC has evidence, which it considers to be credible, from a significant number of the union members within the new bargaining unit that they do not want the union (or unions) to conduct collective bargaining on their behalf;]

(c) membership evidence is produced which leads the CAC to conclude that there are doubts whether a significant number of the union members within the new unit want the union (or unions) to conduct collective bargaining on their behalf.

(5) For the purposes of sub-paragraph (4)(c) membership evidence is—

(a) evidence about the circumstances in which union members became members;

(b) evidence about the length of time for which union members have been members, in a case where the CAC is satisfied that such evidence should be taken into account.

(6) If the CAC issues a declaration under sub-paragraph (2)—

(a) so far as it affects workers in the new unit who fall within the original unit, the declaration shall have effect in place of any declaration that the union is (or unions are) recognised as entitled to conduct collective bargaining on behalf of the original unit;

(b) the method of collective bargaining relating to the original unit shall have effect in relation to the new unit, with any modifications which the CAC considers necessary to take account of the change of bargaining unit and specifies in the declaration.

88.—(1) This paragraph applies if—
(a) the CAC decides both the questions in paragraph 86(2) in the affirmative, and
(b) the CAC is not satisfied that a majority of the workers constituting the new unit are members of the union (or unions).

(2) The CAC must give notice to the parties that it intends to arrange for the holding of a secret ballot in which the workers constituting the new unit are asked whether they want the union (or unions) to conduct collective bargaining on their behalf.

89.—(1) If the CAC gives notice under paragraph 87(3) or 88(2) the union (or unions) may within the notification period notify the CAC that the union does not (or unions do not) want the CAC to arrange for the holding of the ballot; and the notification period is the period of 10 working days starting with the day after that on which the union (or last of the unions) receives the CAC's notice.

(2) If the CAC is so notified—
(a) it must not arrange for the holding of the ballot,
(b) it must inform the parties that it will not arrange for the holding of the ballot, and why,
(c) it must issue a declaration that the bargaining arrangements, so far as relating to workers falling within the new unit, are to cease to have effect on a date specified by it in the declaration, and
(d) the bargaining arrangements shall cease to have effect accordingly.

(3) If the CAC is not so notified it must arrange for the holding of the ballot.

(4) Paragraph 25 applies if the CAC arranges under this paragraph for the holding of a ballot (as well as if the CAC arranges under paragraph 24 for the holding of a ballot).

(5) Paragraphs 26 to 29 apply accordingly, [but as if—
(a) references to the bargaining unit were references to the new unit, and
(b) paragraph 26(4F) to (4H), and the references in paragraph 26(4) and (6) to paragraph 19D, were omitted].

(6) If as a result of the ballot the CAC issues a declaration that the union is (or unions are) recognised as entitled to conduct collective bargaining on behalf of the new unit—
(a) so far as it affects workers in the new unit who fall within the original unit, the declaration shall have effect in place of any declaration that the union is (or unions are) recognised as entitled to conduct collective bargaining on behalf of the original unit;
(b) the method of collective bargaining relating to the original unit shall have effect in relation to the new unit, with any modifications which the CAC considers necessary to take account of the change of bargaining unit and specifies in the declaration.

(7) If as a result of the ballot the CAC issues a declaration that the union is (or unions are) not entitled to be recognised as entitled to conduct collective bargaining on behalf of the new unit—
(a) the CAC must state in the declaration the date on which the bargaining arrangements, so far as relating to workers falling within the new unit, are to cease to have effect, and
(b) the bargaining arrangements shall cease to have effect accordingly.

(8) Paragraphs (a) and (b) of sub-paragraph (6) also apply if the CAC issues a declaration under paragraph 27(2) [or 27D(3)].

[(9) Paragraphs (a) and (b) of sub-paragraph (7) also apply if the CAC issues a declaration under paragraph 27D(4).]

[819]

NOTES

Inserted as noted at the beginning of this Schedule.

Para 83: number in square brackets substituted by the Employment Relations Act 2004, s 57(1), Sch 1, para 23(1), (17), as from 6 April 2005.

Para 87: sub-para (4)(b) substituted by the Employment Relations Act 2004, s 6(2), as from 6 April 2005, except in relation to any application for a decision which was accepted by the CAC under paras 68(5) or 76(5) of this Schedule before that date (see SI 2005/872, art 6).

Para 89: words in square brackets in sub-para (5) substituted, words in square brackets in sub-para (8) inserted, and sub-para (9) added, by the Employment Relations Act 2004, s 57(1), Sch 1, para 23(1), (18)–(20), as from 6 April 2005.

Residual workers

90.—(1) This paragraph applies if—
(a) the CAC decides an appropriate bargaining unit or units under paragraph 70 or 79, and
(b) at least one worker falling within the original unit does not fall within the new unit (or any of the new units).

(2) In such a case—
(a) the CAC must issue a declaration that the bargaining arrangements, so far as relating to the worker or workers mentioned in sub-paragraph (1)(b), are to cease to have effect on a date specified by the CAC in the declaration, and
(b) the bargaining arrangements shall cease to have effect accordingly.

91.—(1) This paragraph applies if—
(a) the CAC has proceeded as stated in paragraphs 83 to 89 with regard to the new unit (if there is one only) or with regard to each new unit (if there are two or more), and
(b) in so doing the CAC has issued one or more declarations under paragraph 83.

(2) The CAC must—
(a) consider each declaration issued under paragraph 83, and
(b) in relation to each declaration, identify each statutory outside bargaining unit which contains at least one worker who also falls within the new unit to which the declaration relates;

and in this paragraph each statutory outside bargaining unit so identified is referred to as a parent unit.

(3) The CAC must then—
(a) consider each parent unit, and
(b) in relation to each parent unit, identify any workers who fall within the parent unit but who do not fall within the new unit (or any of the new units);

and in this paragraph the workers so identified in relation to a parent unit are referred to as a residual unit.

(4) In relation to each residual unit, the CAC must issue a declaration that the outside union is (or outside unions are) recognised as entitled to conduct collective bargaining on its behalf.

(5) But no such declaration shall be issued in relation to a residual unit if the CAC has received an application under paragraph 66 or 75 in relation to its parent unit.

(6) In this paragraph references to the outside union (or to outside unions) in relation to a residual unit are to the union which is (or unions which are) recognised as entitled to conduct collective bargaining on behalf of its parent unit.

(7) If the CAC issues a declaration under sub-paragraph (4)—
(a) the declaration shall have effect in place of the existing declaration that the outside union is (or outside unions are) recognised as entitled to conduct collective bargaining on behalf of the parent unit, so far as the existing declaration relates to the residual unit;
(b) if there is a method of collective bargaining relating to the parent unit, it shall have effect in relation to the residual unit with any modifications which the CAC considers necessary to take account of the change of bargaining unit and specifies in the declaration.

[820]

NOTES

Inserted as noted at the beginning of this Schedule.

Applications under this Part

92.—(1) An application to the CAC under this Part of this Schedule is not admissible unless—
(a) it is made in such form as the CAC specifies, and
(b) it is supported by such documents as the CAC specifies.

(2) An application which is made by a union (or unions) to the CAC under this Part of this Schedule is not admissible unless the union gives (or unions give) to the employer—
(a) notice of the application, and
(b) a copy of the application and any documents supporting it.

(3) An application which is made by an employer to the CAC under this Part of this Schedule is not admissible unless the employer gives to the union (or each of the unions)—
(a) notice of the application, and
(b) a copy of the application and any documents supporting it.

[821]

NOTES

Inserted as noted at the beginning of this Schedule.

Withdrawal of application

93.—(1) If an application under paragraph 66 or 75 is accepted by the CAC, the applicant (or applicants) may not withdraw the application—
(a) after the CAC issues a declaration under paragraph 69(3) or 78(3),
(b) after the CAC decides under paragraph 77(2) or 77(3),
(c) after the CAC issues a declaration under paragraph [83(2)], 85(2), 86(3) or 87(2) in relation to the new unit (where there is only one) or a declaration under any of those paragraphs in relation to any of the new units (where there is more than one),
(d) after the union has (or unions have) notified the CAC under paragraph 89(1) in relation to the new unit (where there is only one) or any of the new units (where there is more than one), or
(e) after the end of the notification period referred to in paragraph 89(1) and relating to the new unit (where there is only one) or any of the new units (where there is more than one).

(2) If an application is withdrawn by the applicant (or applicants)—
(a) the CAC must give notice of the withdrawal to the other party (or parties), and
(b) no further steps are to be taken under this Part of this Schedule.

[822]

NOTES

Inserted as noted at the beginning of this Schedule.

Para 93: number in square brackets in sub-para (1)(c) substituted by the Employment Relations Act 2004, s 57(1), Sch 1, para 23(1), (21), as from 6 April 2005.

Meaning of collective bargaining

94.—(1) This paragraph applies for the purposes of this Part of this Schedule.

(2) Except in relation to paragraphs 69(5), 78(5) and 83(6), the meaning of collective bargaining given by section 178(1) shall not apply.

(3) In relation to a new unit references to collective bargaining are to negotiations relating to the matters which were the subject of collective bargaining in relation to the corresponding original unit; and the corresponding original unit is the unit which was the subject of an application under paragraph 66 or 75 in consequence of which the new unit was agreed by the parties or decided by the CAC.

(4) But if the parties agree matters as the subject of collective bargaining in relation to the new unit, references to collective bargaining in relation to that unit are to negotiations relating to the agreed matters; and this is the case whether the agreement is made before or after the time when the CAC issues a declaration that the union is (or unions are) recognised as entitled to conduct collective bargaining on behalf of the new unit.

(5) In relation to a residual unit in relation to which a declaration is issued under paragraph 91, references to collective bargaining are to negotiations relating to the matters which were the subject of collective bargaining in relation to the corresponding parent unit.

(6) In construing paragraphs 69(3)(c), 78(3)(c), 85(2)(c), 87(6)(b) and 89(6)(b)—

(a) sub-paragraphs (3) and (4) do not apply, and
(b) references to collective bargaining are to negotiations relating to pay, hours and holidays.

[823]

NOTES

Inserted as noted at the beginning of this Schedule.

Method of collective bargaining

95.—(1) This paragraph applies for the purposes of this Part of this Schedule.

(2) Where a method of collective bargaining has effect in relation to a new unit, that method shall have effect as if it were contained in a legally enforceable contract made by the parties.

(3) But if the parties agree in writing—
(a) that sub-paragraph (2) shall not apply, or shall not apply to particular parts of the method, or
(b) to vary or replace the method,
the written agreement shall have effect as a legally enforceable contract made by the parties.

(4) Specific performance shall be the only remedy available for breach of anything which is a legally enforceable contract by virtue of this paragraph.

[824]

NOTES

Inserted as noted at the beginning of this Schedule.

PART IV
DERECOGNITION: GENERAL

Introduction

96.—(1) This Part of this Schedule applies if the CAC has issued a declaration that a union is (or unions are) recognised as entitled to conduct collective bargaining on behalf of a bargaining unit.

(2) In such a case references in this Part of this Schedule to the bargaining arrangements are to the declaration and to the provisions relating to the collective bargaining method.

(3) For this purpose the provisions relating to the collective bargaining method are—
(a) the parties' agreement as to the method by which collective bargaining is to be conducted,
(b) anything effective as, or as if contained in, a legally enforceable contract and relating to the method by which collective bargaining is to be conducted, or
(c) any provision of Part III of this Schedule that a method of collective bargaining is to have effect.

97. For the purposes of this Part of this Schedule the relevant date is the date of the expiry of the period of 3 years starting with the date of the CAC's declaration.

98. References in this Part of this Schedule to the parties are to the employer and the union (or unions) concerned.

[825]

NOTES

Inserted as noted at the beginning of this Schedule.

Employer employs fewer than 21 workers

99.—(1) This paragraph applies if—

(a) the employer believes that he, taken with any associated employer or employers, employed an average of fewer than 21 workers in any period of 13 weeks, and
(b) that period ends on or after the relevant date.

(2) If the employer wishes the bargaining arrangements to cease to have effect, he must give the union (or each of the unions) a notice complying with sub-paragraph (3) and must give a copy of the notice to the CAC.

(3) A notice complies with this sub-paragraph if it—
[(za) is not invalidated by paragraph 99A,]
(a) identifies the bargaining arrangements,
(b) specifies the period of 13 weeks in question,
(c) states the date on which the notice is given,
(d) is given within the period of 5 working days starting with the day after the last day of the specified period of 13 weeks,
(e) states that the employer, taken with any associated employer or employers, employed an average of fewer than 21 workers in the specified period of 13 weeks, and
(f) states that the bargaining arrangements are to cease to have effect on a date which is specified in the notice and which falls after the end of the period of 35 working days starting with the day after that on which the notice is given.

(4) To find the average number of workers employed by the employer, taken with any associated employer or employers, in the specified period of 13 weeks—
(a) take the number of workers employed in each of the 13 weeks (including workers not employed for the whole of the week);
(b) aggregate the 13 numbers;
(c) divide the aggregate by 13.

(5) For the purposes of sub-paragraph (1)(a) any worker employed by an associated company incorporated outside Great Britain must be ignored in relation to a week unless the whole or any part of that week fell within a period during which he ordinarily worked in Great Britain.

(6) For the purposes of sub-paragraph (5) a worker who is employed on board a ship registered in the register maintained under section 8 of the Merchant Shipping Act 1995 shall be treated as ordinarily working in Great Britain unless—
(a) the ship's entry in the register specifies a port outside Great Britain as the port to which the vessel is to be treated as belonging,
(b) the employment is wholly outside Great Britain, or
(c) the worker is not ordinarily resident in Great Britain.

(7) An order made under paragraph 7(6) may also—
(a) provide that sub-paragraphs (1) to (6) of this paragraph and paragraphs [99A] to 103 are not to apply, or are not to apply in specified circumstances, or
(b) vary the number of workers for the time being specified in sub-paragraphs (1)(a) and (3)(e).

[99A.—(1) A notice given for the purposes of paragraph 99(2) ("the notice in question") is invalidated by this paragraph if—
(a) a relevant application was made, or an earlier notice under paragraph 99(2) was given, within the period of 3 years prior to the date when the notice in question was given,
(b) the relevant application, or that earlier notice, and the notice in question relate to the same bargaining unit, and
(c) the CAC accepted the relevant application or (as the case may be) decided under paragraph 100 that the earlier notice under paragraph 99(2) complied with paragraph 99(3).

(2) A relevant application is an application made to the CAC—
(a) by the employer under paragraph 106, 107 or 128, or
(b) by a worker (or workers) under paragraph 112.]

100.—(1) [If an employer gives notice for the purposes of paragraph 99(2),] within the validation period the CAC must decide whether the notice complies with paragraph 99(3).

(2) If the CAC decides that the notice does not comply with paragraph 99(3)—
(a) the CAC must give the parties notice of its decision, and
(b) the employer's notice shall be treated as not having been given.

(3) If the CAC decides that the notice complies with paragraph 99(3) it must give the parties notice of the decision.

(4) The bargaining arrangements shall cease to have effect on the date specified under paragraph 99(3)(f) if—

(a) the CAC gives notice under sub-paragraph (3), and

(b) the union does not (or unions do not) apply to the CAC under paragraph 101.

(5) The validation period is—

(a) the period of 10 working days starting with the day after that on which the CAC receives the copy of the notice, or

(b) such longer period (so starting) as the CAC may specify to the parties by notice containing reasons for the extension.

101.—(1) This paragraph applies if—

(a) the CAC gives notice under paragraph 100(3), and

(b) within the period of 10 working days starting with the day after that on which the notice is given, the union makes (or unions make) an application to the CAC for a decision whether the period of 13 weeks specified under paragraph 99(3)(b) ends on or after the relevant date and whether the statement made under paragraph 99(3)(e) is correct.

(2) An application is not admissible unless—

(a) it is made in such form as the CAC specifies, and

(b) it is supported by such documents as the CAC specifies.

(3) An application is not admissible unless the union gives (or unions give) to the employer—

(a) notice of the application, and

(b) a copy of the application and any documents supporting it.

(4), (5) . . .

102.—(1) The CAC must give notice to the parties of receipt of an application under paragraph 101.

(2) Within the acceptance period the CAC must decide whether the application is admissible within the terms of paragraph 101.

(3) In deciding whether an application is admissible the CAC must consider any evidence which it has been given by the employer or the union (or unions).

(4) If the CAC decides that the application is not admissible—

(a) the CAC must give notice of its decision to the parties,

(b) the CAC must not accept the application,

(c) no further steps are to be taken under this Part of this Schedule, and

(d) the bargaining arrangements shall cease to have effect on the date specified under paragraph 99(3)(f).

(5) If the CAC decides that the application is admissible it must—

(a) accept the application, and

(b) give notice of the acceptance to the parties.

(6) The acceptance period is—

(a) the period of 10 working days starting with the day after that on which the CAC receives the application, or

(b) such longer period (so starting) as the CAC may specify to the parties by notice containing reasons for the extension.

103.—(1) If the CAC accepts an application it—

(a) must give the employer and the union (or unions) an opportunity to put their views on the questions whether the period of 13 weeks specified under paragraph 99(3)(b) ends on or after the relevant date and whether the statement made under paragraph 99(3)(e) is correct;

(b) must decide the questions within the decision period and must give reasons for the decision.

(2) If the CAC decides that the period of 13 weeks specified under paragraph 99(3)(b) ends on or after the relevant date and that the statement made under paragraph 99(3)(e) is correct the bargaining arrangements shall cease to have effect on the termination date.

(3) If the CAC decides that the period of 13 weeks specified under paragraph 99(3)(b) does not end on or after the relevant date or that the statement made under paragraph 99(3)(e) is not correct, the notice under paragraph 99 shall be treated as not having been given.

[(3A) Sub-paragraph (3) does not prevent the notice from being treated for the purposes of the provisions mentioned in sub-paragraph (3B) as having been given.

(3B) Those provisions are—
- (a) paragraphs 109(1), 113(1) and 130(1);
- (b) paragraph 99A(1) in its application to a later notice given for the purposes of paragraph 99(2).]

(4) The decision period is—
- (a) the period of 10 working days starting with the day after that on which the CAC gives notice of acceptance of the application, or
- (b) such longer period (so starting) as the CAC may specify to the parties by notice containing reasons for the extension.

(5) The termination date is the later of—
- (a) the date specified under paragraph 99(3)(f), and
- (b) the day after the last day of the decision period.

[826]

NOTES

Inserted as noted at the beginning of this Schedule.

Para 99: sub-para (3)(za) inserted, and number in square brackets in sub-para (7)(a) substituted, by the Employment Relations Act 2004, s 12(1)–(3), as from 6 April 2005, except in relation to any notice which the employer gave, for the purposes of para 99(2) of this Schedule, to the union (or each of the unions) before that date (see SI 2005/872, art 9).

Para 99A: inserted by the Employment Relations Act 2004, s 12(4), as from 6 April 2005 (subject to the same exception in SI 2005/872, art 9 as noted above).

Para 100: words in square brackets in sub-para (1) inserted by the Employment Relations Act 2004, s 12(5), as from 6 April 2005 (subject to the same exception in SI 2005/872, art 9 as noted above).

Para 101: sub-paras (4), (5) repealed by the Employment Relations Act 2004, ss 12(6), 57(2), Sch 2, as from 6 April 2005 (subject to the same exception in SI 2005/872, art 9 as noted above).

Para 103: sub-paras (3A), (3B) inserted by the Employment Relations Act 2004, s 12(7), as from 6 April 2005 (subject to the same exception in SI 2005/872, art 9 as noted above).

Employer's request to end arrangements

104.—(1) This paragraph and paragraphs 105 to 111 apply if after the relevant date the employer requests the union (or each of the unions) to agree to end the bargaining arrangements.

(2) The request is not valid unless it—
- (a) is in writing,
- (b) is received by the union (or each of the unions),
- (c) identifies the bargaining arrangements, and
- (d) states that it is made under this Schedule.

105.—(1) If before the end of the first period the parties agree to end the bargaining arrangements no further steps are to be taken under this Part of this Schedule.

(2) Sub-paragraph (3) applies if before the end of the first period—
- (a) the union informs the employer that the union does not accept the request but is willing to negotiate, or
- (b) the unions inform the employer that the unions do not accept the request but are willing to negotiate.

(3) The parties may conduct negotiations with a view to agreeing to end the bargaining arrangements.

(4) If such an agreement is made before the end of the second period no further steps are to be taken under this Part of this Schedule.

(5) The employer and the union (or unions) may request ACAS to assist in conducting the negotiations.

(6) The first period is the period of 10 working days starting with the day after—

(a) the day on which the union receives the request, or
(b) the last day on which any of the unions receives the request.

(7) The second period is—
(a) the period of 20 working days starting with the day after that on which the first period ends, or
(b) such longer period (so starting) as the parties may from time to time agree.

106.—(1) This paragraph applies if—
(a) before the end of the first period the union fails (or unions fail) to respond to the request, or
(b) before the end of the first period the union informs the employer that it does not (or unions inform the employer that they do not) accept the request (without indicating a willingness to negotiate).

(2) The employer may apply to the CAC for the holding of a secret ballot to decide whether the bargaining arrangements should be ended.

107.—(1) This paragraph applies if—
(a) the union informs (or unions inform) the employer under paragraph 105(2), and
(b) no agreement is made before the end of the second period.

(2) The employer may apply to the CAC for the holding of a secret ballot to decide whether the bargaining arrangements should be ended.

(3) But no application may be made if within the period of 10 working days starting with the day after that on which the union informs (or unions inform) the employer under paragraph 105(2) the union proposes (or unions propose) that ACAS be requested to assist in conducting the negotiations and—
(a) the employer rejects the proposal, or
(b) the employer fails to accept the proposal within the period of 10 working days starting with the day after that on which the union makes (or unions make) the proposal.

108.—(1) An application under paragraph 106 or 107 is not admissible unless—
(a) it is made in such form as the CAC specifies, and
(b) it is supported by such documents as the CAC specifies.

(2) An application under paragraph 106 or 107 is not admissible unless the employer gives to the union (or each of the unions)—
(a) notice of the application, and
(b) a copy of the application and any documents supporting it.

109.—(1) An application under paragraph 106 or 107 is not admissible if—
(a) a relevant application was made[, or a notice under paragraph 99(2) was given,] within the period of 3 years prior to the date of the application under paragraph 106 or 107,
(b) the relevant application[, or notice under paragraph 99(2),] and the application under paragraph 106 or 107 relate to the same bargaining unit, and
(c) the CAC accepted the relevant application [or (as the case may be) decided under paragraph 100 that the notice complied with paragraph 99(3)].

(2) A relevant application is an application made to the CAC—
(a) …
(b) by the employer under paragraph 106, 107 or 128, or
(c) by a worker (or workers) under paragraph 112.

110.—(1) An application under paragraph 106 or 107 is not admissible unless the CAC decides that—
(a) at least 10 per cent of the workers constituting the bargaining unit favour an end of the bargaining arrangements, and
(b) a majority of the workers constituting the bargaining unit would be likely to favour an end of the bargaining arrangements.

(2) The CAC must give reasons for the decision.

111.—(1) The CAC must give notice to the parties of receipt of an application under paragraph 106 or 107.

(2) Within the acceptance period the CAC must decide whether—
(a) the request is valid within the terms of paragraph 104, and
(b) the application is made in accordance with paragraph 106 or 107 and admissible within the terms of paragraphs 108 to 110.

(3) In deciding those questions the CAC must consider any evidence which it has been given by the employer or the union (or unions).

(4) If the CAC decides that the request is not valid or the application is not made in accordance with paragraph 106 or 107 or is not admissible—
(a) the CAC must give notice of its decision to the parties,
(b) the CAC must not accept the application, and
(c) no further steps are to be taken under this Part of this Schedule.

(5) If the CAC decides that the request is valid and the application is made in accordance with paragraph 106 or 107 and is admissible it must—
(a) accept the application, and
(b) give notice of the acceptance to the parties.

(6) The acceptance period is—
(a) the period of 10 working days starting with the day after that on which the CAC receives the application, or
(b) such longer period (so starting) as the CAC may specify to the parties by notice containing reasons for the extension.

[827]

NOTES

Inserted as noted at the beginning of this Schedule.

Para 109: words in square brackets in sub-para (1) inserted, and sub-para (2)(a) repealed, by the Employment Relations Act 2004, ss 12(8), (9), 57(2), Sch 2, as from 6 April 2005, except in relation to any notice which the employer gave, for the purposes of para 99(2) of this Schedule, to the union (or each of the unions) before that date (see SI 2005/872, art 9).

Workers' application to end arrangements

112.—(1) A worker or workers falling within the bargaining unit may after the relevant date apply to the CAC to have the bargaining arrangements ended.

(2) An application is not admissible unless—
(a) it is made in such form as the CAC specifies, and
(b) it is supported by such documents as the CAC specifies.

(3) An application is not admissible unless the worker gives (or workers give) to the employer and to the union (or each of the unions)—
(a) notice of the application, and
(b) a copy of the application and any documents supporting it.

113.—(1) An application under paragraph 112 is not admissible if—
(a) a relevant application was made[, or a notice under paragraph 99(2) was given,] within the period of 3 years prior to the date of the application under paragraph 112,
(b) the relevant application[, or notice under paragraph 99(2),] and the application under paragraph 112 relate to the same bargaining unit, and
(c) the CAC accepted the relevant application [or (as the case may be) decided under paragraph 100 that the notice complied with paragraph 99(3)].

(2) A relevant application is an application made to the CAC—
(a) …
(b) by the employer under paragraph 106, 107 or 128, or
(c) by a worker (or workers) under paragraph 112.

114.—(1) An application under paragraph 112 is not admissible unless the CAC decides that—
(a) at least 10 per cent of the workers constituting the bargaining unit favour an end of the bargaining arrangements, and
(b) a majority of the workers constituting the bargaining unit would be likely to favour an end of the bargaining arrangements.

(2) The CAC must give reasons for the decision.

115.—(1) The CAC must give notice to the worker (or workers), the employer and the union (or unions) of receipt of an application under paragraph 112.

(2) Within the acceptance period the CAC must decide whether the application is admissible within the terms of paragraphs 112 to 114.

(3) In deciding whether the application is admissible the CAC must consider any evidence which it has been given by the employer, the union (or unions) or any of the workers falling within the bargaining unit.

(4) If the CAC decides that the application is not admissible—
- (a) the CAC must give notice of its decision to the worker (or workers), the employer and the union (or unions),
- (b) the CAC must not accept the application, and
- (c) no further steps are to be taken under this Part of this Schedule.

(5) If the CAC decides that the application is admissible it must—
- (a) accept the application, and
- (b) give notice of the acceptance to the worker (or workers), the employer and the union (or unions).

(6) The acceptance period is—
- (a) the period of 10 working days starting with the day after that on which the CAC receives the application, or
- (b) such longer period (so starting) as the CAC may specify to the worker (or workers), the employer and the union (or unions) by notice containing reasons for the extension.

116.—(1) If the CAC accepts the application, in the negotiation period the CAC must help the employer, the union (or unions) and the worker (or workers) with a view to—
- (a) the employer and the union (or unions) agreeing to end the bargaining arrangements, or
- (b) the worker (or workers) withdrawing the application.

(2) The negotiation period is—
- (a) the period of 20 working days starting with the day after that on which the CAC gives notice of acceptance of the application, or
- (b) such longer period (so starting) as the CAC may decide with the consent of the worker (or workers), the employer and the union (or unions).

[828]

NOTES

Inserted as noted at the beginning of this Schedule.

Para 113: words in square brackets in sub-para (1) inserted, and sub-para (2)(a) repealed, by the Employment Relations Act 2004, ss 12(8), (9), 57(2), Sch 2, as from 6 April 2005, except in relation to any notice which the employer gave, for the purposes of para 99(2) of this Schedule, to the union (or each of the unions) before that date (see SI 2005/872, art 9).

Ballot on derecognition

117.—(1) This paragraph applies if the CAC accepts an application under paragraph 106 or 107.

(2) This paragraph also applies if—
- (a) the CAC accepts an application under paragraph 112, and
- (b) in the period mentioned in paragraph 116(1) there is no agreement or withdrawal as there described.

(3) The CAC must arrange for the holding of a secret ballot in which the workers constituting the bargaining unit are asked whether the bargaining arrangements should be ended.

(4) The ballot must be conducted by a qualified independent person appointed by the CAC.

(5) The ballot must be conducted within—

(a) the period of 20 working days starting with the day after that on which the qualified independent person is appointed, or
(b) such longer period (so starting) as the CAC may decide.

(6) The ballot must be conducted—
(a) at a workplace or workplaces decided by the CAC,
(b) by post, or
(c) by a combination of the methods described in sub-paragraphs (a) and (b),
depending on the CAC's preference.

(7) In deciding how the ballot is to be conducted the CAC must take into account—
(a) the likelihood of the ballot being affected by unfairness or malpractice if it were conducted at a workplace or workplaces;
(b) costs and practicality;
(c) such other matters as the CAC considers appropriate.

(8) The CAC may not decide that the ballot is to be conducted as mentioned in sub-paragraph (6)(c) unless there are special factors making such a decision appropriate; and special factors include—
(a) factors arising from the location of workers or the nature of their employment;
(b) factors put to the CAC by the employer or the union (or unions).

[(8A) If the CAC decides that the ballot must (in whole or in part) be conducted at a workplace (or workplaces), it may require arrangements to be made for workers—
(a) who (but for the arrangements) would be prevented by the CAC's decision from voting by post, and
(b) who are unable, for reasons relating to those workers as individuals, to cast their votes in the ballot at the workplace (or at any of them),
to be given the opportunity (if they request it far enough in advance of the ballot for this to be practicable) to vote by post; and the CAC's imposing such a requirement is not to be treated for the purposes of sub-paragraph (8) as a decision that the ballot be conducted as mentioned in sub-paragraph (6)(c).]

(9) A person is a qualified independent person if—
(a) he satisfies such conditions as may be specified for the purposes of this paragraph by order of the Secretary of State or is himself so specified, and
(b) there are no grounds for believing either that he will carry out any functions conferred on him in relation to the ballot otherwise than competently or that his independence in relation to the ballot might reasonably be called into question.

(10) An order under sub-paragraph (9)(a) shall be made by statutory instrument subject to annulment in pursuance of a resolution of either House of Parliament.

(11) As soon as is reasonably practicable after the CAC is required under sub-paragraph (3) to arrange for the holding of a ballot it must inform the employer and the union (or unions)—
(a) that it is so required;
(b) of the name of the person appointed to conduct the ballot and the date of his appointment;
(c) of the period within which the ballot must be conducted;
(d) whether the ballot is to be conducted by post or at a workplace or workplaces;
(e) of the workplace or workplaces concerned (if the ballot is to be conducted at a workplace or workplaces).

118.—(1) An employer who is informed by the CAC under paragraph 117(11) must comply with the following [five] duties.

(2) The first duty is to co-operate generally, in connection with the ballot, with the union (or unions) and the person appointed to conduct the ballot; and the second and third duties are not to prejudice the generality of this.

(3) The second duty is to give to the union (or unions) such access to the workers constituting the bargaining unit as is reasonable to enable the union (or unions) to inform the workers of the object of the ballot and to seek their support and their opinions on the issues involved.

(4) The third duty is to do the following (so far as it is reasonable to expect the employer to do so)—
(a) to give to the CAC, within the period of 10 working days starting with the day

after that on which the employer is informed under paragraph 117(11), the names and home addresses of the workers constituting the bargaining unit;

(b) to give to the CAC, as soon as is reasonably practicable, the name and home address of any worker who joins the unit after the employer has complied with paragraph (a);

(c) to inform the CAC, as soon as is reasonably practicable, of any worker whose name has been given to the CAC under paragraph (a) or (b) but who ceases to be within the unit.

[(4A) The fourth duty is to refrain from making any offer to any or all of the workers constituting the bargaining unit which—

(a) has or is likely to have the effect of inducing any or all of them not to attend any relevant meeting between the union (or unions) and the workers constituting the bargaining unit, and

(b) is not reasonable in the circumstances.

(4B) The fifth duty is to refrain from taking or threatening to take any action against a worker solely or mainly on the grounds that he—

(a) attended or took part in any relevant meeting between the union (or unions) and the workers constituting the bargaining unit, or

(b) indicated his intention to attend or take part in such a meeting.

(4C) A meeting is a relevant meeting in relation to a worker for the purposes of sub-paragraph (4A) and (4B) if—

(a) it is organised in accordance with any agreement reached concerning the second duty or as a result of a step ordered to be taken under paragraph 119 to remedy a failure to comply with that duty, and

(b) it is one which the employer is, by such an agreement or order as is mentioned in paragraph (a), required to permit the worker to attend.

(4D) Without prejudice to the generality of the second duty imposed by this paragraph, an employer is to be taken to have failed to comply with that duty if—

(a) he refuses a request for a meeting between the union (or unions) and any or all of the workers constituting the bargaining unit to be held in the absence of the employer or any representative of his (other than one who has been invited to attend the meeting) and it is not reasonable in the circumstances for him to do so,

(b) he or a representative of his attends such a meeting without having been invited to do so,

(c) he seeks to record or otherwise be informed of the proceedings at any such meeting and it is not reasonable in the circumstances for him to do so, or

(d) he refuses to give an undertaking that he will not seek to record or otherwise be informed of the proceedings at any such meeting unless it is reasonable in the circumstances for him to do either of those things.

(4E) The fourth and fifth duties do not confer any rights on a worker; but that does not affect any other right which a worker may have.]

(5) As soon as is reasonably practicable after the CAC receives any information under sub-paragraph (4) it must pass it on to the person appointed to conduct the ballot.

(6) If asked to do so by the union (or unions) the person appointed to conduct the ballot must send to any worker—

(a) whose name and home address have been given under sub-paragraph (5), and

(b) who is still within the unit (so far as the person so appointed is aware),

any information supplied by the union (or unions) to the person so appointed.

(7) The duty under sub-paragraph (6) does not apply unless the union bears (or unions bear) the cost of sending the information.

[(8) Each of the powers specified in sub-paragraph (9) shall be taken to include power to issue Codes of Practice—

(a) about reasonable access for the purposes of sub-paragraph (3), and

(b) about the fourth duty imposed by this paragraph.

(9) The powers are—

(a) the power of ACAS under section 199(1);

(b) the power of the Secretary of State under section 203(1)(a).]

119.—(1) If the CAC is satisfied that the employer has failed to fulfil any of the [duties imposed on him] by paragraph 118, and the ballot has not been held, the CAC may order the employer—

(a) to take such steps to remedy the failure as the CAC considers reasonable and specifies in the order, and

(b) to do so within such period as the CAC considers reasonable and specifies in the order.

(2) If—

(a) the ballot has been arranged in consequence of an application under paragraph 106 or 107,

(b) the CAC is satisfied that the employer has failed to comply with an order under sub-paragraph (1), and

(c) the ballot has not been held,

the CAC may refuse the application.

(3) …

(4) If the CAC refuses an application under sub-paragraph (2) it shall take steps to cancel the holding of the ballot; and if the ballot is held it shall have no effect.

[119A.—(1) Each of the parties informed by the CAC under paragraph 117(11) must refrain from using any unfair practice.

(2) A party uses an unfair practice if, with a view to influencing the result of the ballot, the party—

(a) offers to pay money or give money's worth to a worker entitled to vote in the ballot in return for the worker's agreement to vote in a particular way or to abstain from voting,

(b) makes an outcome-specific offer to a worker entitled to vote in the ballot,

(c) coerces or attempts to coerce a worker entitled to vote in the ballot to disclose—

(i) whether he intends to vote or to abstain from voting in the ballot, or

(ii) how he intends to vote, or how he has voted, in the ballot,

(d) dismisses or threatens to dismiss a worker,

(e) takes or threatens to take disciplinary action against a worker,

(f) subjects or threatens to subject a worker to any other detriment, or

(g) uses or attempts to use undue influence on a worker entitled to vote in the ballot.

(3) For the purposes of sub-paragraph (2)(b) an "outcome-specific offer" is an offer to pay money or give money's worth which—

(a) is conditional on—

(i) the issuing by the CAC of a declaration that the bargaining arrangements are to cease to have effect, or

(ii) the refusal by the CAC of an application under paragraph 106, 107 or 112, and

(b) is not conditional on anything which is done or occurs as a result of that declaration or, as the case may be, of that refusal.

(4) The duty imposed by this paragraph does not confer any rights on a worker; but that does not affect any other right which a worker may have.

(5) Each of the following powers shall be taken to include power to issue Codes of Practice about unfair practices for the purposes of this paragraph—

(a) the power of ACAS under section 199(1);

(b) the power of the Secretary of State under section 203(1)(a).

119B.—(1) A party may complain to the CAC that another party has failed to comply with paragraph 119A.

(2) A complaint under sub-paragraph (1) must be made on or before the first working day after—

(a) the date of the ballot, or

(b) if votes may be cast in the ballot on more than one day, the last of those days.

(3) Within the decision period the CAC must decide whether the complaint is well-founded.

(4) A complaint is well-founded if—

(a) the CAC finds that the party complained against used an unfair practice, and

(b) the CAC is satisfied that the use of that practice changed or was likely to change, in the case of a worker entitled to vote in the ballot—
   (i) his intention to vote or to abstain from voting,
   (ii) his intention to vote in a particular way, or
   (iii) how he voted.

(5) The decision period is—
(a) the period of 10 working days starting with the day after that on which the complaint under sub-paragraph (1) was received by the CAC, or
(b) such longer period (so starting) as the CAC may specify to the parties by a notice containing reasons for the extension.

(6) If, at the beginning of the decision period, the ballot has not begun, the CAC may by notice to the parties and the qualified independent person postpone the date on which it is to begin until a date which falls after the end of the decision period.

119C.—(1) This paragraph applies if the CAC decides that a complaint under paragraph 119B is well-founded.

(2) The CAC must, as soon as is reasonably practicable, issue a declaration to that effect.

(3) The CAC may do either or both of the following—
(a) order the party concerned to take any action specified in the order within such period as may be so specified, or
(b) make arrangements for the holding of a secret ballot in which the workers constituting the bargaining unit are asked whether the bargaining arrangements should be ended.

(4) The CAC may give an order or make arrangements under sub-paragraph (3) either at the same time as it issues the declaration under sub-paragraph (2) or at any other time before it acts under paragraph 121.

(5) The action specified in an order under sub-paragraph (3)(a) shall be such as the CAC considers reasonable in order to mitigate the effect of the failure of the party complained against to comply with the duty imposed by paragraph 119A.

(6) The CAC may give more than one order under sub-paragraph (3)(a).

119D.—(1) This paragraph applies if the CAC issues a declaration under paragraph 119C(2) and the declaration states that the unfair practice used consisted of or included—
(a) the use of violence, or
(b) the dismissal of a union official.

(2) This paragraph also applies if the CAC has made an order under paragraph 119C(3)(a) and—
(a) it is satisfied that the party subject to the order has failed to comply with it, or
(b) it makes another declaration under paragraph 119C(2) in relation to a complaint against that party.

(3) If the party concerned is the employer, the CAC may refuse the employer's application under paragraph 106 or 107.

(4) If the party concerned is a union, the CAC may issue a declaration that the bargaining arrangements are to cease to have effect on a date specified by the CAC in the declaration.

(5) If a declaration is issued under sub-paragraph (4) the bargaining arrangements shall cease to have effect accordingly.

(6) The powers conferred by this paragraph are in addition to those conferred by paragraph 119C(3).

119E.—(1) This paragraph applies if the CAC issues a declaration that a complaint under paragraph 119B is well-founded and—
(a) makes arrangements under paragraph 119C(3)(b),
(b) refuses under paragraph 119D(3) or 119H(6) an application under paragraph 106, 107 or 112, or
(c) issues a declaration under paragraph 119D(4) or 119H(5).

(2) If the ballot in connection with which the complaint was made has not been held, the CAC shall take steps to cancel it.

(3) If that ballot is held, it shall have no effect.

119F.—(1) This paragraph applies if the CAC makes arrangements under paragraph 119C(3)(b).

(2) Paragraphs 117(4) to (11) and 118 to 121 apply in relation to those arrangements as they apply in relation to arrangements made under paragraph 117(3) but with the modifications specified in sub-paragraphs (3) to (5).

(3) An employer's duty under paragraph (a) of paragraph 118(4) is limited to—
- (a) giving the CAC the names and home addresses of any workers in the bargaining unit which have not previously been given to it in accordance with that duty;
- (b) giving the CAC the names and home addresses of those workers who have joined the bargaining unit since he last gave the CAC information in accordance with that duty;
- (c) informing the CAC of any change to the name or home address of a worker whose name and home address have previously been given to the CAC in accordance with that duty; and
- (d) informing the CAC of any worker whose name had previously been given to it in accordance with that duty who has ceased to be within the bargaining unit.

(4) Any order given under paragraph 119(1) or 119C(3)(a) for the purposes of the cancelled or ineffectual ballot shall have effect (to the extent that the CAC specifies in a notice to the parties) as if it were made for the purposes of the ballot for which arrangements are made under paragraph 119C(3)(b).

(5) The gross costs of the ballot shall be borne by such of the parties and in such proportions as the CAC may determine and, accordingly, sub-paragraphs (2) and (3) of paragraph 120 shall be omitted and the reference in sub-paragraph (4) of that paragraph to the employer and the union (or each of the unions) shall be construed as a reference to the party or parties which bear the costs in accordance with the CAC's determination.

119G.—(1) Paragraphs 119A to 119C, 119E and 119F apply in relation to an application under paragraph 112 as they apply in relation to an application under paragraph 106 or 107 but with the modifications specified in this paragraph.

(2) References in those paragraphs (and, accordingly, in paragraph 119H(3)) to a party shall be read as including references to the applicant worker or workers; but this is subject to sub-paragraph (3).

(3) The reference in paragraph 119A(1) to a party informed under paragraph 117(11) shall be read as including a reference to the applicant worker or workers.

119H.—(1) This paragraph applies in relation to an application under paragraph 112 in the cases specified in sub-paragraphs (2) and (3).

(2) The first case is where the CAC issues a declaration under paragraph 119C(2) and the declaration states that the unfair practice used consisted of or included—
- (a) the use of violence, or
- (b) the dismissal of a union official.

(3) The second case is where the CAC has made an order under paragraph 119C(3)(a) and—
- (a) it is satisfied that the party subject to the order has failed to comply with it, or
- (b) it makes another declaration under paragraph 119C(2) in relation to a complaint against that party.

(4) If the party concerned is the employer, the CAC may order him to refrain from further campaigning in relation to the ballot.

(5) If the party concerned is a union, the CAC may issue a declaration that the bargaining arrangements are to cease to have effect on a date specified by the CAC in the declaration.

(6) If the party concerned is the applicant worker (or any of the applicant workers), the CAC may refuse the application under paragraph 112.

(7) If a declaration is issued under sub-paragraph (5) the bargaining arrangements shall cease to have effect accordingly.

(8) The powers conferred by this paragraph are in addition to those conferred by paragraph 119C(3).

119I.—(1) This paragraph applies if—
(a) a ballot has been arranged in consequence of an application under paragraph 112,
(b) the CAC has given the employer an order under paragraph 119(1), 119C(3) or 119H(4), and
(c) the ballot for the purposes of which the order was made (or any other ballot for the purposes of which it has effect) has not been held.

(2) The applicant worker (or each of the applicant workers) and the union (or each of the unions) is entitled to enforce obedience to the order.

(3) The order may be enforced—
(a) in England and Wales, in the same way as an order of the county court;
(b) in Scotland, in the same way as an order of the sheriff.]

120.—(1) This paragraph applies if the holding of a ballot has been arranged under paragraph 117(3), whether or not it has been cancelled.

(2) The gross costs of the ballot shall be borne—
(a) as to half, by the employer, and
(b) as to half, by the union (or unions).

(3) If there is more than one union they shall bear their half of the gross costs—
(a) in such proportions as they jointly indicate to the person appointed to conduct the ballot, or
(b) in the absence of such an indication, in equal shares.

(4) The person appointed to conduct the ballot may send to the employer and the union (or each of the unions) a demand stating—
(a) the gross costs of the ballot, and
(b) the amount of the gross costs to be borne by the recipient.

(5) In such a case the recipient must pay the amount stated to the person sending the demand, and must do so within the period of 15 working days starting with the day after that on which the demand is received.

(6) In England and Wales, if the amount stated is not paid in accordance with sub-paragraph (5) it shall, if a county court so orders, be recoverable *by execution issued from that court* or otherwise as if it were payable under an order of that court.

[(6A) *Where an amount is recoverable from a union under sub-paragraph (6) execution may be carried out*, to the same extent and in the same manner as if the union were a body corporate, against any property held in trust for the union other than protected property as defined in section 23(2).]

(7) References to the costs of the ballot are to—
(a) the costs wholly, exclusively and necessarily incurred in connection with the ballot by the person appointed to conduct it,
(b) such reasonable amount as the person appointed to conduct the ballot charges for his services, and
(c) such other costs as the employer and the union (or unions) agree.

121.—(1) As soon as is reasonably practicable after the CAC is informed of the result of a ballot by the person conducting it, the CAC must act under this paragraph.

[(1A) The duty in sub-paragraph (1) does not apply if the CAC makes arrangements under paragraph 119C(3)(b).]

(2) The CAC must inform the employer and the union (or unions) of the result of the ballot.

(3) If the result is that the proposition that the bargaining arrangements should be ended is supported by—
(a) a majority of the workers voting, and
(b) at least 40 per cent of the workers constituting the bargaining unit,
the CAC must issue a declaration that the bargaining arrangements are to cease to have effect on a date specified by the CAC in the declaration.

(4) If the result is otherwise the CAC must refuse the application under paragraph 106, 107 or 112.

(5) If a declaration is issued under sub-paragraph (3) the bargaining arrangements shall cease to have effect accordingly.

(6) The Secretary of State may by order amend sub-paragraph (3) so as to specify a different degree of support; and different provision may be made for different circumstances.

(7) An order under sub-paragraph (6) shall be made by statutory instrument.

(8) No such order shall be made unless a draft of it has been laid before Parliament and approved by a resolution of each House of Parliament.

[829]

NOTES

Inserted as noted at the beginning of this Schedule.

Para 117: sub-para (8A) inserted by the Employment Relations Act 2004, s 8(2), as from 6 April 2005, except where, before that date, the CAC had informed the parties, in accordance with paras 25(9) or 117(11) of this Schedule (see SI 2005/872, art 7).

Para 118: word in square brackets in sub-para (1) substituted, sub-paras (4A)–(4E) inserted, and sub-paras (8), (9) substituted (for original sub-para (8)), by the Employment Relations Act 2004, s 9(6)–(9), as from 1 October 2005, except where, before that date, the CAC had informed the parties, in accordance with paras 25(9) or 117(11) of this Schedule (see SI 2005/2419, art 5).

Para 119: words in square brackets in sub-para (1) substituted, and sub-para (3) repealed, by the Employment Relations Act 2004, ss 9(10), 57, Sch 1, paras 23(1), (22), Sch 2, as from 1 October 2005 (subject to the same exception in SI 2005/2419, art 5 as noted above).

Paras 119A–119I: inserted by the Employment Relations Act 2004, s 13(1), as from 1 October 2005 (subject to the same exception in SI 2005/2419, art 5 as noted above).

Para 120: for the words in italics in sub-para (6) there are substituted the words "under section 85 of the County Courts Act 1984" by the Tribunals, Courts and Enforcement Act 2007, s 62(3), Sch 13, paras 108, 111(1), (2), as from a day to be appointed; sub-para (6A) inserted by the Employment Relations Act 2004, s 57(1), Sch 1, para 23(1), (23), as from 1 October 2005 (subject to the same exception in SI 2005/2419, art 5 as noted above); for the words in italics in sub-para (6A) there are substituted the words "Where a warrant of control is issued under section 85 of the 1984 Act to recover an amount in accordance with sub-paragraph (6), the power conferred by the warrant is exercisable" by the Tribunals, Courts and Enforcement Act 2007, s 62(3), Sch 13, paras 108, 111(1), (3), as from a day to be appointed.

Para 121: sub-para (1A) inserted by the Employment Relations Act 2004, s 13(2), as from 1 October 2005 (subject to the same exception in SI 2005/2419, art 5 as noted above).

Code of Practice: Access and unfair practices during recognition and derecognition ballots (2005) at **[4690]**.

Orders: the Recognition and Derecognition Ballots (Qualified Persons) Order 2000, SI 2000/1306 at **[2631]**.

PART V
DERECOGNITION WHERE RECOGNITION AUTOMATIC

Introduction

122.—(1) This Part of this Schedule applies if—

(a) the CAC has issued a declaration under paragraph [19F(5), 22(2), 27(2) or 27D(3)] that a union is (or unions are) recognised as entitled to conduct collective bargaining on behalf of a bargaining unit, and

(b) the parties have agreed under paragraph 30 or 31 a method by which they will conduct collective bargaining.

(2) In such a case references in this Part of this Schedule to the bargaining arrangements are to—

(a) the declaration, and

(b) the parties' agreement.

123.—(1) This Part of this Schedule also applies if—

(a) the CAC has issued a declaration under paragraph [19F(5), 22(2), 27(2) or 27D(3)] that a union is (or unions are) recognised as entitled to conduct collective bargaining on behalf of a bargaining unit, and

(b) the CAC has specified to the parties under paragraph 31(3) the method by which they are to conduct collective bargaining.

(2) In such a case references in this Part of this Schedule to the bargaining arrangements are to—

(a) the declaration, and

(b) anything effective as, or as if contained in, a legally enforceable contract by virtue of paragraph 31.

124.—(1) This Part of this Schedule also applies if the CAC has issued a declaration under paragraph 87(2) that a union is (or unions are) recognised as entitled to conduct collective bargaining on behalf of a bargaining unit.

(2) In such a case references in this Part of this Schedule to the bargaining arrangements are to—

(a) the declaration, and
(b) paragraph 87(6)(b).

125. For the purposes of this Part of this Schedule the relevant date is the date of the expiry of the period of 3 years starting with the date of the CAC's declaration.

126. References in this Part of this Schedule to the parties are to the employer and the union (or unions) concerned.

[830]

NOTES

Inserted as noted at the beginning of this Schedule.

Paras 122, 123: words in square brackets substituted by the Employment Relations Act 2004, s 57(1), Sch 1, para 23(1), (24), (25), as from 6 April 2005.

Employer's request to end arrangements

127.—(1) The employer may after the relevant date request the union (or each of the unions) to agree to end the bargaining arrangements.

(2) The request is not valid unless it—

(a) is in writing,
(b) is received by the union (or each of the unions),
(c) identifies the bargaining arrangements,
(d) states that it is made under this Schedule, and
(e) states that fewer than half of the workers constituting the bargaining unit are members of the union (or unions).

128.—(1) If before the end of the negotiation period the parties agree to end the bargaining arrangements no further steps are to be taken under this Part of this Schedule.

(2) If no such agreement is made before the end of the negotiation period, the employer may apply to the CAC for the holding of a secret ballot to decide whether the bargaining arrangements should be ended.

(3) The negotiation period is the period of 10 working days starting with the day after—

(a) the day on which the union receives the request, or
(b) the last day on which any of the unions receives the request;

or such longer period (so starting) as the parties may from time to time agree.

129.—(1) An application under paragraph 128 is not admissible unless—

(a) it is made in such form as the CAC specifies, and
(b) it is supported by such documents as the CAC specifies.

(2) An application under paragraph 128 is not admissible unless the employer gives to the union (or each of the unions)—

(a) notice of the application, and
(b) a copy of the application and any documents supporting it.

130.—(1) An application under paragraph 128 is not admissible if—

(a) a relevant application was made[, or a notice under paragraph 99(2) was given,] within the period of 3 years prior to the date of the application under paragraph 128,
(b) the relevant application[, or notice under paragraph 99(2),] and the application under paragraph 128 relate to the same bargaining unit, and

(c) the CAC accepted the relevant application [or (as the case may be) decided under paragraph 100 that the notice complied with paragraph 99(3)].

(2) A relevant application is an application made to the CAC—

(a) . . .

(b) by the employer under paragraph 106, 107 or 128, or

(c) by a worker (or workers) under paragraph 112.

131.—(1) An application under paragraph 128 is not admissible unless the CAC is satisfied that fewer than half of the workers constituting the bargaining unit are members of the union (or unions).

(2) The CAC must give reasons for the decision.

132.—(1) The CAC must give notice to the parties of receipt of an application under paragraph 128.

(2) Within the acceptance period the CAC must decide whether—

(a) the request is valid within the terms of paragraph 127, and

(b) the application is admissible within the terms of paragraphs 129 to 131.

(3) In deciding those questions the CAC must consider any evidence which it has been given by the parties.

(4) If the CAC decides that the request is not valid or the application is not admissible—

(a) the CAC must give notice of its decision to the parties,

(b) the CAC must not accept the application, and

(c) no further steps are to be taken under this Part of this Schedule.

(5) If the CAC decides that the request is valid and the application is admissible it must—

(a) accept the application, and

(b) give notice of the acceptance to the parties.

(6) The acceptance period is—

(a) the period of 10 working days starting with the day after that on which the CAC receives the application, or

(b) such longer period (so starting) as the CAC may specify to the parties by notice containing reasons for the extension.

[831]

NOTES

Inserted as noted at the beginning of this Schedule.

Para 130: words in square brackets in sub-para (1) inserted, and sub-para (2)(a) repealed, by the Employment Relations Act 2004, ss 12(8), (9), 57(2), Sch 2, as from 6 April 2005, except in relation to any notice which the employer gave, for the purposes of para 99(2) of this Schedule, to the union (or each of the unions) before that date (see SI 2005/872, art 9).

Ballot on derecognition

133.—(1) Paragraph 117 applies if the CAC accepts an application under paragraph 128 (as well as in the cases mentioned in paragraph 117(1) and (2)).

(2) Paragraphs 118 to 121 apply accordingly, but as if—

(a) the [references in paragraphs 119(2)(a) and 119D(3)] to paragraph 106 or 107 were to paragraph 106, 107 or 128;

(b) the [references in paragraphs 119A(3)(a)(ii), 119E(1)(b) and 121(4)] to paragraph 106, 107 or 112 were to paragraph 106, 107, 112 or 128.

[832]

NOTES

Inserted as noted at the beginning of this Schedule.

Para 133: words in square brackets in sub-para (2) substituted by the Employment Relations Act 2004, s 57(1), Sch 1, para 23(1), (26), as from 6 April 2005.

PART VI
DERECOGNITION WHERE UNION NOT INDEPENDENT

Introduction

134.—(1) This Part of this Schedule applies if—

(a) an employer and a union (or unions) have agreed that the union is (or unions are) recognised as entitled to conduct collective bargaining on behalf of a group or groups of workers, and

(b) the union does not have (or none of the unions has) a certificate [of independence].

(2) In such a case references in this Part of this Schedule to the bargaining arrangements are to—

(a) the parties' agreement mentioned in sub-paragraph (1)(a), and

(b) any agreement between the parties as to the method by which they will conduct collective bargaining.

135. In this Part of this Schedule—

(a) references to the parties are to the employer and the union (or unions);

(b) references to the bargaining unit are to the group of workers referred to in paragraph 134(1)(a) (or the groups taken together).

136. The meaning of collective bargaining given by section 178(1) shall not apply in relation to this Part of this Schedule.

[833]

NOTES

Inserted as noted at the beginning of this Schedule.

Para 134: words in square brackets in sub-para (1)(b) substituted by the Employment Relations Act 2004, s 50(6), as from 6 April 2005.

Workers' application to end arrangements

137.—(1) A worker or workers falling within the bargaining unit may apply to the CAC to have the bargaining arrangements ended.

(2) An application is not admissible unless—

(a) it is made in such form as the CAC specifies, and

(b) it is supported by such documents as the CAC specifies.

(3) An application is not admissible unless the worker gives (or workers give) to the employer and to the union (or each of the unions)—

(a) notice of the application, and

(b) a copy of the application and any documents supporting it.

138. An application under paragraph 137 is not admissible if the CAC is satisfied that any of the unions has a certificate [of independence].

139.—(1) An application under paragraph 137 is not admissible unless the CAC decides that—

(a) at least 10 per cent of the workers constituting the bargaining unit favour an end of the bargaining arrangements, and

(b) a majority of the workers constituting the bargaining unit would be likely to favour an end of the bargaining arrangements.

(2) The CAC must give reasons for the decision.

140. An application under paragraph 137 is not admissible if the CAC is satisfied that—

(a) the union (or any of the unions) has made an application to the Certification Officer under section 6 for a certificate that it is independent, and

(b) the Certification Officer has not come to a decision on the application (or each of the applications).

141.—(1) The CAC must give notice to the worker (or workers), the employer and the union (or unions) of receipt of an application under paragraph 137.

(2) Within the acceptance period the CAC must decide whether the application is admissible within the terms of paragraphs 137 to 140.

(3) In deciding whether the application is admissible the CAC must consider any evidence which it has been given by the employer, the union (or unions) or any of the workers falling within the bargaining unit.

(4) If the CAC decides that the application is not admissible—
(a) the CAC must give notice of its decision to the worker (or workers), the employer and the union (or unions),
(b) the CAC must not accept the application, and
(c) no further steps are to be taken under this Part of this Schedule.

(5) If the CAC decides that the application is admissible it must—
(a) accept the application, and
(b) give notice of the acceptance to the worker (or workers), the employer and the union (or unions).

(6) The acceptance period is—
(a) the period of 10 working days starting with the day after that on which the CAC receives the application, or
(b) such longer period (so starting) as the CAC may specify to the worker (or workers), the employer and the union (or unions) by notice containing reasons for the extension.

142.—(1) If the CAC accepts the application, in the negotiation period the CAC must help the employer, the union (or unions) and the worker (or workers) with a view to—
(a) the employer and the union (or unions) agreeing to end the bargaining arrangements, or
(b) the worker (or workers) withdrawing the application.

(2) The negotiation period is—
(a) the period of 20 working days starting with the day after that on which the CAC gives notice of acceptance of the application, or
(b) such longer period (so starting) as the CAC may decide with the consent of the worker (or workers), the employer and the union (or unions).

143.—(1) This paragraph applies if—
(a) the CAC accepts an application under paragraph 137,
(b) during the period mentioned in paragraph 142(1) or 145(3) the CAC is satisfied that the union (or each of the unions) has made an application to the Certification Officer under section 6 for a certificate that it is independent, that the application (or each of the applications) to the Certification Officer was made before the application under paragraph 137 and that the Certification Officer has not come to a decision on the application (or each of the applications), and
(c) at the time the CAC is so satisfied there has been no agreement or withdrawal as described in paragraph 142(1) or 145(3).

(2) In such a case paragraph 142(1) or 145(3) shall cease to apply from the time when the CAC is satisfied as mentioned in sub-paragraph (1)(b).

144.—(1) This paragraph applies if the CAC is subsequently satisfied that—
(a) the Certification Officer has come to a decision on the application (or each of the applications) mentioned in paragraph 143(1)(b), and
(b) his decision is that the union (or any of the unions) which made an application under section 6 is independent.

(2) In such a case—
(a) the CAC must give the worker (or workers), the employer and the union (or unions) notice that it is so satisfied, and
(b) the application under paragraph 137 shall be treated as not having been made.

145.—(1) This paragraph applies if the CAC is subsequently satisfied that—
(a) the Certification Officer has come to a decision on the application (or each of the applications) mentioned in paragraph 143(1)(b), and

(b) his decision is that the union (or each of the unions) which made an application under section 6 is not independent.

(2) The CAC must give the worker (or workers), the employer and the union (or unions) notice that it is so satisfied.

(3) In the new negotiation period the CAC must help the employer, the union (or unions) and the worker (or workers) with a view to—

(a) the employer and the union (or unions) agreeing to end the bargaining arrangements, or

(b) the worker (or workers) withdrawing the application.

(4) The new negotiation period is—

(a) the period of 20 working days starting with the day after that on which the CAC gives notice under sub-paragraph (2), or

(b) such longer period (so starting) as the CAC may decide with the consent of the worker (or workers), the employer and the union (or unions).

146.—(1) This paragraph applies if—

(a) the CAC accepts an application under paragraph 137,

(b) paragraph 143 does not apply, and

(c) during the relevant period the CAC is satisfied that a certificate of independence has been issued to the union (or any of the unions) under section 6.

(2) In such a case the relevant period is the period starting with the first day of the negotiation period (as defined in paragraph 142(2)) and ending with the first of the following to occur—

(a) any agreement by the employer and the union (or unions) to end the bargaining arrangements;

(b) any withdrawal of the application by the worker (or workers);

(c) the CAC being informed of the result of a relevant ballot by the person conducting it;

and a relevant ballot is a ballot held by virtue of this Part of this Schedule.

(3) This paragraph also applies if—

(a) the CAC gives notice under paragraph 145(2), and

(b) during the relevant period the CAC is satisfied that a certificate of independence has been issued to the union (or any of the unions) under section 6.

(4) In such a case, the relevant period is the period starting with the first day of the new negotiation period (as defined in paragraph 145(4)) and ending with the first of the following to occur—

(a) any agreement by the employer and the union (or unions) to end the bargaining arrangements;

(b) any withdrawal of the application by the worker (or workers);

(c) the CAC being informed of the result of a relevant ballot by the person conducting it;

and a relevant ballot is a ballot held by virtue of this Part of this Schedule.

(5) If this paragraph applies—

(a) the CAC must give the worker (or workers), the employer and the union (or unions) notice that it is satisfied as mentioned in sub-paragraph (1)(c) or (3)(b), and

(b) the application under paragraph 137 shall be treated as not having been made.

[834]

NOTES

Inserted as noted at the beginning of this Schedule.

Para 138: words in square brackets substituted by the Employment Relations Act 2004, s 50(6), as from 6 April 2005.

Ballot on derecognition

147.—(1) Paragraph 117 applies if—

(a) the CAC accepts an application under paragraph 137, and

(b) in the period mentioned in paragraph 142(1) or 145(3) there is no agreement or withdrawal as there described, (as well as in the cases mentioned in paragraph 117(1) and (2)).

(2) Paragraphs 118 to 121 apply accordingly, but as if—

(a) the [references in paragraphs 119H(1) and 119I(1)(a)] to paragraph 112 were to paragraph 112 or 137;

(b) the [references in paragraphs 119A(3)(a)(ii), 119E(1)(b) and 121(4)] to paragraph 106, 107 or 112 were to paragraph 106, 107, 112 or 137;

(c) the reference in paragraph 119(4) to the CAC refusing an application under paragraph 119(2) included a reference to it being required to give notice under paragraph 146(5).

[835]

NOTES

Inserted as noted at the beginning of this Schedule.

Para 147: words in square brackets in sub-para (2) substituted by the Employment Relations Act 2004, s 57(1), Sch 1, para 23(1), (27), as from 6 April 2005.

Derecognition: other cases

148.—(1) This paragraph applies if as a result of a declaration by the CAC another union is (or other unions are) recognised as entitled to conduct collective bargaining on behalf of a group of workers at least one of whom falls within the bargaining unit.

(2) The CAC must issue a declaration that the bargaining arrangements are to cease to have effect on a date specified by the CAC in the declaration.

(3) If a declaration is issued under sub-paragraph (2) the bargaining arrangements shall cease to have effect accordingly.

(4) It is for the CAC to decide whether sub-paragraph (1) is fulfilled, but in deciding the CAC may take account of the views of any person it believes has an interest in the matter.

[836]

NOTES

Inserted as noted at the beginning of this Schedule.

PART VII
LOSS OF INDEPENDENCE

Introduction

149.—(1) This Part of this Schedule applies if the CAC has issued a declaration that a union is (or unions are) recognised as entitled to conduct collective bargaining on behalf of a bargaining unit.

(2) In such a case references in this Part of this Schedule to the bargaining arrangements are to the declaration and to the provisions relating to the collective bargaining method.

(3) For this purpose the provisions relating to the collective bargaining method are—

(a) the parties' agreement as to the method by which collective bargaining is to be conducted,

(b) anything effective as, or as if contained in, a legally enforceable contract and relating to the method by which collective bargaining is to be conducted, or

(c) any provision of Part III of this Schedule that a method of collective bargaining is to have effect.

150.—(1) This Part of this Schedule also applies if—

(a) the parties have agreed that a union is (or unions are) recognised as entitled to conduct collective bargaining on behalf of a bargaining unit,

(b) the CAC has specified to the parties under paragraph 63(2) the method by which they are to conduct collective bargaining, and

(c) the parties have not agreed in writing to replace the method or that paragraph 63(3) shall not apply.

(2) In such a case references in this Part of this Schedule to the bargaining arrangements are to—
- (a) the parties' agreement mentioned in sub-paragraph (1)(a), and
- (b) anything effective as, or as if contained in, a legally enforceable contract by virtue of paragraph 63.

151. References in this Part of this Schedule to the parties are to the employer and the union (or unions) concerned.

[837]

NOTES

Inserted as noted at the beginning of this Schedule.

Loss of certificate

152.—(1) This paragraph applies if—
- (a) only one union is a party, and
- (b) under section 7 the Certification Officer withdraws the union's certificate of independence.

(2) This paragraph also applies if—
- (a) more than one union is a party, and
- (b) under section 7 the Certification Officer withdraws the certificate of independence of each union (whether different certificates are withdrawn on the same or on different days).

(3) Sub-paragraph (4) shall apply on the day after—
- (a) the day on which the Certification Officer informs the union (or unions) of the withdrawal (or withdrawals), or
- (b) if there is more than one union, and he informs them on different days, the last of those days.

(4) The bargaining arrangements shall cease to have effect; and the parties shall be taken to agree that the union is (or unions are) recognised as entitled to conduct collective bargaining on behalf of the bargaining unit concerned.

[838]

NOTES

Inserted as noted at the beginning of this Schedule.

Certificate re-issued

153.—(1) This paragraph applies if—
- (a) only one union is a party,
- (b) paragraph 152 applies, and
- (c) as a result of an appeal under section 9 against the decision to withdraw the certificate, the Certification Officer issues a certificate that the union is independent.

(2) This paragraph also applies if—
- (a) more than one union is a party,
- (b) paragraph 152 applies, and
- (c) as a result of an appeal under section 9 against a decision to withdraw a certificate, the Certification Officer issues a certificate that any of the unions concerned is independent.

(3) Sub-paragraph (4) shall apply, beginning with the day after—
- (a) the day on which the Certification Officer issues the certificate, or
- (b) if there is more than one union, the day on which he issues the first or only certificate.

(4) The bargaining arrangements shall have effect again; and paragraph 152 shall cease to apply.

[839]

NOTES

Inserted as noted at the beginning of this Schedule.

Miscellaneous

154. Parts III to VI of this Schedule shall not apply in the case of the parties at any time when, by virtue of this Part of this Schedule, the bargaining arrangements do not have effect.

155. If—

(a) by virtue of paragraph 153 the bargaining arrangements have effect again beginning with a particular day, and

(b) in consequence section 70B applies in relation to the bargaining unit concerned,

for the purposes of section 70B(3) that day shall be taken to be the day on which section 70B first applies in relation to the unit.

[840]

NOTES

Inserted as noted at the beginning of this Schedule.

PART VIII
DETRIMENT

Detriment

156.—(1) A worker has a right not to be subjected to any detriment by any act, or any deliberate failure to act, by his employer if the act or failure takes place on any of the grounds set out in sub-paragraph (2).

(2) The grounds are that—

(a) the worker acted with a view to obtaining or preventing recognition of a union (or unions) by the employer under this Schedule;

(b) the worker indicated that he supported or did not support recognition of a union (or unions) by the employer under this Schedule;

(c) the worker acted with a view to securing or preventing the ending under this Schedule of bargaining arrangements;

(d) the worker indicated that he supported or did not support the ending under this Schedule of bargaining arrangements;

(e) the worker influenced or sought to influence the way in which votes were to be cast by other workers in a ballot arranged under this Schedule;

(f) the worker influenced or sought to influence other workers to vote or to abstain from voting in such a ballot;

(g) the worker voted in such a ballot;

(h) the worker proposed to do, failed to do, or proposed to decline to do, any of the things referred to in paragraphs (a) to (g).

(3) A ground does not fall within sub-paragraph (2) if it constitutes an unreasonable act or omission by the worker.

(4) This paragraph does not apply if the worker is an employee and the detriment amounts to dismissal within the meaning of the Employment Rights Act 1996.

(5) A worker may present a complaint to an employment tribunal on the ground that he has been subjected to a detriment in contravention of this paragraph.

(6) Apart from the remedy by way of complaint as mentioned in sub-paragraph (5), a worker has no remedy for infringement of the right conferred on him by this paragraph.

157.—(1) An employment tribunal shall not consider a complaint under paragraph 156 unless it is presented—

(a) before the end of the period of 3 months starting with the date of the act or failure to which the complaint relates or, if that act or failure is part of a series of similar acts or failures (or both), the last of them, or

(b) where the tribunal is satisfied that it was not reasonably practicable for the complaint to be presented before the end of that period, within such further period as it considers reasonable.

(2) For the purposes of sub-paragraph (1)—

(a) where an act extends over a period, the reference to the date of the act is a reference to the last day of that period;

(b) a failure to act shall be treated as done when it was decided on.

(3) For the purposes of sub-paragraph (2), in the absence of evidence establishing the contrary an employer must be taken to decide on a failure to act—

(a) when he does an act inconsistent with doing the failed act, or

(b) if he has done no such inconsistent act, when the period expires within which he might reasonably have been expected to do the failed act if it was to be done.

158. On a complaint under paragraph 156 it shall be for the employer to show the ground on which he acted or failed to act.

159.—(1) If the employment tribunal finds that a complaint under paragraph 156 is well-founded it shall make a declaration to that effect and may make an award of compensation to be paid by the employer to the complainant in respect of the act or failure complained of.

(2) The amount of the compensation awarded shall be such as the tribunal considers just and equitable in all the circumstances having regard to the infringement complained of and to any loss sustained by the complainant which is attributable to the act or failure which infringed his right.

(3) The loss shall be taken to include—

(a) any expenses reasonably incurred by the complainant in consequence of the act or failure complained of, and

(b) loss of any benefit which he might reasonably be expected to have had but for that act or failure.

(4) In ascertaining the loss, the tribunal shall apply the same rule concerning the duty of a person to mitigate his loss as applies to damages recoverable under the common law of England and Wales or Scotland.

(5) If the tribunal finds that the act or failure complained of was to any extent caused or contributed to by action of the complainant, it shall reduce the amount of the compensation by such proportion as it considers just and equitable having regard to that finding.

160.—(1) If the employment tribunal finds that a complaint under paragraph 156 is well-founded and—

(a) the detriment of which the worker has complained is the termination of his worker's contract, but

(b) that contract was not a contract of employment,

any compensation awarded under paragraph 159 must not exceed the limit specified in sub-paragraph (2).

(2) The limit is the total of—

(a) the sum which would be the basic award for unfair dismissal, calculated in accordance with section 119 of the Employment Rights Act 1996, if the worker had been an employee and the contract terminated had been a contract of employment, and

(b) the sum for the time being specified in section 124(1) of that Act which is the limit for a compensatory award to a person calculated in accordance with section 123 of that Act.

[841]

NOTES

Inserted as noted at the beginning of this Schedule.

Conciliation: employment tribunal proceedings and claims which could be the subject of employment tribunal proceedings under or arising out of a contravention, or alleged contravention, of para 156 are proceedings to which the Employment Tribunals Act 1996, s 18 applies; see s 18(1)(f) of that Act at **[975]**, and the Employment Tribunals Act 1996 (Application of Conciliation Provisions) Order 2000, SI 2000/1337 (made under s 18(8)(a), (b)). The standard conciliation period applies to such claims by virtue of the Employment Tribunals (Constitution and Rules of Procedure) Regulations 2004, SI 2004/1861, Sch 1, rule 22(1), (6).

Tribunal jurisdiction: the Employment Act 2002, ss 31, 32, 38 at **[1493]**, **[1494]**, **[1496]** apply to proceedings before the employment tribunal relating to a claim under para 156; see ss 31(1), 32(1), 38(1) of, and Schs 3–5 to, the 2002 Act at **[1508]–[1510]**.

For the circumstances in which the time limit laid down by para 157 (for presenting a complaint under para 156) is extended for a period of three months, see the Employment Act 2002 (Dispute Resolution) Regulations 2004, SI 2004/752, regs 15 and 18 at **[3096]** and **[3098]**.

Dismissal

161.—(1) For the purposes of Part X of the Employment Rights Act 1996 (unfair dismissal) the dismissal of an employee shall be regarded as unfair if the dismissal was made—

(a) for a reason set out in sub-paragraph (2), or

(b) for reasons the main one of which is one of those set out in sub-paragraph (2).

(2) The reasons are that—

(a) the employee acted with a view to obtaining or preventing recognition of a union (or unions) by the employer under this Schedule;

(b) the employee indicated that he supported or did not support recognition of a union (or unions) by the employer under this Schedule;

(c) the employee acted with a view to securing or preventing the ending under this Schedule of bargaining arrangements;

(d) the employee indicated that he supported or did not support the ending under this Schedule of bargaining arrangements;

(e) the employee influenced or sought to influence the way in which votes were to be cast by other workers in a ballot arranged under this Schedule;

(f) the employee influenced or sought to influence other workers to vote or to abstain from voting in such a ballot;

(g) the employee voted in such a ballot;

(h) the employee proposed to do, failed to do, or proposed to decline to do, any of the things referred to in paragraphs (a) to (g).

(3) A reason does not fall within sub-paragraph (2) if it constitutes an unreasonable act or omission by the employee.

[842]

NOTES

Inserted as noted at the beginning of this Schedule.

Selection for redundancy

162. For the purposes of Part X of the Employment Rights Act 1996 (unfair dismissal) the dismissal of an employee shall be regarded as unfair if the reason or principal reason for the dismissal was that he was redundant but it is shown—

(a) that the circumstances constituting the redundancy applied equally to one or more other employees in the same undertaking who held positions similar to that held by him and who have not been dismissed by the employer, and

(b) that the reason (or, if more than one, the principal reason) why he was selected for dismissal was one falling within paragraph 161(2).

[843]

NOTES

Inserted as noted at the beginning of this Schedule.

Employees with fixed-term contracts

163. Section 197(1) of the Employment Rights Act 1996 (fixed-term contracts) does not prevent Part X of that Act from applying to a dismissal which is regarded as unfair by virtue of paragraph 161 or 162.

[844]

NOTES

Inserted as noted at the beginning of this Schedule.

Para 163: repealed by the Employment Relations Act 1999, s 44, Sch 9(3), as from a day to be appointed.

Note that s 197(1) of the 1996 Act was itself repealed by s 44 of, and Sch 9(3) to, the 1999 Act.

Exclusion of requirement as to qualifying period

164. Sections 108 and 109 of the Employment Rights Act 1996 (qualifying period and upper age limit for unfair dismissal protection) do not apply to a dismissal which by virtue of paragraph 161 or 162 is regarded as unfair for the purposes of Part X of that Act.

[845]

NOTES

Inserted as noted at the beginning of this Schedule.

Section 109 of the Employment Rights Act 1996 was repealed by the Employment Equality (Age) Regulations 2006, SI 2006/1031, reg 49(1), Sch 8, Pt 1, paras 21, 25, as from 1 October 2006.

Meaning of worker's contract

165. References in this Part of this Schedule to a worker's contract are to the contract mentioned in paragraph (a) or (b) of section 296(1) or the arrangements for the employment mentioned in paragraph (c) of section 296(1).

[846]

NOTES

Inserted as noted at the beginning of this Schedule.

PART IX
GENERAL

[Rights of appeal against demands for costs

165A.—(1) This paragraph applies where a demand has been made under paragraph 19E(3), 28(4) or 120(4).

(2) The recipient of the demand may appeal against the demand within 4 weeks starting with the day after receipt of the demand.

(3) An appeal under this paragraph lies to an employment tribunal.

(4) On an appeal under this paragraph against a demand under paragraph 19E(3), the tribunal shall dismiss the appeal unless it is shown that—

(a) the amount specified in the demand as the costs of the appointed person is too great, or

(b) the amount specified in the demand as the amount of those costs to be borne by the recipient is too great.

(5) On an appeal under this paragraph against a demand under paragraph 28(4) or paragraph 120(4), the tribunal shall dismiss the appeal unless it is shown that—

(a) the amount specified in the demand as the gross costs of the ballot is too great, or

(b) the amount specified in the demand as the amount of the gross costs to be borne by the recipient is too great.

(6) If an appeal is allowed, the tribunal shall rectify the demand and the demand shall have effect as if it had originally been made as so rectified.

(7) If a person has appealed under this paragraph against a demand and the appeal has not been withdrawn or finally determined, the demand—

(a) is not enforceable until the appeal has been withdrawn or finally determined, but

(b) as from the withdrawal or final determination of the appeal shall be enforceable as if paragraph (a) had not had effect.]

[846A]

NOTES

This Schedule was inserted as noted at the beginning of this Schedule.

Para 165A: inserted by the Employment Relations Act 2004, s 14, as from 6 April 2005, except in relation to any demand which the person appointed to conduct the ballot had sent, under paras 28(4) or 120(4) of this Schedule, to the employer and the union (or each of the unions) before that date (see SI 2005/872, art 10).

Power to amend

166.—[(1) This paragraph applies if the CAC represents to the Secretary of State that a provision of this Schedule has an unsatisfactory effect and should be amended.

(2) The Secretary of State, with a view to rectifying the effect—

(a) may amend the provision by exercising (if applicable) any of the powers conferred on him by paragraphs 7(6), 29(5), 121(6), 166A, 166B, 169A, 169B and 171A, or

(b) may amend the provision by order in such other way as he thinks fit.

(2A) The Secretary of State need not proceed in a way proposed by the CAC (if it proposes one).

(2B) Nothing in this paragraph prevents the Secretary of State from exercising any of the powers mentioned in sub-paragraph (2)(a) in the absence of a representation from the CAC.]

(3) An order under [sub-paragraph (2)(b)] shall be made by statutory instrument.

(4) No such order shall be made unless a draft of it has been laid before Parliament and approved by a resolution of each House of Parliament.

[166A.—(1) This paragraph applies in relation to any provision of paragraph 19D(2), 26(4) or 118(4) which requires the employer to give to the CAC a worker's home address.

(2) The Secretary of State may by order provide that the employer must give to the CAC (in addition to the worker's home address) an address of a specified kind for the worker.

(3) In this paragraph "address" includes any address or number to which information may be sent by any means.

(4) An order under this paragraph may—

(a) amend this Schedule;

(b) include supplementary or incidental provision (including, in particular, provision amending paragraph 19E(1)(a), 26(6)(a) or 118(6)(a));

(c) make different provision for different cases or circumstances.

(5) An order under this paragraph shall be made by statutory instrument.

(6) No such order shall be made unless a draft of it has been laid before Parliament and approved by a resolution of each House of Parliament.]

[166B.—(1) The Secretary of State may by order provide that, during any period beginning and ending with the occurrence of specified events, employers and unions to which the order applies are prohibited from using such practices as are specified as unfair practices in relation to an application under this Schedule of a specified description.

(2) An order under this paragraph may make provision about the consequences of a contravention of any prohibition imposed by the order (including provision modifying the effect of any provision of this Schedule in the event of such a contravention).

(3) An order under this paragraph may confer functions on the CAC

(4) An order under this paragraph may contain provision extending for the purposes of the order either or both of the following powers to issue Codes of Practice—

(a) the power of ACAS under section 199(1);

(b) the power of the Secretary of State under section 203(1)(a).

(5) An order under this paragraph may—

(a) include supplementary or incidental provisions (including provision amending this Schedule), and

(b) make different provision for different cases or circumstances.

(6) An order under this paragraph shall be made by statutory instrument.

(7) No such order shall be made unless a draft of it has been laid before and approved by a resolution of each House of Parliament.

(8) In this paragraph "specified" means specified in an order under this paragraph.]

[847]

NOTES

Inserted as noted at the beginning of this Schedule.

Para 166: sub-paras (1), (2), (2A), (2B) substituted, for original sub-paras (1), (2), and words in square brackets in sub-para (3) substituted, by the Employment Relations Act 2004, s 15, as from 31 December 2004.

Paras 166A, 166B: inserted by the Employment Relations Act 2004, ss 16, 17, as from 6 April 2005.

Guidance

167.—(1) The Secretary of State may issue guidance to the CAC on the way in which it is to exercise its functions under paragraph 22 or 87.

(2) The CAC must take into account any such guidance in exercising those functions.

(3) However, no guidance is to apply with regard to an application made to the CAC before the guidance in question was issued.

(4) The Secretary of State must—

(a) lay before each House of Parliament any guidance issued under this paragraph, and

(b) arrange for any such guidance to be published by such means as appear to him to be most appropriate for drawing it to the attention of persons likely to be affected by it.

[848]

NOTES

Inserted as noted at the beginning of this Schedule.

Method of conducting collective bargaining

168.—(1) After consulting ACAS the Secretary of State may by order specify for the purposes of paragraphs 31(3) and 63(2) a method by which collective bargaining might be conducted.

(2) If such an order is made the CAC—

(a) must take it into account under paragraphs 31(3) and 63(2), but

(b) may depart from the method specified by the order to such extent as the CAC thinks it is appropriate to do so in the circumstances.

(3) An order under this paragraph shall be made by statutory instrument subject to annulment in pursuance of a resolution of either House of Parliament.

[849]

NOTES

Inserted as noted at the beginning of this Schedule.

Orders: the Trade Union Recognition (Method of Collective Bargaining) Order 2000, SI 2000/1300 at **[2628]**.

Directions about certain applications

169.—(1) The Secretary of State may make to the CAC directions as described in sub-paragraph (2) in relation to any case where—

(a) two or more applications are made to the CAC,
(b) each application is a relevant application,
(c) each application relates to the same bargaining unit, and
(d) the CAC has not accepted any of the applications.

(2) The directions are directions as to the order in which the CAC must consider the admissibility of the applications.

(3) The directions may include—
(a) provision to deal with a case where a relevant application is made while the CAC is still considering the admissibility of another one relating to the same bargaining unit;
(b) other incidental provisions.

(4) A relevant application is an application under paragraph 101, 106, 107, 112 or 128. **[850]**

NOTES

Inserted as noted at the beginning of this Schedule.

[Rights of appeal against demands for costs

169A.—(1) The Secretary of State may by order make provision for any case where—
(a) an application has been made, a declaration has been issued, or any other thing has been done under or for the purposes of this Schedule by, to or in relation to a union, or
(b) anything has been done in consequence of anything so done,

and the union amalgamates or transfers all or any of its engagements.

(2) An order under this paragraph may, in particular, make provision for cases where an amalgamated union, or union to which engagements are transferred, does not have a certificate of independence.] **[850A]**

NOTES

This Schedule was inserted as noted at the beginning of this Schedule.
Para 169A: inserted, together with paras 169B, 169C, by the Employment Relations Act 2004, s 18, as from 31 December 2004.

[Effect of change of identity of employer

169B.—(1) The Secretary of State may by order make provision for any case where—
(a) an application has been made, a declaration has been issued, or any other thing has been done under or for the purposes of this Schedule in relation to a group of workers, or
(b) anything has been done in consequence of anything so done,

and the person who was the employer of the workers constituting that group at the time the thing was done is no longer the employer of all of the workers constituting that group (whether as a result of a transfer of the whole or part of an undertaking or business or otherwise).

(2) In this paragraph "group" includes two or more groups taken together.] **[850B]**

NOTES

This Schedule was inserted as noted at the beginning of this Schedule.
Para 169B: inserted as noted to para 169A at **[850A]**.

[Orders under paragraphs 169A and 169B: supplementary

169C.—(1) An order under paragraph 169A or 169B may—
(a) amend this Schedule;

(b) include supplementary, incidental, saving or transitional provisions;
(c) make different provision for different cases or circumstances.

(2) An order under paragraph 169A or 169B shall be made by statutory instrument.

(3) No such order shall be made unless a draft of it has been laid before Parliament and approved by a resolution of each House of Parliament.]

[850C]

NOTES

This Schedule was inserted as noted at the beginning of this Schedule.
Para 169C: inserted as noted to para 169A at **[850A]**.

Notice of declarations

170.—(1) If the CAC issues a declaration under this Schedule it must notify the parties of the declaration and its contents.

(2) The reference here to the parties is to—
(a) the union (or unions) concerned and the employer concerned, and
(b) if the declaration is issued in consequence of an application by a worker or workers, the worker or workers making it.

[851]

NOTES

Inserted as noted at the beginning of this Schedule.

[Supply of information to CAC

170A.—(1) The CAC may, if it considers it necessary to do so to enable or assist it to exercise any of its functions under this Schedule, exercise any or all of the powers conferred in sub-paragraphs (2) to (4).

(2) The CAC may require an employer to supply the CAC case manager, within such period as the CAC may specify, with specified information concerning either or both of the following—
(a) the workers in a specified bargaining unit who work for the employer;
(b) the likelihood of a majority of those workers being in favour of the conduct by a specified union (or specified unions) of collective bargaining on their behalf.

(3) The CAC may require a union to supply the CAC case manager, within such period as the CAC may specify, with specified information concerning either or both of the following—
(a) the workers in a specified bargaining unit who are members of the union;
(b) the likelihood of a majority of the workers in a specified bargaining unit being in favour of the conduct by the union (or by it and other specified unions) of collective bargaining on their behalf.

(4) The CAC may require an applicant worker to supply the CAC case manager, within such period as the CAC may specify, with specified information concerning the likelihood of a majority of the workers in his bargaining unit being in favour of having bargaining arrangements ended.

(5) The recipient of a requirement under this paragraph must, within the specified period, supply the CAC case manager with such of the specified information as is in the recipient's possession.

(6) From the information supplied to him under this paragraph, the CAC case manager must prepare a report and submit it to the CAC.

(7) If an employer, a union or a worker fails to comply with sub-paragraph (5), the report under sub-paragraph (6) must mention that failure; and the CAC may draw an inference against the party concerned.

(8) The CAC must give a copy of the report under sub-paragraph (6) to the employer, to the union (or unions) and, in the case of an application under paragraph 112 or 137, to the applicant worker (or applicant workers).

(9) In this paragraph—

"applicant worker" means a worker who—

(a) falls within a bargaining unit ("his bargaining unit") and

(b) has made an application under paragraph 112 or 137 to have bargaining arrangements ended;

"the CAC case manager" means the member of the staff provided to the CAC by ACAS who is named in the requirement (but the CAC may, by notice given to the recipient of a requirement under this paragraph, change the member of that staff who is to be the CAC case manager for the purposes of that requirement);

"collective bargaining" is to be construed in accordance with paragraph 3; and

"specified" means specified in a requirement under this paragraph.]

[851A]

NOTES

This Schedule was inserted as noted at the beginning of this Schedule.

Para 170A: inserted by the Employment Relations Act 2004, s 19, as from 6 April 2005.

CAC's general duty

171. In exercising functions under this Schedule in any particular case the CAC must have regard to the object of encouraging and promoting fair and efficient practices and arrangements in the workplace, so far as having regard to that object is consistent with applying other provisions of this Schedule in the case concerned.

[852]

NOTES

Inserted as noted at the beginning of this Schedule.

["Pay" and other matters subject to collective bargaining

171A.—(1) In this Schedule "pay" does not include terms relating to a person's membership of or rights under, or his employer's contributions to—

(a) an occupational pension scheme (as defined by section 1 of the Pension Schemes Act 1993), or

(b) a personal pension scheme (as so defined).

(2) The Secretary of State may by order amend sub-paragraph (1).

(3) The Secretary of State may by order—

(a) amend paragraph 3(3), 54(4) or 94(6)(b) by adding specified matters relating to pensions to the matters there specified to which negotiations may relate;

(b) amend paragraph 35(2)(b) or 44(2)(b) by adding specified matters relating to pensions to the core topics there specified.

(4) An order under this paragraph may—

(a) include supplementary, incidental, saving or transitional provisions including provision amending this Schedule, and

(b) make different provision for different cases.

(5) An order under this paragraph may make provision deeming—

(a) the matters to which any pre-commencement declaration of recognition relates, and

(b) the matters to which any pre-commencement method of collective bargaining relates,

to include matters to which a post-commencement declaration of recognition or method of collective bargaining could relate.

(6) In sub-paragraph (5)—

"pre-commencement declaration of recognition" means a declaration of recognition issued by the CAC before the coming into force of the order, "pre-commencement method of collective bargaining" means a method of collective bargaining specified by the CAC before the coming into force of the order,

and references to a post-commencement declaration of recognition or method of collective bargaining shall be construed accordingly.

(7) An order under this paragraph shall be made by statutory instrument; and no such order shall be made unless a draft of it has been laid before Parliament and approved by a resolution of each House of Parliament.]

[852A]

NOTES

This Schedule was inserted as noted at the beginning of this Schedule.

Para 171A: inserted by the Employment Relations Act 2004, s 20, as from 6 April 2005.

General interpretation

172.—(1) References in this Schedule to the CAC are to the Central Arbitration Committee.

(2) For the purposes of this Schedule in its application to a part of Great Britain a working day is a day other than—

(a) a Saturday or a Sunday,
(b) Christmas day or Good Friday, or
(c) a day which is a bank holiday under the Banking and Financial Dealings Act 1971 in that part of Great Britain.]

[853]

NOTES

Inserted as noted at the beginning of this Schedule.

(*Schs 1, 2 contain repeals and consequential amendments; in so far as relevant, these have been incorporated at the appropriate place.*)

SCHEDULE 3
TRANSITIONAL PROVISIONS AND SAVINGS

Section 300(3)

Continuity of the law

1.—(1) The repeal and re-enactment of provisions in this Act does not affect the continuity of the law.

(2) Anything done (including subordinate legislation made), or having effect as done, under a provision reproduced in this Act has effect as if done under the corresponding provision of this Act.

(3) References (express or implied) in this Act or any other enactment, instrument or document to a provision of this Act shall, so far as the context permits, be construed as including, in relation to times, circumstances and purposes before the commencement of this Act, a reference to corresponding earlier provisions.

(4) A reference (express or implied) in any enactment, instrument or other document to a provision reproduced in this Act shall be construed, so far as is required for continuing its effect, and subject to any express amendment made by this Act, as being, or as the case may required including, a reference to the corresponding provision of this Act.

General saving for old transitional provisions and savings

2.—(1) The repeal by this Act of a transitional provision or saving relating to the coming into force of a provision reproduced in this Act does not affect the operation of the transitional provision or saving, in so far as it is not specifically reproduced in this Act but remains capable of having effect in relation to the corresponding provision of this Act.

(2) The repeal by this Act of an enactment previously repealed subject to savings does not affect the continued operation of those savings.

(3) The repeal by this Act of a saving on the previous repeal of an enactment does not affect the operation of the saving in so far as it is not specifically reproduced in this Act but remains capable of having effect.

Effect of repeal of 1946 Act

3. The repeal by this Act of the Trade Disputes and Trade Unions Act 1946 shall not be construed as reviving in any respect the effect of the Trade Disputes and Trade Unions Act 1927.

Pre-1974 references to registered trade unions or employers' associations

4.—(1) Any reference in an enactment passed, or instrument made under an enactment, before 16th September 1974—

(a) to a trade union or employers' association registered under—
  (i) the Trade Union Acts 1871 to 1964, or
  (ii) the Industrial Relations Act 1971, or

(b) to an organisation of workers or an organisation of employers within the meaning of the Industrial Relations Act 1971,

shall be construed as a reference to a trade union or employers' association within the meaning of this Act.

(2) Subsection (1) does not apply to any enactment relating to income tax or corporation tax.

Enforceability of collective agreements

5. Section 179 of this Act (enforceability of collective agreements) does not apply to a collective agreement made on or after 1st December 1971 and before 16th September 1974.

Trade unions and employers' associations ceasing to be incorporated by virtue of 1974 Act

6.—(1) The repeal by this Act of section 19 of the Trade Union and Labour Relations Act 1974 (transitional provisions for trade unions and employers' associations ceasing to be incorporated) does not affect—

(a) the title to property which by virtue of that section vested on 16th September 1974 in "the appropriate trustees" as defined by that section, or

(b) any liability, obligation or right affecting such property which by virtue of that section became a liability, obligation or right of those trustees.

(2) A certificate given by the persons who on that date were the president and general secretary of a trade union or employers' association, or occupied positions equivalent to that of president and general secretary, that the persons named in the certificate are the appropriate trustees of the union or association for the purposes of section 19(2) of the Trade Union and Labour Relations Act 1974 is conclusive evidence that those persons were the appropriate trustees for those purposes.

(3) A document which purports to be such a certificate shall be taken to be such a certificate unless the contrary is proved.

References to former Industrial Arbitration Board

7. Any reference to the former Industrial Arbitration Board in relation to which section 10(2) of the Employment Protection Act 1975 applied immediately before the commencement of this Act shall continue to be construed as a reference to the Central Arbitration Committee.

Effect of political resolution passed before 1984 amendments

8. A resolution under section 3 of the Trade Union Act 1913, or rule made for the purposes of that section, in relation to which section 17(2) of the Trade Union Act 1984 applied immediately before the commencement of this Act shall continue to have effect as if for any reference to the political objects to which section 3 of the 1913 Act formerly applied there were substituted a reference to the objects to which that section applied as amended by the 1984 Act.

Persons elected to trade union office before 1988 amendments

9, 10. (*Spent*.)

Qualification to act as auditor of trade union or employers' association

11.—(1) Nothing in section 34 (eligibility for appointment as auditor) affects the validity of any appointment as auditor of a trade union or employers' association made before 1st October 1991 (when section 389 of the Companies Act 1985 was repealed and replaced by the provisions of Part II of the Companies Act 1989).

(2) A person who is not qualified as mentioned in section 34(1) may act as auditor of a trade union in respect of an accounting period if—

(a) the union was registered under the Trade Union Acts 1871 to 1964 on 30th September 1971,

(b) he acted as its auditor in respect of the last period in relation to which it was required to make an annual return under section 16 of the Trade Union Act 1871,

(c) he has acted as its auditor in respect of every accounting period since that period, and

(d) he retains an authorisation formerly granted by the Board of Trade or the Secretary of State under section 16(1)(b) of the Companies Act 1948 (adequate knowledge and experience, or pre-1947 practice).

12. . . .

Use of existing forms, &c

13. Any document made, served or issued on or after the commencement of this Act which contains a reference to an enactment repealed by this Act shall be construed, except so far as a contrary intention appears, as referring or, as the context may require, including a reference to the corresponding provision of this Act.

Saving for power to vary or revoke

14. The power of the Secretary of State by further order to vary or revoke the Funds for Trade Union Ballots Order 1982 extends to so much of section 115(2)(a) as reproduces the effect of Article 2 of that order.

[854]

NOTES

Para 12: applied to Northern Ireland only and was repealed by the Trade Union and Labour Relations (Northern Ireland) Order 1995, SI 1995/1980.

Note: it is assumed that the word "required" in the second place it occurs in para 1 should read "require".

Companies Act 1948: repealed (see now the Companies Act 1985 and the Companies Act 2006).

Employment Act 1988: ss 12(1), 13–15 of that Act are repealed by s 300(1) of, and Sch 1 to, this Act.

Employment Protection Act 1975: s 10(2) of that Act is repealed by s 300(1) of, and Sch 1 to, this Act.

Industrial Relations Act 1971: repealed by the Trade Union and Labour Relations Act 1974, ss 1, 25(3), Sch 5.

Trade Disputes and Trade Unions Act 1927: repealed by the Trade Disputes and Trade Unions Act 1946, s 1.

Trade Disputes and Trade Unions Act 1946: repealed by s 300(1) of, and Sch 1 to, this Act.

Trade Union Act 1913: s 3 of that Act is repealed by s 300(1) of, and Sch 1 to, this Act.

Trade Union Acts 1871 to 1964: the Acts which were cited together under this collective title were: the Trade Union Act 1871 (repealed); the Trade Union Act Amendment Act 1876 (repealed); the Trade Disputes Act 1906 (repealed); the Trade Union Act 1913 (repealed with a saving); the Trade Union (Amalgamation) Act 1917 (repealed); the Trade Disputes and Trade Unions Act 1927 (repealed); the Societies (Miscellaneous Provisions) Act 1940, s 6 (repealed); and the Trade Union (Amalgamations, etc) Act 1964 (repealed).

Trade Union Act 1984: s 3 was repealed by the Employment Act 1988, ss 14(2), 33(2), Sch 4. The whole Act is repealed by s 300(1) of, and Sch 1 to, this Act.

Trade Union and Labour Relations Act 1974: repealed by s 300(1) of, and Sch 1 to, this Act.

TRADE UNION REFORM AND EMPLOYMENT RIGHTS ACT 1993 (NOTE)

(1993 c 19)

An Act to make further reforms of the law relating to trade unions and industrial relations; to make amendments of the law relating to employment rights and to abolish the right to statutory minimum remuneration; to amend the law relating to the constitution and jurisdiction of industrial tribunals and the Employment Appeal Tribunal; to amend section 56A of the Sex Discrimination Act 1975; to provide for the Secretary of State to have functions of securing the provision of careers services; to make further provision about employment and training functions of Scottish Enterprise and of Highlands and Islands Enterprise; and for connected purposes

[1 July 1993]

NOTES

See *Harvey* Q.

Almost all of this major Act either amends other legislation (principally the Trade Union and Labour Relations (Consolidation) Act 1992) or has since been repealed and re-enacted by the Employment Tribunals Act 1996 and the Employment Rights Act 1996. It is therefore not necessary to reproduce provisions of the Act here. Instead this note summarises the position under the two major categories indicated above, in the following tables.

1 Provisions amending the 1992 Act

Section/Schedule	*Amendments*
1	Amends ss 49, 52
2	Inserts s 51A, amends s 52
3	Introduces Sch 1 (which amends ss 74, 75 and 78 and inserts s 77A)
4	Substitutes s 100 with new ss 100–100E
5	Amends s 99
6	Inserts s 24A
7	Repeals ss 115, 116
8	Amends s 32(3)
9	Inserts s 32A
10	Inserts ss 37A–37E
11	Amends s 45 and inserts s 45A
12	Inserts ss 45B, 45C
13	Amends s 148
14	Substitutes ss 174–177
15	Substitutes s 68 with new ss 68 and 68A

Section/Schedule	Amendments
16	Amends s 65
17	Amends s 230
18	Amends s 226 and inserts s 226A
19	Inserts s 231A
20	Amends s 229 and inserts ss 226B, 226C, 231B
21	Inserts s 234A
22	Inserts ss 235A–235C (ss 235B, 235C repealed by the Employment Relations Act 1999)
34	Amends ss 188, 190, 193, substitutes s 195, repeals s 283 (repealed in part by SI 1995/2587 and the Statute Law (Repeals) Act 2004)
43	Amends ss 209, 249, substitutes s 213 (repealed in part by the Employment Relations Act 1999)
44	Inserts s 251A
Sch 1	Amends ss 74, 75, 78, inserts s 77A
Sch 6 (part)	Amends s 288 (repealed in part by the Employment Rights (Dispute Resolution) Act 1998)

2 Provisions repealed by the Employment Tribunals Act 1996

Section/ Schedule	*Effect of provision*	*Provisions as re-enacted*
36	Amended the Employment Protection (Consolidation) Act 1978, s 128	4(1)–(7), 41(2)
37	Substituted Sch 11, Pt I, para 16 to the 1978 Act	28(2)–(5)
38	Amended s 131 of the 1978 Act	3(1), (3), (5), 8(2), (4)
40	Amended Sch 9, para 1 to the 1978 Act	7(5), 11(1)–(6)
41	Inserted Sch 11, Pt I, para 18A to the 1978 Act	31
42	Inserted s 136A of the 1978 Act	33, 37(3)

3 Provisions repealed by the Employment Rights Act 1996

Section/ Schedule	*Effect of provision*	*Provisions as re-enacted*
23	Substituted the Employment Protection (Consolidation) Act 1978, Part III with ss 33–38A and ss 39–44 (enacted by Sch 2)	71–78, 236(3), 79–83, 85, 236(3)
24	Substituted s 60, amended ss 53, 59, 64 of the 1978 Act	99(1)–(3), 105(1), (2), 108(3), 109(2), 92(4)
25	Introduced Sch 3 (inserted ss 45–47 of the 1978 Act)	66–70, 106(3)

Section/ Schedule	Effect of provision	Provisions as re-enacted
26	Introduced Sch 4 (substituted ss 1–6 of the 1978 Act)	1–7, 198
28	Introduced Sch 5 (inserted ss 22A–C, 57A, 75A, 77–79 and amended ss 57(3), 59(2), 64(4), 71–73 of the 1978 Act)	44, 48, 49, 98(6), 100, 105(3), 108(3), 109(2), 117(3), (4), 118, 119(1), 120, 122(3), 125, 128–132, 236(3).
29	Inserted s 60A, amended ss 59(2), 64(4) of the 1978 Act	104, 105(7), 108(3), 109(2)
30	Amended ss 71, 74, 75 of the 1978 Act	117(2), 123(1), 124(3),(4)
31	Amended s 138, inserted s 138A of the 1978 Act	192(1)–(8), 236(3)
39(1)	Amended s 140 of the 1978 Act	203(2)–(4)
Sch 2	Substituted ss 39–44 of the 1978 Act	79–83, 85, 236(3)
Sch 3	Inserted ss 45–47 of the 1978 Act	66–70, 106(3)
Sch 4	Substituted ss 1–6 of the 1978 Act	1–7, 198
Sch 5	Inserted ss 22A–C, 57A, 75A, 77–79 and amended ss 57(3), 59(2), 64(4), 71–73 of the 1978 Act	44, 48, 49, 98(6), 100, 105(3), 108(3), 109(2), 117(3), (4), 118, 119(1), 120, 122(3), 125, 128–132, 236(3)
Sch 6 (part)	Amended the Wages Act 1986, s 6	203(2)–(4), 231

4 Other provisions not reproduced

Section/ Schedule	Effect of provision	Reason for omission
27	Inserted the Employment Protection (Consolidation) Act 1978, s146(4A)–(4C)	Repealed by SI 1995/31
32	Inserts the Sex Discrimination Act 1986, s 6(4A)–(4D)	Qv at [378]
33	Amended SI 1981/1794	Repealed by SI 2006/246
35	Repealed the Wages Act 1986, Pt II	Repealed by the Statute Law (Repeals) Act 2004
39(2)	Introduces Sch 6	See Sch 6 below
45–47	Amend the Employment and Training Act 1973, Enterprise and the New Towns (Scotland) Act 1990	Outside the scope of this work
48	Interpretation	Unnecessary
49	Introduces Schs 7 and 8	See Schs 7 and 8 below
50	Introduces Sch 9	See Sch 9 below
51	Introduces Sch 10	See Sch 10 below
52	Commencement	Unnecessary
53	Financial provision	Unnecessary
54	Application to Northern Ireland	Outside the scope of this work
55	Short title	Unnecessary

Section/ Schedule	*Effect of provision*	*Reason for omission*
Sch 6 (part)	Amends the Sex Discrimination Act 1975, s 77 and the Race Relations Act 1976, s 72	Qv at [191] and [297]
Sch 7	Miscellaneous amendments	Unnecessary (in so far as relevant to this work such amendments have been incorporated)
Schs 8	Consequential amendments	Unnecessary (in so far as relevant to this work such amendments have been incorporated)
Sch 9	Transitional provisions and savings	Spent
Sch 10	Repeals	Unnecessary (in so far as relevant to this work such repeals have been incorporated)

[855]

PENSION SCHEMES ACT 1993

(1993 c 48)

ARRANGEMENT OF SECTIONS

PART III
CERTIFICATION OF PENSION SCHEMES AND EFFECTS ON MEMBERS' STATE SCHEME RIGHTS AND DUTIES

CHAPTER I
CERTIFICATION

General requirements for certification

PART VII
INSOLVENCY OF EMPLOYERS

CHAPTER II
PAYMENT BY SECRETARY OF STATE OF UNPAID SCHEME CONTRIBUTIONS

PART X
INVESTIGATIONS: THE PENSIONS OMBUDSMAN

An Act to consolidate certain enactments relating to pension schemes with amendments to give effect to recommendations of the Law Commission and the Scottish Law Commission

[5 November 1993]

NOTES

Only certain parts of this Act most relevant to employment law are reproduced. Provisions omitted are not annotated. The provisions reproduced have been extensively amended by the Pensions Acts 1995 and 2004, and the Child Support, Pensions and Social Security Act 2000, and are printed as so amended.

See *Harvey* B8(D), G1(D), Q, R.

PART III
CERTIFICATION OF PENSION SCHEMES AND EFFECTS ON MEMBERS' STATE SCHEME RIGHTS AND DUTIES

CHAPTER I
CERTIFICATION

General requirements for certification

11 Elections as to employments covered by contracting-out certificates

(1) Subject to the provisions of this Part, an employment otherwise satisfying the conditions for inclusion in a contracting-out certificate shall be so included if and so long as the employer so elects and not otherwise.

(2) Subject to subsections (3) and (4), an election may be so made, and an employment so included, either generally or in relation only to a particular description of earners.

(3) Except in such cases as may be prescribed, an employer shall not, in making or abstaining from making any election under this section, discriminate between different earners on any grounds other than the nature of their employment.

(4) If the [Inland Revenue consider] that an employer is contravening subsection (3) in relation to any scheme, [they] may—

(a) refuse to give effect to any election made by him in relation to that scheme; or
(b) cancel any contracting-out certificate held by him in respect of it.

(5) Regulations may make provision—

(a) for regulating the manner in which an employer is to make an election with a view to the issue, variation or surrender of a contracting-out certificate;

(b) for requiring an employer to give a notice of his intentions in respect of making or abstaining from making any such election in relation to any existing or proposed scheme—

(i) to employees in any employment to which the scheme applies or to which it is proposed that it should apply;

(ii) to any independent trade union recognised to any extent for the purpose of collective bargaining in relation to those employees;

(iii) to the trustees and managers of the scheme; and

(iv) to such other persons as may be prescribed;

(c) for requiring an employer, in connection with any such notice, to furnish such information as may be prescribed and to undertake such consultations as may be prescribed with any such trade union as is mentioned in paragraph (b)(ii);

(d) for empowering the [Inland Revenue] to refuse to give effect to an election made by an employer unless [they are] satisfied that he has complied with the requirements of the regulations;

(e) for referring to an [employment tribunal] any question—

(i) whether an organisation is such a trade union as is mentioned in paragraph (b)(ii), or

(ii) whether the requirements of the regulations as to consultation have been complied with.

[856]

NOTES

Sub-s (4): words in square brackets substituted by the Social Security Contributions (Transfer of Functions, etc) Act 1999, s 1(1), Sch 1, para 37.

Sub-s (5): words in first and second pairs of square brackets substituted by the Social Security Contributions (Transfer of Functions, etc) Act 1999, s 1(1), Sch 1, para 37; words in final pair of square brackets substituted by the Employment Rights (Dispute Resolution) Act 1998, s 1(2)(a).

Inland Revenue: a reference to the Inland Revenue is now to be taken as a reference to Her Majesty's Revenue and Customs; see the Commissioners for Revenue and Customs Act 2005, s 50(1), (7).

Regulations: the Occupational Pension Schemes (Contracting-out) Regulations 1996, SI 1996/1172; the Personal and Occupational Pension Schemes (Miscellaneous Amendments) Regulations 1999, SI 1999/3198; the Occupational and Personal Pension Schemes (Contracting-out) (Miscellaneous Amendments) Regulations 2002, SI 2002/681.

PART VII
INSOLVENCY OF EMPLOYERS

CHAPTER II
PAYMENT BY SECRETARY OF STATE OF UNPAID SCHEME CONTRIBUTIONS

123 Interpretation of Chapter II

(1) For the purposes of this Chapter, an employer shall be taken to be insolvent if, but only if, in England and Wales—

(a) he has been adjudged bankrupt or has made a composition or arrangement with his creditors;

(b) he has died and his estate falls to be administered in accordance with an order under section 421 of the Insolvency Act 1986; or

(c) where the employer is a company—

(i) a winding-up order … is made or a resolution for voluntary winding up is passed with respect to it [or the company enters administration],

(ii) a receiver or manager of its undertaking is duly appointed,

(iii) possession is taken, by or on behalf of the holders of any debentures secured by a floating charge, of any property of the company comprised in or subject to the charge, or

(iv) a voluntary arrangement proposed for the purpose of Part I of the Insolvency Act 1986 is approved under that Part.

(2) For the purposes of this Chapter, an employer shall be taken to be insolvent if, but only if, in Scotland—

(a) sequestration of his estate is awarded or he executes a trust deed for his creditors or enters into a composition contract;

(b) he has died and a judicial factor appointed under section 11A of the Judicial Factors (Scotland) Act 1889 is required by this section to divide his insolvent estate among his creditors; or

(c) where the employer is a company—

(i) a winding-up order … is made or a resolution for voluntary winding up is passed with respect to it [or the company enters administration],

(ii) a receiver of its undertaking is duly appointed, or

(iii) a voluntary arrangement proposed for the purpose of Part I of the Insolvency Act 1986 is approved under that Part.

(3) In this Chapter—

"contract of employment", "employee", "employer" and "employment" and other expressions which are defined in [the Employment Rights Act 1996] have the same meaning as in that Act;

"holiday pay" means—

(a) pay in respect of holiday actually taken; or

(b) any accrued holiday pay which under the employee's contract of employment would in the ordinary course have become payable to him in respect of the period of a holiday if his employment with the employer had continued until he became entitled to a holiday;

…

(4) …

(5) Any reference in this Chapter to the resources of a scheme is a reference to the funds out of which the benefits provided by the scheme are from time to time payable.

[857]

NOTES

Sub-ss (1), (2): words omitted from sub-para (c)(i) repealed, and words in square brackets added, by the Enterprise Act 2002 (Insolvency) Order 2003, SI 2003/2096, art 4, Schedule, para 22, as from 15 September 2003, except in relation to cases where a petition for an administration order was presented before that date.

Sub-s (3): words in square brackets substituted by the Employment Rights Act 1996, s 240, Sch 1, para 61(1), (3); definition "occupational pension scheme" repealed by the Pensions Act 2004, ss 319(1), 320, Sch 12, paras 9, 19(a), Sch 13, Pt 1, as from 22 September 2005.

Sub-s (4): repealed by the Pensions Act 2004, ss 319(1), 320, Sch 12, paras 9, 19(b), Sch 13, Pt 1, as from 22 September 2005.

124 Duty of Secretary of State to pay unpaid contributions to schemes

(1) If, on an application made to him in writing by the persons competent to act in respect of an occupational pension scheme or a personal pension scheme, the Secretary of State is satisfied—

(a) that an employer has become insolvent; and

(b) that at the time he did so there remained unpaid relevant contributions falling to be paid by him to the scheme,

then, subject to the provisions of this section and section 125, the Secretary of State shall pay into the resources of the scheme the sum which in his opinion is payable in respect of the unpaid relevant contributions.

(2) In this section and section 125 "relevant contributions" means contributions falling to be paid by an employer to an occupational pension scheme or a personal pension scheme, either on his own account or on behalf of an employee; and for the purposes of this section a contribution shall not be treated as falling to be paid on behalf of an employee unless a sum equal to that amount has been deducted from the pay of the employee by way of a contribution from him.

(3) [Subject to subsection (3A),] the sum payable under this section in respect of unpaid contributions of an employer on his own account to an occupational pension scheme or a personal pension scheme shall be the least of the following amounts—

(a) the balance of relevant contributions remaining unpaid on the date when he became insolvent and payable by the employer on his own account to the scheme in respect of the 12 months immediately preceding that date;

(b) the amount certified by an actuary to be necessary for the purpose of meeting the liability of the scheme on dissolution to pay the benefits provided by the scheme to or in respect of the employees of the employer;

(c) an amount equal to 10 per cent. of the total amount of remuneration paid or payable to those employees in respect of the 12 months immediately preceding the date on which the employer became insolvent.

[(3A) Where the scheme in question is a money purchase scheme, the sum payable under this section by virtue of subsection (3) shall be the lesser of the amounts mentioned in paragraphs (a) and (c) of that subsection.]

(4) For the purposes of subsection (3)(c), "remuneration" includes holiday pay, statutory sick pay, statutory maternity pay under Part V of the Social Security Act 1986 or Part XII of the Social Security Contributions and Benefits Act 1992 [and any payment such as is referred to in section 184(2) of the Employment Rights Act 1996].

(5) Any sum payable under this section in respect of unpaid contributions on behalf of an employee shall not exceed the amount deducted from the pay of the employee in respect of the employee's contributions to the scheme during the 12 months immediately preceding the date on which the employer became insolvent.

[(6) In this section "on his own account", in relation to an employer, means on his own account but to fund benefits for, or in respect of, one or more employees.]

[858]

NOTES

Sub-s (3): words in square brackets inserted by the Pensions Act 1995, s 90.

Sub-s (3A): inserted by the Pensions Act 1995, s 90.

Sub-s (4): words in square brackets substituted by the Employment Rights Act 1996, s 240, Sch 1, para 61(1), (3).

Sub-s (6): inserted by the Pensions Act 2004, s 319(1), Sch 12, paras 9, 20, as from 22 September 2005.

Social Security Act 1986, Pt V: repealed by the Social Security (Consequential Provisions) Act 1992. The relevant provisions of that Part relating to maternity pay were re-enacted in the Social Security Contributions and Benefits Act 1992, Pt XII.

125 Certification of amounts payable under s 124 by insolvency officers

(1) This section applies where one of the officers mentioned in subsection (2) ("the relevant officer") has been or is required to be appointed in connection with an employer's insolvency.

(2) The officers referred to in subsection (1) are—

(a) a trustee in bankruptcy;

(b) a liquidator;

(c) an administrator;

(d) a receiver or manager; or

(e) a trustee under a composition or arrangement between the employer and his creditors or under a trust deed for his creditors executed by the employer;

and in this subsection "trustee", in relation to a composition or arrangement, includes the supervisor of a voluntary arrangement proposed for the purposes of and approved under Part I or VIII of the Insolvency Act 1986.

(3) Subject to subsection (5), where this section applies the Secretary of State shall not make any payment under section 124 in respect of unpaid relevant contributions until he has received a statement from the relevant officer of the amount of relevant contributions which appear to have been unpaid on the date on which the employer became insolvent and to remain unpaid; and the relevant officer shall on request by the Secretary of State provide him as soon as reasonably practicable with such a statement.

(4) Subject to subsection (5), an amount shall be taken to be payable, paid or deducted as mentioned in subsection (3)(a) or (c) or (5) of section 124 only if it is so certified by the relevant officer.

(5) If the Secretary of State is satisfied—

(a) that he does not require a statement under subsection (3) in order to determine the amount of relevant contributions that was unpaid on the date on which the employer became insolvent and remains unpaid, or

(b) that he does not require a certificate under subsection (4) in order to determine the amounts payable, paid or deducted as mentioned in subsection (3)(a) or (c) or (5) of section 124, he may make a payment under that section in respect of the contributions in question without having received such a statement or, as the case may be, such a certificate.

[859]

126 Complaint to [employment tribunal]

(1) Any persons who are competent to act in respect of an occupational pension scheme or a personal pension scheme and who have applied for a payment to be made under section 124 into the resources of the scheme may present a complaint to an [employment tribunal] that—

(a) the Secretary of State has failed to make any such payment; or

(b) any such payment made by him is less than the amount which should have been paid.

(2) Such a complaint must be presented within the period of three months beginning with the date on which the decision of the Secretary of State on that application was communicated to the persons presenting it or, if that is not reasonably practicable, within such further period as is reasonable.

(3) Where an [employment tribunal] finds that the Secretary of State ought to make a payment under section 124, it shall make a declaration to that effect and shall also declare the amount of any such payment which it finds that the Secretary of State ought to make.

[860]

NOTES

Section heading, sub-ss (1), (3): words in square brackets substituted by the Employment Rights (Dispute Resolution) Act 1998, s 1(2)(a).

127 Transfer to Secretary of State of rights and remedies

(1) Where in pursuance of section 124 the Secretary of State makes any payment into the resources of an occupational pension scheme or a personal pension scheme in respect of any contributions to the scheme, any rights and remedies in respect of those contributions belonging to the persons competent to act in respect of the scheme shall, on the making of the payment, become rights and remedies of the Secretary of State.

(2) Where the Secretary of State makes any such payment as is mentioned in subsection (1) and the sum (or any part of the sum) falling to be paid by the employer on account of the contributions in respect of which the payment is made constitutes—

(a) a preferential debt within the meaning of the Insolvency Act 1986 for the purposes of any provision of that Act (including any such provision as applied by an order made under that Act) or any provision of [the Companies Act 2006]; or

(b) a preferred debt within the meaning of the Bankruptcy (Scotland) Act 1985 for the purposes of any provision of that Act (including any such provision as applied by section 11A of the Judicial Factors (Scotland) Act 1889,

then, without prejudice to the generality of subsection (1), there shall be included among the rights and remedies which become rights and remedies of the Secretary of State in accordance with that subsection any right arising under any such provision by reason of the status of that sum (or that part of it) as a preferential or preferred debt.

(3) In computing for the purposes of any provision referred to in subsection (2)(a) or (b) the aggregate amount payable in priority to other creditors of the employer in respect of—

(a) any claim of the Secretary of State to be so paid by virtue of subsection (2); and

(b) any claim by the persons competent to act in respect of the scheme,

any claim falling within paragraph (a) shall be treated as if it were a claim of those persons; but the Secretary of State shall be entitled, as against those persons, to be so paid in respect of any such claim of his (up to the full amount of the claim) before any payment is made to them in respect of any claim falling within paragraph (b).

[861]

NOTES

Sub-s (2): words in square brackets in para (a) substituted by the Companies Act 2006 (Consequential Amendments etc) Order 2008, SI 2008/948, arts 3(1)(b), 6, Sch 1, Pt 2, para 194(1), (2), as from 6 April 2008.

PART X
INVESTIGATIONS: THE PENSIONS OMBUDSMAN

145 The Pensions Ombudsman

(1) For the purpose of conducting investigations in accordance with this Part or any corresponding legislation having effect in Northern Ireland there shall be a commissioner to be known as the Pensions Ombudsman.

[(1A) Provisions conferring power on the Pensions Ombudsman to conduct investigations as mentioned in subsection (1) are to be read as conferring power that—
- (a) in a case of a prescribed description, or
- (b) in a case involving a scheme that is prescribed or is of a prescribed description,

may be exercised whatever the extent of any connections with places outside the United Kingdom.

(1B) In subsection (1A) "scheme" means occupational pension scheme or personal pension scheme.

(1C) Subsection (1A) shall not be taken to prejudice any power of the Pensions Ombudsman apart from that subsection to conduct investigations in a case having connections with places outside the United Kingdom.]

(2) The Pensions Ombudsman shall be appointed by the Secretary of State and shall hold [and vacate] office upon such terms and conditions as the Secretary of State may think fit.

[(3) The Pensions Ombudsman may resign or be removed from office in accordance with those terms and conditions.]

[(4A) The Pensions Ombudsman may (with the approval of the Secretary of State as to numbers) appoint such persons to be employees of his as he thinks fit, on such terms and conditions as to remuneration and other matters as the Pensions Ombudsman may with the approval of the Secretary of State determine.

(4B) The Secretary of State may, on such terms as to payment by the Pensions Ombudsman as the Secretary of State thinks fit, make available to the Pensions Ombudsman such additional staff and such other facilities as he thinks fit.

(4C) Any function of the Pensions Ombudsman, other than the determination of complaints made and disputes referred under this Part, may be performed by any—
- (a) employee appointed by the Pensions Ombudsman under subsection (4A), or
- (b) member of staff made available to him by the Secretary of State under subsection (4B),

who is authorised for that purpose by the Pensions Ombudsman.]

(5) The Secretary of State may—
- (a) pay to or in respect of the Pensions Ombudsman such amounts by way of remuneration, compensation for loss of office, pension, allowances and gratuities, or by way of provision for any such benefits, as the Secretary of State may determine … ; and
- (b) reimburse him in respect of any expenses incurred by him in the performance of his functions.

(6) The Pensions Ombudsman shall prepare a report on the discharge of his functions for each financial year, and shall submit it to the Secretary of State as soon as practicable afterwards.

(7) The Secretary of State shall arrange for the publication of each report submitted to him under subsection (6).

[(8) As soon as is reasonably practicable, the Pensions Ombudsman shall send to the Comptroller and Auditor General a statement of the Pensions Ombudsman's accounts in respect of a financial year.

(9) The Comptroller and Auditor General shall—
- (a) examine, certify and report on a statement received under this section; and
- (b) send a copy of the statement and the report to the Secretary of State who shall lay them before Parliament.

(10) In this section "financial year" means a period of 12 months ending with 31st March.]

[862]

NOTES

Sub-ss (1A)–(1C): inserted by the Pensions Act 2004, s 319(1), Sch 12, paras 9, 23, as from a day to be appointed.

Sub-s (2): words in square brackets inserted by the Pensions Act 2004, s 274(1), as from 17 December 2004.

Sub-s (3): substituted by the Pensions Act 2004, s 274(2), as from 17 December 2004.

Sub-ss (4A)–(4C): substituted, for original sub-s (4), by the Pensions Act 1995, s 156.

Sub-s (5): words omitted repealed by the Pensions Act 1995, ss 173, 177, Sch 6, paras 2, 7, Sch 7, Pt IV.

Sub-ss (8)–(10): added by the Government Resources and Accounts Act 2000 (Audit of Public Bodies) Order 2008, SI 2008/817, arts 9, 10, as from 26 March 2008, in relation to financial years ending on or after 31 March 2008.

[145A Deputy Pensions Ombudsman

(1) The Secretary of State may appoint one or more persons to act as a deputy to the Pensions Ombudsman ("a Deputy Pensions Ombudsman").

(2) Any such appointment is to be upon such terms and conditions as the Secretary of State thinks fit.

(3) A Deputy Pensions Ombudsman—
- (a) is to hold and vacate office in accordance with the terms and conditions of his appointment, and
- (b) may resign or be removed from office in accordance with those terms and conditions.

(4) A Deputy Pensions Ombudsman may perform the functions of the Pensions Ombudsman—
- (a) during any vacancy in that office,
- (b) at any time when the Pensions Ombudsman is for any reason unable to discharge his functions, or
- (c) at any other time, with the consent of the Secretary of State.

(5) References to the Pensions Ombudsman in relation to the performance of his functions are accordingly to be construed as including references to a Deputy Pensions Ombudsman in relation to the performance of those functions.

(6) The Secretary of State may—
- (a) pay to or in respect of a Deputy Pensions Ombudsman such amounts—
  - (i) by way of remuneration, compensation for loss of office, pension, allowances and gratuities, or
  - (ii) by way of provision for any such benefits,

  as the Secretary of State may determine, and
- (b) reimburse the Pensions Ombudsman in respect of any expenses incurred by a Deputy Pensions Ombudsman in the performance of any of the Pensions Ombudsman's functions.]

[862A]

NOTES

Commencement: 17 December 2004.

Inserted by the Pensions Act 2004, s 274(3), as from 17 December 2004.

146 Functions of the Pensions Ombudsman

[(1) The Pensions Ombudsman may investigate and determine the following [matters]—
- (a) a complaint made to him by or on behalf of an actual or potential beneficiary of an occupational or personal pension scheme who alleges that he has sustained injustice in consequence of maladministration in connection with any act or omission of a person responsible for the management of the scheme,
- (b) a complaint made to him—
  - (i) by or on behalf of a person responsible for the management of an occupational pension scheme who in connection with any act or omission of another person responsible for the management of the scheme, alleges maladministration of the scheme, or
  - (ii) by or on behalf of the trustees or managers or an occupational pension

scheme who in connection with any act or omission of any trustee or manager of another such scheme, allege maladministration of the other scheme,

and in any case falling within sub-paragraph (ii) references in this Part to the scheme to which the complaint relates [are references to the other scheme referred to in that sub-paragraph],

[(ba) a complaint made to him by or on behalf of an independent trustee of a trust scheme who, in connection with any act or omission which is an act or omission either—

(i) of trustees of the scheme who are not independent trustees, or

(ii) of former trustees of the scheme who were not independent trustees,

alleges maladministration of the scheme,]

(c) any dispute of fact or law … in relation to an occupational or personal pension scheme between—

(i) a person responsible for the management of the scheme, and

(ii) an actual or potential beneficiary,

and which is referred to him by or on behalf of the actual or potential beneficiary, and

(d) any dispute of fact or law … between the trustees or managers of an occupational pension scheme and—

(i) another person responsible for the management of the scheme, or

(ii) any trustee or manager of another such scheme, [and in a case falling within sub-paragraph (ii) references in this Part to the scheme to which the reference relates are references to each of the schemes,

(e) any dispute not falling within paragraph (f) between different trustees of the same occupational pension scheme,

[(f) any dispute, in relation to a time while section 22 of the Pensions Act 1995 (circumstances in which Regulatory Authority may appoint an independent trustee) applies in relation to an occupational pension scheme, between an independent trustee of the scheme appointed under section 23(1) of that Act and either—

(i) other trustees of the scheme, or

(ii) former trustees of the scheme who were not independent trustees appointed under section 23(1) of that Act, and]

(g) any question relating, in the case of an occupational pension scheme with a sole trustee, to the carrying out of the functions of that trustee.]

[(1A) The Pensions Ombudsman shall not investigate or determine any dispute or question falling within subsection (1)(c) to (g) unless it is referred to him—

(a) in the case of a dispute falling within subsection (1)(c), by or on behalf of the actual or potential beneficiary who is a party to the dispute,

(b) in the case of a dispute falling within subsection (1)(d), by or on behalf of any of the parties to the dispute,

(c) in the case of a dispute falling within subsection (1)(e), by or on behalf of at least half the trustees of the scheme,

(d) in the case of a dispute falling within subsection (1)(f), by or on behalf of the independent trustee who is a party to the dispute,

(e) in the case of a question falling within subsection (1)(g), by or on behalf of the sole trustee.

(1B) For the purposes of this Part, any reference to or determination by the Pensions Ombudsman of a question falling within subsection (1)(g) shall be taken to be the reference or determination of a dispute.]

(2) Complaints and references made to the Pensions Ombudsman must be made to him in writing.

(3) For the purposes of this Part, the following persons (subject to subsection (4)) are responsible for the management of an occupational pension scheme [or a personal pension scheme]—

(a) the trustees or managers, and

(b) the employer;

but, in relation to a person falling within one of those paragraphs, references in this Part to another person responsible for the management of the same scheme are to a person falling within the other paragraph.

(3A) …

(4) Regulations may provide that, subject to any prescribed modifications or exceptions, this Part shall apply in the case of an occupational or personal pension scheme in relation to any prescribed person or body of persons where the person or body—
(a) is not a trustee or manager of employer, but
(b) is concerned with the financing or administration of, or the provision or benefits under, the scheme,

as if for the purposes of this Part he were a person responsible for the management of the scheme.]

[(4A) For the purposes of subsection (4) a person or body of persons is concerned with the administration of an occupational or personal pension scheme where the person or body is responsible for carrying out an act of administration concerned with the scheme.]

(5) The Pensions Ombudsman may investigate a complaint or dispute notwithstanding that it arose, or relates to a matter which arose, before 1st October 1990 (the date on which the provisions under which his office was constituted came into force).

(6) The Pensions Ombudsman shall not investigate or determine a complaint or dispute—
[(a) if, before the making of the complaint or the reference of the dispute—
(i) proceedings in respect of the matters which would be the subject of the investigation have been begun in any court or employment tribunal, and
(ii) those proceedings are proceedings which have not been discontinued or which have been discontinued on the basis of a settlement or compromise binding all the persons by or on whose behalf the complaint or reference is made;]
(b) if the scheme is of a description which is excluded from the jurisdiction of the Pensions Ombudsman by regulations under this subsection; or
(c) if and to the extent that the complaint or dispute, or any matter arising in connection with the complaint or dispute, is of a description which is excluded from the jurisdiction of the Pensions Ombudsman by regulations under this subsection.

[(6A) For the purposes of subsection (6)(c)—
(a) a description of complaint may be framed (in particular) by reference to the person making the complaint or to the scheme concerned (or to both), and
(b) a description of dispute may be framed (in particular) by reference to the person referring the dispute or to the scheme concerned (or to both).]

(7) The persons who, for the purposes of this Part are [actual or potential beneficiaries] in relation to a scheme are—
(a) a member of the scheme,
(b) the [widow, widower or surviving civil partner], or any surviving dependant, of a deceased member of the scheme;
[(ba) a person who is entitled to a pension credit as against the trustees or managers of the scheme;]
(c) where the complaint or dispute relates to the question—
(i) whether a person who claims to be such a person as is mentioned in [paragraph (a), (b) or (ba)] is such a person, or
(ii) whether a person who claims to be entitled to become a member of the scheme is so entitled,

the person so claiming.

(8) In this Part—

"employer", in relation to a pension scheme, includes a person—
(a) who is or has been an employer in relation to the scheme, or
(b) who is or has been treated under section 181(2) as an employer in relation to the scheme for the purposes of any provision of this Act, or under section 176(2) of the Pension Schemes (Northern Ireland) Act 1993 as an employer in relation to the scheme for the purposes of any provision of that Act;

["independent trustee", in relation to a scheme, means—
(a) a trustee of the scheme appointed under [section 23(1) of the Pensions Act 1995 (appointment of independent trustee by the Regulatory Authority)],
(b) a person appointed under section 7(1) of that Act to replace a trustee falling within paragraph (a) or this paragraph;]

"member", in relation to a pension scheme, includes a person—

(a) who is or has been in pensionable service under the scheme, or

(b) who is or has been treated under section 181(4) as a member in relation to the scheme for the purposes of any provision of this Act or under section 176(3) of the Pension Schemes (Northern Ireland) Act 1993 as a member in relation to the scheme for the purposes of any provision of that Act;

"Northern Ireland public service pension scheme" means a public service pension scheme within the meaning of section 176(1) of that Act;

"pensionable service" in this subsection includes pensionable service as defined in section 176(1) of that Act;

"trustees or managers", in relation to a pension scheme which is a public service pension scheme or a Northern Ireland public service pension scheme, includes the scheme's administrators.

[863]

NOTES

Sub-s (1): substituted, together with sub-ss (2), (3), (3A), (4) for original sub-ss (1)–(4), by the Pensions Act 1995, s 157(1), (2); word in first pair of square brackets and words in square brackets in paras (b), (d) substituted, para (ba) inserted, and words omitted repealed, by the Child Support, Pensions and Social Security Act 2000, s 53(1), (2), (9)(a)–(c), Sch 9, Pt III(3); para (f) substituted by the Pensions Act 2004, s 319(1), Sch 12, paras 9, 24(a), as from 6 April 2005.

Sub-ss (1A), (1B): inserted by the Child Support, Pensions and Social Security Act 2000, s 53(1), (4).

Sub-ss (2), (4): substituted as noted above.

Sub-s (3): substituted as noted above; words in square brackets inserted by the Child Support, Pensions and Social Security Act 2000, s 53(1), (5).

Sub-s (3A): substituted as noted above; repealed by the Child Support, Pensions and Social Security Act 2000, s 85, Sch 9, Pt III(3).

Sub-s (4A): inserted by the Pensions Act 2004, s 275, as from 6 April 2005.

Sub-s (6): para (a) substituted by the Child Support, Pensions and Social Security Act 2000, s 53(1), (6), (10).

Sub-s (6A): inserted by the Pensions Act 2004, s 319(1), Sch 12, paras 9, 24(b), as from a day to be appointed.

Sub-s (7): words in first pair of square brackets substituted by the Pensions Act 1995, s 157(1), (3); words in square brackets in para (b) substituted by the Civil Partnership (Pensions and Benefit Payments) (Consequential, etc Provisions) Order 2005, SI 2005/2053, art 2, Schedule, Pt 3, para 16, as from 5 December 2005; para (ba) inserted, and words in square brackets in para (c)(i) substituted, by the Child Support, Pensions and Social Security Act 2000, s 53(1), (7).

Sub-s (8): definition "independent trustee" inserted by the Child Support, Pensions and Social Security Act 2000, s 53(1), (8), and words in square brackets in that definition substituted by the Pensions Act 2004, s 319(1), Sch 12, paras 9, 24(c), as from 6 April 2005.

Regulations: the Personal and Occupational Pension Schemes (Pensions Ombudsman) Regulations 1996, SI 1996/2475 at **[2375]**.

147 Death, insolvency or disability of authorised complainant

(1) Where an [actual or potential beneficiary] dies or is a minor or is otherwise unable to act for himself, then, unless subsection (3) applies—

(a) any complaint or dispute (whenever arising) which the [actual or potential beneficiary] might otherwise have made or referred under this Part may be made or referred by the appropriate person, and

(b) anything in the process of being done by or in relation to the [actual or potential beneficiary] under or by virtue of this Part may be continued by or in relation to the appropriate person,

and any reference in this Part, except this section, to an [actual or potential beneficiary] shall be construed as including a reference to the appropriate person.

(2) For the purposes of subsection (1) "the appropriate person" means—

(a) where the [actual or potential beneficiary] has died, his personal representatives; or

(b) in any other case, a member of [his] family, or some body or individual suitable to represent him.

(3) Where a person is acting as an insolvency practitioner in relation to [a person by whom, or on whose behalf, a complaint or reference has been made under this Part], investigations under this Part shall be regarded for the purposes of the Insolvency Act 1986 and the Bankruptcy (Scotland) Act 1985 as legal proceedings.

(4) In this section "acting as an insolvency practitioner" shall be construed in accordance with section 388 of the Insolvency Act 1986, but disregarding subsection (5) of that section (exclusion of official receiver).

[864]

NOTES

Sub-ss (1)–(3): words in square brackets substituted by the Pensions Act 1995, s 157(1), (4), (5).

148 Staying court proceedings where a complaint is made or a dispute is referred

(1) This section applies where—

(a) complaint has been made or a dispute referred to the Pensions Ombudsman; and

(b) any party to the investigation subsequently commences any legal proceedings in any court against any other party to the investigation in respect of any of the matters which are the subject of the complaint or dispute.

(2) In England and Wales, where this section applies any party to the legal proceedings may at any time after acknowledgement of service, and before delivering any pleadings or taking any other step in the proceedings, apply to that court to stay the proceedings.

(3) In Scotland, where this section applies any party to the legal proceedings may—

(a) if the proceedings are in the Court of Session, at any time—

(i) after appearance has been entered but before defences have been lodged or any other step in the proceedings has been taken; or

(ii) (in procedure by petition) after intimation and service but before answers have been lodged or any other step in the proceedings has been taken; and

(b) if the proceedings are in the sheriff court, at any time—

(i) after notice has been given of intention to defend but before defences have been lodged or any other step in the proceedings has been taken; or

(ii) (in summary cause procedure) after appearance has been made, or notice of intention to appear has been lodged, but before any defence has been stated or any other step in the proceedings has been taken,

apply to the court for a sist of process.

(4) On an application under subsection (2) or (3) the court may make an order staying or, in Scotland, sisting the proceedings if it is satisfied—

(a) that there is no sufficient reason why the matter should not be investigated by the Pensions Ombudsman; and

(b) that the applicant was at the time when the legal proceedings were commenced and still remains ready and willing to do all things necessary to the proper conduct of the investigation.

(5) For the purposes of this section the parties to an investigation are—

[(a) to the person by whom, or on whose behalf, the complaint or reference was made, and

(b) to any person (if different) responsible for the management of the scheme to which the complaint or reference relates;]

[(ba), (bb) …]

(c) any person against whom allegations are made in the complaint or reference; and

(d) any person claiming under a person falling within paragraphs (a) to (c).

[865]

NOTES

Sub-s (5): paras (a), (b) substituted by the Pensions Act 1995, s 157(1), (6); paras (ba), (bb) inserted by the Child Support, Pensions and Social Security Act 2000, s 54(1), (2)(a), and repealed by the Pensions Act 2004, ss 276(2)(a), 320, Sch 13, Pt 1, as from 6 April 2005 (note that these paragraphs were brought into force on 1 March 2002 for the purposes of the making of rules and regulations only, but were never brought into force for remaining purposes).

149 Procedure on an investigation

[(1), (1A), (1B) …]

(2) The Secretary of State may make rules with respect to the procedure which is to be adopted in connection with the making of complaints, the reference of disputes, and the investigation of complaints made and disputes referred, under this Part.

(3) The rules may include provision—

(a) requiring any oral hearing held in connection with such an investigation to take place in public, except in such cases as may be specified in the rules; …

(b) as to the persons entitled to appear and be heard on behalf of parties to an investigation, as defined in section 148(5);

[(ba) …]

(c) for the payment by the Ombudsman of such travelling and other allowances (including compensation for loss of remunerative time) as the Secretary of State may determine, to—

(i) actual or potential beneficiaries of a scheme to which a complaint or reference relates, or

(ii) person appearing and being heard on behalf of such actual or potential beneficiaries,

who attend at the request of the Ombudsman any oral hearing held in connection with an investigation into the complaint or dispute][; …

(d) …]

(4) Subject to any provision made by the rules, the procedure for conducting such an investigation shall be such as the Pensions Ombudsman considers appropriate in the circumstances of the case; and he may, in particular, obtain information from such persons and in such manner, and make such inquiries, as he thinks fit.

[(5) The Pensions Ombudsman may disclose any information which he obtains for the purposes of an investigation under this Part to any person to whom subsection (6) applies, if the Ombudsman considers that the disclosure would enable or assist that person to discharge any of his functions.

(6) This subsection applies to the following—

(a) the Regulatory Authority,

[(b) the Board of the Pension Protection Fund,

(ba) the Ombudsman for the Board of the Pension Protection Fund,]

(c) …

(d) any department of the Government (including the government of Northern Ireland),

(e) the [Financial Services Authority],

(f), (g) …

[(h) a person appointed under—

(i) Part 14 of the Companies Act 1985,

(ii) section 167 of the Financial Services and Markets Act 2000,

(iii) subsection (3) or (5) of section 168 of that Act, or

(iv) section 284 of that Act,

to conduct an investigation;]

(j) an inspector appointed by the Department of Economic Development in Northern Ireland under Part XV of the Companies (Northern Ireland) Order 1986,

[(k) a body designated under section 326(1) of the Financial Services and Markets Act 2000; …

(l) a recognised investment exchange or a recognised clearing house (as defined by section 285 of that Act)];

[(n) a person who, in a member State other than the United Kingdom, has functions corresponding to functions of the Pensions Ombudsman]'

[(o) a body corporate established in accordance with paragraph 2(1) of Schedule 17 to the Financial Services and Markets Act 2000 (the scheme operator of the ombudsman scheme);

(p) an ombudsman as defined in paragraph 1 of that Schedule (interpretation)].

(7) The Secretary of State may by order—

(a) amend subsection (6) by adding any person or removing any person for the time being specified in that subsection, or

(b) restrict the circumstances in which, or impose conditions subject to which, disclosure may be made to any person for the time being specified in that subsection.]

[(8) …]

[866]

NOTES

Sub-ss (1), (1A), (1B): substituted, for original sub-s (1), by the Child Support, Pensions and Social Security Act 2000, s 54(1), (3), (9), and repealed by the Pensions Act 2004, ss 276(2)(b), 320, Sch 13, Pt 1, as from 6 April 2005 (note that these subsections were brought into force on 1 March 2002 for the purposes of the making of rules and regulations only, but were never brought into force for remaining purposes).

Sub-s (3): word omitted from para (a) repealed, and para (c) inserted, by the Pensions Act 1995, ss 158, 177, Sch 7, Pt IV; paras (ba), (d) and the word immediately preceding para (d) inserted, by the Child Support, Pensions and Social Security Act 2000, s 54(1), (4), (5), (9), and repealed by the Pensions Act 2004, ss 276(2)(c), (d), 320, Sch 13, Pt 1, as from 6 April 2005 (note that these paragraphs were brought into force on 1 March 2002 for the purposes of the making of rules and regulations only, but were never brought into force for remaining purposes).

Sub-ss (5), (7): added, together with sub-s (6), by the Pensions Act 1995, s 159(1).

Sub-s (6): added as noted above; paras (b), (ba) substituted for original para (b), and para (n) added, by the Pensions Act 2004, s 319(1), Sch 12, paras 9, 25, as from 6 April 2005; words in square brackets in para (e) substituted by the Bank of England Act 1998, s 23(1), Sch 5, para 69(1), (2); paras (f), (g) repealed, para (h) substituted, and paras (k), (l) substituted for original paras (k)–(m), by the Financial Services and Markets Act 2000 (Consequential Amendments and Repeals) Order 2001, SI 2001/3649, art 123; para (c) and the word omitted from para (k) repealed by the Pensions Act 2004, s 320, Sch 13, Pt 1, as from 6 April 2006; paras (o), (p) added by the Pensions Ombudsman (Disclosure of Information) (Amendment of Specified Persons) Order 2005, SI 2005/2743, art 2, as from 1 November 2005.

Sub-s (8): added by the Child Support, Pensions and Social Security Act 2000, s 54(1), (6), and repealed by the Pensions Act 2004, ss 276(2)(e), 320, Sch 13, Pt 1, as from 6 April 2005 (note that this subsection was brought into force on 1 March 2002 for the purposes of the making of rules and regulations only, but was never brought into force for remaining purposes).

Rules: the Personal and Occupational Pensions (Pensions Ombudsman) Procedure Rules 1995, SI 1995/1053 at **[2285]**.

Orders: the Pensions Ombudsman (Disclosure of Information) (Amendment of Specified Persons) Order 2005, SI 2005/2743.

150 Investigations: further provisions

(1) For the purposes of an investigation under this Part or under any corresponding legislation having effect in Northern Ireland, the Pensions Ombudsman may require—

(a) [any person responsible for the management of the scheme to which the complaint or reference relates], or

(b) any other person who, in his opinion is able to furnish information or produce documents relevant to the investigation,

to furnish any such information or produce any such documents.

(2) For the purposes of any such investigation the Pensions Ombudsman shall have the same powers as the court in respect of the attendance and examination of witnesses (including the administration of oaths and affirmations and the examination of witnesses abroad) and in respect of the production of documents.

(3) No person shall be compelled for the purposes of any such investigation to give any evidence or produce any document which he could not be compelled to give or produce in civil proceedings before the court.

(4) If any person without lawful excuse obstructs the Pensions Ombudsman in the performance of his functions or is guilty of any act or omission in relation to an investigation under this Part which, if that investigation were a proceeding in the court, would constitute contempt of court, the Pensions Ombudsman may certify the offence to the court.

(5) Where an offence is certified under subsection (4) the court may inquire into the matter and, after hearing any witnesses who may be produced against or on behalf of the person charged with the offence and hearing any statement that may be offered in defence, deal with him in any manner in which the court could deal with him if he had committed the like offence in relation to the court.

(6) To assist him in an investigation, the Pensions Ombudsman may obtain advice from any person who in his opinion is qualified to give it and may pay to any such person such fees or allowances as he may with the approval of the Treasury determine.

(7) The Pensions Ombudsman may refer any question of law arising for determination in connection with a complaint or dispute to the High Court or, in Scotland, the Court of Session.

(8) In this section "the court" means—

(a) in England and Wales, a county court;

(b) in Scotland, the sheriff.

(9) Subsections (4) and (5) shall be construed, in their application to Scotland, as if contempt of court were categorised as an offence in Scots law.

[867]

NOTES

Sub-s (1): words in square brackets substituted by the Pensions Act 1995, s 157(1), (8).

151 Determinations of the Pensions Ombudsman

(1) Where the Pensions Ombudsman has conducted an investigation under this Part he shall send a written statement of his determination of the complaint or dispute in question—

[(a) to the person by whom, or on whose behalf, the complaint or reference was made, and

(b) to any person (if different) responsible for the management of the scheme to which the complaint or reference relates][…

(c) …]

and any such statement shall contain the reasons for his determination.

(2) Where the Pensions Ombudsman makes a determination under this Part or under any corresponding legislation having effect in Northern Ireland, he may direct [any person responsible for the management of the scheme to which the complaint or reference relates] to take, or refrain from taking, such steps as he may specify in the statement referred to in subsection (1) or otherwise in writing.

(3) Subject to subsection (4), the determination by the Pensions Ombudsman of a complaint or dispute, and any direction given by him under subsection (2), shall be final and binding on—

[(a) the person by whom, or on whose behalf, the complaint or reference was made,

(b) any person (if different) responsible for the management of the scheme to which the complaint or reference relates,

[(ba), (bb) …]

(c) any person claiming under a person falling within paragraph (a) or (b).]

(4) An appeal on a point of law shall lie to the High Court or, in Scotland, the Court of Session from a determination or direction of the Pensions Ombudsman at the instance of any person falling within paragraphs (a) to (c) of subsection (3).

(5) Any determination or direction of the Pensions Ombudsman shall be enforceable—

(a) in England and Wales, in a county court as if it were a judgment or order of that court, and

(b) in Scotland, [in like manner as an extract registered decree arbitral bearing warrant for execution issued by the sheriff court of any sheriffdom in Scotland].

(6) If the Pensions Ombudsman considers it appropriate to do so in any particular case, he may publish in such form and manner as he thinks fit a report of any investigation under this Part and of the result of that investigation.

(7) For the purposes of the law of defamation, the publication of any matter by the Pensions Ombudsman—

(a) in submitting or publishing a report under section 145(6) or subsection (6) of this section, or

[(aa) in disclosing any information under s 149(5)]

(b) in sending to any person a statement under subsection (1) or a direction under subsection (2),

shall be absolutely privileged.

[868]

NOTES

Sub-s (1): paras (a), (b) substituted by the Pensions Act 1995, s 157(1), (9); para (c) and the word immediately preceding it inserted by the Child Support, Pensions and Social Security Act 2000, s 54(1), (7), (9), and repealed by the Pensions Act 2004, ss 276(2)(f), 320, Sch 13, Pt 1, as from 6 April 2005 (note that this paragraph was brought into force on 1 March 2002 for the purposes of the making of rules and regulations only, but was never brought into force for remaining purposes).

Sub-s (2): words in square brackets substituted by the Pensions Act 1995, s 157(1), (10).

Sub-s (3): paras (a)–(c) substituted by the Pensions Act 1995, s 157(1), (11); paras (ba), (bb) substituted for the original word "and" at the end of para (b) by the Child Support, Pensions and Social

Security Act 2000, s 54(1), (8), (9), and repealed by the Pensions Act 2004, ss 276(2)(g), 320, Sch 13, Pt 1, as from 6 April 2005 (note (i) that these paragraphs were brought into force on 1 March 2002 for the purposes of the making of rules and regulations only, but were never brought into force for remaining purposes; (ii) a consequential amendment to para (c) (ie, the substitution of the words "any of paragraphs (a) to (bb)" for the words "paragraph (a) or (b)") was also brought into force for these limited purposes only and subsequently repealed by the Pensions Act 2004, ss 276(2)(h), 320, Sch 13, Pt 1, as from 6 April 2005).

Sub-s (5): words in square brackets substituted by the Pensions Act 1995, s 173, Sch 6, paras 2, 8.

Sub-s (7): para (aa) inserted by the Pensions Act 1995, s 159(2).

[151A Interest on late payment of benefit

Where under this Part the Pensions Ombudsman directs a person responsible for the management of an occupational or personal pension scheme to make any payment in respect of benefit under the scheme which, in his opinion, ought to have been paid earlier, his direction may also require the payment of interest at the prescribed rate.]

[869]

NOTES

Inserted by the Pensions Act 1995, s 160.

Regulations: the Personal and Occupational Pension Schemes (Pensions Ombudsman) Regulations 1996, SI 1996/2475 at **[2375]**.

PART XI
GENERAL AND MISCELLANEOUS PROVISIONS

Avoidance of certain transactions and provisions

160 Terms of contracts of service or schemes restricting choice to be void

(1) Subject to such exceptions as may be prescribed—

(a) any term of a contract of service (whenever made) or any rule of a personal or occupational pension scheme to the effect that an employed earner must be a member—

(i) of a personal or occupational pension scheme,

(ii) of a particular personal or occupational pension scheme, or

(iii) of one or other of a number of particular personal or occupational pension schemes,

shall be void; and

(b) any such term or rule to the effect that contributions shall be paid by or in respect of an employed earner—

(i) to a particular personal or occupational pension scheme of which the earner is not a member, or

(ii) to one or other of a number of personal or occupational pension schemes of none of which he is a member,

shall be unenforceable for so long as he is not a member of the scheme or any of the schemes.

(2) Subsection (1) shall not be construed so as to have the effect that an employer is required, when he would not otherwise be—

(a) to make contributions to a personal or occupational pension scheme; or

(b) to increase an employed earner's pay in lieu of making contributions to a personal or occupational pension scheme.

[870]

NOTES

Regulations: by virtue of s 189(1) of, and Sch 6, Pt I, para 2(2) to, this Act, the Pension Schemes (Voluntary Contributions Requirements and Voluntary and Compulsory Membership) Regulations 1987, SI 1987/1108 have effect as if made under this section.

161 Provisions excluding Chapter II of Part VII to be void

Any provision in an agreement (whether a contract of employment or not) shall be void in so far as it purports—

(a) to exclude or limit the operation of any provision of Chapter II of Part VII of this Act; or

(b) to preclude any person from presenting a complaint to, or bringing any proceedings before, an [employment tribunal] under that Chapter.

[871]

NOTES

Words in square brackets substituted by the Employment Rights (Dispute Resolution) Act 1998, s 1(2)(a).

PART XII
SUPPLEMENTARY PROVISIONS

Interpretation

181 General interpretation

(1) In this Act, unless the context otherwise requires—

["abolition date" means the day appointed for the commencement of section 15(1) of the Pensions Act 2007;]

. . .

"age", in relation to any person, shall be construed so that—

(a) he is over or under a particular age if he has or, as the case may be, has not attained that age;

(b) he is between two particular ages if he has attained the first but not the second;

"appropriate scheme certificate" and references to an appropriate scheme shall be construed in accordance with section 7;

"Category A retirement pension" and "Category B retirement pension" mean the retirement pensions of those descriptions payable under Part II of the Social Security Contributions and Benefits Act 1992;

["civil recovery order" means an order under section 266 of the Proceeds of Crime Act 2002 or an order under section 276 imposing the requirement mentioned in section 277(3);]

"contract of service" has the same meaning as in section 122(1) of the Social Security Contributions and Benefits Act 1992;

"contracted-out employment" shall be construed in accordance with section 8;

. . .

"contracting-out certificate" and references to a contracted-out scheme and to contracting-out shall be construed in accordance with section 7 [and section 181A];

"contributions equivalent premium" has the meaning given in [section 55(2)];

"earner" and "earnings" shall be construed in accordance with sections 3, 4 and 112 of the Social Security Contributions and Benefits Act 1992;

"earnings factors" shall be construed in accordance with sections 22 and 23 of the Social Security Contributions and Benefits Act 1992;

["employed earner" and "self-employed earner" have the meanings given by section 2 of the Social Security Contributions and Benefits Act 1992;]

"employee" means a person gainfully employed in Great Britain either under a contract of service or in an office (including an elective office) with [general earnings (as defined by section 7 of the Income Tax (Earnings and Pensions) Act 2003)];

"employer" means—

(a) in the case of an employed earner employed under a contract of service, his employer;

(b) in the case of an employed earner employed in an office with emoluments—

(i) such person as may be prescribed in relation to that office; or

(ii) if no person is prescribed, the government department, public authority or body of persons responsible for paying the emoluments of the office;

"employment" includes any trade, business, profession, office or vocation and "employed" shall be construed accordingly except in the expression "employed earner";

. . .

["Financial Services Compensation Scheme" means the Financial Services Compensation Scheme referred to in section 213(2) of the Financial Services and Markets Act 2000;]

["the flat rate introduction year" has the meaning given by section 122 of the Social Security Contributions and Benefits Act 1992;]

"guaranteed minimum pension" has the meaning given in section 8(2);

"independent trade union" has the same meaning as in the Trade Union and Labour Relations (Consolidation) Act 1992;

"[employment tribunal]" means a tribunal established or having effect as if established under [section 1(1) of [the Employment Tribunals Act 1996]];

["HMRC" means the Commissioners for Her Majesty's Revenue and Customs;]

"the Inland Revenue" means the Commissioners of Inland Revenue;

. . .

. . .

"linked qualifying service" has the meaning given in section 179;

"long-term benefit" has the meaning given in section 20(2) of the Social Security Contributions and Benefits Act 1992;

"lower earnings limit" and "upper earnings limit" shall be construed in accordance with section 5 of the Social Security Contributions and Benefits Act 1992 and "current", in relation to those limits, means for the time being in force;

"minimum contributions" shall be construed in accordance with sections 43 to 45;

"minimum payment" has the meaning given in section 8(2);

"modifications" includes additions, omissions and amendments, and related expressions shall be construed accordingly;

"money purchase benefits", in relation to a member of a personal or occupational pension scheme or the [widow, widower or surviving civil partner] of a member of such a scheme, means benefits the rate or amount of which is calculated by reference to a payment or payments made by the member or by any other person in respect of the member and which are not average salary benefits;

"money purchase contracted-out scheme" has the meaning given in section 8(1)(a)(ii);

"money purchase scheme" means a pension scheme under which all the benefits that may be provided are money purchase benefits;

"normal pension age" has the meaning given in section 180;

"occupational pension scheme" has the meaning given in section 1;

["overseas arrangement" means a scheme or arrangement which—

(a) has effect, or is capable of having effect, so as to provide benefits on termination of employment or on death or retirement to or in respect of earners;

(b) is administered wholly or primarily outside Great Britain;

(c) is not an appropriate scheme; and

(d) is not an occupational pension scheme;]

["pension credit" means a credit under section 29(1)(b) of the Welfare Reform and Pensions Act 1999 or under corresponding Northern Ireland legislation;]

["pension debit" means a debit under section 29(1)(a) of the Welfare Reform and Pensions Act 1999;]

["pensionable age"—

(a) so far as any provisions (other than sections 46 to 48) relate to guaranteed minimum pensions, means the age of 65 in the case of a man and the age of 60 in the case of a woman, and

(b) in any other case, has the meaning given by the rules in paragraph 1 of Schedule 4 to the Pensions Act 1995];

"pensionable service" has the meaning given in section 70(2);

. . .

. . .

"personal pension scheme" has the meaning given in section 1;

"prescribe" means prescribe by regulations and "prescribed" shall be construed accordingly;

. . .

"the preservation requirements" has the meaning given in section 69(2);

"primary Class 1 contributions" and "secondary Class 1 contributions" have the same meanings as in the Social Security Contributions and Benefits Act 1992;

"protected rights" has the meaning given in section 10;

"public service pension scheme" has the meaning given in section 1;

. . .

…

"regulations" means regulations made by the Secretary of State under this Act;

["the Regulatory Authority" means the Pensions Regulator;]

"resources", in relation to an occupational pension scheme, means the funds out of which the benefits provided by the scheme are payable from time to time, including the proceeds of any policy of insurance taken out, or annuity contract entered into, for the purposes of the scheme;

"rights", in relation to accrued rights (within the meaning of section 73, 136 or 179) or transfer credits, includes rights to benefit and also options to have benefits paid in a particular form or at a particular time;

["safeguarded rights" has the meaning given in section 68A;]

…

"short service benefit" has the meaning given in section 71(2);

…

…

"tax week" means one of the successive periods in a tax year beginning with the first day of that year and every seventh day thereafter, the last day of a tax year (or, in a leap year, the last two days) being treated accordingly as a separate tax week;

"tax year" means the 12 months beginning with 6th April in any year;

"trade or business", in relation to a public or local authority, includes the exercise and performance of the powers and duties of the authority;

"transfer credits" means rights allowed to an earner under the rules of an occupational pension scheme by reference to[—

(a) a transfer to the scheme of, or transfer payment to the trustees or managers of the scheme in respect of, any of his rights (including transfer credits allowed) under another occupational pension scheme or a personal pension scheme, other than rights attributable (directly or indirectly) to a pension credit, or

(b) a cash transfer sum paid under Chapter 5 of Part 4 in respect of him, to the trustees or managers of the scheme;]

…

["the upper accrual point" has the meaning given by section 122 of the Social Security Contributions and Benefits Act 1992;]

…

"week" means a period of seven days beginning with Sunday;

["working life", in relation to a person, means the period beginning with the tax year in which the person attains the age of 16 and ending with—

(a) the tax year before the one in which the person attains the age of 65 in the case of a man or 60 in the case of a woman, or

(b) if earlier, the tax year before the one in which the person dies].

(2) References to employers in the provisions of this Act (other than sections 123 to 127, 157, [and 160] ("the excluded provisions")) are to be treated, in relation to persons within the application of an occupational pension scheme and qualifying or prospectively qualifying for its benefits, as including references to persons who in relation to them and their employment are treated by regulations as being employers for the purposes of those provisions.

(3) Subject to any such regulations, references to an employer in any of the provisions of this Act (other than the excluded provisions or … , Chapter I of Part IV, Part VIII so far as it applies for the purposes of Chapter I of Part IV, sections … 153(2), 158(1) to (5), 162, 163, … and 176 and …) shall, in relation to an earner employed in an office with emoluments, be construed as references to—

(a) such person as may be prescribed in relation to that office; or

(b) if no person is prescribed, the government department, public authority or body of persons responsible for paying the emoluments of that office.

(4) Regulations may for any purpose of any provision of this Act (other than the excluded provisions or section … 27, 28, 29, 31, 32, *43, 44,* 111, 160, 164, 165 or 169) prescribe the persons who are to be regarded as members or prospective members of an occupational pension scheme and as to the times at which and the circumstances in which a person is to be treated as becoming, or as ceasing to be, a member or prospective member.

(5) In sections 165 and 166—

(a) references to the United Kingdom include references to the territorial waters of the United Kingdom; and

(b) references to Great Britain include references to the territorial waters of the United Kingdom adjacent to Great Britain.

(6) Any reference in section 185 or 186 to an order or regulations under this Act includes a reference to an order or regulations made under any provision of an enactment passed after this Act and directed to be construed as one with it; but this subsection applies only so far as a contrary intention is not expressed in the enactment so passed, and shall be without prejudice to the generality of any such direction.

(7) In the application of section 158 ... to Northern Ireland any reference to a government department is to be taken to be, or to include (as the context may require), a Northern Ireland department.

[872]

NOTES

Sub-s (1) has been amended as follows:

Definition "abolition date" inserted by the Pensions Act 2007, s 15(3)(a), Sch 4, Pt 1, paras 1, 34(1), (2)(a), as from a day to be appointed.

Definitions "accrued rights premium", "the Board", "contracted-out protected rights premium", "limited revaluation premium", "pensioner's rights premium", "personal pension protected rights premium", "state scheme premium", "transfer premium" (omitted) repealed by the Pensions Act 1995, ss 151, 177, Sch 5, para 77(a)(i), Sch 7, Pt III.

Definition "appropriate scheme certificate" substituted by the Pensions Act 2007, s 15(3)(a), Sch 4, Pt 1, paras 1, 34(1), (2)(b), as from a day to be appointed, as follows—

""appropriate scheme" and "appropriate scheme certificate" are to be construed in accordance with section 181A;".

Definition "civil recovery order" inserted by the Proceeds of Crime Act 2002, s 456, Sch 11, paras 1, 22(1), (6).

In definition "contracting-out certificate" words in square brackets inserted by the Pensions Act 2007, s 15(3)(a), Sch 4, Pt 1, paras 1, 34(1), (2)(c), as from a day to be appointed.

In definition "contributions equivalent premium" words in square brackets substituted by the Pensions Act 1995, ss 151, Sch 5, para 77(a).

Definitions "employed earner" and "self-employed earner" substituted, for original definition "employed earner", by the Welfare Reform and Pensions Act 1999, Sch 2, para 3(1)(b).

In definition "employee" words in square brackets substituted by the Income Tax (Earnings and Pensions) Act 2003, s 722, Sch 6, Pt 2, paras 207, 222, for the purposes of income tax for the year 2003–04 and subsequent years of assessment, and for the purposes of corporation tax for accounting periods ending after 5 April 2003.

Definition "equal access requirements" repealed for certain purposes by the Pension Schemes Act 1993, ss 188, 190, Sch 5, Pt II, Sch 7, para 3(i), and repealed for remaining purposes by the Pensions Act 1995, ss 122, 177, Sch 3, para 44(a)(i), Sch 7, Pt I.

Definition "Financial Services Compensation Scheme" inserted by the Financial Services and Markets Act 2000 (Consequential Amendments and Repeals) Order 2001, SI 2001/3649, art 127(a).

Definition "the flat rate introduction year" inserted by the Pensions Act 2007, s 12(4), Sch 1, Pt 7, para 38, as from 26 September 2007.

In definition "employment tribunal" (formerly "industrial tribunal") words in first and third (inner) pairs of square brackets substituted by the Employment Rights (Dispute Resolution) Act 1998, s 1(2)(a), (c); words in second (outer) pair of square brackets substituted by the Employment Tribunals Act 1996, s 43, Sch 1, para 11.

Definition "HMRC" inserted by the Pensions Act 2007, s 15(3)(a), Sch 4, Pt 1, paras 1, 34(1), (2)(a), as from a day to be appointed.

Definition "insurance company" (omitted) repealed by SI 2001/3649, art 127(b).

Definition "minimum contributions" repealed by the Pensions Act 2007, ss 15(3)(a), 27(2), Sch 4, Pt 2, paras 46, 58(1), (2), Sch 7, Pt 7, as from a day to be appointed.

In definition "money purchase benefits" words in square brackets substituted by the Civil Partnership (Pensions and Benefit Payments) (Consequential, etc Provisions) Order 2005, SI 2005/2053, art 2, Schedule, Pt 3, para 18, as from 5 December 2005.

Definition "money purchase contracted-out scheme" substituted by the Pensions Act 2007, s 15(3)(a), Sch 4, Pt 1, paras 1, 34(1), (2)(d), as from a day to be appointed, as follows—

""money purchase contracted-out scheme" is to be construed in accordance with section 181A;".

Definition "overseas arrangement" inserted by the Child Support, Pensions and Social Security Act 2000, s 56, Sch 5, Pt I, para 2(3).

Definition "pension credit" inserted by the Welfare Reform and Pensions Act 1999, s 84(1), Sch 12, Pt I, paras 28, 41(a).

Definition "pension debit" inserted by the Welfare Reform and Pensions Act 1999, s 32(1), (5).

Definition "pensionable age" substituted by the Pensions Act 1995, s 126, Sch 4, para 17.

Definition "the prescribed equivalent" (omitted) repealed by the Welfare Reform and Pensions Act 1999, s 88, Sch 13, Pt VI.

Definitions "the Register" and "the Registrar" (omitted) repealed by the Pensions Act 2004, s 320, Sch 13, Pt 1, as from 6 April 2005.

Definition "the Regulatory Authority" inserted by the Pensions Act 1995, s 122, Sch 3, para 44(a)(ii), and substituted by the Pensions Act 2004, s 7(2)(a), as from 6 April 2005.

Definition "safeguarded rights" inserted by the Welfare Reform and Pensions Act 1999, s 84(1), Sch 12, Pt I, paras 28, 41(b).

Definition "self-employed pension arrangement" (omitted) repealed by the Welfare Reform and Pensions Act 1999, ss 18, 88, Sch 2, para 3(2)(c), Sch 13, Pt I.

Definitions "tax-exemption" and "tax-approval" (omitted) repealed by the Taxation of Pension Schemes (Consequential Amendments) Order 2006, SI 2006/745, art 7, as from 6 April 2006.

In definition "transfer credits" words in square brackets substituted by the Pensions Act 2004, s 319(1), Sch 12, paras 9, 31, as from 6 April 2006.

Definition "the upper accrual point" inserted by the Pensions Act 2007, s 12(4), Sch 1, Pt 7, para 38, as from 26 September 2007.

Definition "voluntary contributions requirements" (omitted) repealed by the Pensions Act 2004, ss 267(3), 320, Sch 13, Pt 1, as 6 April 2006.

Definition "working life" substituted by the Pensions Act 2004, s 282, as from 6 April 2005.

Sub-s (2): words in square brackets substituted by the Pensions Act 1995, s 122, Sch 3, paras 22, 44(b).

Sub-s (3): first words omitted repealed by the Pensions Act 2004, s 320, Sch 13, Pt 1, as from 6 April 2005; other words omitted repealed by the Pensions Act 1995, ss 151, 173, 177, Sch 5, paras 18, 77(b), Sch 6, paras 2, 14, Sch 7, Pts III, IV.

Sub-s (4): number omitted repealed by the Pensions Act 2004, s 320, Sch 13, Pt 1, as from 6 April 2005; numbers in italics repealed by the Pensions Act 2007, ss 15(3)(a), 27(2), Sch 4, Pt 1, paras 1, 34(1), (3), Sch 4, Pt 2, paras 46, 58(1), (3), Sch 7, Pt 7, as from a day to be appointed.

Sub-s (7): words omitted repealed by the Pensions Act 1995, ss 151, 177, Sch 5, paras 18, 77(c), Sch 7, Pt III.

Commissioners of Inland Revenue: a reference to the Commissioners of Inland Revenue is now to be taken as a reference to the Commissioners for Her Majesty's Revenue and Customs; see the Commissioners for Revenue and Customs Act 2005, s 50(1), (7).

Regulations: Regulations made under this section are generally outside the scope of this work.

[181A Interpretation of references to money purchase contracted-out schemes or appropriate schemes after abolition date

(1) This section applies for the interpretation of this Act on and after the abolition date.

(2) An occupational pension scheme was a money purchase contracted-out scheme at a time before the abolition date if, at that time, the scheme was contracted-out by virtue of satisfying section 9(3) (as it then had effect).

(3) A money purchase contracted-out scheme was, at a time before the abolition date, a contracted-out scheme in relation to an earner's employment if it was, at that time, specified in a contracting-out certificate in relation to that employment; and references to the contracting-out of a scheme are, in relation to a money purchase contracted-out scheme, references to its inclusion in such a certificate.

(4) Any reference to a contracting-out certificate is, in relation to a money purchase contracted-out scheme, a reference to a certificate issued by virtue of section 7, as it had effect before the abolition date, in relation to the employment of an earner in employed earner's employment which was contracted-out by reference to that scheme.

(5) Any certificate so issued that was, at a time before the abolition date, in force in respect of an employed earner's employment is to be taken as conclusive that the employment was, at that time, contracted-out employment.

(6) A personal pension scheme was an appropriate scheme at a time before the abolition date if, at that time, there was in force a certificate issued under section 7(1)(b) (as it then had effect) stating that the scheme was an appropriate scheme; and "appropriate scheme certificate" means such a certificate.

(7) Any appropriate scheme certificate in force in relation to a scheme at any time before the abolition date is to be taken as conclusive that the scheme was, at that time, an appropriate scheme.]

[872A]

NOTES

Commencement: to be appointed.

Inserted by the Pensions Act 2007, s 15(3)(a), Sch 4, Pt 1, paras 1, 35, as from a day to be appointed.

---

193 Short title and commencement

(1) This Act may be cited as the Pension Schemes Act 1993.

(2) Subject to the provisions of Schedule 9, this Act shall come into force on such day as the Secretary of State may by order appoint.

(3) As respects the coming into force of—

(a) Part II of Schedule 5 and section 188(1) so far as it relates to it; or

(b) Schedule 7 and section 190 so far as it relates to it,

an order under subsection (2) may appoint different days from the day appointed for the other provisions of this Act or different days for different purposes.

[873]

NOTES

Orders: the Pension Schemes Act 1993 (Commencement No 1) Order 1994, SI 1994/86.

INSOLVENCY ACT 1994 (NOTE)

(1994 c 7)

NOTES

This Act amends ss 44 and 57 of the Insolvency Act 1986 at **[369]** and **[370]**, in each case in relation to contracts of employment adopted on or after 15 March 1994 (see ss 2(4) and 3(5) respectively) and makes corresponding provision for Northern Ireland (s 4, Sch 1). Section 1 amended s 19 of the 1986 Act and is now spent following the substitution of Pt II of the 1986 Act by the Enterprise Act 2002 (subject to certain transitional provisions and savings). The only other provisions are the short title, repeals and extent (s 5 and Sch 2).

See *Harvey* G1(F).

[874]–[889]

PENSIONS ACT 1995

(1995 c 26)

ARRANGEMENT OF SECTIONS

PART I
OCCUPATIONAL PENSIONS

Resolution of disputes

Equal treatment

Treatment of overseas residents etc

Modification of schemes

An Act to amend the law about pensions and for connected purposes

[19 July 1995]

NOTES

This major Act covers a wide range of aspects of pension law. Only those areas of most direct relevance to employment law are reproduced here. Provisions omitted are not annotated.

See *Harvey* B8, Q, R.

PART I
OCCUPATIONAL PENSIONS

Resolution of disputes

[50 Requirement for dispute resolution arrangements

(1) The trustees or managers of an occupational pension scheme must secure that dispute resolution arrangements [complying with the requirements of this section] are made and implemented.

(2) Dispute resolution arrangements are [arrangements] for the resolution of pension disputes.

(3) For this purpose a pension dispute is a dispute which—
(a) is between—
(i) the trustees or managers of a scheme, and
(ii) one or more persons with an interest in the scheme (see section 50A),
(b) is about matters relating to the scheme, and
(c) is not an exempted dispute (see subsection (9)).

(4) The dispute resolution arrangements must provide a procedure—
(a) for any of the parties to the dispute mentioned in subsection (3)(a)(ii) to make an application for a decision to be taken on the matters in dispute ("an application for the resolution of a pension dispute"), and
(b) for the trustees or managers to take that decision.

[(4A) The dispute resolution arrangements may make provision for securing that an application for the resolution of a pension dispute may not be made to the trustees or managers unless—
(a) the matters in dispute have been previously referred to a person of a description specified in the arrangements ("the specified person") in order for him to consider those matters, and
(b) the specified person has given his decision on those matters,

and for enabling the specified person's decision to be confirmed or replaced by the decision taken by the trustees or managers on the application, after reconsidering those matters.]

(5) Where an application for the resolution of a pension dispute is made in accordance with the dispute resolution arrangements, the trustees or managers must—
(a) take the decision required on the matters in dispute within a reasonable period of the receipt of the application by them, and
(b) notify the applicant of the decision within a reasonable period of it having been taken.

[(5A) In a case where a reference is made to the specified person in accordance with provision made under subsection (4A), subsection (5) applies in relation to the specified person as it applies in relation to the trustees or managers in a case where an application for the resolution of a pension dispute is made to them.]

(6) The procedure provided for by the dispute resolution arrangements [in pursuance of subsection (4)] must include the provision required by section 50B.

(7) Dispute resolution arrangements under subsection (1) must, in the case of existing schemes, have effect on and after the date of commencement of this section in relation to applications made on or after that date.

(8) This section does not apply in relation to an occupational pension scheme if—
(a) every member of the scheme is a trustee of the scheme,
(b) the scheme has no more than one member, or
(c) the scheme is of a prescribed description.

(9) For the purposes of this section a dispute is an exempted dispute if—
(a) proceedings in respect of it have been commenced in any court or tribunal,
(b) the Pensions Ombudsman has commenced an investigation in respect of it as a result of a complaint made or a dispute referred to him, or
(c) it is of a prescribed description.

(10) If, in the case of an occupational pension scheme, the dispute resolution arrangements required by this section to be made—
(a) have not been made, or
(b) are not being implemented,

section 10 applies to any of the trustees or managers who have failed to take all reasonable steps to secure that such arrangements are made or implemented.]

[889A]

NOTES

Commencement: 5 March 2008 (for the purpose of making regulations); 6 April 2008 (otherwise).

The original section 50 was substituted by new ss 50, 50A, 50B by the Pensions Act 2004, s 273 (as amended as noted below), as from 5 March 2008 (for the purpose of making regulations), and as from 6 April 2008 (otherwise).

Note that the amendments made to this section, ie, the insertion of the words in square brackets in sub-ss (1), (6), the substitution of the word in square brackets in sub-s (2), and the insertion of sub-ss (4A), (5A), were amendments made to the Pensions Act 2004, s 273 by the Pensions Act 2007, s 16(1)–(6), as from 26 September 2007.

Regulations: the Personal and Occupational Pension Schemes (Miscellaneous Amendments) Regulations 1999, SI 1999/3198; the Stakeholder Pension Schemes Regulations 2000, SI 2000/1403; the Occupational Pension Schemes (Republic of Ireland Schemes Exemption (Revocation) and Tax Exempt Schemes (Miscellaneous Amendments)) Regulations 2006, SI 2006/467; the Occupational Pension Schemes (Internal Dispute Resolution Procedures Consequential and Miscellaneous Amendments) Regulations 2008, SI 2008/649 at **[3474KA]**.

[50A Meaning of "person with an interest in the scheme"

(1) For the purposes of section 50 a person is a person with an interest in an occupational pension scheme if—

(a) he is a member of the scheme,
(b) he is a widow, widower[, surviving civil partner] or surviving dependant of a deceased member of the scheme,
(c) he is a surviving non-dependant beneficiary of a deceased member of the scheme,
(d) he is a prospective member of the scheme,
(e) he has ceased to be within any of the categories of persons referred to in paragraphs (a) to (d), or
(f) he claims to be such a person as is mentioned in paragraphs (a) to (e) and the dispute relates to whether he is such a person.

(2) In subsection (1)(c) a "non-dependant beneficiary", in relation to a deceased member of an occupational pension scheme, means a person who, on the death of the member, is entitled to the payment of benefits under the scheme.

(3) In subsection (1)(d) a "prospective member" means any person who, under the terms of his contract of service or the rules of the scheme—

(a) is able, at his own option, to become a member of the scheme,
(b) will become so able if he continues in the same employment for a sufficiently long period,
(c) will be admitted to the scheme automatically unless he makes an election not to become a member, or
(d) may be admitted to it subject to the consent of his employer.]

[889B]

NOTES

Commencement: 6 April 2008.
Substituted as noted to s 50 at **[889A]**.
Sub-s (1): words in square brackets in para (b) inserted by the Civil Partnership (Pensions and Benefit Payments) (Consequential, etc Provisions) Order 2005, SI 2005/2053, art 2, Schedule, Pt 4, para 21, as from 5 December 2005.

[50B The dispute resolution procedure

(1) The procedure provided for by the dispute resolution arrangements [in pursuance of section 50(4) must (in accordance with section 50(6))] include the following provision.

(2) The procedure must provide that an application for the resolution of a pension dispute under section 50(4) may be made or continued on behalf of a person who is a party to the dispute mentioned in section 50(3)(a)(ii)—

(a) where the person dies, by his personal representative,
(b) where the person is a minor or is otherwise incapable of acting for himself, by a member of his family or some other person suitable to represent him, and
(c) in any other case, by a representative nominated by him.

[(3) The procedure—

(a) must include provision requiring an application to which subsection (3A) applies to be made by the end of such reasonable period as is specified;
(b) may include provision about the time limits for making such other applications for the resolution of pension disputes as are specified.

(3A) This subsection applies to—

(a) any application by a person with an interest in a scheme as mentioned in section 50A(1)(e), and

(b) any application by a person with an interest in a scheme as mentioned in section 50A(1)(f) who is claiming to be such a person as is mentioned in section 50A(1)(e).]

(4) The procedure must include provision about—

(a) the manner in which an application for the resolution of a pension dispute is to be made,

(b) the particulars which must be included in such an application, and

(c) the manner in which any decisions required [in relation to such an application] are to be reached and given.

[(4A) The provision made under subsection (4)(c) may include provision for decisions of the trustees or managers to be taken on their behalf by one or more of their number.]

(5) The procedure must provide that if, after an application for the resolution of a pension dispute has been made, the dispute becomes an exempted dispute within the meaning of section 50(9)(a) or (b), the resolution of the dispute under the procedure ceases.]

[889C]

NOTES

Commencement: 6 April 2008.

Substituted as noted to s 50 at **[889A]**.

Note that the amendments made to this section, ie, the substitution of the words in square brackets in sub-s (1), the insertion of the words in square brackets in sub-s (4), the insertion of sub-s (4A), and the substitution of sub-ss (3), (3A) (for the original sub-s (3)) were amendments made to the Pensions Act 2004, s 273 by the Pensions Act 2007, s 16(1), (7)–(10), as from 26 September 2007.

Equal treatment

62 The equal treatment rule

(1) An occupational pension scheme which does not contain an equal treatment rule shall be treated as including one.

(2) An equal treatment rule is a rule which relates to the terms on which—

(a) persons become members of the scheme, and

(b) members of the scheme are treated.

(3) Subject to subsection (6), an equal treatment rule has the effect that where—

(a) a woman is employed on like work with a man in the same employment,

(b) a woman is employed on work rated as equivalent with that of a man in the same employment, or

(c) a woman is employed on work which, not being work in relation to which paragraph (a) or (b) applies, is, in terms of the demands made on her (for instance under such headings as effort, skill and decision) of equal value to that of a man in the same employment,

but (apart from the rule) any of the terms referred to in subsection (2) is or becomes less favourable to the woman than it is to the man, the term shall be treated as so modified as not to be less favourable.

(4) An equal treatment rule does not operate in relation to any difference as between a woman and a man in the operation of any of the terms referred to in subsection (2) if the trustees or managers of the scheme prove that the difference is genuinely due to a material factor which—

(a) is not the difference of sex, but

(b) is a material difference between the woman's case and the man's case.

(5) References in subsection (4) and sections 63 to 65 to the terms referred to in subsection (2), or the effect of any of those terms, include—

(a) a term which confers on the trustees or managers of an occupational pension scheme, or any other person, a discretion which, in a case within any of paragraphs (a) to (c) of subsection (3)—

(i) may be exercised so as to affect the way in which persons become members of the scheme, or members of the scheme are treated, and

(ii) may (apart from the equal treatment rule) be so exercised in a way less favourable to the woman than to the man, and

(b) the effect of any exercise of such a discretion;

and references to the terms on which members of the scheme are treated are to be read accordingly.

(6) In the case of a term within subsection (5)(a) the effect of an equal treatment rule is that the term shall be treated as so modified as not to permit the discretion to be exercised in a way less favourable to the woman than to the man.

[890]

63 Equal treatment rule: supplementary

(1) The reference in section 62(2) to the terms on which members of a scheme are treated includes those terms as they have effect for the benefit of dependants of members, and the reference in section 62(5) to the way in which members of a scheme are treated includes the way they are treated as it has effect for the benefit of dependants of members.

(2) Where the effect of any of the terms referred to in section 62(2) on persons of the same sex differs according to their [family, marital or civil partnership] status, the effect of the term is to be compared for the purposes of section 62 with its effect on persons of the other sex who have the same status.

(3) An equal treatment rule has effect subject to paragraphs 5 and 6 of Schedule 5 to the Social Security Act 1989 (employment-related-benefit schemes: maternity and family leave provisions).

(4) Section 62 shall be construed as one with section 1 of the Equal Pay Act 1970 (requirement of equal treatment for men and women in the same employment); and sections 2 and 2A of that Act (disputes and enforcement) shall have effect for the purposes of section 62 as if—

(a) references to an equality clause were to an equal treatment rule,

(b) references to employers and employees were to the trustees or managers of the scheme (on the one hand) and the members, or prospective members, of the scheme (on the other),

(c) … and

(d) references to Section 1(2)(c) of the Equal Pay Act 1970 were to section 62(3)(c) of this Act.

(5) Regulations may make provision for the Equal Pay Act 1970 to have effect, in relation to an equal treatment rule, with prescribed modifications; and subsection (4) shall have effect subject to any regulations made by virtue of this subsection.

(6) Section 62, so far as it relates to the terms on which members of a scheme are treated, is to be treated as having had effect in relation to any pensionable service on or after 17th May 1990.

[891]

NOTES

Sub-s (2): words in square brackets substituted by the Civil Partnership (Pensions and Benefit Payments) (Consequential, etc Provisions) Order 2005, SI 2005/2053, art 2, Schedule, Pt 4, para 22, as from 5 December 2005.

Sub-s (4): para (c) repealed by the Occupational Pension Schemes (Equal Treatment) (Amendment) Regulations 2005, SI 2005/1923, reg 3, as from 10 August 2005. Note this repeal applies to proceedings in respect of the terms of an occupational pension scheme if the proceedings are or were instituted on or after that date, unless the last day on which the woman was employed in the employment to which the occupational pension scheme relates fell more than six months before that date (see reg 2 of the 2005 Regulations at **[3321]**).

Regulations: the Occupational Pension Schemes (Equal Treatment) Regulations 1995, SI 1995/3183 at **[2305]**; the Occupational Pension Schemes (Equal Treatment) (Amendment) Regulations 2005, SI 2005/1923 at **[3320]**.

64 Equal treatment rule: exceptions

(1) An equal treatment rule does not operate in relation to any variation as between a woman and a man in the effect of any of the terms referred to in section 62(2) if the variation is permitted by or under any of the provisions of this section.

(2) Where a man and a woman are eligible, in prescribed circumstances, to receive different amounts by way of pension, the variation is permitted by this subsection if, in prescribed circumstances the differences are attributable only to differences between men and

women in the benefits under sections 43 to 55 of the Social Security Contributions and Benefits Act 1992 (State retirement pensions) to which, in prescribed circumstances, they are or would be entitled.

(3) A variation is permitted by this subsection if—

(a) the variation consists of the application of actuarial factors which differ for men and women to the calculation of contributions to a scheme by employers, being factors which fall within a prescribed class or description, or

(b) the variation consists of the application of actuarial factors which differ for men and women to the determination of benefits falling within a prescribed class or description;

and in this subsection "benefits" include any payment or other benefit made to or in respect of a person as a member of the scheme.

(4) Regulations may—

(a) permit further variations, or

(b) amend or repeal subsection (2) or (3);

and regulations made by virtue of this subsection may have effect in relation to pensionable service on or after 17th May 1990 and before the date on which the regulations are made.

[892]

NOTES

Regulations: the Occupational Pension Schemes (Equal Treatment) Regulations 1995, SI 1995/3183 at **[2305]**.

65 Equal treatment rule: consequential alteration of schemes

(1) The trustees or managers of an occupational pension scheme may, if—

(a) they do not (apart from this section) have power to make such alterations to the scheme as may be required to secure conformity with an equal treatment rule, or

(b) they have such power but the procedure for doing so—

(i) is liable to be unduly complex or protracted, or

(ii) involves the obtaining of consents which cannot be obtained, or can only be obtained with undue delay or difficulty,

by resolution make such alterations to the scheme.

(2) The alterations may have effect in relation to a period before the alterations are made.

[893]

66 Equal treatment rule: effect on terms of employment, etc

(1)–(3) …

(4) Regulations may make provision—

(a) for the Equal Pay Act 1970 to have effect, in relation to terms of employment relating to membership of, or rights under, an occupational pension scheme with prescribed modifications, and

(b) for imposing requirements on employers as to the payment of contributions and otherwise in case of their failing or having failed to comply with any such terms.

(5) References in subsection (4) to terms of employment include (where the context permits)—

(a) any collective agreement or pay structure, and

(b) an agricultural wages order within section 5 of the Equal Pay Act 1970.

[894]

NOTES

Sub-s (1): amends the Equal Pay Act 1970, s 6, at **[11]**.

Sub-ss (2), (3): amend the Sex Discrimination Act 1975, ss 4(1), 6, at **[104]**, **[106]**.

Regulations: the Occupational Pension Schemes (Equal Treatment) Regulations 1995, SI 1995/3183 at **[2305]**; the Occupational Pension Schemes (Equal Treatment) (Amendment) Regulations 2005, SI 2005/1923 at **[3320]**.

[Treatment of overseas residents etc

66A Prohibition on different rules for overseas residents etc

(1) This section applies where an occupational pension scheme contains provisions contravening subsection (2) or (3).

(2) Except so far as regulations otherwise provide, provisions of an occupational pension scheme contravene this subsection to the extent that they would (apart from this section) have an effect with respect to—

(a) the entitlement of any person to benefits under the scheme, or

(b) the payment to any person of benefits under the scheme,

which would be different according to whether or not a place outside the United Kingdom is specified by that person as the place to which he requires payments of benefits under the scheme to be made to him.

(3) Except so far as regulations otherwise provide, provisions of an occupational pension scheme contravene this subsection to the extent that they would (apart from this section) have an effect with respect to—

(a) the entitlement of any person to remain a member of the scheme,

(b) the eligibility of any person to remain a person by or in respect of whom contributions are made towards or under the scheme, or

(c) the making by or in respect of any person who is a member of the scheme of any contributions towards or under the scheme,

which would be different according to whether that person works wholly in the United Kingdom or wholly or partly outside the United Kingdom.

(4) Provisions contravening subsection (2) shall have effect, in relation to all times after the coming into force of section 55 of the Child Support, Pensions and Social Security Act 2000, as if they made the same provision in relation to a person who requires payments of benefits to be made to a place outside the United Kingdom as they make in relation to a person in whose case all payments of benefits fall to be made to a place in the United Kingdom.

(5) Provisions contravening subsection (3) shall have effect, in relation to all times after the coming into force of section 55 of the Child Support, Pensions and Social Security Act 2000, as if they made the same provision in relation to persons working wholly or partly outside the United Kingdom as they make in relation to persons working wholly in the United Kingdom.

(6) This section—

(a) shall be without prejudice to any enactment under which any amount is to be or may be deducted, or treated as deducted, from amounts payable by way of benefits under the scheme or treated as so payable; and

(b) shall not apply in relation to so much of any provision of a scheme as is required for securing compliance with the conditions of any [registration], exemption or relief given or available under the Tax Acts.]

[895]

NOTES

Inserted, together with the preceding heading, by the Child Support, Pensions and Social Security Act 2000, s 55.

Sub-s (6): word in square brackets substituted by the Taxation of Pension Schemes (Consequential Amendments) Order 2006, SI 2006/745, art 10(1), (3), as from 6 April 2006.

This section is the domestic implementation of Council Directive 98/49/EC on safeguarding the supplementary pension rights of employed and self-employed persons moving within the Community (at **[3942]**).

Regulations: the Occupational and Personal Pension Schemes (Miscellaneous Amendments) Regulations 2007, SI 2007/814.

Modification of schemes

[67 The subsisting rights provisions

(1) The subsisting rights provisions apply to any power conferred on any person by an occupational pension scheme to modify the scheme, other than a power conferred by—

(a) a public service pension scheme, or
(b) a prescribed scheme or a scheme of a prescribed description.

(2) Any exercise of such a power to make a regulated modification is voidable in accordance with section 67G unless the following are satisfied in respect of the modification—

(a) in the case of each affected member—
 (i) if the modification is a protected modification, the consent requirements (see section 67B),
 (ii) if it is not, either the consent requirements or the actuarial equivalence requirements (see section 67C),
(b) the trustee approval requirement (see section 67E), and
(c) the reporting requirement (see section 67F).

(3) The subsisting rights provisions do not apply in relation to the exercise of a power—

(a) for a purpose connected with debits under section 29(1) of the Welfare Reform and Pensions Act 1999, or
(b) in a prescribed manner.

(4) References in this section and sections 67A to 67I to "the subsisting rights provisions" are to this section and those sections.

(5) Subsection (6) applies in relation to the exercise of a power to which the subsisting rights provisions apply to make a regulated modification where a member of the scheme dies before the requirements mentioned in subsection (2), so far as they apply in his case, have been complied with in respect of the modification if—

(a) before he died he had given his consent to the modification in accordance with section 67B(4)(b), or
(b) before he died, or before the trustees of the scheme had become aware that he had died, the trustees had complied with section 67C(4)(a), (b) and (d) in respect of the modification in his case.

(6) Any of the requirements mentioned in subsection (2), as it applies in respect of the modification—

(a) which is satisfied in the case of the member, or
(b) which would have been satisfied in his case had he not died before it was satisfied,

is to be taken to be satisfied in the case of any survivor of the member in respect of the modification.]

[895A]

NOTES

Commencement: 1 November 2005 (for the purpose of conferring power to make regulations); 6 April 2006 (otherwise).

Substituted together with ss 67A–67I, for original s 67, by the Pensions Act 2004, s 262, as from 1 November 2005 (for the purpose of conferring power to make regulations), and as from 6 April 2006 (otherwise).

Regulations: the Personal and Occupational Pension Schemes (Miscellaneous Amendments) Regulations 1999, SI 1999/3198; the Occupational and Personal Pension Schemes (Contracting-out) (Miscellaneous Amendments) Regulations 2002, SI 2002/681; the Occupational Pension Schemes (Modification of Schemes) Regulations 2006, SI 2006/759.

[67A The subsisting rights provisions: interpretation

(1) In the subsisting rights provisions, each of the following expressions has the meaning given to it by the following provisions of this section—

"regulated modification"
"protected modification"
"detrimental modification"
"affected member"
"subsisting right"
"scheme rules".

(2) "Regulated modification" means a modification which is—

(a) a protected modification, or
(b) a detrimental modification,

or is both.

(3) "Protected modification" means a modification of an occupational pension scheme which—

(a) on taking effect would or might result in any subsisting right of—

(i) a member of the scheme, or

(ii) a survivor of a member of the scheme,

which is not a right or entitlement to money purchase benefits becoming, or being replaced with, a right or entitlement to money purchase benefits under the scheme rules,

(b) would or might result in a reduction in the prevailing rate of any pension in payment under the scheme rules, or

(c) is of a prescribed description.

For the purposes of paragraph (a), the reference in the definition of "money purchase benefits" in section 181(1) of the Pension Schemes Act 1993 to the widow or widower of a member of an occupational pension scheme is to be read as including any other survivor of the member.

(4) "Detrimental modification" means a modification of an occupational pension scheme which on taking effect would or might adversely affect any subsisting right of—

(a) any member of the scheme, or

(b) any survivor of a member of the scheme.

(5) A person is an "affected member"—

(a) in relation to a protected modification within paragraph (a) or (b) of subsection (3), if, at the time the modification takes effect, he is—

(i) a member of the scheme, or

(ii) a survivor of a member of the scheme,

and, on taking effect, the modification would or might affect any of his subsisting rights as mentioned in that paragraph,

(b) in relation to a protected modification within paragraph (c) of that subsection, if he is of a prescribed description, and

(c) in relation to a detrimental modification which is not a protected modification if, at the time the modification takes effect, he is—

(i) a member of the scheme, or

(ii) a survivor of a member of the scheme,

and, on taking effect, the modification would or might adversely affect any of his subsisting rights.

(6) "Subsisting right" means—

(a) in relation to a member of an occupational pension scheme, at any time—

(i) any right which at that time has accrued to or in respect of him to future benefits under the scheme rules, or

(ii) any entitlement to the present payment of a pension or other benefit which he has at that time, under the scheme rules, and

(b) in relation to the survivor of a member of an occupational pension scheme, at any time, any entitlement to benefits, or right to future benefits, which he has at that time under the scheme rules in respect of the member.

For this purpose, "right" includes a pension credit right.

(7) At any time when the pensionable service of a member of an occupational pension scheme is continuing, his subsisting rights are to be determined as if he had opted, immediately before that time, to terminate that service.

(8) "Scheme rules", in relation to a scheme, means—

(a) the rules of the scheme, except so far as overridden by a relevant legislative provision,

(b) the relevant legislative provisions, to the extent that they have effect in relation to the scheme and are not reflected in the rules of the scheme, and

(c) any provision which the rules of the scheme do not contain but which the scheme must contain if it is to conform with the requirements of Chapter 1 of Part 4 of the Pension Schemes Act 1993 (preservation of benefit under occupational pension schemes).

(9) For the purposes of subsection (8)—

(a) "relevant legislative provision" means any provision contained in any of the following provisions—

(i) Schedule 5 to the Social Security Act 1989 (equal treatment for men and women);

(ii) Chapters 2 to 5 of Part 4 of the Pension Schemes Act 1993 (certain protection for early leavers) or regulations made under any of those Chapters;
(iii) Part 4A of that Act (requirements relating to pension credit benefit) or regulations made under that Part;
(iv) section 110(1) of that Act (requirement as to resources for annual increase of guaranteed minimum pensions);
(v) this Part of this Act (occupational pensions) or subordinate legislation made or having effect as if made under this Part;
(vi) section 31 of the Welfare Reform and Pensions Act 1999 (pension debits: reduction of benefit);
(vii) any provision mentioned in section 306(2) of the Pensions Act 2004;

(b) a relevant legislative provision is to be taken to override any of the provisions of the scheme if, and only if, it does so by virtue of any of the following provisions—
(i) paragraph 3 of Schedule 5 to the Social Security Act 1989;
(ii) section 129(1) of the Pension Schemes Act 1993;
(iii) section 117(1) of this Act;
(iv) section 31(4) of the Welfare Reform and Pensions Act 1999;
(v) section 306(1) of the Pensions Act 2004.

(10) For the purposes of this section—
(a) "survivor", in relation to a member of an occupational pension scheme, means a person who—
(i) is the widow or widower of the member, or
(ii) has survived the member and has any entitlement to benefit, or right to future benefits, under the scheme rules in respect of the member, and
(b) a modification would or might adversely affect a person's subsisting right if it would alter the nature or extent of the entitlement or right so that the benefits, or future benefits, to which the entitlement or right relates would or might be less generous.

(11) In the subsisting rights provisions, in relation to—
(a) the exercise of a power to modify an occupational pension scheme to which the subsisting rights provisions apply, or
(b) a modification made, or to be made, in exercise of such a power,

references to "the scheme" are to be read as references to the scheme mentioned in paragraph (a).]

[895AA]

NOTES

Commencement: 1 November 2005 (for the purpose of conferring power to make regulations); 6 April 2006 (otherwise).

Substituted as noted to s 67 at **[895A]**.

[67B The consent requirements

(1) References in the subsisting rights provisions to the consent requirements, in respect of a regulated modification, are to be read in accordance with this section.

(2) The consent requirements apply in the case of an affected member—
(a) if the modification is a protected modification;
(b) if it is not a protected modification, unless the actuarial equivalence requirements apply in his case.

(3) The consent requirements consist of—
(a) the informed consent requirement (see subsection (4)), and
(b) the timing requirement (see subsection (6)).

(4) The informed consent requirement is satisfied in the case of an affected member if before the modification is made—
(a) the trustees have—
(i) given him information in writing adequate to explain the nature of the modification and its effect on him,
(ii) notified him in writing that he may make representations to the trustees about the modification,
(iii) afforded him a reasonable opportunity to make such representations, and

(iv) notified him in writing that the consent requirements apply in his case in respect of the modification, and

(b) after the trustees have complied with paragraph (a)(i), (ii) and (iv), the affected member has given his consent in writing to the modification.

(5) If—

(a) the modification is not a protected modification, and

(b) before the modification is made the trustees notify an affected member in writing that—

(i) if he gives his consent to the modification for the purposes of the consent requirements, those requirements apply in his case in respect of the modification, but

(ii) otherwise, the actuarial equivalence requirements apply in his case in respect of the modification,

the trustees are to be taken to have complied with subsection (4)(a)(iv) in respect of him.

(6) The timing requirement is satisfied in the case of an affected member if the modification takes effect within a reasonable period after the member has given his consent to the modification in accordance with subsection (4)(b).]

[895AB]

NOTES

Commencement: 1 November 2005 (for the purpose of conferring power to make regulations); 6 April 2006 (otherwise).

Substituted as noted to s 67 at **[895A]**.

[67C The actuarial equivalence requirements

(1) References in the subsisting rights provisions to the actuarial equivalence requirements, in respect of a detrimental modification which is not a protected modification, are to be read in accordance with this section and section 67D.

(2) The actuarial equivalence requirements apply in the case of an affected member only if—

(a) the modification is not a protected modification, and

(b) the trustees of the scheme determine that they are to apply in his case.

(3) The actuarial equivalence requirements consist of—

(a) the information requirement (see subsection (4)),

(b) the actuarial value requirement (see subsection (5)), and

(c) the actuarial equivalence statement requirement (see subsection (6)).

(4) The information requirement is satisfied in the case of an affected member if before the modification is made the trustees have taken all reasonable steps to—

(a) give him information in writing adequate to explain the nature of the modification and its effect on him,

(b) notify him in writing that he may make representations to the trustees about the modification,

(c) afford him a reasonable opportunity to make such representations, and

(d) notify him in writing that the actuarial equivalence requirements apply in his case in respect of the modification.

(5) The actuarial value requirement is satisfied in the case of an affected member if before the modification is made the trustees have made such arrangements, or taken such steps, as are adequate to secure that actuarial value will be maintained.

(6) The actuarial equivalence statement requirement is satisfied in the case of an affected member if the trustees have, within a reasonable period beginning with the date on which the modification takes effect, obtained an actuarial equivalence statement relating to the affected member in respect of the modification.

(7) For the purposes of subsection (6) "actuarial equivalence statement" means a statement in writing which—

(a) is given by—

(i) the actuary appointed in relation to the scheme under section 47(1)(b), or

(ii) a person with prescribed qualifications or experience or who is approved by the Secretary of State, and

(b) certifies that actuarial value has been maintained.

(8) For the purposes of subsections (5) and (7) as they apply in relation to an affected member, actuarial value is maintained if the actuarial value, immediately after the time at which the modification takes effect, of the affected member's subsisting rights is equal to or greater than the actuarial value of his subsisting rights immediately before that time.]

[895AC]

NOTES

Commencement: 1 November 2005 (for the purpose of conferring power to make regulations); 6 April 2006 (otherwise).

Substituted as noted to s 67 at **[895A]**.

Regulations: the Occupational Pension Schemes (Modification of Schemes) Regulations 2006, SI 2006/759.

[67D The actuarial equivalence requirements: further provisions

(1) This section applies for the purposes of section 67C.

(2) Where—

(a) the information requirement has been satisfied in the case of an affected member in respect of a proposed modification ("the original modification"),

(b) before the trustees have made a determination, or given their consent, for the purposes of section 67E(1) in relation to the original modification, the original modification has been revised, and

(c) the modification as so revised ("the revised modification") does not differ from the original modification in any material respect,

the information requirement is to be taken to have been satisfied in relation to the revised modification.

(3) The trustees are to be regarded as having taken all reasonable steps to notify an affected member as mentioned in section 67C(4)(d) in respect of a modification if they have taken all reasonable steps to notify him in writing that—

(a) if he gives his consent to the modification for the purposes of the consent requirements, those requirements apply in his case in respect of the modification, but

(b) otherwise, the actuarial equivalence requirements apply in his case in respect of the modification.

(4) Any calculation for the purposes of section 67C of the actuarial value of an affected member's subsisting rights at any time must conform with such requirements as may be prescribed.

(5) Requirements prescribed by regulations under subsection (4) may include requirements for any such calculation to be made in accordance with guidance that [is prepared and from time to time revised by a prescribed body].

(6) Nothing in subsections (6) and (7) of section 67C precludes actuarial equivalence statements relating to—

(a) two or more affected members, or

(b) affected members of any particular description,

in respect of a modification being given in a single document.]

[895AD]

NOTES

Commencement: 1 November 2005 (for the purpose of conferring power to make regulations); 6 April 2006 (otherwise).

Substituted as noted to s 67 at **[895A]**.

Sub-s (5): words in square brackets substituted by the Pensions Act 2007, s 17, Sch 5, para 7, as from 1 November 2007.

Regulations: the Occupational Pension Schemes (Modification of Schemes) Regulations 2006, SI 2006/759; the Occupational and Personal Pension Schemes (Prescribed Bodies) Regulations 2007, SI 2007/60; the Occupational Pension Schemes (Transfer Values) (Amendment) Regulations 2008, SI 2008/1050.

[67E The trustee approval requirement

(1) For the purposes of section 67(2)(b), the trustee approval requirement is satisfied in relation to the exercise of a power to make a regulated modification if—

(a) the trustees of the scheme have determined to exercise the power to make the modification, or

(b) if the power is exercised by another person, the trustees have consented to the exercise of the power to make the modification,

and the making of the determination, or giving of consent, complies with subsections (2) and (3).

(2) The trustees must not make a determination, or give their consent, for the purposes of subsection (1) unless, in the case of each affected member—

(a) if the modification is a protected modification, the informed consent requirement is satisfied (within the meaning of section 67B), or

(b) if it is not a protected modification—

(i) the informed consent requirement is satisfied, or

(ii) the information and actuarial value requirements are satisfied (within the meaning of section 67C),

in respect of the modification.

(3) The trustees must not make a determination, or give their consent, for the purposes of subsection (1) more than a reasonable period after the first consent given by an affected member under section 67B(4)(b) in respect of the modification was given.]

[895AE]

NOTES

Commencement: 1 November 2005 (for the purpose of conferring power to make regulations); 6 April 2006 (otherwise).

Substituted as noted to s 67 at **[895A]**.

[67F The reporting requirement

(1) For the purposes of section 67(2)(c), the reporting requirement is satisfied in relation to the exercise of a power to which the subsisting rights provisions apply to make a regulated modification if the trustees have, in accordance with subsection (2)—

(a) notified each affected member in whose case the consent requirements apply in respect of the modification, and

(b) taken all reasonable steps to notify each affected member in whose case the actuarial equivalence requirements apply in respect of the modification,

that they have made a determination, or given their consent, for the purposes of section 67E(1) in relation to the exercise of the power to make the modification.

(2) The trustees must give (or, where the actuarial equivalence requirements apply, take all reasonable steps to give) the notification—

(a) within a reasonable period beginning with the date of the determination or giving of consent mentioned in subsection (1), and

(b) before the date on which the modification takes effect.]

[895AF]

NOTES

Commencement: 1 November 2005 (for the purpose of conferring power to make regulations); 6 April 2006 (otherwise).

Substituted as noted to s 67 at **[895A]**.

[67G Powers of the Authority: voidable modifications

(1) Subsection (2) applies in relation to a regulated modification made in exercise of a power to which the subsisting rights provisions apply which is voidable by virtue of—

(a) section 67(2), or

(b) section 67H(3).

(2) The Authority may make an order declaring that subsection (6) applies in relation to the regulated modification.

(3) An order under subsection (2) relating to a regulated modification may also declare that subsection (6) applies in relation to—

(a) any other modification of the scheme made by the exercise of the power mentioned in subsection (1), or

(b) the grant of any rights under the scheme (whether by virtue of the attribution of notional periods as pensionable service or otherwise) in connection with the regulated modification.

(4) An order under subsection (2) relating to a regulated modification must specify the affected member or affected members or description of affected members in respect of whom subsection (6) applies ("the specified persons").

(5) An order under subsection (2) relating to a regulated modification may also—

(a) require the trustees to take, within the time specified in the order, such steps as are so specified for the purpose of giving effect to the order;

(b) declare that subsection (7) applies in relation to anything done by the trustees after the time at which the modification would, disregarding the order, have taken effect which—

(i) would not have contravened any provision of the scheme rules if the modification had taken effect at that time, but

(ii) as a result of the modification being void to any extent by virtue of the order, would (but for that subsection) contravene such a provision.

This is without prejudice to section 174(3).

(6) Where the Authority make an order declaring that this subsection applies in relation to a modification of a scheme, or the grant of any rights under the scheme, the modification or grant is void to the extent specified in the order, and in respect of the specified persons, as from the time when it would, disregarding the order, have taken effect.

(7) Where, by virtue of subsection (5)(b), the Authority make an order under subsection (2) declaring that this subsection applies in relation to anything done by the trustees, that thing is to be taken, for such purposes as are specified in the order, not to have contravened any provision of the trust deed or scheme rules.

(8) An order under subsection (2) relating to a regulated modification, or other modification, of a scheme or the grant of any rights under the scheme may be made before or after the time at which the modification or grant would, disregarding the order, have taken effect.]

[895AG]

NOTES

Commencement: 1 November 2005 (for the purpose of conferring power to make regulations); 6 April 2006 (otherwise).

Substituted as noted to s 67 at **[895A]**.

[67H Powers of the Authority to intervene

(1) Subsection (2) applies where the Authority have reasonable grounds to believe that a power to which the subsisting rights provisions apply—

(a) will be exercised, or

(b) has been exercised,

to make a regulated modification in circumstances where the modification will be voidable by virtue of section 67(2).

(2) The Authority may by order—

(a) in a case within subsection (1)(a), direct the person on whom the power is conferred not to exercise the power to make the regulated modification;

(b) require the trustees to take, within the time specified in the order, such steps as are so specified for the purpose of securing that any of the requirements mentioned in section 67(2) is satisfied.

(3) A regulated modification made in exercise of a power to which the subsisting rights provisions apply is voidable in accordance with section 67G if—

(a) the exercise of the power contravened an order under paragraph (a) of subsection (2), or

(b) the trustees fail to comply with a requirement imposed by an order under paragraph (b) of that subsection relating to any exercise of the power to make the modification.]

[895AH]

NOTES

Commencement: 1 November 2005 (for the purpose of conferring power to make regulations); 6 April 2006 (otherwise).

Substituted as noted to s 67 at **[895A]**.

[67I Subsisting rights provisions: civil penalties

(1) Subsections (2) and (3) apply where a regulated modification is voidable by virtue of section 67(2).

(2) Where the modification was made by the exercise of a power—

(a) by the trustees of the scheme, or

(b) by any other person in circumstances which do not fall within subsection (3),

section 10 applies to any trustee who has failed to take all reasonable steps to secure that the modification is not so voidable.

(3) Section 10 applies to any person other than the trustees of the scheme who, without reasonable excuse, exercises a power to make the modification if—

(a) the trustees have not given their consent, for the purposes of section 67E(1), to the exercise of the power to make the modification, or

(b) in the case of any affected member, the timing requirement is not satisfied (within the meaning of section 67B) in respect of the modification.

(4) Where the trustees fail to comply with any requirement imposed, by virtue of subsection (5)(a) of section 67G, by an order under subsection (2) of that section, section 10 applies to any trustee who has failed to take all reasonable steps to secure such compliance.

(5) Where a regulated modification is made by the exercise of a power in contravention of an order under section 67H(2)(a)—

(a) if the power is exercised by the trustees, section 10 applies to any trustee who has failed to take all reasonable steps to secure that the order was not contravened;

(b) section 10 applies to any other person who without reasonable excuse exercises the power in contravention of the order.

(6) Where the trustees fail to comply with any requirement specified in an order under section 67H(2)(b), section 10 applies to any trustee who has failed to take all reasonable steps to secure such compliance.]

[895AI]

NOTES

Commencement: 1 November 2005 (for the purpose of conferring power to make regulations); 6 April 2006 (otherwise).

Substituted as noted to s 67 at **[895A]**.

68 Power of trustees to modify schemes by resolution

(1) The trustees of a trust scheme may by resolution modify the scheme with a view to achieving any of the purposes specified in subsection (2).

(2) The purposes referred to in subsection (1) are—

(a) to extend the class of persons who may receive benefits under the scheme in respect of the death of a member of the scheme,

(b) to enable the scheme to conform with such arrangements as are required by [section 241 of the Pensions Act 2004],

[(c) to enable the scheme to comply with such terms and conditions as may be imposed by the Board of the Pension Protection Fund in relation to any payment made by it under section 185 or 186 of the Pensions Act 2004,]

(d) to enable the scheme to conform with section 37(2), 76(2), 91 or 92,

[(da) to enable the scheme to accommodate persons with pension credits or pension credit rights, and]

(e) prescribed purposes.

(3) No modification may be made by virtue of subsection (2)(a) without the consent of the employer.

(4) Modifications made by virtue of subsection (2)(b) may include in particular—

(a) modification of any limit on the number of, or of any category of, trustees, or

(b) provision for the transfer or vesting of property.

(5) Nothing done by virtue of subsection (2)(d), or any corresponding provisions in force in Northern Ireland, shall be treated as effecting an alteration to the scheme in question for the purposes of section 591B (cessation of approval) of the Taxes Act 1988.

(6) Regulations may provide that this section does not apply to trust schemes falling within a prescribed class or description.

[895B]

NOTES

Sub-s (2): words in square brackets in para (b) substituted by the Pensions Act 2004, s 319(1), Sch 12, paras 34, 56(a), as from 6 April 2006; para (c) substituted by the Pensions Act 2004, s 319(1), Sch 12, paras 34, 56(b), as from 1 September 2005; para (da) substituted (for the word "and" following para (d)) by the Welfare Reform and Pensions Act 1999, s 84(1), Sch 12, Pt I, paras 43, 54.

Regulations: the Occupational Pension Schemes (Winding Up) Regulations 1996, SI 1996/3126; the Occupational Pension Schemes (Deficiency on Winding Up etc) Regulations 1996, SI 1996/3128; the Occupational Pension Schemes (Employer Debt) Regulations 2005, SI 2005/678; the Occupational Pension Schemes (Winding up etc) Regulations 2005, SI 2005/706; the Occupational Pension Schemes (Scheme Funding) Regulations 2005, SI 2005/3377; the Occupational Pension Schemes (Republic of Ireland Schemes Exemption (Revocation) and Tax Exempt Schemes (Miscellaneous Amendments)) Regulations 2006, SI 2006/467; the Occupational Pension Schemes (Modification of Schemes) Regulations 2006, SI 2006/759; the Occupational Pension Schemes (Employer Debt and Miscellaneous Amendments) Regulations 2008, SI 2008/731; the Occupational Pension Schemes (Employer Debt—Apportionment Arrangements) (Amendment) Regulations 2008, SI 2008/1068.

69 Grounds for applying for modifications

(1) The Authority may, on an application made to them by persons competent to do so, make an order in respect of an occupational pension scheme (other than a public service pension scheme)—

(a) authorising the modification of the scheme with a view to achieving any of the purposes mentioned in subsection (3), or
(b) modifying the scheme with a view to achieving any such purpose.

(2) Regulations may make provision [requiring applications under this section to meet prescribed requirements].

(3) The purposes referred to in subsection (1) are—

(a) …
(b) in the case of [a registered pension scheme under section 153 of the Finance Act 2004] which is being wound up, to enable assets remaining after the liabilities of the scheme have been fully discharged to be distributed to the employer, where prescribed requirements in relation to the distribution are satisfied, or
(c) to enable the scheme to be so treated during a prescribed period that an employment to which the scheme applies may be contracted-out employment by reference to it.

(4) The persons competent to make an application under this section are—

(a) in the case of the purposes referred to in paragraph … (b) of subsection (3), the trustees of the scheme, and
(b) in the case of the purposes referred to in paragraph (c) of that subsection—
 (i) the trustees or managers of the scheme,
 (ii) the employer, or
 (iii) any person other than the trustees or managers who has power to alter the rules of the scheme.

(5) An order under subsection (1)(a) must be framed—

(a) if made with a view to achieving … the purposes referred to in [subsection (3)(b)], so as to confer the power of modification on the trustees, and
(b) if made with a view to achieving the purposes referred to in subsection (3)(c), so as to confer the power of modification on such persons (who may include persons who were not parties to the application made to the Authority) as the Authority think appropriate.

(6) Regulations may provide that in prescribed circumstances this section does not apply to occupational pension schemes falling within a prescribed class or description or applies to them with prescribed modifications.

[895C]

NOTES

Sub-s (2): words in square brackets substituted by the Pensions Act 2004, s 319(1), Sch 12, paras 34, 57(a), as from 6 April 2006.

Sub-s (3): para (a) repealed by the Pensions Act 2004, ss 319(1), 320, Sch 12, paras 34, 57(b), Sch 13, Pt 1, as from 6 April 2006; words in square brackets in para (b) substituted by the Taxation of Pension Schemes (Consequential Amendments) Order 2006, SI 2006/745, art 10(1), (4), as from 6 April 2006.

Sub-s (4): words omitted from para (a) repealed by the Pensions Act 2004, ss 319(1), 320, Sch 12, paras 34, 57(c), Sch 13, Pt 1, as from 6 April 2006.

Sub-s (5): words omitted repealed, and words in square brackets substituted, by the Pensions Act 2004, ss 319(1), 320, Sch 12, paras 34, 57(d), Sch 13, Pt 1, as from 6 April 2006.

Regulations: the Occupational Pension Schemes (Republic of Ireland Schemes Exemption (Revocation) and Tax Exempt Schemes (Miscellaneous Amendments)) Regulations 2006, SI 2006/467.

70 Section 69: supplementary

(1) The Authority may not make an order under section 69 unless they are satisfied that the purposes for which the application for the order was made—

(a) cannot be achieved otherwise than by means of such an order, or

(b) can only be achieved in accordance with a procedure which—

(i) is liable to be unduly complex or protracted, or

(ii) involves the obtaining of consents which cannot be obtained, or can only be obtained with undue delay or difficulty.

(2) The extent of the Authority's powers to make such an order is not limited, in relation to any purposes for which they are exercisable, to the minimum necessary to achieve those purposes.

(3) The Authority may not make an order under section 69 with a view to achieving the purpose referred to in subsection (3)(c) of that section unless they are satisfied that it is reasonable in all the circumstances to make it.

[895D]

72 Modification of public service pension schemes

(1) The appropriate authority may make such provision for the modification of a public service pension scheme as could be made in respect of a scheme other than a public service pension scheme by an order of the Authority under section 69(1)(b).

(2) In this section "the appropriate authority", in relation to a scheme, means such Minister of the Crown or government department as may be designated by the Treasury as having responsibility for the particular scheme.

(3) The powers of the appropriate authority under this section are exercisable by means of an order—

(a) directly modifying the scheme (without regard, in the case of a scheme contained in or made under powers conferred by an enactment, to the terms of the enactment or any of its restrictions), or

(b) modifying an enactment under which the scheme was made or by virtue of which it has effect.

(4) Any such order may adapt, amend or repeal any such enactment as is referred to in paragraph (a) or (b) of subsection (3) as that authority thinks appropriate.

[895E]

NOTES

Orders: Orders made under this section relate to specific pension schemes only and are therefore outside the scope of this work.

[Supervision of winding-up

72A Reports to Authority about winding-up

(1) Where—

(a) an occupational pension scheme is being wound up, and

(b) the winding-up is one beginning at a time (whether before or after the passing of this Act) by reference to which regulations provide that it is to be a winding-up to which this section applies, it shall be the duty of the trustees or managers, in accordance with this section, to make periodic reports in writing to the Authority about the progress of the winding-up.

(2) In the case of each winding-up, the first report to be made under this section shall be made—

(a) except in a case to which paragraph (b) applies—

(i) after the end of the prescribed period beginning with the day on which the winding-up began; and

(ii) before the end of the prescribed period that begins with the end of the period that applies for the purposes of sub-paragraph (i);

and

(b) in a case where the winding-up began before the coming into force of the regulations which (for the purposes of subsection (1)(b)) prescribe the time by reference to which the winding-up is one to which this section applies, before such date as may be prescribed by those regulations.

(3) Subject to subsection (4), each subsequent report made under this section in the case of a winding-up shall be made no more than twelve months after the date which (apart from any postponement under subsection (4)) was the latest date for the making of the previous report required to be made in the case of that winding-up.

(4) If, in the case of any report required to be made under subsection (3), the Authority consider (whether on an application made for the purpose or otherwise) that it would be appropriate to do so, they may, at any time before the latest time for the making of that report, postpone that latest time by such period as they think fit.

(5) The latest time for making a report shall not be postponed under subsection (4) by more than twelve months.

(6) Subject to the application of the limit specified in subsection (5) to the cumulative period of the postponements, more than one postponement may be made under subsection (4) in the case of the same report.

(7) A report under this section—

(a) must contain such information and statements as may be prescribed; and

(b) must be made in accordance with the prescribed requirements.

(8) Regulations may—

(a) provide that, in prescribed circumstances, there shall be no obligation to make a report that would otherwise fall to be made under this section;

(b) make provision for the period within which, and the manner in which, applications may be made for a postponement under subsection (4); and

(c) modify subsections (3) and (5) by substituting periods of different lengths for the periods for the time being specified in those subsections.

(9) If there is any failure by the trustees or managers of any scheme to comply with their duty to make a report in accordance with the requirements imposed by or under this section—

(a) …

(b) section 10 applies (irrespective of the description of scheme involved) to any trustee or manager who has failed to take all such steps.]

[895F]

NOTES

Commencement: 1 March 2002 (in so far as relating to sub-ss (1), (2), sub-s (3) (except for the words "Subject to subsection (4)," and "(apart from any postponement under subsection (4))", and sub-ss (7), (8)(a), (9) (for the purposes of making regulations and rules only)); 1 April 2002 (all the provisions noted above for all other purposes); to be appointed (otherwise).

Inserted, together with the preceding heading, by the Child Support, Pensions and Social Security Act 2000, s 49(1) (as to the commencement of this section see the note above).

Sub-s (9): para (a) repealed by the Pensions Act 2004, ss 319(1), 320, Sch 12, paras 34, 59, Sch 13, Pt 1, as from 6 April 2005.

Regulations: the Occupational Pension Schemes (Winding Up Notices and Reports etc) Regulations 2002, SI 2002/459.

[72B Directions by Authority for facilitating winding-up

(1) Subject to the following provisions of this section, the Authority shall have power, at any time after the winding-up of an occupational pension scheme has begun, to give directions under this section if they consider that the giving of the direction is appropriate on any of the grounds set out in subsection (2).

(2) Those grounds are—

(a) that the trustees or managers of the scheme are not taking all the steps in connection with the winding-up that the Authority consider would be being taken if the trustees or managers were acting reasonably;

(b) that steps being taken by the trustees or managers for the purposes of the winding-up involve things being done with what the Authority consider to be unreasonable delay;

(c) that the winding-up is being obstructed or unreasonably delayed by the failure of any person—

(i) to provide information to the trustees or managers;

(ii) to provide information to a person involved in the administration of the scheme;

(iii) to provide information to a person of a prescribed description; or

(iv) to take any step (other than the provision of information) that he has been asked to take by the trustees or managers;

(d) that the winding-up would be likely to be facilitated or accelerated by the taking by any person other than the trustees or managers of any other steps;

(e) that in any prescribed circumstances not falling within paragraphs (a) to (d)—

(i) the provision by any person of any information to the trustees or managers or to any other person, or

(ii) the taking of any other step by any person,

would be likely to facilitate or accelerate the progress of the winding-up.

(3) Except in prescribed circumstances, the power of the Authority to give a direction under this section in the case of a winding-up shall be exercisable only where—

(a) periodic reports about the progress of the winding-up are required to be made under section 72A; and

(b) the first report that has to be made for the purposes of that section in the case of that winding-up either has been made or should have been made.

(4) Regulations may provide that, in prescribed circumstances, the Authority shall not give a direction on the ground set out in subsection (2)(e) except in response to an application made by the trustees or managers of the scheme for the giving of a direction on that ground.

(5) A direction under this section is a direction in writing given to and imposing requirements on—

(a) any or all of the trustees or managers of the scheme;

(b) a person who is involved in its administration; or

(c) a person of a prescribed description.

(6) The requirements that may be imposed by a direction under this section are any requirement for the person to whom it is given, within such period specified in the direction as the Authority may consider reasonable—

(a) to provide the trustees or managers with all such information as may be specified or described in the direction;

(b) to provide a person involved in the administration of the scheme with all such information as may be so specified or described;

(c) to provide a person who is of a prescribed description with all such information as may be so specified or described;

(d) to take such steps (other than the provision of information) as may be so specified or described.

(7) …

(8) Regulations may—

(a) impose limitations on the steps that a person may be required to take by a direction under this section;

(b) …

(9) In this section references, in relation to a scheme, to a person involved in the administration of the scheme are (subject to subsection (10)) references to any person who is so involved otherwise than as—

(a) the employer in relation to that scheme;

(b) a trustee or manager of the scheme;

(c) the auditor of the scheme or its actuary;

(d) a legal adviser of the trustees or managers of the scheme;

(e) a fund manager for the scheme;

(f) a person acting on behalf of a person who is involved in the administration of the scheme;
(g) a person providing services to a person so involved;
(h) a person acting in his capacity as an employee of a person so involved;
(i) a person who would fall within any of paragraphs (f) to (h) if persons acting in relation to the scheme in any capacity mentioned in the preceding paragraphs were treated as involved in the administration of a scheme.

(10) In this section references, in relation to a scheme, to a person involved in the administration of the scheme do not include references to persons of a particular description if regulations provide for persons of that description to be excluded from those references.]

[895G]

NOTES

Inserted, together with s 72C, by the Child Support, Pensions and Social Security Act 2000, s 50.
Sub-s (7): repealed by the Pensions Act 2004, s 320, Sch 13, Pt 1, as from 6 April 2006.
Sub-s (8): para (b) repealed by the Pensions Act 2004, s 320, Sch 13, Pt 1, as from 6 April 2006.
Transitional provisions: for transitional provisions in connection with the continuity of functions, etc, following the transfer of functions from the Authority to the Regulator, see SI 2005/695, arts 5, 6, Sch 3.
Regulations: the Occupational Pension Schemes (Winding Up Notices and Reports etc) Regulations 2002, SI 2002/459.

[72C Duty to comply with directions under s 72B

(1) It shall be the duty of any person to whom a direction is given under section 72B to comply with it.

(2) …

(3) Section 10 applies to any trustee or manager of a scheme who fails, without reasonable excuse, to take all such steps as are reasonable to secure compliance by the trustees or managers of that scheme with any direction given to them under section 72B.

(4) Section 10 applies to any person who—
(a) is a person to whom a direction under section 72B is given otherwise than in the capacity of a trustee or manager; and
(b) without reasonable excuse, fails to comply with that direction.

(5) For the purposes of this section it shall not be a reasonable excuse in relation to any failure to provide information in pursuance of a direction under section 72B that the provision of that information would (but for the duty imposed by subsection (1) of this section) involve a breach by any person of a duty owed to another not to disclose that information.]

[895H]

NOTES

Inserted as noted to s 72B at **[895G]**.
Sub-s (2): repealed by the Pensions Act 2004, ss 319(1), 320, Sch 12, paras 34, 60, Sch 13, Pt 1, as from 6 April 2005.

Winding up

[73 Preferential liabilities on winding up

(1) This section applies where an occupational pension scheme to which this section applies is being wound up to determine the order in which the assets of the scheme are to be applied towards satisfying the liabilities of the scheme in respect of pensions and other benefits.

(2) This section applies to an occupational pension scheme other than a scheme which is—
(a) a money purchase scheme, or
(b) a prescribed scheme or a scheme of a prescribed description.

(3) The assets of the scheme must be applied first towards satisfying the amounts of the liabilities mentioned in subsection (4) and, if the assets are insufficient to satisfy those amounts in full, then—
(a) the assets must be applied first towards satisfying the amounts of the liabilities

mentioned in earlier paragraphs of subsection (4) before the amounts of the liabilities mentioned in later paragraphs, and

(b) where the amounts of the liabilities mentioned in one of those paragraphs cannot be satisfied in full, those amounts must be satisfied in the same proportions.

(4) The liabilities referred to in subsection (3) are—

(a) where—

(i) the trustees or managers of the scheme are entitled to benefits under a relevant pre-1997 contract of insurance entered into in relation to the scheme, and

(ii) either that contract may not be surrendered or the amount payable on surrender does not exceed the liability secured by the contract,

the liability so secured;

(b) any liability for pensions or other benefits to the extent that the amount of the liability does not exceed the corresponding PPF liability, other than a liability within paragraph (a);

(c) any liability for pensions or other benefits which, in the opinion of the trustees or managers, are derived from the payment by any member of voluntary contributions, other than a liability within paragraph (a) or (b);

(d) any other liability in respect of pensions or other benefits.

(5) For the purposes of subsection (4)—

"corresponding PPF liability" in relation to any liability for pensions or other benefits means—

(a) where the liability is to a member of the scheme, the cost of securing benefits for or in respect of the member corresponding to the compensation which would be payable to or in respect of the member in accordance with the pension compensation provisions if the Board of the Pension Protection Fund assumed responsibility for the scheme in accordance with Chapter 3 of Part 2 of the Pensions Act 2004 (pension protection), and

(b) where the liability is to another person in respect of a member of the scheme, the cost of securing benefits for that person corresponding to the compensation which would be payable to that person in respect of the member in accordance with the pension compensation provisions if the Board assumed responsibility for the scheme in accordance with that Chapter;

"relevant pre-1997 contract of insurance" means a contract of insurance which was entered into before 6th April 1997 with a view to securing the whole or part of the scheme's liability for—

(a) any pension or other benefit payable to or in respect of one particular person whose entitlement to payment of a pension or other benefit has arisen, and

(b) any benefit which will be payable in respect of that person on his death.

(6) For the purposes of this section, when determining the corresponding PPF liability in relation to any liability of a scheme to, or in respect of, a member for pensions or other benefits, the pension compensation provisions apply with such modifications as may be prescribed.

(7) Regulations may modify subsection (4).

(8) For the purposes of that subsection—

(a) regulations may prescribe how it is to be determined whether a liability for pensions or other benefits which, in the opinion of the trustees or managers of the scheme, are derived from the payment by any member of voluntary contributions falls within paragraph (a) or (b) of that subsection;

(b) no pension or other benefit which is attributable (directly or indirectly) to a pension credit is to be regarded for the purposes of paragraph (c) of that subsection as derived from the payment of voluntary contributions.

(9) Where, on the commencement of the winding up period, a member becomes a person to whom Chapter 5 of Part 4 of the Pension Schemes Act 1993 (early leavers: cash transfer sums and contribution refunds) applies, that Chapter applies in relation to him with such modifications as may be prescribed.

(10) For the purposes of this section—

"assets" of a scheme to which this section applies do not include any assets representing the value of any rights in respect of money purchase benefits under the scheme rules;

"liabilities" of such a scheme do not include any liabilities in respect of money purchase benefits under the scheme rules;

"the pension compensation provisions" has the same meaning as in Part 2 of the Pensions Act 2004 (see section 162 of that Act);

"scheme rules" has the same meaning as in the Pensions Act 2004 (see section 318 of that Act);

"winding up period", in relation to an occupational pension scheme to which this section applies, means the period which—

(a) begins with the day on which the time immediately after the beginning of the winding up of the scheme falls, and

(b) ends when the winding up of the scheme is completed.]

[895I]

NOTES

Commencement: 10 February 2005 (for the purpose only of conferring power to make regulations, orders or rules); 6 April 2005 (otherwise).

Substituted together with ss 73A, 73B, for original s 73, by the Pensions Act 2004, s 270(1), as from 10 February 2005 (for the purpose only of conferring power to make regulations, orders or rules), and as from 6 April 2005 (otherwise).

Transitional provisions: for transitional provisions in relation to any scheme which (a) was regarded at 6 April 2005 (by virtue of the Occupational Pension Schemes (Winding Up) Regulations 1996, SI 1996/3126, reg 2), as having begun to be wound up for the purposes of those Regulations; or (b) in accordance with s 124(3A)–(3E) of this Act began to wind up before that date, see SI 2005/275, art 2. For other transitional modifications, see reg 3 of the 1996 Regulations (as amended). See also the Pensions Act 2004, ss 319(1), 320, Sch 12, paras 34, 61, Sch 13, Pt 1 (amendments to this section prior to the substitution as noted above).

Regulations: the Occupational Pension Schemes (Winding Up) Regulations 1996, SI 1996/3126; the Personal and Occupational Pension Schemes (Miscellaneous Amendments) Regulations 1999, SI 1999/3198; the Pension Sharing (Consequential and Miscellaneous Amendments) Regulations 2000, SI 2000/2691; the Occupational Pension Schemes (Minimum Funding Requirement and Miscellaneous Amendments) Regulations 2002, SI 2002/380; the Occupational Pension Schemes (Winding Up and Deficiency on Winding Up etc) (Amendment) Regulations 2004, SI 2004/403; the Occupational Pension Schemes (Winding Up, Deficiency on Winding Up and Transfer Values) (Amendment) Regulations 2005, SI 2005/72; the Occupational Pension Schemes (Winding up etc) Regulations 2005, SI 2005/706; the Occupational Pension Schemes (Winding Up) (Modification for Multi-employer Schemes and Miscellaneous Amendments) Regulations 2005, SI 2005/2159; the Occupational Pension Schemes (Republic of Ireland Schemes Exemption (Revocation) and Tax Exempt Schemes (Miscellaneous Amendments)) Regulations 2006, SI 2006/467; the Occupational and Personal Pension Schemes (Miscellaneous Amendments) Regulations 2007, SI 2007/814.

[73A Operation of scheme during winding up period

(1) This section applies where an occupational pension scheme to which section 73 applies is being wound up.

(2) During the winding up period, the trustees or managers of the scheme—

(a) must secure that any pensions or other benefits (other than money purchase benefits) paid to or in respect of a member are reduced, so far as necessary, to reflect the liabilities of the scheme to or in respect of the member which will be satisfied in accordance with section 73, and

(b) may, for the purposes of paragraph (a), take such steps as they consider appropriate (including steps adjusting future payments) to recover any overpayment or pay any shortfall.

(3) During the winding up period—

(a) no benefits may accrue under the scheme rules to, or in respect of, members of the scheme, and

(b) no new members of any class may be admitted to the scheme.

(4) Subsection (3) does not prevent any increase, in a benefit, which would otherwise accrue in accordance with the scheme or any enactment.

(5) Subsection (3) does not prevent the accrual of money purchase benefits to the extent that they are derived from income or capital gains arising from the investment of payments which are made by, or in respect of, a member of the scheme.

(6) Where a person is entitled to a pension credit derived from another person's shareable rights under the scheme, subsection (3) does not prevent the trustees or managers of the scheme discharging their liability in respect of the credit under Chapter 1 of Part 4 of the

Welfare Reform and Pensions Act 1999 (sharing of rights under pension arrangements) by conferring appropriate rights under the scheme on that person.

(7) Regulations may require the trustees or managers of the scheme, in prescribed circumstances—

(a) to adjust the entitlement of a person to a pension or other benefit under the scheme rules where the entitlement arises as a result of a discretionary award which takes effect during the winding up period;

(b) to adjust the entitlement of a person ("the survivor") to a pension or other benefit under the scheme rules where—

(i) a member of the scheme, or a person who was (or might have become) entitled to a pension or other benefit in respect of a member, dies during the winding up period, and

(ii) the survivor's entitlement is to a pension or other benefit in respect of the member (whether arising on the date of that death or subsequently).

(8) Regulations under subsection (7) may, in particular—

(a) prescribe how the required adjustments to entitlement are to be determined and the manner in which they are to be made;

(b) in a case where the commencement of the winding up of the scheme is backdated (whether in accordance with section 154 of the Pensions Act 2004 (requirement to wind up schemes with sufficient assets to meet protected liabilities) or otherwise), require any adjustment to a person's entitlement to be made with effect from the time the award takes effect;

(c) without prejudice to sections 10(3) to (9), 73B(2) and 116, make provision about the consequences of breaching the requirements of the regulations.

(9) If the scheme confers power on any person other than the trustees or managers of the scheme to apply the assets of the scheme in respect of pensions or other benefits (including increases in pensions or benefits), it cannot be exercised by that person but may, subject to the provisions made by or by virtue of this section and sections 73 and 73B, be exercised instead by the trustees or managers.

(10) For the purposes of this section—

"appropriate rights" has the same meaning as in paragraph 5 of Schedule 5 to the Welfare Reform and Pensions Act 1999 (pension credits: mode of discharge);

"discretionary award" means an award of a prescribed description;

"shareable rights" has the same meaning as in Chapter 1 of Part 4 of the Welfare Reform and Pensions Act 1999 (sharing of rights under pension arrangements);

and subsection (10) of section 73 applies as it applies for the purposes of that section.]

[895J]

NOTES

Commencement: 10 February 2005 (for the purpose only of conferring power to make regulations, orders or rules); 6 April 2005 (otherwise).

Substituted as noted to s 73 at **[895I]**.

Regulations: the Occupational Pension Schemes (Winding up etc) Regulations 2005, SI 2005/706.

[73B Sections 73 and 73A: supplementary

(1) Any action taken in contravention of section 73A(3) is void.

(2) If any provision made by or by virtue of the winding up provisions is not complied with in relation to a scheme to which section 73 applies, section 10 applies to any trustee or manager of the scheme who has failed to take all reasonable steps to secure compliance.

(3) For the purposes of subsection (2), when determining whether section 73A(3) has been complied with subsection (1) of this section is to be disregarded.

(4) Regulations may—

(a) prescribe how, for the purposes of the winding up provisions—

(i) the assets and liabilities of a scheme to which section 73 applies, and

(ii) their value or amount,

are to be determined, calculated and verified;

(b) modify any of the winding up provisions as it applies—

(i) to prescribed schemes or prescribed descriptions of schemes;

(ii) in relation to a scheme where only part of the scheme is being wound up;

(iii) in relation to a case where any liability of the scheme in respect of a member has been discharged by virtue of regulations under section 135(4) of the Pensions Act 2004 (power to make regulations permitting discharge of scheme's liabilities during an assessment period).

(5) Without prejudice to the generality of subsection (4), regulations under paragraph (b)(i) of that subsection may, in particular, modify any of the winding up provisions as it applies in relation to a scheme in relation to which there is more than one employer.

(6) The winding up provisions do not apply—

(a) in relation to any liability for an amount by way of pensions or other benefits which a person became entitled to payment of, under the scheme rules, before commencement of the winding up period,

(b) in prescribed circumstances, in relation to any liability in respect of rights of a prescribed description to which a member of the scheme became entitled under the scheme rules by reason of his pensionable service under the scheme terminating before the commencement of the winding up period,

(c) in relation to any liability in respect of rights of prescribed descriptions to which a member of the scheme had become entitled under the scheme rules before the commencement of the winding up period, or

(d) in relation to any liability the discharge of which is validated under section 136 of the Pensions Act 2004 (power to validate actions taken during an assessment period to discharge liabilities of a scheme).

(7) But nothing in subsection (6) prevents the winding up provisions applying in relation to a liability under Chapter 4 of Part 4 of the Pension Schemes Act 1993 (transfer values) which—

(a) arose before the commencement of the winding up of the scheme, and

(b) was not discharged before the commencement of the winding up period.

(8) Regulations may provide that, in prescribed circumstances, where—

(a) an occupational pension scheme to which section 73 applies is being wound up,

(b) a member of the scheme died before the winding up began, and

(c) during the winding up period a person becomes entitled under the scheme rules to a benefit of a prescribed description in respect of the member,

his entitlement to payment of all or part of the benefit is, for the purposes of subsection (6), to be treated as having arisen immediately before the commencement of the winding up period.

(9) If, immediately before the winding up period in relation to an occupational pension scheme to which section 73 applies, a person is entitled to an amount but has postponed payment of it, he is not, for the purposes of subsection (6), to be regarded as having become entitled to payment of the amount before that period.

(10) For the purposes of this section—

(a) "winding up provisions" means this section and sections 73, 73A and 74, and

(b) subsection (10) of section 73 applies as it applies for the purposes of that section.]

[895K]

NOTES

Commencement: 10 February 2005 (for the purpose only of conferring power to make regulations, orders or rules); 6 April 2005 (otherwise).

Substituted as noted to s 73 at **[895I]**.

Regulations: the Occupational Pension Schemes (Winding up etc) Regulations 2005, SI 2005/706; the Occupational Pension Schemes (Winding Up) (Modification for Multi-employer Schemes and Miscellaneous Amendments) Regulations 2005, SI 2005/2159; the Occupational and Personal Pension Schemes (Miscellaneous Amendments) Regulations 2007, SI 2007/814.

74 Discharge of liabilities by insurance, etc

[(1) This section applies where an occupational pension scheme to which section 73 applies is being wound up.]

(2) A liability to or in respect of a member of the scheme in respect of pensions or other benefits ... is to be treated as discharged (to the extent that it would not be so treated apart from this section) if the trustees or managers of the scheme have, in accordance with prescribed arrangements, provided for the discharge of the liability in one or more of the ways mentioned in subsection (3).

(3) The ways referred to in subsection (2) are—

(a) by acquiring transfer credits allowed under the rules of another occupational pension scheme which satisfies prescribed requirements and the trustees or managers of which are able and willing to accept payment in respect of the member,

(b) by acquiring rights allowed under the rules of a personal pension scheme which satisfies prescribed requirements and the trustees or managers of which are able and willing to accept payment in respect of the member's accrued rights [or pension credit rights],

(c) by purchasing one or more annuities which satisfy prescribed requirements from one or more [insurers], being companies willing to accept payment in respect of the member from the trustees or managers,

(d) by subscribing to other pension arrangements which satisfy prescribed requirements,

[(e) by the payment of a cash sum in circumstances where prescribed requirements are met].

(4) If the assets of the scheme are insufficient to satisfy in full the liabilities, as calculated in accordance with the [scheme rules], in respect of pensions and other benefits … the reference in subsection (2) to providing for the discharge of any liability in one or more of the ways mentioned in subsection (3) is to applying any amount available, in accordance with section 73, in one or more of those ways.

(5) Regulations may provide for this section—

(a) to have effect in relation to so much of any liability as may be determined in accordance with the regulations, …

(b) …

[(6) For the purposes of this section—

(a) references to assets of the scheme do not include any assets representing the value of any rights in respect of money purchase benefits under the scheme rules, and

(b) references to liabilities of the scheme do not include any liabilities in respect of money purchase benefits under the scheme rules;

and "scheme rules" has the same meaning as in the Pensions Act 2004 (see section 318 of that Act).]

[895L]

NOTES

Sub-s (1): substituted by the Pensions Act 2004, s 270(2)(a), as from 6 April 2005.

Sub-s (2): words omitted repealed by the Pensions Act 2004, ss 270(2)(b), 320, Sch 13, Pt 1, as from 6 April 2005.

Sub-s (3): words in square brackets in para (b) inserted by the Welfare Reform and Pensions Act 1999, s 84(1), Sch 12, Pt I, paras 43, 56; word in square brackets in para (c) substituted by the Financial Services and Markets Act 2000 (Consequential Amendments and Repeals) Order 2001, SI 2001/3649, art 144; para (e) added by the Pensions Act 2004, s 270(2)(c), as from 10 February 2005 (for the purpose only of conferring power to make regulations, orders or rules), and as from 6 April 2005 (otherwise).

Sub-s (4): words in square brackets substituted, and words omitted repealed, by the Pensions Act 2004, ss 270(2)(d), 320, Sch 13, Pt 1, as from 6 April 2005.

Sub-s (5): para (b) and the word immediately preceding it repealed by the Pensions Act 2004, ss 270(2)(e), 320, Sch 13, Pt 1, as from 6 April 2005.

Sub-s (6): added by the Pensions Act 2004, s 270(2)(f), as from 6 April 2005.

Transitional provisions: for transitional provisions in relation to any scheme which (a) was regarded at 6 April 2005 (by virtue of the Occupational Pension Schemes (Winding Up) Regulations 1996, SI 1996/3126, reg 2), as having begun to be wound up for the purposes of those Regulations; or (b) in accordance with s 124(3A)–(3E) of this Act began to wind up before that date, see SI 2005/275, art 2.

Regulations: the Occupational Pension Schemes (Winding Up) Regulations 1996, SI 1996/3126; the Occupational Pension Schemes (Winding up etc) Regulations 2005, SI 2005/706.

75 Deficiencies in the assets

[(1) This section applies in relation to an occupational pension scheme other than a scheme which is—

(a) a money purchase scheme, or

(b) a prescribed scheme or a scheme of a prescribed description.

(2) If—

(a) at any time which falls—

(i) when a scheme is being wound up, but

(ii) before any relevant event in relation to the employer which occurs while the scheme is being wound up,

the value of the assets of the scheme is less than the amount at that time of the liabilities of the scheme, and

(b) the trustees or managers of the scheme designate that time for the purposes of this subsection (before the occurrence of an event within paragraph (a)(ii)),

an amount equal to the difference shall be treated as a debt due from the employer to the trustees or managers of the scheme.

This is subject to subsection (3).

(3) Subsection (2) applies only if—

(a) either—

(i) no relevant event within subsection (6A)(a) or (b) occurred in relation to the employer during the period beginning with the appointed day and ending with the commencement of the winding up of the scheme, or

(ii) during the period—

(a) beginning with the occurrence of the last such relevant event which occurred during the period mentioned in sub-paragraph (i), and

(b) ending with the commencement of the winding up of the scheme,

a cessation notice was issued in relation to the scheme and became binding, and

(b) no relevant event within subsection (6A)(c) has occurred in relation to the employer during the period mentioned in paragraph (a)(i).

(4) Where—

(a) immediately before a relevant event ("the current event") occurs in relation to the employer the value of the assets of the scheme is less than the amount at that time of the liabilities of the scheme,

(b) the current event—

(i) occurred on or after the appointed day, and

(ii) did not occur in prescribed circumstances,

(c) if the scheme was being wound up immediately before that event, subsection (2) has not applied in relation to the scheme to treat an amount as a debt due from the employer to the trustees or managers of the scheme,

(d) if the current event is within subsection (6A)(a) or (b), either—

(i) no relevant event within subsection (6A)(a) or (b) occurred in relation to the employer during the period beginning with the appointed day and ending immediately before the current event, or

(ii) a cessation event has occurred in relation to the scheme in respect of a cessation notice issued during the period—

(a) beginning with the occurrence of the last such relevant event which occurred during the period mentioned in sub-paragraph (i), and

(b) ending immediately before the current event, and

(e) no relevant event within subsection (6A)(c) has occurred in relation to the employer during the period mentioned in paragraph (d)(i),

an amount equal to the difference shall be treated as a debt due from the employer to the trustees or managers of the scheme.

(4A) Where the current event is within subsection (6A)(a) or (b), the debt under subsection (4) is to be taken, for the purposes of the law relating to insolvency as it applies to the employer, to arise immediately before the occurrence of the current event.

(4B) Subsection (4C) applies if, in a case within subsection (4)—

(a) the current event is within subsection (6A)(a) or (b), and

(b) the scheme was not being wound up immediately before that event.

(4C) Where this subsection applies, the debt due from the employer under subsection (4) is contingent upon—

(a) a scheme failure notice being issued in relation to the scheme after the current event and the following conditions being satisfied—

(i) the scheme failure notice is binding,

(ii) no relevant event within subsection (6A)(c) has occurred in relation to the employer before the scheme failure notice became binding, and

(iii) a cessation event has not occurred in relation to the scheme in respect of a cessation notice issued during the period—

(a) beginning with the occurrence of the current event, and

(b) ending immediately before the issuing of the scheme failure notice, and the occurrence of such a cessation event in respect of a cessation notice issued during that period is not a possibility, or

(b) the commencement of the winding up of the scheme before—

(i) any scheme failure notice or cessation notice issued in relation to the scheme becomes binding, or

(ii) any relevant event within subsection (6A)(c) occurs in relation to the employer.]

(5) For the purposes of [subsections (2) and (4)], the liabilities and assets to be taken into account, and their amount or value, must be determined, calculated and verified by a prescribed person and in the prescribed manner.

(6) In calculating the value of any liabilities for those purposes, a provision of the scheme [rules] which limits the amount of its liabilities by reference to the amount of its assets is to be disregarded.

[In this subsection "scheme rules" has the same meaning as in the Pensions Act 2004 ("the 2004 Act") (see section 318 of that Act).]

[(6A) For the purposes of this section, a relevant event occurs in relation to the employer in relation to an occupational pension scheme if and when—

(a) an insolvency event occurs in relation to the employer,

(b) the trustees or managers of the scheme make an application under subsection (1) of section 129 of the 2004 Act or receive a notice from the Board of the Pension Protection Fund under subsection (5)(a) of that section, or

(c) a resolution is passed for a voluntary winding up of the employer in a case where a declaration of solvency has been made under section 89 of the Insolvency Act 1986 (members' voluntary winding up).

(6B) For the purposes of this section—

(a) a "cessation notice", in the case of a relevant event within subsection (6A)(a), means—

(i) a withdrawal notice issued under section 122(2)(b) of the 2004 Act (scheme rescue has occurred),

(ii) a withdrawal notice issued under section 148 of that Act (no insolvency event has occurred or is likely to occur),

(iii) a notice issued under section 122(4) of that Act (inability to confirm status of scheme) in a case where the notice has become binding and section 148 of that Act does not apply,

(b) a "cessation notice" in the case of a relevant event within subsection (6A)(b), means a withdrawal notice issued under section 130(3) of the 2004 Act (scheme rescue has occurred),

(c) a cessation event occurs in relation to a scheme when a cessation notice in relation to the scheme becomes binding,

(d) the occurrence of a cessation event in relation to a scheme in respect of a cessation notice issued during a particular period ("the specified period") is a possibility until each of the following are no longer reviewable—

(i) any cessation notice which has been issued in relation to the scheme during the specified period,

(ii) any failure to issue such a cessation notice during the specified period,

(iii) any notice which has been issued by the Board under Chapter 2 or 3 of Part 2 of the 2004 Act which is relevant to the issue of a cessation notice in relation to the scheme during the specified period or to such a cessation notice which has been issued during that period becoming binding,

(iv) any failure to issue such a notice as is mentioned in sub-paragraph (iii),

(e) the issue or failure to issue a notice is to be regarded as reviewable—

(i) during the period within which it may be reviewed by virtue of Chapter 6 of Part 2 of the 2004 Act, and

(ii) if the matter is so reviewed, until—

(a) the review and any reconsideration,

(b) any reference to the Ombudsman for the Board of the Pension Protection Fund in respect of the matter, and

(c) any appeal against his determination or directions,

has been finally disposed of, and

(f) a "scheme failure notice" means a scheme failure notice issued under section 122(2)(a) or 130(2) of the 2004 Act (scheme rescue not possible).

(6C) For the purposes of this section—

(a) section 121 of the 2004 Act applies for the purposes of determining if and when an insolvency event has occurred in relation to the employer,

(b) "appointed day" means the day appointed under section 126(2) of the 2004 Act (no pension protection under Chapter 3 of Part 2 of that Act if the scheme begins winding up before the day appointed by the Secretary of State),

(c) references to a relevant event in relation to an employer do not include a relevant event which occurred in relation to him before he became the employer in relation to the scheme,

(d) references to a cessation notice becoming binding are to the notice in question mentioned in subsection (6B)(a) or (b) and issued under Part 2 of the 2004 Act becoming binding within the meaning given by that Part of that Act, and

(e) references to a scheme failure notice becoming binding are to the notice in question mentioned in subsection (6B)(f) and issued under Part 2 of the 2004 Act becoming binding within the meaning given by that Part of that Act.

(6D) Where—

(a) a resolution is passed for a voluntary winding up of the employer in a case where a declaration of solvency has been made under section 89 of the Insolvency Act 1986 (members' voluntary winding up), and

(b) either—

(i) the voluntary winding up of the employer is stayed other than in prescribed circumstances, or

(ii) a meeting of creditors is held in relation to the employer under section 95 of that Act (creditors' meeting which has the effect of converting a members' voluntary winding up into a creditors' voluntary winding up),

this section has effect as if that resolution had never been passed and any debt which arose under this section by virtue of the passing of that resolution shall be treated as if it had never arisen.]

(7) This section does not prejudice any other right or remedy which the trustees or managers may have in respect of a deficiency in the scheme's assets.

(8) A debt due by virtue only of this section shall not be regarded—

(a) as a preferential debt for the purposes of the Insolvency Act 1986, or

(b) as a preferred debt for the purposes of the Bankruptcy (Scotland) Act 1985.

(9) …

(10) Regulations may modify this section as it applies in prescribed circumstances.

[895M]

NOTES

Sub-ss (1)–(4C): substituted, for original sub-ss (1)–(4), by the Pensions Act 2004, s 270(2)(a), as from 10 February 2005 (for the purpose only of conferring power to make regulations, orders or rules), and as from 6 April 2005 (otherwise).

Sub-s (5): words in square brackets substituted by the Pensions Act 2004, s 271(1), (3), as from 6 April 2005.

Sub-s (6): word in square brackets inserted by the Pensions Act 2004, s 271(1), (4), as from 6 April 2005.

Sub-ss (6A)–(6D): inserted by the Pensions Act 2004, s 271(1), (5), as from 10 February 2005 (for the purpose only of conferring power to make regulations, orders or rules), and as from 6 April 2005 (otherwise).

Sub-s (9): repealed by the Pensions Act 2004, ss 271(6), 320, Sch 13, Pt 1, as from 6 April 2005.

Transitional provisions: for transitional provisions in relation to (a) any scheme other than a money purchase scheme in the case of which a debt to the trustees or managers of the scheme has been treated as arising under s 75(1) of this Act before 6 April 2005; (b) any scheme regarded at 6 April 2005 (by virtue of the Occupational Pension Schemes (Winding Up) Regulations 1996, SI 1996/3126, reg 2) as having begun to be wound up for the purposes of those Regulations; or (c) any scheme which in accordance with section 124(3A)–(3E) of this Act began to wind up before that date, see SI 2005/275, art 2.

Regulations: the Occupational Pension Schemes (Minimum Funding Requirement and Actuarial Valuations) Regulations 1996, SI 1996/1536; the Occupational Pension Schemes (Deficiency on Winding Up etc) Regulations 1996, SI 1996/3128; the Personal and Occupational Pension Schemes (Miscellaneous Amendments) (No 2) Regulations 1997, SI 1997/3038; the Personal and Occupational Pension Schemes (Miscellaneous Amendments) Regulations 1999, SI 1999/3198; the Occupational Pension Schemes (Minimum Funding Requirement and Miscellaneous Amendments) Regulations 2002, SI 2002/380; the Occupational Pension Schemes (Winding Up and Deficiency on Winding Up etc) (Amendment) Regulations 2004, SI 2004/403; the Occupational Pension Schemes (Winding Up, Deficiency on Winding Up and Transfer Values) (Amendment) Regulations 2005, SI 2005/72; the Occupational Pension Schemes (Employer Debt) Regulations 2005, SI 2005/678; the Occupational

Pension Schemes (Employer Debt etc) (Amendment) Regulations 2005, SI 2005/2224; the Occupational Pension Schemes (Republic of Ireland Schemes Exemption (Revocation) and Tax Exempt Schemes (Miscellaneous Amendments)) Regulations 2006, SI 2006/467; the Occupational Pension Schemes (Fraud Compensation Levy) Regulations 2006, SI 2006/558; the Occupational and Personal Pension Schemes (Prescribed Bodies) Regulations 2007, SI 2007/60; the Occupational Pension Schemes (Employer Debt and Miscellaneous Amendments) Regulations 2008, SI 2008/731; the Occupational Pension Schemes (Employer Debt—Apportionment Arrangements) (Amendment) Regulations 2008, SI 2008/1068.

General

124 Interpretation of Part I

(1) In this Part—

"active member", in relation to an occupational pension scheme, means a person who is in pensionable service under the scheme,

"the actuary" and "the auditor", in relation to an occupational pension scheme, have the meanings given by section 47,

["the Authority" means the Pensions Regulator,]

["civil partnership status", in relation to a person, means whether that person has previously formed a civil partnership and, if so, whether that civil partnership has ended,]

"the Compensation Board" has the meaning given by section 78(1),

"the compensation provisions" has the meaning given by section 81(3),

"contravention" includes failure to comply,

"deferred member", in relation to an occupational pension scheme, means a person (other than an active or pensioner member) who has accrued rights under the scheme,

"employer", in relation to an occupational pension scheme, means the employer of persons in the description *or category* of employment to which the scheme in question relates (but see section 125(3)),

"equal treatment rule" has the meaning given by section 62,

"firm" means a body corporate or a partnership,

"fund manager", in relation to an occupational pension scheme, means a person who manages the investments held for the purposes of the scheme,

"independent trustee" has the meaning given by section 23(3),

"managers", in relation to an occupational pension scheme other than a trust scheme, means the persons responsible for the management of the scheme,

"member", in relation to an occupational pension scheme, means any active, deferred[, pensioner or pension credit] member (but see section 125(4)),

…

…

…

"normal pension age" has the meaning given by section 180 of the Pension Schemes Act 1993,

"payment schedule" has the meaning given by section 87(2),

["pension credit" means a credit under section 29(1)(b) of the Welfare Reform and Pensions Act 1999" or under corresponding Northern Ireland legislation,

"pension credit member", in relation to an occupational pension scheme, means a person who has rights under the scheme which are attributable (directly or indirectly) to a pension credit,

"pension credit rights", in relation to an occupational pension scheme, means rights to future benefits under the scheme which are attributable (directly or indirectly) to a pension credit,]

"pensionable service", in relation to a member of an occupational pension scheme, means service in any description *or category* of employment to which the scheme relates which qualifies the member (on the assumption that it continues for the appropriate period) for pension or other benefits under the scheme,

"pensioner member", in relation to an occupational pension scheme, means a person who in respect of his pensionable service under the scheme or by reason of transfer credits, is entitled to the present payment of pension or other benefits […],

"prescribed" means prescribed by regulations,

"professional adviser", in relation to a scheme, has the meaning given by section 47,

"public service pension scheme" has the meaning given by section 1 of the Pension Schemes Act 1993, "regulations" means regulations made by the Secretary of State,

"resources", in relation to an occupational pension scheme, means the funds out of which the benefits provided by the scheme are payable from time to time, including the proceeds of any policy of insurance taken out, or annuity contract entered into, for the purposes of the scheme,

"Scottish partnership" means a partnership constituted under the law of Scotland,

"the Taxes Act 1988" means the Income and Corporation Taxes Act 1988,

"transfer credits" means rights allowed to a member under the rules of an occupational pension scheme by reference to[—

(a) a transfer to the scheme of, or transfer payment to the trustees or managers of the scheme in respect of, any of his rights (including transfer credits allowed) under another occupational pension scheme or a personal pension scheme, other than pension credit rights, or

(b) a cash transfer sum paid under Chapter 5 of Part 4 of the Pension Schemes Act 1993 (early leavers) in respect of him, to the trustees or managers of the scheme,]

"trustees or managers", in relation to an occupational pension scheme, means—

(a) in the case of a trust scheme, the trustees of the scheme, and

(b) in any other case, the managers of the scheme,

"trust scheme" means an occupational pension scheme established under a trust.

(2) For the purposes of this Part—

(a) the accrued rights of a member of an occupational pension scheme at any time are the rights which have accrued to or in respect of him at that time to future benefits under the scheme, and

(b) at any time when the pensionable service of a member of an occupational pension scheme is continuing, his accrued rights are to be determined as if he had opted, immediately before that time, to terminate that service;

and references to accrued pension or accrued benefits are to be interpreted accordingly.

[(2A) In subsection (2)(a), the reference to rights which have accrued to or in respect of the member does not include any rights which are pension credit rights.]

(3) In determining what is "pensionable service" for the purposes of this Part—

(a) service notionally attributable for any purpose of the scheme is to be disregarded, and

(b) no account is to be taken of any rules of the scheme by which a period of service can be treated for any purpose as being longer or shorter than it actually is

[but, in its application for the purposes of section 51, paragraph (b) does not affect the operation of any rules of the scheme by virtue of which a period of service is to be rounded up or down by a period of less than a month].

[(3A) In a case of the winding-up of an occupational pension scheme in pursuance of an order of the Authority under section 11 or of an order of a court, the winding-up shall (subject to subsection (3E) [and to sections 28, 154 and 219 of the Pensions Act 2004]) be taken for the purposes of this Part to begin—

(a) if the order provides for a time to be the time when the winding-up begins, at that time; and

(b) in any other case, at the time when the order comes into force.

(3B) In a case of the winding-up of an occupational pension scheme in accordance with a requirement or power contained in the rules of the scheme, the winding-up shall (subject to subsections (3C) to (3E) [and to sections 154 and 219 of the Pensions Act 2004]) be taken for the purposes of this Part to begin—

(a) at the time (if any) which under those rules is the time when the winding-up begins; and

(b) if paragraph (a) does not apply, at the earliest time which is a time fixed by the trustees or managers as the time from which steps for the purposes of the winding-up are to be taken.

(3C) Subsection (3B) shall not require a winding-up of a scheme to be treated as having begun at any time before the end of any period during which effect is being given—

(a) to a determination under section 38 that the scheme is not for the time being to be wound up; or

(b) to a determination in accordance with the rules of the scheme to postpone the commencement of a winding-up.

(3D) In subsection (3B)(b) the reference to the trustees or managers of the scheme shall have effect in relation to any scheme the rules of which provide for a determination that the scheme is to be wound up to be made by persons other than the trustees or managers as including a reference to those other persons.

(3E) Subsections (3A) to (3D) above do not apply for such purposes as may be prescribed.]

(4) In the application of this Part to Scotland, in relation to conviction on indictment, references to imprisonment are to be read as references to imprisonment for a term not exceeding two years.

(5) Subject to the provisions of this Act, expressions used in this Act and in the Pension Schemes Act 1993 have the same meaning in this Act as in that.

[896]

NOTES

Sub-s (1) is amended as follows:

Definition "the Authority" substituted by the Pensions Act 2004, s 7(2)(b), as from 6 April 2005.

Definition "civil partnership status" inserted by the Civil Partnership (Pensions and Benefit Payments) (Consequential, etc Provisions) Order 2005, SI 2005/2053, art 2, Schedule, Pt 4, para 25, as from 5 December 2005.

In definition "employer" words in italics repealed by the Pensions Act 2004, s 320, Sch 13, Pt 1, as from a day to be appointed.

In definition "member" words in square brackets substituted by the Welfare Reform and Pensions Act 1999, s 84(1), Sch 12, Pt I, paras 43, 61(1), (2).

Definitions "member-nominated director" and "member-nominated trustee" (omitted) repealed by the Pensions Act 2004, s 320, Sch 13, Pt 1, as from 6 April 2006.

Definition "the minimum funding requirement" (omitted) repealed by the Pensions Act 2004, s 320, Sch 13, Pt 1, as from 6 April 2007 (for savings see SI 2006/2722, art 3).

Definitions "pension credit", "pension credit member", "pension credit rights" inserted by the Welfare Reform and Pensions Act 1999, s 84(1), Sch 12, Pt I, paras 43, 61(1),(3).

In definition "pensionable service" words in italics repealed by the Pensions Act 2004, s 320, Sch 13, Pt 1, as from a day to be appointed.

In definition "pensioner member" words in square brackets inserted by the Child Support, Pensions and Social Security Act 2000, s 56, Sch 5, Pt I, para 8(3), and repealed by the Taxation of Pension Schemes (Consequential Amendments) Order 2006, SI 2006/745, art 10(1), (7), as from 6 April 2006.

In definition "transfer credits" words in square brackets substituted by the Pensions Act 2004, s 319(1), Sch 12, paras 34, 69(1), (2), as from 6 April 2006.

Sub-s (2A): inserted by the Welfare Reform and Pensions Act 1999, s 84(1), Sch 12, Pt I, paras 43, 61(1), (4).

Sub-s (3): words in square brackets added by the Welfare Reform and Pensions Act 1999, s 18, Sch 2, Pt I, para 18.

Sub-ss (3A), (3B): inserted, together with sub-ss (3C)–(3E), by the Child Support, Pensions and Social Security Act 2000, s 49(2); words in square brackets inserted by the Pensions Act 2004, s 319(1), Sch 12, paras 34, 69(1), (3), (4), as from 6 April 2006.

Sub-ss (3C)–(3E): inserted as noted above.

Transitional provisions: for transitional provisions in connection with the continuity of functions, etc, following the transfer of functions from the Authority to the Regulator, see SI 2005/695, arts 5, 6, Sch 3.

Regulations: the Occupational Pension Schemes (Winding Up Notices and Reports etc) Regulations 2002, SI 2002/459; the Occupational Pension Schemes (Winding Up) (Amendment) Regulations 2004, SI 2004/1140; the Occupational Pension Schemes (Winding up etc) Regulations 2005, SI 2005/706 (all made under sub-s (3E)).

125 Section 124: supplementary

(1) For the purposes of this Part, an occupational pension scheme is salary related if—

(a) the scheme is not a money purchase scheme, and

(b) the scheme does not fall within a prescribed class or description,

and "salary related trust scheme" is to be read accordingly.

(2) Regulations may apply this Part with prescribed modifications to occupational pension schemes—

(a) which are not money purchase schemes, but

(b) where some of the benefits that may be provided are money purchase benefits.

(3) Regulations may, in relation to occupational pension schemes, extend for the purposes of this Part the meaning of "employer" to include[—

(a)] persons who have been the employer in relation to the scheme[;

(b) such other persons as may be prescribed].

(4) For any of the purposes of this Part, regulations may in relation to occupational pension schemes—

(a) extend or restrict the meaning of "member",

(b) determine who is to be treated as a prospective member, and

(c) determine the times at which a person is to be treated as becoming, or as ceasing to be, a member or prospective member.

[897]

NOTES

Sub-s (3): words in square brackets inserted by the Pensions Act 2004, s 240(1), as from a day to be appointed.

Regulations: the Occupational Pension Schemes (Winding Up) Regulations 1996, SI 1996/3126; the Occupational Pension Schemes (Deficiency on Winding Up etc) Regulations 1996, SI 1996/3128; the Occupational Pension Schemes (Reference Scheme and Miscellaneous Amendments) Regulations 1997, SI 1997/819; the Occupational Pension Schemes (Minimum Funding Requirement and Miscellaneous Amendments) Regulations 2002, SI 2002/380; the Occupational Pension Schemes (Employer Debt) Regulations 2005, SI 2005/678; the Occupational Pension Schemes (Independent Trustee) Regulations 2005, SI 2005/703; the Personal and Occupational Pension Schemes (Indexation and Disclosure of Information) (Miscellaneous Amendments) Regulations 2005, SI 2005/704; the Occupational Pension Schemes (Employer Debt etc) (Amendment) Regulations 2005, SI 2005/2224; the Occupational Pension Schemes (Investment) Regulations 2005, SI 2005/3378; the Occupational Pension Schemes (Republic of Ireland Schemes Exemption (Revocation) and Tax Exempt Schemes (Miscellaneous Amendments)) Regulations 2006, SI 2006/467; the Occupational Pension Schemes (Payments to Employer) Regulations 2006, SI 2006/802; the Occupational Pension Schemes (Employer Debt and Miscellaneous Amendments) Regulations 2008, SI 2008/731.

PART IV
MISCELLANEOUS AND SUPPLEMENTAL

General

180 Commencement

(1) Subject to the following provisions, this Act shall come into force on such day as the Secretary of State may by order made by statutory instrument appoint and different days may be appointed for different purposes.

(2)–(4) (*Outside the scope of this work.*)

[898]

NOTES

Orders: the commencement orders relevant to the sections of the Act reproduced here are the Pensions Act 1995 (Commencement No 2) Order 1995, SI 1995/3104; the Pensions Act 1995 (Commencement No 3) Order 1996, SI 1996/778; the Pensions Act 1995 (Commencement No 8) Order 1996, SI 1996/2637; the Pensions Act 1995 (Commencement No 10) Order 1997, SI 1997/664.

181 Short title

This Act may be cited as the Pensions Act 1995.

[899]

DISABILITY DISCRIMINATION ACT 1995

(1995 c 50)

ARRANGEMENT OF SECTIONS

PART I
DISABILITY

PART II
THE EMPLOYMENT FIELD AND MEMBERS OF LOCALLY-ELECTABLE AUTHORITIES

Meaning of "discrimination" and "harassment"

Employment

Contract workers

Office-holders

Occupational pension schemes

Partnerships

Barristers and advocates

Trade and professional bodies

Practical work experience

Relationships between locally-electable authorities and their members

Other unlawful acts

Enforcement etc

Supplementary and general

PART III
DISCRIMINATION IN OTHER AREAS

Goods, facilities and services

Public authorities

Enforcement, etc

PART 5A
PUBLIC AUTHORITIES

PART VII
SUPPLEMENTAL

PART VIII
MISCELLANEOUS

SCHEDULES:

An Act to make it unlawful to discriminate against disabled persons in connection with employment, the provision of goods, facilities and services or the disposal or management of premises; to make provision about the employment of disabled persons; and to establish a National Disability Council

[8 November 1995]

NOTES

In so far as still in force, this Act is reproduced in full except for ss 21F–21J in Pt III (discrimination in relation to private clubs); ss 22–24M, 27 in Pt III (discrimination in relation to premises); Pt IV (ie, ss 28A–31C: education); Pt V (ie, ss 32–49: public transport); Pt 5B (ie, ss 49G–49I: improvements to dwelling houses); ss 67A and 67B in Pt VIII (Exercise of discretion under section 67(5A) and Annual report on rail vehicle exemption orders). The Schedules introduced by the sections listed *ante* are also omitted as outside the scope of this work, as well as Schs 6, 7 (consequential amendments and repeals), and Sch 8 (modification of provisions in their application to Northern Ireland). Note also that amendments made to this Act by the Special Educational Needs and Disability (Northern Ireland) Order 2005, SI 2005/1117 (NI 6) and the Disability Discrimination (Northern Ireland) Order 2006, SI 2006/312 (NI 1) that apply to Northern Ireland only are not reproduced.

Employment Appeal Tribunal: an appeal lies to the Employment Appeal Tribunal on any question of law arising from any decision of, or in any proceedings before, an employment tribunal under or by virtue of this Act; see the Employment Tribunals Act 1996, s 21(1)(e) at **[978]**.

For Regulations relevant to the employment provisions of the Act, see the Disability Discrimination (Meaning of Disability) Regulations 1996, SI 1996/1455 at **[2330]**, and the Disability Discrimination (Employment Field) (Leasehold Premises) Regulations 2004, SI 2004/153 at **[3074]**.

The Codes of Practice issued under s 53 have been replaced by new Codes issued under s 53A; see the Disability Rights Commission Code of Practice on Employment and Occupation at **[4662]**, and the Disability Rights Commission Code of Practice for Trade Organisations and Qualifications Bodies at **[4678]**. For the Guidance issued under s 3 see **[4756]**.

Regulatory functions: the regulatory functions conferred by, or under, this Act are subject to the Legislative and Regulatory Reform Act 2006, ss 21, 22 at **[1783]**, **[1784]**; see the Legislative and Regulatory Reform (Regulatory Functions) Order 2007, SI 2007/3544 (made under s 24(2) of the 2006 Act) for details.

See *Harvey* L3, Q, R, S10, S11.

PART I
DISABILITY

1 Meaning of "disability" and "disabled person"

(1) Subject to the provisions of Schedule 1, a person has a disability for the purposes of this Act if he has a physical or mental impairment which has a substantial and long-term adverse effect on his ability to carry out normal day-to-day activities.

(2) In this Act "disabled person" means a person who has a disability.

[900]

2 Past disabilities

(1) The provisions of this Part and Parts II [to 4] [and 5A] apply in relation to a person who has had a disability as they apply in relation to a person who has that disability.

(2) Those provisions are subject to the modifications made by Schedule 2.

(3) Any regulations or order made under this Act [by the Secretary of State, the Scottish Ministers or the [Welsh Ministers]] may include provision with respect to persons who have had a disability.

(4) In any proceedings under Part [2, 3, 4 or 5A]of this Act, the question whether a person had a disability at a particular time ("the relevant time") shall be determined, for the purposes of this section, as if the provisions of, or made under, this Act in force when the act complained of was done had been in force at the relevant time.

(5) The relevant time may be a time before the passing of this Act.

[901]

NOTES

Sub-s (1): words in first pair of square brackets substituted by the Special Educational Needs and Disability Act 2001, s 38(1), (2)(a); words in second pair of square brackets inserted by the Disability Discrimination Act 2005, s 19(1), Sch 1, Pt 1, paras 1, 2(1), (2), as from 5 December 2005.

Sub-s (3): words in first (outer) pair of square brackets inserted by the Disability Discrimination Act 2005, s 19(1), Sch 1, Pt 1, paras 1, 2(1), (3), as from 30 June 2005; words in second (inner) pair of square brackets substituted by the Government of Wales Act 2006 (Consequential Modifications and Transitional Provisions) Order 2007, SI 2007/1388, art 3, Sch 1, paras 47, 48, as from 25 May 2007.

Sub-s (4): words in square brackets substituted by the Disability Discrimination Act 2005, s 19(1), Sch 1, Pt 1, paras 1, 2(1), (4), as from 4 December 2006.

3 Guidance

[(A1) The Secretary of State may issue guidance about matters to be taken into account in determining whether a person is a disabled person.]

(1) [Without prejudice to the generality of subsection (A1),] the Secretary of State may[, in particular,] issue guidance about the matters to be taken into account in determining—
- (a) whether an impairment has a substantial adverse effect on a person's ability to carry out normal day-to-day activities; or
- (b) whether such an impairment has a long-term effect.

(2) [Without prejudice to the generality of subsection (A1), guidance about the matters mentioned in subsection (1)] may, among other things, give examples of—
- (a) effects which it would be reasonable, in relation to particular activities, to regard for purposes of this Act as substantial adverse effects;
- (b) effects which it would not be reasonable, in relation to particular activities, to regard for such purposes as substantial adverse effects;
- (c) substantial adverse effects which it would be reasonable to regard, for such purposes, as long-term;
- (d) substantial adverse effects which it would not be reasonable to regard, for such purposes, as long-term.

(3) [An adjudicating body] determining, for any purpose of this Act, whether [a person is a disabled person], shall take into account any guidance which appears to it to be relevant.

[(3A) "Adjudicating body" means—
- (a) a court;
- (b) a tribunal; and

(c) any other person who, or body which, may decide a claim under Part 4.]

(4) In preparing a draft of any guidance, the Secretary of State shall consult such persons as he considers appropriate.

(5) Where the Secretary of State proposes to issue any guidance, he shall publish a draft of it, consider any representations that are made to him about the draft and, if he thinks it appropriate, modify his proposals in the light of any of those representations.

(6) If the Secretary of State decides to proceed with any proposed guidance, he shall lay a draft of it before each House of Parliament.

(7) If, within the 40-day period, either House resolves not to approve the draft, the Secretary of State shall take no further steps in relation to the proposed guidance.

(8) If no such resolution is made within the 40-day period, the Secretary of State shall issue the guidance in the form of his draft.

(9) The guidance shall come into force on such date as the Secretary of State may appoint by order.

(10) Subsection (7) does not prevent a new draft of the proposed guidance from being laid before Parliament.

(11) The Secretary of State may—

(a) from time to time revise the whole or part of any guidance and re-issue it;

(b) by order revoke any guidance.

(12) In this section—

"40-day period", in relation to the draft of any proposed guidance, means—

(a) if the draft is laid before one House on a day later than the day on which it is laid before the other House, the period of 40 days beginning with the later of the two days, and

(b) in any other case, the period of 40 days beginning with the day on which the draft is laid before each House,

no account being taken of any period during which Parliament is dissolved or prorogued or during which both Houses are adjourned for more than 4 days; and

"guidance" means guidance issued by the Secretary of State under this section and includes guidance which has been revised and re-issued.

[902]

NOTES

Sub-s (A1): inserted by the Disability Discrimination Act 2005, s 19(1), Sch 1, Pt 1, paras 1, 3(1), (2), as from 30 June 2005.

Sub-s (1): words in square brackets inserted by the Disability Discrimination Act 2005, s 19(1), Sch 1, Pt 1, paras 1, 3(1), (3), as from 30 June 2005.

Sub-s (2): words in square brackets substituted by the Disability Discrimination Act 2005, s 19(1), Sch 1, Pt 1, paras 1, 3(1), (4), as from 30 June 2005.

Sub-s (3): words in first pair of square brackets substituted by the Special Educational Needs and Disability Act 2001, s 38(1), (3); words in second pair of square brackets substituted by the Disability Discrimination Act 2005, s 19(1), Sch 1, Pt 1, paras 1, 3(1), (5), as from 5 December 2005.

Sub-s (3A): inserted by the Special Educational Needs and Disability Act 2001, s 38(1), (4).

Guidance issued under this section: see the Guidance on matters to be taken into account in determining questions relating to the definition of disability (2006) at **[4756]**.

Orders: the Disability Discrimination (Guidance on the Definition of Disability) Appointed Day Order 2006, SI 2006/1005 (appointing 1 May 2006 as the date on which the above Guidance is to have effect); the Disability Discrimination (Guidance on the Definition of Disability) Revocation Order 2006, SI 2006/1007 (revoking, with effect from 1 May 2006, the 1996 Guidance on matters to be taken into account in determining questions relating to the definition of disability).

PART II
[THE EMPLOYMENT FIELD] [AND MEMBERS OF LOCALLY-ELECTABLE AUTHORITIES]

NOTES

This Part is reproduced as amended by the Disability Discrimination Act 1995 (Amendment) Regulations 2003, SI 2003/1673 at **[3032]**, the Disability Discrimination Act 1995 (Pensions) Regulations 2003, SI 2003/2770 at **[3036]**, and the Disability Discrimination Act 2005. The substantive provisions of both sets of 2003 Regulations came into force on 1 October 2004 (there was a limited commencement before that date for the purposes of preparing and bringing into force codes of practice under s 53A of this Act but there were no other transitional provisions except as specifically noted below). The 2003 Regulations implement provisions of Council Directive 2000/78/EC establishing a general framework for equal treatment in employment and occupation at **[3994]**, in so far as the Directive relates to disability discrimination.

Serious Organised Crime Agency: for the application of this Part to a constable or other person seconded to SOCA as a member of its staff, see the Serious Organised Crime and Police Act 2005, s 56(1), (2).

Part heading: words in first pair of square brackets substituted by the Disability Discrimination Act 1995 (Amendment) Regulations 2003, SI 2003/1673, regs 3(1), 4(1), as from 1 October 2004; words in second pair of square brackets inserted by the Disability Discrimination Act 2005, s 19(1), Sch 1, Pt 1, paras 1, 4, as from 5 December 2005.

[Meaning of "discrimination" and "harassment"

3A Meaning of "discrimination"

(1) For the purposes of this Part, a person discriminates against a disabled person if—

(a) for a reason which relates to the disabled person's disability, he treats him less favourably than he treats or would treat others to whom that reason does not or would not apply, and

(b) he cannot show that the treatment in question is justified.

(2) For the purposes of this Part, a person also discriminates against a disabled person if he fails to comply with a duty to make reasonable adjustments imposed on him in relation to the disabled person.

(3) Treatment is justified for the purposes of subsection (1)(b) if, but only if, the reason for it is both material to the circumstances of the particular case and substantial.

(4) But treatment of a disabled person cannot be justified under subsection (3) if it amounts to direct discrimination falling within subsection (5).

(5) A person directly discriminates against a disabled person if, on the ground of the disabled person's disability, he treats the disabled person less favourably than he treats or would treat a person not having that particular disability whose relevant circumstances, including his abilities, are the same as, or not materially different from, those of the disabled person.

(6) If, in a case falling within subsection (1), a person is under a duty to make reasonable adjustments in relation to a disabled person but fails to comply with that duty, his treatment of that person cannot be justified under subsection (3) unless it would have been justified even if he had complied with that duty.]

[902A]

NOTES

Commencement: 1 October 2004.

Inserted, together with the preceding heading and s 3B, by the Disability Discrimination Act 1995 (Amendment) Regulations 2003, SI 2003/1673, regs 3(1), 4(2), as from 1 October 2004.

[3B Meaning of "harassment"

(1) For the purposes of this Part, a person subjects a disabled person to harassment where, for a reason which relates to the disabled person's disability, he engages in unwanted conduct which has the purpose or effect of—

(a) violating the disabled person's dignity, or

(b) creating an intimidating, hostile, degrading, humiliating or offensive environment for him.

(2) Conduct shall be regarded as having the effect referred to in paragraph (a) or (b) of subsection (1) only if, having regard to all the circumstances, including in particular the perception of the disabled person, it should reasonably be considered as having that effect.]

[902B]

NOTES

Commencement: 1 October 2004.

Inserted as noted to s 3A at **[902A]**.

[Employment

4 Employers: discrimination and harassment

(1) It is unlawful for an employer to discriminate against a disabled person—

(a) in the arrangements which he makes for the purpose of determining to whom he should offer employment;

(b) in the terms on which he offers that person employment; or

(c) by refusing to offer, or deliberately not offering, him employment.

(2) It is unlawful for an employer to discriminate against a disabled person whom he employs—

(a) in the terms of employment which he affords him;

(b) in the opportunities which he affords him for promotion, a transfer, training or receiving any other benefit;

(c) by refusing to afford him, or deliberately not affording him, any such opportunity; or

(d) by dismissing him, or subjecting him to any other detriment.

(3) It is also unlawful for an employer, in relation to employment by him, to subject to harassment—

(a) a disabled person whom he employs; or

(b) a disabled person who has applied to him for employment.

(4) Subsection (2) does not apply to benefits of any description if the employer is concerned with the provision (whether or not for payment) of benefits of that description to the public, or to a section of the public which includes the employee in question, unless—

(a) that provision differs in a material respect from the provision of the benefits by the employer to his employees;

(b) the provision of the benefits to the employee in question is regulated by his contract of employment; or

(c) the benefits relate to training.

(5) The reference in subsection (2)(d) to the dismissal of a person includes a reference—

(a) to the termination of that person's employment by the expiration of any period (including a period expiring by reference to an event or circumstance), not being a termination immediately after which the employment is renewed on the same terms; and

(b) to the termination of that person's employment by any act of his (including the giving of notice) in circumstances such that he is entitled to terminate it without notice by reason of the conduct of the employer.

(6) This section applies only in relation to employment at an establishment in Great Britain.]

[903]

NOTES

Commencement: 1 October 2004.

Substituted, together with the preceding heading and ss 4A–4F for the original ss 4–6, by the Disability Discrimination Act 1995 (Amendment) Regulations 2003, SI 2003/1673, regs 3(1), 5, as from 1 October 2004.

Modified, in relation to governing bodies with delegated budgets, by the Education (Modification of Enactments Relating to Employment) (England) Order 2003, SI 2003/1964, art 3, Schedule at **[3035C]**, **[3035G]** and the Education (Modification of Enactments Relating to Employment) (Wales) Order 2006, SI 2006/1073, art 3, Schedule at **[3462B]**, **[3462F]**. Note, however, that there has been no amendment to SI 2003/1964 to reflect the changes in the numbering of sections of this Act by SI 2003/1673 (which substituted ss 4, 4A–4F for the original ss 4, 5, 6), nor the insertion of ss 4G–4K by SI 2003/2770. It is therefore unclear which sections of this Act are actually modified. The 2006 Order (made after the substitutions and insertions noted *ante*) stipulates that ss 4–6, 11, 12, 16, 55, 57 and 58 of the 1995 Act are modified (the same sections as in the 2003 Order).

[4A Employers: duty to make adjustments

(1) Where—

(a) a provision, criterion or practice applied by or on behalf of an employer, or

(b) any physical feature of premises occupied by the employer,

places the disabled person concerned at a substantial disadvantage in comparison with persons who are not disabled, it is the duty of the employer to take such steps as it is reasonable, in all the circumstances of the case, for him to have to take in order to prevent the provision, criterion or practice, or feature, having that effect.

(2) In subsection (1), "the disabled person concerned" means—

(a) in the case of a provision, criterion or practice for determining to whom employment should be offered, any disabled person who is, or has notified the employer that he may be, an applicant for that employment;

(b) in any other case, a disabled person who is—

(i) an applicant for the employment concerned, or

(ii) an employee of the employer concerned.

(3) Nothing in this section imposes any duty on an employer in relation to a disabled person if the employer does not know, and could not reasonably be expected to know—

(a) in the case of an applicant or potential applicant, that the disabled person concerned is, or may be, an applicant for the employment; or

(b) in any case, that that person has a disability and is likely to be affected in the way mentioned in subsection (1).]

[903A]

NOTES

Commencement: 1 October 2004.
Substituted as noted to s 4 at **[903]**.
Modification: see the note to s 4 at **[903]**.

[Contract workers

4B Contract workers

(1) It is unlawful for a principal, in relation to contract work, to discriminate against a disabled person who is a contract worker (a "disabled contract worker")—

(a) in the terms on which he allows him to do that work;

(b) by not allowing him to do it or continue to do it;

(c) in the way he affords him access to any benefits or by refusing or deliberately omitting to afford him access to them; or

(d) by subjecting him to any other detriment.

(2) It is also unlawful for a principal, in relation to contract work, to subject a disabled contract worker to harassment.

(3) Subsection (1) does not apply to benefits of any description if the principal is concerned with the provision (whether or not for payment) of benefits of that description to the public, or to a section of the public which includes the contract worker in question, unless that provision differs in a material respect from the provision of the benefits by the principal to contract workers.

(4) This subsection applies to a disabled contract worker where, by virtue of—

(a) a provision, criterion or practice applied by or on behalf of all or most of the principals to whom he is or might be supplied, or

(b) a physical feature of premises occupied by such persons,

he is likely, on each occasion when he is supplied to a principal to do contract work, to be placed at a substantial disadvantage in comparison with persons who are not disabled which is the same or similar in each case.

(5) Where subsection (4) applies to a disabled contract worker, his employer must take such steps as he would have to take under section 4A if the provision, criterion or practice were applied by him or on his behalf or (as the case may be) if the premises were occupied by him.

(6) Section 4A applies to any principal, in relation to contract work, as if he were, or would be, the employer of the disabled contract worker and as if any contract worker supplied to do work for him were an employee of his.

(7) However, for the purposes of section 4A as applied by subsection (6), a principal is not required to take a step in relation to a disabled contract worker if under that section the disabled contract worker's employer is required to take the step in relation to him.

(8) This section applies only in relation to contract work done at an establishment in Great Britain (the provisions of section 68 about the meaning of "employment at an establishment in Great Britain" applying for the purposes of this subsection with the appropriate modifications).

(9) In this section—

"principal" means a person ("A") who makes work available for doing by individuals who are employed by another person who supplies them under a contract made with A;

"contract work" means work so made available; and

"contract worker" means any individual who is supplied to the principal under such a contract.]

[903B]

NOTES

Commencement: 1 October 2004.

Substituted as noted to s 4 at **[903]**.

Modification: see the note to s 4 at **[903]**.

[Office-holders

4C Office-holders: introductory

(1) Subject to subsection (5), sections 4D and 4E apply to an office or post if—

(a) no relevant provision of this Part applies in relation to an appointment to the office or post; and

(b) one or more of the conditions specified in subsection (3) is satisfied.

(2) The following are relevant provisions of this Part for the purposes of subsection (1)(a): section 4, section 4B, section 6A, section 7A, section 7C[, section 14C and section 15B(3)(b)].

(3) The conditions specified in this subsection are that—

(a) the office or post is one to which persons are appointed to discharge functions personally under the direction of another person, and in respect of which they are entitled to remuneration;

(b) the office or post is one to which appointments are made by a Minister of the Crown, a government department, the [Welsh Ministers, the First Minister for Wales, the Counsel General to the Welsh Assembly Government] or any part of the Scottish Administration;

(c) the office or post is one to which appointments are made on the recommendation of, or subject to the approval of, a person referred to in paragraph (b).

(4) For the purposes of subsection (3)(a) the holder of an office or post—

(a) is to be regarded as discharging his functions under the direction of another person if that other person is entitled to direct him as to when and where he discharges those functions;

(b) is not to be regarded as entitled to remuneration merely because he is entitled to payments—

(i) in respect of expenses incurred by him in carrying out the functions of the office or post, or

(ii) by way of compensation for the loss of income or benefits he would or might have received from any person had he not been carrying out the functions of the office or post.

(5) Sections 4D and 4E do not apply to—

(a) any office of the House of Commons held by a member of it,

(b) a life peerage within the meaning of the Life Peerages Act 1958, or any office of the House of Lords held by a member of it,

(c) any office mentioned in Schedule 2 (Ministerial offices) to the House of Commons Disqualification Act 1975,

(d) the offices of Leader of the Opposition, Chief Opposition Whip or Assistant Opposition Whip within the meaning of the Ministerial and other Salaries Act 1975,

(e) any office of the Scottish Parliament held by a member of it,

(f) a member of the Scottish Executive within the meaning of section 44 of the Scotland Act 1998, or a junior Scottish Minister within the meaning of section 49 of that Act,

(g) any office of the National Assembly for Wales held by a member of it,

[(ga) a member of the Welsh Assembly Government,]

(h) in England, any office of a county council, a London borough council, a district council or a parish council held by a member of it,

(i) in Wales, any office of a county council, a county borough council or a community council held by a member of it,

(j) in relation to a council constituted under section 2 of the Local Government etc (Scotland) Act 1994 or a community council established under section 51 of the Local Government (Scotland) Act 1973, any office of such a council held by a member of it,

(k) any office of the Greater London Authority held by a member of it,

(l) any office of the Common Council of the City of London held by a member of it,

(m) any office of the Council of the Isles of Scilly held by a member of it, or

(n) any office of a political party.]

[903C]

NOTES

Commencement: 1 October 2004.

Substituted as noted to s 4 at **[903]**.

Sub-s (2): words in square brackets substituted by the Disability Discrimination Act 2005, s 19(1), Sch 1, Pt 1, paras 1, 5, as from 5 December 2005.

Sub-s (3): words in square brackets in para (b) substituted by the Government of Wales Act 2006 (Consequential Modifications and Transitional Provisions) Order 2007, SI 2007/1388, art 3, Sch 1, paras 47, 49(1), (2), as from 25 May 2007.

Sub-s (5): para (ga) inserted by SI 2007/1388, art 3, Sch 1, paras 47, 49(1), (3), as from 25 May 2007.

Modification: see the note to s 4 at **[903]**.

4D Office-holders: discrimination and harassment

(1) It is unlawful for a relevant person, in relation to an appointment to an office or post to which this section applies, to discriminate against a disabled person—

(a) in the arrangements which he makes for the purpose of determining who should be offered the appointment;

(b) in the terms on which he offers him the appointment; or

(c) by refusing to offer him the appointment.

(2) It is unlawful for a relevant person, in relation to an appointment to an office or post to which this section applies and which satisfies the condition set out in section 4C(3)(c), to discriminate against a disabled person—

(a) in the arrangements which he makes for the purpose of determining who should be recommended or approved in relation to the appointment; or

(b) in making or refusing to make a recommendation, or giving or refusing to give an approval, in relation to the appointment.

(3) It is unlawful for a relevant person, in relation to a disabled person who has been appointed to an office or post to which this section applies, to discriminate against him—

(a) in the terms of the appointment;

(b) in the opportunities which he affords him for promotion, a transfer, training or receiving any other benefit, or by refusing to afford him any such opportunity;

(c) by terminating the appointment; or

(d) by subjecting him to any other detriment in relation to the appointment.

(4) It is also unlawful for a relevant person, in relation to an office or post to which this section applies, to subject to harassment a disabled person—

(a) who has been appointed to the office or post;

(b) who is seeking or being considered for appointment to the office or post; or

(c) who is seeking or being considered for a recommendation or approval in relation to an appointment to an office or post satisfying the condition set out in section 4C(3)(c).

(5) Subsection (3) does not apply to benefits of any description if the relevant person is concerned with the provision (for payment or not) of benefits of that description to the public, or a section of the public to which the disabled person belongs, unless—

(a) that provision differs in a material respect from the provision of the benefits to persons appointed to offices or posts which are the same as, or not materially different from, that to which the disabled person has been appointed;

(b) the provision of the benefits to the person appointed is regulated by the terms and conditions of his appointment; or

(c) the benefits relate to training.

(6) In subsection (3)(c) the reference to the termination of the appointment includes a reference—

(a) to the termination of the appointment by the expiration of any period (including a period expiring by reference to an event or circumstance), not being a termination immediately after which the appointment is renewed on the same terms and conditions; and

(b) to the termination of the appointment by any act of the person appointed (including the giving of notice) in circumstances such that he is entitled to terminate the appointment by reason of the conduct of the relevant person.

(7) In this section—

(a) references to making a recommendation include references to making a negative recommendation; and

(b) references to refusal include references to deliberate omission.] **[903D]**

NOTES

Commencement: 1 October 2004.
Substituted as noted to s 4 at **[903]**.
Modification: see the note to s 4 at **[903]**.

[4E Office-holders: duty to make adjustments

(1) Where—

(a) a provision, criterion or practice applied by or on behalf of a relevant person, or

(b) any physical feature of premises—

(i) under the control of a relevant person, and

(ii) at or from which the functions of an office or post to which this section applies are performed,

places the disabled person concerned at a substantial disadvantage in comparison with persons who are not disabled, it is the duty of the relevant person to take such steps as it is reasonable, in all the circumstances of the case, for him to have to take in order to prevent the provision, criterion or practice, or feature, having that effect.

(2) In this section, "the disabled person concerned" means—

(a) in the case of a provision, criterion or practice for determining who should be appointed to, or recommended or approved in relation to, an office or post to which this section applies, any disabled person who—

(i) is, or has notified the relevant person that he may be, seeking appointment to, or (as the case may be) seeking a recommendation or approval in relation to, that office or post, or

(ii) is being considered for appointment to, or (as the case may be) for a recommendation or approval in relation to, that office or post;

(b) in any other case, a disabled person—

(i) who is seeking or being considered for appointment to, or a recommendation or approval in relation to, the office or post concerned, or

(ii) who has been appointed to the office or post concerned.

(3) Nothing in this section imposes any duty on the relevant person in relation to a disabled person if the relevant person does not know, and could not reasonably be expected to know—

(a) in the case of a person who is being considered for, or is or may be seeking, appointment to, or a recommendation or approval in relation to, an office or post, that the disabled person concerned—

(i) is, or may be, seeking appointment to, or (as the case may be) seeking a recommendation or approval in relation to, that office or post, or

(ii) is being considered for appointment to, or (as the case may be) for a recommendation or approval in relation to, that office or post; or

(b) in any case, that that person has a disability and is likely to be affected in the way mentioned in subsection (1).]

[903E]

NOTES

Commencement: 1 October 2004.
Substituted as noted to s 4 at **[903]**.
Modification: see the note to s 4 at **[903]**.

[4F Office-holders: supplementary

(1) In sections 4C to 4E, appointment to an office or post does not include election to an office or post.

(2) In sections 4D and 4E, "relevant person" means—

(a) in a case relating to an appointment to an office or post, the person with power to make that appointment;

(b) in a case relating to the making of a recommendation or the giving of an approval in relation to an appointment, a person or body referred to in section 4C(3)(b) with power to make that recommendation or (as the case may be) to give that approval;

(c) in a case relating to a term of an appointment, the person with power to determine that term;

(d) in a case relating to a working condition afforded in relation to an appointment—

(i) the person with power to determine that working condition; or

(ii) where there is no such person, the person with power to make the appointment;

(e) in a case relating to the termination of an appointment, the person with power to terminate the appointment;

(f) in a case relating to the subjection of a disabled person to any other detriment or to harassment, any person or body falling within one or more of paragraphs (a) to (e) in relation to such cases as are there mentioned.

(3) In subsection (2)(d), "working condition" includes—

(a) any opportunity for promotion, a transfer, training or receiving any other benefit; and

(b) any physical feature of premises at or from which the functions of an office or post are performed.]

[903F]

NOTES

Commencement: 1 October 2004.
Substituted as noted to s 4 at **[903]**.
Modification: see the note to s 4 at **[903]**.

[Occupational pension schemes

4G Occupational pension schemes: non-discrimination rule

(1) Every occupational pension scheme shall be taken to include a provision ("the non-discrimination rule") containing the following requirements—

(a) a requirement that the trustees or managers of the scheme refrain from discriminating against a relevant disabled person in carrying out any of their functions in relation to the scheme (including in particular their functions relating to the admission of members to the scheme and the treatment of members of the scheme);

(b) a requirement that the trustees or managers of the scheme do not subject a relevant disabled person to harassment in relation to the scheme.

(2) The other provisions of the scheme are to have effect subject to the non-discrimination rule.

(3) It is unlawful for the trustees or managers of an occupational pension scheme—

(a) to discriminate against a relevant disabled person contrary to requirement (a) of the non-discrimination rule; or

(b) to subject a relevant disabled person to harassment contrary to requirement (b) of the non-discrimination rule.

(4) The non-discrimination rule does not apply in relation to rights accrued, or benefits payable, in respect of periods of service prior to the coming into force of this section (but it does apply to communications with members or prospective members of the scheme in relation to such rights or benefits).

(5) The trustees or managers of an occupational pension scheme may, if—

(a) they do not (apart from this subsection) have power to make such alterations to the scheme as may be required to secure conformity with the non-discrimination rule, or

(b) they have such power but the procedure for doing so—

(i) is liable to be unduly complex or protracted, or

(ii) involves the obtaining of consents which cannot be obtained, or can only be obtained with undue delay or difficulty,

by resolution make such alterations to the scheme.

(6) The alterations referred to in subsection (5) may have effect in relation to a period before the alterations are made (but may not have effect in relation to a period before the coming into force of this section).]

[903G]

NOTES

Commencement: 1 October 2004.

Inserted, together with the preceding heading and ss 4H–4K, by the Disability Discrimination Act 1995 (Pensions) Regulations 2003, SI 2003/2770, regs 2, 3, as from 1 October 2004.

Modification: see the note to s 4 at **[903]**.

[4H Occupational pension schemes: duty to make adjustments

(1) Where—

(a) a provision, criterion or practice (including a scheme rule) applied by or on behalf of the trustees or managers of an occupational pension scheme, or

(b) any physical feature of premises occupied by the trustees or managers,

places a relevant disabled person at a substantial disadvantage in comparison with persons who are not disabled, it is the duty of the trustees or managers to take such steps as it is reasonable, in all the circumstances of the case, for them to have to take in order to prevent the provision, criterion or practice, or feature, having that effect.

(2) The making of alterations to scheme rules is (in addition to the examples set out in section 18B(2)) an example of a step which trustees or managers may have to take in order to comply with the duty set out in subsection (1).

(3) Nothing in subsection (1) imposes any duty on trustees or managers in relation to a disabled person if they do not know, and could not reasonably be expected to know—

(a) that the disabled person is a relevant disabled person; or

(b) that that person has a disability and is likely to be affected in the way mentioned in subsection (1).]

[903H]

NOTES

Commencement: 1 October 2004.

Inserted as noted to s 4G at **[903G]**.

Modification: see the note to s 4 at **[903]**.

[4I Occupational pension schemes: procedure

(1) Where under section 17A a relevant disabled person presents a complaint to an employment tribunal that the trustees or managers of an occupational pension scheme have acted in relation to him in a way which is unlawful under this Part, the employer in relation to that scheme shall, for the purposes of the rules governing procedure, be treated as a party and be entitled to appear and be heard in accordance with those rules.

(2) In this section, "employer", in relation to an occupational pension scheme, has the meaning given by section 124(1) of the Pensions Act 1995 as at the date of coming into force of this section.]

[903I]

NOTES

Commencement: 1 October 2004.
Inserted as noted to s 4G at **[903G]**.
Modification: see the note to s 4 at **[903]**.

[4J Occupational pension schemes: remedies

(1) This section applies where—

(a) under section 17A a relevant disabled person presents to an employment tribunal a complaint that—

(i) the trustees or managers of an occupational pension scheme have acted in relation to him in a way which is unlawful under this Part; or

(ii) an employer has so acted in relation to him;

(b) the complaint relates to—

(i) the terms on which persons become members of an occupational pension scheme, or

(ii) the terms on which members of the scheme are treated;

(c) the disabled person is not a pensioner member of the scheme; and

(d) the tribunal finds that the complaint is well-founded.

(2) The tribunal may, without prejudice to the generality of its power under section 17A(2)(a), make a declaration that the complainant has a right—

(a) (where subsection (1)(b)(i) applies) to be admitted to the scheme in question; or

(b) (where subsection (1)(b)(ii) applies) to membership of the scheme without discrimination.

(3) A declaration under subsection (2)—

(a) may be made in respect of such period as the declaration may specify (but may not be made in respect of any period before the coming into force of this section);

(b) may make such provision as the tribunal considers appropriate as to the terms upon which, or the capacity in which, the disabled person is to enjoy such admission or membership.

(4) The tribunal may not award the disabled person any compensation under section 17A(2)(b) (whether in relation to arrears of benefits or otherwise) other than—

(a) compensation for injury to feelings;

(b) compensation pursuant to section 17A(5).]

[903J]

NOTES

Commencement: 1 October 2004.
Inserted as noted to s 4G at **[903G]**.
Modification: see the note to s 4 at **[903]**.

[4K Occupational pension schemes: supplementary

(1) In their application to communications, sections 4G to 4J apply in relation to a disabled person who is—

(a) entitled to the present payment of dependants' or survivors' benefits under an occupational pension scheme; or

(b) a pension credit member of such a scheme,

as they apply in relation to a disabled person who is a pensioner member of the scheme.

(2) In sections 4G to 4J and in this section—

"active member", "deferred member", "managers", "pension credit member", "pensioner member" and "trustees or managers" have the meanings given by section 124(1) of the Pensions Act 1995 as at the date of coming into force of this section;

"communications" includes—

(i) the provision of information, and

(ii) the operation of a dispute resolution procedure;

"member", in relation to an occupational pension scheme, means any active, deferred or pensioner member;

"non-discrimination rule" means the rule in section 4G(1);

"relevant disabled person", in relation to an occupational pension scheme, means a disabled person who is a member or prospective member of the scheme; and

"prospective member" means any person who, under the terms of his contract of employment or the scheme rules or both—

(i) is able, at his own option, to become a member of the scheme,

(ii) will become so able if he continues in the same employment for a sufficiently long period,

(iii) will be admitted to it automatically unless he makes an election not to become a member, or

(iv) may be admitted to it subject to the consent of his employer.]

[903K]

NOTES

Commencement: 1 October 2004.

Inserted as noted to s 4G at **[903G]**.

Modification: see the note to s 4 at **[903]**.

5, 6 (*Substituted as noted to s 4* at **[903]**.)

[Partnerships

6A Partnerships: discrimination and harassment

(1) It is unlawful for a firm, in relation to a position as partner in the firm, to discriminate against a disabled person—

(a) in the arrangements which they make for the purpose of determining who should be offered that position;

(b) in the terms on which they offer him that position;

(c) by refusing or deliberately omitting to offer him that position; or

(d) in a case where the person already holds that position—

(i) in the way they afford him access to any benefits or by refusing or deliberately omitting to afford him access to them; or

(ii) by expelling him from that position, or subjecting him to any other detriment.

(2) It is also unlawful for a firm, in relation to a position as partner in the firm, to subject to harassment a disabled person who holds or has applied for that position.

(3) Subsection (1) does not apply to benefits of any description if the firm are concerned with the provision (whether or not for payment) of benefits of that description to the public, or to a section of the public which includes the partner in question, unless that provision differs in a material respect from the provision of the benefits to other partners.

(4) The reference in subsection (1)(d)(ii) to the expulsion of a person from a position as partner includes a reference—

(a) to the termination of that person's partnership by the expiration of any period (including a period expiring by reference to an event or circumstance), not being a termination immediately after which the partnership is renewed on the same terms; and

(b) to the termination of that person's partnership by any act of his (including the giving of notice) in circumstances such that he is entitled to terminate it without notice by reason of the conduct of the other partners.]

[904]

NOTES

Commencement: 1 October 2004.

Inserted, together with the preceding heading and ss 6B, 6C, by the Disability Discrimination Act 1995 (Amendment) Regulations 2003, SI 2003/1673, regs 3(1), 6, as from 1 October 2004.

[6B Partnerships: duty to make adjustments

(1) Where—

(a) a provision, criterion or practice applied by or on behalf of a firm, or

(b) any physical feature of premises occupied by the firm,

places the disabled person concerned at a substantial disadvantage in comparison with persons who are not disabled, it is the duty of the firm to take such steps as it is reasonable, in all the circumstances of the case, for them to have to take in order to prevent the provision, criterion or practice, or feature, having that effect.

(2) In this section, "the disabled person concerned" means—

(a) in the case of a provision, criterion or practice for determining to whom the position of partner should be offered, any disabled person who is, or has notified the firm that he may be, a candidate for that position;

(b) in any other case, a disabled person who is—

(i) a partner, or

(ii) a candidate for the position of partner.

(3) Nothing in this section imposes any duty on a firm in relation to a disabled person if the firm do not know, and could not reasonably be expected to know—

(a) in the case of a candidate or potential candidate, that the disabled person concerned is, or may be, a candidate for the position of partner; or

(b) in any case, that that person has a disability and is likely to be affected in the way mentioned in subsection (1).

(4) Where a firm are required by this section to take any steps in relation to the disabled person concerned, the cost of taking those steps shall be treated as an expense of the firm; and the extent to which such cost should be borne by that person, where he is or becomes a partner in the firm, shall not exceed such amount as is reasonable, having regard in particular to the proportion in which he is entitled to share in the firm's profits.]

[905]

NOTES

Commencement: 1 October 2004.
Inserted as noted to s 6A at **[904]**.

[6C Partnerships: supplementary

(1) Sections 6A(1)(a) to (c) and (2) and section 6B apply in relation to persons proposing to form themselves into a partnership as they apply in relation to a firm.

(2) Sections 6A and 6B apply to a limited liability partnership as they apply to a firm; and, in the application of those sections to a limited liability partnership, references to a partner in a firm are references to a member of the limited liability partnership.

(3) In the case of a limited partnership, references in sections 6A and 6B to a partner shall be construed as references to a general partner as defined in section 3 of the Limited Partnerships Act 1907.

(4) In sections 6A and 6B and in this section, "firm" has the meaning given by section 4 of the Partnership Act 1890.]

[906]

NOTES

Commencement: 1 October 2004.
Inserted as noted to s 6A at **[904]**.

7 *(Repealed by the Disability Discrimination Act 1995 (Amendment) Regulations 2003, SI 2003/1673, regs 3(1), 7, as from 1 October 2004.)*

[Barristers and advocates

7A Barristers: discrimination and harassment

(1) It is unlawful for a barrister or a barrister's clerk, in relation to any offer of a pupillage or tenancy, to discriminate against a disabled person—

(a) in the arrangements which are made for the purpose of determining to whom it should be offered;

(b) in respect of any terms on which it is offered; or

(c) by refusing, or deliberately omitting, to offer it to him.

(2) It is unlawful for a barrister or a barrister's clerk, in relation to a disabled pupil or tenant in the set of chambers in question, to discriminate against him—

(a) in respect of any terms applicable to him as a pupil or tenant;

(b) in the opportunities for training, or gaining experience, which are afforded or denied to him;

(c) in the benefits which are afforded or denied to him;

(d) by terminating his pupillage or by subjecting him to any pressure to leave the chambers; or

(e) by subjecting him to any other detriment.

(3) It is unlawful for a barrister or barrister's clerk, in relation to a pupillage or tenancy, to subject to harassment a disabled person who is, or has applied to be, a pupil or tenant in the set of chambers in question.

(4) It is also unlawful for any person, in relation to the giving, withholding or acceptance of instructions to a barrister, to discriminate against a disabled person or to subject him to harassment.

(5) In this section and in section 7B—

"barrister's clerk" includes any person carrying out any of the functions of a barrister's clerk;

"pupil", "pupillage" and "set of chambers" have the meanings commonly associated with their use in the context of barristers practising in independent practice; and

"tenancy" and "tenant" have the meanings commonly associated with their use in the context of barristers practising in independent practice, but they also include reference to any barrister permitted to practise from a set of chambers.]

[907]

NOTES

Commencement: 1 October 2004.

Inserted, together with the preceding heading and ss 7B–7D, by the Disability Discrimination Act 1995 (Amendment) Regulations 2003, SI 2003/1673, regs 3(1), 8, as from 1 October 2004.

[7B Barristers: duty to make adjustments

(1) Where—

(a) a provision, criterion or practice applied by or on behalf of a barrister or barrister's clerk, or

(b) any physical feature of premises occupied by a barrister or a barrister's clerk,

places the disabled person concerned at a substantial disadvantage in comparison with persons who are not disabled, it is the duty of the barrister or barrister's clerk to take such steps as it is reasonable, in all the circumstances of the case, for him to have to take in order to prevent the provision, criterion or practice, or feature, having that effect.

(2) In a case where subsection (1) applies in relation to two or more barristers in a set of chambers, the duty in that subsection is a duty on each of them to take such steps as it is reasonable, in all of the circumstances of the case, for him to have to take.

(3) In this section, "the disabled person concerned" means—

(a) in the case of a provision, criterion or practice for determining to whom a pupillage or tenancy should be offered, any disabled person who is, or has notified the barrister or the barrister's clerk concerned that he may be, an applicant for a pupillage or tenancy;

(b) in any other case, a disabled person who is—

(i) a tenant;

(ii) a pupil; or

(iii) an applicant for a pupillage or tenancy.

(4) Nothing in this section imposes any duty on a barrister or a barrister's clerk in relation to a disabled person if he does not know, and could not reasonably be expected to know—

(a) in the case of an applicant or potential applicant, that the disabled person concerned is, or may be, an applicant for a pupillage or tenancy; or

(b) in any case, that that person has a disability and is likely to be affected in the way mentioned in subsection (1).]

[908]

NOTES

Commencement: 1 October 2004.
Inserted as noted to s 7A at **[907]**.

[7C Advocates: discrimination and harassment

(1) It is unlawful for an advocate, in relation to taking any person as his pupil, to discriminate against a disabled person—

(a) in the arrangements which he makes for the purpose of determining whom he will take as his pupil;
(b) in respect of any terms on which he offers to take the disabled person as his pupil; or
(c) by refusing, or deliberately omitting, to take the disabled person as his pupil.

(2) It is unlawful for an advocate, in relation to a disabled person who is a pupil, to discriminate against him—

(a) in respect of any terms applicable to him as a pupil;
(b) in the opportunities for training, or gaining experience, which are afforded or denied to him;
(c) in the benefits which are afforded or denied to him;
(d) by terminating the relationship or by subjecting him to any pressure to leave; or
(e) by subjecting him to any other detriment.

(3) It is unlawful for an advocate, in relation to taking any person as his pupil, to subject to harassment a disabled person who is, or has applied to be taken as, his pupil.

(4) It is also unlawful for any person, in relation to the giving, withholding or acceptance of instructions to an advocate, to discriminate against a disabled person or to subject him to harassment.

(5) In this section and section 7D—

"advocate" means a member of the Faculty of Advocates practising as such; and
"pupil" has the meaning commonly associated with its use in the context of a person training to be an advocate.]

[909]

NOTES

Commencement: 1 October 2004.
Inserted as noted to s 7A at **[907]**.

[7D Advocates: duty to make adjustments

(1) Where—

(a) a provision, criterion or practice applied by or on behalf of an advocate, or
(b) any physical feature of premises occupied by, and under the control of, an advocate,

places the disabled person concerned at a substantial disadvantage in comparison with persons who are not disabled, it is the duty of the advocate to take such steps as it is reasonable, in all the circumstances of the case, for him to have to take in order to prevent the provision, criterion or practice, or feature, having that effect.

(2) In this section, "the disabled person concerned" means—

(a) in the case of a provision, criterion or practice for determining whom he will take as his pupil, any disabled person who has applied, or has notified the advocate that he may apply, to be taken as a pupil;
(b) in any other case, a disabled person who is—
  (i) an applicant to be taken as the advocate's pupil, or
  (ii) a pupil.

(3) Nothing in this section imposes any duty on an advocate in relation to a disabled person if he does not know, and could not reasonably be expected to know—

(a) in the case of an applicant or potential applicant, that the disabled person concerned is, or may be, applying to be taken as his pupil; or
(b) in any case, that that person has a disability and is likely to be affected in the way mentioned in subsection (1).]

[910]

NOTES

Commencement: 1 October 2004.
Inserted as noted to s 7A at **[907]**.

8–12 *(S 8 renumbered as s 17A (and amended) by the Disability Discrimination Act 1995 (Amendment) Regulations 2003, SI 2003/1673, regs 3(1), 9, as from 1 October 2004 (for s 17A see* **[914]***); s 9 repealed by regs 3(1), 10 of the 2003 Regulations, as from 1 October 2004; s 10 renumbered as s 18C by regs 3(1), 11 of the 2003 Regulations, as from 1 October 2004 (for s 18C see* **[917C]***); ss 11, 12 repealed by regs 3(1), 12 of the 2003 Regulations, as from 1 October 2004.)*

[Trade and professional bodies

13 Trade organisations: discrimination and harassment

(1) It is unlawful for a trade organisation to discriminate against a disabled person—

(a) in the arrangements which it makes for the purpose of determining who should be offered membership of the organisation;

(b) in the terms on which it is prepared to admit him to membership of the organisation; or

(c) by refusing to accept, or deliberately not accepting, his application for membership.

(2) It is unlawful for a trade organisation, in the case of a disabled person who is a member of the organisation, to discriminate against him—

(a) in the way it affords him access to any benefits or by refusing or deliberately omitting to afford him access to them;

(b) by depriving him of membership, or varying the terms on which he is a member; or

(c) by subjecting him to any other detriment.

(3) It is also unlawful for a trade organisation, in relation to membership of that organisation, to subject to harassment a disabled person who—

(a) is a member of the organisation; or

(b) has applied for membership of the organisation.

(4) In this section and section 14 "trade organisation" means—

(a) an organisation of workers;

(b) an organisation of employers; or

(c) any other organisation whose members carry on a particular profession or trade for the purposes of which the organisation exists.]

[911]

NOTES

Commencement: 1 October 2004.
Substituted, together with the preceding heading and ss 14, 14A–14D for the original ss 13–15, by the Disability Discrimination Act 1995 (Amendment) Regulations 2003, SI 2003/1673, regs 3(1), 13, as from 1 October 2004.

[14 Trade organisations: duty to make adjustments

(1) Where—

(a) a provision, criterion or practice applied by or on behalf of a trade organisation, or

(b) any physical feature of premises occupied by the organisation,

places the disabled person concerned at a substantial disadvantage in comparison with persons who are not disabled, it is the duty of the organisation to take such steps as it is reasonable, in all the circumstances of the case, for it to have to take in order to prevent the provision, criterion or practice, or feature, having that effect.

(2) In this section "the disabled person concerned" means—

(a) in the case of a provision, criterion or practice for determining to whom membership should be offered, any disabled person who is, or has notified the organisation that he may be, an applicant for membership;

(b) in any other case, a disabled person who is—

(i) a member of the organisation, or
(ii) an applicant for membership of the organisation.

(3) Nothing in this section imposes any duty on an organisation in relation to a disabled person if the organisation does not know, and could not reasonably be expected to know—
(a) in the case of an applicant or potential applicant, that the disabled person concerned is, or may be, an applicant for membership of the organisation; or
(b) in any case, that that person has a disability and is likely to be affected in the way mentioned in subsection (1).]

[912]

NOTES
Commencement: 1 October 2004.
Substituted as noted to s 13 at **[911]**.

[14A Qualifications bodies: discrimination and harassment

(1) It is unlawful for a qualifications body to discriminate against a disabled person—
(a) in the arrangements which it makes for the purpose of determining upon whom to confer a professional or trade qualification;
(b) in the terms on which it is prepared to confer a professional or trade qualification on him;
(c) by refusing or deliberately omitting to grant any application by him for such a qualification; or
(d) by withdrawing such a qualification from him or varying the terms on which he holds it.

(2) It is also unlawful for a qualifications body, in relation to a professional or trade qualification conferred by it, to subject to harassment a disabled person who holds or applies for such a qualification.

(3) In determining for the purposes of subsection (1) whether the application by a qualifications body of a competence standard to a disabled person constitutes discrimination within the meaning of section 3A, the application of the standard is justified for the purposes of section 3A(1)(b) if, but only if, the qualifications body can show that—
(a) the standard is, or would be, applied equally to persons who do not have his particular disability; and
(b) its application is a proportionate means of achieving a legitimate aim.

(4) For the purposes of subsection (3)—
(a) section 3A(2) (and (6)) does not apply; and
(b) section 3A(4) has effect as if the reference to section 3A(3) were a reference to subsection (3) of this section.

(5) In this section and section 14B—
"qualifications body" means any authority or body which can confer a professional or trade qualification, but it does not include—
(a) a responsible body (within the meaning of Chapter 1 or 2 of Part 4),
(b) a local education authority in England or Wales, or
(c) an education authority (within the meaning of section 135(1) of the Education (Scotland) Act 1980);
"confer" includes renew or extend;
"professional or trade qualification" means an authorisation, qualification, recognition, registration, enrolment, approval or certification which is needed for, or facilitates engagement in, a particular profession or trade;
"competence standard" means an academic, medical or other standard applied by or on behalf of a qualifications body for the purpose of determining whether or not a person has a particular level of competence or ability.]

[912A]

NOTES
Commencement: 1 October 2004.
Substituted as noted to s 13 at **[911]**.

[14B Qualifications bodies: duty to make adjustments

(1) Where—

(a) a provision, criterion or practice, other than a competence standard, applied by or on behalf of a qualifications body; or

(b) any physical feature of premises occupied by a qualifications body,

places the disabled person concerned at a substantial disadvantage in comparison with persons who are not disabled, it is the duty of the qualifications body to take such steps as it is reasonable, in all the circumstances of the case, for it to have to take in order to prevent the provision, criterion or practice, or feature, having that effect.

(2) In this section "the disabled person concerned" means—

(a) in the case of a provision, criterion or practice for determining on whom a professional or trade qualification is to be conferred, any disabled person who is, or has notified the qualifications body that he may be, an applicant for the conferment of that qualification;

(b) in any other case, a disabled person who—

(i) holds a professional or trade qualification conferred by the qualifications body, or

(ii) applies for a professional or trade qualification which it confers.

(3) Nothing in this section imposes a duty on a qualifications body in relation to a disabled person if the body does not know, and could not reasonably be expected to know—

(a) in the case of an applicant or potential applicant, that the disabled person concerned is, or may be, an applicant for the conferment of a professional or trade qualification; or

(b) in any case, that that person has a disability and is likely to be affected in the way mentioned in subsection (1).]

[912B]

NOTES

Commencement: 1 October 2004.
Substituted as noted to s 13 at **[911]**.

[Practical work experience

14C Practical work experience: discrimination and harassment

(1) It is unlawful, in the case of a disabled person seeking or undertaking a work placement, for a placement provider to discriminate against him—

(a) in the arrangements which he makes for the purpose of determining who should be offered a work placement;

(b) in the terms on which he affords him access to any work placement or any facilities concerned with such a placement;

(c) by refusing or deliberately omitting to afford him such access;

(d) by terminating the placement; or

(e) by subjecting him to any other detriment in relation to the placement.

(2) It is also unlawful for a placement provider, in relation to a work placement, to subject to harassment—

(a) a disabled person to whom he is providing a placement; or

(b) a disabled person who has applied to him for a placement.

[(3) This section and section 14D do not apply—

(a) to anything which is unlawful under any provision of section 4, sections 19 to 21A, sections 21F to 21J or Part 4; or

(b) to anything which would be unlawful under any such provision but for the operation of any provision in or made under this Act.]

(4) In this section and section 14D—

"work placement" means practical work experience undertaken for a limited period for the purposes of a person's vocational training;

"placement provider" means any person who provides a work placement to a person whom he does not employ.

(5) This section and section 14D do not apply to a work placement undertaken in any of the naval, military and air forces of the Crown.]

[912C]

NOTES

Commencement: 1 October 2004.

Substituted as noted to s 13 at **[911]**.

Sub-s (3): substituted by the Disability Discrimination Act 2005, s 19(1), Sch 1, Pt 1, paras 1, 6, as from 5 December 2005.

[14D Practical work experience: duty to make adjustments

(1) Where—

(a) a provision, criterion or practice applied by or on behalf of a placement provider, or

(b) any physical feature of premises occupied by the placement provider,

places the disabled person concerned at a substantial disadvantage in comparison with persons who are not disabled, it is the duty of the placement provider to take such steps as it is reasonable, in all the circumstances of the case, for him to have to take in order to prevent the provision, criterion or practice, or feature, having that effect.

(2) In this section, "the disabled person concerned" means—

(a) in the case of a provision, criterion or practice for determining to whom a work placement should be offered, any disabled person who is, or has notified the placement provider that he may be, an applicant for that work placement;

(b) in any other case, a disabled person who is—

(i) an applicant for the work placement concerned, or

(ii) undertaking a work placement with the placement provider.

(3) Nothing in this section imposes any duty on a placement provider in relation to the disabled person concerned if he does not know, and could not reasonably be expected to know—

(a) in the case of an applicant or potential applicant, that the disabled person concerned is, or may be, an applicant for the work placement; or

(b) in any case, that that person has a disability and is likely to be affected in the way mentioned in subsection (1).]

[912D]

NOTES

Commencement: 1 October 2004.

Substituted as noted to s 13 at **[911]**.

15 (*Substituted as noted to s 13 at* **[911]**.)

[Relationships between locally-electable authorities and their members

15A Interpretation of sections 15B and 15C

(1) Sections 15B and 15C apply to the following authorities—

(a) the Greater London Authority;

(b) a county council (in England or Wales);

(c) a county borough council (in Wales);

(d) a district council (in England);

(e) a London borough council;

(f) the Common Council of the City of London;

(g) the Council of the Isles of Scilly;

(h) a council constituted under section 2 of the Local Government etc (Scotland) Act 1994;

(i) a parish council (in England); and

(j) a community council (in Wales or Scotland).

(2) In relation to a member of an authority to which sections 15B and 15C apply, a reference in those sections to his carrying-out of official business is to his doing of anything—

(a) as member of the authority;

(b) as member of any body to which he is appointed by, or is appointed following nomination by, the authority or a group of bodies that includes the authority; or

(c) as member of any other body if it is a public body.

(3) In this section and sections 15B and 15C "member", in relation to the Greater London Authority, means Mayor of London or member of the London Assembly.]

[912E]

NOTES

Commencement: 5 December 2005 (certain purposes); 4 December 2006 (otherwise).

Inserted, together with the preceding heading and ss 15B, 15C, by the Disability Discrimination Act 2005, s 1, as from 5 December 2005 (in so far as relating to s 15B), and as from 4 December 2006 (otherwise).

[15B Authorities and their members: discrimination and harassment

(1) It is unlawful for an authority to which this section applies to discriminate against a disabled person who is a member of the authority—

(a) in the opportunities which it affords the disabled person to receive training, or any other facility, for his carrying-out of official business;

(b) by refusing to afford, or deliberately not affording, the disabled person any such opportunities; or

(c) by subjecting the disabled person to any other detriment in connection with his carrying-out of official business.

(2) It is unlawful for an authority to which this section applies to subject a disabled person who is a member of the authority to harassment in connection with his carrying-out of official business.

(3) A member of an authority to which this section applies is not subjected to a detriment for the purposes of subsection (1)(c) by reason of—

(a) his not being appointed or elected to an office of the authority;

(b) his not being appointed or elected to, or to an office of, a committee or sub-committee of the authority; or

(c) his not being appointed or nominated in exercise of any power of the authority, or of a group of bodies that includes the authority, to appoint, or nominate for appointment, to any body.

(4) Regulations may make provision as to the circumstances in which treatment is to be taken to be justified, or is to be taken not to be justified, for the purposes of section 3A(1)(b) as it has effect for the interpretation of "discriminate" in subsection (1).

(5) Regulations under subsection (4) may (in particular) provide for section 3A(3) to apply with prescribed modifications, or not to apply, for those purposes; but treatment of a disabled person cannot be justified under subsection (4) if it amounts to direct discrimination falling within section 3A(5).

(6) If, in a case falling within section 3A(1) as it has effect for the interpretation of "discriminate" in subsection (1), an authority to which this section applies is under a duty imposed by section 15C in relation to a disabled person but fails to comply with that duty, its treatment of that person cannot be justified under subsection (4) unless it would have been justified even if it had complied with that duty.]

[912F]

NOTES

Commencement: 5 December 2005.

Inserted as noted to s 15A at **[912F]**.

[15C Authorities and their members: duty to make adjustments

(1) Subsection (2) applies where—

(a) a provision, criterion or practice applied by or on behalf of an authority to which this section applies, or

(b) any physical feature of premises occupied by, or under the control of, such an authority,

places a disabled person who is a member of the authority at a substantial disadvantage, in comparison with members of the authority who are not disabled persons, in connection with his carrying-out of official business.

(2) It is the duty of the authority to take such steps as it is reasonable, in all the circumstances of the case, for it to have to take in order to prevent the provision, criterion or practice, or feature, having that effect.

(3) Subsection (2) does not impose any duty on an authority to which this section applies in relation to a member of the authority who is a disabled person if the authority does not know, and could not reasonably be expected to know, that the member—

(a) has a disability; and

(b) is likely to be affected in the way mentioned in subsection (1).

(4) Regulations may make provision, for purposes of this section—

(a) as to circumstances in which a provision, criterion or practice, or physical feature, is to be taken to have the effect mentioned in subsection (1);

(b) as to circumstances in which a provision, criterion or practice, or physical feature, is to be taken not to have the effect mentioned in subsection (1);

(c) as to circumstances in which it is, or as to circumstances in which it is not, reasonable for an authority to have to take steps of a prescribed description;

(d) as to steps which it is always, or as to steps which it is never, reasonable for an authority to have to take;

(e) as to things which are, or as to things which are not, to be treated as physical features.]

[912G]

NOTES

Commencement: 4 December 2006.
Inserted as noted to s 15A at **[912F]**.

16 (*Renumbered as s 18A* (*and amended*) *by the Disability Discrimination Act 1995* (*Amendment*) *Regulations 2003, SI 2003/1673, regs 3*(*1*), *14, as from 1 October 2004* (*for s 18A see* **[917A]**).)

[Other unlawful acts

16A Relationships which have come to an end

(1) This section applies where—

(a) there has been a relevant relationship between a disabled person and another person ("the relevant person"), and

(b) the relationship has come to an end.

(2) In this section a "relevant relationship" is—

(a) a relationship during the course of which an act of discrimination against, or harassment of, one party to the relationship by the other party to it is unlawful under any preceding provision of this Part[, other than sections 15B and 15C]; or

(b) a relationship between a person providing employment services … and a person receiving such services.

(3) It is unlawful for the relevant person—

(a) to discriminate against the disabled person by subjecting him to a detriment, or

(b) to subject the disabled person to harassment,

where the discrimination or harassment arises out of and is closely connected to the relevant relationship.

(4) This subsection applies where—

(a) a provision, criterion or practice applied by the relevant person to the disabled person in relation to any matter arising out of the relevant relationship, or

(b) a physical feature of premises which are occupied by the relevant person,

places the disabled person at a substantial disadvantage in comparison with persons who are not disabled, but are in the same position as the disabled person in relation to the relevant person.

(5) Where subsection (4) applies, it is the duty of the relevant person to take such steps as it is reasonable, in all the circumstances of the case, for him to have to take in order to prevent the provision, practice or criterion, or feature, having that effect.

(6) Nothing in subsection (5) imposes any duty on the relevant person if he does not know, and could not reasonably be expected to know, that the disabled person has a disability and is likely to be affected in the way mentioned in that subsection.

(7) In subsection (2), reference to an act of discrimination or harassment which is unlawful includes, in the case of a relationship which has come to an end before the commencement of this section, reference to such an act which would, after the commencement of this section, be unlawful.]

[913]

NOTES

Commencement: 1 October 2004.

Inserted, together with the preceding heading and ss 16B, 16C, by the Disability Discrimination Act 1995 (Amendment) Regulations 2003, SI 2003/1673, regs 3(1), 15(1), as from 1 October 2004.

Sub-s (2): words in square brackets in para (a) inserted by the Disability Discrimination Act 2005, s 19(1), Sch 1, Pt 1, paras 1, 7(a), as from 5 December 2005 (in so far as relating to s 15B), and as from 4 December 2006 (otherwise); words omitted from para (b) repealed by the Disability Discrimination Act 2005, s 19, Sch 1, Pt 1, paras 1, 7(b), Sch 2, as from 5 December 2005.

[16B Discriminatory advertisements

[(1) It is unlawful for a person to publish or cause to be published an advertisement which—

(a) invites applications for a relevant appointment or benefit; and

(b) indicates, or might reasonably be understood to indicate, that an application will or may be determined to any extent by reference to—

(i) the applicant not having any disability, or any particular disability,

(ii) the applicant not having had any disability, or any particular disability, or

(iii) any reluctance of the person determining the application to comply with a duty to make reasonable adjustments or (in relation to employment services) with the duty imposed by section 21(1) as modified by section 21A(6).]

(2) Subsection (1) does not apply where it would not in fact be unlawful under this Part or, to the extent that it relates to the provision of employment services, Part 3 for an application to be determined in the manner indicated (or understood to be indicated) in the advertisement.

[(2A) A person who publishes an advertisement of the kind described in subsection (1) shall not be subject to any liability under subsection (1) in respect of the publication of the advertisement if he proves—

(a) that the advertisement was published in reliance on a statement made to him by the person who caused it to be published to the effect that, by reason of the operation of subsection (2), the publication would not be unlawful; and

(b) that it was reasonable for him to rely on the statement.

(2B) A person who knowingly or recklessly makes a statement such as is mentioned in subsection (2A)(a) which in a material respect is false or misleading commits an offence, and shall be liable on summary conviction to a fine not exceeding level 5 on the standard scale.]

[(2C) Subsection (1) does not apply in relation to an advertisement so far as it invites persons to apply, in their capacity as members of an authority to which sections 15B and 15C apply, for a relevant appointment or benefit which the authority is intending to make or confer.]

(3) In [this section], "relevant appointment or benefit" means—

(a) any employment, promotion or transfer of employment;

(b) membership of, or a benefit under, an occupational pension scheme;

(c) an appointment to any office or post to which section 4D applies;

(d) any partnership in a firm (within the meaning of section 6A);

(e) any tenancy or pupillage (within the meaning of section 7A or 7C);

(f) any membership of a trade organisation (within the meaning of section 13);

(g) any professional or trade qualification (within the meaning of section 14A);

(h) any work placement (within the meaning of section 14C);

(i) any employment services …

(4) In this section, "advertisement" includes every form of advertisement or notice, whether to the public or not.

[(5) Proceedings in respect of a contravention of subsection (1) may be brought only—

(a) by the Commission for Equality and Human Rights, and
(b) in accordance with section 25 of the Equality Act 2006.]]

[913A]

NOTES

Commencement: 1 October 2004.
Inserted as noted to s 16A at **[913]**.
Sub-s (1): substituted by the Disability Discrimination Act 2005, s 10(1), (2), as from 5 December 2005.
Sub-ss (2A), (2B): inserted by the Disability Discrimination Act 2005, s 10(1), (3), as from 5 December 2005.
Sub-s (2C): inserted by the Disability Discrimination Act 2005, s 19(1), Sch 1, Pt 1, paras 1, 8(1), (2), as from 5 December 2005 (in so far as relating to s 15B), and as from 4 December 2006 (otherwise).
Sub-s (3): words in square brackets substituted, and words omitted from para (i) repealed, by the Disability Discrimination Act 2005, ss 10(1), (4), 19, Sch 1, Pt 1, paras 1, 8(1), (3), Sch 2, as from 5 December 2005.
Sub-s (5): added by the Equality Act 2006, s 40, Sch 3, paras 41, 42, as from 1 October 2007.
Modified as noted to s 4 at **[903]**.
Proceedings in respect of a contravention of subsection (1): see further the Equality Act 2006, ss 25, 26 at **[1668]**, **[1669]**.

[16C Instructions and pressure to discriminate

(1) It is unlawful for a person—

(a) who has authority over another person, or
(b) in accordance with whose wishes that other person is accustomed to act,

to instruct him to do any act which is unlawful under this Part or, to the extent that it relates to the provision of employment services, Part 3, or to procure or attempt to procure the doing by him of any such act.

(2) It is also unlawful to induce, or attempt to induce, a person to do any act which contravenes this Part or, to the extent that it relates to the provision of employment services, Part 3 by—

(a) providing or offering to provide him with any benefit, or
(b) subjecting or threatening to subject him to any detriment.

(3) An attempted inducement is not prevented from falling within subsection (2) because it is not made directly to the person in question, if it is made in such a way that he is likely to hear of it.

[(4) Proceedings in respect of a contravention of this section may be brought only—

(a) by the Commission for Equality and Human Rights, and
(b) in accordance with section 25 of the Equality Act 2006.]]

[913B]

NOTES

Commencement: 1 October 2004.
Inserted as noted to s 16A at **[913]**.
Sub-s (4): added by the Equality Act 2006, s 40, Sch 3, paras 41, 43, as from 1 October 2007.
Proceedings in respect of a contravention of subsection (1): see further the Equality Act 2006, ss 25, 26 at **[1668]**, **[1669]**.

17 (*Repealed by the Disability Discrimination Act 1995 (Pensions) Regulations 2003, SI 2003/2770, regs 2, 4(1), as from 1 October 2004.*)

Enforcement etc

[17A] Enforcement, remedies and procedure

(1) A complaint by any person that another person—

(a) has discriminated against him[, or subjected him to harassment,] in a way which is unlawful under this Part, or
(b) is, by virtue of section 57 or 58, to be treated as having [done so],

may be presented to an [employment tribunal].

[(1A) Subsection (1) does not apply to a complaint under section 14A(1) or (2) of an act in respect of which an appeal, or proceedings in the nature of an appeal, may be brought under any enactment.

(1B) …

(1C) Where, on the hearing of a complaint under subsection (1), the complainant proves facts from which the tribunal could, apart from this subsection, conclude in the absence of an adequate explanation that the respondent has acted in a way which is unlawful under this Part, the tribunal shall uphold the complaint unless the respondent proves that he did not so act.]

(2) Where an [employment tribunal] finds that a complaint presented to it under this section is well-founded, it shall take such of the following steps as it considers just and equitable—

(a) making a declaration as to the rights of the complainant and the respondent in relation to the matters to which the complaint relates;

(b) ordering the respondent to pay compensation to the complainant;

(c) recommending that the respondent take, within a specified period, action appearing to the tribunal to be reasonable, in all the circumstances of the case, for the purpose of obviating or reducing the adverse effect on the complainant of any matter to which the complaint relates.

(3) Where a tribunal orders compensation under subsection (2)(b), the amount of the compensation shall be calculated by applying the principles applicable to the calculation of damages in claims in tort or (in Scotland) in reparation for breach of statutory duty.

(4) For the avoidance of doubt it is hereby declared that compensation in respect of discrimination in a way which is unlawful under this Part may include compensation for injury to feelings whether or not it includes compensation under any other head.

(5) If the respondent to a complaint fails, without reasonable justification, to comply with a recommendation made by an [employment tribunal] under subsection (2)(c) the tribunal may, if it thinks it just and equitable to do so—

(a) increase the amount of compensation required to be paid to the complainant in respect of the complaint, where an order was made under subsection (2)(b); or

(b) make an order under subsection (2)(b).

(6) Regulations may make provision—

(a) for enabling a tribunal, where an amount of compensation falls to be awarded under subsection (2)(b), to include in the award interest on that amount; and

(b) specifying, for cases where a tribunal decides that an award is to include an amount in respect of interest, the manner in which and the periods and rate by reference to which the interest is to be determined.

(7) Regulations may modify the operation of any order made under [section 14 of [the Employment Tribunals Act 1996]] (power to make provision as to interest on sums payable in pursuance of [employment tribunal] decisions) to the extent that it relates to an award of compensation under subsection (2)(b).

(8) Part I of Schedule 3 makes further provision about the enforcement of this Part and about procedure.

[914]–[915]

NOTES

This section was originally s 8. It was renumbered as s 17A (together with the preceding heading) by the Disability Discrimination Act 1995 (Amendment) Regulations 2003, SI 2003/1673, regs 3(1), 9(1), as from 1 October 2004.

Sub-s (1): words in square brackets in para (a) inserted, and words in square brackets in para (b) substituted, by SI 2003/1673, regs 3(1), 9(2)(a), (b), as from 1 October 2004; words in third pair of square brackets substituted by the Employment Rights (Dispute Resolution) Act 1998, s 1(2)(a).

Sub-ss (1A), (1C): inserted, together with sub-s (1B), by SI 2003/1673, regs 3(1), 9(2)(c), as from 1 October 2004. Note that, by virtue of reg 2(1), (4) of those Regulations at **[3033]**, sub-s (1C) applies in relation to a complaint presented to an employment tribunal before 1 October 2004, as well as one presented on or after that date; but it does not affect any case in which a complaint was determined by an employment tribunal before that date.

Sub-s (1B): inserted as noted above; repealed by the Disability Discrimination Act 2005, s 19, Sch 1, Pt 1, paras 1, 9, Sch 2, as from 30 June 2005.

Sub-ss (2), (5): words in square brackets substituted by the Employment Rights (Dispute Resolution) Act 1998, s 1(2)(a).

Sub-s (7): words in first (outer) pair of square brackets substituted by the Employment Tribunals Act 1996, s 43, Sch 1, para 12(1), (2); words in second (inner) pair of square brackets and words in third pair of square brackets substituted by the Employment Rights (Dispute Resolution) Act 1998, s 1(2)(a), (c).

Conciliation: employment tribunal proceedings and claims which could be the subject of employment tribunal proceedings under this section are proceedings to which the Employment Tribunals Act 1996, s 18 applies; see s 18(1)(c) of that Act at **[975]**.

Restriction of publicity in disability cases: the Employment Tribunals Act 1996, s 12 applies to proceedings on a complaint under this section in which evidence of a personal nature is likely to be heard; see s 12(1) of the 1996 Act at **[968]**.

Tribunal jurisdiction: the Employment Act 2002, ss 31, 32, 38, at **[1493]**, **[1494]**, **[1496]** apply to proceedings before the employment tribunal relating to a claim under this section; see ss 31(1), 32(1), 38(1) of, and Schs 3–5 to, the 2002 Act at **[1508]–[1510]**.

For the circumstances in which the normal time limit for presenting a complaint under this section is extended for a period of three months, see the Employment Act 2002 (Dispute Resolution) Regulations 2004, SI 2004/752, regs 15 and 18 at **[3096]** and **[3098]**.

Compensation for dismissal: as to the powers of an employment tribunal to award compensation where any act constitutes both unfair dismissal under the Employment Rights Act 1996, and discrimination under any one or more of the Sex Discrimination Act 1975, the Race Relations Act 1976, the Disability Discrimination Act 1995, the Employment Equality (Sexual Orientation) Regulations 2003, the Employment Equality (Religion or Belief) Regulations 2003, or the Employment Equality (Age) Regulations 2006, see s 126 of the 1996 Act at **[1170]**.

Regulations: the Employment Tribunals (Interest on Awards in Discrimination Cases) Regulations 1996, SI 1996/2803 at **[2390]** (made under this section when numbered as s 8).

17B *(Inserted, together with s 17C, by the Disability Discrimination Act 1995 (Amendment) Regulations 2003, SI 2003/1673, regs 3(1), 16(1), as from 1 October 2004; repealed by the Equality Act 2006, ss 40, 91, Sch 3, paras 41, 44, Sch 4, as from 1 October 2007.)*

[17C Validity of contracts, collective agreements and rules of undertakings

Schedule 3A shall have effect.]

[916]–[917]

NOTES

Commencement: 1 October 2004.

Inserted as noted to s 17B.

[Supplementary and general]

18 *(Repealed by the Disability Discrimination Act 2005, ss 11(1), 19(2), Sch 2, as from 5 December 2005.)*

[18A] Alterations to premises occupied under leases

(1) This section applies where—

(a) [a person to whom a duty to make reasonable adjustments applies] ("the occupier") occupies premises under a lease;

(b) but for this section, the occupier would not be entitled to make a particular alteration to the premises; and

(c) the alteration is one which the occupier proposes to make in order to comply with [that duty].

(2) Except to the extent to which it expressly so provides, the lease shall have effect by virtue of this subsection as if it provided—

(a) for the occupier to be entitled to make the alteration with the written consent of the lessor;

(b) for the occupier to have to make a written application to the lessor for consent if he wishes to make the alteration;

(c) if such an application is made, for the lessor not to withhold his consent unreasonably; and

(d) for the lessor to be entitled to make his consent subject to reasonable conditions.

(3) In this section—

"lease" includes a tenancy, sub-lease or sub-tenancy and an agreement for a lease, tenancy, sub-lease or sub-tenancy; and "sub-lease" and "sub-tenancy" have such meaning as may be prescribed.

(4) If the terms and conditions of a lease—

(a) impose conditions which are to apply if the occupier alters the premises, or

(b) entitle the lessor to impose conditions when consenting to the occupier's altering the premises,

the occupier is to be treated for the purposes of subsection (1) as not being entitled to make the alteration.

(5) Part I of Schedule 4 supplements the provisions of this section.]

[917A]

NOTES

This section was originally s 16. It was renumbered as s 18A (and the original heading preceding s 16 was repealed) by the Disability Discrimination Act 1995 (Amendment) Regulations 2003, SI 2003/1673, regs 3(1), 14(2), as from 1 October 2004.

Sub-s (1): words in square brackets substituted by SI 2003/1673, regs 3(1), 14(3), as from 1 October 2004.

Modified as noted to s 4 at **[903]**.

Sub-leases and sub-tenancies: this section is modified in relation to any case where the occupier occupies premises under a sub-lease or sub-tenancy, by the Disability Discrimination (Employment Field) (Leasehold Premises) Regulations 2004, SI 2004/153, regs 8, 9(a), (b) at **[3080]**, **[3081]**.

Regulations: the Disability Discrimination (Employment Field) (Leasehold Premises) Regulations 2004, SI 2004/153 at **[3074]** (made under this section when numbered as s 16).

[18B Reasonable adjustments: supplementary

(1) In determining whether it is reasonable for a person to have to take a particular step in order to comply with a duty to make reasonable adjustments, regard shall be had, in particular, to—

(a) the extent to which taking the step would prevent the effect in relation to which the duty is imposed;

(b) the extent to which it is practicable for him to take the step;

(c) the financial and other costs which would be incurred by him in taking the step and the extent to which taking it would disrupt any of his activities;

(d) the extent of his financial and other resources;

(e) the availability to him of financial or other assistance with respect to taking the step;

(f) the nature of his activities and the size of his undertaking;

(g) where the step would be taken in relation to a private household, the extent to which taking it would—

(i) disrupt that household, or

(ii) disturb any person residing there.

(2) The following are examples of steps which a person may need to take in relation to a disabled person in order to comply with a duty to make reasonable adjustments—

(a) making adjustments to premises;

(b) allocating some of the disabled person's duties to another person;

(c) transferring him to fill an existing vacancy;

(d) altering his hours of working or training;

(e) assigning him to a different place of work or training;

(f) allowing him to be absent during working or training hours for rehabilitation, assessment or treatment;

(g) giving, or arranging for, training or mentoring (whether for the disabled person or any other person);

(h) acquiring or modifying equipment;

(i) modifying instructions or reference manuals;

(j) modifying procedures for testing or assessment;

(k) providing a reader or interpreter;

(l) providing supervision or other support.

(3) For the purposes of a duty to make reasonable adjustments, where under any binding obligation a person is required to obtain the consent of another person to any alteration of the premises occupied by him—

(a) it is always reasonable for him to have to take steps to obtain that consent; and

(b) it is never reasonable for him to have to make that alteration before that consent is obtained.

(4) The steps referred to in subsection (3)(a) shall not be taken to include an application to a court or tribunal.

(5) In subsection (3), "binding obligation" means a legally binding obligation (not contained in a lease (within the meaning of section 18A(3)) in relation to the premises, whether arising from an agreement or otherwise.

(6) A provision of this Part imposing a duty to make reasonable adjustments applies only for the purpose of determining whether a person has discriminated against a disabled person; and accordingly a breach of any such duty is not actionable as such.]

[917B]

NOTES

Commencement: 1 October 2004.

Inserted by the Disability Discrimination Act 1995 (Amendment) Regulations 2003, SI 2003/1673, regs 3(1), 17(2), as from 1 October 2004.

[18C] Charities and support for particular groups of persons

(1) Nothing in this Part—

(a) affects any charitable instrument which provides for conferring benefits on one or more categories of person determined by reference to any physical or mental capacity; or

(b) makes unlawful any act done by a charity or recognised body in pursuance of any of its charitable purposes, so far as those purposes are connected with persons so determined.

(2) Nothing in this Part prevents—

(a) a person who provides supported employment from treating members of a particular group of disabled persons more favourably than other persons in providing such employment; or

(b) the Secretary of State from agreeing to arrangements for the provision of supported employment which will, or may, have that effect.

(3) In this section—

"charitable instrument" means an enactment or other instrument (whenever taking effect) so far as it relates to charitable purposes;

"charity" has the same meaning as in the Charities Act 1993;

"recognised body" means a body which is a recognised body for the purposes of Part I of the Law Reform (Miscellaneous Provisions) (Scotland) Act 1990; and

"supported employment" means facilities provided, or in respect of which payments are made, under section 15 of the Disabled Persons (Employment) Act 1944.

(4) In the application of this section to England and Wales, "charitable purposes" means purposes which are exclusively charitable according to the law of England and Wales.

(5) In the application of this section to Scotland, "charitable purposes" shall be construed in the same way as if it were contained in the Income Tax Acts.]

[917C]

NOTES

This section was originally s 10. It was renumbered as s 18C by the Disability Discrimination Act 1995 (Amendment) Regulations 2003, SI 2003/1673, regs 3(1), 11, as from 1 October 2004.

[18D Interpretation of Part 2

(1) Subject to any duty to make reasonable adjustments, nothing in this Part is to be taken to require a person to treat a disabled person more favourably than he treats or would treat others.

(2) In this Part—

"benefits"[, except in sections 4G to 4K,] includes facilities and services;

"detriment", except in section 16C(2)(b), does not include conduct of the nature referred to in section 3B (harassment);

"discriminate", "discrimination" and other related expressions are to be construed in accordance with section 3A;

"duty to make reasonable adjustments" means a duty imposed by or under section 4A, 4B(5) or (6), 4E, [4H,] 6B, 7B, 7D, 14, 14B, 14D[, 15C] or 16A(5);

"employer" includes a person who has no employees but is seeking to employ another person;

"harassment" is to be construed in accordance with section 3B;

"physical feature", in relation to any premises, includes [(subject to any provision under section 15C(4)(e))] any of the following (whether permanent or temporary)—

(a) any feature arising from the design or construction of a building on the premises,

(b) any feature on the premises of any approach to, exit from or access to such a building,

(c) any fixtures, fittings, furnishings, furniture, equipment or material in or on the premises,

(d) any other physical element or quality of any land comprised in the premises;

"provision, criterion or practice" includes any arrangements.]

[917D]

NOTES

Commencement: 1 October 2004.

Inserted by the Disability Discrimination Act 1995 (Amendment) Regulations 2003, SI 2003/1673, regs 3(1), 18, as from 1 October 2004.

Sub-s (2): words in square brackets in definition "benefits" and first figure in square brackets in definition "duty to make reasonable adjustments" inserted by the Disability Discrimination Act 1995 (Pensions) Regulations 2003, SI 2003/2770, regs 2, 4(2), as from 1 October 2004; second figure in square brackets in definition "duty to make reasonable adjustments" and words in square brackets in definition "physical feature" inserted by the Disability Discrimination Act 2005, s 19(1), Sch 1, Pt 1, paras 1, 11, as from 4 December 2006.

[18E Premises provided otherwise than in course of a Part 2 relationship

(1) This Part does not apply in relation to the provision, otherwise than in the course of a Part 2 relationship, of premises by the regulated party to the other party.

(2) For the purposes of subsection (1)—

(a) "Part 2 relationship" means a relationship during the course of which an act of discrimination against, or harassment of, one party to the relationship by the other party to it is unlawful under sections 4 to 15C; and

(b) in relation to a Part 2 relationship, "regulated party" means the party whose acts of discrimination, or harassment, are made unlawful by sections 4 to 15C.]

[917E]

NOTES

Commencement: 4 December 2006.

Inserted by the Disability Discrimination Act 2005, s 19(1), Sch 1, Pt 1, paras 1, 12, as from 4 December 2006.

PART III
DISCRIMINATION IN OTHER AREAS

Goods, facilities and services

19 Discrimination in relation to goods, facilities and services

(1) It is unlawful for a provider of services to discriminate against a disabled person—

(a) in refusing to provide, or deliberately not providing, to the disabled person any service which he provides, or is prepared to provide, to members of the public;

(b) in failing to comply with any duty imposed on him by section 21 in circumstances in which the effect of that failure is to make it impossible or unreasonably difficult for the disabled person to make use of any such service;

(c) in the standard of service which he provides to the disabled person or the manner in which he provides it to him; or

(d) in the terms on which he provides a service to the disabled person.

(2) For the purposes of this section and sections 20 [to 21ZA]—

(a) the provision of services includes the provision of any goods or facilities;
(b) a person is "a provider of services" if he is concerned with the provision, in the United Kingdom, of services to the public or to a section of the public; and
(c) it is irrelevant whether a service is provided on payment or without payment.

(3) The following are examples of services to which this section and sections 20 and 21 apply—
(a) access to and use of any place which members of the public are permitted to enter;
(b) access to and use of means of communication;
(c) access to and use of information services;
(d) accommodation in a hotel, boarding house or other similar establishment;
(e) facilities by way of banking or insurance or for grants, loans, credit or finance;
(f) facilities for entertainment, recreation or refreshment;
(g) facilities provided by employment agencies or under section 2 of the Employment and Training Act 1973;
(h) the services of any profession or trade, or any local or other public authority.

(4) In the case of an act which constitutes discrimination by virtue of section 55, this section also applies to discrimination against a person who is not disabled.

[(4A) Subsection (1) does not apply to anything that is governed by Regulation (EC) No 1107/2006 of the European Parliament and of the Council of 5 July 2006 concerning the rights of disabled persons and persons with reduced mobility when travelling by air.]

[(5) Regulations may provide for subsection (1) and section 21(1), (2) and (4) not to apply, or to apply only to a prescribed extent, in relation to a service of a prescribed description.]

[(5A) Nothing in this section or sections 20 to 21A applies to the provision of a service in relation to which discrimination is unlawful under Part 4.]

(6) …

[918]

NOTES

Sub-s (2): words in square brackets substituted by the Disability Discrimination Act 2005, s 19(1), Sch 1, Pt 1, paras 1, 13(1), (2), as from 30 June 2005.

Sub-s (4A): inserted by the Civil Aviation (Access to Air Travel for Disabled Persons and Persons with Reduced Mobility) Regulations 2007, SI 2007/1895, reg 8, as from 26 July 2007.

Sub-s (5): substituted by the Disability Discrimination Act 2005, s 19(1), Sch 1, Pt 1, paras 1, 13(1), (3), as from 30 June 2005.

Sub-s (5A): inserted by the Special Educational Needs and Disability Act 2001, s 38(1), (6); substituted by the Disability Discrimination Act 2005, s 19(1), Sch 1, Pt 1, paras 1, 13(1), (4), as from 4 December 2006.

Sub-s (6): repealed by the Special Educational Needs and Disability Act 2001, ss 38(1), (5)(b), 42(6), Sch 9.

20 Meaning of "discrimination"

(1) For the purposes of section 19, a provider of services discriminates against a disabled person if—
(a) for a reason which relates to the disabled person's disability, he treats him less favourably than he treats or would treat others to whom that reason does not or would not apply; and
(b) he cannot show that the treatment in question is justified.

(2) For the purposes of section 19, a providers of services also discriminates against a disabled person if—
(a) he fails to comply with a section 21 duty imposed on him in relation to the disabled person; and
(b) he cannot show that his failure to comply with that duty is justified.

(3) For the purposes of this section, treatment is justified only if—
(a) in the opinion of the provider of services, one or more of the conditions mentioned in subsection (4) are satisfied; and
(b) it is reasonable, in all the circumstances of the case, for him to hold that opinion.

(4) The conditions are that—
(a) in any case, the treatment is necessary in order not to endanger the health or safety of any person (which may include that of the disabled person);

(b) in any case, the disabled person is incapable of entering into an enforceable agreement, or of giving an informed consent, and for that reason the treatment is reasonable in that case;

(c) in a case falling within section 19(1)(a), the treatment is necessary because the provider of services would otherwise be unable to provide the service to members of the public;

(d) in a case falling within section 19(1)(c) or (d), the treatment is necessary in order for the provider of services to be able to provide the service to the disabled person or to other members of the public;

(e) in a case falling within section 19(1)(d), the difference in the terms on which the service is provided to the disabled person and those on which it is provided to other members of the public reflects the greater cost to the provider of services in providing the service to the disabled person.

(5) Any increase in the cost of providing a service to a disabled person which results from compliance by a provider of services with a section 21 duty shall be disregarded for the purposes of subsection (4)(e).

(6) Regulations may make provision, for purposes of this section, as to circumstances in which—

(a) it is reasonable for a provider of services to hold the opinion mentioned in subsection (3)(a);

(b) it is not reasonable for a provider of services to hold that opinion.

(7) Regulations may make provision for subsection (4)(b) not to apply in prescribed circumstances where—

(a) a person is acting for a disabled person under a power of attorney;

(b) functions conferred by or under [the Mental Capacity Act 2005] are exercisable in relation to a disabled person's property or affairs; or

[(c) powers are exercisable in relation to a disabled person's property or affairs in consequence of the appointment, under the law of Scotland, of a guardian, tutor or judicial factor].

(8) Regulations may make provision, for purposes of this section, as to circumstances (other than those mentioned in subsection (4)) in which treatment is to be taken to be justified.

(9) In subsections (3), (4) and (8) "treatment" includes failure to comply with a section 21 duty.

[919]

NOTES

Sub-s (7): words in square brackets in para (b) substituted by the Mental Capacity Act 2005, s 67(1), Sch 6, para 41, as from 1 October 2007; para (c) substituted by the Disability Discrimination Act 2005, s 19(1), Sch 1, Pt 1, paras 1, 14, as from 30 June 2005.

Regulations: the Disability Discrimination (Service Providers and Public Authorities Carrying Out Functions) Regulations 2005, SI 2005/2901.

21 Duty of providers of services to make adjustments

(1) Where a provider of services has a practice, policy or procedure which makes it impossible or unreasonably difficult for disabled persons to make use of a service which he provides, or is prepared to provide, to other members of the public, it is his duty to take such steps as it is reasonable, in all the circumstances of the case, for him to have to take in order to change that practice, policy or procedure so that it no longer has that effect.

(2) Where a physical feature (for example, one arising from the design or construction of a building or the approach or access to premises) makes it impossible or unreasonably difficult for disabled persons to make use of such a service, it is the duty of the provider of that service to take such steps as it is reasonable, in all the circumstances of the case, for him to have to take in order to—

(a) remove the feature;

(b) alter it so that it no longer has that effect;

(c) provide a reasonable means of avoiding the feature; or

(d) provide a reasonable alternative method of making the service in question available to disabled persons.

(3) Regulations may prescribe—

(a) matters which are to be taken into account in determining whether any provision of a kind mentioned in subsection (2)(c) or (d) is reasonable; and
(b) categories of providers of services to whom subsection (2) does not apply.

(4) Where an auxiliary aid or service (for example, the provision of information on audio tape or of a sign language interpreter) would—
(a) enable disabled persons to make use of a service which a provider of services provides, or is prepared to provide, to members of the public, or
(b) facilitate the use by disabled persons of such a service,
it is the duty of the provider of that service to take such steps as it is reasonable, in all the circumstances of the case, for him to have to take in order to provide that auxiliary aid or service.

(5) Regulations may make provision, for the purposes of this section—
(a) as to circumstances in which it is reasonable for a provider of services to have to take steps of a prescribed description;
(b) as to circumstances in which it is not reasonable for a provider of services to have to take steps of a prescribed description;
(c) as to what is to be included within the meaning of "practice, policy or procedure";
(d) as to what is not to be included within the meaning of that expression;
(e) as to things which are to be treated as physical features;
(f) as to things which are not to be treated as such features;
(g) as to things which are to be treated as auxiliary aids or services;
(h) as to things which are not to be treated as auxiliary aids or services.

(6) Nothing in this section requires a provider of services to take any steps which would fundamentally alter the nature of the service in question or the nature of his trade, profession or business.

(7) Nothing in this section requires a provider of services to take any steps which would cause him to incur expenditure exceeding the prescribed maximum.

(8) Regulations under subsection (7) may provide for the prescribed maximum to be calculated by reference to—
(a) aggregate amounts of expenditure incurred in relation to different cases;
(b) prescribed periods;
(c) services of a prescribed description;
(d) premises of a prescribed description; or
(e) such other criteria as may be prescribed.

(9) Regulations may provide, for the purposes of subsection (7), for expenditure incurred by one provider of services to be treated as incurred by another.

(10) This section imposes duties only for the purpose of determining whether a provider of services has discriminated against a disabled person; and accordingly a breach of any such duty is not actionable as such.

[920]

NOTES

Commencement: 26 April 1999 (sub-ss (3), (5)); 1 October 1999 (sub-ss (1), (2)(d), (4), (6), (10)); 1 October 2004 (otherwise).

Regulations: the Disability Discrimination (Providers of Services) (Adjustment of Premises) Regulations 2001, SI 2001/3253; the Disability Discrimination (Service Providers and Public Authorities Carrying Out Functions) Regulations 2005, SI 2005/2901; the Disability Discrimination (Transport Vehicles) Regulations 2005, SI 2005/3190 (all made under sub-s (5)). As of 6 April 2008 no Regulations had been made under sub-ss (7)–(9).

[21ZA Application of sections 19 to 21 to transport vehicles

(1) Section 19(1) (a), (c) and (d) do not apply in relation to a case where the service is a transport service and, as provider of that service, the provider of services discriminates against a disabled person—
(a) in not providing, or in providing, him with a vehicle; or
(b) in not providing, or in providing, him with services when he is travelling in a vehicle provided in the course of the transport service.

(2) For the purposes of section 21(1), (2) and (4), it is never reasonable for a provider of services, as a provider of a transport service—

(a) to have to take steps which would involve the alteration or removal of a physical feature of a vehicle used in providing the service;
(b) to have to take steps which would—
  (i) affect whether vehicles are provided in the course of the service or what vehicles are so provided, or
  (ii) where a vehicle is provided in the course of the service, affect what happens in the vehicle while someone is travelling in it.

(3) Regulations may provide for subsection (1) or (2) not to apply, or to apply only to a prescribed extent, in relation to vehicles of a prescribed description.

(4) In this section—
"transport service" means a service which (to any extent) involves transport of people by vehicle;
"vehicle" means a vehicle for transporting people by land, air or water, and includes (in particular)—
  (a) a vehicle not having wheels, and
  (b) a vehicle constructed or adapted to carry passengers on a system using a mode of guided transport;
"guided transport" has the same meaning as in the Transport and Works Act 1992.]

[920A]

NOTES

Commencement: 30 June 2005.
Inserted by the Disability Discrimination Act 2005, s 5, as from 30 June 2005.
Regulations: the Disability Discrimination (Transport Vehicles) Regulations 2005, SI 2005/3190.

[21A Employment services

(1) In [this Act], "employment services" means—
(a) vocational guidance;
(b) vocational training; or
(c) services to assist a person to obtain or retain employment, or to establish himself as self-employed.

(2) It is unlawful for a provider of employment services, in relation to such services, to subject to harassment a disabled person—
(a) to whom he is providing such services, or
(b) who has requested him to provide such services;
and section 3B (meaning of "harassment") applies for the purposes of this subsection as it applies for the purposes of Part 2.

(3) In their application to employment services, the preceding provisions of this Part have effect as follows.

(4) Section 19 has effect as if—
(a) after subsection (1)(a), there were inserted the following paragraph—
"(aa) in failing to comply with a duty imposed on him by subsection (1) of section 21 in circumstances in which the effect of that failure is to place the disabled person at a substantial disadvantage in comparison with persons who are not disabled in relation to the provision of the service;";
(b) in subsection (1)(b), for "section 21" there were substituted "subsection (2) or (4) of section 21";
[(c) in subsection (2), for "sections 20 to 21ZA" there is substituted "sections 20 to 21A"].

(5) Section 20 has effect as if—
(a) after subsection (1), there were inserted the following subsection—

"(1A) For the purposes of section 19, a provider of services also discriminates against a disabled person if he fails to comply with a duty imposed on him by subsection (1) of section 21 in relation to the disabled person.";
(b) in subsection (2)(a), for "a section 21 duty imposed" there were substituted "a duty imposed by subsection (2) or (4) of section 21";
(c) after subsection (3), there were inserted the following subsection—

"(3A) But treatment of a disabled person cannot be justified under subsection (3) if it amounts to direct discrimination falling within section 3A(5).".

(6) Section 21 has effect as if—

(a) in subsection (1), for "makes it impossible or unreasonably difficult for disabled persons to make use of" there were substituted "places disabled persons at a substantial disadvantage in comparison with persons who are not disabled in relation to the provision of";

(b) after subsection (1), there were inserted the following subsection—

"(1A) In subsection (1), "practice, policy or procedure" includes a provision or criterion.".]

[921]

NOTES

Commencement: 1 October 2004.

Inserted by the Disability Discrimination Act 1995 (Amendment) Regulations 2003, SI 2003/1673, regs 3(1), 19(1), as from 1 October 2004.

Sub-ss (1), (4): words in square brackets substituted by the Disability Discrimination Act 2005, s 19(1), Sch 1, Pt 1, paras 1, 15, as from 30 June 2005.

[Public authorities

21B Discrimination by public authorities

(1) It is unlawful for a public authority to discriminate against a disabled person in carrying out its functions.

(2) In this section, and sections 21D and 21E, "public authority"—

(a) includes any person certain of whose functions are functions of a public nature; but

(b) does not include any person mentioned in subsection (3).

(3) The persons are—

(a) either House of Parliament;

(b) a person exercising functions in connection with proceedings in Parliament;

(c) the Security Service;

(d) the Secret Intelligence Service;

(e) the Government Communications Headquarters; and

(f) a unit, or part of a unit, of any of the naval, military or air forces of the Crown which is for the time being required by the Secretary of State to assist the Government Communications Headquarters in carrying out its functions.

(4) In relation to a particular act, a person is not a public authority by virtue only of subsection (2)(a) if the nature of the act is private.

(5) Regulations may provide for a person of a prescribed description to be treated as not being a public authority for purposes of this section and sections 21D and 21E.

(6) In the case of an act which constitutes discrimination by virtue of section 55, subsection (1) of this section also applies to discrimination against a person who is not disabled.

(7) Subsection (1)—

(a) does not apply to anything which is unlawful under any provision of this Act other than subsection (1); and

(b) does not, subject to subsections (8) and (9), apply to anything which would be unlawful under any such provision but for the operation of any provision in or made under this Act.

(8) Subsection (1) does apply in relation to a public authority's function of appointing a person to, and in relation to a public authority's functions with respect to a person as holder of, an office or post if—

(a) none of the conditions specified in section 4C(3) is satisfied in relation to the office or post; and

(b) sections 4D and 4E would apply in relation to an appointment to the office or post if any of those conditions was satisfied.

(9) Subsection (1) does apply in relation to a public authority's functions with respect to a person as candidate or prospective candidate for election to, and in relation to a public authority's functions with respect to a person as elected holder of, an office or post if—

(a) the office or post is not membership of a House of Parliament, the Scottish Parliament, the National Assembly for Wales or an authority mentioned in section 15A(1);

(b) none of the conditions specified in section 4C(3) is satisfied in relation to the office or post; and

(c) sections 4D and 4E would apply in relation to an appointment to the office or post if—

(i) any of those conditions was satisfied, and

(ii) section 4F(1) (but not section 4C(5)) was omitted.

(10) Subsections (8) and (9)—

(a) shall not be taken to prejudice the generality of subsection (1); but

(b) are subject to section 21C(5).]

[921A]

NOTES

Commencement: 4 December 2006.

Inserted, together with the preceding heading and ss 21C–21E, by the Disability Discrimination Act 2005, s 2, as from 4 December 2006.

Regulations: as of 6 April 2008, no Regulations had been made under this section.

[21C Exceptions from section 21B(1)

(1) Section 21B(1) does not apply to—

(a) a judicial act (whether done by a court, tribunal or other person); or

(b) an act done on the instructions, or on behalf, of a person acting in a judicial capacity.

(2) Section 21B(1) does not apply to any act of, or relating to, making, confirming or approving—

(a) an Act, an Act of the Scottish Parliament[, a Measure or Act of the National Assembly for Wales] or an Order in Council; or

(b) an instrument made under an Act, or under an Act of the Scottish Parliament, [or under a Measure or Act of the National Assembly for Wales,] by—

(i) a Minister of the Crown;

(ii) a member of the Scottish Executive; or

(iii) the [Welsh Ministers, the First Minister for Wales or the Counsel General to the Welsh Assembly Government].

(3) Section 21B(1) does not apply to any act of, or relating to, imposing conditions or requirements of a kind falling within section 59(1)(c).

(4) Section 21B(1) does not apply to—

(a) a decision not to institute criminal proceedings;

(b) where such a decision is made, an act done for the purpose of enabling the decision to be made;

(c) a decision not to continue criminal proceedings; or

(d) where such a decision is made—

(i) an act done for the purpose of enabling the decision to be made; or

(ii) an act done for the purpose of securing that the proceedings are not continued.

(5) Section 21B(1) does not apply to an act of a prescribed description.]

[921B]

NOTES

Commencement: 4 December 2006.

Inserted as noted to s 21B at **[921A]**.

Sub-s (2): words in square brackets in para (a) and words in first pair of square brackets in para (b) inserted, and words in second pair of square brackets in para (b) substituted, by the Government of Wales Act 2006 (Consequential Modifications and Transitional Provisions) Order 2007, SI 2007/1388, art 3, Sch 1, paras 47, 50, as from 25 May 2007.

[21D Meaning of "discrimination" in section 21B

(1) For the purposes of section 21B(1), a public authority discriminates against a disabled person if—

(a) for a reason which relates to the disabled person's disability, it treats him less favourably than it treats or would treat others to whom that reason does not or would not apply; and

(b) it cannot show that the treatment in question is justified under subsection (3), (5) or (7)(c).

(2) For the purposes of section 21B(1), a public authority also discriminates against a disabled person if—

(a) it fails to comply with a duty imposed on it by section 21E in circumstances in which the effect of that failure is to make it—

(i) impossible or unreasonably difficult for the disabled person to receive any benefit that is or may be conferred, or

(ii) unreasonably adverse for the disabled person to experience being subjected to any detriment to which a person is or may be subjected,

by the carrying-out of a function by the authority; and

(b) it cannot show that its failure to comply with that duty is justified under subsection (3), (5) or (7)(c).

(3) Treatment, or a failure to comply with a duty, is justified under this subsection if—

(a) in the opinion of the public authority, one or more of the conditions specified in subsection (4) are satisfied; and

(b) it is reasonable, in all the circumstances of the case, for it to hold that opinion.

(4) The conditions are—

(a) that the treatment, or non-compliance with the duty, is necessary in order not to endanger the health or safety of any person (which may include that of the disabled person);

(b) that the disabled person is incapable of entering into an enforceable agreement, or of giving an informed consent, and for that reason the treatment, or non-compliance with the duty, is reasonable in the particular case;

(c) that, in the case of treatment mentioned in subsection (1), treating the disabled person equally favourably would in the particular case involve substantial extra costs and, having regard to resources, the extra costs in that particular case would be too great;

(d) that the treatment, or non-compliance with the duty, is necessary for the protection of rights and freedoms of other persons.

(5) Treatment, or a failure to comply with a duty, is justified under this subsection if the acts of the public authority which give rise to the treatment or failure are a proportionate means of achieving a legitimate aim.

(6) Regulations may make provision, for purposes of this section, as to circumstances in which it is, or as to circumstances in which it is not, reasonable for a public authority to hold the opinion mentioned in subsection (3)(a).

(7) Regulations may—

(a) amend or omit a condition specified in subsection (4) or make provision for it not to apply in prescribed circumstances;

(b) amend or omit subsection (5) or make provision for it not to apply in prescribed circumstances;

(c) make provision for purposes of this section (in addition to any provision for the time being made by subsections (3) to (5)) as to circumstances in which treatment, or a failure to comply with a duty, is to be taken to be justified.]

[921C]

NOTES

Commencement: 30 June 2005 (for the purpose only of exercising the power to make regulations); 4 December 2006 (otherwise).

Inserted as noted to s 21B at **[921A]**.

Regulations: the Disability Discrimination (Service Providers and Public Authorities Carrying Out Functions) Regulations 2005, SI 2005/2901.

[21E Duties for purposes of section 21D(2) to make adjustments

(1) Subsection (2) applies where a public authority has a practice, policy or procedure which makes it—

(a) impossible or unreasonably difficult for disabled persons to receive any benefit that is or may be conferred, or

(b) unreasonably adverse for disabled persons to experience being subjected to any detriment to which a person is or may be subjected,

by the carrying-out of a function by the authority.

(2) It is the duty of the authority to take such steps as it is reasonable, in all the circumstances of the case, for the authority to have to take in order to change that practice, policy or procedure so that it no longer has that effect.

(3) Subsection (4) applies where a physical feature makes it—

(a) impossible or unreasonably difficult for disabled persons to receive any benefit that is or may be conferred, or

(b) unreasonably adverse for disabled persons to experience being subjected to any detriment to which a person is or may be subjected,

by the carrying-out of a function by a public authority.

(4) It is the duty of the authority to take such steps as it is reasonable, in all the circumstances of the case, for the authority to have to take in order to—

(a) remove the feature;

(b) alter it so that it no longer has that effect;

(c) provide a reasonable means of avoiding the feature; or

(d) adopt a reasonable alternative method of carrying out the function.

(5) Regulations may prescribe—

(a) matters which are to be taken into account in determining whether any provision of a kind mentioned in subsection (4)(c) or (d) is reasonable;

(b) categories of public authorities to whom subsection (4) does not apply.

(6) Subsection (7) applies where an auxiliary aid or service would—

(a) enable disabled persons to receive, or facilitate the receiving by disabled persons of, any benefit that is or may be conferred, or

(b) reduce the extent to which it is adverse for disabled persons to experience being subjected to any detriment to which a person is or may be subjected,

by the carrying-out of a function by a public authority.

(7) It is the duty of the authority to take such steps as it is reasonable, in all the circumstances of the case, for the authority to have to take in order to provide that auxiliary aid or service.

(8) Regulations may make provision, for purposes of this section—

(a) as to circumstances in which it is, or as to circumstances in which it is not, reasonable for a public authority to have to take steps of a prescribed description;

(b) as to steps which it is always, or as to steps which it is never, reasonable for a public authority to have to take;

(c) as to what is, or as to what is not, to be included within the meaning of "practice, policy or procedure";

(d) as to things which are, or as to things which are not, to be treated as physical features;

(e) as to things which are, or as to things which are not, to be treated as auxiliary aids or services.

(9) Nothing in this section requires a public authority to take any steps which, apart from this section, it has no power to take.

(10) This section imposes duties only for the purposes of determining whether a public authority has, for the purposes of section 21B(1), discriminated against a disabled person; and accordingly a breach of any such duty is not actionable as such.]

[921D]

NOTES

Commencement: 30 June 2005 (for the purpose only of exercising the power to make regulations); 4 December 2006 (otherwise).

Inserted as noted to s 21B at **[921A]**.

Regulations: the Disability Discrimination (Service Providers and Public Authorities Carrying Out Functions) Regulations 2005, SI 2005/2901.

21F–24M *(Ss 21F–21J (Private clubs), ss 22–24M (Premises) outside the scope of this work.)*

Enforcement, etc

25 Enforcement, remedies and procedure

(1) A claim by any person that another person—

(a) has discriminated against him in a way which is unlawful under this Part; or

(b) is by virtue of section 57 or 58 to be treated as having discriminated against him in such a way,

may be made the subject of civil proceedings in the same way as any other claim in tort or (in Scotland) in reparation for breach of statutory duty.

(2) For the avoidance of doubt it is hereby declared that damages in respect of discrimination in a way which is unlawful under this Part may include compensation for injury to feelings whether or not they include compensation under any other head.

(3) Proceedings in England and Wales shall be brought only in a county court.

(4) Proceedings in Scotland shall be brought only in a sheriff court.

(5) The remedies available in such proceedings are those which are available in the High Court or (as the case may be) the Court of Session.

(6) Part II of Schedule 3 makes further provision about the enforcement of this Part and about procedure.

[(6A) Subsection (1) does not apply in relation to a claim by a person that another person—

(a) has discriminated against him in relation to the provision under a group insurance arrangement of facilities by way of insurance; or

(b) is by virtue of section 57 or 58 to be treated as having discriminated against him in relation to the provision under such an arrangement of such facilities.]

[[(7) Subsection (1) does not apply in relation to a claim by a person that another person—

(a) has discriminated against him in relation to the provision of employment services; or

(b) is by virtue of section 57 or 58 to be treated as having discriminated against him in relation to the provision of employment services.

(8) A claim—

(a) of the kind referred to in subsection (6A) or (7), or

(b) by a person that another—

(i) has subjected him to harassment in a way which is unlawful under section 21A(2), or

(ii) is by virtue of section 57 or 58 to be treated as having subjected him to harassment in such a way,

may be presented as a complaint to an employment tribunal.]

(9) Section 17A(1A) to (7) and paragraphs 3 and 4 of Schedule 3 apply in relation to a complaint under subsection (8) as if it were a complaint under section 17A(1) (and paragraphs 6 to 8 of Schedule 3 do not apply in relation to such a complaint).]

[922]

NOTES

Sub-s (6A): inserted by the Disability Discrimination Act 2005, s 11(2), as from 5 December 2005.

Sub-ss (7), (8): added, together with sub-s (9), by the Disability Discrimination Act 1995 (Amendment) Regulations 2003, SI 2003/1673, regs 3(1), 19(2), as from 1 October 2004; substituted by the Disability Discrimination Act 2005, s 19(1), Sch 1, Pt 1, paras 1, 21, as from 5 December 2005.

Sub-s (9): added as noted above.

Conciliation: employment tribunal proceedings and claims which could be the subject of employment tribunal proceedings under sub-s (8) above are proceedings to which the Employment Tribunals Act 1996, s 18 applies; see s 18(1)(c) of that Act at **[975]**. For the powers of Commission for Equality and Human Rights to make arrangements for the provision of conciliation services for disputes in respect of which proceedings have been, or could be, brought under this section,; see the Equality Act 2006, s 27 at **[1670]**.

Restriction of publicity in disability cases: the Employment Tribunals Act 1996, s 12 applies to proceedings on a complaint under sub-s (8) in which evidence of a personal nature is likely to be heard; see s 12(1) of the 1996 Act at **[968]**.

26 Validity and revision of certain agreements

(1) Any term in a contract for the provision of goods, facilities or services or in any other agreement is void so far as it purports to—

(a) require a person to do anything which would contravene any provision of, or made under, this Part,

(b) exclude or limit the operation of any provision of this Part, or

(c) prevent any person from making a claim under this Part.

[(1A) Subsection (1) does not apply to—

(a) any term in a contract for the provision of employment services;

(b) any term in a contract which is a group insurance arrangement; or

(c) a term which—

(i) is in an agreement which is not a contract of either of those kinds, and

(ii) relates to the provision of employment services or the provision under a group insurance arrangement of facilities by way of insurance.]

(2) Paragraphs (b) and (c) of subsection (1) do not apply to an agreement settling a claim to which section 25 applies.

(3) On the application of any person interested in an agreement to which subsection (1) applies, a county court or a sheriff court may make such order as it thinks just for modifying the agreement to take account of the effect of subsection (1).

(4) No such order shall be made unless all persons affected have been—

(a) given notice of the application; and

(b) afforded an opportunity to make representations to the court.

(5) Subsection (4) applies subject to any rules of court providing for that notice to be dispensed with.

(6) An order under subsection (3) may include provision as respects any period before the making of the order.

[923]–[924]

NOTES

Sub-s (1A): inserted by the Disability Discrimination Act 1995 (Amendment) Regulations 2003, SI 2003/1673, regs 3(1), 19(3), as from 1 October 2004; substituted by the Disability Discrimination Act 2005, s 19(1), Sch 1, Pt 1, paras 1, 22, as from 5 December 2005.

27, 28, 28A–49 (*S 27* (*Alterations to premises occupied under leases*) *outside the scope of this work; s 28 repealed by the Equality Act 2006, ss 40, 91, Sch 3, paras 41, 45, Sch 4, as from 1 October 2007; ss 28A–31C* (*Pt IV: Education; including new ss 31ADA, 31ADB as inserted by the Disability Discrimination Act 1995* (*Amendment etc*) (*General Qualifications Bodies*) (*Alteration of Premises and Enforcement*) *Regulations 200, SI 2007/2405, regs 2*(*1*), *3, as from 1 September 2007*), *and ss 32–49* (*Pt V: Public Transport*) *outside the scope of this work.*)

[PART 5A
PUBLIC AUTHORITIES

49A General duty

(1) Every public authority shall in carrying out its functions have due regard to—

(a) the need to eliminate discrimination that is unlawful under this Act;

(b) the need to eliminate harassment of disabled persons that is related to their disabilities;

(c) the need to promote equality of opportunity between disabled persons and other persons;

(d) the need to take steps to take account of disabled persons' disabilities, even where that involves treating disabled persons more favourably than other persons;

(e) the need to promote positive attitudes towards disabled persons; and

(f) the need to encourage participation by disabled persons in public life.

(2) Subsection (1) is without prejudice to any obligation of a public authority to comply with any other provision of this Act.]

[924A]

NOTES

Commencement: 5 December 2005 (sub-s (1) for the purpose only of regulations under s 49D); 4 December 2006 (otherwise).

Inserted, together with the preceding heading and ss 49B–49F, by the Disability Discrimination Act 2005, s 3, as from 5 December 2005 (in so far as relating to sub-s (1) for the purpose only of regulations under s 49D), and as from 4 December 2006 (otherwise).

Assessment and compliance: for the power of the Commission for Equality and Human Rights to assess the extent to which, or the manner in which, a person has complied with a duty under this section and s 49D and, where it thinks that a person has failed to comply with such duty, to give the person a notice requiring him: (i) to comply with the duty, and (ii) to give the Commission (within the period of 28 days beginning with the date on which he receives the notice) written information of steps taken, or proposed, for the purpose of complying with the duty, see the Equality Act 2006, ss 31, 32 at **[1674]**, **[1675]**.

[49B Meaning of "public authority" in Part 5A

(1) In this Part "public authority"—

(a) includes any person certain of whose functions are functions of a public nature; but

(b) does not include—

(i) any person mentioned in section 21B(3);

(ii) the Scottish Parliament; …

(iii) a person, other than the Scottish Parliamentary Corporate Body, exercising functions in connection with proceedings in the Scottish Parliament;

[(iv) the National Assembly for Wales; or

(v) a person, other than the National Assembly for Wales Commission, exercising functions in connection with proceedings in the National Assembly for Wales].

(2) In relation to a particular act, a person is not a public authority by virtue only of subsection (1)(a) if the nature of the act is private.

(3) Regulations may provide for a person of a prescribed description to be treated as not being a public authority for the purposes of this Part.]

[924B]

NOTES

Commencement: 5 December 2005.

Inserted as noted to s 49A at **[924A]**.

Sub-s (1): word omitted from para (b)(ii) repealed, and paras (b)(iv), (v) added, by the Government of Wales Act 2006 (Consequential Modifications and Transitional Provisions) Order 2007, SI 2007/1388, art 3, Sch 1, paras 55, 57, as from 25 May 2007.

Regulations: as of 6 April 2008, no Regulations had been made under this section.

[49C Exceptions from section 49A(1)

(1) Section 49A(1) does not apply to—

(a) a judicial act (whether done by a court, tribunal or other person); or

(b) an act done on the instructions, or on behalf, of a person acting in a judicial capacity.

(2) Section 49A(1) does not apply to any act of, or relating to, making or approving an Act of Parliament, an Act of the Scottish Parliament[, a Measure or Act of the National Assembly for Wales] or an Order in Council.

(3) Section 49A(1)(c) and (d) do not apply to—

(a) an act done in connection with recruitment to any of the naval, military or air forces of the Crown; or

(b) an act done in relation to a person in connection with service by him as a member of any of those forces.

(4) Regulations may provide for [one or more specified paragraphs of section 49A(1)] not to apply to an act of a prescribed description.]

[924C]

NOTES

Commencement: 5 December 2005.

Inserted as noted to s 49A at **[924A]**.

Sub-s (2): words in square brackets inserted by the Government of Wales Act 2006 (Consequential Modifications and Transitional Provisions) Order 2007, SI 2007/1388, art 3, Sch 1, paras 47, 58, as from 25 May 2007.

Sub-s (4): words in square brackets substituted by the Equality Act 2006, s 88, as from 18 April 2006.

Regulations: as of 6 April 2008, no Regulations had been made under this section.

[49D Power to impose specific duties

(1) The Secretary of State may by regulations impose on a public authority, other than a relevant Scottish authority or a cross-border authority, such duties as the Secretary of State considers appropriate for the purpose of ensuring the better performance by that authority of its duty under section 49A(1).

(2) The Secretary of State may by regulations impose on a cross-border authority such duties as the Secretary of State considers appropriate for the purpose of ensuring the better performance by that authority of its duty under section 49A(1) so far as relating to such of its functions as are not Scottish functions.

(3) The Scottish Ministers may by regulations impose on a relevant Scottish authority such duties as the Scottish Ministers consider appropriate for the purpose of ensuring the better performance by that authority of its duty under section 49A(1).

(4) The Scottish Ministers may by regulations impose on a cross-border authority such duties as the Scottish Ministers consider appropriate for the purpose of ensuring the better performance by that authority of its duty under section 49A(1) so far as relating to its Scottish functions.

(5) Before making regulations under any of subsections (1) to (4), the person making the regulations shall consult the [Commission for Equality and Human Rights].

(6) Before making regulations under subsection (1) or (2) in relation to functions exercisable in relation to Wales by a public authority that is not a relevant Welsh authority, the Secretary of State shall consult the [Welsh Ministers].

(7) The Secretary of State shall not make regulations under subsection (1) or (2) in relation to a relevant Welsh authority except with the consent of the [Welsh Ministers].

(8) Before making regulations under subsection (2), the Secretary of State shall consult the Scottish Ministers.

(9) Before making regulations under subsection (4), the Scottish Ministers shall consult the Secretary of State.

(10) In this section—

"relevant Scottish authority" means—

(a) a member of the Scottish executive or a junior Scottish Minister;

(b) the Registrar General of Births, Deaths and Marriages for Scotland, the Keeper of the Registers of Scotland or the Keeper of the Records of Scotland;

(c) any office of a description specified in an Order in Council under section 126(8)(b) of the Scotland Act 1998 (other non-ministerial office in the Scottish Administration); or

(d) a public body, public office or holder of a public office—

(i) which (or who) is not a cross-border authority or the Scottish Parliamentary Corporate Body;

(ii) whose functions are exercisable only in or as regards Scotland; and

(iii) some at least of whose functions do not (within the meaning of the Scotland Act 1998) relate to reserved matters;

"cross-border authority" means a cross-border public authority within the meaning given by section 88(5) of the Scotland Act 1998;

"Scottish functions" means functions which are exercisable in or as regards Scotland and which do not (within the meaning of the Scotland Act 1998) relate to reserved matters;

"relevant Welsh authority" means—

[(a) the National Assembly for Wales Commission;

(aa) the Welsh Ministers, the First Minister for Wales or the Counsel General to the Welsh Assembly Government; or]

(b) a public authority whose functions are exercisable only in relation to Wales.]

[924D]–[929]

NOTES

Commencement: 30 June 2005 (for the purpose of exercising the power to make regulations); 5 December 2005 (otherwise).

Inserted as noted to s 49A at **[924A]**.

Sub-s (5): words in square brackets substituted by the Equality Act 2006, s 40, Sch 3, paras 41, 48, as from 1 October 2007.

Sub-ss (6), (7), (10): words in square brackets substituted by the Government of Wales Act 2006 (Consequential Modifications and Transitional Provisions) Order 2007, SI 2007/1388, art 3, Sch 1, paras 47, 59(1), (2), as from 25 May 2007.

Assessment and compliance: see the note to s 49A at **[924A]**.

Regulations: the Disability Discrimination (Public Authorities) (Statutory Duties) Regulations 2005, SI 2005/2966 at **[3346]**; the Disability Discrimination (Public Authorities) (Statutory Duties) (Scotland) Regulations 2005, SSI 2005/565 at **[3356]**.

49E–49I, 50–52 *(Ss 49E, 49F inserted by the Disability Discrimination Act 2005, s 3, as from 5 December 2005 and repealed by the Equality Act 2006, ss 40, 91, Sch 3, paras 41, 49, Sch 4, as from 1 October 2007; ss 49G–49I (Pt 5B: Improvements to dwelling houses) outside the scope of this work; ss 50–52 (Pt VI: the National Disability Council) repealed by the Disability Rights Commission Act 1999, s 14(2), Sch 5, partly from 25 April 2000, and from 4 December 2006 otherwise.)*

PART VII
SUPPLEMENTAL

53A, 53, 54 *(S 53A inserted (at the beginning of this Part) by the Disability Rights Commission Act 1999, s 9(1), and repealed by the Equality Act 2006, ss 40, 91, Sch 3, paras 41, 52, Sch 4, as from 1 October 2007; ss 53, 54 repealed by the Disability Rights Commission Act 1999, s 14(2), Sch 5, partly from 25 April 2000, and from 4 December 2006 otherwise.)*

55 Victimisation

(1) For the purposes of [Part 2 or Part 4, or Part 3 other than sections 24A to 24L,] a person ("A") discriminates against another person ("B") if—

(a) he treats B less favourably than he treats or would treat other persons whose circumstances are the same as B's; and

(b) he does so for a reason mentioned in subsection (2).

(2) The reasons are that—

(a) B has—

(i) brought proceedings against A or any other person under this Act; or

(ii) given evidence or information in connection with such proceedings brought by any person; or

(iii) otherwise done anything under[, or by reference to,] this Act in relation to A or any other person; or

(iv) alleged that A or any other person has (whether or not the allegation so states) contravened this Act; or

(b) A believes or suspects that B has done or intends to do any of those things.

(3) Where B is a disabled person, or a person who has had a disability, the disability in question shall be disregarded in comparing his circumstances with those of any other person for the purposes of subsection (1)(a).

[(3A) For the purposes of Chapter 1 of Part 4—

(a) references in subsection (2) to B include references to—

(i) a person who is, for the purposes of that Chapter, B's parent; and

(ii) a sibling of B; and

(b) references in that subsection to this Act are, as respects a person mentioned in sub-paragraph (i) or (ii) of paragraph (a), restricted to that Chapter.]

(4) Subsection (1) does not apply to treatment of a person because of an allegation made by him if the allegation was false and not made in good faith.

[(5) In the case of an act which constitutes discrimination by virtue of this section, sections 4, 4B, 4D, [4G,] 6A, 7A, 7C, 13, 14A, 14C[, 15B] and 16A also apply to discrimination against a person who is not disabled.

(6) …]

[930]

NOTES

Sub-s (1): words in square brackets substituted by the Disability Discrimination Act 2005, s 19(1), Sch 1, Pt 1, paras 1, 29(1), (2), as from 4 December 2006.

Sub-s (2): words in square brackets in para (a)(iii) inserted by the Disability Discrimination Act 2005, s 19(1), Sch 1, Pt 1, paras 1, 29(1), (3), as from 5 December 2005.

Sub-s (3A): inserted by the Special Educational Needs and Disability Act 2001, s 38(1), (8).

Sub-s (5): added, together with sub-s (6), by the Disability Discrimination Act 1995 (Amendment) Regulations 2003, SI 2003/1673, regs 3(1), 21, as from 1 October 2004; figure in first pair of square brackets inserted by the Disability Discrimination Act 1995 (Pensions) Regulations 2003, SI 2003/2770, regs 2, 4(3), as from 1 October 2004; figure in second pair of square brackets inserted by the Disability Discrimination Act 2005, s 19(1), Sch 1, Pt 1, paras 1, 29(1), (4), as from 5 December 2005.

Sub-s (6): added as noted above; repealed by the Disability Discrimination Act 2005, s 19, Sch 1, Pt 1, paras 1, 29(1), (5), Sch 2, as from 5 December 2005.

Modified, in relation to governing bodies with delegated budgets, by the Education (Modification of Enactments Relating to Employment) (England) Order 2003, SI 2003/1964, art 3, Schedule at **[3035C]**, **[3035G]** and the Education (Modification of Enactments Relating to Employment) (Wales) Order 2006, SI 2006/1073, art 3, Schedule at **[3462B]**, **[3462F]**.

[56 Help for aggrieved persons in obtaining information etc

(1) For the purposes of this section—

(a) a person who considers that he may have been—

(i) discriminated against in contravention of Part 2 or 3, or

(ii) subjected to harassment in contravention of Part 2 or section 21A(2),

is referred to as "the person aggrieved"; and

(b) a person against whom the person aggrieved may decide to institute, or has instituted, proceedings in respect of such discrimination or harassment is referred to as "the respondent".

(2) With a view to helping the person aggrieved decide whether to institute proceedings and, if he does so, to formulate and present his case in the most effective manner, the Secretary of State shall by order prescribe—

(a) forms by which the person aggrieved may question the respondent on his reasons for doing any relevant act, or on any other matter which is or may be relevant; and

(b) forms by which the respondent may if he so wishes reply to any questions.

(3) Where the person aggrieved questions the respondent in accordance with forms prescribed by an order under subsection (2)—

(a) the question, and any reply by the respondent (whether in accordance with such an order or not), shall be admissible as evidence in any proceedings under Part 2 or 3;

(b) if it appears to the court or tribunal in any such proceedings—

(i) that the respondent deliberately, and without reasonable excuse, omitted to reply within the period of eight weeks beginning with the day on which the question was served on him, or

(ii) that the respondent's reply is evasive or equivocal,

it may draw any inference which it considers it just and equitable to draw, including an inference that the respondent committed an unlawful act.

(4) The Secretary of State may by order—

(a) prescribe the period within which questions must be duly served in order to be admissible under subsection (3)(a); and

(b) prescribe the manner in which a question, and any reply by the respondent, may be duly served.

(5) Rules of court may enable a court entertaining a claim under section 25 to determine, before the date fixed for the hearing of the claim, whether a question or reply is admissible under this section or not.

(6) In proceedings in respect of a section 21B claim, subsection (3)(b) does not apply in relation to a failure to reply, or a particular reply, if the following conditions are met—

(a) that, at the time of doing any relevant act, the respondent was carrying out public investigator functions or was a public prosecutor; and

(b) that the respondent reasonably believes that a reply or (as the case may be) a different reply would be likely to prejudice any criminal investigation, any decision to institute criminal proceedings or any criminal proceedings or would reveal the reasons behind a decision not to institute, or a decision not to continue, criminal proceedings.

(7) Regulations may provide for this section not to have effect, or to have effect with prescribed modifications, in relation to section 21B claims of a prescribed description.

(8) This section is without prejudice to any other enactment or rule of law regulating interlocutory and preliminary matters in proceedings before a county court, the sheriff or an employment tribunal, and has effect subject to any enactment or rule of law regulating the admissibility of evidence in such proceedings.

(9) In this section "section 21B claim" means a claim under section 25 by virtue of section 21B.]

[931]

NOTES

Commencement: 30 June 2005 (for the purpose of exercising any power to make regulations, orders or rules of court); 5 December 2005 (in so far as not already in force, except for sub-ss (6), (7) so far as not already in force, and sub-s (9)); 4 December 2006 (otherwise).

Substituted by the Disability Discrimination Act 2005, s 17, as from such dates and for such purposes as noted above.

Orders: the Disability Discrimination (Questions and Replies) Order 2004, SI 2004/1168 at **[3141]**; the Disability Discrimination (Questions and Replies) Order 2005, SI 2005/2703. Note that SI 2005/2703 applies in relation to cases falling within Part 3 of the Act, with certain exceptions (see art 2).

Regulations: as of 6 April 2008, no Regulations had been made under this section.

57 Aiding unlawful acts

(1) A person who knowingly aids another person to do an [unlawful act] is to be treated for the purposes of this Act as himself doing the same kind of unlawful act.

(2) For the purposes of subsection (1), an employee or agent for whose act the employer or principal is liable under section 58 (or would be so liable but for section 58(5)) shall be taken to have aided the employer or principal to do the act.

(3) For the purposes of this section, a person does not knowingly aid another to do an unlawful act if—

(a) he acts in reliance on a statement made to him by that other person that, because of any provision of this Act, the act would not be unlawful; and

(b) it is reasonable for him to rely on the statement.

(4) A person who knowingly or recklessly makes such a statement which is false or misleading in a material respect is guilty of an offence.

(5) Any person guilty of an offence under subsection (4) shall be liable on summary conviction to a fine not exceeding level 5 on the standard scale.

[(6) "Unlawful act" means an act made unlawful by any provision of this Act other than a provision contained in Chapter 1 of Part 4.]

[932]

NOTES

Sub-s (1): words in square brackets substituted by the Special Educational Needs and Disability Act 2001, s 38(1), (9).

Sub-s (6): added by the Special Educational Needs and Disability Act 2001, s 38(1), (10).

Modified as noted to s 55 at **[930]**.

58 Liability of employers and principals

(1) Anything done by a person in the course of his employment shall be treated for the purposes of this Act as also done by his employer, whether or not it was done with the employer's knowledge or approval.

(2) Anything done by a person as agent for another person with the authority of that other person shall be treated for the purposes of this Act as also done by that other person.

(3) Subsection (2) applies whether the authority was—
(a) express or implied; or
(b) given before or after the act in question was done.

(4) Subsections (1) and (2) do not apply in relation to an offence under section 57(4).

(5) In proceedings under this Act against any person in respect of an act alleged to have been done by an employee of his, it shall be a defence for that person to prove that he took such steps as were reasonably practicable to prevent the employee from—
(a) doing that act; or
(b) doing, in the course of his employment, acts of that description.

[933]

NOTES

Modified as noted to s 55 at **[930]**.

Serious Organised Crime Agency: for the application of this section to any constable or other person who has been seconded to SOCA to serve as a member of its staff, see the Serious Organised Crime and Police Act 2005, s 56(3), (4).

59 Statutory authority and national security etc

(1) Nothing in this Act makes unlawful any act done—
(a) in pursuance of any enactment; or
[(b) in pursuance of any instrument made under any enactment by—
(i) a Minister of the Crown,
(ii) a member of the Scottish Executive, …
(iii) the National Assembly for Wales [constituted by the Government of Wales Act 1998, or
(iv) the Welsh Ministers, the First Minister for Wales or the Counsel General to the Welsh Assembly Government]; or
(c) to comply with any condition or requirement—
(i) imposed by a Minister of the Crown (whether before or after the passing of this Act) by virtue of any enactment,
(ii) imposed by a member of the Scottish Executive (whether before or after the coming into force of this sub-paragraph) by virtue of any enactment, …
(iii) imposed by the National Assembly for Wales [constituted by the Government of Wales Act 1998] (whether before or after the coming into force of this sub-paragraph) by virtue of any enactment[, or
(iv) imposed by the Welsh Ministers, the First Minister for Wales or the Counsel General to the Welsh Assembly Government].]

(2) In subsection (1) "enactment" includes one passed or made after the date on which this Act is passed and "instrument" includes one made after that date.

[(2A) Nothing in—
(a) Part 2 of this Act, or
(b) Part 3 of this Act to the extent that it relates to the provision of employment services,

makes unlawful any act done for the purpose of safeguarding national security if the doing of the act was justified by that purpose.]

(3) Nothing in [any other provision of] this Act makes unlawful any act done for the purpose of safeguarding national security.

[934]

NOTES

Sub-s (1): paras (b), (c) substituted by the Disability Discrimination Act 2005, s 19(1), Sch 1, Pt 1, paras 1, 30, as from 30 June 2005; other words in square brackets inserted, and words omitted repealed, by the Government of Wales Act 2006 (Consequential Modifications and Transitional Provisions) Order 2007, SI 2007/1388, art 3, Sch 1, paras 47, 61, as from 25 May 2007.

Sub-s (2A): inserted by the Disability Discrimination Act 1995 (Amendment) Regulations 2003, SI 2003/1673, regs 3(1), 23(a), as from 1 October 2004.

Sub-s (3): words in square brackets inserted by SI 2003/1673, regs 3(1), 23(b), as from 1 October 2004.

[59A National security

(1) Rules of court may make provision for enabling a county court or sheriff court in which a claim is brought in respect of alleged discrimination contrary to this Act (including

anything treated by virtue of this Act as amounting to discrimination contrary to this Act), where the court considers it expedient in the interests of national security—

(a) to exclude from all or part of the proceedings—
  (i) the claimant;
  (ii) the claimant's representatives;
  (iii) any assessors;
(b) to permit a claimant or representative who has been excluded to make a statement to the court before the commencement of the proceedings, or the part of the proceedings, from which he is excluded;
(c) to take steps to keep secret all or part of the reasons for the court's decision in the proceedings.

(2) The Attorney General or, in Scotland, the Advocate General for Scotland, may appoint a person to represent the interests of a claimant in, or in any part of, proceedings from which the claimant or his representatives are excluded by virtue of subsection (1).

(3) A person may be appointed under subsection (2) only—
(a) in relation to proceedings in England and Wales, if he has a general qualification (within the meaning of section 71 of the Courts and Legal Services Act 1990 (c 41)), or
(b) in relation to proceedings in Scotland, if he is—
  (i) an advocate, or
  (ii) qualified to practice as a solicitor in Scotland.

(4) A person appointed under subsection (2) shall not be responsible to the person whose interests he is appointed to represent.]

[934A]

NOTES

Commencement: 18 April 2006.
Inserted by the Equality Act 2006, s 89, as from 18 April 2006.

PART VIII
MISCELLANEOUS

60 Appointment by Secretary of State of advisers

(1) The Secretary of State may appoint such persons as he thinks fit to advise or assist him in connection with matters relating to the employment of disabled persons and persons who have had a disability.

(2) Persons may be appointed by the Secretary of State to act generally or in relation to a particular area or locality.

(3) The Secretary of State may pay to any person appointed under this section such allowances and compensation for loss of earnings as he considers appropriate.

(4) The approval of the Treasury is required for any payment under this section.

(5) In subsection (1) "employment" includes self-employment.

(6) The Secretary of State may by order—
(a) provide for section 17 of, and Schedule 2 to, the Disabled Persons (Employment) Act 1944 (national advisory council and district advisory committees) to cease to have effect—
  (i) so far as concerns the national advisory council; or
  (ii) so far as concerns district advisory committees; or
(b) repeal that section and Schedule.

(7) At any time before the coming into force of an order under paragraph (b) of subsection (6), section 17 of the Act of 1944 shall have effect as if in subsection (1), after "disabled persons" in each case there were inserted ", and persons who have had a disability," and as if at the end of the section there were added—

"(3) For the purposes of this section—
(a) a person is a disabled person if he is a disabled person for the purposes of the Disability Discrimination Act 1995; and
(b) "disability" has the same meaning as in that Act."

(8) At any time before the coming into force of an order under paragraph (a)(i) or (b) of subsection (6), section 16 of the Chronically Sick and Disabled Persons Act 1970 (which extends the functions of the national advisory council) shall have effect as if after "disabled persons" in each case there were inserted ", and persons who have had a disability," and as if at the end of the section there were added—

"(2) For the purposes of this section—
(a) a person is a disabled person if he is a disabled person for the purposes of the Disability Discrimination Act 1995; and
(b) "disability" has the same meaning as in that Act."

[935]

NOTES

Orders: the Disability Discrimination (Abolition of District Advisory Committees) Order 1997, SI 1997/536; the Disability Discrimination (Repeal of section 17 of, and Schedule 2 to, the Disabled Persons (Employment) Act, 1944) Order 1998, SI 1998/565.

61 Amendment of the Disabled Persons (Employment) Act 1944

(1)–(7) ...

(8) Any provision of subordinate legislation in which "disabled person" is defined by reference to the Act of 1944 shall be construed as if that expression had the same meaning as in this Act.

(9) Subsection (8) does not prevent the further amendment of any such provision by subordinate legislation.

[936]

NOTES

Sub-ss (1)–(7): amend the Disabled Persons (Employment) Act 1944, s 15(1), (2), 16, insert s 15(2A), (5A) of that Act, and repeal ss 1, 6–14, 19, 21.

62, 63 (*Repealed by the Employment Tribunals Act 1996, s 45, Sch 3, Pt I; the equivalent provisions in that Act are ss 12, 32 respectively at* **[968]**, **[989]**.)

64 Application to Crown etc

[(A1) The following provisions bind the Crown—
(a) sections 21B to 21E and Part 5A, and
(b) the other provisions of this Act so far as applying for the purposes of provisions mentioned in paragraph (a);

and sections 57 and 58 shall apply for purposes of provisions mentioned in paragraph (a) as if service as a Crown servant were employment by the Crown.]

(1) This Act[, other than the provisions mentioned in paragraphs (a) and (b) of subsection (A1),] applies—
(a) to an act done by or for purposes of a Minister of the Crown or government department, or
(b) to an act done on behalf of the Crown by a statutory body, or a person holding a statutory office,

as it applies to an act done by a private person.

(2) ... Part II applies to service—
(a) for purposes of a Minister of the Crown or government department, other than service of a person holding a statutory office, or
(b) on behalf of the Crown for purposes of a person holding a statutory office or purposes of a statutory body,

as it applies to employment by a private person.

[(2A) Subsections [(A1) to] (2) have effect subject to section 64A.]

(3) The provisions of Parts II to IV of the 1947 Act apply to proceedings against the Crown under this Act as they apply to Crown proceedings in England and Wales ...

(4) The provisions of Part V of the 1947 Act apply to proceedings against the Crown under this Act as they apply to proceedings in Scotland which by virtue of that Part are treated

as civil proceedings by or against the Crown; but the proviso to section 44 of that Act (removal of proceedings from the sheriff court to the Court of Session) does not apply.

(5), (6) …

(7) … Part II does not apply to service in any of the naval, military or air forces of the Crown.

(8) In this section—

"the 1947 Act" means the Crown Proceedings Act 1947;

…

"Crown proceedings" means proceedings which, by virtue of section 23 of the 1947 Act, are treated for the purposes of Part II of that Act as civil proceedings by or against the Crown;

…

…

…

…

"service for purposes of a Minister of the Crown or government department" does not include service in any office for the time being mentioned in Schedule 2 (Ministerial offices) to the House of Commons Disqualification Act 1975;

"statutory body" means a body set up by or under an enactment;

"statutory office" means an office so set up; *and*

…

[937]

NOTES

Sub-s (A1): inserted by the Disability Discrimination Act 2005, s 19(1), Sch 1, Pt 1, paras 1, 31(1), (2), as from 5 December 2005 (in so far as relating to Pt 5A), and as from 4 December 2006 (otherwise).

Sub-s (1): words in square brackets inserted by the Disability Discrimination Act 2005, s 19(1), Sch 1, Pt 1, paras 1, 31(1), (3), as from 5 December 2005 (in so far as relating to Pt 5A), and as from 4 December 2006 (otherwise).

Sub-ss (2), (7): words omitted repealed by the Disability Discrimination Act 1995 (Amendment) Regulations 2003, SI 2003/1673, regs 3(1), 24(a), (d), as from 1 October 2004.

Sub-s (2A): inserted by SI 2003/1673, regs 3(1), 24(b), as from 1 October 2004; words in square brackets substituted by the Disability Discrimination Act 2005, s 19(1), Sch 1, Pt 1, paras 1, 31(1), (4), as from 5 December 2005 (in so far as relating to Pt 5A), and as from 4 December 2006 (otherwise).

Sub-s (3): words omitted repealed by the Civil Procedure (Modification of Crown Proceedings Act 1947) Order 2005, SI 2005/2712, art 3, Sch 2, para 3, as from 1 October 2005.

Sub-ss (5), (6): repealed by SI 2003/1673, regs 3(1), 24(c), as from 1 October 2004.

Sub-s (8): definitions "British Transport Police", "fire brigade", "Ministry of Defence Police", "prison officer", "Royal Parks Constabulary", and "United Kingdom Atomic Energy Authority Constabulary" (and the word immediately preceding that definition) (omitted) repealed by SI 2003/1673, regs 3(1), 24(e), as from 1 October 2004.

[64A Police

(1) For the purposes of Part 2, the holding of the office of constable shall be treated as employment—

(a) by the chief officer of police as respects any act done by him in relation to a constable or that office;

(b) by the police authority as respects any act done by them in relation to a constable or that office.

(2) For the purposes of section 58—

(a) the holding of the office of constable shall be treated as employment by the chief officer of police (and as not being employment by any other person); and

(b) anything done by a person holding such an office in the performance, or purported performance, of his functions shall be treated as done in the course of that employment.

(3) There shall be paid out of the police fund—

(a) any compensation, costs or expenses awarded against a chief officer of police in any proceedings brought against him under Part 2 [or 3], and any costs or expenses incurred by him in any such proceedings so far as not recovered by him in the proceedings; and

(b) any sum required by a chief officer of police for the settlement of any claim made against him under Part 2 [or 3] if the settlement is approved by the police authority.

(4) Any proceedings under Part 2 [or 3] which, by virtue of [this section], would lie against a chief officer of police shall be brought against—

(a) the chief officer of police for the time being, or

(b) in the case of a vacancy in that office, against the person for the time being performing the functions of that office;

and references in subsection (3) to the chief officer of police shall be construed accordingly.

(5) A police authority may, in such cases and to such extent as appear to it to be appropriate, pay out of the police fund—

(a) any compensation, costs or expenses awarded in proceedings under Part 2 [or 3] of this Act against a person under the direction and control of the chief officer of police;

(b) any costs or expenses incurred and not recovered by such a person in such proceedings; and

(c) any sum required in connection with the settlement of a claim that has or might have given rise to such proceedings.

(6) Subsections (1) and (2) apply to a police cadet and appointment as a police cadet as they apply to a constable and the office of constable.

(7) Subject to subsection (8), in this section—

"chief officer of police"—

(a) in relation to a person appointed, or an appointment falling to be made, under a specified Act, has the same meaning as in the Police Act 1996,

(b) …

(c) in relation to a person appointed, or an appointment falling to be made, under the Police (Scotland) Act 1967, means the chief constable of the relevant police force,

(d) in relation to any other person or appointment means the officer or other person who has the direction and control of the body of constables or cadets in question;

"police authority"—

(a) in relation to a person appointed, or an appointment falling to be made, under a specified Act, has the same meaning as in the Police Act 1996,

(b) …

(c) in relation to a person appointed, or an appointment falling to be made, under the Police (Scotland) Act 1967, has the meaning given in that Act,

(d) in relation to any other person or appointment, means the authority by whom the person in question is or on appointment would be paid;

"police cadet" means any person appointed to undergo training with a view to becoming a constable;

"police fund"—

(a) in relation to a chief officer of police within paragraph (a) of the above definition of that term, has the same meaning as in the Police Act 1996,

(b) …

(c) in any other case means money provided by the police authority;

"specified Act" means the Metropolitan Police Act 1829, the City of London Police Act 1839 or the Police Act 1996.

(8) In relation to a constable of a force who is not under the direction and control of the chief officer of police for that force, references in this section to the chief officer of police are references to the chief officer of the force under whose direction and control he is, and references in this section to the police authority are references to the relevant police authority for that force.]

[938]

NOTES

Commencement: 1 October 2004.

Inserted by the Disability Discrimination Act 1995 (Amendment) Regulations 2003, SI 2003/1673, regs 3(1), 25, as from 1 October 2004.

Sub-ss (3), (5): words in square brackets inserted by the Disability Discrimination Act 2005, s 4(1), (2), as from 5 December 2005.

Sub-s (4):words in first pair of square brackets inserted, and words in second pair of square brackets substituted, by the Disability Discrimination Act 2005, s 4, as from 5 December 2005.

Sub-s (7): para (b) of definitions "chief officer of police", "police authority" and "police fund" repealed by the Serious Organised Crime and Police Act 2005, ss 59, 174(2), Sch 4, paras 64, 65(1), (2), Sch 17, Pt 2, as from 1 April 2006.

65 Application to Parliament

(1) This Act applies to an act done by or for purposes of the House of Lords or the House of Commons as it applies to an act done by a private person.

(2) For the purposes of the application of Part II in relation to the House of Commons, the Corporate Officer of that House shall be treated as the employer of a person who is (or would be) a relevant member of the House of Commons staff for the purposes of [section 195 of the Employment Rights Act 1996].

(3) Except as provided in subsection (4), for the purposes of the application of sections 19 to 21, the provider of services is—

(a) as respects the House of Lords, the Corporate Officer of that House; and

(b) as respects the House of Commons, the Corporate Officer of that House.

(4) Where the service in question is access to and use of any place in the Palace of Westminster which members of the public are permitted to enter, the Corporate Officers of both Houses jointly are the provider of that service.

(5) Nothing in any rule of law or the law or practice of Parliament prevents proceedings being instituted before an [employment tribunal] under [Part 2 or 3] or before any court under Part III.

[939]–[940]

NOTES

Sub-s (2): words in square brackets substituted by the Employment Rights Act 1996, s 240, Sch 1, para 69(1), (3).

Sub-s (5): words in first pair of square brackets substituted by the Employment Rights (Dispute Resolution) Act 1998, s 1(2)(a); words in second pair of square brackets substituted by the Disability Discrimination Act 2005, s 19(1), Sch 1, Pt 1, paras 1, 32, as from 5 December 2005.

66 *(Repealed by the Disability Discrimination Act 1995 (Amendment) Regulations 2003, SI 2003/1673, regs 3(1), 26, as from 1 October 2004. For equivalent provisions inserted by SI 2003/1673 as from that date, see ss 4C–4F at* **[903C]–[903F]**.)

67 Regulations and orders

(1) Any power under this Act [of the Secretary of State, the Scottish Ministers or the [Welsh Ministers]] to make regulations or orders shall be exercisable by statutory instrument.

(2) Any such power may be exercised to make different provision for different cases, including different provision for different areas or localities.

(3) Any such power includes power—

(a) to make such incidental, supplemental, consequential or transitional provision as appears to the [person by whom the power is exercisable] to be expedient; and

(b) to provide for a person to exercise a discretion in dealing with any matter.

[(3A) Where regulations under section 21D(7)(b) provide for the omission of section 21D(5), the provision that may be made by the regulations in exercise of the power conferred by subsection (3)(a) includes provision amending section 21D for the purpose of omitting references to section 21D(5).

(3B) The provision that may be made by regulations under section 21G(5)(b) in exercise of the power conferred by subsection (3)(a) includes provision amending or repealing section 21G(4).

(3C) The provision that may be made by regulations under any of subsections (1) to (4) of section 49D in exercise of the power conferred by subsection (3)(a) includes provision amending or repealing an enactment.]

[(4) Subsection (4A) applies to—

(a) the first regulations to be made under section 21H(1);

(b) the first regulations to be made under each of subsections (1), (2) and (4) of section 31AE;

(c) regulations under section 31AE(1), (2) or (4) that amend this Act;

(d) regulations under section 31AE(1) that make provision as to remedies;

(e) regulations under section 47J(3);

(f) regulations under section 49D(1) or (2) that, in exercise of the power under subsection (3)(a), amend or repeal an enactment contained in an Act[, in an Act of the Scottish Parliament, or in a Measure or Act of the National Assembly for Wales];

(g) regulations under section 67A(3);

(h) regulations under paragraph 6A(2) of Schedule 1.

(4A) No regulations to which this subsection applies shall be made unless a draft of the statutory instrument containing the regulations (whether containing the regulations alone or with other provisions) has been laid before, and approved by a resolution of, each House of Parliament.

(4B) Subsection (4C) applies to regulations under section 49D(3) or (4) that, in exercise of the power under subsection (3)(a), amend or repeal any enactment contained in an Act or in an Act of the Scottish Parliament.

(4C) No regulations to which this subsection applies shall be made unless a draft of the statutory instrument containing the regulations (whether containing the regulations alone or with other provisions) has been laid before, and approved by a resolution of, the Scottish Parliament.

(4D) A statutory instrument—

(a) that—

(i) contains regulations under section 49D(3) or (4), and

(ii) is not subject to the requirement in subsection (4C) that a draft of the instrument be laid before, and approved by, the Scottish Parliament, or

(b) that contains regulations or an order made by the Scottish Ministers under section 33,

shall be subject to annulment in pursuance of a resolution of the Scottish Parliament.

(5) A statutory instrument—

(a) that—

(i) contains regulations made by the Secretary of State under this Act, and

(ii) is not subject to the requirement in subsection (4A) that a draft of the instrument be laid before, and approved by a resolution of, each House of Parliament, or

(b) that contains an order made by the Secretary of State under this Act that is not an order under section 3(9), 47(1), … or 70(3),

shall be subject to annulment in pursuance of a resolution of either House of Parliament.

(5A) A statutory instrument that contains an order under section 47(1), if made without a draft having been laid before, and approved by a resolution of, each House of Parliament, shall be subject to annulment in pursuance of a resolution of either House, but the exercise of the discretion conferred by this subsection is subject to section 67A.]

(6) Subsection (1) does not require an order under section 43 which applies only to a specified vehicle, or to vehicles of a specified person, to be made by statutory instrument but such an order shall be as capable of being amended or revoked as an order which is made by statutory instrument.

(7) Nothing in section 34(4), 40(6) or 46(5) affects the powers conferred by subsections (2) and (3).

[941]

NOTES

Sub-s (1): words in first (outer) pair of square brackets inserted by the Disability Discrimination Act 2005, s 19(1), Sch 1, Pt 1, paras 1, 33(1), (2), as from 30 June 2005; words in second (inner) pair of square brackets substituted by the Government of Wales Act 2006 (Consequential Modifications and Transitional Provisions) Order 2007, SI 2007/1388, art 3, Sch 1, paras 47, 62(1), (2), as from 25 May 2007.

Sub-s (3): words in square brackets in para (a) substituted by the Disability Discrimination Act 2005, s 19(1), Sch 1, Pt 1, paras 1, 33(1), (3), as from 30 June 2005.

Sub-ss (3A)–(3C): inserted by the Disability Discrimination Act 2005, s 19(1), Sch 1, Pt 1, paras 1, 33(1), (4), as from 30 June 2005 (for the purpose of exercising the power to make regulations), and as from 5 December 2005 (otherwise).

Sub-ss (4), (4A)–(4D), (5), (5A): substituted, for original sub-ss (4), (5), by the Disability Discrimination Act 2005, s 19(1), Sch 1, Pt 1, paras 1, 33(1), (5), as from 30 June 2005 (for the purpose of exercising the power to make regulations), and as from 5 December 2005 (otherwise); words in square brackets in sub-s (4)(f) substituted by SI 2007/1388, art 3, Sch 1, paras 47, 62(1), (3), as from 25 May 2007; figure omitted from sub-s (5)(b) repealed by the Equality Act 2006, ss 40, 91, Sch 3, paras 41, 44, Sch 4, as from 1 October 2007.

67A, 67B *(S 67A (Exercise of discretion under s 67(5A) in connection with the making of any particular order under s 47(1)), s 67B (Annual report on vehicle exemption orders) outside the scope of this work.)*

68 Interpretation

(1) In this Act—

"accessibility certificate" means a certificate issued under section 41(1)(a);

"act" includes a deliberate omission;

"approval certificate" means a certificate issued under section 42(4);

...

"conciliation officer" means a person designated under section 211 of the Trade Union and Labour Relations (Consolidation) Act 1992;

["criminal investigation" has the meaning given in subsection (1A);]

["criminal proceedings" includes—

(*a*) *proceedings on dealing summarily with a charge under the Army Act 1955 or the Air Force Act 1955 or on summary trial under the Naval Discipline Act 1957;*

(*b*) *proceedings before a summary appeal court constituted under any of those Acts;*

(*c*) *proceedings before a court-martial constituted under any of those Acts or a disciplinary court constituted under section 52G of the Naval Discipline Act 1957;*

(*d*) *proceedings before the Courts-Martial Appeal Court; and*

(*e*) *proceedings before a Standing Civilian Court;]*

"employment" means, subject to any prescribed provision, employment under a contract of service or of apprenticeship or a contract personally to do any work, and related expressions are to be construed accordingly;

["employment at an establishment in Great Britain" is to be construed in accordance with subsections (2) to (4A);]

["employment services" has the meaning given in section 21A(1);]

"enactment" includes subordinate legislation and any Order in Council[, and … includes an enactment comprised in, or in an instrument made under, an Act of the Scottish Parliament];

["Great Britain" includes such of the territorial waters of the United Kingdom as are adjacent to Great Britain;]

["group insurance arrangement" means an arrangement between an employer and another for the provision by the other of facilities by way of insurance to the employer's employees or to any class of those employees;]

"licensing authority"[, except in section 37A,] means—

(a) in relation to the area to which the Metropolitan Public Carriage Act 1869 applies, the Secretary of State or the holder of any office for the time being designated by the Secretary of State; or

(b) in relation to any other area in England and Wales, the authority responsible for licensing taxis in that area;

"mental impairment" does not have the same meaning as in the Mental Health Act 1983 … but the fact that an impairment would be a mental impairment for the purposes of [that Act] does not prevent it from being a mental impairment for the purposes of this Act;

["Minister of the Crown" includes the Treasury and the Defence Council;]

"occupational pension scheme" has the same meaning as in the Pension Schemes Act 1993;

"premises" includes land of any description;

"prescribed" means prescribed by regulations[, except in section 28D (where it has the meaning given by section 28D(17))];

"profession" includes any vocation or occupation;

"provider of services" has the meaning given in section 19(2)(b);

["public investigator functions" has the meaning given in subsection (1B);]

"public service vehicle" and "regulated public service vehicle" have the meaning given in section 40;

"PSV accessibility regulations" means regulations made under section 40(1);
"rail vehicle" and "regulated rail vehicle" have the meaning given in section 46;
["rail vehicle accessibility compliance certificate" has the meaning given in section 47A(3);]
"rail vehicle accessibility regulations" means regulations made under section 46(1);
"regulations" means regulations made by the Secretary of State[, except in sections 2(3), 28D, 28L(6), 28Q(7), 33, 49D … and 67 (provisions where the meaning of "regulations" is apparent)];
…
"section 21 duty" means any duty imposed by or under section 21;
"subordinate legislation" has the same meaning as in section 21 of the Interpretation Act 1978;
"taxi" and "regulated taxi" have the meaning given in section 32;
"taxi accessibility regulations" means regulations made under section 32(1);
"trade" includes any business;
"trade organisation" has the meaning given in section 13;
"vehicle examiner" means an examiner appointed under section 66A of the Road Traffic Act 1988.

[(1A) In this Act "criminal investigation" means—

(a) any investigation which a person in carrying out functions to which section 21B(1) applies has a duty to conduct with a view to it being ascertained whether a person should be charged with, or in Scotland prosecuted for, an offence, or whether a person charged with or prosecuted for an offence is guilty of it;

(b) any investigation which is conducted by a person in carrying out functions to which section 21B(1) applies and which in the circumstances may lead to a decision by that person to institute criminal proceedings which the person has power to conduct; or

(c) any investigation which is conducted by a person in carrying out functions to which section 21B(1) applies and which in the circumstances may lead to a decision by that person to make a report to the procurator fiscal for the purpose of enabling him to determine whether criminal proceedings should be instituted.

(1B) In this Act "public investigator functions" means functions of conducting criminal investigations or charging offenders.

(1C) In subsections (1A) and (1B)—
"offence" includes *any offence of a kind triable by court-martial under the Army Act 1955, the Air Force Act 1955 or the Naval Discipline Act 1957*, and
"offender" is to be construed accordingly.]

[(2) Employment (including employment on board a ship to which subsection (2B) applies or on an aircraft or hovercraft to which subsection (2C) applies) is to be regarded as being employment at an establishment in Great Britain if the employee—

(a) does his work wholly or partly in Great Britain; or
(b) does his work wholly outside Great Britain and subsection (2A) applies.

(2A) This subsection applies if—

(a) the employer has a place of business at an establishment in Great Britain;
(b) the work is for the purposes of the business carried on at the establishment; and
(c) the employee is ordinarily resident in Great Britain—
    (i) at the time when he applies for or is offered the employment, or
    (ii) at any time during the course of the employment.

(2B) This subsection applies to a ship if—

(a) it is registered at a port of registry in Great Britain; or
(b) it belongs to or is possessed by Her Majesty in right of the Government of the United Kingdom.

(2C) This subsection applies to an aircraft or hovercraft if—

(a) it is—
    (i) registered in the United Kingdom, and
    (ii) operated by a person who has his principal place of business, or is ordinarily resident, in Great Britain; or
(b) it belongs to or is possessed by Her Majesty in right of the Government of the United Kingdom.

(2D) The following are not to be regarded as being employment at an establishment in Great Britain—

(a) employment on board a ship to which subsection (2B) does not apply;

(b) employment on an aircraft or hovercraft to which subsection (2C) does not apply.]

(4) Employment of a prescribed kind, or in prescribed circumstances, is to be regarded as not being employment at an establishment in Great Britain.

[(4A) For the purposes of determining if employment concerned with the exploration of the sea bed or sub-soil or the exploitation of their natural resources is outside Great Britain, subsections (2)(a) and (b), (2A) and (2C) of this section each have effect as if "Great Britain" had the same meaning as that given to the last reference to Great Britain in section 10(1) of the Sex Discrimination Act 1975 by section 10(5) of that Act read with the Sex Discrimination and Equal Pay (Offshore Employment) Order 1987.]

(5) ...

[942]

NOTES

Sub-s (1) is amended as follows:

Definition "benefits" (omitted) repealed by the Disability Discrimination Act 1995 (Amendment) Regulations 2003, SI 2003/1673, regs 3(1), 27(a)(i), as from 1 October 2004.

Definitions "criminal investigation", "criminal proceedings" and "public investigator functions" inserted by the Disability Discrimination Act 2005, s 19(1), Sch 1, Pt 1, paras 1, 34(1), (2), as from 4 December 2006; definition "criminal proceedings" subsequently substituted by the Armed Forces Act 2006, s 378(1), Sch 16, para 134(a), as from a day to be appointed, as follows—

""criminal proceedings" includes service law proceedings (as defined by section 324(5) of the Armed Forces Act 2006);".

Definition "employment at an establishment in Great Britain" substituted by SI 2003/1673, regs 3(1), 27(a)(ii), as from 1 October 2004.

Definitions "employment services" and "group insurance arrangement" inserted by the Disability Discrimination Act 2005, ss 11(3), 19(1), Sch 1, Pt 1, paras 1, 34(1), (2), as from 5 December 2005.

In definition "enactment" words in square brackets inserted by the Scotland Act 1998 (Consequential Modifications) Order 2000, SI 2000/2040, arts 1(1), 2(1), Schedule, Pt I, para 18; words omitted repealed by the Disability Discrimination Act 2005, s 19, Sch 1, Pt 1, paras 1, 34(1), (3), Sch 2, as from 5 December 2005.

Definition "Great Britain" inserted by SI 2003/1673, regs 3(1), 27(a)(iii), as from 1 October 2004.

In definition "licensing authority" words in square brackets inserted by the Private Hire Vehicles (Carriage of Guide Dogs etc) Act 2002, s 5, as from 31 December 2003.

In definition "mental impairment" words omitted repealed, and words in square brackets substituted, by the Disability Discrimination Act 2005, s 19, Sch 1, Pt 1, paras 1, 34(1), (4), Sch 2, as from 5 December 2005.

Definition "Minister of the Crown" substituted by SI 2003/1673, regs 3(1), 27(a)(iv), as from 1 October 2004.

In definition "prescribed" words in square brackets inserted by the Disability Discrimination Act 2005, s 19(1), Sch 1, Pt 1, paras 1, 34(1), (5), as from 30 June 2005.

Definition "rail vehicle accessibility compliance certificate" inserted by the Disability Discrimination Act 2005, s 7(3), as from a day to be appointed.

In definition "regulations" words in square brackets inserted by the Disability Discrimination Act 2005, s 19(1), Sch 1, Pt 1, paras 1, 34(1), (6), as from 10 October 2005; words omitted repealed by the Equality Act 2006, ss 40, 91, Sch 3, paras 41, 54, Sch 4, as from 1 October 2007.

Definition "section 6 duty" (omitted) repealed by SI 2003/1673, regs 3(1), 27(a)(i), as from 1 October 2004.

Definition "section 15 duty" (omitted) repealed by SI 2003/1673, regs 3(1), 27(a)(i), as from 1 October 2004.

Sub-ss (1A), (1B): inserted, together with sub-s (1C), by the Disability Discrimination Act 2005, s 19(1), Sch 1, Pt 1, paras 1, 34(1), (7), as from 4 December 2006.

Sub-s (1C): inserted as noted above; for the words in italics in the definition "offence" there are substituted the words "any service offence within the meaning of the Armed Forces Act 2006" by the Armed Forces Act 2006, s 378(1), Sch 16, para 134(b), as from a day to be appointed.

Sub-ss (2), (2A)–(2D): substituted, for original sub-ss (2), (3), by SI 2003/1673, regs 3(1), 27(b), as from 1 October 2004.

Sub-s (4A): inserted by SI 2003/1673, regs 3(1), 27(c), as from 1 October 2004.

Sub-s (5): repealed by SI 2003/1673, regs 3(1), 27(d), as from 1 October 2004.

69 Financial provisions

There shall be paid out of money provided by Parliament—

(a) any expenditure incurred by a Minister of the Crown under this Act;

(b) any increase attributable to this Act in the sums payable out of money so provided under or by virtue of any other enactment.

[943]

70 Short title, commencement, extent etc

(1) This Act may be cited as the Disability Discrimination Act 1995.

(2) This section (apart from subsections (4), (5) and (7)) comes into force on the passing of this Act.

(3) The other provisions of this Act come into force on such day as the Secretary of State may by order appoint and different days may be appointed for different purposes.

(4) Schedule 6 makes consequential amendments.

(5) The repeals set out in Schedule 7 shall have effect.

[(5A) Sections 7A, [7B and 49G] extend to England and Wales only

(5B) Sections 7C and 7D extend to Scotland only.]

(6) [Subject to subsections (5A) and (5B), this Act extends to England and Wales, Scotland and Northern Ireland;] but in their application to Northern Ireland the provisions of this Act mentioned in Schedule 8 shall have effect subject to the modifications set out in that Schedule.

(7) …

(8) Consultations which are required by any provision of this Act to be held by the Secretary of State may be held by him before the coming into force of that provision.

[944]

NOTES

Sub-s (5A): inserted, together with sub-s (5B), by the Disability Discrimination Act 1995 (Amendment) Regulations 2003, SI 2003/1673, regs 3(1), 28(a), as from 1 October 2004; words in square brackets substituted by Equality Act 2006, s 40, Sch 3, paras 41, 55, as from 1 October 2007.

Sub-s (5B): inserted as noted above.

Sub-s (6): words in square brackets substituted by SI 2003/1673, regs 3(1), 28(b), as from 1 October 2004.

Sub-s (7): amends the House of Commons Disqualification Act 1975, Sch 1, Pt II, and the Northern Ireland Assembly Disqualification Act 1975, Sch 1, Pt II; repealed in part by the Disability Rights Commission Act 1999, s 14(2), Sch 5.

Orders: the Disability Discrimination Act 1995 (Commencement No 1) Order 1995, SI 1995/3330; the Disability Discrimination Act 1995 (Commencement No 2) Order 1996, SI 1996/1336; the Disability Discrimination Act 1995 (Commencement No 3 and Saving and Transitional Provisions) Order 1996, SI 1996/1474; the Disability Discrimination Act 1995 (Commencement No 4) Order 1996, SI 1996/3003; the Disability Discrimination Act 1995 (Commencement No 5) Order 1998, SI 1998/1282; the Disability Discrimination Act 1995 (Commencement No 6) Order 1999, SI 1999/1190; the Disability Discrimination Act 1995 (Commencement No 7) Order 2000, SI 2000/1969; the Disability Discrimination Act 1995 (Commencement No 8) Order 2000, SI 2000/2989; the Disability Discrimination Act 1995 (Commencement No 9) Order 2001, SI 2001/2030; the Disability Discrimination Act 1995 (Commencement No 10) (Scotland) Order 2003, SI 2003/215; the Disability Discrimination Act 1995 (Commencement No 11) Order 2005, SI 2005/1122.

SCHEDULES

SCHEDULE 1
PROVISIONS SUPPLEMENTING SECTION 1

Section 1(1)

Impairment

1.—(1) …

(2) Regulations may make provision, for the purposes of this Act—

(a) for conditions of a prescribed description to be treated as amounting to impairments;

(b) for conditions of a prescribed description to be treated as not amounting to impairments.

(3) Regulations made under sub-paragraph (2) may make provision as to the meaning of "condition" for the purposes of those regulations.

Long-term effects

2.—(1) The effect of an impairment is a long-term effect if—
(a) it has lasted at least 12 months;
(b) the period for which it lasts is likely to be at least 12 months; or
(c) it is likely to last for the rest of the life of the person affected.

(2) Where an impairment ceases to have a substantial adverse effect on a person's ability to carry out normal day-to-day activities, it is to be treated as continuing to have that effect if that effect is likely to recur.

(3) For the purposes of sub-paragraph (2), the likelihood of an effect recurring shall be disregarded in prescribed circumstances.

(4) Regulations may prescribe circumstances in which, for the purposes of this Act—
(a) an effect which would not otherwise be a long-term effect is to be treated as such an effect; or
(b) an effect which would otherwise be a long-term effect is to be treated as not being such an effect.

Severe disfigurement

3.—(1) An impairment which consists of a severe disfigurement is to be treated as having a substantial adverse effect on the ability of the person concerned to carry out normal day-to-day activities.

(2) Regulations may provide that in prescribed circumstances a severe disfigurement is not to be treated as having that effect.

(3) Regulations under sub-paragraph (2) may, in particular, make provision with respect to deliberately acquired disfigurements.

Normal day-to-day activities

4.—(1) An impairment is to be taken to affect the ability of the person concerned to carry out normal day-to-day activities only if it affects one of the following—
(a) mobility;
(b) manual dexterity;
(c) physical co-ordination;
(d) continence;
(e) ability to lift, carry or otherwise move everyday objects;
(f) speech, hearing or eyesight;
(g) memory or ability to concentrate, learn or understand; or
(h) perception of the risk of physical danger.

(2) Regulations may prescribe—
(a) circumstances in which an impairment which does not have an effect falling within sub-paragraph (1) is to be taken to affect the ability of the person concerned to carry out normal day-to-day activities;
(b) circumstances in which an impairment which has an effect falling within sub-paragraph (1) is to be taken not to affect the ability of the person concerned to carry out normal day-to-day activities.

Substantial adverse effects

5. Regulations may make provision for the purposes of this Act—
(a) for an effect of a prescribed kind on the ability of a person to carry out normal day-to-day activities to be treated as a substantial adverse effect;
(b) for an effect of a prescribed kind on the ability of a person to carry out normal day-to-day activities to be treated as not being a substantial adverse effect.

Effect of medical treatment

6.—(1) An impairment which would be likely to have a substantial adverse effect on the ability of the person concerned to carry out normal day-to-day activities, but for the fact that measures are being taken to treat or correct it, is to be treated as having that effect.

(2) In sub-paragraph (1) "measures" includes, in particular, medical treatment and the use of a prosthesis or other aid.

(3) Sub-paragraph (1) does not apply—

(a) in relation to the impairment of a person's sight, to the extent that the impairment is, in his case, correctable by spectacles or contact lenses or in such other ways as may be prescribed; or

(b) in relation to such other impairments as may be prescribed, in such circumstances as may be prescribed.

[6A.—(1) Subject to sub-paragraph (2), a person who has cancer, HIV infection or multiple sclerosis is to be deemed to have a disability, and hence to be a disabled person.

(2) Regulations may provide for sub-paragraph (1) not to apply in the case of a person who has cancer if he has cancer of a prescribed description.

(3) A description of cancer prescribed under sub-paragraph (2) may (in particular) be framed by reference to consequences for a person of his having it.]

Persons deemed to be disabled

7.—(1) Sub-paragraph (2) applies to any person whose name is, both on 12th January 1995 and on the date when this paragraph comes into force, in the register of disabled persons maintained under section 6 of the Disabled Persons (Employment) Act 1944.

(2) That person is to be deemed—

(a) during the initial period, to have a disability, and hence to be a disabled person; and

(b) afterwards, to have had a disability and hence to have been a disabled person during that period.

(3) A certificate of registration shall be conclusive evidence, in relation to the person with respect to whom it was issued, of the matters certified.

(4) Unless the contrary is shown, any document purporting to be a certificate of registration shall be taken to be such a certificate and to have been validly issued.

(5) Regulations may provide for prescribed descriptions of person to be deemed to have disabilities, and hence to be disabled persons, for the purposes of this Act.

[(5A) The generality of sub-paragraph (5) shall not be taken to be prejudiced by the other provisions of this Schedule.]

(6) Regulations may prescribe circumstances in which a person who has been deemed to be a disabled person by the provisions of sub-paragraph (1) or regulations made under sub-paragraph (5) is to be treated as no longer being deemed to be such a person.

(7) In this paragraph—

"certificate of registration" means a certificate issued under regulations made under section 6 of the Act of 1944; and

"initial period" means the period of three years beginning with the date on which this paragraph comes into force.

Progressive conditions

8.—(1) Where—

(a) a person has a progressive condition (such as cancer, multiple sclerosis or muscular dystrophy or [HIV infection]),

(b) as a result of that condition, he has an impairment which has (or had) an effect on his ability to carry out normal day-to-day activities, but

(c) that effect is not (or was not) a substantial adverse effect,

he shall be taken to have an impairment which has such a substantial adverse effect if the condition is likely to result in his having such an impairment.

(2) Regulations may make provision, for the purposes of this paragraph—

(a) for conditions of a prescribed description to be treated as being progressive;

(b) for conditions of a prescribed description to be treated as not being progressive.

[Interpretation

9. In this Schedule "HIV infection" means infection by a virus capable of causing the Acquired Immune Deficiency Syndrome.]

[945]

NOTES

Para 1: sub-para (1) repealed by the Disability Discrimination Act 2005, ss 18(1), (2), 19(2), Sch 2, as from 5 December 2005.

Para 6A: inserted by the Disability Discrimination Act 2005, s 18(1), (3), as from 30 June 2005 (for the purpose of exercising the power to make regulations), and as from 5 December 2005 (otherwise).

Para 7: sub-para (5A) inserted by the Disability Discrimination Act 2005, s 18(1), (4), as from 30 June 2005 (for the purpose of exercising the power to make regulations), and as from 5 December 2005 (otherwise).

Para 8: words in square brackets in sub-para (1)(a) substituted by the Disability Discrimination Act 2005, s 19(1), Sch 1, Pt 1, paras 1, 36, as from 5 December 2005.

Para 9: inserted by the Disability Discrimination Act 2005, s 18(1), (5), as from 5 December 2005.

Disabled Persons (Employment) Act 1944, s 6: repealed by ss 61(7)(b), 70(5) of, and Sch 7 to, this Act.

Orders: Disability Discrimination (Meaning of Disability) Regulations 1996, SI 1996/1455 at **[2330]**; the Disability Discrimination (Blind and Partially Sighted Persons) Regulations 2003, SI 2003/712 at **[2891]**.

See also Guidance on matters to be taken into account in determining questions relating to the definition of disability (2006), issued under s 3 at **[4756]**.

SCHEDULE 2
PAST DISABILITIES

Section 2(2)

1. The modifications referred to in section 2 are as follows.

2. References in Parts II [to 4] [and 5A] to a disabled person are to be read as references to a person who has had a disability.

[2A. References in Chapter 1 of Part 4 to a disabled pupil are to be read as references to a pupil who has had a disability.

2B. References in Chapter 2 of Part 4 to a disabled student are to be read as references to a student who has had a disability.]

[2C. In [sections 3A(5) and 31AB(8)], after "not having that particular disability" insert "and who has not had that particular disability".]

[3. In sections 4A(1), 4B(4), 4E(1), [4H(1),] 6B(1), 7B(1), 7D(1), 14(1), 14B(1), 14D(1)[, 15C(1)] and 16A(4), section 21A(4)(a) (in the words to be read as section 19(1)(aa)) and section 21A(6)(a) (in the words to be substituted in section 21(1)), [and section 31AD(1)(d), (2)(c) and (3),] after "not disabled" (in each place it occurs) insert "and who have not had a disability".]

[4. In sections 4A(3)(b), 4E(3)(b), [4H(3)(b),] 6B(3)(b), 7B(4)(b), 7D(3)(b), 14(3)(b), 14B(3)(b), 14D(3)(b)[, 15C(3)(a)][, 16A(6) and 31AD(4)(b),] for "has" (in each place it occurs) substitute "has had".]

[4ZA In section 24(3)(e)(i) and (f)(i), after "having" insert "had".

4ZB In sections 24D(2)(a) and 24J(3)(b), for "did not have" substitute "had not had".]

[4A. In section 28B(3)(a) and (4), after "disabled" insert "or that he had had a disability".

4B. In section 28C(1), in paragraphs (a) and (b), after "not disabled" insert "and who have not had a disability".

[4C. In section 28S

(a) in subsection (3)(a), after "disabled" insert "or that he had had a disability",

(b) in subsection (6)(a), after "who do not have" insert "and have not had", and

(c) in subsection (10), for "that particular disability" substitute "and who has not had that particular disability and".]

4D. In [subsections (1), (1A), (1B), (1C) and (1D)] of section 28T, after "not disabled" insert "and who have not had a disability".

4E. In [subsection (1) of that section] as substituted by paragraphs 2 [9, 14 and 21] of Schedule 4C, after "not disabled" insert "and who have not had a disability".]

5. For paragraph 2(1) to (3) of Schedule 1, substitute—

"(1) The effect of an impairment is a long-term effect if it has lasted for at least 12 months.

(2) Where an impairment ceases to have a substantial adverse effect on a person's ability to carry out normal day-to-day activities, it is to be treated as continuing to have that effect if that effect recurs.

(3) For the purposes of sub-paragraph (2), the recurrence of an effect shall be disregarded in prescribed circumstances."

[946]

NOTES

Para 2: words in first pair of square brackets substituted by the Special Educational Needs and Disability Act 2001, s 38(1), (11); words in second pair of square brackets inserted by the Disability Discrimination Act 2005, s 19(1), Sch 1, Pt 1, paras 1, 37(1), (2), as from 5 December 2005.

Paras 2A, 2B: inserted by the Special Educational Needs and Disability Act 2001, s 38(1), (12).

Para 2C: inserted by the Disability Discrimination Act 1995 (Amendment) Regulations 2003, SI 2003/1673, regs 3(1), 29(1)(a), as from as from 1 October 2004; words in square brackets substituted by the Disability Discrimination Act 2005, s 19(1), Sch 1, Pt 1, paras 1, 37(1), (3), as from 1 September 2007.

Para 3: substituted by SI 2003/1673, regs 3(1), 29(1)(b), as from 1 October 2004; figure in first pair of square brackets inserted by the Disability Discrimination Act 1995 (Pensions) Regulations 2003, SI 2003/2770, regs 2, 4(4), as from 1 October 2004; figure in second pair of square brackets inserted by the Disability Discrimination Act 2005, s 19(1), Sch 1, Pt 1, paras 1, 37(1), (4)(a), as from 4 December 2006, and words in final pair of square brackets inserted by s 19(1) of, and Sch 1, Pt 1, paras 1, 37(1), (4)(b) to, the 2005 Act, as from 1 September 2007.

Para 4: substituted by SI 2003/1673, regs 3(1), 29(1)(c), as from 1 October 2004; figure in first pair of square brackets inserted by the Disability Discrimination Act 1995 (Pensions) Regulations 2003, SI 2003/2770, regs 2, 4(4), as from 1 October 2004; figure in second pair of square brackets inserted by the Disability Discrimination Act 2005, s 19(1), Sch 1, Pt 1, paras 1, 37(1), (5)(a), as from 4 December 2006, and words in final pair of square brackets substituted, by s 19(1) of, and Sch 1, Pt 1, paras 37(1), (5)(b) to, the 2005 Act, as from 1 September 2007.

Paras 4ZA, 4ZB: inserted by the Disability Discrimination Act 2005, s 19(1), Sch 1, Pt 1, paras 1, 37(1), (6), as from 4 December 2006.

Paras 4A–4E: inserted by the Special Educational Needs and Disability Act 2001, s 38(1), (13); para 4C, and the words in square brackets in paras 4D, 4E, substituted by the Disability Discrimination Act 1995 (Amendment) (Further and Higher Education) Regulations 2006, SI 2006/1721, regs 4(1), 18, as from 30 June 2006 (so far as enabling anything to be done for the purposes of preparing and bringing into force, on or after 1 September 2006, a code of practice under s 53A of this Act), and as from 1 September 2006 (otherwise).

SCHEDULE 3
ENFORCEMENT AND PROCEDURE

Sections [17A(8)] and 25(6)

PART I
EMPLOYMENT

Conciliation

1. …

Restriction on proceedings for breach of Part II

2.—[(1) Except as provided by Part 2, no civil or criminal proceedings may be brought against any person in respect of an act merely because the act is unlawful under that Part.]

(2) Sub-paragraph (1) does not prevent the making of an application for judicial review [or the investigation or determination of any matter in accordance with Part 10 (investigations) of the Pension Schemes Act 1993 by the Pensions Ombudsman].

[(3) Sub-paragraph (1) does not prevent the bringing of proceedings in respect of an offence under section 16B(2B).]

Period within which proceedings must be brought

3.—(1) An [employment tribunal] shall not consider a complaint under [section 17A or 25(8)] unless it is presented before the end of the period of three months beginning when the act complained of was done.

(2) A tribunal may consider any such complaint which is out of time if, in all the circumstances of the case, it considers that it is just and equitable to do so.

(3) For the purposes of sub-paragraph (1)—

(a) where an unlawful act … is attributable to a term in a contract, that act is to be treated as extending throughout the duration of the contract;

(b) any act extending over a period shall be treated as done at the end of that period; and

(c) a deliberate omission shall be treated as done when the person in question decided upon it.

(4) In the absence of evidence establishing the contrary, a person shall be taken for the purposes of this paragraph to decide upon an omission—

(a) when he does an act inconsistent with doing the omitted act; or

(b) if he has done no such inconsistent act, when the period expires within which he might reasonably have been expected to do the omitted act if it was to be done.

Evidence

4.—(1) In any proceedings under [section 17A or 25(8)], a certificate signed by or on behalf of a Minister of the Crown and certifying—

(a) that any conditions or requirements specified in the certificate were imposed by a Minister of the Crown and were in operation at a time or throughout a time so specified, …

(b) …

shall be conclusive evidence of the matters certified.

[(1A) In any proceedings under section 17A or 25(8), a certificate signed by or on behalf of the Scottish Ministers and certifying that any conditions or requirements specified in the certificate—

(a) were imposed by a member of the Scottish Executive, and

(b) were in operation at a time or throughout a time so specified,

shall be conclusive evidence of the matters certified.

(1B) In any proceedings under section 17A or 25(8), a certificate signed by or on behalf of the [Welsh Ministers] and certifying that any conditions or requirements specified in the certificate—

(a) were imposed by the Assembly, and

(b) were in operation at a time or throughout a time so specified,

shall be conclusive evidence of the matters certified.]

(2) A document purporting to be such a certificate [as is mentioned in sub-paragraph (1), (1A) or (1B)] shall be received in evidence and, unless the contrary is proved, be deemed to be such a certificate.

[947]

NOTES

Schedule enabling power: number in square brackets substituted by virtue of the Disability Discrimination Act 1995 (Amendment) Regulations 2003, SI 2003/1673, regs 3(1), 29(2)(a), as from 1 October 2004.

Para 1: repealed by the Employment Tribunals Act 1996, s 45, Sch 3, Pt I; the equivalent provision is s 18(1)–(3), (6), (7) of the 1996 Act at **[975]**.)

Para 2: sub-para (1) substituted by SI 2003/1673, regs 3(1), 29(2)(b), as from 1 October 2004; words in square brackets in sub-para (2) inserted by the Disability Discrimination Act 1995 (Pensions) Regulations 2003, SI 2003/2770, regs 2, 4(5), as from 1 October 2004; sub-para (3) added by the Disability Discrimination Act 2005, s 19(1), Sch 1, Pt 1, paras 1, 38(1), (2), as from 5 December 2005.

Para 3: words in first pair of square brackets substituted by the Employment Rights (Dispute Resolution) Act 1998, s 1(2)(a); words in second pair of square brackets substituted, and words omitted repealed, by SI 2003/1673, regs 3(1), 29(2)(e), as from 1 October 2004.

Para 4 is amended as follows:

Words in square brackets in sub-para (1) substituted by SI 2003/1673, regs 3(1), 29(2)(c), (d), as from 1 October 2004.

Sub-para (1)(b) and the word immediately preceding it repealed by the Employment Relations Act 1999, ss 41, 44, Sch 8, para 7, Sch 9(12).

Sub-paras (1A), (1B), and words in square brackets in sub-para (2), inserted by the Disability Discrimination Act 2005, s 19(1), Sch 1, Pt 1, paras 1, 38(1), (3), (4), as from 30 June 2005.

Words in square brackets in sub-para (1B) substituted by the Government of Wales Act 2006 (Consequential Modifications and Transitional Provisions) Order 2007, SI 2007/1388, art 3, Sch 1, paras 47, 63(1), (2), as from 25 May 2007.

For the circumstances in which the normal time limit for presenting a complaint under s 17A is extended for a period of three months, see the Employment Act 2002 (Dispute Resolution) Regulations 2004, SI 2004/752, regs 15 and 18 at **[3096]** and **[3098]**.

PART II
DISCRIMINATION IN OTHER AREAS

Restriction on proceedings for breach of Part III

5.—(1) Except as provided by section 25 no civil or criminal proceedings may be brought against any person in respect of an act merely because the act is unlawful under Part III.

(2) Sub-paragraph (1) does not prevent the making of an application for judicial review.

Period within which proceedings must be brought

6.—(1) A county court or a sheriff court shall not consider a claim under section 25 unless proceedings in respect of the claim are instituted before the end of the period of six months beginning when the act complained of was done.

[(2) Where, in relation to proceedings or prospective proceedings under section 25, the dispute concerned is referred for conciliation in pursuance of arrangements under section 27 of the Equality Act 2006 before the end of the period of six months mentioned in sub-paragraph (1), the period allowed by that sub-paragraph shall be extended by three months.]

(3) A court may consider any claim under section 25 which is out of time if, in all the circumstances of the case, it considers that it is just and equitable to do so.

(4) For the purposes of sub-paragraph (1)—

(a) where an unlawful act of discrimination is attributable to a term in a contract, that act is to be treated as extending throughout the duration of the contract;

(b) any act extending over a period shall be treated as done at the end of that period; and

(c) a deliberate omission shall be treated as done when the person in question decided upon it.

(5) In the absence of evidence establishing the contrary, a person shall be taken for the purposes of this paragraph to decide upon an omission—

(a) when he does an act inconsistent with doing the omitted act; or

(b) if he has done no such inconsistent act, when the period expires within which he might reasonably have been expected to do the omitted act if it was to be done.

[Staying or sisting proceedings on section 21B claim affecting criminal matters

6A.—(1) Sub-paragraph (2) applies where a party to proceedings under section 25 which have arisen by virtue of section 21B(1) has applied for a stay or sist of those proceedings on the grounds of prejudice to—

(a) particular criminal proceedings;

(b) a criminal investigation; or
(c) a decision to institute criminal proceedings.

(2) The court shall grant the stay or sist unless it is satisfied that the continuance of the proceedings under section 25 would not result in the prejudice alleged.

Restriction of remedies for section 21B claim relating to criminal matters

6B.—(1) Sub-paragraph (2) applies to a remedy other than—
(a) damages; or
(b) a declaration or, in Scotland, a declarator.

(2) In proceedings under section 25, the remedy shall be obtainable in respect of a relevant discriminatory act only if the court is satisfied that—
(a) no criminal investigation,
(b) no decision to institute criminal proceedings, and
(c) no criminal proceedings,
would be prejudiced by the remedy.

(3) In sub-paragraph (2) "relevant discriminatory act" means an act—
(a) which is done, or by virtue of section 57 or 58 is treated as done, by a person—
(i) in carrying out public investigator functions, or
(ii) in carrying out functions as a public prosecutor; and
(b) which is unlawful by virtue of section 21B(1).]

Compensation for injury to feelings

7.— In any proceedings under section 25, the amount of any damages awarded as compensation for injury to feelings shall not exceed the prescribed amount.

Evidence

8.—(1) In any proceedings under section 25, a certificate signed by or on behalf of a Minister of the Crown and certifying—
(a) that any conditions or requirements specified in the certificate were imposed by a Minister of the Crown and were in operation at a time or throughout a time so specified, or
(b) that an act specified in the certificate was done for the purpose of safeguarding national security,
shall be conclusive evidence of the matters certified.

(2) A document purporting to be such a certificate shall be received in evidence and, unless the contrary is proved, be deemed to be such a certificate.

[(3) In any proceedings under section 25, a certificate signed by or on behalf of the Scottish Ministers and certifying that any conditions or requirements specified in the certificate—
(a) were imposed by a member of the Scottish Executive, and
(b) were in operation at a time or throughout a time so specified,
shall be conclusive evidence of the matters certified.

(4) In any proceedings under section 25, a certificate signed by or on behalf of the [Welsh Ministers] and certifying that any conditions or requirements specified in the certificate—
(a) were imposed by the [National Assembly for Wales constituted by the Government of Wales Act 1998, the Welsh Ministers, the First Minister for Wales or the Counsel General to the Welsh Assembly Government], and
(b) were in operation at a time or throughout a time so specified,
shall be conclusive evidence of the matters certified.

(5) A document purporting to be such a certificate as is mentioned in sub-paragraph (3) or (4) shall be received in evidence and, unless the contrary is proved, be deemed to be such a certificate.]

[948]

NOTES

Para 6: sub-para (2) substituted by the Equality Act 2006, ss 40, Sch 3, paras 41, 56(1), as from 1 October 2007.

Paras 6A, 6B: inserted by the Disability Discrimination Act 2005, s 19(1), Sch 1, Pt 1, paras 1, 38(1), (5), as from 4 December 2006.

Para 8: sub-paras (3)–(5) added by the Disability Discrimination Act 2005, s 19(1), Sch 1, Pt 1, paras 1, 38(1), (6), as from 30 June 2005; words in square brackets in sub-para (4) substituted by the Government of Wales Act 2006 (Consequential Modifications and Transitional Provisions) Order 2007, SI 2007/1388, art 3, Sch 1, paras 47, 63(1), (3), as from 25 May 2007.

Regulations: as of 6 April 2008, no Regulations had been made under para 7.

(Sch 3, Pts 3, 4 (discrimination in schools and in further and higher education institutions), as added by the Special Educational Needs and Disability Act 2001, ss 19(2), 30(2), Sch 3 are outside the scope of this work; Sch 3, Pt 5 (discrimination in general qualification bodies) as added by the Disability Discrimination Act 1995 (Amendment etc) (General Qualifications Bodies) (Alteration of Premises and Enforcement) Regulations 2007, SI 2007/2405, regs 2(1), 4(1), (3), as from 1 September 2007 is also outside the scope of this work.)

[SCHEDULE 3A
VALIDITY OF CONTRACTS, COLLECTIVE AGREEMENTS AND RULES OF UNDERTAKINGS

Section 17C

PART 1
VALIDITY AND REVISION OF CONTRACTS

1.—(1) A term of a contract is void where—

(a) the making of the contract is, by reason of the inclusion of the term, unlawful by virtue of this Part of this Act;

(b) it is included in furtherance of an act which is unlawful by virtue of this Part of this Act; or

(c) it provides for the doing of an act which is unlawful by virtue of this Part of this Act.

(2) Sub-paragraph (1) does not apply to a term the inclusion of which constitutes, or is in furtherance of, or provides for, unlawful discrimination against, or harassment of, a party to the contract, but the term shall be unenforceable against that party.

(3) A term in a contract which purports to exclude or limit any provision of this Part of this Act is unenforceable by any person in whose favour the term would operate apart from this paragraph.

(4) Sub-paragraphs (1), (2) and (3) apply whether the contract was entered into before or after the date on which this Schedule comes into force; but in the case of a contract made before that date, those sub-paragraphs do not apply in relation to any period before that date.

2.—(1) Paragraph 1(3) does not apply—

(a) to a contract settling a complaint to which section 17A(1) or 25(8) applies where the contract is made with the assistance of a conciliation officer (within the meaning of the Trade Union and Labour Relations (Consolidation) Act 1992); or

(b) to a contract settling a complaint to which section 17A(1) or 25(8) applies if the conditions regulating compromise contracts under this Schedule are satisfied in relation to the contract.

(2) The conditions regulating compromise contracts under this Schedule are that—

(a) the contract must be in writing;

(b) the contract must relate to the particular complaint;

(c) the complainant must have received advice from a relevant independent adviser as to the terms and effect of the proposed contract and in particular its effect on his ability to pursue a complaint before an employment tribunal;

(d) there must be in force, when the adviser gives the advice, a contract of insurance, or an indemnity provided for members of a profession or professional body, covering the risk of a claim by the complainant in respect of loss arising in consequence of the advice;

(e) the contract must identify the adviser; and

(f) the contract must state that the conditions regulating compromise contracts under this Schedule are satisfied.

(3) A person is a relevant independent adviser for the purposes of sub-paragraph (2)(c)—
(a) if he is a qualified lawyer;
(b) if he is an officer, official, employee or member of an independent trade union who has been certified in writing by the trade union as competent to give advice and as authorised to do so on behalf of the trade union; …
(c) if he works at an advice centre (whether as an employee or a volunteer) and has been certified in writing by the centre as competent to give advice and as authorised to do so on behalf of the centre[; or
(d) if he is a person of a description specified in an order made by the Secretary of State].

(4) But a person is not a relevant independent adviser for the purposes of sub-paragraph (2)(c) in relation to the complainant—
(a) if he is, is employed by or is acting in the matter for the other party or a person who is connected with the other party;
(b) in the case of a person within sub-paragraph (3)(b) or (c), if the trade union or advice centre is the other party or a person who is connected with the other party; or
(c) in the case of a person within sub-paragraph (3)(c), if the complainant makes a payment for the advice received from him.

(5) In sub-paragraph (3)(a) "qualified lawyer" means—
(a) as respects England and Wales, *a barrister (whether in practice as such or employed to give legal advice), a solicitor who holds a practising certificate, or a person other than a barrister or solicitor who is an authorised advocate or authorised litigator (within the meaning of the Courts and Legal Services Act 1990); and*
(b) as respects Scotland, an advocate (whether in practice as such or employed to give legal advice), or a solicitor who holds a practising certificate.

(6) In sub-paragraph (3)(b) "independent trade union" has the same meaning as in the Trade Union and Labour Relations (Consolidation) Act 1992.

(7) For the purposes of sub-paragraph (4)(a) any two persons are to be treated as connected—
(a) if one is a company of which the other (directly or indirectly) has control; or
(b) if both are companies of which a third person (directly or indirectly) has control.

(8) An agreement under which the parties agree to submit a dispute to arbitration—
(a) shall be regarded for the purposes of sub-paragraph (1)(a) and (b) as being a contract settling a complaint if—
(i) the dispute is covered by a scheme having effect by virtue of an order under section 212A of the Trade Union and Labour Relations (Consolidation) Act 1992, and
(ii) the agreement is to submit it to arbitration in accordance with the scheme; but
(b) shall be regarded as neither being nor including such a contract in any other case.

3.—(1) On the application of a disabled person interested in a contract to which paragraph 1(1) or (2) applies, a county court or a sheriff court may make such order as it thinks fit for—
(a) removing or modifying any term rendered void by paragraph 1(1), or
(b) removing or modifying any term made unenforceable by paragraph 1(2);

but such an order shall not be made unless all persons affected have been given notice in writing of the application (except where under rules of court notice may be dispensed with) and have been afforded an opportunity to make representations to the court.

(2) An order under sub-paragraph (1) may include provision as respects any period before the making of the order (but after the coming into force of this Schedule).]

[949]

NOTES

Commencement: 1 October 2004.

Inserted by the Disability Discrimination Act 1995 (Amendment) Regulations 2003, SI 2003/1673, regs 3(1), 16(2), Schedule, as from 1 October 2004.

Para 2: word omitted from sub-para (3)(b) repealed, and sub-para (3)(d) and the word immediately preceding it added, by the Disability Discrimination Act 2005, s 19, Sch 1, Pt 1, paras 1, 39(1), (2), Sch 2, as from 30 June 2005; for the words in italics in sub-para (5)(a) there are substituted the words "a person who, for the purposes of the Legal Services Act 2007, is an authorised person in relation to an activity which constitutes the exercise of a right of audience or the conduct of litigation (within the meaning of that Act); and" by the Legal Services Act 2007, s 208(1), Sch 21, para 118, as from a day to be appointed.

This Part of the Schedule replaces equivalent provisions formerly in s 9 of this Act. However, prior to its amendment by the Disability Discrimination Act 2005 (as noted above), it did not contain provision for Orders specifying descriptions of persons who may be relevant independent advisers, as did the former s 9(4)(d). Therefore, following the insertion of this Schedule by SI 2003/1673 it was not clear whether the Compromise Agreements (Description of Person) Order 2004, SI 2004/754 (or the amending SI 2004/2515) which so far as relevant to this Act were made under the power conferred by s 9(4)(d), continued to have effect following the repeal of s 9(4)(d) without replacement. The situation was clarified by the Compromise Agreements (Description of Person) Order 2005, SI 2005/2364 which provides that a Fellow of the Institute of Legal Executives employed by a solicitors' practice is specified for the purposes of para 2(3)(d) above. Accordingly, SI 2004/754 (and the amending SI 2004/2515) have lapsed in so far as relevant to this Act.

Orders: the Compromise Agreements (Description of Person) Order 2005, SI 2005/2364.

[PART 2
COLLECTIVE AGREEMENTS AND RULES OF UNDERTAKINGS

4.—(1) This Part of this Schedule applies to—

(a) any term of a collective agreement, including an agreement which was not intended, or is presumed not to have been intended, to be a legally enforceable contract;

(b) any rule made by an employer for application to all or any of the persons who are employed by him or who apply to be, or are, considered by him for employment;

(c) any rule made by a trade organisation (within the meaning of section 13) or a qualifications body (within the meaning of section 14A) for application to—

(i) all or any of its members or prospective members; or

(ii) all or any of the persons on whom it has conferred authorisations or qualifications or who are seeking the authorisations or qualifications which it has power to confer.

(2) Any term or rule to which this Part of this Schedule applies is void where—

(a) the making of the collective agreement is, by reason of the inclusion of the term, unlawful by virtue of this Part of this Act;

(b) the term or rule is included in furtherance of an act which is unlawful by virtue of this Part of this Act; or

(c) the term or rule provides for the doing of an act which is unlawful by virtue of this Part of this Act.

(3) Sub-paragraph (2) applies whether the agreement was entered into, or the rule made, before or after the date on which this Schedule comes into force; but in the case of an agreement entered into, or a rule made, before the date on which this Schedule comes into force, that sub-paragraph does not apply in relation to any period before that date.

5. A disabled person to whom this paragraph applies may present a complaint to an employment tribunal that a term or rule is void by virtue of paragraph 4 if he has reason to believe—

(a) that the term or rule may at some future time have effect in relation to him; and

(b) where he alleges that it is void by virtue of paragraph 4(2)(c), that—

(i) an act for the doing of which it provides, may at some such time be done in relation to him, and

(ii) the act would be unlawful by virtue of this Part of this Act if done in relation to him in present circumstances.

6. In the case of a complaint about—

(a) a term of a collective agreement made by or on behalf of—

(i) an employer,

(ii) an organisation of employers of which an employer is a member, or

(iii) an association of such organisations of one of which an employer is a member, or

(b) a rule made by an employer within the meaning of paragraph 4(1)(b),

paragraph 5 applies to any disabled person who is, or is genuinely and actively seeking to become, one of his employees.

7. In the case of a complaint about a rule made by an organisation or body to which paragraph 4(1)(c) applies, paragraph 5 applies to any disabled person—
- (a) who is, or is genuinely and actively seeking to become, a member of the organisation or body;
- (b) on whom the organisation or body has conferred an authorisation or qualification; or
- (c) who is genuinely and actively seeking an authorisation or qualification which the organisation or body has power to confer.

8.—(1) When an employment tribunal finds that a complaint presented to it under paragraph 5 is well-founded the tribunal shall make an order declaring that the term or rule is void.

(2) An order under sub-paragraph (1) may include provision as respects any period before the making of the order (but after the coming into force of this Schedule).

9. The avoidance by virtue of paragraph 4(2) of any term or rule which provides for any person to be discriminated against shall be without prejudice to the following rights (except in so far as they enable any person to require another person to be treated less favourably than himself), namely—
- (a) such of the rights of the person to be discriminated against, and
- (b) such of the rights of any person who will be treated more favourably in direct or indirect consequence of the discrimination,

as are conferred by or in respect of a contract made or modified wholly or partly in pursuance of, or by reference to, that term or rule.]

[950]

NOTES

Commencement: 1 October 2004.
Inserted as noted to Pt 1 at **[949]**.

[PART 3
INTERPRETATION

10. In this Schedule "collective agreement" means any agreement relating to one or more of the matters mentioned in section 178(2) of the Trade Union and Labour Relations (Consolidation) Act 1992 (meaning of trade dispute), being an agreement made by or on behalf of one or more employers or one or more organisations of employers or associations of such organisations with one or more organisations of workers or associations of such organisations.

[11. Any reference in this Schedule to this Part of this Act shall be taken to include a reference to Part 3 of this Act, to the extent that it relates to—
- (a) the provision of employment services; or
- (b) the provision under a group insurance arrangement of facilities by way of insurance.

12. Where a term to which section 26(1A)(c) applies is a term in an agreement which is not a contract, Part 1 of this Schedule shall have effect as if the agreement were a contract.]

[951]

NOTES

Commencement: 1 October 2004.
Inserted as noted to Pt 1 at **[949]**.
Paras 11, 12: substituted, for original para 11, by the Disability Discrimination Act 2005, s 19(1), Sch 1, Pt 1, paras 1, 39(1), (3), as from 5 December 2005.

SCHEDULE 4
PREMISES OCCUPIED UNDER LEASES

Sections [18A(5)] and 27(5)

PART I
OCCUPATION BY [EMPLOYER ETC]

Failure to obtain consent to alteration

1. If any question arises as to whether the occupier has failed to comply with [any duty to make reasonable adjustments], by failing to make a particular alteration to the premises, any constraint attributable to the fact that he occupies the premises under a lease is to be ignored unless he has applied to the lessor in writing for consent to the making of the alteration.

Joining lessors in proceedings under [section 17A ...]

2.—(1) In any proceedings [on a complaint under section 17A], in a case to which [section 18A] applies, the complainant or the occupier may ask the tribunal hearing the complaint to direct that the lessor be joined or sisted as a party to the proceedings.

(2) The request shall be granted if it is made before the hearing of the complaint begins.

(3) The tribunal may refuse the request if it is made after the hearing of the complaint begins.

(4) The request may not be granted if it is made after the tribunal has determined the complaint.

(5) Where a lessor has been so joined or sisted as a party to the proceedings, the tribunal may determine—

(a) whether the lessor has—

(i) refused consent to the alteration, or

(ii) consented subject to one or more conditions, and

(b) if so, whether the refusal or any of the conditions was unreasonable.

(6) If, under sub-paragraph (5), the tribunal determines that the refusal or any of the conditions was unreasonable it may take one or more of the following steps—

(a) make such declaration as it considers appropriate;

(b) make an order authorising the occupier to make the alteration specified in the order;

(c) order the lessor to pay compensation to the complainant.

(7) An order under sub-paragraph (6)(b) may require the occupier to comply with conditions specified in the order.

(8) Any step taken by the tribunal under sub-paragraph (6) may be in substitution for, or in addition to, any step taken by the tribunal under [section 17A(2)].

(9) If the tribunal orders the lessor to pay compensation it may not make an order under [section 17A(2)] ordering the occupier to do so.

Regulations

3. Regulations may make provision as to circumstances in which—

(a) a lessor is to be taken, for the purposes of [section 18A] and this Part of this Schedule to have—

(i) withheld his consent;

(ii) withheld his consent unreasonably;

(iii) acted reasonably in withholding his consent;

(b) a condition subject to which a lessor has given his consent is to be taken to be reasonable;

(c) a condition subject to which a lessor has given his consent is to be taken to be unreasonable.

Sub-leases etc

4. The Secretary of State may by regulations make provision supplementing, or modifying, the provision made by [section 18A] or any provision made by or under this Part of this Schedule in relation to cases where the occupier occupies premises under a sub-lease or sub-tenancy.

[952]

NOTES

Schedule enabling power: number in square brackets substituted by the Disability Discrimination Act 1995 (Amendment) Regulations 2003, SI 2003/1673, regs 3(1), 29(3)(a), as from 1 October 2004.

Part heading: words in square brackets substituted by SI 2003/1673, regs 3(1), 29(3)(b), as from 1 October 2004.

Paras 1, 3, 4: words in square brackets substituted by SI 2003/1673, regs 3(1), 29(3)(c), (g), as from 1 October 2004.

Para 2: words in square brackets in the heading substituted by SI 2003/1673, regs 3(1), 29(3)(d), as from 1 October 2004; words omitted from the heading repealed, and words in first pair of square brackets in sub-para (1) substituted, by the Disability Discrimination Act 2005, s 19(1), Sch 1, Pt 1, paras 1, 40(1), (2), as from 5 December 2005; words in second pair of square brackets in sub-para (1), and words in square brackets in sub-paras (8), (9), substituted by SI 2003/1673, regs 3(1), 29(3)(e), as from 1 October 2004.

Sub-leases and sub-tenancies: this Part is modified in relation to any case where the occupier occupies premises under a sub-lease or sub-tenancy, by the Disability Discrimination (Employment Field) (Leasehold Premises) Regulations 2004, SI 2004/153, reg 9 at **[3081]**.

Regulations: the Disability Discrimination (Employment Field) (Leasehold Premises) Regulations 2004, SI 2004/153 at **[3074]**.

PART II
OCCUPATION BY [PERSONS SUBJECT TO A DUTY UNDER SECTION 21, 21E OR 21H]

Failure to obtain consent to alteration

5. If any question arises as to whether the occupier has failed to comply with the section 21 duty [or a duty imposed under section 21E or 21H], by failing to make a particular alteration to premises, any constraint attributable to the fact that he occupies the premises under a lease is to be ignored unless he has applied to the lessor in writing for consent to the making of the alteration.

Reference to court

6.—(1) If the occupier has applied in writing to the lessor for consent to the alteration and—

(a) that consent has been refused, or
(b) the lessor has made his consent subject to one or more conditions,

the occupier or a disabled person who has an interest in the proposed alteration to the premises being made, may refer the matter to a county court or, in Scotland, to the sheriff.

(2) In the following provisions of this Schedule "court" includes "sheriff".

(3) On such a reference the court shall determine whether the lessor's refusal was unreasonable or (as the case may be) whether the condition is, or any of the conditions are, unreasonable.

(4) If the court determines—

(a) that the lessor's refusal was unreasonable, or
(b) that the condition is, or any of the conditions are, unreasonable,

it may make such declaration as it considers appropriate or an order authorising the occupier to make the alteration specified in the order.

(5) An order under sub-paragraph (4) may require the occupier to comply with conditions specified in the order.

Joining lessors in proceedings under section 25

7.—(1) In any proceedings on a claim [under section 25 in a case to which section 27 applies, other than a claim presented as a complaint under section 25(8),] the plaintiff, the pursuer or the occupier concerned may ask the court to direct that the lessor be joined or sisted as a party to the proceedings.

(2) The request shall be granted if it is made before the hearing of the claim begins.

(3) The court may refuse the request if it is made after the hearing of the claim begins.

(4) The request may not be granted if it is made after the court has determined the claim.

(5) Where a lessor has been so joined or sisted as a party to the proceedings, the court may determine—
- (a) whether the lessor has—
  - (i) refused consent to the alteration, or
  - (ii) consented subject to one or more conditions, and
- (b) if so, whether the refusal or any of the conditions was unreasonable.

(6) If, under sub-paragraph (5), the court determines that the refusal or any of the conditions was unreasonable it may take one or more of the following steps—
- (a) make such declaration as it considers appropriate;
- (b) make an order authorising the occupier to make the alteration specified in the order;
- (c) order the lessor to pay compensation to the complainant.

(7) An order under sub-paragraph (6)(b) may require the occupier to comply with conditions specified in the order.

(8) If the court orders the lessor to pay compensation it may not order the occupier to do so.

[Joining lessors in proceedings relating to group insurance or employment services

7A.—(1) In any proceedings on a complaint under section 25(8) in a case to which section 27 applies, the complainant or the occupier may ask the tribunal hearing the complaint to direct that the lessor be joined or sisted as a party to the proceedings.

(2) The request shall be granted if it is made before the hearing of the complaint begins.

(3) The tribunal may refuse the request if it is made after the hearing of the complaint begins.

(4) The request may not be granted if it is made after the tribunal has determined the complaint.

(5) Where a lessor has been so joined or sisted as a party to the proceedings, the tribunal may determine—
- (a) whether the lessor has—
  - (i) refused consent to the alteration, or
  - (ii) consented subject to one or more conditions; and
- (b) if so, whether the refusal or any of the conditions was unreasonable.

(6) If, under sub-paragraph (5), the tribunal determines that the refusal or any of the conditions was unreasonable it may take one or more of the following steps—
- (a) make such declaration as it considers appropriate;
- (b) make an order authorising the occupier to make the alteration specified in the order;
- (c) order the lessor to pay compensation to the complainant.

(7) An order under sub-paragraph (6)(b) may require the occupier to comply with conditions specified in the order.

(8) Any step taken by the tribunal under sub-paragraph (6) may be in substitution for, or in addition to, any step taken by the tribunal under section 17A(2).

(9) If the tribunal orders the lessor to pay compensation it may not make an order under section 17A(2) ordering the occupier to do so.]

Regulations

8. Regulations may make provision as to circumstances in which—
(a) a lessor is to be taken, for the purposes of section 27 and this Part of this Schedule to have—
(i) withheld his consent;
(ii) withheld his consent unreasonably;
(iii) acted reasonably in withholding his consent;
(b) a condition subject to which a lessor has given his consent is to be taken to be reasonable;
(c) a condition subject to which a lessor has given his consent is to be taken to be unreasonable.

Sub-leases etc

9. The Secretary of State may by regulations make provision supplementing, or modifying, the provision made by section 27 or any provision made by or under this Part of this Schedule in relation to cases where the occupier occupies premises under a sub-lease or sub-tenancy.
[953]

NOTES

Part heading: words in square brackets substituted by the Disability Discrimination Act 2005, s 19(1), Sch 1, Pt 1, paras 1, 40(1), (3), as from 4 December 2006.

Para 5: words in square brackets inserted by the Disability Discrimination Act 2005, s 19(1), Sch 1, Pt 1, paras 1, 40(1), (4), as from 4 December 2006.

Para 7: words in square brackets in sub-para (1) substituted by the Disability Discrimination Act 2005, s 19(1), Sch 1, Pt 1, paras 1, 40(1), (5), as from 5 December 2005.

Para 7A: inserted by the Disability Discrimination Act 2005, s 19(1), Sch 1, Pt 1, paras 1, 40(1), (6), as from 5 December 2005.

Sub-leases and sub-tenancies: this Part is modified in relation to any case where the occupier occupies premises under a sub-lease or sub-tenancy, by the Disability Discrimination (Providers of Services) (Adjustment of Premises) Regulations 2001, SI 2001/3253, reg 9.

Regulations: the Disability Discrimination (Providers of Services) (Adjustment of Premises) Regulations 2001, SI 2001/3253; the Disability Discrimination (Service Providers and Public Authorities Carrying Out Functions) Regulations 2005, SI 2005/2901.

(*The remaining provisions of this Act are as follows (and are outside the scope of this work): Sch 4, Pt 3 (Occupation by educational institutions), as added by the Special Educational Needs and Disability Act 2001, s 31(2), Sch 6; Sch 4, Pt 4 (occupation by general qualification bodies), as added by the Disability Discrimination Act 1995 (Amendment etc) (General Qualifications Bodies) (Alteration of Premises and Enforcement) Regulations 2007, SI 2007/2405, regs 2(1), 6(1), (3), as from 1 September 2007; Schs 4A, 4B, 4C (Responsible bodies for schools and educational institutions and modification of Pt 4, Chap 2)), as inserted by the Special Educational Needs and Disability Act 2001, ss 11(2), 26(2), 29, Schs 2, 4, 5; Sch 6 (consequential amendments); Sch 7 (repeals); Sch 8 (modifications in relation to Northern Ireland); Sch 5 was repealed by the Disability Rights Commission Act 1999, s 14(2), Sch 5.*)

[EMPLOYMENT TRIBUNALS ACT 1996]

(1996 c 17)

ARRANGEMENT OF SECTIONS

PART I
EMPLOYMENT TRIBUNALS

Introductory

Jurisdiction

Membership etc

Procedure

Recoupment of social security benefits

Conciliation

PART II
THE EMPLOYMENT APPEAL TRIBUNAL

Introductory

Jurisdiction

Membership etc

An Act to consolidate enactments relating to [employment tribunals] and the Employment Appeal Tribunal

[22 May 1996]

NOTES

Title: substituted by the Employment Rights (Dispute Resolution) Act 1998, s 1(2)(c).

Long title: words in square brackets substituted by virtue of the Employment Rights (Dispute Resolution) Act 1998, s 1(2)(b).

This Act is the first separate legislation devoted to the constitution, powers and procedure of Employment Tribunals and the Employment Appeal Tribunal. It consolidates provisions mainly in the Employment Protection (Consolidation) Act 1978 but also widely scattered in other Acts. A Destination Table, showing where previous statutory provisions consolidated by this Act are now to be found, is printed after the Act.

As to the further power to amend this Act, see the Employment Relations Act 2004, s 42(1), (4)(d) at **[1616]**.

Employment Appeal Tribunal: an appeal lies to the Employment Appeal Tribunal on any question of law arising from any decision of, or in any proceedings before, an employment tribunal under or by virtue of this Act; see s 21(1)(g) at **[978]**.

Employment Judges: a person who is a member of a panel of chairmen of employment tribunals which is appointed in accordance with regulations under s 1(1) of this Act may be referred to as an Employment Judge; see s 3A at **[956A]** (as inserted by the Tribunals, Courts and Enforcement Act 2007, s 48(1), Sch 8, paras 35, 36, as from 1 December 2007).

The Tribunals, Courts and Enforcement Act 2007, s 2 (at **[1815]**) makes provision for the appointment of a Senior President of Tribunals who has certain functions with respect to employment tribunals and the representation of their members; see also Sch 1, Pt 4 to that Act.

By the Tribunals, Courts and Enforcement Act 2007, Sch 6, Pt 6, an employment tribunal is a scheduled tribunal for the purposes of s 35 of that Act (at **[1817]**), under which the Lord Chancellor has powers relating to the transfer of Ministerial responsibilities for scheduled tribunals.

For the power of the Lord Chancellor to provide for a function of a scheduled tribunal (as specified in Sch 6, Pts 1–4 to the 2007 Act) to be transferred to an employment tribunal, see the Tribunals, Courts and Enforcement Act 2007, s 30(1)(f), (h), (i), (2)–(9).

By the Administrative Justice and Tribunals Council (Listed Tribunals) Order 2007, SI 2007/2951 (made under the Tribunals, Courts and Enforcement Act 2007, Sch 7, para 25(2)), an employment tribunal is a listed tribunal for the purposes of Sch 7 to the 2007 Act (oversight by the Administrative Justice and Tribunals Council).

See *Harvey* Q. R. T.

PART I
[EMPLOYMENT TRIBUNALS]

NOTES

The Part heading was substituted by the Employment Rights (Dispute Resolution) Act 1998, s 1(2)(b).

Introductory

1 [Employment tribunals]

(1) The Secretary of State may by regulations make provision for the establishment of tribunals to be known as [employment tribunals].

(2) Regulations made wholly or partly under section 128(1) of the Employment Protection (Consolidation) Act 1978 and in force immediately before this Act comes into force shall, so far as made under that provision, continue to have effect (until revoked) as if made under subsection (1); …

[954]

NOTES

Section heading, sub-s (1): words in square brackets substituted by the Employment Rights (Dispute Resolution) Act 1998, s 1(2)(b).

Sub-s (2): words omitted repealed by the Employment Rights (Dispute Resolution) Act 1998, s 15, Sch 2.

Employment Protection (Consolidation) Act 1978, s 128(1): repealed by this Act.

Regulations: the Employment Tribunals (Constitution and Rules of Procedure) Regulations 2004, SI 2004/1861 at **[3151]** which revoke and replace (subject to transitional provisions in reg 20 of the 2004 Regulations at **[3170]**) the Employment Tribunals (Constitution and Rules of Procedure) Regulations 2001, SI 2001/1171, and the Employment Tribunals (Constitution and Rules of Procedure) (Scotland) Regulations 2001, SI 2001/1170 (the Regulations continued in force by sub-s (2) were revoked and replaced by the 2001 Regulations).

Jurisdiction

2 Enactments conferring jurisdiction on [employment tribunals]

[Employment tribunals] shall exercise the jurisdiction conferred on them by or by virtue of this Act or any other Act, whether passed before or after this Act.

[955]

NOTES

Words in square brackets substituted by the Employment Rights (Dispute Resolution) Act 1998, s 1(2)(b).

3 Power to confer further jurisdiction on [employment tribunals]

(1) The appropriate Minister may by order provide that proceedings in respect of—

(a) any claim to which this section applies, or

(b) any claim to which this section applies and which is of a description specified in the order,

may, subject to such exceptions (if any) as may be so specified, be brought before an [employment tribunal].

(2) Subject to subsection (3), this section applies to—

(a) a claim for damages for breach of a contract of employment or other contract connected with employment,

(b) a claim for a sum due under such a contract, and

(c) a claim for the recovery of a sum in pursuance of any enactment relating to the terms or performance of such a contract,

if the claim is such that a court in England and Wales or Scotland would under the law for the time being in force have jurisdiction to hear and determine an action in respect of the claim.

(3) This section does not apply to a claim for damages, or for a sum due, in respect of personal injuries.

(4) Any jurisdiction conferred on an [employment tribunal] by virtue of this section in respect of any claim is exercisable concurrently with any court in England and Wales or in Scotland which has jurisdiction to hear and determine an action in respect of the claim.

(5) In this section—

"appropriate Minister", as respects a claim in respect of which an action could be heard and determined by a court in England and Wales, means the Lord Chancellor and, as respects a claim in respect of which an action could be heard and determined by a court in Scotland, means the [Secretary of State], and

"personal injuries" includes any disease and any impairment of a person's physical or mental condition.

(6) In this section a reference to breach of a contract includes a reference to breach of—

(a) a term implied in a contract by or under any enactment or otherwise,

(b) a term of a contract as modified by or under any enactment or otherwise, and

(c) a term which, although not contained in a contract, is incorporated in the contract by another term of the contract.

[956]

NOTES

Section heading, sub-ss (1), (4): words in square brackets substituted by the Employment Rights (Dispute Resolution) Act 1998, s 1(2)(a), (b).

Sub-s (5): words in square brackets in definition "appropriate Minister" substituted by virtue of the Transfer of Functions (Lord Advocate and Secretary of State) Order 1999, SI 1999/678, art 2(1), Schedule.

Transfer of functions: functions under this section are transferred, in so far as they are exercisable in or as regards Scotland, to the Scottish Ministers, by the Scotland Act 1998 (Transfer of Functions to the Scottish Ministers etc) Order 1999, SI 1999/1750, art 2, Sch 1.

Conciliation: employment tribunal proceedings and claims which could be the subject of employment tribunal proceedings which are proceedings in respect of which an employment tribunal has jurisdiction by virtue of this section are proceedings to which s 18(1)(e) of this Act at **[975]** applies.

Orders: as of 6 April 2008 no Orders had been made under this section but, by virtue of s 44 of, and Sch 2, Pt I, paras 1–4 to, this Act, the Employment Tribunals Extension of Jurisdiction (England and Wales) Order 1994, SI 1994/1623 at **[2252]**, and the Employment Tribunals Extension of Jurisdiction (Scotland) Order 1994, SI 1994/1624 at **[2262]**, have effect as if made under this section.

[3A Meaning of "Employment Judge"

A person who is a member of a panel of chairmen of employment tribunals which is appointed in accordance with regulations under section 1(1) may be referred to as an Employment Judge.]

[956A]

NOTES

Commencement: 1 December 2007.

Inserted by the Tribunals, Courts and Enforcement Act 2007, s 48(1), Sch 8, paras 35, 36, as from 1 December 2007.

Membership etc

4 Composition of a tribunal

(1) Subject to the following provisions of this section [and to section 7(3A)], proceedings before an [employment tribunal] shall be heard by—

(a) the person who, in accordance with regulations made under section 1(1), is the chairman, and

(b) two other members, or (with the consent of the parties) one other member, selected as the other members (or member) in accordance with regulations so made.

(2) Subject to subsection (5), the proceedings specified in subsection (3) shall be heard by the person mentioned in subsection (1)(a) alone [or alone by any Employment Judge who, in accordance with regulations made under section 1(1), is a member of the tribunal].

(3) The proceedings referred to in subsection (2) are—

(a) proceedings [on a complaint under section 68A[, 87] or 192 of the Trade Union and Labour Relations (Consolidation) Act 1992 or] on an application under section 161, 165 or 166 of [that Act],

(b) proceedings on a complaint under section 126 of the Pension Schemes Act 1993,

(c) proceedings [on a reference under section 11, 163 or 170 of the Employment Rights Act 1996,] on a complaint under section 23[, 34] or 188 of [that Act, on a complaint under section 70(1) of that Act relating to section 64 of that Act,] on an application under section 128, 131 or 132 of that [Act or for an appointment under section 206(4) of that] Act,

[(ca) proceedings on a complaint under [regulation 15(10) of the Transfer of Undertakings (Protection of Employment) Regulations 2006],]

[(cc) proceedings on a complaint under section 11 of the National Minimum Wage Act 1998;

(cd) proceedings on an appeal under section 19 or 22 of the National Minimum Wage Act 1998;]

(d) proceedings in respect of which an [employment tribunal] has jurisdiction by virtue of section 3 of this Act,

(e) proceedings in which the parties have given their written consent to the proceedings being heard in accordance with subsection (2) (whether or not they have subsequently withdrawn it),

(f) … and

(g) proceedings in which the person (or, where more than one, each of the persons) against whom the proceedings are brought does not, or has ceased to, contest the case.

(4) The Secretary of State [and the Lord Chancellor, acting jointly,] may by order amend the provisions of subsection (3).

(5) Proceedings specified in subsection (3) shall be heard in accordance with subsection (1) if a person who, in accordance with regulations made under section 1(1), may be the chairman of an [employment tribunal], having regard to—

(a) whether there is a likelihood of a dispute arising on the facts which makes it desirable for the proceedings to be heard in accordance with subsection (1),

(b) whether there is a likelihood of an issue of law arising which would make it desirable for the proceedings to be heard in accordance with subsection (2),

(c) any views of any of the parties as to whether or not the proceedings ought to be heard in accordance with either of those subsections, and

(d) whether there are other proceedings which might be heard concurrently but which are not proceedings specified in subsection (3),

decides at any stage of the proceedings that the proceedings are to be heard in accordance with subsection (1).

(6) Where (in accordance with the following provisions of this Part) the Secretary of State makes [employment tribunal] procedure regulations, the regulations may provide that [any act which is required or authorised by the regulations to be done by an employment tribunal and is of a description specified by the regulations for the purposes of this subsection may] be done by the person mentioned in subsection (1)(a) alone [or alone by any Employment Judge who, in accordance with regulations made under section 1(1), is a member of the tribunal].

[(6A) Subsection (6) in particular enables employment tribunal procedure regulations to provide that—

(a) the determination of proceedings in accordance with regulations under section 7(3A), (3B) or (3C)(a),

(b) the carrying-out of pre-hearing reviews in accordance with regulations under subsection (1) of section 9 (including the exercise of powers in connection with such reviews in accordance with regulations under paragraph (b) of that subsection), or

(c) the hearing and determination of a preliminary issue in accordance with regulations under section 9(4) (where it involves hearing witnesses other than the parties or their representatives as well as where, in accordance with regulations under section 7(3C)(b), it does not),

may be done by the person mentioned in subsection (1)(a) alone [or alone by any Employment Judge who, in accordance with regulations made under section 1(1), is a member of the tribunal].]

[(6B) Employment tribunal procedure regulations may (subject to subsection (6C)) also provide that any act which—

(a) by virtue of subsection (6) may be done by the person mentioned in subsection (1)(a) alone [or alone by any Employment Judge who, in accordance with regulations made under section 1(1), is a member of the tribunal], and

(b) is of a description specified by the regulations for the purposes of this subsection,

may be done by a person appointed as a legal officer in accordance with regulations under section 1(1); and any act so done shall be treated as done by an employment tribunal.

(6C) But regulations under subsection (6B) may not specify—

(a) the determination of any proceedings, other than proceedings in which the parties have agreed the terms of the determination or in which the person bringing the proceedings has given notice of the withdrawal of the case, or

(b) the carrying-out of pre-hearing reviews in accordance with regulations under section 9(1).]

(7) . . .

[957]

NOTES

Sub-s (1): words in square brackets substituted by the Employment Rights (Dispute Resolution) Act 1998, ss 1(2)(a), 15, Sch 1, para 12(1), (2); para (b) substituted by s 4 of the 1998 Act, as from a day to be appointed, as follows—

"(b) two other members selected as the other members in accordance with regulations so made or, with appropriate consent, one other member selected as the other member in accordance with regulations so made;

and in paragraph (b) "appropriate consent" means either consent given at the beginning of the hearing by such of the parties as are then present in person or represented, or consent given by each of the parties.".

Sub-s (2): words in square brackets inserted by the Tribunals, Courts and Enforcement Act 2007, s 48(1), Sch 8, paras 35, 37, as from 1 December 2007.

Sub-s (3): in para (a) words in first (outer) pair of square brackets and words in second (inner) pair of square brackets inserted, and words in final pair of square brackets substituted, and in para (c) words in first, second and final pairs of square brackets inserted, and words in third pair of square brackets substituted, by the Employment Rights (Dispute Resolution) Act 1998, ss 3(1)–(3), 15, Sch 1, para 12(1), (3); para (ca) inserted, in para (d) words in square brackets substituted, and para (f) repealed, by the Employment Rights (Dispute Resolution) Act 1998, ss 1(2)(a), 3(1), (4), (5), 15, Sch 1, para 12, Sch 2; words in square brackets in para (ca) substituted by the Transfer of Undertakings (Protection of Employment) Regulations 2006, SI 2006/246, reg 20, Sch 2, para 8, as from 6 April 2006 (for transitional provisions in relation to a relevant transfer, etc, that took place before that date, see reg 21 of the 2006 Regulations at **[3395]**); paras (cc), (cd) inserted by the National Minimum Wage Act 1998, s 27(1).

Sub-s (4): words in square brackets inserted by the Tribunals, Courts and Enforcement Act 2007, s 48(1), Sch 8, paras 35, 38, as from 1 December 2007.

Sub-s (5): words in square brackets substituted by the Employment Rights (Dispute Resolution) Act 1998, ss 1(2)(a), 15, Sch 1, para 12(1), (4).

Sub-s (6): words in first and second pairs of square brackets substituted by the Employment Rights (Dispute Resolution) Act 1998, ss 1(2)(a), 15, Sch 1, para 12(1), (4); words in final pair of square brackets inserted by the Tribunals, Courts and Enforcement Act 2007, s 48(1), Sch 8, paras 35, 37, as from 1 December 2007.

Sub-ss (6A)–(6C): inserted by the Employment Rights (Dispute Resolution) Act 1998, ss 3(6), 5; words in square brackets in sub-ss (6A), (6B) inserted by the Tribunals, Courts and Enforcement Act 2007, s 48(1), Sch 8, paras 35, 37, as from 1 December 2007.

Sub-s (7): repealed by the Employment Relations Act 1999, ss 41, 44, Sch 8, para 2, Sch 9(12), as from 16 July 2001.

This section is modified for the purposes of national security proceedings by the Employment Tribunals (Constitution and Rules of Procedure) Regulations 2004, SI 2004/1861, reg 12 at **[3162]**.

Regulations: the Employment Tribunals (Constitution and Rules of Procedure) Regulations 2004, SI 2004/1861 at **[3151]**.

Orders: as of 6 April 2008, no Orders had been made under sub-s (4) or the provisions consolidated therein.

5 Remuneration, fees and allowances

(1) The Secretary of State may pay to—

(a) the [President of the Employment Tribunals (England and Wales)],

(b) the [President of the Employment Tribunals (Scotland)], …

[(c) any person who is an Employment Judge on a full-time basis, and]

[(d) any person who is a legal officer appointed in accordance with such regulations,]

such remuneration as he may with the consent of the Treasury determine.

(2) The Secretary of State may pay to—

(a) members of [employment tribunals],

(b) any assessors appointed for the purposes of proceedings before [employment tribunals], and

(c) any persons required for the purposes of section 2A(1)(b) of the Equal Pay Act 1970 to prepare reports,

such fees and allowances as he may with the consent of the Treasury determine.

(3) The Secretary of State may pay to any other persons such allowances as he may with the consent of the Treasury determine for the purposes of, or in connection with, their attendance at [employment tribunals].

[958]

NOTES

Sub-s (1): words in first and second pairs of square brackets substituted, word omitted from para (b) repealed, and para (d) inserted, by the Employment Rights (Dispute Resolution) Act 1998, ss 1(2)(d), (e), 15, Sch 1, para 13, Sch 2; para (c) substituted by the Tribunals, Courts and Enforcement Act 2007, s 48(1), Sch 8, paras 35, 39, as from 1 December 2007.

Sub-ss (2), (3): words in square brackets substituted by the Employment Rights (Dispute Resolution) Act 1998, s 1(2)(b).

[5A Training etc

The Senior President of Tribunals is responsible, within the resources made available by the Lord Chancellor, for the maintenance of appropriate arrangements for the training, guidance and welfare of members of panels of members of employment tribunals (in their capacities as members of such panels, whether or not panels of chairmen).]

[958A]

NOTES

Commencement: to be appointed.

Inserted, together with ss 5B–5D. by the Tribunals, Courts and Enforcement Act 2007, s 48(1), Sch 8, paras 35, 40, as from a day to be appointed.

[5B Members of employment tribunals: removal from office

(1) Any power by which the President of the Employment Tribunals (England and Wales) may be removed from that office may be exercised only with the concurrence of the Lord Chief Justice of England and Wales.

(2) Any power by which the President of the Employment Tribunals (Scotland) may be removed from that office may be exercised only with the concurrence of the Lord President of the Court of Session.

(3) Any power by which a member of a panel may be removed from membership of the panel—

(a) may, if the person exercises functions wholly or mainly in Scotland, be exercised only with the concurrence of the Lord President of the Court of Session;

(b) may, if paragraph (a) does not apply, be exercised only with the concurrence of the Lord Chief Justice of England and Wales.

(4) In subsection (3) "panel" means—

(a) a panel of chairmen of employment tribunals, or

(b) any other panel of members of employment tribunals,

which is appointed in accordance with regulations made under section 1(1).

(5) The Lord Chief Justice of England and Wales may nominate a judicial office holder (as defined in section 109(4) of the Constitutional Reform Act 2005) to exercise his functions under this section.

(6) The Lord President of the Court of Session may nominate a judge of the Court of Session who is a member of the First or Second Division of the Inner House of that Court to exercise his functions under this section.]

[958B]

NOTES

Commencement: to be appointed.
Inserted as noted to s 5A at **[958A]**.

[5C Oaths

(1) Subsection (2) applies to a person ("the appointee")—

(a) who is appointed—

(i) as President of the Employment Tribunals (England and Wales),

(ii) as President of the Employment Tribunals (Scotland), or

(iii) as a member of a panel (as defined in section 5B(4)), and

(b) who has not previously taken the required oaths after accepting another office.

(2) The appointee must take the required oaths before—

(a) the Senior President of Tribunals, or

(b) an eligible person who is nominated by the Senior President of Tribunals for the purpose of taking the oaths from the appointee.

(3) If the appointee is a President or panel member appointed before the coming into force of this section, the requirement in subsection (2) applies in relation to the appointee from the coming into force of this section.

(4) A person is eligible for the purposes of subsection (2)(b) if one or more of the following paragraphs applies to him—

(a) he holds high judicial office (as defined in section 60(2) of the Constitutional Reform Act 2005);

(b) he holds judicial office (as defined in section 109(4) of that Act);

(c) he holds (in Scotland) the office of sheriff.

(5) In this section "the required oaths" means—

(a) the oath of allegiance, and

(b) the judicial oath,

as set out in the Promissory Oaths Act 1868.]

[958C]

NOTES

Commencement: to be appointed.
Inserted as noted to s 5A at **[958A]**.

[5D Judicial assistance

(1) Subsection (2) applies where regulations under section 1(1) make provision for a relevant tribunal judge, or a relevant judge, to be able by virtue of his office to act as a member of a panel of members of employment tribunals.

(2) The provision has effect only if—

(a) the persons in relation to whom the provision operates have to be persons nominated for the purposes of the provision by the Senior President of Tribunals,

(b) its operation in relation to a panel established for England and Wales in any particular case requires the consent of the President of Employment Tribunals (England and Wales),

(c) its operation in relation to a panel established for Scotland in any particular case requires the consent of the President of Employment Tribunals (Scotland),

(d) its operation as respects a particular relevant judge requires—

(i) the consent of the relevant judge, and

(ii) the appropriate consent (see subsection (3)), and

(e) it operates as respects a relevant tribunal judge or a relevant judge only for the purpose of enabling him to act as a member of a panel of chairmen of employment tribunals.

(3) In subsection (2)(d)(ii) "the appropriate consent" means—

(a) the consent of the Lord Chief Justice of England and Wales where the relevant judge is—

(i) an ordinary judge of the Court of Appeal in England and Wales,

(ii) a puisne judge of the High Court in England and Wales,

(iii) a circuit judge,

(iv) a district judge in England and Wales, or

(v) a District Judge (Magistrates' Courts);

(b) the consent of the Lord President of the Court of Session where the relevant judge is—

(i) a judge of the Court of Session, or

(ii) a sheriff;

(c) the consent of the Lord Chief Justice of Northern Ireland where the relevant judge is—

(i) a Lord Justice of Appeal in Northern Ireland,

(ii) a puisne judge of the High Court in Northern Ireland,

(iii) a county court judge in Northern Ireland, or

(iv) a district judge in Northern Ireland.

(4) In this section—

(a) "relevant tribunal judge" means—

(i) a person who is a judge of the First-tier Tribunal by virtue of appointment under paragraph 1(1) of Schedule 2 to the Tribunals, Courts and Enforcement Act 2007,

(ii) a transferred-in judge of the First-tier Tribunal,

(iii) a person who is a judge of the Upper Tribunal by virtue of appointment under paragraph 1(1) of Schedule 3 to that Act,

(iv) a transferred-in judge of the Upper Tribunal,

(v) a deputy judge of the Upper Tribunal, or

(vi) a person who is the Chamber President of a chamber of the First-tier Tribunal, or of a chamber of the Upper Tribunal, and does not fall within any of sub-paragraphs (i) to (v);

(b) "relevant judge" means a person who—

(i) is an ordinary judge of the Court of Appeal in England and Wales (including the vice-president, if any, of either division of that Court),

(ii) is a Lord Justice of Appeal in Northern Ireland,

(iii) is a judge of the Court of Session,

(iv) is a puisne judge of the High Court in England and Wales or Northern Ireland,

(v) is a circuit judge,

(vi) is a sheriff in Scotland,
(vii) is a county court judge in Northern Ireland,
(viii) is a district judge in England and Wales or Northern Ireland, or
(ix) is a District Judge (Magistrates' Courts).

(5) References in subsection (4)(b)(iii) to (ix) to office-holders do not include deputies or temporary office-holders.]

[958D]

NOTES

Commencement: to be appointed.
Inserted as noted to s 5A at **[958A]**.

Procedure

6 Conduct of hearings

(1) A person may appear before an [employment tribunal] in person or be represented by—

(a) counsel or a solicitor,
(b) a representative of a trade union or an employers' association, or
(c) any other person whom he desires to represent him.

(2) [The Arbitration Act 1996] does not apply to any proceedings before an [employment tribunal].

[959]

NOTES

Sub-s (1): words in square brackets substituted by the Employment Rights (Dispute Resolution) Act 1998, s 1(2)(a).

Sub-s (2): words in first pair of square brackets substituted by the Arbitration Act 1996, s 107(1), Sch 3, para 62; words in second pair of square brackets substituted by the Employment Rights (Dispute Resolution) Act 1998, s 1(2)(a).

7 [Employment tribunal] procedure regulations

(1) The Secretary of State may by regulations ("[employment tribunal] procedure regulations") make such provision as appears to him to be necessary or expedient with respect to proceedings before [employment tribunals].

(2) Proceedings before [employment tribunals] shall be instituted in accordance with [employment tribunal] procedure regulations.

(3) [Employment tribunal] procedure regulations may, in particular, include provision—

(a) for determining by which tribunal any proceedings are to be determined,
(b) for enabling an [employment tribunal] to hear and determine proceedings brought by virtue of section 3 concurrently with proceedings brought before the tribunal otherwise than by virtue of that section,
(c) for treating the Secretary of State (either generally or in such circumstances as may be prescribed by the regulations) as a party to any proceedings before an [employment tribunal] (where he would not otherwise be a party to them) and entitling him to appear and to be heard accordingly,
(d) for requiring persons to attend to give evidence and produce documents and for authorising the administration of oaths to witnesses,
(e) for enabling an [employment tribunal], on the application of any party to the proceedings before it or of its own motion, to order—
(i) in England and Wales, such discovery or inspection of documents, or the furnishing of such further particulars, as might be ordered by a county court on application by a party to proceedings before it, or
(ii) in Scotland, such recovery or inspection of documents as might be ordered by a sheriff,
(f) for prescribing the procedure to be followed in any proceedings before an [employment tribunal], including provision—
(i) …
[(ia) for postponing fixing a time and place for a hearing, or postponing a time

fixed for a hearing, for such period as may be determined in accordance with the regulations for the purpose of giving an opportunity for the proceedings to be settled by way of conciliation and withdrawn, and]

(ii) for enabling an [employment tribunal] to review its decisions, and revoke or vary its orders and awards, in such circumstances as may be determined in accordance with the regulations,

(g) for the appointment of one or more assessors for the purposes of any proceedings before an [employment tribunal], where the proceedings are brought under an enactment which provides for one or more assessors to be appointed,

(h) for authorising an [employment tribunal] to require persons to furnish information and produce documents to a person required for the purposes of section 2A(1)(b) of the Equal Pay Act 1970 to prepare a report, and

(j) for the registration and proof of decisions, orders and awards of [employment tribunals].

[(3ZA) Employment tribunal procedure regulations may—

(a) authorise the Secretary of State to prescribe, or prescribe requirements in relation to, any form which is required by such regulations to be used for the purpose of instituting, or entering an appearance to, proceedings before employment tribunals,

(b) authorise the Secretary of State to prescribe requirements in relation to documents to be supplied with any such form, and

(c) make provision about the publication of anything prescribed under authority conferred by virtue of this subsection.]

[(3A) Employment tribunal procedure regulations may authorise the determination of proceedings without any hearing in such circumstances as the regulations may prescribe.]

(3B) Employment tribunal procedure regulations may authorise the determination of proceedings without hearing anyone other than the person or persons by whom the proceedings are brought (or his or their representatives) where—

(a) the person (or, where more than one, each of the persons) against whom the proceedings are brought has done nothing to contest the case, or

(b) it appears from the application made by the person (or, where more than one, each of the persons) bringing the proceedings that he is not (or they are not) seeking any relief which an employment tribunal has power to give or that he is not (or they are not) entitled to any such relief.

(3C) Employment tribunal procedure regulations may authorise the determination of proceedings without hearing anyone other than the person or persons by whom, and the person or persons against whom, the proceedings are brought (or his or their representatives) where—

(a) an employment tribunal is on undisputed facts bound by the decision of a court in another case to dismiss the case of the person or persons by whom, or of the person or persons against whom, the proceedings are brought, or

(b) the proceedings relate only to a preliminary issue which may be heard and determined in accordance with regulations under section 9(4).]

(4) A person who without reasonable excuse fails to comply with—

(a) any requirement imposed by virtue of subsection (3)(d) or (h), or

(b) any requirement with respect to the discovery, recovery or inspection of documents imposed by virtue of subsection (3)(e)[, or

(c) any requirement imposed by virtue of employment tribunal procedure regulations to give written answers for the purpose of facilitating the determination of proceedings as mentioned in subsection (3A), (3B) or (3C),]

is guilty of an offence and liable on summary conviction to a fine not exceeding level 3 on the standard scale.

(5) Subject to any regulations under section 11(1)(a), [employment tribunal] procedure regulations may include provision authorising or requiring an [employment tribunal], in circumstances specified in the regulations, to send notice or a copy of—

(a) any document specified in the regulations which relates to any proceedings before the tribunal, or

(b) any decision, order or award of the tribunal,

to any government department or other person or body so specified.

(6) Where in accordance with [employment tribunal] procedure regulations an [employment tribunal] determines in the same proceedings—

(a) a complaint presented under section 111 of the Employment Rights Act 1996, and

(b) a question referred under section 163 of that Act,

subsection (2) of that section has no effect for the purposes of the proceedings in so far as they relate to the complaint under section 111.

[960]

NOTES

Section heading, sub-ss (1), (2), (5), (6): words in square brackets substituted by the Employment Rights (Dispute Resolution) Act 1998, s 1(2)(a), (b).

Sub-s (3): sub-para (f)(ia) inserted by the Employment Act 2002, s 24(1), as from 9 July 2004; other words in square brackets substituted, and sub-para (f)(i) repealed, by the Employment Rights (Dispute Resolution) Act 1998, ss 1(2)(a), (b), 15, Sch 1, para 14(1), (2), Sch 2.

Sub-s (3ZA): inserted by the Employment Act 2002, s 25, as from 9 July 2004.

Sub-ss (3A), (3B): inserted, together with sub-s (3C), by the Employment Rights (Dispute Resolution) Act 1998, s 2;.

Sub-s (3C): inserted as noted above; substituted by the Employment Act 2002, s 26, as from 9 July 2004.

Sub-s (4): para (c) and the word immediately preceding it inserted by the Employment Rights (Dispute Resolution) Act 1998, s 15, Sch 1, para 14(1), (3).

Note: sub-s (3) did not contain a para (i) in the Queen's Printer's copy of this Act.

Regulations: the Employment Tribunals (Enforcement of Orders in Other Jurisdictions) (Scotland) Regulations 2002, SI 2002/2972; the Employment Tribunals (Constitution and Rules of Procedure) Regulations 2004, SI 2004/1861 at **[3151]**.

[7A Practice directions

[(A1) The Senior President of Tribunals may make directions about the procedure of employment tribunals.]

(1) Employment tribunal procedure regulations may include provision—

(a) enabling the [territorial] President to make directions about the procedure of employment tribunals, including directions about the exercise by tribunals of powers under such regulations,

(b) for securing compliance with *such directions*, and

(c) about the publication of *such directions*.

(2) Employment tribunal procedure regulations may, instead of providing for any matter, refer to provision made or to be made about that matter by directions made *by the President*.

[(2A) The power under subsection (A1) includes—

(a) power to vary or revoke directions made in exercise of the power, and

(b) power to make different provision for different purposes (including different provision for different areas).

(2B) Directions under subsection (A1) may not be made without the approval of the Lord Chancellor.

(2C) Directions under subsection (1)(a) may not be made without the approval of—

(a) the Senior President of Tribunals, and

(b) the Lord Chancellor.

(2D) Subsections (2B) and (2C)(b) do not apply to directions to the extent that they consist of guidance about any of the following—

(a) the application or interpretation of the law;

(b) the making of decisions by members of an employment tribunal.

(2E) Subsections (2B) and (2C)(b) do not apply to directions to the extent that they consist of criteria for determining which members of employment tribunals may be selected to decide particular categories of matter; but the directions may, to that extent, be made only after consulting the Lord Chancellor.]

(3) In this section, references to the [territorial] President are to a person appointed in accordance with regulations under section 1(1) as—

(a) President of the Employment Tribunals (England and Wales), or

(b) President of the Employment Tribunals (Scotland).]

[961]

NOTES

Commencement: 9 July 2004.

Inserted by the Employment Act 2002, s 27, as from 9 July 2004.

Sub-ss (A1), (2A)–(2E): inserted by the Tribunals, Courts and Enforcement Act 2007, s 48(1), Sch 8, paras 35, 41(1), (2), (5), as from a day to be appointed.

Sub-s (1): word in square brackets in para (a) inserted, and for the words in italics in paras (b), (c) there are substituted the words "directions under subsection (A1) or paragraph (a)", by the Tribunals, Courts and Enforcement Act 2007, s 48(1), Sch 8, paras 35, 41(1), (3), as from a day to be appointed.

Sub-s (2): for the words in italics there are substituted the words "under subsection (A1) or (1)(a)" by the Tribunals, Courts and Enforcement Act 2007, s 48(1), Sch 8, paras 35, 41(1), (4), as from a day to be appointed.

Sub-s (3): word in square brackets inserted by the Tribunals, Courts and Enforcement Act 2007, s 48(1), Sch 8, paras 35, 41(1), (6), as from a day to be appointed.

Regulations: the Employment Tribunals (Constitution and Rules of Procedure) Regulations 2004, SI 2004/1861 at **[3151]**.

[7B Mediation

(1) Employment tribunal procedure regulations may include provision enabling practice directions to provide for members to act as mediators in relation to disputed matters in a case that is the subject of proceedings.

(2) The provision that may be included in employment tribunal procedure regulations by virtue of subsection (1) includes provision for enabling practice directions to provide for a member to act as mediator in relation to disputed matters in a case even though the member has been selected to decide matters in the case.

(3) Once a member has begun to act as mediator in relation to a disputed matter in a case that is the subject of proceedings, the member may decide matters in the case only with the consent of the parties.

(4) Staff appointed under section 40(1) of the Tribunals, Courts and Enforcement Act 2007 (staff for employment and other tribunals) may, subject to their terms of appointment, act as mediators in relation to disputed matters in a case that is the subject of proceedings.

(5) Before making a practice direction that makes provision in relation to mediation, the person making the direction must consult the Advisory, Conciliation and Arbitration Service.

(6) In this section—

"member" means a member of a panel of members of employment tribunals (whether or not a panel of chairmen);

"practice direction" means a direction under section 7A;

"proceedings" means proceedings before an employment tribunal.]

[961A]

NOTES

Commencement: to be appointed.

Inserted by the Tribunals, Courts and Enforcement Act 2007, s 48(1), Sch 8, paras 35, 42, as from a day to be appointed.

8 Procedure in contract cases

(1) Where in proceedings brought by virtue of section 3 an [employment tribunal] finds that the whole or part of a sum claimed in the proceedings is due, the tribunal shall order the respondent to the proceedings to pay the amount which it finds due.

(2) An order under section 3 may provide that an [employment tribunal] shall not in proceedings in respect of a claim, or a number of claims relating to the same contract, order the payment of an amount exceeding such sum as may be specified in the order as the maximum amount which an [employment tribunal] may order to be paid in relation to a claim or in relation to a contract.

(3) An order under section 3 may include provisions—

(a) as to the manner in which and time within which proceedings are to be brought by virtue of that section, and

(b) modifying any other enactment.

(4) An order under that section may make different provision in relation to proceedings in respect of different descriptions of claims.

[962]

NOTES

Sub-ss (1), (2): words in square brackets substituted by the Employment Rights (Dispute Resolution) Act 1998, s 1(2)(a).

The sum specified for the purposes of sub-s (2) is £25,000, see the Employment Tribunals Extension of Jurisdiction (England and Wales) Order 1994, SI 1994/1623, art 10 at **[2261]**, and the Employment Tribunals Extension of Jurisdiction (Scotland) Order 1994, SI 1994/1624, art 10 at **[2271]**.

9 Pre-hearing reviews and preliminary matters

(1) [Employment tribunal] procedure regulations may include provision—

(*a*) *for authorising the carrying-out by an [employment tribunal] of a preliminary consideration of any proceedings before it (a "pre-hearing review"), and*

(b) for enabling such powers to be exercised in connection with a pre-hearing review as may be prescribed by the regulations.

(2) Such regulations may in particular include provision—

(a) for authorising any tribunal carrying out a pre-hearing review under the regulations to make, in circumstances specified in the regulations, an order requiring a party to the proceedings in question, if he wishes to continue to participate in those proceedings, to pay a deposit of an amount not exceeding [£500], and

(b) for prescribing—

(i) the manner in which the amount of any such deposit is to be determined in any particular case,

(ii) the consequences of non-payment of any such deposit, and

(iii) the circumstances in which any such deposit, or any part of it, may be refunded to the party who paid it or be paid over to another party to the proceedings.

[(2A) Regulations under subsection (1)(b), so far as relating to striking out, may not provide for striking out on a ground which does not apply outside a pre-hearing review.]

(3) The Secretary of State may from time to time by order substitute for the sum specified in subsection (2)(a) such other sum as is specified in the order.

(4) [Employment tribunal] procedure regulations may also include provision for authorising an [employment tribunal] to hear and determine [separately any preliminary issue of a description prescribed by the regulations which is raised by any case].

[963]

NOTES

Sub-s (1): words in square brackets substituted by the Employment Rights (Dispute Resolution) Act 1998, s 1(2)(a); para (a) substituted by the Employment Act 2002, s 28(1), (2), as from a day to be appointed, as follows—

"(a) for authorising an employment tribunal to carry out a review of any proceedings before it at any time before a hearing held for the purpose of determining them (a "pre-hearing review"),".

Sub-s (2): sum in square brackets in para (a) substituted by the Employment Tribunals (Increase of Maximum Deposit) Order 2001, SI 2001/237, art 2.

Sub-s (2A): inserted by the Employment Act 2002, s 28(1), (3), as from 9 July 2004.

Sub-s (4): words in square brackets substituted by the Employment Rights (Dispute Resolution) Act 1998, ss 1(2)(a), 15, Sch 1, para 15.

Regulations: the Employment Tribunals (Constitution and Rules of Procedure) Regulations 2004, SI 2004/1861 at **[3151]**.

Orders: the Employment Tribunals (Increase of Maximum Deposit) Order 2001, SI 2001/237 (superseded by SI 2004/1861, Sch 1, rule 20 at **[3171]**).

[10 National security

(1) If on a complaint under—

[(a) section 145A, 145B or 146 of the Trade Union and Labour Relations (Consolidation) Act 1992 (inducements and detriments in respect of trade union membership etc),] or

(b) section 111 of the Employment Rights Act 1996 (unfair dismissal),

it is shown that the action complained of was taken for the purpose of safeguarding national security, the employment tribunal shall dismiss the complaint.

(2) Employment tribunal procedure regulations may make provision about the composition of the tribunal (including provision disapplying or modifying section 4) for the purposes of proceedings in relation to which—

(a) a direction is given under subsection (3), or
(b) an order is made under subsection (4).

(3) A direction may be given under this subsection by a Minister of the Crown if—

(a) it relates to particular Crown employment proceedings, and
(b) the Minister considers it expedient in the interests of national security.

(4) An order may be made under this subsection by the President or a Regional Chairman in relation to particular proceedings if he considers it expedient in the interests of national security.

(5) Employment tribunal procedure regulations may make provision enabling a Minister of the Crown, if he considers it expedient in the interests of national security—

(a) to direct a tribunal to sit in private for all or part of particular Crown employment proceedings;
(b) to direct a tribunal to exclude the applicant from all or part of particular Crown employment proceedings;
(c) to direct a tribunal to exclude the applicant's representatives from all or part of particular Crown employment proceedings;
(d) to direct a tribunal to take steps to conceal the identity of a particular witness in particular Crown employment proceedings;
(e) to direct a tribunal to take steps to keep secret all or part of the reasons for its decision in particular Crown employment proceedings.

[(6) Employment tribunal procedure regulations may enable a tribunal, if it considers it expedient in the interests of national security, to do in relation to particular proceedings before it anything of a kind which, by virtue of subsection (5), employment tribunal procedure regulations may enable a Minister of the Crown to direct a tribunal to do in relation to particular Crown employment proceedings.]

(7) In relation to cases where a person has been excluded by virtue of subsection (5)(b) or (c) or (6), employment tribunal procedure regulations may make provision—

(a) for the appointment by the Attorney General, or by the Advocate General for Scotland, of a person to represent the interests of the applicant;
(b) about the publication and registration of reasons for the tribunal's decision;
(c) permitting an excluded person to make a statement to the tribunal before the commencement of the proceedings, or the part of the proceedings, from which he is excluded.

(8) Proceedings are Crown employment proceedings for the purposes of this section if the employment to which the complaint relates—

(a) is Crown employment, or
(b) is connected with the performance of functions on behalf of the Crown.

(9) The reference in subsection (4) to the President or a Regional Chairman is to a person appointed in accordance with regulations under section 1(1) as—

(a) a Regional Chairman,
(b) President of the Employment Tribunals (England and Wales), or
(c) President of the Employment Tribunals (Scotland).]

[964]

NOTES

Substituted, together with ss 10A, 10B for original s 10, by the Employment Relations Act 1999, s 41, Sch 8, para 3.

Sub-s (1): para (a) substituted by the Employment Relations Act 2004, s 57(1), Sch 1, para 24, as from 1 October 2004, except in relation to cases where the act or failure to act to which the complaint relates was done before that date, or where the act or failure to act to which the complaint relates is part of a series and the first act or failure in the series was done before that date (see SI 2004/2566, art 6).

Sub-s (6): substituted by the Employment Relations Act 2004, s 36, as from 31 December 2004.

Regulations: the Employment Tribunals (Constitution and Rules of Procedure) Regulations 2004, SI 2004/1861 at **[3151]**.

[10A Confidential information

(1) Employment tribunal procedure regulations may enable an employment tribunal to sit in private for the purpose of hearing evidence from any person which in the opinion of the tribunal is likely to consist of—

(a) information which he could not disclose without contravening a prohibition imposed by or by virtue of any enactment,

(b) information which has been communicated to him in confidence or which he has otherwise obtained in consequence of the confidence reposed in him by another person, or

(c) information the disclosure of which would, for reasons other than its effect on negotiations with respect to any of the matters mentioned in section 178(2) of the Trade Union and Labour Relations (Consolidation) Act 1992, cause substantial injury to any undertaking of his or in which he works.

(2) The reference in subsection (1)(c) to any undertaking of a person or in which he works shall be construed—

(a) in relation to a person in Crown employment, as a reference to the national interest,

(b) in relation to a person who is a relevant member of the House of Lords staff, as a reference to the national interest or (if the case so requires) the interests of the House of Lords, and

(c) in relation to a person who is a relevant member of the House of Commons staff, as a reference to the national interest or (if the case so requires) the interests of the House of Commons.]

[965]

NOTES

Substituted as noted to s 10 at **[964]**.

Regulations: the Employment Tribunals (Constitution and Rules of Procedure) Regulations 2004, SI 2004/1861 at **[3151]**.

[10B Restriction of publicity in cases involving national security

(1) This section applies where a tribunal has been directed under section 10(5) or has determined under section 10(6)—

(a) to take steps to conceal the identity of a particular witness, or

(b) to take steps to keep secret all or part of the reasons for its decision.

(2) It is an offence to publish—

(a) anything likely to lead to the identification of the witness, or

(b) the reasons for the tribunal's decision or the part of its reasons which it is directed or has determined to keep secret.

(3) A person guilty of an offence under this section is liable on summary conviction to a fine not exceeding level 5 on the standard scale.

(4) Where a person is charged with an offence under this section it is a defence to prove that at the time of the alleged offence he was not aware, and neither suspected nor had reason to suspect, that the publication in question was of, or included, the matter in question.

(5) Where an offence under this section committed by a body corporate is proved to have been committed with the consent or connivance of, or to be attributable to any neglect on the part of—

(a) a director, manager, secretary or other similar officer of the body corporate, or

(b) a person purporting to act in any such capacity,

he as well as the body corporate is guilty of the offence and liable to be proceeded against and punished accordingly.

(6) A reference in this section to publication includes a reference to inclusion in a programme which is included in a programme service, within the meaning of the Broadcasting Act 1990.]

[966]

NOTES

Substituted as noted to s 10 at **[964]**.

11 Restriction of publicity in cases involving sexual misconduct

(1) [Employment tribunal] procedure regulations may include provision—

(a) for cases involving allegations of the commission of sexual offences, for securing that the registration or other making available of documents or decisions shall be so effected as to prevent the identification of any person affected by or making the allegation, and provision—

(b) for cases involving allegations of sexual misconduct, enabling an [employment tribunal], on the application of any party to proceedings before it or of its own motion, to make a restricted reporting order having effect (if not revoked earlier) until the promulgation of the decision of the tribunal.

(2) If any identifying matter is published or included in a relevant programme in contravention of a restricted reporting order—

(a) in the case of publication in a newspaper or periodical, any proprietor, any editor and any publisher of the newspaper or periodical,

(b) in the case of publication in any other form, the person publishing the matter, and

(c) in the case of matter included in a relevant programme—

(i) any body corporate engaged in providing the service in which the programme is included, and

(ii) any person having functions in relation to the programme corresponding to those of an editor of a newspaper,

shall be guilty of an offence and liable on summary conviction to a fine not exceeding level 5 on the standard scale.

(3) Where a person is charged with an offence under subsection (2) it is a defence to prove that at the time of the alleged offence he was not aware, and neither suspected nor had reason to suspect, that the publication or programme in question was of, or included, the matter in question.

(4) Where an offence under subsection (2) committed by a body corporate is proved to have been committed with the consent or connivance of, or to be attributable to any neglect on the part of—

(a) a director, manager, secretary or other similar officer of the body corporate, or

(b) a person purporting to act in any such capacity,

he as well as the body corporate is guilty of the offence and liable to be proceeded against and punished accordingly.

(5) In relation to a body corporate whose affairs are managed by its members "director", in subsection (4), means a member of the body corporate.

(6) In this section—

"identifying matter", in relation to a person, means any matter likely to lead members of the public to identify him as a person affected by, or as the person making, the allegation,

"relevant programme" has the same meaning as in the Sexual Offences (Amendment) Act 1992,

"restricted reporting order" means an order—

(a) made in exercise of a power conferred by regulations made by virtue of this section, and

(b) prohibiting the publication in Great Britain of identifying matter in a written publication available to the public or its inclusion in a relevant programme for reception in Great Britain,

"sexual misconduct" means the commission of a sexual offence, sexual harassment or other adverse conduct (of whatever nature) related to sex, and conduct is related to sex whether the relationship with sex lies in the character of the conduct or in its having reference to the sex or sexual orientation of the person at whom the conduct is directed,

"sexual offence" means any offence to which section 4 of the Sexual Offences (Amendment) Act 1976, the Sexual Offences (Amendment) Act 1992 or section 274(2) of the Criminal Procedure (Scotland) Act 1995 applies (offences under the Sexual Offences Act 1956, Part I of the Criminal Law (Consolidation) (Scotland) Act 1995 and certain other enactments), and

"written publication" has the same meaning as in the Sexual Offences (Amendment) Act 1992.

[967]

NOTES

Sub-s (1): words in square brackets substituted by the Employment Rights (Dispute Resolution) Act 1998, s 1(2)(a).

Sexual Offences (Amendment) Act 1976, s 4: repealed by Youth Justice and Criminal Evidence Act 1999, ss 48, 67(3), Sch 2, para 4, Sch 6.

Regulations: the Employment Tribunals (Constitution and Rules of Procedure) Regulations 2004, SI 2004/1861 at **[3151]**.

12 Restriction of publicity in disability cases

(1) This section applies to proceedings on a complaint under [section 17A or 25(8)] of the Disability Discrimination Act 1995 in which evidence of a personal nature is likely to be heard by the [employment tribunal] hearing the complaint.

(2) [Employment tribunal] procedure regulations may include provision in relation to proceedings to which this section applies for—

(a) enabling an [employment tribunal], on the application of the complainant or of its own motion, to make a restricted reporting order having effect (if not revoked earlier) until the promulgation of the decision of the tribunal, and

(b) where a restricted reporting order is made in relation to a complaint which is being dealt with by the tribunal together with any other proceedings, enabling the tribunal to direct that the order is to apply also in relation to those other proceedings or such part of them as the tribunal may direct.

(3) If any identifying matter is published or included in a relevant programme in contravention of a restricted reporting order—

(a) in the case of publication in a newspaper or periodical, any proprietor, any editor and any publisher of the newspaper or periodical,

(b) in the case of publication in any other form, the person publishing the matter, and

(c) in the case of matter included in a relevant programme—

(i) any body corporate engaged in providing the service in which the programme is included, and

(ii) any person having functions in relation to the programme corresponding to those of an editor of a newspaper,

shall be guilty of an offence and liable on summary conviction to a fine not exceeding level 5 on the standard scale.

(4) Where a person is charged with an offence under subsection (3), it is a defence to prove that at the time of the alleged offence he was not aware, and neither suspected nor had reason to suspect, that the publication or programme in question was of, or included, the matter in question.

(5) Where an offence under subsection (3) committed by a body corporate is proved to have been committed with the consent or connivance of, or to be attributable to any neglect on the part of—

(a) a director, manager, secretary or other similar officer of the body corporate, or

(b) a person purporting to act in any such capacity,

he as well as the body corporate is guilty of the offence and liable to be proceeded against and punished accordingly.

(6) In relation to a body corporate whose affairs are managed by its members "director", in subsection (5), means a member of the body corporate.

(7) In this section—

"evidence of a personal nature" means any evidence of a medical, or other intimate, nature which might reasonably be assumed to be likely to cause significant embarrassment to the complainant if reported,

"identifying matter" means any matter likely to lead members of the public to identify the complainant or such other persons (if any) as may be named in the order,

"promulgation" has such meaning as may be prescribed by regulations made by virtue of this section,

"relevant programme" means a programme included in a programme service, within the meaning of the Broadcasting Act 1990,

"restricted reporting order" means an order—

(a) made in exercise of a power conferred by regulations made by virtue of this section, and

(b) prohibiting the publication in Great Britain of identifying matter in a written publication available to the public or its inclusion in a relevant programme for reception in Great Britain, and

"written publication" includes a film, a sound track and any other record in permanent form but does not include an indictment or other document prepared for use in particular legal proceedings.

[968]

NOTES

Sub-s (1): words in first pair of square brackets substituted by the Disability Discrimination Act 1995 (Amendment) Regulations 2003, SI 2003/1673, regs 3(2), 31(2), as from 1 October 2004; words in second pair of square brackets substituted by the Employment Rights (Dispute Resolution) Act 1998, s 1(2)(a).

Sub-s (2): words in square brackets substituted by the Employment Rights (Dispute Resolution) Act 1998, s 1(2)(a).

Regulations: the Employment Tribunals (Constitution and Rules of Procedure) Regulations 2004, SI 2004/1861 at **[3151]**.

13 Costs and expenses

[(1) Employment tribunal procedure regulations may include provision—

(a) for the award of costs or expenses;

(b) for the award of any allowances payable under section 5(2)(c) or (3).

(1A) Regulations under subsection (1) may include provision authorising an employment tribunal to have regard to a person's ability to pay when considering the making of an award against him under such regulations.

(1B) Employment tribunal procedure regulations may include provision for authorising an employment tribunal

(a) to disallow all or part of the costs or expenses of a representative of a party to proceedings before it by reason of that representative's conduct of the proceedings;

(b) to order a representative of a party to proceedings before it to meet all or part of the costs or expenses incurred by a party by reason of the representative's conduct of the proceedings;

(c) to order a representative of a party to proceedings before it to meet all or part of any allowances payable by the Secretary of State under section 5(2)(c) or (3) by reason of the representative's conduct of the proceedings.

(1C) Employment tribunal procedure regulations may also include provision for taxing or otherwise settling the costs or expenses referred to in subsection (1)(a) or (1B)(b) (and, in particular in England and Wales, for enabling the amount of such costs to be assessed by way of detailed assessment in a county court).]

(2) In relation to proceedings under section 111 of the Employment Rights Act 1996—

(a) where the employee has expressed a wish to be reinstated or re-engaged which has been communicated to the employer at least seven days before the hearing of the complaint, …

(b) …

[employment tribunal] procedure regulations shall include provision for requiring the employer to pay the costs or expenses of any postponement or adjournment of the hearing caused by his failure, without a special reason, to adduce reasonable evidence as to the availability of the job from which the complainant was dismissed … or of comparable or suitable employment.

[969]

NOTES

Sub-ss (1), (1A)–(1C): substituted, for original sub-s (1), by the Employment Act 2002, s 22(1), as from 9 July 2004.

Sub-s (2): words in square brackets substituted by the Employment Rights (Dispute Resolution) Act 1998, s 1(2)(a); words omitted repealed by the Employment Relations Act 1999, ss 9, 44, Sch 4, Pt III, paras 1, 4, Sch 9(2).

Regulations: the Employment Tribunals (Constitution and Rules of Procedure) Regulations 2004, SI 2004/1861 at **[3151]**.

[13A Payments in respect of preparation time

(1) Employment tribunal procedure regulations may include provision for authorising an employment tribunal to order a party to proceedings before it to make a payment to any other party in respect of time spent in preparing that other party's case.

(2) Regulations under subsection (1) may include provision authorising an employment tribunal to have regard to a person's ability to pay when considering the making of an order against him under such regulations.

(3) If employment tribunal procedure regulations include—

(a) provision of the kind mentioned in subsection (1), and

(b) provision of the kind mentioned in section 13(1)(a),

they shall also include provision to prevent an employment tribunal exercising its powers under both kinds of provision in favour of the same person in the same proceedings.]

[970]

NOTES

Commencement: 9 July 2004.

Inserted by the Employment Act 2002, s 22(2), as from 9 July 2004.

Regulations: the Employment Tribunals (Constitution and Rules of Procedure) Regulations 2004, SI 2004/1861 at **[3151]**.

14 Interest

(1) The Secretary of State may by order made with the approval of the Treasury provide that sums payable in pursuance of decisions of [employment tribunals] shall carry interest at such rate and between such times as may be prescribed by the order.

(2) Any interest due by virtue of such an order shall be recoverable as a sum payable in pursuance of the decision.

(3) The power conferred by subsection (1) includes power—

(a) to specify cases or circumstances in which interest is not payable,

(b) to provide that interest is payable only on sums exceeding a specified amount or falling between specified amounts,

(c) to make provision for the manner in which and the periods by reference to which interest is to be calculated and paid,

(d) to provide that any enactment—

(i) does or does not apply in relation to interest payable by virtue of subsection (1), or

(ii) applies to it with such modifications as may be specified in the order,

(e) to make provision for cases where sums are payable in pursuance of decisions or awards made on appeal from [employment tribunals],

(f) to make such incidental or supplemental provision as the Secretary of State considers necessary.

(4) In particular, an order under subsection (1) may provide that the rate of interest shall be the rate specified in section 17 of the Judgments Act 1838 as that enactment has effect from time to time.

[971]

NOTES

Sub-ss (1), (3): words in square brackets substituted by the Employment Rights (Dispute Resolution) Act 1998, s 1(2)(b).

Orders: as of 6 April 2008 no Orders had been made under this section but, by virtue of s 44 of, and Sch 2, Pt I, paras 1–4 to, this Act, the Employment Tribunals (Interest) Order 1990, SI 1990/479 at **[2164]** has effect as if made under this section.

15 Enforcement

(1) Any sum payable in pursuance of a decision of an [employment tribunal] in England and Wales which has been registered in accordance with [employment tribunal] procedure regulations *shall, if a county court so orders, be recoverable by execution issued from the county court or otherwise as if it were payable under an order of that court.*

(2) Any order for the payment of any sum made by an [employment tribunal] in Scotland (or any copy of such an order certified by the Secretary of the Tribunals) may be enforced as if it were an extract registered decree arbitral bearing a warrant for execution issued by the sheriff court of any sheriffdom in Scotland.

(3) In this section a reference to a decision or order of an [employment tribunal]—

(a) does not include a decision or order which, on being reviewed, has been revoked by the tribunal, and

(b) in relation to a decision or order which on being reviewed, has been varied by the tribunal, shall be construed as a reference to the decision or order as so varied.

[972]

NOTES

Sub-s (1) is amended as follows:

For the words "shall, if a county court so orders," to the end of the subsection there are substituted the words "shall be recoverable by execution issued from a county court or otherwise as if it were payable under an order of a county court" by the Tribunals, Courts and Enforcement Act 2007, s 48(1), Sch 8, paras 35, 43, as from a day to be appointed.

For the words "by execution issued from the county court" there are substituted the words "under section 85 of the County Courts Act 1984" by the Tribunals, Courts and Enforcement Act 2007, s 62(3), Sch 13, para 125, as from a day to be appointed.

Words in square brackets in sub-s (1) and words in square brackets in sub-ss (2), (3) substituted by the Employment Rights (Dispute Resolution) Act 1998, s 1(2)(a).

Recoupment of social security benefits

16 Power to provide for recoupment of benefits

(1) This section applies to payments which are the subject of proceedings before [employment tribunals] and which are—

(a) payments of wages or compensation for loss of wages,

(b) payments by employers to employees under sections 146 to 151, sections 168 to 173 or section 192 of the Trade Union and Labour Relations (Consolidation) Act 1992,

(c) payments by employers to employees under—

(i) Part III, V, VI or VII,

(ii) section 93, or

(iii) Part X,

of the Employment Rights Act 1996, or

(d) payments by employers to employees of a nature similar to, or for a purpose corresponding to the purpose of, payments within paragraph (b) or (c),

and to payments of remuneration under a protective award under section 189 of the Trade Union and Labour Relations (Consolidation) Act 1992.

(2) The Secretary of State may by regulations make with respect to payments to which this section applies provision for any or all of the purposes specified in subsection (3).

(3) The purposes referred to in subsection (2) are—

(a) enabling the Secretary of State to recover from an employer, by way of total or partial recoupment of jobseeker's allowance [income support or income-related employment and support allowance]—

(i) a sum not exceeding the amount of the prescribed element of the monetary award, or

(ii) in the case of a protective award, the amount of the remuneration,

(b) requiring or authorising an [employment tribunal] to order the payment of such a sum, by way of total or partial recoupment of [jobseeker's allowance, income support or income-related employment and support allowance], to the Secretary of State instead of to an employee, and

(c) requiring an [employment tribunal] to order the payment to an employee of only the excess of the prescribed element of the monetary award over the amount of any jobseeker's allowance [income support or income-related employment and support allowance] shown to the tribunal to have been paid to the employee and enabling the Secretary of State to recover from the employer, by way of total or partial recoupment of the benefit, a sum not exceeding that amount.

(4) Regulations under this section may be framed—

(a) so as to apply to all payments to which this section applies or to one or more classes of those payments, and

[(b) so as to apply to all or any of the benefits mentioned in subsection (3)].

(5) Regulations under this section may—

(a) confer powers and impose duties on [employment tribunals] or … other persons,

(b) impose on an employer to whom a monetary award or protective award relates a duty—

(i) to furnish particulars connected with the award, and

(ii) to suspend payments in pursuance of the award during any period prescribed by the regulations,

(c) provide for an employer who pays a sum to the Secretary of State in pursuance of this section to be relieved from any liability to pay the sum to another person,

[(cc) provide for the determination by the Secretary of State of any issue arising as to the total or partial recoupment in pursuance of the regulations of a jobseeker's allowance, unemployment benefit, [income support or income-related employment and support allowance],

(d) confer on an employee a right of appeal to an appeal tribunal constituted under Chapter I of Part I of the Social Security Act 1998 against any decision of the Secretary of State on any such issue, and]

(e) provide for the proof in proceedings before [employment tribunals] (whether by certificate or in any other manner) of any amount of jobseeker's allowance, [income support or income-related employment and support allowance] paid to an employee.

(6) Regulations under this section may make different provision for different cases.

[973]

NOTES

Sub-s (1): words in square brackets substituted by the Employment Rights (Dispute Resolution) Act 1998, s 1(2)(b).

Sub-s (3): words "employment tribunal" in square brackets substituted by the Employment Rights (Dispute Resolution) Act 1998, s 1(2)(a); other words in square brackets substituted by the Welfare Reform Act 2007, s 28, Sch 3, Pt 1, para 15(1), (2)(a), (b), as from 18 March 2008.

Sub-s (4): para (b) substituted by the Welfare Reform Act 2007, s 28, Sch 3, Pt 1, para 15(1), (2)(c), as from 18 March 2008.

Sub-s (5): words in square brackets in para (a), and words in first pair of square brackets in para (e), substituted by the Employment Rights (Dispute Resolution) Act 1998, s 1(2)(b); words omitted from para (a) repealed, and paras (cc), (d) substituted for original para (d), by the Social Security Act 1998, s 86, Sch 7, para 147, Sch 8; words in square brackets in para (cc), and words in second pair of square brackets in para (e), substituted by the Welfare Reform Act 2007, s 28, Sch 3, Pt 1, para 15(1), (2)(a), as 18 March 2008.

Regulations: the Employment Protection (Recoupment of Jobseeker's Allowance and Income Support) Regulations 1996, SI 1996/2349 at **[2364]**.

17 Recoupment: further provisions

(1) Where in pursuance of any regulations under section 16 a sum has been recovered by or paid to the Secretary of State by way of total or partial recoupment of jobseeker's allowance *or income support*—

(a) no sum shall be recoverable under Part III or V of the Social Security Administration Act 1992, and

(b) no abatement, payment or reduction shall be made by reference to the jobseeker's allowance *or income support* recouped.

(2) Any amount found to have been duly recovered by or paid to the Secretary of State in pursuance of regulations under section 16 by way of total or partial recoupment of jobseeker's allowance shall be paid into the National Insurance Fund.

(3) In section 16—

"monetary award" means the amount which is awarded, or ordered to be paid, to the employee by the tribunal or would be so awarded or ordered apart from any provision of regulations under that section, and

"the prescribed element", in relation to any monetary award, means so much of that award as is attributable to such matters as may be prescribed by regulations under that section.

(4) In section 16 "income-based jobseeker's allowance" has the same meaning as in the Jobseekers Act 1995.

[(5) In this section and section 16 "income-related employment and support allowance" means an income-related allowance under Part 1 of the Welfare Reform Act 2007 (employment and support allowance).]

[974]

NOTES

Sub-s (1): for the words in italics there are substituted the words "income support or income-related employment and support allowance" by the Welfare Reform Act 2007, s 28, Sch 3, Pt 1, para 15(1), (3), as from 27 October 2008.

Sub-s (5): added by the Welfare Reform Act 2007, s 28, Sch 3, Pt 1, para 15(1), (4), as from 18 March 2008 (for the purpose of making regulations), and as from 27 October 2008 (otherwise).

Conciliation

18 Conciliation

(1) This section applies in the case of [employment tribunal] proceedings and claims which could be the subject of [employment tribunal] proceedings—

(a) under—
  (i) section 2(1) of the Equal Pay Act 1970,
  (ii) section 63 of the Sex Discrimination Act 1975, or
  (iii) section 54 of the Race Relations Act 1976,

(b) arising out of a contravention, or alleged contravention, of section 64, 68[, 86], 137, 138, [145A, 145B,] 146, 168, [168A,] 169, 170, 174, 188 or 190 of the Trade Union and Labour Relations (Consolidation) Act 1992,

(c) under [section 17A or 25(8)] of the Disability Discrimination Act 1995,

(d) [under or] arising out of a contravention, or alleged contravention, of section 8, 13, 15, 18(1), 21(1), 28[, [80G(1), 80H(1)(b),] [80(1),] 92 or 135,] or of Part V, VI, VII or X, of the Employment Rights Act 1996,

[(dd) under or by virtue of section 11, 18, 20(1)(a) or 24 of the National Minimum Wage Act 1998;]

(e) which are proceedings in respect of which an [employment tribunal] has jurisdiction by virtue of section 3 of this Act, …

(f) [under or] arising out of a contravention, or alleged contravention, of a provision specified by an order under subsection (8)(b) as a provision to which this paragraph applies […

(ff) under regulation 30 of the Working Time Regulations 1998,] […

(g) under regulation 27 or 32 of the Transnational Information and Consultation of Employees Regulations 1999,][…

(h) arising out of a contravention, or alleged contravention of regulation [5(1) or] 7(2) of the Part-time Workers (Prevention of Less Favourable Treatment) Regulations 2000,]

[(i) arising out of a contravention, or alleged contravention of regulation 3 or 6(2) of the Fixed-term Employees (Prevention of Less Favourable Treatment) Regulations 2002; …

(j) under regulation 9 of those Regulations], […

(k) under regulation 28 of the Employment Equality (Sexual Orientation) Regulations 2003], […

(l) under regulation 28 of the Employment Equality (Religion or Belief) Regulations 2003],

[(m) under regulation 18 of the Merchant Shipping (Working Time: Inland Waterways) Regulations 2003] […

(n) under regulation 41 or 45 of the European Public Limited-Liability Company Regulations 2004,]

[[(o)] under regulation 19 of the Fishing Vessels (Working Time: Sea-fishermen) Regulations 2004], […

(p) under regulation 29 or 33 of the Information and Consultation of Employees Regulations 2004], […

(q) under paragraph 4 or 8 of the Schedule to the Occupational and Personal Pension Schemes (Consultation by Employers and Miscellaneous Amendment) Regulations 2006], […

(r) under regulation 36 of the Employment Equality (Age) Regulations 2006][, …
(s) under regulation 30 or 34 of the European Cooperative Society (Involvement of Employees) Regulations 2006], [or
(t) under regulation 45 or 51 of the Companies (Cross-Border Mergers) Regulations 2007].

(2) Where an application has been presented to an [employment tribunal], and a copy of it has been sent to a conciliation officer, it is the duty of the conciliation officer—

(a) if he is requested to do so by the person by whom and the person against whom the proceedings are brought, or
(b) if, in the absence of any such request, the conciliation officer considers that he could act under this subsection with a reasonable prospect of success,

to endeavour to promote a settlement of the proceedings without their being determined by an [employment tribunal].

[(2A) Where employment tribunal procedure regulations include provision postponing the fixing of a time and place for a hearing for the purpose of giving an opportunity for the proceedings to be settled by way of conciliation and withdrawn, subsection (2) shall have effect from the end of the postponement to confer a power on the conciliation officer, instead of imposing a duty.]

(3) Where at any time—

(a) a person claims that action has been taken in respect of which proceedings could be brought by him before an [employment tribunal], but
(b) before any application relating to that action has been presented by him a request is made to a conciliation officer (whether by that person or by the person against whom the proceedings could be instituted) to make his services available to them,

the conciliation officer shall act in accordance with subsection (2) as if an application had been presented to an [employment tribunal].

(4) Where a person who has presented a complaint to an [employment tribunal] under section 111 of the Employment Rights Act 1996 has ceased to be employed by the employer against whom the complaint was made, the conciliation officer shall (for the purpose of promoting a settlement of the complaint in accordance with subsection (2)) in particular—

(a) seek to promote the reinstatement or re-engagement of the complainant by the employer, or by a successor of the employer or by an associated employer, on terms appearing to the conciliation officer to be equitable, or
(b) where the complainant does not wish to be reinstated or re-engaged, or where reinstatement or re-engagement is not practicable, and the parties desire the conciliation officer to act, seek to promote agreement between them as to a sum by way of compensation to be paid by the employer to the complainant.

(5) Where at any time—

(a) a person claims that action has been taken in respect of which a complaint could be presented by him to an [employment tribunal] under section 111 of the Employment Rights Act 1996, but
(b) before any complaint relating to that action has been presented by him a request is made to a conciliation officer (whether by that person or by the employer) to make his services available to them,

the conciliation officer shall act in accordance with subsection (4) as if a complaint had been presented to an [employment tribunal] under section 111.

(6) In proceeding under this section a conciliation officer shall, where appropriate, have regard to the desirability of encouraging the use of other procedures available for the settlement of grievances.

(7) Anything communicated to a conciliation officer in connection with the performance of his functions under this section shall not be admissible in evidence in any proceedings before an [employment tribunal], except with the consent of the person who communicated it to that officer.

(8) The Secretary of State [and the Lord Chancellor, acting jointly,] may by order—

(a) direct that further provisions of the Employment Rights Act 1996 be added to the list in subsection (1)(d), or
(b) specify a provision of any other Act as a provision to which subsection (1)(f) applies.

[975]

NOTES

Sub-s (1) has been amended as follows:

Words "employment tribunal" in square brackets (in every place they occur) substituted by the Employment Rights (Dispute Resolution) Act 1998, s 1(2)(a).

In para (b) figure ", 86" in square brackets inserted by the Employment Rights (Dispute Resolution) Act 1998, s 15, Sch 1, para 16.

In para (b) figures "145A, 145B," in square brackets inserted by the Employment Relations Act 2004, s 57(1), Sch 1, para 25, as from 1 October 2004, except in relation to cases where the act or failure to act to which the complaint relates was done before that date, or where the act or failure to act to which the complaint relates is part of a series and the first act or failure in the series occurred before that date (see SI 2004/2566, art 6).

In para (b) figure "168A," in square brackets inserted by the Employment Act 2002, s 53, Sch 7, para 23(1), (2)(a), as from 27 April 2003.

In para (c) words in square brackets substituted by the Disability Discrimination Act 1995 (Amendment) Regulations 2003, SI 2003/1673, regs 3(2), 31(2), as from 1 October 2004.

In para (d) words "under or" and reference to "80G(1), 80H(1)(b)," in square brackets inserted by the Employment Act 2002, s 53, Sch 7, para 23(1), (2)(b).

In para (d) figure ", 80(1)" in square brackets inserted by virtue of the Employment Tribunals (Application of Conciliation Provisions) Order 2000, SI 2000/1337, art 2.

In para (d) words ", 92 or 135," in square brackets substituted by the Employment Rights (Dispute Resolution) Act 1998, s 11(1).

Para (dd) inserted by the National Minimum Wage Act 1998, s 30(1).

Word omitted from para (e) repealed by the Working Time Regulations 1998, SI 1998/1833, reg 33(a).

Words in square brackets in para (f) inserted by the Employment Act 2002, s 53, Sch 7, para 23(1), (2)(c).

Word omitted from para (f) repealed by the Transnational Information and Consultation of Employees Regulations 1999, SI 1999/3323, reg 33(1)(a).

Para (ff) inserted by SI 1998/1833, reg 33(b).

Word omitted from para (ff) repealed by the Part-time Workers (Prevention of Less Favourable Treatment) Regulations 2000, SI 2000/1551, reg 10, Schedule, para 1(a)(i).

Para (g) and the word immediately preceding it added by SI 1999/3323, reg 33(1)(b).

Word omitted from para (g) repealed by the Fixed-term Employees (Prevention of Less Favourable Treatment) Regulations 2002, SI 2002/2034, reg 11, Sch 2, Pt 1, para 2(a)(i).

Para (h) and the word immediately preceding it added by SI 2000/1551, reg 10, Schedule, para 1(a)(ii).

In para (h) words "5(1) or" in square brackets inserted by the Part-time Workers (Prevention of Less Favourable Treatment) Regulations 2001, SI 2001/1107, reg 2.

Para (i) added by SI 2002/2034, reg 11, Sch 2, Pt 1, para 2(a)(ii).

Word omitted from para (i) repealed by the Employment Equality (Sexual Orientation) Regulations 2003, SI 2003/1661, reg 39, Sch 5, para 1(a)(i), as from 1 December 2003.

Para (j) added by SI 2002/2034, reg 11, Sch 2, Pt 1, para 2(a)(ii).

Word omitted from para (j) repealed by the Employment Equality (Religion or Belief) Regulations 2003, SI 2003/1660, reg 39(2), Sch 5, para 1(a)(i), as from 2 December 2003.

Para (k) and the word immediately preceding it added by SI 2003/1661, reg 39, Sch 5, para 1(a)(ii), as from 1 December 2003.

Word omitted from para (k) repealed by the Merchant Shipping (Working Time: Inland Waterways) Regulations 2003, SI 2003/3049, reg 20, Sch 2, para 2(1), (2), as from 24 December 2003.

Para (l) and the word immediately preceding it added by SI 2003/1660, reg 39(5), Sch 5, para 1(a)(ii), as from 2 December 2003.

Para (m) added by SI 2003/3049, reg 20, Sch 2, para 2(1), (2), as from 24 December 2003.

Word omitted from para (m) repealed by the Information and Consultation of Employees Regulations 2004, SI 2004/3426, reg 34(a), as from 6 April 2005.

Para (n) and the word immediately preceding it added by the European Public Limited-Liability Company Regulations 2004, SI 2004/2326, reg 46, as from 8 October 2004.

Para (o) added by the Fishing Vessels (Working Time: Sea-fishermen) Regulations 2004, SI 2004/1713, reg 21, Sch 2, para 1(1), (2), as from 16 August 2004. Note that this paragraph was originally added as para (n) and was redesignated as para (o) by SI 2004/3426, reg 34(b), as from 6 April 2005.

Para (p) and the word immediately preceding it added by SI 2004/3426, reg 34(c), as from 6 April 2005.

Para (q) and the word immediately preceding it added, and word omitted from para (o) repealed, by the Occupational and Personal Pension Schemes (Consultation by Employers and Miscellaneous Amendment) Regulations 2006, SI 2006/349, reg 17, Schedule, para 9, as from 6 April 2006.

Para (r) and the word immediately preceding it added, and word omitted from para (p) repealed, by the Employment Equality (Age) Regulations 2006, SI 2006/1031, reg 49(1), Sch 8, Pt 1, paras 18, 19(1), (2), as from 1 October 2006.

Para (s) and the word immediately preceding it added, and word omitted from para (q) repealed, by the European Cooperative Society (Involvement of Employees) Regulations 2006, SI 2006/2059, reg 35, as from 18 August 2006.

Para (t) and the word immediately preceding it added, and word omitted from para (r) repealed, by the Companies (Cross-Border Mergers) Regulations 2007, SI 2007/2974, reg 52, as from 15 December 2007.

Sub-ss (2), (3)–(5), (7): words in square brackets substituted by the Employment Rights (Dispute Resolution) Act 1998, s 1(2)(a).

Sub-s (2A): inserted by the Employment Act 2002, s 24(2), as from 9 July 2004.

Sub-s (8): words in square brackets inserted by the Tribunals, Courts and Enforcement Act 2007, s 48(1), Sch 8, paras 35, 38, as from 1 December 2007.

Orders: the Employment Tribunals Act (Application of Conciliation Provisions) Order 2000, SI 2000/1299 (revoked due to a drafting error by SI 2000/1336 without coming into force); the Employment Tribunals Act (Application of Conciliation Provisions) Order 2000 (Revocation) Order 2000, SI 2000/1336; the Employment Tribunals Act 1996 (Application of Conciliation Provisions) Order 2000, SI 2000/1337 (which amends sub-s (1)(d) as noted above and specifies that the Trade Union and Labour Relations (Consolidation) Act 1992,s 70B, Sch 1, para 156 are provisions to which sub-s (1)(f) above applies).

19 Conciliation procedure

[(1)] [Employment tribunal] procedure regulations shall include in relation to [employment tribunal] proceedings in the case of which any enactment makes provision for conciliation—

(a) provisions requiring a copy of the application by which the proceedings are instituted, and a copy of any notice relating to it which is lodged by or on behalf of the person against whom the proceedings are brought, to be sent to a conciliation officer, [and]

(b) provisions securing that the applicant and the person against whom the proceedings are brought are notified that the services of a conciliation officer are available to them, …

(c) …

[(2) If employment tribunal procedure regulations include provision postponing the fixing of a time and place for a hearing for the purpose of giving an opportunity for the proceedings to be settled by way of conciliation and withdrawn, they shall also include provision for the parties to proceedings to which the provision for postponement applies to be notified that the services of a conciliation officer may no longer be available to them after the end of the postponement.]

[976]

NOTES

Sub-s (1): numbered as such by the Employment Act 2002, s 24(4), as from 9 July 2004; word omitted from para (b) and the whole of para (c) repealed by ss 24(3), 54 of, and Sch 8 to, the 2002 Act, as from 6 April 2003; word "and" in square brackets inserted by s 53 of, and Sch 7, para 23(1), (3) to, the 2002 Act, as from 1 October 2004; other words in square brackets substituted by the Employment Rights (Dispute Resolution) Act 1998, s 1(2)(a).

Sub-s (2): added by the Employment Act 2002, s 24(4), as from 9 July 2004.

Regulations: the Employment Tribunals (Constitution and Rules of Procedure) Regulations 2004, SI 2004/1861 at **[3151]**.

[19A Conciliation: recovery of sums payable under compromises

(1) Subsections (3) to (6) apply if—

(a) a conciliation officer—

(i) has taken action under section 18 in a case, and

(ii) issues a certificate in writing stating that a compromise has been reached in the case, and

(b) all of the terms of the compromise are set out—

(i) in a single relevant document, or

(ii) in a combination of two or more relevant documents.

(2) A document is a "relevant document" for the purposes of subsection (1) if—

(a) it is the certificate, or

(b) it is a document that is referred to in the certificate or that is referred to in a document that is within this paragraph.

(3) Any sum payable by a person under the terms of the compromise (a "compromise sum") shall, subject to subsections (4) to (7), be recoverable—

(a) in England and Wales, by execution issued from a county court or otherwise as if the sum were payable under an order of that court;

(b) in Scotland, by diligence as if the certificate were an extract registered decree arbitral bearing a warrant for execution issued by the sheriff court of any sheriffdom in Scotland.

(4) A compromise sum is not recoverable under subsection (3) if—

(a) the person by whom it is payable applies for a declaration that the sum would not be recoverable from him under the general law of contract, and
(b) that declaration is made.

(5) If rules of court so provide, a compromise sum is not recoverable under subsection (3) during the period—
(a) beginning with the issue of the certificate, and
(b) ending at such time as may be specified in, or determined under, rules of court.

(6) If the terms of the compromise provide for the person to whom a compromise sum is payable to do anything in addition to discontinuing or not starting proceedings, that sum is recoverable by him under subsection (3)—
(a) in England and Wales, only if a county court so orders;
(b) in Scotland, only if the sheriff so orders.

(7) Once an application has been made for a declaration under subsection (4) in relation to a sum, no further reliance may be placed on subsection (3) for the recovery of the sum while the application is pending.

(8) An application for a declaration under subsection (4) may be made to an employment tribunal, a county court or the sheriff.

(9) Employment tribunal procedure regulations may (in particular) make provision as to the time within which an application to an employment tribunal for a declaration under subsection (4) is to be made.

(10) Rules of court may make provision as to—
(a) the time within which an application to a county court for a declaration under subsection (4) is to be made;
(b) the time within which an application to the sheriff for a declaration under subsection (4) is to be made;
(c) when an application (whether made to a county court, the sheriff or an employment tribunal) for a declaration under subsection (4) is pending for the purposes of subsection (7).

(11) Nothing in this section shall be taken to prejudice any rights or remedies that a person has apart from this section.

(12) In this section "compromise" (except in the phrase "compromise sum") means a settlement, or compromise, to avoid proceedings or bring proceedings to an end.]

[976A]

NOTES

Commencement: to be appointed.
Inserted by the Tribunals, Courts and Enforcement Act 2007, s 142, as from a day to be appointed.

PART II
THE EMPLOYMENT APPEAL TRIBUNAL

Introductory

20 The Appeal Tribunal

(1) The Employment Appeal Tribunal ("the Appeal Tribunal") shall continue in existence.

(2) The Appeal Tribunal shall have a central office in London but may sit at any time and in any place in Great Britain.

(3) The Appeal Tribunal shall be a superior court of record and shall have an official seal which shall be judicially noticed.

[(4) Subsection (2) is subject to regulation 34 of the Transnational Information and Consultation of Employees Regulations [1999,] [regulation 46(1) of the European Public Limited-Liability Company Regulations] [2004,] [regulation 36(1) of the Information and Consultation of Employees Regulations] [2004,] [regulation 37(1) of the European Cooperative Society (Involvement of Employees) Regulations 2006] [and regulation 58(1) of the Companies (Cross-Border Mergers) Regulations 2007].]

[977]

NOTES

Sub-s (4): added by the Transnational Information and Consultation of Employees Regulations 1999, SI 1999/3323, reg 35(1), (2), and subsequently amended as follows:

Entry relating to the European Public Limited-Liability Company Regulations inserted by the European Public Limited-Liability Company Regulations 2004, SI 2004/2326, reg 48(2), as from 8 October 2004.

Entry relating to the Information and Consultation of Employees Regulations inserted by the Information and Consultation of Employees Regulations 2004, SI 2004/3426, reg 36(2), as from 6 April 2005.

Entry relating to the European Cooperative Society (Involvement of Employees) Regulations inserted by the European Cooperative Society (Involvement of Employees) Regulations 2006, SI 2006/2059, reg 37, as from 18 August 2006.

Entry relating to the Companies (Cross-Border Mergers) Regulations inserted by the Companies (Cross-Border Mergers) Regulations 2007, SI 2007/2974, reg 58(2)(b), as from 15 December 2007.

The other amendments in sub-s (4) are purely grammatical changes made by the same Regulations noted above, ie, the substitution of a particular year and the word "and", with the same year and a comma.

Jurisdiction

21 Jurisdiction of Appeal Tribunal

(1) An appeal lies to the Appeal Tribunal on any question of law arising from any decision of, or arising in any proceedings before, an [employment tribunal] under or by virtue of—

(a) the Equal Pay Act 1970,
(b) the Sex Discrimination Act 1975,
(c) the Race Relations Act 1976,
(d) the Trade Union and Labour Relations (Consolidation) Act 1992,
(e) the Disability Discrimination Act 1995, …
(f) the Employment Rights Act 1996, […
[(ff) …]
[(fg) …]
[(g) this Act,
(ga) the National Minimum Wage Act 1998,
(gb) the Employment Relations Act 1999],
[(gc) the Equality Act 2006,]
[(h) the Working Time Regulations 1998, …
(i) the Transnational Information and Consultation of Employees Regulations 1999]; […
(j) the Part-time Workers (Prevention of Less Favourable Treatment) Regulations 2000,][…
(k) the Fixed-term Employees (Prevention of Less Favourable Treatment) Regulations 2002,][…
(l) the Employment Equality (Sexual Orientation) Regulations 2003,][…
(m) the Employment Equality (Religion or Belief) Regulations 2003],
[(n) the Merchant Shipping (Working Time: Inland Waterways) Regulations 2003], […
(o) the European Public Limited-Liability Company Regulations 2004],
[[(p)] the Fishing Vessels (Working Time: Sea-fishermen) Regulations 2004], […
(q) the Information and Consultation of Employees Regulations 2004], […
(r) the Schedule to the Occupational and Personal Pension Schemes (Consultation by Employers and Miscellaneous Amendment) Regulations 2006], […
(s) the Employment Equality (Age) Regulations 2006][, …
(t) the European Cooperative Society (Involvement of Employees) Regulations 2006], [or
(u) the Companies (Cross-Border Mergers) Regulations 2007].

(2) No appeal shall lie except to the Appeal Tribunal from any decision of an [employment tribunal] under or by virtue of the Acts listed [or the Regulations referred to] in subsection (1).

(3) Subsection (1) does not affect any provision contained in, or made under, any Act which provides for an appeal to lie to the Appeal Tribunal (whether from an [employment tribunal], the Certification Officer or any other person or body) otherwise than on a question to which that subsection applies.

[(4) The Appeal Tribunal also has any jurisdiction in respect of matters other than appeals which is conferred on it by or under—

(a) the Trade Union and Labour Relations (Consolidation) Act 1992,

(b) this Act, or

(c) any other Act].

[978]

NOTES

Sub-s (1) has been amended as follows:

Words in first pair of square brackets substituted by the Employment Rights (Dispute Resolution) Act 1998, s 1(2)(a).

Word omitted from para (e) repealed by the Employment Rights (Dispute Resolution) Act 1998, s 15, Sch 2.

Word omitted from para (f) repealed by the National Minimum Wage Act 1998, s 53, Sch 3.

Para (ff) originally inserted by the National Minimum Wage Act 1998, s 29 (see further the notes below).

Para (fg) inserted by the Tax Credits Act 1999, s 7, Sch 3, para 5; repealed by the Tax Credits Act 2002, s 60, Sch 6, as from 6 April 2003.

Para (g) added by the Employment Rights (Dispute Resolution) Act 1998, s 15, Sch 1, para 17(1), (2) (see further the notes below).

Paras (g), (ga), (gb) substituted, for the original para (ff) (as inserted as noted above) and the original para (g) (as inserted as noted above), by the Employment Relations Act 2004, s 38, as from 1 October 2004.

Para (gc) inserted by the Equality Act 2006, s 40, Sch 3, para 57, as from 30 April 2007.

Paras (h), (i) substituted (for words that appeared in the original para (g) (as inserted as noted above)) by the Transnational Information and Consultation of Employees Regulations 1999, SI 1999/3323, reg 35(1), (3).

Word omitted from para (h) repealed, and para (j) and the word immediately preceding it added, by the Part-time Workers (Prevention of Less Favourable Treatment) Regulations 2000, SI 2000/1551, reg 10, Schedule, para 1(b).

Word omitted from para (i) repealed, and para (k) and the word immediately preceding it added, by the Fixed-term Employees (Prevention of Less Favourable Treatment) Regulations 2002, SI 2002/2034, reg 11, Sch 2, Pt 1, para 2(b).

Word omitted from para (j) repealed, and para (l) and the word immediately preceding it added, by the Employment Equality (Sexual Orientation) Regulations 2003, SI 2003/1661, reg 39, Sch 5, para 1(b), as from 1 December 2003.

Word omitted from para (k) repealed, and para (m) and the word immediately preceding it added, by the Employment Equality (Religion or Belief) Regulations 2003, SI 2003/1660, reg 39(2), Sch 5, para 1(b), as from 1 December 2003.

Word omitted from para (l) repealed, and para (n) added, by the Merchant Shipping (Working Time: Inland Waterways) Regulations 2003, SI 2003/3049, reg 20, Sch 2, para 2(1), (3), as from 24 December 2003.

Word omitted from para (n) repealed by the Information and Consultation of Employees Regulations 2004, SI 2004/3426, reg 37(a), as from 6 April 2005.

Para (o) and the word immediately preceding it added by the European Public Limited-Liability Company Regulations 2004, SI 2004/2326, reg 49, as from 8 October 2004.

Para (p) inserted by the Fishing Vessels (Working Time: Sea-fishermen) Regulations 2004, SI 2004/1713, reg 21, Sch 2, para 1(1), (3), as from 16 August 2004. Note that this paragraph was originally added as para (o) and was redesignated as para (p) by SI 2004/3426, reg 37(b), as from 6 April 2005.

Para (q) and the word immediately preceding it added by SI 2004/3426, reg 37(c), as from 6 April 2005.

Para (r) and the word immediately preceding it added, and word omitted from para (p) repealed, by the Occupational and Personal Pension Schemes (Consultation by Employers and Miscellaneous Amendment) Regulations 2006, SI 2006/349, reg 17, Schedule, para 10, as from 6 April 2006.

Para (s) and the word immediately preceding it added, and word omitted from para (q) repealed, by the Employment Equality (Age) Regulations 2006, SI 2006/1031, reg 49(1), Sch 8, Pt 1, paras 18, 20, as from 1 October 2006.

Para (t) and the word immediately preceding it added, and word omitted from para (r) repealed, by the European Cooperative Society (Involvement of Employees) Regulations 2006, SI 2006/2059, reg 38, as from 18 August 2006.

Para (u) and the word immediately preceding it added, and word omitted from para (s) repealed, by the Companies (Cross-Border Mergers) Regulations 2007, SI 2007/2974, reg 59, as from 15 December 2007.

Sub-s (2): words in first pair of square brackets substituted by the Employment Rights (Dispute Resolution) Act 1998, s 1(2)(a); words in second pair of square brackets inserted by SI 1998/1833, reg 34(b).

Sub-s (3): words square brackets substituted by the Employment Rights (Dispute Resolution) Act 1998, s 1(2)(a).

Sub-s (4): added by the Employment Rights (Dispute Resolution) Act 1998, s 15, Sch 1, para 17(1), (3).

See also as a source of authority to hear appeals, the Transfer of Undertakings (Protection of Employment) Regulations 2006, SI 2006/246, reg 16(2) at **[3391]**.

Membership etc

22 Membership of Appeal Tribunal

(1) The Appeal Tribunal shall consist of—

(a) such number of judges as may be nominated from time to time [by the Lord Chief Justice, after consulting the Lord Chancellor,] from the judges ... of the High Court and the Court of Appeal,

(b) at least one judge of the Court of Session nominated from time to time by the Lord President of the Court of Session, and

(c) such number of other members as may be appointed from time to time by Her Majesty on the joint recommendation of the Lord Chancellor and the Secretary of State ("appointed members").

(2) The appointed members shall be persons who appear to the Lord Chancellor and the Secretary of State to have special knowledge or experience of industrial relations either—

(a) as representatives of employers, or

(b) as representatives of workers (within the meaning of the Trade Union and Labour Relations (Consolidation) Act 1992).

(3) The [Lord Chief Justice shall] appoint one of the judges nominated under subsection (1) to be the President of the Appeal Tribunal.

[(3A) The Lord Chief Justice must not make an appointment under subsection (3) unless—

(a) he has consulted the Lord Chancellor, and

(b) the Lord President of the Court of Session agrees.]

(4) No judge shall be nominated a member of the Appeal Tribunal except with his consent.

[(5) The Lord Chief Justice may nominate a judicial office holder (as defined in section 109(4) of the Constitutional Reform Act 2005) to exercise his functions under this section.

(6) The Lord President of the Court of Session may nominate a judge of the Court of Session who is a member of the First or Second Division of the Inner House of that Court to exercise his functions under subsection (3A)(b).]

[979]

NOTES

Sub-s (1): words in square brackets substituted, and words omitted repealed, by the Constitutional Reform Act 2005, ss 15, 146, Sch 4, Pt 1, paras 245, 246(1), (2), Sch 18, Pt 2, as from 3 April 2006.

Sub-s (3): words in square brackets substituted by the Constitutional Reform Act 2005, s 15, Sch 4, Pt 1, paras 245, 246(1), (3), as from 3 April 2006.

Sub-ss (3A), (5), (6): inserted and added respectively by the Constitutional Reform Act 2005, s 15, Sch 4, Pt 1, paras 245, 246(1), (4), (5), as from 3 April 2006.

23 Temporary membership

(1) At any time when—

(a) the office of President of the Appeal Tribunal is vacant, or

(b) the person holding that office is temporarily absent or otherwise unable to act as the President of the Appeal Tribunal,

the [Lord Chief Justice] may nominate another judge nominated under section 22(1)(a) to act temporarily in his place.

(2) At any time when a judge of the Appeal Tribunal nominated under paragraph (a) or (b) of subsection (1) of section 22 is temporarily absent or otherwise unable to act as a member of the Appeal Tribunal—

(a) in the case of a judge nominated under paragraph (a) of that subsection, the [Lord Chief Justice] may nominate another judge who is qualified to be nominated under that paragraph to act temporarily in his place, and

(b) in the case of a judge nominated under paragraph (b) of that subsection, the Lord President of the Court of Session may nominate another judge who is qualified to be nominated under that paragraph to act temporarily in his place.

(3) At any time when an appointed member of the Appeal Tribunal is temporarily absent or otherwise unable to act as a member of the Appeal Tribunal, the Lord Chancellor and the

Secretary of State may jointly appoint a person appearing to them to have the qualifications for appointment as an appointed member to act temporarily in his place.

(4) A person nominated or appointed to act temporarily in place of the President or any other member of the Appeal Tribunal, when so acting, has all the functions of the person in whose place he acts.

(5) No judge shall be nominated to act temporarily as a member of the Appeal Tribunal except with his consent.

[(6) The functions conferred on the Lord Chief Justice by the preceding provisions of this section may be exercised only after consulting the Lord Chancellor.

(7) The functions conferred on the Lord Chancellor by subsection (3) may be exercised only after consultation with the Lord Chief Justice.

(8) The Lord Chief Justice may nominate a judicial office holder (as defined in section 109(4) of the Constitutional Reform Act 2005) to exercise his functions under this section.]

[980]

NOTES

Sub-ss (1), (2): words in square brackets substituted by the Constitutional Reform Act 2005, s 15, Sch 4, Pt 1, paras 245, 247(1)–(3), as from 3 April 2006.

Sub-ss (6)–(8): added by the Constitutional Reform Act 2005, s 15, Sch 4, Pt 1, paras 245, 247(1), (4), as from 3 April 2006.

24 Temporary additional judicial membership

[(1) This section applies if both of the following conditions are met—

(a) the Lord Chancellor thinks that it is expedient, after consulting the Lord Chief Justice, for a qualified person to be appointed to be a temporary additional judge of the Appeal Tribunal in order to facilitate in England and Wales the disposal of business in the Appeal Tribunal;

(b) the Lord Chancellor requests the Lord Chief Justice to make such an appointment.

(1A) The Lord Chief Justice may, after consulting the Lord Chancellor, appoint a qualified person as mentioned in subsection (1)(a).

(1B) An appointment under this section is—

(a) for such period, or

(b) on such occasions,

as the Lord Chief Justice determines, after consulting the Lord Chancellor.]

(2) In [this section] "qualified person" means a person who—

(a) is qualified for appointment as a judge of the High Court under section 10 of the *Supreme Court Act 1981*, or

(b) has held office as a judge of the High Court or the Court of Appeal.

(3) A person appointed to be a temporary additional judge of the Appeal Tribunal has all the functions of a judge nominated under section 22(1)(a).

[(4) The Lord Chief Justice may nominate a judicial office holder (as defined in section 109(4) of the Constitutional Reform Act 2005) to exercise his functions under this section.]

[981]

NOTES

Sub-ss (1), (1A), (1B): substituted, for original sub-s (1), by the Constitutional Reform Act 2005, s 15, Sch 4, Pt 1, paras 245, 248(1), (2), as from 3 April 2006.

Sub-s (2): words in square brackets substituted by the Constitutional Reform Act 2005, s 15, Sch 4, Pt 1, paras 245, 248(1), (3), as from 3 April 2006; for the words in italics there are substituted the words "Senior Courts Act 1981" by the Constitutional Reform Act 2005, s 59, Sch 11, Pt 1, para 1(2), as from a day to be appointed.

Sub-s (4): added by the Constitutional Reform Act 2005, s 15, Sch 4, Pt 1, paras 245, 248(1), (4), as from 3 April 2006.

[24A Training etc of members of Appeal Tribunal

The Senior President of Tribunals is responsible, within the resources made available by the Lord Chancellor, for the maintenance of appropriate arrangements for the training, guidance and welfare of judges, and other members, of the Appeal Tribunal (in their capacities as members of the Appeal Tribunal).]

[981A]

NOTES

Commencement: to be appointed.

Inserted, together with s 24B, by the Tribunals, Courts and Enforcement Act 2007, s 48(1), Sch 8, paras 35, 44, as from a day to be appointed.

[24B Oaths

(1) Subsection (2) applies to a person ("the appointee")—

(a) who is appointed under section 22(1)(c) or 23(3), or

(b) who is appointed under section 24(1A) and—

(i) falls when appointed within paragraph (a), but not paragraph (b), of section 24(2), and

(ii) has not previously taken the required oaths after accepting another office.

(2) The appointee must take the required oaths before—

(a) the Senior President of Tribunals, or

(b) an eligible person who is nominated by the Senior President of Tribunals for the purpose of taking the oaths from the appointee.

(3) If the appointee is a member of the Appeal Tribunal appointed before the coming into force of this section, the requirement in subsection (2) applies in relation to the appointee from the coming into force of this section.

(4) A person is eligible for the purposes of subsection (2)(b) if one or more of the following paragraphs applies to him—

(a) he holds high judicial office (as defined in section 60(2) of the Constitutional Reform Act 2005);

(b) he holds judicial office (as defined in section 109(4) of that Act);

(c) he holds (in Scotland) the office of sheriff.

(5) In this section "the required oaths" means—

(a) the oath of allegiance, and

(b) the judicial oath,

as set out in the Promissory Oaths Act 1868.]

[981B]

NOTES

Commencement: to be appointed.

Inserted as noted to s 24A at **[981A]**.

25 Tenure of appointed members

(1) Subject to subsections (2) to (4), an appointed member shall hold and vacate office in accordance with the terms of his appointment.

(2) An appointed member—

(a) may at any time resign his membership by notice in writing addressed to the Lord Chancellor and the Secretary of State, and

(b) shall vacate his office on the day on which he attains the age of seventy.

(3) Subsection (2)(b) is subject to section 26(4) to (6) of the Judicial Pensions and Retirement Act 1993 (Lord Chancellor's power to authorise continuance of office up to the age of seventy-five).

(4) If the Lord Chancellor, after consultation with the Secretary of State, is satisfied that an appointed member—

(a) has been absent from sittings of the Appeal Tribunal for a period longer than six consecutive months without the permission of the President of the Appeal Tribunal,

(b) has become bankrupt or made an arrangement with his creditors, or has had his estate sequestrated or made a trust deed for behoof of his creditors or a composition contract,

(c) is incapacitated by physical or mental illness, or

(d) is otherwise unable or unfit to discharge the functions of a member,

the Lord Chancellor may declare his office as a member to be vacant and shall notify the declaration in such manner as the Lord Chancellor thinks fit; and when the Lord Chancellor does so, the office becomes vacant.

[(5) The Lord Chancellor may declare an appointed member's office vacant under subsection (4) only with the concurrence of the appropriate senior judge.

(6) The appropriate senior judge is the Lord Chief Justice of England and Wales, unless the member whose office is to be declared vacant exercises functions wholly or mainly in Scotland, in which case it is the Lord President of the Court of Session.]

[982]

NOTES

Sub-ss (5), (6): added by the Constitutional Reform Act 2005, s 15, Sch 4, Pt 1, paras 245, 249, as from 3 April 2006.

26 Staff

The Secretary of State may appoint such officers and servants of the Appeal Tribunal as he may determine, subject to the approval of the Minister for the Civil Service as to numbers and terms and conditions of service.

[983]

NOTES

Repealed by the Tribunals, Courts and Enforcement Act 2007, s 146, Sch 23, Pt 1, as from a day to be appointed.

27 Remuneration, pensions and allowances

(1) The Secretary of State shall pay—

(a) the appointed members, [and]

(b) any person appointed to act temporarily in the place of an appointed member, *and*

(c) the officers and servants of the Appeal Tribunal,

such remuneration and such travelling and other allowances as he may, with the relevant approval, determine; and for this purpose the relevant approval is that of the Treasury in the case of persons within paragraph (a) or (b) *and the Minister for the Civil Service in the case of persons within paragraph (c)*.

(2) A person appointed to be a temporary additional judge of the Appeal Tribunal shall be paid such remuneration and allowances as the Lord Chancellor may, with the approval of the Treasury, determine.

(3) If the Secretary of State determines, with the approval of the Treasury, that this subsection applies in the case of an appointed member, the Secretary of State shall—

(a) pay such pension, allowance or gratuity to or in respect of that person on his retirement or death, or

(b) make to the member such payments towards the provision of a pension, allowance or gratuity for his retirement or death,

as the Secretary of State may, with the approval of the Treasury, determine.

(4) Where—

(a) a person ceases to be an appointed member otherwise than on his retirement or death, and

(b) it appears to the Secretary of State that there are special circumstances which make it right for him to receive compensation,

the Secretary of State may make to him a payment of such amount as the Secretary of State may, with the approval of the Treasury, determine.

[984]

NOTES

Sub-s (1): word in square brackets inserted, and words in italics repealed, by the Tribunals, Courts and Enforcement Act 2007, ss 48(1), 146, Sch 8, paras 35, 45, Sch 23, Pt 1, as from a day to be appointed.

28 Composition of Appeal Tribunal

(1) The Appeal Tribunal may sit, in accordance with directions given by the President of the Appeal Tribunal, either as a single tribunal or in two or more divisions concurrently.

(2) Subject to subsections (3) to (5), proceedings before the Appeal Tribunal shall be heard by a judge and either two or four appointed members, so that in either case there is an equal number—

(a) of persons whose knowledge or experience of industrial relations is as representatives of employers, and

(b) of persons whose knowledge or experience of industrial relations is as representatives of workers.

(3) With the consent of the parties, proceedings before the Appeal Tribunal may be heard by a judge and one appointed member or by a judge and three appointed members.

(4) Proceedings on an appeal on a *question arising from any decision of, or arising in any proceedings before, an [employment tribunal] consisting of the person mentioned in section 4(1)(a) alone* shall be heard by a judge alone unless a judge directs that the proceedings shall be heard in accordance with subsections (2) and (3).

[(4A) In subsection (4) "chairman-alone question" means—

(a) a question arising from any decision of an employment tribunal that is a decision of—

(i) the person mentioned in section 4(1)(a) acting alone, or

(ii) any Employment Judge acting alone, or

(b) a question arising in any proceedings before an employment tribunal that are proceedings before—

(i) the person mentioned in section 4(1)(a) alone, or

(ii) any Employment Judge alone.]

(5) …

[985]

NOTES

Sub-s (4): words in square brackets substituted by the Employment Rights (Dispute Resolution) Act 1998, s 1(2)(a); for the words in italics there are substituted the words "chairman-alone question" by the Tribunals, Courts and Enforcement Act 2007, s 48(1), Sch 8, paras 35, 46(1), (2), as from a day to be appointed.

Sub-s (4A): inserted by the Tribunals, Courts and Enforcement Act 2007, s 48(1), Sch 8, paras 35, 46(1), (3), as from a day to be appointed.

Sub-s (5): repealed by the Employment Relations Act 1999, ss 41, 44, Sch 8, para 4, Sch 9(12). There has been no corresponding amendment to sub-s (2).

Procedure

29 Conduct of hearings

(1) A person may appear before the Appeal Tribunal in person or be represented by—

(a) counsel or a solicitor,

(b) a representative of a trade union or an employers' association, or

(c) any other person whom he desires to represent him.

(2) The Appeal Tribunal has in relation to—

(a) the attendance and examination of witnesses,

(b) the production and inspection of documents, and

(c) all other matters incidental to its jurisdiction,

the same powers, rights, privileges and authority (in England and Wales) as the High Court and (in Scotland) as the Court of Session.

[986]

[29A Practice directions

(1) Directions about the procedure of the Appeal Tribunal may be given—

(a) by the Senior President of Tribunals, or

(b) by the President of the Appeal Tribunal.

(2) A power under subsection (1) includes—

(a) power to vary or revoke directions given in exercise of the power, and

(b) power to make different provision for different purposes.

(3) Directions under subsection (1)(a) may not be given without the approval of the Lord Chancellor.

(4) Directions under subsection (1)(b) may not be given without the approval of—

(a) the Senior President of Tribunals, and

(b) the Lord Chancellor.

(5) Subsection (1) does not prejudice any power apart from that subsection to give directions about the procedure of the Appeal Tribunal.

(6) Directions may not be given in exercise of any such power as is mentioned in subsection (5) without the approval of—

(a) the Senior President of Tribunals, and

(b) the Lord Chancellor.

(7) Subsections (3), (4)(b) and (6)(b) do not apply to directions to the extent that they consist of guidance about any of the following—

(a) the application or interpretation of the law;

(b) the making of decisions by members of the Appeal Tribunal.

(8) Subsections (3), (4)(b) and (6)(b) do not apply to directions to the extent that they consist of criteria for determining which members of the Appeal Tribunal may be chosen to decide particular categories of matter; but the directions may, to that extent, be given only after consulting the Lord Chancellor.

(9) Subsections (4) and (6) do not apply to directions given in a particular case for the purposes of that case only.

(10) Subsection (6) does not apply to directions under section 28(1).]

[986A]

NOTES

Commencement: to be appointed.

Inserted by the Tribunals, Courts and Enforcement Act 2007, s 48(1), Sch 8, paras 35, 47, as from a day to be appointed.

30 Appeal Tribunal procedure rules

(1) The Lord Chancellor, after consultation with the Lord President of the Court of Session, shall make rules ("Appeal Tribunal procedure rules") with respect to proceedings before the Appeal Tribunal.

(2) Appeal Tribunal procedure rules may, in particular, include provision—

(a) with respect to the manner in which, and the time within which, an appeal may be brought,

(b) with respect to the manner in which any application [or complaint] to the Appeal Tribunal may be made,

(c) for requiring persons to attend to give evidence and produce documents and for authorising the administration of oaths to witnesses,

(d) for requiring or enabling the Appeal Tribunal to sit in private in circumstances in which an [employment tribunal] is required or empowered to sit in private by virtue of [section 10A] of this Act,

(e) … and

(f) for interlocutory matters arising on any appeal or application to the Appeal Tribunal to be dealt with otherwise than in accordance with section 28(2) to (5) of this Act.

[(2A) Appeal Tribunal procedure rules may make provision of a kind which may be made by employment tribunal procedure regulations under section 10(2), (5), (6) or (7).

(2B) For the purposes of subsection (2A)—

(a) the reference in section 10(2) to section 4 shall be treated as a reference to section 28, and

(b) the reference in section 10(4) to the President or a Regional Chairman shall be treated as a reference to a judge of the Appeal Tribunal.

(2C) Section 10B shall have effect in relation to a direction to or determination of the Appeal Tribunal as it has effect in relation to a direction to or determination of an employment tribunal.]

(3) Subject to Appeal Tribunal procedure rules [and directions under section 28(1) or 29A(1)], the Appeal Tribunal has power to regulate its own procedure.

[987]

NOTES

Sub-s (2): words in square brackets in para (b) inserted by the Transnational Information and Consultation of Employees Regulations 1999, SI 1999/3323, reg 35(1), (4); in para (d) words in first pair of square brackets substituted by the Employment Rights (Dispute Resolution) Act 1998, s 1(2)(a), and words in second pair of square brackets substituted by the Employment Relations Act 1999, s 41, Sch 8, para 5(1), (2); para (e) repealed by the Employment Relations Act 2004, s 57, Sch 1, para 26, Sch 2, as from 31 December 2004, except in relation to the case of any award made on an application to the EAT, under the Trade Union and Labour Relations (Consolidation) Act 1992, ss 67 or 176, which requires registration or proof on or after that date (see SI 2004/3342, art 11).

Sub-ss (2A)–(2C): inserted by the Employment Relations Act 1999, s 41, Sch 8, para 5(1), (3).

Sub-s (3): words in square brackets inserted by the Tribunals, Courts and Enforcement Act 2007, s 48(1), Sch 8, paras 35, 48, as from a day to be appointed.

Rules: by virtue of s 44 of, and Sch 2, Pt I, paras 1–4 to, this Act, the Employment Appeal Tribunal Rules 1993, SI 1993/2854 at **[2188]** have effect as if made under this section. These Rules have subsequently been amended by Rules made under this section; see in particular SI 1996/3216, SI 2001/1128 (as amended by SI 2001/1476), SI 2004/2526 and SI 2005/1871.

31 Restriction of publicity in cases involving sexual misconduct

(1) Appeal Tribunal procedure rules may, as respects proceedings to which this section applies, include provision—

(a) for cases involving allegations of the commission of sexual offences, for securing that the registration or other making available of documents or divisions shall be so effected as to prevent the identification of any person affected by or making the allegation, and

(b) for cases involving allegations of sexual misconduct, enabling the Appeal Tribunal, on the application of any party to the proceedings before it or of its own motion, to make a restricted reporting order having effect (if not revoked earlier) until the promulgation of the decision of the Appeal Tribunal.

(2) This section applies to—

(a) proceedings on an appeal against a decision of an [employment tribunal] to make, or not to make, a restricted reporting order, and

(b) proceedings on an appeal against any interlocutory decision of an [employment tribunal] in proceedings in which the [employment tribunal] has made a restricted reporting order which it has not revoked.

(3) If any identifying matter is published or included in a relevant programme in contravention of a restricted reporting order—

(a) in the case of publication in a newspaper or periodical, any proprietor, any editor and any publisher of the newspaper or periodical,

(b) in the case of publication in any other form, the person publishing the matter, and

(c) in the case of matter included in a relevant programme—

(i) any body corporate engaged in providing the service in which the programme is included, and

(ii) any person having functions in relation to the programme corresponding to those of an editor of a newspaper,

shall be guilty of an offence and liable on summary conviction to a fine not exceeding level 5 on the standard scale.

(4) Where a person is charged with an offence under subsection (3) it is a defence to prove that at the time of the alleged offence he was not aware, and neither suspected nor had reason to suspect, that the publication or programme in question was of, or included, the matter in question.

(5) Where an offence under subsection (3) committed by a body corporate is proved to have been committed with the consent or connivance of, or to be attributable to any neglect on the part of—

(a) a director, manager, secretary or other similar officer of the body corporate, or

(b) a person purporting to act in any such capacity,

he as well as the body corporate is guilty of the offence and liable to be proceeded against and punished accordingly.

(6) In relation to a body corporate whose affairs are managed by its members "director", in subsection (5), means a member of the body corporate.

(7) "Restricted reporting order" means—

(a) in subsections (1) and (3), an order—

(i) made in exercise of a power conferred by rules made by virtue of this section, and

(ii) prohibiting the publication in Great Britain of identifying matter in a written publication available to the public or its inclusion in a relevant programme for reception in Great Britain, and

(b) in subsection (2), an order which is a restricted reporting order for the purposes of section 11.

(8) In this section—

"identifying matter", in relation to a person, means any matter likely to lead members of the public to identify him as a person affected by, or as the person making, the allegation,

"relevant programme" has the same meaning as in the Sexual Offences (Amendment) Act 1992,

"sexual misconduct" means the commission of a sexual offence, sexual harassment or other adverse conduct (of whatever nature) related to sex, and conduct is related to sex whether the relationship with sex lies in the character of the conduct or in its having reference to the sex or sexual orientation of the person at whom the conduct is directed,

"sexual offence" means any offence to which section 4 of the Sexual Offences (Amendment) Act 1976, the Sexual Offences (Amendment) Act 1992 or section 274(2) of the Criminal Procedure (Scotland) Act 1995 applies (offences under the Sexual Offences Act 1956, Part I of the Criminal Law (Consolidation) (Scotland) Act 1995 and certain other enactments), and

"written publication" has the same meaning as in the Sexual Offences (Amendment) Act 1992.

[988]

NOTES

Sub-s (2): words in square brackets substituted by the Employment Rights (Dispute Resolution) Act 1998, s 1(2)(a).

Sexual Offences (Amendment) Act 1976, s 4: repealed by Youth Justice and Criminal Evidence Act 1999, ss 48, 67(3), Sch 2, para 4, Sch 6.

Rules: see the note to s 30 at **[987]**.

32 Restriction of publicity in disability cases

(1) This section applies to proceedings—

(a) on an appeal against a decision of an [employment tribunal] to make, or not to make, a restricted reporting order, or

(b) on an appeal against any interlocutory decision of an [employment tribunal] in proceedings in which the [employment tribunal] has made a restricted reporting order which it has not revoked.

(2) Appeal Tribunal procedure rules may, as respects proceedings to which this section applies, include provision for—

(a) enabling the Appeal Tribunal, on the application of the complainant or of its own motion, to make a restricted reporting order having effect (if not revoked earlier) until the promulgation of the decision of the Appeal Tribunal, and

(b) where a restricted reporting order is made in relation to an appeal which is being dealt with by the Appeal Tribunal together with any other proceedings, enabling the Appeal Tribunal to direct that the order is to apply also in relation to those other proceedings or such part of them as the Appeal Tribunal may direct.

(3) If any identifying matter is published or included in a relevant programme in contravention of a restricted reporting order—

(a) in the case of publication in a newspaper or periodical, any proprietor, any editor and any publisher of the newspaper or periodical,

(b) in the case of publication in any other form, the person publishing the matter, and

(c) in the case of matter included in a relevant programme—

(i) any body corporate engaged in providing the service in which the programme is included, and

(ii) any person having functions in relation to the programme corresponding to those of an editor of a newspaper,

shall be guilty of an offence and liable on summary conviction to a fine not exceeding level 5 on the standard scale.

(4) Where a person is charged with an offence under subsection (3), it is a defence to prove that at the time of the alleged offence he was not aware, and neither suspected nor had reason to suspect, that the publication or programme in question was of, or included, the matter in question.

(5) Where an offence under subsection (3) committed by a body corporate is proved to have been committed with the consent or connivance of, or to be attributable to any neglect on the part of—

(a) a director, manager, secretary or other similar officer of the body corporate, or

(b) a person purporting to act in any such capacity,

he as well as the body corporate is guilty of the offence and liable to be proceeded against and punished accordingly.

(6) In relation to a body corporate whose affairs are managed by its members "director", in subsection (5), means a member of the body corporate.

(7) "Restricted reporting order" means—

(a) in subsection (1), an order which is a restricted reporting order for the purposes of section 12, and

(b) in subsections (2) and (3), an order—

(i) made in exercise of a power conferred by rules made by virtue of this section, and

(ii) prohibiting the publication in Great Britain of identifying matter in a written publication available to the public or its inclusion in a relevant programme for reception in Great Britain.

(8) In this section—

"complainant" means the person who made the complaint to which the proceedings before the Appeal Tribunal relate,

"identifying matter" means any matter likely to lead members of the public to identify the complainant or such other persons (if any) as may be named in the order,

"promulgation" has such meaning as may be prescribed by rules made by virtue of this section,

"relevant programme" means a programme included in a programme service, within the meaning of the Broadcasting Act 1990, and

"written publication" includes a film, a sound track and any other record in permanent form but does not include an indictment or other document prepared for use in particular legal proceedings.

[989]

NOTES

Sub-s (1): words in square brackets substituted by the Employment Rights (Dispute Resolution) Act 1998, s 1(2)(a).

Rules: see the note to s 30 at **[987]**.

33 Restriction of vexatious proceedings

(1) If, on an application made by the Attorney General or the Lord Advocate under this section, the Appeal Tribunal is satisfied that a person has habitually and persistently and without any reasonable ground—

(a) instituted vexatious proceedings, whether [before the Certification Officer,] in an [employment tribunal] or before the Appeal Tribunal, and whether against the same person or against different persons, or

(b) made vexatious applications in any proceedings, whether [before the Certification Officer,] in an [employment tribunal] or before the Appeal Tribunal,

the Appeal Tribunal may, after hearing the person or giving him an opportunity of being heard, make a restriction of proceedings order.

(2) A "restriction of proceedings order" is an order that—

(a) no proceedings shall without the leave of the Appeal Tribunal be instituted [before the Certification Officer,] in any [employment tribunal] or before the Appeal Tribunal by the person against whom the order is made,

(b) any proceedings instituted by him [before the Certification Officer,] in any [employment tribunal] or before the Appeal Tribunal before the making of the order shall not be continued by him without the leave of the Appeal Tribunal, and

(c) no application (other than one for leave under this section) is to be made by him in any proceedings [before the Certification Officer,] in any [employment tribunal] or before the Appeal Tribunal without the leave of the Appeal Tribunal.

(3) A restriction of proceedings order may provide that it is to cease to have effect at the end of a specified period, but otherwise it remains in force indefinitely.

(4) Leave for the institution or continuance of, or for the making of an application in, any proceedings [before the Certification Officer,] in an [employment tribunal] or before the Appeal Tribunal by a person who is the subject of a restriction of proceedings order shall not be given unless the Appeal Tribunal is satisfied—

(a) that the proceedings or application are not an abuse of [process], and

(b) that there are reasonable grounds for the proceedings or application.

(5) A copy of a restriction of proceedings order shall be published in the London Gazette and the Edinburgh Gazette.

[990]

NOTES

Sub-s (1): words in first pair of square brackets in paras (a), (b) inserted by the Employment Relations Act 2004, s 49(1)–(3), as from 6 April 2005; words in second pair of square brackets in those paragraphs substituted by the Employment Rights (Dispute Resolution) Act 1998, s 1(2)(a).

Sub-s (2): words in first pair of square brackets in paras (a)–(c) inserted by the Employment Relations Act 2004, s 49(1), (4)–(6), as from 6 April 2005; words in second pair of square brackets in those paragraphs substituted by the Employment Rights (Dispute Resolution) Act 1998, s 1(2)(a).

Sub-s (4): words in first pair of square brackets inserted, and word in third pair of square brackets substituted, by the Employment Relations Act 2004, s 49(1), (7), as from 6 April 2005; words in second pair of square brackets substituted by the Employment Rights (Dispute Resolution) Act 1998, s 1(2)(a).

[34 Costs and expenses

(1) Appeal Tribunal procedure rules may include provision for the award of costs or expenses.

(2) Rules under subsection (1) may include provision authorising the Appeal Tribunal to have regard to a person's ability to pay when considering the making of an award against him under such rules.

(3) Appeal Tribunal procedure rules may include provision for authorising the Appeal Tribunal—

(a) to disallow all or part of the costs or expenses of a representative of a party to proceedings before it by reason of that representative's conduct of the proceedings;

(b) to order a representative of a party to proceedings before it to meet all or part of the costs or expenses incurred by a party by reason of the representative's conduct of the proceedings.

(4) Appeal Tribunal procedure rules may also include provision for taxing or otherwise settling the costs or expenses referred to in subsection (1) or (3)(b) (and, in particular in England and Wales, for enabling the amount of such costs to be assessed by way of detailed assessment in the High Court).]

[991]

NOTES

Commencement: 9 July 2004.

Substituted by the Employment Act 2002, s 23, as from 9 July 2004.

Rules: see the note to s 30 at **[987]**.

Decisions and further appeals

35 Powers of Appeal Tribunal

(1) For the purpose of disposing of an appeal, the Appeal Tribunal may—

(a) exercise any of the powers of the body or officer from whom the appeal was brought, or

(b) remit the case to that body or officer.

(2) Any decision or award of the Appeal Tribunal on an appeal has the same effect, and may be enforced in the same manner, as a decision or award of the body or officer from whom the appeal was brought.

[992]

36 Enforcement of decisions etc

(1)–(3) …

(4) No person shall be punished for contempt of the Appeal Tribunal except by, or with the consent of, a judge.

(5) A magistrates' court shall not remit the whole or part of a fine imposed by the Appeal Tribunal unless it has the consent of a judge who is a member of the Appeal Tribunal.

[993]

NOTES

Sub-ss (1)–(3): repealed by the Employment Relations Act 2004, s 57, Sch 1, para 27, Sch 2, as from 31 December 2004, except in relation to the case of any sum payable in pursuance of an award of the EAT, under the Trade Union and Labour Relations (Consolidation) Act 1992, ss 67 or 176, which was outstanding on or after that date (see SI 2004/3342, art 12).

37 Appeals from Appeal Tribunal

(1) Subject to subsection (3), an appeal on any question of law lies from any decision or order of the Appeal Tribunal to the relevant appeal court with the leave of the Appeal Tribunal or of the relevant appeal court.

(2) In subsection (1) the "relevant appeal court" means—

(a) in the case of proceedings in England and Wales, the Court of Appeal, and

(b) in the case of proceedings in Scotland, the Court of Session.

(3) No appeal lies from a decision of the Appeal Tribunal refusing leave for the institution or continuance of, or for the making of an application in, proceedings by a person who is the subject of a restriction of proceedings order made under section 33.

(4) This section is without prejudice to section 13 of the Administration of Justice Act 1960 (appeal in case of contempt of court).

[994]

PART III
SUPPLEMENTARY

Crown employment and Parliamentary staff

38 Crown employment

(1) This Act has effect in relation to Crown employment and persons in Crown employment as it has effect in relation to other employment and other employees.

(2) In this Act "Crown employment" means employment under or for the purposes of a government department or any officer or body exercising on behalf of the Crown functions conferred by a statutory provision.

(3) For the purposes of the application of this Act in relation to Crown employment in accordance with subsection (1)—

(a) references to an employee shall be construed as references to a person in Crown employment, and

(b) references to a contract of employment shall be construed as references to the terms of employment of a person in Crown employment.

(4) Subsection (1) applies to—

(a) service as a member of the naval, military or air forces of the Crown, and

(b) employment by an association established for the purposes of Part XI of the Reserve Forces Act 1996;

but Her Majesty may by Order in Council make any provision of this Act apply to service as a member of the naval, military or air forces of the Crown subject to such exceptions and modifications as may be specified in the Order in Council.

[995]

NOTES

Sub-s (4) has effect, by virtue of Sch 2, Pt II, para 9, and until the relevant commencement date as defined in para 9(2), as if the subsection set out in para 9(1) were substituted for sub-s (4) of this section: see Sch 2, Pt II, para 9 at **[1004]** and the notes thereto.

39 Parliamentary staff

(1) This Act has effect in relation to employment as a relevant member of the House of Lords staff or a relevant member of the House of Commons staff as it has effect in relation to other employment.

(2) Nothing in any rule of law or the law or practice of Parliament prevents a relevant member of the House of Lords staff or a relevant member of the House of Commons staff from bringing before an [employment tribunal] proceedings of any description which could be brought before such a tribunal by a person who is not a relevant member of the House of Lords staff or a relevant member of the House of Commons staff.

(3) For the purposes of the application of this Act in relation to a relevant member of the House of Commons staff—

(a) references to an employee shall be construed as references to a relevant member of the House of Commons staff, and

(b) references to a contract of employment shall be construed as including references to the terms of employment of a relevant member of the House of Commons staff.

(4) In this Act "relevant member of the House of Lords staff" means any person who is employed under a contract of employment with the Corporate Officer of the House of Lords.

(5) In this Act "relevant member of the House of Commons staff" has the same meaning as in section 195 of the Employment Rights Act 1996; and (subject to an Order in Council under subsection (12) of that section)—

(a) subsections (6) and (7) of that section have effect for determining who is the employer of a relevant member of the House of Commons staff for the purposes of this Act, and

(b) subsection (8) of that section applies in relation to proceedings brought by virtue of this section.

[996]

NOTES

Sub-s (2): words in square brackets substituted by the Employment Rights (Dispute Resolution) Act 1998, s 1(2)(a).

General

40 Power to amend Act

(1) The Secretary of State [and the Lord Chancellor, acting jointly,] may by order—

(a) provide that any provision of this Act to which this section applies and which is specified in the order shall not apply to persons, or to employments, of such classes as may be prescribed in the order, or

(b) provide that any provision of this Act to which this section applies shall apply to persons or employments of such classes as may be prescribed in the order subject to such exceptions and modifications as may be so prescribed.

(2) This section applies to sections 3, 8, 16 and 17 and to section 18 so far as deriving from section 133 of the Employment Protection (Consolidation) Act 1978.

[997]

NOTES

Sub-s (1): words in square brackets inserted by the Tribunals, Courts and Enforcement Act 2007, s 48(1), Sch 8, paras 35, 38, as from 1 December 2007.

Orders: as of 6 April 2008 no Orders had been made under this section but, by virtue of s 44 of, and Sch 2, Pt I, paras 1–4 to, this Act, the Redundancy Payments (National Health Service) (Modification) Order 1993, SI 1993/3167, and the Employment Protection (Continuity of Employment of National Health Service Employees) (Modification) Order 1996, SI 1996/1023, have effect as if made under this section.

41 Orders, regulations and rules

(1) Any power conferred by this Act on a Minister of the Crown to make an order, and any power conferred by this Act to make regulations or rules, is exercisable by statutory instrument.

(2) No recommendation shall be made to Her Majesty to make an Order in Council under section 38(4), and no order shall be made under section 3, 4(4) or 40, unless a draft of the Order in Council or order has been laid before Parliament and approved by a resolution of each House of Parliament.

(3) A statutory instrument containing—

(a) an order made by a Minister of the Crown under any other provision of this Act except Part II of Schedule 2, or

(b) regulations or rules made under this Act,

is subject to annulment in pursuance of a resolution of either House of Parliament.

(4) Any power conferred by this Act which is exercisable by statutory instrument includes power to make such incidental, supplementary or transitional provision as appears to the Minister exercising the power to be necessary or expedient.

[998]

42 Interpretation

(1) In this Act—

"the Appeal Tribunal" means the Employment Appeal Tribunal,

"Appeal Tribunal procedure rules" shall be construed in accordance with section 30(1),

"appointed member" shall be construed in accordance with section 22(1)(c),

["Certification Officer" shall be construed in accordance with section 254 of the Trade Union and Labour Relations (Consolidation) Act 1992,]

"conciliation officer" means an officer designated by the Advisory, Conciliation and Arbitration Service under section 211 of the Trade Union and Labour Relations (Consolidation) Act 1992,

"contract of employment" means a contract of service or apprenticeship, whether express or implied, and (if it is express) whether oral or in writing,

"employee" means an individual who has entered into or works under (or, where the employment has ceased, worked under) a contract of employment,

"employer", in relation to an employee, means the person by whom the employee is (or, where the employment has ceased, was) employed,

"employers' association" has the same meaning as in the Trade Union and Labour Relations (Consolidation) Act 1992,

"employment" means employment under a contract of employment and "employed" shall be construed accordingly,

"[employment tribunal] procedure regulations" shall be construed in accordance with section 7(1),

"statutory provision" means a provision, whether of a general or a special nature, contained in, or in any document made or issued under, any Act, whether of a general or special nature,

"successor", in relation to the employer of an employee, means (subject to subsection (2)) a person who in consequence of a change occurring (whether by virtue of a sale or other disposition or by operation of law) in the ownership of the undertaking, or of the part of the undertaking, for the purposes of which the employee was employed, has become the owner of the undertaking or part, and "trade union" has the meaning given by section 1 of the Trade Union and Labour Relations (Consolidation) Act 1992.

(2) The definition of "successor" in subsection (1) has effect (subject to the necessary modifications) in relation to a case where—

(a) the person by whom an undertaking or part of an undertaking is owned immediately before a change is one of the persons by whom (whether as partners, trustees or otherwise) it is owned immediately after the change, or

(b) the persons by whom an undertaking or part of an undertaking is owned immediately before a change (whether as partners, trustees or otherwise) include the persons by whom, or include one or more of the persons by whom, it is owned immediately after the change,

as it has effect where the previous owner and the new owner are wholly different persons.

(3) For the purposes of this Act any two employers shall be treated as associated if—

(a) one is a company of which the other (directly or indirectly) has control, or

(b) both are companies of which a third person (directly or indirectly) has control;

and "associated employer" shall be construed accordingly.

[999]

NOTES

Sub-s (1): definition "Certification Officer" inserted by the Employment Relations Act 2004, s 49(8), as from 6 April 2005; in definition "employment tribunal procedure regulations" words in square brackets substituted by the Employment Rights (Dispute Resolution) Act 1998, s 1(2)(a).

Final provisions

43–45 (*S 43 introduces Sch 1* (*consequential amendments*), *s 44 introduces Sch 2* (*transitional provisions, savings and transitory provisions*), *s 45 introduces Sch 3* (*repeals and revocations*).)

46 Commencement

This Act shall come into force at the end of the period of three months beginning with the day on which it is passed.

[1000]

47 Extent

This Act does not extend to Northern Ireland.

[1001]

48 Short title

This Act may be cited as the [Employment Tribunals Act 1996].

[1002]

NOTES

Words in square brackets substituted by the Employment Rights (Dispute Resolution) Act 1998, s 1(2)(c).

SCHEDULES

(*Sch 1* (*Consequential amendments; in so far as relevant to this work, these amendments have been incorporated at the appropriate place*).)

SCHEDULE 2
TRANSITIONAL PROVISIONS, SAVINGS AND TRANSITORY PROVISIONS

Section 44

PART I
TRANSITIONAL PROVISIONS AND SAVINGS

1. The substitution of this Act for the provisions repealed or revoked by this Act does not affect the continuity of the law.

2. Anything done, or having effect as done, (including the making of subordinate legislation) under or for the purposes of any provision repealed or revoked by this Act has effect as if done under or for the purposes of any corresponding provision of this Act.

3. Any reference (express or implied) in this Act or any other enactment, or in any instrument or document, to a provision of this Act is (so far as the context permits) to be read as (according to the context) being or including in relation to times, circumstances and purposes before the commencement of this Act a reference to the corresponding provision repealed or revoked by this Act.

4.—(1) Any reference (express or implied) in any enactment, or in any instrument or document, to a provision repealed or revoked by this Act is (so far as the context permits) to be read as (according to the context) being or including in relation to times, circumstances and purposes after the commencement of this Act a reference to the corresponding provision of this Act.

(2) In particular, where a power conferred by an Act is expressed to be exercisable in relation to enactments contained in Acts passed before or in the same Session as the Act conferring the power, the power is also exercisable in relation to provisions of this Act which reproduce such enactments.

5. Paragraphs 1 to 4 have effect in place of section 17(2) of the Interpretation Act 1978 (but are without prejudice to any other provision of that Act).

6. The repeal by the Act of section 130 of, and Schedule 10 to, the Employment Protection (Consolidation) Act 1978 (jurisdiction of referees under specified provisions to be exercised by [employment tribunals]) does not affect—

(a) the operation of those provisions in relation to any question which may arise after the commencement of this Act, or

(b) the continued operation of those provisions after the commencement of this Act in relation to any question which has arisen before that commencement.

[1003]

NOTES

Para 6: words in square brackets substituted by the Employment Rights (Dispute Resolution) Act 1998, s 1(2)(b).

PART II
TRANSITORY PROVISIONS

7, 8. *(Spent.)*

Armed forces

9.—(1) If section 31 of the Trade Union Reform and Employment Rights Act 1993 has not come into force before the commencement of this Act, section 38 shall have effect until the relevant commencement date as if for subsection (4) there were substituted—

"(4) Subsection (1)—

(a) does not apply to service as a member of the naval, military or air forces of the Crown, but

(b) does apply to employment by an association established for the purposes of Part XI of the Reserve Forces Act 1996.".

(2) The reference in sub-paragraph (1) to the relevant commencement date is a reference—

(a) if an order has been made before the commencement of this Act appointing a day after that commencement as the day on which section 31 of the Trade Union Reform and Employment Rights Act 1993 is to come into force, to the day so appointed, and

(b) otherwise, to such day as the Secretary of State may by order appoint.

10. *(Spent.)*

[1004]

NOTES

Para 9: the Trade Union Reform and Employment Rights Act 1993, s 31 was repealed (never having been brought into force) by the Employment Rights Act 1996, s 242, Sch 3, Pt I, and replaced by s 192 of that Act at **[1236]**. The said s 192 had not been brought into force as of 6 April 2008, and is the subject of transitional provisions as noted to that section.

"Relevant commencement date": no such Order as is mentioned in para 9(2)(a) was made, and as of 6 April 2008 no Order had been made under para 9(2)(b).

(*Sch 3* (*repeals and revocations*) *in so far as relevant to this work, these have been incorporated at the appropriate place.*)

EMPLOYMENT TRIBUNALS ACT 1996; DESTINATION TABLE

DESTINATION TABLE

This table shows in column (1) the enactments repealed by the Employment Tribunals Act 1996 and in column (2) the provisions of that Act corresponding thereto.

In certain cases the enactment in column (1), though having a corresponding provision in column (2) is not, or not wholly, repealed as it is still required, or partly required, for the purposes of other legislation.

A "dash" in the right hand column means that the repealed provision to which it corresponds in the left hand column is spent, unnecessary or for some other reason not specifically reproduced.

(1)	(2)
Betting, Gaming and Lotteries Act 1963 (c 2)	Employment Tribunals Act 1996 (c 17)
Sch 5A, para 21	s 18(1)
Sex Discrimination Act 1975 (c 65)	Employment Tribunals Act 1996 (c 17)
s 64(1)	s 18(2)
s 64(2)	s 18(3)
s 64(3)	s 18(6)
s 64(4)	s 18(7)
Race Relations Act 1976 (c 74)	Employment Tribunals Act 1996 (c 17)
s 55(1)	s 18(2)
s 55(2)	s 18(3)
s 55(3)	s 18(6)
s 55(4)	s 18(7)
Employment Protection (Consolidation) Act 1978 (c 44)	Employment Tribunals Act 1996 (c 17)
s 128(1)	ss 1(1), 2
s 128(2)	Spent
s 128(2A), (2B)	s 4(1), (2)
s 128(2C)	s 4(3)
s 128(2D), (2F)	s 4(4), (5)
s 128(2E)	s 41(2)
s 128(4)	s 7(2)
s 128(5), (6)	s 4(6), (7)
s 130	Sch 2, para 6
s 131(1)	s 3(1)
s 131(2)	s 3(2)
s 131(3)	s 3(3)
s 131(4)	s 8(1)
s 131(4A)	s 8(2)
s 131(5)	s 8(3)
s 131(5A)	s 8(4)
s 131(6)	s 3(4)
s 131(7)	s 3(5), (6)
s 131(8)	s 41(2)
s 132(1)	s 16(1)
s 132(2)	s 16(2), (3)
s 132(3)	s 16(4)–(6)
Employment Protection (Consolidation) Act 1978 (c 44)	Employment Tribunals Act 1996 (c 17)
s 132(4)	s 17(1)
s 132(5)	s 17(2)
s 132(6)	s 17(3), (4)
s 133(1)	s 18(1)
s 133(2)	s 18(2)
s 133(3)	s 18(3)
s 133(4)	s 18(2), (3)
s 133(5)	s 18(6)
s 133(6)	s 18(7)
s 133(7)	s 18(8)
s 134(1)	s 18(1), (2)
s 134(2)	s 18(4)
s 134(3)	s 18(3), (5)
s 134(4)	s 18(6)
s 134(5)	s 18(7)
s 135(1)	s 20(1)
s 135(2)–(5)	s 22
s 135(6)	Spent
s 136(1)	s 21(1)
s 136(2), (3)	Rep 1992 c 52, s 300(1), Sch 1
s 136(4)	s 37(1), (2), (4)
s 136(5)	s 21(2)
s 136A(1)–(4)	s 33(1)–(4)
s 136A(5)	s 37(3)
s 136A(6)	s 33(5)
s 138(1)†	s 38(1)
s 138(2)†	s 38(2)
s 138(3)†	s 38(4)
s 138(7)(a), (b)†	s 38(3)
s 138(7)(c)†	s 10(6)
s 138(7)(e)	s 10(3)(a)
s 138A(2)(b)†	s 38(4)
s 138A(6)†	s 41(2)
s 139(1)*	ss 10(3), (6), 39(1), (3)
s 139(2)†	s 39(2)
s 139A(1)†	s 39(1)
s 139A(2)†	s 39(2)

† Not repealed (provisions of the 1978 Act not repealed by this Act were repealed by the Employment Rights Act 1996 (qv below)

* Repealed in part

(1) Employment Protection (Consolidation) Act 1978 (c 44)	(2) Employment Tribunals Act 1996 (c 17)
s 139A(3)(a)	s 10(3)(b)
s 139A(5)†	s 39(4)
s 149(1), (2)†	s 40(1), (2)
s 149(4)†	s 41(2)
s 153(1)†	s 42(1)
s 153(4)†	s 42(3)
s 153(4A)†	s 42(2)
s 154(1)†	s 41(1)
s 154(2), (3)†	s 41(3), (4)
Sch 9, para 1(1)	s 7(1)
Sch 9, para 1(2)(a)–(g), (j)	s 7(3)(a)–(g), (j)
Sch 9, para 1(2)(h), (i)	s 13(1)
Sch 9, para 1(2)(ga)	s 7(3)(h)
Sch 9, para 1(3)	s 19
Sch 9, para 1(4)	s 13(2)
Sch 9, para 1(4A)	s 10(1)
Sch 9, para 1(5)	s 10(2)
Sch 9, para 1(5A)	s 11(1), (6)
Sch 9, para 1(6)	s 7(5)
Sch 9, para 1(7)	s 7(4)
Sch 9, para 1(8)–(11)	s 11(2)–(5)
Sch 9, para 1A(1)	s 9(1)
Sch 9, para 1A(2)	s 9(2)
Sch 9, para 1A(3)	s 9(3)
Sch 9, para 1B	s 9(4)
Sch 9, para 2(1)	s 10(4)
Sch 9, para 2(2)	s 10(5)
Sch 9, para 3	Rep 1990 c 38, s 16(2), Sch 3
Sch 9, para 4	s 6(2)
Sch 9, para 5	s 7(6)
Sch 9, para 6	s 6(1)
Sch 9, para 6A	s 14
Sch 9, para 7(1)–(3)	s 15(1)–(3)
Sch 9, para 8	Rep 1993 c 19, s 51, Sch 10
Sch 9, para 9	s 5(1)
Sch 9, para 10	s 5(2), (3)
Sch 9, para 11	Rep 1981 c 20, s 36, Sch 4
Sch 10	Sch 2, para 6
Sch 11, para 1	s 25(1)
Sch 11, para 2	s 25(2), (3)
Sch 11, para 3	s 25(4)
Sch 11, para 4	s 23(1)
Sch 11, paras 5, 6	s 23(2)
Sch 11, para 7	s 23(3)
Sch 11, para 8(1), (2)	s 24(1), (2)
Sch 11, para 9	s 23(4)
Sch 11, para 10	s 24(3)
Sch 11, para 11	s 23(5)
Sch 11, para 12	s 20(3)
Sch 11, paras 13, 14	s 20(2)
Sch 11, para 15	s 28(1)
Sch 11, para 16	s 28(2)–(5)
Sch 11, para 17(1), (2)	s 30(1), (3)
Sch 11, para 18	s 30(2)
Sch 11, para 18A	s 31
Sch 11, para 19	s 34
Sch 11, para 20	s 29(1)
Sch 11, para 21	s 35
Sch 11, para 21A	s 36(1)–(3)
Sch 11, para 22(1)	s 29(2)
Sch 11, para 22(2)	s 36(4)
Sch 11, para 23(1)	Rep 1981 c 49, s 16(6)
Sch 11, para 23(2)	s 36(5)
Sch 11, para 23(3)	Spent
Sch 11, para 24	s 26
Sch 11, para 25	s 27(1)
Sch 11, paras 26–28	s 27(2)–(4)
Sch 15, para 18	Spent
Sch 16*	Spent (so far as relevant)
Social Security Act 1980 (c 30)	**Employment Tribunals Act 1996 (c 17)**
Sch 4, para 13	s 16(5)
Employment Act 1980 (c 42)	**Employment Tribunals Act 1996 (c 17)**
Sch 1, para 16	s 7(2)
Sch 1, para 17	s 18(1)
Sch 1, para 18	s 18(3), (5)
Sch 1, para 19†	s 21(2)
Sch 1, para 26	s 7(3)(a)
Sch 1, para 27	s 15(2)
Sch 1, para 28	s 30(2)
Sch 1, para 29	s 36(1), (2)
Contempt of Court Act 1981 (c 49)	**Employment Tribunals Act 1996 (c 17)**
s 16(6)	—
Supreme Court Act 1981 (c 54)	**Employment Tribunals Act 1996 (c 17)**
Sch 5*	s 24(2)

† Not repealed (provisions of the 1978 Act not repealed by this Act were repealed by the Employment Rights Act 1996 (qv below)

* Repealed in part

(1)	(2)
Employment Act 1982 (c 46)	**Employment Tribunals Act 1996 (c 17)**
Sch 3, Pt I, para 7	s 14
Sch 3, Pt I, para 8(1)	s 30(2)
Sch 3, Pt I, para 8(2)	Spent
Sch 3, Pt I, para 9	s 36(3)
Wages Act 1986 (c 48)	**Employment Tribunals Act 1996 (c 17)**
Sch 4, para 9	s 18(1)
Sch 4, para 10	s 21(1)
Social Security Act 1986 (c 50)	**Employment Tribunals Act 1996 (c 17)**
Sch 10, Pt II, para 50(a)	s 16(3)
Sch 10, Pt II, para 50(b)	s 16(4), (5)
Sch 10, Pt II, para 50(c)	s 17(1)
Employment Act 1988 (c 19)†	**Employment Tribunals Act 1996 (c 17)**
Sch 3, Pt I, para 2(3)	s 18(1)
Sch 3, Pt I, para 2(4)	s 21(2)
Sch 3, Pt I, para 2(5)	s 36(1)
Employment Act 1989 (c 38)	**Employment Tribunals Act 1996 (c 17)**
s 20	s 9(1)–(3)
Sch 6, para 26	s 7(3)(e)
Social Security (Consequential Provisions) Act 1992 (c 6)	**Employment Tribunals Act 1996 (c 17)**
Sch 2, para 50(1)	s 17(1)
Sch 2, para 50(2)	Spent
Trade Union and Labour Relations (Consolidation) Act 1992 (c 52)	**Employment Tribunals Act 1996 (c 17)**
s 290	s 18(1)
s 291(2), (3)	s 21(1), (2)
Sch 2, para 19	s 16(1)
Sch 2, para 20	s 22(2)
Sch 2, para 21(1)†	—
Sch 2, para 21(2)(b)†, (d)†, (f)†	s 42(1)
Sch 2, para 21(3)†	s 42(2)
Sch 2, para 24(1), (2)	s 10(4)
Sch 2, para 25(a)	s 30(2)
Sch 2, para 25(b)	s 36(1), (3)
Sch 3, para 1(4)†	s 10(2)
Judicial Pensions and Retirement Act 1993 (c 8)	**Employment Tribunals Act 1996 (c 17)**
Sch 6, para 30	s 25(2), (3)
Trade Union Reform and Employment Rights Act 1993 (c 19)	**Employment Tribunals Act 1996 (c 17)**
s 31(1)†	s 38(4)
s 31(2)†	ss 38(4), 41(2)
s 36(1)	Unnecessary
s 36(2)	ss 4(1)–(5), 41(2)
s 36(3)	s 4(6), (7)
s 37	s 28(2)–(5)
s 38(a)	s 3(1)
s 38(b)	s 3(3)
s 38(c)	s 8(2)
s 38(d)	s 8(4)
s 38(e)	s 3(5)
s 40(1)	Unnecessary
s 40(2)	s 11(1), (6)
s 40(3)	s 7(5)
s 40(4)	s 11(2)–(6)
s 41	s 31
s 42	ss 33, 37(3)
Sch 7, para 6(a)	s 10(1)
Sch 7, para 6(b)	s 10(5)
Sch 7, para 7	s 30(2)
Sch 7, para 11†	ss 10(3), 39(1), (2), (4)
Sch 8, para 19	s 16(1)
Sch 8, para 20	s 18(1)
Sch 8, para 28(a)	s 13(2)
Sch 8, para 28(b)	s 9(1)
Sch 8, para 28(c)	s 9(4)
Sch 8, paras 29, 30	s 30(2)
Sch 8, para 86	s 18(1)
Sch 8, para 87	Spent
Pension Schemes Act 1993 (c 48)	**Employment Tribunals Act 1996 (c 17)**
Sch 8, para 11(2)	s 4(3)(b)
Sunday Trading Act 1994 (c 20)	**Employment Tribunals Act 1996 (c 17)**
Sch 4, para 21	s 18(1)
Deregulation and Contracting Out Act 1994 (c 40)	**Employment Tribunals Act 1996 (c 17)**
Sch 8†	s 18(1)
Jobseekers Act 1995 (c 18)	**Employment Tribunals Act 1996 (c 17)**
Sch 2, para 2(1)	Unnecessary
Sch 2, para 2(2)	ss 16(3), (4), 17(2)
Sch 2, para 2(3)	s 16(5)
Sch 2, para 2(4)	s 17(1)
Sch 2, para 2(5)	s 17(3), (4)

† Not repealed

* Repealed in part

(1)	(2)	(1)	(2)
Pensions Act 1995 (c 26)	Employment Tribunals Act 1996 (c 17)	Reserve Forces Act 1996 (c 14)	Employment Rights Act 1996 (c 18)
Sch 3, para 8	s 18(1)	Sch 10, para 17†	s 38(4)
Sch 3, para 9	s 21(1)		
Disability Discrimination Act 1995 (c 50)	Employment Tribunals Act 1996 (c 17)	Equal Pay (Amendment) Regulations 1983, SI 1983/1794	Employment Tribunals Act 1996 (c 17)
s 62	s 12	Reg 3	ss 5(2), 7(3)(h), (4)
s 63(1), (2)	s 32(1), (2)	Collective Redundancies and Transfer of Undertakings (Protection of Employment) (Amendment) Regulations 1995, SI 1995/2587	Employment Tribunals Act 1996 (c 17)
s 63(3)	s 32(3)–(6)		
s 63(4), (5)	s 32(7)		
s 63(6)	s 32(8)		
Sch 3, Pt I, para 1(1)	s 18(2)		
Sch 3, Pt I, para 1(2)	s 18(3)		
Sch 3, Pt I, para 1(3)	s 18(6)		
Sch 3, Pt I, para 1(4)	s 18(7)	Regs 12(3), 13(3)	s 18(1)
Sch 6, para 2	s 21(1)	Reg 14(4)*	s 10(5)

† Not repealed

* Repealed in part

[1005]

EMPLOYMENT RIGHTS ACT 1996

(1996 c 18)

ARRANGEMENT OF SECTIONS

PART I
EMPLOYMENT PARTICULARS

Right to statements of employment particulars

Right to itemised pay statement

Enforcement

PART II
PROTECTION OF WAGES

Deductions by employer

Payments to employer

Cash shortages and stock deficiencies in retail employment

Enforcement

Supplementary

PART III
GUARANTEE PAYMENTS

PART IV
SUNDAY WORKING FOR SHOP AND BETTING WORKERS

Protected shop workers and betting workers

Opting-out of Sunday work

PART IVA
PROTECTED DISCLOSURES

PART V
PROTECTION FROM SUFFERING DETRIMENT IN EMPLOYMENT

Rights not to suffer detriment

Enforcement

Application to police of rights relating to health and safety

PART VI
TIME OFF WORK

Public duties

Looking for work and making arrangements for training

Ante-natal care

Dependants

Occupational pension scheme trustees

Employee representatives

PART VII
SUSPENSION FROM WORK

Suspension on medical grounds

Suspension on maternity grounds

General

PART VIII

CHAPTER I
MATERNITY LEAVE

CHAPTER IA
ADOPTION LEAVE

CHAPTER II
PARENTAL LEAVE

CHAPTER III
PATERNITY LEAVE

PART VIIIA
FLEXIBLE WORKING

PART IX
TERMINATION OF EMPLOYMENT

Minimum period of notice

Written statement of reasons for dismissal

PART X
UNFAIR DISMISSAL

CHAPTER I
RIGHT NOT TO BE UNFAIRLY DISMISSED

The right

Dismissal

Fairness

Retirement

Other dismissals

Exclusion of right

CHAPTER II
REMEDIES FOR UNFAIR DISMISSAL

Introductory

Orders for reinstatement or re-engagement

Compensation

Interim relief

CHAPTER III
SUPPLEMENTARY

PART XI
REDUNDANCY PAYMENTS ETC

CHAPTER I
RIGHT TO REDUNDANCY PAYMENT

CHAPTER II
RIGHT ON DISMISSAL BY REASON OF REDUNDANCY

Dismissal by reason of redundancy

Exclusions

Supplementary

CHAPTER III
RIGHT BY REASON OF LAY-OFF OR SHORT-TIME

Lay-off and short-time

Exclusions

Supplementary

CHAPTER IV
GENERAL EXCLUSIONS FROM RIGHT

CHAPTER V
OTHER PROVISIONS ABOUT REDUNDANCY PAYMENTS

CHAPTER VI
PAYMENTS BY SECRETARY OF STATE

CHAPTER VII
SUPPLEMENTARY

Application of Part to particular cases

Death of employer or employee

Equivalent payments

Other supplementary provisions

PART XII
INSOLVENCY OF EMPLOYERS

PART XIII
MISCELLANEOUS

CHAPTER I
PARTICULAR TYPES OF EMPLOYMENT

Crown employment etc

Parliamentary staff

Excluded classes of employment

Offshore employment

CHAPTER II
OTHER MISCELLANEOUS MATTERS

Restrictions on disclosure of information

Contracting out etc and remedies

General provisions about death of employer or employee

Modifications of Act

PART XIV
INTERPRETATION

CHAPTER I
CONTINUOUS EMPLOYMENT

CHAPTER II
WEEK'S PAY

Introductory

Employments with normal working hours

Employments with no normal working hours

The calculation date

Maximum amount of week's pay

Miscellaneous

CHAPTER III
OTHER INTERPRETATION PROVISIONS

PART XV
GENERAL AND SUPPLEMENTARY

General

Final provisions

SCHEDULES:

An Act to consolidate enactments relating to employment rights

[22 May 1996]

NOTES

This Act consolidates the individual employment legislation contained principally in the Employment Protection (Consolidation) Act 1978 (as extensively and repeatedly amended) and unrepealed provisions of the Wages Act 1986. It also incorporates relevant provisions in a number of other Acts as detailed in the Destination Table printed immediately following the text of the Act at **[1285]**. Provisions of the 1978 Act relating to employment tribunals and the Employment Appeal Tribunal were separately consolidated into the Employment Tribunals Act 1996 at **[954]** et seq.

The Act came into force on 22 August 1996, subject to transitional provisions in Sch 2, Pt II relating to consolidation of legislation not yet in force. Commencement details are not given for individual sections unless affected by Sch 2 or subsequently inserted by other legislation with effect on or after 6 April 2003. The whole of the Act is printed (as in force on 6 April 2008) except for ss 238 and 239, which apply to Northern Ireland and the Isle of Man, Schedules 1 and 3, which enact consequential amendments and repeals, and the sections (240 and 242) introducing them. Other provisions omitted are those repealed by subsequent legislation (as noted to each such provision). As to the further power to amend this Act, see the Employment Relations Act 2004, s 42(1), (4)(d) at **[1616]**.

Employment Appeal Tribunal: an appeal lies to the Employment Appeal Tribunal on any question of law arising from any decision of, or in any proceedings before, an employment tribunal under or by virtue of this Act; see the Employment Tribunals Act 1996, s 21(1)(f) at **[978]**.

See *Harvey* Q, R, T, U.

PART I
EMPLOYMENT PARTICULARS

Right to statements of employment particulars

1 Statement of initial employment particulars

(1) Where an employee begins employment with an employer, the employer shall give to the employee a written statement of particulars of employment.

(2) The statement may (subject to section 2(4)) be given in instalments and (whether or not given in instalments) shall be given not later than two months after the beginning of the employment.

(3) The statement shall contain particulars of—
- (a) the names of the employer and employee,
- (b) the date when the employment began, and
- (c) the date on which the employee's period of continuous employment began (taking into account any employment with a previous employer which counts towards that period).

(4) The statement shall also contain particulars, as at a specified date not more than seven days before the statement (or the instalment containing them) is given, of—
- (a) the scale or rate of remuneration or the method of calculating remuneration,
- (b) the intervals at which remuneration is paid (that is, weekly, monthly or other specified intervals),
- (c) any terms and conditions relating to hours of work (including any terms and conditions relating to normal working hours),
- (d) any terms and conditions relating to any of the following—
  - (i) entitlement to holidays, including public holidays, and holiday pay (the particulars given being sufficient to enable the employee's entitlement, including any entitlement to accrued holiday pay on the termination of employment, to be precisely calculated),
  - (ii) incapacity for work due to sickness or injury, including any provision for sick pay, and
  - (iii) pensions and pension schemes,

(e) the length of notice which the employee is obliged to give and entitled to receive to terminate his contract of employment,
(f) the title of the job which the employee is employed to do or a brief description of the work for which he is employed,
(g) where the employment is not intended to be permanent, the period for which it is expected to continue or, if it is for a fixed term, the date when it is to end,
(h) either the place of work or, where the employee is required or permitted to work at various places, an indication of that and of the address of the employer,
(j) any collective agreements which directly affect the terms and conditions of the employment including, where the employer is not a party, the persons by whom they were made, and
(k) where the employee is required to work outside the United Kingdom for a period of more than one month—
(i) the period for which he is to work outside the United Kingdom,
(ii) the currency in which remuneration is to be paid while he is working outside the United Kingdom,
(iii) any additional remuneration payable to him, and any benefits to be provided to or in respect of him, by reason of his being required to work outside the United Kingdom, and
(iv) any terms and conditions relating to his return to the United Kingdom.

(5) Subsection (4)(d)(iii) does not apply to an employee of a body or authority if—
(a) the employee's pension rights depend on the terms of a pension scheme established under any provision contained in or having effect under any Act, and
(b) any such provision requires the body or authority to give to a new employee information concerning the employee's pension rights or the determination of questions affecting those rights.

[1006]

NOTES

Failure to give statement: as to the powers of the employment tribunal in proceedings to which the Employment Act 2002, Sch 5 at **[1510]** applies, see s 38 of that Act at **[1496]**.

Note: sub-s (4) did not contain a para (i) in the Queen's Printer's copy of this Act.

2 Statement of initial particulars: supplementary

(1) If, in the case of a statement under section 1, there are no particulars to be entered under any of the heads of paragraph (d) or (k) of subsection (4) of that section, or under any of the other paragraphs of subsection (3) or (4) of that section, that fact shall be stated.

(2) A statement under section 1 may refer the employee for particulars of any of the matters specified in subsection (4)(d)(ii) and (iii) of that section to the provisions of some other document which is reasonably accessible to the employee.

(3) A statement under section 1 may refer the employee for particulars of either of the matters specified in subsection (4)(e) of that section to the law or to the provisions of any collective agreement directly affecting the terms and conditions of the employment which is reasonably accessible to the employee.

(4) The particulars required by section 1(3) and (4)(a) to (c), (d)(i), (f) and (h) shall be included in a single document.

(5) Where before the end of the period of two months after the beginning of an employee's employment the employee is to begin to work outside the United Kingdom for a period of more than one month, the statement under section 1 shall be given to him not later than the time when he leaves the United Kingdom in order to begin so to work.

(6) A statement shall be given to a person under section 1 even if his employment ends before the end of the period within which the statement is required to be given.

[1007]

3 Note about disciplinary procedures and pensions

(1) A statement under section 1 shall include a note—
(a) specifying any disciplinary rules applicable to the employee or referring the employee to the provisions of a document specifying such rules which is reasonably accessible to the employee,

[(aa) specifying any procedure applicable to the taking of disciplinary decisions relating to the employee, or to a decision to dismiss the employee, or referring the employee to the provisions of a document specifying such a procedure which is reasonably accessible to the employee,]

(b) specifying (by description or otherwise)—

(i) a person to whom the employee can apply if dissatisfied with any disciplinary decision relating to him [or any decision to dismiss him], and

(ii) a person to whom the employee can apply for the purpose of seeking redress of any grievance relating to his employment, and the manner in which any such application should be made, and

(c) where there are further steps consequent on any such application, explaining those steps or referring to the provisions of a document explaining them which is reasonably accessible to the employee.

(2) Subsection (1) does not apply to rules, disciplinary decisions, [decisions to dismiss,] grievances or procedures relating to health or safety at work.

(3), (4) …

(5) The note shall also state whether there is in force a contracting-out certificate (issued in accordance with Chapter 1 of Part III of the Pension Schemes Act 1993) stating that the employment is contracted-out employment (for the purposes of that Part of that Act).

[1008]

NOTES

Sub-ss (1), (2): words in square brackets inserted by the Employment Act 2002, s 35, as from 1 October 2004.

Sub-ss (3), (4): repealed by the Employment Act 2002, ss 36, 54, Sch 8, as from 1 October 2004.

4 Statement of changes

(1) If, after the material date, there is a change in any of the matters particulars of which are required by sections 1 to 3 to be included or referred to in a statement under section 1, the employer shall give to the employee a written statement containing particulars of the change.

(2) For the purposes of subsection (1)—

(a) in relation to a matter particulars of which are included or referred to in a statement given under section 1 otherwise than in instalments, the material date is the date to which the statement relates,

(b) in relation to a matter particulars of which—

(i) are included or referred to in an instalment of a statement given under section 1, or

(ii) are required by section 2(4) to be included in a single document but are not included in an instalment of a statement given under section 1 which does include other particulars to which that provision applies,

the material date is the date to which the instalment relates, and

(c) in relation to any other matter, the material date is the date by which a statement under section 1 is required to be given.

(3) A statement under subsection (1) shall be given at the earliest opportunity and, in any event, not later than—

(a) one month after the change in question, or

(b) where that change results from the employee being required to work outside the United Kingdom for a period of more than one month, the time when he leaves the United Kingdom in order to begin so to work, if that is earlier.

(4) A statement under subsection (1) may refer the employee to the provisions of some other document which is reasonably accessible to the employee for a change in any of the matters specified in sections 1(4)(d)(ii) and (iii) and 3(1)(a) and (c).

(5) A statement under subsection (1) may refer the employee for a change in either of the matters specified in section 1(4)(e) to the law or to the provisions of any collective agreement directly affecting the terms and conditions of the employment which is reasonably accessible to the employee.

(6) Where, after an employer has given to an employee a statement under section 1, either—

(a) the name of the employer (whether an individual or a body corporate or partnership) is changed without any change in the identity of the employer, or

(b) the identity of the employer is changed in circumstances in which the continuity of the employee's period of employment is not broken,

and subsection (7) applies in relation to the change, the person who is the employer immediately after the change is not required to give to the employee a statement under section 1; but the change shall be treated as a change falling within subsection (1) of this section.

(7) This subsection applies in relation to a change if it does not involve any change in any of the matters (other than the names of the parties) particulars of which are required by sections 1 to 3 to be included or referred to in the statement under section 1.

(8) A statement under subsection (1) which informs an employee of a change such as is referred to in subsection (6)(b) shall specify the date on which the employee's period of continuous employment began.

[1009]

NOTES

Failure to give statement of changes: as to the powers of the employment tribunal in proceedings to which the Employment Act 2002, Sch 5 at **[1510]** applies, see s 38 of that Act at **[1496]**.

5 Exclusion from rights to statements

(1) Sections 1 to 4 apply to an employee who at any time comes or ceases to come within the exceptions from those sections provided by [section] 199, and under section 209, as if his employment with his employer terminated or began at that time.

(2) The fact that section 1 is directed by subsection (1) to apply to an employee as if his employment began on his ceasing to come within the exceptions referred to in that subsection does not affect the obligation under section 1(3)(b) to specify the date on which his employment actually began.

[1010]

NOTES

Sub-s (1): word in square brackets substituted by the Employment Relations Act 1999, s 32(3).

6 Reasonably accessible document or collective agreement

In sections 2 to 4 references to a document or collective agreement which is reasonably accessible to an employee are references to a document or collective agreement which—

(a) the employee has reasonable opportunities of reading in the course of his employment, or

(b) is made reasonably accessible to the employee in some other way.

[1011]

7 Power to require particulars of further matters

The Secretary of State may by order provide that section 1 shall have effect as if particulars of such further matters as may be specified in the order were included in the particulars required by that section; and, for that purpose, the order may include such provisions amending that section as appear to the Secretary of State to be expedient.

[1012]

NOTES

Orders: as of 6 April 2008 no Orders had been made under this section.

[7A Use of alternative documents to give particulars

(1) Subsections (2) and (3) apply where—

(a) an employer gives an employee a document in writing in the form of a contract of employment or letter of engagement,

(b) the document contains information which, were the document in the form of a statement under section 1, would meet the employer's obligation under that section in relation to the matters mentioned in subsections (3) and (4)(a) to (c), (d)(i), (f) and (h) of that section, and

(c) the document is given after the beginning of the employment and before the end of the period for giving a statement under that section.

(2) The employer's duty under section 1 in relation to any matter shall be treated as met if the document given to the employee contains information which, were the document in the form of a statement under that section, would meet the employer's obligation under that section in relation to that matter.

(3) The employer's duty under section 3 shall be treated as met if the document given to the employee contains information which, were the document in the form of a statement under section 1 and the information included in the form of a note, would meet the employer's obligation under section 3.

(4) For the purposes of this section a document to which subsection (1)(a) applies shall be treated, in relation to information in respect of any of the matters mentioned in section 1(4), as specifying the date on which the document is given to the employee as the date as at which the information applies.

(5) Where subsection (2) applies in relation to any matter, the date on which the document by virtue of which that subsection applies is given to the employee shall be the material date in relation to that matter for the purposes of section 4(1).

(6) Where subsection (3) applies, the date on which the document by virtue of which that subsection applies is given to the employee shall be the material date for the purposes of section 4(1) in relation to the matters of which particulars are required to be given under section 3.

(7) The reference in section 4(6) to an employer having given a statement under section 1 shall be treated as including his having given a document by virtue of which his duty to give such a statement is treated as met.]

[1013]

NOTES

Commencement: 1 October 2004.
Inserted, together with s 7B, by the Employment Act 2002, s 37, as from 1 October 2004.

[7B Giving of alternative documents before start of employment

A document in the form of a contract of employment or letter of engagement given by an employer to an employee before the beginning of the employee's employment with the employer shall, when the employment begins, be treated for the purposes of section 7A as having been given at that time.]

[1014]

NOTES

Commencement: 1 October 2004.
Inserted as noted to s 7A at **[1013]**.

Right to itemised pay statement

8 Itemised pay statement

(1) An employee has the right to be given by his employer, at or before the time at which any payment of wages or salary is made to him, a written itemised pay statement.

(2) The statement shall contain particulars of—
(a) the gross amount of the wages or salary,
(b) the amounts of any variable, and (subject to section 9) any fixed, deductions from that gross amount and the purposes for which they are made,
(c) the net amount of wages or salary payable, and
(d) where different parts of the net amount are paid in different ways, the amount and method of payment of each part-payment.

[1015]

NOTES

Conciliation: employment tribunal proceedings and claims which could be the subject of employment tribunal proceedings under this section are proceedings to which the Employment Tribunals Act 1996, s 18 applies; see s 18(1)(d) of that Act at **[975]**. The short conciliation period applies to such proceedings by virtue of the Employment Tribunals (Constitution and Rules of Procedure) Regulations 2004, SI 2004/1861, Sch 1, rule 22(5).

9 Standing statement of fixed deductions

(1) A pay statement given in accordance with section 8 need not contain separate particulars of a fixed deduction if—

(a) it contains instead an aggregate amount of fixed deductions, including that deduction, and

(b) the employer has given to the employee, at or before the time at which the pay statement is given, a standing statement of fixed deductions which satisfies subsection (2).

(2) A standing statement of fixed deductions satisfies this subsection if—

(a) it is in writing,

(b) it contains, in relation to each deduction comprised in the aggregate amount of deductions, particulars of—

(i) the amount of the deduction,

(ii) the intervals at which the deduction is to be made, and

(iii) the purpose for which it is made, and

(c) it is (in accordance with subsection (5)) effective at the date on which the pay statement is given.

(3) A standing statement of fixed deductions may be amended, whether by—

(a) addition of a new deduction,

(b) a change in the particulars, or

(c) cancellation of an existing deduction,

by notice in writing, containing particulars of the amendment, given by the employer to the employee.

(4) An employer who has given to an employee a standing statement of fixed deductions shall—

(a) within the period of twelve months beginning with the date on which the first standing statement was given, and

(b) at intervals of not more than twelve months afterwards,

re-issue it in a consolidated form incorporating any amendments notified in accordance with subsection (3).

(5) For the purposes of subsection (2)(c) a standing statement of fixed deductions—

(a) becomes effective on the date on which it is given to the employee, and

(b) ceases to be effective at the end of the period of twelve months beginning with that date or, where it is re-issued in accordance with subsection (4), with the end of the period of twelve months beginning with the date of the last re-issue.

[1016]

10 Power to amend provisions about pay and standing statements

The Secretary of State may by order—

(a) vary the provisions of sections 8 and 9 as to the particulars which must be included in a pay statement or a standing statement of fixed deductions by adding items to, or removing items from, the particulars listed in those sections or by amending any such particulars, and

(b) vary the provisions of subsections (4) and (5) of section 9 so as to shorten or extend the periods of twelve months referred to in those subsections, or those periods as varied from time to time under this section.

[1017]

NOTES

Orders: as of 6 April 2008 no Orders had been made under this section.

Enforcement

11 References to [employment tribunals]

(1) Where an employer does not give an employee a statement as required by section 1, 4 or 8 (either because he gives him no statement or because the statement he gives does not

comply with what is required), the employee may require a reference to be made to an [employment tribunal] to determine what particulars ought to have been included or referred to in a statement so as to comply with the requirements of the section concerned.

(2) Where—

(a) a statement purporting to be a statement under section 1 or 4, or a pay statement or a standing statement of fixed deductions purporting to comply with section 8 or 9, has been given to an employee, and

(b) a question arises as to the particulars which ought to have been included or referred to in the statement so as to comply with the requirements of this Part,

either the employer or the employee may require the question to be referred to and determined by an [employment tribunal].

(3) For the purposes of this section—

(a) a question as to the particulars which ought to have been included in the note required by section 3 to be included in the statement under section 1 does not include any question whether the employment is, has been or will be contracted-out employment (for the purposes of Part III of the Pension Schemes Act 1993), and

(b) a question as to the particulars which ought to have been included in a pay statement or standing statement of fixed deductions does not include a question solely as to the accuracy of an amount stated in any such particulars.

(4) An [employment tribunal] shall not consider a reference under this section in a case where the employment to which the reference relates has ceased unless an application requiring the reference to be made was made—

(a) before the end of the period of three months beginning with the date on which the employment ceased, or

(b) within such further period as the tribunal considers reasonable in a case where it is satisfied that it was not reasonably practicable for the application to be made before the end of that period of three months.

[1018]

NOTES

Section heading, sub-ss (1), (2), (4): words in square brackets substituted by the Employment Rights (Dispute Resolution) Act 1998, s 1(2)(a), (b).

Conciliation: employment tribunal proceedings under this section in respect of a breach of s 8 of this Act and claims which could be the subject of such proceedings (but not proceedings or claims in relation to a breach of ss 1 or 4) are proceedings to which the Employment Tribunals Act 1996, s 18 applies; see s 18(1)(d) of that Act at **[975]**. The short conciliation period applies by virtue of the Employment Tribunals (Constitution and Rules of Procedure) Regulations 2004, SI 2004/1861, Sch 1, rule 22(5).

12 Determination of references

(1) Where, on a reference under section 11(1), an [employment tribunal] determines particulars as being those which ought to have been included or referred to in a statement given under section 1 or 4, the employer shall be deemed to have given to the employee a statement in which those particulars were included, or referred to, as specified in the decision of the tribunal.

(2) On determining a reference under section 11(2) relating to a statement purporting to be a statement under section 1 or 4, an [employment tribunal] may—

(a) confirm the particulars as included or referred to in the statement given by the employer,

(b) amend those particulars, or

(c) substitute other particulars for them,

as the tribunal may determine to be appropriate; and the statement shall be deemed to have been given by the employer to the employee in accordance with the decision of the tribunal.

(3) Where on a reference under section 11 an [employment tribunal] finds—

(a) that an employer has failed to give an employee any pay statement in accordance with section 8, or

(b) that a pay statement or standing statement of fixed deductions does not, in relation to a deduction, contain the particulars required to be included in that statement by that section or section 9,

the tribunal shall make a declaration to that effect.

(4) Where on a reference in the case of which subsection (3) applies the tribunal further finds that any unnotified deductions have been made (from the pay of the employee during the period of thirteen weeks immediately preceding the date of the application for the reference (whether or not the deductions were made in breach of the contract of employment), the tribunal may order the employer to pay the employee a sum not exceeding the aggregate of the unnotified deductions so made.

(5) For the purposes of subsection (4) a deduction is an unnotified deduction if it is made without the employer giving the employee, in any pay statement or standing statement of fixed deductions, the particulars of the deduction required by section 8 or 9.

[1019]

NOTES

Sub-ss (1)–(3): words in square brackets substituted by the Employment Rights (Dispute Resolution) Act 1998, s 1(2)(a).

See further, as to remedies following a reference under s 11(1) or (2), the notes to ss 1, 4 at **[1006]**, **[1009]**.

PART II
PROTECTION OF WAGES

Deductions by employer

13 Right not to suffer unauthorised deductions

(1) An employer shall not make a deduction from wages of a worker employed by him unless—

(a) the deduction is required or authorised to be made by virtue of a statutory provision or a relevant provision of the worker's contract, or

(b) the worker has previously signified in writing his agreement or consent to the making of the deduction.

(2) In this section "relevant provision", in relation to a worker's contract, means a provision of the contract comprised—

(a) in one or more written terms of the contract of which the employer has given the worker a copy on an occasion prior to the employer making the deduction in question, or

(b) in one or more terms of the contract (whether express or implied and, if express, whether oral or in writing) the existence and effect, or combined effect, of which in relation to the worker the employer has notified to the worker in writing on such an occasion.

(3) Where the total amount of wages paid on any occasion by an employer to a worker employed by him is less than the total amount of the wages properly payable by him to the worker on that occasion (after deductions), the amount of the deficiency shall be treated for the purposes of this Part as a deduction made by the employer from the worker's wages on that occasion.

(4) Subsection (3) does not apply in so far as the deficiency is attributable to an error of any description on the part of the employer affecting the computation by him of the gross amount of the wages properly payable by him to the worker on that occasion.

(5) For the purposes of this section a relevant provision of a worker's contract having effect by virtue of a variation of the contract does not operate to authorise the making of a deduction on account of any conduct of the worker, or any other event occurring, before the variation took effect.

(6) For the purposes of this section an agreement or consent signified by a worker does not operate to authorise the making of a deduction on account of any conduct of the worker, or any other event occurring, before the agreement or consent was signified.

(7) This section does not affect any other statutory provision by virtue of which a sum payable to a worker by his employer but not constituting "wages" within the meaning of this Part is not to be subject to a deduction at the instance of the employer.

[1020]

NOTES

Conciliation: employment tribunal proceedings and claims which could be the subject of employment tribunal proceedings under this section are proceedings to which the Employment Tribunals Act 1996, s 18 applies; see s 18(1)(d) of that Act at **[975]**. The short conciliation period applies to such proceedings by virtue of the Employment Tribunals (Constitution and Rules of Procedure) Regulations 2004, SI 2004/1861, Sch 1, rule 22(5).

14 Excepted deductions

(1) Section 13 does not apply to a deduction from a worker's wages made by his employer where the purpose of the deduction is the reimbursement of the employer in respect of—

(a) an overpayment of wages, or

(b) an overpayment in respect of expenses incurred by the worker in carrying out his employment,

made (for any reason) by the employer to the worker.

(2) Section 13 does not apply to a deduction from a worker's wages made by his employer in consequence of any disciplinary proceedings if those proceedings were held by virtue of a statutory provision.

(3) Section 13 does not apply to a deduction from a worker's wages made by his employer in pursuance of a requirement imposed on the employer by a statutory provision to deduct and pay over to a public authority amounts determined by that authority as being due to it from the worker if the deduction is made in accordance with the relevant determination of that authority.

(4) Section 13 does not apply to a deduction from a worker's wages made by his employer in pursuance of any arrangements which have been established—

(a) in accordance with a relevant provision of his contract to the inclusion of which in the contract the worker has signified his agreement or consent in writing, or

(b) otherwise with the prior agreement or consent of the worker signified in writing,

and under which the employer is to deduct and pay over to a third person amounts notified to the employer by that person as being due to him from the worker, if the deduction is made in accordance with the relevant notification by that person.

(5) Section 13 does not apply to a deduction from a worker's wages made by his employer where the worker has taken part in a strike or other industrial action and the deduction is made by the employer on account of the worker's having taken part in that strike or other action.

(6) Section 13 does not apply to a deduction from a worker's wages made by his employer with his prior agreement or consent signified in writing where the purpose of the deduction is the satisfaction (whether wholly or in part) of an order of a court or tribunal requiring the payment of an amount by the worker to the employer.

[1021]

Payments to employer

15 Right not to have to make payments to employer

(1) An employer shall not receive a payment from a worker employed by him unless—

(a) the payment is required or authorised to be made by virtue of a statutory provision or a relevant provision of the worker's contract, or

(b) the worker has previously signified in writing his agreement or consent to the making of the payment.

(2) In this section "relevant provision", in relation to a worker's contract, means a provision of the contract comprised—

(a) in one or more written terms of the contract of which the employer has given the worker a copy on an occasion prior to the employer receiving the payment in question, or

(b) in one or more terms of the contract (whether express or implied and, if express, whether oral or in writing) the existence and effect, or combined effect, of which in relation to the worker the employer has notified to the worker in writing on such an occasion.

(3) For the purposes of this section a relevant provision of a worker's contract having effect by virtue of a variation of the contract does not operate to authorise the receipt of a payment on account of any conduct of the worker, or any other event occurring, before the variation took affect.

(4) For the purposes of this section an agreement or consent signified by a worker does not operate to authorise the receipt of a payment on account of any conduct of the worker, or any other event occurring, before the agreement or consent was signified.

(5) Any reference in this Part to an employer receiving a payment from a worker employed by him is a reference to his receiving such a payment in his capacity as the worker's employer.

[1022]

NOTES

Conciliation: employment tribunal proceedings and claims which could be the subject of employment tribunal proceedings under this section are proceedings to which the Employment Tribunals Act 1996, s 18 applies; see s 18(1)(d) of that Act at **[975]**. The short conciliation period applies to such proceedings by virtue of the Employment Tribunals (Constitution and Rules of Procedure) Regulations 2004, SI 2004/1861, Sch 1, rule 22(5).

16 Excepted payments

(1) Section 15 does not apply to a payment received from a worker by his employer where the purpose of the payment is the reimbursement of the employer in respect of—

(a) an overpayment of wages, or
(b) an overpayment in respect of expenses incurred by the worker in carrying out his employment,

made (for any reason) by the employer to the worker.

(2) Section 15 does not apply to a payment received from a worker by his employer in consequence of any disciplinary proceedings if those proceedings were held by virtue of a statutory provision.

(3) Section 15 does not apply to a payment received from a worker by his employer where the worker has taken part in a strike or other industrial action and the payment has been required by the employer on account of the worker's having taken part in that strike or other action.

(4) Section 15 does not apply to a payment received from a worker by his employer where the purpose of the payment is the satisfaction (whether wholly or in part) of an order of a court or tribunal requiring the payment of an amount by the worker to the employer.

[1023]

Cash shortages and stock deficiencies in retail employment

17 Introductory

(1) In the following provisions of this Part—

"cash shortage" means a deficit arising in relation to amounts received in connection with retail transactions, and

"stock deficiency" means a stock deficiency arising in the course of retail transactions.

(2) In the following provisions of this Part "retail employment", in relation to a worker, means employment involving (whether or not on a regular basis)—

(a) the carrying out by the worker of retail transactions directly with members of the public or with fellow workers or other individuals in their personal capacities, or
(b) the collection by the worker of amounts payable in connection with retail transactions carried out by other persons directly with members of the public or with fellow workers or other individuals in their personal capacities.

(3) References in this section to a "retail transaction" are to the sale or supply of goods or the supply of services (including financial services).

(4) References in the following provisions of this Part to a deduction made from wages of a worker in retail employment, or to a payment received from such a worker by his employer, on account of a cash shortage or stock deficiency include references to a deduction or payment so made or received on account of—

(a) any dishonesty or other conduct on the part of the worker which resulted in any such shortage or deficiency, or

(b) any other event in respect of which he (whether or not together with any other workers) has any contractual liability and which so resulted,

in each case whether or not the amount of the deduction or payment is designed to reflect the exact amount of the shortage or deficiency.

(5) References in the following provisions of this Part to the recovery from a worker of an amount in respect of a cash shortage or stock deficiency accordingly include references to the recovery from him of an amount in respect of any such conduct or event as is mentioned in subsection (4)(a) or (b).

(6) In the following provisions of this Part "pay day", in relation to a worker, means a day on which wages are payable to the worker.

[1024]

18 Limits on amount and time of deductions

(1) Where (in accordance with section 13) the employer of a worker in retail employment makes, on account of one or more cash shortages or stock deficiencies, a deduction or deductions from wages payable to the worker on a pay day, the amount or aggregate amount of the deduction or deductions shall not exceed one-tenth of the gross amount of the wages payable to the worker on that day.

(2) Where the employer of a worker in retail employment makes a deduction from the worker's wages on account of a cash shortage or stock deficiency, the employer shall not be treated as making the deduction in accordance with section 13 unless (in addition to the requirements of that section being satisfied with respect to the deduction)—

(a) the deduction is made, or

(b) in the case of a deduction which is one of a series of deductions relating to the shortage or deficiency, the first deduction in the series was made,

not later than the end of the relevant period.

(3) In subsection (2) "the relevant-period" means the period of twelve months beginning with the date when the employer established the existence of the shortage or deficiency or (if earlier) the date when he ought reasonably to have done so.

[1025]

NOTES

Conciliation: employment tribunal proceedings and claims which could be the subject of employment tribunal proceedings under sub-s (1) are proceedings to which the Employment Tribunals Act 1996, s 18 applies; see s 18(1)(d) of that Act at **[975]**. The short conciliation period applies to such proceedings by virtue of the Employment Tribunals (Constitution and Rules of Procedure) Regulations 2004, SI 2004/1861, Sch 1, rule 22(5).

19 Wages determined by reference to shortages etc

(1) This section applies where—

(a) by virtue of an agreement between a worker in retail employment and his employer, the amount of the worker's wages or any part of them is or may be determined by reference to the incidence of cash shortages or stock deficiencies, and

(b) the gross amount of the wages payable to the worker on any pay day is, on account of any such shortages or deficiencies, less than the gross amount of the wages that would have been payable to him on that day if there had been no such shortages or deficiencies.

(2) The amount representing the difference between the two amounts referred to in subsection (1)(b) shall be treated for the purposes of this Part as a deduction from the wages payable to the worker on that day made by the employer on account of the cash shortages or stock deficiencies in question.

(3) The second of the amounts referred to in subsection (1)(b) shall be treated for the purposes of this Part (except subsection (1)) as the gross amount of the wages payable to him on that day.

(4) Accordingly—

(a) section 13, and

(b) if the requirements of section 13 and subsection (2) of section 18 are satisfied, subsection (1) of section 18,

have effect in relation to the amount referred to in subsection (2) of this section.

[1026]

20 Limits on method and timing of payments

(1) Where the employer of a worker in retail employment receives from the worker a payment on account of a cash shortage or stock deficiency, the employer shall not be treated as receiving the payment in accordance with section 15 unless (in addition to the requirements of that section being satisfied with respect to the payment) he has previously—

(a) notified the worker in writing of the worker's total liability to him in respect of that shortage or deficiency, and

(b) required the worker to make the payment by means of a demand for payment made in accordance with the following provisions of this section.

(2) A demand for payment made by the employer of a worker in retail employment in respect of a cash shortage or stock deficiency—

(a) shall be made in writing, and

(b) shall be made on one of the worker's pay days.

(3) A demand for payment in respect of a particular cash shortage or stock deficiency, or (in the case of a series of such demands) the first such demand, shall not be made—

(a) earlier than the first pay day of the worker following the date when he is notified of his total liability in respect of the shortage or deficiency in pursuance of subsection (1)(a) or, where he is so notified on a pay day, earlier than that day, or

(b) later than the end of the period of twelve months beginning with the date when the employer established the existence of the shortage or deficiency or (if earlier) the date when he ought reasonably to have done so.

(4) For the purposes of this Part a demand for payment shall be treated as made by the employer on one of a worker's pay days if it is given to the worker or posted to, or left at, his last known address—

(a) on that pay day, or

(b) in the case of a pay day which is not a working day of the employer's business, on the first such working day following that pay day.

(5) Legal proceedings by the employer of a worker in retail employment for the recovery from the worker of an amount in respect of a cash shortage or stock deficiency shall not be instituted by the employer after the end of the period referred to in subsection (3)(b) unless the employer has within that period made a demand for payment in respect of that amount in accordance with this section.

[1027]

21 Limit on amount of payments

(1) Where the employer of a worker in retail employment makes on any pay day one or more demands for payment in accordance with section 20, the amount or aggregate amount required to be paid by the worker in pursuance of the demand or demands shall not exceed—

(a) one-tenth of the gross amount of the wages payable to the worker on that day, or

(b) where one or more deductions falling within section 18(1) are made by the employer from those wages, such amount as represents the balance of that one-tenth after subtracting the amount or aggregate amount of the deduction or deductions.

(2) Once an amount has been required to be paid by means of a demand for payment made in accordance with section 20 on any pay day, that amount shall not be taken into account under subsection (1) as it applies to any subsequent pay day, even though the employer is obliged to make further requests for it to be paid.

(3) Where in any legal proceedings the court finds that the employer of a worker in retail employment is (in accordance with section 15 as it applies apart from section 20(1)) entitled to recover an amount from the worker in respect of a cash shortage or stock deficiency, the court shall, in ordering the payment by the worker to the employer of that amount, make such provision as appears to the court to be necessary to ensure that it is paid by the worker at a rate not exceeding that at which it could be recovered from him by the employer in accordance with this section.

[1028]

NOTES

Conciliation: employment tribunal proceedings and claims which could be the subject of employment tribunal proceedings under sub-s (1) are proceedings to which the Employment Tribunals Act 1996, s 18 applies; see s 18(1)(d) of that Act at **[975]**. The short conciliation period applies to such proceedings by virtue of the Employment Tribunals (Constitution and Rules of Procedure) Regulations 2004, SI 2004/1861, Sch 1, rule 22(5).

22 Final instalments of wages

(1) In this section "final instalment of wages", in relation to a worker, means—

(a) the amount of wages payable to the worker which consists of or includes an amount payable by way of contractual remuneration in respect of the last of the periods for which he is employed under his contract prior to its termination for any reason (but excluding any wages referable to any earlier such period), or

(b) where an amount in lieu of notice is paid to the worker later than the amount referred to in paragraph (a), the amount so paid,

in each case whether the amount in question is paid before or after the termination of the worker's contract.

(2) Section 18(1) does not operate to restrict the amount of any deductions which may (in accordance with section 13(1)) be made by the employer of a worker in retail employment from the worker's final instalment of wages.

(3) Nothing in section 20 or 21 applies to a payment falling within section 20(1) which is made on or after the day on which any such worker's final instalment of wages is paid; but (even if the requirements of section 15 would otherwise be satisfied with respect to it) his employer shall not be treated as receiving any such payment in accordance with that section if the payment was first required to be made after the end of the period referred to in section 20(3)(b).

(4) Section 21(3) does not apply to an amount which is to be paid by a worker on or after the day on which his final instalment of wages is paid.

[1029]

Enforcement

23 Complaints to [employment tribunals]

(1) A worker may present a complaint to an [employment tribunal]—

(a) that his employer has made a deduction from his wages in contravention of section 13 (including a deduction made in contravention of that section as it applies by virtue of section 18(2)),

(b) that his employer has received from him a payment in contravention of section 15 (including a payment received in contravention of that section as it applies by virtue of section 20(1)),

(c) that his employer has recovered from his wages by means of one or more deductions falling within section 18(1) an amount or aggregate amount exceeding the limit applying to the deduction or deductions under that provision, or

(d) that his employer has received from him in pursuance of one or more demands for payment made (in accordance with section 20) on a particular pay day, a payment or payments of an amount or aggregate amount exceeding the limit applying to the demand or demands under section 21(1).

(2) Subject to subsection (4), an [employment tribunal] shall not consider a complaint under this section unless it is presented before the end of the period of three months beginning with—

(a) in the case of a complaint relating to a deduction by the employer, the date of payment of the wages from which the deduction was made, or

(b) in the case of a complaint relating to a payment received by the employer, the date when the payment was received.

(3) Where a complaint is brought under this section in respect of—

(a) a series of deductions or payments, or

(b) a number of payments falling within subsection (1)(d) and made in pursuance of demands for payment subject to the same limit under section 21(1) but received by the employer on different dates, the references in subsection (2) to the deduction or payment are to the last deduction or payment in the series or to the last of the payments so received.

(4) Where the [employment tribunal] is satisfied that it was not reasonably practicable for a complaint under this section to be presented before the end of the relevant period of three months, the tribunal may consider the complaint if it is presented within such further period as the tribunal considers reasonable.

[(5) No complaint shall be presented under this section in respect of any deduction made in contravention of section 86 of the Trade Union and Labour Relations (Consolidation) Act 1992 (deduction of political fund contribution where certificate of exemption or objection has been given).]

[1030]

NOTES

Section heading, sub-ss (1), (2), (4): words in square brackets substituted by the Employment Rights (Dispute Resolution) Act 1998, s 1(2)(a), (b).

Sub-s (5): added by the Employment Rights (Dispute Resolution) Act 1998, s 15, Sch 1, para 18.

Conciliation: employment tribunal proceedings under this section in respect of a breach of any of ss 13, 15, 18(1) or 21(1) of this Act and claims which could be the subject of such proceedings are proceedings to which the Employment Tribunals Act 1996, s 18 applies; see s 18(1)(d) of that Act at **[975]**. The short conciliation period applies to such proceedings by virtue of the Employment Tribunals (Constitution and Rules of Procedure) Regulations 2004, SI 2004/1861, Sch 1, rule 22(5).

Tribunal jurisdiction: the Employment Act 2002, ss 31, 32, 38, at **[1493]**, **[1494]**, **[1496]** apply to proceedings before the employment tribunal relating to a claim under this section; see ss 31(1), 32(1), 38(1) of, and Schs 3–5 to, the 2002 Act at **[1508]**–**[1510]**.

For the circumstances in which the normal time limit for presenting a complaint under this section is extended for a period of three months, see the Employment Act 2002 (Dispute Resolution) Regulations 2004, SI 2004/752, regs 15 and 18 at **[3096]** and **[3098]**.

24 Determination of complaints

Where a tribunal finds a complaint under section 23 well-founded, it shall make a declaration to that effect and shall order the employer—

(a) in the case of a complaint under section 23(1)(a), to pay to the worker the amount of any deduction made in contravention of section 13,

(b) in the case of a complaint under section 23(1)(b), to repay to the worker the amount of any payment received in contravention of section 15,

(c) in the case of a complaint under section 23(1)(c), to pay to the worker any amount recovered from him in excess of the limit mentioned in that provision, and

(d) in the case of a complaint under section 23(1)(d), to repay to the worker any amount received from him in excess of the limit mentioned in that provision.

[1031]

25 Determinations: supplementary

(1) Where, in the case of any complaint under section 23(1)(a), a tribunal finds that, although neither of the conditions set out in section 13(1)(a) and (b) was satisfied with respect to the whole amount of the deduction, one of those conditions was satisfied with respect to any lesser amount, the amount of the deduction shall for the purposes of section 24(a) be treated as reduced by the amount with respect to which that condition was satisfied.

(2) Where, in the case of any complaint under section 23(1)(b), a tribunal finds that, although neither of the conditions set out in section 15(1)(a) and (b) was satisfied with respect to the whole amount of the payment, one of those conditions was satisfied with respect to any lesser amount, the amount of the payment shall for the purposes of section 24(b) be treated as reduced by the amount with respect to which that condition was satisfied.

(3) An employer shall not under section 24 be ordered by a tribunal to pay or repay to a worker any amount in respect of a deduction or payment, or in respect of any combination of deductions or payments, in so far as it appears to the tribunal that he has already paid or repaid any such amount to the worker.

(4) Where a tribunal has under section 24 ordered an employer to pay or repay to a worker any amount in respect of a particular deduction or payment falling within section 23(1)(a) to (d), the amount which the employer is entitled to recover (by whatever means) in respect of the matter in relation to which the deduction or payment was originally made or received shall be treated as reduced by that amount.

(5) Where a tribunal has under section 24 ordered an employer to pay or repay to a worker any amount in respect of any combination of deductions or payments falling within section 23(1)(c) or (d), the aggregate amount which the employer is entitled to recover (by whatever means) in respect of the cash shortages or stock deficiencies in relation to which the deductions or payments were originally made or required to be made shall be treated as reduced by that amount.

[1032]

26 Complaints and other remedies

Section 23 does not affect the jurisdiction of an [employment tribunal] to consider a reference under section 11 in relation to any deduction from the wages of a worker; but the aggregate of any amounts ordered by an [employment tribunal] to be paid under section 12(4) and under section 24 (whether on the same or different occasions) in respect of a particular deduction shall not exceed the amount of the deduction.

[1033]

NOTES

Words in square brackets substituted by the Employment Rights (Dispute Resolution) Act 1998, s 1(2)(a).

Supplementary

27 Meaning of "wages" etc

(1) In this Part "wages", in relation to a worker, means any sums payable to the worker in connection with his employment, including—

(a) any fee, bonus, commission, holiday pay or other emolument referable to his employment, whether payable under his contract or otherwise,
(b) statutory sick pay under Part XI of the Social Security Contributions and Benefits Act 1992,
(c) statutory maternity pay under Part XII of that Act,
[(ca) *statutory paternity pay* under Part 12ZA of that Act,
(cb) statutory adoption pay under Part 12ZB of that Act,]
(d) a guarantee payment (under section 28 of this Act),
(e) any payment for time off under Part VI of this Act or section 169 of the Trade Union and Labour Relations (Consolidation) Act 1992 (payment for time off for carrying out trade union duties etc),
(f) remuneration on suspension on medical grounds under section 64 of this Act and remuneration on suspension on maternity grounds under section 68 of this Act,
(g) any sum payable in pursuance of an order for reinstatement or re-engagement under section 113 of this Act,
(h) any sum payable in pursuance of an order for the continuation of a contract of employment under section 130 of this Act or section 164 of the Trade Union and Labour Relations (Consolidation) Act 1992, and
(j) remuneration under a protective award under section 189 of that Act,

but excluding any payments within subsection (2).

(2) Those payments are—

(a) any payment by way of an advance under an agreement for a loan or by way of an advance of wages (but without prejudice to the application of section 13 to any deduction made from the worker's wages in respect of any such advance),
(b) any payment in respect of expenses incurred by the worker in carrying out his employment,
(c) any payment by way of a pension, allowance or gratuity in connection with the worker's retirement or as compensation for loss of office,
(d) any payment referable to the worker's redundancy, and
(e) any payment to the worker otherwise than in his capacity as a worker.

(3) Where any payment in the nature of a non-contractual bonus is (for any reason) made to a worker by his employer, the amount of the payment shall for the purposes of this Part—

(a) be treated as wages of the worker, and
(b) be treated as payable to him as such on the day on which the payment is made.

(4) In this Part "gross amount", in relation to any wages payable to a worker, means the total amount of those wages before deductions of whatever nature.

(5) For the purposes of this Part any monetary value attaching to any payment or benefit in kind furnished to a worker by his employer shall not be treated as wages of the worker except in the case of any voucher, stamp or similar document which is—

(a) of a fixed value expressed in monetary terms, and

(b) capable of being exchanged (whether on its own or together with other vouchers, stamps or documents, and whether immediately or only after a time) for money, goods or services (or for any combination of two or more of those things).

[1034]

NOTES

Sub-s (1): paras (ca), (cb) inserted by the Employment Act 2002, s 53, Sch 7, paras 24, 25; for the words in italics in para (ca) there are substituted the words "ordinary statutory paternity pay or additional statutory paternity pay" by the Work and Families Act 2006, s 11(1), Sch 1, para 29, as from a day to be appointed.

Note: sub-s (1) did not contain a para (i) in the Queen's Printer's copy of this Act.

PART III
GUARANTEE PAYMENTS

28 Right to guarantee payment

(1) Where throughout a day during any part of which an employee would normally be required to work in accordance with his contract of employment the employee is not provided with work by his employer by reason of—

(a) a diminution in the requirements of the employer's business for work of the kind which the employee is employed to do, or

(b) any other occurrence affecting the normal working of the employer's business in relation to work of the kind which the employee is employed to do,

the employee is entitled to be paid by his employer an amount in respect of that day.

(2) In this Act a payment to which an employee is entitled under subsection (1) is referred to as a guarantee payment.

(3) In this Part—

(a) a day falling within subsection (1) is referred to as a "workless day", and

(b) "workless period" has a corresponding meaning.

(4) In this Part "day" means the period of twenty-four hours from midnight to midnight.

(5) Where a period of employment begun on any day extends, or would normally extend, over midnight into the following day—

(a) if the employment before midnight is, or would normally be, of longer duration than that after midnight, the period of employment shall be treated as falling wholly on the first day, and

(b) in any other case, the period of employment shall be treated as falling wholly on the second day.

[1035]

NOTES

Conciliation: employment tribunal proceedings and claims which could be the subject of employment tribunal proceedings under this section are proceedings to which the Employment Tribunals Act 1996, s 18 applies; see s 18(1)(d) of that Act at **[975]**. The short conciliation period applies to such proceedings by virtue of the Employment Tribunals (Constitution and Rules of Procedure) Regulations 2004, SI 2004/1861, Sch 1, rule 22(5).

29 Exclusions from right to guarantee payment

(1) An employee is not entitled to a guarantee payment unless he has been continuously employed for a period of not less than one month ending with the day before that in respect of which the guarantee payment is claimed.

(2) …

(3) An employee is not entitled to a guarantee payment in respect of a workless day if the failure to provide him with work for that day occurs in consequence of a strike, lock-out or other industrial action involving any employee of his employer or of an associated employer.

(4) An employee is not entitled to a guarantee payment in respect of a workless day if—

(a) his employer has offered to provide alternative work for that day which is suitable in all the circumstances (whether or not it is work which the employee is under his contract employed to perform), and

(b) the employee has unreasonably refused that offer.

(5) An employee is not entitled to a guarantee payment if he does not comply with reasonable requirements imposed by his employer with a view to ensuring that his services are available.

[1036]

NOTES

Sub-s (2): repealed by the Fixed-term Employees (Prevention of Less Favourable Treatment) Regulations 2002, SI 2002/2034, reg 11, Sch 2, Pt 1, para 3(1), (2).

30 Calculation of guarantee payment

(1) Subject to section 31, the amount of a guarantee payment payable to an employee in respect of any day is the sum produced by multiplying the number of normal working hours on the day by the guaranteed hourly rate; and, accordingly, no guarantee payment is payable to an employee in whose case there are no normal working hours on the day in question.

(2) The guaranteed hourly rate, in relation to an employee, is the amount of one week's pay divided by the number of normal working hours in a week for that employee when employed under the contract of employment in force on the day in respect of which the guarantee payment is payable.

(3) But where the number of normal working hours differs from week to week or over a longer period, the amount of one week's pay shall be divided instead by—

(a) the average number of normal working hours calculated by dividing by twelve the total number of the employee's normal working hours during the period of twelve weeks ending with the last complete week before the day in respect of which the guarantee payment is payable, or

(b) where the employee has not been employed for a sufficient period to enable the calculation to be made under paragraph (a), a number which fairly represents the number of normal working hours in a week having regard to such of the considerations specified in subsection (4) as are appropriate in the circumstances.

(4) The considerations referred to in subsection (3)(b) are—

(a) the average number of normal working hours in a week which the employee could expect in accordance with the terms of his contract, and

(b) the average number of normal working hours of other employees engaged in relevant comparable employment with the same employer.

(5) If in any case an employee's contract has been varied, or a new contract has been entered into, in connection with a period of short-time working, subsections (2) and (3) have effect as if for the references to the day in respect of which the guarantee payment is payable there were substituted references to the last day on which the original contract was in force.

[1037]

31 Limits on amount of and entitlement to guarantee payment

(1) The amount of a guarantee payment payable to an employee in respect of any day shall not exceed [£20.40].

(2) An employee is not entitled to guarantee payments in respect of more than the specified number of days in any period of three months.

(3) The specified number of days for the purposes of subsection (2) is the number of days, not exceeding five, on which the employee normally works in a week under the contract of employment in force on the day in respect of which the guarantee payment is claimed.

(4) But where that number of days varies from week to week or over a longer period, the specified number of days is instead—

(a) the average number of such days, not exceeding five, calculated by dividing by twelve the total number of such days during the period of twelve weeks ending with the last complete week before the day in respect of which the guarantee payment is claimed, and rounding up the resulting figure to the next whole number, or

(b) where the employee has not been employed for a sufficient period to enable the calculation to be made under paragraph (a), a number which fairly represents the number of the employee's normal working days in a week, not exceeding five, having regard to such of the considerations specified in subsection (5) as are appropriate in the circumstances.

(5) The considerations referred to in subsection (4)(b) are—

(a) the average number of normal working days in a week which the employee could expect in accordance with the terms of his contract, and

(b) the average number of such days of other employees engaged in relevant comparable employment with the same employer.

(6) If in any case an employee's contract has been varied, or a new contract has been entered into, in connection with a period of short-time working, subsections (3) and (4) have effect as if for the references to the day in respect of which the guarantee payment is claimed there were substituted references to the last day on which the original contract was in force.

[(7) The Secretary of State may by order vary—

(a) the length of the period specified in subsection (2);

(b) a limit specified in subsection (3) or (4).]

[1038]

NOTES

Sub-s (1): sum in square brackets substituted by the Employment Rights (Increase of Limits) Order 2007, SI 2007/3570, art 3, Schedule, as from 1 February 2008, in relation to any case where the appropriate date falls on or after that date (see SI 2007/3570, art 4 at **[3474H]**). The previous sum was £19.60 (see SI 2006/3045). This sum may be varied by the Secretary of State, see the Employment Relations Act 1999, s 34(1)(a), (3)(a) at **[1445]**.

Sub-s (7): substituted by the Employment Relations Act 1999, s 35, as from 25 October 1999.

32 Contractual remuneration

(1) A right to a guarantee payment does not affect any right of an employee in relation to remuneration under his contract of employment ("contractual remuneration").

(2) Any contractual remuneration paid to an employee in respect of a workless day goes towards discharging any liability of the employer to pay a guarantee payment in respect of that day; and, conversely, any guarantee payment paid in respect of a day goes towards discharging any liability of the employer to pay contractual remuneration in respect of that day.

(3) For the purposes of subsection (2), contractual remuneration shall be treated as paid in respect of a workless day—

(a) where it is expressed to be calculated or payable by reference to that day or any part of that day, to the extent that it is so expressed, and

(b) in any other case, to the extent that it represents guaranteed remuneration, rather than remuneration for work actually done, and is referable to that day when apportioned rateably between that day and any other workless period falling within the period in respect of which the remuneration is paid.

[1039]

33 Power to modify provisions about guarantee payments

The Secretary of State may by order provide that in relation to any description of employees the provisions of—

(a) sections 28(4) and (5), 30, 31(3) to (5) (as originally enacted or as varied under section 31(7)) and 32, and

(b) so far as they apply for the purposes of those provisions, Chapter II of Part XIV and section 234,

shall have effect subject to such modifications and adaptations as may be prescribed by the order.

[1040]

NOTES

Orders: as of 6 April 2008 no Orders had been made under this section.

34 Complaints to [employment tribunals]

(1) An employee may present a complaint to an [employment tribunal] that his employer has failed to pay the whole or any part of a guarantee payment to which the employee is entitled.

(2) An [employment tribunal] shall not consider a complaint relating to a guarantee payment in respect of any day unless the complaint is presented to the tribunal—

(a) before the end of the period of three months beginning with that day, or

(b) within such further period as the tribunal considers reasonable in a case where it is satisfied that it was not reasonably practicable for the complaint to be presented before the end of that period of three months.

(3) Where an [employment tribunal] finds a complaint under this section well-founded, the tribunal shall order the employer to pay to the employee the amount of guarantee payment which it finds is due to him.

[1041]

NOTES

Words in square brackets substituted by the Employment Rights (Dispute Resolution) Act 1998, s 1(2)(a), (b).

Conciliation: employment tribunal proceedings under this section in respect of a breach of s 28 of this Act and claims which could be the subject of such proceedings are proceedings to which the Employment Tribunals Act 1996, s 18 applies; see s 18(1)(d) of that Act at **[975]**. The short conciliation period applies to such proceedings by virtue of the Employment Tribunals (Constitution and Rules of Procedure) Regulations 2004, SI 2004/1861, Sch 1, rule 22(5).

35 Exemption orders

(1) Where—

(a) at any time there is in force a collective agreement, or an agricultural wages order, under which employees to whom the agreement or order relates have a right to guaranteed remuneration, and

(b) on the application of all the parties to the agreement, or of the Board making the order, the appropriate Minister (having regard to the provisions of the agreement or order) is satisfied that section 28 should not apply to those employees,

he may make an order under this section excluding those employees from the operation of that section.

(2) In subsection (1) "agricultural wages order" means an order made under—

(a) section 3 of the Agricultural Wages Act 1948, or

(b) section 3 of the Agricultural Wages (Scotland) Act 1949.

(3) In subsection (1) "the appropriate Minister" means—

(a) in relation to a collective agreement or to an order such as is referred to in subsection (2)(b), the Secretary of State, and

(b) in relation to an order such as is referred to in subsection (2)(a), the [Secretary of State].

(4) The Secretary of State shall not make an order under this section in respect of an agreement unless—

(a) the agreement provides for procedures to be followed (whether by arbitration or otherwise) in cases where an employee claims that his employer has failed to pay the whole or any part of any guaranteed remuneration to which the employee is entitled under the agreement and those procedures include a right to arbitration or adjudication by an independent referee or body in cases where (by reason of an equality of votes or otherwise) a decision cannot otherwise be reached, or

(b) the agreement indicates that an employee to whom the agreement relates may present a complaint to an [employment tribunal] that his employer has failed to pay the whole or any part of any guaranteed remuneration to which the employee is entitled under the agreement.

(5) Where an order under this section is in force in respect of an agreement indicating as described in paragraph (b) of subsection (4) an [employment tribunal] shall have jurisdiction over a complaint such as is mentioned in that paragraph as if it were a complaint falling within section 34.

(6) An order varying or revoking an earlier order under this section may be made in pursuance of an application by all or any of the parties to the agreement in question, or the Board which made the order in question, or in the absence of such an application.

[1042]

NOTES

Sub-s (3): words in square brackets substituted by the Ministry of Agriculture, Fisheries and Food (Dissolution) Order 2002, SI 2002/794, art 5(1), Sch 1, para 37.

Sub-ss (4), (5): words in square brackets substituted by the Employment Rights (Dispute Resolution) Act 1998, s 1(2)(a).

Orders: as of 6 April 2008 no Orders had been made under this section. However, the following Guarantee Payments Exemption Orders in force at that date have effect as if made hereunder by virtue of s 241 of, and Sch 2, Pt I, paras 1–4 to, this Act: No 1 (SI 1977/156) Federation of Civil Engineering Contracts; No 2 (SI 1977/157) National Federation of Demolition Contractors; No 5 (SI 1977/902) British Footwear Manufacturers' Federation; No 6 (SI 1977/1096) Steeplejacks and Lightning Conductor Engineers; No 7 (SI 1977/1158) Paper and Board Industry; No 8 (SI 1977/1322) Smiths Food Group; No 9 (SI 1977/1349) British Leather Federation; No 10 (SI 1977/1522) Fibreboard Packing Case Industry; No 11 (SI 1977/1523) Henry Wiggin & Co Ltd; No 12 (SI 1977/1583) Refractory Users Federation; No 13 (SI 1977/1601) Multiwall Sack Manufacturers; No 14 (SI 1977/2032) Tudor Food Products; No 15 (SI 1978/153) British Carton Association; No 16 (SI 1978/429) Henry Wiggin & Co; No 17 (SI 1978/737) NJC for Workshops for the Blind; No 18 (SI 1978/826) Employers' Federation of Card Clothing Manufacturers; No 19 (SI 1979/1403) NJC for the Motor Vehicle Repair Industry; No 21 (SI 1981/6) Plant Hire Working Rule Agreement; No 23 (SI 1987/1757) National Agreement for Wire and Wire Rope Industries (revoking No 4); No 24 (SI 1989/1326) Rowntree Mackintosh Confectionery Ltd (revoking No 22 as amended); No 25 (SI 1989/1575) Building and Allied Trades Joint Industrial Council (revoking No 20); No 26 (SI 1989/2163) Airflow Streamlines; No 27 (SI 1990/927) G & G Kynock plc; No 28 (SI 1990/2330) Bridon Ropes Ltd; No 30 (SI 1996/2132) National Joint Council for the Building Industry.

PART IV
SUNDAY WORKING FOR SHOP AND BETTING WORKERS

Protected shop workers and betting workers

36 Protected shop workers and betting workers

(1) Subject to subsection (5), a shop worker or betting worker is to be regarded as "protected" for the purposes of any provision of this Act if (and only if) subsection (2) or (3) applies to him.

(2) This subsection applies to a shop worker or betting worker if—

(a) on the day before the relevant commencement date he was employed as a shop worker or a betting worker but not to work only on Sunday,

(b) he has been continuously employed during the period beginning with that day and ending with the day which, in relation to the provision concerned, is the appropriate date, and

(c) throughout that period, or throughout every part of it during which his relations with his employer were governed by a contract of employment, he was a shop worker or a betting worker.

(3) This subsection applies to any shop worker or betting worker whose contract of employment is such that under it he—

(a) is not, and may not be, required to work on Sunday, and

(b) could not be so required even if the provisions of this Part were disregarded.

(4) Where on the day before the relevant commencement date an employee's relations with his employer had ceased to be governed by a contract of employment, he shall be regarded as satisfying subsection (2)(a) if—

(a) that day fell in a week which counts as a period of employment with that employer under section 212(2) or (3) or under regulations under section 219, and

(b) on the last day before the relevant commencement date on which his relations with his employer were governed by a contract of employment, the employee was employed as a shop worker or a betting worker but not to work only on Sunday.

(5) A shop worker is not a protected shop worker, and a betting worker is not a protected betting worker, if—

(a) he has given his employer an opting-in notice on or after the relevant commencement date, and

(b) after giving the notice, he has expressly agreed with his employer to do shop work, or betting work, on Sunday or on a particular Sunday.

(6) In this Act "opting-in notice", in relation to a shop worker or a betting worker, means written notice, signed and dated by the shop worker or betting worker, in which the shop worker or betting worker expressly states that he wishes to work on Sunday or that he does not object to Sunday working.

(7) [Subject to subsection (8),] in this Act "the relevant commencement date" means—

(a) in relation to a shop worker, 26th August 1994, and

(b) in relation to a betting worker, 3rd January 1995.

[(8) In any provision of this Act which applies to Scotland by virtue of section 1(5) of the Sunday Working (Scotland) Act 2003 (extension to Scotland of provisions which refer to shop workers and betting workers), "the relevant commencement date" means, in relation to Scotland, the date on which that section came into force.]

[1043]

NOTES

Sub-s (7): words in square brackets inserted by the Sunday Working (Scotland) Act 2003, s 1(1), (2)(a), as from 6 April 2004.

Sub-s (8): added by the Sunday Working (Scotland) Act 2003, s 1(1), (2)(b), as from 6 April 2004.

Relevant commencement date: the Sunday Working (Scotland) Act 2003, s 1 came into force on 6 April 2004 (see SI 2004/958).

37 Contractual requirements relating to Sunday work

(1) Any contract of employment under which a shop worker or betting worker who satisfies section 36(2)(a) was employed on the day or before the relevant commencement date is unenforceable to the extent that it—

(a) requires the shop worker to do shop work, or the betting worker to do betting work, on Sunday on or after that date, or

(b) requires the employer to provide the shop worker with shop work, or the betting worker with betting work, on Sunday on or after that date.

(2) Subject to subsection (3), any agreement entered into after the relevant commencement date between a protected shop worker, or a protected betting worker, and his employer is unenforceable to the extent that it—

(a) requires the shop worker to do shop work, or the betting worker to do betting work, on Sunday, or

(b) requires the employer to provide the shop worker with shop work, or the betting worker with betting work, on Sunday.

(3) Where, after giving an opting-in notice, a protected shop worker or a protected betting worker expressly agrees with his employer to do shop work or betting work on Sunday or on a particular Sunday (and so ceases to be protected), his contract of employment shall be taken to be varied to the extent necessary to give effect to the terms of the agreement.

(4) …

(5) For the purposes of section 36(2)(b), the appropriate date—

(a) in relation to subsections (2) and (3) of this section, is the day on which the agreement is entered into, …

(b) …

[1044]

NOTES

Sub-s (4): repealed by the Employment Relations Act 1999, ss 9, 44, Sch 4, Pt III, paras 1, 5, 6(a), Sch 9(2).

Sub-s (5): word omitted from para (a), and para (b) repealed, by the Employment Relations Act 1999, ss 9, 44, Sch 4, Pt III, paras 1, 5, 6(b), (c), Sch 9(2).

38 Contracts with guaranteed hours

(1) This section applies where—

(a) under the contract of employment under which a shop worker or betting worker who satisfies section 36(2)(a) was employed on the day before the relevant commencement date, the employer is, or may be, required to provide him with shop work, or betting work, for a specified number of hours each week,

(b) under the contract the shop worker or betting worker was, or might have been, required to work on Sunday before that date, and

(c) the shop worker has done shop work, or the betting worker betting work, on Sunday in that employment (whether or not before that day) but has, on or after that date, ceased to do so.

(2) So long as the shop worker remains a protected shop worker, or the betting worker remains a protected betting worker, the contract shall not be regarded as requiring the employer to provide him with shop work, or betting work, on weekdays in excess of the hours normally worked by the shop worker or betting worker on weekdays before he ceased to do shop work, or betting work, on Sunday.

(3) For the purposes of section 36(2)(b), the appropriate date in relation to this section is any time in relation to which the contract is to be enforced.

[1045]

39 Reduction of pay etc

(1) This section applies where—

(a) under the contract of employment under which a shop worker or betting worker who satisfies section 36(2)(a) was employed on the day before the relevant commencement date, the shop worker or betting worker was, or might have been, required to work on Sunday before the relevant commencement date,

(b) the shop worker has done shop work, or the betting worker has done betting work, on Sunday in that employment (whether or not before that date) but has, on or after that date, ceased to do so, and

(c) it is not apparent from the contract what part of the remuneration payable, or of any other benefit accruing, to the shop worker or betting worker was intended to be attributable to shop work, or betting work, on Sunday.

(2) So long as the shop worker remains a protected shop worker, or the betting worker remains a protected betting worker, the contract shall be regarded as enabling the employer to reduce the amount of remuneration paid, or the extent of the other benefit provided, to the shop worker or betting worker in respect of any period by the relevant proportion.

(3) In subsection (2) "the relevant proportion" means the proportion which the hours of shop work, or betting work, which (apart from this Part) the shop worker, or betting worker, could have been required to do on Sunday in the period ("the contractual Sunday hours") bears to the aggregate of those hours and the hours of work actually done by the shop worker, or betting worker, in the period.

(4) Where, under the contract of employment, the hours of work actually done on weekdays in any period would be taken into account determining the contractual Sunday hours, they shall be taken into account in determining the contractual Sunday hours for the purposes of subsection (3).

(5) For the purposes of section 36(2)(b), the appropriate date in relation to this section is the end of the period in respect of which the remuneration is paid or the benefit accrues.

[1046]

Opting-out of Sunday work

40 Notice of objection to Sunday working

(1) A shop worker or betting worker to whom this section applies may at any time give his employer written notice, signed and dated by the shop worker or betting worker, to the effect that he objects to Sunday working.

(2) In this Act "opting-out notice" means a notice given under subsection (1) by a shop worker or betting worker to whom this section applies.

(3) This section applies to any shop worker or betting worker under his contract of employment—

(a) is or may be required to work on Sunday (whether or not a result of previously giving an opting-in notice), but
(b) is not employed to work only on Sunday.

[1047]

41 Opted-out shop workers and betting workers

(1) Subject to subsection (2), a shop worker or betting worker is regarded as "opted-out" for the purposes of any provision of this (and only if)—
(a) he has given his employer an opting-out notice,
(b) he has been continuously employed during the period beginning with the day on which the notice was given and ending with the day which, in relation to the provision concerned, is the appropriate date, and
(c) throughout that period, or throughout every part of it during which his relations with his employer were governed by a contract of employment, he was a shop worker or a betting worker.

(2) A shop worker is not an opted-out shop worker, and a betting worker is not an opted out betting worker, if—
(a) after giving the opting-out notice concerned, he has given his employer an opting-in notice, and
(b) after giving the opting-in notice, he has expressly agreed with his employer to do shop work, or betting work, on Sunday or on a particular Sunday.

(3) In this Act "notice period", in relation to an opted-out shop worker or an opted-out betting worker, means, subject to section 42(2), the period of three months beginning with the day on which the opting-out notice concerned was given.

[1048]

42 Explanatory statement

(1) Where a person becomes a shop worker or betting worker to whom section 40 applies, his employer shall, before the end of the period two months beginning with the day on which that person becomes such worker, give him a written statement in the prescribed form.

(2) If—
(a) an employer fails to comply with subsection (1) in relation to any shop worker or betting worker, and
(b) the shop worker or betting worker, on giving the employer an opting-out notice, becomes an opted-out shop worker or an opted-out betting worker,

section 41(3) has effect in relation to the shop worker or betting worker with the substitution for "three months" of "one month".

(3) An employer shall not be regarded as failing to comply with subsection (1) in any case where, before the end of the period referred to that subsection, the shop worker or betting worker has given him an opting-out notice.

(4) Subject to subsection (6), the prescribed form in the case of a shop worker is as follows—

"STATUTORY RIGHTS IN RELATION TO SUNDAY SHOP WORK

You have become employed as a shop worker and are or can be required under your contract of employment to do the Sunday work your contract provides for.

However, if you wish, you can give a notice, as described in the next paragraph, to your employer and you will then have the right not to work in or about a shop on any Sunday on which the shop is open once three months have passed from the date on which you gave the notice.

Your notice must—
be in writing;
be signed and dated by you;
say that you object to Sunday working.

For three months after you give the notice, your employer can still require you to do all the Sunday work your contract provides for. After the three month period has ended, you have the right to complain to an [employment tribunal] if, because of your refusal to work on Sundays on which the shop is open, your employer—

dismisses you, or
does something else detrimental to you, for example, failing to promote you.

Once you have the rights described, you can surrender them only by giving your employer a further notice, signed and dated by you, saying that you wish to work on Sunday or that you do not object to Sunday working and then agreeing with your employer to work on Sundays or on a particular Sunday.".

(5) Subject to subsection (6), the prescribed form in the case of betting worker is as follows—

"STATUTORY RIGHTS IN RELATION TO SUNDAY BETTING WORK

You have become employed under a contract of employment under which you are or can be required to do Sunday betting work that is to say, work—
at a track on a Sunday on which your employer is taking bets at the track, or
in a licensed betting office on a Sunday on which it is open for business.

However, if you wish, you can give a notice, as described in the next paragraph, to your employer and you will then have the right not to do Sunday betting work once three months have passed from the date on which you gave the notice.

Your notice must—
be in writing;
be signed and dated by you;
say that you object to doing Sunday betting work.

For three months after you give the notice, your employer can still require you to do all the Sunday betting work your contract provides for. After the three month period has ended, you have the right to complain to an [employment tribunal] if, because of your refusal to do Sunday betting work, your employer—
dismisses you, or
does something else detrimental to you, for example, failing to promote you.

Once you have the rights described, you can surrender them only by giving your employer a further notice, signed and dated by you, saying that you wish to do Sunday betting work or that you do not object to doing Sunday betting work and then agreeing with your employer to do such work on Sundays or on a particular Sunday.".

(6) The Secretary of State may by order amend the prescribed forms set out in subsections (4) and (5).

[1049]

NOTES

Sub-ss (4), (5): words in square brackets substituted by the Employment Rights (Dispute Resolution) Act 1998, s 1(2)(a).

Orders: as of 6 April 2008 no Orders had been made under sub-s (6).

43 Contractual requirements relating to Sunday work

(1) Where a shop worker or betting worker gives his employer an opting-out notice, the contract of employment under which he was employed immediately before he gave that notice becomes unenforceable to the extent that it—

(a) requires the shop worker to do shop work, or the betting worker to do betting work, on Sunday after the end of the notice period, or
(b) requires the employer to provide the shop worker with shop work, or the betting worker with betting work, on Sunday after the end of that period.

(2) Subject to subsection (3), any agreement entered into between an opted-out shop worker, or an opted-out betting worker, and his employer is unenforceable to the extent that it—

(a) requires the shop worker to do shop work, or the betting worker to do betting work, on Sunday after the end of the notice period, or
(b) requires the employer to provide the shop worker with shop work, or the betting worker with betting work, on Sunday after the end of that period.

(3) Where, after giving an opting-in notice, an opted-out shop worker an opted-out betting worker expressly agrees with his employer to do shop work or betting work on Sunday

or on a particular Sunday (and so ceases to be opted-out), his contract of employment shall be taken to be varied to the extent necessary to give effect to the terms of the agreement.

(4) …

(5) For the purposes of section 41(1)(b), the appropriate date—

(a) in relation to subsections (2) and (3) of this section, is the day on which the agreement is entered into, …

(b) …

[1050]

NOTES

Sub-s (4): repealed by the Employment Relations Act 1999, ss 9, 44, Sch 4, Pt III, paras 1, 5, 7(a), Sch 9(2).

Sub-s (5): word omitted from para (a), and para (b), repealed by the Employment Relations Act 1999, ss 9, Sch 4, Pt III, paras 1, 5, 7(b), (c), Sch 9(2).

[PART IVA
PROTECTED DISCLOSURES

NOTES

Grievance procedure: as to the circumstances in which the grievance procedures set out in the Employment Act 2002, Sch 2, Pt 2 at **[1505]**, are applicable to the kinds of disclosure dealt with in this Part of this Act, see s 29 of, and Sch 2, Pt 4, para 15 to, the 2002 Act at **[1491]**, **[1507]**.

43A Meaning of "protected disclosure"

In this Act a "protected disclosure" means a qualifying disclosure (as defined by section 43B) which is made by a worker in accordance with any of sections 43C to 43H.]

[1051]

NOTES

Inserted, together with ss 43A–43L, by the Public Interest Disclosure Act 1998, s 1.

[43B Disclosures qualifying for protection

(1) In this Part a "qualifying disclosure" means any disclosure of information which, in the reasonable belief of the worker making the disclosure, tends to show one or more of the following—

(a) that a criminal offence has been committed, is being committed or is likely to be committed,

(b) that a person has failed, is failing or is likely to fail to comply with any legal obligation to which he is subject,

(c) that a miscarriage of justice has occurred, is occurring or is likely to occur,

(d) that the health or safety of any individual has been, is being or is likely to be endangered,

(e) that the environment has been, is being or is likely to be damaged, or

(f) that information tending to show any matter falling within any one of the preceding paragraphs has been, or is likely to be deliberately concealed.

(2) For the purposes of subsection (1), it is immaterial whether the relevant failure occurred, occurs or would occur in the United Kingdom or elsewhere, and whether the law applying to it is that of the United Kingdom or of any other country or territory.

(3) A disclosure of information is not a qualifying disclosure if the person making the disclosure commits an offence by making it.

(4) A disclosure of information in respect of which a claim to legal professional privilege (or, in Scotland, to confidentiality as between client and professional legal adviser) could be maintained in legal proceedings is not a qualifying disclosure if it is made by a person to whom the information had been disclosed in the course of obtaining legal advice.

(5) In this Part "the relevant failure", in relation to a qualifying disclosure, means the matter falling within paragraphs (a) to (f) of subsection (1).]

[1052]

NOTES

Inserted as noted to s 43A at **[1051]**.

[43C Disclosure to employer or other responsible person

(1) A qualifying disclosure is made in accordance with this section if the worker makes the disclosure in good faith—

(a) to his employer, or

(b) where the worker reasonably believes that the relevant failure relates solely or mainly to—

(i) the conduct of a person other than his employer, or

(ii) any other matter for which a person other than his employer has legal responsibility,

to that other person.

(2) A worker who, in accordance with a procedure whose use by him is authorised by his employer, makes a qualifying disclosure to a person other than his employer, is to be treated for the purposes of this Part as making the qualifying disclosure to his employer.]

[1053]

NOTES

Inserted as noted to s 43A at **[1051]**.

[43D Disclosure to legal adviser

A qualifying disclosure is made in accordance with this section if it is made in the course of obtaining legal advice.]

[1054]

NOTES

Inserted as noted to s 43A at **[1051]**.

[43E Disclosure to Minister of the Crown

A qualifying disclosure is made in accordance with this section if—

(a) the worker's employer is—

(i) an individual appointed under any enactment [(including any enactment comprised in, or in an instrument made under, an Act of the Scottish Parliament)] by a Minister of the Crown [or a member of the Scottish Executive], or

(ii) a body any of whose members are so appointed, and

(b) the disclosure is made in good faith to a Minister of the Crown [or a member of the Scottish Executive].]

[1055]

NOTES

Inserted as noted to s 43A at **[1051]**.

Words in square brackets inserted by the Scotland Act 1998 (Consequential Modifications) Order 2000, SI 2000/2040, arts 1(1), 2(1), Schedule, Pt I, para 19.

[43F Disclosure to prescribed person

(1) A qualifying disclosure is made in accordance with this section if the worker—

(a) makes the disclosure in good faith to a person prescribed by an order made by the Secretary of State for the purposes of this section, and

(b) reasonably believes—

(i) that the relevant failure falls within any description of matters in respect of which that person is so prescribed, and

(ii) that the information disclosed, and any allegation contained in it, are substantially true.

(2) An order prescribing persons for the purposes of this section may specify persons or descriptions of persons, and shall specify the descriptions of matters in respect of which each person, or persons of each description, is or are prescribed.]

[1056]

NOTES

Inserted as noted to s 43A at **[1051]**.
Orders: the Public Interest Disclosure (Prescribed Persons) Order 1999, SI 1999/1549 at **[2512]**.

[43G Disclosure in other cases

(1) A qualifying disclosure is made in accordance with this section if—
- (a) the worker makes the disclosure in good faith,
- (b) he reasonably believes that the information disclosed, and any allegation contained in it, are substantially true,
- (c) he does not make the disclosure for purposes of personal gain,
- (d) any of the conditions in subsection (2) is met, and
- (e) in all the circumstances of the case, it is reasonable for him to make the disclosure.

(2) The conditions referred to in subsection (1)(d) are—
- (a) that, at the time he makes the disclosure, the worker reasonably believes that he will be subjected to a detriment by his employer if he makes a disclosure to his employer or in accordance with section 43F,
- (b) that, in a case where no person is prescribed for the purposes of section 43F in relation to the relevant failure, the worker reasonably believes that it is likely that evidence relating to the relevant failure will be concealed or destroyed if he makes a disclosure to his employer, or
- (c) that the worker has previously made a disclosure of substantially the same information—
  - (i) to his employer, or
  - (ii) in accordance with section 43F.

(3) In determining for the purposes of subsection (1)(e) whether it is reasonable for the worker to make the disclosure, regard shall be had, in particular, to—
- (a) the identity of the person to whom the disclosure is made,
- (b) the seriousness of the relevant failure,
- (c) whether the relevant failure is continuing or is likely to occur in the future,
- (d) whether the disclosure is made in breach of a duty of confidentiality owed by the employer to any other person,
- (e) in a case falling within subsection (2)(c)(i) or (ii), any action which the employer or the person to whom the previous disclosure in accordance with section 43F was made has taken or might reasonably be expected to have taken as a result of the previous disclosure, and
- (f) in a case falling within subsection (2)(c)(i), whether in making the disclosure to the employer the worker complied with any procedure whose use by him was authorised by the employer.

(4) For the purposes of this section a subsequent disclosure may be regarded as a disclosure of substantially the same information as that disclosed by a previous disclosure as mentioned in subsection (2)(c) even though the subsequent disclosure extends to information about action taken or not taken by any person as a result of the previous disclosure.]

[1057]

NOTES

Inserted as noted to s 43A at **[1051]**.

[43H Disclosure of exceptionally serious failure

(1) A qualifying disclosure is made in accordance with this section if—
- (a) the worker makes the disclosure in good faith,
- (b) he reasonably believes that the information disclosed, and any allegation contained in it, are substantially true,
- (c) he does not make the disclosure for purposes of personal gain,
- (d) the relevant failure is of an exceptionally serious nature, and
- (e) in all the circumstances of the case, it is reasonable for him to make the disclosure.

(2) In determining for the purposes of subsection (1)(e) whether it is reasonable for the worker to make the disclosure, regard shall be had, in particular, to the identity of the person to whom the disclosure is made.]

[1058]

NOTES

Inserted as noted to s 43A at **[1051]**.

[43J Contractual duties of confidentiality

(1) Any provision in an agreement to which this section applies is void in so far as it purports to preclude the worker from making a protected disclosure.

(2) This section applies to any agreement between a worker and his employer (whether a worker's contract or not), including an agreement to refrain from instituting or continuing any proceedings under this Act or any proceedings for breach of contract.]

[1059]

NOTES

Inserted as noted to s 43A at **[1051]**.

[43K Extension of meaning of "worker" etc for Part IVA

(1) For the purposes of this Part "worker" includes an individual who is not a worker as defined by section 230(3) but who—

(a) works or worked for a person in circumstances in which—

(i) he is or was introduced or supplied to do that work by a third person, and

(ii) the terms on which he is or was engaged to do the work are or were in practice substantially determined not by him but by the person for whom hc works or worked, by the third person or by both of them,

(b) contracts or contracted with a person, for the purposes of that person's business, for the execution of work to be done in a place not under the control or management of that person and would fall within section 230(3)(b) if for "personally" in that provision there were substituted "(whether personally or otherwise)",

[(ba) works or worked as a person performing services under a contract entered into by him with a Primary Care Trust [under section 84 or 100 of the National Health Service Act 2006 or with a Local Health Board under section 42 or 57 of the National Health Service (Wales) Act 2006] [or with a Primary Care Trust under section 117 of that Act],]

[(bb) works or worked as a person performing services under a contract entered into by him with a Health Board under section 17J of the National Health Service (Scotland) Act 1978,]

(c) works or worked as a person providing ... general dental services, general ophthalmic services or pharmaceutical services in accordance with arrangements made—

(i) by a [Primary Care Trust [under section 126 of the National Health Service Act 2006,] or] [Local Health Board] under [section 71 or 80 of the National Health Service (Wales) Act 2006], or

(ii) by a Health Board under section ... 25, *26 or 27* of the National Health Service (Scotland) Act 1978, or

[(ca) works or worked as a person performing services under a contract entered into by him with a Health Board under section 17Q of the National Health Service (Scotland) Act 1978,]

(d) is or was provided with work experience provided pursuant to a training course or programme or with training for employment (or with both) otherwise than—

(i) under a contract of employment, or

(ii) by an educational establishment on a course run by that establishment;

and any reference to a worker's contract, to employment or to a worker being "employed" shall be construed accordingly.

(2) For the purposes of this Part "employer" includes—

(a) in relation to a worker falling within paragraph (a) of subsection (1), the person who substantially determines or determined the terms on which he is or was engaged, [(aa) in relation to a worker falling within paragraph (ba) of that subsection, the Primary Care Trust or Local Health Board referred to in that paragraph,]

[(ab) in relation to a worker falling within paragraph (bb) of that subsection, the Health Board referred to in that paragraph,]

(b) in relation to a worker falling within paragraph (c) of that subsection, the authority or board referred to in that paragraph, and

[(ba) in relation to a worker falling within paragraph (ca) of that subsection, the Health Board referred to in that paragraph, and]

(c) in relation to a worker falling within paragraph (d) of that subsection, the person providing the work experience or training.

(3) In this section "educational establishment" includes any university, college, school or other educational establishment.]

[1060]

NOTES

Inserted as noted to s 43A at **[1051]**.

Sub-s (1) is amended as follows:

Para (ba) inserted by the Health and Social Care (Community Health and Standards) Act 2003, s 184, Sch 11, para 65(1), (2), as from 1 April 2004.

Words in first pair of square brackets in para (ba) substituted by the National Health Service (Consequential Provisions) Act 2006, s 2, Sch 1, paras 177, 178(a), as from 1 March 2007.

Words in second pair of square brackets in para (ba) inserted by the Health Act 2006, s 80(1), Sch 8, para 37 (as amended by the National Health Service (Consequential Provisions) Act 2006, s 2, Sch 1, paras 281, 294), as from a day to be appointed.

Para (bb) inserted, and first words omitted from para (c) and the figure omitted from para (c)(ii) repealed, by the Primary Medical Services (Scotland) Act 2004 (Consequential Modifications) Order 2004, SI 2004/957, art 2, Schedule, para 8(a), as from 1 April 2004.

Words in first (outer) pair of square brackets in para (c)(i) inserted by the National Health Service Reform and Health Care Professions Act 2002, s 2(5), Sch 2, Pt 2, para 63.

Words in second (inner) pair of square brackets in para (c)(i) inserted, and words in final pair of square brackets on that paragraph substituted, by the National Health Service (Consequential Provisions) Act 2006, s 2, Sch 1, paras 177, 178(b), as from 1 March 2007.

Words in third pair of square brackets in para (c)(i) substituted by the References to Health Authorities Order 2007, SI 2007/961, art 3, Schedule, para 27(1), (2), as from 1 April 2007.

For the words in italics in para (c)(ii) there are substituted the words "or 26", and para (ca) is inserted, by the Smoking, Health and Social Care (Scotland) Act 2005 (Consequential Modifications) (England, Wales and Northern Ireland) Order 2006, SI 2006/1056, art 2, Schedule, Pt 1, para 7(a), as from a day to be appointed.

Sub-s (2): para (aa) inserted by the Health and Social Care (Community Health and Standards) Act 2003, s 184, Sch 11, para 65(1), (3), as from 1 April 2004; para (ab) inserted by SI 2004/957, art 2, Schedule, para 8(b), as from 1 April 2004; para (ba) inserted by SI 2006/1056, art 2, Schedule, Pt 1, para 7(b), as from a day to be appointed.

Transitional provisions and miscellaneous:

The General Medical Services and Personal Medical Services Transitional and Consequential Provisions Order 2004, SI 2004/865, art 109(1), (2)(d), and the General Medical Services Transitional and Consequential Provisions (Wales) (No 2) Order 2004, SI 2004/1016, art 85(1), (2)(d) (both made under the Health and Social Care (Community Health and Standards) Act 2003, ss 176, 195(1), 200, 201) provide that until such time as default contracts entered into pursuant s 176(3) of the 2003 Act cease to exist, any reference to a general medical services contract or to a contract under the National Health Service Act 1977, s 28Q shall include a reference to a default contract.

[43KA Application of this Part and related provisions to police

(1) For the purposes of—

(a) this Part,

(b) section 47B and sections 48 and 49 so far as relating to that section, and

(c) section 103A and the other provisions of Part 10 so far as relating to the right not to be unfairly dismissed in a case where the dismissal is unfair by virtue of section 103A,

a person who holds, otherwise than under a contract of employment, the office of constable or an appointment as a police cadet shall be treated as an employee employed by the relevant officer under a contract of employment; and any reference to a worker being "employed" and to his "employer" shall be construed accordingly.

(2) In this section "the relevant officer" means—

(a) in relation to a member of a police force or a special constable appointed for a police area, the chief officer of police;

[(b) in relation to a member of a police force seconded to the Serious Organised Crime Agency to serve as a member of its staff, that Agency; and]

(d) in relation to any other person holding the office of constable or an appointment as police cadet, the person who has the direction and control of the body of constables or cadets in question.]

[1061]

NOTES

Commencement: 1 April 2004.

Inserted by the Police Reform Act 2002, s 37(1), as from 1 April 2004.

Sub-s (2): para (b) substituted, for original paras (b), (c), by the Serious Organised Crime and Police Act 2005, s 59, Sch 4, paras 84, 85, as from 1 April 2006.

[43L Other interpretative provisions

(1) In this Part—

"qualifying disclosure" has the meaning given by section 43B;

"the relevant failure", in relation to a qualifying disclosure, has the meaning given by section 43B(5).

(2) In determining for the purposes of this Part whether a person makes a disclosure for purposes of personal gain, there shall be disregarded any reward payable by or under any enactment.

(3) Any reference in this Part to the disclosure of information shall have effect, in relation to any case where the person receiving the information is already aware of it, as a reference to bringing the information to his attention.]

[1062]

NOTES

Inserted as noted to s 43A at **[1051]**.

PART V
PROTECTION FROM SUFFERING DETRIMENT IN EMPLOYMENT

NOTES

Conciliation: employment tribunal proceedings and claims which could be the subject of employment tribunal proceedings under this Part are proceedings to which the Employment Tribunals Act 1996, s 18 applies; see s 18(1)(d) of that Act at **[975]**. The standard conciliation period applies to such proceedings, except those brought under s 47B (for which there is no fixed conciliation period) by virtue of the Employment Tribunals (Constitution and Rules of Procedure) Regulations 2004, SI 2004/1861, Sch 1, rule 22(1), (5).

Rights not to suffer detriment

[43M Jury service

(1) An employee has the right not to be subjected to any detriment by any act, or any deliberate failure to act, by his employer on the ground that the employee—

(a) has been summoned under the Juries Act 1974, the Coroners Act 1988, the Court of Session Act 1988 or the Criminal Procedure (Scotland) Act 1995 to attend for service as a juror, or

(b) has been absent from work because he attended at any place in pursuance of being so summoned.

(2) This section does not apply where the detriment in question amounts to dismissal within the meaning of Part 10.

(3) For the purposes of this section, an employee is not to be regarded as having been subjected to a detriment by a failure to pay remuneration in respect of a relevant period unless under his contract of employment he is entitled to be paid that remuneration.

(4) In subsection (3) "a relevant period" means any period during which the employee is absent from work because of his attendance at any place in pursuance of being summoned as mentioned in subsection (1)(a).]

[1062A]

NOTES

Commencement: 6 April 2005.

Inserted by the Employment Relations Act 2004, s 40(1), as from 6 April 2005, except in relation to cases of detriment where the act or deliberate failure to act is before that date (see SI 2005/872, art 13).

44 Health and safety cases

(1) An employee has the right not to be subjected to any detriment by any act, or any deliberate failure to act, by his employer done on the ground that—

(a) having been designated by the employer to carry out activities in connection with preventing or reducing risks to health and safety at work, the employee carried out (or proposed to carry out) any such activities,

(b) being a representative of workers on matters of health and safety at work or member of a safety committee—

(i) in accordance with arrangements established under or by virtue of any enactment, or

(ii) by reason of being acknowledged as such by the employer,

the employee performed (or proposed to perform) any functions as such a representative or a member of such committee,

[(ba) the employee took part (or proposed to take part) in consultation with the employer pursuant to the Health and Safety (Consultation with Employees) Regulations 1996 or in an election of representatives of employee safety within the meaning of those Regulations (whether as a candidate or otherwise),]

(c) being an employee at a place where—

(i) there was no such representative or safety committee, or

(ii) there was such a representative or safety committee but it was not reasonably practicable for the employee to raise the matter by those means,

he brought to his employer's attention, by reasonable means, circumstances connected with his work which he reasonably believed were harmful or potentially harmful to health or safety,

(d) in circumstances of danger which the employee reasonable believed to be serious and imminent and which he could no reasonably have been expected to avert, he left (or proposed to leave) or (while the danger persisted) refused to return to his place of work or any dangerous part of his place of work, or

(e) in circumstances of danger which the employee reasonably believed to be serious and imminent, he took (or proposed to take) appropriate steps to protect himself or other persons from the danger.

(2) For the purposes of subsection (1)(e) whether steps which employee took (or proposed to take) were appropriate is to be judged by reference to all the circumstances including, in particular, his knowledge and the facilities and advice available to him at the time.

(3) An employee is not to be regarded as having been subjected to a detriment on the ground specified in subsection (1)(e) if the employer shows that it was (or would have been) so negligent for the employee to take the steps which he took (or proposed to take) that a reasonable employer might have treated him as the employer did.

(4) … this section does not apply where the detriment in question amounts to dismissal (within the meaning of [Part X]).

[1063]

NOTES

Sub-s (1): para (ba) inserted by the Health and Safety (Consultation with Employees) Regulations 1996, SI 1996/1513, reg 8.

Sub-s (4): words omitted repealed, and words in square brackets substituted, by the Employment Relations Act 1999, ss 18(2), 44, Sch 9(3).

45 Sunday working for shop and betting workers

(1) An employee who is—

(a) a protected shop worker or an opted-out shop worker, or

(b) a protected betting worker or an opted-out betting worker, has the right not to be subjected to any detriment by any act, or any deliberate failure to act, by his employer done on the ground that he employee refused (or proposed to refuse) to do shop work, or betting work, on Sunday or on a particular Sunday.

(2) Subsection (1) does not apply to anything done in relation to an opted-out shop worker or an opted-out betting worker on the ground that he refused (or proposed to refuse) to do shop work, or betting work, on any Sunday or Sundays falling before the end of the notice period.

(3) An employee who is a shop worker or a betting worker has the right not to be subjected to any detriment by any act, or any deliberate failure to act, by his employer done on the ground that the employee gave (or proposed to give) an opting-out notice to his employer.

(4) Subsections (1) and (3) do not apply where the detriment in question amounts to dismissal (within the meaning of Part X).

(5) For the purposes of this section a shop worker or betting worker who does not work on Sunday or on a particular Sunday is not to be regarded as having been subjected to any detriment by—

(a) a failure to pay remuneration in respect of shop work, or betting work, on a Sunday which he has not done,

(b) a failure to provide him with any other benefit, where that failure results from the application (in relation to a Sunday on which the employee has not done shop work, or betting work) of a contractual term under which the extent of that benefit varies according to the number of hours worked by the employee or the remuneration of the employee, or

(c) a failure to provide him with any work, remuneration or other benefit which by virtue of section 38 or 39 the employer is not obliged to provide.

(6) Where an employer offers to pay a sum specified in the offer to any or more employees

(a) who are protected shop workers or opted-out shop workers or protected betting workers or opted-out betting workers, or

(b) who under their contracts of employment are not obliged to do shop work, or betting work, on Sunday,

if they agree to do shop work, or betting work, on Sunday or on a particular Sunday subsections (7) and (8) apply.

(7) An employee to whom the offer is not made is not to be regarded for the purposes of this section as having been subjected to any detriment by any failure to make the offer to him or to pay him the sum specified in the offer.

(8) An employee who does not accept the offer is not to be regarded for the purposes of this section as having been subjected to any detriment by any failure to pay him the sum specified in the offer.

(9) For the purposes of section 36(2)(b) or 41(1)(b), the appropriate date in relation to this section is the date of the act or failure to act.

(10) For the purposes of subsection (9)—

(a) where an act extends over a period, the "date of the act" means the first day of that period, and

(b) a deliberate failure to act shall be treated as done when it was decided on;

and, in the absence of evidence establishing the contrary, an employee shall be taken to decide on a failure to act when he does an act inconsistent with doing the failed act or, if he has done no such inconsistent act, when the period expires within which he might reasonably have been expected to do the failed act if it was to be done.

[1064]

[45A Working time cases

(1) A worker has the right not to be subjected to any detriment by any act, or any deliberate failure to act, by his employer done on the ground that the worker—

(a) refused (or proposed to refuse) to comply with a requirement which the employer imposed (or proposed to impose) in contravention of the Working Time Regulations 1998,

(b) refused (or proposed to refuse) to forgo a right conferred on him by those Regulations,

(c) failed to sign a workforce agreement for the purposes of those Regulations, or to enter into, or agree to vary or extend, any other agreement with his employer which is provided for in those Regulations,

(d) being—

(i) a representative of members of the workforce for the purposes of Schedule 1 to those Regulations, or

(ii) a candidate in an election in which any person elected will, on being elected, be such a representative,

performed (or proposed to perform) any functions or activities as such a representative or candidate,

(e) brought proceedings against the employer to enforce a right conferred on him by those Regulations, or

(f) alleged that the employer had infringed such a right.

(2) It is immaterial for the purposes of subsection (1)(e) or (f)—

(a) whether or not the worker has the right, or

(b) whether or not the right has been infringed,

but, for those provisions to apply, the claim to the right and that it has been infringed must be made in good faith.

(3) It is sufficient for subsection (1)(f) to apply that the worker, without specifying the right, made it reasonably clear to the employer what the right claimed to have been infringed was.

(4) This section does not apply where a worker is an employee and the detriment in question amounts to dismissal within the meaning of Part X …]

[(5) A reference in this section to the Working Time Regulations 1998 includes a reference to—

[(a)] the Merchant Shipping (Working Time: Inland Waterways) Regulations 2003;

[(b) the Fishing Vessels (Working Time: Sea-fishermen) Regulations 2004].]

[1065]

NOTES

Inserted by the Working Time Regulations 1998, SI 1998/1833, regs 2(1), 31(1).

Sub-s (4): words omitted repealed by the Employment Relations Act 1999, ss 18(3), 44, Sch 9(3).

Sub-s (5): added by the Merchant Shipping (Working Time: Inland Waterways) Regulations 2003, SI 2003/3049, reg 20, Sch 2, para 3(1), (2), as from 24 December 2003; the letter "(a)" and para (b) inserted by the Fishing Vessels (Working Time: Sea-fishermen) Regulations 2004, SI 2004/1713, reg 21, Sch 2, para 2(1), (2)(b), as from 16 August 2004.

46 Trustees of occupational pension schemes

(1) An employee has the right not to be subjected to any detriment by any act, or any deliberate failure to act, by his employer done on the ground that, being a trustee of a relevant occupational pension scheme which relates to his employment, the employee performed (or propose to perform) any functions as such a trustee.

(2) … this section does not apply where the detriment in question amounts to dismissal (within the meaning of [Part X]).

[(2A) This section applies to an employee who is a director of a company which is a trustee of a relevant occupational pension scheme as it applies to an employee who is a trustee of such a scheme (references to such a trustee being read for this purpose as references to such a director).]

(3) In this section "relevant occupational pension scheme" means an occupational pension scheme (as defined in section 1 of the Pension Schemes Act 1993) established under a trust.

[1066]

NOTES

Sub-s (2): words omitted repealed, and words in square brackets substituted, by the Employment Relations Act 1999, ss 18(2), 44, Sch 9(3).

Sub-s (2A): inserted by the Welfare Reform and Pensions Act 1999, s 18, Sch 2, para 19(1), (2).

By s 6(1) of the Welfare Reform and Pensions Act 1999, this section applies to an employee who is (or is a director of a company which is) a trustee of a scheme designated by his employer under s 3(2) of that Act as it applies to employees who are trustees, or directors of companies which are trustees of a relevant occupational pension scheme.

47 Employee representatives

(1) An employee has the right not to be subjected to any detriment by any act, or any deliberate failure to act, by his employer done on the ground that, being—

(a) an employee representative for the purposes of Chapter II of Part IV of the Trade Union and Labour Relation (Consolidation) Act 1992 (redundancies) or [regulations 9, 13 and 15 of the Transfer of Undertakings (Protection of Employment) Regulations 2006], or

(b) a candidate in an election in which any person elected will, on being elected, be such an employee representative,

he performed (or proposed to perform) any functions or activities as such an employee representative or candidate.

[(1A) An employee has the right not to be subjected to any detriment by any act, or by any deliberate failure to act, by his employer done on the ground of his participation in an election of employee representatives for the purposes of Chapter II of Part IV of the Trade Union and Labour Relations (Consolidation) Act 1992 (redundancies) or [regulations 9, 13 and 15 of the Transfer of Undertakings (Protection of Employment) Regulations 2006].]

(2) … this section does not apply where the detriment in question amounts to dismissal (within the meaning of [Part X]).

[1067]

NOTES

Sub-s (1): words in square brackets in para (a) substituted by the Transfer of Undertakings (Protection of Employment) Regulations 2006, SI 2006/246, reg 20, Sch 2, para 10, as from 6 April 2006 (for transitional provisions in relation to a relevant transfer, etc, that took place before that date, see reg 21 of the 2006 Regulations at **[3395]**).

Sub-s (1A): inserted by the Collective Redundancies and Transfer of Undertakings (Protection of Employment) (Amendment) Regulations 1999, SI 1999/1925, reg 12; words in square brackets substituted by SI 2006/246, reg 20, Sch 2, para 10, as from 6 April 2006 (for transitional provisions in relation to a relevant transfer, etc, that took place before that date, see reg 21 of the 2006 Regulations at **[3395]**).

Sub-s (2): words omitted repealed, and words in square brackets substituted, by the Employment Relations Act 1999, ss 18(2), 44, Sch 9(3).

[47A Employees exercising the right to time off work for study or training

(1) An employee has the right not to be subjected to any detriment by any act, or any deliberate failure to act, by his employer or the principal (within the meaning of section 63A(3)) done on the ground that, being a person entitled to—

(a) time off under section 63A(1) or (3), and

(b) remuneration under section 63B(1) in respect of that time taken off,

the employee exercised (or proposed to exercise) that right or received (or sought to receive) such remuneration.

(2) … this section does not apply where the detriment in question amounts to dismissal (within the meaning of [Part X]).]

[1068]

NOTES

Inserted by the Teaching and Higher Education Act 1998, s 44(1), Sch 3, para 10.

Sub-s (2): words omitted repealed, and words in square brackets substituted, by the Employment Relations Act 1999, ss 18(2), 44, Sch 9(3).

[47B Protected disclosures

(1) A worker has the right not to be subjected to any detriment by any act, or any deliberate failure to act, by his employer done on the ground that the worker has made a protected disclosure.

(2) … this section does not apply where—

(a) the worker is an employee, and
(b) the detriment in question amounts to dismissal (within the meaning of [Part X]).

(3) For the purposes of this section, and of sections 48 and 49 so far as relating to this section, "worker", "worker's contract", "employment" and "employer" have the extended meaning given by section 43K.]

[1069]

NOTES

Inserted by the Public Interest Disclosure Act 1998, ss 2, 18(2).

Sub-s (2): words omitted repealed, and words in square brackets substituted, by the Employment Relations Act 1999, ss 18(2), Sch 9(3).

[47C Leave for family and domestic reasons

(1) An employee has the right not to be subjected to any detriment by any act, or any deliberate failure to act, by his employer done for a prescribed reason.

(2) A prescribed reason is one which is prescribed by regulations made by the Secretary of State and which relates to—
(a) pregnancy, childbirth or maternity,
(b) ordinary, compulsory or additional maternity leave,
[(ba) ordinary or additional adoption leave,]
(c) parental leave,
[(ca) paternity leave, or]
(d) time off under section 57A.

(3) A reason prescribed under this section in relation to parental leave may relate to action which an employee takes, agrees to take or refuses to take under or in respect of a collective or workforce agreement.

(4) Regulations under this section may make different provision for different cases or circumstances.]

[1070]

NOTES

Inserted by the Employment Relations Act 1999, s 9, Sch 4, Pt III, paras 1, 5, 8.

Sub-s (2): para (ba) inserted, and para (ca) substituted for the original word "or" at the end of para (c), by the Employment Act 2002, s 53, Sch 7, paras 24, 26; para (ca) further substituted by the Work and Families Act 2006, s 11(1), Sch 1, para 30, as from a day to be appointed, as follows—

"(ca) ordinary or additional paternity leave, or".

Regulations: the Maternity and Parental Leave etc Regulations 1999, SI 1999/3312 at **[2553]**; the Paternity and Adoption Leave Regulations 2002, SI 2002/2788 at **[2752]**; the Paternity and Adoption Leave (Adoptions from Overseas) Regulations 2003, SI 2003/921.

[47D Tax credits

(1) An employee has the right not to be subjected to any detriment by any act, or any deliberate failure to act, by his employer, done on the ground that—
(a) any action was taken, or was proposed to be taken, by or on behalf of the employee with a view to enforcing, or otherwise securing the benefit of, a right conferred on the employee by regulations under section 25 of the Tax Credits Act 2002,
(b) a penalty was imposed on the employer, or proceedings for a penalty were brought against him, under that Act, as a result of action taken by or on behalf of the employee for the purpose of enforcing, or otherwise securing the benefit of, such a right, or
(c) the employee is entitled, or will or may be entitled, to working tax credit.

(2) It is immaterial for the purposes of subsection (1)(a) or (b)—
(a) whether or not the employee has the right, or
(b) whether or not the right has been infringed,

but, for those provisions to apply, the claim to the right and (if applicable) the claim that it has been infringed must be made in good faith.

(3) Subsections (1) and (2) apply to a person who is not an employee within the meaning of this Act but who is an employee within the meaning of section 25 of the Tax Credits

Act 2002, with references to his employer in those subsections (and sections 48(2) and (4) and 49(1)) being construed in accordance with that section.

(4) Subsections (1) and (2) do not apply to an employee if the detriment in question amounts to dismissal (within the meaning of Part 10).]

[1071]

NOTES

Inserted by the Tax Credits Act 2002, s 27, Sch 1, paras 1(1), (2).

[47E Flexible working

(1) An employee has the right not to be subjected to any detriment by any act, or any deliberate failure to act, by his employer done on the ground that the employee—

- (a) made (or proposed to make) an application under section 80F,
- (b) exercised (or proposed to exercise) a right conferred on him under section 80G,
- (c) brought proceedings against the employer under section 80H, or
- (d) alleged the existence of any circumstance which would constitute a ground for bringing such proceedings.

(2) This section does not apply where the detriment in question amounts to dismissal within the meaning of Part 10.]

[1072]

NOTES

Inserted by the Employment Act 2002, s 47(1), (3), with effect only in relation to an act or failure to act which takes place on or after 6 April 2003 (see SI 2002/2866, Sch 3, para 7).

Note: in the Queen's Printer's copy of the Employment Act 2002, this section was originally numbered as s 47D. In a correction slip, issued in December 2002, the section number was changed to s 47E to take account of the fact that a s 47D had already been inserted by the Tax Credits Act 2002.

Enforcement

48 Complaints to [employment tribunals]

(1) An employee may present a complaint to an [employment tribunal] that he has been subjected to a detriment in contravention of section [43M,] 44, 45, [46, 47[, 47A[, 47C or [47E]]]].

[(1ZA) A worker may present a complaint to an employment tribunal that he has been subjected to a detriment in contravention of section 45A.]

[(1A) A worker may present a complaint to an employment tribunal that he has been subjected to a detriment in contravention of section 47B.]

[(1B) A person may present a complaint to an employment tribunal that he has been subjected to a detriment in contravention of section 47D.]

(2) On such a complaint it is for the employer to show the ground on which any act, or deliberate failure to act, was done.

(3) An [employment tribunal] shall not consider a complaint under this section unless it is presented—

- (a) before the end of the period of three months beginning with the date of the act or failure to act to which the complaint relates or, where that act or failure is part of a series of similar acts or failures, the last of them, or
- (b) within such further period as the tribunal considers reasonable in a case where it is satisfied that it was not reasonably practicable for the complaint to be presented before the end of that period of three months.

(4) For the purposes of subsection (3)—

- (a) where an act extends over a period, the "date of the act" means the last day of that period, and
- (b) a deliberate failure to act shall be treated as done when it was decided on;

and, in the absence of evidence establishing the contrary, an employer shall be taken to decide on a failure to act when he does an act inconsistent with doing the failed act or, if he has done no such inconsistent act, when the period expires within which he might reasonably have been expected do the failed act if it was to be done.

[(5) In this section and section 49 any reference to the employer includes, where a person complains that he has been subjected to a detriment in contravention of section 47A, the principal (within the meaning of section 63A(3)).]

[1073]

NOTES

Section heading, sub-s (3): words in square brackets substituted by the Employment Rights (Dispute Resolution) Act 1998, s 1(2)(a), (b).

Sub-s (1) is amended as follows:

Words in first pair of square brackets substituted by the Employment Rights (Dispute Resolution) Act 1998, s 1(2)(a).

Figure "43M," in square brackets inserted by the Employment Relations Act 2004, s 40(2), as from 6 April 2005, except in relation to cases of detriment where the act or deliberate failure to act is before that date (see SI 2005/872, art 13).

Figures "46, 47" in square brackets substituted by the Teaching and Higher Education Act 1998, s 44(1), Sch 3, para 11(a).

Figure ", 47A" in square brackets substituted by the Employment Relations Act 1999, s 9, Sch 4, Pt III, paras 5, 9.

Words in square brackets beginning ", 47C or" substituted by the Employment Act 2002, s 53, Sch 7, paras 24, 27.

Figure "47E" in square brackets substituted by the Employment Relations Act 2004, s 41(3), as from 6 April 2005, except in relation to cases of detriment where the act or deliberate failure to act is before that date (see SI 2005/872, art 13).

Sub-s (1ZA): inserted by the Working Time Regulations 1998, SI 1998/1833, regs 2(1), 31(2).

Sub-s (1A): inserted by the Public Interest Disclosure Act 1998, ss 3, 18(2).

Sub-s (1B): inserted by the Tax Credits Act 2002, s 27, Sch 1, para 1(1), (3).

Sub-s (5): added by the Teaching and Higher Education Act 1998, s 44(1), Sch 3, para 11(b).

Conciliation: employment tribunal proceedings under this section in respect of a breach of any of the sections listed in sub-ss (1)–(1B) above and claims which could be the subject of such proceedings are proceedings to which the Employment Tribunals Act 1996, s 18 applies; see s 18(1)(d) of that Act at **[975]**. The standard conciliation period applies to such proceedings, except those brought under s 47B (for which there is no fixed conciliation period) by virtue of the Employment Tribunals (Constitution and Rules of Procedure) Regulations 2004, SI 2004/1861, Sch 1, rule 22(1), (5).

Tribunal jurisdiction: the Employment Act 2002, ss 31, 32, 38, at **[1493]**, **[1494]**, **[1496]** apply to proceedings before the employment tribunal relating to a claim under this section; see ss 31(1), 32(1), 38(1) of, and Schs 3–5 to, the 2002 Act at **[1508]–[1510]**.

For the circumstances in which the normal time limit for presenting a complaint under this section is extended for a period of three months, see the Employment Act 2002 (Dispute Resolution) Regulations 2004, SI 2004/752, regs 15 and 18 at **[3096]** and **[3098]**.

49 Remedies

(1) Where an [employment tribunal] finds a complaint under section 48 well-founded, the tribunal—

(a) shall make a declaration to that effect, and

(b) may make an award of compensation to be paid by the employer to the complainant in respect of the act or failure to act to which the complaint relates.

(2) [Subject to [subsections (5A) and (6)]] The amount of the compensation awarded shall be such as the tribunal considers just and equitable in all the circumstances having regard to—

(a) the infringement to which the complaint relates, and

(b) any loss which is attributable to the act, or failure to act, which infringed the complainant's right.

(3) The loss shall be taken to include—

(a) any expenses reasonably incurred by the complainant in consequence of the act, or failure to act, to which the complaint relates, and

(b) loss of any benefit which he might reasonably be expected to have had but for that act or failure to act.

(4) In ascertaining the loss the tribunal shall apply the same rule concerning the duty of a person to mitigate his loss as applies to damages recoverable under the common law of England and Wales or (as the case may be) Scotland.

(5) Where the tribunal finds that the act, or failure to act, to which the complaint relates was to any extent caused or contributed to by action of the complainant, it shall reduce the amount of the compensation by such proportion as it considers just and equitable having regard to that finding.

[(5A) Where—

(a) the complaint is made under section 48 (1ZA),

(b) the detriment to which the worker is subjected is the termination of his worker's contract, and

(c) that contract is not a contract of employment,

any compensation must not exceed the compensation that would be payable under Chapter II of Part X if the worker had been an employee and had been dismissed for the reason specified in section 101A.]

[(6) Where—

(a) the complaint is made under section 48(1A),

(b) the detriment to which the worker is subjected is the termination of his worker's contract, and

(c) that contract is not a contract of employment,

any compensation must not exceed the compensation that would be payable under Chapter II of Part X if the worker had been an employee and had been dismissed for the reason specified in section 103A.]

[(7) Where—

(a) the complaint is made under section 48(1B) by a person who is not an employee, and

(b) the detriment to which he is subjected is the termination of his contract with the person who is his employer for the purposes of section 25 of the Tax Credits Act 2002,

any compensation must not exceed the compensation that would be payable under Chapter 2 of Part 10 if the complainant had been an employee and had been dismissed for the reason specified in section 104B.]

[1074]

NOTES

Sub-s (1): words in square brackets substituted by the Employment Rights (Dispute Resolution) Act 1998, s 1(2)(a).

Sub-s (2): words in first (outer) pair of square brackets inserted by the Public Interest Disclosure Act 1998, ss 4(1), (2), 18(2); words in second (inner) pair of square brackets substituted by the Working Time Regulations 1998, SI 1998/1833, regs 2(1), 31(3)(a).

Sub-s (5A): inserted by the Working Time Regulations 1998, SI 1998/1833, regs 2(1), 31(3)(b).

Sub-s (6): added by the Public Interest Disclosure Act 1998, ss 4(1), (3), 18(2).

Sub-s (7): added by the Tax Credits Act 2002, s 27, Sch 1, para 1(1), (4).

[Application to police of rights relating to health and safety

49A Application to police of section 44 and related provisions

(1) For the purposes of section 44, and of sections 48 and 49 so far as relating to that section, the holding, otherwise than under a contract of employment, of the office of constable or an appointment as police cadet shall be treated as employment by the relevant officer under a contract of employment.

[(2) In this section "the relevant officer", in relation to—

(a) a person holding the office of constable, or

(b) a person holding an appointment as a police cadet,

means the person who under section 51A of the Health and Safety at Work etc Act 1974 is to be treated as his employer for the purposes of Part 1 of that Act.]

[1075]

NOTES

Inserted by the Police (Health and Safety) Act 1997, s 3.

Sub-s (2): substituted by the Serious Organised Crime and Police Act 2005, s 158(1), (2)(a), (3), (5), as from 7 April 2005, with effect for the purposes of any proceedings in or before a court or tribunal that are commenced on or after that date as if this substitution had come into force on 1 July 1998.

Note: this section was amended by the Police Reform Act 2002, s 95, as from a day to be appointed. Those amendments lapsed following the repeal of that section without being brought into force, by the Serious Organised Crime and Police Act 2005, ss 158(4)(a), 174(2), Sch 17, Pt 1, as from 7 April 2005.

PART VI
TIME OFF WORK

NOTES

Conciliation: employment tribunal proceedings and claims which could be the subject of employment tribunal proceedings under this Part are proceedings to which the Employment Tribunals Act 1996, s 18 applies; see s 18(1)(d) of that Act at **[975]**. By virtue of the Employment Tribunals (Constitution and Rules of Procedure) Regulations 2004, SI 2004/1861, Sch 1, rule 22(1), (5), (6), the short conciliation period applies to all such proceedings brought under ss 51, 54 and 57; proceedings under ss 57B, 60, 63 and 63C are subject to the standard conciliation period.

Public duties

50 Right to time off for public duties

(1) An employer shall permit an employee of his who is a justice of the peace to take time off during the employee's working hours for the purpose of performing any of the duties of his office.

(2) An employer shall permit an employee of his who is a member of—

(a) a local authority,
(b) a statutory tribunal,
[(c) a police authority established under section 3 of the Police Act 1996 or the Metropolitan Police Authority,]
[(ca) …]
(d) [an independent monitoring board for a prison] or a prison visiting committee,
(e) a relevant health body,
(f) a relevant education body, …
(g) the Environment Agency or the Scottish Environment Protection Agency, [or
[(h) Scottish Water or a Water Customer Consultation Panel,]]

to take time off during the employee's working hours for the purposes specified in subsection (3).

(3) The purposes referred to in subsection (2) are—

(a) attendance at a meeting of the body or any of its committees or sub-committees, and
(b) the doing of any other thing approved by the body, or anything of a class so approved, for the purpose of the discharge of the functions of the body or of any of its committees or sub-committees[, and
(c) in the case of a local authority which are operating executive arrangements—
 (i) attendance at a meeting of the executive of that local authority or committee of that executive; and
 (ii) the doing of any other thing, by an individual member of that executive, for the purposes of the discharge of any function which is to any extent the responsibility of that executive.]

(4) The amount of time off which an employee is to be permitted to take under this section, and the occasions on which and any condition subject to which time off may be so taken, are those that are reasonable in all the circumstances having regard, in particular, to—

(a) how much time off is required for the performance of the duties of the office or as a member of the body in question, and how much time off is required for the performance of the particular duty,
(b) how much time off the employee has already been permitted under this section or sections 168 and 170 of the Trade Union and Labour Relations (Consolidation) Act 1992 (time off trade union duties and activities), and
(c) the circumstances of the employer's business and the effect of the employee's absence on the running of that business.

(5) In subsection (2)(a) "a local authority" means—

(a) a local authority within the meaning of the Local Government Act 1972,

(b) a council constituted under section 2 of the Local Government etc (Scotland) Act 1994,
(c) the Common Council of the City of London,
(d) a National Park authority, or
(e) the Broads Authority.

(6) …

(7) In subsection (2)(d)—
(a) ["independent monitoring board" means a board] appointed under section 6(2) of the Prison Act 1952, and
(b) "a prison visiting committee" means a visiting committee appointed under section 19(3) of the Prisons (Scotland) Act 1989 or constituted by virtue of rules made under section 39 (as read with section 8(1)) of that Act.

(8) In subsection (2)(e) "a relevant health body" means—
(a) a National Health Service trust established under [section 25 of the National Health Service Act 2006, section 18 of the National Health Service (Wales) Act 2006] or the National Health Service (Scotland) Act 1978,
[(ab) an NHS foundation trust,]
(b) a [Strategic Health Authority established under section 13 of the National Health Service Act 2006, a] [Local Health Board established under section 11 of the National Health Service (Wales) Act 2006] … [, a Special Health Authority established under [section 28 of the National Health Service Act 2006 or section 22 of the National Health Service (Wales) Act 2006] or a Primary Care Trust established under] [section 18 of the National Health Service Act 2006], or
(c) a Health Board constituted under section 2 of the National Health Service (Scotland) Act 1978.

(9) In subsection (2)(f) "a relevant education body" means—
(a) a managing or governing body of an educational establishment maintained by a local education authority,
(b) a governing body of a … further education corporation or higher education corporation,
(c) a school council appointed under section 125(1) of the Local Government (Scotland) Act 1973,
[(d) a parent council within the meaning of section 5(2) of the Scottish Schools (Parental Involvement) Act 2006,]
(e) …
(f) a board of management of a college of further education within the meaning of section 36(1) of the Further and Higher Education (Scotland) Act 1992,
(g) a governing body of a central institution within the meaning of section 135(1) of the Education (Scotland) Act 1980, …
(h) a governing body of a designated institution within the meaning of Part II of the Further and Higher Education (Scotland) Act 1992,
[(i) the General Teaching Council for England, or
(j) the General Teaching Council for Wales.]

[(9A) In subsection (3)(c) of this section "executive" and "executive arrangements" have the same meaning as in Part II of the Local Government Act 2000.]

(10) The Secretary of State may by order—
(a) modify the provisions of subsections (1) and (2) and (5) to (9) by adding any office or body, removing any office or body or altering the description of any office or body, or
(b) modify the provisions of subsection (3).

(11) For the purposes of this section the working hours of an employee shall be taken to be any time when, in accordance with his contract of employment, the employee is required to be at work.

[1076]

NOTES

Sub-s (2) is amended as follows:

Para (c) substituted by the Police and Justice Act 2006, s 52, Sch 14, para 31, as from 1 April 2007.

Para (ca) inserted by the Police Act 1997, s 134(1), Sch 9, para 88, and repealed by the Serious Organised Crime and Police Act 2005, ss 59, 174(2), Sch 4, paras 84, 86, Sch 17, Pt 2, as from 1 April 2006.

Words in square brackets in para (d) substituted by the Offender Management Act 2007, s 39, Sch 3, Pt 2, para 8(a), as from 1 November 2007.

Word omitted from para (f) repealed, and para (h) and the word immediately preceding it added, by the Time Off for Public Duties Order 2000, SI 2000/1737, art 2.

Para (h) substituted by the Water Industry (Scotland) Act 2002 (Consequential Modifications) Order 2004, SI 2004/1822, art 2, Schedule, Pt 1, para 18, as from 14 July 2004.

Sub-s (3): para (c) and the word immediately preceding it inserted, in relation to England, by the Local Authorities (Executive and Alternative Arrangements) (Modification of Enactments and Other Provisions) (England) Order 2001, SI 2001/2237, art 30(a), and in relation to Wales, by the Local Authorities (Executive and Alternative Arrangements) (Modification of Enactments and Other Provisions) (Wales) Order 2002, SI 2002/808, arts 2(o), 29(a).

Sub-s (6): repealed by the Police and Justice Act 2006, s 52, Sch 15, Pt 1, as from 1 April 2007. Note that this subsection provided that the reference in sub-s (2) to a member of a police authority is to a person appointed as such a member under Schedule 2 to the Police Act 1996. See also SI 2007/709, art 7 which provides that, notwithstanding the repeal of this subsection, it shall continue to have effect until 31 March 2008.

Sub-s (7): words in square brackets in para (a) substituted by the Offender Management Act 2007, s 39, Sch 3, Pt 2, para 8(b), as from 1 November 2007.

Sub-s (8) is amended as follows:

Words in square brackets in para (a) substituted by the National Health Service (Consequential Provisions) Act 2006, s 2, Sch 1, paras 177, 179(a), as from 1 March 2007.

Para (ab) inserted by the Health and Social Care (Community Health and Standards) Act 2003, s 34, Sch 4, paras 99, 100, as from 1 April 2004.

Words in first, fourth (inner), and fifth pairs of square brackets in para (b) substituted, and words omitted from that paragraph repealed, by the National Health Service (Consequential Provisions) Act 2006, s 2, Sch 1, paras 177, 179(b), as from 1 March 2007; words in second pair of square brackets in para (b) substituted by the References to Health Authorities Order 2007, SI 2007/961, art 3, Schedule, para 27(1), (3), as from 1 April 2007; words in third (outer) pair of square brackets in para (b) substituted by the Health Act 1999 (Supplementary, Consequential etc Provisions) Order 2000, SI 2000/90, art 3(1), Sch 1, para 30(1), (2).

Sub-s (9): words omitted from para (b) repealed by the School Standards and Framework Act 1998, s 140(3), Sch 31; para (d) substituted by the Time Off for Public Duties (Parent Councils) Order 2007, SI 2007/1837, art 2, as from 1 August 2007; para (e) repealed by the Standards in Scotland's Schools etc Act 2000, s 60(2), Sch 3, as from 31 December 2004; word omitted from para (g) repealed, and paras (i), (j) added, by the Time Off for Public Duties (No 2) Order 2000, SI 2000/2463, art 2.

Sub-s (9A): inserted, in relation to England, by SI 2001/2237, art 30(b), as from 11 July 2001, and in relation to Wales, by SI 2002/808, arts 2(o), 29(b).

Local Government (Scotland) Act 1973, s 125: repealed by the Self-Governing Schools etc (Scotland) Act 1989, s 82(2), Sch 11.

Orders: the Time Off for Public Duties Order 2000, SI 2000/1737; the Time Off for Public Duties (No 2) Order 2000, SI 2000/2463; the Time Off for Public Duties (Parent Councils) Order 2007, SI 2007/1837.

51 Complaints to [employment tribunals]

(1) An employee may present a complaint to an [employment tribunal] that his employer has failed to permit him to take time off as required by section 50.

(2) An [employment tribunal] shall not consider a complaint under this section that an employer has failed to permit an employee to take time off unless it is presented—

(a) before the end of the period of three months beginning with the date on which the failure occurred, or

(b) within such further period as the tribunal considers reasonable in a case where it is satisfied that it was not reasonably practicable for the complaint to be presented before the end of that period of three months.

(3) Where an [employment tribunal] finds a complaint under this section well-founded, the tribunal—

(a) shall make a declaration to that effect, and

(b) may make an award of compensation to be paid by the employer to the employee.

(4) The amount of the compensation shall be such as the tribunal considers just and equitable in all the circumstances having regard to—

(a) the employer's default in failing to permit time off to be taken by the employee, and

(b) any loss sustained by the employee which is attributable to the matters to which the complaint relates.

[1077]

NOTES

Section heading, sub-ss (1)–(3): words in square brackets substituted by the Employment Rights (Dispute Resolution) Act 1998, s 1(2)(a), (b).

Conciliation: employment tribunal proceedings under this section in respect of a breach of s 50 of this Act and claims which could be the subject of such proceedings are proceedings to which the Employment Tribunals Act 1996, s 18 applies; see s 18(1)(d) of that Act at **[975]**. The short conciliation period applies to such proceedings by virtue of the Employment Tribunals (Constitution and Rules of Procedure) Regulations 2004, SI 2004/1861, Sch 1, rule 22(5).

Looking for work and making arrangements for training

52 Right to time off to look for work or arrange training

(1) An employee who is given notice of dismissal by reason of redundancy is entitled to be permitted by his employer to take reasonable time off during the employee's working hours before the end of his notice in order to—

(a) look for new employment, or

(b) make arrangements for training for future employment.

(2) An employee is not entitled to take time off under this section unless, on whichever is the later of—

(a) the date on which the notice is due to expire, and

(b) the date on which it would expire were it the notice required to be given by section 86(1),

he will have been (or would have been) continuously employed for period of two years or more.

(3) For the purposes of this section the working hours of an employee shall be taken to be any time when, in accordance with his contract of employment, the employee is required to be at work.

[1078]

53 Right to remuneration for time off under section 52

(1) An employee who is permitted to take time off under section 52 is entitled to be paid remuneration by his employer for the period of absence at the appropriate hourly rate.

(2) The appropriate hourly rate, in relation to an employee, is the amount of one week's pay divided by the number of normal working hours in a week for that employee when employed under the contract of employment in force on the day when the notice of dismissal was given.

(3) But where the number of normal working hours differs from week to week or over a longer period, the amount of one week's pay shall be divided instead by the average number of normal working hours calculated by dividing by twelve the total number of the employee's normal working hours during the period of twelve weeks ending with the last complete week before the day on which the notice was given.

(4) If an employer unreasonably refuses to permit an employee to take time off from work as required by section 52, the employee is entitled to be paid an amount equal to the remuneration to which he would have been entitled under subsection (1) if he had been permitted to take the time off.

(5) The amount of an employer's liability to pay remuneration under subsection (1) shall not exceed, in respect of the notice period of any employee, forty per cent of a week's pay of that employee.

(6) A right to any amount under subsection (1) or (4) does not affect any right of an employee in relation to remuneration under his contract of employment ("contractual remuneration").

(7) Any contractual remuneration paid to an employee in respect of a period of time off under section 52 goes towards discharging any liability of the employer to pay remuneration under subsection (1) in respect of that period; and, conversely, any payment of remuneration under subsection (1) in respect of a period goes towards discharging any liability the employer to pay contractual remuneration in respect of that period.

[1079]

54 Complaints to [employment tribunals]

(1) An employee may present a complaint to an [employment tribunal] that his employer—

(a) has unreasonably refused to permit him to take time off as required by section 52, or
(b) has failed to pay the whole or any part of any amount to which the employee is entitled under section 53(1) or (4).

(2) An [employment tribunal] shall not consider a complaint under this section unless it is presented—
(a) before the end of the period of three months beginning with the date on which it is alleged that the time off should have been permitted, or
(b) within such further period as the tribunal considers reasonable in a case where it is satisfied that it was not reasonably practicable for the complaint to be presented before the end of that period of three months.

(3) Where an [employment tribunal] finds a complaint under this section well-founded, the tribunal shall—
(a) make a declaration to that effect, and
(b) order the employer to pay to the employee the amount which it finds due to him.

(4) The amount which may be ordered by a tribunal to be paid by an employer under subsection (3) (or, where the employer is liable to pay remuneration under section 53, the aggregate of that amount and the amount of that liability) shall not exceed, in respect of the notice period of any employee, forty per cent of a week's pay of that employee.

[1080]

NOTES

Section heading, sub-ss (1)–(3): words in square brackets substituted by the Employment Rights (Dispute Resolution) Act 1998, s 1(2)(a), (b).

Conciliation: employment tribunal proceedings under this section in respect of a breach of ss 52, 53(1), (4) and claims which could be the subject of such proceedings are proceedings to which the Employment Tribunals Act 1996, s 18 applies; see s 18(1)(d) of that Act at **[975]**. The short conciliation period applies to such proceedings by virtue of the Employment Tribunals (Constitution and Rules of Procedure) Regulations 2004, SI 2004/1861, Sch 1, rule 22(5).

Ante-natal care

55 Right to time off for ante-natal care

(1) An employee who—
(a) is pregnant, and
(b) has, on the advice of a registered medical practitioner, registered midwife or [registered nurse], made an appointment to attend at any place for the purpose of receiving ante-natal care,

is entitled to be permitted by her employer to take time off during the employee's working hours in order to enable her to keep the appointment.

(2) An employee is not entitled to take time off under this section to keep an appointment unless, if her employer requests her to do so, she produces for his inspection—
(a) a certificate from a registered medical practitioner, registered midwife or [registered nurse] stating that the employee is pregnant, and
(b) an appointment card or some other document showing that the appointment has been made.

(3) Subsection (2) does not apply where the employee's appointment is the first appointment during her pregnancy for which she seek permission to take time off in accordance with subsection (1).

(4) For the purposes of this section the working hours of an employee shall be taken to be any time when, in accordance with her contract of employment, the employee is required to be at work.

[(5) References in this section to a registered nurse are to such a nurse—
(a) who is also registered in the Specialist Community Public Health Nurses' Part of the register maintained under article 5 of the Nursing and Midwifery Order 2001, and
(b) whose entry in that Part of the register is annotated to show that he holds a qualification in health visiting.]

[1081]

NOTES

Sub-ss (1), (2): words in square brackets substituted by the Nursing and Midwifery Order 2001, SI 2002/253, art 54(3), Sch 5, para 13, as from 1 August 2004.

Sub-s (5): added by the Health Act 1999 (Consequential Amendments) (Nursing and Midwifery) Order 2004, SI 2004/1771, art 3, Schedule, Pt 1, para 3, as from 1 August 2004.

56 Right to remuneration for time off under section 55

(1) An employee who is permitted to take time off under section 55 is entitled to be paid remuneration by her employer for the period of absence at the appropriate hourly rate.

(2) The appropriate hourly rate, in relation to an employee, is the amount of one week's pay divided by the number of normal working hours in a week for that employee when employed under the contract of employment in force on the day when the time off is taken.

(3) But where the number of normal working hours differs from week to week or over a longer period, the amount of one week's pay shall be divided instead by—

- (a) the average number of normal working hours calculated by dividing by twelve the total number of the employee's normal working hours during the period of twelve weeks ending with the last complete week before the day on which the time off taken, or
- (b) where the employee has not been employed for a sufficient period to enable the calculation to be made under paragraph (a), a number which fairly represents the number of normal working hours in a week having regard to such of the considerations specified in subsection (4) as are appropriate in the circumstances.

(4) The considerations referred to in subsection (3)(b) are—

- (a) the average number of normal working hours in a week which the employee could expect in accordance with the terms of her contract, and
- (b) the average number of normal working hours of other employees engaged in relevant comparable employment with the same employer.

(5) A right to any amount under subsection (1) does not affect any right of an employee in relation to remuneration under her contract of employment ("contractual remuneration").

(6) Any contractual remuneration paid to an employee in respect of a period of time off under section 55 goes towards discharging any liability of the employer to pay remuneration under subsection (1) in respect of that period; and, conversely, any payment of remuneration under subsection (1) in respect of a period goes towards discharging any liability of the employer to pay contractual remuneration in respect of that period.

[1082]

57 Complaints to [employment tribunals]

(1) An employee may present a complaint to an [employment tribunal] that her employer—

- (a) has unreasonably refused to permit her to take time off as required by section 55, or
- (b) has failed to pay the whole or any part of any amount to which the employee is entitled under section 56.

(2) An [employment tribunal] shall not consider a complaint under this action unless it is presented—

- (a) before the end of the period of three months beginning with the date of the appointment concerned, or
- (b) within such further period as the tribunal considers reasonable in a case where it is satisfied that it was not reasonably practicable for the complaint to be presented before the end of that period of three months.

(3) Where an [employment tribunal] finds a complaint under this section well-founded, the tribunal shall make a declaration to that effect.

(4) If the complaint is that the employer has unreasonably refused to permit the employee to take time off, the tribunal shall also order the employer to pay to the employee an amount equal to the remuneration to which she would have been entitled under section 56 if the employer had not refused.

(5) If the complaint is that the employer has failed to pay the employee the whole or part of any amount to which she is entitled under section 56, the tribunal shall also order the employer to pay to the employee the amount which it finds due to her.

[1083]

NOTES

Section heading, sub-ss (1)–(3): words in square brackets substituted by the Employment Rights (Dispute Resolution) Act 1998, s 1(2)(a), (b).

Conciliation: employment tribunal proceedings under this section in respect of a breach of ss 55, 56 and claims which could be the subject of such proceedings are proceedings to which the Employment Tribunals Act 1996, s 18 applies; see s 18(1)(d) of that Act at **[975]**. The short conciliation period applies to such proceedings by virtue of the Employment Tribunals (Constitution and Rules of Procedure) Regulations 2004, SI 2004/1861, Sch 1, rule 22(5).

[Dependants

57A Time off for dependants

(1) An employee is entitled to be permitted by his employer to take a reasonable amount of time off during the employee's working hours in order to take action which is necessary—

(a) to provide assistance on an occasion when a dependant falls ill, gives birth or is injured or assaulted,

(b) to make arrangements for the provision of care for a dependant who is ill or injured,

(c) in consequence of the death of a dependant,

(d) because of the unexpected disruption or termination of arrangements for the care of a dependant, or

(e) to deal with an incident which involves a child of the employee and which occurs unexpectedly in a period during which an educational establishment which the child attends is responsible for him.

(2) Subsection (1) does not apply unless the employee—

(a) tells his employer the reason for his absence as soon as reasonably practicable, and

(b) except where paragraph (a) cannot be complied with until after the employee has returned to work, tells his employer for how long he expects to be absent.

(3) Subject to subsections (4) and (5), for the purposes of this section "dependant" means, in relation to an employee—

(a) a spouse [or civil partner],

(b) a child,

(c) a parent,

(d) a person who lives in the same household as the employee, otherwise than by reason of being his employee, tenant, lodger or boarder.

(4) For the purposes of subsection (1)(a) or (b) "dependant" includes, in addition to the persons mentioned in subsection (3), any person who reasonably relies on the employee—

(a) for assistance on an occasion when the person falls ill or is injured or assaulted, or

(b) to make arrangements for the provision of care in the event of illness or injury.

(5) For the purposes of subsection (1)(d) "dependant" includes, in addition to the persons mentioned in subsection (3), any person who reasonably relies on the employee to make arrangements for the provision of care.

(6) A reference in this section to illness or injury includes a reference to mental illness or injury.]

[1084]

NOTES

Inserted, together with preceding heading and s 57B, by the Employment Relations Act 1999, s 8, Sch 4, Pt II.

Sub-s (3): words in square brackets in para (a) inserted by the Civil Partnership Act 2004, s 261(1), Sch 27, para 151, as from 5 December 2005.

[57B Complaint to employment tribunal

(1) An employee may present a complaint to an employment tribunal that his employer has unreasonably refused to permit him to take time off as required by section 57A.

(2) An employment tribunal shall not consider a complaint under this section unless it is presented—

(a) before the end of the period of three months beginning with the date when the refusal occurred, or

(b) within such further period as the tribunal considers reasonable in a case where it is satisfied that it was not reasonably practicable for the complaint to be presented before the end of that period of three months.

(3) Where an employment tribunal finds a complaint under subsection (1) well-founded, it—

(a) shall make a declaration to that effect, and

(b) may make an award of compensation to be paid by the employer to the employee.

(4) The amount of compensation shall be such as the tribunal considers just and equitable in all the circumstances having regard to—

(a) the employer's default in refusing to permit time off to be taken by the employee, and

(b) any loss sustained by the employee which is attributable to the matters complained of.]

[1085]

NOTES

Inserted as noted to s 57A at **[1084]**.

Conciliation: employment tribunal proceedings under this section in respect of a breach of s 57A and claims which could be the subject of such proceedings are proceedings to which the Employment Tribunals Act 1996, s 18 applies; see s 18(1)(d) of that Act at **[975]**. The standard conciliation period applies to such proceedings by virtue of the Employment Tribunals (Constitution and Rules of Procedure) Regulations 2004, SI 2004/1861, Sch 1, rule 22(1), (6).

Occupational pension scheme trustees

58 Right to time off for pension scheme trustees

(1) The employer in relation to a relevant occupational pension scheme shall permit an employee of his who is a trustee of the scheme to the time off during the employee's working hours for the purpose of—

(a) performing any of his duties as such a trustee, or

(b) undergoing training relevant to the performance of those duties.

(2) The amount of time off which an employee is to be permitted to take under this section and the purposes for which, the occasions on which and any conditions subject to which time off may be so taken are those that are reasonable in all the circumstances having regard, in particular, to—

(a) how much time off is required for the performance of the duties of a trustee of the scheme and the undergoing of relevant training, and how much time off is required for performing the particular duty or for undergoing the particular training, and

(b) the circumstances of the employer's business and the effect of the employee's absence on the running of that business.

[(2A) This section applies to an employee who is a director of a company which is a trustee of a relevant occupational pension scheme as it applies to an employee who is a trustee of such a scheme (references to such a trustee being read for this purpose as references to such a director).]

(3) In this section—

(a) "relevant occupational pension scheme" means an occupational pension scheme (as defined in section 1 of the Pension Schemes Act 1993) established under a trust, and

(b) references to the employer, in relation to such a scheme, are to an employer of persons in the description *or category* of employment to which the scheme relates[, and

(c) references to training are to training on the employer's premises or elsewhere.]

(4) For the purposes of this section the working hours of an employee shall be taken to be any time when, in accordance with his contract of employment, the employee is required to be at work.

[1086]

NOTES

Sub-s (2A): inserted by the Welfare Reform and Pensions Act 1999, s 18, Sch 2, para 19(1), (3).

Sub-s (3): words in italics in para (b) repealed by the Pensions Act 2004, s 320, Sch 13, Pt 1, as from a day to be appointed; para (c) and word immediately preceding it added by the Teaching and Higher Education Act 1998, s 44(1), Sch 3, para 12.

By s 6(2) of the Welfare Reform and Pensions Act 1999, this section shall apply to the employer in relation to a designated scheme as it applies to the employer in relation to a relevant occupational pension scheme.

59 Right to payment for time off under section 58

(1) An employer who permits an employee to take time off under section 58 shall pay him for the time taken off pursuant to the permission.

(2) Where the employee's remuneration for the work he would ordinarily have been doing during that time does not vary with the amount of work done, he must be paid as if he had worked at that work for the whole of that time.

(3) Where the employee's remuneration for the work he would ordinarily have been doing during that time varies with the amount of work done, he must be paid an amount calculated by reference to the average hourly earnings for that work.

(4) The average hourly earnings mentioned in subsection (3) are—

(a) those of the employee concerned, or

(b) if no fair estimate can be made of those earnings, the average hourly earnings for work of that description of persons in comparable employment with the same employer or, if there are no such persons, a figure of average hourly earnings which is reasonable in the circumstances.

(5) A right to be paid an amount under subsection (1) does not affect any right of an employee in relation to remuneration under his contract of employment ("contractual remuneration").

(6) Any contractual remuneration paid to an employee in respect of a period of time off under section 58 goes towards discharging any liability of the employer under subsection (1) in respect of that period; and, conversely, any payment under subsection (1) in respect of a period goes towards discharging any liability of the employer to pay contractual remuneration in respect of that period.

[1087]

60 Complaints to [employment tribunals]

(1) An employee may present a complaint to an [employment tribunal] that his employer—

(a) has failed to permit him to take time off as required by section 58, or

(b) has failed to pay him in accordance with section 59.

(2) An [employment tribunal] shall not consider a complaint under this section unless it is presented—

(a) before the end of the period of three months beginning with the date when the failure occurred, or

(b) within such further period as the tribunal considers reasonable in a case where it is satisfied that it was not reasonably practicable for the complaint to be presented before the end of that period of three months.

(3) Where an [employment tribunal] finds a complaint under subsection (1)(a) well-founded, the tribunal—

(a) shall make a declaration to that effect, and

(b) may make an award of compensation to be paid by the employer to the employee.

(4) The amount of the compensation shall be such as the tribunal considers just and equitable in all the circumstances having regard to—

(a) the employer's default in failing to permit time off to be taken by the employee, and

(b) any loss sustained by the employee which is attributable to the matters complained of.

(5) Where on a complaint under subsection (1)(b) an [employment tribunal] finds that an employer has failed to pay an employee in accordance with section 59, it shall order the employer to pay the amount which it finds to be due.

[1088]

NOTES

Section heading, sub-ss (1)–(3), (5): words in square brackets substituted by the Employment Rights (Dispute Resolution) Act 1998, s 1(2)(a), (b).

Conciliation: employment tribunal proceedings under this section in respect of a breach of ss 58, 59 and claims which could be the subject of such proceedings are proceedings to which the Employment Tribunals Act 1996, s 18 applies; see s 18(1)(d) of that Act at **[975]**. The standard conciliation period applies to such proceedings by virtue of the Employment Tribunals (Constitution and Rules of Procedure) Regulations 2004, SI 2004/1861, Sch 1, rule 22(1), (6).

Employee representatives

61 Right to time off for employee representatives

(1) An employee who is—

(a) an employee representative for the purposes of Chapter II of Part IV of the Trade Union and Labour Relations (Consolidation) Act 1992 (redundancies) or [regulations 9, 13 and 15 of the Transfer of Undertakings (Protection of Employment) Regulations 2006], or

(b) a candidate in an election in which any person elected will, on being elected, be such an employee representative,

is entitled to be permitted by his employer to take reasonable time off during the employee's working hours in order to perform his functions as such an employee representative or candidate [or in order to undergo training to perform such functions].

(2) For the purposes of this section the working hours of an employee shall be taken to be any time when, in accordance with his contract of employment, the employee is required to be at work.

[1089]

NOTES

Sub-s (1): words in square brackets in para (a) substituted by the Transfer of Undertakings (Protection of Employment) Regulations 2006, SI 2006/246, reg 20, Sch 2, para 10, as from 6 April 2006 (for transitional provisions in relation to a relevant transfer, etc, that took place before that date, see reg 21 of the 2006 Regulations at **[3395]**); words in second pair of square brackets added by the Collective Redundancies and Transfer of Undertakings (Protection of Employment) (Amendment) Regulations 1999, SI 1999/1925, reg 15.

62 Right to remuneration for time off under section 61

(1) An employee who is permitted to take time off under section 61 is entitled to be paid remuneration by his employer for the time taken off at the appropriate hourly rate.

(2) The appropriate hourly rate, in relation to an employee, is the amount of one week's pay divided by the number of normal working hours in a week for that employee when employed under the contract of employment in force on the day when the time off is taken.

(3) But where the number of normal working hours differs from week to week or over a longer period, the amount of one week's pay shall be divided instead by—

(a) the average number of normal working hours calculated by dividing by twelve the total number of the employee's normal working hours during the period of twelve weeks ending with the last complete week before the day on which the time off is taken, or

(b) where the employee has not been employed for a sufficient period to enable the calculation to be made under paragraph (a), a number which fairly represents the number of normal working hours in a week having regard to such of the considerations specified in subsection (4) as are appropriate in the circumstances.

(4) The considerations referred to in subsection (3)(b) are—

(a) the average number of normal working hours in a week which the employee could expect in accordance with the terms of his contract, and

(b) the average number of normal working hours of other employees engaged in relevant comparable employment with the same employer.

(5) A right to any amount under subsection (1) does not affect any right of an employee in relation to remuneration under his contract of employment ("contractual remuneration").

(6) Any contractual remuneration paid to an employee in respect of a period of time off under section 61 goes towards discharging any liability of the employer to pay remuneration under subsection (1) in respect of that period; and, conversely, any payment of remuneration under subsection (1) in respect of a period goes towards discharging any liability of the employer to pay contractual remuneration in respect of that period.

[1090]

63 Complaints to [employment tribunals]

(1) An employee may present a complaint to an [employment tribunal] that his employer—

(a) has unreasonably refused to permit him to take time off as required by section 61, or

(b) has failed to pay the whole or any part of any amount to which the employee is entitled under section 62.

(2) An [employment tribunal] shall not consider a complaint under this section unless it is presented—

(a) before the end of the period of three months beginning with the day on which the time off was taken or on which it is alleged the time off should have been permitted, or

(b) within such further period as the tribunal considers reasonable in a case where it is satisfied that it was not reasonably practicable for the complaint to be presented before the end of that period of three months.

(3) Where an [employment tribunal] finds a complaint under this section well-founded, the tribunal shall make a declaration to that effect.

(4) If the complaint is that the employer has unreasonably refused to permit the employee to take time off, the tribunal shall also order the employer to pay to the employee an amount equal to the remuneration to which he would have been entitled under section 62 if the employer had not refused.

(5) If the complaint is that the employer has failed to pay the employee the whole or part of any amount to which he is entitled under section 62, the tribunal shall also order the employer to pay to the employee the amount which it finds due to him.

[1091]

NOTES

Section heading, sub-ss (1)–(3): words in square brackets substituted by the Employment Rights (Dispute Resolution) Act 1998, s 1(2)(a), (b).

Conciliation: employment tribunal proceedings under this section in respect of a breach of ss 61, 62 and claims which could be the subject of such proceedings are proceedings to which the Employment Tribunals Act 1996, s 18 applies; see s 18(1)(d) of that Act at **[975]**. The standard conciliation period applies to such proceedings by virtue of the Employment Tribunals (Constitution and Rules of Procedure) Regulations 2004, SI 2004/1861, Sch 1, rule 22(1), (6).

[63A Right to time off for young person for study or training

(1) An employee who—

(a) is aged 16 or 17,

(b) is not receiving full-time secondary or further education, and

(c) has not attained such standard of achievement as is prescribed by regulations made by the Secretary of State,

is entitled to be permitted by his employer to take time off during the employee's working hours in order to undertake study or training leading to a relevant qualification.

(2) In this section—

(a) "secondary education"—

(i) in relation to England and Wales, has the same meaning as in the Education Act 1996, and
(ii) in relation to Scotland, has the same meaning as in section 135(2)(b) of the Education (Scotland) Act 1980;

(b) "further education"—
(i) in relation to England and Wales, [has the same meaning as in the Education Act 1996,] and
(ii) in relation to Scotland, has the same meaning as in section 1(3) of the Further and Higher Education (Scotland) Act 1992; and

(c) "relevant qualification" means an external qualification the attainment of which—
(i) would contribute to the attainment of the standard prescribed for the purposes of subsection (1)(c), and
(ii) would be likely to enhance the employee's employment prospects (whether with his employer or otherwise);

and for the purposes of paragraph (c) "external qualification" means an academic or vocational qualification awarded or authenticated by such person or body as may be specified in or under regulations made by the Secretary of State.

(3) An employee who—
(a) satisfies the requirements of paragraphs (a) to (c) of subsection (1), and
(b) is for the time being supplied by his employer to another person ("the principal") to perform work in accordance with a contract made between the employer and the principal,

is entitled to be permitted by the principal to take time off during the employee's working hours in order to undertake study or training leading to a relevant qualification.

(4) Where an employee—
(a) is aged 18,
(b) is undertaking study or training leading to a relevant qualification, and
(c) began such study or training before attaining that age,

subsections (1) and (3) shall apply to the employee, in relation to that study or training, as if "or 18" were inserted at the end of subsection (1)(a).

(5) The amount of time off which an employee is to be permitted to take under this section, and the occasions on which and any conditions subject to which time off may be so taken, are those that are reasonable in all the circumstances having regard, in particular, to—
(a) the requirements of the employee's study or training, and
(b) the circumstances of the business of the employer or the principal and the effect of the employee's time off on the running of that business.

(6) Regulations made for the purposes of subsections (1)(c) and (2) may make different provision for different cases, and in particular may make different provision in relation to England, Wales and Scotland respectively.

(7) References in this section to study or training are references to study or training on the premises of the employer or (as the case may be) principal or elsewhere.

(8) For the purposes of this section the working hours of an employee shall be taken to be any time when, in accordance with his contract of employment, the employee is required to be at work.]

[1092]

NOTES

Inserted by the Teaching and Higher Education Act 1998, s 32.

Sub-s (2): words in square brackets substituted by the Learning and Skills Act 2000, s 149, Sch 9, paras 1, 50.

Transfer of functions: functions under sub-ss (1)(c) and (2) are transferred, in so far as they are exercisable in or as regards Scotland, to the Scottish Ministers subject to the requirement that they are exercisable only after consultation with the Secretary of State, by the Scotland Act 1998 (Transfer of Functions to the Scottish Ministers etc) Order 1999, SI 1999/1750, art 2, Sch 1.

Regulations: the Right to Time Off for Study or Training (Scotland) Regulations 1999, SI 1999/1058; the Right to Time Off for Study or Training Regulations 2001, SI 2001/2801.

[63B Right to remuneration for time off under section 63A

(1) An employee who is permitted to take time off under section 63A is entitled to be paid remuneration by his employer for the time taken off at the appropriate hourly rate.

(2) The appropriate hourly rate, in relation to an employee, is the amount of one week's pay divided by the number of normal working hours in a week for that employee when employed under the contract of employment in force on the day when the time off is taken.

(3) But where the number of normal working hours differs from week to week or over a longer period, the amount of one week's pay shall be divided instead by—

(a) the average number of normal working hours calculated by dividing by twelve the total number of the employee's working hours during the period of twelve weeks ending with the last complete week before the day on which the time off is taken, or

(b) where the employee has not been employed for a sufficient period to enable the calculation to be made under paragraph (a), a number which fairly represents the number of normal working hours in a week having regard to such of the considerations specified in subsection (4) as are appropriate in the circumstances.

(4) The considerations referred to in subsection (3)(b) are—

(a) the average number of normal working hours in a week which the employee could expect in accordance with the terms of his contract, and

(b) the average number of normal working hours of other employees engaged in relevant comparable employment with the same employer.

(5) A right to any amount under subsection (1) does not affect any right of an employee in relation to remuneration under his contract of employment ("contractual remuneration").

(6) Any contractual remuneration paid to an employee in respect of a period of time off under section 63A goes towards discharging any liability of the employer to pay remuneration under subsection (1) in respect of that period; and, conversely, any payment of remuneration under subsection (1) in respect of a period goes towards discharging any liability of the employer to pay contractual remuneration in respect of that period.]

[1093]

NOTES

Inserted, together with s 63C, by the Teaching and Higher Education Act 1998, s 33.

[63C Complaints to employment tribunals

(1) An employee may present a complaint to an employment tribunal that—

(a) his employer, or the principal referred to in subsection (3) of section 63A, has unreasonably refused to permit him to take time off as required by that section, or

(b) his employer has failed to pay the whole or any part of any amount to which the employee is entitled under section 63B.

(2) An employment tribunal shall not consider a complaint under this section unless it is presented—

(a) before the end of the period of three months beginning with the day on which the time off was taken or on which it is alleged the time off should have been permitted, or

(b) within such further period as the tribunal considers reasonable in a case where it is satisfied that it was not reasonably practicable for the complaint to be presented before the end of that period of three months.

(3) Where an employment tribunal finds a complaint under this section well-founded, the tribunal shall make a declaration to that effect.

(4) If the complaint is that the employer or the principal has unreasonably refused to permit the employee to take time off, the tribunal shall also order the employer or the principal, as the case may be, to pay to the employee an amount equal to the remuneration to which he would have been entitled under section 63B if the employer or the principal had not refused.

(5) If the complaint is that the employer has failed to pay the employee the whole or part of any amount to which he is entitled under section 63B, the tribunal shall also order the employer to pay to the employee the amount which it finds due to him.]

[1094]

NOTES

Inserted as noted to s 63B at **[1093]**.

Conciliation: employment tribunal proceedings under this section in respect of a breach of ss 63A, 63B and claims which could be the subject of such proceedings are proceedings to which the Employment Tribunals Act 1996, s 18 applies; see s 18(1) of that Act at **[975]**. The standard conciliation period applies to such proceedings by virtue of the Employment Tribunals (Constitution and Rules of Procedure) Regulations 2004, SI 2004/1861, Sch 1, rule 22(1), (6).

PART VII
SUSPENSION FROM WORK

NOTES

Conciliation: employment tribunal proceedings and claims which could be the subject of employment tribunal proceedings under this Part are proceedings to which the Employment Tribunals Act 1996, s 18 applies; see s 18(1)(d) of that Act at **[975]**. The short conciliation period applies to such proceedings by virtue of the Employment Tribunals (Constitution and Rules of Procedure) Regulations 2004, SI 2004/1861, Sch 1, rule 22(5).

Suspension on medical grounds

64 Right to remuneration on suspension on medical grounds

(1) An employee who is suspended from work by his employer on medical grounds is entitled to be paid by his employer remuneration while he is so suspended for a period not exceeding twenty-six weeks.

(2) For the purposes of this Part an employee is suspended from work on medical grounds if he is suspended from work in consequence of—

(a) a requirement imposed by or under a provision of an enactment or of an instrument made under an enactment, or

(b) a recommendation in a provision of a code of practice issued or approved under section 16 of the Health and Safety at Work etc Act 1974,

and the provision is for the time being specified in subsection (3).

(3) The provisions referred to in subsection (2) are—

Regulation 16 of the Control of Lead at Work Regulations 1980,

[Regulation 24 of the Ionising Radiations Regulations 1999 (SI 1999/3232)], and

Regulation 11 of the Control of Substances Hazardous to Health Regulations 1988.

(4) The Secretary of State may by order add provisions to or remove provisions from the list of provisions specified in subsection (3).

(5) For the purposes of this Part an employee shall be regarded as suspended from work on medical grounds only if and for so long as he—

(a) continues to be employed by his employer, but

(b) is not provided with work or does not perform the work he normally performed before the suspension.

[1095]

NOTES

Sub-s (3): words in square brackets substituted by the Ionising Radiations Regulations 1999, SI 1999/3232, reg 41(1), Sch 9, para 2.

Control of Lead at Work Regulations 1980, SI 1980/1248: revoked and replaced by the Control of Lead at Work Regulations 1998, SI 1998/543 (revoked). See now, the Control of Substances Hazardous to Health Regulations 2002, SI 2002/2677.

The reference to the Control of Substances Hazardous to Health Regulations 1988 is an apparent drafting error as these regulations had been revoked and replaced by the (largely consolidating) Control of Substances Hazardous to Health Regulations 1994, SI 1994/3246. See now, the Control of Substances Hazardous to Health Regulations 2002, SI 2002/2677.

65 Exclusions from right to remuneration

(1) An employee is not entitled to remuneration under section 64 unless he has been continuously employed for a period of not less than one month ending with the day before that on which the suspension begins.

(2) …

(3) An employee is not entitled to remuneration under section 64 in respect of any period during which he is incapable of work by reason of disease or bodily or mental disablement.

(4) An employee is not entitled to remuneration under section 64 in respect of any period if—

(a) his employer has offered to provide him with suitable alternative work during the period (whether or not it is work which the employee is under his contract, or was under the contract in force before the suspension, employed to perform) and the employee has unreasonably refused to perform that work, or

(b) he does not comply with reasonable requirements imposed by his employer with a view to ensuring that his services are available.

[1096]

NOTES

Sub-s (2): repealed by the Fixed-term Employees (Prevention of Less Favourable Treatment) Regulations 2002, SI 2002/2034, reg 11, Sch 2, Pt 1, para 3(1), (3).

Suspension on maternity grounds

66 Meaning of suspension on maternity grounds

(1) For the purposes of this Part an employee is suspended from work on maternity grounds if, in consequence of any relevant requirement or relevant recommendation, she is suspended from work by her employer on the ground that she is pregnant, has recently given birth or is breastfeeding a child.

(2) In subsection (1)—

"relevant requirement" means a requirement imposed by or under a specified provision of an enactment or of an instrument made under an enactment, and

"relevant recommendation" means a recommendation in a specified provision of a code of practice issued or approved under section 16 of the Health and Safety at Work etc Act 1974;

and in this subsection "specified provision" means a provision for the time being specified in an order made by the Secretary of State under this subsection.

(3) For the purposes of this Part an employee shall be regarded as suspended from work on maternity grounds only if and for so long as she—

(a) continues to be employed by her employer, but

(b) is not provided with work or (disregarding alternative work for the purposes of section 67) does not perform the work she normally performed before the suspension.

[1097]

NOTES

Modified, in relation to governing bodies with delegated budgets, by the Education (Modification of Enactments Relating to Employment) (England) Order 2003, SI 2003/1964, art 3, Schedule at **[3035C]**, **[3035G]** and the Education (Modification of Enactments Relating to Employment) (Wales) Order 2006, SI 2006/1073, art 3, Schedule at **[3462B]**, **[3462F]**.

Orders: the Suspension from Work on Maternity Grounds (Merchant Shipping and Fishing Vessels) Order 1998, SI 1998/587, specifying regs 8(3) and 9(2) of the Merchant Shipping and Fishing Vessels (Health and Safety at Work) Regulations 1997, SI 1997/2962, for the purposes of s 66(2). Also, by virtue of s 241 of, and Sch 2, Pt I, paras 1–4 to, this Act, the Suspension from Work (on Maternity Grounds) Order 1994, SI 1994/2930 has effect as if made under this section.

67 Right to offer of alternative work

(1) Where an employer has available suitable alternative work for an employee, the employee has a right to be offered to be provided with the alternative work before being suspended from work on maternity grounds.

(2) For alternative work to be suitable for an employee for the purposes of this section—

(a) the work must be of a kind which is both suitable in relation to her and appropriate for her to do in the circumstances, and

(b) the terms and conditions applicable to her for performing the work, if they differ from the corresponding terms and conditions applicable to her for performing the work she normally performs under her contract of employment, must not be substantially less favourable to her than those corresponding terms and conditions.

[1098]

NOTES

Modified as noted to s 66 at **[1097]**.

68 Right to remuneration

(1) An employee who is suspended from work on maternity grounds is entitled to be paid remuneration by her employer while she is so suspended.

(2) An employee is not entitled to remuneration under this section in respect of any period if—

(a) her employer has offered to provide her during the period with work which is suitable alternative work for her for the purposes of section 67, and

(b) the employee has unreasonably refused to perform that work.

[1099]

NOTES

Modified as noted to s 66 at **[1097]**.

General

69 Calculation of remuneration

(1) The amount of remuneration payable by an employer to an employee under section 64 or 68 is a week's pay in respect of each week of the period of suspension; and if in any week remuneration is payable in respect of only part of that week the amount of a week's pay shall be reduced proportionately.

(2) A right to remuneration under section 64 or 68 does not affect any right of an employee in relation to remuneration under the employee's contract of employment ("contractual remuneration").

(3) Any contractual remuneration paid by an employer to an employee in respect of any period goes towards discharging the employer's liability under section 64 or 68 in respect of that period; and, conversely, any payment of remuneration in discharge of an employer's liability under section 64 or 68 in respect of any period goes towards discharging any obligation of the employer to pay contractual remuneration in respect of that period.

[1100]

70 Complaints to [employment tribunals]

(1) An employee may present a complaint to an [employment tribunal] that his or her employer has failed to pay the whole or any part of remuneration to which the employee is entitled under section 64 or 68.

(2) An [employment tribunal] shall not consider a complaint under subsection (1) relating to remuneration in respect of any day unless it is presented—

(a) before the end of the period of three months beginning with that day, or

(b) within such further period as the tribunal considers reasonable in a case where it is satisfied that it was not reasonably practicable for the complaint to be presented within that period of three months.

(3) Where an [employment tribunal] finds a complaint under subsection (1) well-founded, the tribunal shall order the employer to pay the employee the amount of remuneration which it finds is due to him or her.

(4) An employee may present a complaint to an [employment tribunal] that in contravention of section 67 her employer has failed to offer to provide her with work.

(5) An [employment tribunal] shall not consider a complaint under subsection (4) unless it is presented—

(a) before the end of the period of three months beginning with the first day of the suspension, or

(b) within such further period as the tribunal considers reasonable in a case where it is satisfied that it was not reasonably practicable for the complaint to be presented within that period of three months.

(6) Where an [employment tribunal] finds a complaint under subsection (4) well-founded, the tribunal may make an award of compensation to be paid by the employer to the employee.

(7) The amount of the compensation shall be such as the tribunal considers just and equitable in all the circumstances having regard to—

(a) the infringement of the employee's right under section 67 by the failure on the part of the employer to which the complaint relates, and

(b) any loss sustained by the employee which is attributable to that failure.

[1101]

NOTES

Section heading, sub-ss (1)–(6): words in square brackets substituted by the Employment Rights (Dispute Resolution) Act 1998, s 1(2)(a), (b).

Conciliation: see the note at the beginning of this Part.

Modified as noted to s 66 at **[1097]**.

[PART VIII

CHAPTER I
MATERNITY LEAVE]

NOTES

A new Pt VIII (ss 71–75, 76–80) was substituted for the original Pt VIII (ss 71–85) by the Employment Relations Act 1999, s 7, Sch 4, Pt I. Subsequently, various amendments have been made to this Part, including the insertion of ss 75A–75D and 80A–80E.

[71 Ordinary maternity leave

(1) An employee may, provided that she satisfies any conditions which may be prescribed, be absent from work at any time during an ordinary maternity leave period.

(2) An ordinary maternity leave period is a period calculated in accordance with regulations made by the Secretary of State.

[(3) Regulations under subsection (2)—

(a) shall secure that, where an employee has a right to leave under this section, she is entitled to an ordinary maternity leave period of at least 26 weeks;

(b) may allow an employee to choose, subject to prescribed restrictions, the date on which an ordinary maternity leave period starts;

(c) may specify circumstances in which an employee may work for her employer during an ordinary maternity leave period without bringing the period to an end.]

(4) Subject to section 74, an employee who exercises her right under subsection (1)—

(a) is entitled[, for such purposes and to such extent as may be prescribed,] to the benefit of the terms and conditions of employment which would have applied if she had not been absent,

(b) is bound[, for such purposes and to such extent as may be prescribed,] by any obligations arising under those terms and conditions (except in so far as they are inconsistent with subsection (1)), and

[(c) is entitled to return from leave to a job of a prescribed kind].

(5) In subsection (4)(a) "terms and conditions of employment"—

(a) includes matters connected with an employee's employment whether or not they arise under her contract of employment, but

(b) does not include terms and conditions about remuneration.

(6) The Secretary of State may make regulations specifying matters which are, or are not, to be treated as remuneration for the purposes of this section.

[(7) The Secretary of State may make regulations making provision, in relation to the right to return under subsection (4)(c) above, about—

(a) seniority, pension rights and similar rights;
(b) terms and conditions of employment on return.]]

[1102]

NOTES

Substituted as noted following the Part heading above.

Sub-s (3): substituted by the Work and Families Act 2006, s 11(1), Sch 1, para 31, as from 27 June 2006 (for the purpose of the power to prescribe matters by regulations), and as from 1 October 2006 (otherwise).

Sub-s (4): words in square brackets in paras (a), (b) inserted, and para (c) substituted, by the Employment Act 2002, s 17(1), (2) (with effect in relation to employees whose expected week of childbirth begins on or after 6 April 2003).

Sub-s (7): substituted by the Employment Act 2002, s 17(1), (3) (with effect in relation to employees whose expected week of childbirth begins on or after 6 April 2003).

Modified as noted to s 66 at **[1097]**.

Regulations: the Maternity and Parental Leave etc Regulations 1999, SI 1999/3312 at **[2553]**.

[72 Compulsory maternity leave

(1) An employer shall not permit an employee who satisfies prescribed conditions to work during a compulsory maternity leave period.

(2) A compulsory maternity leave period is a period calculated in accordance with regulations made by the Secretary of State.

(3) Regulations under subsection (2) shall secure—
(a) that no compulsory leave period is less than two weeks, and
(b) that every compulsory maternity leave period falls within an ordinary maternity leave period.

(4) Subject to subsection (5), any provision of or made under the Health and Safety at Work etc Act 1974 shall apply in relation to the prohibition under subsection (1) as if it were imposed by regulations under section 15 of that Act.

(5) Section 33(1)(c) of the 1974 Act shall not apply in relation to the prohibition under subsection (1); and an employer who contravenes that subsection shall be—
(a) guilty of an offence, and
(b) liable on summary conviction to a fine not exceeding level 2 on the standard scale.]

[1103]

NOTES

Substituted as noted following the Part heading above.

Regulations: the Maternity and Parental Leave etc Regulations 1999, SI 1999/3312 at **[2553]**.

[73 Additional maternity leave

(1) An employee who satisfies prescribed conditions may be absent from work at any time during an additional maternity leave period.

(2) An additional maternity leave period is a period calculated in accordance with regulations made by the Secretary of State.

[(3) Regulations under subsection (2)—
(a) may allow an employee to choose, subject to prescribed restrictions, the date on which an additional maternity leave period ends;
(b) may specify circumstances in which an employee may work for her employer during an additional maternity leave period without bringing the period to an end.]

(4) Subject to section 74, an employee who exercises her right under subsection (1)—
(a) is entitled, for such purposes and to such extent as may be prescribed, to the benefit of the terms and conditions of employment which would have applied if she had not been absent,
(b) is bound, for such purposes and to such extent as may be prescribed, by obligations arising under those terms and conditions (except in so far as they are inconsistent with subsection (1)), and
(c) is entitled to return from leave to a job of a prescribed kind.

(5) In subsection (4)(a) "terms and conditions of employment"—

(a) includes matters connected with an employee's employment whether or not they arise under her contract of employment, but
(b) does not include terms and conditions about remuneration.

[(5A) In subsection (4)(c), the reference to return from leave includes, where appropriate, a reference to a continuous period of absence attributable partly to additional maternity leave and partly to ordinary maternity leave.]

(6) The Secretary of State may make regulations specifying matters which are, or are not, to be treated as remuneration for the purposes of this section.

(7) The Secretary of State may make regulations making provision, in relation to the right to return under subsection (4)(c), about—
(a) seniority, pension rights and similar rights;
(b) terms and conditions of employment on return.]

[1104]

NOTES

Substituted as noted following the Part heading above.

Sub-s (3): substituted by the Work and Families Act 2006, s 11(1), Sch 1, para 32, as from 27 June 2006 (for the purpose of the power to prescribe matters by regulations), and as from 1 October 2006 (otherwise).

Sub-s (5A): inserted by the Employment Act 2002, s 17(1), (4) (with effect in relation to employees whose expected week of childbirth began on or after 6 April 2003).

Regulations: the Maternity and Parental Leave etc Regulations 1999, SI 1999/3312 at **[2553]**.

[74 Redundancy and dismissal

(1) Regulations under section 71 or 73 may make provision about redundancy during an ordinary or additional maternity leave period.

(2) Regulations under section 71 or 73 may make provision about dismissal (other than by reason of redundancy) during an ordinary or additional maternity leave period.

(3) Regulations made by virtue of subsection (1) or (2) may include—
(a) provision requiring an employer to offer alternative employment;
(b) provision for the consequences of failure to comply with the regulations (which may include provision for a dismissal to be treated as unfair for the purposes of Part X).

(4) Regulations under section [71 or] 73 may make provision—
(a) for section [71(4)(c) or] 73(4)(c) not to apply in specified cases, and
(b) about dismissal at the conclusion of an [ordinary or] additional maternity leave period.]

[1105]

NOTES

Substituted as noted following the Part heading above.

Sub-s (4): words in square brackets inserted by the Employment Act 2002, s 17(1), (5) (with effect in relation to employees whose expected week of childbirth began on or after 6 April 2003).

[75 Sections 71 to 73: supplemental

(1) Regulations under section 71, 72 or 73 may—
(a) make provision about notices to be given, evidence to be produced and other procedures to be followed by employees and employers;
(b) make provision for the consequences of failure to give notices, to produce evidence or to comply with other procedural requirements;
(c) make provision for the consequences of failure to act in accordance with a notice given by virtue of paragraph (a);
(d) make special provision for cases where an employee has a right which corresponds to a right under this Chapter and which arises under her contract of employment or otherwise;
(e) make provision modifying the effect of Chapter II of Part XIV (calculation of a week's pay) in relation to an employee who is or has been absent from work on ordinary or additional maternity leave;
(f) make provision applying, modifying or excluding an enactment, in such

circumstances as may be specified and subject to any conditions specified, in relation to a person entitled to ordinary, compulsory or additional maternity leave;

(g) make different provision for different cases or circumstances.

(2) In sections 71 to 73 "prescribed" means prescribed by regulations made by the Secretary of State.]

[1106]

NOTES

Substituted as noted following the Part heading above.

[CHAPTER IA
ADOPTION LEAVE

75A Ordinary adoption leave

(1) An employee who satisfies prescribed conditions may be absent from work at any time during an ordinary adoption leave period.

(2) An ordinary adoption leave period is a period calculated in accordance with regulations made by the Secretary of State.

[(2A) Regulations under subsection (2) may specify circumstances in which an employee may work for his employer during an ordinary adoption leave period without bringing the period to an end.]

(3) Subject to section 75C, an employee who exercises his right under subsection (1)—

(a) is entitled, for such purposes and to such extent as may be prescribed, to the benefit of the terms and conditions of employment which would have applied if he had not been absent,

(b) is bound, for such purposes and to such extent as may be prescribed, by any obligations arising under those terms and conditions (except in so far as they are inconsistent with subsection (1)), and

(c) is entitled to return from leave to a job of a prescribed kind.

(4) In subsection (3)(a) "terms and conditions of employment"—

(a) includes matters connected with an employee's employment whether or not they arise under his contract of employment, but

(b) does not include terms and conditions about remuneration.

(5) In subsection (3)(c), the reference to return from leave includes, where appropriate, a reference to a continuous period of absence attributable partly to ordinary adoption leave and partly to maternity leave.

(6) The Secretary of State may make regulations specifying matters which are, or are not, to be treated as remuneration for the purposes of this section.

(7) The Secretary of State may make regulations making provision, in relation to the right to return under subsection (3)(c), about—

(a) seniority, pension rights and similar rights;

(b) terms and conditions of employment on return.]

[1107]

NOTES

Chapter IA (ss 75A–75D) inserted by the Employment Act 2002, s 3.

Sub-s (2A): inserted by the Work and Families Act 2006, s 11(1), Sch 1, para 33, as from 27 June 2006 (for the purpose of the power to prescribe matters by regulations), and as from 1 October 2006 (otherwise).

Regulations: the Paternity and Adoption Leave Regulations 2002, SI 2002/2788 at **[2752]**; the Paternity and Adoption Leave (Adoptions from Overseas) Regulations 2003, SI 2003/921.

[75B Additional adoption leave

(1) An employee who satisfies prescribed conditions may be absent from work at any time during an additional adoption leave period.

(2) An additional adoption leave period is a period calculated in accordance with regulations made by the Secretary of State.

[(3) Regulations under subsection (2)—
(a) may allow an employee to choose, subject to prescribed restrictions, the date on which an additional adoption leave period ends;
(b) may specify circumstances in which an employee may work for his employer during an additional adoption leave period without bringing the period to an end.]

(4) Subject to section 75C, an employee who exercises his right under subsection (1)—
(a) is entitled, for such purposes and to such extent as may be prescribed, to the benefit of the terms and conditions of employment which would have applied if he had not been absent,
(b) is bound, for such purposes and to such extent as may be prescribed, by obligations arising under those terms and conditions (except in so far as they are inconsistent with subsection (1)), and
(c) is entitled to return from leave to a job of a prescribed kind.

(5) In subsection (4)(a) "terms and conditions of employment"—
(a) includes matters connected with an employee's employment whether or not they arise under his contract of employment, but
(b) does not include terms and conditions about remuneration.

(6) In subsection (4)(c), the reference to return from leave includes, where appropriate, a reference to a continuous period of absence attributable partly to additional adoption leave and partly to—
(a) maternity leave, or
(b) ordinary adoption leave,

or to both.

(7) The Secretary of State may make regulations specifying matters which are, or are not, to be treated as remuneration for the purposes of this section.

(8) The Secretary of State may make regulations making provision, in relation to the right to return under subsection (4)(c), about—
(a) seniority, pension rights and similar rights;
(b) terms and conditions of employment on return.]

[1108]

NOTES

Inserted as noted to s 75A at **[1107]**.

Sub-s (3): substituted by the Work and Families Act 2006, s 11(1), Sch 1, para 34, as from 27 June 2006 (for the purpose of the power to prescribe matters by regulations), and as from 1 October 2006 (otherwise).

Regulations: the Paternity and Adoption Leave Regulations 2002, SI 2002/2788 at **[2752]**; the Paternity and Adoption Leave (Adoptions from Overseas) Regulations 2003, SI 2003/921.

[75C Redundancy and dismissal

(1) Regulations under section 75A or 75B may make provision about—
(a) redundancy, or
(b) dismissal (other than by reason of redundancy),

during an ordinary or additional adoption leave period.

(2) Regulations made by virtue of subsection (1) may include—
(a) provision requiring an employer to offer alternative employment;
(b) provision for the consequences of failure to comply with the regulations (which may include provision for a dismissal to be treated as unfair for the purposes of Part 10).

(3) Regulations under section 75A or 75B may make provision—
(a) for section 75A(3)(c) or 75B(4)(c) not to apply in specified cases, and
(b) about dismissal at the conclusion of an ordinary or additional adoption leave period.]

[1109]

NOTES

Inserted as noted to s 75A at **[1107]**.

Regulations: the Paternity and Adoption Leave Regulations 2002, SI 2002/2788 at **[2752]**; the Paternity and Adoption Leave (Adoptions from Overseas) Regulations 2003, SI 2003/921.

[75D Chapter 1A: supplemental

(1) Regulations under section 75A or 75B may—

(a) make provision about notices to be given, evidence to be produced and other procedures to be followed by employees and employers;

(b) make provision requiring employers or employees to keep records;

(c) make provision for the consequences of failure to give notices, to produce evidence, to keep records or to comply with other procedural requirements;

(d) make provision for the consequences of failure to act in accordance with a notice given by virtue of paragraph (a);

(e) make special provision for cases where an employee has a right which corresponds to a right under this Chapter and which arises under his contract of employment or otherwise;

(f) make provision modifying the effect of Chapter 2 of Part 14 (calculation of a week's pay) in relation to an employee who is or has been absent from work on ordinary or additional adoption leave;

(g) make provision applying, modifying or excluding an enactment, in such circumstances as may be specified and subject to any conditions specified, in relation to a person entitled to ordinary or additional adoption leave;

(h) make different provision for different cases or circumstances.

(2) In sections 75A and 75B "prescribed" means prescribed by regulations made by the Secretary of State.]

[1110]

NOTES

Inserted as noted to s 75A at **[1107]**.

[CHAPTER II
PARENTAL LEAVE

76 Entitlement to parental leave

(1) The Secretary of State shall make regulations entitling an employee who satisfies specified conditions—

(a) as to duration of employment, and

(b) as to having, or expecting to have, responsibility for a child,

to be absent from work on parental leave for the purpose of caring for a child.

(2) The regulations shall include provision for determining—

(a) the extent of an employee's entitlement to parental leave in respect of a child;

(b) when parental leave may be taken.

(3) Provision under subsection (2)(a) shall secure that where an employee is entitled to parental leave in respect of a child he is entitled to a period or total period of leave of at least three months; but this subsection is without prejudice to any provision which may be made by the regulations for cases in which—

(a) a person ceases to satisfy conditions under subsection (1);

(b) an entitlement to parental leave is transferred.

(4) Provision under subsection (2)(b) may, in particular, refer to—

(a) a child's age, or

(b) a specified period of time starting from a specified event.

(5) Regulations under subsection (1) may—

(a) specify things which are, or are not, to be taken as done for the purpose of caring for a child;

(b) require parental leave to be taken as a single period of absence in all cases or in specified cases;

(c) require parental leave to be taken as a series of periods of absence in all cases or in specified cases;

(d) require all or specified parts of a period of parental leave to be taken at or by specified times;

(e) make provision about the postponement by an employer of a period of parental leave which an employee wishes to take;

(f) specify a minimum or maximum period of absence which may be taken as part of a period of parental leave.

(g) specify a maximum aggregate of periods of parental leave which may be taken during a specified period of time.]

[1111]

NOTES

Substituted as noted following the Part heading above.

Regulations: the Maternity and Parental Leave etc Regulations 1999, SI 1999/3312 at **[2553]**.

[77 Rights during and after parental leave

(1) Regulations under section 76 shall provide—

(a) that an employee who is absent on parental leave is entitled, for such purposes and to such extent as may be prescribed, to the benefit of the terms and conditions of employment which would have applied if he had not been absent,

(b) that an employee who is absent on parental leave is bound, for such purposes and to such extent as may be prescribed, by any obligations arising under those terms and conditions (except in so far as they are inconsistent with section 76(1)), and

(c) that an employee who is absent on parental leave is entitled, subject to section 78(1), to return from leave to a job of such kind as the regulations may specify.

(2) In subsection (1)(a) "terms and conditions of employment"—

(a) includes matters connected with an employee's employment whether or not they arise under a contract of employment, but

(b) does not include terms and conditions about remuneration.

(3) Regulations under section 76 may specify matters which are, or are not, to be treated as remuneration for the purposes of subsection (2)(b) above.

(4) The regulations may make provision, in relation to the right to return mentioned in subsection (1)(c), about—

(a) seniority, pension rights and similar rights;

(b) terms and conditions of employment on return.]

[1112]

NOTES

Substituted as noted following the Part heading above.

[78 Special cases

(1) Regulations under section 76 may make provision—

(a) about redundancy during a period of parental leave;

(b) about dismissal (other than by reason of redundancy) during a period of parental leave.

(2) Provision by virtue of subsection (1) may include—

(a) provision requiring an employer to offer alternative employment;

(b) provision for the consequences of failure to comply with the regulations (which may include provision for a dismissal to be treated as unfair for the purposes of Part X).

(3) Regulations under section 76 may provide for an employee to be entitled to choose to exercise all or part of his entitlement to parental leave—

(a) by varying the terms of his contract of employment as to hours of work, or

(b) by varying his normal working practice as to hours of work,

in a way specified in or permitted by the regulations for a period specified in the regulations.

(4) Provision by virtue of subsection (3)—

(a) may restrict an entitlement to specified circumstances;

(b) may make an entitlement subject to specified conditions (which may include conditions relating to obtaining the employer's consent);

(c) may include consequential and incidental provision.

(5) Regulations under section 76 may make provision permitting all or part of an employee's entitlement to parental leave in respect of a child to be transferred to another employee in specified circumstances.

(6) The reference in section 77(1)(c) to absence on parental leave includes, where appropriate, a reference to a continuous period of absence attributable partly [to parental leave and partly to—

(a) maternity leave, or

(b) adoption leave,

or to both].

(7) Regulations under section 76 may provide for specified provisions of the regulations not to apply in relation to an employee if any provision of his contract of employment—

(a) confers an entitlement to absence from work for the purpose of caring for a child, and

(b) incorporates or operates by reference to all or part of a collective agreement, or workforce agreement, of a kind specified in the regulations.]

[1113]

NOTES

Substituted as noted following the Part heading above.

Sub-s (6): words in square brackets substituted by the Employment Act 2002, s 53, Sch 7, paras 24, 28.

[79 Supplemental

(1) Regulations under section 76 may, in particular—

(a) make provision about notices to be given and evidence to be produced by employees to employers, by employers to employees, and by employers to other employers;

(b) make provision requiring employers or employees to keep records;

(c) make provision about other procedures to be followed by employees and employers;

(d) make provision (including provision creating criminal offences) specifying the consequences of failure to give notices, to produce evidence, to keep records or to comply with other procedural requirements;

(e) make provision specifying the consequences of failure to act in accordance with a notice given by virtue of paragraph (a);

(f) make special provision for cases where an employee has a right which corresponds to a right conferred by the regulations and which arises under his contract of employment or otherwise;

(g) make provision applying, modifying or excluding an enactment, in such circumstances as may be specified and subject to any conditions specified, in relation to a person entitled to parental leave;

(h) make different provision for different cases or circumstances.

(2) The regulations may make provision modifying the effect of Chapter II of Part XIV (calculation of a week's pay) in relation to an employee who is or has been absent from work on parental leave.

(3) Without prejudice to the generality of section 76, the regulations may make any provision which appears to the Secretary of State to be necessary or expedient—

(a) for the purpose of implementing Council Directive 96/34/EC on the framework agreement on parental leave, or

(b) for the purpose of dealing with any matter arising out of or related to the United Kingdom's obligations under that Directive.]

[1114]

NOTES

Substituted as noted following the Part heading above.

[80 Complaint to employment tribunal

(1) An employee may present a complaint to an employment tribunal that his employer—

(a) has unreasonably postponed a period of parental leave requested by the employee, or

(b) has prevented or attempted to prevent the employee from taking parental leave.

(2) An employment tribunal shall not consider a complaint under this section unless it is presented—

(a) before the end of the period of three months beginning with the date (or last date) of the matters complained of, or

(b) within such further period as the tribunal considers reasonable in a case where it is satisfied that it was not reasonably practicable for the complaint to be presented before the end of that period of three months.

(3) Where an employment tribunal finds a complaint under this section well-founded it—

(a) shall make a declaration to that effect, and

(b) may make an award of compensation to be paid by the employer to the employee.

(4) The amount of compensation shall be such as the tribunal considers just and equitable in all the circumstances having regard to—

(a) the employer's behaviour, and

(b) any loss sustained by the employee which is attributable to the matters complained of.]

[1115]

NOTES

Substituted as noted following the Part heading above.

Conciliation: employment tribunal proceedings and claims which could be the subject of employment tribunal proceedings under sub-s (1) are proceedings to which the Employment Tribunals Act 1996, s 18 applies; see s 18(1)(d) of that Act at **[975]**. The standard conciliation period applies to such proceedings by virtue of the Employment Tribunals (Constitution and Rules of Procedure) Regulations 2004, SI 2004/1861, Sch 1, rule 22(1), (6).

[CHAPTER III
PATERNITY LEAVE

80A Entitlement to [ordinary] paternity leave: birth

(1) The Secretary of State shall make regulations entitling an employee who satisfies specified conditions—

(a) as to duration of employment,

(b) as to relationship with a newborn, or expected, child, and

(c) as to relationship with the child's mother,

to be absent from work on leave under this section for the purpose of caring for the child or supporting the mother.

(2) The regulations shall include provision for determining—

(a) the extent of an employee's entitlement to leave under this section in respect of a child;

(b) when leave under this section may be taken.

(3) Provision under subsection (2)(a) shall secure that where an employee is entitled to leave under this section in respect of a child he is entitled to at least two weeks' leave.

(4) Provision under subsection (2)(b) shall secure that leave under this section must be taken before the end of a period of at least 56 days beginning with the date of the child's birth.

(5) Regulations under subsection (1) may—

(a) specify things which are, or are not, to be taken as done for the purpose of caring for a child or supporting the child's mother;

(b) make provision excluding the right to be absent on leave under this section in respect of a child where more than one child is born as a result of the same pregnancy;

(c) make provision about how leave under this section may be taken.

(6) Where more than one child is born as a result of the same pregnancy, the reference in subsection (4) to the date of the child's birth shall be read as a reference to the date of birth of the first child born as a result of the pregnancy.

(7) In this section—

"newborn child" includes a child stillborn after twenty-four weeks of pregnancy;

"week" means any period of seven days.]

[1116]

NOTES

Chapter III (ss 80A–80E) inserted by the Employment Act 2002, s 1.

Section heading: word in square brackets inserted by the Work and Families Act 2006, s 11(1), Sch 1, para 35, as from a day to be appointed.

Regulations: the Paternity and Adoption Leave Regulations 2002, SI 2002/2788 at **[2752]**.

[80AA Entitlement to additional paternity leave: birth

(1) The Secretary of State may make regulations entitling an employee who satisfies specified conditions—
- (a) as to duration of employment,
- (b) as to relationship with a child, and
- (c) as to relationship with the child's mother,

to be absent from work on leave under this section for the purpose of caring for the child, at a time when the child's mother satisfies any conditions prescribed under subsection (2).

(2) The conditions that may be prescribed under this subsection are conditions relating to any one or more of the following—
- (a) any employment or self-employment of the child's mother;
- (b) her entitlement (or lack of entitlement) to leave under this Part or to statutory maternity pay or maternity allowance;
- (c) whether, and to what extent, she is exercising or has exercised any such entitlement.

(3) Any regulations under this section shall include provision for determining—
- (a) the extent of an employee's entitlement to leave under this section in respect of a child;
- (b) when leave under this section may be taken.

(4) Provision under subsection (3)(a) shall secure that an employee is not entitled to more than 26 weeks' leave in respect of a child.

(5) Provision under subsection (3)(b) shall secure that leave under this section—
- (a) may not be taken before the end of a specified period beginning with the date of the child's birth, but
- (b) must be taken before the end of the period of twelve months beginning with that date.

(6) Subsections (4) and (5)(a) do not limit the provision that may be made under subsection (3) in relation to cases where the child's mother has died before the end of the period mentioned in subsection (5)(b).

(7) Regulations under subsection (1) may—
- (a) specify things which are, or are not, to be taken as done for the purpose of caring for a child;
- (b) make provision excluding the right to be absent on leave under this section in respect of a child where more than one child is born as a result of the same pregnancy;
- (c) specify a minimum period which may be taken as leave under this section;
- (d) make provision about how leave under this section may be taken;
- (e) specify circumstances in which an employee may work for his employer during a period of leave under this section without bringing the period of leave to an end.

(8) Where more than one child is born as a result of the same pregnancy, the reference in subsection (5) to the date of the child's birth shall be read as a reference to the date of birth of the first child born as a result of the pregnancy.

(9) In this section "week" means any period of seven days.]

[1116A]

NOTES

Commencement: to be appointed.

Inserted by the Work and Families Act 2006, s 3, as from a day to be appointed.

[80B Entitlement to [ordinary] paternity leave: adoption

(1) The Secretary of State shall make regulations entitling an employee who satisfies specified conditions—

(a) as to duration of employment,
(b) as to relationship with a child placed, or expected to be placed, for adoption under the law of any part of the United Kingdom, and
(c) as to relationship with a person with whom the child is, or is expected to be, so placed for adoption,

to be absent from work on leave under this section for the purpose of caring for the child or supporting the person by reference to whom he satisfies the condition under paragraph (c).

(2) The regulations shall include provision for determining—
(a) the extent of an employee's entitlement to leave under this section in respect of a child;
(b) when leave under this section may be taken.

(3) Provision under subsection (2)(a) shall secure that where an employee is entitled to leave under this section in respect of a child he is entitled to at least two weeks' leave.

(4) Provision under subsection (2)(b) shall secure that leave under this section must be taken before the end of a period of at least 56 days beginning with the date of the child's placement for adoption.

(5) Regulations under subsection (1) may—
(a) specify things which are, or are not, to be taken as done for the purpose of caring for a child or supporting a person with whom a child is placed for adoption;
(b) make provision excluding the right to be absent on leave under this section in the case of an employee who exercises a right to be absent from work on adoption leave;
(c) make provision excluding the right to be absent on leave under this section in respect of a child where more than one child is placed for adoption as part of the same arrangement;
(d) make provision about how leave under this section may be taken.

(6) Where more than one child is placed for adoption as part of the same arrangement, the reference in subsection (4) to the date of the child's placement shall be read as a reference to the date of placement of the first child to be placed as part of the arrangement.

(7) In this section, "week" means any period of seven days.

(8) The Secretary of State may by regulations provide for this section to have effect in relation to cases which involve adoption, but not the placement of a child for adoption under the law of any part of the United Kingdom, with such modifications as the regulations may prescribe.]

[1117]

NOTES

Inserted as noted to s 80A at **[1116]**.

Section heading: word in square brackets inserted by the Work and Families Act 2006, s 11(1), Sch 1, para 36, as from a day to be appointed.

Modified, in relation to adoptions from overseas, by the Employment Rights Act 1996 (Application of Section 80B to Adoptions from Overseas) Regulations 2003, SI 2003/920.

Regulations: the Paternity and Adoption Leave Regulations 2002, SI 2002/2788 at **[2752]**; the Employment Rights Act 1996 (Application of Section 80B to Adoptions from Overseas) Regulations 2003, SI 2003/920; the Paternity and Adoption Leave (Adoptions from Overseas) Regulations 2003, SI 2003/921.

[80BB Entitlement to additional paternity leave: adoption

(1) The Secretary of State may make regulations entitling an employee who satisfies specified conditions—
(a) as to duration of employment,
(b) as to relationship with a child placed for adoption under the law of any part of the United Kingdom, and
(c) as to relationship with a person with whom the child is so placed for adoption ("the adopter"),

to be absent from work on leave under this section for the purpose of caring for the child, at a time when the adopter satisfies any conditions prescribed under subsection (2).

(2) The conditions that may be prescribed under this subsection are conditions relating to any one or more of the following—

(a) any employment or self-employment of the adopter;
(b) the adopter's entitlement (or lack of entitlement) to leave under this Part or to statutory adoption pay;
(c) whether, and to what extent, the adopter is exercising or has exercised any such entitlement.

(3) Any regulations under this section shall include provision for determining—
(a) the extent of an employee's entitlement to leave under this section in respect of a child;
(b) when leave under this section may be taken.

(4) Provision under subsection (3)(a) shall secure that an employee is not entitled to more than 26 weeks' leave in respect of a child.

(5) Provision under subsection (3)(b) shall secure that leave under this section—
(a) may not be taken before the end of a specified period beginning with the date of the child's placement for adoption, but
(b) must be taken before the end of the period of twelve months beginning with that date.

(6) Subsections (4) and (5)(a) do not limit the provision that may be made under subsection (3) in relation to cases where the adopter has died before the end of the period mentioned in subsection (5)(b).

(7) Regulations under subsection (1) may—
(a) specify things which are, or are not, to be taken as done for the purpose of caring for a child;
(b) make provision excluding the right to be absent on leave under this section in the case of an employee who exercises a right to be absent from work on adoption leave;
(c) make provision excluding the right to be absent on leave under this section in respect of a child where more than one child is placed for adoption as part of the same arrangement;
(d) specify a minimum period which may be taken as leave under this section;
(e) make provision about how leave under this section may be taken;
(f) specify circumstances in which an employee may work for his employer during a period of leave under this section without bringing the period of leave to an end.

(8) Where more than one child is placed for adoption as part of the same arrangement, the reference in subsection (5) to the date of the child's placement shall be read as a reference to the date of placement of the first child to be placed as part of the arrangement.

(9) In this section "week" means any period of seven days.

(10) The Secretary of State may by regulations provide for this section to have effect in relation to cases which involve adoption, but not the placement of a child for adoption under the law of any part of the United Kingdom, with such modifications as the regulations may prescribe.]

[1117A]

NOTES

Commencement: to be appointed.
Inserted by the Work and Families Act 2006, s 4, as from a day to be appointed.

[80C Rights during and after paternity leave

(1) Regulations under section 80A [or 80AA] shall provide—
(a) that an employee who is absent on leave under that section is entitled, for such purposes and to such extent as the regulations may prescribe, to the benefit of the terms and conditions of employment which would have applied if he had not been absent;
(b) that an employee who is absent on leave under that section is bound, for such purposes and to such extent as the regulations may prescribe, by obligations arising under those terms and conditions (except in so far as they are inconsistent with subsection (1) of that section), and
(c) that an employee who is absent on leave under that section is entitled to return from leave to a job of a kind prescribed by regulations, subject to section 80D(1).

(2) The reference in subsection (1)(c) to absence on leave under section 80A [or 80AA] includes, where appropriate, a reference to a continuous period of absence attributable partly to leave under that section and partly to any one or more of the following—

[(za) leave under the other section,]
(a) maternity leave,
(b) adoption leave, and
(c) parental leave.

(3) Subsection (1) shall apply to regulations under section 80B *as it applies to regulations under section 80A*.

(4) In the application of subsection (1)(c) to regulations under section 80B [or 80BB], the reference to absence on leave under that section includes, where appropriate, a reference to a continuous period of absence attributable partly to leave under that section and partly to any one or more of the following—

[(za) leave under the other section,]
(a) maternity leave,
(b) adoption leave,
(c) parental leave, and
(d) leave under section 80A [or 80AA].

(5) In subsection (1)(a), "terms and conditions of employment"—
(a) includes matters connected with an employee's employment whether or not they arise under his contract of employment, but
(b) does not include terms and conditions about remuneration.

(6) Regulations under *section 80A or 80B* may specify matters which are, or are not, to be treated as remuneration for the purposes of this section.

(7) Regulations under *section 80A or 80B* may make provision, in relation to the right to return mentioned in subsection (1)(c), about—
(a) seniority, pension rights and similar rights;
(b) terms and conditions of employment on return.]

[1118]

NOTES

Inserted as noted to s 80A at **[1116]**.

Sub-ss (1), (2), (4): words and figures in square brackets inserted by the Work and Families Act 2006, s 5(1)–(3), (5), as from a day to be appointed.

Sub-s (3): for the words in italics there are substituted the words "or 80BB as it applies to regulations under section 80A or 80AA" by the Work and Families Act 2006, s 5(1), (4), as from a day to be appointed.

Sub-ss (6), (7): for the words in italics there are substituted the words "any of sections 80A to 80BB" by the Work and Families Act 2006, s 5(1), (6), as from a day to be appointed.

[80D Special cases

(1) Regulations under section *80A or 80B* may make provision about—
(a) redundancy, or
(b) dismissal (other than by reason of redundancy),

during a period of leave under that section.

(2) Provision by virtue of subsection (1) may include—
(a) provision requiring an employer to offer alternative employment;
(b) provision for the consequences of failure to comply with the regulations (which may include provision for a dismissal to be treated as unfair for the purposes of Part 10).]

[1119]

NOTES

Inserted as noted to s 80A at **[1116]**.

Sub-s (1): for the words in italics there are substituted the words "80A, 80AA, 80B or 80BB" by the Work and Families Act 2006, s 11(1), Sch 1, para 37, as from a day to be appointed.

[80E Chapter 3: supplemental

[(1)] Regulations under *section 80A or 80B* may—

(a) make provision about notices to be given, evidence to be produced and other procedures to be followed by employees and employers;
(b) make provision requiring employers or employees to keep records;
(c) make provision for the consequences of failure to give notices, to produce evidence, to keep records or to comply with other procedural requirements;
(d) make provision for the consequences of failure to act in accordance with a notice given by virtue of paragraph (a);
(e) make special provision for cases where an employee has a right which corresponds to a right under *section 80A or 80B* and which arises under his contract of employment or otherwise;
(f) make provision modifying the effect of Chapter 2 of Part 14 (calculation of a week's pay) in relation to an employee who is or has been absent from work on leave under *section 80A or 80B*;
(g) make provision applying, modifying or excluding an enactment, in such circumstances as may be specified and subject to any conditions which may be specified, in relation to a person entitled to take leave under *section 80A or 80B*;
(h) make different provision for different cases or circumstances.

[(2) The persons on whom duties may be imposed by regulations under section 80AA or 80BB include not only employees exercising rights by virtue of that section and their employers but also—
(a) in the case of section 80AA, the mother of the child in question and any employer or former employer of hers, and
(b) in the case of section 80BB, the person by reference to whom the condition in subsection (1)(c) of that section is satisfied and any employer or former employer of that person.]]

[1120]

NOTES

Inserted as noted to s 80A at **[1116]**.

Sub-s (1) numbered as such, for the words in italics in that subsection there are substituted the words "any of sections 80A to 80BB", and sub-s (2) added by the Work and Families Act 2006, s 11(1), Sch 1, para 38(1), (3), as from a day to be appointed.

[PART VIIIA
FLEXIBLE WORKING

80F Statutory right to request contract variation

(1) A qualifying employee may apply to his employer for a change in his terms and conditions of employment if—
(a) the change relates to—
(i) the hours he is required to work,
(ii) the times when he is required to work,
(iii) where, as between his home and a place of business of his employer, he is required to work, or
(iv) such other aspect of his terms and conditions of employment as the Secretary of State may specify by regulations, and
[(b) his purpose in applying for the change is to enable him to care for someone who, at the time of application, is—
(i) a child who has not reached the prescribed age or falls within a prescribed description and in respect of whom (in either case) the employee satisfies prescribed conditions as to relationship, or
(ii) a person aged 18 or over who falls within a prescribed description and in respect of whom the employee satisfies prescribed conditions as to relationship].

(2) An application under this section must—
(a) state that it is such an application,
(b) specify the change applied for and the date on which it is proposed the change should become effective,
(c) explain what effect, if any, the employee thinks making the change applied for would have on his employer and how, in his opinion, any such effect might be dealt with, and

(d) explain how the employee meets, in respect of the [child or other person to be cared for, the conditions as to relationship mentioned in subsection (1)(b)(i) or (ii)].

(3) …

(4) If an employee has made an application under this section, he may not make a further application under this section to the same employer before the end of the period of twelve months beginning with the date on which the previous application was made.

(5) The Secretary of State may by regulations make provision about—

(a) the form of applications under this section, and
(b) when such an application is to be taken as made.

(6), (7) …

(8) For the purposes of this section, an employee is—

(a) a qualifying employee if he—
  (i) satisfies such conditions as to duration of employment as the Secretary of State may specify by regulations, and
  (ii) is not an agency worker;
(b) an agency worker if he is supplied by a person ("the agent") to do work for another ("the principal") under a contract or other arrangement made between the agent and the principal.]

[(9) Regulations under this section may make different provision for different cases.

(10) In this section—

"child" means a person aged under 18;

"prescribed" means prescribed by regulations made by the Secretary of State.]

[1121]

NOTES

Part VIIIA (ss 80F–80I) inserted by the Employment Act 2002, s 47(1), (2).

Sub-s (1): para (b) substituted by the Work and Families Act 2006, s 12(1), (2), as from 6 April 2007.

Sub-s (2): words in square brackets in para (d) substituted by the Work and Families Act 2006, s 12(1), (3), as from 6 April 2007.

Sub-ss (3), (6), (7): repealed by the Work and Families Act 2006, ss 12(1), (4), 15, Sch 2, as from 6 April 2007.

Sub-ss (9), (10): added by the Work and Families Act 2006, s 12(1), (5), as from 6 April 2007.

Regulations: the Flexible Working (Eligibility, Complaints and Remedies) Regulations 2002, SI 2002/3236 at **[2875]** (made under sub-ss (1)(b), (5), (8)(a)).

Orders: as of the date of its repeal, no Orders had been made under sub-s (6).

[80G Employer's duties in relation to application under section 80F

(1) An employer to whom an application under section 80F is made—

(a) shall deal with the application in accordance with regulations made by the Secretary of State, and
(b) shall only refuse the application because he considers that one or more of the following grounds applies—
  (i) the burden of additional costs,
  (ii) detrimental effect on ability to meet customer demand,
  (iii) inability to re-organise work among existing staff,
  (iv) inability to recruit additional staff,
  (v) detrimental impact on quality,
  (vi) detrimental impact on performance,
  (vii) insufficiency of work during the periods the employee proposes to work,
  (viii) planned structural changes, and
  (ix) such other grounds as the Secretary of State may specify by regulations.

(2) Regulations under subsection (1)(a) shall include—

(a) provision for the holding of a meeting between the employer and the employee to discuss an application under section 80F within twenty eight days after the date the application is made;
(b) provision for the giving by the employer to the employee of notice of his decision on the application within fourteen days after the date of the meeting under paragraph (a);

(c) provision for notice under paragraph (b) of a decision to refuse the application to state the grounds for the decision;

(d) provision for the employee to have a right, if he is dissatisfied with the employer's decision, to appeal against it within fourteen days after the date on which notice under paragraph (b) is given;

(e) provision about the procedure for exercising the right of appeal under paragraph (d), including provision requiring the employee to set out the grounds of appeal;

(f) provision for notice under paragraph (b) to include such information as the regulations may specify relating to the right of appeal under paragraph (d);

(g) provision for the holding, within fourteen days after the date on which notice of appeal is given by the employee, of a meeting between the employer and the employee to discuss the appeal;

(h) provision for the employer to give the employee notice of his decision on any appeal within fourteen days after the date of the meeting under paragraph (g);

(i) provision for notice under paragraph (h) of a decision to dismiss an appeal to state the grounds for the decision;

(j) provision for a statement under paragraph (c) or (i) to contain a sufficient explanation of the grounds for the decision;

(k) provision for the employee to have a right to be accompanied at meetings under paragraph (a) or (g) by a person of such description as the regulations may specify;

(l) provision for postponement in relation to any meeting under paragraph (a) or (g) which a companion under paragraph (k) is not available to attend;

(m) provision in relation to companions under paragraph (k) corresponding to section 10(6) and (7) of the Employment Relations Act 1999 (c 26) (right to paid time off to act as companion, etc);

(n) provision, in relation to the rights under paragraphs (k) and (l), for the application (with or without modification) of sections 11 to 13 of the Employment Relations Act 1999 (provisions ancillary to right to be accompanied under section 10 of that Act).

(3) Regulations under subsection (1)(a) may include—

(a) provision for any requirement of the regulations not to apply where an application is disposed of by agreement or withdrawn;

(b) provision for extension of a time limit where the employer and employee agree, or in such other circumstances as the regulations may specify;

(c) provision for applications to be treated as withdrawn in specified circumstances;

and may make different provision for different cases.

(4) The Secretary of State may by order amend subsection (2).]

[1122]

NOTES

Inserted as noted to s 80F at **[1121]**.

Conciliation: employment tribunal proceedings and claims which could be the subject of employment tribunal proceedings under sub-s (1) are proceedings to which the Employment Tribunals Act 1996, s 18 applies; see s 18(1)(d) of that Act at **[975]**. The standard conciliation period applies to such proceedings by virtue of the Employment Tribunals (Constitution and Rules of Procedure) Regulations 2004, SI 2004/1861, Sch 1, rule 22(1), (6).

Regulations: the Flexible Working (Procedural Requirements) Regulations 2002, SI 2002/3207 at **[2858]**.

[80H Complaints to employment tribunals

(1) An employee who makes an application under section 80F may present a complaint to an employment tribunal—

(a) that his employer has failed in relation to the application to comply with section 80G(1), or

(b) that a decision by his employer to reject the application was based on incorrect facts.

(2) No complaint under this section may be made in respect of an application which has been disposed of by agreement or withdrawn.

(3) In the case of an application which has not been disposed of by agreement or withdrawn, no complaint under this section may be made until the employer—

(a) notifies the employee of a decision to reject the application on appeal, or
(b) commits a breach of regulations under section 80G(1)(a) of such description as the Secretary of State may specify by regulations.

(4) No complaint under this section may be made in respect of failure to comply with provision included in regulations under subsection (1)(a) of section 80G because of subsection (2)(k), (l) or (m) of that section.

(5) An employment tribunal shall not consider a complaint under this section unless it is presented—
(a) before the end of the period of three months beginning with the relevant date, or
(b) within such further period as the tribunal considers reasonable in a case where it is satisfied that it was not reasonably practicable for the complaint to be presented before the end of that period of three months.

(6) In subsection (5)(a), the reference to the relevant date is—
(a) in the case of a complaint permitted by subsection (3)(a), the date on which the employee is notified of the decision on the appeal, and
(b) in the case of a complaint permitted by subsection (3)(b), the date on which the breach concerned was committed.]

[1123]

NOTES

Inserted as noted to s 80F at **[1121]**.

Conciliation: employment tribunal proceedings and claims which could be the subject of employment tribunal proceedings under sub-s (1)(b) are proceedings to which the Employment Tribunals Act 1996, s 18 applies; see s 18(1)(d) of that Act at **[975]**. The standard conciliation period applies to such proceedings by virtue of the Employment Tribunals (Constitution and Rules of Procedure) Regulations 2004, SI 2004/1861, Sch 1, rule 22(1), (6).

Regulations: the Flexible Working (Eligibility, Complaints and Remedies) Regulations 2002, SI 2002/3236 at **[2875]**.

[80I Remedies

(1) Where an employment tribunal finds a complaint under section 80H well-founded it shall make a declaration to that effect and may—
(a) make an order for reconsideration of the application, and
(b) make an award of compensation to be paid by the employer to the employee.

(2) The amount of compensation shall be such amount, not exceeding the permitted maximum, as the tribunal considers just and equitable in all the circumstances.

(3) For the purposes of subsection (2), the permitted maximum is such number of weeks' pay as the Secretary of State may specify by regulations.

(4) Where an employment tribunal makes an order under subsection (1)(a), section 80G, and the regulations under that section, shall apply as if the application had been made on the date of the order.]

[1124]

NOTES

Inserted as noted to s 80F at **[1121]**.

Regulations: the Flexible Working (Eligibility, Complaints and Remedies) Regulations 2002, SI 2002/3236 at **[2875]**.

PART IX
TERMINATION OF EMPLOYMENT

Minimum period of notice

86 Rights of employer and employee to minimum notice

(1) The notice required to be given by an employer to terminate the contract of employment of a person who has been continuously employed for one month or more—
(a) is not less than one week's notice if his period of continuous employment is less than two years,

(b) is not less than one week's notice for each year of continuous employment if his period of continuous employment is two years or more but less than twelve years, and

(c) is not less than twelve weeks' notice if his period of continuous employment is twelve years or more.

(2) The notice required to be given by an employee who has been continuously employed for one month or more to terminate his contract of employment is not less than one week.

(3) Any provision for shorter notice in any contract of employment with a person who has been continuously employed for one month or more has effect subject to subsections (1) and (2); but this section does not prevent either party from waiving his right to notice on any occasion or from accepting a payment in lieu of notice.

(4) Any contract of employment of a person who has been continuously employed for three months or more which is a contract for a term certain of one month or less shall have effect as if it were for an indefinite period; and, accordingly, subsections (1) and (2) apply to the contract.

(5) …

(6) This section does not affect any right of either party to a contract of employment to treat the contract as terminable without notice by reason of the conduct of the other party.

[1125]

NOTES

Sub-s (5): repealed by the Fixed-term Employees (Prevention of Less Favourable Treatment) Regulations 2002, SI 2002/2034, reg 11, Sch 2, Pt 1, para 3(1), (4).

87 Rights of employee in period of notice

(1) If an employer gives notice to terminate the contract of employment of a person who has been continuously employed for one month or more, the provisions of sections 88 to 91 have effect as respects the liability of the employer for the period of notice required by section 86(1).

(2) If an employee who has been continuously employed for one month or more gives notice to terminate his contract of employment, the provisions of sections 88 to 91 have effect as respects the liability of the employer for the period of notice required by section 86(2).

(3) In sections 88 to 91 "period of notice" means—

(a) where notice is given by an employer, the period of notice required by section 86(1), and

(b) where notice is given by an employee, the period of notice required by section 86(2).

(4) This section does not apply in relation to a notice given by the employer or the employee if the notice to be given by the employer to terminate the contract must be at least one week more than the notice required by section 86(1).

[1126]

88 Employments with normal working hours

(1) If an employee has normal working hours under the contract of employment in force during the period of notice and during any part of those normal working hours—

(a) the employee is ready and willing to work but no work is provided for him by his employer,

(b) the employee is incapable of work because of sickness or injury,

(c) the employee is absent from work wholly or partly because of pregnancy or childbirth [or on [adoption leave, parental leave or *paternity leave*]], or

(d) the employee is absent from work in accordance with the terms of his employment relating to holidays,

the employer is liable to pay the employee for the part of normal working hours covered by any of paragraphs (a), (b), (c) and (d) a sum not less than the amount of remuneration for that part of normal working hours calculated at the average hourly rate of remuneration produced by dividing a week's pay by the number of normal working hours.

(2) Any payments made to the employee by his employer in respect of the relevant part of the period of notice (whether by way of sick pay, statutory sick pay, maternity pay, statutory maternity pay, [paternity pay, *statutory paternity pay*, adoption pay, statutory adoption pay,] holiday pay or otherwise) go towards meeting the employer's liability under this section.

(3) Where notice was given by the employee, the employer's liability under this section does not arise unless and until the employee leaves the service of the employer in pursuance of the notice.

[1127]

NOTES

Sub-s (1): words in first (outer) pair of square brackets in para (c) inserted by the Employment Relations Act 1999, s 9, Sch 4, Pt III, paras 1, 5, 10; words in second (inner) pair of square brackets in para (c) substituted by the Employment Act 2002, s 53, Sch 7, paras 24, 29(1), (2); for the words in italics there are substituted the words "ordinary or additional paternity leave" by the Work and Families Act 2006, s 11(1), Sch 1, para 39(1), (2), as from a day to be appointed.

Sub-s (2): words in square brackets inserted by the Employment Act 2002, s 53, Sch 7, paras 24, 29(1), (3); for the words in italics there are substituted the words "ordinary statutory paternity pay, additional statutory paternity pay" by the Work and Families Act 2006, s 11(1), Sch 1, para 39(1), (3), as from a day to be appointed.

89 Employments without normal working hours

(1) If an employee does not have normal working hours under the contract of employment in force in the period of notice, the employer is liable to pay the employee for each week of the period of notice a sum not less than a week's pay.

(2) The employer's liability under this section is conditional on the employee being ready and willing to do work of a reasonable nature and amount to earn a week's pay.

(3) Subsection (2) does not apply—

- (a) in respect of any period during which the employee is incapable of work because of sickness or injury,
- (b) in respect of any period during which the employee is absent from work wholly or partly because of pregnancy or childbirth [or on [adoption leave, parental leave or *paternity leave*]], or
- (c) in respect of any period during which the employee is absent from work in accordance with the terms of his employment relating to holidays.

(4) Any payment made to an employee by his employer in respect of a period within subsection (3) (whether by way of sick pay, statutory sick pay, maternity pay, statutory maternity pay, [paternity pay, *statutory paternity pay*, adoption pay, statutory adoption pay,] holiday pay or otherwise) shall be taken into account for the purposes of this section as if it were remuneration paid by the employer in respect of that period.

(5) Where notice was given by the employee, the employer's liability under this section does not arise unless and until the employee leaves the service of the employer in pursuance of the notice.

[1128]

NOTES

Sub-s (3): words in first (outer) pair of square brackets in para (b) inserted by the Employment Relations Act 1999, s 9, Sch 4, Pt III, paras 1, 5, 11; words in second (inner) pair of square brackets in para (b) substituted by the Employment Act 2002, s 53, Sch 7, paras 24, 30(1), (2); for the words in italics there are substituted the words "ordinary or additional paternity leave" by the Work and Families Act 2006, s 11(1), Sch 1, para 40(1), (2), as from a day to be appointed.

Sub-s (4): words in square brackets inserted by the Employment Act 2002, s 53, Sch 7, paras 24, 30(1), (3); for the words in italics there are substituted the words "ordinary statutory paternity pay, additional statutory paternity pay" by the Work and Families Act 2006, s 11(1), Sch 1, para 40(1), (3), as from a day to be appointed.

90 Short-term incapacity benefit and industrial injury benefit

(1) This section has effect where the arrangements in force relating to the employment are such that—

- (a) payments by way of sick pay are made by the employer to employees to whom the arrangements apply, in cases where any such employees are incapable of work because of sickness or injury, and

(b) in calculating any payment so made to any such employee an amount representing, or treated as representing, short-term incapacity benefit or industrial injury benefit is taken into account, whether by way of deduction or by way of calculating the payment as a supplement to that amount.

(2) If—

(a) during any part of the period of notice the employee is incapable of work because of sickness or injury,

(b) one or more payments by way of sick pay are made to him by the employer in respect of that part of the period of notice, and

(c) in calculating any such payment such an amount as is referred to in paragraph (b) of subsection (1) is taken into account as mentioned in that paragraph,

for the purposes of section 88 or 89 the amount so taken into account shall be treated as having been paid by the employer to the employee by way of sick pay in respect of that part of that period, and shall go towards meeting the liability of the employer under that section accordingly.

[1129]

91 Supplementary

(1) An employer is not liable under section 88 or 89 to make any payment in respect of a period during which an employee is absent from work with the leave of the employer granted at the request of the employee, including any period of time off taken in accordance with—

(a) Part VI of this Act, or

(b) section 168 or 170 of the Trade Union and Labour Relations (Consolidation) Act 1992 (trade union duties and activities).

(2) No payment is due under section 88 or 89 in consequence of a notice to terminate a contract given by an employee if, after the notice is given and on or before the termination of the contract, the employee takes part in a strike of employees of the employer.

(3) If, during the period of notice, the employer breaks the contract of employment, payments received under section 88 or 89 in respect of the part of the period after the breach go towards mitigating the damages recoverable by the employee for loss of earnings in that part of the period of notice.

(4) If, during the period of notice, the employee breaks the contract and the employer rightfully treats the breach as terminating the contract, no payment is due to the employee under section 88 or 89 in respect of the part of the period falling after the termination of the contract.

(5) If an employer fails to give the notice required by section 86, the rights conferred by sections 87 to 90 and this section shall be taken into account in assessing his liability for breach of the contract.

(6) Sections 86 to 90 and this section apply in relation to a contract all or any of the terms of which are terms which take effect by virtue of any provision contained in or having effect under an Act (whether public or local) as in relation to any other contract; and the reference in this subsection to an Act includes, subject to any express provision to the contrary, an Act passed after this Act.

[1130]

Written statement of reasons for dismissal

92 Right to written statement of reasons for dismissal

(1) An employee is entitled to be provided by his employer with a written statement giving particulars of the reasons for the employee's dismissal—

(a) if the employee is given by the employer notice of termination of his contract of employment,

(b) if the employee's contract of employment is terminated by the employer without notice, or

[(c) if the employee is employed under a limited-term contract and the contract terminates by virtue of the limiting event without being renewed under the same contract].

(2) Subject to [subsections (4) and (4A)], an employee is entitled to a written statement under this section only if he makes a request for one; and a statement shall be provided within fourteen days of such a request.

(3) Subject to [subsections (4) and (4A)], an employee is not entitled to a written statement under this section unless on the effective date of termination he has been, or will have been, continuously employed for a period of not less than [one year] ending with that date.

(4) An employee is entitled to a written statement under this section without having to request it and irrespective of whether she has been continuously employed for any period if she is dismissed—

(a) at any time while she is pregnant, or

(b) after childbirth in circumstances in which her [ordinary or additional maternity leave period] ends by reason of the dismissal.

[(4A) An employee who is dismissed while absent from work during an ordinary or additional adoption leave period is entitled to a written statement under this section without having to request it and irrespective of whether he has been continuously employed for any period if he is dismissed in circumstances in which that period ends by reason of the dismissal.]

(5) A written statement under this section is admissible in evidence in any proceedings.

(6) Subject to subsection (7), in this section "the effective date of termination"—

(a) in relation to an employee whose contract of employment is terminated by notice, means the date on which the notice expires,

(b) in relation to an employee whose contract of employment is terminated without notice, means the date on which the termination takes effect, and

[(c) in relation to an employee who is employed under a limited-term contract which terminates by virtue of the limiting event without being renewed under the same contract, means the date on which the termination takes effect].

(7) Where—

(a) the contract of employment is terminated by the employer, and

(b) the notice required by section 86 to be given by an employer would, if duly given on the material date, expire on a date later than the effective date of termination (as defined by subsection (6)),

the later date is the effective date of termination.

(8) In subsection (7)(b) "the material date" means—

(a) the date when notice of termination was given by the employer, or

(b) where no notice was given, the date when the contract of employment was terminated by the employer.

[1131]

NOTES

Sub-s (1): para (c) substituted by the Fixed-term Employees (Prevention of Less Favourable Treatment) Regulations 2002, SI 2002/2034, reg 11, Sch 2, Pt 1, para 3(1), (5).

Sub-s (2): words in square brackets substituted by the Employment Act 2002, s 53, Sch 7, paras 24, 31.

Sub-s (3): words in first pair of square brackets substituted by the Employment Act 2002, s 53, Sch 7, paras 24, 31; words in second pair of square brackets substituted by the Unfair Dismissal and Statement of Reasons for Dismissal (Variation of Qualifying Period) Order 1999, SI 1999/1436, arts 2, 5.

Sub-s (4): words in square brackets substituted by the Employment Relations Act 1999, s 9, Sch 4, Pt III, paras 1, 5, 12.

Sub-s (4A): inserted by the Employment Act 2002, s 53, Sch 7, paras 24, 31.

Sub-s (6): para (c) substituted by the Employment Relations Act 2004, s 57(1), Sch 1, para 28, as from 6 April 2005.

Modified as noted to s 66 at **[1097]**.

Conciliation: employment tribunal proceedings and claims which could be the subject of employment tribunal proceedings under this section are proceedings to which the Employment Tribunals Act 1996, s 18 applies; see s 18(1)(d) of that Act at **[975]**. The standard conciliation period applies to such proceedings by virtue of the Employment Tribunals (Constitution and Rules of Procedure) Regulations 2004, SI 2004/1861, Sch 1, rule 22(1), (6).

93 Complaints to [employment tribunal]

(1) A complaint may be presented to an [employment tribunal] by an employee on the ground that—

(a) the employer unreasonably failed to provide a written statement under section 92, or

(b) the particulars of reasons given in purported compliance with that section are inadequate or untrue.

(2) Where an [employment tribunal] finds a complaint under this section well-founded, the tribunal—

(a) may make a declaration as to what it finds the employer's reasons were for dismissing the employee, and

(b) shall make an award that the employer pay to the employee a sum equal to the amount of two weeks' pay.

(3) An [employment tribunal] shall not consider a complaint under this section relating to the reasons for a dismissal unless it is presented to the tribunal at such a time that the tribunal would, in accordance with section 111, consider a complaint of unfair dismissal in respect of that dismissal presented at the same time.

[1132]

NOTES

Words in square brackets substituted by the Employment Rights (Dispute Resolution) Act 1998, s 1(2)(a).

Conciliation: employment tribunal proceedings under this section in respect of a breach of s 92 of this Act and claims which could be the subject of such proceedings are proceedings to which the Employment Tribunals Act 1996, s 18 applies; see s 18(1)(d) of that Act at **[975]**. The standard conciliation period applies to such proceedings by virtue of the Employment Tribunals (Constitution and Rules of Procedure) Regulations 2004, SI 2004/1861, Sch 1, rule 22(1), (6).

Modified as noted to s 66 at **[1097]**.

PART X
UNFAIR DISMISSAL

NOTES

This Part (ss 94–134A) is modified, in relation to governing bodies with delegated budgets, by the Education (Modification of Enactments Relating to Employment) (England) Order 2003, SI 2003/1964, art 3, Schedule at **[3035C]**, **[3035G]** and the Education (Modification of Enactments Relating to Employment) (Wales) Order 2006, SI 2006/1073, art 3, Schedule at **[3462B]**, **[3462F]**.

Conciliation: employment tribunal proceedings and claims which could be the subject of employment tribunal proceedings under this Part are proceedings to which the Employment Tribunals Act 1996, s 18 applies; see s 18(1)(d) of that Act at **[975]**. The standard conciliation period applies to such proceedings by virtue of the Employment Tribunals (Constitution and Rules of Procedure) Regulations 2004, SI 2004/1861, Sch 1, rule 22(1), (6), except where it is claimed that a dismissal was automatically unfair by virtue of ss 103A or 105(6A); in such cases there is no fixed conciliation period by virtue of SI 2004/1861, Sch 1, rule 22(1).

CHAPTER I
RIGHT NOT TO BE UNFAIRLY DISMISSED

The right

94 The right

(1) An employee has the right not to be unfairly dismissed by his employer.

(2) Subsection (1) has effect subject to the following provisions of this Part (in particular sections 108 to 110) and to the provisions of the Trade Union and Labour Relations (Consolidation) Act 1992 (in particular sections 237 to 239).

[1133]

Dismissal

95 Circumstances in which an employee is dismissed

(1) For the purposes of this Part an employee is dismissed by his employer if (and, subject to subsection (2) … , only if)—

(a) the contract under which he is employed is terminated by the employer (whether with or without notice),

[(b) he is employed under a limited-term contract and that contract terminates by virtue of the limiting event without being renewed under the same contract, or]

(c) the employee terminates the contract under which he is employed (with or without notice) in circumstances in which he is entitled to terminate it without notice by reason of the employer's conduct.

(2) An employee shall be taken to be dismissed by his employer for the purposes of this Part if—

(a) the employer gives notice to the employee to terminate his contract of employment, and

(b) at a time within the period of that notice the employee gives notice to the employer to terminate the contract of employment on a date earlier than the date on which the employer's notice is due to expire;

and the reason for the dismissal is to be taken to be the reason for which the employer's notice is given.

[1134]

NOTES

Sub-s (1): words omitted repealed by the Employment Relations Act 2004, s 57, Sch 1, para 29, Sch 2, as from 6 April 2005; para (b) substituted by the Fixed-term Employees (Prevention of Less Favourable Treatment) Regulations 2002, SI 2002/2034, reg 11, Sch 2, para 3(1), (7) (note that SI 2002/2034 purports to insert this paragraph).

96 (*Repealed by the Employment Relations Act 1999, ss 9, 44, Sch 4, Pt III, paras 1, 5, 13, Sch 9*(2).)

97 Effective date of termination

(1) Subject to the following provisions of this section, in this Part "the effective date of termination"—

(a) in relation to an employee whose contract of employment is terminated by notice, whether given by his employer or by the employee, means the date on which the notice expires,

(b) in relation to an employee whose contract of employment is terminated without notice, means the date on which the termination takes effect, and

[(c) in relation to an employee who is employed under a limited-term contract which terminates by virtue of the limiting event without being renewed under the same contract, means the date on which the termination takes effect].

(2) Where—

(a) the contract of employment is terminated by the employer, and

(b) the notice required by section 86 to be given by an employer would, if duly given on the material date, expire on a date later than the effective date of termination (as defined by subsection (1)),

for the purposes of sections 108(1), 119(1) and 227(3) the later date is the effective date of termination.

(3) In subsection (2)(b) "the material date" means—

(a) the date when notice of termination was given by the employer, or

(b) where no notice was given, the date when the contract of employment was terminated by the employer.

(4) Where—

(a) the contract of employment is terminated by the employee,

(b) the material date does not fall during a period of notice given by the employer to terminate that contract, and

(c) had the contract been terminated not by the employee but by notice given on the material date by the employer, that notice would have been required by section 86 to expire on a date later than the effective date of termination (as defined by subsection (1)),

for the purposes of sections 108(1), 119(1) and 227(3) the later date is the effective date of termination.

(5) In subsection (4) "the material date" means—

(a) the date when notice of termination was given by the employee, or

(b) where no notice was given, the date when the contract of employment was terminated by the employee.

(6) …

[1135]

NOTES

Sub-s (1): para (c) substituted by the Fixed-term Employees (Prevention of Less Favourable Treatment) Regulations 2002, SI 2002/2034, reg 11, Sch 2, para 3(1), (8).

Sub-s (6): repealed by the Employment Relations Act 1999, ss 9, 44, Sch 4, Pt III, paras 1, 5, 14, Sch 9(2).

Fairness

98 General

(1) In determining for the purposes of this Part whether the dismissal of an employee is fair or unfair, it is for the employer to show—

(a) the reason (or, if more than one, the principal reason) for the dismissal, and

(b) that it is either a reason falling within subsection (2) or some other substantial reason of a kind such as to justify the dismissal of an employee holding the position which the employee held.

(2) A reason falls within this subsection if it—

(a) relates to the capability or qualifications of the employee for performing work of the kind which he was employed by the employer to do,

(b) relates to the conduct of the employee,

[(ba) is retirement of the employee,]

(c) is that the employee was redundant, or

(d) is that the employee could not continue to work in the position which he held without contravention (either on his part or on that of his employer) of a duty or restriction imposed by or under an enactment.

[(2A) Subsections (1) and (2) are subject to sections 98ZA to 98ZF.]

(3) In subsection (2)(a)—

(a) "capability", in relation to an employee, means his capability assessed by reference to skill, aptitude, health or any other physical or mental quality, and

(b) "qualifications", in relation to an employee, means any degree, diploma or other academic, technical or professional qualification relevant to the position which he held.

[(3A) In any case where the employer has fulfilled the requirements of subsection (1) by showing that the reason (or the principal reason) for the dismissal is retirement of the employee, the question whether the dismissal is fair or unfair shall be determined in accordance with section 98ZG.]

(4) [In any other case where] the employer has fulfilled the requirements of subsection (1), the determination of the question whether the dismissal is fair or unfair (having regard to the reason shown by the employer)—

(a) depends on whether in the circumstances (including the size and administrative resources of the employer's undertaking) the employer acted reasonably or unreasonably in treating it as a sufficient reason for dismissing the employee, and

(b) shall be determined in accordance with equity and the substantial merits of the case.

(5) …

(6) [Subsection (4)] [is] subject to—

(a) sections [98A] to 107 of this Act, and

(b) sections 152, 153[, 238 and 238A] of the Trade Union and Labour Relations (Consolidation) Act 1992 (dismissal on ground of trade union membership or activities or in connection with industrial action).

[1136]

NOTES

Sub-s (2): para (ba) inserted by the Employment Equality (Age) Regulations 2006, SI 2006/1031, reg 49(1), Sch 8, Pt 1, paras 21, 22(1), (2), as from 1 October 2006.

Sub-ss (2A), (3A): inserted by SI 2006/1031, reg 49(1), Sch 8, Pt 1, paras 21, 22(1), (3), (4), as from 1 October 2006.

Sub-s (4): words in square brackets substituted by SI 2006/1031, reg 49(1), Sch 8, Pt 1, paras 21, 22(1), (5), as from 1 October 2006.

Sub-s (5): repealed by the Employment Relations Act 1999, ss 9, Sch 4, Pt III, paras 1, 5, 15(a), Sch 9(2).

Sub-s (6): words in first pair of square brackets substituted by the Employment Relations Act 1999, s 9, Sch 4, Pt III, paras 1, 5, 15(b); word in second pair of square brackets and figure in third pair of square brackets substituted by the Employment Act 2002, s 53, Sch 7, paras 24, 32, as from 1 October 2004; words in fourth pair of square brackets substituted by the Employment Relations Act 2004, s 57(1), Sch 1, para 30, as from 6 April 2005, except in relation to a dismissal where the effective date of termination (as defined in s 97 of this Act) occurred before that date (see SI 2005/872, art 12).

[Retirement

98ZA No normal retirement age: dismissal before 65

(1) This section applies to the dismissal of an employee if—

(a) the employee has no normal retirement age, and

(b) the operative date of termination falls before the date when the employee reaches the age of 65.

(2) Retirement of the employee shall not be taken to be the reason (or a reason) for the dismissal.]

[1136A]

NOTES

Commencement: 1 October 2006.

Inserted, together with the preceding heading, ss 98ZB–98ZH and the heading preceding s 98A, by the Employment Equality (Age) Regulations 2006, SI 2006/1031, reg 49(1), Sch 8, Pt 1, paras 21, 23, as from 1 October 2006.

[98ZB No normal retirement age: dismissal at or after 65

(1) This section applies to the dismissal of an employee if—

(a) the employee has no normal retirement age, and

(b) the operative date of termination falls on or after the date when the employee reaches the age of 65.

(2) In a case where—

(a) the employer has notified the employee in accordance with paragraph 2 of Schedule 6 to the 2006 Regulations, and

(b) the contract of employment terminates on the intended date of retirement,

retirement of the employee shall be taken to be the only reason for the dismissal by the employer and any other reason shall be disregarded.

(3) In a case where—

(a) the employer has notified the employee in accordance with paragraph 2 of Schedule 6 to the 2006 Regulations, but

(b) the contract of employment terminates before the intended date of retirement,

retirement of the employee shall not be taken to be the reason (or a reason) for dismissal.

(4) In a case where—

(a) the employer has not notified the employee in accordance with paragraph 2 of Schedule 6 to the 2006 Regulations, and

(b) there is an intended date of retirement in relation to the dismissal, but

(c) the contract of employment terminates before the intended date of retirement,

retirement of the employee shall not be taken to be the reason (or a reason) for dismissal.

(5) In all other cases where the employer has not notified the employee in accordance with paragraph 2 of Schedule 6 to the 2006 Regulations, particular regard shall be had to the matters in section 98ZF when determining the reason (or principal reason) for dismissal.]

[1136B]

NOTES

Commencement: 1 October 2006.

Inserted as noted to s 98ZA at **[1136A]**.

For transitional provisions affecting the application of Sch 6 to the Employment Equality (Age) Regulations 2006, SI 2006/1031 where the employer gave notice of dismissal expiring before 1 April 2007, see Sch 7 to those Regulations at **[3460]**.

[98ZC Normal retirement age: dismissal before retirement age

(1) This section applies to the dismissal of an employee if—

(a) the employee has a normal retirement age, and

(b) the operative date of termination falls before the date when the employee reaches the normal retirement age.

(2) Retirement of the employee shall not be taken to be the reason (or a reason) for the dismissal.]

[1136C]

NOTES

Commencement: 1 October 2006.

Inserted as noted to s 98ZA at **[1136A]**.

[98ZD Normal retirement age 65 or higher: dismissal at or after retirement age

(1) This section applies to the dismissal of an employee if—

(a) the employee has a normal retirement age,

(b) the normal retirement age is 65 or higher, and

(c) the operative date of termination falls on or after the date when the employee reaches the normal retirement age.

(2) In a case where—

(a) the employer has notified the employee in accordance with paragraph 2 of Schedule 6 to the 2006 Regulations, and

(b) the contract of employment terminates on the intended date of retirement,

retirement of the employee shall be taken to be the only reason for the dismissal by the employer and any other reason shall be disregarded.

(3) In a case where—

(a) the employer has notified the employee in accordance with paragraph 2 of Schedule 6 to the 2006 Regulations, but

(b) the contract of employment terminates before the intended date of retirement,

retirement of the employee shall not be taken to be the reason (or a reason) for dismissal.

(4) In a case where—

(a) the employer has not notified the employee in accordance with paragraph 2 of Schedule 6 to the 2006 Regulations, and

(b) there is an intended date of retirement in relation to the dismissal, but

(c) the contract of employment terminates before the intended date of retirement,

retirement of the employee shall not be taken to be the reason (or a reason) for dismissal.

(5) In all other cases where the employer has not notified the employee in accordance with paragraph 2 of Schedule 6 to the 2006 Regulations, particular regard shall be had to the matters in section 98ZF when determining the reason (or principal reason) for dismissal.]

[1136D]

NOTES

Commencement: 1 October 2006.

Inserted as noted to s 98ZA at **[1136A]**.

Transitional provisions: see the note to s 98ZB at **[1136B]**.

[98ZE Normal retirement age below 65: dismissal at or after retirement age

(1) This section applies to the dismissal of an employee if—

(a) the employee has a normal retirement age,

(b) the normal retirement age is below 65, and

(c) the operative date of termination falls on or after the date when the employee reaches the normal retirement age.

(2) If it is unlawful discrimination under the 2006 Regulations for the employee to have that normal retirement age, retirement of the employee shall not be taken to be the reason (or a reason) for dismissal.

(3) Subsections (4) to (7) apply if it is not unlawful discrimination under the 2006 Regulations for the employee to have that normal retirement age.

(4) In a case where—

(a) the employer has notified the employee in accordance with paragraph 2 of Schedule 6 to the 2006 Regulations, and

(b) the contract of employment terminates on the intended date of retirement,

retirement of the employee shall be taken to be the only reason for dismissal by the employer and any other reason shall be disregarded.

(5) In a case where—

(a) the employer has notified the employee in accordance with paragraph 2 of Schedule 6 to the 2006 Regulations, but

(b) the contract of employment terminates before the intended date of retirement,

retirement of the employee shall not be taken to be the reason (or a reason) for dismissal.

(6) In a case where—

(a) the employer has not notified the employee in accordance with paragraph 2 of Schedule 6 to the 2006 Regulations, and

(b) there is an intended date of retirement in relation to the dismissal, but

(c) the contract of employment terminates before the intended date of retirement,

retirement of the employee shall not be taken to be the reason (or a reason) for dismissal.

(7) In all other cases where the employer has not notified the employee in accordance with paragraph 2 of Schedule 6 to the 2006 Regulations, particular regard shall be had to the matters in section 98ZF when determining the reason (or principal reason) for dismissal]

[1136E]

NOTES

Commencement: 1 October 2006.
Inserted as noted to s 98ZA at **[1136A]**.
Transitional provisions: see the note to s 98ZB at **[1136B]**.

[98ZF Reason for dismissal: particular matters

(1) These are the matters to which particular regard is to be had in accordance with section 98ZB(5), 98ZD(5) or 98ZE(7)—

(a) whether or not the employer has notified the employee in accordance with paragraph 4 of Schedule 6 to the 2006 Regulations;

(b) if the employer has notified the employee in accordance with that paragraph, how long before the notified retirement date the notification was given;

(c) whether or not the employer has followed, or sought to follow, the procedures in paragraph 7 of Schedule 6 to the 2006 Regulations.

(2) In subsection (1)(b) "notified retirement date" means the date notified to the employee in accordance with paragraph 4 of Schedule 6 to the 2006 Regulations as the date on which the employer intends to retire the employee.]

[1136F]

NOTES

Commencement: 1 October 2006.
Inserted as noted to s 98ZA at **[1136A]**.
Transitional provisions: see the note to s 98ZB at **[1136B]**.

[98ZG Retirement dismissals: fairness

(1) This section applies if the reason (or principal reason) for a dismissal is retirement of the employee.

(2) The employee shall be regarded as unfairly dismissed if, and only if, there has been a failure on the part of the employer to comply with an obligation imposed on him by any of the following provisions of Schedule 6 to the 2006 Regulations—

(a) paragraph 4 (notification of retirement, if not already given under paragraph 2),
(b) paragraphs 6 and 7 (duty to consider employee's request not to be retired),
(c) paragraph 8 (duty to consider appeal against decision to refuse request not to be retired).]

[1136G]

NOTES

Commencement: 1 October 2006.
Inserted as noted to s 98ZA at **[1136A]**.
Transitional provisions: see the note to s 98ZB at **[1136B]**.

[98ZH Interpretation

In sections 98ZA to 98ZG—

"2006 Regulations" means the Employment Equality (Age) Regulations 2006;

"intended date of retirement" means the date which, by virtue of paragraph 1(2) of Schedule 6 to the 2006 Regulations, is the intended date of retirement in relation to a particular dismissal;

"normal retirement age", in relation to an employee, means the age at which employees in the employer's undertaking who hold, or have held, the same kind of position as the employee are normally required to retire;

"operative date of termination" means—

(a) where the employer terminates the employee's contract of employment by notice, the date on which the notice expires, or
(b) where the employer terminates the contract of employment without notice, the date on which the termination takes effect.]

[1136H]

NOTES

Commencement: 1 October 2006.
Inserted as noted to s 98ZA at **[1136A]**.

[Other dismissals]

[98A Procedural fairness

(1) An employee who is dismissed shall be regarded for the purposes of this Part as unfairly dismissed if—

(a) one of the procedures set out in Part 1 of Schedule 2 to the Employment Act 2002 (dismissal and disciplinary procedures) applies in relation to the dismissal,
(b) the procedure has not been completed, and
(c) the non-completion of the procedure is wholly or mainly attributable to failure by the employer to comply with its requirements.

(2) Subject to subsection (1), failure by an employer to follow a procedure in relation to the dismissal of an employee shall not be regarded for the purposes of section 98(4)(a) as by itself making the employer's action unreasonable if he shows that he would have decided to dismiss the employee if he had followed the procedure.

(3) For the purposes of this section, any question as to the application of a procedure set out in Part 1 of Schedule 2 to the Employment Act 2002, completion of such a procedure or failure to comply with the requirements of such a procedure shall be determined by reference to regulations under section 31 of that Act.]

[1137]

NOTES

Commencement: 1 October 2004.
Heading preceding this section inserted as noted to s 98ZA at **[1136A]**.
Inserted by the Employment Act 2002, s 34(1), (2), as from 1 October 2004. For transitional provisions as to the applicability of Sch 2, Pt 1 to the 2002 Act, see SI 2004/752, reg 18 at **[3098]**.

[98B Jury Service

(1) An employee who is dismissed shall be regarded for the purposes of this Part as unfairly dismissed if the reason (or, if more than one, the principal reason) for the dismissal is that the employee—

(a) has been summoned under the Juries Act 1974, the Coroners Act 1988, the Court of Session Act 1988 or the Criminal Procedure (Scotland) Act 1995 to attend for service as a juror, or

(b) has been absent from work because he attended at any place in pursuance of being so summoned.

(2) Subsection (1) does not apply in relation to an employee who is dismissed if the employer shows—

(a) that the circumstances were such that the employee's absence in pursuance of being so summoned was likely to cause substantial injury to the employer's undertaking,

(b) that the employer brought those circumstances to the attention of the employee,

(c) that the employee refused or failed to apply to the appropriate officer for excusal from or a deferral of the obligation to attend in pursuance of being so summoned, and

(d) that the refusal or failure was not reasonable.

(3) In paragraph (c) of subsection (2) "the appropriate officer" means—

(a) in the case of a person who has been summoned under the Juries Act 1974, the officer designated for the purposes of section 8, 9 or, as the case may be, 9A of that Act;

(b) in the case of a person who has been summoned under the Coroners Act 1988, a person who is the appropriate officer for the purposes of any rules made under subsection (1) of section 32 of that Act by virtue of subsection (2) of that section;

(c) in the case of a person who has been summoned under the Court of Session Act 1988, either—

(i) the clerk of court issuing the citation to attend for jury service; or

(ii) the clerk of the court before which the person is cited to attend for jury service;

(d) in the case of a person who has been summoned under the Criminal Procedure (Scotland) Act 1995, either—

(i) the clerk of court issuing the citation to attend for jury service; or

(ii) the clerk of the court before which the person has been cited to attend for jury service;

and references in that paragraph to a refusal or failure to apply include references to a refusal or failure to give a notice under section 1(2)(b) of the Law Reform (Miscellaneous Provisions) (Scotland) Act 1980.]

[1137A]

NOTES

Commencement: 6 April 2005.

Inserted by the Employment Relations Act 2004, s 40(3), as from 6 April 2005, except in relation to any dismissal where the effective date of termination (within the meaning of s 97 of this Act) was before that date (see SI 2005/872, art 13).

[99 Leave for family reasons

(1) An employee who is dismissed shall be regarded for the purposes of this Part as unfairly dismissed if—

(a) the reason or principal reason for the dismissal is of a prescribed kind, or

(b) the dismissal takes place in prescribed circumstances.

(2) In this section "prescribed" means prescribed by regulations made by the Secretary of State.

(3) A reason or set of circumstances prescribed under this section must relate to—

(a) pregnancy, childbirth or maternity,

(b) ordinary, compulsory or additional maternity leave,

[(ba) ordinary or additional adoption leave,]

(c) parental leave,

[(ca) paternity leave, or]

(d) time off under section 57A;

and it may also relate to redundancy or other factors.

(4) A reason or set of circumstances prescribed under subsection (1) satisfies subsection (3)(c) or (d) if it relates to action which an employee—

(a) takes,

(b) agrees to take, or

(c) refuses to take,

under or in respect of a collective or workforce agreement which deals with parental leave.

(5) Regulations under this section may—

(a) make different provision for different cases or circumstances

(b) apply any enactment, in such circumstances as may be specified and subject to any conditions specified, in relation to persons regarded as unfairly dismissed by reason of this section.]

[1138]

NOTES

Substituted by the Employment Relations Act 1999, s 9, Sch 4, Pt III, paras 1, 5, 16.

Sub-s (3): para (ba) inserted, and para (ca) substituted for original word "or" at the end of para (c), by the Employment Act 2002, s 53, Sch 7, paras 24, 33, as from 8 December 2002; para (ca) further substituted by the Work and Families Act 2006, s 11(1), Sch 1, para 41, as from a day to be appointed, as follows—

"(ca) ordinary or additional paternity leave, or".

Regulations: the Maternity and Parental Leave etc Regulations 1999, SI 1999/3312 at **[2553]**; the Paternity and Adoption Leave Regulations 2002, SI 2002/2788 at **[2752]**; the Paternity and Adoption Leave (Adoptions from Overseas) Regulations 2003, SI 2003/921.

100 Health and safety cases

(1) An employee who is dismissed shall be regarded for the purposes of this Part as unfairly dismissed if the reason (or, if more than one, the principal reason) for the dismissal is that—

(a) having been designated by the employer to carry out activities in connection with preventing or reducing risks to health and safety at work, the employee carried out (or proposed to carry out) any such activities,

(b) being a representative of workers on matters of health and safety at work or member of a safety committee—

(i) in accordance with arrangements established under or by virtue of any enactment, or

(ii) by reason of being acknowledged as such by the employer,

the employee performed (or proposed to perform) any functions as such a representative or a member of such a committee,

[(ba) the employee took part (or proposed to take part) in consultation with the employer pursuant to the Health and Safety (Consultation with Employees) Regulations 1996 or in the election of representatives of employee safety within the meaning of those Regulations (whether as a candidate or otherwise),]

(c) being an employee at a place where—

(i) there was no such representative or safety committee, or

(ii) there was such a representative or safety committee but it was not reasonably practicable for the employee to raise the matter by those means,

he brought to his employer's attention, by reasonable means, circumstances connected with his work which he reasonably believed were harmful or potentially harmful to health or safety,

(d) in circumstances of danger which the employee reasonably believed to be serious and imminent and which he could not reasonably have been expected to avert, he left (or proposed to leave) or (while the danger persisted) refused to return to his place of work or any dangerous part of his place of work, or

(e) in circumstances of danger which the employee reasonably believed to be serious and imminent, he took (or proposed to take) appropriate steps to protect himself or other persons from the danger.

(2) For the purposes of subsection (1)(e) whether steps which an employee took (or proposed to take) were appropriate is to be judged by reference to all the circumstances including, in particular, his knowledge and the facilities and advice available to him at the time.

(3) Where the reason (or, if more than one, the principal reason) for the dismissal of an employee is that specified in subsection (1)(e), he shall not be regarded as unfairly dismissed if the employer shows that it was (or would have been) so negligent for the employee to take the steps which he took (or proposed to take) that a reasonable employer might have dismissed him for taking (or proposing to take) them.

[1139]

NOTES

Sub-s (1): para (ba) inserted by the Health and Safety (Consultation with Employees) Regulations 1996, SI 1996/1513, reg 8.

101 Shop workers and betting workers who refuse Sunday work

(1) Where an employee who is—

(a) a protected shop worker or an opted-out shop worker, or

(b) a protected betting worker or an opted-out betting worker,

is dismissed, he shall be regarded for the purposes of this Part as unfairly dismissed if the reason (or, if more than one, the principal reason) for the dismissal is that he refused (or proposed to refuse) to do shop work, or betting work, on Sunday or on a particular Sunday.

(2) Subsection (1) does not apply in relation to an opted-out shop worker or an opted-out betting worker where the reason (or principal reason) for the dismissal is that he refused (or proposed to refuse) to do shop work, or betting work, on any Sunday or Sundays falling before the end of the notice period.

(3) A shop worker or betting worker who is dismissed shall be regarded for the purposes of this Part as unfairly dismissed if the reason (or, if more than one, the principal reason) for the dismissal is that the shop worker or betting worker gave (or proposed to give) an opting-out notice to the employer.

(4) For the purposes of section 36(2)(b) or 41(1)(b), the appropriate date in relation to this section is the effective date of termination.

[1140]

[101A Working time cases

[(1)] An employee who is dismissed shall be regarded for the purposes of this Part as unfairly dismissed if the reason (or, if more than one, the principal reason) for the dismissal is that the employee—

(a) refused (or proposed to refuse) to comply with a requirement which the employer imposed (or proposed to impose) in contravention of the Working Time Regulations 1998,

(b) refused (or proposed to refuse) to forgo a right conferred on him by those Regulations,

(c) failed to sign a workforce agreement for the purposes of those Regulations, or to enter into, or agree to vary or extend, any other agreement with his employer which is provided for in those Regulations, or

(d) being—

(i) a representative of members of the workforce for the purposes of Schedule 1 to those Regulations, or

(ii) a candidate in an election in which any person elected will, on being elected, be such a representative,

performed (or proposed to perform) any functions or activities as such a representative or candidate.]

[(2) A reference in this section to the Working Time Regulations 1998 includes a reference to—

[(a)] the Merchant Shipping (Working Time: Inland Waterways) Regulations 2003;]

[(b) the Fishing Vessels (Working Time: Sea-fishermen) Regulations 2004].]

[1141]

NOTES

Inserted by the Working Time Regulations 1998, SI 1998/1833, regs 2(1), 32(1).

Sub-s (1): numbered as such by the Merchant Shipping (Working Time: Inland Waterways) Regulations 2003, SI 2003/3049, reg 20, Sch 2, para 3(1), (3), as from 24 December 2003.

Sub-s (2): added by SI 2003/3049, reg 20, Sch 2, para 3(1), (3), as from 24 December 2003; letter "(a)" in square brackets and para (b) added by the Fishing Vessels (Working Time: Sea-fishermen) Regulations 2004, SI 2004/1713, reg 21, Sch 2, para 2(1), (3)(a), as from 16 August 2004.

102 Trustees of occupational pension schemes

(1) An employee who is dismissed shall be regarded for the purposes of this Part as unfairly dismissed if the reason (or, if more than one, the principal reason) for the dismissal is that, being a trustee of a relevant occupational pension scheme which relates to his employment, the employee performed (or proposed to perform) any functions as such a trustee.

[(1A) This section applies to an employee who is a director of a company which is a trustee of a relevant occupational pension scheme as it applies to an employee who is a trustee of such a scheme (references to such a trustee being read for this purpose as references to such a director).]

(2) In this section "relevant occupational pension scheme" means an occupational pension scheme (as defined in section 1 of the Pension Schemes Act 1993) established under a trust.

[1142]

NOTES

Sub-s (1A): inserted by the Welfare Reform and Pensions Act 1999, s 18, Sch 2, para 19(1), (4).

By s 6(1) of the Welfare Reform and Pensions Act 1999, this section applies to an employee who is (or is a director of a company which is) a trustee of a scheme designated by his employer under s 3(2) of that Act as it applies to employees who are trustees, or directors of companies which are trustees of a relevant occupational pension scheme.

103 Employee representatives

[(1)] An employee who is dismissed shall be regarded for the purposes of this Part as unfairly dismissed if the reason (or, if more than one, the principal reason) for the dismissal is that the employee, being—

(a) an employee representative for the purposes of Chapter II of Part IV of the Trade Union and Labour Relations (Consolidation) Act 1992 (redundancies) or [regulations 9, 13 and 15 of the Transfer of Undertakings (Protection of Employment) Regulations 2006], or

(b) a candidate in an election in which any person elected will, on being elected, be such an employee representative,

performed (or proposed to perform) any functions or activities as such an employee representative or candidate.

[(2) An employee who is dismissed shall be regarded for the purposes of this Part as unfairly dismissed if the reason (or, if more than one, the principal reason) for the dismissal is that the employee took part in an election of employee representatives for the purposes of Chapter II of Part IV of the Trade Union and Labour Relations (Consolidation) Act 1992 (redundancies) or [regulations 9, 13 and 15 of the Transfer of Undertakings (Protection of Employment) Regulations 2006].]

[1143]

NOTES

Sub-s (1): numbered as such by the Collective Redundancies and Transfer of Undertakings (Protection of Employment) (Amendment) Regulations 1999, SI 1999/1925, reg 13; words in square brackets in para (a) substituted by the Transfer of Undertakings (Protection of Employment) Regulations 2006, SI 2006/246, reg 20, Sch 2, para 10, as from 6 April 2006 (for transitional provisions in relation to a relevant transfer, etc, that took place before that date, see reg 21 of the 2006 Regulations at **[3395]**).

Sub-s (2): added by SI 1999/1925, reg 13; words in square brackets substituted by SI 2006/246, reg 20, Sch 2, para 10, as from 6 April 2006 (for transitional provisions in relation to a relevant transfer, etc, that took place before that date, see reg 21 of the 2006 Regulations at **[3395]**).

[103A Protected disclosure

An employee who is dismissed shall be regarded for the purposes of this Part as unfairly dismissed if the reason (or, if more than one, the principal reason) for the dismissal is that the employee made a protected disclosure.]

[1144]

NOTES
Inserted by the Public Interest Disclosure Act 1998, ss 5, 18(2).

104 Assertion of statutory right

(1) An employee who is dismissed shall be regarded for the purposes of this Part as unfairly dismissed if the reason (or, if more than one, the principal reason) for the dismissal is that the employee—

(a) brought proceedings against the employer to enforce a right of his which is a relevant statutory right, or

(b) alleged that the employer had infringed a right of his which is a relevant statutory right.

(2) It is immaterial for the purposes of subsection (1)—

(a) whether or not the employee has the right, or

(b) whether or not the right has been infringed;

but, for that subsection to apply, the claim to the right and that it has been infringed must be made in good faith.

(3) It is sufficient for subsection (1) to apply that the employee, without specifying the right, made it reasonably clear to the employer what the right claimed to have been infringed was.

(4) The following are relevant statutory rights for the purposes of this section—

(a) any right conferred by this Act for which the remedy for its infringement is by way of a complaint or reference to an [employment tribunal],

(b) the right conferred by section 86 of this Act, …

(c) the rights conferred by sections 68, 86, [145A, 145B,] 146, 168, [168A,] 169 and 170 of the Trade Union and Labour Relations (Consolidation) Act 1992 (deductions from pay, union activities and time off) […

[(d) the rights conferred by the Working Time Regulations 1998, the Merchant Shipping (Working Time: Inland Waterway) Regulations 2003 or the Fishing Vessels (Working Time: Sea-fishermen) Regulations 2004]][, and

(e) the rights conferred by the Transfer of Undertakings (Protection of Employment) Regulations 2006].

[(5) In this section any reference to an employer includes, where the right in question is conferred by section 63A, the principal (within the meaning of section 63A(3)).]

[1145]

NOTES
Sub-s (4): words in square brackets in para (a) substituted by the Employment Rights (Dispute Resolution) Act 1998, s 1(2)(a); word omitted from para (b) repealed, and para (d) and word immediately preceding it added, by the Working Time Regulations 1998, SI 1998/1833, regs 2(1), 32(2); first figures in square brackets in para (c) inserted by the Employment Relations Act 2004, s 57(1), Sch 1, para 31, as from 1 October 2004, except in relation to cases where the act or failure to act to which the complaint relates was done before that date, or where the act or failure to act to which the complaint relates is part of a series and the first act or failure in the series was done before that date (see SI 2004/2566, art 6); second figure in square brackets in para (c) inserted by the Employment Act 2002, s 53, Sch 7, paras 24, 34, as from 27 April 2003; para (d) subsequently substituted by the Fishing Vessels (Working Time: Sea-fishermen) Regulations 2004, SI 2004/1713, reg 21, Sch 2, para 2(1), (4), as from 16 August 2004; word omitted from para (c) repealed, and para (e) and the word immediately preceding it added, by the Transfer of Undertakings (Protection of Employment) Regulations 2006, SI 2006/246, reg 19, as from 6 April 2006 (for transitional provisions in relation to a relevant transfer, etc, that took place before that date, see reg 21 of the 2006 Regulations at **[3395]**).

Sub-s (5): added by the Teaching and Higher Education Act 1998, s 44(1), Sch 3, para 13.

[104A The national minimum wage

(1) An employee who is dismissed shall be regarded for the purposes of this Part as unfairly dismissed if the reason (or, if more than one, the principal reason) for the dismissal is that—

(a) any action was taken, or was proposed to be taken, by or on behalf of the employee with a view to enforcing, or otherwise securing the benefit of, a right of the employee's to which this section applies; or

(b) the employer was prosecuted for an offence under section 31 of the National

Minimum Wage Act 1998 as a result of action taken by or on behalf of the employee for the purpose of enforcing, or otherwise securing the benefit of, a right of the employee's to which this section applies; or

(c) the employee qualifies, or will or might qualify, for the national minimum wage or for a particular rate of national minimum wage.

(2) It is immaterial for the purposes of paragraph (a) or (b) of subsection (1) above—

(a) whether or not the employee has the right, or

(b) whether or not the right has been infringed,

but, for that subsection to apply, the claim to the right and, if applicable, the claim that it has been infringed must be made in good faith.

(3) The following are the rights to which this section applies—

(a) any right conferred by, or by virtue of, any provision of the National Minimum Wage Act 1998 for which the remedy for its infringement is by way of a complaint to an employment tribunal; and

(b) any right conferred by section 17 of the National Minimum Wage Act 1998 (worker receiving less than national minimum wage entitled to additional remuneration).]

[1146]

NOTES

Inserted by the National Minimum Wage Act 1998, s 25(1).

Agricultural workers: as to the application of this section to agricultural workers, see the Agricultural Wages Act 1948, s 3A, and the Agricultural Wages (Scotland) Act 1949, s 3A.

[104B Tax credits

(1) An employee who is dismissed shall be regarded for the purposes of this Part as unfairly dismissed if the reason (or, if more than one, the principal reason) for the dismissal is that—

(a) any action was taken, or was proposed to be taken, by or on behalf of the employee with a view to enforcing, or otherwise securing the benefit of, a right conferred on the employee by regulations under section 25 of the Tax Credits Act 2002,

(b) a penalty was imposed on the employer, or proceedings for a penalty were brought against him, under that Act, as a result of action taken by or on behalf of the employee for the purpose of enforcing, or otherwise securing the benefit of, such a right, or

(c) the employee is entitled, or will or may be entitled, to working tax credit.

(2) It is immaterial for the purposes of subsection (1)(a) or (b)—

(a) whether or not the employee has the right, or

(b) whether or not the right has been infringed,

but, for those provisions to apply, the claim to the right and (if applicable) the claim that it has been infringed must be made in good faith.]

[1147]

NOTES

Inserted by the Tax Credits Act 1999, s 7, Sch 3, para 3(1); substituted by the Tax Credits Act 2002, s 27, Sch 1, para 3(1), (2).

[104C Flexible working

An employee who is dismissed shall be regarded for the purposes of this Part as unfairly dismissed if the reason (or, if more than one, the principal reason) for the dismissal is that the employee—

(a) made (or proposed to make) an application under section 80F,

(b) exercised (or proposed to exercise) a right conferred on him under section 80G,

(c) brought proceedings against the employer under section 80H, or

(d) alleged the existence of any circumstance which would constitute a ground for bringing such proceedings.]

[1148]

NOTES

Inserted by the Employment Act 2002, s 47(1), (4).

105 Redundancy

(1) An employee who is dismissed shall be regarded for the purposes of this Part as unfairly dismissed if—

(a) the reason (or, if more than one, the principal reason) for the dismissal is that the employee was redundant,

(b) it is shown that the circumstances constituting the redundancy applied equally to one or more other employees in the same undertaking who held positions similar to that held by the employee and who have not been dismissed by the employer, and

[(c) it is shown that any of subsections [(2A) to (7K)] applies].

(2) …

[(2A) This subsection applies if the reason (or, if more than one, the principal reason) for which the employee was selected for dismissal was one of those specified in subsection (1) of section 98B (unless the case is one to which subsection (2) of that section applies).]

(3) This subsection applies if the reason (or, if more than one, the principal reason) for which the employee was selected for dismissal was one of those specified in subsection (1) of section 100 (read with subsections (2) and (3) of that section).

(4) This subsection applies if either—

(a) the employee was a protected shop worker or an opted-out shop worker, or a protected betting worker or an opted-out betting worker, and the reason (or, if more than one, the principal reason) for which the employee was selected for dismissal was that specified in subsection (1) of section 101 (read with subsection (2) of that section), or

(b) the employee was a shop worker or a betting worker and the reason (or, if more than one, the principal reason) for which the employee was selected for dismissal was that specified in subsection (3) of that section.

[(4A) This subsection applies if the reason (or, if more than one, the principal reason) for which the employee was selected for dismissal was one of those specified in section 101A.]

(5) This subsection applies if the reason (or, if more than one, the principal reason) for which the employee was selected for dismissal was that specified in section 102(1).

(6) This subsection applies if the reason (or, if more than one, the principal reason) for which the employee was selected for dismissal was that specified in section 103.

[(6A) This subsection applies if the reason (or, if more than one, the principal reason) for which the employee was selected for dismissal was that specified in section 103A.]

(7) This subsection applies if the reason (or, if more than one, the principal reason) for which the employee was selected for dismissal was one of those specified in subsection (1) of section 104 (read with subsections (2) and (3) of that section).

[(7A) This subsection applies if the reason (or, if more than one, the principal reason) for which the employee was selected for dismissal was one of those specified in subsection (1) of section 104A (read with subsection (2) of that section).]

[(7B) This subsection applies if the reason (or, if more than one, the principal reason) for which the employee was selected for dismissal was one of those specified in subsection (1) of section 104B (read with subsection (2) of that section).]

[(7BA) This subsection applies if the reason (or, if more than one, the principal reason) for which the employee was selected for dismissal was one of those specified in section 104C.]

[(7C) This subsection applies if—

(a) the reason (or, if more than one, the principal reason) for which the employee was selected for dismissal was the reason mentioned in section 238A(2) of the Trade Union and Labour Relations (Consolidation) Act 1992 (participation in official industrial action), and

(b) subsection (3), (4) or (5) of that section applies to the dismissal.]

[(7D) This subsection applies if the reason (or, if more than one, the principal reason) for which the employee was selected for dismissal was one specified in paragraph (3) or (6) of regulation 28 of the Transnational Information and Consultation of Employees Regulations 1999 (read with paragraphs (4) and (7) of that regulation).]

[(7E) This subsection applies if the reason (or, if more than one, the principal reason) for which the employee was selected for dismissal was one specified in paragraph (3) of regulation 7 of the Part-time Workers (Prevention of Less Favourable Treatment) Regulations 2000 (unless the case is one to which paragraph (4) of that regulation applies).]

[(7F) This subsection applies if the reason (or, if more than one, the principal reason) for which the employee was selected for dismissal was one specified in paragraph (3) of regulation 6 of the Fixed-term Employees (Prevention of Less Favourable Treatment) Regulations 2002 (unless the case is one to which paragraph (4) of that regulation applies).]

[(7G) This subsection applies if the reason (or, if more than one, the principal reason) for which the employee was selected for dismissal was one specified in paragraph (3) or (6) of regulation 42 of the European Public Limited-Liability Company Regulations 2004 (read with paragraphs (4) and (7) of that regulation).]

[(7H) This subsection applies if the reason (or, if more than one, the principal reason) for which the employee was selected for dismissal was one specified in paragraph (3) or (6) of regulation 30 of the Information and Consultation of Employees Regulations 2004 (read with paragraphs (4) and (7) of that regulation).]

[(7I) This subsection applies if the reason (or, if more than one, the principal reason) for which the employee was selected for dismissal was one specified in paragraph 5(3) or (5) of the Schedule to the Occupational and Personal Pension Schemes (Consultation by Employers and Miscellaneous Amendment) Regulations 2006 (read with paragraph 5(6) of that Schedule).]

[(7IA) This subsection applies if the reason (or, if more than one, the principal reason) for which the employee was selected for dismissal was that he—

(a) exercised or sought to exercise his right to be accompanied in accordance with paragraph 9 of Schedule 6 to the Employment Equality (Age) Regulations 2006, or

(b) accompanied or sought to accompany an employee pursuant to a request under that paragraph.]

[(7J) This subsection applies if the reason (or, if more than one, the principal reason) for which the employee was selected for dismissal was one specified in paragraph (3) or (6) of regulation 31 of the European Cooperative Society (Involvement of Employees) Regulations 2006 (read with paragraphs (4) and (7) of that regulation).]

[(7K) This subsection applies if the reason (or, if more than one, the principal reason) for which the employee was selected for dismissal was one specified in—

(a) paragraph (2) of regulation 46 of the Companies (Cross-Border Mergers) Regulations 2007 (read with paragraphs (3) and (4) of that regulation); or

(b) paragraph (2) of regulation 47 of the Companies (Cross-Border Mergers) Regulations 2007 (read with paragraph (3) of that regulation).]

(8) For the purposes of section 36(2)(b) or 41(1)(b), the appropriate date in relation to this section is the effective date of termination.

(9) In this Part "redundancy case" means a case where paragraphs (a) and (b) of subsection (1) of this section are satisfied.

[1149]

NOTES

Sub-s (1): para (c) substituted by the European Cooperative Society (Involvement of Employees) Regulations 2006, SI 2006/2059, reg 32(1)(a), as from 18 August 2006; words in square brackets in para (c) substituted by the Companies (Cross-Border Mergers) Regulations 2007, SI 2007/2974, reg 48(1)(a), as from 15 December 2007.

Sub-s (2): repealed by the Employment Relations Act 1999, ss 9, Sch 4, Pt III, paras 1, 5, 17, Sch 9(2).

Sub-s (2A): inserted by the Employment Relations Act 2004, s 40(5), as from 6 April 2005, except in relation to any dismissal where the effective date of termination (within the meaning of s 97 of this Act) was before that date (see SI 2005/872, art 13).

Sub-s (4A): inserted by the Working Time Regulations 1998, SI 1998/1833, regs 2(1), 32(3).

Sub-s (6A): inserted by the Public Interest Disclosure Act 1998, ss 6, 18(2).

Sub-s (7A): inserted by the National Minimum Wage Act 1998, s 25(2).

Sub-s (7B): inserted by the Tax Credits Act 1999, s 7, Sch 3, para 3(2).

Sub-s (7BA): inserted by the Employment Relations Act 2004, s 41(4), as from 6 April 2005 (subject to the same exception in SI 2005/872, art 13 as noted above).
Sub-s (7C): inserted by the Employment Relations Act 1999, s 16, Sch 5, para 5(1), (3).
Sub-s (7D): inserted by the Transnational Information and Consultation of Employees Regulations 1999, SI 1999/3323, reg 29(1).
Sub-s (7E): inserted by the Part-time Workers (Prevention of Less Favourable Treatment) Regulations 2000, SI 2000/1551, reg 10, Schedule, para 2(1).
Sub-s (7F): inserted by the Fixed-term Employees (Prevention of Less Favourable Treatment) Regulations 2002, SI 2002/2034, reg 11, Sch 2, Pt 1, para 3(1), (10).
Sub-s (7G): inserted by the European Public Limited-Liability Company Regulations 2004, SI 2004/2326, reg 43(1)(b), as from 8 October 2004.
Sub-s (7H): inserted by the Information and Consultation of Employees Regulations 2004, SI 2004/3426, reg 31(1)(b), as from 6 April 2005.
Sub-s (7I): inserted by the Occupational and Personal Pension Schemes (Consultation by Employers and Miscellaneous Amendment) Regulations 2006, SI 2006/349, reg 17, Schedule, para 6(1)(b), as from 6 April 2006.
Sub-s (7IA): inserted by the Employment Equality (Age) (Consequential Amendments) Regulations 2007, SI 2007/825, reg 3, as from 6 April 2007.
Sub-s (7J): inserted by SI 2006/2059, reg 32(1)(b), as from 18 August 2006.
Sub-s (7K): inserted by SI 2007/2974, reg 48(1)(b), as from 15 December 2007.

106 Replacements

(1) Where this section applies to an employee he shall be regarded for the purposes of section 98(1)(b) as having been dismissed for a substantial reason of a kind such as to justify the dismissal of an employee holding the position which the employee held.

(2) This section applies to an employee where—

(a) on engaging him the employer informs him in writing that his employment will be terminated on the resumption of work by another employee who is, or will be, absent wholly or partly because of pregnancy or childbirth, [or on adoption leave] [or leave under section 80AA or 80BB (additional paternity leave)] and

(b) the employer dismisses him in order to make it possible to give work to the other employee.

(3) This section also applies to an employee where—

(a) on engaging him the employer informs him in writing that his employment will be terminated on the end of a suspension of another employee from work on medical grounds or maternity grounds (within the meaning of Part VII), and

(b) the employer dismisses him in order to make it possible to allow the resumption of work by the other employee.

(4) Subsection (1) does not affect the operation of section 98(4) in a case to which this section applies.

[1150]

NOTES

Sub-s (2): words in first pair of square brackets in para (a) inserted by the Employment Act 2002, s 53, Sch 7, paras 24, 35; words in second pair of square brackets in that paragraph inserted by the Work and Families Act 2006, s 11(1), Sch 1, para 42, as from a day to be appointed.

107 Pressure on employer to dismiss unfairly

(1) This section applies where there falls to be determined for the purposes of this Part a question—

(a) as to the reason, or principal reason, for which an employee was dismissed,

(b) whether the reason or principal reason for which an employee was dismissed was a reason fulfilling the requirement of section 98(1)(b), or

(c) whether an employer acted reasonably in treating the reason or principal reason for which an employee was dismissed as a sufficient reason for dismissing him.

(2) In determining the question no account shall be taken of any pressure which by calling, organising, procuring or financing a strike or other industrial action, or threatening to do so, was exercised on the employer to dismiss the employee; and the question shall be determined as if no such pressure had been exercised.

[1151]

Exclusion of right

108 Qualifying period of employment

(1) Section 94 does not apply to the dismissal of an employee unless he has been continuously employed for a period of not less than [one year] ending with the effective date of termination.

(2) If an employee is dismissed by reason of any such requirement or recommendation as is referred to in section 64(2), subsection (1) has effect in relation to that dismissal as if for the words ["one year"] there were substituted the words "one month".

(3) Subsection (1) does not apply if—

(a) …

[(aa) subsection (1) of section 98B (read with subsection (2) of that section) applies,]

[(b) subsection (1) of section 99 (read with any regulations made under that section) applies,]

(c) subsection (1) of section 100 (read with subsections (2) and (3) of that section) applies,

(d) subsection (1) of section 101 (read with subsection (2) of that section) or subsection (3) of that section applies,

[(dd) section 101A applies,]

(e) section 102 applies,

(f) section 103 applies,

[(ff) section 103A applies,]

(g) subsection (1) of section 104 (read with subsections (2) and (3) of that section) applies, …

[(gg) subsection (1) of section 104A (read with subsection (2) of that section) applies, …]

[(gh) subsection (1) of section 104B (read with subsection (2) of that section) applies, …]

[(gi) section 104C applies,]

(h) section 105 applies, […

(hh) paragraph (3) or (6) of regulation 28 of the Transnational Information and Consultation of Employees Regulations 1999 (read with paragraphs (4) and (7) of that regulation) applies], […

(i) paragraph (1) of regulation 7 of the Part-time Workers (Prevention of Less Favourable Treatment) Regulations 2000 applies], […

(j) paragraph (1) of regulation 6 of the Fixed-term Employees (Prevention of Less Favourable Treatment) Regulations 2002 applies], […

(k) paragraph (3) or (6) of regulation 42 of the European Public Limited-Liability Company Regulations 2004 applies]; […

(l) paragraph (3) or (6) of regulation 30 of the Information and Consultation of Employees Regulations 2004 (read with paragraphs (4) and (7) of that regulation) applies] [, …

(m) paragraph 5(3) or (5) of the Schedule to the Occupational and Personal Pension Schemes (Consultation by Employers and Miscellaneous Amendment) Regulations 2006 (read with paragraph 5(6) of that Schedule) applies] [, …

(n) paragraph (a) or (b) of paragraph 13(5) of Schedule 6 to the Employment Equality (Age) Regulations 2006 applies][, …

(o) paragraph (3) or (6) of regulation 31 of the European Cooperative Society (Involvement of Employees) Regulations 2006 (read with paragraphs (4) and (7) of that regulation) applies], [or

(p) regulation 46 or 47 of the Companies (Cross-Border Mergers) Regulations 2007 applies].

[1152]–[1153]

NOTES

Sub-ss (1), (2): words in square brackets substituted by the Unfair Dismissal and Statement of Reasons for Dismissal (Variation of Qualifying Period) Order 1999, SI 1999/1436, arts 3–5.

Sub-s (3) is amended as follows:

Para (a) repealed by the Employment Relations Act 1999, ss 9, 44, Sch 4, Pt III, paras 1, 5, 18, Sch 9(2).

Para (aa) inserted by the Employment Relations Act 2004, s 40(6), as from 6 April 2005, except in relation to any dismissal where the effective date of termination (within the meaning of s 97 of this Act) occurred before that date (see SI 2005/872, art 13).

Para (b) substituted by the Employment Relations Act 2004, s 57(1), Sch 1, para 32, as from 6 April 2005, except in relation to a dismissal where the effective date of termination (within the meaning of s 97 of this Act) occurred before that date (see SI 2005/872, art 12).

Para (dd) inserted by the Working Time Regulations 1998, SI 1998/1833, regs 2(1), 32(4).

Para (ff) inserted by the Public Interest Disclosure Act 1998, ss 7(1), 18(2).

Word omitted from para (g) repealed, and para (gg) inserted, by the National Minimum Wage Act 1998, ss 25(3), 53, Sch 3.

Word omitted from para (gg) repealed, and para (gh) inserted, by the Tax Credits Act 1999, ss 7, 19(4), Sch 3, para 3(3), Sch 6.

Word omitted from para (gh) repealed, and para (hh) and the word immediately preceding it inserted, by the Transnational Information and Consultation of Employees Regulations 1999, SI 1999/3323, reg 29(2).

Para (gi) inserted by the Employment Relations Act 2004, s 41(5), as from 6 April 2005, except in relation to any dismissal where the effective date of termination (within the meaning of s 97 of this Act) occurred before that date (see SI 2005/872, art 13).

Word omitted from para (h) repealed, and para (i) and the word immediately preceding it added, by the Part-time Workers (Prevention of Less Favourable Treatment) Regulations 2000, SI 2000/1551, reg 10, Schedule, para 2(2).

Word omitted from para (hh) repealed, and para (j) and the word immediately preceding it added, by the Fixed-term Employees (Prevention of Less Favourable Treatment) Regulations 2002, SI 2002/2034, reg 11, Sch 2, Pt 1, para 3(1), (11).

Word omitted from para (i) repealed, and para (k) and the word immediately preceding it added, by the European Public Limited-Liability Company Regulations 2004, SI 2004/2326, reg 43(2), as from 8 October 2004.

Word omitted from para (j) repealed, and para (l) and the word immediately preceding it added, by the Information and Consultation of Employees Regulations 2004, SI 2004/3426, reg 31(2), as from 6 April 2005.

Word omitted from para (k) repealed, and para (m) and the word immediately preceding it added, by the Occupational and Personal Pension Schemes (Consultation by Employers and Miscellaneous Amendment) Regulations 2006, SI 2006/349, reg 17, Schedule, para 6(2), as from 6 April 2006.

Word omitted from para (l) repealed, and para (n) and the word immediately preceding it added, by the Employment Equality (Age) Regulations 2006, SI 2006/1031, reg 49(1), Sch 8, Pt 1, paras 21, 24, as from 1 October 2006.

Word omitted from para (m) repealed, and para (o) and the word immediately preceding it added, by the European Cooperative Society (Involvement of Employees) Regulations 2006, SI 2006/2059, reg 32(2), as from 18 August 2006.

Word omitted from para (n) repealed, and para (p) and the word immediately preceding it added, by the Companies (Cross-Border Mergers) Regulations 2007, SI 2007/2974, reg 48(2), as from 15 December 2007.

Exclusion: this section is excluded in relation to dismissal on grounds related to union membership or activities; see the Trade Union and Labour Relations (Consolidation) Act 1992, s 154 at **[640]**.

109 (*Repealed by the Employment Equality (Age) Regulations 2006, SI 2006/1031, reg 49(1), Sch 8, Pt 1, paras 21, 25, as from 1 October 2006.*)

110 Dismissal procedures agreements

(1) Where a dismissal procedures agreement is designated by an order under subsection (3) which is for the time being in force—

(a) the provisions of that agreement relating to dismissal shall have effect in substitution for any rights under section 94, and

(b) accordingly, section 94 does not apply to the dismissal of an employee from any employment if it is employment to which, and he is an employee to whom, those provisions of the agreement apply.

[(2) But if the agreement includes provision that it does not apply to dismissals of particular descriptions, subsection (1) does not apply in relation to a dismissal of any such description.]

(3) An order designating a dismissal procedures agreement may be made by the Secretary of State, on an application being made to him jointly by all the parties to the agreement, if he is satisfied that—

(a) every trade union which is a party to the agreement is an independent trade union,

(b) the agreement provides for procedures to be followed in cases where an employee claims that he has been, or is in the course of being, unfairly dismissed,

(c) those procedures are available without discrimination to all employees falling within any description to which the agreement applies,

(d) the remedies provided by the agreement in respect of unfair dismissal are on the whole as beneficial as (but not necessarily identical with) those provided in respect of unfair dismissal by this Part,

[(e) the agreement includes provision either for arbitration in every case or for—

(i) arbitration where (by reason of equality of votes or for any other reason) a decision under the agreement cannot otherwise be reached, and
(ii) a right to submit to arbitration any question of law arising out of such a decision, and]

(f) the provisions of the agreement are such that it can be determined with reasonable certainty whether or not a particular employee is one to whom the agreement applies.

[(3A) The Secretary of State may by order amend subsection (3) so as to add to the conditions specified in that subsection such conditions as he may specify in the order.]

(4) If at any time when an order under subsection (3) is in force in relation to a dismissal procedures agreement the Secretary of State is satisfied, whether on an application made to him by any of the parties to the agreement or otherwise, either—

(a) that it is the desire of all the parties to the agreement that the order should be revoked, or
(b) that the agreement no longer satisfies all the conditions specified in subsection (3),

the Secretary of State shall revoke the order by an order under this subsection.

(5) The transitional provisions which may be made in an order under subsection (4) include, in particular, provisions directing—

(a) that an employee—
(i) shall not be excluded from his right under section 94 where the effective date of termination falls within a transitional period which ends with the date on which the order takes effect and which is specified in the order, and
(ii) shall have an extended time for presenting a complaint under section 111 in respect of a dismissal where the effective date of termination falls within that period, and
(b) that, where the effective date of termination falls within such a transitional period, an [employment tribunal] shall, in determining any complaint of unfair dismissal presented by an employee to whom the dismissal procedures agreement applies, have regard to such considerations as are specified in the order (in addition to those specified in this Part and section 10(4) and (5) of [the Employment Tribunals Act 1996]).

[(6) Where an award is made under a designated dismissal procedures agreement—

(a) in England and Wales it may be enforced, by leave of a county court, in the same manner as a judgment of the court to the same effect and, where leave is given, judgment may be entered in terms of the award, and
(b) in Scotland it may be recorded for execution in the Books of Council and Session and shall be enforceable accordingly.

[1154]

NOTES

Sub-s (2): substituted by the Employment Rights (Dispute Resolution) Act 1998, s 12(1), (5).

Sub-s (3): words in square brackets substituted by the Employment Rights (Dispute Resolution) Act 1998, s 12(2), (5).

Sub-s (3A): inserted by the Employment Act 2002, s 44, as from a day to be appointed.

Sub-s (5): words in square brackets substituted by the Employment Rights (Dispute Resolution) Act 1998, s 1(2)(a), (b).

Sub-s (6): added by the Employment Rights (Dispute Resolution) Act 1998, s 12(3), (5).

The only Order under the provisions re-enacted in this section (not made as a statutory instrument) is in relation to the electrical contracting industry. This order was revoked with effect from 1 June 2001 by the Dismissal Procedures Agreement Designation (Electrical Contracting Industry) Order 1991 Revocation Order 2001 (SI 2001/1752), subject to transitional provisions.

CHAPTER II
REMEDIES FOR UNFAIR DISMISSAL

Introductory

111 Complaints to [employment tribunal]

(1) A complaint may be presented to an [employment tribunal] against an employer by any person that he was unfairly dismissed by the employer.

(2) Subject to subsection (3), an [employment tribunal] shall not consider a complaint under this section unless it is presented to the tribunal—

(a) before the end of the period of three months beginning with the effective date of termination, or

(b) within such further period as the tribunal considers reasonable in a case where it is satisfied that it was not reasonably practicable for the complaint to be presented before the end of that period of three months.

(3) Where a dismissal is with notice, an [employment tribunal] shall consider a complaint under this section if it is presented after the notice is given but before the effective date of termination.

(4) In relation to a complaint which is presented as mentioned in subsection (3), the provisions of this Act, so far as they relate to unfair dismissal, have effect as if—

(a) references to a complaint by a person that he was unfairly dismissed by his employer included references to a complaint by a person that his employer has given him notice in such circumstances that he will be unfairly dismissed when the notice expires,

(b) references to reinstatement included references to the withdrawal of the notice by the employer,

(c) references to the effective date of termination included references to the date which would be the effective date of termination on the expiry of the notice, and

(d) references to an employee ceasing to be employed included references to an employee having been given notice of dismissal.

[1155]

NOTES

Section heading, sub-ss (1)–(3): words in square brackets substituted by the Employment Rights (Dispute Resolution) Act 1998, s 1(2)(a).

Conciliation: employment tribunal proceedings under this section in respect of a complaint of unfair dismissal and claims which could be the subject of such proceedings are proceedings to which the Employment Tribunals Act 1996, s 18 applies; see s 18(1)(d) of that Act at **[975]**. The standard conciliation period applies to such proceedings by virtue of the Employment Tribunals (Constitution and Rules of Procedure) Regulations 2004, SI 2004/1861, Sch 1, rule 22(1), (6), except where it is claimed that a dismissal was automatically unfair by virtue of ss 103A or 105(6A); in such cases there is no fixed conciliation period by virtue of SI 2004/1861, Sch 1, rule 22(1).

Tribunal jurisdiction: the Employment Act 2002, ss 31, 32, 38 at **[1493]**, **[1494]**, **[1496]** apply to proceedings before the employment tribunal relating to a claim under this section; see ss 31(1), 32(1), 38(1) of, and Schs 3–5 to, the 2002 Act at **[1508]–[1510]**.

For the circumstances in which the normal time limit for presenting a complaint under this section is extended for a period of three months, see the Employment Act 2002 (Dispute Resolution) Regulations 2004, SI 2004/752, regs 15 and 18 at **[3096]** and **[3098]**.

112 The remedies: orders and compensation

(1) This section applies where, on a complaint under section 111, an [employment tribunal] finds that the grounds of the complaint are well-founded.

(2) The tribunal shall—

(a) explain to the complainant what orders may be made under section 113 and in what circumstances they may be made, and

(b) ask him whether he wishes the tribunal to make such an order.

(3) If the complainant expresses such a wish, the tribunal may make an order under section 113.

(4) If no order is made under section 113, the tribunal shall make an award of compensation for unfair dismissal (calculated in accordance with sections 118 to [126] […]) to be paid by the employer to the employee.

[(5) Where—

(a) an employee is regarded as unfairly dismissed by virtue of section [98ZG or] 98A(1) (whether or not his dismissal is unfair or regarded as unfair for any other reason), and

(b) an order is made in respect of the employee under section 113,

the employment tribunal shall, subject to subsection (6), also make an award of four weeks' pay to be paid by the employer to the employee.

(6) An employment tribunal shall not be required to make an award under subsection (5) if it considers that such an award would result in injustice to the employer.]

[1156]

NOTES

Sub-s (1): words in square brackets substituted by the Employment Rights (Dispute Resolution) Act 1998, s 1(2)(a).

Sub-s (4): figure in square brackets substituted by the Employment Act 2002, s 53, Sch 7, paras 24, 36, as from 1 October 2004; words omitted (originally inserted by the Public Interest Disclosure Act 1998, s 8(1)) repealed by the Employment Relations Act 1999, s 44, Sch 9(11).

Sub-s (5): added, together with sub-s (6), by the Employment Act 2002, s 34(1), (3), as from 1 October 2004; figure in square brackets inserted by the Employment Equality (Age) Regulations 2006, SI 2006/1031, reg 49(1), Sch 8, Pt 1, paras 21, 26, as from 1 October 2006.

Sub-s (6): added as noted above.

Orders for Reinstatement or Re-engagement

113 The orders

An order under this section may be—

(a) an order for reinstatement (in accordance with section 114), or

(b) an order for re-engagement (in accordance with section 115),

as the tribunal may decide.

[1157]

114 Order for reinstatement

(1) An order for reinstatement is an order that the employer shall treat the complainant in all respects as if he had not been dismissed.

(2) On making an order for reinstatement the tribunal shall specify—

(a) any amount payable by the employer in respect of any benefit which the complainant might reasonably be expected to have had but for the dismissal (including arrears of pay) for the period between the date of termination of employment and the date of reinstatement,

(b) any rights and privileges (including seniority and pension rights) which must be restored to the employee, and

(c) the date by which the order must be complied with.

(3) If the complainant would have benefited from an improvement in his terms and conditions of employment had he not been dismissed, an order for reinstatement shall require him to be treated as if he had benefited from that improvement from the date on which he would have done so but for being dismissed.

(4) In calculating for the purposes of subsection (2)(a) any amount payable by the employer, the tribunal shall take into account, so as to reduce the employer's liability, any sums received by the complainant in respect of the period between the date of termination of employment and the date of reinstatement by way of—

(a) wages in lieu of notice or ex gratia payments paid by the employer, or

(b) remuneration paid in respect of employment with another employer,

and such other benefits as the tribunal thinks appropriate in the circumstances.

(5) …

[1158]

NOTES

Sub-s (5): repealed by the Employment Relations Act 1999, ss 9, 44, Sch 4, Pt III, paras 1, 5, 20, Sch 9(2).

115 Order for re-engagement

(1) An order for re-engagement is an order, on such terms as the tribunal may decide, that the complainant be engaged by the employer, or by a successor of the employer or by an associated employer, in employment comparable to that from which he was dismissed or other suitable employment.

(2) On making an order for re-engagement the tribunal shall specify the terms on which re-engagement is to take place, including—

(a) the identity of the employer,

(b) the nature of the employment,

(c) the remuneration for the employment,

(d) any amount payable by the employer in respect of any benefit which the complainant might reasonably be expected to have had but for the dismissal (including arrears of pay) for the period between the date of termination of employment and the date of re-engagement,

(e) any rights and privileges (including seniority and pension rights) which must be restored to the employee, and

(f) the date by which the order must be complied with.

(3) In calculating for the purposes of subsection (2)(d) any amount payable by the employer, the tribunal shall take into account, so as to reduce the employer's liability, any sums received by the complainant in respect of the period between the date of termination of employment and the date of re-engagement by way of—

(a) wages in lieu of notice or ex gratia payments paid by the employer, or

(b) remuneration paid in respect of employment with another employer,

and such other benefits as the tribunal thinks appropriate in the circumstances.

(4) …

[1159]

NOTES

Sub-s (4): repealed by the Employment Relations Act 1999, ss 9, 44, Sch 4, Pt III, paras 1, 5, 21, Sch 9(2).

116 Choice of order and its terms

(1) In exercising its discretion under section 113 the tribunal shall first consider whether to make an order for reinstatement and in so doing shall take into account—

(a) whether the complainant wishes to be reinstated,

(b) whether it is practicable for the employer to comply with an order for reinstatement, and

(c) where the complainant caused or contributed to some extent to the dismissal, whether it would be just to order his reinstatement.

(2) If the tribunal decides not to make an order for reinstatement it shall then consider whether to make an order for re-engagement and, if so, on what terms.

(3) In so doing the tribunal shall take into account—

(a) any wish expressed by the complainant as to the nature of the order to be made,

(b) whether it is practicable for the employer (or a successor or an associated employer) to comply with an order for re-engagement, and

(c) where the complainant caused or contributed to some extent to the dismissal, whether it would be just to order his re-engagement and (if so) on what terms.

(4) Except in a case where the tribunal takes into account contributory fault under subsection (3)(c) it shall, if it orders re-engagement, do so on terms which are, so far as is reasonably practicable, as favourable as an order for reinstatement.

(5) Where in any case an employer has engaged a permanent replacement for a dismissed employee, the tribunal shall not take that fact into account in determining, for the purposes of subsection (1)(b) or (3)(b), whether it is practicable to comply with an order for reinstatement or re-engagement.

(6) Subsection (5) does not apply where the employer shows—

(a) that it was not practicable for him to arrange for the dismissed employee's work to be done without engaging a permanent replacement, or

(b) that—

(i) he engaged the replacement after the lapse of a reasonable period, without having heard from the dismissed employee that he wished to be reinstated or re-engaged, and

(ii) when the employer engaged the replacement it was no longer reasonable for him to arrange for the dismissed employee's work to be done except by a permanent replacement.

[1160]

117 Enforcement of order and compensation

(1) An [employment tribunal] shall make an award of compensation, to be paid by the employer to the employee, if—

(a) an order under section 113 is made and the complainant is reinstated or re-engaged, but

(b) the terms of the order are not fully complied with.

(2) Subject to section 124 […], the amount of the compensation shall be such as the tribunal thinks fit having regard to the loss sustained by the complainant in consequence of the failure to comply fully with the terms of the order.

[(2A) There shall be deducted from any award under subsection (1) the amount of any award made under section 112(5) at the time of the order under section 113.]

(3) Subject to subsections (1) and (2) […], if an order under section 113 is made but the complainant is not reinstated or re-engaged in accordance with the order, the tribunal shall make—

(a) an award of compensation for unfair dismissal (calculated in accordance with sections 118 to [126]), and

(b) except where this paragraph does not apply, an additional award of compensation of [an amount not less than twenty-six nor more than fifty-two weeks' pay],

to be paid by the employer to the employee.

(4) Subsection (3)(b) does not apply where—

(a) the employer satisfies the tribunal that it was not practicable to comply with the order, …

(b) …

(5), (6) …

(7) Where in any case an employer has engaged a permanent replacement for a dismissed employee, the tribunal shall not take that fact into account in determining for the purposes of subsection (4)(a) whether it was practicable to comply with the order for reinstatement or re-engagement unless the employer shows that it was not practicable for him to arrange for the dismissed employee's work to be done without engaging a permanent replacement.

(8) Where in any case an [employment tribunal] finds that the complainant has unreasonably prevented an order under section 113 from being complied with, in making an award of compensation for unfair dismissal … it shall take that conduct into account as a failure on the part of the complainant to mitigate his loss.

[1161]

NOTES

Sub-s (1): words in square brackets substituted by the Employment Rights (Dispute Resolution) Act 1998, s 1(2)(a).

Sub-s (2): words omitted (originally inserted by the Public Interest Disclosure Act 1998, s 8(2)(a)) repealed by the Employment Relations Act 1999, s 44, Sch 9(11).

Sub-s (2A): inserted by the Employment Act 2002, s 34(1), (4), as from 1 October 2004.

Sub-s (3): words omitted (originally inserted by the Public Interest Disclosure Act 1998, s 8(2)(b)) repealed by the Employment Relations Act 1999, s 44, Sch 9(11); figure in square brackets in para (a) substituted by the Employment Act 2002, s 53, Sch 7, paras 24, 37, as from 1 October 2004; words in square brackets in para (b) substituted by the Employment Relations Act 1999, s 33(2).

Sub-s (4): para (b) and word immediately preceding it repealed by the Employment Relations Act 1999, ss 33(1)(a), 44, Sch 9(10).

Sub-ss (5), (6): repealed by the Employment Relations Act 1999, ss 33(2), 44, Sch 9(10).

Sub-s (8): words in square brackets substituted, and words omitted repealed, by the Employment Rights (Dispute Resolution) Act 1998, ss 1(2)(a), 15, Sch 2.

Modifications: for modifications in relation to arbitration schemes for unfair dismissal cases, see the ACAS Arbitration Scheme (Great Britain) Order 2004, SI 2004/753 at **[3099]**.

Compensation

118 General

(1) […] where a tribunal makes an award of compensation for unfair dismissal under section 112(4) or 117(3)(a) the award shall consist of—

(a) a basic award (calculated in accordance with sections 119 to 122 and 126), and

(b) a compensatory award (calculated in accordance with sections 123, 124, [124A and 126]).

(2), (3), [(4)] …

[1162]

NOTES

Sub-s (1): words omitted (originally inserted by the Public Interest Disclosure Act 1998, s 8(3)) repealed by the Employment Relations Act 1999, s 44, Sch 9(11); words in square brackets in para (b) substituted by the Employment Act 2002, s 53, Sch 7, paras 24, 38, as from 1 October 2004.

Sub-ss (2), (3): repealed by the Employment Relations Act 1999, ss 33(1)(a), 44, Sch 9(10).

Sub-s (4): added by the Employment Rights (Dispute Resolution) Act 1998, s 15, Sch 1, para 21(1), (3); repealed by the Employment Act 2002, s 54, Sch 8(1), as from 1 November 2004.

119 Basic award

(1) Subject to the provisions of this section, sections 120 to 122 and section 126, the amount of the basic award shall be calculated by—

(a) determining the period, ending with the effective date of termination, during which the employee has been continuously employed,

(b) reckoning backwards from the end of that period the number of years of employment falling within that period, and

(c) allowing the appropriate amount for each of those years of employment.

(2) In subsection (1)(c) "the appropriate amount" means—

(a) one and a half weeks' pay for a year of employment in which the employee was not below the age of forty-one,

(b) one week's pay for a year of employment (not within paragraph (a)) in which he was not below the age of twenty-two, and

(c) half a week's pay for a year of employment not within paragraph (a) or (b).

(3) Where twenty years of employment have been reckoned under subsection (1), no account shall be taken under that subsection of any year of employment earlier than those twenty years.

(4)–(6) …

[1163]

NOTES

Sub-ss (4), (5): repealed by the Employment Equality (Age) Regulations 2006, SI 2006/1031, reg 49(1), Sch 8, Pt 1, paras 21, 27, as from 1 October 2006.

Sub-s (6): repealed by the Employment Relations Act 1999, ss 9, 44, Sch 4, Pt III, paras 1, 5, 23, Sch 9(2).

120 Basic award: minimum in certain cases

(1) The amount of the basic award (before any reduction under section 122) shall not be less than [£4,400] where the reason (or, if more than one, the principal reason)—

(a) in a redundancy case, for selecting the employee for dismissal, or

(b) otherwise, for the dismissal,

is one of those specified in section 100(1)(a) and (b), [101A(d),] 102(1) or 103.

[(1A) Where—

(a) an employee is regarded as unfairly dismissed by virtue of section [98ZG or] 98A(1) (whether or not his dismissal is unfair or regarded as unfair for any other reason),

(b) an award of compensation falls to be made under section [98ZG or] 112(4), and

(c) the amount of the award under section [98ZG or] 118(1)(a), before any reduction under section 122(3A) or (4), is less than the amount of four weeks' pay,

the employment tribunal shall, subject to subsection (1B), increase the award under section [98ZG or] 118(1)(a) to the amount of four weeks' pay.

(1B) An employment tribunal shall not be required by subsection (1A) to increase the amount of an award if it considers that the increase would result in injustice to the employer.]

(2) …

[1164]

NOTES

Sub-s (1): sum in first pair of square brackets substituted by the Employment Rights (Increase of Limits) Order 2007, SI 2007/3570, art 3, Schedule, as from 1 February 2008, in relation to any case where the appropriate date falls on or after that date (see SI 2007/3570, art 4 at **[3474H]**). The previous sum was £4,200 (see SI 2006/3045). This sum may be varied by the Secretary of State (see the Employment Relations Act 1999, s 34(1)(a), (3)(a) at **[1445]**); figure in second pair of square brackets inserted by the Working Time Regulations 1998, SI 1998/1833, regs 2(1), 32(5).

Sub-s (1A): inserted, together with sub-s (1B), by the Employment Act 2002, s 34(1), (6), as from 1 October 2004; figures in square brackets inserted by the Employment Equality (Age) Regulations 2006, SI 2006/1031, reg 49(1), Sch 8, Pt 1, paras 21, 28, as from 1 October 2006.

Sub-s (1B): inserted as noted above.

Sub-s (2): repealed by the Employment Relations Act 1999, ss 36(1)(a), 44, Sch 9(10).

121 Basic award of two weeks' pay in certain cases

The amount of the basic award shall be two weeks' pay where the tribunal finds that the reason (or, where there is more than one, the principal reason) for the dismissal of the employee is that he was redundant and the employee—

(a) by virtue of section 138 is not regarded as dismissed for the purposes of Part XI, or

(b) by virtue of section 141 is not, or (if he were otherwise entitled) would not be, entitled to a redundancy payment.

[1165]

122 Basic award: reductions

(1) Where the tribunal finds that the complainant has unreasonably refused an offer by the employer which (if accepted) would have the effect of reinstating the complainant in his employment in all respects as if he had not been dismissed, the tribunal shall reduce or further reduce the amount of the basic award to such extent as it considers just and equitable having regard to that finding.

(2) Where the tribunal considers that any conduct of the complainant before the dismissal (or, where the dismissal was with notice, before the notice was given) was such that it would be just and equitable to reduce or further reduce the amount of the basic award to any extent, the tribunal shall reduce or further reduce that amount accordingly.

(3) Subsection (2) does not apply in a redundancy case unless the reason for selecting the employee for dismissal was one of those specified in section 100(1)(a) and (b), [101A(d),] 102(1) or 103; and in such a case subsection (2) applies only to so much of the basic award as is payable because of section 120.

[(3A) Where the complainant has been awarded any amount in respect of the dismissal under a designated dismissal procedures agreement, the tribunal shall reduce or further reduce the amount of the basic award to such extent as it considers just and equitable having regard to that award.]

(4) The amount of the basic award shall be reduced or further reduced by the amount of—

(a) any redundancy payment awarded by the tribunal under Part XI in respect of the same dismissal, or

(b) any payment made by the employer to the employee on the ground that the dismissal was by reason of redundancy (whether in pursuance of Part XI or otherwise).

[1166]

NOTES

Sub-s (3): figure in square brackets inserted by the Working Time Regulations 1998, SI 1998/1833, regs 2(1), 32(5).

Sub-s (3A): inserted by the Employment Rights (Dispute Resolution) Act 1998, s 15, Sch 1, para 22.

123 Compensatory award

(1) Subject to the provisions of this section and sections 124[, 124A and 126], the amount of the compensatory award shall be such amount as the tribunal considers just and equitable in all the circumstances having regard to the loss sustained by the complainant in consequence of the dismissal in so far as that loss is attributable to action taken by the employer.

(2) The loss referred to in subsection (1) shall be taken to include—

(a) any expenses reasonably incurred by the complainant in consequence of the dismissal, and

(b) subject to subsection (3), loss of any benefit which he might reasonably be expected to have had but for the dismissal.

(3) The loss referred to in subsection (1) shall be taken to include in respect of any loss of—

(a) any entitlement or potential entitlement to a payment on account of dismissal by reason of redundancy (whether in pursuance of Part XI or otherwise), or

(b) any expectation of such a payment,

only the loss referable to the amount (if any) by which the amount of that payment would have exceeded the amount of a basic award (apart from any reduction under section 122) in respect of the same dismissal.

(4) In ascertaining the loss referred to in subsection (1) the tribunal shall apply the same rule concerning the duty of a person to mitigate his loss as applies to damages recoverable under the common law of England and Wales or (as the case may be) Scotland.

(5) In determining, for the purposes of subsection (1), how far any loss sustained by the complainant was attributable to action taken by the employer, no account shall be taken of any pressure which by—

(a) calling, organising, procuring or financing a strike or other industrial action, or

(b) threatening to do so,

was exercised on the employer to dismiss the employee; and that question shall be determined as if no such pressure had been exercised.

(6) Where the tribunal finds that the dismissal was to any extent caused or contributed to by any action of the complainant, it shall reduce the amount of the compensatory award by such proportion as it considers just and equitable having regard to that finding.

(7) If the amount of any payment made by the employer to the employee on the ground that the dismissal was by reason of redundancy (whether in pursuance of Part XI or otherwise) exceeds the amount of the basic award which would be payable but for section 122(4), that excess goes to reduce the amount of the compensatory award.

[(8) Where the amount of the compensatory award falls to be calculated for the purposes of an award under section 117(3)(a), there shall be deducted from the compensatory award any award made under section 112(5) at the time of the order under section 113.]

[1167]

NOTES

Sub-s (1): words in square brackets substituted by the Employment Act 2002, s 53, Sch 7, paras 24, 39, as from 1 October 2004.

Sub-s (8): added by the Employment Act 2002, s 34(1), (5), as from 1 October 2004.

124 Limit of compensatory award etc

(1) The amount of—

(a) any compensation awarded to a person under section 117(1) and (2), or

(b) a compensatory award to a person calculated in accordance with section 123,

shall not exceed [£63,000].

[(1A) Subsection (1) shall not apply to compensation awarded, or a compensatory award made, to a person in a case where he is regarded as unfairly dismissed by virtue of section 100, 103A, 105(3) or 105(6A).]

(2) …

(3) In the case of compensation awarded to a person under section 117(1) and (2), the limit imposed by this section may be exceeded to the extent necessary to enable the award fully to reflect the amount specified as payable under section 114(2)(a) or section 115(2)(d).

(4) Where—

(a) a compensatory award is an award under paragraph (a) of subsection (3) of section 117, and

(b) an additional award falls to be made under paragraph (b) of that subsection, the limit imposed by this section on the compensatory award may be exceeded to the extent necessary to enable the aggregate of the compensatory and additional awards fully to reflect the amount specified as payable under section 114(2)(a) or section 115(2)(d).

(5) The limit imposed by this section applies to the amount which the [employment tribunal] would, apart from this section, award in respect of the subject matter of the complaint after taking into account—

(a) any payment made by the respondent to the complainant in respect of that matter, and

(b) any reduction in the amount of the award required by any enactment or rule of law.

[1168]

NOTES

Sub-s (1): sum in square brackets substituted by the Employment Rights (Increase of Limits) Order 2007, SI 2007/3570, art 3, Schedule, as from 1 February 2008, in relation to any case where the appropriate date falls on or after that date (see SI 2007/3570, art 4 at **[3474H]**). The previous sum was £60,600 (see SI 2006/3045). This sum may be varied by the Secretary of State (see the Employment Relations Act 1999, s 34(1)(a), (3)(b), at **[1341]**). Sums for periods prior to 1 February 2007 were £58,400 as from 1 February 2006 (SI 2005/3352), £56,800 as from 1 February 2005 (SI 2004/2989), and £55,000 as from 1 February 2004 (SI 2003/3038) in each case where the appropriate date fell after the commencement date).

Sub-s (1A): inserted by the Employment Relations Act 1999, s 37(1).

Sub-s (2): repealed by the Employment Relations Act 1999, ss 36(1)(a), 44, Sch 9(10).

Sub-s (5): words in square brackets substituted by the Employment Rights (Dispute Resolution) Act 1998, s 1(2)(a).

[124A Adjustments under the Employment Act 2002

Where an award of compensation for unfair dismissal falls to be—

(a) reduced or increased under section 31 of the Employment Act 2002 (non-completion of statutory procedures), or

(b) increased under section 38 of that Act (failure to give statement of employment particulars),

the adjustment shall be in the amount awarded under section 118(1)(b) and shall be applied immediately before any reduction under section 123(6) or (7).]

[1169]

NOTES

Commencement: 1 October 2004.

Inserted by the Employment Act 2002, s 39, as from 1 October 2004.

125 (*Repealed by the Employment Relations Act 1999, ss 33(1)(a), 44, Sch 9(10).*)

126 Acts which are both unfair dismissal and discrimination

(1) This section applies where compensation falls to be awarded in respect of any act both under—

(a) the provisions of this Act relating to unfair dismissal, and

[(b) any one or more of the following—

(i) the Sex Discrimination Act 1975;

(ii) the Race Relations Act 1976;

(iii) the Disability Discrimination Act 1995;

(iv) the Employment Equality (Sexual Orientation) Regulations 2003;

(v) the Employment Equality (Religion or Belief) Regulations 2003;

(vi) the Employment Equality (Age) Regulations 2006].

(2) An [employment tribunal] shall not award compensation under any one of those … Acts in respect of any loss or other matter which is or has been taken into account under [any other of them] by the tribunal (or another [employment tribunal]) in awarding compensation on the same or another complaint in respect of that act.

[1170]–[1171]

NOTES

Sub-s (1): para (b) substituted by the Employment Equality (Age) Regulations 2006, SI 2006/1031, reg 49(1), Sch 8, Pt 1, paras 21, 29, as from 1 October 2006.

Sub-s (2): words in square brackets substituted, and word omitted repealed, by the Employment Rights (Dispute Resolution) Act 1998, ss 1(2)(a), 14(2), (4), 15, Sch 2.

Note: the reference to 'Acts' in the section heading has not been amended despite the terms of the amended sub-s (1)(b) above.

127, 127A, 127B (*S 127 repealed by the Employment Relations Act 1999, ss 9, 44, Sch 4, Pt III, paras 1, 5, 24, Sch 9(2); s 127A inserted by the Employment Rights (Dispute Resolution) Act 1998, s 13, and repealed by the Employment Act 2002, ss 53, 54, Sch 7, paras 24, 40, Sch 8(1), as from 1 October 2004; s 127B inserted by the Public Interest Disclosure Act 1998, ss 8(4), 18(2), and repealed by the Employment Relations Act 1999, ss 37(2), 44, Sch 9(11).*)

Interim relief

128 Interim relief pending determination of complaint

(1) An employee who presents a complaint to an [employment tribunal]—

(a) that he has been unfairly dismissed by his employer, and

(b) that the reason (or, if more than one, the principal reason) for the dismissal is one of those specified in section 100(1)(a) and (b), [101A(d),] 102(1)[, 103 or 103A] [or in paragraph 161(2) of Schedule A1 to the Trade Union and Labour Relations (Consolidation) Act 1992],

may apply to the tribunal for interim relief.

(2) The tribunal shall not entertain an application for interim relief unless it is presented to the tribunal before the end of the period of seven days immediately following the effective date of termination (whether before, on or after that date).

(3) The tribunal shall determine the application for interim relief as soon as practicable after receiving the application.

(4) The tribunal shall give to the employer not later than seven days before the date of the hearing a copy of the application together with notice of the date, time and place of the hearing.

(5) The tribunal shall not exercise any power it has of postponing the hearing of an application for interim relief except where it is satisfied that special circumstances exist which justify it in doing so.

[1172]

NOTES

Sub-s (1): words in first pair of square brackets substituted by the Employment Rights (Dispute Resolution) Act 1998, s 1(2)(a); figure in second pair of square brackets inserted by the Working Time Regulations 1998, SI 1998/1833, regs 2(1), 32(5); words in third pair of square brackets substituted by the Public Interest Disclosure Act 1998, s 9; words in final pair of square brackets inserted by the Employment Relations Act 1999, s 6. Note that the Queen's Printer's copy of the 1999 Act provides that the words in the final pair of square brackets should be inserted after the figure "103". It is assumed that this is an error and that the words should be correctly inserted after the figure "103A".

129 Procedure on hearing of application and making of order

(1) This section applies where, on hearing an employee's application for interim relief, it appears to the tribunal that it is likely that on determining the complaint to which the application relates the tribunal will find that the reason (or, if more than one, the principal reason) for his dismissal is one of those specified in section 100(1)(a) and (b), [101A(d),] 102(1)[, 103 or 103A] [or in paragraph 161(2) of Schedule A1 to the Trade Union and Labour Relations (Consolidation) Act 1992].

(2) The tribunal shall announce its findings and explain to both parties (if present)—

(a) what powers the tribunal may exercise on the application, and

(b) in what circumstances it will exercise them.

(3) The tribunal shall ask the employer (if present) whether he is willing, pending the determination or settlement of the complaint—

(a) to reinstate the employee (that is, to treat him in all respects as if he had not been dismissed), or

(b) if not, to re-engage him in another job on terms and conditions not less favourable than those which would have been applicable to him if he had not been dismissed.

(4) For the purposes of subsection (3)(b) "terms and conditions not less favourable than those which would have been applicable to him if he had not been dismissed" means, as regards seniority, pension rights and other similar rights, that the period prior to the dismissal should be regarded as continuous with his employment following the dismissal.

(5) If the employer states that he is willing to reinstate the employee, the tribunal shall make an order to that effect.

(6) If the employer—

(a) states that he is willing to re-engage the employee in another job, and
(b) specifies the terms and conditions on which he is willing to do so,

the tribunal shall ask the employee whether he is willing to accept the job on those terms and conditions.

(7) If the employee is willing to accept the job on those terms and conditions, the tribunal shall make an order to that effect.

(8) If the employee is not willing to accept the job on those terms and conditions—

(a) where the tribunal is of the opinion that the refusal is reasonable, the tribunal shall make an order for the continuation of his contract of employment, and
(b) otherwise, the tribunal shall make no order.

(9) If on the hearing of an application for interim relief the employer—

(a) fails to attend before the tribunal, or
(b) states that he is unwilling either to reinstate or re-engage the employee as mentioned in subsection (3),

the tribunal shall make an order for the continuation of the employee's contract of employment.

[1173]

NOTES

Sub-s (1): figure in first pair of square brackets inserted by the Working Time Regulations 1998, SI 1998/1833, regs 2(1), 32(5); words in second pair of square brackets substituted by the Public Interest Disclosure Act 1998, s 9; words in third pair of square brackets inserted by the Employment Relations Act 1999, s 6. Note that the Queen's Printer's copy of the 1999 Act provides that the words in the third pair of square brackets should be inserted after the figure "103". It is assumed that this is an error and that the words should be correctly inserted after the figure "103A".

130 Order for continuation of contract of employment

(1) An order under section 129 for the continuation of a contract of employment is an order that the contract of employment continue in force—

(a) for the purposes of pay or any other benefit derived from the employment, seniority, pension rights and other similar matters, and
(b) for the purposes of determining for any purpose the period for which the employee has been continuously employed,

from the date of its termination (whether before or after the making of the order) until the determination or settlement of the complaint.

(2) Where the tribunal makes such an order it shall specify in the order the amount which is to be paid by the employer to the employee by way of pay in respect of each normal pay period, or part of any such period, falling between the date of dismissal and the determination or settlement of the complaint.

(3) Subject to the following provisions, the amount so specified shall be that which the employee could reasonably have been expected to earn during that period, or part, and shall be paid—

(a) in the case of a payment for any such period falling wholly or partly after the making of the order, on the normal pay day for that period, and
(b) in the case of a payment for any past period, within such time as may be specified in the order.

(4) If an amount is payable in respect only of part of a normal pay period, the amount shall be calculated by reference to the whole period and reduced proportionately.

(5) Any payment made to an employee by an employer under his contract of employment, or by way of damages for breach of that contract, in respect of a normal pay period, or part of any such period, goes towards discharging the employer's liability in respect of that period under subsection (2); and, conversely, any payment under that subsection in respect of a period goes towards discharging any liability of the employer under, or in respect of breach of, the contract of employment in respect of that period.

(6) If an employee, on or after being dismissed by his employer, receives a lump sum which, or part of which, is in lieu of wages but is not referable to any normal pay period, the tribunal shall take the payment into account in determining the amount of pay to be payable in pursuance of any such order.

(7) For the purposes of this section, the amount which an employee could reasonably have been expected to earn, his normal pay period and the normal pay day for each such period shall be determined as if he had not been dismissed.

[1174]

131 Application for variation or revocation of order

(1) At any time between—

(a) the making of an order under section 129, and

(b) the determination or settlement of the complaint,

the employer or the employee may apply to an [employment tribunal] for the revocation or variation of the order on the ground of a relevant change of circumstances since the making of the order.

(2) Sections 128 and 129 apply in relation to such an application as in relation to an original application for interim relief except that, in the case of an application by the employer, section 128(4) has effect with the substitution of a reference to the employee for the reference to the employer.

[1175]

NOTES

Sub-s (1): words in square brackets substituted by the Employment Rights (Dispute Resolution) Act 1998, s 1(2)(a).

132 Consequence of failure to comply with order

(1) If, on the application of an employee, an [employment tribunal] is satisfied that the employer has not complied with the terms of an order for the reinstatement or re-engagement of the employee under section 129(5) or (7), the tribunal shall—

(a) make an order for the continuation of the employee's contract of employment, and

(b) order the employer to pay compensation to the employee.

(2) Compensation under subsection (1)(b) shall be of such amount as the tribunal considers just and equitable in all the circumstances having regard—

(a) to the infringement of the employee's right to be reinstated or re-engaged in pursuance of the order, and

(b) to any loss suffered by the employee in consequence of the non-compliance.

(3) Section 130 applies to an order under subsection (1)(a) as in relation to an order under section 129.

(4) If on the application of an employee an [employment tribunal] is satisfied that the employer has not complied with the terms of an order for the continuation of a contract of employment subsection (5) or (6) applies.

(5) Where the non-compliance consists of a failure to pay an amount by way of pay specified in the order—

(a) the tribunal shall determine the amount owed by the employer on the date of the determination, and

(b) if on that date the tribunal also determines the employee's complaint that he has been unfairly dismissed, it shall specify that amount separately from any other sum awarded to the employee.

(6) In any other case, the tribunal shall order the employer to pay the employee such compensation as the tribunal considers just and equitable in all the circumstances having regard to any loss suffered by the employee in consequence of the non-compliance.

[1176]

NOTES

Sub-ss (1), (4): words in square brackets substituted by the Employment Rights (Dispute Resolution) Act 1998, s 1(2)(a).

CHAPTER III
SUPPLEMENTARY

133 Death of employer or employee

(1) Where—

(a) an employer has given notice to an employee to terminate his contract of employment, and

(b) before that termination the employee or the employer dies,

this Part applies as if the contract had been duly terminated by the employer by notice expiring on the date of the death.

(2) Where—

(a) an employee's contract of employment has been terminated,

(b) by virtue of subsection (2) or (4) of section 97 a date later than the effective date of termination as defined in subsection (1) of that section is to be treated for certain purposes as the effective date of termination, and

(c) the employer or the employee dies before that date,

subsection (2) or (4) of section 97 applies as if the notice referred to in that subsection as required by section 86 expired on the date of the death.

(3) Where an employee has died, sections 113 to 116 do not apply; and, accordingly, if the [employment tribunal] finds that the grounds of the complaint are well-founded, the case shall be treated as falling within section 112(4) as a case in which no order is made under section 113.

(4) Subsection (3) does not prejudice an order for reinstatement or re-engagement made before the employee's death.

(5) Where an order for reinstatement or re-engagement has been made and the employee dies before the order is complied with—

(a) if the employer has before the death refused to reinstate or re-engage the employee in accordance with the order, subsections (3) to (6) of section 117 apply, and an award shall be made under subsection (3)(b) of that section, unless the employer satisfies the tribunal that it was not practicable at the time of the refusal to comply with the order, and

(b) if there has been no such refusal, subsections (1) and (2) of that section apply if the employer fails to comply with any ancillary terms of the order which remain capable of fulfilment after the employee's death as they would apply to such a failure to comply fully with the terms of an order where the employee had been reinstated or re-engaged.

[1177]

NOTES

Sub-s (3): words in square brackets substituted by the Employment Rights (Dispute Resolution) Act 1998, s 1(2)(a).

134 Teachers in aided schools

(1) Where a teacher in [a foundation, voluntary aided or foundation special school is dismissed by the governing body of the school in pursuance of a requirement of the local education authority under [paragraph 7 of Schedule 2 to the Education Act 2002]], this Part has effect in relation to the dismissal as if—

(a) the local education authority had at all material times been the teacher's employer,

(b) the local education authority had dismissed him, and

(c) the reason or principal reason for which they did so had been the reason or principal reason for which they required his dismissal.

(2) For the purposes of a complaint under section 111 as it has effect by virtue of subsection (1)—

(a) section 117(4)(a) applies as if for the words "not practicable to comply" there were substituted the words "not practicable for the local education authority to permit compliance", and
(b) section 123(5) applies as if the references in it to the employer were to the local education authority.

[1178]

NOTES

Sub-s (1): words in first (outer) pair of square brackets substituted by the School Standards and Framework Act 1998, s 140(1), Sch 30, para 55; words in second (inner) pair of square brackets substituted by the Education Act 2002, s 215(1), Sch 21, para 30, as from 1 September 2003 (in relation to England), and as from 1 April 2006 (in relation to Wales).

[134A Application to police

(1) For the purposes of section 100, and of the other provisions of this Part so far as relating to the right not to be unfairly dismissed in a case where the dismissal is unfair by virtue of section 100, the holding, otherwise than under a contract of employment, of the office of constable or an appointment as police cadet shall be treated as employment by the relevant officer under a contract of employment.

[(2) In this section "the relevant officer", in relation to—
(a) a person holding the office of constable, or
(b) a person holding an appointment as a police cadet,

means the person who under section 51A of the Health and Safety at Work etc Act 1974 is to be treated as his employer for the purposes of Part 1 of that Act.]

[(3) Subsection (1) does not apply to the holding of the office of constable by a member of a police force on secondment to the Serious Organised Crime Agency.]]

[1179]

NOTES

Inserted by the Police (Health and Safety) Act 1997, s 4.

Sub-s (2): substituted by the Serious Organised Crime and Police Act 2005, s 158(1), (2)(b), (3), (5), as from 7 April 2005, with effect for the purposes of any proceedings in or before a court or tribunal commenced on or after that date as if this substitution had come into force on 1 July 1998.

Sub-s (3): added by the Serious Organised Crime and Police Act 2005, s 59, Sch 4, paras 84, 87, as from 1 April 2006.

Note: this section was amended by the Police Reform Act 2002, s 95, as from a day to be appointed. Those amendments lapsed following the repeal of that section without being brought into force, by the Serious Organised Crime and Police Act 2005, ss 158(4)(a), 174(2), Sch 17, Pt 1, as from 7 April 2005.

PART XI
REDUNDANCY PAYMENTS ETC

CHAPTER I
RIGHT TO REDUNDANCY PAYMENT

135 The right

(1) An employer shall pay a redundancy payment to any employee of his if the employee—
(a) is dismissed by the employer by reason of redundancy, or
(b) is eligible for a redundancy payment by reason of being laid off or kept on short-time.

(2) Subsection (1) has effect subject to the following provisions of this Part (including, in particular, sections 140 to 144, 149 to 152, 155 to 161 and 164).

[1180]

NOTES

Conciliation: employment tribunal proceedings and claims which could be the subject of employment tribunal proceedings under this section are proceedings to which the Employment Tribunals Act 1996, s 18 applies; see s 18(1)(d) of that Act at **[975]**. The short conciliation period applies to such claims by virtue of the Employment Tribunals (Constitution and Rules of Procedure) Regulations 2004, SI 2004/1861, Sch 1, rule 22(5).

CHAPTER II
RIGHT ON DISMISSAL BY REASON OF REDUNDANCY

Dismissal by reason of redundancy

136 Circumstances in which an employee is dismissed

(1) Subject to the provisions of this section and sections 137 and 138, for the purposes of this Part an employee is dismissed by his employer if (and only if)—

(a) the contract under which he is employed by the employer is terminated by the employer (whether with or without notice),

[(b) he is employed under a limited term contract and that contract terminates by virtue of the limiting event without being renewed under the same contract, or]

(c) the employee terminates the contract under which he is employed (with or without notice) in circumstances in which he is entitled to terminate it without notice by reason of the employer's conduct.

(2) Subsection (1)(c) does not apply if the employee terminates the contract without notice in circumstances in which he is entitled to do so by reason of a lock-out by the employer.

(3) An employee shall be taken to be dismissed by his employer for the purposes of this Part if—

(a) the employer gives notice to the employee to terminate his contract of employment, and

(b) at a time within the obligatory period of notice the employee gives notice in writing to the employer to terminate the contract of employment on a date earlier than the date on which the employer's notice is due to expire.

(4) In this Part the "obligatory period of notice", in relation to notice given by an employer to terminate an employee's contract of employment, means—

(a) the actual period of the notice in a case where the period beginning at the time when the notice is given and ending at the time when it expires is equal to the minimum period which (by virtue of any enactment or otherwise) is required to be given by the employer to terminate the contract of employment, and

(b) the period which—

(i) is equal to the minimum period referred to in paragraph (a), and

(ii) ends at the time when the notice expires,

in any other case.

(5) Where in accordance with any enactment or rule of law—

(a) an act on the part of an employer, or

(b) an event affecting an employer (including, in the case of an individual, his death),

operates to terminate a contract under which an employee is employed by him, the act or event shall be taken for the purposes of this Part to be a termination of the contract by the employer.

[1181]

NOTES

Sub-s (1): para (b) substituted by the Fixed-term Employees (Prevention of Less Favourable Treatment) Regulations 2002, SI 2002/2034, reg 11, Sch 2, Pt 1, para 3(1), (13).

---

137 (*Repealed by the Employment Relations Act 1999, ss 9, 44, Sch 4, Pt III, paras 1, 5, 25, Sch 9*(2).)

138 No dismissal in cases of renewal of contract or re-engagement

(1) Where—

(a) an employee's contract of employment is renewed, or he is re-engaged under a new contract of employment in pursuance of an offer (whether in writing or not) made before the end of his employment under the previous contract, and

(b) the renewal or re-engagement takes effect either immediately on, or after an interval of not more than four weeks after, the end of that employment,

the employee shall not be regarded for the purposes of this Part as dismissed by his employer by reason of the ending of his employment under the previous contract.

(2) Subsection (1) does not apply if—

(a) the provisions of the contract as renewed, or of the new contract, as to—

(i) the capacity and place in which the employee is employed, and

(ii) the other terms and conditions of his employment,

differ (wholly or in part) from the corresponding provisions of the previous contract, and

(b) during the period specified in subsection (3)—

(i) the employee (for whatever reason) terminates the renewed or new contract, or gives notice to terminate it and it is in consequence terminated, or

(ii) the employer, for a reason connected with or arising out of any difference between the renewed or new contract and the previous contract, terminates the renewed or new contract, or gives notice to terminate it and it is in consequence terminated.

(3) The period referred to in subsection (2)(b) is the period—

(a) beginning at the end of the employee's employment under the previous contract, and

(b) ending with—

(i) the period of four weeks beginning with the date on which the employee starts work under the renewed or new contract, or

(ii) such longer period as may be agreed in accordance with subsection (6) for the purpose of retraining the employee for employment under that contract;

and is in this Part referred to as the "trial period".

(4) Where subsection (2) applies, for the purposes of this Part—

(a) the employee shall be regarded as dismissed on the date on which his employment under the previous contract (or, if there has been more than one trial period, the original contract) ended, and

(b) the reason for the dismissal shall be taken to be the reason for which the employee was then dismissed, or would have been dismissed had the offer (or original offer) of renewed or new employment not been made, or the reason which resulted in that offer being made.

(5) Subsection (2) does not apply if the employee's contract of employment is again renewed, or he is again re-engaged under a new contract of employment, in circumstances such that subsection (1) again applies.

(6) For the purposes of subsection (3)(b)(ii) a period of retraining is agreed in accordance with this subsection only if the agreement—

(a) is made between the employer and the employee or his representative before the employee starts work under the contract as renewed, or the new contract,

(b) is in writing,

(c) specifies the date on which the period of retraining ends, and

(d) specifies the terms and conditions of employment which will apply in the employee's case after the end of that period.

[1182]

139 Redundancy

(1) For the purposes of this Act an employee who is dismissed shall be taken to be dismissed by reason of redundancy if the dismissal is wholly or mainly attributable to—

(a) the fact that his employer has ceased or intends to cease—

(i) to carry on the business for the purposes of which the employee was employed by him, or

(ii) to carry on that business in the place where the employee was so employed, or

(b) the fact that the requirements of that business—

(i) for employees to carry out work of a particular kind, or

(ii) for employees to carry out work of a particular kind in the place where the employee was employed by the employer,

have ceased or diminished or are expected to cease or diminish.

(2) For the purposes of subsection (1) the business of the employer together with the business or businesses of his associated employers shall be treated as one (unless either of the conditions specified in paragraphs (a) and (b) of that subsection would be satisfied without so treating them).

(3) For the purposes of subsection (1) the activities carried on by a local education authority with respect to the schools maintained by it, and the activities carried on by the

[governing bodies] of those schools, shall be treated as one business (unless either of the conditions specified in paragraphs (a) and (b) of that subsection would be satisfied without so treating them).

(4) Where—

(a) the contract under which a person is employed is treated by section 136(5) as terminated by his employer by reason of an act or event, and

(b) the employee's contract is not renewed and he is not re-engaged under a new contract of employment,

he shall be taken for the purposes of this Act to be dismissed by reason of redundancy if the circumstances in which his contract is not renewed, and he is not re-engaged, are wholly or mainly attributable to either of the facts stated in paragraphs (a) and (b) of subsection (1).

(5) In its application to a case within subsection (4), paragraph (a)(i) of subsection (1) has effect as if the reference in that subsection to the employer included a reference to any person to whom, in consequence of the act or event, power to dispose of the business has passed.

(6) In subsection (1) "cease" and "diminish" mean cease and diminish either permanently or temporarily and for whatever reason.

[1183]

NOTES

Sub-s (3): words in square brackets substituted by the Education Act 2002, s 215(1), Sch 21, para 31.

Exclusions

140 Summary dismissal

(1) Subject to subsections (2) and (3), an employee is not entitled to a redundancy payment by reason of dismissal where his employer, being entitled to terminate his contract of employment without notice by reason of the employee's conduct, terminates it either—

(a) without notice,

(b) by giving shorter notice than that which, in the absence of conduct entitling the employer to terminate the contract without notice, the employer would be required to give to terminate the contract, or

(c) by giving notice which includes, or is accompanied by, a statement in writing that the employer would, by reason of the employee's conduct, be entitled to terminate the contract without notice.

(2) Where an employee who—

(a) has been given notice by his employer to terminate his contract of employment, or

(b) has given notice to his employer under section 148(1) indicating his intention to claim a redundancy payment in respect of lay-off or short-time,

takes part in a strike at any relevant time in circumstances which entitle the employer to treat the contract of employment as terminable without notice, subsection (1) does not apply if the employer terminates the contract by reason of his taking part in the strike.

(3) Where the contract of employment of an employee who—

(a) has been given notice by his employer to terminate his contract of employment, or

(b) has given notice to his employer under section 148(1) indicating his intention to claim a redundancy payment in respect of lay-off or short-time,

is terminated as mentioned in subsection (1) at any relevant time otherwise than by reason of his taking part in a strike, an [employment tribunal] may determine that the employer is liable to make an appropriate payment to the employee if on a reference to the tribunal it appears to the tribunal, in the circumstances of the case, to be just and equitable that the employee should receive it.

(4) In subsection (3) "appropriate payment" means—

(a) the whole of the redundancy payment to which the employee would have been entitled apart from subsection (1), or

(b) such part of that redundancy payment as the tribunal thinks fit.

(5) In this section "relevant time"—

(a) in the case of an employee who has been given notice by his employer to terminate his contract of employment, means any time within the obligatory period of notice, and
(b) in the case of an employee who has given notice to his employer under section 148(1), means any time after the service of the notice.

[1184]

NOTES

Sub-s (3): words in square brackets substituted by the Employment Rights (Dispute Resolution) Act 1998, s 1(2)(a).

141 Renewal of contract or re-engagement

(1) This section applies where an offer (whether in writing or not) is made to an employee before the end of his employment—

(a) to renew his contract of employment, or
(b) to re-engage him under a new contract of employment,

with renewal or re-engagement to take effect either immediately on, or after an interval of not more than four weeks after, the end of his employment.

(2) Where subsection (3) is satisfied, the employee is not entitled to a redundancy payment if he unreasonably refuses the offer.

(3) This subsection is satisfied where—

(a) the provisions of the contract as renewed, or of the new contract, as to—
(i) the capacity and place in which the employee would be employed, and
(ii) the other terms and conditions of his employment,

would not differ from the corresponding provisions of the previous contract, or

(b) those provisions of the contract as renewed, or of the new contract, would differ from the corresponding provisions of the previous contract but the offer constitutes an offer of suitable employment in relation to the employee.

(4) The employee is not entitled to a redundancy payment if—

(a) his contract of employment is renewed, or he is re-engaged under a new contract of employment, in pursuance of the offer,
(b) the provisions of the contract as renewed or new contract as to the capacity or place in which he is employed or the other terms and conditions of his employment differ (wholly or in part) from the corresponding provisions of the previous contract,
(c) the employment is suitable in relation to him, and
(d) during the trial period he unreasonably terminates the contract, or unreasonably gives notice to terminate it and it is in consequence terminated.

[1185]

142 Employee anticipating expiry of employer's notice

(1) Subject to subsection (3), an employee is not entitled to a redundancy payment where—

(a) he is taken to be dismissed by virtue of section 136(3) by reason of giving to his employer notice terminating his contract of employment on a date earlier than the date on which notice by the employer terminating the contract is due to expire,
(b) before the employee's notice is due to expire, the employer gives him a notice such as is specified in subsection (2), and
(c) the employee does not comply with the requirements of that notice.

(2) The employer's notice referred to in subsection (1)(b) is a notice in writing—

(a) requiring the employee to withdraw his notice terminating the contract of employment and to continue in employment until the date on which the employer's notice terminating the contract expires, and
(b) stating that, unless he does so, the employer will contest any liability to pay to him a redundancy payment in respect of the termination of his contract of employment.

(3) An [employment tribunal] may determine that the employer is liable to make an appropriate payment to the employee if on a reference to the tribunal it appears to the tribunal, having regard to—

(a) the reasons for which the employee seeks to leave the employment, and

(b) the reasons for which the employer requires him to continue in it,

to be just and equitable that the employee should receive the payment.

(4) In subsection (3) "appropriate payment" means—

(a) the whole of the redundancy payment to which the employee would have been entitled apart from subsection (1), or

(b) such part of that redundancy payment as the tribunal thinks fit.

[1186]

NOTES

Sub-s (3): words in square brackets substituted by the Employment Rights (Dispute Resolution) Act 1998, s 1(2)(a).

143 Strike during currency of employer's notice

(1) This section applies where—

(a) an employer has given notice to an employee to terminate his contract of employment ("notice of termination"),

(b) after the notice is given the employee begins to take part in a strike of employees of the employer, and

(c) the employer serves on the employee a notice of extension.

(2) A notice of extension is a notice in writing which—

(a) requests the employee to agree to extend the contract of employment beyond the time of expiry by a period comprising as many available days as the number of working days lost by striking ("the proposed period of extension"),

(b) indicates the reasons for which the employer makes that request, and

(c) states that the employer will contest any liability to pay the employee a redundancy payment in respect of the dismissal effected by the notice of termination unless either—

(i) the employee complies with the request, or

(ii) the employer is satisfied that, in consequence of sickness or injury or otherwise, the employee is unable to comply with it or that (even though he is able to comply with it) it is reasonable in the circumstances for him not to do so.

(3) Subject to subsections (4) and (5), if the employee does not comply with the request contained in the notice of extension, he is not entitled to a redundancy payment by reason of the dismissal effected by the notice of termination.

(4) Subsection (3) does not apply if the employer agrees to pay a redundancy payment to the employee in respect of the dismissal effected by the notice of termination even though he has not complied with the request contained in the notice of extension.

(5) An [employment tribunal] may determine that the employer is liable to make an appropriate payment to the employee if on a reference to the tribunal it appears to the tribunal that—

(a) the employee has not complied with the request contained in the notice of extension and the employer has not agreed to pay a redundancy payment in respect of the dismissal effected by the notice of termination, but

(b) either the employee was unable to comply with the request or it was reasonable in the circumstances for him not to comply with it.

(6) In subsection (5) "appropriate payment" means—

(a) the whole of the redundancy payment to which the employee would have been entitled apart from subsection (3), or

(b) such part of that redundancy payment as the tribunal thinks fit.

(7) If the employee—

(a) complies with the request contained in the notice of extension, or

(b) does not comply with it but attends at his proper or usual place of work and is ready and willing to work on one or more (but not all) of the available days within the proposed period of extension,

the notice of termination has effect, and shall be deemed at all material times to have had effect, as if the period specified in it had been appropriately extended; and sections 87 to 91 accordingly apply as if the period of notice required by section 86 were extended to a corresponding extent.

(8) In subsection (7) "appropriately extended" means—

(a) in a case within paragraph (a) of that subsection, extended beyond the time of expiry by an additional period equal to the proposed period of extension, and

(b) in a case within paragraph (b) of that subsection, extended beyond the time of expiry up to the end of the day (or last of the days) on which he attends at his proper or usual place of work and is ready and willing to work.

[1187]

NOTES

Sub-s (5): words in square brackets substituted by the Employment Rights (Dispute Resolution) Act 1998, s 1(2)(a).

144 Provisions supplementary to section 143

(1) For the purposes of section 143 an employee complies with the request contained in a notice of extension if, but only if, on each available day within the proposed period of extension, he—

(a) attends at his proper or usual place of work, and

(b) is ready and willing to work,

whether or not he has signified his agreement to the request in any other way.

(2) The reference in section 143(2) to the number of working days lost by striking is a reference to the number of working days in the period—

(a) beginning with the date of service of the notice of termination, and

(b) ending with the time of expiry,

which are days on which the employee in question takes part in a strike of employees of his employer.

(3) In section 143 and this section—

"available day", in relation to an employee, means a working day beginning at or after the time of expiry which is a day on which he is not taking part in a strike of employees of the employer,

"available day within the proposed period of extension" means an available day which begins before the end of the proposed period of extension,

"time of expiry", in relation to a notice of termination, means the time at which the notice would expire apart from section 143, and

"working day", in relation to an employee, means a day on which, in accordance with his contract of employment, he is normally required to work.

(4) Neither the service of a notice of extension nor any extension by virtue of section 143(7) of the period specified in a notice of termination affects—

(a) any right either of the employer or of the employee to terminate the contract of employment (whether before, at or after the time of expiry) by a further notice or without notice, or

(b) the operation of this Part in relation to any such termination of the contract of employment.

[1188]

Supplementary

145 The relevant date

(1) For the purposes of the provisions of this Act relating to redundancy payments "the relevant date" in relation to the dismissal of an employee has the meaning given by this section.

(2) Subject to the following provisions of this section, "the relevant date"—

(a) in relation to an employee whose contract of employment is terminated by notice, whether given by his employer or by the employee, means the date on which the notice expires,

(b) in relation to an employee whose contract of employment is terminated without notice, means the date on which the termination takes effect, and

[(c) in relation to an employee who is employed under a limited-term contract which terminates by virtue of the limiting event without being renewed under the same contract, means the date on which the termination takes effect].

(3) Where the employee is taken to be dismissed by virtue of section 136(3) the "relevant date" means the date on which the employee's notice to terminate his contract of employment expires.

(4) Where the employee is regarded by virtue of section 138(4) as having been dismissed on the date on which his employment under an earlier contract ended, "the relevant date" means—

(a) for the purposes of section 164(1), the date which is the relevant date as defined by subsection (2) in relation to the renewed or new contract or, where there has been more than one trial period, the last such contract, and
(b) for the purposes of any other provision, the date which is the relevant date as defined by subsection (2) in relation to the previous contract or, where there has been more than one such trial period, the original contract.

(5) Where—

(a) the contract of employment is terminated by the employer, and
(b) the notice required by section 86 to be given by an employer would, if duly given on the material date, expire on a date later than the relevant date (as defined by the previous provisions of this section),

for the purposes of sections 155, 162(1) and 227(3) the later date is the relevant date.

(6) In subsection (5)(b) "the material date" means—

(a) the date when notice of termination was given by the employer, or
(b) where no notice was given, the date when the contract of employment was terminated by the employer.

(7) …

[1189]

NOTES

Sub-s (2): para (c) substituted by the Fixed-term Employees (Prevention of Less Favourable Treatment) Regulations 2002, SI 2002/2034, reg 11, Sch 2, Pt 1, para 3(1), (14).

Sub-s (7): repealed by the Employment Relations Act 1999, ss 9, 44, Sch 4, Pt III, paras 1, 5, 26, Sch 9(2).

146 Provisions supplementing sections 138 and 141

(1) In sections 138 and 141—

(a) references to re-engagement are to re-engagement by the employer or an associated employer, and

(b) references to an offer are to an offer made by the employer or an associated employer.

(2) For the purposes of the application of section 138(1) or 141(1) to a contract under which the employment ends on a Friday, Saturday or Sunday—

(a) the renewal or re-engagement shall be treated as taking effect immediately on the ending of the employment under the previous contract if it takes effect on or before the next Monday after that Friday, Saturday or Sunday, and

(b) the interval of four weeks to which those provisions refer shall be calculated as if the employment had ended on that next Monday.

(3) …

[1190]

NOTES

Sub-s (3): repealed by the Employment Relations Act 1999, ss 9, 44, Sch 4, Pt III, paras 1, 5, 27, Sch 9(2).

Modification: this section is modified in relation to any person to whom the Redundancy Payments (Continuity of Employment in Local Government, etc) (Modification) Order 1999, SI 1999/2277 applies for the purposes of determining that person's entitlement to a redundancy payment under the this Act and the amount of such payment; see arts 2, 3 of, and Sch 2, Pt I to, the 1999 Order at **[2519]**, **[2520]**, **[2524]**.

CHAPTER III
RIGHT BY REASON OF LAY-OFF OR SHORT-TIME

Lay-off and short-time

147 Meaning of "lay-off" and "short-time"

(1) For the purposes of this Part an employee shall be taken to be laid off for a week if—

(a) he is employed under a contract on terms and conditions such that his remuneration under the contract depends on his being provided by the employer with work of the kind which he is employed to do, but

(b) he is not entitled to any remuneration under the contract in respect of the week because the employer does not provide such work for him.

(2) For the purposes of this Part an employee shall be taken to be kept on short-time for a week if by reason of a diminution in the work provided for the employee by his employer (being work of a kind which under his contract the employee is employed to do) the employee's remuneration for the week is less than half a week's pay.

[1191]

148 Eligibility by reason of lay-off or short-time

(1) Subject to the following provisions of this Part, for the purposes of this Part an employee is eligible for a redundancy payment by reason of being laid off or kept on short-time if—

(a) he gives notice in writing to his employer indicating (in whatever terms) his intention to claim a redundancy payment in respect of lay-off or short-time (referred to in this Part as "notice of intention to claim"), and

(b) before the service of the notice he has been laid off or kept on short-time in circumstances in which subsection (2) applies.

(2) This subsection applies if the employee has been laid off or kept on short-time—

(a) for four or more consecutive weeks of which the last before the service of the notice ended on, or not more than four weeks before, the date of service of the notice, or

(b) for a series of six or more weeks (of which not more than three were consecutive) within a period of thirteen weeks, where the last week of the series before the service of the notice ended on, or not more than four weeks before, the date of service of the notice.

[1192]

Exclusions

149 Counter-notices

Where an employee gives to his employer notice of intention to claim but—

(a) the employer gives to the employee, within seven days after the service of that notice, notice in writing (referred to in this Part as a "counter-notice") that he will contest any liability to pay to the employee a redundancy payment in pursuance of the employee's notice, and

(b) the employer does not withdraw the counter-notice by a subsequent notice in writing,

the employee is not entitled to a redundancy payment in pursuance of his notice of intention to claim except in accordance with a decision of an [employment tribunal].

[1193]

NOTES

Words in square brackets substituted by the Employment Rights (Dispute Resolution) Act 1998, s 1(2)(a).

150 Resignation

(1) An employee is not entitled to a redundancy payment by reason of being laid off or kept on short-time unless he terminates his contract of employment by giving such period of notice as is required for the purposes of this section before the end of the relevant period.

(2) The period of notice required for the purposes of this section—

(a) where the employee is required by his contract of employment to give more than one week's notice to terminate the contract, is the minimum period which he is required to give, and

(b) otherwise, is one week.

(3) In subsection (1) "the relevant period"—

(a) if the employer does not give a counter-notice within seven days after the service of the notice of intention to claim, is three weeks after the end of those seven days,

(b) if the employer gives a counter-notice within that period of seven days but withdraws it by a subsequent notice in writing, is three weeks after the service of the notice of withdrawal, and

(c) if—

(i) the employer gives a counter-notice within that period of seven days, and does not so withdraw it, and

(ii) a question as to the right of the employee to a redundancy payment in pursuance of the notice of intention to claim is referred to an [employment tribunal],

is three weeks after the tribunal has notified to the employee its decision on that reference.

(4) For the purposes of subsection (3)(c) no account shall be taken of—

(a) any appeal against the decision of the tribunal, or

(b) any proceedings or decision in consequence of any such appeal.

[1194]

NOTES

Sub-s (3): words in square brackets substituted by the Employment Rights (Dispute Resolution) Act 1998, s 1(2)(a).

151 Dismissal

(1) An employee is not entitled to a redundancy payment by reason of being laid off or kept on short-time if he is dismissed by his employer.

(2) Subsection (1) does not prejudice any right of the employee to a redundancy payment in respect of the dismissal.

[1195]

152 Likelihood of full employment

(1) An employee is not entitled to a redundancy payment in pursuance of a notice of intention to claim if—

(a) on the date of service of the notice it was reasonably to be expected that the employee (if he continued to be employed by the same employer) would, not later than four weeks after that date, enter on a period of employment of not less than thirteen weeks during which he would not be laid off or kept on short-time for any week, and

(b) the employer gives a counter-notice to the employee within seven days after the service of the notice of intention to claim.

(2) Subsection (1) does not apply where the employee—

(a) continues or has continued, during the next four weeks after the date of service of the notice of intention to claim, to be employed by the same employer, and

(b) is or has been laid off or kept on short-time for each of those weeks.

[1196]

Supplementary

153 The relevant date

For the purposes of the provisions of this Act relating to redundancy payments "the relevant date" in relation to a notice of intention to claim or a right to a redundancy payment in pursuance of such a notice—

(a) in a case falling within paragraph (a) of subsection (2) of section 148, means the date on which of the last of the four or more consecutive weeks before the service of the notice came to an end, and

(b) in a case falling within paragraph (b) of that subsection, means the date on which the last of the series of six or more weeks before the service of the notice came to an end.

[1197]

154 Provisions supplementing sections 148 and 152

For the purposes of sections 148(2) and 152(2)—

(a) it is immaterial whether a series of weeks consists wholly of weeks for which the employee is laid off or wholly of weeks for which he is kept on short-time or partly of the one and partly of the other, and

(b) no account shall be taken of any week for which an employee is laid off or kept on short-time where the lay-off or short-time is wholly or mainly attributable to a strike or a lock-out (whether or not in the trade or industry in which the employee is employed and whether in Great Britain or elsewhere).

[1198]

CHAPTER IV
GENERAL EXCLUSIONS FROM RIGHT

155 Qualifying period of employment

An employee does not have any right to a redundancy payment unless he has been continuously employed for a period of not less than two years ending with the relevant date.

[1199]–[1200]

NOTES

Modified as noted to s 146 at **[1190]**.

156 (*Repealed by the Employment Equality (Age) Regulations 2006, SI 2006/1031, reg 49(1), Sch 8, Pt 1, paras 21, 30, 33, as from 1 October 2006, except in relation to any case where the relevant date by virtue of s 153 of this Act fell before that date.*)

157 Exemption orders

(1) Where an order under this section is in force in respect of an agreement covered by this section, an employee who, immediately before the relevant date, is an employee to whom the agreement applies does not have any right to a redundancy payment.

(2) An agreement is covered by this section if it is an agreement between—

(a) one or more employers or organisations of employers, and

(b) one or more trade unions representing employees,

under which employees to whom the agreement applies have a right in certain circumstances to payments on the termination of their contracts of employment.

(3) Where, on the application of all the parties to an agreement covered by this section, the Secretary of State is satisfied, having regard to the provisions of the agreement, that the employees to whom the agreement applies should not have any right to a redundancy payment, he may make an order under this section in respect of the agreement.

(4) The Secretary of State shall not make an order under this section in respect of an agreement unless the agreement indicates (in whatever terms) the willingness of the parties to it to submit to an [employment tribunal] any question arising under the agreement as to—

(a) the right of an employee to a payment on the termination of his employment, or

(b) the amount of such a payment.

(5) An order revoking an earlier order under this section may be made in pursuance of an application by all or any of the parties to the agreement in question or in the absence of such an application.

(6) …

[1201]–[1202]

NOTES

Sub-s (4): words in square brackets substituted by the Employment Rights (Dispute Resolution) Act 1998, s 1(2)(a).

Sub-s (6): repealed by the Employment Relations Act 1999, ss 9, 44, Sch 4, Pt III, paras 1, 5, 29, Sch 9(2).

Orders: as of 6 April 2008 no Orders had been made under this section but, by virtue of s 241 of, and Sch 2, Pt I, paras 1–4 to, this Act, the Redundancy Payments (Exemption) (No 1) Order 1969, SI 1969/207, the Redundancy Payments (Exemption) (No 1) Order 1970, SI 1970/354, and the Redundancy Payments (Exemption) Order 1980, SI 1980/1052, have effect as if made under this section.

158 *(Repealed by the Employment Equality (Age) Regulations 2006, SI 2006/1031, reg 49(1), Sch 8, Pt 1, paras 21, 31, 33, as from 1 October 2006, except in relation to any case where the relevant date by virtue of s 153 of this Act fell before that date.)*

159 Public offices etc

A person does not have any right to a redundancy payment in respect of any employment which—

(a) is employment in a public office within the meaning of section 39 of the Superannuation Act 1965, or

(b) is for the purposes of pensions and other superannuation benefits treated (whether by virtue of that Act or otherwise) as service in the civil service of the State.

[1203]

160 Overseas government employment

(1) A person does not have any right to a redundancy payment in respect of employment in any capacity under the Government of an overseas territory.

(2) The reference in subsection (1) to the Government of an overseas territory includes a reference to—

(a) a Government constituted for two or more overseas territories, and

(b) any authority established for the purpose of providing or administering services which are common to, or relate to matters of common interest to, two or more overseas territories.

(3) In this section references to an overseas territory are to any territory or country outside the United Kingdom.

[1204]

161 Domestic servants

(1) A person does not have any right to a redundancy payment in respect of employment as a domestic servant in a private household where the employer is the parent (or step-parent), grandparent, child (or step-child), grandchild or brother or sister (or half-brother or half-sister) of the employee.

(2) Subject to that, the provisions of this Part apply to an employee who is employed as a domestic servant in a private household as if—

(a) the household were a business, and

(b) the maintenance of the household were the carrying on of that business by the employer.

[1205]

NOTES

Step-parent; step-child: references to a step-parent or step-child include relationships arising through civil partnership; see the Civil Partnership Act 2004, ss 246, 247, Sch 21, para 42.

CHAPTER V
OTHER PROVISIONS ABOUT REDUNDANCY PAYMENTS

162 Amount of a redundancy payment

(1) The amount of a redundancy payment shall be calculated by—

(a) determining the period, ending with the relevant date, during which the employee has been continuously employed,

(b) reckoning backwards from the end of that period the number of years of employment falling within that period, and

(c) allowing the appropriate amount for each of those years of employment.

(2) In subsection (1)(c) "the appropriate amount" means—

(a) one and a half weeks' pay for a year of employment in which the employee was not below the age of forty-one,

(b) one week's pay for a year of employment (not within paragraph (a)) in which he was not below the age of twenty-two, and

(c) half a week's pay for each year of employment not within paragraph (a) or (b).

(3) Where twenty years of employment have been reckoned under subsection (1), no account shall be taken under that subsection of any year of employment earlier than those twenty years.

(4), (5) …

(6) [Subsections (1) to (3)] apply for the purposes of any provision of this Part by virtue of which an [employment tribunal] may determine that an employer is liable to pay to an employee—

(a) the whole of the redundancy payment to which the employee would have had a right apart from some other provision, or

(b) such part of the redundancy payment to which the employee would have had a right apart from some other provision as the tribunal thinks fit,

as if any reference to the amount of a redundancy payment were to the amount of the redundancy payment to which the employee would have been entitled apart from that other provision.

(7), (8) …

[1206]

NOTES

Sub-ss (4), (5), (8): repealed by the Employment Equality (Age) Regulations 2006, SI 2006/1031, reg 49(1), Sch 8, Pt 1, paras 21, 32(1), (2), 33, as from 1 October 2006, except in relation to any case where the relevant date by virtue of s 153 of this Act fell before that date.

Sub-s (6): words in first pair of square brackets substituted by SI 2006/1031, reg 49(1), Sch 8, Pt 1, paras 21, 32(1), (3), as from 1 October 2006, except in relation to any case where the relevant date by virtue of s 153 of this Act fell before that date; words in second pair of square brackets substituted by the Employment Rights (Dispute Resolution) Act 1998, s 1(2)(a).

Sub-s (7): repealed by the Employment Relations Act 1999, ss 9, 44, Sch 4, Pt III, paras 1, 5, 30, Sch 9(2).

Modified as noted to s 146 at **[1190]**.

163 References to [employment tribunals]

(1) Any question arising under this Part as to—

(a) the right of an employee to a redundancy payment, or

(b) the amount of a redundancy payment,

shall be referred to and determined by an [employment tribunal].

(2) For the purposes of any such reference, an employee who has been dismissed by his employer shall, unless the contrary is proved, be presumed to have been so dismissed by reason of redundancy.

(3) Any question whether an employee will become entitled to a redundancy payment if he is not dismissed by his employer and he terminates his contract of employment as mentioned in section 150(1) shall for the purposes of this Part be taken to be a question as to the right of the employee to a redundancy payment.

(4) Where an order under section 157 is in force in respect of an agreement, this section has effect in relation to any question arising under the agreement as to the right of an employee to a payment on the termination of his employment, or as to the amount of such a payment, as if the payment were a redundancy payment and the question arose under this Part.

[1207]

NOTES

Section heading, sub-s (1): words in square brackets substituted by the Employment Rights (Dispute Resolution) Act 1998, s 1(2)(a), (b).

Conciliation: employment tribunal proceedings under this section in respect of the right to, or amount of, a redundancy payment and claims which could be the subject of such proceedings are proceedings to which the Employment Tribunals Act 1996, s 18 applies; see s 18(1)(d) of that Act at **[975]**. The short conciliation period applies to such claims by virtue of the Employment Tribunals (Constitution and Rules of Procedure) Regulations 2004, SI 2004/1861, Sch 1, rule 22(5).

Tribunal jurisdiction: the Employment Act 2002, ss 31, 32, 38 at **[1493]**, **[1494]**, **[1496]** apply to proceedings before the employment tribunal relating to a claim under this section; see ss 31(1), 32(1), 38(1) of, and Schs 3–5 to, the 2002 Act at **[1508]**–**[1510]**.

For the circumstances in which the normal time limit for presenting a claim under this section is extended for a period of three months, see the Employment Act 2002 (Dispute Resolution) Regulations 2004, SI 2004/752, regs 15 and 18 at **[3096]** and **[3098]**.

164 Claims for redundancy payment

(1) An employee does not have any right to a redundancy payment unless, before the end of the period of six months beginning with the relevant date—

(a) the payment has been agreed and paid,

(b) the employee has made a claim for the payment by notice in writing given to the employer,

(c) a question as to the employee's right to, or the amount of, the payment has been referred to an [employment tribunal], or

(d) a complaint relating to his dismissal has been presented by the employee under section 111.

(2) An employee is not deprived of his right to a redundancy payment by subsection (1) if, during the period of six months immediately following the period mentioned in that subsection, the employee—

(a) makes a claim for the payment by notice in writing given to the employer,

(b) refers to an [employment tribunal] a question as to his right to, or the amount of, the payment, or

(c) presents a complaint relating to his dismissal under section 111,

and it appears to the tribunal to be just and equitable that the employee should receive a redundancy payment.

(3) In determining under subsection (2) whether it is just and equitable that an employee should receive a redundancy payment an [employment tribunal] shall have regard to—

(a) the reason shown by the employee for his failure to take any such step as is referred to in subsection (2) within the period mentioned in subsection (1), and

(b) all the other relevant circumstances.

[1208]

NOTES

Words in square brackets substituted by the Employment Rights (Dispute Resolution) Act 1998, s 1(2)(a).

Conciliation: see the note to s 163 at **[1207]**.

Extension of time limit: see the note to s 163 at **[1207]**.

165 Written particulars of redundancy payment

(1) On making any redundancy payment, otherwise than in pursuance of a decision of a tribunal which specifies the amount of the payment to be made, the employer shall give to the employee a written statement indicating how the amount of the payment has been calculated.

(2) An employer who without reasonable excuse fails to comply with subsection (1) is guilty of an offence and liable on summary conviction to a fine not exceeding level 1 on the standard scale.

(3) If an employer fails to comply with the requirements of subsection (1), the employee may by notice in writing to the employer require him to give to the employee a written statement complying with those requirements within such period (not being less than one week beginning with the day on which the notice is given) as may be specified in the notice.

(4) An employer who without reasonable excuse fails to comply with a notice under subsection (3) is guilty of an offence and liable on summary conviction to a fine not exceeding level 3 on the standard scale.

[1209]

CHAPTER VI
PAYMENTS BY SECRETARY OF STATE

166 Applications for payments

(1) Where an employee claims that his employer is liable to pay to him an employer's payment and either—

(a) that the employee has taken all reasonable steps, other than legal proceedings, to recover the payment from the employer and the employer has refused or failed to pay it, or has paid part of it and has refused or failed to pay the balance, or

(b) that the employer is insolvent and the whole or part of the payment remains unpaid,

the employee may apply to the Secretary of State for a payment under this section.

(2) In this Part "employer's payment", in relation to an employee, means—

(a) a redundancy payment which his employer is liable to pay to him under this Part, …

[(aa) a payment which his employer is liable to make to him under an agreement to refrain from instituting or continuing proceedings for a contravention or alleged contravention of section 135 which has effect by virtue of section 203(2)(e) or (f), or]

(b) a payment which his employer is, under an agreement in respect of which an order is in force under section 157, liable to make to him on the termination of his contract of employment.

(3) In relation to any case where (in accordance with any provision of this Part) an [employment tribunal] determines that an employer is liable to pay part (but not the whole) of a redundancy payment the reference in subsection (2)(a) to a redundancy payment is to the part of the redundancy payment.

(4) In subsection (1)(a) "legal proceedings"—

(a) does not include any proceedings before an [employment tribunal], but

(b) includes any proceedings to enforce a decision or award of an [employment tribunal].

(5) An employer is insolvent for the purposes of subsection (1)(b)—

(a) where the employer is an individual, if (but only if) subsection (6) is satisfied, …

(b) where the employer is a company, if (but only if) subsection (7) is satisfied [, and

(c) where the employer is a limited liability partnership, if (but only if) subsection (8) is satisfied.]

(6) This subsection is satisfied in the case of an employer who is an individual—

(a) in England and Wales if—

(i) he has been adjudged bankrupt or has made a composition or arrangement with his creditors, or

(ii) he has died and his estate falls to be administered in accordance with an order under section 421 of the Insolvency Act 1986, and

(b) in Scotland if—

(i) sequestration of his estate has been awarded or he has executed a trust deed for his creditors or has entered into a composition contract, or

(ii) he has died and a judicial factor appointed under section 11A of the Judicial Factors (Scotland) Act 1889 is required by that section to divide his insolvent estate among his creditors.

(7) This subsection is satisfied in the case of an employer which is a company—

(a) if a winding up order … has been made, or a resolution for voluntary winding up has been passed, with respect to the company,

[(aa) if the company is in administration for the purposes of the Insolvency Act 1986,]

(b) if a receiver or (in England and Wales only) a manager of the company's undertaking has been duly appointed, or (in England and Wales only) possession has been taken, by or on behalf of the holders of any debentures secured by a floating charge, of any property of the company comprised in or subject to the charge, or

(c) if a voluntary arrangement proposed in the case of the company for the purposes of Part I of the Insolvency Act 1986 has been approved under that Part of that Act.

[(8) This subsection is satisfied in the case of an employer which is a limited liability partnership—

(a) if a winding-up order, an administration order or a determination for a voluntary winding-up has been made with respect to the limited liability partnership,

(b) if a receiver or (in England and Wales only) a manager of the undertaking of the limited liability partnership has been duly appointed, or (in England and Wales only) possession has been taken, by or on behalf of the holders of any debentures secured by a floating charge, of any property of the limited liability partnership comprised in or subject to the charge, or

(c) if a voluntary arrangement proposed in the case of the limited liability partnership for the purpose of Part I of the Insolvency Act 1986 has been approved under that Part of that Act.]

[1210]

NOTES

Sub-s (2): word omitted from para (a) repealed, and para (aa) inserted, by the Employment Rights (Dispute Resolution) Act 1998, ss 11(2), 15, Sch 2.

Sub-ss (3), (4): words in square brackets substituted by the Employment Rights (Dispute Resolution) Act 1998, s 1(2)(a).

Sub-s (5): word omitted from para (a) repealed, and para (c) and word immediately preceding it added, by the Limited Liability Partnerships Regulations 2001, SI 2001/1090, reg 9, Sch 5, para 18(1), (2).

Sub-s (7): words omitted from para (a) repealed, and para (aa) inserted, by the Enterprise Act 2002, ss 248(3), 278(2), Sch 17, para 49(1), (2), Sch 26, as from 15 September 2003, except in relation to cases where a petition for an administration order was presented before that date, and subject to savings in relation to special administration regimes (within the meaning of s 249 of the 2002 Act).

Sub-s (8): added by SI 2001/1090, reg 9, Sch 5, para 18(1), (3).

167 Making of payments

(1) Where, on an application under section 166 by an employee in relation to an employer's payment, the Secretary of State is satisfied that the requirements specified in subsection (2) are met, he shall pay to the employee out of the National Insurance Fund a sum calculated in accordance with section 168 but reduced by so much (if any) of the employer's payment as has already been paid.

(2) The requirements referred to in subsection (1) are—

(a) that the employee is entitled to the employer's payment, and

(b) that one of the conditions specified in paragraphs (a) and (b) of subsection (1) of section 166 is fulfilled,

and, in a case where the employer's payment is a payment such as is mentioned in subsection (2)(b) of that section, that the employee's right to the payment arises by virtue of a period of continuous employment (computed in accordance with the provisions of the agreement in question) which is not less than two years.

(3) Where under this section the Secretary of State pays a sum to an employee in respect of an employer's payment—

(a) all rights and remedies of the employee with respect to the employer's payment, or (if the Secretary of State has paid only part of it) all the rights and remedies of the employee with respect to that part of the employer's payment, are transferred to and vest in the Secretary of State, and

(b) any decision of an [employment tribunal] requiring the employer's payment to be paid to the employee has effect as if it required that payment, or that part of it which the Secretary of State has paid, to be paid to the Secretary of State.

(4) Any money recovered by the Secretary of State by virtue of subsection (3) shall be paid into the National Insurance Fund.

[1211]

NOTES

Sub-s (3): words in square brackets substituted by the Employment Rights (Dispute Resolution) Act 1998, s 1(2)(a).

168 Amount of payments

(1) The sum payable to an employee by the Secretary of State under section 167—

(a) where the employer's payment to which the employee's application under section 166 relates is a redundancy payment or a part of a redundancy payment, is a sum equal to the amount of the redundancy payment or part, …

[(aa) where the employer's payment to which the employee's application under section 166 relates is a payment which his employer is liable to make to him under an agreement having effect by virtue of section 203(2)(e) or (f), is a sum equal to the amount of the employer's payment or of any redundancy payment which the employer would have been liable to pay to the employee but for the agreement, whichever is less, and]

(b) where the employer's payment to which the employee's application under section 166 relates is a payment which the employer is liable to make under an agreement in respect of which an order is in force under section 157, is a sum equal to the amount of the employer's payment or of the relevant redundancy payment, whichever is less.

(2) The reference in subsection (1)(b) to the amount of the relevant redundancy payment is to the amount of the redundancy payment which the employer would have been liable to pay to the employee on the assumptions specified in subsection (3).

(3) The assumptions referred to in subsection (2) are that—

(a) the order in force in respect of the agreement had not been made,

(b) the circumstances in which the employer's payment is payable had been such that the employer was liable to pay a redundancy payment to the employee in those circumstances,

(c) the relevant date, in relation to any such redundancy payment, had been the date on which the termination of the employee's contract of employment is treated as having taken effect for the purposes of the agreement, and

(d) in so far as the provisions of the agreement relating to the circumstances in which the continuity of an employee's period of employment is to be treated as broken, and the weeks which are to count in computing a period of employment, are inconsistent with the provisions of Chapter I of Part XIV, the provisions of the agreement were substituted for those provisions.

[1212]

NOTES

Sub-s (1): word omitted from para (a) repealed, and para (aa) inserted, by the Employment Rights (Dispute Resolution) Act 1998, ss 11(3), 15, Sch 2.

169 Information relating to applications for payments

(1) Where an employee makes an application to the Secretary of State under section 166, the Secretary of State may, by notice in writing given to the employer, require the employer—

(a) to provide the Secretary of State with such information, and

(b) to produce for examination on behalf of the Secretary of State documents in his custody or under his control of such description,

as the Secretary of State may reasonably require for the purpose of determining whether the application is well-founded.

(2) Where a person on whom a notice is served under subsection (1) fails without reasonable excuse to comply with a requirement imposed by the notice, he is guilty of an offence and liable on summary conviction to a fine not exceeding level 3 on the standard scale.

(3) A person is guilty of an offence if—

(a) in providing any information required by a notice under subsection (1), he makes a statement which he knows to be false in a material particular or recklessly makes a statement which is false in a material particular, or

(b) he produces for examination in accordance with a notice under subsection (1) a document which to his knowledge has been wilfully falsified.

(4) A person guilty of an offence under subsection (3) is liable—

(a) on summary conviction, to a fine not exceeding the statutory maximum or to imprisonment for a term not exceeding three months, or to both, or

(b) on conviction on indictment, to a fine or to imprisonment for a term not exceeding two years, or to both.

[1213]

170 References to [employment tribunals]

(1) Where on an application made to the Secretary of State for a payment under section 166 it is claimed that an employer is liable to pay an employer's payment, there shall be referred to an [employment tribunal]—

(a) any question as to the liability of the employer to pay the employer's payment, and

(b) any question as to the amount of the sum payable in accordance with section 168.

(2) For the purposes of any reference under this section an employee who has been dismissed by his employer shall, unless the contrary is proved, be presumed to have been so dismissed by reason of redundancy.

[1214]

NOTES

Section heading, sub-s (1): words in square brackets substituted by the Employment Rights (Dispute Resolution) Act 1998, s 1(2)(a), (b).

CHAPTER VII
SUPPLEMENTARY

Application of Part to particular cases

171 Employment not under contract of employment

(1) The Secretary of State may by regulations provide that, subject to such exceptions and modifications as may be prescribed by the regulations, this Part and the provisions of this Act supplementary to this part have effect in relation to any employment of a description to which this section applies as may be so prescribed as if—

(a) it were employment under a contract of employment,

(b) any person engaged in employment of that description were an employee, and

(c) such person as may be determined by or under the regulations were his employer.

(2) This section applies to employment of any description which—

(a) is employment in the case of which secondary Class 1 contributions are payable under Part I of the Social Security Contributions and Benefits Act 1992 in respect of persons engaged in it, but

(b) is not employment under a contract of service or of apprenticeship or employment of any description falling within subsection (3).

(3) The following descriptions of employment fall within this subsection—

(a) any employment such as is mentioned in section 159 (whether as originally enacted or as modified by an order under section 209(1)),

(b) any employment remunerated out of the revenue of the Duchy of Lancaster or the Duchy of Cornwall,

(c) any employment remunerated out of the Queen's Civil List, and

(d) any employment remunerated out of Her Majesty's Privy Purse.

[1215]

NOTES

Regulations: as of 6 April 2008 no Regulations had been made under this section but, by virtue of s 241 of, and Sch 2, Pt I, paras 1–4 to, this Act, the Redundancy Payments Office Holders Regulations 1965, SI 1965/2007, have effect as if made under this section.

172 Termination of employment by statute

(1) The Secretary of State may by regulations provide that, subject to such exceptions and modifications as may be prescribed by the regulations, this Part has effect in relation to any person who by virtue of any statutory provisions—

(a) is transferred to, and becomes a member of, a body specified in those provisions, but

(b) at a time so specified ceases to be a member of that body unless before that time certain conditions so specified have been fulfilled,

as if the cessation of his membership of that body by virtue of those provisions were dismissal by his employer by reason of redundancy.

(2) The power conferred by subsection (1) is exercisable whether or not membership of the body in question constitutes employment within the meaning of section 230(5); and, where that membership does not constitute such employment, that power may be exercised in addition to any power exercisable under section 171.

[1216]

NOTES

Regulations: as of 6 April 2008 no Regulations had been made under this section but, by virtue of s 241 of, and Sch 2, Pt I, paras 1–4 to, this Act, the Redundancy Payments Termination of Employment Regulations 1965, SI 1965/2022 (concerning chief constables and chief or assistant chief fire officers), have effect as if made under this section.

173 Employees paid by person other than employer

(1) For the purposes of the operation of the provisions of this Part (and Chapter I of Part XIV) in relation to any employee whose remuneration is, by virtue of any statutory provision, payable to him by a person other than his employer, each of the references to the employer specified in subsection (2) shall be construed as a reference to the person by whom the remuneration is payable.

(2) The references referred to in subsection (1) are the first reference in section 135(1), the third reference in section 140(3), the first reference in section 142(3) and the first reference in section 143(2)(c) and the references in sections 142(2)(b), 143(4) and (5), 149(a) and (b), 150(3), 152(1)(b), 158(4), 162(6), 164 to 169, 170(1) and 214(5).

[1217]

Death of employer or employee

174 Death of employer: dismissal

(1) Where the contract of employment of an employee is taken for the purposes of this Part to be terminated by his employer by reason of the employer's death, this Part has effect in accordance with the following provisions of this section.

(2) Section 138 applies as if—

(a) in subsection (1)(a), for the words "in pursuance" onwards there were substituted "by a personal representative of the deceased employer",

(b) in subsection (1)(b), for the words "either immediately" onwards there were substituted "not later than eight weeks after the death of the deceased employer", and

(c) in subsections (2)(b) and (6)(a), for the word "employer" there were substituted "personal representative of the deceased employer".

(3) Section 141(1) applies as if—

(a) for the words "before the end of his employment" there were substituted "by a personal representative of the deceased employer", and

(b) for the words "either immediately" onwards there were substituted "not later than eight weeks after the death of the deceased employer."

(4) For the purposes of section 141—

(a) provisions of the contract as renewed, or of the new contract, do not differ from the corresponding provisions of the contract in force immediately before the death of the deceased employer by reason only that the personal representative would be substituted for the deceased employer as the employer, and

(b) no account shall be taken of that substitution in determining whether refusal of the offer was unreasonable or whether the employee acted reasonably in terminating or giving notice to terminate the new or renewed employment.

(5) Section 146 has effect as if—

(a) subsection (1) were omitted, and

(b) in subsection (2), paragraph (a) were omitted and, in paragraph (b), for the word "four" there were substituted "eight".

(6) For the purposes of the application of this Part (in accordance with section 161(2)) in relation to an employee who was employed as a domestic servant in a private household, references in this section and sections 175 and 218(4) and (5) to a personal representative

include a person to whom the management of the household has passed, otherwise than in pursuance of a sale or other disposition for valuable consideration, in consequence of the death of the employer.

[1218]

175 Death of employer: lay-off and short-time

(1) Where an employee is laid off or kept on short-time and his employer dies, this Part has effect in accordance with the following provisions of this section.

(2) Where the employee—
- (a) has been laid off or kept on short-time for one or more weeks before the death of the employer,
- (b) has not given the deceased employer notice of intention to claim before the employer's death,
- (c) after the employer's death has his contract of employment renewed, or is re-engaged under a new contract, by a personal representative of the deceased employer, and
- (d) after renewal or re-engagement is laid off or kept on short-time for one or more weeks by the personal representative,

the week in which the employer died and the first week of the employee's employment by the personal representative shall be treated for the purposes of Chapter III as consecutive weeks (and references to four weeks or thirteen weeks shall be construed accordingly).

(3) The following provisions of this section apply where—
- (a) the employee has given the deceased employer notice of intention to claim before the employer's death,
- (b) the employer's death occurred before the end of the period of four weeks after the service of the notice, and
- (c) the employee has not terminated his contract of employment by notice expiring before the employer's death.

(4) If the contract of employment is not renewed, and the employee is not re-engaged under a new contract, by a personal representative of the deceased employer before the end of the period of four weeks after the service of the notice of intention to claim—
- (a) sections 149 and 152 do not apply, but
- (b) (subject to that) Chapter III applies as if the employer had not died and the employee had terminated the contract of employment by a week's notice, or by the minimum notice which he is required to give to terminate the contract (if longer than a week), expiring at the end of that period.

(5) If—
- (a) the contract of employment is renewed, or the employee is re-engaged under a new contract, by a personal representative of the deceased employer before the end of the period of four weeks after the service of the notice of intention to claim, and
- (b) the employee was laid off or kept on short-time by the deceased employer for one or more of those weeks and is laid off or kept on short-time by the personal representative for the week, or for the next two or more weeks, following the renewal or re-engagement,

subsection (6) has effect.

(6) Where this subsection has effect Chapter III applies as if—
- (a) all the weeks mentioned in subsection (5) were consecutive weeks during which the employee was employed (but laid off or kept on short-time) by the same employer, and
- (b) the periods specified by section 150(3)(a) and (b) as the relevant period were extended by any week or weeks any part of which was after the death of the employer and before the date on which the renewal or re-engagement took effect.

[1219]

176 Death of employee

(1) Where an employee whose employer has given him notice to terminate his contract of employment dies before the notice expires, this part applies as if the contract had been duly terminated by the employer by notice expiring on the date of the employee's death.

(2) Where—

(a) an employee's contract of employment has been terminated by the employer,
(b) (by virtue of subsection (5) of section 145) a date later than the relevant date as defined by the previous provisions of that section is the relevant date for the purposes of certain provisions of this Act, and
(c) the employee dies before that date,

that subsection applies as if the notice to which it refers would have expired on the employee's death.

(3) Where—
(a) an employer has given notice to an employee to terminate his contract of employment and has offered to renew his contract of employment or to re-engage him under a new contract, and
(b) the employee dies without having accepted or refused the offer and without the offer having been withdrawn,

section 141(2) applies as if for the words "he unreasonably refuses" there were substituted "it would have been unreasonable on his part to refuse".

(4) Where an employee's contract of employment has been renewed or he has been re-engaged under a new contract—
(a) if he dies during the trial period without having terminated, or given notice to terminate, the contract, section 141(4) applies as if for paragraph (d) there were substituted—
"(d) it would have been unreasonable for the employee during the trial period to terminate or give notice to terminate the contract.", and
(b) if during that trial period he gives notice to terminate the contract but dies before the notice expires, sections 138(2) and 141(4) apply as if the notice had expired (and the contract had been terminated by its expiry) on the date of the employee's death.

(5) Where in the circumstances specified in paragraphs (a) and (b) of subsection (3) of section 136 the employee dies before the notice given by him under paragraph (b) of that subsection expires—
(a) if he dies before his employer has given him a notice such as is specified in subsection (2) of section 142, subsections (3) and (4) of that section apply as if the employer had given him such a notice and he had not complied with it, and
(b) if he dies after his employer has given him such a notice, that section applies as if the employee had not died but did not comply with the notice.

(6) Where an employee has given notice of intention to claim—
(a) if he dies before he has given notice to terminate his contract of employment and before the relevant period (as defined in subsection (3) of section 150) has expired, that section does not apply, and
(b) if he dies within the period of seven days after the service of the notice of intention to claim, and before the employer has given a counter-notice, Chapter III applies as if the employer had given a counter-notice within that period of seven days.

(7) Where a claim for a redundancy payment is made by a personal representative of a deceased employee—
(a) if the employee died before the end of the period of six months beginning with the relevant date, subsection (1) of section 164, and
(b) if the employee died after the end of the period of six months beginning with the relevant date but before the end of the following period of six months, subsection (2) of that section,

applies as if for the words "six months" there were substituted "one year".

[1220]

Equivalent payments

177 References to [employment tribunals]

(1) Where the terms and conditions (whether or not they constitute a contract of employment) on which a person is employed in employment of any description mentioned in section 171(3) include provision—
(a) for the making of a payment to which this section applies, and

(b) for referring to an [employment tribunal] any question as to the right of any person to such a payment in respect of that employment or as to the amount of such a payment,

the question shall be referred to and determined by an [employment tribunal].

(2) This section applies to any payment by way of compensation for loss of employment of any description mentioned in section 171(3) which is payable in accordance with arrangements falling within subsection (3).

(3) The arrangements which fall within this subsection are arrangements made with the approval of the Treasury (or, in the case of persons whose service is for the purposes of pensions and other superannuation benefits treated as service in the civil service of the State, of the Minister for the Civil Service) for securing that a payment will be made—

(a) in circumstances which in the opinion of the Treasury (or Minister) correspond (subject to the appropriate modifications) to those in which a right to a redundancy payment would have accrued if the provisions of this Part (apart from section 159 and this section) applied, and

(b) on a scale which in the opinion of the Treasury (or Minister), taking into account any sums payable in accordance with—

(i) a scheme made under section 1 of the Superannuation Act 1972, or

(ii) the Superannuation Act 1965 as it continues to have effect by virtue of section 23(1) of the Superannuation Act 1972,

to or in respect of the person losing the employment in question, corresponds (subject to the appropriate modifications) to that on which a redundancy payment would have been payable if those provisions applied.

[1221]

NOTES

Section heading, sub-s (1): words in square brackets substituted by the Employment Rights (Dispute Resolution) Act 1998, s 1(2)(a), (b).

Other supplementary provisions

178 Old statutory compensation schemes

(1) The Secretary of State may make provision by regulations for securing that where—

(a) (apart from this section) a person is entitled to compensation under a statutory provision to which this section applies, and

(b) the circumstances are such that he is also entitled to a redundancy payment,

the amount of the redundancy payment shall be set off against the compensation to which he would be entitled apart from this section; and any statutory provision to which any such regulations apply shall have effect subject to the regulations.

(2) This section applies to any statutory provision—

(a) which was in force immediately before 6th December 1965, and

(b) under which the holders of such situations, places or employments as are specified in that provision are, or may become, entitled to compensation for loss of employment, or for loss or diminution of emoluments or of pension rights, in consequence of the operation of any other statutory provision referred to in that provision.

[1222]

NOTES

Regulations: as of 6 April 2008 no Regulations had been made under this section but, by virtue of s 241 of, and Sch 2, Pt I, paras 1–4 to, this Act, the Redundancy Payments Statutory Compensation Regulations 1965, SI 1965/1988, have effect as if made under this section.

179 Notices

(1) Any notice which under this Part is required or authorised to be given by an employer to an employee may be given by being delivered to the employee, or left for him at his usual or last-known place of residence, or sent by post addressed to him at that place.

(2) Any notice which under this Part is required or authorised to be given by an employee to an employer may be given either by the employee himself or by a person authorised by him to act on his behalf, and (whether given by or on behalf of the employee)—

(a) may be given by being delivered to the employer, or sent by post addressed to him at the place where the employee is or was employed by him, or

(b) if arrangements have been made by the employer, may be given by being delivered to a person designated by the employer in pursuance of the arrangements, left for such a person at a place so designated or sent by post to such a person at an address so designated.

(3) In this section any reference to the delivery of a notice includes, in relation to a notice which is not required by this Part to be in writing, a reference to the oral communication of the notice.

(4) Any notice which, in accordance with any provision of this section, is left for a person at a place referred to in that provision shall, unless the contrary is proved, be presumed to have been received by him on the day on which it was left there.

(5) Nothing in subsection (1) or (2) affects the capacity of an employer to act by a servant or agent for the purposes of any provision of this Part (including either of those subsections).

(6) In relation to an employee to whom section 173 applies, this section has effect as if—

(a) any reference in subsection (1) or (2) to a notice required or authorised to be given by or to an employer included a reference to a notice which, by virtue of that section, is required or authorised to be given by or to the person by whom the remuneration is payable,

(b) in relation to a notice required or authorised to be given to that person, any reference to the employer in paragraph (a) or (b) of subsection (2) were a reference to that person, and

(c) the reference to an employer in subsection (5) included a reference to that person.

[1223]

180 Offences

(1) Where an offence under this Part committed by a body corporate is proved—

(a) to have been committed with the consent or connivance of, or

(b) to be attributable to any neglect on the part of,

any director, manager, secretary or other similar officer of the body corporate, or any person who was purporting to act in any such capacity, he (as well as the body corporate) is guilty of the offence and liable to be proceeded against and punished accordingly.

(2) In this section "director", in relation to a body corporate established by or under any enactment for the purpose of carrying on under national ownership any industry or part of an industry or undertaking, being a body corporate whose affairs are managed by its members, means a member of that body corporate.

[1224]

181 Interpretation

(1) In this Part—

"counter-notice" shall be construed in accordance with section 149(a),

"dismissal" and "dismissed" shall be construed in accordance with sections 136 to 138,

"employer's payment" has the meaning given by section 166,

"notice of intention to claim" shall be construed in accordance with section 148(1),

"obligatory period of notice" has the meaning given by section 136(4), and

"trial period" shall be construed in accordance with section 138(3).

(2) In this Part—

(a) references to an employee being laid off or being eligible for a redundancy payment by reason of being laid off, and

(b) references to an employee being kept on short-time or being eligible for a redundancy payment by reason of being kept on short-time,

shall be construed in accordance with sections 147 and 148.

[1225]

PART XII
INSOLVENCY OF EMPLOYERS

182 Employee's rights on insolvency of employer

If, on an application made to him in writing by an employee, the Secretary of State is satisfied that—

(a) the employee's employer has become insolvent,
(b) the employee's employment has been terminated, and
(c) on the appropriate date the employee was entitled to be paid the whole or part of any debt to which this Part applies,

the Secretary of State shall, subject to section 186, pay the employee out of the National Insurance Fund the amount to which, in the opinion of the Secretary of State, the employee is entitled in respect of the debt.

[1226]

183 Insolvency

(1) An employer has become insolvent for the purposes of this Part—

(a) where the employer is an individual, if (but only if) subsection (2) is satisfied, …
(b) where the employer is a company, if (but only if) subsection (3) is satisfied [, and
(c) where the employer is a limited liability partnership, if (but only if) subsection (4) is satisfied].

(2) This subsection is satisfied in the case of an employer who is an individual—

(a) in England and Wales if—
[(ai) a moratorium period under a debt relief order applies in relation to him,]
(i) he has been adjudged bankrupt or has made a composition or arrangement with his creditors, or
(ii) he has died and his estate falls to be administered in accordance with an order under section 421 of the Insolvency Act 1986, and
(b) in Scotland if—
(i) sequestration of his estate has been awarded or he has executed a trust deed for his creditors or has entered into a composition contract, or
(ii) he has died and a judicial factor appointed under section 11A of the Judicial Factors (Scotland) Act 1889 is required by that section to divide his insolvent estate among his creditors.

(3) This subsection is satisfied in the case of an employer which is a company—

(a) if a winding up order … has been made, or a resolution for voluntary winding up has been passed, with respect to the company,
[(aa) if the company is in administration for the purposes of the Insolvency Act 1986,]
(b) if a receiver or (in England and Wales only) a manager of the company's undertaking has been duly appointed, or (in England and Wales only) possession has been taken, by or on behalf of the holders of any debentures secured by a floating charge, of any property of the company comprised in or subject to the charge, or
(c) if a voluntary arrangement proposed in the case of the company for the purposes of Part I of the Insolvency Act 1986 has been approved under that Part of that Act.

[(4) This subsection is satisfied in the case of an employer which is a limited liability partnership—

(a) if a winding-up order, an administration order or a determination for a voluntary winding-up has been made with respect to the limited liability partnership,
(b) if a receiver or (in England and Wales only) a manager of the undertaking of the limited liability partnership has been duly appointed, or (in England and Wales only) possession has been taken, by or on behalf of the holders of any debentures secured by a floating charge, of any property of the limited liability partnership comprised in or subject to the charge, or
(c) if a voluntary arrangement proposed in the case of the limited liability partnership for the purposes of Part I of the Insolvency Act 1986 has been approved under that Part of that Act.]

[1227]

NOTES

Sub-s (1): word omitted from para (a) repealed, and para (c) and word immediately preceding it added, by the Limited Liability Partnership Regulations, SI 2001/1090, reg 9, Sch 5, para 19(1), (2).

Sub-s (2): sub-para (a)(ai) inserted by the Tribunals, Courts and Enforcement Act 2007, s 108(3), Sch 20, Pt 2, para 17, as from a day to be appointed.

Sub-s (3): words omitted from para (a) repealed, and para (aa) inserted, by the Enterprise Act 2002, ss 248(3), 278(2), Sch 17, para 49(1), (3), Sch 26, as from 15 September 2003, except in relation to cases where a petition for an administration order was presented before that date, and subject to savings in relation to special administration regimes (within the meaning of s 249 of the 2002 Act).

Sub-s (4): added by SI 2001/1090, reg 9, Sch 5, para 19(1), (3).

184 Debts to which Part applies

(1) This Part applies to the following debts—

(a) any arrears of pay in respect of one or more (but not more than eight) weeks,

(b) any amount which the employer is liable to pay the employee for the period of notice required by section 86(1) or (2) or for any failure of the employer to give the period of notice required by section 86(1),

(c) any holiday pay—

(i) in respect of a period or periods of holiday not exceeding six weeks in all, and

(ii) to which the employee became entitled during the twelve months ending with the appropriate date,

(d) any basic award of compensation for unfair dismissal [or so much of an award under a designated dismissal procedures agreement as does not exceed any basic award of compensation for unfair dismissal to which the employee would be entitled but for the agreement], and

(e) any reasonable sum by way of reimbursement of the whole or part of any fee or premium paid by an apprentice or articled clerk.

(2) For the purposes of subsection (1)(a) the following amounts shall be treated as arrears of pay—

(a) a guarantee payment,

(b) any payment for time off under Part VI of this Act or section 169 of the Trade Union and Labour Relations (Consolidation) Act 1992 (payment for time off for carrying out trade union duties etc),

(c) remuneration on suspension on medical grounds under section 64 of this Act and remuneration on suspension on maternity grounds under section 68 of this Act, and

(d) remuneration under a protective award under section 189 of the Trade Union and Labour Relations (Consolidation) Act 1992.

(3) In subsection (1)(c) "holiday pay", in relation to an employee, means—

(a) pay in respect of a holiday actually taken by the employee, or

(b) any accrued holiday pay which, under the employee's contract of employment, would in the ordinary course have become payable to him in respect of the period of a holiday if his employment with the employer had continued until he became entitled to a holiday.

(4) A sum shall be taken to be reasonable for the purposes of subsection (1)(e) in a case where a trustee in bankruptcy, or (in Scotland) a permanent or interim trustee (within the meaning of the Bankruptcy (Scotland) Act 1985), or liquidator has been or is required to be appointed—

(a) as respects England and Wales, if it is admitted to be reasonable by the trustee in bankruptcy or liquidator under section 348 of the Insolvency Act 1986 (effect of bankruptcy on apprenticeships etc), whether as originally enacted or as applied to the winding up of a company by rules under section 411 of that Act, and

(b) as respects Scotland, if it is accepted by the permanent or interim trustee or liquidator for the purposes of the sequestration or winding up.

[1228]

NOTES

Sub-s (1): words in square brackets in para (d) inserted by the Employment Rights (Dispute Resolution) Act 1998, s 12(4).

185 The appropriate date

In this Part "the appropriate date"—

(a) in relation to arrears of pay (not being remuneration under a protective award made under section 189 of the Trade Union and Labour Relations (Consolidation) Act 1992) and to holiday pay, means the date on which the employer became insolvent,

(b) in relation to a basic award of compensation for unfair dismissal and to remuneration under a protective award so made, means whichever is the latest of—

(i) the date on which the employer became insolvent,

(ii) the date of the termination of the employee's employment, and

(iii) the date on which the award was made, and

(c) in relation to any other debt to which this Part applies, means whichever is the later of—

(i) the date on which the employer became insolvent, and

(ii) the date of the termination of the employee's employment.

[1229]

186 Limit on amount payable under section 182

(1) The total amount payable to an employee in respect of any debt to which this Part applies, where the amount of the debt is referable to a period of time, shall not exceed—

(a) [£330] in respect of any one week, or

(b) in respect of a shorter period, an amount bearing the same proportion to [£290] as that shorter period bears to a week.

(2) …

[1230]

NOTES

Sub-s (1): sums in square brackets substituted by the Employment Rights (Increase of Limits) Order 2007, SI 2007/3570, art 3, Schedule, as from 1 February 2008, in relation to any case where the appropriate date falls on or after that date (see SI 2007/3570, art 4 at **[3474II]**). The previous sum was £310 (see SI 2006/3045). This sum may be varied by the Secretary of State (see the Employment Relations Act 1999, s 34(1)(a), (3)(a) at **[1445]**). See also the Work and Families Act 2006, s 14 at **[1699]** (Secretary of State's additional 'one-off' power to alter the sum in sub-s (1) above). Sums for periods prior to 1 February 2007 were £290 as from 1 February 2006 (SI 2005/3352), £280 as from 1 February 2005 (SI 2004/2989), and £270 as from 1 February 2004 (SI 2003/3038) in each case where the appropriate date fell after the commencement date).

Sub-s (2): repealed by the Employment Relations Act 1999, ss 36(1)(a), 44, Sch 9(10).

187 Role of relevant officer

(1) Where a relevant officer has been, or is required to be, appointed in connection with an employer's insolvency, the Secretary of State shall not make a payment under section 182 in respect of a debt until he has received a statement from the relevant officer of the amount of that debt which appears to have been owed to the employee on the appropriate date and to remain unpaid.

(2) If the Secretary of State is satisfied that he does not require a statement under subsection (1) in order to determine the amount of a debt which was owed to the employee on the appropriate date and remains unpaid, he may make a payment under section 182 in respect of the debt without having received such a statement.

(3) A relevant officer shall, on request by the Secretary of State, provide him with a statement for the purposes of subsection (1) as soon as is reasonably practicable.

(4) The following are relevant officers for the purposes of this section—

(a) a trustee in bankruptcy or a permanent or interim trustee (within the meaning of the Bankruptcy (Scotland) Act 1985),

(b) a liquidator,

(c) an administrator,

(d) a receiver or manager,

(e) a trustee under a composition or arrangement between the employer and his creditors, and

(f) a trustee under a trust deed for his creditors executed by the employer.

(5) In subsection (4)(e) "trustee" includes the supervisor of a voluntary arrangement proposed for the purposes of, and approved under, Part I or VIII of the Insolvency Act 1986.

[1231]

188 Complaints to [employment tribunals]

(1) A person who has applied for a payment under section 182 may present a complaint to an [employment tribunal]—

(a) that the Secretary of State has failed to make any such payment, or

(b) that any such payment made by him is less than the amount which should have been paid.

(2) An [employment tribunal] shall not consider a complaint under subsection (1) unless it is presented—

(a) before the end of the period of three months beginning with the date on which the decision of the Secretary of State on the application was communicated to the applicant, or

(b) within such further period as the tribunal considers reasonable in a case where it is not reasonably practicable for the complaint to be presented before the end of that period of three months.

(3) Where an [employment tribunal] finds that the Secretary of State ought to make a payment under section 182, the tribunal shall—

(a) make a declaration to that effect, and

(b) declare the amount of any such payment which it finds the Secretary of State ought to make.

[1232]

NOTES

Words in square brackets substituted by the Employment Rights (Dispute Resolution) Act 1998, s 1(2)(a), (b).

---

189 Transfer to Secretary of State of rights and remedies

(1) Where, in pursuance of section 182, the Secretary of State makes a payment to an employee in respect of a debt to which this Part applies—

(a) on the making of the payment any rights and remedies of the employee in respect of the debt (or, if the Secretary of State has paid only part of it, in respect of that part) become rights and remedies of the Secretary of State, and

(b) any decision of an [employment tribunal] requiring an employer to pay that debt to the employee has the effect that the debt (or the part of it which the Secretary of State has paid) is to be paid to the Secretary of State.

(2) Where a debt (or any part of a debt) in respect of which the Secretary of State has made a payment in pursuance of section 182 constitutes—

(a) a preferential debt within the meaning of the Insolvency Act 1986 for the purposes of any provision of that Act (including any such provision as applied by any order made under that Act) or any provision of [the Companies Act 2006], or

(b) a preferred debt within the meaning of the Bankruptcy (Scotland) Act 1985 for the purposes of any provision of that Act (including any such provision as applied by section 11A of the Judicial Factors (Scotland) Act 1889),

the rights which become rights of the Secretary of State in accordance with subsection (1) include any right arising under any such provision by reason of the status of the debt (or that part of it) as a preferential or preferred debt.

(3) In computing for the purposes of any provision mentioned in subsection (2)(a) or (b) the aggregate amount payable in priority to other creditors of the employer in respect of—

(a) any claim of the Secretary of State to be paid in priority to other creditors of the employer by virtue of subsection (2), and

(b) any claim by the employee to be so paid made in his own right,

any claim of the Secretary of State to be so paid by virtue of subsection (2) shall be treated as if it were a claim of the employee.

(4) …

(5) Any sum recovered by the Secretary of State in exercising any right, or pursuing any remedy, which is his by virtue of this section shall be paid into the National Insurance Fund.

[1233]

NOTES

Sub-s (1): words in square brackets substituted by the Employment Rights (Dispute Resolution) Act 1998, s 1(2)(a).

Sub-s (2): words in square brackets in para (a) substituted by the Companies Act 2006 (Consequential Amendments etc) Order 2008, SI 2008/948, arts 3(1)(b), 6, Sch 1, Pt 2, para 201, as from 6 April 2008.

Sub-s (4): repealed by the Enterprise Act 2002, ss 248(3), 278(2), Sch 17, para 49(1), (4), Sch 26, as from 15 September 2003, except in relation to cases where a petition for an administration order was presented before that date, and subject to savings in relation to special administration regimes (within the meaning of s 249 of the 2002 Act).

190 Power to obtain information

(1) Where an application is made to the Secretary of State under section 182 in respect of a debt owed by an employer, the Secretary of State may require—

(a) the employer to provide him with such information as he may reasonably require for the purpose of determining whether the application is well-founded, and

(b) any person having the custody or control of any relevant records or other documents to produce for examination on behalf of the Secretary of State any such document in that person's custody or under his control which is of such a description as the Secretary of State may require.

(2) Any such requirement—

(a) shall be made by notice in writing given to the person on whom the requirement is imposed, and

(b) may be varied or revoked by a subsequent notice so given.

(3) If a person refuses or wilfully neglects to furnish any information or produce any document which he has been required to furnish or produce by a notice under this section he is guilty of an offence and liable on summary conviction to a fine not exceeding level 3 on the standard scale.

(4) If a person, in purporting to comply with a requirement of a notice under this section, knowingly or recklessly makes any false statement he is guilty of an offence and liable on summary conviction to a fine not exceeding level 5 on the standard scale.

(5) Where an offence under this section committed by a body corporate is proved—

(a) to have been committed with the consent or connivance of, or

(b) to be attributable to any neglect on the part of,

any director, manager, secretary or other similar officer of the body corporate, or any person who was purporting to act in any such capacity, he (as well as the body corporate) is guilty of the offence and liable to be proceeded against and punished accordingly.

(6) Where the affairs of a body corporate are managed by its members, subsection (5) applies in relation to the acts and defaults of a member in connection with his functions of management as if he were a director of the body corporate.

[1234]

PART XIII
MISCELLANEOUS

CHAPTER I
PARTICULAR TYPES OF EMPLOYMENT

Crown employment etc

191 Crown employment

(1) Subject to sections 192 and 193, the provisions of this Act to which this section applies have effect in relation to Crown employment and persons in Crown employment as they have effect in relation to other employment and other employees or workers.

(2) This section applies to—

(a) Parts I to III,

[(aa) Part IVA,]

(b) Part V, apart from section 45,

[(c) Parts 6 to 8A,]

(d) in Part IX, sections 92 and 93,
(e) Part X, apart from section 101, and
(f) this Part and Parts XIV and XV.

(3) In this Act "Crown employment" means employment under or for the purposes of a government department or any officer or body exercising on behalf of the Crown functions conferred by a statutory provision.

(4) For the purposes of the application of provisions of this Act in relation to Crown employment in accordance with subsection (1)—

(a) references to an employee or a worker shall be construed as references to a person in Crown employment,
(b) references to a contract of employment, or a worker's contract, shall be construed as references to the terms of employment of a person in Crown employment,
(c) references to dismissal, or to the termination of a worker's contract, shall be construed as references to the termination of Crown employment,
(d) references to redundancy shall be construed as references to the existence of such circumstances as are treated, in accordance with any arrangements falling within section 177(3) for the time being in force, as equivalent to redundancy in relation to Crown employment, …
[(da) the reference in section 98B(2)(a) to the employer's undertaking shall be construed as a reference to the national interest, and]
(e) [any other reference] to an undertaking shall be construed—
  (i) in relation to a Minister of the Crown, as references to his functions or (as the context may require) to the department of which he is in charge, and
  (ii) in relation to a government department, officer or body, as references to the functions of the department, officer or body or (as the context may require) to the department, officer or body.

(5) Where the terms of employment of a person in Crown employment restrict his right to take part in—

(a) certain political activities, or
(b) activities which may conflict with his official functions,

nothing in section 50 requires him to be allowed time off work for public duties connected with any such activities.

(6) Sections 159 and 160 are without prejudice to any exemption or immunity of the Crown.

[1235]

NOTES

Sub-s (2): para (aa) inserted by the Public Interest Disclosure Act 1998, ss 10, 18(2); para (c) substituted by the Employment Act 2002, s 53, Sch 7, paras 24, 41.

Sub-s (4): word omitted from para (d) repealed, para (da) inserted, and words in square brackets in para (e) substituted, by the Employment Relations Act 2004, s 57, Sch 1, para 34, Sch 2, as from 6 April 2005.

192 Armed forces

(1) Section 191—

(a) applies to service as a member of the naval, military or air forces of the Crown but subject to the following provisions of this section, and
(b) applies to employment by an association established for the purposes of Part XI of the Reserve Forces Act 1996.

(2) The provisions of this Act which have effect by virtue of section 191 in relation to service as a member of the naval, military or air forces of the Crown are—

(a) Part I,
[(aa) in Part V, [sections [43M,] 45A, 47C and 47D] and sections 48 and 49 so far as relating to [those sections],
[(ab) section 47C,]
(b) in Part VI, sections [55 to 57B],
(c) Parts VII and VIII,
(d) in Part IX, sections 92 and 93,
(e) Part X, apart from sections [98B(2) and (3),] 100 to 103[, 104C] and 134, and
(f) this Part and Parts XIV and XV.

(3) Her Majesty may by Order in Council—

(a) amend subsection (2) by making additions to, or omissions from, the provisions for the time being specified in that subsection, and

(b) make any provision for the time being so specified apply to service as a member of the naval, military or air forces of the Crown subject to such exceptions and modifications as may be specified in the Order in Council,

but no provision contained in Part II may be added to the provisions for the time being specified in subsection (2).

(4) Modifications made by an Order in Council under subsection (3) may include provision precluding the making of a complaint or reference to any [employment tribunal] unless[—

(a) the person aggrieved has made [a service complaint]; and

(b) the Defence Council have made a determination with respect to the [service complaint]].

[(5) Where modifications made by an Order in Council under subsection (3) include provision such as is mentioned in subsection (4), the Order in Council shall also include provision—

(a) enabling a complaint or reference to be made to an [employment tribunal] in such circumstances as may be specified in the Order, notwithstanding that provision such as is mentioned in subsection (4) would otherwise preclude the making of the complaint or reference; and

(b) where a complaint or reference is made to an [employment tribunal] by virtue of provision such as is mentioned in paragraph (a), enabling [the service complaint procedures] to continue after the complaint or reference is made.]

[(6A) In subsections (4) and (5)—

"service complaint" means a complaint under section 334 of the Armed Forces Act 2006;

"the service complaint procedures" means the procedures prescribed by regulations under that section.]

(7) No provision shall be made by virtue of subsection (4) which has the effect of substituting a period longer than six months for any period specified as the normal period for a complaint or reference.

(8) In subsection (7) "the normal period for a complaint or reference", in relation to any matter within the jurisdiction of an [employment tribunal], means the period specified in the relevant enactment as the period within which the complaint or reference must be made (disregarding any provision permitting an extension of that period at the discretion of the tribunal).

[1236]

NOTES

Commencement: to be appointed (see the note below).

By Sch 2, para 16 to this Act, s 192 has effect until a day to be appointed by order under sub-para (2)(b) of para 16 in the terms set out in para 16(1) at **[1284]**. This section, although not in force, has been amended as follows—

Sub-s (2): para (aa) inserted by the Working Time Regulations 1998, SI 1998/1833, regs 2(1), 31(4); words in first (outer) and final pairs of square brackets in para (aa) substituted by the Tax Credits Act 2002, s 27, Sch 1, para 1(1), (5); figure in second (inner) pair of square paragraphs in para (aa) inserted by the Employment Relations Act 2004, s 57(1), Sch 1, para 35(a), as from 6 April 2005; para (ab) inserted, and words in square brackets in para (b) substituted, by the Employment Relations Act 1999, s 9, Sch 4, Pt III, paras 1, 5, 31; para (ab) repealed by the Tax Credits Act 2002, s 60, Sch 6, as from a day to be appointed; words in first pair of square brackets in para (e) inserted by the Employment Relations Act 2004, s 57(1), Sch 1, para 35(b), as from 6 April 2005; figure in second pair of square brackets in para (e) inserted by the Employment Act 2002, s 53, Sch 7, paras 24, 42.

Sub-s (4): words in first pair of square brackets substituted by the Employment Rights (Dispute Resolution) Act 1998, s 1(2)(a); words in second (outer) pair of square brackets substituted by the Armed Forces Act 1996, s 26(1), (2); words in square brackets in paras (a), (b) substituted by the Armed Forces Act 2006, s 378(1), Sch 16, para 136(a), as from 1 January 2008.

Sub-s (5): substituted by the Armed Forces Act 1996, s 26(1), (3); words "employment tribunal" in square brackets substituted by the Employment Rights (Dispute Resolution) Act 1998, s 1(2)(a); other words in square brackets substituted by the Armed Forces Act 2006, s 378(1), Sch 16, para 136(b), as from 1 January 2008.

Sub-s (6A): substituted, for original sub-s (6), by the Armed Forces Act 2006, s 378(1), Sch 16, para 136(c), as from 1 January 2008.

Sub-s (8): words in square brackets substituted by the Employment Rights (Dispute Resolution) Act 1998, s 1(2)(a).

[193 National security

Part IVA and section 47B of this Act do not apply in relation to employment for the purposes of—

(a) the Security Service,
(b) the Secret Intelligence Service, or
(c) the Government Communications Headquarters.]

[1237]

NOTES

Substituted by the Employment Relations Act 1999, s 41, Sch 8, para 1.

Parliamentary staff

194 House of Lords staff

(1) The provisions of this Act to which this section applies have effect in relation to employment as a relevant member of the House of Lords staff as they have effect in relation to other employment.

(2) This section applies to—

(a) Part I,
(b) Part III,
(c) in Part V, [sections [43M,] 44, 45A[, 47[, 47C] [47D and 47E]]], and sections 48 and 49 so far as relating to those sections,
(d) Part VI, apart from sections 58 to 60,
[(e) Parts VII, VIII and VIIIA,]
(f) in Part IX, sections 92 and 93,
(g) Part X, apart from sections 101 and 102, and
(h) this Part and Parts XIV and XV.

[(2A) For the purposes of the application of section 98B(2) in relation to a relevant member of the House of Lords staff, the reference to the employer's undertaking shall be construed as a reference to the national interest or, if the case so requires, the interests of the House of Lords.]

(3) For the purposes of the application of [the other provisions] of this Act to which this section applies in relation to a relevant member of the House of Lords staff references to an undertaking shall be construed as references to the House of Lords.

(4) Nothing in any rule of law or the law or practice of Parliament prevents a relevant member of the House of Lords staff from bringing before the High Court or a county court—

(a) a claim arising out of or relating to a contract of employment or any other contract connected with employment, or
(b) a claim in tort arising in connection with employment.

(5) Where the terms of the contract of employment of a relevant member of the House of Lords staff restrict his right to take part in—

(a) certain political activities, or
(b) activities which may conflict with his official functions,

nothing in section 50 requires him to be allowed time off work for public duties connected with any such activities.

(6) In this section "relevant member of the House of Lords staff" means any person who is employed under a contract of employment with the Corporate Officer of the House of Lords.

(7) For the purposes of the application of—

(a) the provisions of this Act to which this section applies, or
(b) a claim within subsection (4),

in relation to a person continuously employed in or for the purposes of the House of Lords up to the time when he became so employed under a contract of employment with the Corporate

Officer of the House of Lords, his employment shall not be treated as having been terminated by reason only of a change in his employer before or at that time.

[1238]

NOTES

Sub-s (2) is amended as follows:

Words in first (outer) pair of square brackets in para (c) substituted by the Working Time Regulations 1998, SI 1998/1833, regs 2(1), 31(5).

Figure "43M," in square brackets in para (c) inserted by the Employment Relations Act 2004, s 57(1), Sch 1, para 36(1), (2), as from 6 April 2005.

Figure ", 47" in square brackets in para (c) substituted by the Employment Relations Act 1999, s 9, Sch 4, Pt II, paras 1, 5, 32.

Figure ", 47C" in square brackets in para (c) substituted by both the Tax Credits Act 2002, s 27, Sch 1, para 1(1), (6)(a), and the Employment Act 2002, s 53, Sch 7, paras 24, 43(a).

Words ", 47D and 47E" in square brackets in para (c) substituted by the Employment Relations Act 2004, s 41(7), as from 6 April 2005, except in relation to cases of detriment where the act or deliberate failure to act occurred before that date (see SI 2005/872, art 13).

Para (e) substituted by the Employment Act 2002, s 53, Sch 7, paras 24, 43(b).

Sub-s (2A): inserted by the Employment Relations Act 2004, s 57(1), Sch 1, para 36(1), (3), as from 6 April 2005.

Sub-s (3): words in square brackets substituted by the Employment Relations Act 2004, s 57(1), Sch 1, para 36(1), (4), as from 6 April 2005.

195 House of Commons staff

(1) The provisions of this Act to which this section applies have in effect in relation to employment as a relevant member of the House of Commons staff as they have effect in relation to other employment.

(2) This section applies to—

(a) Part I,
(b) Part III,
(c) in Part V, [sections [43M,] 44, 45A[, 47[, 47C] [47D and 47E]]], and sections 48 and 49 so far as relating to those sections,
(d) Part VI, apart from sections 58 to 60,
[(e) Parts VII, VIII and VIIIA,]
(f) in Part IX, sections 92 and 93,
(g) Part X, apart from sections 101 and 102, and
(h) this Part and Parts XIV and XV.

[(2A) For the purposes of the application of section 98B(2) in relation to a relevant member of the House of Commons staff, the reference to the employer's undertaking shall be construed as a reference to the national interest or, if the case so requires, the interests of the House of Commons.]

(3) For the purposes of the application of the provisions of this Act to which this section applies in relation to a relevant member of the House of Commons staff—

(a) references to an employee shall be construed as references to a relevant member of the House of Commons staff,
(b) references to a contract of employment shall be construed as including references to the terms of employment of a relevant member of the House of Commons staff,
(c) references to dismissal shall be construed as including references to the termination of the employment of a relevant member of the House of Commons staff, and
(d) references to an undertaking [(other than in section 98B)] shall be construed as references to the House of Commons.

(4) Nothing in any rule of law or the law or practice of Parliament prevents a relevant member of the House of Commons staff from bringing before the High Court or a county court—

(a) a claim arising out of or relating to a contract of employment or any other contract connected with employment, or
(b) a claim in tort arising in connection with employment.

(5) In this section "relevant member of the House of Commons staff" means any person—

(a) who was appointed by the House of Commons Commission or is employed in the refreshment department, or
(b) who is a member of the Speaker's personal staff.

(6) Subject to subsection (7), for the purposes of—
(a) the provisions of this Act to which this section applies,
(b) Part XI (where applicable to relevant members of the House of Commons staff), and
(c) a claim within subsection (4),

the House of Commons Commission is the employer of staff appointed by the Commission and the Speaker is the employer of his personal staff and of any person employed in the refreshment department and not appointed by the Commission.

(7) Where the House of Commons Commission or the Speaker designates a person to be treated for all or any of the purposes mentioned in subsection (6) as the employer of any description of staff (other than the Speaker's personal staff), the person so designated shall be treated for those purposes as their employer.

(8) Where any proceedings are brought by virtue of this section against—
(a) the House of Commons Commission,
(b) the Speaker, or
(c) any person designated under subsection (7),

the person against whom the proceedings are brought may apply to the court or [employment tribunal] concerned to have some other person against whom the proceedings could at the time of the application be properly brought substituted for him as a party to the proceedings.

(9) For the purposes mentioned in subsection (6)—
(a) a person's employment in or for the purposes of the House of Commons shall not (provided he continues to be employed in such employment) be treated as terminated by reason only of a change in his employer, and
(b) (provided he so continues) his first appointment to such employment shall be deemed after the change to have been made by his employer for the time being.

(10) In accordance with subsection (9)—
(a) an employee shall be treated for the purposes mentioned in subsection (6) as being continuously employed by his employer for the time being from the commencement of his employment until its termination, and
(b) anything done by or in relation to his employer for the time being in respect of his employment before the change shall be so treated as having been done by or in relation to the person who is his employer for the time being after the change.

(11) In subsections (9) and (10) "employer for the time being", in relation to a person who has ceased to be employed in or for the purposes of the House of Commons, means the person who was his employer immediately before he ceased to be so employed, except that where some other person would have been his employer for the time being if he had not ceased to be so employed it means that other person.

(12) If the House of Commons resolves at any time that any provision of subsections (5) to (8) should be amended in its application to any member of the staff of that House, Her Majesty may by Order in Council amend that provision accordingly.

[1239]

NOTES

Sub-s (2) is amended as follows:

Words in first (outer) pair of square brackets in para (c) substituted by the Working Time Regulations 1998, SI 1998/1833, regs 2(1), 31(5).

Figure "43M," in square brackets in para (c) inserted by the Employment Relations Act 2004, s 57(1), Sch 1, para 36(1), (2), as from 6 April 2005.

Figure ", 47" in square brackets in para (c) substituted by the Employment Relations Act 1999, s 9, Sch 4, Pt II, paras 1, 5, 33.

Figure ", 47C" in square brackets in para (c) substituted by both the Tax Credits Act 2002, s 27, Sch 1, para 1(1), (6)(a), and the Employment Act 2002, s 53, Sch 7, paras 24, 43(a).

Words ", 47D and 47E" in square brackets in para (c) substituted by the Employment Relations Act 2004, s 41(7), as from 6 April 2005, except in relation to cases of detriment where the act or deliberate failure to act occurred before that date (see SI 2005/872, art 13).

Para (e) substituted by the Employment Act 2002, s 53, Sch 7, paras 24, 43(b).

Sub-s (2A): inserted by the Employment Relations Act 2004, s 57(1), Sch 1, para 37(1), (3), as from 6 April 2005.

Sub-s (3): words in square brackets in para (d) inserted by the Employment Relations Act 2004, s 57(1), Sch 1, para 37(1), (4), as from 6 April 2005.

Sub-s (8): words in square brackets substituted by the Employment Rights (Dispute Resolution) Act 1998, s 1(2)(a).

Excluded classes of employment

196, 197 (*S 196 repealed by the Employment Relations Act 1999, ss 32(3), 44, Sch 9(9); s 197 repealed by the Fixed-term Employees (Prevention of Less Favourable Treatment) Regulations 2002, SI 2002/2034, reg 11, Sch 2, Pt 1, para 3(1), (15), subject to transitional provisions in Sch 2, Pt 2, para 5 thereto at* **[2751]** (*sub-ss (1), (2) had been repealed previously by the Employment Relations Act 1999, ss 32(3), 44, Sch 9(9).*)

198 Short-term employment

Sections 1 to 7 do not apply to an employee if his employment continues for less than one month.

[1240]

199 Mariners

(1) Sections 1 to 7, Part II and sections 86 to 91 do not apply to a person employed as a seaman in a ship registered in the United Kingdom under a crew agreement the provisions and form of which are of a kind approved by the Secretary of State.

(2) Sections 8 to 10, Part III, sections 44, 45, 47, [47C, [47E,] 50 to 57B] and 61 to 63, [Parts VII, VIII and VIIIA], sections 92 and 93 and … Parts X to XII do not apply to employment as master, or as a member of the crew, of a fishing vessel where the employee is remunerated only by a share in the profits or gross earnings of the vessel.

(3) …

(4) Sections 8 to 10 and 50 to 54 and Part XII do not apply to employment as a merchant seaman.

(5) In subsection (4) "employment as a merchant seaman"—

(a) does not include employment in the fishing industry or employment on board a ship otherwise than by the owner, manager or charterer of that ship except employment as a radio officer, but

(b) subject to that, includes—

(i) employment as a master or a member of the crew of any ship,

(ii) employment as a trainee undergoing training for the sea service, and

(iii) employment in or about a ship in port by the owner, manager or charterer of the ship to do work of the kind ordinarily done by a merchant seaman on a ship while it is in port.

(6) …

[(7) The provisions mentioned in subsection (8) apply to employment on board a ship registered in the register maintained under section 8 of the Merchant Shipping Act 1995 if and only if—

(a) the ship's entry in the register specifies a port in Great Britain as the port to which the vessel is to be treated as belonging,

(b) under his contract of employment the person employed does not work wholly outside Great Britain, and

(c) the person employed is ordinarily resident in Great Britain.

(8) The provisions are—

(a) sections 8 to 10,

(b) Parts II, III and V,

(c) Part VI, apart from sections 58 to 60,

[(d) Parts VII, VIII and VIIIA,]

(e) sections 92 and 93, and

(f) Part X.]

[1241]

NOTES

Sub-s (2): words in first (outer) pair of square brackets substituted, and words omitted repealed, by the Employment Relations Act 1999, ss 9, 44, Sch 4, Pt III, paras 1, 5, 34(a), (b), Sch 9(2); figure in second (inner) pair of square brackets originally inserted by the Employment Act 2002, s 53, Sch 7, paras 24, 44(1), (2)(a), and substituted by the Employment Relations Act 2004, s 41(8), as from 6 April 2005, except in relation to cases of detriment where the act or deliberate failure to act occurred before that date (see SI 2005/872, art 13); words in third pair of square brackets substituted by the Employment Act 2002, s 53, Sch 7, paras 24, 44(1), (2)(b).

Sub-s (3): repealed by the Employment Relations Act 1999, ss 9, 44, Sch 4, Pt III, paras 1, 5, 34(c), Sch 9(2).
Sub-s (6): repealed by the Fixed-term Employees (Prevention of Less Favourable Treatment) Regulations 2002, SI 2002/2034, reg 11, Sch 2, Pt 1, para 3(1), (16), subject to transitional provisions in Sch 2, Pt 2, para 5 thereto at **[2751]**.
Sub-s (7): added by the Employment Relations Act 1999, s 32(4).
Sub-s (8): added by the Employment Relations Act 1999, s 32(4); para (d) substituted by the Employment Act 2002, s 53, Sch 7, paras 24, 44(1), (3).

200 Police officers

(1) Sections 8 to 10, Part III[…], sections … , [43M,] 45, [45A,] 47[…], [47C,] 50 [to 57B] and 61 to 63, Parts VII and VIII, sections 92 and 93 [and], Part X [(except sections 100[, 103A] and 134A and the other provisions of that Part so far as relating to the right not to be unfairly dismissed in a case where the dismissal is unfair by virtue of section 100 [or 103A])] … do not apply to employment under a contract of employment in police service or to persons engaged in such employment.

(2) In subsection (1) "police service" means—

(a) service as a member of a constabulary maintained by virtue of an enactment, or

(b) subject to section 126 of the Criminal Justice and Public Order Act 1994 (prison staff not to be regarded as in police service), service in any other capacity by virtue of which a person has the powers or privileges of a constable.

[1242]

NOTES

Sub-s (1) is amended as follows:
First and third words omitted originally inserted by the Public Interest Disclosure Act 1998, ss 13, 18(2), and repealed by the Police Reform Act 2002, ss 37(2)(a), 107, Sch 8, as from 1 April 2004.
Second word omitted repealed by the Police (Health and Safety) Act 1997, s 6(2)(a).
Figure "43M," in square brackets inserted by the Employment Relations Act 2004, s 57(1), Sch 1, para 38, as from 6 April 2005.
Figure "45A," in square brackets inserted by the Working Time Regulations 1998, SI 1998/1833, reg 31(6).
Figure "47C," in square brackets and the word "and" in square brackets inserted by the Employment Relations Act 1999, s 9, Sch 4, Pt III, paras 5, 35(a), (c).
Words "to 57B" in square brackets substituted by the Employment Relations Act 1999, s 9, Sch 4, Pt III, paras 5, 35(b).
Words in square brackets beginning with the words "(except sections 100" inserted by the Police (Health and Safety) Act 1997, s 6(2)(b).
Figure ", 103A" in square brackets and words "or 103A" in square brackets inserted by the Police Reform Act 2002, s 37(2)(b), (c), as from 1 April 2004.
Final words omitted repealed by the Employment Relations Act 1999, ss 9, 44, Sch 4, Pt III, paras 5, 35(d), Sch 9, Table 2.

Offshore employment

201 Power to extend employment legislation to offshore employment

(1) In this section "offshore employment" means employment for the purposes of activities—

(a) in the territorial waters of the United Kingdom,

(b) connected with the exploration of the sea-bed or subsoil, or the exploitation of their natural resources, in the United Kingdom sector of the continental shelf, or

(c) connected with the exploration or exploitation, in a foreign sector of the continental shelf, of a cross-boundary petroleum field.

(2) Her Majesty may by Order in Council provide that—

(a) the provisions of this Act, and

(b) any Northern Ireland legislation making provision for purposes corresponding to any of the purposes of this Act,

apply, to such extent and for such purposes as may be specified in the Order (with or without modification), to or in relation to a person in offshore employment.

(3) An Order in Council under this section—

(a) may make different provision for different cases,

(b) may provide that all or any of the provisions referred to in subsection (2), as applied by such an Order in Council, apply—
  (i) to individuals whether or not they are British subjects, and
  (ii) to bodies corporate whether or not they are incorporated under the law of a part of the United Kingdom,

and apply even where the application may affect their activities outside the United Kingdom,

(c) may make provision for conferring jurisdiction on any court or class of court specified in the Order in Council, or on [employment tribunals], in respect of offences, causes of action or other matters arising in connection with offshore employment,

(d) may (without prejudice to subsection (2) and paragraph (a)) provide that the provisions referred to in subsection (2), as applied by the Order in Council, apply in relation to any person in employment in a part of the areas referred to in subsection (1)(a) and (b),

(e) may exclude from the operation of section 3 of the Territorial Waters Jurisdiction Act 1878 (consents required for prosecutions) proceedings for offences under the provisions referred to in subsection (2) in connection with offshore employment,

(f) may provide that such proceedings shall not be brought without such consent as may be required by the Order in Council,

(g) may (without prejudice to subsection (2)) modify or exclude the operation of any or all of sections … 199 and 215(2) to (6) or of any corresponding Northern Ireland legislation.

(4) Any jurisdiction conferred on a court or tribunal under this section is without prejudice to jurisdiction exercisable apart from this section by that or any other court or tribunal.

(5) In this section—

"cross-boundary petroleum field" means a petroleum field that extends across the boundary between the United Kingdom sector of the continental shelf and a foreign sector of the continental shelf,

"foreign sector of the continental shelf" means an area outside the territorial waters of any state, within which rights with respect to the sea-bed and subsoil and their natural resources are exercisable by a state other than the United Kingdom,

"petroleum field" means a geological structure identified as an oil or gas field by the Order in Council concerned, and

"United Kingdom sector of the continental shelf" means the area designated under section 1(7) of the Continental Shelf Act 1964.

[1243]

NOTES

Sub-s (1): substituted by the Petroleum Act 1998, s 50, Sch 4, para 40(1), (2), as from a day to be appointed, as follows—

"(1) In this section "offshore employment" means employment for the purposes of—
  (a) any activities in the territorial sea adjacent to the United Kingdom, or
  (b) any such activities as are mentioned in section 11(2) of the Petroleum Act 1998 in waters within subsection (8)(b) or (c) of that section.".

Sub-s (3): words in square brackets in para (c) substituted by the Employment Rights (Dispute Resolution) Act 1998, s 1(2)(b); figure omitted from para (g) repealed by the Employment Relations Act 1999, s 44, Sch 9(9).

Sub-s (5): repealed by the Petroleum Act 1998, ss 50, 51(1), Sch 4, para 40(1), (3), Sch 5, Pt I, as from a day to be appointed.

Orders: the Employment Relations (Offshore Employment) Order 2000, SI 2000/1828. Also, by virtue of s 241 of, and Sch 2, Pt I, paras 1–4 to, this Act, the Employment Protection (Offshore Employment) Order 1976, SI 1976/766, has effect as if made under this section.

CHAPTER II
OTHER MISCELLANEOUS MATTERS

Restrictions on disclosure of information

202 National security

(1) Where in the opinion of any Minister of the Crown the disclosure of any information would be contrary to the interests of national security—

(a) nothing in any of the provisions to which this section applies requires any person to disclose the information, and

(b) no person shall disclose the information in any proceedings in any court or tribunal relating to any of those provisions.

(2) This section applies to—

(a) Part I, so far as it relates to employment particulars,

(b) in Part V, [sections [43M,] 44, 45A[, 47 and 47C]], and sections 48 and 49 so far as relating to those sections,

(c) in Part VI, sections [55 to 57B] and 61 to 63,

(d) in Part VII, sections 66 to 68, and sections 69 and 70 so far as relating to those sections,

(e) Part VIII,

(f) in Part IX, sections 92 and 93 where they apply by virtue of section 92(4),

(g) Part X so far as relating to a dismissal which is treated as unfair—

[(i) by section [98B,] 99, 100, 101A(d) or 103, or by section 104 in its application in relation to time off under section 57A.]

(ii) by subsection (1) of section 105 by reason of the application of subsection [(2A)], (3) or (6) of that section [or by reason of the application of subsection (4A) in so far as it applies where the reason (or, if more than one, the principal reason) for which an employee was selected for dismissal was that specified in section 101A(d)], and

(h) this Part and Parts XIV and XV (so far as relating to any of the provisions in paragraphs (a) to (g)).

[1244]

NOTES

Sub-s (2) is amended as follows:

Words in first (outer) pair of square brackets in para (b) substituted by the Working Time Regulations 1998, SI 1998/1833, reg 31(5).

Figure "43M," in square brackets in para (b) inserted by the Employment Relations Act 2004, s 57(1), Sch 1, para 39(1), (2), as from 6 April 2005.

Words ", 47 and 47C" in square brackets in para (b) substituted by the Employment Relations Act 1999, s 9, Sch 4, Pt III, paras 5, 36(a).

Words in square brackets in para (c) substituted by the Employment Relations Act 1999, s 9, Sch 4, Pt III, paras 5, 36(b).

Para (g)(i) substituted by the Employment Relations Act 1999, s 9, Sch 4, Pt III, paras 5, 36(c).

Figure "98B," in square brackets in para (g)(i) inserted by the Employment Relations Act 2004, s 57(1), Sch 1, para 39(1), (3)(a), as from 6 April 2005.

Figure "(2A)" in square brackets in para (g)(ii) substituted by the Employment Relations Act 2004, s 57(1), Sch 1, para 39(1), (3)(b), as from 6 April 2005.

Words in second pair of square brackets in para (g)(ii) inserted by SI 1998/1833, reg 32(6).

Contracting out etc and remedies

203 Restrictions on contracting out

(1) Any provision in an agreement (whether a contract of employment or not) is void in so far as it purports—

(a) to exclude or limit the operation of any provision of this Act, or

(b) to preclude a person from bringing any proceedings under this Act before an [employment tribunal].

(2) Subsection (1)—

(a) does not apply to any provision in a collective agreement excluding rights under section 28 if an order under section 35 is for the time being in force in respect of it,

(b) does not apply to any provision in a dismissal procedures agreement excluding the right under section 94 if that provision is not to have effect unless an order under section 110 is for the time being in force in respect of it,

(c) does not apply to any provision in an agreement if an order under section 157 is for the time being in force in respect of it,

(d) …

(e) does not apply to any agreement to refrain from instituting or continuing proceedings where a conciliation officer has taken action under section 18 of [the Employment Tribunals Act 1996], and

(f) does not apply to any agreement to refrain from instituting or continuing … any proceedings within [the following provisions of section 18(1) of the Employment Tribunals Act 1996 (cases where conciliation available)—
  (i) paragraph (d) (proceedings under this Act),
  (ii) paragraph (h) (proceedings arising out of the Part-time Workers (Prevention of Less Favourable Treatment) Regulations 2000,)]
  [(iii) paragraph (i) (proceedings arising out of the Fixed-term Employees (Prevention of Less Favourable Treatment) Regulations 2002),
  (iv) paragraph (j) (proceedings under those Regulations),]

if the conditions regulating compromise agreements under this Act are satisfied in relation to the agreement.

(3) For the purposes of subsection (2)(f) the conditions regulating compromise agreements under this Act are that—
(a) the agreement must be in writing,
(b) the agreement must relate to the particular [proceedings],
(c) the employee or worker must have received [advice from a relevant independent adviser] as to the terms and effect of the proposed agreement and, in particular, its effect on his ability to pursue his rights before an [employment tribunal],
(d) there must be in force, when the adviser gives the advice, a [contract of insurance, or an indemnity provided for members of a professional body,] covering the risk of a claim by the employee or worker in respect of loss arising in consequence of the advice,
(e) the agreement must identify the adviser, and
(f) the agreement must state that the conditions regulating compromise agreements under this Act are satisfied.

[(3A) A person is a relevant independent adviser for the purposes of subsection (3)(c)—
(a) if he is a qualified lawyer,
(b) if he is an officer, official, employee or member of an independent trade union who has been certified in writing by the trade union as competent to give advice and as authorised to do so on behalf of the trade union,
(c) if he works at an advice centre (whether as an employee or a volunteer) and has been certified in writing by the centre as competent to give advice and as authorised to do so on behalf of the centre, or
(d) if he is a person of a description specified in an order made by the Secretary of State.

(3B) But a person is not a relevant independent adviser for the purposes of subsection (3)(c) in relation to the employee or worker—
(a) if he is, is employed by or is acting in the matter for the employer or an associated employer,
(b) in the case of a person within subsection (3A)(b) or (c), if the trade union or advice centre is the employer or an associated employer,
(c) in the case of a person within subsection (3A)(c), if the employee or worker makes a payment for the advice received from him, or
(d) in the case of a person of a description specified in an order under subsection (3A)(d), if any condition specified in the order in relation to the giving of advice by persons of that description is not satisfied.

(4) In subsection (3A)(a) "qualified lawyer" means—
(a) as respects England and Wales, *a barrister (whether in practice as such or employed to give legal advice), a solicitor who holds a practising certificate, or a person other than a barrister or solicitor who is an authorised advocate or authorised litigator (within the meaning of the Courts and Legal Services Act 1990), and*
(b) as respects Scotland, an advocate (whether in practice as such or employed to give legal advice), or a solicitor who holds a practising certificate.]

[(5) An agreement under which the parties agree to submit a dispute to arbitration—
(a) shall be regarded for the purposes of subsection (2)(e) and (f) as being an agreement to refrain from instituting or continuing proceedings if—
  (i) the dispute is covered by a scheme having effect by virtue of an order under section 212A of the Trade Union and Labour Relations (Consolidation) Act 1992, and
  (ii) the agreement is to submit it to arbitration in accordance with the scheme, but

(b) shall be regarded as neither being nor including such an agreement in any other case.]

[1245]

NOTES

Sub-s (1): words in square brackets substituted by the Employment Rights (Dispute Resolution) Act 1998, s 1(2)(a).

Sub-s (2): para (d) repealed, and paras (f)(iii), (iv) inserted, by the Fixed-term Employees (Prevention of Less Favourable Treatment) Regulations 2002, SI 2002/2034, reg 11, Sch 2, Pt 1, para 3(1), (17), subject to transitional provisions in Sch 2, Pt 2, para 5 thereto at **[2751]**; words in square brackets in para (e) substituted, and words omitted from para (f) repealed, by the Employment Rights (Dispute Resolution) Act 1998, ss 1(2)(c), 15, 44, Schs 2, 9(3); words in first pair of square brackets in para (f) substituted by the Part-time Workers (Prevention of Less Favourable Treatment) Regulations 2001, SI 2001/1107, reg 3.

Sub-s (3): words in square brackets substituted by the Employment Rights (Dispute Resolution) Act 1998, ss 1(2)(a), 9(1), (2)(e), 10(1), (2)(e), 15, Sch 1, para 24(1), (2).

Sub-ss (3A), (3B), (4): substituted, for original sub-s (4), by the Employment Rights (Dispute Resolution) Act 1998, s 15, Sch 1, para 24(1), (3). For the words in italics in sub-s (4) there are substituted the words "a person who, for the purposes of the Legal Services Act 2007, is an authorised person in relation to an activity which constitutes the exercise of a right of audience or the conduct of litigation (within the meaning of that Act), and" by the Legal Services Act 2007, s 208(1), Sch 21, para 120, as from a day to be appointed.

Sub-s (5): added by the Employment Rights (Dispute Resolution) Act 1998, s 8(5).

Orders: the Compromise Agreements (Description of Person) Order 2004, SI 2004/754 at **[3138]**.

204 Law governing employment

(1) For the purposes of this Act it is immaterial whether the law which (apart from this Act) governs any person's employment is the law of the United Kingdom, or of a part of the United Kingdom, or not.

(2) …

[1246]

NOTES

Sub-s (2): repealed by the Employment Relations Act 1999, s 44, Sch 9(9).

205 Remedy for infringement of certain rights

(1) The remedy of an employee for infringement of any of the rights conferred by section 8, Part III, Parts V to VIII, section 92, Part X and Part XII is, where provision is made for a complaint or the reference of a question to an [employment tribunal], by way of such a complaint or reference and not otherwise.

[(1ZA) In relation to the right conferred by section 45A, the reference in subsection (1) to an employee has effect as a reference to a worker.]

[(1A) In relation to the right conferred by section 47B, the reference in subsection (1) to an employee has effect as a reference to a worker.]

(2) The remedy of a worker in respect of any contravention of section 13, 15, 18(1) or 21(1) is by way of a complaint under section 23 and not otherwise.

[1247]

NOTES

Sub-s (1): words in square brackets substituted by the Employment Rights (Dispute Resolution) Act 1998, s 1(2)(a).

Sub-s (1ZA): inserted by the Working Time Regulations 1998, SI 1998/1833, regs 2(1), 31(7).

Sub-s (1A): inserted by the Public Interest Disclosure Act 1998, ss 14, 18(2).

General provisions about death of employer or employee

206 Institution or continuance of tribunal proceedings

(1) Where an employer has died, any tribunal proceedings arising under any of the provisions of this Act to which this section applies may be defended by a personal representative of the deceased employer.

(2) This section and section 207 apply to—
- (a) Part I, so far as it relates to itemised pay statements,
- (b) Part III,
- (c) Part V,
- (d) Part VI, apart from sections 58 to 60,
- (e) Parts VII and VIII,
- (f) in Part IX, sections 92 and 93, and
- (g) Parts X to XII.

(3) Where an employee has died, any tribunal proceedings arising under any of the provisions of this Act to which this section applies may be instituted or continued by a personal representative of the deceased employee.

(4) If there is no personal representative of a deceased employee, any tribunal proceedings arising under any of the provisions of this Act to which this section applies may be instituted or continued on behalf of the estate of the deceased employee by any appropriate person appointed by the [employment tribunal].

(5) In subsection (4) "appropriate person" means a person who is—
- (a) authorised by the employee before his death to act in connection with the proceedings, or
- (b) the widow or widower, [surviving civil partner,] child, parent or brother or sister of the deceased employee;

and in Part XI and the following provisions of this section and section 207 references to a personal representative include a person appointed under subsection (4).

(6) In a case where proceedings are instituted or continued by virtue of subsection (4), any award made by the [employment tribunal] shall be—
- (a) made in such terms, and
- (b) enforceable in such manner,

as the Secretary of State may by regulations provide.

(7) Any reference in the provisions of this Act to which this section applies to the doing of anything by or in relation to an employer or employee includes a reference to the doing of the thing by or in relation to a personal representative of the deceased employer or employee.

(8) Any reference in the provisions of this Act to which this section applies to a thing required or authorised to be done by or in relation to an employer or employee includes a reference to a thing required or authorised to be done by or in relation to a personal representative of the deceased employer or employee.

(9) Subsections (7) and (8) do not prevent a reference to a successor of an employer including a personal representative of a deceased employer.

[1248]

NOTES

Sub-ss (4), (6): words in square brackets substituted by the Employment Rights (Dispute Resolution) Act 1998, s 1(2)(a).

Sub-s (5): words in square brackets in para (b) inserted by the Civil Partnership Act 2004 (Overseas Relationships and Consequential, etc Amendments) Order 2005, SI 2005/3129, art 4(4), Sch 4, para 11, as from 5 December 2005.

Regulations: as of 6 April 2008 no Regulations had been made under this section but, by virtue of s 241 of, and Sch 2, Pt I, paras 1–4 to, this Act, the Employment Tribunal Awards (Enforcement in case of Death) Regulations 1976, SI 1976/663, have effect as if made under this section.

207 Rights and liabilities accruing after death

(1) Any right arising under any of the provisions of this Act to which this section applies which accrues after the death of an employee devolves as if it had accrued before his death.

(2) Where an [employment tribunal] determines under any provision of Part XI that an employer is liable to pay to a personal representative of a deceased employee—
- (a) the whole of a redundancy payment to which he would have been entitled but for some provision of Part XI or section 206, or
- (b) such part of such a redundancy payment as the tribunal thinks fit,

the reference in subsection (1) to a right includes any right to receive it.

(3) Where—

(a) by virtue of any of the provisions to which this section applies a personal representative is liable to pay any amount, and
(b) the liability has not accrued before the death of the employer,

it shall be treated as a liability of the deceased employer which had accrued immediately before his death.

[1249]

NOTES

Sub-s (2): words in square brackets substituted by the Employment Rights (Dispute Resolution) Act 1998, s 1(2)(a).

Modifications of Act

208 (*Repealed by the Employment Relations Act 1999, ss 36(2), 44, Sch 9(10).*)

209 Powers to amend Act

(1) The Secretary of State may by order—
(a) provide that any provision of this Act, other than any to which this paragraph does not apply, which is specified in the order shall not apply to persons, or to employments, of such classes as may be prescribed in the order,
(b) provide that any provision of this Act, other than any to which this paragraph does not apply, shall apply to persons or employments of such classes as may be prescribed in the order subject to such exceptions and modifications as may be so prescribed, or
(c) vary, or exclude the operation of, any of the provisions to which this paragraph applies.

(2) Subsection (1)(a) does not apply to—
(a) Parts II and IV,
(b) in Part V, sections 45 and 46, and sections 48 and 49 so far as relating to those sections,
(c) in Part VI, sections 58 to 60,
(d) in Part IX, sections 87(3), 88 to 90, 91(1) to (4) and (6) and 92(6) to (8),
(e) in Part X, sections 95, 97(1) to (5), 98(1) to (4) and (6), 100, 101, [101A,] 102, 103, 105, 107, 110, 111, 120(2), 124(1), (2) and (5), 125(7) and 134,
(f) in Part XI, sections 143, 144, 160(2) and (3), 166 to 173 and 177 to 180,
(g) in Part XIII, sections … ,
(h) Chapter I of Part XIV, or
(j) in Part XV, section 236(3) so far as relating to sections 120(2), 124(2) and 125(7).

(3) Subsection (1)(b) does not apply to—
(a) any of the provisions to which subsection (1)(a) does not apply,
(b) sections 1 to 7, or
(c) the provisions of sections 86 to 91 not specified in subsection (2).

(4) The provision which may be made by virtue of paragraph (b) of subsection (1) in relation to section 94 does not include provision for application subject to exceptions or modifications; but this subsection does not prejudice paragraph (a) of that subsection.

(5) Subsection (1)(c) applies to sections 29(2), 65(2), 86(5), 92(3), 108(1), … 159, 160(1) … and 199(1), (2), (4) and (5).

(6), (7) …

(8) The provisions of this section are without prejudice to any other power of the Secretary of State to amend, vary or repeal any provision of this Act or to extend or restrict its operation in relation to any person or employment.

[1250]

NOTES

Sub-s (2): figure in square brackets in para (e) inserted by the Working Time Regulations 1998, SI 1998/1833, regs 2(1), 32(7); words omitted from para (g) repealed by the Employment Relations Act 1999, s 44, Sch 9(3), (9) (it is unclear why the whole of para (g) was not repealed).

Sub-s (5): first words omitted repealed by the Employment Equality (Age) Regulations 2006, SI 2006/1031, reg 49(1), Sch 8, Pt 1, paras 21, 34, as from 1 October 2006; second words omitted repealed by the Employment Relations Act 1999, s 44, Sch 9(9).

Sub-s (6): repealed by the Employment Relations Act 1999, ss 9, 44, Sch 4, Pt III, paras 1, 5, 37, Sch 9(2).

Sub-s (7): repealed by the Employment Relations Act 1999, ss 23(6), 44, Sch 9(4).

Orders: the Unfair Dismissal and Statement of Reasons for Dismissal (Variation of Qualifying Period) Order 1999, SI 1999/1436; the Redundancy Payments (Continuity of Employment in Local Government, etc) (Modification) Order 1999, SI 1999/2277 at **[2518]**. Also, by virtue of s 241 of, and Sch 2, Pt I, paras 1–4 to, this Act, the following Orders have effect as if made under this section: the Redundancy Payments (National Health Service) (Modification) Order 1993, SI 1993/3167; the Employment Protection (Continuity of Employment of National Health Service Employees) (Modification) Order 1996, SI 1996/1023.

PART XIV
INTERPRETATION

CHAPTER I
CONTINUOUS EMPLOYMENT

210 Introductory

(1) References in any provision of this Act to a period of continuous employment are (unless provision is expressly made to the contrary) to a period computed in accordance with this Chapter.

(2) In any provision of this Act which refers to a period of continuous employment expressed in months or years—

(a) a month means a calendar month, and

(b) a year means a year of twelve calendar months.

(3) In computing an employee's period of continuous employment for the purposes of any provision of this Act, any question—

(a) whether the employee's employment is of a kind counting towards a period of continuous employment, or

(b) whether periods (consecutive or otherwise) are to be treated as forming a single period of continuous employment,

shall be determined week by week; but where it is necessary to compute the length of an employee's period of employment it shall be computed in months and years of twelve months in accordance with section 211.

(4) Subject to sections 215 to 217, a week which does not count in computing the length of a period of continuous employment breaks continuity of employment.

(5) A person's employment during any period shall, unless the contrary is shown, be presumed to have been continuous.

[1251]

211 Period of continuous employment

(1) An employee's period of continuous employment for the purposes of any provision of this Act—

(a) (subject to [subsection] (3)) begins with the day on which the employee starts work, and

(b) ends with the day by reference to which the length of the employee's period of continuous employment is to be ascertained for the purposes of the provision.

(2) …

(3) If an employee's period of continuous employment includes one or more periods which (by virtue of section 215, 216 or 217) while not counting in computing the length of the period do not break continuity of employment, the beginning of the period shall be treated as postponed by the number of days falling within that intervening period, or the aggregate number of days falling within those periods, calculated in accordance with the section in question.

[1252]

NOTES

Sub-s (1): word in square brackets in para (a) substituted by the Employment Equality (Age) Regulations 2006, SI 2006/1031, reg 49(1), Sch 8, Pt 1, paras 21, 35(1), (2), as from 1 October 2006.

Sub-s (2): repealed by SI 2006/1031, reg 49(1), Sch 8, Pt 1, paras 21, 35(1), (3), as from 1 October 2006.

212 Weeks counting in computing period

(1) Any week during the whole or part of which an employee's relations with his employer are governed by a contract of employment counts in computing the employee's period of employment.

(2) …

(3) Subject to subsection (4), any week (not within subsection (1)) during the whole or part of which an employee is—

(a) incapable of work in consequence of sickness or injury,
(b) absent from work on account of a temporary cessation of work, [or]
(c) absent from work in circumstances such that, by arrangement or custom, he is regarded as continuing in the employment of his employer for any purpose, …
(d) …

counts in computing the employee's period of employment.

(4) Not more than twenty-six weeks count under subsection (3)(a) … between any periods falling under subsection (1).

[1253]

NOTES

Sub-s (2): repealed by the Employment Relations Act 1999, ss 9, 44, Sch 4, Pt III, paras 1, 5, 38(1), (2), Sch 9(2).

Sub-s (3): word in square brackets in para (b) inserted, and para (d) and word immediately preceding repealed, by the Employment Relations Act 1999, ss 9, 44, Sch 4, Pt III, paras 1, 5, 38(1), (3), Sch 9(2).

Sub-s (4): words omitted repealed by the Employment Relations Act 1999, ss 9, Sch 4, Pt III, paras 1, 5, 38(1), (4), Sch 9(2).

213 Intervals in employment

(1) Where in the case of an employee a date later than the date which would be the effective date of termination by virtue of subsection (1) of section 97 is treated for certain purposes as the effective date of termination by virtue of subsection (2) or (4) of that section, the period of the interval between the two dates counts as a period of employment in ascertaining for the purposes of section 108(1) or 119(1) the period for which the employee has been continuously employed.

(2) Where an employee is by virtue of section 138(1) regarded for the purposes of Part XI as not having been dismissed by reason of a renewal or re-engagement taking effect after an interval, the period of the interval counts as a period of employment in ascertaining for the purposes of section 155 or 162(1) the period for which the employee has been continuously employed (except so far as it is to be disregarded under section 214 or 215).

(3) Where in the case of an employee a date later than the date which would be the relevant date by virtue of subsections (2) to (4) of section 145 is treated for certain purposes as the relevant date by virtue of subsection (5) of that section, the period of the interval between the two dates counts as a period of employment in ascertaining for the purposes of section 155 or 162(1) the period for which the employee has been continuously employed (except so far as it is to be disregarded under section 214 or 215).

[1254]

214 Special provisions for redundancy payments

(1) This section applies where a period of continuous employment has to be determined in relation to an employee for the purposes of the application of section 155 or 162(1).

(2) The continuity of a period of employment is broken where—

(a) a redundancy payment has previously been paid to the employee (whether in respect of dismissal or in respect of lay-off or short-time), and
(b) the contract of employment under which the employee was employed was

renewed (whether by the same or another employer) or the employee was re-engaged under a new contract of employment (whether by the same or another employer).

(3) The continuity of a period of employment is also broken where—

(a) a payment has been made to the employee (whether in respect of the termination of his employment or lay-off or short-time) in accordance with a scheme under section 1 of the Superannuation Act 1972 or arrangements falling within section 177(3), and

(b) he commenced new, or renewed, employment.

(4) The date on which the person's continuity of employment is broken by virtue of this section—

(a) if the employment was under a contract of employment, is the date which was the relevant date in relation to the payment mentioned in subsection (2)(a) or (3)(a), and

(b) if the employment was otherwise than under a contract of employment, is the date which would have been the relevant date in relation to the payment mentioned in subsection (2)(a) or (3)(a) had the employment been under a contract of employment.

(5) For the purposes of this section a redundancy payment shall be treated as having been paid if—

(a) the whole of the payment has been paid to the employee by the employer,

(b) a tribunal has determined liability and found that the employer must pay part (but not all) of the redundancy payment and the employer has paid that part, or

(c) the Secretary of State has paid a sum to the employee in respect of the redundancy payment under section 167.

[1255]

215 Employment abroad etc

(1) This Chapter applies to a period of employment—

(a) (subject to the following provisions of this section) even where during the period the employee was engaged in work wholly or mainly outside Great Britain, and

(b) even where the employee was excluded by or under this Act from any right conferred by this Act.

(2) For the purposes of sections 155 and 162(1) a week of employment does not count in computing a period of employment if the employee—

(a) was employed outside Great Britain during the whole or part of the week, and

(b) was not during that week an employed earner for the purposes of the Social Security Contributions and Benefits Act 1992 in respect of whom a secondary Class 1 contribution was payable under that Act (whether or not the contribution was in fact paid).

(3) Where by virtue of subsection (2) a week of employment does not count in computing a period of employment, the continuity of the period is not broken by reason only that the week does not count in computing the period; and the number of days which, for the purposes of section 211(3), fall within the intervening period is seven for each week within this subsection.

(4) Any question arising under subsection (2) whether—

(a) a person was an employed earner for the purposes of the Social Security Contributions and Benefits Act 1992, or

(b) if so, whether a secondary Class 1 contribution was payable in respect of him under that Act,

shall be determined by [an officer of the Commissioners of Inland Revenue].

[(5) Part II of the Social Security Contributions (Transfer of Functions, etc) Act 1999 (decisions and appeals) shall apply in relation to the determination of any issue by the Inland Revenue under subsection (4) as if it were a decision falling within section 8(1) of that Act.]

(6) Subsection (2) does not apply in relation to a person who is—

(a) employed as a master or seaman in a British ship, and

(b) ordinarily resident in Great Britain.

[1256]

NOTES

Sub-s (4): words in square brackets substituted by the Social Security Contributions (Transfer of Functions, etc) Act 1999, s 18, Sch 7, para 21(1), (2).

Sub-s (5): substituted by the Social Security Contributions (Transfer of Functions, etc) Act 1999, s 18, Sch 7, para 21(1), (3).

Commissioners of Inland Revenue: a reference to the Commissioners of Inland Revenue is now to be taken as a reference to the Commissioners for Her Majesty's Revenue and Customs; see the Commissioners for Revenue and Customs Act 2005, s 50(1), (7).

216 Industrial disputes

(1) A week does not count under section 212 if during the week, or any part of the week, the employee takes part in a strike.

(2) The continuity of an employee's period of employment is not broken by a week which does not count under this Chapter (whether or not by virtue only of subsection (1)) if during the week, or any part of the week, the employee takes part in a strike; and the number of days which, for the purposes of section 211(3), fall within the intervening period is the number of days between the last working day before the strike and the day on which work was resumed.

(3) The continuity of an employee's period of employment is not broken by a week if during the week, or any part of the week, the employee is absent from work because of a lock-out by the employer; and the number of days which, for the purposes of section 211(3), fall within the intervening period is the number of days between the last working day before the lock-out and the day on which work was resumed.

[1257]

217 Reinstatement after military service

(1) If a person who is entitled to apply to his former employer under the Reserve Forces (Safeguard of Employment) Act 1985 enters the employment of the employer not later than the end of the six month period mentioned in section 1(4)(b) of that Act, his period of service in the armed forces of the Crown in the circumstances specified in section 1(1) of that Act does not break his continuity of employment.

(2) In the case of such a person the number of days which, for the purposes of section 211(3), fall within the intervening period is the number of days between the last day of his previous period of employment with the employer (or, if there was more than one such period, the last of them) and the first day of the period of employment beginning in the six month period.

[1258]

218 Change of employer

(1) Subject to the provisions of this section, this Chapter relates only to employment by the one employer.

(2) If a trade or business, or an undertaking (whether or not established by or under an Act), is transferred from one person to another—

(a) the period of employment of an employee in the trade or business or undertaking at the time of the transfer counts as a period of employment with the transferee, and

(b) the transfer does not break the continuity of the period of employment.

(3) If by or under an Act (whether public or local and whether passed before or after this Act) a contract of employment between any body corporate and an employee is modified and some other body corporate is substituted as the employer—

(a) the employee's period of employment at the time when the modification takes effect counts as a period of employment with the second body corporate, and

(b) the change of employer does not break the continuity of the period of employment.

(4) If on the death of an employer the employee is taken into the employment of the personal representatives or trustees of the deceased—

(a) the employee's period of employment at the time of the death counts as a period of employment with the employer's personal representatives or trustees, and

(b) the death does not break the continuity of the period of employment.

(5) If there is a change in the partners, personal representatives or trustees who employ any person—

(a) the employee's period of employment at the time of the change counts as a period of employment with the partners, personal representatives or trustees after the change, and

(b) the change does not break the continuity of the period of employment.

(6) If an employee of an employer is taken into the employment of another employer who, at the time when the employee enters the second employer's employment, is an associated employer of the first employer—

(a) the employee's period of employment at that time counts as a period of employment with the second employer, and

(b) the change of employer does not break the continuity of the period of employment.

(7) If an employee of the [governing body] of a school maintained by a local education authority is taken into the employment of the authority or an employee of a local education authority is taken into the employment of the [governing body] of a school maintained by the authority—

(a) his period of employment at the time of the change of employer counts as a period of employment with the second employer, and

(b) the change does not break the continuity of the period of employment.

(8) If a person employed in relevant employment by a health service employer is taken into relevant employment by another such employer, his period of employment at the time of the change of employer counts as a period of employment with the second employer and the change does not break the continuity of the period of employment.

(9) For the purposes of subsection (8) employment is relevant employment if it is employment of a description—

(a) in which persons are engaged while undergoing professional training which involves their being employed successively by a number of different health service employers, and

(b) which is specified in an order made by the Secretary of State.

(10) The following are health service employers for the purposes of subsections (8) and (9)—

(a) [Strategic Health Authorities [established under section 13 of the National Health Service Act 2006]] … ,

(b) Special Health Authorities established under [section 28 of that Act or section 22 of the National Health Service (Wales) Act 2006],

[(bb) Primary Care Trusts established under [section 18 of the National Health Service Act 2006],]

(c) National Health Service trusts established under [that Act or the National Health Service (Wales) Act 2006],

[(ca) NHS foundation trusts,]

[(cb) Local Health Boards established under section 11 of the National Health Service (Wales) Act 2006,]

(d) …

[(dd) the Health Protection Agency] …

(e) …

[1259]

NOTES

Sub-s (7): words in square brackets substituted by the Education Act 2002, s 215(1), Sch 21, para 32.

Sub-s (10) is amended as follows:

Words in first (outer) pair of square brackets in para (a) substituted by the National Health Service Reform and Health Care Professions Act 2002 (Supplementary, Consequential etc Provisions) Regulations 2002, SI 2002/2469, reg 4, Sch 1, para 22(1), (3); words in second (inner) pair of square brackets in para (a) inserted by the National Health Service (Consequential Provisions) Act 2006, s 2, Sch 1, paras 177, 180(a), as from 1 March 2007; words omitted from para (a) repealed by a combination of the National Health Service (Consequential Provisions) Act 2006, s 2, Sch 1, paras 177, 180(a), as from 1 March 2007, and the References to Health Authorities Order 2007, SI 2007/961, art 3, Schedule, para 27(1), (4), as from 1 April 2007.

Words in square brackets in para (b) substituted by the National Health Service (Consequential Provisions) Act 2006, s 2, Sch 1, paras 177, 180(b), as from 1 March 2007.

Para (bb) inserted by the Health Act 1999 (Supplementary, Consequential etc Provisions) Order 2000, SI 2000/90, art 3(1), Sch 1, para 30(1), (3); words in square brackets substituted by the National Health Service (Consequential Provisions) Act 2006, s 2, Sch 1, paras 177, 180(c), as from 1 March 2007.

Words in square brackets in para (c) substituted by the National Health Service (Consequential Provisions) Act 2006, s 2, Sch 1, paras 177, 180(d), as from 1 March 2007.

Para (ca) inserted by the Health and Social Care (Community Health and Standards) Act 2003, s 34, Sch 4, paras 99, 101, as from 1 April 2004.

Para (cb) inserted by SI 2007/961, art 3, Schedule, para 27(1), (4), as from 1 April 2007.

Para (d) and para (e) (and the word immediately preceding para (e)) repealed by the Health and Social Care (Community Health and Standards) Act 2003, ss 190(2), 196, Sch 13, para 8, Sch 14, Pts 4, 7, as from 1 April 2006 and 1 April 2005 respectively.

Para (dd) inserted by the Health Protection Agency Act 2004, s 11(1), Sch 3, para 13, as from 1 April 2005.

Orders: as of 6 April 2008 no Orders had been made under this section but, by virtue of s 241 of, and Sch 2, Pt I, paras 1–4 to, this Act, the Employment Protection (National Health Service) Order 1996, SI 1996/638, has effect as if made under this section.

219 Reinstatement or re-engagement of dismissed employee

(1) Regulations made by the Secretary of State may make provision—

(a) for preserving the continuity of a person's period of employment for the purposes of this Chapter or for the purposes of this Chapter as applied by or under any other enactment specified in the regulations, or

(b) for modifying or excluding the operation of section 214 subject to the recovery of any such payment as is mentioned in that section,

in cases where … a dismissed employee is reinstated [re-engaged or otherwise re-employed] by his employer or by a successor or associated employer of that employer [in any circumstances prescribed by the regulations].

(2)–(4) …

[1260]

NOTES

Sub-s (1): words omitted repealed, words in first pair of square brackets substituted, and words in second pair of square brackets inserted, by the Employment Rights (Dispute Resolution) Act 1998, s 15, Sch 1, para 25(1), (2), Sch 2.

Sub-ss (2)–(4): repealed by the Employment Rights (Dispute Resolution) Act 1998, s 15, Sch 1, para 25(1), (3), Sch 2.

Regulations: the Employment Protection (Continuity of Employment) Regulations 1996, SI 1996/3147 at **[2398]**.

CHAPTER II
A WEEK'S PAY

Introductory

220 Introductory

The amount of a week's pay of an employee shall be calculated for the purposes of this Act in accordance with this Chapter.

[1261]

Employments with normal working hours

221 General

(1) This section and sections 222 and 223 apply where there are normal working hours for the employee when employed under the contract of employment in force on the calculation date.

(2) Subject to section 222, if the employee's remuneration for employment in normal working hours (whether by the hour or week or other period) does not vary with the amount of work done in the period, the amount of a week's pay is the amount which is payable by the employer under the contract of employment in force on the calculation date if the employee works throughout his normal working hours in a week.

(3) Subject to section 222, if the employee's remuneration for employment in normal working hours (whether by the hour or week or other period) does vary with the amount of

work done in the period, the amount of a week's pay is the amount of remuneration for the number of normal working hours in a week calculated at the average hourly rate of remuneration payable by the employer to the employee in respect of the period of twelve weeks ending—

(a) where the calculation date is the last day of a week, with that week, and

(b) otherwise, with the last complete week before the calculation date.

(4) In this section references to remuneration varying with the amount of work done includes remuneration which may include any commission or similar payment which varies in amount.

(5) This section is subject to sections 227 and 228.

[1262]

222 Remuneration varying according to time of work

(1) This section applies if the employee is required under the contract of employment in force on the calculation date to work during normal working hours on days of the week, or at times of the day, which differ from week to week or over a longer period so that the remuneration payable for, or apportionable to, any week varies according to the incidence of those days or times.

(2) The amount of a week's pay is the amount of remuneration for the average number of weekly normal working hours at the average hourly rate of remuneration.

(3) For the purposes of subsection (2)—

(a) the average number of weekly hours is calculated by dividing by twelve the total number of the employee's normal working hours during the relevant period of twelve weeks, and

(b) the average hourly rate of remuneration is the average hourly rate of remuneration payable by the employer to the employee in respect of the relevant period of twelve weeks.

(4) In subsection (3) "the relevant period of twelve weeks" means the period of twelve weeks ending—

(a) where the calculation date is the last day of a week, with that week, and

(b) otherwise, with the last complete week before the calculation date.

(5) This section is subject to sections 227 and 228.

[1263]

223 Supplementary

(1) For the purposes of sections 221 and 222, in arriving at the average hourly rate of remuneration, only—

(a) the hours when the employee was working, and

(b) the remuneration payable for, or apportionable to, those hours,

shall be brought in.

(2) If for any of the twelve weeks mentioned in sections 221 and 222 no remuneration within subsection (1)(b) was payable by the employer to the employee, account shall be taken of remuneration in earlier weeks so as to bring up to twelve the number of weeks of which account is taken.

(3) Where—

(a) in arriving at the average hourly rate of remuneration, account has to be taken of remuneration payable for, or apportionable to, work done in hours other than normal working hours, and

(b) the amount of that remuneration was greater than it would have been if the work had been done in normal working hours (or, in a case within section 234(3), in normal working hours falling within the number of hours without overtime),

account shall be taken of that remuneration as if the work had been done in such hours and the amount of that remuneration had been reduced accordingly.

[1264]

Employments with no normal working hours

224 Employments with no normal working hours

(1) This section applies where there are no normal working hours for the employee when employed under the contract of employment in force on the calculation date.

(2) The amount of a week's pay is the amount of the employee's average weekly remuneration in the period of twelve weeks ending—

(a) where the calculation date is the last day of a week, with that week, and

(b) otherwise, with the last complete week before the calculation date.

(3) In arriving at the average weekly remuneration no account shall be taken of a week in which no remuneration was payable by the employer to the employee and remuneration in earlier weeks shall be brought in so as to bring up to twelve the number of weeks of which account is taken.

(4) This section is subject to sections 227 and 228.

[1265]

The calculation date

225 Rights during employment

(1) Where the calculation is for the purposes of section 30, the calculation date is—

(a) where the employee's contract has been varied, or a new contract entered into, in connection with a period of short-time working, the last day on which the original contract was in force, and

(b) otherwise, the day in respect of which the guarantee payment is payable.

(2) Where the calculation is for the purposes of section 53 or 54, the calculation date is the day on which the employer's notice was given.

(3) Where the calculation is for the purposes of section 56, the calculation date is the day of the appointment.

(4) Where the calculation is for the purposes of section 62, the calculation date is the day on which the time off was taken or on which it is alleged the time off should have been permitted.

[(4A) Where the calculation is for the purposes of section 63B, the calculation date is the day on which the time off was taken or on which it is alleged the time off should have been permitted.]

(5) Where the calculation is for the purposes of section 69—

(a) in the case of an employee suspended on medical grounds, the calculation date is the day before that on which the suspension begins, and

(b) in the case of an employee suspended on maternity grounds, the calculation date is—

[(i) where the day before that on which the suspension begins falls during a period of ordinary or additional maternity leave, the day before the beginning of that period,]

(ii) otherwise, the day before that on which the suspension begins.

[(6) Where the calculation is for the purposes of section 80I, the calculation date is the day on which the application under section 80F was made.]

[1266]

NOTES

Sub-s (4A): inserted by the Teaching and Higher Education Act 1998, s 44(1), Sch 3, paras 10, 14.

Sub-s (5): para (b)(i) substituted by the Employment Relations Act 1999, s 9, Sch 4, Pt III, paras 1, 5, 39.

Sub-s (6): added by the Employment Act 2002, s 53, Sch 7, paras 24, 45.

226 Rights on termination

(1) Where the calculation is for the purposes of section 88 or 89, the calculation date is the day immediately preceding the first day of the period of notice required by section 86(1) or (2).

(2) Where the calculation is for the purposes of section 93, 117 or 125, the calculation date is—

(a) if the dismissal was with notice, the date on which the employer's notice was given, and

(b) otherwise, the effective date of termination.

(3) Where the calculation is for the purposes of section [112, 119, 120 or 121], the calculation date is—

(a) …

(b) if by virtue of subsection (2) or (4) of section 97 a date later than the effective date of termination as defined in subsection (1) of that section is to be treated for certain purposes as the effective date of termination, the effective date of termination as so defined, and

(c) otherwise, the date specified in subsection (6).

(4) Where the calculation is for the purposes of section 147(2), the

calculation date is the day immediately preceding the first of the four, or six, weeks referred to in section 148(2).

(5) Where the calculation is for the purposes of section 162, the calculation date is—

(a) …

(b) if by virtue of subsection (5) of section 145 a date is to be treated for certain purposes as the relevant date which is later than the relevant date as defined by the previous provisions of that section, the relevant date as so defined, and

(c) otherwise, the date specified in subsection (6).

(6) The date referred to in subsections (3)(c) and (5)(c) is the date on which notice would have been given had—

(a) the contract been terminable by notice and been terminated by the employer giving such notice as is required by section 86 to terminate the contract, and

(b) the notice expired on the effective date of termination, or the relevant date,

(whether or not those conditions were in fact fulfilled).

[1267]

NOTES

Sub-s (3): words in square brackets by the Employment Act 2002, s 53, Sch 7, paras 24, 46, as from 1 October 2004; para (a) repealed by the Employment Relations Act 1999, ss 9, 44, Sch 4, Pt III, paras 1, 5, 40, Sch 9(2).

Sub-s (5): para (a) repealed by the Employment Relations Act 1999, ss 9, 44, Sch 4, Pt III, paras 1, 5, 40, Sch 9(2).

Maximum amount of week's pay

227 Maximum amount

(1) For the purpose of calculating—

[(za) an award of compensation under section 80I(1)(b),]

(a) a basic award of compensation for unfair dismissal,

(b) an additional award of compensation for unfair dismissal,

[(ba) an award under section 112(5), or]

(c) a redundancy payment,

the amount of a week's pay shall not exceed [£330].

(2)–(4) …

[1268]

NOTES

Sub-s (1): para (za) inserted by the Employment Act 2002, s 53, Sch 7, paras 24, 47(1), (2), and para (ba) substituted (for the original word "or" at the end of para (b)) by s 53 of, and Sch 7, paras 24, 47(1), (3) to, the 2002 Act, as from 1 November 2004; sum in square brackets substituted by the Employment Rights (Increase of Limits) Order 2007, SI 2007/3570, art 3, Schedule, as from 1 February 2008, in relation to any case where the appropriate date falls on or after that date (see SI 2007/3570, art 4 at **[3474H]**). The previous sum was £310 (see SI 2006/3045). This sum may be varied by the Secretary of State (see the Employment Relations Act 1999, s 34(1)(a), (3)(a) at **[1445]**). See also the Work and Families Act 2006, s 14 at **[1699]** (Secretary of State's additional 'one-off' power to alter the sum in sub-s (1) above). Sums for periods prior to 1 February 2007 were £290 as from 1 February 2006

(SI 2005/3352), £280 as from 1 February 2005 (SI 2004/2989), and £270 as from 1 February 2004 (SI 2003/3038) in each case where the appropriate date fell after the commencement date).

Sub-ss (2)–(4): repealed by the Employment Relations Act 1999, ss 36(1)(a), 44, Sch 9(10).

Miscellaneous

228 New employments and other special cases

(1) In any case in which the employee has not been employed for a sufficient period to enable a calculation to be made under the preceding provisions of this Chapter, the amount of a week's pay is the amount which fairly represents a week's pay.

(2) In determining that amount the [employment tribunal]—

(a) shall apply as nearly as may be such of the preceding provisions of this Chapter as it considers appropriate, and

(b) may have regard to such of the considerations specified in subsection (3) as it thinks fit.

(3) The considerations referred to in subsection (2)(b) are—

(a) any remuneration received by the employee in respect of the employment in question,

(b) the amount offered to the employee as remuneration in respect of the employment in question,

(c) the remuneration received by other persons engaged in relevant comparable employment with the same employer, and

(d) the remuneration received by other persons engaged in relevant comparable employment with other employers.

(4) The Secretary of State may by regulations provide that in cases prescribed by the regulations the amount of a week's pay shall be calculated in such manner as may be so prescribed.

[1269]

NOTES

Sub-s (2): words in square brackets substituted by the Employment Rights (Dispute Resolution) Act 1998, s 1(2)(a).

Regulations: as of 6 April 2008 no Regulations had been made under this section.

229 Supplementary

(1) In arriving at—

(a) an average hourly rate of remuneration, or

(b) average weekly remuneration,

under this Chapter, account shall be taken of work for a former employer within the period for which the average is to be taken if, by virtue of Chapter I of this Part, a period of employment with the former employer counts as part of the employee's continuous period of employment.

(2) Where under this Chapter account is to be taken of remuneration or other payments for a period which does not coincide with the periods for which the remuneration or other payments are calculated, the remuneration or other payments shall be apportioned in such manner as may be just.

[1270]

CHAPTER III
OTHER INTERPRETATION PROVISIONS

230 Employees, workers etc

(1) In this Act "employee" means an individual who has entered into or works under (or, where the employment has ceased, worked under) a contract of employment.

(2) In this Act "contract of employment" means a contract of service or apprenticeship, whether express or implied, and (if it is express) whether oral or in writing.

(3) In this Act "worker" (except in the phrases "shop worker" and "betting worker") means an individual who has entered into or works under (or, where the employment has ceased, worked under)—

(a) a contract of employment, or

(b) any other contract, whether express or implied and (if it is express) whether oral or in writing, whereby the individual undertakes to do or perform personally any work or services for another party to the contract whose status is not by virtue of the contract that of a client or customer of any profession or business undertaking carried on by the individual;

and any reference to a worker's contract shall be construed accordingly.

(4) In this Act "employer", in relation to an employee or a worker, means the person by whom the employee or worker is (or, where the employment has ceased, was) employed.

(5) In this Act "employment"—

(a) in relation to an employee, means (except for the purposes of section 171) employment under a contract of employment, and

(b) in relation to a worker, means employment under his contract;

and "employed" shall be construed accordingly.

[(6) This section has effect subject to sections 43K and 47B(3); and for the purposes of Part XIII so far as relating to Part IVA or section 47B, "worker", "worker's contract" and, in relation to a worker, "employer", "employment" and "employed" have the extended meaning given by section 43K.]

[1271]

NOTES

Sub-s (6): added by the Public Interest Disclosure Act 1998, ss 15(1), 18(2).

231 Associated employers

For the purposes of this Act any two employers shall be treated as associated if—

(a) one is a company of which the other (directly or indirectly) has control, or

(b) both are companies of which a third person (directly or indirectly) has control;

and "associated employer" shall be construed accordingly.

[1272]

232 Shop workers

(1) In this Act "shop worker" means an employee who, under his contract of employment, is or may be required to do shop work.

(2) In this Act "shop work" means work in or about a shop … on a day on which the shop is open for the serving of customers.

(3) Subject to subsection (4), in this Act "shop" includes any premises where any retail trade or business is carried on.

(4) Where premises are used mainly for purposes other than those of retail trade or business and would not (apart from subsection (3)) be regarded as a shop, only such part of the premises as—

(a) is used wholly or mainly for the purposes of retail trade or business, or

(b) is used both for the purposes of retail trade or business and for the purposes of wholesale trade and is used wholly or mainly for those two purposes considered together,

is to be regarded as a shop for the purposes of this Act.

(5) In subsection (4)(b) "wholesale trade" means the sale of goods for use or resale in the course of a business or the hire of goods for use in the course of a business.

(6) In this section "retail trade or business" includes—

(a) the business of a barber or hairdresser,

(b) the business of hiring goods otherwise than for use in the course of a trade or business, and

(c) retail sales by auction,

but does not include catering business or the sale at theatres and places of amusement of programmes, catalogues and similar items.

(7) In subsection (6) "catering business" means—

(a) the sale of meals, refreshments or [alcohol] [(in Scotland, alcoholic liquor)] for consumption on the premises on which they are sold, or

(b) the sale of meals or refreshments prepared to order for immediate consumption off the premises;

and in paragraph (a) ["alcohol" has the same meaning as in the Licensing Act 2003] [and "alcoholic liquor" the same meaning as in the Licensing (Scotland) Act 1976].

(8) In this Act—

"notice period", in relation to an opted-out shop worker, has the meaning given by section 41(3),

"opted-out", in relation to a shop worker, shall be construed in accordance with section 41(1) and (2),

"opting-in notice", in relation to a shop worker, has the meaning given by section 36(6),

"opting-out notice", in relation to a shop worker, has the meaning given by section 40(2), and

"protected", in relation to a shop worker, shall be construed in accordance with section 36(1) to (5).

[1273]

NOTES

Sub-s (2): words omitted repealed by the Sunday Working (Scotland) Act 2003, s 1(1), (3)(a), as from 6 April 2004.

Sub-s (7): words in first and third pairs of square brackets substituted by the Licensing Act 2003, s 198(1), Sch 6, para 114, as from 11 November 2005; words in second and fourth pairs of square brackets inserted by the Sunday Working (Scotland) Act 2003, s 1(1), (3)(b), as from 6 April 2004.

[233 Betting workers

(1) In this Act "betting worker" means an employee who under his contract of employment is or may be required to do betting work.

(2) In this Act "betting work" means—

(a) work which consists of or includes dealing with betting transactions at a track in England or Wales and which is carried out for a person who holds a general betting operating licence, a pool betting operating licence or a horse-race pool betting operating licence, and

(b) work on premises in respect of which a betting premises licence has effect at a time when the premises are used for betting transactions.

(3) In subsection (2) "betting transactions" includes the collection or payment of winnings.

(4) Expressions used in this section and in the Gambling Act 2005 have the same meaning in this section as in that Act.

(5) In this Act—

"notice period", in relation to an opted-out betting worker, has the meaning given by section 41(3),

"opted-out", in relation to a betting worker, shall be construed in accordance with section 41(1) and (2),

"opting-in notice", in relation to a betting worker, has the meaning given by section 36(6),

"opting-out notice", in relation to a betting worker, has the meaning given by section 40(2), and

"protected", in relation to a betting worker, shall be construed in accordance with section 36(1) to (5).]

[1274]

NOTES

Commencement: 1 September 2007.

Substituted by the Gambling Act 2005, s 356(1), Sch 16, Pt 2, para 11, as from 1 September 2007.

234 Normal working hours

(1) Where an employee is entitled to overtime pay when employed for more than a fixed number of hours in a week or other period, there are for the purposes of this Act normal working hours in his case.

(2) Subject to subsection (3), the normal working hours in such a case are the fixed number of hours.

(3) Where in such a case—

(a) the contract of employment fixes the number, or minimum number, of hours of employment in a week or other period (whether or not it also provides for the reduction of that number or minimum in certain circumstances), and

(b) that number or minimum number of hours exceeds the number of hours without overtime,

the normal working hours are that number or minimum number of hours (and not the number of hours without overtime).

[1275]

235 Other definitions

(1) In this Act, except in so far as the context otherwise requires—

"act" and "action" each includes omission and references to doing an act or taking action shall be construed accordingly,

"basic award of compensation for unfair dismissal" shall be construed in accordance with section 118,

"business" includes a trade or profession and includes any activity carried on by a body of persons (whether corporate or unincorporated),

"childbirth" means the birth of a living child or the birth of a child whether living or dead after twenty-four weeks of pregnancy,

"collective agreement" has the meaning given by section 178(1) and (2) of the Trade Union and Labour Relations (Consolidation) Act 1992,

"conciliation officer" means an officer designated by the Advisory, Conciliation and Arbitration Service under section 211 of that Act,

"dismissal procedures agreement" means an agreement in writing with respect to procedures relating to dismissal made by or on behalf of one or more independent trade unions and one or more employers or employers' associations,

"employers' association" has the same meaning as in the Trade Union and Labour Relations (Consolidation) Act 1992,

"expected week of childbirth" means the week, beginning with midnight between Saturday and Sunday, in which it is expected that childbirth will occur,

"guarantee payment" has the meaning given by section 28,

"independent trade union" means a trade union which—

(a) is not under the domination or control of an employer or a group of employers or of one or more employers' associations, and

(b) is not liable to interference by an employer or any such group or association (arising out of the provision of financial or material support or by any other means whatever) tending towards such control,

"job", in relation to an employee, means the nature of the work which he is employed to do in accordance with his contract and the capacity and place in which he is so employed,

. . .

["paternity leave" means leave under section 80A or 80B,]

"position", in relation to an employee, means the following matters taken as a whole—

(a) his status as an employee,

(b) the nature of his work, and

(c) his terms and conditions of employment,

["protected disclosure" has the meaning given by section 43A,]

"redundancy payment" has the meaning given by Part XI,

"relevant date" has the meaning given by sections 145 and 153,

"renewal" includes extension, and any reference to renewing a contract or a fixed term shall be construed accordingly,

"statutory provision" means a provision, whether of a general or a special nature, contained in, or in any document made or issued under, any Act, whether of a general or special nature,

"successor", in relation to the employer of an employee, means (subject to subsection (2)) a person who in consequence of a change occurring (whether by virtue of a sale or other disposition or by operation of law) in the ownership of the undertaking, or of the part of the undertaking, for the purposes of which the employee was employed, has become the owner of the undertaking or part, "trade union" has the meaning given by section 1 of the Trade Union and Labour Relations (Consolidation) Act 1992,

"week"—

(a) in Chapter I of this Part means a week ending with Saturday, and

(b) otherwise, except in [sections 80A, 80B and 86], means, in relation to an employee whose remuneration is calculated weekly by a week ending with a day other than Saturday, a week ending with that other day and, in relation to any other employee, a week ending with Saturday.

(2) The definition of "successor" in subsection (1) has effect (subject to the necessary modifications) in relation to a case where—

(a) the person by whom an undertaking or part of an undertaking is owned immediately before a change is one of the persons by whom (whether as partners, trustees or otherwise) it is owned immediately after the change, or

(b) the persons by whom an undertaking or part of an undertaking is owned immediately before a change (whether as partners, trustees or otherwise) include the persons by whom, or include one or more of the persons by whom, it is owned immediately after the change,

as it has effect where the previous owner and the new owner are wholly different persons.

[(2A) For the purposes of this Act a contract of employment is a "limited-term contract" if—

(a) the employment under the contract is not intended to be permanent, and

(b) provision is accordingly made in the contract for it to terminate by virtue of a limiting event.

(2B) In this Act, "limiting event", in relation to a contract of employment means—

(a) in the case of a contract for a fixed-term, the expiry of the term,

(b) in the case of a contract made in contemplation of the performance of a specific task, the performance of the task, and

(c) in the case of a contract which provides for its termination on the occurrence of an event (or the failure of an event to occur), the occurrence of the event (or the failure of the event to occur).]

(3) References in this Act to redundancy, dismissal by reason of redundancy and similar expressions shall be construed in accordance with section 139.

(4) In sections 136(2), 154 and 216(3) and paragraph 14 of Schedule 2 "lock-out" means—

(a) the closing of a place of employment,

(b) the suspension of work, or

(c) the refusal by an employer to continue to employ any number of persons employed by him in consequence of a dispute,

done with a view to compelling persons employed by the employer, or to aid another employer in compelling persons employed by him, to accept terms or conditions of or affecting employment.

(5) In sections 91(2), 140(2) and (3), 143(1), 144(2) and (3), 154 and 216(1) and (2) and paragraph 14 of Schedule 2 "strike" means—

(a) the cessation of work by a body of employed persons acting in combination, or

(b) a concerted refusal, or a refusal under a common understanding, of any number of employed persons to continue to work for an employer in consequence of a dispute,

done as a means of compelling their employer or any employed person or body of employed persons, or to aid other employees in compelling their employer or any employed person or body of employed persons, to accept or not to accept terms or conditions of or affecting employment.

[1276]

NOTES

Sub-s (1) is amended as follows:

Definitions omitted repealed by the Employment Relations Act 1999, ss 9, 44, Sch 4, Pt III, paras 1, 5, 41, Sch 9(2).

Definition "paternity leave" inserted, and words in square brackets in definition "week" substituted, by the Employment Act 2002, s 53, Sch 7, paras 24, 48.

Definition "paternity leave" subsequently substituted by the Work and Families Act 2006, s 11(1), Sch 1, para 43, as from a day to be appointed, as follows—

""ordinary or additional paternity leave" means leave under any of sections 80A to 80BB,".

Definition "protected disclosure" inserted by the Public Interest Disclosure Act 1998, ss 15(2), 18(2).
Sub-ss (2A), (2B): inserted by the Fixed-term Employees (Prevention of Less Favourable Treatment) Regulations 2002, SI 2002/2034, reg 11, Sch 2, Pt 1, para 3(1), (18).

PART XV
GENERAL AND SUPPLEMENTARY

General

236 Orders and regulations

(1) Any power conferred by any provision of this Act to make any order (other than an Order in Council) or regulations is exercisable by statutory instrument.

(2) A statutory instrument made under any power conferred by this Act to make an Order in Council or other order or regulations, except—

(a) an Order in Council or other order [or regulations] to which subsection (3) applies,

(b) an order under section 35 or Part II of Schedule 2, or

(c) an order made in accordance with section 208,

is subject to annulment in pursuance of a resolution of either House of Parliament.

(3) No recommendation shall be made to Her Majesty to make an Order in Council under section 192(3), and no order [or regulations] shall be made under section [47C, 71, 72, 73, [75A, 75B,] 76, *[80A, 80B, 80G,]* 99,] *120(2), 124(2)* or 125(7) or (subject to subsection (4)) section 209, unless a draft of the Order in Council[, order or regulations] has been laid before Parliament and approved by a resolution of each House of Parliament.

(4) Subsection (3) does not apply to an order under section 209(1)(b) which specifies only provisions contained in Part XI.

(5) Any power conferred by this Act which is exercisable by statutory instrument includes power to make such incidental, supplementary or transitional provisions as appear to the authority exercising the power to be necessary or expedient.

[1277]

NOTES

Sub-s (2): words in square brackets in para (a) inserted by the Employment Relations Act 1999, s 9, Sch 4, Pt III, paras 1, 5, 42(1), (2); para (c) repealed by the Employment Relations Act 1999, s 44, Sch 9(10), as from a day to be appointed.
Sub-s (3): words in first pair of square brackets inserted, and words in second (outer) and final pairs of square brackets substituted, by the Employment Relations Act 1999, s 44, Sch 4, Pt III, paras 1, 5, 42(1), (3); words in third and fourth (inner) pairs of square brackets inserted by the Employment Act 2002, s 53, Sch 7, paras 24, 49; for the first figures in italics there are substituted the figures "80A, 80AA, 80B, 80BB, 80G" by the Work and Families Act 2006, s 11(1), Sch 1, para 44, as from a day to be appointed; second figures in italics repealed by the Employment Relations Act 1999, s 9, Sch 9(10), as from a day to be appointed.

237 Financial provisions

There shall be paid out of the National Insurance Fund into the Consolidated Fund sums equal to the amount of—

(a) any expenses incurred by the Secretary of State in consequence of Part XI, and

(b) any expenses incurred by the Secretary of State (or by persons acting on his behalf) in exercising his functions under Part XII.

[1278]

238, 239 *(S 238—provision for arrangements for co-ordinating provisions of Northern Ireland legislation corresponding to this Act (previously contained in s 157 of the 1978 Act), and s 239—provision for arrangements for co-ordinating provisions of Isle of Man legislation corresponding to this Act (previously contained in s 158 of the 1978 Act) outside the scope of this work.)*

Final provisions

240 (*Introduces Sch 1* (*consequential amendments*).)

241 Transitionals, savings and transitory provisions

Schedule 2 (transitional provisions, savings and transitory provisions) shall have effect.

[1279]

242 (*Introduces Sch 3* (*repeals and revocations*).)

243 Commencement

This Act shall come into force at the end of the period of three months beginning with the day on which it is passed.

[1280]

244 Extent

(1) Subject to the following provisions, this Act extends to England and Wales and Scotland but not to Northern Ireland.

(2) [Sections 36(2) and (4), 37(1) and (5), 38 and 39] extend to England and Wales only.

(3) Sections 201 and 238 (and sections 236 and 243, this section and section 245) extend to Northern Ireland (as well as to England and Wales and Scotland).

(4) Sections 240 and 242 and Schedules 1 and 3 have the same extent as the provisions amended or repealed by this Act.

[1281]

NOTES

Sub-s (2): words in square brackets substituted by the Sunday Working (Scotland) Act 2003, s 1(1), (5), as from 6 April 2004.

245 Short title

This Act may be cited as the Employment Rights Act 1996.

[1282]

SCHEDULES

(*Schedule 1* (*consequential amendments*) *in so far as these are within the scope of this work, they have been incorporated at the appropriate place.*)

SCHEDULE 2
TRANSITIONAL PROVISIONS, SAVINGS AND TRANSITORY PROVISIONS

Section 241

PART I
TRANSITIONAL PROVISIONS AND SAVINGS

General transitionals and savings

1. The substitution of this Act for the provisions repealed or revoked by this Act does not affect the continuity of the law.

2.—(1) Anything done, or having effect as done, (including the making of subordinate legislation) under or for the purposes of any provision repealed or revoked by this Act has effect as if done under or for the purposes of any corresponding provision of this Act.

(2) Sub-paragraph (1) does not apply to the making of any subordinate legislation to the extent that it is reproduced in this Act.

3. Any reference (express or implied) in this Act or any other enactment, or in any instrument or document, to a provision of this Act is (so far as the context permits) to be read

as (according to the context) being or including in relation to times, circumstances and purposes before the commencement of this Act a reference to the corresponding provision repealed or revoked by this Act.

4.—(1) Any reference (express or implied) in any enactment, or in any instrument or document, to a provision repealed or revoked by this Act is (so far as the context permits) to be read as (according to the context) being or including in relation to times, circumstances and purposes after the commencement of this Act a reference to the corresponding provision of this Act.

(2) In particular, where a power conferred by an Act is expressed to be exercisable in relation to enactments contained in Acts passed before or in the same Session as the Act conferring the power, the power is also exercisable in relation to provisions of this Act which reproduce such enactments.

5. Paragraphs 1 to 4 have effect in place of section 17(2) of the Interpretation Act 1978 (but are without prejudice to any other provision of that Act).

Preservation of old transitionals and savings

6.—(1) The repeal by this Act of an enactment previously repealed subject to savings (whether or not in the repealing enactment) does not affect the continued operation of those savings.

(2) The repeal by this Act of a saving made on the previous repeal of an enactment does not affect the operation of the saving in so far as it remains capable of having effect.

(3) Where the purpose of an enactment repealed by this Act was to secure that the substitution of the provisions of the Act containing that enactment for provisions repealed by that Act did not affect the continuity of the law, the enactment repealed by this Act continues to have effect in so far as it is capable of doing so.

Employment particulars

7.—(1) In this paragraph "pre-TURERA employee" means an employee whose employment with his employer began before 30th November 1993 (the day on which section 26 of the Trade Union Reform and Employment Rights Act 1993 came into force), whether or not the provisions of sections 1 to 6 of the Employment Protection (Consolidation) Act 1978, as they had effect before the substitution made by that section, applied to him before that date.

(2) Subject to the following provisions of this paragraph, sections 1 to 7 of this Act do not apply to a pre-TURERA employee (but the provisions of sections 1 to 6 of the Employment Protection (Consolidation) Act 1978, as they had effect before the substitution made by section 26 of the Trade Union Reform and Employment Rights Act 1993, continue in force in his case).

(3) Where a pre-TURERA employee, at any time—

(a) on or after the day on which this Act comes into force, and

(b) either before the end of his employment or within the period of three months beginning with the day on which his employment ends,

requests from his employer a statement under section 1 of this Act, the employer shall (subject to section 5 and any other provision disapplying or having the effect of disapplying sections 1 to 4) be treated as being required by section 1 to give him a written statement under that section not later than two months after the request is made; and section 4 of this Act shall (subject to that) apply in relation to the employee after he makes the request.

(4) An employer is not required to give an employee a statement under section 1 pursuant to sub-paragraph (3)—

(a) on more than one occasion, or

(b) if he has already given him a statement pursuant to paragraph 3(3) of Schedule 9 to the Trade Union Reform and Employment Rights Act 1993.

(5) Where—

(a) on or after the day on which this Act comes into force there is in the case of a pre-TURERA employee a change in any of the matters particulars of which would, had he been given a statement of particulars on 30th November 1993 under section 1 of the Employment Protection (Consolidation) Act 1978 (as substituted by section 26 of the Trade Union Reform and Employment Rights Act 1993), have been included or referred to in the statement, and

(b) he has not previously requested a statement under sub-paragraph (3) or paragraph 3(3) of Schedule 9 to the Trade Union Reform and Employment Rights Act 1993,

subsections (1) and (6) of section 4 of this Act shall be treated (subject to section 5 and any other provision disapplying or having the effect of disapplying section 4) as requiring his employer to give him a written statement containing particulars of the change at the time specified in subsection (3) of section 4; and the other provisions of section 4 apply accordingly.

Monetary limits in old cases

8. In relation to any case in which (but for this Act) a limit lower than that set by Article 3 of the Employment Protection (Increase of Limits) Order 1995 would have applied in accordance with Article 4 of that Order, this Act has effect as if it reproduced that lower limit.

Shop workers and betting workers to whom old maternity provisions applied

9.—(1) This paragraph applies where an employee exercised a right to return to work under Part III of the Employment Protection (Consolidation) Act 1978 at a time when the amendments of that Part made by the Trade Union Reform and Employment Rights Act 1993 did not have effect in her case (so that her right was a right to return to work in the job in which she was employed under the original contract of employment).

(2) Section 36(4) shall have effect as if for paragraph (b) there were substituted—

"(b) under her original contract of employment, she was a shop worker, or a betting worker, but was not employed to work only on Sunday."

(3) If the employee was employed as a shop worker under her original contract of employment, she shall not be regarded as failing to satisfy the condition in section 36(2)(a) or (c) or 41(1)(c) merely because during her pregnancy she was employed under a different contract of employment by virtue of section 60(2) of the Employment Protection (Consolidation) Act 1978 (as it had effect before the commencement of section 24 of the Trade Union Reform and Employment Rights Act 1993) or otherwise by reason of her pregnancy.

(4) In this paragraph, and in section 36(4)(b) as substituted by sub-paragraph (2), "original contract of employment" has the meaning given by section 153(1) of the Employment Protection (Consolidation) Act 1978 as originally enacted.

Validity of provisions deriving from certain regulations

10. Any question as to the validity of any of sections 47, 61, 62, 63 and 103, which derive from the Collective Redundancies and Transfer of Undertakings (Protection of Employment) (Amendment) Regulations 1995 made under subsection (2) of section 2 of the European Communities Act 1972, shall be determined as if those provisions were contained in regulations made under that subsection.

Unfair dismissal

11. Part X does not apply to a dismissal from employment under a contract for a fixed term of two years or more (not being a contract of apprenticeship) if—

(a) the contract was made before 28th February 1972, and

(b) the dismissal consists only of the expiry of that term without its being renewed.

Redundancy payments

12.—(1) Section 135 does not apply to an employee who immediately before the relevant date is employed under a contract for a fixed term of two years or more (not being a contract of apprenticeship) if the contract was made before 6th December 1965.

(2) Section 197(3) does not apply if the contract was made before 6th December 1965.

Periods of employment

13.—(1) The reference in section 215(2)(b) to a person being an employed earner for the purposes of the Social Security Contributions and Benefits Act 1992 in respect of whom a secondary Class 1 contribution was payable under that Act (whether or not it was in fact paid) shall be construed—

(a) as respects a week of employment after 1st June 1976 and before 1st July 1992, as a reference to a person being an employed earner for the purposes of the Social Security Act 1975 in respect of whom a secondary Class 1 contribution was payable under that Act (whether or not it was in fact paid),

(b) as respects a week of employment after 6th April 1975 and before 1st June 1976, as a reference to a person being an employed earner for the purposes of the Social Security Act 1975, and

(c) as respects a week of employment before 6th April 1975, as a reference to a person being an employee in respect of whom an employer's contribution was payable in respect of the corresponding contribution week (whether or not it was in fact paid).

(2) For the purposes of the application of sub-paragraph (1) to a week of employment where the corresponding contribution week began before 5th July 1948, an employer's contribution shall be treated as payable as mentioned in that sub-paragraph if such a contribution would have been so payable had the statutory provisions relating to national insurance in force on 5th July 1948 been in force in that contribution week.

(3) The references in subsection (4) of section 215 to the Social Security Contributions and Benefits Act 1992 include the Social Security Act 1975; and that subsection applies to any question arising whether an employer's contribution was or would have been payable as mentioned in sub-paragraph (1) or (2).

(4) In this paragraph—

"employer's contribution" has the same meaning as in the National Insurance Act 1965, and

"corresponding contribution week", in relation to a week of employment, means a contribution week (within the meaning of that Act) of which so much as falls within the period beginning with midnight between Sunday and Monday and ending with Saturday also falls within that week of employment.

14.—(1) Subject to paragraph 13 and sub-paragraphs (2) and (3) of this paragraph, Chapter I of Part XIV applies to periods before this Act comes into force as it applies to later periods.

(2) If, during the whole or any part of a week beginning before 6th July 1964, an employee was absent from work—

(a) because he was taking part in a strike, or

(b) because of a lock-out by his employer,

the week counts as a period of employment.

(3) Any week which counted as a period of employment in the computation of a period of employment for the purposes of the Employment Protection (Consolidation) Act 1978 counts as a period of employment for the purposes of this Act; and any week which did not break the continuity of a person's employment for the purposes of that Act shall not break the continuity of a period of employment for the purposes of this Act.

[1283]

PART II
TRANSITORY PROVISIONS

15. …

Armed forces

16.—(1) If section 31 of the Trade Union Reform and Employment Rights Act 1993 has not come into force before the commencement of this Act, this Act shall have effect until the relevant commencement date as if for section 192 there were substituted—

"192 Armed forces

(1) Section 191—

(a) does not apply to service as a member of the naval, military or air forces of the Crown, but

(b) does apply to employment by an association established for the purposes of Part XI of the Reserve Forces Act 1996."

(2) The reference in sub-paragraph (1) to the relevant commencement date is a reference—

(a) if an order has been made before the commencement of this Act appointing a day after that commencement as the day on which section 31 of the Trade Union Reform and Employment Rights Act 1993 is to come into force, to the day so appointed, and

(b) otherwise, to such day as the Secretary of State may by order appoint.

17.—(1) If Part XI of the Reserve Forces Act 1996 has not come into force before the commencement of this Act, section 192 of this Act shall have effect until the relevant commencement date as if for "Part XI of the Reserve Forces Act 1996" there were substituted "Part VI of the Reserve Forces Act 1980".

(2) The reference in sub-paragraph (1) to the relevant commencement date is a reference—

(a) if an order has been made before the commencement of this Act appointing a day after that commencement as the day on which Part XI of the Reserve Forces Act 1996 is to come into force, to the day so appointed, and

(b) otherwise, to such day as the Secretary of State may by order appoint.

Disability discrimination

18. …

[1284]

NOTES

Para 15: repealed by the Statute Law (Repeals) Act 2004, as from 22 July 2004 (it was previously spent).

Para 16: s 31 of the 1993 Act was not brought into force prior to its repeal by Sch 3 to this Act, and as of 6 April 2008 no Orders had been made under para 16(2)(b); therefore, s 192 of the 1996 Act has effect as stated in para 16(1) until a date to be appointed by Order under para 16(2)(b).

Para 17: the Reserve Forces Act 1996, Pt XI was brought into force on 1 April 1997 by the Reserve Forces Act 1996 (Commencement No 1) Order 1997, SI 1997/305. That Order was made on 19 February 1997 (ie, after the commencement of this Act on 22 August 1996). As of 6 April 2008 no Orders had been made under para 17(2)(b).

Para 18: repealed by the Employment Rights (Dispute Resolution) Act 1998, s 15, Sch 2.

(*Sch 3* (*repeals and revocations*) *in so far as these are within the scope of this work, they have been incorporated at the appropriate place.*)

EMPLOYMENT RIGHTS ACT 1996, DESTINATION TABLE

DESTINATION TABLE

This table shows in column (1) the enactments repealed by the Employment Rights Act 1996 and in column (2) the provisions of that Act corresponding thereto.

In certain cases the enactment in column (1), though having a corresponding provision in column (2) is not, or not wholly, repealed as it is still required, or partly required, for the purposes of other legislation.

(1)	(2)
Betting, Gaming and Lotteries Act 1963 (c 2)	
s 31A	Unnecessary
Sch 5A, para 1(1)	ss 36(7), 45(4), 233(1)–(4), (6)
Sch 5A, para 1(2)	ss 210(1)–(3), 230(1), (2), (4), (5), 235(1)
Sch 5A, para 1(3)	s 210(3)
Sch 5A, para 1(4)	s 96(6)
Sch 5A, para 2(1)–(3)	s 36(1)–(3)
Sch 5A, para 2(4)(a)	ss 101(4), 105(8)
Sch 5A, para 2(4)(b)	s 45(9)
Sch 5A, para 2(4)(c), (d)	s 37(5)
Sch 5A, para 2(4)(e)	s 38(3)
Sch 5A, para 2(4)(f)	s 39(5)
Sch 5A, para 2(5)	Spent
Sch 5A, para 2(6)	s 45(10)
Sch 5A, para 2(7)	s 36(4)
Sch 5A, para 3(1), (2)	s 36(5), (6)
Sch 5A, para 4(1)	s 40(3)
Sch 5A, para 4(2)	s 40(1)
Sch 5A, para 4(3)	s 40(2)
Sch 5A, para 5(1)	s 41(1)
Sch 5A, para 5(2)(a)	ss 101(4), 105(8)
Sch 5A, para 5(2)(b)	s 45(9)
Sch 5A, para 5(2)(c), (d)	s 43(5)
Sch 5A, para 5(3)	Spent
Sch 5A, para 5(4)	s 45(10)
Sch 5A, para 5(5)	s 41(2)
Sch 5A, para 6	s 41(3)
Sch 5A, para 7(1)–(3)	s 101(1)–(3)
Sch 5A, para 7(4)	s 197(2)
Sch 5A, para 8	s 105(1), (4)
Sch 5A, para 9	ss 108(3), 109(2)
Sch 5A, para 10(1)–(3)	s 45(1)–(3)
Sch 5A, para 10(4)	s 45(4)
Sch 5A, para 10(5)	s 45(5)
Betting, Gaming and Lotteries Act 1963 (c 2)	
Sch 5A, para 10(6)	s 45(6)–(8)
Sch 5A, para 11(1)–(3)	s 42(1)–(3)
Sch 5A, para 11(4)	s 42(5)
Sch 5A, para 11(5)	s 42(6)
Sch 5A, para 11(6)	s 236(1), (2)
Sch 5A, para 12(1)–(4)	s 37(1)–(4)
Sch 5A, para 13(1)–(4)	s 43(1)–(4)
Sch 5A, para 14	s 38(1), (2)
Sch 5A, para 15(1)	s 39(1)–(3)
Sch 5A, para 15(2)	s 39(4)
Sch 5A, para 16	s 48(1)
Sch 5A, para 17(1)	s 203(1)
Sch 5A, para 17(2)	s 203(2)
Sch 5A, para 18	Sch 2, para 9
Sch 5A, para 19	s 104(4)
Sch 5A, para 20	s 110(2)
Sch 5A, para 22	s 196(2), (3), 205(1), 206(2)
Post Office Act 1969 (c 48)	
Sch 9, para 33	Spent
Atomic Energy Act 1971 (c 11)	
s 10(1)	Spent
Race Relations Act 1976 (c 74)	
Sch 2, paras 11(1)*, (2), (3), (5), 12, 13	Spent
Employment Protection (Consolidation) Act 1978 (c 44)	
s 1(1)	s 1(1), (2)
s 1(2)–(4)	s 1(3)–(5)
s 2(1)	s 2(1)
s 2(2)(a)	ss 2(2), 6
s 2(2)(b), (3)	ss 2(3), 6
s 2(4)–(6)	s 2(4)–(6)

* Repealed in part

(1)	(2)	(1)	(2)
Employment Protection (Consolidation) Act 1978 (c 44)		**Employment Protection (Consolidation) Act 1978 (c 44)**	
s 3(1)(a)–(c)	ss 3(1), 6	s 18(4)	s 35(4), (5)
s 3(1)(d)	s 3(5)	s 18(5)	s 35(6)
s 3(2)–(4)	s 3(2)–(4)	s 19(1)	s 64(1)–(3)
s 4(1), (2)	s 4(1)–(3)	s 19(2)	s 64(5)
s 4(3)(a)	ss 4(4), 6	s 19(3)	s 64(4)
s 4(3)(b), (4)	ss 4(5), 6	s 20	s 65
s 4(5)	s 4(6), (7)	s 21(1)	s 69(1)
s 4(6)	s 4(8)	s 21(2)	s 69(2)
s 5(1)(a)	s 198	s 21(3)	s 69(3)
s 5(1)(b)	Rep SI 1995/31	s 22(1)	s 70(1)
s 5(2)	s 5(1)	s 22(2)	s 70(2)
s 5(3)	s 5(2)	s 22(3)	s 70(3)
s 6	s 7	s 22A	s 44
s 8	s 8	s 22AA	s 47
s 9(1)	s 9(1), (2)	s 22B(1)	s 48(1)
s 9(2)–(4)	s 9(3)–(5)	s 22B(2)–(4)	s 48(2)–(4)
s 10	s 10	s 22C	s 49
s 11(1)	s 11(1)	s 29(1)(a)	s 50(1)
s 11(2)	s 11(2)	s 29(1)(b)	s 50(2)(a)
s 11(3)	Rep 1993 c 19, s 51, Sch 10	s 29(1)(ba), (bb)	s 50(5)
		s 29(1)(bc)	s 50(2)(c), (6)
s 11(4)	s 11(3)	s 29(1)(c)	s 50(2)(b)
s 11(5), (6)	s 12(1), (2)	s 29(1)(cc)	s 50(2)(d), (7)
s 11(7)	Rep 1993 c 19, s 51, Sch 10	s 29(1)(d)	s 50(2)(e), (8)
		s 29(1)(e), (ee), (ef)	s 50(2)(f), (9)
s 11(8)	s 12(3)–(5)	s 29(1)(f)	s 50(2)(g)
s 11(9)	s 11(4)	s 29(2)(a)	s 50(5)
s 12(1)	s 28(1)–(3)	s 29(2)(b)	s 50(2)(e), (8)
s 12(2)	s 28(4), (5)	s 29(2)(c)	s 50(9) (Unnecessary in part)
s 13(1), (2)	s 29(1), (2)		
s 13(3)	s 29(3)	s 29(2)(d)	Rep SI 1996/973
s 13(4)	s 29(4), (5)	s 29(3)	s 50(3)
s 14(1)	s 30(1)	s 29(4)	s 50(4)
s 14(2)	s 30(2)–(4)	s 29(5)	s 50(10)
s 14(3)	s 30(5)	s 29(6)	s 51(1)
s 15(1)	s 31(1)	s 30(1)	s 51(2)
s 15(2)	s 31(2)	s 30(2)	s 51(3), (4)
s 15(3)	s 31(3)–(5)	s 30(3)	Rep1992 c 52, s 300(1), (2), Sch 1, Sch 2, para 12
s 15(4)	s 31(6)		
s 15(5)	s 31(7)	s 31(1), (2)	s 52(1), (2)
s 16(1)–(3)	s 32(1)–(3)	s 31(3)	s 53(1)
s 16(4)	s 33	s 31(4)	s 53(2), (3)
s 17(1)–(3)	s 34(1)–(3)	s 31(5)	s 53(4)
s 18(1)–(3)	s 35(1)–(3)	s 31(6)–(8)	s 54(1)–(3)

* Repealed in part

(1) Employment Protection (Consolidation) Act 1978 (c 44)	(2)	(1) Employment Protection (Consolidation) Act 1978 (c 44)	(2)
s 31(9)	ss 53(5), 54(4)	s 47(3)	s 69(1)
s 31(10), (11)	s 53(6), (7)	s 47(4)	s 69(2)
s 31A(1)–(3)	s 55(1)–(3)	s 47(5)	s 69(3)
s 31A(4)	s 56(1)	s 47(6)	s 70(1)
s 31A(5)	s 56(2)–(4)	s 47(7)	s 70(2)
s 31A(6), (7)	s 57(1), (2)	s 47(8)	s 70(3)
s 31A(8)	s 57(3)–(5)	s 49(1)–(4)	s 86(1)–(4)
s 31A(9), (10)	s 56(5), (6)	s 49(4A)	s 86(5)
s 31A(11)	Spent	s 49(5)	s 86(6)
s 31AA(1)	s 61(1)	s 49(6)	s 235(1)
s 31AA(2), (3)	ss 62, 63	s 50(1), (2)	s 87(1), (2)
s 32	ss 50(11), 52(3), 55(4), 61(2)	s 50(3)	s 87(4)
		s 51	s 91(5)
s 33	s 71	s 52	s 91(6)
s 34(1)–(3)	s 72	s 53(1)	s 92(1), (2)
s 34(4)	s 236(3)	s 53(2)	s 92(3)
s 35(1)	s 73(1)	s 53(2A)	s 92(4)
s 35(2)	s 73(2), (4)	s 53(3)	s 92(5)
s 35(3)	s 73(3)	s 53(4)	s 93(1), (2)
s 35(4)	s 73(5)	s 53(5)	s 93(3)
s 35(5)	s 236(3)	s 54	s 94
s 36	s 74	s 55(1), (2)	s 95(1)
s 37	s 75	s 55(3)	s 95(2)
s 37A	s 76	s 55(4)	s 97(1)
s 38(1)	s 77(1), (2)	s 55(5)	ss 92(7), 97(2)
s 38(2)	s 77(3)	s 55(6)	s 97(4)
s 38A	s 78	s 55(7)(a)	s 97(3)
s 39(1)–(3)	s 79	s 55(7)(b)	s 97(5)
s 39(4)	s 236(3)	s 56	s 96(1)
s 40	s 80	s 56A	s 96(2)–(5)
s 41(1)	s 81(1), (2)	s 57(1), (2)	s 98(1), (2)
s 41(2)	s 81(3)	s 57(3)	s 98(4)–(6)
s 42(1), (2)	s 82(1), (2)	s 57(4)	s 98(3)
s 42(3)	s 82(3), (4)	s 57A	s 100
s 42(4)–(6)	s 82(5)–(7)	s 57AA	s 103
s 42(7)	s 82(8), (9)	s 59(1)	s 105(1), (4)
s 43(1), (2)	Unnecessary	s 59(2)	s 105(2), (3), (6), (7)
s 43(3), (4)	s 83	s 59(3)	s 105(9)
s 44	s 85	s 60	s 99(1)–(3)
s 45(1), (3)	s 66(1), (2)	s 60A(1)–(3)	s 104(1)–(3)
s 45(2)	s 66(3)	s 60A(4)	s 104(4)
s 46(1), (2)	s 67	s 61	s 106
s 46(3)–(6)	s 70(4)–(7)	s 63	s 107
s 47(1), (2)	s 68	s 64(1)(a)	s 108(1)

* Repealed in part

(1) Employment Protection (Consolidation) Act 1978 (c 44)	(2)
s 64(1)(b)	s 109(1)
s 64(2)	s 108(2)
s 64(3)–(5)	ss 108(3), 109(2)
s 64A	Rep 1993 c 19, ss 49(1), 51, Sch 7, para 2, Sch 10
s 65(1), (2)	s 110(3)
s 65(3)	s 110(1)
s 65(4)	s 110(2)
s 66(1)	Rep 1980 c 42, s 20(2), (3), Sch 1, para 13, Sch 2
s 66(2)	s 110(4)
s 66(3)	s 110(5)
s 67(1), (2)	s 111(1), (2)
s 67(3)	Rep 1992 c 52, s 300(1), Sch 1
s 67(4)	s 111(3), (4)
s 68	s 112
s 69(1)	ss 113, 115(1), (2)
s 69(2)	s 114(1), (2)
s 69(3)	s 114(3)
s 69(4)	s 115(1), (2)
s 69(5)	s 116(1)
s 69(6)	s 116(2)–(4)
s 70(1)	s 116(5), (6)
s 70(2)	ss 114(4), 115(3)
s 71(1)	s 117(1), (2)
s 71(1A)	s 124(3)
s 71(2), (2A), (2B)	s 117(3)–(5)
s 71(3)	s 117(6)
s 71(4)	s 117(7)
s 71(5)	s 117(8)
s 72(1)	s 118(1)
s 72(2), (3)	s 118(2), (3)
s 73(1), (3)	s 119(1), (2)
s 73(2)	s 121
s 73(4)	s 119(3)
s 73(4A), (4B)	Rep 1992 c 52, s 300(1), Sch 1
s 73(5), (6)	s 119(4), (5)
s 73(6A), (6B)	s 120(1)
s 73(6C)	s 120(2)
s 73(6D)	s 236(3)

(1) Employment Protection (Consolidation) Act 1978 (c 44)	(2)
s 73(7)	Rep 1982 c 46, ss 4, 21(3), Sch 4
s 73(7A)	s 122(1)
s 73(7B)	s 122(2)
s 73(7C)	s 122(3)
s 73(8)	Rep 1980 c 42, ss 9(5), 20(3), Sch 2
s 73(9)	s 122(4)
s 74(1)–(7)	s 123
s 74(8)	s 124(4)
s 75(1)	s 124(1)
s 75(2)	ss 124(2), 236(3)
s 75(3)	s 124(5)
s 75A(1)–(7)	s 125
s 75A(8)	s 236(3)
s 76(1)	s 126
s 76(2)	Rep 1994 c 10, ss 1(2), 3(2), Schedule
s 77	s 128
s 77A(1)	s 129(1)
s 77A(2)	s 129(2), (3)
s 77A(3)	s 129(4)
s 77A(4)	s 129(5)
s 77A(5)	s 129(6)–(8)
s 77A(6)	s 129(9)
s 78	s 130
s 78A	s 131
s 79(1)	s 132(1), (2)
s 79(2)	s 132(3)
s 79(3)	s 132(4)
s 79(4), (5)	s 132(5)
s 79(6)	s 132(6)
s 80	s 134
s 81(1)	ss 135, 155, 162(1), (2)
s 81(2)	s 139(1), (2)
s 81(2A)	s 139(3)
s 81(3)	s 139(6)
s 81(4)	s 155
s 82(1)	s 156(1)
s 82(2)	s 140(1)
s 82(3)	s 141(1)
s 82(4)	s 146(2)
s 82(5)	s 141(2), (3)
s 82(6)	s 141(4)

* Repealed in part

(1)	(2)	(1)	(2)
Employment Protection (Consolidation) Act 1978 (c 44)		Employment Protection (Consolidation) Act 1978 (c 44)	
s 82(7)	s 146(1)	s 98(3)	s 158(4)
s 83	s 136(1), (2)	s 99(1)	ss 159, 191(6)
s 84(1)	s 138(1)	s 99(2)	s 160(1)
s 84(2)	s 146(2)	s 100	s 161
s 84(3), (6)	s 138(2), (4), (5)	s 101(1)	s 164(1)
s 84(4)	s 138(3)	s 101(2)	s 164(2), (3)
s 84(5)	s 138(6)	s 102(1), (2)	s 165(1), (2)
s 84(7)	s 146(1)	s 102(3)	s 165(3), (4)
s 85(1), (2)	s 136(3)	s 106(1)	s 166(1)
s 85(3)	s 142(1), (2)	s 106(1A), (1B)	s 166(2), (3)
s 85(4)	s 142(3), (4)	s 106(2)	s 167(1), (2)
s 85(5)	s 136(4)	s 106(3)	s 167(3), (4)
s 86	s 137(1)	s 106(4)	Rep 1989 c 38, s 29(3), (4), Sch 6, para 21, Sch 7, Pt II
s 87	s 147		
s 88(1)	s 148		
s 88(2)	ss 150(1), (2), 151	s 106(5), (6)	s 166(5)–(7)
s 88(3)	s 152(1)	s 106(7)	s 166(4)
s 88(4)	ss 149, 152(1)	s 107(1)–(3)	s 169(1)–(3)
s 89(1)	s 152(2)	s 107(4), (5)	s 169(4)
s 89(2), (3)	s 154	s 108	s 170
s 89(4)	s 149	s 110(1), (2)	s 143(1), (2)
s 89(5)	s 150(3)	s 110(3)	s 144(1)
s 89(6)	s 150(4)	s 110(4)	s 143(7), (8)
s 90(1)	s 145(1)–(4)	s 110(5)	s 143(3), (4)
s 90(2)	s 153	s 110(6)	s 143(5), (6)
s 90(3)	s 145(5), (6)	s 110(7)	s 144(4)
s 91(1)–(3)	s 163(1)–(3)	s 110(8)	s 144(2)
s 92(1)	s 140(2)	s 110(9)	s 144(3)
s 92(2)	s 140(5)	s 111(1)	s 171(3)
s 92(3)	s 140(3), (4)	s 111(2)	Spent
s 92(4)	s 136(1), (2)	s 111(3)	s 177(3)
s 92(5)	s 235(4), (5)	s 111(4)–(6)	Spent
s 93(1)	s 136(5)	s 112(1)	s 177(2)
s 93(2)	s 139(4)	s 112(2)	s 177(1)
s 93(3)	s 139(5)	s 114	s 160(2), (3)
s 93(4)	Rep 1993 c 19, s 51, Sch 10	s 115(1)	s 171(2)
		s 115(2)	s 171(1)
s 96(1)	s 157(2), (3)	s 115(3)	Spent
s 96(2)	s 157(4)	s 116	s 172
s 96(3)(a)	s 157(1)	s 117(1), (2), (4)	s 173
s 96(3)(b)	s 163(4)	s 117(2A), (2B)	Rep 1989 c 38, s 29(4), Sch 7, Pt II
s 96(4)	s 157(5)		
s 98(1)	s 158(1), (2)	s 117(3)	s 179(6)
s 98(2)	s 158(3)	s 118(1)	s 178(2)

* Repealed in part

(1) Employment Protection (Consolidation) Act 1978 (c 44)	(2)
s 118(2)	s 178(1)
s 119(1)–(5)	s 179(1)–(5)
s 120	s 180
s 122(1)	s 182
s 122(2)	s 185
s 122(3)	s 184(1)
s 122(4)	ss 27(1), 184(2)
s 122(5)	s 186(1)
s 122(6)	s 186(2)
s 122(7), (8)	s 184(4)
s 122(9), (10)	s 187(1), (3)–(5)
s 122(11)	s 187(2)
s 124(1)	s 188(1), (2)
s 124(2)	Rep 1993 c 48, s 188(1), Sch 5, Pt I
s 124(3)	s 188(3)
s 125(1), (2)	s 189(1), (2)
s 125(2A)	s 189(3), (4)
s 125(3), (3A), (3B)	Rep 1993 c 48, s 188(1), Sch 5, Pt I
s 125(4)	s 189(5)
s 126(1)–(4)	s 190(1)–(4)
s 127(1), (2)	s 183
s 127(3)	s 184(3)
s 129	s 205(1)
s 137(1)	s 201(2)
s 137(2)	s 201(1), (5)
s 137(3)	s 201(3)
s 137(4)	s 201(4)
s 137(5)	s 201(5)
s 138(1)	s 191(1), (2)
s 138(2)	s 191(3)
s 138(3)	s 192(1)
s 138(4)	s 193
s 138(5)	Rep 1990 c 19, s 66(2), Sch 10
s 138(7)*	s 191(4)
s 138(8)	s 191(5)
s 138A(1)–(4)	s 192(2)–(5)
s 138A(5)	s 192(7)
s 138A(6)	s 236(3)
s 138A(7)	s 192(6), (8)
s 139(1)*	s 195(1)–(3)
s 139(2), (3)	s 195(4), (5)

(1) Employment Protection (Consolidation) Act 1978 (c 44)	(2)
s 139(4)–(6)	s 195(6)–(8)
s 139(7)	s 195(9), (10)
s 139(8), (9)	s 195(11), (12)
s 139A(1)	s 194(1), (2)
s 139A(2)	s 194(4)
s 139A(3)(b)	s 194(3)
s 139A(4)	s 194(5)
s 139A(5)	s 194(4), (6)
s 139A(6)	s 194(7)
s 140(1)	s 203(1)
s 140(2)	s 203(2)
s 140(3), (4)	s 203(3), (4)
s 141(1)	s 196(1)
s 141(2)	s 196(2), (3)
s 141(2A)	s 196(7)
s 141(3), (4)	s 196(6)
s 141(5)	s 196(5)
s 142(1)	s 197(1)
s 142(2)–(4)	s 197(3)–(5)
s 144(1)	s 199(1)
s 144(2)	s 199(2)
s 144(3)	s 199(6)
s 144(4), (5)	s 199(4), (5)
s 146(1)	Rep 1982 c 46, s 21, Sch 3, Pt I, para 6, Sch 4
s 146(2)	s 200(1)
s 146(3)	s 200(2)
s 146(4)–(8)	Rep SI 1995/31
s 146A	s 202
s 148(1)–(5)	s 208(1)–(5)
s 148(6)	s 208(6), (7)
s 149(1)	s 209(1), (4), (5)
s 149(2)	s 209(2), (3)
s 149(2A)	s 209(7)
s 149(3)	s 209(8)
s 149(4)	s 236(3)
s 149(5)	s 236(4)
s 150	Unnecessary
s 151(1)	s 210(1), (2)
s 151(2)	s 210(3)
s 151(3)–(5)	s 211
s 151(6)(a)	s 215(3)
s 151(6)(b)	s 216(2), (3)

* Repealed in part

(1)	(2)
Employment Protection (Consolidation) Act 1978 (c 44)	
s 151(6)(c)	s 217
s 152	—
s 153(1)	ss 230(1), (2), (4), (5), 235(1) (Unnecessary in part)
s 153(2)	s 235(3)
s 153(3)	Rep 1993 c 19, s 51, Sch 10
s 153(4)	s 231
s 153(4A)	s 235(2)
s 153(5)	s 204
s 153(6), (7)	Unnecessary
s 154(1), (2)	s 236(1), (2)
s 154(3)	s 236(5)
s 154(4)	Unnecessary
s 155(1), (2)	s 190(5), (6)
s 156(1)	Rep 1986 c 50, s 86(2), Sch 11
s 156(2)	s 237 (Spent in part)
s 156(3)	Spent
s 157(1)	s 238(1), (2)
s 157(2)	Rep 1990 c 38, s 16(2), Sch 3
s 157(3)	s 238(3)–(5)
s 157(4)	s 238(6)
s 158(1), (2)	s 239(1), (2)
s 158(3)	s 239(3), (4)
s 158(4)	s 239(5)
ss 159, 160	Unnecessary
Sch 1	s 64(1)–(3)
Sch 2, Pt I, para 1	ss 97(6), 98(4)–(6), 99(4), 108(3), 109(2), 110(2), 114(5), 115(4), 119(6)
Sch 2, Pt I, para 2(1)	s 98(4)–(6)
Sch 2, Pt I, para 2(2)	s 99(4)
Sch 2, Pt I, para 2(3)(a)	s 97(6)
Sch 2, Pt I, para 2(3)(b)	ss 114(5), 115(4)
Sch 2, Pt I, para 2(4)	ss 97(6), 108(3), 109(2), 110(2), 119(6), 196(4), 199(3), 226(3), 227(3), (4)
Sch 2, Pt I, para 2(5)	s 226(3)
Sch 2, Pt II, para 3	Unnecessary
Sch 2, Pt II, para 4(1)(a)	s 145(7)
Sch 2, Pt II, para 4(1)(b), (c)	s 146(3)
Sch 2, Pt II, para 4(2)	s 137(1)
Sch 2, Pt II, para 4(3)	ss 156(2), 157(6), 162(7), 199(3), 226(5), 227(3), (4)
Sch 2, Pt II, para 4(4)	s 226(5)
Sch 2, Pt II, para 5	s 137(2)
Sch 2, Pt III, para 6(1) (2)	s 84(1)
Sch 2, Pt III, para 6(3)	ss 108(3), 109(2), 110(2), 196(4), 199(3)
Sch 2, Pt III, para 6(4)(a)	s 127
Sch 2, Pt III, para 6(4)(b)	s 84(2)
Sch 2, Pt III, para 7(1)	s 209(6)
Sch 2, Pt III, para 7(2)	s 236(3)
Sch 3, para 1	s 87(3)
Sch 3, para 2(1)	s 88(1)
Sch 3, para 2(2)	s 88(2)
Sch 3, para 2(3)	s 88(3)
Sch 3, para 3(1), (2)	s 89(1), (2)
Sch 3, para 3(3)	s 89(3), (4)
Sch 3, para 3(4)	s 89(5)
Sch 3, para 4	s 90
Sch 3, para 5	s 91(1)
Sch 3, para 6	s 91(2)
Sch 3, para 7	s 91(3), (4)
Sch 4, paras 1, 2	s 162(1), (2)
Sch 4, para 3	s 162(3)
Sch 4, para 4	s 162(4), (5)
Sch 4, para 5	s 162(6)
Sch 4, para 6	s 162(8)
Sch 4, para 7	Rep 1982 c 46, ss 20, 21(3), Sch 2, para 6(5), Sch 4
Sch 7	s 168
Sch 8	s 173
Sch 12, Pt I, para 1	s 206(2)
Sch 12, Pt I, para 2	s 206(1), (3)
Sch 12, Pt I, para 3(1)	s 206(4), (5)
Sch 12, Pt I, para 3(2)	s 206(6)
Sch 12, Pt I, para 4(1)	s 206(7), (8)
Sch 12, Pt I, para 4(2)	s 206(9)

* Repealed in part

(1)	(2)	(1)	(2)
Employment Protection (Consolidation) Act 1978 (c 44)		Employment Protection (Consolidation) Act 1978 (c 44)	
Sch 12, Pt I, para 5	s 207(1)	Sch 13, para 14(3)	s 215(3)
Sch 12, Pt I, para 6	s 207(3)	Sch 13, para 14(4)	s 215(4), (5)
Sch 12, Pt II, paras 7, 8	s 133(1)	Sch 13, para 14(5)	cf Sch 2, Pt I, para 13
Sch 12, Pt II, para 9	s 133(2)	Sch 13, para 14(6)	s 215(6)
Sch 12, Pt II, para 10	s 133(3), (4)	Sch 13, para 15(1)	s 216(1)
Sch 12, Pt II, para 11	s 133(5)	Sch 13, para 15(2), (3)	s 216(2)
Sch 12, Pt III, para 12	ss 174(1), 175(1), (2)	Sch 13, para 15(4)	s 216(3)
Sch 12, Pt III, para 13	Rep 1993 c 19, s 51, Sch 10	Sch 13, para 16(1)	s 217
		Sch 13, para 16(2)	Rep 1985 c 17, s 21, Sch 5
Sch 12, Pt III, paras 14, 15	s 174(2), (3), (5)	Sch 13, para 17(1)	s 218(1)
Sch 12, Pt III, para 16	s 174(4)	Sch 13, para 17(2)–(5)	s 218(2)–(5)
Sch 12, Pt III, para 17	s 175(1), (2)	Sch 13, para 18	s 218(6)
		Sch 13, para 18A	s 218(7)
Sch 12, Pt III, paras 18, 19	s 175(3), (4)	Sch 13, para 18B	s 218(8)–(10)
		Sch 13, para 19(1)	s 191(1), (2)
Sch 12, Pt III, para 20(1), (2)	s 175(5), (6)	Sch 13, para 19(2)	s 191(3)
Sch 12, Pt III, para 21	s 174(6)	Sch 13, para 19(3)	s 192(1)
		Sch 13, para 19(4)	Rep SI 1995/31
Sch 12, Pt IV, para 22(1), (2)	s 176(1), (2)	Sch 13, para 19(5)	s 191(4)
Sch 12, Pt IV, para 23(1)	s 176(3)	Sch 13, para 20	s 219
		Sch 13, paras 21, 22	Cf Sch 2, para 14(1), (2)
Sch 12, Pt IV, paras 23(2), 24	s 176(4)	Sch 13, para 23	Saved, Sch 2, para 6
		Sch 13, para 24(1)	s 235(1), (4), (5)
Sch 12, Pt IV, paras 25–27	s 176(5)–(7)	Sch 13, para 24(2)	Rep SI 1995/31
Sch 12, Pt IV, para 28	s 207(2)	Sch 14, Pt I, para 1	s 234(1), (2)
Sch 13, para 1(1)	s 210(4)	Sch 14, Pt I, para 2	s 234(3)
Sch 13, para 1(2)	s 215(1)	Sch 14, Pt II, para 3	s 221(1)–(4)
Sch 13, para 1(3)	s 210(5)	Sch 14, Pt II, para 4(1), (2)	s 222(1), (2)
Sch 13, para 3	Rep SI 1995/31 (there was no para 2)		
Sch 13, para 4	s 212(1)	Sch 14, Pt II, para 4(3), (4)	s 222(3), (4)
Sch 13, paras 5–8	Rep SI 1995/31	Sch 14, Pt II, para 5(1)	s 223(1), (2)
Sch 13, para 9(1), (2)	s 212(3), (4)		
Sch 13, para 10	s 212(2)	Sch 14, Pt II, para 5(2), (3)	s 223(3)
Sch 13, para 11(1)	s 213(1)	Sch 14, Pt II, para 6	s 224(1)–(3)
Sch 13, para 11(2), (3)	s 213(2), (3)		
Sch 13, para 12(1), (2)	s 214(1)–(4)	Sch 14, Pt II, para 7(1)(a)	s 225(1)
Sch 13, para 12(3)	s 214(5)		
Sch 13, para 13	Rep 1982 c 46, s 21, Sch 4	Sch 14, Pt II, para 7(1)(b)	s 225(5)
		Sch 14, Pt II, para 7(1)(c)	s 225(2)
Sch 13, para 14(1)(a), (b)(ia)	s 215(2)		
		Sch 14, Pt II, para 7(1)(cc)	s 225(3)
Sch 13, para 14(1)(b)(i)–(iii), (2)	Cf Sch 2, Pt I, para 13		

* Repealed in part

(1)	(2)
Employment Protection (Consolidation) Act 1978 (c 44)	
Sch 14, Pt II, para 7(1)(ccc)	s 225(4)
Sch 14, Pt II, para 7(1)(d)	Rep 1986 c 50, s 86(2), Sch 11
Sch 14, Pt II, para 7(1)(e)	s 226(1)
Sch 14, Pt II, para 7(1)(ea)	s 225(5)
Sch 14, Pt II, para 7(1)(f), (g)	s 226(2)
Sch 14, Pt II, para 7(1)(h)	s 226(3)
Sch 14, Pt II, para 7(1)(i)	s 226(3), (6)
Sch 14, Pt II, para 7(1)(ia), (ib)	s 226(2)
Sch 14, Pt II, para 7(1)(j)	s 226(4)
Sch 14, Pt II, para 7(1)(k)	s 226(5)
Sch 14, Pt II, para 7(1)(l)	s 226(5), (6)
Sch 14, Pt II, para 7(2)	s 226(6)
Sch 14, Pt II, para 8(1), (2)	s 227(1), (2)
Sch 14, Pt II, para 8(3), (4)	s 227(3), (4)
Sch 14, Pt II, para 9	s 228(1)–(3)
Sch 14, Pt II, para 10	s 229(1)
Sch 14, Pt II, para 11	s 229(2)
Sch 14, Pt II, para 12	s 228(4)
Sch 15	Superseded by Sch 2; repealed in part; spent in part
Sch 16	Superseded by Sch 1; repealed in part; spent in part
Sch 17	Spent
Reserve Forces Act 1980 (c 9)	
Sch 9, para 17	s 192(1)
Education Act 1980 (c 20)	
Sch 1, para 30	Unnecessary
Employment Act 1980 (c 42)	
s 6	s 98(4)–(6)
s 8(2)	s 197(1)
s 9(1)	Unnecessary
s 9(2)	s 119(1)
s 9(3)	s 119(2)
s 9(4)	s 122(1), (2)
s 9(5)	Spent
s 12	s 96(2)–(5)
s 13	ss 55(1)–(3), 56, 57
s 14(1), (2)	s 31(2)
ss 20, 21	Spent in part; unnecessary in part
Sch 1, para 1	Spent
Sch 1, para 8	s 31(7)
Sch 1, para 11	s 96(1)
Sch 1, para 13(a)	Spent
Sch 1, para 13(b)	s 110(4)
Sch 1, para 20	Spent
Sch 1, para 22	Spent in part; otherwise unnecessary
Sch 1, para 23	s 98(4)–(6)
Sch 1, para 25	Spent
Sch 1, para 31	s 212(2)
Sch 1, para 33	s 225(3)
Sch 2	Spent
Magistrates' Courts Act 1980 (c 43)	
Sch 7, para 175	s 169(4)
Finance Act 1980 (c 48)	
Sch 19, para 5(4)	Spent
New Towns Act 1981 (c 64)	
s 54(6)	Spent
Civil Aviation Act 1982 (c 16)	
Sch 3, paras 6, 8(1)	Spent
Oil and Gas Enterprise Act 1982 (c 23)	
Sch 3, para 40	Unnecessary
Social Security and Housing Benefits Act 1982 (c 24)	
Sch 2, para 13	ss 88(2), 89(3), (4)

* Repealed in part

(1)	(2)
Employment Act 1982 (c 46)	
ss 20, 21(2), (3)	Spent in part; otherwise unnecessary
Sch 2, para 1	s 29(1), (2)
Sch 2, para 2	s 65
Sch 2, para 3(1)	ss 86(1)–(3), 87(1), (2)
Sch 2, para 3(2)	s 86(4)
Sch 2, para 3(3)	s 86(5)
Sch 2, para 4	s 92(3)
Sch 2, para 5(1)(a)	Spent
Sch 2, para 5(1)(b)	s 108(2)
Sch 2, para 5(2)	Spent
Sch 2, para 6(2)	Spent
Sch 2, para 6(4)	s 167(2)
Sch 2, para 6(5)	Spent
Sch 2, para 7(1)	ss 210(1)–(3), 211, 215(3), 216(2), (3), 217
Sch 2, para 7(2)	ss 210(4), (5), 215(1)
Sch 2, para 9(1)	s 209(2), (5)
Sch 2, para 9(2)	s 238(1), (2)
Sch 3, Pt I, para 1	ss 92(7), 97(2)–(5)
Sch 3, Pt I, para 2(1)	s 139(3)
Sch 3, Pt I, para 2(2)	s 218(1)
Sch 3, Pt I, para 2(3)	s 218(7)
Sch 3, Pt I, para 4	s 184(1)
Sch 3, Pt I, para 6	Spent
Sch 3, Pt II, para 15	s 29(3)
Sch 3, Pt II, para 21	s 112
Sch 3, Pt II, para 22	s 117(3), (8)
Sch 3, Pt II, para 23	s 123(3)
Sch 3, Pt II, para 25	s 209(2)
Sch 3, Pt II, para 26	Unnecessary
Sch 3, Pt II, para 27(1)	Spent
Sch 3, Pt II, para 28	s 133(1)
Sch 3, Pt II, para 29	s 213(1)
Sch 3, Pt II, para 30(1)	s 227(3)
Sch 3, Pt II, para 30(2)(a), (b)	s 226(3)
Sch 3, Pt II, para 30(3)	s 227(3)
Sch 4	Spent
Water Act 1983 (c 23)	
Sch 2, Pt I, para 8(1)(b)	Spent
Health and Social Services and Social Security Adjudications Act 1983 (c 41)	
Sch 9, Pt I, para 25	Spent
Mental Health (Scotland) Act 1984 (c 36)	
s 126(2)(c)	Spent
Reserve Forces (Safeguard of Employment) Act 1985 (c 17)	
Sch 4, para 6	s 217
Local Government Act 1985 (c 51)	
ss 53*, 55*, 59*	Spent
Insolvency Act 1985 (c 65)	
s 218(1)	Unnecessary
s 218(2)	s 182
s 218(3)	s 185
s 218(4)	ss 27(1), 184(2)
s 218(5)	s 184(4)
s 218(6)(a)	s 187(4)
s 218(6)(b)	s 187(5)
Sch 8, para 31(1)	Unnecessary
Sch 8, para 31(2)(a)	s 166(6)
Sch 8, para 31(2)(b)	s 166(7)
Sch 8, para 31(5)(a)	s 183(2)
Sch 8, para 31(5)(b)	s 183(3)
Bankruptcy (Scotland) Act 1985 (c 66)	
Sch 7, Pt I, para 14(1), (2), (4)	ss 16(6), 183(2), 184(4)
Housing (Consequential Provisions) Act 1986 (c 71)	
Sch 4, para 7(2)(a)	Spent
Insolvency Act 1986 (c 45)	
Sch 14*	ss 166(6), (7), 183(2), (3), 184(4), 187(5)
Legal Aid (Scotland) Act 1986 (c 47)	
Sch 1, para 10(2)(a)*	Spent
Wages Act 1986 (c 48)	
s 1(1)	s 13(1)
s 1(2)	s 15(1)
s 1(3)	ss 13(2), 15(2)
s 1(4)	ss 13(5), (6), 15(3), (4)
s 1(5)(a)	ss 14(1), 16(1)

* Repealed in part

(1)	(2)	(1)	(2)
Wages Act 1986 (c 48)		Wages Act 1986 (c 48)	
s 1(5)(b)	ss 14(2), 16(2)	s 9(5)	s 191(4)
s 1(5)(c)	s 14(3)	s 10	s 201
s 1(5)(d)	s 14(4)	s 11	Spent
s 1(5)(e)	ss 14(5), 16(3)	ss 28, 29	Unnecessary; spent
s 1(5)(f)	ss 14(6), 16(4)	s 30(1)	s 196(2), (3)
s 1(6)	s 13(7)	s 30(2)	s 191(5)
s 2(1)	s 18(1)	s 30(3)	s 199(1)
s 2(2)	s 17(1)–(3), (6)	ss 32, 33	Spent in part; otherwise unnecessary
s 2(3)	s 18(2), (3)		
s 2(4)	s 19(1)	Sch 1	Spent
s 2(5)	s 19(2)–(4)	Sch 4, para 4	Superseded by Sch 1, para 3
s 3(1)–(3)	s 20(1)–(3)		
s 3(4), (5)	s 21(1), (2)	Sch 5	Spent
s 3(6)	s 20(4)	Sch 6, para 10	Unnecessary
s 4(1)–(3)	s 22(1)–(3)	Social Security Act 1986 (c 50)	
s 4(4)	s 20(5)		
s 4(5)	ss 21(3), 22(4)	Sch 10, Pt IV, para 76	Spent
s 4(6)	s 17(4), (5)	Sch 10, Pt IV, para 81	s 27(1)
s 5(1)	s 23(1)	Sex Discrimination Act 1986 (c 59)	
s 5(2)	s 23(2), (4)		
s 5(3)	s 23(3)	s 3(1)	s 109(1)
s 5(3A)	Rep 1992 c 52, s 300(1), Sch 1	s 3(2)	s 119(4)
		s 3(3)	Spent
s 5(4)	s 24	Housing (Scotland) Act 1987 (c 26)	
s 5(5)	s 25(1), (2)		
s 5(6)–(8)	s 25(3)–(5)	Sch 22, Pt II, para 10(2)(a)	Spent
s 6(1)	s 205(2)		
s 6(2)	s 26	Income and Corporation Taxes Act 1988 (c 1)	
s 6(3)	s 203(1), (2)		
s 6(4), (5)	s 203(3), (4)	ss 150(b), 579*, 580(2)	Spent
s 6(6)	s 231	Norfolk and Suffolk Broads Act 1988 (c 4)	
s 7(1)	s 27(1)		
s 7(2), (3)	s 27(2), (3)	Sch 6, para 19	s 50(5)
s 7(4)	s 27(5)	Dartford-Thurrock Crossing Act 1988 (c 20)	
s 8(1)	ss 27(4), 230(3)–(5), 235(1) (Unnecessary in part)	Sch 5, Pt I, para 2(2)	Spent
s 8(2)	s 230(3)	Legal Aid Act 1988 (c 34)	
s 8(3), (4)	s 13(3), (4)		
s 8(5)	s 15(5)	Sch 7, para 7(3)*	Spent
s 9(1)	s 191(1), (2)	Education Reform Act 1988 (c 40)	
s 9(2)	s 191(3)		
s 9(3)	Rep 1993 c 19, s 51, Sch 10	s 173*	Spent
		s 178(1), (2)	Spent
s 9(4)	s 192(1)		

* Repealed in part

(1)	(2)
Education Reform Act 1988 (c 40)	
Sch 12, Pt I, para 23	s 50(2)(f), (9)
Sch 12, Pt III, para 80...	s 50(2)(f), (9)
Housing (Scotland) Act 1988 (c 26)	
Sch 1, para 12(2)	Spent
Housing Act 1988 (c 50)	
Sch 5, para 19(2)*	Spent
Dock Work Act 1989 (c 13)	
s 6(2)............................	Spent
s 7(4)............................	s 199(3)
Sch 2, paras 6, 7	Spent
Water Act 1989 (c 15)	
s 194(7)*......................	Unnecessary
Sch 25, para 56	s 50(2)(g)
Electricity Act 1989 (c 29)	
s 56(2)...........................	Spent
Employment Act 1989 (c 38)	
s 15(1)...........................	s 92(3)
s 15(2)...........................	s 209(5)
s 16(1)...........................	s 156(1)
s 16(2)...........................	s 162(5)
s 17	Spent
s 18(1)...........................	Unnecessary
s 18(2)...........................	s 187(2)
s 18(3)...........................	Spent
s 19(1)...........................	s 189(2)–(4)
ss 27(1)*, 29(1)*, 30(3)(f)	Spent
Sch 6, para 21(1)	Spent
Sch 6, para 21(2)	s 166(2), (3)
Sch 6, para 21(3)	s 167(2)
Sch 6, para 21(4)	Spent
Sch 6, para 22	s 170
Sch 6, para 23	s 183(2)
Sch 6, para 24	Unnecessary
Sch 6, para 25	s 168
Sch 9, paras 3–5	Spent
Self-Governing Schools etc (Scotland) Act 1989 (c 39)	
Sch 10, para 7	s 50(9)
National Health Service and Community Care Act 1990 (c 19)	
Sch 9, para 20	s 50(2)(e), (8)
Enterprise and New Towns (Scotland) Act 1990 (c 35)	
Sch 1, para 17(2)	Spent
Employment Act 1990 (c 38)	
ss 13(1), (2), (4), 16, 17*	Spent in part; otherwise unnecessary
Sch 2, para 1(1)	Spent
Sch 2, para 1(3)	s 167(1), (4)
Sch 2, para 1(4)	ss 182, 189(5)
Sch 2, para 1(5)(a)........	s 237
Sch 2, para 1(5)(b)	Spent
Sch 2, para 1(6)	s 239(2)
Sch 3	Spent
Environmental Protection Act 1990 (c 43)	
Sch 10, para 16*	Spent
Natural Heritage (Scotland) Act 1991 (c 28)	
Sch 4, para 5*	Spent
Social Security (Consequential Provisions) Act 1992 (c 6)	
Sch 2, para 51(1)	s 215(2), (4), (5)
Sch 2, para 74	s 27(1)
Further and Higher Education Act 1992 (c 13)	
Sch 8, Pt II, para 89	s 50(2)(f), (9)
Trade Union and Labour Relations (Consolidation) Act 1992 (c 52)	
Sch 2, para 11	s 50(4)
Sch 2, para 12(a)	s 51(2)
Sch 2, para 12(b)	s 51(3), (4)
Sch 2, para 12(c)	Spent

* Repealed in part

(1)	(2)
Trade Union and Labour Relations (Consolidation) Act 1992 (c 52)	
Sch 2, para 13	ss 50(11), 52(3), 55(4), 61(2)
Sch 2, para 14	s 98(4)–(6)
Sch 2, para 15†	s 117(4)
Sch 2, para 16	s 118(1)
Sch 2, para 17	s 122(3)
Sch 2, para 18	ss 27(1), 184(2), 185
Sch 2, para 21(1)	Spent
Sch 2, para 21(2)	s 235(1)
Sch 2, para 21(3)	s 235(2)
Sch 2, para 22	s 98(4)–(6)
Sch 2, para 23	s 91(1)
Sch 2, paras 29(2), 30, 33	Unnecessary
Sch 2, para 34(1), (2)	s 27(1)
Trade Union Reform and Employment Rights Act 1993 (c 19)	
s 23(1)	Unnecessary
s 23(2)	ss 71, 72, 73, 74, 75, 76, 77, 78, 236(3)
s 24(1)	s 99(1)–(3)
s 24(2)	s 105(1)–(3), (6), (7)
s 24(3)	ss 108(3), 109(2)
s 24(4)	s 92(4)
ss 25, 26, 28	Unnecessary
s 29(1)	s 104
s 29(2)	s 105(7)
s 29(3)	ss 108(3), 109(2)
s 30(1)	Unnecessary
s 30(2)(a)	s 117(1), (2)
s 30(2)(b)	s 124(3)
s 30(3)(a)	s 123(1)
s 30(3)(b)	s 124(4)
s 30(4)	Unnecessary
s 31(1)	s 192(1)
s 31(2)	ss 192(2)–(8), 236(3)
s 39(1)(a)	s 203(2)
s 39(1)(b)	s 203(3), (4)
s 39(2)*	Unnecessary
s 54*	Spent
Sch 2	ss 79, 80, 81, 82, 83, 85, 236(3)
Sch 3	ss 66, 67, 68, 69, 70

(1)	(2)
Trade Union Reform and Employment Rights Act 1993 (c 19)	
Sch 4	ss 1–7, 198
Sch 5, para 1	ss 44, 48(1), 49
Sch 5, para 2	s 98(4)–(6)
Sch 5, para 3	s 100
Sch 5, para 4	s 105(3)
Sch 5, para 5	ss 108(3), 109(2)
Sch 5, para 6(a)	s 117(3)
Sch 5, para 6(b)	s 117(4)
Sch 5, para 7	s 118(2), (3)
Sch 5, para 8(a)	s 119(1)
Sch 5, para 8(b)	ss 120, 236(3)
Sch 5, para 8(c)	s 122(3)
Sch 5, para 9	ss 125, 236(3)
Sch 5, para 10	ss 128, 129, 130, 131, 132
Sch 6, para 3(a)	s 203(2)
Sch 6, para 3(b)	ss 203(3), (4), 231
Sch 7, para 2	Spent
Sch 7, para 3(a)	Spent
Sch 7, para 3(b)	s 193(1), (2)
Sch 7, para 4	Spent
Sch 7, para 5	s 202
Sch 7, para 11	s 194
Sch 7, para 13	s 209(7)
Sch 7, para 14(a)–(c)	s 219(2)
Sch 7, para 14(d)	s 219(2)–(4)
Sch 7, para 16(a)	s 236(3)
Sch 7, para 16(b)	s 236(4)
Sch 8, para 10(a)	s 11(1)
Sch 8, para 10(b)	s 11(3)
Sch 8, para 10(c)	s 11(4)
Sch 8, para 11	s 93(1), (2)
Sch 8, para 12	s 96(1)
Sch 8, para 13	s 96(2)–(5)
Sch 8, para 14(a)	s 105(1), (4)
Sch 8, para 14(b)	Rep 1994 c 40, s 81(1), Sch 17
Sch 8, para 14(c)	s 105(9)
Sch 8, para 15	s 106(2), (3)
Sch 8, para 16	s 110(2)
Sch 8, para 17	s 137(1)
Sch 8, para 18	ss 27(1), 184(2)
Sch 8, para 21	s 203(2)
Sch 8, para 22	s 196(1)

* Repealed in part

(1)	(2)
Trade Union Reform and Employment Rights Act 1993 (c 19)	
Sch 8, para 23	s 199(1)
Sch 8, para 24	s 209(2)
Sch 8, para 25(a)(i)–(iv)	s 235(1)
Sch 8, para 25(a)(v)	Unnecessary
Sch 8, para 25(b)	s 204
Sch 8, para 26(a)(i)	s 98(4)–(6)
Sch 8, para 26(a)(ii)	s 99(4)
Sch 8, para 26(a)(iii)	s 226(3)
Sch 8, para 26(b)(i)	s 146(3)
Sch 8, para 26(b)(ii)	s 226(5)
Sch 8, para 26(c)	s 137(2)
Sch 8, para 26(d)	s 84(1)
Sch 8, para 26(e)	s 209(6)
Sch 8, para 27(a)(i), (ii)	s 88(1)
Sch 8, para 27(a)(iii)	s 88(2)
Sch 8, para 27(b)	s 89(3), (4)
Sch 8, para 31(a)	s 212(3)
Sch 8, para 31(b)	s 212(2)
Sch 8, para 32(a)	s 225(5)
Sch 8, para 32(b)	s 226(2)
Sch 8, para 35	Unnecessary
Sch 8, para 36	ss 196(2), (3), 199(1)
Sch 8, paras 37, 67	Unnecessary
Sch 9, para 3	Unnecessary
Pension Schemes Act 1993 (c 48)	
s 164(6)	Spent
Sch 8, para 11(1)	s 11(3)
Sch 8, para 45(a)	Unnecessary
Race Relations (Remedies) Act 1994 (c 10)	
s 1(2)	Spent
Social Security (Incapacity for Work) Act 1994 (c 18)	
Sch 1, Pt II, para 54	s 90(1)
Sunday Trading Act 1994 (c 20)	
Sch 4, para 1(1)	ss 36(7), 45(4), 232(1)–(3), (6)–(8)
Sch 4, para 1(2), (3)	s 232(4), (5)
Sch 4, para 1(4)	ss 210(1)–(3), 230(1), (2), (4), (5), 235(1)

(1)	(2)
Sunday Trading Act 1994 (c 20)	
Sch 4, para 1(5)	s 210(3)
Sch 4, para 1(6)	s 96(6)
Sch 4, para 2(1)–(3)	s 36(1)–(3)
Sch 4, para 2(4)(a)	ss 101(4), 105(8)
Sch 4, para 2(4)(b)	s 45(9)
Sch 4, para 2(4)(c), (d)	s 37(5)
Sch 4, para 2(4)(e)	s 38(3)
Sch 4, para 2(4)(f)	s 39(5)
Sch 4, para 2(5)	Unnecessary
Sch 4, para 2(6)	s 45(10)
Sch 4, para 2(7)	s 36(4)
Sch 4, para 3(1), (2)	s 36(5), (6)
Sch 4, para 4(1)	s 40(3)
Sch 4, para 4(2)	s 40(1)
Sch 4, para 4(3)	s 40(2)
Sch 4, para 5(1)	s 41(1)
Sch 4, para 5(2)(a)	ss 101(4), 105(8)
Sch 4, para 5(2)(b)	s 45(9)
Sch 4, para 5(2)(c), (d)	s 43(5)
Sch 4, para 5(3)	Unnecessary
Sch 4, para 5(4)	s 45(10)
Sch 4, para 5(5)	s 41(2)
Sch 4, para 6	s 41(3)
Sch 4, para 7(1)–(3)	s 101(1)–(3)
Sch 4, para 7(4)	s 197(2)
Sch 4, para 8	s 105(1), (4)
Sch 4, para 9	ss 108(3), 109(2)
Sch 4, para 10(1)–(3)	s 45(1)–(3)
Sch 4, para 10(4)	s 45(4)
Sch 4, para 10(5)	s 45(5)
Sch 4, para 10(6)	s 45(6)–(8)
Sch 4, para 11(1)–(3)	s 42(1)–(3)
Sch 4, para 11(4)	s 42(4)
Sch 4, para 11(5)	s 42(6)
Sch 4, para 11(6)	s 236(1), (2)
Sch 4, para 12(1)–(4)	s 37(1)–(4)
Sch 4, para 13(1)–(4)	s 43(1)–(4)
Sch 4, para 14	s 38(1), (2)
Sch 4, para 15(1)	s 39(1)–(3)
Sch 4, para 15(2)	s 39(4)
Sch 4, para 16	s 48(1)
Sch 4, para 17(1)	s 203(1)
Sch 4, para 17(2)	s 203(2)
Sch 4, para 18	Sch 2, para 9 (spent in part)

* Repealed in part

(1)	(2)
Sunday Trading Act 1994 (c 20)	
Sch 4, para 19	s 104(4)
Sch 4, para 20	s 110(2)
Sch 4, para 22	ss 196(2), (3), 205(1), 206(2)
Deregulation and Contracting Out Act 1994 (c 40)	
ss 20(3), (5), 36(1)	Unnecessary or spent
Sch 8	ss 36, 37, 38, 39, 40, 41, 42(1)–(3), (5), (6), 43, 45, 48(1), 96(6), 101, 104(4), 105(1), (4), (8), 108(3), 109(2), 110(2), 196(2), (3), 197(2), 203(1), (2), 205(1), 206(2), 210(1)–(3), 230(1), (2), (4), (5), 233(1)–(4), (6), 235(1), 236(1), (2)
Health Authorities Act 1995 (c 17)	
Sch 1, Pt III, para 103	ss 50(8), 218(1), (8)–(10)
Environment Act 1995 (c 25)	
Sch 7, para 11(3)*	s 50(5)
Pensions Act 1995 (c 26)	
s 42(1)	s 58(1)
s 42(2)	s 58(2)
s 42(3)	s 60(1)
s 42(4)	s 58(4)
s 43(1)–(4)	s 59(1)–(4)
s 43(5)	s 59(5), (6)
s 43(6)	s 60(1)
s 44	s 60(2)
s 45(1)–(3)	s 60(3)–(5)
s 45(4)	s 205(1)
s 46(1), (2)	s 46(1), (2)
s 46(3)	s 48(1)
s 46(4)(a)	s 205(1)
s 46(4)(b)	s 196(2), (3)
s 46(4)(c)	s 206(2)
s 46(5)	s 102(1)

(1)	(2)
Pensions Act 1995 (c 26)	
s 46(6)	s 105(1), (5)
s 46(7)	ss 108(3), 109(2)
s 46(8)	s 203(1)
s 46(9)	s 203(2)
s 46(10)	s 46(2)
s 46(11)	ss 230(1), (2), (4), (5), 235(1)
s 124(1)†	s 58(3)
Sch 3, para 1	Unnecessary
Sch 3, para 2	s 104(4)
Sch 3, para 3	s 117(4)
Sch 3, para 4	s 118(3)
Sch 3, para 5	s 120(1)
Sch 3, para 6	s 128(1)
Sch 3, para 7	s 129(1)
Sch 3, para 10	s 191(1), (2)
Disability Discrimination Act 1995 (c 50)	
Sch 6, para 3(a)	s 219(3)
Sch 6, para 3(b)	s 219(2)
Sch 6, para 3(c)	s 219(4)
Reserve Forces Act 1996 (c 14)	
Sch 10, para 17	s 192(1)
Employment Protection (Medical Suspension) Order 1980, SI 1980/1581	s 64(1)–(3)
Insolvency of Employer (Excluded Classes) Regulations 1983, SI 1983/624	
Reg 3	ss 196(2), (3), (7), 200(1)
Employment Protection (Medical Suspension) Order 1985, SI 1985/1787	s 64(1)–(3)
Employment Protection (Medical Suspension) Order 1988, SI 1988/1746	s 64(1)–(3)

* Repealed in part

(1)	(2)
Time Off for Public Duties Order 1990, SI 1990/1870	s 50(2)(d), (7)
Sex Discrimination and Equal Pay (Remedies) Regulations 1993, SI 1993/2798*	
Sch 1, para 1*, 2	Spent
Employment Protection (Part-time Employees) Regulations 1995, SI 1995/31	
Regs 1–3, 4(1)	Spent
Reg 4(2)	s 210(4)
Regs 5, 6, Schedule	Spent
Insolvency of Employer (Excluded Classes) Regulations 1995, SI 1995/278	
Regs 1, 2	Unnecessary
Reg 3	s 196(7)
Reg 4	Spent
Reg 5	Unnecessary
Time Off for Public Duties Order 1995, SI 1995/694	s 50(2)(c), (6)
Collective Redundancies and Transfer of Undertakings (Protection of Employment) (Amendment) Regulations 1995, SI 1995/2587	
Reg 12(1)	s 47

(1)	(2)
Collective Redundancies and Transfer of Undertakings (Protection of Employment) (Amendment) Regulations 1995, SI 1995/2587	
Reg 12(2)	s 48(1)
Reg 12(4)	s 209(7)
Reg 13(1)	s 61(1)
Reg 13(2)	s 61(2)
Reg 13(4)	s 193(1), (2)
Reg 13(5)	s 202(2)
Reg 13(6)	s 225(4)
Reg 14(1)	s 103
Reg 14(2)	ss 105(6), 108(3), 109(2)
Reg 14(3)	ss 117(4), 118(3), 120(1), 128, 129(1)
Reg 14(4)	ss 193(1), (2), 202(2)
Reg 14(5)	s 192(2)
Reg 14(6)	s 209(2)
Reg 14(7)	Unnecessary
Environment Act 1995 (Consequential Amendments) Regulations 1996, SI 1996/593	
Sch 1, para 19	s 50(2)(g)
Environment Act 1995 (Consequential and Transitional Provisions) (Scotland) Regulations 1996, SI 1996/973	
Schedule, para 4(1)	Unnecessary
Schedule, para 4(2)(a)	s 50(2)(g)
Schedule, para 4(2)(b)	Unnecessary

* Repealed in part

[1285]

ARMED FORCES ACT 1996 (NOTE)

(1996 c 46)

NOTES

Sections 21, 23, 24, 26 amend the Sex Discrimination Act 1975, ss 76, 85 at **[190]**, **[199]**; the Race Relations Act 1976, ss 68, 74, 75 at **[289]**, **[301]**, **[302]**; the Equal Pay Act 1970, s 1 at **[5]** (and s 7A of that Act), and the Employment Rights Act 1996, s 192 at **[1236]**. The relevant amendments are incorporated in the text of the sections concerned. Other provisions of the Act are outside the scope of this work.

See *Harvey* L2(A), Q.

[1286]

ASYLUM AND IMMIGRATION ACT 1996 (NOTE)

(1996 c 49)

NOTES

Only ss 8 (Restrictions on employment), 8A (Code of practice) and 13 (Short title, etc) were reproduced in the fifteenth edition of this work. Sections 8 and 8A were repealed by the Immigration, Asylum and Nationality Act 2006, ss 26, 61, Sch 3, as from 29 February 2008, except in relation to employment which commenced before that date (see the transitional provisions note to s 15 of the 2006 Act at **[1696A]**). Section 13, although still in force, is now outside the scope of this work.

[1287]–[1289]

PROTECTION FROM HARASSMENT ACT 1997

(1997 c 40)

ARRANGEMENT OF SECTIONS

England and Wales

Scotland

General

An Act to make provision for protecting persons from harassment and similar conduct

[21 March 1997]

NOTES

Regulatory functions: the regulatory functions conferred by, or under, this Act are subject to the Legislative and Regulatory Reform Act 2006, ss 21, 22 at **[1783]**, **[1784]**; see the Legislative and Regulatory Reform (Regulatory Functions) Order 2007, SI 2007/3544 (made under s 24(2) of the 2006 Act) for details.

See *Harvey* L1(A).

England and Wales

1 Prohibition of harassment

(1) A person must not pursue a course of conduct—

(a) which amounts to harassment of another, and

(b) which he knows or ought to know amounts to harassment of the other.

[(1A) A person must not pursue a course of conduct—

(a) which involves harassment of two or more persons, and
(b) which he knows or ought to know involves harassment of those persons, and
(c) by which he intends to persuade any person (whether or not one of those mentioned above)—
  (i) not to do something that he is entitled or required to do, or
  (ii) to do something that he is not under any obligation to do.]

(2) For the purposes of this section, the person whose course of conduct is in question ought to know that it amounts to [or involves] harassment of another if a reasonable person in possession of the same information would think the course of conduct amounted to [or involved] harassment of the other.

(3) Subsection (1) [or (1A)] does not apply to a course of conduct if the person who pursued it shows—
(a) that it was pursued for the purpose of preventing or detecting crime,
(b) that it was pursued under any enactment or rule of law or to comply with any condition or requirement imposed by any person under any enactment, or
(c) that in the particular circumstances the pursuit of the course of conduct was reasonable.

[1290]

NOTES

Sub-s (1A): inserted by the Serious Organised Crime and Police Act 2005, s 125(1), (2)(a), as from 1 July 2005.

Sub-ss (2), (3): words in square brackets inserted by the Serious Organised Crime and Police Act 2005, s 125(1), (2)(b), (c), as from 1 July 2005.

2 Offence of harassment

(1) A person who pursues a course of conduct in breach of [section 1(1) or (1A)] is guilty of an offence.

(2) A person guilty of an offence under this section is liable on summary conviction to imprisonment for a term not exceeding six months, or a fine not exceeding level 5 on the standard scale, or both.

(3) …

[1291]

NOTES

Sub-s (1): words in square brackets substituted by the Serious Organised Crime and Police Act 2005, s 125(1), (3), as from 1 July 2005.

Sub-s (3): repealed by the Police Reform Act 2002, s 107(2), Sch 8.

3 Civil remedy

(1) An actual or apprehended breach of [section 1(1)] may be the subject of a claim in civil proceedings by the person who is or may be the victim of the course of conduct in question.

(2) On such a claim, damages may be awarded for (among other things) any anxiety caused by the harassment and any financial loss resulting from the harassment.

(3) Where—
(a) in such proceedings the High Court or a county court grants an injunction for the purpose of restraining the defendant from pursuing any conduct which amounts to harassment, and
(b) the plaintiff considers that the defendant has done anything which he is prohibited from doing by the injunction,

the plaintiff may apply for the issue of a warrant for the arrest of the defendant.

(4) An application under subsection (3) may be made—
(a) where the injunction was granted by the High Court, to a judge of that court, and
(b) where the injunction was granted by a county court, to a judge or district judge of that or any other county court.

(5) The judge or district judge to whom an application under subsection (3) is made may only issue a warrant if—

(a) the application is substantiated on oath, and
(b) the judge or district judge has reasonable grounds for believing that the defendant has done anything which he is prohibited from doing by the injunction.

(6) Where—
(a) the High Court or a county court grants an injunction for the purpose mentioned in subsection (3)(a), and
(b) without reasonable excuse the defendant does anything which he is prohibited from doing by the injunction,

he is guilty of an offence.

(7) Where a person is convicted of an offence under subsection (6) in respect of any conduct, that conduct is not punishable as a contempt of court.

(8) A person cannot be convicted of an offence under subsection (6) in respect of any conduct which has been punished as a contempt of court.

(9) A person guilty of an offence under subsection (6) is liable—
(a) on conviction on indictment, to imprisonment for a term not exceeding five years, or a fine, or both, or
(b) on summary conviction, to imprisonment for a term not exceeding six months, or a fine not exceeding the statutory maximum, or both.

[1292]

NOTES

Sub-s (1): words in square brackets substituted by the Serious Organised Crime and Police Act 2005, s 125(1), (4), as from 1 July 2005.

[3A Injunctions to protect persons from harassment within section 1(1A)

(1) This section applies where there is an actual or apprehended breach of section 1(1A) by any person ("the relevant person").

(2) In such a case—
(a) any person who is or may be a victim of the course of conduct in question, or
(b) any person who is or may be a person falling within section 1(1A)(c),

may apply to the High Court or a county court for an injunction restraining the relevant person from pursuing any conduct which amounts to harassment in relation to any person or persons mentioned or described in the injunction.

(3) Section 3(3) to (9) apply in relation to an injunction granted under subsection (2) above as they apply in relation to an injunction granted as mentioned in section 3(3)(a).]

[1292A]

NOTES

Commencement: 1 July 2005.
Inserted by the Serious Organised Crime and Police Act 2005, s 125(1), (5), as from 1 July 2005.

4 Putting people in fear of violence

(1) A person whose course of conduct causes another to fear, on at least two occasions, that violence will be used against him is guilty of an offence if he knows or ought to know that his course of conduct will cause the other so to fear on each of those occasions.

(2) For the purposes of this section, the person whose course of conduct is in question ought to know that it will cause another to fear that violence will be used against him on any occasion if a reasonable person in possession of the same information would think the course of conduct would cause the other so to fear on that occasion.

(3) It is a defence for a person charged with an offence under this section to show that—
(a) his course of conduct was pursued for the purpose of preventing or detecting crime,
(b) his course of conduct was pursued under any enactment or rule of law or to comply with any condition or requirement imposed by any person under any enactment, or
(c) the pursuit of his course of conduct was reasonable for the protection of himself or another or for the protection of his or another's property.

(4) A person guilty of an offence under this section is liable—

(a) on conviction on indictment, to imprisonment for a term not exceeding five years, or a fine, or both, or

(b) on summary conviction, to imprisonment for a term not exceeding six months, or a fine not exceeding the statutory maximum, or both.

(5) If on the trial on indictment of a person charged with an offence under this section the jury find him not guilty of the offence charged, they may find him guilty of an offence under section 2.

(6) The Crown Court has the same powers and duties in relation to a person who is by virtue of subsection (5) convicted before it of an offence under section 2 as a magistrates' court would have on convicting him of the offence.

[1293]

5 Restraining orders [on conviction]

(1) A court sentencing or otherwise dealing with a person ("the defendant") convicted of an offence *under section 2 or 4* may (as well as sentencing him or dealing with him in any other way) make an order under this section.

(2) The order may, for the purpose of protecting the victim [or victims] of the offence, or any other person mentioned in the order, from *further* conduct which—

(a) amounts to harassment, or

(b) will cause a fear of violence,

prohibit the defendant from doing anything described in the order.

(3) The order may have effect for a specified period or until further order.

[(3A) In proceedings under this section both the prosecution and the defence may lead, as further evidence, any evidence that would be admissible in proceedings for an injunction under section 3.]

(4) The prosecutor, the defendant or any other person mentioned in the order may apply to the court which made the order for it to be varied or discharged by a further order.

[(4A) Any person mentioned in the order is entitled to be heard on the hearing of an application under subsection (4).]

(5) If without reasonable excuse the defendant does anything which he is prohibited from doing by an order under this section, he is guilty of an offence.

(6) A person guilty of an offence under this section is liable—

(a) on conviction on indictment, to imprisonment for a term not exceeding five years, or a fine, or both, or

(b) on summary conviction, to imprisonment for a term not exceeding six months, or a fine not exceeding the statutory maximum, or both.

[(7) A court dealing with a person for an offence under this section may vary or discharge the order in question by a further order.]

[1294]

NOTES

Section heading: words in square brackets added by the Domestic Violence, Crime and Victims Act 2004, s 58(1), Sch 10, para 43(1), (2), as from a day to be appointed, except in relation to cases where the acquittal (or, where s 5A(5) applies, the allowing of the appeal) occurs before the commencement of this amendment (see Sch 12, para 5(3)).

Sub-s (1): words in italics repealed by the Domestic Violence, Crime and Victims Act 2004, ss 12(1), 58(2), Sch 11, as from a day to be appointed, except in relation to cases where the conviction occurs before the commencement of this amendment (see Sch 12, para 5(1)).

Sub-s (2): words in square brackets inserted by the Serious Organised Crime and Police Act 2005, s 125(1), (6), as from 1 July 2005; word in italics repealed by the Domestic Violence, Crime and Victims Act 2004, s 58(1), (2), Sch 10, para 43(1), (3), Sch 11, as from a day to be appointed, except in relation to cases where the conviction occurs before the commencement of this amendment (see Sch 12, para 5(1)).

Sub-s (3A): inserted by the Domestic Violence, Crime and Victims Act 2004, s 12(2), as from a day to be appointed, in relation to applications made on or after the commencement of this amendment (see Sch 12, para 5(2)).

Sub-s (4A): inserted by the Domestic Violence, Crime and Victims Act 2004, s 12(3), as from a day to be appointed.

Sub-s (7): added by the Domestic Violence, Crime and Victims Act 2004, s 12(4), as from a day to be appointed, except in relation to cases where the acquittal (or, where s 5A(5) applies, the allowing of the appeal) occurs before the commencement of this amendment (see Sch 12, para 5(3)).

[5A Restraining orders on acquittal

(1) A court before which a person ("the defendant") is acquitted of an offence may, if it considers it necessary to do so to protect a person from harassment by the defendant, make an order prohibiting the defendant from doing anything described in the order.

(2) Subsections (3) to (7) of section 5 apply to an order under this section as they apply to an order under that one.

(3) Where the Court of Appeal allow an appeal against conviction they may remit the case to the Crown Court to consider whether to proceed under this section.

(4) Where—

(a) the Crown Court allows an appeal against conviction, or

(b) a case is remitted to the Crown Court under subsection (3),

the reference in subsection (1) to a court before which a person is acquitted of an offence is to be read as referring to that court.

(5) A person made subject to an order under this section has the same right of appeal against the order as if—

(a) he had been convicted of the offence in question before the court which made the order, and

(b) the order had been made under section 5.]

[1294A]

NOTES

Commencement: to be appointed.

Inserted by the Domestic Violence, Crime and Victims Act 2004, s 12(5), as from a day to be appointed.

6 (*Amends the Limitation Act 1980, s 11 at* **[352G]**.)

7 Interpretation of this group of sections

(1) This section applies for the interpretation of *sections 1 to 5*.

(2) References to harassing a person include alarming the person or causing the person distress.

[(3) A "course of conduct" must involve—

(a) in the case of conduct in relation to a single person (see section 1(1)), conduct on at least two occasions in relation to that person, or

(b) in the case of conduct in relation to two or more persons (see section 1(1A)), conduct on at least one occasion in relation to each of those persons.]

[(3A) A person's conduct on any occasion shall be taken, if aided, abetted, counselled or procured by another—

(a) to be conduct on that occasion of the other (as well as conduct of the person whose conduct it is); and

(b) to be conduct in relation to which the other's knowledge and purpose, and what he ought to have known, are the same as they were in relation to what was contemplated or reasonably foreseeable at the time of the aiding, abetting, counselling or procuring.]

(4) "Conduct" includes speech.

[(5) References to a person, in the context of the harassment of a person, are references to a person who is an individual.]

[1295]

NOTES

Sub-s (1): for the words in italics there are substituted the words "sections 1 to 5A" by the Domestic Violence, Crime and Victims Act 2004, s 58(1), Sch 10, para 44, as from a day to be appointed, except in relation to cases where the acquittal (or, where s 5A(5) applies, the allowing of the appeal) occurs before the commencement of this amendment (see Sch 12, para 5(3)).

Sub-s (3): substituted by the Serious Organised Crime and Police Act 2005, s 125(1), (7)(a), as from 1 July 2005.

Sub-s (3A): inserted by the Criminal Justice and Police Act 2001, s 44(1), in relation to any aiding, abetting, counselling or procuring that takes place after 1 August 2001.

Sub-s (5): added by the Serious Organised Crime and Police Act 2005, s 125(1), (7)(b), as from 1 July 2005.

Scotland

8 Harassment

(1) Every individual has a right to be free from harassment and, accordingly, a person must not pursue a course of conduct which amounts to harassment of another and—

(a) is intended to amount to harassment of that person; or

(b) occurs in circumstances where it would appear to a reasonable person that it would amount to harassment of that person.

(2) An actual or apprehended breach of subsection (1) may be the subject of a claim in civil proceedings by the person who is or may be the victim of the course of conduct in question; and any such claim shall be known as an action of harassment.

(3) For the purposes of this section—

"conduct" includes speech;

"harassment" of a person includes causing the person alarm or distress; and

a course of conduct must involve conduct on at least two occasions.

(4) It shall be a defence to any action of harassment to show that the course of conduct complained of—

(a) was authorised by, under or by virtue of any enactment or rule of law;

(b) was pursued for the purpose of preventing or detecting crime; or

(c) was, in the particular circumstances, reasonable.

(5) In an action of harassment the court may, without prejudice to any other remedies which it may grant—

(a) award damages;

(b) grant—

(i) interdict or interim interdict;

(ii) if it is satisfied that it is appropriate for it to do so in order to protect the person from further harassment, an order, to be known as a "non-harassment order", requiring the defender to refrain from such conduct in relation to the pursuer as may be specified in the order for such period (which includes an indeterminate period) as may be so specified,

but a person may not be subjected to the same prohibitions in an interdict or interim interdict and a non-harassment order at the same time.

(6) The damages which may be awarded in an action of harassment include damages for any anxiety caused by the harassment and any financial loss resulting from it.

(7) Without prejudice to any right to seek review of any interlocutor, a person against whom a non-harassment order has been made, or the person for whose protection the order was made, may apply to the court by which the order was made for revocation of or a variation of the order and, on any such application, the court may revoke the order or vary it in such manner as it considers appropriate.

(8) In section 10(1) of the Damages (Scotland) Act 1976 (interpretation), in the definition of "personal injuries", after "to reputation" there is inserted ", or injury resulting from harassment actionable under section 8 of the Protection from Harassment Act 1997".

[1296]

9 Breach of non-harassment order

(1) Any person who is … in breach of a non-harassment order made under section 8 is guilty of an offence and liable—

(a) on conviction on indictment, to imprisonment for a term not exceeding five years or to a fine, or to both such imprisonment and such fine; and

(b) on summary conviction, to imprisonment for a period not exceeding six months or to a fine not exceeding the statutory maximum, or to both such imprisonment and such fine.

(2) A breach of a non-harassment order shall not be punishable other than in accordance with subsection (1).

[(3) A constable may arrest without warrant any person he reasonably believes is committing or has committed an offence under subsection (1).

(4) Subsection (3) is without prejudice to any power of arrest conferred by law apart from that subsection.]

[1297]

NOTES

Sub-s (1): words omitted repealed by the Criminal Justice (Scotland) Act 2003, s 49(2)(a), as from 27 June 2003.

Sub-ss (3), (4): added by the Criminal Justice (Scotland) Act 2003, s 49(2)(b), as from 27 June 2003.

10–13 (*Outside the scope of this work.*)

14 Extent

(1) Sections 1 to 7 extend to England and Wales only.

(2) Sections 8 to 11 extend to Scotland only.

(3) This Act (except section 13) does not extend to Northern Ireland.

[1298]

15 Commencement

(1) Sections 1, 2, 4, 5 and 7 to 12 are to come into force on such day as the Secretary of State may by order made by statutory instrument appoint.

(2) Sections 3 and 6 are to come into force on such day as the Lord Chancellor may by order made by statutory instrument appoint.

(3) Different days may be appointed under this section for different purposes.

[1299]

NOTES

Orders: the Protection from Harassment Act 1997 (Commencement) (No 1) Order 1997, SI 1997/1418; the Protection from Harassment Act 1997 (Commencement) (No 2) Order 1997, SI 1997/1498; the Protection from Harassment Act 1997 (Commencement) (No 3) Order 1998, SI 1998/1902.

16 Short title

This Act may be cited as the Protection from Harassment Act 1997.

[1300]–[1302]

EMPLOYMENT RIGHTS (DISPUTE RESOLUTION) ACT 1998

(1998 c 8)

An Act to rename industrial tribunals and amend the law relating to those tribunals; to amend the law relating to dismissal procedures agreements and other alternative methods of resolving disputes about employment rights; to provide for the adjustment of awards of compensation for unfair dismissal in cases where no use is made of internal procedures for appealing against dismissal; to make provision about cases involving both unfair dismissal and disability discrimination; and for connected purposes

[8 April 1998]

NOTES

Most of this Act comprises amendments to the Employment Tribunals Act 1996 and related legislation. The relevant amendments are incorporated in the text and noted below. Where these are enabling provisions any Orders are noted to the text of the provisions as inserted or amended.

See *Harvey* Q, R.

PART I
EMPLOYMENT TRIBUNALS

Renaming of tribunals

1 Industrial tribunals to be known as employment tribunals

(1) Industrial tribunals are renamed employment tribunals.

(2) Accordingly, the Industrial Tribunals Act 1996 may be cited as the Employment Tribunals Act 1996; and (wherever they occur in any enactment)—

(a) for the words "industrial tribunal" substitute "employment tribunal",
(b) for the words "industrial tribunals" substitute "employment tribunals",
(c) for the words "the Industrial Tribunals Act 1996" substitute "the Employment Tribunals Act 1996",
(d) for the words "President of the Industrial Tribunals (England and Wales)" substitute "President of the Employment Tribunals (England and Wales)", and
(e) for the words "President of the Industrial Tribunals (Scotland)" substitute "President of the Employment Tribunals (Scotland)".

[1303]

2–6 (*S 2 inserts the Employment Tribunals Act 1996, s 7(3A)–(3C) at* **[960]**; *s 3 amends s 4(3) and inserts s 4(6A) of the 1996 Act at* **[957]**; *s 4 substitutes s 4(1)(b) of the 1996 Act at* **[957]**; *s 5 inserts s 4(6B), (6C) of the 1996 Act at* **[957]**; *s 6 substitutes the Trade Union and Labour Relations (Consolidation) Act 1992, s 87 at* **[574]**.)

PART II
OTHER METHODS OF DISPUTE RESOLUTION

7–12 (*S 7 inserts the Trade Union and Labour Relations (Consolidation) Act 1992, s 212A at* **[698]**; *s 8 inserts the Sex Discrimination Act 1975, s 77(4D) at* **[191]**, *the Race Relations Act 1976, s 72(4D) at* **[297]**, *s 288(6) of the 1992 Act at* **[782]**, *the Employment Rights Act 1996, s 203(5) at* **[1245]**, *and amended the Disability Discrimination Act 1995, s 9 (repealed); s 9 amends s 77(4A) of the 1975 Act at* **[191]**, *s 72(4A) of the 1976 Act at* **[297]**, *s 288(2B) of the 1992 Act at* **[782]**, *s 203(3) of the 1996 Act at* **[1245]**, *and amended the Disability Discrimination Act 1995, s 9 (repealed); s 10 makes further amendments to each of the subsections noted to s 9 above; s 11 amends the Employment Tribunals Act 1996, s 18(1) at* **[975]**, *and the Employment Rights Act 1996, ss 166(2) and 168(1) at* **[1210]**, **[1212]**; *s 12 amends ss 110 and 184 of that Act at* **[1154]** *and* **[1228]**.)

PART III
AWARDS OF COMPENSATION

13, 14 (*S 13 inserted the Employment Rights Act 1996, s 127A (repealed), and was itself repealed by the Employment Act 2002, s 54, Sch 8, as from 1 November 2004; s 14(1) (repealed) originally amended s 117 of the 1996 Act; s 14(2) amends s 126 of the 1996 Act, at* **[1170]**.)

PART IV
SUPPLEMENTARY AND GENERAL

15, 16 (*S 15 introduces Sch 1 (minor and consequential amendments) and Sch 2 (repeals); s 16 relates to Northern Ireland.*)

17 Commencement, transitional provisions and savings

(1) The provisions of this Act (apart from section 16, this section and section 18 and paragraph 17(2) of Schedule 1) shall not come into force until such day as the Secretary of State may by order made by statutory instrument appoint; and different days may be appointed for different purposes.

(2) An order under subsection (1) may contain such transitional provisions and savings as appear to the Secretary of State to be appropriate.

(3) The amendment made by paragraph 17(2) of Schedule 1 shall be deemed always to have had effect.

(4) …

[1304]

NOTES

Sub-s (4): repealed by the Statute Law (Repeals) Act 2004, as from 22 July 2004.

Orders: the Employment Rights (Dispute Resolution) Act 1998 (Commencement No 1 and Transitional and Saving Provisions) Order 1998, SI 1998/1658.

18 Short title

This Act may be cited as the Employment Rights (Dispute Resolution) Act 1998.

[1305]

(Schs 1 and 2 (minor and consequential amendments and repeals) are not reproduced. In so far as they amend or repeal any provision reproduced in this work, that amendment (etc) has been incorporated at the appropriate place.)

PUBLIC INTEREST DISCLOSURE ACT 1998

(1998 c 23)

An Act to protect individuals who make certain disclosures of information in the public interest; to allow such individuals to bring action in respect of victimisation; and for connected purposes

[2 July 1998]

NOTES

This Act consists almost entirely of provisions adding to or amending existing legislation, principally the Employment Rights Act 1996. The provisions so added or amended are incorporated at the relevant point in the text and are noted below. The provisions of the Act not brought into force at Royal Assent (see s 18(4) below) were brought into force on 2 July 1999 (SI 1999/1547). See also the Public Interest Disclosure (Prescribed Persons) Order 1999, SI 1999/1549, as amended (principally by SI 2003/1993) at **[2512]** (made under the Employment Rights Act 1996, s 43F, as inserted by s 1 of this Act).

See *Harvey* A3(B), DII(H), Q, S.

1–17 *(S 1 inserts the Employment Rights Act 1996, Pt IVA (ss 43A–43L) at* **[1051]–[1062]***, s 2 inserts 47B of the 1996 Act at* **[1069]***; s 3 inserts s 48(1A) of the 1996 Act at* **[1073]***; s 4 amends s 49 of the 1996 Act at* **[1074]***; s 5 inserts s 103A of the 1996 Act at* **[1144]***; s 6 inserts s 105(6A) of the 1996 Act at* **[1149]***; s 7 amends ss 108(3) of the 1996 Act at* **[1152]** *and amended s 109 of that Act (repealed); s 8 (repealed) originally amended ss 112(4), 117(2), (3) and 118(1), and inserted s 127B, of the 1996 Act; s 9 amends s 128(1) and 129(1) of the 1996 Act at* **[1172]** *and* **[1173]***; s 10 amends s 191(2) of the 1996 Act at* **[1235]***; s 11 (repealed) originally amended s 193 of the 1996 Act; s 12 amended s 196 of the 1996 Act (repealed); s 13 amended s 200(1) of the 1996 Act, and was repealed by the Police Reform Act 2002, ss 37(3), 107(2), Sch 8, as from 1 April 2004; s 14 inserts s 205(1A) of the 1996 Act at* **[1247]***; s 15 inserts s 230(6) and amends s 235 of the 1996 Act at* **[1271]**, **[1276]***; s 16 amends the Trade Union and Labour Relations (Consolidation) Act 1992, s 237(1A) at* **[734]***; s 17 (Northern Ireland) outside the scope of this work.)*

18 Short title, interpretation, commencement and extent

(1) This Act may be cited as the Public Interest Disclosure Act 1998.

(2) In this Act "the 1996 Act" means the Employment Rights Act 1996.

(3) Subject to subsection (4), this Act shall come into force on such day or days as the Secretary of State may by order made by statutory instrument appoint, and different days may be appointed for different purposes.

(4) The following provisions shall come into force on the passing of this Act—

(a) section 1 so far as relating to the power to make an order under section 43F of the 1996 Act,

(b) …
(c) section 17, and
(d) this section.

(5) This Act, except section 17, does not extend to Northern Ireland.

[1306]

NOTES

Sub-s (4): para (b) repealed by the Employment Relations Act 1999, s 44, Sch 9(11).
Orders: the Public Interest Disclosure Act 1998 (Commencement) Order 1999, SI 1999/1547.

SCHOOL STANDARDS AND FRAMEWORK ACT 1998

(1998 c 31)

An Act to make new provision with respect to school education and the provision of nursery education otherwise than at school; to enable arrangements to be made for the provision of further education for young persons partly at schools and partly at further education institutions; to make provision with respect to the Education Assets Board; and for connected purposes

[24 July 1998]

NOTES

This is a major Act most parts of which are outside the scope of this work and are therefore omitted. Provisions omitted are not annotated. The provisions reproduced here only apply to England and Wales. They re-enact with amendments equivalent provisions of the Education Act 1996, which are repealed. Sections 54–57 of, and Schs 16, 17 to, this Act (staffing of schools) were repealed by the Education Act 2002, as from 1 September 2003 (in relation to England) and as from 1 April 2006 (in relation to Wales). See now ss 35–37 of the 2002 Act at **[1510A]–[1510C]** and Regulations made thereunder.

PART II
NEW FRAMEWORK FOR MAINTAINED SCHOOLS

CHAPTER V
STAFFING AND CONDUCT OF SCHOOLS

Appointment and dismissal of teachers of religious education

58 Appointment and dismissal of certain teachers at schools with a religious character

(1) In this section—
(a) subsections (2) to (6) apply to a foundation or voluntary controlled school which has a religious character; and
(b) subsection (7) applies (subject to subsection (8)) to a voluntary aided school which has a religious character;

and references in this Chapter to a school which has (or does not have) a religious character shall be construed in accordance with section 69(3).

(2) Where the number of [teachers at] a school to which this subsection applies is more than two, [the teachers shall] include persons who—
(a) are selected for their fitness and competence to give religious education as is required in accordance with arrangements under paragraph 3(3) of Schedule 19 (arrangements for religious education in accordance with the school's trust deed or with the tenets of the school's specified religion or religious denomination), and
(b) are specifically appointed to do so.

(3) The number of reserved teachers in such a school shall not exceed one-fifth of [the total number of teachers], including the head teacher (and for this purpose, where [the total number of teachers] is not a multiple of five, it shall be treated as if it were the next higher multiple of five).

(4) *The head teacher of such a school shall not, [while he remains] head teacher of the school, be a reserved teacher.*

(5) Where the appropriate body propose to appoint a person to be a reserved teacher in such a school, that body—

(a) shall consult the foundation governors, and

(b) shall not so appoint that person unless the foundation governors are satisfied as to his fitness and competence to give such religious education as is mentioned in subsection (2)(a).

(6) If the foundation governors of such a school consider that a reserved teacher has failed to give such religious education efficiently and suitably, they [may—

(a) in the case of a teacher who is an employee, require the appropriate body to dismiss him from employment as a reserved teacher at the school, and

(b) in the case of a teacher who is engaged otherwise than under a contract of employment, require the governing body to terminate his engagement].

(7) If a teacher appointed to give religious education in a school to which this subsection applies fails to give such education efficiently and suitably, he may be dismissed on that ground by the governing body without the consent of the local education authority.

(8) Subsection (7) does not apply—

(a) where the school has a delegated budget, or

(b) to religious education in accordance with an agreed syllabus.

(9) In this section—

"the appropriate body" means—

(a) in relation to a foundation school, the governing body, and

(b) in relation to a voluntary controlled school, the local education authority;

"reserved teacher", in relation to a foundation or voluntary controlled school, means a person employed [or engaged] at the school in pursuance of subsection (2).

[1307]

NOTES

Sub-ss (2), (3), (6): words in square brackets substituted by the Education Act 2002, s 40, Sch 3, paras 1, 6(1)–(3), (5), as from 1 September 2003 (in relation to England), and as from 1 April 2006 (in relation to Wales).

Sub-s (4): repealed by the Education and Inspections Act 2006, ss 37(1), 184, Sch 18, Pt 6, as from a day to be appointed; words in square brackets substituted by the Education Act 2002, s 40, Sch 3, paras 1, 6(1), (4), as from 1 September 2003 (in relation to England), and as from 1 April 2006 (in relation to Wales).

Sub-s (9): in definition "reserved teacher" words in square brackets inserted by the Education Act 2002, s 40, Sch 3, para 6(1), (6), as from 1 September 2003 (in relation to England), and as from 1 April 2006 (in relation to Wales).

Religious opinions etc of staff

59 Staff at community, secular foundation or voluntary, or special school

(1) This section applies to—

(a) a community school or a community or foundation special school, or

(b) a foundation or voluntary school which does not have a religious character.

(2) No person shall be disqualified by reason of his religious opinions, or of his attending or omitting to attend religious worship—

(a) from being a teacher at the school, or

(b) from being employed [or engaged] for the purposes of the school otherwise than as a teacher.

(3) No teacher at the school shall be required to give religious education.

(4) No teacher at the school shall receive any less remuneration or be deprived of, or disqualified for, any promotion or other advantage—

(a) by reason of the fact that he does or does not give religious education, or

(b) by reason of his religious opinions or of his attending or omitting to attend religious worship.

[1308]

NOTES

Sub-s (2): words in square brackets inserted by the Education Act 2002, s 40, Sch 3, para 7, as from 1 September 2003 (in relation to England), and as from 1 April 2006 (in relation to Wales).

60 Staff at foundation or voluntary school with religious character

(1) This section applies to a foundation or voluntary school which has a religious character.

(2) If the school is a foundation or voluntary controlled school, then (subject to subsections (3) and (4) below) section 59(2) to (4) shall apply to the school as they apply to a foundation or voluntary controlled school which does not have a religious character.

(3) Section 59(2) to (4) shall not so apply in relation to a reserved teacher at the school; and instead subsection (5) below shall apply in relation to such a teacher as it applies in relation to a teacher at a voluntary aided school.

(4) In connection with the appointment of a person to be head teacher of the school (whether foundation or voluntary controlled) [in a case where the head teacher is not to be a reserved teacher] regard may be had to that person's ability and fitness to preserve and develop the religious character of the school.

(5) If the school is a voluntary aided school—

(a) preference may be given, in connection with the appointment, remuneration or promotion of teachers at the school, to persons—

(i) whose religious opinions are in accordance with the tenets of the religion or religious denomination specified in relation to the school under section 69(4), or

(ii) who attend religious worship in accordance with those tenets, or

(iii) who give, or are willing to give, religious education at the school in accordance with those tenets; and

(b) regard may be had, in connection with the termination of the employment [or engagement] of any teacher at the school, to any conduct on his part which is incompatible with the precepts, or with the upholding of the tenets, of the religion or religious denomination so specified.

(6) If the school is a voluntary aided school [in Wales], no person shall be disqualified by reason of his religious opinions, or of his attending or omitting to attend religious worship, from being employed [or engaged] for the purposes of the school otherwise than as a teacher.

(7) Where immediately before the appointed day a teacher at a school which on that day becomes a school to which this section applies enjoyed, by virtue of section 304 or 305 of the Education Act 1996 (religious opinions of staff etc), any rights not conferred on him by this section as a teacher at a school to which it applies, he shall continue to enjoy those rights (in addition to those conferred by this section) until he ceases to be employed as a teacher at the school.

(8) In this section "reserved teacher", in relation to a foundation or voluntary controlled school, means a person employed at the school in pursuance of section 58(2).

[1309]

NOTES

Sub-s (4): words in square brackets inserted by the Education and Inspections Act 2006, s 37(2)(a), as from a day to be appointed.

Sub-s (5): words in square brackets in para (b) inserted by the Education Act 2002, s 40, Sch 3, para 8(1), (2), as from 1 September 2003 (in relation to England), and as from 1 April 2006 (in relation to Wales).

Sub-s (6): words in first pair of square brackets inserted by the Education and Inspections Act 2006, s 37(2)(b), as from a day to be appointed; words in second pair of square brackets inserted by the Education Act 2002, s 40, Sch 3, para 8, as from 1 September 2003 (in relation to England), and as from 1 April 2006 (in relation to Wales).

PART VII
MISCELLANEOUS AND GENERAL

Final provisions

145 Short title, commencement and extent

(1) This Act may be cited as the School Standards and Framework Act 1998.

(2) (*Outside the scope of this work.*)

(3) Subject to subsections (4) and (5), this Act shall come into force on such day as the Secretary of State may by order appoint; and different days may be appointed for different provisions and for different purposes.

(4), (5) (*Outside the scope of this work.*)

(6) Subject to subsections (7) and (8), this Act extends to England and Wales only.

(7)–(9) (*Outside the scope of this work.*)

[1310]

NOTES

Orders: the commencement order relevant to the provisions reproduced here is the School Standards and Framework Act 1998 (Commencement No 7 and Saving and Transitional Provisions) Order 1999, SI 1999/2323.

DATA PROTECTION ACT 1998

(1998 c 29)

ARRANGEMENT OF SECTIONS

PART I
PRELIMINARY

PART II
RIGHTS OF DATA SUBJECTS AND OTHERS

PART IV
EXEMPTIONS

PART V
ENFORCEMENT

PART VI
MISCELLANEOUS AND GENERAL

Functions of Commissioner

Records obtained under data subject's right of access

General

SCHEDULES:

An Act to make new provision for the regulation of the processing of information relating to individuals, including the obtaining, holding, use or disclosure of such information

[16 July 1998]

NOTES

This Act is the domestic implementation of Council Directive 95/46/EC on data protection at **[3871]**. The Directive required the domestic implementation of any necessary legislation by 24 October 1998 but this date was not achieved and the substantive provisions of the Act (other than those which came into force at Royal Assent by virtue of s 75(2) at **[1340]**) were brought into force on 1 March 2000 (SI 2000/183). Much of the Act relates to aspects of data protection in areas other than employment. Only those provisions of this Act relevant to employment law are reproduced. Provisions not reproduced are not annotated.

PART I
PRELIMINARY

1 Basic interpretative provisions

(1) In this Act, unless the context otherwise requires—

"data" means information which—

(a) is being processed by means of equipment operating automatically in response to instructions given for that purpose,

(b) is recorded with the intention that it should be processed by means of such equipment,

(c) is recorded as part of a relevant filing system or with the intention that it should form part of a relevant filing system, …

(d) does not fall within paragraph (a), (b) or (c) but forms part of an accessible record as defined by section 68, [or

(e) is recorded information held by a public authority and does not fall within any of paragraphs (a) to (d);]

"data controller" means, subject to subsection (4), a person who (either alone or jointly or in common with other persons) determines the purposes for which and the manner in which any personal data are, or are to be, processed;

"data processor", in relation to personal data, means any person (other than an employee of the data controller) who processes the data on behalf of the data controller;

"data subject" means an individual who is the subject of personal data;

"personal data" means data which relate to a living individual who can be identified—

(a) from those data, or

(b) from those data and other information which is in the possession of, or is likely to come into the possession of, the data controller,

and includes any expression of opinion about the individual and any indication of the intentions of the data controller or any other person in respect of the individual;

"processing", in relation to information or data, means obtaining, recording or holding the information or data or carrying out any operation or set of operations on the information or data, including—

(a) organisation, adaptation or alteration of the information or data,

(b) retrieval, consultation or use of the information or data,

(c) disclosure of the information or data by transmission, dissemination or otherwise making available, or

(d) alignment, combination, blocking, erasure or destruction of the information or data;

["public authority" means a public authority as defined by the Freedom of Information Act 2000 or a Scottish public authority as defined by the Freedom of Information (Scotland) Act 2002;]

"relevant filing system" means any set of information relating to individuals to the extent that, although the information is not processed by means of equipment operating automatically in response to instructions given for that purpose, the set is structured, either by reference to individuals or by reference to criteria relating to individuals, in such a way that specific information relating to a particular individual is readily accessible.

(2) In this Act, unless the context otherwise requires—

(a) "obtaining" or "recording", in relation to personal data, includes obtaining or recording the information to be contained in the data, and

(b) "using" or "disclosing", in relation to personal data, includes using or disclosing the information contained in the data.

(3) In determining for the purposes of this Act whether any information is recorded with the intention—

(a) that it should be processed by means of equipment operating automatically in response to instructions given for that purpose, or

(b) that it should form part of a relevant filing system,

it is immaterial that it is intended to be so processed or to form part of such a system only after being transferred to a country or territory outside the European Economic Area.

(4) Where personal data are processed only for purposes for which they are required by or under any enactment to be processed, the person on whom the obligation to process the data is imposed by or under that enactment is for the purposes of this Act the data controller.

[(5) In paragraph (e) of the definition of "data" in subsection (1), the reference to information "held" by a public authority shall be construed in accordance with section 3(2) of the Freedom of Information Act 2000.

(6) Where—

[(a)] section 7 of the Freedom of Information Act 2000 prevents Parts I to V of that Act [or

(b) section 7(1) of the Freedom of Information (Scotland) Act 2002 prevents that Act,] from applying to certain information held by a public authority, that information is not to be treated for the purposes of paragraph (e) of the definition of "data" in subsection (1) as held by a public authority.]

[1311]

NOTES

Sub-s (1): in definition "data" word omitted from para (c) repealed, and para (e) and the word immediately preceding it added, by the Freedom of Information Act 2000, ss 68(1), (2), 86, Sch 8, Pt III, as from 1 January 2005; definition "public authority" inserted by s 68(1), (2) of the 2000 Act, as from 1 January 2005, and substituted by the Freedom of Information (Scotland) Act 2002 (Consequential Modifications) Order 2004, SI 2004/3089, art 2(1), (2)(a), as from the same date.

Sub-ss (5), (6): added by the Freedom of Information Act 2000, s 68(1), (3), as from 1 January 2005; words in square brackets inserted by SI 2004/3089, art 2(1), (2)(b), (c), as from 1 January 2005.

2 Sensitive personal data

In this Act "sensitive personal data" means personal data consisting of information as to—

(a) the racial or ethnic origin of the data subject,
(b) his political opinions,
(c) his religious beliefs or other beliefs of a similar nature,
(d) whether he is a member of a trade union (within the meaning of the Trade Union and Labour Relations (Consolidation) Act 1992,
(e) his physical or mental health or condition,
(f) his sexual life,
(g) the commission or alleged commission by him of any offence, or
(h) any proceedings for any offence committed or alleged to have been committed by him, the disposal of such proceedings or the sentence of any court in such proceedings.

[1312]

3 The special purposes

In this Act "the special purposes" means any one or more of the following—

(a) the purposes of journalism,
(b) artistic purposes, and
(c) literary purposes.

[1313]

4 The data protection principles

(1) References in this Act to the data protection principles are to the principles set out in Part I of Schedule 1.

(2) Those principles are to be interpreted in accordance with Part II of Schedule 1.

(3) Schedule 2 (which applies to all personal data) and Schedule 3 (which applies only to sensitive personal data) set out conditions applying for the purposes of the first principle; and Schedule 4 sets out cases in which the eighth principle does not apply.

(4) Subject to section 27(1), it shall be the duty of a data controller to comply with the data protection principles in relation to all personal data with respect to which he is the data controller.

[1314]

5 Application of Act

(1) Except as otherwise provided by or under section 54, this Act applies to a data controller in respect of any data only if—

(a) the data controller is established in the United Kingdom and the data are processed in the context of that establishment, or
(b) the data controller is established neither in the United Kingdom nor in any other EEA State but uses equipment in the United Kingdom for processing the data otherwise than for the purposes of transit through the United Kingdom.

(2) A data controller falling within subsection (1)(b) must nominate for the purposes of this Act a representative established in the United Kingdom.

(3) For the purposes of subsections (1) and (2), each of the following is to be treated as established in the United Kingdom—

(a) an individual who is ordinarily resident in the United Kingdom,
(b) a body incorporated under the law of, or of any part of, the United Kingdom,
(c) a partnership or other unincorporated association formed under the law of any part of the United Kingdom, and
(d) any person who does not fall within paragraph (a), (b) or (c) but maintains in the United Kingdom—
(i) an office, branch or agency through which he carries on any activity, or
(ii) a regular practice;

and the reference to establishment in any other EEA State has a corresponding meaning.

[1315]

6 The Commissioner and the Tribunal

[(1) For the purposes of this Act and of the Freedom of Information Act 2000 there shall be an officer known as the Information Commissioner (in this Act referred to as "the Commissioner").]

(2) The Commissioner shall be appointed by Her Majesty by Letters Patent.

[(3) For the purposes of this Act and of the Freedom of Information Act 2000 there shall be a tribunal known as the Information Tribunal (in this Act referred to as "the Tribunal").]

(4) The Tribunal shall consist of—
(a) a chairman appointed by the Lord Chancellor after consultation with the [Secretary of State],
(b) such number of deputy chairmen so appointed as the Lord Chancellor may determine, and
(c) such number of other members appointed by the [Secretary of State] as he may determine.

(5) The members of the Tribunal appointed under subsection (4)(a) and (b) shall be—
(a) persons who have a 7 year general qualification, within the meaning of section 71 of the Courts and Legal Services Act 1990,
(b) advocates or solicitors in Scotland of at least *7* years' standing, or
(c) members of the bar of Northern Ireland or *solicitors of the Supreme Court of Northern Ireland* of at least *7* years' standing.

(6) The members of the Tribunal appointed under subsection (4)(c) shall be—
(a) persons to represent the interests of data subjects,
[(aa) persons to represent the interests of those who make requests for information under the Freedom of Information Act 2000,]
(b) persons to represent the interests of data controllers[, and
(bb) persons to represent the interests of public authorities.]

(7) Schedule 5 has effect in relation to the Commissioner and the Tribunal.

[1316]

NOTES

Sub-s (1): substituted by the Freedom of Information Act 2000, s 18(4), Sch 2, Pt I, para 13(1), (2).

Sub-s (3): substituted by the Freedom of Information Act 2000, s 18(4), Sch 2, Pt I, para 13(1), (3).

Sub-s (4): words in square brackets in para (a) substituted by virtue of the Transfer of Functions (Lord Advocate and Secretary of State) Order 1999, SI 1999/678, art 2(1), Schedule; words in square brackets in para (c) substituted by the Secretary of State for Constitutional Affairs Order 2003, SI 2003/1887, art 9, Sch 2, para 9(1)(a), as from 19 August 2003.

Sub-s (5) is amended as follows:

Para (a) substituted by the Tribunals, Courts and Enforcement Act 2007, s 50, Sch 10, Pt 1, para 30(1), (2), as from a day to be appointed, as follows—

"(a) persons who satisfy the judicial-appointment eligibility condition on a 5-year basis,".

For the figure "7" in italics in paras (b), (c) there is substituted the figure "5" by the Tribunals, Courts and Enforcement Act 2007, s 50, Sch 10, Pt 1, para 30(1), (3), as from a day to be appointed.

For the words in italics in para (c) there are substituted the words "solicitors of the Court of Judicature of Northern Ireland" by the Constitutional Reform Act 2005, s 59(5), Sch 11, Pt 3, para 5, as from a day to be appointed.

Sub-s (6): para (aa) substituted for original word "and" at the end of para (a), and para (bb) and the word immediately preceding it added, by the Freedom of Information Act 2000, s 18(4), Sch 2, Pt II, para 16.

Transfer of functions: functions of the Secretary of State under sub-s (4)(a), (b) are transferred, in so far as they are exercisable in or as regards Scotland, to the Scottish Ministers, by the Scotland Act 1998 (Transfer of Functions to the Scottish Ministers etc) Order 1999, SI 1999/1750, art 2, Sch 1.

PART II
RIGHTS OF DATA SUBJECTS AND OTHERS

7 Right of access to personal data

(1) Subject to the following provisions of this section and to [sections 8, 9 and 9A], an individual is entitled—

(a) to be informed by any data controller whether personal data of which that individual is the data subject are being processed by or on behalf of that data controller,

(b) if that is the case, to be given by the data controller a description of—

(i) the personal data of which that individual is the data subject,

(ii) the purposes for which they are being or are to be processed, and

(iii) the recipients or classes of recipients to whom they are or may be disclosed,

(c) to have communicated to him in an intelligible form—

(i) the information constituting any personal data of which that individual is the data subject, and

(ii) any information available to the data controller as to the source of those data, and

(d) where the processing by automatic means of personal data of which that individual is the data subject for the purpose of evaluating matters relating to him such as, for example, his performance at work, his creditworthiness, his reliability or his conduct, has constituted or is likely to constitute the sole basis for any decision significantly affecting him, to be informed by the data controller of the logic involved in that decision-taking.

(2) A data controller is not obliged to supply any information under subsection (1) unless he has received—

(a) a request in writing, and

(b) except in prescribed cases, such fee (not exceeding the prescribed maximum) as he may require.

[(3) Where a data controller—

(a) reasonably requires further information in order to satisfy himself as to the identity of the person making a request under this section and to locate the information which that person seeks, and

(b) has informed him of that requirement,

the data controller is not obliged to comply with the request unless he is supplied with that further information.]

(4) Where a data controller cannot comply with the request without disclosing information relating to another individual who can be identified from that information, he is not obliged to comply with the request unless—

(a) the other individual has consented to the disclosure of the information to the person making the request, or

(b) it is reasonable in all the circumstances to comply with the request without the consent of the other individual.

(5) In subsection (4) the reference to information relating to another individual includes a reference to information identifying that individual as the source of the information sought by the request; and that subsection is not to be construed as excusing a data controller from communicating so much of the information sought by the request as can be communicated without disclosing the identity of the other individual concerned, whether by the omission of names or other identifying particulars or otherwise.

(6) In determining for the purposes of subsection (4)(b) whether it is reasonable in all the circumstances to comply with the request without the consent of the other individual concerned, regard shall be had, in particular, to—

(a) any duty of confidentiality owed to the other individual,

(b) any steps taken by the data controller with a view to seeking the consent of the other individual,

(c) whether the other individual is capable of giving consent, and

(d) any express refusal of consent by the other individual.

(7) An individual making a request under this section may, in such cases as may be prescribed, specify that his request is limited to personal data of any prescribed description.

(8) Subject to subsection (4), a data controller shall comply with a request under this section promptly and in any event before the end of the prescribed period beginning with the relevant day.

(9) If a court is satisfied on the application of any person who has made a request under the foregoing provisions of this section that the data controller in question has failed to comply with the request in contravention of those provisions, the court may order him to comply with the request.

(10) In this section—

"prescribed" means prescribed by the [Secretary of State] by regulations;

"the prescribed maximum" means such amount as may be prescribed;

"the prescribed period" means forty days or such other period as may be prescribed;

"the relevant day", in relation to a request under this section, means the day on which the data controller receives the request or, if later, the first day on which the data controller has both the required fee and the information referred to in subsection (3).

(11) Different amounts or periods may be prescribed under this section in relation to different cases.

[1317]

NOTES

Sub-s (1): words in square brackets substituted by the Freedom of Information Act 2000, s 69(1), as from 1 January 2005.

Sub-s (3): substituted by the Freedom of Information Act 2000, s 73, Sch 6, para 1.

Sub-s (10): words in square brackets substituted by the Secretary of State for Constitutional Affairs Order 2003, SI 2003/1887, art 9, Sch 2, para 9(1)(a), as from 19 August 2003.

Regulations: the Data Protection (Subject Access) (Fees and Miscellaneous Provisions) Regulations 2000, SI 2000/191. See also, for further exemptions from this section: the Data Protection (Subject Access Modification) (Health) Order 2000, SI 2000/413; the Data Protection (Subject Access Modification) (Education) Order 2000, SI 2000/414; the Data Protection (Subject Access Modification) (Social Work) Order 2000, SI 2000/415; the Data Protection (Miscellaneous Subject Access Exemptions) Order 2000, SI 2000/419, which modify s 7 in relation to data to which the respective orders apply. See also s 9 of this Act (application of s 7 where data controller is a credit reference agency), s 9A (limited exemptions in relation to data held by public authorities), and Sch 7 at **[1345]** (miscellaneous exemptions).

8 Provisions supplementary to section 7

(1) The [Secretary of State] may by regulations provide that, in such cases as may be prescribed, a request for information under any provision of subsection (1) of section 7 is to be treated as extending also to information under other provisions of that subsection.

(2) The obligation imposed by section 7(1)(c)(i) must be complied with by supplying the data subject with a copy of the information in permanent form unless—

(a) the supply of such a copy is not possible or would involve disproportionate effort, or

(b) the data subject agrees otherwise;

and where any of the information referred to in section 7(1)(c)(i) is expressed in terms which are not intelligible without explanation the copy must be accompanied by an explanation of those terms.

(3) Where a data controller has previously complied with a request made under section 7 by an individual, the data controller is not obliged to comply with a subsequent identical or similar request under that section by that individual unless a reasonable interval has elapsed between compliance with the previous request and the making of the current request.

(4) In determining for the purposes of subsection (3) whether requests under section 7 are made at reasonable intervals, regard shall be had to the nature of the data, the purpose for which the data are processed and the frequency with which the data are altered.

(5) Section 7(1)(d) is not to be regarded as requiring the provision of information as to the logic involved in any decision-taking if, and to the extent that, the information constitutes a trade secret.

(6) The information to be supplied pursuant to a request under section 7 must be supplied by reference to the data in question at the time when the request is received, except that it may take account of any amendment or deletion made between that time and the time when the information is supplied, being an amendment or deletion that would have been made regardless of the receipt of the request.

(7) For the purposes of section 7(4) and (5) another individual can be identified from the information being disclosed if he can be identified from that information, or from that and any other information which, in the reasonable belief of the data controller, is likely to be in, or to come into, the possession of the data subject making the request.

[1318]

NOTES

Sub-s (1): words in square brackets substituted by the Secretary of State for Constitutional Affairs Order 2003, SI 2003/1887, art 9, Sch 2, para 9(1)(a), as from 19 August 2003.

Regulations: the Data Protection (Subject Access) (Fees and Miscellaneous Provisions) Regulations 2000, SI 2000/191.

10 Right to prevent processing likely to cause damage or distress

(1) Subject to subsection (2), an individual is entitled at any time by notice in writing to a data controller to require the data controller at the end of such period as is reasonable in the circumstances to cease, or not to begin, processing, or processing for a specified purpose or in a specified manner, any personal data in respect of which he is the data subject, on the ground that, for specified reasons—

(a) the processing of those data or their processing for that purpose or in that manner is causing or is likely to cause substantial damage or substantial distress to him or to another, and

(b) that damage or distress is or would be unwarranted.

(2) Subsection (1) does not apply—

(a) in a case where any of the conditions in paragraphs 1 to 4 of Schedule 2 is met, or

(b) in such other cases as may be prescribed by the [Secretary of State] by order.

(3) The data controller must within twenty-one days of receiving a notice under subsection (1) ("the data subject notice") give the individual who gave it a written notice—

(a) stating that he has complied or intends to comply with the data subject notice, or

(b) stating his reasons for regarding the data subject notice as to any extent unjustified and the extent (if any) to which he has complied or intends to comply with it.

(4) If a court is satisfied, on the application of any person who has given a notice under subsection (1) which appears to the court to be justified (or to be justified to any extent), that the data controller in question has failed to comply with the notice, the court may order him to take such steps for complying with the notice (or for complying with it to that extent) as the court thinks fit.

(5) The failure by a data subject to exercise the right conferred by subsection (1) or section 11(1) does not affect any other right conferred on him by this Part.

[1319]

NOTES

Sub-s (2): words in square brackets substituted by the Secretary of State for Constitutional Affairs Order 2003, SI 2003/1887, art 9, Sch 2, para 9(1)(a), as from 19 August 2003.

Orders: as of 6 April 2008 no Orders had been made under this section.

12 Rights in relation to automated decision-taking

(1) An individual is entitled at any time, by notice in writing to any data controller, to require the data controller to ensure that no decision taken by or on behalf of the data controller which significantly affects that individual is based solely on the processing by automatic means of personal data in respect of which that individual is the data subject for the purpose of evaluating matters relating to him such as, for example, his performance at work, his creditworthiness, his reliability or his conduct.

(2) Where, in a case where no notice under subsection (1) has effect, a decision which significantly affects an individual is based solely on such processing as is mentioned in subsection (1)—

(a) the data controller must as soon as reasonably practicable notify the individual that the decision was taken on that basis, and

(b) the individual is entitled, within twenty-one days of receiving that notification from the data controller, by notice in writing to require the data controller to reconsider the decision or to take a new decision otherwise than on that basis.

(3) The data controller must, within twenty-one days of receiving a notice under subsection (2)(b) ("the data subject notice") give the individual a written notice specifying the steps that he intends to take to comply with the data subject notice.

(4) A notice under subsection (1) does not have effect in relation to an exempt decision; and nothing in subsection (2) applies to an exempt decision.

(5) In subsection (4) "exempt decision" means any decision—
(a) in respect of which the condition in subsection (6) and the condition in subsection (7) are met, or
(b) which is made in such other circumstances as may be prescribed by the [Secretary of State] by order.

(6) The condition in this subsection is that the decision—
(a) is taken in the course of steps taken—
(i) for the purpose of considering whether to enter into a contract with the data subject,
(ii) with a view to entering into such a contract, or
(iii) in the course of performing such a contract, or
(b) is authorised or required by or under any enactment.

(7) The condition in this subsection is that either—
(a) the effect of the decision is to grant a request of the data subject, or
(b) steps have been taken to safeguard the legitimate interests of the data subject (for example, by allowing him to make representations).

(8) If a court is satisfied on the application of a data subject that a person taking a decision in respect of him ("the responsible person") has failed to comply with subsection (1) or (2)(b), the court may order the responsible person to reconsider the decision, or to take a new decision which is not based solely on such processing as is mentioned in subsection (1).

(9) An order under subsection (8) shall not affect the rights of any person other than the data subject and the responsible person.

[1320]–[1321]

NOTES

Sub-s (5): words in square brackets substituted by the Secretary of State for Constitutional Affairs Order 2003, SI 2003/1887, art 9, Sch 2, para 9(1)(a), as from 19 August 2003.

Orders: as of 6 April 2008 no Orders had been made under this section.

12A *(By virtue of Sch 13, para 1 to this Act, this section ceased to have effect on 23 October 2007.)*

13 Compensation for failure to comply with certain requirements

(1) An individual who suffers damage by reason of any contravention by a data controller of any of the requirements of this Act is entitled to compensation from the data controller for that damage.

(2) An individual who suffers distress by reason of any contravention by a data controller of any of the requirements of this Act is entitled to compensation from the data controller for that distress if—
(a) the individual also suffers damage by reason of the contravention, or
(b) the contravention relates to the processing of personal data for the special purposes.

(3) In proceedings brought against a person by virtue of this section it is a defence to prove that he had taken such care as in all the circumstances was reasonably required to comply with the requirement concerned.

[1322]

14 Rectification, blocking, erasure and destruction

(1) If a court is satisfied on the application of a data subject that personal data of which the applicant is the subject are inaccurate, the court may order the data controller to rectify, block, erase or destroy those data and any other personal data in respect of which he is the data controller and which contain an expression of opinion which appears to the court to be based on the inaccurate data.

(2) Subsection (1) applies whether or not the data accurately record information received or obtained by the data controller from the data subject or a third party but where the data accurately record such information, then—

(a) if the requirements mentioned in paragraph 7 of Part II of Schedule 1 have been complied with, the court may, instead of making an order under subsection (1), make an order requiring the data to be supplemented by such statement of the true facts relating to the matters dealt with by the data as the court may approve, and

(b) if all or any of those requirements have not been complied with, the court may, instead of making an order under that subsection, make such order as it thinks fit for securing compliance with those requirements with or without a further order requiring the data to be supplemented by such a statement as is mentioned in paragraph (a).

(3) Where the court—

(a) makes an order under subsection (1), or

(b) is satisfied on the application of a data subject that personal data of which he was the data subject and which have been rectified, blocked, erased or destroyed were inaccurate,

it may, where it considers it reasonably practicable, order the data controller to notify third parties to whom the data have been disclosed of the rectification, blocking, erasure or destruction.

(4) If a court is satisfied on the application of a data subject—

(a) that he has suffered damage by reason of any contravention by a data controller of any of the requirements of this Act in respect of any personal data, in circumstances entitling him to compensation under section 13, and

(b) that there is a substantial risk of further contravention in respect of those data in such circumstances,

the court may order the rectification, blocking, erasure or destruction of any of those data.

(5) Where the court makes an order under subsection (4) it may, where it considers it reasonably practicable, order the data controller to notify third parties to whom the data have been disclosed of the rectification, blocking, erasure or destruction.

(6) In determining whether it is reasonably practicable to require such notification as is mentioned in subsection (3) or (5) the court shall have regard, in particular, to the number of persons who would have to be notified.

[1323]

15 Jurisdiction and procedure

(1) The jurisdiction conferred by sections 7 to 14 is exercisable by the High Court or a county court or, in Scotland, by the Court of Session or the sheriff.

(2) For the purpose of determining any question whether an applicant under subsection (9) of section 7 is entitled to the information which he seeks (including any question whether any relevant data are exempt from that section by virtue of Part IV) a court may require the information constituting any data processed by or on behalf of the data controller and any information as to the logic involved in any decision-taking as mentioned in section 7(1)(d) to be made available for its own inspection but shall not, pending the determination of that question in the applicant's favour, require the information sought by the applicant to be disclosed to him or his representatives whether by discovery (or, in Scotland, recovery) or otherwise.

[1324]

PART IV
EXEMPTIONS

27 Preliminary

(1) References in any of the data protection principles or any provision of Parts II and III to personal data or to the processing of personal data do not include references to data or processing which by virtue of this Part are exempt from that principle or other provision.

(2) In this Part "the subject information provisions" means—

(a) the first data protection principle to the extent to which it requires compliance with paragraph 2 of Part II of Schedule 1, and

(b) section 7.

(3) In this Part "the non-disclosure provisions" means the provisions specified in subsection (4) to the extent to which they are inconsistent with the disclosure in question.

(4) The provisions referred to in subsection (3) are—
(a) the first data protection principle, except to the extent to which it requires compliance with the conditions in Schedules 2 and 3,
(b) the second, third, fourth and fifth data protection principles, and
(c) sections 10 and 14(1) to (3).

(5) Except as provided by this Part, the subject information provisions shall have effect notwithstanding any enactment or rule of law prohibiting or restricting the disclosure, or authorising the withholding, of information.

[1325]

[33A Manual data held by public authorities

(1) Personal data falling within paragraph (e) of the definition of "data" in section 1(1) are exempt from—
(a) the first, second, third, fifth, seventh and eighth data protection principles,
(b) the sixth data protection principle except so far as it relates to the rights conferred on data subjects by sections 7 and 14,
(c) sections 10 to 12,
(d) section 13, except so far as it relates to damage caused by a contravention of section 7 or of the fourth data protection principle and to any distress which is also suffered by reason of that contravention,
(e) Part III, and
(f) section 55.

(2) Personal data which fall within paragraph (e) of the definition of "data" in section 1(1) and relate to appointments or removals, pay, discipline, superannuation or other personnel matters, in relation to—
(a) service in any of the armed forces of the Crown,
(b) service in any office or employment under the Crown or under any public authority, or
(c) service in any office or employment, or under any contract for services, in respect of which power to take action, or to determine or approve the action taken, in such matters is vested in Her Majesty, any Minister of the Crown, the National Assembly for Wales, any Northern Ireland Minister (within the meaning of the Freedom of Information Act 2000) or any public authority,

are also exempt from the remaining data protection principles and the remaining provisions of Part II.]

[1325A]

NOTES

Commencement: 1 January 2005.

Inserted by the Freedom of Information Act 2000, s 70(1), as from 1 January 2005.

As to the meaning of employment by or under the Crown, see also the National Assembly for Wales Commission (Crown Status) Order 2007, SI 2007/1118, art 5.

35 Disclosures required by law or made in connection with legal proceedings etc

(1) Personal data are exempt from the non-disclosure provisions where the disclosure is required by or under any enactment, by any rule of law or by the order of a court.

(2) Personal data are exempt from the non-disclosure provisions where the disclosure is necessary—
(a) for the purpose of, or in connection with, any legal proceedings (including prospective legal proceedings), or
(b) for the purpose of obtaining legal advice,

or is otherwise necessary for the purposes of establishing, exercising or defending legal rights.

[1326]

37 Miscellaneous exemptions

Schedule 7 (which confers further miscellaneous exemptions) has effect.

[1327]–[1328]

PART V
ENFORCEMENT

40 Enforcement notices

(1) If the Commissioner is satisfied that a data controller has contravened or is contravening any of the data protection principles, the Commissioner may serve him with a notice (in this Act referred to as "an enforcement notice") requiring him, for complying with the principle or principles in question, to do either or both of the following—

(a) to take within such time as may be specified in the notice, or to refrain from taking after such time as may be so specified, such steps as are so specified, or

(b) to refrain from processing any personal data, or any personal data of a description specified in the notice, or to refrain from processing them for a purpose so specified or in a manner so specified, after such time as may be so specified.

(2) In deciding whether to serve an enforcement notice, the Commissioner shall consider whether the contravention has caused or is likely to cause any person damage or distress.

(3) An enforcement notice in respect of a contravention of the fourth data protection principle which requires the data controller to rectify, block, erase or destroy any inaccurate data may also require the data controller to rectify, block, erase or destroy any other data held by him and containing an expression of opinion which appears to the Commissioner to be based on the inaccurate data.

(4) An enforcement notice in respect of a contravention of the fourth data protection principle, in the case of data which accurately record information received or obtained by the data controller from the data subject or a third party, may require the data controller either—

(a) to rectify, block, erase or destroy any inaccurate data and any other data held by him and containing an expression of opinion as mentioned in subsection (3), or

(b) to take such steps as are specified in the notice for securing compliance with the requirements specified in paragraph 7 of Part II of Schedule 1 and, if the Commissioner thinks fit, for supplementing the data with such statement of the true facts relating to the matters dealt with by the data as the Commissioner may approve.

(5) Where—

(a) an enforcement notice requires the data controller to rectify, block, erase or destroy any personal data, or

(b) the Commissioner is satisfied that personal data which have been rectified, blocked, erased or destroyed had been processed in contravention of any of the data protection principles,

an enforcement notice may, if reasonably practicable, require the data controller to notify third parties to whom the data have been disclosed of the rectification, blocking, erasure or destruction; and in determining whether it is reasonably practicable to require such notification regard shall be had, in particular, to the number of persons who would have to be notified.

(6) An enforcement notice must contain—

(a) a statement of the data protection principle or principles which the Commissioner is satisfied have been or are being contravened and his reasons for reaching that conclusion, and

(b) particulars of the rights of appeal conferred by section 48.

(7) Subject to subsection (8), an enforcement notice must not require any of the provisions of the notice to be complied with before the end of the period within which an appeal can be brought against the notice and, if such an appeal is brought, the notice need not be complied with pending the determination or withdrawal of the appeal.

(8) If by reason of special circumstances the Commissioner considers that an enforcement notice should be complied with as a matter of urgency he may include in the notice a statement to that effect and a statement of his reasons for reaching that conclusion; and in that event subsection (7) shall not apply but the notice must not require the provisions of the notice to be complied with before the end of the period of seven days beginning with the day on which the notice is served.

(9) Notification regulations (as defined by section 16(2)) may make provision as to the effect of the service of an enforcement notice on any entry in the register maintained under section 19 which relates to the person on whom the notice is served.

(10) This section has effect subject to section 46(1).

[1329]

NOTES

Regulations: as of 6 April 2008 no Regulations had been made under this section.

41 Cancellation of enforcement notice

(1) If the Commissioner considers that all or any of the provisions of an enforcement notice need not be complied with in order to ensure compliance with the data protection principle or principles to which it relates, he may cancel or vary the notice by written notice to the person on whom it was served.

(2) A person on whom an enforcement notice has been served may, at any time after the expiry of the period during which an appeal can be brought against that notice, apply in writing to the Commissioner for the cancellation or variation of that notice on the ground that, by reason of a change of circumstances, all or any of the provisions of that notice need not be complied with in order to ensure compliance with the data protection principle or principles to which that notice relates.

[1330]

42 Request for assessment

(1) A request may be made to the Commissioner by or on behalf of any person who is, or believes himself to be, directly affected by any processing of personal data for an assessment as to whether it is likely or unlikely that the processing has been or is being carried out in compliance with the provisions of this Act.

(2) On receiving a request under this section, the Commissioner shall make an assessment in such manner as appears to him to be appropriate, unless he has not been supplied with such information as he may reasonably require in order to—

- (a) satisfy himself as to the identity of the person making the request, and
- (b) enable him to identify the processing in question.

(3) The matters to which the Commissioner may have regard in determining in what manner it is appropriate to make an assessment include—

- (a) the extent to which the request appears to him to raise a matter of substance,
- (b) any undue delay in making the request, and
- (c) whether or not the person making the request is entitled to make an application under section 7 in respect of the personal data in question.

(4) Where the Commissioner has received a request under this section he shall notify the person who made the request—

- (a) whether he has made an assessment as a result of the request, and
- (b) to the extent that he considers appropriate, having regard in particular to any exemption from section 7 applying in relation to the personal data concerned, of any view formed or action taken as a result of the request.

[1331]

47 Failure to comply with notice

(1) A person who fails to comply with an enforcement notice, an information notice or a special information notice is guilty of an offence.

(2) A person who, in purported compliance with an information notice or a special information notice—

- (a) makes a statement which he knows to be false in a material respect, or
- (b) recklessly makes a statement which is false in a material respect,

is guilty of an offence.

(3) It is a defence for a person charged with an offence under subsection (1) to prove that he exercised all due diligence to comply with the notice in question.

[1332]

48 Rights of appeal

(1) A person on whom an enforcement notice, an information notice or a special information notice has been served may appeal to the Tribunal against the notice.

(2) A person on whom an enforcement notice has been served may appeal to the Tribunal against the refusal of an application under section 41(2) for cancellation or variation of the notice.

(3) Where an enforcement notice, an information notice or a special information notice contains a statement by the Commissioner in accordance with section 40(8), 43(5) or 44(6) then, whether or not the person appeals against the notice, he may appeal against—

(a) the Commissioner's decision to include the statement in the notice, or
(b) the effect of the inclusion of the statement as respects any part of the notice.

(4) A data controller in respect of whom a determination has been made under section 45 may appeal to the Tribunal against the determination.

(5) Schedule 6 has effect in relation to appeals under this section and the proceedings of the Tribunal in respect of any such appeal.

[1333]

NOTES

As to appeals generally, see the Information Tribunal (Enforcement Appeals) Rules 2005, SI 2005/14.

49 Determination of appeals

(1) If on an appeal under section 48(1) the Tribunal considers—

(a) that the notice against which the appeal is brought is not in accordance with the law, or

(b) to the extent that the notice involved an exercise of discretion by the Commissioner, that he ought to have exercised his discretion differently,

the Tribunal shall allow the appeal or substitute such other notice or decision as could have been served or made by the Commissioner; and in any other case the Tribunal shall dismiss the appeal.

(2) On such an appeal, the Tribunal may review any determination of fact on which the notice in question was based.

(3) If on an appeal under section 48(2) the Tribunal considers that the enforcement notice ought to be cancelled or varied by reason of a change in circumstances, the Tribunal shall cancel or vary the notice.

(4) On an appeal under subsection (3) of section 48 the Tribunal may direct—

(a) that the notice in question shall have effect as if it did not contain any such statement as is mentioned in that subsection, or

(b) that the inclusion of the statement shall not have effect in relation to any part of the notice,

and may make such modifications in the notice as may be required for giving effect to the direction.

(5) On an appeal under section 48(4), the Tribunal may cancel the determination of the Commissioner.

(6) Any party to an appeal to the Tribunal under section 48 may appeal from the decision of the Tribunal on a point of law to the appropriate court; and that court shall be—

(a) the High Court of Justice in England if the address of the person who was the appellant before the Tribunal is in England or Wales,

(b) the Court of Session if that address is in Scotland, and

(c) the High Court of Justice in Northern Ireland if that address is in Northern Ireland.

(7) For the purposes of subsection (6)—

(a) the address of a registered company is that of its registered office, and

(b) the address of a person (other than a registered company) carrying on a business is that of his principal place of business in the United Kingdom.

[1334]

NOTES

As to appeals generally, see the Information Tribunal (Enforcement Appeals) Rules 2005, SI 2005/14.

PART VI
MISCELLANEOUS AND GENERAL

Functions of Commissioner

51 General duties of Commissioner

(1) It shall be the duty of the Commissioner to promote the following of good practice by data controllers and, in particular, so to perform his functions under this Act as to promote the observance of the requirements of this Act by data controllers.

(2) The Commissioner shall arrange for the dissemination in such form and manner as he considers appropriate of such information as it may appear to him expedient to give to the public about the operation of this Act, about good practice, and about other matters within the scope of his functions under this Act, and may give advice to any person as to any of those matters.

(3) Where—

(a) the [Secretary of State] so directs by order, or

(b) the Commissioner considers it appropriate to do so,

the Commissioner shall, after such consultation with trade associations, data subjects or persons representing data subjects as appears to him to be appropriate, prepare and disseminate to such persons as he considers appropriate codes of practice for guidance as to good practice.

(4) The Commissioner shall also—

(a) where he considers it appropriate to do so, encourage trade associations to prepare, and to disseminate to their members, such codes of practice, and

(b) where any trade association submits a code of practice to him for his consideration, consider the code and, after such consultation with data subjects or persons representing data subjects as appears to him to be appropriate, notify the trade association whether in his opinion the code promotes the following of good practice.

(5) An order under subsection (3) shall describe the personal data or processing to which the code of practice is to relate, and may also describe the persons or classes of persons to whom it is to relate.

(6) The Commissioner shall arrange for the dissemination in such form and manner as he considers appropriate of—

(a) any Community finding as defined by paragraph 15(2) of Part II of Schedule 1,

(b) any decision of the European Commission, under the procedure provided for in Article 31(2) of the Data Protection Directive, which is made for the purposes of Article 26(3) or (4) of the Directive, and

(c) such other information as it may appear to him to be expedient to give to data controllers in relation to any personal data about the protection of the rights and freedoms of data subjects in relation to the processing of personal data in countries and territories outside the European Economic Area.

(7) The Commissioner may, with the consent of the data controller, assess any processing of personal data for the following of good practice and shall inform the data controller of the results of the assessment.

(8) The Commissioner may charge such sums as he may with the consent of the [Secretary of State] determine for any services provided by the Commissioner by virtue of this Part.

(9) In this section—

"good practice" means such practice in the processing of personal data as appears to the Commissioner to be desirable having regard to the interests of data subjects and others, and includes (but is not limited to) compliance with the requirements of this Act;

"trade association" includes any body representing data controllers.

[1335]

NOTES

Sub-ss (3), (8): words in square brackets substituted by the Secretary of State for Constitutional Affairs Order 2003, SI 2003/1887, art 9, Sch 2, para 9(1)(a), as from 19 August 2003.

Codes of Practice: see the Employment Practices Data Protection Code at **[4706]** issued by the Information Commissioner under this section. Note that unlike other statutory provisions authorising the making of codes of practice, this section has no provision requiring an Order to bring the code into effect.

Orders: as of 6 April 2008 no Orders had been made under this section.

52 Reports and codes of practice to be laid before Parliament

(1) The Commissioner shall lay annually before each House of Parliament a general report on the exercise of his functions under this Act.

(2) The Commissioner may from time to time lay before each House of Parliament such other reports with respect to those functions as he thinks fit.

(3) The Commissioner shall lay before each House of Parliament any code of practice prepared under section 51(3) for complying with a direction of the [Secretary of State], unless the code is included in any report laid under subsection (1) or (2).

[1336]

NOTES

Sub-s (3): words in square brackets substituted by the Secretary of State for Constitutional Affairs Order 2003, SI 2003/1887, art 9, Sch 2, para 9(1)(a), as from 19 August 2003.

Codes of Practice: see the note to s 51 at **[1335]**.

Records obtained under data subject's right of access

56 Prohibition of requirement as to production of certain records

(1) A person must not, in connection with—

(a) the recruitment of another person as an employee,

(b) the continued employment of another person, or

(c) any contract for the provision of services to him by another person,

require that other person or a third party to supply him with a relevant record or to produce a relevant record to him.

(2) A person concerned with the provision (for payment or not) of goods, facilities or services to the public or a section of the public must not, as a condition of providing or offering to provide any goods, facilities or services to another person, require that other person or a third party to supply him with a relevant record or to produce a relevant record to him.

(3) Subsections (1) and (2) do not apply to a person who shows—

(a) that the imposition of the requirement was required or authorised by or under any enactment, by any rule of law or by the order of a court, or

(b) that in the particular circumstances the imposition of the requirement was justified as being in the public interest.

(4) Having regard to the provisions of Part V of the Police Act 1997 (certificates of criminal records etc), the imposition of the requirement referred to in subsection (1) or (2) is not to be regarded as being justified as being in the public interest on the ground that it would assist in the prevention or detection of crime.

(5) A person who contravenes subsection (1) or (2) is guilty of an offence.

(6) In this section "a relevant record" means any record which—

(a) has been or is to be obtained by a data subject from any data controller specified in the first column of the Table below in the exercise of the right conferred by section 7, and

(b) contains information relating to any matter specified in relation to that data controller in the second column,

and includes a copy of such a record or a part of such a record.

Table

Data controller	*Subject-matter*
1. Any of the following persons— (a) a chief officer of police of a police force in England and Wales. (b) a chief constable of a police force in Scotland. (c) the [Chief Constable of the Police Service of Northern Ireland]. [(d) the Director General of the Serious Organised Crime Agency.]	(a) Convictions. (b) Cautions.
2. The Secretary of State.	(a) Convictions. (b) Cautions. (c) His functions under [section 92 of the Powers of Criminal Courts (Sentencing) Act 2000], section 205(2) or 208 of the Criminal Procedure (Scotland) Act 1995 or section 73 of the Children and Young Persons Act (Northern Ireland) 1968 in relation to any person sentenced to detention. (d) His functions under the Prison Act 1952, the Prisons (Scotland) Act 1989 or the Prison Act (Northern Ireland) 1953 in relation to any person imprisoned or detained. (e) His functions under the Social Security Contributions and Benefits Act 1992, the Social Security Administration Act 1992 or the Jobseekers Act 1995. (f) His functions under Part V of the Police Act 1997. [(g) His functions under the Safeguarding Vulnerable Groups Act 2006 [or the Safeguarding Vulnerable Groups (Northern Ireland) Order 2007].]
3. The Department of Health and Social Services for Northern Ireland.	Its functions under the Social Security Contributions and Benefits (Northern Ireland) Act 1992, the Social Security Administration (Northern Ireland) Act 1992 or the Jobseekers (Northern Ireland) Order 1995.
[4 The Independent Barring Board.	Its functions under the Safeguarding Vulnerable Groups Act 2006 [or the Safeguarding Vulnerable Groups (Northern Ireland) Order 2007].]

[(6A) A record is not a relevant record to the extent that it relates, or is to relate, only to personal data falling within paragraph (e) of the definition of "data" in section 1(1).]

(7) In the Table in subsection (6)—

"caution" means a caution given to any person in England and Wales or Northern Ireland in respect of an offence which, at the time when the caution is given, is admitted;

"conviction" has the same meaning as in the Rehabilitation of Offenders Act 1974 or the Rehabilitation of Offenders (Northern Ireland) Order 1978.

(8) The [Secretary of State] may by order amend—
(a) the Table in subsection (6), and
(b) subsection (7).

(9) For the purposes of this section a record which states that a data controller is not processing any personal data relating to a particular matter shall be taken to be a record containing information relating to that matter.

(10) In this section "employee" means an individual who—
(a) works under a contract of employment, as defined by section 230(2) of the Employment Rights Act 1996, or
(b) holds any office,

whether or not he is entitled to remuneration; and "employment" shall be construed accordingly.

[1337]

NOTES

Sub-s (6): words in square brackets in sub-para 1(c) of the table substituted by the Police (Northern Ireland) Act 2000, s 78(2)(a); sub-para 1(d) of the table substituted, for original sub-paras 1(d), (e), by the Serious Organised Crime and Police Act 2005, Sch 4, para 112, as from 1 April 2006; sub-para (2)(g) of the table, and para 4 of the table, inserted by the Safeguarding Vulnerable Groups Act 2006, s 63(1), Sch 9, Pt 2, para 15(1), (2), as from a day to be appointed; words in square brackets in those entries inserted by the Safeguarding Vulnerable Groups (Northern Ireland) Order 2007, SI 2007/1351, art 60, Sch 7, para 4(1), as from a day to be appointed; words in square brackets in sub-para 2(c) of the table substituted by the Powers of Criminal Courts (Sentencing) Act 2000, s 165(1), Sch 9, para 191, as from 25 August 2000.

Sub-s (6A): inserted by the Freedom of Information Act 2000, s 68(4), as from 1 January 2005.

Sub-s (8): words in square brackets substituted by the Secretary of State for Constitutional Affairs Order 2003, SI 2003/1887, art 9, Sch 2, para 9(1)(a), as from 19 August 2003.

Orders: as of 6 April 2007 no Orders had been made under this section.

57 Avoidance of certain contractual terms relating to health records

(1) Any term or condition of a contract is void in so far as it purports to require an individual—
(a) to supply any other person with a record to which this section applies, or with a copy of such a record or a part of such a record, or
(b) to produce to any other person such a record, copy or part.

(2) This section applies to any record which—
(a) has been or is to be obtained by a data subject in the exercise of the right conferred by section 7, and
(b) consists of the information contained in any health record as defined by section 68(2).

[1338]–[1339]

General

75 Short title, commencement and extent

(1) This Act may be cited as the Data Protection Act 1998.

(2) The following provisions of this Act—
(a) sections 1 to 3,
(b) section 25(1) and (4),
(c) section 26,
(d) sections 67 to 71,
(e) this section,
(f) paragraph 17 of Schedule 5,
(g) Schedule 11,
(h) Schedule 12, and
(i) so much of any other provision of this Act as confers any power to make subordinate legislation,

shall come into force on the day on which this Act is passed.

(3) The remaining provisions of this Act shall come into force on such day as the [Secretary of State] may by order appoint; and different days may be appointed for different purposes.

(4) The day appointed under subsection (3) for the coming into force of section 56 must not be earlier than the first day on which sections 112, 113 and 115 of the Police Act 1997 (which provide for the issue by the Secretary of State of criminal conviction certificates, criminal record certificates and enhanced criminal record certificates) are all in force.

[(4A) Subsection (4) does not apply to section 56 so far as that section relates to a record containing information relating to—

(a) the Secretary of State's functions under the Safeguarding Vulnerable Groups Act 2006 [or the Safeguarding Vulnerable Groups (Northern Ireland) Order 2007], or

(b) the Independent Barring Board's functions under that Act [or that Order].]

(5) Subject to subsection (6), this Act extends to Northern Ireland.

(6) Any amendment, repeal or revocation made by Schedule 15 or 16 has the same extent as that of the enactment or instrument to which it relates.

[1340]

NOTES

Sub-s (3): words in square brackets substituted by the Secretary of State for Constitutional Affairs Order 2003, SI 2003/1887, art 9, Sch 2, para 9(1)(a), as from 19 August 2003.

Sub-s (4A): inserted by the Safeguarding Vulnerable Groups Act 2006, s 63(1), Sch 9, Pt 2, para 15(1), (3), as from a day to be appointed; words in square brackets inserted by the Safeguarding Vulnerable Groups (Northern Ireland) Order 2007, SI 2007/1351, art 60, Sch 7, para 4(2), as from a day to be appointed.

Orders: the Data Protection Act 1998 (Commencement) Order 2000, SI 2000/183.

SCHEDULES

SCHEDULE 1
THE DATA PROTECTION PRINCIPLES

PART I
THE PRINCIPLES

1. Personal data shall be processed fairly and lawfully and, in particular, shall not be processed unless—

(a) at least one of the conditions in Schedule 2 is met, and

(b) in the case of sensitive personal data, at least one of the conditions in Schedule 3 is also met.

2. Personal data shall be obtained only for one or more specified and lawful purposes, and shall not be further processed in any manner incompatible with that purpose or those purposes.

3. Personal data shall be adequate, relevant and not excessive in relation to the purpose or purposes for which they are processed.

4. Personal data shall be accurate and, where necessary, kept up to date.

5. Personal data processed for any purpose or purposes shall not be kept for longer than is necessary for that purpose or those purposes.

6. Personal data shall be processed in accordance with the rights of data subjects under this Act.

7. Appropriate technical and organisational measures shall be taken against unauthorised or unlawful processing of personal data and against accidental loss or destruction of, or damage to, personal data.

8. Personal data shall not be transferred to a country or territory outside the European Economic Area unless that country or territory ensures an adequate level of protection for the rights and freedoms of data subjects in relation to the processing of personal data.

[1341]

PART II
INTERPRETATION OF THE PRINCIPLES IN PART I

The first principle

1.—(1) In determining for the purposes of the first principle whether personal data are processed fairly, regard is to be had to the method by which they are obtained, including in particular whether any person from whom they are obtained is deceived or misled as to the purpose or purposes for which they are to be processed.

(2) Subject to paragraph 2, for the purposes of the first principle data are to be treated as obtained fairly if they consist of information obtained from a person who—
- (a) is authorised by or under any enactment to supply it, or
- (b) is required to supply it by or under any enactment or by any convention or other instrument imposing an international obligation on the United Kingdom.

2.—(1) Subject to paragraph 3, for the purposes of the first principle personal data are not to be treated as processed fairly unless—
- (a) in the case of data obtained from the data subject, the data controller ensures so far as practicable that the data subject has, is provided with, or has made readily available to him, the information specified in sub-paragraph (3), and
- (b) in any other case, the data controller ensures so far as practicable that, before the relevant time or as soon as practicable after that time, the data subject has, is provided with, or has made readily available to him, the information specified in sub-paragraph (3).

(2) In sub-paragraph (1)(b) "the relevant time" means—
- (a) the time when the data controller first processes the data, or
- (b) in a case where at that time disclosure to a third party within a reasonable period is envisaged—
  - (i) if the data are in fact disclosed to such a person within that period, the time when the data are first disclosed,
  - (ii) if within that period the data controller becomes, or ought to become, aware that the data are unlikely to be disclosed to such a person within that period, the time when the data controller does become, or ought to become, so aware, or
  - (iii) in any other case, the end of that period.

(3) The information referred to in sub-paragraph (1) is as follows, namely—
- (a) the identity of the data controller,
- (b) if he has nominated a representative for the purposes of this Act, the identity of that representative,
- (c) the purpose or purposes for which the data are intended to be processed, and
- (d) any further information which is necessary, having regard to the specific circumstances in which the data are or are to be processed, to enable processing in respect of the data subject to be fair.

3.—(1) Paragraph 2(1)(b) does not apply where either of the primary conditions in sub-paragraph (2), together with such further conditions as may be prescribed by the [Secretary of State] by order, are met.

(2) The primary conditions referred to in sub-paragraph (1) are—
- (a) that the provision of that information would involve a disproportionate effort, or
- (b) that the recording of the information to be contained in the data by, or the disclosure of the data by, the data controller is necessary for compliance with any legal obligation to which the data controller is subject, other than an obligation imposed by contract.

4.—(1) Personal data which contain a general identifier falling within a description prescribed by the [Secretary of State] by order are not to be treated as processed fairly and lawfully unless they are processed in compliance with any conditions so prescribed in relation to general identifiers of that description.

(2) In sub-paragraph (1) "a general identifier" means any identifier (such as, for example, a number or code used for identification purposes) which—
- (a) relates to an individual, and
- (b) forms part of a set of similar identifiers which is of general application.

The second principle

5. The purpose or purposes for which personal data are obtained may in particular be specified—
- (a) in a notice given for the purposes of paragraph 2 by the data controller to the data subject, or
- (b) in a notification given to the Commissioner under Part III of this Act.

6. In determining whether any disclosure of personal data is compatible with the purpose or purposes for which the data were obtained, regard is to be had to the purpose or purposes for which the personal data are intended to be processed by any person to whom they are disclosed.

The fourth principle

7. The fourth principle is not to be regarded as being contravened by reason of any inaccuracy in personal data which accurately record information obtained by the data controller from the data subject or a third party in a case where—
- (a) having regard to the purpose or purposes for which the data were obtained and further processed, the data controller has taken reasonable steps to ensure the accuracy of the data, and
- (b) if the data subject has notified the data controller of the data subject's view that the data are inaccurate, the data indicate that fact.

The sixth principle

8. A person is to be regarded as contravening the sixth principle if, but only if—
- (a) he contravenes section 7 by failing to supply information in accordance with that section,
- (b) he contravenes section 10 by failing to comply with a notice given under subsection (1) of that section to the extent that the notice is justified or by failing to give a notice under subsection (3) of that section,
- (c) he contravenes section 11 by failing to comply with a notice given under subsection (1) of that section, or
- (d) he contravenes section 12 by failing to comply with a notice given under subsection (1) or (2)(b) of that section or by failing to give a notification under subsection (2)(a) of that section or a notice under subsection (3) of that section.

The seventh principle

9. Having regard to the state of technological development and the cost of implementing any measures, the measures must ensure a level of security appropriate to—
- (a) the harm that might result from such unauthorised or unlawful processing or accidental loss, destruction or damage as are mentioned in the seventh principle, and
- (b) the nature of the data to be protected.

10. The data controller must take reasonable steps to ensure the reliability of any employees of his who have access to the personal data.

11. Where processing of personal data is carried out by a data processor on behalf of a data controller, the data controller must in order to comply with the seventh principle—

(a) choose a data processor providing sufficient guarantees in respect of the technical and organisational security measures governing the processing to be carried out, and
(b) take reasonable steps to ensure compliance with those measures.

12. Where processing of personal data is carried out by a data processor on behalf of a data controller, the data controller is not to be regarded as complying with the seventh principle unless—
(a) the processing is carried out under a contract—
(i) which is made or evidenced in writing, and
(ii) under which the data processor is to act only on instructions from the data controller, and
(b) the contract requires the data processor to comply with obligations equivalent to those imposed on a data controller by the seventh principle.

The eighth principle

13. An adequate level of protection is one which is adequate in all the circumstances of the case, having regard in particular to—
(a) the nature of the personal data,
(b) the country or territory of origin of the information contained in the data,
(c) the country or territory of final destination of that information,
(d) the purposes for which and period during which the data are intended to be processed,
(e) the law in force in the country or territory in question,
(f) the international obligations of that country or territory,
(g) any relevant codes of conduct or other rules which are enforceable in that country or territory (whether generally or by arrangement in particular cases), and
(h) any security measures taken in respect of the data in that country or territory.

14. The eighth principle does not apply to a transfer falling within any paragraph of Schedule 4, except in such circumstances and to such extent as the [Secretary of State] may by order provide.

15.—(1) Where—
(a) in any proceedings under this Act any question arises as to whether the requirement of the eighth principle as to an adequate level of protection is met in relation to the transfer of any personal data to a country or territory outside the European Economic Area, and
(b) a Community finding has been made in relation to transfers of the kind in question,

that question is to be determined in accordance with that finding.

(2) In sub-paragraph (1) "Community finding" means a finding of the European Commission, under the procedure provided for in Article 31(2) of the Data Protection Directive, that a country or territory outside the European Economic Area does, or does not, ensure an adequate level of protection within the meaning of Article 25(2) of the Directive.
[1342]

NOTES

Paras 3, 4, 14: words in square brackets substituted by the Secretary of State for Constitutional Affairs Order 2003, SI 2003/1887, art 9, Sch 2, para 9(1)(b), as from 19 August 2003.

Orders: the Data Protection (Conditions under Paragraph 3 of Part II of Schedule 1) Order 2000, SI 2000/185.

SCHEDULE 2
CONDITIONS RELEVANT FOR PURPOSES OF THE FIRST PRINCIPLE: PROCESSING OF ANY PERSONAL DATA

Section 4(3)

1. The data subject has given his consent to the processing.

2. The processing is necessary—
(a) for the performance of a contract to which the data subject is a party, or

(b) for the taking of steps at the request of the data subject with a view to entering into a contract.

3. The processing is necessary for compliance with any legal obligation to which the data controller is subject, other than an obligation imposed by contract.

4. The processing is necessary in order to protect the vital interests of the data subject.

5. The processing is necessary—
(a) for the administration of justice,
[(aa) for the exercise of any functions of either House of Parliament,]
(b) for the exercise of any functions conferred on any person by or under any enactment,
(c) for the exercise of any functions of the Crown, a Minister of the Crown or a government department, or
(d) for the exercise of any other functions of a public nature exercised in the public interest by any person.

6.—(1) The processing is necessary for the purposes of legitimate interests pursued by the data controller or by the third party or parties to whom the data are disclosed, except where the processing is unwarranted in any particular case by reason of prejudice to the rights and freedoms or legitimate interests of the data subject.

(2) The [Secretary of State] may by order specify particular circumstances in which this condition is, or is not, to be taken to be satisfied.

[1343]

NOTES

Para 5: sub-para (aa) inserted by the Freedom of Information Act 2000, s 73, Sch 6, para 4, as from 1 January 2005.

Para 6: words in square brackets substituted by the Secretary of State for Constitutional Affairs Order 2003, SI 2003/1887, art 9, Sch 2, para 9(1)(b), as from 19 August 2003.

By virtue of the Northern Ireland Assembly Commission (Crown Status) Order 1999, SI 1999/3145, art 9(3)(b), the functions of the Commission are treated as functions of the Crown for the purposes of para 5.

As to the meaning of government department, see also the National Assembly for Wales Commission (Crown Status) Order 2007, SI 2007/1118, art 5.

Orders: as of 6 April 2008 no Orders had been made under para 6.

SCHEDULE 3
CONDITIONS RELEVANT FOR PURPOSES OF THE FIRST PRINCIPLE: PROCESSING OF SENSITIVE PERSONAL DATA

Section 4(3)

1. The data subject has given his explicit consent to the processing of the personal data.

2.—(1) The processing is necessary for the purposes of exercising or performing any right or obligation which is conferred or imposed by law on the data controller in connection with employment.

(2) The [Secretary of State] may by order—
(a) exclude the application of sub-paragraph (1) in such cases as may be specified, or
(b) provide that, in such cases as may be specified, the condition in subparagraph (1) is not to be regarded as satisfied unless such further conditions as may be specified in the order are also satisfied.

3. The processing is necessary—
(a) in order to protect the vital interests of the data subject or another person, in a case where—
(i) consent cannot be given by or on behalf of the data subject, or
(ii) the data controller cannot reasonably be expected to obtain the consent of the data subject, or
(b) in order to protect the vital interests of another person, in a case where consent by or on behalf of the data subject has been unreasonably withheld.

4. The processing—

(a) is carried out in the course of its legitimate activities by any body or association which—
  (i) is not established or conducted for profit, and
  (ii) exists for political, philosophical religious or trade-union purposes,
(b) is carried out with appropriate safeguards for the rights and freedoms of data subjects,
(c) relates only to individuals who either are members of the body or association or have regular contact with it in connection with its purposes, and
(d) does not involve disclosure of the personal data to a third party without the consent of the data subject.

5. The information contained in the personal data has been made public as a result of steps deliberately taken by the data subject.

6. The processing—
(a) is necessary for the purpose of, or in connection with, any legal proceedings (including prospective legal proceedings),
(b) is necessary for the purpose of obtaining legal advice, or
(c) is otherwise necessary for the purposes of establishing, exercising or defending legal rights.

7.—(1) The processing is necessary—
(a) for the administration of justice,
[(aa) for the exercise of any functions of either House of Parliament,]
(b) for the exercise of any functions conferred on any person by or under an enactment, or
(c) for the exercise of any functions of the Crown, a Minister of the Crown or a government department.

(2) The [Secretary of State] may by order—
(a) exclude the application of sub-paragraph (1) in such cases as may be specified, or
(b) provide that, in such cases as may be specified, the condition in subparagraph (1) is not to be regarded as satisfied unless such further conditions as may be specified in the order are also satisfied.

[7A.—(1) The processing—
(a) is either—
  (i) the disclosure of sensitive personal data by a person as a member of an anti-fraud organisation or otherwise in accordance with any arrangements made by such an organisation; or
  (ii) any other processing by that person or another person of sensitive personal data so disclosed; and
(b) is necessary for the purposes of preventing fraud or a particular kind of fraud.

(2) In this paragraph "an anti-fraud organisation" means any unincorporated association, body corporate or other person which enables or facilitates any sharing of information to prevent fraud or a particular kind of fraud or which has any of these functions as its purpose or one of its purposes.]

8.—(1) The processing is necessary for medical purposes and is undertaken by—
(a) a health professional, or
(b) a person who in the circumstances owes a duty of confidentiality which is equivalent to that which would arise if that person were a health professional.

(2) In this paragraph "medical purposes" includes the purposes of preventative medicine, medical diagnosis, medical research, the provision of care and treatment and the management of healthcare services.

9.—(1) The processing—
(a) is of sensitive personal data consisting of information as to racial or ethnic origin,
(b) is necessary for the purpose of identifying or keeping under review the existence or absence of equality of opportunity or treatment between persons of different racial or ethnic origins, with a view to enabling such equality to be promoted or maintained, and
(c) is carried out with appropriate safeguards for the rights and freedoms of data subjects.

(2) The [Secretary of State] may by order specify circumstances in which processing falling within sub-paragraph (1)(a) and (b) is, or is not, to be taken for the purposes of sub-paragraph (1)(c) to be carried out with appropriate safeguards for the rights and freedoms of data subjects.

10. The personal data are processed in circumstances specified in an order made by the [Secretary of State] for the purposes of this paragraph

[1344]

NOTES

Paras 2, 9, 10: words in square brackets substituted by the Secretary of State for Constitutional Affairs Order 2003, SI 2003/1887, art 9, Sch 2, para 9(1)(b), as from 19 August 2003.

Para 7: sub-para (1)(aa) inserted by the Freedom of Information Act 2000, s 73, Sch 6, para 5, as from 1 January 2005; words in square brackets in sub-para (2) substituted by SI 2003/1887, art 9, Sch 2, para 9(1)(b), as from 19 August 2003.

Para 7A: inserted by the Serious Crime Act 2007, s 72, as from a day to be appointed.

By virtue of the Northern Ireland Assembly Commission (Crown Status) Order 1999, SI 1999/3145, art 9(3)(b), the functions of the Commission are treated as functions of the Crown for the purposes of para 7.

As to the meaning of government department, see also the National Assembly for Wales Commission (Crown Status) Order 2007, SI 2007/1118, art 5.

Orders: the Data Protection (Processing of Sensitive Personal Data) Order 2000, SI 2000/417 at **[2622]**; the Data Protection (Processing of Sensitive Personal Data) (Elected Representatives) Order 2002, SI 2002/2905; the Data Protection (Processing of Sensitive Personal Data) Order 2006, SI 2006/2068.

SCHEDULE 7
MISCELLANEOUS EXEMPTIONS

Section 37

Confidential references given by the data controller

1. Personal data are exempt from section 7 if they consist of a reference given or to be given in confidence by the data controller for the purposes of—
   - (a) the education, training or employment, or prospective education, training or employment, of the data subject,
   - (b) the appointment, or prospective appointment, of the data subject to any office, or
   - (c) the provision, or prospective provision, by the data subject of any service.

Judicial appointments and honours

2, 3. (*Outside the scope of this work.*)

Crown employment and Crown or Ministerial appointments

4.—[(1)] The [Secretary of State] may by order exempt from the subject information provisions personal data processed for the purposes of assessing any person's suitability for—
   - (a) employment by or under the Crown, or
   - (b) any office to which appointments are made by Her Majesty, by a Minister of the Crown or by a [Northern Ireland authority].

[(2) In this paragraph "Northern Ireland authority" means the First Minister, the deputy First Minister, a Northern Ireland Minister or a Northern Ireland department.]

Management forecasts etc

5. Personal data processed for the purposes of management forecasting or management planning to assist the data controller in the conduct of any business or other activity are exempt from the subject information provisions in any case to the extent to which the application of those provisions would be likely to prejudice the conduct of that business or other activity.

6. (*Outside the scope of this work.*)

Negotiations

7. Personal data which consist of records of the intentions of the data controller in relation to any negotiations with the data subject are exempt from the subject information provisions in any case to the extent to which the application of those provisions would be likely to prejudice those negotiations.

8–10. (*Outside the scope of this work.*)

Self-incrimination

11.—(1) A person need not comply with any request or order under section 7 to the extent that compliance would, by revealing evidence of the commission of any offence other than an offence under this Act, expose him to proceedings for that offence.

(2) Information disclosed by any person in compliance with any request or order under section 7 shall not be admissible against him in proceedings for an offence under this Act.

[1345]—[1348]

NOTES

Para 4: sub-para (1) numbered as such, words in second pair of square brackets in that sub-paragraph substituted, and sub-para (2) added, by the Northern Ireland Act 1998, s 99, Sch 13, para 21; words in first pair of square brackets in sub-para (1) substituted by the Secretary of State for Constitutional Affairs Order 2003, SI 2003/1887, art 9, Sch 2, para 9(1)(e), as from 19 August 2003.

By virtue of the Northern Ireland Assembly Commission (Crown Status) Order 1999, SI 1999/3145, art 9(3)(d), employment by or under the Commission is treated as employment by or under the Crown for the purposes of para 4.

As to the meaning of employment by or under the Crown, see also the National Assembly for Wales Commission (Crown Status) Order 2007, SI 2007/1118, art 5.

Orders: the Data Protection (Corporate Finance Exemption) Order 2000, SI 2000/184; the Data Protection (Crown Appointments) Order 2000, SI 2000/416.

(*Sch 8: following the expiry on 24 October 2007 of Sch 8, Pt III (Exemptions available after 23rd October 2001 but before 24th October 2007) this Schedule is, in so far as still in force, outside the scope of this work.*)

NATIONAL MINIMUM WAGE ACT 1998

(1998 c 39)

ARRANGEMENT OF SECTIONS

Entitlement to the national minimum wage

Regulations relating to the national minimum wage

Records

Officers

Information

Enforcement

Rights not to suffer unfair dismissal or other detriment

Offences

Special classes of person

Extensions

Exclusions

An Act to make provision for and in connection with a national minimum wage; to provide for the amendment of certain enactments relating to the remuneration of persons employed in agriculture; and for connected purposes

[31 July 1998]

NOTES

This Act is reproduced in full apart from ss 5–8 (which relate to the Low Pay Commission), 25–27, 29 and 30 (amendments to other Acts, incorporated therein), 46 and 47 (which relate to agricultural wages), 50 (publicity for the National Minimum Wage) and 53 (repeals and revocations) and Schs 1–3 (the Low Pay Commission, agricultural wages and repeals and revocations). The principal Regulations under this Act are the National Minimum Wage Regulations 1999, SI 1999/584 at **[2465]**. The obligation to pay the national minimum wage came into effect on 1 April 1999 (and all provisions of this Act not previously in force came into effect on that date, except as noted to the relevant provisions below).

Employment Appeal Tribunal: an appeal lies to the Employment Appeal Tribunal on any question of law arising from any decision of, or in any proceedings before, an employment tribunal under or by virtue of this Act; see the Employment Tribunals Act 1996, s 21(1)(ga) at **[978]**.

See *Harvey* B, Q.

Entitlement to the national minimum wage

1 Workers to be paid at least the minimum wage

(1) A person who qualifies for the national minimum wage shall be remunerated by his employer in respect of his work in any pay reference period at a rate which is not less than the national minimum wage.

(2) A person qualifies for the national minimum wage if he is an individual who—

(a) is a worker;

(b) is working, or ordinarily works, in the United Kingdom under his contract; and

(c) has ceased to be of compulsory school age.

(3) The national minimum wage shall be such single hourly rate as the Secretary of State may from time to time prescribe.

(4) For the purposes of this Act a "pay reference period" is such period as the Secretary of State may prescribe for the purpose.

(5) Subsections (1) to (4) above are subject to the following provisions of this Act.

[1349]

NOTES

Regulations: the National Minimum Wage Regulations 1999, SI 1999/584 at **[2465]**. Regulation 11 thereof at **[2475]**, prescribes £5.52 an hour as the single hourly rate of the national minimum wage, as from 1 October 2007. The previous rates were: £3.60 (from 1 April 1999); £3.70 (from 1 October 2000); £4.10 (from 1 October 2001); £4.20 (from 1 October 2002); £4.50 (from 1 October 2003); £4.85 (from

1 October 2004); £5.05 (from 1 October 2005); £5.35 (from 1 October 2006). For provisions as to, and the current rates applicable for, those who do not qualify for the single hourly rate, see regs 12, 13 of the 1999 Regulations at **[2476]**, **[2477]**.

Regulations relating to the national minimum wage

2 Determination of hourly rate of remuneration

(1) The Secretary of State may by regulations make provision for determining what is the hourly rate at which a person is to be regarded for the purposes of this Act as remunerated by his employer in respect of his work in any pay reference period.

(2) The regulations may make provision for determining the hourly rate in cases where—
- (a) the remuneration, to the extent that it is at a periodic rate, is at a single rate;
- (b) the remuneration is, in whole or in part, at different rates applicable at different times or in different circumstances;
- (c) the remuneration is, in whole or in part, otherwise than at a periodic rate or rates;
- (d) the remuneration consists, in whole or in part, of benefits in kind.

(3) The regulations may make provision with respect to—
- (a) circumstances in which, times at which, or the time for which, a person is to be treated as, or as not, working, and the extent to which a person is to be so treated;
- (b) the treatment of periods of paid or unpaid absence from, or lack of, work and of remuneration in respect of such periods.

(4) The provision that may be made by virtue of paragraph (a) of subsection (3) above includes provision for or in connection with—
- (a) treating a person as, or as not, working for a maximum or minimum time, or for a proportion of the time, in any period;
- (b) determining any matter to which that paragraph relates by reference to the terms of an agreement.

(5) The regulations may make provision with respect to—
- (a) what is to be treated as, or as not, forming part of a person's remuneration, and the extent to which it is to be so treated;
- (b) the valuation of benefits in kind;
- (c) the treatment of deductions from earnings;
- (d) the treatment of any charges or expenses which a person is required to bear.

(6) The regulations may make provision with respect to—
- (a) the attribution to a period, or the apportionment between two or more periods, of the whole or any part of any remuneration or work, whether or not the remuneration is received or the work is done within the period or periods in question;
- (b) the aggregation of the whole or any part of the remuneration for different periods;
- (c) the time at which remuneration is to be treated as received or accruing.

(7) Subsections (2) to (6) above are without prejudice to the generality of subsection (1) above.

(8) No provision shall be made under this section which treats the same circumstances differently in relation to—
- (a) different areas;
- (b) different sectors of employment;
- (c) undertakings of different sizes;
- (d) persons of different ages; or
- (e) persons of different occupations.

[1350]

NOTES

Regulations: the National Minimum Wage Regulations 1999, SI 1999/584 at **[2465]**.

3 Exclusion of, and modifications for, certain classes of person

(1) This section applies to persons who have not attained the age of 26.

[(1A) This section also applies to persons who have attained the age of 26 who are—

(a) within the first six months after the commencement of their employment with an employer by whom they have not previously been employed;
(b) participating in a scheme under which shelter is provided in return for work;
(c) participating in a scheme designed to provide training, work experience or temporary work;
(d) participating in a scheme to assist in the seeking or obtaining of work; …
(e) [undertaking] a course of higher education requiring attendance for a period of work experience; [or
(f) undertaking a course of further education requiring attendance for a period of work experience].]

(2) The Secretary of State may by regulations make provision in relation to any of the persons to whom this section applies—
(a) preventing them being persons who qualify for the national minimum wage; or
(b) prescribing an hourly rate for the national minimum wage other than the single hourly rate for the time being prescribed under section 1(3) above.

(3) No provision shall be made under subsection (2) above which treats persons differently in relation to—
(a) different areas;
(b) different sectors of employment;
(c) undertakings of different sizes; or
(d) different occupations.

(4) If any description of persons who have attained the age of 26 is added by regulations under section 4 below to the descriptions of person to whom this section applies, no provision shall be made under subsection (2) above which treats persons of that description differently in relation to different ages over 26.

[1351]

NOTES

Sub-s (1A): inserted by the National Minimum Wage Act 1998 (Amendment) Regulations 1999, SI 1999/583, reg 2; word omitted from para (d) repealed, word in square brackets in para (e) substituted, and para (f) (and the word immediately preceding it) inserted, by the National Minimum Wage Act 1998 (Amendment) Regulations 2007, SI 2007/2042, reg 2, as from 17 July 2007.

Regulations: the National Minimum Wage Regulations 1999, SI 1999/584 at **[2465]**.

4 Power to add to the persons to whom section 3 applies

(1) The Secretary of State may by regulations amend section 3 above by adding descriptions of persons who have attained the age of 26 to the descriptions of person to whom that section applies.

(2) No amendment shall be made under subsection (1) above which treats persons differently in relation to—
(a) different areas;
(b) different sectors of employment;
(c) undertakings of different sizes;
(d) different ages over 26; or
(e) different occupations.

[1352]

NOTES

Regulations: National Minimum Wage Act 1998 (Amendment) Regulations 1999, SI 1999/583; the National Minimum Wage Act 1998 (Amendment) Regulations 2007, SI 2007/2042.

5–8 (*(Establishment of, and references to, the Low Pay Commission) outside the scope of this work.*)

Records

9 Duty of employers to keep records

For the purposes of this Act, the Secretary of State may by regulations make provision requiring employers—

(a) to keep, in such form and manner as may be prescribed, such records as may be prescribed; and
(b) to preserve those records for such period as may be prescribed.

[1353]

NOTES

Regulations: the National Minimum Wage Regulations 1999, SI 1999/584 at **[2465]**.

10 Worker's right of access to records

(1) A worker may, in accordance with the following provisions of this section,—
(a) require his employer to produce any relevant records; and
(b) inspect and examine those records and copy any part of them.

(2) The rights conferred by subsection (1) above are exercisable only if the worker believes on reasonable grounds that he is or may be being, or has or may have been, remunerated for any pay reference period by his employer at a rate which is less than the national minimum wage.

(3) The rights conferred by subsection (1) above are exercisable only for the purpose of establishing whether or not the worker is being, or has been, remunerated for any pay reference period by his employer at a rate which is less than the national minimum wage.

(4) The rights conferred by subsection (1) above are exercisable—
(a) by the worker alone; or
(b) by the worker accompanied by such other person as the worker may think fit.

(5) The rights conferred by subsection (1) above are exercisable only if the worker gives notice (a "production notice") to his employer requesting the production of any relevant records relating to such period as may be described in the notice.

(6) If the worker intends to exercise the right conferred by subsection (4)(b) above, the production notice must contain a statement of that intention.

(7) Where a production notice is given, the employer shall give the worker reasonable notice of the place and time at which the relevant records will be produced.

(8) The place at which the relevant records are produced must be—
(a) the worker's place of work; or
(b) any other place at which it is reasonable, in all the circumstances, for the worker to attend to inspect the relevant records; or
(c) such other place as may be agreed between the worker and the employer.

(9) The relevant records must be produced—
(a) before the end of the period of fourteen days following the date of receipt of the production notice; or
(b) at such later time as may be agreed during that period between the worker and the employer.

(10) In this section—

"records" means records which the worker's employer is required to keep and, at the time of receipt of the production notice, preserve in accordance with section 9 above;

"relevant records" means such parts of, or such extracts from, any records as are relevant to establishing whether or not the worker has, for any pay reference period to which the records relate, been remunerated by the employer at a rate which is at least equal to the national minimum wage.

[1354]

11 Failure of employer to allow access to records

(1) A complaint may be presented to an employment tribunal by a worker on the ground that the employer—
(a) failed to produce some or all of the relevant records in accordance with subsections (8) and (9) of section 10 above; or
(b) failed to allow the worker to exercise some or all of the rights conferred by subsection (1)(b) or (4)(b) of that section.

(2) Where an employment tribunal finds a complaint under this section well-founded, the tribunal shall—

(a) make a declaration to that effect; and
(b) make an award that the employer pay to the worker a sum equal to 80 times the hourly amount of the national minimum wage (as in force when the award is made).

(3) An employment tribunal shall not consider a complaint under this section unless it is presented to the tribunal before the expiry of the period of three months following—
(a) the end of the period of fourteen days mentioned in paragraph (a) of subsection (9) of section 10 above; or
(b) in a case where a later day was agreed under paragraph (b) of that subsection, that later day.

(4) Where the employment tribunal is satisfied that it was not reasonably practicable for a complaint under this section to be presented before the expiry of the period of three months mentioned in subsection (3) above, the tribunal may consider the complaint if it is presented within such further period as the tribunal considers reasonable.

(5) Expressions used in this section and in section 10 above have the same meaning in this section as they have in that section.

[1355]

NOTES

Conciliation: employment tribunal proceedings and claims which could be the subject of employment tribunal proceedings under or by virtue of this section are proceedings to which the Employment Tribunals Act 1996, s 18 applies; see s 18(1)(dd) of that Act at **[975]**. The standard conciliation period applies to such proceedings by virtue of the Employment Tribunals (Constitution and Rules of Procedure) Regulations 2004, SI 2004/1861, Sch 1, rule 22(1), (6).

12 Employer to provide worker with national minimum wage statement

(1) Regulations may make provision for the purpose of conferring on a worker the right to be given by his employer, at or before the time at which any payment of remuneration is made to the worker, a written statement.

(2) The regulations may make provision with respect to the contents of any such statement and may, in particular, require it to contain—
(a) prescribed information relating to this Act or any regulations under it; or
(b) prescribed information for the purpose of assisting the worker to determine whether he has been remunerated at a rate at least equal to the national minimum wage during the period to which the payment of remuneration relates.

(3) Any statement required to be given under this section to a worker by his employer may, if the worker is an employee, be included in the written itemised pay statement required to be given to him by his employer under section 8 of the Employment Rights Act 1996 or Article 40 of the Employment Rights (Northern Ireland) Order 1996, as the case may be.

(4) The regulations may make provision for the purpose of applying—
(a) sections 11 and 12 of the Employment Rights Act 1996 (references to employment tribunals and determination of references), or
(b) in relation to Northern Ireland, Articles 43 and 44 of the Employment Rights (Northern Ireland) Order 1996 (references to industrial tribunals and determination of references),

in relation to a worker and any such statement as is mentioned in subsection (1) above as they apply in relation to an employee and a statement required to be given to him by his employer under section 8 of that Act or Article 40 of that Order, as the case may be.

[1356]

NOTES

Regulations: as of 6 April 2008 no Regulations had been made under this section.

Officers

13 Appointment of officers

(1) The Secretary of State—
(a) may appoint officers to act for the purposes of this Act; and

(b) may, instead of or in addition to appointing any officers under this section, arrange with any Minister of the Crown or government department, or any body performing functions on behalf of the Crown, that officers of that Minister, department or body shall act for those purposes.

(2) When acting for the purposes of this Act, an officer shall, if so required, produce some duly authenticated document showing his authority so to act.

(3) If it appears to an officer that any person with whom he is dealing while acting for the purposes of this Act does not know that he is an officer so acting, the officer shall identify himself as such to that person.

[1357]

14 Powers of officers

(1) An officer acting for the purposes of this Act shall have power for the performance of his duties—

(a) to require the production by a relevant person of any records required to be kept and preserved in accordance with regulations under section 9 above and to inspect and examine those records and to copy any material part of them;

(b) to require a relevant person to furnish to him (either alone or in the presence of any other person, as the officer thinks fit) an explanation of any such records;

(c) to require a relevant person to furnish to him (either alone or in the presence of any other person, as the officer thinks fit) any additional information known to the relevant person which might reasonably be needed in order to establish whether this Act, or any enforcement notice under section 19 below, is being or has been complied with;

(d) at all reasonable times to enter any relevant premises in order to exercise any power conferred on the officer by paragraphs (a) to (c) above.

(2) No person shall be required under paragraph (b) or (c) of subsection (above to answer any question or furnish any information which might incriminate the person or, if [married or a civil partner, the person's spouse or civil partner].

(3) The powers conferred by subsection (1) above include power, on reasonable written notice, to require a relevant person—

(a) to produce any such records as are mentioned in paragraph (a) of that subsection to an officer at such time and place as may be specified in the notice; or

(b) to attend before an officer at such time and place as may be specified in the notice to furnish any such explanation or additional information as is mentioned in paragraph (b) or (c) of that subsection.

(4) In this section "relevant person" means any person whom an officer acting for the purposes of this Act has reasonable cause to believe to be—

(a) the employer of a worker;

(b) a person who for the purposes of section 34 below is the agent or the principal;

(c) a person who supplies work to an individual who qualifies for the national minimum wage;

(d) a worker, servant or agent of a person falling within paragraph (a), (b) or (c) above; or

(e) a person who qualifies for the national minimum wage.

(5) In this section "relevant premises" means any premises which an officer acting for the purposes of this Act has reasonable cause to believe to be—

(a) premises at which an employer carries on business;

(b) premises which an employer uses in connection with his business (including any place used, in connection with that business, for giving out work to home workers, within the meaning of section 35 below); or

(c) premises of a person who for the purposes of section 34 below is the agent or the principal.

[1358]

NOTES

Para (2): words in square brackets substituted by the Civil Partnership Act 2004, s 261(1), Sch 27, para 155, as from 5 December 2005.

Information

15 Information obtained by officers

(1) This section applies to any information obtained by an officer acting for the purposes of this Act, whether by virtue of paragraph (a) or paragraph (b) of section 13(1) above.

(2) Information to which this section applies vests in the Secretary of State.

(3) Information to which this section applies may be used for any purpose relating to this Act by—

(a) the Secretary of State; or

(b) any relevant authority whose officer obtained the information.

(4) Information to which this section applies—

(a) may be supplied by, or with the authorisation of, the Secretary of State to any relevant authority for any purpose relating to this Act; and

(b) may be used by the recipient for any purpose relating to this Act.

(5) Information supplied under subsection (4) above—

(a) shall not be supplied by the recipient to any other person or body unless it is supplied for the purposes of any civil or criminal proceedings relating to this Act; and

(b) shall not be supplied in those circumstances without the authorisation of the Secretary of State.

[(6) This section—

(a) does not limit the circumstances in which information may be supplied or used apart from this section; and

(b) is subject to section 148 of the Finance Act 2000 (use of minimum wage information).]

[(6A) Nothing in this section prevents a disclosure in accordance with section 16A below.]

(7) Subsection (2) above does not affect the title or rights of—

(a) any person whose property the information was immediately before it was obtained as mentioned in subsection (1) above; or

(b) any person claiming title or rights through or under such a person otherwise than by virtue of any power conferred by or under this Act.

(8) In this section "relevant authority" means any Minister of the Crown who, or government department or other body which, is party to arrangements made with the Secretary of State which are in force under section 13(1)(b) above.

[1359]

NOTES

Sub-s (6): substituted by the Finance Act 2000, s 148(4).

Sub-s (6A): inserted by the Employment Relations Act 2004, s 57(1), Sch 1, para 40, as from 6 April 2005.

See further, as to the information to which this section applies, the Employment Relations Act 1999, s 39 at **[1448]**.

16 Information obtained by agricultural wages officers

(1) This section applies to information which has been obtained by an officer acting for the purposes of any of the agricultural wages legislation.

(2) Information to which this section applies may, with the authorisation of the relevant authority, be supplied to the Secretary of State for use for any purpose relating to this Act.

(3) Information supplied under subsection (2) above may be supplied by the recipient to any Minister of the Crown, government department or other body if—

(a) arrangements made between the recipient and that Minister, department or body under section 13(1)(b) above are in force; and

(b) the information is supplied for any purpose relating to this Act.

(4) Except as provided by subsection (3) above, information supplied under subsection (2) or (3) above—

(a) shall not be supplied by the recipient to any other person or body unless it is supplied for the purposes of any civil or criminal proceedings relating to this Act; and

(b) shall not be supplied in those circumstances without the authorisation of the relevant authority.

(5) This section does not limit the circumstances in which information may be supplied or used apart from this section.

[(5A) Nothing in this section prevents a disclosure in accordance with section 16A below.]

(6) In this section—

"the agricultural wages legislation" means—

(a) the Agricultural Wages Act 1948;

(b) the Agricultural Wages (Scotland) Act 1949; and

(c) the Agricultural Wages (Regulation) (Northern Ireland) Order 1977;

"relevant authority" means—

(a) in relation to information obtained by an officer acting in England, the Minister of Agriculture, Fisheries and Food;

(b) in relation to information obtained by an officer acting in Wales, the Minister of the Crown with the function of appointing officers under section 12 of the Agricultural Wages Act 1948 in relation to Wales;

(c) in relation to information obtained by an officer acting in an area which is partly in England and partly in Wales, the Ministers mentioned in paragraphs (a) and (b) above acting jointly;

(d) in relation to information obtained by an officer acting in Scotland, the Minister of the Crown with the function of appointing officers under section 12 of the Agricultural Wages (Scotland) Act 1949; and

(e) in relation to information obtained by an officer acting in Northern Ireland, the Department of Agriculture for Northern Ireland.

[1360]

NOTES

Sub-s (5A): inserted by the Employment Relations Act 2004, s 57(1), Sch 1, para 41, as from 6 April 2005.

Transfer of functions in relation to Wales: as to the transfer of functions under this section from Ministers of the Crown to the National Assembly for Wales, see the National Assembly for Wales (Transfer of Functions) Order 1999, SI 1999/672.

See further the Employment Relations Act 1999, s 39 at **[1448]**.

[16A Disclosure of information by officers

(1) Subsection (2) applies to information obtained for the purposes of the relevant legislation by an enforcement officer so far as that information relates to an identifiable worker or agency worker.

(2) In order to enable or assist him to act for the purposes of the relevant legislation, the enforcement officer may disclose all or any of the information to the worker or, as the case may be, agency worker concerned.

(3) Subsection (4) applies to information obtained for the purposes of the relevant legislation by an enforcement officer so far as that information relates to an identifiable employer or person who is the agent or the principal for the purposes of section 34 below.

(4) In order to enable or assist him to act for the purposes of the relevant legislation, the officer may disclose all or any of the information to the employer, the agent or, as the case may be, the principal concerned.

(5) In this section—

"agency worker" shall be construed in accordance with section 34 below;

"enforcement officer" means—

(a) an officer acting for the purposes of this Act, whether by virtue of paragraph (a) or (b) of section 13(1) above;

(b) an officer acting for the purposes of the Agricultural Wages Act 1948; or

(c) an officer acting for the purposes of the Agricultural Wages (Regulation) (Northern Ireland) Order 1977;

"the relevant legislation" means—

(a) in relation to an enforcement officer acting for the purposes of this Act, this Act;
(b) in relation to an enforcement officer acting for the purposes of the Agricultural Wages Act 1948, that Act; and
(c) in relation to an enforcement officer acting for the purposes of the Agricultural Wages (Regulation) (Northern Ireland) Order 1977, that Order.]

[1360A]

NOTES

Commencement: 6 April 2005.

Inserted by the Employment Relations Act 2004, s 44, as from 6 April 2005, except in relation to any information which was obtained by an enforcement officer for the purposes of the relevant legislation before that date (see SI 2005/872, art 14).

Enforcement

17 Non-compliance: worker entitled to additional remuneration

(1) If a worker who qualifies for the national minimum wage is remunerated for any pay reference period by his employer at a rate which is less than the national minimum wage, the worker shall be taken to be entitled under his contract to be paid, as additional remuneration in respect of that period, the amount described in subsection (2) below.

(2) That amount is the difference between—
(a) the relevant remuneration received by the worker for the pay reference period; and
(b) the relevant remuneration which the worker would have received for that period had he been remunerated by the employer at a rate equal to the national minimum wage.

(3) In subsection (2) above, "relevant remuneration" means remuneration which falls to be brought into account for the purposes of regulations under section 2 above.

[1361]

18 Enforcement in the case of special classes of worker

(1) If the persons who are the worker and the employer for the purposes of section 17 above would not (apart from this section) fall to be regarded as the worker and the employer for the purposes of—
(a) Part II of the Employment Rights Act 1996 (protection of wages), or
(b) in relation to Northern Ireland, Part IV of the Employment Rights (Northern Ireland) Order 1996,

they shall be so regarded for the purposes of the application of that Part in relation to the entitlement conferred by that section.

(2) In the application by virtue of subsection (1) above of—
(a) Part II of the Employment Rights Act 1996, or
(b) Part IV of the Employment Rights (Northern Ireland) Order 1996,

in a case where there is or was, for the purposes of that Part, no worker's contract between the persons who are the worker and the employer for the purposes of section 17 above, it shall be assumed that there is or, as the case may be, was such a contract.

(3) For the purpose of enabling the amount described as additional remuneration in subsection (1) of section 17 above to be recovered in civil proceedings on a claim in contract in a case where in fact there is or was no worker's contract between the persons who are the worker and the employer for the purposes of that section, it shall be assumed for the purpose of any civil proceedings, so far as relating to that amount, that there is or, as the case may be, was such a contract.

[1362]

NOTES

Conciliation: employment tribunal proceedings and claims which could be the subject of employment tribunal proceedings by virtue of this section are proceedings to which the Employment Tribunals Act 1996, s 18 applies; see s 18(1)(dd) of that Act at **[975]**. The standard conciliation period applies to such proceedings by virtue of the Employment Tribunals (Constitution and Rules of Procedure) Regulations 2004, SI 2004/1861, Sch 1, rule 22(1), (6).

19 Power of officer to issue enforcement notice

(1) If an officer acting for the purposes of this Act is of the opinion that a worker who qualifies for the national minimum wage has not been remunerated for any pay reference period by his employer at a rate at least equal to the national minimum wage, the officer may serve a notice (an "enforcement notice") on the employer requiring the employer to remunerate the worker for pay reference periods ending on or after the date of the notice at a rate equal to the national minimum wage.

(2) An enforcement notice may also require the employer to pay to the worker within such time as may be specified in the notice the sum due to the worker under section 17 above in respect of the employer's previous failure to remunerate the worker at a rate at least equal to the national minimum wage.

[(2A) If an officer acting for the purposes of this Act is of the opinion that a worker who has at any time qualified for the national minimum wage has not been remunerated for any pay reference period (whether ending before or after the coming into force of this subsection) by his employer at a rate at least equal to the national minimum wage, the officer may serve on the employer an enforcement notice which imposes a requirement under subsection (2) above in relation to the worker, whether or not a requirement under subsection (1) above is, or may be, imposed in relation to that worker (or any other worker to whom the notice relates).

(2B) An enforcement notice may not impose a requirement under subsection (2) above in respect of any pay reference period ending more than 6 years before the date on which the notice is served.]

[(2C) Where an enforcement notice imposes a requirement under subsection (2) above, the amount specified in the notice as the sum due to the worker under section 17 above need not include any sum so due to him in respect of any very recent pay reference period (although the amount so specified may include any such sum).

(2D) In subsection (2C) above a "very recent" pay reference period means a pay reference period ending less than 3 months before the date on which the notice is served.]

(3) [An] enforcement notice may relate to more than one worker (and, where it does so, may be so framed as to relate to workers specified in the notice or to workers of a description so specified).

(4) A person on whom an enforcement notice is served may appeal against the notice before the end of the period of four weeks following the date of service of the notice.

(5) An appeal under subsection (4) above lies to an employment tribunal.

(6) On an appeal under subsection (4) above, the employment tribunal shall dismiss the appeal unless it is established—

- (a) that, in the case of the worker or workers to whom the enforcement notice relates, the facts are such that an officer who was aware of them would have had no reason to serve any enforcement notice on the appellant; or
- (b) where the enforcement notice relates to two or more workers, that the facts are such that an officer who was aware of them would have had no reason to include some of the workers in any enforcement notice served on the appellant; or
- (c) where the enforcement notice imposes a requirement under subsection (2) above in relation to a worker,—
  - (i) that no sum was due to the worker under section 17 above; or
  - (ii) that the amount specified in the notice as the sum due to the worker under that section is [too great, or];
  - [(iii) that the notice contravenes subsection (2B) above;]

and in this subsection any reference to a worker includes a reference to a person whom the enforcement notice purports to treat as a worker.

(7) Where an appeal is allowed by virtue of paragraph (a) of subsection (6) above, the employment tribunal shall rescind the enforcement notice.

(8) If, in a case where subsection (7) above does not apply, an appeal is allowed by virtue of paragraph (b) or (c) of subsection (6) above—

- (a) the employment tribunal shall rectify the enforcement notice; and
- (b) the enforcement notice shall have effect as if it had originally been served as so rectified.

(9) The powers of an employment tribunal in allowing an appeal in a case where subsection (8) above applies shall include power to rectify, as the tribunal may consider appropriate in consequence of its decision on the appeal, any penalty notice which has been served under section 21 below in respect of the enforcement notice.

(10) Where a penalty notice is rectified under subsection (9) above, it shall have effect as if it had originally been served as so rectified.

[1363]

NOTES

Sub-ss (2A), (2B): inserted by the National Minimum Wage (Enforcement Notices) Act 2003, s 1, as from 8 July 2003.

Sub-ss (2C), (2D): inserted by the Employment Relations Act 2004, s 45(1), (2), (4), as from 6 April 2005, except in relation to any enforcement notice which was issued before that date (see SI 2005/872, art 15).

Sub-s (3): word in square brackets substituted by the Employment Relations Act 2004, s 45(1), (3), (4), as from 6 April 2005.

Sub-s (6): words in square brackets in sub-para (c)(ii) substituted, and sub-para (c)(iii) inserted, by the Employment Relations Act 2004, s 46(2), (4), as from 6 April 2005 (for transitional provisions see SI 2005/872, art 15).

See further, the Employment Relations Act 2004, ss 45(4), 46(4) which provide that nothing in those sections affects this section as it has effect for the purposes of the Agricultural Wages (Scotland) Act 1949.

20 Non-compliance: power of officer to sue on behalf of worker

(1) If an enforcement notice is not complied with in whole or in part, an officer acting for the purposes of this Act may, on behalf of any worker to whom the notice relates,—

(a) present a complaint under section 23(1)(a) of the Employment Rights Act 1996 (deductions from worker's wages in contravention of section 13 of that Act) to an employment tribunal in respect of any sums due to the worker by virtue of section 17 above; or

(b) in relation to Northern Ireland, present a complaint under Article 55(1)(a) of the Employment Rights (Northern Ireland) Order 1996 (deductions from worker's wages in contravention of Article 45 of that Order) to an industrial tribunal in respect of any sums due to the worker by virtue of section 17 above; or

(c) commence other civil proceedings for the recovery, on a claim in contract, of any sums due to the worker by virtue of section 17 above.

(2) The powers conferred by subsection (1) above for the recovery of sums due from an employer to a worker shall not be in derogation of any right which the worker may have to recover such sums by civil proceedings.

[1364]

NOTES

Conciliation: employment tribunal proceedings and claims which could be the subject of employment tribunal proceedings under or by virtue of sub-s (1)(a) above are proceedings to which the Employment Tribunals Act 1996, s 18 applies; see s 18(1)(dd) of that Act at **[975]**. The standard conciliation period applies to such proceedings by virtue of the Employment Tribunals (Constitution and Rules of Procedure) Regulations 2004, SI 2004/1861, Sch 1, rule 22(1), (6).

See further the notes to the Employment Rights Act 1996, s 23 at **[1030]** as to the application to proceedings under that section of the Employment Act 2002, ss 31, 32 and 38 and of the Employment Act 2002 (Dispute Resolution) Regulations 2004, SI 2004/752, regs 15 and 18.

21 Financial penalty for non-compliance

(1) If an officer acting for the purposes of this Act is satisfied that a person on whom an enforcement notice has been served has failed, in whole or in part, to comply with the notice, the officer may serve on that person a notice (a "penalty notice") requiring the person to pay a financial penalty to the Secretary of State.

(2) A penalty notice must state—

(a) the amount of the financial penalty;

(b) the time within which the financial penalty is to be paid (which must not be less than four weeks from the date of service of the notice);

(c) the period to which the financial penalty relates;

(d) the respects in which the officer is of the opinion that the enforcement notice has not been complied with; and

(e) the calculation of the amount of the financial penalty.

(3) The amount of the financial penalty shall be calculated at a rate equal to twice the hourly amount of the national minimum wage (as in force at the date of the penalty notice) in respect of each worker to whom the failure to comply relates for each day during which the failure to comply has continued in respect of the worker.

(4) The Secretary of State may by regulations from time to time amend the multiplier for the time being specified in subsection (3) above in relation to the hourly amount of the national minimum wage.

(5) A financial penalty under this section—

(a) in England and Wales, shall be recoverable, if a county court so orders, *by execution issued from the county court* or otherwise as if it were payable under an order of that court;

(b) in Scotland, may be enforced in the same manner as an extract registered decree arbitral bearing a warrant for execution issued by the sheriff court of any sheriffdom in Scotland;

(c) in Northern Ireland, shall be recoverable, if the county court so orders, as if it were payable under an order of that court.

(6) Where a person has appealed under subsection (4) of section 19 above against an enforcement notice and the appeal has not been withdrawn or finally determined, then, notwithstanding the appeal,—

(a) the enforcement notice shall have effect; and

(b) an officer may serve a penalty notice in respect of the enforcement notice.

(7) If, in a case falling within subsection (6) above, an officer serves a penalty notice in respect of the enforcement notice, the penalty notice—

(a) shall not be enforceable until the appeal has been withdrawn or finally determined; and

(b) shall be of no effect if the enforcement notice is rescinded as a result of the appeal; but

(c) subject to paragraph (b) above and section 22(4) and (6)(a) below, as from the withdrawal or final determination of the appeal shall be enforceable as if paragraph (a) above had not had effect.

(8) Any sums received by the Secretary of State by virtue of this section shall be paid into the Consolidated Fund.

[1365]

NOTES

Sub-s (5): for the words in italics in para (a) there are substituted the words "under section 85 of the County Courts Act 1984" by the Tribunals, Courts and Enforcement Act 2007, s 62(3), Sch 13, para 128, as from a day to be appointed.

Regulations: as of 6 April 2008 no Regulations had been made under this section.

22 Appeals against penalty notices

(1) A person on whom a penalty notice is served may appeal against the notice before the end of the period of four weeks following the date of service of the notice.

(2) An appeal under subsection (1) above lies to an employment tribunal.

(3) On an appeal under subsection (1) above, the employment tribunal shall dismiss the appeal unless it is shown—

(a) that, in the case of each of the allegations of failure to comply with the enforcement notice, the facts are such that an officer who was aware of them would have had no reason to serve any penalty notice on the appellant; or

[(b) that the amount of the financial penalty is too great because the penalty notice is incorrect in some of the particulars which affect that amount; or

(c) that the amount of the financial penalty is too great because its calculation is incorrect;]

and for the purposes of any appeal relating to a penalty notice, the enforcement notice in question shall (subject to rescission or rectification on any appeal brought under section 19 above) be taken to be correct.

(4) Where an appeal is allowed by virtue of paragraph (a) of subsection (3) above, the employment tribunal shall rescind the penalty notice.

(5) If, in a case where subsection (4) above does not apply, an appeal is allowed by virtue of paragraph (b) or (c) of subsection (3) above—
(a) the employment tribunal shall rectify the penalty notice; and
(b) the penalty notice shall have effect as if it had originally been served as so rectified.

(6) Where a person has appealed under subsection (1) above against a penalty notice and the appeal has not been withdrawn or finally determined, the penalty notice—
(a) shall not be enforceable until the appeal has been withdrawn or finally determined; but
(b) subject to subsection (4) above and section 21(7)(a) and (b) above, as from the withdrawal or final determination of the appeal shall be enforceable as if paragraph (a) above had not had effect.

[1366]

NOTES

Sub-s (3): paras (b), (c) substituted by the Employment Relations Act 2004, s 46(3), (4), as from 6 April 2005, except in relation to any enforcement notice which was issued before that date (see SI 2005/872, art 15).

[22A Withdrawal of enforcement notice

(1) Where an enforcement notice has been served (and has not already been withdrawn or rescinded), an officer acting for the purposes of this Act may withdraw the enforcement notice by serving notice of the withdrawal on the employer.

(2) Subsection (3) applies if an enforcement notice is withdrawn and either—
(a) no new enforcement notice is served in accordance with section 22B; or
(b) a new enforcement notice is so served, but the notice of withdrawal states that subsection (3) applies.

(3) If an enforcement notice is withdrawn and this subsection applies,—
(a) after the withdrawal no penalty notice may be served under section 21 in respect of any non-compliance with the enforcement notice before it was withdrawn;
(b) if any penalty notice was so served before the withdrawal, it ceases to have effect and any appeal against it must be dismissed;
(c) any sum paid or recovered in respect of any such penalty notice must be repaid to the employer with interest at the appropriate rate running from the date when the sum was paid or recovered;
(d) any appeal against the enforcement notice must be dismissed;
(e) after the withdrawal no complaint may be presented or other civil proceedings commenced by virtue of section 20 in reliance on any non-compliance with the enforcement notice before it was withdrawn;
(f) any complaint or proceedings so presented or commenced before the withdrawal may be proceeded with despite the withdrawal.

(4) In subsection (3)(c) "the appropriate rate" means the rate that, on the date the sum was paid or recovered, was specified in section 17 of the Judgments Act 1838.

(5) Where subsection (3) applies the notice of withdrawal must indicate the effect of that subsection (but a failure to do so does not make the withdrawal ineffective).

(6) Section 21(6) has effect subject to this section and sections 22B and 22C.]

[1366A]

NOTES

Commencement: 6 April 2005.

Inserted, together with ss 22B–22F, by the Employment Relations Act 2004, s 46(1), as from 6 April 2005, except in relation to any enforcement notice which was issued before that date (see SI 2005/872, art 15).

[22B Replacement of enforcement notice

(1) This section applies if an officer withdraws an enforcement notice.

(2) The officer may at the same time as he serves the notice of withdrawal (and if he is of the opinion mentioned in section 19(1) or (2A)) serve on the employer a new enforcement notice under section 19 relating to some or all of the workers to whom the old enforcement notice related.

(3) The new enforcement notice may not relate to any workers to whom the old enforcement notice did not relate (but this is without prejudice to any power that arises apart from this section to serve an enforcement notice relating to those workers).

(4) If the new enforcement notice contravenes subsection (3)—

(a) the case shall be treated as falling within paragraph (b) (or, if none of the workers included in the old enforcement notice is included in the new enforcement notice, paragraph (a)) of section 19(6); and

(b) the new enforcement notice is not to be treated for the purposes of sections 22A(2), 22C(1) and 22D(1) as served in accordance with this section.

(5) If the new enforcement notice includes a requirement under section 19(2) as respects a worker, it must relate to the sum due to the worker under section 17 in respect of the employer's failure previous to the new notice to remunerate the worker as mentioned in section 19(2) (regardless of whether that failure occurred to any extent before or after the service of the old notice).

(6) Subsection (5) is subject to section 19(2B) to (2D) as they apply in relation to the new enforcement notice; but section 19(2B) applies in relation to that notice as if the reference to 6 years before the date on which the notice is served were a reference to 6 years before the date on which the old notice was served.

(7) The new enforcement notice must—

(a) indicate the differences between it and the old enforcement notice that it is reasonable for the officer to consider are material; and

(b) unless the notice of withdrawal states that section 22A(3) applies, indicate the effect of sections 22C and 22D.

(8) A failure to comply with subsection (7) does not make the new enforcement notice ineffective, but a notice that does not comply with that subsection is not to be treated for the purposes of sections 22A(2), 22C(1) and 22D(1) as served in accordance with this section.

(9) The reference in subsection (1) to an enforcement notice does not include an enforcement notice served by virtue of this section.]

[1366B]

NOTES

Commencement: 6 April 2005.
Inserted as noted to s 22A at **[1366A]**.

[22C Effect of replacement on penalties where section 22A(3) not applied

(1) If an enforcement notice is withdrawn and a new enforcement notice is served in accordance with section 22B, this section applies unless the notice withdrawing the old enforcement notice states that section 22A(3) applies.

(2) Where this section applies, subject to subsections (3) and (5) the withdrawal of the old enforcement notice does not affect—

(a) any penalty notice that before the withdrawal was served under section 21 in respect of any non-compliance with the old enforcement notice;

(b) the power under section 21 to serve a penalty notice in respect of any non-compliance with the old enforcement notice before it was withdrawn.

(3) If—

(a) before the withdrawal of the old enforcement notice a penalty notice was served which included an amount for a day's non-compliance with the old enforcement notice as respects a worker, and

(b) that amount could not validly have been included in the penalty notice if the old enforcement notice had been as it should have been according to the new enforcement notice,

the penalty notice shall be treated as withdrawn under section 22E at the same time as the old enforcement notice is withdrawn.

(4) Where subsection (3) applies, section 22F (power to replace penalty notice) applies—

(a) as if the cases mentioned in section 22F(1) as cases in which that section applies included the case where a penalty notice is by virtue of this section treated as withdrawn; and

(b) as if the references in section 22F(2) to the amount and particulars that the officer considers should have been stated in the penalty notice were to the amount and particulars that he considers should have been so stated if the old enforcement notice had been as it should have been.

(5) A penalty notice served by virtue of subsection (2)(b) must not include an amount for a day's non-compliance with the old enforcement notice as respects a worker if, had the old enforcement notice been as it should have been according to the new enforcement notice, that amount could not validly have been included in the penalty notice.

(6) The words after paragraph (c) in section 22(3) shall not apply for the purposes of any appeal against a penalty notice continued in effect by virtue of subsection (2)(a) above or served by virtue of subsection (2)(b) above.]

[1366C]

NOTES

Commencement: 6 April 2005.
Inserted as noted to s 22A at **[1366A]**.

[22D Effect of replacement on appeals and civil proceedings where section 22A(3) not applied

(1) If an enforcement notice is withdrawn and a new enforcement notice is served in accordance with section 22B, this section applies unless the notice withdrawing the old enforcement notice states that section 22A(3) applies.

(2) If an appeal has been made under section 19(4) against the old enforcement notice and the appeal has not been withdrawn or finally determined before the time when that notice is withdrawn—

(a) that appeal ("the earlier appeal") shall have effect after that time as if it were against the new enforcement notice; and

(b) the employer may exercise his right of appeal under section 19(4) against the new enforcement notice only if he withdraws the earlier appeal.

(3) If an appeal is made under section 19(4) against the new enforcement notice (or by virtue of subsection (2) above has effect as if so made), section 19(9) and paragraphs (a) to (c) of section 21(7) apply in relation to any penalty notice—

(a) continued in effect by virtue of section 22C(2)(a), or

(b) served by virtue of section 22C(2)(b),

as they apply in relation to penalty notices served in respect of the new enforcement notice.

(4) Where this section applies—

(a) after the withdrawal of the old enforcement notice no complaint may be presented or other civil proceedings commenced by virtue of section 20 in reliance on any non-compliance with that notice before it was withdrawn;

(b) any complaint or proceedings so presented or commenced before the withdrawal of the old enforcement notice may be proceeded with despite the withdrawal and replacement of that notice.]

[1366D]

NOTES

Commencement: 6 April 2005.
Inserted as noted to s 22A at **[1366A]**.

[22E Withdrawal of penalty notice

(1) Where a penalty notice has been served on a person ("the employer") (and has not already been withdrawn or rescinded), an officer acting for the purposes of this Act may withdraw the penalty notice if he is of the opinion—

(a) that, in the case of each of the allegations of failure to comply with the enforcement notice in respect of which the penalty notice was served, the facts are such that an officer who was aware of them would have had no reason to serve any penalty notice on the employer; or

(b) that the amount of the financial penalty is too great because the penalty notice is incorrect in some of the particulars which affect that amount; or

(c) that the amount of the financial penalty is too great because its calculation is incorrect.

(2) The withdrawal shall be effected by serving notice of the withdrawal on the employer.

(3) If a penalty notice is withdrawn and is not replaced under section 22F—

(a) any sum already paid or recovered in respect of the penalty notice must be repaid to the employer with interest at the appropriate rate running from the date when the sum was paid or recovered;

(b) any appeal against the notice must be dismissed.

(4) In subsection (3)(a) "the appropriate rate" means the rate that, on the date the sum was paid or recovered, was specified in section 17 of the Judgments Act 1838.]

[1366E]

NOTES

Commencement: 6 April 2005.
Inserted as noted to s 22A at **[1366A]**.

[22F Replacement of penalty notice with notice imposing lower penalty

(1) This section applies if a penalty notice is withdrawn because the officer is of the opinion mentioned in section 22E(1)(b) or (c).

(2) The officer may, at the same time as that notice is withdrawn, serve by way of replacement a new penalty notice under section 21 in which—

(a) the amount of the financial penalty is the amount (which must be less than that in the old penalty notice) that the officer now considers should have been the amount stated in the old penalty notice; and

(b) the particulars stated under section 21(2)(c) to (e) are as he now considers they should have been in that notice.

(3) The new penalty notice must indicate—

(a) the differences between it and the old penalty notice that it is reasonable for the officer to consider are material, and

(b) the effect of subsections (4) to (7),

but a failure to comply with this subsection does not make the new penalty notice ineffective.

(4) If a sum was paid or recovered in respect of the old penalty notice—

(a) an amount equal to that sum (or, if more than one, the total of those sums) shall be treated as having been paid in respect of the new penalty notice; and

(b) any amount by which that sum (or total) exceeds the amount payable under the new penalty notice must be repaid to the employer with interest at the appropriate rate running from the date when the sum (or, if more than one, the first of them) was paid or recovered.

(5) In subsection (4)(b) "the appropriate rate" means the rate that, on the date mentioned in subsection (4)(b), was specified in section 17 of the Judgments Act 1838.

(6) Subsection (7) applies where—

(a) a new penalty notice is served by virtue of this section; and

(b) an appeal has been made under section 22(1) against the old penalty notice and has not been withdrawn or finally determined before the time when that notice is withdrawn.

(7) In such a case—

(a) that appeal ("the earlier appeal") shall have effect after that time as if it were against the new penalty notice; and

(b) the employer may exercise his right of appeal under section 22 against the new penalty notice only if he withdraws the earlier appeal.

(8) The reference in subsection (1) to a penalty notice does not include a penalty notice served by virtue of this section.

(9) This section is without prejudice to any power arising apart from this section to serve two or more penalty notices in respect of the same enforcement notice.]

[1366F]

NOTES
Commencement: 6 April 2005.
Inserted as noted to s 22A at **[1366A]**.

Rights not to suffer unfair dismissal or other detriment

23 The right not to suffer detriment

(1) A worker has the right not to be subjected to any detriment by any act, or any deliberate failure to act, by his employer, done on the ground that—

(a) any action was taken, or was proposed to be taken, by or on behalf of the worker with a view to enforcing, or otherwise securing the benefit of, a right of the worker's to which this section applies; or

(b) the employer was prosecuted for an offence under section 31 below as a result of action taken by or on behalf of the worker for the purpose of enforcing, or otherwise securing the benefit of, a right of the worker's to which this section applies; or

(c) the worker qualifies, or will or might qualify, for the national minimum wage or for a particular rate of national minimum wage.

(2) It is immaterial for the purposes of paragraph (a) or (b) of subsection (1) above—

(a) whether or not the worker has the right, or

(b) whether or not the right has been infringed,

but, for that subsection to apply, the claim to the right and, if applicable, the claim that it has been infringed must be made in good faith.

(3) The following are the rights to which this section applies—

(a) any right conferred by, or by virtue of, any provision of this Act for which the remedy for its infringement is by way of a complaint to an employment tribunal; and

(b) any right conferred by section 17 above.

[(4) This section does not apply where the detriment in question amounts to dismissal within the meaning of—

(a) Part X of the Employment Rights Act 1996 (unfair dismissal), or

(b) Part XI of the Employment Rights (Northern Ireland) Order 1996 (corresponding provision for Northern Ireland),

…]

[1367]

NOTES
Sub-s (4): substituted by the Employment Relations Act 1999, s 18(4); words omitted repealed by the Employment Relations (Northern Ireland) Order 1999, SI 1999/2790, arts 20(5)(a), 40, Sch 9(3).

24 Enforcement of the right

(1) A worker may present a complaint to an employment tribunal that he has been subjected to a detriment in contravention of section 23 above.

(2) Subject to the following provisions of this section, the provisions of—

(a) sections 48(2) to (4) and 49 of the Employment Rights Act 1996 (complaints to employment tribunals and remedies), or

(b) in relation to Northern Ireland, Articles 71(2) to (4) and 72 of the Employment Rights (Northern Ireland) Order 1996 (complaints to industrial tribunals and remedies),

shall apply in relation to a complaint under this section as they apply in relation to a complaint under section 48 of that Act or Article 71 of that Order (as the case may be), but taking references in those provisions to the employer as references to the employer within the meaning of section 23(1) above.

(3) Where—

(a) the detriment to which the worker is subjected is the termination of his worker's contract, but

(b) that contract is not a contract of employment,

any compensation awarded under section 49 of the Employment Rights Act 1996 or Article 72 of the Employment Rights (Northern Ireland) Order 1996 by virtue of subsection (2) above must not exceed the limit specified in subsection (4) below.

(4) The limit mentioned in subsection (3) above is the total of—

(a) the sum which would be the basic award for unfair dismissal, calculated in accordance with section 119 of the Employment Rights Act 1996 or Article 153 of the Employment Rights (Northern Ireland) Order 1996 (as the case may be), if the worker had been an employee and the contract terminated had been a contract of employment; and

(b) the sum for the time being specified in section 124(1) of that Act or Article 158(1) of that Order (as the case may be) which is the limit for a compensatory award to a person calculated in accordance with section 123 of that Act or Article 157 of that Order (as the case may be).

(5) Where the worker has been working under arrangements which do not fall to be regarded as a worker's contract for the purposes of—

(a) the Employment Rights Act 1996, or

(b) in relation to Northern Ireland, the Employment Rights (Northern Ireland) Order 1996,

he shall be treated for the purposes of subsections (3) and (4) above as if any arrangements under which he has been working constituted a worker's contract falling within section 230(3)(b) of that Act or Article 3(3)(b) of that Order (as the case may be).

[1368]

NOTES

Conciliation: employment tribunal proceedings and claims which could be the subject of employment tribunal proceedings under or by virtue of this section are proceedings to which the Employment Tribunals Act 1996, s 18 applies; see s 18(1)(dd) of that Act at **[975]**. The standard conciliation period applies to such proceedings by virtue of the Employment Tribunals (Constitution and Rules of Procedure) Regulations 2004, SI 2004/1861, Sch 1, rule 22(1), (6).

Tribunal jurisdiction: the Employment Act 2002, ss 31, 32, 38, at **[1493]**, **[1494]**, **[1496]** apply to proceedings before the employment tribunal relating to a claim under this section; see ss 31(1), 32(1), 38(1) of, and Schs 3–5 to, the 2002 Act at **[1508]**–**[1510]**.

For the circumstances in which the normal time limit for presenting a complaint under this section is extended for a period of three months, see the Employment Act 2002 (Dispute Resolution) Regulations 2004, SI 2004/752, regs 15 and 18 at **[3096]** and **[3098]**.

25, 26 (*S 25 inserts the Employment Rights Act 1996, s 104A at* **[1146]**, *and amends ss 105, 108 of that Act at* **[1149]**, **[1152]**, *and amended s 109* (*repealed*)*; s 26 applies to Northern Ireland* (*outside the scope of this work*).)

Civil procedure, evidence and appeals

27 (*Sub-s* (*1*) *amends the Employment Tribunals Act 1996, s 4(3) at* **[957]**; *sub-s* (*2*) *applies to Northern Ireland* (*outside the scope of this work*).)

28 Reversal of burden of proof

(1) Where in any civil proceedings any question arises as to whether an individual qualifies or qualified at any time for the national minimum wage, it shall be presumed that the individual qualifies or, as the case may be, qualified at that time for the national minimum wage unless the contrary is established.

(2) Where—

(a) a complaint is made—

(i) to an employment tribunal under section 23(1)(a) of the Employment Rights Act 1996 (unauthorised deductions from wages), or

(ii) to an industrial tribunal under Article 55(1)(a) of the Employment Rights (Northern Ireland) Order 1996, and

(b) the complaint relates in whole or in part to the deduction of the amount described as additional remuneration in section 17(1) above,

it shall be presumed for the purposes of the complaint, so far as relating to the deduction of that amount, that the worker in question was remunerated at a rate less than the national minimum wage unless the contrary is established.

(3) Where in any civil proceedings a person seeks to recover on a claim in contract the amount described as additional remuneration in section 17(1) above, it shall be presumed for the purposes of the proceedings, so far as relating to that amount, that the worker in question was remunerated at a rate less than the national minimum wage unless the contrary is established.

[1369]

29 (*Amends the Employment Tribunals Act 1996, s 21*(*1*) *at* **[978]**.)

Conciliation

30 (*Sub-s* (*1*) *amends the Employment Tribunals Act 1996, s 18*(*1*) *at* **[975]**; *sub-s* (*2*) *applies to Northern Ireland* (*outside the scope of this work*).)

Offences

31 Offences

(1) If the employer of a worker who qualifies for the national minimum wage refuses or wilfully neglects to remunerate the worker for any pay reference period at a rate which is at least equal to the national minimum wage, that employer is guilty of an offence.

(2) If a person who is required to keep or preserve any record in accordance with regulations under section 9 above fails to do so, that person is guilty of an offence.

(3) If a person makes, or knowingly causes or allows to be made, in a record required to be kept in accordance with regulations under section 9 above any entry which he knows to be false in a material particular, that person is guilty of an offence.

(4) If a person, for purposes connected with the provisions of this Act, produces or furnishes, or knowingly causes or allows to be produced or furnished, any record or information which he knows to be false in a material particular, that person is guilty of an offence.

(5) If a person—

(a) intentionally delays or obstructs an officer acting for the purposes of this Act in the exercise of any power conferred by this Act, or

(b) refuses or neglects to answer any question, furnish any information or produce any document when required to do so under section 14(1) above,

that person is guilty of an offence.

(6) Where the commission by any person of an offence under subsection (1) or (2) above is due to the act or default of some other person, that other person is also guilty of the offence.

(7) A person may be charged with and convicted of an offence by virtue of subsection (6) above whether or not proceedings are taken against any other person.

(8) In any proceedings for an offence under subsection (1) or (2) above it shall be a defence for the person charged to prove that he exercised all due diligence and took all reasonable precautions to secure that the provisions of this Act, and of any relevant regulations made under it, were complied with by himself and by any person under his control.

(9) A person guilty of an offence under this section shall be liable on summary conviction to a fine not exceeding level 5 on the standard scale.

[1370]

32 Offences by bodies corporate etc

(1) This section applies to any offence under this Act.

(2) If an offence committed by a body corporate is proved—

(a) to have been committed with the consent or connivance of an officer of the body, or

(b) to be attributable to any neglect on the part of such an officer,

the officer as well as the body corporate is guilty of the offence and liable to be proceeded against and punished accordingly.

(3) In subsection (2) above "officer", in relation to a body corporate, means a director, manager, secretary or other similar officer of the body, or a person purporting to act in any such capacity.

(4) If the affairs of a body corporate are managed by its members, subsection (2) above applies in relation to the acts and defaults of a member in connection with his functions of management as if he were a director of the body corporate.

(5) If an offence committed by a partnership in Scotland is proved—
 (a) to have been committed with the consent or connivance of a partner, or
 (b) to be attributable to any neglect on the part of a partner,
the partner as well as the partnership is guilty of the offence and liable to be proceeded against and punished accordingly.

(6) In subsection (5) above, "partner" includes a person purporting to act as a partner.

[1371]

33 Proceedings for offences

(1) The persons who may conduct proceedings for an offence under this Act—
 (*a*) *in England and Wales, before a magistrates' court, or*
 (b) in Northern Ireland, before a court of summary jurisdiction,
shall include any person authorised for the purpose by the Secretary of State even if that person is not a barrister or solicitor.

[(1A) The persons who may conduct proceedings for an offence under this Act in England and Wales, before a magistrates' court, shall include any person authorised for the purpose by the Secretary of State.]

(2) In England and Wales or Northern Ireland, proceedings for an offence under this Act may be begun at any time within whichever of the following periods expires the later, that is to say—
 (a) the period of 6 months from the date on which evidence, sufficient in the opinion of the Secretary of State to justify a prosecution for the offence, comes to the knowledge of the Secretary of State, or
 (b) the period of 12 months from the commission of the offence,
notwithstanding anything in any other enactment (including an enactment comprised in Northern Ireland legislation) or in any instrument made under an enactment.

(3) For the purposes of subsection (2) above, a certificate purporting to be signed by or on behalf of the Secretary of State as to the date on which such evidence as is mentioned in paragraph (a) of that subsection came to the knowledge of the Secretary of State shall be conclusive evidence of that date.

(4) In Scotland, proceedings for an offence under this Act may, notwithstanding anything in section 136 of the Criminal Procedure (Scotland) Act 1995, be commenced at any time within—
 (a) the period of 6 months from the date on which evidence, sufficient in the opinion of the procurator fiscal to justify proceedings, comes to the knowledge of the procurator fiscal, or
 (b) the period of 12 months from the commission of the offence,
whichever period expires the later.

(5) For the purposes of subsection (4) above—
 (a) a certificate purporting to be signed by or on behalf of the procurator fiscal as to the date on which such evidence as is mentioned above came to the knowledge of the procurator fiscal shall be conclusive evidence of that date; and
 (b) subsection (3) of section 136 of the said Act of 1995 (date of commencement of proceedings) shall have effect as it has effect for the purposes of that section.

[1372]

NOTES

Sub-s (1): para (a) repealed by the Legal Services Act 2007, ss 208(1), 210, Sch 21, paras 124, 125(a), Sch 23, as from a day to be appointed.

Sub-s (1A): inserted by the Legal Services Act 2007, s 208(1), Sch 21, paras 124, 125(b), as from a day to be appointed.

Special classes of person

34 Agency workers who are not otherwise "workers"

(1) This section applies in any case where an individual ("the agency worker")—

(a) is supplied by a person ("the agent") to do work for another ("the principal") under a contract or other arrangements made between the agent and the principal; but

(b) is not, as respects that work, a worker, because of the absence of a worker's contract between the individual and the agent or the principal; and

(c) is not a party to a contract under which he undertakes to do the work for another party to the contract whose status is, by virtue of the contract, that of a client or customer of any profession or business undertaking carried on by the individual.

(2) In a case where this section applies, the other provisions of this Act shall have effect as if there were a worker's contract for the doing of the work by the agency worker made between the agency worker and—

(a) whichever of the agent and the principal is responsible for paying the agency worker in respect of the work; or

(b) if neither the agent nor the principal is so responsible, whichever of them pays the agency worker in respect of the work.

[1373]

35 Home workers who are not otherwise "workers"

(1) In determining for the purposes of this Act whether a home worker is or is not a worker, section 54(3)(b) below shall have effect as if for the word "personally" there were substituted "(whether personally or otherwise)".

(2) In this section "home worker" means an individual who contracts with a person, for the purposes of that person's business, for the execution of work to be done in a place not under the control or management of that person.

[1374]

36 Crown employment

(1) Subject to section 37 below, the provisions of this Act have effect in relation to Crown employment and persons in Crown employment as they have effect in relation to other employment and other workers.

(2) In this Act, subject to section 37 below, "Crown employment" means employment under or for the purposes of a government department or any officer or body exercising on behalf of the Crown functions conferred by statutory provision.

(3) For the purposes of the application of the other provisions of this Act in relation to Crown employment in accordance with subsection (1) above—

(a) references to an employee or a worker shall be construed as references to a person in Crown employment;

(b) references to a contract of employment or a worker's contract shall be construed as references to the terms of employment of a person in Crown employment; and

(c) references to dismissal, or to the termination of a worker's contract, shall be construed as references to the termination of Crown employment.

[1375]

37 Armed forces

(1) A person serving as a member of the naval, military or air forces of the Crown does not qualify for the national minimum wage in respect of that service.

(2) Section 36 above applies to employment by an association established for the purposes of Part XI of the Reserve Forces Act 1996, notwithstanding anything in subsection (1) above.

[1376]

38 House of Lords staff

(1) Apart from section 21 above, the provisions of this Act have effect in relation to employment as a relevant member of the House of Lords staff as they have effect in relation to other employment.

(2) Nothing in any rule of law or the law or practice of Parliament prevents a relevant member of the House of Lords staff from bringing before the High Court or a county court any claim under this Act.

(3) In this section "relevant member of the House of Lords staff" means any person who is employed under a worker's contract with the Corporate Officer of the House of Lords.

[1377]

39 House of Commons staff

(1) Apart from section 21 above, the provisions of this Act have effect in relation to employment as a relevant member of the House of Commons staff as they have effect in relation to other employment.

(2) Nothing in any rule of law or the law or practice of Parliament prevents a relevant member of the House of Commons staff from bringing before the High Court or a county court any claim under this Act.

(3) In this section "relevant member of the House of Commons staff" means any person—

(a) who was appointed by the House of Commons Commission; or
(b) who is a member of the Speaker's personal staff.

[1378]

40 Mariners

For the purposes of this Act, an individual employed to work on board a ship registered in the United Kingdom under Part II of the Merchant Shipping Act 1995 shall be treated as an individual who under his contract ordinarily works in the United Kingdom unless—

(a) the employment is wholly outside the United Kingdom; or
(b) the person is not ordinarily resident in the United Kingdom;

and related expressions shall be construed accordingly.

[1379]

Extensions

41 Power to apply Act to individuals who are not otherwise "workers"

The Secretary of State may by regulations make provision for this Act to apply, with or without modifications, as if—

(a) any individual of a prescribed description who would not otherwise be a worker for the purposes of this Act were a worker for those purposes;
(b) there were in the case of any such individual a worker's contract of a prescribed description under which the individual works; and
(c) a person of a prescribed description were the employer under that contract.

[1380]

NOTES

Regulations: as of 6 April 2008 no Regulations had been made under this section.

42 Power to apply Act to offshore employment

(1) In this section "offshore employment" means employment for the purposes of activities—

(a) in the territorial waters of the United Kingdom, or
(b) connected with the exploration of the sea-bed or subsoil, or the exploitation of their natural resources, in the United Kingdom sector of the continental shelf, or
(c) connected with the exploration or exploitation, in a foreign sector of the continental shelf, of a cross-boundary petroleum field.

(2) Her Majesty may by Order in Council provide that the provisions of this Act apply, to such extent and for such purposes as may be specified in the Order (with or without modification), to or in relation to a person in offshore employment.

(3) An Order in Council under this section—

(a) may provide that all or any of the provisions of this Act, as applied by such an Order in Council, apply—

(i) to individuals whether or not they are British subjects, and
(ii) to bodies corporate whether or not they are incorporated under the law of a part of the United Kingdom,

and apply even where the application may affect their activities outside the United Kingdom,

(b) may make provision for conferring jurisdiction on any court or class of court specified in the Order in Council, or on employment tribunals, in respect of offences, causes of action or other matters arising in connection with offshore employment,
(c) may (without prejudice to subsection (2) above) provide that the provisions of this Act, as applied by the Order in Council, apply in relation to any person in employment in a part of the areas referred to in subsection (1)(a) and (b) above,
(d) may exclude from the operation of section 3 of the Territorial Waters Jurisdiction Act 1878 (consents required for prosecutions) proceedings for offences under this Act in connection with offshore employment,
(e) may provide that such proceedings shall not be brought without such consent as may be required by the Order in Council,
(f) may (without prejudice to subsection (2) above) modify or exclude the operation of sections 1(2)(b) and 40 above.

(4) Any jurisdiction conferred on a court or tribunal under this section is without prejudice to jurisdiction exercisable apart from this section by that or any other court or tribunal.

(5) In this section—

"cross-boundary petroleum field" means a petroleum field that extends across the boundary between the United Kingdom sector of the continental shelf and a foreign sector of the continental shelf,

"foreign sector of the continental shelf" means an area outside the territorial waters of any state, within which rights with respect to the sea-bed and subsoil and their natural resources are exercisable by a state other than the United Kingdom,

"petroleum field" means a geological structure identified as an oil or gas field by the Order in Council concerned, and

"United Kingdom sector of the continental shelf" means the area designated under section 1(7) of the Continental Shelf Act 1964.

[1381]

NOTES

Orders: the National Minimum Wage (Offshore Employment) Order 1999, SI 1999/1128.

Exclusions

43 Share fishermen

A person—

(a) employed as master, or as a member of the crew, of a fishing vessel, and
(b) remunerated, in respect of that employment, only by a share in the profits or gross earnings of the vessel,

does not qualify for the national minimum wage in respect of that employment.

[1382]

44 Voluntary workers

(1) A worker employed by a charity, a voluntary organisation, an associated fund-raising body or a statutory body does not qualify for the national minimum wage in respect of that employment if he receives, and under the terms of his employment (apart from this Act) is entitled to,—

(a) no monetary payments of any description, or no monetary payments except in respect of expenses—
  (i) actually incurred in the performance of his duties; or
  (ii) reasonably estimated as likely to be or to have been so incurred; and
(b) no benefits in kind of any description, or no benefits in kind other than the provision of some or all of his subsistence or of such accommodation as is reasonable in the circumstances of the employment.

(2) A person who would satisfy the conditions in subsection (1) above but for receiving monetary payments made solely for the purpose of providing him with means of subsistence shall be taken to satisfy those conditions if—

(a) he is employed to do the work in question as a result of arrangements made between a charity acting in pursuance of its charitable purposes and the body for which the work is done; and

(b) the work is done for a charity, a voluntary organisation, an associated fund-raising body or a statutory body.

(3) For the purposes of subsection (1)(b) above—

(a) any training (other than that which a person necessarily acquires in the course of doing his work) shall be taken to be a benefit in kind; but

(b) there shall be left out of account any training provided for the sole or main purpose of improving the worker's ability to perform the work which he has agreed to do.

(4) In this section—

"associated fund-raising body" means a body of persons the profits of which are applied wholly for the purposes of a charity or voluntary organisation;

"charity" means a body of persons, or the trustees of a trust, established for charitable purposes only;

"receive", in relation to a monetary payment or a benefit in kind, means receive in respect of, or otherwise in connection with, the employment in question (whether or not under the terms of the employment);

"statutory body" means a body established by or under an enactment (including an enactment comprised in Northern Ireland legislation);

"subsistence" means such subsistence as is reasonable in the circumstances of the employment in question, and does not include accommodation;

"voluntary organisation" means a body of persons, or the trustees of a trust, which is established only for charitable purposes (whether or not those purposes are charitable within the meaning of any rule of law), benevolent purposes or philanthropic purposes, but which is not a charity.

[1383]

[44A Religious and other communities: resident workers

(1) A residential member of a community to which this section applies does not qualify for the national minimum wage in respect of employment by the community.

(2) Subject to subsection (3), this section applies to a community if—

(a) it is a charity or is established by a charity,

(b) a purpose of the community is to practise or advance a belief of a religious or similar nature, and

(c) all or some of its members live together for that purpose.

(3) This section does not apply to a community which—

(a) is an independent school, or

(b) provides a course of further or higher education.

(4) The residential members of a community are those who live together as mentioned in subsection (2)(c).

(5) In this section—

(a) "charity" has the same meaning as in section 44, and

(b) "independent school" has the same meaning as in section 463 of the Education Act 1996 (in England and Wales), section 135 of the Education (Scotland) Act 1980 (in Scotland) and Article 2 of the Education and Libraries (Northern Ireland) Order 1986 (in Northern Ireland).

(6) In this section "course of further or higher education" means—

(a) in England and Wales, a course of a description referred to in Schedule 6 to the Education Reform Act 1988 or Schedule 2 to the Further and Higher Education Act 1992;

(b) in Scotland, a course or programme of a description mentioned in or falling within section 6(1) or 38 of the Further and Higher Education (Scotland) Act 1992;

(c) in Northern Ireland, a course of a description referred to in Schedule 1 to the Further Education (Northern Ireland) Order 1997 or a course providing further education within the meaning of Article 3 of that Order.]

[1384]

NOTES

Inserted by the Employment Relations Act 1999, s 22.

45 Prisoners

(1) A prisoner does not qualify for the national minimum wage in respect of any work which he does in pursuance of prison rules.

(2) In this section—

"prisoner" means a person detained in, or on temporary release from, a prison;

"prison" includes any other institution to which prison rules apply;

"prison rules" means—

(a) in relation to England and Wales, rules made under section 47 of the Prison Act 1952;

(b) in relation to Scotland, rules made under section 39 of the Prisons (Scotland) Act 1989; and

(c) in relation to Northern Ireland, rules made under section 13 of the Prison Act (Northern Ireland) 1953.

[1385]

[45A Persons discharging fines by unpaid work

A person does not qualify for the national minimum wage in respect of any work that he does in pursuance of a work order under Schedule 6 to the Courts Act 2003 (discharge of fines by unpaid work).]

[1386]

NOTES

Commencement: 1 April 2005.

Inserted by the Courts Act 2003, s 109(1), Sch 8, para 382, as from 1 April 2005.

[45B Immigration: detained persons

Section 153A of the Immigration and Asylum Act 1999 (c 33) (persons detained in removal centres) disqualifies certain persons for the national minimum wage.]

[1386A]

NOTES

Commencement: 31 August 2006.

Inserted by the Immigration, Asylum and Nationality Act 2006, s 59(2), as from 31 August 2006.

46, 47 (*Agricultural workers: outside the scope of this work.*)

Miscellaneous

48 Application of Act to superior employers

Where—

(a) the immediate employer of a worker is himself in the employment of some other person, and

(b) the worker is employed on the premises of that other person,

that other person shall be deemed for the purposes of this Act to be the employer of the worker jointly with the immediate employer.

[1387]

49 Restrictions on contracting out

(1) Any provision in any agreement (whether a worker's contract or not) is void in so far as it purports—

(a) to exclude or limit the operation of any provision of this Act; or

(b) to preclude a person from bringing proceedings under this Act before an employment tribunal.

(2) Subsection (1) above does not apply to any agreement to refrain from instituting or continuing proceedings where a conciliation officer has taken action under—

(a) section 18 of the Employment Tribunals Act 1996 (conciliation), or

(b) in relation to Northern Ireland, Article 20 of the Industrial Tribunals (Northern Ireland) Order 1996.

(3) Subsection (1) above does not apply to any agreement to refrain from instituting or continuing before an employment tribunal any proceedings within—

(a) section 18(1)(dd) of the Employment Tribunals Act 1996 (proceedings under or by virtue of this Act where conciliation is available), or

(b) in relation to Northern Ireland, Article 20(1)(cc) of the Industrial Tribunals (Northern Ireland) Order 1996,

if the conditions regulating compromise agreements under this Act are satisfied in relation to the agreement.

(4) For the purposes of subsection (3) above the conditions regulating compromise agreements under this Act are that—

(a) the agreement must be in writing,

(b) the agreement must relate to the particular proceedings,

(c) the employee or worker must have received advice from a relevant independent adviser as to the terms and effect of the proposed agreement and, in particular, its effect on his ability to pursue his rights before an employment tribunal,

(d) there must be in force, when the adviser gives the advice, a contract of insurance, or an indemnity provided for members of a profession or a professional body, covering the risk of a claim by the employee or worker in respect of loss arising in consequence of the advice,

(e) the agreement must identify the adviser, and

(f) the agreement must state that the conditions regulating compromise agreements under this Act are satisfied.

(5) A person is a relevant independent adviser for the purposes of subsection (4)(c) above—

(a) if he is a qualified lawyer,

(b) if he is an officer, official, employee or member of an independent trade union who has been certified in writing by the trade union as competent to give advice and as authorised to do so on behalf of the trade union,

(c) if he works at an advice centre (whether as an employee or a volunteer) and has been certified in writing by the centre as competent to give advice and as authorised to do so on behalf of the centre, or

(d) if he is a person of a description specified in an order made by the Secretary of State.

(6) But a person is not a relevant independent adviser for the purposes of subsection (4)(c) above in relation to the employee or worker—

(a) if he is employed by, or is acting in the matter for, the employer or an associated employer,

(b) in the case of a person within subsection (5)(b) or (c) above, if the trade union or advice centre is the employer or an associated employer,

(c) in the case of a person within subsection (5)(c) above, if the employee or worker makes a payment for the advice received from him, or

(d) in the case of a person of a description specified in an order under subsection (5)(d) above, if any condition specified in the order in relation to the giving of advice by persons of that description is not satisfied.

(7) In this section "qualified lawyer" means—

(*a*) *as respects England and Wales—*

(i) a barrister (whether in practice as such or employed to give legal advice);

(ii) a solicitor who holds a practising certificate; or

(iii) a person other than a barrister or solicitor who is an authorised advocate or authorised litigator (within the meaning of the Courts and Legal Services Act 1990);

(b) as respects Scotland—

(i) an advocate (whether in practice as such or employed to give legal advice); or

(ii) a solicitor who holds a practising certificate; and

(c) as respects Northern Ireland—

(i) a barrister (whether in practice as such or employed to give legal advice); or

(ii) a solicitor who holds a practising certificate.

(8) For the purposes of this section any two employers shall be treated as associated if—

(a) one is a company of which the other (directly or indirectly) has control; or

(b) both are companies of which a third person (directly or indirectly) has control;

and "associated employer" shall be construed accordingly.

(9)–(11) (*Apply to Northern Ireland: outside the scope of this work.*)

[1388]

NOTES

Sub-s (7): para (a) substituted by the Legal Services Act 2007, s 208(1), Sch 21, paras 124, 126, as from a day to be appointed, as follows—

"(a) as regards England and Wales, a person who, for the purposes of the Legal Services Act 2007, is an authorised person in relation to an activity which constitutes the exercise of a right of audience or the conduct of litigation (within the meaning of that Act);".

Orders: the Compromise Agreements (Description of Person) Order 2004, SI 2004/754 at **[3138]**.

50 ((*Publicity for the Act and Regulations*) *outside the scope of this work.*)

Supplementary

51 Regulations and orders

(1) Except to the extent that this Act makes provision to the contrary, any power conferred by this Act to make an Order in Council, regulations or an order includes power—

(a) to make different provision for different cases or for different descriptions of person; and

(b) to make incidental, consequential, supplemental or transitional provision and savings.

(2) Paragraph (a) of subsection (1) above does not have effect in relation to regulations under section 1(3) above or an order under section 49 above.

(3) No recommendation shall be made to Her Majesty to make an Order in Council under any provision of this Act unless a draft of the Order in Council has been laid before Parliament and approved by a resolution of each House of Parliament.

(4) Any power of a Minister of the Crown to make regulations or an order under this Act shall be exercisable by statutory instrument.

(5) A statutory instrument containing (whether alone or with other provisions) regulations under this Act shall not be made unless a draft of the instrument has been laid before, and approved by a resolution of, each House of Parliament.

(6) Subsection (5) above shall not have effect in relation to a statutory instrument if the only regulations under this Act which the instrument contains are regulations under section 21 or 47(2) or (4) above.

(7) A statutory instrument—

(a) which contains (whether alone or with other provisions) any regulations under section 21 or 47(2) or (4) above or an order under section 49 above, and

(b) which is not subject to any requirement that a draft of the instrument be laid before, and approved by a resolution of, each House of Parliament,

shall be subject to annulment in pursuance of a resolution of either House of Parliament.

(8) The power—

(a) of the Department of Economic Development to make an order under section 26(6) above, or

(b) of the Department of Agriculture for Northern Ireland to make regulations under section 47 above,

shall be exercisable by statutory rule for the purposes of the Statutory Rules (Northern Ireland) Order 1979; and any such order or regulations shall be subject to negative resolution within the meaning of section 41(6) of the Interpretation Act (Northern Ireland) 1954.

[1389]

52 Expenses

There shall be paid out of money provided by Parliament—

(a) any expenditure incurred under this Act by a Minister of the Crown or government department or by a body performing functions on behalf of the Crown; and

(b) any increase attributable to the provisions of this Act in the sums payable out of such money under any other Act.

[1390]

53 (*Introduces Sch 3* (*repeals and revocations*).)

54 Meaning of "worker", "employee" etc

(1) In this Act "employee" means an individual who has entered into or works under (or, where the employment has ceased, worked under) a contract of employment.

(2) In this Act "contract of employment" means a contract of service or apprenticeship, whether express or implied, and (if it is express) whether oral or in writing.

(3) In this Act "worker" (except in the phrases "agency worker" and "home worker") means an individual who has entered into or works under (or, where the employment has ceased, worked under)—

(a) a contract of employment; or

(b) any other contract, whether express or implied and (if it is express) whether oral or in writing, whereby the individual undertakes to do or perform personally any work or services for another party to the contract whose status is not by virtue of the contract that of a client or customer of any profession or business undertaking carried on by the individual;

and any reference to a worker's contract shall be construed accordingly.

(4) In this Act "employer", in relation to an employee or a worker, means the person by whom the employee or worker is (or, where the employment has ceased, was) employed.

(5) In this Act "employment"—

(a) in relation to an employee, means employment under a contract of employment; and

(b) in relation to a worker, means employment under his contract;

and "employed" shall be construed accordingly.

[1391]

55 Interpretation

(1) In this Act, unless the context otherwise requires,—

"civil proceedings" means proceedings before an employment tribunal or civil proceedings before any other court;

"enforcement notice" shall be construed in accordance with section 19 above;

"government department" includes a Northern Ireland department, except in section 52(a) above;

"industrial tribunal" means a tribunal established under Article 3 of the Industrial Tribunals (Northern Ireland) Order 1996;

"notice" means notice in writing;

"pay reference period" shall be construed in accordance with section 1(4) above;

"penalty notice" shall be construed in accordance with section 21 above;

"person who qualifies for the national minimum wage" shall be construed in accordance with section 1(2) above; and related expressions shall be construed accordingly;

"prescribe" means prescribe by regulations;

"regulations" means regulations made by the Secretary of State, except in the case of regulations under section 47(2) or (4) above made by the Secretary of State and the Minister of Agriculture, Fisheries and Food acting jointly or by the Department of Agriculture for Northern Ireland.

(2) Any reference in this Act to a person being remunerated for a pay reference period is a reference to the person being remunerated by his employer in respect of his work in that pay reference period.

(3) Any reference in this Act to doing work includes a reference to performing services; and "work" and other related expressions shall be construed accordingly.

(4) For the purposes of this Act, a person ceases to be of compulsory school age in Scotland when he ceases to be of school age in accordance with sections 31 and 33 of the Education (Scotland) Act 1980.

(5) Any reference in this Act to a person ceasing to be of compulsory school age shall, in relation to Northern Ireland, be construed in accordance with Article 46 of the Education and Libraries (Northern Ireland) Order 1986.

(6) Any reference in this Act to an employment tribunal shall, in relation to Northern Ireland, be construed as a reference to an industrial tribunal.

[1392]

56 Short title, commencement and extent

(1) This Act may be cited as the National Minimum Wage Act 1998.

(2) Apart from this section and any powers to make an Order in Council or regulations or an order (which accordingly come into force on the day on which this Act is passed) the provisions of this Act shall come into force on such day or days as the Secretary of State may by order appoint; and different days may be appointed for different purposes.

(3) This Act extends to Northern Ireland.

[1393]

NOTES

Orders: the National Minimum Wage Act 1998 (Commencement No 1 and Transitional Provisions) Order 1998, SI 1998/2574; the National Minimum Wage Act 1998 (Commencement No 2 and Transitional Provisions) Order 1999, SI 1999/685.

Sch 1 (provisions as to the Low Pay Commission), and Sch 2 (amendments to agricultural wages legislation) outside the scope of this work; Sch 3 contains repeals and revocations only and, in so far as relevant to this work, these have been incorporated at the appropriate place.)

HUMAN RIGHTS ACT 1998

(1998 c 42)

ARRANGEMENT OF SECTIONS

Introduction

Legislation

Public authorities

Remedial action

An Act to give further effect to rights and freedoms guaranteed under the European Convention on Human Rights; to make provision with respect to holders of certain judicial offices who become judges of the European Court of Human Rights; and for connected purposes

[9 November 1998]

NOTES

Only certain provisions of this Act are included: those omitted are outside the scope of this work for reasons given in notes thereto.

See *Harvey* L1(A), M, N, Q, R.

Introduction

1 The Convention Rights

(1) In this Act "the Convention rights" means the rights and fundamental freedoms set out in—

(a) Articles 2 to 12 and 14 of the Convention,
(b) Articles 1 to 3 of the First Protocol, and
(c) [Article 1 of the Thirteenth Protocol],

as read with Articles 16 to 18 of the Convention.

(2) Those Articles are to have effect for the purposes of this Act subject to any designated derogation or reservation (as to which see sections 14 and 15).

(3) The Articles are set out in Schedule 1.

(4) The [Secretary of State] may by order make such amendments to this Act as he considers appropriate to reflect the effect, in relation to the United Kingdom, of a protocol.

(5) In subsection (4) "protocol" means a protocol to the Convention—

(a) which the United Kingdom has ratified; or
(b) which the United Kingdom has signed with a view to ratification.

(6) No amendment may be made by an order under subsection (4) so as to come into force before the protocol concerned is in force in relation to the United Kingdom.

[1394]

NOTES

Sub-s (1): words in square brackets in para (c) substituted by the Human Rights Act 1998 (Amendment) Order 2004, SI 2004/1574, art 2(1), as from 22 June 2004.

Sub-s (4): words in square brackets substituted by the Secretary of State for Constitutional Affairs Order 2003, SI 2003/1887, art 9, Sch 2, para 10(1), as from 19 August 2003.
Orders: the Human Rights Act 1998 (Amendment) Order 2004, SI 2004/1574.

2 Interpretation of Convention rights

(1) A court or tribunal determining a question which has arisen in connection with a Convention right must take into account any—

(a) judgment, decision, declaration or advisory opinion of the European Court of Human Rights,
(b) opinion of the Commission given in a report adopted under Article 31 of the Convention,
(c) decision of the Commission in connection with Article 26 or 27(2) of the Convention, or
(d) decision of the Committee of Ministers taken under Article 46 of the Convention,

whenever made or given, so far as, in the opinion of the court or tribunal, it is relevant to the proceedings in which that question has arisen.

(2) Evidence of any judgment, decision, declaration or opinion of which account may have to be taken under this section is to be given in proceedings before any court or tribunal in such manner as may be provided by rules.

(3) In this section "rules" means rules of court or, in the case of proceedings before a tribunal, rules made for the purposes of this section—

(a) by ... [the Lord Chancellor or] the Secretary of State, in relation to any proceedings outside Scotland;
(b) by the Secretary of State, in relation to proceedings in Scotland; or
(c) by a Northern Ireland department, in relation to proceedings before a tribunal in Northern Ireland—
  (i) which deals with transferred matters; and
  (ii) for which no rules made under paragraph (a) are in force.

[1395]

NOTES

Sub-s (3): words omitted from para (a) repealed by the Secretary of State for Constitutional Affairs Order 2003, SI 2003/1887, art 9, Sch 2, para 10(2), as from 19 August 2003; words in square brackets in para (a) inserted by the Transfer of Functions (Lord Chancellor and Secretary of State) Order 2005, SI 2005/3429, art 8, Schedule, para 3, as from 12 January 2006.
Rules: the Act of Adjournal (Criminal Procedure Rules Amendment No 2) (Human Rights Act 1998) 2000, SSI 2000/315; the Act of Sederunt (Rules of the Court of Session Amendment No 6) (Human Rights Act 1998) 2000, SSI 2000/316.

Legislation

3 Interpretation of legislation

(1) So far as it is possible to do so, primary legislation and subordinate legislation must be read and given effect in a way which is compatible with the Convention rights.

(2) This section—

(a) applies to primary legislation and subordinate legislation whenever enacted;
(b) does not affect the validity, continuing operation or enforcement of any incompatible primary legislation; and
(c) does not affect the validity, continuing operation or enforcement of any incompatible subordinate legislation if (disregarding any possibility of revocation) primary legislation prevents removal of the incompatibility.

[1396]

4 Declaration of incompatibility

(1) Subsection (2) applies in any proceedings in which a court determines whether a provision of primary legislation is compatible with a Convention right.

(2) If the court is satisfied that the provision is incompatible with a Convention right, it may make a declaration of that incompatibility.

(3) Subsection (4) applies in any proceedings in which a court determines whether a provision of subordinate legislation, made in the exercise of a power conferred by primary legislation, is compatible with a Convention right.

(4) If the court is satisfied—

(a) that the provision is incompatible with a Convention right, and

(b) that (disregarding any possibility of revocation) the primary legislation concerned prevents removal of the incompatibility,

it may make a declaration of that incompatibility.

(5) In this section "court" means—

(*a*) *the House of Lords;*

(b) the Judicial Committee of the Privy Council;

(c) the *Courts-Martial Appeal Court;*

(d) in Scotland, the High Court of Justiciary sitting otherwise than as a trial court or the Court of Session;

(e) in England and Wales or Northern Ireland, the High Court or the Court of Appeal;

[(f) the Court of Protection, in any matter being dealt with by the President of the Family Division, the Vice-Chancellor or a puisne judge of the High Court].

(6) A declaration under this section ("a declaration of incompatibility")—

(a) does not affect the validity, continuing operation or enforcement of the provision in respect of which it is given; and

(b) is not binding on the parties to the proceedings in which it is made.

[1397]

NOTES

Sub-s (5) is amended as follows:

Para (a) substituted by the Constitutional Reform Act 2005, s 40, Sch 9, Pt 1, para 66(1), (2), as from a day to be appointed, as follows—

"(a) the Supreme Court;".

For the words in italics in para (c) there are substituted the words "Court Martial Appeal Court" by the Armed Forces Act 2006, s 378(1), Sch 16, para 156, as from a day to be appointed.

Para (f) added by the Mental Capacity Act 2005, s 67(1), Sch 6, para 43, as from 1 October 2007.

5 (*Right of Crown to intervene in certain proceedings* (*outside the scope of this work*).)

Public authorities

6 Acts of public authorities

(1) It is unlawful for a public authority to act in a way which is incompatible with a Convention right.

(2) Subsection (1) does not apply to an act if—

(a) as the result of one or more provisions of primary legislation, the authority could not have acted differently; or

(b) in the case of one or more provisions of, or made under, primary legislation which cannot be read or given effect in a way which is compatible with the Convention rights, the authority was acting so as to give effect to or enforce those provisions.

(3) In this section "public authority" includes—

(a) a court or tribunal, and

(b) any person certain of whose functions are functions of a public nature,

but does not include either House of Parliament or a person exercising functions in connection with proceedings in Parliament.

(4) In subsection (3) "Parliament" does not include the House of Lords in its judicial capacity.

(5) In relation to a particular act, a person is not a public authority by virtue only of subsection (3)(b) if the nature of the act is private.

(6) "An act" includes a failure to act but does not include a failure to—

(a) introduce in, or lay before, Parliament a proposal for legislation; or

(b) make any primary legislation or remedial order.

[1398]

NOTES

Sub-s (4): repealed by the Constitutional Reform Act 2005, ss 40, 146, Sch 9, Pt 1, para 66(1), (4), Sch 18, Pt 5, as from a day to be appointed.

7 Proceedings

(1) A person who claims that a public authority has acted (or proposes to act) in a way which is made unlawful by section 6(1) may—

(a) bring proceedings against the authority under this Act in the appropriate court or tribunal, or

(b) rely on the Convention right or rights concerned in any legal proceedings,

but only if he is (or would be) a victim of the unlawful act.

(2) In subsection (1)(a) "appropriate court or tribunal" means such court or tribunal as may be determined in accordance with rules; and proceedings against an authority include a counterclaim or similar proceeding.

(3) If the proceedings are brought on an application for judicial review, the applicant is to be taken to have a sufficient interest in relation to the unlawful act only if he is, or would be, a victim of that act.

(4) If the proceedings are made by way of a petition for judicial review in Scotland, the applicant shall be taken to have title and interest to sue in relation to the unlawful act only if he is, or would be, a victim of that act.

(5) Proceedings under subsection (1)(a) must be brought before the end of—

(a) the period of one year beginning with the date on which the act complained of took place; or

(b) such longer period as the court or tribunal considers equitable having regard to all the circumstances,

but that is subject to any rule imposing a stricter time limit in relation to the procedure in question.

(6) In subsection (1)(b) "legal proceedings" includes—

(a) proceedings brought by or at the instigation of a public authority; and

(b) an appeal against the decision of a court or tribunal.

(7) For the purposes of this section, a person is a victim of an unlawful act only if he would be a victim for the purposes of Article 34 of the Convention if proceedings were brought in the European Court of Human Rights in respect of that act.

(8) Nothing in this Act creates a criminal offence.

(9) In this section "rules" means—

(a) in relation to proceedings before a court or tribunal outside Scotland, rules made by … [the Lord Chancellor or] the Secretary of State for the purposes of this section or rules of court,

(b) in relation to proceedings before a court or tribunal in Scotland, rules made by the Secretary of State for those purposes,

(c) in relation to proceedings before a tribunal in Northern Ireland—

(i) which deals with transferred matters; and

(ii) for which no rules made under paragraph (a) are in force,

rules made by a Northern Ireland department for those purposes,

and includes provision made by order under section 1 of the Courts and Legal Services Act 1990.

(10) In making rules, regard must be had to section 9.

(11) The Minister who has power to make rules in relation to a particular tribunal may, to the extent he considers it necessary to ensure that the tribunal can provide an appropriate remedy in relation to an act (or proposed act) of a public authority which is (or would be) unlawful as a result of section 6(1), by order add to—

(a) the relief or remedies which the tribunal may grant; or

(b) the grounds on which it may grant any of them.

(12) An order made under subsection (11) may contain such incidental, supplemental, consequential or transitional provision as the Minister making it considers appropriate.

(13) "The Minister" includes the Northern Ireland department concerned.

[1399]

NOTES

Sub-s (9): words omitted from para (a) repealed by the Secretary of State for Constitutional Affairs Order 2003, SI 2003/1887, art 9, Sch 2, para 10(2), as from 19 August 2003; words in square brackets in para (a) inserted by the Transfer of Functions (Lord Chancellor and Secretary of State) Order 2005, SI 2005/3429, art 8, Schedule, para 3, as from 12 January 2006.

Rules: the Human Rights Act 1998 (Jurisdiction) (Scotland) Rules 2000, SSI 2000/301; the Proscribed Organisations Appeal Commission (Human Rights Act Proceedings) Rules 2001, SI 2001/127.

Orders: as of 6 April 2008 no Orders had been made under sub-s (11).

8 Judicial remedies

(1) In relation to any act (or proposed act) of a public authority which the court finds is (or would be) unlawful, it may grant such relief or remedy, or make such order, within its powers as it considers just and appropriate.

(2) But damages may be awarded only by a court which has power to award damages, or to order the payment of compensation, in civil proceedings.

(3) No award of damages is to be made unless, taking account of all the circumstances of the case, including—

- (a) any other relief or remedy granted, or order made, in relation to the act in question (by that or any other court), and
- (b) the consequences of any decision (of that or any other court) in respect of that act,

the court is satisfied that the award is necessary to afford just satisfaction to the person in whose favour it is made.

(4) In determining—

- (a) whether to award damages, or
- (b) the amount of an award,

the court must take into account the principles applied by the European Court of Human Rights in relation to the award of compensation under Article 41 of the Convention.

(5) A public authority against which damages are awarded is to be treated—

- (a) in Scotland, for the purposes of section 3 of the Law Reform (Miscellaneous Provisions) (Scotland) Act 1940 as if the award were made in an action of damages in which the authority has been found liable in respect of loss or damage to the person to whom the award is made;
- (b) for the purposes of the Civil Liability (Contribution) Act 1978 as liable in respect of damage suffered by the person to whom the award is made.

(6) In this section—

"court" includes a tribunal;

"damages" means damages for an unlawful act of a public authority; and

"unlawful" means unlawful under section 6(1).

[1400]

9 (*Proceedings and remedies in respect of judicial acts* (*outside the scope of this work*).)

Remedial action

10 Power to take remedial action

(1) This section applies if—

- (a) a provision of legislation has been declared under section 4 to be incompatible with a Convention right and, if an appeal lies—
  - (i) all persons who may appeal have stated in writing that they do not intend to do so;
  - (ii) the time for bringing an appeal has expired and no appeal has been brought within that time; or
  - (iii) an appeal brought within that time has been determined or abandoned; or
- (b) it appears to a Minister of the Crown or Her Majesty in Council that, having regard to a finding of the European Court of Human Rights made after the coming

into force of this section in proceedings against the United Kingdom, a provision of legislation is incompatible with an obligation of the United Kingdom arising from the Convention.

(2) If a Minister of the Crown considers that there are compelling reasons for proceeding under this section, he may by order make such amendments to the legislation as he considers necessary to remove the incompatibility.

(3) If, in the case of subordinate legislation, a Minister of the Crown considers—

(a) that it is necessary to amend the primary legislation under which the subordinate legislation in question was made, in order to enable the incompatibility to be removed, and

(b) that there are compelling reasons for proceeding under this section,

he may by order make such amendments to the primary legislation as he considers necessary.

(4) This section also applies where the provision in question is in subordinate legislation and has been quashed, or declared invalid, by reason of incompatibility with a Convention right and the Minister proposes to proceed under paragraph 2(b) of Schedule 2.

(5) If the legislation is an Order in Council, the power conferred by subsection (2) or (3) is exercisable by Her Majesty in Council.

(6) In this section "legislation" does not include a Measure of the Church Assembly or of the General Synod of the Church of England.

(7) Schedule 2 makes further provision about remedial orders.

[1401]

NOTES

Orders: the Mental Health Act 1983 (Remedial) Order 2001, SI 2001/3712; the Naval Discipline Act 1957 (Remedial) Order 2004, SI 2004/66; Marriage Act 1949 (Remedial) Order 2007, SI 2007/438.

Other rights and proceedings

11 Safeguard for existing human rights

A person's reliance on a Convention right does not restrict—

(a) any other right or freedom conferred on him by or under any law having effect in any part of the United Kingdom; or

(b) his right to make any claim or bring any proceedings which he could make or bring apart from sections 7 to 9.

[1402]

12 (*Restrictions on grant of relief affecting freedom of expression* (*outside the scope of this work*).)

13 Freedom of thought, conscience and religion

(1) If a court's determination of any question arising under this Act might affect the exercise by a religious organisation (itself or its members collectively) of the Convention right to freedom of thought, conscience and religion, it must have particular regard to the importance of that right.

(2) In this section "court" includes a tribunal.

[1403]

14–18 (*Ss 14–17* (*derogations and reservations*), *s 18* (*appointment of judges of the European Court of Human Rights*) *outside the scope of this work.*)

Parliamentary procedure

19 Statements of compatibility

(1) A Minister of the Crown in charge of a Bill in either House of Parliament must, before Second Reading of the Bill—

(a) make a statement to the effect that in his view the provisions of the Bill are compatible with the Convention rights ("a statement of compatibility"); or

(b) make a statement to the effect that although he is unable to make a statement of compatibility the government nevertheless wishes the House to proceed with the Bill.

(2) The statement must be in writing and be published in such manner as the Minister making it considers appropriate.

[1404]

Supplemental

20 Orders etc under this Act

(1) Any power of a Minister of the Crown to make an order under this Act is exercisable by statutory instrument.

(2) The power of … [the Lord Chancellor or] the Secretary of State to make rules (other than rules of court) under section 2(3) or 7(9) is exercisable by statutory instrument.

(3) Any statutory instrument made under section 14, 15 or 16(7) must be laid before Parliament.

(4) No order may be made by … [the Lord Chancellor or] the Secretary of State under section 1(4), 7(11) or 16(2) unless a draft of the order has been laid before, and approved by, each House of Parliament.

(5) Any statutory instrument made under section 18(7) or Schedule 4, or to which subsection (2) applies, shall be subject to annulment in pursuance of a resolution of either House of Parliament.

(6) The power of a Northern Ireland department to make—

(a) rules under section 2(3)(c) or 7(9)(c), or

(b) an order under section 7(11),

is exercisable by statutory rule for the purposes of the Statutory Rules (Northern Ireland) Order 1979.

(7) Any rules made under section 2(3)(c) or 7(9)(c) shall be subject to negative resolution; and section 41(6) of the Interpretation Act (Northern Ireland) 1954 (meaning of "subject to negative resolution") shall apply as if the power to make the rules were conferred by an Act of the Northern Ireland Assembly.

(8) No order may be made by a Northern Ireland department under section 7(11) unless a draft of the order has been laid before, and approved by, the Northern Ireland Assembly.

[1405]

NOTES

Sub-ss (2), (4): words omitted repealed by the Secretary of State for Constitutional Affairs Order 2003, SI 2003/1887, art 9, Sch 2, para 10(2), as from 19 August 2003; words in square brackets inserted by the Transfer of Functions (Lord Chancellor and Secretary of State) Order 2005, SI 2005/3429, art 8, Schedule, para 3, as from 12 January 2006.

21 Interpretation, etc

(1) In this Act—

"amend" includes repeal and apply (with or without modifications);

"the appropriate Minister" means the Minister of the Crown having charge of the appropriate authorised government department (within the meaning of the Crown Proceedings Act 1947);

"the Commission" means the European Commission of Human Rights;

"the Convention" means the Convention for the Protection of Human Rights and Fundamental Freedoms, agreed by the Council of Europe at Rome on 4th November 1950 as it has effect for the time being in relation to the United Kingdom;

"declaration of incompatibility" means a declaration under section 4;

"Minister of the Crown" has the same meaning as in the Ministers of the Crown Act 1975;

"Northern Ireland Minister" includes the First Minister and the deputy First Minister in Northern Ireland;

"primary legislation" means any—
(a) public general Act;
(b) local and personal Act;
(c) private Act;
(d) Measure of the Church Assembly;
(e) Measure of the General Synod of the Church of England;
(f) Order in Council—
(i) made in exercise of Her Majesty's Royal Prerogative;
(ii) made under section 38(1)(a) of the Northern Ireland Constitution Act 1973 or the corresponding provision of the Northern Ireland Act 1998; or
(iii) amending an Act of a kind mentioned in paragraph (a), (b) or (c);

and includes an order or other instrument made under primary legislation (otherwise than by the [Welsh Ministers, the First Minister for Wales, the Counsel General to the Welsh Assembly Government], a member of the Scottish Executive, a Northern Ireland Minister or a Northern Ireland department) to the extent to which it operates to bring one or more provisions of that legislation into force or amends any primary legislation;

"the First Protocol" means the protocol to the Convention agreed at Paris on 20th March 1952;

…

"the Eleventh Protocol" means the protocol to the Convention (restructuring the control machinery established by the Convention) agreed at Strasbourg on 11th May 1994;

["the Thirteenth Protocol" means the protocol to the Convention (concerning the abolition of the death penalty in all circumstances) agreed at Vilnius on 3rd May 2002;]

"remedial order" means an order under section 10;

"subordinate legislation" means any—
(a) Order in Council other than one—
(i) made in exercise of Her Majesty's Royal Prerogative;
(ii) made under section 38(1)(a) of the Northern Ireland Constitution Act 1973 or the corresponding provision of the Northern Ireland Act 1998; or
(iii) amending an Act of a kind mentioned in the definition of primary legislation;
(b) Act of the Scottish Parliament;
[(ba) Measure of the National Assembly for Wales;
(bb) Act of the National Assembly for Wales;]
(c) Act of the Parliament of Northern Ireland;
(d) Measure of the Assembly established under section 1 of the Northern Ireland Assembly Act 1973;
(e) Act of the Northern Ireland Assembly;
(f) order, rules, regulations, scheme, warrant, byelaw or other instrument made under primary legislation (except to the extent to which it operates to bring one or more provisions of that legislation into force or amends any primary legislation);
(g) order, rules, regulations, scheme, warrant, byelaw or other instrument made under legislation mentioned in paragraph (b), (c), (d) or (e) or made under an Order in Council applying only to Northern Ireland;
(h) order, rules, regulations, scheme, warrant, byelaw or other instrument made by a member of the Scottish Executive[, Welsh Ministers, the First Minister for Wales, the Counsel General to the Welsh Assembly Government], a Northern Ireland Minister or a Northern Ireland department in exercise of prerogative or other executive functions of Her Majesty which are exercisable by such a person on behalf of Her Majesty;

"transferred matters" has the same meaning as in the Northern Ireland Act 1998; and

"tribunal" means any tribunal in which legal proceedings may be brought.

(2) The references in paragraphs (b) and (c) of section 2(1) to Articles are to Articles of the Convention as they had effect immediately before the coming into force of the Eleventh Protocol.

(3) The reference in paragraph (d) of section 2(1) to Article 46 includes a reference to Articles 32 and 54 of the Convention as they had effect immediately before the coming into force of the Eleventh Protocol.

(4) The references in section 2(1) to a report or decision of the Commission or a decision of the Committee of Ministers include references to a report or decision made as provided by paragraphs 3, 4 and 6 of Article 5 of the Eleventh Protocol (transitional provisions).

(5) Any liability under the Army Act 1955, the Air Force Act 1955 or the Naval Discipline Act 1957 to suffer death for an offence is replaced by a liability to imprisonment for life or any less punishment authorised by those Acts; and those Acts shall accordingly have effect with the necessary modifications.

[1406]

NOTES

Sub-s (1) is amended as follows:

Words in square brackets in the definition "primary legislation" substituted by the Government of Wales Act 2006, s 160(1), Sch 10, para 56(1), (2), as from 25 May 2007.

Definition "the Sixth Protocol" (omitted) repealed, and definition "the Thirteenth Protocol" inserted, by the Human Rights Act 1998 (Amendment) Order 2004, SI 2004/1574, art 2(2), as from 22 June 2004.

In definition "subordinate legislation" paras (ba), (bb) inserted, and words in square brackets in para (h) inserted, by the Government of Wales Act 2006, s 160(1), Sch 10, para 56(1), (3), (4), as from 25 May 2007.

Sub-s (5): repealed by the Armed Forces Act 2006, s 378(2), Sch 17, as from a day to be appointed.

22 Short title, commencement, application and extent

(1) This Act may be cited as the Human Rights Act 1998.

(2) Sections 18, 20 and 21(5) and this section come into force on the passing of this Act.

(3) The other provisions of this Act come into force on such day as the Secretary of State may by order appoint; and different days may be appointed for different purposes.

(4) Paragraph (b) of subsection (1) of section 7 applies to proceedings brought by or at the instigation of a public authority whenever the act in question took place; but otherwise that subsection does not apply to an act taking place before the coming into force of that section.

(5) This Act binds the Crown.

(6) This Act extends to Northern Ireland.

(7) Section 21(5), so far as it relates to any provision contained in the Army Act 1955, the Air Force Act 1955 or the Naval Discipline Act 1957, extends to any place to which that provision extends.

[1407]

NOTES

Sub-s (7): repealed by the Armed Forces Act 2006, s 378(2), Sch 17, as from a day to be appointed.

Orders: the Human Rights Act 1998 (Commencement) Order 1998, SI 1998/2882; the Human Rights Act 1998 (Commencement No 2) Order 2000, SI 2000/1851.

SCHEDULES

SCHEDULE 1
THE ARTICLES

Section 1(3)

PART I
THE CONVENTION

RIGHTS AND FREEDOMS

Article 2
Right to life

1. Everyone's right to life shall be protected by law. No one shall be deprived of his life intentionally save in the execution of a sentence of a court following his conviction of a crime for which this penalty is provided by law.

2. Deprivation of life shall not be regarded as inflicted in contravention of this Article when it results from the use of force which is no more than absolutely necessary:
 (a) in defence of any person from unlawful violence;
 (b) in order to effect a lawful arrest or to prevent the escape of a person lawfully detained;
 (c) in action lawfully taken for the purpose of quelling a riot or insurrection.

Article 3
Prohibition of torture

No one shall be subjected to torture or to inhuman or degrading treatment or punishment.

Article 4
Prohibition of slavery and forced labour

1. No one shall be held in slavery or servitude.

2. No one shall be required to perform forced or compulsory labour.

3. For the purpose of this Article the term "forced or compulsory labour" shall not include:
 (a) any work required to be done in the ordinary course of detention imposed according to the provisions of Article 5 of this Convention or during conditional release from such detention;
 (b) any service of a military character or, in case of conscientious objectors in countries where they are recognised, service exacted instead of compulsory military service;
 (c) any service exacted in case of an emergency or calamity threatening the life or well-being of the community;
 (d) any work or service which forms part of normal civic obligations.

Article 5
Right to liberty and security

1. Everyone has the right to liberty and security of person. No one shall be deprived of his liberty save in the following cases and in accordance with a procedure prescribed by law:
 (a) the lawful detention of a person after conviction by a competent court;
 (b) the lawful arrest or detention of a person for non-compliance with the lawful order of a court or in order to secure the fulfilment of any obligation prescribed by law;
 (c) the lawful arrest or detention of a person effected for the purpose of bringing him before the competent legal authority on reasonable suspicion of having committed an offence or when it is reasonably considered necessary to prevent his committing an offence or fleeing after having done so;
 (d) the detention of a minor by lawful order for the purpose of educational supervision or his lawful detention for the purpose of bringing him before the competent legal authority;
 (e) the lawful detention of persons for the prevention of the spreading of infectious diseases, of persons of unsound mind, alcoholics or drug addicts or vagrants;
 (f) the lawful arrest or detention of a person to prevent his effecting an unauthorised entry into the country or of a person against whom action is being taken with a view to deportation or extradition.

2. Everyone who is arrested shall be informed promptly, in a language which he understands, of the reasons for his arrest and of any charge against him.

3. Everyone arrested or detained in accordance with the provisions of paragraph 1(c) of this Article shall be brought promptly before a judge or other officer authorised by law to exercise judicial power and shall be entitled to trial within a reasonable time or to release pending trial. Release may be conditioned by guarantees to appear for trial.

4. Everyone who is deprived of his liberty by arrest or detention shall be entitled to take proceedings by which the lawfulness of his detention shall be decided speedily by a court and his release ordered if the detention is not lawful.

5. Everyone who has been the victim of arrest or detention in contravention of the provisions of this Article shall have an enforceable right to compensation.

Article 6
Right to a fair trial

1. In the determination of his civil rights and obligations or of any criminal charge against him, everyone is entitled to a fair and public hearing within a reasonable time by an independent and impartial tribunal established by law. Judgment shall be pronounced publicly but the press and public may be excluded from all or part of the trial in the interest of morals, public order or national security in a democratic society, where the interests of juveniles or the protection of the private life of the parties so require, or to the extent strictly necessary in the opinion of the court in special circumstances where publicity would prejudice the interests of justice.

2. Everyone charged with a criminal offence shall be presumed innocent until proved guilty according to law.

3. Everyone charged with a criminal offence has the following minimum rights:

(a) to be informed promptly, in a language which he understands and in detail, of the nature and cause of the accusation against him;
(b) to have adequate time and facilities for the preparation of his defence;
(c) to defend himself in person or through legal assistance of his own choosing or, if he has not sufficient means to pay for legal assistance, to be given it free when the interests of justice so require;
(d) to examine or have examined witnesses against him and to obtain the attendance and examination of witnesses on his behalf under the same conditions as witnesses against him;
(e) to have the free assistance of an interpreter if he cannot understand or speak the language used in court.

Article 7
No punishment without law

1. No one shall be held guilty of any criminal offence on account of any act or omission which did not constitute a criminal offence under national or international law at the time when it was committed. Nor shall a heavier penalty be imposed than the one that was applicable at the time the criminal offence was committed.

2. This Article shall not prejudice the trial and punishment of any person for any act or omission which, at the time when it was committed, was criminal according to the general principles of law recognised by civilised nations.

Article 8
Right to respect for private and family life

1. Everyone has the right to respect for his private and family life, his home and his correspondence.

2. There shall be no interference by a public authority with the exercise of this right except such as is in accordance with the law and is necessary in a democratic society in the interests of national security, public safety or the economic well-being of the country, for the prevention of disorder or crime, for the protection of health or morals, or for the protection of the rights and freedoms of others.

Article 9
Freedom of thought, conscience and religion

1. Everyone has the right to freedom of thought, conscience and religion; this right includes freedom to change his religion or belief and freedom, either alone or in community with others and in public or private, to manifest his religion or belief, in worship, teaching, practice and observance.

2. Freedom to manifest one's religion or beliefs shall be subject only to such limitations as are prescribed by law and are necessary in a democratic society in the interests of public safety, for the protection of public order, health or morals, or for the protection of the rights and freedoms of others.

Article 10
Freedom of expression

1. Everyone has the right to freedom of expression. This right shall include freedom to hold opinions and to receive and impart information and ideas without interference by public authority and regardless of frontiers. This Article shall not prevent States from requiring the licensing of broadcasting, television or cinema enterprises.

2. The exercise of these freedoms, since it carries with it duties and responsibilities, may be subject to such formalities, conditions, restrictions or penalties as are prescribed by law and are necessary in a democratic society, in the interests of national security, territorial integrity or public safety, for the prevention of disorder or crime, for the protection of health or morals, for the protection of the reputation or rights of others, for preventing the disclosure of information received in confidence, or for maintaining the authority and impartiality of the judiciary.

Article 11
Freedom of assembly and association

1. Everyone has the right to freedom of peaceful assembly and to freedom of association with others, including the right to form and to join trade unions for the protection of his interests.

2. No restrictions shall be placed on the exercise of these rights other than such as are prescribed by law and are necessary in a democratic society in the interests of national security or public safety, for the prevention of disorder or crime, for the protection of health or morals or for the protection of the rights and freedoms of others. This Article shall not prevent the imposition of lawful restrictions on the exercise of these rights by members of the armed forces, of the police or of the administration of the State.

Article 12
Right to marry

Men and women of marriageable age have the right to marry and to found a family, according to the national laws governing the exercise of this right.

Article 14
Prohibition of discrimination

The enjoyment of the rights and freedoms set forth in this Convention shall be secured without discrimination on any ground such as sex, race, colour, language, religion, political or other opinion, national or social origin, association with a national minority, property, birth or other status.

Article 16
Restrictions on political activity of aliens

Nothing in Articles 10, 11 and 14 shall be regarded as preventing the High Contracting Parties from imposing restrictions on the political activity of aliens.

Article 17
Prohibition of abuse of rights

Nothing in this Convention may be interpreted as implying for any State, group or person any right to engage in any activity or perform any act aimed at the destruction of any of the rights and freedoms set forth herein or at their limitation to a greater extent than is provided for in the Convention.

Article 18
Limitation on use of restrictions on rights

The restrictions permitted under this Convention to the said rights and freedoms shall not be applied for any purpose other than those for which they have been prescribed.

[1408]

PART II
THE FIRST PROTOCOL

Article 1
Protection of property

Every natural or legal person is entitled to the peaceful enjoyment of his possessions. No one shall be deprived of his possessions except in the public interest and subject to the conditions provided for by law and by the general principles of international law.

The preceding provisions shall not, however, in any way impair the right of a State to enforce such laws as it deems necessary to control the use of property in accordance with the general interest or to secure the payment of taxes or other contributions or penalties.

Article 2
Right to education

No person shall be denied the right to education. In the exercise of any functions which it assumes in relation to education and to teaching, the State shall respect the right of parents to ensure such education and teaching in conformity with their own religious and philosophical convictions.

Article 3
Right to free elections

The High Contracting Parties undertake to hold free elections at reasonable intervals by secret ballot, under conditions which will ensure the free expression of the opinion of the people in the choice of the legislature.

[1409]

[PART III
ARTICLE 1 OF THE THIRTEENTH PROTOCOL

Abolition of the Death Penalty

The death penalty shall be abolished. No one shall be condemned to such penalty or executed.]

[1410]–[1411]

NOTES

Commencement: 22 June 2004.

Substituted by the Human Rights Act 1998 (Amendment) Order 2004, SI 2004/1574, art 2(3), as from 22 June 2004.

(*Sch 2* (*remedial orders*), *Sch 3* (*derogations and reservations*), *Sch 4* (*judicial pensions*) *outside the scope of this work.*)

DISABILITY RIGHTS COMMISSION ACT 1999 (NOTE)

(1999 c 17)

NOTES

This Act was repealed by the Equality Act 2006, ss 40, 91, Sch 3, para 59, Sch 4, as from 1 October 2007. For transitional provisions relating to the discharge by the Commission for Equality and Human Rights of the former functions of the Disability Rights Commission, see the Equality Act 2006 (Dissolution of Commissions and Consequential and Transitional Provisions) Order 2007, SI 2007/2602, art 5 at **[3473O]**.

[1412]–[1430]

EMPLOYMENT RELATIONS ACT 1999

(1999 c 26)

ARRANGEMENT OF SECTIONS

Trade unions

Disciplinary and grievance hearings

Other rights of individuals

Miscellaneous

General

An Act to amend the law relating to employment, to trade unions and to employment agencies and businesses

[27 July 1999]

NOTES

Much of this Act amends other legislation; the amendments are incorporated therein so far as within the scope of this work, and noted below. The Act is otherwise printed in full except where (and for the reasons) noted.

Employment Appeal Tribunal: an appeal lies to the Employment Appeal Tribunal on any question of law arising from any decision of, or in any proceedings before, an employment tribunal under or by virtue of this Act; see the Employment Tribunals Act 1996, s 21(1)(gb) at **[978]**.

See *Harvey* A11, 16.

Trade unions

1, 2 (*S 1 adds the Trade Union and Labour Relations* (*Consolidation*) *Act 1992, Pt I, Ch VA* (*s 70A*) *and Sch A1, at* **[553]**, **[795]**; *s 2 introduces Sch 2* (*Detriment related to trade union membership*).)

3 Blacklists

(1) The Secretary of State may make regulations prohibiting the compilation of lists which—

(a) contain details of members of trade unions or persons who have taken part in the activities of trade unions, and

(b) are compiled with a view to being used by employers or employment agencies for the purposes of discrimination in relation to recruitment or in relation to the treatment of workers.

(2) The Secretary of State may make regulations prohibiting—

(a) the use of lists to which subsection (1) applies;

(b) the sale or supply of lists to which subsection (1) applies.

(3) Regulations under this section may, in particular—

(a) confer jurisdiction (including exclusive jurisdiction) on employment tribunals and on the Employment Appeal Tribunal;

(b) include provision for or about the grant and enforcement of specified remedies by courts and tribunals;

(c) include provision for the making of awards of compensation calculated in accordance with the regulations;

(d) include provision permitting proceedings to be brought by trade unions on behalf of members in specified circumstances;

(e) include provision about cases where an employee is dismissed by his employer and the reason or principal reason for the dismissal, or why the employee was selected for dismissal, relates to a list to which subsection (1) applies;

(f) create criminal offences;

(g) in specified cases or circumstances, extend liability for a criminal offence created under paragraph (f) to a person who aids the commission of the offence or to a person who is an agent, principal, employee, employer or officer of a person who commits the offence;

(h) provide for specified obligations or offences not to apply in specified circumstances;

(i) include supplemental, incidental, consequential and transitional provision, including provision amending an enactment;

(j) make different provision for different cases or circumstances.

(4) Regulations under this section creating an offence may not provide for it to be punishable—

(a) by imprisonment,

(b) by a fine in excess of level 5 on the standard scale in the case of an offence triable only summarily, or

(c) by a fine in excess of the statutory maximum in the case of summary conviction for an offence triable either way.

(5) In this section—

"list" includes any index or other set of items whether recorded electronically or by any other means, and

"worker" has the meaning given by section 13.

(6) Subject to subsection (5), expressions used in this section and in the Trade Union and Labour Relations (Consolidation) Act 1992 have the same meaning in this section as in that Act.

[1431]

NOTES

Regulations: as of 6 April 2008 no Regulations had been made under this section.

4–9 *(S 4 introduces Sch 3 (Ballots and notices); s 5 inserts the Trade Union and Labour Relations (Consolidation) Act 1992, ss 70B, 70C at* **[554], [555]***; s 6 amends the Employment Rights Act 1996, ss 128(1), 129(1) at* **[1172], [1173]***; s 7 substitutes Pt VIII of the 1996 Act at* **[1102]** *et seq; s 8 inserts ss 57A, 57B in the 1996 Act at* **[1084], [1085]***; s 9 introduces Sch 4, Pt III to this Act (amendments consequential on ss 7, 8).)*

Disciplinary and grievance hearings

10 Right to be accompanied

(1) This section applies where a worker—

(a) is required or invited by his employer to attend a disciplinary or grievance hearing, and

(b) reasonably requests to be accompanied at the hearing.

[(2A) Where this section applies, the employer must permit the worker to be accompanied at the hearing by one companion who—

(a) is chosen by the worker; and

(b) is within subsection (3).

(2B) The employer must permit the worker's companion to—

(a) address the hearing in order to do any or all of the following—

(i) put the worker's case;

(ii) sum up that case;

(iii) respond on the worker's behalf to any view expressed at the hearing;

(b) confer with the worker during the hearing.

(2C) Subsection (2B) does not require the employer to permit the worker's companion to—

(a) answer questions on behalf of the worker;

(b) address the hearing if the worker indicates at it that he does not wish his companion to do so; or

(c) use the powers conferred by that subsection in a way that prevents the employer from explaining his case or prevents any other person at the hearing from making his contribution to it.]

(3) A person is within this subsection if he is—

(a) employed by a trade union of which he is an official within the meaning of sections 1 and 119 of the Trade Union and Labour Relations (Consolidation) Act 1992,

(b) an official of a trade union (within that meaning) whom the union has reasonably certified in writing as having experience of, or as having received training in, acting as a worker's companion at disciplinary or grievance hearings, or

(c) another of the employer's workers.

(4) If—

(a) a worker has a right under this section to be accompanied at a hearing,

(b) his chosen companion will not be available at the time proposed for the hearing by the employer, and

(c) the worker proposes an alternative time which satisfies subsection (5),

the employer must postpone the hearing to the time proposed by the worker.

(5) An alternative time must—

(a) be reasonable, and

(b) fall before the end of the period of five working days beginning with the first working day after the day proposed by the employer.

(6) An employer shall permit a worker to take time off during working hours for the purpose of accompanying another of the employer's workers in accordance with a request under subsection (1)(b).

(7) Sections 168(3) and (4), 169 and 171 to 173 of the Trade Union and Labour Relations (Consolidation) Act 1992 (time off for carrying out trade union duties) shall apply in relation to subsection (6) above as they apply in relation to section 168(1) of that Act.

[1432]

NOTES

Sub-ss (2A)–(2C): substituted, for original sub-s (2), by the Employment Relations Act 2004, s 37(1), as from 1 October 2004, except in relation to any disciplinary or grievance hearing occurring on or after that date which the worker was required or invited to attend before that date (see SI 2004/2566, art 8).

See also the ACAS Code of Practice 1: Disciplinary and Grievance Procedures (2004) at **[4653]**.

11 Complaint to employment tribunal

(1) A worker may present a complaint to an employment tribunal that his employer has failed, or threatened to fail, to comply with section [10(2A), (2B)] or (4).

(2) A tribunal shall not consider a complaint under this section in relation to a failure or threat unless the complaint is presented—

- (a) before the end of the period of three months beginning with the date of the failure or threat, or
- (b) within such further period as the tribunal considers reasonable in a case where it is satisfied that it was not reasonably practicable for the complaint to be presented before the end of that period of three months.

(3) Where a tribunal finds that a complaint under this section is well-founded it shall order the employer to pay compensation to the worker of an amount not exceeding two weeks' pay.

(4) Chapter II of Part XIV of the Employment Rights Act 1996 (calculation of a week's pay) shall apply for the purposes of subsection (3); and in applying that Chapter the calculation date shall be taken to be—

- (a) in the case of a claim which is made in the course of a claim for unfair dismissal, the date on which the employer's notice of dismissal was given or, if there was no notice, the effective date of termination, and
- (b) in any other case, the date on which the relevant hearing took place (or was to have taken place).

(5) The limit in section 227(1) of the Employment Rights Act 1996 (maximum amount of week's pay) shall apply for the purposes of subsection (3) above.

(6) ...

[1433]

NOTES

Sub-s (1): figures in square brackets substituted by the Employment Relations Act 2004, s 37(2), as from 1 October 2004, except in relation to any disciplinary or grievance hearing occurring on or after that date which the worker was required or invited to attend before that date (see SI 2004/2566, art 8).

Sub-s (6): repealed by the Employment Act 2002, s 54, Sch 8, as from 1 November 2004.

Conciliation: by virtue of s 14 of this Act at **[1436]**, this section (and ss 10, 12 and 13) is treated as a provision of Part V of the Employment Rights .Act 1996 for the purposes of the Employment Tribunals Act 1996, s 18. The standard conciliation period applies to such proceedings by virtue of the Employment Tribunals (Constitution and Rules of Procedure) Regulations 2004, SI 2004/1861, Sch 1, rule 22(1), (6).

Application: as to the power of the Secretary of State to make Regulations under the Employment Rights Act 1996, s 80G(1) making provision for the application of this section (with or without modifications) and ss 12, 13 of this Act to requests made by qualifying employees under s 80F of that Act, see s 80G(1), (2)(n) of the 1996 Act at **[1122]**.

12 Detriment and dismissal

(1) A worker has the right not to be subjected to any detriment by any act, or any deliberate failure to act, by his employer done on the ground that he—

- (a) exercised or sought to exercise the right under section [10(2A), (2B)] or (4), or
- (b) accompanied or sought to accompany another worker (whether of the same employer or not) pursuant to a request under that section.

(2) Section 48 of the Employment Rights Act 1996 shall apply in relation to contraventions of subsection (1) above as it applies in relation to contraventions of certain sections of that Act.

(3) A worker who is dismissed shall be regarded for the purposes of Part X of the Employment Rights Act 1996 as unfairly dismissed if the reason (or, if more than one, the principal reason) for the dismissal is that he—

(a) exercised or sought to exercise the right under section [10(2A), (2B)] or (4), or

(b) accompanied or sought to accompany another worker (whether of the same employer or not) pursuant to a request under that section.

(4) Sections 108 and 109 of that Act (qualifying period of employment and upper age limit) shall not apply in relation to subsection (3) above.

(5) Sections 128 to 132 of that Act (interim relief) shall apply in relation to dismissal for the reason specified in subsection (3)(a) or (b) above as they apply in relation to dismissal for a reason specified in section 128(1)(b) of that Act.

(6) In the application of Chapter II of Part X of that Act in relation to subsection (3) above, a reference to an employee shall be taken as a reference to a worker.

[(7) References in this section to a worker having accompanied or sought to accompany another worker include references to his having exercised or sought to exercise any of the powers conferred by section 10(2A) or (2B).]

[1434]

NOTES

Sub-ss (1), (3): figures in square brackets substituted by the Employment Relations Act 2004, s 37(3)(a), as from 1 October 2004, except in relation to any disciplinary or grievance hearing occurring on or after that date which the worker was required or invited to attend before that date (see SI 2004/2566, art 8).

Sub-s (7): added by the Employment Relations Act 2004, s 37(3)(b), as from 1 October 2004 (subject to the same exception in SI 2004/2566, art 8 as noted above).

Application: see the note to s 11 at **[1433]**.

13 Interpretation

(1) In sections 10 to 12 and this section "worker" means an individual who is—

(a) a worker within the meaning of section 230(3) of the Employment Rights Act 1996,

(b) an agency worker,

(c) a home worker,

(d) a person in Crown employment within the meaning of section 191 of that Act, other than a member of the naval, military, air or reserve forces of the Crown, or

(e) employed as a relevant member of the House of Lords staff or the House of Commons staff within the meaning of section 194(6) or 195(5) of that Act.

(2) In subsection (1) "agency worker" means an individual who—

(a) is supplied by a person ("the agent") to do work for another ("the principal") by arrangement between the agent and the principal,

(b) is not a party to a worker's contract, within the meaning of section 230(3) of that Act, relating to that work, and

(c) is not a party to a contract relating to that work under which he undertakes to do the work for another party to the contract whose status is, by virtue of the contract, that of a client or customer of any professional or business undertaking carried on by the individual;

and, for the purposes of sections 10 to 12, both the agent and the principal are employers of an agency worker.

(3) In subsection (1) "home worker" means an individual who—

(a) contracts with a person, for the purposes of the person's business, for the execution of work to be done in a place not under the person's control or management, and

(b) is not a party to a contract relating to that work under which the work is to be executed for another party to the contract whose status is, by virtue of the contract, that of a client or customer of any professional or business undertaking carried on by the individual;

and, for the purposes of sections 10 to 12, the person mentioned in paragraph (a) is the home worker's employer.

(4) For the purposes of section 10 a disciplinary hearing is a hearing which could result in—

(a) the administration of a formal warning to a worker by his employer,
(b) the taking of some other action in respect of a worker by his employer, or
(c) the confirmation of a warning issued or some other action taken.

(5) For the purposes of section 10 a grievance hearing is a hearing which concerns the performance of a duty by an employer in relation to a worker.

(6) For the purposes of section 10(5)(b) in its application to a part of Great Britain a working day is a day other than—

(a) a Saturday or a Sunday,
(b) Christmas Day or Good Friday, or
(c) a day which is a bank holiday under the Banking and Financial Dealings Act 1971 in that part of Great Britain.

[1435]

NOTES

A hearing: a meeting held for the purposes of the Employment Act 2002, Sch 2, is a hearing for the purposes of sub-ss (4), (5) of this section; see s 29, Sch 2, Pt 4, para 14 to the 2002 Act at **[1491]**, **[1507]**.

Application: see the note to s 11 at **[1433]**.

14 Contracting out and conciliation

Sections 10 to 13 of this Act shall be treated as provisions of Part V of the Employment Rights Act 1996 for the purposes of—

(a) section 203(1), (2)(e) and (f), (3) and (4) of that Act (restrictions on contracting out), and
(b) section 18(1)(d) of the Employment Tribunals Act 1996 (conciliation).

[1436]

15 National security employees

Sections 10 to 13 of this Act shall not apply in relation to a person employed for the purposes of—

(a) the Security Service,
(b) the Secret Intelligence Service, or
(c) the Government Communications Headquarters.

[1437]–[1438]

Other rights of individuals

16–18 (*S 16 introduces Sch 5* (*Unfair dismissal of striking workers*)*; s 17 repealed by the Employment Relations Act 2004, ss 31*(*8*)*, 57*(*2*)*, Sch 2, as from 1 October 2004; s 18*(*1*)*–*(*4*) *amend the Employment Rights Act 1996, ss 44*(*4*)*, 45A*(*4*)*, 46*(*2*)*, 47*(*2*)*, 47A*(*2*)*, 47B*(*2*)*, at* **[1063]**, **[1065]**, **[1066]**, **[1067]**, **[1068]**, **[1069]**, *amended s 197* (*repealed*)*, and substitute the National Minimum Wage Act 1998, s 23*(*4*) *at* **[1367]**; *s 18*(*5*) *repealed by the Tax Credits Act 2002, s 60, Sch 6, as from 8 April 2003* (*subject to transitional provisions and savings in SI 2003/962*)*; s 18*(*6*) *repealed by Sch 9 to this Act.*)

19 Part-time work: discrimination

(1) The Secretary of State shall make regulations for the purpose of securing that persons in part-time employment are treated, for such purposes and to such extent as the regulations may specify, no less favourably than persons in full-time employment.

(2) The regulations may—

(a) specify classes of person who are to be taken to be, or not to be, in part-time employment;
(b) specify classes of person who are to be taken to be, or not to be, in full-time employment;
(c) specify circumstances in which persons in part-time employment are to be taken to be, or not to be, treated less favourably than persons in full-time employment;

(d) make provision which has effect in relation to persons in part-time employment generally or provision which has effect only in relation to specified classes of persons in part-time employment.

(3) The regulations may—

(a) confer jurisdiction (including exclusive jurisdiction) on employment tribunals and on the Employment Appeal Tribunal;

(b) create criminal offences in relation to specified acts or omissions by an employer, by an organisation of employers, by an organisation of workers or by an organisation existing for the purposes of a profession or trade carried on by the organisation's members;

(c) in specified cases or circumstances, extend liability for a criminal offence created under paragraph (b) to a person who aids the commission of the offence or to a person who is an agent, principal, employee, employer or officer of a person who commits the offence;

(d) provide for specified obligations or offences not to apply in specified circumstances;

(e) make provision about notices or information to be given, evidence to be produced and other procedures to be followed;

(f) amend, apply with or without modifications, or make provision similar to any provision of the Employment Rights Act 1996 (including, in particular, Parts V, X and XIII) or the Trade Union and Labour Relations (Consolidation) Act 1992;

(g) provide for the provisions of specified agreements to have effect in place of provisions of the regulations to such extent and in such circumstances as may be specified;

(h) include supplemental, incidental, consequential and transitional provision, including provision amending an enactment;

(i) make different provision for different cases or circumstances.

(4) Without prejudice to the generality of this section the regulations may make any provision which appears to the Secretary of State to be necessary or expedient—

(a) for the purpose of implementing Council Directive 97/81/EC on the framework agreement on part-time work in its application to terms and conditions of employment;

(b) for the purpose of dealing with any matter arising out of or related to the United Kingdom's obligations under that Directive;

(c) for the purpose of any matter dealt with by the framework agreement or for the purpose of applying the provisions of the framework agreement to any matter relating to part-time workers.

(5) Regulations under this section which create an offence—

(a) shall provide for it to be triable summarily only, and

(b) may not provide for it to be punishable by imprisonment or by a fine in excess of level 5 on the standard scale.

[1439]

NOTES

Regulations: the Part-time Workers (Prevention of Less Favourable Treatment) Regulations 2000, SI 2000/1551 at **[2637]**; the Part-time Workers (Prevention of Less Favourable Treatment) Regulations 2001, SI 2001/1107.

---

20 Part-time work: code of practice

(1) The Secretary of State may issue codes of practice containing guidance for the purpose of—

(a) eliminating discrimination in the field of employment against part-time workers;

(b) facilitating the development of opportunities for part-time work;

(c) facilitating the flexible organisation of working time taking into account the needs of workers and employers;

(d) any matter dealt with in the framework agreement on part-time work annexed to Council Directive 97/81/EC.

(2) The Secretary of State may revise a code and issue the whole or part of the revised code.

(3) A person's failure to observe a provision of a code does not make him liable to any proceedings.

(4) A code—
 (a) is admissible in evidence in proceedings before an employment tribunal, and
 (b) shall be taken into account by an employment tribunal in any case in which it appears to the tribunal to be relevant.

[1440]

NOTES
Codes of Practice: as of 6 April 2008 no codes had been issued under this section.

21 Code of practice: supplemental

(1) Before issuing or revising a code of practice under section 20 the Secretary of State shall consult such persons as he considers appropriate.

(2) Before issuing a code the Secretary of State shall—
 (a) publish a draft code,
 (b) consider any representations made to him about the draft,
 (c) if he thinks it appropriate, modify the draft in the light of any representations made to him.

(3) If, having followed the procedure under subsection (2), the Secretary of State decides to issue a code, he shall lay a draft code before each House of Parliament.

(4) If the draft code is approved by resolution of each House of Parliament, the Secretary of State shall issue the code in the form of the draft.

(5) In this section and section 20(3) and (4)—
 (a) a reference to a code includes a reference to a revised code,
 (b) a reference to a draft code includes a reference to a draft revision, and
 (c) a reference to issuing a code includes a reference to issuing part of a revised code.

[1441]

22 (*Inserts the National Minimum Wage Act 1998, s 44A at* **[1384]**.)

23 Power to confer rights on individuals

(1) This section applies to any right conferred on an individual against an employer (however defined) under or by virtue of any of the following—
 (a) the Trade Union and Labour Relations (Consolidation) Act 1992;
 (b) the Employment Rights Act 1996;
 [(ba) the Employment Act 2002;]
 (c) this Act;
 (d) any instrument made under section 2(2) of the European Communities Act 1972.

(2) The Secretary of State may by order make provision which has the effect of conferring any such right on individuals who are of a specified description.

(3) The reference in subsection (2) to individuals includes a reference to individuals expressly excluded from exercising the right.

(4) An order under this section may—
 (a) provide that individuals are to be treated as parties to workers' contracts or contracts of employment;
 (b) make provision as to who are to be regarded as the employers of individuals;
 (c) make provision which has the effect of modifying the operation of any right as conferred on individuals by the order;
 (d) include such consequential, incidental or supplementary provisions as the Secretary of State thinks fit.

(5) An order under this section may make provision in such way as the Secretary of State thinks fit …

[(5A) The ways in which an order under this section may make provision include, in particular—
 (a) amending any enactment;
 (b) excluding or applying (whether with or without amendment) any enactment.

(5B) In subsection (5A) "enactment" includes an enactment comprised in subordinate legislation made under an Act.]

(6) Section 209(7) of the Employment Rights Act 1996 (which is superseded by this section) shall be omitted.

(7) Any order made or having effect as if made under section 209(7), so far as effective immediately before the commencement of this section, shall have effect as if made under this section.

[1442]–[1443]

NOTES

Sub-s (1): para (ba) inserted by the Employment Act 2002, s 53, Sch 7, para 54.

Sub-s (5): words omitted repealed by a combination of the Employment Act 2002, s 41, and the Employment Relations Act 2004, ss 39(1), (2), 57(2), Sch 2, as from 31 December 2004.

Sub-ss (5A), (5B): inserted by the Employment Relations Act 2004, s 39(1), (3), as from 31 December 2004.

Orders: as of 6 April 2008 no Orders had been made under this section. As to Orders made or having effect as if made under the Employment Rights Act 1996, s 209(7) (and therefore having effect as if made under this section by virtue of sub-s (7) above) see the note to s 209 of the 1996 Act at **[1250]**.

CAC, ACAS, Commissioners and Certification Officer

24–29 (*S 24 amends the Trade Union and Labour Relations* (*Consolidation*) *Act 1992, s 260 at* **[761]**; *s 25 inserts ss 263*(*7*) *and 263A and amends s 264 of that Act at* **[764]**, **[765]**, **[766]**; *s 26 amends s 209 of that Act at* **[694]**; *s 27 amends ss 253*(*1*) *and 265*(*1*) *of that Act at* **[752]**, **[767]**; *s 28*(*1*), (*2*) *abolished the office of Commissioner for the Rights of Trade Union Members and the office of Commissioner for Protection Against Unlawful Industrial Action and repealed the Trade Union and Labour Relations* (*Consolidation*) *Act 1992, Pt I, Ch VIII, ss 235B, 235C and 266–271, and were themselves repealed by the Statute Law* (*Repeals*) *Act 2004, as from 22 July 2004; s 28*(*3*) *amends s 32A of the 1992 Act at* **[502]**; *s 29 introduces Sch 6* (*the Certification Officer*).)

Miscellaneous

30 Partnerships at work

(1) The Secretary of State may spend money or provide money to other persons for the purpose of encouraging and helping employers (or their representatives) and employees (or their representatives) to improve the way they work together.

(2) Money may be provided in such way as the Secretary of State thinks fit (whether as grants or otherwise) and on such terms as he thinks fit (whether as to repayment or otherwise).

[1444]

31–33 (*S 31 introduces Sch 7* (*employment agencies*); *s 32 amends the Trade Union and Labour Relations* (*Consolidation*) *Act 1992, s 285*(*1*) *at* **[779]**, *inserts s 278*(*3A*) *of the 1992 Act at* **[774]**, *repeals the Employment Rights Act 1996, s 196 and inserts s 199*(*7*), (*8*) *of the 1996 Act at* **[1241]**; *s 33*(*1*) *repealed the Employment Rights Act 1996, ss 117*(*4*)(*b*), *118*(*2*), (*3*), *125 and the Trade Union and Labour Relations* (*Consolidation*) *Act 1992, ss 157, 158, and was repealed by the Statute Law* (*Repeals*) *Act 2004, as from 22 July 2004; s 33*(*2*), (*3*) *amend s 117*(*3*) *of the 1996 Act at* **[1161]**, *and the Employment Rights* (*Dispute Resolution*) *Act 1998, s 14, and were repealed in part by the Statute Law* (*Repeals*) *Act 2004, as from 22 July 2004.*)

34 Indexation of amounts, &c

(1) This section applies to the sums specified in the following of provisions—

(a) section 31(1) of the Employment Rights Act 1996 (guarantee payments: limits);
(b) section 120(1) of that Act (unfair dismissal: minimum amount of basic award);
(c) section 124(1) of that Act (unfair dismissal: limit of compensatory award);
(d) section 186(1)(a) and (b) of that Act (employee's rights on insolvency of employer: maximum amount payable);
(e) section 227(1) of that Act (maximum amount of a week's pay for purposes of certain calculations);
[(ea) section 145E(3) of the Trade Union and Labour Relations (Consolidation) Act 1992 (unlawful inducements: amount of award);

(f) section 156(1) of that Act (unfair dismissal: minimum basic award);]

(g) section [176(6A)] of that Act (right to membership of trade union: remedies).

(2) If the retail prices index for September of a year is higher or lower than the index for the previous September, the Secretary of State shall as soon as practicable make an order in relation to each sum mentioned in subsection (1)—

(a) increasing each sum, if the new index is higher, or

(b) decreasing each sum, if the new index is lower,

by the same percentage as the amount of the increase or decrease of the index.

(3) In making the calculation required by subsection (2) the Secretary of State shall—

(a) in the case of the sum mentioned in subsection (1)(a), round the result up to the nearest 10 pence,

(b) in the case of the sums mentioned in subsection (1)(b), (c), [(ea),] (f) and (g), round the result up to the nearest £100, and

(c) in the case of the sums mentioned in subsection (1)(d) and (e), round the result up to the nearest £10.

(4) For the sum specified in section 124(1) of the Employment Rights Act 1996 (unfair dismissal: limit of compensatory award) there shall be substituted the sum of £50,000 (subject to subsection (2) above).

(5) In this section "the retail prices index" means—

(a) the general index of retail prices (for all items) published by the [Statistics Board], or

(b) where that index is not published for a month, any substituted index or figures published by [the Board].

(6) An order under this section—

(a) shall be made by statutory instrument,

(b) may include transitional provision, and

(c) shall be laid before Parliament after being made.

[1445]

NOTES

Sub-s (1): paras (ea), (f) substituted, for original para (f), by the Employment Relations Act 2004, s 57(1), Sch 1, para 42(1), (2), as from 1 October 2004, except in relation to cases where the act or failure to act to which the complaint relates was done before that date, or where the act or failure to act to which the complaint relates is part of a series and the first act or failure in the series was done before that date (see SI 2004/2566, art 6); figure in square brackets in para (g) substituted by s 57(1) of, and Sch 1, para 42(1), (3) to, the 2004 Act, as from 31 December 2004.

Sub-s (3): words in square brackets in para (b) inserted by the Employment Relations Act 2004, s 57(1), Sch 1, para 42(1), (4), as from 1 October 2004 (subject to the same exception in SI 2004/2566, art 6 as noted above).

Sub-s (5): words in square brackets substituted by the Statistics and Registration Service Act 2007, s 60(1), Sch 3, para 11, as from 1 April 2008.

See further, as to the 'one-off' power of the Secretary of State to increase the sums specified in ss 186(1)(a), (b), 227(1) of the 1996 Act, the Work and Families Act 2006, s 14 at **[1699]**.

Orders: the current Order is the Employment Rights (Increase of Limits) Order 2007, SI 2007/3570 at **[3474E]**.

35 (*Substitutes the Employment Rights Act 1996, s 31(7) at* **[1038]**.)

36 Sections 33 to 35: consequential

(1), (2) ...

(3) An increase effected, before section 34 comes into force, by virtue of a provision repealed by this section shall continue to have effect notwithstanding this section (but subject to section 34(2) and (4)).

[1446]

NOTES

Sub-ss (1), (2): repeal the Employment Rights Act 1996, ss 120(2), 124(2), 186(2), 208, 227(2)–(4), and the Trade Union and Labour Relations (Consolidation) Act 1992, ss 159, 176(7), (8).

37 (*S 37(1) inserts the Employment Rights Act 1996, s 124(1A) at* **[1168]**; *s 37(2) repealed s 127B of that Act, and was repealed by the Statute Law (Repeals) Act 2004, as from 22 July 2004.*)

38 Transfer of undertakings

(1) This section applies where regulations under section 2(2) of the European Communities Act 1972 (general implementation of Treaties) make provision for the purpose of implementing, or for a purpose concerning, a Community obligation of the United Kingdom which relates to the treatment of employees on the transfer of an undertaking or business or part of an undertaking or business.

(2) The Secretary of State may by regulations make the same or similar provision in relation to the treatment of employees in circumstances other than those to which the Community obligation applies (including circumstances in which there is no transfer, or no transfer to which the Community obligation applies).

(3) Regulations under this section shall be subject to annulment in pursuance of a resolution of either House of Parliament.

[1447]

NOTES

Regulations: the Transfer of Undertakings (Protection of Employment) (Rent Officer Service) Regulations 1999, SI 1999/2511; the Transfer of Undertakings (Protection of Employment) (Transfer to OFCOM) Regulations 2003, SI 2003/2715; the Transfer of Undertakings (Protection of Employment) Regulations 2006, SI 2006/246 at **[3376]**.

39 Minimum wage: information

(1) Information obtained by a revenue official in the course of carrying out a function of the Commissioners of Inland Revenue may be—

(a) supplied by the Commissioners of Inland Revenue to the Secretary of State for any purpose relating to the National Minimum Wage Act 1998;

(b) supplied by the Secretary of State with the authority of the Commissioners of Inland Revenue to any person acting under section 13(1)(b) of that Act;

(c) supplied by the Secretary of State with the authority of the Commissioners of Inland Revenue to an officer acting for the purposes of any of the agricultural wages legislation.

(2) In this section—

"revenue official" means an officer of the Commissioners of Inland Revenue appointed under section 4 of the Inland Revenue Regulation Act 1890 (appointment of collectors, officers and other persons), and

"the agricultural wages legislation" has the same meaning as in section 16 of the National Minimum Wage Act 1998 (agricultural wages officers).

[1448]

NOTES

Commissioners of Inland Revenue: a reference to the Commissioners of Inland Revenue is now to be taken as a reference to the Commissioners for Her Majesty's Revenue and Customs; see the Commissioners for Revenue and Customs Act 2005, s 50(1), (7).

Inland Revenue Regulation Act 1890, s 4: repealed by the Commissioners for Revenue and Customs Act 2005, ss 50(6), 52(2), Sch 4, para 5, Sch 5.

40, 41 (*S 40 repealed by the Education Act 2002, s 215(2), Sch 22, Pt 3, as from 1 September 2003 (in relation to England) and as from 1 April 2006 (in relation to Wales); s 41 introduces Sch 8 (national security).*)

General

42 Orders and regulations

(1) Any power to make an order or regulations under this Act shall be exercised by statutory instrument.

(2) No order or regulations shall be made under section 3, 17, 19 or 23 unless a draft has been laid before, and approved by resolution of, each House of Parliament.

[1449]

43 Finance

There shall be paid out of money provided by Parliament—

(a) any increase attributable to this Act in the sums so payable under any other enactment;

(b) any other expenditure of the Secretary of State under this Act.

[1450]

44 (*Introduces Sch 9* (*repeals*).)

45 Commencement

(1) The preceding provisions of this Act shall come into force in accordance with provision made by the Secretary of State by order made by statutory instrument.

(2) An order under this section—

(a) may make different provision for different purposes;

(b) may include supplementary, incidental, saving or transitional provisions.

[1451]

NOTES

Orders: the Employment Relations Act 1999 (Commencement No 1 and Transitional Provisions) Order 1999, SI 1999/2509; the Employment Relations Act 1999 (Commencement No 2 and Transitional and Saving Provisions) Order 1999, SI 1999/2830; the Employment Relations Act 1999 (Commencement No 3 and Transitional Provision) Order 1999, SI 1999/3374; the Employment Relations Act 1999 (Commencement No 4 and Transitional Provision) Order 2000, SI 2000/420; the Employment Relations Act 1999 (Commencement No 5 and Transitional Provision) Order 2000, SI 2000/875; the Employment Relations Act 1999 (Commencement No 6 and Transitional Provisions) Order 2000, SI 2000/1338; the Employment Relations Act 1999 (Commencement No 7 and Transitional Provisions) Order 2000, SI 2000/2242; the Employment Relations Act 1999 (Commencement No 8) Order 2001, SI 2001/1187; the Employment Relations Act 1999 (Commencement No 8) (Amendment) Order 2001, SI 2001/1461; the Employment Relations Act 1999 (Commencement No 9) Order 2003, SI 2003/3357.

46 Extent

(1) Any amendment or repeal in this Act has the same extent as the provision amended or repealed.

(2) An Order in Council under paragraph 1(1)(b) of Schedule 1 to the Northern Ireland Act 1974 (legislation for Northern Ireland in the interim period) which contains a statement that it is made only for purposes corresponding to any of the purposes of this Act—

(a) shall not be subject to paragraph 1(4) and (5) of that Schedule (affirmative resolution of both Houses of Parliament), but

(b) shall be subject to annulment in pursuance of a resolution of either House of Parliament.

(3) Apart from sections 39 and 45 and subject to subsection (1), the preceding sections of this Act shall not extend to Northern Ireland.

[1452]

NOTES

Northern Ireland Act 1974: repealed by the Northern Ireland Act 1998, s 100(2), Sch 15.

47 Citation

This Act may be cited as the Employment Relations Act 1999.

[1453]–[1464]

(*In so far as still in force, the Schedules make the following amendments: Sch 1 sets out new Sch A1 to the Trade Union and Labour Relations* (*Consolidation*) *Act 1992 at* **[795]** *et seq*; *Sch 2 amends ss 146–150 of the 1992 Act at* **[632]–[636]**; *Sch 3 inserts ss 232A, 232B of the 1992 Act at* **[726]**, **[727]**, *and amends other sections of that Act as noted to the sections concerned; Sch 4, Pt I sets out new Pt VIII of the Employment Rights Act 1996 at* **[1102]** *et* *seq; Sch 4, Pt II inserts ss 57A, 57B of the 1996 Act at* **[1084]**, **[1085]**; *Sch 4, Pt III inserts s 47C of that Act at* **[1070]**, *amends and repeals various provisions of that Act (as noted to the provisions concerned), and amends the Trade Union and Labour Relations (Consolidation) Act 1992 and the Employment Tribunals Act 1996 (as noted to the provisions concerned); Sch 5 inserts the Trade Union and Labour Relations (Consolidation) Act 1992, s 238A at* **[736]**, *and amends ss 238 and 239 of that Act at* **[735]**, **[737]**, *and the Employment Rights Act 1996, s 105 at* **[1149]**; *Sch 6 inserts the Trade Union and Labour Relations (Consolidation) Act 1992, ss 45D, 56A, 72A, 108A–108C, 256A, 256B at* **[524]**, **[537]**, **[558]**, **[600]**–**[602]**, **[756]**, **[757]**, *and amends other sections of that Act (as noted to the sections concerned); Sch 7 (Employment Agencies) amends the Employment Agencies Act 1973 at* **[25]** *et seq; Sch 8 substitutes or amends provisions of the Employment Rights Act 1996, the Employment Tribunals Act 1996, the Race Relations Act 1976, and the Disability Discrimination Act 1995 (as noted to the provisions concerned); Sch 9 contains repeals and, in so far as relevant to this work, these have been incorporated at the appropriate place.)*

CONTRACTS (RIGHTS OF THIRD PARTIES) ACT 1999

(1999 c 31)

ARRANGEMENT OF SECTIONS

An Act to make provision for the enforcement of contractual terms by third parties

[11 November 1999]

NOTES

As to the commencement and application of this Act, see s 10(2), (3) at **[1473]**.

1 Right of third party to enforce contractual term

(1) Subject to the provisions of this Act, a person who is not a party to a contract (a "third party") may in his own right enforce a term of the contract if—

(a) the contract expressly provides that he may, or

(b) subject to subsection (2), the term purports to confer a benefit on him.

(2) Subsection (1)(b) does not apply if on a proper construction of the contract it appears that the parties did not intend the term to be enforceable by the third party.

(3) The third party must be expressly identified in the contract by name, as a member of a class or as answering a particular description but need not be in existence when the contract is entered into.

(4) This section does not confer a right on a third party to enforce a term of a contract otherwise than subject to and in accordance with any other relevant terms of the contract.

(5) For the purpose of exercising his right to enforce a term of the contract, there shall be available to the third party any remedy that would have been available to him in an action for breach of contract if he had been a party to the contract (and the rules relating to damages, injunctions, specific performance and other relief shall apply accordingly).

(6) Where a term of a contract excludes or limits liability in relation to any matter references in this Act to the third party enforcing the term shall be construed as references to his availing himself of the exclusion or limitation.

(7) In this Act, in relation to a term of a contract which is enforceable by a third party—

"the promisor" means the party to the contract against whom the term is enforceable by the third party, and

"the promisee" means the party to the contract by whom the term is enforceable against the promisor.

[1465]

2 Variation and rescission of contract

(1) Subject to the provisions of this section, where a third party has a right under section 1 to enforce a term of the contract, the parties to the contract may not, by agreement, rescind the contract, or vary it in such a way as to extinguish or alter his entitlement under that right, without his consent if—

(a) the third party has communicated his assent to the term to the promisor,

(b) the promisor is aware that the third party has relied on the term, or

(c) the promisor can reasonably be expected to have foreseen that the third party would rely on the term and the third party has in fact relied on it.

(2) The assent referred to in subsection (1)(a)—

(a) may be by words or conduct, and

(b) if sent to the promisor by post or other means, shall not be regarded as communicated to the promisor until received by him.

(3) Subsection (1) is subject to any express term of the contract under which—

(a) the parties to the contract may by agreement rescind or vary the contract without the consent of the third party, or

(b) the consent of the third party is required in circumstances specified in the contract instead of those set out in subsection (1)(a) to (c).

(4) Where the consent of a third party is required under subsection (1) or (3), the court or arbitral tribunal may, on the application of the parties to the contract, dispense with his consent if satisfied—

(a) that his consent cannot be obtained because his whereabouts cannot reasonably be ascertained, or

(b) that he is mentally incapable of giving his consent.

(5) The court or arbitral tribunal may, on the application of the parties to a contract, dispense with any consent that may be required under subsection (1)(c) if satisfied that it cannot reasonably be ascertained whether or not the third party has in fact relied on the term.

(6) If the court or arbitral tribunal dispenses with a third party's consent, it may impose such conditions as it thinks fit, including a condition requiring the payment of compensation to the third party.

(7) The jurisdiction conferred on the court by subsections (4) to (6) is exercisable by both the High Court and a county court.

[1466]

3 Defences etc available to promisor

(1) Subsections (2) to (5) apply where, in reliance on section 1, proceedings for the enforcement of a term of a contract are brought by a third party.

(2) The promisor shall have available to him by way of defence or set-off any matter that—

(a) arises from or in connection with the contract and is relevant to the term, and

(b) would have been available to him by way of defence or set-off if the proceedings had been brought by the promisee.

(3) The promisor shall also have available to him by way of defence or set-off any matter if—

(a) an express term of the contract provides for it to be available to him in proceedings brought by the third party, and

(b) it would have been available to him by way of defence or set-off if the proceedings had been brought by the promisee.

(4) The promisor shall also have available to him—

(a) by way of defence or set-off any matter, and

(b) by way of counterclaim any matter not arising from the contract, that would have been available to him by way of defence or set-off or, as the case may be, by way of counterclaim against the third party if the third party had been a party to the contract.

(5) Subsections (2) and (4) are subject to any express term of the contract as to the matters that are not to be available to the promisor by way of defence, set-off or counterclaim.

(6) Where in any proceedings brought against him a third party seeks in reliance on section 1 to enforce a term of a contract (including, in particular, a term purporting to exclude or limit liability), he may not do so if he could not have done so (whether by reason of any particular circumstances relating to him or otherwise) had he been a party to the contract.

[1467]

4 Enforcement of contract by promisee

Section 1 does not affect any right of the promisee to enforce any term of the contract.

[1468]

5 Protection of party promisor from double liability

Where under section 1 a term of a contract is enforceable by a third party, and the promisee has recovered from the promisor a sum in respect of—

(a) the third party's loss in respect of the term, or

(b) the expense to the promisee of making good to the third party the default of the promisor,

then, in any proceedings brought in reliance on that section by the third party, the court or arbitral tribunal shall reduce any award to the third party to such extent as it thinks appropriate to take account of the sum recovered by the promisee.

[1469]

6 Exceptions

(1) Section 1 confers no rights on a third party in the case of a contract on a bill of exchange, promissory note or other negotiable instrument.

(2) Section 1 confers no rights on a third party in the case of any contract binding on a company and its members under section 14 of the Companies Act 1985.

[(2A) Section 1 confers no rights on a third party in the case of any incorporation document of a limited liability partnership agreement as defined in the Limited Liability Partnerships Regulations 2001 (SI 2001/1090).]

(3) Section 1 confers no right on a third party to enforce—

(a) any term of a contract of employment against an employee,

(b) any term of a worker's contract against a worker (including a home worker), or

(c) any term of a relevant contract against an agency worker.

(4) In subsection (3)—

(a) "contract of employment", "employee", "worker's contract", and "worker" have the meaning given by section 54 of the National Minimum Wage Act 1998,

(b) "home worker" has the meaning given by section 35(2) of that Act,

(c) "agency worker" has the same meaning as in section 34(1) of that Act, and

(d) "relevant contract" means a contract entered into, in a case where section 34 of that Act applies, by the agency worker as respects work falling within subsection (1)(a) of that section.

(5)–(8) ((*Carriage of goods and cargo*) *outside the scope of this work.*)

[1470]

NOTES

Sub-s (2A): inserted by the Limited Liability Partnerships Regulations 2001, SI 2001/1090, reg 9(1), Sch 5, para 20.

7 Supplementary provisions relating to third party

(1) Section 1 does not affect any right or remedy of a third party that exists or is available apart from this Act.

(2) Section 2(2) of the Unfair Contract Terms Act 1977 (restriction on exclusion etc of liability for negligence) shall not apply where the negligence consists of the breach of an obligation arising from a term of a contract and the person seeking to enforce it is a third party acting in reliance on section 1.

(3) In sections 5 and 8 of the Limitation Act 1980 the references to an action founded on a simple contract and an action upon a specialty shall respectively include references to an action brought in reliance on section 1 relating to a simple contract and an action brought in reliance on that section relating to specialty.

(4) A third party shall not, by virtue of section 1(5) or 3(4) or (6), be treated as a party to the contract for the purposes of any other Act (or any instrument made under any other Act). **[1471]**

8 Arbitration provisions

(1) Where—

(a) a right under section 1 to enforce a term ("the substantive term") is subject to a term providing for the submission of disputes to arbitration ("the arbitration agreement"), and

(b) the arbitration agreement is an agreement in writing for the purposes of Part I of the Arbitration Act 1996,

the third party shall be treated for the purposes of that Act as a party to the arbitration agreement as regards disputes between himself and the promisor relating to the enforcement of the substantive term by the third party.

(2) Where—

(a) a third party has a right under section 1 to enforce a term providing for one or more descriptions of dispute between the third party and the promisor to be submitted to arbitration ("the arbitration agreement"),

(b) the arbitration agreement is an agreement in writing for the purposes of Part I of the Arbitration Act 1996, and

(c) the third party does not fall to be treated under subsection (1) as a party to the arbitration agreement,

the third party shall, if he exercises the right, be treated for the purposes of that Act as a party to the arbitration agreement in relation to the matter with respect to which the right is exercised, and be treated as having been so immediately before the exercise of the right. **[1472]**

9 (*Applies to Northern Ireland* (*outside the scope of this work*).)

10 Short title, commencement and extent

(1) This Act may be cited as the Contracts (Rights of Third Parties) Act 1999.

(2) This Act comes into force on the day on which it is passed but, subject to subsection (3), does not apply in relation to a contract entered into before the end of the period of six months beginning with that day.

(3) The restriction in subsection (2) does not apply in relation to a contract which—

(a) is entered into on or after the day on which this Act is passed, and

(b) expressly provides for the application of this Act.

(4) This Act extends as follows—

(a) section 9 extends to Northern Ireland only;

(b) the remaining provisions extend to England and Wales and Northern Ireland only. **[1473]**

REGULATION OF INVESTIGATORY POWERS ACT 2000

(2000 c 23)

An Act to make provision for and about the interception of communications, the acquisition and disclosure of data relating to communications, the carrying out of surveillance, the use of covert human intelligence sources and the acquisition of the means by which electronic data protected by encryption or passwords may be decrypted or accessed; to provide for Commissioners and a tribunal with functions and jurisdiction in relation to those matters, to entries on and interferences with property or with wireless telegraphy and to the carrying out of their functions by the Security Service, the Secret Intelligence Service and the Government Communications Headquarters; and for connected purposes

[28 July 2000]

NOTES

Only those provisions of this Act relevant to employment law are reproduced. Provisions not reproduced are not annotated.

1 Unlawful interception

(1) It shall be an offence for a person intentionally and without lawful authority to intercept, at any place in the United Kingdom, any communication in the course of its transmission by means of—

(a) a public postal service; or
(b) a public telecommunication system.

(2) It shall be an offence for a person—

(a) intentionally and without lawful authority, and
(b) otherwise than in circumstances in which his conduct is excluded by subsection (6) from criminal liability under this subsection,

to intercept, at any place in the United Kingdom, any communication in the course of its transmission by means of a private telecommunication system.

(3) Any interception of a communication which is carried out at any place in the United Kingdom by, or with the express or implied consent of, a person having the right to control the operation or the use of a private telecommunication system shall be actionable at the suit or instance of the sender or recipient, or intended recipient, of the communication if it is without lawful authority and is either—

(a) an interception of that communication in the course of its transmission by means of that private system; or
(b) an interception of that communication in the course of its transmission, by means of a public telecommunication system, to or from apparatus comprised in that private telecommunication system.

(4) Where the United Kingdom is a party to an international agreement which—

(a) relates to the provision of mutual assistance in connection with, or in the form of, the interception of communications,
(b) requires the issue of a warrant, order or equivalent instrument in cases in which assistance is given, and
(c) is designated for the purposes of this subsection by an order made by the Secretary of State,

it shall be the duty of the Secretary of State to secure that no request for assistance in accordance with the agreement is made on behalf of a person in the United Kingdom to the competent authorities of a country or territory outside the United Kingdom except with lawful authority.

(5) Conduct has lawful authority for the purposes of this section if, and only if—

(a) it is authorised by or under section 3 or 4;
(b) it takes place in accordance with a warrant under section 5 ("an interception warrant"); or
(c) it is in exercise, in relation to any stored communication, of any statutory power that is exercised (apart from this section) for the purpose of obtaining information or of taking possession of any document or other property;

and conduct (whether or not prohibited by this section) which has lawful authority for the purposes of this section by virtue of paragraph (a) or (b) shall also be taken to be lawful for all other purposes.

(6) The circumstances in which a person makes an interception of a communication in the course of its transmission by means of a private telecommunication system are such that his conduct is excluded from criminal liability under subsection (2) if—

(a) he is a person with a right to control the operation or the use of the system; or
(b) he has the express or implied consent of such a person to make the interception.

(7) A person who is guilty of an offence under subsection (1) or (2) shall be liable—

(a) on conviction on indictment, to imprisonment for a term not exceeding two years or to a fine, or to both;

(b) on summary conviction, to a fine not exceeding the statutory maximum.

(8) No proceedings for any offence which is an offence by virtue of this section shall be instituted—

(a) in England and Wales, except by or with the consent of the Director of Public Prosecutions;

(b) in Northern Ireland, except by or with the consent of the Director of Public Prosecutions for Northern Ireland.

[1474]

NOTES

Regulations: the Regulation of Investigatory Powers (Designation of an International Agreement) Order 2004, SI 2004/158.

2 Meaning and location of "interception" etc

(1) In this Act—

"postal service" means any service which—

(a) consists in the following, or in any one or more of them, namely, the collection, sorting, conveyance, distribution and delivery (whether in the United Kingdom or elsewhere) of postal items; and

(b) is offered or provided as a service the main purpose of which, or one of the main purposes of which, is to make available, or to facilitate, a means of transmission from place to place of postal items containing communications;

"private telecommunication system" means any telecommunication system which, without itself being a public telecommunication system, is a system in relation to which the following conditions are satisfied—

(a) it is attached, directly or indirectly and whether or not for the purposes of the communication in question, to a public telecommunication system; and

(b) there is apparatus comprised in the system which is both located in the United Kingdom and used (with or without other apparatus) for making the attachment to the public telecommunication system;

"public postal service" means any postal service which is offered or provided to, or to a substantial section of, the public in any one or more parts of the United Kingdom;

"public telecommunications service" means any telecommunications service which is offered or provided to, or to a substantial section of, the public in any one or more parts of the United Kingdom;

"public telecommunication system" means any such parts of a telecommunication system by means of which any public telecommunications service is provided as are located in the United Kingdom;

"telecommunications service" means any service that consists in the provision of access to, and of facilities for making use of, any telecommunication system (whether or not one provided by the person providing the service); and

"telecommunication system" means any system (including the apparatus comprised in it) which exists (whether wholly or partly in the United Kingdom or elsewhere) for the purpose of facilitating the transmission of communications by any means involving the use of electrical or electro-magnetic energy.

(2) For the purposes of this Act, but subject to the following provisions of this section, a person intercepts a communication in the course of its transmission by means of a telecommunication system if, and only if, he—

(a) so modifies or interferes with the system, or its operation,

(b) so monitors transmissions made by means of the system, or

(c) so monitors transmissions made by wireless telegraphy to or from apparatus comprised in the system,

as to make some or all of the contents of the communication available, while being transmitted, to a person other than the sender or intended recipient of the communication.

(3) References in this Act to the interception of a communication do not include references to the interception of any communication broadcast for general reception.

(4) For the purposes of this Act the interception of a communication takes place in the United Kingdom if, and only if, the modification, interference or monitoring or, in the case of a postal item, the interception is effected by conduct within the United Kingdom and the communication is either—

(a) intercepted in the course of its transmission by means of a public postal service or public telecommunication system; or

(b) intercepted in the course of its transmission by means of a private telecommunication system in a case in which the sender or intended recipient of the communication is in the United Kingdom.

(5) References in this Act to the interception of a communication in the course of its transmission by means of a postal service or telecommunication system do not include references to—

(a) any conduct that takes place in relation only to so much of the communication as consists in any traffic data comprised in or attached to a communication (whether by the sender or otherwise) for the purposes of any postal service or telecommunication system by means of which it is being or may be transmitted; or

(b) any such conduct, in connection with conduct falling within paragraph (a), as gives a person who is neither the sender nor the intended recipient only so much access to a communication as is necessary for the purpose of identifying traffic data so comprised or attached.

(6) For the purposes of this section references to the modification of a telecommunication system include references to the attachment of any apparatus to, or other modification of or interference with—

(a) any part of the system; or

(b) any wireless telegraphy apparatus used for making transmissions to or from apparatus comprised in the system.

(7) For the purposes of this section the times while a communication is being transmitted by means of a telecommunication system shall be taken to include any time when the system by means of which the communication is being, or has been, transmitted is used for storing it in a manner that enables the intended recipient to collect it or otherwise to have access to it.

(8) For the purposes of this section the cases in which any contents of a communication are to be taken to be made available to a person while being transmitted shall include any case in which any of the contents of the communication, while being transmitted, are diverted or recorded so as to be available to a person subsequently.

(9) In this section "traffic data", in relation to any communication, means—

(a) any data identifying, or purporting to identify, any person, apparatus or location to or from which the communication is or may be transmitted,

(b) any data identifying or selecting, or purporting to identify or select, apparatus through which, or by means of which, the communication is or may be transmitted,

(c) any data comprising signals for the actuation of apparatus used for the purposes of a telecommunication system for effecting (in whole or in part) the transmission of any communication, and

(d) any data identifying the data or other data as data comprised in or attached to a particular communication,

but that expression includes data identifying a computer file or computer program access to which is obtained, or which is run, by means of the communication to the extent only that the file or program is identified by reference to the apparatus in which it is stored.

(10) In this section—

(a) references, in relation to traffic data comprising signals for the actuation of apparatus, to a telecommunication system by means of which a communication is being or may be transmitted include references to any telecommunication system in which that apparatus is comprised; and

(b) references to traffic data being attached to a communication include references to the data and the communication being logically associated with each other;

and in this section "data", in relation to a postal item, means anything written on the outside of the item.

(11) In this section "postal item" means any letter, postcard or other such thing in writing as may be used by the sender for imparting information to the recipient, or any packet or parcel.

[1475]

3 Lawful interception without an interception warrant

(1) Conduct by any person consisting in the interception of a communication is authorised by this section if the communication is one which, or which that person has reasonable grounds for believing, is both—

(a) a communication sent by a person who has consented to the interception; and
(b) a communication the intended recipient of which has so consented.

(2) Conduct by any person consisting in the interception of a communication is authorised by this section if—

(a) the communication is one sent by, or intended for, a person who has consented to the interception; and
(b) surveillance by means of that interception has been authorised under Part II.

(3) Conduct consisting in the interception of a communication is authorised by this section if—

(a) it is conduct by or on behalf of a person who provides a postal service or a telecommunications service; and
(b) it takes place for purposes connected with the provision or operation of that service or with the enforcement, in relation to that service, of any enactment relating to the use of postal services or telecommunications services.

(4) Conduct by any person consisting in the interception of a communication in the course of its transmission by means of wireless telegraphy is authorised by this section if it takes place—

(a) with the authority of a designated person under [section 48 of the Wireless Telegraphy Act 2006 (interception and disclosure of wireless telegraphy messages)]; and
(b) for purposes connected with anything falling within subsection (5).

(5) Each of the following falls within this subsection—

[(a) the grant of wireless telegraphy licences under the Wireless Telegraphy Act 2006;]
(b) the prevention or detection of anything which constitutes interference with wireless telegraphy; and
(c) the enforcement of[—
(i) any provision of Part 2 (other than Chapter 2 and sections 27 to 31) or Part 3 of that Act, or
(ii) any enactment not falling within sub-paragraph (i),]

that relates to such interference.

[1476]

NOTES

Sub-ss (4), (5): words in square brackets substituted by the Wireless Telegraphy Act 2006, s 123, Sch 7, paras 21, 22, as from 8 February 2007.

4 Power to provide for lawful interception

(1) Conduct by any person ("the interceptor") consisting in the interception of a communication in the course of its transmission by means of a telecommunication system is authorised by this section if—

(a) the interception is carried out for the purpose of obtaining information about the communications of a person who, or who the interceptor has reasonable grounds for believing, is in a country or territory outside the United Kingdom;
(b) the interception relates to the use of a telecommunications service provided to persons in that country or territory which is either—
(i) a public telecommunications service; or
(ii) a telecommunications service that would be a public telecommunications service if the persons to whom it is offered or provided were members of the public in a part of the United Kingdom;
(c) the person who provides that service (whether the interceptor or another person) is required by the law of that country or territory to carry out, secure or facilitate the interception in question;

(d) the situation is one in relation to which such further conditions as may be prescribed by regulations made by the Secretary of State are required to be satisfied before conduct may be treated as authorised by virtue of this subsection; and

(e) the conditions so prescribed are satisfied in relation to that situation.

(2) Subject to subsection (3), the Secretary of State may by regulations authorise any such conduct described in the regulations as appears to him to constitute a legitimate practice reasonably required for the purpose, in connection with the carrying on of any business, of monitoring or keeping a record of—

(a) communications by means of which transactions are entered into in the course of that business; or

(b) other communications relating to that business or taking place in the course of its being carried on.

(3) Nothing in any regulations under subsection (2) shall authorise the interception of any communication except in the course of its transmission using apparatus or services provided by or to the person carrying on the business for use wholly or partly in connection with that business.

(4) Conduct taking place in a prison is authorised by this section if it is conduct in exercise of any power conferred by or under any rules made under section 47 of the Prison Act 1952, section 39 of the Prisons (Scotland) Act 1989 or section 13 of the Prison Act (Northern Ireland) 1953 (prison rules).

(5) Conduct taking place in any hospital premises where high security psychiatric services are provided is authorised by this section if it is conduct in pursuance of, and in accordance with, any direction given under [section 8 of the National Health Service Act 2006, or section 19 or 23 of the National Health Service (Wales) Act 2006] (directions as to the carrying out of their functions by health bodies) to the body providing those services at those premises.

(6) Conduct taking place in a state hospital is authorised by this section if it is conduct in pursuance of, and in accordance with, any direction given to the State Hospitals Board for Scotland under section 2(5) of the National Health Service (Scotland) Act 1978 (regulations and directions as to the exercise of their functions by health boards) as applied by Article 5(1) of and the Schedule to The State Hospitals Board for Scotland Order 1995 (which applies certain provisions of that Act of 1978 to the State Hospitals Board).

(7) In this section references to a business include references to any activities of a government department, of any public authority or of any person or office holder on whom functions are conferred by or under any enactment.

(8) In this section—

"government department" includes any part of the Scottish Administration, a Northern Ireland department and [the Welsh Assembly Government];

"high security psychiatric services" has the same meaning as in [section 4 of the National Health Service Act 2006];

"hospital premises" has the same meaning as in section 4(3) of that Act; and

"state hospital" has the same meaning as in the National Health Service (Scotland) Act 1978.

(9) In this section "prison" means—

(a) any prison, young offender institution, young offenders centre or remand centre which is under the general superintendence of, or is provided by, the Secretary of State under the Prison Act 1952 or the Prison Act (Northern Ireland) 1953, or

(b) any prison, young offenders institution or remand centre which is under the general superintendence of the Scottish Ministers under the Prisons (Scotland) Act 1989,

and includes any contracted out prison, within the meaning of Part IV of the Criminal Justice Act 1991 or section 106(4) of the Criminal Justice and Public Order Act 1994, and any legalised police cells within the meaning of section 14 of the Prisons (Scotland) Act 1989.

[1477]

NOTES

Sub-s (5): words in square brackets substituted by the National Health Service (Consequential Provisions) Act 2006, s 2, Sch 1, paras 207, 208(a), as from 1 March 2007.

Sub-s (8): words in square brackets in definition "government department" substituted by the Government of Wales Act 2006 (Consequential Modifications and Transitional Provisions) Order 2007, SI 2007/1388, art 3, Sch 1, paras 76(1), (2), as from 25 May 2007; words in square brackets in definition "high security psychiatric services" substituted by the National Health Service (Consequential Provisions) Act 2006, s 2, Sch 1, paras 207, 208(b), as from 1 March 2007.

Regulations: the Telecommunications (Lawful Business Practice) (Interception of Communications) Regulations 2000, SI 2000/2699 at **[2655]**; the Regulation of Investigatory Powers (Conditions for the Lawful Interception of Persons outside the United Kingdom) Regulations 2004, SI 2004/157.

PART V
MISCELLANEOUS AND SUPPLEMENTAL

83 Short title, commencement and extent

(1) This Act may be cited as the Regulation of Investigatory Powers Act 2000.

(2) The provisions of this Act, other than this section, shall come into force on such day as the Secretary of State may by order appoint; and different days may be appointed under this subsection for different purposes.

(3) This Act extends to Northern Ireland.

[1478]–[1487]

NOTES

Orders: the commencement order relevant to the provisions reproduced here is the Regulation of Investigatory Powers Act 2000 (Commencement No 1 and Transitional Provisions) Order 2000, SI 2000/2543.

EMPLOYMENT ACT 2002

(2002 c 22)

ARRANGEMENT OF SECTIONS

PART 1
STATUTORY LEAVE AND PAY

CHAPTER 1
PATERNITY AND ADOPTION

Administration and enforcement: pay

PART 3
DISPUTE RESOLUTION ETC

Statutory procedures

Employment particulars

General

PART 4
MISCELLANEOUS AND GENERAL

Miscellaneous

General

SCHEDULES:

An Act to make provision for statutory rights to paternity and adoption leave and pay; to amend the law relating to statutory maternity leave and pay; to amend the Employment Tribunals Act 1996; to make provision for the use of statutory procedures in relation to employment disputes; to amend the law relating to particulars of employment; to make provision about compromise agreements; to make provision for questionnaires in relation to equal pay; to make provision in connection with trade union learning representatives; to amend section 110 of the Employment Rights Act 1996; to make provision about fixed-term work; to make provision about flexible working; to amend the law relating to maternity allowance; to make provision for work-focused interviews for partners of benefit claimants; to make provision about the use of information for, or relating to, employment and training; and for connected purposes

[8 July 2002]

NOTES

Most of this major Act consists of amendments and additions to other legislation, principally the Employment Rights Act 1996 and the Social Security Contributions and Benefits Act 1992. These are cross referenced. The Act is otherwise printed in full save for those provisions that either have been repealed or are outside the scope of this work.

Note also that ss 29–34 of this Act, together with Schs 2–4, will be repealed, as from a date to be appointed, following the enactment of Employment Bill 2007.

PART 1
STATUTORY LEAVE AND PAY

CHAPTER 1
PATERNITY AND ADOPTION

1–4 (*S 1 inserts the Employment Rights Act 1996, ss 80A, 80B, 80C–80E at* **[1116]** *et seq; s 2 inserts the Social Security Contributions and Benefits Act 1992, ss 171ZA–171ZE,*

171ZF–171ZK at **[441]** *et seq; s 3 inserts the Employment Rights Act 1996, ss 75A–75D at* **[1107]** *et seq; s 4 inserts the Social Security Contributions and Benefits Act 1992, ss 171ZL–171ZT at* **[452]** *et seq.)*

Administration and enforcement: pay

5, 6 (*S 5 repealed by the Commissioners for Revenue and Customs Act 2005, ss 50(6), 52(2), Sch 4, para 93, Sch 5, as from 18 April 2005; s 6 (financial arrangements) outside the scope of this work.*)

7 Funding of employers' liabilities

(1) The Secretary of State shall by regulations make provision for the payment by employers of *statutory paternity pay* and statutory adoption pay to be funded by the Board to such extent as the regulations may specify.

(2) Regulations under subsection (1) shall—

- (a) make provision for a person who has made a payment of *statutory paternity pay* or statutory adoption pay to be entitled, except in such circumstances as the regulations may provide, to recover an amount equal to the sum of—
  - (i) the aggregate of such of those payments as qualify for small employers' relief; and
  - (ii) an amount equal to 92 per cent of the aggregate of such of those payments as do not so qualify; and
- (b) include provision for a person who has made a payment of *statutory paternity pay* or statutory adoption pay qualifying for small employers' relief to be entitled, except in such circumstances as the regulations may provide, to recover an additional amount equal to the amount to which the person would have been entitled under section 167(2)(b) of the Social Security Contributions and Benefits Act 1992 (corresponding provision for statutory maternity pay) had the payment been a payment of statutory maternity pay.

(3) For the purposes of subsection (2), *a payment of statutory paternity pay* or statutory adoption pay qualifies for small employers' relief if it would have so qualified were it a payment of statutory maternity pay, treating the period for which the payment is made, *in the case of statutory paternity pay*, or the payee's adoption pay period, in the case of statutory adoption pay, as the maternity pay period.

(4) Regulations under subsection (1) may, in particular—

- (a) make provision for funding in advance as well as in arrear;
- (b) make provision for funding, or the recovery of amounts due under provision made by virtue of subsection (2)(b), by means of deductions from such amounts for which employers are accountable to the Board as the regulations may provide, or otherwise;
- (c) make provision for the recovery by the Board of any sums overpaid to employers under the regulations.

(5) Where in accordance with any provision of regulations under subsection (1) an amount has been deducted from an employer's contributions payments, the amount so deducted shall (except in such cases as the Secretary of State may by regulations provide) be treated for the purposes of any provision made by or under any enactment in relation to primary or secondary Class 1 contributions—

- (a) as having been paid (on such date as may be determined in accordance with the regulations), and
- (b) as having been received by the Board,

towards discharging the employer's liability in respect of such contributions.

(6) Regulations under this section must be made with the concurrence of the Board.

(7) In this section, "contributions payments", in relation to an employer, means any payments which the employer is required, by or under any enactment, to make in discharge of any liability in respect of primary or secondary Class 1 contributions.

[1488]

NOTES

Sub-ss (1), (2): for the words in italics there are substituted the words "ordinary statutory paternity pay, additional statutory paternity pay" by the Work and Families Act 2006, s 11(1), Sch 1, para 50(1)–(3), as from a day to be appointed.

Sub-s (3): for the first words in italics there are substituted the words "a payment of ordinary statutory paternity pay, additional statutory paternity pay", and for the second words in italics there are substituted the words "in the case of ordinary statutory paternity pay or additional statutory paternity pay", by the Work and Families Act 2006, s 11(1), Sch 1, para 50(1), (4), as from a day to be appointed.

Regulations: the Statutory Paternity Pay and Statutory Adoption Pay (Administration) Regulations 2002, SI 2002/2820 at **[2787]**; the Statutory Paternity Pay (Adoption) and Statutory Adoption Pay (Adoptions from Overseas) (Administration) Regulations 2003, SI 2003/1192.

8 Regulations about payment

(1) The Secretary of State may make regulations with respect to the payment by employers of *statutory paternity pay* and statutory adoption pay.

(2) Regulations under subsection (1) may, in particular, include provision—

(a) about the records to be kept by employers in relation to payments of *statutory paternity pay* and statutory adoption pay, including the length of time for which they are to be retained;

(b) for the production of wages sheets and other documents and records to officers of the Board for the purpose of enabling them to satisfy themselves that *statutory paternity pay* and statutory adoption pay have been paid and are being paid, in accordance with the regulations, to employees who are entitled to them;

(c) for requiring employers to provide information to employees (in their itemised pay statements or otherwise);

(d) for requiring employers to make returns to the Board containing such particulars with respect to payments of *statutory paternity pay* and statutory adoption pay as the regulations may provide.

(3) Regulations under subsection (1) must be made with the concurrence of the Board.

[1489]

NOTES

Sub-ss (1), (2): for the words in italics there are substituted the words "ordinary statutory paternity pay, additional statutory paternity pay" by the Work and Families Act 2006, s 11(1), Sch 1, para 51, as from a day to be appointed.

Regulations: the Statutory Paternity Pay and Statutory Adoption Pay (Administration) Regulations 2002, SI 2002/2820 at **[2787]**; the Statutory Paternity Pay (Adoption) and Statutory Adoption Pay (Adoptions from Overseas) (Administration) Regulations 2003, SI 2003/1192.

9–15 (*S 9 amends the Social Security Contributions (Transfer of Functions, etc) Act 1999; ss 10–15 (powers to require information, penalties and supply and use of information) outside the scope of this work.*)

16 Interpretation

In sections 5 to 15—

"the Board" means the Commissioners of Inland Revenue;

"the Department" means the Department for Social Development or the Department for Employment and Learning;

"employer" and "employee" have the same meanings as in Parts 12ZA and 12ZB of the Social Security Contributions and Benefits Act 1992.

[1490]

NOTES

Commissioners of Inland Revenue: a reference to the Commissioners of Inland Revenue is now to be taken as a reference to the Commissioners for Her Majesty's Revenue and Customs; see the Commissioners for Revenue and Customs Act 2005, s 50(1), (7).

17–28 (*S 17 amends the Employment Rights Act 1996, ss 71, 73, 74 at* **[1102]**, **[1104]**, **[1105]**; *s 18 amended the Social Security Contributions and Benefits Act 1992, s 165, and was repealed by the Work and Families Act 2006, s 15, Sch 2, as from 1 October 2006.; s 19 substitutes s 166 of the 1992 Act at* **[435]**; *s 20 amends s 164 of the 1992 Act at* **[433]**; *s 21(1) substitutes s 167 of the 1992 Act at* **[436]**; *s 21(2) (Northern Ireland) outside the scope of this work; s 22 amends the Employment Tribunals Act 1996, s 13 at* **[969]** *and inserts s 13A of that Act, at* **[970]**; *s 23 substitutes s 34 of that Act at* **[991]**; *s 24 amends ss 7, 18, 19 of that Act at* **[960]**, **[975]**, **[976]**; *ss 25, 26 amend s 7 of that Act at* **[960]**; *s 27 inserts s 7A of that Act at* **[961]**; *s 28 amends s 9 of that Act at* **[963]**.)

PART 3
DISPUTE RESOLUTION ETC

Statutory procedures

29 Statutory dispute resolution procedures

(1) Schedule 2 (which sets out the statutory dispute resolution procedures) shall have effect.

(2) The Secretary of State may by order—
- (a) amend Schedule 2;
- (b) make provision for the Schedule to apply, with or without modifications, as if—
  - (i) any individual of a description specified in the order who would not otherwise be an employee for the purposes of the Schedule were an employee for those purposes; and
  - (ii) a person of a description specified in the order were, in the case of any such individual, the individual's employer for those purposes.

(3) Before making an order under this section, the Secretary of State must consult the Advisory, Conciliation and Arbitration Service.

[1491]

NOTES

Commencement: 27 April 2003 (sub-ss (2), (3)); 1 October 2004 (otherwise).

Modified, in relation to governing bodies with delegated budgets, by the Education (Modification of Enactments Relating to Employment) (England) Order 2003, SI 2003/1964, art 3, Schedule at **[3035C]**, **[3035G]** and the Education (Modification of Enactments Relating to Employment) (Wales) Order 2006, SI 2006/1073, art 3, Schedule at **[3462B]**, **[3462F]**.

Orders: as of 6 April 2008 no Orders had been made under this section.

30 Contracts of employment

(1) Every contract of employment shall have effect to require the employer and employee to comply, in relation to any matter to which a statutory procedure applies, with the requirements of the procedure.

(2) Subsection (1) shall have effect notwithstanding any agreement to the contrary, but does not affect so much of an agreement to follow a particular procedure as requires the employer or employee to comply with a requirement which is additional to, and not inconsistent with, the requirements of the statutory procedure.

(3) The Secretary of State may for the purpose of this section by regulations make provision about the application of the statutory procedures.

(4) In this section, "contract of employment" has the same meaning as in the Employment Rights Act 1996 (c 18).

[1492]

NOTES

Commencement: 27 April 2003 (sub-s (3)); to be appointed (otherwise).

Modified as noted to s 29 at **[1491]**.

Regulations: as of 6 April 2008 no Regulations had been made under this section.

31 Non-completion of statutory procedure: adjustment of awards

(1) This section applies to proceedings before an employment tribunal relating to a claim under any of the jurisdictions listed in Schedule 3 by an employee.

(2) If, in the case of proceedings to which this section applies, it appears to the employment tribunal that—
- (a) the claim to which the proceedings relate concerns a matter to which one of the statutory procedures applies,
- (b) the statutory procedure was not completed before the proceedings were begun, and
- (c) the non-completion of the statutory procedure was wholly or mainly attributable to failure by the employee—

(i) to comply with a requirement of the procedure, or
(ii) to exercise a right of appeal under it,

it must, subject to subsection (4), reduce any award which it makes to the employee by 10 per cent, and may, if it considers it just and equitable in all the circumstances to do so, reduce it by a further amount, but not so as to make a total reduction of more than 50 per cent.

(3) If, in the case of proceedings to which this section applies, it appears to the employment tribunal that—

(a) the claim to which the proceedings relate concerns a matter to which one of the statutory procedures applies,
(b) the statutory procedure was not completed before the proceedings were begun, and
(c) the non-completion of the statutory procedure was wholly or mainly attributable to failure by the employer to comply with a requirement of the procedure,

it must, subject to subsection (4), increase any award which it makes to the employee by 10 per cent and may, if it considers it just and equitable in all the circumstances to do so, increase it by a further amount, but not so as to make a total increase of more than 50 per cent.

(4) The duty under subsection (2) or (3) to make a reduction or increase of 10 per cent does not apply if there are exceptional circumstances which would make a reduction or increase of that percentage unjust or inequitable, in which case the tribunal may make no reduction or increase or a reduction or increase of such lesser percentage as it considers just and equitable in all the circumstances.

(5) Where an award falls to be adjusted under this section and under section 38, the adjustment under this section shall be made before the adjustment under that section.

(6) The Secretary of State may for the purposes of this section by regulations—

(a) make provision about the application of the statutory procedures;
(b) make provision about when a statutory procedure is to be taken to be completed;
(c) make provision about what constitutes compliance with a requirement of a statutory procedure;
(d) make provision about circumstances in which a person is to be treated as not subject to, or as having complied with, such a requirement;
(e) make provision for a statutory procedure to have effect in such circumstances as may be specified by the regulations with such modifications as may be so specified;
(f) make provision about when an employee is required to exercise a right of appeal under a statutory procedure.

(7) The Secretary of State may by order—

(a) amend Schedule 3 for the purpose of—
  (i) adding a jurisdiction to the list in that Schedule, or
  (ii) removing a jurisdiction from that list;
(b) make provision, in relation to a jurisdiction listed in Schedule 3, for this section not to apply to proceedings relating to claims of a description specified in the order;
(c) make provision for this section to apply, with or without modifications, as if—
  (i) any individual of a description specified in the order who would not otherwise be an employee for the purposes of this section were an employee for those purposes, and
  (ii) a person of a description specified in the order were, in the case of any such individual, the individual's employer for those purposes.

[1493]

NOTES

Commencement: 27 April 2003 (sub-ss (6), (7)); 1 October 2004 (otherwise, subject to transitional provisions as noted below).

Modified as noted to s 29 at **[1491]**.

Transitional provisions: this section does not apply in relation to a grievance where the employee presented a complaint to the employment tribunal about that grievance prior to 1 October 2004 (see SI 2004/1717, art 3). For further transitional provisions affecting the application of this section, see SI 2004/752, reg 18 at **[3098]**.

Regulations: the Employment Act 2002 (Dispute Resolution) Regulations 2004, SI 2004/752 at **[3082]**.

Orders: the Employment Act 2002 (Amendment of Schedules 3, 4 and 5) Order 2007, SI 2007/30 at **[3470]**.

32 Complaints about grievances

(1) This section applies to the jurisdictions listed in Schedule 4.

(2) An employee shall not present a complaint to an employment tribunal under a jurisdiction to which this section applies if—

(a) it concerns a matter in relation to which the requirement in paragraph 6 or 9 of Schedule 2 applies, and

(b) the requirement has not been complied with.

(3) An employee shall not present a complaint to an employment tribunal under a jurisdiction to which this section applies if—

(a) it concerns a matter in relation to which the requirement in paragraph 6 or 9 of Schedule 2 has been complied with, and

(b) less than 28 days have passed since the day on which the requirement was complied with.

(4) An employee shall not present a complaint to an employment tribunal under a jurisdiction to which this section applies if—

(a) it concerns a matter in relation to which the requirement in paragraph 6 or 9 of Schedule 2 has been complied with, and

(b) the day on which the requirement was complied with was more than one month after the end of the original time limit for making the complaint.

(5) In such circumstances as the Secretary of State may specify by regulations, an employment tribunal may direct that subsection (4) shall not apply in relation to a particular matter.

(6) An employment tribunal shall be prevented from considering a complaint presented in breach of subsections (2) to (4), but only if—

(a) the breach is apparent to the tribunal from the information supplied to it by the employee in connection with the bringing of the proceedings, or

(b) the tribunal is satisfied of the breach as a result of his employer raising the issue of compliance with those provisions in accordance with regulations under section 7 of the Employment Tribunals Act 1996 (c 17) (employment tribunal procedure regulations).

(7) The Secretary of State may for the purposes of this section by regulations—

(a) make provision about the application of the procedures set out in Part 2 of Schedule 2;

(b) make provision about what constitutes compliance with paragraph 6 or 9 of that Schedule;

(c) make provision about circumstances in which a person is to be treated as having complied with paragraph 6 or 9 of that Schedule;

(d) make provision for paragraph 6 or 9 of that Schedule to have effect in such circumstances as may be specified by the regulations with such modifications as may be so specified.

(8) The Secretary of State may by order—

(a) amend, repeal or replace any of subsections (2) to (4);

(b) amend Schedule 4;

(c) make provision for this section to apply, with or without modifications, as if—

(i) any individual of a description specified in the order who would not otherwise be an employee for the purposes of this section were an employee for those purposes, and

(ii) a person of a description specified in the order were, in the case of any such individual, the individual's employer for those purposes.

(9) Before making an order under subsection (8)(a), the Secretary of State must consult the Advisory, Conciliation and Arbitration Service.

(10) In its application to orders under subsection (8)(a), section 51(1)(b) includes power to amend this section.

[1494]

NOTES

Commencement: 27 April 2003 (sub-ss (7)–(10)); 1 October 2004 (otherwise, subject to transitional provisions as noted below).

Modified as noted to s 29 at **[1491]**.

Transitional provisions: this section does not apply in relation to a grievance where the employee presented a complaint to the employment tribunal about that grievance prior to 1 October 2004 (see SI 2004/1717, art 3). For further transitional provisions affecting the application of this section, see SI 2004/752, reg 18 at **[3098]**.

Regulations: the Employment Act 2002 (Dispute Resolution) Regulations 2004, SI 2004/752 at **[3082]** (made under sub-s (7)).

Orders: the Employment Act 2002 (Amendment of Schedules 3, 4 and 5) Order 2007, SI 2007/30 at **[3470]** (made under sub-s (8)).

Regulations: as of 6 April 2008, no Regulations had been made under sub-s (5).

33 Consequential adjustment of time limits

(1) The Secretary of State may, in relation to a jurisdiction listed in Schedule 3 or 4, by regulations make provision about the time limit for beginning proceedings in respect of a claim concerning a matter to which a statutory procedure applies.

(2) Regulations under this section may, in particular—

(a) make provision extending, or authorising the extension of, the time for beginning proceedings,

(b) make provision about the exercise of a discretion to extend the time for beginning proceedings, or

(c) make provision treating proceedings begun out of time as begun within time.

[1495]

NOTES

Commencement: 27 April 2003.

Regulations: the Employment Act 2002 (Dispute Resolution) Regulations 2004, SI 2004/752 at **[3082]**.

34 (*Inserts the Employment Rights Act 1996, s 98A at* **[1137]***, and amends ss 112, 117, 120, 123 of that Act at* **[1156]**, **[1161]**, **[1164]**, **[1167]**.)

Employment particulars

35–37 (*S 35 amends the Employment Rights Act 1996, s 3 at* **[1008]***; s 36 repeals s 3(3), (4) of the 1996 Act at* **[1008]***; s 37 inserts ss 7A, 7B of the 1996 Act at* **[1013]**, **[1014]**.)

38 Failure to give statement of employment particulars etc

(1) This section applies to proceedings before an employment tribunal relating to a claim by an employee under any of the jurisdictions listed in Schedule 5.

(2) If in the case of proceedings to which this section applies—

(a) the employment tribunal finds in favour of the employee, but makes no award to him in respect of the claim to which the proceedings relate, and

(b) when the proceedings were begun the employer was in breach of his duty to the employee under section 1(1) or 4(1) of the Employment Rights Act 1996 (c 18) (duty to give a written statement of initial employment particulars or of particulars of change),

the tribunal must, subject to subsection (5), make an award of the minimum amount to be paid by the employer to the employee and may, if it considers it just and equitable in all the circumstances, award the higher amount instead.

(3) If in the case of proceedings to which this section applies—

(a) the employment tribunal makes an award to the employee in respect of the claim to which the proceedings relate, and

(b) when the proceedings were begun the employer was in breach of his duty to the employee under section 1(1) or 4(1) of the Employment Rights Act 1996,

the tribunal must, subject to subsection (5), increase the award by the minimum amount and may, if it considers it just and equitable in all the circumstances, increase the award by the higher amount instead.

(4) In subsections (2) and (3)—

(a) references to the minimum amount are to an amount equal to two weeks' pay, and

(b) references to the higher amount are to an amount equal to four weeks' pay.

(5) The duty under subsection (2) or (3) does not apply if there are exceptional circumstances which would make an award or increase under that subsection unjust or inequitable.

(6) The amount of a week's pay of an employee shall—

(a) be calculated for the purposes of this section in accordance with Chapter 2 of Part 14 of the Employment Rights Act 1996 (c 18), and

(b) not exceed the amount for the time being specified in section 227 of that Act (maximum amount of week's pay).

(7) For the purposes of Chapter 2 of Part 14 of the Employment Rights Act 1996 as applied by subsection (6), the calculation date shall be taken to be—

(a) if the employee was employed by the employer on the date the proceedings were begun, that date, and

(b) if he was not, the effective date of termination as defined by section 97 of that Act.

(8) The Secretary of State may by order—

(a) amend Schedule 5 for the purpose of—

(i) adding a jurisdiction to the list in that Schedule, or

(ii) removing a jurisdiction from that list;

(b) make provision, in relation to a jurisdiction listed in Schedule 5, for this section not to apply to proceedings relating to claims of a description specified in the order;

(c) make provision for this section to apply, with or without modifications, as if—

(i) any individual of a description specified in the order who would not otherwise be an employee for the purposes of this section were an employee for those purposes, and

(ii) a person of a description specified in the order were, in the case of any such individual, the individual's employer for those purposes.

[1496]

NOTES

Commencement: 1 October 2004.

Orders: the Employment Act 2002 (Amendment of Schedules 3, 4 and 5) Order 2007, SI 2007/30 at **[3470]**.

General

39 (*Inserts the Employment Rights Act 1996, s 124A at* **[1169]**.)

40 Interpretation of Part 3

In this Part—

"employer" and "employee" have the same meanings as in the Employment Rights Act 1996 (c 18);

"statutory procedure" means a procedure set out in Schedule 2.

[1497]

NOTES

Commencement: 1 October 2004.

PART 4

MISCELLANEOUS AND GENERAL

Miscellaneous

41–44 (*S 41 repealed by the Employment Relations Act 2004, s 57(2), Sch 2, as from 6 April 2005; s 42 inserts the Equal Pay Act 1970, s 7B at* **[16]**; *s 43 inserts the Trade Union and Labour Relations (Consolidation) Act 1992, s 168A at* **[652]**, *and amends ss 169, 170, 173, 199, 200, 203 of that Act at* **[653]**, **[654]**, **[657]**, **[684]**, **[685]**, **[688]**; *s 44 amends the Employment Rights Act 1996, s 110 at* **[1154]**.)

45 Fixed-term work

(1) The Secretary of State shall make regulations—

(a) for the purpose of securing that employees in fixed-term employment are treated, for such purposes and to such extent as the regulations may specify, no less favourably than employees in permanent employment, and

(b) for the purpose of preventing abuse arising from the use of successive periods of fixed-term employment.

(2) The regulations may—

(a) specify classes of employee who are to be taken to be, or not to be, in fixed-term employment;

(b) specify classes of employee who are to be taken to be, or not to be, in permanent employment;

(c) specify circumstances in which employees in fixed-term employment are to be taken to be, or not to be, treated less favourably than employees in permanent employment;

(d) specify circumstances in which periods of fixed-term employment are to be taken to be, or not to be, successive;

(e) specify circumstances in which fixed-term employment is to have effect as permanent employment;

(f) make provision which has effect in relation to employees in fixed-term employment generally or provision which has effect only in relation to specified classes of employee in fixed-term employment.

(3) The regulations may—

(a) confer jurisdiction (including exclusive jurisdiction) on employment tribunals;

(b) provide for specified obligations not to apply in specified circumstances;

(c) make provision about notices or information to be given, evidence to be produced and other procedures to be followed;

(d) amend, apply with or without modifications, or make provision similar to any provision of—

(i) the Employment Rights Act 1996 (c 18) (including, in particular, Parts 5, 10 and 13),

(ii) the Trade Union and Labour Relations (Consolidation) Act 1992 (c 52), or

(iii) the Social Security Contributions and Benefits Act 1992 (c 4);

(e) provide for the provisions of specified agreements to have effect in place of provisions of the regulations to such extent and in such circumstances as may be specified.

(4) Without prejudice to the generality of this section, the regulations may make any provision in relation to employees which appears to the Secretary of State to be necessary or expedient—

(a) for the purpose of implementing Council Directive 99/70/EC on the framework agreement on fixed-term work in its application to terms and conditions of employment;

(b) for the purpose of dealing with any matter arising out of or related to the United Kingdom's obligations under that Directive;

(c) for the purpose of any matter dealt with by the framework agreement or for the purpose of applying the provisions of the framework agreement to any matter relating to fixed term workers.

(5) In its application to this section, section 51(1)(b) includes power to amend an enactment.

(6) In this section—

(a) "employee" means an individual who has entered into or works under (or, where the employment has ceased, worked under) a contract of employment, and

(b) "contract of employment" means a contract of service or apprenticeship, whether express or implied, and (if it is express) whether oral or in writing.

[1498]

NOTES

Commencement: 8 July 2002.

Regulations: the Fixed-term Employees (Prevention of Less Favourable Treatment) Regulations 2002, SI 2002/2034 at **[2730]**.

46–50 (*S 46 applies to Northern Ireland only; s 47 inserts the Employment Rights Act 1996, ss 47E, 80F–80I, 104C at* **[1072]**, **[1121]–[1124]**, **[1148]**; *s 48* (*Rate of maternity allowance*), *s 49* (*Work-focused interviews for partners*), *s 50* (*introduces Sch 6* (*Use of information for, or relating to, employment and training*)) *outside the scope of this work.*)

General

51 Orders and regulations

(1) Any power of the Secretary of State to make orders or regulations under this Act includes power—

(a) to make different provision for different cases or circumstances;

(b) to make such incidental, supplementary, consequential or transitional provision as the Secretary of State thinks fit.

(2) Any power of the Secretary of State to make orders or regulations under this Act is exercisable by statutory instrument.

(3) No order may be made under this Act unless a draft of the order has been laid before and approved by resolution of each House of Parliament.

(4) No regulations may be made under section 30, 31, 32, 33 or 45 unless a draft of the regulations has been laid before and approved by resolution of each House of Parliament.

(5) A statutory instrument containing regulations under any other provision of this Act shall be subject to annulment in pursuance of a resolution of either House of Parliament.

(6) This section does not apply to orders under section 55(2).

[1499]

52 Financial provisions

(1) There shall be paid out of money provided by Parliament—

(a) any expenses incurred by a Minister of the Crown or government department in consequence of this Act, and

(b) any increase attributable to this Act in the sums so provided under any other Act.

(2) There shall be paid into the Consolidated Fund any increase attributable to this Act in the sums payable into that Fund under any other Act.

[1500]

53 Minor and consequential amendments

Schedule 7 (which makes minor and consequential amendments) has effect.

[1501]

NOTES

Commencement: 31 July 2002 (certain purposes); 9 September 2002 (certain purposes); 24 November 2002 (certain purposes); 8 December 2002 (certain purposes); 6 April 2003 (certain purposes); 27 April 2003 (certain purposes); 5 July 2003 (certain purposes); 1 October 2004 (certain purposes); 1 November 2004 (otherwise).

54 Repeals and revocations

The enactments and instruments specified in Schedule 8 are hereby repealed or revoked to the extent specified there.

[1502]

NOTES

Commencement: 9 September 2002 (certain purposes); 24 November 2002 (certain purposes); 6 April 2003 (certain purposes); 1 October 2004 (certain purposes); 1 November 2004 (otherwise).

55 Short title etc

(1) This Act may be cited as the Employment Act 2002.

(2) This Act, except sections 45, 46, 51 and 52 and this section, shall come into force on such day as the Secretary of State may by order made by statutory instrument appoint, and different days may be so appointed for different purposes.

(3) An order under subsection (2) may contain such transitional provisions and savings as the Secretary of State considers necessary or expedient in connection with the coming into force of any of the provisions of this Act.

(4) The Secretary of State may by regulations make such transitional provisions and savings as he considers necessary or expedient for the purposes of or in connection with—

(a) the coming into force of section 19 or 48, or Schedule 7 so far as relating to any amendment made in consequence of either of those sections; or

(b) the operation of any enactment amended by any of those provisions during any period when the amendment is not wholly in force.

(5) Subject to subsections (6) and (7), this Act extends to England and Wales and Scotland only.

(6)–(8) (*Apply to Northern Ireland only.*)

[1503]

NOTES

Orders: the Employment Act 2002 (Commencement No 1) Order 2002, SI 2002/1989; the Employment Act 2002 (Commencement No 2) Order 2002, SI 2002/2256; the Employment Act 2002 (Commencement No 3 and Transitional and Saving Provisions) Order 2002, SI 2002/2866; the Employment Act 2002 (Commencement No 4 and Transitional Provisions) Order 2003, SI 2003/1190; the Employment Act 2002 (Commencement No 5) Order 2003, SI 2003/1666; the Employment Act 2002 (Commencement No 6 and Transitional Provision) Order 2004, SI 2004/1717; the Employment Act 2002 (Commencement No 7) Order 2004, SI 2004/2185; the Employment Act 2002 (Commencement No 8) Order 2004, SI 2004/2822.

SCHEDULES

(*Sch 1 (Penalties: procedure and appeals) outside the scope of this work.*)

SCHEDULE 2
STATUTORY DISPUTE RESOLUTION PROCEDURES

Section 29

NOTES

Transitional provisions: this Schedule does not apply in relation to a grievance where the employee presented a complaint to the employment tribunal about that grievance prior to 1 October 2004 (see SI 2004/1717, art 3). For further transitional provisions affecting the application of this Schedule, see SI 2004/752, reg 18 at **[3098]**.

PART 1
DISMISSAL AND DISCIPLINARY PROCEDURES

CHAPTER 1
STANDARD PROCEDURE

Step 1: statement of grounds for action and invitation to meeting

1.—(1) The employer must set out in writing the employee's alleged conduct or characteristics, or other circumstances, which lead him to contemplate dismissing or taking disciplinary action against the employee.

(2) The employer must send the statement or a copy of it to the employee and invite the employee to attend a meeting to discuss the matter.

Step 2: meeting

2.—(1) The meeting must take place before action is taken, except in the case where the disciplinary action consists of suspension.

(2) The meeting must not take place unless—

(a) the employer has informed the employee what the basis was for including in the statement under paragraph 1(1) the ground or grounds given in it, and

(b) the employee has had a reasonable opportunity to consider his response to that information.

(3) The employee must take all reasonable steps to attend the meeting.

(4) After the meeting, the employer must inform the employee of his decision and notify him of the right to appeal against the decision if he is not satisfied with it.

Step 3: appeal

3.—(1) If the employee does wish to appeal, he must inform the employer.

(2) If the employee informs the employer of his wish to appeal, the employer must invite him to attend a further meeting.

(3) The employee must take all reasonable steps to attend the meeting.

(4) The appeal meeting need not take place before the dismissal or disciplinary action takes effect.

(5) After the appeal meeting, the employer must inform the employee of his final decision.

CHAPTER 2
MODIFIED PROCEDURE

Step 1: statement of grounds for action

4. The employer must—
 (a) set out in writing—
  (i) the employee's alleged misconduct which has led to the dismissal,
  (ii) what the basis was for thinking at the time of the dismissal that the employee was guilty of the alleged misconduct, and
  (iii) the employee's right to appeal against dismissal, and
 (b) send the statement or a copy of it to the employee.

Step 2: appeal

5.—(1) If the employee does wish to appeal, he must inform the employer.

(2) If the employee informs the employer of his wish to appeal, the employer must invite him to attend a meeting.

(3) The employee must take all reasonable steps to attend the meeting.

(4) After the appeal meeting, the employer must inform the employee of his final decision.

[1504]

NOTES

Commencement: 1 October 2004 (subject to transitional provisions as noted below).
Modified as noted to s 29 at **[1491]**.

PART 2
GRIEVANCE PROCEDURES

CHAPTER 1
STANDARD PROCEDURE

Step 1: statement of grievance

6. The employee must set out the grievance in writing and send the statement or a copy of it to the employer.

Step 2: meeting

7.—(1) The employer must invite the employee to attend a meeting to discuss the grievance.

(2) The meeting must not take place unless—

(a) the employee has informed the employer what the basis for the grievance was when he made the statement under paragraph 6, and

(b) the employer has had a reasonable opportunity to consider his response to that information.

(3) The employee must take all reasonable steps to attend the meeting.

(4) After the meeting, the employer must inform the employee of his decision as to his response to the grievance and notify him of the right to appeal against the decision if he is not satisfied with it.

Step 3: appeal

8.—(1) If the employee does wish to appeal, he must inform the employer.

(2) If the employee informs the employer of his wish to appeal, the employer must invite him to attend a further meeting.

(3) The employee must take all reasonable steps to attend the meeting.

(4) After the appeal meeting, the employer must inform the employee of his final decision.

CHAPTER 2
MODIFIED PROCEDURE

Step 1: statement of grievance

9. The employee must—

(a) set out in writing—

(i) the grievance, and

(ii) the basis for it, and

(b) send the statement or a copy of it to the employer.

Step 2: response

10. The employer must set out his response in writing and send the statement or a copy of it to the employee.

[1505]

NOTES

Commencement: 1 October 2004 (subject to transitional provisions as noted to Part 1 at **[1504]**).
Modified as noted to s 29 at **[1491]**.

PART 3
GENERAL REQUIREMENTS

Introductory

11. The following requirements apply to each of the procedures set out above (so far as applicable).

Timetable

12. Each step and action under the procedure must be taken without unreasonable delay.

Meetings

13.—(1) Timing and location of meetings must be reasonable.

(2) Meetings must be conducted in a manner that enables both employer and employee to explain their cases.

(3) In the case of appeal meetings which are not the first meeting, the employer should, as far as is reasonably practicable, be represented by a more senior manager than attended the first meeting (unless the most senior manager attended that meeting).

[1506]

NOTES

Commencement: 1 October 2004 (subject to transitional provisions as noted to Part 1 at **[1504]**).
Modified as noted to s 29 at **[1491]**.

PART 4
SUPPLEMENTARY

Status of meetings

14. A meeting held for the purposes of this Schedule is a hearing for the purposes of section 13(4) and (5) of the Employment Relations Act 1999 (c 26) (definition of "disciplinary hearing" and "grievance hearing" in relation to the right to be accompanied under section 10 of that Act).

Scope of grievance procedures

15.—(1) The procedures set out in Part 2 are only applicable to matters raised by an employee with his employer as a grievance.

(2) Accordingly, those procedures are only applicable to the kind of disclosure dealt with in Part 4A of the Employment Rights Act 1996 (c 18) (protected disclosures of information) if information is disclosed by an employee to his employer in circumstances where—

(a) the information relates to a matter which the employee could raise as a grievance with his employer, and

(b) it is the intention of the employee that the disclosure should constitute the raising of the matter with his employer as a grievance.

[1507]

NOTES

Commencement: 1 October 2004 (subject to transitional provisions as noted to Part 1 at **[1504]**).
Modified as noted to s 29 at **[1491]**.

SCHEDULE 3
TRIBUNAL JURISDICTIONS TO WHICH SECTION 31 APPLIES

Section 31

Section 2 of the Equal Pay Act 1970 (c 41) (equality clauses)

Section 63 of the Sex Discrimination Act 1975 (c 65) (discrimination in the employment field)

Section 54 of the Race Relations Act 1976 (c 74) (discrimination in the employment field)

[Section 145A of the Trade Union and Labour Relations (Consolidation) Act 1992 (inducements relating to union membership or activities)

Section 145B of that Act (inducements relating to collective bargaining)

Section 146 of that Act (detriment in relation to union membership and activities)]

Paragraph 156 of Schedule A1 to that Act (detriment in relation to union recognition rights)

[Section 17A of the Disability Discrimination Act 1995] (c 50) (discrimination in the employment field)

Section 23 of the Employment Rights Act 1996 (c 18) (unauthorised deductions and payments)

Section 48 of that Act (detriment in employment)

Section 111 of that Act (unfair dismissal)

Section 163 of that Act (redundancy payments)

Section 24 of the National Minimum Wage Act 1998 (c 39) (detriment in relation to national minimum wage)

…

The Employment Tribunals Extension of Jurisdiction (England and Wales) Order 1994 (SI 1994/1623) (breach of employment contract and termination)

The Employment Tribunals Extension of Jurisdiction (Scotland) Order 1994 (SI 1994/1624) (corresponding provision for Scotland)

Regulation 30 of the Working Time Regulations 1998 (SI 1998/1833) (breach of regulations)

Regulation 32 of the Transnational Information and Consultation of Employees Regulations 1999 (SI 1999/3323) (detriment relating to European Works Councils)

[Regulation 28 of the Employment Equality (Sexual Orientation) Regulations 2003 (discrimination in the employment field)]

[Regulation 28 of the Employment Equality (Religion or Belief) Regulations 2003 (discrimination in the employment field)].

[Regulation 45 of the European Public Limited-Liability Company Regulations 2004 (SI 2004/2326) (detriment in employment)

Regulation 33 of the Information and Consultation of Employees Regulations 2004 (SI 2004/3426) (detriment in employment)

Paragraph 8 of the Schedule to the Occupational and Personal Pension Schemes (Consultation by Employers and Miscellaneous Amendment) Regulations 2006 (SI 2006/349) (detriment in employment)]

[Regulation 36 of the Employment Equality (Age) Regulations 2006 (discrimination in the employment field)]

[Regulation 34 of the European Cooperative Society (Involvement of Employees) Regulations 2006 (detriment in relation to involvement in a European Cooperative Society)]

[Regulation 51 of the Companies (Cross-Border Mergers) Regulations 2007 (detriment in relation to special negotiating body or employee participation)]

[1508]

NOTES

Commencement: 1 October 2004.

Entries relating to the Trade Union and Labour Relations (Consolidation) Act 1992 substituted by the Employment Relations Act 2004, s 57(1), Sch 1, para 43, as from 1 October 2004, except in relation to cases where the act or failure to act to which the complaint relates was done before that date, or where the act or failure to act to which the complaint relates is part of a series and the first act or failure in the series was done before that date (see SI 2004/2566, art 6).

In the entry relating to the Disability Discrimination Act 1995, words in square brackets substituted by the Disability Discrimination Act 1995 (Amendment) Regulations 2003, SI 2003/1673, regs 3(2), 31(3), as from 1 October 2004.

Entry relating to the Tax Credits Act 1999 repealed by the Tax Credits Act 2002, s 60, Sch 6, as from 8 April 2003 (subject to savings and transitional provisions in SI 2003/962).

Entry relating to the Employment Equality (Sexual Orientation) Regulations 2003 inserted by the Employment Equality (Sexual Orientation) Regulations 2003, SI 2003/1661, reg 39, Sch 5, para 4(a), as from 1 December 2003.

Entry relating to the Employment Equality (Religion or Belief) Regulations 2003 inserted by the Employment Equality (Religion or Belief) Regulations 2003, SI 2003/1660, reg 39(2), Sch 5, para 4(a), as from 2 December 2003.

Entries relating to the European Public Limited-Liability Company Regulations 2004, the Information and Consultation of Employees Regulations 2004, and the Occupational and Personal Pension Schemes (Consultation by Employers and Miscellaneous Amendment) Regulations 2006 inserted by the Employment Act 2002 (Amendment of Schedules 3, 4 and 5) Order 2007, SI 2007/30, art 2, as from 6 April 2007 (for transitional provisions see art 3 of the 2007 Order at **[3470A]**).

Entry relating to the Employment Equality (Age) Regulations 2006 inserted by the Employment Equality (Age) Regulations 2006, SI 2006/1031, reg 49(1), Sch 8, Pt 1, para 36(1), (2), as from 1 October 2006.

Entry relating to the European Cooperative Society (Involvement of Employees) Regulations 2006 inserted by the European Cooperative Society (Involvement of Employees) Regulations 2006, SI 2006/2059, reg 34(4)(a), as from 18 August 2006.

Entry relating to the Companies (Cross-Border Mergers) Regulations 2007 inserted by the Companies (Cross-Border Mergers) Regulations 2007, SI 2007/2974, reg 63(a), as from 15 December 2007.

Modified as noted to s 29 at **[1491]**.

SCHEDULE 4
TRIBUNAL JURISDICTIONS TO WHICH SECTION 32 APPLIES

Section 32

Section 2 of the Equal Pay Act 1970 (c 41) (equality clauses)

Section 63 of the Sex Discrimination Act 1975 (c 65) (discrimination in the employment field)

Section 54 of the Race Relations Act 1976 (c 74) (discrimination in the employment field)

[Section 145A of the Trade Union and Labour Relations (Consolidation) Act 1992 (inducements relating to union membership or activities)

Section 145B of that Act (inducements relating to collective bargaining)

Section 146 of that Act (detriment in relation to union membership and activities)]

Paragraph 156 of Schedule A1 to that Act (detriment in relation to union recognition rights)

[Section 17A of the Disability Discrimination Act 1995] (c 50) (discrimination in the employment field)

Section 23 of the Employment Rights Act 1996 (c 18) (unauthorised deductions and payments)

Section 48 of that Act (detriment in employment)

Section 111 of that Act (unfair dismissal)

Section 163 of that Act (redundancy payments)

Section 24 of the National Minimum Wage Act 1998 (c 39) (detriment in relation to national minimum wage)

…

Regulation 30 of the Working Time Regulations 1998 (SI 1998/1833) (breach of regulations)

Regulation 32 of the Transnational Information and Consultation of Employees Regulations 1999 (SI 1999/3323) (detriment relating to European Works Councils)

[Regulation 28 of the Employment Equality (Sexual Orientation) Regulations 2003 (discrimination in the employment field)]

[Regulation 28 of the Employment Equality (Religion or Belief) Regulations 2003 (discrimination in the employment field)].

[Regulation 45 of the European Public Limited-Liability Company Regulations 2004 (SI 2004/2326) (detriment in employment)

Regulation 33 of the Information and Consultation of Employees Regulations 2004 (SI 2004/3426) (detriment in employment)

Paragraph 8 of the Schedule to the Occupational and Personal Pension Schemes (Consultation by Employers and Miscellaneous Amendment) Regulations 2006 (SI 2006/349) (detriment in employment)]

[Regulation 36 of the Employment Equality (Age) Regulations 2006 (discrimination in the employment field)]

[Regulation 34 of the European Cooperative Society (Involvement of Employees) Regulations 2006 (detriment in relation to involvement in a European Cooperative Society)]

[Regulation 51 of the Companies (Cross-Border Mergers) Regulations 2007 (detriment in relation to special negotiating body or employee participation)]

[1509]

NOTES

Commencement: 1 October 2004.

Entries relating to the Trade Union and Labour Relations (Consolidation) Act 1992 substituted by the Employment Relations Act 2004, s 57(1), Sch 1, para 43, as from 1 October 2004, except in relation to cases where the act or failure to act to which the complaint relates was done before that date, or where the act or failure to act to which the complaint relates is part of a series and the first act or failure in the series was done before that date (see SI 2004/2566, art 6).

In the entry relating to the Disability Discrimination Act 1995, words in square brackets substituted by the Disability Discrimination Act 1995 (Amendment) Regulations 2003, SI 2003/1673, regs 3(2), 31(3), as from 1 October 2004.

Entry relating to the Tax Credits Act 1999 repealed by the Tax Credits Act 2002, s 60, Sch 6, as from 8 April 2003 (subject to savings and transitional provisions in SI 2003/962).

Entry relating to the Employment Equality (Sexual Orientation) Regulations 2003 inserted by the Employment Equality (Sexual Orientation) Regulations 2003, SI 2003/1661, reg 39, Sch 5, para 4(b), as from 1 December 2003.

Entry relating to the Employment Equality (Religion or Belief) Regulations 2003 inserted by the Employment Equality (Religion or Belief) Regulations 2003, SI 2003/1660, reg 39(2), Sch 5, para 4(b), as from 2 December 2003.

Entries relating to the European Public Limited-Liability Company Regulations 2004, the Information and Consultation of Employees Regulations 2004, and the Occupational and Personal Pension Schemes (Consultation by Employers and Miscellaneous Amendment) Regulations 2006 inserted by the Employment Act 2002 (Amendment of Schedules 3, 4 and 5) Order 2007, SI 2007/30, art 2, as from 6 April 2007 (for transitional provisions see art 3 of the 2007 Order at **[3470A]**).

Entry relating to the Employment Equality (Age) Regulations 2006 inserted by the Employment Equality (Age) Regulations 2006, SI 2006/1031, reg 49(1), Sch 8, Pt 1, para 36(1), (2), as from 1 October 2006.

Entry relating to the European Cooperative Society (Involvement of Employees) Regulations 2006 inserted by the European Cooperative Society (Involvement of Employees) Regulations 2006, SI 2006/2059, reg 34(4), as from 18 August 2006.

Entry relating to the Companies (Cross-Border Mergers) Regulations 2007 inserted by the Companies (Cross-Border Mergers) Regulations 2007, SI 2007/2974, reg 63(b), as from 15 December 2007.

Modified as noted to s 29 at **[1491]**.

SCHEDULE 5
TRIBUNAL JURISDICTIONS TO WHICH SECTION 38 APPLIES

Section 38

Section 2 of the Equal Pay Act 1970 (equality clauses)

Section 63 of the Sex Discrimination Act 1975 (c 65) (discrimination in the employment field)

Section 54 of the Race Relations Act 1976 (c 74) (discrimination in the employment field)

[Section 145A of the Trade Union and Labour Relations (Consolidation) Act 1992 (inducements relating to union membership or activities)

Section 145B of that Act (inducements relating to collective bargaining)

Section 146 of that Act (detriment in relation to union membership and activities)]

Paragraph 156 of Schedule A1 to that Act (detriment in relation to union recognition rights)

[Section 17A of the Disability Discrimination Act 1995] (c 50) (discrimination in the employment field)

Section 23 of the Employment Rights Act 1996 (c 18) (unauthorised deductions and payments)

Section 48 of that Act (detriment in employment)

Section 111 of that Act (unfair dismissal)

Section 163 of that Act (redundancy payments)

Section 24 of the National Minimum Wage Act 1998 (c 39) (detriment in relation to national minimum wage)

…

The Employment Tribunal Extension of Jurisdiction (England and Wales) Order 1994 (SI 1994/1623) (breach of employment contract and termination)

The Employment Tribunal Extension of Jurisdiction (Scotland) Order 1994 (SI 1994/1624) (corresponding provision for Scotland)

Regulation 30 of the Working Time Regulations 1998 (SI 1998/1833) (breach of regulations)

Regulation 32 of the Transnational Information and Consultation of Employees Regulations 1999 (SI 1999/3323) (detriment relating to European Works Councils)

[Regulation 28 of the Employment Equality (Sexual Orientation) Regulations 2003 (discrimination in the employment field)]

[Regulation 28 of the Employment Equality (Religion or Belief) Regulations 2003 (discrimination in the employment field)]

[Regulation 45 of the European Public Limited-Liability Company Regulations 2004 (SI 2004/2326) (detriment in employment)

Regulation 33 of the Information and Consultation of Employees Regulations 2004 (SI 2004/3426) (detriment in employment)

Paragraph 8 of the Schedule to the Occupational and Personal Pension Schemes (Consultation by Employers and Miscellaneous Amendment) Regulations 2006 (SI 2006/349) (detriment in employment)]

[Regulation 36 of the Employment Equality (Age) Regulations 2006 (discrimination in the employment field)]

[Regulation 34 of the European Cooperative Society (Involvement of Employees) Regulations 2006 (detriment in relation to involvement in a European Cooperative Society)]

[Regulation 51 of the Companies (Cross-Border Mergers) Regulations 2007 (detriment in relation to special negotiating body or employee participation)]

[1510]

NOTES

Commencement: 1 October 2004.

Entries relating to the Trade Union and Labour Relations (Consolidation) Act 1992 substituted by the Employment Relations Act 2004, s 57(1), Sch 1, para 43, as from 1 October 2004, except in relation to cases where the act or failure to act to which the complaint relates was done before that date, or where the act or failure to act to which the complaint relates is part of a series and the first act or failure in the series was done before that date (see SI 2004/2566, art 6).

In the entry relating to the Disability Discrimination Act 1995, words in square brackets substituted by the Disability Discrimination Act 1995 (Amendment) Regulations 2003, SI 2003/1673, regs 3(2), 31(3), as from 1 October 2004.

Entry relating to the Tax Credits Act 1999 repealed by the Tax Credits Act 2002, s 60, Sch 6, as from 8 April 2003 (subject to savings and transitional provisions in SI 2003/962).

Entry relating to the Employment Equality (Sexual Orientation) Regulations 2003 inserted by the Employment Equality (Sexual Orientation) Regulations 2003, SI 2003/1661, reg 39, Sch 5, para 4(c), as from 1 December 2003.

Entry relating to the Employment Equality (Religion or Belief) Regulations 2003 inserted by the Employment Equality (Religion or Belief) Regulations 2003, SI 2003/1660, reg 39(2), Sch 5, para 4(c), as from 2 December 2003.

Entries relating to the European Public Limited-Liability Company Regulations 2004, the Information and Consultation of Employees Regulations 2004, and the Occupational and Personal Pension Schemes (Consultation by Employers and Miscellaneous Amendment) Regulations 2006 inserted by the Employment Act 2002 (Amendment of Schedules 3, 4 and 5) Order 2007, SI 2007/30, art 2, as from 6 April 2007 (for transitional provisions see art 3 of the 2007 Order at **[3470A]**).

Entry relating to the Employment Equality (Age) Regulations 2006 inserted by the Employment Equality (Age) Regulations 2006, SI 2006/1031, reg 49(1), Sch 8, Pt 1, para 36(1), (2), as from 1 October 2006.

Entry relating to the European Cooperative Society (Involvement of Employees) Regulations 2006 inserted by the European Cooperative Society (Involvement of Employees) Regulations 2006, SI 2006/2059, reg 34(4), as from 18 August 2006.

Entry relating to the Companies (Cross-Border Mergers) Regulations 2007 inserted by the Companies (Cross-Border Mergers) Regulations 2007, SI 2007/2974, reg 63(c), as from 15 December 2007.

(Sch 6 (Miscellaneous amendments concerning the use of information for, or relating to, employment and training) outside the scope of this work; Schs 7 and 8 contain minor and consequential amendments and repeals respectively and, where relevant to this work, have been incorporated at the appropriate place.)

EDUCATION ACT 2002

(2002 c 32)

An Act to make provision about education, training and childcare

[24 July 2002]

NOTES

Most of this Act covers matters outside the scope of this work, and only those provisions most directly relevant to employment law are printed. For reasons of space, the subject matter of sections not printed is not annotated. The provisions printed here apply only to England and Wales.

PART 3
MAINTAINED SCHOOLS

CHAPTER 1
GOVERNMENT OF MAINTAINED SCHOOLS

35 Staffing of community, voluntary controlled, community special and maintained nursery schools

(1) This section applies to—

(a) community schools,

(b) voluntary controlled schools,

(c) community special schools, and

(d) maintained nursery schools.

(2) Any teacher or other member of staff who is appointed to work under a contract of employment at a school to which this section applies is to be employed by the local education authority.

(3) The teaching staff of any school to which this section applies shall include—

(a) a person appointed as head teacher, or

(b) a person appointed to carry out the functions of the head teacher of the school—

(i) pending the appointment of a head teacher, or

(ii) in the absence of the head teacher.

(4) Regulations may make further provision with respect to the staffing of schools to which this section applies.

(5) Regulations under subsection (4) may, in particular—

(a) make provision with respect to the appointment, discipline, suspension and dismissal of teachers and other staff,

(b) make provision with respect to the appointment of teachers and other staff to work at a school otherwise than under a contract of employment,

(c) make provision with respect to staff employed, or engaged otherwise than under a contract of employment, wholly or partly for the purposes of—

(i) the provision of facilities and services under section 27, or

(ii) any other activities which are not school activities but are carried on the school premises under the management or control of the governing body, and

(d) confer functions on local education authorities, governing bodies and head teachers.

(6) In relation to teachers at a voluntary controlled school who are reserved teachers within the meaning of section 58 of the School Standards and Framework Act 1998 (c 31) (appointment and dismissal of certain teachers at schools with a religious character), regulations under subsection (4) shall have effect subject to the provisions of that section.

(7) If at any time a school to which this section applies does not have a delegated budget by virtue of any suspension under section 17 of, or Schedule 15 to, the School Standards and Framework Act 1998—

(a) regulations under subsection (4) shall not apply, and

(b) the provisions of Part 1 of Schedule 2 shall apply instead.

(8) In discharging any function conferred by regulations under subsection (4), a local education authority or the governing body or head teacher of a maintained school shall have regard to any guidance given from time to time—

(a) in relation to England, by the Secretary of State, or

(b) in relation to Wales, by the National Assembly for Wales.

[1510A]

NOTES

Commencement: 1 April 2003 (sub-ss (4), (5) in relation to England); 1 September 2003 (sub-ss (1)–(3), (6)–(8) in relation to England); 1 April 2006 (in relation to Wales).

Regulations: the School Staffing (England) Regulations 2003, SI 2003/1963 at **[3034B]**; the Staffing of Maintained Schools (Wales) Regulations 2006, SI 2006/873; the School Governance (Federations) (England) Regulations 2007, SI 2007/960.

36 Staffing of foundation, voluntary aided and foundation special schools

(1) This section applies to—

(a) foundation schools,

(b) voluntary aided schools, and

(c) foundation special schools.

(2) Except as provided by regulations under subsection (4), any teacher or other member of staff who is appointed to work under a contract of employment at a school to which this section applies is to be employed by the governing body of the school.

(3) The teaching staff of any school to which this section applies shall include—

(a) a person appointed as head teacher, or

(b) a person appointed to carry out the functions of the head teacher of the school—

(i) pending the appointment of a head teacher, or

(ii) in the absence of the head teacher.

(4) Regulations may make further provision with respect to the staffing of schools to which this section applies.

(5) Regulations under subsection (4) may, in particular—

(a) make provision with respect to the appointment, discipline, suspension and dismissal of teachers and other staff,

(b) make provision with respect to the appointment of teachers and other staff to work at a school otherwise than under a contract of employment,

(c) make provision with respect to staff employed, or engaged otherwise than under a contract of employment, wholly or partly for the purposes of—

(i) the provision of facilities and services under section 27, or

(ii) any other activities which are not school activities but are carried on the school premises under the management or control of the governing body,

(d) enable teachers and other staff to be employed by the local education authority in prescribed cases, and

(e) confer functions on local education authorities, governing bodies and head teachers.

(6) Regulations under subsection (4) shall have effect subject to section 58 of the School Standards and Framework Act 1998 (c 31) (appointment and dismissal of certain teachers at schools with a religious character).

(7) If at any time a school to which this section applies does not have a delegated budget by virtue of any suspension under section 17 of, or Schedule 15 to, the School Standards and Framework Act 1998, regulations under subsection (4) shall have effect subject to the provisions of Part 2 of Schedule 2.

(8) In discharging any function conferred by regulations under subsection (4), a local education authority or the governing body or head teacher of a maintained school shall have regard to any guidance given from time to time—

(a) in relation to England, by the Secretary of State, or

(b) in relation to Wales, by the National Assembly for Wales.

[1510B]

NOTES

Commencement: 1 April 2003 (sub-ss (4), (5) in relation to England); 1 September 2003 (sub-ss (1)–(3), (6)–(8) in relation to England); 1 April 2006 (in relation to Wales).

Regulations: the School Staffing (England) Regulations 2003, SI 2003/1963 at **[3034B]**; the Staffing of Maintained Schools (Wales) Regulations 2006, SI 2006/873; the School Governance (Federations) (England) Regulations 2007, SI 2007/960.

37 Payments in respect of dismissal, etc

(1) It shall be for the governing body of a maintained school to determine—

(a) whether any payment should be made by the local education authority in respect of the dismissal, or for the purpose of securing the resignation, of any member of the staff of the school, and

(b) the amount of any such payment.

(2) Subsection (1) does not, however, apply in relation to a payment which the local education authority are required to make—

(a) by virtue of any contract other than one made in contemplation of the impending dismissal or resignation of the member of staff concerned, or

(b) under any statutory provision.

(3) The local education authority—

(a) shall take such steps as may be required for giving effect to any determination of the governing body under subsection (1), and

(b) shall not make, or agree to make, a payment in relation to which that subsection applies except in accordance with such a determination.

(4) Subject to subsection (7), costs incurred by the local education authority in respect of any premature retirement of a member of the staff of a maintained school shall be met from the school's budget share for one or more *financial years* except in so far as the authority agree with the governing body in writing (whether before or after the retirement occurs) that they shall not be so met.

(5) Subject to subsection (7), costs incurred by the local education authority in respect of the dismissal, or for the purpose of securing the resignation, of any member of the staff of a maintained school shall not be met from the school's budget share for any *financial year* except in so far as the authority have good reason for deducting those costs, or any part of those costs, from that share.

(6) The fact that the authority have a policy precluding dismissal of their employees by reason of redundancy is not to be regarded as a good reason for the purposes of subsection (5); and in this subsection the reference to dismissal by reason of redundancy shall be read in accordance with section 139 of the Employment Rights Act 1996 (c 18).

(7) Where a local education authority incur costs—

(a) in respect of any premature retirement of any member of the staff of a maintained school who is employed for community purposes, or

(b) in respect of the dismissal, or for the purpose of securing the resignation, of any member of the staff of a maintained school who is employed for those purposes,

they shall recover those costs from the governing body except in so far as the authority agree with the governing body in writing (whether before or after the retirement, dismissal or resignation occurs) that they shall not be so recoverable.

(8) Any amount payable by virtue of subsection (7) by the governing body of a maintained school to the local education authority shall not be met by the governing body out of the school's budget share for any *financial year*.

(9) Where a person is employed partly for community purposes and partly for other purposes, any payment or costs in respect of that person is to be apportioned between the two purposes; and the preceding provisions of this section shall apply separately to each part of the payment or costs.

(10) Regulations may make provision with respect to the recovery from governing bodies of amounts payable by virtue of subsection (7).

(11) Subsections (1) to (6) do not apply to a maintained school at any time when the school does not have a delegated budget by virtue of any suspension under section 17 of, or Schedule 15 to, the School Standards and Framework Act 1998 (c 31).

(12) In this section "community purposes" means the purposes of the provision of facilities or services under section 27.

[1510C]

NOTES

Commencement: 1 October 2002 (in relation to England); 1 April 2006 (in relation to Wales).

Sub-s (4): for the words in italics there are substituted the words "funding periods" by the Education Act 2005, s 117, Sch 18, para 14(1), (2), as from 1 November 2005 (in relation to England), and as from a day to be appointed (in relation to Wales).

Sub-ss (5), (8): for the words in italics there are substituted the words "funding period" by the Education Act 2005, s 117, Sch 18, para 14(1), (3), as from 1 November 2005 (in relation to England), and as from a day to be appointed (in relation to Wales).

Sub-s (12): substituted by the Education Act 2005, s 117, Sch 18, para 14(1), (4), as from 1 November 2005 (in relation to England), and as from a day to be appointed (in relation to Wales), as follows—

"(12) In this section—

"community purposes" means the purposes of the provision of facilities or services under section 27;

"funding period" has the meaning given by section 45(1B) of the School Standards and Framework Act 1998.".

PART 11
MISCELLANEOUS AND GENERAL

General

216 Commencement

(1) The following provisions shall come into force on the day on which this Act is passed

(*outside the scope of this work*),

this section and section 217.

(2), (3) (*Outside the scope of this work.*)

(4) Subject to subsections (1) to (3), this Act shall come into force—

(a) except in relation to Wales, in accordance with provision made by the Secretary of State by order, and

(b) in relation to Wales, in accordance with provision made by the National Assembly for Wales by order.

(5) An order under this section may—

(a) make provision generally or for specified purposes only,

(b) make different provision for different purposes, and

(c) contain such transitional provisions and savings as the person making the order thinks fit.

[1510D]

NOTES

Orders: Commencement orders made under this section are outside the scope of this work.

217 Short title and extent

(1) This Act may be cited as the Education Act 2002.

(2) This Act shall be included in the list of Education Acts set out in section 578 of the Education Act 1996 (c 56).

(3) Any amendment or repeal in this Act has the same extent as the provision amended or repealed.

(4) Except as provided by subsection (3), this Act extends to England and Wales only.

[1510E]

INCOME TAX (EARNINGS AND PENSIONS) ACT 2003

(2003 c 1)

ARRANGEMENT OF SECTIONS

PART 1
OVERVIEW

PART 2
EMPLOYMENT INCOME: CHARGE TO TAX

CHAPTER 1
INTRODUCTION

CHAPTER 8
APPLICATION OF PROVISIONS TO WORKERS UNDER ARRANGEMENTS MADE BY INTERMEDIARIES

Application of this Chapter

The deemed employment payment

Supplementary provisions

CHAPTER 9
MANAGED SERVICE COMPANIES

Application of this Chapter

The deemed employment payment

Supplementary provisions

PART 3
EMPLOYMENT INCOME: EARNINGS AND BENEFITS ETC TREATED AS EARNINGS

CHAPTER 1
EARNINGS

CHAPTER 2
TAXABLE BENEFITS: THE BENEFITS CODE

The benefits code

CHAPTER 3
TAXABLE BENEFITS: EXPENSES PAYMENTS

CHAPTER 5
TAXABLE BENEFITS: LIVING ACCOMMODATION

Living accommodation

Exceptions

CHAPTER 6
TAXABLE BENEFITS: CARS, VANS AND RELATED BENEFITS

General

CHAPTER 10
TAXABLE BENEFITS: RESIDUAL LIABILITY TO CHARGE

Introduction

General rule for deduction of employee's expenses

Travel expenses

PART 6
EMPLOYMENT INCOME: INCOME WHICH IS NOT EARNINGS OR SHARE-RELATED

CHAPTER 3
PAYMENTS AND BENEFITS ON TERMINATION OF EMPLOYMENT ETC

Preliminary

Payments and benefits treated as employment income

Exceptions and reductions

General and supplementary provisions

PART 11
PAY AS YOU EARN

CHAPTER 2
PAYE: GENERAL

CHAPTER 5
PAYE SETTLEMENT AGREEMENTS

PART 13
SUPPLEMENTARY PROVISIONS

Amendments, repeals, citation etc

An Act to restate, with minor changes, certain enactments relating to income tax on employment income, pension income and social security income; and for connected purposes

[6 March 2003]

NOTES

This substantial Act is essentially a re-enactment of the provisions of the Income and Corporation Taxes Act 1988 (referred to in this Act as ICTA) and later legislation, so far as relating to the taxation of earnings and pensions. Most of this Act covers matters outside the scope of this work, and only those provisions most directly relevant to employment law are printed. For reasons of space, the subject matter of sections not printed is not annotated. The provisions printed here, unless noted otherwise, came into force on 6 April 2003 and have effect for the purposes of income tax for the year 2003–04 and subsequent years of assessment, and for the purposes of corporation tax for accounting periods ending after 5 April 2003. This Act is reproduced as amended by the Income Tax Act 2007, as from 6 April 2007, with effect for the purposes of income tax for the year 2007–08 and subsequent tax years, and for the purposes of corporation tax for accounting periods ending after 5 April 2007 (see s 1034(1)). For transitional provisions and savings see s 1034(2) of, and Sch 2 to, the 2007 Act.

PART 1
OVERVIEW

1 Overview of contents of this Act

(1) This Act imposes charges to income tax on—

(a) employment income (see Parts 2 to 7),

(b) pension income (see Part 9), and

(c) social security income (see Part 10).

(2) …

(3) This Act also—

(a) confers certain reliefs in respect of liabilities of former employees (see Part 8),

(b) provides for the assessment, collection and recovery of income tax in respect of employment, pension or social security income that is PAYE income (see Part 11), and

(c) allows deductions to be made from such income in respect of payroll giving (see Part 12).

[1511]

NOTES

Sub-s (2): repealed by the Income Tax Act 2007, ss 1027, 1031, Sch 1, Pt 2, paras 425, 426, Sch 3, Pt 1, as from 6 April 2007 (for effect and transitional provisions see the introductory note to this Act).

PART 2
EMPLOYMENT INCOME: CHARGE TO TAX

CHAPTER 1
INTRODUCTION

3 Structure of employment income Parts

(1) The structure of the employment income Parts is as follows—

this Part imposes the charge to tax on employment income, and sets out—

(a) how the amount charged to tax for a tax year is to be calculated, and

(b) who is liable for the tax charged;

Part 3 sets out what are earnings and provides for amounts to be treated as earnings;

Part 4 deals with exemptions from the charge to tax under this Part (and, in some cases, from other charges to tax);

Part 5 deals with deductions from taxable earnings;

Part 6 deals with employment income other than earnings or share-related income; and

Part 7 deals with [income and exemptions relating to securities and securities options acquired in connection with an employment].

(2) In this Act "the employment income Parts" means this Part and Parts 3 to 7.

[1512]

NOTES

Sub-s (1): words in square brackets substituted by the Finance Act 2003, s 140, Sch 22, paras 1, 16(1), as from 16 April 2003.

4 "Employment" for the purposes of the employment income Parts

(1) In the employment income Parts "employment" includes in particular—

(a) any employment under a contract of service,

(b) any employment under a contract of apprenticeship, and

(c) any employment in the service of the Crown.

(2) In those Parts "employed", "employee" and "employer" have corresponding meanings.

[1513]

5 Application to offices and office-holders

(1) The provisions of the employment income Parts that are expressed to apply to employments apply equally to offices, unless otherwise indicated.

(2) In those provisions as they apply to an office—

(a) references to being employed are to being the holder of the office;

(b) "employee" means the office-holder;

(c) "employer" means the person under whom the office-holder holds office.

(3) In the employment income Parts "office" includes in particular any position which has an existence independent of the person who holds it and may be filled by successive holders.

[1514]

CHAPTER 8
APPLICATION OF PROVISIONS TO WORKERS UNDER ARRANGEMENTS MADE BY INTERMEDIARIES

Application of this Chapter

49 Engagements to which this Chapter applies

(1) This Chapter applies where—

(a) an individual ("the worker") personally performs, or is under an obligation personally to perform, services [for another person] ("the client"),

(b) the services are provided not under a contract directly between the client and the worker but under arrangements involving a third party ("the intermediary"), and

(c) the circumstances are such that, if the services were provided under a contract directly between the client and the worker, the worker would be regarded for income tax purposes as an employee of the client.

(2) …

(3) The reference in subsection (1)(b) to a "third party" includes a partnership or unincorporated body of which the worker is a member.

(4) The circumstances referred to in subsection (1)(c) include the terms on which the services are provided, having regard to the terms of the contracts forming part of the arrangements under which the services are provided.

(5) In this Chapter "engagement to which this Chapter applies" means any such provision of services as is mentioned in subsection (1).

[1515]

NOTES

Sub-s (1): words in square brackets in para (a) substituted by the Finance Act 2003, s 136(1), (2), in relation to services performed or due to be performed on or after 10 April 2003.

Sub-s (2): repealed by the Finance Act 2003, ss 216, 136(1), (3)(a), Sch 43, Pt 3(1), in relation to services performed or due to be performed on or after 10 April 2003.

50 Worker treated as receiving earnings from employment

(1) If, in the case of an engagement to which this Chapter applies, in any tax year—

(a) the conditions specified in section 51, 52 or 53 are met in relation to the intermediary, and

(b) the worker, or an associate of the worker—

(i) receives from the intermediary, directly or indirectly, a payment or benefit that is not employment income, or

(ii) has rights which entitle, or which in any circumstances would entitle, the worker or associate to receive from the intermediary, directly or indirectly, any such payment or benefit,

the intermediary is treated as making to the worker, and the worker is treated as receiving, in that year a payment which is to be treated as earnings from an employment ("the deemed employment payment").

(2) A single payment is treated as made in respect of all engagements in relation to which the intermediary is treated as making a payment to the worker in the tax year.

(3) The deemed employment payment is treated as made at the end of the tax year, unless section 57 applies (earlier date of deemed payment in certain cases).

(4) In this Chapter "the relevant engagements", in relation to a deemed employment payment, means the engagements mentioned in subsection (2).

[1516]

51 Conditions of liability where intermediary is a company

(1) Where the intermediary is a company the conditions are that the intermediary is not an associated company of the client that falls within subsection (2) and either—

(a) the worker has a material interest in the intermediary, or

(b) the payment or benefit mentioned in section 50(1)(b)—

(i) is received or receivable by the worker directly from the intermediary, and

(ii) can reasonably be taken to represent remuneration for services provided by the worker to the client.

(2) An associated company of the client falls within this subsection if it is such a company by reason of the intermediary and the client being under the control—

(a) of the worker, or

(b) of the worker and other persons.

(3) A worker is treated as having a material interest in a company if—

(a) the worker, alone or with one or more associates of the worker, or

(b) an associate of the worker, with or without other such associates,

has a material interest in the company.

(4) For this purpose a material interest means—

(a) beneficial ownership of, or the ability to control, directly or through the medium of other companies or by any other indirect means, more than 5% of the ordinary share capital of the company; or

(b) possession of, or entitlement to acquire, rights entitling the holder to receive more than 5% of any distributions that may be made by the company; or

(c) where the company is a close company, possession of, or entitlement to acquire, rights that would in the event of the winding up of the company, or in any other circumstances, entitle the holder to receive more than 5% of the assets that would then be available for distribution among the participators.

(5) In subsection (4)(c) "participator" has the meaning given by section 417(1) of ICTA.

[1517]

52 Conditions of liability where intermediary is a partnership

(1) Where the intermediary is a partnership the conditions are as follows.

(2) In relation to any payment or benefit received or receivable by the worker as a member of the partnership the conditions are—

(a) that the worker, alone or with one or more relatives, is entitled to 60% or more of the profits of the partnership; or

(b) that most of the profits of the partnership concerned derive from the provision of services under engagements to which this Chapter applies—

(i) to a single client, or

(ii) to a single client together with associates of that client; or

(c) that under the profit sharing arrangements the income of any of the partners is based on the amount of income generated by that partner by the provision of services under engagements to which this Chapter applies.

In paragraph (a) "relative" means [spouse or civil partner], parent or child or remoter relation in the direct line, or brother or sister.

(3) In relation to any payment or benefit received or receivable by the worker otherwise than as a member of the partnership, the conditions are that the payment or benefit—

(a) is received or receivable by the worker directly from the intermediary, and

(b) can reasonably be taken to represent remuneration for services provided by the worker to the client.

[1518]

NOTES

Sub-s (2): words in square brackets substituted by the Tax and Civil Partnership Regulations 2005, SI 2005/3229, regs 137, 138, as from 5 December 2005.

53 Conditions of liability where intermediary is an individual

Where the intermediary is an individual the conditions are that the payment or benefit—

(a) is received or receivable by the worker directly from the intermediary, and

(b) can reasonably be taken to represent remuneration for services provided by the worker to the client.

[1519]

The deemed employment payment

54 Calculation of deemed employment payment

(1) The amount of the deemed employment payment for a tax year ("the year") is the amount resulting from the following steps—

Step 1

Find (applying section 55) the total amount of all payments and benefits received by the intermediary in the year in respect of the relevant engagements, and reduce that amount by 5%.

Step 2

Add (applying that section) the amount of any payments and benefits received by the worker in the year in respect of the relevant engagements, otherwise than from the intermediary, that—

(a) are not chargeable to income tax as employment income, and

(b) would be so chargeable if the worker were employed by the client.

Step 3

Deduct (applying Chapters 1 to 5 of Part 5) the amount of any expenses met in the year by the intermediary that would have been deductible from the taxable earnings from the employment if—

(a) the worker had been employed by the client, and

(b) the expenses had been met by the worker out of those earnings.

If the result at this or any later point is nil or a negative amount, there is no deemed employment payment.

Step 4

Deduct the amount of any capital allowances in respect of expenditure incurred by the intermediary that could have been deducted from employment income under section 262 of CAA 2001 (employments and offices) if the worker had been employed by the client and had incurred the expenditure.

Step 5

Deduct any contributions made in the year for the benefit of the worker by the intermediary to a [registered pension scheme] that if made by an employer for the benefit of an employee would not be chargeable to income tax as income of the employee.

This does not apply to excess contributions made and later repaid.

Step 6

Deduct the amount of any employer's national insurance contributions paid by the intermediary for the year in respect of the worker.

Step 7

Deduct the amount of any payments and benefits received in the year by the worker from the intermediary—

(a) in respect of which the worker is chargeable to income tax as employment income, and

(b) which do not represent items in respect of which a deduction was made under step 3.

Step 8

Assume that the result of step 7 represents an amount together with employer's national insurance contributions on it, and deduct what (on that assumption) would be the amount of those contributions.

The result is the deemed employment payment.

(2) If [section 61 of the Finance Act 2004] applies (sub-contractors in the construction industry: payments to be made under deduction), the intermediary is treated for the purposes of step 1 of subsection (1) as receiving the amount that would have been received had no deduction been made under that section.

(3) In step 3 of subsection (1), the reference to expenses met by the intermediary includes—

(a) expenses met by the worker and reimbursed by the intermediary, and

(b) where the intermediary is a partnership and the worker is a member of the partnership, expenses met by the worker for and on behalf of the partnership.

(4) In step 3 of subsection (1), the expenses deductible include the amount of any mileage allowance relief for the year which the worker would have been entitled to in respect of the use of a vehicle falling within subsection (5) if—

(a) the worker had been employed by the client, and

(b) the vehicle had not been a company vehicle (within the meaning of Chapter 2 of Part 4).

(5) A vehicle falls within this subsection if—

(a) it is provided by the intermediary for the worker, or

(b) where the intermediary is a partnership and the worker is a member of the partnership, it is provided by the worker for the purposes of the business of the partnership.

(6) Where, on the assumptions mentioned in paragraphs (a) and (b) of step 3 of subsection (1), the deductibility of the expenses is determined under sections 337 to 342 (travel expenses), the duties performed under the relevant engagements are treated as duties of a continuous employment with the intermediary.

(7) In step 7 of subsection (1), the amounts deductible include any payments received in the year from the intermediary that—

(a) are exempt from income tax by virtue of section 229 or 233 (mileage allowance payments and passenger payments), and

(b) do not represent items in respect of which a deduction was made under step 3.

(8) For the purposes of subsection (1) any necessary apportionment is to be made on a just and reasonable basis of amounts received by the intermediary that are referable—

(a) to the services of more than one worker, or

(b) partly to the services of the worker and partly to other matters.

[1520]

NOTES

Sub-s (1): words in square brackets in step 5 substituted by the Finance Act 2004, s 281(1), Sch 35, paras 54, 56, as from 6 April 2006 (for transitional provisions, see Sch 36 to the 2004 Act).

Sub-s (2): words in square brackets substituted by the Finance Act 2004, s 76, Sch 12, para 17, in relation to payments made on or after 6 April 2007 under contracts relating to construction operations (see SI 2006/3240 and s 77 of the 2004 Act). The previous reference was to "section 559 of ICTA".

See further, the Pension Protection Fund (Tax) Regulations 2006, SI 2006/575, reg 39 which provides as follows—

"39. Step 5 of section 54(1) of ITEPA 2003 (calculation of deemed employment payment under arrangements made by intermediaries) applies in relation to a payment, by the intermediary, of any sum in respect of any of the Pensions Act levies in the same way as it applies in relation to any contributions that may be deducted under that step.".

55 Application of rules relating to earnings from employment

(1) The following provisions apply in relation to the calculation of the deemed employment payment.

(2) A "payment or benefit" means anything that, if received by an employee for performing the duties of an employment, would be earnings from the employment.

(3) The amount of a payment or benefit is taken to be—

(a) in the case of a payment or cash benefit, the amount received, and

(b) in the case of a non-cash benefit, the cash equivalent of the benefit.

(4) The cash equivalent of a non-cash benefit is taken to be—

(a) the amount that would be earnings if the benefit were earnings from an employment, or

(b) in the case of living accommodation, whichever is the greater of that amount and the cash equivalent determined in accordance with section 398(2).

(5) A payment or benefit is treated as received—

(a) in the case of a payment or cash benefit, when payment is made of or on account of the payment or benefit;

(b) in the case of a non-cash benefit that is calculated by reference to a period within the tax year, at the end of that period;

(c) in the case of a non-cash benefit that is not so calculated, when it would have been treated as received for the purposes of Chapter 4 or 5 of this Part (see section 19 or 32) if—

(i) the worker had been an employee, and

(ii) the benefit had been provided by reason of the employment.

[1521]

56 Application of Income Tax Acts in relation to deemed employment

(1) The Income Tax Acts (in particular, the PAYE provisions) apply in relation to the deemed employment payment as follows.

(2) They apply as if—
(a) the worker were employed by the intermediary, and
(b) the relevant engagements were undertaken by the worker in the course of performing the duties of that employment.

(3) The deemed employment payment is treated in particular—
(a) as taxable earnings from the employment for the purpose of securing that any deductions under Chapters 2 to 6 of Part 5 do not exceed the deemed employment payment; and
(b) as taxable earnings from the employment for the purposes of section 232.

(4) The worker is not chargeable to tax in respect of the deemed employment payment if, or to the extent that, by reason of any combination of the factors mentioned in subsection (5), the worker would not be chargeable to tax if—
(a) the client employed the worker,
(b) the worker performed the services in the course of that employment, and
(c) the deemed employment payment were a payment by the client of earnings from that employment.

(5) The factors are—
(a) the worker being resident, ordinarily resident or domiciled outside the United Kingdom,
(b) the client being resident or ordinarily resident outside the United Kingdom, and
(c) the services in question being provided outside the United Kingdom.

(6) Where the intermediary is a partnership or unincorporated association, the deemed employment payment is treated as received by the worker in the worker's personal capacity and not as income of the partnership or association.

(7) Where—
(a) the worker is resident in the United Kingdom, [and]
(b) the services in question are provided in the United Kingdom, …
(c) …

the intermediary is treated as having a place of business in the United Kingdom, whether or not it in fact does so.

(8) …

[1522]

NOTES

Sub-s (7): word in square brackets in para (a) inserted, and para (c) and the word immediately preceding it repealed, by the Finance Act 2003, ss 136(1), (3)(b)(ii), 216, Sch 43, Pt 3(1), in relation to services performed or due to be performed on or after 10 April 2003.

Sub-s (8): repealed by the Finance Act 2004, s 326, Sch 42, Pt 3, as from 6 April 2006. Note that this subsection was also amended by s 281(1) of, and Sch 35, paras 54, 57 to, the 2004 Act as from the same date. For transitional provisions in relation to this repeal, see Sch 36 to the 2004 Act.

Supplementary provisions

57 Earlier date of deemed employment payment in certain cases

(1) If in any tax year—
(a) a deemed employment payment is treated as made, and
(b) before the date on which the payment would be treated as made under section 50(2) any relevant event (as defined below) occurs in relation to the intermediary,

the deemed employment payment for that year is treated as having been made immediately before that event or, if there is more than one, immediately before the first of them.

(2) Where the intermediary is a company the following are relevant events—
(a) the company ceasing to trade;
(b) where the worker is a member of the company, the worker ceasing to be such a member;
(c) where the worker holds an office with the company, the worker ceasing to hold such an office;
(d) where the worker is employed by the company, the worker ceasing to be so employed.

(3) Where the intermediary is a partnership the following are relevant events—
(a) the dissolution of the partnership or the partnership ceasing to trade or a partner ceasing to act as such;
(b) where the worker is employed by the partnership, the worker ceasing to be so employed.

(4) Where the intermediary is an individual and the worker is employed by the intermediary, it is a relevant event if the worker ceases to be so employed.

(5) The fact that the deemed employment payment is treated as made before the end of the tax year does not affect what receipts and other matters are taken into account in calculating its amount.

[1523]

58 Relief in case of distributions by intermediary

(1) A claim for relief may be made under this section where the intermediary—
(a) is a company,
(b) is treated as making a deemed employment payment in any tax year, and
(c) either in that tax year (whether before or after that payment is treated as made), or in a subsequent tax year, makes a distribution (a "relevant distribution").

(2) A claim for relief under this section must be made—
(a) by the intermediary by notice to [an officer of Revenue and Customs], and
(b) within 5 years after the 31st January following the tax year in which the distribution is made.

(3) If on a claim being made [an officer of Revenue and Customs] [is] satisfied that relief should be given in order to avoid a double charge to tax, [the officer] must direct the giving of such relief by way of amending any assessment, by discharge or repayment of tax, or otherwise, as appears to [the officer] appropriate.

(4) Relief under this section is given by setting the amount of the deemed employment payment against the relevant distribution so as to reduce the distribution.

(5) In the case of more than one relevant distribution, [an officer of Revenue and Customs] must exercise the power conferred by this section so as to secure that so far as practicable relief is given by setting the amount of a deemed employment payment—
(a) against relevant distributions of the same tax year before those of other years,
(b) against relevant distributions received by the worker before those received by another person, and
(c) against relevant distributions of earlier years before those of later years.

(6) Where the amount of a relevant distribution is reduced under this section, the amount of any associated tax credit is reduced accordingly.

[1524]

NOTES

Sub-ss (2), (3), (5):words in square brackets substituted by the Commissioners for Revenue and Customs Act 2005, s 50(6), Sch 4, paras 101, 102(1), 103(1)(a), 105, as from 18 April 2005.

---

59 Provisions applicable to multiple intermediaries

(1) The provisions of this section apply where in the case of an engagement to which this Chapter applies the arrangements involve more than one relevant intermediary.

(2) All relevant intermediaries in relation to the engagement are jointly and severally liable, subject to subsection (3), to account for any amount required under the PAYE provisions to be deducted from a deemed employment payment treated as made by any of them—
(a) in respect of that engagement, or
(b) in respect of that engagement together with other engagements.

(3) An intermediary is not so liable if it has not received any payment or benefit in respect of that engagement or any such other engagement as is mentioned in subsection (2)(b).

(4) Subsection (5) applies where a payment or benefit has been made or provided, directly or indirectly, from one relevant intermediary to another in respect of the engagement.

(5) In that case, the amount taken into account in relation to any intermediary in step 1 or step 2 of section 54(1) is reduced to such extent as is necessary to avoid double-counting having regard to the amount so taken into account in relation to any other intermediary.

(6) Except as provided by subsections (2) to (5), the provisions of this Chapter apply separately in relation to each relevant intermediary.

(7) In this section "relevant intermediary" means an intermediary in relation to which the conditions specified in section 51, 52 or 53 are met.

[1525]

60 Meaning of "associate"

(1) In this Chapter "associate"—

(a) in relation to an individual, has the meaning given by section 417(3) and (4) of ICTA, subject to the following provisions of this section;

(b) in relation to a company, means a person connected with the company; and

(c) in relation to a partnership, means any associate of a member of the partnership.

(2) Where an individual has an interest in shares or obligations of the company as a beneficiary of an employee benefit trust, the trustees are not regarded as associates of the individual by reason only of that interest except in the following circumstances.

(3) The exception is where—

(a) the individual, either alone or with any one or more associates of the individual, or

(b) any associate of the individual, with or without other such associates,

has at any time on or after 14th March 1989 been the beneficial owner of, or able (directly or through the medium of other companies or by any other indirect means) to control more than 5% of the ordinary share capital of the company.

(4) In subsection (3) "associate" does not include the trustees of an employee benefit trust as a result only of the individual's having an interest in shares or obligations of the trust.

(5) Sections 549 to 554 (attribution of interests in companies to beneficiaries of employee benefit trusts) apply for the purposes of subsection (3) as they apply for the purposes of the provisions listed in section 549(2).

(6) In this section "employee benefit trust" has the meaning given by sections 550 and 551.

[1526]

61 Interpretation

(1) In this Chapter—

"associate" has the meaning given by section 60;

"associated company" has the meaning given by section 416 of ICTA;

"business" means any trade, profession or vocation and includes a [UK property business or] Schedule A business;

"company" means a body corporate or unincorporated association, and does not include a partnership;

"employer's national insurance contributions" means secondary Class 1 or Class 1A national insurance contributions;

"engagement to which this Chapter applies" has the meaning given by section 49(5);

"national insurance contributions" means contributions under Part 1 of SSCBA 1992 or Part 1 of SSCB(NI)A 1992;

"PAYE provisions" means the provisions of Part 11 or PAYE regulations;

"the relevant engagements" has the meaning given by section 50(4).

(2) References in this Chapter to payments or benefits received or receivable from a partnership or unincorporated association include payments or benefits to which a person is or may be entitled in the person's capacity as a member of the partnership or association.

(3) For the purposes of this Chapter—

(a) anything done by or in relation to an associate of an intermediary is treated as done by or in relation to the intermediary, and

(b) a payment or other benefit provided to a member of an individual's family or household is treated as provided to the individual.

(4) For the purposes of this Chapter a man and a woman living together as husband and wife are treated as if they were married to each other.

[(5) For the purposes of this Chapter two people of the same sex living together as if they were civil partners of each other are treated as if they were civil partners of each other.

For the purposes of this Chapter, two people of the same sex are to be regarded as living together as if they were civil partners if, but only if, they would be regarded as living together as husband and wife were they instead two people of the opposite sex.]

[1527]

NOTES

Sub-s (1): in definition "business" words in square brackets inserted the Income Tax (Trading and Other Income) Act 2005, s 882, Sch 1, Pt 2, paras 584, 586, for the purposes of income tax for the year 2005–06 and subsequent tax years, and for the purposes of corporation tax for accounting periods ending after 5 April 2005.

Sub-s (5): added by the Tax and Civil Partnership Regulations 2005, SI 2005/3229, regs 137, 139, as from 5 December 2005.

'SSCBA 1992' and 'SSCB(NI)A 1992': the Social Security Contributions and Benefits Act 1992 and the Social Security Contributions and Benefits (Northern Ireland) Act 1992, respectively.

[CHAPTER 9
MANAGED SERVICE COMPANIES

Application of this Chapter

61A Scope of this Chapter

(1) This Chapter has effect with respect to the provision of services by a managed service company.

(2) Nothing in this Chapter—
- (a) affects the operation of Chapter 7 of this Part (agency workers), or
- (b) applies to payments or transfers to which section 966(3) or (4) of ITA 2007 applies (visiting performers: duty to deduct and account for sums representing income tax).]

[1527A]

NOTES

Commencement: 6 April 2007.

Chapter 9 (ss 61A–61J) was inserted by the Finance Act 2007, s 25(1), Sch 3, Pt 1, paras 1, 4, with retrospective effect from 6 April 2007.

[61B Meaning of "managed service company"

(1) A company is a "managed service company" if—
- (a) its business consists wholly or mainly of providing (directly or indirectly) the services of an individual to other persons,
- (b) payments are made (directly or indirectly) to the individual (or associates of the individual) of an amount equal to the greater part or all of the consideration for the provision of the services,
- (c) the way in which those payments are made would result in the individual (or associates) receiving payments of an amount (net of tax and national insurance) exceeding that which would be received (net of tax and national insurance) if every payment in respect of the services were employment income of the individual, and
- (d) a person who carries on a business of promoting or facilitating the use of companies to provide the services of individuals ("an MSC provider") is involved with the company.

(2) An MSC provider is "involved with the company" if the MSC provider or an associate of the MSC provider—
- (a) benefits financially on an ongoing basis from the provision of the services of the individual,
- (b) influences or controls the provision of those services,
- (c) influences or controls the way in which payments to the individual (or associates of the individual) are made,
- (d) influences or controls the company's finances or any of its activities, or

(e) gives or promotes an undertaking to make good any tax loss.

(3) A person does not fall within subsection (1)(d) merely by virtue of providing legal or accountancy services in a professional capacity.

(4) A person does not fall within subsection (1)(d) merely by virtue of carrying on a business consisting only of placing individuals with persons who wish to obtain their services (including by contracting with companies which provide their services).

(5) Subsection (4) does not apply if the person or an associate of the person—

(a) does anything within subsection (2)(c) or (e), or

(b) does anything within subsection (2)(d) other than influencing the company's finances or activities by doing anything within subsection (2)(b).]

[1527B]

NOTES

Commencement: 6 April 2007.

Inserted as noted to s 61A at **[1527A]**.

[61C Section 61B: supplementary

(1) The Treasury may by order provide that persons of a prescribed description do not fall within section 61B(1)(d).

(2) An order under subsection (1) may be made so as to have effect in relation to the whole of the tax year in which it is made.

(3) In section 61B and this section, "company" means a body corporate or partnership.

(4) References in section 61B to an associate of a person ("P") include a person who, for the purpose of securing that the individual's services are provided by a company, acts in concert with P (or with P and other persons).

(5) In section 61B(2)(e), "undertaking to make good any tax loss" means an undertaking (in any terms) to make good (in whole or in part, and by any means) any cost to the individual or an associate of the individual resulting from a relevant provision, or a particular kind of relevant provision, applying in relation to payments made to the individual or associate.

(6) In subsection (5) "relevant provision" means—

(a) a provision of the Tax Acts,

(b) an enactment relating to national insurance, or

(c) a provision of subordinate legislation made under any such provision or enactment.]

[1527C]

NOTES

Commencement: 6 April 2007.

Inserted as noted to s 61A at **[1527A]**.

[The deemed employment payment

61D Worker treated as receiving earnings from employment

(1) This section applies if—

(a) the services of an individual ("the worker") are provided (directly or indirectly) by a managed service company ("the MSC"),

(b) the worker, or an associate of the worker, receives (from any person) a payment or benefit which can reasonably be taken to be in respect of the services, and

(c) the payment or benefit is not earnings (within Chapter 1 of Part 3) received by the worker directly from the MSC.

(2) The MSC is treated as making to the worker, and the worker is treated as receiving, a payment which is to be treated as earnings from an employment ("the deemed employment payment").

(3) The deemed employment payment is treated as made at the time the payment or benefit mentioned in subsection (1)(b) is received.

(4) In this Chapter—
"the worker" has the meaning given by subsection (1),
"the relevant services" means the services mentioned in that subsection, and
"the client" means the person to whom the relevant services are provided.

(5) Section 61F supplements this section.]

[1527D]

NOTES

Commencement: 6 April 2007.
Inserted as noted to s 61A at **[1527A]**.

[61E Calculation of deemed employment payment

(1) The amount of the deemed employment payment is the amount resulting from the following steps—

Step 1 Find (applying section 61F) the amount of the payment or benefit mentioned in section 61D(1)(b).

Step 2 Deduct (applying Chapters 1 to 5 of Part 5) the amount of any expenses met by the worker that would have been deductible from the taxable earnings from the employment if—

(a) the worker had been employed by the client to provide the relevant services, and
(b) the expenses had been met by the worker out of those earnings.

If the result at this point is nil or a negative amount, there is no deemed employment payment.

Step 3 Assume that the result of step 2 represents an amount together with employer's national insurance contributions on it, and deduct what (on that assumption) would be the amount of those contributions.

The result is the deemed employment payment.

(2) In step 2 of subsection (1), the reference to expenses met by the worker includes, where the MSC is a partnership and the worker is a member of the partnership, expenses met by the worker for and on behalf of the partnership.

(3) In step 2 of subsection (1), the expenses deductible include the amount of any mileage allowance relief which the worker would have been entitled to in respect of the use of a vehicle falling within subsection (4) if—

(a) the worker had been employed by the client to provide the relevant services, and
(b) the vehicle had not been a company vehicle (within the meaning of Chapter 2 of Part 4).

(4) A vehicle falls within this subsection if—

(a) it is provided by the MSC for the worker, or
(b) where the MSC is a partnership and the worker is a member of the partnership, it is provided by the worker for the purposes of the business of the partnership.

(5) For the purposes of subsection (1) any necessary apportionment of payments or benefits that are referable partly to the provision of the relevant services and partly to other matters is to be made on a just and reasonable basis.]

[1527E]

NOTES

Commencement: 6 April 2007.
Inserted as noted to s 61A at **[1527A]**.

[61F Sections 61D and 61E: application of rules relating to earnings from employment

(1) The following provisions apply for the purposes of sections 61D and 61E.

(2) A "payment or benefit" means anything that, if received by an employee for performing the duties of an employment, would be general earnings from the employment.

(3) The amount of a payment or benefit is taken to be—

(a) in the case of a payment or cash benefit, the amount received, and
(b) in the case of a non-cash benefit, the cash equivalent of the benefit.

(4) The cash equivalent of a non-cash benefit is taken to be—
(a) the amount that would be general earnings if the benefit were general earnings from an employment, or
(b) in the case of living accommodation, whichever is the greater of that amount and the cash equivalent determined in accordance with section 398(2).

(5) A payment or benefit is treated as received—
(a) in the case of a payment or cash benefit, when payment is made of or on account of the payment or benefit;
(b) in the case of a non-cash benefit, when it would have been treated as received for the purposes of Chapter 4 or 5 of this Part (see section 19 or 32) if—
(i) the worker had been an employee, and
(ii) the benefit had been provided by reason of the employment.]

[1527F]

NOTES

Commencement: 6 April 2007.
Inserted as noted to s 61A at **[1527A]**.

[61G Application of Income Tax Acts in relation to deemed employment

(1) The Income Tax Acts (in particular, the PAYE provisions) apply in relation to the deemed employment payment as follows.

(2) They apply as if—
(a) the worker were employed by the MSC to provide the relevant services, and
(b) the deemed employment payment were a payment by the MSC of earnings from that employment;

but this is subject to subsection (3).

(3) No deduction under Part 5 (deductions allowed from employment income) or section 232 (mileage allowance relief) may be made from the deemed employment payment.

(4) The worker is not chargeable to tax in respect of the deemed employment payment if, or to the extent that, by reason of any combination of the factors mentioned in subsection (5), the worker would not be chargeable to tax if—
(a) the worker were employed by the client to perform the relevant services, and
(b) the deemed employment payment were a payment by the client of earnings from that employment.

(5) The factors are—
(a) the worker being resident, ordinarily resident or domiciled outside the United Kingdom,
(b) the client being resident or ordinarily resident outside the United Kingdom, and
(c) the relevant services being provided outside the United Kingdom.

(6) Where the MSC is a partnership and the worker is a member of the partnership, the deemed employment payment is treated as received by the worker in the worker's personal capacity and not as income of the partnership.

(7) Where—
(a) the worker is resident in the United Kingdom, and
(b) the relevant services are provided in the United Kingdom,

the MSC is treated as having a place of business in the United Kingdom, whether or not it in fact does so.]

[1527G]

NOTES

Commencement: 6 April 2007.
Inserted as noted to s 61A at **[1527A]**.

[Supplementary provisions

61H Relief in case of distributions by managed service company

(1) A claim for relief may be made under this section where the MSC—

(a) is a body corporate,

(b) is treated as making a deemed employment payment in any tax year, and

(c) either in that tax year (whether before or after that payment is treated as made), or in a subsequent tax year, makes a distribution (a "relevant distribution").

(2) A claim for relief under this section must be made—

(a) by the MSC by notice to an officer of Revenue and Customs, and

(b) within 5 years after 31st January following the tax year in which the distribution is made.

(3) If on a claim being made an officer of Revenue and Customs is satisfied that relief should be given in order to avoid a double charge to tax, the officer must direct the giving of such relief by way of amending any assessment, by discharge or repayment of tax, or otherwise, as appears to the officer appropriate.

(4) Relief under this section is given by setting the amount of the deemed employment payment against the relevant distribution so as to reduce the distribution.

(5) In the case of more than one relevant distribution, an officer of Revenue and Customs must exercise the power conferred by this section so as to secure that so far as practicable relief is given by setting the amount of a deemed employment payment—

(a) against relevant distributions of the same tax year before those of other years,

(b) against relevant distributions received by the worker before those received by another person, and

(c) against relevant distributions of earlier years before those of later years.

(6) Where the amount of a relevant distribution is reduced under this section, the amount of any associated tax credit is reduced accordingly.]

[1527H]

NOTES

Commencement: 6 April 2007.
Inserted as noted to s 61A at **[1527A]**.

[61I Meaning of "associate"

(1) Subsections (2) to (4) apply for the purposes of this Chapter.

(2) "Associate", in relation to an individual, means—

(a) a member of the individual's family or household,

(b) a relative of the individual,

(c) a partner of the individual, or

(d) the trustee of any settlement in relation to which the individual, or a relative of the individual or member of the individual's family (living or dead), is or was a settlor.

(3) "Associate", in relation to a company, means a person connected with the company.

(4) "Associate", in relation to a partnership, means any associate of a member of the partnership.

(5) If—

(a) a managed service company ("the MSC") is a partnership, and

(b) a person is an associate of another person by virtue only of being a member of the partnership,

the person is to be treated, for the purposes of this Chapter as it applies in relation to the MSC, as if the person were not an associate of that other person.

(6) In subsection (2), "relative" means ancestor, lineal descendant, brother or sister.

(7) For the purposes of subsection (2)—

(a) a man and woman living together as husband and wife are treated as if they were married to each other, and

(b) two persons of the same sex living together as if they were civil partners of each other are treated as if they were civil partners of each other.]

[1527I]

NOTES
Commencement: 6 April 2007.
Inserted as noted to s 61A at **[1527A]**.

[61J Interpretation of Chapter

(1) In this Chapter—
"associate" has the meaning given by section 61I,
"business" means any trade, profession or vocation,
"the client" has the meaning given by section 61D(4),
"employer's national insurance contributions" means secondary Class 1 or Class 1A national insurance contributions,
"managed service company" has the meaning given by section 61B,
"national insurance contributions" means contributions under Part 1 of SSCBA 1992 or Part 1 of SSCB(NI)A 1992,
"PAYE provisions" means the provisions of Part 11 or PAYE regulations,
"the relevant services" has the meaning given by section 61D(4), and
"the worker" has the meaning given by section 61D(4).

(2) Nothing in section 995 of ITA 2007 (meaning of control) applies for the purposes of this Chapter.]

[1527J]

NOTES
Commencement: 6 April 2007.
Inserted as noted to s 61A at **[1527A]**.

PART 3
EMPLOYMENT INCOME: EARNINGS AND BENEFITS ETC TREATED AS EARNINGS

CHAPTER 1
EARNINGS

62 Earnings

(1) This section explains what is meant by "earnings" in the employment income Parts.

(2) In those Parts "earnings", in relation to an employment, means—
(a) any salary, wages or fee,
(b) any gratuity or other profit or incidental benefit of any kind obtained by the employee if it is money or money's worth, or
(c) anything else that constitutes an emolument of the employment.

(3) For the purposes of subsection (2) "money's worth" means something that is—
(a) of direct monetary value to the employee, or
(b) capable of being converted into money or something of direct monetary value to the employee.

(4) Subsection (1) does not affect the operation of statutory provisions that provide for amounts to be treated as earnings (and see section 721(7)).

[1528]

CHAPTER 2
TAXABLE BENEFITS: THE BENEFITS CODE

The benefits code

63 The benefits code

(1) In the employment income Parts "the benefits code" means—
this Chapter,
Chapter 3 (expenses payments),
Chapter 4 (vouchers and credit-tokens),

Chapter 5 (living accommodation),
Chapter 6 (cars, vans and related benefits),
Chapter 7 (loans),
…
…
Chapter 10 (residual liability to charge), and
Chapter 11 (exclusion of lower-paid employments from parts of benefits code).

(2) If an employment is an excluded employment, the general effect of section 216(1) (provisions not applicable to lower-paid employments) is that only the following Chapters apply to the employment—

this Chapter,
Chapter 4 (vouchers and credit-tokens),
Chapter 5 (living accommodation), and
Chapter 11 (exclusion of lower-paid employments from parts of benefits code).

(3) Section 216(5) and (6) explain and restrict the effect of section 216(1).

(4) In the benefits code "excluded employment" means an employment to which the exclusion in section 216(1) applies.

[1529]

NOTES

Sub-s (1): entries relating to Chapters 8 and 9 repealed by the Finance Act 2003, ss 140, 216, Sch 22, paras 1, 20(1), Sch 43, Pt 3(4), in relation to shares, and interests in shares, acquired on or after 16 April 2003.

CHAPTER 3
TAXABLE BENEFITS: EXPENSES PAYMENTS

70 Sums in respect of expenses

(1) This Chapter applies to a sum paid to an employee in a tax year if the sum—

(a) is paid to the employee in respect of expenses, and
(b) is so paid by reason of the employment.

(2) This Chapter applies to a sum paid away by an employee in a tax year if the sum—

(a) was put at the employee's disposal in respect of expenses,
(b) was so put by reason of the employment, and
(c) is paid away by the employee in respect of expenses.

(3) For the purposes of this Chapter it does not matter whether the employment is held at the time when the sum is paid or paid away so long as it is held at some point in the tax year in which the sum is paid or paid away.

(4) References in this Chapter to an employee accordingly include a prospective or former employee.

(5) This Chapter does not apply to the extent that the sum constitutes earnings from the employment by virtue of any other provision.

[1530]

71 Meaning of paid or put at disposal by reason of the employment

(1) If an employer pays a sum in respect of expenses to an employee it is to be treated as paid by reason of the employment unless—

(a) the employer is an individual, and
(b) the payment is made in the normal course of the employer's domestic, family or personal relationships.

(2) If an employer puts a sum at an employee's disposal in respect of expenses it is to be treated as put at the employee's disposal by reason of the employment unless—

(a) the employer is an individual, and
(b) the sum is put at the employee's disposal in the normal course of the employer's domestic, family or personal relationships.

[1531]

72 Sums in respect of expenses treated as earnings

(1) If this Chapter applies to a sum, the sum is to be treated as earnings from the employment for the tax year in which it is paid or paid away.

(2) Subsection (1) does not prevent the making of a deduction allowed under any of the provisions listed in subsection (3).

(3) The provisions are—
section 336 (deductions for expenses: the general rule);
section 337 (travel in performance of duties);
section 338 (travel for necessary attendance);
section 340 (travel between group employments);
section 341 (travel at start or finish of overseas employment);
section 342 (travel between employments where duties performed abroad);
section 343 (deduction for professional membership fees);
section 344 (deduction for annual subscriptions);
section 346 (deduction for employee liabilities);
section 351 (expenses of ministers of religion);
section 353 (deductions from earnings charged on remittance).

[1532]

CHAPTER 5
TAXABLE BENEFITS: LIVING ACCOMMODATION

Living accommodation

97 Living accommodation to which this Chapter applies

(1) This Chapter applies to living accommodation provided for—
(a) an employee, or
(b) a member of an employee's family or household,
by reason of the employment.

(2) Living accommodation provided for any of those persons by the employer is to be regarded as provided by reason of the employment unless—
(a) the employer is an individual, and
(b) the provision is made in the normal course of the employer's domestic, family or personal relationships.

[1533]

Exceptions

98 Accommodation provided by local authority

This Chapter does not apply to living accommodation provided for an employee if—
(a) the employer is a local authority,
(b) it is provided for the employee by the authority, and
(c) the terms on which it is provided are no more favourable than those on which similar accommodation is provided by the authority for persons who are not their employees but whose circumstances are otherwise similar to those of the employee.

[1534]

99 Accommodation provided for performance of duties

(1) This Chapter does not apply to living accommodation provided for an employee if it is necessary for the proper performance of the employee's duties that the employee should reside in it.

(2) This Chapter does not apply to living accommodation provided for an employee if—
(a) it is provided for the better performance of the duties of the employment, and
(b) the employment is one of the kinds of employment in the case of which it is customary for employers to provide living accommodation for employees.

(3) But if the accommodation is provided by a company and the employee ("E") is a director of the company or of an associated company, the exception in subsection (1) or (2) only applies if, in the case of each company of which E is a director—

(a) E has no material interest in the company, and

(b) either—

(i) E's employment is as a full-time working director, or

(ii) the company is non-profit-making or is established for charitable purposes only.

(4) "Non-profit-making" means that the company does not carry on a trade and its functions do not consist wholly or mainly in the holding of investments or other property.

(5) A company is "associated" with another if—

(a) one has control of the other, or

(b) both are under the control of the same person.

[1535]

CHAPTER 6
TAXABLE BENEFITS: CARS, VANS AND RELATED BENEFITS

General

114 Cars, vans and related benefits

(1) This Chapter applies to a car or a van in relation to a particular tax year if in that year the car or van—

(a) is made available (without any transfer of the property in it) to an employee or a member of the employee's family or household,

(b) is so made available by reason of the employment (see section 117), and

(c) is available for the employee's or member's private use (see section 118).

(2) Where this Chapter applies to a car or van—

(a) sections 120 to 148 provide for the cash equivalent of the benefit of the car to be treated as earnings,

(b) sections 149 to 153 provide for the cash equivalent of the benefit of any fuel provided for the car to be treated as earnings, …

(c) sections 154 to [159] provide for the cash equivalent of the benefit of the van to be treated as earnings[; and

(d) sections 160 to 164 provide for the cash equivalent of the benefit of any fuel provided for the van to be treated as earnings in certain circumstances].

(3) This Chapter does not apply if an amount constitutes earnings from the employment in respect of the benefit of the car or van by virtue of any other provision (see section 119).

[(3A) This Chapter does not apply to a van in relation to a tax year if the private use of the van during the tax year by the employee or member of the employee's family or household is insignificant.]

(4) The following provisions of this Chapter provide for further exceptions—

section 167 (pooled cars);

section 168 (pooled vans);

section 169 (car available to more than one member of family or household employed by same employer);

[section 169A (van available to more than one member of family or household employed by same employer)].

[1536]

NOTES

Sub-s (2): word omitted from para (b) repealed, figure in square brackets in para (c) substituted, and para (d) and the word immediately preceding it added, by the Finance Act 2004, ss 80(1), 326, Sch 14, paras 1, 2(1)–(3), Sch 42, Pt 2(9), with effect for the year 2005–06 and subsequent years of assessment.

Sub-s (3A): inserted by the Finance Act 2004, s 80(1), Sch 14, paras 1, 2(1), (4), with effect for the year 2005–06 and subsequent years of assessment.

Sub-s (4): words in square brackets added by the Finance Act 2004, s 80(1), Sch 14, paras 1, 2(1), (4), with effect for the year 2005–06 and subsequent years of assessment.

115 Meaning of "car" and "van"

(1) In this Chapter—

"car" means a mechanically propelled road vehicle which is not—

(a) a goods vehicle,

(b) a motor cycle,

(c) an invalid carriage, or

(d) a vehicle of a type not commonly used as a private vehicle and unsuitable to be so used;

"van" means a mechanically propelled road vehicle which—

(a) is a goods vehicle, and

(b) has a design weight not exceeding 3,500 kilograms,

and which is not a motor cycle.

(2) For the purposes of subsection (1)—

"design weight" means the weight which a vehicle is designed or adapted not to exceed when in normal use and travelling on a road laden;

"goods vehicle" means a vehicle of a construction primarily suited for the conveyance of goods or burden of any description;

"invalid carriage" has the meaning given by section 185(1) of the Road Traffic Act 1988 (c 52);

"motor cycle" has the meaning given by section 185(1) of the Road Traffic Act 1988.

[1537]

116 Meaning of when car or van is available to employee

(1) For the purposes of this Chapter a car or van is available to an employee at a particular time if it is then made available, by reason of the employment and without any transfer of the property in it, to the employee or a member of the employee's family or household.

(2) References in this Chapter to—

(a) the time when a car [or van] is first made available to an employee are to the earliest time when the car [or van] is made available as mentioned in subsection (1), and

(b) the last day in a year on which a car [or van] is available to an employee are to the last day in the year on which the car [or van] is made available as mentioned in subsection (1).

(3) This section does not apply to section 138 (automatic car for a disabled employee).

[1538]

NOTES

Sub-s (2): words in square brackets inserted by the Finance Act 2004, s 80(1), Sch 14, paras 1, 3, with effect for the year 2005–06 and subsequent years of assessment.

117 Meaning of car or van made available by reason of employment

For the purposes of this Chapter a car or van made available by an employer to an employee or a member of the employee's family or household is to be regarded as made available by reason of the employment unless—

(a) the employer is an individual, and

(b) it is so made available in the normal course of the employer's domestic, family or personal relationships.

[1539]

118 Availability for private use

(1) For the purposes of this Chapter a car or van made available in a tax year to an employee or a member of the employee's family or household is to be treated as available for the employee's or member's private use unless in that year—

(a) the terms on which it is made available prohibit such use, and

(b) it is not so used.

(2) In this Chapter "private use", in relation to a car or van made available to an employee or a member of the employee's family or household, means any use other than for the employee's business travel (see section 171(1)).

[1540]

CHAPTER 10
TAXABLE BENEFITS: RESIDUAL LIABILITY TO CHARGE

Introduction

201 Employment-related benefits

(1) This Chapter applies to employment-related benefits.

(2) In this Chapter—

"benefit" means a benefit or facility of any kind;

"employment-related benefit" means a benefit, other than an excluded benefit, which is provided in a tax year—

(a) for an employee, or

(b) for a member of an employee's family or household,

by reason of the employment.

For the definition of "excluded benefit" see section 202.

(3) A benefit provided by an employer is to be regarded as provided by reason of the employment unless—

(a) the employer is an individual, and

(b) the provision is made in the normal course of the employer's domestic, family or personal relationships.

(4) For the purposes of this Chapter it does not matter whether the employment is held at the time when the benefit is provided so long as it is held at some point in the tax year in which the benefit is provided.

(5) References in this Chapter to an employee accordingly include a prospective or former employee.

[1541]

202 Excluded benefits

(1) A benefit is an "excluded benefit" for the purposes of this Chapter if—

(a) any of Chapters 3 to 9 of the benefits code applies to the benefit,

(b) any of those Chapters would apply to the benefit but for an exception, or

(c) the benefit consists in the right to receive, or the prospect of receiving, sums treated as earnings under section 221 (payments where employee absent because of sickness or disability).

(2) In this section "exception", in relation to the application of a Chapter of the benefits code to a benefit, means any enactment in the Chapter which provides that the Chapter does not apply to the benefit.

But for this purpose section 86 (transport vouchers under pre-26th March 1982 arrangements) is not an exception.

[1542]

Cash equivalent of benefit treated as earnings

203 Cash equivalent of benefit treated as earnings

(1) The cash equivalent of an employment-related benefit is to be treated as earnings from the employment for the tax year in which it is provided.

(2) The cash equivalent of an employment-related benefit is the cost of the benefit less any part of that cost made good by the employee to the persons providing the benefit.

(3) The cost of an employment-related benefit is determined in accordance with section 204 unless—

(a) section 205 provides that the cost is to be determined in accordance with that section, or

(b) section 206 provides that the cost is to be determined in accordance with that section.

[1543]

Determination of the cost of the benefit

204 Cost of the benefit: basic rule

The cost of an employment-related benefit is the expense incurred in or in connection with provision of the benefit (including a proper proportion of any expense relating partly to provision of the benefit and partly to other matters).

[1544]

Supplementary provisions

210 Power to exempt minor benefits

(1) The Treasury may make provision by regulations for exempting from the application of this Chapter such minor benefits as may be specified in the regulations.

(2) An exemption conferred by such regulations is conditional on the benefit being made available to the employer's employees generally on similar terms.

[1545]

NOTES

Regulations: the Income Tax (Benefits in Kind) (Exemption for Welfare Counselling) Regulations 2000, SI 2000/2080, the Income Tax (Exemption of Minor Benefits) Regulations 2002, SI 2002/205, and the Income Tax (Benefits in Kind) (Exemption for Employment Costs resulting from Disability) Regulations 2002, all have effect as if made under this section by virtue of s 723(2) of, and Sch 7, para 3 to, this Act.

CHAPTER 11
TAXABLE BENEFITS: EXCLUSION OF LOWER-PAID EMPLOYMENTS FROM PARTS OF BENEFITS CODE

Introduction

216 Provisions not applicable to lower-paid employments

(1) The Chapters of the benefits code listed in subsection (4) do not apply to an employment in relation to a tax year if—
 (a) it is lower-paid employment in relation to that year (see section 217), and
 (b) condition A or B is met.

(2) Condition A is that the employee is not employed as a director of a company.

(3) Condition B is that the employee is employed as a director of a company but has no material interest in the company and either—
 (a) the employment is as a full-time working director, or
 (b) the company is non-profit-making or is established for charitable purposes only.

"Non-profit-making" means that the company does not carry on a trade and its functions do not consist wholly or mainly in the holding of investments or other property.

(4) The Chapters referred to in subsection (1) are—
Chapter 3 (taxable benefits: expenses payments);
Chapter 6 (taxable benefits: cars, vans and related benefits);
Chapter 7 (taxable benefits: loans);
…
…
Chapter 10 (taxable benefits: residual liability to charge).

(5) Subsection (1)—
 (a) means that in any of those Chapters a reference to an employee does not include an employee whose employment is within the exclusion in that subsection, if the context is such that the reference is to an employee in relation to whom the Chapter applies, but
 (b) does not restrict the meaning of references to employees in other contexts.

(6) Subsection (1) has effect subject to—
section 188(2) (discharge of loan: where employment becomes lower-paid),

…

… and

section 220 (employment in two or more related employments).

[1546]

NOTES

Sub-s (4): entries relating to Chapters 8 and 9 repealed by the Finance Act 2003, ss 140, 216, Sch 22, paras 1, 24(1), (2), Sch 43, Pt 3(4), in relation to shares, and interests in shares, acquired on or after 16 April 2003.

Sub-s (6): entries relating to sections 195(3) and 199(4) repealed by the Finance Act 2003, ss 140, 216, Sch 22, paras 1, 24(1), (3), Sch 43, Pt 3(4), in relation to shares, and interests in shares, acquired on or after 16 April 2003.

"Employment", "employed", "employee" and "employer": in relation to times before 6 April 2003, references in the benefits code to "employment", "employed", "employee" and "employer" are to be read in accordance with Sch 7, Pt 3, para 17 to this Act.

PART 4
EMPLOYMENT INCOME: EXEMPTIONS

CHAPTER 10
EXEMPTIONS: TERMINATION OF EMPLOYMENT

Redundancy payments

309 Limited exemptions for statutory redundancy payments

(1) No liability to income tax in respect of earnings arises by virtue of a redundancy payment or an approved contractual payment, except where subsection (2) applies.

(2) Where an approved contractual payment exceeds the amount which would have been due if a redundancy payment had been payable, the excess is liable to income tax.

(3) No liability to income tax in respect of employment income other than earnings arises by virtue of a redundancy payment or an approved contractual payment, except where it does so by virtue of Chapter 3 of Part 6 (payments and benefits on termination of employment etc).

(4) For the purposes of this section—

(a) a statutory payment in respect of a redundancy payment is to be treated as paid on account of the redundancy payment, and

(b) a statutory payment in respect of an approved contractual payment is to be treated as paid on account of the approved contractual payment.

(5) In this section—

"approved contractual payment" means a payment to a person on the termination of the person's employment under an agreement in respect of which an order is in force under section 157 of ERA 1996 or Article 192 of ER(NI)O 1996,

"redundancy payment" means a redundancy payment under Part 11 of ERA 1996 or Part 12 of ER(NI)O 1996, and

"statutory payment" means a payment under section 167(1) of ERA 1996 or Article 202(1) of ER(NI)O 1996.

(6) In subsection (5) "employment", in relation to a person, has the meaning given in section 230(5) of ERA 1996 or Article 3(5) of ER(NI)O 1996.

[1547]

NOTES

'ERA 1996' and 'ER(NI)O 1996': the Employment Rights Act 1996 and the Employment Rights (Northern Ireland) Order 1996, respectively.

Outplacement benefits

310 Counselling and other outplacement services

(1) No liability to income tax arises in respect of—

(a) the provision of services to a person in connection with the cessation of the person's employment, or
(b) the payment or reimbursement of—
  (i) fees for such provision, or
  (ii) travelling expenses incurred in connection with such provision,

if conditions A to D and, in the case of travel expenses, condition E are met.

(2) Condition A is that the only or main purpose of the provision of the services is to enable the person to do either or both of the following—
(a) to adjust to the cessation of the employment, or
(b) to find other gainful employment (including self-employment).

(3) Condition B is that the services consist wholly of any or all of the following—
(a) giving advice and guidance,
(b) imparting or improving skills,
(c) providing or making available the use of office equipment or similar facilities.

(4) Condition C is that the person has been employed … in the employment which is ceasing throughout the period of 2 years ending—
(a) at the time when the services begin to be provided, or
(b) if earlier, at the time when the employment ceases.

(5) Condition D is that the opportunity to receive the services, on similar terms as to payment or reimbursement of any expenses incurred in connection with their provision, is available—
(a) generally to employees or former employees of the person's employer in that employment, or
(b) to a particular class or classes of them.

(6) Condition E is that the travel expenses are expenses—
(a) in respect of which, on the assumptions in subsection (7), mileage allowance relief under Chapter 2 of this Part would be available if no mileage allowance payments had been made, or
(b) which, on those assumptions, would be deductible under Part 5.

(7) The assumptions are—
(a) that receiving the services is one of the duties of the employee's employment,
(b) that the employee incurs and pays the expenses, and
(c) if the employment has in fact ceased, that it continues.

(8) In this section "mileage allowance payments" has the meaning given by section 229(2).

[1548]

NOTES

Sub-s (4): words omitted repealed by the Finance Act 2005, ss 18(1), (2), 104, Sch 11, Pt 2(1), in relation to the year 2005–06 and subsequent years of assessment.

PART 5
EMPLOYMENT INCOME: DEDUCTIONS ALLOWED FROM EARNINGS

CHAPTER 1
DEDUCTIONS ALLOWED FROM EARNINGS: GENERAL RULES

Introduction

327 Deductions from earnings: general

(1) This Part provides for deductions that are allowed from the taxable earnings from an employment in a tax year in calculating the net taxable earnings from the employment in the tax year for the purposes of Part 2 (see section 11(1)).

(2) In this Part, unless otherwise indicated by the context—
(a) references to the earnings from which deductions are allowed are references to the taxable earnings mentioned in subsection (1), and
(b) references to the tax year are references to the tax year mentioned there.

(3) The deductions for which this Part provides are those allowed under—
Chapter 2 (deductions for employee's expenses),
Chapter 3 (deductions from benefits code earnings),
Chapter 4 (fixed allowances for employee's expenses),
Chapter 5 (deductions for earnings representing benefits or reimbursed expenses), and
Chapter 6 (deductions from seafarers' earnings).

(4) Further provision about deductions from earnings is made in—
section 232 (giving effect to mileage allowance relief),
…
section 262 of CAA 2001 (capital allowances to be given effect by treating them as deductions from earnings).

(5) Further provision about deductions from income including earnings is made in—
Part 12 (payroll giving),
[and sections 188 to 194 of FA 2004 (contributions to registered pension schemes)]

[1549]

NOTES

Sub-s (4): words omitted repealed by the Finance Act 2004, ss 281, 326, Sch 35, paras 54, 60(1), (2), Sch 42, Pt 3, as from 6 April 2006 (for transitional provisions, see Sch 36 to the 2004 Act).

Sub-s (5): words in square brackets substituted by the Finance Act 2004, s 281(1), Sch 35, paras 54, 60(1), (3), as from 6 April 2006 (for transitional provisions, see Sch 36 to the 2004 Act).

CHAPTER 2
DEDUCTIONS FOR EMPLOYEE'S EXPENSES

Introduction

333 Scope of this Chapter: expenses paid by the employee

(1) A deduction from a person's earnings for an amount is allowed under the following provisions of this Chapter only if the amount—

(a) is paid by the person, or

(b) is paid on the person's behalf by someone else and is included in the earnings.

(2) In the following provisions of this Chapter, in relation to a deduction from a person's earnings, references to the person paying an amount include references to the amount being paid on the person's behalf by someone else if or to the extent that the amount is included in the earnings.

(3) Subsection (1)(b) does not apply to the deductions under—

(a) section 351(2) and (3) (expenses of ministers of religion), and

(b) section 355 (deductions for corresponding payments by non-domiciled employees with foreign employers),

and subsection (2) does not apply in the case of those deductions.

(4) Chapter 3 of this Part provides for deductions where—

(a) a person's earnings include an amount treated as earnings under Chapter 4, 5 or 10 of Part 3 (taxable benefits: vouchers etc, living accommodation and residual liability to charge), and

(b) an amount in respect of the benefit in question would be deductible under this Chapter if the person had incurred and paid it.

[1550]

334 Effect of reimbursement etc

(1) For the purposes of this Chapter, a person may be regarded as paying an amount despite—

(a) its reimbursement, or

(b) any other payment from another person in respect of the amount.

(2) But where a reimbursement or such other payment is made in respect of an amount, a deduction for the amount is allowed under the following provisions of this Chapter only if or to the extent that—

(a) the reimbursement, or

(b) so much of the other payment as relates to the amount,

is included in the person's earnings.

(3) This section does not apply to a deduction allowed under section 351 (expenses of ministers of religion).

(4) This section is to be disregarded for the purposes of the deductibility provisions.

[1551]

General rule for deduction of employee's expenses

336 Deductions for expenses: the general rule

(1) The general rule is that a deduction from earnings is allowed for an amount if—

(a) the employee is obliged to incur and pay it as holder of the employment, and

(b) the amount is incurred wholly, exclusively and necessarily in the performance of the duties of the employment.

(2) The following provisions of this Chapter contain additional rules allowing deductions for particular kinds of expenses and rules preventing particular kinds of deductions.

(3) No deduction is allowed under this section for an amount that is deductible under sections 337 to 342 (travel expenses).

[1552]

Travel expenses

337 Travel in performance of duties

(1) A deduction from earnings is allowed for travel expenses if—

(a) the employee is obliged to incur and pay them as holder of the employment, and

(b) the expenses are necessarily incurred on travelling in the performance of the duties of the employment.

(2) This section needs to be read with section 359 (disallowance of travel expenses: mileage allowances and reliefs).

[1553]

338 Travel for necessary attendance

(1) A deduction from earnings is allowed for travel expenses if—

(a) the employee is obliged to incur and pay them as holder of the employment, and

(b) the expenses are attributable to the employee's necessary attendance at any place in the performance of the duties of the employment.

(2) Subsection (1) does not apply to the expenses of ordinary commuting or travel between any two places that is for practical purposes substantially ordinary commuting.

(3) In this section "ordinary commuting" means travel between—

(a) the employee's home and a permanent workplace, or

(b) a place that is not a workplace and a permanent workplace.

(4) Subsection (1) does not apply to the expenses of private travel or travel between any two places that is for practical purposes substantially private travel.

(5) In subsection (4) "private travel" means travel between—

(a) the employee's home and a place that is not a workplace, or

(b) two places neither of which is a workplace.

(6) This section needs to be read with section 359 (disallowance of travel expenses: mileage allowances and reliefs).

[1554]

339 Meaning of "workplace" and "permanent workplace"

(1) In this Part "workplace", in relation to an employment, means a place at which the employee's attendance is necessary in the performance of the duties of the employment.

(2) In this Part "permanent workplace", in relation to an employment, means a place which—

(a) the employee regularly attends in the performance of the duties of the employment, and

(b) is not a temporary workplace.

This is subject to subsections (4) and (8).

(3) In subsection (2) "temporary workplace", in relation to an employment, means a place which the employee attends in the performance of the duties of the employment—

(a) for the purpose of performing a task of limited duration, or

(b) for some other temporary purpose.

This is subject to subsections (4) and (5).

(4) A place which the employee regularly attends in the performance of the duties of the employment is treated as a permanent workplace and not a temporary workplace if—

(a) it forms the base from which those duties are performed, or

(b) the tasks to be carried out in the performance of those duties are allocated there.

(5) A place is not regarded as a temporary workplace if the employee's attendance is—

(a) in the course of a period of continuous work at that place—

(i) lasting more than 24 months, or

(ii) comprising all or almost all of the period for which the employee is likely to hold the employment, or

(b) at a time when it is reasonable to assume that it will be in the course of such a period.

(6) For the purposes of subsection (5), a period is a period of continuous work at a place if over the period the duties of the employment are performed to a significant extent at the place.

(7) An actual or contemplated modification of the place at which duties are performed is to be disregarded for the purposes of subsections (5) and (6) if it does not, or would not, have any substantial effect on the employee's journey, or expenses of travelling, to and from the place where they are performed.

(8) An employee is treated as having a permanent workplace consisting of an area if—

(a) the duties of the employment are defined by reference to an area (whether or not they also require attendance at places outside it),

(b) in the performance of those duties the employee attends different places within the area,

(c) none of the places the employee attends in the performance of those duties is a permanent workplace, and

(d) the area would be a permanent workplace if subsections (2), (3), (5), (6) and (7) referred to the area where they refer to a place.

[1555]

PART 6
EMPLOYMENT INCOME: INCOME WHICH IS NOT EARNINGS OR SHARE-RELATED

CHAPTER 3
PAYMENTS AND BENEFITS ON TERMINATION OF EMPLOYMENT ETC

Preliminary

401 Application of this Chapter

(1) This Chapter applies to payments and other benefits which are received directly or indirectly in consideration or in consequence of, or otherwise in connection with—

(a) the termination of a person's employment,

(b) a change in the duties of a person's employment, or

(c) a change in the earnings from a person's employment,

by the person, or the person's spouse [or civil partner], blood relative, dependant or personal representatives.

(2) Subsection (1) is subject to subsection (3) and sections 405 to 413 (exceptions for certain payments and benefits).

(3) This Chapter does not apply to any payment or other benefit chargeable to income tax apart from this Chapter.

(4) For the purposes of this Chapter—

(a) a payment or other benefit which is provided on behalf of, or to the order of, the employee or former employee is treated as received by the employee or former employee, and

(b) in relation to a payment or other benefit—

(i) any reference to the employee or former employee is to the person mentioned in subsection (1), and

(ii) any reference to the employer or former employer is to be read accordingly.

[1556]

NOTES

Sub-s (1): words in square brackets inserted by the Tax and Civil Partnership Regulations 2005, SI 2005/3229, regs 137, 152, as from 5 December 2005.

402 Meaning of "benefit"

(1) In this Chapter "benefit" includes anything in respect of which, were it received for performance of the duties of the employment, an amount—

(a) would be taxable earnings from the employment, or

(b) would be such earnings apart from an earnings-only exemption.

This is subject to subsections (2) to (4).

(2) In this Chapter "benefit" does not include a benefit received in connection with the termination of a person's employment that is a benefit which, were it received for performance of the duties of the employment, would fall within—

(a) section 239(4) (exemption of benefits connected with taxable cars and vans and exempt heavy goods vehicles), so far as that section applies to a benefit connected with a car or van,

(b) section 269 (exemption where benefits or money obtained in connection with taxable car or van or exempt heavy goods vehicle),

(c) section 319 (mobile telephones), or

(d) section 320 (limited exemption for computer equipment).

(3) In this Chapter "benefit" does not include a benefit received in connection with any change in the duties of, or earnings from, a person's employment to the extent that it is a benefit which, were it received for performance of the duties of the employment, would fall within section 271(1) (limited exemption of removal benefits and expenses).

(4) The right to receive a payment or benefit is not itself a benefit for the purposes of this Chapter.

[1557]

Payments and benefits treated as employment income

403 Charge on payment or other benefit

(1) The amount of a payment or benefit to which this Chapter applies counts as employment income of the employee or former employee for the relevant tax year if and to the extent that it exceeds the £30,000 threshold.

(2) In this section "the relevant tax year" means the tax year in which the payment or other benefit is received.

(3) For the purposes of this Chapter—

(a) a cash benefit is treated as received—

(i) when it is paid or a payment is made on account of it, or

(ii) when the recipient becomes entitled to require payment of or on account of it, and

(b) a non-cash benefit is treated as received when it is used or enjoyed.

(4) For the purposes of this Chapter the amount of a payment or benefit in respect of an employee or former employee exceeds the £30,000 threshold if and to the extent that, when it is aggregated with other such payments or benefits to which this Chapter applies, it exceeds £30,000 according to the rules in section 404 (how the £30,000 threshold applies).

(5) If it is received after the death of the employee or former employee—

(a) the amount of a payment or benefit to which this Chapter applies counts as the employment income of the personal representatives for the relevant year if or to the extent that it exceeds £30,000 according to the rules in section 404, and

(b) the tax is accordingly to be assessed and charged on them and is a debt due from and payable out of the estate.

(6) In this Chapter references to the taxable person are to the person in relation to whom subsection (1) or (5) provides for an amount to count as employment income.

[1558]

NOTES

Note: this section does not apply in relation to payments or other benefits received on or after 6 April 2003 that were brought into charge to tax before 6 April 1998 (see Sch 7, Pt 6, paras 42, 43 to this Act).

404 How the £30,000 threshold applies

(1) For the purpose of the £30,000 threshold in section 403(4) and (5), the payments and other benefits provided in respect of an employee or former employee which are to be aggregated are those provided—

(a) in respect of the same employment,

(b) in respect of different employments with the same employer, and

(c) in respect of employments with employers who are associated.

(2) For this purpose employers are "associated" if on a termination or change date—

(a) one of them is under the control of the other, or

(b) one of them is under the control of a third person who on that termination or change date or another such date controls or is under the control of the other.

(3) In subsection (2)—

(a) references to an employer, or to a person controlling or controlled by an employer, include the successors of the employer or person, and

(b) "termination or change date" means a date on which a termination or change occurs in connection with which a payment or other benefit to which this Chapter applies is received in respect of the employee or former employee.

(4) If payments and other benefits are received in different tax years, the £30,000 is set against the amount of payments and other benefits received in earlier years before those received in later years.

(5) If more than one payment or other benefit is received in a tax year in which the threshold is exceeded—

(a) the £30,000 (or the balance of it) is set against the amounts of cash benefits as they are received, and

(b) any balance at the end of the year is set against the aggregate amount of non-cash benefits received in the year.

[1559]

[404A Amounts charged to be treated as highest part of total income

(1) A payment or other benefit which counts as a person's employment income as a result of section 403 is treated as the highest part of the person's total income.

(2) Subsection (1) has effect for all income tax purposes except the purposes of sections 535 to 537 of ITTOIA 2005 (gains from contracts for life insurance etc: top slicing relief).

(3) See section 1012 of ITA 2007 (relationship between highest part rules) for the relationship between—

(a) the rule in subsection (1), and

(b) other rules requiring particular income to be treated as the highest part of a person's total income]

[1559A]

NOTES

Commencement: 6 April 2007.

Inserted by the Income Tax Act 2007, s 1027, Sch 1, Pt 2, paras 425, 437, as from 6 April 2007 (for effect and transitional provisions see the introductory note to this Act).

ITTOIA 2005: the Income Tax (Trading and Other Income) Act 2005.

ITA 2007: the Income Tax Act 2007.

Exceptions and reductions

405 Exception for certain payments exempted when received as earnings

(1) This Chapter does not apply to any payment received in connection with the termination of a person's employment which, were it received for the performance of the duties of the employment, would fall within section 308 (exemption of contributions to approved personal pension arrangements).

(2) This Chapter does not apply to any payment received in connection with any change in the duties of, or earnings from, a person's employment to the extent that, were it received for the performance of the duties of the employment, it would fall within section 271(1) (limited exemption of removal benefits and expenses).

[1560]

406 Exception for death or disability payments and benefits

This Chapter does not apply to a payment or other benefit provided—

(a) in connection with the termination of employment by the death of an employee, or

(b) on account of injury to, or disability of, an employee.

[1561]

407 Exception for payments and benefits under tax-exempt pension schemes

(1) This Chapter does not apply to a payment or other benefit provided under a tax-exempt pension scheme if—

(a) the payment or other benefit is by way of compensation—

(i) for loss of employment, or

(ii) for loss or diminution of earnings, and

the loss or diminution is due to ill-health, or

(b) the payment or other benefit is properly regarded as earned by past service.

(2) For this purpose "tax-exempt pension scheme" means—

[(a) a registered pension scheme,

(aa) a scheme set up by a government outside the United Kingdom for the benefit of employees or primarily for their benefit, or]

(b) any such scheme or fund as was described in section 221(1) and (2) of ICTA 1970 (schemes to which payments could be made without charge to tax under section 220 of ICTA 1970).

(3) …

[1562]

NOTES

Sub-s (2): paras (a), (aa) substituted, for original para (a), by the Finance Act 2004, s 281(1), Sch 35, paras 54, 62(1), (2), as from 6 April 2006 (for transitional provisions, see Sch 36 to the 2004 Act).

Sub-s (3): repealed by the Finance Act 2004, ss 281(1), 326, Sch 35, paras 54, 62(1), (3), Sch 42, Pt 3, as from 6 April 2006 (for transitional provisions, see Sch 36 to the 2004 Act).

ICTA 1970: the Income and Corporation Taxes Act 1970 (repealed).

408 Exception for contributions to [registered pension schemes]

(1) This Chapter does not apply to a contribution to a [registered pension scheme] if the contribution is made—

(a) as part of an arrangement relating to the termination of a person's employment, and

(b) in order to provide benefits for the person in accordance with the terms of the scheme or approved personal pension arrangements.

(2) …

[1563]

NOTES

Section heading, sub-s (1): words in square brackets substituted by the Finance Act 2004, s 281(1), Sch 35, paras 54, 63(1), (2), (4), as from 6 April 2006 (for transitional provisions, see Sch 36 to the 2004 Act).

Sub-s (2): repealed by the Finance Act 2004, ss 281(1), 326, Sch 35, paras 54, 63(1), (3), Sch 42, Pt 3, as from 6 April 2006 (for transitional provisions, see Sch 36 to the 2004 Act).

409 Exception for payments and benefits in respect of employee liabilities and indemnity insurance

(1) This Chapter does not apply to a payment or other benefit received by an individual if or to the extent that—

(a) in the case of a cash benefit, it is provided for meeting the cost of a deductible amount, or

(b) in the case of a non-cash benefit, it is or represents a benefit equivalent to the cost of paying a deductible amount.

(2) For the purposes of this section "deductible amount" means an amount which meets conditions A to C.

(3) Condition A is that the amount is paid by the individual.

(4) Condition B is that a deduction for the amount would have been allowed under section 346 from earnings from the relevant employment, if the individual still held the employment when the amount was paid.

(5) Condition C is that the amount is paid at a time which falls within the run-off period.

(6) In this section and section 410—

"relevant employment" means the employment mentioned in section 401(1);

"run-off period" means the period which—

(a) starts with the day on which the relevant employment terminated, and

(b) ends with the last day of the sixth tax year following the tax year in which the period started.

[1564]

410 Exception for payments and benefits in respect of employee liabilities and indemnity insurance: individual deceased

(1) This Chapter does not apply to a payment or other benefit received by an individual's personal representatives if or to the extent that—

(a) in the case of a cash benefit, it is provided for meeting the cost of a deductible amount, or

(b) in the case of a non-cash benefit, it is or represents a benefit equivalent to the cost of paying a deductible amount.

(2) For the purposes of this section "deductible amount" means an amount which meets conditions A to C.

(3) Condition A is that the amount is paid by the individual's personal representatives.

(4) Condition B is that a deduction for the amount would have been allowed under section 346 from earnings from the relevant employment, if—

(a) the individual had not died,

(b) the amount had been paid by the individual, and

(c) the individual still held the employment when the amount was paid.

(5) Condition C is that the amount is paid at a time which falls within the run-off period.

[1565]

411 Exception for payments and benefits for forces

[(1)] This Chapter does not apply to a payment or other benefit provided—

(a) under a Royal Warrant, Queen's Order or Order in Council relating to members of Her Majesty's forces, or

(b) by way of payment in commutation of annual or other periodical payments authorised by any such Warrant or Order.

[(2) This Chapter does not apply to a payment or other benefit provided under a scheme established by an order under section 1(1) of the Armed Forces (Pensions and Compensation) Act 2004.]

[1566]

NOTES

Sub-s (1) numbered as such, and sub-s (2) added, by the Finance Act 2007, s 63, with effect for the tax year 2006–07 and subsequent tax years.

412 Exception for payments and benefits provided by foreign governments etc

(1) This Chapter does not apply to—

(a) a benefit provided under a pension scheme administered by the government of an overseas territory within the Commonwealth, or

(b) a payment of compensation for loss of career, interruption of service or disturbance made—

(i) in connection with any change in the constitution of any such overseas territory, and

(ii) to a person who was employed in the public service of the territory before the change.

(2) References in subsection (1) to—

(a) an overseas territory,

(b) the government of such a territory, and

(c) employment in the public service of such a territory,

have the meanings given in section 615 of ICTA.

[1567]

413 Exception in certain cases of foreign service

(1) This Chapter does not apply if the service of the employee or former employee in the employment in respect of which the payment or other benefit is received included foreign service comprising—

(a) three-quarters or more of the whole period of service ending with the date of the termination or change in question, or

(b) if the period of service ending with that date exceeded 10 years, the whole of the last 10 years, or

(c) if the period of service ending with that date exceeded 20 years, one-half or more of that period, including any 10 of the last 20 years.

(2) In subsection (1) "foreign service" means service to which subsection (3), (4) or (6) applies.

(3) This subsection applies to service in or after the tax year 2003–04 such that—

(a) the earnings from the employment were not general earnings to which section 15 or 21 applies (earnings for year when employee resident and ordinarily resident in UK), or would not have been had there been any, or

(b) a deduction equal to the whole amount of the earnings from the employment was or would have been allowable under Chapter 6 of Part 5 (deductions from seafarers' earnings).

(4) This subsection applies to service before the tax year 2003–04 and after the tax year 1973–74 such that—

(a) the emoluments from the employment were not chargeable under Case I of Schedule E, or would not have been so chargeable had there been any, or

(b) a deduction equal to the whole amount of the emoluments from the employment was or would have been allowable under a foreign earnings deduction provision.

(5) In subsection (4) "foreign earnings deduction provision" means—

(a) paragraph 1 of Schedule 2 to FA 1974,

(b) paragraph 1 of Schedule 7 to FA 1977, or

(c) section 192A or 193(1) of ICTA.

(6) This subsection applies to service before the tax year 1974–75 such that tax was not chargeable in respect of the emoluments of the employment—

(a) in the tax year 1956–57 or later, under Case I of Schedule E, or

(b) in earlier tax years, under Schedule E,

or it would not have been so chargeable had there been any such emoluments.

[1568]

414 Reduction in other cases of foreign service

(1) This section applies if—

(a) the service of the employee or former employee in the employment in respect of which the payment or other benefit is received includes foreign service, and

(b) section 413 (exception in certain cases of foreign service) does not apply.

(2) The taxable person may claim relief in the form of a proportionate reduction of the amount that would otherwise count as employment income under this Chapter.

(3) The proportion is that which the length of the foreign service bears to the whole length of service in the employment before the date of the termination or change in question.

(4) A person's entitlement to relief under this section is limited as mentioned in subsection (5) if the person is entitled—

(a) to deduct, retain or satisfy income tax out of a payment which the person is liable to make, or

(b) to charge any income tax against another person.

(5) The relief must not reduce the amount of income tax for which the person is liable below the amount the person is entitled so to deduct, retain, satisfy or charge.

(6) In this section "foreign service" has the same meaning as in section 413(2).

[1569]

General and supplementary provisions

415 Valuation of benefits

(1) In the case of a cash benefit, for the purposes of this Chapter the amount of a payment or other benefit is taken to be the amount received.

(2) In the case of a non-cash benefit, for the purposes of this Chapter the amount of a payment or other benefit is taken to be the greater of—

(a) the amount of earnings (as defined in Chapter 1 of Part 3) that the benefit would give rise to if it were received by an employee within section 15 for performance of the duties of an employment (money's worth), and

(b) the cash equivalent of the benefit under the benefits code if it were so received and the code applied to it.

(3) For the purposes of subsection (2), the benefits code has effect with the modifications in subsections (4), (6) and (7).

(4) References in the benefits code to the employee are to be taken as references to the taxable person and any other person by whom the benefit is received.

(5) For the purposes of subsection (4), section 401(4)(a) is to be disregarded.

(6) References in the benefits code to the employer are to be taken as including references to the former employer.

(7) Where—

(a) section 106 (cash equivalent: cost of accommodation over £75,000) applies, and

(b) the sum referred to in section 105(2)(b) (the sum made good) exceeds the amount referred to in section 105(2)(a) (the rental value),

the amount to be subtracted under paragraph (b) of step 4 of the calculation in section 106(2) is that excess (and not only the excess rent referred to there).

[1570]

416 Notional interest treated as paid if amount charged for beneficial loan

(1) This section applies if an amount ("the taxable amount") consisting of, or including, an amount representing the benefit of a loan counts as a person's employment income in a tax year under section 403.

(2) That person is to be treated for the purposes of the Tax Acts (other than this Chapter) as having paid interest on the loan in the tax year equal to the lesser of—

(a) the amount representing the cash equivalent of the loan, and

(b) the taxable amount.

(3) The interest is to be treated—

(a) as accruing during the period in the tax year during which the loan is outstanding, and

(b) as paid at the end of the period.

(4) The interest is not to be treated—

(a) as income of the person making the loan, or

(b) as relevant loan interest to which section 369 of ICTA applies (mortgage interest payable under deduction of tax).

[1571]

PART 11
PAY AS YOU EARN

CHAPTER 2
PAYE: GENERAL

684 PAYE regulations

(1) [The Commissioners for Her Majesty's Revenue and Customs] must make regulations ("PAYE regulations") with respect to the assessment, charge, collection and recovery of income tax in respect of all PAYE income.

(2) PAYE regulations may, in particular, include any such provision as is set out in the following list.

LIST OF PROVISIONS

1. Provision—

(a) for requiring persons making payments of, or on account of, PAYE income to make, at the [relevant time], deductions or repayments of income tax calculated by reference to tax tables prepared by [the Commissioners for Her Majesty's Revenue and Customs], and

(b) for making persons who are required to make any such deductions or repayments accountable to or, as the case may be, entitled to repayment from the Board.

["The relevant time" is—

(a) if the payment is a notional payment for the purposes of section 710 and the person is treated by virtue of any Act as making it at a time before the date on which the Act is passed, that date, and

(b) in any other case, the time when the payment is made.]

[1A. Provision—

(a) for deductions to be made, if and to the extent that the payee does not object, with a view to securing that income tax payable in respect of any income of a payee for a tax year which is not PAYE income is deducted from PAYE income of the payee paid during that year; and

(b) as to the circumstances and manner in which a payee may object to the making of deductions.

2. Provision—

(a) for repayments or deductions to be made, if and to the extent that the payee does not object, in respect of any amounts overpaid or remaining unpaid (or treated as overpaid or remaining unpaid) on account of—

(i) income tax in respect of income for a previous tax year, or

(ii) capital gains tax in respect of chargeable gains for such a year; and

(b) as to the circumstances in which repayments or deductions may be made, and the circumstances and manner in which a payee may object to the making of repayments or deductions.]

3. Provision for the production to, and inspection by, persons authorised by the Board of wages sheets and other documents and records for the purposes of satisfying themselves that income tax has been and is being deducted, repaid and accounted for in accordance with the regulations.

4. Provision for requiring an employer or former employer to provide any information, within a prescribed time, about payments or other benefits provided or to be provided, including those provided or to be provided in connection with—
   (a) the termination of a person's employment, or
   (b) a change in the duties of or general earnings from a person's employment.

[4A. Provision authorising the recovery from the payee rather than the payer of any amount that [an officer of Revenue and Customs] considers should have been deducted by the payer.]

5. Provision for the way in which any matters provided for by the regulations are to be proved.

6. Provision—
   (a) for requiring the payment of interest on sums due to the Board which are not paid by the due date,
   (b) for determining the date (being not less than 14 days after the end of the tax year in respect of which the sums are due) from which such interest is to be calculated, and
   (c) for enabling the repayment or remission of such interest.

7. Provision for requiring the payment of interest on sums due from the Board and for determining the date from which such interest is to be calculated.

[7A. Provision for excluding payments of such description as may be specified from the operation of the regulations in such circumstances as may be specified.

8. Provision for the making of decisions by [Her Majesty's Revenue and Customs] as to any matter required to be decided for the purposes of the regulations and for appeals against such decisions.]

9. Provision for appeals with respect to matters arising under the regulations which would otherwise not be the subject of an appeal.

10. Different provision for different cases or classes of case.

11. Any incidental, consequential, supplementary and transitional provision which appears to the Board to be expedient.

(3) The deductions of income tax required to be made by PAYE regulations under item 1 in the above list may be required to be made at the basic rate or other rates in such cases or classes of case as may be provided by the regulations.

(4) Interest required to be paid by PAYE regulations under item 6 or 7 in the above list must be paid without any deduction of income tax and may not be taken into account in computing any income, profits or losses for any tax purposes.

(5) PAYE regulations must not affect any right of appeal to the General or Special Commissioners which a person would have apart from the regulations.

(6) It does not matter for the purposes of PAYE regulations that income is wholly or partly income for a tax year other than that in which the payment is made.

(7) PAYE regulations have effect despite anything in the Income Tax Acts.

[(7A) Nothing in PAYE regulations may be read—
   (a) as preventing the making of arrangements for the collection of tax in such manner as may be agreed by, or on behalf of, the payer and [an officer of Revenue and Customs], or
   (b) as requiring the payer to comply with the regulations in circumstances in which [an officer of Revenue and Customs] is satisfied that it is unnecessary or not appropriate for the payer to do so

(7B) References in this section and section 685 to income tax in respect of PAYE income are references to income tax in respect of that income if reasonable assumptions are (when necessary) made about other income.

(7C) In this section and section 685—
"payer" means any person paying PAYE income and "payee" means any person in receipt of such income;
"specified" means specified in PAYE regulations.]

(8) In this Act and any other enactment (whenever passed) "PAYE regulations" means regulations under this section.

[1572]

NOTES

Sub-s (1): words in square brackets substituted by the Commissioners for Revenue and Customs Act 2005, s 50(6), Sch 4, paras 101, 102(2), as from 18 April 2005.

Sub-s (2) is amended as follows:

Words in first pair of square brackets in Item 1 substituted, and words in final pair of square brackets in Item 1 inserted, by the Finance Act 2006, s 94(1), (3), as from 19 July 2006 (for effect in relation to notional payments treated by virtue of that Act as made before that date see s 94(5) of that Act).

Words in second pair of square brackets in Item 1, and words in square brackets in Items 4A, and 8 substituted, by the Commissioners for Revenue and Customs Act 2005, s 50(6), Sch 4, paras 101, 102(1), (2), 117, as from 18 April 2005.

Items 1A, 2 substituted for original Item 2, Item 4A inserted, and Items 7A, 8 substituted for original Item 8, by the Finance Act 2003, s 145(1), as from 10 July 2003.

Sub-s (7A): inserted, together with sub-ss (7B), (7C), by the Finance Act 2003, s 145(2), as from 10 July 2003; words in square brackets substituted by the Commissioners for Revenue and Customs Act 2005, s 50(6), Sch 4, paras 101, 102(1), as from 18 April 2005.

Sub-ss (7B), (7C): inserted as noted above.

Regulations: the Income Tax (Pay As You Earn) Regulations 2003, SI 2003/2682 (as amended).

685 Tax tables

(1) [The Commissioners for Her Majesty's Revenue and Customs] must construct tax tables with a view to securing that so far as possible—

(a) the total income tax payable in respect of PAYE income for any tax year is deducted from PAYE income paid during that year, and

(b) the income tax deductible or repayable on the occasion of any payment of, or on account of, PAYE income is such that the following proportions are the same—

(i) the proportion which the total net income tax deducted since the beginning of the tax year bears to the total income tax payable for the year, and

(ii) the proportion which the part of the tax year which ends with the date of the payment bears to the whole year.

(2) References in subsection (1) to the total income tax payable for the year are to be read as references to the total income tax estimated to be payable for the year in respect of the income in question—

(a) subject to a provisional deduction for allowances and reliefs, and

[(b) subject to an adjustment in respect of amounts required to be deducted or repaid by PAYE regulations made under item 1A or 2 in the list in section 684(2)].

(3) For the purpose of estimating the total income tax payable as mentioned in subsection (1)(a), it may be assumed, in relation to any payment of, or on account of, PAYE income, that the following proportions will be the same—

(a) the proportion which the income paid in the part of the tax year which ends with the making of the payment bears to the income for the whole year, and

(b) the proportion which that part of the tax year bears to the whole year.

[(4) PAYE regulations may make provision, where it appears to [an officer of Revenue and Customs] that it is impracticable for a payer to deduct tax by reference to tax tables—

(a) for deductions to be made by the payer in accordance with other arrangements agreed as mentioned in section 684(7A)(a), or

(b) for the payee to be required to keep records and make payments and returns as if he were the payer.]

[1573]

NOTES

Sub-s (1): words in square brackets substituted by the Commissioners for Revenue and Customs Act 2005, s 50(6), Sch 4, paras 101, 102(2), as from 18 April 2005.

Sub-s (2): para (b) substituted by the Finance Act 2003, s 145(3), as from 10 July 2003.

Sub-s (4): added by the Finance Act 2003, s 145(4), as from 10 July 2003; words in square brackets substituted by the Commissioners for Revenue and Customs Act 2005, s 50(6), Sch 4, paras 101, 102(1), as from 18 April 2005.

Regulations: the Income Tax (Pay As You Earn) Regulations 2003, SI 2003/2682 (as amended).

686 Meaning of "payment"

(1) For the purposes of PAYE regulations, a payment of, or on account of, PAYE income of a person is treated as made at the earliest of the following times—

Rule 1

The time when the payment is made.

Rule 2

The time when the person becomes entitled to the payment.

Rule 3

If the person is a director of a company and the income is income from employment with the company (whether or not as director), whichever is the earliest of—

- (a) the time when sums on account of the income are credited in the company's accounts or records (whether or not there is any restriction on the right to draw the sums);
- (b) if the amount of the income for a period is determined before the period ends, the time when the period ends;
- (c) if the amount of the income for a period is not determined until after the period has ended, the time when the amount is determined.

[But this is subject to subsection (5) (PAYE pension income: social security pension lump sums).]

(2) Rule 3 applies if the person is a director of the company at any time in the tax year in which the time mentioned falls.

(3) In this section "director" means—

- (a) in relation to a company whose affairs are managed by a board of directors or similar body, a member of that board or body,
- (b) in relation to a company whose affairs are managed by a single director or other person, that director or person, and
- (c) in relation to a company whose affairs are managed by the members themselves, a member of the company,

and includes any person in accordance with whose directions or instructions the company's directors (as defined above) are accustomed to act.

(4) For the purposes of subsection (3) a person is not regarded as a person in accordance with whose directions or instructions the company's directors are accustomed to act merely because the directors act on advice given by that person in a professional capacity.

[(5) For the purposes of PAYE regulations, a payment of, or on account of, an amount which is PAYE pension income of a person by virtue of section 683(3A) (social security pension lump sums) is to be treated as made at the time when the payment is made.]

[1574]

NOTES

Sub-s (1): words in square brackets added by the Finance (No 2) Act 2005, s 10(1), (5), as from 20 July 2005.

Sub-s (5): added by the Finance (No 2) Act 2005, s 10(1), (6), as from 20 July 2005.

CHAPTER 5
PAYE SETTLEMENT AGREEMENTS

703 Introduction

This Chapter provides—

- (a) for employers to make agreements with [an officer of Revenue and Customs] ("PAYE settlement agreements") under which they agree to be accountable to the [Commissioners] for sums in respect of income tax on general earnings of their employees; and
- (b) for such earnings to be treated for certain purposes of the Income Tax Acts as excluded from the employees' income.

[1575]

NOTES

Words in square brackets in para (a) substituted by the Commissioners for Revenue and Customs Act 2005, s 50(6), Sch 4, paras 101, 102(1), (3)(j), as from 18 April 2005.

704 Sums payable by employers under agreements

(1) PAYE regulations may provide—

(a) for a person to make a PAYE settlement agreement with [an officer of Revenue and Customs]; and

(b) to such extent as may be prescribed, for that person's accountability, and the sums to be accounted for, in respect of income tax on general earnings of that person's employees to be determined—

(i) in accordance with the agreement, and

(ii) not in accordance with PAYE regulations which would apply apart from this Chapter.

(2) Without prejudice to the generality of section 684(2), any power of the [Commissioners] to make PAYE regulations with respect to sums falling to be accounted for under such regulations includes power to make the corresponding provision with respect to sums falling to be accounted for in accordance with a PAYE settlement agreement.

[1576]

NOTES

Sub-ss (1), (2): words in square brackets substituted by the Commissioners for Revenue and Customs Act 2005, s 50(6), Sch 4, paras 101, 102(1), (3)(k), as from 18 April 2005.

Regulations: the Income Tax (Pay As You Earn) Regulations 2003, SI 2003/2682 (as amended).

705 Approximations allowed in calculations

PAYE regulations may provide for a PAYE settlement agreement to allow sums which an employer is to account for—

(a) to be computed, if two or more persons hold employments to which the agreement relates, by reference to a number of those persons all taken together;

(b) to include sums representing income tax on an estimated amount taken to be the aggregate of the amounts of PAYE income consisting of—

(i) taxable benefits provided or made available by reason of the employments to which the agreement relates, and

(ii) expenses paid to the persons holding those employments; and

(c) to be computed in a manner under which they do not necessarily represent an amount of income tax which would be payable (apart from the agreement) by persons holding employments to which the agreement relates.

[1577]

NOTES

Regulations: the Income Tax (Pay As You Earn) Regulations 2003, SI 2003/2682 (as amended).

706 Exclusion of general earnings from income etc

PAYE regulations may provide—

(a) that sums accountable for by an employer under a PAYE settlement agreement, or any other sums, are not to be treated for any prescribed purpose as tax deducted from general earnings;

(b) that an employee is to have no right to be treated as having paid tax in respect of sums accountable for by the employer under such an agreement;

(c) that an employee is to be treated, except—

(i) for the purposes of the obligations imposed on the employer by such an agreement, and

(ii) to such further extent as may be prescribed,

as relieved from any prescribed obligations of the employee under the Income Tax Acts in respect of general earnings from an employment to which the agreement relates; and

(d) that such earnings are to be treated as excluded from the employee's income for such further purposes of the Income Tax Acts, and to such extent, as may be prescribed.

[1578]

NOTES

Regulations: the Income Tax (Pay As You Earn) Regulations 2003, SI 2003/2682 (as amended).

707 Interpretation of this Chapter

In this Chapter—

"employment" means any employment the general earnings from which are (or, apart from any regulations made by virtue of [this Chapter], would be) PAYE income and related expressions are to be construed accordingly;

"prescribed" means prescribed by PAYE regulations;

"taxable benefit", in relation to an employee, means any benefit provided or made available, otherwise than in the form of a payment of money, to the employee, or to a person who is a member of the employee's family or household.

[1579]

NOTES

In definition "employment" words in square brackets substituted by the Finance Act 2003, s 145(5), as from 10 July 2003.

PART 13
SUPPLEMENTARY PROVISIONS

Amendments, repeals, citation etc

723 Commencement and transitional provisions and savings

(1) This Act comes into force on 6th April 2003 and has effect—

(a) for the purposes of income tax, for the tax year 2003–04 and subsequent tax years, and

(b) for the purposes of corporation tax, for accounting periods ending after 5th April 2003.

(2) Subsection (1) is subject to Schedule 7, which contains transitional provisions and savings.

[1580]

725 Citation

This Act may be cited as the Income Tax (Earnings and Pensions) Act 2003.

[1581]

NATIONAL MINIMUM WAGE (ENFORCEMENT NOTICES) ACT 2003 (NOTE)

(2003 c 8)

NOTES

This Act amends the National Minimum Wage 1998, s 19 by inserting sub-ss (2A), (2B) at **[1363]**.

[1582]

SUNDAY WORKING (SCOTLAND) ACT 2003 (NOTE)

(2003 c 18)

NOTES

This Act extends to Scotland provisions of the Employment Rights Act 1996 relating to Sunday working by shop workers and betting shop workers. Section 1 amends ss 36, 232, 233, 234 of the 1996

Act at **[1043]**, **[1273]**, **[1274]**, **[1275]**, as from 6 April 2004 (see SI 2004/958). The remaining provisions are outside the scope of this work and therefore not printed.

[1583]

LOCAL GOVERNMENT ACT 2003

(2003 c 26)

An Act to make provision about finance, and other provision, in connection with local and certain other authorities; to provide for changing the dates of local elections in 2004; to amend the Audit Commission Act 1998; and for connected purposes

[18 September 2003]

NOTES

Most of this Act covers matters outside the scope of this work, and only those provisions most directly relevant to employment law are printed. For reasons of space, the subject matter of sections not printed is not annotated. All provisions of the Act printed here apply to England, Wales and Scotland, except where the contrary appears.

PART 8
MISCELLANEOUS AND GENERAL

CHAPTER 1
MISCELLANEOUS

Contracting-out

101 Staff transfer matters: general

(1) In exercising a power to contract with a person for the provision of services, [a relevant authority] must—

(a) deal with matters affecting—

(i) who will be the employer of existing staff if a contract is entered into and carried out, or

(ii) what will be the terms and conditions of employment of existing staff, or the arrangements for their pensions, if their employer changes as a result of a contract being entered into and carried out,

in accordance with directions given to it by the appropriate person;

(b) have regard to guidance issued to it by the appropriate person on matters relating to the employment or pensions of existing staff.

(2) In subsection (1), references to existing staff, in relation to a contract for the provision of services, are to staff who before the contract is carried out are engaged in the provision of any of the services.

(3) Where the provision of any services under a contract with [a relevant authority] for their provision is to cease in circumstances where they are to be provided instead by members of the authority's staff, the authority shall comply with directions given to it by the appropriate person for the purpose of requiring it to offer employment to staff who, before the services cease to be provided under the contract, are engaged in the provision of any of the services.

(4) The duties under Part 1 of the Local Government Act 1999 (c 27) (best value) of a best value authority have effect subject to subsections (1) and (3).

(5) The duties under sections 1 and 2 of the Local Government in Scotland Act 2003 (asp 1) (best value) of a relevant authority have effect subject to subsections (1) and (3).

(6) Directions given, or guidance issued, for the purposes of subsection (1) or (3)—

(a) may be addressed to—

(i) [all relevant authorities], or

(ii) authorities of a particular description;

(b) may be different for different cases or authorities.

[(7) For the purposes of this section, the Secretary of State is the "appropriate person" in relation to a police authority for a police area in Wales.]

[(7A) In this section, in relation to England and Wales, "relevant authority" means—
(a) a best value authority;
(b) a parish council;
(c) a parish meeting of a parish which does not have a separate parish council; or
(d) a community council.]

(8) In this section[, in relation to Scotland]—
"appropriate person" … means the Scottish Ministers; and
"relevant authority" means—
(a) a council constituted under section 2 of the Local Government etc (Scotland) Act 1994 (c 39),
(b) the Strathclyde Passenger Transport Authority, or
(c) any other body to which Part 1 of the Local Government in Scotland Act 2003 (asp 1) (best value and accountability) applies.

[1584]

NOTES

Commencement: 18 November 2003 (so far as relating to England and to a best value authority in Wales mentioned in sub-s (7)); 27 November 2003 (so far as relating to a best value authority in Wales, other than one mentioned in sub-s (7)); to be appointed (so far as relating to Scotland).

Sub-ss (1), (3), (6): words in square brackets substituted by the Local Government and Public Involvement in Health Act 2007, s 136(3), Sch 7, para 3(1), (9)(a), (b), as from 1 April 2008.

Sub-s (7): substituted by the Local Government and Public Involvement in Health Act 2007, s 144(2), Sch 8, Pt 2, para 25(1), (4), as from 1 April 2008.

Sub-s (7A): inserted by the Local Government and Public Involvement in Health Act 2007, s 136(3), Sch 7, para 3(1), (9)(c), as from 1 April 2008.

Sub-s (8): words in square brackets inserted, and words omitted repealed, by the Local Government and Public Involvement in Health Act 2007, s 136(3), Sch 7, para 3(1), (9)(d), as from 1 April 2008.

See further, the Office of the Deputy Prime Minister's Code of Practice on Workforce Matters in Local Authority Service Contracts (February 2003) at **[5044]**.

102 Staff transfer matters: pensions

(1) The appropriate person shall exercise his power to give directions under section 101(1) so as to secure that where a local authority is contracting with a person ("the contractor") for the provision of services that are to be provided under a contract instead of by employees of the authority, it does so on terms—
(a) that require the contractor, in the event of there being any transferring employees, to secure pension protection for each of them, and
(b) that, so far as relating to the securing of pension protection for a transferring employee, are enforceable by the employee.

(2) For the purposes of subsection (1)—
(a) "transferring employee" means an employee of the authority whose contract of employment becomes, by virtue of the application of the TUPE regulations in relation to what is done for the purposes of carrying out the contract between the authority and the contractor, a contract of employment with someone other than the authority, and
(b) "pension protection" is secured for a transferring employee if after that change in his employer he has, as an employee of his new employer, rights to acquire pension benefits and those rights—
(i) are the same as, or
(ii) under the directions count as being broadly comparable to or better than,
those that he had as an employee of the authority.

(3) The appropriate person shall exercise his power to give directions under section 101(1) so as to secure that where—
(a) a local authority has contracted with a person ("the first contractor") for the provision of services,
(b) the application of the TUPE regulations in relation to what was done for the purposes of carrying out the contract between the authority and the first contractor resulted in employees of the authority ("the original employees") becoming employees of someone other than the authority, and
(c) the authority is contracting with a person ("the subsequent contractor") for the provision of any of the services,

the authority contracts with the subsequent contractor on terms satisfying the requirements of subsection (4).

(4) Those requirements are that the terms—
(a) require the subsequent contractor, in the event of there being any transferring original employees, to secure pension protection for each of them, and
(b) so far as relating to the securing of pension protection for an original employee, are enforceable by the employee.

(5) For the purposes of subsection (4)—
(a) "transferring original employee" means an original employee—
(i) whose contract of employment becomes, by virtue of the application of the TUPE regulations in relation to what is done for the purposes of carrying out the contract between the authority and the subsequent contractor, a contract of employment with someone other than his existing employer, and
(ii) whose contract of employment on each occasion when an intervening contract was carried out became, by virtue of the application of the TUPE regulations in relation to what was done for the purposes of carrying out the intervening contract, a contract of employment with someone other than his existing employer;
(b) "pension protection" is secured for a transferring original employee if after the change in his employer mentioned in paragraph (a)(i) he has, as an employee of his new employer, rights to acquire pension benefits and those rights—
(i) are the same as, or
(ii) under the directions count as being broadly comparable to or better than,
those that he had before that change.

(6) In subsection (5)(a)(ii), "intervening contract" means a contract with the authority for the provision, at times after they are provided under the contract with the first contractor and before they are to be provided under a contract with the subsequent contractor, of the services to be provided under the contract with the subsequent contractor.

(7) Any expression used in this section, and in the TUPE regulations, has in this section the meaning that it has in the TUPE regulations.

[(7A) In this section, in relation to England, "local authority" means—
(a) a county council in England, a district council, a London borough council, a parish council or a parish meeting of a parish which does not have a separate parish council;
(b) the Council of the Isles of Scilly;
(c) the Common Council of the City of London in its capacity as a local authority; and
(d) the Greater London Authority so far as it exercises its functions through the Mayor.

(7B) In this section, in relation to Wales, "local authority" means a county council, county borough council or community council in Wales.]

(8) In this section[, in relation to Scotland]—
"appropriate person" … means the Scottish Ministers;
"local authority"—
(a) …
(b) … means a council constituted under section 2 of the Local Government etc (Scotland) Act 1994 (c 39);

[(9) In this section,]
"the TUPE regulations" means the [Transfer of Undertakings (Protection of Employment) Regulations 2006], or any regulations replacing those regulations, as from time to time amended.

[1585]

NOTES

Commencement: 27 November 2003 (in relation to Wales); 1 April 2004 (in relation to England); to be appointed (in relation to Scotland).

Sub-ss (7A), (7B): inserted by the Local Government and Public Involvement in Health Act 2007, s 136(3), Sch 7, para 3(1), (10), as from 1 April 2008.

Sub-s (8): words in square brackets inserted, and words omitted repealed, by the Local Government and Public Involvement in Health Act 2007, s 136(3), Sch 7, para 3(1), (11)(a)–(c), as from 1 April 2008.

Sub-s (9): numbered as such, and words "In this section," in square brackets inserted, by the Local Government and Public Involvement in Health Act 2007, s 136(3), Sch 7, para 3(1), (11)(d), as from 1 April 2008; words in square brackets in definition "the TUPE regulations" substituted by the Transfer of Undertakings (Protection of Employment) Regulations 2006, SI 2006/246, Sch 2, para 1(i), as from 6 April 2006 (for transitional provisions in relation to a relevant transfer, etc, that took place before that date, see reg 21 of the 2006 Regulations at **[3395]**).

See further, the Office of the Deputy Prime Minister's Code of Practice on Workforce Matters in Local Authority Service Contracts (February 2003) at **[5044]**.

CHAPTER 2
GENERAL

124 General interpretation

In this Act—

"appropriate person" means—

(a) in relation to England, the Secretary of State, and

(b) in relation to Wales, the National Assembly for Wales;

"best value authority" means an authority or body which is a best value authority for the purposes of Part 1 of the Local Government Act 1999 (c 27);

"financial year" means a period of 12 months beginning with 1st April;

"valuation tribunal" means a tribunal established under Schedule 11 to the Local Government Finance Act 1988 (c 41).

[1585A]

NOTES

Commencement: 18 September 2003.

Definition "valuation tribunal" repealed by the Local Government and Public Involvement in Health Act 2007, ss 220(1), 241, Sch 16, paras 10, 12, Sch 18, Pt 17, as from a day to be appointed.

128 Commencement

(1) The following provisions shall come into force on the day on which this Act is passed—

(a) this section and sections 30, 34, 35, 72, 73, 103, 104, 110, 114, 121, 123, 124 and 129;

(b), (c) (*outside the scope of this work.*)

(2) (*Outside the scope of this work.*)

(3) The following provisions shall come into force on such day as the Secretary of State may by order appoint—

(a) (*outside the scope of this work*);

(b) section 101, so far as relating to England and so far as relating to a best value authority in Wales mentioned in subsection (7) of that section;

(c)–(f) (*outside the scope of this work.*)

(4) The following provisions shall come into force on such day as the National Assembly for Wales may by order appoint—

(a), (b) (*outside the scope of this work*);

(c) section 101, so far as relating to a best value authority in Wales, other than one mentioned in subsection (7) of that section;

(d)–(g) (*outside the scope of this work.*)

(5) So far as relating to Scotland, sections 101 and 102 shall come into force on such day as the Scottish Ministers may by order appoint.

(6) The remaining provisions of this Act—

(a) so far as relating to England, shall come into force on such day as the Secretary of State may by order appoint, and

(b) so far as relating to Wales, shall come into force on such day as the National Assembly for Wales may by order appoint.

(7) Power to make orders under this section is exercisable by statutory instrument.

(8) Orders under this section may make different provision for different purposes.

(9) A person who has power under this section to appoint a day for the coming into force of a provision may by order make in connection with the coming into force of that provision such transitional provision or saving as the person considers necessary or expedient.

[1586]

NOTES

Commencement: 18 September 2003.

Orders: the commencement orders relevant to the sections reproduced here are the Local Government Act 2003 (Commencement No 1 and Transitional Provisions and Savings) Order 2003, SI 2003/2938, and the Local Government Act 2003 (Commencement) (Wales) Order 2003, SI 2003/3034.

129 Short title and extent

(1) This Act may be cited as the Local Government Act 2003.

(2) Subject to the following provisions, this Act extends to England and Wales only.

(3) Sections 83(2), 101 and 102 extend also to Scotland.

(4) The following provisions extend also to Scotland, Northern Ireland and Gibraltar—
- (a) sections 103, 104 and 128,
- (b) this section, and
- (c) *(outside the scope of this work.)*

(5)–(8) *(Outside the scope of this work.)*

[1587]–[1590]

NOTES

Commencement: 18 September 2003.

GENDER RECOGNITION ACT 2004

(2004 c 7)

ARRANGEMENT OF SECTIONS

Consequences of issue of gender recognition certificate etc

Supplementary

SCHEDULES

An Act to make provision for and in connection with change of gender

[1 July 2004]

NOTES

Most of this Act covers matters outside the scope of this work, and only those provisions most directly relevant to employment law are printed. For reasons of space, the subject matter of sections not printed is not annotated. Amendments made to provisions included in this Handbook are noted to the appropriate provisions. The provisions reproduced here apply to the whole of the United Kingdom (s 28). All provisions which did not come into force on Royal assent came into force on 4 April 2005 (SI 2005/54).

Consequences of issue of gender recognition certificate etc

9 General

(1) Where a full gender recognition certificate is issued to a person, the person's gender becomes for all purposes the acquired gender (so that, if the acquired gender is the male gender, the person's sex becomes that of a man and, if it is the female gender, the person's sex becomes that of a woman).

(2) Subsection (1) does not affect things done, or events occurring, before the certificate is issued; but it does operate for the interpretation of enactments passed, and instruments and other documents made, before the certificate is issued (as well as those passed or made afterwards).

(3) Subsection (1) is subject to provision made by this Act or any other enactment or any subordinate legislation.

[1591]

NOTES

Commencement: 4 April 2005.

13 Social security benefits and pensions

Schedule 5 (entitlement to benefits and pensions) has effect.

[1592]

NOTES

Commencement: 4 April 2005.

15 Succession etc

The fact that a person's gender has become the acquired gender under this Act does not affect the disposal or devolution of property under a will or other instrument made before the appointed day.

[1593]

NOTES

Commencement: 4 April 2005.

19 Sport

(1) A body responsible for regulating the participation of persons as competitors in an event or events involving a gender-affected sport may, if subsection (2) is satisfied, prohibit or restrict the participation as competitors in the event or events of persons whose gender has become the acquired gender under this Act.

(2) This subsection is satisfied if the prohibition or restriction is necessary to secure—
- (a) fair competition, or
- (b) the safety of competitors,

at the event or events.

(3) "Sport" means a sport, game or other activity of a competitive nature.

(4) A sport is a gender-affected sport if the physical strength, stamina or physique of average persons of one gender would put them at a disadvantage to average persons of the other gender as competitors in events involving the sport.

(5) This section does not affect—
- (a) section 44 of the Sex Discrimination Act 1975 (c 65) (exception from Parts 2 to 4 of that Act for acts related to sport), or
- (b) Article 45 of the Sex Discrimination (Northern Ireland) Order 1976 (SI 1976/1042 (NI 15)) (corresponding provision for Northern Ireland).

[1594]

NOTES

Commencement: 4 April 2005.

Supplementary

29 Short title

This Act may be cited as the Gender Recognition Act 2004.

[1595]

NOTES

Commencement: 1 July 2004.

SCHEDULES

SCHEDULE 5
BENEFITS AND PENSIONS

Section 13

PART 1
INTRODUCTORY

1. This Schedule applies where a full gender recognition certificate is issued to a person.

[1596]

NOTES

Commencement: 4 April 2005.

PART 3
OCCUPATIONAL PENSION SCHEMES

14 Guaranteed minimum pensions etc: Great Britain

(1) In this paragraph "the 1993 Act" means the Pension Schemes Act 1993 (c 48); and expressions used in this paragraph and in that Act have the same meaning in this paragraph as in that Act.

(2) The fact that the person's gender has become the acquired gender does not affect the operation of section 14 of the 1993 Act (guaranteed minimum) in relation to the person, except to the extent that its operation depends on section 16 of the 1993 Act (revaluation); and sub-paragraphs (3) and (5) have effect subject to that.

(3) If (immediately before the certificate is issued) the person is a woman who is entitled to a guaranteed minimum pension but has not attained the age of 65—

(a) the person is for the purposes of section 13 of the 1993 Act and the guaranteed minimum pension provisions to be treated after it is issued as not having attained pensionable age (so that the entitlement ceases) but as attaining pensionable age on subsequently attaining the age of 65, and

(b) in a case where the person's guaranteed minimum pension has commenced before the certificate is issued, it is to be treated for the purposes of Chapter 3 of Part 4 of the 1993 Act (anti-franking) as if it had not.

(4) But sub-paragraph (3)(a) does not—

(a) affect any pension previously paid to the person, or

(b) prevent section 15 of the 1993 Act (increase of guaranteed minimum where commencement of guaranteed minimum pension postponed) operating to increase the person's guaranteed minimum by reason of a postponement of the commencement of the person's guaranteed minimum pension for a period ending before the certificate is issued.

(5) If (immediately before the certificate is issued) the person is a man who—

(a) has attained the age of 60, but

(b) has not attained the age of 65,

the person is to be treated for the purposes of section 13 of the 1993 Act and the guaranteed minimum pension provisions as attaining pensionable age when it is issued.

(6) If at that time the person has attained the age of 65, the fact that the person's gender has become the acquired gender does not affect the person's pensionable age for those purposes.

(7) The fact that the person's gender has become the acquired gender does not affect any guaranteed minimum pension to which the person is entitled as a widow or widower immediately before the certificate is issued (except in consequence of the operation of the previous provisions of this Schedule).

(8) If a transaction to which section 19 of the 1993 Act applies which is carried out before the certificate is issued discharges a liability to provide a guaranteed minimum pension for or in respect of the person, it continues to do so afterwards.

(9) "The guaranteed minimum pension provision" means so much of the 1993 Act (apart from section 13) and of any other enactment as relates to guaranteed minimum pensions.

15. (*Applies to Northern Ireland only.*)

16 Equivalent pension benefits: Great Britain

(1) The provision that may be made by regulations under paragraph 15 of Schedule 3 to the Social Security (Consequential Provisions) Act 1992 (c 6) (power to retain provisions repealed by Social Security Act 1973 (c 38), with or without modification, for transitional purposes) includes provision modifying the preserved equivalent pension benefits provisions in consequence of this Act.

(2) "The preserved equivalent pension benefits provisions" are the provisions of the National Insurance Act 1965 (c 51) relating to equivalent pension benefits continued in force, with or without modification, by regulations having effect as if made under that paragraph.

17. (*Applies to Northern Ireland only.*)

[1597]

NOTES

Commencement: 4 April 2005.

HIGHER EDUCATION ACT 2004

(2004 c 8)

An Act to make provision about research in the arts and humanities and about complaints by students against institutions providing higher education; to make provision about fees payable by students in higher education; to provide for the appointment of a Director of Fair Access to Higher Education; to make provision about grants and loans to students in higher or further education; to limit the jurisdiction of visitors of institutions providing higher education; and for connected purposes

[1 July 2004]

NOTES

Most of this Act covers matters outside the scope of this work, and only s 46 and the short title are reproduced here. For reasons of space, the subject matter of sections not printed is not annotated. Section 46 came into force on 1 January 2005 in relation to both England and Wales (SI 2004/2781 and SI 2004/3144) and applies to England and Wales only (s 53).

PART 5
MISCELLANEOUS AND GENERAL

Staff disputes: jurisdiction of visitor

46 Exclusion of visitor's jurisdiction in relation to staff disputes

(1) The visitor of a qualifying institution has no jurisdiction in respect of—

(a) any dispute relating to a member of staff which concerns his appointment or employment or the termination of his appointment or employment,

(b) any other dispute between a member of staff and the qualifying institution in respect of which proceedings could be brought before any court or tribunal, or

(c) any dispute as to the application of the statutes or other internal laws of the institution in relation to a matter falling within paragraph (a) or (b).

(2) In subsection (1) "qualifying institution" has the meaning given by section 11.

(3) In determining whether a dispute falls within subsection (1)(b) it is to be assumed that the visitor does not have jurisdiction to determine the dispute.

(4) Section 206 of the Education Reform Act 1988 (c 40) (which is superseded by subsection (1)) shall cease to have effect.

[1598]

NOTES

Commencement: 1 January 2005

Note for the purposes of this section that s 11 of this Act in Pt 2 provides as follows—

"11 Qualifying institutions

In this Part "qualifying institution" means any of the following institutions in England or Wales—

(a) a university (whether or not receiving financial support under section 65 of the 1992 Act) whose entitlement to grant awards is conferred or confirmed by—

(i) an Act of Parliament,

(ii) a Royal Charter, or

(iii) an order under section 76 of the 1992 Act;

(b) a constituent college, school or hall or other institution of a university falling within paragraph (a);

(c) an institution conducted by a higher education corporation;

(d) a designated institution, as defined by section 72(3) of the 1992 Act.".

General

54 Short title, etc

(1) This Act may be cited as the Higher Education Act 2004.

(2) This Act is to be included in the list of Education Acts set out in section 578 of the Education Act 1996 (c 56).

[1599]

NOTES

Commencement: 1 July 2004.

GANGMASTERS (LICENSING) ACT 2004

(2004 c 11)

ARRANGEMENT OF SECTIONS

Scope of Act

An Act to make provision for the licensing of activities involving the supply or use of workers in connection with agricultural work, the gathering of wild creatures and wild plants, the harvesting of fish from fish farms, and certain processing and packaging; and for connected purposes

[8 July 2004]

1, 2 ((*The Gangmasters Licensing Authority*) *outside the scope of this work.*)

Scope of Act

3 Work to which this Act applies

(1) The work to which this Act applies is—

(a) agricultural work,
(b) gathering shellfish, and
(c) processing or packaging—
  (i) any produce derived from agricultural work, or
  (ii) shellfish, fish or products derived from shellfish or fish.

This is subject to any provision made by regulations under subsection (5) below and to section 5 (territorial scope of application).

(2) In subsection (1)(a) "agricultural work" means work in agriculture.

(3) In this Act "agriculture" includes—

(a) dairy-farming,
(b) the production for the purposes of any trade, business or other undertaking (whether carried on for profit or not) of consumable produce,
(c) the use of land as grazing, meadow or pasture land,
(d) the use of land as an orchard or as osier land or woodland, and
(e) the use of land for market gardens or nursery grounds.

In paragraph (b) "consumable produce" means produce grown for sale, consumption or other use after severance from the land on which it is grown.

(4) In this Act "shellfish" means crustaceans and molluscs of any kind, and includes any part of a shellfish and any (or any part of any) brood, ware, halfware or spat of shellfish, and any spawn of shellfish, and the shell, or any part of the shell, of a shellfish.

(5) The Secretary of State may by regulations make provision—
(a) excluding work of a prescribed description from being work to which this Act applies;
(b) including work of the following nature as being work to which this Act applies—
(i) the gathering (by any manner) of wild creatures, or wild plants, of a prescribed description and the processing and packaging of anything so gathered, and
(ii) the harvesting of fish from a fish farm (within the meaning of the Diseases of Fish Act 1937 (c 33)).

[1600]

NOTES

Commencement: 1 December 2004.
Regulations: as of 6 April 2008 no Regulations had been made under this section.

4 Acting as a gangmaster

(1) This section defines what is meant in this Act by a person acting as a gangmaster.

(2) A person ("A") acts as a gangmaster if he supplies a worker to do work to which this Act applies for another person ("B").

(3) For the purposes of subsection (2) it does not matter—
(a) whether the worker works under a contract with A or is supplied to him by another person,
(b) whether the worker is supplied directly under arrangements between A and B or indirectly under arrangements involving one or more intermediaries,
(c) whether A supplies the worker himself or procures that the worker is supplied,
(d) whether the work is done under the control of A, B or an intermediary,
(e) whether the work done for B is for the purposes of a business carried on by him or in connection with services provided by him to another person.

(4) A person ("A") acts as a gangmaster if he uses a worker to do work to which this Act applies in connection with services provided by him to another person.

(5) A person ("A") acts as a gangmaster if he uses a worker to do any of the following work to which this Act applies for the purposes of a business carried on by him—
(a) harvesting or otherwise gathering agricultural produce following—
(i) a sale, assignment or lease of produce to A, or
(ii) the making of any other agreement with A,
where the sale, assignment, lease or other agreement was entered into for the purpose of enabling the harvesting or gathering to take place;
(b) gathering shellfish;
(c) processing or packaging agricultural produce harvested or gathered as mentioned in paragraph (a).

In this subsection "agricultural produce" means any produce derived from agriculture.

(6) For the purposes of subsection (4) or (5) A shall be treated as using a worker to do work to which this Act applies if he makes arrangements under which the worker does the work—
(a) whether the worker works for A (or for another) or on his own account, and
(b) whether or not he works under a contract (with A or another).

(7) Regulations under section 3(5)(b) may provide for the application of subsections (5) and (6) above in relation to work that is work to which this Act applies by virtue of the regulations.

[1601]

NOTES

Commencement: 1 December 2004.

5 Territorial scope of application

(1) The work to which this Act applies is work—
(a) in the United Kingdom,

(b) on any portion of the shore or bed of the sea, or of an estuary or tidal river, adjacent to the United Kingdom, whether above or below (or partly above and partly below) the low water mark, or

(c) in UK coastal waters.

(2) In subsection (1)(c) "UK coastal waters" means waters adjacent to the United Kingdom to a distance of six miles measured from the baselines from which the breadth of the territorial sea is measured.

In this subsection "miles" means international nautical miles of 1,852 metres.

(3) The provisions of this Act apply where a person acts as a gangmaster, whether in the United Kingdom or elsewhere, in relation to work to which this Act applies.

[1602]

NOTES

Commencement: 1 December 2004.

Licensing

6 Prohibition of unlicensed activities

(1) A person shall not act as a gangmaster except under the authority of a licence.

(2) Regulations made by the Secretary of State may specify circumstances in which a licence is not required.

[1603]

NOTES

Commencement: 1 December 2004 (sub-s (2)); 1 October 2006 (sub-s (1), for purposes related to work falling within s 3(1)(a), (c)); 6 April 2007 (sub-s (1), for purposes related to work falling within s 3(1)(b)).

Regulations: the Gangmasters Licensing (Exclusions) Regulations 2006, SI 2006/658.

7 Grant of licence

(1) The Authority may grant a licence if it thinks fit.

(2) A licence shall describe the activities authorised by it and shall be granted for such period as the Authority thinks fit.

(3) A licence authorises activities—

(a) by the holder of the licence, and

(b) by persons employed or engaged by the holder of the licence who are named or otherwise specified in the licence.

(4) In the case of a licence held otherwise than by an individual, the reference in subsection (3)(a) to activities by the holder of the licence shall be read as a reference only to such activities as are mentioned in whichever of the following provisions applies—

section 20(2) (body corporate);

section 21(2) (unincorporated association);

section 22(4) (partnership that is regarded as a legal person under the law of the country or territory under which it is formed).

(5) A licence shall be granted subject to such conditions as the Authority considers appropriate.

[1604]

NOTES

Commencement: 1 April 2005.

8 General power of Authority to make rules

(1) The Authority may make such rules as it thinks fit in connection with the licensing of persons acting as gangmasters.

(2) The rules may, in particular—

(a) prescribe the form and contents of applications for licences and other documents to be filed in connection with applications;
(b) regulate the procedure to be followed in connection with applications and authorise the rectification of procedural irregularities;
(c) prescribe time limits for doing anything required to be done in connection with an application and provide for the extension of any period so prescribed;
(d) prescribe the requirements which must be met before a licence is granted;
(e) provide for the manner in which the meeting of those requirements is to be verified;
(f) allow for the grant of licences on a provisional basis before it is determined whether the requirements for the grant of a licence are met and for the withdrawal of such licences (if appropriate) if it appears that those requirements are not met;
(g) prescribe the form of licences and the information to be contained in them;
(h) require the payment of such fees as may be prescribed or determined in accordance with the rules;
(i) provide that licences are to be granted subject to conditions requiring the licence holder—
    (i) to produce, in prescribed circumstances, evidence in a prescribed form of his being licensed, and
    (ii) to comply with any prescribed requirements relating to the recruitment, use and supply of workers.

(3) The Authority must consult the Secretary of State before making any rules about fees.

(4) In subsection (2) "prescribed" means prescribed by the rules.

[1605]

NOTES

Commencement: 1 April 2005.

Rules: the Gangmasters (Licensing Conditions) (No 2) Rules 2006, SI 2006/2373 (revoking and replacing the Gangmasters (Licensing Conditions) Rules 2006, SI 2006/660).

9 Modification, revocation or transfer of licence

(1) The Authority may by notice in writing to the licensee modify or revoke any licence granted to him (including any of the conditions of that licence)—
(a) with the consent of the licensee, or
(b) where it appears to him that a condition of the licence or any requirement of this Act has not been complied with.

(2) The modifications that may be made include one suspending the effect of the licence for such period as the Authority may determine.

(3) A licence may be transferred with the written consent of the Authority and in such other cases as may be determined by the Authority.

[1606]

NOTES

Commencement: 1 April 2005.

10 Appeals

(1) The Secretary of State shall by regulations make provision for an appeal against any decision of the Authority—
(a) to refuse an application for a licence,
(b) as to the conditions to which the grant of the licence is subject,
(c) to refuse consent to the transfer of a licence, or
(d) to modify or revoke a licence.

(2) The regulations shall make provision—
(a) for and in connection with the appointment of a person to hear and determine such appeals (including provision for the payment of remuneration and allowances to such a person), and
(b) as to the procedure to be followed in connection with an appeal.

[1607]

NOTES

Commencement: 1 December 2004.

Regulations: the Gangmasters (Appeals) Regulations 2006, SI 2006/662.

11 Register of licences

(1) The Authority shall establish and maintain a register of persons licensed under this Act.

(2) The register shall contain such particulars as the Authority may determine of every person who for the time being holds a licence or whose activities are authorised by a licence (whether or not they are named in the licence).

(3) The Authority shall ensure that appropriate arrangements are in force for allowing members of the public to inspect the contents of the register.

[1608]

NOTES

Commencement: 1 October 2006.

Offences

12 Offences: acting as a gangmaster, being in possession of false documents etc

(1) A person commits an offence if he acts as a gangmaster in contravention of section 6 (prohibition of unlicensed activities).

For this purpose a person acting as a gangmaster does not contravene section 6 by reason only of the fact that he breaches a condition of the licence which authorises him to so act.

(2) A person commits an offence if he has in his possession or under his control—

(a) a relevant document that is false and that he knows or believes to be false,

(b) a relevant document that was improperly obtained and that he knows or believes to have been improperly obtained, or

(c) a relevant document that relates to someone else,

with the intention of inducing another person to believe that he or another person acting as a gangmaster in contravention of section 6 is acting under the authority of a licence.

(3) A person guilty of an offence under subsection (1) or (2) is liable on summary conviction—

(a) in England and Wales, to imprisonment for a term not exceeding twelve months, or to a fine not exceeding the statutory maximum, or to both;

(b) in Scotland or Northern Ireland, to imprisonment for a term not exceeding six months, or to a fine not exceeding the statutory maximum, or to both.

In relation to an offence committed before the commencement of section 154(1) of the Criminal Justice Act 2003 (c 44), for "twelve months" in paragraph (a) substitute "six months".

(4) A person guilty of an offence under subsection (1) or (2) is liable on conviction on indictment to imprisonment for a term not exceeding ten years, or to a fine, or to both.

(5) For the purposes of this section—

(a) except in Scotland, a document is false only if it is false within the meaning of Part 1 of the Forgery and Counterfeiting Act 1981 (c 45) (see section 9(1) of that Act), and

(b) a document was improperly obtained if false information was provided, in or in connection with the application for its issue or an application for its modification, to the person who issued it or (as the case may be) to a person entitled to modify it,

and references to the making of a false document include references to the modification of a document so that it becomes false.

(6) In this section "relevant document" means—

(a) a licence, or
(b) any document issued by the Authority in connection with a licence.

[1609]

NOTES

Commencement: 1 October 2006 (for purposes related to work falling within s 3(1)(a), (c)); 6 April 2007 (for purposes related to work falling within s 3(1)(b)).

13 Offences: entering into arrangements with gangmasters

(1) A person commits an offence if—

(a) he enters into arrangements under which a person ("the gangmaster") supplies him with workers or services, and
(b) the gangmaster in supplying the workers or services contravenes section 6 (prohibition of unlicensed activities).

(2) In proceedings against a person for an offence under subsection (1) it is a defence for him to prove that he—

(a) took all reasonable steps to satisfy himself that the gangmaster was acting under the authority of a valid licence, and
(b) did not know, and had no reasonable grounds for suspecting that the gangmaster was not the holder of a valid licence.

(3) The Secretary of State may by regulations make provision as to what constitutes "reasonable steps" for the purposes of subsection (2)(a).

(4) A person guilty of an offence under subsection (1) is liable—

(a) on summary conviction in England and Wales, to imprisonment for a term not exceeding 51 weeks, or to a fine not exceeding the statutory maximum, or to both,
(b) on summary conviction in Scotland or Northern Ireland, to imprisonment for a term not exceeding six months, or to a fine not exceeding the statutory maximum, or to both.

In relation to an offence committed before the commencement of section 281(5) of the Criminal Justice Act 2003 (c 44), for "51 weeks" in paragraph (a) substitute "six months".

[1610]

NOTES

Commencement: 1 October 2006 (sub-s (3)); 1 December 2006 (sub-ss (1), (2), (4), for purposes related to work falling within s 3(1)(a), (c)); 6 April 2007 (sub-ss (1), (2), (4), for purposes related to work falling within s 3(1)(b)).

Regulations: as of 6 April 2008 no Regulations had been made under sub-s (3).

14 Offences: supplementary provisions

(1) An enforcement officer (see section 15) has the powers of arrest mentioned in subsection (2) (in addition to powers under [section 24A] of the Police and Criminal Evidence Act 1984 (c 60)) in relation to any of the following offences—

(a) an offence under section 12(1) or (2),
(b) conspiring to commit any such offence,
(c) attempting to commit any such offence,
(d) inciting, aiding, abetting, counselling or procuring the commission of any such offence.

(2) Those powers are as follows—

(a) if he has reasonable grounds for suspecting that such an offence has been committed, he may arrest without warrant anyone whom he has reasonable grounds for suspecting to be guilty of the offence;
(b) he may arrest without warrant—
    (i) anyone who is about to commit such an offence;
    (ii) anyone whom he has reasonable grounds for suspecting to be about to commit such an offence.

(3) Subsections (1) and (2) do not apply in Scotland.

(4) …

[1611]

NOTES

Commencement: 1 October 2006.

Sub-s (1): words in square brackets substituted by the Serious Organised Crime and Police Act 2005, s 111, Sch 7, Pt 4, para 62(a), as from 1 January 2006.

Sub-s (4): amends the Proceeds of Crime Act 2002, Schs 2, 4, 5.

Attempt, conspiracy or incitement to commit an offence: see the Serious Crime Act 2007, s 63(1), (2), Sch 6, Pt 1, para 50 which provides that any reference however expressed to (or to conduct amounting to) the offence abolished by s 59 of the 2007 Act (abolition of common law offence of inciting the commission of another offence) has effect as a reference to (or to conduct amounting to) the offences of encouraging or assisting the commission of an offence.

15–22 (*Ss 15–19* (*Enforcement*), *ss 20–22* (*supplementary*) *outside the scope of this work.*)

Miscellaneous and general

23–25 (*S 23* (*Annual report*), *s 24* (*financial provision*), *s 25* (*general provisions about the making of Regulations, etc*) *outside the scope of this work.*)

26 Meaning of "worker"

(1) In this Act "worker" means an individual who does work to which this Act applies.

(2) A person is not prevented from being a worker for the purposes of this Act by reason of the fact that he has no right to be, or to work, in the United Kingdom.

[1612]

NOTES

Commencement: 1 December 2004.

27 Exclusion of provisions relating to employment agencies and businesses

(1) The Employment Agencies Act 1973 (c 35) does not apply to an employment agency or an employment business in so far as it consists of activities for which a licence is required under this Act.

(2) In subsection (1) "employment agency" and "employment business" have the same meaning as in that Act.

[1613]

NOTES

Commencement: 1 October 2006 (for purposes related to work falling within s 3(1)(a), (c)); 6 April 2007 (for purposes related to work falling within s 3(1)(b)).

28 ((*Application to Northern Ireland*) *Outside the scope of this work.*)

29 Commencement and transitional provision

(1) The provisions of this Act come into force on such day as the Secretary of State may by order appoint.

(2) Different days may be appointed for different purposes and for different areas.

(3) The Secretary of State may by order make such transitional provision as he considers appropriate in connection with the coming into force of any provision of this Act.

[1614]

NOTES

Commencement: to be appointed.

Orders: the Gangmasters (Licensing) Act 2004 (Commencement No 1) Order 2004, SI 2004/2857; the Gangmasters (Licensing) Act 2004 (Commencement No 2) Order 2005, SI 2005/447; the Gangmasters (Licensing) Act 2004 (Commencement No 3) Order 2006, SI 2006/2406; the Gangmasters (Licensing) Act 2004 (Commencement No 4) Order 2006, SI 2006/2906; the Gangmasters (Licensing) Act 2004 (Commencement No 5) Order 2007, SI 2007/695.

For the statutory basis of orders made under a section not yet in force, see the Interpretation Act 1978, s 13 (anticipatory exercise of powers).

30 Short title and extent

(1) This Act may be cited as the Gangmasters (Licensing) Act 2004.

(2) This Act extends to England and Wales, Scotland and Northern Ireland.

[1615]

NOTES

Commencement: 1 December 2004.

(Sch 1 (Consequential amendments), Sch 2 (Application to Northern Ireland) outside the scope of this work.)

EMPLOYMENT RELATIONS ACT 2004

(2004 c 24)

An Act to amend the law relating to the recognition of trade unions and the taking of industrial action; to make provision about means of voting in ballots under the Trade Union and Labour Relations (Consolidation) Act 1992; to amend provisions of that Act relating to rights of members and non-members of trade unions and to make other provision about rights of trade union members, employees and workers; to make further provision concerning the enforcement of legislation relating to minimum wages; to make further provision about proceedings before and appeals from the Certification Officer; to make further provision about the amalgamation of trade unions; to make provision facilitating the administration of trade unions and the carrying out by them of their functions; and for connected purposes

[16 September 2004]

1–28 *(Pt 1 (ss 1–21: Union Recognition) inserts the Trade Union and Labour Relations (Consolidation) Act 1992, s 210A at* **[685A]***, and amends Sch A1 to the 1992 Act at* **[795]** *et seq; Pt 2 (ss 22–28: Law Relating to Industrial Action) contains various amendments to the 1992 Act (these amendments have been incorporated at the appropriate place.))*

PART 3
RIGHTS OF TRADE UNION MEMBERS, WORKERS AND EMPLOYEES

29–34 *(Insert the Trade Union and Labour Relations (Consolidation) Act 1992, s 145A–145F at* **[631A]** *et seq, amend ss 67, 146, 148, 151, 152, 174, 176 of the 1992 Act at* **[548]**, **[632]**, **[634]**, **[637]**, **[638]**, **[658]**, **[660]**, *and repeal the Employment Relations Act 1999, s 17.)*

Other rights of workers and employees

35–41 *(Substitute the Trade Union and Labour Relations (Consolidation) Act 1992, s 154 at* **[640]**, *and amend ss 237, 238 of that Act at* **[734]**,**[735]**, *amend the Employment Tribunals Act 1996, ss 10, 21 at* **[964]**, **[978]**, *amend the Employment Relations Act 1999, ss 10–12, 23 at* **[1432]**–**[1434]**, **[1442]**, *insert the Employment Rights Act 1996, ss 43M, 98B at* **[1062A]**, **[1137A]**, *amend ss 48, 105, 108, 194, 195, 199 of that Act at* **[1073]**, **[1149]**, **[1152]**, **[1238]**, **[1239]**, **[1241]**, *and amended s 109 (repealed))*

42 Information and consultation: Great Britain

(1) The Secretary of State may make regulations for the purpose of conferring on employees of an employer to whom the regulations apply, or on representatives of those employees, rights—

(a) to be informed by the employer about prescribed matters;
(b) to be consulted by the employer about prescribed matters.

(2) Regulations made under subsection (1) must make provision as to the employers to whom the regulations apply which may include provision—

(a) applying the regulations by reference to factors including the number of employees in the United Kingdom in the employer's undertaking;

(b) as to the method by which the number of employees in an employer's undertaking is to be calculated; and

(c) applying the regulations to different descriptions of employer with effect from different dates.

(3) Regulations made under subsection (1) may make provision—

(a) as to the circumstances in which the rights mentioned in subsection (1) arise and the extent of those rights;

(b) for and about the initiation and conduct of negotiations between employers to whom the regulations apply and their employees for the purposes of reaching an agreement satisfying prescribed conditions about the provision of information to the employees, and consultation of them (whether that provision or consultation is to be direct or through representatives);

(c) about the representatives the employees may have for the purposes of the regulations and the method by which those representatives are to be selected;

(d) as to the resolution of disputes and the enforcement of obligations imposed by the regulations or by an agreement of the kind mentioned in paragraph (b).

(4) Regulations made under subsection (1) may—

(a) confer jurisdiction (including exclusive jurisdiction) on employment tribunals and on the Employment Appeal Tribunal;

(b) confer functions on the Central Arbitration Committee;

(c) require or authorise the holding of ballots;

(d) amend, apply with or without modifications, or make provision similar to any provision of the Employment Rights Act 1996 (c 18) (including, in particular, Parts 5, 10 and 13), the Employment Tribunals Act 1996 (c 17) or the 1992 Act;

(e) include supplemental, incidental, consequential and transitional provision, including provision amending any enactment;

(f) make different provision for different cases or circumstances.

(5) Regulations made under subsection (1) may make any provision which appears to the Secretary of State to be necessary or expedient—

(a) for the purpose of implementing Directive 2002/14/EC of the European Parliament and of the Council of 11 March 2002 establishing a general framework for informing and consulting employees in the European Community;

(b) for the purpose of dealing with any matter arising out of or related to the United Kingdom's obligations under that Directive.

(6) Nothing in subsections (2) to (5) prejudices the generality of this section.

(7) Regulations under this section shall be made by statutory instrument.

(8) No such regulations may be made unless a draft of the regulations has been laid before Parliament and approved by a resolution of each House of Parliament.

(9) In this section "prescribed" means prescribed by regulations under this section.

[1616]

NOTES

Commencement: 16 September 2004.

Regulations: the Information and Consultation of Employees Regulations 2004, SI 2004/3426 at **[3254]**.

43–51 (*S 43* (*Information and consultation: Northern Ireland*) *outside the scope of this work; ss 44–47* (*Pt 4 Enforcement of Minimum Wage Legislation*) *amend the National Minimum Wage Act 1998, ss 19, 22 at* **[1363]**, **[1366]**, *insert ss 16A, 22A–22F of that Act at* **[1360A]**, **[1366A]**–**[1366F]**, *and contain miscellaneous amendments to agricultural wages legislation that are outside the scope of this work; ss 48–51* (*Pt 5 The Certification Officer*) *insert the Trade Union and Labour Relations* (*Consolidation*) *Act 1992, ss 101A, 101B, 256ZA at* **[592A]**, **[592B]**, **[755A]**, *amend ss 9, 98, 126, 133, 256A, 298, 299 of, and Sch A1 to, that Act at* **[477]**, **[584]**, **[612]**, **[619]**, **[756]**, **[789]**, **[790]**, **[795]**, *and amend the Employment Tribunals Act 1996, ss 33, 42 at* **[990]**, **[999]**.)

PART 6
MISCELLANEOUS

52, 53 (*Amend the Trade Union and Labour Relations (Consolidation) Act 1992, ss 34, 36, 37, 46 at* **[504]**, **[506]**, **[507]**, **[525]**.)

54 Means of voting in ballots and elections

(1) The Secretary of State may by order provide, in relation to any description of ballot or election authorised or required by the 1992 Act, that any ballot or election of that description is to be conducted by such one or more permissible means as the responsible person determines.

(2) A "permissible means" is a means of voting that the order provides is permissible for that description of ballot or election.

(3) "The responsible person" is a person specified, or of a description specified, by the order.

(4) An order under this section may—

(a) include provision about the determinations that may be made by the responsible person, including provision requiring specified factors to be taken into account, or specified criteria to be applied, in making a determination;

(b) allow the determination of different means of voting for voters in different circumstances;

(c) allow a determination to be such that voters have a choice of means of voting.

(5) The means that an order specifies as permissible means must, in the case of any description of ballot or election, include (or consist of) postal voting.

(6) An order under this section may—

(a) include supplemental, incidental and consequential provisions;

(b) make different provision for different cases or circumstances.

(7) An order under this section may—

(a) modify the provisions of the 1992 Act;

(b) exclude or apply (with or without modifications) any provision of that Act;

(c) make provision as respects any ballot or election conducted by specified means which is similar to any provision of that Act relating to ballots or elections.

(8) The power to make an order under this section is exercisable by statutory instrument.

(9) No order may be made under this section unless a draft of the order has been laid before Parliament and approved by a resolution of each House.

(10) The Secretary of State shall not make an order under this section which provides that a means of voting is permissible for a description of ballot or election unless he considers—

(a) that a ballot or election of that description conducted by that means could, if particular conditions were satisfied, meet the required standard; and

(b) that, in relation to any ballot or election of that description held after the order comes into force, the responsible person will not be permitted to determine that that means must or may be used by any voters unless he has taken specified factors into account or applied specified criteria.

(11) In specifying in an order under this section factors to be taken into account or criteria to be applied by the responsible person, the Secretary of State must have regard to the need for ballots and elections to meet the required standard.

(12) For the purposes of subsections (10) and (11) a ballot or election meets "the required standard" if it is such that—

(a) those entitled to vote have an opportunity to do so;

(b) votes cast are secret;

(c) the risk of any unfairness or malpractice is minimised.

(13) In this section "specified" means specified in an order under this section.

[1617]

NOTES

Commencement: 31 December 2004.
Orders: as of 6 April 2008, no Orders had been made under this section.

55 (*Inserts the Trade Union and Labour Relations* (*Consolidation*) *Act 1992, ss 116A, 118*(*8*) *at* **[602A]**, **[604]**.)

PART 7
SUPPLEMENTARY PROVISIONS

56 Meaning of "the 1992 Act"

In this Act "the 1992 Act" means the Trade Union and Labour Relations (Consolidation) Act 1992 (c 52).

[1618]

NOTES

Commencement: 16 September 2004.

57, 58 (*S 57 introduces Schs 1, 2* (*Minor and consequential amendments and repeals*); *s 58* (*Corresponding provision for Northern Ireland*) *outside the scope of this work.*)

59 Citation, commencement and extent

(1) This Act may be cited as the Employment Relations Act 2004.

(2) This section and sections 42, 43, 56 and 58 shall come into force on the day on which this Act is passed.

(3) The other provisions of this Act shall not come into force until such day as the Secretary of State may by order made by statutory instrument appoint, and different days may be appointed for different purposes.

(4) An order under subsection (3) may contain such transitional provisions and savings as the Secretary of State considers necessary or expedient in connection with the coming into force of any of the provisions of this Act.

(5) Subject to subsections (6) and (7), this Act extends to England and Wales and to Scotland.

(6) Any amendment by this Act of an enactment (including an enactment contained in Northern Ireland legislation) has the same extent as the enactment amended.

(7) Sections 43 and 58 extend to Northern Ireland only.

[1619]

NOTES

Commencement: 16 September 2004.
Orders: the Employment Relations Act 2004 (Commencement No 1 and Transitional Provisions) Order 2004, SI 2004/2566; the Employment Relations Act 2004 (Commencement No 2 and Transitional Provisions) Order 2004, SI 2004/3342; the Employment Relations Act 2004 (Commencement No 3 and Transitional Provisions) Order 2005, SI 2005/872; the Employment Relations Act 2004 (Commencement No 4 and Transitional Provisions) Order 2005, SI 2005/2419.

(*Schs 1, 2 contain minor and consequential amendments and repeals; in so far as these are relevant to this work, they have been taken in at the appropriate place.*)

PENSIONS ACT 2004

(2004 c 35)

ARRANGEMENT OF SECTIONS

An Act to make provision relating to pensions and financial planning for retirement and provision relating to entitlement to bereavement payments, and for connected purposes

[18 November 2004]

NOTES

Most of this Act covers matters outside the scope of this work, and only those provisions most directly relevant to employment law are printed. For reasons of space, the subject matter of sections not printed is not annotated. Amendments made to provisions included in this Handbook are noted to the appropriate provisions. The substantive provisions reproduced here apply to Great Britain only (s 323), and come into force in accordance with provision made by the Secretary of State by order (s 322(1)).

PART 4
FINANCIAL PLANNING AND RETIREMENT

Employee information and advice

238 Information and advice to employees

(1) Regulations may require employers to take action for the purpose of enabling employees to obtain information and advice about pensions and saving for retirement.

(2) Regulations under subsection (1) may in particular—

(a) provide that they are to apply in relation to employers of a prescribed description and employees of a prescribed description;

(b) make different provision for different descriptions of employers and employees;

(c) make provision as to the action to be taken by employers (including the frequency at which, and the time and place at which, action is to be taken);

(d) make provision as to the description of information and advice in relation to which requirements apply;

(e) make provision about the description of person authorised to provide any such information and advice.

(3) Employers to whom regulations under subsection (1) apply must provide information to the Regulator about the action taken by them for the purpose of complying with the regulations.

(4) Regulations may make provision as to—

(a) the information to be provided under subsection (3);

(b) the form and manner in which the information is to be provided;

(c) the period within which the information is to be provided.

(5) Section 10 of the Pensions Act 1995 (c 26) (civil penalties) applies to any person who, without reasonable excuse, fails to comply with subsection (3).

(6) In this section "employer" means any employer, whether or not resident or incorporated in any part of the United Kingdom.

[1620]

NOTES

Commencement: to be appointed.

PART 5
OCCUPATIONAL AND PERSONAL PENSION SCHEMES:
MISCELLANEOUS PROVISIONS

Requirements for member-nominated trustees and directors

241 Requirement for member-nominated trustees

(1) The trustees of an occupational trust scheme must secure—

(a) that, within a reasonable period of the commencement date, arrangements are in place which provide for at least one-third of the total number of trustees to be member-nominated trustees, and

(b) that those arrangements are implemented.

(2) "Member-nominated trustees" are trustees of an occupational trust scheme who—

(a) are nominated as the result of a process in which at least the following are eligible to participate—

(i) all the active members of the scheme or an organisation which adequately represents the active members, and

(ii) all the pensioner members of the scheme or an organisation which adequately represents the pensioner members, and

(b) are selected as a result of a process which involves some or all of the members of the scheme.

(3) The "commencement date", in relation to a scheme, is—

(a) the date upon which this section first applies in relation to the scheme, or

(b) in the case of a scheme to which this section has ceased to apply and then reapplies, the date on which the section reapplies to it.

(4) The arrangements may provide for a greater number of member-nominated trustees than that required to satisfy the one-third minimum mentioned in subsection (1)(a) only if the employer has approved the greater number.

(5) The arrangements—

(a) must provide for the nomination and selection process to take place within a reasonable period of any requirement arising under the arrangements to appoint a member-nominated trustee,

(b) must provide, where a vacancy is not filled because insufficient nominations are received, for the nomination and selection process to be repeated at reasonable intervals until the vacancy is filled,

(c) must provide that where the employer so requires, a person who is not a member of the scheme must have the employer's approval to qualify for selection as a member-nominated trustee, and

(d) subject to paragraph (c), may provide that, where the number of nominations received is equal to or less than the number of appointments required, the nominees are deemed to be selected.

(6) The arrangements must provide that the removal of a member-nominated trustee requires the agreement of all the other trustees.

(7) Nothing in the arrangements or in the provisions of the scheme may exclude member-nominated trustees from the exercise of functions exercisable by other trustees by reason only of the fact that they are member-nominated trustees.

(8) This section does not apply in relation to an occupational trust scheme if—

(a) every member of the scheme is a trustee of the scheme and no other person is such a trustee,

(b) every trustee of the scheme is a company, or

(c) the scheme is of a prescribed description.

(9) If, in the case of an occupational trust scheme, the arrangements required by subsection (1)—

(a) are not in place as required by subsection (1)(a), or

(b) are not being implemented,

section 10 of the Pensions Act 1995 (c 26) (civil penalties) applies to any trustee who has failed to take all reasonable steps to secure compliance.

[1621]

NOTES

Commencement: 1 November 2005 (for the purpose of conferring power to make Regulations); 6 April 2006 (otherwise).

Regulations: the Occupational Pension Schemes (Member-nominated Trustees and Directors) Regulations 2006, SI 2006/714 at **[3396]**; the Occupational and Personal Pension Schemes (Miscellaneous Amendments) Regulations 2007, SI 2007/814.

---

242 Requirement for member-nominated directors of corporate trustees

(1) Where a company is a trustee of an occupational trust scheme and every trustee of the scheme is a company, the company must secure—

(a) that, within a reasonable period of the commencement date, arrangements are in place which provide for at least one-third of the total number of directors of the company to be member-nominated directors, and

(b) that those arrangements are implemented.

(2) "Member-nominated directors" are directors of the company in question who—

(a) are nominated as the result of a process in which at least the following are eligible to participate—

(i) all the active members of the occupational trust scheme or an organisation which adequately represents the active members, and

(ii) all the pensioner members of the occupational trust scheme or an organisation which adequately represents the pensioner members, and

(b) are selected as a result of a process which involves some or all of the members of that scheme.

(3) The "commencement date", in relation to a company, is—

(a) the date upon which this section first applies in relation to the company, or

(b) in the case of a company to which this section has ceased to apply and then reapplies, the date on which the section reapplies to it.

(4) The arrangements may provide for a greater number of member-nominated directors than that required to satisfy the one-third minimum mentioned in subsection (1)(a) only if the employer has approved the greater number.

(5) The arrangements—

(a) must provide for the nomination and selection process to take place within a reasonable period of any requirement arising under the arrangements to appoint a member-nominated director,

(b) must provide, where a vacancy is not filled because insufficient nominations are received, for the nomination and selection process to be repeated at reasonable intervals until the vacancy is filled,

(c) must provide that where the employer so requires, a person who is not a member of the scheme must have the employer's approval to qualify for selection as a member-nominated director, and

(d) subject to paragraph (c), may provide that, where the number of nominations received is equal to or less than the number of appointments required, the nominees are deemed to be selected.

(6) The arrangements must provide that the removal of a member-nominated director requires the agreement of all the other directors.

(7) Nothing in the arrangements may exclude member-nominated directors from the exercise of functions exercisable by other directors by reason only of the fact that they are member-nominated directors.

(8) Where the same company is a trustee of two or more occupational trust schemes by reference to each of which this section applies to the company, then, subject to subsection (9), the preceding provisions of this section have effect as if—

(a) the schemes were a single scheme,

(b) the members of each of the schemes were members of that single scheme, and

(c) the references to "the employer" were references to all the employers in relation to the schemes.

(9) Where, apart from this subsection, subsection (8) would apply in relation to a company, the company may elect that subsection (8)

(a) is not to apply as mentioned in that subsection, or

(b) is to apply but only in relation to some of the schemes to which it would otherwise apply.

(10) This section does not apply in relation to an occupational trust scheme if the scheme is of a prescribed description.

(11) If, in the case of a company which is a trustee of an occupational trust scheme, the arrangements required by subsection (1)—

(a) are not in place as required by subsection (1)(a), or

(b) are not being implemented,

section 10 of the Pensions Act 1995 (c 26) (civil penalties) applies to the company.

[1622]

NOTES

Commencement: 1 November 2005 (for the purpose of conferring power to make Regulations); 6 April 2006 (otherwise).

Regulations: the Occupational Pension Schemes (Member-nominated Trustees and Directors) Regulations 2006, SI 2006/714 at **[3396]**; the Occupational and Personal Pension Schemes (Miscellaneous Amendments) Regulations 2007, SI 2007/814.

243 Member-nominated trustees and directors: supplementary

(1) The Secretary of State may, by order, amend sections 241(1)(a) and (4) and 242(1)(a) and (4) by substituting, in each of those provisions, "one-half" for "one-third".

(2) Regulations may modify sections 241 and 242 (including any of the provisions mentioned in subsection (1)) in their application to prescribed cases.

(3) In sections 241 and 242—

"company" means a company within the meaning given by section 735(1) of the Companies Act 1985 (c 6) or a company which may be wound up under Part 5 of the Insolvency Act 1986 (c 45) (unregistered companies);

"occupational trust scheme" means an occupational pension scheme established under a trust.

[1623]

NOTES

Commencement: 1 November 2005.

Regulations: the Occupational Pension Schemes (Member-nominated Trustees and Directors) Regulations 2006, SI 2006/714 at **[3396]**.

Pension protection on transfer of employment

257 Conditions for pension protection

(1) This section applies in relation to a person ("the employee") where—

[(a) there is a relevant transfer within the meaning of the TUPE regulations,]

(b) by virtue of the transfer the employee ceases to be employed by the transferor and becomes employed by the transferee, and

(c) at the time immediately before the employee becomes employed by the transferee—

(i) there is an occupational pension scheme ("the scheme") in relation to which the transferor is the employer, and

(ii) one of subsections (2), (3) and (4) applies.

(2) This subsection applies where—

(a) the employee is an active member of the scheme, and

(b) if any of the benefits that may be provided under the scheme are money purchase benefits—

(i) the transferor is required to make contributions to the scheme in respect of the employee, or

(ii) the transferor is not so required but has made one or more such contributions.

(3) This subsection applies where—

(a) the employee is not an active member of the scheme but is eligible to be such a member, and

(b) if any of the benefits that may be provided under the scheme are money purchase benefits, the transferor would have been required to make contributions to the scheme in respect of the employee if the employee had been an active member of it.

(4) This subsection applies where—

(a) the employee is not an active member of the scheme, nor eligible to be such a member, but would have been an active member of the scheme or eligible to be such a member if, after the date on which he became employed by the transferor, he had been employed by the transferor for a longer period, and

(b) if any of the benefits that may be provided under the scheme are money purchase benefits, the transferor would have been required to make contributions to the scheme in respect of the employee if the employee had been an active member of it.

(5) For the purposes of this section, the condition in subsection (1)(c) is to be regarded as satisfied in any case where it would have been satisfied but for any action taken by the transferor by reason of the transfer.

(6) …

(7) In the case of a scheme which is contracted-out by virtue of section 9 of the Pension Schemes Act 1993 (c 48), the references in subsections (2)(b), (3)(b) and (4)(b) to contributions mean contributions other than minimum payments (within the meaning of that Act).

(8) In this section—

the "TUPE Regulations" means the [Transfer of Undertakings (Protection of Employment) Regulations 2006];

references to the transferor include any associate of the transferor, and section 435 of the Insolvency Act 1986 (c 45) applies for the purposes of this section as it applies for the purposes of that Act.

[1624]

NOTES

Commencement: 6 April 2005.

Sub-s (1): para (a) substituted by the Transfer of Undertakings (Protection of Employment) Regulations 2006, SI 2006/246, reg 20(3), Sch 2, paras 13(1), (2), as from 6 April 2006 (for transitional provisions in relation to a relevant transfer, etc, that took place before that date, see reg 21 of the 2006 Regulations at **[3395]**).

Sub-s (6): repealed by SI 2006/246, reg 20(3), Sch 2, paras 13(1), (3), as from 6 April 2006 (for transitional provisions see the note above).

Sub-s (7): repealed by the Pensions Act 2007, ss 15(3)(a), 27(2), Sch 4, Pt 1, para 41, Sch 7, Pt 6, as from a day to be appointed.

Sub-s (8): words in square brackets in definition "TUPE Regulations" substituted by SI 2006/246, reg 20(3), Sch 2, paras 13(1), (4), as from 6 April 2006 (for transitional provisions see the note above).

258 Form of protection

(1) In a case where section 257 applies, it is a condition of the employee's contract of employment with the transferee that the requirements in subsection (2) or the requirement in subsection (3) are complied with.

(2) The requirements in this subsection are that—

(a) the transferee secures that, as from the relevant time, the employee is, or is eligible to be, an active member of an occupational pension scheme in relation to which the transferee is the employer, and

(b) in a case where the scheme is a money purchase scheme, as from the relevant time—

(i) the transferee makes relevant contributions to the scheme in respect of the employee, or

(ii) if the employee is not an active member of the scheme but is eligible to be such a member, the transferee would be required to make such contributions if the employee were an active member, and

(c) in a case where the scheme is not a money purchase scheme, as from the relevant time the scheme—

(i) satisfies the statutory standard referred to in section 12A of the Pension Schemes Act 1993 (c 48), or

(ii) if regulations so provide, complies with such other requirements as may be prescribed.

(3) The requirement in this subsection is that, as from the relevant time, the transferee makes relevant contributions to a stakeholder pension scheme of which the employee is a member.

(4) The requirement in subsection (3) is for the purposes of this section to be regarded as complied with by the transferee during any period in relation to which the condition in subsection (5) is satisfied.

(5) The condition in this subsection is that the transferee has offered to make relevant contributions to a stakeholder pension scheme of which the employee is eligible to be a member (and the transferee has not withdrawn the offer).

(6) Subsection (1) does not apply in relation to a contract if or to the extent that the employee and the transferee so agree at any time after the time when the employee becomes employed by the transferee.

(7) In this section—

"the relevant time" means—

(a) in a case where section 257 applies by virtue of the application of subsection (2) or (3) of that section, the time when the employee becomes employed by the transferee;

(b) in a case where that section applies by virtue of the application of subsection (4) of that section, the time at which the employee would have been a member of the scheme referred to in subsection (1)(c)(i) of that section or (if earlier) would have been eligible to be such a member;

"relevant contributions" means such contributions in respect of such period or periods as may be prescribed;

"stakeholder pension scheme" means a pension scheme which is registered under section 2 of the Welfare Reform and Pensions Act 1999 (c 30).

[1625]

NOTES

Commencement: 10 February 2005 (sub-s (2)(c)(ii) and the definition of "relevant contributions" in sub-s (7) (for the purpose of conferring power to make regulations, orders or rules only)); 6 April 2005 (otherwise).

Regulations: the Transfer of Employment (Pension Protection) Regulations 2005, SI 2005/649 at **[3295]**.

Consultation by employers

259 Consultation by employers: occupational pension schemes

(1) Regulations may require any prescribed person who is the employer in relation to an occupational pension scheme and who—

(a) proposes to make a prescribed decision in relation to the scheme, or

(b) has been notified by the trustees or managers of the scheme that they propose to make a prescribed decision in relation to the scheme,

to consult prescribed persons in the prescribed manner before the decision is made.

(2) Regulations may require the trustees or managers of an occupational pension scheme not to make a prescribed decision in relation to the scheme unless—

(a) they have notified the employer of the proposed decision, and

(b) they are satisfied that the employer has undertaken any consultation required by virtue of subsection (1).

(3) The validity of any decision made in relation to an occupational pension scheme is not affected by any failure to comply with regulations under this section.

(4) Section 261 contains further provisions about regulations under this section.

[1626]

NOTES

Commencement: 1 January 2006 (for the purpose of making regulations); 6 April 2006 (otherwise).

Multi-employer Schemes: this section and s 261 are modified, in relation to multi-employer schemes, by the Occupational Pension Schemes (Consultation by Employers) (Modification for Multi-employer Schemes) Regulations 2006, SI 2006/16, reg 2, so that any reference in those sections to the trustees or managers of an occupational pension scheme is to be treated as if it included a reference to any other person who under the rules of a multi-employer scheme has power to make a decision in relation to the scheme.

Regulations: the Occupational and Personal Pension Schemes (Consultation by Employers and Miscellaneous Amendment) Regulations 2006, SI 2006/349 at **[3395A]**; the Occupational and Personal Pension Schemes (Miscellaneous Amendments) Regulations 2006, SI 2006/778; the Occupational and Personal Pension Schemes (Miscellaneous Amendments) Regulations 2007, SI 2007/814.

260 Consultation by employers: personal pension schemes

(1) Regulations may require any prescribed person who—

(a) is the employer in relation to a personal pension scheme where direct payment arrangements exist in respect of one or more members of the scheme who are his employees, and

(b) proposes to make a prescribed decision affecting the application of the direct payment arrangements in relation to those employees,

to consult prescribed persons in the prescribed manner before he makes the decision.

(2) The validity of any decision prescribed for the purposes of subsection (1)(b) is not affected by any failure to comply with regulations under this section.

(3) Section 261 contains further provisions about regulations under this section.

[1627]

NOTES

Commencement: 1 January 2006 (for the purpose of making regulations); 6 April 2006 (otherwise).

Regulations: the Occupational and Personal Pension Schemes (Consultation by Employers and Miscellaneous Amendment) Regulations 2006, SI 2006/349 at **[3395A]**; the Occupational and Personal Pension Schemes (Miscellaneous Amendments) Regulations 2006, SI 2006/778.

261 Further provisions about regulations relating to consultation

(1) In this section "consultation regulations" means regulations under section 259 or 260.

(2) Consultation regulations may—

(a) make provision about the time to be allowed for consultation;

(b) prescribe the information which must be provided to the persons who are required to be consulted;

(c) confer a discretion on the employer in prescribed cases as to the persons who are to be consulted;

(d) make provision about the representatives the employees may have for the purposes of the regulations and the methods by which those representatives are to be selected;

(e) require or authorise the holding of ballots;

(f) amend, apply with or without modifications, or make provision similar to, any provision of the Employment Rights Act 1996 (c 18) (including, in particular, Parts 5, 10 and 13), the Employment Tribunals Act 1996 (c 17) or the Trade Union and Labour Relations (Consolidation) Act 1992 (c 52);

(g) enable any requirement for consultation imposed by the regulations to be waived or relaxed by order of the Regulator;

(h) require the employer to communicate to the trustees and managers of the scheme any representations received by the employer in response to any consultation required by the regulations.

(3) Persons on whom obligations are imposed by consultation regulations, either as employers or as the trustees or managers of occupational pension schemes, must, if so required by the Regulator, provide information to the Regulator about the action taken by them for the purpose of complying with the regulations.

(4) Consultation regulations may make provision as to—

(a) the information to be provided under subsection (3);

(b) the form and manner in which the information is to be provided;

(c) the period within which the information is to be provided.

(5) Nothing in consultation regulations is to be regarded as affecting any duty to consult arising otherwise than under the regulations.

[1628]

NOTES

Commencement: 1 January 2006 (for the purpose of making regulations); 6 April 2006 (otherwise).

Multi-employer Schemes: see the note to s 59 at **[1626]**.

Regulations: the Occupational and Personal Pension Schemes (Consultation by Employers and Miscellaneous Amendment) Regulations 2006, SI 2006/349 at **[3395A]**.

PART 9

MISCELLANEOUS AND SUPPLEMENTARY

Miscellaneous and Supplementary

325 Short title

This Act may be cited as the Pensions Act 2004.

[1629]

NOTES

Commencement: 18 November 2004.

DISABILITY DISCRIMINATION ACT 2005 (NOTE)

(2005 c 13)

NOTES

This Act is largely amending. The main amendments are to the Disability Discrimination Act 1995 (at **[900]** et seq) though many of these relate to areas that are outside the scope of this work. Amendments to provisions of the 1995 Act that are within the scope of this work have been incorporated into the text at the appropriate points. There were also minor amendments to the Disability Rights Commission Act 1999 (repealed by the Equality Act 2006, ss 40, 91, Sch 3, para 59, Sch 4, as from 1 October 2007), as well as other legislation that is, again, outside the scope of this work.

[1630]

SMOKING, HEALTH AND SOCIAL CARE (SCOTLAND) ACT 2005

(2005 asp 13)

ARRANGEMENT OF SECTIONS

PART 1
SMOKING: PROHIBITION AND CONTROL

PART 7
GENERAL

An Act of the Scottish Parliament to prohibit smoking in certain wholly or substantially enclosed places; to enable the Scottish Ministers by order to vary the minimum age limit of those to whom tobacco may be sold; to make provision in relation to general dental services, general ophthalmic services, personal dental services, pharmaceutical care services and detection of vision problems in children; to make provision in relation to disqualification by the NHS Tribunal; to enable the Scottish Ministers to establish a scheme for the making of payments to certain persons infected with hepatitis C as a result of NHS treatment and to certain persons infected with the virus by transmission of it from a person infected with it as a result of such treatment; to amend the Regulation of Care (Scotland) Act 2001 as respects what constitutes an independent health care service, the implementation of certain decisions by the Scottish Commission for the Regulation of Care or the Scottish Social Services Council, the provision of information to the Council and the minimum frequency of inspection of care services by the Commission; to make provision providing further time for applications to be made for registration of child care agencies and housing support services under the Regulation of Care (Scotland) Act 2001 and provide authorisation for the payment of certain grants to such services while not registered under that Act; to amend the Adults with Incapacity (Scotland) Act 2000 as respects authorisation of medical treatment; to amend the Public Health (Scotland) Act 1897 to introduce a right of appeal in certain cases under that Act; to enable the Scottish Ministers to form, participate in and provide assistance to companies for the purpose of providing facilities or services for persons exercising functions under the National Health Service (Scotland) Act 1978 or of making money available to the health service in Scotland; to amend the rules as to membership of and other matters relating to the Scottish Hospital Endowments Research Trust; and for connected purposes

[5 August 2005]

NOTES

Only those provisions of this Act relevant to employment law are reproduced. Provisions not reproduced are not annotated.

PART 1
SMOKING: PROHIBITION AND CONTROL

1 Offence of permitting others to smoke in no-smoking premises

(1) A person who, having the management or control of no-smoking premises, knowingly permits another to smoke there commits an offence.

(2) A person accused of an offence under this section is to be regarded as having knowingly permitted another to smoke in no-smoking premises if that person ought to have known that the other person was smoking there.

(3) It is a defence for an accused charged with an offence under this section to prove—

- (a) that the accused (or any employee or agent of the accused) took all reasonable precautions and exercised all due diligence not to commit the offence; or
- (b) that there were no lawful and reasonably practicable means by which the accused could prevent the other person from smoking in the no-smoking premises.

(4) A person guilty of an offence under this section is liable, on summary conviction, to a fine not exceeding level 4 on the standard scale.

[1631]

NOTES

Commencement: 26 March 2006 (at 0600 hours)

2 Offence of smoking in no-smoking premises

(1) A person who smokes in no-smoking premises commits an offence.

(2) It is a defence for an accused charged with an offence under this section to prove that the accused did not know, and could not reasonably be expected to have known, that the place in which it is alleged that the accused was smoking was no-smoking premises.

(3) A person guilty of an offence under this section is liable, on summary conviction, to a fine not exceeding level 3 on the standard scale.

[1632]

NOTES

Commencement: 26 March 2006 (at 0600 hours).

3 Display of warning notices in and on no-smoking premises

(1) If notices are not conspicuously displayed—

- (a) in, on or near no-smoking premises so as to be visible to and legible by persons in and persons approaching the premises; and
- (b) stating—
  - (i) that the premises are no-smoking premises; and
  - (ii) that it is an offence to smoke there or knowingly to permit smoking there,

the person having the management or control of the premises commits an offence.

(2) It is a defence for an accused charged with an offence under this section to prove that the accused (or any employee or agent of the accused) took all reasonable precautions and exercised all due diligence not to commit the offence.

(3) The Scottish Ministers may, after consulting such persons as they consider appropriate, by regulations provide further as to the manner of display, form and content of the notices referred to in subsection (1) and that any such provision is to be treated, for the purposes of that subsection, as if incorporated in it.

(4) A person guilty of an offence under this section is liable, on summary conviction, to a fine not exceeding level 3 on the standard scale.

[1633]

NOTES

Commencement: 1 November 2005 (sub-s (3)); 26 March 2006 (at 0600 hours) (otherwise).

Regulations: the Prohibition of Smoking in Certain Premises (Scotland) Regulations 2006, SSI 2006/90 at **[3370]**.

4 Meaning of "smoke" and "no-smoking premises"

(1) In this Part, "smoke" means smoke tobacco, any substance or mixture which includes it or any other substance or mixture; and a person is to be taken as smoking if the person is holding or otherwise in possession or control of lit tobacco, of any lit substance or mixture which includes tobacco or of any other lit substance or mixture which is in a form or in a receptacle in which it can be smoked.

(2) In this Part, "no-smoking premises" means such premises or such classes of premises, being premises of a kind mentioned in subsection (4), as are prescribed by regulations made by the Scottish Ministers after consulting such persons as they consider appropriate on a draft of the regulations.

(3) Regulations under subsection (2) may prescribe premises or parts of premises or classes of premises or parts of premises which are excluded from the definition of "no-smoking premises".

(4) The kind of premises referred to in subsection (2) is premises which are wholly or substantially enclosed and—

(a) to which the public or a section of the public has access;
(b) which are being used wholly or mainly as a place of work;
(c) which are being used by and for the purposes of a club or other unincorporated association; or
(d) which are being used wholly or mainly for the provision of education or of health or care services.

(5) In subsection (4)(b), the reference to work includes work undertaken for no financial advantage.

(6) Regulations under subsection (2) may, for the purposes of that subsection, define or elaborate the meaning of any of the expressions—

(a) "premises";
(b) "wholly or substantially enclosed";
(c) "the public"; and
(d) "has access".

(7) Regulations under subsection (2) may define or elaborate the meaning of "premises"—

(a) by reference to the person or class of person who owns or occupies them;
(b) so as to include vehicles, vessels, trains and other means of transport (except aircraft), or such, or such classes, of them as are specified in the regulations.

(8) The Scottish Ministers may, by regulations, after consulting such persons as they consider appropriate on a draft of the regulations, modify subsection (4) so as—

(a) to add a kind of premises to; or
(b) remove a kind of premises (but not the kind referred to in paragraph (a) of that subsection) from,

those in that subsection.

(9) Regulations made by virtue of subsection (7)(b) may provide as to how the statement referred to in section 3(1)(b) is to be expressed in the case of each of the means of transport referred to in the regulations and that any such provision is to be treated, for the purposes of that section, as if incorporated in it.

[1634]

NOTES

Commencement: the Smoking, Health and Social Care (Scotland) Act 2005 (Commencement No 1) Order 2005, SSI 2005/492 provides that sub-ss (2), (3), (7) of this section come into force on 1 November 2005 (see Sch 2 to that Order) and that the remaining subsections come into force on 26 March 2006 (at 0600 hours) (see art 3(d) of that Order). However, the Smoking, Health and Social Care (Scotland) Act 2005 (Commencement No 2) Order 2005, SSI 2005/642 provides that sub-ss (6), (8), (9) above come into force on 16 December 2005 (see art 2 of that Order), and the Smoking, Health and Social Care (Scotland) Act 2005 (Commencement No 3) Order 2006, SSI 2006/47 provides that this section, in so far as not already in force, shall come into force on 7 February 2006 (see art 2 of that Order).

Regulations: the Prohibition of Smoking in Certain Premises (Scotland) Regulations 2006, SSI 2006/90 at **[3370]**.

5 Proceeding for offences under sections 1 to 3

(1) Summary proceedings in pursuance of section 1, 2 or 3 may be commenced at any time within the period of 6 months from the date on which evidence sufficient in the opinion of the Lord Advocate to justify the proceedings comes to the Lord Advocate's knowledge.

(2) Subsection (3) of section 136 of the Criminal Procedure (Scotland) Act 1995 (c 46) (date of commencement of summary proceedings) has effect for the purposes of subsection (1) as it has effect for the purposes of that section.

(3) For the purposes of subsection (1), a certificate of the Lord Advocate as to the date on which the evidence in question came to the Lord Advocate's knowledge is conclusive evidence of the date on which it did so.

[1635]

NOTES

Commencement: 26 March 2006 (at 0600 hours).

6 Fixed penalties

(1) Schedule 1 (which provides as to fixed penalties for offences under this Part) has effect.

(2) Schedule 1 does not extend to an offence under section 1 or 3 committed otherwise than by a natural person.

[1636]

NOTES

Commencement: 1 November 2005 (in so far as relating to Sch 1, paras 2, 4(1), 5(2), 12); 26 March 2006 (at 0600 hours) (otherwise).

Note: Sch 1 contains further provisions with regard to fixed penalties for offences under ss 1–3. Paras 1, 2 of the Schedule provide that an authorised officer of a council and a constable may, if having reason to believe that a person is committing or has committed an offence under ss 1–3 in no-smoking premises, give that person a fixed penalty notice in relation to that offence within a certain time-period to be prescribed. Para 3 gives details as to the contents of the notice (the amount of the penalty and the period within which it may be paid; the discounted penalty; methods of payment; consequences of not making a payment, etc). Para 4 provides for the amount of the penalty (to be prescribed) and the period for payment (29 days). Para 5 provides that a discounted amount is payable if payment is made within 15 days. Para 6 provides that no proceedings for the offence may be commenced before the end of the period for payment of the penalty or if the penalty is paid within that time. Para 7 provides that a person to whom a fixed penalty notice has been given may, before the expiry of the period for payment of the penalty, give notice requesting a hearing in respect of the offence; the council must hold such a hearing. Paras 8–11 deal with the council's power to withdraw a notice, the effect of prosecution on a notice, and recovery, etc, of unpaid penalties. Paras 12, 13 provide that the Scottish Ministers may make regulations concerning the application by councils of fixed penalties paid under this schedule, the keeping of accounts, and the circumstances in which they may be given (etc). For the amounts prescribed for fixed penalties see the Prohibition of Smoking in Certain Premises (Scotland) Regulations 2006, SSI 2006/90, reg 4 at **[3373]**.

7 Powers to enter and require identification

(1) An authorised officer of the appropriate council may enter and search any no-smoking premises in order to ascertain whether an offence under section 1, 2 or 3 has been or is being committed there.

(2) A power under this section may be exercised, if need be, by force.

(3) A person who—

(a) an authorised officer of a council reasonably believes—

(i) is committing or has committed an offence under section 1, 2 or 3; or

(ii) has information relating to such an offence; and

(b) fails without reasonable excuse to supply the officer with the person's name and address on being so required by the officer,

commits an offence.

(4) A person guilty of an offence under subsection (3) is liable, on summary conviction, to a fine not exceeding level 3 on the standard scale.

(5) In this section—

"authorised" means authorised for the purposes of this section by the appropriate council;

"the appropriate council" means, in relation to no-smoking premises, the council of the area in which those premises are.

[1637]

NOTES

Commencement: 26 March 2006 (at 0600 hours).

8 Bodies corporate etc

(1) Where an offence under this Part which has been committed by a body corporate other than a council is proved to have been committed with the consent or connivance of, or to be attributable to, any neglect on the part of—

(a) a director, manager or secretary, member or other similar officer of the body corporate; or

(b) any person who was purporting to act in any such capacity,

that person, as well as the body corporate, is guilty of the offence and liable to be proceeded against and punished accordingly.

(2) Where an offence under this Part which has been committed by a council is proved to have been committed with the consent or connivance of, or to be attributable to any neglect on the part of—

(a) an officer or member of the council; or

(b) any person who was purporting to act in any such capacity,

that person, as well as the council, is guilty of the offence and liable to be proceeded against and punished accordingly.

(3) Where an offence under this Part which has been committed by a Scottish partnership is proved to have been committed with the consent or connivance of, or to be attributable to any neglect on the part of—

(a) a partner; or

(b) any person who was purporting to act in any such capacity,

that person, as well as the partnership, is guilty of the offence and liable to be proceeded against and punished accordingly.

(4) Where an offence under this Part which has been committed by an unincorporated association other than a Scottish partnership is proved to have been committed with the consent or connivance of, or to be attributable to any neglect on the part of—

(a) a person who is concerned in the management or control of the association; or

(b) any person who was purporting to act in any such capacity,

that person, as well as the unincorporated association, is guilty of the offence and liable to be proceeded against and punished accordingly.

[1638]

NOTES

Commencement: 26 March 2006 (at 0600 hours).

PART 7
GENERAL

39 Ancillary provision

(1) The Scottish Ministers may by order make such incidental, supplemental, consequential, transitional, transitory or saving provision as they consider necessary or expedient for the purposes, or in consequence, of this Act.

(2) An order under this section may—

(a) make different provision for different purposes;

(b) modify any enactment, instrument or document.

[1639]

NOTES

Commencement: 5 August 2005

Orders: the Smoking, Health and Social Care (Scotland) Act 2005 (Consequential Amendments) Order 2006, SSI 2006/95.

Regulations: the National Health Service (Pharmaceutical Services) (Scotland) Amendment Regulations 2006, SSI 2006/143.

40 Regulations or orders

(1) Any power conferred by this Act on the Scottish Ministers to make orders or regulations—

(a) must be exercised by statutory instrument;

(b) may be exercised so as to make different provision for different purposes.

(2) A statutory instrument containing an order or regulations made under this Act (except an order under section 43(3)) is, subject to subsection (3), subject to annulment in pursuance of a resolution of the Parliament.

(3) A statutory instrument containing—

(a) regulations under section 3(3) or 4(2) or (8) or paragraph 2, 4(1), 5(2), 12 or 13 of schedule 1 or an order under section 9 or 33(4)(e);

(b) an order under section 39 containing provisions which add to, replace or omit any part of the text of an Act,

is not to be made unless a draft of the instrument has been laid before, and approved by resolution of, the Parliament.

[1640]

NOTES

Commencement: 5 August 2005.

41 Interpretation

In this Act—

"the 1978 Act" means the National Health Service (Scotland) Act 1978 (c 29);

"the 2001 Act" means the Regulation of Care (Scotland) Act 2001 (asp 8);

"council" means a council constituted under section 2 of the Local Government etc (Scotland) Act 1994 (c 39);

"prescribed" means prescribed by regulations made by the Scottish Ministers.

[1641]–[1642]

NOTES

Commencement: 6 August 2005.

43 Short title and commencement

(1) This Act may be cited as the Smoking, Health and Social Care (Scotland) Act 2005.

(2) Sections 33, 34, 41 and (in so far as it relates to paragraph 2(2) and (4) of schedule 2) 42 and paragraph 2(2) and (4) of schedule 2 come into force on the day after Royal Assent.

(3) The remaining provisions of this Act, except this section and sections 39 and 40, come into force on such day as the Scottish Ministers may by order appoint, and an order under this section appointing a day for sections 1 to 10 or schedule 1 may specify the time in the day for the commencement of those provisions.

(4) Different days may be appointed under subsection (3) for different purposes.

[1643]

NOTES

Commencement: 5 August 2005.

Orders: the Smoking, Health and Social Care (Scotland) Act 2005 (Commencement No 1) Order 2005, SSI 2005/492, the Smoking, Health and Social Care (Scotland) Act 2005 (Commencement No 2) Order 2005, SSI 2005/642, the Smoking, Health and Social Care (Scotland) Act 2005 (Commencement

No 3) Order 2006, SSI 2006/47; the Smoking, Health and Social Care (Scotland) Act 2005 (Commencement No 4) Order 2006, SSI 2006/121; the Smoking, Health and Social Care (Scotland) Act 2005 (Commencement No 5) Order 2007, SSI 2007/218.

(*As to Sch 1 (fixed penalty notices), see the note to s 6 at* **[1636]**; *Sch 2 (minor and consequential amendments), Sch 3 (repeals) outside the scope of this work.*)

EQUALITY ACT 2006

(2006 c 3)

ARRANGEMENT OF SECTIONS

PART 1
THE COMMISSION FOR EQUALITY AND HUMAN RIGHTS

The Commission

Duties

General powers

Enforcement powers

Interpretation

Dissolution of Existing Commissions

Miscellaneous

PART 3
DISCRIMINATION ON GROUNDS OF SEXUAL ORIENTATION

PART 5
GENERAL

SCHEDULES:

An Act to make provision for the establishment of the Commission for Equality and Human Rights; to dissolve the Equal Opportunities Commission, the Commission for Racial Equality and the Disability Rights Commission; to make provision about discrimination on grounds of religion or belief; to enable provision to be made about discrimination on grounds of sexual orientation; to impose duties relating to sex discrimination on persons performing public functions; to amend the Disability Discrimination Act 1995; and for connected purposes

[16 February 2006]

NOTES

Part 1 of this Act, which establishes the Commission for Equality and Human Rights, is reproduced in full. Only those other provisions of most relevance to employment law are reproduced.

Regulatory functions: the regulatory functions conferred by, or under, this Act are subject to the Legislative and Regulatory Reform Act 2006, ss 21, 22 at **[1783]**, **[1784]**; see the Legislative and Regulatory Reform (Regulatory Functions) Order 2007, SI 2007/3544 (made under s 24(2) of the 2006 Act) for details.

As to the transfer of the functions of the Secretary of State for Trade and Industry under Part 1 of this Act to the Secretary of State for Communities and Local Government, see the Secretary of State for Communities and Local Government Order 2006, SI 2006/1926, arts 7(1), (2), (3)(c), 8. Note also that by the Transfer of Functions (Equality) Order 2007, SI 2007/2914, art 3(1), (2)(f), the functions of the

Secretary of State under this Act (except s 66(2) and Sch 2, para 14(4) are transferred to the Lord Privy Seal, as from 12 October 2007 (however note that, presumably by oversight, amendments have not been made to ss 36–38, 41, 42 or 93 to reflect this transfer).

PART 1
THE COMMISSION FOR EQUALITY AND HUMAN RIGHTS

The Commission

1 Establishment

There shall be a body corporate known as the Commission for Equality and Human Rights.

[1644]

NOTES

Commencement: 18 April 2006.

2 Constitution, &c

Schedule 1 (constitution of the Commission, proceedings, money, &c) shall have effect.

[1645]

NOTES

Commencement: 18 April 2006.

3 General duty

The Commission shall exercise its functions under this Part with a view to encouraging and supporting the development of a society in which—

(a) people's ability to achieve their potential is not limited by prejudice or discrimination,

(b) there is respect for and protection of each individual's human rights,

(c) there is respect for the dignity and worth of each individual,

(d) each individual has an equal opportunity to participate in society, and

(e) there is mutual respect between groups based on understanding and valuing of diversity and on shared respect for equality and human rights.

[1646]

NOTES

Commencement: 18 April 2006.

4 Strategic plan

(1) The Commission shall prepare a plan showing—

(a) activities or classes of activity to be undertaken by the Commission in pursuance of its functions under this Act,

(b) an expected timetable for each activity or class, and

(c) priorities for different activities or classes, or principles to be applied in determining priorities.

(2) The Commission shall review the plan—

(a) at least once during the period of three years beginning with its completion,

(b) at least once during each period of three years beginning with the completion of a review, and

(c) at such other times as the Commission thinks appropriate.

(3) If the Commission thinks it appropriate as a result of a review, the Commission shall revise the plan.

(4) The Commission shall send the plan and each revision to the [Minister], who shall lay a copy before Parliament.

(5) The Commission shall publish the plan and each revision.

[1647]

NOTES

Commencement: 18 April 2006.

Sub-s (4): word in square brackets substituted by the Transfer of Functions (Equality) Order 2007, SI 2007/2914, art 8, Schedule, para 16(a), as from 12 October 2007.

5 Strategic plan: consultation

Before preparing or reviewing a plan in accordance with section 4 the Commission shall—

- (a) consult such persons having knowledge or experience relevant to the Commission's functions as the Commission thinks appropriate,
- (b) consult such other persons as the Commission thinks appropriate,
- (c) issue a general invitation to make representations, in a manner likely in the Commission's opinion to bring the invitation to the attention of as large a class of persons who may wish to make representations as is reasonably practicable, and
- (d) take account of any representations made.

[1648]

NOTES

Commencement: 18 April 2006.

6 Disclosure

(1) A person who is or was a Commissioner, an Investigating Commissioner, an employee of the Commission or a member of a committee established by the Commission commits an offence if he discloses information to which this section applies unless subsection (3) authorises the disclosure.

(2) This section applies to information acquired by the Commission—

- (a) by way of representations made in relation to, or otherwise in the course of, an inquiry under section 16,
- (b) by way of representations made in relation to, or otherwise in the course of, an investigation under section 20,
- (c) by way of representations made in relation to, or otherwise in the course of, an assessment under section 31,
- (d) by way of representations made in relation to, or otherwise in connection with, a notice under section 32, or
- (e) from a person with whom the Commission enters into, or considers entering into, an agreement under section 23.

(3) This subsection authorises a disclosure made—

- (a) for the purpose of the exercise of a function of the Commission under any of sections 16, 20, 21, 24, 25, 31 and 32,
- (b) in a report of an inquiry, investigation or assessment published by the Commission,
- (c) in pursuance of an order of a court or tribunal,
- (d) with the consent of each person to whom the disclosed information relates,
- (e) in a manner that ensures that no person to whom the disclosed information relates can be identified,
- (f) for the purpose of civil or criminal proceedings to which the Commission is party, or
- (g) if the information was acquired by the Commission more than 70 years before the date of the disclosure.

(4) But subsection (3) does not authorise, nor may the Commission make, a disclosure of information provided by or relating to an intelligence service unless the service has authorised the disclosure.

(5) In subsection (4) "intelligence service" means—

- (a) the Security Service,
- (b) the Secret Intelligence Service, and
- (c) the Government Communications Headquarters.

(6) A person guilty of an offence under subsection (1) shall be liable on summary conviction to a fine not exceeding level 5 on the standard scale.

[1649]

NOTES

Commencement: 1 October 2007.

Discloses information: in so far as it authorises the disclosure of information, this section is subject to the Anti-terrorism, Crime and Security Act 2001, s 17; see Sch 4, Pt 1 to that Act.

7 Scotland: human rights

(1) The Commission shall not take human rights action in relation to a matter if the Scottish Parliament has legislative competence to enable a person to take action of that kind in relation to that matter.

(2) In subsection (1) "human rights action" means action taken—
- (a) in accordance with section 9(1), and
- (b) under, by virtue of or in pursuance of—
  - (i) section 11(1) in so far as it relates to the Human Rights Act 1998 (c 42),
  - (ii) section 11(2)(c) or (d),
  - (iii) section 12,
  - (iv) section 13,
  - (v) section 16,
  - (vi) section 17, or
  - (vii) section 30.

(3) Despite section 9(4), the Commission shall not, in the course of fulfilling a duty under section 8 or 10, consider the question whether a person's human rights have been contravened if the Scottish Parliament has legislative competence to enable a person to consider that question.

(4) Subsections (1) and (3) shall not prevent the Commission from taking action with the consent (whether general or specific) of a person if—
- (a) the person is established by Act of the Scottish Parliament, and
- (b) the person's principal duties relate to human rights and are similar to any of the Commission's duties under section 9.

(5) Subsections (1) and (3) shall not prevent the Commission from relying on section 13(1)(f) so as to act jointly or cooperate (but not assist) for a purpose relating to human rights and connected with Scotland.

[1650]

NOTES

Commencement: 1 October 2007.

Duties

8 Equality and diversity

(1) The Commission shall, by exercising the powers conferred by this Part—
- (a) promote understanding of the importance of equality and diversity,
- (b) encourage good practice in relation to equality and diversity,
- (c) promote equality of opportunity,
- (d) promote awareness and understanding of rights under the equality enactments,
- (e) enforce the equality enactments,
- (f) work towards the elimination of unlawful discrimination, and
- (g) work towards the elimination of unlawful harassment.

(2) In subsection (1)—

"diversity" means the fact that individuals are different,

"equality" means equality between individuals, and

"unlawful" is to be construed in accordance with section 34.

(3) In promoting equality of opportunity between disabled persons and others, the Commission may, in particular, promote the favourable treatment of disabled persons.

(4) In this Part "disabled person" means a person who—
- (a) is a disabled person within the meaning of the Disability Discrimination Act 1995 (c 50), or

(b) has been a disabled person within that meaning (whether or not at a time when that Act had effect).

[1651]

NOTES

Commencement: 1 October 2007.

9 Human rights

(1) The Commission shall, by exercising the powers conferred by this Part—

(a) promote understanding of the importance of human rights,

(b) encourage good practice in relation to human rights,

(c) promote awareness, understanding and protection of human rights, and

(d) encourage public authorities to comply with section 6 of the Human Rights Act 1998 (c 42) (compliance with Convention rights).

(2) In this Part "human rights" means—

(a) the Convention rights within the meaning given by section 1 of the Human Rights Act 1998, and

(b) other human rights.

(3) In determining what action to take in pursuance of this section the Commission shall have particular regard to the importance of exercising the powers conferred by this Part in relation to the Convention rights.

(4) In fulfilling a duty under section 8 or 10 the Commission shall take account of any relevant human rights.

(5) A reference in this Part (including this section) to human rights does not exclude any matter by reason only of its being a matter to which section 8 or 10 relates.

[1652]

NOTES

Commencement: 1 October 2007.

10 Groups

(1) The Commission shall, by exercising the powers conferred by this Part—

(a) promote understanding of the importance of good relations—

(i) between members of different groups, and

(ii) between members of groups and others,

(b) encourage good practice in relation to relations—

(i) between members of different groups, and

(ii) between members of groups and others,

(c) work towards the elimination of prejudice against, hatred of and hostility towards members of groups, and

(d) work towards enabling members of groups to participate in society.

(2) In this Part "group" means a group or class of persons who share a common attribute in respect of any of the following matters—

(a) age,

(b) disability,

(c) gender,

(d) proposed, commenced or completed reassignment of gender (within the meaning given by section 82(1) of the Sex Discrimination Act 1975 (c 65)),

(e) race,

(f) religion or belief, and

(g) sexual orientation.

(3) For the purposes of this Part a reference to a group (as defined in subsection (2)) includes a reference to a smaller group or smaller class, within a group, of persons who share a common attribute (in addition to the attribute by reference to which the group is defined) in respect of any of the matters specified in subsection (2)(a) to (g).

(4) In determining what action to take in pursuance of this section the Commission shall have particular regard to the importance of exercising the powers conferred by this Part in relation to groups defined by reference to race, religion or belief.

(5) The Commission may, in taking action in pursuance of subsection (1) in respect of groups defined by reference to disability and others, promote or encourage the favourable treatment of disabled persons.

(6) The [Minister] may by order amend the list in subsection (2) so as to—
(a) add an entry, or
(b) vary an entry.

(7) This section is without prejudice to the generality of section 8.

[1653]

NOTES

Commencement: 1 October 2007

Sub-s (6): word in square brackets substituted by the Transfer of Functions (Equality) Order 2007, SI 2007/2914, art 8, Schedule, para 16(b), as from 12 October 2007.

Orders: as of 6 April 2008 no Orders had been made under this section.

11 Monitoring the law

(1) The Commission shall monitor the effectiveness of the equality and human rights enactments.

(2) The Commission may—
(a) advise central government about the effectiveness of any of the equality and human rights enactments;
(b) recommend to central government the amendment, repeal, consolidation (with or without amendments) or replication (with or without amendments) of any of the equality and human rights enactments;
(c) advise central or devolved government about the effect of an enactment (including an enactment in or under an Act of the Scottish Parliament);
(d) advise central or devolved government about the likely effect of a proposed change of law.

(3) In this section—
(a) "central government" means Her Majesty's Government,
(b) "devolved government" means—
(i) the Scottish Ministers, and
(ii) the National Assembly for Wales, and
(c) a reference to the equality enactments shall be treated as including a reference to any provision of this Act.

[1654]

NOTES

Commencement: 1 October 2007.

Sub-s (3): words in square brackets in para (b)(ii) substituted by the Government of Wales Act 2006 (Consequential Modifications and Transitional Provisions) Order 2007, SI 2007/1388, art 3, Sch 1, paras 112, 113. as from 25 May 2007.

12 Monitoring progress

(1) The Commission shall from time to time identify—
(a) changes in society that have occurred or are expected to occur and are relevant to the aim specified in section 3,
(b) results at which to aim for the purpose of encouraging and supporting the development of the society described in section 3 ("outcomes"), and
(c) factors by reference to which progress towards those results may be measured ("indicators").

(2) In identifying outcomes and indicators the Commission shall—
(a) consult such persons having knowledge or experience relevant to the Commission's functions as the Commission thinks appropriate,
(b) consult such other persons as the Commission thinks appropriate,
(c) issue a general invitation to make representations, in a manner likely in the Commission's opinion to bring the invitation to the attention of as large a class of persons who may wish to make representations as is reasonably practicable, and
(d) take account of any representations made.

(3) The Commission shall from time to time monitor progress towards each identified outcome by reference to any relevant identified indicator.

(4) The Commission shall publish a report on progress towards the identified outcomes by reference to the identified indicators—

(a) within the period of three years beginning with the date on which this section comes into force, and

(b) within each period of three years beginning with the date on which a report is published under this subsection.

(5) The Commission shall send each report to the [Minister], who shall lay a copy before Parliament.

[1655]

NOTES

Commencement: 1 October 2007

Sub-s (5): word in square brackets substituted by the Transfer of Functions (Equality) Order 2007, SI 2007/2914, art 8, Schedule, para 16(b), as from 12 October 2007.

General powers

13 Information, advice, &c

(1) In pursuance of its duties under sections 8 to 10 the Commission may—

(a) publish or otherwise disseminate ideas or information;

(b) undertake research;

(c) provide education or training;

(d) give advice or guidance (whether about the effect or operation of an enactment or otherwise);

(e) arrange for a person to do anything within paragraphs (a) to (d);

(f) act jointly with, co-operate with or assist a person doing anything within paragraphs (a) to (d).

(2) The reference to giving advice in subsection (1)(d) does not include a reference to preparing, or assisting in the preparation of, a document to be used for the purpose of legal proceedings.

[1656]

NOTES

Commencement: 1 October 2007.

14 Codes of practice

(1) The Commission may issue a code of practice in connection with a matter addressed by any of the following—

(a) the Equal Pay Act 1970 (c 41),

(b) Parts 2 to 4 and section 76A of the Sex Discrimination Act 1975 (c 65) or an order under section 76B or 76C of that Act,

(c) Parts 2 to 4 and section 71 of the Race Relations Act 1976 (c 74),

(d) Parts 2 to 4 and 5A of the Disability Discrimination Act 1995 (c 50) except for sections 28D and 28E (accessibility in schools),

(e) Part 2 of this Act,

(f) regulations under Part 3 of this Act,

(g) Parts 2 and 3 of the Employment Equality (Sexual Orientation) Regulations 2003 (SI 2003/1661), …

(h) Parts 2 and 3 of the Employment Equality (Religion or Belief) Regulations 2003 (SI 2003/1660)[, and

(i) Parts 2 and 3 of the Employment Equality (Age) Regulations 2006].

(2) A code of practice under subsection (1) shall contain provision designed—

(a) to ensure or facilitate compliance with a provision or enactment listed in subsection (1), or

(b) to promote equality of opportunity.

(3) The Commission may issue a code of practice giving practical guidance to landlords and tenants in England or Wales about—

(a) circumstances in which a tenant requires the consent of his landlord to make a relevant improvement, within the meaning of section 49G(7) of the Disability Discrimination Act 1995 (c 50) (improvements), to a dwelling house,

(b) reasonableness in relation to that consent, and

(c) the application in relation to relevant improvements (within that meaning) to dwelling houses of—

(i) section 19(2) of the Landlord and Tenant Act 1927 (c 36) (consent to improvements),

(ii) sections 81 to 85 of the Housing Act 1980 (c 51) (tenant's improvements),

(iii) sections 97 to 99 of the Housing Act 1985 (c 68) (tenant's improvements), and

(iv) section 49G of the Disability Discrimination Act 1995.

(4) The Commission may issue a code of practice giving practical guidance to landlords and tenants of houses (within the meaning of the Housing (Scotland) Act 2006 (asp 01)) in Scotland about—

(a) circumstances in which the tenant requires the consent of the landlord to carry out work in relation to the house for the purpose of making the house suitable for the accommodation, welfare or employment of any disabled person who occupies, or intends to occupy, the house as a sole or main residence,

(b) circumstances in which it is unreasonable to withhold that consent,

(c) circumstances in which any condition imposed on the granting of that consent is unreasonable, and

(d) the application in relation to such work of—

(i) sections 28 to 31 and 34(6) of the Housing (Scotland) Act 2001 (asp 10), and

(ii) sections 52, 53 and 64(6) of the Housing (Scotland) Act 2006 (asp 01).

(5) The Commission shall comply with a direction of the [Minister] to issue a code under this section in connection with a specified matter if—

(a) the matter is not listed in subsection (1), but

(b) the [Minister] expects to add it by order under section 15(6).

(6) Before issuing a code under this section the Commission shall—

(a) publish proposals, and

(b) consult such persons as it thinks appropriate.

(7) Before issuing a code under this section the Commission shall submit a draft to the [Minister], who shall—

(a) if he approves the draft—

(i) notify the Commission, and

(ii) lay a copy before Parliament, or

(b) otherwise, give the Commission written reasons why he does not approve the draft.

(8) Where a draft is laid before Parliament under subsection (7)(a)(ii), if neither House passes a resolution disapproving the draft within 40 days—

(a) the Commission may issue the code in the form of the draft, and

(b) it shall come into force in accordance with provision made by the [Minister] by order.

(9) If, or in so far as, a code relates to a duty imposed by or under section 76A, 76B or 76C of the Sex Discrimination Act 1975 (c 65), section 71 of the Race Relations Act 1976 (c 74) or section 49A or 49D of the Disability Discrimination Act 1995 (c 50) (public authorities: general anti-discrimination duties) the [Minister] shall consult the Scottish Ministers and the [Welsh Ministers] before—

(a) approving a draft under subsection (7)(a) above, or

(b) making an order under subsection (8)(b) above.

(10) In relation to a code of practice under subsection (4), the [Minister] shall consult the Scottish Ministers before—

(a) approving a draft under subsection (7)(a) above, or

(b) making an order under subsection (8)(b) above.

[1657]

NOTES

Commencement: 1 October 2007

Sub-s (1): word omitted from para (g) repealed, and para (i) and the word immediately preceding it added, by the Employment Equality (Age) Regulations 2006, SI 2006/1031, reg 49(1), Sch 8, Pt 1, paras 37, 38, as from 1 October 2006.

Sub-ss (5), (7), (8), (10): words in square brackets substituted by the Transfer of Functions (Equality) Order 2007, SI 2007/2914, art 8, Schedule, para 16(d), as from 12 October 2007.

Sub-s (9): word in first pair of square brackets substituted by SI 2007/2914, art 8, Schedule, para 16(d), as from 12 October 2007; words in second pair of square brackets substituted by the Government of Wales Act 2006 (Consequential Modifications and Transitional Provisions) Order 2007, SI 2007/1388, art 3, Sch 1, paras 112, 114, as from 25 May 2007.

Orders: as of 6 April 2008 no Orders had been made under this section.

15 Codes of practice: supplemental

(1) The Commission may revise a code issued under section 14; and a reference in this section or in that section to the issue of a code shall be treated as including a reference to the revision of a code.

(2) The 40 day period specified in section 14(8)—
- (a) shall begin with the date on which the draft is laid before both Houses (or, if laid before each House on a different date, with the later date), and
- (b) shall be taken not to include a period during which—
  - (i) Parliament is prorogued or dissolved, or
  - (ii) both Houses are adjourned for more than four days.

(3) A code issued under section 14 may be revoked by the [Minister], at the request of the Commission, by order.

(4) A failure to comply with a provision of a code shall not of itself make a person liable to criminal or civil proceedings; but a code—
- (a) shall be admissible in evidence in criminal or civil proceedings, and
- (b) shall be taken into account by a court or tribunal in any case in which it appears to the court or tribunal to be relevant.

(5) Subsection (4)(b) does not apply in relation to a code issued under section 14(4).

(6) The [Minister] may by order amend section 14 so as to vary the range of matters that codes of practice under that section may address.

[1658]

NOTES

Commencement: 1 October 2007

Sub-ss (3), (6): words in square brackets substituted by the Transfer of Functions (Equality) Order 2007, SI 2007/2914, art 8, Schedule, para 16(e), as from 12 October 2007.

Orders: as of 6 April 2008 no Orders had been made under this section.

16 Inquiries

(1) The Commission may conduct an inquiry into a matter relating to any of the Commission's duties under sections 8, 9 and 10.

(2) If in the course of an inquiry the Commission begins to suspect that a person may have committed an unlawful act—
- (a) in continuing the inquiry the Commission shall, so far as possible, avoid further consideration of whether or not the person has committed an unlawful act,
- (b) the Commission may commence an investigation into that question under section 20,
- (c) the Commission may use information or evidence acquired in the course of the inquiry for the purpose of the investigation, and
- (d) the Commission shall so far as possible ensure (whether by aborting or suspending the inquiry or otherwise) that any aspects of the inquiry which concern the person investigated, or may require his involvement, are not pursued while the investigation is in progress.

(3) The report of an inquiry—
- (a) may not state (whether expressly or by necessary implication) that a specified or identifiable person has committed an unlawful act, and

(b) shall not otherwise refer to the activities of a specified or identifiable person unless the Commission thinks that the reference—
  (i) will not harm the person, or
  (ii) is necessary in order for the report adequately to reflect the results of the inquiry.

(4) Subsections (2) and (3) shall not prevent an inquiry from considering or reporting a matter relating to human rights (whether or not a necessary implication arises in relation to the equality enactments).

(5) Before settling a report of an inquiry which records findings which in the Commission's opinion are of an adverse nature and relate (whether expressly or by necessary implication) to a specified or identifiable person the Commission shall—

(a) send a draft of the report to the person,

(b) specify a period of at least 28 days during which he may make written representations about the draft, and

(c) consider any representations made.

(6) Schedule 2 makes supplemental provision about inquiries.

[1659]

NOTES

Commencement: 1 October 2007.

17 Grants

(1) In pursuance of any of its duties under sections 8 to 10 the Commission may make grants to another person.

(2) A grant under subsection (1) may be made subject to conditions (which may, in particular, include conditions as to repayment).

(3) A power under this Part to co-operate with or assist a person may not be exercised by the provision of financial assistance otherwise than in accordance with this section.

[1660]

NOTES

Commencement: 1 October 2007.

18 Human rights

In pursuance of its duties under section 9 the Commission may (without prejudice to the generality of section 13) co-operate with persons interested in human rights within the United Kingdom or elsewhere.

[1661]

NOTES

Commencement: 1 October 2007.

19 Groups

(1) In pursuance of its duties under section 10 the Commission may do anything specified in this section (without prejudice to the generality of section 13).

(2) The Commission may make, co-operate with or assist in arrangements—

(a) for the monitoring of kinds of crime affecting certain groups;

(b) designed to prevent or reduce crime within or affecting certain groups;

(c) for activities (whether social, recreational, sporting, civic, educational or otherwise) designed to involve members of groups.

[1662]

NOTES

Commencement: 1 October 2007.

Enforcement powers

20 Investigations

(1) The Commission may investigate whether or not a person—

(a) has committed an unlawful act,

(b) has complied with a requirement imposed by an unlawful act notice under section 21, or

(c) has complied with an undertaking given under section 23.

(2) The Commission may conduct an investigation under subsection (1)(a) only if it suspects that the person concerned may have committed an unlawful act.

(3) A suspicion for the purposes of subsection (2) may (but need not) be based on the results of, or a matter arising during the course of, an inquiry under section 16.

(4) Before settling a report of an investigation recording a finding that a person has committed an unlawful act or has failed to comply with a requirement or undertaking the Commission shall—

(a) send a draft of the report to the person,

(b) specify a period of at least 28 days during which he may make written representations about the draft, and

(c) consider any representations made.

(5) Schedule 2 makes supplemental provision about investigations.

[1663]

NOTES

Commencement: 1 October 2007.

21 Unlawful act notice

(1) The Commission may give a person a notice under this section (an "unlawful act notice") if—

(a) he is or has been the subject of an investigation under section 20(1)(a), and

(b) the Commission is satisfied that he has committed an unlawful act.

(2) A notice must specify—

(a) the unlawful act, and

(b) the provision of the equality enactments by virtue of which the act is unlawful.

(3) A notice must inform the recipient of the effect of—

(a) subsections (5) to (7),

(b) section 20(1)(b), and

(c) section 24(1).

(4) A notice may—

(a) require the person to whom the notice is given to prepare an action plan for the purpose of avoiding repetition or continuation of the unlawful act;

(b) recommend action to be taken by the person for that purpose.

(5) A person who is given a notice may, within the period of six weeks beginning with the day on which the notice is given, appeal to the appropriate court or tribunal on the grounds—

(a) that he has not committed the unlawful act specified in the notice, or

(b) that a requirement for the preparation of an action plan imposed under subsection (4)(a) is unreasonable.

(6) On an appeal under subsection (5) the court or tribunal may—

(a) affirm a notice;

(b) annul a notice;

(c) vary a notice;

(d) affirm a requirement;

(e) annul a requirement;

(f) vary a requirement;

(g) make an order for costs or expenses.

(7) In subsection (5) "the appropriate court or tribunal" means—

(a) an employment tribunal, if a claim in respect of the alleged unlawful act could be made to it, or

(b) a county court (in England and Wales) or the sheriff (in Scotland), if a claim in respect of the alleged unlawful act could be made to it or to him.

[1664]

NOTES

Commencement: 1 October 2007.

Modification: see the Equality Act 2006 (Dissolution of Commissions and Consequential and Transitional Provisions) Order 2007, SI 2007/2602, art 5(3) at **[3473O]**, which provides as follows—

"(3) Section 21(1)(a) of the 2006 Act shall apply in relation to an investigation under section 57 of the 1975 Act or section 48 of the 1976 Act as if, after "section 20(1)(a)", there were inserted "of this Act, section 57 of the Sex Discrimination Act 1975 or section 48 of the Race Relations Act 1976".".

22 Action plans

(1) This section applies where a person has been given a notice under section 21 which requires him (under section 21(4)(a)) to prepare an action plan.

(2) The notice must specify a time by which the person must give the Commission a first draft plan.

(3) After receiving a first draft plan from a person the Commission shall—

(a) approve it, or

(b) give the person a notice which—

(i) states that the draft is not adequate,

(ii) requires the person to give the Commission a revised draft by a specified time, and

(iii) may make recommendations about the content of the revised draft.

(4) Subsection (3) shall apply in relation to a revised draft plan as it applies in relation to a first draft plan.

(5) An action plan comes into force—

(a) if the period of six weeks beginning with the date on which a first draft or revised draft is given to the Commission expires without the Commission—

(i) giving a notice under subsection (3)(b), or

(ii) applying for an order under subsection (6)(b), or

(b) upon a court's declining to make an order under subsection (6)(b) in relation to a revised draft of the plan.

(6) The Commission may apply to a county court (in England and Wales) or to the sheriff (in Scotland)—

(a) for an order requiring a person to give the Commission a first draft plan by a time specified in the order,

(b) for an order requiring a person who has given the Commission a revised draft plan to prepare and give to the Commission a further revised draft plan—

(i) by a time specified in the order, and

(ii) in accordance with any directions about the plan's content specified in the order, or

(c) during the period of five years beginning with the date on which an action plan prepared by a person comes into force, for an order requiring the person—

(i) to act in accordance with the action plan, or

(ii) to take specified action for a similar purpose.

(7) An action plan may be varied by agreement between the Commission and the person who prepared it.

(8) Paragraphs 10 to 14 of Schedule 2 apply (but omitting references to oral evidence) in relation to consideration by the Commission of the adequacy of a draft action plan as they apply in relation to the conduct of an inquiry.

(9) A person commits an offence if without reasonable excuse he fails to comply with an order under subsection (6); and a person guilty of an offence under this subsection shall be liable on summary conviction to a fine not exceeding level 5 on the standard scale.

[1665]

NOTES

Commencement: 1 October 2007.

23 Agreements

(1) The Commission may enter into an agreement with a person under which—

(a) the person undertakes—

(i) not to commit an unlawful act of a specified kind, and

(ii) to take, or refrain from taking, other specified action (which may include the preparation of a plan for the purpose of avoiding an unlawful act), and

(b) the Commission undertakes not to proceed against the person under section 20 or 21 in respect of any unlawful act of the kind specified under paragraph (a)(i).

(2) The Commission may enter into an agreement with a person under this section only if it thinks that the person has committed an unlawful act.

(3) But a person shall not be taken to admit to the commission of an unlawful act by reason only of entering into an agreement under this section.

(4) An agreement under this section—

(a) may be entered into whether or not the person is or has been the subject of an investigation under section 20,

(b) may include incidental or supplemental provision (which may include provision for termination in specified circumstances), and

(c) may be varied or terminated by agreement of the parties.

(5) This section shall apply in relation to the breach of a duty specified in section 34(2) as it applies in relation to the commission of an unlawful act; and for that purpose the reference in subsection (1)(b) above to section 20 or 21 shall be taken as a reference to section 32.

[1666]

NOTES

Commencement: 1 October 2007.

24 Applications to court

(1) If the Commission thinks that a person is likely to commit an unlawful act, it may apply—

(a) in England and Wales, to a county court for an injunction restraining the person from committing the act, or

(b) in Scotland, to the sheriff for an interdict prohibiting the person from committing the act.

(2) Subsection (3) applies if the Commission thinks that a party to an agreement under section 23 has failed to comply, or is likely not to comply, with an undertaking under the agreement.

(3) The Commission may apply to a county court (in England and Wales) or to the sheriff (in Scotland) for an order requiring the person—

(a) to comply with his undertaking, and

(b) to take such other action as the court or the sheriff may specify.

[1667]

NOTES

Commencement: 1 October 2007.

25 Application to restrain unlawful advertising, pressure, &c

(1) This section applies to an act which is unlawful under any of the following—

(a) sections 38 to 40 of the Sex Discrimination Act 1975 (c 65) (advertising; and instructions or pressure to discriminate),

(b) sections 29 to 31 of the Race Relations Act 1976 (c 74) (advertising; and instructions or pressure to discriminate),

(c) sections 16B and 16C of the Disability Discrimination Act 1995 (c 50) (advertising; and instructions or pressure to discriminate),

[(ca) sections 28UB and 28UC of that Act (advertising; and instructions or pressure to discriminate),] and

(d) sections 54 and 55 below (religious discrimination: advertising; and instructions or pressure to discriminate)[, and

(e) regulations 10 and 11 of the Equality Act (Sexual Orientation) Regulations 2007].

(2) Legal proceedings in relation to action to which this section applies—

(a) may be brought by the Commission in accordance with this section, and

(b) may not be brought by anyone else.

(3) Where the Commission thinks that a person has done an act to which this section applies the Commission may—

(a) present a complaint to an employment tribunal, where the act is alleged to be unlawful by reference to—

(i) Part 2 of the Sex Discrimination Act 1975,

(ii) Part 2 of the Race Relations Act 1976,

(iii) Part 2 of the Disability Discrimination Act 1995,

(iv) Part 3 of that Act in so far as it relates to employment services, or

(v) Part 2 of this Act, or

(b) in any other case, apply to a county court (in England and Wales) or the sheriff (in Scotland).

(4) On a complaint or application under subsection (3) in respect of an alleged act to which this section applies, the tribunal, court or sheriff shall determine whether the allegation is correct.

(5) The Commission may apply to a county court (in England and Wales) for an injunction restraining a person from doing an act to which this section applies where—

(a) either—

(i) a tribunal or court has determined under subsection (4) that the person has done an act to which this section applies, or

(ii) the Commission thinks that the person has done an act to which this section applies, and

(b) the Commission thinks that if unrestrained the person is likely to do another act to which this section applies.

(6) The Commission may apply to the sheriff (in Scotland) for an interdict prohibiting a person from doing an act to which this section applies where—

(a) either—

(i) a tribunal or the sheriff has determined under subsection (4) that the person has done an act to which this section applies, or

(ii) the Commission thinks that the person has done an act to which this section applies, and

(b) the Commission thinks that without an interdict the person is likely to do another act to which this section applies.

(7) Subsection (1) does not apply to an act which constitutes an offence.

[1668]

NOTES

Commencement: 1 October 2007.

Sub-s (1): para (ca) inserted by the Disability Discrimination Act 1995 (Amendment) (Further and Higher Education) Regulations 2006, SI 2006/1721, regs 4(1), 22, as from 1 September 2006; para (e) and the word immediately preceding it added by the Equality Act (Sexual Orientation) Regulations 2007, SI 2007/1263, reg 32, as from 30 April 2007.

26 Section 25: supplemental

(1) A complaint or application under section 25(3) may be presented or made only—

(a) within the period of six months beginning with the date (or last date) on which the alleged unlawful act occurred, or

(b) with the permission of the tribunal, court or sheriff.

(2) A determination under section 25(4) shall not be relied upon by a county court or the sheriff in proceedings under section 25(5) or (6) while an appeal against the determination—

(a) is pending, or

(b) may be brought (disregarding the possibility of an appeal out of time with permission).

(3) An application under section 25(5) or (6) may be made only—

(a) within the period of five years beginning with the date (or last date) on which the unlawful act referred to in that subsection occurred, or

(b) with the permission of the court or sheriff.

[1669]

NOTES

Commencement: 1 October 2007.

27 Conciliation

(1) The Commission may make arrangements for the provision of conciliation services for disputes in respect of which proceedings have been or could be brought under or by virtue of—

(a) section 66 of the Sex Discrimination Act 1975 (c 65) (civil proceedings),

(b) section 57 of the Race Relations Act 1976 (c 74) (civil proceedings),

(c) section 25, 28I, 28N, 28V[, 31ADA] or 31AE(1) of the Disability Discrimination Act 1995 (c 50) (civil proceedings),

(d) section 66 below,

(e) a provision of regulations under Part 3 of this Act corresponding to section 66 below,

(f) regulation 31 of the Employment Equality (Religion or Belief) Regulations 2003 (SI 2003/1660) (civil proceedings), …

(g) regulation 31 of the Employment Equality (Sexual Orientation) Regulations 2003 (SI 2003/1661) (civil proceedings)[, or

(h) regulation 39 of the Employment Equality (Age) Regulations 2006 (Jurisdiction of County and Sheriff Courts)].

[(1A) The Commission may make arrangements for the provision of conciliation services for disputes in respect of which proceedings have been or could be brought in England and Wales or Scotland under regulation 9 of the Civil Aviation (Access to Air Travel for Disabled Persons and Persons with Reduced Mobility) Regulations 2007 (civil proceedings).]

(2) The Commission may make arrangements for the provision of conciliation services for disputes about a landlord's reasonableness in relation to consent to the making of an improvement to a dwelling in England or Wales where the improvement would be likely to facilitate the enjoyment of the premises by the tenant or another lawful occupier having regard to a disability.

(3) The Commission may make arrangements for the provision of conciliation services for disputes about whether—

(a) it is unreasonable for a landlord of a house (within the meaning of the Housing (Scotland) Act 2006 (asp 01)) in Scotland to withhold consent to the carrying out of work in relation to the house for the purpose of making the house suitable for the accommodation, welfare or employment of any disabled person who occupies, or intends to occupy, the house as a sole or main residence, or

(b) any condition imposed by such a landlord on consenting to the carrying out of such work is unreasonable.

(4) The Commission shall aim to exercise the powers in subsections (1) to (3) so as to ensure that, so far as is reasonably practicable, conciliation services are available to parties who want them.

(5) Information communicated to a person providing conciliation services in accordance with arrangements under this section may not be adduced in legal proceedings without the consent of the person who communicated the information.

(6) None of the following shall participate in the provision of conciliation services for which arrangements are made under this section—

(a) a Commissioner,

(b) a member of the Commission's staff,

(c) a member of a committee established by the Commission, and

(d) an Investigating Commissioner.

(7) The Commission shall make administrative arrangements designed to secure that information in connection with conciliation services provided in accordance with arrangements made under this section is not disclosed to—

(a) a Commissioner, or

(b) a member of the Commission's staff.

(8) But subsection (7) shall not apply to a disclosure—

(a) made with the consent of the parties to the dispute to which it relates,

(b) which does not identify individuals or enable them to be identified, or

(c) of information without which arrangements under this section cannot be made.

(9) In this section "conciliation services" means a service which is provided—

(a) by a person who is not party to a dispute,

(b) to the parties to the dispute, and

(c) with the aim of enabling the dispute to be settled by agreement and without legal proceedings.

(10) The [Minister] may by order amend this section so as to vary the range of disputes in respect of which the Commission may make arrangements for the provision of conciliation services.

[1670]

NOTES

Commencement: 1 October 2007.

Sub-s (1): figure in square brackets in para (c) inserted by the Disability Discrimination Act 1995 (Amendment etc) (General Qualifications Bodies) (Alteration of Premises and Enforcement) Regulations 2007, SI 2007/2405, regs 2(2), 7, as from 1 September 2007; word omitted from para (f) repealed, and para (h) and the word immediately preceding it added, by the Employment Equality (Age) Regulations 2006, SI 2006/1031, reg 49(1), Sch 8, Pt 1, paras 37, 39, as from 1 October 2006.

Sub-s (1A): inserted by the Civil Aviation (Access to Air Travel for Disabled Persons and Persons with Reduced Mobility) Regulations 2007, SI 2007/1895, reg 10, as from 1 October 2007.

Sub-s (10): word in square brackets substituted by the Transfer of Functions (Equality) Order 2007, SI 2007/2914, art 8, Schedule, para 16(f), as from 12 October 2007.

Orders: as of 6 April 2008 no Orders had been made under this section.

28 Legal assistance

(1) The Commission may assist an individual who is or may become party to legal proceedings if—

(a) the proceedings relate or may relate (wholly or partly) to a provision of the equality enactments, and

(b) the individual alleges that he has been the victim of behaviour contrary to a provision of the equality enactments.

(2) The Commission may assist an individual who is or may become party to legal proceedings in England and Wales if and in so far as the proceedings concern or may concern the question of a landlord's reasonableness in relation to consent to the making of an improvement to a dwelling where the improvement would be likely to facilitate the enjoyment of the premises by the tenant or another lawful occupier having regard to a disability.

(3) The Commission may assist an individual who is or may become a party to legal proceedings in Scotland if and in so far as the proceedings concern or may concern the question whether—

(a) it is unreasonable for a landlord to withhold consent to the carrying out of work in relation to a house (within the meaning of the Housing (Scotland) Act 2006 (asp 01)) for the purpose of making the house suitable for the accommodation, welfare or employment of any disabled person who occupies, or intends to occupy, the house as a sole or main residence, or

(b) any condition imposed by a landlord on consenting to the carrying out of such work is unreasonable.

(4) In giving assistance under this section the Commission may provide or arrange for the provision of—

(a) legal advice;

(b) legal representation;

(c) facilities for the settlement of a dispute;

(d) any other form of assistance.

(5) Assistance may not be given under subsection (1) in relation to alleged behaviour contrary to a provision of Part V of the Disability Discrimination Act 1995 (c 50) (public transport).

(6) Where proceedings relate or may relate partly to a provision of the equality enactments and partly to other matters—

(a) assistance may be given under subsection (1) in respect of any aspect of the proceedings while they relate to a provision of the equality enactments, but

(b) if the proceedings cease to relate to a provision of the equality enactments, assistance may not be continued under subsection (1) in respect of the proceedings (except in so far as it is permitted by virtue of subsection (7) or (8)).

(7) The Lord Chancellor may by order disapply subsection (6)(b), and enable the Commission to give assistance under subsection (1), in respect of legal proceedings which—

(a) when instituted, related (wholly or partly) to a provision of the equality enactments,

(b) have ceased to relate to the provision of the equality enactments, and

(c) relate (wholly or partly) to any of the Convention rights within the meaning given by section 1 of the Human Rights Act 1998 (c 42).

(8) The [Minister] may by order enable the Commission to give assistance under this section in respect of legal proceedings in the course of which an individual who is or has been a disabled person relies or proposes to rely on a matter relating to his disability; but an order under this subsection may not permit assistance in relation to alleged behaviour contrary to a provision of Part V of the Disability Discrimination Act 1995 (c 50).

(9) An order under subsection (7) or (8) may make provision generally or only in relation to proceedings of a specified kind or description (which in the case of an order under subsection (7) may, in particular, refer to specified provisions of the equality enactments) or in relation to specified circumstances.

(10) This section is without prejudice to the effect of any restriction imposed, in respect of representation—

(a) by virtue of an enactment (including an enactment in or under an Act of the Scottish Parliament), or

(b) in accordance with the practice of a court.

(11) A legislative provision which requires insurance or an indemnity in respect of advice given in connection with a compromise contract or agreement shall not apply to advice provided by the Commission under this section.

(12) A reference in this section to a provision of the equality enactments includes a reference to a provision of Community law which—

(a) relates to discrimination on grounds of sex (including reassignment of gender), racial origin, ethnic origin, religion, belief, disability, age or sexual orientation, and

(b) confers rights on individuals.

(13) In its application by virtue of subsection (12), subsection (1)(b) shall have effect as if it referred to an allegation by an individual that he is disadvantaged by—

(a) an enactment (including an enactment in or under an Act of the Scottish Parliament) which is contrary to a provision of Community law, or

(b) a failure by the United Kingdom to implement a right as required by Community law.

[1671]

NOTES

Commencement: 1 October 2007.

Sub-s (8): word in square brackets substituted by the Transfer of Functions (Equality) Order 2007, SI 2007/2914, art 8, Schedule, para 16(g), as from 12 October 2007.

Orders: as of 6 April 2008 no Orders had been made under this section.

29 Legal assistance: costs

(1) This section applies where—

(a) the Commission has assisted an individual under section 28 in relation to proceedings, and

(b) the individual becomes entitled to some or all of his costs in the proceedings (whether by virtue of an award or by virtue of an agreement).

(2) The Commission's expenses in providing the assistance—
(a) shall be charged on sums paid to the individual by way of costs, and
(b) may be enforced as a debt due to the Commission.

(3) A requirement to pay money to the Commission under subsection (2) ranks, in England and Wales, after a requirement imposed by virtue of section 11(4)(f) of the Access to Justice Act 1999 (c 22) (recovery of costs in funded cases).

(4) Subsection (2), in its application to Scotland, shall not affect the operation of section 17(2A) of the Legal Aid (Scotland) Act 1986 (c 47) (requirement in certain cases to pay to the Scottish Legal Aid Board sums recovered under awards of, or agreements as to, expenses).

(5) For the purposes of subsection (2) the Commission's expenses shall be calculated in accordance with such provision (if any) as the [Minister] makes for the purpose by regulations; and regulations may, in particular, provide for the apportionment of expenditure incurred by the Commission—
(a) partly for one purpose and partly for another, or
(b) for general purposes.

(6) In the application of this section to Scotland a reference to costs shall be taken as a reference to expenses.

[1672]

NOTES

Commencement: 1 October 2007.
Sub-s (5): word in square brackets substituted by the Transfer of Functions (Equality) Order 2007, SI 2007/2914, art 8, Schedule, para 16(h), as from 12 October 2007.
Orders: as of 6 April 2008 no Regulations had been made under this section.

30 Judicial review and other legal proceedings

(1) The Commission shall have capacity to institute or intervene in legal proceedings, whether for judicial review or otherwise, if it appears to the Commission that the proceedings are relevant to a matter in connection with which the Commission has a function.

(2) The Commission shall be taken to have title and interest in relation to the subject matter of any legal proceedings in Scotland which it has capacity to institute, or in which it has capacity to intervene, by virtue of subsection (1).

(3) The Commission may, in the course of legal proceedings for judicial review which it institutes (or in which it intervenes), rely on section 7(1)(b) of the Human Rights Act 1998 (c 42) (breach of Convention rights); and for that purpose—
(a) the Commission need not be a victim or potential victim of the unlawful act to which the proceedings relate,
(b) the Commission may act only if there is or would be one or more victims of the unlawful act,
(c) section 7(3) and (4) of that Act shall not apply, and
(d) no award of damages may be made to the Commission (whether or not the exception in section 8(3) of that Act applies);

and an expression used in this subsection and in section 7 of the Human Rights Act 1998 has the same meaning in this subsection as in that section.

(4) Subsections (1) and (2)—
(a) do not create a cause of action, and
(b) are, except as provided by subsection (3), subject to any limitation or restriction imposed by virtue of an enactment (including an enactment in or under an Act of the Scottish Parliament) or in accordance with the practice of a court.

[1673]

NOTES

Commencement: 1 October 2007.

31 Public sector duties: assessment

(1) The Commission may assess the extent to which or the manner in which a person has complied with a duty under or by virtue of—

(a) section 76A, 76B or 76C of the Sex Discrimination Act 1975 (c 65) (public authorities: duty to eliminate discrimination, &c),

(b) section 71 of the Race Relations Act 1976 (c 74) (public authorities: duty to eliminate discrimination, &c), or

(c) section 49A or 49D of the Disability Discrimination Act 1995 (c 50) (public authorities: duty to eliminate discrimination, &c).

(2) Schedule 2 makes supplemental provision about assessments.

(3) This section is without prejudice to the generality of sections 16 and 20.

[1674]

NOTES

Commencement: 1 October 2007.

32 Public sector duties: compliance notice

(1) This section applies where the Commission thinks that a person has failed to comply with a duty under or by virtue of—

(a) section 76A, 76B or 76C of the Sex Discrimination Act 1975 (public authorities: duty to eliminate discrimination, &c),

(b) section 71 of the Race Relations Act 1976 (public authorities: duty to eliminate discrimination, &c), or

(c) section 49A or 49D of the Disability Discrimination Act 1995 (public authorities: duty to eliminate discrimination, &c).

(2) The Commission may give the person a notice requiring him—

(a) to comply with the duty, and

(b) to give the Commission, within the period of 28 days beginning with the date on which he receives the notice, written information of steps taken or proposed for the purpose of complying with the duty.

(3) A notice under this section may require a person to give the Commission information required by the Commission for the purposes of assessing compliance with the duty; in which case the notice shall specify—

(a) the period within which the information is to be given (which shall begin with the date on which the notice is received and shall not exceed three months), and

(b) the manner and form in which the information is to be given.

(4) The Commission may not give a notice under this section in respect of a duty under section 76A of the Sex Discrimination Act 1975, section 71(1) of the Race Relations Act 1976 or section 49A of the Disability Discrimination Act 1995 unless—

(a) the Commission has carried out an assessment under section 31 above, and

(b) the notice relates to the results of the assessment.

(5) A person who receives a notice under this section shall comply with it.

(6) But a notice under this section shall not oblige a person to give information—

(a) that he is prohibited from disclosing by virtue of an enactment, or

(b) that he could not be compelled to give in proceedings before the High Court or the Court of Session.

(7) Paragraphs 11 and 14 of Schedule 2 shall have effect (with any necessary modifications) in relation to a requirement imposed by a notice under this section as they have effect in relation to a requirement imposed by a notice under paragraph 9 of that Schedule.

(8) If the Commission thinks that a person, to whom a notice under this section has been given, has failed to comply with a requirement of the notice, the Commission may apply to the court for an order requiring the person to comply.

(9) In subsection (8) "the court" means—

(a) where the notice related to a duty under section 76A of the Sex Discrimination Act 1975 (c 65), section 71(1) of the Race Relations Act 1976 (c 74) or section 49A of the Disability Discrimination Act 1995 (c 50), the High Court (in England and Wales) or (in Scotland) the Court of Session, and

(b) in any other case, a county court (in England and Wales) or the sheriff (in Scotland).

(10) A notice under this section shall specify a time before which the Commission may not make an application under subsection (8) in respect of the notice.

(11) Legal proceedings in relation to a duty by virtue of section 76B or 76C of the Sex Discrimination Act 1975, section 71(2) of the Race Relations Act 1976 or section 49D of the Disability Discrimination Act 1995—

(a) may be brought by the Commission in accordance with subsection (8) above, and

(b) may not be brought in any other way.

[1675]

NOTES

Commencement: 1 October 2007.

Modification: see the Equality Act 2006 (Dissolution of Commissions and Consequential and Transitional Provisions) Order 2007, SI 2007/2602, art 5(4) at **[3473O]**, which provides as follows—

"(4) Section 32(8) of the 2006 Act shall apply in relation to notices issued under section 76D of the 1975 Act (specific duties: enforcement) or section 71D of the 1976 Act (general statutory duty: compliance notices) as if, after "this section", there were inserted ", section 76D of the Sex Discrimination Act 1975 or section 71D of the Race Relations Act 1976".".

Interpretation

33 Equality and human rights enactments

(1) In this Part "the equality enactments" means—

(a) the Equal Pay Act 1970 (c 41),

(b) the Sex Discrimination Act 1975,

(c) the Race Relations Act 1976,

(d) the Disability Discrimination Act 1995,

(e) Part 2 of this Act,

(f) regulations under Part 3 of this Act,

(g) the Employment Equality (Sexual Orientation) Regulations 2003 (SI 2003/1661), …

(h) the Employment Equality (Religion or Belief) Regulations 2003 (SI 2003/1660)[, and

(i) the Employment Equality (Age) Regulations 2006].

(2) In this Part "the equality and human rights enactments" means the equality enactments and the Human Rights Act 1998 (c 42).

(3) The [Minister] may by order amend the list in subsection (1) so as to—

(a) add an entry,

(b) remove an entry, or

(c) vary an entry.

[1676]

NOTES

Commencement: 18 April 2006.

Sub-s (1): word omitted from para (g) repealed, and para (i) and the word immediately preceding it added, by the Employment Equality (Age) Regulations 2006, SI 2006/1031, reg 49(1), Sch 8, Pt 1, paras 37, 40, as from 1 October 2006.

Sub-s (3): word in square brackets substituted by the Transfer of Functions (Equality) Order 2007, SI 2007/2914, art 8, Schedule, para 16(i), as from 12 October 2007.

Orders: as of 6 April 2008 no Orders had been made under this section.

34 Unlawful

(1) In this Part (except section 30(3)) "unlawful" means contrary to a provision of the equality enactments.

(2) But action is not unlawful for the purposes of this Part by reason only of the fact that it contravenes a duty under or by virtue of—

(a) section 76A, 76B or 76C of the Sex Discrimination Act 1975 (c 65) (public authorities: duty to eliminate discrimination, &c),

(b) section 71 of the Race Relations Act 1976 (c 74) (public authorities: duty to eliminate discrimination, &c), or

(c) any of the following provisions of the Disability Discrimination Act 1995 (c 50)—
  (i) Part 5 (public transport),
  (ii) sections 49A and 49D (public authorities), and
  (iii) section 49G (consent to tenant's improvements).

[1677]

NOTES

Commencement: 18 April 2006.

35 General

In this Part—

"act" includes deliberate omission,

"groups" has the meaning given by section 10,

"the Commission" means the Commission for Equality and Human Rights,

"disabled person" has the meaning given by section 8,

"human rights" has the meaning given by section 9,

["the Minister" means the Lord Privy Seal;]

"race" includes colour, nationality, ethnic origin and national origin,

"religion or belief" has the same meaning as in Part 2 (as defined by section 44), and

"sexual orientation" means an individual's sexual orientation towards—
  (a) persons of the same sex as him or her,
  (b) persons of the opposite sex, or
  (c) both.

[1678]

NOTES

Commencement: 18 April 2006.

Definition "the Minister" inserted by the Transfer of Functions (Equality) Order 2007, SI 2007/2914, art 8, Schedule, para 15(1), as from 12 October 2007.

Dissolution of Existing Commissions

36 Dissolution

(1) The Secretary of State may by order provide for—
  (a) any of the former Commissions to cease to exist, or
  (b) the removal from any of the former Commissions of a specified function.

(2) In this Part "the former Commissions" means—
  (a) the Equal Opportunities Commission,
  (b) the Commission for Racial Equality, and
  (c) the Disability Rights Commission.

(3) The Secretary of State shall by exercising the power under subsection (1) ensure that each of the former Commissions ceases to exist not later than the end of 31st March 2009.

[1679]

NOTES

Commencement: 18 April 2006.

"The Secretary of State": see the note on transfer of functions immediately before Part 1 of this Act.

Orders: the Equality Act 2006 (Dissolution of Commissions and Consequential and Transitional Provisions) Order 2007, SI 2007/2602 at **[3473K]**.

37 Transfer of property, &c

(1) An order under section 36(1) in respect of any of the former Commissions may provide for the transfer to the Commission for Equality and Human Rights of specified property, rights and liabilities of the former Commission.

(2) The Secretary of State may give a former Commission any direction that the Secretary of State thinks appropriate in connection with the dissolution of the former Commission or the establishment of the Commission for Equality and Human Rights; and a direction may, in particular, require the former Commission—

(a) to provide information in connection with property, rights or liabilities;
(b) to provide information in connection with the exercise of functions;
(c) to transfer specified property, rights and liabilities to a specified person;
(d) to make property, staff or facilities available, on such terms or conditions as may be specified in the direction, to the Commission for Equality and Human Rights;
(e) not to take action of a specified kind or in specified circumstances.

(3) The Secretary of State may direct a former Commission to prepare a scheme for the transfer of specified property, rights and liabilities to—
(a) the Commission for Equality and Human Rights, or
(b) another person specified in the direction.

(4) If the Secretary of State gives a direction under subsection (3)—
(a) the former Commission shall prepare a scheme in accordance with the direction, having consulted either the Commission for Equality and Human Rights or the person specified under subsection (3)(b), and
(b) the scheme shall have effect—
(i) when approved by the Secretary of State, and
(ii) subject to any modifications made by him, having consulted the former Commission and either the Commission for Equality and Human Rights or the person specified under subsection (3)(b).

(5) Where a former Commission ceases to exist by virtue of section 36(1)(a), its property, rights and liabilities shall by virtue of this subsection vest in the Commission for Equality and Human Rights (and this subsection operates in addition to any transfer provided for by virtue of subsection (1) above).

(6) An order, direction or scheme under or by virtue of this section may, in particular—
(a) specify property, rights or liabilities;
(b) specify a class or description of property, rights or liabilities;
(c) specify property, rights or liabilities to a specified extent.

[1680]

NOTES

Commencement: 18 April 2006.
"The Secretary of State": see the note on transfer of functions immediately before Part 1 of this Act.

38 Transfer of property: supplemental

(1) A direction under section 37—
(a) shall be in writing,
(b) may be given only following consultation with the former Commission to which the direction relates and, where the Secretary of State thinks it appropriate, the Commission for Equality and Human Rights, and
(c) may be varied or revoked by a further direction.

(2) In so far as is appropriate as a consequence of a transfer effected by or by virtue of section 37—
(a) anything done by or in relation to any of the former Commissions which has effect immediately before the transfer shall continue to have effect as if done by or in relation to the Commission for Equality and Human Rights, and
(b) anything (including any legal proceedings) which immediately before the transfer is in the process of being done by or in relation to any of the former Commissions may be continued by or in relation to the Commission for Equality and Human Rights.

(3) In so far as is appropriate in consequence of a transfer effected by or by virtue of section 37 a reference to any of the former Commissions in an agreement, instrument or other document shall be treated as a reference to the Commission for Equality and Human Rights.

(4) Section 37, and a direction, scheme or order under or by virtue of that section, shall operate in relation to property, rights or liabilities—
(a) whether or not they would otherwise be capable of being transferred,
(b) without any instrument or other formality being required, and
(c) irrespective of any requirement for consent that would otherwise apply.

(5) A scheme or order under or by virtue of section 37 which relates to rights or liabilities under a contract of employment—

(a) must provide for the application of the [Transfer of Undertakings (Protection of Employment) Regulations 2006], and

(b) must provide that for any purpose relating to an employee of a former commission who becomes an employee of the Commission for Equality and Human Rights by virtue of the scheme or order—

(i) a period of employment with the former commission shall be treated as a period of employment with the Commission for Equality and Human Rights, and

(ii) the transfer to that Commission shall not be treated as a break in service.

[1681]

NOTES

Commencement: 18 April 2006.

Sub-s (5): the Transfer of Undertakings (Protection of Employment) Regulations 2006, SI 2006/246, reg 20, Sch 2, para 1(l) provides that the words "Transfer of Undertakings (Protection of Employment) Regulations 2006" should be substituted for the words "Transfer of Undertakings (Protection of Employment) Regulations 1981 (SI 1981/1794)" in s 39(5) of this Act (as from 6 April 2006). It appears that this is a drafting error as the words in question occur in sub-s (5) of this section and not in s 39(5). The amendment has been taken in above (for transitional provisions in relation to a relevant transfer, etc, that took place before 6 April 2006, see reg 21 of the 2006 Regulations at **[3395]**).

"The Secretary of State": see the note on transfer of functions immediately before Part 1 of this Act.

Miscellaneous

39 Orders and regulations

(1) An order of a Minister of the Crown under this Part and regulations under this Part shall be made by statutory instrument.

(2) An order of a Minister of the Crown under this Part and regulations under this Part—

(a) may make provision generally or only for specified purposes,

(b) may make different provision for different purposes, and

(c) may include transitional, incidental or consequential provision.

(3) An order or regulations under any of the following provisions shall be subject to annulment in pursuance of a resolution of either House of Parliament—

(a) section 15(3),

(b) section 28,

(c) section 29,

(d) section 36, and

(e) Part 5 of Schedule 1.

(4) An order under section 10(6), 15(6), 27(10) or 33(3)—

(a) may, in particular, make consequential amendment of an enactment (including this Act and including an enactment in or under an Act of the Scottish Parliament), and

(b) may not be made unless a draft has been laid before and approved by resolution of each House of Parliament.

(5) An incidental provision included in an order or regulations by virtue of subsection (2)(c) may, in particular, impose a requirement for consent to action under or by virtue of the order or regulations.

[1682]–[1683]

NOTES

Commencement: 18 April 2006.

40 (*Introduces Sch 3* (*consequential amendments*).)

41 Transitional: the Commission

(1) If an order under section 93 provides for any of sections 1 to 3 and Schedule 1 to come into force (to any extent) at a time before any of sections 8 to 32 come into force (to any extent)—

(a) the period between that time and the commencement of any of sections 8 to 32 (to any extent) is the "transitional period" for the purposes of this section, and

(b) the following provisions of this section shall have effect.

(2) During the transitional period the minimum number of Commissioners shall be five (and not as provided by paragraph 1 of Schedule 1).

(3) The Secretary of State shall, as soon as is reasonably practicable after making the first appointments under that paragraph, appoint as additional members of the Commission (to be known as Transition Commissioners)—

(a) a commissioner of the Equal Opportunities Commission nominated by its chairman,

(b) a commissioner of the Commission for Racial Equality nominated by its chairman, and

(c) a commissioner of the Disability Rights Commission nominated by its chairman.

(4) A person may nominate himself as a Transition Commissioner.

(5) If a Transition Commissioner ceases to be a commissioner of the Commission whose chairman nominated him—

(a) he shall cease to be a Transition Commissioner,

(b) the chairman of that Commission shall nominate a replacement, and

(c) the Secretary of State shall appoint the nominated replacement.

(6) A person shall hold appointment as a Transition Commissioner until a time specified by order of the Secretary of State (subject to subsection (5)); and the Secretary of State shall specify a time which in his opinion is not more than two years after the time when, by virtue of section 36, the Commission whose chairman nominated the Transition Commissioner—

(a) ceases to exist, or

(b) loses its principal functions.

(7) In all other respects the provisions of this Part apply in relation to a Transition Commissioner as in relation to another Commissioner.

[1684]

NOTES

Commencement: 16 February 2006.

"The Secretary of State": see the note on transfer of functions immediately before Part 1 of this Act.

Orders: Equality Act 2006 (Termination of Appointments) Order 2007, SI 2007/2604.

42 Transitional: functions of the dissolved Commissions

(1) An order under section 36(1)(a) or (b) may—

(a) provide for a former Commission to continue to exercise a function in respect of a transitional case of a kind specified;

(b) provide for the Commission for Equality and Human Rights to exercise a function of a former Commission in respect of a transitional case of a kind specified.

(2) An order under section 93 commencing a provision of Schedule 3 or 4 may include a saving or a consequential or incidental provision for the purpose of the operation of provision made by virtue of subsection (1) above; and the saving, consequential or incidental provision may, in particular, include provision applying, disapplying or modifying the application of a provision of this Act or of another enactment (including an enactment in or under an Act of the Scottish Parliament).

(3) A code of practice issued by a Commission dissolved by virtue of section 36, or which relates to a function of a Commission removed by virtue of section 36(1)(b)—

(a) shall continue to have effect until revoked by the Secretary of State, at the request of the Commission for Equality and Human Rights, by order made by statutory instrument, and

(b) may be revised by the Commission for Equality and Human Rights as if it had been issued under section 14.

(4) Consultation undertaken by a former Commission in relation to the issue or revision of a code of practice may be relied upon by the Commission for Equality and Human Rights for a purpose of section 14.

(5) An order under subsection (3)(a) shall be subject to annulment in pursuance of a resolution of either House of Parliament.

[1685]

NOTES

Commencement: 16 February 2006.

"The Secretary of State": see the note on transfer of functions immediately before Part 1 of this Act.

Orders: the Equality Act 2006 (Dissolution of Commissions and Consequential and Transitional Provisions) Order 2007, SI 2007/2602 at **[3473K]**.

43–80 *(S 43(1) inserts the Disability Discrimination Act 1995, s 49I (Conciliation of disputes: rented housing in Scotland) and is outside the scope of this work; s 43(2) amended s 53A) of the 1995 Act (repealed); 43(3) amends the Disability Rights Commission Act 1999, s 7 (repealed); ss 44–80 (Pt 2: Discrimination on grounds of religion or belief in relation to goods, facilities and services) omitted for reasons of space.)*

PART 3
DISCRIMINATION ON GROUNDS OF SEXUAL ORIENTATION

81 Regulations

(1) The [Minister] may by regulations make provision about discrimination or harassment on grounds of sexual orientation.

(2) In subsection (1) "sexual orientation" has the meaning given by section 35.

(3) The regulations may, in particular—
- (a) make provision of a kind similar to Part 2 of this Act;
- (b) define discrimination;
- (c) define harassment;
- (d) make provision for enforcement (which may, in particular, include provision—
  - (i) creating a criminal offence of a kind similar to, and with the same maximum penalties as, an offence created by an enactment relating to discrimination or equality;
  - (ii) about validity and revision of contracts;
  - (iii) about discriminatory advertisements;
  - (iv) about instructing or causing discrimination or harassment);
- (e) provide for exceptions (whether or not of a kind similar to those provided for by Part 2 of this Act or any other enactment relating to discrimination or equality);
- (f) make provision which applies generally or only in specified cases or circumstances;
- (g) make different provision for different cases or circumstances;
- (h) include incidental or consequential provision (which may include provision amending an enactment);
- (i) include transitional provision.

(4) The regulations—
- (a) shall be made by statutory instrument, and
- (b) may not be made unless a draft has been laid before and approved by resolution of each House of Parliament.

(5) In subsection (3)(h) "enactment" includes an enactment in or under an Act of the Scottish Parliament.

[(6) In this section "the Minister" means the Lord Privy Seal.]

[1686]

NOTES

Commencement: 18 April 2006.

Sub-s (1): word in square brackets substituted by the Transfer of Functions (Equality) Order 2007, SI 2007/2914, art 8, Schedule, para 16(n).

Sub-s (6): added by SI 2007/2914, art 8, Schedule, para 15(3), as from 12 October 2007.

Regulations: the Equality Act (Sexual Orientation) Regulations 2007, SI 2007/1263.

82–90 *(S 82 (Regulations for Northern Ireland) outside the scope of this work; ss 83–90 (Pt 4) contain various amendments to the Sex Discrimination Act 1975, the Race Relations Act 1976, and the Disability Discrimination Act 1995 which have been incorporated at the appropriate place.)*

PART 5
GENERAL

91 (*Introduces Schedule 4* (*Repeals*).)

92 Crown application

This Act applies (except as is otherwise expressly provided) to—
(a) Ministers of the Crown,
(b) government departments,
(c) office-holders in the Scottish Administration (within the meaning of section 126(7) of the Scotland Act 1998 (c 46)),
[(ca) the Welsh Ministers, the First Minister for Wales and the Counsel General to the Welsh Assembly Government,] and
(d) other agents of the Crown.

[1687]

NOTES
Commencement: 18 April 2006.
Para (ca) inserted by the Government of Wales Act 2006 (Consequential Modifications and Transitional Provisions) Order 2007, SI 2007/1388, art 3, Sch 1, paras 112, 119, as from 25 May 2007.

93 Commencement

(1) The preceding provisions of this Act, except for sections 41, 42 and 86, shall come into force in accordance with provision made by the Secretary of State by order.

(2) An order under subsection (1)—
(a) shall be made by statutory instrument,
(b) may make provision generally or only for a specified purpose,
(c) may make different provision for different purposes, and
(d) may include transitional provisions and savings.

[1688]

NOTES
Commencement: 16 February 2006.
"The Secretary of State": see the note on transfer of functions immediately before Part 1 of this Act.
Orders: the Equality Act 2006 (Commencement No 1) Order 2006, SI 2006/1082; the Equality Act 2006 (Commencement No 2) Order 2007, SI 2007/1092; the Equality Act 2006 (Commencement No 3 and Savings) Order 2007, SI 2007/2603 at **[3473P]**.

94 Extent

(1) This Act extends only to—
(a) England and Wales, and
(b) Scotland.

(2) But—
(a) section 82 extends only to Northern Ireland, and
(b) except as provided by subsection (3), an amendment of an enactment by this Act shall have the same extent as the enactment amended (or as the relevant part of the enactment amended).

(3) Paragraphs 36 to 38 and 41 to 56 of Schedule 3 (which amend the Estate Agents Act 1979 (c 38) and the Disability Discrimination Act 1995 (c 50)), together with corresponding entries in Schedule 4, shall not extend to Northern Ireland.

[1689]

NOTES
Commencement: 16 February 2006.

95 Short title

This Act may be cited as the Equality Act 2006.

[1690]

NOTES

Commencement: 16 February 2006.

SCHEDULES

SCHEDULE 1
THE COMMISSION: CONSTITUTION, &C

Section 2

PART 1
CONSTITUTION

Membership

1.—(1) The [Minister] shall appoint not less than 10 or more than 15 individuals as members of the Commission (to be known as Commissioners).

(2) The chief executive of the Commission (appointed under paragraph 7 below) shall be a Commissioner *ex officio*.

2.—(1) In appointing Commissioners the [Minister] shall—
- (a) appoint an individual only if the [Minister] thinks that the individual—
  - (i) has experience or knowledge relating to a relevant matter, or
  - (ii) is suitable for appointment for some other special reason, and
- (b) have regard to the desirability of the Commissioners together having experience and knowledge relating to the relevant matters.

(2) For the purposes of sub-paragraph (1) the relevant matters are those matters in respect of which the Commission has functions including, in particular—
- (a) discrimination (whether on grounds of age, disability, gender, gender reassignment, race, religion or belief, sexual orientation or otherwise), and
- (b) human rights.

(3) The [Minister] shall ensure that the Commission includes—
- (a) a Commissioner appointed under paragraph 1(1) who is (or has been) a disabled person,
- (b) a Commissioner appointed under paragraph 1(1), with the consent of the Scottish Ministers, who knows about conditions in Scotland, and
- (c) a Commissioner appointed under paragraph 1(1), with the consent of the [Welsh Ministers], who knows about conditions in Wales.

(4) A person may not be appointed for the purpose of satisfying more than one paragraph of sub-paragraph (3).

Tenure

3.—(1) A Commissioner shall hold and vacate office in accordance with the terms of his appointment (subject to this Schedule).

(2) The appointment of a Commissioner must be expressed to be for a specified period of not less than two years or more than five years.

(3) A Commissioner whose period of membership has expired may be re-appointed.

(4) A Commissioner may resign by notice in writing to the [Minister].

(5) The [Minister] may dismiss a Commissioner who is, in the opinion of the [Minister], unable, unfit or unwilling to perform his functions.

(6) This paragraph does not apply to the chief executive.

Chairman

4.—(1) The [Minister] shall appoint—

(a) a Commissioner as Chairman, and
(b) one or more Commissioners as deputy Chairman.

(2) The Chairman shall—
(a) preside over meetings of the Commission,
(b) perform such functions as may be specified in the terms of his appointment, and
(c) perform such other functions as may be assigned to him by the Commission.

(3) A deputy Chairman—
(a) may act for the Chairman when he is unavailable, and
(b) shall perform—
(i) such functions as may be specified in the terms of his appointment, and
(ii) such other functions as the Chairman may delegate or assign to him.

(4) The Chairman or a deputy Chairman—
(a) shall vacate office if he ceases to be a Commissioner,
(b) may resign by notice in writing to the [Minister], and
(c) otherwise, shall hold and vacate office in accordance with the terms of his appointment (and may be reappointed).

(5) If the Chairman resigns he shall cease to be a Commissioner (but he may be reappointed as a Commissioner).

(6) The chief executive may not be appointed Chairman or deputy Chairman.

[1691]

NOTES

Commencement: 18 April 2006.

Paras 1, 3, 4: words in square brackets substituted by the Transfer of Functions (Equality) Order 2007, SI 2007/2914, art 8, Schedule, para 16(o), as from 12 October 2007.

Para 2: words in square brackets in sub-para (1), and word in first pair of square brackets in sub-para (3) substituted by SI 2007/2914, art 8, Schedule, para 16(o), as from 12 October 2007; words in second pair of square brackets in sub-para (3) substituted by the Government of Wales Act 2006 (Consequential Modifications and Transitional Provisions) Order 2007, SI 2007/1388, art 3, Sch 1, paras 112, 120, as from 25 May 2007.

PART 2
PROCEEDINGS

Procedure

5. The Commission may regulate its own proceedings (subject to this Schedule).

6.—(1) The Commission shall determine a quorum for its meetings.

(2) At least five Commissioners must participate in the process by which a determination under sub-paragraph (1) is made.

Staff

7.—(1) The Commission—
(a) shall appoint a chief executive, and
(b) may appoint other staff.

(2) A person may be appointed under sub-paragraph (1)(a) only with the consent of the [Minister].

(3) An appointment may be made under sub-paragraph (1)(b) only if consistent with arrangements determined by the Commission and approved by the [Minister] as to—
(a) numbers, and
(b) terms and conditions of appointment.

8. …

Investigating Commissioners

9.—(1) The Commission may appoint one or more Investigating Commissioners.

(2) An Investigating Commissioner may be appointed only—
(a) for the purpose of having delegated to him by the Commission the function of taking action of a kind listed in sub-paragraph (3), and
(b) with the consent of the [Minister].

(3) The kinds of action referred to in sub-paragraph (2)(a) are—
(a) carrying out an inquiry under section 16,
(b) carrying out an investigation under section 20,
(c) giving an unlawful act notice under section 21, and
(d) entering into an agreement under section 23.

(4) An Investigating Commissioner is not a Commissioner; but paragraphs 3(1), (4) and (5) and 33 apply to him as if he were (and with the substitution of references to the Commission for references to the [Minister]).

Delegation

10.—(1) The Commission may delegate a function—
(a) to a Commissioner,
(b) to staff, or
(c) in accordance with paragraph 9, to an Investigating Commissioner.

(2) Paragraphs 15, 21, 22, 29, 30 and 52 make provision about delegation to committees.

Committees

11.—(1) The Commission may establish one or more committees (to be known as advisory committees) to advise—
(a) the Commission, or
(b) an Investigating Commissioner.

(2) An advisory committee may include any of the following—
(a) Commissioners;
(b) staff;
(c) other non-Commissioners.

12.—(1) The Commission may establish one or more committees to whom the Commission may delegate functions (to be known as decision-making committees).

(2) A decision-making committee may include any of the following—
(a) Commissioners;
(b) staff;
(c) other non-Commissioners.

(3) The Commission shall ensure that the Chairman of each decision-making committee is a Commissioner.

(4) In allocating its resources the Commission shall ensure that each decision-making committee receives a share sufficient to enable it to exercise its functions.

13. A member of a committee shall hold and vacate office in accordance with the terms of his appointment by the Commission (which may include provision for dismissal).

14. The Commission—
(a) may, to any extent, regulate the proceedings of a committee (and may, in particular, determine a quorum for meetings),
(b) may, to any extent, permit a committee to regulate its own proceedings (and may, in particular, enable a committee to determine a quorum for meetings), and
(c) may dissolve a committee.

15.—(1) The Commission may delegate a function to a decision-making committee.

(2) This paragraph is subject to paragraphs 21, 22, 29, 30 and 52.

Scotland Committee

16.—(1) The Commission shall establish a decision-making committee to be known as the Scotland Committee.

(2) The Commission shall ensure that the Scotland Committee is established before any of sections 8 to 12 comes into force (to any extent).

17. The Commission shall appoint as the Chairman of the Scotland Committee a Commissioner appointed for the purpose of satisfying paragraph 2(3)(b).

18. The Commission shall appoint each member of the Scotland Committee for a period of not less than two years or more than 5 years, subject to the possibilities of—
(a) reappointment, and
(b) dismissal in accordance with the terms of appointment.

19. The Scotland Committee shall advise the Commission about the exercise of the Commission's functions in so far as they affect Scotland.

20. Before exercising a function in a manner which in the opinion of the Commission is likely to affect persons in Scotland, the Commission shall consult the Scotland Committee.

21.—(1) The power under section 13—
(a) shall be treated by virtue of this paragraph as having been delegated by the Commission to the Scotland Committee in so far as its exercise, in the opinion of the Commission, affects Scotland, and
(b) to that extent shall not be exercisable by the Commission.

(2) Sub-paragraph (1) shall not apply to the power under section 13 in so far as it is treated as delegated to the Disability Committee in accordance with paragraph 52.

(3) Sub-paragraph (1) shall not prevent the Commission from making arrangements under section 13(1)(d) or (e) for the provision of advice or guidance to persons anywhere in Great Britain.

22.—(1) The power under section 11(2)(c)—
(a) shall be treated by virtue of this paragraph as having been delegated by the Commission to the Scotland Committee in so far as it concerns the giving of advice to devolved government about enactments which, in the opinion of the Commission, affect only Scotland, and
(b) to that extent shall not be exercisable by the Commission.

(2) The power under section 11(2)(d)—
(a) shall be treated by virtue of this paragraph as having been delegated by the Commission to the Scotland Committee in so far as it concerns the giving of advice to devolved government about proposed changes in the law which, in the opinion of the Commission, would affect only Scotland, and
(b) to that extent shall not be exercisable by the Commission.

(3) Sub-paragraphs (1) and (2) shall not apply to the powers under section 11(2)(c) and (d) in so far as they are treated as delegated to the Disability Committee in accordance with paragraph 52.

23. In allocating its resources the Commission shall ensure that the Scotland Committee receives a share sufficient to enable it to exercise its functions.

Wales Committee

24.—(1) The Commission shall establish a decision-making committee to be known as the Wales Committee.

(2) The Commission shall ensure that the Wales Committee is established before any of sections 8 to 12 comes into force (to any extent).

25. The Commission shall appoint as the Chairman of the Wales Committee a Commissioner appointed for the purpose of satisfying paragraph 2(3)(c).

26. The Commission shall appoint each member of the Wales Committee for a period of not less than two years or more than 5 years, subject to the possibilities of—
   (a) reappointment, and
   (b) dismissal in accordance with the terms of appointment.

27. The Wales Committee shall advise the Commission about the exercise of its functions in so far as they affect Wales.

28. Before exercising a function in a manner which in the opinion of the Commission is likely to affect persons in Wales, the Commission shall consult the Wales Committee.

29.—(1) The power under section 13—
   (a) shall be treated by virtue of this paragraph as having been delegated by the Commission to the Wales Committee in so far as its exercise, in the opinion of the Commission, affects Wales, and
   (b) to that extent shall not be exercisable by the Commission.

(2) Sub-paragraph (1) does not apply to the power under section 13 in so far as it is treated as delegated to the Disability Committee in accordance with paragraph 52.

(3) Sub-paragraph (1) shall not prevent the Commission from making arrangements under section 13(1)(d) or (e) for the provision of advice or guidance to persons anywhere in Great Britain.

30.—(1) The power under section 11(2)(c)—
   (a) shall be treated by virtue of this paragraph as having been delegated by the Commission to the Wales Committee in so far as it concerns the giving of advice to devolved government about enactments which, in the opinion of the Commission, affect only Wales, and
   (b) to that extent shall not be exercisable by the Commission.

(2) The power under section 11(2)(d)—
   (a) shall be treated by virtue of this paragraph as having been delegated by the Commission to the Wales Committee in so far as it concerns the giving of advice to devolved government about proposed changes in the law which, in the opinion of the Commission, would affect only Wales, and
   (b) to that extent shall not be exercisable by the Commission.

(3) Sub-paragraphs (1) and (2) shall not apply to the powers under section 11(2)(c) and (d) in so far as they are treated as delegated to the Disability Committee in accordance with paragraph 52.

31. In allocating its resources the Commission shall ensure that the Wales Committee receives a share sufficient to enable it to exercise its functions.

Annual report

32.—(1) The Commission shall for each financial year prepare a report on the performance of its functions in that year (to be known as its annual report).

(2) An annual report shall, in particular, indicate in what manner and to what extent the Commission's performance of its functions has accorded to the plan under section 4.

(3) The matters addressed by an annual report shall, in particular, include the Commission's activities in relation to—
   (a) Scotland, and
   (b) Wales.

(4) The Commission shall send each annual report to the [Minister] within such period, beginning with the end of the financial year to which the report relates, as he may specify.

(5) The [Minister] shall lay before Parliament a copy of each annual report received under sub-paragraph (4).

(6) The Commission shall send a copy of each annual report to—
   (a) the Scottish Parliament, and
   (b) the National Assembly for Wales.

Savings

33. The validity of proceedings of the Commission shall not be affected by—
(a) a vacancy (whether for Commissioner, Chairman, deputy Chairman or chief executive), or
(b) a defect in relation to an appointment.

34. The validity of proceedings of a committee of the Commission shall not be affected by—
(a) a vacancy (including a vacancy in the office of Chairman), or
(b) a defect in relation to an appointment (including a defect in relation to the office of Chairman).

[1692]

NOTES

Commencement: 18 April 2006.

Paras 7, 9, 32: words in square brackets substituted by the Transfer of Functions (Equality) Order 2007, SI 2007/2914, art 8, Schedule, para 16(o), as from 12 October 2007

Para 8: amends the Employers' Liability (Compulsory Insurance) Act 1969, s 3.

Modification: see the Equality Act 2006 (Dissolution of Commissions and Consequential and Transitional Provisions) Order 2007, SI 2007/2602, art 5(2) at **[3473O]**, which provides that in its application to any investigation to which para (1)(f) of that article applies (ie, under ss 57–60 of the 1975 Act and ss 48–51 of the 1976 Act), para 9(3)(b) above shall have effect as if, after "section 20", there were inserted "of this Act, section 57 of the Sex Discrimination Act 1975 or section 48 of the Race Relations Act 1976".

PART 3
MONEY

Remuneration, &c

35.—(1) The Commission may pay to the Chairman, a deputy Chairman or another Commissioner—
(a) such remuneration as the [Minister] may determine, and
(b) such travelling and other allowances as the [Minister] may determine.

(2) The Commission may pay to or in respect of the Chairman, a deputy Chairman or another Commissioner such sums as the [Minister] may determine by way of, or in respect of, pensions, allowances or gratuities.

(3) If the [Minister] thinks that there are special circumstances that make it right for a person ceasing to hold office as Chairman, deputy Chairman or Commissioner to receive compensation, the Commission may pay to him such compensation as the [Minister] may determine.

(4) This paragraph does not apply to the Chief Executive.

36.—(1) The Commission may pay sums to or in respect of a member or former member of staff by way of or in respect of—
(a) remuneration,
(b) allowances,
(c) pensions,
(d) gratuities, or
(e) compensation for loss of employment.

(2) …

(3) The Commission shall pay to the Minister for the Civil Service such sums as he may determine in respect of any increase attributable to sub-paragraph (2) in the sums payable out of money provided by Parliament under the Superannuation Act 1972 (c 11).

37.—(1) The Commission may, with the approval of the [Minister], pay sums to or in respect of a member or former member of an advisory or decision-making committee by way of or in respect of—
(a) remuneration,
(b) allowances, or

(c) gratuities.

(2) This paragraph does not apply in relation to a person who is a member of staff of the Commission.

(3) Approval for the purposes of sub-paragraph (1) may be general or specific.

Funding by [Minister]

38. The [Minister] shall pay to the Commission such sums as appear to the [Minister] reasonably sufficient for the purpose of enabling the Commission to perform its functions.

Charging

39. The Commission may make a charge for a service provided under section 13 or 27.

Accounts

40.—(1) The Commission shall—
(a) keep proper accounting records, and
(b) prepare a statement of accounts in respect of each financial year in such form as the [Minister] may direct.

(2) The Commission shall send a copy of a statement under sub-paragraph (1)(b) to—
(a) the [Minister], and
(b) the Comptroller and Auditor General.

(3) A copy of a statement must be sent under sub-paragraph (2) within such period, beginning with the end of the financial year to which the statement relates, as the [Minister] may direct.

(4) The Comptroller and Auditor General shall—
(a) examine, certify and report on a statement received under this paragraph, and
(b) lay a copy of the statement and his report before Parliament.

(5) The [Minister] may make a direction under sub-paragraph (1)(b) only with the consent of the Treasury.

Financial year

41.—(1) The financial year of the Commission shall be the period of 12 months ending with 31st March.

(2) But the first financial year of the Commission shall be the period—
(a) beginning with the coming into force of section 1, and
(b) ending with—
(i) the following 31st March, if that section comes into force on 1st April, and
(ii) the second following 31st March, in any other case.

[1693]

NOTES

Commencement: 18 April 2006.

Paras 35, 37, 38, 40: words in square brackets substituted by the Transfer of Functions (Equality) Order 2007, SI 2007/2914, art 8, Schedule, para 16(o), as from 12 October 2007

Para 36: sub-para (2) amends the Superannuation Act 1972, Sch 1.

PART 4
STATUS, &C

Status

42.—(1) The Commission shall not—

(a) be regarded as the servant or agent of the Crown, or
(b) enjoy any status, immunity or privilege of the Crown.

(2) Service as Commissioner, Investigating Commissioner or employee of the Commission is not employment in the civil service of the State.

(3) The [Minister] shall have regard to the desirability of ensuring that the Commission is under as few constraints as reasonably possible in determining—
(a) its activities,
(b) its timetables, and
(c) its priorities.

Supervision

43. …

Disqualifications

44, 45. …

46. A Commissioner or Investigating Commissioner, and a member of a decision-making committee of the Commission, shall be disqualified from being a member of the National Assembly for Wales.

Records

47, 48. …

[1694]

NOTES

Commencement: 18 April 2006.

Para 42: word in square brackets substituted by the Transfer of Functions (Equality) Order 2007, SI 2007/2914, art 8, Schedule, para 16(o), as from 12 October 2007.

Paras 43–45, 47, 48: amend the Parliamentary Commissioner Act 1967, Sch 2, the House of Commons Disqualification Act 1975, Sch 1, Pts II, III, the Northern Ireland Assembly Disqualification Act 1975, Sch 1, Pts II, III, the Public Records Act 1958, Sch 1, and the Freedom of Information Act 2000, Sch 1, Pt VI.

PART 5
DISABILITY COMMITTEE

Establishment

49.—(1) The Commission shall establish a decision-making committee to be known as the Disability Committee.

(2) The Commission shall ensure that the Disability Committee is established before either section 8 or section 10, in so far as they relate to disability, comes into force (to any extent).

Membership

50.—(1) The Commission shall ensure that—
(a) there are not less than 7 or more than 9 members of the Disability Committee,
(b) at least one half of the members are (or have been) disabled persons, and
(c) the Chairman is (or has been) a disabled person.

(2) The Transition Commissioner nominated by the chairman of the Disability Rights Commission may not be a member of the Disability Committee.

51.— The appointment of each member of the Disability Committee shall be for a period of not less than two years or more than 5 years, subject to the possibilities of—

(a) reappointment,

(b) dismissal in accordance with the terms of appointment, and

(c) the lapsing of the appointment upon the dissolution of the Committee.

Functions

52.—(1) The Commission shall by virtue of this paragraph be treated as having delegated to the Disability Committee—

(a) the Commission's duty under section 8 in so far as it relates to disability matters and may be fulfilled by the exercise of the powers conferred by or referred to in—

(i) section 11,

(ii) section 13(1)(a), (c) or (d) (or paragraph (e) or (f) in so far as it relates to paragraph (a), (c) or (d)),

(iii) section 14,

(iv) section 15,

(v) section 19, in so far as it relates to disability,

(vi) section 27,

(vii) section 28, or

(viii) section 30,

(b) the Commission's duty under section 10 in so far as it relates to disability and may be fulfilled by the exercise of those powers, and

(c) those powers in so far as they are or may be exercised for the purpose of disability matters.

(2) Delegation under this paragraph shall not prevent the exercise by the Commission of a power, or the fulfilment by the Commission of a duty, by action which relates partly to disability matters and partly to other matters.

(3) In this paragraph "disability matters" means—

(a) matters provided for in Parts 1, 3, 4, 5 and 5B of the Disability Discrimination Act 1995 (c 50),

(b) sections 8 and 10 above, in so far as they relate to disability, and

(c) matters addressed in sections 14(3) and (4), 27(2) and (3) and 28(2) and (3).

(4) Before exercising a power to which paragraph 21(2) or 22(3) applies the Disability Committee shall consult the Scotland Committee.

(5) Before exercising a power to which paragraph 29(2) or 30(3) applies the Disability Committee shall consult the Wales Committee.

53. Before exercising a power or fulfilling a duty wholly or partly in relation to a matter affecting disabled persons (including, in particular, any matter provided for in Part 2 of the Disability Discrimination Act 1995 (c 50)) the Commission shall consult the Disability Committee.

54. The Disability Committee shall advise the Commission about the exercise of the Commission's functions in so far as they affect disabled persons (including, in particular, in so far as they relate to any matter provided for in Part 2 of the Disability Discrimination Act 1995).

Resources

55. In allocating its resources the Commission shall ensure that the Disability Committee receives a share sufficient to enable it to exercise its functions.

Report

56.—(1) The Disability Committee shall for each financial year of the Commission submit to the Commission a report on the Committee's activities in that year.

(2) The Commission shall incorporate each report of the Disability Committee under sub-paragraph (1) into the relevant annual report of the Commission.

5-year review

57. The Commission shall arrange for a review of the activities of the Disability Committee to be conducted as soon as is reasonably practicable after the end of the period of five years beginning with the date of the commencement for all purposes of sections 8 and 10 in so far as they relate to disability.

58. The following may not participate in the review (although those conducting the review may seek views from any of the following)—
- (a) a Commissioner or former Commissioner,
- (b) staff or former staff of the Commission,
- (c) a person who is or has been an Investigating Commissioner, and
- (d) a person who is or has been a member of a committee established by the Commission.

59. The Commission shall ensure—
- (a) that those conducting the review consult disabled persons and other persons whom they think likely to have an interest,
- (b) that those conducting the review submit a report to the Commission which, in particular, recommends for how long the Disability Committee should continue in existence, and
- (c) that the report is published.

60. As soon as is reasonably practicable after receiving a report under paragraph 59 the Commission shall recommend to the [Minister] for how long the Disability Committee should continue in existence.

61. As soon as is reasonably practicable after receiving a recommendation under paragraph 60 the [Minister] shall by order—
- (a) dissolve the Disability Committee with effect from such time as shall be specified in the order, and
- (b) repeal this Part of this Schedule with effect from that time.

62. An order under paragraph 61 may include provision about—
- (a) the conduct of the business of the Disability Committee before its dissolution;
- (b) the conduct of the Commission after the dissolution of the Disability Committee in relation to functions formerly delegated to that committee.

63. The dissolution of the Disability Committee is without prejudice to any power of the Commission under this Schedule—
- (a) to establish a committee, or
- (b) to delegate to a committee.

64. The Disability Committee may not be dissolved under paragraph 14(c).

[1695]

NOTES

Commencement: 18 April 2006.

Paras 60, 61: words in square brackets substituted by the Transfer of Functions (Equality) Order 2007, SI 2007/2914, art 8, Schedule, para 16(o), as from 12 October 2007

Orders: as of 6 April 2008 no Orders had been made under this Part of this Schedule.

SCHEDULE 2
INQUIRIES, INVESTIGATIONS AND ASSESSMENTS

Sections 16, 20 and 31

Introduction

1. This Schedule applies to—
- (a) inquiries under section 16,
- (b) investigations under section 20, and
- (c) assessments under section 31.

Terms of reference

2. Before conducting an inquiry the Commission shall—
   (a) publish the terms of reference of the inquiry in a manner that the Commission thinks is likely to bring the inquiry to the attention of persons whom it concerns or who are likely to be interested in it, and
   (b) in particular, give notice of the terms of reference to any persons specified in them.

3. Before conducting an investigation the Commission shall—
   (a) prepare terms of reference specifying the person to be investigated and the nature of the unlawful act which the Commission suspects,
   (b) give the person to be investigated notice of the proposed terms of reference,
   (c) give the person to be investigated an opportunity to make representations about the proposed terms of reference,
   (d) consider any representations made, and
   (e) publish the terms of reference once settled.

4. Before conducting an assessment of a person's compliance with a duty the Commission shall—
   (a) prepare terms of reference,
   (b) give the person notice of the proposed terms of reference,
   (c) give the person an opportunity to make representations about the proposed terms of reference,
   (d) consider any representations made, and
   (e) publish the terms of reference once settled.

5. Paragraphs 2 to 4 shall apply in relation to revised terms of reference as they apply in relation to original terms of reference.

Representations

6.—(1) The Commission shall make arrangements for giving persons an opportunity to make representations in relation to inquiries, investigations and assessments.

(2) In particular, in the course of an investigation, inquiry or assessment the Commission must give any person specified in the terms of reference an opportunity to make representations.

7. Arrangements under paragraph 6 may (but need not) include arrangements for oral representations.

8.—(1) The Commission shall consider representations made in relation to an inquiry, investigation or assessment.

(2) But the Commission may, where they think it appropriate, refuse to consider representations—
   (a) made neither by nor on behalf of a person specified in the terms of reference, or
   (b) made on behalf of a person specified in the terms of reference by a person who is not *a barrister, an advocate or a solicitor*.

[(2A) "Relevant lawyer" means—
   (a) an advocate or solicitor in Scotland, or
   (b) a person who, for the purposes of the Legal Services Act 2007, is an authorised person in relation to an activity which constitutes the exercise of a right of audience or the conduct of litigation (within the meaning of that Act).]

(3) If the Commission refuse to consider representations in reliance on sub-paragraph (2) they shall give the person who makes them written notice of the Commission's decision and the reasons for it.

Evidence

9. In the course of an inquiry, investigation or assessment the Commission may give a notice under this paragraph to any person.

10.—(1) A notice given to a person under paragraph 9 may require him—
(a) to provide information in his possession,
(b) to produce documents in his possession, or
(c) to give oral evidence.

(2) A notice under paragraph 9 may include provision about—
(a) the form of information, documents or evidence;
(b) timing.

(3) A notice under paragraph 9—
(a) may not require a person to provide information that he is prohibited from disclosing by virtue of an enactment,
(b) may not require a person to do anything that he could not be compelled to do in proceedings before the High Court or the Court of Session, and
(c) may not require a person to attend at a place unless the Commission undertakes to pay the expenses of his journey.

11. The recipient of a notice under paragraph 9 may apply to a county court (in England and Wales) or to the sheriff (in Scotland) to have the notice cancelled on the grounds that the requirement imposed by the notice is—
(a) unnecessary having regard to the purpose of the inquiry, investigation or assessment to which the notice relates, or
(b) otherwise unreasonable.

12.—(1) Sub-paragraph (2) applies where the Commission thinks that a person—
(a) has failed without reasonable excuse to comply with a notice under paragraph 9, or
(b) is likely to fail without reasonable excuse to comply with a notice under paragraph 9.

(2) The Commission may apply to a county court (in England and Wales) or to the sheriff (in Scotland) for an order requiring a person to take such steps as may be specified in the order to comply with the notice.

13.—(1) A person commits an offence if without reasonable excuse he—
(a) fails to comply with a notice under paragraph 9 or an order under paragraph 12(2),
(b) falsifies anything provided or produced in accordance with a notice under paragraph 9 or an order under paragraph 12(2), or
(c) makes a false statement in giving oral evidence in accordance with a notice under paragraph 9.

(2) A person who is guilty of an offence under this paragraph shall be liable on summary conviction to a fine not exceeding level 5 on the standard scale.

14.—(1) Where a person is given a notice under paragraph 9 he shall disregard it, and notify the Commission that he is disregarding it, in so far as he thinks it would require him—
(a) to disclose sensitive information within the meaning of paragraph 4 of Schedule 3 to the Intelligence Services Act 1994 (c 13) (Intelligence and Security Committee),
(b) to disclose information which might lead to the identification of an employee or agent of an intelligence service (other than one whose identity is already known to the Commission),
(c) to disclose information which might provide details of processes used in recruiting, selecting or training employees or agents of an intelligence service,
(d) to disclose information which might provide details of, or cannot practicably be separated from, information falling within any of paragraphs (a) to (c), or
(e) to make a disclosure of information relating to an intelligence service which would prejudice the interests of national security.

(2) In sub-paragraph (1) "intelligence service" means—
(a) the Security Service,
(b) the Secret Intelligence Service, and
(c) the Government Communications Headquarters.

(3) Where in response to a notice under paragraph 9 a person gives a notice to the Commission under sub-paragraph (1) above—
(a) paragraphs 12 and 13 shall not apply in relation to that part of the notice under paragraph 9 to which the notice under sub-paragraph (1) above relates,

(b) the Commission may apply to the tribunal established by section 65 of the Regulation of Investigatory Powers Act 2000 (c 23) for an order requiring the person to take such steps as may be specified in the order to comply with the notice,

(c) the following provisions of that Act shall apply in relation to proceedings under this paragraph as they apply in relation to proceedings under that Act (with any necessary modifications)—

(i) section 67(7), (8) and (10) to (12) (determination),

(ii) section 68 (procedure), and

(iii) section 69 (rules), and

(d) the tribunal shall determine proceedings under this paragraph by considering the opinion of the person who gave the notice under sub-paragraph (1) above in accordance with the principles that would be applied by a court on an application for judicial review of the giving of the notice.

(4) Where the Commission receives information or documents from or relating to an intelligence service in response to a notice under paragraph 9, the Commission shall store and use the information or documents in accordance with any arrangements specified by the Secretary of State.

(5) The recipient of a notice under paragraph 9 may apply to the High Court (in England and Wales) or the Court of Session (in Scotland) to have the notice cancelled on the grounds that the requirement imposed by the notice is undesirable for reasons of national security, other than for the reason that it would require a disclosure of a kind to which sub-paragraph (1) above applies.

Reports

15. The Commission shall publish a report of its findings on an inquiry, investigation or assessment.

Recommendations

16.—(1) The Commission may make recommendations—

(a) as part of a report of an inquiry, investigation or assessment under paragraph 15, or

(b) in respect of a matter arising in the course of an inquiry, investigation or assessment.

(2) A recommendation may be addressed to any class of person.

Effect of report

17.—(1) A court or tribunal—

(a) may have regard to a finding of the report of an inquiry, investigation or assessment, but

(b) shall not treat it as conclusive.

18. A person to whom a recommendation in the report of an inquiry, investigation or assessment is addressed shall have regard to it.

Courts and tribunals

19. An inquiry, investigation or assessment may not question (whether expressly or by necessary implication) the findings of a court or tribunal.

Intelligence services

20.—(1) An inquiry may not consider—

(a) whether an intelligence service has acted (or is acting) in a way which is incompatible with a person's human rights, or

(b) other matters concerning human rights in relation to an intelligence service.

(2) In this paragraph "intelligence service" has the same meaning as in paragraph 14.

[1696]

NOTES

Commencement: 1 October 2007.

Para 8: for the words in italics in sub-para (2)(b) there are substituted the words "a relevant lawyer", and sub-para (2A) is added, by the Legal Services Act 2007, s 208(1), Sch 21, para 152, as from a day to be appointed.

(Sch 3 (Amendments Consequential on Part 1): paras 1–5, 36–39, 58, 60–63 contain various amendments to enactments that are outside the scope of this work; paras 6–20 amend the Sex Discrimination Act 1975, ss 37–40, 76, 81, 82, Sch 2 at **[147]–[150]**, **[190]**, **[195]**, **[196]**, **[204]**, *and repeal ss 53–61, 67–73, 75, 76D, 76E of, and Sch 3 to, that Act; paras 21–35 amend the Race Relations Act 1976, ss 28–31, 68, 74, 78, Sch 1A, Pt II at* **[247]–[250]**, **[289]**, **[301]**, **[310]**, **[315]**, *and repeal ss 43–52, 58–64, 66, 71C–71E of, and Sch 1 to, that Act; para 40 amends the Employment Act 1989, s 28 at* **[410]**; *paras 41–56 amend the Disability Discrimination Act 1995, ss 16B, 16C, 49D, 67, 68, 70, Sch 3, Pt II at* **[913A]**, **[913B]**, **[924D]**, **[941]**, **[942]**, **[944]**, **[948]**, *and repeal ss 17B, 28, 49E, 49F, 53 (and contain other amendments and repeals of provisions not reproduced in this Handbook); para 57 amends the Employment Tribunals Act 1996, s 21 at* **[978]**; *para 59 repeals the Disability Rights Commission Act 1999; Sch 4 contains repeals only and, in so far as relevant to this Handbook, they have been incorporated at the appropriate place.)*

IMMIGRATION, ASYLUM AND NATIONALITY ACT 2006

(2006 c 13)

ARRANGEMENT OF SECTIONS

Employment

An Act to make provision about immigration, asylum and nationality; and for connected purposes

[30 March 2006]

NOTES

Only those provisions of this Act relevant to employment law are reproduced. Provisions not reproduced are not annotated. The provisions reproduced here extend to the whole of the United Kingdom (s 63). As to the commencement of the provisions reproduced here, see the notes thereto.

Employment

15 Penalty

(1) It is contrary to this section to employ an adult subject to immigration control if—

(a) he has not been granted leave to enter or remain in the United Kingdom, or

(b) his leave to enter or remain in the United Kingdom—
(i) is invalid,
(ii) has ceased to have effect (whether by reason of curtailment, revocation, cancellation, passage of time or otherwise), or
(iii) is subject to a condition preventing him from accepting the employment.

(2) The Secretary of State may give an employer who acts contrary to this section a notice requiring him to pay a penalty of a specified amount not exceeding the prescribed maximum.

(3) An employer is excused from paying a penalty if he shows that he complied with any prescribed requirements in relation to the employment.

(4) But the excuse in subsection (3) shall not apply to an employer who knew, at any time during the period of the employment, that it was contrary to this section.

(5) The Secretary of State may give a penalty notice without having established whether subsection (3) applies.

(6) A penalty notice must—
(a) state why the Secretary of State thinks the employer is liable to the penalty,
(b) state the amount of the penalty,
(c) specify a date, at least 28 days after the date specified in the notice as the date on which it is given, before which the penalty must be paid,
(d) specify how the penalty must be paid,
(e) explain how the employer may object to the penalty, and
(f) explain how the Secretary of State may enforce the penalty.

(7) An order prescribing requirements for the purposes of subsection (3) may, in particular—
(a) require the production to an employer of a document of a specified description;
(b) require the production to an employer of one document of each of a number of specified descriptions;
(c) require an employer to take specified steps to verify, retain, copy or record the content of a document produced to him in accordance with the order;
(d) require action to be taken before employment begins;
(e) require action to be taken at specified intervals or on specified occasions during the course of employment.

[1696A]

NOTES

Commencement: 5 November 2007 (for the purposes of making an Order under sub-ss (2), (3), (7)); 29 February 2008 (otherwise).

Transitional provisions: the Immigration, Asylum and Nationality Act 2006 (Commencement No 8 and Transitional and Saving Provisions) Order 2008, SI 2008/310, art 5 provides as follows (note that by virtue of art 1 of that Order, "the 2006 Act" is this Act, and "the 1996 Act" is the Asylum and Immigration Act 1996)—

"5.—(1) Notwithstanding the commencement of section 26 of the 2006 Act (repeal) the following provisions and instruments continue to have effect in relation to employment which commenced before 29th February 2008, including employment which continued on or after that date—
(a) sections 8 (restrictions on employment) and 8A (code of practice) of the 1996 Act;
(b) any Code of Practice in force immediately before 29th February 2008 under section 8A of the 1996 Act;
(c) the Immigration (Restrictions on Employment) Order 2004; and
(d) the Immigration (Restrictions on Employment) (Code of Practice) Order 2001.

(2) Sections 15 to 18, 21, 22, 24, 25 and 26 of the 2006 Act are of no effect in relation to employment of a kind mentioned in paragraph (1)."

Orders: the Immigration (Restrictions on Employment) Order 2007, SI 2007/3290 at **[3473S]**; the Immigration (Employment of Adults Subject to Immigration Control) (Maximum Penalty) Order 2008, SI 2008/132 at **[3474J]**.

16 Objection

(1) This section applies where an employer to whom a penalty notice is given objects on the ground that—
(a) he is not liable to the imposition of a penalty,
(b) he is excused payment by virtue of section 15(3), or
(c) the amount of the penalty is too high.

(2) The employer may give a notice of objection to the Secretary of State.

(3) A notice of objection must—
(a) be in writing,
(b) give the objector's reasons,
(c) be given in the prescribed manner, and
(d) be given before the end of the prescribed period.

(4) Where the Secretary of State receives a notice of objection to a penalty he shall consider it and—
(a) cancel the penalty,
(b) reduce the penalty,
(c) increase the penalty, or
(d) determine to take no action.

(5) Where the Secretary of State considers a notice of objection he shall—
(a) have regard to the code of practice under section 19 (in so far as the objection relates to the amount of the penalty),
(b) inform the objector of his decision before the end of the prescribed period or such longer period as he may agree with the objector,
(c) if he increases the penalty, issue a new penalty notice under section 15, and
(d) if he reduces the penalty, notify the objector of the reduced amount.

[1696B]

NOTES

Commencement: 5 November 2007 (for the purposes of making an Order under sub-ss (3), (5)); 29 February 2008 (otherwise).

Transitional provisions: see the note to s 15 at **[1696A]**.

Orders: the Immigration (Restrictions on Employment) Order 2007, SI 2007/3290 at **[3473S]**.

---

17 Appeal

(1) An employer to whom a penalty notice is given may appeal to the court on the ground that—
(a) he is not liable to the imposition of a penalty,
(b) he is excused payment by virtue of section 15(3), or
(c) the amount of the penalty is too high.

(2) The court may—
(a) allow the appeal and cancel the penalty,
(b) allow the appeal and reduce the penalty, or
(c) dismiss the appeal.

(3) An appeal shall be a re-hearing of the Secretary of State's decision to impose a penalty and shall be determined having regard to—
(a) the code of practice under section 19 that has effect at the time of the appeal (in so far as the appeal relates to the amount of the penalty), and
(b) any other matters which the court thinks relevant (which may include matters of which the Secretary of State was unaware);

and this subsection has effect despite any provision of rules of court.

(4) An appeal must be brought within the period of 28 days beginning with—
(a) the date specified in the penalty notice as the date upon which it is given, or
(b) if the employer gives a notice of objection and the Secretary of State reduces the penalty, the date specified in the notice of reduction as the date upon which it is given, or
(c) if the employer gives a notice of objection and the Secretary of State determines to take no action, the date specified in the notice of that determination as the date upon which it is given.

(5) An appeal may be brought by an employer whether or not—
(a) he has given a notice of objection under section 16;
(b) the penalty has been increased or reduced under that section.

(6) In this section "the court" means—
(a) where the employer has his principal place of business in England and Wales, a county court,

(b) where the employer has his principal place of business in Scotland, the sheriff, and

(c) where the employer has his principal place of business in Northern Ireland, a county court.

[1696C]

NOTES

Commencement: 29 February 2008.

Transitional provisions: see the note to s 15 at **[1696A]**.

18 Enforcement

(1) A sum payable to the Secretary of State as a penalty under section 15 may be recovered by the Secretary of State as a debt due to him.

(2) In proceedings for the enforcement of a penalty no question may be raised as to—

(a) liability to the imposition of the penalty,

(b) the application of the excuse in section 15(3), or

(c) the amount of the penalty.

(3) Money paid to the Secretary of State by way of penalty shall be paid into the Consolidated Fund.

[1696D]

NOTES

Commencement: 29 February 2008.

Transitional provisions: see the note to s 15 at **[1696A]**.

19 Code of practice

(1) The Secretary of State shall issue a code of practice specifying factors to be considered by him in determining the amount of a penalty imposed under section 15.

(2) The code—

(a) shall not be issued unless a draft has been laid before Parliament, and

(b) shall come into force in accordance with provision made by order of the Secretary of State.

(3) The Secretary of State shall from time to time review the code and may revise and re-issue it following a review; and a reference in this section to the code includes a reference to the code as revised.

[1696E]

NOTES

Commencement: 31 August 2006.

Orders: the Immigration (Restrictions on Employment) Order 2007, SI 2007/3290 at **[3473S]**.

Code of practice: see the code of practice (Civil Penalties for Employers) at **[4766]**.

20 Orders

(1) An order of the Secretary of State under section 15, 16 or 19—

(a) may make provision which applies generally or only in specified circumstances,

(b) may make different provision for different circumstances,

(c) may include transitional or incidental provision, and

(d) shall be made by statutory instrument.

(2) An order under section 15(2) may not be made unless a draft has been laid before and approved by resolution of each House of Parliament.

(3) Any other order shall be subject to annulment in pursuance of a resolution of either House of Parliament.

[1696F]

NOTES

Commencement: 5 November 2007.

21 Offence

(1) A person commits an offence if he employs another ("the employee") knowing that the employee is an adult subject to immigration control and that—

(a) he has not been granted leave to enter or remain in the United Kingdom, or

(b) his leave to enter or remain in the United Kingdom—
  (i) is invalid,
  (ii) has ceased to have effect (whether by reason of curtailment, revocation, cancellation, passage of time or otherwise), or
  (iii) is subject to a condition preventing him from accepting the employment.

(2) A person guilty of an offence under this section shall be liable—

(a) on conviction on indictment—
  (i) to imprisonment for a term not exceeding two years,
  (ii) to a fine, or
  (iii) to both, or

(b) on summary conviction—
  (i) to imprisonment for a term not exceeding 12 months in England and Wales or 6 months in Scotland or Northern Ireland,
  (ii) to a fine not exceeding the statutory maximum, or
  (iii) to both.

(3) An offence under this section shall be treated as—

(a) a relevant offence for the purpose of sections 28B and 28D of the Immigration Act 1971 (c 77) (search, entry and arrest), and

(b) an offence under Part III of that Act (criminal proceedings) for the purposes of sections 28E, 28G and 28H (search after arrest).

(4) In relation to a conviction occurring before the commencement of section 154(1) of the Criminal Justice Act 2003 (c 44) (general limit on magistrates' powers to imprison) the reference to 12 months in subsection (2)(b)(i) shall be taken as a reference to 6 months.

[1696G]

NOTES

Commencement: 29 February 2008.
Transitional provisions: see the note to s 15 at **[1696A]**.

22 Offence: bodies corporate, &c

(1) For the purposes of section 21(1) a body (whether corporate or not) shall be treated as knowing a fact about an employee if a person who has responsibility within the body for an aspect of the employment knows the fact.

(2) If an offence under section 21(1) is committed by a body corporate with the consent or connivance of an officer of the body, the officer, as well as the body, shall be treated as having committed the offence.

(3) In subsection (2) a reference to an officer of a body includes a reference to—

(a) a director, manager or secretary,

(b) a person purporting to act as a director, manager or secretary, and

(c) if the affairs of the body are managed by its members, a member.

(4) Where an offence under section 21(1) is committed by a partnership (whether or not a limited partnership) subsection (2) above shall have effect, but as if a reference to an officer of the body were a reference to—

(a) a partner, and

(b) a person purporting to act as a partner.

[1696H]

NOTES

Commencement: 29 February 2008.
Transitional provisions: see the note to s 15 at **[1696A]**.

23 Discrimination: code of practice

(1) The Secretary of State shall issue a code of practice specifying what an employer should or should not do in order to ensure that, while avoiding liability to a penalty under section 15 and while avoiding the commission of an offence under section 21, he also avoids contravening—

(a) the Race Relations Act 1976 (c 74), or
(b) the Race Relations (Northern Ireland) Order 1997 (SI 869 (NI 6)).

(2) Before issuing the code the Secretary of State shall—

(a) consult—
 (i) the Commission for Equality and Human Rights,
 (ii) the Equality Commission for Northern Ireland,
 (iii) such bodies representing employers as he thinks appropriate, and
 (iv) such bodies representing workers as he thinks appropriate,
(b) publish a draft code (after that consultation),
(c) consider any representations made about the published draft, and
(d) lay a draft code before Parliament (after considering representations under paragraph (c) and with or without modifications to reflect the representations).

(3) The code shall come into force in accordance with provision made by order of the Secretary of State; and an order—

(a) may include transitional provision,
(b) shall be made by statutory instrument, and
(c) shall be subject to annulment in pursuance of a resolution of either House of Parliament.

(4) A breach of the code—

(a) shall not make a person liable to civil or criminal proceedings, but
(b) may be taken into account by a court or tribunal.

(5) The Secretary of State shall from time to time review the code and may revise and re-issue it following a review; and a reference in this section to the code includes a reference to the code as revised.

(6) Until the dissolution of the Commission for Racial Equality, the reference in subsection (2)(a)(i) to the Commission for Equality and Human Rights shall be treated as a reference to the Commission for Racial Equality.

[1696I]

NOTES

Commencement: 31 August 2006.

Code of practice: see the code of practice (Guidance for Employers on the Avoidance of Unlawful Discrimination in Employment Practice while Seeking to Prevent Illegal Working) at **[4772]**.

24 Temporary admission, &c

Where a person is at large in the United Kingdom by virtue of paragraph 21(1) of Schedule 2 to the Immigration Act 1971 (c 77) (temporary admission or release from detention)—

(a) he shall be treated for the purposes of sections 15(1) and 21(1) as if he had been granted leave to enter the United Kingdom, and
(b) any restriction as to employment imposed under paragraph 21(2) shall be treated for those purposes as a condition of leave.

[1696J]

NOTES

Commencement: 29 February 2008.

Transitional provisions: see the note to s 15 at **[1696A]**.

25 Interpretation

In sections 15 to 24—

(a) "adult" means a person who has attained the age of 16,
(b) a reference to employment is to employment under a contract of service or apprenticeship, whether express or implied and whether oral or written,

(c) a person is subject to immigration control if under the Immigration Act 1971 he requires leave to enter or remain in the United Kingdom, and

(d) "prescribed" means prescribed by order of the Secretary of State.

[1696K]

NOTES

Commencement: 5 November 2007.
Transitional provisions: see the note to s 15 at **[1696A]**.

26 Repeal

Sections 8 and 8A of the Asylum and Immigration Act 1996 (c 49) (restrictions on employment) shall cease to have effect.

[1696L]

NOTES

Commencement: 29 February 2008.
Transitional provisions: see the note to s 15 at **[1696A]**.

WORK AND FAMILIES ACT 2006

(2006 c 18)

ARRANGEMENT OF SECTIONS

An Act to make provision about statutory rights to leave and pay in connection with the birth or adoption of children; to amend section 80F of the Employment Rights Act 1996; to make provision about workers' entitlement to annual leave; to provide for the increase in the sums specified in section 186(1) and 227(1) of that Act; and for connected purposes

[21 June 2006]

1–10 (*S 1 amends the Social Security Contributions and Benefits Act 1992, s 165(1) at* **[434]**; *s 2 amends s 171ZN(2) of the 1992 Act at* **[454]**; *ss 3, 4 add the Employment Rights Act 1996, ss 80AA, 80BB, at* **[1116A], [1117A]**; *s 5 amends s 80C of the 1996 Act at* **[1118]**; *ss 6–10 add ss 171ZEA–171ZEE of the 1992 Act at* **[445A]–[445E]**.)

Leave and pay related to birth or adoption: further amendments

11 Leave and pay related to birth or adoption: further amendments

(1) Schedule 1 (which contains further amendments relating to statutory leave and pay) has effect.

(2) Any reference to statutory paternity pay in any instrument or document made before the commencement of paragraphs 12 and 13 of Schedule 1 is to be read, in relation to any time after that commencement, as a reference to ordinary statutory paternity pay.

(3) Any reference to ordinary statutory paternity pay in any enactment (including this Act and any enactment amended by this Act) or any instrument or document is to be read, in relation to any time before the commencement of paragraphs 12 and 13 of Schedule 1, as a reference to statutory paternity pay.

[1697]

NOTES

Commencement: 27 June 2006 (specified paragraphs of Sch 1 (see SI 2006/1682)); 1 October 2006 (specified paragraphs of Sch 1 (see SI 2006/1682 and SI 2006/2232)); to be appointed (sub-s (1) otherwise and sub-ss (2), (3)).

Miscellaneous provisions about employment rights

12 (*Amends the Employment Rights Act 1996, s 80F at* **[1121]**.)

13 Annual leave

(1) The Secretary of State may by regulations make provision conferring on workers the right, except in prescribed cases, to a prescribed amount of annual leave in each leave year, as defined for the purposes of the regulations.

(2) The regulations may in particular—

(a) make provision for determining the amount of annual leave to which workers are to be entitled;

(b) make provision for determining the amount of pay in respect of any period of leave which is required by the regulations to be paid leave;

(c) make provision enabling a worker to elect when to take leave to which he is entitled by virtue of the regulations, subject to any provision of the regulations enabling his employer to require him to take, or not to take, that leave at a particular time;

(d) make provision for the payment of compensation in prescribed cases to a worker who has not taken leave to which he is entitled;

(e) make provision as to the relationship between the rights conferred by the regulations and a worker's rights to leave, pay or compensation under any contract or under any Act or subordinate legislation;

(f) enable a worker to present a complaint to an employment tribunal that his employer has refused to permit him to exercise any right he has under the regulations, or has failed to pay him any amount due to him under the regulations;

(g) make, in connection with any right conferred by the regulations (including any right to payment), any other provision which is the same as or similar to any provision made, in connection with any right relating to annual leave conferred in pursuance of any Community obligation, by any regulations under section 2(2) of the 1972 Act made at any time before the day on which the first regulations under this section are made.

(3) Regulations under this section may make provision as to—

(a) who is to be treated as a worker for the purposes of the regulations, and

(b) who is to be treated as the worker's employer.

(4) Regulations under this section may in particular—

(a) make provision applying to—

(i) Crown employment and persons in Crown employment;

(ii) service as a member of the armed forces;

(b) make provision conferring rights to and in connection with annual leave on persons falling within any other categories of persons on whom any Community obligation of the United Kingdom requires a right to annual leave to be conferred.

(5) Regulations under this section may not make provision in relation to the subject-matter of the Agricultural Wages (Scotland) Act 1949 (c 30) (as that Act had effect on 1st July 1999).

(6) Regulations under this section—

(a) are to be made by statutory instrument;

(b) may make different provision for different cases;

(c) may contain incidental, supplemental, consequential, transitional or saving provision, including provision amending any Act or subordinate legislation.

(7) No statutory instrument containing regulations under this section may be made unless a draft of the instrument has been laid before, and approved by a resolution of, each House of Parliament.

(8) In this section—

"the 1972 Act" means the European Communities Act 1972 (c 68);

"the armed forces" means any of the naval, military or air forces of the Crown;

"Crown employment" has the meaning given by section 191(3) of ERA 1996;

"subordinate legislation" has the same meaning as in the Interpretation Act 1978 (c 30).

[1698]

NOTES

Commencement: 1 October 2006.

Regulations: the Working Time (Amendment) Regulations 2007, SI 2007/2079 amending the Working Time Regulations 1998, SI 1998/1833 at **[2411]**.

14 Increase of maximum amount of a week's pay for certain purposes

(1) This section applies to the sums specified in the following provisions—

(a) section 186(1)(a) and (b) of ERA 1996 (employee's rights on insolvency of employer: maximum amount payable);

(b) section 227(1) of ERA 1996 (maximum amount of a week's pay for the purposes of certain provisions of the Act relating to awards of compensation and redundancy payments).

(2) The Secretary of State may, on one occasion only, by order substitute for each of the sums mentioned in subsection (1) such higher sum as may be specified in the order.

(3) An order under this section—

(a) is to be made by statutory instrument;

(b) may include transitional provision;

(c) may exclude, on a single occasion specified in the order under this section, any duty to make an order under section 34 of the 1999 Act (indexation of certain amounts, &c), so far as relating to the sums mentioned in subsection (1).

(4) Subject to any provision made under subsection (3)(c), this section does not affect the operation of section 34 of the 1999 Act in relation to the sums substituted by the order under this section in the provisions mentioned in subsection (1).

(5) No statutory instrument containing an order under this section may be made unless a draft of the instrument has been laid before, and approved by a resolution of, each House of Parliament.

(6) In this section "the 1999 Act" means the Employment Relations Act 1999 (c 26).

[1699]

NOTES

Commencement: 1 October 2006.

Orders: as of 6 April 2008, no Orders had been made under this section.

Supplementary

15 (*Introduces Sch 2* (*repeals*).)

16 Interpretation

In this Act—

"ERA 1996" means the Employment Rights Act 1996 (c 18);

"SSCBA 1992" means the Social Security Contributions and Benefits Act 1992 (c 4).

[1700]–[1701]

NOTES

Commencement: 21 June 2006.

17 ((*Corresponding provision for Northern Ireland*) *outside the scope of this work.*)

18 Financial provisions

(1) There shall be paid out of money provided by Parliament—

(a) any expenses incurred by a Minister of the Crown or government department under this Act, and

(b) any increase attributable to this Act in the sums which under any other Act are payable out of money so provided.

(2) There shall be paid into the Consolidated Fund any increase attributable to this Act in the sums payable into that Fund under any other Act.

[1702]

NOTES

Commencement: 21 June 2006.

19 Commencement

(1) Sections 16 to 18, this section and section 20 come into force on the day on which this Act is passed.

(2) The other provisions of this Act come into force in accordance with provision made by the Secretary of State by order made by statutory instrument.

(3) An order under this section—

(a) may make different provision for different purposes;

(b) may include supplementary, incidental, saving or transitional provisions.

[1703]

NOTES

Commencement: 21 June 2006.

Orders: the Work and Families Act 2006 (Commencement No 1) Order 2006, SI 2006/1682; the Work and Families Act 2006 (Commencement No 2) Order 2006, SI 2006/2232.

20 Short title and extent

(1) This Act may be cited as the Work and Families Act 2006.

(2) Subject to subsection (3), this Act extends to England and Wales and Scotland only.

(3) The following provisions extend also to Northern Ireland—

(a) this section and sections 17 to 19;

(b) paragraphs 2, 45, 49, and 55 to 61 of Schedule 1, and section 11 so far as relating to those paragraphs;

(c) the entry in Schedule 2 relating to the Income Tax (Earnings and Pensions) Act 2003 (c 1), and section 15 so far as relating to that entry.

[1704]–[1705]

NOTES

Commencement: 21 June 2006.

SCHEDULES

(*Sch 1* (*Leave and pay related to birth or adoptions: further amendments*) *contains various consequential amendments to the Social Security Act 1989, the Finance Act 1989, the Social*

Security Contributions and Benefits Act 1992, the Social Security Administration Act 1992, the Employment Rights Act 1996, the Finance Act 1997, the Social Security Contributions (Transfer of Functions, etc) Act 1999, the Finance Act 1999, the Employment Act 2002, the Proceeds of Crime Act 2002, the Income Tax (Earnings and Pensions) Act 2003, and the Commissioners for Revenue and Customs Act 2005; in so far as relevant to this work, these have been incorporated at the appropriate place. Sch 2 repeals certain provisions in the Social Security Contributions and Benefits Act 1992, the Employment Rights Act 1996, the Employment Act 2002, and the Income Tax (Earnings and Pensions) Act 2003 (incorporated as appropriate).)

HEALTH ACT 2006

(2006 c 28)

ARRANGEMENT OF ARTICLES

PART 1
SMOKING

CHAPTER 1
SMOKE-FREE PREMISES, PLACES AND VEHICLES

Introduction

Smoke-free premises, etc

No-smoking signs

Offences relating to smoking in smoke-free premises, etc

Fixed penalties

Enforcement

Interpretation, etc

PART 7
FINAL PROVISIONS

Offences

General

SCHEDULES:

An Act to make provision for the prohibition of smoking in certain premises, places and vehicles and for amending the minimum age of persons to whom tobacco may be sold; to make provision in relation to the prevention and control of health care associated infections; to make provision in relation to the management and use of controlled drugs; to make provision in relation to the supervision of certain dealings with medicinal products and the running of pharmacy premises, and about orders under the Medicines Act 1968 and orders amending that Act under the Health Act 1999; to make further provision about the National Health Service in England and Wales and about the recovery of National Health Service costs; to make provision for the establishment and functions of the Appointments Commission; to make further provision about the exercise of social care training functions; and for connected purposes

[19 July 2006]

NOTES

Only certain provisions of this Act are directly relevant to employment law, and accordingly, only those provisions of most relevance have been included in this work. For reasons of space, the subject matter of the sections and Schedules omitted is not annotated.

Note that the subordinate legislation made under the sections printed here in some case applies only to England, or to Wales; some applies to both. Accordingly, the extent of each measure is given in the notes below. This Act applies only to England and Wales. The equivalent provisions for Scotland are in the Smoking, Health and Social Care (Scotland) Act 2005 at **[1631]**.

Regulatory functions: the regulatory functions conferred by, or under, this Act are subject to the Legislative and Regulatory Reform Act 2006, ss 21, 22 at **[1783]**, **[1784]**; see the Legislative and Regulatory Reform (Regulatory Functions) Order 2007, SI 2007/3544 (made under s 24(2) of the 2006 Act) for details.

PART 1
SMOKING

CHAPTER 1
SMOKE-FREE PREMISES, PLACES AND VEHICLES

Introduction

1 Introduction

(1) This Chapter makes provision for the prohibition of smoking in certain premises, places and vehicles which are smoke-free by virtue of this Chapter.

(2) In this Chapter—

(a) "smoking" refers to smoking tobacco or anything which contains tobacco, or smoking any other substance, and
(b) smoking includes being in possession of lit tobacco or of anything lit which contains tobacco, or being in possession of any other lit substance in a form in which it could be smoked.

(3) In this Chapter, "smoke" and other related expressions are to be read in accordance with subsection (2).

[1706]

NOTES

Commencement: 2 April 2007 (in relation to Wales); 1 July 2007 (in relation to England).

Smoke-free premises, etc

2 Smoke-free premises

(1) Premises are smoke-free if they are open to the public.

But unless the premises also fall within subsection (2), they are smoke-free only when open to the public.

(2) Premises are smoke-free if they are used as a place of work—
(a) by more than one person (even if the persons who work there do so at different times, or only intermittently), or
(b) where members of the public might attend for the purpose of seeking or receiving goods or services from the person or persons working there (even if members of the public are not always present).

They are smoke-free all the time.

(3) If only part of the premises is open to the public or (as the case may be) used as a place of work mentioned in subsection (2), the premises are smoke-free only to that extent.

(4) In any case, premises are smoke-free only in those areas which are enclosed or substantially enclosed.

(5) The appropriate national authority may specify in regulations what "enclosed" and "substantially enclosed" mean.

(6) Section 3 provides for some premises, or areas of premises, not to be smoke-free despite this section.

(7) Premises are "open to the public" if the public or a section of the public has access to them, whether by invitation or not, and whether on payment or not.

(8) "Work", in subsection (2), includes voluntary work.

[1707]

NOTES

Commencement: 19 July 2006 (in so far as this section confers any power to make regulations); 2 April 2007 (in relation to Wales for remaining purposes); 1 July 2007 (in relation to England for remaining purposes).

"The appropriate national authority": see s 82(1) at **[1722]**.

Regulations: the Smoke-free (Premises and Enforcement) Regulations 2006, SI 2006/3368 (these Regulations apply to England only); the Smoke-free Premises etc (Wales) Regulations 2007, SI 2007/787 (these Regulations apply to Wales only).

3 Smoke-free premises: exemptions

(1) The appropriate national authority may make regulations providing for specified descriptions of premises, or specified areas within specified descriptions of premises, not to be smoke-free despite section 2.

(2) Descriptions of premises which may be specified under subsection (1) include, in particular, any premises where a person has his home, or is living whether permanently or temporarily (including hotels, care homes, and prisons and other places where a person may be detained).

(3) The power to make regulations under subsection (1) is not exercisable so as to specify any description of—

(a) premises in respect of which a premises licence under the Licensing Act 2003 (c 17) authorising the sale by retail of alcohol for consumption on the premises has effect,

(b) premises in respect of which a club premises certificate (within the meaning of section 60 of that Act) has effect.

(4) But subsection (3) does not prevent the exercise of that power so as to specify any area, within a specified description of premises mentioned in subsection (3), where a person has his home, or is living whether permanently or temporarily.

(5) For the purpose of making provision for those participating as performers in a performance, or in a performance of a specified description, not to be prevented from smoking if the artistic integrity of the performance makes it appropriate for them to smoke—

(a) the power in subsection (1) also includes power to provide for specified descriptions of premises or specified areas within such premises not to be smoke-free in relation only to such performers, and

(b) subsection (3) does not prevent the exercise of that power as so extended.

(6) The regulations may provide, in relation to any description of premises or areas of premises specified in the regulations, that the premises or areas are not smoke-free—

(a) in specified circumstances,

(b) if specified conditions are satisfied, or

(c) at specified times,

or any combination of those.

(7) The conditions may include conditions requiring the designation in accordance with the regulations, by the person in charge of the premises, of any rooms in which smoking is to be permitted.

(8) For the purposes of subsection (5), the references to a performance—

(a) include, for example, the performance of a play, or a performance given in connection with the making of a film or television programme, and

(b) if the regulations so provide, include a rehearsal.

[1708]

NOTES

Commencement: 19 July 2006 (in so far as this section confers any power to make regulations); 2 April 2007 (in relation to Wales for remaining purposes); 1 July 2007 (in relation to England for remaining purposes).

"The appropriate national authority": see s 82(1) at **[1722]**.

Regulations: the Smoke-free (Exemptions and Vehicles) Regulations 2007, SI 2007/765; the Smoke-free Premises etc (Wales) Regulations 2007, SI 2007/787 (these Regulations apply to England only).

4 Additional smoke-free places

(1) The appropriate national authority may make regulations designating as smoke-free any place or description of place that is not smoke-free under section 2.

(2) The place, or places falling within the description, need not be enclosed or substantially enclosed.

(3) The appropriate national authority may designate a place or description of place under this section only if in the authority's opinion there is a significant risk that, without a designation, persons present there would be exposed to significant quantities of smoke.

(4) The regulations may provide for such places, or places falling within the description, to be smoke-free only—

(a) in specified circumstances,

(b) at specified times,

(c) if specified conditions are satisfied,

(d) in specified areas,

or any combination of those.

[1709]

NOTES

Commencement: 19 July 2006.

"The appropriate national authority": see s 82(1) at **[1722]**.

Regulations: as of 6 April 2008, no Regulations had been made under this section.

5 Vehicles

(1) The appropriate national authority may make regulations providing for vehicles to be smoke-free.

(2) The regulations may in particular make provision—

(a) for the descriptions of vehicle which are to be smoke-free,

(b) for the circumstances in which they are to be smoke-free,

(c) for them to be smoke-free only in specified areas, or except in specified areas,

(d) for exemptions.

(3) The power to make regulations under this section is not exercisable in relation to—

(a) any ship or hovercraft in relation to which regulations could be made under section 85 of the Merchant Shipping Act 1995 (c 21) (safety and health on ships), including that section as applied by any Order in Council under section 1(1)(h) of the Hovercraft Act 1968 (c 59), or

(b) persons on any such ship or hovercraft.

(4) …

(5) In this Chapter, "vehicle" means every type of vehicle, including train, vessel, aircraft and hovercraft.

[1710]

NOTES

Commencement: 19 July 2006 (in so far as this section confers any power to make regulations); 2 April 2007 (in relation to Wales for remaining purposes); 1 July 2007 (in relation to England for remaining purposes).

Sub-s (4): amends the Merchant Shipping Act 1995, s 85.

"The appropriate national authority": see s 82(1) at **[1722]**.

Regulations: the Smoke-free (Exemptions and Vehicles) Regulations 2007, SI 2007/765 (these Regulations apply to England only); the Smoke-free Premises etc (Wales) Regulations 2007, SI 2007/787 (these Regulations apply to Wales only).

No-smoking signs

6 No-smoking signs

(1) It is the duty of any person who occupies or is concerned in the management of smoke-free premises to make sure that no-smoking signs complying with the requirements of this section are displayed in those premises in accordance with the requirements of this section.

(2) Regulations made by the appropriate national authority may provide for a duty corresponding to that mentioned in subsection (1) in relation to—

(a) places which are smoke-free by virtue of section 4,

(b) vehicles which are smoke-free by virtue of section 5.

The duty is to be imposed on persons, or on persons of a description, specified in the regulations.

(3) The signs must be displayed in accordance with any requirements contained in regulations made by the appropriate national authority.

(4) The signs must conform to any requirements specified in regulations made by the appropriate national authority (for example, requirements as to content, size, design, colour, or wording).

(5) A person who fails to comply with the duty in subsection (1), or any corresponding duty in regulations under subsection (2), commits an offence.

(6) It is a defence for a person charged with an offence under subsection (5) to show—

(a) that he did not know, and could not reasonably have been expected to know, that the premises were smoke-free (or, as the case may be, that the place or vehicle was smoke-free), or

(b) that he did not know, and could not reasonably have been expected to know, that no-smoking signs complying with the requirements of this section were not being displayed in accordance with the requirements of this section, or

(c) that on other grounds it was reasonable for him not to comply with the duty.

(7) If a person charged with an offence under subsection (5) relies on a defence in subsection (6), and evidence is adduced which is sufficient to raise an issue with respect to that defence, the court must assume that the defence is satisfied unless the prosecution proves beyond reasonable doubt that it is not.

(8) A person guilty of an offence under subsection (5) is liable on summary conviction to a fine not exceeding a level on the standard scale specified in regulations made by the Secretary of State.

(9) The references in this section, however expressed, to premises, places or vehicles which are smoke-free, are to those premises, places or vehicles so far as they are smoke-free under or by virtue of this Chapter (and references to smoke-free premises include premises which by virtue of regulations under section 3(5) are smoke-free except in relation to performers).

[1711]

NOTES

Commencement: 19 July 2006 (in so far as this section confers any power to make regulations); 2 April 2007 (in relation to Wales for remaining purposes); 1 July 2007 (in relation to England for remaining purposes).

"The appropriate national authority": see s 82(1) at **[1722]**.

Regulations: the Smoke-free (Penalties and Discounted Amounts) Regulations 2007, SI 2007/764 (these Regulations apply to England and Wales); the Smoke-free Premises etc (Wales) Regulations 2007, SI 2007/787 (these Regulations apply to Wales only); the Smoke-free (Signs) Regulations 2007, SI 2007/923 (these Regulations apply to England only).

Offences relating to smoking in smoke-free premises, etc

7 Offence of smoking in smoke-free place

(1) In this section, a "smoke-free place" means any of the following—

(a) premises, so far as they are smoke-free under or by virtue of sections 2 and 3 (including premises which by virtue of regulations under section 3(5) are smoke-free except in relation to performers),

(b) a place, so far as it is smoke-free by virtue of section 4,

(c) a vehicle, so far as it is smoke-free by virtue of section 5.

(2) A person who smokes in a smoke-free place commits an offence.

(3) But a person who smokes in premises which are not smoke-free in relation to performers by virtue of regulations under section 3(5) does not commit an offence if he is such a performer.

(4) It is a defence for a person charged with an offence under subsection (2) to show that he did not know, and could not reasonably have been expected to know, that it was a smoke-free place.

(5) If a person charged with an offence under this section relies on a defence in subsection (4), and evidence is adduced which is sufficient to raise an issue with respect to that defence, the court must assume that the defence is satisfied unless the prosecution proves beyond reasonable doubt that it is not.

(6) A person guilty of an offence under this section is liable on summary conviction to a fine not exceeding a level on the standard scale specified in regulations made by the Secretary of State.

[1712]

NOTES

Commencement: 19 July 2006 (in so far as this section confers any power to make regulations); 2 April 2007 (in relation to Wales for remaining purposes); 1 July 2007 (in relation to England for remaining purposes).

Regulations: the Smoke-free (Penalties and Discounted Amounts) Regulations 2007, SI 2007/764 (these Regulations apply to England and Wales).

8 Offence of failing to prevent smoking in smoke-free place

(1) It is the duty of any person who controls or is concerned in the management of smoke-free premises to cause a person smoking there to stop smoking.

(2) The reference in subsection (1) to a person smoking does not include a performer in relation to whom the premises are not smoke-free by virtue of regulations under section 3(5).

(3) Regulations made by the appropriate national authority may provide for a duty corresponding to that mentioned in subsection (1) in relation to—

(a) places which are smoke-free by virtue of section 4,

(b) vehicles which are smoke-free by virtue of section 5.

The duty is to be imposed on persons, or on persons of a description, specified in the regulations.

(4) A person who fails to comply with the duty in subsection (1), or any corresponding duty in regulations under subsection (3), commits an offence.

(5) It is a defence for a person charged with an offence under subsection (4) to show—

(a) that he took reasonable steps to cause the person in question to stop smoking, or

(b) that he did not know, and could not reasonably have been expected to know, that the person in question was smoking, or

(c) that on other grounds it was reasonable for him not to comply with the duty.

(6) If a person charged with an offence under this section relies on a defence in subsection (5), and evidence is adduced which is sufficient to raise an issue with respect to that defence, the court must assume that the defence is satisfied unless the prosecution proves beyond reasonable doubt that it is not.

(7) A person guilty of an offence under this section is liable on summary conviction to a fine not exceeding a level on the standard scale specified in regulations made by the Secretary of State.

(8) The references in this section, however expressed, to premises, places or vehicles which are smoke-free, are to those premises, places or vehicles so far as they are smoke-free under or by virtue of this Chapter (and references to smoke-free premises include premises which by virtue of regulations under section 3(5) are smoke-free except in relation to performers).

[1713]

NOTES

Commencement: 19 July 2006 (in so far as this section confers any power to make regulations); 2 April 2007 (in relation to Wales for remaining purposes); 1 July 2007 (in relation to England for remaining purposes).

"The appropriate national authority": see s 82(1) at **[1722]**.

Regulations: the Smoke-free (Vehicle Operators and Penalty Notices) Regulations 2007, SI 2007/760 (these Regulations apply to England only); the Smoke-free (Penalties and Discounted Amounts) Regulations 2007, SI 2007/764 (these Regulations apply to England and Wales); the Smoke-free Premises etc (Wales) Regulations 2007, SI 2007/787 (these Regulations apply to Wales only).

Fixed penalties

9 Fixed penalties

(1) An authorised officer of an enforcement authority (see section 10) who has reason to believe that a person has committed an offence under section 6(5) or 7(2) on premises, or in a place or vehicle, in relation to which the authorised officer has functions may give him a penalty notice in respect of the offence.

(2) A penalty notice is a notice offering a person the opportunity to discharge any liability to conviction for the offence to which the notice relates by paying a penalty in accordance with this Chapter.

(3) Schedule 1 makes further provision about fixed penalties.

[1714]

NOTES

Commencement: 2 April 2007 (in relation to Wales); 1 July 2007 (in relation to England).

Enforcement

10 Enforcement

(1) The appropriate national authority may make regulations designating the bodies or descriptions of body which are to be enforcement authorities for the purposes of this Chapter.

(2) The regulations—

(a) must specify the descriptions of premises, place or vehicle in relation to which an enforcement authority has enforcement functions,

(b) may provide for a case being dealt with by one enforcement authority to be transferred (or further transferred, or transferred back) to, and taken over by, another enforcement authority.

(3) It is the duty of an enforcement authority to enforce, as respects the premises, places and vehicles in relation to which it has enforcement functions, the provisions of this Chapter and regulations made under it.

(4) The appropriate national authority may direct, in relation to cases of a particular description or a particular case, that any duty imposed on an enforcement authority by subsection (3) is to be discharged instead by the appropriate national authority.

(5) In this Chapter, "authorised officer", in relation to an enforcement authority, means any person (whether or not an officer of the authority) who is authorised by it in writing, either generally or specially, to act in matters arising under this Chapter.

(6) If regulations under this section so provide, no person is to be so authorised unless he has such qualifications as are prescribed by the regulations.

(7) Schedule 2 makes provision about powers of entry, etc

[1715]

NOTES

Commencement: 19 July 2006 (in so far as this section confers any power to make regulations); 2 April 2007 (in relation to Wales for remaining purposes); 1 July 2007 (in relation to England for remaining purposes).

"The appropriate national authority": see s 82(1) at **[1722]**.

Regulations: the Smoke-free (Premises and Enforcement) Regulations 2006, SI 2006/3368 (these Regulations apply to England only); the Smoke-free Premises etc (Wales) Regulations 2007, SI 2007/787 (these Regulations apply to Wales only).

11 Obstruction etc of officers

(1) Any person who intentionally obstructs an authorised officer of an enforcement authority, acting in the exercise of his functions under or by virtue of this Chapter, commits an offence.

(2) Any person who without reasonable cause fails to give to an authorised officer of an enforcement authority, acting in the exercise of his functions under or by virtue of this Chapter, any facilities, assistance or information which the authorised officer reasonably requires of him for the performance of those functions commits an offence.

(3) A person commits an offence if, in purported compliance with any requirement of an authorised officer mentioned in subsection (2)—

(a) he makes a statement which is false or misleading, and

(b) he either knows that it is false or misleading or is reckless as to whether it is false or misleading.

"False or misleading" means false or misleading in a material particular.

(4) A person guilty of an offence under this section is liable on summary conviction to a fine not exceeding level 3 on the standard scale.

(5) If a direction of the appropriate national authority has effect under section 10(4), this section has effect, in relation to any case or case of a description specified in the direction, as if references to an authorised officer of an enforcement authority were to a person acting on behalf of the appropriate national authority.

[1716]

NOTES

Commencement: 2 April 2007 (in relation to Wales); 1 July 2007 (in relation to England).
"The appropriate national authority": see s 82(1) at **[1722]**.

Interpretation, etc

12 Interpretation and territorial sea

(1) In this Chapter—

"authorised officer" has the meaning given by section 10(5),

"premises" includes a tent, and (if not a ship within the meaning of the Merchant Shipping Act 1995 (c 21)) a moveable structure and an offshore installation (as defined in regulation 3 of the Offshore Installations and Pipeline Works (Management and Administration) Regulations 1995 (SI 1995/738)),

"specified", in relation to regulations, means specified in the regulations,

"vehicle" is to be construed in accordance with section 5(5).

(2) The appropriate national authority may by order provide for the definition of "premises" in subsection (1) to be read as if a reference to another enactment were substituted for the reference to regulation 3 of the Offshore Installations and Pipeline Works (Management and Administration) Regulations 1995.

(3) This Chapter—

(a) has effect in relation to the territorial sea adjacent to England as it has effect in relation to England, and

(b) has effect in relation to the territorial sea adjacent to Wales as it has effect in relation to Wales.

(4) The following have effect for the purposes of subsection (3) if or in so far as expressed to apply for the general or residual purposes of the Act in question or for the purposes of this section—

(a) an Order in Council under section 126(2) of the Scotland Act 1998 (c 46),

(b) an order or Order in Council under or by virtue of section [158(3) and (4) of the Government of Wales Act 2006].

[1717]

NOTES

Commencement: 19 July 2006 (for the purpose of making orders or regulations); 2 April 2007 (in relation to Wales for remaining purposes); 1 July 2007 (in relation to England for remaining purposes).

Sub-s (4): words in square brackets in para (b) substituted by the Government of Wales Act 2006 (Consequential Modifications and Transitional Provisions) Order 2007, SI 2007/1388, art 3, Sch 1, para 123, as from 25 May 2007.

"The appropriate national authority": see s 82(1) at **[1722]**.

Orders: as of 6 April 2008, no Orders had been made under this section.

PART 7
FINAL PROVISIONS

Offences

76 Offences by bodies corporate etc

(1) If an offence committed by a body corporate is proved—

(a) to have been committed with the consent or connivance of an officer, or

(b) to be attributable to any neglect on his part,

the officer as well as the body corporate is guilty of the offence and liable to be proceeded against and punished accordingly.

(2) In subsection (1) "officer", in relation to the body corporate, means a director, manager, secretary or other similar officer of the body, or a person purporting to act in any such capacity.

(3) If the affairs of a body corporate are managed by its members, subsection (1) applies in relation to the acts and defaults of a member in connection with his functions of management as if he were a director of the body corporate.

(4) If an offence committed by a partnership is proved—

(a) to have been committed with the consent or connivance of a partner, or

(b) to be attributable to any neglect on his part,

the partner as well as the partnership is guilty of the offence and liable to be proceeded against and punished accordingly.

(5) In subsection (4) "partner" includes a person purporting to act as a partner.

(6) If an offence committed by an unincorporated association (other than a partnership) is proved—

(a) to have been committed with the consent or connivance of an officer of the association or a member of its governing body, or

(b) to be attributable to any neglect on the part of such an officer or member,

the officer or member as well as the association is guilty of the offence and liable to be proceeded against and punished accordingly.

(7) In this section and section 77 "offence" means an offence under any provision of this Act.

[1718]

NOTES

Commencement: 1 February 2007 (in relation to Wales and in so far as relating to offences under Chapter 3 of Part 4); 2 April 2007 (in relation to Wales and in so far as relating to offences under Chapter 1 of Part 1); 1 July 2007 (in relation to England and in so far as relating to offences under Part 1); 22 April 2008 (in so far as they relate to offences under Chapter 3 of Part 4, except so far as they relate to the Welsh Ministers' counter fraud functions in relation to the health service in Wales or to offences committed in relation to those functions) and as from the same date (in relation to England and Scotland so far as they relate to offences under Chapter 1 of Part 3 (including offences created in regulations under that chapter)); to be appointed (otherwise).

77 Offences committed by partnerships and other unincorporated associations

(1) Proceedings for an offence alleged to have been committed by a partnership shall be brought in the name of the partnership (and not in that of any of the partners).

(2) Proceedings for an offence alleged to have been committed by an unincorporated association (other than a partnership) shall be brought in the name of the association (and not in that of any of its members).

(3) Rules of court relating to the service of documents shall have effect as if the partnership or unincorporated association were a body corporate.

(4) In proceedings for an offence brought against a partnership or an unincorporated association, the following provisions apply as they apply in relation to a body corporate—

(a) section 33 of the Criminal Justice Act 1925 (c 86) and Schedule 3 to the Magistrates' Courts Act 1980 (c 43);

(b) sections 70 and 143 of the Criminal Procedure (Scotland) Act 1995 (c 46);

(c) section 18 of the Criminal Justice Act (Northern Ireland) 1945 (c 15 (NI)) and Schedule 4 to the Magistrates' Courts (Northern Ireland) Order 1981 (SI 1981/1675 (NI 26)).

(5) A fine imposed on a partnership on its conviction for an offence is to be paid out of the partnership assets.

(6) A fine imposed on an unincorporated association on its conviction for an offence is to be paid out of the funds of the association.

(7) Subsections (1) and (2) are not to be read as prejudicing any liability of a partner, officer or member under section 76(4) or (6).

[1719]

NOTES

Commencement: 1 February 2007 (in relation to Wales and in so far as relating to offences under Chapter 3 of Part 4); 2 April 2007 (in relation to Wales and in so far as relating to offences under Chapter 1 of Part 1); 1 July 2007 (in relation to England and in so far as relating to offences under Part 1); 22 April 2008 (in so far as they relate to offences under Chapter 3 of Part 4, except so far as they relate to the Welsh Ministers' counter fraud functions in relation to the health service in Wales or to offences committed in relation to those functions) and as from the same date (in relation to England and Scotland so far as they relate to offences under Chapter 1 of Part 3 (including offences created in regulations under that chapter)); to be appointed (otherwise).

78 Penalties for offences: transitional modification for England and Wales

(1) This section contains transitional modifications in respect of penalties for certain offences committed in England and Wales.

(2) In relation to an offence committed before the commencement of section 154(1) of the Criminal Justice Act 2003 (c 44) (general limit on magistrates' courts power to impose imprisonment), the references in [section 21(2)(b)] of this Act to periods of imprisonment of 12 months are to be read as references to periods of imprisonment of 6 months.

(3) In relation to an offence committed before the commencement of section 281(5) of the Criminal Justice Act 2003 (alteration of penalties for summary offences), the references in sections 52(2)(a) and 53(2)(b) of this Act to periods of imprisonment of 51 weeks are to be read as references to periods of imprisonment of 3 months.

[1720]

NOTES

Commencement: 1 February 2007 (in relation to Wales and in so far as relating to offences under Chapter 3 of Part 4); 2 April 2007 (in relation to Wales and in so far as relating to offences under Chapter 1 of Part 1); 22 April 2008 (in so far as they relate to offences under Chapter 3 of Part 4, except so far as they relate to the Welsh Ministers' counter fraud functions in relation to the health service in Wales or to offences committed in relation to those functions) and as from the same date (in relation to England so far as they relate to offences under Chapter 1 of Part 3 (including offences created in regulations under that chapter)); to be appointed (otherwise).

Sub-s (2): words in square brackets substituted by the National Health Service (Consequential Provisions) Act 2006, s 2, Sch 1, paras 281, 289, as from 1 March 2007.

Sub-s (3): repealed by the National Health Service (Consequential Provisions) Act 2006, s 6, Sch 4, as from 1 March 2007 (certain purposes), and as from a day to be appointed (otherwise) (see s 8(2), (4)–(6) of the 2006 Act).

General

79 Orders and regulations

(1) Subject to subsection (2), any power to make an order or regulations under this Act is exercisable by statutory instrument.

(2) Any power of the Department of Health, Social Services and Public Safety to make an order or regulations under this Act is exercisable by statutory rule for the purposes of the Statutory Rules (Northern Ireland) Order 1979 (SI 1979/1573 (NI 12)).

(3) Any power to make an order or regulations under this Act—

- (a) may be exercised so as to make different provision for different cases or descriptions of case or different purposes or areas, and
- (b) includes power to make such incidental, supplementary, consequential, transitory, transitional or saving provision as the authority making the order or regulations considers appropriate.

(4) No statutory instrument containing—

- (a) regulations under section 3, 4, 5, 6(8), 7(6) or 8(7),
- (b) an order under section 13,
- (c) regulations under section 17 which amend or repeal any provision of an Act or an Act of the Scottish Parliament,
- (d) an order under section 45(7),
- (e) an order under section 75 or 80(3) which amends or repeals any provision of an Act or an Act of the Scottish Parliament, or

(f) regulations under paragraph 5 or 8 of Schedule 1,

may be made by the Secretary of State unless a draft of the instrument has been laid before, and approved by a resolution of, each House of Parliament.

(5) Otherwise, a statutory instrument containing any order or regulations made by the Secretary of State under this Act (other than an order under section 83) is to be subject to annulment in pursuance of a resolution of either House of Parliament.

(6) No statutory instrument containing an order under section 80(4) which amends or repeals any provision of an Act or an Act of the Scottish Parliament may be made by the Scottish Ministers unless a draft of the instrument has been laid before, and approved by a resolution of, the Scottish Parliament.

(7) Otherwise, a statutory instrument containing an order under section 80(4) is to be subject to annulment in pursuance of a resolution of the Scottish Parliament.

(8) A statutory rule containing regulations made by the Department of Health, Social Services and Public Safety under section 17 which amend or repeal any provision of an Act is to be subject to affirmative resolution within the meaning of section 41(4) of the Interpretation Act (Northern Ireland) 1954 (c 33 (NI)).

(9) Otherwise, a statutory rule containing regulations made by the Department of Health, Social Services and Public Safety under Chapter 1 of Part 3 is to be subject to negative resolution within the meaning of section 41(6) of the Interpretation Act (Northern Ireland) 1954.

[1721]

NOTES

Commencement: 19 July 2006.

82 Interpretation

(1) In this Act—

…

"the 2003 Act" means the Health and Social Care (Community Health and Standards) Act 2003 (c 43);

["the 2006 Act" means the National Health Service Act 2006;]

"the appropriate national authority" means—

(a) in relation to England, the Secretary of State, and

(b) in relation to Wales, the National Assembly for Wales;

"the health service"—

(a) in relation to England and Wales, has the same meaning as in [the 2006 Act],

(b) in relation to Scotland, has the same meaning as in the National Health Service (Scotland) Act 1978 (c 29), and

(c) in relation to Northern Ireland, means health services within the meaning given by Article 2(2) of the Health and Personal Social Services (Northern Ireland) Order 1972 (SI 1972/1265 (NI 14)).

(2) In this Act "enactment" includes—

(a) any provision of subordinate legislation (within the meaning of the Interpretation Act 1978 (c 30)), and

(b) (in sections 17(5)(f) and 80(8)) any provision made by or under an Act of the Scottish Parliament or Northern Ireland legislation,

and references to enactments include enactments passed or made after the passing of this Act.

(3) Subsection (2) applies except where the context otherwise requires.

[1722]

NOTES

Commencement: 19 July 2006.

Sub-s (1): definition "the 1977 Act" repealed, definition "the 2006 Act" inserted, and words in square brackets in definition "the health service" substituted, by the National Health Service (Consequential Provisions) Act 2006, s 2, Sch 1, paras 281, 290, as from 1 March 2007.

Note: that the Assembly Commission shall be treated as a Crown body for the purposes of Chapter 1 of Part I of this Act (see SI 2007/1353).

83 Commencement

(1) The following provisions come into force on the day on which this Act is passed—
- (a) sections 74 and 75,
- (b) sections 79, 80(3) to (8), 81 and 82, this section and section 84,
- (c) paragraphs 36, 53 and 54 of Schedule 8,
- (d) section 80(1) so far as relating to those paragraphs, and
- (e) (except for section 36(2)) any other provision of this Act so far as it—
  - (i) confers power to make an order or regulations, or
  - (ii) defines any expression relevant to the exercise of any such power.

Subsections (2)(b) and (3) to (6) have effect subject to paragraph (e).

(2) The following provisions come into force on such day as the Scottish Ministers may by order appoint—
- (a) section 36(2), and
- (b) so far as extending to Scotland—
  - (i) section 73,
  - (ii) paragraph 55 of Schedule 8, and
  - (iii) section 80(1) so far as relating to that paragraph.

(3) Part 5 comes into force on such day as the Secretary of State, after consulting the National Assembly for Wales, may by order appoint.

(4) The following provisions come into force in relation to Wales on such day as the National Assembly for Wales may by order appoint—
- (a) Chapter 1 of Part 1 and sections 76 and 77 so far as relating to offences under that Chapter, and
- (b) paragraph 24(a) of Schedule 8 and section 80(1) so far as relating to that paragraph.

(5) The following provisions come into force on such day as the National Assembly for Wales may by order appoint—
- (a) Chapter 1 of Part 3 and sections 76 to 78 so far as relating to the Assembly's functions under that Chapter (see section 24) or to offences committed in relation to those functions,
- (b) Chapter 1 of Part 4 so far as relating to the Assembly's functions under sections 42 and 42B of the 1977 Act,
- (c) Chapter 3 of Part 4 and sections 76 to 78 so far as relating to the Assembly's counter fraud functions in relation to the health service in Wales (see section 44) or to offences committed in relation to those functions,
- (d) section 56, Schedule 3 and paragraph 44 of Schedule 8 so far as relating to Welsh NHS bodies,
- (e) paragraphs 43 and 62 of Schedule 8,
- (f) so far as relating to Welsh NHS bodies, any provision of Schedule 9 which repeals or revokes an enactment amending or repealing section 98 of the 1977 Act, and
- (g) section 80(1) and (2) so far as relating to the provisions in paragraphs (d), (e) and (f).

In this subsection "Welsh NHS body" has the meaning given by paragraph 2 of the Schedule 12B inserted by Schedule 3.

(6) The following provisions come into force on such day as the Department of Health, Social Services and Public Safety may by order appoint—
- (a) Chapter 1 of Part 3 so far as relating to the functions of the Department of Health, Social Services and Public Safety under that Chapter (see section 24), and
- (b) sections 76 and 77 so far as relating to offences committed in relation to those functions.

(7) Otherwise, this Act comes into force on such day as the Secretary of State may by order appoint.

(8) Different days may be appointed for different provisions, different purposes or different areas.

[1723]

NOTES

Commencement: 19 July 2006.

Orders: the Health Act 2006 (Commencement No 1 and Transitional Provisions) Order 2006, SI 2006/2603; the Health Act 2006 (Commencement No 2) Order 2006, SI 2006/3125; the Health Act 2006 (Commencement No 1) (Scotland) Order 2007, SSI 2007/9; the Health Act 2006 (Commencement No 1 and Transitional Provisions) (Wales) Order 2007, SI 2007/204; the Health Act 2006 (Commencement No 3) Order 2007, SI 2007/1375; the Health Act 2006 (Commencement No 4) Order 2008, SI 2008/1147.

84 Short title and extent

(1) This Act may be cited as the Health Act 2006.

(2) Subject to subsections (3) and (4), this Act extends to England and Wales only.

(3) The following provisions extend also to Scotland and Northern Ireland—
- (a) Chapter 1 of Part 3,
- (b) Part 5, and
- (c) sections 75, 76, 77, 79 to 83 and this section.

(4) Any amendment, repeal or revocation made by this Act has the same extent as the enactment to which it relates.

[1724]

NOTES

Commencement: 19 July 2006.

SCHEDULES

SCHEDULE 1
FIXED PENALTIES

Section 9

Contents of penalty notice

1. A penalty notice must—
   - (a) state the alleged offence, and
   - (b) give such particulars of the circumstances alleged to constitute it as are necessary for giving reasonable information about it.

2.—(1) A penalty notice must also state—
- (a) the name and address of the enforcement authority on whose behalf the authorised officer was acting when he gave the notice,
- (b) the amount of the penalty and the period for its payment,
- (c) the discounted amount and the period for its payment,
- (d) the consequences of not paying the penalty or the discounted amount before the end of the period mentioned in paragraph (b) or (c),
- (e) the person to whom and the address at which payment may be made,
- (f) by what method payment may be made,
- (g) the person to whom and the address at which any representations relating to the notice may be made.

(2) The person mentioned in sub-paragraph (1)(e) and (g) must be the enforcement authority referred to in sub-paragraph (1)(a).

3. A penalty notice must also—
   - (a) inform the person to whom it is given of his right to be tried for the alleged offence, and
   - (b) explain how that right may be exercised.

4. A penalty notice must be in a form specified in regulations made by the appropriate national authority.

Amount of penalty and period for payment

5. The penalty is such amount as the Secretary of State may specify in regulations.

6. The period for payment of the penalty is the period of 29 days beginning with the day on which the notice is given.

Discounted amount and period for payment

7.—(1) A discounted amount is payable instead of the amount specified in regulations under paragraph 5 if payment is made before the end of the period for payment of the discounted amount.

(2) That period is the period of 15 days beginning with the day on which the notice is given, unless the 15th day is not a working day.

(3) If the 15th day is not a working day, that period is the period beginning with the day on which the notice is given and ending immediately after the first working day following the 15th day.

(4) In this paragraph, "working day" means any day which is not Saturday, Sunday, Christmas Day, Good Friday or a day which is a bank holiday in England and Wales under the Banking and Financial Dealings Act 1971 (c 80).

8. The discounted amount is such amount as the Secretary of State may specify in regulations.

Effect of notice and payment

9.—(1) Proceedings for the offence in respect of which a penalty notice was given may not be brought before the end of the period for payment of the penalty.

(2) Sub-paragraph (1) does not apply if the person to whom the notice was given has asked in accordance with paragraphs 14 and 15 to be tried for the alleged offence.

10. If the penalty is paid in accordance with the penalty notice before the end of the period mentioned in paragraph 9(1), no proceedings for the offence may be brought, and paragraph 14 does not apply.

11. If the discounted amount is paid in accordance with the penalty notice before the end of the period for payment of the discounted amount, no proceedings for the offence may be brought, and paragraph 14 does not apply.

12. If proceedings have been brought pursuant to a request under paragraph 14, but then the penalty or discounted amount is paid as mentioned in paragraph 10 or 11, those proceedings may not be continued.

13. In any proceedings, a certificate is evidence of the facts which it states if it—

(a) purports to be signed by or on behalf of the person responsible for the financial affairs of the enforcement authority on whose behalf the authorised officer who gave a penalty notice was acting, and

(b) states that payment of the penalty or discounted amount in pursuance of the notice was or was not received by a date specified in the certificate.

Trial

14. If the person to whom a penalty notice has been given asks to be tried for the alleged offence, proceedings may be brought against him.

15. Any request to be tried must be made—

(a) by notice given to the enforcement authority in question before the end of the period for payment of the penalty,

(b) in the manner specified in the penalty notice.

Withdrawal of notices

16.—(1) This paragraph applies if an enforcement authority considers that a penalty notice which an authorised officer acting on its behalf has given to a person ("P") ought not to have been given.

(2) The enforcement authority may give notice to P withdrawing the penalty notice.

(3) If it does so—

(a) it must repay any amount which has been paid by way of penalty in pursuance of the penalty notice, and

(b) no proceedings may be brought or continued against P for the offence in question. **[1725]**

NOTES

Commencement: 19 July 2006 (in so far as this Schedule confers any power to make regulations); 2 April 2007 (in relation to Wales for remaining purposes); 1 July 2007 (in relation to England for remaining purposes).

"The appropriate national authority": see s 82(1) at **[1722]**.

Regulations: the Smoke-free (Vehicle Operators and Penalty Notices) Regulations 2007, SI 2007/760; the Smoke-free (Penalties and Discounted Amounts) Regulations 2007, SI 2007/764; the Smoke-free Premises etc (Wales) Regulations 2007, SI 2007/787.

SCHEDULE 2
POWERS OF ENTRY, ETC

Section 10

1. In this Schedule—

"authorised officer" means authorised officer of an enforcement authority,

"premises" includes any place and any vehicle.

2. An authorised officer has the right to do any of the following, on production (if required) of his written authority—

(a) at any reasonable hour, enter any premises (other than premises used only as a private dwelling house not open to the public) which he considers it is necessary for him to enter for the purpose of the proper exercise of his functions by virtue of Chapter 1 of Part 1 of this Act,

(b) there carry out such inspections and examinations as he considers necessary for that purpose,

(c) if he considers it necessary for that purpose, require the production of any substance or product, and inspect it, and take and retain samples of or extracts from it,

(d) take possession of any substance or product on the premises, and retain it for as long as he considers necessary for that purpose,

(e) require any person to give him such information, or afford him such facilities and assistance, as he considers necessary for that purpose.

3. An authorised officer may, if he considers it necessary for the purpose of the proper exercise of his functions by virtue of Chapter 1 of Part 1 of this Act, arrange for any substance, product, sample or extract mentioned in paragraph 2(c) or (d) to be analysed.

4. An authorised officer may make such purchases and secure the provision of such services as he considers necessary for the purpose of the proper exercise of his functions by virtue of Chapter 1 of Part 1 of this Act.

5. A person may not be required under paragraph 2 to give any information which he would be entitled to refuse to give in proceedings in the High Court on grounds of legal professional privilege.

6.—(1) A justice of the peace may exercise the power in sub-paragraph (3) if he is satisfied on sworn information in writing—

(a) that for the purpose of the proper exercise of the functions of an enforcement authority under Chapter 1 of Part 1 of this Act there are reasonable grounds for entry into any premises other than premises used only as a private dwelling house not open to the public, and

(b) of either or both of the matters mentioned in sub-paragraph (2).

(2) The matters are—

(a) that admission to the premises has been, or is likely to be, refused, and that notice of intention to apply for a warrant under this Schedule has been given to the occupier or a person who reasonably appears to the enforcement authority to be concerned in the management of the premises,

(b) that an application for admission, or the giving of such notice, would defeat the object of the entry, or that the premises are unoccupied, or that the occupier is temporarily absent and it might defeat the object of the entry to await his return.

(3) The justice may by warrant signed by him authorise any authorised officer to enter the premises, if need be by force.

(4) Such a warrant continues in force until the end of the period of one month beginning with the date on which the justice signs it.

7. An authorised officer entering any premises by virtue of paragraph 2, or of a warrant under paragraph 6, may take with him such other persons and such equipment as he considers necessary.

8. If premises which an authorised officer is authorised to enter by a warrant under paragraph 6 are unoccupied, or if the occupier is temporarily absent, then on leaving them that officer must leave the premises as effectively secured against unauthorised entry as he found them.

9. If by virtue of paragraph 2(d) an authorised officer takes possession of anything, he must leave on the premises from which it was taken a statement giving particulars of what he has taken and stating that he has taken possession of it.

10. If a direction of the appropriate national authority has effect under section 10(4), this Schedule has effect, in relation to any case or case of a description specified in the direction, as if references to an authorised officer were to a person acting on behalf of the appropriate national authority.

[1726]

NOTES

Commencement: 2 April 2007 (in relation to Wales); 1 July 2007 (in relation to England).

COMPENSATION ACT 2006

(2006 c 29)

ARRANGEMENT OF ARTICLES

PART 1
STANDARD OF CARE

PART 2
CLAIMS MANAGEMENT SERVICES

PART 3
GENERAL

An Act to specify certain factors that may be taken into account by a court determining a claim in negligence or breach of statutory duty; to make provision about damages for mesothelioma; and to make provision for the regulation of claims management services

[25 July 2006]

PART 1
STANDARD OF CARE

1 Deterrent effect of potential liability

A court considering a claim in negligence or breach of statutory duty may, in determining whether the defendant should have taken particular steps to meet a standard of care (whether by taking precautions against a risk or otherwise), have regard to whether a requirement to take those steps might—

(a) prevent a desirable activity from being undertaken at all, to a particular extent or in a particular way, or

(b) discourage persons from undertaking functions in connection with a desirable activity.

[1727]

NOTES

Commencement: 25 July 2006.

2 Apologies, offers of treatment or other redress

An apology, an offer of treatment or other redress, shall not of itself amount to an admission of negligence or breach of statutory duty.

[1728]

NOTES

Commencement: 25 July 2006.

3 (*S 3* (*Mesothelioma: damages*) *outside the scope of this work.*)

PART 2
CLAIMS MANAGEMENT SERVICES

4 Provision of regulated claims management services

(1) A person may not provide regulated claims management services unless—

(a) he is an authorised person,

(b) he is an exempt person,

(c) the requirement for authorisation has been waived in relation to him in accordance with regulations under section 9, or

(d) he is an individual acting otherwise than in the course of a business.

(2) In this Part—

(a) "authorised person" means a person authorised by the Regulator under section 5(1)(a),

(b) "claims management services" means advice or other services in relation to the making of a claim,

(c) "claim" means a claim for compensation, restitution, repayment or any other remedy or relief in respect of loss or damage or in respect of an obligation, whether the claim is made or could be made—

(i) by way of legal proceedings,

(ii) in accordance with a scheme of regulation (whether voluntary or compulsory), or

(iii) in pursuance of a voluntary undertaking,

(d) "exempt person" has the meaning given by section 6(5), and

(e) services are regulated if they are—

(i) of a kind prescribed by order of the Secretary of State, or

(ii) provided in cases or circumstances of a kind prescribed by order of the Secretary of State.

[(2A) The Secretary of State may not make an order under subsection (2)(e) unless—

(a) it is made in accordance with a recommendation made by the Legal Services Board, or

(b) the Secretary of State has consulted the Legal Services Board about the making of the order.]

(3) For the purposes of this section—

(a) a reference to the provision of services includes, in particular, a reference to—

(i) the provision of financial services or assistance,

(ii) the provision of services by way of or in relation to legal representation,

(iii) referring or introducing one person to another, and

(iv) making inquiries, and

(b) a person does not provide claims management services by reason only of giving, or preparing to give, evidence (whether or not expert evidence).

(4) For the purposes of subsection (1)(d) an individual acts in the course of a business if, in particular—

(a) he acts in the course of an employment, or

(b) he otherwise receives or hopes to receive money or money's worth as a result of his action.

(5) The Secretary of State may by order provide that a claim for a specified benefit shall be treated as a claim for the purposes of this Part.

(6) The Secretary of State may specify a benefit under subsection (5) only if it appears to him to be a United Kingdom social security benefit designed to provide compensation for industrial injury.

[1729]

NOTES

Commencement: 1 December 2006 (sub-ss (2), (3), (5), (6)); 23 April 2007 (otherwise).

Sub-s (2A): inserted by the Legal Services Act 2007, s 187, Sch 19, paras 1, 2, as from a day to be appointed.

Orders: the Compensation (Regulated Claims Management Services) Order 2006, SI 2006/3319 at **[3469]**; the Compensation (Specification of Benefits) Order 2006, SI 2006/3321.

---

5 The Regulator

(1) The Secretary of State may by order designate a person ("the Regulator")—

(a) to authorise persons to provide regulated claims management services,

(b) to regulate the conduct of authorised persons, and

(c) to exercise such other functions as are conferred on the Regulator by or under this Part.

[(1A) The Secretary of State may designate a person only on the recommendation of the Legal Services Board.]

(2) *The Secretary of State may designate a person* only if satisfied that the person—

(a) is competent to perform the functions of the Regulator,

(b) will make arrangements to avoid any conflict of interest between the person's functions as Regulator and any other functions, and

(c) will promote the interests of persons using regulated claims management services (including, in particular, by—

(i) setting and monitoring standards of competence and professional conduct for persons providing regulated claims management services,

(ii) promoting good practice by persons providing regulated claims management services, in particular in relation to the provision of information about charges and other matters to persons using or considering using the services,

(iii) promoting practices likely to facilitate competition between different providers of regulated claims management services, and

(iv) ensuring that arrangements are made for the protection of persons using regulated claims management services (including arrangements for the handling of complaints about the conduct of authorised persons)).

(3) If the Secretary of State thinks that no existing person (whether an individual or a body corporate or unincorporate) is suitable for designation under subsection (1), he may by order establish a person for the purpose of being designated.

(4) The Regulator shall—

(a) comply with any directions given to him by the *Secretary of State*;

(b) have regard to any guidance given to him by the *Secretary of State*;

(c) have regard to any code of practice issued to him by the Secretary of State;

(d) try to meet any targets set for him by the *Secretary of State*;

(e) provide the *Secretary of State* with any report or information requested (but this paragraph does not require or permit disclosure of information in contravention of any other enactment).

(5) The Secretary of State shall lay before Parliament any code of practice issued by him to the Regulator.

(6) The Secretary of State may pay grants to the Regulator (which may be on terms or conditions, including terms and conditions as to repayment with or without interest).

(7) A reference in this Part to the Regulator includes a reference to a person acting on behalf of the Regulator or with his authority.

(8) The Secretary of State may[, on the recommendation of the Legal Services Board,] by order revoke a person's designation under subsection (1).

(9) While no person is designated under subsection (1) the *Secretary of State* shall exercise functions of the Regulator.

(10) The Secretary of State may[, on the recommendation of the Legal Services Board,] by order transfer (whether for a period of time specified in the order or otherwise) a function of the Regulator to the *Secretary of State*.

[(11) In discharging any function by virtue of subsection (9) or (10), the Legal Services Board must take such steps as are necessary to ensure an appropriate financial and organisational separation between the activities of the Board that relate to the carrying out of those functions and the other activities of the Board.]

[1730]

NOTES

Commencement: 1 December 2006.

Sub-s (1A): inserted by the Legal Services Act 2007, s 187, Sch 19, paras 1, 3(1), (2), as from a day to be appointed.

Sub-s (2): for the words in italics there are substituted the words "The Legal Services Board may recommend a person for designation" by the Legal Services Act 2007, s 187, Sch 19, paras 1, 3(1), (3), as from a day to be appointed.

Sub-s (3): repealed by the Legal Services Act 2007, ss 187, 210, Sch 19, paras 1, 3(1), (4), Sch 23, as from a day to be appointed.

Sub-s (4): for the words "Secretary of State" in italics in paras (a), (b), (d), (e) there are substituted the words "Legal Services Board", and para (c) is repealed, by the Legal Services Act 2007, ss 187, 210, Sch 19, paras 1, 3(1), (5), Sch 23, as from a day to be appointed.

Sub-s (8): words in square brackets inserted by the Legal Services Act 2007, s 187, Sch 19, paras 1, 3(1), (6), as from a day to be appointed.

Sub-s (9): for the words in italics there are substituted the words "Legal Services Board" by the Legal Services Act 2007, s 187, Sch 19, paras 1, 3(1), (7), as from a day to be appointed.

Sub-s (10): words in square brackets inserted, and for the words in italics there are substituted the words "Legal Services Board", by the Legal Services Act 2007, s 187, Sch 19, paras 1, 3(1), (8), as from a day to be appointed.

Sub-s (11): added by the Legal Services Act 2007, s 187, Sch 19, paras 1, 3(1), (9), as from a day to be appointed.

6 Exemptions

(1) The Secretary of State may by order provide that section 4(1) shall not prevent the provision of regulated claims management services by a person who is a member of a specified body.

(2) The Secretary of State may by order provide that section 4(1) shall not prevent the provision of regulated claims management services—

(a) by a specified person or class of person,

(b) in specified circumstances, or

(c) by a specified person or class of person in specified circumstances.

(3) Provision by virtue of subsection (1) or (2) may be expressed to have effect subject to compliance with specified conditions.

[(3A) The Secretary of State may not make an order under subsection (1) or (2) unless—

(a) it is made in accordance with a recommendation made by the Legal Services Board, or

(b) the Secretary of State has consulted the Legal Services Board about the making of the order.]

(4) Section 4(1) shall not prevent the provision of regulated claims management services by a person who is established or appointed by virtue of an enactment.

(5) For the purposes of this Part a person is "exempt" if, or in so far as, section 4(1) does not, by virtue of this section, prevent him from providing regulated claims management services.

[1731]

NOTES

Commencement: 1 December 2006.

Sub-s (3A): inserted by the Legal Services Act 2007, s 187, Sch 19, paras 1, 4, as from a day to be appointed.

Orders: the Compensation (Exemptions) Order 2007, SI 2007/209 at **[3471]**.

7 Enforcement: offence

(1) A person commits an offence if he contravenes section 4(1).

(2) A person who is guilty of an offence under subsection (1) shall be liable—

(a) on conviction on indictment—

(i) to imprisonment for a term not exceeding two years,

(ii) to a fine, or

(iii) to both, or

(b) on summary conviction—

(i) to imprisonment for a term not exceeding [12 months],

(ii) to a fine not exceeding [the statutory maximum], or

(iii) to both.

[(3) In relation to an offence committed before the commencement of section 154(1) of the Criminal Justice Act 2003 the reference in subsection (2)(b)(i) to 12 months is to be read as a reference to 6 months.]

[1732]

NOTES

Commencement: 23 April 2007.

Sub-s (2): words in square brackets substituted by the Legal Services Act 2007, s 187, Sch 19, paras 1, 5(1), (2), as from 7 March 2008.

Sub-s (3): substituted by the Legal Services Act 2007, s 187, Sch 19, paras 1, 5(1), (3), as from 7 March 2008.

8 Enforcement: the Regulator

(1) The Regulator may apply to the court for an injunction restraining a person from providing regulated claims management services if he is not—

(a) an authorised person,

(b) an exempt person, or

(c) the subject of a waiver in accordance with regulations under section 9.

(2) In subsection (1) "the court" means the High Court or a county court.

(3) The Regulator may—

(a) investigate whether an offence has been committed under this Part;

(b) institute criminal proceedings in respect of an offence under this Part.

(4) For the purpose of investigating whether an offence has been committed under this Part the Regulator may require the provision of information or documents.

(5) On an application by the Regulator a judge of the High Court, Circuit judge or justice of the peace may issue a warrant authorising the Regulator[—

(a)] to enter and search premises on which a person conducts or is alleged to conduct regulated claims management business, for the purposes of investigating whether an offence has been committed under this Part[, and

(b) to take possession of any written or electronic records found on the search for the purposes of subsection (6)].

(6) The Regulator may take copies of written or electronic records found on a search by virtue of subsection (5) for a purpose specified in subsection (3)(a) or (b).

(7) In subsections (4) to (6) a reference to the Regulator includes a reference to a person authorised by him in writing.

(8) The Secretary of State shall make regulations—

(a) specifying matters of which a judge or justice of the peace must be satisfied, or to which he must have regard, before issuing a warrant under subsection (5), and

(b) regulating the exercise of a power under or by virtue of subsection (4) or (5) (whether by restricting the circumstances in which a power may be exercised, by specifying conditions to be complied with in the exercise of a power, or otherwise).

[(9) The Secretary of State may not make regulations under subsection (8) unless—

(a) they are made in accordance with a recommendation made by the Legal Services Board, or

(b) the Secretary of State has consulted the Legal Services Board about the making of the regulations.]

[1733]

NOTES

Commencement: 1 December 2006 (sub-s (8)); 23 April 2007 (otherwise).

Sub-s (5): words in square brackets inserted by the Legal Services Act 2007, s 187, Sch 19, paras 1, 6(1), (2)(a), as from a day to be appointed.

Sub-s (9): inserted by the Legal Services Act 2007, s 187, Sch 19, paras 1, 6(1), (3), as from a day to be appointed.

Regulations: the Compensation (Claims Management Services) Regulations 2006, SI 2006/3322.

9 Regulations

(1) The Secretary of State shall make regulations about—

(a) authorisations under section 5(1);

(b) the functions of the Regulator.

(2) The Schedule specifies particular provision that may be made by the regulations.

[(2A) The Secretary of State may not make regulations under this section unless—

(a) they are made in accordance with a recommendation made by the Legal Services Board, or

(b) the Secretary of State has consulted the Legal Services Board about the making of the regulations.]

(3) Transitional provision of regulations under this section may, in particular, make provision about the extent to which functions under this Part or under the regulations may be exercised in respect of matters arising before the commencement of a provision made by or by virtue of this Part.

[1734]

NOTES

Commencement: 1 December 2006.

Sub-s (2A): inserted by the Legal Services Act 2007, s 187, Sch 19, paras 1, 7, as from a day to be appointed.
Regulations: the Compensation (Claims Management Services) Regulations 2006, SI 2006/3322.

10 Obstructing the Regulator

(1) A person commits an offence if without reasonable excuse he obstructs the Regulator in the exercise of a power—
(a) under section 8(4) to (6), or
(b) by virtue of paragraph 14 of the Schedule.

(2) A person who is guilty of an offence under subsection (1) shall be liable on summary conviction to a fine not exceeding level 5 on the standard scale.

[1735]

NOTES

Commencement: 23 April 2007.

11 Pretending to be authorised, &c

(1) A person commits an offence if he falsely holds himself out as being—
(a) an authorised person,
(b) an exempt person, or
(c) the subject of a waiver in accordance with regulations under section 9.

(2) A person commits an offence if—
(a) he offers to provide regulated claims management services, and
(b) provision by him of those services would constitute an offence under this Part.

(3) For the purposes of subsection (2) a person offers to provide services if he—
(a) makes an offer to a particular person or class of person,
(b) makes arrangements for an advertisement in which he offers to provide services, or
(c) makes arrangements for an advertisement in which he is described or presented as competent to provide services.

(4) A person who is guilty of an offence under subsection (1) or (2) shall be liable—
(a) on conviction on indictment—
(i) to imprisonment for a term not exceeding two years,
(ii) to a fine, or
(iii) to both, or
(b) on summary conviction—
(i) to imprisonment for a term not exceeding [12 months],
(ii) to a fine not exceeding [the statutory maximum], or
(iii) to both.

(5) Where a person commits an offence under this section by causing material to be displayed or made accessible, he shall be treated as committing the offence on each day during any part of which the material is displayed or made accessible.

[(6) In relation to an offence committed before the commencement of section 154(1) of the Criminal Justice Act 2003 the reference in subsection (4)(b)(i) to 12 months is to be read as a reference to 6 months.]

[1736]

NOTES

Commencement: 23 April 2007.
Sub-s (4): words in square brackets substituted by the Legal Services Act 2007, s 187, Sch 19, paras 1, 8(1), (2)(a), as from 7 March 2008.
Sub-s (6): substituted by the Legal Services Act 2007, s 187, Sch 19, paras 1, 8(1), (3), as from 7 March 2008.

12 The Claims Management Services Tribunal

(1) There shall be a tribunal to be known as the Claims Management Services Tribunal.

(2) The Tribunal shall be constituted as follows—

(a) members of the Financial Services and Markets Tribunal shall also be members of the Claims Management Services Tribunal,
(b) the President of the Financial Services and Markets Tribunal shall also act as President of the Claims Management Services Tribunal,
(c) the Deputy President of the Financial Services and Markets Tribunal shall also act as Deputy President of the Claims Management Services Tribunal, and
(d) the panel of chairmen of the Financial Services and Markets Tribunal shall also be the panel of chairmen of the Claims Management Services Tribunal.

(3) An appeal or reference to the Tribunal shall be heard by a member of the panel of chairmen—
(a) selected in accordance with arrangements made by the President, and
(b) sitting alone or, in accordance with those arrangements, with one or two members of the lay panel;

and a chairman who sits with one other member shall have a casting vote.

(4) The Lord Chancellor may make rules about the proceedings of the Tribunal; and the rules—
(a) shall include provision about timing of references and appeals,
(b) shall include provision for the suspension of decisions of the Regulator while an appeal could be brought or is pending,
(c) shall include provision about the making of interim orders,
(d) shall enable the Tribunal to suspend or further suspend (wholly or partly) the effect of a decision of the Regulator,
(e) shall permit the Regulator to apply for the termination of the suspension of a decision of his,
(f) may include provision about evidence,
(g) may include provision about any other matter of a kind for which rules under section 132 of the Financial Services and Markets Act 2000 (c 8) (the Financial Services and Markets Tribunal) may make provision,
(h) may include transitional, consequential or incidental provision,
(i) may make provision generally or only for specified cases or circumstances,
(j) may make different provision for different cases or circumstances,
(k) shall be made by statutory instrument, and
(l) shall be subject to annulment in pursuance of a resolution of either House of Parliament.

(5) The following provisions of Schedule 13 to the Financial Services and Markets Act 2000 shall have effect, with any necessary modifications, in relation to the Claims Management Services Tribunal—
(a) paragraph 5 (remuneration and allowances),
(b) paragraph 6 (staff),
(c) paragraph 7(3) and (4) (composition),
(d) paragraph 8 (sittings),
(e) paragraph 10 (practice directions),
(f) paragraph 11 (evidence), and
(g) paragraph 12(1) to (3) (decisions).

(6) …

[1737]

NOTES

Commencement: 23 January 2007.
Sub-s (6): amends the Tribunals and Inquiries Act 1992, Sch 1, Pt I.
Rules: the Claims Management Services Tribunal Rules 2007, SI 2007/90.

13 Appeals and references to Tribunal

(1) A person may appeal to the Claims Management Services Tribunal if the Regulator—
(a) refuses the person's application for authorisation,
(b) grants the person authorisation on terms or subject to conditions,
(c) imposes conditions on the person's authorisation,
(d) suspends the person's authorisation, or
(e) cancels the person's authorisation.

(2) The Regulator may refer to the Tribunal (with or without findings of fact or recommendations)—

(a) a complaint about the professional conduct of an authorised person, or

(b) the question whether an authorised person has complied with a rule of professional conduct.

(3) On a reference or appeal under this section the Tribunal—

(a) may take any decision on an application for authorisation that the Regulator could have taken;

(b) may impose or remove conditions on a person's authorisation;

(c) may suspend a person's authorisation;

(d) may cancel a person's authorisation;

(e) may remit a matter to the Regulator;

(f) may not award costs.

(4) An authorised person may appeal to the Court of Appeal [on a point of law arising from] a decision of the Tribunal.

[1738]

NOTES

Commencement: 23 January 2007 (sub-ss (1), (3), (4)); to be appointed (otherwise).

Sub-s (4): words in square brackets substituted by the Legal Services Act 2007, s 187, Sch 19, paras 1, 9, as from 7 March 2008.

14 Interpretation

In this Part—

"action" includes omission,

"authorised person" has the meaning given by section 4,

"claim" has the meaning given by section 4,

"claims management services" has the meaning given by section 4,

"exempt person" has the meaning given by section 6(5),

"regulated claims management services" shall be construed in accordance with section 4(2)(e),

"specified", in relation to an order or regulations, means specified in the order or regulations, and

"the Regulator" means (subject to section 5(7)) the person designated under section 5(1) or, where no person is designated or in so far as is necessary having regard to any order under section 5(10), the *Secretary of State*.

[1739]

NOTES

Commencement: 1 December 2006.

For the words in italics in the definition "the Regulator" there are substituted the words "Legal Services Board" by the Legal Services Act 2007, s 187, Sch 19, paras 1, 10, as from a day to be appointed.

15 Orders and regulations

(1) An order or regulations under this Part—

(a) may make provision that applies generally or only in specified cases or circumstances,

(b) may make different provision for different cases or circumstances, and

(c) may include transitional, incidental or consequential provision.

(2) An order or regulations under this Part shall be made by statutory instrument.

(3) An order under section 4(2)(e)—

(a) may not be made unless the Secretary of State has consulted—

(i) the Office of Fair Trading, and

(ii) such other persons as he thinks appropriate, and

(b) may not be made unless a draft has been laid before and approved by resolution of each House of Parliament.

(4) An order under section 4(5) may not be made unless a draft has been laid before, and approved by resolution of, each House of Parliament.

(5) An order under section 5 may not be made unless a draft has been laid before, and approved by resolution of, each House of Parliament.

(6) An order under section 5(3) may include provision—
- *(a) for the appointment of members;*
- *(b) for funding;*
- *(c) for dissolution (which may include provision enabling the Secretary of State to make provision for the transfer of property, rights and liabilities).*

(7) The first order made under section 6 may not be made unless a draft has been laid before, and approved by resolution of, each House of Parliament.

(8) An order under section 6 which has the effect of removing or restricting an exemption from section 4(1) may not be made unless a draft has been laid before, and approved by resolution of, each House of Parliament.

(9) Any other order under section 6 shall be subject to annulment in pursuance of a resolution of either House of Parliament.

(10) Regulations under section 8 or 9 may not be made unless a draft has been laid before, and approved by resolution of, each House of Parliament.

[1740]

NOTES

Commencement: 1 December 2006.
Sub-s (6): repealed by the Legal Services Act 2007, s 210, Sch 23, as from a day to be appointed.

PART 3
GENERAL

16 Commencement

(1) The preceding provisions of this Act, other than sections 1, 2 and 3, shall come into force in accordance with provision made by order of the Secretary of State.

(2) An order under subsection (1)—
- (a) may make provision generally or only for specified purposes,
- (b) may make different provision for different purposes,
- (c) may make transitional, consequential or incidental provision, and
- (d) shall be made by statutory instrument.

(3) Section 3 shall be treated as having always had effect.

(4) But the section shall have no effect in relation to—
- (a) a claim which is settled before 3rd May 2006 (whether or not legal proceedings in relation to the claim have been instituted), or
- (b) legal proceedings which are determined before that date.

(5) Where a claim is settled on or after that date and before the date on which this Act is passed, a party to the settlement may apply to a relevant court to have the settlement varied; and—
- (a) a court is a relevant court for that purpose if it had, or would have had, jurisdiction to determine the claim by way of legal proceedings,
- (b) an application shall be brought as an application in, or by way of, proceedings on the claim, and
- (c) a court to which an application is made shall vary the settlement to such extent (if any) as appears appropriate to reflect the effect of section 3.

(6) Where legal proceedings are determined on or after that date and before the date on which this Act is passed, a party to the proceedings may apply to the court to vary the determination; and—
- (a) "the court" means the court which determined the proceedings,
- (b) the application shall be treated as an application in the proceedings, and
- (c) the court shall vary the determination to such extent (if any) as appears appropriate to reflect the effect of section 3.

[1741]

NOTES

Commencement: 25 July 2006.

Orders: the Compensation Act 2006 (Commencement No 1) Order 2006; the Compensation Act 2006 (Commencement No 2) Order 2007, SI 2007/94; the Compensation Act 2006 (Commencement No 3) Order 2007, SI 2007/922.

17 Extent

(1) This Act shall extend to England and Wales only.

(2) But section 3 (and section 16(3) to (6)) shall extend to—
- (a) England and Wales,
- (b) Scotland, and
- (c) Northern Ireland.

[1742]

NOTES

Commencement: 25 July 2006.

18 Short title

This Act may be cited as the Compensation Act 2006.

[1743]

NOTES

Commencement: 25 July 2006.

SCHEDULE
CLAIMS MANAGEMENT REGULATIONS

Section 9

Introduction

1. In this Schedule "regulations" means regulations under section 9.

2. Regulations made by virtue of a provision of this Schedule may confer a discretion on the Regulator.

Waiver of requirement for authorisation

3.—(1) Regulations may permit the Regulator to waive the requirement for authorisation, as mentioned in section 4(1)(c), in specified cases or circumstances.

(2) Regulations by virtue of this sub-paragraph may permit waiver in relation to a person only—
- (a) if the Secretary of State intends to exempt the person under section 6, and
- (b) for a single period not exceeding six months.

(3) The regulations may, in particular, permit or require the Regulator to provide for waiver to be subject to a condition of a kind specified in the regulations.

Grant of authorisations

4.—(1) Regulations shall prescribe the procedure for applying to the Regulator for authorisation.

(2) Regulations may, in particular, require the provision of information or documents relating to the applicant or to any person who appears to the Regulator to be connected with the applicant.

5.—(1) Regulations shall require the Regulator not to grant an application for authorisation unless satisfied of the applicant's competence and suitability to provide regulated claims management services of the kind to which the application relates.

(2) For that purpose the Regulator shall apply such criteria, and have regard to such matters, as the regulations shall specify.

(3) Regulations by virtue of sub-paragraph (2) may, in particular—
- (a) refer to a provision of directions, *guidance or a code given or issued* under section 5(4);
- (b) relate to persons who are or are expected to be employed or engaged by, or otherwise connected with, the applicant;
- (c) relate to—
  - (i) criminal records;
  - (ii) proceedings in any court or tribunal;
  - (iii) proceedings of a body exercising functions in relation to a trade or profession;
  - (iv) financial circumstances;
  - (v) management structure;
  - (vi) actual or proposed connections or arrangements with other persons;
  - (vii) qualifications;
  - (viii) actual or proposed arrangements for training;
  - (ix) arrangements for accounting;
  - (x) practice or proposed practice in relation to the provision of information about fees;
  - (xi) arrangements or proposed arrangements for holding clients' money;
  - (xii) arrangements or proposed arrangements for insurance.

6. Regulations may—
- (a) provide for authorisation to be on specified terms or subject to compliance with specified conditions;
- (b) permit the Regulator to grant authorisation on terms or subject to conditions;
- (c) permit the Regulator to grant an application for authorisation only to a specified extent or only in relation to specified matters, cases or circumstances.

7. Regulations may—
- (a) enable the Regulator to charge—
  - (i) fees in connection with applications for, or the grant of, authorisation;
  - (ii) periodic fees for authorised persons;
- (b) specify the consequences of failure to pay fees;
- (c) permit the charging of different fees for different cases or circumstances (which may, in particular, be defined wholly or partly by reference to turnover or other criteria relating to an authorised person's business);
- (d) permit the waiver, reduction or repayment of fees in specified circumstances;
- (e) provide for the amount of fees to be prescribed or controlled by the *Secretary of State*;
- (f) make provision for the manner in which fees are to be accounted for;
- (g) make provision for the application of income from fees (which may, in respect of a time when the Secretary of State is exercising functions of the Regulator under section 5(9) or (10), include provision permitting or requiring payment into the Consolidated Fund [after consultation with the Secretary of State]).

Conduct of authorised persons

8.—(1) Regulations shall require the Regulator to prescribe rules for the professional conduct of authorised persons.

(2) Regulations under sub-paragraph (1) shall include provision—
- (a) about the manner in which rules are to be prepared and published (which may, in particular, include provision requiring—
  - (i) consultation;
  - (ii) the submission of a draft to the *Secretary of State* for approval);
- (b) about the consequences of failure to comply with the rules (which may, in particular, include—
  - (i) provision for rules to be treated as conditions of authorisations;
  - (ii) provision enabling the Regulator to impose conditions on, suspend or cancel authorisations).

9.—(1) Regulations shall enable the Regulator to issue one or more codes of practice about the professional conduct of authorised persons.

(2) Regulations under sub-paragraph (1) shall include provision—

(a) about the manner in which a code is to be prepared and published (which may, in particular, include provision requiring—

(i) consultation;

(ii) the submission of a draft to the *Secretary of State* for approval);

(b) about the consequences of failure to comply with a code (which may, in particular—

(i) provide for compliance with a code to be treated as a condition of authorisations;

(ii) enable the Regulator to impose conditions on, suspend or cancel authorisations).

10.—(1) Regulations shall provide for the Regulator to investigate complaints about the professional conduct of an authorised person.

(2) Regulations under sub-paragraph (1) shall enable the Regulator to—

(a) impose conditions on a person's authorisation;

(b) suspend a person's authorisation;

(c) cancel a person's authorisation.

11.—(1) Regulations may require, or permit the Regulator to require, an authorised person to take out a policy of professional indemnity insurance in respect of his actions in the course of providing or purporting to provide regulated claims management services.

(2) Regulations under sub-paragraph (1) may, in particular—

(a) make provision about the level or nature of insurance cover to be provided by the policy;

(b) include provision about failure to comply (which may, in particular, provide for compliance to be treated as a condition of authorisations or enable the Regulator to impose conditions on, suspend or cancel authorisations).

12.—(1) Regulations may require the Regulator to establish a scheme to compensate a client of an authorised person where—

(a) money is paid to the authorised person in complete or partial satisfaction of the client's claim, and

(b) the client is unable to obtain all or part of the money because the authorised person becomes insolvent or is otherwise unable or unwilling to pay.

(2) In particular, regulations may make provision—

(a) about the purchase of bonds or other forms of insurance or indemnity;

(b) about the funding of the scheme (which may include the application of part of fees charged in accordance with paragraph 7 and may not include payments, or other financial assistance, by a Minister of the Crown);

(c) about procedure in connection with compensation (including criteria to be applied);

(d) about the amount of compensation.

Enforcement

13. Regulations may permit or require the Regulator to take action of a specified kind for the purpose of assessing compliance with terms or conditions of authorisations.

14.—(1) Regulations may enable the Regulator, for the purpose of investigating a complaint about the activities of an authorised person or for the purpose of assessing compliance with terms and conditions of an authorisation, to require the provision of information or documents.

(2) The Regulations may provide that on an application by the Regulator a judge of the High Court, Circuit judge or justice of the peace may issue a warrant authorising the Regulator *to enter and search premises on which a person conducts or is alleged to conduct regulated claims management business, for the purpose of—*

(a) investigating a complaint about the activities of an authorised person, or

(b) assessing compliance with terms and conditions of an authorisation.

(3) Regulations may enable the Regulator to take copies of written or electronic records found on a search by virtue of sub-paragraph (2) for a purpose specified in that subsection.

(4) Regulations may enable the Regulator to impose conditions on, suspend or cancel a person's authorisation if—

(a) a requirement imposed by virtue of sub-paragraph (1) is not complied with, or

(b) an attempt to exercise a power by virtue of sub-paragraph (2) or (3) is obstructed.

(5) In this paragraph a reference to the Regulator includes a reference to a person authorised by him in writing.

(6) Regulations shall—

(a) specify matters of which a judge or justice of the peace must be satisfied, or to which he must have regard, before issuing a warrant under sub-paragraph (2),

(b) regulate the exercise of a power under or by virtue of sub-paragraph (1), (2) or (3) (whether by restricting the circumstances in which a power may be exercised, by specifying conditions to be complied with in the exercise of a power, or otherwise).

15. Regulations may make provision about the exercise by the Regulator of a power under section 8.

[1744]

NOTES

Commencement: 1 December 2006.

Para 5: for the words in italics in sub-para (3)(a) there are substituted the words "or guidance given" by the Legal Services Act 2007, s 187, Sch 19, paras 1, 11(1), (2), as from a day to be appointed.

Para 7: for the words in italics in sub-paras (e) and (g) there are substituted the words "Legal Services Board", and the words in square brackets in sub-para (g) are inserted, by the Legal Services Act 2007, s 187, Sch 19, paras 1, 11(1), (3), as from a day to be appointed.

Paras 8, 9: for the words in italics in sub-para (2)(a) there are substituted the words "Legal Services Board" by the Legal Services Act 2007, s 187, Sch 19, paras 1, 11(1), (4), (5), as from a day to be appointed.

Para 14: for the words in italics in sub-para (2) there are substituted the following words by the Legal Services Act 2007, s 187, Sch 19, paras 1, 11(1), (6), as from a day to be appointed—

"(a) to enter and search premises on which a person conducts or is alleged to conduct regulated claims management business, for the purposes of—

(i) investigating a complaint about the activities of an authorised person, or

(ii) assessing compliance with terms and conditions of an authorisation, and

(b) to take possession of written or electronic records found on the search for the purposes of taking copies in accordance with regulations under sub-paragraph (3).".

COMPANIES ACT 2006

(2006 c 46)

NOTES

Only certain sections of this Act are directly relevant to employment law, and accordingly, only those sections of most relevance have been included in this work. For reasons of space, the subject matter of the sections and Schedules omitted is not annotated.

Interpretation of provisions in this Act: the Companies Act 2006 (Commencement No 1, Transitional Provisions and Savings) Order 2006, SI 2006/3428, art 6 provides as set out below. Note that the similar provision is also made by the Companies Act 2006 (Commencement No 2, Consequential Amendments, Transitional Provisions and Savings) Order 2007, SI 2007/1093, art 4, the Companies Act 2006 (Commencement No 3, Consequential Amendments, Transitional Provisions and Savings) Order 2007, SI 2007/2194, art 7, the Companies Act 2006 (Commencement No 4 and Commencement No 3 (Amendment)) Order 2007, SI 2007/2607, art 3, and the Companies Act 2006 (Commencement No 5, Transitional Provisions and Savings) Order 2007, SI 2007/3495, art 7—

"4 Interpretation of provisions brought into force

Where an expression in a provision brought into force by this Order (or in an adaptation made by this Order of such a provision)—

(a) is defined in the 1985 Act or the 1986 Order ("the old definition"); and

(b) is defined in the Companies Act 2006 by another provision that is not yet in force for the purposes of the provision brought into force ("the new definition"),

the expression has, for the purposes of the provision brought into force (or the adaptation), the meaning given by the old definition until the new definition is brought into force for the purposes of that provision.".

Civil Procedure Rules: the Civil Procedure Rules 1998, SI 1998/3132, rule 49 (as amended), states that those Rules apply to proceedings under this Act subject to the provisions of the relevant practice direction which applies to those proceedings.

ARRANGEMENT OF SECTIONS

PART 10
A COMPANY'S DIRECTORS

CHAPTER 1
APPOINTMENT AND REMOVAL OF DIRECTORS

Requirement to have directors

Appointment

Removal

CHAPTER 2
GENERAL DUTIES OF DIRECTORS

Introductory

The general duties

Supplementary provisions

CHAPTER 3
DECLARATION OF INTEREST IN EXISTING TRANSACTION OR ARRANGEMENT

CHAPTER 4
TRANSACTIONS WITH DIRECTORS REQUIRING APPROVAL OF MEMBERS

Service contracts

Payments for loss of office

Supplementary

CHAPTER 5
DIRECTORS' SERVICE CONTRACTS

CHAPTER 7
DIRECTORS' LIABILITIES

Provision protecting directors from liability

CHAPTER 9
SUPPLEMENTARY PROVISIONS

Provision for employees on cessation or transfer of business

PART 15
ACCOUNTS AND REPORTS

CHAPTER 5
DIRECTORS' REPORT

Directors' report

CHAPTER 6
QUOTED COMPANIES: DIRECTORS' REMUNERATION REPORT

PART 47
FINAL PROVISIONS

An Act to reform company law and restate the greater part of the enactments relating to companies; to make other provision relating to companies and other forms of business organisation; to make provision about directors' disqualification, business names, auditors and actuaries; to amend Part 9 of the Enterprise Act 2002; and for connected purposes

[8 November 2006]

PART 10
A COMPANY'S DIRECTORS

CHAPTER 1
APPOINTMENT AND REMOVAL OF DIRECTORS

Requirement to have directors

154 Companies required to have directors

(1) A private company must have at least one director.

(2) A public company must have at least two directors.

[1745]

NOTES

Commencement: 1 October 2007.

155 Companies required to have at least one director who is a natural person

(1) A company must have at least one director who is a natural person.

(2) This requirement is met if the office of director is held by a natural person as a corporation sole or otherwise by virtue of an office.

[1746]

NOTES

Commencement: 1 October 2008.

Transitional provisions: Sch 4, Pt 3, para 46 to the Companies Act 2006 (Commencement No 5, Transitional Provisions and Savings) Order 2007, SI 2007/3495 provides as follows—

"Requirement to have at least one director who is a natural person (*s 155*)

46. If on 8th November 2006—
   (a) none of a company's directors were natural persons, and
   (b) section 282 of the 1985 Act or Article 290 of the 1986 Order (requirement as to number of directors) was complied with in relation to the company,

section 155 of the Companies Act 2006 (companies required to have at least one director who is a natural person) does not apply to the company until 1st October 2010.".

Appointment

160 Appointment of directors of public company to be voted on individually

(1) At a general meeting of a public company a motion for the appointment of two or more persons as directors of the company by a single resolution must not be made unless a resolution that it should be so made has first been agreed to by the meeting without any vote being given against it.

(2) A resolution moved in contravention of this section is void, whether or not its being so moved was objected to at the time.

But where a resolution so moved is passed, no provision for the automatic reappointment of retiring directors in default of another appointment applies.

(3) For the purposes of this section a motion for approving a person's appointment, or for nominating a person for appointment, is treated as a motion for his appointment.

(4) Nothing in this section applies to a resolution amending the company's articles.

[1747]

NOTES

Commencement: 1 October 2007.

161 Validity of acts of directors

(1) The acts of a person acting as a director are valid notwithstanding that it is afterwards discovered—
   (a) that there was a defect in his appointment;
   (b) that he was disqualified from holding office;
   (c) that he had ceased to hold office;
   (d) that he was not entitled to vote on the matter in question.

(2) This applies even if the resolution for his appointment is void under section 160 (appointment of directors of public company to be voted on individually).

[1748]

NOTES

Commencement: 1 October 2007.

Transitional provisions: Sch 3, para 4 to the Companies Act 2006 (Commencement No 3, Consequential Amendments, Transitional Provisions and Savings) Order 2007, SI 2007/2194 provides as follows—

"4 Validity of acts of directors (s 161)

(1) Section 161 of the Companies Act 2006 (validity of acts of directors) applies to acts done on or after 1st October 2007.

(2) Section 285 of the 1985 Act (validity of acts of director or manager) or Article 293 of the 1986 Order (validity of acts of director) continues to apply to acts done before that date.".

Removal

168 Resolution to remove director

(1) A company may by ordinary resolution at a meeting remove a director before the expiration of his period of office, notwithstanding anything in any agreement between it and him.

(2) Special notice is required of a resolution to remove a director under this section or to appoint somebody instead of a director so removed at the meeting at which he is removed.

(3) A vacancy created by the removal of a director under this section, if not filled at the meeting at which he is removed, may be filled as a casual vacancy.

(4) A person appointed director in place of a person removed under this section is treated, for the purpose of determining the time at which he or any other director is to retire, as if he had become director on the day on which the person in whose place he is appointed was last appointed a director.

(5) This section is not to be taken—

(a) as depriving a person removed under it of compensation or damages payable to him in respect of the termination of his appointment as director or of any appointment terminating with that as director, or

(b) as derogating from any power to remove a director that may exist apart from this section.

[1749]

NOTES

Commencement: 1 October 2007.

169 Director's right to protest against removal

(1) On receipt of notice of an intended resolution to remove a director under section 168, the company must forthwith send a copy of the notice to the director concerned.

(2) The director (whether or not a member of the company) is entitled to be heard on the resolution at the meeting.

(3) Where notice is given of an intended resolution to remove a director under that section, and the director concerned makes with respect to it representations in writing to the company (not exceeding a reasonable length) and requests their notification to members of the company, the company shall, unless the representations are received by it too late for it to do so—

(a) in any notice of the resolution given to members of the company state the fact of the representations having been made; and

(b) send a copy of the representations to every member of the company to whom notice of the meeting is sent (whether before or after receipt of the representations by the company).

(4) If a copy of the representations is not sent as required by subsection (3) because received too late or because of the company's default, the director may (without prejudice to his right to be heard orally) require that the representations shall be read out at the meeting.

(5) Copies of the representations need not be sent out and the representations need not be read out at the meeting if, on the application either of the company or of any other person who claims to be aggrieved, the court is satisfied that the rights conferred by this section are being abused.

(6) The court may order the company's costs (in Scotland, expenses) on an application under subsection (5) to be paid in whole or in part by the director, notwithstanding that he is not a party to the application.

[1750]

NOTES

Commencement: 1 October 2007.

Transitional provisions: Sch 3, para 5 to the Companies Act 2006 (Commencement No 3, Consequential Amendments, Transitional Provisions and Savings) Order 2007, SI 2007/2194 provides as follows—

"**5 Removal of directors (ss 168 and 169**)

(1) Section 169(5) of the Companies Act 2006 (circumstances in which representations need not be sent out or read out at the meeting) applies where the representations are received by the company on or after 1st October 2007.

(2) Section 304(4) of the 1985 Act or Article 312(4) of the 1986 Order continues to apply where the representations are received by the company before that date.".

CHAPTER 2
GENERAL DUTIES OF DIRECTORS

Introductory

170 Scope and nature of general duties

(1) The general duties specified in sections 171 to 177 are owed by a director of a company to the company.

(2) A person who ceases to be a director continues to be subject—
- (a) to the duty in section 175 (duty to avoid conflicts of interest) as regards the exploitation of any property, information or opportunity of which he became aware at a time when he was a director, and
- (b) to the duty in section 176 (duty not to accept benefits from third parties) as regards things done or omitted by him before he ceased to be a director.

To that extent those duties apply to a former director as to a director, subject to any necessary adaptations.

(3) The general duties are based on certain common law rules and equitable principles as they apply in relation to directors and have effect in place of those rules and principles as regards the duties owed to a company by a director.

(4) The general duties shall be interpreted and applied in the same way as common law rules or equitable principles, and regard shall be had to the corresponding common law rules and equitable principles in interpreting and applying the general duties.

(5) The general duties apply to shadow directors where, and to the extent that, the corresponding common law rules or equitable principles so apply.

[1750A]

NOTES

Commencement: 1 October 2007.

Transitional adaptations: art 6 of the Companies Act 2006 (Commencement No 3, Consequential Amendments, Transitional Provisions and Savings) Order 2007, SI 2007/2194 provides that the provisions brought into force by that Order shall have effect subject to any transitional adaptations specified in Sch 1 to that Order. Schedule 1, para 6 to the Order provides as follows (note, however, that this paragraph is revoked by the Companies Act 2006 (Commencement No 5, Transitional Provisions and Savings) Order 2007, SI 2007/3495, art 10(2), (3), as from 1 October 2008 (subject to any transitional provisions and savings as apply, in accordance with Sch 4 to that Order, in relation to the repeal of the provisions of the 1985 Act referred to in the adaptation; see art 10 thereto))—

"6 General duties of directors (**ss 170 to 181**)

(1) Section 170 (scope and nature of general duties) has effect with the following adaptations.

(2) In subsection (1), for "177" substitute "174".

(3) Omit subsection (2).

(4) In subsection (3) after "The general duties" insert "in sections 171 to 174".".

The general duties

171 Duty to act within powers

A director of a company must—
- (a) act in accordance with the company's constitution, and
- (b) only exercise powers for the purposes for which they are conferred.

[1750B]

NOTES

Commencement: 1 October 2007.

172 Duty to promote the success of the company

(1) A director of a company must act in the way he considers, in good faith, would be most likely to promote the success of the company for the benefit of its members as a whole, and in doing so have regard (amongst other matters) to—

(a) the likely consequences of any decision in the long term,
(b) the interests of the company's employees,
(c) the need to foster the company's business relationships with suppliers, customers and others,
(d) the impact of the company's operations on the community and the environment,
(e) the desirability of the company maintaining a reputation for high standards of business conduct, and
(f) the need to act fairly as between members of the company.

(2) Where or to the extent that the purposes of the company consist of or include purposes other than the benefit of its members, subsection (1) has effect as if the reference to promoting the success of the company for the benefit of its members were to achieving those purposes.

(3) The duty imposed by this section has effect subject to any enactment or rule of law requiring directors, in certain circumstances, to consider or act in the interests of creditors of the company.

[1750C]

NOTES
Commencement: 1 October 2007.

173 Duty to exercise independent judgment

(1) A director of a company must exercise independent judgment.

(2) This duty is not infringed by his acting—
(a) in accordance with an agreement duly entered into by the company that restricts the future exercise of discretion by its directors, or
(b) in a way authorised by the company's constitution.

[1750D]

NOTES
Commencement: 1 October 2007.

174 Duty to exercise reasonable care, skill and diligence

(1) A director of a company must exercise reasonable care, skill and diligence.

(2) This means the care, skill and diligence that would be exercised by a reasonably diligent person with—
(a) the general knowledge, skill and experience that may reasonably be expected of a person carrying out the functions carried out by the director in relation to the company, and
(b) the general knowledge, skill and experience that the director has.

[1750E]

NOTES
Commencement: 1 October 2007.

175 Duty to avoid conflicts of interest

(1) A director of a company must avoid a situation in which he has, or can have, a direct or indirect interest that conflicts, or possibly may conflict, with the interests of the company.

(2) This applies in particular to the exploitation of any property, information or opportunity (and it is immaterial whether the company could take advantage of the property, information or opportunity).

(3) This duty does not apply to a conflict of interest arising in relation to a transaction or arrangement with the company.

(4) This duty is not infringed—
(a) if the situation cannot reasonably be regarded as likely to give rise to a conflict of interest; or
(b) if the matter has been authorised by the directors.

(5) Authorisation may be given by the directors—

(a) where the company is a private company and nothing in the company's constitution invalidates such authorisation, by the matter being proposed to and authorised by the directors; or

(b) where the company is a public company and its constitution includes provision enabling the directors to authorise the matter, by the matter being proposed to and authorised by them in accordance with the constitution.

(6) The authorisation is effective only if—

(a) any requirement as to the quorum at the meeting at which the matter is considered is met without counting the director in question or any other interested director, and

(b) the matter was agreed to without their voting or would have been agreed to if their votes had not been counted.

(7) Any reference in this section to a conflict of interest includes a conflict of interest and duty and a conflict of duties.

[1750F]

NOTES

Commencement: 1 October 2008.

Transitional provisions: Sch 4, Pt 3, para 47 to the Companies Act 2006 (Commencement No 5, Transitional Provisions and Savings) Order 2007, SI 2007/3495 provides as follows—

"Duty of directors to avoid conflicts of interest (s 175)

47.—(1) Section 175 of the Companies Act 2006 (duty to avoid conflicts of interest) applies where the situation described in subsection (1) of that section arises on or after 1st October 2008.

(2) The law that applied before that date continues to apply to such a situation that arose before that date.

(3) Section 175(5)(a) of that Act (private companies: authorisation by directors) applies—

(a) to companies incorporated on or after 1st October 2008, and

(b) to companies incorporated before that date where the members of the company have resolved (before, on or after 1st October 2008) that authorisation may be given in accordance with that provision.

(4) Chapter 3 of Part 3 of the Companies Act 2006 (resolutions and agreements affecting a company's constitution) applies to any such resolution.

(5) For the purposes of section 30 of that Act (copies of resolutions to be forwarded to registrar) such a resolution passed before 1st October 2008 is treated as if passed on that date.".

176 Duty not to accept benefits from third parties

(1) A director of a company must not accept a benefit from a third party conferred by reason of—

(a) his being a director, or

(b) his doing (or not doing) anything as director.

(2) A "third party" means a person other than the company, an associated body corporate or a person acting on behalf of the company or an associated body corporate.

(3) Benefits received by a director from a person by whom his services (as a director or otherwise) are provided to the company are not regarded as conferred by a third party.

(4) This duty is not infringed if the acceptance of the benefit cannot reasonably be regarded as likely to give rise to a conflict of interest.

(5) Any reference in this section to a conflict of interest includes a conflict of interest and duty and a conflict of duties.

[1750G]

NOTES

Commencement: 1 October 2008.

177 Duty to declare interest in proposed transaction or arrangement

(1) If a director of a company is in any way, directly or indirectly, interested in a proposed transaction or arrangement with the company, he must declare the nature and extent of that interest to the other directors.

(2) The declaration may (but need not) be made—
(a) at a meeting of the directors, or
(b) by notice to the directors in accordance with—
(i) section 184 (notice in writing), or
(ii) section 185 (general notice).

(3) If a declaration of interest under this section proves to be, or becomes, inaccurate or incomplete, a further declaration must be made.

(4) Any declaration required by this section must be made before the company enters into the transaction or arrangement.

(5) This section does not require a declaration of an interest of which the director is not aware or where the director is not aware of the transaction or arrangement in question.

For this purpose a director is treated as being aware of matters of which he ought reasonably to be aware.

(6) A director need not declare an interest—
(a) if it cannot reasonably be regarded as likely to give rise to a conflict of interest;
(b) if, or to the extent that, the other directors are already aware of it (and for this purpose the other directors are treated as aware of anything of which they ought reasonably to be aware); or
(c) if, or to the extent that, it concerns terms of his service contract that have been or are to be considered—
(i) by a meeting of the directors, or
(ii) by a committee of the directors appointed for the purpose under the company's constitution.

[1750H]

NOTES

Commencement: 1 October 2008.

Transitional provisions: Sch 4, Pt 3, para 48 to the Companies Act 2006 (Commencement No 5, Transitional Provisions and Savings) Order 2007, SI 2007/3495 provides as follows—

"*Declaration by directors of interest in proposed transaction or arrangement* (*s 177*)

48.—(1) Section 177(1) of the Companies Act 2006 (duty of director to declare interest in proposed transaction or arrangement) applies where the duty to declare an interest arises on or after 1st October 2008.

(2) Section 317 of the 1985 Act or Article 325 of the 1986 Order continues to apply in relation to a duty arising before that date.

(3) For the purposes of section 177(3) of the Companies Act 2006 (previous declaration under that section proving or becoming inadequate), a declaration of interest in relation to a proposed transaction or arrangement made before 1st October 2008 under section 317 of the 1985 Act or Article 325 of the 1986 Order is treated on and after that date as if made under section 177 of the Companies Act 2006.".

Supplementary provisions

178 Civil consequences of breach of general duties

(1) The consequences of breach (or threatened breach) of sections 171 to 177 are the same as would apply if the corresponding common law rule or equitable principle applied.

(2) The duties in those sections (with the exception of section 174 (duty to exercise reasonable care, skill and diligence)) are, accordingly, enforceable in the same way as any other fiduciary duty owed to a company by its directors.

[1750I]

NOTES

Commencement: 1 October 2007.

Transitional adaptations: art 6 of the Companies Act 2006 (Commencement No 3, Consequential Amendments, Transitional Provisions and Savings) Order 2007, SI 2007/2194 provides that the provisions brought into force by that Order shall have effect subject to any transitional adaptations specified in Sch 1 to that Order. Schedule 1, para 7 to the Order provides as follows (note, however, that this paragraph is revoked by the Companies Act 2006 (Commencement No 5, Transitional Provisions and Savings) Order 2007, SI 2007/3495, art 10(2), (3), as from 1 October 2008 (subject to any transitional provisions and savings as apply, in accordance with Sch 4 to that Order, in relation to the repeal of the provisions of the 1985 Act referred to in the adaptation; see art 10 thereto))—

"7.—(1) Section 178 (civil consequences of breach of general duties) has effect with the following adaptation.

(2) In subsection (1), for "177" substitute "174".".

179 Cases within more than one of the general duties

Except as otherwise provided, more than one of the general duties may apply in any given case.

[1751]

NOTES

Commencement: 1 October 2007.

180 Consent, approval or authorisation by members

(1) In a case where—

(a) section 175 (duty to avoid conflicts of interest) is complied with by authorisation by the directors, or

(b) section 177 (duty to declare interest in proposed transaction or arrangement) is complied with,

the transaction or arrangement is not liable to be set aside by virtue of any common law rule or equitable principle requiring the consent or approval of the members of the company.

This is without prejudice to any enactment, or provision of the company's constitution, requiring such consent or approval.

(2) The application of the general duties is not affected by the fact that the case also falls within Chapter 4 (transactions requiring approval of members), except that where that Chapter applies and— (a) approval is given under that Chapter, or (b) the matter is one as to which it is provided that approval is not needed, it is not necessary also to comply with section 175 (duty to avoid conflicts of interest) or section 176 (duty not to accept benefits from third parties).

(3) Compliance with the general duties does not remove the need for approval under any applicable provision of Chapter 4 (transactions requiring approval of members).

(4) The general duties—

(a) have effect subject to any rule of law enabling the company to give authority, specifically or generally, for anything to be done (or omitted) by the directors, or any of them, that would otherwise be a breach of duty, and

(b) where the company's articles contain provisions for dealing with conflicts of interest, are not infringed by anything done (or omitted) by the directors, or any of them, in accordance with those provisions.

(5) Otherwise, the general duties have effect (except as otherwise provided or the context otherwise requires) notwithstanding any enactment or rule of law.

[1752]

NOTES

Commencement: 1 October 2007.

Transitional provisions: Sch 4, Pt 3, para 49 to the Companies Act 2006 (Commencement No 5, Transitional Provisions and Savings) Order 2007, SI 2007/3495 provides as follows—

"*General duties of directors: approval by members* (*s 180*(2))

49. The reference in section 180(2) of the Companies Act 2006 (exclusion of general duties where approval of members given) to approval given under Chapter 4 of Part 10 of that Act (transactions requiring approval of members) includes approval given by a resolution passed before 1st October 2007

that is effective by virtue of paragraph 6(2), 7(2), 8(2) or 12(2) of Schedule 3 to the Companies Act 2006 (Commencement No 3, Consequential Amendments, Transitional Provisions and Savings) Order 2007.".

Transitional adaptations: art 6 of the Companies Act 2006 (Commencement No 3, Consequential Amendments, Transitional Provisions and Savings) Order 2007, SI 2007/2194 provides that the provisions brought into force by that Order shall have effect subject to any transitional adaptations specified in Sch 1 to that Order. Schedule 1, para 8 to the Order provides as follows (note, however, that this paragraph is revoked by the Companies Act 2006 (Commencement No 5, Transitional Provisions and Savings) Order 2007, SI 2007/3495, art 10(2), (3), as from 1 October 2008 (subject to any transitional provisions and savings as apply, in accordance with Sch 4 to that Order, in relation to the repeal of the provisions of the 1985 Act referred to in the adaptation; see art 10 thereto))—

"8.—(1) Section 180 (consent, approval or authorisation by members) has effect with the following adaptations.

(2) Omit subsection (1).

(3) In subsection (2), omit the words from ", except that" to the end.

(4) In subsection (4), omit paragraph (b).".

181 Modification of provisions in relation to charitable companies

(1) In their application to a company that is a charity, the provisions of this Chapter have effect subject to this section.

(2) Section 175 (duty to avoid conflicts of interest) has effect as if—

(a) for subsection (3) (which disapplies the duty to avoid conflicts of interest in the case of a transaction or arrangement with the company) there were substituted—

"(3) This duty does not apply to a conflict of interest arising in relation to a transaction or arrangement with the company if or to the extent that the company's articles allow that duty to be so disapplied, which they may do only in relation to descriptions of transaction or arrangement specified in the company's articles.";

(b) for subsection (5) (which specifies how directors of a company may give authority under that section for a transaction or arrangement) there were substituted—

"(5) Authorisation may be given by the directors where the company's constitution includes provision enabling them to authorise the matter, by the matter being proposed to and authorised by them in accordance with the constitution.".

(3) Section 180(2)(b) (which disapplies certain duties under this Chapter in relation to cases excepted from requirement to obtain approval by members under Chapter 4) applies only if or to the extent that the company's articles allow those duties to be so disapplied, which they may do only in relation to descriptions of transaction or arrangement specified in the company's articles.

(4) (*Inserts the Charities Act 1993, s 26(5A)* (*outside the scope of this work*).)

(5) This section does not extend to Scotland.

[1752A]

NOTES

Commencement: 1 October 2007.

Transitional adaptations: art 6 of the Companies Act 2006 (Commencement No 3, Consequential Amendments, Transitional Provisions and Savings) Order 2007, SI 2007/2194 provides that the provisions brought into force by that Order shall have effect subject to any transitional adaptations specified in Sch 1 to that Order. Schedule 1, para 9 to the Order provides as follows (note, however, that this paragraph is revoked by the Companies Act 2006 (Commencement No 5, Transitional Provisions and Savings) Order 2007, SI 2007/3495, art 10(2), (3), as from 1 October 2008 (subject to any transitional provisions and savings as apply, in accordance with Sch 4 to that Order, in relation to the repeal of the provisions of the 1985 Act referred to in the adaptation; see art 10 thereto))—

"9.—(1) Section 181 (modification of provisions in relation to charitable companies) has effect with the following modifications.

(2) Omit subsections (2) and (3).".".

CHAPTER 3
DECLARATION OF INTEREST IN EXISTING TRANSACTION OR ARRANGEMENT

182 Declaration of interest in existing transaction or arrangement

(1) Where a director of a company is in any way, directly or indirectly, interested in a transaction or arrangement that has been entered into by the company, he must declare the nature and extent of the interest to the other directors in accordance with this section.

This section does not apply if or to the extent that the interest has been declared under section 177 (duty to declare interest in proposed transaction or arrangement).

(2) The declaration must be made—
- (a) at a meeting of the directors, or
- (b) by notice in writing (see section 184), or
- (c) by general notice (see section 185).

(3) If a declaration of interest under this section proves to be, or becomes, inaccurate or incomplete, a further declaration must be made.

(4) Any declaration required by this section must be made as soon as is reasonably practicable.

Failure to comply with this requirement does not affect the underlying duty to make the declaration.

(5) This section does not require a declaration of an interest of which the director is not aware or where the director is not aware of the transaction or arrangement in question.

For this purpose a director is treated as being aware of matters of which he ought reasonably to be aware.

(6) A director need not declare an interest under this section—
- (a) if it cannot reasonably be regarded as likely to give rise to a conflict of interest;
- (b) if, or to the extent that, the other directors are already aware of it (and for this purpose the other directors are treated as aware of anything of which they ought reasonably to be aware); or
- (c) if, or to the extent that, it concerns terms of his service contract that have been or are to be considered—
  - (i) by a meeting of the directors, or
  - (ii) by a committee of the directors appointed for the purpose under the company's constitution.

[1753]

NOTES

Commencement: 1 October 2008.

Transitional provisions: Sch 4, Pt 3, para 50 to the Companies Act 2006 (Commencement No 5, Transitional Provisions and Savings) Order 2007, SI 2007/3495 provides as follows—

"*Declaration of interest in existing transaction or arrangement* (*ss 182 to 187*)

50.—(1) Sections 182 to 187 of the Companies Act 2006 (declaration by director of interest in existing transaction or arrangement) apply in relation to transactions or arrangements entered into by a company on or after 1st October 2008.

(2) Section 317 of the 1985 Act or Article 325 of the 1986 Order continues to apply in relation to transactions or arrangements entered into before that date.

(3) For the purposes of section 182(1) of the Companies Act 2006 (declaration of interest in existing transaction not previously declared under section 177), a declaration of interest made before 1st October 2008 under section 317 of the 1985 Act or Article 325 of the 1986 Order is treated on and after that date as if made under section 177.

(4) For the purposes of section 182(3) of the Companies Act 2006 (previous declaration under that section proving or becoming inadequate), a declaration of interest made before 1st October 2008 under section 317 of the 1985 Act or Article 325 of the 1986 Order is treated on and after that date as if made under section 182.".

183 Offence of failure to declare interest

(1) A director who fails to comply with the requirements of section 182 (declaration of interest in existing transaction or arrangement) commits an offence.

(2) A person guilty of an offence under this section is liable—
- (a) on conviction on indictment, to a fine;
- (b) on summary conviction, to a fine not exceeding the statutory maximum.

[1754]

NOTES

Commencement: 1 October 2008.

Transitional provisions: see the note to s 182 at **[1753]**.

184 Declaration made by notice in writing

(1) This section applies to a declaration of interest made by notice in writing.

(2) The director must send the notice to the other directors.

(3) The notice may be sent in hard copy form or, if the recipient has agreed to receive it in electronic form, in an agreed electronic form.

(4) The notice may be sent—
- (a) by hand or by post, or
- (b) if the recipient has agreed to receive it by electronic means, by agreed electronic means.

(5) Where a director declares an interest by notice in writing in accordance with this section—
- (a) the making of the declaration is deemed to form part of the proceedings at the next meeting of the directors after the notice is given, and
- (b) the provisions of section 248 (minutes of meetings of directors) apply as if the declaration had been made at that meeting.

[1755]

NOTES

Commencement: 1 October 2008.
Transitional provisions: see the note to s 182 at **[1753]**.

185 General notice treated as sufficient declaration

(1) General notice in accordance with this section is a sufficient declaration of interest in relation to the matters to which it relates.

(2) General notice is notice given to the directors of a company to the effect that the director—
- (a) has an interest (as member, officer, employee or otherwise) in a specified body corporate or firm and is to be regarded as interested in any transaction or arrangement that may, after the date of the notice, be made with that body corporate or firm, or
- (b) is connected with a specified person (other than a body corporate or firm) and is to be regarded as interested in any transaction or arrangement that may, after the date of the notice, be made with that person.

(3) The notice must state the nature and extent of the director's interest in the body corporate or firm or, as the case may be, the nature of his connection with the person.

(4) General notice is not effective unless—
- (a) it is given at a meeting of the directors, or
- (b) the director takes reasonable steps to secure that it is brought up and read at the next meeting of the directors after it is given.

[1756]

NOTES

Commencement: 1 October 2008.
Transitional provisions: see the note to s 182 at **[1753]**.

CHAPTER 4
TRANSACTIONS WITH DIRECTORS REQUIRING APPROVAL OF MEMBERS

Service contracts

188 Directors' long-term service contracts: requirement of members' approval

(1) This section applies to provision under which the guaranteed term of a director's employment—
- (a) with the company of which he is a director, or
- (b) where he is the director of a holding company, within the group consisting of that company and its subsidiaries,

is, or may be, longer than two years.

(2) A company may not agree to such provision unless it has been approved—

(a) by resolution of the members of the company, and

(b) in the case of a director of a holding company, by resolution of the members of that company.

(3) The guaranteed term of a director's employment is—

(a) the period (if any) during which the director's employment—

(i) is to continue, or may be continued otherwise than at the instance of the company (whether under the original agreement or under a new agreement entered into in pursuance of it), and

(ii) cannot be terminated by the company by notice, or can be so terminated only in specified circumstances, or

(b) in the case of employment terminable by the company by notice, the period of notice required to be given,

or, in the case of employment having a period within paragraph (a) and a period within paragraph (b), the aggregate of those periods.

(4) If more than six months before the end of the guaranteed term of a director's employment the company enters into a further service contract (otherwise than in pursuance of a right conferred, by or under the original contract, on the other party to it), this section applies as if there were added to the guaranteed term of the new contract the unexpired period of the guaranteed term of the original contract.

(5) A resolution approving provision to which this section applies must not be passed unless a memorandum setting out the proposed contract incorporating the provision is made available to members—

(a) in the case of a written resolution, by being sent or submitted to every eligible member at or before the time at which the proposed resolution is sent or submitted to him;

(b) in the case of a resolution at a meeting, by being made available for inspection by members of the company both—

(i) at the company's registered office for not less than 15 days ending with the date of the meeting, and

(ii) at the meeting itself.

(6) No approval is required under this section on the part of the members of a body corporate that—

(a) is not a UK-registered company, or

(b) is a wholly-owned subsidiary of another body corporate.

(7) In this section "employment" means any employment under a director's service contract.

[1757]

NOTES

Commencement: 1 October 2007.

Transitional provisions: Sch 3, para 6 to the Companies Act 2006 (Commencement No 3, Consequential Amendments, Transitional Provisions and Savings) Order 2007, SI 2007/2194 provides as follows—

"**6 Transactions requiring members' approval: directors' long-term service contracts (ss 188 and 189)**

(1) Sections 188 and 189 of the Companies Act 2006 (directors' long-term service contracts: requirement of members' approval) apply to agreements made on or after 1st October 2007.

(2) A resolution passed before that date approving the provision made by such an agreement is effective for the purposes of those sections if it complies with the requirements of those sections.

(3) Section 188(4) (addition of unexpired period of earlier contract in determining guaranteed period under new contract) applies whether the original contract (within the meaning of that provision) was entered into before or after that date.

(4) Section 319 of the 1985 Act or Article 327 of the 1986 Order continues to apply to agreements made before that date.".

189 Directors' long-term service contracts: civil consequences of contravention

If a company agrees to provision in contravention of section 188 (directors' long-term service contracts: requirement of members' approval)—

(a) the provision is void, to the extent of the contravention, and

(b) the contract is deemed to contain a term entitling the company to terminate it at any time by the giving of reasonable notice.

[1758]

NOTES

Commencement: 1 October 2007.

Transitional provisions: see the note to s 188 at **[1757]**.

Payments for loss of office

215 Payments for loss of office

(1) In this Chapter a "payment for loss of office" means a payment made to a director or past director of a company—

(a) by way of compensation for loss of office as director of the company,

(b) by way of compensation for loss, while director of the company or in connection with his ceasing to be a director of it, of—

(i) any other office or employment in connection with the management of the affairs of the company, or

(ii) any office (as director or otherwise) or employment in connection with the management of the affairs of any subsidiary undertaking of the company,

(c) as consideration for or in connection with his retirement from his office as director of the company, or

(d) as consideration for or in connection with his retirement, while director of the company or in connection with his ceasing to be a director of it, from—

(i) any other office or employment in connection with the management of the affairs of the company, or

(ii) any office (as director or otherwise) or employment in connection with the management of the affairs of any subsidiary undertaking of the company.

(2) The references to compensation and consideration include benefits otherwise than in cash and references in this Chapter to payment have a corresponding meaning.

(3) For the purposes of sections 217 to 221 (payments requiring members' approval)—

(a) payment to a person connected with a director, or

(b) payment to any person at the direction of, or for the benefit of, a director or a person connected with him,

is treated as payment to the director.

(4) References in those sections to payment by a person include payment by another person at the direction of, or on behalf of, the person referred to.

[1759]

NOTES

Commencement: 1 October 2007.

Transitional provisions: Sch 3, para 12 to the Companies Act 2006 (Commencement No 3, Consequential Amendments, Transitional Provisions and Savings) Order 2007, SI 2007/2194 provides as follows—

"**12 Transactions requiring members' approval: payments for loss of office (ss 215 to 222)**

(1) Sections 215 to 222 of the Companies Act 2006 (payments for loss of office: requirement of members' approval) apply in relation to any such loss of office or employment as is mentioned in section 215(1)(a) or (b), or any such retirement as is mentioned in section 215(1)(c) or (d), occurring on or after 1st October 2007.

(2) A resolution passed before that date approving a payment is effective for the purposes of those sections if it complies with the requirements of those sections.

(3) Sections 312 to 316 of the 1985 Act or Articles 320 to 324 of the 1986 Order continue to apply in relation to loss of office or retirement within the meaning of those provisions occurring before that date.

(4) For the purposes of this paragraph loss of office or retirement is regarded as occurring—

(a) in the case of a directorship, when the person ceases to be a director;

(b) in the case of any other office, when the person ceases to hold that office;

(c) in the case of employment, when the employment comes to an end.".

216 Amounts taken to be payments for loss of office

(1) This section applies where in connection with any such transfer as is mentioned in section 218 or 219 (payment in connection with transfer of undertaking, property or shares) a director of the company—

(a) is to cease to hold office, or

(b) is to cease to be the holder of—

(i) any other office or employment in connection with the management of the affairs of the company, or

(ii) any office (as director or otherwise) or employment in connection with the management of the affairs of any subsidiary undertaking of the company.

(2) If in connection with any such transfer—

(a) the price to be paid to the director for any shares in the company held by him is in excess of the price which could at the time have been obtained by other holders of like shares, or

(b) any valuable consideration is given to the director by a person other than the company,

the excess or, as the case may be, the money value of the consideration is taken for the purposes of those sections to have been a payment for loss of office.

[1760]

NOTES

Commencement: 1 October 2007.

Transitional provisions: see the note to s 215 at **[1759]**.

217 Payment by company: requirement of members' approval

(1) A company may not make a payment for loss of office to a director of the company unless the payment has been approved by a resolution of the members of the company.

(2) A company may not make a payment for loss of office to a director of its holding company unless the payment has been approved by a resolution of the members of each of those companies.

(3) A resolution approving a payment to which this section applies must not be passed unless a memorandum setting out particulars of the proposed payment (including its amount) is made available to the members of the company whose approval is sought—

(a) in the case of a written resolution, by being sent or submitted to every eligible member at or before the time at which the proposed resolution is sent or submitted to him;

(b) in the case of a resolution at a meeting, by being made available for inspection by the members both—

(i) at the company's registered office for not less than 15 days ending with the date of the meeting, and

(ii) at the meeting itself.

(4) No approval is required under this section on the part of the members of a body corporate that—

(a) is not a UK-registered company, or

(b) is a wholly-owned subsidiary of another body corporate.

[1761]

NOTES

Commencement: 1 October 2007.

Transitional provisions: see the note to s 215 at **[1759]**.

218 Payment in connection with transfer of undertaking etc: requirement of members' approval

(1) No payment for loss of office may be made by any person to a director of a company in connection with the transfer of the whole or any part of the undertaking or property of the company unless the payment has been approved by a resolution of the members of the company.

(2) No payment for loss of office may be made by any person to a director of a company in connection with the transfer of the whole or any part of the undertaking or property of a subsidiary of the company unless the payment has been approved by a resolution of the members of each of the companies.

(3) A resolution approving a payment to which this section applies must not be passed unless a memorandum setting out particulars of the proposed payment (including its amount) is made available to the members of the company whose approval is sought—

(a) in the case of a written resolution, by being sent or submitted to every eligible member at or before the time at which the proposed resolution is sent or submitted to him;

(b) in the case of a resolution at a meeting, by being made available for inspection by the members both—

(i) at the company's registered office for not less than 15 days ending with the date of the meeting, and

(ii) at the meeting itself.

(4) No approval is required under this section on the part of the members of a body corporate that—

(a) is not a UK-registered company, or

(b) is a wholly-owned subsidiary of another body corporate.

(5) A payment made in pursuance of an arrangement—

(a) entered into as part of the agreement for the transfer in question, or within one year before or two years after that agreement, and

(b) to which the company whose undertaking or property is transferred, or any person to whom the transfer is made, is privy,

is presumed, except in so far as the contrary is shown, to be a payment to which this section applies.

[1762]

NOTES

Commencement: 1 October 2007.

Transitional provisions: see the note to s 215 at **[1759]**.

219 Payment in connection with share transfer: requirement of members' approval

(1) No payment for loss of office may be made by any person to a director of a company in connection with a transfer of shares in the company, or in a subsidiary of the company, resulting from a takeover bid unless the payment has been approved by a resolution of the relevant shareholders.

(2) The relevant shareholders are the holders of the shares to which the bid relates and any holders of shares of the same class as any of those shares.

(3) A resolution approving a payment to which this section applies must not be passed unless a memorandum setting out particulars of the proposed payment (including its amount) is made available to the members of the company whose approval is sought—

(a) in the case of a written resolution, by being sent or submitted to every eligible member at or before the time at which the proposed resolution is sent or submitted to him;

(b) in the case of a resolution at a meeting, by being made available for inspection by the members both—

(i) at the company's registered office for not less than 15 days ending with the date of the meeting, and

(ii) at the meeting itself.

(4) Neither the person making the offer, nor any associate of his (as defined in section 988), is entitled to vote on the resolution, but—

(a) where the resolution is proposed as a written resolution, they are entitled (if they would otherwise be so entitled) to be sent a copy of it, and

(b) at any meeting to consider the resolution they are entitled (if they would otherwise be so entitled) to be given notice of the meeting, to attend and speak and if present (in person or by proxy) to count towards the quorum.

(5) If at a meeting to consider the resolution a quorum is not present, and after the meeting has been adjourned to a later date a quorum is again not present, the payment is (for the purposes of this section) deemed to have been approved.

(6) No approval is required under this section on the part of shareholders in a body corporate that—

(a) is not a UK-registered company, or

(b) is a wholly-owned subsidiary of another body corporate.

(7) A payment made in pursuance of an arrangement—

(a) entered into as part of the agreement for the transfer in question, or within one year before or two years after that agreement, and

(b) to which the company whose shares are the subject of the bid, or any person to whom the transfer is made, is privy,

is presumed, except in so far as the contrary is shown, to be a payment to which this section applies.

[1763]

NOTES

Commencement: 1 October 2007.

Transitional provisions: see the note to s 215 at **[1759]**.

220 Exception for payments in discharge of legal obligations etc

(1) Approval is not required under section 217, 218 or 219 (payments requiring members' approval) for a payment made in good faith—

(a) in discharge of an existing legal obligation (as defined below),

(b) by way of damages for breach of such an obligation,

(c) by way of settlement or compromise of any claim arising in connection with the termination of a person's office or employment, or

(d) by way of pension in respect of past services.

(2) In relation to a payment within section 217 (payment by company) an existing legal obligation means an obligation of the company, or any body corporate associated with it, that was not entered into in connection with, or in consequence of, the event giving rise to the payment for loss of office.

(3) In relation to a payment within section 218 or 219 (payment in connection with transfer of undertaking, property or shares) an existing legal obligation means an obligation of the person making the payment that was not entered into for the purposes of, in connection with or in consequence of, the transfer in question.

(4) In the case of a payment within both section 217 and section 218, or within both section 217 and section 219, subsection (2) above applies and not subsection (3).

(5) A payment part of which falls within subsection (1) above and part of which does not is treated as if the parts were separate payments.

[1764]

NOTES

Commencement: 1 October 2007.

Transitional provisions: see the note to s 215 at **[1759]**.

221 Exception for small payments

(1) Approval is not required under section 217, 218 or 219 (payments requiring members' approval) if—

(a) the payment in question is made by the company or any of its subsidiaries, and

(b) the amount or value of the payment, together with the amount or value of any other relevant payments, does not exceed £200.

(2) For this purpose "other relevant payments" are payments for loss of office in relation to which the following conditions are met.

(3) Where the payment in question is one to which section 217 (payment by company) applies, the conditions are that the other payment was or is paid—

(a) by the company making the payment in question or any of its subsidiaries,
(b) to the director to whom that payment is made, and
(c) in connection with the same event.

(4) Where the payment in question is one to which section 218 or 219 applies (payment in connection with transfer of undertaking, property or shares), the conditions are that the other payment was (or is) paid in connection with the same transfer—

(a) to the director to whom the payment in question was made, and
(b) by the company making the payment or any of its subsidiaries.

[1765]

NOTES

Commencement: 1 October 2007.
Transitional provisions: see the note to s 215 at **[1759]**.

222 Payments made without approval: civil consequences

(1) If a payment is made in contravention of section 217 (payment by company)—

(a) it is held by the recipient on trust for the company making the payment, and
(b) any director who authorised the payment is jointly and severally liable to indemnify the company that made the payment for any loss resulting from it.

(2) If a payment is made in contravention of section 218 (payment in connection with transfer of undertaking etc), it is held by the recipient on trust for the company whose undertaking or property is or is proposed to be transferred.

(3) If a payment is made in contravention of section 219 (payment in connection with share transfer)—

(a) it is held by the recipient on trust for persons who have sold their shares as a result of the offer made, and
(b) the expenses incurred by the recipient in distributing that sum amongst those persons shall be borne by him and not retained out of that sum.

(4) If a payment is in contravention of section 217 and section 218, subsection (2) of this section applies rather than subsection (1).

(5) If a payment is in contravention of section 217 and section 219, subsection (3) of this section applies rather than subsection (1), unless the court directs otherwise.

[1766]

NOTES

Commencement: 1 October 2007.
Transitional provisions: see the note to s 215 at **[1759]**.

Supplementary

223 Transactions requiring members' approval: application of provisions to shadow directors

(1) For the purposes of—

(a) sections 188 and 189 (directors' service contracts),
(b) sections 190 to 196 (property transactions),
(c) sections 197 to 214 (loans etc), and
(d) sections 215 to 222 (payments for loss of office),

a shadow director is treated as a director.

(2) Any reference in those provisions to loss of office as a director does not apply in relation to loss of a person's status as a shadow director.

[1767]

NOTES

Commencement: 1 October 2007.

CHAPTER 5
DIRECTORS' SERVICE CONTRACTS

227 Directors' service contracts

(1) For the purposes of this Part a director's "service contract", in relation to a company, means a contract under which—

(a) a director of the company undertakes personally to perform services (as director or otherwise) for the company, or for a subsidiary of the company, or

(b) services (as director or otherwise) that a director of the company undertakes personally to perform are made available by a third party to the company, or to a subsidiary of the company.

(2) The provisions of this Part relating to directors' service contracts apply to the terms of a person's appointment as a director of a company.

They are not restricted to contracts for the performance of services outside the scope of the ordinary duties of a director.

[1768]

NOTES

Commencement: 1 October 2007.

228 Copy of contract or memorandum of terms to be available for inspection

(1) A company must keep available for inspection—

(a) a copy of every director's service contract with the company or with a subsidiary of the company, or

(b) if the contract is not in writing, a written memorandum setting out the terms of the contract.

(2) All the copies and memoranda must be kept available for inspection at—

(a) the company's registered office, or

(b) a place specified in regulations under section 1136.

(3) The copies and memoranda must be retained by the company for at least one year from the date of termination or expiry of the contract and must be kept available for inspection during that time.

(4) The company must give notice to the registrar—

(a) of the place at which the copies and memoranda are kept available for inspection, and

(b) of any change in that place,

unless they have at all times been kept at the company's registered office.

(5) If default is made in complying with subsection (1), (2) or (3), or default is made for 14 days in complying with subsection (4), an offence is committed by every officer of the company who is in default.

(6) A person guilty of an offence under this section is liable on summary conviction to a fine not exceeding level 3 on the standard scale and, for continued contravention, a daily default fine not exceeding one-tenth of level 3 on the standard scale.

(7) The provisions of this section apply to a variation of a director's service contract as they apply to the original contract.

[1769]

NOTES

Commencement: 1 October 2007.

Transitional provisions: Sch 3, para 13 to the Companies Act 2006 (Commencement No 3, Consequential Amendments, Transitional Provisions and Savings) Order 2007, SI 2007/2194 (as amended (by the substitution of the words in square brackets in para (2)) by the Companies Act 2006 (Commencement No 5, Transitional Provisions and Savings) Order 2007, SI 2007/3495, art 11, Sch 5, para 2(1), (3), as from 14 January 2008) provides as follows—

"13 Directors' service contracts (ss 227 to 230)

(1) Sections 228 to 230 of the Companies Act 2006 (directors' service contracts) apply to—

(a) contracts within section 227(1) of that Act entered into on or after 1st October 2007,

(b) appointments within section 227(2) of that Act made on or after that date, and

(c) contracts to which section 318(1) of the 1985 Act or Article 326(1) of the 1986 Order applied immediately before that date.

(2) Until regulations under section 1136 of the Companies Act 2006 [come into force] specifying a place for the purposes of section 228(2)(b), the copies and memoranda referred to in section 228 may be kept by a company—

(a) at any place where its register of members is kept, or

(b) at its principal place of business,

provided that place is situated in the part of the United Kingdom in which the company is registered.

(3) Until section 1068(1) of the Companies Act 2006 comes into force the notice referred to in section 228(4) must be given on the form prescribed for the purposes of section 318(4) of the 1985 Act or Article 326(4) of the 1986 Order.

(4) The provisions of section 318 of the 1985 Act or Article 326 of the 1986 Order continue to apply in relation to—

(a) any default before 1st October 2007 in complying with section 318(1) or (5) or Article 326(1) or (5);

(b) any request for inspection under section 318(7) or Article 326(7) made before that date;

(c) any duty to give notice under section 318(4) or Article 326(4) arising before that date.".

229 Right of member to inspect and request copy

(1) Every copy or memorandum required to be kept under section 228 must be open to inspection by any member of the company without charge.

(2) Any member of the company is entitled, on request and on payment of such fee as may be prescribed, to be provided with a copy of any such copy or memorandum.

The copy must be provided within seven days after the request is received by the company.

(3) If an inspection required under subsection (1) is refused, or default is made in complying with subsection (2), an offence is committed by every officer of the company who is in default.

(4) A person guilty of an offence under this section is liable on summary conviction to a fine not exceeding level 3 on the standard scale and, for continued contravention, a daily default fine not exceeding one-tenth of level 3 on the standard scale.

(5) In the case of any such refusal or default the court may by order compel an immediate inspection or, as the case may be, direct that the copy required be sent to the person requiring it.

[1770]

NOTES

Commencement: 20 January 2007 (for the purpose of enabling the exercise of powers to make Orders or Regulations by statutory instrument); 1 October 2007 (otherwise).

Transitional provisions: see the note to s 228 at **[1769]**.

Regulations: the Companies (Fees for Inspection and Copying of Company Records) Regulations 2007, SI 2007/2612.

230 Directors' service contracts: application of provisions to shadow directors

A shadow director is treated as a director for the purposes of the provisions of this Chapter.

[1771]

NOTES

Commencement: 1 October 2007.

Transitional provisions: see the note to s 228 at **[1769]**.

CHAPTER 7
DIRECTORS' LIABILITIES

Provision protecting directors from liability

232 Provisions protecting directors from liability

(1) Any provision that purports to exempt a director of a company (to any extent) from any liability that would otherwise attach to him in connection with any negligence, default, breach of duty or breach of trust in relation to the company is void.

(2) Any provision by which a company directly or indirectly provides an indemnity (to any extent) for a director of the company, or of an associated company, against any liability attaching to him in connection with any negligence, default, breach of duty or breach of trust in relation to the company of which he is a director is void, except as permitted by—

(a) section 233 (provision of insurance),
(b) section 234 (qualifying third party indemnity provision), or
(c) section 235 (qualifying pension scheme indemnity provision).

(3) This section applies to any provision, whether contained in a company's articles or in any contract with the company or otherwise.

(4) Nothing in this section prevents a company's articles from making such provision as has previously been lawful for dealing with conflicts of interest.

[1772]

NOTES

Commencement: 1 October 2007.
Transitional provisions: Sch 3, para 15 to the Companies Act 2006 (Commencement No 3, Consequential Amendments, Transitional Provisions and Savings) Order 2007, SI 2007/2194 provides as follows—

"Directors' liabilities (ss 232 to 239)

15.—(1) Sections 232 to 236 of the Companies Act 2006 (restrictions on provision protecting directors from liability) apply to any provision made on or after 1st October 2007.

(2) Sections 309A, 309B and 309C(1) to (3) and (6) of the 1985 Act or Article 318 of the 1986 Order (so far as it relates to directors) continue to apply in relation to any provision to which they applied immediately before that date.".

233 Provision of insurance

Section 232(2) (voidness of provisions for indemnifying directors) does not prevent a company from purchasing and maintaining for a director of the company, or of an associated company, insurance against any such liability as is mentioned in that subsection.

[1773]

NOTES

Commencement: 1 October 2007.
Transitional provisions: see the note to s 232 at **[1772]**.

234 Qualifying third party indemnity provision

(1) Section 232(2) (voidness of provisions for indemnifying directors) does not apply to qualifying third party indemnity provision.

(2) Third party indemnity provision means provision for indemnity against liability incurred by the director to a person other than the company or an associated company.

Such provision is qualifying third party indemnity provision if the following requirements are met.

(3) The provision must not provide any indemnity against—

(a) any liability of the director to pay—
  (i) a fine imposed in criminal proceedings, or

(ii) a sum payable to a regulatory authority by way of a penalty in respect of non-compliance with any requirement of a regulatory nature (however arising); or

(b) any liability incurred by the director—

(i) in defending criminal proceedings in which he is convicted, or

(ii) in defending civil proceedings brought by the company, or an associated company, in which judgment is given against him, or

(iii) in connection with an application for relief (see subsection (6)) in which the court refuses to grant him relief.

(4) The references in subsection (3)(b) to a conviction, judgment or refusal of relief are to the final decision in the proceedings.

(5) For this purpose—

(a) a conviction, judgment or refusal of relief becomes final—

(i) if not appealed against, at the end of the period for bringing an appeal, or

(ii) if appealed against, at the time when the appeal (or any further appeal) is disposed of; and

(b) an appeal is disposed of—

(i) if it is determined and the period for bringing any further appeal has ended, or

(ii) if it is abandoned or otherwise ceases to have effect.

(6) The reference in subsection (3)(b)(iii) to an application for relief is to an application for relief under—

section 661(3) or (4) (power of court to grant relief in case of acquisition of shares by innocent nominee), or

section 1157 (general power of court to grant relief in case of honest and reasonable conduct).

[1774]

NOTES

Commencement: 1 October 2007.

Transitional provisions: see the note to s 232 at **[1772]**.

Transitional adaptations: art 6 of the Companies Act 2006 (Commencement No 3, Consequential Amendments, Transitional Provisions and Savings) Order 2007, SI 2007/2194 provides that the provisions brought into force by that Order shall have effect subject to any transitional adaptations specified in Sch 1 to that Order. Schedule 1, para 12 to the Order provides as follows (note, however, that para 12 is revoked by the Companies Act 2006 (Commencement No 5, Transitional Provisions and Savings) Order 2007, SI 2007/3495, art 10(2), (3), as from 1 October 2008 (subject to any transitional provisions and savings as apply, in accordance with Sch 4 to that Order, in relation to the repeal of the provisions of the 1985 Act referred to in the adaptation; see art 10 thereto), and is also revoked by virtue of the Companies Act 2006 (Commencement No 6, Saving and Commencement Nos 3 and 5 (Amendment)) Order 2008, SI 2008/674, art 5, Sch 3, para 1(1)(a), as from the same date))—

"12 Directors' liabilities (ss 232 to 239)

(1) Section 234 (qualifying third party indemnity provision) has effect with the following adaptation.

(2) In subsection (6), for the words from "section 661(3)" to the end substitute—

"section 144(3) or (4) of the Companies Act 1985 or Article 154(3) or (4) of the Companies (Northern Ireland) Order 1986 (acquisition of shares by innocent nominee), or

section 727 of the Companies Act 1985 or Article 675 of the Companies (Northern Ireland) Order 1986 (general power to grant relief in case of honest and reasonable conduct).".".

The Companies Act 2006 (Commencement No 6, Saving and Commencement Nos 3 and 5 (Amendment)) Order 2008, SI 2008/674, art 5, Sch 3, para 1(1)(b) provides that this section shall have effect with the transitional adaptation provided for in Sch 3, para 1(2). That sub-paragraph reads as follows—

"(2) In section 205(5) and section 234(6), for the words from "section 661(3)" to "innocent nominee)" substitute "section 144(3) or (4) of the Companies Act 1985 or Article 154(3) or (4) of the Companies (Northern Ireland) Order 1986 (acquisition of shares by innocent nominee)".".

Note that the above transitional adaptation replaces the transitional adaptation contained in the Companies Act 2006 (Commencement No 5, Transitional Provisions and Savings) Order 2007, SI 2007/3495, Sch 1, para 2, which was due to come into force on 6 April 2008. That paragraph was also revoked by SI 2008/674, art 5, Sch 3, para 5, as from 6 April 2008.

235 Qualifying pension scheme indemnity provision

(1) Section 232(2) (voidness of provisions for indemnifying directors) does not apply to qualifying pension scheme indemnity provision.

(2) Pension scheme indemnity provision means provision indemnifying a director of a company that is a trustee of an occupational pension scheme against liability incurred in connection with the company's activities as trustee of the scheme.

Such provision is qualifying pension scheme indemnity provision if the following requirements are met.

(3) The provision must not provide any indemnity against—

(a) any liability of the director to pay—
  (i) a fine imposed in criminal proceedings, or
  (ii) a sum payable to a regulatory authority by way of a penalty in respect of non-compliance with any requirement of a regulatory nature (however arising); or

(b) any liability incurred by the director in defending criminal proceedings in which he is convicted.

(4) The reference in subsection (3)(b) to a conviction is to the final decision in the proceedings.

(5) For this purpose—

(a) a conviction becomes final—
  (i) if not appealed against, at the end of the period for bringing an appeal, or
  (ii) if appealed against, at the time when the appeal (or any further appeal) is disposed of; and

(b) an appeal is disposed of—
  (i) if it is determined and the period for bringing any further appeal has ended, or
  (ii) if it is abandoned or otherwise ceases to have effect.

(6) In this section "occupational pension scheme" means an occupational pension scheme as defined in section 150(5) of the Finance Act 2004 (c 12) that is established under a trust.

[1774A]

NOTES

Commencement: 1 October 2007.
Transitional provisions: see the note to s 232 at **[1772]**.

236 Qualifying indemnity provision to be disclosed in directors' report

(1) This section requires disclosure in the directors' report of—

(a) qualifying third party indemnity provision, and
(b) qualifying pension scheme indemnity provision.

Such provision is referred to in this section as "qualifying indemnity provision".

(2) If when a directors' report is approved any qualifying indemnity provision (whether made by the company or otherwise) is in force for the benefit of one or more directors of the company, the report must state that such provision is in force.

(3) If at any time during the financial year to which a directors' report relates any such provision was in force for the benefit of one or more persons who were then directors of the company, the report must state that such provision was in force.

(4) If when a directors' report is approved qualifying indemnity provision made by the company is in force for the benefit of one or more directors of an associated company, the report must state that such provision is in force.

(5) If at any time during the financial year to which a directors' report relates any such provision was in force for the benefit of one or more persons who were then directors of an associated company, the report must state that such provision was in force.

[1774B]

NOTES

Commencement: 1 October 2007.

Transitional provisions: see the note to s 232 at **[1772]**.

CHAPTER 9
SUPPLEMENTARY PROVISIONS

Provision for employees on cessation or transfer of business

247 Power to make provision for employees on cessation or transfer of business

(1) The powers of the directors of a company include (if they would not otherwise do so) power to make provision for the benefit of persons employed or formerly employed by the company, or any of its subsidiaries, in connection with the cessation or the transfer to any person of the whole or part of the undertaking of the company or that subsidiary.

(2) This power is exercisable notwithstanding the general duty imposed by section 172 (duty to promote the success of the company).

(3) In the case of a company that is a charity it is exercisable notwithstanding any restrictions on the directors' powers (or the company's capacity) flowing from the objects of the company.

(4) The power may only be exercised if sanctioned—

(a) by a resolution of the company, or

(b) by a resolution of the directors,

in accordance with the following provisions.

(5) A resolution of the directors—

(a) must be authorised by the company's articles, and

(b) is not sufficient sanction for payments to or for the benefit of directors, former directors or shadow directors.

(6) Any other requirements of the company's articles as to the exercise of the power conferred by this section must be complied with.

(7) Any payment under this section must be made—

(a) before the commencement of any winding up of the company, and

(b) out of profits of the company that are available for dividend.

[1775]

NOTES

Commencement: to be appointed.

Note: the Companies Act 2006 (Commencement No 3, Consequential Amendments, Transitional Provisions and Savings) Order 2007, SI 2007/2194, art 2(1)(d) originally provided that this section would come into force on 1 October 2007 (subject to transitional provisions in Sch 3, para 18 to that Order). Article 2(1)(d) was subsequently amended by the Companies Act 2006 (Commencement No 4 and Commencement No 3 (Amendment)) Order 2007, SI 2007/2607, art 4(1) (with effect from 30 September 2007) so that the commencement of this section on 1 October 2007 was reversed. The transitional provisions in Sch 3, para 18 were revoked at the same time.

PART 15
ACCOUNTS AND REPORTS

CHAPTER 5
DIRECTORS' REPORT

Directors' report

416 Contents of directors' report: general

(1) The directors' report for a financial year must state—

(a) the names of the persons who, at any time during the financial year, were directors of the company, and

(b) the principal activities of the company in the course of the year.

(2) In relation to a group directors' report subsection (1)(b) has effect as if the reference to the company was to the undertakings included in the consolidation.

(3) Except in the case of a company [entitled to the small companies exemption], the report must state the amount (if any) that the directors recommend should be paid by way of dividend.

(4) The Secretary of State may make provision by regulations as to other matters that must be disclosed in a directors' report.

Without prejudice to the generality of this power, the regulations may make any such provision as was formerly made by Schedule 7 to the Companies Act 1985.

[1776]

NOTES

Commencement: 20 January 2007 (for the purpose of enabling the exercise of powers to make Orders or Regulations by statutory instrument); 6 April 2008 (otherwise).

Sub-s (3): words in square brackets substituted by the Companies Act 2006 (Amendment) (Accounts and Reports) Regulations 2008, SI 2008/393, reg 6(3), as from 6 April 2008, in relation to financial years beginning on or after that date.

Transitional provisions: Sch 4, Pt 1, para 6 to the Companies Act 2006 (Commencement No 5, Transitional Provisions and Savings) Order 2007, SI 2007/3495 provides as follows—

"*Accounts and reports* (*ss 380 to 389, 393 to 416, 418 to 462 and 464 to 474*)

6.—(1) Sections 380 to 389, 393 to 416, 418 to 462 and 464 to 474 of the Companies Act 2006 (accounts and reports) apply to accounts and reports for financial years beginning on or after 6th April 2008.

(2) The corresponding provisions of the 1985 Act or the 1986 Order continue to apply to accounts and reports for financial years beginning before that date.".

Regulations: the Small Companies and Groups (Accounts and Directors' Report) Regulations 2008, SI 2008/409; the Large and Medium-sized Companies and Groups (Accounts and Reports) Regulations 2008, SI 2008/410.

CHAPTER 6
QUOTED COMPANIES: DIRECTORS' REMUNERATION REPORT

420 Duty to prepare directors' remuneration report

(1) The directors of a quoted company must prepare a directors' remuneration report for each financial year of the company.

(2) In the case of failure to comply with the requirement to prepare a directors' remuneration report, every person who—

(a) was a director of the company immediately before the end of the period for filing accounts and reports for the financial year in question, and

(b) failed to take all reasonable steps for securing compliance with that requirement,

commits an offence.

(3) A person guilty of an offence under this section is liable—

(a) on conviction on indictment, to a fine;

(b) on summary conviction, to a fine not exceeding the statutory maximum.

[1777]

NOTES

Commencement: 6 April 2008.

Transitional provisions: see the note to s 416 at **[1776]**.

421 Contents of directors' remuneration report

(1) The Secretary of State may make provision by regulations as to—

(a) the information that must be contained in a directors' remuneration report,

(b) how information is to be set out in the report, and

(c) what is to be the auditable part of the report.

(2) Without prejudice to the generality of this power, the regulations may make any such provision as was made, immediately before the commencement of this Part, by Schedule 7A to the Companies Act 1985 (c 6).

(3) It is the duty of—
(a) any director of a company, and
(b) any person who is or has at any time in the preceding five years been a director of the company,

to give notice to the company of such matters relating to himself as may be necessary for the purposes of regulations under this section.

(4) A person who makes default in complying with subsection (3) commits an offence and is liable on summary conviction to a fine not exceeding level 3 on the standard scale.

[1778]

NOTES

Commencement: 6 April 2008.
Transitional provisions: see the note to s 416 at **[1776]**.
Regulations: the Large and Medium-sized Companies and Groups (Accounts and Reports) Regulations 2008, SI 2008/410.

422 Approval and signing of directors' remuneration report

(1) The directors' remuneration report must be approved by the board of directors and signed on behalf of the board by a director or the secretary of the company.

(2) If a directors' remuneration report is approved that does not comply with the requirements of this Act, every director of the company who—
(a) knew that it did not comply, or was reckless as to whether it complied, and
(b) failed to take reasonable steps to secure compliance with those requirements or, as the case may be, to prevent the report from being approved,

commits an offence.

(3) A person guilty of an offence under this section is liable—
(a) on conviction on indictment, to a fine;
(b) on summary conviction, to a fine not exceeding the statutory maximum.

[1779]

NOTES

Commencement: 6 April 2008.
Transitional provisions: see the note to s 416 at **[1776]**.

PART 47
FINAL PROVISIONS

1298 Short title

The short title of this Act is the Companies Act 2006.

[1780]

NOTES

Commencement: 8 November 2006.

1299 Extent

Except as otherwise provided (or the context otherwise requires), the provisions of this Act extend to the whole of the United Kingdom.

[1781]

NOTES

Commencement: 8 November 2006.

1300 Commencement

(1) The following provisions come into force on the day this Act is passed—

(a) Part 43 (transparency obligations and related matters), except the amendment in paragraph 11(2) of Schedule 15 of the definition of "regulated market" in Part 6 of the Financial Services and Markets Act 2000 (c 8),

(b) in Part 44 (miscellaneous provisions)—
section 1274 (grants to bodies concerned with actuarial standards etc), and
section 1276 (application of provisions to Scotland and Northern Ireland),

(c) Part 46 (general supplementary provisions), except section 1295 and Schedule 16 (repeals), and

(d) this Part.

(2) The other provisions of this Act come into force on such day as may be appointed by order of the Secretary of State or the Treasury.

[1782]

NOTES

Commencement: 8 November 2006.

Orders: the Companies Act 2006 (Commencement No 1, Transitional Provisions and Savings) Order 2006, SI 2006/3428; the Companies Act 2006 (Commencement No 2, Consequential Amendments, Transitional Provisions and Savings) Order 2007, SI 2007/1093; the Companies Act 2006 (Commencement No 3, Consequential Amendments, Transitional Provisions and Savings) Order 2007, SI 2007/2194; the Companies Act 2006 (Commencement No 4 and Commencement No 3 (Amendment)) Order 2007, SI 2007/2607; the Companies Act 2006 (Commencement No 5, Transitional Provisions and Savings) Order 2007, SI 2007/3495; the Companies Act 2006 (Commencement No 6, Saving and Commencement Nos 3 and 5 (Amendment)) Order 2008, SI 2008/674.

LEGISLATIVE AND REGULATORY REFORM ACT 2006

(2006 c 51)

An Act to enable provision to be made for the purpose of removing or reducing burdens resulting from legislation and promoting regulatory principles; to make provision about the exercise of regulatory functions; to make provision about the interpretation of legislation relating to the European Communities and the European Economic Area; to make provision relating to section 2(2) of the European Communities Act 1972; and for connected purposes

[8 November 2006]

NOTES

Only those provisions of this Act relevant to employment law are reproduced. Provisions not reproduced are not annotated. The provisions reproduced here extend to the whole of the United Kingdom (s 34) and the entire Act came into force on 8 January 2007 (s 33).

PART 2
REGULATORS

Exercise of regulatory functions

21 Principles

(1) Any person exercising a regulatory function to which this section applies must have regard to the principles in subsection (2) in the exercise of the function.

(2) Those principles are that—

(a) regulatory activities should be carried out in a way which is transparent, accountable, proportionate and consistent;

(b) regulatory activities should be targeted only at cases in which action is needed.

(3) The duty in subsection (1) is subject to any other requirement affecting the exercise of the regulatory function.

[1783]

NOTES
Commencement: 8 January 2007.

22 Code of practice

(1) A Minister of the Crown may issue and from time to time revise a code of practice in relation to the exercise of regulatory functions.

(2) Any person exercising a regulatory function to which this section applies must, except in a case where subsection (3) applies, have regard to the code in determining any general policy or principles by reference to which the person exercises the function.

(3) Any person exercising a regulatory function to which this section applies which is a function of setting standards or giving guidance generally in relation to the exercise of other regulatory functions must have regard to the code in the exercise of the function.

(4) The duties in subsections (2) and (3) are subject to any other requirement affecting the exercise of the regulatory function.

[1784]

NOTES
Commencement: 8 January 2007.

23 Code of practice: procedure

(1) Where a Minister of the Crown proposes to issue or revise a code of practice under section 22, he shall prepare a draft of the code (or revised code).

(2) The Minister shall, in preparing the draft, seek to secure that it is consistent with the principles specified in section 21(2).

(3) The Minister shall consult the following about the draft—
(a) persons appearing to him to be representative of persons exercising regulatory functions;
(b) such other persons as he considers appropriate.

(4) If the Minister determines to proceed with the draft (either in its original form or with modifications) he shall lay the draft before Parliament.

(5) Where the draft laid before Parliament under subsection (4) is approved by resolution of each House of Parliament, the Minister may issue the code (or revised code).

(6) A code (or revised code) issued under subsection (5) shall come into force on such date as the Minister may by order made by statutory instrument appoint.

[1785]

NOTES
Commencement: 8 January 2007.
Orders: the Legislative and Regulatory Reform Code of Practice (Appointed Day) Order 2007, SI 2007/3548.

24 Functions to which sections 21 and 22 apply

(1) Sections 21 and 22 apply to regulatory functions specified under this section.

(2) A Minister of the Crown may by order in accordance with this section specify regulatory functions as functions to which sections 21 and 22 apply.

(3) A Minister may not under subsection (2) specify—
(a) a regulatory function so far as exercisable in Scotland, if or to the extent that the function relates to matters which are not reserved matters;
(b) a regulatory function so far as exercisable in Northern Ireland, if or to the extent that the function relates to matters which are transferred matters; or
(c) a regulatory function exercisable only in or as regards Wales.

(4) [The Welsh Ministers] may by order in accordance with this section specify regulatory functions exercisable only in or as regards Wales as functions to which sections 21 and 22 apply.

(5) An order under this section may not specify regulatory functions conferred on or exercisable by any of the following—

(a) the Gas and Electricity Markets Authority;
(b) the Office of Communications;
(c) the Office of Rail Regulation;
(d) the Postal Services Commission;
(e) the Water Services Regulation Authority.

(6) Before making an order under this section, the authority making the order must consult the following—

(a) any person (other than the authority) whose functions are to be specified in the order;
(b) such other persons as the authority considers appropriate.

(7) An order under this section may make such consequential, supplementary, incidental, or transitional provision (including provision amending any enactment) as the authority making it considers appropriate; and may make different provision for different purposes.

(8) An order under this section must be made by statutory instrument.

(9) A Minister of the Crown may not make a statutory instrument containing an order under this section unless a draft has been laid before, and approved by resolution of, each House of Parliament.

[(9A) The Welsh Ministers may not make a statutory instrument containing an order under this section unless a draft has been laid before, and approved by resolution of, the Assembly.]

(10) In this section—

"reserved matter" and "Scotland" have the same meanings as in the Scotland Act 1998 (c 46);

"transferred matter" and "Northern Ireland" have the same meanings as in the Northern Ireland Act 1998 (c 47);

"Wales" has the same meaning as in the [Government of Wales Act 2006].

[1786]

NOTES

Commencement: 8 January 2007.

Sub-ss (4), (10): words in square brackets substituted by the Government of Wales Act 2006 (Consequential Modifications and Transitional Provisions) Order 2007, SI 2007/1388, art 3, Sch 1, paras 143, 148(a), (c), as from 25 May 2007.

Sub-s (9A): inserted by SI 2007/1388, art 3, Sch 1, paras 143, 148(b), as from 25 May 2007.

Orders: the Legislative and Regulatory Reform (Regulatory Functions) Order 2007, SI 2007/3544

CORPORATE MANSLAUGHTER AND CORPORATE HOMICIDE ACT 2007

(2007 c 19)

ARRANGEMENT OF SECTIONS

Corporate manslaughter and corporate homicide

Relevant duty of care

Gross breach

Remedial orders and publicity orders

Application to particular categories of organisation

Miscellaneous

General and supplemental

SCHEDULES:

An Act to create a new offence that, in England and Wales or Northern Ireland, is to be called corporate manslaughter and, in Scotland, is to be called corporate homicide; and to make provision in connection with that offence

[26 July 2007]

Corporate manslaughter and corporate homicide

1 The offence

(1) An organisation to which this section applies is guilty of an offence if the way in which its activities are managed or organised—

(a) causes a person's death, and

(b) amounts to a gross breach of a relevant duty of care owed by the organisation to the deceased.

(2) The organisations to which this section applies are—

(a) a corporation;

(b) a department or other body listed in Schedule 1;

(c) a police force;

(d) a partnership, or a trade union or employers' association, that is an employer.

(3) An organisation is guilty of an offence under this section only if the way in which its activities are managed or organised by its senior management is a substantial element in the breach referred to in subsection (1).

(4) For the purposes of this Act—

(a) "relevant duty of care" has the meaning given by section 2, read with sections 3 to 7;

(b) a breach of a duty of care by an organisation is a "gross" breach if the conduct alleged to amount to a breach of that duty falls far below what can reasonably be expected of the organisation in the circumstances;

(c) "senior management", in relation to an organisation, means the persons who play significant roles in—

(i) the making of decisions about how the whole or a substantial part of its activities are to be managed or organised, or

(ii) the actual managing or organising of the whole or a substantial part of those activities.

(5) The offence under this section is called—

(a) corporate manslaughter, in so far as it is an offence under the law of England and Wales or Northern Ireland;

(b) corporate homicide, in so far as it is an offence under the law of Scotland.

(6) An organisation that is guilty of corporate manslaughter or corporate homicide is liable on conviction on indictment to a fine.

(7) The offence of corporate homicide is indictable only in the High Court of Justiciary. **[1787]**

NOTES

Commencement: 6 April 2008 (except in relation to anything done or omitted before that date; see s 27(3) *post*).

Relevant duty of care

2 Meaning of "relevant duty of care"

(1) A "relevant duty of care", in relation to an organisation, means any of the following duties owed by it under the law of negligence—

(a) a duty owed to its employees or to other persons working for the organisation or performing services for it;

(b) a duty owed as occupier of premises;

(c) a duty owed in connection with—

(i) the supply by the organisation of goods or services (whether for consideration or not),

(ii) the carrying on by the organisation of any construction or maintenance operations,

(iii) the carrying on by the organisation of any other activity on a commercial basis, or

(iv) the use or keeping by the organisation of any plant, vehicle or other thing;

(d) a duty owed to a person who, by reason of being a person within subsection (2), is someone for whose safety the organisation is responsible.

(2) A person is within this subsection if—

(a) he is detained at a custodial institution or in a custody area at a court or police station;

(b) he is detained at a removal centre or short-term holding facility;

(c) he is being transported in a vehicle, or being held in any premises, in pursuance of prison escort arrangements or immigration escort arrangements;

(d) he is living in secure accommodation in which he has been placed;

(e) he is a detained patient.

(3) Subsection (1) is subject to sections 3 to 7.

(4) A reference in subsection (1) to a duty owed under the law of negligence includes a reference to a duty that would be owed under the law of negligence but for any statutory provision under which liability is imposed in place of liability under that law.

(5) For the purposes of this Act, whether a particular organisation owes a duty of care to a particular individual is a question of law.

The judge must make any findings of fact necessary to decide that question.

(6) For the purposes of this Act there is to be disregarded—

(a) any rule of the common law that has the effect of preventing a duty of care from being owed by one person to another by reason of the fact that they are jointly engaged in unlawful conduct;

(b) any such rule that has the effect of preventing a duty of care from being owed to a person by reason of his acceptance of a risk of harm.

(7) In this section—

"construction or maintenance operations" means operations of any of the following descriptions—

(a) construction, installation, alteration, extension, improvement, repair, maintenance, decoration, cleaning, demolition or dismantling of—

(i) any building or structure,

(ii) anything else that forms, or is to form, part of the land, or

(iii) any plant, vehicle or other thing;

(b) operations that form an integral part of, or are preparatory to, or are for rendering complete, any operations within paragraph (a);

"custodial institution" means a prison, a young offender institution, a secure training centre, a young offenders institution, a young offenders centre, a juvenile justice centre or a remand centre;

"detained patient" means—

(a) a person who is detained in any premises under—

(i) Part 2 or 3 of the Mental Health Act 1983 (c 20) ("the 1983 Act"), or

(ii) Part 2 or 3 of the Mental Health (Northern Ireland) Order 1986 (SI 1986/595 (NI 4)) ("the 1986 Order");

(b) a person who (otherwise than by reason of being detained as mentioned in paragraph (a)) is deemed to be in legal custody by—

(i) section 137 of the 1983 Act,

(ii) Article 131 of the 1986 Order, or

(iii) article 11 of the Mental Health (Care and Treatment) (Scotland) Act 2003 (Consequential Provisions) Order 2005 (SI 2005/2078);

(c) a person who is detained in any premises, or is otherwise in custody, under the Mental Health (Care and Treatment) (Scotland) Act 2003 (asp 13) or Part 6 of the Criminal Procedure (Scotland) Act 1995 (c 46) or who is detained in a hospital under section 200 of that Act of 1995;

"immigration escort arrangements" means arrangements made under section 156 of the Immigration and Asylum Act 1999 (c 33);

"the law of negligence" includes—

(a) in relation to England and Wales, the Occupiers' Liability Act 1957 (c 31), the Defective Premises Act 1972 (c 35) and the Occupiers' Liability Act 1984 (c 3);

(b) in relation to Scotland, the Occupiers' Liability (Scotland) Act 1960 (c 30);

(c) in relation to Northern Ireland, the Occupiers' Liability Act (Northern Ireland) 1957 (c 25), the Defective Premises (Northern Ireland) Order 1975 (SI 1975/1039 (NI 9)), the Occupiers' Liability (Northern Ireland) Order 1987 (SI 1987/1280 (NI 15)) and the Defective Premises (Landlord's Liability) Act (Northern Ireland) 2001 (c 10);

"prison escort arrangements" means arrangements made under section 80 of the Criminal Justice Act 1991 (c 53) or under section 102 or 118 of the Criminal Justice and Public Order Act 1994 (c 33);

"removal centre" and "short-term holding facility" have the meaning given by section 147 of the Immigration and Asylum Act 1999;

"secure accommodation" means accommodation, not consisting of or forming part of a custodial institution, provided for the purpose of restricting the liberty of persons under the age of 18.

[1788]

NOTES

Commencement: 6 April 2008 (sub-ss (1)(a)–(c), (2)–(7)); to be appointed (otherwise).

Transitional provisions: the Corporate Manslaughter and Corporate Homicide Act 2007 (Commencement No 1) Order 2008, art 2 provides as follows—

"2.—(1) Apart from the provisions mentioned in paragraph (2), the Corporate Manslaughter and Corporate Homicide Act 2007 shall, to the extent that it is not already in force, come into force on 6th April 2008.

(2) Those provisions are—
(a) section 2(1)(d) (duty owed to a person in custody etc to be a relevant duty of care);
(b) section 10 (power to order conviction etc to be publicised).

(3) In relation to anything done or omitted before section 2(1)(d) comes into force—
(a) section 20 (abolition of the common law offence of manslaughter by gross negligence in its application to corporations and other organisations) does not apply to an offence committed by the breach of any such duty as is referred to in section 2(1)(d);
(b) section 2 has effect with the omission of—
(i) subsection (2), and
(ii) the definitions in subsection (7) of expressions used in subsection (2),
except that those provisions have effect for the purposes of paragraph (a) above.
(c) sections 3(2), 5(3) and 7(1) have effect as if "section 2(1)(a) or (b)" were substituted for "section 2(1)(a), (b) or (d)".".

3 Public policy decisions, exclusively public functions and statutory inspections

(1) Any duty of care owed by a public authority in respect of a decision as to matters of public policy (including in particular the allocation of public resources or the weighing of competing public interests) is not a "relevant duty of care".

(2) Any duty of care owed in respect of things done in the exercise of an exclusively public function is not a "relevant duty of care" unless it falls within section 2(1)(a), (b) or (d).

(3) Any duty of care owed by a public authority in respect of inspections carried out in the exercise of a statutory function is not a "relevant duty of care" unless it falls within section 2(1)(a) or (b).

(4) In this section—

"exclusively public function" means a function that falls within the prerogative of the Crown or is, by its nature, exercisable only with authority conferred—
(a) by the exercise of that prerogative, or
(b) by or under a statutory provision;

"statutory function" means a function conferred by or under a statutory provision.

[1789]

NOTES

Commencement: 6 April 2008.
Transitional provisions: see the note to s 2 at **[1788]**.

4 Military activities

(1) Any duty of care owed by the Ministry of Defence in respect of—
(a) operations within subsection (2),
(b) activities carried on in preparation for, or directly in support of, such operations, or
(c) training of a hazardous nature, or training carried out in a hazardous way, which it is considered needs to be carried out, or carried out in that way, in order to improve or maintain the effectiveness of the armed forces with respect to such operations,

is not a "relevant duty of care".

(2) The operations within this subsection are operations, including peacekeeping operations and operations for dealing with terrorism, civil unrest or serious public disorder, in the course of which members of the armed forces come under attack or face the threat of attack or violent resistance.

(3) Any duty of care owed by the Ministry of Defence in respect of activities carried on by members of the special forces is not a "relevant duty of care".

(4) In this section "the special forces" means those units of the armed forces the maintenance of whose capabilities is the responsibility of the Director of Special Forces or which are for the time being subject to the operational command of that Director.

[1790]

NOTES
Commencement: 6 April 2008.

5 Policing and law enforcement

(1) Any duty of care owed by a public authority in respect of—
(a) operations within subsection (2),
(b) activities carried on in preparation for, or directly in support of, such operations, or
(c) training of a hazardous nature, or training carried out in a hazardous way, which it is considered needs to be carried out, or carried out in that way, in order to improve or maintain the effectiveness of officers or employees of the public authority with respect to such operations,

is not a "relevant duty of care".

(2) Operations are within this subsection if—
(a) they are operations for dealing with terrorism, civil unrest or serious disorder,
(b) they involve the carrying on of policing or law-enforcement activities, and
(c) officers or employees of the public authority in question come under attack, or face the threat of attack or violent resistance, in the course of the operations.

(3) Any duty of care owed by a public authority in respect of other policing or law-enforcement activities is not a "relevant duty of care" unless it falls within section 2(1)(a), (b) or (d).

(4) In this section "policing or law-enforcement activities" includes—
(a) activities carried on in the exercise of functions that are—
(i) functions of police forces, or
(ii) functions of the same or a similar nature exercisable by public authorities other than police forces;
(b) activities carried on in the exercise of functions of constables employed by a public authority;
(c) activities carried on in the exercise of functions exercisable under Chapter 4 of Part 2 of the Serious Organised Crime and Police Act 2005 (c 15) (protection of witnesses and other persons);
(d) activities carried on to enforce any provision contained in or made under the Immigration Acts.

[1791]

NOTES
Commencement: 6 April 2008.
Transitional provisions: see the note to s 2 at **[1788]**.

6 Emergencies

(1) Any duty of care owed by an organisation within subsection (2) in respect of the way in which it responds to emergency circumstances is not a "relevant duty of care" unless it falls within section 2(1)(a) or (b).

(2) The organisations within this subsection are—
(a) a fire and rescue authority in England and Wales;
(b) a fire and rescue authority or joint fire and rescue board in Scotland;
(c) the Northern Ireland Fire and Rescue Service Board;
(d) any other organisation providing a service of responding to emergency circumstances either—
(i) in pursuance of arrangements made with an organisation within paragraph (a), (b) or (c), or
(ii) (if not in pursuance of such arrangements) otherwise than on a commercial basis;
(e) a relevant NHS body;
(f) an organisation providing ambulance services in pursuance of arrangements—
(i) made by, or at the request of, a relevant NHS body, or
(ii) made with the Secretary of State or with the Welsh Ministers;

(g) an organisation providing services for the transport of organs, blood, equipment or personnel in pursuance of arrangements of the kind mentioned in paragraph (f);

(h) an organisation providing a rescue service;

(i) the armed forces.

(3) For the purposes of subsection (1), the way in which an organisation responds to emergency circumstances does not include the way in which—

(a) medical treatment is carried out, or

(b) decisions within subsection (4) are made.

(4) The decisions within this subsection are decisions as to the carrying out of medical treatment, other than decisions as to the order in which persons are to be given such treatment.

(5) Any duty of care owed in respect of the carrying out, or attempted carrying out, of a rescue operation at sea in emergency circumstances is not a "relevant duty of care" unless it falls within section 2(1)(a) or (b).

(6) Any duty of care owed in respect of action taken—

(a) in order to comply with a direction under Schedule 3A to the Merchant Shipping Act 1995 (c 21) (safety directions), or

(b) by virtue of paragraph 4 of that Schedule (action in lieu of direction),

is not a "relevant duty of care" unless it falls within section 2(1)(a) or (b).

(7) In this section—

"emergency circumstances" means circumstances that are present or imminent and—

(a) are causing, or are likely to cause, serious harm or a worsening of such harm, or

(b) are likely to cause the death of a person;

"medical treatment" includes any treatment or procedure of a medical or similar nature;

"relevant NHS body" means—

(a) a Strategic Health Authority, Primary Care Trust, NHS trust, Special Health Authority or NHS foundation trust in England;

(b) a Local Health Board, NHS trust or Special Health Authority in Wales;

(c) a Health Board or Special Health Board in Scotland, or the Common Services Agency for the Scottish Health Service;

(d) a Health and Social Services trust or Health and Social Services Board in Northern Ireland;

"serious harm" means—

(a) serious injury to or the serious illness (including mental illness) of a person;

(b) serious harm to the environment (including the life and health of plants and animals);

(c) serious harm to any building or other property.

(8) A reference in this section to emergency circumstances includes a reference to circumstances that are believed to be emergency circumstances.

[1792]

NOTES

Commencement: 6 April 2008.

7 Child-protection and probation functions

(1) A duty of care to which this section applies is not a "relevant duty of care" unless it falls within section 2(1)(a), (b) or (d).

(2) This section applies to any duty of care that a local authority or other public authority owes in respect of the exercise by it of functions conferred by or under—

(a) Parts 4 and 5 of the Children Act 1989 (c 41),

(b) Part 2 of the Children (Scotland) Act 1995 (c 36), or

(c) Parts 5 and 6 of the Children (Northern Ireland) Order 1995 (SI 1995/755 (NI 2)).

(3) This section also applies to any duty of care that a local probation board[, a provider of probation services] or other public authority owes in respect of the exercise by it of functions conferred by or under—

(a) Chapter 1 of Part 1 of the Criminal Justice and Court Services Act 2000 (c 43),

[(aa) section 13 of the Offender Management Act 2007 (c 21),]

(b) section 27 of the Social Work (Scotland) Act 1968 (c 49), or

(c) Article 4 of the Probation Board (Northern Ireland) Order 1982 (SI 1982/713 (NI 10)).

[(4) This section also applies to any duty of care that a provider of probation services owes in respect of the carrying out by it of activities in pursuance of arrangements under section 3 of the Offender Management Act 2007.]

[1793]

NOTES

Commencement: 6 April 2008.

Sub-s (3): words in first pair of square brackets and para (aa) inserted by the Offender Management Act 2007 (Consequential Amendments) Order 2008, SI 2008/912, art 3, Sch 1, Pt 1, para 25(1), (2)(a), as from 1 April 2008.

Sub-s (4): added by SI 2008/912, art 3, Sch 1, Pt 1, para 25(1), (2)(b), as from 1 April 2008.

Transitional provisions: see the note to s 2 at **[1788]**.

Gross breach

8 Factors for jury

(1) This section applies where—

(a) it is established that an organisation owed a relevant duty of care to a person, and

(b) it falls to the jury to decide whether there was a gross breach of that duty.

(2) The jury must consider whether the evidence shows that the organisation failed to comply with any health and safety legislation that relates to the alleged breach, and if so—

(a) how serious that failure was;

(b) how much of a risk of death it posed.

(3) The jury may also—

(a) consider the extent to which the evidence shows that there were attitudes, policies, systems or accepted practices within the organisation that were likely to have encouraged any such failure as is mentioned in subsection (2), or to have produced tolerance of it;

(b) have regard to any health and safety guidance that relates to the alleged breach.

(4) This section does not prevent the jury from having regard to any other matters they consider relevant.

(5) In this section "health and safety guidance" means any code, guidance, manual or similar publication that is concerned with health and safety matters and is made or issued (under a statutory provision or otherwise) by an authority responsible for the enforcement of any health and safety legislation.

[1794]

NOTES

Commencement: 6 April 2008.

Remedial orders and publicity orders

9 Power to order breach etc to be remedied

(1) A court before which an organisation is convicted of corporate manslaughter or corporate homicide may make an order (a "remedial order") requiring the organisation to take specified steps to remedy—

(a) the breach mentioned in section 1(1) ("the relevant breach");

(b) any matter that appears to the court to have resulted from the relevant breach and to have been a cause of the death;

(c) any deficiency, as regards health and safety matters, in the organisation's policies, systems or practices of which the relevant breach appears to the court to be an indication.

(2) A remedial order may be made only on an application by the prosecution specifying the terms of the proposed order.

Any such order must be on such terms (whether those proposed or others) as the court considers appropriate having regard to any representations made, and any evidence adduced, in relation to that matter by the prosecution or on behalf of the organisation.

(3) Before making an application for a remedial order the prosecution must consult such enforcement authority or authorities as it considers appropriate having regard to the nature of the relevant breach.

(4) A remedial order—

(a) must specify a period within which the steps referred to in subsection (1) are to be taken;

(b) may require the organisation to supply to an enforcement authority consulted under subsection (3), within a specified period, evidence that those steps have been taken.

A period specified under this subsection may be extended or further extended by order of the court on an application made before the end of that period or extended period.

(5) An organisation that fails to comply with a remedial order is guilty of an offence, and liable on conviction on indictment to a fine.

[1795]

NOTES

Commencement: 6 April 2008.

10 Power to order conviction etc to be publicised

(1) A court before which an organisation is convicted of corporate manslaughter or corporate homicide may make an order (a "publicity order") requiring the organisation to publicise in a specified manner—

(a) the fact that it has been convicted of the offence;

(b) specified particulars of the offence;

(c) the amount of any fine imposed;

(d) the terms of any remedial order made.

(2) In deciding on the terms of a publicity order that it is proposing to make, the court must—

(a) ascertain the views of such enforcement authority or authorities (if any) as it considers appropriate, and

(b) have regard to any representations made by the prosecution or on behalf of the organisation.

(3) A publicity order—

(a) must specify a period within which the requirements referred to in subsection (1) are to be complied with;

(b) may require the organisation to supply to any enforcement authority whose views have been ascertained under subsection (2), within a specified period, evidence that those requirements have been complied with.

(4) An organisation that fails to comply with a publicity order is guilty of an offence, and liable on conviction on indictment to a fine.

[1796]

NOTES

Commencement: to be appointed.

Application to particular categories of organisation

11 Application to Crown bodies

(1) An organisation that is a servant or agent of the Crown is not immune from prosecution under this Act for that reason.

(2) For the purposes of this Act—

(a) a department or other body listed in Schedule 1, or

(b) a corporation that is a servant or agent of the Crown,

is to be treated as owing whatever duties of care it would owe if it were a corporation that was not a servant or agent of the Crown.

(3) For the purposes of section 2—

(a) a person who is—

(i) employed by or under the Crown for the purposes of a department or other body listed in Schedule 1, or

(ii) employed by a person whose staff constitute a body listed in that Schedule,

is to be treated as employed by that department or body;

(b) any premises occupied for the purposes of—

(i) a department or other body listed in Schedule 1, or

(ii) a person whose staff constitute a body listed in that Schedule,

are to be treated as occupied by that department or body.

(4) For the purposes of sections 2 to 7 anything done purportedly by a department or other body listed in Schedule 1, although in law by the Crown or by the holder of a particular office, is to be treated as done by the department or other body itself.

(5) Subsections (3)(a)(i), (3)(b)(i) and (4) apply in relation to a Northern Ireland department as they apply in relation to a department or other body listed in Schedule 1.
[1797]

NOTES

Commencement: 6 April 2008.

12 Application to armed forces

(1) In this Act "the armed forces" means any of the naval, military or air forces of the Crown raised under the law of the United Kingdom.

(2) For the purposes of section 2 a person who is a member of the armed forces is to be treated as employed by the Ministry of Defence.

(3) A reference in this Act to members of the armed forces includes a reference to—

(a) members of the reserve forces (within the meaning given by section 1(2) of the Reserve Forces Act 1996 (c 14)) when in service or undertaking training or duties;

(b) persons serving on Her Majesty's vessels (within the meaning given by section 132(1) of the Naval Discipline Act 1957 (c 53)).
[1798]

NOTES

Commencement: 6 April 2008.

13 Application to police forces

(1) In this Act "police force" means—

(a) a police force within the meaning of—

(i) the Police Act 1996 (c 16), or

(ii) the Police (Scotland) Act 1967 (c 77);

(b) the Police Service of Northern Ireland;

(c) the Police Service of Northern Ireland Reserve;

(d) the British Transport Police Force;

(e) the Civil Nuclear Constabulary;

(f) the Ministry of Defence Police.

(2) For the purposes of this Act a police force is to be treated as owing whatever duties of care it would owe if it were a body corporate.

(3) For the purposes of section 2—

(a) a member of a police force is to be treated as employed by that force;

(b) a special constable appointed for a police area in England and Wales is to be treated as employed by the police force maintained by the police authority for that area;

(c) a special constable appointed for a police force mentioned in paragraph (d) or (f) of subsection (1) is to be treated as employed by that force;

(d) a police cadet undergoing training with a view to becoming a member of a police force mentioned in paragraph (a) or (d) of subsection (1) is to be treated as employed by that force;

(e) a police trainee appointed under section 39 of the Police (Northern Ireland) Act 2000 (c 32) or a police cadet appointed under section 42 of that Act is to be treated as employed by the Police Service of Northern Ireland;

(f) a police reserve trainee appointed under section 40 of that Act is to be treated as employed by the Police Service of Northern Ireland Reserve;

(g) a member of a police force seconded to the Serious Organised Crime Agency or the National Policing Improvement Agency to serve as a member of its staff is to be treated as employed by that Agency.

(4) A reference in subsection (3) to a member of a police force is to be read, in the case of a force mentioned in paragraph (a)(ii) of subsection (1), as a reference to a constable of that force.

(5) For the purposes of section 2 any premises occupied for the purposes of a police force are to be treated as occupied by that force.

(6) For the purposes of sections 2 to 7 anything that would be regarded as done by a police force if the force were a body corporate is to be so regarded.

(7) Where—

(a) by virtue of subsection (3) a person is treated for the purposes of section 2 as employed by a police force, and

(b) by virtue of any other statutory provision (whenever made) he is, or is treated as, employed by another organisation,

the person is to be treated for those purposes as employed by both the force and the other organisation.

[1799]

NOTES

Commencement: 6 April 2008.

14 Application to partnerships

(1) For the purposes of this Act a partnership is to be treated as owing whatever duties of care it would owe if it were a body corporate.

(2) Proceedings for an offence under this Act alleged to have been committed by a partnership are to be brought in the name of the partnership (and not in that of any of its members).

(3) A fine imposed on a partnership on its conviction of an offence under this Act is to be paid out of the funds of the partnership.

(4) This section does not apply to a partnership that is a legal person under the law by which it is governed.

[1800]

NOTES

Commencement: 6 April 2008.

Miscellaneous

15 ((*Procedure, evidence and sentencing*) *outside the scope of this work.*)

16 Transfer of functions

(1) This section applies where—

(a) a person's death has occurred, or is alleged to have occurred, in connection with the carrying out of functions by a relevant public organisation, and

(b) subsequently there is a transfer of those functions, with the result that they are still carried out but no longer by that organisation.

(2) In this section "relevant public organisation" means—

(a) a department or other body listed in Schedule 1;
(b) a corporation that is a servant or agent of the Crown;
(c) a police force.

(3) Any proceedings instituted against a relevant public organisation after the transfer for an offence under this Act in respect of the person's death are to be instituted against—
(a) the relevant public organisation, if any, by which the functions mentioned in subsection (1) are currently carried out;
(b) if no such organisation currently carries out the functions, the relevant public organisation by which the functions were last carried out.

This is subject to subsection (4).

(4) If an order made by the Secretary of State so provides in relation to a particular transfer of functions, the proceedings referred to in subsection (3) may be instituted, or (if they have already been instituted) may be continued, against—
(a) the organisation mentioned in subsection (1), or
(b) such relevant public organisation (other than the one mentioned in subsection (1) or the one mentioned in subsection (3)(a) or (b)) as may be specified in the order.

(5) If the transfer occurs while proceedings for an offence under this Act in respect of the person's death are in progress against a relevant public organisation, the proceedings are to be continued against—
(a) the relevant public organisation, if any, by which the functions mentioned in subsection (1) are carried out as a result of the transfer;
(b) if as a result of the transfer no such organisation carries out the functions, the same organisation as before.

This is subject to subsection (6).

(6) If an order made by the Secretary of State so provides in relation to a particular transfer of functions, the proceedings referred to in subsection (5) may be continued against—
(a) the organisation mentioned in subsection (1), or
(b) such relevant public organisation (other than the one mentioned in subsection (1) or the one mentioned in subsection (5)(a) or (b)) as may be specified in the order.

(7) An order under subsection (4) or (6) is subject to negative resolution procedure.

[1801]

NOTES

Commencement: 6 April 2008.

17 DPP's consent required for proceedings

Proceedings for an offence of corporate manslaughter—
(a) may not be instituted in England and Wales without the consent of the Director of Public Prosecutions;
(b) may not be instituted in Northern Ireland without the consent of the Director of Public Prosecutions for Northern Ireland.

[1802]

NOTES

Commencement: 6 April 2008.

18 No individual liability

(1) An individual cannot be guilty of aiding, abetting, counselling or procuring the commission of an offence of corporate manslaughter.

[(1A) An individual cannot be guilty of an offence under Part 2 of the Serious Crime Act 2007 (encouraging or assisting crime) by reference to an offence of corporate manslaughter.]

(2) An individual cannot be guilty of aiding, abetting, counselling or procuring, or being art and part in, the commission of an offence of corporate homicide.

[1803]

NOTES

Commencement: 6 April 2008.

Sub-s (1A): inserted, in relation to England, Wales and Northern Ireland, by the Serious Crime Act 2007, s 62 as from a day to be appointed.

19 Convictions under this Act and under health and safety legislation

(1) Where in the same proceedings there is—

(a) a charge of corporate manslaughter or corporate homicide arising out of a particular set of circumstances, and

(b) a charge against the same defendant of a health and safety offence arising out of some or all of those circumstances,

the jury may, if the interests of justice so require, be invited to return a verdict on each charge.

(2) An organisation that has been convicted of corporate manslaughter or corporate homicide arising out of a particular set of circumstances may, if the interests of justice so require, be charged with a health and safety offence arising out of some or all of those circumstances.

(3) In this section "health and safety offence" means an offence under any health and safety legislation.

[1804]

NOTES

Commencement: 6 April 2008.

20 Abolition of liability of corporations for manslaughter at common law

The common law offence of manslaughter by gross negligence is abolished in its application to corporations, and in any application it has to other organisations to which section 1 applies.

[1805]

NOTES

Commencement: 6 April 2008 (except in relation to any liability, investigation, legal proceeding or penalty for, or in respect of, an offence committed wholly or partly before that date; see s 27(4), (5) *post*).

Transitional provisions: see the note to s 2 at **[1788]**.

General and supplemental

21 Power to extend section 1 to other organisations

(1) The Secretary of State may by order amend section 1 so as to extend the categories of organisation to which that section applies.

(2) An order under this section may make any amendment to this Act that is incidental or supplemental to, or consequential on, an amendment made by virtue of subsection (1).

(3) An order under this section is subject to affirmative resolution procedure.

[1806]

NOTES

Commencement: 6 April 2008.

22 Power to amend Schedule 1

(1) The Secretary of State may amend Schedule 1 by order.

(2) A statutory instrument containing an order under this section is subject to affirmative resolution procedure, unless the only amendments to Schedule 1 that it makes are amendments within subsection (3).

In that case the instrument is subject to negative resolution procedure.

(3) An amendment is within this subsection if—

(a) it is consequential on a department or other body listed in Schedule 1 changing its name,

(b) in the case of an amendment adding a department or other body to Schedule 1, it is consequential on the transfer to the department or other body of functions all of which were previously exercisable by one or more organisations to which section 1 applies, or

(c) in the case of an amendment removing a department or other body from Schedule 1, it is consequential on—

(i) the abolition of the department or other body, or

(ii) the transfer of all the functions of the department or other body to one or more organisations to which section 1 applies.

[1807]

NOTES

Commencement: 6 April 2008.

Orders: the Corporate Manslaughter and Corporate Homicide Act 2007 (Amendment of Schedule 1) Order 2008, SI 2008/396.

23, 24 (*S 23 (Power to extend section 2(2)), s 24 (Orders) outside the scope of this work.*)

25 Interpretation

In this Act—

"armed forces" has the meaning given by section 12(1);

"corporation" does not include a corporation sole but includes any body corporate wherever incorporated;

"employee" means an individual who works under a contract of employment or apprenticeship (whether express or implied and, if express, whether oral or in writing), and related expressions are to be construed accordingly; see also sections 11(3)(a), 12(2) and 13(3) (which apply for the purposes of section 2);

"employers' association" has the meaning given by section 122 of the Trade Union and Labour Relations (Consolidation) Act 1992 (c 52) or Article 4 of the Industrial Relations (Northern Ireland) Order 1992 (SI 1992/807 (NI 5));

"enforcement authority" means an authority responsible for the enforcement of any health and safety legislation;

"health and safety legislation" means any statutory provision dealing with health and safety matters, including in particular provision contained in the Health and Safety at Work etc Act 1974 (c 37) or the Health and Safety at Work (Northern Ireland) Order 1978 (SI 1978/1039 (NI 9));

"member", in relation to the armed forces, is to be read in accordance with section 12(3);

"partnership" means—

(a) a partnership within the Partnership Act 1890 (c 39), or

(b) a limited partnership registered under the Limited Partnerships Act 1907 (c 24),

or a firm or entity of a similar character formed under the law of a country or territory outside the United Kingdom;

"police force" has the meaning given by section 13(1);

"premises" includes land, buildings and moveable structures;

"public authority" has the same meaning as in section 6 of the Human Rights Act 1998 (c 42) (disregarding subsections (3)(a) and (4) of that section);

"publicity order" means an order under section 10(1);

"remedial order" means an order under section 9(1);

"statutory provision", except in section 15, means provision contained in, or in an instrument made under, any Act, any Act of the Scottish Parliament or any Northern Ireland legislation;

"trade union" has the meaning given by section 1 of the Trade Union and Labour Relations (Consolidation) Act 1992 (c 52) or Article 3 of the Industrial Relations (Northern Ireland) Order 1992 (SI 1992/807 (NI 5)).

[1808]

NOTES

Commencement: 6 April 2008.

26 (*Introduces Sch 2* (*Minor and consequential amendments*).)

27 Commencement and savings

(1) The preceding provisions of this Act come into force in accordance with provision made by order by the Secretary of State.

(2) An order bringing into force paragraph (d) of section 2(1) is subject to affirmative resolution procedure.

(3) Section 1 does not apply in relation to anything done or omitted before the commencement of that section.

(4) Section 20 does not affect any liability, investigation, legal proceeding or penalty for or in respect of an offence committed wholly or partly before the commencement of that section.

(5) For the purposes of subsection (4) an offence is committed wholly or partly before the commencement of section 20 if any of the conduct or events alleged to constitute the offence occurred before that commencement.

[1809]

NOTES

Commencement: 26 July 2007.

Orders: the Corporate Manslaughter and Corporate Homicide Act 2007 (Commencement No 1) Order 2008, SI 2008/401.

28 Extent and territorial application

(1) Subject to subsection (2), this Act extends to England and Wales, Scotland and Northern Ireland.

(2) An amendment made by this Act extends to the same part or parts of the United Kingdom as the provision to which it relates.

(3) Section 1 applies if the harm resulting in death is sustained in the United Kingdom or—

(a) within the seaward limits of the territorial sea adjacent to the United Kingdom;

(b) on a ship registered under Part 2 of the Merchant Shipping Act 1995 (c 21);

(c) on a British-controlled aircraft as defined in section 92 of the Civil Aviation Act 1982 (c 16);

(d) on a British-controlled hovercraft within the meaning of that section as applied in relation to hovercraft by virtue of provision made under the Hovercraft Act 1968 (c 59);

(e) in any place to which an Order in Council under section 10(1) of the Petroleum Act 1998 (c 17) applies (criminal jurisdiction in relation to offshore activities).

(4) For the purposes of subsection (3)(b) to (d) harm sustained on a ship, aircraft or hovercraft includes harm sustained by a person who—

(a) is then no longer on board the ship, aircraft or hovercraft in consequence of the wrecking of it or of some other mishap affecting it or occurring on it, and

(b) sustains the harm in consequence of that event.

[1810]

NOTES

Commencement: 26 July 2007.

29 Short title

This Act may be cited as the Corporate Manslaughter and Corporate Homicide Act 2007.

[1811]

NOTES

Commencement: 26 July 2007.

SCHEDULES

SCHEDULE 1
LIST OF GOVERNMENT DEPARTMENTS ETC

Section 1

Assets Recovery Agency

Attorney General's Office

Cabinet Office

Central Office of Information

Crown Office and Procurator Fiscal Service

Crown Prosecution Service

[Department for Business, Enterprise and Regulatory Reform

Department for Children, Schools and Families]

Department for Communities and Local Government

…

Department for Culture, Media and Sport

…

Department for Environment, Food and Rural Affairs

[Department for Innovation, Universities and Skills]

Department for International Development

Department for Transport

Department for Work and Pensions

Department of Health

…

Export Credits Guarantee Department

Foreign and Commonwealth Office

Forestry Commission

General Register Office for Scotland

Government Actuary's Department

Her Majesty's Land Registry

Her Majesty's Revenue and Customs

Her Majesty's Treasury

Home Office

Ministry of Defence

[Ministry of Justice (including the Scotland Office and the Wales Office)]

National Archives

National Archives of Scotland

National Audit Office

National Savings and Investments

National School of Government

Northern Ireland Audit Office

Northern Ireland Court Service

Northern Ireland Office

Office for National Statistics

…

Office of Her Majesty's Chief Inspector of Education and Training in Wales

Ordnance Survey

...

Public Prosecution Service for Northern Ireland

Registers of Scotland Executive Agency

Revenue and Customs Prosecutions Office

Royal Mint

Scottish Executive

Serious Fraud Office

Treasury Solicitor's Department

UK Trade and Investment

Welsh Assembly Government

[1812]

NOTES

Commencement: 6 April 2008.

Entry "Assets Recovery Agency" repealed by the Serious Crime Act 2007, s 74(2)(g), Sch 8, Pt 7, para 178, as from a day to be appointed.

Other entries in square brackets inserted, and entries omitted repealed, by the Corporate Manslaughter and Corporate Homicide Act 2007 (Amendment of Schedule 1) Order 2008, SI 2008/396, art 2, as from 6 April 2008.

(*Sch 2* (*Minor and Consequential Amendments*) *contains amendments to enactments that are outside the scope of this work.*)

STATISTICS AND REGISTRATION SERVICE ACT 2007

(2007 c 18)

An Act to establish and make provision about the Statistics Board; to make provision about offices and office-holders under the Registration Service Act 1953; and for connected purposes

[26 July 2007]

NOTES

Only s 69 of this Act is relevant to employment law. Provisions not reproduced are not annotated. Section 69 extends to England and Wales only (s 75) and came into force on 1 December 2007 (see SI 2007/3388).

PART 2
REGISTRATION SERVICE

69 Employment status of officials

(1) On commencement of this section, every person who immediately before commencement of this section holds a relevant office becomes an employee of the relevant local authority.

(2) The relevant offices are—

(a) superintendent registrar of births, deaths and marriages appointed under section 6 of the Registration Service Act 1953;

(b) registrar of births and deaths appointed under that section;

(c) deputy superintendent registrar of births, deaths and marriages appointed under section 8 of that Act;

(d) deputy registrar of births and deaths appointed under that section.

(3) The terms and conditions of appointment of the holder of a relevant office have effect from commencement of this section (subject to any necessary modifications) as the terms and conditions of his employment with the relevant local authority.

(4) On commencement of this section any liabilities incurred by the holder of a relevant office in connection with the exercise of his functions are transferred to the relevant local authority.

(5) Any period which ends immediately before commencement of this section during which a person was continuously—

(a) the holder of a relevant office (whether in respect of the same or different relevant offices), or

(b) the holder of a relevant office (whether in respect of the same or different relevant offices) or an employee of a local authority,

must be treated as a period of continuous employment with the relevant local authority.

(6) If, immediately before commencement of this section, the holder of a relevant office was a member of a pension scheme established in pursuance of regulations under sections 7 and 12 of the Superannuation Act 1972 (c 11), he continues to be a member of the scheme by virtue of his becoming an employee of the relevant local authority.

(7) For the purposes of this section, the "relevant local authority" is—

(a) in relation to the holder of a relevant office falling within subsection (2)(a) or (b), the local authority by which he was appointed;

(b) in relation to the holder of a relevant office falling within subsection (2)(c) or (d), the local authority which appointed the superintendent registrar of births, deaths and marriages or registrar of births and deaths by whom he was appointed.

(8) For the purposes of this section, each of the following is a local authority—

(a) a county council in England;

(b) a district council in England for an area without a county council;

(c) a London borough council;

(d) the Common Council of the City of London;

(e) the Council of the Isles of Scilly;

(f) a county or county borough council in Wales.

[1813]

NOTES

Commencement: 1 December 2007.

TRIBUNALS, COURTS AND ENFORCEMENT ACT 2007

(2007 c 15)

ARRANGEMENT OF SECTIONS

PART 1
TRIBUNALS AND INQUIRIES

CHAPTER 1
TRIBUNAL JUDICIARY: INDEPENDENCE AND SENIOR PRESIDENT

CHAPTER 2
FIRST-TIER TRIBUNAL AND UPPER TRIBUNAL

Establishment

CHAPTER 3
TRANSFER OF TRIBUNAL FUNCTIONS

CHAPTER 4
ADMINISTRATIVE MATTERS IN RESPECT OF CERTAIN TRIBUNALS

An Act to make provision about tribunals and inquiries; to establish an Administrative Justice and Tribunals Council; to amend the law relating to judicial appointments and appointments to the Law Commission; to amend the law relating to the enforcement of judgments and debts; to make further provision about the management and relief of debt; to make provision protecting cultural objects from seizure or forfeiture in certain circumstances; to amend the law relating to the taking of possession of land affected by compulsory purchase; to alter the powers of the High Court in judicial review applications; and for connected purposes

[19 July 2007]

NOTES

Only those provisions of this Act relevant to employment law are reproduced. Provisions not reproduced are not annotated. The provisions reproduced here extend to the whole of the United Kingdom (s 147). As to the commencement of the provisions reproduced here, see the notes thereto.

PART 1
TRIBUNALS AND INQUIRIES

CHAPTER 1
TRIBUNAL JUDICIARY: INDEPENDENCE AND SENIOR PRESIDENT

1 Independence of tribunal judiciary

In section 3 of the Constitutional Reform Act 2005 (c 4) (guarantee of continued judicial independence), after subsection (7) insert—

"(7A) In this section "the judiciary" also includes every person who—

(a) holds an office listed in Schedule 14 or holds an office listed in subsection (7B), and

(b) but for this subsection would not be a member of the judiciary for the purposes of this section.

(7B) The offices are those of—

(a) Senior President of Tribunals;

(b) President of Employment Tribunals (Scotland);

(c) Vice President of Employment Tribunals (Scotland);

(d) member of a panel of chairmen of Employment Tribunals (Scotland);

(e) member of a panel of members of employment tribunals that is not a panel of chairmen;

(f) adjudicator appointed under section 5 of the Criminal Injuries Compensation Act 1995."

[1814]

NOTES

Commencement: 19 September 2007.

2 Senior President of Tribunals

(1) Her Majesty may, on the recommendation of the Lord Chancellor, appoint a person to the office of Senior President of Tribunals.

(2) Schedule 1 makes further provision about the Senior President of Tribunals and about recommendations for appointment under subsection (1).

(3) A holder of the office of Senior President of Tribunals must, in carrying out the functions of that office, have regard to—
- (a) the need for tribunals to be accessible,
- (b) the need for proceedings before tribunals—
  - (i) to be fair, and
  - (ii) to be handled quickly and efficiently,
- (c) the need for members of tribunals to be experts in the subject-matter of, or the law to be applied in, cases in which they decide matters, and
- (d) the need to develop innovative methods of resolving disputes that are of a type that may be brought before tribunals.

(4) In subsection (3) "tribunals" means—
- (a) the First-tier Tribunal,
- (b) the Upper Tribunal,
- (c) employment tribunals,
- (d) the Employment Appeal Tribunal, and
- (e) the Asylum and Immigration Tribunal.

[1815]

NOTES

Commencement: 19 September 2007.

CHAPTER 2
FIRST-TIER TRIBUNAL AND UPPER TRIBUNAL

Establishment

3 The First-tier Tribunal and the Upper Tribunal

(1) There is to be a tribunal, known as the First-tier Tribunal, for the purpose of exercising the functions conferred on it under or by virtue of this Act or any other Act.

(2) There is to be a tribunal, known as the Upper Tribunal, for the purpose of exercising the functions conferred on it under or by virtue of this Act or any other Act.

(3) Each of the First-tier Tribunal, and the Upper Tribunal, is to consist of its judges and other members.

(4) The Senior President of Tribunals is to preside over both of the First-tier Tribunal and the Upper Tribunal.

(5) The Upper Tribunal is to be a superior court of record.

[1816]

NOTES

Commencement: to be appointed.

CHAPTER 3
TRANSFER OF TRIBUNAL FUNCTIONS

35 Transfer of Ministerial responsibilities for certain tribunals

(1) The Lord Chancellor may by order—
- (a) transfer any relevant function, so far as that function is exercisable by a Minister of the Crown—
  - (i) to the Lord Chancellor, or
  - (ii) to two (or more) Ministers of the Crown of whom one is the Lord Chancellor;
- (b) provide for any relevant function that is exercisable by a Minister of the Crown

other than the Lord Chancellor to be exercisable by the other Minister of the Crown concurrently with the Lord Chancellor;

(c) provide for any relevant function that is exercisable by the Lord Chancellor concurrently with another Minister of the Crown to cease to be exercisable by the other Minister of the Crown.

(2) In this section "relevant function" means a function, in relation to a scheduled tribunal, which relates—

(a) to the operation of the tribunal (including, in particular, its membership, administration, staff, accommodation and funding, and payments to its members or staff), or

(b) to the provision of expenses and allowances to persons attending the tribunal or attending elsewhere in connection with proceedings before the tribunal.

(3) In subsection (2) "scheduled tribunal" means a tribunal in a list in Schedule 6 that has effect for the purposes of this section.

(4) A relevant function may not be transferred under subsection (1) if, or to the extent that, the provision conferring the function—

(a) would be within the legislative competence of the Scottish Parliament if it were included in an Act of that Parliament, or

(b) would be within the legislative competence of the Northern Ireland Assembly if it were included in an Act of that Assembly.

(5) Subsection (4) does not apply to any relevant function of the Secretary of State—

(a) under section 41 of the Consumer Credit Act 1974 (c 39) (appeals), or

(b) under section 7 of the Estate Agents Act 1979 (c 38) (appeals).

(6) Any reference in subsection (1) to a Minister of the Crown includes a reference to a Minister of the Crown acting jointly.

(7) An order under subsection (1)—

(a) may relate to a function either wholly or in cases (including cases framed by reference to areas) specified in the order;

(b) may include provision for the purposes of, or in consequence of, or for giving full effect to, the transfer or (as the case may be) other change as regards exercise;

(c) may include such incidental, supplementary, transitional or consequential provision or savings as the Lord Chancellor thinks fit;

(d) may include provision for the transfer of any property, rights or liabilities of the person who loses functions or whose functions become shared with the Lord Chancellor.

(8) An order under subsection (1), so far as it—

(a) provides under paragraph (a) for the transfer of a function, or

(b) provides under paragraph (b) for a function to become exercisable by the Lord Chancellor, or

(c) provides under paragraph (c) for a function to cease to be exercisable by a Minister of the Crown other than the Lord Chancellor,

may not, after that transfer or other change has taken place, be revoked by another order under that subsection.

(9) Section 1 of the 1975 Act (power to transfer Ministerial functions) does not apply to a function of the Lord Chancellor—

(a) so far as it is a function transferred to the Lord Chancellor under subsection (1)(a),

(b) so far as it is a function exercisable by the Lord Chancellor as a result of provision under subsection (1)(b), or

(c) so far as it is a function that has become exercisable by the Lord Chancellor alone as a result of provision under subsection (1)(c).

(10) In this section—

"Minister of the Crown" has the meaning given by section 8(1) of the 1975 Act but includes the Commissioners for Her Majesty's Revenue and Customs;

"the 1975 Act" means the Ministers of the Crown Act 1975 (c 26).

[1817]

NOTES

Commencement: 19 September 2007.

36 Transfer of powers to make procedural rules for certain tribunals

(1) The Lord Chancellor may by order transfer any power to make procedural rules for a scheduled tribunal to—
(a) himself, or
(b) the Tribunal Procedure Committee.

(2) A power may not be transferred under subsection (1) if, or to the extent that, the provision conferring the power—
(a) would be within the legislative competence of the Scottish Parliament if it were included in an Act of that Parliament, or
(b) would be within the legislative competence of the Northern Ireland Assembly if it were included in an Act of that Assembly.

(3) Subsection (2) does not apply to—
(a) power conferred by section 40A(3) *or 41(2)* of the Consumer Credit Act 1974 (c 39) (power to make provision with respect to appeals), or
(b) power conferred by section 7(3) of the Estate Agents Act 1979 (c 38) (duty of Secretary of State to make regulations with respect to appeals under section 7(1) of that Act).

(4) An order under subsection (1)(b)—
(a) may not alter any parliamentary procedure relating to the making of the procedural rules concerned, but
(b) may otherwise include provision for the purpose of assimilating the procedure for making them to the procedure for making Tribunal Procedure Rules.

(5) An order under subsection (1)(b) may include provision requiring the Tribunal Procedure Committee to make procedural rules for purposes notified to it by the Lord Chancellor.

(6) An order under this section—
(a) may relate to a power either wholly or in cases (including cases framed by reference to areas) specified in the order;
(b) may include provision for the purposes of or in consequence of, or for giving full effect to, the transfer;
(c) may include such incidental, supplementary, transitional or consequential provision or savings as the Lord Chancellor thinks fit.

(7) A power to make procedural rules for a tribunal that is exercisable by the Tribunal Procedure Committee by virtue of an order under this section must be exercised by the committee with a view to securing—
(a) that the system for deciding matters within the jurisdiction of that tribunal is accessible and fair,
(b) that proceedings before that tribunal are handled quickly and efficiently,
(c) that the rules are both simple and simply expressed, and
(d) that the rules where appropriate confer on persons who are, or who are members of, that tribunal responsibility for ensuring that proceedings before that tribunal are handled quickly and efficiently.

(8) In this section—
"procedural rules", in relation to a tribunal, means provision (whether called rules or not) regulating practice or procedure before the tribunal;
"scheduled tribunal" means a tribunal in a list in Schedule 6 that has effect for the purposes of this section.

[1818]

NOTES

Commencement: 19 September 2007.
Sub-s (3): in para (a) words "or 41(2)" in italics repealed by s 146 of, and Sch 23, Pt 1 to, this Act, as from a day to be appointed.

CHAPTER 4
ADMINISTRATIVE MATTERS IN RESPECT OF CERTAIN TRIBUNALS

39 The general duty

(1) The Lord Chancellor is under a duty to ensure that there is an efficient and effective system to support the carrying on of the business of—

(a) the First-tier Tribunal,
(b) the Upper Tribunal,
(c) employment tribunals,
(d) the Employment Appeal Tribunal, and
(e) the Asylum and Immigration Tribunal,

and that appropriate services are provided for those tribunals (referred to in this section and in sections 40 and 41 as "the tribunals").

(2) Any reference in this section, or in section 40 or 41, to the Lord Chancellor's general duty in relation to the tribunals is to his duty under subsection (1).

(3) The Lord Chancellor must annually prepare and lay before each House of Parliament a report as to the way in which he has discharged his general duty in relation to the tribunals. **[1819]**

NOTES

Commencement: 19 September 2007.

40 Tribunal staff and services

(1) The Lord Chancellor may appoint such staff as appear to him appropriate for the purpose of discharging his general duty in relation to the tribunals.

(2) Subject to subsections (3) and (4), the Lord Chancellor may enter into such contracts with other persons for the provision, by them or their sub-contractors, of staff or services as appear to him appropriate for the purpose of discharging his general duty in relation to the tribunals.

(3) The Lord Chancellor may not enter into contracts for the provision of staff to discharge functions which involve making judicial decisions or exercising any judicial discretion.

(4) The Lord Chancellor may not enter into contracts for the provision of staff to carry out the administrative work of the tribunals unless an order made by the Lord Chancellor authorises him to do so.

(5) Before making an order under subsection (4) the Lord Chancellor must consult the Senior President of Tribunals as to what effect (if any) the order might have on the proper and efficient administration of justice.

(6) An order under subsection (4) may authorise the Lord Chancellor to enter into contracts for the provision of staff to discharge functions—
(a) wholly or to the extent specified in the order,
(b) generally or in cases or areas specified in the order, and
(c) unconditionally or subject to the fulfilment of conditions specified in the order. **[1820]**

NOTES

Commencement: 19 September 2007.

41 Provision of accommodation

(1) The Lord Chancellor may provide, equip, maintain and manage such tribunal buildings, offices and other accommodation as appear to him appropriate for the purpose of discharging his general duty in relation to the tribunals.

(2) The Lord Chancellor may enter into such arrangements for the provision, equipment, maintenance or management of tribunal buildings, offices or other accommodation as appear to him appropriate for the purpose of discharging his general duty in relation to the tribunals.

(3) The powers under—
(a) section 2 of the Commissioners of Works Act 1852 (c 28) (acquisition by agreement), and
(b) section 228(1) of the Town and Country Planning Act 1990 (c 8) (compulsory acquisition),

to acquire land necessary for the public service are to be treated as including power to acquire land for the purpose of its provision under arrangements entered into under subsection (2).

(4) In this section "tribunal building" means any place where any of the tribunals sits, including the precincts of any building in which it sits.

[1821]

NOTES

Commencement: 19 September 2007.

43 Report by Senior President of Tribunals

(1) Each year the Senior President of Tribunals must give the Lord Chancellor a report covering, in relation to relevant tribunal cases—

(a) matters that the Senior President of Tribunals wishes to bring to the attention of the Lord Chancellor, and

(b) matters that the Lord Chancellor has asked the Senior President of Tribunals to cover in the report.

(2) The Lord Chancellor must publish each report given to him under subsection (1).

(3) In this section "relevant tribunal cases" means—

(a) cases coming before the First-tier Tribunal,

(b) cases coming before the Upper Tribunal,

(c) cases coming before the Employment Appeal Tribunal, …

(d) cases coming before employment tribunals[, and

(e) cases coming before the Asylum and Immigration Tribunal].

[1822]–[2000]

NOTES

Commencement: to be appointed.

Sub-s (3): word omitted from para (c) repealed, and para (e) (and the word immediately preceding it) inserted, by the UK Borders Act 2007, ss 56(1), 58, Schedule, as from 1 April 2008.

PART 2
STATUTORY INSTRUMENTS

REDUNDANCY PAYMENTS PENSIONS REGULATIONS 1965

(SI 1965/1932)

NOTES

Made: 10 November 1965.

Authority: Redundancy Payments Act 1965, s 14 (repealed); Employment Protection (Consolidation) Act 1978, s 98 (repealed). These Regulations now have effect as if made under the Employment Rights Act 1996, s 158.

Commencement: 6 December 1965.

See *Harvey* E14, R.

ARRANGEMENT OF REGULATIONS

SCHEDULES:

1 Citation and commencement

These Regulations may be cited as the Redundancy Payments Pensions Regulations 1965 and shall come into operation on 6th December 1965.

[2001]

2 Interpretation

(1) The Interpretation Act 1889 applies to the interpretation of these Regulations as it applies to the Interpretation of an Act of Parliament.

(2) In these Regulations, unless the context otherwise requires, the following expressions have the meanings hereby assigned to them respectively, that is to say—

"the Act" means the Redundancy Payments Act 1965;

"employee" has the meaning assigned to it in subsection (1) of section 25 of the Act and includes any person in respect of whom the Act has effect as if he were an employee within the meaning of that subsection;

"employer" has the meaning assigned to it in subsection (1) of section 25 of the Act and includes any person in respect of whom the Act has effect as if he were an employer within the meaning of that subsection;

"the Minister" means the Minister of Labour;

"pension" has the meaning assigned to it in Regulation 3 and includes any part of a pension;

"pensioned employee" means an employee who has a right or claim to a pension of a kind referred to in Regulation 4;

"tribunal" means a tribunal established under section 12 of the Industrial Training Act 1964;

"week" means a week ending with Saturday.

[2002]

NOTES

Interpretation Act 1889: see now the Interpretation Act 1978.

Redundancy Payments Act 1965: repealed by the Statute Law (Repeals) Act 1989.

"Subsection (1) of section 25": see now the Employment Rights Act 1996, s 230(1), (4).

"Section 12 of the Industrial Training Act 1964": now s 1 of the Employment Tribunals Act 1996.

3 Meaning of "pension"

(1) Subject to the provisions of this Regulation, in these Regulations "pension" means a periodical payment or lump sum by way of pension, gratuity or superannuation allowance as respects which the Minister is satisfied that it is to be paid in accordance with any scheme or arrangement having for its object or one of its objects to make provision in respect of persons serving in particular employments for providing them with retirement benefits and (except in the case of such a lump sum which had been paid to the employee) that—

(a) the scheme or arrangement is established by Act of Parliament or of the Parliament of Northern Ireland, or other instrument having the force of law; or

(b) the benefits under the scheme or arrangement are secured by an irrevocable trust which is subject to the laws of any part of Great Britain; or

(c) the benefits under the scheme or arrangement are secured by a contract of assurance or an annuity contract which is made with—

(i) an insurance company to which the Insurance Companies Act 1958 applies; or

(ii) a registered friendly society; or

(iii) an industrial and provident society registered under the Industrial and Provident Societies Act 1893; or

(d) the benefits under the scheme or arrangement are secured by any regulation or other instrument (not being a regulation or instrument having the force of law) made with the authority of a Minister of the Crown or with the consent of the Treasury for the purpose of authorising the payment to persons not employed in the Civil Service of the State of such pensions, gratuities or other like benefits as might have been granted to persons so employed; or

(e) the scheme or arrangement is established by an enactment or other instrument having the force of law in any part of the Commonwealth outside the United Kingdom;

and that the provision made to enable benefits to be paid (taking into account any additional resources which could and would be provided by the employer, or any person connected with the employer, to meet any deficiency) is adequate to ensure payment in full of the benefits aforesaid.

(2) If in any case the Minister is satisfied that benefits under the scheme or arrangement are wholly or mainly provided for the benefit of persons not resident in Great Britain he may if he thinks fit and subject to such conditions, if any, as he thinks proper, waive the requirement contained in sub-paragraph (b) of the foregoing paragraph in respect of a scheme or arrangement the benefits under which are secured by an irrevocable trust or the requirements of heads (i), (ii) or (iii) of sub-paragraph (c) thereof in the case of a scheme or arrangement the benefits under which are secured by a contract of assurance or an annuity contract.

(3) In these Regulations "pension" does not include—

(a) a payment to an employee which consists solely of a return of his own contributions, with or without interest;

(b) that part of a payment to an employee which is attributable solely to additional voluntary contributions by that employee made in accordance with the scheme or arrangement;

(c) a periodical payment or lump sum, in so far as that payment or lump sum represents such compensation as is mentioned in section 47(1) of the Act (which relates to statutory compensation schemes) and is payable under a statutory provision, whether made or passed before, on or after the appointed day.

[2003]

NOTES

"Section 47(1) of the Act": see now the Employment Rights Act 1996, s 178 (formerly the Employment Protection (Consolidation) Act 1978, s 118).

4 Application of Regulations

(1) These Regulations apply in any case where an employee who is entitled, or but for these Regulations, would be entitled to a redundancy payment from an employer has a right or claim to a pension for himself which—

(a) is to be paid by reference to the employee's last period of continuous employment with that employer;

(i) if it is a lump sum is to be paid, or
(ii) if it is a periodical payment is to begin to accrue,

at the time when the employee leaves the employment with that employer or within 90 weeks thereafter; and

(c) in so far as it consists of periodical payments satisfies the conditions specified in the next following paragraph.

(2) The conditions referred to in the preceding paragraph are that the Minister is satisfied that the pension is payable for life and is not capable of being terminated or suspended except for—

(a) the operation of any provision for the termination or suspension of the pension—
(i) upon the commutation thereof; or
(ii) upon assignment, charge or other alienation (whether by operation of law or otherwise), or any attempt thereat; or
(iii) in case of mental disorder or inability to act (if there is provision enabling the pension in either of these circumstances to be paid or applied at discretion for the maintenance or support of the pensioner's spouse or of other persons dependent on him);

(b) the operation of any provision for the suspension of the pension during imprisonment or detention in legal custody or upon resumption of employment with the employer or of any other provision for the suspension of the pension during employment, being a provision contained in or made under any of the enactments specified in Schedule 5 to the National Insurance Act 1965, or in subsection (6) of section 62 of that Act (which relate to certain statutory superannuation schemes) or a provision of the Superannuation Acts 1934 to 1950, and any Act amending those Acts, as applied by any enactment or other instrument having the force of law or by any instrument referred to in sub-paragraphs (d) or (e) of Regulation 3(1) of these Regulations;

(c) the operation of section 2 of the Forfeiture Act 1870, (which provides, in certain cases of persons convicted of treason or felony, for the termination of a pension or superannuation allowance payable by the public or out of any public fund).

[2004]

NOTES

"Section 47(1) of the Act": see now the Employment Rights Act 1996, s 178 (formerly the Employment Protection (Consolidation) Act 1978, s 118).

Felony: the distinction between felonies and misdemeanours was abolished by the Criminal Law Act 1967, s 1(1).

---

5 Exclusion or reduction of redundancy payments

(1) An employer of a pensioned employee may, by notice in writing to that employee, claim to—

(a) exclude the right of the employee to the redundancy payment to which he would otherwise be entitled; or

(b) reduce the amount thereof,

in accordance with or to the extent permitted by Schedule 1 to these Regulations and in such a case the employee shall not be entitled to a redundancy payment or, as the case may be, shall be entitled only to the reduced amount thereof.

(2) The notice in writing referred to in paragraph (1) of this Regulation shall contain a written statement explaining how the right of the pensioned employee to the redundancy payment has been excluded or, as the case may be, how the amount of the redundancy payment has been reduced by reason of the pension and specifying the amount of any redundancy payment so reduced.

(3) The provisions of this Regulation are without prejudice to the right of an employee to apply to a tribunal to determine any question as to his right to a redundancy payment or as to the amount of such payment.

[2005]

6 Employees paid by person other than employer

(1) This Regulation applies to any employee whose remuneration is, by virtue of any statutory provision, payable to him by a person other than his employer.

(2) For the purposes of the operation, in relation to employees to whom this Regulation applies, of the provisions of these Regulations specified in column 1 of Schedule 2 to these Regulations, any reference to the employer which is specified in column 2 of that Schedule shall be construed as a reference to the person responsible for paying the remuneration.

[2006]

SCHEDULES

SCHEDULE 1
EXCLUSION OF OR REDUCTION IN THE AMOUNT OF A REDUNDANCY PAYMENT BY REASON OF A PENSION

Regulation 5(1)

1.—(1) An employer of a pensioned employee may exclude the right of that employee to the redundancy payment to which he would otherwise be entitled under the Act by reason of his employment with the employer if the pension to which he has a right or claim by reference to that employment amounts in the annual value thereof to at least one-third of the employee's annual pay and is one as respects which—

(a) in so far as it consists of periodical payments the employee has a right or claim for the payments to begin to accrue, and

(b) in so far as it consists of a lump sum the employee has a right or claim for it to be paid,

immediately the employee ceases to be employed by the employer.

(2) An employer of a pensioned employee may reduce by an amount, not exceeding the appropriate proportion, the amount of the redundancy payment to which that employee would otherwise be entitled under the Act by reason of his employment with the employer if the pension to which he has a right or claim by reference to that employment is one as respects which—

(a) in so far as it consists of periodical payments the employee has a right or claim for the payments to begin to accrue, and

(b) in so far as it consists of a lump sum the employee has a right or claim for it to be paid,

immediately the employee ceases to be employed by the employer.

2. In a case in which the preceding paragraph of this Schedule does not apply but in which a pensioned employee has a right or claim to a pension as respects which—

(a) in so far as it consists of periodical payments the employee has a right or claim for the payments to begin to accrue, and

(b) in so far as it consists of a lump sum the employee has a right or claim for it to be paid,

at some time (not exceeding 90 weeks) later than the time when the pensioned employee ceases to be employed by him, an employer of that employee may reduce the amount of the redundancy payment by an amount not exceeding the appropriate proportion:

Provided that to the reduced payment so ascertained there shall be added the weekly value of the pension for each week that is to elapse between the cessation of the pensioned employee's employment with the employer and the time when the pensioned employee has a right or claim for the pension to begin to accrue or, as the case may be, to be paid; so however that the total payment due to the pensioned employee under this paragraph shall not exceed the amount of the redundancy payment to which he would be entitled apart from these Regulations.

3. For the purposes of this Schedule—

"appropriate proportion" means the proportion which the annual value of the pension to the employee bears to one-third of that employee's annual pay;

"annual pay" means the amount of a week's pay of the employee, calculated in accordance with paragraph 5 of Schedule 1 to the Act, multiplied by 52, any fraction of a pound in the product being disregarded;

"annual value of the pension" means—

(a) in the case of a pension to which the employee has a right or claim which consists of periodical payments—

(i) where the pension is payable at intervals of seven days the amount of the first payment multiplied by 52, any fraction of a pound in the product being disregarded if the pension consists wholly of periodical payments;

(ii) where the pension is payable at other than intervals of seven days the amount which would accrue during the 12 calendar months beginning with the day on which the pension begins to accrue and assuming that the value of the pension does not change, any fraction of a pound being disregarded if the pension consists wholly of periodical payments;

(b) in the case of a pension to which the employee has a right or claim which consists of a lump sum, one-tenth of the amount of such lump sum, any fraction of a pound being disregarded if the pension consists wholly of a lump sum;

(c) in the case of a pension to which the employee has a right or claim which consists partly of periodical payments and partly of a lump sum, the total annual value ascertained in accordance with sub-paragraph (a) and sub-paragraph (b) of this paragraph, any fraction of a pound in that total being disregarded;

"weekly value of the pension" means the amount, not exceeding one-third of one week's value of the employee (calculated in accordance with paragraph 5 of Schedule 1 to the Act), obtained by dividing the annual value of the pension by 52.

[2007]

NOTES

"Paragraph 5 of Schedule 1 to the Act": see now the Employment Rights Act 1996, ss 225–227 (formerly the Employment Protection (Consolidation) Act 1978, Sch 14, paras 7, 8).

SCHEDULE 2

Regulation 6

Provisions of Regulations	Reference to be construed as reference to the person responsible for paying the remuneration
Regulation 3(1).	The references to "employer".
Regulation 4(1).	The first reference to "employer".
Regulation 5(1).	The reference to "employer".
Schedule 1, paragraph 1(1).	The first reference to "employer".
Schedule 1, paragraph 1(2).	The first reference to "employer".
Schedule 1, paragraph 2.	The first reference to "employer".

[2008]

TRADE UNIONS AND EMPLOYERS' ASSOCIATIONS (AMALGAMATIONS, ETC) REGULATIONS 1975

(SI 1975/536)

NOTES

Made: 26 March 1975.

Authority: originally made under the Trade Union (Amalgamations, etc) Act 1964, s 7 (repealed); now has effect under the Trade Union and Labour Relations (Consolidation) Act 1992, s 108.

Commencement: 12 May 1975.

ARRANGEMENT OF REGULATIONS

SCHEDULES:

1 Citation, commencement and revocation

(1) These Regulations may be cited as the Trade Unions and Employers' Associations (Amalgamations, etc) Regulations 1975 and shall come into operation on 12th May 1975.

(2) …

[2008A]

NOTES

Para (2): revokes the Employers' and Workers' Organisations (Amalgamations, etc) Regulations 1971, SI 1971/1542.

2 Interpretation

(1) The Interpretation Act 1889 shall apply to these Regulations as it applies to an Act of Parliament.

(2) For the purposes of these Regulations, unless the context otherwise requires, the following expressions shall have the meanings hereby assigned to them respectively, that is to say—

"the 1964 Act" means the Trade Union (Amalgamations, etc) Act 1964;

"the 1974 Act" means the Trade Union and Labour Relations Act 1974;

["the Certification Officer" means the officer appointed under section 7(1) of the Employment Protection Act 1975 or any assistant certification officer appointed under section 7(4) of the said Act to whom, in accordance with section 7(5) of the said Act, functions have been delegated in relation to any matter authorised or required to be dealt with under these Regulations];

"duly authenticated" means bearing the signature of [the Certification Officer] and the date of the signature;

"organisation" means any trade union as defined in section 28(1) of the 1974 Act, or any employers' association as defined in section 28(2) of the 1974 Act which is not a corporate body;

"Northern Ireland union" has the meaning assigned to it by section 10(5) of the 1964 Act.

[2008B]

NOTES

Para (2): definition "the Certification Officer" substituted by the Trade Unions and Employers' Associations (Amalgamations, etc) (Amendment) Regulations 1978, SI 1978/1344. As to the appointment of Certification Officers, see now the Trade Union and Labour Relations (Consolidation) Act 1992, s 254.

Interpretation Act 1889: see now the Interpretation Act 1978.

Trade Union (Amalgamations, etc) Act 1964; Trade Union and Labour Relations Act 1974: repealed and replaced by the Trade Union and Labour Relations (Consolidation) Act 1992.

3 Approval of proposed instruments and notices

(1) An application pursuant to section 1(4) of the 1964 Act for approval of a proposed instrument of amalgamation or transfer shall be submitted to [the Certification Officer]—

(a) in the case of a proposed instrument of amalgamation, by one of the amalgamating organisations; and

(b) in the case of a proposed instrument of transfer, by the transferor organisation, and the application shall be accompanied by two copies of the proposed instrument both of which shall be signed as required by paragraph 6 of Schedule 1 or, as the case may be, paragraph 4 of Schedule 2 to these Regulations [by the fee prescribed by Regulation 11(1)], and by copies of the current rules of the organisations which are parties to the instrument.

(2) An application pursuant to section 1(4) of the 1964 Act for approval of a proposed notice to be supplied to members of an organisation in accordance with section 1(2)(d) of that Act shall be accompanied by two copies of the proposed notice.

(3) [The Certification Officer] shall signify his approval of such instrument or notice by returning to the applicant organisation one of the copies endorsed with the word "Approved" and duly authenticated.

[2008C]

NOTES

Para (1): words in first pair of square brackets substituted by the Trade Unions and Employers' Associations (Amalgamations, etc) (Amendment) Regulations 1978, SI 1978/1344; words in second pair of square brackets substituted by the Certification Officer (Amendment of Fees) Regulations 1988, SI 1988/310, reg 2.

Para (3): words in square brackets substituted by SI 1978/1344.

4 Contents of instrument of amalgamation or transfer

(1) Subject to Regulation 5 an instrument of amalgamation shall contain the particulars and information specified in Schedule 1 to these Regulations.

(2) Subject to Regulation 5 an instrument of transfer shall contain the particulars and information specified in Schedule 2 to these Regulations.

[2008D]

5 Regulation 4 shall not apply to any instrument of amalgamation or instrument of transfer which, before the coming into operation of these Regulations, has been approved by the Chief [Certification Officer] of Trade Unions and Employers' Associations or by any assistant registrar appointed by him for the purpose of section 8 of the 1964 Act.

[2008E]

NOTES

Words in square brackets substituted by the Trade Unions and Employers' Associations (Amalgamations, etc) (Amendment) Regulations 1978, SI 1978/1344.

6 Application for registration of instruments

(1) An application pursuant to section 1(5) of the 1964 Act for registration of an instrument of amalgamation shall be signed by three members of the committee of management or other governing body and the secretary of each of the amalgamating organisations and shall be submitted to [the Certification Officer] in the form to be provided by him for that purpose. The application shall be accompanied by two copies of the instrument and two copies of the proposed rules of the amalgamated organisation and by a statutory declaration from each of the amalgamating organisations in the form to be provided by [the Certification Officer] for that purpose. Each copy of the proposed rules shall be signed by the secretary of each of the amalgamating organisations.

(2) An application pursuant to section 1(5) of the 1964 Act for registration of an instrument of transfer shall be signed by three members of the committee of management or other governing body and the secretary of each of the organisations concerned and shall be submitted to [the Certification Officer] by the transferee organisation in the form to be provided by him for that purpose. The application shall be accompanied by two copies of the instrument and by statutory declarations made by the secretary of the transferor organisation and the secretary of the transferee organisation in the forms to be provided by [the Certification Officer] for that purpose. The application shall also be accompanied by two copies of any amendments to the rules of the transferee organisation made since the date of the application for approval of the proposed instrument of transfer under Regulation 3(1).

(3) In any case where he considers it desirable with a view to ensuring that adequate publicity is given to the date by which complaints must be made to him, under section 4 of the 1964 Act, as to the validity of a resolution approving an instrument of amalgamation or transfer, [the Certification Officer] may, not later than seven days after the date on which he

receives the application for registration of the instrument, require notice to be given or published in such manner, in such form, and on or before such date, as he may direct of the fact that the application for registration has been or is to be made to him.

[2008F]

NOTES

Words in square brackets substituted by the Trade Unions and Employers' Associations (Amalgamations, etc) (Amendment) Regulations 1978, SI 1978/1344.

7 Registration of instruments

(1) Before registering an instrument of amalgamation, [the Certification Officer] shall satisfy himself that the proposed rules of the amalgamated organisation are in no way inconsistent with the terms of the said instrument.

(2) Upon registering the instrument [the Certification Officer] shall send to the address specified for that purpose on the form of application for registration one copy of the instrument endorsed with the word "Registered" and duly authenticated.

[2008G]

NOTES

Words in square brackets substituted by the Trade Unions and Employers' Associations (Amalgamations, etc) (Amendment) Regulations 1978, SI 1978/1344.

8—(1) Before registering an instrument of transfer [the Certification Officer] shall satisfy himself that the rules of the transferee organisation are in no way inconsistent with the terms of the said instrument.

(2) Upon registering the instrument [the Certification Officer] shall send to the transferee organisation one copy of the instrument endorsed with the word "Registered" and duly authenticated.

[2008H]

NOTES

Words in square brackets substituted by the Trade Unions and Employers' Associations (Amalgamations, etc) (Amendment) Regulations 1978, SI 1978/1344.

9 Approval of change of name

(1) An application by an organisation pursuant to section 6(2) of the 1964 Act for the approval of a change of name shall be signed by three members of the committee of management or other governing body and the secretary of the organisation and shall be submitted to [the Certification Officer] in duplicate in the form to be provided by him for that purpose.

(2) The application shall be accompanied by a statutory declaration as to the manner in which the change of name was effected by the secretary of the organisation in the form to be provided by [the Certification Officer] for the purpose.

(3) Upon approving the change of name [the Certification Officer] shall return to the organisation one copy of the application endorsed with the word "Approved" and duly authenticated.

[2008I]

NOTES

Words in square brackets substituted by the Trade Unions and Employers' Associations (Amalgamations, etc) (Amendment) Regulations 1978, SI 1978/1344.

10 Amalgamations of transfers involving Northern Ireland Unions

Where a Northern Ireland union is a party to an amalgamation or transfer of engagements, these Regulations shall have effect subject to the following modifications, that is to say:—

(a) Regulations 3 and 6(3) shall not apply to a Northern Ireland union;

(b) Regulation 4(2) shall not apply to an instrument of transferor if the transfer organisation is a Northern Ireland union;

(c) Regulation 6 shall not require any statutory declaration from a Northern Ireland union;

(d) the application to the Certification Officer under Regulation 6(2) for the registration of an instrument of transfer shall be submitted by the transferor organisation of the transferee organisation is a Northern Ireland union.

[2008J]

[11 Fees

(1) The fee referred to in Regulation 3(1) (fee to accompany an application for approval of a proposed instrument of amalgamation or transfer) shall be [£1850].

(2) The following fees shall be payable in advance—

For approval of a change of name	[£96]
For every inspection on the same day of documents kept by the Certification Officer under the 1964 Act relating to one and the same organisation	[£19].]

[2008K]

NOTES

Substituted by the Certification Officer (Amendment of Fees) Regulations 1988, SI 1988/310, reg 2.

Sums in square brackets substituted by the Certification Officer (Amendment of Fees) Regulations 2005, SI 2005/713, regs 2, 3, as from 6 April 2005.

[12 A fee of [£41] shall be payable for the entry of an amalgamated organisation on the list of trade unions or employers' associations maintained by the Certification Officer under section 8 of the 1974 Act where each of the amalgamating organisations is already entered on the list.]

[2008L]

NOTES

Substituted by the Trade Unions and Employers' Associations (Amalgamations, etc) (Amendment) Regulations 1978, SI 1978/1344.

Sum in square brackets substituted by the Certification Officer (Amendment of Fees) Regulations 2005, SI 2005/713, regs 4, as from 6 April 2005.

SCHEDULES

SCHEDULE 1
CONTENTS OF INSTRUMENT OF AMALGAMATION

Regulation 4(1)

1. The instrument shall state that it is an instrument of amalgamation between the organisations named therein as the amalgamating organisations, and that upon the coming into operation of the instrument the members of the amalgamating organisations will become members of the amalgamated organisation and be subject to that organisation's rules.

2. The instrument shall either set out the proposed rules of the amalgamated organisation or state who are the persons authorised to draw up those rules.

3. If the instrument does not set out the proposed rules it shall contain a summary of what those rules will provide with regard to the following matters:—

(i) the name and principal purposes of the amalgamated organisation;

(ii) the conditions of admission to membership;

(iii) the structure of the amalgamated organisation;

(iv) the method of appointing and removing its governing body and principal officials and of altering its rules;

(v) the contributions and benefits applicable to members of the amalgamating organisations.

4. The instrument shall specify property held for the benefit of any of the amalgamating organisations or for the benefit of a branch of any of those organisations which is not to be vested in the appropriate trustees as defined in section 5(3) of the 1964 Act, and shall state the proposed disposition of any such property.

5. Without prejudice to section 1(5) of the 1964 Act, the instrument shall state the date on which it is to take effect.

6. The instrument shall be signed by three members of the committee of management or other governing body and the secretary of each of the amalgamating organisations.

[2008M]

SCHEDULE 2
CONTENTS OF INSTRUMENT OF TRANSFER

Regulation 4(2)

1. The instrument shall state that it is an instrument of transfer of the engagements of the organisation named therein as the transferor organisation to the organisation named therein as the transferee organisation, and that upon the coming into operation of the instrument the members of the transferor organisation will become members of the transferee organisation and be subject to that organisation's rules.

2. The instrument shall:—
   (i) state what contributions and benefits will be applicable to members of the transferor organisation under the transferee organisation's rules;
   (ii) if members of the transferor organisation are to be allocated to a branch or section or to branches or sections of the transferee organisation, give particulars of such allocation or the method by which it is to be decided;
   (iii) state whether before registration of the instrument the transferee organisation's rules are to be altered in their application to members of the transferor organisation and, if so, the effect of any alterations;
   (iv) without prejudice to section 1(5) of the 1964 Act, state the date on which the instrument is to take effect.

3. The instrument shall specify any property held for the benefit of the transferor organisation or for the benefit of a branch of the transferor organisation which is not to be vested in the appropriate trustees as defined in section 5(3) of the 1964 Act, and shall state the proposed disposition of any such property.

4. The instrument shall be signed by three members of the committee of management or other governing body and the secretary of each of the organisations.

[2008N]

REHABILITATION OF OFFENDERS ACT 1974 (EXCEPTIONS) ORDER 1975

(SI 1975/1023)

NOTES

Made: 24 June 1975.
Authority: Rehabilitation of Offenders Act 1974, ss 4(4), 7(4).
Commencement: 1 July 1975.
Note: this Order was revoked in relation to Scotland by the Rehabilitation of Offenders Act 1974 (Exclusions and Exceptions) (Scotland) Order 2003, SSI 2003/231, art 6(a), as from 29 March 2003. The 2003 Scottish Order is printed at **[2881A]**. The Order remains in force for England and Wales. Amendments made to this Order before 29 March 2003 which applied to Scotland only have now been omitted from the Order as reproduced here.
See *Harvey* DI(9), (13), R.

1 This Order may be cited as the Rehabilitation of Offenders Act 1974 (Exceptions) Order 1975 and shall come into operation on 1st July 1975.

[2009]

NOTES

Revoked in relation to Scotland as noted at the beginning of this Order.

2—[(1) In this Order, except where the context otherwise requires—

["the 2000 Act" means the Financial Services and Markets Act 2000;]

"the Act" means the Rehabilitation of Offenders Act 1974;

["administration of justice offence" means—

(a) the offence of perverting the course of justice,

(b) any offence under section 51 of the Criminal Justice and Public Order Act 1994 (intimidation etc of witnesses, jurors and others),

(c) an offence under section 1, 2, 6 or 7 of the Perjury Act 1911 (perjury),

or any offence committed under the law of any part of the United Kingdom (other than England or Wales) or of any other country where the conduct which constitutes the offence would, if it all took place in England or Wales, constitute one or more of the offences specified by paragraph (a) to (c);]

["adoption agency" has the meaning given to it by section 1 of the Adoption Act 1976;]

["associate", in relation to a person ("A"), means someone who is a controller, director or manager of A or, where A is a partnership, any partner of A;]

. . .

["child minding" means—

(a) until section 79 of the Care Standards Act 2000 comes into force, acting as a child minder within the meaning of section 71 of the Children Act 1989; and

(b) when section 79 of the Care Standards Act 2000 is in force, child minding within the meaning of section 79A of the Children Act 1989;]

["collective investment scheme" has the meaning given by section 235 of the 2000 Act;]

["the competent authority for listing" means the competent authority for the purposes of Part VI of the 2000 Act (listing);]

["contracting authority" means a contracting authority within the meaning of Article 1(9) of Directive 2004/18/EC;]

["contracting entity" means a contracting entity within the meaning of Article 2(2) of Directive 2004/17/EC;]

["controller" has the meaning given by section 422 of the 2000 Act;]

["Council" has the meaning given to it by section 54 of the Care Standards Act 2000;]

["Council of Lloyd's" means the council constituted by section 3 of Lloyd's Act 1982;]

["day care" means—

(a) until section 79 of the Care Standards Act 2000 comes into force, day care for which registration is required by section 78(1) of the Children Act 1989; and

(b) when section 79 of the Care Standards Act 2000 is in force, day care for which registration is required by section 79D(5) of the Children Act 1989;]

["day care premises" means any premises on which day care is provided, but does not include any part of the premises where children are not looked after;]

["Directive 2004/17/EC" means Directive 2004/17/EC of the European Parliament and of the Council of 31 March 2004;]

["Directive 2004/18/EC" means Directive 2004/18/EC of the European Parliament and of the Council of 31 March 2004;]

["director" has the meaning given by section 417 of the 2000 Act;]

["key worker", in relation to any body ("A"), means any individual who is likely, in the course of the duties of his office or employment—

(a) where A is the Authority, to play a significant role in the decision making process of the Authority in relation to the exercise of the Authority's public functions (within the meaning of section 349(5) of the 2000 Act) under any provision of the 2000 Act other than Part VI, or to support directly such a person;

(b) where A is the competent authority for listing, to play a significant role in the decision making process of the competent authority for listing in relation to the exercise of its functions under Part VI of the 2000 Act, or to support directly such a person;]

["manager" has the meaning given by section 423 of the 2000 Act;]

["open-ended investment company" has the meaning given by section 236 of the 2000 Act]

[Part IV permission" has the meaning given by section 40(4) of the 2000 Act;]

["relevant collective investment scheme" means a collective investment scheme which is recognised under section 264 (schemes constituted in other EEA States), 270 (schemes authorised in designated countries or territories) or 272 (individually recognised overseas schemes) of the 2000 Act;]

…

["taxi driver licence" means a licence granted under—

[(i) section 46 of the Town Police Clauses Act 1847;]

(ii) section 8 of the Metropolitan Public Carriage Act 1869;

(iii) section 9 of the Plymouth City Council Act 1975;

(iv) section 51 of the Local Government (Miscellaneous Provisions) Act 1976; or

(v) section 13 of the Private Hire Vehicles (London) Act 1998;]

["trustee", in relation to a unit trust scheme, has the meaning given by section 237 of the 2000 Act;]

["UK recognised clearing house" means a clearing house in relation to which a recognition order under section 290 of the 2000 Act, otherwise than by virtue of section 292(2) of that Act (overseas clearing houses), is in force;]

["UK recognised investment exchange" means an investment exchange in relation to which a recognition order under section 290 of the 2000 Act, otherwise than by virtue of section 292(2) of that Act (overseas investment exchanges), is in force;]

["work" includes—

(a) work of any kind, whether paid or unpaid, and whether under a contract of service or apprenticeship, under a contract for services, or otherwise than under a contract; and

(b) an office established by or by virtue of an enactment;]

["work with children" means work of the kind described in paragraph 14 of Schedule 1 to this Order;]

…

(2) Where, by virtue of this Order, the operation of any of the provisions of the Act is excluded in relation to spent convictions the exclusion shall be taken to extend to spent convictions for offences of every description …].

(3) Part IV of Schedule 1 to this Order shall have effect for the interpretation of expressions used in that Schedule.

(4) In this Order a reference to any enactment shall be construed as a reference to that enactment as amended, extended or applied by or under any other enactment.

(5) The Interpretation Act 1889 shall apply to the interpretation of this Order as it applies to the interpretation of an Act of Parliament.

[2010]

NOTES

Revoked in relation to Scotland as noted at the beginning of this Order.

Para (1) is amended as follows:

Substituted, together with para (2), by the Rehabilitation of Offenders Act 1974 (Exceptions) (Amendment No 2) Order 1986, SI 1986/2268, art 2(1), Schedule, para 1.

Definitions "the 2000 Act", "administration of justice offence", "associate", "collective investment scheme", "the competent authority for listing", "controller", "Council of Lloyd's", "director", "key worker", "manager", "open-ended investment company", "relevant collective investment scheme", "trustee", "UK recognised clearing house", and "UK recognised investment exchange" inserted by the Rehabilitation of Offenders Act 1974 (Exceptions) (Amendment) (No 2) Order 2001, SI 2001/3816, arts 2, 3(1).

Definitions "adoption agency", "child minding", "day care", "day care premises", "work", and "work with children" inserted by the Rehabilitation of Offenders Act 1974 (Exceptions) (Amendment) Order 2001, SI 2001/1192, arts 2, 3.

Definition "the Building Societies Commission" (omitted) revoked by SI 2001/3816, arts 2, 3(3).

Definitions "contracting authority", "contracting entity", "Directive 2004/17/EC", and "Directive 2004/18/EC" inserted by the Rehabilitation of Offenders Act 1974 (Exceptions) (Amendment) (England and Wales) Order 2006, SI 2006/2143, arts 2, 3(b), as from 26 July 2006.

Definition "Council" inserted by the Rehabilitation of Offenders Act 1974 (Exceptions) (Amendment) (England and Wales) Order 2003, SI 2003/965, arts 2, 3(a).

Definition "Part IV permission" inserted by SI 2001/3816, arts 2, 3(1).

Definition "relevant offence" (omitted) revoked by the Rehabilitation of Offenders Act 1974 (Exceptions) (Amendment) (England and Wales) Order 2007, SI 2007/2149, arts 2, 3(1), as from 22 July 2007.

Definition "taxi driver licence" inserted by SI 2003/965, arts 2, 3(a); para (i) substituted by SI 2006/2143, arts 2, 3(a), as from 26 July 2006.

Final words omitted revoked by SI 2001/3816, arts 2, 3(3).
Para (2): substituted as noted above; words omitted revoked by SI 2007/2149, arts 2, 3(2), as from 22 July 2007.
Adoption Act 1976, s 1: repealed by the Adoption and Children Act 2002, s 139(3), Sch 5. As to the meaning of "adoption agency", see now s 2(1) of the 2002 Act.
Interpretation Act 1889: repealed and replaced by the Interpretation Act 1978.

3 None of the provisions of section 4(2) of the Act shall apply in relation to—

(a) any question asked by or on behalf of any person, in the course of the duties of his office or employment, in order to assess the suitability—

(i) of the person to whom the question relates for admission to any of the professions specified in Part I of Schedule 1 to this Order; or

[(ii) of the person to whom the question relates for any office or employment specified in Part II of the said Schedule 1 or for any other work specified in paragraph [13, 14, 20, 21, 35, 36, 37, 40 or 43] of Part II of the said Schedule 1; or]

(iii) of the person to whom the question relates or of any other person to pursue any occupation specified in Part III of the said Schedule 1 or to pursue it subject to a particular condition or restriction; or

(iv) of the person to whom the question relates or of any other person to hold a licence, certificate or permit of a kind specified in Schedule 2 to this Order or to hold it subject to a particular condition or restriction,

where the person questioned is informed at the time the question is asked that, by virtue of this Order, spent convictions are to be disclosed;

[(aa) any question asked by or on behalf of any person, in the course of the duties of his work, in order to assess the suitability of a person to work with children, where—

(i) the question relates to the person whose suitability is being assessed;

(ii) the person whose suitability is being assessed lives on the premises where his work with children would normally take place and the question relates to a person living in the same household as him;

(iii) the person whose suitability is being assessed lives on the premises where his work with children would normally take place and the question relates to a person who regularly works on those premises at a time when the work with children usually takes place; or

(iv) the work for which the person's suitability is being assessed is child minding which would normally take place on premises other than premises where that person lives and the question relates to a person who lives on those other premises or to a person who regularly works on them at a time when the child minding takes place,

and where the person to whom the question relates is informed at the time the question is asked that, by virtue of this Order, spent convictions are to be disclosed;]

[(ab) …]

(b) any question asked by or on behalf of any person, in the course of his duties as a person employed in the service of the Crown, the United Kingdom Atomic Energy Authority, [or] … [the Financial Services Authority] in order to assess, for the purpose of safeguarding national security, the suitability of the person to whom the question relates or of any other person for any office or employment where the person questioned is informed at the time the question is asked that, by virtue of this Order, spent convictions are to be disclosed for the purpose of safeguarding national security;

[(bb) any question asked by or on behalf of

(i) the Civil Aviation Authority,

(ii) any other person authorised to provide air traffic services under section 4 or section 5 of the Transport Act 2000 (in any case where such person is a company, an "authorised company"),

(iii) any company which is a subsidiary (within the meaning given by section 736(1) of the Companies Act 1985) of an authorised company, or

(iv) any company of which an authorised company is a subsidiary,

where, in the case of sub-paragraphs (iii) and (iv) of this paragraph the question is put in relation to the provision of air traffic services, and in all cases, where the question is put in order to assess, for the purpose of safeguarding national security, the suitability of the person to whom the question relates or of any other person for any office or employment where the person questioned is informed at the time the question is asked that, by virtue of this Order, spent convictions are to be disclosed for the purpose of safeguarding national security;]

[(e) any question asked by or on behalf of any person in the course of his duties as a person employed by an adoption agency for the purpose of assessing the suitability of any person to adopt children in general or a child in particular where—

(i) the question relates to the person whose suitability is being assessed; or

(ii) the question relates to a person over the age of 18 living in the same household as the person whose suitability is being assessed,

and where the person to whom the question relates is informed at the time the question is asked that, by virtue of this Order, spent convictions are to be disclosed;

(f) any question asked by or on behalf of any person, in the course of the duties of his work, in order to assess the suitability of a person to provide day care where—

(i) the question relates to the person whose suitability is being assessed; or

(ii) the question relates to a person who lives on the premises which are or are proposed to be day care premises,

and where the person to whom the question relates is informed at the time the question is asked that, by virtue of this Order, spent convictions are to be disclosed];

[(g) any question asked by, or on behalf of, the person listed in the second column of any entry in the table below to the extent that it relates to a conviction … (or any circumstances ancillary to … a conviction) of any individual, but only if—

(i) the person questioned is informed at the time the question is asked that, by virtue of this Order, spent convictions … are to be disclosed; and

(ii) the question is asked in order to assess the suitability of the individual to whom the question relates to have the status specified in the first column of that entry.

Status			*Questioner*
1	A person with Part IV permission.		The Financial Services Authority.
2	(a)	An approved person (within the meaning of Part V of the 2000 Act (performance of regulated activities)).	The Financial Services Authority or the authorised person (within the meaning of section 31(2) of the 2000 Act) or the applicant for Part IV permission who made the application for the Authority's approval under section 59 of the 2000 Act in relation to the person mentioned in sub-paragraph (a) of the first column.
	(b)	An associate of the person (whether or not an individual) mentioned in sub-paragraph (a).	
3	(a)	The manager or trustee of an authorised unit trust scheme, within the meaning of section 237 of the 2000 Act.	The Financial Services Authority or the unit trust scheme mentioned in the first column.
	(b)	An associate of the person (whether or not an individual) mentioned in sub-paragraph (a).	
4	(a)	A director of an open-ended investment company.	The Financial Services Authority or the open-ended investment company mentioned in the first column.
	(b)	An associate of the person (whether or not an individual) mentioned in sub-paragraph (a).	
5	An associate of the operator or trustee of a relevant collective investment scheme.		The Financial Services Authority or the collective investment scheme mentioned in the first column.

	Status	*Questioner*
6	An associate of a UK recognised investment exchange or UK recognised clearing house.	The Financial Services Authority or the investment exchange or clearing house mentioned in the first column.
7	A controller of a person with Part IV permission.	The Financial Services Authority or the person with Part IV permission mentioned in the first column.
8	(a) A person who carries on a regulated activity (within the meaning of section 22 of the 2000 Act) but to whom the general prohibition does not apply by virtue of section 327 of the 2000 Act (exemption from the general prohibition for members of a designated professional body).	(a) The Financial Services Authority.
	(b) An associate of the person (whether or not an individual) mentioned in sub-paragraph (a).	(b) In the case of a person mentioned in sub-paragraph (b) of the first column, the person mentioned in sub-paragraph (a) of that column.
9	A key worker of the Financial Services Authority.	The Financial Services Authority.
10	An ombudsman (within the meaning of Schedule 17 to the 2000 Act) of the Financial Ombudsman Service.	The scheme operator (within the meaning of section 225 of the 2000 Act) of the Financial Ombudsman Service.
11	An associate of the issuer of securities which have been admitted to the official list maintained by the competent authority for listing under section 74 of the 2000 Act.	The competent authority for listing.
12	A sponsor (within the meaning of section 88(2) of the 2000 Act).	The competent authority for listing.
13	A key worker of the competent authority for listing.	The competent authority for listing.
14	An associate of a person who has Part IV permission and who is admitted to Lloyd's as an underwriting agent (within the meaning of section 2 of Lloyd's Act 1982).	(a) The Council of Lloyd's. (b) The person with Part IV permission specified in the first column (or a person applying for such permission).
15	An associate of the Council of Lloyd's.	The Council of Lloyd's.
16	(a) Any member of a UK recognised investment exchange or UK recognised clearing house.	(a) The UK recognised investment exchange or UK recognised clearing house specified in the first column.
	(b) Any associate of the person (whether or not an individual) mentioned in sub-paragraph (a).	(b) In the case of a person mentioned in sub-paragraph (b) of the first column, the person mentioned in sub-paragraph (a) of that column];

[(h) any question asked by or on behalf of the National Lottery Commission for the purpose of determining whether to grant or revoke a licence under Part I of the National Lottery etc Act 1993 where the question relates to an individual—

(i) who manages the business or any part of the business carried on under the licence (or who is likely to do so if the licence is granted), or

(ii) for whose benefit that business is carried on (or is likely to be carried on if the licence is granted),

and where the person to whom the question relates is informed at the time that the question is asked that, by virtue of this Order, spent convictions are to be disclosed];

[(i) any question asked by or on behalf of the Council for the purpose of determining whether or not to grant an application for registration under Part IV of the Care Standards Act 2000, where the person questioned is informed at the time the question is asked that, by virtue of this Order, spent convictions are to be disclosed];

[(j) any question asked by or on behalf of a contracting authority or contracting entity in relation to a conviction within the meaning of Article 45(1) of Directive 2004/18/EC which is a spent conviction (or any circumstances ancillary to such a conviction) for the purpose of determining whether or not to treat a person as ineligible:

(i) for the purposes of regulation 23 of the Public Contracts Regulations 2006 or regulation 23 of the Utilities Contracts Regulations 2006; or

(ii) to participate in a design contest for the purposes of regulation 33 of the Public Contracts Regulations 2006 or regulation 34 of the Utilities Contracts Regulations 2006,

where the person questioned is informed at the time the question is asked that, by virtue of this Order, convictions within the meaning of Article 45(1) of Directive 2004/18/EC which are spent convictions are to be disclosed;

(k) any question asked, by or on behalf of the Football Association[, Football League] or Football Association Premier League in order to assess the suitability of the person to whom the question relates or of any other person to be approved as able to undertake, in the course of acting as a steward at a sports ground at which football matches are played or as a supervisor or manager of such a person, licensable conduct within the meaning of the Private Security Industry Act 2001 without a licence issued under that Act, in accordance with … section 4 of that Act];

[(l) any question asked by the Secretary of State for the purpose of considering the suitability of an individual to have access to information released under sections 113A and 113B of the Police Act 1997].

[2011]

NOTES

Revoked in relation to Scotland as noted at the beginning of this Order.

Para (a): sub-para (ii) substituted by the Rehabilitation of Offenders Act 1974 (Exceptions) (Amendment) Order 2001, SI 2001/1192, arts 2, 4(1); words in square brackets in sub-para (ii) substituted by the Rehabilitation of Offenders Act 1974 (Exceptions) (Amendment) (England and Wales) Order 2007, SI 2007/2149, arts 2, 4(1), as from 22 July 2007.

Para (aa): inserted by the Rehabilitation of Offenders Act 1974 (Exceptions) (Amendment) Order 1986, SI 1986/1249, art 2, Schedule; substituted by SI 2001/1192, arts 2, 4(2).

Para (ab): inserted by the Rehabilitation of Offenders Act 1974 (Exceptions) (Amendment No 2) Order 1986, SI 1986/2268, art 2(1), Schedule, para 2; revoked by the Rehabilitation of Offenders Act 1974 (Exceptions) (Amendment) (No 2) Order 2001, SI 2001/3816, arts 2, 4(1), (2).

Para (b): word in first pair of square brackets inserted by the Postal Services Act 2000 (Consequential Modifications No 1) Order 2001, SI 2001/1149, art 3(1), Sch 1, para 41; words omitted revoked by a combination of SI 2002/441, arts 2, 3(2) and SI 2001/1149, art 3(2), Sch 2; words in second pair of square brackets inserted by SI 2001/3816, arts 2, 4(1), (3).

Para (bb): inserted by SI 2002/441, arts 2, 3(3), as from a day to be appointed (ie, the day on which the Police Act 1997, s 133(d) comes into force in England and Wales).

Paras (e), (f): added by SI 2001/1192, arts 2, 4(3). Note that SI 2001/1192 purports to insert these paragraphs after para (d) but it is understood that this is a drafting error as this article does not contain a para (d).

Para (g): added by SI 2001/3816, arts 2, 4(1), (4); words omitted revoked by SI 2007/2149, arts 2, 4(2), (3), as from 22 July 2007.

Para (h): added by SI 2002/441, arts 2, 3(4).

Para (i): added by SI 2003/965, arts 2, 5.

Para (j): added, together with para (k), by the Rehabilitation of Offenders Act 1974 (Exceptions) (Amendment) (England and Wales) Order 2006, SI 2006/2143, arts 2, 4, as from 26 July 2006.

Para (k): added as noted above; words in square brackets inserted, and words omitted revoked, by the Rehabilitation of Offenders Act 1974 (Exceptions) (Amendment No 2) (England and Wales) Order 2006, SI 2006/3290, art 2, as from 7 December 2006.

Para (l): added by SI 2007/2149, arts 2, 4(4), as from 22 July 2007.

4 Paragraph (b) of section 4(3) of the Act shall not apply in relation to—

(a) the dismissal or exclusion of any person from any profession specified in Part I of Schedule 1 to this Order;

[(b) any office, employment or occupation specified in Part II or Part III of the said Schedule 1 or any other work specified in paragraph [13, 14, 20, 21, 35, 36, 37, 40 or 43] of Part II of the said Schedule 1;]

(c) any action taken for the purpose of safeguarding national security;

[(d) any decision by the Financial Services Authority—

(i) to refuse an application for Part IV permission under the 2000 Act,

(ii) to vary or to cancel such permission (or to refuse to vary or cancel such permission) or to impose a requirement under section 43 of that Act or,

(iii) to make, or to refuse to vary or revoke, an order under section 56 of that Act (prohibition orders),

(iv) to refuse an application for the Authority's approval under section 59 of that Act or to withdraw such approval,

(v) to refuse to make, or to revoke, an order declaring a unit trust scheme to be an authorised unit trust scheme under section 243 of the 2000 Act or to refuse to give its approval under section 251 of the 2000 Act to a proposal to replace the manager or trustee of such a scheme,

(vi) to give a direction under section 257 of the 2000 Act (authorised unit trust schemes), or to vary (or to refuse to vary or revoke) such a direction,

(vii) to refuse to make, or to revoke, an authorisation order under regulation 14 of the Open-Ended Investment Companies Regulations 2001 or to refuse to give its approval under regulation 21 of those Regulations to a proposal to replace a director or to appoint an additional director of an open-ended investment company,

(viii) to give a direction to an open-ended investment company under regulation 25 of those Regulations or to vary (or refuse to vary or revoke) such a direction,

(ix) to refuse to give its approval to a collective investment scheme being recognised under section 270 of the 2000 Act or to direct that such a scheme cease to be recognised by virtue of that section or to refuse to make, or to revoke, an order declaring a collective investment scheme to be a recognised scheme under section 272 of that Act,

(x) to refuse to make, or to revoke, a recognition order under section 290 of the 2000 Act, otherwise than by virtue of section 292(2) of that Act, or to give a direction to a UK recognised investment exchange or UK recognised clearing house under section 296 of the 2000 Act,

(xi) to make, or to refuse to vary or to revoke, an order under section 329 (orders in respect of members of a designated professional body in relation to the general prohibition), or

(xii) to dismiss, fail to promote or exclude a person from being a key worker of the Authority,

by reason of, or partly by reason of, a spent conviction of an individual …, or of any circumstances ancillary to such a conviction or of a failure (whether or not by that individual) to disclose such a conviction or any such circumstances;

(e) any decision by the scheme operator (within the meaning of section 225 of the 2000 Act) of the Financial Ombudsman Service to dismiss, or not to appoint, an individual as, an ombudsman (within the meaning of Schedule 17 to the 2000 Act) of the Financial Ombudsman Service by reason of, or partly by reason of, his spent conviction …, or of any circumstances ancillary to such a conviction or of a failure (whether or not by that individual) to disclose such a conviction or any such circumstances;

(f) any decision of the competent authority for listing—

(i) to refuse an application for listing under Part VI of the 2000 Act or to discontinue or suspend the listing of any securities under section 77 of that Act,

(ii) to refuse to grant a person's application for approval as a sponsor under section 88 of the 2000 Act or to cancel such approval, or

(iii) to dismiss, fail to promote or exclude a person from being a key worker of the competent authority for listing,

by reason of, or partly by reason of, a spent conviction of an individual …, or of any circumstances ancillary to such a conviction or of a failure (whether or not by that individual) to disclose such a conviction or any such circumstances;

(g) any decision of anyone who is specified in any of sub-paragraphs 2 to 4 or 5 to 7 of the second column of the table in article 3(g), other than the Authority, to dismiss an individual who has, or to fail to promote or exclude an individual who is seeking to obtain, the status specified in the corresponding entry in the first column of that table (but not, where applicable, the status of being an associate of another person), by reason of, or partly by reason of, a spent conviction of that individual or of his associate ..., or of any circumstances ancillary to such a conviction or of a failure (whether or not by that individual) to disclose such a conviction or any such circumstances;

(h) any decision of anyone who is specified in sub-paragraph 8(a), 14(a) or 16(a) of the second column of the table in article 3(g) to dismiss an individual who has, or to fail to promote or exclude an individual who is seeking to obtain, the status specified in the corresponding entry in sub-paragraph (b) of the first column of that table (associate), by reason of, or partly by reason of, a spent conviction of that individual ..., or of any circumstances ancillary to such a conviction or of a failure (whether or not by that individual) to disclose such a conviction or any such circumstances;

(i) any decision of the Council of Lloyd's—

(i) to refuse to admit any person as, or to exclude, an underwriting agent (within the meaning of section 2 of Lloyd's Act 1982), where that person has, or who has applied for, Part IV permission, or

(ii) to dismiss, or to exclude a person from being, an associate of the Council of Lloyd's,

by reason of, or partly by reason of, a spent conviction of an individual ..., or of any circumstances ancillary to such a conviction or of a failure (whether or not by that individual) to disclose such a conviction or any such circumstances;

(j) any decision of a UK recognised investment exchange or UK recognised clearing house to refuse to admit any person as, or to exclude, a member by reason of, or partly by reason of, a spent conviction of an individual ..., or of any circumstances ancillary to such a conviction or of a failure (whether or not by that individual) to disclose such a conviction or any such circumstances;]

[(k) any decision by the Council to refuse to grant an application for registration under Part IV of the Care Standards Act 2000 or to suspend, remove or refuse to restore a person's registration under that Part;

(l) any decision to refuse to grant a taxi driver licence, to grant such a licence subject to conditions or to suspend, revoke or refuse to renew such a licence;

(m) any decision by the Security Industry Authority to refuse to grant a licence under section 8 of the Private Security Industry Act 2001, to grant such a licence subject to conditions, to modify such a licence (including any of the conditions of that licence) or to revoke such a licence];

[(n) any decision by the Football Association[, Football League] or Football Association Premier League to refuse to approve a person as able to undertake, in the course of acting as a steward at a sports ground at which football matches are played or as a supervisor or manager of such a person, licensable conduct within the meaning of the Private Security Industry Act 2001 without a licence issued under that Act, in accordance with ... section 4 of that Act].

[2012]

NOTES

Revoked in relation to Scotland as noted at the beginning of this Order.

Para (b): substituted by the Rehabilitation of Offenders Act 1974 (Exceptions) (Amendment) Order 2001, SI 2001/1192, arts 2, 5; words in square brackets substituted by the Rehabilitation of Offenders Act 1974 (Exceptions) (Amendment) (England and Wales) Order 2007, SI 2007/2149, arts 2, 5(2), as from 22 July 2007.

Para (d): inserted by the Rehabilitation of Offenders Act 1974 (Exceptions) (Amendment No 2) Order 1986, SI 1986/2268, art 2(1), Schedule, para 3, and substituted (by new paras (d)–(j)) by the Rehabilitation of Offenders Act 1974 (Exceptions) (Amendment) (No 2) Order 2001, SI 2001/3816, arts 2, 5; words omitted revoked by SI 2007/2149, arts 2, 5(1), as from 22 July 2007.

Paras (e)–(j): substituted as noted above; words omitted revoked by SI 2007/2149, arts 2, 5(1), as from 22 July 2007.

Paras (k)–(m): added by SI 2003/965, arts 2, 7.

Para (n): added by the Rehabilitation of Offenders Act 1974 (Exceptions) (Amendment) (England and Wales) Order 2006, SI 2006/2143, arts 2, 5, as from 26 July 2006; words in square brackets inserted, and words omitted revoked, by the Rehabilitation of Offenders Act 1974 (Exceptions) (Amendment No 2) (England and Wales) Order 2006, SI 2006/3290, art 2, as from 7 December 2006.

[5—(1) Section 4(1) of the Act shall not—

(a) apply in relation to any proceedings specified in Schedule 3 to this Order;

(b) apply in relation to any proceedings specified in paragraph (2) below to the extent that there falls to be determined therein any issue relating to a person's spent conviction … or to circumstances ancillary thereto;

(c) prevent, in any proceedings specified in paragraph (2) below, the admission or requirement of any evidence relating to a person's spent conviction … or to circumstances ancillary thereto.

[(2) The proceedings referred to in paragraph (1) above are any proceedings with respect to a decision or proposed decision of the kind specified in article 4(d) to (j).]]

[2013]

NOTES

Revoked in relation to Scotland as noted at the beginning of this Order.

Substituted by the Rehabilitation of Offenders Act 1974 (Exceptions) (Amendment No 2) Order 1986, SI 1986/2268, art 2(1), Schedule, para 4.

Para (1): words omitted revoked by the Rehabilitation of Offenders Act 1974 (Exceptions) (Amendment) (England and Wales) Order 2007, SI 2007/2149, arts 2, 6, as from 22 July 2007.

Para (2): substituted by the Rehabilitation of Offenders Act 1974 (Exceptions) (Amendment) (No 2) Order 2001, SI 2001/3816, arts 2, 6.

SCHEDULES

SCHEDULE 1
[EXCEPTED PROFESSIONS, OFFICES, EMPLOYMENTS, WORK AND OCCUPATIONS]

Article 2(3), 3, 4

PART I
PROFESSIONS

1. Medical practitioner.

2. Barrister (in England and Wales), advocate (in Scotland), solicitor.

3. Chartered accountant, certified accountant.

4. Dentist, dental hygienist, [dental therapist].

5. Veterinary surgeon.

6. Nurse, midwife.

7. [optometrist], dispensing optician.

[8. Registered pharmacist.

8A. Registered pharmacy technician.]

9. Registered teacher (in Scotland).

10. Any profession to which the [Health Professions Order 2001] applies and which is undertaken following registration under that Act.

[11. Registered osteopath.]

[12. Registered chiropractor.]

[13. Chartered psychologist.

14. Actuary.

15. Registered foreign lawyer.

16. Legal executive.

17. Receiver appointed by the Court of Protection.]

[18. Home inspector.]

[2014]

NOTES

Revoked in relation to Scotland as noted at the beginning of this Order.

Schedule heading: substituted by the Rehabilitation of Offenders Act 1974 (Exceptions) (Amendment) Order 2001, SI 2001/1192, arts 2, 6(1).

Para 4: words in square brackets substituted by the Dentists Act 1984 (Amendment) Order 2005, SI 2005/2011, art 49, Sch 6, Pt II, para 7, as from 31 July 2006.

Para 7: words in square brackets substituted by the Opticians Act 1989 (Amendment) Order 2005, SI 2005/848, art 28, Sch 1, Pt 3, para 14, as from 30 June 2005.

Para 8: the original para 8 (pharmaceutical chemist) was substituted by new paras 8, 8A, by the Pharmacists and Pharmacy Technicians Order 2007, SI 2007/289, art 67, Sch 1, Pt 2, para 12(a), as from 30 March 2007 (in so far as relating to the new para 8), and as from a day to be appointed (in so far as relating to para 8A).

Para 8A: see the para 8 note above.

Para 10: words in square brackets substituted by the Health Professions Order 2001 (Consequential Amendments) Order 2003, SI 2003/1590, art 3, Schedule, Pt 2, para 26, as from 9 July 2003.

Para 11: added by the Osteopaths Act 1993, s 39(2).

Para 12: added by the Chiropractors Act 1994, s 40(2).

Paras 13–17: added by the Rehabilitation of Offenders Act 1974 (Exceptions) (Amendment) Order 2002, SI 2002/441, arts 2, 5(1).

Para 18: added by the Rehabilitation of Offenders Act 1974 (Exceptions) (Amendment) (England and Wales) Order 2006, SI 2006/2143, arts 2, 6, as from 26 July 2006.

Solicitor: the reference to a solicitor should now be read as including a reference to a registered European lawyer, see the European Communities (Lawyer's Practice) Regulations 2000, SI 2000/1119, reg 37(3), Sch 4, para 19.

PART II
[OFFICES, EMPLOYMENTS AND WORK]

1. Judicial appointments.

[2. The Director of Public Prosecutions and any office or employment in the Crown Prosecution Service.]

3. …

[4. [Designated officers for magistrates' courts, for justices of the peace or for local justice areas], justices' clerks [and assistants to justices' clerks].]

5. Clerks (including depute and assistant clerks) and officers of the High Court of Justiciary, the Court of Session and the district court, sheriff clerks (including sheriff clerks depute) and their clerks and assistants.

6. Constables, persons appointed as police cadets to undergo training with a view to becoming constables and persons employed for the purposes of, or to assist the constables of, a police force established under any enactment; naval, military and air force police.

7. Any employment which is concerned with the administration of, or is otherwise normally carried out wholly or partly within the precincts of, a prison, remand centre, [removal centre, short-term holding facility,] [young offender institution] or young offenders institution, and members of boards of visitors appointed under section 6 of the Prison Act 1952 or of visiting committees appointed under section 7 of the Prisons (Scotland) Act 1952.

8. Traffic wardens appointed under section 81 of the Road Traffic Regulation Act 1967 or section 9 of the Police (Scotland) Act 1967.

9. Probation officers appointed under Schedule 3 to the Powers of Criminal Courts Act 1973.

10, 11. …

[12. Any office or employment which is concerned with:

(a) the provision of care services to vulnerable adults; or

(b) the representation of, or advocacy services for, vulnerable adults by a service that has been approved by the Secretary of State or created under any enactment;

and which is of such a kind as to enable a person, in the course of his normal duties, to have access to vulnerable adults in receipt of such services.]

[13. Any employment or other work which is concerned with the provision of health services and which is of such a kind as to enable the holder of that employment or the person engaged in that work to have access to persons in receipt of such services in the course of his normal duties.]

[14. Any work which is—

(a) work in a regulated position; or

(b) work in a further education institution where the normal duties of that work involve regular contact with persons aged under 18.]

[15. Any employment in the Royal Society for the Prevention of Cruelty to Animals where the person employed or working, as part of his duties, may carry out the [humane] killing of animals.

16. Any office or employment in the Serious Fraud Office.

17. Any office or employment in the [Serious Organised Crime Agency].

[18. The Commissioners for Her Majesty's Revenue and Customs and any office or employment in their service.

18A. The Director and any office or employment in the Revenue and Customs Prosecutions Office.]

19. Any employment which is concerned with the monitoring, for the purposes of child protection, of communications by means of the internet.]

[20. Any employment or other work which is normally carried out in premises approved under section 9 of the Criminal Justice and Court Services Act 2000.

21. Any employment or other work which is normally carried out in a hospital used only for the provision of high security psychiatric services.]

[22. An individual designated under section 2 of the Traffic Management Act 2004.

23. Judges' clerks, secretaries and legal secretaries within the meaning of section 98 of the Supreme Court Act 1981.

24. Court officers and court contractors, who in the course of their work, have face to face contact with judges of the Supreme Court, or access to such judges' lodgings.

25. Persons who in the course of their work have regular access to personal information relating to an identified or identifiable member of the judiciary.

26. Court officers and court contractors, who, in the course of their work, attend either the Royal Courts of Justice or the Central Criminal Court.

27. Court security officers, and tribunal security officers.

28. Court contractors, who, in the course of their work, have unsupervised access to court-houses, offices and other accommodation used in relation to the courts.

29. Contractors, sub-contractors, and any person acting under the authority of such a contractor or sub-contractor, who, in the course of their work, have unsupervised access to tribunal buildings, offices and other accommodation used in relation to tribunals.

30. The following persons—
(a) Court officers who execute county court warrants;
(b) High Court enforcement officers;
(c) sheriffs and under-sheriffs;
(d) tipstaffs;
(e) any other persons who execute High Court writs or warrants who act under the authority of a person listed at (a) to (d);
(f) persons who execute writs of sequestration;
(g) civilian enforcement officers as defined in section 125A of the Magistrates' Courts Act 1980;
(h) persons who are authorised to execute warrants under section 125B(1) of the Magistrates' Courts Act 1980 , and any other person, (other than a constable), who is authorised to execute a warrant under section 125(2) of the 1980 Act;
(i) persons who execute clamping orders, as defined in paragraph 38(2) of Schedule 5 to the Courts Act 2003.

31. The Official Solicitor and his deputy.

32. Persons appointed to the office of Public Trustee or deputy Public Trustee, and officers of the Public Trustee.

33. Court officers and court contractors who exercise functions in connection with the administration and management of funds in court including the deposit, payment, delivery and transfer in, into and out of any court of funds in court and regulating the evidence of such deposit, payment, delivery or transfer and court officers and court contractors, who receive payments in pursuance of a conviction or order of a magistrates' court.]

[34. People working in [the Department for Children, Schools and Families], the Office for Standards in Education, Children's Services and Skills or in the Government Offices for the English Regions with access to sensitive or personal information about children or vulnerable adults.

35. Any office, employment or other work which is concerned with the establishment or operation of a database under section 12 of the Children Act 2004, and which is of such a kind as to enable the holder of that office or employment, or the person engaged in that work, to have access to information included in the database.

36. Any office, employment or other work which is of such a kind that the person is or may be permitted or required to be given access to a database under section 12 of the Children Act 2004.

37. Any work which is normally concerned with the provision of any form of information, advice or guidance wholly or mainly to children which relates to their physical, emotional or educational well-being and is provided by means of telephone or other form of electronic communication including the internet and mobile telephone text messaging.

38. The chairman, other members, and members of staff (including any person seconded to serve as a member of staff) of the Independent Barring Board.

39. Staff working within the Public Guardianship Office, (to be known as the Office of the Public Guardian from October 2007), with access to data relating to children and vulnerable adults.

40. The Commissioner for Older People in Wales, and his deputy, and any person appointed by the Commissioner to assist him in the discharge of his functions or authorised to discharge his functions on his behalf.

41. The Commissioners for the Gambling Commission and any office or employment in their service.

42. Individuals seeking authorisation from the Secretary of State for the Home Department to become authorised search officers.

43. Any employment or other work where the normal duties

(a) involve caring for, training, supervising, or being solely in charge of, persons aged under 18 serving in the naval, military or air forces of the Crown; or

(b) include supervising or managing a person employed or working in a capacity referred to in paragraph (a).]

[2015]

NOTES

Revoked in relation to Scotland as noted at the beginning of this Order.

Schedule heading: see note to Pt I at **[2014]**.

Part heading: substituted by the Rehabilitation of Offenders Act 1974 (Exceptions) (Amendment) Order 2001, SI 2001/1192, arts 2, 6(21).

Para 2: substituted by the Rehabilitation of Offenders Act 1974 (Exceptions) (Amendment) Order 2002, SI 2002/441, arts 2, 5(2)(a), (b).

Para 3: revoked by the Rehabilitation of Offenders Act 1974 (Exceptions) (Amendment) (England and Wales) Order 2006, SI 2006/2143, arts 2, 7(a), as from 26 July 2006.

Para 4: substituted by SI 2001/1192, arts 2, 6(3); words in first pair of square brackets substituted by the Courts Act 2003 (Consequential Provisions) (No 2) Order 2005, SI 2005/617, art 2, Schedule, para 55, as from 1 April 2005; words in second pair of square brackets substituted by SI 2006/2143, arts 2, 7(b)(i), as from 26 July 2006.

Para 7: words in first pair of square brackets inserted by SI 2006/2143, arts 2, 7(b)(ii), as from 26 July 2006; words in second pair of square brackets substituted by virtue of the Criminal Justice Act 1988, s 123(6), Sch 8, paras 1, 3.

Paras 10, 11: revoked by the Rehabilitation of Offenders Act 1974 (Exceptions) (Amendment) Order 1986, SI 1986/1249, art 2, Schedule.

Para 12: substituted by SI 2006/2143, arts 2, 7(c), as from 26 July 2006.

Para 13: substituted by SI 2001/1192, arts 2, 6(4).

Para 14: substituted, for original paras 14, 15, by SI 1986/1249, art 2, Schedule; further substituted by SI 2001/1192, arts 2, 6(5).

Para 15: added (together with paras 16, 17, 18, 19) by SI 2002/441, arts 2, 5(2)(c); word in square brackets inserted by SI 2006/2143, arts 2, 7(b)(iii), as from 26 July 2006.

Paras 16, 19: added as noted above.

Para 17: added as noted above; words in square brackets substituted by the Serious Organised Crime and Police Act 2005 (Consequential and Supplementary Amendments to Secondary Legislation) Order 2006, SI 2006/594, art 2, Schedule, para 2, as from 1 April 2006.

Paras 18, 18A: para 18 originally added as noted above; subsequently substituted by new paras 18, 18A by SI 2006/2143, arts 2, 7(d), as from 26 July 2006.

Paras 20, 21: added by the Rehabilitation of Offenders Act 1974 (Exceptions) (Amendment) (England and Wales) Order 2003, SI 2003/965, arts 2, 8.

Paras 22–33: added by SI 2006/2143, arts 2, 7(e), as from 26 July 2006.

Paras 34–43: added by the Rehabilitation of Offenders Act 1974 (Exceptions) (Amendment) (England and Wales) Order 2007, SI 2007/2149, arts 2, 7, as from 22 July 2007; words in square brackets in para 34 substituted by the Secretaries of State for Children, Schools and Families, for Innovation, Universities and Skills and for Business, Enterprise and Regulatory Reform Order 2007, SI 2007/3224, art 15, Schedule, Pt 2, para 11, as from 12 December 2007.

Road Traffic Regulation Act 1967, s 81: repealed by the Road Traffic Regulation Act 1984, and replaced by s 95 thereof.

Powers of Criminal Courts Act 1973, Sch 3: repealed by the Probation Service Act 1993, and replaced by s 4 thereof; s 4 was in turn been repealed by the Criminal Justice and Court Services Act 2000, s 75, Sch 8. As to the National Probation Service for England and Wales, see now Chapter I of Pt I of the 2000 Act.

PART III
REGULATED OCCUPATIONS

1. Firearms dealer.

2. Any occupation in respect of which an application to the Gaming Board for Great Britain for a licence, certificate or registration is required by or under any enactment.

3. …

4. *Dealer in securities.*

5. *Manager or trustee under a unit trust scheme.*

6. Any occupation which is concerned with—

(a) the management of a place in respect of which the approval of the Secretary of State is required by section 1 of the Abortion Act 1967; or

(b) in England and Wales, carrying on a nursing home in respect of which registration is required by section 187 of the Public Health Act 1936 or section 14 of the Mental Health Act 1959; or

(c) in Scotland, carrying on a nursing home in respect of which registration is required under section 1 of the Nursing Homes Registration (Scotland) Act 1938 or a private hospital in respect of which registration is required under section 15 of the Mental Health (Scotland) Act 1960.

7. Any occupation which is concerned with carrying on an establishment in respect of which registration is required by section 37 of the National Assistance Act 1948 or section 61 of the Social Work (Scotland) Act 1968.

8. Any occupation in respect of which the holder, as occupier of premises on which explosives are kept, is required [pursuant to regulations 4 and 7 of the Control of Explosives Regulations 1991 to obtain from the chief officer of police a valid explosives certificate certifying him to be a fit person to acquire or acquire and keep explosives].

[9. …]

[2016]

NOTES

Revoked in relation to Scotland as noted at the beginning of this Order.

Schedule heading: see note to Pt I at **[2014]**.

Para 3: revoked by the Rehabilitation of Offenders Act 1974 (Exceptions) (Amendment) (No 2) Order 2001, SI 2001/3816, arts 2, 7(a).

Paras 4, 5: revoked by the Rehabilitation of Offenders Act 1974 (Exceptions) (Amendment No 2) Order 1986, SI 1986/2268, art 2(2)(a), as from the date on which the Financial Services Act 1986, s 189, Sch 14 is brought into force for the purposes of this revocation. Note, however, that the 1986 Act was repealed by the Financial Services and Markets Act 2000 (Consequential Amendments and Repeals) Order 2001, SI 2001/3649, art 3(1)(c), as from 1 December 2001, without ever having been brought into force for these purposes.

Para 8: words in square brackets substituted by the Manufacture and Storage of Explosives Regulations 2005, SI 2005/1082, reg 28(1), Sch 5, Pt 2, para 27(1), (2), as from 26 April 2005.

Para 9: added by the Rehabilitation of Offenders Act 1974 (Exceptions) (Amendment) Order 2002, SI 2002/441, arts 2, 5(3)(a); revoked by the Rehabilitation of Offenders Act 1974 (Exceptions) (Amendment) (England and Wales) Order 2003, SI 2003/965, arts 2, 9.

Gaming Board for Great Britain: functions, etc, transferred to the Gambling Commission by the Gambling Act 2005, s 21, Sch 5.

Public Health Act 1936, s 187, Mental Health Act 1959, s 14, National Assistance Act 1948, s 37: repealed.

PART IV
INTERPRETATION

In this Schedule—

["actuary" means a member of the Institute of Actuaries or a member or student of the Faculty of Actuaries;

["assistants to justices' clerks" has the meaning given by section 27(5) of the Courts Act 2003;]

["authorised search officer" means a person authorised to carry out searches in accordance with sections 40 and 41 of the Immigration, Asylum and Nationality Act 2006;]

"care services" means

(i) accommodation and nursing or personal care in a care home (where "care home" has the same meaning as in the Care Standards Act 2000);

(ii) personal care or nursing or support for a person to live independently in his own home;

(iii) social care services; or

(iv) any services provided in an establishment catering for a person with learning difficulties;]

"certified accountant" means a member of the Association of Certified Accountants;

"chartered accountant" means a member of the Institute of Chartered Accountants in England and Wales or of the Institute of Chartered Accountants of Scotland;

["chartered psychologist" means a psychologist included in the British Psychological Society's Register of Chartered Psychologists;]

["child" means a person under the age of eighteen (and "children" is to be construed accordingly);]

["court contractor" means a person who has entered into a contract with the Lord Chancellor under section 2(4) of the Courts Act 2003, such a person's sub-contractor, and persons acting under the authority of such a contractor or sub-contractor for the purpose of discharging the Lord Chancellor's general duty in relation to the courts;]

["court officer" means a person appointed by the Lord Chancellor under section 2(1) of the Courts Act 2003;]

["court security officers" has the meaning given by section 51 of the Courts Act 2003;]

"dealer in securities" means a person dealing in securities within the meaning of section 26(1) of the Prevention of Fraud (Investments) Act 1958;

"firearms dealer" has the meaning assigned to that expression by section 57(4) of the Firearms Act 1968;

["funds in court" has the meaning given by section 47 of the Administration of Justice Act 1982;]

"further education" has the meaning assigned to that expression by section 41 of the Education Act 1944 or, in Scotland, section 4 of the Education (Scotland) Act 1962;

["further education institution" has the meaning given to it by paragraph 3 of the Education (Restriction of Employment) Regulations 2000;]

"health services" means services provided under the National Health Service Acts 1946 to 1973 or the National Health Service (Scotland) Acts 1947 to 1973 and similar services provided otherwise than under the National Health Service;

["high security psychiatric services" has the meaning given by section 4 of the National Health Service Act 1977;]

["home inspector" means a person who is a member of a certification scheme approved by the Secretary of State in accordance with section 164(3) of the Housing Act 2004;]

. . .

["judges of the Supreme Court" means the Lord Chief Justice, the Master of the Rolls, the President of the Queen's Bench Division, the President of the Family Division, the Chancellor of the High Court, the Lords Justices of Appeal and the puisne judges of the High Court;]

"judicial appointment" means an appointment to any office by virtue of which the holder has power (whether alone or with others) under any enactment or rule of law to determine any question affecting the rights, privileges, obligations or liabilities of any person;

["legal executive" means a fellow of the Institute of Legal Executives;]

["members of the judiciary" means persons appointed to any office by virtue of which the holder has power (whether alone or with others) under any enactment or rule of law to determine any question affecting the rights, privileges, obligations or liabilities of any person;]

["personal information" means any information which is of a personal or confidential nature and is not in the public domain and it includes information in any form but excludes anything disclosed for the purposes of proceedings in a particular cause or matter;]

"proprietor" and "independent school" have the meanings assigned to those expressions by section 114(1) of the Education Act 1944 or, in Scotland, section 145 of the Education (Scotland) Act 1962;

["registered chiropractor" has the meaning given by section 43 of the Chiropractors Act 1994.]

["registered foreign lawyer" has the meaning given by section 89 of the Courts and Legal Services Act 1990;]

["registered osteopath" has the meaning given by section 41 of the Osteopaths Act 1993.]

["registered pharmacist" means a person who is registered in the register maintained under article 10(1) of the Pharmacists and Pharmacy Technicians Order 2007;

"registered pharmacy technician" means a person who is registered in the register maintained under article 21(1) of the Pharmacists and Pharmacy Technicians Order 2007;]

"registered teacher" means a teacher registered under the Teaching Council (Scotland) Act 1965 and includes a provisionally registered teacher;

["regulated position" means a position which is a regulated position for the purposes of Part II of the Criminal Justice and Court Services Act 2000;]

["removal centre" and "short-term holding facility" have the meaning given by section 147 of the Immigration and Asylum Act 1999;]

"school" has the meaning assigned to that expression by section 114(1) of the Education Act 1944 or, in Scotland, section 145 of the Education (Scotland) Act 1962;

...

[...]

"teacher" includes a warden of a community centre, leader of a youth club or similar institution, youth worker and, in Scotland, youth and community worker;

["tribunal security officers" means persons who, in the course of their work, guard tribunal buildings, offices and other accommodation used in relation to tribunals against unauthorised access or occupation, against outbreaks of disorder or against damage;]

["tribunals" means any person exercising the judicial power of the State, that is not a court listed in section 1(1) of the Courts Act 2003;]

"unit trust scheme" has the meaning assigned to that expression by section 26(1) of the Prevention of Fraud (Investments) Act 1958 and, in relation thereto, "manager" and "trustee" shall be construed in accordance with section 26(3) of that Act

["vulnerable adult" means a person aged 18 or over who has a condition of the following type:

(i) a substantial learning or physical disability;

(ii) a physical or mental illness or mental disorder, chronic or otherwise, including an addiction to alcohol or drugs; or

(iii) a significant reduction in physical or mental capacity].

[2017]–[2025]

NOTES

Revoked in relation to Scotland as noted at the beginning of this Order.

Schedule heading: see note to Pt I at **[2014]**.

Definitions "actuary", "care services", "chartered psychologist", "legal executive", "registered foreign lawyer", and "vulnerable adult" inserted by the Rehabilitation of Offenders Act 1974 (Exceptions) (Amendment) Order 2002, SI 2002/441, arts 2, 5(4).

Definitions "assistants to justices' clerks", "court contractor", "court officer", "court security officers", "funds in court", "home inspector", "judges of the Supreme Court", "members of the judiciary", "personal information", "removal centre", "short-term holding facility", "tribunal security officers", and "tribunals" inserted by the Rehabilitation of Offenders Act 1974 (Exceptions) (Amendment) (England and Wales) Order 2006, SI 2006/2143, arts 2, 8, as from 26 July 2006.

Definitions "authorised search officer" and "child" inserted by the Rehabilitation of Offenders Act 1974 (Exceptions) (Amendment) (England and Wales) Order 2007, SI 2007/2149, arts 2, 8, as from 22 July 2007.

Definitions "dealer in securities" and "unit trust scheme" revoked by the Rehabilitation of Offenders Act 1974 (Exceptions) (Amendment No 2) Order 1986, SI 1986/2268, art 2(2)(a), as from the date on which the Financial Services Act 1986, s 189, Sch 14 is brought into force for the purposes of this revocation (note, however, that the 1986 Act was repealed by the Financial Services and Markets Act 2000 (Consequential Amendments and Repeals) Order 2001, SI 2001/3649, art 3(1)(c), as from 1 December 2001, without ever having been brought into force for these purposes).

Definitions "further education institution" and "regulated position" inserted by the Rehabilitation of Offenders Act 1974 (Exceptions) (Amendment) Order 2001, SI 2001/1192, arts 2, 6(6)(a), (b).

Definition "high security psychiatric services" inserted by the Rehabilitation of Offenders Act 1974 (Exceptions) (Amendment) (England and Wales) Order 2003, SI 2003/965, arts 2, 10(a).

Definition "insurance company" (omitted) revoked by the Rehabilitation of Offenders Act 1974 (Exceptions) (Amendment) (No 2) Order 2001, SI 2001/3816, arts 2, 7(b).

Definition "registered chiropractor" inserted by the Chiropractors Act 1994, s 40(4).

Definition "registered osteopath" inserted by the Osteopaths Act 1993, s 39(4).

Definitions "registered pharmacist" and "registered pharmacy technician" inserted by the Pharmacists and Pharmacy Technicians Order 2007, SI 2007/289, art 67, Sch 1, Pt 2, para 12(b), as from 30 March 2007 (in so far as relating to "registered pharmacist"), and as from a day to be appointed (in so far as relating to "registered pharmacy technician").

Definition "social services" (omitted) revoked by SI 2002/441, arts 2, 5(4)(e).

Definition "taxi driver" inserted by SI 2002/441, arts 2, 5(4), and revoked by SI 2003/965, arts 2, 10(b).

Prevention of Fraud (Investments) Act 1958: repealed by the Financial Services Act 1986, s 212, Sch 17 (now itself repealed).

Education Act 1944, ss 41, 114(1): repealed by the Education Act 1996, s 582(2), Sch 38, Pt I.

National Health Service Acts 1946 to 1973: repealed and consolidated in the National Health Service Act 1977. The 1977 Act has either been repealed, or is prospectively repealed, by the National Health Service (Consequential Provisions) Act 2006. See now, generally, the National Health Service Act 2006 and the National Health Service (Wales) Act 2006.

Education (Restriction of Employment) Regulations 2000: revoked by the Education (Prohibition from Teaching or Working with Children) Regulations 2003, SI 2003/1184.

(Schs 2, 3 outside the scope of this work.)

SEX DISCRIMINATION (QUESTIONS AND REPLIES) ORDER 1975

(SI 1975/2048)

NOTES

Made: 5 December 1975.
Authority: Sex Discrimination Act 1975, ss 74, 81(4).
Commencement: 29 December 1975.
See *Harvey* L1, R.

ARRANGEMENT OF ARTICLES

1 Citation and operation

This Order may be cited as the Sex Discrimination (Questions and Replies) Order 1975 and shall come into operation on 29th December 1975.

[2026]

2 Interpretation

(1) In this Order "the Act" means the Sex Discrimination Act 1975.

(2) In this Order any reference to a court is a reference to a county court in England or Wales or a sheriff court in Scotland and any reference to a tribunal is a reference to an [employment tribunal].

(3) The Interpretation Act 1889 shall apply to the interpretation of this Order as it applies to the interpretation of an Act of Parliament.

[2027]

NOTES

Para (2): words in square brackets substituted by the Employment Rights (Dispute Resolution) Act 1998, s 1(2)(a).
Interpretation Act 1889: see now the Interpretation Act 1978.

3 Forms for asking and answering questions

The forms respectively set out in Schedules 1 and 2 to this Order or forms to the like effect with such variation as the circumstances may require are, respectively, hereby prescribed as forms—

(a) by which a person aggrieved may question a respondent as mentioned in subsection (1)(a) of section 74 of the Act;

(b) by which a respondent may if he so wishes reply to such questions as mentioned in subsection (1)(b) of that section.

[2028]

4 Period for service of questions—court cases

In proceedings before a court, a question shall only be admissible as evidence in pursuance of section 74(2)(a) of the Act—

[(a) where it was served before those proceedings had been instituted, if it was so served during—
    (i) the period of six months beginning when the act complained of was done, or
    (ii) in a case to which section 66(5) of the Act applies, the period of eight months so beginning;]

(b) where it was served when those proceedings had been instituted, if it was served with the leave of, and within a period specified by, the court.

[2029]

NOTES

Para (a): substituted by the Sex Discrimination (Questions and Replies) (Amendment) Order 1977, SI 1977/844, art 2.

5 Period for service of questions—tribunal cases

In proceedings before a tribunal, a question shall only be admissible as evidence in pursuance of section 74(2)(a) of the Act—

[(a) where it was served before a complaint had been presented to a tribunal, if it was so served—
    (i) within the period of three months beginning when the act complained of was done; or
    (ii) where the period under section 76 of the Act within which proceedings must be brought is extended by regulation 15 of the Employment Act 2002 (Dispute Resolution) Regulations 2004, within that extended period;]

(b) where it was served when a complaint had been presented to a tribunal, either if it was so served within the period of twenty-one days beginning with the day on which the complaint was presented or if it was so served later with leave given, and within a period specified, by a direction of a tribunal.

[2030]

NOTES

Para (a) substituted by the Employment Act 2002 (Dispute Resolution) Regulations 2004, SI 2004/752, reg 17(a), as from 1 October 2004 (for transitional provisions and effect see reg 18 of those Regulations at **[3098]**).

6 Manner of service of questions and replies

A question and any reply thereto may be served on the respondent or, as the case may be, on the person aggrieved—

(a) by delivering it to him; or

(b) by sending it by post to him at his usual or last-known residence or place of business; or

(c) where the person to be served is a body corporate or is a trade union or employers' association within the meaning of the Trade Union and Labour Relations Act 1974, by delivering it to the secretary or clerk of the body, union or association at its registered or principal office or by sending it by post to the secretary or clerk at that office; or

(d) where the person to be served is acting by a solicitor, by delivering it at, or by sending it by post to, the solicitor's address for service; or

(e) where the person to be served is the person aggrieved, by delivering the reply, or sending it by post, to him at his address for reply as stated by him in the document containing the questions.

[2031]

NOTES

Solicitors: references to solicitors are modified so as to include references to recognised bodies within the meaning of the Administration of Justice Act 1985, s 9, by the Solicitors' Incorporated Practices Order 1991, SI 1991/2684, arts 3–5, Sch 1.

"Trade union or employers' association": definitions now contained in the Trade Union and Labour Relations (Consolidation) Act 1992, ss 1, 122.

SCHEDULES

SCHEDULE 1
THE SEX DISCRIMINATION ACT 1975 S 74(1)(A) QUESTIONNAIRE OF PERSON AGGRIEVED

To .... (*name of person to be questioned*) of ....
.... (*address*)

1—(1) I .... (*name of questioner*) of .... (*address*) consider that you may have discriminated against me contrary to the Sex Discrimination Act 1975.

(2) (*Give date, approximate time and a factual description of the treatment received and of the circumstances leading up to the treatment.*)

(3) I consider that this treatment may have been unlawful [because .... (*complete if you wish to give reasons, otherwise delete*)].

2 Do you agree that the statement in paragraph 1(2) above is an accurate description of what happened? If not, in what respect do you disagree or what is your version of what happened?

3 Do you accept that your treatment of me was unlawful discrimination by you against me?
If not—
(a) why not,
(b) for what reason did I receive the treatment accorded to me, and
(c) how far did my sex or marital status affect your treatment of me?

4 (*Any other questions you wish to ask.*)

5 My address for any reply you may wish to give to the questions raised above is [that set out in paragraph 1(1) above] [the following address ....].

.... (*signature of person questioned*)

.... (*date*)

N.B.—By virtue of section 74 of the Act this questionnaire and any reply are (subject to the provisions of the section) admissible in proceedings under the Act and a court or tribunal may draw any such inference as is just and equitable from a failure without reasonable excuse to reply within a reasonable period, or from an evasive or equivocal reply, including an inference that the person questioned has discriminated unlawfully.

[2032]

NOTES

As to what is a 'reasonable period' for a reply, see the Sex Discrimination Act 1975, s 74(2A) at **[188]**.

SCHEDULE 2
THE SEX DISCRIMINATION ACT 1975 S 74(1)(B) REPLY BY RESPONDENT

To .... (*name of questioner*) of ....
.... (*address*)

1 I .... (*name of person questioned*) of .... (*address*) hereby acknowledge receipt of the questionnaire signed by you and dated .... which was served on me on .... (*date*).

2 [I agree that the statement in paragraph 1(2) of the questionnaire is an accurate description of what happened.]

[I disagree with the statement in paragraph 1(2) of the questionnaire in that ....]

3 I accept/dispute that my treatment of you was unlawful discrimination by me against you.

[My reasons for so disputing are ....
The reason why you received the treatment accorded to you and the answers to the other questions in paragraph 3 of the questionnaire are ....]

4 (*Replies to questions in paragraph 4 of the questionnaire.*)

[5 I have deleted (in whole or in part) the paragraph(s) numbered .... above, since I am unable/unwilling to reply to the relevant questions in the correspondingly numbered paragraph(s) of the questionnaire for the following reasons ....
....]

.... (*signature of person questioned*)

.... (*date*)

[2033]

SAFETY REPRESENTATIVES AND SAFETY COMMITTEES REGULATIONS 1977

(SI 1977/500)

NOTES

Made: 16 March 1997.

Authority: Health and Safety at Work etc Act 1974, ss 2(4), (7), 15(1), (3)(b), (5)(b), 80(1), (4), 82(3)(a).

Commencement: 1 October 1978.

See also the Health and Safety Commission Codes of Practice 'Safety Representatives and Safety Committees' (1978) and 'Time off for the Training of Safety Representatives' (1978) at **[4501]** and **[4502]** respectively. As to the abolition of the Health and Safety Commission, see the note 'The Health and Safety Executive' at **[2038]**.

ARRANGEMENT OF REGULATIONS

SCHEDULES:

1 Citation and commencement

These Regulations may be cited as the Safety Representatives and Safety Committees Regulations 1977 and shall come into operation on 1st October 1978.

[2034]

2 Interpretation

(1) In these Regulations, unless the context otherwise requires—

"the 1974 Act" means the Health and Safety at Work etc Act 1974 as amended by the 1975 Act;

"the 1975 Act" means the Employment Protection Act 1975;

"employee" has the meaning assigned by section 53(1) of the 1974 Act and "employer" shall be construed accordingly;

"recognised trade union" [...] means an independent trade union as defined in section 30(1) of the Trade Union and Labour Relations Act 1974 which the employer concerned recognises for the purpose of negotiations relating to or connected with one or more of the matters specified in section 29(1) of that Act in relation to persons employed by him or as to which the Advisory, Conciliation and Arbitration Service has made a recommendation for recognition under the 1975 Act which is operative within the meaning of section 15 of that Act;

"safety representative" means a person appointed under Regulation 3(1) of these Regulations to be a safety representative;

"welfare at work" means those aspects of welfare at work which are the subject of health and safety regulations or of any of the existing statutory provisions within the meaning of section 53(1) of the 1974 Act;

"workplace" in relation to a safety representative means any place or places where the group or groups of employees he is appointed to represent are likely to work or which they are likely to frequent in the course of their employment or incidentally to it.

(2) The Interpretation Act 1889 shall apply to the interpretation of these Regulations as it applies to the interpretation of an Act of Parliament.

(3) These Regulations shall not be construed as giving any person a right to inspect any place, article, substance or document which is the subject of restrictions on the grounds of national security unless he satisfies any test or requirement imposed on those grounds by or on behalf of the Crown.

[2035]–[2036]

NOTES

Para (1): in definition "recognised trade union" words in square brackets inserted by the Police (Health and Safety) Regulations 1999, SI 1999/860, reg 3(1), (2), and revoked by the Serious Organised Crime and Police Act 2005 (Consequential and Supplementary Amendments to Secondary Legislation) Order 2006, SI 2006/594, art 2, Schedule, para 3(1), (2)(a), as from 1 April 2006. Note that the Queen's Printer's copy of SI 2006/594 actually provides that the words be omitted from the definition "regional trade union".

Employment Protection Act 1975: largely repealed and consolidated in the Trade Union and Labour Relations (Consolidation) Act 1992.

Trade Union and Labour Relations Act 1974: see now the Trade Union and Labour Relations (Consolidation) Act 1992. As to s 29(1) of the 1974 Act, see s 218 of the 1992 Act, and as to s 30(1) of the 1974 Act, see s 5 of the 1992 Act.

The reference in the definition of "recognised trade union" to the 1975 Act is now otiose, the relevant provisions of the 1975 Act having been repealed by the Employment Act 1980.

Interpretation Act 1889: see now the Interpretation Act 1978.

2A (*Inserted by the Police* (*Health and Safety*) *Regulations 1999, SI 1999/860, reg 3(1), (3); revoked by the Serious Organised Crime and Police Act 2005* (*Consequential and Supplementary Amendments to Secondary Legislation*) *Order 2006, SI 2006/594, art 2, Schedule, para 3(1), (2)(a), as from 1 April 2006.*)

3 Appointment of safety representatives

(1) For the purposes of section 2(4) of the 1974 Act, a recognised trade union may appoint safety representatives from amongst the employees in all cases where one or more employees are employed by an employer by whom it is recognised, …

(2) Where the employer has been notified in writing by or on behalf of a trade union of the names of the persons appointed as safety representatives under this Regulation and the group or groups of employees they represent, each such safety representative shall have the functions set out in Regulation 4 below.

(3) A person shall cease to be a safety representative for the purposes of these Regulations when—

(a) the trade union which appointed him notifies the employer in writing that his appointment has been terminated; or

(b) he ceases to be employed at the workplace but if he was appointed to represent employees at more than one workplace he shall not cease by virtue of this sub-paragraph to be a safety representative so long as he continues to be employed at any one of them; or

(c) he resigns.

(4) A person appointed under paragraph (1) above as a safety representative shall so far as is reasonably practicable either have been employed by his employer throughout the preceding two years or have had at least two years experience in similar employment.

[2037]

NOTES

Para (1): words omitted revoked by the Health and Safety (Consultation with Employees) Regulations 1996, SI 1996/1513, reg 13.

4 Functions of safety representatives

(1) In addition to his function under section 2(4) of the 1974 Act to represent the employees in consultations with the employer under section 2(6) of the 1974 Act (which requires every employer to consult safety representatives with a view to the making and maintenance of arrangements which will enable him and his employees to cooperate effectively in promoting and developing measures to ensure the health and safety at work of the employees and in checking the effectiveness of such measures), each safety representative shall have the following functions—

(a) to investigate potential hazards and dangerous occurrences at the workplace (whether or not they are drawn to his attention by the employees he represents) and to examine the causes of accidents at the workplace;

(b) to investigate complaints by any employee he represents relating to that employee's health, safety or welfare at work;

(c) to make representations to the employer on matters arising out of sub-paragraphs (a) and (b) above;

(d) to make representations to the employer on general matters affecting the health, safety or welfare at work of the employees at the workplace;

(e) to carry out inspections in accordance with Regulations 5, 6 and 7 below;

(f) to represent the employees he was appointed to represent in consultations at the workplace with inspectors of the Health and Safety Executive and of any other enforcing authority;

(g) to receive information from inspectors in accordance with section 28(8) of the 1974 Act; and

(h) to attend meetings of safety committees where he attends in his capacity as a safety representative in connection with any of the above functions;

but, without prejudice to sections 7 and 8 of the 1974 Act, no function given to a safety representative by this paragraph shall be construed as imposing any duty on him.

(2) An employer shall permit a safety representative to take such time off with pay during the employee's working hours as shall be necessary for the purposes of—

(a) performing his functions under section 2(4) of the 1974 Act and paragraph (1)(a) to (h) above;

(b) undergoing such training in aspects of those functions as may be reasonable in all the circumstances having regard to any relevant provisions of a code of practice relating to time off for training approved for the time being by the [the Health and Safety Executive] under section 16 of the 1974 Act.

In this paragraph "with pay" means with pay in accordance with [Schedule 2] to these Regulations.

[2038]

NOTES

Para (2): words in first pair of square brackets substituted by the Legislative Reform (Health and Safety Executive) Order 2008, SI 2008/960, art 22, Sch 3, as from 1 April 2008 (see further the note below); words in second pair of square brackets substituted by the Police (Health and Safety) Regulations 1999, SI 1999/860, reg 3(1), (4).

The Health and Safety Executive: as to the abolition of the Health and Safety Commission and the Health and Safety Executive (with effect from 1 April 2008) and their replacement with a single Health and Safety Executive exercising the combined functions of those bodies, see the Legislative Reform (Health and Safety Executive) Order 2008, SI 2008/960 (at **[3474L]**), and the amendments made by that Order to the Health and Safety at Work etc Act 1974 (at **[30]** et seq). For transitional provisions in relation to the abolition of the former bodies and the establishment of the new Health and Safety Executive, see art 21 of, and Sch 2 to, the 2008 Order at **[3474N]**, **[3474O]**.

[4A Employer's duty to consult and provide facilities and assistance

(1) Without prejudice to the generality of section 2(6) of the Health and Safety at Work etc Act 1974, every employer shall consult safety representatives in good time with regard to—

(a) the introduction of any measure at the workplace which may substantially affect the health and safety of the employees the safety representatives concerned represent;

(b) his arrangements for appointing or, as the case may be, nominating persons in accordance with [regulations 7(1) and 8(1)(b) of the Management of Health and Safety at Work Regulations 1999] [or article 13(3)(b) of the Regulatory Reform (Fire Safety) Order 2005];

(c) any health and safety information he is required to provide to the employees the safety representatives concerned represent by or under the relevant statutory provisions;

(d) the planning and organisation of any health and safety training he is required to provide to the employees the safety representatives concerned represent by or under the relevant statutory provisions; and

(e) the health and safety consequences for the employees the safety representatives concerned represent of the introduction (including the planning thereof) of new technologies into the workplace.

(2) Without prejudice to regulations 5 and 6 of these Regulations, every employer shall provide such facilities and assistance as safety representatives may reasonably require for the purpose of carrying out their functions under section 2(4) of the 1974 Act and under these Regulations.]

[2039]

NOTES

Inserted by the Management of Health and Safety at Work Regulations 1992, SI 1992/2051, reg 17, Schedule.

Para (1): words in first pair of square brackets in sub-para (b) substituted by the Management of Health and Safety at Work Regulations 1999, SI 1999/3242, reg 29(2), Sch 2; words in second pair of square brackets in sub-para (b) originally inserted by the Fire Precautions (Workplace) Regulations 1997, SI 1997/1840, reg 21(1), and substituted by the Regulatory Reform (Fire Safety) Order 2005, SI 2005/1541, art 41(1), as from 1 October 2006, in relation to England and Wales only. A corresponding amendment has been made in relation to Scotland by the Fire (Scotland) Act 2005 (Consequential Modifications and Savings) (No 2) Order 2006, SSI 2006/457, which provides that the words should now read "or regulation 12(3)(b) of the Fire Safety (Scotland) Regulations 2006".

---

5 Inspections of the workplace

(1) Safety representatives shall be entitled to inspect the workplace or a part of it if they have given the employer or his representative reasonable notice in writing of their intention to do so and have not inspected it, or that part of it, as the case may be, in the previous three months; and may carry out more frequent inspections by agreement with the employer.

(2) Where there has been a substantial change in the conditions of work (whether because of the introduction of new machinery or otherwise) or new information has been published by … the Health and Safety Executive relevant to the hazards of the workplace since the last inspection under this Regulation, the safety representatives after consultation with the employer shall be entitled to carry out a further inspection of the part of the workplace concerned notwithstanding that three months have not elapsed since the last inspection.

(3) The employer shall provide such facilities and assistance as the safety representatives may reasonably require (including facilities for independent investigation by them and private discussion with the employees) for the purpose of carrying out an inspection under this Regulation, but nothing in this paragraph shall preclude the employer or his representative from being present in the workplace during the inspection.

(4) An inspection carried out under section 123 of the Mines and Quarries Act 1954 [or regulation 40 of the Quarries Regulations 1999] shall count as an inspection under this Regulation.

[2040]

NOTES

Para (2): words omitted revoked by the Legislative Reform (Health and Safety Executive) Order 2008, SI 2008/960, art 22, Sch 3, as from 1 April 2008 (see further the note 'The Health and Safety Executive' at **[2038]**).

Para (4): words in square brackets inserted by the Quarries Regulations 1999, SI 1999/2024, reg 48(1), Sch 5, Pt II.

6 Inspections following notifiable accidents, occurrences and diseases

(1) Where there has been a notifiable accident or dangerous occurrence in a workplace or a notifiable disease has been contracted there and—

(a) it is safe for an inspection to be carried out; and

(b) the interests of employees in the group or groups which safety representatives are appointed to represent might be involved,

those safety representatives may carry out an inspection of the part of the workplace concerned and so far as is necessary for the purpose of determining the cause they may inspect any other part of the workplace; where it is reasonably practicable to do so they shall notify the employer or his representative of their intention to carry out the inspection.

(2) The employer shall provide such facilities and assistance as the safety representatives may reasonably require (including facilities for independent investigation by them and private discussion with the employees) for the purpose of carrying out an inspection under this Regulation; but nothing in this paragraph shall preclude the employer or his representative from being present in the workplace during the inspection.

(3) In this Regulation "notifiable accident or dangerous occurrence" and "notifiable disease" mean any accident, dangerous occurrence or disease, as the case may be, notice of which is required to be given by virtue of any of the relevant statutory provisions within the meaning of section 53(1) of the 1974 Act.

[2041]

7 Inspection of documents and provision of information

(1) Safety representatives shall for the performance of their functions under section 2(4) of the 1974 Act and under Regulations, if they have given the employer reasonable notice, be entitled to inspect and take copies of any document relevant to the workplace or to the employees the safety representatives represent which the employer is required to keep by virtue of any relevant statutory provision within the meaning of section 53(1) of the 1974 Act except a document consisting of or relating to any health record of an identifiable individual.

(2) An employer shall make available to safety representatives the information, within the employer's knowledge, necessary to enable them to fulfil their functions except—

(a) any information the disclosure of which would be against the interests of national security; or

(b) any information which he could not disclose without contravening a prohibition imposed by or under an enactment; or

(c) any information relating specifically to an individual, unless he has consented to its being disclosed; or

(d) any information the disclosure of which would, for reasons other than its effect on health, safety or welfare at work, cause substantial injury to the employer's undertaking or, where the information was supplied to him by some other person, to the undertaking of that other person; or

(e) any information obtained by the employer for the purpose of bringing, prosecuting or defending any legal proceedings.

(3) Paragraph (2) above does not require an employer to produce or allow inspection of any document or part of a document which is not related to health, safety or welfare.

[2042]

8 Cases where safety representatives need not be employees

(1) In the cases mentioned in paragraph (2) below safety representatives appointed under Regulation 3(1) of these Regulations need not be employees of the employer concerned; and section 2(4) of the 1974 Act shall be modified accordingly.

(2) The said cases are those in which the employees in the group or groups the safety representatives are appointed to represent are members of the British Actors' Equity Association or of the Musicians' Union.

(3) Regulations 3(3)(b) and (4) and 4(2) of these Regulations shall not apply to safety representatives appointed by virtue of this Regulation and in the case of safety representatives to be so appointed Regulation 3(1) shall have effect as if the words "from amongst the employees" were omitted.

[2043]

9 Safety committees

(1) For the purposes of section 2(7) of the 1974 Act (which requires an employer in prescribed cases to establish a safety committee if requested to do so by safety representatives) the prescribed cases shall be any cases in which at least two safety representatives request the employer in writing to establish a safety committee.

(2) Where an employer is requested to establish a safety committee in a case prescribed in paragraph (1) above, he shall establish it in accordance with the following provisions—

(a) he shall consult with the safety representatives who made the request and with the representatives of recognised trade unions whose members work in any workplace in respect of which he proposes that the committee should function;

(b) the employer shall post a notice stating the composition of the committee and the workplace or workplaces to be covered by it in a place where it may be easily read by the employees;

(c) the committee shall be established not later than three months after the request for it.

[2044]

10 Power of [the Health and Safety Executive] to grant exemptions

The [the Health and Safety Executive] may grant exemptions from any requirement imposed by these Regulations and any such exemption may be unconditional or subject to such conditions as the Commission may impose and may be with or without a limit of time.

[2045]

NOTES

Words in square brackets substituted by the Legislative Reform (Health and Safety Executive) Order 2008, SI 2008/960, art 22, Sch 3, as from 1 April 2008 (see further the note 'The Health and Safety Executive' at **[2038]**).

11 Provisions as to [employment tribunals]

(1) A safety representative may, in accordance with the jurisdiction conferred on [employment tribunals] by paragraph 16(2) of Schedule 1 to the Trade Union and Labour Relations Act 1974, present a complaint to an [employment tribunal] that—

(a) the employer has failed to permit him to take time off in accordance with Regulation 4(2) of these Regulations; or

(b) the employer has failed to pay him in accordance with Regulation 4(2) of and the Schedule to these Regulations.

(2) An [employment tribunal] shall not consider a complaint under paragraph (1) above unless it is presented within three months of the date when the failure occurred or within such further period as the tribunal considers reasonable in a case where it is satisfied that it was not reasonably practicable for the complaint to be presented within the period of three months.

(3) Where an [employment tribunal] finds a complaint under paragraph (1)(a) above well-founded the tribunal shall make a declaration to that effect and may make an award of compensation to be paid by the employer to the employee which shall be of such amount as the tribunal considers just and equitable in all the circumstances having regard to the employer's default in failing to permit time off to be taken by the employee and to any loss sustained by the employee which is attributable to the matters complained of.

(4) Where on a complaint under paragraph (1)(b) above an [employment tribunal] finds that the employer has failed to pay the employee the whole or part of the amount required to be paid under paragraph (1)(b), the tribunal shall order the employer to pay the employee the amount which it finds due to him.

(5) …

[2046]–[2047]

NOTES

Words in square brackets substituted by the Employment Rights (Dispute Resolution) Act 1998, s 1(2)(a), (b).

Para (5): amended the Trade Union and Labour Relations Act 1974, Sch 1, para 16 (and is now spent).

1974 Act: the references to the 1974 Act in para (1) have been superseded; the jurisdiction of industrial tribunals (now employment tribunals) is now conferred by the Employment Tribunals Act 1996, s 2.

SCHEDULES

(Sch 1 inserted by the Police (Health and Safety) Regulations 1999, SI 1999/860, reg 3(1), (5); revoked by the Serious Organised Crime and Police Act 2005 (Consequential and Supplementary Amendments to Secondary Legislation) Order 2006, SI 2006/594, art 2, Schedule, para 3(1), (2)(a), as from 1 April 2006.)

[SCHEDULE 2]
PAY FOR TIME OFF ALLOWED TO SAFETY REPRESENTATIVES

Regulation 4(2)

1. Subject to paragraph 3 below, where a safety representative is permitted to take time off in accordance with Regulation 4(2) of these Regulations, his employer shall pay him—
   (a) where the safety representative's remuneration for the work he would ordinarily have been doing during that time does not vary with the amount of work done, as if he had worked at that work for the whole of that time;
   (b) where the safety representative's remuneration for that work varies with the amount of work done, an amount calculated by reference to the average hourly earnings for that work (ascertained in accordance with paragraph 2 below).

2. The average hourly earnings referred to in paragraph 1(b) above are the average hourly earnings of the safety representative concerned or, if no fair estimate can be made of those earnings, the average hourly earnings for work of that description of persons in comparable employment with the same employer or, if there are no such persons, a figure of average hourly earnings which is reasonable in the circumstances.

3. Any payment to a safety representative by an employer in respect of a period of time off—
   (a) if it is a payment which discharges any liability which the employer may have under section 57 of the 1975 Act in respect of that period, shall also discharge his liability in respect of the same period under Regulation 4(2) of these Regulations;
   (b) if it is a payment under any contractual obligation, shall go towards discharging the employer's liability in respect of the same period under Regulation 4(2) of these Regulations;
   (c) if it is a payment under Regulation 4(2) of these Regulations shall go towards discharging any liability of the employer to pay contractual remuneration in respect of the same period.

[2048]–[2056]

NOTES

Original Schedule renumbered as Schedule 2 by the Police (Health and Safety) Regulations 1999, SI 1999/860, reg 3(1), (6).

"Section 57": see now the Trade Union and Labour Relations (Consolidation) Act 1992, s 169.

RACE RELATIONS (QUESTIONS AND REPLIES) ORDER 1977

(SI 1977/842)

NOTES

Made: 13 May 1977.
Authority: Race Relations Act 1976, ss 65, 74(3).
Commencement: 13 June 1977.
See *Harvey* L2, R.

ARRANGEMENT OF ARTICLES

SCHEDULES:

1 Citation and operation

This Order may be cited as the Race Relations (Questions and Replies) Order 1977 and shall come into operation on 13th June 1977.

[2057]

2 Interpretation

(1) In this Order "the Act" means the Race Relations Act 1976.

(2) In this Order any reference to a court is a reference to a county court in England or Wales designated for the time being for the purposes of the Act by an order made by the Lord Chancellor under section 67(1) of the Act or a sheriff court in Scotland and any reference to a tribunal is a reference to an [employment tribunal].

(3) The Interpretation Act 1889 shall apply to the interpretation of this Order as it applies to the interpretation of an Act of Parliament.

[2058]

NOTES

Para (2): words in square brackets substituted by the Employment Rights (Dispute Resolution) Act 1998, s 1(2)(a).

Interpretation Act 1889: see now the Interpretation Act 1978.

3 Forms for asking and answering questions

The forms respectively set out in Schedules 1 and 2 to this Order or forms to the like effect with such variation as the circumstances may require are, respectively, hereby prescribed as forms—

(a) by which a person aggrieved may question a respondent as mentioned in subsection (1)(a) of section 65 of the Act;

(b) by which a respondent may if he so wishes reply to such questions as mentioned in subsection (1)(b) of that section.

[2059]

4 Period for service of questions—court cases

In proceedings before a court, a question shall only be admissible as evidence in pursuance of section 65(2)(a) of the Act—

(a) where it was served before those proceedings had been instituted, if it was so served during—

(i) the period of six months beginning when the act complained of was done, or

(ii) in a case to which section 57(5) of the Act applies, the period of eight months so beginning;

(b) where it was served when those proceedings had been instituted, if it was served with the leave of, and within a period specified by, the court.

[2060]

5 Period for service of questions—tribunal cases

In proceedings before a tribunal, a question shall only be admissible as evidence in pursuance of section 65(2)(a) of the Act—

[(a) where it was served before a complaint had been presented to a tribunal, if it was so served—

(i) within the period of three months beginning when the act complained of was done; or

(ii) where the period under section 76 of the Act within which proceedings must be brought is extended by regulation 15 of the Employment Act 2002 (Dispute Resolution) Regulations 2004, within that extended period;]

(b) where it was served when a complaint had been presented to a tribunal, either if it was so served within the period of twenty-one days beginning with the day on which the complaint was presented or if it was so served later with leave given, and within a period specified, by a direction of a tribunal.

[2061]

NOTES

Para (a) substituted by the Employment Act 2002 (Dispute Resolution) Regulations 2004, SI 2004/752, reg 17(b), as from 1 October 2004 (for transitional provisions and effect see reg 18 of those Regulations at **[3098]**).

6 Manner of service of questions and replies

A question and any reply thereto may be served on the respondent or, as the case may be, on the person aggrieved—

(a) by delivering it to him; or

(b) by sending it by post to him at his usual or last-known residence or place of business; or

(c) where the person to be served is a body corporate or is a trade union or employers' association within the meaning of the Trade Union and Labour Relations Act 1974, by delivering it to the secretary or clerk of the body, union or association at its registered or principal office or by sending it by post to the secretary or clerk at that office; or

(d) where the person to be served is acting by a solicitor, by delivering it at, or by sending it by post to, the solicitor's address for service; or

(e) where the person to be served is the person aggrieved, by delivering the reply, or sending it by post, to him at his address for reply as stated by him in the document containing the questions.

[2062]

NOTES

Solicitors: references to solicitors are modified so as to include references to recognised bodies within the meaning of the Administration of Justice Act 1985, s 9, by the Solicitors' Incorporated Practices Order 1991, SI 1991/2684, arts 3–5, Sch 1.

"Trade union or employers' association": definitions now contained in the Trade Union and Labour Relations (Consolidation) Act 1992, ss 1, 122.

SCHEDULES

SCHEDULE 1
THE RACE RELATIONS ACT 1976 S 65(1)(A)

Article 3

QUESTIONNAIRE OF PERSON AGGRIEVED

To ....(*name of person to be questioned*)

of .... (*address*)

1.—(1) I .... (*name of questioner*) of .... (*address*) consider that you may have discriminated against me contrary to the Race Relations Act 1976.

(2) (*Give date, approximate time and a factual description of the treatment received and of the circumstances leading up to the treatment.*)

(3) I consider that this treatment may have been unlawful [because ....

....

(*complete if you wish to give reasons, otherwise delete*)].

2. Do you agree that the statement in paragraph 1(2) above is an accurate description of what happened? If not, in what respect do you disagree or what is your version of what happened?

3. Do you accept that your treatment of me was unlawful discrimination by you against me? If not—
   (a) why not,
   [(b) for what reason did I receive the treatment accorded to me, and
   (c) how far did considerations of colour, race, nationality (including citizenship) or ethnic or national origins affect your treatment of me?

4. (*Any other questions you wish to ask.*)

5. My address for any reply you may wish to give to the questions raised above is [that set out in paragraph 1(1) above] [the following address ....].

.... (*signature of person questioned*)

.... (*date*)

N.B.—By virtue of section 65 of the Act this questionnaire and any reply are (subject to the provisions of the section) admissible in proceedings under the Act and a court or tribunal may draw any such inference as is just and equitable from a failure without reasonable excuse to reply within a reasonable period, or from an evasive or equivocal reply, including an inference that the person questioned has discriminated unlawfully.

[2063]

NOTES

By the Race Relations Act 1976, s 65(2)(b) at **[286]** (as amended by the Race Relations Act 1976 (Amendment) Regulations 2003, SI 2003/1626, regs 2, 47, with effect from 19 July 2003, in relation to any questionnaire served on or after that date) the period of eight weeks from the date of service of a question applies in place of a reasonable period where the question relates to discrimination on grounds of race or ethnic or national origin, or harassment; the form of questionnaire in this Schedule has not been amended to reflect this.

SCHEDULE 2
THE RACE RELATIONS ACT 1976 S 65(1)(B)

Article 3

REPLY BY RESPONDENT

To .... (*name of questioner*) of ....

.... (*address*).

1. I .... (*name of person questioned*) of .... (*address*) hereby acknowledge receipt of the questionnaire signed by you and dated .... which was served on me on .... (*date*).

2. [I agree that the statement in paragraph 1(2) of the questionnaire is an accurate description of what happened.] [I disagree with the statement in paragraph 1(2) of the questionnaire in that ....]

3. I accept/dispute that my treatment of you was unlawful discrimination by me against you.

[My reasons for so disputing are ....

....

The reason why you received the treatment accorded to you and the answers to the other questions in paragraph 3 of the questionnaire are ....

....]

4. (*Replies to questions in paragraph 4 of the questionnaire.*)

[5. I have deleted (in whole or in part) the paragraph(s) numbered .... above, since I am unable/unwilling to reply to the relevant questions in the correspondingly numbered paragraph(s) of the questionnaire for the following reasons ....]

.... (*signature of person questioned*)

.... (*date*)

[2064]

TRANSFER OF UNDERTAKINGS (PROTECTION OF EMPLOYMENT) REGULATIONS 1981 (NOTE)

(SI 1981/1794)

NOTES

These Regulations were revoked and replaced by the Transfer of Undertakings (Protection of Employment) Regulations 2006, SI 2006/246, as from 6 April 2006. The 2006 Regulations are at **[3376]**. By virtue of reg 21 of the 2006 Regulations (at **[3395]**), these Regulations continue to apply to: (a) a relevant transfer (within the meaning of these Regulations) that took place before 6 April 2006; and (b) a transfer, not falling within (a) above, that took place before 6 April 2006 and is regarded by virtue of any enactment as a relevant transfer (within the meaning of these Regulations).

[2065]–[2079]

STATUTORY SICK PAY (GENERAL) REGULATIONS 1982

(SI 1982/894)

NOTES

Made: 30 June 1982.

Authority: Social Security and Housing Benefits Act 1982, ss 1(3), (4), 3(5), (7), 4(2), 5(5), 6(1), 8(1)–(3), 17(4), 18(1), 20, 26(1), (3)–(5), Sch 1, para 1, Sch 2, paras 2(3), 3(2) (repealed). These Regulations now have effect as if made under the Social Security Contributions and Benefits Act 1992, ss 151(4)–(6), 153(5), (6), (10), 154(2), 155(5), 156(1), 163(1), (3)–(5), Sch 12, paras 2(3), 3(2), and the Social Security Administration Act 1992, ss 5, 130(1), (2), (3)(c)(i), (4), by virtue of the Social Security (Consequential Provisions) Act 1992, s 2(2).

Commencement: 6 April 1983.

Transfer of functions: the functions of the Secretary of State conferred by regs 9A–9C, 10, 14 were transferred to the Commissioners of Inland Revenue by the Social Security Contributions (Transfer of Functions, etc) Act 1999, s 1(2), Sch 2. Note also that a reference to the Commissioners of Inland Revenue is now to be taken as a reference to the Commissioners for Her Majesty's Revenue and Customs; see the Commissioners for Revenue and Customs Act 2005, s 50(1), (7).

See *Harvey* H1, R.

ARRANGEMENT OF REGULATIONS

1 Citation, commencement and interpretation

(1) These regulations may be cited as the Statutory Sick Pay (General) Regulations 1982, and shall come into operation on 6th April 1983.

(2) In these regulations—

"the Act" means the Social Security and Housing Benefits Act 1982;

["the Contributions and Benefits Act" means the Social Security Contributions and Benefits Act 1992;]

["income tax month" means the period beginning on the 6th day of any calendar month and ending on the 5th day of the following calendar month;]

"Part I" means Part I of the Act;

and other expressions, unless the context otherwise requires, have the same meanings as in Part I.

(3) Unless the context otherwise requires, any reference—

(a) in these regulations to a numbered section or Schedule is a reference to the section or Schedule, as the case may be, of or to the Act bearing that number;

(b) in these regulations to a numbered regulation is a reference to the regulation bearing that number in these regulations; and

(c) in any of these regulations to a numbered paragraph is a reference to the paragraph bearing that number in that regulation.

[2080]

NOTES

Para (2): definition "the Contributions and Benefits Act" inserted by the Social Security (Miscellaneous Provisions) Amendment Regulations 1992, SI 1992/2595, reg 14; definition "income tax month" inserted by the Social Security Contributions, Statutory Maternity Pay and Statutory Sick Pay (Miscellaneous Amendments) Regulations 1996, SI 1996/777, reg 2(1), (2).

Social Security and Housing Benefits Act 1982: largely repealed by the Social Security (Consequential Provisions) Act 1992; see now the Social Security Administration Act 1992 and the Social Security Contributions and Benefits Act 1992.

2 Persons deemed incapable of work

(1) A person who is not incapable of work of which he can reasonably be expected to do under a particular contract of service may be deemed to be incapable of work of such a kind by reason of some specific disease or bodily or mental disablement for any day on which either—

(a)

(i) he is under medical care in respect of a disease or disablement as aforesaid,

(ii) it is stated by a registered medical practitioner that for precautionary or convalescent reasons consequential on such disease or disablement he should abstain from work, or from work of such a kind, and

(iii) he does not work under that contract of service, or

[(b) he is—

(i) excluded or abstains from work, or from work of such a kind, pursuant to a request or notice in writing lawfully made under an enactment; or

(ii) otherwise prevented from working pursuant to an enactment,

by reason of his being a carrier, or having been in contact with a case, of a relevant disease].

(2) A person who at the commencement of any day is, or thereafter on that day becomes, incapable of work of such a kind by reason of some specific disease or bodily or mental disablement, and

(a) on that day, under that contract of service, does no work, or no work except during a shift which ends on that day having begun on the previous day; and

(b) does no work under that contract of service during a shift which begins on that day and ends on the next,

shall be deemed to be incapable of work of such a kind by reason of that disease or bodily or mental disablement throughout that day.

[(3) For the purposes of paragraph (1)(b)—

"enactment" includes an enactment comprised in, or in an instrument made under—

(a) an Act; or

(b) an Act of the Scottish Parliament; and

"relevant disease" means—

(a) in England and Wales, any disease, food poisoning, infection, infectious disease or notifiable disease—

(i) to which section 20(1) of the Public Health (Control of Disease) Act 1984 (stopping of work to prevent spread of disease) applies; or

(ii) to which—

(aa) regulation 3 (public health enactments applied to certain diseases) of, and Schedule 1 to,

(bb) regulation 9(1) (provisions for preventing the spread of typhus and relapsing fever) of, and Schedule 3 to, or

(cc) regulation 9(2) (provisions for preventing the spread of food poisoning and food borne infections) of, and Schedule 4 to,

the Public Health (Infectious Diseases) Regulations 1988 applies; or

(iii) to which regulations 8 and 9 (examination, etc of persons on aircraft and powers in respect of persons leaving aircraft) of the Public Health (Aircraft) Regulations 1979 applies; or

(iv) to which regulations 9 and 10 (examination, etc of persons on ships and powers in respect of certain persons on ships) of the Public Health (Ships) Regulations 1979 applies; and

(b) in Scotland, any food poisoning or infectious disease—

(i) to which section 71(1) of the Health Services and Public Health Act 1968 (compensation for stopping employment to prevent spread of disease in Scotland) applies;

(ii) to which—

(aa) regulations 8 and 9 (examination, etc of persons on aircraft and powers in respect of persons leaving aircraft) of the Public Health (Aircraft) (Scotland) Regulations 1971; or

(bb) regulations 9 and 10 (examination, etc of persons on ships and powers in respect of certain persons on ships) of the Public Health (Ships) (Scotland) Regulations 1971,

applies.]

[2081]

NOTES

Para (1): sub-para (b) substituted by the Statutory Sick Pay (General) Amendment Regulations 2006, SI 2006/799, reg 2(1), (2), as from 10 April 2006.

Para (3): added by SI 2006/799, reg 2(1), (3), as from 10 April 2006.

2A *(Spent; this regulation was inserted by the Statutory Sick Pay (General) Amendment Regulations 1986, SI 1986/477, reg 2, and amended the Social Security and Housing Benefits Act 1982, s 2(3), which was repealed by the Social Security (Consequential Provisions) Act 1992, s 3(1), Sch 1.)*

3 Period of entitlement ending or not arising

(1) In a case where an employee is detained in legal custody or sentenced to a term of imprisonment (except where the sentence is suspended) on a day which in relation to him falls within a period of entitlement, that period shall end with that day.

(2) A period of entitlement shall not arise in relation to a period of incapacity for work where at any time on the first day of that period of incapacity for work the employee in question is in legal custody or sentenced to or undergoing a term of imprisonment (except where the sentence is suspended).

[(2A) A period of entitlement in respect of an employee who was entitled to incapacity benefit, maternity allowance or severe disablement allowance shall not arise in relation to any day within a period of incapacity for work beginning with the first day on which paragraph 2(d) of Schedule 11 to the Contributions and Benefits Act ceases to have effect where the employee in question is a person to whom regulation 13A of the Social Security (Incapacity for Work) (General) Regulations 1995 (welfare to work beneficiary) applies.]

[(2B) Paragraph (2A) shall not apply, in the case of an employee who was entitled to incapacity benefit, where paragraph 2(d)(i) of Schedule 11 to the Contributions and Benefits Act ceases to have effect by virtue of paragraph 5A of that Schedule.]

[(3) A period of entitlement as between an employee and his employer shall end after 3 years if it has not otherwise ended in accordance with [section 153(2) of the Contributions and Benefits Act] or with regulations (other than this paragraph) made under [section 153(6) of the Contributions and Benefits Act.]

[[(4) Where a period of entitlement is current as between an employee and her employer and the employee—

(a) is pregnant or has been confined; and

(b) is incapable of work wholly or partly because of pregnancy or confinement on any day which falls on or after the beginning of the [4th week] before the expected week of confinement; and

(c) is not by virtue of that pregnancy or confinement entitled to statutory maternity pay under Part XII of the Contributions and Benefits Act or to maternity allowance under section 35 of that Act;

the period of entitlement shall end on that day or, if earlier, on the day she was confined.

(5) Where an employee—

(a) is pregnant or has been confined; and

(b) is incapable of work wholly or partly because of pregnancy or confinement on any day which falls on or after the beginning of the [4th week] before the expected week of confinement; and

(c) is not by virtue of that pregnancy or confinement entitled to statutory maternity pay under Part XII of the Contributions and Benefits Act or to maternity allowance under section 35 of that Act;

a period of entitlement as between her and her employer shall not arise in relation to a period of incapacity for work where the first day in that period falls within 18 weeks of the beginning of the week containing the day referred to at (b) above or, if earlier, of the week in which she was confined.]

(6) In paragraphs (4) and (5) "confinement" and "confined" have the same meanings as in [section 171 of the Contributions and Benefits Act.]]

[2082]

NOTES

Para (2A): inserted by the Social Security (Welfare to Work) Regulations 1998, SI 1998/2231, reg 6.

Para (2B): inserted by the Employment Equality (Age) (Consequential Amendments) Regulations 2007, SI 2007/825, reg 5(1), (2), as from 6 April 2007.

Para (3): added by the Statutory Sick Pay (General) Amendment Regulations 1986, SI 1986/477, reg 3; words in square brackets substituted by the Social Security Maternity Benefits and Statutory Sick Pay (Amendment) Regulations 1994, SI 1994/1367, reg 9(1), (2).

Paras (4), (5): added by the Statutory Sick Pay (General) Amendment (No 2) Regulations 1987, SI 1987/868, reg 2, and substituted by SI 1994/1367, reg 9(1), (3), (4); words in square brackets substituted by the Social Security, Statutory Maternity Pay and Statutory Sick Pay (Miscellaneous Amendments) Regulations 2002, SI 2002/2690, reg 13 (with effect in relation to those women whose expected week of confinement commenced on or after 6 April 2003).

Para (6): added by SI 1987/868, reg 2; words in square brackets substituted by SI 1994/1367, reg 9(1), (5).

[3A Maximum entitlement to Statutory Sick Pay in a period of entitlement

(1) For the purpose of determining whether an employee's maximum entitlement to statutory sick pay has been reached in a period of entitlement as between him and an employer of his, days falling within a previous period of entitlement as between the employee and any person who is or has in the past been an employer of his are, subject to paragraph (3), to be counted in the circumstances specified in paragraph (2).

(2) The circumstances specified for the purpose of paragraph (1) are—

(a) the period of entitlement as between the employee and his employer arose not more than 8 weeks after the last day in respect of which a person who is or has in the past been an employer of his was liable to make to him a payment of statutory sick pay; and either

(b) the employee has provided his employer with a statement issued in accordance with regulation 15A by a previous employer of his—

(i) on or before the seventh day after the first qualifying day in the period of entitlement, or

(ii) within such longer period as the employer may require,

so however that where an employee shows good cause for delay in providing the statement, he may provide it later than the time specified in heads (i) and (ii) above but not later than the ninety-first day after the first qualifying day in the period of entitlement; or

(c) the employer has himself issued such a statement to the employee.

(3) Where an employee provides his employer with more than one statement or the employer himself issued more than one statement such as is referred to in paragraph (2), the employer shall have regard to one only of those statements and if the number of weeks specified in the statements is not the same he shall have regard to the statement which specifies the greatest number of weeks.

(4) For the purposes of paragraph (2)(b) a statement enclosed in an envelope which is properly addressed and sent by prepaid post shall be deemed to have been provided on the day which it was posted.

(5) The employer shall return the statement to the employee where—

(a) a period of entitlement does not arise as between the employee and his employer, or

(b) the employee leaves his employment with the employer within eight weeks of its commencement, and the employer is not himself required to provide the employee with a statement in accordance with regulation 15A,

and in such cases regulation 13(2) shall not apply to him.]

[2083]

NOTES

Inserted by the Statutory Sick Pay (General) Amendment Regulations 1986, SI 1986/477, reg 4.

4 Contract of service ended for the purpose of avoiding liability for statutory sick pay

(1) The provisions of this regulation apply in any case where an employer's contract of service with an employee is brought to an end by the employer solely or mainly for the purpose of avoiding liability for statutory sick pay.

(2) Where a period of entitlement is current on the day on which the contract is brought to an end, the employer shall be liable to pay statutory sick pay to the employee until the occurrence of an event which, if the contract had still been current, would have caused the period of entitlement to come to an end under section 3(2)(a), (b) or (d) or regulation 3(1) [of these regulations or regulation 10(2) of the Statutory Sick Pay (Mariners, Airmen and Persons Abroad) Regulations 1982], or (if earlier) until the date on which the contract would have expired.

[2084]

NOTES

Para (2): words in square brackets inserted by the Statutory Sick Pay (Mariners, Airmen and Persons Abroad) Regulations 1982, SI 1982/1349, reg 10(3).

5 Qualifying days

(1) In this regulation "week" means a period of 7 consecutive days beginning with Sunday.

(2) Where an employee and an employer of his have not agreed which day or days in any week are or were qualifying days [or where in any week the only day or days are or were such as are referred to in paragraph (3)], the qualifying day or days in that week shall be—

(a) the day or days on which it is agreed between the employer and the employee that the employee is or was required to work (if not incapable) for that employer or, if it is so agreed that there is or was no such day,

(b) the Wednesday, or, if there is no such agreement between the employer and employee as mentioned in sub-paragraph (a),

(c) every day, except that or those (if any) on which it is agreed between the employer and the employee that none of that employer's employees are or were required to work (any agreement that all days are or were such days being ignored).

[(3) No effect shall be given to any agreement between an employee and his employer to treat as qualifying days—

(a) any day where the day is identified, whether expressly or otherwise, by reference to that or another day being a day of incapacity for work in relation to the employee's contract of service with an employer;

(b) any day identified, whether expressly or otherwise, by reference to a period of entitlement or to a period of incapacity for work.]

[2085]

NOTES

Para (2): words in square brackets inserted by the Statutory Sick Pay (General) Amendment Regulations 1985, SI 1985/126, reg 2.

Para (3): added by SI 1985/126, reg 2.

6 Calculation of entitlement limit

(1) Where an employee's entitlement to statutory sick pay is calculated by reference to different weekly rates in the same period of entitlement … , the entitlement limit shall be calculated in the manner described in paragraphs (2) and (3), or, as the case may be, (4) and (5); and where a number referred to in paragraph (2)(b) or (d) or (4)(a)(ii) or (d)(ii) is not a whole number [of thousandths, it shall be rounded up to the next thousandth].

(2) For the purpose of determining whether an employee has reached his maximum entitlement to statutory sick pay in respect of a period of entitlement, there shall be calculated—

(a) the amount of statutory sick pay to which the employee became entitled during the part of the period of entitlement before the change in the weekly rate;

(b) the number by which the weekly rate (before the change) must be multiplied in order to produce the amount mentioned in sub-paragraph (a);

(c) the amount of statutory sick pay to which the employee has so far become entitled during the part of the period of entitlement after the change in the weekly rate; and

(d) the number by which the weekly rate (after the change) must be multiplied in order to produce the amount mentioned in sub-paragraph (c);

(e) the sum of the amounts mentioned in sub-paragraphs (a) and (c); and

(f) the sum of the numbers mentioned in sub-paragraphs (b) and (d).

(3) When the sum mentioned in paragraph (2)(f) reaches [28], the sum mentioned in paragraph (2)(e) reaches the entitlement limit.

(4), (5) …

[2086]

NOTES

Para (1): words omitted revoked by the Statutory Sick Pay (General) Amendment Regulations 1986, SI 1986/477, reg 9; words in square brackets substituted by the Statutory Sick Pay (General) Amendment Regulations 1984, SI 1984/385, reg 2.

Para (3): number in square brackets substituted by SI 1986/477, reg 9.

Paras (4), (5): revoked by SI 1986/477, reg 9.

7 Time and manner of notification of incapacity for work

(1) Subject to paragraph (2), notice of any day of incapacity for work shall be given by or on behalf of an employee to his employer—

(a) in a case where the employer has decided on a time limit (not being one which requires the notice to be given earlier than … the first qualifying day in the period of incapacity for work which includes that day of incapacity for work [or by a specified time during that qualifying day]) and taken reasonable steps to make it known to the employee, within that time limit; and

(b) in any other case, on or before the seventh day after that day of incapacity for work.

(2) Notice of any day of incapacity for work may be given [one month] later than as provided by paragraph (1) where there is good cause for giving it later [or if in the particular circumstances that is not practicable, as soon as it is reasonably practicable thereafter], so however that it shall in any event be given on or before the 91st day after that day.

(3) A notice contained in a letter which is properly addressed and sent by prepaid post shall be deemed to have been given on the day on which it was posted.

(4) Notice of any day of incapacity for work shall be given by or on behalf of an employee to his employer—

(a) in a case where the employer has decided on a manner in which it is to be given (not being a manner which imposes a requirement such as is specified in paragraph (5)) and taken reasonable steps to make it known to the employee, in that manner; and

(b) in any other case, in any manner, so however that unless otherwise agreed between the employer and employee it shall be given in writing.

(5) The requirements mentioned in paragraph (4)(a) are that notice shall be given—

(a) personally;
(b) in the form of medical evidence;
(c) more than one in every 7 days during a period of entitlement;
(d) on a document supplied by the employer; or
(e) on a printed form.

[2087]

NOTES

Para (1): words omitted revoked, and words in square brackets inserted, by the Statutory Sick Pay (General) Amendment Regulations 1984, SI 1984/385, reg 2.

Para (2): words in square brackets inserted by the Social Security Contributions, Statutory Maternity Pay and Statutory Sick Pay (Miscellaneous Amendments) Regulations 1996, SI 1996/777, reg 2(1), (3).

8 Manner in which statutory sick pay may not be paid

Statutory sick pay may not be paid in kind or by way of the provision of board or lodging or of services or other facilities.

[2088]

9 Time limits for paying statutory sick pay

(1) In this regulation, "pay day" means a day on which it has been agreed, or it is the normal practice, between an employer and an employee of his, that payments by way of remuneration are to be made, or, where there is no such agreement or normal practice, the last day of a calendar month.

(2) In any case where—

(a) a decision has been made by an [adjudication officer], [social security appeal tribunal] or Commissioner in proceedings under Part I that an employee is entitled to an amount of statutory sick pay; and

(b) the time for bringing an appeal against the decision has expired and either—
 (i) no such appeal has been brought; or
 (ii) such an appeal has been brought and has been finally disposed of,

that amount of statutory sick pay is to be paid within the time specified in paragraph (3).

(3) Subject to paragraphs (4) and (5), the employer is required to pay the amount not later than the first pay day after—

(a) where an appeal has been brought, the day on which the employer receives notification that it has been finally disposed of;

(b) where leave to appeal has been refused and there remains no further opportunity to apply for leave, the day on which the employer receives notification of the refusal; and

(c) in any other case, the day on which the time for bringing an appeal expires.

(4) Subject to paragraph (5), where it is impracticable, in view of the employer's methods of accounting for and paying remuneration, for the requirement of payment referred to in paragraph (3) to be met by the pay day referred to in that paragraph, it shall be met not later than the next following pay day.

(5) Where the employer would not have remunerated the employee for his work on the day of incapacity for work in question (if it had not been a day of incapacity for work) as early as the pay day specified in paragraph (3) or (if it applies) paragraph (4), the requirement of payment shall be met on the first day on which the employee would have been remunerated for his work on that day.

[2089]

NOTES

Para (2): words in square brackets substituted by virtue of the Health and Social Services and Social Security Adjudications Act 1983, s 25, Sch 8, Pt I, para 1(1), (3)(a).

[9A Liability of the [Commissioners of Inland Revenue] for payments of statutory sick pay

(1) Notwithstanding the provisions of section 1 of the Act and subject to paragraph (4), where—

(a) an adjudicating authority has determined that an employer is liable to make payments of statutory sick pay to an employee, and

(b) the time for appealing against that determination has expired, and

(c) no appeal against the determination has been lodged or leave to appeal against the determination is required and has been refused,

then for any day of incapacity for work in respect of which it was determined the employer was liable to make those payments, and for any further days of incapacity for work which fall within the same spell of incapacity for work and in respect of which the employer was liable to make payments of statutory sick pay to that employee, the liability to make payments of statutory sick pay in respect of those days shall, to the extent that payment has not been made by the employer, be that of the [Commissioners of Inland Revenue] and not the employer.

(2) For the purposes of this regulation a spell of incapacity for work consists of consecutive days of incapacity for work with no day of the week disregarded.

(3) In paragraph (1) above "adjudicating authority" means, as the case may be, the Chief or other adjudication officer, a Social Security Appeal Tribunal or the Chief or any other Social Security Commissioner.

(4) This regulation shall not apply to any liability of an employer to make a payment of statutory sick pay where the day of incapacity for work in respect of which the liability arose falls within a period of entitlement which commenced before 6th April 1987.]

[2090]

NOTES

Inserted by the Statutory Sick Pay (General) Amendment Regulations 1987, SI 1987/372, reg 2.

Words in square brackets substituted by virtue of the Social Security Contributions (Transfer of Functions, etc) Act 1999, s 1(2), Sch 2.

Commissioners of Inland Revenue: a reference to the Commissioners of Inland Revenue is now to be taken as a reference to the Commissioners for Her Majesty's Revenue and Customs; see the Commissioners for Revenue and Customs Act 2005, s 50(1), (7).

[9B Insolvency of employer

(1) Notwithstanding the provisions of section 1 of the Act and subject to paragraph (3), any liability arising under Part I of the Act to make a payment of statutory sick pay in respect of a day of incapacity for work in relation to an employee's contract of service with his employer shall be that of the [Commissioners of Inland Revenue] and not that of the employer where the employer is insolvent on that day.

(2) For the purposes of paragraph (1) an employer shall be taken to be insolvent if, and only if—

(a) in England and Wales—

(i) he has been adjudged bankrupt or has made a composition or arrangement with his creditors;

(ii) he has died and his estate falls to be administered in accordance with an order under section 421 of the Insolvency Act 1986; or

(iii) where an employer is a company, a winding-up order … is made or a resolution for voluntary winding-up is passed with respect to it [or it enters administration], or a receiver or manager of its undertaking is duly appointed, or possession is taken by or on behalf of the holders of any debentures secured by a floating charge, or any property of the company comprised in or subject to the charge or a voluntary arrangement proposed for the purposes of Part I of the Insolvency Act 1986 is approved under that Part;

(b) in Scotland—

(i) an award of sequestration is made on his estate or he executes a trust deed for his creditors or enters into a composition contract;

(ii) he has died and a judicial factor appointed under section 11A of the Judicial Factors (Scotland) Act 1889 is required by that section to divide his insolvent estate among his creditors; or

(iii) where the employer is a company, a winding-up order … is made or a resolution for voluntary winding-up is passed with respect to it [or it enters administration] or a receiver of its undertaking is duly appointed or a voluntary arrangement proposed for the purposes of Part I of the Insolvency Act 1986 is approved under that Part.

(3) This regulation shall not apply where the employer became insolvent before 6th April 1987].

[2091]

NOTES

Inserted by the Statutory Sick Pay (General) Amendment Regulations 1987, SI 1987/372, reg 2.

Para (1): words in square brackets substituted by virtue of the Social Security Contributions (Transfer of Functions, etc) Act 1999, s 1(2), Sch 2.

Para (2): words omitted revoked, and words in square brackets inserted, by the Enterprise Act 2002 (Insolvency) Order 2003, SI 2003/2096, art 5, Schedule, Pt 2, para 42, as from 15 September 2003, except in relation to any case where a petition for an administration order was presented before that date.

Commissioners of Inland Revenue: a reference to the Commissioners of Inland Revenue is now to be taken as a reference to the Commissioners for Her Majesty's Revenue and Customs; see the Commissioners for Revenue and Customs Act 2005, s 50(1), (7).

[9C Payments by the [Commissioners of Inland Revenue]

Where the [Commissioners of Inland Revenue became] liable in accordance with regulation 9A or 9B to make payments of statutory sick pay to a person, the first payment shall be made as soon as reasonably practicable after he becomes so liable, and payments thereafter shall be made at weekly intervals, by means of an instrument of payment[, instrument for benefit payment] or by such other means as appears to the [Commissioners of Inland Revenue] to be appropriate in the circumstances of the particular case.]

[2092]

NOTES

Inserted by the Statutory Sick Pay (General) Amendment Regulations 1987, SI 1987/372, reg 2.

Words "Commissioners of Inland Revenue" and "Commissioners of Inland Revenue became" in square brackets substituted by virtue of the Social Security Contributions (Transfer of Functions, etc) Act 1999, s 1(2), Sch 2; other words in square brackets inserted by the Social Security (Claims and Payments Etc) Amendment Regulations 1996, SI 1996/672, reg 3.

Commissioners of Inland Revenue: a reference to the Commissioners of Inland Revenue is now to be taken as a reference to the Commissioners for Her Majesty's Revenue and Customs; see the Commissioners for Revenue and Customs Act 2005, s 50(1), (7).

10 Persons unable to act

(1) Where in the case of any employee—

(a) statutory sick pay is payable to him or he is alleged to be entitled to it;

(b) he is unable for the time being to act; and

(c) either—

(i) no receiver has been appointed by the Court of Protection with power to receive statutory sick pay on his behalf, or

(ii) in Scotland, his estate is not being administered by any tutor, curator or other guardian acting or appointed in terms of law,

the [Commissioners of Inland Revenue] may, upon written application to [them] by a person who, if a natural person, is over the age of 18, appoint that person to exercise, on behalf of the employee, any right to which he may be entitled under Part I and to deal on his behalf with any sums payable to him.

(2) Where the [Commissioners of Inland Revenue have] made an appointment under paragraph (1)—

(a) [they] may at any time in [their] absolute discretion revoke it;

(b) the person appointed may resign his office after having given one month's notice in writing to the [Commissioners of Inland Revenue] of his intention to do so; and

(c) the appointment shall terminate when the [Commissioners of Inland Revenue are] notified that a receiver or other person to whom paragraph (1)(c) applies has been appointed.

(3) Anything required by Part I to be done by or to any employee who is unable to act may be done by or to the person appointed under this regulation to act on his behalf, and the receipt of the person so appointed shall be a good discharge to the employee's employer for any sum paid.

[2093]

NOTES

Words in square brackets substituted by virtue of the Social Security Contributions (Transfer of Functions, etc) Act 1999, s 1(2), Sch 2.

Commissioners of Inland Revenue: a reference to the Commissioners of Inland Revenue is now to be taken as a reference to the Commissioners for Her Majesty's Revenue and Customs; see the Commissioners for Revenue and Customs Act 2005, s 50(1), (7).

11 Rounding to avoid fractional amounts

Where any payment of statutory sick pay is made and the statutory sick pay due for the period for which the payment purports to be made includes a fraction of a penny, the payment shall be rounded up to the next whole number of pence.

[2094]

12 Days not to be treated as, or as parts of, periods of interruption of employment

In a case to which paragraph 3 of Schedule 2 applies, the day of incapacity for work mentioned in sub-paragraph (1)(b) of that paragraph shall not be, or form part of, a period of interruption of employment where it is a day which, by virtue of section 17(1) or (2) of the Social Security Act 1975 or any regulations made thereunder, is not to be treated as a day of incapacity for work.

[2095]

NOTES

"Section 17(1) or (2) of the Social Security Act 1975": see now the Social Security Contributions and Benefits Act 1992, s 57(1), (3).

13 Records to be maintained by employers

[(1)] Every employer shall maintain for 3 years after the end of each tax year a record, in relation to each employee of his, of—

(a) any day in that tax year which was one of 4 or more consecutive days on which, according to information supplied by or on behalf of the employee, the employee was incapable by reason of some specific disease or bodily or mental disablement of doing work which he could reasonably be expected to do under any contract of service between him and the employer, whether or not he would normally have been expected to work on that day; [and

(b) any payment of statutory sick pay made in respect of any day recorded under sub-paragraph (a).]

[(1A) For the purposes of paragraph (1)(b) only, the employer is not to be regarded as having made a payment of statutory sick pay where, in respect of any day recorded under paragraph (1)(a), the employee is entitled to receive, and does in fact receive, a payment or payments by way of contractual remuneration from his employer which, in aggregate, equal or exceed the amount of statutory sick pay payable in respect of that day.]

[(2)–(5) …]

[2096]

NOTES

Para (1): numbered as such by the Statutory Sick Pay (General) Amendment Regulations 1986, SI 1986/477, reg 5; sub-para (b) and the word immediately preceding it substituted, for original sub-paras (b)–(d), by the Social Security Contributions, Statutory Maternity Pay and Statutory Sick Pay (Miscellaneous Amendments) Regulations 1996, SI 1996/777, reg 2(1), (4)(a).

Para (1A): inserted by the Statutory Sick Pay (General) Amendment Regulations 1996, SI 1996/3042, reg 2.
Paras (2)–(5): added by SI 1986/477, reg 5, and revoked by SI 1996/777, reg 2(1), (4)(b).

[13A Production of employer's records

(1) An authorised officer of the Commissioners of Inland Revenue may by notice require an employer to produce to him at the place of keeping such records as are in the employer's possession or power and as (in the officer's reasonable opinion) contain, or may contain, information relevant to satisfy him that statutory sick pay has been paid and is being paid in accordance with these regulations to employees or former employees who are entitled to it.

(2) A notice referred to in paragraph (1) shall be in writing and the employer shall produce the records referred to in that paragraph within 30 days after the date of such a notice.

(3) The production of records in pursuance of this regulation shall be without prejudice to any lien which a third party may have in respect of those records.

(4) References in this regulation to "records" means—
(a) any wage sheet or deductions working sheet; or
(b) any other document which relates to the calculation or payment of statutory sick pay to his employees or former employees,
whether kept in written form, electronically, or otherwise.

(5) In paragraph (1), "place of keeping" means such place in Great Britain that an employer and an authorised officer may agree upon, or, in the absence of such agreement—
(a) any place in Great Britain where records referred to in paragraph (1) are normally kept; or
(b) if there is no such place, the employer's principal place of business in Great Britain.]

[2096A]

NOTES

Commencement: 6 April 2005.
Inserted by the Statutory Maternity Pay (General) and Statutory Sick Pay (General) (Amendment) Regulations 2005, SI 2005/989, reg 3(1), (2), as from 6 April 2005.
Commissioners of Inland Revenue: a reference to the Commissioners of Inland Revenue is now to be taken as a reference to the Commissioners for Her Majesty's Revenue and Customs; see the Commissioners for Revenue and Customs Act 2005, s 50(1), (7).

14 Provision of information in connection with determination of questions

Any person claiming to be entitled to statutory sick pay, or any other person who is a party to proceedings arising under Part I, shall, if he receives notification from the [Commissioners of Inland Revenue] that any information is required from him for the determination of any question arising in connection therewith, furnish that information to the [Commissioners of Inland Revenue] within 10 days of receiving that notification.

[2097]

NOTES

Words in square brackets substituted by virtue of the Social Security Contributions (Transfer of Functions, etc) Act 1999, s 1(2), Sch 2.
Commissioners of Inland Revenue: a reference to the Commissioners of Inland Revenue is now to be taken as a reference to the Commissioners for Her Majesty's Revenue and Customs; see the Commissioners for Revenue and Customs Act 2005, s 50(1), (7).

15 Provision of information by employers to employees

(1) [Subject to paragraph (1A),] in a case which falls within paragraph (a), (b) or (c) of section 18(3) (provision of information by employers in connection with the making of claims for [short-term incapacity] and other benefits), the employer shall furnish to his employee, in writing on a form approved by the Secretary of State for the purpose [or in a form in which it can be processed by equipment operating automatically in response to instructions given for that purpose], the information specified in paragraph (2), (3) or (4) below respectively within the time specified in the appropriate one of those paragraphs.

[(1A) For the purposes of paragraph (1), where, in the particular circumstances of a case, it is not practicable for the employer to furnish the information within the specified time mentioned in paragraph (2), (3), (4)(b)(ii) or (5), he shall, not later than the first pay day within the meaning of regulation 9(1) immediately following the relevant specified time, furnish the information to his employee.]

(2) In a case which falls within paragraph (a) (no period of entitlement arising in relation to a period of incapacity for work) of section 18(3)—

(a) the information mentioned in paragraph (1) is a statement of all the reasons why, under the provisions of paragraph 1 of Schedule 1 and regulations made thereunder, a period of entitlement does not arise; and

(b) it shall be furnished not more than 7 days after the day on which the employer is notified by or on behalf of the employee of the employee's incapacity for work on the fourth day of the period of incapacity for work.

(3) In a case which falls within paragraph (b) (period of entitlement ending but period of incapacity for work continuing) of section 18(3)—

[(a) the information mentioned in paragraph (1) above is a statement informing the employee of—

(i) the reason why the period of entitlement ended;

(ii) the date of the first day in the period of entitlement or where the employer has taken into account days falling within a previous period of entitlement as between the employee and a person who is or was an employer of his, the date of the first day in that previous period of entitlement;

(iii) the date of the last day in respect of which the employer is or was liable to make a payment of statutory sick pay to him;

(iv) the number of qualifying days falling within the last week (beginning with Sunday) in the period of entitlement in which the employer is or was liable to make to him a payment of statutory sick pay; and either

(v) where the period of entitlement ends otherwise than by virtue of section 3(2)(b) of the Act, the number of weeks (a week being 7 days beginning with Sunday) and days in respect of which the employer was liable to make a payment of statutory sick pay to him in that period of entitlement; or

(vi) where the period of entitlement ends otherwise than by virtue of section 3(2)(b) of the Act and where the employee provided the employer with a statement issued to him in accordance with regulation 15A by a person who is or was an employer of his, the number of weeks (a week being 7 days beginning with Sunday) and days in respect of which he and the previous employer were together liable to make a payment of statutory sick pay to him; and

(b) the statement shall be furnished not more than 7 days after the day on which the period of entitlement ended, or if earlier, on the day on which it is already required to be furnished under paragraph (4).]

(4) In a case which falls within paragraph (c) (period of entitlement expected to end before period of incapacity for work ends, on certain assumptions) of section 18(3)—

[(a) the information mentioned in paragraph (1) above is a statement informing the employee of—

(i) the reason why the period of entitlement is expected to end;

(ii) the date of the first day in the period of entitlement or where the employer has taken into account days of incapacity for work in a previous period of entitlement as between the employee and a person who is or was an employer of his, the date of the first day in that previous period of entitlement;

(iii) the date of the last day in respect of which the employer is or was expected to be liable to make a payment of statutory sick pay to him;

(iv) the number of qualifying days falling within the last week (beginning with Sunday) in the period of entitlement in which the employer is or was expected to be liable to make to him a payment of statutory sick pay; and either

(v) where the period of entitlement is expected to end otherwise than by virtue of section 3(2)(b) of the Act, the number of weeks (a week being 7 days beginning with Sunday) and days in respect of which the employer will have been liable to make a payment of statutory sick pay to him in that period of entitlement; or

(vi) where the period of entitlement is expected to end otherwise than by virtue of section 3(2)(b) of the Act and where the employee provided the employer with a statement issued to him in accordance with regulation 15A by a person who is or was an employer of his, the number of weeks (a week being 7 days beginning with Sunday) and days in respect of which he and the previous employer were together liable to make a payment of statutory sick pay to him; and

(b) the statement shall be furnished—

(i) in a case where the period of entitlement is expected to end in accordance with section 3(2)(b) of the Act (maximum entitled to statutory sick pay), on or before the 42nd day before the period of entitlement is expected to end, or

(ii) in any other case, on or before the seventh day before the period of entitlement is expected to end,

…]

(5) For the purposes of section 18(3)(c)(i) (period for which the period of incapacity for work is to be assumed to continue to run) the prescribed period shall be 14 days.

[2098]

NOTES

Para (1): words in first and third pairs of square brackets inserted by the Social Security Contributions, Statutory Maternity Pay and Statutory Sick Pay (Miscellaneous Amendments) Regulations 1996, SI 1996/777, reg 2(1), (5)(a); words in second pair of square brackets substituted by the Social Security (Incapacity Benefit) (Consequential and Transitional Amendments and Savings) Regulations 1995, SI 1995/829, reg 15.

Para (1A): inserted by SI 1996/777, reg 2(1), (5)(b).

Para (3): sub-paras (a), (b) substituted by the Statutory Sick Pay (General) Amendment Regulations 1986, SI 1986/477, reg 6.

Para (4): sub-paras (a), (b) substituted by SI 1986/477, reg 6; words omitted from sub-para (b) revoked by SI 1996/777, reg 2(1), (5)(c).

"Section 18(3)": see now the Social Security Administration Act 1992, s 130(2), (3).

[15A Statements relating to the payment of Statutory Sick Pay

(1) Subject to the provisions of this regulation, where—

(a) an employee is about to leave his employment with his employer, or has been employed by him in the past,

(b) the period of entitlement as between the employee and that employer will come or has come to an end within the period of 8 weeks ending with the day on which the employee's contract of service with the employer concerned expires or is brought to an end, and

[(c) the employer is or was liable to make a payment of statutory sick pay to the employee in respect of any week within that period, and for this purpose a week includes any days rounded up to a week in accordance with paragraph (4),][and

(d) the employee requests one or more statements in relation to the payment of statutory sick pay,]

the employer shall provide the employee with [one or more statements in writing containing the information specified in paragraph (2) within 7 days of the employee making the request under sub-paragraph (d), or where it is not practicable, not later than his first pay day within the meaning of regulation 9(1) which would have fallen within the next income tax month immediately following that request.]

(2) The information mentioned in paragraph (1) is—

(a) the date of the first day of the period of entitlement;

(b) the number of weeks (a week being 7 days beginning with Sunday) … in respect of which the employer was liable to make a payment of statutory sick pay to the employee in that period of entitlement;

(c) the date of the last day in respect of which the employer was liable to make to the employee a payment of statutory sick pay;

(d) the date the statement was made by the employer; and

(e) the full name, address and, if there is one, telephone number of the employer making the statement.

(3) For the purposes of paragraph (2)(a) and (b) above, the period of entitlement includes any previous period of entitlement relevant for the purposes of regulation 3A (maximum entitlement to statutory sick pay in a period of entitlement).

(4) For the purposes of this regulation, where the total number of days in the period of entitlement in respect of which the employer is or was liable to make the employee a payment in respect of statutory sick pay amounts in aggregate to less than a complete week or number of weeks, then the number of weeks shall be determined by disregarding the remainder where it is 3 days or less and if it is not by rounding them up to a week.

(5) Where a question arises under Part I of the 1982 Act as to or in connection with entitlement to statutory sick pay, a written statement or, as the case may be, a revised written statement containing the information specified in paragraph (2) shall be provided by the employer to the employee within 7 days of the question being determined.

(6) A question is determined for the purpose of paragraph (5) when the time for appealing from a decision of an adjudication officer, a local tribunal or a Commissioner, as the case may be, has expired or leave to appeal has been refused.

(7) …

(8) An employer may, at the request of a person who is or was employed by him, provide a second copy of the statement if he is satisfied that the person making the request has a need for it.]

[2099]

NOTES

Inserted by the Statutory Sick Pay (General) Amendment Regulations 1986, SI 1986/477, reg 7.

Para (1): sub-para (c) substituted by the Statutory Sick Pay (General) Amendment (No 2) Regulations 1987, SI 1987/868, reg 3(a); sub-para (d) and the word immediately preceding it added, and other words in square brackets substituted, by the Social Security Contributions, Statutory Maternity Pay and Statutory Sick Pay (Miscellaneous Amendments) Regulations 1996, SI 1996/777, reg 2(1), (6)(a).

Para (2): words omitted revoked by SI 1987/868, reg 3(b).

Para (7): revoked by SI 1996/777, reg 2(1), (6)(b).

16 Meaning of "employee"

(1) [Subject to paragraph (1ZA),] in a case where, and in so far as, a person … is treated as an employed earner by virtue of the Social Security (Categorisation of Earners) Regulations 1978, he shall be treated as an employee for the purposes of Part I and in a case where, and in so far as, such a person is treated otherwise than as an employed earner by virtue of those regulations, he shall not be treated as an employee for the purposes of Part I.

[(1ZA) Paragraph (1) shall have effect in relation to a person who—

(a) is under the age of 16; and

(b) would or, as the case may be, would not have been treated as an employed earner by virtue of the Social Security (Categorisation of Earners) Regulations 1978 had he been over that age,

as it has effect in relation to a person who is or, as the case may be, is not so treated.]

[(1A) Any person who is in employed earner's employment within the meaning of the Social Security Act 1975 under a contract of apprenticeship shall be treated as an employee for the purposes of Part I.]

(2) A person who is in employed earner's employment within the meaning of the Social Security Act 1975 but whose employer—

(a) does not fulfil the conditions prescribed in regulation 119(1)(b) of the Social Security (Contributions) Regulations 1979 as to residence or presence in Great Britain, or

(b) is a person who, by reason of any international treaty to which the United Kingdom is a party or of any international convention binding the United Kingdom—

(i) is exempt from the provisions of the Social Security Act 1975, or

(ii) is a person against whom the provisions of that Act are not enforceable,

shall not be treated as an employee for the purposes of Part I.

[2100]

NOTES

Para (1): words in square brackets inserted, and words omitted revoked, by the Employment Equality (Age) Regulations 2006, SI 2006/1031, reg 49(1), Sch 8, Pt 2, paras 49, 50(1), (2), as from 1 October 2006.

Para (1ZA): inserted by SI 2006/1031, reg 49(1), Sch 8, Pt 2, paras 49, 50(1), (3), as from 1 October 2006; substituted by the Employment Equality (Age) (Consequential Amendments) Regulations 2007, SI 2007/825, reg 5(1), (3), as from 6 April 2007.

Para (1A): inserted by the Statutory Sick Pay (Compensation of Employers) and Miscellaneous Provisions Regulations 1983, SI 1983/376, reg 5(2).

Social Security Act 1975: see now the Social Security Contributions and Benefits Act 1992.

17 Meaning of "earnings"

(1) …

[(2) For the purposes of section 163(2) of the Contributions and Benefits Act, the expression "earnings" refers to gross earnings and includes any remuneration or profit derived from a person's employment except any payment or amount which is—

(a) excluded [or disregarded in the calculation of a person's earnings under regulation 25, 27 or 123 of, or Schedule 3 to, the Social Security (Contributions) Regulations 2001] [(or would have been so excluded had he not been under the age of 16)];

(b) a chargeable emolument under section 10A of the Social Security Contributions and Benefits Act 1992, except where, in consequence of such a chargeable emolument being excluded from earnings, a person would not be entitled to statutory sick pay [(or where such a payment or amount would have been so excluded and in consequence he would not have been entitled to statutory sick pay had he not been under the age of 16)].]

[(2A) …]

(3) For the purposes of [section 163(2) of the Contributions and Benefits Act] the expression "earnings" includes also—

[(za) any amount retrospectively treated as earnings by regulations made by virtue of section 4B(2) of the Contributions and Benefits Act;]

(a) any sum payable by way of maternity pay or payable by the Secretary of State in pursuance of section 40 of the Employment Protection (Consolidation) Act 1978 in respect of maternity pay;

(b) any sum which is payable by the Secretary of State by virtue of section 122(3)(a) of that Act in respect of arrears of pay and which by virtue of section 42(1) of that Act is to go towards discharging a liability to pay maternity pay;

(c) any sum payable in respect of arrears of pay in pursuance of an order for re-instatement or re-engagement under that Act;

(d) any sum payable by way of pay in pursuance of an order under the Act for the continuation of a contract of employment;

(e) any sum payable by way of remuneration in pursuance of a protective award under the Employment Protection Act 1975;

(f) any sum payable to any employee under the Temporary Short-time Working Compensation Scheme administered under powers conferred by the Employment Subsidies Act 1978;

(g) any sum paid in satisfaction of any entitlement to statutory sick pay;

[(h) any sum payable by way of statutory maternity pay under Part V of the Social Security Act 1986, including sums payable in accordance with regulations made under section 46(8)(b) of that Act];

[(i) any sum payable by way of statutory paternity pay, including any sums payable in accordance with regulations made under section 171ZD(3) of the Contributions and Benefits Act;

(j) any sum payable by way of statutory adoption pay, including any sums payable in accordance with regulations made under section 171ZM(3) of the Contributions and Benefits Act].

(4), (5) …

[2101]

NOTES

Paras (1), (4), (5): revoked by the Social Security (Miscellaneous Provisions) Amendment Regulations 1992, SI 1992/2595, reg 15.

Para (2): substituted by the Social Security Contributions, Statutory Maternity Pay and Statutory Sick Pay (Miscellaneous Amendments) Regulations 1999, SI 1999/567, reg 13; words in first pair of square brackets in sub-para (a) substituted by the Social Security, Occupational Pension Schemes and Statutory Payments (Consequential Provisions) Regulations 2007, SI 2007/1154, reg 5(1), (2), as from 6 April 2007 with retrospective effect from 2 December 2004; words in second pair of square brackets in sub-para (a) and words in square brackets in sub-para (b) inserted by the Employment Equality (Age) Regulations 2006, SI 2006/1031, reg 49(1), Sch 8, Pt 2, para 51, as from 1 October 2006.

Para (2A): inserted by the Statutory Sick Pay (Compensation of Employers) and Miscellaneous Provisions Regulations 1983, SI 1983/376, reg 5(3); revoked by SI 1992/2595, reg 15.

Para (3): words in first pair of square brackets substituted by the Social Security, Statutory Maternity Pay and Statutory Sick Pay (Miscellaneous Amendments) Regulations 2002, SI 2002/2690, reg 14(a); sub-para (za) inserted by SI 2007/1154, reg 5(1), (3), as from 6 April 2007 with retrospective effect from 2 December 2004; sub-para (h) added by the Statutory Sick Pay (General) Amendment (No 2) Regulations 1987, SI 1987/868, reg 4(b); sub-paras (i), (j) added by SI 2002/2690, reg 14(b).

Statutory paternity pay: the Work and Families Act 2006, s 11(2) at **[1697]** provides that any reference to statutory paternity pay in any instrument or document made before the commencement of paras 12 and 13 of Sch 1 to that Act is to be read, in relation to any time after that commencement, as a reference to ordinary statutory paternity pay. As of 6 April 2008, Sch 1, paras 12, 13 had not been brought into force.

"Section 40 of the Employment Protection (Consolidation) Act 1978": s 40 as then in force was repealed by the Social Security Act 1986: see now the Social Security Contributions and Benefits Act 1992, Pt XII.

"Section 122(3)(a) of that Act": see now the Employment Rights Act 1996, s 184(1).

"Section 42(1) of that Act": see now the Employment Rights Act 1996, s 82(1).

"Employment Protection Act 1975": relevant provisions are now contained in the Trade Union and Labour Relations (Consolidation) Act 1992, s 188 et seq.

"Part V of the Social Security Act 1986": see now the Social Security Contributions and Benefits Act 1992, Pt XII.

18 Payments to be treated or not to be treated as contractual remuneration

For the purposes of paragraph 2(1) and (2) of Schedule 2 to the Act, those things which are included within the expression "earnings" by regulation 17 (except paragraph (3)(g) thereof) shall be, and those things which are excluded from that expression by that regulation shall not be, treated as contractual remuneration.

[2102]

19 Normal weekly earnings

(1) For the purposes of section 26(2) and (4), an employee's normal weekly earnings shall be determined in accordance with the provisions of this regulation.

(2) In this regulation—

"the critical date" means the first day of the period of entitlement in relation to which a person's normal weekly earnings fall to be determined, or, in a case to which paragraph 2(c) of Schedule 1 applies, the relevant date within the meaning of Schedule 1;

"normal pay day" means a day on which the terms of an employee's contract of service require him to be paid, or the practice in his employment is for him to be paid, if any payment is due to him; and

"day of payment" means a day on which the employee was paid.

(3) Subject to paragraph (4), the relevant period (referred to in section 26(2)) is the period between—

(a) the last normal pay day to fall before the critical date; and

(b) the last normal pay day to fall at least 8 weeks earlier than the normal pay day mentioned in sub-paragraph (a),

including the normal pay day mentioned in sub-paragraph (a) but excluding that first mentioned in sub-paragraph (b).

(4) In a case where an employee has no identifiable normal pay day, paragraph (3) shall have effect as if the words "day of payment" were substituted for the words "normal pay day" in each place where they occur.

(5) In a case where an employee has normal pay days at intervals of or approximating to one or more calendar months (including intervals of or approximating to a year) his normal weekly earnings shall be calculated by dividing his earnings in the relevant period by the number of calendar months in that period (or, if it is not a whole number, the nearest whole number), multiplying the result by 12 and dividing by 52.

(6) In a case to which paragraph (5) does not apply and the relevant period is not an exact number of weeks, the employee's normal weekly earnings shall be calculated by dividing his earnings in the relevant period by the number of days in the relevant period and multiplying the result by 7.

(7) In a case where the normal pay day mentioned in sub-paragraph (a) of paragraph (3) exists but that first mentioned in sub-paragraph (b) of that paragraph does not yet exist, the employee's normal weekly earnings shall be calculated as if the period for which all the earnings under his contract of service received by him before the critical date represented payment were the relevant period.

(8) In a case where neither of the normal pay days mentioned in paragraph (3) yet exists, the employee's normal weekly earnings shall be the remuneration to which he is entitled, in accordance with the terms of his contract of service, for, as the case may be—

(a) a week's work; or

(b) a number of calendar months' work, divided by that number of months, multiplied by 12 and divided by 52.

[2103]

20 Treatment of one or more employers as one

(1) In a case where the earnings paid to an employee in respect of 2 or more employments are aggregated and treated as a single payment of earnings under regulation 12(1) of the Social Security (Contributions) Regulations 1979, the employers of the employee in respect of those employments shall be treated as one for all purposes of Part I.

(2) Where 2 or more employers are treated as one under the provisions of paragraph (1), liability for the statutory sick pay payable by them to the employee shall be apportioned between them in such proportions as they may agree or, in default of agreement, in the proportions which the employee's earnings from each employment bear to the amount of the aggregated earnings.

(3) [Subject to paragraphs (4) and (5)] where a contract of service ("the current contract") was preceded by a contract of service entered into between the same employer and employee ("the previous contract"), and the interval between the date on which the previous contract ceased to have effect and that on which the current contract came into force was not more than 8 weeks, then for the purposes of establishing the employee's maximum entitlement within the meaning of section 5 (limitation on entitlement to statutory sick pay in any one period of entitlement or tax year), the provisions of Part I shall not have effect as if the employer were a different employer in relation to each of those contracts of service.

[(4) Where a contract of service ("the current contract") was preceded by two or more contracts of service entered into between the same employer and employee ("the previous contracts") and the previous contracts—

(a) existed concurrently for at least part of their length, and

(b) the intervals between the dates on which each of the previous contracts ceased to have effect and that on which the current contract came into force was not more than 8 weeks,

then for the purposes of establishing the employee's maximum entitlement within the meaning of section 5 the provisions of Part I shall not have effect as if the employer were a different employer in relation to the current contract and whichever of the previous contracts was the contract by virtue of which the employer had become liable to pay the greatest proportion of statutory sick pay in respect of any tax year or period of entitlement.

(5) If, in any case to which paragraph (4) applies, the same proportion of the employer's liability for statutory sick pay becomes due under each of the previous contracts, then for the purpose of establishing the employee's maximum entitlement within the meaning of section 5, the provisions of Part I shall have effect in relation to only one of the previous contracts.]

[2104]

NOTES

Para (3): words in square brackets inserted by the Statutory Sick Pay (Compensation of Employers) and Miscellaneous Provisions Regulations 1983, SI 1983/376, reg 3(4).

Paras (4), (5): added by SI 1983/376, reg 3(4).

21 Treatment of more than one contract of service as one

Where 2 or more contracts of service exist concurrently between one employer and one employee, they shall be treated as one for all purposes of Part I except where, by virtue of regulation 11 of the Social Security (Contributions) Regulations 1979, the earnings from those contracts of service are not aggregated for the purposes of earnings-related contributions.

[2105]

[21A Election to be treated as different employers not to apply to recovery of statutory sick pay

(1) Paragraph (2) below applies for the purposes of section 159A of the Contributions and Benefits Act (power to provide for recovery by employers of sums paid by way of statutory sick pay) and of any order made under that section.

(2) Where an employer has made 2 or more elections under regulation 3 of the Income Tax (Employments) Regulations 1993 to be treated as a different employer in respect of each of the groups of employees specified in the election, the different employers covered by each of those elections shall be treated as one employer.]

[2106]–[2107]

NOTES

Inserted by the Statutory Sick Pay Percentage Threshold Order 1995, SI 1995/513, art 3.

22 (*Revoked by the Statutory Maternity Pay (General) and Statutory Sick Pay (General) (Amendment) Regulations 2005, SI 2005/989, reg 3(1), (3), as from 6 April 2005 (immediately before the coming into force of the National Insurance Contributions and Statutory Payments Act 2004, s 9(4) on that date.*)

STATUTORY SICK PAY (MEDICAL EVIDENCE) REGULATIONS 1985

(SI 1985/1604)

NOTES

Made: 22 October 1985.

Authority: Social Security and Housing Benefits Act 1982, s 17(2A), as inserted by the Social Security Act 1985, s 20 (repealed). By virtue of the Social Security (Consequential Provisions) Act 1992, s 2(2), these Regulations now have effect as if made under the Social Security Administration Act 1992, s 14(2).

Commencement: 6 April 1986.

See *Harvey* H1, R.

ARRANGEMENT OF REGULATIONS

SCHEDULES:

1 Citation, commencement and interpretation

(1) These regulations may be cited as the Statutory Sick Pay (Medical Evidence) Regulations 1985 and shall come into operation on 6th April 1986.

(2) In these regulations, unless the context otherwise requires—

"the 1982 Act" means the Social Security and Housing Benefits Act 1982;

"signature" means, in relation to a statement given in accordance with these regulations, the name by which the person giving that statement is usually known (any name other than the surname being either in full or otherwise indicated) written by that person in his own handwriting; and "signed" shall be construed accordingly.

(3) ...

[2108]

NOTES

Para (3): revoked by the Social Security (Miscellaneous Provisions) Amendment Regulations 1992, SI 1992/247, reg 6(1), (2).

Social Security and Housing Benefits Act 1982: largely repealed by the Social Security (Consequential Provisions) Act 1992; see now the Social Security Administration Act 1992 and the Social Security Contributions and Benefits Act 1992.

2 Medical information

[(1) Medical information required under section 17(2) of the 1982 Act relating to incapacity for work shall be provided either—

(a) in the form of a statement given by a doctor in accordance with the rules set out in Part I of Schedule 1 to these Regulations on the form set out in Part II of that Schedule; or

(b) where the doctor—

(i) has not given a statement under sub-paragraph (a) of this paragraph since the patient was examined and wishes to give such a statement but more than one day has passed since the examination; or

(ii) advises that the patient should refrain from work on the basis of a written report from another doctor,

by means of a special statement given in accordance with the rules set out in Part I of Schedule 1A to these Regulations on the form set out in Part II of that Schedule; or

(c) by such other means as may be sufficient in the circumstances of any particular case.]

(2) An employee shall not be required under section 17(2) of the 1982 Act to provide medical information in respect of the first 7 days in any spell of incapacity for work; and for this purpose "spell of incapacity" means a continuous period of incapacity for work which is immediately preceded by a day on which the claimant either worked or was not incapable of work.

[2109]

NOTES

Para (1): substituted by the Social Security (Miscellaneous Provisions) Amendment Regulations 1992, SI 1992/247, reg 6(1), (2).

"Section 17(2) of the 1982 Act": see now the Social Security Administration Act 1992, s 14(1).

SCHEDULES

SCHEDULE [1]

Regulation 1(3)

PART I
RULES

1. In these rules, unless the context otherwise requires—

"patient" means the person in respect of whom a statement is given in accordance with these rules;

"doctor" means a registered medical practitioner not being the patient;

"2 weeks" means any period of 14 consecutive days.

2. The doctor's statement shall be in the form set out in Part II of this Schedule.

[3. Where the patient—

(a) is on the list of a person providing primary medical services under the National

Health Service Act 1977 or the National Health Service (Scotland) Act 1978 and is being attended by a doctor performing such services; or

(b) is on the list of a doctor, or list held jointly by two or more doctors performing personal medical services in connection with a pilot scheme under the National Health Service (Primary Care) Act 1997 and is being attended by such a doctor,

the doctor's statement shall be on the form provided by the Secretary of State for the purpose and shall be signed by the attending doctor.]

4. In any other case, the doctor's statement shall be on a form provided by the Secretary of State for the purpose and shall be signed by the doctor attending the patient.

5. Every doctor's statement shall be completed in ink or other indelible substance and shall contain the following particulars—

(a) the patient's name;
(b) the date of the examination on which the doctor's statement is based;
(c) the diagnosis of the patient's disorder in respect of which the doctor is advising the patient to refrain from work or, as the case may be, which has caused the patient's absence from work;
(d) the date on which the doctor's statement is given;
(e) the address of the doctor,

and shall bear, opposite the words "Doctor's signature", the signature of the doctor making the statement written after there have been entered the patient's name and the doctor's diagnosis.

6. Subject to rules 7 and 8 below, the diagnosis of the disorder in respect of which the doctor is advising the patient to refrain from work or, as the case may be, which has caused the patient's absence from work shall be specified as precisely as the doctor's knowledge of the patient's condition at the time of the examination permits.

7. The diagnosis may be specified less precisely where, in the doctor's opinion, a disclosure of the precise disorder would be prejudicial to the patient's well-being, or to the patient's position with his employer.

8. In the case of an initial examination by a doctor in respect of a disorder stated by the patient to have caused incapacity for work, where—

(a) there are no clinical signs of that disorder, and
(b) in the doctor's opinion, the patient need not refrain from work,

instead of specifying a diagnosis "unspecified" may be entered.

9. A doctor's statement must be given on a date not later than one day after the date of the examination on which it is based, and no further doctor's statement based on the same examination shall be furnished other than a doctor's statement by way of replacement of an original which has been lost or mislaid, in which case it shall be clearly marked "duplicate".

10. Where, in the doctor's opinion, the patient will become fit to resume work on a day not later than 2 weeks after the date of the examination on which the doctor's statement is based, the doctor's statement shall specify that day.

11. Subject to rules 12 and 13 below, the doctor's statement shall specify the minimum period during which, in the doctor's opinion, the patient should, by reason of his disorder, refrain from work.

12. The period specified shall begin on the date of the examination on which the doctor's statement is based and shall not exceed 6 months unless the patient has, on the advice of a doctor, refrained from work for at least 6 months immediately preceding that date.

13. Where—

(a) the patient has, on the advice of a doctor, refrained from work for at least 6 months immediately preceding the date of the examination on which the doctor's statement is based, and
(b) in the doctor's opinion, it will be necessary for the patient to refrain from work for the foreseeable future,

instead of specifying a period, the doctor may, having regard to the circumstances of the particular case, enter, after the word "until", the words "further notice".

14. The notes set out in Part III of this Schedule shall accompany the form of doctor's statement provided by the Secretary of State.

[2110]

NOTES

Original Schedule numbered as Sch 1 by the Social Security (Miscellaneous Provisions) Amendment Regulations 1992, SI 1992/247, reg 6(1), (4).

Para 3: substituted, in relation to England, by the General Medical Services and Personal Medical Services Transitional and Consequential Provisions Order 2004, SI 2004/865, art 119, Sch 1, para 3, as from 1 April 2004. A similar amendment was made, in relation to Wales, by the General Medical Services Transitional and Consequential Provisions (Wales) (No 2) Order 2004, SI 2004/1016, art 95, Sch 1, para 3, also from 1 April 2004 The substituted paragraph in relation to Wales is the same as the one reproduced above apart from the omission of "(a)", the word "or" at the end of sub-para (a), and the whole of sub-para (b).

PART II
FORM OF DOCTOR'S STATEMENT

DOCTOR'S STATEMENT

In confidence to

Mr/Mrs/Miss ....

I examined you today/yesterday and advised you that—

(a) you need not refrain from work (b) you should refrain from work

for ....

OR until ....

Diagnosis of your disorder causing absence from work..........

Doctor's remarks ....

Doctor's signature .... Date of signing ....

[2111]

NOTES

Original Schedule numbered as Sch 1 by the Social Security (Miscellaneous Provisions) Amendment Regulations 1992, SI 1992/247, reg 6(1), (4).

PART III
NOTES

The following notes shall accompany the form of doctor's statement provided by the Secretary of State—

On the doctor's statement—

(1) After the words "you should refrain from work for", the period entered must not exceed 6 months unless the patient has, on the advice of a doctor, already refrained from work for a continuous period of 6 months.

(2) After the words "you should refrain from work until"—

(a) if the patient is being given a date when he can return to work, the date entered should not be more than 2 weeks after the date of the examination;

(b) if the patient has already been incapable of work for at least 6 months and recovery of capacity for work in the foreseeable future is not expected, "further notice" may be entered.

[2112]

NOTES

Original Schedule numbered as Sch 1 by the Social Security (Miscellaneous Provisions) Amendment Regulations 1992, SI 1992/247, reg 6(1), (4).

[SCHEDULE 1A

Regulation 2(1)

PART I
RULES

1. In these rules, unless the context otherwise requires—
"patient" means the person in respect of whom a statement is given in accordance with these rules;
"doctor" means a registered medical practitioner not being the patient;
"special statement" means the form prescribed in Part II of this Schedule.

2. Where a doctor advises a patient to refrain from work on the basis of a written report which he has received from another doctor or where a doctor has not issued a statement since the claimant was examined and he wishes to issue a statement more than a day after the examination he shall use the special statement.

3. The special statement shall be completed in the manner described in paragraph 5 of Part I to Schedule 1.

4. Subject to rules 5 and 6 below, the diagnosis of the patient's disorder in respect of which the doctor is advising the patient to refrain from work or as the case may be, which has caused the patient's absence from work shall be specified as precisely as the doctor's knowledge of the patient's condition permits.

5. The diagnosis may be specified less precisely where in the doctor's opinion, a disclosure of the precise disorder would be prejudicial to the patient's well being, or to the patient's position with his employer.

6. In a case of a disorder stated by the patient to have caused incapacity for work, where—
(a) no clinical signs have been found of that disorder, and
(b) in the doctor's opinion, the patient need not refrain from work,
instead of specifying a diagnosis "unspecified" may be entered.

7. Part B of the special statement must only be given on a date not later than one month after the date of the written report on which the special statement is based and that part shall only be used where the patient is being advised to refrain from work for a specified period of not more than one month.]

[2113]

NOTES

Added by the Social Security (Miscellaneous Provisions) Amendment Regulations 1992, SI 1992/247, reg 6(1), (5), Sch 2.

PART II
FORM OF SPECIAL STATEMENT

FOR SOCIAL SECURITY AND STATUTORY	Special Statement
SICK PAY PURPOSES ONLY	by the Doctor

In confidence to

Mr/Mrs/Miss/Ms ....

(A) I examined you on the following dates	(B) I have not examined you but, on the basis of a recent written report from—
....	Doctor ....(Name if known)
....	....
of..	....
....	....

and advised you that you should refrain from work ....(Address)

From ....to ....

I have advised you that you should refrain from work for/until ....

Diagnosis of your disorder causing absence from work ....

Doctor's remarks..

Doctor's signature............................ Date of signing...

The special circumstances in which this form may be used are described in the handbook "Medical Evidence for Social Security and Statutory Sick Pay purposes".]

[2114]

NOTES

Added by the Social Security (Miscellaneous Provisions) Amendment Regulations 1992, SI 1992/247, reg 6(1), (5), Sch 2.

STATUTORY MATERNITY PAY (GENERAL) REGULATIONS 1986

(SI 1986/1960)

NOTES

Made: 17 November 1986.

Authority: Social Security Act 1986, ss 46(4), (7), (8), 47(1), (3), (6), (7), 48(3), (6), 50(1), (2), (4), (5), 51(1)(g), (k), (n), (r), (4), 54(1), 83(1), 84(1), Sch 4, paras 6, 8, 12(3) (repealed apart from ss 54(1), 83(1), 84(1)). By virtue of the Social Security (Consequential Provisions) Act 1992, s 2(2), these Regulations now have effect as if made under the Social Security Contributions and Benefits Act 1992, ss 164(4), (8), (9), 165(1), (3), (7), 166(3), (6), 171(1), (2), (5), (6), Sch 13, and the Social Security Administration Act 1992, ss 5, 132.

Commencement: 6 April 1987.

Transfer of functions: the functions of the Secretary of State conferred by regs 7, 25, 30, 31 have been transferred to the Commissioners of Inland Revenue by the Social Security Contributions (Transfer of Functions, etc) Act 1999, s 1(2), Sch 2. Note also that a reference to the Commissioners of Inland Revenue is now to be taken as a reference to the Commissioners for Her Majesty's Revenue and Customs; see the Commissioners for Revenue and Customs Act 2005, s 50(1), (7).

See *Harvey* G1(E), R.

ARRANGEMENT OF REGULATIONS

PART I
INTRODUCTION

PART II
ENTITLEMENT

PART II
CONTINUOUS EMPLOYMENT AND NORMAL WORKING HOURS

PART IV
GENERAL PROVISIONS

PART V
ADMINISTRATION

PART VI
PAYMENT

PART I
INTRODUCTION

1 Citation, commencement and interpretation

(1) These regulations may be cited as the Statutory Maternity Pay (General) Regulations 1986 and shall come into operation in the case of regulations 1, 22 and 23 on 15th March 1987, and in the case of the remainder of the regulations on 6th April 1987.

(2) In these regulations, unless the context otherwise requires—

"the 1975 Act" means the Social Security Act 1975;

"the 1978 Act" means the Employment Protection (Consolidation) Act 1978;

"the 1986 Act" means the Social Security Act 1986;

["the Contributions and Benefits Act" means the Social Security Contributions and Benefits Act 1992];

["statutory maternity leave" means ordinary maternity leave and any additional maternity leave under, respectively, sections 71 and 73 of the Employment Rights Act 1996].

(3) Unless the context otherwise requires, any references in these regulations to—
(a) a numbered regulation is a reference to the regulation bearing that number in these regulations and any reference in a regulation to a numbered paragraph is a reference to the paragraph of that regulation bearing that number;
(b) any provision made by or contained in an enactment or instrument shall be construed as a reference to that provision as amended or extended by any enactment or instrument and as including a reference to any provision which it re-enacts or replaces, or which may re-enact or replace it, with or without modifications.

[2115]

NOTES

Para (2): definition "the Contributions and Benefits Act" added by the Social Security (Miscellaneous Provisions) Amendment (No 2) Regulations 1992, SI 1992/2595, reg 12; definition "statutory maternity leave" added by the Statutory Maternity Pay (General) (Amendment) Regulations 2005, SI 2005/729, reg 2, as from 6 April 2005.

Social Security Act 1975, Social Security Act 1986: largely repealed and consolidated in the Social Security Contributions and Benefits Act 1992 and the Social Security Administration Act 1992.

Employment Protection (Consolidation) Act 1978: repealed and largely consolidated in the Trade Union and Labour Relations (Consolidation) Act 1992, the Employment Rights Act 1996 and the Employment Tribunals Act 1996.

PART II
ENTITLEMENT

[2 The Maternity Pay Period

(1) Subject to paragraphs (3) to (5), where—
(a) a woman gives notice to her employer of the date from which she expects his liability to pay her statutory maternity pay to begin; and
(b) in conformity with that notice ceases to work for him in a week which is later than the 12th week before the expected week of confinement,

the first day of the maternity pay period shall be the day on which she expects his liability to pay her statutory maternity pay to begin in conformity with that notice provided that day is not later than the day immediately following the day on which she is confined.

(2) The maternity pay period shall be a period of 39 consecutive weeks.

(3) In a case where a woman is confined—
(a) before the 11th week before the expected week of confinement; or
(b) after the 12th week before the expected week of confinement and the confinement occurs on a day which precedes that mentioned in a notice given to her employer as being the day on which she expects his liability to pay her statutory maternity pay to begin,

section 165 of the Contributions and Benefits Act shall have effect so that the first day of the maternity pay period shall be the day following the day on which she is so confined.

(4) In a case where a woman is absent from work wholly or partly because of pregnancy or confinement on any day—
(a) which falls on or after the beginning of the 4th week before the expected week of confinement; but
(b) not later than the day immediately following the day on which she is confined,

the first day of the maternity pay period shall be the day following the day on which she is so absent.

(5) In a case where a woman leaves her employment—
(a) at any time falling after the beginning of the 11th week before the expected week of confinement and before the start of the maternity pay period, but
(b) not later than the day on which she is confined,

the first day of the maternity pay period shall be the day following the day on which she leaves her employment.]

[2116]

NOTES

Commencement: 1 October 2006 (with effect in relation to those women whose expected week of confinement commences on or after 1 April 2007).

Substituted by the Statutory Maternity Pay, Social Security (Maternity Allowance) and Social Security (Overlapping Benefits) (Amendment) Regulations 2006, SI 2006/2379, reg 3(1), (2), as from 1 October 2006 (with effect in relation to those women whose expected week of confinement commences on or after 1 April 2007; see SI 2006/2379, reg 1(2)).

3 Contract of service ended for the purpose of avoiding liability for statutory maternity pay

(1) A former employer shall be liable to make payments of statutory maternity pay to any woman who was employed by him for a continuous period of at least 8 weeks and whose contract of service with him was brought to an end by the former employer solely or mainly for the purpose of avoiding liability for statutory maternity pay.

(2) In order to determine the amount payable by the former employer—

(a) the woman shall be deemed for the purposes of Part V of the 1986 Act to have been employed by him from the date her employment with him ended until the end of the week immediately preceding the 14th week before the expected week of confinement on the same terms and conditions of employment as those subsisting immediately before her employment ended, and

(b) her normal weekly earnings for the period of 8 weeks immediately preceding the 14th week before the expected week of confinement shall for those purposes be calculated by reference to her normal weekly earnings for the period of 8 weeks ending with the last day in respect of which she was paid under her former contract of service.

[2117]

NOTES

"Part V of the 1986 Act": see now the Social Security Contributions and Benefits Act 1992, Pt XII.

4 Modification of entitlement provisions

(1) …

(2) In relation to a woman in employed earner's employment who was confined before the 14th week before the expected week of confinement [section 164(2)(a) and (b) of the Contributions and Benefits Act] shall have effect as if for the conditions there set out, there was substituted the conditions that—

(a) she would but for her confinement have been in employed earner's employment with an employer for a continuous period of at least 26 weeks ending with the week immediately preceding the 14th week before the expected week of confinement, and

(b) her normal weekly earnings for the period of 8 weeks ending with the week immediately preceding the week of her confinement are not less than the lower earnings limit in force under [section 5(1)(a) of the Contributions and Benefits Act] immediately before the commencement of the week of her confinement.

[(3) In relation to a woman to whom paragraph (2) applies, section 166 of the Contributions and Benefits Act shall be modified so that subsection (2) has effect as if the reference to the period of 8 weeks immediately preceding the 14th week before the expected week of confinement was a reference to the period of 8 weeks immediately preceding the week in which her confinement occurred.]

[2118]

NOTES

Para (1): revoked by the Social Security Maternity Benefits and Statutory Sick Pay (Amendment) Regulations 1994, SI 1994/1367, reg 3(1), (2).

Para (2): words in square brackets substituted by SI 1994/1367, reg 3(1), (3).

Para (3): added by the Statutory Maternity Pay (General) Amendment Regulations 1988, SI 1988/532, reg 2; substituted by SI 1994/1367, reg 3(1), (4).

"Lower earnings limit": this is currently £90 per week, as from 6 April 2008: see the Social Security (Contributions) Regulations 2001, SI 2001/1004, reg 10(a) (as amended by the Social Security (Contributions) (Amendment) Regulations 2008, SI 2008/133, regs 2, 3(b)). The previous sum was £87 (as from 6 April 2007; see the Social Security (Contributions) (Amendment) Regulations 2006, SI 2007/118, regs 2, 3(b), which also amended reg 10 of the 2001 Regulations).

5 Treatment of more than one contract of service as one

Where 2 or more contracts of service exist concurrently between one employer and one employee, they shall be treated as one for the purposes of Part V of the 1986 Act, except where, by virtue of regulation 11 of the Social Security (Contributions) Regulations 1979 the earnings from those contracts of service are not aggregated for the purposes of earnings-related contributions.

[2119]

NOTES

"Part V of the 1986 Act": see now the Social Security Contributions and Benefits Act 1992, Pt XII.

[6 Prescribed rate of statutory maternity pay

The rate of statutory maternity pay prescribed under section 166(1)(b) of the Contributions and Benefits Act is a weekly rate of [£117.18].]

[2120]

NOTES

Commencement: 6 April 2003.

Substituted by the Social Security, Statutory Maternity Pay and Statutory Sick Pay (Miscellaneous Amendments) Regulations 2002, SI 2002/2690, reg 3, as from 6 April 2003.

Sum in square brackets substituted by the Social Security Benefits Up-rating Order 2008, SI 2008/632, art 10, as from 6 April 2008 (except for the purpose of determining the rate of maternity allowance in accordance with Social Security Contributions and Benefits Act 1992, s 35A(1), for which purpose it came into force on 7 April 2008). The previous amount was £112.75, as from 1 April 2007 and 9 April 2007 respectively (see the Social Security Benefits Up-rating Order 2007, SI 2007/688, art 10). Prior to those dates the amount was £108.80 (see SI 2006/645, art 10)

7 Liability of [Commissioners of Inland Revenue] to pay statutory maternity pay

(1) Where—

(a) an adjudicating authority has determined that an employer is liable to make payments of statutory maternity pay to a woman, and

(b) the time for appealing against that determination has expired, and

(c) no appeal against the determination has been lodged or leave to appeal against the determination is required and has been refused,

then for any week in respect of which the employer was liable to make payments of statutory maternity pay but did not do so, and for any subsequent weeks in the maternity pay period the liability to make those payments shall, notwithstanding section 46(3) of the 1986 Act, be that of the [Commissioners of Inland Revenue] and not the employer.

(2) In paragraph (1) adjudicating authority means, as the case may be, the Chief or any other adjudication officer, a Social Security Appeal Tribunal or the Chief or any other Social Security Commissioner.

(3) Liability to make payments of statutory maternity pay shall, notwithstanding section 46(3) of the 1986 Act, be a liability of the [Commissioners of Inland Revenue] and not the employer as from the week in which the employer first becomes insolvent until the end of the maternity pay period.

(4) For the purposes of paragraph (3) an employer shall be taken to be insolvent if, and only if—

(a) in England and Wales—

(i) he has been adjudged bankrupt or has made a composition or arrangement with his creditors;

(ii) he has died and his estate falls to be administered in accordance with an order under section 421 of the Insolvency Act 1986; or

(iii) where an employer is a company, a winding-up order … is made or a resolution for voluntary winding-up is passed with respect to it [or it enters administration], or a receiver or manager of its undertaking is duly appointed, or possession is taken by or on behalf of the holders of any debentures secured by a floating charge, of any property of the company comprised in or subject to the charge or a voluntary arrangement proposed for the purposes of Part I of the Insolvency Act 1986 is approved under that Part;

(b) in Scotland—
  (i) an award of sequestration is made on his estate or he executes a trust deed for his creditors or enters into a composition contract;
  (ii) he has died and a judicial factor appointed under section 11A of the Judicial Factors (Scotland) Act 1889 is required by that section to divide his insolvent estate among his creditors; or
  (iii) where the employer is a company, a winding-up order … is made or a resolution for voluntary winding-up is passed with respect to it [or it enters administration] or a receiver of its undertaking is duly appointed or a voluntary arrangement proposed for the purposes of Part I of the Insolvency Act 1986 is approved under that Part.

[2121]

NOTES

Regulation heading, paras (1), (3): words in square brackets substituted by virtue of the Social Security Contributions (Transfer of Functions, etc) Act 1999, s 1(2), Sch 2.

Para (4): words omitted revoked, and words in square brackets inserted, by the Enterprise Act 2002 (Insolvency) Order 2003, SI 2003/2096, art 5, Schedule, Pt 2, para 44, as from 15 September 2003, except in relation to any case where a petition for an administration order was presented before that date.

Commissioners of Inland Revenue: a reference to the Commissioners of Inland Revenue is now to be taken as a reference to the Commissioners for Her Majesty's Revenue and Customs; see the Commissioners for Revenue and Customs Act 2005, s 50(1), (7).

"Section 46(3) of the 1986 Act": see now the Social Security Contributions and Benefits Act 1992, s 164(3).

8 Work after confinement

(1) Where in the week immediately preceding the 14th week before the expected week of confinement a woman had 2 or more employers but one or more of them were not liable to make payments to her of statutory maternity pay ("non-liable employer"), section 47(6) of the 1986 Act shall not apply in respect of any week after the week of confinement but within the maternity pay period in which she works only for a non-liable employer.

(2) Where after her confinement a woman—
  (a) works for an employer who is not liable to pay her statutory maternity pay and is not a non-liable employer, but
  (b) before the end of her maternity pay period ceases to work for that employer,

the person who before she commenced work was liable to make payments of statutory maternity pay to her shall, notwithstanding section 46 of the 1986 Act, not be liable to make such payments to her for any weeks in the maternity pay period after she ceases work.

[2122]

NOTES

"Section 47(6) of the 1986 Act": see now the Social Security Contributions and Benefits Act 1992, s 165(6); as to s 46 of the 1986 Act, see now s 164 of the 1992 Act.

9 No liability to pay statutory maternity pay

Notwithstanding the provisions of section 46(1) of the 1986 Act, no liability to make payments of statutory maternity pay to a woman shall arise in respect of a week within the maternity pay period for any part of which she is detained in legal custody or sentenced to a term of imprisonment (except where the sentence is suspended), or of any subsequent week within that period.

[2123]

NOTES

"Section 46(1) of the 1986 Act": see now the Social Security Contributions and Benefits Act 1992, s 164(1).

[9A Working for not more than 10 days in the Maternity Pay Period

In a case where a woman does any work under a contract of service with her employer on any day, but for not more than 10 days (whether consecutive or not), during her maternity pay period, statutory maternity pay shall continue to be payable to the employee by the employer.]

[2123A]

NOTES

Commencement: 1 October 2006 (with effect in relation to those women whose expected week of confinement commences on or after 1 April 2007).

Inserted by the Statutory Maternity Pay, Social Security (Maternity Allowance) and Social Security (Overlapping Benefits) (Amendment) Regulations 2006, SI 2006/2379, reg 3(1), (3), as from 1 October 2006 (with effect in relation to those women whose expected week of confinement commences on or after 1 April 2007; see SI 2006/2379, reg 1(2)).

10 Death of woman

An employer shall not be liable to make payments of statutory maternity pay in respect of a woman for any week within the maternity pay period which falls after the week in which she dies.

[2124]

PART III
CONTINUOUS EMPLOYMENT AND NORMAL WORKING HOURS

11 Continuous employment

(1) Subject to the following provisions of this regulation, where in any week a woman is, for the whole or part of the week,—

(a) incapable of work in consequence of sickness or injury, or

(b) absent from work on account of a temporary cessation of work, or

(c) absent from work in circumstances such that, by arrangement or custom, she is regarded as continuing in the employment of her employer for all or any purpose, or

(d) absent from work wholly or partly because of pregnancy or confinement, [or]

[(e) absent from work in consequence of taking paternity leave, adoption leave or parental leave under Part 8 of the Employment Rights Act 1996,]

and returns to work for her employer after the incapacity for or absence from work, that week shall be treated for the purposes of Part V of the 1986 Act as part of a continuous period of employment with that employer, notwithstanding that no contract of service exists with that employer in respect of that week.

(2) Incapacity for work which lasts for more than 26 consecutive weeks shall not count for the purposes of paragraph (1)(a).

(3) Paragraph (1)(d) shall only apply to a woman who—

(a) has a contract of service with the same employer both before and after the confinement but not during any period of absence from work due to her confinement and the period between those contracts does not exceed 26 weeks, or

(b) returns to work in accordance with section 45(1) of the 1978 Act or in pursuance of an offer made in circumstances described in section 56A(2) of that Act after a period of absence from work wholly or partly occasioned by pregnancy or confinement.

[(3A) Where a woman who is pregnant—

(a) is an employee in an employed earner's employment in which the custom is for the employer—

(i) to offer work for a fixed period of not more than 26 consecutive weeks;

(ii) to offer work for such period on 2 or more occasions in a year for periods which do not overlap; and

(iii) to offer the work available to those persons who had worked for him during the last or a recent such period, but

(b) is absent from work—

(i) wholly or partly because of the pregnancy or her confinement, or

(ii) because of incapacity arising from some specific disease or bodily or mental disablement,

then in her case paragraph (1) shall apply as if the words "and returns to work for an employer after the incapacity for or absence from work" were omitted and paragraph (4) shall not apply.]

(4) Where a woman is employed under a contract of service for part only of the week immediately preceding the 14th week before the expected week of confinement, the whole of that week shall count in computing any period of continuous employment for the purposes of Part V of the 1986 Act.

[2125]

NOTES

Para (1): word in square brackets in sub-para (d) added by the Social Security, Statutory Maternity Pay and Statutory Sick Pay (Miscellaneous Amendments) Regulations 2002, SI 2002/2690, reg 4(a) (with effect in relation to those women whose expected week of confinement commenced on or after 6 April 2003); para (e) added by reg 4(b) of the 2002 Regulations (with effect in relation to those women whose expected week of confinement commenced on or after 6 April 2003).

Para (3A): inserted by the Statutory Maternity Pay (General) Amendment Regulations 1990, SI 1990/622, reg 2.

"Part V of the 1986 Act": see now the Social Security Contributions and Benefits Act 1992, Pt XII.

"Section 45(1) of the 1978 Act": see now the Employment Rights Act 1996, s 79.

"Section 56A(2) of that Act": replaced by the Employment Rights Act 1996, s 96(3) (repealed).

12 Continuous employment and unfair dismissal

(1) This regulation applies to a woman in relation to whose dismissal an action is commenced which consists—

(a) of the presentation by her of a complaint under section 67(1) of the 1978 Act; or

(b) of her making a claim in accordance with a dismissals procedure agreement designated by an order under section 65 of that Act; or

(c) of any action taken by a conciliation officer under section 134(3) of that Act; [or

(d) of a decision arising out of the use of a statutory dispute resolution procedure contained in Schedule 2 to the Employment Act 2002 in a case where, in accordance with the Employment Act 2002 (Dispute Resolution) Regulations 2004, such a procedure applies].

(2) If in consequence of an action of the kind specified in paragraph (1) a woman is reinstated or re-engaged by her employer or by a successor or associated employer of that employer the continuity of her employment shall be preserved for the purposes of Part V of the 1986 Act and any week which falls within the interval beginning with the effective date of termination and ending with the date of reinstatement or re-engagement, as the case may be, shall count in the computation of her period of continuous employment.

(3) In this regulation—

"successor" and "dismissals procedure agreement" have the same meanings as in section 30(3) and (4) of the Trade Union and Labour Relations Act 1974, and

"associated employer" shall be construed in accordance with section 153(4) of the 1978 Act.

[2126]

NOTES

Para (1): sub-para (d) and the word immediately preceding it inserted by the Statutory Maternity Pay (General) and Statutory Paternity Pay and Statutory Adoption Pay (General) (Amendment) Regulations 2005, SI 2005/358, reg 3, as from 6 April 2005, in relation to a reinstatement or re-engagement of employment occurring on or after that date.

"Section 67(1) of the 1978 Act": see now the Employment Rights Act 1996, s 111(1).

"Section 65 of that Act": see now the Employment Rights Act 1996, s 110.

"Section 134(3) of that Act": see now the Employment Tribunals Act 1996, s 18(5).

"Part V of the 1986 Act": see now the Social Security Contributions and Benefits Act 1992, Pt XII.

"Section 30(3) and (4) of the Trade Union and Labour Relations Act 1974": see now the Employment Rights Act 1996, s 235.

"Section 153(4) of the 1978 Act": see now the Employment Rights Act 1996, s 231 and the Employment Tribunals Act 1996, s 42(3).

13 Continuous employment and stoppages of work

(1) Where for any week or part of a week a woman does no work because there is, within the meaning of section 19 of the 1975 Act a stoppage of work due to a trade dispute at her place of employment the continuity of her employment shall, subject to paragraph (2), be treated as continuing throughout the stoppage but, subject to paragraph (3), no such week shall count in the computation of her period of employment.

(2) Subject to paragraph (3), where during the stoppage of work a woman is dismissed from her employment, the continuity of her employment shall not be treated in accordance with paragraph (1) as continuing beyond the commencement of the day she stopped work.

(3) The provisions of paragraph (1) to the extent that they provide that a week in which a stoppage of work occurred shall not count in the computation of a period of employment, and paragraph (2) shall not apply to a woman who proves that at no time did she have a direct interest in the trade dispute in question.

[2127]

NOTES

"Section 19 of the 1975 Act": replaced by the Social Security Contributions and Benefits Act 1992, s 27 (repealed); see now the Jobseekers Act 1995, s 14.

14 Change of employer

A woman's employment shall, notwithstanding the change of employer, be treated as continuous employment with the second employer where—

(a) the employer's trade or business or an undertaking (whether or not it is an undertaking established by or under an Act of Parliament) is transferred from one person to another;

(b) by or under an Act of Parliament, whether public or local and whenever passed, a contract of employment between any body corporate and the woman is modified and some other body corporate is substituted as her employer;

(c) on the death of her employer, the woman is taken into the employment of the personal representatives or trustees of the deceased;

(d) the woman is employed by partners, personal representatives or trustees and there is a change in the partners, or, as the case may be, personal representatives or trustees;

(e) the woman is taken into the employment of an employer who is, at the time she entered his employment, an associated employer of her previous employer, and for this purpose "associated employer" shall be construed in accordance with section 153(4) of the 1978 Act;

(f) on the termination of her employment with an employer she is taken into the employment of another employer and [those employers are the governors of a school maintained by a local education authority and that authority].

[2128]

NOTES

Para (f): words in square brackets substituted by the Statutory Maternity Pay (General) Amendment Regulations 1990, SI 1990/622, reg 3.

"Section 153(4) of the 1978 Act": see now the Employment Rights Act 1996, s 231 and the Employment Tribunals Act 1996, s 42(3).

15 Reinstatement after service with the armed forces etc

If a woman who is entitled to apply to her former employer under the Reserve Forces (Safeguard of Employment) Act 1985 enters the employment of that employer not later than the 6 month period mentioned in section 1(4)(b) of that Act, her previous period of employment with that employer (or if there was more than one such period, the last of those periods) and the period of employment beginning in the said period of 6 months shall be treated as continuous.

[2129]

16 Normal working weeks

(1) For the purposes of section 48(5) of the 1986 Act, a woman's contract of service shall be treated as not normally involving or having involved employment for less than 16 hours weekly where she is normally employed for 16 hours or more weekly.

(2) Where a woman's relations with her employer were governed for a continuous period of at least 2 years by a contract of service which normally involved employment for not less than 16 hours weekly and this period was followed by a further period, ending with the week immediately preceding the 14th week before the expected week of confinement, in which her relations with that employer were governed by a contract of service which normally involved

employment for less than 16 hours, but not less than 8 hours weekly, then her contract of service shall be treated for the purpose of section 48(5) of the 1986 Act as not normally involving or having involved employment for less than 16 hours weekly.

(3) Where a woman's relations with her employer are or were governed for a continuous period of at least 2 years by a contract of service which involved

(a) for not more than 26 weeks in that period, employment for 8 hours or more but less than 16 hours weekly, and

(b) for the whole of the remainder of that period employment for not less than 16 hours weekly,

the contract of service shall be treated for the purposes of section 48(5) of the 1986 Act as not normally involving or having involved employment for less than 16 hours weekly.

[2130]

NOTES

"Section 48(5) of the 1986 Act": replaced by the Social Security Contributions and Benefits Act 1992, s 166(5) (subsequently repealed by the Maternity Allowance and Statutory Maternity Pay Regulations 1994, SI 1994/1230, reg 4(4)).

[16A Meaning of "week"

Where a woman has been in employed earner's employment with the same employer in each of 26 consecutive weeks (but no more than 26 weeks) ending with the week immediately preceding the 14th week before the expected week of confinement then for the purpose of determining whether that employment amounts to a continuous period of at least 26 weeks, the first of those 26 weeks shall be a period commencing on the first day of her employment with the employer and ending at midnight on the first Saturday thereafter or on that day where her first day is a Saturday.]

[2131]

NOTES

Inserted by the Statutory Maternity Pay (General) Amendment Regulations 1990, SI 1990/622, reg 4.

PART IV
GENERAL PROVISIONS

17 Meaning of "employee"

(1) [Subject to paragraph (1A),] in a case where, and in so far as, a woman … is treated as an employed earner by virtue of the Social Security (Categorisation of Earners) Regulations 1978 she shall be treated as an employee for the purposes of Part V of the 1986 Act and in a case where, and in so far as, such a woman is treated otherwise than as an employed earner by virtue of those regulations, she shall not be treated as an employee for the purposes of Part V.

[(1A) Paragraph (1) shall have effect in relation to a woman who—

(a) is under the age of 16; and

(b) would or, as the case may be, would not have been treated as an employed earner by virtue of the Social Security (Categorisation of Earners) Regulations 1978 had she been over that age,

as it has effect in relation to a woman who is, or, as the case may be, is not so treated.]

(2) Any woman who is in employed earner's employment within the meaning of the 1975 Act under a contract of apprenticeship shall be treated as an employee for the purposes of Part V.

(3) A woman who is in employed earner's employment within the meaning of the 1975 Act but whose employer—

(a) does not fulfil the conditions prescribed in regulation 119(1)(b) of the Social Security (Contributions) Regulations 1979 as to residence or presence in Great Britain, or

(b) is a woman who, by reason of any international treaty to which the United Kingdom is a party or of any international convention binding the United Kingdom—

(i) is exempt from the provisions of the 1975 Act, or
(ii) is a woman against whom the provisions of that Act are not enforceable,

shall not be treated as an employee for the purposes of Part V of the 1986 Act.

[2132]

NOTES

Para (1): words in square brackets inserted, and words omitted revoked, by the Employment Equality (Age) Regulations 2006, SI 2006/1031, reg 49(1), Sch 8, Pt 2, paras 52, 53(1), (2), as from 1 October 2006.

Para (1A): inserted by SI 2006/1031, reg 49(1), Sch 8, Pt 2, paras 52, 53(1), (3), as from 1 October 2006; substituted by the Employment Equality (Age) (Consequential Amendments) Regulations 2007, SI 2007/825, reg 6, as from 6 April 2007.

"Part V of the 1986 Act": see now the Social Security Contributions and Benefits Act 1992, Pt XII.

18 Treatment of two or more employers as one

(1) In a case where the earnings paid to a woman in respect of 2 or more employments are aggregated and treated as a single payment of earnings under regulation 12(1) of the Social Security (Contributions) Regulations 1979, the employers of the woman in respect of those employments shall be treated as one for all purposes of Part V of the 1986 Act.

(2) Where 2 or more employers are treated as one under the provisions of paragraph (1), liability for statutory maternity pay payable by them to a woman shall be apportioned between them in such proportions as they may agree or, in default of agreement, in the proportions which the woman's earnings from each employment bear to the amount of the aggregated earnings.

[2133]

NOTES

"Part V of the 1986 Act": see now the Social Security Contributions and Benefits Act 1992, Pt XII.

19 Payments to be treated as contractual remuneration

For the purposes of paragraph 12(1) and (2) of Schedule 4 to the 1986 Act, the payments which are to be treated as contractual remuneration are sums payable under the contract of service—

(a) by way of remuneration;
(b) for incapacity for work due to sickness or injury, and
(c) by reason of pregnancy or confinement.

[2134]

NOTES

"1986 Act, Sch 4, para 12": see now the Social Security Contributions and Benefits Act 1992, Sch 13, para 3.

20 Meaning of "earnings"

(1) …

[(2) For the purposes of section 171(4) of the Contributions and Benefits Act, the expression "earnings" refers to gross earnings and includes any remuneration or profit derived from a woman's employment except any payment or amount which is—

(a) excluded [or disregarded in the calculation of a person's earnings under regulation 25, 27 or 123 of, or Schedule 3 to, the Social Security (Contributions) Regulations 2001] (payments to be disregarded and payments to directors to be disregarded respectively) [(or would have been so excluded had she not been under the age of 16)];
(b) a chargeable emolument under section 10A of the Social Security Contributions and Benefits Act 1992, except where, in consequence of such a chargeable emolument being excluded from earnings, a woman would not be entitled to statutory maternity pay [(or where such a payment or amount would have been so excluded and in consequence she would not have been entitled to statutory maternity pay had she not been under the age of 16)].]

(3) …

(4) For the purposes of [section 171(4) of the Contributions and Benefits Act] the expression "earnings" includes also—

[(za) any amount retrospectively treated as earnings by regulations made by virtue of section 4B(2) of the Contributions and Benefits Act;]

(a) any sum payable in respect of arrears of pay in pursuance of an order for reinstatement or re-engagement under the 1978 Act;

(b) any sum payable by way of pay in pursuance of an order under the 1978 Act for the continuation of a contract of employment;

(c) any sum payable by way of remuneration in pursuance of a protective award under the Employment Protection Act 1975;

(d) any sum payable by way of statutory sick pay, including sums payable in accordance with regulations made under section 1(5) of the Social Security and Housing Benefits Act 1982;

[(e) any sum payable by way of statutory maternity pay, including sums payable in accordance with regulations made under section 164(9)(b) of the Contributions and Benefits Act;

(f) any sum payable by way of statutory paternity pay, including sums payable in accordance with regulations made under section 171ZD(3) of the Contributions and Benefits Act;

(g) any sum payable by way of statutory adoption pay, including sums payable in accordance with regulations made under section 171ZM(3) of the Contributions and Benefits Act].

(5), (6) …

[2135]

NOTES

Paras (1), (3), (5), (6): revoked by the Social Security (Miscellaneous Provisions) Amendment (No 2) Regulations 1992, SI 1992/2595, reg 13(1), (2), (4).

Para (2): substituted by the Social Security Contributions, Statutory Maternity Pay and Statutory Sick Pay (Miscellaneous Amendments) Regulations 1999, SI 1999/567, reg 12; words in first pair of square brackets in sub-para (a) substituted by the Social Security, Occupational Pension Schemes and Statutory Payments (Consequential Provisions) Regulations 2007, SI 2007/1154, reg 4(1), (2), as from 6 April 2007 with retrospective effect from 2 December 2004; words in second pair of square brackets in sub-para (a) and words in square brackets in sub-para (b) inserted by the Employment Equality (Age) Regulations 2006, SI 2006/1031, reg 49(1), Sch 8, Pt 2, paras 52, 54, as from 1 October 2006 (in relation to any case where the expected week of confinement begins on or after 14 January 2007).

Para (4): words in first pair of square brackets substituted by the Social Security, Statutory Maternity Pay and Statutory Sick Pay (Miscellaneous Amendments) Regulations 2002, SI 2002/2690, reg 5(a); sub-para (za) inserted by SI 2007/1154, reg 4(1), (3), as from 6 April 2007 with retrospective effect from 2 December 2004; paras (e)–(g) added by reg 5(b) of the 2002 Regulations.

Statutory paternity pay: the Work and Families Act 2006, s 11(2) at **[1697]** provides that any reference to statutory paternity pay in any instrument or document made before the commencement of paras 12 and 13 of Sch 1 to that Act is to be read, in relation to any time after that commencement, as a reference to ordinary statutory paternity pay. As of 6 April 2008, Sch 1, paras 12, 13 had not been brought into force.

"Protective award under the Employment Protection Act 1975": see now the Trade Union and Labour Relations (Consolidation) Act 1992, ss 189–191.

"Section 1(5) of the Social Security and Housing Benefits Act 1982": see now the Social Security Contributions and Benefits Act 1992, s 151(4)–(6).

21 Normal weekly earnings

(1) For the purposes of [Part XII of the Contributions and Benefits Act], a woman's normal weekly earnings shall be calculated in accordance with the following provisions of this regulation.

(2) In this regulation—

"the appropriate date" means the first day of the 14th week before the expected week of confinement, or the first day in the week in which the woman is confined, whichever is the earlier, …

"normal pay day" means a day on which the terms of a woman's contract of service require her to be paid, or the practice in her employment is for her to be paid, if any payment is due to her; and

"day of payment" means a day on which the woman was paid.

(3) Subject to paragraph (4), the relevant period for the purposes of [section 171(4) of the Contributions and Benefits Act] is the period between—

(a) the last normal pay day to fall before the appropriate date; and

(b) the last normal pay day to fall at least 8 weeks earlier than the normal pay day mentioned in sub-paragraph (a),

including the normal pay day mentioned in sub-paragraph (a) but excluding that first mentioned in sub-paragraph (b).

(4) In a case where a woman has no identifiable normal pay day, paragraph (3) shall have effect as if the words "day of payment" were substituted for the words "normal pay day" in each place where they occur.

(5) In a case where a woman has normal pay days at intervals of or approximating to one or more calendar months (including intervals of or approximating to a year) her normal weekly earnings shall be calculated by dividing her earnings in the relevant period by the number of calendar months in that period (or, if it is not a whole number, the nearest whole number), multiplying the result by 12 and dividing by 52.

(6) In a case to which paragraph (5) does not apply and the relevant period is not an exact number of weeks, the woman's normal weekly earnings shall be calculated by dividing her earnings in the relevant period by the number of days in the relevant period and multiplying the result by 7.

[(7) In any case where—

(a) a woman is awarded a pay increase (or would have been awarded such an increase had she not then been absent on statutory maternity leave); and

(b) that pay increase applies to the whole or any part of the period between the beginning of the relevant period and the end of her period of statutory maternity leave,

her normal weekly earnings shall be calculated as if such an increase applied in each week of the relevant period.]

[2136]

NOTES

Paras (1), (3): words in square brackets substituted by the Social Security Maternity Benefits and Statutory Sick Pay (Amendment) Regulations 1994, SI 1994/1367, reg 5(1), (2), (4).

Para (2): words omitted revoked by SI 1994/1367, reg 5(1), (3).

Para (7): added by the Statutory Maternity Pay (General) Amendment Regulations 1996, SI 1996/1335, reg 2, and substituted by the Statutory Maternity Pay (General) (Amendment) Regulations 2005, SI 2005/729, reg 3, as from 6 April 2005.

21A (*Inserted by the Statutory Maternity Pay* (*General*) *Amendment Regulations 1988, SI 1988/532, reg 3; revoked by the Social Security, Statutory Maternity Pay and Statutory Sick Pay* (*Miscellaneous Amendments*) *Regulations 2002, SI 2002/2690, reg 6.*)

[21B Effect of maternity allowance on statutory maternity pay

Where a woman, in any week which falls within the maternity pay period, is—

(a) in receipt of maternity allowance pursuant to the provisions of sections 35 and 35A of the Contributions and Benefits Act; and

(b) entitled to receive statutory maternity pay in consequence of[—

(i) receiving a pay increase referred to in regulation 21(7), or

(ii) being treated as having been paid retrospective earnings under regulation 20(4)(za)],

the employer shall not be liable to make payments of statutory maternity pay in respect of such a week unless, and to the extent by which, the rate of statutory maternity pay exceeds the rate of maternity allowance received by her in that week.]

[2137]

NOTES

Commencement: 6 April 2005.

Inserted by the Statutory Maternity Pay (General) Amendment Regulations 1996, SI 1996/1335, reg 3, and substituted by the Statutory Maternity Pay (General) (Amendment) Regulations 2005, SI 2005/729, reg 4, as from 6 April 2005.

Sub-paras (b)(i), (ii) substituted by the Social Security, Occupational Pension Schemes and Statutory Payments (Consequential Provisions) Regulations 2007, SI 2007/1154, reg 4(1), (4), as from 6 April 2007 with retrospective effect from 2 December 2004.

PART V
ADMINISTRATION

22 Evidence of expected week of confinement or of confinement

(1) A woman shall in accordance with the following provisions of this regulation, provide the person who is liable to pay her statutory maternity pay with evidence as to—

(a) the week in which the expected date of confinement occurs, and

(b) where her entitlement to statutory maternity pay depends upon the fact of her confinement, the week in which she was confined.

(2) For the purpose of paragraph (1)(b) a certificate of birth shall be sufficient evidence that the woman was confined in the week in which the birth occurred.

(3) The evidence shall be submitted to the person who will be liable to make payments of statutory maternity pay not later than the end of the third week of the maternity pay period so however that where the woman has good cause the evidence may be submitted later than that date but not later than the end of the 13th week of the maternity pay period.

(4) For the purposes of paragraph (3) evidence contained in an envelope which is properly addressed and sent by prepaid post shall be deemed to have been submitted on the day on which it was posted.

[2138]

23 Notice of absence from work

(1) Where a woman is confined before the beginning of the 14th week before the expected week of confinement, she shall be entitled to payments of statutory maternity pay only if—

(a) she gives notice to the person who will be liable to pay it [of the date on which she was confined], and

(b) that notice is given within [28 days] of the date she was confined or if in the particular circumstances that is not practicable, as soon as is reasonably practicable thereafter; and

(c) where the person so requests, the notice is in writing.

(2) Where a woman is confined before the date stated in a notice provided in accordance with [section 164(4) of the Contributions and Benefits Act] as being the date her absence from work is due to begin, she shall be entitled to payments of statutory maternity pay only if—

(a) she gives a further notice to the person who will be liable to pay it specifying the date she was confined and the date her absence from work … began, and

(b) that further notice is given within [28 days] of the date she was confined or if in the particular circumstances that is not practicable, as soon as is reasonably practicable thereafter; and

(c) where the person so requests, the notice is in writing.

(3) For the purposes of this regulation, a notice contained in an envelope which is properly addressed and sent by prepaid post shall be deemed to be given on the date on which it is posted.

[(4) Subject to paragraph (5), section 164(4) of the Contributions and Benefits Act (statutory maternity pay-entitlement and liability to pay) shall not have effect in the case of a woman who leaves her employment with the person who will be liable to pay her statutory maternity pay after the beginning of the week immediately preceding the 14th week before the expected week of confinement.]

[(5) A woman who is exempted from section 164(4) of the Contributions and Benefits Act by paragraph (4) but who is confined before the 11th week before the expected week of confinement shall only be entitled to statutory maternity pay if she gives the person who will be liable to pay it notice specifying the date she was confined.]

[2139]

NOTES

Para (1): words in square brackets substituted by the Social Security, Statutory Maternity Pay and Statutory Sick Pay (Miscellaneous Amendments) Regulations 2002, SI 2002/2690, reg 6(1), (2) (with effect in relation to those women whose expected week of confinement commenced on or after 6 April 2003).

Para (2): words in first pair of square brackets substituted by the Social Security Maternity Benefits and Statutory Sick Pay (Amendment) Regulations 1994, SI 1994/1367, reg 6(1), (2); words omitted revoked, and words in second pair of square brackets substituted, by SI 2002/2690, reg 6(1), (3) (with effect in relation to those women whose expected week of confinement commenced on or after 6 April 2003).

Para (4): substituted by SI 2002/2690, reg 6(1), (4) (with effect in relation to those women whose expected week of confinement commenced on or after 6 April 2003).

Para (5): substituted by SI 1994/1367, reg 6(1), (3).

24 Notification of employment after confinement

A woman who after the date of confinement but within the maternity pay period commences work in employed earner's employment with a person who is not liable to make payments of statutory maternity pay to her and is not a non-liable employer for the purposes of regulation 8(1), shall within 7 days of the day she commenced work inform any person who is so liable of the date she commenced work.

[2140]

25 Provision of information in connection with determination of questions

Any woman claiming to be entitled to statutory maternity pay, or any other person who is a party to proceedings arising under the 1986 Act relating to statutory maternity pay, shall, if she receives notification from the [Commissioners of Inland Revenue] that any information is required from her for the determination of any question arising in connection therewith, furnish that information to the [Commissioners of Inland Revenue] within 10 days of receiving that notification.

[2141]

NOTES

Words in square brackets substituted by virtue of the Social Security Contributions (Transfer of Functions, etc) Act 1999, s 1(2), Sch 2.

Commissioners of Inland Revenue: a reference to the Commissioners of Inland Revenue is now to be taken as a reference to the Commissioners for Her Majesty's Revenue and Customs; see the Commissioners for Revenue and Customs Act 2005, s 50(1), (7).

[25A Provision of information relating to claims for certain other benefits

(1) Where an employer who has been given notice in accordance with [section 164(4)(a) or (9)(ea) of the Contributions and Benefits Act] or regulation 23 by a woman who is or has been an employee—

(a) decides that he has no liability to make payments of statutory maternity pay to her, or

(b) has made one or more payments of statutory maternity pay to her but decides, before the end of the maternity pay period and for a reason specified in paragraph (3), that he has no liability to make further payments to her,

then, in connection with the making of a claim by the woman for a maternity allowance or incapacity benefit, he shall furnish her with the information specified in the following provisions of this regulation.

(2) Where the employer decides he has no liability to make payments of statutory maternity pay to the woman, he shall furnish her with details of the decision and the reasons for it.

(3) Where the employer decides he has no liability to make further payments of statutory maternity pay to the woman because … she has within the maternity pay period been detained in legal custody or sentenced to a term of imprisonment which was not suspended, … he shall furnish her with—

(a) details of his decision and the reasons for it; and

(b) details of the last week in respect of which a liability to pay statutory maternity pay arose and the total number of weeks within the maternity pay period in which such a liability arose.

(4) The employer shall—

(a) return to the woman any maternity certificate provided by her in support of the notice referred to in paragraph (1); and

(b) comply with any requirements imposed by the preceding provisions of this regulation—

(i) in a case to which paragraph (2) applies, within 7 days of the decision being made, or, if earlier, within [28 days] of the day the woman gave notice of her intended absence or of her confinement if that had occurred; or

(ii) in a case to which paragraph (3) refers, within 7 days of being notified of the woman's detention or sentence …

(5) In this regulation, "incapacity benefit" means [incapacity benefit] or a severe disablement allowance.]

[2142]

NOTES

Inserted by the Statutory Maternity Pay (General) Amendment Regulations 1990, SI 1990/622, reg 7.

Para (1): words in square brackets substituted by the Social Security, Statutory Maternity Pay and Statutory Sick Pay (Miscellaneous Amendments) Regulations 2002, SI 2002/2690, reg 8(1), (2) (with effect in relation to those women whose expected week of confinement commenced on or after 6 April 2003).

Para (3): words omitted revoked by SI 2002/2690, reg 8(1), (3) (with effect in relation to those women whose expected week of confinement commenced on or after 6 April 2003).

Para (4): words in square brackets substituted, and words omitted revoked, by SI 2002/2690, reg 8(1), (4) (with effect in relation to those women whose expected week of confinement commenced on or after 6 April 2003).

Para (5): words in square brackets substituted by the Social Security (Incapacity Benefit) (Consequential and Transitional Amendments and Savings) Regulations 1995, SI 1995/829, reg 18(1), (3).

26 Records to be maintained by employers

(1) Every employer shall maintain for 3 years after the end of the tax year in which the maternity pay period ends a record in relation to any woman who is or was an employee of his of—

(a) the date of the first day of absence from work wholly or partly because of pregnancy or confinement as notified by her and, if different, the date of the first day when such absence commenced;

(b) the weeks in that tax year in which statutory maternity pay was paid and the amount paid in each week, and

(c) any week in that tax year which was within her maternity pay period but for which no payment of statutory maternity pay was made to her and the reasons no payment was made.

(2) Except where he was not liable to make a payment of statutory maternity pay and subject to paragraphs (3) and (4), every employer shall retain for 3 years after the end of the tax year in which the maternity pay period ends any medical certificate or other evidence relating to the expected week of confinement, or as the case may be, the confinement which was provided to him by a woman who is or was an employee of his.

(3) Where an employer returns a medical certificate to an employee of his for the purpose of enabling her to make a claim for benefit under the 1975 Act, it shall be sufficient for the purposes of paragraph (2) if he retains a copy of that certificate.

(4) An employer shall not retain any certificate of birth provided to him as evidence of confinement by a woman who is or was an employee of his, but shall retain a record of the date of birth.

[2143]

[26A Production of employer's records

(1) An authorised officer of the Commissioners of Inland Revenue may by notice require an employer to produce to him at the place of keeping such records as are in the employer's possession or power and as (in the officer's reasonable opinion) contain, or may contain, information relevant to satisfy him that statutory maternity pay has been paid and is being paid in accordance with these regulations to employees or former employees who are entitled to it.

(2) A notice referred to in paragraph (1) shall be in writing and the employer shall produce the records referred to in that paragraph within 30 days after the date of such a notice.

(3) The production of records in pursuance of this regulation shall be without prejudice to any lien which a third party may have in respect of those records.

(4) References in this regulation to "records" means—

(a) any wage sheet or deductions working sheet; or

(b) any other document which relates to the calculation or payment of statutory maternity pay to his employees or former employees, whether kept in written form, electronically, or otherwise.

(5) In paragraph (1), "place of keeping" means such place in Great Britain that an employer and an authorised officer may agree upon, or, in the absence of such agreement—

(a) any place in Great Britain where records referred to in paragraph (1) are normally kept; or

(b) if there is no such place, the employer's principal place of business in Great Britain.]

[2143A]

NOTES

Commencement: 6 April 2005.

Inserted by the Statutory Maternity Pay (General) and Statutory Sick Pay (General) (Amendment) Regulations 2005, SI 2005/989, reg 2(1), (2), as from 6 April 2005.

Commissioners of Inland Revenue: a reference to the Commissioners of Inland Revenue is now to be taken as a reference to the Commissioners for Her Majesty's Revenue and Customs; see the Commissioners for Revenue and Customs Act 2005, s 50(1), (7).

PART VI
PAYMENT

27 Payment of statutory maternity pay

Payment of statutory maternity pay may be made in a like manner to payments of remuneration but shall not include payments in kind or by way of the provision of board or lodgings or of services or other facilities.

[2144]

[28 Rounding to avoid fractional amounts

Where any payment of statutory maternity pay is paid for any week or part of a week and the amount due includes a fraction of a penny, the payment shall be rounded up to the next whole number of pence.]

[2145]

NOTES

Commencement: 1 October 2006 (with effect in relation to those women whose expected week of confinement commences on or after 1 April 2007).

Substituted by the Statutory Maternity Pay, Social Security (Maternity Allowance) and Social Security (Overlapping Benefits) (Amendment) Regulations 2006, SI 2006/2379, reg 3(1), (4), as from 1 October 2006 (with effect in relation to those women whose expected week of confinement commences on or after 1 April 2007; see SI 2006/2379, reg 1(2)).

29 Time when statutory maternity pay is to be paid

(1) In this regulation, "pay day" means a day on which it has been agreed, or it is the normal practice between an employer or former employer and a woman who is or was an employee of his, that payments by way of remuneration are to be made, or, where there is no such agreement or normal practice, the last day of a calendar month.

(2) In any case where—

(a) a decision has been made by an adjudication officer, appeal tribunal or Commissioner in proceedings under Part III of the 1975 Act as a result of which a woman is entitled to an amount of statutory maternity pay; and

(b) the time for bringing an appeal against the decision has expired and either—

(i) no such appeal has been brought; or

(ii) such an appeal has been brought and has been finally disposed of,

that amount of statutory maternity pay shall be paid within the time specified in paragraph (3).

(3) Subject to paragraphs (4) and (5), the employer or former employer shall pay the amount not later than the first pay day after—

(a) where an appeal has been brought, the day on which the employer or former employer receives notification that it has been finally disposed of;

(b) where leave to appeal has been refused and there remains no further opportunity to apply for leave, the day on which the employer or former employer receives notification of the refusal; and

(c) in any other case, the day on which the time for bringing an appeal expires.

(4) Subject to paragraph (5), where it is impracticable, in view of the employer's or former employer's methods of accounting for and paying remuneration, for the requirement of payment referred to in paragraph (3) to be met by the pay day referred to in that paragraph, it shall be met not later than the next following pay day.

(5) Where the employer or former employer would not have remunerated the woman for her work in the week in question as early as the pay day specified in paragraph (3) or (if it applies) paragraph (4), the requirement of payment shall be met on the first day on which the woman would have been remunerated for her work in that week.

[2146]

30 Payments by the [Commissioners of Inland Revenue]

Where the [Commissioners of Inland Revenue become] liable in accordance with regulation 7 to make payments of statutory maternity pay to a woman, the first payment shall be made as soon as reasonably practicable after he becomes so liable, and payments thereafter shall be made at weekly intervals, by means of an instrument of payment or by such other means as appears to the [Commissioners of Inland Revenue] to be appropriate in the circumstances of any particular case.

[2147]

NOTES

Words in square brackets substituted by virtue of the Social Security Contributions (Transfer of Functions, etc) Act 1999, s 1(2), Sch 2.

Commissioners of Inland Revenue: a reference to the Commissioners of Inland Revenue is now to be taken as a reference to the Commissioners for Her Majesty's Revenue and Customs; see the Commissioners for Revenue and Customs Act 2005, s 50(1), (7).

31 Persons unable to act

(1) Where in the case of any woman—

(a) statutory maternity pay is payable to her or she is alleged to be entitled to it;

(b) she is unable for the time being to act; and

(c) either—

(i) no receiver has been appointed by the Court of Protection with power to receive statutory maternity pay on her behalf, or

(ii) in Scotland, her estate is not being administered by any tutor, curator or other guardian acting or appointed in terms of law,

the [Commissioners of Inland Revenue] may, upon written application to him by a person who, if a natural person, is over the age of 18, appoint that person to exercise, on behalf of the woman any right to which she may be entitled under Part V of the 1986 Act and to deal on her behalf with any sums payable to her.

(2) Where the [Commissioners of Inland Revenue have] made an appointment under paragraph (1)—

(a) [they] may at any time in [their] absolute discretion revoke it;

(b) the person appointed may resign his office after having given one month's notice in writing to the [Commissioners of Inland Revenue] of his intention to do so; and

(c) the appointment shall terminate when the [Commissioners of Inland Revenue are] notified that a receiver or other person to whom paragraph (1)(c) applies has been appointed.

(3) Anything required by Part V of the 1986 Act to be done by or to any woman who is unable to act may be done by or to the person appointed under this regulation to act on her behalf, and the receipt of the person so appointed shall be a good discharge to the woman's employer or former employer for any sum paid.

[2148]–[2149]

NOTES

Paras (1), (2): words in square brackets substituted by virtue of the Social Security Contributions (Transfer of Functions, etc) Act 1999, s 1(2), Sch 2.

Commissioners of Inland Revenue: a reference to the Commissioners of Inland Revenue is now to be taken as a reference to the Commissioners for Her Majesty's Revenue and Customs; see the Commissioners for Revenue and Customs Act 2005, s 50(1), (7).

"Part V of the 1986 Act": see now the Social Security Contributions and Benefits Act 1992, Pt XII.

32 *(Reg 32 (Pt V) revoked by the Statutory Maternity Pay (General) and Statutory Sick Pay (General) (Amendment) Regulations 2005, SI 2005/989, reg 2(1), (3), as from 6 April 2005 (immediately before the coming into force of the National Insurance Contributions and Statutory Payments Act 2004, s 9(4) on that date.)*

STATUTORY MATERNITY PAY (MEDICAL EVIDENCE) REGULATIONS 1987

(SI 1987/235)

NOTES

Made: 19 February 1987.

Authority: Social Security Act 1986, ss 49 (repealed), 84(1), Sch 4, para 6 (repealed). These Regulations now have effect as if made under the Social Security Administration Act 1992, s 15(1), by virtue of the Social Security (Consequential Provisions) Act 1992, s 2(2).

Commencement: 15 March 1987.

See *Harvey* J, R.

1 Citation, commencement and interpretation

(1) These regulations may be cited as the Statutory Maternity Pay (Medical Evidence) Regulations 1987 and shall come into force on 15th March 1987.

(2) In these regulations, unless the context otherwise requires—

"the Act" means the Social Security Act 1986;

["registered midwife" means a midwife who is registered as a midwife with the Nursing and Midwifery Council under the Nursing and Midwifery Order 2001;]

"doctor" means a registered medical practitioner;

["Primary Care Trust" means a Primary Care Trust established under section 16A of the National Health Service Act 1977;]

"signature" means, in relation to any statement or certificate given in accordance with these regulations, the name by which the person giving that statement or certificate, as the case may be, is usually known (any name other than the surname being either in full or otherwise indicated) written by that person in his own handwriting; and "signed" shall be construed accordingly.

[2150]

NOTES

Para (2): definition "registered midwife" substituted by the Nursing and Midwifery Order 2001 (Consequential Amendments) Order 2002, SI 2002/881, art 2, Schedule, para 2, as from 17 April 2002; definition "Primary Care Trust" inserted by the National Health Service Reform and Health Care Professions Act 2002 (Supplementary, Consequential etc Provisions) Regulations 2002, SI 2002/2469, reg 11, Sch 8, as from 1 October 2002.

Social Security Act 1986: largely repealed and consolidated in the Social Security Contributions and Benefits Act 1992 and the Social Security Administration Act 1992.

2 Evidence of pregnancy and confinement

The evidence as to pregnancy and the expected date of confinement which a woman is required to provide to a person who is liable to pay her statutory maternity pay shall be furnished in the form of a maternity certificate given by a doctor or by a registered midwife, not earlier than the beginning of the [20th week] before the expected week of confinement, in accordance with the rules set out in Part I of the Schedule to these regulations—

(a) in the appropriate form as set out in Part II of that Schedule, or

(b) in a form substantially to the like effect with such variations as the circumstances may require.

[2151]

NOTES

Words in square brackets substituted by the Social Security (Medical Evidence) and Statutory Maternity Pay (Medical Evidence) (Amendment) Regulations 2001, SI 2001/2931, reg 3(1), (2).

SCHEDULE

Regulation 2

PART I
RULES

1. In these rules any reference to a woman is a reference to the woman in respect of whom a maternity certificate is given in accordance with these rules.

2. A maternity certificate shall be given by a doctor or registered midwife attending the woman and shall not be given by the woman herself.

3. The maternity certificate shall be on a form provided by the Secretary of State for the purpose and the wording shall be that set out in the appropriate part of the form specified in Part II of this Schedule.

4. Every maternity certificate shall be completed in ink or other indelible substance and shall contain the following particulars—

(a) the woman's name;

(b) the week in which the woman is expected to be confined or, if the maternity certificate is given after confinement, the date of that confinement and the date the confinement was expected to take place … ;

(c) the date of the examination on which the maternity certificate is based;

(d) the date on which the maternity certificate is signed; and

[(e) the address of the doctor or where the maternity certificate is signed by a registered midwife the personal identification number given to her on her registration in … the register maintained by the Nursing and Midwifery Council [("NMC") under article 5 of] the Nursing and Midwifery Order 2001 and the expiry date of that registration,]

and shall bear opposite the word "Signature", the signature of the person giving the maternity certificate written after there has been entered on the maternity certificate the woman's name and the expected date or, as the case may be, the date of the confinement.

5. After a maternity certificate has been given, no further maternity certificate based on the same examination shall be furnished other than a maternity certificate by way of replacement of an original which has been lost or mislaid, in which case it shall be clearly marked "duplicate".

[2152]

NOTES

Para 4: words omitted from sub-para (b) revoked by the Social Security (Miscellaneous Provisions) Amendment Regulations 1991, SI 1991/2284, reg 23; sub-para (e) substituted by the Nursing and Midwifery Order 2001 (Consequential Amendments) Order 2002, SI 2002/881, art 2, Schedule, para 3; words omitted from sub-para (e) revoked, and words in square brackets in that paragraph substituted, by the Health Act 1999 (Consequential Amendments) (Nursing and Midwifery) Order 2004, SI 2004/1771, art 3, Schedule, Pt 2, para 51(a), as from 1 August 2004.

[PART II
FORM OF CERTIFICATE

MATERNITY CERTIFICATE

Please fill in this form in ink

Name of patient ....

Fill in this part if you are giving the certificate before the confinement.

Do not fill this in more [than 20 weeks] before the week the baby is expected.

Fill in this part if you are giving the certificate after the confinement.

I certify that I examined you on the date given below. In my opinion you can expect to have your baby in the week that includes......... /.......... /..........

Weeks means a period of 7 days starting on a Sunday and ending on a Saturday

Date of examination......... /......... /........

Date of signing....... ./........ /........

Signature...

I certify that I attended you in connection with the birth which took place on.......... /......... /......... when you were delivered of a child [ ] children.

Registered midwives

Please give your [NMC] Personal Identification Number and the expiry date of your registration with the [NMC].

Doctors

Please stamp your name and address here if the form has not been stamped by the [Primary Care Trust or Local Health Board in whose medical performers list you are included (or, in Scotland, by the Health Board in whose primary medical services performers list you are included)]

[2153]

NOTES

Substituted by the Social Security (Miscellaneous Provisions) Amendment Regulations 1991, SI 1991/2284, reg 24.

Words in square brackets in the left column substituted by the Social Security (Medical Evidence) and Statutory Maternity Pay (Medical Evidence) (Amendment) Regulations 2001, SI 2001/2931, reg 3(1), (3); "NMC" in square brackets in both places it occurs in the right column substituted by the Health Act 1999 (Consequential Amendments) (Nursing and Midwifery) Order 2004, SI 2004/1771, art 3, Schedule, Pt 2, para 51(b), as from 1 August 2004; final words in square brackets in the right column substituted, in relation to England and Scotland, by the General Medical Services and Personal Medical Services Transitional and Consequential Provisions Order 2004, SI 2004/865, art 119, Sch 1, para 5, as from 1 April 2004 (subject to transitional provisions in art 107 of that Order), and in relation to Wales by the General Medical Services Transitional and Consequential Provisions (Wales) (No 2) Order 2004, SI 2004/1016, art 95, Sch 1, para 5, as from the same date (subject to transitional provisions in art 83 of that Order). See also the General Medical Services and Section 17C Agreements (Transitional and other Ancillary Provisions) (Scotland) Order 2004, SSI 2004/163, art 94 for the same transitional provisions in relation to Scotland.

HEALTH AND SAFETY INFORMATION FOR EMPLOYEES REGULATIONS 1989

(SI 1989/682)

NOTES

Made: 18 April 1989.

Authority: Health and Safety at Work etc Act 1974, s 15(1), (2), (3)(a), (4)(a), (5)(b), (6)(b), Sch 3, para 15(1).

Commencement: 18 October 1989.

See *Harvey* N22(D).

ARRANGEMENT OF REGULATIONS

1 Citation and commencement

These Regulations may be cited as the Health and Safety Information for Employees Regulations 1989 and shall come into force on 18th October 1989.

[2154]

2 Interpretation and application

(1) In these Regulations, unless the context otherwise requires—

"the 1974" Act means the Health and Safety at Work etc Act 1974;

["the 1995 Order" means the Health and Safety at Work etc Act 1974 (Application outside Great Britain) Order 1995;]

"the approved poster" and "the approved leaflet" have the meanings assigned by regulation 3;

"employment medical advisory service" means the employment medical advisory service referred to in section 55 of the 1974 Act;

"ship" has the meaning assigned to it by section 742 of the Merchant Shipping Act 1894.

(2) Any reference in these Regulations to the enforcing authority for premises is a reference to the enforcing authority which has responsibility for the enforcement of section 2 of the 1974 Act in relation to the main activity carried on in those premises.

(3) Any reference in these Regulations to—

(a) a numbered regulation is a reference to the regulation so numbered in these Regulations;

(b) a numbered paragraph is a reference to the paragraph so numbered in the regulation in which the reference appears.

(4) These Regulations shall have effect for the purpose of providing information to employees relating to health, safety and welfare but they shall not apply in relation to the master and crew of a sea going ship [(except to the extent that the master and crew are engaging in activities falling within articles 4, 5 and 6 of the 1995 Order)].

[(5) These Regulations shall, subject to paragraph (4) apply to and in relation to the premises and activities outside Great Britain to which sections 1 to 59 and 80 and 82 of the Health and Safety at Work etc Act 1974 apply by virtue of the 1995 Order as they apply to premises and activities within Great Britain.]

[2155]

NOTES

Para (1): definition "the 1995 Order" inserted by the Health and Safety Information for Employees (Modifications and Repeals) Regulations 1995, SI 1995/2923, reg 2(a)(i).

Para (4): words in square brackets added by SI 1995/2923, reg 2(a)(ii).

Para (5): added by SI 1995/2923, reg 2(a)(iii).

The Health and Safety at Work etc Act 1974 (Application outside Great Britain) Order 1995, SI 1995/263: revoked and replaced by the Health and Safety at Work etc Act 1974 (Application outside Great Britain) Order 2001, SI 2001/2127.

3 Meaning of and revisions to the approved poster and leaflet

(1) In these Regulations "the approved poster" or "the approved leaflet" means, respectively, a poster or leaflet in the form approved and published for the purposes of these Regulations by the Health and Safety Executive, as revised from time to time in accordance with paragraph (2).

(2) The Health and Safety Executive may approve a revision (in whole or in part) to the form of poster or leaflet; and where it does so it shall publish the revised form of poster or leaflet and issue a notice in writing specifying the date the revision was approved.

(3) Such a revision shall not take effect until nine months after the date of its approval, but during that time the employer may use the approved poster or the approved leaflet incorporating that revision for the purposes of regulation 4(1).

[(4) The Health and Safety Executive may approve a particular form of poster or leaflet for use in relation to a particular employment or class of employment and where any such form has been approved the Executive shall publish it and issue a notice in writing specifying the date that form was approved and the particular employment or class of employment in respect of which it is approved.

(5) Where a particular form of poster or leaflet has been approved under paragraph (4) then paragraphs (2) and (3) shall apply to the revision of that particular form as they apply to the revision of an approved poster or an approved leaflet save that the notice in writing issued under paragraph (2) in respect of the revised form shall also specify the employment or class of employment in respect of which the revised form is approved.

(6) An employer may, in respect of employment for which a particular poster or leaflet has been approved under paragraph (4), comply with the requirements of regulation 4(1) by displaying that particular form of poster or giving that particular form of leaflet and in connection with any such compliance regulation 4 shall be construed as if the references to the approved poster and the approved leaflet in that regulation were references to the particular form of poster and the particular form of leaflet approved under paragraph (4) and as if the reference in regulation 4(3) to revision pursuant to regulation 3(2) were a reference to a revision pursuant to regulation 3(5).]

[2156]

NOTES

Paras (4)–(6): added by the Health and Safety Information for Employees (Modifications and Repeals) Regulations 1995, SI 1995/2923, reg 2(b).

Health and Safety Executive: as to the abolition of the Health and Safety Commission and the Health and Safety Executive (with effect from 1 April 2008) and their replacement with a single Health and Safety Executive exercising the combined functions of those bodies, see the Legislative Reform (Health and Safety Executive) Order 2008, SI 2008/960 (at **[3474L]**), and the amendments made by that Order to the Health and Safety at Work etc Act 1974 (at **[30]** et seq). For transitional provisions in relation to the abolition of the former bodies and the establishment of the new Health and Safety Executive, see art 21 of, and Sch 2 to, the 2008 Order at **[3474N]**, **[3474O]**.

4 Provision of poster or leaflet

(1) An employer shall, in relation to each of his employees—

(a) ensure that the approved poster is kept displayed in a readable condition—

(i) at a place which is reasonably accessible to the employee while he is at work, and

(ii) in such a position in that place as to be easily seen and read by that employee; or

(b) give to the employee the approved leaflet.

(2) An employer shall be treated as having complied with paragraph (1)(b) from the date these Regulations come into force or the date the employee commences employment with him (if later) if he gives to the employee the approved leaflet as soon as is reasonably practicable after that date.

(3) Where the form of poster or leaflet is revised pursuant to regulation 3(2), then on or before the date the revision takes effect—

(a) an employer relying on compliance with paragraph (1)(a) shall ensure that the approved poster displayed is the one as revised;

(b) an employer relying on compliance with paragraph (1)(b) shall either give to the employees concerned fresh approved leaflets (as so revised) or bring the revision to their notice in writing.

[2157]

5 Provision of further information

(1) An employer relying on compliance with regulation 4(1)(a) shall, subject to paragraph (2), ensure that the following information is clearly and indelibly written on the poster in the appropriate space—

(a) the name of the enforcing authority for the premises where the poster is displayed and the address of the office of that authority for the area in which those premises are situated; and

(b) the address of the office of the employment medical advisory service for the area in which those premises are situated.

(2) Where there is a change in any of the matters referred to in paragraph (1) it shall be sufficient compliance with that paragraph for the corresponding amendment to the poster to be made within six months from the date thereof.

(3) An employer who gives to his employee a leaflet pursuant to regulation 4(1)(b) shall give with the leaflet a written notice containing—

(a) the name of the enforcing authority for the premises where the employee works, and the address of the office of that authority for the area in which those premises are situated; and

(b) the address of the office of the employment medical advisory service for the area in which those premises are situated.

(4) Where the employee works in more than one location he shall, for the purposes of paragraph (3), be treated as working at the premises from which his work is administered, and if his work is administered from two or more premises, the employer may choose any one of them for the purpose of complying with that paragraph.

(5) Where an employer relies on compliance with regulation 4(1)(b) and there is a change in any of the matters referred to in paragraph (3) the employer shall within six months of the date thereof give to the employee a written notice specifying the change.

[2158]

6 Exemption certificates

(1) Subject to paragraph (2) the Health and Safety Executive may, by a certificate in writing, exempt any person or class of persons from all or any of the requirements imposed by these Regulations and any such exemption may be granted subject to conditions and to a limit of time and may be revoked in writing at any time.

(2) The Executive shall not grant any such exemption unless, having regard to the circumstances of the case, and in particular to—

(a) the conditions if any, which it proposes to attach to the exemption; and

(b) any other requirements imposed by or under any enactment which apply to the case;

it is satisfied that the health, safety and welfare of persons who are likely to be affected by the exemption will not be prejudiced in consequence of it.

[2159]

NOTES

Health and Safety Executive: see the note at **[2156]**.

7 Defence

In any proceedings for an offence for a contravention of these Regulations it shall be a defence for the accused to prove that he took all reasonable precautions and exercised all due diligence to avoid the commission of that offence.

[2160]

8 (*Introduces the repeals, revocations and modifications set out in the Schedule.*)

(*Schedule* (*Repeals, revocations and modifications*) *outside the scope of this work.*)

SEX DISCRIMINATION ACT 1975 (EXEMPTION OF SPECIAL TREATMENT FOR LONE PARENTS) ORDER 1989

(SI 1989/2140)

NOTES

Made: 17 November 1989.
Authority: Employment Act 1989, ss 8, 28.
Commencement: 19 December 1989.
See *Harvey* L1, R.

1 Citation and commencement

This Order may be cited as the Sex Discrimination Act 1975 (Exemption of Special Treatment for Lone Parents) Order 1989 and shall come into force on 19th December 1989.

[2161]

2 Interpretation

In this Order—

"child of that lone parent" means a person who for the purposes of any regulations made in pursuance of section 20(1)(a) of the Social Security Act 1986 is—

(a) a child or young person for whom that lone parent is responsible, and
(b) a member of the same household as that lone parent; and

"Employment Training" means the arrangements known by that name made under section 2 of the Employment and Training Act 1973 [or section 2 of the Enterprise and New Towns (Scotland) Act 1990].

[2162]

NOTES

In definition "Employment Training" words in square brackets added by the Enterprise (Scotland) Consequential Amendments Order 1991, SI 1991/387, art 2, Schedule.

Social Security Act 1986: largely repealed and consolidated in the Social Security Contributions and Benefits Act 1992 and the Social Security Administration Act 1992. As to s 20(1)(a) of the 1986 Act, see now the Social Security Contributions and Benefits Act 1992, s 123(1).

3 Exemption of Special Treatment

With respect to Employment Training, section 8 of the Employment Act 1989 shall apply to any special treatment afforded—

(a) by the making of any payment, in connection with the participation of a lone parent in Employment Training, to a person having the care of a child of that lone parent, or
(b) by the fixing of any special condition for the participation of lone parents in Employment Training.

[2163]

[EMPLOYMENT TRIBUNALS] (INTEREST) ORDER 1990

(SI 1990/479)

NOTES

Made: 6 March 1990.

Authority: Employment Protection (Consolidation) Act 1978, Sch 9, paras 1, 6A (repealed). These Regulations now have effect as if made under the Employment Tribunals Act 1996, s 14.

Commencement: 1 April 1990.

Title: words in square brackets substituted by the Employment Rights (Dispute Resolution) Act 1998, s 1(2)(b).

By virtue of the Employment Tribunals (Interest on Awards in Discrimination Cases) Regulations 1996, SI 1996/2803 at **[2390]** (as amended), this Order applies to (i) an award, under the Equal Pay Act 1970, of arrears of remuneration or damages, or (ii) an Order under the Sex Discrimination Act 1975, s 65(1)(b), the Race Relations Act 1976, s 56(1)(b), the Disability Discrimination Act 1995, s 8(2)(b), the Employment Equality (Sexual Orientation) Regulations 2003, reg 30(1)(b), the Employment Equality (Religion or Belief) Regulations 2003, reg 30(1)(b), and the Employment Equality (Age) Regulations 2006, reg 38(1)(b), for payment of compensation as if (a) references to the calculation day were references to the day immediately following the relevant decision day (as defined in art 2(3) of this Order) and accordingly (subject to (b) below) interest is to accrue under this Order from that day onwards (including that day) and (b) (notwithstanding (a) above) no interest is to be payable by virtue of this Order if payment of the full amount of the award (including any interest awarded under reg 2 of SI 1996/2803) is made within 14 days after the relevant decision day. Note that the Disability Discrimination Act 1995, s 8(2)(b) is now s 17A(2)(b) following the amendments made to that Act by the Disability Discrimination Act 1995 (Amendment) Regulations 2003, SI 2003/1673. However, no consequential amendment has been made to SI 1996/2803 to take account of this.

See *Harvey* T(A)27.

ARRANGEMENT OF ARTICLES

1 Citation, commencement and transitional provisions

(1) This Order may be cited as the [Employment Tribunals] (Interest) Order 1990 and shall come into force on 1st April 1990.

(2) Where a relevant decision day or a day to be treated as if it were a relevant decision day would, but for this paragraph of this Article, fall on a day before 1st April 1990, the relevant decision day or day to be treated as if it were that day shall be 1st April 1990.

[2164]

NOTES

Para (1): words in square brackets substituted by the Employment Rights (Dispute Resolution) Act 1998, s 1(2)(b).

2 Interpretation

(1) In this Order, except in so far as the context otherwise requires—

"appellate court" means the Employment Appeal Tribunal, the High Court, the Court of Appeal, the Court of Session or the House of Lords as the case may be;

"the calculation day" in relation to a relevant decision means the day immediately following the expiry of the period of 42 days beginning with the relevant decision day;

"interest" means simple interest which accrues from day to day;

"relevant decision" in relation to a tribunal means any award or other determination of the tribunal by virtue of which one party to proceedings before the tribunal is required to pay a sum of money, excluding a sum representing costs or expenses, to another party to those proceedings;

"Rules of Procedure" means rules having effect in relation to proceedings before a tribunal by virtue of any regulations or order made pursuant to an enactment;

"the stipulated rate of interest" has the meaning assigned to it in Article 4 below;

"tribunal" means in England and Wales an [employment tribunal] (England and Wales) established in pursuance of the Industrial Tribunals (England and Wales) Regulations 1965 and in Scotland an [employment tribunal] (Scotland) established in pursuance of the Industrial Tribunals (Scotland) Regulations 1965.

(2) For the purposes of this Order a sum of money is required to be paid by one party to proceedings to another such party if, and only if, an amount of money required to be so paid is—

(a) specified in an award or other determination of a tribunal or, as the case may be, in an order or decision of an appellate court; or

(b) otherwise ascertainable solely by reference to the terms of such an award or determination or, as the case may be, solely by reference to the terms of such an order or decision,

but where a tribunal or, as the case may be, appellate court has made a declaration as to entitlement under a contract nothing in this Order shall be taken to provide for interest to be payable on any payment under that contract in respect of which no obligation to make the payment has arisen under that contract before the declaration was made.

(3) In this Order, except in so far as the context otherwise requires, "decision day" means the day signified by the date recording the sending of the document which is sent to the parties recording an award or other determination of a tribunal and "relevant decision day", subject to Article 5, 6 and 7 below, means the day so signified in relation to a relevant decision.

(4) In this Order "party" includes the Secretary of State where he has elected to appear as if he were a party in accordance with a Rule of Procedure entitling him so to elect.

[2165]

NOTES

Para (1): in definition "tribunal" words in square brackets substituted by the Employment Rights (Dispute Resolution) Act 1998, s 1(2)(a).

Industrial Tribunals (England and Wales) Regulations 1965, Industrial Tribunals (Scotland) Regulations 1965: see now the Employment Tribunals (Constitution and Rules of Procedure) Regulations 2004, SI 2004/1861 at **[3151]**.

3 Computation of interest

(1) Subject to paragraphs (2) and (3) of this Article and to Article 11 below, where the whole or any part of a sum of money payable by virtue of a relevant decision of a tribunal remains unpaid on the calculation day the sum of money remaining unpaid on the calculation day shall carry interest at the stipulated rate of interest from the calculation day (including that day).

(2) Where, after the calculation day, a party pays to another party some but not all of such a sum of money remaining unpaid on the calculation day, then beginning with the day on which the payment is made interest shall continue to accrue only on that part of the sum of money which then remains unpaid.

(3) For the purposes of the computation of interest under this Order, there shall be disregarded—

(a) any part of a sum of money which pursuant to the Employment Protection (Recoupment of Unemployment Benefit and Supplementary Benefit) Regulations 1977 has been claimed by the Secretary of State in a recoupment notice; and

(b) any part of a sum of money which the party required to pay the sum of money is required, by virtue of any provision contained in or having effect under any enactment, to deduct and pay over to a public authority in respect of income tax or contributions under Part I of the Social Security Act 1975.

[2166]

NOTES

Employment Protection (Recoupment of Unemployment Benefit and Supplementary Benefit) Regulations 1977 (SI 1977/674): revoked and replaced by the Employment Protection (Recoupment of Jobseeker's Allowance and Income Support) Regulations 1996, SI 1996/2349 at **[2364]**.

Social Security Act 1975, Pt I: repealed by the Social Security (Consequential Provisions) Act 1992, and replaced by the Social Security Contributions and Benefits Act 1992, Pt I.

4 Rate of interest

The stipulated rate of interest shall be the rate of interest specified in section 17 of the Judgments Act 1838 on the relevant decision day.

[2167]

NOTES

The specified rate is (as at 6 April 2008) 8% per annum. This has been the rate since 1 April 1993 (see SI 1993/564 which amends the Judgments Act 1838, s 17).

5 Reviews

Where a tribunal reviews its decision pursuant to the Rules of Procedure and the effect of the review, or of any re-hearing which takes place as a result of the review, is that a sum of money payable by one party to another party is confirmed or varied the relevant decision day shall be the decision day of the decision which is the subject of the review.

[2168]

6 Decisions on remission to a tribunal

Where an appellate court remits a matter to a tribunal for re-assessment of the sum of money which would have been payable by virtue of a previous relevant decision or by virtue of an order of another appellate court, the relevant decision day shall be the decision day of that previous relevant decision or the day on which the other appellate court promulgated its order, as the case may be.

[2169]

7 Appeals from relevant decisions

Where, on an appeal from a relevant decision, or on a further appeal arising from a relevant decision an appellate court makes an order which confirms or varies the sum of money which would have been payable by virtue of that relevant decision if there had been no appeal, the relevant decision day shall be the decision day of that relevant decision.

[2170]

8 Other appeals

(1) This Article applies in relation to any order made by an appellate court on an appeal from a determination of any issue by a tribunal which is not a relevant decision, or on any further appeal arising from such a determination, where the effect of the order is that for the first time in relation to that issue one party to the proceedings is required to pay a sum of money, other than a sum representing costs or expenses, to another party to the proceedings.

(2) Where this Article applies in relation to an order, Articles 3 and 4 above shall apply to the sum of money payable by virtue of the order as if it was a sum of money payable by virtue of a relevant decision and as if the day on which the appellate court promulgated the order was the relevant decision day.

[2171]

9 Where, on an appeal from an order in relation to which Article 8 applies or on a further appeal arising from such an order, an appellate court makes an order which confirms or varies the sum of money which would have been payable by virtue of the order in relation to which Article 8 applies if there had been no appeal, the day to be treated as the relevant decision day shall be the day on which the order in relation to which Article 8 applies was promulgated.

[2172]

10 Reviews by the Employment Appeal Tribunal

Where the Employment Appeal Tribunal reviews an order to which Article 8 above applies, the day to be treated as the relevant decision day shall be the day on which the order reviewed was promulgated.

[2173]

11 Variations of the sum of money on appeal etc

Where a sum of money payable by virtue of a relevant decision is varied under one of the procedures referred to in Articles 5, 6 and 7 above, or a sum of money treated as being so payable by virtue of Article 8 above is varied under one of the procedures referred to in Articles 6, 9 and 10 above, the reference in paragraph (1) of Article 3 above, to a sum of money payable by virtue of a relevant decision shall be treated as if it were a reference to that sum as so varied.

[2174]

12 Notices

(1) Where a decision of a tribunal is a relevant decision and a copy of a document recording that decision is sent to all parties entitled to receive that decision, it shall be the duty of the Secretary of the Central Office of the [Employment Tribunals] (England and Wales) or the Secretary of the Central Office of the [Employment Tribunals] (Scotland), as the case may be, to cause a notice containing the matters detailed in paragraph (2) below to accompany that document.

(2) The notice referred to in paragraph (1) above shall specify the decision day, the stipulated rate of interest and the calculation day in respect of the decision concerned.

(3) The failure to discharge the duty under paragraph (1) above correctly or at all shall have no effect on the liability of one party to pay to another party any sum of money which is payable by virtue of this Order.

[2175]

NOTES

Para (1): words in square brackets substituted by virtue of the Employment Rights (Dispute Resolution) Act 1998, s 1.

SEX DISCRIMINATION ACT 1975 (EXEMPTION OF SPECIAL TREATMENT FOR LONE PARENTS) ORDER 1991

(SI 1991/2813)

NOTES

Made: 12 December 1991.
Authority: Employment Act 1989, ss 8, 28.
Commencement: 14 January 1992.
See *Harvey* L1, R.

1 Citation and commencement

This Order may be cited as the Sex Discrimination Act 1975 (Exemption of Special Treatment for Lone Parents) Order 1991 and shall come into force on 14th January 1992.

[2176]

2 Interpretation

In this Order—

"the Council" means the National Council for One Parent Families;

"the Return to Work Programme" means arrangements known by that name made under section 2 of the Employment and Training Act 1973 for the provision by or on behalf of the Council of training and other assistance to persons wishing to obtain employment.

[2177]

3 Exemption of special treatment

With respect to the Return to Work Programme, section 8 of the Employment Act 1989 shall apply to any special treatment afforded to or in respect of lone parents—

(a) by the fixing of any special condition for participation in the Programme, or

(b) by the making of any payment in respect of the care of a child of a lone parent while that lone parent is participating in the Programme.

[2178]

TRADE UNION BALLOTS AND ELECTIONS (INDEPENDENT SCRUTINEER QUALIFICATIONS) ORDER 1993

(SI 1993/1909)

NOTES

Made: 27 July 1993.
Authority: Trade Union and Labour Relations (Consolidation) Act 1992, ss 49(2), 75(2), 100A(2), 226B(2).
Commencement: 30 August 1993.
See *Harvey* M7(A), Q, R.

1 Citation, commencement and interpretation

(1) This Order may be cited as the Trade Union Ballots and Elections (Independent Scrutineer Qualifications) Order 1993 and shall come into force on 30 August 1993.

(2) In this Order, unless the context otherwise requires—

"an individual potentially qualified to be a scrutineer" means an individual who satisfies the requirement specified in either paragraph (a) of article 3 or paragraph (a) of article 4;

"the 1992 Act" means the Trade Union and Labour Relations (Consolidation) Act 1992;

"the relevant provisions" means the provisions of sections 49(2)(a), 75(2)(a), 100A(2)(a) and 226B(2)(a) of the 1992 Act.

[2179]

2 Qualifications

An individual satisfies the condition specified for the purposes of the relevant provisions in relation to a ballot or election, (as the case may be), if he satisfies the condition specified in article 3 or 4.

[2180]

3 An individual satisfies this condition if—

(a) he has in force a practising certificate issued by the Law Society of England and Wales or the Law Society of Scotland; and

(b) he is not disqualified from satisfying this condition by virtue of article 5.

[2181]

4 An individual satisfies this condition if—

(a) he is qualified to be an auditor of a trade union by virtue of section 34(1) of the 1992 Act; and

(b) he is not disqualified from satisfying this condition by virtue of article 5.

[2182]

5—(1) An individual potentially qualified to be a scrutineer does not satisfy the condition specified in article 3 or 4 if he or any existing partner of his has—

(a) during the preceding 12 months, been a member, an officer or an employee of the trade union proposing to hold the ballot or election; or

(b) in acting at any time as a scrutineer for any trade union, knowingly permitted any member, officer or employee of the trade union to assist him in carrying out any of the functions referred to in sections 49(3), 75(3), 100A(3) and 226B(1) of the 1992 Act.

(2) References in this article to an officer shall be construed as not including an auditor.

[2183]

6 A partnership satisfies the condition specified for the purposes of the relevant provisions in relation to a ballot or election, (as the case may be), if—

(a) every member of the partnership is an individual potentially qualified to be a scrutineer; and

(b) no member of the partnership is disqualified from being a scrutineer by virtue of article 5.

[2184]

[7 Persons specified by name

The following persons are specified for the purpose of the relevant provisions—

Electoral Reform (Ballot Services) Limited;

Election.com Limited;

Popularis Limited; and

Involvement and Participation Association.]

[2185]

NOTES

Substituted by the Trade Union Ballots and Elections (Independent Scrutineer Qualifications) Order 1993 (Amendment) Order 2002, SI 2002/2267, art 2.

8 (*Revokes the Trade Union Ballots and Elections (Independent Scrutineer Qualifications) Order 1988, SI 1988/2117.*)

[EMPLOYMENT TRIBUNALS] (CONSTITUTION AND RULES OF PROCEDURE) REGULATIONS 1993 (NOTE)

(SI 1993/2687)

NOTES

These Regulations were revoked and replaced by the Employment Tribunals (Constitution and Rules of Procedure) Regulations 2001, SI 2001/1171, as from 16 July 2001. The 2001 Regulations were in turn revoked and replaced by the Employment Tribunals (Constitution and Rules of Procedure) Regulations 2004, SI 2004/1861 at **[3151]**.

[2186]

[EMPLOYMENT TRIBUNALS] (CONSTITUTION AND RULES OF PROCEDURE) (SCOTLAND) REGULATIONS 1993 (NOTE)

(SI 1993/2688)

NOTES

These Regulations were revoked and replaced by the Employment Tribunals (Constitution and Rules of Procedure) (Scotland) Regulations 2001, SI 2001/1170, as from 16 July 2001. The 2001 Regulations were in turn revoked and replaced by the Employment Tribunals (Constitution and Rules of Procedure) Regulations 2004, SI 2004/1861 at **[3151]**.

[2187]

EMPLOYMENT APPEAL TRIBUNAL RULES 1993

(SI 1993/2854)

NOTES

Made: 23 November 1993.

Authority: Employment Protection (Consolidation) Act 1978, s 154(3), Sch 11, paras 17(1), 18, 18A(1), 19(1) (repealed). These rules have effect as if made under the Employment Tribunals Act 1996, ss 30(1), (2), 31, 34, 41(4).

Commencement: 16 December 1993.

The rules were extensively amended by the Employment Appeal Tribunal (Amendment) Rules 2001, SI 2001/1128, as amended by SI 2001/1476 (substituting a commencement date of 16 July 2001 for the original date of 18 April 2001), and were further amended by the Employment Appeal Tribunal (Amendment) Rules 2004, SI 2004/2526, as from 1 October 2004 (for transitional provisions see the notes to the individual rules subject to such transitional provisions). The amendments made by SI 2004/2526 apply, except where the notes indicate otherwise, to appeals whenever commenced. These rules were further amended by the Employment Appeal Tribunal (Amendment) Rules 2005, SI 2005/1871, as from 1 October 2005. Further amendments are noted below.

See also the Employment Appeal Tribunal Practice Direction 2008 at **[5014]**.

See *Harvey* D1, Q, R, T(B), U3.

ARRANGEMENT OF RULES

1 Citation and commencement

(1) These Rules may be cited as the Employment Appeal Tribunal Rules 1993 and shall come into force on 16th December 1993.

(2) As from that date the Employment Appeal Tribunal Rules 1980, the Employment Appeal Tribunal (Amendment) Rules 1985 and the Employment Appeal Tribunal (Amendment) Rules 1988 shall be revoked.

[2188]

[2 Interpretation

(1) In these rules—

"the 1992 Act" means the Trade Union and Labour Relations (Consolidation) Act 1992;

"the 1996 Act" means the Employment Tribunals Act 1996;

"the 1999 Regulations" means the Transnational Information and Consultation of Employees Regulations 1999;

["the 2004 Regulations" means the European and Public Limited-Liability Company Regulations 2004;]

["the Information and Consultation Regulations" means the Information and Consultation of Employees Regulations 2004;]

["the 2007 Regulations" means the Companies (Cross-Border Mergers) Regulations 2007;]

"the Appeal Tribunal" means the Employment Appeal Tribunal established under section 87 of the Employment Protection Act 1975 and continued in existence under section 20(1) of the 1996 Act and includes the President, a judge, a member or the Registrar acting on behalf of the Tribunal;

"the CAC" means the Central Arbitration Committee;

"the Certification Officer" means the person appointed to be the Certification Officer under section 254(2) of the 1992 Act;

"costs officer" means any officer of the Appeal Tribunal authorised by the President to assess costs or expenses;

"Crown employment proceedings" has the meaning given by section 10(8) of the 1996 Act;

["document" includes a document delivered by way of electronic communication;]

["electronic communication" shall have the meaning given to it by section 15(1) of the Electronic Communications Act 2000;]

"excluded person" means, in relation to any proceedings, a person who has been excluded from all or part of the proceedings by virtue of—

(a) a direction of a Minister of the Crown under rule 30A(1)(b) or (c); or

(b) an order of the Appeal Tribunal under rule 30A(2)(a) read with rule 30A(1)(b) or (c);

"judge" means a judge of the Appeal Tribunal nominated under section 22(1)(a) or (b) of the 1996 Act and includes a judge nominated under section 23(2) of, or a judge appointed under section 24(1) of, the 1996 Act to be a temporary additional judge of the Appeal Tribunal;

["legal representative" shall mean a person, including a person who is a party's employee, who—

(a) has a general qualification within the meaning of the Courts and Legal Services Act 1990;

(b) is an advocate or solicitor in Scotland; or

(c) is a member of the Bar of Northern Ireland or a *Solicitor of the Supreme Court of Northern Ireland*;]

"member" means a member of the Appeal Tribunal appointed under section 22(1)(c) of the 1996 Act and includes a member appointed under section 23(3) of the 1996 Act to act temporarily in the place of a member appointed under that section;

["national security proceedings" shall have the meaning given to it in regulation 2 of the Employment Tribunals (Constitution and Rules of Procedure) Regulations 2004;]

"the President" means the judge appointed under section 22(3) of the 1996 Act to be President of the Appeal Tribunal and includes a judge nominated under section 23(1) of the 1996 Act to act temporarily in his place;

"the Registrar" means the person appointed to be Registrar of the Appeal Tribunal and includes any officer of the Tribunal authorised by the President to act on behalf of the Registrar;

"the Secretary of Employment Tribunals" means the person acting for the time being as the Secretary of the Central Office of the Employment Tribunals (England and Wales) or, as may be appropriate, of the Central Office of the Employment Tribunals (Scotland);

"special advocate" means a person appointed pursuant to rule 30A(4);

["writing" includes writing delivered by means of electronic communication].

(2) …

(3) Any reference in these Rules to a person who was the [claimant] or, as the case may be, the respondent in the proceedings before an employment tribunal includes, where those proceedings are still continuing, a reference to a person who is the [claimant] or, as the case may be, is the respondent in those proceedings.]

[2189]

NOTES

Substituted by the Employment Appeal Tribunal (Amendment) Rules 2001, SI 2001/1128, r 2, in relation to all proceedings irrespective of when those proceedings were commenced.

Para (1): definitions "the 2004 Regulations", "document", "electronic communication", "legal representative", "national security proceedings", and "writing" inserted by the Employment Appeal Tribunal (Amendment) Rules 2004, SI 2004/2526, r 2(1), as from 1 October 2004; definition "the Information and Consultation Regulations" inserted by the Information and Consultation of Employees Regulations 2004, SI 2004/3426, reg 41(a), as from 6 April 2005; definition "the 2007 Regulations" inserted by the Companies (Cross-Border Mergers) Regulations 2007, SI 2007/2974, reg 64(1), as from 15 December 2007; in definition "legal representative" for the words in italics there are substituted the

words "Solicitor of the Court of Judicature of Northern Ireland" by the Constitutional Reform Act 2005, s 59(5), Sch 11, Pt 3, para 5, as from a day to be appointed.
Para (2): revoked by SI 2004/2526, r 2(2), as from 1 October 2004.
Para (3): words in square brackets substituted by SI 2004/2526, r 2(3), as from 1 October 2004.

[2A—(1) The overriding objective of these Rules is to enable the Appeal Tribunal to deal with cases justly.

(2) Dealing with a case justly includes, so far as practicable —

(a) ensuring that the parties are on an equal footing;
(b) dealing with the case in ways which are proportionate to the importance and complexity of the issues;
(c) ensuring that it is dealt with expeditiously and fairly; and
(d) saving expense.

(3) The parties shall assist the Appeal Tribunal to further the overriding objective.]

[2189A]

NOTES

Commencement: 1 October 2004.
Inserted by the Employment Appeal Tribunal (Amendment) Rules 2004, SI 2004/2526, r 3, as from 1 October 2004.

[3 Institution of Appeal

(1) Every appeal to the Appeal Tribunal shall, subject to paragraphs (2) and (4), be instituted by serving on the Tribunal the following documents—

(a) a notice of appeal in, or substantially in, accordance with Form 1, 1A or 2 in the Schedule to these rules;
[(b) in the case of an appeal from a judgment of an employment tribunal a copy of any claim and response in the proceedings before the employment tribunal or an explanation as to why either is not included; and]
[(c) in the case of an appeal from a judgment of an employment tribunal a copy of the written record of the judgment of the employment tribunal which is subject to appeal and the written reasons for the judgment, or an explanation as to why written reasons are not included;] and
(d) in the case of an appeal made pursuant to regulation 38(8) of the 1999 Regulations [or regulation 47(6) of the 2004 Regulations] [or regulation 35(6) of the Information and Consultation Regulations] [or regulation 57(6) of the 2007 Regulations] from a declaration or order of the CAC, a copy of that declaration or order[; and]
[(e) in the case of an appeal from an order of an employment tribunal a copy of the written record of the order of the employment tribunal which is subject to appeal and (if available) the written reasons for the order;
(f) in the case of an appeal from a decision or order of the Certification Officer a copy of the decision or order of the Certification Officer which is subject to appeal and the written reasons for that decision or order.]

[(2) In an appeal from a judgment or order of the employment tribunal in relation to national security proceedings where the appellant was the claimant—

(i) the appellant shall not be required by virtue of paragraph (1)(b) to serve on the Appeal Tribunal a copy of the response if the response was not disclosed to the appellant; and
(ii) the appellant shall not be required by virtue of paragraph (1)(c) or (e) to serve on the Appeal Tribunal a copy of the written reasons for the judgment or order if the written reasons were not sent to the appellant but if a document containing edited reasons was sent to the appellant, he shall serve a copy of that document on the Appeal Tribunal.]

(3) The period within which an appeal to the Appeal Tribunal may be instituted is—

[(a) in the case of an appeal from a judgment of the employment tribunal—
  (i) where the written reasons for the judgment subject to appeal—
    (aa) were requested orally at the hearing before the employment tribunal or in writing within 14 days of the date on which the written record of the judgment was sent to the parties; or
    (bb) were reserved and given in writing by the employment tribunal

42 days from the date on which the written reasons were sent to the parties;

(ii) in an appeal from a judgment given in relation to national security proceedings, where there is a document containing edited reasons for the judgment subject to appeal, 42 days from the date on which that document was sent to the parties; or

(iii) where the written reasons for the judgment subject to appeal—

(aa) were not requested orally at the hearing before the employment tribunal or in writing within 14 days of the date on which the written record of the judgment was sent to the parties; and

(bb) were not reserved and given in writing by the employment tribunal

42 days from the date on which the written record of the judgment was sent to the parties;]

[(b) in the case of an appeal from an order of an employment tribunal, 42 days from the date of the order;]

(c) in the case of an appeal from a decision of the Certification Officer, 42 days from the date on which the written record of that decision was sent to the appellant;

(d) in the case of an appeal from a declaration or order of the CAC under regulation 38(8) of the 1999 Regulations [or regulation 47(6) of the 2004 Regulations] [or regulation 35(6) of the Information and Consultation Regulations] [or regulation 57(6) of the 2007 Regulations], 42 days from the date on which the written notification of that declaration or order was sent to the appellant.

(4) In the case of [an appeal from a judgment or order of the employment tribunal in relation to national security proceedings], the appellant shall not set out the grounds of appeal in his notice of appeal and shall not append to his notice of appeal the [written reasons for the judgment] of the tribunal.

(5) In [an appeal from the employment tribunal in relation to national security proceedings] in relation to which the appellant was the respondent in the proceedings before the employment tribunal, the appellant shall, within the period described in paragraph (3)(a), provide to the Appeal Tribunal a document setting out the grounds on which the appeal is brought.

(6) In [an appeal from the employment tribunal in relation to national security proceedings] in relation to which the appellant was the [claimant] in the proceedings before the employment tribunal—

(a) the appellant may, within the period described in [paragraph 3(a)(ii) or (iii) or paragraph 3(b), whichever is applicable,] provide to the Appeal Tribunal a document setting out the grounds on which the appeal is brought; and

(b) a special advocate appointed in respect of the appellant may, within the period described in [paragraph 3(a)(ii) or (iii) or paragraph 3(b), whichever is applicable,] or within 21 days of his appointment, whichever is later, provide to the Appeal Tribunal a document setting out the grounds on which the appeal is brought or providing supplementary grounds of appeal.

[(7) Where it appears to a judge or the Registrar that a notice of appeal or a document provided under paragraph (5) or (6)—

(a) discloses no reasonable grounds for bringing the appeal; or

(b) is an abuse of the Appeal Tribunal's process or is otherwise likely to obstruct the just disposal of proceedings,

he shall notify the Appellant or special advocate accordingly informing him of the reasons for his opinion and, subject to paragraphs (8) and (10), no further action shall be taken on the notice of appeal or document provided under paragraph (5) or (6).]

[(7A) In paragraphs (7) and (10) reference to a notice of appeal or a document provided under paragraph (5) or (6) includes reference to part of a notice of appeal or document provided under paragraph (5) or (6).]

(8) Where notification has been given under paragraph (7), the appellant or the special advocate, as the case may be, may serve a fresh notice of appeal, or a fresh document under paragraph (5) or (6), within the time remaining under paragraph (3) or (6) or within 28 days from the date on which [the notification given under paragraph (7)] was sent to him, whichever is the longer period.

(9) Where the appellant or the special advocate serves a fresh notice of appeal or a fresh document under paragraph (8), [a judge or the Registrar] shall consider such fresh notice of appeal or document with regard to jurisdiction as though it were an original notice of appeal

lodged pursuant to paragraphs (1) and (3), or as though it were an original document provided pursuant to paragraph (5) or (6), as the case may be.]

[(10) Where notification has been given under paragraph (7) and within 28 days of the date the notification was sent, an appellant or special advocate expresses dissatisfaction in writing with the reasons given by the judge or Registrar for his opinion, he is entitled to have the matter heard before a judge who shall make a direction as to whether any further action should be taken on the notice of appeal or document under paragraph (5) or (6).]

[2190]

NOTES

Substituted by the Employment Appeal Tribunal (Amendment) Rules 2001, SI 2001/1128, r 3, in relation to all proceedings irrespective of when those proceedings were commenced.

Para (1): sub-paras (b), (c) substituted, words in first pair of square brackets in sub-para (d) inserted, word in final pair of square brackets in that paragraph substituted, and sub-paras (e), (f) inserted, by the Employment Appeal Tribunal (Amendment) Rules 2004, SI 2004/2526, r 4(1), as from 1 October 2004 (subject to transitional provisions, in r 26(1) of those Rules, in relation to any proceedings commenced in an employment tribunal prior to 1 October 2004); words in second pair of square brackets in sub-para (d) inserted by the Information and Consultation of Employees Regulations 2004, SI 2004/3426, reg 41(b), as from 6 April 2005; words in third pair of square brackets in sub-para (d) inserted by the Companies (Cross-Border Mergers) Regulations 2007, SI 2007/2974, reg 64(2), as from 15 December 2007.

Paras (2), (7), (10): substituted by SI 2004/2526, r 4(2), (6), (11), as from 1 October 2004 (subject to transitional provisions as noted above).

Para (3): sub-paras (a), (b) substituted, and words in first pair of square brackets in sub-para (d) inserted, by SI 2004/2526, r 4(3), as from 1 October 2004 (subject to transitional provisions as noted above); words in second pair of square brackets in sub-para (d) inserted by SI 2004/3426, reg 41(b), as from 6 April 2005; words in third pair of square brackets in sub-para (d) inserted by SI 2007/2974, reg 64(2), as from 15 December 2007.

Paras (4)–(6), (8), (9): words in square brackets substituted by SI 2004/2526, r 4(4)–(6), (9), (10), as from 1 October 2004 (subject to transitional provisions as noted above).

Para (7A): inserted by SI 2004/2526, r 4(8), as from 1 October 2004 (subject to transitional provisions as noted above).

4 Service of notice of appeal

[(1)] On receipt of notice under rule 3, the Registrar shall seal the notice with the Appeal Tribunal's seal and shall serve a sealed copy on the appellant and on—

- (a) every person who, in accordance with rule 5, is a respondent to the appeal; and
- (b) the Secretary of [Employment Tribunals] in the case of an appeal from an [employment tribunal]; or
- (c) the Certification Officer in the case of an appeal from any of his decisions; or
- (d) the Secretary of State in the case of an appeal under … Chapter II of Part IV of the 1992 Act [or Part XI of the Employment Rights Act 1996] to which he is not a respondent[; or
- (e) the Chairman of the CAC in the case of an appeal from the CAC under regulation 38(8) of the 1999 Regulations [or regulation 47(6) of the 2004 Regulations] [or regulation 35(6) of the Information and Consultation Regulations] [or regulation 57(6) of the 2007 Regulations]].

[(2) On receipt of a document provided under rule 3(5)—

- (a) the Registrar shall not send the document to a person in respect of whom a Minister of the Crown has informed the Registrar that he wishes to address the Appeal Tribunal in accordance with rule 30A(3) with a view to the Appeal Tribunal making an order applicable to this stage of the proceedings under rule 30A(2)(a) read with 30A(1)(b) or (c) (exclusion of a party or his representative), at any time before the Appeal Tribunal decides whether or not to make such an order; but if it decides not to make such an order, the Registrar shall, subject to sub-paragraph (b), send the document to such a person 14 days after the Appeal Tribunal's decision not to make the order; and
- (b) the Registrar shall not send a copy of the document to an excluded person, but if a special advocate is appointed in respect of such a person, the Registrar shall send a copy of the document to the special advocate.

(3) On receipt of a document provided under rule 3(6)(a) or (b), the Registrar shall not send a copy of the document to an excluded person, but shall send a copy of the document to the respondent.]

[2191]

NOTES

Para (1): numbered as such, words omitted from sub-para (d) revoked, words in square brackets in that paragraph inserted, and para (e) and the word immediately preceding it added, by the Employment Appeal Tribunal (Amendment) Rules 2001, SI 2001/1128, r 4(a)–(d), in relation to all proceedings irrespective of when those proceedings were commenced; words in square brackets in sub-para (b) substituted by the Employment Rights (Dispute Resolution) Act 1998, s 1(2)(a), (b); words in first pair of square brackets in sub-para (e) inserted by the Employment Appeal Tribunal (Amendment) Rules 2004, SI 2004/2526, r 5, as from 1 October 2004; words in second pair of square brackets in sub-para (e) inserted by the Information and Consultation of Employees Regulations 2004, SI 2004/3426, reg 41(b), as from 6 April 2005; words in third pair of square brackets in sub-para (e) inserted by the Companies (Cross-Border Mergers) Regulations 2007, SI 2007/2974, reg 64(2), as from 15 December 2007.

Paras (2), (3): added by SI 2001/1128, r 4(d), in relation to all proceedings irrespective of when those proceedings were commenced.

5 Respondents to appeals

The respondents to an appeal shall be—

(a) in the case of an appeal from an [employment tribunal] or of an appeal made pursuant to [section 45D, 56A, 95, 104 or 108C] of the 1992 Act from a decision of the Certification Officer, the parties (other than the appellant) to the proceedings before the [employment tribunal] or the Certification Officer;

(b) in the case of an appeal made pursuant to [section 9 or 126] of the 1992 Act from a decision of the Certification Officer, that Officer;

[(c) in the case of an appeal made pursuant to regulation 38(8) of the 1999 Regulations [or regulation 47(6) of the 2004 Regulations] [or regulation 35(6) of the Information and Consultation Regulations] [or regulation 57(6) of the 2007 Regulations] from a declaration or order of the CAC, the parties (other than the appellant) to the proceedings before the CAC]

[2192]

NOTES

Words in first and third pairs of square brackets substituted by the Employment Rights (Dispute Resolution) Act 1998, s 1(2)(a); words in second and fourth pairs of square brackets substituted, and para (c) added, by the Employment Appeal Tribunal (Amendment) Rules 2001, SI 2001/1128, r 5, in relation to all proceedings irrespective of when those proceedings were commenced; words in first pair of square brackets in sub-para (c) inserted by the Employment Appeal Tribunal (Amendment) Rules 2004, SI 2004/2526, r 6, as from 1 October 2004; words in second pair of square brackets in sub-para (c) inserted by the Information and Consultation of Employees Regulations 2004, SI 2004/3426, reg 41(b), as from 6 April 2005; words in third pair of square brackets in sub-para (c) inserted by the Companies (Cross-Border Mergers) Regulations 2007, SI 2007/2974, reg 64(2), as from 15 December 2007.

6 Respondent's answer and notice of cross-appeal

(1) The Registrar shall, as soon as practicable, notify every respondent of the date appointed by the Appeal Tribunal by which any answer under this rule must be delivered.

(2) A respondent who wishes to resist an appeal shall, [subject to paragraph (6), and] within the time appointed under paragraph (1) of this rule, deliver to the Appeal Tribunal an answer in writing in, or substantially in, accordance with Form 3 in the Schedule to these Rules, setting out the grounds on which he relies, so, however, that it shall be sufficient for a respondent to an appeal referred to in rule 5(a) [or 5(c)] who wishes to rely on any ground which is the same as a ground relied on by the [employment tribunal][, the Certification Officer or the CAC] for making the [judgment,] decision[, declaration] or order appealed from to state that fact in his answer.

(3) A respondent who wishes to cross-appeal may [subject to paragraph (6),] do so by including in his answer a statement of the grounds of his cross-appeal, and in that event an appellant who wishes to resist the cross-appeal shall, within a time to be appointed by the Appeal Tribunal, deliver to the Tribunal a reply in writing setting out the grounds on which he relies.

(4) The Registrar shall serve a copy of every answer and reply to a cross-appeal on every party other than the party by whom it was delivered.

(5) Where the respondent does not wish to resist an appeal, the parties may deliver to the Appeal Tribunal an agreed draft of an order allowing the appeal and the Tribunal may, if it thinks it right to do so, make an order allowing the appeal in the terms agreed.

[(6) In [an appeal from the employment tribunal in relation to national security proceedings], the respondent shall not set out the grounds on which he relies in his answer to an appeal, nor include in his answer a statement of the grounds of any cross-appeal.

(7) In [an appeal from the employment tribunal in relation to national security proceedings] in relation to which the respondent was not the [claimant] in the proceedings before the employment tribunal, the respondent shall, within the time appointed under paragraph (1), provide to the Registrar a document, setting out the grounds on which he intends to resist the appeal, and may include in that document a statement of the grounds of any cross-appeal.

(8) In [an appeal from the employment tribunal in relation to national security proceedings] in relation to which the respondent was the [claimant] in the proceedings before the employment tribunal—

(a) the respondent may, within the time appointed under paragraph (1) provide to the Registrar a document, setting out the grounds on which he intends to resist the appeal, and may include in that document a statement of the grounds of any cross-appeal; and

(b) a special advocate appointed in respect of the respondent may, within the time appointed under paragraph (1), or within 21 days of his appointment, whichever is the later, provide to the Registrar a document, setting out the grounds, or the supplementary grounds, on which the respondent intends to resist the appeal, and may include in that document a statement of the grounds, or the supplementary grounds, of any cross-appeal.

(9) In [an appeal from the employment tribunal in relation to national security proceedings], if the respondent, or any special advocate appointed in respect of a respondent, provides in the document containing grounds for resisting an appeal a statement of grounds of cross-appeal and the appellant wishes to resist the cross-appeal—

(a) where the appellant was not the [claimant] in the proceedings before the employment tribunal, the appellant shall within a time to be appointed by the Appeal Tribunal deliver to the Tribunal a reply in writing setting out the grounds on which he relies; and

(b) where the appellant was the [claimant] in the proceedings before the employment tribunal, the appellant, or any special advocate appointed in respect of him, may within a time to be appointed by the Appeal Tribunal deliver to the Tribunal a reply in writing setting out the grounds on which the appellant relies.

(10) Any document provided under paragraph (7) or (9)(a) shall be treated by the Registrar in accordance with rule 4(2), as though it were a document received under rule 3(5).

(11) Any document provided under paragraph (8) or (9)(b) shall be treated by the Registrar in accordance with rule 4(3), as though it were a document received under rule 3(6)(a) or (b).]

[(12) Where it appears to a judge or the Registrar that a statement of grounds of cross-appeal contained in respondent's answer or document provided under paragraph (7) or (8)—

(a) discloses no reasonable grounds for bringing the cross-appeal; or

(b) is an abuse of the Appeal Tribunal's process or is otherwise likely to obstruct the just disposal of proceedings,

he shall notify the appellant or special advocate accordingly informing him of the reasons for his opinion and, subject to paragraphs (14) and (16), no further action shall be taken on the statement of grounds of cross-appeal.

(13) In paragraphs (12) and (16) reference to a statement of grounds of cross-appeal includes reference to part of a statement of grounds of cross-appeal.

(14) Where notification has been given under paragraph (12), the respondent or special advocate, as the case may be, may serve a fresh statement of grounds of cross-appeal before the time appointed under paragraph (1) or within 28 days from the date on which the notification given under paragraph (12) was sent to him, whichever is the longer.

(15) Where the respondent or special advocate serves a fresh statement of grounds of cross-appeal, a judge or the Registrar shall consider such statement with regard to jurisdiction as though it was contained in the original Respondent's answer or document provided under (7) or (8).

(16) Where notification has been given under paragraph (12) and within 28 days of the date the notification was sent, a respondent or special advocate expresses dissatisfaction in writing with the reasons given by the judge or Registrar for his opinion, he is entitled to have the matter heard before a judge who shall make a direction as to whether any further action should be taken on the statement of grounds of cross-appeal.]

[2193]

NOTES

Para (2): words in first, second and sixth pair of square brackets inserted, and words in fourth pair of square brackets substituted, by the Employment Appeal Tribunal (Amendment) Rules 2001, SI 2001/1128, r 6(a), (b), in relation to all proceedings irrespective of when those proceedings were commenced; words in third pair of square brackets substituted by the Employment Rights (Dispute Resolution) Act 1998, s 1(2)(a); word in fifth pair of square brackets inserted by the Employment Appeal Tribunal (Amendment) Rules 2004, SI 2004/2526, r 7(1)(a), as from 1 October 2004.

Para (3): words in square brackets substituted by SI 2001/1128, r 6(b), in relation to all proceedings irrespective of when those proceedings were commenced.

Paras (6)–(9): added, together with paras (10), (11), by SI 2001/1128, r 6(c), in relation to all proceedings irrespective of when those proceedings were commenced; words in square brackets substituted by SI 2004/2526, r 7(1)(b), (c), as from 1 October 2004.

Paras (10), (11): added as noted above.

Paras (12)–(16): added by SI 2004/2526, r 7(2), as from 1 October 2004.

7 Disposal of appeal

(1) The Registrar shall, as soon as practicable, give notice of the arrangements made by the Appeal Tribunal for hearing the appeal to—

- (a) every party to the proceedings; and
- (b) the Secretary of [Employment Tribunals] in the case of an appeal from an [employment tribunal]; or
- (c) the Certification Officer in the case of an appeal from one of his decisions; or
- (d) the Secretary of State in the case of an appeal under [Part XI of the Employment Rights Act 1996] or Chapter II of Part IV of the 1992 Act to which he is not a respondent[; or
- (e) the Chairman of the CAC in the case of an appeal from a declaration or order of, or arising in any proceedings before, the CAC under regulation 38(8) of the 1999 Regulations [or regulation 47(6) of the 2004 Regulations] [or regulation 35(6) of the Information and Consultation Regulations] [or regulation 57(6) of the 2007 Regulations]].

(2) Any such notice shall state the date appointed by the Appeal Tribunal by which any [interim] application must be made.

[2194]

NOTES

Para (1): words in square brackets in sub-para (b) substituted by the Employment Rights (Dispute Resolution) Act 1998, s 1(2)(a), (b); words in square brackets in sub-para (d) substituted, and sub-para (e) and word immediately preceding it added, by the Employment Appeal Tribunal (Amendment) Rules 2001, SI 2001/1128, r 7, in relation to all proceedings irrespective of when those proceedings were commenced; words in first pair of square brackets in sub-para (e) inserted by the Employment Appeal Tribunal (Amendment) Rules 2004, SI 2004/2526, r 8(1), as from 1 October 2004; words in second pair of square brackets in sub-para (e) inserted by the Information and Consultation of Employees Regulations 2004, SI 2004/3426, reg 41(b), as from 6 April 2005; words in third pair of square brackets in sub-para (e) inserted by the Companies (Cross-Border Mergers) Regulations 2007, SI 2007/2974, reg 64(2), as from 15 December 2007.

Para (2): word in square brackets substituted by SI 2004/2526, r 8(2), as from 1 October 2004.

8 Application in respect of exclusion or expulsion from, or unjustifiable discipline by, a trade union

Every application under section 67 or 176 of the 1992 Act to the Appeal Tribunal for—

- (a) an award of compensation for exclusion or expulsion from a trade union; or
- (b) one or both of the following, that is to say—
  - (i) an award of compensation for unjustifiable discipline;
  - (ii) an order that the union pay to the applicant an amount equal to any sum which he has paid in pursuance of any such determination as is mentioned in section 64(2)(b) of the 1992 Act;

shall be made in writing in, or substantially in, accordance with Form 4 in the Schedule to these Rules and shall be served on the Appeal Tribunal together with a copy of the decision or order declaring that the applicant's complaint against the trade union was well-founded.

[2195]

9 If on receipt of an application under rule 8(a) it becomes clear that at the time the application was made the applicant had been admitted or re-admitted to membership of the union against which the complaint was made, the Registrar shall forward the application to the Central Office of [Employment Tribunals].

[2196]

NOTES

Words in square brackets substituted by the Employment Rights (Dispute Resolution) Act 1998, s 1(2)(b).

10 Service of application under rule 8

On receipt of an application under rule 8, the Registrar shall seal it with the Appeal Tribunal's seal and shall serve a sealed copy on the applicant and on the respondent trade union and the Secretary of [Employment Tribunals].

[2197]

NOTES

Words in square brackets substituted by the Employment Rights (Dispute Resolution) Act 1998, s 1(2)(b).

11 Appearance by respondent trade union

(1) Subject to paragraph (2) of this rule, a respondent trade union wishing to resist an application under rule 8 shall within 14 days of receiving the sealed copy of the application enter an appearance in, or substantially in, accordance with Form 5 in the Schedule to these Rules and setting out the grounds on which the union relies.

(2) Paragraph (1) above shall not require a respondent trade union to enter an appearance where the application is before the Appeal Tribunal by virtue of having been transferred there by an [employment tribunal] and, prior to that transfer, the respondent had entered an appearance to the proceedings before the [employment tribunal].

[2198]

NOTES

Para (2): words in square brackets substituted by the Employment Rights (Dispute Resolution) Act 1998, s 1(2)(a).

12 On receipt of the notice of appearance under rule 11 the Registrar shall serve a copy of it on the applicant.

[2199]

13 Application for restriction of proceedings order

Every application to the Appeal Tribunal by the Attorney General or the Lord Advocate under [section 33 of the 1996 Act] for a restriction of proceedings order shall be made in writing in, or substantially in, accordance with Form 6 in the Schedule to these Rules, accompanied by an affidavit in support, and shall be served on the Tribunal.

[2200]

NOTES

Words in square brackets substituted by the Employment Appeal Tribunal (Amendment) Rules 2001, SI 2001/1128, r 8, in relation to all proceedings irrespective of when those proceedings were commenced.

14 Service of application under rule 13

On receipt of an application under rule 13, the Registrar shall seal it with the Appeal Tribunal's seal and shall serve a sealed copy on the Attorney General or the Lord Advocate, as the case may be, on the Secretary of [Employment Tribunals] and on the person named in the application.

[2201]

NOTES

Words in square brackets substituted by the Employment Rights (Dispute Resolution) Act 1998, s 1(2)(b).

15 Appearance by person named in application under rule 13

A person named in an application under rule 13 who wishes to resist the application shall within 14 days of receiving the sealed copy of the application enter an appearance in, or substantially in, accordance with Form 7 in the Schedule to these Rules, accompanied by an affidavit in support.

[2202]

16 On receipt of the notice of appearance under rule 15 the Registrar shall serve a copy of it on the Attorney General or the Lord Advocate, as the case may be.

[2203]

[16A Complaints under regulations 20 and 21 of the 1999 Regulations

Every complaint under regulation 20 or 21 of the 1999 Regulations shall be made by way of application in writing in, or substantially in, accordance with Form 4A in the Schedule to these Rules and shall be served on the Appeal Tribunal.]

[2204]

NOTES

Inserted, together with rr 16B–16D, by the Employment Appeal Tribunal (Amendment) Rules 2001, SI 2001/1128, r 9, in relation to all proceedings irrespective of when those proceedings were commenced.

[16AA Applications under regulation 33(6) of the 2004 Regulations

Every application under regulation 33(6) of the 2004 Regulations [or regulation 22(6) of the Information and Consultation Regulations] [or regulation 53(6) of the 2007 Regulations] shall be made by way of application in writing in, or substantially in, accordance with Form 4B in the Schedule to these Rules and shall be served on the Appeal Tribunal together with a copy of the declaration referred to in regulation 33(4) of [the 2004 Regulations or regulation 22(4) of the Information and Consultation Regulations] [or regulation 53(4) of the 2007 Regulations], or an explanation as to why none is included.]

[2204A]

NOTES

Commencement: 1 October 2004.

Inserted by the Employment Appeal Tribunal (Amendment) Rules 2004, SI 2004/2526, r 9, as from 1 October 2004.

Words in first pair of square brackets inserted, and words in third pair of square brackets substituted, by the Information and Consultation of Employees Regulations 2004, SI 2004/3426, reg 41(c), as from 6 April 2005; other words in square brackets inserted by the Companies (Cross-Border Mergers) Regulations 2007, SI 2007/2974, reg 64(3), as from 15 December 2007.

[16B Service of application under rule 16A

On receipt of an application under rule 16A [or 16AA], the Registrar shall seal it with the Appeal Tribunal's seal and shall serve a sealed copy on the applicant and on the respondent.]

[2205]

NOTES

Inserted as noted to r 16A at **[2204]**.

Words in square brackets inserted by the Employment Appeal Tribunal (Amendment) Rules 2004, SI 2004/2526, r 10, as from 1 October 2004.

[16C Appearance by respondent

A respondent wishing to resist an application under rule 16A [or 16AA] shall within 14 days of receiving the sealed copy of the application enter an appearance in, or substantially in, accordance with Form 5A in the Schedule to these Rules and setting out the grounds on which the respondent relies.]

[2206]

NOTES

Inserted as noted to r 16A at **[2204]**.

Words in square brackets inserted by the Employment Appeal Tribunal (Amendment) Rules 2004, SI 2004/2526, r 10, as from 1 October 2004.

[16D On receipt of the notice of appearance under rule 16C the Registrar shall serve a copy of it on the applicant.]

[2207]

NOTES

Inserted as noted to r 16A at **[2204]**.

17 Disposal of application

(1) The Registrar shall, as soon as practicable, give notice to the parties to an application under rule 8[, 13[, 16A or 16AA]] of the arrangements made by the Appeal Tribunal for hearing the application.

(2) Any such notice shall state the date appointed by the Appeal Tribunal by which any [interim] application must be made.

[2208]

NOTES

Sub-s (1): words in first (outer) pair of square brackets substituted by the Employment Appeal Tribunal (Amendment) Rules 2001, SI 2001/1128, r 10, in relation to all proceedings irrespective of when those proceedings were commenced; words in second (inner) pair of square brackets substituted by the Employment Appeal Tribunal (Amendment) Rules 2004, SI 2004/2526, r 11, as from 1 October 2004.

Para (2): word in square brackets substituted by SI 2004/2526, r 12, as from 1 October 2004.

18 Joinder of parties

The Appeal Tribunal may, on the application of any person or of its own motion, direct that any person not already a party to the proceedings be added as a party, or that any party to proceedings shall cease to be a party, and in either case may give such consequential directions as it considers necessary.

[2209]

19 [Interim] applications

(1) An [interim] application may be made to the Appeal Tribunal by giving notice in writing specifying the direction or order sought.

(2) On receipt of a notice under paragraph (1) of this rule, the Registrar shall serve a copy on every other party to the proceedings who appears to him to be concerned in the matter to which the notice relates and shall notify the applicant and every such party of the arrangements made by the Appeal Tribunal for disposing of the application.

[2210]

NOTES

Words in square brackets substituted by the Employment Appeal Tribunal (Amendment) Rules 2004, SI 2004/2526, r 12, as from 1 October 2004.

[20 Disposal of interim applications

(1) Every interim application made to the Appeal Tribunal shall be considered in the first place by the Registrar who shall have regard to rule 2A (the overriding objective) and, where applicable, to rule 23(5).

(2) Subject to sub-paragraphs (3) and (4), every interim application shall be disposed of by the Registrar except that any matter which he thinks should properly be decided by the President or a judge shall be referred by him to the President or judge who may dispose of it himself or refer it in whole or part to the Appeal Tribunal as required to be constituted by section 28 of the 1996 Act or refer it back to the Registrar with such directions as he thinks fit.

(3) Every interim application for a restricted reporting order shall be disposed of by the President or a judge or, if he so directs, the application shall be referred to the Appeal Tribunal as required to be constituted by section 28 of the 1996 Act who shall dispose of it.

(4) Every interim application for permission to institute or continue or to make a claim or application in any proceedings before an employment tribunal or the Appeal Tribunal, pursuant to section 33(4) of the 1996 Act, shall be disposed of by the President or a judge, or, if he so directs, the application shall be referred to the Appeal Tribunal as required to be constituted by section 28 of the 1996 Act who shall dispose of it.]

[2211]

NOTES

Commencement: 1 October 2004.

Substituted by the Employment Appeal Tribunal (Amendment) Rules 2004, SI 2004/2526, r 13, as from 1 October 2004.

21 Appeals from Registrar

(1) Where an application is disposed of by the Registrar in pursuance of rule 20(2) any party aggrieved by his decision may appeal to a judge and in that case … the judge may determine the appeal himself or refer it in whole or in part to the Appeal Tribunal as required to be constituted by [section 28 of the 1996 Act].

(2) Notice of appeal under paragraph (1) of this rule may be given to the Appeal Tribunal, either orally or in writing, within five days of the decision appealed from and the Registrar shall notify every other party who appears to him to be concerned in the appeal and shall inform every such party and the appellant of the arrangements made by the Tribunal for disposing of the appeal.

[2212]

NOTES

Para (1): words omitted revoked, and words in square brackets substituted, by the Employment Appeal Tribunal (Amendment) Rules 2001, SI 2001/1128, r 12, in relation to all proceedings irrespective of when those proceedings were commenced.

22 Hearing of interlocutory applications

(1) The Appeal Tribunal may, subject to [any direction of a Minister of the Crown under rule 30A(1) or order of the Appeal Tribunal under rule 30A(2)(a) read with rule 30A(1),] and, where applicable, to rule 23(6), sit either in private or in public for the hearing of any [interim] application.

(2) …

[2213]

NOTES

Para (1): words in first pair of square brackets substituted by the Employment Appeal Tribunal (Amendment) Rules 2001, SI 2001/1128, r 13(a), in relation to all proceedings irrespective of when those proceedings were commenced; word in second pair of square brackets substituted by the Employment Appeal Tribunal (Amendment) Rules 2004, SI 2004/2526, r 14, as from 1 October 2004.

Para (2): revoked by SI 2001/1128, r 13(b), in relation to all proceedings irrespective of when those proceedings were commenced.

23 Cases involving allegations of sexual misconduct or the commission of sexual offences

(1) This rule applies to any proceedings to which [section 31 of the 1996 Act] applies.

(2) In any such proceedings where the appeal appears to involve allegations of the commission of a sexual offence, the Registrar shall omit from any register kept by the Appeal Tribunal, which is available to the public, or delete from any order, judgment or other

document, which is available to the public, any identifying matter which is likely to lead members of the public to identify any person affected by or making such an allegation.

(3) In any proceedings to which this rule applies where the appeal involves allegations of sexual misconduct the Appeal Tribunal may at any time before promulgation of its decision either on the application of a party or of its own motion make a restricted reporting order having effect, if not revoked earlier by the Appeal Tribunal, until the promulgation of its decision.

(4) A restricted reporting order shall specify the persons who may not be identified.

[(5) Subject to paragraph (5A) the Appeal Tribunal shall not make a full restricted reporting order unless it has given each party to the proceedings an opportunity to advance oral argument at a hearing, if they so wish.]

[(5A) The Appeal Tribunal may make a temporary restricted reporting order without a hearing.

(5B) Where a temporary restricted reporting order has been made the Registrar shall inform the parties to the proceedings in writing as soon as possible of:

(a) the fact that the order has been made; and

(b) their right to apply to have the temporary restricted reporting order revoked or converted into a full restricted reporting order within 14 days of the temporary order being made.

(5C) If no such application is made under subparagraph (5B)(b) within the 14 days, the temporary restricted reporting order shall lapse and cease to have any effect on the fifteenth day after it was made. When such an application is made the temporary restricted reporting order shall continue to have effect until the Hearing at which the application is considered.]

(6) Any … hearing shall, subject to [any direction of a Minister of the Crown under rule 30A(1) or order of the Appeal Tribunal under rule 30A(2)(a) read with rule 30A(1),] or unless the Appeal Tribunal decides for any of the reasons mentioned in rule 29(2) to sit in private to hear evidence, be held in public.

(7) The Appeal Tribunal may revoke a restricted reporting order at any time where it thinks fit.

(8) Where the Appeal Tribunal makes a restricted reporting order, the Registrar shall ensure that a notice of that fact is displayed on the notice board of the Appeal Tribunal at the office in which the proceedings in question are being dealt with, on the door of the room in which those proceedings are taking place and with any list of the proceedings taking place before the Appeal Tribunal.

(9) In this rule, "promulgation of its decision" means the date recorded as being the date on which the Appeal Tribunal's order finally disposing of the appeal is sent to the parties.

[2214]

NOTES

Para (1): words in square brackets substituted by the Employment Appeal Tribunal (Amendment) Rules 2001, SI 2001/1128, r 14(a), in relation to all proceedings irrespective of when those proceedings were commenced.

Para (5): substituted by the Employment Appeal Tribunal (Amendment) Rules 2004, SI 2004/2526, r 15(1), as from 1 October 2004.

Paras (5A)–(5C): inserted by SI 2004/2526, r 15(2), as from 1 October 2004.

Para (6): word omitted revoked by SI 2004/2526, r 15(3), as from 1 October 2004; words in square brackets substituted by SI 2001/1128, r 14(b), in relation to all proceedings irrespective of when those proceedings were commenced.

[23A Restricted reporting orders in disability cases

(1) This rule applies to proceedings to which section 32(1) of [the [1996 Act]] applies.

(2) In proceedings to which this rule applies the Appeal Tribunal may, on the application of the complainant or of its own motion, make a restricted reporting order having effect, if not revoked earlier by the Appeal Tribunal, until the promulgation of its decision.

(3) Where the Appeal Tribunal makes a restricted reporting order under paragraph (2) of this rule in relation to an appeal which is being dealt with by the Appeal Tribunal together with any other proceedings, the Appeal Tribunal may direct that the order is to apply also in relation to those other proceedings or such part of them as it may direct.

(4) Paragraphs (5) to (9) of rule 23 apply in relation to the making of a restricted reporting order under this rule as they apply in relation to the making of a restricted reporting order under that rule.]

[2215]

NOTES

Inserted by the Employment Appeal Tribunal (Amendment) Rules 1996, SI 1996/3216, r 2.

Para (1): word in first (outer) pair of square brackets substituted by the Employment Rights (Dispute Resolution) Act 1998, s 1(2)(c); words in second (inner) pair of square brackets substituted by the Employment Appeal Tribunal (Amendment) Rules 2001, SI 2001/1128, r 15, in relation to all proceedings irrespective of when those proceedings were commenced.

24 Appointment for direction

(1) Where it appears to the Appeal Tribunal that the future conduct of any proceedings would thereby be facilitated, the Tribunal may (either of its own motion or on application) at any stage in the proceedings appoint a date for a meeting for directions as to their future conduct and thereupon the following provisions of this rule shall apply.

(2) The Registrar shall give to every party in the proceedings notice of the date appointed under paragraph (1) of this rule and any party applying for directions shall, if practicable, before that date give to the Appeal Tribunal particulars of any direction for which he asks.

(3) The Registrar shall take such steps as may be practicable to inform every party of any directions applied for by any other party.

(4) On the date appointed under paragraph (1) of this rule, the Appeal Tribunal shall consider every application for directions made by any party and any written representations relating to the application submitted to the Tribunal and shall give such directions as it thinks fit for the purpose of securing the just, expeditious and economical disposal of the proceedings, including, where appropriate, directions in pursuance of rule 36, for the purpose of ensuring that the parties are enabled to avail themselves of opportunities for conciliation.

(5) Without prejudice to the generality of paragraph (4) of this rule, the Appeal Tribunal may give such directions as it thinks fit as to—

(a) the amendment of any notice, answer or other document;
(b) the admission of any facts or documents;
(c) the admission in evidence of any documents;
(d) the mode in which evidence is to be given at the hearing;
(e) the consolidation of the proceedings with any other proceedings pending before the Tribunal;
(f) the place and date of the hearing.

(6) An application for further directions or for the variation of any directions already given may be made in accordance with rule 19.

[2216]

25 Appeal Tribunal's power to give directions

The Appeal Tribunal may either of its own motion or on application, at any stage of the proceedings, give any party directions as to any steps to be taken by him in relation to the proceedings.

[2217]

26 Default by parties

If a respondent to any proceedings fails to deliver an answer or, in the case of an application made under section 67 or 176 of the 1992 Act[, section 33 of the 1996 Act[,] regulation 20 or 21 of the 1999 Regulations], [… regulation 33 of the 2004 Regulations] [… regulation 22 of the Information and Consultation Regulations] [or regulation 53 the 2007 Regulations], a notice of appearance within the time appointed under these Rules, or if any party fails to comply with an order or direction of the Appeal Tribunal, the Tribunal may order that he be debarred from taking any further part in the proceedings, or may make such other order as it thinks just.

[2218]

NOTES

Words in first pair of square brackets substituted by the Employment Appeal Tribunal (Amendment) Rules 2001, SI 2001/1128, r 16, in relation to all proceedings irrespective of when those proceedings were commenced; the comma in the second (inner) pair of square brackets was substituted (for the original word "or"), and the words in the third pair of square brackets were inserted, by the Employment Appeal Tribunal (Amendment) Rules 2004, SI 2004/2526, r 17, as from 1 October 2004; first word omitted revoked, and words in penultimate pair of square brackets inserted, by the Information and Consultation of Employees Regulations 2004, SI 2004/3426, reg 41(d), as from 6 April 2005; second word omitted revoked, and words in final pair of square brackets inserted, by the Companies (Cross-Border Mergers) Regulations 2007, SI 2007/2974, reg 64(4), as from 15 December 2007.

27 Attendance of witnesses and production of documents

(1) The Appeal Tribunal may, on the application of any party, order any person to attend before the Tribunal as a witness or to produce any document.

[(1A) Where—

(a) a Minister has at any stage issued a direction under rule 30A(1)(b) or (c) (exclusion of a party or his representative), or the Appeal Tribunal has at any stage made an order under rule 30A(2)(a) read with rule 30A(1)(b) or (c); and

(b) the Appeal Tribunal is considering whether to impose, or has imposed, a requirement under paragraph (1) on any person,

the Minister (whether or not he is a party to the proceedings) may make an application to the Appeal Tribunal objecting to the imposition of a requirement under paragraph (1) or, where a requirement has been imposed, an application to vary or set aside the requirement, as the case may be. The Appeal Tribunal shall hear and determine the Minister's application in private and the Minister shall be entitled to address the Appeal Tribunal thereon. The application shall be made by notice to the Registrar and the Registrar shall give notice of the application to each party.]

(2) No person to whom an order is directed under paragraph (1) of this rule shall be treated as having failed to obey that order unless at the time at which the order was served on him there was tendered to him a sufficient sum of money to cover his costs of attending before the Appeal Tribunal.

[2219]

NOTES

Para (1A): inserted by the Employment Appeal Tribunal (Amendment) Rules 2001, SI 2001/1128, r 17, in relation to all proceedings irrespective of when those proceedings were commenced.

28 Oaths

The Appeal Tribunal may, either of its own motion or on application, require any evidence to be given on oath.

[2220]

29 Oral hearings

(1) Subject to paragraph (2) of this rule and to [any direction of a Minister of the Crown under rule 30A(1)(a) or order of the Appeal Tribunal under rule 30A(2)(a) read with rule 30A(1)(a),] an oral hearing at which any proceedings before the Appeal Tribunal are finally disposed of shall take place in public before, where applicable, such members of the Tribunal as (subject to [section 28 of the 1996 Act]) the President may nominate for the purpose.

[(2) Notwithstanding paragraph (1), the Appeal Tribunal may sit in private for the purpose of hearing evidence from any person which in the opinion of the Tribunal is likely to consist of—

(a) information which he could not disclose without contravening a prohibition imposed by or by virtue of any enactment;

(b) information which has been communicated to him in confidence or which he has otherwise obtained in consequence of the confidence reposed in him by another person; or

(c) information the disclosure of which would, for reasons other than its effect on negotiations with respect to any of the matters mentioned in section 178(2) of the 1992 Act, cause substantial injury to any undertaking of his or in which he works.]

[2221]

NOTES

Para (1): words in square brackets substituted by the Employment Appeal Tribunal (Amendment) Rules 2001, SI 2001/1128, r 18(a), in relation to all proceedings irrespective of when those proceedings were commenced.

Para (2): substituted by SI 2001/1128, r 18(b), in relation to all proceedings irrespective of when those proceedings were commenced.

[30 Duty of Appeal Tribunal concerning disclosure of information

When exercising its functions, the Appeal Tribunal shall ensure that information is not disclosed contrary to the interests of national security.]

[2222]

NOTES

Substituted, together with r 30A, for original r 30, by the Employment Appeal Tribunal (Amendment) Rules 2001, SI 2001/1128, r 19, in relation to all proceedings irrespective of when those proceedings were commenced.

[30A Proceedings in cases concerning national security

(1) A Minister of the Crown (whether or not he is a party to the proceedings) may, if he considers it expedient in the interests of national security, direct the Appeal Tribunal by notice to the Registrar to—

(a) sit in private for all or part of particular Crown employment proceedings;

(b) exclude any party who was the [claimant] in the proceedings before the employment tribunal from all or part of particular Crown employment proceedings;

(c) exclude the representatives of any party who was the [claimant] in the proceedings before the employment tribunal from all or part of particular Crown employment proceedings;

(d) take steps to conceal the identity of a particular witness in particular Crown employment proceedings.

(2) The Appeal Tribunal may, if it considers it expedient in the interests of national security, by order—

(a) do [in relation to particular proceedings before it] anything of a kind which the Appeal Tribunal can be required to do [in relation to particular Crown employment proceedings] by direction under paragraph (1) of this rule;

(b) direct any person to whom any document (including any decision or record of the proceedings) has been provided for the purposes of the proceedings not to disclose any such document or the content thereof—

(i) to any excluded person;

(ii) in any case in which a direction has been given under paragraph (1)(a) or an order has been made under paragraph (2)(a) read with paragraph (1)(a), to any person excluded from all or part of the proceedings by virtue of such direction or order; or

(iii) in any case in which a Minister of the Crown has informed the Registrar in accordance with paragraph (3) that he wishes to address the Appeal Tribunal with a view to the Tribunal making an order under paragraph (2)(a) read with paragraph (1)(b) or (c), to any person who may be excluded from all or part of the proceedings by virtue of such an order, if an order is made, at any time before the Appeal Tribunal decides whether or not to make such an order;

(c) take steps to keep secret all or part of the reasons for any order it makes.

The Appeal Tribunal shall keep under review any order it makes under this paragraph.

(3) In any proceedings in which a Minister of the Crown considers that it would be appropriate for the Appeal Tribunal to make an order as referred to in paragraph (2), he shall (whether or not he is a party to the proceedings) be entitled to appear before and to address the Appeal Tribunal thereon. The Minister shall inform the Registrar by notice that he wishes to address the Appeal Tribunal and the Registrar shall copy the notice to the parties.

(4) In any proceedings in which there is an excluded person, the Appeal Tribunal shall inform the Attorney General or, in the case of an appeal from an employment tribunal in

Scotland, the Advocate General for Scotland, of the proceedings before it with a view to the Attorney General (or, as the case may be, the Advocate General), if he thinks it fit to do so, appointing a special advocate to represent the interests of the person who was the [claimant] in the proceedings before the employment tribunal in respect of those parts of the proceedings from which—

(a) any representative of his is excluded;

(b) both he and his representative are excluded; or

(c) he is excluded, where he does not have a representative.

(5) A special advocate shall have a general qualification within the meaning of section 71 of the Courts and Legal Services Act 1990, or, in the case of an appeal from an employment tribunal in Scotland, shall be—

(a) an advocate; or

(b) a solicitor who has by virtue of section 25A of the Solicitors (Scotland) Act 1980 rights of audience in the Court of Session or the High Court of Justiciary.

(6) Where the excluded person is a party to the proceedings, he shall be permitted to make a statement to the Appeal Tribunal before the commencement of the proceedings, or the part of the proceedings, from which he is excluded.

(7) Except in accordance with paragraphs (8) to (10), the special advocate may not communicate directly or indirectly with any person (including an excluded person)—

(a) (except in the case of the Appeal Tribunal or the party who was the respondent in the proceedings before the employment tribunal) on any matter contained in the documents referred to in rule 3(5), 3(6), 6(7) or 6(8)(b); or

(b) (except in the case of a person who was present) on any matter discussed or referred to during any part of the proceedings in which the Appeal Tribunal sat in private pursuant to a direction of the Minister under paragraph (1)(a) or an order of the Appeal Tribunal under paragraph (2)(a) read with paragraph (1)(a).

(8) The special advocate may apply for directions from the Appeal Tribunal authorising him to seek instructions from, or otherwise to communicate with, an excluded person—

(a) on any matter contained in the documents referred to in rule 3(5), 3(6), 6(7) or 6(8)(b); or

(b) on any matter discussed or referred to during any part of the proceedings in which the Appeal Tribunal sat in private as referred to in paragraph (7)(b).

(9) An application under paragraph (8) shall be made by presenting to the Registrar a notice of application, which shall state the title of the proceedings and set out the grounds of the application.

(10) The Registrar shall notify the Minister of an application for directions under paragraph (8) and the Minister shall be entitled to address the Appeal Tribunal on the application.

(11) In these rules, in any case in which a special advocate has been appointed in respect of a party, any reference to a party shall (save in those references specified in paragraph (12)) include the special advocate.

(12) The references mentioned in paragraph (11) are those in rules 5 and 18, the first and second references in rule 27(1A), paragraphs (1) and (6) of this rule, the first reference in paragraph (3) of this rule, rule 34(1), the reference in item 4 of Form 1, and in item 4 of Form 1A, in the Schedule to these Rules.]

[2223]

NOTES

Substituted as noted to r 30 at **[2222]**.

Paras (1), (4): words in square brackets substituted by the Employment Appeal Tribunal (Amendment) Rules 2004, SI 2004/2526, r 16, as from 1 October 2004.

Para (2): words in square brackets in sub-para (a) inserted by the Employment Appeal Tribunal (Amendment) Rules 2005, SI 2005/1871, r 2, as from 1 October 2005.

31 Drawing up, reasons for, and enforcement of orders

(1) Every order of the Appeal Tribunal shall be drawn up by the Registrar and a copy, sealed with the seal of the Tribunal, shall be served by the Registrar on every party to the proceedings to which it relates and—

(a) in the case of an order disposing of an appeal from an [employment tribunal] or of an order under [section 33 of the 1996 Act] on the Secretary of the [Employment Tribunals]; …

(b) in the case of an order disposing of an appeal from the Certification Officer, on that Officer.

[(c) in the case of an order imposing a penalty notice under regulation 20 or 21 of the 1999 Regulations, [… regulation 33 of the 2004 Regulations] [or regulation 22 of the Information and Consultation Regulations] [… regulation 53 the 2007 Regulations], on the Secretary of State; or

(d) in the case of an order disposing of an appeal from the CAC made under regulation 38(8) of the 1999 Regulations, on the Chairman of the CAC.]

(2) [Subject to rule 31A,] the Appeal Tribunal shall, on the application of any party made within 14 days after the making of an order finally disposing of any proceedings, give its reasons in writing for the order unless it was made after the delivery of a reasoned judgment.

(3) Subject to any order made by the Court of Appeal or Court of Session and to any directions given by the Appeal Tribunal, an appeal from the Tribunal shall not suspend the enforcement of any order made by it.

[2224]

NOTES

Para (1): words in first and third pairs of square brackets in sub-para (a) substituted by the Employment Rights (Dispute Resolution) Act 1998, s 1(2)(a), (b); words in second pair of square brackets in sub-para (a) substituted, word omitted revoked, and sub-paras (c), (d) added, by the Employment Appeal Tribunal (Amendment) Rules 2001, SI 2001/1128, r 20(a)–(c), in relation to all proceedings irrespective of when those proceedings were commenced; words in first pair of square brackets in sub-para (c) inserted by the Employment Appeal Tribunal (Amendment) Rules 2004, SI 2004/2526, r 18, as from 1 October 2004; first word omitted revoked, and words in second pair of square brackets in sub-para (c) inserted, by the Information and Consultation of Employees Regulations 2004, SI 2004/3426, reg 41(d), as from 6 April 2005; second word omitted revoked, and words in final pair of square brackets inserted, by the Companies (Cross-Border Mergers) Regulations 2007, SI 2007/2974, reg 64(4), as from 15 December 2007.

Para (2): words in square brackets inserted by SI 2001/1128, r 20(d), in relation to all proceedings irrespective of when those proceedings were commenced.

[31A Reasons for orders in cases concerning national security

(1) Paragraphs (1) to (5) of this rule apply to the document setting out the reasons for the Appeal Tribunal's order prepared under rule 31(2) or any reasoned judgment of the Appeal Tribunal as referred to in rule 31(2), in any particular Crown employment proceedings in which a direction of a Minister of the Crown has been given under rule 30A(1)(a), (b) or (c) or an order of the Appeal Tribunal has been made under rule 30A(2)(a) read with rule 30A(1)(a), (b) or (c).

(2) Before the Appeal Tribunal gives its reasons in writing for any order or delivers any reasoned judgment, the Registrar shall send a copy of the reasons or judgment to the Minister.

(3) If the Minister considers it expedient in the interests of national security, he may—

(a) direct the Appeal Tribunal that the document containing its reasons for any order or its reasoned judgment shall not be disclosed to any person who was excluded from all or part of the proceedings and to prepare a further document setting out the reasons for its order, or a further reasoned judgment, but with the omission of such reasons as are specified in the direction; or

(b) direct the Appeal Tribunal that the document containing its reasons for any order or its reasoned judgment shall not be disclosed to any person who was excluded from all or part of the proceedings, but that no further document setting out the Appeal Tribunal's reasons for its order or further reasoned judgment should be prepared.

(4) Where the Minister has directed the Appeal Tribunal in accordance with paragraph (3)(a), the document prepared pursuant to that direction shall be marked in each place where an omission has been made. The document may then be given by the Registrar to the parties.

(5) The Registrar shall send the document prepared pursuant to a direction of the Minister in accordance with paragraph (3)(a) and the full document without the omissions made pursuant to that direction—

(a) to whichever of the appellant and the respondent was not the [claimant] in the proceedings before the employment tribunal;
(b) if he was not an excluded person, to the person who was the [claimant] in the proceedings before the employment tribunal and, if he was not an excluded person, to his representative;
(c) if applicable, to the special advocate; and
(d) where there are proceedings before a superior court relating to the order in question, to that court.

(6) Where the Appeal Tribunal intends to take steps under rule 30A(2)(c) to keep secret all or part of the reasons for any order it makes, it shall send the full reasons for its order to the persons listed in sub-paragraphs (a) to (d) of paragraph (5), as appropriate.]

[2225]

NOTES

Inserted by the Employment Appeal Tribunal (Amendment) Rules 2001, SI 2001/1128, r 21, in relation to all proceedings irrespective of when those proceedings were commenced.

Para (5): words in square brackets in sub-paras (a), (b) substituted by the Employment Appeal Tribunal (Amendment) Rules 2004, SI 2004/2526, r 16, as from 1 October 2004.

32 Registration and proof of awards in respect of exclusion or expulsion from, or unjustifiable discipline by, a trade union

(1) This rule applies where an application has been made to the Appeal Tribunal under section 67 or 176 of the 1992 Act.

(2) Without prejudice to rule 31, where the Appeal Tribunal makes an order in respect of an application to which this rule applies, and that order—
(a) makes an award of compensation, or
(b) is or includes an order of the kind referred to in rule 8(b)(ii),

or both, the Registrar shall as soon as may be enter a copy of the order, sealed with the seal of the Tribunal, into a register kept by the Tribunal (in this rule referred to as "the Register").

(3) The production in any proceedings in any court of a document, purporting to be certified by the Registrar to be a true copy of an entry in the Register of an order to which this rule applies shall, unless the contrary is proved, be sufficient evidence of the document and of the facts stated therein.

[2226]

33 Review of decisions and correction of errors

(1) The Appeal Tribunal may, either of its own motion or on application, review any order made by it and may, on such review, revoke or vary that order on the grounds that—
(a) the order was wrongly made as the result of an error on the part of the Tribunal or its staff;
(b) a party did not receive proper notice of the proceedings leading to the order; or
(c) the interests of justice require such review.

(2) An application under paragraph (1) above shall be made within 14 days of the date of the order.

(3) A clerical mistake in any order arising from an accidental slip or omission may at any time be corrected by, or on the authority of, a judge or member.

[(4) The decision to grant or refuse an application for review may be made by a judge.]

[2227]

NOTES

Para (4): added by the Employment Appeal Tribunal (Amendment) Rules 2004, SI 2004/2526, r 19, as from 1 October 2004.

[34 General power to make costs or expenses orders

(1) In the circumstances listed in rule 34A the Appeal Tribunal may make an order ("a costs order") that a party or a special advocate, ("the paying party") make a payment in respect of the costs incurred by another party or a special advocate ("the receiving party").

(2) For the purposes of these Rules "costs" includes fees, charges, disbursements and expenses incurred by or on behalf of a party or special advocate in relation to the proceedings, including the reimbursement allowed to a litigant in person under rule 34D. In Scotland, all references to costs or costs orders (except in the expression "wasted costs") shall be read as references to expenses or orders for expenses.

(3) A costs order may be made against or in favour of a respondent who has not had an answer accepted in the proceedings in relation to the conduct of any part which he has taken in the proceedings.

(4) A party or special advocate may apply to the Appeal Tribunal for a costs order to be made at any time during the proceedings. An application may also be made at the end of a hearing, or in writing to the Registrar within 14 days of the date on which the order of the Appeal Tribunal finally disposing of the proceedings was sent to the parties.

(5) No costs order shall be made unless the Registrar has sent notice to the party or special advocate against whom the order may be made giving him the opportunity to give reasons why the order should not be made. This paragraph shall not be taken to require the Registrar to send notice to the party or special advocate if the party or special advocate has been given an opportunity to give reasons orally to the Appeal Tribunal as to why the order should not be made.

(6) Where the Appeal Tribunal makes a costs order it shall provide written reasons for doing so if a request for written reasons is made within 21 days of the date of the costs order. The Registrar shall send a copy of the written reasons to all the parties to the proceedings.]

[2228]

NOTES

Commencement: 1 October 2004.

Substituted by the Employment Appeal Tribunal (Amendment) Rules 2004, SI 2004/2526, r 20, as from 1 October 2004.

[34A When a costs or expenses order may be made

(1) Where it appears to the Appeal Tribunal that any proceedings brought by the paying party were unnecessary, improper, vexatious or misconceived or that there has been unreasonable delay or other unreasonable conduct in the bringing or conducting of proceedings by the paying party, the Appeal Tribunal may make a costs order against the paying party.

(2) The Appeal Tribunal may in particular make a costs order against the paying party when—

(a) he has not complied with a direction of the Appeal Tribunal;
(b) he has amended its notice of appeal, document provided under rule 3 sub-paragraphs (5) or (6), Respondent's answer or statement of grounds of cross-appeal, or document provided under rule 6 sub-paragraphs (7) or (8); or
(c) he has caused an adjournment of proceedings.

(3) Nothing in paragraph (2) shall restrict the Appeal Tribunal's discretion to award costs under paragraph (1).]

[2228A]

NOTES

Commencement: 1 October 2004.

Inserted, together with rr 34B–34D, by the Employment Appeal Tribunal (Amendment) Rules 2004, SI 2004/2526, r 21, as from 1 October 2004. This rule, and rr 34B, 34D, apply irrespective of when the proceedings in the Appeal Tribunal were commenced.

[34B The amount of a costs or expenses order

(1) Subject to sub-paragraphs (2) and (3) the amount of a costs order against the paying party can be determined in the following ways:

(a) the Appeal Tribunal may specify the sum which the paying party must pay to the receiving party;
(b) the parties may agree on a sum to be paid by the paying party to the receiving party and if they do so the costs order shall be for the sum agreed; or
(c) the Appeal Tribunal may order the paying party to pay the receiving party the

whole or a specified part of the costs of the receiving party with the amount to be paid being determined by way of detailed assessment in the High Court in accordance with the Civil Procedure Rules 1998 or in Scotland the Appeal Tribunal may direct that it be taxed by the Auditor of the Court of Session, from whose decision an appeal shall lie to a judge.

(2) The Appeal Tribunal may have regard to the paying party's ability to pay when considering the amount of a costs order.

(3) The costs of an assisted person in England and Wales shall be determined by detailed assessment in accordance with the Civil Procedure Rules.]

[2228B]

NOTES

Commencement: 1 October 2004.
Inserted as noted to r 34A at **[2228A]**.

[34C Personal liability of representatives for costs

(1) The Appeal Tribunal may make a wasted costs order against a party's representative.

(2) In a wasted costs order the Appeal Tribunal may disallow or order the representative of a party to meet the whole or part of any wasted costs of any party, including an order that the representative repay to his client any costs which have already been paid.

(3) "Wasted costs" means any costs incurred by a party (including the representative's own client and any party who does not have a legal representative):

(a) as a result of any improper, unreasonable or negligent act or omission on the part of any representative; or

(b) which, in the light of any such act or omission occurring after they were incurred, the Appeal Tribunal considers it reasonable to expect that party to pay.

(4) In this rule "representative" means a party's legal or other representative or any employee of such representative, but it does not include a representative who is not acting in pursuit of profit with regard to the proceedings. A person is considered to be acting in pursuit of profit if he is acting on a conditional fee arrangement.

(5) Before making a wasted costs order, the Appeal Tribunal shall give the representative a reasonable opportunity to make oral or written representations as to reasons why such an order should not be made. The Appeal Tribunal may also have regard to the representative's ability to pay when considering whether it shall make a wasted costs order or how much that order should be.

(6) When the Appeal Tribunal makes a wasted costs order, it must specify in the order the amount to be disallowed or paid.

(7) The Registrar shall inform the representative's client in writing—

(a) of any proceedings under this rule; or

(b) of any order made under this rule against the party's representative.

(8) Where the Appeal Tribunal makes a wasted costs order it shall provide written reasons for doing so if a request is made for written reasons within 21 days of the date of the wasted costs order. The Registrar shall send a copy of the written reasons to all parties to the proceedings.]

[2228C]

NOTES

Commencement: 1 October 2004.
Inserted as noted to r 34A at **[2228A]**. This rule does not apply to proceedings in the Appeal Tribunal which were commenced before 1 October 2004 (see SI 2004/2526, r 26(2)).

[34D Litigants in person and party litigants

(1) This rule applies where the Appeal Tribunal makes a costs order in favour of a party who is a litigant in person.

(2) The costs allowed under this rule must not exceed, except in the case of a disbursement, two-thirds of the amount which would have been allowed if the litigant in person had been represented by a legal representative.

(3) The litigant in person shall be allowed—

(a) costs for the same categories of—

(i) work; and

(ii) disbursements,

which would have been allowed if the work had been done or the disbursements had been made by a legal representative on the litigant in person's behalf;

(b) the payments reasonably made by him for legal services relating to the conduct of the proceedings;

(c) the costs of obtaining expert assistance in assessing the costs claim; and

(d) other expenses incurred by him in relation to the proceedings.

(4) The amount of costs to be allowed to the litigant in person for any item of work claimed shall be—

(a) where the litigant in person can prove financial loss, the amount that he can prove he had lost for the time reasonably spent on doing the work; or

(b) where the litigant in person cannot prove financial loss, an amount for the time which the Tribunal considers reasonably spent on doing the work at the rate of £25.00 per hour;

(5) For the year commencing 6th April 2006 the hourly rate of £25.00 shall be increased by the sum of £1.00 and for each subsequent year commencing on 6 April, the hourly rate for the previous year shall also be increased by the sum of £1.00.

(6) A litigant in person who is allowed costs for attending at court to conduct his case is not entitled to a witness allowance in respect of such attendance in addition to those costs.

(7) For the purpose of this rule, a litigant in person includes—

(a) a company or other corporation which is acting without a legal representative; and

(b) in England and Wales a barrister, solicitor, solicitor's employee or other authorised litigator (as defined in the Courts and Legal Services Act), who is acting for himself; and

(c) in Scotland, an advocate or solicitor (within the meaning of the Solicitors (Scotland) Act 1980) who is acting for himself.

(8) In the application of this rule to Scotland, references to a litigant in person shall be read as references to a party litigant.]

[2228D]

NOTES

Commencement: 1 October 2004.

Inserted as noted to r 34A at **[2228A]**.

35 Service of documents

(1) Any notice or other document required or authorised by these Rules to be served on, or delivered to, any person may be sent to him by post to his address for service or, where no address for service has been given, to his registered office, principal place of business, head or main office or last known address, as the case may be, and any notice or other document required or authorised to be served on, or delivered to, the Appeal Tribunal may be sent by post or delivered to the Registrar—

(a) in the case of a notice instituting proceedings, at the central office or any other office of the Tribunal; or

(b) in any other case, at the office of the Tribunal in which the proceedings in question are being dealt with in accordance with rule 38(2).

(2) Any notice or other document required or authorised to be served on, or delivered to, an unincorporated body may be sent to its secretary, manager or other similar officer.

(3) Every document served by post shall be assumed, in the absence of evidence to the contrary, to have been delivered in the normal course of post.

(4) The Appeal Tribunal may inform itself in such manner as it thinks fit of the posting of any document by an officer of the Tribunal.

(5) The Appeal Tribunal may direct that service of any document be dispensed with or be effected otherwise than in the manner prescribed by these Rules.

[2229]

36 Conciliation

Where at any stage of any proceedings it appears to the Appeal Tribunal that there is a reasonable prospect of agreement being reached between the parties [or of disposal of the appeal or a part of it by consensual means], the Tribunal may take such steps as it thinks fit to enable the parties to avail themselves of any opportunities for conciliation, whether by adjourning any proceedings or otherwise.

[2230]

NOTES

Words in square brackets inserted by the Employment Appeal Tribunal (Amendment) Rules 2004, SI 2004/2526, r 22, as from 1 October 2004.

37 Time

(1) The time prescribed by these Rules or by order of the Appeal Tribunal for doing any act may be extended (whether it has already expired or not) or abridged, and the date appointed for any purpose may be altered, by order of the Tribunal.

[(1A) Where an act is required to be done on or before a particular day it shall be done by 4 pm on that day.]

(2) Where the last day for the doing of any act falls on a day on which the appropriate office of the Tribunal is closed and by reason thereof the act cannot be done on that day, it may be done on the next day on which that office is open.

(3) An application for an extension of the time prescribed for the doing of an act, including the institution of an appeal under rule 3, shall be heard and determined as an [interim] application under rule 20.

[(4) An application for an extension of the time prescribed for the institution of an appeal under rule 3 shall not be heard until the notice of the appeal has been served on the Appeal Tribunal.]

[2231]

NOTES

Para (1A): inserted by the Employment Appeal Tribunal (Amendment) Rules 2004, SI 2004/2526, r 23(1), as from 1 October 2004.

Para (3): word in square brackets substituted by SI 2004/2526, r 23(2), as from 1 October 2004.

Para (4): added by the Employment Appeal Tribunal (Amendment) Rules 2001, SI 2001/1128, r 23, in relation to all proceedings irrespective of when those proceedings were commenced.

38 Tribunal offices and allocation of business

(1) The central office and any other office of the Appeal Tribunal shall be open at such times as the President may direct.

(2) Any proceedings before the Tribunal may be dealt with at the central office or at such other office as the President may direct.

[2232]

39 Non-compliance with, and waiver of, rules

(1) Failure to comply with any requirements of these Rules shall not invalidate any proceedings unless the Appeal Tribunal otherwise directs.

(2) The Tribunal may, if it considers that to do so would lead to the more expeditious or economical disposal of any proceedings or would otherwise be desirable in the interests of justice, dispense with the taking of any step required or authorised by these Rules, or may direct that any such steps be taken in some manner other than that prescribed by these Rules.

(3) The powers of the Tribunal under paragraph (2) extend to authorising the institution of an appeal notwithstanding that the period prescribed in rule 3(2) may not have commenced.

[2233]

40 Transitional provisions

(1) Where, prior to 16th December 1993, an [employment tribunal] has given full written reasons for its decision or order, those reasons shall be treated as extended written reasons for the purposes of rule 3(1)(c) and rule 3(2) and for the purposes of Form 1 in the Schedule to these Rules.

(2) Anything validly done under or pursuant to the Employment Appeal Tribunal Rules 1980 shall be treated as having been done validly for the purposes of these Rules, whether or not what was done could have been done under or pursuant to these Rules.

[2234]

NOTES

Para (1): words in square brackets substituted by the Employment Rights (Dispute Resolution) Act 1998, s 1(2)(a).

Employment Appeal Tribunal Rules 1980, SI 1980/2035: revoked by r 1(2) of these Rules.

SCHEDULE

[FORM 1

Rule 3

Notice of Appeal from Decision of Employment Tribunal

1. The appellant is (*name and address of appellant*).

2. Any communication relating to this appeal may be sent to the appellant at (*appellant's address for service, including telephone number if any*).

3. The appellant appeals from (*here give particulars of the judgment, decision or order of the employment tribunal from which the appeal is brought including the location of the employment tribunal and the date*).

4. The parties to the proceedings before the employment tribunal, other than the appellant, were (*name and addresses of other parties to the proceedings resulting in judgment, decision or order appealed from*).

5. Copies of—
   - (a) the written record of the employment tribunal's judgment, decision or order and the written reasons of the employment tribunal;
   - (b) the claim (ET1);
   - (c) the response (ET3); and/or (*where relevant*)
   - (d) an explanation as to why any of these documents are not included;

are attached to this notice.

6. If the appellant has made an application to the employment tribunal for a review of its judgment or decision, copies of—
   - (a) the review application;
   - (b) the judgment;
   - (c) the written reasons of the employment tribunal in respect of that review application; and /or;
   - (d) a statement by or on behalf of the appellant, if such be the case, that a judgment is awaited

are attached to this Notice. If any of these documents exist but cannot be included, then a written explanation must be given.

7. The grounds upon which this appeal is brought are that the employment tribunal erred in law in that (*here set out in paragraphs the various grounds of appeal*).

Date ....

Signed ....

NB. The details entered on your Notice of Appeal must be legible and suitable for photocopying or electronic scanning. The use of black ink or typescript is recommended.]

[2235]

NOTES

Substituted by the Employment Appeal Tribunal (Amendment) Rules 2005, SI 2005/1871, r 3(a), as from 1 October 2005.

[FORM 1A

Rule 3

Notice of Appeal from the CAC Made Pursuant to Regulation 38(8) of the Transnational Information and Consultation of Employees Regulations 1999, [… regulation 47(6) of the European Public Limited-Liability Company Regulations 2004] [… regulation 35(6) of the Information and Consultation of Employees Regulations 2004] [or regulation 57(6) of the Companies (Cross-Border Mergers) Regulations 2007]

1. The appellant is (*name and address of appellant*).

2. Any communication relating to this appeal may be sent to the appellant at (*appellant's address for service, including telephone number if any*).

3. The appellant appeals from (*here give particulars of the decision, declaration or order of the CAC from which the appeal is brought including the date*).

4. The parties to the proceedings before the CAC, other than the appellant, were (*names and addresses of other parties to the proceedings resulting in decision appealed from*).

5. A copy of the CAC's decision, declaration or order appealed from is attached to this notice.

6. The grounds upon which this appeal is brought are that the CAC erred in law in that (*here set out in paragraphs the various grounds of appeal*).

Date ....

Signed ....]

[2236]

NOTES

Inserted by the Employment Appeal Tribunal (Amendment) Rules 2001, SI 2001/1128, r 24, in relation to all proceedings irrespective of when those proceedings were commenced.

Words in first pair of square brackets in the heading inserted by the Employment Appeal Tribunal (Amendment) Rules 2004, SI 2004/2526, r 25(1), as from 1 October 2004; first word omitted from the heading revoked, and words in second pair of square brackets inserted, by the Information and Consultation of Employees Regulations 2004, SI 2004/3426, reg 41(e), as from 6 April 2005; second word omitted revoked, and words in final pair of square brackets added, by the Companies (Cross-Border Mergers) Regulations 2007, SI 2007/2974, reg 64(5), as from 15 December 2007.

FORM 2

Rule 3

Notice of Appeal from Decision of Certification Officer

1. The appellant is (*name and address of appellant*).

2. Any communication relating to this appeal may be sent to the appellant at (*appellant's address for service, including telephone number if any*).

3. The appellant appeals from

(*here give particulars of the order or decision of the Certification Officer from which the appeal is brought*).

4. The appellant's grounds of appeal are:

(*here state the grounds of appeal*).

5. A copy of the Certification Officer's decision is attached to this notice.

Date ....

Signed...

[2237]

FORM 3

Rule 6

Respondent's Answer

1. The respondent is (*name and address of respondent*).

2. Any communication relating to this appeal may be sent to the respondent at (*respondent's address for service, including telephone number if any*).

3. The respondent intends to resist the appeal of (here give the name of appellant). The grounds on which the respondent will rely are (the grounds relied upon by the [employment tribunal]/Certification Officer for making the [judgment,] decision or order appealed from) (and) (the following grounds):

(*here set out any grounds which differ from those relied upon by the [employment tribunal] or Certification Officer, as the case may be*).

4. The respondent cross-appeals from

(*here give particulars of the decision appealed from*).

5. The respondent's grounds of appeal are:

(*here state the grounds of appeal*).

Date ....

Signed...

[2238]

NOTES

Para 3: words in first and third pairs of square brackets substituted by the Employment Rights (Dispute Resolution) Act 1998, s 1(2)(a); word in second pair of square brackets inserted by the Employment Appeal Tribunal (Amendment) Rules 2005, SI 2005/1871, r 3(b)(ii), as from 1 October 2005.

FORM 4

Rule 8

Application to the Employment Appeal Tribunal for Compensation for Exclusion or Expulsion from a Trade Union or for Compensation or an Order in respect of Unjustifiable Discipline

1. My name is

My address is

2. Any communication relating to this application may be sent to me at

(*state address for service, including telephone number, if any*).

3. My complaint against (*state the name and address of the trade union*) was declared to be well-founded by (*state tribunal*) on (*give date of decision or order*).

4. (*Where the application relates to exclusion or expulsion from a trade union*) I have not been admitted/re-admitted* to membership of the above-named trade union and hereby apply for compensation on the following grounds.

(*Where the application relates to unjustifiable discipline*) The determination infringing my right not to be unjustifiably disciplined has not been revoked./ The trade union has failed to take all the steps necessary for securing the reversal of things done for the purpose of giving effect to the determination.*

(*Delete as appropriate)

Date ....

Signed...

NB.—A copy of the decision or order declaring the complaint against the trade union to be well-founded must be enclosed with this application.

[2239]

[FORM 4A

Rule 16A

Application under Regulation 20 or 21 of the Transnational Information and Consultation of Employees Regulations 1999

1. The applicant is (*name and address of applicant*).

2. Any communication relating to this application may be sent to the applicant at (*state address for service, including telephone number, if any*).

3. The application is made against (*state identity or, where applicable, identities of respondents*) who is/are, or is/are representative of, the central or local management/the European Works Council/one or more information and consultation representatives (*delete what does not apply*).

4. The address(es) of the respondent(s) is/are

5. My complaint against the respondent(s) is that it/they failed to comply with its/their obligations under regulation 20 or 21 of the Transnational Information and Consultation of Employees Regulations 1999 as follows (*give particulars, set out in paragraphs and making reference to the specific provisions in the 1999 Regulations alleged to have been breached*).

Date ....

Signed ....]

[2240]

NOTES

Inserted by the Employment Appeal Tribunal (Amendment) Rules 2001, SI 2001/1128, r 25, in relation to all proceedings irrespective of when those proceedings were commenced.

[FORM 4B

Rule 16AA

Applications under Regulation 33 of the European Public Limited–Liability Company Regulations 2004 [or regulation 22 of the Information and Consultation of Employees Regulations 2004] [or regulation 53 of the Companies (Cross-Border Mergers) Regulations 2007]

1. The applicant's name is (*name and address of applicant*)

2. Any communication relating to this application may be sent to the applicant at (*applicant's address for service, including telephone number if any*).

3. The application is made against (*state identity of respondent*)

4. The address of the respondent is

5. The Central Arbitration Committee made a declaration in my favour on [ ] (*insert date*) and I request the Employment Tribunal to issue a penalty notice in accordance with regulation 33 of the European Public Limited–Liability Company Regulations 2004 [or regulation 22 of the Information and Consultation of Employees Regulations 2004 [or regulation 53 of the Companies (Cross-Border Mergers) Regulations 2007] (*delete which does not apply*)].

Date ....

Signed ....]

[2240A]

NOTES

Commencement: 1 October 2004.

Inserted by the Employment Appeal Tribunal (Amendment) Rules 2004, SI 2004/2526, r 25(2), as from 1 October 2004.

Words in first pair of square brackets in the heading, and first (outer) pair of square brackets in para 5, inserted by the Information and Consultation of Employees Regulations 2004, SI 2004/3426, reg 41(f), as from 6 April 2005; words in second pair of square brackets in the heading, and second (inner) pair of square brackets in para 5, inserted by the Companies (Cross-Border Mergers) Regulations 2007, SI 2007/2974, reg 64(6), as from 15 December 2007.

FORM 5

Rule 11

Notice of appearance to Application to Employment Appeal Tribunal for Compensation for Exclusion or Expulsion from a Trade Union or for Compensation or an Order in respect of Unjustifiable Discipline

1. The respondent trade union is (*name and address of union*).

2. Any communication relating to this application may be sent to the respondent at (*respondent's address for service, including telephone number, if any*).

3. The respondent intends to resist the application of (*here give name of the applicant*).

The grounds on which the respondent will rely are as follows:

4. (*Where the application relates to exclusion or expulsion from the trade union, state whether or not the applicant had been admitted or re-admitted to membership on or before the date of application.*)

(*Where the application relates to unjustifiable discipline, state whether—*

(*a*) *the determination infringing the applicant's right not to be unjustifiably disciplined has been revoked; and*

(*b*) *the trade union has taken all the steps necessary for securing the reversal of anything done for the purpose of giving effect to the determination.*)

Date ....

Signed..

Position in union ....

[2241]

[FORM 5A

Rule 16C

Notice of appearance to Employment Appeal Tribunal under Regulation 20 or 21 of the Transnational Information and Consultation of Employees Regulations 1999

1. The respondent is (*name and address of respondent*).

2. Any communication relating to this application may be sent to the respondent at (*respondent's address for service, including telephone number, if any*).

3. The respondent intends to resist the application of (*here give the name or description of the applicant*).

The grounds on which the respondent will rely are as follows: (*give particulars, set out in paragraphs and making reference to the specific provisions in the Transnational Information and Consultation of Employees Regulations 1999 alleged to have been breached*).

Date ....

Signed...

Position in respondent company or undertaking:...

(*Where appropriate give position in respondent central or local management or position held in relation to respondent Works Council*).]

[2242]

NOTES

Inserted by the Employment Appeal Tribunal (Amendment) Rules 2001, SI 2001/1128, r 26, in relation to all proceedings irrespective of when those proceedings were commenced.

FORM 6

Rule 13

Application to the Employment Appeal Tribunal Under [section 33 of the 1996 Act] for a Restriction of Proceedings Order

1. The applicant is (*the Attorney General/Lord Advocate*).

2. Any communication relating to this application may be sent to the applicant at (*state address for service, including telephone number*).

3. The application is for a restriction of proceedings order to be made against (*state the name and address of the person against whom the order is sought*).

4. An affidavit in support of the application is attached.

Date ....

Signed...

[2243]

NOTES

Words in square brackets substituted by SI 2001/1128, r 27, in relation to all proceedings irrespective of when those proceedings were commenced.

FORM 7

Rule 15

Notice of appearance to Application to the Employment Appeal Tribunal under [section 33 of the 1996 Act] for a Restriction of Proceedings Order

1. The respondent is (*state name and address of respondent*).

2. Any communication relating to this application may be sent to the respondent at (*respondent's address for service, including telephone number, if any*).

3. The respondent intends to resist the application. An affidavit in support is attached to this notice.

Date ....

Signed...

[2244]

NOTES

Words in square brackets substituted by SI 2001/1128, r 27, in relation to all proceedings irrespective of when those proceedings were commenced.

REDUNDANCY PAYMENTS (NATIONAL HEALTH SERVICE) (MODIFICATION) ORDER 1993

(SI 1993/3167)

NOTES

Made: 16 December 1993.

Authority: Employment Protection (Consolidation) Act 1978, ss 149(1)(b), 154(3) (repealed). This Order now has effect as if made under the Employment Rights Act 1996, ss 209(1)(b), 236(5).

Commencement: 13 January 1994.

See *Harvey* R.

ARRANGEMENT OF ARTICLES

SCHEDULES:

1 Citation, commencement and interpretation

(1) This Order may be cited as the Redundancy Payments (National Health Service) (Modification) Order 1993 and shall come into force on 13th January 1994.

(2) In this Order, unless the context otherwise requires—

(a) "relevant event" means any event occurring on or after the coming into force of this Order on the happening of which an employee may become entitled to a redundancy payment in accordance with the provisions of the 1978 Act;

(b) "the 1978 Act" means the Employment Protection (Consolidation) Act 1978.

[2245]

NOTES

Employment Protection (Consolidation) Act 1978: repealed and largely consolidated in the Trade Union and Labour Relations (Consolidation) Act 1992, the Employment Rights Act 1996 and the Employment Tribunals Act 1996.

2 Application of order

This Order applies to any person who immediately before the occurrence of the relevant event is employed by an employer described in Schedule 1 to this Order, for the purposes of determining that person's entitlement to a redundancy payment under the 1978 Act and the amount of such payment.

[2246]

NOTES

"The 1978 Act": as to redundancy payments, etc see now the Employment Rights Act 1996, Pt XI (ss 135–181).

3 Application of certain redundancy payments provisions with modifications

In relation to any person to whom this Order applies the provisions of the 1978 Act mentioned in Schedule 2 to this Order shall have effect subject to the modifications specified in that Schedule.

[2247]

4 Transitional, supplementary and incidental provisions

(1) Any reference to the 1978 Act in any enactment shall have effect as a reference to that Act as modified by this Order in relation to persons to whom this Order applies.

(2) Any document which refers, whether specifically or by means of a general description, to an enactment which is modified by any provision of this Order shall, except so far as the context otherwise requires, be construed as referring, or as including a reference, to that provision.

(3) Where a period of employment of a person to whom this Order applies falls to be computed in accordance with the provisions of the 1978 Act as modified by this Order, the provisions of this Order shall have effect in relation to any period whether falling wholly or partly before or after the coming into force of this Order.

[2248]

SCHEDULES

SCHEDULE 1
EMPLOYMENT TO WHICH THIS ORDER APPLIES: EMPLOYERS IMMEDIATELY BEFORE THE RELEVANT EVENT

Article 2

[1. a Strategic Health Authority or Health Authority established under section 8 of the National Health Service Act 1977 ("the 1977 Act");

1A. a Special Health Authority established under section 11 of the 1977 Act;]

2. a National Health Service trust established by an order made under section 5(1) of the National Health Service and Community Care Act 1990;

[2ZA. an NHS foundation trust within the meaning of section 1(1) of the Health and Social Care (Community Health and Standards) Act 2003;]

[2A. a Primary Care Trust established under section 16A of the 1977 Act;]

3. a Family Health Services Authority (formerly called a Family Practitioner Committee) established by an order made under section 10(1) of the 1977 Act;

4. the Dental Practice Board (formerly called the Dental Estimates Board) constituted by regulations made under section 37(1) of the 1977 Act;

5. …

6. a Health Board or a special Health Board constituted under section 2(1)(a) or section 2(1)(b) respectively of the National Health Service (Scotland) Act 1978 (hereinafter in this Schedule referred to as "the 1978 Act");

7. …

8. the Common Services Agency for the Scottish Health Service established under section 10 of the 1978 Act;

9. a National Health Service trust established under section 12A(1) of the 1978 Act;

10. the Scottish Dental Practice Board (formerly called the Scottish Dental Estimates Board) constituted by regulations made under section 4 of the 1978 Act.

[2249]

NOTES

Paras 1, 1A: substituted, for original para 1, by the National Health Service Reform and Health Care Professions Act 2002 (Supplementary, Consequential etc Provisions) Regulations 2002, SI 2002/2469, reg 4, Sch 1, Pt 2, para 61.

Para 2ZA: inserted by the Health and Social Care (Community Health and Standards) Act 2003 (Supplementary and Consequential Provision) (NHS Foundation Trusts) Order 2004, SI 2004/696, art 3(1), Sch 1, para 14, as from 1 April 2004.

Para 2A: inserted by the Health Act 1999 (Supplementary, Consequential etc Provisions) (No 2) Order 2000, SI 2000/694, art 3, Schedule, Pt II, para 6.

Para 5: revoked by the Health and Social Care (Community Health and Standards) Act 2003 (Public Health Laboratory Service Board) (Consequential Provisions) Order 2005, SI 2005/1622, art 3, Schedule, as from 15 July 2005.

Para 7: revoked by the Mental Health (Care and Treatment) (Scotland) Act 2003 (Consequential Provisions) Order 2005, SI 2005/2078, art 15, Sch 2, para 16 (in relation to England and Wales), as from 5 October 2005, and by the Mental Health (Care and Treatment) (Scotland) Act 2003 (Modification of Subordinate Legislation) Order 2005, SSI 2005/445, art 2, Schedule, para 20 (in relation to Scotland), as from the same date.

SCHEDULE 2
MODIFICATIONS TO CERTAIN REDUNDANCY PAYMENTS PROVISIONS OF THE 1978 ACT

Article 3

1. Section 81 of the 1978 Act shall have effect as if:—
   (a) in subsection (1) for the words "has been continuously employed for the requisite period" there were substituted the words "has been employed in relevant health service for the requisite period" and for the words "Schedules 4, 13 and 14" there were substituted the words "Schedule 4, as modified by the Redundancy Payments (National Health Service) (Modification) Order 1993, and Schedules 13 and 14";
   (b) after subsection (4) there were inserted the following subsection:—
   "(5) In this section and Schedule 4—
   (a) "relevant health service" means—
   (i) continuous employment by an employer referred to in the Appendix to Schedule 2 to the Redundancy Payments (National Health Service) (Modification) Order 1993, or
   (ii) where immediately before the relevant event a person has been successively employed by two or more employers referred to in the Appendix to Schedule 2 to the said Order, such aggregate period of service with such employers as would be continuous employment if they were a single employer;
   (b) "relevant event" means any event occurring on or after the coming into force of the Redundancy Payments (National Health Service) (Modification) Order 1993 on the happening of which an employee may become entitled to a redundancy payment in accordance with this Act.".

2. Section 82 of the 1978 Act shall have effect as if immediately after subsection (7) there were inserted—

   "(7A) Any reference in this section to re-engagement by the employer shall be construed as including a reference to re-engagement by any employer referred to in the Appendix to Schedule 2 to the Redundancy Payments (National Health Service) (Modification) Order 1993 and any reference in this section to an offer by the employer shall be construed as including a reference to an offer made by any such employer."

3. Section 84 of the 1978 Act shall have effect as if immediately after subsection (7) thereof there were inserted the following subsection—

   "(7A) Any reference in this section to re-engagement by the employer shall be construed as including a reference to re-engagement by any employer referred to in the Appendix to Schedule 2 to the Redundancy Payments (National Health Service) (Modification) Order 1993 and any reference in this section to an offer made by the employer shall be construed as including a reference to an offer made by any such employer."

4. Schedule 4 to the 1978 Act shall have effect as if for paragraph 1 there were substituted the following paragraph—

"1. The amount of a redundancy payment to which an employee is entitled in any case to which the Redundancy Payments (National Health Service) (Modification) Order 1993 applies shall, subject to the following provisions of this Schedule, be calculated by reference to the period ending with the relevant date during which he has been employed in relevant health service."

5. Schedule 6 to the 1978 Act shall have effect as if in paragraph 1 for the words "Schedule 4" there were substituted the words "Schedule 4 as modified by the Redundancy Payments (National Health Service) (Modification) Order 1993".

[2250]

NOTES

"The 1978 Act": for provisions as to redundancy payments, etc see now the Employment Rights Act 1996, Pt XI (ss 135–181). The equivalent provisions in the 1996 Act to those referred to are: s 81(1) and (4): now ss 135, 155, 162(1), (2), and 155 respectively, of the 1996 Act; s 82(7): now s 146(1); s 84(7): now s 146(1); Sch 4, para 1: now s 162(1); Sch 6: repealed by the Employment Act 1989, s 17, Sch 7.

APPENDIX
EMPLOYERS WITH WHICH EMPLOYMENT MAY CONSTITUTE RELEVANT HEALTH SERVICE

Any employer described in Schedule 1 whether or not in existence at the time of the relevant event.

[2251]

[EMPLOYMENT TRIBUNALS] EXTENSION OF JURISDICTION (ENGLAND AND WALES) ORDER 1994

(SI 1994/1623)

NOTES

Made: 11 July 1994.

Authority: Employment Protection (Consolidation) Act 1978, ss 131(1), (4A), (5), (5A), 154(3) (repealed). This Order now has effect as if made under the Employment Tribunals Act 1996, ss 3(1), 8(2)–(4), 41(4).

Commencement: 12 July 1994.

Title: words in square brackets substituted by the Employment Rights (Dispute Resolution) Act 1998, s 1(2)(b).

This Order applies only to England and Wales. For the equivalent Scottish Order, see the Employment Tribunals Extension of Jurisdiction (Scotland) Order 1994, SI 1994/1624 at **[2262]**.

Tribunal jurisdiction: the Employment Act 2002, ss 31, 38, at **[1493]**, **[1496]** apply to proceedings before the employment tribunal relating to a claim under this Order; see ss 31(1), 38(1) of, and Schs 3, 5 to, the 2002 Act at **[1508]**, **[1510]**. Note, however, that s 32 of the 2002 Act does not apply to such proceedings; see Sch 4 to the 2002 Act at **[1509]**.

Conciliation: proceedings in respect of which an employment tribunal has jurisdiction by virtue of the Employment Tribunals Act 1996, s 3 are proceedings to which s 18 of that Act applies; see s 18(1)(e) at **[975]**. The short conciliation period applies to such proceedings by virtue of the Employment Tribunals (Constitution and Rules of Procedure) Regulations 2004, SI 2004/1861, Sch 1, rule 22(5).

For the circumstances in which the normal time limit for presenting complaints under this Order is extended for a period of three months, see the Employment Act 2002 (Dispute Resolution) Regulations 2004, SI 2004/752, regs 15 and 18 at **[3096]** and **[3098]**, and art 7(ba) of this Order at **[2258]**.

See *Harvey* T(A), U2.

ARRANGEMENT OF ARTICLES

1 Citation, commencement and interpretation

(1) This Order may be cited as the [Employment Tribunals] Extension of Jurisdiction (England and Wales) Order 1994 and comes into force on the first day after it is made.

(2) In this Order—

"contract claim" means a claim in respect of which proceedings may be brought before an [employment tribunal] by virtue of article 3 or 4; and

"the 1978 Act" means the Employment Protection (Consolidation) Act 1978.

[2252]

NOTES

Words in square brackets substituted by the Employment Rights (Dispute Resolution) Act 1998, s 1(2)(a), (b).

Employment Protection (Consolidation) Act 1978: repealed and largely consolidated in the Trade Union and Labour Relations (Consolidation) Act 1992, the Employment Rights Act 1996 and the Employment Tribunals Act 1996.

2 Transitional provision

This Order does not enable proceedings in respect of a contract claim to be brought before an [employment tribunal] unless—

(a) the effective date of termination (as defined in section 55(4) of the 1978 Act) in respect of the contract giving rise to the claim, or

(b) where there is no effective date of termination, the last day upon which the employee works in the employment which has terminated,

occurs on or after the day on which the Order comes into force.

[2253]

NOTES

Words in square brackets substituted by the Employment Rights (Dispute Resolution) Act 1998, s 1(2)(a).

"Section 55(4) of the 1978 Act": see now the Employment Rights Act 1996, s 97(1).

3 Extension of jurisdiction

Proceedings may be brought before an [employment tribunal] in respect of a claim of an employee for the recovery of damages or any other sum (other than a claim for damages, or for a sum due, in respect of personal injuries) if—

(a) the claim is one to which section 131(2) of the 1978 Act applies and which a court in England and Wales would under the law for the time being in force have jurisdiction to hear and determine;

(b) the claim is not one to which article 5 applies; and

(c) the claim arises or is outstanding on the termination of the employee's employment.

[2254]

NOTES

Words in square brackets substituted by the Employment Rights (Dispute Resolution) Act 1998, s 1(2)(a).

"Section 131(2) of the 1978 Act": see now the Employment Tribunals Act 1996, s 3(2).

4 Proceedings may be brought before an [employment tribunal] in respect of a claim of an employer for the recovery of damages or any other sum (other than a claim for damages, or for a sum due, in respect of personal injuries) if—

(a) the claim is one to which section 131(2) of the 1978 Act applies and which a court in England and Wales would under the law for the time being in force have jurisdiction to hear and determine;

(b) the claim is not one to which article 5 applies;

(c) the claim arises or is outstanding on the termination of the employment of the employee against whom it is made; and

(d) proceedings in respect of a claim of that employee have been brought before an [employment tribunal] by virtue of this Order.

[2255]

NOTES

Words in square brackets substituted by the Employment Rights (Dispute Resolution) Act 1998, s 1(2)(a).

"Section 131(2) of the 1978 Act": see now the Employment Tribunals Act 1996, s 3(2).

5 This article applies to a claim for breach of a contractual term of any of the following descriptions—

(a) a term requiring the employer to provide living accommodation for the employee;
(b) a term imposing an obligation on the employer or the employee in connection with the provision of living accommodation;
(c) a term relating to intellectual property;
(d) a term imposing an obligation of confidence;
(e) a term which is a covenant in restraint of trade.

In this article, "intellectual property" includes copyright, rights in performances, moral rights, design right, registered designs, patents and trade marks.

[2256]

6 Manner in which proceedings may be brought

Proceedings on a contract claim may be brought before an [employment tribunal] by presenting a complaint to an [employment tribunal].

[2257]

NOTES

Words in square brackets substituted by the Employment Rights (Dispute Resolution) Act 1998, s 1(2)(a).

7 Time within which proceedings may be brought

An [employment tribunal] shall not entertain a complaint in respect of an employee's contract claim unless it is presented—

(a) within the period of three months beginning with the effective date of termination of the contract giving rise to the claim, or
(b) where there is no effective date of termination, within the period of three months beginning with the last day upon which the employee worked in the employment which has terminated, or
[(ba) where the period within which a complaint must be presented in accordance with paragraph (a) or (b) is extended by regulation 15 of the Employment Act 2002 (Dispute Resolution) Regulations 2004, the period within which the complaint must be presented shall be the extended period rather than the period in paragraph (a) or (b)],
(c) where the tribunal is satisfied that it was not reasonably practicable for the complaint to be presented within whichever of those periods is applicable, within such further period as the tribunal considers reasonable.

[2258]

NOTES

Words in first pair of square brackets substituted by the Employment Rights (Dispute Resolution) Act 1998, s 1(2)(a); para (ba) inserted by the Employment Act 2002 (Dispute Resolution) Regulations 2004, SI 2004/752, reg 17(c), as from 1 October 2004 (for transitional provisions and effect see reg 18 at **[3098]**). See also the note below.

Note: the text of this provision has been changed following the comments of Underhill J in *HM Prison Service v Barua* [2007] IRLR 4. In setting out this article in the text of his judgment, Underhill J commented—

"I have reproduced this as it appears in Butterworths Employment Law Handbook, but it is in fact unclear whether the "or" at the end of para (ba) should not appear at the end of para (b) instead; reg 17(c) of the 2004 Regulations, which inserts para (ba) into the 1994 Order, is arguably ambiguous on this point. Either way, however, although the lay-out is clumsy it is clear that para (ba) is intended as a qualification to paras (a) and (b)".

Accordingly, the "or" that followed para (ba) of this article in the fourteenth edition of this work has been moved to the end of para (b).

8 An [employment tribunal] shall not entertain a complaint in respect of an employer's contract claim unless—

(a) it is presented at a time when there is before the tribunal a complaint in respect of a contract claim of a particular employee which has not been settled or withdrawn;
(b) it arises out of a contract with that employee; and
(c) it is presented—
  (i) within the period of six weeks beginning with the day, or if more than one the last of the days, on which the employer (or other person who is the respondent party to the employee's contract claim) received from the tribunal a copy of an originating application in respect of a contract claim of that employee; or
  (ii) where the tribunal is satisfied that it was not reasonably practicable for the complaint to be presented within that period, within such further period as the tribunal considers reasonable.

[2259]

NOTES

Words in square brackets substituted by the Employment Rights (Dispute Resolution) Act 1998, s 1(2)(a).

9 Death and bankruptcy

(1) Where proceedings in respect of a contract claim have been brought before an [employment tribunal] and an employee or employer party to them dies before their conclusion, the proceedings shall not abate by reason of the death and the tribunal may, if it thinks it necessary in order to ensure that all matters in dispute may be effectually and completely determined and adjudicated upon, order the personal representatives of the deceased party, or other persons whom the tribunal considers appropriate, to be made parties and the proceedings to be carried on as if they had been substituted for the deceased party.

(2) Where proceedings in respect of a contract claim have been brought before an [employment tribunal] and the employee or employer who is the applicant party to them becomes bankrupt before their conclusion, the proceedings shall not abate by reason of the bankruptcy and the tribunal may, if it thinks it necessary in order to ensure that all matters in dispute may be effectually and completely adjudicated upon, order the person in whom the interest of the bankrupt party has vested to be made a party and the proceedings to be carried on as if he had been substituted for the bankrupt party.

[2260]

NOTES

Words in square brackets substituted by the Employment Rights (Dispute Resolution) Act 1998, s 1(2)(a).

10 Limit on payment to be ordered

An [employment tribunal] shall not in proceedings in respect of a contract claim, or in respect of a number of contract claims relating to the same contract, order the payment of an amount exceeding £25,000.

[2261]

NOTES

Words in square brackets substituted by the Employment Rights (Dispute Resolution) Act 1998, s 1(2)(a).

[EMPLOYMENT TRIBUNALS] EXTENSION OF JURISDICTION (SCOTLAND) ORDER 1994

(SI 1994/1624)

NOTES

Made: 11 July 1994.

Authority: Employment Protection (Consolidation) Act 1978, ss 131(1), (4A), (5), (5A), 154(3) (repealed). This Order now has effect as if made under the Employment Tribunals Act 1996, ss 3(1), 8(2)–(4), 41(4).

Commencement: 12 July 1994.

Title: words in square brackets substituted by the Employment Rights (Dispute Resolution) Act 1998, s 1(2)(b).

This Order applies only to Scotland. For the equivalent Order applying to England and Wales, see the Employment Tribunals Extension of Jurisdiction (England and Wales) Order 1994, SI 1994/1623 at **[2252]**.

Tribunal jurisdiction: the Employment Act 2002, ss 31, 38 at **[1493]**, **[1496]** apply to proceedings before the employment tribunal relating to a claim under this Order; see ss 31(1), 38(1) of, and Schs 3, 5 to, the 2002 Act at **[1508]**, **[1510]**. Note, however, that s 32 of the 2002 Act does not apply to such proceedings; see Sch 4 to the 2002 Act at **[1509]**.

Conciliation: proceedings in respect of which an employment tribunal has jurisdiction by virtue of the Employment Tribunals Act 1996, s 3 are proceedings to which s 18 of that Act applies; see s 18(1)(e) at **[975]**. The short conciliation period applies to such proceedings by virtue of the Employment Tribunals (Constitution and Rules of Procedure) Regulations 2004, SI 2004/1861, Sch 1, rule 22(5).

For the circumstances in which the normal time limit for presenting complaints under this Order is extended for a period of three months, see the Employment Act 2002 (Dispute Resolution) Regulations 2004, SI 2004/752, regs 15 and 18 at **[3096]** and **[3098]**, and art 7(ba) of this Order at **[2268]**.

See *Harvey* T(A), U2.

ARRANGEMENT OF ARTICLES

1 Citation, commencement and interpretation

(1) This Order may be cited as the [Employment Tribunals] Extension of Jurisdiction (Scotland) Order 1994 and comes into force on the first day after it is made.

(2) In this Order—

"contract claim" means a claim in respect of which proceedings may be brought before an [employment tribunal] by virtue of article 3 or 4; and

"the 1978 Act" means the Employment Protection (Consolidation) Act 1978.

[2262]

NOTES

Words in square brackets substituted by the Employment Rights (Dispute Resolution) Act 1998, s 1(2)(a), (b).

Employment Protection (Consolidation) Act 1978: repealed and largely consolidated in the Trade Union and Labour Relations (Consolidation) Act 1992, the Employment Rights Act 1996 and the Employment Tribunals Act 1996.

2 Transitional provision

This Order does not enable proceedings in respect of a contract claim to be brought before an [employment tribunal] unless—

(a) the effective date of termination (as defined in section 55(4) of the 1978 Act) in respect of the contract giving rise to the claim, or

(b) where there is no effective date of termination, the last day upon which the employee works in the employment which has terminated,

occurs on or after the day on which the Order comes into force.

[2263]

NOTES

Words in square brackets substituted by the Employment Rights (Dispute Resolution) Act 1998, s 1(2)(a).

"Section 55(4) of the 1978 Act": see now the Employment Rights Act 1996, s 97(1).

3 Extension of jurisdiction

Proceedings may be brought before an [employment tribunal] in respect of a claim of an employee for the recovery of damages or any other sum (other than a claim for damages, or for a sum due, in respect of personal injuries) if—

(a) the claim is one to which section 131(2) of the 1978 Act applies and which a court in Scotland would under the law for the time being in force have jurisdiction to hear and determine;
(b) the claim is not one to which article 5 applies; and
(c) the claim arises or is outstanding on the termination of the employee's employment.

[2264]

NOTES

Words in square brackets substituted by the Employment Rights (Dispute Resolution) Act 1998, s 1(2)(a).

"Section 131(2) of the 1978 Act": see now the Employment Tribunals Act 1996, s 3(2).

4 Proceedings may be brought before an [employment tribunal] in respect of a claim of an employer for the recovery of damages or any other sum (other than a claim for damages, or for a sum due, in respect of personal injuries) if—

(a) the claim is one to which section 131(2) of the 1978 Act applies and which a court in Scotland would under the law for the time being in force have jurisdiction to hear and determine;
(b) the claim is not one to which article 5 applies;
(c) the claim arises or is outstanding on the termination of the employment of the employee against whom it is made; and
(d) proceedings in respect of a claim of that employee have been brought before an [employment tribunal] by virtue of this Order.

[2265]

NOTES

Words in square brackets substituted by the Employment Rights (Dispute Resolution) Act 1998, s 1(2)(a).

"Section 131(2) of the 1978 Act": see now the Employment Tribunals Act 1996, s 3(2).

5 This article applies to a claim for breach of a contractual term of any of the following descriptions—

(a) a term requiring the employer to provide living accommodation for the employee;
(b) a term imposing an obligation on the employer or the employee in connection with the provision of living accommodation;
(c) a term relating to intellectual property;
(d) a term imposing an obligation of confidence;
(e) a term which is a covenant in restraint of trade.

In this article, "intellectual property" includes copyright, rights in performances, moral rights, design right, registered designs, patents and trade marks.

[2266]

6 Manner in which proceedings may be brought

Proceedings on a contract claim may be brought before an [employment tribunal] by presenting a complaint to an [employment tribunal].

[2267]

NOTES

Words in square brackets substituted by the Employment Rights (Dispute Resolution) Act 1998, s 1(2)(a).

7 Time within which proceedings may be brought

An [employment tribunal] shall not entertain a complaint in respect of an employee's contract claim unless it is presented—

(a) within the period of three months beginning with the effective date of termination of the contract giving rise to the claim, or
(b) where there is no effective date of termination, within the period of three months beginning with the last day upon which the employee worked in the employment which has terminated, or
[(ba) where the period within which a complaint must be presented in accordance with

paragraph (a) or (b) is extended by regulation 15 of the Employment Act 2002 (Dispute Resolution) Regulations 2004, the period within which the complaint must be presented shall be the extended period rather than the period in paragraph (a) or (b),]

(c) where the tribunal is satisfied that it was not reasonably practicable for the complaint to be presented within whichever of those periods is applicable, within such further period as the tribunal considers reasonable.

[2268]

NOTES

Words in first pair of square brackets substituted by the Employment Rights (Dispute Resolution) Act 1998, s 1(2)(a); para (ba) inserted by the Employment Act 2002 (Dispute Resolution) Regulations 2004, SI 2004/752, reg 17(d), as from 1 October 2004 (for transitional provisions and effect see reg 18 at **[3098]**).

See also the comments of Underhill J as set out in the notes to art 7 of the English equivalent of this article at **[2258]**. Those comments are equally applicable here and the word "or" has been moved accordingly.

8 An [employment tribunal] shall not entertain a complaint in respect of an employer's contract claim unless—

(a) it is presented at a time when there is before the tribunal a complaint in respect of a contract claim of a particular employee which has not been settled or withdrawn;

(b) it arises out of a contract with that employee; and

(c) it is presented—

   (i) within the period of six weeks beginning with the day, or if more than one the last of the days, on which the employer (or other person who is the respondent party to the employee's contract claim) received from the tribunal a copy of an originating application in respect of a contract claim of that employee; or

   (ii) where the tribunal is satisfied that it was not reasonably practicable for the complaint to be presented within that period, within such further period as the tribunal considers reasonable.

[2269]

NOTES

Words in square brackets substituted by the Employment Rights (Dispute Resolution) Act 1998, s 1(2)(a).

9 Death and legal incapacity

Where proceedings in respect of a contract claim have been brought before an [employment tribunal] and an employee or employer party to them dies or comes under legal incapacity before the conclusion of the proceedings, the tribunal may order any person who represents that party or his estate to be made a party to the proceedings in place of the party who has died or come under legal incapacity and the proceedings to be carried on accordingly.

[2270]

NOTES

Words in square brackets substituted by the Employment Rights (Dispute Resolution) Act 1998, s 1(2)(a).

10 Limit on payment to be ordered

An [employment tribunal] shall not in proceedings in respect of a contract claim, or in respect of a number of contract claims relating to the same contract, order the payment of an amount exceeding £25,000.

[2271]

NOTES

Words in square brackets substituted by the Employment Rights (Dispute Resolution) Act 1998, s 1(2)(a).

STATUTORY MATERNITY PAY (COMPENSATION OF EMPLOYERS) AND MISCELLANEOUS AMENDMENT REGULATIONS 1994 (NOTE)

(SI 1994/1882)

NOTES

These Regulations, which were reproduced in the fifteenth edition of this work, have been omitted for reasons of space.

The Regulations are printed in *Harvey* at **R[817]**.

[2272]–[2280]

STATUTORY SICK PAY PERCENTAGE THRESHOLD ORDER 1995 (NOTE)

(SI 1995/512)

NOTES

This Order, which was reproduced in the fifteenth edition of this work, has been omitted for reasons of space.

The Order is printed in *Harvey* at **R[845]**.

[2281]–[2284]

PERSONAL AND OCCUPATIONAL PENSION SCHEMES (PENSIONS OMBUDSMAN) (PROCEDURE) RULES 1995

(SI 1995/1053)

NOTES

Made: 10 April 1995.
Authority: Pension Schemes Act 1993, s 149(2), (3).
Commencement: 10 May 1995.
See *Harvey* B8.

ARRANGEMENT OF RULES

1 Citation, commencement and interpretation

(1) These Rules may be cited as the Personal and Occupational Pension Schemes (Pensions Ombudsman) (Procedure) Rules 1995 and shall come into force on 10th May 1995.

(2) In these Rules—

"complaint" means a complaint falling within [section 146(1)(a) and (b)] of the Pension Schemes Act (complaint of maladministration);

["complainant" means a person by or in respect of whom the complaint is made or dispute is referred under section 146(1) of the Pension Schemes Act;]

"dispute" means a dispute falling within [section 146(1)(c) and (d)] of the Pension Schemes Act (dispute of fact or law);

"party to the investigation" means, as the case may be, [the complainant] or the respondent (as defined in these Rules) and "party" and "parties" shall be construed accordingly;

"the Pension Schemes Act" means the Pension Schemes Act 1993;

"respondent" means—

[(a) a person responsible for the management of a personal or an occupational pension scheme, or

(b) any other person to whom Part X of the Pension Schemes Act applies as it applies to a person responsible for the management of a personal or an occupational pension scheme]

to whom the complaint or dispute relates.

[2285]

NOTES

Para (2): words in square brackets in definitions "complaint", "dispute" and "party to the investigation" substituted, definition "complainant" inserted, and sub-paras (a), (b) of definition "respondent" substituted, by the Personal and Occupational Pension Schemes (Pensions Ombudsman) (Procedure) Amendment Rules 1996, SI 1996/2638, r 2(1), (2).

2 Provision of details of complaint made or dispute referred

(1) [A complainant] shall give details of the complaint made or dispute referred in writing.

(2) The details shall include—

(a) the name and address of [the complainant];

(b) the name and address of the respondent;

(c) the facts relating to the complaint or dispute;

(d) whether or not the complaint or dispute has been brought to the attention of the Occupational Pensions Advisory Service Limited;

(e) the name, address and profession of the representative (if any) of [the complainant] and whether such address is the address for correspondence to the complainant for the purposes of the investigation.

[2286]

NOTES

Paras (1), (2): words in square brackets substituted by the Personal and Occupational Pension Schemes (Pensions Ombudsman) (Procedure) Amendment Rules 1996, SI 1996/2638, r 2(2).

3 Amendment of details and delivery of supplementary statement

[The complainant] may with the leave of the Pensions Ombudsman (which leave shall not be unreasonably refused) at any time—

(a) submit a supplementary statement;

(b) amend the details of his complaint or dispute or his supplementary statement.

[2287]

NOTES

Words in square brackets substituted by the Personal and Occupational Pension Schemes (Pensions Ombudsman) (Procedure) Amendment Rules 1996, SI 1996/2638, r 2(2).

4 Withdrawal of complaint or dispute

[The complainant] may withdraw his complaint or dispute—

(a) at any time before the end of fourteen days from the date he receives a copy of the reply referred to in paragraph (3) of rule 6 by sending to the office of the Pensions Ombudsman a notice stating he so withdraws signed by him or his representative; or

(b) thereafter with the leave of the Pensions Ombudsman which leave shall not be unreasonably refused.

[2288]

NOTES

Words in square brackets substituted by the Personal and Occupational Pension Schemes (Pensions Ombudsman) (Procedure) Amendment Rules 1996, SI 1996/2638, r 2(2).

5 Acknowledgement and supply of copy documents by Pensions Ombudsman

(1) Upon receiving details of a complaint or dispute the Pensions Ombudsman shall send to [the complainant] or his representative an acknowledgement of receipt.

(2) Where the Pensions Ombudsman proposes to investigate the complaint or dispute, he shall forthwith supply a copy of the details of the complaint or dispute together with any amendments or supplementary statements, written representations or other documents received from [the complainant] or his representative to the respondent.

(3) Where the Pensions Ombudsman does not propose to investigate the complaint or dispute, he shall forthwith inform [the complainant] or his representative that he does not propose to conduct an investigation.

[2289]

NOTES

Words in square brackets substituted by the Personal and Occupational Pension Schemes (Pensions Ombudsman) (Procedure) Amendment Rules 1996, SI 1996/2638, r 2(2).

6 Action by the respondent on receipt of a complaint or dispute

(1) Upon receiving a copy of the details of a complaint or dispute the respondent shall deliver to the Pensions Ombudsman a written reply acknowledging receipt of the details and stating—

(a) the facts relating to the complaint or dispute, whether or not the respondent opposes the allegations made in the complaint or dispute and any details on which it relies in opposing those allegations;

(b) whether in the opinion of the respondent, any other person has a direct interest in the subject matter of the complaint or dispute and if so the name and address of such other person;

(c) the name, address and profession of the representative (if any) of the respondent and whether such address is the address for correspondence to the respondent for the purposes of the investigation.

(2) The respondent shall deliver to the Pensions Ombudsman a sufficient number of additional copies of the reply to enable the Pensions Ombudsman to provide a copy to [the complainant] and any other person named by the respondent as having a direct interest in the subject matter of the complaint or dispute.

(3) Every such reply shall be signed by or on behalf of the respondent and shall be delivered at the office of the Pensions Ombudsman not later than twenty-one days after the date on which the copy of the details of the complaint or dispute was received by the respondent from the Pensions Ombudsman.

(4) The respondent may in its reply, or in a separate notice to the Pensions Ombudsman submitted within the twenty-one day period referred to in paragraph (3) request—

(a) further particulars of the complaint or dispute;

(b) a determination of any question as a preliminary issue.

[2290]

NOTES

Para (2): words in square brackets substituted by the Personal and Occupational Pension Schemes (Pensions Ombudsman) (Procedure) Amendment Rules 1996, SI 1996/2638, r 2(2).

7 Amendment of reply by the respondent

(1) The respondent may with the leave of the Pensions Ombudsman (which leave shall not be unreasonably refused) at any time—

(a) submit a supplementary statement;

(b) amend any reply or supplementary statement.

(2) The respondent shall deliver to the Pensions Ombudsman a sufficient number of additional copies of any amended reply or supplementary statement to enable the Pensions Ombudsman to provide a copy to [the complainant] and any other person named by the respondent as having a direct interest in the subject matter of the complaint or dispute.

[2291]

NOTES

Para (2): words in square brackets substituted by the Personal and Occupational Pension Schemes (Pensions Ombudsman) (Procedure) Amendment Rules 1996, SI 1996/2638, r 2(2).

8 Failure to reply and absence of opposition

If no reply is received by the Pensions Ombudsman within the period referred to in paragraph (3) of rule 6 or any extension of that period allowed by the Pensions Ombudsman, or if the respondent states in writing that it does not oppose or withdraws its opposition to the allegations the Pensions Ombudsman may, in any such case where there is no other opposition to the allegations, determine the complaint or dispute forthwith.

[2292]

9 Disclosure of documents and other material

(1) [The complainant] and respondent shall send or deliver to the Pensions Ombudsman by such date as the Pensions Ombudsman may specify a copy of any document or other material on which he intends to rely.

(2) The respondent shall, subject to paragraph (3), in addition send to the Pensions Ombudsman a sufficient number of copies of any such document or other material to which paragraph (1) applies to enable the Pensions Ombudsman to provide a copy to any other party to the investigation.

(3) The respondent need not send the additional copies referred to in paragraph (2) where the document or material or a copy thereof is already in the possession of the other parties or the Pensions Ombudsman already holds a sufficient number of copies.

(4) Where a document or other material is obtained by the Pensions Ombudsman pursuant to a request made by him to any party to the investigation, the Pensions Ombudsman shall supply a copy to each of the other parties to the investigation.

(5) It shall be a condition of the supply of any document under this rule that a party to the investigation shall use the document supplied only for the purposes of the investigation.

[2293]

NOTES

Para (1): words in square brackets substituted by the Personal and Occupational Pension Schemes (Pensions Ombudsman) (Procedure) Amendment Rules 1996, SI 1996/2638, r 2(2).

10 Notice of requirements in the event of an oral hearing

(1) Where the Pensions Ombudsman considers it appropriate for an oral hearing to be held in connection with any investigation conducted by him, he shall, with due regard to the convenience of the parties to the investigation, fix the time and place of any such hearing and, not less than twenty-one days before the date so fixed (or such shorter time as the parties agree), send to each party a notice of the time and place of such hearing.

(2) The Pensions Ombudsman shall include in or with the notice of hearing—

(a) information as to attendance at the hearing of the parties and witnesses, the bringing of documents and the right to representation by another person;

(b) a statement explaining—

(i) the right of any party to the investigation, who does not attend and is not represented, to make representations in writing; and

(ii) the possible consequences of non-attendance.

(3) The Pensions Ombudsman may, if it is necessary in the circumstances, alter the time and place of any oral hearing and he shall give the parties not less than seven days (or such shorter time as the parties agree) notice of any such alteration, provided that any altered hearing date shall not (unless the parties agree) be before the date notified under paragraph (1) of this rule.

(4) Where the Pensions Ombudsman adjourns any oral hearing, providing that the time and place of the reconvening of the hearing are announced before the adjournment, no further notice shall be required.

[2294]

11 Action of party to the investigation in relation to any hearing

(1) Each party to the investigation shall inform the Pensions Ombudsman whether or not he intends to attend or be represented at the hearing and whether or not he intends to call witnesses.

(2) If any party to the investigation does not intend to attend or be represented at the hearing, he may send to the Pensions Ombudsman additional written representations.

[2295]

12 Hearings to be in public subject to exceptions

(1) All hearings by the Pensions Ombudsman shall be in public except where by reason of the disclosure of any matter that relates to intimate personal or financial circumstances, is commercially sensitive, consists of information communicated or obtained in confidence or concerns national security, it is just and reasonable for the hearing or any part thereof to be in private.

(2) A member of the Council on Tribunals or of the Scottish Committee of that Council shall be entitled to attend the hearing whether it is in public or in private.

(3) The Pensions Ombudsman, with the consent of the parties to the investigation, may permit any other person to attend any hearing which is held in private.

(4) Any person whose conduct has disrupted or is likely to disrupt the hearing may be excluded by the Pensions Ombudsman.

[2296]

13 Failure of parties to the investigation to attend any hearing

(1) If a party to the investigation fails to attend or be represented at a hearing of which he has been duly notified, the Pensions Ombudsman may—

(a) conduct the hearing and determine the complaint or dispute in the party's absence; or

(b) adjourn the hearing.

(2) Before deciding to dispose of any case in the absence of a party, the Pensions Ombudsman shall consider any representations in writing submitted by that party in response to the notice of hearing.

[2297]

14 Representation at any hearing

At any hearing, any party to the investigation, if an individual, may conduct his case himself (with assistance from any person if he wishes) or may appear and be represented by any person whether or not legally qualified, provided that, if in any particular case there are good and sufficient reasons for doing so, the Pensions Ombudsman may refuse to permit a particular person to assist or represent the party at the hearing.

[2298]

15 Procedure at any hearing

(1) At the beginning of any hearing the Pensions Ombudsman shall explain the order of proceeding which he proposes to adopt.

(2) Subject to this rule, the Pensions Ombudsman shall conduct the hearing in such manner as he considers appropriate to the clarification of the issues before him and generally to the just handling of the investigation; he shall so far as seems appropriate seek to avoid formality in the hearing.

(3) The parties to the investigation shall be heard in such order as the Pensions Ombudsman shall determine. They shall be entitled to give evidence, to call witnesses, to question any party to the investigation or witnesses and to address the Pensions Ombudsman both on the evidence and generally on the subject matter of the investigation.

(4) Evidence before the Pensions Ombudsman may be given orally or where the Pensions Ombudsman considers appropriate, by affidavit or written statement, but the Pensions Ombudsman may, if it is appropriate, at any stage of the hearing require the personal attendance of any deponent or maker of a written statement.

(5) The Pensions Ombudsman may receive evidence of any fact which appears to him to be relevant notwithstanding that such evidence would be inadmissible in proceedings before a court of law, but shall not refuse to admit any evidence which is admissible at law and is relevant.

[2299]

[15A Payment of travel and subsistence expenses and compensation for lost earnings

(1) Where the Pensions Ombudsman considers it appropriate for an oral hearing to be held in connection with an investigation conducted by him, he may, having regard to the particular circumstances of the case, make payments in respect of allowances, fees and expenses in accordance with the following provisions of this rule.

(2) In this rule, "specified" in relation to any amount means the amount determined by the Secretary of State from time to time and notified by him to the Pensions Ombudsman.

(3) Sub-paragraphs (a) to (c) of paragraph (4) apply only in respect of complaints or disputes in which the complainant is an actual or potential beneficiary of a personal or an occupational pension scheme.

(4) Subject to paragraph (3), travelling expenses actually and reasonably incurred may be paid to the following—

- (a) in a case where the complainant attends the hearing, that person;
- (b) in a case where the complainant cannot, for reasons of ill health or incapacity, attend the hearing but is represented at the hearing by a relative or friend who is not receiving any form of remuneration in connection with his involvement in the complaint or dispute, that relative or friend;
- (c) in a case where the complainant requires, for reasons of ill health or incapacity, to be accompanied at the hearing by an attendant, that attendant;
- (d) a witness, other than a medical or other expert witness, attending the hearing where an application has been made in writing to the Pensions Ombudsman and the Pensions Ombudsman certifies that, in the circumstances of the case, the attendance of the witness is necessary or desirable.

(5) An allowance in respect of day and, where applicable, overnight subsistence may be paid at the specified rate to the persons and in the circumstances mentioned in paragraph (4).

(6) An allowance in respect of travel and subsistence expenses may be paid in advance of a hearing to the persons and in the circumstances mentioned in paragraph (4) where the Pensions Ombudsman is satisfied that such persons would not otherwise be able to attend the hearing.

(7) Compensation in respect of lost earnings may be paid, subject to the specified daily maximum, to the persons and in the circumstances mentioned in paragraph (4) where the Pensions Ombudsman is satisfied that—

- (a) by attending the hearing, such persons have experienced an interruption in employment which results in a reduction in their gross earnings; and
- (b) had such persons not attended the hearing, their gross earnings in respect of the period of interruption of employment would not have been less than the amount claimed.

(8) A claim for travel and subsistence expenses or, as the case may be, for compensation in respect of lost earnings must be made in writing to the Pensions Ombudsman and must be accompanied by full particulars and evidence of the expenses and lost earnings claimed.

(9) In any case where the Pensions Ombudsman considers it appropriate to hold an oral hearing in connection with an investigation conducted by him, he must immediately provide to an actual or potential beneficiary and, on request, to any other person full particulars of the arrangements made for the payment of specified travel and subsistence expenses, including information about advance payments and compensation in respect of lost earnings.]

[2300]

NOTES

Inserted by the Personal and Occupational Pension Schemes (Pensions Ombudsman) (Procedure) Amendment Rules 1996, SI 1996/2638, r 2(3).

16 Miscellaneous powers of the Pensions Ombudsman

(1) The Pensions Ombudsman may—

(a) extend the time appointed by or under these Rules for doing any act, notwithstanding that the time appointed may have expired;

(b) subject to paragraph (2) below, at any stage of the investigation order to be struck out or amended any written representation on the grounds that it is scandalous, frivolous or vexatious;

(c) subject to paragraph (2) below, order the discontinuance of an investigation if he considers it appropriate to do so.

(2) Before making any order under paragraph (1)(b) or (c) above, the Pensions Ombudsman shall send notice to the party to the investigation against whom it is proposed that any such order should be made giving him an opportunity to show cause why such an order should not be made.

[2301]

17 Irregularities

(1) Any irregularity resulting from failure to comply with any provisions of these Rules shall not of itself render the proceedings void.

(2) Clerical mistakes in any written statement of a determination (including any direction made under section 151(2) of the Pension Schemes Act) or errors arising in such a document from an accidental slip or omission, may be corrected by the Pensions Ombudsman by certificate under his hand.

[2302]

18 Method of sending or delivering documents etc

(1) Any document required or authorised by these Rules to be sent or delivered to any person shall be duly sent or delivered to that person:—

(a) if it is sent to him at his proper address by post;

(b) if it is sent to him at that address by facsimile or other similar means which produce a document containing a text of the communication, in which event the document shall be regarded as sent when it is received in a legible form;

(c) if it is delivered to him or left at his proper address.

(2) The proper address for the Pensions Ombudsman is the address of the office of the Pensions Ombudsman.

(3) The proper address of any other person to whom any such document is to be sent or delivered shall be the address given by that person or, if none, the last known address of that person or, in the case of an incorporated company or body, the registered or principal office of that company or body.

[2303]

19 Substituted service

If any person to whom any document is required to be sent or delivered for the purpose of these Rules cannot be found or has died and has no known personal representative, or is out of the United Kingdom, or if for any other reason service on him cannot be readily effected, the Pensions Ombudsman may dispense with service on such person or may make an order for substituted service on such other person in such other form (whether by advertisement in a newspaper or otherwise) as is reasonable.

[2304]

OCCUPATIONAL PENSION SCHEMES (EQUAL TREATMENT) REGULATIONS 1995

(SI 1995/3183)

NOTES

Made: 7 December 1995.
Authority: Pensions Act 1995, ss 63(5), 64(2), (3), 66(4), 124(1), 174(2), (3).
Commencement: 1 January 1996.

These Regulations modify and supplement the Equal Pay Act 1970 and apply it to certain pension claims. In view of their complexity and specialist application and for ease of understanding, the Regulations are reproduced in full, including the provisions which amend the Equal Pay Act 1970.

See *Harvey* B7, B8, F1(G), Q, R, S.

ARRANGEMENT OF REGULATIONS

1 Citation, commencement and interpretation

(1) These Regulations may be cited as the Occupational Pension Schemes (Equal Treatment) Regulations 1995 and shall come into force on 1st January 1996.

(2) In these Regulations, unless the context otherwise requires—

"the Pensions Act" means the Pensions Act 1995;

"Category A retirement pension" has the same meaning as in Part II of the Contributions and Benefits Act;

"the Contributions and Benefits Act" means the Social Security Contributions and Benefits Act 1992;

"equality clause" shall be construed in accordance with section 1(2) of the Equal Pay Act;

"the Equal Pay Act" means the Equal Pay Act 1970;

"pensionable age" shall be construed in accordance with section 122(1) of the Contributions and Benefits Act;

"pensionable service" includes any service in respect of which transfer credits have been allowed by the scheme;

"pensioner member" includes a person who is entitled to the present payment of pension or other benefits derived through a member;

"salary-related contracted-out scheme" means an occupational pension scheme which is contracted-out by virtue of satisfying section 9(2) of the Pension Schemes Act 1993 and includes a scheme which was formerly a salary-related contracted-out scheme which is subject to supervision in accordance with section 53 of that Act;

"scheme" means an occupational pension scheme.

[2305]

NOTES

"Pensionable age": the definition of pensionable age in s 122(1) was substituted by the Pensions Act 1995, Sch 4, para 13, which provides that it has the meaning given by the rules in Sch 4, para 1, to that Act.

2 Application of the Equal Pay Act to the equal treatment rule

[(1)] In addition to the modifications made to the Equal Pay Act by the Pensions Act, the Equal Pay Act shall have effect for the purposes of sections 62 to 64 of the Pensions Act in relation to an equal treatment rule—

[(a) subject to the further modifications made in paragraph (2) below and in regulations 3 to 7 below,]

(b) as if references to remuneration were to benefits, and

(c) as if expressions used in the Pensions Act and in the Equal Pay Act have the same meaning as in the Pensions Act.

[(2) Section 2ZA of the Equal Pay Act shall have effect in relation to an equal treatment rule as if—

(a) for subsection (1) there were substituted—

"(1) This section applies for the purpose of determining the qualifying date, in relation to relevant proceedings in respect of a woman, for the purposes of section 2(4) above.

(1A) In subsection (1) above "relevant proceedings" means proceedings in respect of the terms on which—

(a) persons become members of an occupational pension scheme, or

(b) members of an occupational pension scheme are treated."; and

(b) in subsection (2)—

(i) in paragraph (a) of the definition of "concealment case", the reference to the employer was a reference to the employer or the trustees or managers of the scheme, and

(ii) in paragraph (c) of the definition of "disability case", the reference to the employer was a reference to the employer or the trustees or managers of the scheme.]

[2306]

NOTES

Para (1): numbered as such, and sub-para (a) substituted, by the Occupational Pension Schemes (Equal Treatment) (Amendment) Regulations 2005, SI 2005/1923, regs 4, 5(1)(a), (b), as from 10 August 2005 (for effect see the note below).

Para (2): added by SI 2005/1923, regs 4, 5(1)(c), as from 10 August 2005 (for effect see the note below).

Note: the amendments made by SI 2005/1923 (above) apply to proceedings in respect of the terms of an occupational pension scheme if the proceedings are instituted on or after 10 August 2005, unless the last day on which the woman was employed in the employment to which the occupational pension scheme relates fell more than six months before that date (see reg 2 of the 2005 Regulations at **[3321]**).

3 Modification of the Equal Pay Act: no power to make financial awards in relation to the equal treatment rule

In the case of a claim made in respect of a failure to comply with an equal treatment rule, other than a claim to which regulation 7 below applies, section 2 of the Equal Pay Act shall have effect as if for subsection (5) there were substituted—

"(5) A woman shall not be entitled, in proceedings brought in respect of a failure to comply with an equal treatment rule (including proceedings before an [employment tribunal]), to be awarded any payment by way of arrears of benefits, damages or any other financial award.".

[2307]

NOTES

Words in square brackets substituted by the Employment Rights (Dispute Resolution) Act 1998, s 1(2)(a).

4 Modification of the Equal Pay Act: employer to have right to appear and be heard in proceedings for breach of an equal treatment rule

In the case of a claim made in respect of a failure to comply with an equal treatment rule, section 2 of the Equal Pay Act shall have effect as if after subsection (5) there were inserted—

"(5A) In any proceedings brought before an [employment tribunal] by a woman in respect of a failure to comply with an equal treatment rule, the employer shall, for the purposes of the rules governing procedure, be treated as a party and be entitled to appear and be heard in accordance with those rules.".

[2308]

NOTES

Words in square brackets substituted by the Employment Rights (Dispute Resolution) Act 1998, s 1(2)(a).

[5 Power for a court or employment tribunal to declare right to admission to scheme

Where a claim to which regulation 3 applies relates to the terms on which persons become members of the scheme, section 2 of the Equal Pay Act shall have effect as if, after subsection (5A) (as inserted by regulation 4), there were added—

"(6A) Where a court or employment tribunal finds that there has been a breach of an equal treatment rule which relates to the terms on which persons become members of the scheme (including any terms concerning the age or length of service needed for becoming a member of the scheme), the court or tribunal may declare that a woman has the right to be admitted to the scheme with effect from such date as it may specify provided that, in any case, that date is not earlier than 8th April 1976.".]

[2309]

NOTES

Commencement: 10 August 2005.

Substituted by the Occupational Pension Schemes (Equal Treatment) (Amendment) Regulations 2005, SI 2005/1923, regs 4, 5(2), as from 10 August 2005 (for effect see the note to reg 2 at **[2306]**).

6 Power for a court or [employment tribunal] to declare right to equal treatment for members and employer's duty to provide additional resources

Where a claim to which regulation 3 applies relates to the terms on which members of the scheme are treated, section 2 of the Equal Pay Act shall have effect as if the following subsections were added after subsection (5A) (as inserted by regulation 4)—

"(6B) Where a court or [employment tribunal] finds that there has been a breach of an equal treatment rule which relates to the terms on which members of a scheme are treated—

(a) the court or tribunal may declare that a member has a right to equal treatment in respect of such a period as it may specify provided that the period does not begin before 17th May 1990, and

(b) if the court or tribunal declares that a member has a right to equal treatment in relation to a period falling before the date of the declaration, the employer shall provide any such resources to the scheme as are specified in subsection (7B) below.

(7B) The resources referred to in subsection (6B)(b) above are such additional resources, if any, as may be necessary for the scheme to secure to the member, without contribution or further contribution by the member or by other members of the scheme, the same accrued rights in respect of the period falling before the date of the declaration as if that member had been treated equally in respect of that period.".

[2310]

NOTES

Words in square brackets substituted by the Employment Rights (Dispute Resolution) Act 1998, s 1(2)(a).

[7 Power for a court or employment tribunal to make a financial award for equal treatment claims by pensioner members and employer's duty to provide additional resources

(1) This regulation applies in the case of a claim by a pensioner member of a scheme in respect of a failure to comply with an equal treatment rule which relates to the terms on which the member is treated.

(2) Section 2 of the Equal Pay Act shall have effect as if—

(a) for subsection (5) there were substituted—

"(5) A woman who is a pensioner member shall not be entitled, in proceedings brought in respect of a failure to comply with an equal treatment rule (including proceedings before an employment tribunal), to be awarded any payment by way of arrears of benefits or damages or any other financial award—

(a) in proceedings in England and Wales, in respect of a time earlier than the arrears date (determined in accordance with section 2ZB below), and

(b) in proceedings in Scotland, in respect of a time before the period determined in accordance with section 2ZC below."; and

(b) the following subsections were added after subsection (5A) (as inserted by regulation 4)—

"(6C) Where a court or employment tribunal awards a payment by way of arrears of benefits or damages, or makes any other financial award, the employer shall provide any such resources to the scheme as are specified in subsection (7C) below.

(7C) The resources referred to in subsection (6C) above are such additional resources, if any, as may be necessary for the scheme to secure to the pensioner member the payment of the amount awarded or other financial award made, without contribution or further contribution by the pensioner member or by other members of the scheme.".

(3) Section 2ZB of the Equal Pay Act shall have effect as if—

(a) for subsection (1) there were substituted—

"(1) This section applies for the purpose of determining the arrears date, in relation to an award of any payment by way of arrears of benefits or damages or any other financial award in relevant proceedings in England and Wales in respect of a woman, for the purposes of section 2(5)(a) above.

(1A) In subsection (1) above "relevant proceedings" means proceedings in respect of the terms on which members of an occupational pension scheme are treated."; and

(b) in subsection (2), the reference in the definition of "concealment case" to the employer were a reference to the employer or the trustees or managers of the scheme.

(4) Section 2ZC of the Equal Pay Act shall have effect as if—

(a) for subsection (1) there were substituted—

"(1) This section applies, in relation to an award of any payment by way of arrears of benefits or damages or any other financial award in relevant proceedings in Scotland in respect of a woman, for the purposes of determining the period mentioned in section 2(5)(b) above.

(1A) In subsection (1) above "relevant proceedings" means proceedings in respect of the terms on which members of an occupational pension scheme are treated."; and

(b) in subsection (2)(a), the reference to the employer or any person acting on his behalf was a reference to the employer, the trustees or managers of the scheme or any person acting on his or their behalf.]

[2311]

NOTES

Commencement: 10 August 2005.

Substituted by the Occupational Pension Schemes (Equal Treatment) (Amendment) Regulations 2005, SI 2005/1923, regs 4, 5(3), as from 10 August 2005 (for effect see the note to reg 2 at **[2306]**).

8 Application of the Equal Pay Act to terms of employment relating to pension rights

The Equal Pay Act shall have effect in relation to terms of employment relating to membership of and rights under a scheme—

(a) subject to the modifications made in regulations 9 to 12 below,

(b) as if references to remuneration were to benefits, and

(c) as if expressions used in the Pensions Act and in the Equal Pay Act have the same meaning as in the Pensions Act.

[2312]

9 Modification of the Equal Pay Act: no power to award damages in relation to an equality clause in connection with pension rights

In the case of a claim made in respect of a breach of an equality clause which relates to membership of or rights under a scheme, other than a claim to which regulation 12 applies, section 2 of the Equal Pay Act shall have effect as if for subsection (5) there were substituted—

"(5) A woman shall not be entitled, in proceedings brought in respect of a failure to comply with an equality clause (including proceedings before an [employment tribunal]), to be awarded any payment by way of arrears of benefits or damages.".

[2313]

NOTES

Words in square brackets substituted by the Employment Rights (Dispute Resolution) Act 1998, s 1(2)(a).

[10 Power for a court or employment tribunal to declare right to admission to scheme for breach of term in contract of employment in relation to access claims

Where a claim to which regulation 9 applies relates to the terms on which persons become members of the scheme, section 2 of the Equal Pay Act shall have effect as if, after subsection (5) (as modified by regulation 9), there were added—

"(6D) Where a court or employment tribunal finds that there has been a breach of an equality clause which relates to the terms on which persons become members of the scheme (including any terms concerning the age or length of service needed for becoming a member of the scheme), the court or tribunal may declare that a woman has a right to be admitted to the scheme with effect from such date as it may specify provided that, in any case, that date is not earlier than 8th April 1976.".]

[2314]

NOTES

Commencement: 10 August 2005.

Substituted by the Occupational Pension Schemes (Equal Treatment) (Amendment) Regulations 2005, SI 2005/1923, regs 4, 6, as from 10 August 2005 (for effect see the note to reg 2 at **[2306]**).

11 Power for a court or [employment tribunal] to declare right to equal treatment for members and employer's duty to provide additional resources for breach of term in contract of employment

Where a claim to which regulation 9 applies relates to the terms on which members of a scheme are treated, section 2 of the Equal Pay Act shall have effect as if the following subsections were added after subsection (5) (as modified by regulation 9)—

"(6E) Where a court or [employment tribunal] finds that there has been a breach of an equality clause which relates to the terms on which members of a scheme are treated—

(a) the court or tribunal may declare that a member has a right to equal treatment in respect of such a period as it may specify provided that the period does not begin before 17th May 1990, and

(b) if the court or tribunal declares that a member has a right to equal treatment in relation to a period falling before the date of the declaration, the employer shall provide any such resources to the scheme as are specified in subsection (7E) below.

(7E) The resources referred to in subsection (6E)(b) above are such additional resources, if any, as may be necessary for the scheme to secure to the member, without contribution or further contribution by the member or by other members of the scheme, the same accrued rights in respect of the period falling before the date of the declaration as if that member had been treated equally in respect of that period.".

[2315]

NOTES

Words in square brackets substituted by the Employment Rights (Dispute Resolution) Act 1998, s 1(2)(a).

12 Power for a court or [employment tribunal] to award payment of arrears or damages in breach of contract of employment claims by pensioner members and employer's duty to provide additional resources

In the case of a claim by a pensioner member, in respect of a failure to comply with an equality clause which relates to the terms on which the member is treated, section 2 of the Equal Pay Act shall have effect as if the following subsections were added after subsection (5)—

"(6F) Where the court or tribunal awards a payment by way of arrears of benefits or damages, the employer shall provide any such resources to the scheme as are specified in subsection (7F) below.

(7F) The resources referred to in subsection (6F) above are such additional resources, if any, as may be necessary for the scheme to secure the payment of those arrears of benefits or damages to the member, without contribution or further contribution by the member or by other members of the scheme.".

[2316]

NOTES

Words in square brackets substituted by the Employment Rights (Dispute Resolution) Act 1998, s 1(2)(a).

13 Exceptions to the equal treatment rule: bridging pensions

The following circumstances are prescribed for the purposes of section 64(2) of the Pensions Act—

(a) the man is in receipt of a pension from the scheme and has not attained pensionable age but would have attained pensionable age if he were a woman; and

(b) an additional amount of pension is paid to the man which does not exceed the amount of Category A retirement pension that would be payable to a woman with earnings the same as the man's earnings in respect of his period of pensionable service under the scheme (assuming that the requirements for entitlement to Category A retirement pension were satisfied and a claim made).

[2317]

14 Exceptions to the equal treatment rule: effect of indexation

(1) The following circumstances are prescribed for the purposes of section 64(2) of the Pensions Act—

(a) the scheme is a salary-related contracted-out scheme under which the annual rate of a pension payable to or in respect of a member is increased by more than it would have been increased had the recipient been of the other sex; and

(b) the amount by which the pension increase exceeds any increase that would have applied had the member been of the other sex, does not exceed the relevant amount.

(2) In this regulation, the relevant amount means the amount by which X exceeds Y where—

X is the amount by which the additional pension of a Category A retirement pension attributable to the member's earnings factors during his period of pensionable service under the scheme would have been increased following an order made under section 150(9) of the Social Security Administration Act 1992 if the member had been of the other sex; and

Y is the amount (if any) by which the member's entitlement to the additional pension of a Category A retirement pension attributable to his earnings factors during his period of pensionable service under the scheme is increased following an order made under section 150(9) of the Social Security Administration Act 1992.

[2318]

15 Exceptions to the equal treatment rule: use of actuarial factors which differ for men and women

(1) The factors prescribed for the purposes of section 64(3)(a) of the Pensions Act (equal treatment rule: exception relating to the application of actuarial factors which differ for men and women to employers' contributions) are actuarial factors which differ for men and women in respect of the differences in the average life expectancy of men and women and which are determined with a view to providing equal periodical pension benefits for men and women.

(2) The following benefits are prescribed for the purposes of section 64(3)(b) of the Pensions Act (equal treatment rule: exception relating to the application of actuarial factors which differ for men and women to the determination of prescribed benefits)—

(a) a lump sum payment which consists of a commuted periodical pension or part of such a pension;

(b) a periodical pension granted in exchange for a lump sum payment;

(c) money purchase benefits within the meaning of section 181(1) of the Pension Schemes Act 1993;

(d) transfer credits and any rights allowed to a member by reference to a transfer from a personal pension scheme;

(e) a transfer payment including a cash equivalent within the meaning of section 94 of the Pension Schemes Act 1993;

(f) a periodical pension payable in respect of a member who opts to take such benefits before normal pension age or in respect of a member who defers taking such benefits until after normal pension age;

(g) benefits payable to another person in exchange for part of a member's benefits and the part of the member's benefits given up for that purpose;

(h) benefits provided in respect of a member's voluntary contributions within the meaning of section 111 of the Pension Schemes Act 1993.

[2319]

OCCUPATIONAL PENSION SCHEMES (INTERNAL DISPUTE RESOLUTION PROCEDURES) REGULATIONS 1996

(SI 1996/1270)

NOTES

These Regulations were revoked by the Occupational Pension Schemes (Internal Dispute Resolution Procedures Consequential and Miscellaneous Amendments) Regulations 2008, SI 2008/649, reg 7, as from 6 April 2008, subject to transitional provisions in relation to cases already being considered before that date (see reg 5 of the 2008 Regulations at **[3474KE]**). Much of the detail formerly contained in these Regulations is now contained in the Pensions Act 1995 ss 50, 50A, 50B at **[889A]** et seq.

[2320]–[2329]

DISABILITY DISCRIMINATION (MEANING OF DISABILITY) REGULATIONS 1996

(SI 1996/1455)

NOTES

Made: 4 June 1996.
Authority: Disability Discrimination Act 1995, s 1(1), Sch 1, paras 1(2), 2(4), 3(2), (3), 4(2)(a), 5(a).
Commencement: 30 July 1996.

See also the Guidance on matters to be taken into account in determining questions relating to the definition of disability (2006) at **[4756]**.
See *Harvey* L3, Q, R, S.

ARRANGEMENT OF REGULATIONS

1 Citation and commencement

These Regulations may be cited as the Disability Discrimination (Meaning of Disability) Regulations 1996 and shall come into force on 30th July 1996.

[2330]

2 Interpretation

In these Regulations—

"the Act" means the Disability Discrimination Act 1995; and
"addiction" includes a dependency.

[2331]

3 Addictions

(1) Subject to paragraph (2) below, addiction to alcohol, nicotine or any other substance is to be treated as not amounting to an impairment for the purposes of the Act.

(2) Paragraph (1) above does not apply to addiction which was originally the result of administration of medically prescribed drugs or other medical treatment.

[2332]

4 Other conditions not to be treated as impairments

(1) For the purposes of the Act the following conditions are to be treated as not amounting to impairments—

(a) a tendency to set fires,
(b) a tendency to steal,
(c) a tendency to physical or sexual abuse of other persons,
(d) exhibitionism, and
(e) voyeurism.

(2) Subject to paragraph (3) below for the purposes of the Act the condition known as seasonal allergic rhinitis shall be treated as not amounting to an impairment.

(3) Paragraph (2) above shall not prevent that condition from being taken into account for the purposes of the Act where it aggravates the effect of another condition.

[2333]

5 Tattoos and piercings

For the purposes of paragraph 3 of Schedule 1 to the Act a severe disfigurement is not to be treated as having a substantial adverse effect on the ability of the person concerned to carry out normal day-to-day activities if it consists of—

(a) a tattoo (which has not been removed), or
(b) a piercing of the body for decorative or other non-medical purposes, including any object attached through the piercing for such purposes.

[2334]

6 Babies and young children

For the purposes of the Act where a child under six years of age has an impairment which does not have an effect falling within paragraph 4(1) of Schedule 1 to the Act that impairment is to be taken to have a substantial and long-term adverse effect on the ability of that child to carry out normal day-to-day activities where it would normally have a substantial and long-term adverse effect on the ability of a person aged 6 years or over to carry out normal day-to-day activities.

[2335]

DISABILITY DISCRIMINATION (EMPLOYMENT) REGULATIONS 1996 (NOTE)

(SI 1996/1456)

NOTES

These Regulations were revoked and partly replaced by the Disability Discrimination (Employment Field) (Leasehold Premises) Regulations 2004, SI 2004/153 (at **[3074]**), as from 1 October 2004.

See *Harvey* L3, R.

[2336]–[2350]

HEALTH AND SAFETY (CONSULTATION WITH EMPLOYEES) REGULATIONS 1996

(SI 1996/1513)

NOTES

Made: 10 June 1996.
Authority: European Communities Act 1972, s 2(2).
Commencement: 1 October 1996.
See *Harvey* R.

ARRANGEMENT OF REGULATIONS

SCHEDULES:

1 Citation, extent and commencement

These Regulations, which extend to Great Britain, may be cited as the Health and Safety (Consultation with Employees) Regulations 1996 and shall come into force on 1st October 1996.

[2351]

2 Interpretation

(1) In these Regulations, unless the context otherwise requires—

"the 1974 Act" means the Health and Safety at Work etc Act 1974;

"the 1977 Regulations" means the Safety Representatives and Safety Committees Regulations 1977;

"employee" has the meaning assigned to it by section 53(1) of the 1974 Act but shall not include a person employed as a domestic servant in a private household; and "employer" shall be construed accordingly;

"the relevant statutory provisions" has the meaning assigned to it by section 53(1) of the 1974 Act;

"representatives of employee safety" shall be construed in accordance with regulation 4(1)(b);

"safety representative" has the meaning assigned to it by regulation 2(1) of the 1977 Regulations;

"workplace" means, in relation to an employee, any place or places where that employee is likely to work or which he is likely to frequent in the course of his employment or incidentally to it and, in relation to a representative of employee safety, any place or places where the employees he represents are likely so to work or frequent.

(2) Any reference in these Regulations to consulting employees directly or consulting representatives of employee safety is a reference to consulting them pursuant to regulation 3 and regulation 4(1)(a) or (b), as the case may be.

(3) Unless the context otherwise requires, any reference in these Regulations to—

(a) a numbered regulation or schedule is a reference to the regulation or schedule in these Regulations so numbered; and

(b) a numbered paragraph is a reference to the paragraph so numbered in the regulation or schedule in which the reference appears.

[2352]

3 Duty of employer to consult

Where there are employees who are not represented by safety representatives under the 1977 Regulations, the employer shall consult those employees in good time on matters relating to their health and safety at work and, in particular, with regard to—

(a) the introduction of any measure at the workplace which may substantially affect the health and safety of those employees;

(b) his arrangements for appointing or, as the case may be, nominating persons in accordance with [regulations 7(1) and 8(1)(b) of the Management of Health and Safety at Work Regulations 1999] [or article 13(3)(b) of the Regulatory Reform (Fire Safety) Order 2005]];

(c) any health and safety information he is required to provide to those employees by or under the relevant statutory provisions;

(d) the planning and organisation of any health and safety training he is required to provide to those employees by or under the relevant statutory provisions; and

(e) the health and safety consequences for those employees of the introduction (including the planning thereof) of new technologies into the workplace.

[2353]

NOTES

Para (b): words in first pair of square brackets substituted by the Management of Health and Safety at Work Regulations 1999, SI 1999/3242, reg 29(2), Sch 2; words in second pair of square brackets originally inserted by the Fire Precautions (Workplace) Regulations 1997, SI 1997/1840, reg 21(1), and substituted by the Regulatory Reform (Fire Safety) Order 2005, SI 2005/1541, art 41(2), as from 1 April 2006, in relation to England and Wales only. A corresponding amendment has been made in relation to Scotland by the Fire (Scotland) Act 2005 (Consequential Modifications and Savings) (No 2) Order 2006, SSI 2006/457, which provides that the words should now read "or regulation 12(3)(b) of the Fire Safety (Scotland) Regulations 2006".

4 Persons to be consulted

(1) The consultation required by regulation 3 is consultation with either—

(a) the employees directly; or

(b) in respect of any group of employees, one or more persons in that group who were elected, by the employees in that group at the time of the election, to represent that group for the purposes of such consultation (and any such persons are in these Regulations referred to as "representatives of employee safety").

(2) Where an employer consults representatives of employee safety he shall inform the employees represented by those representatives of—

(a) the names of those representatives; and
(b) the group of employees represented by those representatives.

(3) An employer shall not consult a person as a representative of employee safety if—
(a) that person has notified the employer that he does not intend to represent the group of employees for the purposes of such consultation;
(b) that person has ceased to be employed in the group of employees which he represents;
(c) the period for which that person was elected has expired without that person being re-elected; or
(d) that person has become incapacitated from carrying out his functions under these regulations;

and where pursuant to this paragraph an employer discontinues consultation with that person he shall inform the employees in the group concerned of that fact.

(4) Where an employer who has been consulting representatives of employee safety decides to consult employees directly he shall inform the employees and the representatives of that fact.

[2354]

5 Duty of employer to provide information

(1) Where an employer consults employees directly he shall, subject to paragraph (3), make available to those employees such information, within the employer's knowledge, as is necessary to enable them to participate fully and effectively in the consultation.

(2) Where an employer consults representatives of employee safety he shall, subject to paragraph (3), make available to those representatives such information, within the employer's knowledge, as is—
(a) necessary to enable them to participate fully and effectively in the consultation and in the carrying out of their functions under these Regulations;
(b) contained in any record which he is required to keep by regulation 7 of the Reporting of Injuries, Diseases and Dangerous Occurrences Regulations 1995 and which relates to the workplace or the group of employees represented by those representatives.

(3) Nothing in paragraph (1) or (2) shall require an employer to make available any information—
(a) the disclosure of which would be against the interests of national security;
(b) which he could not disclose without contravening a prohibition imposed by or under any enactment;
(c) relating specifically to an individual, unless he has consented to its being disclosed;
(d) the disclosure of which would, for reasons other than its effect on health or safety, cause substantial injury to the employer's undertaking or, where the information was supplied to him by some other person, to the undertaking of that other person; or
(e) obtained by the employer for the purpose of bringing, prosecuting or defending any legal proceedings;

or to provide or allow the inspection of any document or part of a document which is not related to health or safety.

[2355]

6 Functions of representatives of employee safety

Where an employer consults representatives of employee safety each of those representatives shall, for the period for which that representative is so consulted, have the following functions—
(a) to make representations to the employer on potential hazards and dangerous occurrences at the workplace which affect, or could affect, the group of employees he represents;
(b) to make representations to the employer on general matters affecting the health and safety at work of the group of employees he represents and, in particular, on such matters as he is consulted about by the employer under regulation 3; and
(c) to represent the group of employees he represents in consultations at the workplace with inspectors appointed under section 19(l) of the 1974 Act.

[2356]

7 Training, time off and facilities for representatives of employee safety and time off for candidates

(1) Where an employer consults representatives of employee safety, he shall—

(a) ensure that each of those representatives is provided with such training in respect of that representative's functions under these Regulations as is reasonable in all the circumstances and the employer shall meet any reasonable costs associated with such training including travel and subsistence costs; and

(b) permit each of those representatives to take such time off with pay during that representative's working hours as shall be necessary for the purpose of that representative performing his functions under these Regulations or undergoing any training pursuant to paragraph (l)(a).

(2) An employer shall permit a candidate standing for election as a representative of employee safety reasonable time off with pay during that person's working hours in order to perform his functions as such a candidate.

(3) Schedule 1 (pay for time off) and Schedule 2 (provisions as to [employment tribunals]) shall have effect.

(4) An employer shall provide such other facilities and assistance as a representative of employee safety may reasonably require for the purpose of carrying out his functions under these Regulations.

[2357]

NOTES

Para (3): words in square brackets substituted by the Employment Rights (Dispute Resolution) Act 1998, s 1(2)(b).

8 (*Inserts the Employment Rights Act 1996, ss 44(1)(ba), 100(1)(ba) at* **[1063]**, **[1139]**.)

9 Exclusion of civil liability

Breach of a duty imposed by these Regulations shall, subject to regulation 7(3) and Schedule 2, not confer any right of action in any civil proceedings.

[2358]

10 Application of health and safety legislation

Sections 16 to 21, 23, 24, 26, 28, 33, 34, 36 to 39, 42(1) to (3) and 46 of the 1974 Act, the Health and Safety (Enforcing Authority) Regulations 1989 and the Health and Safety (Training for Employment) Regulations 1990 shall apply as if any references therein to health and safety regulations or to the relevant statutory provisions included references to these Regulations.

[2359]

NOTES

Health and Safety (Enforcing Authority) Regulations 1989: revoked and replaced by the Health and Safety (Enforcing Authority) Regulations 1998, SI 1998/494.

11 Application to the Crown and armed forces

(1) Section 48 of the 1974 Act shall, subject to paragraph (2), apply in respect of these Regulations as it applies in respect of regulations made under Part I of that Act.

(2) These Regulations shall apply in respect of members of the armed forces of the Crown subject to the following—

(a) references to "representatives of employee safety" (in regulation 4(1)(b) and elsewhere) shall, in respect of any group of employees, be references to one or more persons in that group who were appointed by the employer to represent that group for the purposes of such consultation;

(b) references to "elected" and "re-elected" in regulation 4(3)(c) shall be, respectively, references to "appointed" and "re-appointed"; and

(c) regulation 7(l)(b), (2) and (3) shall not apply.

[2360]

12 Disapplication to sea-going ships

These Regulations shall not apply to or in relation to the master or crew of a seagoing ship or to the employer of such persons in respect of the normal ship-board activities of a ship's crew under the direction of the master.

[2361]

13 (*Amends the Safety Representatives and Safety Committees Regulations 1977, SI 1977/500, reg 3(1) at* **[2037]**.)

SCHEDULES

SCHEDULE 1
PAY FOR TIME OFF

Regulation 7(3)

1. Subject to paragraph 3 below, where a person is permitted to take time off in accordance with regulation 7(l)(b) or 7(2), his employer shall pay him—
   (a) where the person's remuneration for the work he would ordinarily have been doing during that time does not vary with the amount of work done, as if he had worked at that work for the whole of that time;
   (b) where the person's remuneration for that work varies with the amount of work done, an amount calculated by reference to the average hourly earnings for that work (ascertained in accordance with paragraph 2).

2. The average hourly earnings referred to in paragraph 1(b) are the average hourly earnings of the person concerned or, if no fair estimate can be made of those earnings, the average hourly earnings for work of that description of persons in comparable employment with the same employer or, if there are no such persons, a figure of average hourly earnings which is reasonable in all the circumstances.

3. Any payment to a person by an employer in respect of a period of time off—
   (a) if it is a payment which discharges any liability which the employer may have under sections 168 or 169 of the Trade Union and Labour Relations (Consolidation) Act 1992, in respect of that period, shall also discharge his liability in respect of the same period under regulation 7(l)(b) or 7(2);
   (b) if it is a payment under any contractual obligation, shall go towards discharging the employer's liability in respect of the same period under regulation 7(l)(b) or 7(2);
   (c) if it is a payment under regulation 7(l)(b) or 7(2), shall go towards discharging any liability of the employer to pay contractual remuneration in respect of the same period.

[2362]

SCHEDULE 2
PROVISIONS AS TO [EMPLOYMENT TRIBUNALS]

Regulation 7(3)

1. An [employment tribunal] shall have jurisdiction to determine complaints in accordance with the following provisions of this Schedule.

2. A person (referred to in this Schedule as the "complainant") may present a complaint to an [employment tribunal] that—
   (a) his employer has failed to permit him to take time off in accordance with regulation 7(1)(b) or 7(2); or
   (b) his employer has failed to pay him in accordance with regulation 7(1)(b) or 7(2) and Schedule 1.

3. An [employment tribunal] shall not consider a complaint under paragraph 2 unless it is presented within three months of the date when the failure occurred or within such further period as the tribunal considers reasonable in a case where it is satisfied that it was not reasonably practicable for the complaint to be presented within the period of three months.

4. Where an [employment tribunal] finds a complaint under paragraph 2(a) well-founded the tribunal shall make a declaration to that effect and may make an award of compensation to

be paid by the employer to the complainant which shall be of such amount as the tribunal considers just and equitable in all the circumstances having regard to the employer's default in failing to permit time off to be taken by the complainant and to any loss sustained by the complainant which is attributable to the matters complained of.

5. Where on a complaint under paragraph 2(b) an [employment tribunal] finds that the employer has failed to pay the complainant the whole or part of the amount required to be paid in accordance with regulation 7(1)(b) or 7(2) and Schedule 1, the tribunal shall order the employer to pay the complainant the amount which it finds due to him.

[2363]

NOTES

Words in square brackets substituted by the Employment Rights (Dispute Resolution) Act 1998, s 1(2)(a), (b).

EMPLOYMENT PROTECTION (RECOUPMENT OF JOBSEEKER'S ALLOWANCE AND INCOME SUPPORT) REGULATIONS 1996

(SI 1996/2349)

NOTES

Made: 10 September 1996.

Authority: Employment Tribunals Act 1996, ss 16, 41(4); Social Security Administration Act 1992, s 58(1) (repealed subject to certain exceptions). Now has effect wholly under the Employment Tribunals Act 1996, ss 16, 41(4) (as amended by the Social Security Act 1998, s 86, Sch 7, para 147, Sch 8).

Commencement: 7 October 1996.

See *Harvey* DI(18D), Q, R.

ARRANGEMENT OF REGULATIONS

PART I
INTRODUCTORY

PART II
EMPLOYMENT TRIBUNAL PROCEEDINGS

PART III
RECOUPMENT OF BENEFIT

PART IV
DETERMINATION OF BENEFIT RECOUPED

PART I
INTRODUCTORY

1 Citation and Commencement

These Regulations may be cited as the Employment Protection (Recoupment of Jobseeker's Allowance and Income Support) Regulations 1996 and shall come into force on 7th October 1996.

[2364]

2 Interpretation

(1) In these Regulations, unless the context otherwise requires, the following expressions have the meanings hereby assigned to them respectively, that is to say—

"the 1992 Act" means the Trade Union and Labour Relations (Consolidation) Act 1992;

"the 1996 Act" means the Employment Rights Act 1996;

"prescribed element" has the meaning assigned to it in Regulation 3 below and the Schedule to these Regulations;

"protected period" has the same meaning as in section 189(5) of the 1992 Act;

"protective award" has the same meaning as in section 189(3) of the 1992 Act;

"recoupable benefit" means any jobseeker's allowance or income support as the case may be, which is recoupable under these Regulations;

"recoupment notice" means a notice under these Regulations;

"Secretary of the Tribunals" means the Secretary of the Central Office of the [Employment Tribunals] (England and Wales) or, as the case may require, the Secretary of the Central Office of the [Employment Tribunals] (Scotland) for the time being.

(2) In the Schedule to these Regulations references to sections are references to sections of the 1996 Act unless otherwise indicated and references in column 3 of the table to the conclusion of the tribunal proceedings are references to the conclusion of the proceedings mentioned in the corresponding entry in column 2.

(3) For the purposes of these Regulations (and in particular for the purposes of any calculations to be made by an [employment tribunal] as respects the prescribed element) the conclusion of the tribunal proceedings shall be taken to occur—

(a) where the [employment tribunal] at the hearing announces the effect of its decision to the parties, on the date on which that announcement is made;

(b) in any other case, on the date on which the decision of the tribunal is sent to the parties.

(4) References to parties in relevant [employment tribunal] proceedings shall be taken to include references to persons appearing on behalf of parties in a representative capacity.

(5) References in these Regulations to anything done, or to be done, in, or in consequence of, any tribunal proceedings include references to anything done, or to be done, in, or in consequence of any such proceedings as are in the nature of a review, or re-hearing or a further hearing consequent on an appeal.

[2365]

NOTES

Paras (1), (3), (4): words in square brackets substituted by the Employment Rights (Dispute Resolution) Act 1998, s 1(2)(a), (b).

PART II
[EMPLOYMENT TRIBUNAL] PROCEEDINGS

3 Application to payments and proceedings

(1) Subject to paragraph (2) below these Regulations apply—

(a) to the payments described in column 1 of the table contained in the Schedule to these Regulations, being, in each case, payments which are the subject of [employment tribunal] proceedings of the kind described in the corresponding entry in column 2 and the prescribed element in relation to each such payment is so much of the relevant monetary award as is attributable to the matter described in the corresponding entry in column 3; and

(b) to payments of remuneration in pursuance of a protective award.

(2) The payments to which these Regulations apply by virtue of paragraph (1)(a) above include payments in proceedings under section 192 of the 1992 Act and, accordingly, where an order is made on an employee's complaint under that section, the relevant protective award shall, as respects that employee and to the appropriate extent, be taken to be subsumed in the order made under section 192 so that the provisions of these Regulations relating to monetary awards shall apply to payments under that order to the exclusion of the provisions relating to protective awards, but without prejudice to anything done under the latter in connection with the relevant protective award before the making of the order under section 192.

[2366]

NOTES

Words in square brackets in para (1) and in the heading preceding this regulation substituted by the Employment Rights (Dispute Resolution) Act 1998, s 1(2)(a).

4 Duties of the [employment tribunals] and of the Secretary of the Tribunals in respect of monetary awards

(1) Where these Regulations apply, no regard shall be had, in assessing the amount of a monetary award, to the amount of any jobseeker's allowance or any income support which may have been paid to or claimed by the employee for a period which coincides with any part of a period to which the prescribed element is attributable.

(2) Where the [employment tribunal] in arriving at a monetary award makes a reduction on account of the employee's contributory fault or on account of any limit imposed by or under the 1992 Act or 1996 Act, a proportionate reduction shall be made in arriving at the amount of the prescribed element.

(3) Subject to the following provisions of this Regulation it shall be the duty of the [employment tribunal] to set out in any decision which includes a monetary award the following particulars—

(a) the monetary award;
(b) the amount of the prescribed element, if any;
(c) the dates of the period to which the prescribed element is attributable;
(d) the amount, if any, by which the monetary award exceeds the prescribed element.

(4) Where the [employment tribunal] at the hearing announces to the parties the effect of a decision which includes a monetary award it shall inform those parties at the same time of the amount of any prescribed element included in the monetary award and shall explain the effect of Regulations 7 and 8 below in relation to the prescribed element.

(5) Where the [employment tribunal] has made such an announcement as is described in paragraph (4) above the Secretary of the Tribunals shall forthwith notify the Secretary of State that the tribunal has decided to make a monetary award including a prescribed element and shall notify him of the particulars set out in paragraph (3) above.

(6) As soon as reasonably practicable after the Secretary of the Tribunals has sent a copy of a decision containing the particulars set out in paragraph (3) above to the parties he shall send a copy of that decision to the Secretary of State.

(7) In addition to containing the particulars required under paragraph (3) above, any such decision as is mentioned in that paragraph shall contain a statement explaining the effect of Regulations 7 and 8 below in relation to the prescribed element.

(8) The requirements of paragraphs (3) to (7) above do not apply where the tribunal is satisfied that in respect of each day falling within the period to which the prescribed element relates the employee has neither received nor claimed jobseeker's allowance or income support.

[2367]

NOTES

Words in square brackets substituted by the Employment Rights (Dispute Resolution) Act 1998, s 1(2)(a), (b).

5 Duties of the [employment tribunals] and of the Secretary of the Tribunals in respect of protective awards

(1) Where, on a complaint under section 189 of the 1992 Act, an [employment tribunal]—

(a) at the hearing announces to the parties the effect of a decision to make a protective award; or

(b) (where it has made no such announcement) sends a decision to make such an award to the parties;

the Secretary of the Tribunals shall forthwith notify the Secretary of State of the following particulars relating to the award—

(i) where the [employment tribunal] has made such an announcement as is described in paragraph (1)(a) above, the date of the hearing or where it has made no such announcement, the date on which the decision was sent to the parties;

(ii) the location of the tribunal;

(iii) the name and address of the employer;

(iv) the description of the employees to whom the award relates; and

(v) the dates of the protected period.

(2)

(a) Where an [employment tribunal] makes such an announcement as is described in paragraph (1)(a) above in the presence of the employer or his representative it shall advise him of his duties under Regulation 6 below and shall explain the effect of Regulations 7 and 8 below in relation to remuneration under the protective award.

(b) Without prejudice to (a) above any decision of an [employment tribunal] to make a protective award under section 189 of the 1992 Act shall contain a statement advising the employer of his duties under Regulation 6 below and an explanation of the effect of Regulations 7 and 8 below in relation to remuneration under the protective award.

[2368]

NOTES

Words in square brackets substituted by the Employment Rights (Dispute Resolution) Act 1998, s 1(2)(a), (b).

6 Duties of the employer to give information about protective awards

(1) Where an [employment tribunal] makes a protective award under section 189 of the 1992 Act against an employer, the employer shall give to the Secretary of State the following information in writing—

(a) the name, address and national insurance number of every employee to whom the award relates; and

(b) the date of termination (or proposed termination) of the employment of each such employee.

(2) Subject to paragraph (3) below the employer shall comply with paragraph (1) above within the period of ten days commencing on the day on which the [employment tribunal] at the hearing announces to the parties the effect of a decision to make a protective award or (in the case where no such announcement is made) on the day on which the relevant decision is sent to the parties.

(3) Where, in any case, it is not reasonably practicable for the employer to comply with paragraph (1) above within the period applicable under paragraph (2) above he shall comply as soon as reasonably practicable after the expiration of that period.

[2369]

NOTES

Words in square brackets substituted by the Employment Rights (Dispute Resolution) Act 1998, s 1(2)(a).

PART III
RECOUPMENT OF BENEFIT

7 Postponement of Awards

(1) This Regulation shall have effect for the purpose of postponing relevant awards in order to enable the Secretary of State to initiate recoupment under Regulation 8 below.

(2) Accordingly—

(a) so much of the monetary award as consists of the prescribed element;

(b) payment of any remuneration to which an employee would otherwise be entitled under a protective award,

shall be treated as stayed (in Scotland, sisted) as respects the relevant employee until—

(i) the Secretary of State has served a recoupment notice on the employer; or

(ii) the Secretary of State has notified the employer in writing that he does not intend to serve a recoupment notice.

(3) The stay or sist under paragraph (2) above is without prejudice to the right of an employee under section 192 of the 1992 Act to present a complaint to an [employment tribunal] of his employer's failure to pay remuneration under a protective award and Regulation 3(2) above has effect as respects any such complaint and as respects any order made under section 192(3) of that Act.

[2370]

NOTES

Para (3): words in square brackets substituted by the Employment Rights (Dispute Resolution) Act 1998, s 1(2)(a).

8 Recoupment of Benefit

(1) Recoupment shall be initiated by the Secretary of State serving on the employer a recoupment notice claiming by way of total or partial recoupment of jobseeker's allowance or income support the appropriate amount, computed, as the case may require, under paragraph (2) or (3) below.

(2) In the case of monetary awards the appropriate amount shall be whichever is the less of the following two sums—

(a) the amount of the prescribed element (less any tax or social security contributions which fall to be deducted therefrom by the employer); or

(b) the amount paid by way of or paid as on account of jobseeker's allowance or income support to the employee for any period which coincides with any part of the period to which the prescribed element is attributable.

(3) In the case of remuneration under a protective award the appropriate amount shall be whichever is the less of the following two sums—

(a) the amount (less any tax or social security contributions which fall to be deducted therefrom by the employer) accrued due to the employee in respect of so much of the protected period as falls before the date on which the Secretary of State receives from the employer the information required under Regulation 6 above; or

(b) the amount paid by way of or paid as on account of jobseeker's allowance or income support to the employee for any period which coincides with any part of the protected period falling before the date described in (a) above.

(4) A recoupment notice shall be served on the employer by post or otherwise and copies shall likewise be sent to the employee and, if requested, to the Secretary of the Tribunals.

(5) The Secretary of State shall serve a recoupment notice on the employer, or notify the employer that he does not intend to serve such a notice, within the period applicable, as the case may require, under paragraph (6) or (7) below, or as soon as practicable thereafter.

(6) In the case of a monetary award the period shall be—

(a) in any case in which the tribunal at the hearing announces to the parties the effect of its decision as described in Regulation 4(4) above, the period ending 21 days after the conclusion of the hearing or the period ending 9 days after the decision has been sent to the parties, whichever is the later; or

(b) in any other case, the period ending 21 days after the decision has been sent to the parties.

(7) In the case of a protective award the period shall be the period ending 21 days after the Secretary of State has received from the employer the information required under Regulation 6 above.

(8) A recoupment notice served on an employer shall operate as an instruction to the employer to pay, by way of deduction out of the sum due under the award, the recoupable amount to the Secretary of State and it shall be the duty of the employer to comply with the

notice. The employer's duty under this paragraph shall not affect his obligation to pay any balance that may be due to the employee under the relevant award.

(9) The duty imposed on the employer by service of the recoupment notice shall not be discharged by payment of the recoupable amount to the employee during the postponement period or thereafter if a recoupment notice is served on the employer during the said period.

(10) Payment by the employer to the Secretary of State under this Regulation shall be a complete discharge in favour of the employer as against the employee in respect of any sum so paid but without prejudice to any rights of the employee under Regulation 10 below.

(11) The recoupable amount shall be recoverable by the Secretary of State from the employer as a debt.

[2371]

9 Order made in secondary proceedings

(1) In the application of any of the above provisions in the case of—

(a) proceedings for an award under section 192 of the 1992 Act; or

(b) proceedings in the nature of a review, a re-hearing or a further hearing consequent on an appeal,

it shall be the duty of the [employment tribunal] or, as the case may require, the Secretary of State, to take the appropriate account of anything done under or in consequence of these Regulations in relation to any award made in the original proceedings.

(2) For the purposes of this Regulation the original proceedings are—

(a) where paragraph (1)(a) above applies the proceedings under section 189 of the 1992 Act; or

(b) where paragraph (1)(b) above applies the proceedings in respect of which the re-hearing, the review or the further hearing consequent on an appeal takes place.

[2372]

NOTES

Para (1): words in square brackets substituted by the Employment Rights (Dispute Resolution) Act 1998, s 1(2)(a).

PART IV

DETERMINATION … OF BENEFIT RECOUPED

10 Provisions relating to determination of amount paid by way of or paid as on account of benefit

(1) Without prejudice to the right of the Secretary of State to recover from an employer the recoupable benefit, an employee on whom a copy of a recoupment notice has been served in accordance with Regulation 8 above may, within 21 days of the date on which such notice was served on him or within such further time as the Secretary of State may for special reasons allow, give notice in writing to the Secretary of State that he does not accept that the amount specified in the recoupment notice in respect of jobseeker's allowance or income support is correct.

[(2) Where an employee has given notice in writing to the Secretary of State under paragraph (1) above that he does not accept that an amount specified in the recoupment notice is correct, the Secretary of State shall make a decision as to the amount of jobseeker's allowance or, as the case may be, income support paid in respect of the period to which the prescribed element is attributable or, as appropriate, in respect of so much of the protected period as falls before the date on which the employer complies with Regulation 6 above.

(2A) The Secretary of State may revise either upon application made for the purpose or on his own initiative a decision under paragraph (2) above.

(2B) The employee shall have a right of appeal to an appeal tribunal constituted under Chapter I of Part I of the 1998 Act against a decision of the Secretary of State whether as originally made under paragraph (2) or as revised under paragraph (2A) above.

(2C) The Social Security and Child Support (Decisions and Appeals) Regulations 1999 shall apply for the purposes of paragraphs (2A) and (2B) above as though a decision of the Secretary of State under paragraph (2A) above were made under section 9 of the 1998 Act and any appeal from such a decision were made under section 12 of that Act.

(2D) In this Regulation "the 1998 Act" means the Social Security Act 1998.

(3) Where the Secretary of State recovers too much money from an employer under these Regulations the Secretary of State shall pay to the employee an amount equal to the excess.]

(4) In any case where, after the Secretary of State has recovered from an employer any amount by way of recoupment of benefit, the decision given by the [employment tribunal] in consequence of which such recoupment took place is set aside or varied on appeal or on a re-hearing by the [employment tribunal], the Secretary of State shall make such repayment to the employer or payment to the employee of the whole or part of the amount recovered as he is satisfied should properly be made having regard to the decision given on appeal or re-hearing.

[2373]

NOTES

The words omitted from the heading preceding this regulation were revoked, and paras (2), (2A)–(2D), (3), were substituted for original paras (2), (3), by the Social Security Act 1998 (Commencement No 12 and Consequential and Transitional Provisions) Order 1999, SI 1999/3178, art 3(1), (14), Sch 14.

Para (4): words in square brackets substituted by the Employment Rights (Dispute Resolution) Act 1998, s 1(2)(a).

11 *(Revokes the Employment Protection (Recoupment of Unemployment Benefit and Supplementary Benefit) Regulations 1977, SI 1977/674.)*

SCHEDULE
TABLE RELATING TO MONETARY AWARDS

Regulation 3

Column 1 *Payment*	*Column 2* *Proceedings*	*Column 3* *Matter to which prescribed element is attributable*
1. Guarantee payments under section 28.	1. Complaint under section 34.	1. Any amount found to be due to the employee and ordered to be paid under section 34(3) for a period before the conclusion of the tribunal proceedings.
2. Payments under any collective agreement having regard to which the appropriate Minister has made an exemption order under section 35.	2. Complaint under section 35(4).	2. Any amount found to be due to the employee and ordered to be paid under section 34(3), as applied by section 35(4), for a period before the conclusion of the tribunal proceedings.
3. Payments of remuneration in respect of a period of suspension on medical grounds under section 64 and section 108(2).	3. Complaint under section 70.	3. Any amount found to be due to the employee and ordered to be paid under section 70(3) for a period before the conclusion of the tribunal proceedings.
4. Payments of remuneration in respect of a period of suspension on maternity grounds under section 68.	4. Complaint under section 70.	4. Any amount found to be due to the employee and ordered to be paid under section 70(3) for a period before the conclusion of the tribunal proceedings.

Column 1 *Payment*	*Column 2* *Proceedings*	*Column 3* *Matter to which prescribed element is attributable*
5. Payments under an order for reinstatement under section 114(1).	5. Complaint of unfair dismissal under section 111(1).	5. Any amount ordered to be paid under section 114(2)(a) in respect of arrears of pay for a period before the conclusion of the tribunal proceedings.
6. Payments under an order for re-engagement under section 117(8).	6. Complaint of unfair dismissal under section 111(1).	6. Any amount ordered to be paid under section 115(2)(d) in respect of arrears of pay for a period before the conclusion of the tribunal proceedings.
7. Payments under an award of compensation for unfair dismissal in cases falling under section 112(4) (cases where no order for reinstatement or re-engagement has been made).	7. Complaint of unfair dismissal under section 111(1).	7. Any amount ordered to be paid and calculated under section 123 in respect of compensation for loss of wages for a period before the conclusion of the tribunal proceedings.
8. Payments under an award of compensation for unfair dismissal under section 117(3) where reinstatement order not complied with.	8. Proceedings in respect of non-compliance with order.	8. Any amount ordered to be paid and calculated under section 123 in respect of compensation for loss of wages for a period before the conclusion of the tribunal proceedings.
9. Payments under an award of compensation for unfair dismissal under section 117(3) where re-engagement order not complied with.	9. Proceedings in respect of non-compliance with order.	9. Any amount ordered to be paid and calculated under section 123 in respect of compensation for loss of wages for a period before the conclusion of the tribunal proceedings.
10. Payments under an interim order for reinstatement under section 163(4) of the 1992 Act.	10. Proceedings on an application for an order for interim relief under section 161(1) of the 1992 Act.	10. Any amount found to be due to the complainant and ordered to be paid in respect of arrears of pay for the period between the date of termination of employment and the conclusion of the tribunal proceedings.
11. Payments under an interim order for re-engagement under section 163(5)(a) of the 1992 Act.	11. Proceedings on an application for an order for interim relief under section 161(1) of the 1992 Act.	11. Any amount found to be due to the complainant and ordered to be paid in respect of arrears of pay for the period between the date of termination of employment and the conclusion of the tribunal proceedings.

Column 1 Payment	Column 2 Proceedings	Column 3 Matter to which prescribed element is attributable
12. Payments under an order for the continuation of a contract of employment under section 163(5)(b) of the 1992 Act where employee reasonably refuses re-engagement.	12. Proceedings on an application for an order for interim relief under section 161(1) of the 1992 Act.	12. Any amount found to be due to the complainant and ordered to be paid in respect of arrears of pay for the period between the date of termination of employment and the conclusion of the tribunal proceedings.
13. Payments under an order for the continuation of a contract of employment under section 163(6) of the 1992 Act where employer fails to attend or is unwilling to reinstate or re-engage.	13. Proceedings on an application for an order for interim relief under section 161(1) of the 1992 Act.	13. Any amount found to be due to the complainant and ordered to be paid in respect of arrears of pay for the period between the date of termination of employment and the conclusion of the tribunal proceedings.
14. Payments under an order for the continuation of a contract of employment under sections 166(1) and (2) of the 1992 Act where reinstatement or re-engagement order not complied with.	14. Proceedings in respect of non-compliance with order.	14. Any amount ordered to be paid to the employee by way of compensation under section 166(1)(b) of the 1992 Act for loss of wages for the period between the date of termination of employment and the conclusion of the tribunal proceedings.
15. Payments under an order for compensation under sections 166(3)(5) of the 1992 Act where order for the continuation of contract of employment not complied with.	15. Proceedings in respect of non-compliance with order.	15. Any amount ordered to be paid to the employee by way of compensation under section 166(3)(4) of the 1992 Act for loss of wages for the period between the date of termination of employment and the conclusion of the tribunal proceedings.
16. Payments under an order under section 192(3) of the 1992 Act on employer's default in respect of remuneration due to employee under protective award.	16. Complaint under section 192(1) of the 1992 Act.	16. Any amount ordered to be paid to the employee in respect of so much of the relevant protected period as falls before the date of the conclusion of the tribunal proceedings.

[2374]

PERSONAL AND OCCUPATIONAL PENSION SCHEMES (PENSIONS OMBUDSMAN) REGULATIONS 1996

(SI 1996/2475)

NOTES

Made: 25 September 1996.
Authority: Pension Schemes Act 1993, ss 146(4), (6)(b), (c), 151A, 181(1), 182(2), (3).
Commencement: 6 April 1997.
See *Harvey* B8(D).

ARRANGEMENT OF REGULATIONS

1 Citation, commencement and interpretation

(1) These Regulations may be cited as the Personal and Occupational Pension Schemes (Pensions Ombudsman) Regulations 1996 and shall come into force on 6th April 1997.

(2) In these Regulations—

"the 1993 Act" means the Pension Schemes Act 1993;

"the 1995 Act" means the Pensions Act 1995;

["administrator"—

(a) in relation to an occupational pension scheme, means any person concerned with the administration of the scheme, other than a person responsible for the management of the scheme (as defined in section 146(3) of the 1993 Act for the purposes of Part X of that Act), and

(b) in relation to a personal pension scheme, means any person concerned with the administration of the scheme, other than—

(i) a person responsible for the management of the scheme (as defined in section 146(3A) of that Act for the purposes of that Part), or

(ii) a person who is or has been the employer of any member who is or has been an employed earner;]

"actual or potential beneficiaries" has the same meaning as in section 146(7) of the 1993 Act;

"complaint" means a complaint falling within section 146(1)(a) or (b) of the 1993 Act (complaint of maladministration); and

"dispute" means a dispute falling within section 146(1)(c) or (d) of the 1993 Act (disputes of fact or law).

[2375]

NOTES

Definition "administrator" substituted by the Personal and Occupational Pension Schemes (Miscellaneous Amendments) Regulations 1997, SI 1997/786, reg 3, Sch 1, para 15(1), (2).

[1A Persons entitled to benefits to be regarded as members for the purposes of section 146(7) of the 1993 Act

For the purposes of section 146(7) of the 1993 Act (persons who are actual or potential beneficiaries) a person shall be regarded as a member of a scheme if he is, or has been, entitled to the payment of benefits under it.]

[2376]

NOTES

Inserted by the Personal and Occupational Pension Schemes (Miscellaneous Amendments) (No 2) Regulations 1997, SI 1997/3038, reg 9(1), (2).

2 Jurisdiction in relation to administrators

(1) The Pensions Ombudsman may investigate and determine a complaint concerning the administration of a personal or an occupational pension scheme made to him by or in respect of an actual or potential beneficiary of the scheme who alleges that he has sustained injustice in consequence of maladministration in connection with an act or omission of an administrator of the scheme.

(2) Where the Pensions Ombudsman commences an investigation under paragraph (1) above, the provisions of Part X of the 1993 Act (the Pensions Ombudsman) shall apply in relation to the administrator as they would apply in relation to a person responsible for the management of the scheme.

[2377]

3 Exclusion from jurisdiction: Use of internal disputes procedure

(1) In a case to which section 50 of the 1995 Act applies (internal dispute resolution), the Pensions Ombudsman shall not, subject to paragraph (2) below, investigate or determine a complaint or dispute concerning an occupational pension scheme unless written notice of a decision in respect of that complaint or dispute has first been issued by the trustees or managers of the scheme under [section 50(5)(b)] of that Act.

(2) Where, in a case to which section 50 of the 1995 Act applies, an application concerning a complaint or dispute has been made to an occupational pension scheme under the arrangements required by that section, the Pensions Ombudsman may investigate and determine that complaint or dispute in advance of written notice of a decision being issued in respect of it under [section 50(5)(b)] of that Act provided he is satisfied that—

(a) there is no real prospect of a notice being issued within a reasonable period from the date on which the complaint or dispute was received by him in writing; and

(b) it is reasonable in the circumstances that he should investigate and determine the complaint or dispute.

[2378]

NOTES

Words in square brackets substituted by the Occupational Pension Schemes (Internal Dispute Resolution Procedures Consequential and Miscellaneous Amendments) Regulations 2008, SI 2008/649, reg 6(2), as from 6 April 2008.

4 Exclusions from jurisdiction

[(1) The Pensions Ombudsman shall not investigate or determine any complaint or dispute which can be [(and is in fact)] dealt with under the compulsory jurisdiction of the ombudsman scheme provided for by Part 16 of the Financial Services and Markets Act 2000, other than a complaint or dispute relating to the management of a personal pension scheme.]

(2) For the purposes of the investigation or determination of any complaint or dispute, the Pensions Ombudsman shall not make any findings of fact to the effect that a person responsible for the management of an occupational pension scheme has failed to comply with the requirements under the following provisions of the 1995 Act—

(a) sections 16 to 21 (requirement for member nominated trustees),

(b) sections 37 and 76 (payment of surplus or excess assets to the employer),

(c) section 40 (restriction on employer related investments),

(d) section 47(1)(a) and (b) (requirement to appoint professional advisers),

(e) section 49 (requirement to keep books and records),

(f) sections 56 to 61 (the minimum funding requirement and schedules of contributions), and

(g) sections 87 and 88 (requirement for money purchase schemes to keep schedules of payments),

[or the requirements under Part 3 of the Pensions Act 2004].

[2379]

NOTES

Para (1): substituted by the Financial Services and Markets Act 2000 (Consequential Amendments and Repeals) Order 2001, SI 2001/3649, art 539; words in square brackets inserted by the Financial Services and Markets Act 2000 (Consequential Amendments) Order 2002, SI 2002/1555, art 37.

Para (2): words in square brackets inserted by the Occupational Pension Schemes (Scheme Funding) Regulations 2005, SI 2005/3377, reg 20(1), Sch 3, para 6, as from 30 December 2005.

5 Time limit for making complaints and referring disputes

(1) Subject to paragraphs (2) and (3) below, the Pensions Ombudsman shall not investigate a complaint or dispute if the act or omission which is the subject thereof occurred more than 3 years before the date on which the complaint or dispute was received by him in writing.

(2) Where, at the date of its occurrence, the person by or in respect of whom the complaint is made or the dispute is referred was, in the opinion of the Pensions Ombudsman, unaware of the act or omission referred to in paragraph (1) above, the period of 3 years shall begin on the earliest date on which that person knew or ought reasonably to have known of its occurrence.

(3) Where, in the opinion of the Pensions Ombudsman, it was reasonable for a complaint not to be made or a dispute not to be referred before the end of the period allowed under paragraphs (1) and (2) above, the Pensions Ombudsman may investigate and determine that complaint or dispute if it is received by him in writing within such further period as he considers reasonable.

[2380]

6 Payment of interest on late paid benefit

(1) For the purposes of section 151A of the 1993 Act (interest on late payment of benefit), the prescribed rate of interest shall be the base rate for the time being quoted by the reference banks.

(2) In paragraph (1) above—

(a) "base rate" means the rate for the time being quoted by the reference banks as applicable to sterling deposits or, where there is for the time being more than one such base rate, the rate which, when the base rate quoted by each bank is ranked in a descending sequence of four, is first in the sequence; and

[(b) "reference banks" means the four largest persons for the time being who—

(i) have permission under Part 4 of the Financial Services and Markets Act 2000 to accept deposits,

(ii) are incorporated in the United Kingdom and carrying on there a regulated activity of accepting deposits, and

(iii) quote a base rate applicable to sterling deposits].

[(3) Paragraph (2)(b) must be read with—

(a) section 22 of the Financial Services and Markets Act 2000;

(b) any relevant order under that section; and

(c) Schedule 2 to that Act.]

[2381]

NOTES

Para (2): sub-para (b) substituted by the Financial Services and Markets Act 2000 (Consequential Amendments and Repeals) Order 2001, SI 2001/3649, art 540(1).

Para (3): added by SI 2001/3649, art 540(2).

7 (*Revokes the Personal and Occupational Pension Schemes* (*Pensions Ombudsman*) *Regulations 1991, SI 1991/588, the Personal and Occupational Pension Schemes* (*Pensions Ombudsman*) *Amendment Regulations 1996, SI 1996/1271, and the Occupational and Personal Pension Schemes* (*Consequential Amendments*) *Regulations 1994, SI 1994/1062, Sch 2, para 32.*)

8 Saving

Anything done under, or by virtue of, any regulation revoked by these Regulations, if it could have been done under or for the purpose of the corresponding provision of these Regulations, shall be deemed to have been done under or by virtue of the corresponding provision of these Regulations and anything begun under, or by virtue of, any such regulation may be continued under these Regulations as if begun under these Regulations.

[2382]

DISABILITY DISCRIMINATION (QUESTIONS AND REPLIES) ORDER 1996 (NOTE)

(SI 1996/2793)

NOTES

This Order was revoked and replaced by the Disability Discrimination (Questions and Replies) Order 2004, SI 2004/1168 (at **[3141]**) as from 1 October 2004.

[2383]–[2389]

[EMPLOYMENT TRIBUNALS] (INTEREST ON AWARDS IN DISCRIMINATION CASES) REGULATIONS 1996

(SI 1996/2803)

NOTES

Made: 5 November 1996.

Authority: European Communities Act 1972, s 2(2); Race Relations Act 1976, s 56(5), (6); Disability Discrimination Act 1995, s 17A(6), (7). Note that these Regulations were originally made under s 8(6), (7) of the Disability Discrimination Act 1995, but s 8 was renumbered as s 17 by the Disability Discrimination Act 1995 (Amendment) Regulations 2003, SI 2003/1673.

Commencement: 2 December 1996.

Title: words in square brackets substituted by the Employment Rights (Dispute Resolution) Act 1998, s 1(2)(b).

See *Harvey* T(A27).

ARRANGEMENT OF REGULATIONS

1 Citation, commencement, interpretation and revocation

(1) These Regulations may be cited as the [Employment Tribunals] (Interest on Awards in Discrimination Cases) Regulations 1996 and shall come into force on 2nd December 1996.

(2) In these Regulations—

"the 1970 Act" means the Equal Pay Act 1970;

"the 1975 Act" means the Sex Discrimination Act 1975;

"the 1976 Act" means the Race Relations Act 1976;

"the 1995 Act" means the Disability Discrimination Act 1995 and;

"an award under the relevant legislation" means—

(a) an award under the 1970 Act of arrears of remuneration or damages, or

(b) an order under section 65(1)(b) of the 1975 Act, section 56(1)(b) of the 1976 Act … section 8(2)(b) of the 1995 Act [… regulation 30(1)(b) of the Employment Equality (Sexual Orientation) Regulations 2003] [… regulation 30(1)(b) of the Employment Equality (Religion or Belief) Regulations 2003] [or regulation 38(1)(b) of the Employment Equality (Age) Regulations 2006] for payment of compensation,

but does not include an award of costs under rule 12 in Schedule 1 to the [Employment Tribunals] (Constitution and Rules of Procedure) Regulations 1993, or of expenses under rule 12 in Schedule 1 to the [Employment Tribunals] (Constitution and Rules of Procedure) (Scotland) Regulations 1993, even if the award of costs or expenses is made in the same proceedings as an award under the 1970 Act or such an order.

(3) …

[2390]

NOTES

Para (1): words in square brackets substituted by the Employment Rights (Dispute Resolution) Act 1998, s 1(2)(b).

Para (2): in definition "an award under the relevant legislation" first words omitted from para (b) revoked, and words in first pair of square brackets in that paragraph inserted, by the Employment Equality (Sexual Orientation) Regulations 2003, SI 2003/1661, reg 39, Sch 5, para 3, as from 1 December 2003; second words omitted from para (b) of that definition revoked, and words in second pair of square brackets in that paragraph inserted, by the Employment Equality (Religion or Belief) Regulations 2003, SI 2003/1660, reg 39(2), Sch 5, para 3, as from 2 December 2003; final words omitted from para (b) of that definition revoked, and words in final pair of square brackets in that paragraph inserted, by the Employment Equality (Age) Regulations 2006, SI 2006/1031, SI 2006/1031, reg 49(1), Sch 8, Pt 2, para 56(1), (2)(a), as from 1 October 2006; other words in square brackets in that definition substituted by the Employment Rights (Dispute Resolution) Act 1998, s 1(2)(b).

Para (3): revokes the Sex Discrimination and Equal Pay (Remedies) Regulations 1993, SI 1993/2978, and the Race Relations (Interest on Awards) Regulations 1994, SI 1994/1748.

Employment Tribunals (Constitution and Rules of Procedure) Regulations 1993, SI 1993/2867; Employment Tribunals (Constitution and Rules of Procedure) (Scotland) Regulations 1993, SI 1993/2688: revoked and replaced; see now, the Employment Tribunals (Constitution and Rules of Procedure) Regulations 2004, SI 2004/1861 at **[3151]**.

"An award under the relevant legislation": note that the Disability Discrimination Act 1995, s 8(2)(b) is now s 17A(2)(b) following the amendments made to the 1995 Act by the Disability Discrimination Act 1995 (Amendment) Regulations 2003, SI 2003/1673. However, no consequential amendment has been made to this regulation to take account of this.

2 Interest on awards

(1) Where, at any time after the commencement of these Regulations, an [employment tribunal] makes an award under the relevant legislation—

(a) it may, subject to the following provisions of these Regulations, include interest on the sums awarded; and

(b) it shall consider whether to do so, without the need for any application by a party in the proceedings.

(2) Nothing in paragraph (1) shall prevent the tribunal from making an award or decision, with regard to interest, in terms which have been agreed between the parties.

[2391]

NOTES

Para (1): words in square brackets substituted by the Employment Rights (Dispute Resolution) Act 1998, s 1(2)(a).

3 Rate of interest

(1) Interest shall be calculated as simple interest which accrues from day to day.

(2) Subject to paragraph (3), the rate of interest to be applied shall be, in England and Wales, the rate from time to time prescribed for the Special Investment Account under rule 27(1) of the Court Funds Rules 1987 and, in Scotland, the rate fixed, for the time being, by the Act of Sederunt (Interest in Sheriff Court Decrees or Extracts) 1975.

(3) Where the rate of interest in paragraph (2) has varied during a period for which interest is to be calculated, the tribunal may, if it so desires in the interests of simplicity, apply such median or average of those rates as seems to it appropriate.

[2392]

NOTES

Court Funds Rules 1987: ie, SI 1987/821 as amended (most recently by the Court Funds (Amendment No 2) Rules 2007, SI 2007/2617).

Rate of interest: the rate of interest currently prescribed for England and Wales is 6 per cent (as from 1 March 2002); the previous rate was 7 per cent (as from 1 August 1999).

4 Calculation of interest

(1) In this regulation and regulations 5 and 6, "day of calculation" means the day on which the amount of interest is calculated by the tribunal.

(2) In regulation 6, "mid-point date" means the day which falls half-way through the period mentioned in paragraph (3) or, where the number of days in that period is even, the first day of the second half of the period.

(3) The period referred to in paragraph (2) is the period beginning on the date, in the case of an award under the 1970 Act, of the contravention and, in other cases, of the act of discrimination complained of, and ending on the day of calculation.

[2393]

5 No interest shall be included in respect of any sum awarded for a loss or matter which will occur after the day of calculation or in respect of any time before the contravention or act of discrimination complained of.

[2394]

6—(1) Subject to the following paragraphs of this regulation—

(a) in the case of any sum for injury to feelings, interest shall be for the period beginning on the date of the contravention or act of discrimination complained of and ending on the day of calculation;

(b) in the case of all other sums of damages or compensation (other than any sum referred to in regulation 5) and all arrears of remuneration, interest shall be for the period beginning on the mid-point date and ending on the day of calculation.

(2) Where any payment has been made before the day of calculation to the complainant by or on behalf of the respondent in respect of the subject matter of the award, interest in respect of that part of the award covered by the payment shall be calculated as if the references in paragraph (1), and in the definition of "mid-point date" in regulation 4, to the day of calculation were to the date on which the payment was made.

(3) Where the tribunal considers that in the circumstances, whether relating to the case as a whole or to a particular sum in an award, serious injustice would be caused if interest were to be awarded in respect of the period or periods in paragraphs (1) or (2), it may—

(a) calculate interest, or as the case may be interest on the particular sum, for such different period, or

(b) calculate interest for such different periods in respect of various sums in the award,

as it considers appropriate in the circumstances, having regard to the provisions of these Regulations.

[2395]

7 Decision in writing

(1) The tribunal's written statement of reasons for its decision shall contain a statement of the total amount of any interest awarded under regulation 2 and, unless this amount has been agreed between the parties, either a table showing how it has been calculated or a description of the manner in which it has been calculated.

(2) The tribunal's written statement of reasons shall include reasons for any decision not to award interest under regulation 2.

[2396]

8 Interest for period after award

(1) The [Employment Tribunals] (Interest) Order 1990 shall apply in relation to an award under the relevant legislation (whether or not including interest under regulation 2) as if references in that Order to the calculation day were references to the day immediately following the relevant decision day (as defined in Article 2(3) of the Order) and accordingly interest shall accrue under the Order from that day onwards (including that day).

(2) Notwithstanding paragraph (1), no interest shall be payable by virtue of that Order if payment of the full amount of the award (including any interest under regulation 2) is made within 14 days after the relevant decision day.

[2397]

NOTES

Para (1): words in square brackets substituted by the Employment Rights (Dispute Resolution) Act 1998, s 1(2)(b).

EMPLOYMENT PROTECTION (CONTINUITY OF EMPLOYMENT) REGULATIONS 1996

(SI 1996/3147)

NOTES

Made: 16 December 1996.
Authority: Employment Rights Act 1996, s 219.
Commencement: 13 January 1997.
See *Harvey* CI(1C), R.

1 Citation, commencement and revocation

(1) These Regulations may be cited as the Employment Protection (Continuity of Employment) Regulations 1996 and shall come into force on 13th January 1997.

(2) The Employment Protection (Continuity of Employment) Regulations 1993 are revoked.

[2398]

2 Application

These Regulations apply to any action taken in relation to the dismissal of an employee which consists of—

(a) his making a claim in accordance with a dismissal procedures agreement designated by an order under section 110 of the Employment Rights Act 1996,

(b) the presentation by him of a relevant complaint of dismissal,

(c) any action taken by a conciliation officer under section 18 of [the Employment Tribunals Act 1996], ...

(d) the making of a relevant compromise contract[, ...

(e) the making of an agreement to submit a dispute to arbitration in accordance with a scheme having effect by virtue of an order under section 212A of the Trade Union and Labour Relations (Consolidation) Act 1992,][...

(f) a decision taken arising out of the use of a statutory dispute resolution procedure contained in Schedule 2 to the Employment Act 2002 in a case where, in accordance with the Employment Act 2002 (Dispute Resolution) Regulations 2004, such a procedure applies][, or

(g) a decision taken arising out of the use of the statutory duty to consider procedure contained in Schedule 6 to the Employment Equality (Age) Regulations 2006].

[2399]

NOTES

Words in square brackets in para (c) substituted by the Employment Rights (Dispute Resolution) Act 1998, s 1(2)(c).

Word omitted from para (c) revoked, and para (e) and the word immediately preceding it added, by the Employment Protection (Continuity of Employment) (Amendment) Regulations 2001, SI 2001/1188, reg 2.

Word omitted from para (d) revoked, and para (f) and the word immediately preceding it added, by the Employment Act 2002 (Dispute Resolution) Regulations 2004, SI 2004/752, reg 17(e), as from 1 October 2004 (for transitional provisions and effect see reg 18 at **[3098]**).

Word omitted from para (e) revoked, and para (g) and the word immediately preceding it added, by the Employment Equality (Age) Regulations 2006, SI 2006/1031, reg 49(1), Sch 8, Pt 2, para 57, as from 1 October 2006.

Relevant complaint of dismissal; relevant compromise contract: these were defined in the Employment Rights Act 1996, s 219(3), (4) (repealed by the Employment Rights (Dispute Resolution) Act 1998, s 15, Sch 1, para 25, Sch 2).

3 Continuity of employment where employee re-engaged

(1) The provisions of this regulation shall have effect to preserve the continuity of a person's period of employment for the purposes of—

(a) Chapter I of Part XIV of the Employment Rights Act 1996 (continuous employment), and

(b) that Chapter as applied by subsection (2) of section 282 of the Trade Union and Labour Relations (Consolidation) Act 1992 for the purposes of that section.

(2) If in consequence of any action to which these Regulations apply a dismissed employee is reinstated or re-employed by his employer or by a successor or associated employer of the employer—

(a) the continuity of that employee's period of employment shall be preserved, and

(b) the period beginning with the date on which the dismissal takes effect and ending with the date of reinstatement or re-engagement shall count in the computation of the employee's period of continuous employment.

[2400]

4 Exclusion of operation of section 214 of the Employment Rights Act 1996 where redundancy or equivalent payment repaid

(1) Section 214 of the Employment Rights Act 1996 (continuity broken where employee re-employed after the making of a redundancy payment or equivalent payment) shall not apply where—

(a) in consequence of any action to which these Regulations apply a dismissed employee is reinstated or re-employed by his employer or by a successor or associated employer of the employer,

(b) the terms upon which he is so reinstated or re-engaged include provision for him to repay the amount of a redundancy payment or an equivalent payment paid in respect of the relevant dismissal, and

(c) that provision is complied with.

(2) For the purposes of this regulation the cases in which a redundancy payment shall be treated as having been paid are the cases mentioned in section 214(5) of the Employment Rights Act 1996.

[2401]

RACE RELATIONS (COMPLAINTS TO [EMPLOYMENT TRIBUNALS]) (ARMED FORCES) REGULATIONS 1997

(SI 1997/2161)

NOTES

Made: 29 August 1997.
Authority: Race Relations Act 1976, s 75(9A), (10)(aa).
Commencement: 1 October 1997.
Title: words in square brackets substituted by the Employment Rights (Dispute Resolution) Act 1998, s 1(2)(b).
See Harvey L2(A).

1 These Regulations may be cited as the Race Relations (Complaints to [Employment Tribunals]) (Armed Forces) Regulations 1997 and shall come into force on 1st October 1997.

[2402]

NOTES

Words in square brackets substituted by the Employment Rights (Dispute Resolution) Act 1998, s 1(2)(b).

2—(1) A person may present a complaint to an [employment tribunal] under section 54 of the Race Relations Act 1976, notwithstanding that section 75(9) of that Act would otherwise preclude the presentation of such a complaint, where—

(a) he has made a complaint in respect of the same matter to an officer under the service redress procedures; and

(b) that complaint has not been withdrawn.

(2) For the purposes of paragraph (1)(b) above, a person shall be treated as having withdrawn his complaint if, having made a complaint to an officer under the service redress procedures, he fails to submit that complaint to the Defence Council under those procedures.

[2403]

NOTES

Para (1): words in square brackets substituted by the Employment Rights (Dispute Resolution) Act 1998, s 1(2)(a).

EQUAL PAY (COMPLAINTS TO [EMPLOYMENT TRIBUNALS]) (ARMED FORCES) REGULATIONS 1997 (NOTE)

(SI 1997/2162)

NOTES

These Regulations, which were reproduced in the fifteenth edition of this work, have been omitted for reasons of space.

[2404]–[2405]

SEX DISCRIMINATION (COMPLAINTS TO [EMPLOYMENT TRIBUNALS]) (ARMED FORCES) REGULATIONS 1997

(SI 1997/2163)

NOTES

Made: 29 August 1997.
Authority: Sex Discrimination Act 1975, s 85(9C), (9E).
Commencement: 1 October 1997.
Title: words in square brackets substituted by the Employment Rights (Dispute Resolution) Act 1998, s 1(2)(b).

1 These Regulations may be cited as the Sex Discrimination (Complaints to [Employment Tribunals]) (Armed Forces) Regulations 1997 and shall come into force on 1st October 1997.
[2406]

NOTES

Words in square brackets substituted by the Employment Rights (Dispute Resolution) Act 1998, s 1(2)(b).

2—(1) A person may present a complaint to an [employment tribunal] under section 63 of the Sex Discrimination Act 1975, notwithstanding that section 85(9B) of that Act would otherwise preclude the presentation of such a complaint, where—

(a) he has made a complaint in respect of the same matter to an officer under the service redress procedures; and
(b) that complaint has not been withdrawn.

(2) For the purpose of paragraph (1)(b) above, a person shall be treated as having withdrawn his complaint if, having made a complaint to an officer under the service redress procedures, he fails to submit that complaint to the Defence Council under those procedures.
[2407]–[2410]

NOTES

Para (1): words in square brackets substituted by the Employment Rights (Dispute Resolution) Act 1998, s 1(2)(a).

WORKING TIME REGULATIONS 1998

(SI 1998/1833)

NOTES

Made: 30 July 1998.
Authority: European Communities Act 1972, s 2(2).

Commencement: 1 October 1998.

These Regulations are the domestic implementation of Council Directive 93/104/EC on working time at **[3834]**, and (in part) of Council Directive 94/33/EC on the protection of young people at work at **[3835]**. As to the 1993 Council Directive, see now Council Directive 2003/88/EC concerning certain aspects of the organisation of working time at **[4090]**, which consolidates the 1993 Directive and a subsequent amending Directive, as from 2 August 2004.

Conciliation: employment tribunal proceedings and claims which could be the subject of employment tribunal proceedings under reg 30 of these Regulations are proceedings to which the Employment Tribunals Act 1996, s 18 applies; see s 18(1)(ff) of that Act, at **[975]**. The short conciliation period applies in relation to claims made in relation to regs 13, 14(2) or 16(1); otherwise the standard conciliation period applies: see the Employment Tribunals (Constitution and Rules of Procedure) Regulations 2004, SI 2004/1861, Sch 1, rule 22(5), (6), as amended by SI 2005/1865.

Employment Appeal Tribunal: an appeal lies to the Employment Appeal Tribunal on any question of law arising from any decision of, or in any proceedings before, an employment tribunal under or by virtue of these Regulations; see the Employment Tribunals Act 1996, s 21(1)(h) at **[978]**.

See *Harvey* A9, B1(B), DII, R, T(A), U2.

ARRANGEMENT OF REGULATIONS

PART I
GENERAL

PART II
RIGHTS AND OBLIGATIONS CONCERNING WORKING TIME

PART III
EXCEPTIONS

PART IV
MISCELLANEOUS

PART V
SPECIAL CLASSES OF PERSON

SCHEDULES:

PART I
GENERAL

1 Citation, commencement and extent

(1) These Regulations may be cited as the Working Time Regulations 1998 and shall come into force on 1st October 1998.

(2) These Regulations extend to Great Britain only.

[2411]

2 Interpretation

(1) In these Regulations—

"the 1996 Act" means the Employment Rights Act 1996;

"adult worker" means a worker who has attained the age of 18;

"the armed forces" means any of the naval, military and air forces of the Crown;

"calendar year" means the period of twelve months beginning with 1st January in any year;

"the civil protection services" includes the police, fire brigades and ambulance services, the security and intelligence services, customs and immigration officers, the prison service, the coastguard, and lifeboat crew and other voluntary rescue services;

"collective agreement" means a collective agreement within the meaning of section 178 of the Trade Union and Labour Relations (Consolidation) Act 1992, the trade union parties to which are independent trade unions within the meaning of section 5 of that Act;

"day" means a period of 24 hours beginning at midnight;

"employer", in relation to a worker, means the person by whom the worker is (or, where the employment has ceased, was) employed;

"employment", in relation to a worker, means employment under his contract, and "employed" shall be construed accordingly;

["fishing vessel" has the same meaning as in section 313 of the Merchant Shipping Act 1995;

"mobile worker" means any worker employed as a member of travelling or flying personnel by an undertaking which operates transport services for passengers or goods by road or air;]

"night time", in relation to a worker, means a period—

(a) the duration of which is not less than seven hours, and

(b) which includes the period between midnight and 5 am,

which is determined for the purposes of these Regulations by a relevant agreement, or, in default of such a determination, the period between 11 pm and 6 am;

"night work" means work during night time;

"night worker" means a worker—

(a) who, as a normal course, works at least three hours of his daily working time during night time, or

(b) who is likely, during night time, to work at least such proportion of his annual working time as may be specified for the purposes of these Regulations in a collective agreement or a workforce agreement;

and, for the purpose of paragraph (a) of this definition, a person works hours as a normal course (without prejudice to the generality of that expression) if he works such hours on the majority of days on which he works;

["offshore work" means work performed mainly on or from offshore installations (including drilling rigs), directly or indirectly in connection with the exploration, extraction or exploitation of mineral resources, including hydrocarbons, and diving in connection with such activities, whether performed from an offshore installation or a vessel[, including any such work performed in the territorial waters of the United Kingdom adjacent to Great Britain or in any area (except one or part of one in which the law of Northern Ireland applies) designated under section 1(7) of the Continental Shelf Act 1964];]

"relevant agreement", in relation to a worker, means a workforce agreement which applies to him, any provision of a collective agreement which forms part of a contract between him and his employer, or any other agreement in writing which is legally enforceable as between the worker and his employer;

"relevant training" means work experience provided pursuant to a training course or programme, training for employment, or both, other than work experience or training—

(a) the immediate provider of which is an educational institution or a person whose main business is the provision of training, and

(b) which is provided on a course run by that institution or person;

"rest period", in relation to a worker, means a period which is not working time, other than a rest break or leave to which the worker is entitled under these Regulations;

["the restricted period", in relation to a worker, means the period between 10 pm and 6 am or, where the worker's contract provides for him to work after 10 pm, the period between 11 pm and 7 am;]

["ship" has the same meaning as in section 313 of the Merchant Shipping Act 1995;]

"worker" means an individual who has entered into or works under (or, where the employment has ceased, worked under)—

(a) a contract of employment; or

(b) any other contract, whether express or implied and (if it is express) whether oral or in writing, whereby the individual undertakes to do or perform personally any work or services for another party to the contract whose status is not by virtue of the contract that of a client or customer of any profession or business undertaking carried on by the individual;

and any reference to a worker's contract shall be construed accordingly;

"worker employed in agriculture" has the same meaning as in the Agricultural Wages Act 1948 or the Agricultural Wages (Scotland) Act 1949, and a reference to a worker partly employed in agriculture is to a worker employed in agriculture whose employer also employs him for non-agricultural purposes;

"workforce agreement" means an agreement between an employer and workers employed by him or their representatives in respect of which the conditions set out in Schedule 1 to these Regulations are satisfied;

"working time", in relation to a worker, means—

(a) any period during which he is working, at his employer's disposal and carrying out his activity or duties,

(b) any period during which he is receiving relevant training, and

(c) any additional period which is to be treated as working time for the purpose of these Regulations under a relevant agreement;

and "work" shall be construed accordingly;

"Working Time Directive" means Council Directive 93/104/EC of 23rd November 1993 concerning certain aspects of the organization of working time;

"young worker" means a worker who has attained the age of 15 but not the age of 18 and who, as respects England and Wales, is over compulsory school age (construed in accordance with section 8 of the Education Act 1996) and, as respects Scotland, is over school age (construed in accordance with section 31 of the Education (Scotland) Act 1980), and

"Young Workers Directive" means Council Directive 94/33/EC of 22nd June 1994 on the protection of young people at work.

(2) In the absence of a definition in these Regulations, words and expressions used in particular provisions which are also used in corresponding provisions of the Working Time Directive or the Young Workers Directive have the same meaning as they have in those corresponding provisions.

(3) In these Regulations—

(a) a reference to a numbered regulation is to the regulation in these Regulations bearing that number;

(b) a reference in a regulation to a numbered paragraph is to the paragraph in that regulation bearing that number; and

(c) a reference in a paragraph to a lettered sub-paragraph is to the sub-paragraph in that paragraph bearing that letter.

[2412]

NOTES

Para (1): definitions "fishing vessel", "mobile worker", "offshore work", and "ship" inserted by the Working Time (Amendment) Regulations 2003, SI 2003/1684, regs 2, 3, as from 1 August 2003; words in square brackets in definition "offshore work" inserted by the Working Time (Amendment) (No 2) Regulations 2006, SI 2006/2389, reg 2, as from 1 October 2006; definition "the restricted period" inserted by the Working Time (Amendment) Regulations 2002, SI 2002/3128, regs 2, 3.

PART II
RIGHTS AND OBLIGATIONS CONCERNING WORKING TIME

3 General

[(1)] The provisions of this Part have effect subject to the exceptions provided for in Part III of these Regulations.

[(2) Where, in this Part, separate provision is made as respects the same matter in relation to workers generally and to young workers, the provision relating to workers generally applies only to adult workers and those young workers to whom, by virtue of any exception in Part 3, the provision relating to young workers does not apply.]

[2413]

NOTES

Para (1) numbered as such, and para (2) added, by the Working Time (Amendment) Regulations 2002, SI 2002/3128, regs 2, 4.

4 Maximum weekly working time

(1) [Unless his employer has first obtained the worker's agreement in writing to perform such work], a worker's working time, including overtime, in any reference period which is applicable in his case shall not exceed an average of 48 hours for each seven days.

(2) An employer shall take all reasonable steps, in keeping with the need to protect the health and safety of workers, to ensure that the limit specified in paragraph (1) is complied with in the case of each worker employed by him in relation to whom it applies [and shall keep up-to-date records of all workers who carry out work to which it does not apply by reason of the fact that the employer has obtained the worker's agreement as mentioned in paragraph (1)].

(3) Subject to paragraphs (4) and (5) and any agreement under regulation 23(b), the reference periods which apply in the case of a worker are—

(a) where a relevant agreement provides for the application of this regulation in relation to successive periods of 17 weeks, each such period, or

(b) in any other case, any period of 17 weeks in the course of his employment.

(4) Where a worker has worked for his employer for less than 17 weeks, the reference period applicable in his case is the period that has elapsed since he started work for his employer.

(5) Paragraphs (3) and (4) shall apply to a worker who is excluded from the scope of certain provisions of these Regulations by regulation 21 as if for each reference to 17 weeks there were substituted a reference to 26 weeks.

(6) For the purposes of this regulation, a worker's average working time for each seven days during a reference period shall be determined according to the formula—

A + B / C

where—

A is the aggregate number of hours comprised in the worker's working time during the course of the reference period;

B is the aggregate number of hours comprised in his working time during the course of the period beginning immediately after the end of the reference period and ending when the number of days in that subsequent period on which he has worked equals the number of excluded days during the reference period; and

C is the number of weeks in the reference period.

(7) In paragraph (6), "excluded days" means days comprised in—

(a) any period of annual leave taken by the worker in exercise of his entitlement under regulation 13;

(b) any period of sick leave taken by the worker;

(c) any period of maternity [paternity, adoption or parental] leave taken by the worker; and

(d) any period in respect of which the limit specified in paragraph (1) did not apply in relation to the worker [by reason of the fact that the employer has obtained the worker's agreement as mentioned in paragraph (1)].

[2414]

NOTES

Para (1): words in square brackets substituted by the Working Time Regulations 1999, SI 1999/3372, regs 1(1), 3(1)(a).

Para (2): words in square brackets added by SI 1999/3372, regs 1(1), 3(1)(b).

Para (7): words in first pair of square brackets inserted by the Working Time (Amendment) Regulations 2002, SI 2002/3128, regs 2, 5; words in second pair of square brackets substituted by the Working Time Regulations 1999, SI 1999/3372, regs 1(1), 3(1)(a), (c).

5 Agreement to exclude the maximum

(1) …

(2) An agreement for the purposes of [regulation 4]—

(a) may either relate to a specified period or apply indefinitely; and

(b) subject to any provision in the agreement for a different period of notice, shall be terminable by the worker by giving not less than seven days' notice to his employer in writing.

(3) Where an agreement for the purposes of [regulation 4] makes provision for the termination of the agreement after a period of notice, the notice period provided for shall not exceed three months.

(4) …

[2415]

NOTES

Paras (1), (4): revoked by the Working Time Regulations 1999, SI 1999/3372, regs 1(1), 3(2)(a).

Paras (2), (3): words in square brackets substituted by SI 1999/3372, regs 1(1), 3(2)(b).

[5A Maximum working time for young workers

(1) A young worker's working time shall not exceed—

(a) eight hours a day, or

(b) 40 hours a week.

(2) If, on any day, or, as the case may be, during any week, a young worker is employed by more than one employer, his working time shall be determined for the purpose of paragraph (1) by aggregating the number of hours worked by him for each employer.

(3) For the purposes of paragraphs (1) and (2), a week starts at midnight between Sunday and Monday.

(4) An employer shall take all reasonable steps, in keeping with the need to protect the health and safety of workers, to ensure that the limits specified in paragraph (1) are complied with in the case of each worker employed by him in relation to whom they apply.]

[2416]

NOTES

Inserted by the Working Time (Amendment) Regulations 2002, SI 2002/3128, regs 2, 6.

6 Length of night work

(1) A night worker's normal hours of work in any reference period which is applicable in his case shall not exceed an average of eight hours for each 24 hours.

(2) An employer shall take all reasonable steps, in keeping with the need to protect the health and safety of workers, to ensure that the limit specified in paragraph (1) is complied with in the case of each night worker employed by him.

(3) The reference periods which apply in the case of a night worker are—

(a) where a relevant agreement provides for the application of this regulation in relation to successive periods of 17 weeks, each such period, or

(b) in any other case, any period of 17 weeks in the course of his employment.

(4) Where a worker has worked for his employer for less than 17 weeks, the reference period applicable in his case is the period that has elapsed since he started work for his employer.

(5) For the purposes of this regulation, a night worker's average normal hours of work for each 24 hours during a reference period shall be determined according to the formula—

A / B – C

where—

A is the number of hours during the reference period which are normal working hours for that worker;

B is the number of days during the reference period, and

C is the total number of hours during the reference period comprised in rest periods spent by the worker in pursuance of his entitlement under regulation 11, divided by 24.

(6) …

(7) An employer shall ensure that no night worker employed by him whose work involves special hazards or heavy physical or mental strain works for more than eight hours in any 24-hour period during which the night worker performs night work.

(8) For the purposes of paragraph (7), the work of a night worker shall be regarded as involving special hazards or heavy physical or mental strain if—

(a) it is identified as such in—

(i) a collective agreement, or

(ii) a workforce agreement,

which takes account of the specific effects and hazards of night work, or

(b) it is recognised in a risk assessment made by the employer under [regulation 3 of the Management of Health and Safety at Work Regulations 1999] as involving a significant risk to the health or safety of workers employed by him.

[2417]

NOTES

Para (6): revoked by the Working Time (Amendment) Regulations 2002, SI 2002/3128, regs 2, 7.

Para (8): words in square brackets substituted by the Management of Health and Safety at Work Regulations 1999, SI 1999/3242, reg 29(2), Sch 2.

[6A Night work by young workers

An employer shall ensure that no young worker employed by him works during the restricted period.]

[2418]

NOTES

Inserted by the Working Time (Amendment) Regulations 2002, SI 2002/3128, regs 2, 8.

7 Health assessment and transfer of night workers to day work

(1) An employer—

(a) shall not assign an adult worker to work which is to be undertaken during periods such that the worker will become a night worker unless—

(i) the employer has ensured that the worker will have the opportunity of a free health assessment before he takes up the assignment; or

(ii) the worker had a health assessment before being assigned to work to be undertaken during such periods on an earlier occasion, and the employer has no reason to believe that that assessment is no longer valid, and

(b) shall ensure that each night worker employed by him has the opportunity of a free health assessment at regular intervals of whatever duration may be appropriate in his case.

(2) Subject to paragraph (4), an employer—

(a) shall not assign a young worker to work during [the restricted period] unless—

(i) the employer has ensured that the young worker will have the opportunity of a free assessment of his health and capacities before he takes up the assignment; or

(ii) the young worker had an assessment of his health and capacities before being assigned to work during the restricted period on an earlier occasion, and the employer has no reason to believe that that assessment is no longer valid; and

(b) shall ensure that each young worker employed by him and assigned to work during the restricted period has the opportunity of a free assessment of his health and capacities at regular intervals of whatever duration may be appropriate in his case.

(3) For the purposes of paragraphs (1) and (2), an assessment is free if it is at no cost to the worker to whom it relates.

(4) The requirements in paragraph (2) do not apply in a case where the work a young worker is assigned to do is of an exceptional nature.

(5) No person shall disclose an assessment made for the purposes of this regulation to any person other than the worker to whom it relates, unless—

(a) the worker has given his consent in writing to the disclosure, or

(b) the disclosure is confined to a statement that the assessment shows the worker to be fit—

(i) in a case where paragraph (1)(a)(i) or (2)(a)(i) applies, to take up an assignment, or

(ii) in a case where paragraph (1)(b) or (2)(b) applies, to continue to undertake an assignment.

(6) Where—

(a) a registered medical practitioner has advised an employer that a worker employed by the employer is suffering from health problems which the practitioner considers to be connected with the fact that the worker performs night work, and

(b) it is possible for the employer to transfer the worker to work—

(i) to which the worker is suited, and

(ii) which is to be undertaken during periods such that the worker will cease to be a night worker,

the employer shall transfer the worker accordingly.

[2419]

NOTES

Para (2): words in square brackets substituted by the Working Time (Amendment) Regulations 2002, SI 2002/3128, regs 2, 9.

8 Pattern of work

Where the pattern according to which an employer organizes work is such as to put the health and safety of a worker employed by him at risk, in particular because the work is monotonous or the work-rate is predetermined, the employer shall ensure that the worker is given adequate rest breaks.

[2420]

9 Records

An employer shall—

(a) keep records which are adequate to show whether the limits specified in regulations 4(1)[, 5A(1)] and 6(1) and (7) and the requirements in regulations [6A and] 7(1) and (2) are being complied with in the case of each worker employed by him in relation to whom they apply; and

(b) retain such records for two years from the date on which they were made.

[2421]

NOTES

Words in square brackets inserted by the Working Time (Amendment) Regulations 2002, SI 2002/3128, regs 2, 10.

10 Daily rest

(1) [A worker] is entitled to a rest period of not less than eleven consecutive hours in each 24-hour period during which he works for his employer.

(2) Subject to paragraph (3), a young worker is entitled to a rest period of not less than twelve consecutive hours in each 24-hour period during which he works for his employer.

(3) The minimum rest period provided for in paragraph (2) may be interrupted in the case of activities involving periods of work that are split up over the day or of short duration.

[2422]

NOTES

Para (1): words in square brackets substituted by the Working Time (Amendment) Regulations 2002, SI 2002/3128, regs 2, 11.

11 Weekly rest period

(1) Subject to paragraph (2), [a worker] is entitled to an uninterrupted rest period of not less than 24 hours in each seven-day period during which he works for his employer.

(2) If his employer so determines, [a worker] shall be entitled to either—

(a) two uninterrupted rest periods each of not less than 24 hours in each 14-day period during which he works for his employer; or

(b) one uninterrupted rest period of not less than 48 hours in each such 14-day period,

in place of the entitlement provided for in paragraph (1).

(3) Subject to paragraph (8), a young worker is entitled to a rest period of not less than 48 hours in each seven-day period during which he works for his employer.

(4) For the purpose of paragraphs (1) to (3), a seven-day period or (as the case may be) 14-day period shall be taken to begin—

(a) at such times on such days as may be provided for the purposes of this regulation in a relevant agreement; or

(b) where there are no provisions of a relevant agreement which apply, at the start of each week or (as the case may be) every other week.

(5) In a case where, in accordance with paragraph (4), 14-day periods are to be taken to begin at the start of every other week, the first such period applicable in the case of a particular worker shall be taken to begin—

(a) if the worker's employment began on or before the date on which these Regulations come into force, on 5th October 1998; or

(b) if the worker's employment begins after the date on which these Regulations come into force, at the start of the week in which that employment begins.

(6) For the purposes of paragraphs (4) and (5), a week starts at midnight between Sunday and Monday.

(7) The minimum rest period to which [a worker] is entitled under paragraph (1) or (2) shall not include any part of a rest period to which the worker is entitled under regulation 10(1), except where this is justified by objective or technical reasons or reasons concerning the organization of work.

(8) The minimum rest period to which a young worker is entitled under paragraph (3)—

(a) may be interrupted in the case of activities involving periods of work that are split up over the day or are of short duration; and

(b) may be reduced where this is justified by technical or organization reasons, but not to less than 36 consecutive hours.

[2423]

NOTES

Paras (1), (2), (7): words in square brackets substituted by the Working Time (Amendment) Regulations 2002, SI 2002/3128, regs 2, 12.

12 Rest breaks

(1) Where [a worker's] daily working time is more than six hours, he is entitled to a rest break.

(2) The details of the rest break to which [a worker] is entitled under paragraph (1), including its duration and the terms on which it is granted, shall be in accordance with any provisions for the purposes of this regulation which are contained in a collective agreement or a workforce agreement.

(3) Subject to the provisions of any applicable collective agreement or workforce agreement, the rest break provided for in paragraph (1) is an uninterrupted period of not less than 20 minutes, and the worker is entitled to spend it away from his workstation if he has one.

(4) Where a young worker's daily working time is more than four and a half hours, he is entitled to a rest break of at least 30 minutes, which shall be consecutive if possible, and he is entitled to spend it away from his workstation if he has one.

(5) If, on any day, a young worker is employed by more than one employer, his daily working time shall be determined for the purpose of paragraph (4) by aggregating the number of hours worked by him for each employer.

[2424]

NOTES

Paras (1), (2): words in square brackets substituted by the Working Time (Amendment) Regulations 2002, SI 2002/3128, regs 2, 13.

13 Entitlement to annual leave

[(1) Subject to paragraph (5), a worker is entitled to four weeks' annual leave in each leave year.]

(2) …

(3) A worker's leave year, for the purposes of this regulation, begins—

(a) on such date during the calendar year as may be provided for in a relevant agreement; or

(b) where there are no provisions of a relevant agreement which apply—

(i) if the worker's employment began on or before 1st October 1998, on that date and each subsequent anniversary of that date; or

(ii) if the worker's employment begins after 1st October 1998, on the date on which that employment begins and each subsequent anniversary of that date.

(4) Paragraph (3) does not apply to a worker to whom Schedule 2 applies (workers employed in agriculture) except where, in the case of a worker partly employed in agriculture, a relevant agreement so provides.

(5) Where the date on which a worker's employment begins is later than the date on which (by virtue of a relevant agreement) his first leave year begins, the leave to which he is entitled in that leave year is a proportion of the period applicable under [paragraph (1)] equal to the proportion of that leave year remaining on the date on which his employment begins.

(6)–(8) …

(9) Leave to which a worker is entitled under this regulation may be taken in instalments, but—

- (a) it may only be taken in the leave year in respect of which it is due, and
- (b) it may not be replaced by a payment in lieu except where the worker's employment is terminated.

[2425]

NOTES

Para (1): substituted by the Working Time (Amendment) Regulations 2001, SI 2001/3256, art 2(1), (2).

Paras (2), (7), (8): revoked by SI 2001/3256, art 2(1), (3), (6).

Para (5): words in square brackets substituted by SI 2001/3256, art 2(1), (4).

Para (6): revoked by the Working Time (Amendment) Regulations 2007, SI 2007/2079, reg 2(1), (4), as from 1 October 2007.

Para (6): words omitted revoked by SI 2001/3256, art 2(1), (5).

[13A Entitlement to additional annual leave

(1) Subject to regulation 26A and paragraphs (3) and (5), a worker is entitled in each leave year to a period of additional leave determined in accordance with paragraph (2).

(2) The period of additional leave to which a worker is entitled under paragraph (1) is—

- (a) in any leave year beginning on or after 1st October 2007 but before 1st April 2008, 0.8 weeks;
- (b) in any leave year beginning before 1st October 2007, a proportion of 0.8 weeks equivalent to the proportion of the year beginning on 1st October 2007 which would have elapsed at the end of that leave year;
- (c) in any leave year beginning on 1st April 2008, 0.8 weeks;
- (d) in any leave year beginning after 1st April 2008 but before 1st April 2009, 0.8 weeks and a proportion of another 0.8 weeks equivalent to the proportion of the year beginning on 1st April 2009 which would have elapsed at the end of that leave year;
- (e) in any leave year beginning on or after 1st April 2009, 1.6 weeks.

(3) The aggregate entitlement provided for in paragraph (2) and regulation 13(1) is subject to a maximum of 28 days.

(4) A worker's leave year begins for the purposes of this regulation on the same date as the worker's leave year begins for the purposes of regulation 13.

(5) Where the date on which a worker's employment begins is later than the date on which his first leave year begins, the additional leave to which he is entitled in that leave year is a proportion of the period applicable under paragraph (2) equal to the proportion of that leave year remaining on the date on which his employment begins.

(6) Leave to which a worker is entitled under this regulation may be taken in instalments, but it may not be replaced by a payment in lieu except where—

- (a) the worker's employment is terminated; or
- (b) the leave is an entitlement that arises under paragraph (2)(a), (b) or (c); or
- (c) the leave is an entitlement to 0.8 weeks that arises under paragraph (2)(d) in respect of that part of the leave year which would have elapsed before 1st April 2009.

(7) A relevant agreement may provide for any leave to which a worker is entitled under this regulation to be carried forward into the leave year immediately following the leave year in respect of which it is due.

(8) This regulation does not apply to workers to whom the Agricultural Wages (Scotland) Act 1949 applies (as that Act had effect on 1 July 1999).]

[2425A]

NOTES

Commencement: 1 October 2007.

Inserted by the Working Time (Amendment) Regulations 2007, SI 2007/2079, reg 2(1), (2), as from 1 October 2007.

14 Compensation related to entitlement to leave

(1) This regulation applies where—

(a) a worker's employment is terminated during the course of his leave year, and

(b) on the date on which the termination takes effect ("the termination date"), the proportion he has taken of the leave to which he is entitled in the leave year under [regulation 13] [and regulation 13A] differs from the proportion of the leave year which has expired.

(2) Where the proportion of leave taken by the worker is less than the proportion of the leave year which has expired, his employer shall make him a payment in lieu of leave in accordance with paragraph (3).

(3) The payment due under paragraph (2) shall be—

(a) such sum as may be provided for the purposes of this regulation in a relevant agreement, or

(b) where there are no provisions of a relevant agreement which apply, a sum equal to the amount that would be due to the worker under regulation 16 in respect of a period of leave determined according to the formula—

(A x B) – C

where—

A is the period of leave to which the worker is entitled under [regulation 13] [and regulation 13A];

B is the proportion of the worker's leave year which expired before the termination date, and

C is the period of leave taken by the worker between the start of the leave year and the termination date.

(4) A relevant agreement may provide that, where the proportion of leave taken by the worker exceeds the proportion of the leave year which has expired, he shall compensate his employer, whether by a payment, by undertaking additional work or otherwise.

[2426]

NOTES

Paras (1), (3): words in first pair of square brackets substituted by the Working Time (Amendment) Regulations 2001, SI 2001/3256, art 3; words in second pair of square brackets inserted by the Working Time (Amendment) Regulations 2007, SI 2007/2079, reg 2(1), (5), as from 1 October 2007.

15 Dates on which leave is taken

(1) A worker may take leave to which he is entitled under [regulation 13] [and regulation 13A] on such days as he may elect by giving notice to his employer in accordance with paragraph (3), subject to any requirement imposed on him by his employer under paragraph (2).

(2) A worker's employer may require the worker—

(a) to take leave to which the worker is entitled under [regulation 13] [or regulation 13A]; or

(b) not to take such leave,

on particular days, by giving notice to the worker in accordance with paragraph (3).

(3) A notice under paragraph (1) or (2)—

(a) may relate to all or part of the leave to which a worker is entitled in a leave year;

(b) shall specify the days on which leave is or (as the case may be) is not to be taken and, where the leave on a particular day is to be in respect of only part of the day, its duration; and

(c) shall be given to the employer or, as the case may be, the worker before the relevant date.

(4) The relevant date, for the purposes of paragraph (3), is the date—

(a) in the case of a notice under paragraph (1) or (2)(a), twice as many days in advance of the earliest day specified in the notice as the number of days or part-days to which the notice relates, and

(b) in the case of a notice under paragraph (2)(b), as many days in advance of the earliest day so specified as the number of days or part-days to which the notice relates.

(5) Any right or obligation under paragraphs (1) to (4) may be varied or excluded by a relevant agreement.

(6) This regulation does not apply to a worker to whom Schedule 2 applies (workers employed in agriculture) except where, in the case of a worker partly employed in agriculture, a relevant agreement so provides.

[2427]

NOTES

Paras (1), (2): words in first pair of square brackets substituted by the Working Time (Amendment) Regulations 2001, SI 2001/3256, art 3; words in second pair of square brackets inserted by the Working Time (Amendment) Regulations 2007, SI 2007/2079, reg 2(1), (5), (6), as from 1 October 2007.

[15A Leave during the first year of employment

(1) During the first year of his employment, the amount of leave a worker may take at any time in exercise of his entitlement under regulation 13 [or regulation 13A] is limited to the amount which is deemed to have accrued in his case at that time under paragraph (2) [or (2A)], as modified under paragraph (3) in a case where that paragraph applies, less the amount of leave (if any) that he has already taken during that year.

(2) For the purposes of paragraph (1), [in the case of workers to whom the Agricultural Wages (Scotland) Act 1949 applies,] leave is deemed to accrue over the course of the worker's first year of employment, at the rate of one twelfth of the amount specified in regulation 13(1) on the first day of each month of that year.

[(2A) Except where paragraph (2) applies, for the purposes of paragraph (1), leave is deemed to accrue over the course of the worker's first year of employment, at the rate of one-twelfth of the amount specified in regulation 13(1) and regulation 13A(2), subject to the limit contained in regulation 13A(3), on the first day of each month of that year.]

(3) Where the amount of leave that has accrued in a particular case includes a fraction of a day other than a half-day, the fraction shall be treated as a half-day if it is less than a half-day and as a whole day if it is more than a half-day.

(4) This regulation does not apply to a worker whose employment began on or before 25th October 2001.]

[2428]

NOTES

Inserted by the Working Time (Amendment) Regulations 2001, SI 2001/3256, art 4.

Paras (1), (2): words in square brackets inserted by the Working Time (Amendment) Regulations 2007, SI 2007/2079, reg 2(1), (6)–(8), as from 1 October 2007.

Para (2A): inserted by SI 2007/2079, reg 2(1), (9), as from 1 October 2007.

16 Payment in respect of periods of leave

(1) A worker is entitled to be paid in respect of any period of annual leave to which he is entitled under regulation 13 [and regulation 13A], at the rate of a week's pay in respect of each week of leave.

(2) Sections 221 to 224 of the 1996 Act shall apply for the purpose of determining the amount of a week's pay for the purposes of this regulation, subject to the modifications set out in paragraph (3).

(3) The provisions referred to in paragraph (2) shall apply—

(a) as if references to the employee were references to the worker;

(b) as if references to the employee's contract of employment were references to the worker's contract;

(c) as if the calculation date were the first day of the period of leave in question; and

(d) as if the references to sections 227 and 228 did not apply.

(4) A right to payment under paragraph (1) does not affect any right of a worker to remuneration under his contract ("contractual remuneration").

(5) Any contractual remuneration paid to a worker in respect of a period of leave goes towards discharging any liability of the employer to make payments under this regulation in respect of that period; and, conversely, any payment of remuneration under this regulation in respect of a period goes towards discharging any liability of the employer to pay contractual remuneration in respect of that period.

[2429]

NOTES

Para (1): words in square brackets inserted by the Working Time (Amendment) Regulations 2007, SI 2007/2079, reg 2(1), (5), as from 1 October 2007.

17 Entitlements under other provisions

Where during any period a worker is entitled to a rest period, rest break or annual leave both under a provision of these Regulations and under a separate provision (including a provision of his contract), he may not exercise the two rights separately, but may, in taking a rest period, break or leave during that period, take advantage of whichever right is, in any particular respect, the more favourable.

[2430]

PART III
EXCEPTIONS

[18 Excluded sectors

[(1) These Regulations do not apply—

(a) to workers to whom the European Agreement on the organisation of working time of seafarers dated 30th September 1998 and put into effect by Council Directive 1999/63/EC of 21st June 1999 applies;

[(b) to workers to whom the Fishing Vessels (Working Time: Sea-fishermen) Regulations 2004 apply;] or

[(c) to workers to whom the Merchant Shipping (Working Time: Inland Waterways) Regulations 2003 apply].

(2) Regulations 4(1) and (2), 6(1), (2) and (7), 7(1) and (6), 8, 10(1), 11(1) and (2), 12(1), 13[, 13A] and 16 do not apply—

(a) where characteristics peculiar to certain specific services such as the armed forces or the police, or to certain specific activities in the civil protection services, inevitably conflict with the provisions of these Regulations;

(b) to workers to whom the European Agreement on the organisation of working time of mobile staff in civil aviation concluded on 22nd March 2000 and implemented by Council Directive 2000/79/EC of 27th November 2000 applies; or

(c) to the activities of workers who are doctors in training.

(3) Paragraph (2)(c) has effect only until 31st July 2004.

(4) Regulations 4(1) and (2), 6(1), (2) and (7), 8, 10(1), 11(1) and (2) and 12(1) do not apply to workers to whom Directive 2002/15/EC of the European Parliament and of the Council on the organisation of the working time of persons performing mobile road transport activities, dated 11th March 2002 applies.]

[2431]

NOTES

Commencement: 1 August 2003.

Substituted by the Working Time (Amendment) Regulations 2003, SI 2003/1684, regs 2, 4, as from 1 August 2003.

Para (1): sub-para (b) substituted by the Fishing Vessels (Working Time: Sea-fishermen) Regulations 2004, SI 2004/1713, reg 21, Sch 2, para 5, as from 16 August 2004; sub-para (c) substituted by the Merchant Shipping (Working Time: Inland Waterways) Regulations 2003, SI 2003/3049, reg 20, Sch 2, para 6, as from 1 December 2003.

Para (2): figure in square brackets inserted by the Working Time (Amendment) Regulations 2007, SI 2007/2079, reg 2(1), (10), as from 1 October 2007.

19 Domestic service

Regulations 4(1) and (2), [5A(1) and (4),] 6(1), (2) and (7), [6A,] 7(1), (2) and (6) and 8 do not apply in relation to a worker employed as a domestic servant in a private household.

[2432]

NOTES

Words in square brackets inserted by the Working Time (Amendment) Regulations 2002, SI 2002/3128, regs 2, 14.

20 Unmeasured working time

[(1)] Regulations 4(1) and (2), 6(1), (2) and (7), 10(1), 11(1) and (2) and 12(1) do not apply in relation to a worker where, on account of the specific characteristics of the activity in which he is engaged, the duration of his working time is not measured or predetermined or can be determined by the worker himself, as may be the case for—

(a) managing executives or other persons with autonomous decision-taking powers;
(b) family workers; or
(c) workers officiating at religious ceremonies in churches and religious communities.

[(2) ...]

[2433]

NOTES

Para (1): numbered as such by the Working Time Regulations 1999, SI 1999/3372, regs 1(1), 4.
Para (2): added by SI 1999/3372, regs 1(1), 4, and revoked by the Working Time (Amendment) Regulations 2006, SI 2006/99, reg 2, as from 6 April 2006.

21 Other special cases

Subject to regulation 24, regulations 6(1), (2) and (7), 10(1), 11(1) and (2) and 12(1) do not apply in relation to a worker—

(a) where the worker's activities are such that his place of work and place of residence are distant from one another[, including cases where the worker is employed in offshore work,] or his different places of work are distant from one another;
(b) where the worker is engaged in security and surveillance activities requiring a permanent presence in order to protect property and persons, as may be the case for security guards and caretakers or security firms;
(c) where the worker's activities involve the need for continuity of service or production, as may be the case in relation to—
  (i) services relating to the reception, treatment or care provided by hospitals or similar establishments [(including the activities of doctors in training)], residential institutions and prisons;
  (ii) work at docks or airports;
  (iii) press, radio, television, cinematographic production, postal and telecommunications services and civil protection services;
  (iv) gas, water and electricity production, transmission and distribution, household refuse collection and incineration;
  (v) industries in which work cannot be interrupted on technical grounds;
  (vi) research and development activities;
  (vii) agriculture;
  [(viii) the carriage of passengers on regular urban transport services;]
(d) where there is a foreseeable surge of activity, as may be the case in relation to—
  (i) agriculture;
  (ii) tourism; and
  (iii) postal services;
(e) where the worker's activities are affected by—
  (i) an occurrence due to unusual and unforeseeable circumstances, beyond the control of the worker's employer;
  (ii) exceptional events, the consequences of which could not have been avoided despite the exercise of all due care by the employer; or
  (iii) an accident or the imminent risk of an accident;
[(f) where the worker works in railway transport and—

(i) his activities are intermittent;
(ii) he spends his working time on board trains; or
(iii) his activities are linked to transport timetables and to ensuring the continuity and regularity of traffic].

[2434]

NOTES

Words in square brackets in paras (a), (c)(i) inserted, and paras (c)(viii), (f) added, by the Working Time (Amendment) Regulations 2003, SI 2003/1684, regs 2, 5, as from 1 August 2003.

22 Shift workers

(1) Subject to regulation 24—
(a) regulation 10(1) does not apply in relation to a shift worker when he changes shift and cannot take a daily rest period between the end of one shift and the start of the next one;
(b) paragraphs (1) and (2) of regulation 11 do not apply in relation to a shift worker when he changes shift and cannot take a weekly rest period between the end of one shift and the start of the next one; and
(c) neither regulation 10(1) nor paragraphs (1) and (2) of regulation 11 apply to workers engaged in activities involving periods of work split up over the day, as may be the case for cleaning staff.

(2) For the purposes of this regulation—
"shift worker" means any worker whose work schedule is part of shift work; and
"shift work" means any method of organizing work in shifts whereby workers succeed each other at the same workstations according to a certain pattern, including a rotating pattern, and which may be continuous or discontinuous, entailing the need for workers to work at different times over a given period of days or weeks.

[2435]

23 Collective and workforce agreements

A collective agreement or a workforce agreement may—
(a) modify or exclude the application of regulations 6(1) to (3) and (7), 10(1), 11(1) and (2) and 12(1), and
(b) for objective or technical reasons or reasons concerning the organization of work, modify the application of regulation 4(3) and (4) by the substitution, for each reference to 17 weeks, of a different period, being a period not exceeding 52 weeks,

in relation to particular workers or groups of workers.

[2436]

24 Compensatory rest

Where the application of any provision of these Regulations is excluded by regulation 21 or 22, or is modified or excluded by means of a collective agreement or a workforce agreement under regulation 23(a), and a worker is accordingly required by his employer to work during a period which would otherwise be a rest period or rest break—
(a) his employer shall wherever possible allow him to take an equivalent period of compensatory rest, and
(b) in exceptional cases in which it is not possible, for objective reasons, to grant such a period of rest, his employer shall afford him such protection as may be appropriate in order to safeguard the worker's health and safety.

[2437]

[24A Mobile workers

(1) Regulations 6(1), (2) and (7), 10(1), 11(1) and (2) and 12(1) do not apply to a mobile worker in relation to whom the application of those regulations is not excluded by any provision of regulation 18.

(2) A mobile worker, to whom paragraph (1) applies, is entitled to adequate rest, except where the worker's activities are affected by any of the matters referred to in regulation 21(e).

(3) For the purposes of this regulation, "adequate rest" means that a worker has regular rest periods, the duration of which are expressed in units of time and which are sufficiently

long and continuous to ensure that, as a result of fatigue or other irregular working patterns, he does not cause injury to himself, to fellow workers or to others and that he does not damage his health, either in the short term or in the longer term.]

[2438]

NOTES

Commencement: 1 August 2003.

Inserted by the Working Time (Amendment) Regulations 2003, SI 2003/1684, regs 2, 6, as from 1 August 2003.

25 Workers in the armed forces

(1) Regulation 9 does not apply in relation to a worker serving as a member of the armed forces.

(2) Regulations [5A, 6A,] 10(2) and 11(3) do not apply in relation to a young worker serving as a member of the armed forces.

(3) In a case where a young worker is accordingly required to work during [the restricted period, or is not permitted the minimum rest period provided for in regulation 10(2) or 11(3),] he shall be allowed an appropriate period of compensatory rest.

[2439]

NOTES

Para (2): figures in square brackets inserted by the Working Time (Amendment) Regulations 2002, SI 2002/3128, regs 2, 15(a), as from 6 April 2003.

Para (3): words in square brackets substituted by SI 2002/3128, regs 2, 15(b), as from 6 April 2003.

[25A Doctors in training

(1) Paragraph (1) of regulation 4 is modified in its application to workers who are doctors in training as follows—

(a) for the reference to 48 hours there is substituted a reference to 58 hours with effect from 1st August 2004 until 31st July 2007;

(b) for the reference to 48 hours there is substituted a reference to 56 hours with effect from 1st August 2007 until 31st July 2009.

(2) In the case of workers who are doctors in training, paragraphs (3)–(5) of regulation 4 shall not apply and paragraphs (3) and (4) of this regulation shall apply in their place.

(3) Subject to paragraph (4), the reference period which applies in the case of a worker who is a doctor in training is, with effect from 1st August 2004—

(a) where a relevant agreement provides for the application of this regulation in relation to successive periods of 26 weeks, each such period; and

(b) in any other case, any period of 26 weeks in the course of his employment.

(4) Where a doctor in training has worked for his employer for less than 26 weeks, the reference period applicable in his case is the period that has elapsed since he started work for his employer.]

[2440]

NOTES

Commencement: 1 August 2004.

Inserted by the Working Time (Amendment) Regulations 2003, SI 2003/1684, regs 2, 7, as from 1 August 2004.

[25B Workers employed in offshore work

(1) In the case of workers employed in offshore work, paragraphs (3)–(5) of regulation 4 shall not apply and paragraphs (2) and (3) of this regulation shall apply in their place.

(2) Subject to paragraph (3), the reference period which applies in the case of workers employed in offshore work is—

(a) where a relevant agreement provides for the application of this regulation in relation to successive periods of 52 weeks, each such period; and

(b) in any other case, any period of 52 weeks in the course of his employment.

(3) Where a worker employed in offshore work has worked for his employer for less than 52 weeks, the reference period applicable in his case is the period that has elapsed since he started work for his employer.]

[2441]

NOTES

Commencement: 1 August 2003.

Inserted by the Working Time (Amendment) Regulations 2003, SI 2003/1684, regs 2, 8, as from 1 August 2003.

26 (*Revoked by the Working Time (Amendment) Regulations 2003, SI 2003/1684, regs 2, 9, as from 1 August 2003.*)

[26A Entitlement to additional annual leave under a relevant agreement

(1) Regulation 13A does not apply in relation to a worker whose employer, as at 1st October 2007 and by virtue of a relevant agreement, provides each worker employed by him with an annual leave entitlement of 1.6 weeks or 8 days (whichever is the lesser) in addition to each worker's entitlement under regulation 13, provided that such additional annual leave—

(a) may not be replaced by a payment in lieu except in relation to a worker whose employment is terminated;

(b) may not be carried forward into a leave year other than that which immediately follows the leave year in respect of which the leave is due; and

(c) is leave for which the worker is entitled to be paid at not less than the rate of a week's pay in respect of each week of leave, calculated in accordance with sections 221 to 224 of the 1996 Act, modified such that—

 (i) references to the employee are references to the worker;

 (ii) references to the employee's contract of employment are references to the worker's contract;

 (iii) the calculation date is the first day of the period of leave in question; and

 (iv) the references to sections 227 and 228 do not apply.

(2) Notwithstanding paragraph (1), any additional annual leave in excess of 1.6 weeks or 8 days (whichever is the lesser) to which a worker is entitled, shall not be subject to the conditions of that paragraph.

(3) This regulation shall cease to apply to a worker from the day when an employer ceases to provide additional annual leave in accordance with the conditions in paragraph (1).

(4) This regulation does not apply to workers to whom the Agricultural Wages (Scotland) Act 1949 applies (as that Act had effect on 1 July 1999).]

[2441A]

NOTES

Commencement: 1 October 2007.

Inserted by the Working Time (Amendment) Regulations 2007, SI 2007/2079, reg 2(1), (3), as from 1 October 2007.

27 Young workers: force majeure

(1) Regulations [5A, 6A,] 10(2) and 12(4) do not apply in relation to a young worker where his employer requires him to undertake work which no adult worker is available to perform and which—

(a) is occasioned by either—

 (i) an occurrence due to unusual and unforeseeable circumstances, beyond the employer's control, or

 (ii) exceptional events, the consequences of which could not have been avoided despite the exercise of all due care by the employer;

(b) is of a temporary nature; and

(c) must be performed immediately.

(2) Where the application of regulation [5A, 6A,] 10(2) or 12(4) is excluded by paragraph (1), and a young worker is accordingly required to work during a period which would otherwise be a rest period or rest break, his employer shall allow him to take an equivalent period of compensatory rest within the following three weeks.

[2442]

NOTES

Figures in square brackets inserted by the Working Time (Amendment) Regulations 2002, SI 2002/3128, regs 2, 18.

[27A Other exceptions relating to young workers

(1) Regulation 5A does not apply in relation to a young worker where—

(a) the young worker's employer requires him to undertake work which is necessary either to maintain continuity of service or production or to respond to a surge in demand for a service or product;

(b) no adult worker is available to perform the work, and

(c) performing the work would not adversely affect the young worker's education or training.

(2) Regulation 6A does not apply in relation to a young worker employed—

(a) in a hospital or similar establishment, or

(b) in connection with cultural, artistic, sporting or advertising activities,

in the circumstances referred to in paragraph (1).

(3) Regulation 6A does not apply, except in so far as it prohibits work between midnight and 4 am, in relation to a young worker employed in—

(a) agriculture;

(b) retail trading;

(c) postal or newspaper deliveries;

(d) a catering business;

(e) a hotel, public house, restaurant, bar or similar establishment, or

(f) a bakery,

in the circumstances referred to in paragraph (1).

(4) Where the application of regulation 6A is excluded by paragraph (2) or (3), and a young worker is accordingly required to work during a period which would otherwise be a rest period or rest break—

(a) he shall be supervised by an adult worker where such supervision is necessary for the young worker's protection, and

(b) he shall be allowed an equivalent period of compensatory rest.]

[2443]

NOTES

Inserted by the Working Time (Amendment) Regulations 2002, SI 2002/3128, regs 2, 17.

PART IV
MISCELLANEOUS

[28 Enforcement

(1) In this regulation, regulations 29–29E and Schedule 3—

"the 1974 Act" means the Health and Safety at Work etc Act 1974;

"the Civil Aviation Authority" means the authority referred to in section 2(1) of the Civil Aviation Act 1982;

"code of practice" includes a standard, a specification and any other documentary form of practical guidance;

…

"enforcement authority" means the Executive, a local authority, the Civil Aviation Authority[,VOSA or the Office of Rail Regulation];

"the Executive" means the Health and Safety Executive referred to in [section 10(1)] of the 1974 Act;

"local authority" means—

(a) in relation to England, a county council so far as they are the council for an area for which there are no district councils, a district council, a London borough council, the Common Council of the City of London, the Sub-Treasurer of the Inner Temple or the Under-Treasurer of the Middle Temple;

(b) in relation to Wales, a county council or a county borough council;

(c) in relation to Scotland, a council constituted under section 2 of the Local Government etc (Scotland) Act 1994;

"premises" includes any place and, in particular, includes—

(a) any vehicle, vessel, aircraft or hovercraft;

(b) any installation on land (including the foreshore and other land intermittently covered by water), any offshore installation, and any other installation (whether floating, or resting on the seabed or the subsoil thereof, or resting on other land covered with water or the subsoil thereof) and

(c) any tent or movable structure;

"relevant civil aviation worker" means a mobile worker who works mainly on board civil aircraft, excluding any worker to whom regulation 18(2)(b) applies;

"the relevant requirements" means the following provisions—

(a) regulations 4(2), 5A(4), 6(2) and (7), 6A, 7(1), (2) and (6), 8, 9 and 27A(4)(a);

(b) regulation 24, in so far as it applies where regulation 6(1), (2) or (7) is modified or excluded, and

(c) regulation 24A(2), in so far as it applies where regulations 6(1), (2) or (7) is excluded;

"relevant road transport worker" means a mobile worker to whom one or more of the following applies—

(a) Council Regulation (EEC) 3820/85,

(b) the European Agreement concerning the Work of Crews of Vehicles engaged in International Road Transport (AETR) of 1st July 1970, and

(c) the United Kingdom domestic driver's hours code, which is set out in Part VI of the Transport Act 1968;

"the relevant statutory provisions" means—

(a) the provisions of the 1974 Act and of any regulations made under powers contained in that Act; and

(b) while and to the extent that they remain in force, the provisions of the Acts mentioned in Schedule 1 to the 1974 Act and which are specified in the third column of that Schedule and the regulations, orders or other instruments of a legislative character made or having effect under a provision so specified; and

"VOSA" means the Vehicle and Operator Services Agency.

(2) It shall be the duty of the Executive to make adequate arrangements for the enforcement of the relevant requirements except to the extent that—

(a) a local authority is made responsible for their enforcement by paragraph (3);

(b) the Civil Aviation Authority is made responsible for their enforcement by paragraph (5); …

(c) VOSA is made responsible for their enforcement by paragraph (6);

[(d) the Office of Rail Regulation is made responsible for their enforcement by paragraph (3A)].

(3) Where the relevant requirements apply in relation to workers employed in premises in respect of which a local authority is responsible, under the Health and Safety (Enforcing Authority) Regulations 1998, for enforcing any of the relevant statutory provisions, it shall be the duty of that authority to enforce those requirements.

[(3A) Where the relevant requirements apply in relation to workers employed in the carrying out of any of the activities specified in regulation 3(2) of the Health and Safety (Enforcing Authority for Railways and Other Guided Transport Systems) Regulations 2006 it shall be the duty of the Office of Rail Regulation to enforce those requirements.]

(4) The duty imposed on local authorities by paragraph (3) shall be performed in accordance with such guidance as may be given to them by [the Executive].

(5) It shall be the duty of the Civil Aviation Authority to enforce the relevant requirements in relation to relevant civil aviation workers.

(6) It shall be the duty of VOSA to enforce the relevant requirements in relation to relevant road transport workers.

(7) The provisions of Schedule 3 shall apply in relation to the enforcement of the relevant requirements.

(8) …]

[2444]

NOTES

Commencement: 1 August 2003.

Substituted by the Working Time (Amendment) Regulations 2003, SI 2003/1684, regs 2, 10, as from 1 August 2003.

Para (1) is amended as follows:

Definition "the Commission" revoked by the Legislative Reform (Health and Safety Executive) Order 2008, SI 2008/960, art 22, Sch 3, as from 1 April 2008 (see further the note 'The Health and Safety Executive' at **[2038]**).

Words in square brackets in definition "enforcement authority" substituted by the Health and Safety (Enforcing Authority for Railways and Other Guided Transport Systems) Regulations 2006, SI 2006/557, reg 6, Schedule, para 7(a), as from 1 April 2006 (for transitional provisions in connection with the transfer of health and safety functions in relation to the operation of railways, etc, from the Health and Safety Executive to the Office of Rail Regulation, see reg 7 thereof).

Words in square brackets in definition "the Executive" substituted by SI 2008/960, art 22, Sch 3, as from 1 April 2008 (see further the note 'The Health and Safety Executive' at **[2038]**).

Para (2): word omitted from sub-para (b) revoked, and sub-para (d) added, by SI 2006/557, reg 6, Schedule, para 7(b)(ii), as from 1 April 2006 (as to transitional provisions, see the note above).

Para (3A): inserted by SI 2006/557, reg 6, Schedule, para 7(c), as from 1 April 2006 (as to transitional provisions, see the note above).

Para (4): words in square brackets substituted by SI 2008/960, art 22, Sch 3, as from 1 April 2008 (see further the note 'The Health and Safety Executive' at **[2038]**).

Para (8): revoked by SI 2008/960, art 22, Sch 3, as from 1 April 2008 (see further the note 'The Health and Safety Executive' at **[2038]**).

[29 Offences

[(1) An employer who fails to comply with any of the relevant requirements shall be guilty of an offence.

(2) The provisions of paragraph (3) shall apply where an inspector is exercising or has exercised any power conferred by Schedule 3.

(3) It is an offence for a person—

(a) to contravene any requirement imposed by the inspector under paragraph 2 of Schedule 3;

(b) to prevent or attempt to prevent any other person from appearing before the inspector or from answering any question to which the inspector may by virtue of paragraph 2(2)(e) of Schedule 3 require an answer;

(c) to contravene any requirement or prohibition imposed by an improvement notice or a prohibition notice (including any such notice as is modified on appeal);

(d) intentionally to obstruct the inspector in the exercise or performance of his powers or duties;

(e) to use or disclose any information in contravention of paragraph 8 of Schedule 3;

(f) to make a statement which he knows to be false or recklessly to make a statement which is false, where the statement is made in purported compliance with a requirement to furnish any information imposed by or under these Regulations.

(4) An employer guilty of an offence under paragraph (1) shall be liable—

(a) on summary conviction, to a fine not exceeding the statutory maximum;

(b) on conviction on indictment, to a fine.

(5) A person guilty of an offence under paragraph (3) shall be liable to the penalty prescribed in relation to that provision by paragraphs (6), (7) or (8) as the case may be.

(6) A person guilty of an offence under sub-paragraph (3)(a), (b) or (d) shall be liable on summary conviction to a fine not exceeding level 5 on the standard scale.

(7) A person guilty of an offence under sub-paragraph (3)(c) shall be liable—

(a) on summary conviction, to imprisonment for a term not exceeding three months, or a fine not exceeding the statutory maximum;

(b) on conviction on indictment, to imprisonment for a term not exceeding two years, or a fine, or both.

(8) A person guilty of an offence under any of the sub-paragraphs of paragraph (3) not falling within paragraphs (6) or (7) above, shall be liable—

(a) on summary conviction, to a fine not exceeding the statutory maximum;

(b) on conviction on indictment—

(i) if the offence is under sub-paragraph (3)(e), to imprisonment for a term not exceeding two years or a fine or both;

(ii) if the offence is not one to which the preceding sub-paragraph applies, to a fine.

(9) The provisions set out in regulations 29A–29E below shall apply in relation to the offences provided for in paragraphs (1) and (3).]

[2445]

NOTES

Commencement: 1 August 2003.

Substituted, together with regs 29A–29E for original reg 29, by the Working Time (Amendment) Regulations 2003, SI 2003/1684, regs 2, 10, as from 1 August 2003.

[29A Offences due to fault of other person

Where the commission by any person of an offence is due to the act or default of some other person, that other person shall be guilty of the offence, and a person may be charged with and convicted of the offence by virtue of this paragraph whether or not proceedings are taken against the first-mentioned person.]

[2446]

NOTES

Commencement: 1 August 2003.

Substituted as noted to reg 29 at **[2445]**.

[29B Offences by bodies corporate

(1) Where an offence committed by a body corporate is proved to have been committed with the consent or connivance of, or to have been attributable to any neglect on the part of, any director, manager, secretary or other similar officer of the body corporate or a person who was purporting to act in any such capacity, he as well as the body corporate shall be guilty of that offence and shall be liable to be proceeded against and punished accordingly.

(2) Where the affairs of a body corporate are managed by its members, the preceding paragraph shall apply in relation to the acts and defaults of a member in connection with his functions of management as if he were a director of the body corporate.]

[2447]

NOTES

Commencement: 1 August 2003.

Substituted as noted to reg 29 at **[2445]**.

[29C Restriction on institution of proceedings in England and Wales

Proceedings for an offence shall not, in England and Wales, be instituted except by an inspector or by or with the consent of the Director of Public Prosecutions.]

[2448]

NOTES

Commencement: 1 August 2003.

Substituted as noted to reg 29 at **[2445]**.

[29D Prosecutions by inspectors

(1) An inspector, if authorised in that behalf by an enforcement authority, may, although not of counsel or a solicitor, prosecute before a magistrate's court proceedings for an offence under these Regulations.

(2) This regulation shall not apply to Scotland.]

[2449]

NOTES

Commencement: 1 August 2003.
Substituted as noted to reg 29 at **[2445]**.

[29E Power of court to order cause of offence to be remedied

(1) Where a person is convicted of an offence in respect of any matters which appear to the court to be matters which it is in his power to remedy, the court may, in addition to or instead of imposing any punishment, order him, within such time as may be fixed by the order, to take such steps as may be specified in the order for remedying the said matters.

(2) The time fixed by an order under paragraph (1) may be extended or further extended by order of the court on an application made before the end of that time as originally fixed or as extended under this paragraph, as the case may be.

(3) Where a person is ordered under paragraph (1) to remedy any matters, that person shall not be liable under these Regulations in respect of those matters in so far as they continue during the time fixed by the order or any further time allowed under paragraph (2).]

[2450]

NOTES

Commencement: 1 August 2003.
Substituted as noted to reg 29 at **[2445]**.

30 Remedies

(1) A worker may present a complaint to an employment tribunal that his employer—

(a) has refused to permit him to exercise any right he has under—

[(i) regulation 10(1) or (2), 11(1), (2) or (3), 12(1) or (4), 13 or 13A;]

(ii) regulation 24, in so far as it applies where regulation 10(1), 11(1) or (2) or 12(1) is modified or excluded; ...

[(iii) regulation 24A, in so far as it applies where regulation 10(1), 11(1) or (2) or 12(1) is excluded; or

(iv) regulation 25(3), 27A(4)(b) or 27(2); or]

(b) has failed to pay him the whole or any part of any amount due to him under regulation 14(2) or 16(1).

(2) An employment tribunal shall not consider a complaint under this regulation unless it is presented—

(a) before the end of the period of three months (or, in a case to which regulation 38(2) applies, six months) beginning with the date on which it is alleged that the exercise of the right should have been permitted (or in the case of a rest period or leave extending over more than one day, the date on which it should have been permitted to begin) or, as the case may be, the payment should have been made;

(b) within such further period as the tribunal considers reasonable in a case where it is satisfied that it was not reasonably practicable for the complaint to be presented before the end of that period of three or, as the case may be, six months.

[(2A) Where the period within which a complaint must be presented in accordance with paragraph (2) is extended by regulation 15 of the Employment Act 2002 (Dispute Resolution) Regulations 2004, the period within which the complaint must be presented shall be the extended period rather than the period in paragraph (2).]

(3) Where an employment tribunal finds a complaint under paragraph (1)(a) well-founded, the tribunal—

(a) shall make a declaration to that effect, and

(b) may make an award of compensation to be paid by the employer to the worker.

(4) The amount of the compensation shall be such as the tribunal considers just and equitable in all the circumstances having regard to—

(a) the employer's default in refusing to permit the worker to exercise his right, and

(b) any loss sustained by the worker which is attributable to the matters complained of.

(5) Where on a complaint under paragraph (1)(b) an employment tribunal finds that an employer has failed to pay a worker in accordance with regulation 14(2) or 16(1), it shall order the employer to pay to the worker the amount which it finds to be due to him.

[2451]

NOTES

Para (1): sub-para (a)(i) substituted by the Working Time (Amendment) Regulations 2007, SI 2007/2079, reg 2(1), (11), as from 1 October 2007; word omitted from sub-para (a)(ii) revoked, and sub-paras (a)(iii), (iv) substituted for original sub-para (a)(iii), by the Working Time (Amendment) Regulations 2003, SI 2003/1684, regs 2, 11, as from 1 August 2003.

Para (2A): inserted by the Employment Act 2002 (Dispute Resolution) Regulations 2004, SI 2004/752, reg 17(f), as from 1 October 2004 (for transitional provisions and effect see reg 18 at **[3098]**).

Conciliation: employment tribunal proceedings and claims which could be the subject of employment tribunal proceedings under this regulation are proceedings to which the Employment Tribunals Act 1996, s 18 applies; see s 18(1)(ff) of that Act, at **[975]**. The short conciliation period applies to such proceedings to the extent that they relate to regs 13, 14(2) and/or 16(1) of these Regulations only; see the Employment Tribunals (Constitution and Rules of Procedure) Regulations 2004, SI 2004/1861, Sch 1, rule 22(1), (5) (as amended by SI 2005/1865, reg 2, as from 1 October 2005). In other cases, the standard conciliation period applies; see SI 2004/1861, Sch 1, rule 22(1), (6).

Tribunal jurisdiction: the Employment Act 2002, ss 31, 32, 38, at **[1493]**, **[1494]**, **[1496]** apply to proceedings before the employment tribunal relating to a claim under this regulation; see ss 31(1), 32(1), 38(1) of, and Schs 3–5 to, the 2002 Act at **[1508]**–**[1510]**.

For the circumstances in which the normal time limit for presenting complaints under this regulation is extended for a period of three months, see the Employment Act 2002 (Dispute Resolution) Regulations 2004, SI 2004/752, regs 15 and 18 at **[3096]** and **[3098]**.

31–34 (*Reg 31 inserts the Employment Rights Act 1996, ss 45A, 48(1ZA), 49(5A), 205(1ZA) at* **[1065]**, **[1073]**, **[1074]**, **[1247]**, *and amends ss 49(2), 192(2), 194(2), 195(2), 200(1), and 202(2) of that Act at* **[1074]**, **[1236]**, **[1238]**, **[1239]**, **[1242]** *and* **[1244]**; *reg 32 (i) inserts the Employment Rights Act 1996, ss 101A, 105(4A) at* **[1141]**, **[1149]**, *(ii) amends ss 104(4), 108(3), 117(4), 118(3), 120(1), 122(3), 128(1), 129(1), 202(2) and 209(2) of that Act at* **[1145]**, **[1152]**, **[1161]**, **[1162]**, **[1164]**, **[1166]**, **[1172]**, **[1173]**, **[1244]** *and* **[1250]**, *(iii) amends the Trade Union and Labour Relations (Consolidation) Act 1992, ss 237(1A) and 238(2A) at* **[734]** *and* **[735]**, *(iv) amends the Employment Tribunals Act 1996, s 10(5) at* **[964]**, *and (v) amended s 109 of the 1996 Act (repealed); reg 33 amends the Employment Tribunals Act 1996, s 18(1) at* **[975]**; *reg 34 amends the Employment Tribunals Act 1996, s 21(1), (2) at* **[978]**.)

35 Restrictions on contracting out

(1) Any provision in an agreement (whether a contract of employment or not) is void in so far as it purports—

(a) to exclude or limit the operation of any provision of these Regulations, save in so far as these Regulations provide for an agreement to have that effect, or

(b) to preclude a person from bringing proceedings under these Regulations before an employment tribunal.

(2) Paragraph (1) does not apply to—

(a) any agreement to refrain from instituting or continuing proceedings where a conciliation officer has taken action under section 18 of the Employment Tribunals Act 1996 (conciliation); or

(b) any agreement to refrain from instituting or continuing proceedings within section 18(1)(ff) of the Employment Tribunals Act 1996 (proceedings under these Regulations where conciliation is available), if the conditions regulating compromise agreements under these Regulations are satisfied in relation to the agreement.

(3) For the purposes of paragraph (2)(b) the conditions regulating compromise agreements under these Regulations are that—

(a) the agreement must be in writing,

(b) the agreement must relate to the particular complaint,

(c) the worker must have received advice from a relevant independent adviser as to the terms and effect of the proposed agreement and, in particular, its effect on his ability to pursue his rights before an employment tribunal,

(d) there must be in force, when the adviser gives the advice, a contract of insurance, or an indemnity provided for members of a profession or professional body, covering the risk of a claim by the worker in respect of loss arising in consequence of the advice,

(e) the agreement must identify the adviser, and
(f) the agreement must state that the conditions regulating compromise agreements under these Regulations are satisfied.

(4) A person is a relevant independent adviser for the purposes of paragraph (3)(c)—
(a) if he is a qualified lawyer,
(b) if he is an officer, official, employee or member of an independent trade union who has been certified in writing by the trade union as competent to give advice and as authorised to do so on behalf of the trade union, or
(c) if he works at an advice centre (whether as an employee or as a volunteer) and has been certified in writing by the centre as competent to give advice and as authorised to do so on behalf of the centre.

(5) But a person is not a relevant independent adviser for the purposes of paragraph (3)(c) in relation to the worker—
(a) if he, is employed by or is acting in the matter for the employer or an associated employer,
(b) in the case of a person within paragraph (4)(b) or (c), if the trade union or advice centre is the employer or an associated employer, or
(c) in the case of a person within paragraph (4)(c), if the worker makes a payment for the advice received from him.

(6) In paragraph (4)(a), "qualified lawyer" means—
(a) as respects England and Wales, a barrister (whether in practice as such or employed to give legal advice), a solicitor who holds a practising certificate, or a person other than a barrister or solicitor who is an authorised advocate or authorised litigator (within the meaning of the Courts and Legal Services Act 1990); and
(b) as respects Scotland, an advocate (whether in practice as such or employed to give legal advice), or a solicitor who holds a practising certificate.

[(6A) A person shall be treated as being a qualified lawyer within paragraph (6)(a) if he is a Fellow of the Institute of Legal Executives employed by a solicitors' practice.]

(7) For the purposes of paragraph (5) any two employers shall be treated as associated if—
(a) one is a company of which the other (directly or indirectly) has control; or
(b) both are companies of which a third person (directly or indirectly) has control; and "associated employer" shall be construed accordingly.

[2452]

NOTES

Para (6A): inserted by the Working Time Regulations 1998 (Amendment) Regulations 2004, SI 2004/2516, reg 2, as from 1 October 2004.

[35A—(1) The Secretary of State shall, after consulting persons appearing to him to represent the two sides of industry, arrange for the publication, in such form and manner as he considers appropriate, of information and advice concerning the operation of these Regulations.

(2) The information and advice shall be such as appear to him best calculated to enable employers and workers affected by these Regulations to understand their respective rights and obligations under them.]

[2453]

NOTES

Inserted by the Working Time Regulations 1999, SI 1999/3372, regs 1(1), 5.

PART V
SPECIAL CLASSES OF PERSON

36 Agency workers not otherwise "workers"

(1) This regulation applies in any case where an individual ("the agency worker")—

(a) is supplied by a person ("the agent") to do work for another ("the principal") under a contract or other arrangements made between the agent and the principal; but

(b) is not, as respects that work, a worker, because of the absence of a worker's contract between the individual and the agent or the principal; and

(c) is not a party to a contract under which he undertakes to do the work for another party to the contract whose status is, by virtue of the contract, that of a client or customer of any profession or business undertaking carried on by the individual.

(2) In a case where this regulation applies, the other provisions of these Regulations shall have effect as if there were a worker's contract for the doing of the work by the agency worker made between the agency worker and—

(a) whichever of the agent and the principal is responsible for paying the agency worker in respect of the work; or

(b) if neither the agent nor the principal is so responsible, whichever of them pays the agency worker in respect of the work,

and as if that person were the agency worker's employer.

[2454]

37 Crown employment

(1) Subject to paragraph (4) and regulation 38, these Regulations have effect in relation to Crown employment and persons in Crown employment as they have effect in relation to other employment and other workers.

(2) In paragraph (1) "Crown employment" means employment under or for the purposes of a government department or any officer or body exercising on behalf of the Crown functions conferred by a statutory provision.

(3) For the purposes of the application of the provisions of these Regulations in relation to Crown employment in accordance with paragraph (1)—

(a) references to a worker shall be construed as references to a person in Crown employment; and

(b) references to a worker's contract shall be construed as references to the terms of employment of a person in Crown employment.

(4) No act or omission by the Crown which is an offence under regulation 29 shall make the Crown criminally liable, but the High Court or, in Scotland, the Court of Session may, on the application of a person appearing to the Court to have an interest, declare any such act or omission unlawful.

[2455]

38 Armed forces

(1) Regulation 37 applies—

(a) subject to paragraph (2), to service as a member of the armed forces, and

(b) to employment by an association established for the purposes of Part XI of the Reserve Forces Act 1996.

(2) No complaint concerning the service of any person as a member of the armed forces may be presented to an employment tribunal under regulation 30 unless—

(a) that person has made a complaint in respect of the same matter to an officer under the service redress procedures, and

(b) that complaint has not been withdrawn.

(3) For the purpose of paragraph (2)(b), a person shall be treated as having withdrawn his complaint if, having made a complaint to an officer under the service redress procedures, he fails to submit the complaint to the Defence Council under those procedures.

(4) Where a complaint of the kind referred to in paragraph (2) is presented to an employment tribunal, the service redress procedures may continue after the complaint is presented.

(5) In this regulation, "the service redress procedures" means the procedures, excluding those which relate to the making of a report on a complaint to Her Majesty, referred to in section 180 of the Army Act 1955, section 180 of the Air Force Act 1955 and section 130 of the Naval Discipline Act 1957.

[2456]

39 House of Lords staff

(1) These Regulations have effect in relation to employment as a relevant member of the House of Lords staff as they have effect in relation to other employment.

(2) Nothing in any rule of law or the law or practice of Parliament prevents a relevant member of the House of Lords staff from presenting a complaint to an employment tribunal under regulation 30.

(3) In this regulation "relevant member of the House of Lords staff" means any person who is employed under a worker's contract with the Corporate Officer of the House of Lords.

[2457]

40 House of Commons staff

(1) These Regulations have effect in relation to employment as a relevant member of the House of Commons staff as they have effect in relation to other employment.

(2) For the purposes of the application of the provisions of these Regulations in relation to a relevant member of the House of Commons staff—

(a) references to a worker shall be construed as references to a relevant member of the House of Commons staff; and

(b) references to a worker's contract shall be construed as references to the terms of employment of a relevant member of the House of Commons staff.

(3) Nothing in any rule of law or the law or practice of Parliament prevents a relevant member of the House of Commons staff from presenting a complaint to an employment tribunal under regulation 30.

(4) In this regulation "relevant member of the House of Commons staff" means any person—

(a) who was appointed by the House of Commons Commission; or

(b) who is a member of the Speaker's personal staff.

[2458]

41 Police service

(1) [Subject to paragraph (1A),] for the purposes of these Regulations, the holding, otherwise than under a contract of employment, of the office of constable or an appointment as a police cadet shall be treated as employment, under a worker's contract, by the relevant officer.

[(1A) For the purposes of these Regulations, any constable who has been seconded to the Serious Organised Crime Agency to serve as a member of its staff shall be treated as employed by the Serious Organised Crime Agency.]

(2) Any matter relating to the employment of a worker which may be provided for the purposes of these Regulations in a workforce agreement may be provided for the same purposes in relation to the service of a person holding the office of constable or an appointment as a police cadet by an agreement between the relevant officer and a joint branch board.

(3) In this regulation—

"a joint branch board" means a joint branch board constituted in accordance with regulation 7(3) of the Police Federation Regulations 1969 or regulation 7(3) of the Police Federation (Scotland) Regulations 1985, and

"the relevant officer" means—

(a) in relation to a member of a police force or a special constable or police cadet appointed for a police area, the chief officer of police (or, in Scotland, the chief constable);

(b) …

(c) in relation to any other person holding the office of constable or an appointment as a police cadet, the person who has the direction and control of the body of constables or cadets in question.

[(4) For the purposes of these Regulations the relevant officer, as defined by paragraph (3), shall be treated as a corporation sole.

(5) Where, in a case in which the relevant officer, as so defined, is guilty of an offence under these Regulations, it is proved—

(a) that the office-holder personally consented to the commission of the offence;
(b) that he personally connived in its commission; or
(c) that the commission of the offence was attributable to personal neglect on his part,

the office-holder (as well as the corporation sole) shall be guilty of an offence and shall be liable to be proceeded against and punished accordingly.

(6) In paragraph (5) above "the office-holder", in relation to the relevant officer, means an individual who, at the time of the consent, connivance or neglect—
(a) held the office or other position mentioned in paragraph (3) above as the office or position of that officer; or
(b) was for the time being responsible for exercising and performing the powers and duties of that office or position.

(7) In the application of this regulation to Scotland—
(a) paragraph (4) shall have effect as if for the words "corporation sole" there were substituted "distinct juristic person (that is to say, as a juristic person distinct from the individual who for the time being is the office-holder)";
(b) paragraph (5) shall have effect as if for the words "corporation sole" there were substituted "juristic person"; and
(c) paragraph (6) shall have effect as if for the words "paragraph (5)" there were substituted "paragraphs (4) and (5)".]

[2459]

NOTES

Para (1): words in square brackets inserted by the Serious Organised Crime and Police Act 2005 (Consequential and Supplementary Amendments to Secondary Legislation) Order 2006, SI 2006/594, art 2, Schedule, para 16(1), (2), as from 1 April 2006.

Para (1A): inserted by SI 2006/594, art 2, Schedule, para 16(1), (3), as from 1 April 2006.

Para (3): para (b) of definition "the relevant officer" revoked by SI 2006/594, art 2, Schedule, para 16(1), (4), as from 1 April 2006.

Paras (4)–(7): added by the Working Time Regulations 1998 (Amendment) Order 2005, SI 2005/2241, art 2, as from 1 September 2005, except that no person shall be liable by virtue of para (5) above in respect of anything occurring before that date (see SI 2005/2241, art 3).

42 Non-employed trainees

For the purposes of these Regulations, a person receiving relevant training, otherwise than under a contract of employment, shall be regarded as a worker, and the person whose undertaking is providing the training shall be regarded as his employer.

[2460]

43 Agricultural workers

The provisions of Schedule 2 have effect in relation to workers employed in agriculture.

[2461]

SCHEDULES

SCHEDULE 1
WORKFORCE AGREEMENTS

Regulation 2

1. An agreement is a workforce agreement for the purposes of these Regulations if the following conditions are satisfied—
(a) the agreement is in writing;
(b) it has effect for a specified period not exceeding five years;
(c) it applies either—
(i) to all of the relevant members of the workforce, or
(ii) to all of the relevant members of the workforce who belong to a particular group;
(d) the agreement is signed—
(i) in the case of an agreement of the kind referred to in sub-paragraph (c)(i), by the representatives of the workforce, and in the case of an agreement of the kind referred to in sub-paragraph (c)(ii) by the representatives of the group to which the agreement applies (excluding, in either case, any representative not a relevant member of the workforce on the date on which the agreement was first made available for signature), or

(ii) if the employer employed 20 or fewer workers on the date referred to in sub-paragraph (d)(i), either by the appropriate representatives in accordance with that sub-paragraph or by the majority of the workers employed by him;

(e) before the agreement was made available for signature, the employer provided all the workers to whom it was intended to apply on the date on which it came into effect with copies of the text of the agreement and such guidance as those workers might reasonably require in order to understand it fully.

2. For the purposes of this Schedule—

"a particular group" is a group of the relevant members of a workforce who undertake a particular function, work at a particular workplace or belong to a particular department or unit within their employer's business;

"relevant members of the workforce" are all of the workers employed by a particular employer, excluding any worker whose terms and conditions of employment are provided for, wholly or in part, in a collective agreement;

"representatives of the workforce" are workers duly elected to represent the relevant members of the workforce, "representatives of the group" are workers duly elected to represent the members of a particular group, and representatives are "duly elected" if the election at which they were elected satisfied the requirements of paragraph 3 of this Schedule.

3. The requirements concerning elections referred to in paragraph 2 are that—

(a) the number of representatives to be elected is determined by the employer;

(b) the candidates for election as representatives of the workforce are relevant members of the workforce, and the candidates for election as representatives of a group are members of the group;

(c) no worker who is eligible to be a candidate is unreasonably excluded from standing for election;

(d) all the relevant members of the workforce are entitled to vote for representatives of the workforce, and all the members of a particular group are entitled to vote for representatives of the group;

(e) the workers entitled to vote may vote for as many candidates as there are representatives to be elected;

(f) the election is conducted so as to secure that—

(i) so far as is reasonably practicable, those voting do so in secret, and

(ii) the votes given at the election are fairly and accurately counted.

[2462]

SCHEDULE 2
WORKERS EMPLOYED IN AGRICULTURE

Regulations 13(4), 15(6) and 43

1. Except where, in the case of a worker partly employed in agriculture, different provision is made by a relevant agreement—

(a) for the purposes of regulation 13 [and regulation 13A], the leave year of a worker employed in agriculture begins on 6th April each year or such other date as may be specified in an agricultural wages order which applies to him; and

(b) the dates on which leave is taken by a worker employed in agriculture shall be determined in accordance with an agricultural wages order which applies to him.

2. Where, in the case referred to in paragraph 1 above, a relevant agreement makes provision different from sub-paragraph (a) or (b) of that paragraph—

(a) neither section 11 of the Agricultural Wages Act 1948 nor section 11 of the Agricultural Wages (Scotland) Act 1949 shall apply to that provision; and

(b) an employer giving effect to that provision shall not thereby be taken to have failed to comply with the requirements of an agricultural wages order.

3. In this Schedule, "an agricultural wages order" means an order under section 3 of the Agricultural Wages Act 1948 or section 3 of the Agricultural Wages (Scotland) Act 1949.

[2463]

NOTES

Para 1: words in square brackets in sub-para (a) inserted by the Working Time (Amendment) Regulations 2007, SI 2007/2079, reg 2(1), (5), as from 1 October 2007.

[SCHEDULE 3
ENFORCEMENT

Regulation 28(7)

1 Appointment of inspectors

(1) Each enforcement authority may appoint as inspectors (under whatever title it may from time to time determine) such persons having suitable qualifications as it thinks necessary for carrying into effect these Regulations within its field of responsibility, and may terminate any appointment made under this paragraph.

(2) Every appointment of a person as an inspector under this paragraph shall be made by an instrument in writing specifying which of the powers conferred on inspectors by these Regulations are to be exercisable by the person appointed; and an inspector shall in right of his appointment under this paragraph—

(a) be entitled to exercise only such of those powers as are so specified; and

(b) be entitled to exercise the powers so specified only within the field of responsibility of the authority which appointed him.

(3) So much of an inspector's instrument of appointment as specifies the powers which he is entitled to exercise may be varied by the enforcement authority which appointed him.

(4) An inspector shall, if so required when exercising or seeking to exercise any power conferred on him by these Regulations, produce his instrument of appointment or a duly authenticated copy thereof.

2 Powers of inspectors

(1) Subject to the provisions of paragraph 1 and this sub-paragraph, an inspector may, for the purpose of carrying into effect these Regulations within the field of responsibility of the enforcement authority which appointed him, exercise the powers set out in sub-paragraph (2) below.

(2) The powers of an inspector referred to in the preceding sub-paragraph are the following, namely—

(a) at any reasonable time (or, in a situation which in his opinion is or may be dangerous, at any time) to enter any premises which he has reason to believe it is necessary for him to enter for the purpose mentioned in sub-paragraph (1) above;

(b) to take with him a constable if he has reasonable cause to apprehend any serious obstruction in the execution of his duty;

(c) without prejudice to the preceding sub-paragraph, on entering any premises by virtue of paragraph (a) above to take with him—

  (i) any other person duly authorised by the inspector's enforcement authority; and

  (ii) any equipment or materials required for any purpose for which the power of entry is being exercised;

(d) to make such examination and investigation as may in any circumstances be necessary for the purpose mentioned in sub-paragraph (1) above;

(e) to require any person whom he has reasonable cause to believe to be able to give any information relevant to any examination or investigation under paragraph (d) above to answer (in the absence of persons other than a person nominated by him to be present and any persons whom the inspector may allow to be present) such questions as the inspector thinks fit to ask and to sign a declaration of the truth of his answers;

(f) to require the production of, inspect, and take copies of or of any entry in—

  (i) any records which by virtue of these Regulations are required to be kept, and

  (ii) any other books, records or documents which it is necessary for him to see for the purposes of any examination or investigation under paragraph (d) above;

(g) to require any person to afford him such facilities and assistance with respect to any matters or things within that person's control or in relation to which that person has responsibilities as are necessary to enable the inspector to exercise any of the powers conferred on him by this paragraph;

(h) any other power which is necessary for the purpose mentioned in sub-paragraph (1) above.

(3) No answer given by a person in pursuance of a requirement imposed under sub-paragraph (2)(e) above shall be admissible in evidence against that person or the husband or wife of that person in any proceedings.

(4) Nothing in this paragraph shall be taken to compel the production by any person of a document of which he would on grounds of legal professional privilege be entitled to withhold production on an order for discovery in an action in the High Court or, as the case may be, on an order for the production of documents in an action in the Court of Session.

3 Improvement notices

If an inspector is of the opinion that a person—

(a) is contravening one or more of these Regulations; or

(b) has contravened one or more of these Regulations in circumstances that make it likely that the contravention will continue or be repeated,

he may serve on him a notice (in this Schedule referred to as "an improvement notice") stating that he is of that opinion, specifying the provision or provisions as to which he is of that opinion, giving particulars of the reasons why he is of that opinion, and requiring that person to remedy the contravention or, as the case may be, the matters occasioning it within such period (ending not earlier than the period within which an appeal against the notice can be brought under paragraph 6) as may be specified in the notice.

4 Prohibition notices

(1) This paragraph applies to any activities which are being or are likely to be carried on by or under the control of any person, being activities to or in relation to which any of these Regulations apply or will, if the activities are so carried on, apply.

(2) If as regards any activities to which this paragraph applies an inspector is of the opinion that, as carried on or likely to be carried on by or under the control of the person in question, the activities involve or, as the case may be, will involve a risk of serious personal injury, the inspector may serve on that person a notice (in this Schedule referred to as "a prohibition notice").

(3) A prohibition notice shall—

(a) state that the inspector is of the said opinion;

(b) specify the matters which in his opinion give or, as the case may be, will give rise to the said risk;

(c) where in his opinion any of those matters involves or, as the case may be, will involve a contravention of any of these Regulations, state that he is of that opinion, specify the regulation or regulations as to which he is of that opinion, and give particulars of the reasons why he is of that opinion; and

(d) direct that the activities to which the notice relates shall not be carried on by or under the control of the person on whom the notice is served unless the matters specified in the notice in pursuance of paragraph (b) above and any associated contraventions of provisions so specified in pursuance of paragraph (c) above have been remedied.

(4) A direction contained in a prohibition notice in pursuance of sub-paragraph (3)(d) above shall take effect—

(a) at the end of the period specified in the notice; or

(b) if the notice so declares, immediately.

5 Provisions supplementary to paragraphs 3 and 4

(1) In this paragraph "a notice" means an improvement notice or a prohibition notice.

(2) A notice may (but need not) include directions as to the measures to be taken to remedy any contravention or matter to which the notice relates; and any such directions—

(a) may be framed to any extent by reference to any approved code of practice; and

(b) may be framed so as to afford the person on whom the notice is served a choice between different ways of remedying the contravention or matter.

(3) Where an improvement notice or a prohibition notice which is not to take immediate effect has been served—

(a) the notice may be withdrawn by an inspector at any time before the end of the period specified therein in pursuance of paragraph 3 or paragraph 4(4) as the case may be; and

(b) the period so specified may be extended or further extended by an inspector at any time when an appeal against the notice is not pending.

6 Appeal against improvement or prohibition notice

(1) In this paragraph "a notice" means an improvement or a prohibition notice.

(2) A person on whom a notice is served may within 21 days from the date of its service appeal to an employment tribunal; and on such an appeal the tribunal may either cancel or affirm the notice and, if it affirms it, may do so either in its original form or with such modifications as the tribunal may in the circumstances think fit.

(3) Where an appeal under this paragraph is brought against a notice within the period allowed under the preceding sub-paragraph, then—

(a) in the case of an improvement notice, the bringing of the appeal shall have the effect of suspending the operation of the notice until the appeal is finally disposed of or, if the appeal is withdrawn, until the withdrawal of the appeal;

(b) in the case of a prohibition notice, the bringing of the appeal shall have the like effect if, but only if, on the application of the appellant the tribunal so directs (and then only from the giving of the direction).

(4) One or more assessors may be appointed for the purposes of any proceedings brought before an employment tribunal under this paragraph.

7 Power of enforcement authority to indemnify inspectors

Where an action has been brought against an inspector in respect of an act done in the execution or purported execution of these Regulations and the circumstances are such that he is not legally entitled to require the enforcement authority to indemnify him, that authority may, nevertheless, indemnify him against the whole or part of any damages and costs or expenses which he may have been ordered to pay or may have incurred, if the authority is satisfied that the inspector honestly believed that the act complained of was within his powers and that his duty as an inspector required or entitled him to do it.

8 Restrictions on disclosure of information

(1) In this and the two following sub-paragraphs—

(a) "relevant information" means information obtained by an inspector in pursuance of a requirement imposed under paragraph 2(2)(e) or (f); and

(b) "the recipient", in relation to any relevant information, means the person by whom that information was so obtained or to whom that information was so furnished, as the case may be.

(2) Subject to the following sub-paragraph, no relevant information shall be disclosed without the consent of the person by whom it was furnished.

(3) The preceding sub-paragraph shall not apply to—

(a) disclosure of information to the Commission, a government department or any enforcement authority;

(b) without prejudice to paragraph (a) above, disclosure by the recipient of information to any person for the purpose of any function conferred on the recipient by or under any of the relevant statutory provisions or under these Regulations;

(c) without prejudice to paragraph (a) above, disclosure by the recipient of information to—

(i) an officer of a local authority who is authorised by that authority to receive it; or

(ii) a constable authorised by a chief officer of police to receive it; or

(d) disclosure by the recipient of information in a form calculated to prevent it from being identified as relating to a particular person or case.

(4) In the preceding sub-paragraph any reference to the Commission, a government department or an enforcement authority includes respectively a reference to an officer of that body or authority (including in the case of an enforcement authority, any inspector appointed by it), and also, in the case of a reference to the Commission, includes a reference to—

(a) a person performing any functions of the Commission or the Executive on its behalf by virtue of section 13(1)(a) of the 1974 Act;

(b) an officer of a body which is so performing any such functions; and

(c) an adviser appointed in pursuance of section 13(1)(d) of the 1974 Act.

(5) A person to whom information is disclosed in pursuance of sub-paragraph (3) above shall not use the information for a purpose other than—

(a) in a case falling within sub-paragraph (3)(a), a purpose of the Commission, of the government department, or of the enforcement authority in question in connection with these Regulations or with the relevant statutory provisions, as the case may be;

(b) in the case of information given to an officer of a body which is a local authority, the purposes of the body in connection with the relevant statutory provisions or any enactment whatsoever relating to working time, public health, public safety or the protection of the environment;

(c) in the case of information given to a constable, the purposes of the police in connection with these Regulations, the relevant statutory provisions or any enactment whatsoever relating to working time, public health, public safety or the safety of the State.

(6) A person shall not disclose any information obtained by him as a result of the exercise of any power conferred by paragraph 2 of this Schedule (including in particular any information with respect to any trade secret obtained by him in any premises entered by him by virtue of any such power) except—

(a) for the purposes of his functions;

(b) for the purposes of any legal proceedings; or

(c) with the relevant consent.

In this sub-paragraph "the relevant consent" means the consent of the person who furnished it, and, in any other case, the consent of a person having responsibilities in relation to the premises where the information was obtained.

(7) Notwithstanding anything in the preceding sub-paragraph an inspector shall, in circumstances in which it is necessary to do so for the purpose of assisting in keeping persons (or the representatives of persons) employed at any premises adequately informed about matters affecting their health, safety and welfare or working time, give to such persons or their representatives the following descriptions of information, that is to say—

(a) factual information obtained by him as mentioned in that sub-paragraph which relates to those premises or anything which was or is therein or was or is being done therein; and

(b) information with respect to any action which he has taken or proposes to take in or in connection with those premises in the performance of his functions;

and, where an inspector does as aforesaid, he shall give the like information to the employer of the first-mentioned persons.

(8) Notwithstanding anything in sub-paragraph (6) above, a person who has obtained such information as is referred to in that sub-paragraph may furnish to a person who appears to him to be likely to be a party to any civil proceedings arising out of any accident, occurrence, situation or other matter, a written statement of the relevant facts observed by him in the course of exercising any of the powers referred to in that sub-paragraph.]

[2464]

NOTES

Commencement: 1 August 2003.

Added by the Working Time (Amendment) Regulations 2003, SI 2003/1684, regs 2, 12, as from 1 August 2003.

NATIONAL MINIMUM WAGE REGULATIONS 1999

(SI 1999/584)

NOTES

Made: 6 March 1999.

Authority: National Minimum Wage Act 1998, ss 1(3), (4), 2, 3, 9, 51.

Commencement: 1 April 1999.

See Harvey B2(1), Q, R.

ARRANGEMENT OF REGULATIONS

PART I
GENERAL AND INTERPRETATION

PART II
THE RATE OF THE NATIONAL MINIMUM WAGE

The rate and exclusions

PART III
WORKING TIME FOR THE PURPOSES OF THE NATIONAL MINIMUM WAGE

Provisions in relation to working time

PART IV
REMUNERATION COUNTING TOWARDS THE NATIONAL MINIMUM WAGE

PART V
RECORDS

PART I
GENERAL AND INTERPRETATION

1 Citation and commencement

These Regulations may be cited as the National Minimum Wage Regulations 1999 and shall come into force on 1st April 1999.

[2465]

Interpretation

2 General interpretative provisions

(1) In these Regulations—

"the Act" means the National Minimum Wage Act 1998;

"allowance", other than in regulation 8(b), means any payment paid by the employer to a worker attributable to a particular aspect of his working arrangements or to his working or personal circumstances that is not consolidated into his standard pay, but does not include an allowance designed to refund a worker in respect of expenses incurred by him in connection with his employment;

"arrangements made by the Government" means—

(a) in England and Wales, arrangements made by the Secretary of State under section 2 of the Employment and Training Act 1973,

(b) in Scotland, arrangements made by the Secretary of State under section 2 of the Employment and Training Act 1973 or by Scottish Enterprise or Highlands and Islands Enterprise under section 2 of the Enterprise and New Towns (Scotland) Act 1990,

(c) in Northern Ireland, arrangements made by the Department of Economic Development under section 1 of the Employment and Training Act (Northern Ireland) 1950;

"employer" has the meaning given to it by section 54(4) of the Act but, in relation to a worker (as defined in section 54(3) of the Act), includes in addition, except in paragraph (6) of regulation 12—

(a) an agent or principal in relation to whom, by virtue of section 34(2) of the Act, the provisions of the Act have effect as if there were a worker's contract between him and an agency worker for the doing of work by the agency worker, and

(b) an employer of a home worker who is a worker by virtue of section 35 of the Act;

"performance bonus" means a performance bonus or other merit payment attributable to the quality or amount of work done in the course of more than one pay reference period, and not therefore payable directly in respect of work done in specific hours;

"the total of reductions" means the total of reductions determined in accordance with regulations 31 to 37;

"the total of remuneration" means the total of money payments determined in accordance with regulation 30;

"pay reference period" has the meaning assigned to it by regulation 10;

"worker" has the same meaning as in section 54(3) of the Act but, except in [paragraphs (3)[, (5)] and (6)] of regulation 12, includes in addition—

(a) an agency worker in relation to whom, by virtue of section 34(2) of the Act, the provisions of the Act have effect as if there were a worker's contract for the doing of his work between him and an agent or principal; and

(b) a home worker who is a worker by virtue of section 35 of the Act.

(2) In these Regulations "work" does not include work (of whatever description) relating to the employer's family household done by a worker where the conditions in sub-paragraphs (a) or (b) are satisfied.

(a) The conditions to be satisfied under this sub-paragraph are—

(i) that the worker resides in the family home of the employer for whom he works,

(ii) that the worker is not a member of that family, but is treated as such, in particular as regards to the provision of accommodation and meals and the sharing of tasks and leisure activities;

(iii) that the worker is neither liable to any deduction, nor to make any payment to the employer, or any other person, in respect of the provision of the living accommodation or meals; and

(iv) that, had the work been done by a member of the employer's family, it would not be treated as being performed under a worker's contract or as being work because the conditions in sub-paragraph (b) would be satisfied.

(b) The conditions to be satisfied under this sub-paragraph are—

(i) that the worker is a member of the employer's family,

(ii) that the worker resides in the family home of the employer,

(iii) that the worker shares in the tasks and activities of the family,

and that the work is done in that context.

(3) In these Regulations "work" does not include work (of whatever description) relating to an employer's family business, done by a worker who satisfies the conditions in paragraph (4).

(4) The conditions to be satisfied under this paragraph are—

(i) that the worker is a member of the employer's family,

(ii) that the worker resides in the family home of the employer,

(iii) that the worker participates in the running of the family business,

and that the work is done in that context.

[2466]

NOTES

Para (1): words in first (outer) pair of square brackets in definition "worker" substituted by the National Minimum Wage Regulations 1999 (Amendment) Regulations 2000, SI 2000/1989, reg 2; figure in second (inner) pair of square brackets substituted by the National Minimum Wage Regulations 1999 (Amendment) Regulations 2001, SI 2001/1108, reg 2.

3 The meaning of time work

In these Regulations "time work" means—

(a) work that is paid for under a worker's contract by reference to the time for which a worker works and is not salaried hours work;

(b) work that is paid for under a worker's contract by reference to a measure of the output of the worker per hour or other period of time during the whole of which the worker is required to work, and is not salaried hours work; and

(c) work that would fall within paragraph (b) but for the fact that the worker is paid by reference to the length of the period of time alone when his output does not exceed a particular level.

[2467]

4 The meaning of salaried hours work

(1) In these Regulations "salaried hours work" means work—

(a) that is done under a contract to do salaried hours work; and

(b) that falls within paragraph (6) below.

(2) A contract to do salaried hours work is a contract under which a worker—

(a) is entitled to be paid for an ascertainable basic number of hours in a year (referred to in this regulation as "the basic hours"); and

(b) is entitled, in respect of hours that consist of or include the basic hours, to be paid an annual salary—

(i) by equal weekly or monthly instalments of wages, or

(ii) by monthly instalments of wages that vary but have the result that the worker is entitled to be paid an equal amount in each quarter,

regardless of the number of hours in respect of which the worker is entitled to the annual salary that are actually worked by him (if any) in any particular week or month; and

(c) has, in respect of those hours, no entitlement to any payment other than his annual salary or no such entitlement other than an entitlement to a performance bonus.

(3) A contract that satisfies the conditions in paragraph (2) does so—

(a) whether or not all the basic hours are working hours;

(b) whether or not the worker can be required under his contract to work, or does in fact work, any hours in addition to the total of hours in respect of which he is entitled to his annual salary, and regardless of any payments made in respect of those additional hours.

(4) Circumstances having the result that in practice a worker may not be or is not paid by equal instalments of wages, or by an equal amount in each quarter, for hours in respect of which he is entitled under his contract only to his annual salary do not prevent the contract from being a contract for salaried hours work, for example—

(a) that a worker may be awarded a performance bonus,

(b) that the amount of a worker's annual salary may be varied,

(c) that by virtue of regulation 22 or 23 the worker is entitled to the national minimum wage in respect of hours in addition to his basic hours when, under his contract, there is no entitlement to any payment in addition to his annual salary for those additional hours (or to no payment in addition other than a performance bonus), and

(d) that the worker's employment may start or terminate during a week or month with the result that the worker is paid a proportionate amount of his annual salary for the week or month in question.

(5) The fact that, by reason of an absence from work for hours in respect of which his annual salary is normally payable, a worker is entitled under his contract, in respect of those hours, to be paid less than he would be but for the absence or to no payment does not prevent the worker's contract from being a contract for salaried hours work.

(6) The work done under a contract to do salaried hours work that falls within this paragraph, and is therefore salaried hours work, is work in respect of which the worker is entitled to no payment in addition to his annual salary, or to no payment in addition to his annual salary other than a performance bonus.

(7) References in regulation 22 to work or hours of work in respect of which a worker is entitled to no payment other than his annual salary refer also to work or hours of work in respect of which the only payment to which the worker is entitled other than his annual salary is payment of a performance bonus.

[2468]

5 The meaning of output work

In these Regulations "output work" means work that is paid for under a worker's contract that is not time work and, but for the effect of the Act and these Regulations or anything done pursuant to these Regulations, would be paid for under that contract wholly by reference to the number of pieces made or processed by the worker, or wholly by reference to some other measure of output such as the number or value of sales made or transactions completed by the worker or as a result of his work.

[2469]

6 The meaning of unmeasured work

In these Regulations "unmeasured work" means any other work that is not time work, salaried hours work or output work including, in particular, work in respect of which there are no specified hours and the worker is required to work when needed or when work is available.

[2470]

7 Travelling

A worker is to be treated as travelling for the purposes of regulations 15(2), 16(2) and (5)(b), 17(1), 18(1) and 19(1)(b) if—

(a) he is in the course of a journey by a mode of transport or is making a journey on foot;

(b) he is waiting at a place of departure to begin his journey by a mode of transport;

(c) where his journey is broken, he is waiting at a place of departure for his journey to re-commence either by the same or another mode of transport, except for any time during such a period he spends in taking a rest break; or

(d) he is waiting at the end of a journey, in the case of regulations 15(2), 16(2), 17(1) and 18(1), for the purpose of carrying out his duties, or, in the case of regulations 16(5)(b) and 19(1)(b), to receive training, except for any time before he is due to carry out his duties or receive training which he spends in taking a rest break.

[2471]

8 The meaning of payments

References in these Regulations to payments paid by the employer to the worker are references to payments paid by the employer to the worker in his capacity as a worker before any deductions are made, excluding—

(a) any payment by way of an advance under an agreement for a loan or by way of an advance of wages;

(b) any payment by way of a pension, by way of an allowance or gratuity in connection with the worker's retirement or as compensation for loss of office;

(c) any payment of an award made by a court or tribunal or to settle proceedings which have been or might be brought before a court or tribunal, other than the payment of an amount due under the worker's contract;

(d) any payment referable to the worker's redundancy;

(e) any payment by way of an award under a suggestions scheme.

[2472]

9 Benefits in kind not to count as payments

For the purposes of these Regulations the following shall not be treated as payments by the employer to the worker—

(a) any benefit in kind provided to the worker, whether or not a monetary value is attached to the benefit, other than living accommodation;

(b) any voucher, stamp or similar document capable of being exchanged for money, goods or services (or for any combination of those things) provided by the employer to the worker.

[2473]

10 The pay reference period

(1) The pay reference period is a month or, in the case of a worker who is paid wages by reference to a period shorter than a month, that period.

(2) When a worker's contract terminates regulations 14 and 30 to 37 shall be applied in relation to payments made in the period of a month beginning with the day immediately following the last day on which the worker worked under the contract as if such payments had been made in the worker's final pay reference period.

[2474]

PART II
THE RATE OF THE NATIONAL MINIMUM WAGE

The rate and exclusions

11 The rate of the national minimum wage

The single hourly rate of the national minimum wage is [£5.52].

[2475]

NOTES

Sum in square brackets substituted by the National Minimum Wage Regulations 1999 (Amendment) Regulations 2007, SI 2007/2318, reg 2, as from 1 October 2007. The previous sum (applicable as respects any pay reference period beginning on or after 1 October 2006) was £5.35 (see SI 2006/2001). Prior to that date, the sums were £5.05 (from 1 October 2005: see SI 2005/2019), £4.85 (from 1 October 2004: see SI 2004/1930), £4.50 (from 1 October 2003: see SI 2003/1923), £4.20 (from 1 October 2002: see SI 2002/1999), £4.10 (from 1 October 2001: see SI 2001/2673), £3.70 (from 1 October 2000: see SI 2000/1989), and £3.60 (from 1 April 1999).

12 Workers who do not qualify for the national minimum wage

(1) …

(2) A worker who—

(a) …

(b) is employed under a contract of apprenticeship or, in accordance with paragraph (3), is to be treated as employed under a contract of apprenticeship, and

(c) is within the first 12 months after the commencement of that employment or has not attained the age of 19,

does not qualify for the national minimum wage in respect of work done for his employer under that contract.

[(3) A person is to be treated for the purposes of paragraph (2)(b) as a worker who is employed under a contract of apprenticeship if, and only if, he is—

(a) a worker within the meaning given by section 54(3) of the Act; and

(b) engaged—

[(i) in England, under the Government arrangements known, at 1st October 2004, as Apprenticeships or Advanced Apprenticeships;]

(ii) in Scotland, under the Government arrangements known, at 1st October [2004], as Skillseekers or Modern Apprenticeships and the arrangements are for the purpose of gaining a Scottish Vocational Qualification at Level 2 or 3 or a National Vocational Qualification at Level 2 or 3; or

(iii) in Northern Ireland, under the Government arrangements known, at 1st October [2004], as Jobskills Traineeships or Modern Apprenticeships;

(iv) in Wales, under the Government arrangements known, at 1st October 2004, as Modern Apprenticeships or Foundation Modern Apprenticeships].]

(4) For the purposes of paragraph (2)(c) a worker does not commence employment with an employer where he has previously been employed by another employer and continuity of employment is preserved between the two employments by or under any enactment.

[(4A) A worker who is participating in a scheme provided to him—

(a) in England, under the Government arrangements known, at 1st October 2004, as Entry to Employment [or under the Government arrangements known at 1st October 2007, as Programme Led Apprenticeships],

(b) in Scotland, under the Government arrangements known, at 1st October 2004, as Get Ready for Work,

(c) in Northern Ireland, under the Government arrangements known, at 1st October 2004, as Access,

(d) in Wales, under the Government arrangements known, at 1st October 2004, as Skillbuild,

does not qualify for the national minimum wage in respect of work done for his employer as part of the scheme.]

(5) A [person] who is participating in a scheme, designed to provide him with training, work experience or temporary work, or to assist him in seeking or obtaining work, which is … —

[(a) a scheme provided to him under Government arrangements that are not specified in paragraph (3)(b) [or (4A)],

(b) a scheme provided to him under Government arrangements that are specified in paragraph (3)(b), unless the person is a worker within the meaning given by section 54(3) of the Act by virtue of his participation in the scheme, or

(c) a scheme, not being one provided to him under Government arrangements, funded in whole or in part under the European Social Fund,]

does not qualify for the national minimum wage in respect of work done for his employer as part of that scheme except to the extent that paragraph (6) or (7) otherwise provides.

(6) Paragraph (5) does not apply to a [person who is a worker within the meaning given by section 54(3) of the Act and] is participating in a scheme falling within sub-paragraph (a) of paragraph (5) if he is employed by the employer for whom he works under the scheme, unless the worker is engaged, for a period not exceeding three weeks, in a trial period of work with a prospective employer under [Government arrangements].

(7) Paragraph (5) does not apply to an employee who is participating in a scheme falling within sub-paragraph [(c)] of paragraph (5) if he is employed by the employer for whom he works under the scheme, unless the employee is engaged, for a period not exceeding three weeks, in a trial period of work with a prospective employer under [Government arrangements].

[(8)A worker who is [undertaking] a higher education course, and before the course ends is required, as part of that course, to attend a period of work experience not exceeding one year, does not qualify for the national minimum wage in respect of work done for his employer as part of that course.]

(9) For the purposes of paragraph (8) [and paragraph (9B)] a "higher education course" means—

(a) in England and Wales, a course of a description referred to in Schedule 6 to the Education Reform Act 1988;

(b) in Scotland, a course of a description falling within [the definition of "fundable higher education" as defined in section 5(3), (4) and (5) of the Further and Higher Education (Scotland) Act 2005];

(c) in Northern Ireland, a course of a description referred to in Schedule 1 to the Further Education (Northern Ireland) Order 1997.

[(9A) A worker who is undertaking a further education course and before the course ends is required, as part of that course, to attend a period of work experience not exceeding one year, does not qualify for the national minimum wage in respect of work done for his employer as part of that course.

(9B) For the purposes of paragraph (9A) "a further education course" means—

(a) in England, a full-time or part-time course of education that is suitable to the requirements of persons who are over compulsory school age and that—

(i) is funded by the Learning and Skills Council for England,

(ii) is funded by a local authority,

(iii) leads to a qualification that is accredited by the Qualifications and Curriculum Authority pursuant to section 24 of the Education Act 1997, or

(iv) leads to a qualification that is approved pursuant to section 98 of the Learning and Skills Act 2000,

except that it does not include a higher education course;

(b) in Wales, a full-time or part-time course of education that is suitable to the requirements of persons who are over compulsory school age and that—

(i) is funded by the Welsh Ministers,

(ii) is funded by a local authority,

(iii) leads to a qualification that is accredited by the Welsh Ministers pursuant to section 30 of the Education Act 1997, or

(iv) leads to a qualification that is approved pursuant to section 99 of the Learning and Skills Act 2000,

except that it does not include a higher education course;

(c) in Scotland, a course of "fundable further education" as defined in section 5(1) and 5(2) of the Further and Higher Education (Scotland) Act 2005;

(d) in Northern Ireland, a full-time or part-time course of education or training as defined in article 3(1) and 3(2) of the Further Education (Northern Ireland) Order 1997;

(9C) In paragraph (9B)(a) and (9B)(b) "compulsory school age" has the same meaning given by section 8 of the Education Act 1996.]

(10) A worker who satisfies the condition set out in paragraph (11) and is participating in a scheme which satisfies the conditions set out in paragraph (12), under which he is provided with shelter and other benefits (which may include money benefits) in return for performing work, does not qualify for the national minimum wage in respect of work performed for his employer under that scheme.

(11) A worker satisfies the condition referred to in paragraph (10) if, immediately before his entry into the scheme—

(a) he was either homeless or residing in a hostel for homeless persons; and

(b) he—

(i) was in receipt of, or entitled to, income support or income-based job seekers' allowance, or

(ii) was not entitled to receive either of those benefits only because he was not habitually resident in the United Kingdom.

(12) A scheme satisfies this paragraph if—

(a) the arrangements under which the scheme operates prevent the person operating the scheme or any other person from making a profit out of the provision of the scheme, other than one which may only be applied in running the scheme or other schemes satisfying the requirements of this paragraph or, where the person operating the scheme is a charity, for a purpose, being a purpose of the charity, relating to the alleviation of poverty;

(b) every person participating in the scheme satisfies the condition set out in paragraph (11), or would satisfy it if he were a worker;

(c) the accommodation available under the scheme is provided by the person operating the scheme or under arrangements made between that person and another person; and

(d) the work done under the scheme is both provided by, and performed for, the person operating the scheme.

[(13) A worker who is participating in the second phase of the European Community Leonardo da Vinci programme (established pursuant to Council Decision 99/382/EC), does not qualify for the national minimum wage in respect of work done for his employer as part of that scheme.]

[(14) A worker who is participating in the European Community Leonardo da Vinci programme (established pursuant to Decision No 1720/2006/EC of the European Parliament and the Council of the European Union establishing an action programme in the field of lifelong learning), does not qualify for the national minimum wage in respect of work done for his employer as part of that scheme.

(15) A worker who is participating in the European Community Youth in Action Programme (established pursuant to Decision No 1719/2006/EC of the European Parliament and the Council of the European Union, does not qualify for the national minimum wage in respect of work done for his employer as part of that programme.]

[2476]

NOTES

Para (1): revoked by the National Minimum Wage Regulations 1999 (Amendment) (No 2) Regulations 2004, SI 2004/1930, reg 3(a), as from 1 October 2004, except in relation to any pay reference period beginning before that date (see SI 2004/1930, reg 7(1)).

Para (2): sub-para (a) revoked by the Employment Equality (Age) Regulations 2006, SI 2006/1031, reg 49(1), Sch 8, Pt 2, para 58(1), (2), (5), as from 1 October 2006 (except in relation to any case where, before that date, a worker within the meaning of para (2) above has attained the age of 26).

Para (3): substituted by the National Minimum Wage Regulations 1999 (Amendment) Regulations 2000, SI 2000/1989, reg 4(1); sub-para (b)(i) and the year "2004" in sub-paras (b)(ii), (iii) substituted, and sub-para (b)(iv) added, by SI 2004/1930, reg 3(b), as from 1 October 2004.

Para (4A): inserted by SI 2004/1930, reg 3(c), as from 1 October 2004, except in relation to any person who began his participation in the scheme provided to him under the Government arrangements before that date (see SI 2004/1930, reg 7(2)); words in square brackets inserted by the National Minimum Wage Regulations 1999 (Amendment) Regulations 2007, SI 2007/2318, reg 3(1), (2), as from 1 October 2007, except in relation to any pay reference period beginning before that date (see SI 2007/2318, reg 9).

Para (5): words "or (4A)" in square brackets in sub-para (a) inserted by SI 2004/1930, reg 3(d), as from 1 October 2004; other words in square brackets substituted, and word omitted revoked, by the National Minimum Wage Regulations 1999 (Amendment) Regulations 2001, SI 2001/1108, regs 3, 4.

Para (6): words in first pair of square brackets substituted by SI 2000/1989, reg 4(2); words in second pair of square brackets substituted by SI 2001/1108, reg 5.

Para (7): words in square brackets substituted by SI 2001/1108, reg 6.

Para (8): substituted by SI 2000/1989, regs 4(3); words in square brackets substituted by SI 2007/2318, reg 3(1), (3), as from 1 October 2007, except in relation to any pay reference period beginning before that date (see SI 2007/2318, reg 9).

Para (9): words in first pair of square brackets inserted, and words in second pair of square brackets substituted, by SI 2007/2318, reg 3(1), (4), as from 1 October 2007, except in relation to any pay reference period beginning before that date (see SI 2007/2318, reg 9).

Paras (9A)–(9C), (14), (15): inserted and added respectively by SI 2007/2318, reg 3(1), (5), (6), as from 1 October 2007, except in relation to any pay reference period beginning before that date (see SI 2007/2318, reg 9).

Para (13): added by the National Minimum Wage Regulations 1999 (Amendment) Regulations 2005, SI 2005/2019, reg 3, as from 1 October 2005, except in relation to any pay reference period beginning before that date.

13 Workers who qualify for the national minimum wage at a different rate

(1) The hourly rate of the national minimum wage is [£4.60] for a worker who has attained the age of 18 but not the age of 22.

[(1A) The hourly rate of the national minimum wage is [£3.40] for a worker who has not attained the age of 18.]

(2)–(6) …

(7) [Paragraphs (1) and (1A) do] not apply in relation to a worker who, by virtue of regulation 12, does not qualify for the national minimum wage.

[2477]

NOTES

Para (1): sum in square brackets substituted by the National Minimum Wage Regulations 1999 (Amendment) Regulations 2007, SI 2007/2318, reg 4(a), as from 1 October 2007. The previous sum (applicable as respects any pay reference period beginning on or after 1 October 2006) was £4.45 (see SI 2006/2001).Prior to that date, the sums were £4.25 (from 1 October 2005: see SI 2005/2019); £4.10 (from 1 October 2004: see SI 2004/1930); £3.80 (from 1 October 2003: see SI 2003/1923); £3.60 (from 1 October 2002: see SI 2002/1999); £3.50 (from 1 October 2001: see SI 2001/2673); £3.20 (from 1 October 2000: see SI 2000/1411); £3.00 (from 1 April 1999).

Para (1A): inserted by the National Minimum Wage Regulations 1999 (Amendment) (No 2) Regulations 2004, SI 2004/1930, reg 4(b), as from 1 October 2004, except in relation to any pay reference period beginning before that date (see SI 2004/1930, reg 7(1)); sum in square brackets substituted by SI 2007/2318, reg 4(b), as from 1 October 2007. The previous sum (applicable as respects any pay reference period beginning on or after 1 October 2006) was £3.30 (see SI 2006/2001). Prior to that date, the sum was £3.00 (from 1 October 2004: see SI 2004/1930).

Paras (2)–(6): revoked by the Employment Equality (Age) Regulations 2006, SI 2006/1031, reg 49(1), Sch 8, Pt 2, para 58(1), (3), as from 1 October 2006.

Para (7): words in square brackets substituted by SI 2006/2001, reg 2(1), (3)(c), as from 1 October 2006.

Calculation of the hourly rate

14 Method of determining whether the national minimum wage has been paid

(1) The hourly rate paid to a worker in a pay reference period shall be determined by dividing the total calculated in accordance with paragraph (2) by the number of hours specified in paragraph (3).

(2) The total referred to in paragraph (1) shall be calculated by subtracting from the total of remuneration in the pay reference period determined under regulation 30, the total of reductions determined under regulations 31 to 37.

(3) The hours referred to in paragraph (1) are the total number of hours of time work, salaried hours work, output work and unmeasured work worked by the worker in the pay reference period that have been ascertained in accordance with regulations 20 to [29A].

[2478]

NOTES

Para (3): figure in square brackets substituted by the National Minimum Wage Regulations 1999 (Amendment) Regulations 2000, SI 2000/1989, regs 5, 10(1).

[14A Determining the applicable national minimum rate

The hourly rate at which a worker is entitled to be remunerated in respect of his work in any pay reference period is the rate, prescribed by regulations, that is in force on the first day of that period.]

[2479]

NOTES

Inserted by the National Minimum Wage Regulations 1999 (Amendment) Regulations 2002, SI 2002/1999, reg 2.

PART III

WORKING TIME FOR THE PURPOSES OF THE NATIONAL MINIMUM WAGE

Provisions in relation to working time

15 Provisions in relation to time work

[(1) Subject to paragraph (1A), time work includes time when a worker is available at or near a place of work for the purpose of doing time work and is required to be available for such work except where—

(a) the worker's home is at or near the place of work; and

(b) the time is time the worker is entitled to spend at home.

(1A) In relation to a worker who by arrangement sleeps at or near a place of work and is provided with suitable facilities for sleeping, time during the hours he is permitted to use those facilities for the purpose of sleeping shall only be treated as being time work when the worker is awake for the purpose of working.

(2) Time when a worker is travelling for the purpose of duties carried out by him in the course of time work shall be treated as being time work except where—

(a) the travelling is incidental to the duties carried out in the course of time work, the time work is not assignment work and the time is time when the worker would not otherwise be working; or

(b) the travelling is between the worker's home, or an address where he is temporarily residing other than for the purposes of performing work, and his place of work or a place where an assignment is carried out.

(3) For the purposes of paragraph (2)(a)—

(a) travelling is incidental to the duties carried out by a worker unless duties involved in his work are necessarily carried out in the course of the travelling, as in the case of a worker driving a bus, serving in a bar on a train or whose main duty is to transport items from one place to another, and

(b) time work is assignment work if it consists of assignments of work to be carried out at a different places between which the worker is obliged to travel that are not places occupied by the worker's employer.]

(4) Where a worker's hours of work vary either as to their length or in respect of the time at which they are performed and, as a result, it is uncertain in relation to particular time when the worker is travelling whether he would otherwise be working, that time shall be treated, for the purposes of paragraph (2)(a), as time when he would otherwise be working.

(5) Except as mentioned in paragraph (2) and regulation 19, time work does not include time when a worker is absent from work.

(6) A worker engaged in taking industrial action in the course of time work shall be treated as being absent from work for the time during which he is so engaged.

(7) Where a worker is entitled to a rest break in the course of time work, the period of the break shall be treated as time when the worker is absent from work; but a worker shall not be treated as being entitled to any rest breaks during time which is required to be treated as time work by paragraph (2).

[2480]

NOTES

Paras (1), (1A), (2), (3): substituted, for original paras (1)–(3), by the National Minimum Wage Regulations 1999 (Amendment) Regulations 2000, SI 2000/1989, regs 6, 10(1).

16 Provisions in relation to salaried hours work

[(1) Subject to paragraph (1A), time when a worker is available at or near a place of work for the purpose of doing salaried hours work and is required to be available for such work shall be treated as being working hours for the purpose of and to the extent mentioned in regulation 22(3)(d) and (4)(b) except where—

(a) the worker's home is at or near the place or work; and

(b) the time is time the worker is entitled to spend at home.

(1A) In relation to a worker who by arrangement sleeps at or near a place of work and is provided with suitable facilities for sleeping, time during the hours he is permitted to use those facilities for the purpose of sleeping shall only be treated as being salaried hours work when the worker is awake for the purpose of working.

(2) Time when a worker is travelling for the purpose of duties carried out by him in the course of salaried hours work shall be treated as being working hours for the purpose of and to the extent mentioned in regulation 22(3)(d) and (4)(b) except where—

(a) the travelling is incidental to the duties carried out in the course of salaried hours work, the salaried hours work is not assignment work and the time is time when the worker would not otherwise be working; or

(b) the travelling is between the worker's home, or an address where he is temporarily residing other than for the purposes of performing work, and his place of work or a place where an assignment is carried out.

(3) For the purposes of paragraph (2)(a)—

(a) travelling is incidental to the duties carried out by a worker unless duties involved in his work are necessarily carried out in the course of the travelling, as in the case of a worker driving a bus, serving in a bar on a train or whose main duty is to transport items from one place to another, and

(b) salaried hours work is assignment work if it consists of assignments of work to be carried out at different places between which the worker is obliged to travel that are not places occupied by the worker's employer.]

(4) Where a worker's hours of work vary either as to their length or in respect of the time at which they are performed and, as a result, it is uncertain in relation to particular time when the worker is travelling whether he would otherwise be working, that time shall be treated, for the purposes of paragraph (2)(a), as time when he would otherwise be working.

(5) Time when a worker is—

(a) attending at a place other than his normal place of work, when he would otherwise be working, for the purpose of receiving training wholly or mainly in connection with salaried hours work that has been approved by his employer,

(b) travelling, when he would otherwise be working, between a place of work and a place where he is receiving such training, or

(c) receiving such training at his normal place of work,

shall be treated as working hours for the purpose of and to the extent mentioned in regulation 22(3)(d) and (4)(b).

[2481]

NOTES

Paras (1), (1A), (2), (3): substituted, for original paras (1)–(3), by the National Minimum Wage Regulations 1999 (Amendment) Regulations 2000, SI 2000/1989, regs 7, 10(1).

17 Provisions in relation to output work

(1) Time spent by a worker in travelling for the purposes of doing output work shall be treated as time spent doing output work except for time spent travelling between his home, or a place where he is temporarily residing, and—

(a) premises from which he works; or

(b) except in the case of a worker whose work consists in producing tangible items at his home, premises to which he reports.

(2) A worker shall not be treated as doing output work, for the purpose of regulation 24, during time when he is engaged in taking industrial action nor as having worked, for the purpose of regulation 26, during such time.

[2482]

18 Provisions in relation to unmeasured work

(1) Time when a worker is travelling for the purpose of unmeasured work shall be treated as being unmeasured work.

(2) A worker shall not be treated as carrying out his contractual duties to do unmeasured work, for the purpose of regulation 27, during time when he is engaged in taking industrial action, nor as being available to carry out those duties, for the purpose of regulation 29, during such time.

[2483]

19 Time spent on training to be time work

(1) Time when a worker is—

(a) attending at a place other than his normal place of work, when he would otherwise be working, for the purpose of receiving training that has been approved by his employer,

(b) travelling, when he would otherwise be working, between a place of work and a place where he is receiving such training, or

(c) receiving such training at his normal place of work,

shall be treated as time work.

(2) Where a worker's hours of work vary either as to their length or in respect of the time at which they are performed and, as a result, it is uncertain in relation to particular time when the worker is attending at a place or travelling, whether he would otherwise be working, that time shall be treated for the purposes of paragraph (1)(a) or, as the case may be, (1)(b) as time when he would otherwise be working.

(3) Paragraph (1) does not apply in relation to training wholly or mainly in connection with salaried hours work

[2484]

The hours worked in a pay reference period

20 Time work

The time work worked by a worker in a pay reference period shall be the total number of hours of time work done by him in the pay reference period.

[2485]

21 Salaried hours work

(1) In this regulation, "the basic hours" means the basic number of hours in a year in respect of which a worker is entitled under his contract to his annual salary as ascertained in accordance with his contract on the first day of the pay reference period in question.

(2) Except as mentioned in paragraph (3) and regulations 22 and 23, the salaried hours work worked by a worker in a pay reference period shall be the basic hours divided by—

(a) where the pay reference period is a week, 52;

(b) where the pay reference period is a month, 12; and

(c) where the pay reference period is any other period, by the figure obtained by dividing 365 by the number of days in the pay reference period (including non-working days).

(3) Where in a pay reference period—

(a) a worker is absent from work for a number of hours in respect of which his annual salary is payable, and

(b) is, for that reason, entitled to be paid less and is paid less than the normal proportion of his annual salary in respect of the pay reference period,

the salaried hours work worked by the worker in the pay reference period shall be the number of hours determined under paragraph (2) in relation to the pay reference period reduced by the number of hours referred to in sub-paragraph (a) of this paragraph.

(4) Hours in a pay reference period during which a worker is engaged in taking industrial action and in respect of which his annual salary is or, but for his engagement in the action, would be payable, shall be regarded as satisfying the requirements in sub-paragraphs (a)

and (b) of paragraph (3) whether or not the worker's entitlement to the normal proportion of his annual salary is affected by his engagement in the action and whether or not he is paid any amount in respect of those hours.

[2486]

22 Determining the hours of salaried hours work where the basic hours have been exceeded

(1) Where in any calculation year the total of the hours referred to in paragraph (3) exceeds the basic hours, this regulation, and not regulation 21, applies for the purpose of determining the salaried hours work worked by a worker in the pay reference period during which the basic hours are exceeded and in the subsequent pay reference periods (if any) in the calculation year.

(2) In this regulation and regulation 23—

"the basic hours" means—

(a) in a calculation year when the basic number of hours in respect of which the worker is entitled under his contract to his annual salary is not varied, that basic number;

(b) in a calculation year when that basic number of hours is varied—

(i) where the basic hours are determined in respect of the calculation year before the only or first variation takes effect, the basic number of hours ignoring the effect of the variation,

(ii) where the basic hours are determined after a variation has taken effect, the sum of the following numbers of hours—

(aa) for the period beginning with the day on which the variation in question takes effect until the end of the year, the proportion of the basic number of hours in respect of which the worker would be entitled to his annual salary, in accordance with that variation, in a year of 365 days, which the number of days in the period bears to 365,

(bb) for the period starting with the beginning of the year and ending with the day before the day on which the only or first variation took effect, the proportion of the basic number of hours in respect of which the worker would be entitled to his annual salary, before the variation, in a year of 365 days, which the number of days in the period bears to 365, and

(cc) where there has been more than one variation, for each period beginning with the day on which a particular variation took effect and ending on the last day before the next variation took effect, the proportion of the basic number of hours in respect of which the worker would be entitled to his annual salary, in accordance with the earlier variation, in a year of 365 days, which the number of days in the period bears to 365,

but in applying [regulation 21] for the purposes of paragraphs (5)(a) and (b)(i) and (6)(a) the definition of "the basic hours" in regulation 21(1) shall be used;

"calculation year" means—

(a) in the case of a worker employed by an employer when these Regulations come into force, for so long as he continues in that employment, the year beginning on the day these Regulations come into force, and each subsequent year beginning on the anniversary of that day;

(b) in the case of a worker whose annual salary is payable monthly and who becomes employed by an employer after these Regulations come into force, for so long as he continues in the same employment—

(i) where the worker becomes employed on the first day of a month, the year beginning with the first day of that month and each subsequent year beginning on the anniversary of that day,

(ii) where the worker becomes employed on any other day of a month, the period beginning with that day and ending with the day before the first anniversary of the first day of the next month, and each year beginning on that anniversary or on a subsequent anniversary of the first day of that month;

(c) in the case of a worker whose annual salary is payable weekly and who becomes employed by an employer after these Regulations come into force, for so long as he continues in the same employment, the year beginning with the first day of his employment and each subsequent year beginning on the anniversary of that day.

(3) In determining for the purposes of paragraph (1) whether the basic hours have been exceeded by a worker in any calculation year and, if so, when they were exceeded, the following hours in that year shall be taken into account—

(a) the number of the worker's working hours that fell within the basic hours,

(b) the number of hours for which the worker has been absent from work that fell within the basic hours,

(c) any hours worked by the worker outside the basic hours in respect of which the worker had no entitlement under his contract to any payment other than his annual salary,

(d) time required to be treated as working hours by regulation 16, to the extent that such time consisted of hours in respect of which the worker had no entitlement under his contract to his annual salary or to any other payment,

but excluding the number of hours, if any, during which the worker was engaged in taking industrial action.

(4) In that part of the pay reference period during which the basic hours are exceeded which is referred to in paragraph (5)(b) and in each subsequent pay reference period (if any) in the calculation year, a worker shall be treated as working for the sum of the following—

(a) the number of hours in the pay reference period that would have fallen to be taken into account under paragraph (3)(a) if the basic hours had not been exceeded, but excluding any time during those hours in which the worker was engaged in taking industrial action, and

(b) time required to be treated as working hours by regulation 16, to the extent that such time consists of hours in respect of which the worker is not entitled under his contract to his annual salary or to any other payment,

and the number of hours determined under this paragraph is referred to in paragraphs (5) and (6) and in regulation 23(3) as "the actual working hours".

(5) The salaried hours work worked by a worker in the pay reference period during which the basic hours are exceeded shall be the sum of the following—

(a) in relation to the part of the pay reference period before the day on which the basic hours are exceeded, the number of hours that result from applying regulation 21 to the part as if it were a pay reference period containing the number of days in the part; and

(b) in relation to the part of the pay reference period beginning with the day on which the basic hours are exceeded, the sum of—

  (i) the number of hours that result from applying regulation 21(2) to the part as if it were a pay reference period containing the number of days in the part, but ignoring any reduction required by regulation 21(3), and

  (ii) the actual working hours in that part.

(6) The salaried hours work worked by a worker in each subsequent pay reference period until the end of the calculation year shall be the sum of—

(a) the number of hours that result from applying regulation 21(2) in relation to the pay reference period, but ignoring any reduction required by regulation 21(3); and

(b) the actual working hours in the pay reference period.

[2487]

NOTES

Para (2): words in square brackets in definition "basic hours" substituted by the National Minimum Wage Regulations 1999 (Amendment) Regulations 2000, SI 2000/1989, reg 8.

23 Determining the hours of salaried hours work in certain cases where the employment terminates

(1) This regulation applies, in the circumstances specified in paragraphs (2) and (3), to the final pay reference period of a worker whose employment terminates in the course of a calculation year and in cases where the employment of a worker is treated as being terminated by virtue of paragraph (4).

(2) Where the basic hours have not been exceeded at the end of the final pay reference period but, at the end of that pay reference period, the total of the hours to be taken into

account under regulation 22(3) since the beginning of the calculation year (the "A" hours) exceeds the total of the number of hours determined in accordance with regulation 21 in relation to all of the pay reference periods (including the final pay reference period) since the beginning of the calculation year (the "B" hours), the salaried hours work worked by the worker in that pay reference period shall be regarded as including (in addition to the number of hours determined in relation to the pay reference period in accordance with regulation 21) the number of hours by which the "A" hours exceed the "B" hours.

(3) Where the basic hours have been exceeded at any time during the calculation year before the end of the final pay reference period, the salaried hours work worked by the worker in that pay reference period shall be regarded as including (in addition to the number of hours determined in relation to the pay reference period in accordance with regulation 22(5) or, as the case may be, (6)) the number of hours that result from applying regulation 21(2) in relation to the period beginning with the day immediately following the last day of the worker's final pay reference period and ending at the end of the calculation year ("the subsequent period"), as if—

(a) the whole of the subsequent period was a single pay reference period (containing the number of days in it), and

(b) the worker had continued to be employed under his contract to do salaried hours work for the whole of the subsequent period and had not been absent from work during it for any hours in respect of which regulation 21(3) requires a reduction.

(4) Where a worker's contract is varied so that any salaried hours work required to be done under the contract becomes work that is not salaried hours work, this regulation shall apply as if—

(a) the employment of the worker had been terminated; and

(b) the last day of the worker's final pay reference period had fallen on the day before the day on which the variation took effect.

[2488]

[24 Output work

[(1) The output work of a worker in a pay reference period relating to a type of piece produced or a type of task performed shall be the number of hours spent by the worker during the pay reference period in producing that type of piece, or performing that type of task, except where the output work relating to that type of piece or task is rated output work.

(2) Output work is rated output work if—

(a) it satisfies the conditions in paragraph (1) of regulation 25, and

(b) it is work in respect of which the employer has given the worker a notice that satisfies the requirements of paragraph (2) of regulation 25.]

[2489]

NOTES

Commencement: 1 October 2004.

Substituted, together with regs 25, 26, 26A for original regs 24–26, by the National Minimum Wage Regulations 1999 (Amendment) Regulations 2004, SI 2004/1161, reg 2, as from 1 October 2004, except in relation to any pay reference period beginning before that date (see SI 2004/1161, reg 4(1)).

Transitional provisions: SI 2004/1161, reg 4(2) provides that for the purposes of the application of the regulations substituted into these Regulations by SI 2004/1161, reg 2, in relation to a pay reference period beginning on or after 1 October 2004, it shall be irrelevant whether the satisfactory test or satisfactory estimate required by reg 26A of these Regulations was conducted or made before or after 1 October 2004.

[25 Rated output work: conditions and notice

(1) The conditions referred to in regulation 24(2)(a) are—

(a) that the output work relating to the type of piece in question ("the subject piece") or the type of task in question ("the subject task") is work in respect of which the worker's contract does not set any normal, minimum or maximum working hours;

(b) that the employer does not in practice determine or control the hours worked by the worker in relation to the subject piece or the subject task; and

(c) that the employer has determined the mean hourly output rate, as defined in paragraph (3) of regulation 26, for the subject piece or the subject task.

(2) A notice satisfies the requirements of this paragraph if—

(a) it was given in writing to the worker at any time before the beginning of the pay reference period (whether or not it was given before the beginning of, and had effect in relation to, any earlier pay reference periods); and

(b) it contains statements conveying the following information—

(i) that it is being given to inform the worker that, for the purpose of securing compliance with the national minimum wage legislation, he will be treated, in respect of, as appropriate, his production of the subject piece or his performance of the subject task during the pay reference period, as working for a certain period of time;

(ii) that, for the purpose of determining the period of time the worker will be treated as working, the employer has conducted a test or, where applicable, made an estimate of the average speed at which workers employed by the employer produce the subject piece or perform the subject task, as appropriate;

(iii) what the mean hourly output rate for the subject piece or the subject task is;

(iv) the rate to be paid to the worker for the production of a single subject piece or the performance of a single subject task, as appropriate; and

(v) the telephone number of the national minimum wage helpline, which number is identified as being the national minimum wage helpline number.]

[2490]

NOTES

Commencement: 1 October 2004.
Substituted as noted to reg 24 at **[2489]**.
Transitional provisions: see the note to reg 24 at **[2489]**.

[26 Rated output work: determination of hours worked

(1) Where output work is rated output work consisting of the production of subject pieces, the number of hours of output work spent by the worker in producing subject pieces during the pay reference period shall be treated as being [120 per cent of] the number of hours that a worker producing the subject pieces at the mean hourly output rate would have taken to produce the number of subject pieces produced by the worker in the pay reference period.

(2) Where output work is rated output work consisting of the performance of subject tasks, the number of hours of output work spent by the worker in performing subject tasks during the pay reference period shall be treated as being [120 per cent of] the number of hours that a worker performing at the mean hourly output rate would have taken to perform the number of subject tasks performed by the worker in the pay reference period.

(3) In this regulation and in regulations 25 and 26A, "mean hourly output rate" means the average number (including any fraction) of—

(a) subject pieces, or fraction of a subject piece, produced in an hour by workers of the employer producing the subject piece, or

(b) subject tasks, or fraction of a subject task, performed in an hour by workers of the employer performing the subject task,

as determined in accordance with regulation 26A.]

[2491]

NOTES

Commencement: 1 October 2004.
Substituted as noted to reg 24 at **[2489]**.
Paras (1), (2): words in square brackets inserted by the National Minimum Wage Regulations 1999 (Amendment) Regulations 2004, SI 2004/1161, reg 3, as from 6 April 2005, except in relation to any pay reference period beginning before that date (see SI 2004/1161, reg 4(1)).
Transitional provisions: see the note to reg 24 at **[2489]**.

[26A Rated output work: determining the mean hourly output rate

(1) To determine the mean hourly output rate for a subject piece or a subject task, the employer must—

(a) conduct a satisfactory test, in accordance with paragraph (2), of the speed at which every worker in one of the groups specified in that paragraph produces the subject piece or performs the subject task, and then divide the total number of subject pieces or subject tasks (or the fraction of a subject piece or subject task) that all the workers in the group tested have produced or performed per hour during the period of the test by the number of workers in the group tested, or

(b) make a satisfactory estimate, in accordance with paragraph (3), of the average speed, in terms of pieces or tasks per hour, at which the workers producing the subject piece or performing the subject task are likely to produce that piece or perform that task.

(2) The permitted groups for the purposes of the test mentioned in paragraph (1)(a) are—

(a) all of the workers of the employer who produce the subject piece or perform the subject task, or

(b) a sample of those workers of the employer that, in respect of the speed at which the workers in the sample work, is representative of all those workers,

and a test is satisfactory only if all the workers in the group are tested in working circumstances similar to those in which the worker is or will be producing the subject piece or performing the subject task.

(3) Subject to paragraph (4), an estimate is satisfactory for the purposes of paragraph (1)(b) if the employer has—

(a) tested the average speed, in terms of pieces or tasks per hour, at which a sample of workers of the employer working in similar working circumstances to the worker produce a piece or perform a task that is reasonably similar to the subject piece or subject task and, in making the estimate, has fairly adjusted that average speed to take account of the increased or decreased time involved in production of the subject piece or performance of the subject task, or

(b) tested the average speed, in terms of pieces or tasks per hour, at which a sample of workers of the employer working in different working circumstances from the worker produce the subject piece or perform the subject task and, in making the estimate, has fairly adjusted that average speed to take account of the increased or decreased time involved in producing the subject piece or performing the subject task in the same working circumstances as the worker,

and if the sample of workers tested is, so far as reasonably practicable, representative, in respect of the speed at which they work, of the speed at which the workers who produce the subject piece or perform the subject task work.

(4) Where a satisfactory test has been conducted or a satisfactory estimate has been made, subsequent changes in the number or identity of the workers of the employer who produce the subject piece or perform the subject task do not require the employer to conduct a further satisfactory test or make a further satisfactory estimate unless the employer has reason to believe that the changes materially affect the mean hourly output rate.]

[2491A]

NOTES

Commencement: 1 October 2004.
Substituted as noted to reg 24 at **[2489]**.
Transitional provisions: see the note to reg 24 at **[2489]**.

27 Unmeasured work

Unless the condition in regulation 28(1) is satisfied, the unmeasured work worked by a worker in a pay reference period shall be the total of the number of hours spent by him during the pay reference period in carrying out the contractual duties required of him under his contract to do such work.

[2492]

28 "Daily average" agreements for unmeasured work

(1) The condition referred to in regulation 27 is that there is an agreement in writing between the worker and his employer, made at any time before the beginning of the pay reference period, determining the average daily number of hours the worker is likely to spend in carrying out the duties required of him under his contract to do unmeasured work on days when he is available to carry out those duties for the full amount of time contemplated by the contract.

(2) The condition in paragraph (1) is not satisfied if the employer cannot show that the average daily number of hours determined is a realistic average.

(3) Unless otherwise agreed the agreement referred to in paragraph (1) has effect solely for the purpose of determining the amount of unmeasured work the worker is to be treated as having worked for the purpose of these Regulations and does not vary the worker's contract.

[2493]

29 Determining the hours of unmeasured work where there is a "daily average" agreement

(1) In paragraph (2) the term "ascertained hours" means the number of hours of unmeasured work that would have been worked by the worker in a pay reference period if he had worked—

(a) on each day worked by him in the pay reference period on which he was available to carry out his duties for at least the full amount of time contemplated by the contract, for the average daily number of hours specified in the agreement referred to in regulation 28(1); and

(b) on each day worked by him in the pay reference period on which he was available to carry out his duties for only part of that amount of time, for the proportion of that average number of hours which the part bears to the full amount of time contemplated by the contract.

(2) Where the condition in regulation 28(1) is satisfied the hours of unmeasured work worked by a worker in the pay reference period shall be treated as being the ascertained hours.

[2494]

[29A Special provision where payment for work due only on submission of record

Where at the time of the making of a determination under regulation 14 any work done by a worker in the pay reference period in question is work in respect of which—

(a) the worker is not entitled to payment until a record of the work has been submitted to the employer, and

(b) no such record has been submitted to the employer,

the number of hours attributable to that work shall be excluded from the total number of hours referred to in paragraph (3) of regulation 14 in making the determination.]

[2495]

NOTES

Inserted by the National Minimum Wage Regulations 1999 (Amendment) Regulations 2000, SI 2000/1989, regs 9, 10(1).

PART IV

REMUNERATION COUNTING TOWARDS THE NATIONAL MINIMUM WAGE

30 Payments to the worker to be taken into account

The total of remuneration in a pay reference period shall be calculated by adding together—

(a) all money payments paid by the employer to the worker in the pay reference period;

(b) any money payments paid by the employer to the worker in the following pay reference period in respect of the pay reference period (whether in respect of work or not);

(c) any money payment paid by the employer to the worker later than the end of the following pay reference period in respect of work done in the pay reference period, being work in respect of which—

(i) the worker is under an obligation to complete a record of the amount of work done,

(ii) the worker is not entitled to payment until the completed record has been submitted by him to the employer, and

(iii) the worker has failed to submit a record before the fourth working day before the end of that following pay reference period,

provided that the payment is paid in either the pay reference period in which the record is submitted to the employer or the pay reference period after that;

(d) where the employer has provided the worker with living accommodation during the pay reference period, but in respect of that provision is neither entitled to make any deduction from the wages of the worker nor to receive any payment from him, the amount determined in accordance with regulation 36.

[2496]

31 Reductions from payments to be taken into account

(1) The total of reductions required to be subtracted from the total of remuneration shall be calculated by adding together—

(a) any money payments paid by the employer to the worker in the pay reference period that, by virtue of regulation 30(b) or (c), are required to be included in the total of remuneration for an earlier pay reference period;

(b) in the case of—

(i) work other than salaried hours work, any money payments paid by the employer to the worker in respect of periods when the worker was absent from work or engaged in taking industrial action;

(ii) salaried hours work, any money payment paid by the employer to the worker attributable to the hours (if any) by which the number of hours determined under regulation 21(2) is required to be reduced under regulation 21(3) (worker entitled to less than normal proportion of annual salary because of absence from work), whether under the direct application of those regulations or the application of them required by regulation 22(5)(a);

(c) any money payments paid by the employer to the worker in respect of—

(i) time work worked by him in the pay reference period involving particular duties that is paid for at a higher rate per hour than the lowest rate per hour payable to the worker in respect of time work worked by him involving those duties during the pay reference period, to the extent that the total of those payments exceeds the total of the money payments that would have been payable in respect of the work if that lowest rate per hour had been applicable to the work;

(ii) particular output work worked by him in the pay reference period that is paid for at a higher rate than the normal rate applicable to that work by reason of the work being done at a particular time or in particular circumstances, to the extent that the total of those payments exceeds the total of the money payments that would have been payable in respect of the work if the normal rate had been applicable to the work;

(d) any money payment paid by the employer to the worker by way of an allowance other than an allowance attributable to the performance of the worker in carrying out his work;

(e) any money payment paid by the employer to the worker representing amounts paid by customers by way of a service charge, tip, gratuity or cover charge that is not paid through the payroll;

(f) any money payment paid by the employer to the worker to meet a payment by the worker that would fall within regulation 34(1)(b) (payments by workers on account of expenditure in connection with their employment to persons other than their employer) but for the worker's payment being met or designed to be met by the employer;

(g) any deduction falling within regulation 32;

(h) any payment made by or due from the worker in the pay reference period falling within regulation 34;

(i) the amount of any deduction the employer is entitled to make, or payment he is entitled to receive from the worker, in respect of the provision of living accommodation by him to the worker in the pay reference period, as adjusted, where applicable, in accordance with regulation 37, to the extent that it exceeds the amount determined in accordance with regulation 36.

(2) To the extent that any payment or deduction is required to be subtracted from the total of remuneration by virtue of more than one sub-paragraph of paragraph (1), it shall be subtracted only once.

[(3) Any payment made to or deduction by a local housing authority or a registered social landlord in respect of the provision of living accommodation shall be exempted from the operation of sub-paragraph (i) of paragraph (1), except where the living accommodation is provided to the worker in connection with his employment with the local housing authority or registered social landlord.

(4) For the purposes of paragraph (3), "local housing authority" means—

(a) in England and Wales, a local housing authority as defined in Part 1 of the Housing Act 1985 and shall in addition include county councils;

(b) in Scotland, a local authority landlord as defined in section 11(3) of the Housing (Scotland) Act 2001;

(c) in Northern Ireland, the Northern Ireland Housing Executive.

(5) For the purposes of paragraph (3), "registered social landlord" means—

(a) in England and Wales, a social landlord registered under Part 1 of the Housing Act 1996 and shall in addition include subsidiaries or associates as defined in that Act;

(b) in Scotland, a body registered in the register maintained under section 57 of the of the Housing (Scotland) Act 2001;

(c) in Northern Ireland, a housing association registered under Chapter II of Part II of the Housing (Northern Ireland) Order 1992.]

[2496A]

NOTES

Paras (3)–(5): added by the National Minimum Wage Regulations 1999 (Amendment) Regulations 2007, SI 2007/2318, reg 5, as from 1 October 2007, except in relation to any pay reference period beginning before that date (see SI 2007/2318, reg 9).

32 Deductions to be subtracted under regulation 31(1)(g)

(1) The deductions required to be subtracted from the total of remuneration by regulation 31(1)(g) are—

(a) any deduction in respect of the worker's expenditure in connection with his employment;

(b) any deduction made by the employer for his own use and benefit (and accordingly not attributable to any amount paid or payable by the employer to any other person on behalf of the worker), except one specified in regulation 33.

(2) To the extent that any deduction is required to be subtracted by virtue of both sub-paragraphs of paragraph (1), it shall be subtracted only once.

[2497]

33 Deductions not to be subtracted under regulation 31(1)(g)

The deductions excepted from the operation of regulation 32(1)(b) are—

(a) any deduction in respect of conduct of the worker, or any other event, in respect of which he (whether together with any other workers or not) is contractually liable;

(b) any deduction on account of an advance under an agreement for a loan or an advance of wages;

(c) any deduction made to recover an accidental overpayment of wages made to the worker;

(d) any deduction in respect of the purchase by the worker of any shares, other securities or share option, or of any share in a partnership[; or

(e) any deduction in respect of the provision of living accommodation which is exempted from regulation 31(1)(i) by regulation 31(3)].

[2498]

NOTES

Para (e) and the word immediately preceding it inserted by the National Minimum Wage Regulations 1999 (Amendment) Regulations 2007, SI 2007/2318, reg 6, as from 1 October 2007.

34 Payments made by or due from a worker to be subtracted under regulation 31(1)(h)

(1) The payments made by or due from the worker required to be subtracted from the total of remuneration by regulation 31(1)(h) are—

(a) any payment due from the worker to the employer in the pay reference period on account of the worker's expenditure in connection with his employment;

(b) any payment paid in the pay reference period on account of the worker's expenditure in connection with his employment to the extent that the expenditure consists of a payment to a person other than the employer and is not met, or designed to be met, by a payment paid to him by the employer;

(c) any other payment due from the worker to the employer in the pay reference period that the employer retains or is entitled to retain for his own use and benefit except for a payment required to be left out of account by regulation 35.

(2) To the extent that any payment is required to be subtracted by virtue of more than one sub-paragraph of paragraph (1), it shall be subtracted only once.

[2499]

35 Payments not to be subtracted under regulation 31(1)(h)

The payments excepted from the operation of regulation 34(1)(c) are—

(a) any payment in respect of conduct of the worker, or any other event, in respect of which he (whether together with any other workers or not) is contractually liable;

(b) any payment on account of an advance under an agreement for a loan or an advance of wages;

(c) any payment made to refund the employer in respect of an accidental overpayment of wages made by the employer to the worker;

(d) any payment in respect of the purchase by the worker of any shares, other securities or share option, or of any share in a partnership;

(e) any payment in respect of the purchase by the worker of any goods or services from the employer, unless the purchase is made in order to comply with a requirement in the worker's contract or any other requirement imposed on him by the employer in connection with his employment[; or

(f) any payment in respect of the provision of living accommodation which is exempted from regulation 31(1)(i) by regulation 31(3)].

[2500]

NOTES

Para (f) and the word immediately preceding it inserted by the National Minimum Wage Regulations 1999 (Amendment) Regulations 2007, SI 2007/2318, reg 7, as from 1 October 2007.

36 Amount permitted to be taken into account where living accommodation is provided

[(1) The amount referred to in regulations 30(d) and 31(1)(i) is the amount resulting from multiplying the number of days in the pay reference period for which accommodation was provided by [£4.30].]

(2) For the purposes of paragraph (1), living accommodation is provided for a day only if it is provided for the whole of a day from midnight to midnight.

[2501]

NOTES

Para (1): substituted by the National Minimum Wage Regulations 1999 (Amendment) Regulations 2003, SI 2003/1923, reg 4, as from 1 October 2003, except in relation to any pay reference period beginning before that date.

Sum in square brackets in para (1) substituted by the National Minimum Wage Regulations 1999 (Amendment) Regulations 2007, SI 2007/2318, reg 8, as from 1 October 2007. The previous daily rate, as from 1 October 2006 was £4.15 (see SI 2006/2001, reg 2). Prior to that date, the sums were £3.90 (as from 1 October 2005: see SI 2005/2019); £3.75 (as from 1 October 2004: see SI 2004/1930); £3.50 (from 1 October 2003: see SI 2003/1923); £3.25 (from 1 October 2002: see SI 2001/2763); £2.85 (from 1 April 1999).

[36A Determining the applicable living accommodation amount

Any amounts required to be determined for the purpose of regulations 30(d) or 31(1)(i) of these regulations in respect of any pay reference period shall be determined in accordance with the regulations as they are in force on the first day of the pay reference period.]

[2502]

NOTES

Commencement: 1 October 2003.

Inserted by the National Minimum Wage Regulations 1999 (Amendment) Regulations 2003, SI 2003/1923, reg 5, as from 1 October 2003.

37 Adjusted deductions and payments in respect of living accommodation

(1) Where an employer is entitled to make deductions or receive payments in respect of the provision of living accommodation to a worker and in a pay reference period—

(a) a worker is absent from work for a day or more when, but for his absence, he would be expected to perform time work (for example because he is sick or taking a holiday),

(b) during that period of absence he is paid, for the hours of time work for which he is absent, an amount not less than the amount to which he would have been entitled under these Regulations, but for his absence,

(c) the hours of time work worked by the worker in the pay reference period are, by reason of his absence, less than they would be in a pay reference period containing the same number of working days in which the worker worked for the normal number of working hours (and for no additional hours), and

(d) the amount of the deduction the employer is entitled to make or payment he is entitled to receive in respect of the provision of living accommodation to the worker during the pay reference period does not increase by reason of the worker's absence from work,

the provisions of paragraph (2) shall apply.

(2) For the purposes of regulation 31(1)(i), the amount of the deduction the employer is entitled to make or payment he is entitled to receive in respect of the provision of living accommodation shall be adjusted by multiplying that amount by the number of hours of time work actually worked by the worker in the pay reference period (as determined in accordance with regulation 20) and dividing the figure so obtained by the total number of hours of time work the worker would have worked in the pay reference period (including the hours of time work actually worked) but for his absence.

[2503]

PART V
RECORDS

38 Records to be kept by an employer

(1) The employer of a worker who qualifies for the national minimum wage shall keep in respect of that worker records sufficient to establish that he is remunerating the worker at a rate at least equal to the national minimum wage.

(2) The records required to be kept under paragraph (1) shall be in a form which enables the information kept about a worker in respect of a pay reference period to be produced in a single document.

(3) The employer of a worker who qualifies for the national minimum wage who has entered into any agreement with the worker referred to in regulations 13(2)(d) (accredited training) … or 28(1) (unmeasured work), shall keep a copy of that agreement.

[(3A) The employer of a worker who qualifies for the national minimum wage who has given the worker a notice in accordance with regulation 24(2)(b), shall keep a copy of that notice and a copy of such data as is necessary to show how he has determined the rates referred to in paragraphs (iii) and (iv) of regulation 25(2)(b).]

((4) The employer of a worker who qualifies for an agricultural minimum rate of wages shall, in addition to the records he is required to keep under [paragraphs (1), (3), and (3A),] keep in respect of that worker records sufficient to establish that he is remunerating the worker at a rate at least equal to any agricultural minimum rate of wages applicable to the worker.

(5) In paragraph (4), "agricultural minimum rate of wages" means—

(a) in England and Wales, a minimum rate of wages fixed under section 3(1)(a) of the Agricultural Wages Act 1948;

(b) in Scotland, a minimum rate of wages fixed under section 3(1)(a) of the Agricultural Wages (Scotland) Act 1949;

(c) in Northern Ireland, a minimum rate of wages fixed under Article 4(1) of the Agricultural Wages (Regulation) (Northern Ireland) Order 1977.

(6) Where under paragraph (4) an employer is required to keep records in respect of a worker in addition to those he is required to keep under paragraph (1), those additional records shall be in a form which enables the information kept under paragraph (4) about a worker in respect of a pay reference period to be produced in a single document.

(7) The records required to be kept by this regulation shall be kept by the employer for a period of three years beginning with the day upon which the pay reference period immediately following that to which they relate ends.

(8) The records required to be kept by this regulation may be kept by means of a computer.

[2504]

NOTES

Para (3): words omitted revoked by the National Minimum Wage Regulations 1999 (Amendment) (No 2) Regulations 2004, SI 2004/1930, reg 6(a), as from 1 October 2004, except in relation to any pay reference period beginning before that date (see SI 2004/1930, reg 7(1)).

Para (3A): inserted by SI 2004/1930, reg 6(b) as from 1 October 2004, except in relation to any pay reference period beginning before that date (see SI 2004/1930, reg 7(1)).

Para (4): words in square brackets substituted by SI 2004/1930, reg 6(c), except in relation to any pay reference period beginning before that date (see SI 2004/1930, reg 7(1)).

Transitional provisions: SI 2004/1930, reg 7(3) provides that notwithstanding the revocation of the words in para (3) above, the duty of the employer to keep records imposed prior to the revocation by virtue of the omitted words shall continue for the period of three years referred to in para (7) above.

POLICE (HEALTH AND SAFETY) REGULATIONS 1999

(SI 1999/860)

NOTES

Made: 17 March 1999.

Authority: Health and Safety at Work etc Act 1974, ss 2(4), 15(1), (2), (8), 51A(4), 82(3)(a), Sch 3, paras 1(1)(a), (2), 11.

Commencement: 14 April 1999.

1 Citation and commencement

These Regulations may be cited as the Police (Health and Safety) Regulations 1999 and shall come into force on 14th April 1999.

[2505]

2 Amendment to the meaning of "employee" and "at work" in regulations made under Part I of the Health and Safety at Work etc Act 1974

For the purposes of regulations made under Part I of the 1974 Act before the coming into force of the Police (Health and Safety) Act 1997—

(a) a person who, otherwise than under a contract of employment, holds the office of constable or an appointment as police cadet shall be treated as an employee of the relevant officer referred to in section 51A of the 1974 Act; and

(b) a person holding the office of constable shall be treated as at work throughout the time when he is on duty but not otherwise,

and any reference to an "employee" and "at work" in those regulations shall have effect accordingly.

[2506]

3–5 (*Reg 3 amended the Safety Representatives and Safety Committees Regulations 1977, SI 1977/500, reg 2(1), and inserted reg 2A (revoked) and is now spent; regs 4, 5 amend the Personal Protective Equipment at Work Regulations 1992, SI 1992/2966, and the Provision and Use of Work Equipment Regulations 1998, SI 1998/2306.*)

(*The Schedule set out the Safety Representatives and Safety Committees Regulations 1977, SI 1977/500, Sch 1 (revoked) and is now spent.*)

RIGHT TO TIME OFF FOR STUDY OR TRAINING (SCOTLAND) REGULATIONS 1999 (NOTE)

(SI 1999/1058)

NOTES

These Regulations, which were reproduced in the fifteenth edition of this work, have been omitted for reasons of space.

[2507]–[2511]

PUBLIC INTEREST DISCLOSURE (PRESCRIBED PERSONS) ORDER 1999

(SI 1999/1549)

NOTES

Made: 5 June 1999.
Authority: Employment Rights Act 1996, s 43F.
Commencement: 2 July 1999.

The principal provision of this Order, the Schedule, was substituted in its entirety by the Public Interest Disclosure (Prescribed Persons) (Amendment) Order 2003, SI 2003/1993, art 2, as from 1 October 2003. It is printed as so substituted (and subsequently amended).

See Harvey A7, R.

1 Citation and commencement

This Order may be cited as the Public Interest Disclosure (Prescribed Persons) Order 1999 and shall come into force on 2nd July 1999.

[2512]

2 Prescribed Persons

(1) The persons and descriptions of persons prescribed for the purposes of section 43F of the Employment Rights Act 1996 are the persons and descriptions of persons specified in the first column of the Schedule.

(2) The descriptions of matters in respect of which each person, or persons of each description, specified in the first column of the Schedule is or are prescribed are the descriptions of matters respectively specified opposite them in the second column of the Schedule.

[2513]

[SCHEDULE

Article 2

First Column *Persons and descriptions of people*	*Second Column* *Descriptions of matters*
Accounts Commission for Scotland and auditors appointed by the Commission to audit the accounts of local government bodies.	The proper conduct of public business, value for money, fraud and corruption in local government bodies.
Audit Commission for England and Wales and auditors appointed by the Commission to audit the accounts of local government, and health service, bodies.	The proper conduct of public business, value for money, fraud and corruption in local government, and health service, bodies.

First Column *Persons and descriptions of people*	*Second Column* *Descriptions of matters*
Certification Officer.	Fraud, and other irregularities, relating to the financial affairs of trade unions and employers' associations.
Charity Commissioners for England and Wales.	The proper administration of charities and of funds given or held for charitable purposes.
The Scottish Ministers.	The proper administration of charities and of funds given or held for charitable purposes.
Chief Executive of the Criminal Cases Review Commission.	Actual or potential miscarriages of justice.
Chief Executive of the Scottish Criminal Cases Review Commission.	Actual or potential miscarriages of justice.
Civil Aviation Authority.	Compliance with the requirements of civil aviation legislation, including aviation safety.
[Office of Communications.	Matters relating to— (a) the provision of electronic communications networks and services and the use of the electro-magnetic spectrum; (b) broadcasting and the provision of television and radio services; (c) media ownership and control; and (d) competition in communications markets.]
The competent authority under Part IV of the Financial Services and Markets Act 2000.	The listing of securities on a stock exchange; prospectuses on offers of transferable securities to the public.
Commissioners of Customs and Excise.	Value added tax, insurance premium tax, excise duties and landfill tax. The import and export of prohibited or restricted goods.
Commissioners of the Inland Revenue.	Income tax, corporation tax, capital gains tax, petroleum revenue tax, inheritance tax, stamp duties, national insurance contributions, statutory maternity pay, statutory sick pay, tax credits, child benefits, collection of student loans and the enforcement of the national minimum wage.
Comptroller and Auditor General of the National Audit Office.	The proper conduct of public business, value for money, fraud and corruption in relation to the provision of centrally-funded public services.
Auditor General for Wales.	The proper conduct of public business, value for money, fraud and corruption in relation to the provision of public services.
Auditor General for Scotland and persons appointed by or on his behalf under the Public Finance and Accountability (Scotland) Act 2000 to act as auditors or examiners for the purposes of sections 21 to 24 of that Act.	The proper conduct of public business, value for money, fraud and corruption in relation to the provision of public services.
Audit Scotland.	The proper conduct of public business, value for money, fraud and corruption in public bodies.

First Column *Persons and descriptions of people*	*Second Column* *Descriptions of matters*
[Gas and Electricity Markets Authority.	The generation, transmission, distribution and supply of electricity, participation in the operation of an electricity interconnector (as defined in section 4(3E) of the Electricity Act 1989) and activities ancillary to these matters. The transportation, shipping and supply of gas through pipes, participation in the operation of a gas interconnector (as defined in section 5(8) of the Gas Act 1986) and activities ancillary to these matters.]
…	…
…	…
…	…
[Water Services Regulation Authority].	The supply of water and the provision of sewerage services.
[Convener of the Water Customer Consultation Panels and any member of those Panels.	The supply of water and the provision of sewerage services.
Water Industry Commission for Scotland.	The supply of water and the provision of sewerage services.]
Water Industry Commissioner for Scotland.	The supply of water and the provision of sewerage services.
Director of the Serious Fraud Office.	Serious or complex fraud.
Lord Advocate, Scotland.	Serious or complex fraud.
Environment Agency.	Acts or omissions which have an actual or potential effect on the environment or the management or regulation of the environment, including those relating to pollution, abstraction of water, flooding, the flow in rivers, inland fisheries and migratory salmon or trout.
Scottish Environment Protection Agency.	Acts or omissions which have an actual or potential effect on the environment or the management or regulation of the environment, including those relating to flood warning systems and pollution.
Food Standards Agency.	Matters which may affect the health of any member of the public in relation to the consumption of food and other matters concerning the protection of the interests of consumers in relation to food.

First Column *Persons and descriptions of people*	*Second Column* *Descriptions of matters*
Financial Services Authority	The carrying on of investment business or of insurance business; the operation of banks and building societies, deposit-taking businesses and wholesale money market regimes; the operation of friendly societies, benevolent societies, working men's clubs, specially authorised societies, and industrial and provident societies; the functioning of financial markets, investment exchanges and clearing houses; money laundering, financial crime, and other serious financial misconduct, in connection with activities regulated by the Financial Services Authority.
General Social Care Council.	Matters relating to the registration of social care workers under the Care Standards Act 2000.
Care Council for Wales.	Matters relating to the registration of social care workers under the Care Standards Act 2000.
Scottish Social Services Council.	Matters relating to the registration of the social services workforce by the Scottish Social Services Council.
[Children's Commissioner	Matters relating to the views and interests of children.
Commissioner for Children and Young People in Scotland	Matters relating to promoting and safeguarding the rights of children and young people.]
Children's Commissioner for Wales.	Matters relating to the rights and welfare of children.
Health and Safety Executive.	Matters which may affect the health or safety of any individual at work; matters, which may affect the health and safety of any member of the public, arising out of or in connection with the activities of persons at work.
Housing Corporation.	The registration and operation of registered social landlords, including their administration of public and private funds and management of their housing stock.
Local authorities which are responsible for the enforcement of health and safety legislation.	Matters which may affect the health or safety of any individual at work; matters, which may affect the health and safety of any member of the public, arising out of or in connection with the activities of persons at work.
[Independent Police Complaints Commission.	Matters relating to the conduct of a person serving with the police (as defined in section 12(7) of the Police Reform Act 2002) or of any other person in relation to whose conduct the Independent Police Complaints Commission exercises functions in or under any legislation.]

First Column *Persons and descriptions of people*	*Second Column* *Descriptions of matters*
Information Commissioner.	Compliance with the requirements of legislation relating to data protection and to freedom of information.
Scottish Information Commissioner.	Compliance with the requirements of legislation relating to freedom of information.
[Commission for Healthcare Audit and Inspection.	Matters connected with—
	(a) the provision of health care for the purposes of the National Health Service (where "health care" has the same meaning as in section 45(2) of the Health and Social Care (Community Health and Standards) Act 2003);
	(b) the provision of independent health services within the meaning of section 5A(8) of the Care Standards Act 2000; or
	(c) any activities not covered by (a) and (b) in relation to which the Commission for Healthcare Audit and Inspection exercises its functions.
Commission for Social Care Inspection.	Matters relating to the provision of regulated social care services as defined in the Care Standards Act 2000, and the inspection and performance assessment of English local authority social services as defined in section 148 of the Health and Social Care (Community Health and Standards) Act 2003.]
[National Assembly for Wales.	Matters relating to the provision of Part II services as defined in section 8 of the Care Standards Act 2000 and the Children Act 1989.
	Matters relating to the inspection and performance assessment of Welsh local authority social services as defined in section 148 of the Health and Social Care (Community Heath and Standards) Act 2003.
	Matters relating to the review of, and investigation into, the provision of health care by and for Welsh NHS bodies as defined under the Health and Social Care (Community Health and Standards) Act 2003.
	The registration and operation of registered social landlords, including their administration of public and private funds and management of their housing stock.]
Scottish Commission for the Regulation of Care.	Matters relating to the provision of care services, as defined in the Regulation of Care (Scotland) Act 2001.

First Column *Persons and descriptions of people*	*Second Column* *Descriptions of matters*
Occupational Pensions Regulatory Authority.	Matters relating to occupational pension schemes and other private pension arrangements.
Office of Fair Trading.	Matters concerning the sale of goods or the supply of services, which adversely affect the interests of consumers.
	Competition affecting markets in the United Kingdom.
[Office of Rail Regulation.]	The provision and supply of railway services.
Standards Board for England.	Breaches by a member or co-opted member of a relevant authority (as defined in section 49(6) of the Local Government Act 2000) of that authority's code of conduct.
Local Commissioner in Wales.	Breaches by a member or co-opted member of a relevant authority (as defined in section 49(6) of the Local Government Act 2000) of that authority's code of conduct.
Standards Commission for Scotland and the Chief Investigating Officer.	Breaches by a councillor or a member of a devolved public body (as defined in section 28 of the Ethical Standards in Public Life etc (Scotland) Act 2000) of the code of conduct applicable to that councillor or member under that Act.
Treasury.	The carrying on of insurance business.
[Secretary of State for Business, Enterprise and Regulatory Reform.].	Fraud, and other misconduct, in relation to companies, investment business, insurance business, or multi-level marketing schemes (and similar trading schemes); insider dealing.
	Consumer safety.
Secretary of State for Transport.	Compliance with merchant shipping law, including maritime safety.
Local authorities which are responsible for the enforcement of consumer protection legislation.	Compliance with the requirements of consumer protection legislation.
Local authorities which are responsible for the enforcement of food standards.	Compliance with the requirements of food safety legislation.
A person ("person A") carrying out functions, by virtue of legislation, relating to relevant failures falling within one or more matters within a description of matters in respect of which another person ("person B") is prescribed by this Order, where person B was previously responsible for carrying out the same or substantially similar functions and has ceased to be so responsible.	Matters falling within the description of matters in respect of which person B is prescribed by this Order, to the extent that those matters relate to functions currently carried out by person A.]

[2514]

NOTES

Commencement: 1 October 2003.

Substituted by the Public Interest Disclosure (Prescribed Persons) (Amendment) Order 2003, SI 2003/1993, art 2, Schedule, as from 1 October 2003.

Entry relating to the "Office of Communications" inserted by the Public Interest Disclosure (Prescribed Persons) (Amendment) Order 2005, SI 2005/2464, arts 2, 3(1), Schedule, as from 1 October 2005.

Entry relating to the "Gas and Electricity Markets Authority" inserted by SI 2005/2464, arts 2, 3(3), Schedule, as from 1 October 2005.

Entries relating to the "Director General of Electricity Supply", "Director General of Gas Supply", and "Director General of Telecommunications" revoked by SI 2005/2464, arts 2, 3(2), (4), as from 1 October 2005.

Entry "Water Services Regulation Authority" in Column 1 substituted (for original entry "Director General of Water Services") by the Water Act 2003 (Consequential and Supplementary Provisions) Regulations 2005, SI 2005/2035, reg 17, as from 1 April 2006.

Entries relating to the "Convener of the Water Customer Consultation Panels" and the "Water Industry Commission for Scotland" inserted by the Water Services etc (Scotland) Act 2005 (Consequential Provisions and Modifications) Order 2005, SI 2005/3172, art 11, Schedule, Pt 2, para 5, as from 11 November 2005.

Entries relating to the "Children's Commissioner" and the "Commissioner for Children and Young People in Scotland" inserted by the Public Interest Disclosure (Prescribed Persons) (Amendment) Order 2008, SI 2008/531, arts 2, 3, Schedule, as from 6 April 2008.

Entry relating to the "Independent Police Complaints Commission" inserted by the Public Interest Disclosure (Prescribed Persons) (Amendment) Order 2004, SI 2004/3265, art 2, Schedule, as from 1 January 2005.

Entries relating to the "Commission for Healthcare Audit and Inspection" and the "Commission for Social Care Inspection" substituted, for entry relating to the "Commission for Healthcare Audit and Inspection or the Commission for Social Care Inspection" (formerly "National Care Standards Commission"), by SI 2005/2464, arts 2, 3(5), Schedule, as from 1 October 2005.

Entry relating to the "National Assembly for Wales" substituted by SI 2005/2464, arts 2, 3(6), Schedule, as from 1 October 2005.

Entry "Pensions Regulator" in Column 1 substituted (for original entry "Occupational Pensions Regulatory Authority") by SI 2005/2464, arts 2, 3(7), as from 1 October 2005.

Entry "Office of Rail Regulation" in Column 1 substituted (for original entry "Rail Regulator") by the Railways and Transport Safety Act 2003, s 16(4), (5), Sch 3, para 4, as from 5 July 2004.

Words "Secretary of State for Business, Enterprise and Regulatory Reform" substituted, for original words "Secretary of State for Trade and Industry" by the Secretaries of State for Children, Schools and Families, for Innovation, Universities and Skills and for Business, Enterprise and Regulatory Reform Order 2007, SI 2007/3224, art 15, Schedule, Pt 2, para 25, as from 12 December 2007.

Commissioners of Inland Revenue; Commissioners of Customs and Excise: references to the Commissioners of Inland Revenue and the Commissioners of Customs and Excise are now to be taken as a reference to the Commissioners for Her Majesty's Revenue and Customs; see the Commissioners for Revenue and Customs Act 2005, s 50(1), (7).

Charity Commissioners: as to the abolition of the office of Charity Commissioner for England and Wales, the establishment of the Charity Commission for England and Wales, and the transfer of the functions, rights, liabilities, etc from the Charity Commissioners to the Charity Commission, see the Charities Act 2006, s 6.

Health and Safety Executive: see the note at **[2156]**.

DISABILITY DISCRIMINATION (DESCRIPTION OF INSURANCE SERVICES) REGULATIONS 1999 (NOTE)

(SI 1999/2114)

NOTES

These Regulations were made under the Disability Discrimination Act 1995, ss 18(3), 68(1), and lapsed on the repeal of s 18 of the 1995 Act (insurance services) by the Disability Discrimination Act 2005, ss 11(1), 19(2), Sch 2, as from 5 December 2005.

[2515]–[2516]

EDUCATION (MODIFICATION OF ENACTMENTS RELATING TO EMPLOYMENT) ORDER 1999 (NOTE)

(SI 1999/2256)

NOTES

This Order modified various statutory provisions relating to employment to take account of the requirement contained in the School Standards and Framework Act 1998 for local education authorities to delegate financial management of schools to their governing bodies. It was revoked and replaced, in relation to England, by the Education (Modification of Enactments Relating to Employment) (England) Order 2003, SI 2003/1964 (at **[3035A]**), as from 1 September 2003, and was revoked and replaced, in relation to Wales, by the Education (Modification of Enactments Relating to Employment) (Wales) Order 2006, SI 2006/1073 (at **[3461]**), as from 12 May 2006.

[2517]

REDUNDANCY PAYMENTS (CONTINUITY OF EMPLOYMENT IN LOCAL GOVERNMENT, ETC) (MODIFICATION) ORDER 1999

(SI 1999/2277)

NOTES

Made: 11 August 1999.
Authority: Employment Rights Act 1996, ss 209(1)(b), 236.
Commencement: 1 September 1999.

ARRANGEMENT OF ARTICLES

SCHEDULES:

1 Citation, commencement and interpretation

(1) This Order may be cited as the Redundancy Payments (Continuity of Employment in Local Government, etc) (Modification) Order 1999 and shall come into force on 1st September 1999.

(2) In this Order—

(a) "the 1983 Order" means the Redundancy Payments (Local Government) (Modification) Order 1983;
(b) "the 1972 Act" means the Local Government Act 1972;
(c) "the 1978 Act" means the Employment Protection (Consolidation) Act 1978;
(d) "the 1980 Act" means the Education (Scotland) Act 1980;
(e) "the 1985 Act" means the Local Government Act 1985;
(f) "the 1988 Act" means the Education Reform Act 1988;
(g) "the 1992 Act" means the Further and Higher Education Act 1992;
(h) "the 1994 Act" means the Local Government etc (Scotland) Act 1994;
(i) "the 1996 Act" means the Employment Rights Act 1996;
(j) "the 1998 Act" means the School Standards and Framework Act 1998;

(k) "the Education Act" means the Education Act 1996.

(3) Subject to paragraph (4) below, in this Order "relevant event" in relation to a person means any event occurring on or after the day on which this Order comes into force on the happening of which that person may become entitled to a redundancy payment in accordance with the 1996 Act.

(4) Where an event has occurred on or after 21st June 1998 but before the day on which this Order comes into force, on the happening of which a person employed immediately before that event by the English Sports Council may have become entitled to a redundancy payment in accordance with the 1996 Act, "relevant event" in this Order includes that event in relation to that person.

[2518]

2 Application of this Order

(1) This Order applies to any person who immediately before the occurrence of a relevant event is employed by an employer specified in Schedule 1 to this Order.

(2) Where a person commenced employment with a Further Education Funding Council established by section 1 of the 1992 Act before 1st April 1996 and left that employment either—

(a) before that date, or

(b) by reason of a relevant event after the date on which this Order comes into force,

this Order applies to that person as if that Council were specified in Schedule 1 to this Order.

[2519]

3 Modification of certain redundancy payments provisions

In relation to any person to whom this Order applies, the provisions of the 1996 Act mentioned in Part I of Schedule 2 to this Order shall, for the purposes of determining that person's entitlement to a redundancy payment under the 1996 Act and the amount of such payment, have effect subject to the modifications specified in that Part.

[2520]

4 Revocation

The Orders specified in Schedule 3 to this Order are revoked.

[2521]

5 Transitional, supplementary and incidental provisions

(1) In relation to a person to whom this Order applies—

(a) any reference to the 1996 Act in any enactment shall have effect as a reference to that Act as modified by this Order; and

(b) any document which refers, whether specifically or by means of a general description, to the 1996 Act shall, except so far as the context otherwise requires, be construed as referring to that Act as modified by this Order.

(2) Where a period of employment of a person to whom this Order applies falls to be calculated in accordance with the provisions of the 1996 Act as modified by this Order, the provisions of this Order shall have effect in relation to that calculation whether the period in question falls wholly or partly before or wholly after this Order comes into force.

(3) Notwithstanding the revocation by article 4 above of the Orders specified in Schedule 3 to this Order, in relation to determining any person's entitlement to a redundancy payment following an event which occurred before the date on which this Order comes into force (or, in the case of a person such as is referred to in paragraph (4) of article 1, before the date referred to in that paragraph), and which would have been a relevant event if it had occurred on or after that date, the 1983 Order shall continue to have effect as it had effect on the date of that event.

[2522]

SCHEDULES

SCHEDULE 1
EMPLOYMENT TO WHICH THIS ORDER APPLIES: EMPLOYERS IMMEDIATELY BEFORE THE RELEVANT EVENT

Article 2

Section 1—Local Government

1. In relation to England, a county council, a district council, a London borough council, the Common Council of the City of London, the Council of the Isles of Scilly; in relation to Wales, a county council or a county borough council, established under section 20 of the 1972 Act.

2. A council constituted under section 2 of the 1994 Act.

3. In relation to England, a parish council, a common parish council, a parish meeting; in relation to Wales, a community council, a common community council.

4. Any authority established by an order under section 10 of the 1985 Act.

5. A joint board or joint body constituted by or under any enactment for the purposes of exercising the functions of two or more bodies described in any of paragraphs 1 to 4 above.

6. Any other authority or body, not specified in any of paragraphs 1 to 4 above, established by or under any enactment for the purpose of exercising the functions of, or advising, one or more of the bodies specified in paragraphs 1 to 4 above.

[6A. The Greater London Authority.

6B. Transport for London.]

[6C. A functional body as defined in section 424 of the Greater London Authority Act 1999 but excluding Transport for London.

6D. The London Transport Users' Committee established under section 247 of the 1999 Act.

6E. The Cultural Strategy Group for London established under section 375 of that Act.]

7. Any committee (including a joint committee) established by or under any enactment for the purpose of exercising the functions of, or advising, one or more of the bodies specified in any of paragraphs 1 to 6 above.

8. Any two or more bodies described in any of paragraphs 1 to 7 above acting jointly or as a combined authority.

9. Any association which is representative of any two or more authorities described in any of paragraphs 1 to 4 above.

10. Any committee established by one or more of the associations described in paragraph 9 above for the purpose of exercising the functions of, or advising, one or more of such associations.

11. An association which is representative of one or more of the associations described in paragraph 9 above and of another body or other bodies, and included in whose objects is the assembling and dissemination of information and advising with regard to conditions of service in local government service and generally.

12. An organisation which is representative of an association or associations described in paragraph 9 above and employees' organisations and among whose objects is the negotiation of pay and conditions of service in local government service.

13. A National Park authority established under section 63 of the Environment Act 1995.

14. A residuary body established by section 57(1)(b) of the 1985 Act.

15. The Residuary Body for Wales (Corff Gweddilliol Cymru).

16. The Accounts Commission for Scotland.

17. The Commission for Local Administration in England.

18. The Commission for Local Administration in Wales.

19. The Commission for Local Administration in Scotland.

20. The Local Government Management Board.

21. Employers Organisation for Local Government.

22. Improvement and Development Agency for Local Government.

Section 2—Planning and development

1. One North East.

2. Yorkshire Forward.

3. North West Development Agency (NWDA).

4. Advantage West Midlands.

[4A. Dewsbury Partnership Limited.]

5. East Midlands Development Agency (EMDA).

6. East of England Development Agency (EEDA).

7. South East of England Development Agency (SEEDA).

[7A. SEERA Limited.]

8. South West of England Development Agency (SWERDA).

9. A development corporation within the meaning of the New Towns Act 1981.

10. An Urban Development Corporation established under section 135 of the Local Government Planning and Land Act 1980.

11. A housing action trust established under Part III of the Housing Act 1988.

12. The Broads Authority, established under the Norfolk and Suffolk Broads Act 1988.

13. The Commission for the New Towns.

14. The Countryside Commission for Scotland.

15. The Development Board for Rural Wales.

16. The Edinburgh New Town Conservation Committee.

17. The Housing Corporation.

18. Huddersfield Pride Limited.

19. Scottish Enterprise, established under the Enterprise and New Towns (Scotland) Act 1990.

20. Scottish Homes, established under the Housing (Scotland) Act 1988.

21. Springfield Horseshoe Housing Management Co-operative Limited.

22. Housing for Wales (Tai Cymru).

23. …

24. Batley Action Limited.

25. Bethnal Green City Challenge Company Limited.

26. The Blackburn City Challenge Partnership Board.

27. Bolton City Challenge Partnership Limited.

28. Bradford City Challenge Limited.

29. Brixton Challenge Company Limited.

30. Community North (Sunderland) Limited.

31. Dalston City Partnership Limited.

32. Deptford City Challenge Limited.

33. Derby Pride Limited.

34. Douglas Valley Partnership Limited.

35. Harlesden City Challenge Limited.

36. Hulme Regeneration Limited.

37. Leicester City Challenge Limited.

[37A. Manchester Investment and Development Agency Service Limited (MIDAS).]

38. Newcastle West End Partnership Limited.

39. Newtown South Aston City Challenge Limited.

40. North Kensington City Challenge Company Limited.

41. North Tyneside City Challenge Partnership Limited.

42. Stratford Development Partnership Limited.

43. Wolverhampton City Challenge Limited.

44. The Urban Regeneration Agency established under Part III of the Leasehold Reform, Housing and Urban Development Act 1993.

[45. Pennine Housing 2000 Limited.

46. Twin Valley Homes Limited.

47. Urban Futures London Limited.]

[48. Aire-Wharfe Community Housing Trust Limited.

49. Bradford Building Services Limited.

50. Bradford Community Housing Trust Limited.

51. Bradford West City Community Housing Trust Limited.

52. Coast & County Housing Limited.

53. Dumfries and Galloway Housing Partnership Limited.

54. East Bradford Community Housing Trust Limited.

55. Knowsley Housing Trust.

56. North Bradford Community Housing Trust Limited.

57. Northern Housing Consortium Limited.

58. Shipley Community Housing Trust Limited.

59. South Bradford Community Housing Trust Limited.

60. Sunderland Housing Group.]

Section 3—Education

1. The governing body of a further education establishment for the time being mainly dependent for its maintenance on assistance from local education authorities, or grants under section 485 of the Education Act or on such assistance and grants taken together.

2. The governing body of an aided school within the meaning of the Education Act.

3. The governing body of a foundation school, voluntary aided school or foundation special school within the meaning of the 1998 Act.

4. The managers of a grant-aided school as defined in section 135(1) of the 1980 Act.

5. The governing body of a central institution as defined in section 135(1) of the 1980 Act other than a college of agriculture.

6. The governing body of a College of Education as defined in section 135(1) of the 1980 Act.

7. The managers, other than a local authority, of a school which before any direction made by the Secretary of State under paragraph 2(1) of Schedule 7 to the Social Work (Scotland) Act 1968 was a school which immediately before the commencement of Part III of that Act was approved under section 83 of the Children and Young Persons (Scotland) Act 1937 if the employee was employed by those managers at the date the direction became effective.

8. A person carrying on a city technology college[, a city college for the technology of the arts or [an Academy]] established under an agreement with the Secretary of State under section 482 of the Education Act.

9. A company formed to manage a college of further education by virtue of section 65(1) of the Self-Governing Schools etc (Scotland) Act 1989.

10. The board of management of a self-governing school as defined in section 80(1) of the Self-Governing Schools etc (Scotland) Act 1989.

11. A further education corporation established under section 15 or 16 of the 1992 Act or in respect of which an order has been made under section 47 of that Act.

12. The governing body of an institution which is a designated institution for the purposes of Part I of the 1992 Act or, in the case of such an institution conducted by a company, that company.

13. The board of management of a college of further education, established under Part I of the Further and Higher Education (Scotland) Act 1992.

14. The governing body of a designated institution within the meaning of section 44(2) of the Further and Higher Education (Scotland) Act 1992.

15. A higher education corporation established under section 121 or 122 of the 1988 Act or in respect of which an order has been made under section 122A of that Act.

16. The governing body of an institution designated under section 129 of the 1988 Act or, in the case of such an institution conducted by a company, that company.

17. An Education Action Forum established under sections 10 and 11 of the 1998 Act.

18. The governing body of a grant-maintained school.

19. The governing body of a grant-maintained special school.

20. The Central Council for Education and Training in Social Work.

21. The Centre for Information on Language Teaching and Research.

[21A. The Centre for Literacy in Primary Education.

21B. Connexions Lancashire Limited.]

22. Cwmni Cynnal.

23. The General Teaching Council for Scotland, established under the Teaching Council (Scotland) Act 1965.

24. The National Institute of Adult Continuing Education (England and Wales).

25. Newbattle Abbey College.

26. The Scottish Community Education Council.

27. Scottish Consultative Council on the Curriculum.

28. The Scottish Council for Educational Technology.

29. The Scottish Council for Research in Education.

30. The Scottish Examination Board.

31. The Scottish Vocational Education Council.

[32. Shetland Arts Trust.

33. VT Four S Limited.]

Section 4—Careers guidance

1. Argyll & Bute Careers Partnership Limited.

2. Calderdale and Kirklees Careers Service Partnership Limited.

3. Cambridgeshire Careers Guidance Limited.

4. Capital Careers Limited.

5. Career Connections Limited.

6. Career Decisions Limited.

7. Career Development Edinburgh and Lothians.

8. Career Path (Northamptonshire) Limited.

9. Careerpaths (Cardiff and Vale) Limited.

10. Careers and Education Business Partnership.

11. Careers Central Limited.

[11A. Careers Enterprise (Futures) Limited.]

12. Careers Partnership Limited.

13. Careers Service Lancashire Area West Limited.

14. Central Careers Limited.

15. Cornwall and Devon Careers Limited.

[15A. Coventry, Solihull and Warwickshire Partnership Limited.]

16. Derbyshire Careers Service Limited.

17. East Lancashire Careers Services Limited.

18. Education Business Partnership (Wigan) Limited.

19. Essex Careers and Business Partnership Limited.

20. Future Steps Limited.

21. Futures Careers Limited.

22. Grampian Careers.

23. Guidance Enterprises Group Limited.

24. GuideLine Career Services Limited.

25. Gwent Careers Service Partnership Limited.

26. Hereford and Worcester Careers Service Limited.

27. Hertfordshire Careers Services Limited.

28. Highland Careers Services Limited.

29. The Humberside Partnership.

30. Learning Partnership West.

31. Leeds Careers Guidance.

32. Leicestershire Careers and Guidance Services Limited.

33. Lifetime Careers Barnsley, Doncaster and Rotherham Limited.

34. Lifetime Careers Bolton, Bury and Rochdale Limited.

35. Lifetime Careers Brent and Harrow Limited.

36. Lifetime Careers Stockport and High Peak Limited.

37. Lifetime Careers Wiltshire Limited.

38. Lincolnshire Careers and Guidance Services Limited.

[38A. London South Bank Careers.]

39. Mid Glamorgan Careers Limited.

40. Norfolk Careers Services Limited.

41. North East Wales Careers Service Company Limited.

[41A. Oldham Education Business and Guidance Services.]

42. Orkney Opportunities Centre.

43. Prospects Careers Services Limited.

44. Quality Careers Services Limited.

45. St Helens Careers Service Limited.

46. Sheffield Careers Guidance Services.

47. Shropshire Careers Service Limited.

48. Suffolk Careers Limited.

49. Tayside Careers Limited.

50. West Glamorgan Careers and Education Business Company Limited.

Section 5—Public transport

1. A Passenger Transport Executive established under section 9(1) of the Transport Act 1968.

2. A metropolitan county passenger transport authority established by section 28 of the 1985 Act.

3. The Forth Road Bridge Joint Board.

4. The Tay Road Bridge Joint Board.

Section 6—Police, fire and civil defence

1. A fire authority constituted by a combination scheme made under the Fire Services Act 1947.

[1A. A fire and rescue authority constituted by a scheme under section 2 of the Fire and Rescue Services Act 2004 or a scheme to which section 4 of that Act applies.]

2. A police authority … within the meaning of the Police Act 1996.

3. A [metropolitan county fire and rescue authority] established by section 26 of the 1985 Act.

4. …

Section 7—Sports Councils

1. The English Sports Council.

2. The Scottish Sports Council.

3. The Sports Council for Wales.

4. The United Kingdom Sports Council.

Section 8—Social services

1. Coverage Care Limited.

[1A. Forfarshire Society for the Blind.

1B. Harlow Welfare Rights & Advice.]

2. The Humberside Independent Care Association.

[2A. New Charter Building Company Limited.

2B. New Charter Housing Trust Limited.]

3. Quantum Care Limited.

4. Sandwell Community Caring Trust Limited.

[4ZA. The Scottish Commission for the Regulation of Care.

4ZB. The Scottish Social Services Council.

4ZC. Shetland Council of Social Services.]

[4A. Shetland Welfare Trust.

4AA. Tynedale Housing Company Limited.]

5. Waltham Forest Specialist Housing Consortium Limited.

6. The Wrekin Housing Trust Limited.

Section 9—Museums

1. The Board of Governors of the Museum of London.

2. The Board of Trustees of The National Museums and Galleries on Merseyside.

3. Coventry Museum of British Road Transport.

4. The Geffrye Museum Trust.

5. The Horniman Public Museum and Public Park Trust.

6. National Coal Mining Museum for England Trust Limited.

7. The Scottish Museums Council.

Section 10—Miscellaneous bodies

[1. A valuation tribunal in Wales established under the Local Government Finance Act 1988.]

2. …

3. An area tourist board established by virtue of an order made under section 172, 173 or 174 of the 1994 Act.

4. A probation committee within the meaning of the Probation Service Act 1993.

[4A. A local probation board within the meaning of the Criminal Justice and Court Services Act 2000.]

[4B. a probation trust.]

5. A magistrates' courts committee or the Committee of Magistrates for the Inner London Area, within the meaning of the Justices of the Peace Act 1979.

[5A. A body designated as a Care Trust under section 45 of the Health and Social Care Act 2001.]

[6. Blyth Valley Arts and Leisure Limited.

6A. The Business Shop—Angus Limited.

6B. The Care Standards Inspectorate for Wales.

6C. The Children and Family Court Advisory and Support Service.]

7. CIP (Hounslow) Limited.

[7A. Clackmannanshire Leisure.]

8. Community Initiative Partnerships.

[8A. Coventry Sports Trust Limited.]

[8B. CV One Limited.]

9. Derwentside Leisure Limited.

[9ZA. East End Partnership Limited.]

[9A. Edinburgh Leisure.

9AA. Enfield Leisure Centres Limited.]

10. The Environment Agency.

11. Greenwich Leisure Limited.

[11A. Herefordshire Community Leisure Trust.]

12. Hounslow Cultural and Community Services.

13. Hounslow Sports and Recreation Services.

[13A. The Islesburgh Trust.

13B. Kirklees Active Leisure Trust.]

14. The Land Authority for Wales.

15. Leisure Tynedale.

16. The Lee Valley Regional Park Authority.

17. The London Pensions Fund Authority.

[17A. The National Care Standards Commission.]

[17B. The Commission for Healthcare Audit and Inspection.

17C. The Commission for Social Care Inspection.]

18. National Mobility Services Trust Limited.

19. New Park Village TMC Limited.

[19A. Oldham Community Leisure Limited.

19B. Renfrewshire Leisure Limited.

19C. Salford Community Leisure Limited.

19D. Sandwell Sport and Leisure Trust.]

20. The Scottish Children's Reporter Administration established under section 128 of the 1994 Act.

21. The Scottish Environment Protection Agency.

[22. Scottish Water.]

[22A. Shetland Recreational Trust.]

23. The South Yorkshire Pensions Authority.

[24A. Tameside Sports Trust.

24B. Tees Active Limited.

24C. The Valuation Tribunal Service.

24D. The Water Industry Commissioner for Scotland.]

25. West Lothian Leisure Limited.

[26. Wigan Leisure and Culture Trust.]

[2523]

NOTES

Section 1: paras 6A–6E inserted by the London Government (Continuity of Employment) Order 2000, SI 2000/1042, art 4(1)–(3).

Section 2: paras 4A, 37A, 48–60 inserted and added respectively by the Redundancy Payments (Continuity of Employment in Local Government, etc) (Modification) (Amendment) Order 2004,

SI 2004/1682, art 2(1), (2), as from 1 August 2004; para 7A inserted by the Redundancy Payments (Continuity of Employment in Local Government, etc) (Modification) (Amendment) Order 2001, SI 2001/866, art 2(1), (2); para 23 revoked by the Welsh Development Agency (Transfer of Functions to the National Assembly for Wales and Abolition) Order 2005, SI 2005/3226, art 7(1)(b), Sch 2, Pt 1, para 4, as from 1 April 2006; paras 45–47 added by the Redundancy Payments (Continuity of Employment in Local Government, etc) (Modification) (Amendment) Order 2002, SI 2002/532, art 2(1), (2)(a).

Section 3: words in first (outer) pair of square brackets in para 8 substituted by SI 2001/866, art 2(1), (3); words in second (inner) pair of square brackets in para 8 substituted, and paras 21A, 21B, 32, 33 inserted and added respectively, by SI 2004/1682, art 2(1), (3), as from 1 August 2004.

Section 4: para 11A inserted by SI 2001/866, art 2(1), (7); paras 15A, 41A inserted by SI 2004/1682, art 2(1), (4), as from 1 August 2004; para 38A inserted by SI 2002/532, art 2(1), (3).

Section 6: para 1A inserted by the Fire and Rescue Services Act 2004 (Consequential Amendments) (England) Order 2004, SI 2004/3168, art 50, as from 30 December 2004, in relation to England only, and by the Fire and Rescue Services Act 2004 (Consequential Amendments) (Wales) Order 2005, SI 2005/2929, art 50, as from 25 October 2005, in relation to Wales only; words omitted from para 2 and the whole of para 4 revoked by SI 2000/1042, art 4(4); words in square brackets in para 3 substituted by the Civil Contingencies Act 2004, s 32(1), Sch 2, Pt 1, para 10(1), (2), as from 1 April 2005.

Section 8: paras 1A, 1B, 4ZA–4ZC inserted by SI 2004/1682, art 2(1), (5), as from 1 August 2004; paras 2A, 2B inserted by SI 2001/866, art 2(1), (5); paras 4A, 4AA substituted, for para 4A (as inserted by SI 2001/866, art 2(1), (5)), by SI 2002/532, art 2(1), (4)(a).

Section 10: paras 1, 22 substituted, para 2 revoked, paras 4A, 8B, 9ZA, 11A, 13A, 13B, 19A–19D, 22A, 24A–24D, 26 inserted, and paras 6, 6A–6C substituted, for para 6 (as originally enacted), para 6A (as inserted by SI 2001/866, art 2(1), (6)(a)), and para 6AA (as inserted by SI 2002/532, art 2(1), (5)(b)), by SI 2004/1682, art 2(1), (6), as from 1 August 2004; para 4B inserted by the Offender Management Act 2007 (Consequential Amendments) Order 2008, SI 2008/912, art 3, Sch 2, para 1, as from 1 April 2008; paras 5A, 7A, 8A, 17A inserted, and paras 9A, 9AA substituted, for para 9A (as inserted by SI 2001/866, art 2(1), (6)(b)), by SI 2002/532, art 2(1), (5); paras 17B, 17C inserted by the Health and Social Care (Community Health and Standards) Act 2003 (Commission for Healthcare Audit and Inspection and Commission for Social Care Inspection) (Transitional and Consequential Provisions) Order 2004, SI 2004/664, art 2, Sch 1, para 2, as from 1 April 2004.

The Commission for Local Administration in Wales was abolished by the Public Services Ombudsman (Wales) Act 2005, s 36(1) on 1 April 2006; for further effect see SI 2005/2800, arts 6, 7.

SCHEDULE 2

PART I
MODIFICATIONS TO CERTAIN REDUNDANCY PAYMENTS PROVISIONS OF THE 1996 ACT

Article 3

1. Section 146 of the 1996 Act shall have effect as if immediately after subsection (1) there were inserted—

SI 1999/2277 "(1A) The reference in subsection (1) to re-engagement by the employer includes a reference to re-engagement by any employer specified in Part II of Schedule 2 to the Redundancy Payments (Continuity of Employment in Local Government, etc) (Modification) Order 1999 and the reference in subsection (1) to an offer made by the employer includes a reference to an offer made by any employer so specified."

2. Section 155 of the 1996 Act shall have effect as if—

for the words "continuously employed" there were substituted the words "employed in relevant service";

the provisions of that section modified as provided in sub-paragraph (a) were subsection (1) of that section; and

after that subsection there were inserted the following subsections—

SI 1999/2277 "(2) In subsection (1) "relevant service" means

(a) continuous employment by an employer specified in Part II of Schedule 2 to the Redundancy Payments (Continuity of Employment in Local Government, etc) (Modification) Order 1999 ("the 1999 Order"), or

(b) where immediately before the relevant event a person has been successively employed by two or more employers specified in Part II of that Schedule, such aggregate period of service with such employers as would be continuous employment if they were a single employer.

(3) In subsection (2)(b) "relevant event" has the same meaning as in the 1999 Order."

3. Section 162 of the 1996 Act shall have effect as if—

for the words "continuously employed" in subsection (1)(a) there were substituted the words "employed in relevant service"; and

after subsection (1) there were inserted the following subsections—

SI 1999/2277 "(1A) In subsection (1)(a) "relevant service" means—

(a) continuous employment by an employer specified in Part II of Schedule 2 to the Redundancy Payments (Continuity of Employment in Local Government, etc) (Modification) Order 1999 ("the 1999 Order"), or

(b) where immediately before the relevant event a person has been successively employed by two or more employers specified in Part II of that Schedule, such aggregate period of service with such employers as would be continuous employment if they were a single employer.

(1B) In subsection (1A)(b) "relevant event" has the same meaning as in the 1999 Order."

[2524]

PART II
EMPLOYERS WITH WHOM EMPLOYMENT MAY CONSTITUTE RELEVANT SERVICE

Section 1

Any employer specified in Schedule 1 to this Order whether or not in existence at the time of the relevant event.

Section 2—Local government

1. The Greater London Council.

2. The London Residuary Body established by section 57(1)(a) of the 1985 Act.

3. The council of an administrative county, county borough (other than one established under section 20 of the 1972 Act), metropolitan borough or county district.

4. A regional council, islands council or district council established by or under the Local Government (Scotland) Act 1973.

5. The council of a county, county of a city, large burgh, small burgh or district ceasing to exist after 15th May 1975.

6. Any joint board or joint body constituted by or under any enactment for the purpose of exercising the functions of two or more of the bodies described in any of paragraphs 1 to 5 above, and any special planning board within the meaning of paragraph 3 of Schedule 17 to the 1972 Act.

7. Any other body, not specified in any of paragraphs 1 to 6 above, established by or under any enactment for the purpose of exercising the functions of, or advising, one or more of the bodies specified in any of paragraphs 1 to 6 above.

8. Any committee (including a joint committee) established by or under any enactment for the purpose of exercising the functions of, or advising, one or more of the bodies described in any of paragraphs 1 to 6 above.

9. Any two or more bodies described in any of paragraphs 1 to 8 above acting jointly or as a combined authority.

10. Any association which was representative of any two or more bodies described in any of paragraphs 1 to 5 above.

11. Any committee established by one or more of the associations described in paragraph 10 above for the purpose of exercising the functions of, or advising, one or more of such associations.

12. An organisation which was representative of an association or associations described in paragraph 10 above and employees' organisations and among whose objects was to negotiate pay and conditions of service in local government service.

13. The council of a county or district in Wales ceasing to exist after 31st March 1996.

14. The Local Government Training Board.

Section 3—Planning and development

1. A development corporation within the meaning of the New Towns Act 1946 or the New Towns Act 1965.

2. A development corporation established under section 2 of the New Towns (Scotland) Act 1968.

3. The Scottish Development Agency.

4. The Scottish Special Housing Association.

5. The English Industrial Estates Corporation established by the Local Employment Act 1960.

Section 4—Education

1. The governing body of an aided school within the meaning of the Education Act.

2. The governing body of a grant-maintained school.

3. The governing body of a grant-maintained special school.

4. The proprietor (within the meaning of section 579(1) of the Education Act) of a school for the time being recognised as a grammar school for the purposes of regulation 4(1) of the Direct Grant Schools Regulations 1959, being a school in relation to which, before 1st January 1976, the Secretary of State was satisfied as mentioned in regulation 3(1) of the Direct Grant Grammar Schools (Cessation of Grant) Regulations 1975.

5. The proprietor (within the meaning of section 114(1) of the Education Act 1944) of a school not falling within paragraph 1 of this section which throughout the period of employment was recognised as a grammar school or, as the case may be, as a direct grant grammar school for the purposes of regulation 4(1) of the Direct Grant Schools Regulations 1959, of Part IV of the Schools Grant Regulations 1951 or of Part IV of the Primary and Secondary Schools (Grant Conditions) Regulations 1945.

6. The managers of a school which during the period of employment was approved under section 83 of the Children and Young Persons (Scotland) Act 1937.

7. The managers of a school which during the period of employment was a grant-aided school within the meaning of section 143(1) of the Education (Scotland) Act 1946, section 145(22) of the Education (Scotland) Act 1962 or section 135(1) of the 1980 Act.

8. The managers of a school which during the period of employment was a school which, immediately before the commencement of Part III of the Social Work (Scotland) Act 1968, was approved under section 83 of the Children and Young Persons (Scotland) Act 1937.

9. An institution within the PCFC funding sector, within the meaning of section 132(6) of the 1988 Act.

10. The Further Education Staff College.

11. The Inner London Education Authority, known as the Inner London Interim Education Authority for a period prior to the abolition date as defined in section 1(2) of the 1985 Act.

12. The National Advisory Body for Public Sector Higher Education.

13. The Polytechnics and College Funding Council as established by section 132 of the 1988 Act.

14. The Scottish Association for National Certificates and Diplomas.

15. The Scottish Business Education Council.

16. The Scottish Council for Commercial, Administrative and Professional Education.

17. The Scottish Technical Education Council.

18. The Secretary of State for Defence in relation only to employees in schools administered by the Service Children's Education Authority.

19. The Secretary of State for Education and Employment[, the Secretary of State for Education and Skills or the Secretary of State for Children, Schools and Families], in relation only to teachers employed under contract in the European School established under Article 1 of the Statute of the European School and in schools designated as European Schools under Article 1 of the Protocol to that Statute.

[20. A person who, during the period of employment, performed a function of a local education authority pursuant to a direction given by the Secretary of State under section 497A(4) of the Education Act 1996.]

Section 5—Careers guidance

1. Black Country Careers Services Limited.

2. Buckinghamshire Careers Service Limited.

3. Kent Careers and Guidance Service Limited.

Section 6—[Police, fire and civil defence]

[1.] A previous police authority in relation to which Schedule 11 to the Police Act 1964 had effect or which was the police authority for an area or district which was before 1st April 1947 or after 31st March 1946 a separate police area or, in Scotland, a previous police authority for an area which was before 16th May 1975 a separate or combined police area.

[2. The London Fire and Civil Defence Authority.]

Section 7—Sports Councils

The Sports Council.

Section 8—Social services

A person or body of persons responsible for the management of an assisted community home within the meaning of section 36 of the Children and Young Persons Act 1969 or of an approved institution within the meaning of section 46 of that Act.

Section 9—Miscellaneous

1. A regional water board established under section 5 of the Water (Scotland) Act 1967.

2. A river purification board established under section 2 of the Rivers (Prevention of Pollution) (Scotland) Act 1951.

3. A river purification board established under section 135 of the Local Government (Scotland) Act 1973.

4. A local valuation panel constituted under the Local Government Act 1948 or established under the General Rate Act 1967.

[4A. A valuation tribunal in England established under the Local Government Finance Act 1988.]

5. The Central Scotland Water Development Board.

6. The Scottish Industrial Estates Corporation (formerly the Industrial Estates Management Corporation for Scotland) established by section 8 of the Local Employment Act 1960.

7. The Small Industries Council for Rural Areas of Scotland, being a company which was dissolved by section 15(5) of the Scottish Development Agency Act 1975 and was until then registered under the Companies Acts from time to time in force.

8. The Welsh Industrial Estates Corporation (formerly the Industrial Estates Management Corporation for Wales) established by section 8 of the Local Employment Act 1960.

[2525]

NOTES

Section 4: words in square brackets in para 19 substituted (for words originally inserted by SI 2002/1397, art 12, Schedule, Pt II, para 33) by the Secretaries of State for Children, Schools and Families, for Innovation, Universities and Skills and for Business, Enterprise and Regulatory Reform Order 2007, SI 2007/3224, art 15, Schedule, Pt 2, para 26, as from 12 December 2007; para 20 added by the Redundancy Payments (Continuity of Employment in Local Government, etc) (Modification) (Amendment) Order 2001, SI 2001/866, art 2(1), (7).

Section 6: words in square brackets in the heading substituted, para 1 numbered as such, and para 2 added, by the London Government (Continuity of Employment) Order 2000, SI 2000/1042, art 4(1), (5).

Section 9: para 4A inserted by the Redundancy Payments (Continuity of Employment in Local Government, etc) (Modification) (Amendment) Order 2004, SI 2004/1682, art 2(1), (7), as from 1 August 2004.

(*Sch 3 (revocations) outside the scope of this work.*)

MANAGEMENT OF HEALTH AND SAFETY AT WORK REGULATIONS 1999

(SI 1999/3242)

NOTES

Made: 3 December 1999.

Authority: European Communities Act 1972, s 2(2), Health and Safety at Work etc Act 1974, ss 15(1), (2), (3)(a), (5), (9), 47(2), 52(2), (3), 80(1), 82(3)(a), Sch 3, paras 6(1), 7, 8(1), 10, 14, 15, 16.

Commencement: 29 December 1999.

These Regulations revoke and replace the Management of Health and Safety at Work Regulations 1992, SI 1992/2051, and are the continuing domestic implementation of Council Directive 89/391 at **[3773]** and, in part, Council Directive 92/85 at **[3817]**.

See also the Code of Practice "Management of Health and Safety at Work" (not printed in this work) issued in conjunction with the 1992 Regulations by the Health and Safety Commission under the Health and Safety at Work, etc Act 1974, s 16. As to the abolition of the Health and Safety Commission, see the note 'The Health and Safety Executive' at **[2038]**.

ARRANGEMENT OF REGULATIONS

SCHEDULES:

1 Citation, commencement and interpretation

(1) These Regulations may be cited as the Management of Health and Safety at Work Regulations 1999 and shall come into force on 29th December 1999.

(2) In these Regulations—

"the 1996 Act" means the Employment Rights Act 1996;

"the assessment" means, in the case of an employer or self-employed person, the assessment made or changed by him in accordance with regulation 3;

"child"—

(a) as respects England and Wales, means a person who is not over compulsory school age, construed in accordance with section 8 of the Education Act 1996; and

(b) as respects Scotland, means a person who is not over school age, construed in accordance with section 31 of the Education (Scotland) Act 1980;

"employment business" means a business (whether or not carried on with a view to profit and whether or not carried on in conjunction with any other business) which supplies persons (other than seafarers) who are employed in it to work for and under the control of other persons in any capacity:

"fixed-term contract of employment" means a contract of employment for a specific term which is fixed in advance or which can be ascertained in advance by reference to some relevant circumstance;

"given birth" means delivered a living child or, after twenty-four weeks of pregnancy, a stillborn child;

"new or expectant mother" means an employee who is pregnant; who has given birth within the previous six months; or who is breastfeeding;

"the preventive and protective measures" means the measures which have been identified by the employer or by the self-employed person in consequence of the assessment as the measures he needs to take to comply with the requirements and prohibitions imposed upon him by or under the relevant statutory provisions …;

"young person" means any person who has not attained the age of eighteen.

(3) Any reference in these Regulations to—

(a) a numbered regulation or Schedule is a reference to the regulation or Schedule in these Regulations so numbered; or

(b) a numbered paragraph is a reference to the paragraph so numbered in the regulation in which the reference appears.

[2526]

NOTES

Para (2): words omitted from the definition "the preventive and protective measures" revoked by the Regulatory Reform (Fire Safety) Order 2005, SI 2005/1541, art 53(2), Sch 5, as from 1 October 2006 (in relation to England and Wales), and by the Fire (Scotland) Act 2005 (Consequential Modifications and Savings) (No 2) Order 2006, SSI 2006/457, art 2(2), Sch 2, as from 1 October 2006 (in relation to Scotland).

Note: the date of the commencement of the amendment made by SI 2005/1541 above was changed from 1 April 2006 to 1 October 2006 by the Regulatory Reform (Fire Safety) Subordinate Provisions Order 2006, SI 2006/484, art 2.

[2 Disapplication of these Regulations

(1) These Regulations shall not apply to or in relation to the master or crew of a ship, or to the employer of such persons, in respect of the normal ship-board activities of a ship's crew which are carried out solely by the crew under the direction of the master.

(2) Regulations 3(4), (5), 10(2) and 19 shall not apply to occasional work or short-term work involving work regarded as not being harmful, damaging or dangerous to young people in a family undertaking.

(3) In this regulation—

"normal ship-board activities" include—

(a) the construction, reconstruction or conversion of a ship outside, but not inside, Great Britain; and

(b) the repair of a ship save repair when carried out in dry dock;

"ship" includes every description of vessel used in navigation, other than a ship belonging to Her Majesty which forms part of Her Majesty's Navy.]

[2527]

NOTES

Commencement: 27 October 2003.

Substituted by the Management of Health and Safety at Work and Fire Precautions (Workplace) (Amendment) Regulations 2003, SI 2003/2457, regs 2, 3, as from 27 October 2003.

3 Risk assessment

(1) Every employer shall make a suitable and sufficient assessment of—

(a) the risks to the health and safety of his employees to which they are exposed whilst they are at work; and

(b) the risks to the health and safety of persons not in his employment arising out of or in connection with the conduct by him of his undertaking,

for the purpose of identifying the measures he needs to take to comply with the requirements and prohibitions imposed upon him by or under the relevant statutory provisions …

(2) Every self-employed person shall make a suitable and sufficient assessment of—

(a) the risks to his own health and safety to which he is exposed whilst he is at work; and

(b) the risks to the health and safety of persons not in his employment arising out of or in connection with the conduct by him of his undertaking, for the purpose of identifying the measures he needs to take to comply with the requirements and prohibitions imposed upon him by or under the relevant statutory provisions.

(3) Any assessment such as is referred to in paragraph (1) or (2) shall be reviewed by the employer or self-employed person who made it if—

(a) there is reason to suspect that it is no longer valid; or

(b) there has been a significant change in the matters to which it relates;

and where as a result of any such review changes to an assessment are required, the employer or self-employed person concerned shall make them.

(4) An employer shall not employ a young person unless he has, in relation to risks to the health and safety of young persons, made or reviewed an assessment in accordance with paragraphs (1) and (5).

(5) In making or reviewing the assessment, an employer who employs or is to employ a young person shall take particular account of—

(a) the inexperience, lack of awareness of risks and immaturity of young persons;

(b) the fitting-out and layout of the workplace and the workstation;

(c) the nature, degree and duration of exposure to physical, biological and chemical agents;

(d) the form, range, and use of work equipment and the way in which it is handled;

(e) the organisation of processes and activities;

(f) the extent of the health and safety training provided or to be provided to young persons; and

(g) risks from agents, processes and work listed in the Annex to Council Directive 94/33/EC on the protection of young people at work.

(6) Where the employer employs five or more employees, he shall record—

(a) the significant findings of the assessment; and

(b) any group of his employees identified by it as being especially at risk.

[2528]

NOTES

Para (1): words omitted revoked by the Regulatory Reform (Fire Safety) Order 2005, SI 2005/1541, art 53(2), Sch 5, as from 1 October 2006 (in relation to England and Wales), and by the Fire (Scotland) Act 2005 (Consequential Modifications and Savings) (No 2) Order 2006, SSI 2006/457, art 2(2), Sch 2, as from 1 October 2006 (in relation to Scotland).

Note: the date of the commencement of the amendment made by SI 2005/1541 above was changed from 1 April 2006 to 1 October 2006 by the Regulatory Reform (Fire Safety) Subordinate Provisions Order 2006, SI 2006/484, art 2.

As to the layout of this regulation, see the Management of Health and Safety at Work and Fire Precautions (Workplace) (Amendment) Regulations 2003, SI 2003/2457, reg 4 which provides as follows—

"In regulation 3(3) the words "and where" to the end shall follow and not appear in sub-paragraph (b).".

4 Principles of prevention to be applied

Where an employer implements any preventive and protective measures he shall do so on the basis of the principles specified in Schedule 1 to these Regulations.

[2529]

5 Health and safety arrangements

(1) Every employer shall make and give effect to such arrangements as are appropriate, having regard to the nature of his activities and the size of his undertaking, for the effective planning, organisation, control, monitoring and review of the preventive and protective measures.

(2) Where the employer employs five or more employees, he shall record the arrangements referred to in paragraph (1).

[2530]

6 Health surveillance

Every employer shall ensure that his employees are provided with such health surveillance as is appropriate having regard to the risks to their health and safety which are identified by the assessment.

[2531]

7 Health and safety assistance

(1) Every employer shall, subject to paragraphs (6) and (7), appoint one or more competent persons to assist him in undertaking the measures he needs to take to comply with the requirements and prohibitions imposed upon him by or under the relevant statutory provisions …

(2) Where an employer appoints persons in accordance with paragraph (1), he shall make arrangements for ensuring adequate co-operation between them.

(3) The employer shall ensure that the number of persons appointed under paragraph (1), the time available for them to fulfil their functions and the means at their disposal are adequate having regard to the size of his undertaking, the risks to which his employees are exposed and the distribution of those risks throughout the undertaking.

(4) The employer shall ensure that—

(a) any person appointed by him in accordance with paragraph (1) who is not in his employment—

(i) is informed of the factors known by him to affect, or suspected by him of affecting, the health and safety of any other person who may be affected by the conduct of his undertaking, and

(ii) has access to the information referred to in regulation 10; and

(b) any person appointed by him in accordance with paragraph (1) is given such information about any person working in his undertaking who is—

(i) employed by him under a fixed-term contract of employment, or

(ii) employed in an employment business,

as is necessary to enable that person properly to carry out the function specified in that paragraph.

(5) A person shall be regarded as competent for the purposes of paragraphs (1) and (8) where he has sufficient training and experience or knowledge and other qualities to enable him properly to assist in undertaking the measures referred to in paragraph (1).

(6) Paragraph (1) shall not apply to a self-employed employer who is not in partnership with any other person where he has sufficient training and experience or knowledge and other qualities properly to undertake the measures referred to in that paragraph himself.

(7) Paragraph (1) shall not apply to individuals who are employers and who are together carrying on business in partnership where at least one of the individuals concerned has sufficient training and experience or knowledge and other qualities—

(a) properly to undertake the measures he needs to take to comply with the requirements and prohibitions imposed upon him by or under the relevant statutory provisions; and

(b) properly to assist his fellow partners in undertaking the measures they need to take to comply with the requirements and prohibitions imposed upon them by or under the relevant statutory provisions.

(8) Where there is a competent person in the employer's employment, that person shall be appointed for the purposes of paragraph (1) in preference to a competent person not in his employment.

[2532]

NOTES

Para (1): words omitted revoked by the Regulatory Reform (Fire Safety) Order 2005, SI 2005/1541, art 53(2), Sch 5, as from 1 October 2006 (in relation to England and Wales), and by the Fire (Scotland) Act 2005 (Consequential Modifications and Savings) (No 2) Order 2006, SSI 2006/457, art 2(2), Sch 2, as from 1 October 2006 (in relation to Scotland).

Note: the date of the commencement of the amendment made by SI 2005/1541 above was changed from 1 April 2006 to 1 October 2006 by the Regulatory Reform (Fire Safety) Subordinate Provisions Order 2006, SI 2006/484, art 2.

8 Procedures for serious and imminent danger and for danger areas

(1) Every employer shall—

(a) establish and where necessary give effect to appropriate procedures to be followed in the event of serious and imminent danger to persons at work in his undertaking;

(b) nominate a sufficient number of competent persons to implement those procedures in so far as they relate to the evacuation from premises of persons at work in his undertaking; and

(c) ensure that none of his employees has access to any area occupied by him to which it is necessary to restrict access on grounds of health and safety unless the employee concerned has received adequate health and safety instruction.

(2) Without prejudice to the generality of paragraph (1)(a), the procedures referred to in that sub-paragraph shall—

(a) so far as is practicable, require any persons at work who are exposed to serious and imminent danger to be informed of the nature of the hazard and of the steps taken or to be taken to protect them from it;

(b) enable the persons concerned (if necessary by taking appropriate steps in the absence of guidance or instruction and in the light of their knowledge and the technical means at their disposal) to stop work and immediately proceed to a place of safety in the event of their being exposed to serious, imminent and unavoidable danger; and

(c) save in exceptional cases for reasons duly substantiated (which cases and reasons shall be specified in those procedures), require the persons concerned to be prevented from resuming work in any situation where there is still a serious and imminent danger.

(3) A person shall be regarded as competent for the purposes of paragraph (1)(b) where he has sufficient training and experience or knowledge and other qualities to enable him properly to implement the evacuation procedures referred to in that sub-paragraph.

[2533]

9 Contacts with external services

Every employer shall ensure that any necessary contacts with external services are arranged, particularly as regards first-aid, emergency medical care and rescue work.

[2534]

10 Information for employees

(1) Every employer shall provide his employees with comprehensible and relevant information on—

(a) the risks to their health and safety identified by the assessment;

(b) the preventive and protective measures;

(c) the procedures referred to in regulation 8(1)(a) …;

(d) the identity of those persons nominated by him in accordance with regulation 8(1)(b) …; and

(e) the risks notified to him in accordance with regulation 11(1)(c).

(2) Every employer shall, before employing a child, provide a parent of the child with comprehensible and relevant information on—

(a) the risks to his health and safety identified by the assessment;

(b) the preventive and protective measures; and

(c) the risks notified to him in accordance with regulation 11(1)(c).

(3) The reference in paragraph (2) to a parent of the child includes—

(a) in England and Wales, a person who has parental responsibility, within the meaning of section 3 of the Children Act 1989, for him; and

(b) in Scotland, a person who has parental rights, within the meaning of section 8 of the Law Reform (Parent and Child) (Scotland) Act 1986 for him.

[2535]

NOTES

Para (1): words omitted from sub-paras (c), (d) revoked by the Regulatory Reform (Fire Safety) Order 2005, SI 2005/1541, art 53(2), Sch 5, as from 1 October 2006 (in relation to England and Wales), and by the Fire (Scotland) Act 2005 (Consequential Modifications and Savings) (No 2) Order 2006, SSI 2006/457, art 2(2), Sch 2, as from 1 October 2006 (in relation to Scotland).

Note: the date of the commencement of the amendment made by SI 2005/1541 above was changed from 1 April 2006 to 1 October 2006 by the Regulatory Reform (Fire Safety) Subordinate Provisions Order 2006, SI 2006/484, art 2.

11 Co-operation and co-ordination

(1) Where two or more employers share a workplace (whether on a temporary or a permanent basis) each such employer shall—

(a) co-operate with the other employers concerned so far as is necessary to enable them to comply with the requirements and prohibitions imposed upon them by or under the relevant statutory provisions … ;

(b) (taking into account the nature of his activities) take all reasonable steps to co-ordinate the measures he takes to comply with the requirements and prohibitions imposed upon him by or under the relevant statutory provisions … with the measures the other employers concerned are taking to comply with the requirements and prohibitions imposed upon them by that legislation; and

(c) take all reasonable steps to inform the other employers concerned of the risks to their employees' health and safety arising out of or in connection with the conduct by him of his undertaking.

(2) Paragraph (1) … shall apply to employers sharing a workplace with self-employed persons and to self-employed persons sharing a workplace with other self-employed persons as it applies to employers sharing a workplace with other employers; and the references in that paragraph to employers and the reference in the said paragraph to their employees shall be construed accordingly.

[2536]

NOTES

Paras (1), (2): words omitted revoked by the Regulatory Reform (Fire Safety) Order 2005, SI 2005/1541, art 53(2), Sch 5, as from 1 October 2006 (in relation to England and Wales), and by the Fire (Scotland) Act 2005 (Consequential Modifications and Savings) (No 2) Order 2006, SSI 2006/457, art 2(2), Sch 2, as from 1 October 2006 (in relation to Scotland).

Note: the date of the commencement of the amendment made by SI 2005/1541 above was changed from 1 April 2006 to 1 October 2006 by the Regulatory Reform (Fire Safety) Subordinate Provisions Order 2006, SI 2006/484, art 2.

12 Persons working in host employers' or self-employed persons' undertakings

(1) Every employer and every self-employed person shall ensure that the employer of any employees from an outside undertaking who are working in his undertaking is provided with comprehensible information on—

(a) the risks to those employees' health and safety arising out of or in connection with the conduct by that first-mentioned employer or by that self-employed person of his undertaking; and

(b) the measures taken by that first-mentioned employer or by that self-employed person in compliance with the requirements and prohibitions imposed upon him by or under the relevant statutory provisions … in so far as the said requirements and prohibitions relate to those employees.

(2) Paragraph (1) … shall apply to a self-employed person who is working in the undertaking of an employer or a self-employed person as it applies to employees from an outside undertaking who are working therein; and the reference in that paragraph to the employer of any employees from an outside undertaking who are working in the undertaking of an employer or a self-employed person and the references in the said paragraph to employees from an outside undertaking who are working in the undertaking of an employer or a self-employed person shall be construed accordingly.

(3) Every employer shall ensure that any person working in his undertaking who is not his employee and every self-employed person (not being an employer) shall ensure that any person working in his undertaking is provided with appropriate instructions and comprehensible information regarding any risks to that person's health and safety which arise out of the conduct by that employer or self-employed person of his undertaking.

(4) Every employer shall—

(a) ensure that the employer of any employees from an outside undertaking who are working in his undertaking is provided with sufficient information to enable that second-mentioned employer to identify any person nominated by that first mentioned employer in accordance with regulation 8(1)(b) to implement evacuation procedures as far as those employees are concerned; and

(b) take all reasonable steps to ensure that any employees from an outside undertaking who are working in his undertaking receive sufficient information to enable them to identify any person nominated by him in accordance with regulation 8(1)(b) to implement evacuation procedures as far as they are concerned.

(5) Paragraph (4) shall apply to a self-employed person who is working in an employer's undertaking as it applies to employees from an outside undertaking who are working therein; and the reference in that paragraph to the employer of any employees from an outside undertaking who are working in an employer's undertaking and the references in the said paragraph to employees from an outside undertaking who are working in an employer's undertaking shall be construed accordingly.

[2537]

NOTES

Paras (1), (2): words omitted revoked by the Regulatory Reform (Fire Safety) Order 2005, SI 2005/1541, art 53(2), Sch 5, as from 1 October 2006 (in relation to England and Wales), and by the Fire (Scotland) Act 2005 (Consequential Modifications and Savings) (No 2) Order 2006, SSI 2006/457, art 2(2), Sch 2, as from 1 October 2006 (in relation to Scotland).

Note: the date of the commencement of the amendment made by SI 2005/1541 above was changed from 1 April 2006 to 1 October 2006 by the Regulatory Reform (Fire Safety) Subordinate Provisions Order 2006, SI 2006/484, art 2.

13 Capabilities and training

(1) Every employer shall, in entrusting tasks to his employees, take into account their capabilities as regards health and safety.

(2) Every employer shall ensure that his employees are provided with adequate health and safety training—

(a) on their being recruited into the employer's undertaking; and

(b) on their being exposed to new or increased risks because of—

(i) their being transferred or given a change of responsibilities within the employer's undertaking,

(ii) the introduction of new work equipment into or a change respecting work equipment already in use within the employer's undertaking,

(iii) the introduction of new technology into the employer's undertaking, or

(iv) the introduction of a new system of work into or a change respecting a system of work already in use within the employer's undertaking.

(3) The training referred to in paragraph (2) shall—

(a) be repeated periodically where appropriate;

(b) be adapted to take account of any new or changed risks to the health and safety of the employees concerned; and

(c) take place during working hours.

[2538]

14 Employees' duties

(1) Every employee shall use any machinery, equipment, dangerous substance, transport equipment, means of production or safety device provided to him by his employer in accordance both with any training in the use of the equipment concerned which has been received by him and the instructions respecting that use which have been provided to him by the said employer in compliance with the requirements and prohibitions imposed upon that employer by or under the relevant statutory provisions.

(2) Every employee shall inform his employer or any other employee of that employer with specific responsibility for the health and safety of his fellow employees—

(a) of any work situation which a person with the first-mentioned employee's training and instruction would reasonably consider represented a serious and immediate danger to health and safety; and

(b) of any matter which a person with the first-mentioned employee's training and instruction would reasonably consider represented a shortcoming in the employer's protection arrangements for health and safety,

in so far as that situation or matter either affects the health and safety of that first mentioned employee or arises out of or in connection with his own activities at work, and has not previously been reported to his employer or to any other employee of that employer in accordance with this paragraph.

[2539]

15 Temporary workers

(1) Every employer shall provide any person whom he has employed under a fixed-term contract of employment with comprehensible information on—

(a) any special occupational qualifications or skills required to be held by that employee if he is to carry out his work safely; and

(b) any health surveillance required to be provided to that employee by or under any of the relevant statutory provisions,

and shall provide the said information before the employee concerned commences his duties.

(2) Every employer and every self-employed person shall provide any person employed in an employment business who is to carry out work in his undertaking with comprehensible information on—

(a) any special occupational qualifications or skills required to be held by that employee if he is to carry out his work safely; and

(b) health surveillance required to be provided to that employee by or under any of the relevant statutory provisions.

(3) Every employer and every self-employed person shall ensure that every person carrying on an employment business whose employees are to carry out work in his undertaking is provided with comprehensible information on—

(a) any special occupational qualifications or skills required to be held by those employees if they are to carry out their work safely; and

(b) the specific features of the jobs to be filled by those employees (in so far as those features are likely to affect their health and safety);

and the person carrying on the employment business concerned shall ensure that the information so provided is given to the said employees.

[2540]

16 Risk assessment in respect of new or expectant mothers

(1) Where—

(a) the persons working in an undertaking include women of child-bearing age; and

(b) the work is of a kind which could involve risk, by reason of her condition, to the health and safety of a new or expectant mother, or to that of her baby, from any processes or working conditions, or physical, biological or chemical agents, including those specified in Annexes I and II of Council Directive 92/85/EEC on the introduction of measures to encourage improvements in the safety and health at work of pregnant workers and workers who have recently given birth or are breastfeeding,

the assessment required by regulation 3(1) shall also include an assessment of such risk.

(2) Where, in the case of an individual employee, the taking of any other action the employer is required to take under the relevant statutory provisions would not avoid the risk referred to in paragraph (1) the employer shall, if it is reasonable to do so, and would avoid such risks, alter her working conditions or hours of work.

(3) If it is not reasonable to alter the working conditions or hours of work, or if it would not avoid such risk, the employer shall, subject to section 67 of the 1996 Act suspend the employee from work for so long as is necessary to avoid such risk.

(4) In paragraphs (1) to (3) references to risk, in relation to risk from any infectious or contagious disease, are references to a level of risk at work which is in addition to the level to which a new or expectant mother may be expected to be exposed outside the workplace.

[2541]

17 Certificate from registered medical practitioner in respect of new or expectant mothers

Where—

(a) a new or expectant mother works at night; and

(b) a certificate from a registered medical practitioner or a registered midwife shows that it is necessary for her health or safety that she should not be at work for any period of such work identified in the certificate,

the employer shall, subject to section 67 of the 1996 Act, suspend her from work for so long as is necessary for her health or safety.

[2542]

18 Notification by new or expectant mothers

(1) Nothing in paragraph (2) or (3) of regulation 16 shall require the employer to take any action in relation to an employee until she has notified the employer in writing that she is pregnant, has given birth within the previous six months, or is breastfeeding.

(2) Nothing in paragraph (2) or (3) of regulation 16 or in regulation 17 shall require the employer to maintain action taken in relation to an employee—

(a) in a case—

(i) to which regulation 16(2) or (3) relates; and

(ii) where the employee has notified her employer that she is pregnant, where she has failed, within a reasonable time of being requested to do so in writing by her employer, to produce for the employer's inspection a certificate from a registered medical practitioner or a registered midwife showing that she is pregnant;

(b) once the employer knows that she is no longer a new or expectant mother; or

(c) if the employer cannot establish whether she remains a new or expectant mother.

[2543]

19 Protection of young persons

(1) Every employer shall ensure that young persons employed by him are protected at work from any risks to their health or safety which are a consequence of their lack of experience, or absence of awareness of existing or potential risks or the fact that young persons have not yet fully matured.

(2) Subject to paragraph (3), no employer shall employ a young person for work—

(a) which is beyond his physical or psychological capacity;

(b) involving harmful exposure to agents which are toxic or carcinogenic, cause heritable genetic damage or harm to the unborn child or which in any other way chronically affect human health;

(c) involving harmful exposure to radiation;

(d) involving the risk of accidents which it may reasonably be assumed cannot be recognised or avoided by young persons owing to their insufficient attention to safety or lack of experience or training; or

(e) in which there is a risk to health from—

(i) extreme cold or heat;

(ii) noise; or

(iii) vibration,

and in determining whether work will involve harm or risks for the purposes of this paragraph, regard shall be had to the results of the assessment.

(3) Nothing in paragraph (2) shall prevent the employment of a young person who is no longer a child for work—

(a) where it is necessary for his training;

(b) where the young person will be supervised by a competent person; and

(c) where any risk will be reduced to the lowest level that is reasonably practicable.

(4) …

[2544]

NOTES

Para (4): revoked by the Management of Health and Safety at Work and Fire Precautions (Workplace) (Amendment) Regulations 2003, SI 2003/2457, regs 2, 5, as from 27 October 2003.

20 Exemption certificates

(1) The Secretary of State for Defence may, in the interests of national security, by a certificate in writing exempt—

(a) any of the home forces, any visiting force or any headquarters from those requirements of these Regulations which impose obligations other than those in regulations 16–18 on employers; or

(b) any member of the home forces, any member of a visiting force or any member of a headquarters from the requirements imposed by regulation 14;

and any exemption such as is specified in sub-paragraph (a) or (b) of this paragraph may be granted subject to conditions and to a limit of time and may be revoked by the said Secretary of State by a further certificate in writing at any time.

(2) In this regulation—

(a) "the home forces" has the same meaning as in section 12(1) of the Visiting Forces Act 1952;

(b) "headquarters" means a headquarters for the time being specified in Schedule 2 to the Visiting Forces and International Headquarters (Application of Law) Order 1999;

(c) "member of a headquarters" has the same meaning as in paragraph 1(1) of the Schedule to the International Headquarters and Defence Organisations Act 1964; and

(d) "visiting force" has the same meaning as it does for the purposes of any provision of Part I of the Visiting Forces Act 1952.

[2545]

21 Provisions as to liability

Nothing in the relevant statutory provisions shall operate so as to afford an employer a defence in any criminal proceedings for a contravention of those provisions by reason of any act or default of—

(a) an employee of his, or

(b) a person appointed by him under regulation 7.

[2546]

[22 Restriction of civil liability for breach of statutory duty

(1) Breach of a duty imposed on an employer by these Regulations shall not confer a right of action in any civil proceedings insofar as that duty applies for the protection of a third party.

(2) Breach of a duty imposed on an employee by regulation 14 shall not confer a right of action in any civil proceedings insofar as that duty applies for the protection of a third party.

(3) In this regulation, "third party", in relation to the undertaking, means any person who may be affected by that undertaking other than the employer whose undertaking it is and persons in his employment.]

[2547]

NOTES

Commencement: 6 April 2006.

Substituted by the Management of Health and Safety at Work (Amendment) Regulations 2006, SI 2006/438, reg 2, as from 6 April 2006.

23 Extension outside Great Britain

(1) These Regulations shall, subject to regulation 2, apply to and in relation to the premises and activities outside Great Britain to which sections 1 to 59 and 80 to 82 of the Health and Safety at Work etc Act 1974 apply by virtue of the Health and Safety at Work etc Act 1974 (Application Outside Great Britain) Order 1995 as they apply within Great Britain.

(2) For the purposes of Part I of the 1974 Act, the meaning of "at work" shall be extended so that an employee or a self-employed person shall be treated as being at work throughout the time that he is present at the premises to and in relation to which these Regulations apply by virtue of paragraph (1); and, in that connection, these Regulations shall have effect subject to the extension effected by this paragraph.

[2548]–[2549]

NOTES

The Health and Safety at Work etc Act 1974 (Application outside Great Britain) Order 1995, SI 1995/263 was revoked and replaced by the Health and Safety at Work etc Act 1974 (Application outside Great Britain) Order 2001, SI 2001/2127.

24–28 *(Reg 24 revokes the Health and Safety (First-Aid) Regulations 1981, SI 1981/917, reg 6; reg 25 amends the Offshore Installations and Pipeline Works (First-Aid) Regulations 1989, SI 1989/1671, reg 7; reg 26 amends the Mines Miscellaneous Health and Safety Provisions Regulations 1995, SI 1995/2005, reg 4; reg 27 revoked by the Construction (Design and Management) Regulations 2007, SI 2007/320, reg 48(1), Sch 4, as from 6 April 2007; reg 28 revoked by the Regulatory Reform (Fire Safety) Order 2005, SI 2005/1541, art 53(2), Sch 5, as from 1 October 2006 (in relation to England and Wales), and by the Fire (Scotland) Act 2005 (Consequential Modifications and Savings) (No 2) Order 2006, SSI 2006/457, art 2(2), Sch 2, as from 1 October 2006 (in relation to Scotland). Note that the* *date of the commencement of the amendment made by SI 2005/1541 above was changed from 1 April 2006 to 1 October 2006 by the Regulatory Reform (Fire Safety) Subordinate Provisions Order 2006, SI 2006/484, art 2.*)

29 Revocations and consequential amendments

(1) The Management of Health and Safety at Work Regulations 1992, the Management of Health and Safety at Work (Amendment) Regulations 1994, the Health and Safety (Young Persons) Regulations 1997 and Part III of the Fire Precautions (Workplace) Regulations 1997 are hereby revoked.

(2) The instruments specified in column 1 of Schedule 2 shall be amended in accordance with the corresponding provisions in column 3 of that Schedule.

[2550]

30 Transitional provision

The substitution of provisions in these Regulations for provisions of the Management of Health and Safety at Work Regulations 1992 shall not affect the continuity of the law; and accordingly anything done under or for the purposes of such provision of the 1992 Regulations shall have effect as if done under or for the purposes of any corresponding provision of these Regulations.

[2551]

SCHEDULES

SCHEDULE 1
GENERAL PRINCIPLES OF PREVENTION

Regulation 4

(This Schedule specifies the general principles of prevention set out in Article 6(2) of Council Directive 89/391/EEC)

(a) avoiding risks;
(b) evaluating the risks which cannot be avoided;
(c) combating the risks at source;
(d) adapting the work to the individual, especially as regards the design of workplaces, the choice of work equipment and the choice of working and production methods, with a view, in particular, to alleviating monotonous work and work at a predetermined work-rate and to reducing their effect on health;
(e) adapting to technical progress;
(f) replacing the dangerous by the non-dangerous or the less dangerous;
(g) developing a coherent overall prevention policy which covers technology, organisation of work, working conditions, social relationships and the influence of factors relating to the working environment;
(h) giving collective protective measures priority over individual protective measures; and
(i) giving appropriate instructions to employees.

[2552]

(*Sch 2* (*consequential amendments*) *in so far as these are within the scope of this work, they have been incorporated at the appropriate place.*)

MATERNITY AND PARENTAL LEAVE ETC REGULATIONS 1999

(SI 1999/3312)

NOTES

Made: 10 December 1999.

Authority: Employment Rights Act 1996, ss 47C(2), (3), 71(1)–(3), (6), 72(1), (2), 73(1), (2), (4), (7), 74(1), (3), (4), 75(1), 76(1), (2), (5), 77(1), (4), 78(1), (2), (7), 79(1), (2), 99(1).

Commencement: 15 December 1999. For transitional provisions affecting Pt II, Pt III, and regs 19 and 20, see reg 3 (further transitional provisions in reg 13(3) have subsequently been revoked by SI 2001/4010, as noted to that regulation).

These Regulations, so far as relating to parental leave, are the domestic implementation of EC Directive 96/34 at **[3905]**, as extended to the UK by Directive 97/75 at **[3919]**.
See *Harvey* DII, J18, Q, R.

ARRANGEMENT OF REGULATIONS

PART I
GENERAL

PART II
MATERNITY LEAVE

PART III
PARENTAL LEAVE

PART IV
PROVISIONS APPLICABLE IN RELATION TO MORE THAN ONE KIND OF ABSENCE

SCHEDULES:

PART I
GENERAL

1 Citation and commencement

These Regulations may be cited as the Maternity and Parental Leave etc Regulations 1999 and shall come into force on 15th December 1999.

[2553]

2 Interpretation

(1) In these Regulations—

"the 1996 Act" means the Employment Rights Act 1996;

["additional adoption leave" means leave under section 75B of the 1996 Act;]

"additional maternity leave" means leave under section 73 of the 1996 Act;

"business" includes a trade or profession and includes any activity carried on by a body of persons (whether corporate or unincorporated);

"child" means a person under the age of eighteen;

"childbirth" means the birth of a living child or the birth of a child whether living or dead after 24 weeks of pregnancy;

"collective agreement" means a collective agreement within the meaning of section 178 of the Trade Union and Labour Relations (Consolidation) Act 1992, the trade union parties to which are independent trade unions within the meaning of section 5 of that Act;

"contract of employment" means a contract of service or apprenticeship, whether express or implied, and (if it is express) whether oral or in writing;

"disability living allowance" means the disability living allowance provided for in Part III of the Social Security Contributions and Benefits Act 1992;

"employee" means an individual who has entered into or works under (or, where the employment has ceased, worked under) a contract of employment;

"employer" means the person by whom an employee is (or, where the employment has ceased, was) employed;

"expected week of childbirth" means the week, beginning with midnight between Saturday and Sunday, in which it is expected that childbirth will occur, and "week of childbirth" means the week, beginning with midnight between Saturday and Sunday, in which childbirth occurs;

"job", in relation to an employee returning after … maternity leave or parental leave, means the nature of the work which she is employed to do in accordance with her contract and the capacity and place in which she is so employed;

"ordinary maternity leave" means leave under section 71 of the 1996 Act;

"parental leave" means leave under regulation 13(1);

"parental responsibility" has the meaning given by section 3 of the Children Act 1989, and "parental responsibilities" has the meaning given by section 1(3) of the Children (Scotland) Act 1995;

["statutory leave" means leave provided for in Part 8 of the 1996 Act;]

["statutory maternity leave" means ordinary maternity leave and additional maternity leave;

"statutory maternity leave period" means the period during which the employee is on statutory maternity leave;]

"workforce agreement" means an agreement between an employer and his employees or their representatives in respect of which the conditions set out in Schedule 1 to these Regulations are satisfied.

(2) A reference in any provision of these Regulations to a period of continuous employment is to a period computed in accordance with Chapter I of Part XIV of the 1996 Act, as if that provision were a provision of that Act.

(3) For the purposes of these Regulations any two employers shall be treated as associated if—

(a) one is a company of which the other (directly or indirectly) has control; or

(b) both are companies of which a third person (directly or indirectly) has control;

and "associated employer" shall be construed accordingly.

(4) In these Regulations, unless the context otherwise requires,—

(a) a reference to a numbered regulation or schedule is to the regulation or schedule in these Regulations bearing that number;

(b) a reference in a regulation or schedule to a numbered paragraph is to the paragraph in that regulation or schedule bearing that number, and

(c) a reference in a paragraph to a lettered sub-paragraph is to the sub-paragraph in that paragraph bearing that letter.

[2554]

NOTES

Para (1): definitions "additional adoption leave" and "statutory leave" inserted, and word omitted from definition "job" revoked, by the Maternity and Parental Leave (Amendment) Regulations 2002,

SI 2002/2789, regs 3, 4; definitions "statutory maternity leave" and "statutory maternity leave period" inserted by the Maternity and Parental Leave etc and the Paternity and Adoption Leave (Amendment) Regulations 2006, SI 2006/2014, regs 3, 4, as from 1 October 2006 (with effect only in relation to employees whose expected week of childbirth begins on or after 1 April 2007: see SI 2006/2014, reg 2(1) at **[3463A]**).

3 Application

(1) The provisions of Part II of these Regulations have effect only in relation to employees whose expected week of childbirth begins on or after 30th April 2000.

(2) Regulation 19 (protection from detriment) has effect only in relation to an act or failure to act which takes place on or after 15th December 1999.

(3) For the purposes of paragraph (2)—

(a) where an act extends over a period, the reference to the date of the act is a reference to the last day of that period, and

(b) a failure to act is to be treated as done when it was decided on.

(4) For the purposes of paragraph (3), in the absence of evidence establishing the contrary an employer shall be taken to decide on a failure to act—

(a) when he does an act inconsistent with doing the failed act, or

(b) if he has done no such inconsistent act, when the period expires within which he might reasonably have been expected to do the failed act if it was to be done.

(5) Regulation 20 (unfair dismissal) has effect only in relation to dismissals where the effective date of termination (within the meaning of section 97 of the 1996 Act) falls on or after 15th December 1999.

[2555]

PART II
MATERNITY LEAVE

4 Entitlement to ordinary maternity leave [and to additional maternity leave]

(1) An employee is entitled to ordinary maternity leave [and to additional maternity leave] provided that she satisfies the following conditions—

(a) [no later than the end of the fifteenth week before her expected week of childbirth], or, if that is not reasonably practicable, as soon as is reasonably practicable, she notifies her employer of—

(i) her pregnancy;

(ii) the expected week of childbirth, and

(iii) the date on which she intends her ordinary maternity leave period to start,

and

(b) if requested to do so by her employer, she produces for his inspection a certificate from—

(i) a registered medical practitioner, or

(ii) a registered midwife,

stating the expected week of childbirth.

[(1A) An employee who has notified her employer under paragraph (1)(a)(iii) of the date on which she intends her ordinary maternity leave period to start may subsequently vary that date, provided that she notifies her employer of the variation at least—

(a) 28 days before the date varied, or

(b) 28 days before the new date,

whichever is the earlier, or, if that is not reasonably practicable, as soon as is reasonably practicable.]

(2) [Notification under paragraph (1)(a)(iii) or (1A)]—

(a) shall be given in writing, if the employer so requests, and

(b) shall not specify a date earlier than the beginning of the eleventh week before the expected week of childbirth.

(3) Where, by virtue of regulation 6(1)(b), an employee's ordinary maternity leave period commences with [the day which follows] the first day after the beginning of [the fourth week] before the expected week of childbirth on which she is absent from work wholly or partly because of pregnancy—

(a) paragraph (1) does not require her to notify her employer of the date specified in that paragraph, but

(b) (whether or not she has notified him of that date) she is not entitled to ordinary maternity leave [or to additional maternity leave] unless she notifies him as soon as is reasonably practicable that she is absent from work wholly or partly because of pregnancy [and of the date on which her absence on that account began].

(4) Where, by virtue of regulation 6(2), an employee's ordinary maternity leave period commences [on the day which follows] the day on which childbirth occurs—

(a) paragraph (1) does not require her to notify her employer of the date specified in that paragraph, but

(b) (whether or not she has notified him of that date) she is not entitled to ordinary maternity leave [or to additional maternity leave] unless she notifies him as soon as is reasonably practicable after the birth that she has given birth [and of the date on which the birth occurred].

(5) The notification provided for in paragraphs (3)(b) and (4)(b) shall be given in writing, if the employer so requests.

[2556]–[2557]

NOTES

Regulation heading: words in square brackets added by the Maternity and Parental Leave etc and the Paternity and Adoption Leave (Amendment) Regulations 2006, SI 2006/2014, regs 3, 5(a), as from 1 October 2006 (with effect only in relation to employees whose expected week of childbirth begins on or after 1 April 2007: see SI 2006/2014, reg 2(1) at **[3463A]**).

Para (1): words in first pair of square brackets inserted by SI 2006/2014, regs 3, 5(a), as from 1 October 2006 (with effect only in relation to employees whose expected week of childbirth begins on or after 1 April 2007: see SI 2006/2014, reg 2(1) at **[3463A]**); words in second pair of square brackets substituted by the Maternity and Parental Leave (Amendment) Regulations 2002, SI 2002/2789, regs 3, 5(a) (with effect in relation to employees whose expected week of childbirth begins on or after 6 April 2003).

Para (1A): inserted by SI 2002/2789, regs 3, 5(b) (with effect in relation to employees whose expected week of childbirth begins on or after 6 April 2003).

Para (2): words in square brackets substituted by SI 2002/2789, regs 3, 5(c) (with effect in relation to employees whose expected week of childbirth begins on or after 6 April 2003).

Para (3): words in first and final pairs of square brackets inserted, and words in second pair of square brackets substituted, by SI 2002/2789, regs 3, 5(d) (with effect in relation to employees whose expected week of childbirth begins on or after 6 April 2003); words in third pair of square brackets inserted by SI 2006/2014, regs 3, 5(b), as from 1 October 2006 (with effect only in relation to employees whose expected week of childbirth begins on or after 1 April 2007: see SI 2006/2014, reg 2(1) at **[3463A]**).

Para (4): words in first pair of square brackets substituted, and words in third pair of square brackets inserted, by SI 2002/2789, regs 3, 5(e) (with effect in relation to employees whose expected week of childbirth begins on or after 6 April 2003); words in second pair of square brackets inserted by SI 2006/2014, regs 3, 5(b), as from 1 October 2006 (with effect only in relation to employees whose expected week of childbirth begins on or after 1 April 2007: see SI 2006/2014, reg 2(1) at **[3463A]**).

5 (*Revoked by the Maternity and Parental Leave etc and the Paternity and Adoption Leave (Amendment) Regulations 2006, SI 2006/2014, regs 3, 6, as from 1 October 2006 (with effect only in relation to employees whose expected week of childbirth begins on or after 1 April 2007: see SI 2006/2014, reg 2(1) at* **[3463A]**).)

6 Commencement of maternity leave periods

(1) Subject to paragraph (2), an employee's ordinary maternity leave period commences with the earlier of—

(a) the date which … she notifies to her employer[, in accordance with regulation 4,] as the date on which she intends her ordinary maternity leave period to start, [or, if by virtue of the provision for variation in that regulation she has notified more than one such date, the last date she notifies,] and

(b) [the day which follows] the first day after the beginning of [the fourth week] before the expected week of childbirth on which she is absent from work wholly or partly because of pregnancy.

(2) Where the employee's ordinary maternity leave period has not commenced by virtue of paragraph (1) when childbirth occurs, her ordinary maternity leave period commences [on the day which follows] the day on which childbirth occurs.

(3) An employee's additional maternity leave period commences on the day after the last day of her ordinary maternity leave period.

[2558]

NOTES

Para (1): words omitted revoked, words in first, second and third pairs of square brackets inserted, and words in fourth pair of square brackets substituted, by the Maternity and Parental Leave (Amendment) Regulations 2002, SI 2002/2789, regs 3, 7(a), (b) (with effect in relation to employees whose expected week of childbirth begins on or after 6 April 2003).

Para (2): words in square brackets substituted by SI 2002/2789, regs 3, 7(c) (with effect in relation to employees whose expected week of childbirth begins on or after 6 April 2003).

7 Duration of maternity leave periods

(1) Subject to paragraphs (2) and (5), an employee's ordinary maternity leave period continues for the period of [26 weeks] from its commencement, or until the end of the compulsory maternity leave period provided for in regulation 8 if later.

(2) Subject to paragraph (5), where any requirement imposed by or under any relevant statutory provision prohibits the employee from working for any period after the end of the period determined under paragraph (1) by reason of her having recently given birth, her ordinary maternity leave period continues until the end of that later period.

(3) In paragraph (2), "relevant statutory provision" means a provision of—

(a) an enactment, or

(b) an instrument under an enactment,

other than a provision for the time being specified in an order under section 66(2) of the 1996 Act.

(4) Subject to paragraph (5), where an employee is entitled to additional maternity leave her additional maternity leave period continues until the end of the period of [26 weeks from the day on which it commenced].

(5) Where the employee is dismissed after the commencement of an ordinary or additional maternity leave period but before the time when (apart from this paragraph) that period would end, the period ends at the time of the dismissal.

[(6) An employer who is notified under any provision of regulation 4 of the date on which, by virtue of any provision of regulation 6, an employee's ordinary maternity leave period will commence or has commenced shall notify the employee of the date on which [her additional maternity leave period shall end]—

(a), (b) …

(7) The notification provided for in paragraph (6) shall be given to the employee—

(a) where the employer is notified under regulation 4(1)(a)(iii), (3)(b) or (4)(b), within 28 days of the date on which he received the notification;

(b) where the employer is notified under regulation 4(1A), within 28 days of the date on which the employee's ordinary maternity leave period commenced.]

[2559]

NOTES

Paras (1), (4): words in square brackets substituted by the Maternity and Parental Leave (Amendment) Regulations 2002, SI 2002/2789, regs 3, 8(a), (b) (with effect in relation to employees whose expected week of childbirth begins on or after 6 April 2003).

Para (6): added, together with para (7), by SI 2002/2789, regs 3, 8(c) (with effect in relation to employees whose expected week of childbirth begins on or after 6 April 2003); words in square brackets inserted, and paras (a), (b) revoked, by the Maternity and Parental Leave etc and the Paternity and Adoption Leave (Amendment) Regulations 2006, SI 2006/2014, regs 3, 7, as from 1 October 2006 (with effect only in relation to employees whose expected week of childbirth begins on or after 1 April 2007: see SI 2006/2014, reg 2(1) at **[3463A]**).

Para (7): added as noted above.

8 Compulsory maternity leave

The prohibition in section 72 of the 1996 Act, against permitting an employee who satisfies prescribed conditions to work during a particular period (referred to as a "compulsory maternity leave period"), applies—

(a) in relation to an employee who is entitled to ordinary maternity leave, and

(b) in respect of the period of two weeks which commences with the day on which childbirth occurs.

[2560]

[9 Application of terms and conditions during ordinary maternity leave

(1) An employee who takes ordinary maternity leave—

(a) is entitled, during the period of leave, to the benefit of all of the terms and conditions of employment which would have applied if she had not been absent, and

(b) is bound, during that period, by any obligations arising under those terms and conditions, subject only to the exception in section 71(4)(b) of the 1996 Act.

(2) In paragraph (1)(a), "terms and conditions" has the meaning given by section 71(5) of the 1996 Act, and accordingly does not include terms and conditions about remuneration.

(3) For the purposes of section 71 of the 1996 Act, only sums payable to an employee by way of wages or salary are to be treated as remuneration.]

[2561]

NOTES

Substituted by the Maternity and Parental Leave (Amendment) Regulations 2002, SI 2002/2789, regs 3, 9 (with effect in relation to employees whose expected week of childbirth begins on or after 6 April 2003).

---

10 Redundancy during maternity leave

(1) This regulation applies where, during an employee's ordinary or additional maternity leave period, it is not practicable by reason of redundancy for her employer to continue to employ her under her existing contract of employment.

(2) Where there is a suitable available vacancy, the employee is entitled to be offered (before the end of her employment under her existing contract) alternative employment with her employer or his successor, or an associated employer, under a new contract of employment which complies with paragraph (3) (and takes effect immediately on the ending of her employment under the previous contract).

(3) The new contract of employment must be such that—

(a) the work to be done under it is of a kind which is both suitable in relation to the employee and appropriate for her to do in the circumstances, and

(b) its provisions as to the capacity and place in which she is to be employed, and as to the other terms and conditions of her employment, are not substantially less favourable to her than if she had continued to be employed under the previous contract.

[2562]

11 Requirement to notify intention to return during a maternity leave period

[(1) An employee who intends to return to work earlier than the end of her additional maternity leave period, shall give to her employer not less than 8 weeks' notice of the date on which she intends to return.]

(2) If an employee attempts to return to work earlier than the end of [her additional maternity leave period] without complying with paragraph (1), her employer is entitled to postpone her return to a date such as will secure, subject to paragraph (3), that he has [8 weeks'] notice of her return.

[(2A) An employee who complies with her obligations in paragraph (1) or whose employer has postponed her return in the circumstances described in paragraph (2), and who then decides to return to work—

(a) earlier than the original return date, must give her employer not less than 8 weeks' notice of the date on which she now intends to return;

(b) later than the original return date, must give her employer not less than 8 weeks' notice ending with the original return date.

(2B) In paragraph (2A) the "original return date" means the date which the employee notified to her employer as the date of her return to work under paragraph (1), or the date to which her return was postponed by her employer under paragraph (2).]

(3) An employer is not entitled under paragraph (2) to postpone an employee's return to work to a date after the end of the relevant maternity leave period.

(4) If an employee whose return to work has been postponed under paragraph (2) has been notified that she is not to return to work before the date to which her return was

postponed, the employer is under no contractual obligation to pay her remuneration until the date to which her return was postponed if she returns to work before that date.

[(5) This regulation does not apply in a case where the employer did not notify the employee in accordance with regulation 7(6) and (7) of the date on which [her additional maternity leave period] would end.]

[2563]

NOTES

Para (1): substituted by the Maternity and Parental Leave etc and the Paternity and Adoption Leave (Amendment) Regulations 2006, SI 2006/2014, regs 3, 8(a), as from 1 October 2006 (with effect only in relation to employees whose expected week of childbirth begins on or after 1 April 2007: see SI 2006/2014, reg 2(1) at **[3463A]**).

Para (2): words in square brackets substituted by SI 2006/2014, regs 3, 8(b), as from 1 October 2006 (with effect only in relation to employees whose expected week of childbirth begins on or after 1 April 2007: see SI 2006/2014, reg 2(1) at **[3463A]**).

Paras (2A), (2B): inserted by SI 2006/2014, regs 3, 8(c), as from 1 October 2006 (with effect only in relation to employees whose expected week of childbirth begins on or after 1 April 2007: see SI 2006/2014, reg 2(1) at **[3463A]**).

Para (5): added by SI 2002/2789, regs 3, 10(c) (with effect in relation to employees whose expected week of childbirth begins on or after 6 April 2003); words in square brackets substituted by SI 2006/2014, regs 3, 8(d), as from 1 October 2006 (with effect only in relation to employees whose expected week of childbirth begins on or after 1 April 2007: see SI 2006/2014, reg 2(1) at **[3463A]**).

12 *(Revoked by the Maternity and Parental Leave (Amendment) Regulations 2002, SI 2002/2789, regs 3, 11 (with effect in relation to employees whose expected week of childbirth begins on or after 6 April 2003).)*

[12A Work during maternity leave period

[(1) Subject to paragraph (5), an employee may carry out up to 10 days' work for her employer during her statutory maternity leave period without bringing her maternity leave to an end.

(2) For the purposes of this regulation, any work carried out on any day shall constitute a day's work.

(3) Subject to paragraph (4), for the purposes of this regulation, work means any work done under the contract of employment and may include training or any activity undertaken for the purposes of keeping in touch with the workplace.

(4) Reasonable contact from time to time between an employee and her employer which either party is entitled to make during a maternity leave period (for example to discuss an employee's return to work) shall not bring that period to an end.

(5) Paragraph (1) shall not apply in relation to any work carried out by the employee at any time from childbirth to the end of the period of two weeks which commences with the day on which childbirth occurs.

(6) This regulation does not confer any right on an employer to require that any work be carried out during the statutory maternity leave period, nor any right on an employee to work during the statutory maternity leave period.

(7) Any days' work carried out under this regulation shall not have the effect of extending the total duration of the statutory maternity leave period.]

[2563A]

NOTES

Commencement: 1 October 2006 (with effect only in relation to employees whose expected week of childbirth begins on or after 1 April 2007).

Inserted by the Maternity and Parental Leave etc and the Paternity and Adoption Leave (Amendment) Regulations 2006, SI 2006/2014, regs 3, 9, as from 1 October 2006 (with effect only in relation to employees whose expected week of childbirth begins on or after 1 April 2007: see SI 2006/2014, reg 2(1) at **[3463A]**).

PART III
PARENTAL LEAVE

13 Entitlement to parental leave

(1) An employee who—

(a) has been continuously employed for a period of not less than a year [or is to be treated as having been so employed by virtue of paragraph (1A)]; and

(b) has, or expects to have, responsibility for a child,

is entitled, in accordance with these Regulations, to be absent from work on parental leave for the purpose of caring for that child.

[(1A) If, in a case where regulation 15(2) or (3) applies—

(a) the employee was employed, during the period between 15th December 1998 and 9th January 2002, by a person other than the person who was his employer on 9th January 2002, and

(b) the period of his employment by that person (or, if he was employed by more than one person during that period, any such person) was not less than a year,

then, for the purposes of paragraph (1), he shall be treated as having been continuously employed for a period of not less than a year.]

(2) An employee has responsibility for a child, for the purposes of paragraph (1), if—

(a) he has parental responsibility or, in Scotland, parental responsibilities for the child; or

(b) he has been registered as the child's father under any provision of section 10(1) or 10A(1) of the Births and Deaths Registration Act 1953 or of section 18(1) or (2) of the Registration of Births, Deaths and Marriages (Scotland) Act 1965.

(3) …

[2564]

NOTES

Para (1): words in square brackets in sub-para (a) inserted by the Maternity and Parental Leave (Amendment) Regulations 2001, SI 2001/4010, regs 2, 3(a).

Para (1A): inserted by SI 2001/4010, regs 2, 3(b).

Para (3): revoked by SI 2001/4010, regs 2, 3(c).

14 Extent of entitlement

(1) [Except in the case referred to in paragraph (1A), an employee is entitled] to thirteen weeks' leave in respect of any individual child.

[(1A) An employee is entitled to eighteen weeks' leave in respect of a child who is entitled to a disability living allowance.]

(2) Where the period for which an employee is normally required, under his contract of employment, to work in the course of a week does not vary, a week's leave for the employee is a period of absence from work which is equal in duration to the period for which he is normally required to work.

(3) Where the period for which an employee is normally required, under his contract of employment, to work in the course of a week varies from week to week or over a longer period, or where he is normally required under his contract to work in some weeks but not in others, a week's leave for the employee is a period of absence from work which is equal in duration to the period calculated by dividing the total of the periods for which he is normally required to work in a year by 52.

(4) Where an employee takes leave in periods shorter than the period which constitutes, for him, a week's leave under whichever of paragraphs (2) and (3) is applicable in his case, he completes a week's leave when the aggregate of the periods of leave he has taken equals the period constituting a week's leave for him under the applicable paragraph.

[2565]

NOTES

Para (1): words in square brackets substituted by the Maternity and Parental Leave (Amendment) Regulations 2001, SI 2001/4010, regs 2, 4(a).

Para (1A): inserted by SI 2001/4010, regs 2, 4(b).

[15 When parental leave may be taken

(1) Except in the cases referred to in paragraphs (2)–(4), an employee may not exercise any entitlement to parental leave in respect of a child after the date of the child's fifth birthday or, in the case of a child placed with the employee for adoption by him, on or after—

(a) the fifth anniversary of the date on which the placement began, or

(b) the date of the child's eighteenth birthday,

whichever is the earlier.

(2) In the case of child—

(a) born before 15th December 1999, whose fifth birthday was or is on or after that date, or

(b) placed with the employee for adoption by him before 15th December 1999, the fifth anniversary of whose placement was or is on or after that date,

not being a case to which paragraph (3) or (4) applies, any entitlement to parental leave may not be exercised after 31st March 2005.

(3) In the case of a child who is entitled to a disability living allowance, any entitlement to parental leave may not be exercised on or after the date of the child's eighteenth birthday.

(4) In a case where—

(a) the provisions set out in Schedule 2 apply, and

(b) the employee was unable to take leave in respect of a child within the time permitted in the case of that child under paragraphs (1) or (2) because the employer postponed the period of leave under paragraph 6 of that Schedule,

the entitlement to leave is exercisable until the end of the period to which the leave was postponed.]

[2566]

NOTES

Substituted by the Maternity and Parental Leave (Amendment) Regulations 2001, SI 2001/4010, regs 2, 5.

16 Default provisions in respect of parental leave

The provisions set out in Schedule 2 apply in relation to parental leave in the case of an employee whose contract of employment does not include a provision which—

(a) confers an entitlement to absence from work for the purpose of caring for a child, and

(b) incorporates or operates by reference to all or part of a collective agreement or workforce agreement.

[2567]

PART IV
PROVISIONS APPLICABLE IN RELATION TO MORE THAN ONE KIND OF ABSENCE

17 Application of terms and conditions during periods of leave

An employee who takes additional maternity leave or parental leave—

(a) is entitled, during the period of leave, to the benefit of her employer's implied obligation to her of trust and confidence and any terms and conditions of her employment relating to—

(i) notice of the termination of the employment contract by her employer;

(ii) compensation in the event of redundancy, or

(iii) disciplinary or grievance procedures;

(b) is bound, during that period, by her implied obligation to her employer of good faith and any terms and conditions of her employment relating to—

(i) notice of the termination of the employment contract by her;

(ii) the disclosure of confidential information;

(iii) the acceptance of gifts or other benefits, or

(iv) the employee's participation in any other business.

[2568]

[18 Right to return after maternity or parental leave

(1) An employee who returns to work after a period of ordinary maternity leave, or a period of parental leave of four weeks or less, which was—

(a) an isolated period of leave, or

(b) the last of two or more consecutive periods of statutory leave which did not include any period of additional maternity leave or additional adoption leave, or a period of parental leave of more than four weeks,

is entitled to return to the job in which she was employed before her absence.

(2) An employee who returns to work after—

(a) a period of additional maternity leave, or a period of parental leave of more than four weeks, whether or not preceded by another period of statutory leave, or

(b) a period of ordinary maternity leave, or a period of parental leave of four weeks or less, not falling within the description in paragraph (1)(a) or (b) above,

is entitled to return from leave to the job in which she was employed before her absence or, if it is not reasonably practicable for the employer to permit her to return to that job, to another job which is both suitable for her and appropriate for her to do in the circumstances.

(3) The reference in paragraphs (1) and (2) to the job in which an employee was employed before her absence is a reference to the job in which she was employed—

(a) if her return is from an isolated period of statutory leave, immediately before that period began;

(b) if her return is from consecutive periods of statutory leave, immediately before the first such period.

(4) This regulation does not apply where regulation 10 applies.]

[2569]

NOTES

Substituted, together with reg 18A, for original reg 18, by the Maternity and Parental Leave (Amendment) Regulations 2002, SI 2002/2789, regs 3, 12 (with effect in so far as it relates to maternity leave in relation to employees whose expected week of childbirth begins on or after 6 April 2003, and, in so far as it relates to parental leave, with effect only in relation to employees returning from a period of leave beginning on or after that date).

[18A Incidents of the right to return

(1) An employee's right to return under regulation 18(1) or (2) is a right to return—

(a) with her seniority, pension rights and similar rights—

(i) in a case where the employee is returning from additional maternity leave, or consecutive periods of statutory leave which included a period of additional maternity leave or additional adoption leave, as they would have been if the period or periods of her employment prior to her additional maternity leave or (as the case may be) additional adoption leave were continuous with the period of employment following it;

(ii) in any other case, as they would have been if she had not been absent, and

(b) on terms and conditions not less favourable than those which would have applied if she had not been absent.

(2) The provision in paragraph (1)(a)(i) concerning the treatment of periods of additional maternity leave or additional adoption leave is subject to the requirements of paragraphs 5 and 6 of Schedule 5 to the Social Security Act 1989 (equal treatment under pension schemes: maternity absence and family leave).

(3) The provisions in paragraph (1)(a)(ii) and (b) for an employee to be treated as if she had not been absent refer to her absence—

(a) if her return is from an isolated period of statutory leave, since the beginning of that period;

(b) if her return is from consecutive periods of statutory leave, since the beginning of the first such period.]

[2570]

NOTES

Substituted as noted to reg 18 at **[2569]**.

---

19 Protection from detriment

(1) An employee is entitled under section 47C of the 1996 Act not to be subjected to any detriment by any act, or any deliberate failure to act, by her employer done for any of the reasons specified in paragraph (2).

(2) The reasons referred to in paragraph (1) are that the employee—

(a) is pregnant;

(b) has given birth to a child;

(c) is the subject of a relevant requirement, or a relevant recommendation, as defined by section 66(2) of the 1996 Act;

(d) took, sought to take or availed herself of the benefits of, ordinary maternity leave;

(e) took or sought to take—

(i) additional maternity leave;

(ii) parental leave, or

(iii) time off under section 57A of the 1996 Act;

[(ee) failed to return after a period of ordinary or additional maternity leave in a case where—

(i) the employer did not notify her, in accordance with regulation 7(6) and (7) or otherwise, of the date on which the period in question would end, and she reasonably believed that that period had not ended, or

(ii) the employer gave her less than 28 days' notice of the date on which the period in question would end, and it was not reasonably practicable for her to return on that date;]

[(eee) undertook, considered undertaking or refused to undertake work in accordance with regulation 12A;]

(f) declined to sign a workforce agreement for the purpose of these Regulations, or

(g) being—

(i) a representative of members of the workforce for the purposes of Schedule 1, or

(ii) a candidate in an election in which any person elected will, on being elected, become such a representative,

performed (or proposed to perform) any functions or activities as such a representative or candidate.

(3) For the purposes of paragraph (2)(d), a woman avails herself of the benefits of ordinary maternity leave if, during her ordinary maternity leave period, she avails herself of the benefit of any of the terms and conditions of her employment preserved by section 71 of the 1996 Act [and regulation 9] during that period.

(4) Paragraph (1) does not apply in a case where the detriment in question amounts to dismissal within the meaning of Part X of the 1996 Act.

(5) Paragraph (2)(b) only applies where the act or failure to act takes place during the employee's ordinary or additional maternity leave period.

(6) For the purposes of paragraph (5)—

(a) where an act extends over a period, the reference to the date of the act is a reference to the last day of that period, and

(b) a failure to act is to be treated as done when it was decided on.

(7) For the purposes of paragraph (6), in the absence of evidence establishing the contrary an employer shall be taken to decide on a failure to act—

(a) when he does an act inconsistent with doing the failed act, or

(b) if he has done no such inconsistent act, when the period expires within which he might reasonably have been expected to do the failed act if it were to be done.

[2571]

NOTES

Para (2): sub-para (ee) inserted by the Maternity and Parental Leave (Amendment) Regulations 2002, SI 2002/2789, regs 3, 13(a) (with effect in relation to employees whose expected week of childbirth begins on or after 6 April 2003); para (eee) inserted by the Maternity and Parental Leave etc and the Paternity and Adoption Leave (Amendment) Regulations 2006, SI 2006/2014, regs 3, 10, as from 1 October 2006 (with effect only in relation to employees whose expected week of childbirth begins on or after 1 April 2007: see SI 2006/2014, reg 2(1) at **[3463A]**).

Para (3): words in square brackets inserted by SI 2002/2789, regs 3, 13(b) (with effect in relation to employees whose expected week of childbirth begins on or after 6 April 2003).

20 Unfair dismissal

(1) An employee who is dismissed is entitled under section 99 of the 1996 Act to be regarded for the purposes of Part X of that Act as unfairly dismissed if—

(a) the reason or principal reason for the dismissal is of a kind specified in paragraph (3), or

(b) the reason or principal reason for the dismissal is that the employee is redundant, and regulation 10 has not been complied with.

(2) An employee who is dismissed shall also be regarded for the purposes of Part X of the 1996 Act as unfairly dismissed if—

(a) the reason (or, if more than one, the principal reason) for the dismissal is that the employee was redundant;

(b) it is shown that the circumstances constituting the redundancy applied equally to one or more employees in the same undertaking who held positions similar to that held by the employee and who have not been dismissed by the employer, and

(c) it is shown that the reason (or, if more than one, the principal reason) for which the employee was selected for dismissal was a reason of a kind specified in paragraph (3).

(3) The kinds of reason referred to in paragraphs (1) and (2) are reasons connected with—

(a) the pregnancy of the employee;

(b) the fact that the employee has given birth to a child;

(c) the application of a relevant requirement, or a relevant recommendation, as defined by section 66(2) of the 1996 Act;

(d) the fact that she took, sought to take or availed herself of the benefits of, ordinary maternity leave;

(e) the fact that she took or sought to take—

(i) additional maternity leave;

(ii) parental leave, or

(iii) time off under section 57A of the 1996 Act;

[(ee) the fact that she failed to return after a period of ordinary or additional maternity leave in a case where—

(i) the employer did not notify her, in accordance with regulation 7(6) and (7) or otherwise, of the date on which the period in question would end, and she reasonably believed that that period had not ended, or

(ii) the employer gave her less than 28 days' notice of the date on which the period in question would end, and it was not reasonably practicable for her to return on that date;]

[(eee) the fact that she undertook, considered undertaking or refused to undertake work in accordance with regulation 12A;]

(f) the fact that she declined to sign a workforce agreement for the purposes of these Regulations, or

(g) the fact that the employee, being—

(i) a representative of members of the workforce for the purposes of Schedule 1, or

(ii) a candidate in an election in which any person elected will, on being elected, become such a representative,

performed (or proposed to perform) any functions or activities as such a representative or candidate.

(4) Paragraphs (1)(b) and (3)(b) only apply where the dismissal ends the employee's ordinary or additional maternity leave period.

(5) Paragraph (3) of regulation 19 applies for the purposes of paragraph (3)(d) as it applies for the purpose of paragraph (2)(d) of that regulation.

(6) …

(7) Paragraph (1) does not apply in relation to an employee if—

(a) it is not reasonably practicable for a reason other than redundancy for the employer (who may be the same employer or a successor of his) to permit her to return to a job which is both suitable for her and appropriate for her to do in the circumstances;

(b) an associated employer offers her a job of that kind, and

(c) she accepts or unreasonably refuses that offer.

(8) Where on a complaint of unfair dismissal any question arises as to whether the operation of paragraph (1) is excluded by the provisions of paragraph … (7), it is for the employer to show that the provisions in question were satisfied in relation to the complainant.
[2572]

NOTES

Para (3): sub-para (ee) inserted by the Maternity and Parental Leave (Amendment) Regulations 2002, SI 2002/2789, regs 3, 14 (with effect in relation to employees whose expected week of childbirth begins on or after 6 April 2003); para (eee) inserted by the Maternity and Parental Leave etc and the Paternity and Adoption Leave (Amendment) Regulations 2006, SI 2006/2014, regs 3, 11(a), as from 1 October 2006 (with effect only in relation to employees whose expected week of childbirth begins on or after 1 April 2007: see SI 2006/2014, reg 2(1) at **[3463A]**).

Para (6): revoked by SI 2006/2014, regs 3, 11(b), as from 1 October 2006 (with effect only in relation to employees whose expected week of childbirth begins on or after 1 April 2007: see SI 2006/2014, reg 2(1) at **[3463A]**).

Para (8): words omitted revoked by SI 2006/2014, regs 3, 11(c), as from 1 October 2006 (with effect only in relation to employees whose expected week of childbirth begins on or after 1 April 2007: see SI 2006/2014, reg 2(1) at **[3463A]**).

21 Contractual rights to maternity or parental leave

(1) This regulation applies where an employee is entitled to—
- (a) ordinary maternity leave;
- (b) additional maternity leave, or
- (c) parental leave,

(referred to in paragraph (2) as a "statutory right") and also to a right which corresponds to that right and which arises under the employee's contract of employment or otherwise.

(2) In a case where this regulation applies—
- (a) the employee may not exercise the statutory right and the corresponding right separately but may, in taking the leave for which the two rights provide, take advantage of whichever right is, in any particular respect, the more favourable, and
- (b) the provisions of the 1996 Act and of these Regulations relating to the statutory right apply, subject to any modifications necessary to give effect to any more favourable contractual terms, to the exercise of the composite right described in sub-paragraph (a) as they apply to the exercise of the statutory right.

[2573]

22 Calculation of a week's pay

Where—
- (a) under Chapter II of Part XIV of the 1996 Act, the amount of a week's pay of an employee falls to be calculated by reference to the average rate of remuneration, or the average amount of remuneration, payable to the employee in respect of a period of twelve weeks ending on a particular date (referred to as "the calculation date");
- (b) during a week in that period, the employee was absent from work on ordinary or additional maternity leave or parental leave, and
- (c) remuneration is payable to the employee in respect of that week under her contract of employment, but the amount payable is less than the amount that would be payable if she were working,

that week shall be disregarded for the purpose of the calculation and account shall be taken of remuneration in earlier weeks so as to bring up to twelve the number of weeks of which account is taken.

[2574]

SCHEDULES

SCHEDULE 1
WORKFORCE AGREEMENTS

Regulation 2(1)

1. An agreement is a workforce agreement for the purposes of these Regulations if the following conditions are satisfied—
- (a) the agreement is in writing;

(b) it has effect for a specified period not exceeding five years;
(c) it applies either—
(i) to all of the relevant members of the workforce, or
(ii) to all of the relevant members of the workforce who belong to a particular group;
(d) the agreement is signed—
(i) in the case of an agreement of the kind referred to in sub-paragraph (c)(i), by the representatives of the workforce, and in the case of an agreement of the kind referred to in sub-paragraph (c)(ii), by the representatives of the group to which the agreement applies (excluding, in either case, any representative not a relevant member of the workforce on the date on which the agreement was first made available for signature), or
(ii) if the employer employed 20 or fewer employees on the date referred to in sub-paragraph (d)(i), either by the appropriate representatives in accordance with that sub-paragraph or by the majority of the employees employed by him;

and
(e) before the agreement was made available for signature, the employer provided all the employees to whom it was intended to apply on the date on which it came into effect with copies of the text of the agreement and such guidance as those employees might reasonably require in order to understand it in full.

2. For the purposes of this Schedule—
"a particular group" is a group of the relevant members of a workforce who undertake a particular function, work at a particular workplace or belong to a particular department or unit within their employer's business;
"relevant members of the workforce" are all of the employees employed by a particular employer, excluding any employee whose terms and conditions of employment are provided for, wholly or in part, in a collective agreement;
"representatives of the workforce" are employees duly elected to represent the relevant members of the workforce, "representatives of the group" are employees duly elected to represent the members of a particular group, and representatives are "duly elected" if the election at which they were elected satisfied the requirements of paragraph 3 of this Schedule.

3. The requirements concerning elections referred to in paragraph 2 are that—
(a) the number of representatives to be elected is determined by the employer;
(b) the candidates for election as representatives of the workforce are relevant members of the workforce, and the candidates for election as representatives of a group are members of the group;
(c) no employee who is eligible to be a candidate is unreasonably excluded from standing for election;
(d) all the relevant members of the workforce are entitled to vote for representatives of the workforce, and all the members of a particular group are entitled to vote for representatives of the group;
(e) the employees entitled to vote may vote for as many candidates as there are representatives to be elected, and
(f) the election is conducted so as to secure that—
(i) so far as is reasonably practicable, those voting do so in secret, and
(ii) the votes given at the election are fairly and accurately counted.

[2575]

SCHEDULE 2
DEFAULT PROVISIONS IN RESPECT OF PARENTAL LEAVE

Regulation 16

Conditions of entitlement

1. An employee may not exercise any entitlement to parental leave unless—
(a) he has complied with any request made by his employer to produce for the employer's inspection evidence of his entitlement, of the kind described in paragraph 2;
(b) he has given his employer notice, in accordance with whichever of paragraphs 3 to 5 is applicable, of the period of leave he proposes to take, and

(c) in a case where paragraph 6 applies, his employer has not postponed the period of leave in accordance with that paragraph.

2. The evidence to be produced for the purpose of paragraph 1(a) is such evidence as may reasonably be required of—

(a) the employee's responsibility or expected responsibility for the child in respect of whom the employee proposes to take parental leave;

(b) the child's date of birth or, in the case of a child who was placed with the employee for adoption, the date on which the placement began, and

(c) in a case where the employee's right to exercise an entitlement to parental leave under regulation 15, or to take a particular period of leave under paragraph 7, depends upon whether the child is entitled to a disability living allowance, the child's entitlement to that allowance.

[2A. Where regulation 13(1A) applies, and the employee's entitlement to parental leave arises out of a period of employment by a person other than the person who was his employer on 9th January 2002, the employee may not exercise the entitlement unless he has given his employer notice of that period of employment, and provided him with such evidence of it as the employer may reasonably require.]

Notice to be given to employer

3. Except in a case where paragraph 4 or 5 applies, the notice required for the purpose of paragraph 1(b) is notice which—

(a) specifies the dates on which the period of leave is to begin and end, and

(b) is given to the employer at least 21 days before the date on which that period is to begin.

4. Where the employee is the father of the child in respect of whom the leave is to be taken, and the period of leave is to begin on the date on which the child is born, the notice required for the purpose of paragraph 1(b) is notice which—

(a) specifies the expected week of childbirth and the duration of the period of leave, and

(b) is given to the employer at least 21 days before the beginning of the expected week of childbirth.

5. Where the child in respect of whom the leave is to be taken is to be placed with the employee for adoption by him and the leave is to begin on the date of the placement, the notice required for the purpose of paragraph 1(b) is notice which—

(a) specifies the week in which the placement is expected to occur and the duration of the period of leave, and

(b) is given to the employer at least 21 days before the beginning of that week, or, if that is not reasonably practicable, as soon as is reasonably practicable.

Postponement of leave

6. An employer may postpone a period of parental leave where—

(a) neither paragraph 4 nor paragraph 5 applies, and the employee has accordingly given the employer notice in accordance with paragraph 3;

(b) the employer considers that the operation of his business would be unduly disrupted if the employee took leave during the period identified in his notice;

(c) the employer agrees to permit the employee to take a period of leave—

  (i) of the same duration as the period identified in the employee's notice, …

  (ii) beginning on a date determined by the employer after consulting the employee, which is no later than six months after the commencement of that period; [and

  (iii) ending before the date of the child's eighteenth birthday.]

(d) the employer gives the employee notice in writing of the postponement which—

  (i) states the reason for it, and

  (ii) specifies the dates on which the period of leave the employer agrees to permit the employee to take will begin and end,

and

(e) that notice is given to the employee not more than seven days after the employee's notice was given to the employer.

Minimum periods of leave

7. An employee may not take parental leave in a period other than the period which constitutes a week's leave for him under regulation 14 or a multiple of that period, except in a case where the child in respect of whom leave is taken is entitled to a disability living allowance.

Maximum annual leave allowance

8. An employee may not take more than four weeks' leave in respect of any individual child during a particular year.

9. For the purposes of paragraph 8, a year is the period of twelve months beginning—
(a) except where sub-paragraph (b) applies, on the date on which the employee first became entitled to take parental leave in respect of the child in question, or
(b) in a case where the employee's entitlement has been interrupted at the end of a period of continuous employment, on the date on which the employee most recently became entitled to take parental leave in respect of that child,

and each successive period of twelve months beginning on the anniversary of that date.

[2576]

NOTES

Para 2A: inserted by the Maternity and Parental Leave (Amendment) Regulations 2001, SI 2001/4010, regs 2, 6(a).

Para 6: word omitted from sub-para (c)(i) revoked, and sub-para (c)(ii) and word immediately preceding it added, by SI 2001/4010, regs 2, 6(b).

TRANSNATIONAL INFORMATION AND CONSULTATION OF EMPLOYEES REGULATIONS 1999

(SI 1999/3323)

NOTES

Made: 12 December 1999.

Authority: European Communities Act 1972, s 2(2).

Commencement: 15 January 2000.

These Regulations are the domestic implementation for the UK of EC Directive 94/45 at **[3854]**, as extended to the UK by EC Directive 97/74 at **[3919]**.

Employment Appeal Tribunal: an appeal lies to the Employment Appeal Tribunal on any question of law arising from any decision of, or in any proceedings before, an employment tribunal under or by virtue of reg 27 or 32; see the Employment Tribunals Act 1996, s 21(1)(i) at **[978]**.

Conciliation: employment tribunal proceedings and claims which could be the subject of employment tribunal proceedings under regs 27, 32 are proceedings to which the Employment Tribunals Act 1996, s 18 applies; see s 18(1)(g) of that Act at **[975]**. The standard conciliation period applies to such claims by virtue of the Employment Tribunals (Constitution and Rules of Procedure) Regulations 2004, SI 2004/1861, Sch 1, rule 22(1), (6).

See *Harvey* N10(F), P2, R, T(B).

ARRANGEMENT OF REGULATIONS

PART I
GENERAL

PART II
EMPLOYEE NUMBERS & REQUEST TO NEGOTIATE ESTABLISHMENT OF A EUROPEAN WORKS COUNCIL OR INFORMATION AND CONSULTATION PROCEDURE

PART III
SPECIAL NEGOTIATING BODY

PART IV
EUROPEAN WORKS COUNCIL AND INFORMATION AND CONSULTATION PROCEDURE

PART V
COMPLIANCE AND ENFORCEMENT

PART VI
CONFIDENTIAL INFORMATION

PART VII
PROTECTIONS FOR MEMBERS OF A EUROPEAN WORKS COUNCIL, ETC

PART VIII
MISCELLANEOUS

The Appeal Tribunal, Industrial Court, CAC, ACAS and the Labour Relations Agency

PART I
GENERAL

1 Citation, commencement and extent

(1) These Regulations may be cited as the Transnational Information and Consultation of Employees Regulations 1999 and shall come into force on 15th January 2000.

(2) These Regulations extend to Northern Ireland.

[2577]

2 Interpretation

(1) In these Regulations—

"the 1996 Act" means the Employment Rights Act 1996;

"the 1996 Order" means the Employment Rights (Northern Ireland) Order 1996;

"ACAS" means the Advisory, Conciliation and Arbitration Service;

"Appeal Tribunal" means the Employment Appeal Tribunal;

"CAC" means the Central Arbitration Committee;

"central management" means—

(a) the central management of a Community-scale undertaking, or

(b) in the case of a Community-scale group of undertakings, the central management of the controlling undertaking,

or, where appropriate, the central management of an undertaking or group of undertakings that could be or is claimed to be a Community-scale undertaking or Community-scale group of undertakings;

"Community-scale undertaking" means an undertaking with at least 1000 employees within the Member States and at least 150 employees in each of at least two Member States;

"Community-scale group of undertakings" means a group of undertakings which has—

(a) at least 1000 employees within the Member States,

(b) at least two group undertakings in different Member States, and

(c) at least one group undertaking with at least 150 employees in one Member State and at least one other group undertaking with at least 150 employees in another Member State;

"consultation" means the exchange of views and establishment of dialogue between members of a European Works Council in the context of a European Works Council, or information and consultation representatives in the context of an information and consultation procedure, and central management or any more appropriate level of management;

"contract of employment" means a contract of service or apprenticeship, whether express or implied, and (if it is express) whether oral or in writing;

"controlled undertaking" has the meaning assigned to it by regulation 3;

"controlling undertaking" has the meaning assigned to it by regulation 3;

"employee" means an individual who has entered into or works under a contract of employment and in Part VII and regulation 41 includes, where the employment has ceased, an individual who worked under a contract of employment;

"employees' representatives" means—

(a) if the employees are of a description in respect of which an independent trade union is recognised by their employer for the purpose of collective bargaining, representatives of the trade union who normally take part as negotiators in the collective bargaining process, and

(b) any other employee representatives elected or appointed by employees to positions in which they are expected to receive, on behalf of the employees, information—

(i) which is relevant to the terms and conditions of employment of the employees, or

(ii) about the activities of the undertaking which may significantly affect the interests of the employees,

but excluding representatives who are expected to receive information relevant only to a specific aspect of the terms and conditions or interests of the employees, such as health and safety or collective redundancies;

"European Works Council" means the council, established under and in accordance with—

(a) regulation 17, or regulation 18 and the provisions of the Schedule, or

(b) where appropriate, the provisions of the law or practice of a Member State other than the United Kingdom which are designed to give effect to Article 6 of, or Article 7 of and the Annex to, the Transnational Information and Consultation Directive,

with the purpose of informing and consulting employees;

"Extension Directive" means Council Directive 97/74/EC of 15 December 1997 extending, to the United Kingdom, the Transnational Information and Consultation Directive;

"group of undertakings" means a controlling undertaking and its controlled undertakings;

"group undertaking" means an undertaking which is part of a Community-scale group of undertakings;

"independent trade union" has the same meaning as in the Trade Union and Labour Relations (Consolidation) Act 1992, or in Northern Ireland the 1996 Order;

"information and consultation procedure" means one or more information and consultation procedures agreed under—

(a) regulation 17, or

(b) where appropriate, the provisions of the law or practice of a Member State other than the United Kingdom which are designed to give effect to Article 6(3) of the Transnational Information and Consultation Directive;

"information and consultation representative" means a person who represents employees in the context of an information and consultation procedure;

"local management" means the management of one or more establishments in a Community-scale undertaking or of one or more undertakings in a Community-scale group of undertakings which is not the central management;

"Member State" means a state which is a Contracting Party to the Agreement on the European Economic Area signed at Oporto on 2nd May 1992 as adjusted by the Protocol signed at Brussels on 17th March 1993;

"special negotiating body" means the body established for the purposes of negotiating with central management an agreement for a European Works Council or an information and consultation procedure;

"Transnational Information and Consultation Directive" means Council Directive 94/45/EC of 22 September 1994 on the establishment of a European Works Council or a procedure in Community-scale undertakings and Community-scale groups of undertakings for the purposes of informing and consulting employees;

"UK management" means the management which is, or would be, subject to the obligation in regulation 13(2) or paragraph 4(1) of the Schedule, being either the central management in the United Kingdom or the local management in the United Kingdom;

"UK member of the special negotiating body" means a member of the special negotiating body who represents UK employees for the purposes of negotiating with central management an agreement for a European Works Council or an information and consultation procedure.

(2) To the extent that the Transnational Information and Consultation Directive and the Extension Directive permit the establishment of more than one European Works Council in a Community-scale undertaking or Community-scale group of undertakings, these Regulations shall be construed accordingly.

(3) In paragraphs (1) and (4) of this regulation and in regulations 6, 13 to 15 and paragraphs 3 to 5 of the Schedule, references to "UK employees" are references to employees who are employed in the United Kingdom by a Community-scale undertaking or Community-scale group of undertakings.

(4) In regulations 13 and 15 and paragraphs 3 and 4 of the Schedule, references to "UK employees' representatives" are references to employees' representatives who represent UK employees.

(5) In the absence of a definition in these Regulations, words and expressions used in particular regulations and particular paragraphs of the Schedule to these Regulations which are also used in the provisions of the Transnational Information and Consultation Directive or the Extension Directive to which they are designed to give effect have the same meaning as they have in those provisions.

[2578]

3 Controlled and Controlling Undertaking

(1) In these Regulations "controlling undertaking" means an undertaking which can exercise a dominant influence over another undertaking by virtue, for example, of ownership, financial participation or the rules which govern it and "controlled undertaking" means an undertaking over which such a dominant influence can be exercised.

(2) The ability of an undertaking to exercise a dominant influence over another undertaking shall be presumed, unless the contrary is proved, when in relation to another undertaking it directly or indirectly—

(a) can appoint more than half of the members of that undertaking's administrative, management or supervisory body;

(b) controls a majority of the votes attached to that undertaking's issued share capital; or

(c) holds a majority of that undertaking's subscribed capital.

(3) In applying the criteria in paragraph (2), a controlling undertaking's rights as regards voting and appointment shall include—

(a) the rights of its other controlled undertakings; and

(b) the rights of any person or body acting in his or its own name but on behalf of the controlling undertaking or of any other of the controlling undertaking's controlled undertakings.

(4) Notwithstanding paragraphs (1) and (2) an undertaking shall not be a controlling undertaking of another undertaking in which it has holdings where the first undertaking is a company referred to in Article 3(5)(a) or (c) of Council Regulation [(EC) No 139/2004 of 20 January 2004] on the control of concentrations between undertakings.

(5) A dominant influence shall not be presumed to be exercised solely by virtue of the fact that an office holder is exercising functions, according to the law of a Member State, relating to liquidation, winding-up, insolvency, cessation of payments, compositions of creditors or analogous proceedings.

(6) Where the law governing an undertaking is the law of a Member State, the law applicable in order to determine whether an undertaking is a controlling undertaking shall be the law of that Member State.

(7) Where the law governing an undertaking is not that of a Member State the law applicable shall be the law of the Member State within whose territory—

(a) the representative of the undertaking is situated; or

(b) in the absence of such a representative, the management of the group undertaking which employs the greatest number of employees is situated.

(8) If two or more undertakings (whether situated in the same or in different Member States) meet one or more of the criteria in paragraph (2) in relation to another undertaking, the criteria shall be applied in the order listed in relation to each of the first-mentioned undertakings and that which meets the criterion that is highest in the order listed shall be presumed, unless the contrary is proved, to exercise a dominant influence over the undertaking in question.

[2579]

NOTES

Para (4): words in square brackets substituted by the EC Merger Control (Consequential Amendments) Regulations 2004, SI 2004/1079, reg 2, Schedule, para 4, as from 1 May 2004.

4 Circumstances in which provisions of these Regulations apply

(1) Subject to paragraph (2) the provisions of regulations 7 to 41 and of regulation 46 shall apply in relation to a Community-scale undertaking or Community-scale group of undertakings only where, in accordance with regulation 5, the central management is situated in the United Kingdom.

(2) The following regulations shall apply in relation to a Community-scale undertaking or Community-scale group of undertakings whether or not the central management is situated in the United Kingdom—

(a) regulations 7 and 8(1), (2) and (4) (provision of information on employee numbers);
(b) regulations 13 to 15 (UK members of the special negotiating body);
(c) regulation 18 to the extent it applies paragraphs 3 to 5 of the Schedule (UK members of the European Works Council);
(d) regulations 23(1) to (5) (breach of statutory duty);
(e) regulations 25 to 33 (protections for members of a European Works Council, etc);
(f) regulations 34 to 39 (enforcement bodies) to the extent they relate to applications made or complaints presented under any of the other regulations referred to in this paragraph;
(g) regulations 40 and 41 (restrictions on contracting out).

[2580]

5 The central management

(1) The central management shall be responsible for creating the conditions and means necessary for the setting up of a European Works Council or an information and consultation procedure in a Community-scale undertaking or Community-scale group of undertakings where—

(a) the central management is situated in the United Kingdom;
(b) the central management is not situated in a Member State and the representative agent of the central management (to be designated if necessary) is situated in the United Kingdom; or
(c) neither the central management nor the representative agent (whether or not as a result of being designated) is situated in a Member State and—
  (i) in the case of a Community-scale undertaking, there are employed in an establishment, which is situated in the United Kingdom, more employees than are employed in any other establishment which is situated in a Member State, or
  (ii) in the case of a Community-scale group of undertakings, there are employed in a group undertaking, which is situated in the United Kingdom, more employees than are employed in any other group undertaking which is situated in a Member State,

and the central management initiates, or by virtue of regulation 9(1) is required to initiate, negotiations for a European Works Council or information and consultation procedure.

(2) Where the circumstances described in paragraph (1)(b) or (1)(c) apply, the central management shall be treated, for the purposes of these Regulations, as being situated in the United Kingdom and—

(a) the representative agent referred to in paragraph (1)(b); or

(b) the management of the establishment referred to in paragraph (1)(c)(i) or of the group undertaking, referred to in paragraph (1)(c)(ii),

shall be treated, respectively, as being the central management.

[2581]

PART II
EMPLOYEE NUMBERS & REQUEST TO NEGOTIATE ESTABLISHMENT OF A EUROPEAN WORKS COUNCIL OR INFORMATION AND CONSULTATION PROCEDURE

6 Calculation of numbers of employees

(1) For the purposes of determining whether an undertaking is a Community-scale undertaking or a group of undertakings is a Community-scale group of undertakings, the number of employees employed by the undertaking, or group of undertakings, shall be determined—

(a) in the case of UK employees, by ascertaining the average number of employees employed during a two year period, calculated in accordance with paragraph (2) below;

(b) in the case of employees in another Member State, by ascertaining the average number of employees employed during a two year period, calculated in accordance with the provisions of the law or practice of that Member State which is designed to give effect to the Transnational Information and Consultation Directive.

(2) Subject to paragraph (3), the average number of UK employees is to be ascertained by—

(a) determining the number of UK employees in each month in the two year period preceding the relevant date (whether they were employed throughout the month or not);

(b) adding together all of the monthly numbers, and

dividing the number so determined by 24.

(3) For the purposes of the calculation in paragraph 2(a) if for the whole of a month within the two year period an employee works under a contract by virtue of which he would have worked for 75 hours or less in that month—

(a) were the month to have contained 21 working days;

(b) were the employee to have had no absences from work; and

(c) were the employee to have worked no overtime,

the employee may be counted as half a person for the month in question, if the UK management so decides.

(4) For the purposes of this regulation, regulations 7 to 10 and regulation 20 "relevant date" means—

(a) where a request under regulation 7 is made and no valid request under regulation 9 has been made, the last day of the month preceding the month in which the request under regulation 7 is made; and

(b) where a valid request under regulation 9 is made (whether or not a request under regulation 7 has been made), the last day of the month preceding the month in which the request under regulation 9 is made.

(5) Where appropriate, the references in paragraph (4) to regulations 7 and 9 shall be read, instead, as references to the provisions of the law or practice of a Member State other than the United Kingdom which are designed to give effect to, respectively, Article 11(2) and Article 5(1) of the Transnational Information and Consultation Directive.

[2582]

7 Entitlement to information

(1) An employee or an employees' representative may request information from the management of an establishment, or of an undertaking, in the United Kingdom for the purpose of determining whether, in the case of an establishment, it is part of a Community-scale undertaking or Community-scale group of undertakings or, in the case of an undertaking, it is a Community-scale undertaking or is part of a Community-scale group of undertakings.

(2) In this regulation and regulation 8, the management of an establishment or undertaking to which a request under paragraph (1) is made is referred to as the "recipient".

(3) The recipient must provide the employee or employees' representative who has made the request with information on the average number of employees employed by the undertaking, or as the case may be the group of undertakings, in the United Kingdom and in each of the other Member States in the last two years.

[2583]

8 Complaint of failure to provide information

(1) An employee or employees' representative who has requested information under regulation 7 may present a complaint to the CAC that—

(a) the recipient has failed to provide the information referred to in regulation 7(3); or

(b) the information which has been provided by the recipient is false or incomplete in a material particular.

(2) Where the CAC finds the complaint well-founded it shall make an order requiring the recipient to disclose information to the complainant which order shall specify—

(a) the information in respect of which the CAC finds that the complaint is well-founded and which is to be disclosed to the complainant;

(b) the date (or if more than one, the earliest date) on which the recipient refused or failed to disclose information, or disclosed false or incomplete information;

(c) a date (not being less than one week from the date of the order) by which the recipient must disclose the information specified in the order.

(3) If the CAC considers that, from the information it has obtained in considering the complaint, it is beyond doubt that the undertaking is, or that the establishment is part of, a Community-scale undertaking or that the establishment or undertaking is part of a Community-scale group of undertakings, it may make a declaration to that effect.

(4) The CAC shall not consider a complaint presented under this regulation unless it is made after the expiry of a period of one month beginning on the date on which the complainant made his request for information under regulation 7.

[2584]

9 Request to negotiate an agreement for a European Works Council or information and consultation procedure

(1) The central management shall initiate negotiations for the establishment of a European Works Council or an information and consultation procedure where—

(a) a valid request has been made by employees or employees' representatives; and

(b) on the relevant date the undertaking is a Community-scale undertaking or the group of undertakings is a Community-scale group of undertakings.

(2) A valid request may consist of—

(a) a single request made by at least 100 employees, or employees' representatives who represent at least that number, in at least two undertakings or establishments in at least two different Member States; or

(b) a number of separate requests made on the same or different days by employees, or by employees' representatives, which when taken together mean that at least 100 employees, or employees' representatives who represent at least that number, in at least two undertakings or establishments in at least two different Member States have made requests.

(3) To amount to a valid request the single request referred to in paragraph (2)(a) or each separate request referred to in paragraph (2)(b) must—

(a) be in writing;

(b) be sent to—

  (i) the central management, or

  (ii) the local management;

(c) specify the date on which it was sent; and

(d) where appropriate, be made after the expiry of a period of two years, commencing on the date of a decision under regulation 16(3) (unless the special negotiating body and central management have otherwise agreed).

(4) The date on which a valid request is made is—

(a) where it consists of a single request satisfying paragraph 2(a) or of separate requests made on the same day satisfying paragraph 2(b), the date on which the request is or requests are sent; and

(b) where it consists of separate requests made on different days satisfying paragraph 2(b), the date of the sending of the request which resulted in that paragraph being satisfied.

(5) The central management may initiate the negotiations referred to in paragraph (1) on its own initiative.

[2585]

10 Dispute as to whether valid request made or whether obligation in regulation 9(1) applies

(1) If the central management considers that a request (or separate request) did not satisfy any requirement of regulation 9(2) or (3) it may apply to the CAC for a declaration as to whether the request satisfied the requirement.

(2) The CAC shall only consider an application for a declaration made under paragraph (1) if—

(a) the application is made within a three month period beginning on the date when a request, or if more than one the first request, was made for the purposes of regulation 9, whether or not that request satisfied the requirements of regulations 9(2) and (3);

(b) the application is made before the central management takes any step to initiate negotiations for the establishment of a European Works Council or an information and consultation procedure; and

(c) at the time when the application is made, there has been no application by the central management for a declaration under paragraph (3).

(3) If the central management considers for any reason that the obligation in regulation 9(1) did not apply to it on the relevant date, it may, within a period of three months commencing on the date on which the valid request was made, apply to the CAC for a declaration as to whether that obligation applied to it on the relevant date.

(4) Where the date on which the valid request was made is a date falling before the date of any declaration made pursuant to an application made under this regulation the operation of the periods of time specified in paragraphs (1)(b) and (1)(c) of regulation 18 shall be suspended for a period of time—

(a) commencing on the date of the application; and

(b) ending on the date of the declaration.

(5) If on an application for a declaration under this regulation the CAC does not make any declaration in favour of the central management and considers that the central management has, in making the application or conducting the proceedings, acted frivolously, vexatiously, or otherwise unreasonably, the CAC shall make a declaration to the effect that paragraph (4) does not apply.

[2586]

PART III
SPECIAL NEGOTIATING BODY

11 Functions of the special negotiating body

The special negotiating body shall have the task of determining, with the central management, by written agreement, the scope, composition, functions, and term of office of a European Works Council or the arrangements for implementing an information and consultation procedure.

[2587]

12 Composition of the special negotiating body

(1) The special negotiating body shall be constituted in accordance with paragraphs (2) and (3) below.

(2) There shall be on the special negotiating body at least one member representing each Member State in which the Community-scale undertaking has one or more establishments, or in which the Community-scale group of undertakings has its controlling undertaking or one or more controlled undertakings.

(3) There shall be on the special negotiating body the following additional members—

(a) one additional member from a Member State in which there are employed 25 per cent or more but less than 50 per cent of the employees of the undertaking or group of undertakings who are employed in the Member States;

(b) two additional members from a Member State in which there are employed 50 per cent or more but less than 75 per cent of the employees of the undertaking or group of undertakings who are employed in the Member States;

(c) three additional members from a Member State in which there are employed 75 per cent or more of the employees of the undertaking or group of undertakings who are employed in the Member States.

(4) The special negotiating body shall inform the central management and local managements of the composition of the special negotiating body.

[2588]

13 Ballot arrangements

(1) Subject to regulation 15, the UK members of the special negotiating body shall be elected by a ballot of the UK employees.

(2) The UK management must arrange for the holding of a ballot of employees referred to in paragraph (1), which satisfies the requirements specified in paragraph (3).

(3) The requirements referred to in paragraph (2) are that—

(a) the ballot of the UK employees must comprise a single ballot but may instead, if the UK management so decides, comprise separate ballots of employees in such constituencies as the UK management may determine where—

(i) the number of UK members of the special negotiating body to be elected is more than one, and

(ii) the UK management considers that if separate ballots were held for those constituencies, the UK members of the special negotiating body to be elected would better reflect the interests of the UK employees as a whole than if a single ballot were held;

(b) a UK employee who is an employee of the Community-scale undertaking or the Community-scale group of undertakings on the day on which votes may be cast in the ballot, or if the votes may be cast on more than one day, on the first day of those days, is entitled to vote in the ballot of the UK employees;

(c) any UK employee, or UK employees' representative, who is an employee of, or an employees' representative in, the Community-scale undertaking or Community scale group of undertakings immediately before the latest time at which a person may become a candidate in the ballot, is entitled to stand in the ballot of the UK employees as a candidate for election as a UK member of the special negotiating body;

(d) the UK management must, in accordance with paragraph (7), appoint an independent ballot supervisor to supervise the conduct of the ballot of the UK employees but may instead, where there are to be separate ballots, appoint more than one independent ballot supervisor in accordance with that paragraph, each of whom is to supervise such of the separate ballots as the UK management may determine, provided that each separate ballot is supervised by a supervisor;

(e) after the UK management has formulated proposals as to the arrangements for the ballot of the UK employees and before it has published the final arrangements under sub-paragraph (f) it must, so far as reasonably practicable, consult with the UK employees' representatives on the proposed arrangements for the ballot of the UK employees;

(f) the UK management must publish the final arrangements for the ballot of the UK employees in such manner as to bring them to the attention of, so far as reasonably practicable, the UK employees and the UK employees' representatives.

(4) Any UK employee or UK employees' representative who believes that the arrangements for the ballot of the UK employees are defective may, within a period of 21 days beginning on the date on which the UK management published the final arrangements under sub-paragraph (f), present a complaint to the CAC.

(5) Where the CAC finds the complaint well-founded it shall make a declaration to that effect and may make an order requiring the UK management to modify the arrangements it has made for the ballot of the UK employees or to satisfy the requirements in sub-paragraph (e) or (f) of paragraph (3).

(6) An order under paragraph (5) shall specify the modifications to the arrangements which the UK management is required to make and the requirements which it must satisfy.

(7) A person is an independent ballot supervisor for the purposes of paragraph (3)(d) if the UK management reasonably believes that he will carry out any functions conferred on him in relation to the ballot competently and has no reasonable grounds for believing that his independence in relation to the ballot might reasonably be called into question.

(8) For the purposes of paragraph (4) the arrangements for the ballot of the UK employees are defective if—

(a) any of the requirements specified in sub-paragraphs (b) to (f) of paragraph (3) is not satisfied; or

(b) in a case where the ballot is to comprise separate ballots, the constituencies determined by the UK management do not reflect adequately the interests of the UK employees as a whole.

[2589]

14 Conduct of ballot

(1) The UK management must—

(a) ensure that a ballot supervisor appointed under regulation 13(3)(d) carries out his functions under this regulation and that there is no interference with his carrying out of those functions from the UK management, or the central management (where it is not also the UK management); and

(b) comply with all reasonable requests made by a ballot supervisor for the purposes of, or in connection with, the carrying out of those functions.

(2) A ballot supervisor's appointment shall require that he—

(a) supervises the conduct of the ballot, or the separate ballots he is being appointed to supervise, in accordance with the arrangements for the ballot of the UK employees published by the UK management under regulation 13(3)(f) or, where appropriate, in accordance with the arrangements as required to be modified by an order made as a result of a complaint presented under regulation 13(4);

(b) does not conduct the ballot or any of the separate ballots before the UK management has satisfied the requirement specified in regulation 13(3)(e) and—

(i) where no complaint has been presented under regulation 13(4), before the expiry of a period of 21 days beginning on the date on which the UK management published its arrangements under regulation 13(3)(f); or

(ii) where a complaint has been presented under regulation 13(4), before the complaint has been determined and, where appropriate, the arrangements have been modified as required by an order made as a result of the complaint;

(c) conducts the ballot, or each separate ballot, so as to secure that—

(i) so far as reasonably practicable, those entitled to vote are given the opportunity to vote,

(ii) so far as reasonably practicable, those entitled to stand as candidates are given the opportunity to stand,

(iii) so far as is reasonably practicable, those voting are able to do so in secret, and

(iv) the votes given in the ballot are fairly and accurately counted.

(3) As soon as reasonably practicable after the holding of the ballot, the ballot supervisor must publish the results of the ballot in such manner as to make them available to the UK management and, so far as reasonably practicable, the UK employees entitled to vote in the ballot and the persons who stood as candidates in the ballot.

(4) A ballot supervisor shall publish a report ("an ineffective ballot report") where he considers (whether or not on the basis of representations made to him by another person) that—

(a) any of the requirements referred to in paragraph (2) was not satisfied with the result that the outcome of the ballot would have been different; or

(b) there was interference with the carrying out of his functions or a failure by management to comply with all reasonable requests made by him with the result that he was unable to form a proper judgment as to whether each of the requirements referred to in paragraph (2) was satisfied in relation to the ballot.

(5) Where a ballot supervisor publishes an ineffective ballot report the report must be published within a period of one month commencing on the date on which the ballot supervisor publishes the results of the ballot under paragraph (3).

(6) A ballot supervisor shall publish an ineffective ballot report in such manner as to make it available to the UK management and, so far as reasonably practicable, the UK employees entitled to vote in the ballot and the persons who stood as candidates in the ballot.

(7) Where a ballot supervisor publishes an ineffective ballot report then—

(a) if there has been a single ballot or an ineffective ballot report has been published in respect of every separate ballot, the outcome of the ballot or ballots shall have no effect and the UK management shall again be under the obligation in regulation 13(2);

(b) if there have been separate ballots and sub-paragraph (a) does not apply—

(i) the UK management shall arrange for the separate ballot or ballots in respect of which an ineffective ballot report was issued to be reheld in accordance with regulation 13 and this regulation, and

(ii) no such ballot shall have effect until it has been reheld and no ineffective ballot report has been published in respect of it.

(8) All costs relating to the holding of a ballot, including payments made to a ballot supervisor for supervising the conduct of the ballot, shall be borne by the central management (whether or not an ineffective ballot report has been made).

[2590]

15 Consultative Committee

(1) Where a consultative committee exists—

(a) no UK member of the special negotiating body shall be elected by a ballot of the UK employees, except in the circumstances specified in paragraphs (2), (3) or (9) below; and

(b) the committee shall be entitled to nominate from its number the UK members of the special negotiating body.

(2) Where the consultative committee fails to nominate any UK members of the special negotiating body, all of the UK members of the special negotiating body shall be elected by a ballot of the UK employees in accordance with regulations 13 and 14.

(3) Where the consultative committee nominates such number of persons to be a UK member, or UK members, of the special negotiating body, which number is less or more than the number of UK members of the special negotiating body required, the consultative committee shall be treated as having failed to have nominated any UK members of the special negotiating body.

(4) In this regulation, “a consultative committee” means a body of persons—

(a) whose normal functions include or comprise the carrying out of an information and consultation function;

(b) which is able to carry out its information and consultation function without interference from the UK management, or from the central management (where it is not also the UK management);

(c) which, in carrying out its information and consultation function, represents all the UK employees; and

(d) which consists wholly of persons who were elected by a ballot (which may have consisted of a number of separate ballots) in which all the employees who, at the time, were UK employees were entitled to vote.

(5) In paragraph (4) “information and consultation function” means the function of—

(a) receiving, on behalf of all the UK employees, information which may significantly affect the interests of the UK employees, but excluding information which is relevant only to a specific aspect of the interests of the employees, such as health and safety or collective redundancies; and

(b) being consulted by the UK management or the central management (where it is not also the UK management) on the information referred to in sub-paragraph (a) above.

(6) The consultative committee must publish the names of the persons whom it has nominated to be UK members of the special negotiating body in such manner as to bring them to the attention of the UK management and, so far as reasonably practicable, the UK employees and UK employees’ representatives.

(7) Where the UK management, a UK employee or a UK employees' representative believes that—

(a) the consultative committee does not satisfy the requirements in paragraph (4) above; or

(b) any of the persons nominated by the consultative committee is not entitled to be nominated,

it, or as the case may be he, may, within a period of 21 days beginning on the date on which the consultative committee published under paragraph (6) the names of persons nominated, present a complaint to the CAC.

(8) Where the CAC finds the complaint well-founded it shall make a declaration to that effect.

(9) Where the CAC has made a declaration under paragraph (8)—

(a) no nomination made by the consultative committee shall have effect; and

(b) all of the UK members of the special negotiating body shall be elected by a ballot of the UK employees in accordance with regulations 13 and 14.

(10) Where the consultative committee nominates any person to be a UK member of the special negotiating body, that nomination shall have effect after—

(a) where no complaint has been presented under paragraph (7), the expiry of a period of 21 days beginning on the date on which the consultative committee published under paragraph (6) the names of persons nominated; or

(b) where a complaint has been presented under paragraph (7), the complaint has been determined without a declaration under paragraph (8) having been made.

[2591]

PART IV
EUROPEAN WORKS COUNCIL AND INFORMATION AND CONSULTATION PROCEDURE

16 Negotiation procedure

(1) With a view to concluding an agreement referred to in regulation 17 the central management must convene a meeting with the special negotiating body and must inform local managements accordingly.

(2) Subject to paragraph (3), the special negotiating body shall take decisions by a majority of the votes cast by its members and each member of the special negotiating body is to have one vote.

(3) The special negotiating body may decide not to open negotiations with central management or to terminate negotiations. Any such decision must be taken by at least two thirds of the votes cast by its members.

(4) Any decision made under paragraph (3) shall have the following effects—

(a) the procedure to negotiate and conclude the agreement referred to in regulation 17 shall cease from the date of the decision; and

(b) a purported request made under regulation 9 less than two years after the date of the decision shall not be treated as such a request, unless the special negotiating body and the central management otherwise agree.

(5) For the purpose of the negotiations, the special negotiating body may be assisted by experts of its choice.

(6) The central management shall pay for any reasonable expenses relating to the negotiations that are necessary to enable the special negotiating body to carry out its functions in an appropriate manner; but where the special negotiating body is assisted by more than one expert the central management is not required to pay such expenses in respect of more than one of them.

[2592]

17 Content and scope of a European Works Council agreement and information and consultation procedure

(1) The central management and the special negotiating body are under a duty to negotiate in a spirit of cooperation with a view to reaching a written agreement on the detailed arrangements for the information and consultation of employees in a Community-scale undertaking or Community-scale group of undertakings.

(2) In this regulation and regulations 18 and 20, the central management and the special negotiating body are referred to as "the parties".

(3) The parties may decide in writing to establish an information and consultation procedure instead of a European Works Council.

(4) Without prejudice to the autonomy of the parties, where the parties decide to proceed with the establishment of a European Works Council, the agreement establishing it shall determine—

(a) the undertakings of the Community-scale group of undertakings or the establishments of the Community-scale undertaking which are covered by the agreement;

(b) the composition of the European Works Council, the number of members, the allocation of seats and the term of office of the members;

(c) the functions and the procedure for information and consultation of the European Works Council;

(d) the venue, frequency and duration of meetings of the European Works Council;

(e) the financial and material resources to be allocated to the European Works Council; and

(f) the duration of the agreement and the procedure for its renegotiation.

(5) If the parties decide to establish an information and consultation procedure instead of a European Works Council—

(a) the agreement establishing the procedure must specify a method by which the information and consultation representatives are to enjoy the right to meet to discuss the information conveyed to them; and

(b) the information conveyed to the information and consultation representatives shall relate in particular to transnational questions which significantly affect the interests of the employees.

(6) An agreement referred to in paragraph (4) or (5) is not to be subject to the provisions of the Schedule, except to the extent that the parties provide in the agreement that any of those requirements are to apply.

(7) Where a Community-scale group of undertakings comprises one or more undertakings or groups of undertakings which are themselves Community-scale undertakings or Community-scale groups of undertakings, the European Works Council shall be established at the level of the first-mentioned Community-scale group of undertakings, unless an agreement referred to in paragraph (4) provides otherwise.

(8) Unless a wider scope is provided for in an agreement referred to in paragraph (1), the powers and competence of a European Works Council and the scope of an information and consultation procedure shall, in the case of a Community-scale undertaking, cover all the establishments located within the Member States and, in the case of a Community-scale group of undertakings, all group undertakings located within the Member States.

[2593]

18 Subsidiary requirements

(1) The provisions of the Schedule shall apply if—

(a) the parties so agree;

(b) within the period of six months beginning on the date on which a valid request referred to in regulation 9 was made, the central management refuses to commence negotiations; or

(c) after the expiry of a period of three years beginning on the date on which a valid request referred to in regulation 9 was made, the parties have failed to conclude an agreement under regulation 17 and the special negotiating body has not taken the decision under regulation 16(3).

[2594]

19 Cooperation

(1) The central management and the European Works Council are under a duty to work in a spirit of cooperation with due regard to their reciprocal rights and obligations.

(2) The duty in paragraph (1) shall apply also to the central management and information and consultation representatives.

[2595]

PART V
COMPLIANCE AND ENFORCEMENT

20 Failure to establish European Works Council or information and consultation procedure

(1) A complaint may be presented to the Appeal Tribunal by a relevant applicant who considers—

(a) that the parties have reached agreement on the establishment of a European Works Council or an information and consultation procedure, or that regulation 18 applies; and

(b) that, because of a failure of the central management, the European Works Council or information and consultation procedure has not been established at all, or has not been established fully in accordance with the terms of the agreement under regulation 17 or, as the case may be, in accordance with the provisions of the Schedule.

(2) In this regulation "failure" means an act or omission and a failure by the local management shall be treated as a failure by the central management.

(3) In this regulation "relevant applicant" means—

(a) in a case where a special negotiating body exists, the special negotiating body; or

(b) in a case where a special negotiating body does not exist, an employee, employees' representative, or person who was a member of the special negotiating body (if that body existed previously).

(4) Where the Appeal Tribunal finds the complaint well-founded it shall make a decision to that effect and may make an order requiring the central management to take such steps as are necessary to establish the European Works Council or information and consultation procedure in accordance with the terms of the agreement under regulation 17 or, as the case may be, to establish a European Works Council in accordance with the provisions of the Schedule.

(5) The Appeal Tribunal shall not find a complaint under this regulation to be well-founded where—

(a) the central management made no application in relation to the request under regulation 10(1), or where the request consisted of separate requests was unable by reason of the time limit in sub-paragraph (a) of that regulation to make an application under the regulation in relation to a particular request, and shows that the request was not a valid request because a requirement of regulation 9(2) or (3) was not satisfied; or

(b) the central management made no application under regulation 10(3) but shows that the obligation in regulation 9(1) did not, for any reason, apply to it on the relevant date.

(6) An order under paragraph (4) shall specify—

(a) the steps which the central management is required to take;

(b) the date of the failure of the central management; and

(c) the period within which the order must be complied with.

(7) If the Appeal Tribunal makes a decision under paragraph (4) above it shall issue a written penalty notice to the central management requiring it to pay a penalty to the Secretary of State in respect of the failure.

(8) Paragraph (7) shall not apply if the Appeal Tribunal is satisfied, on hearing the representations of the central management, that the failure resulted from a reason beyond the central management's control or that it has some other reasonable excuse for its failure.

(9) Regulation 22 shall apply in respect of a penalty notice issued under this regulation.

(10) No order of the Appeal Tribunal under this regulation shall have the effect of suspending or altering the effect of any act done or of any agreement made by the central management or the local management.

[2596]

21 Disputes about operation of European Works Council or information and consultation procedure

(1) Where—

(a) a European Works Council or information and consultation procedure has been established under regulation 17; or

(b) a European Works Council has been established by virtue of regulation 18,

a complaint may be presented to the Appeal Tribunal by a relevant applicant who considers that, because of the failure of a defaulter, the terms of the agreement under regulation 17 or, as the case may be, the provisions of the Schedule, have not been complied with.

(2) In this regulation, "failure" means an act or omission and a failure by the local management shall be treated as a failure by the central management.

(3) In this regulation "relevant applicant" means—

(a) in the case of a failure concerning a European Works Council, either the central management or the European Works Council; or

(b) in the case of a failure concerning an information and consultation procedure, either the central management or any one or more of the information and consultation representatives,

and "defaulter" means the persons mentioned in sub-paragraph (a) or (b) against whom the complaint is presented.

(4) Where the Appeal Tribunal finds the complaint well-founded it shall make a decision to that effect and may make an order requiring the defaulter to take such steps as are necessary to comply with the terms of the agreement under regulation 17 or, as the case may be, the provisions of the Schedule.

(5) An order made under paragraph (4) shall specify—

(a) the steps which the defaulter is required to take;

(b) the date of the failure; and

(c) the period within which the order must be complied with.

(6) If the Appeal Tribunal makes a decision under paragraph (4) and the defaulter in question is the central management, the Appeal Tribunal shall issue a written penalty notice to the central management requiring it to pay a penalty to the Secretary of State in respect of the failure.

(7) Paragraph (6) shall not apply if the Appeal Tribunal is satisfied, on hearing the representations of the central management, that the failure resulted from a reason beyond the central management's control or that it has some other reasonable excuse for its failure.

(8) Regulation 22 shall apply in respect of a penalty notice issued under this regulation.

(9) No order of the Appeal Tribunal under this regulation shall have the effect of suspending or altering the effect of any act done or of any agreement made by the central management or the local management.

[2597]

22 Penalties

(1) A penalty notice issued under regulation 20 or 21 shall specify—

(a) the amount of the penalty which is payable;

(b) the date before which the penalty must be paid; and

(c) the failure and period to which the penalty relates.

(2) No penalty set by the Appeal Tribunal under this regulation may exceed £75,000.

(3) When setting the amount of the penalty, the Appeal Tribunal shall take into account—

(a) the gravity of the failure;

(b) the period of time over which the failure occurred;

(c) the reason for the failure;

(d) the number of employees affected by the failure; and

(e) the number of employees of the Community-scale undertaking or Community-scale group of undertakings in the Member States.

(4) The date specified under paragraph (1)(b) above must not be earlier than the end of the period within which an appeal against a decision or order made by the Appeal Tribunal under regulation 20 or 21 may be made.

(5) If the specified date in a penalty notice has passed and—

(a) the period during which an appeal may be made has expired without an appeal having been made; or

(b) such an appeal has been made and determined,

the Secretary of State may recover from the central management, as a civil debt due to him, any amount payable under the penalty notice which remains outstanding.

(6) The making of an appeal suspends the effect of a penalty notice.

(7) Any sums received by the Secretary of State under regulation 20 or 21 or this regulation shall be paid into the Consolidated Fund.

[2598]

PART VI
CONFIDENTIAL INFORMATION

23 Breach of statutory duty

(1) A person who is or at any time was—

(a) a member of a special negotiating body or a European Works Council;

(b) an information and consultation representative; or

(c) an expert assisting a special negotiating body, a European Works Council or its select committee, or information and consultation representatives,

shall not disclose any information or document which is or has been in his possession by virtue of his position as described in sub-paragraph (a), (b) or (c) of this paragraph, which the central management has entrusted to him on terms requiring it to be held in confidence.

(2) In this regulation and in regulation 24, a person specified in paragraph (1)(a), (b) or (c) of this regulation is referred to as a "recipient".

(3) The obligation to comply with paragraph (1) is a duty owed to the central management, and a breach of the duty is actionable accordingly (subject to the defences and other incidents applying to actions for breach of statutory duty).

(4) Paragraph (3) shall not affect the liability which any person may incur, nor affect any right which any person may have, apart from paragraph (3).

(5) No action shall lie under paragraph (3) where the recipient reasonably believed the disclosure to be a "protected disclosure" within the meaning given to that expression by section 43A of the 1996 Act or, as the case may be, Article 67A of the 1996 Order.

(6) A recipient whom the central management (which is situated in the United Kingdom) has entrusted with any information or document on terms requiring it to be held in confidence may apply to the CAC for a declaration as to whether it was reasonable for the central management to impose such a requirement.

(7) If the CAC considers that the disclosure of the information or document by the recipient would not, or would not be likely to, prejudice or cause serious harm to the undertaking, it shall make a declaration that it was not reasonable for the central management to require the recipient to hold the information or document in confidence.

(8) If a declaration is made under paragraph (7), the information or document shall not at any time thereafter be regarded as having been entrusted to the recipient who made the application under paragraph (6), or to any other recipient, on terms requiring it to be held in confidence.

[2599]

24 Withholding of information by central management

(1) The central management is not required to disclose any information or document to a recipient when the nature of the information or document is such that, according to objective criteria, the disclosure of the information or document would seriously harm the functioning of, or would be prejudicial to, the undertaking or group of undertakings concerned.

(2) Where there is a dispute between the central management and a recipient as to whether the nature of the information or document which the central management has failed to provide is such as is described in paragraph (1), the central management or a recipient may apply to the CAC for a declaration as to whether the information or document is of such a nature.

(3) If the CAC makes a declaration that the disclosure of the information or document in question would not, according to objective criteria, seriously harm the functioning of, or be

prejudicial to, the undertaking or group of undertakings concerned, the CAC shall order the central management to disclose the information or document.

(4) An order under paragraph (3) above shall specify—

(a) the information or document to be disclosed;

(b) the recipient or recipients to whom the information or document is to be disclosed;

(c) any terms on which the information or document is to be disclosed; and

(d) the date before which the information or document is to be disclosed.

[2600]

PART VII

PROTECTIONS FOR MEMBERS OF A EUROPEAN WORKS COUNCIL, ETC

25 Right to time off for members of a European Works Council, etc

(1) An employee who is—

(a) a member of a special negotiating body;

(b) a member of a European Works Council;

(c) an information and consultation representative; or

(d) a candidate in an election in which any person elected will, on being elected, be such a member or representative,

is entitled to be permitted by his employer to take reasonable time off during the employee's working hours in order to perform his functions as such a member, representative or candidate.

(2) For the purposes of this regulation the working hours of an employee shall be taken to be any time when, in accordance with his contract of employment, the employee is required to be at work.

[2601]

26 Right to remuneration for time off under regulation 25

(1) An employee who is permitted to take time off under regulation 25 is entitled to be paid remuneration by his employer for the time taken off at the appropriate hourly rate.

(2) Chapter II of Part XIV of the 1996 Act (a week's pay) and, in relation to Northern Ireland, Chapter IV of Part I of the 1996 Order shall apply in relation to this regulation as they apply, respectively, in relation to section 62 of the 1996 Act and Article 90 of the 1996 Order.

(3) The appropriate hourly rate, in relation to an employee, is the amount of one week's pay divided by the number of normal working hours in a week for that employee when employed under the contract of employment in force on the day when the time is taken.

(4) But where the number of normal working hours differs from week to week or over a longer period, the amount of one week's pay shall be divided instead by—

(a) the average number of normal working hours calculated by dividing by twelve the total number of the employee's normal working hours during the period of twelve weeks ending with the last complete week before the day on which the time off is taken; or

(b) where the employee has not been employed for a sufficient period to enable the calculation to be made under sub-paragraph (a), a number which fairly represents the number of normal working hours in a week having regard to such of the considerations specified in paragraph (5) as are appropriate in the circumstances.

(5) The considerations referred to in paragraph (4)(b) are—

(a) the average number of normal working hours in a week which the employee could expect in accordance with the terms of his contract; and

(b) the average number of normal working hours of other employees engaged in relevant comparable employment with the same employer.

(6) A right to any amount under paragraph (1) does not affect any right of an employee in relation to remuneration under his contract of employment ("contractual remuneration").

(7) Any contractual remuneration paid to an employee in respect of a period of time off under regulation 25 goes towards discharging any liability of the employer to pay remuneration under paragraph (1) in respect of that period, and, conversely, any payment of

remuneration under paragraph (1) in respect of a period goes towards discharging any liability of the employer to pay contractual remuneration in respect of that period.

[2602]

27 Right to time off: complaints to tribunals

(1) An employee may present a complaint, in Great Britain to an employment tribunal and in Northern Ireland to an industrial tribunal, that his employer—

(a) has unreasonably refused to permit him to take time off as required by regulation 25; or

(b) has failed to pay the whole or any part of any amount to which the employee is entitled under regulation 26.

(2) A tribunal shall not consider a complaint under this regulation unless it is presented—

(a) before the end of the period of three months beginning with the day on which the time off was taken or on which it is alleged the time off should have been permitted; or

(b) within such further period as the tribunal considers reasonable in a case where it is satisfied that it was not reasonably practicable for the complaint to be presented before the end of that period of three months.

(3) Where a tribunal finds a complaint under this regulation well-founded, the tribunal shall make a declaration to that effect.

(4) If the complaint is that the employer has unreasonably refused to permit the employee to take time off, the tribunal shall also order the employer to pay to the employee an amount equal to the remuneration to which he would have been entitled under regulation 26 if the employer had not refused.

(5) If the complaint is that the employer has failed to pay the employee the whole or part of any amount to which he is entitled under regulation 26, the tribunal shall also order the employer to pay to the employee the amount which it finds due to him.

[2603]

NOTES

Conciliation: employment tribunal proceedings and claims which could be the subject of employment tribunal proceedings under this regulation are proceedings to which the Employment Tribunals Act 1996, s 18 applies; see s 18(1)(g) of that Act at **[975]**. The standard conciliation period applies to such proceedings by virtue of the Employment Tribunals (Constitution and Rules of Procedure) Regulations 2004, SI 2004/1861, Sch 1, rule 22(1), (6).

28 Unfair dismissal

(1) An employee who is dismissed and to whom paragraph (2) or (5) applies shall be regarded, if the reason (or, if more than one, the principal reason) for the dismissal is a reason specified in, respectively, paragraph (3) or (6), as unfairly dismissed for the purposes of Part X of the 1996 Act and of Part XI of the 1996 Order.

(2) This paragraph applies to an employee who is—

(a) a member of a special negotiating body;

(b) a member of a European Works Council;

(c) an information and consultation representative; or

(d) a candidate in an election in which any person elected will, on being elected, be such a member or representative.

(3) The reason is that—

(a) the employee performed any functions or activities as such a member, representative or candidate; or

(b) the employee or a person acting on his behalf made a request to exercise an entitlement conferred on the employee by regulation 25 or 26;

or proposed to do so.

(4) The reason in paragraph (3)(a) does not apply where the reason (or principal reason) for the dismissal is that in the performance, or purported performance, of the employee's functions or activities he has disclosed any information or document in breach of the duty in regulation 23(1), unless the employee reasonably believed the disclosure to be a "protected

disclosure" within the meaning given to that expression by section 43A of the 1996 Act or, as the case may be, by Article 67A of the 1996 Order.

(5) This paragraph applies to any employee whether or not he is an employee to whom paragraph (2) applies.

(6) The reasons are that the employee—

(a) took, or proposed to take, any proceedings before an employment tribunal or industrial tribunal to enforce a right or secure an entitlement conferred on him by these Regulations;

(b) exercised, or proposed to exercise, any entitlement to apply or complain to the Appeal Tribunal or the CAC, or in Northern Ireland the Industrial Court, conferred by these Regulations;

(c) requested, or proposed to request, information in accordance with regulation 7;

(d) acted with a view to securing that a special negotiating body, a European Works Council or an information and consultation procedure did or did not come into existence;

(e) indicated that he supported or did not support the coming into existence of a special negotiating body, a European Works Council or an information and consultation procedure;

(f) stood as a candidate in an election in which any person elected would, on being elected, be a member of a special negotiating body or of a European Works Council or an information and consultation representative;

(g) influenced or sought to influence the way in which votes were to be cast by other employees in a ballot arranged under these Regulations;

(h) voted in such a ballot;

(i) expressed doubts, whether to a ballot supervisor or otherwise, as to whether such a ballot had been properly conducted; or

(j) proposed to do, failed to do, or proposed to decline to do, any of the things mentioned in sub-paragraphs (d) to (i).

(7) It is immaterial for the purposes of paragraph (6)(a)—

(a) whether or not the employee has the right; or

(b) whether or not the right has been infringed;

but for that paragraph to apply, the claim to the right and, if applicable, the claim that it has been infringed must be made in good faith.

[2604]

29, 30 (*Reg 29 amends the Employment Rights Act 1996, ss 105, 108 at* **[1149]**, **[1152]**, *and amended s 109 (repealed); reg 30 applies to Northern Ireland and is outside the scope of this work.*)

31 Detriment

(1) An employee to whom paragraph (2) or (5) applies has the right not to be subjected to any detriment by any act, or deliberate failure to act, by his employer, done on a ground specified in, respectively, paragraph (3) or (6).

(2) This paragraph applies to an employee who is—

(a) a member of a special negotiating body;

(b) a member of a European Works Council;

(c) an information and consultation representative; or

(d) a candidate in an election in which any person elected will, on being elected, be such a member or representative.

(3) The ground is that—

(a) the employee performed any functions or activities as such a member, representative or candidate; or

(b) the employee or a person acting on his behalf made a request to exercise an entitlement conferred on the employee by regulation 25 or 26;

or proposed to do so.

(4) The ground in paragraph (3)(a) does not apply where the ground for the subjection to detriment is that in the performance, or purported performance, of the employee's functions or activities he has disclosed any information or document in breach of the duty in regulation 23(1), unless the employee reasonably believed the disclosure to be a "protected

disclosure" within the meaning given to that expression by section 43A of the 1996 Act or, as the case may be, Article 67A of the 1996 Order.

(5) This paragraph applies to any employee, whether or not he is an employee to whom paragraph (2) applies.

(6) The grounds are that the employee—

(a) took, or proposed to take, any proceedings before an employment tribunal or industrial tribunal to enforce a right or secure an entitlement conferred on him by these Regulations;

(b) exercised, or proposed to exercise, any entitlement to apply or complain to the Appeal Tribunal, the CAC, or in Northern Ireland the Industrial Court, conferred by these Regulations;

(c) requested, or proposed to request, information in accordance with regulation 7;

(d) acted with a view to securing that a special negotiating body, a European Works Council or an information and consultation procedure did or did not come into existence;

(e) indicated that he supported or did not support the coming into existence of a special negotiating body, a European Works Council or an information and consultation procedure;

(f) stood as a candidate in an election in which any person elected would, on being elected, be a member of a special negotiating body or of a European Works Council or an information and consultation representative;

(g) influenced or sought to influence the way in which votes were to be cast by other employees in a ballot arranged under these Regulations;

(h) voted in such a ballot;

(i) expressed doubts, whether to a ballot supervisor or otherwise, as to whether such a ballot had been properly conducted; or

(j) proposed to do, failed to do, or proposed to decline to do, any of the things mentioned in sub-paragraphs (d) to (i).

(7) It is immaterial for the purposes of paragraph (6)(a)—

(a) whether or not the employee has the right; or

(b) whether or not the right has been infringed;

but for that paragraph to apply, the claim to the right and, if applicable, the claim that it has been infringed must be made in good faith.

[2605]

32 Detriment: enforcement and subsidiary provisions

(1) An employee may present a complaint, in Great Britain to an employment tribunal and in Northern Ireland to an industrial tribunal, that he has been subjected to a detriment in contravention of regulation 31.

(2) The provisions of—

(a) sections 48(2) to (4) and 49 of the 1996 Act (complaints to employment tribunals and remedies); or

(b) in relation to Northern Ireland, Articles 71(2) to (4) and 72 of the 1996 Order (complaints to industrial tribunals and remedies);

shall apply in relation to a complaint under this regulation as they apply in relation to a complaint under section 48 of that Act or Article 71 of that Order (as the case may be), but taking references in those provisions to the employer as references to the employer within the meaning of regulation 31(1) above.

(3) Regulation 31 does not apply where the detriment in question amounts to dismissal.

[2606]

NOTES

Conciliation: employment tribunal proceedings and claims which could be the subject of employment tribunal proceedings under this regulation are proceedings to which the Employment Tribunals Act 1996, s 18 applies; see s 18(1)(g) of that Act at **[975]**. The standard conciliation period applies to such proceedings by virtue of the Employment Tribunals (Constitution and Rules of Procedure) Regulations 2004, SI 2004/1861, Sch 1, rule 22(1), (6).

Tribunal jurisdiction: the Employment Act 2002, ss 31, 32, 38, at **[1493]**, **[1494]**, **[1496]** apply to proceedings before the employment tribunal relating to a claim under this regulation; see ss 31(1), 32(1), 38(1) of, and Schs 3–5 to, the 2002 Act at **[1508]**–**[1510]**.

For the circumstances in which the normal time limit for presenting a complaint under this regulation is extended for a period of three months, see the Employment Act 2002 (Dispute Resolution) Regulations 2004, SI 2004/752, regs 15 and 18 at **[3096]** and **[3098]**.

33 (*Para (1) amends the Employment Tribunals Act 1996, s 18 at* **[975]**; *para (2) applies to Northern Ireland and is outside the scope of this work.*)

PART VIII
MISCELLANEOUS

The Appeal Tribunal, Industrial Court, CAC, ACAS and the Labour Relations Agency

34 Appeal Tribunal: jurisdiction

(1) Any proceedings before the Appeal Tribunal arising under these Regulations, other than proceedings before the Appeal Tribunal under paragraph (i) of section 21(1) of the Employment Tribunals Act 1996, shall—

(a) where the central management is situated in England and Wales, be in England and Wales;

(b) where the central management is situated in Scotland, be in Scotland.

(2) Paragraph (1) shall apply to proceedings before the Appeal Tribunal arising under regulation 8 as if for the words "central management" there were substituted the words "recipient (within the meaning given to that term by regulation 7)".

(3) Paragraph (1) shall apply to proceedings before the Appeal Tribunal arising under regulation 13 or 15 or paragraph 4 of the Schedule as if for the words "central management" there were substituted the words "UK management".

[2607]

35 (*Amends the Employment Tribunals Act 1996, ss 20, 21, 30 at* **[977]**, **[978]**, **[987]**.)

36 Industrial Court: jurisdiction

(1) Where the central management is situated in Northern Ireland, any complaint under regulation 20 or 21 shall be presented to the Industrial Court instead of to the Appeal Tribunal and references in those regulations and in regulation 22 to the Appeal Tribunal shall be read as references to the Industrial Court.

(2) Where the central management is situated in Northern Ireland, any application under regulation 10, 23 or 24 shall be made to the Industrial Court instead of to the CAC, and references in those regulations to the CAC shall be read as references to the Industrial Court.

(3) Where the recipient (within the meaning given to that term by regulation 7) is situated in Northern Ireland, any complaint under regulation 8 shall be presented to the Industrial Court instead of to the CAC, and references in regulation 8 to the CAC shall be read as references to the Industrial Court.

(4) Where the UK management is situated in Northern Ireland, any complaint under regulation 13 or 15 or paragraph 4 of the Schedule shall be presented to the Industrial Court instead of to the CAC, and references in those regulations or that paragraph to the CAC shall be read as references to the Industrial Court.

[2608]

37 Industrial Court: proceedings

(1) Where under these Regulations a person presents a complaint or makes an application to the Industrial Court, the complaint or application must be in writing and in such form as the Court may require.

(2) In its consideration of an application or complaint under these Regulations, the Industrial Court shall make such enquiries as it sees fit and give any person whom it considers has a proper interest in the application or complaint an opportunity to be heard.

(3) A decision, declaration or order made by the Industrial Court under these Regulations—

(a) must be in writing and state the reasons for the Court's findings; and

(b) may be relied on and enforced as if it were a decision, declaration or order made by the High Court in Northern Ireland.

(4) An appeal lies to the Court of Appeal in Northern Ireland on any question of law arising from a decision, declaration or order of, or arising in any proceedings before, the Industrial Court under these Regulations.

[2609]

38 CAC: proceedings

(1) Where under these Regulations a person presents a complaint or makes an application to the CAC the complaint or application must be in writing and in such form as the CAC may require.

(2) In its consideration of an application or complaint under these Regulations, the CAC shall make such enquiries as it sees fit and give any person whom it considers has a proper interest in the application or complaint an opportunity to be heard.

(3) Where the central management is situated in England and Wales—

(a) a declaration or order made by the CAC under these Regulations may be relied on as if it were a declaration or order made by the High Court in England and Wales; and

(b) an order made by the CAC under these Regulations may be enforced in the same way as an order of the High Court in England and Wales.

(4) Where the central management is situated in Scotland—

(a) a declaration or order made by the CAC under these Regulations may be relied on as if it were a declaration or order made by the Court of Session; and

(b) an order made by the CAC under these Regulations may be enforced in the same way as an order of the Court of Session.

(5) Paragraphs (3) and (4) shall apply to an order made under regulation 8 as if for the words "central management" there were substituted the word "recipient".

(6) Paragraphs (3) and (4) shall apply, as appropriate, to a declaration or order made under regulation 13 or 15 or paragraph 4 of the Schedule as if for the words "central management" there were substituted the words "UK management".

(7) A declaration or order made by the CAC under these Regulations must be in writing and state the reasons for the CAC's findings.

(8) An appeal lies to the Appeal Tribunal on any question of law arising from any declaration or order of, or arising in any proceedings before, the CAC under these Regulations.

[2610]

39 ACAS and the Labour Relations Agency

(1) If on receipt of an application or complaint under these Regulations the CAC, the Appeal Tribunal, or as the case may be the Industrial Court, is of the opinion that it is reasonably likely to be settled by conciliation, it shall refer the application or complaint to ACAS or to the Labour Relations Agency and shall notify the applicant or complainant and any persons whom it considers have a proper interest in the application or complaint accordingly, whereupon ACAS, or as the case may be the Labour Relations Agency, shall seek to promote a settlement of the matter.

(2) If an application or complaint so referred is not settled or withdrawn and ACAS, or as the case may be the Labour Relations Agency, is of the opinion that further attempts at conciliation are unlikely to result in a settlement, it shall inform the CAC, the Appeal Tribunal, or as the case may be the Industrial Court, of its opinion.

(3) If the application or complaint is not referred to ACAS or to the Labour Relations Agency, or if it is so referred, on ACAS, or as the case may be the Labour Relations Agency, informing the CAC, the Appeal Tribunal, or as the case may be the Industrial Court, of its opinion that further attempts at conciliation are unlikely to result in a settlement, the CAC, the Appeal Tribunal, or as the case may be the Industrial Court, shall proceed to hear and determine the application or complaint.

[2611]

Restrictions on contracting out

40 Restrictions on contracting out: general

(1) Any provision in any agreement (whether an employee's contract or not) is void in so far as it purports—

(a) to exclude or limit the operation of any provision of these Regulations other than a provision of Part VII; or

(b) to preclude a person from bringing any proceedings before the Appeal Tribunal or the CAC, or in Northern Ireland the Industrial Court, under any provision of these Regulations other than a provision of Part VII.

(2) Paragraph (1) does not apply to any agreement to refrain from continuing any proceedings referred to in sub-paragraph (b) of that paragraph made after the proceedings have been instituted.

[2612]

41 Restrictions on contracting out: Part VII

(1) Any provision in any agreement (whether an employee's contract or not) is void in so far as it purports—

(a) to exclude or limit the operation of any provision of Part VII of these Regulations; or

(b) to preclude a person from bringing any proceedings before an employment tribunal, or in Northern Ireland an industrial tribunal, under that Part.

(2) Paragraph (1) does not apply to any agreement to refrain from instituting or continuing proceedings before an employment tribunal or, in Northern Ireland, an industrial tribunal where—

(a) a conciliation officer has taken action under section 18 of the Employment Tribunals Act 1996 (conciliation); or

(b) in relation to Northern Ireland, the Labour Relations Agency has taken action under Article 20 of the Industrial Tribunals (Northern Ireland) Order 1996 (conciliation).

(3) Paragraph (1) does not apply to any agreement to refrain from instituting or continuing before an employment tribunal, or in Northern Ireland an industrial tribunal, proceedings within—

(a) section 18(1)(g) of the Employment Tribunals Act 1996 (proceedings under these Regulations where conciliation is available); or

(b) in relation to Northern Ireland, Article 20(1)(g) of the Industrial Tribunals (Northern Ireland) Order 1996,

if the conditions regulating compromise agreements under these Regulations are satisfied in relation to the agreement.

(4) For the purposes of paragraph (3) the conditions regulating compromise agreements are that—

(a) the agreement must be in writing;

(b) the agreement must relate to the particular proceedings;

(c) the employee must have received advice from a relevant independent adviser as to the terms and effect of the proposed agreement and, in particular, its effect on his ability to pursue his rights before an employment tribunal or, in Northern Ireland, an industrial tribunal;

(d) there must be in force, when the adviser gives the advice, a contract of insurance, or an indemnity provided for members of a profession or professional body, covering the risk of a claim by the employee in respect of loss arising in consequence of the advice;

(e) the agreement must identify the adviser; and

(f) the agreement must state that the conditions in sub-paragraphs (a) to (e) are satisfied.

(5) A person is a relevant independent adviser for the purposes of paragraph (4)(c)—

(a) if he is a qualified lawyer;

(b) if he is an officer, official, employee or member of an independent trade union who has been certified in writing by the trade union as competent to give advice and as authorised to do so on behalf of the trade union; or

(c) if he works at an advice centre (whether as an employee or as a volunteer) and has been certified in writing by the centre as competent to give advice and as authorised to do so on behalf of the centre.

(6) But a person is not a relevant independent adviser for the purposes of paragraph (4)(c) in relation to the employee—

(a) if he is, is employed by or is acting in the matter for the employer or an associated employer;

(b) in the case of a person within paragraph (5)(b) or (c), if the trade union or advice centre is the employer or an associated employer; or

(c) in the case of a person within paragraph (5)(c), if the employee makes a payment for the advice received from him.

(7) In paragraph (5)(a), "qualified lawyer" means—

(a) as respects England and Wales, a barrister (whether in practice as such or employed to give legal advice), a solicitor who holds a practising certificate, or a person other than a barrister or solicitor who is an authorised advocate or authorised litigator (within the meaning of the Courts and Legal Services Act 1990);

(b) as respects Scotland, an advocate (whether in practice as such or employed to give legal advice) or a solicitor who holds a practising certificate; and

(c) as respects Northern Ireland, a barrister (whether in practice as such or employed to give legal advice) or a solicitor who holds a practising certificate.

[(7A) A person shall be treated as being a qualified lawyer within paragraph (7)(a) if he is a Fellow of the Institute of Legal Executives employed by a solicitors' practice.]

(8) For the purposes of paragraph (6) any two employers shall be treated as associated if—

(a) one is a company of which the other (directly or indirectly) has control; or

(b) both are companies of which a third person (directly or indirectly) has control;

and "associated employer" shall be construed accordingly.

[2613]

NOTES

Para (7A): inserted by the Transnational Information and Consultation of Employees Regulations 1999 (Amendment) Regulations 2004, SI 2004/2518, reg 2, as from 1 October 2004.

PART IX
EXCEPTIONS

42 Article 6 agreements

(1) Where, in accordance with regulation 5, the central management is situated in the United Kingdom and, immediately before the date on which these Regulations come into force an Article 6 agreement is in force, those provisions referred to in regulation 4(1) which apply only where the central management is situated in the United Kingdom shall only apply if—

(a) the parties to the Article 6 agreement agree or have agreed (whether before or after these Regulations come into force) to the effect that the provisions of these Regulations which would have applied in respect of the agreement had it been made under regulation 17 should apply in respect of the Article 6 agreement; or

(b) the Article 6 agreement ceases to have effect.

(2) In paragraph (1) and regulation 47 "Article 6 agreement" means an agreement for the establishment of a European Works Council or information and consultation procedure made under the provisions of the law or practice of a Member State other than the United Kingdom which are designed to give effect to Article 6 of the Transnational Information and Consultation Directive.

(3) Where paragraph (1)(a) applies these Regulations shall apply as if the Article 6 agreement had been made under regulation 17.

[2614]

43 Article 7 European Works Councils

(1) Where, in accordance with regulation 5, the central management is situated in the United Kingdom, and immediately before the date these Regulations come into force an

Article 7 European Works Council exists, those provisions referred to in regulation 4(1) which apply only where the central management is situated in the United Kingdom shall only apply if—

(a) the central management and European Works Council agree or have agreed (whether before or after these Regulations come into force) to the effect that the provisions of these Regulations which would have applied in respect of the European Works Council had it been made, by virtue of regulation 18, under these Regulations should apply in respect of the Article 7 European Works Council; or

(b) the European Works Council decides, under the provisions of the law or practice of a Member State other than the United Kingdom which are designed to give effect to paragraph 1(f) of the Annex to the Transnational Information and Consultation Directive, to negotiate an agreement for a European Works Council or an information and consultation procedure.

(2) In paragraph (1) and regulations 47 and 48 "Article 7 European Works Council" means a European Works Council established under the provisions of the law or practice of a Member State other than the United Kingdom which are designed to give effect to Article 7 of, and the Annex to, the Transnational Information and Consultation Directive.

(3) Where paragraph (1)(a) or (b) applies these Regulations shall apply, subject to the modifications referred to in paragraphs (4) to (6) of regulation 48, as if the Article 7 European Works Council had been established, by virtue of regulation 18, under these Regulations and, in a case where paragraph (1)(b) applies, as if a decision had been taken under paragraph 10(2) of the Schedule.

[2615]

44 Article 3 agreements

(1) None of the obligations in these Regulations applies to a Community-scale undertaking or Community-scale group of undertakings where the conditions specified in Article 3 of the Extension Directive are satisfied.

(2) The conditions referred to in paragraph (1) above are that—

(a) an agreement is in force which—

(i) is in force immediately before 16th December 1999;

(ii) covers the entire workforce in the Member States; and

(iii) provides for the transnational information and consultation of employees, and

(b) the obligation (whether arising under these Regulations or under the national law or practice of any other Member State), to initiate negotiations for the establishment of a European Works Council or information and consultation procedure would, but for this paragraph, have applied to the Community-scale undertaking or Community-scale group of undertakings solely as a result of the Extension Directive.

(3) If an agreement when taken together with one or more other agreements satisfies the requirements specified in paragraph (2)(a) that agreement, when taken together with such other agreements, shall be treated as an agreement for the purposes of that paragraph.

[2616]

45 Article 13 agreements

(1) None of the obligations in these Regulations applies to a Community-scale undertaking or Community-scale group of undertakings where the conditions specified in Article 13 of the Transnational Information and Consultation Directive are satisfied.

(2) The conditions referred to in paragraph (1) are that an agreement is in force which—

(a) was in force immediately before whichever is the earlier of 23rd September 1996 and the day after the date on which the national law or practice giving effect to the Transnational Information and Consultation Directive came into force in the Member State (other than the United Kingdom) whose national law governs the agreement;

(b) covers the entire workforce in the Member States; and

(c) provides for the transnational information and consultation of employees.

(3) If an agreement when taken together with one or more other agreements satisfies the requirements specified in paragraph (2) that agreement, when taken together with such other agreements, shall be treated as an agreement for the purposes of that paragraph.

[2617]

46 Merchant Navy

(1) Subject to paragraph (3), no long haul crew member shall be—

(a) a member of a special negotiating body;

(b) a member of a European Works Council; or

(c) an information and consultation representative.

(2) In paragraph (1), a "long haul crew member" means a person who is a member of a merchant navy crew other than—

(a) a ferry worker; or

(b) a person who normally works on voyages the duration of which is less than 48 hours.

(3) Paragraph (1) shall not apply where the central management decides that the long haul crew member in question shall be permitted to be, as the case may be, a member of a special negotiating body or of a European Works Council, or an information and consultation representative.

(4) Where paragraph (1) applies, no long haul crew member shall—

(a) stand as a candidate for election as a member of a special negotiating body or of a European Works Council, or as an information and consultation representative; or

(b) be appointed or nominated to be a member of a special negotiating body or of a European Works Council, or an information and consultation representative.

[2618]

[46A—(1) These regulations do not apply to an SE that is—

(a) a Community-scale undertaking, or

(b) a controlling undertaking of a Community-scale group of undertakings,

except where the special negotiating body has taken the decision referred to in regulation 29 of the European Public Limited-Liability Company Regulations 2004 (decision not to open, or to terminate, negotiations).

(2) In this regulation an "SE" means a company established in accordance with the European Public Limited-Liability Company Regulations 2004.]

[2618A]

NOTES

Commencement: 8 October 2004.

Inserted by the European Public Limited-Liability Company Regulations 2004, SI 2004/2326, reg 53, as from 8 October 2004.

[46B—[(1) These regulations do not apply to an SCE that is—

(a) a Community-scale undertaking, or

(b) a controlling undertaking of a Community-scale group of undertakings,

except where the special negotiating body has taken the decision referred to in regulation 19 of, or paragraph 13 of Schedule 1 to, the European Cooperative Society (Involvement of Employees) Regulations 2006 (decision not to open, or to terminate, negotiations).

(2) In this regulation an "SCE" means a European Cooperative Society established in accordance with the European Cooperative Society Regulations 2006.]

[2618B]

NOTES

Commencement: 18 August 2006.

Inserted by the European Cooperative Society (Involvement of Employees) Regulations 2006, SI 2006/2059, reg 42, as from 18 August 2006.

PART X
TRANSITIONALS

47 Transitionals: special negotiating body

(1) Where immediately before the date on which these Regulations come into force—

(a) a special negotiating body has been validly requested or established under the provisions of the law or practice of a Member State other than the United Kingdom which is designed to give effect to the Transnational Information and Consultation Directive;

(b) no Article 6 agreement is in force; and

(c) no Article 7 European Works Council has been established—

paragraphs (2) and (3) shall apply.

(2) Where the central management is situated in the United Kingdom these Regulations shall apply, with the modifications specified in paragraphs (4) to (6), as if a valid request had been made under regulation 9 and, where appropriate, as if the special negotiating body had been established under these Regulations.

(3) Where the central management is not situated in the United Kingdom the regulations referred to in regulation 4(2) shall apply with the modifications specified in paragraphs (5) and (6) of this regulation.

(4) Regulation 12 shall apply in respect of the composition of the special negotiating body only to the extent that it determines the number of UK members on the special negotiating body but shall not affect in any way the number of non-UK members on the special negotiating body.

(5) Where, as a result of the implementation of the Extension Directive by a Member State (including the United Kingdom) there are required to be UK members on the special negotiating body and immediately before the date on which these Regulations come into force—

(a) no person has been designated to attend meetings of the special negotiating body as a representative of employees in the United Kingdom; or

(b) one or more persons have been designated to attend meetings of the special negotiating body as a representative of employees in the United Kingdom,

then in the case mentioned in sub-paragraph (a), the UK members of the special negotiating body shall be elected or appointed in accordance with regulations 13 to 15, and in the case mentioned in sub-paragraph (b), the person or persons shall be treated as from the date on which these Regulations come into force as a UK member of the special negotiating body who has been elected or appointed in accordance with regulations 13 to 15.

(6) Where the number of persons referred to in paragraph (5)(b) is—

(a) in a case where regulation 12 applies, less than the number of UK members of the special negotiating body required by that regulation, or

(b) in a case where regulation 12 does not apply, less than the number of UK members of the special negotiating body required by the provisions of the law or practice of the Member State under which the special negotiating body was established,

the additional number of UK members of the special negotiating body needed to secure compliance with regulation 12 or, as the case may be, the law or practice of the Member State referred to in sub-paragraph (b) of this paragraph shall be elected or appointed in accordance with regulations 13 to 15.

[2619]

48 Transitionals: Article 7 European Works Councils

(1) Where, immediately before the date on which these Regulations come into force, a European Works Council has been established under the provisions of the law or practice of a Member State other than the United Kingdom, which are designed to give effect to Article 7 of, and the Annex to, the Transnational Information and Consultation Directive, paragraphs (2) and (3) shall apply.

(2) Where the central management is situated in the United Kingdom and regulation 43(1) (a) or 43(1)(b) applies these Regulations shall apply with the modifications specified in paragraphs (4) to (6) as if the European Works Council had been established under these Regulations.

(3) Where the central management is not situated in the United Kingdom, or is situated in the United Kingdom but neither regulation 43(1)(a) nor 43(1)(b) applies, the regulations referred to in regulation 4(2) shall apply with the modifications specified in paragraphs (5) and (6) of this regulation.

(4) Paragraph 2 of the Schedule shall apply in respect of the composition of the European Works Council only to the extent that it determines the number of UK members on the European Works Council but shall not affect in any way the number of non-UK members on the European Works Council.

(5) Where, as a result of the implementation of the Extension Directive by a Member State (including the United Kingdom), there are required to be UK members on the European Works Council and immediately before the date on which these Regulations come into force—

- (a) no person has been designated to attend meetings of the European Works Council as a representative of employees in the United Kingdom; or
- (b) one or more persons have been designated to attend meetings of the European Works Council as a representative of employees in the United Kingdom,

then in the case mentioned in sub-paragraph (a), the UK members of the European Works Council shall be appointed or elected in accordance with paragraphs 3 to 5 of the Schedule, and in the case mentioned in sub-paragraph (b), the person or persons shall be treated as from the date on which these Regulations come into force as a UK member of the European Works Council who has been elected or appointed in accordance with paragraphs 3 to 5 of the Schedule.

(6) Where the number of persons referred to in paragraph (5)(b) is—

- (a) in a case where paragraph 2 of the Schedule applies, less than the number of UK members of the European Works Council required by that paragraph; or
- (b) in a case where paragraph 2 of the Schedule does not apply, less than the number of UK members of the European Works Council required by the law or practice of the Member State under which the European Works Council was established,

the additional number of UK members needed to secure compliance with paragraph 2 or, as the case may be, the law or practice of the Member State referred to in sub-paragraph (b) of this paragraph shall be elected or appointed in accordance with paragraphs 3 to 5 of the Schedule.

[2620]

SCHEDULE
SUBSIDIARY REQUIREMENTS

Regulation 18

1 Establishment of European Works Council

A European Works Council shall be established in the Community-scale undertaking or Community-scale group of undertakings in accordance with the provisions in this Schedule.

2 Composition of the European Works Council

(1) The European Works Council shall comprise a minimum of three, and a maximum of 30, members.

(2) Subject to sub-paragraph (1), the European Works Council shall be constituted in accordance with sub-paragraphs (3) and (4) below.

(3) There shall be on the European Works Council at least one member representing each Member State in which the Community-scale undertaking has one or more establishments, or in which the Community-scale group of undertakings has its controlling undertaking or one or more controlled undertakings.

(4) There shall be on the European Works Council the following additional members—

- (a) one additional member from a Member State in which there are employed 25 per cent or more but less than 50 per cent of the employees of the undertaking or group of undertakings who are employed in the Member States;
- (b) two additional members from a Member State in which there are employed 50 per cent or more but less than 75 per cent of the employees of the undertaking or group of undertakings who are employed in the Member States;
- (c) three additional members from a Member State in which there are employed 75 per cent or more of the employees of the undertaking or group of undertakings who are employed in the Member States.

(5) The European Works Council shall inform the central management and any more appropriate level of management of the composition of the European Works Council.

(6) Where the European Works Council decides its size so warrants, it shall elect from among its members a select committee comprising no more than three members who are to act on behalf of the European Works Council.

3 Appointment or election of UK members of the European Works Council

(1) The UK members of the European Works Council must be UK employees and—

(a) in a case where all of those employees are represented by UK employees' representatives, shall be elected or appointed by such employees' representatives;

(b) in a case where not all of those employees are represented by UK employees' representatives, shall be elected by ballot.

(2) For the purposes of this paragraph all of the UK employees are represented by UK employees' representatives if each of the employees referred to in sub-paragraph (1) is a UK employee—

(a) in respect of which an independent trade union is recognised by his employer for the purpose of collective bargaining; or

(b) who has elected or appointed an employees' representative for the purpose of receiving, on the employee's behalf, information—

(i) which is relevant to the employee's terms and conditions of employment; or

(ii) about the activities of the undertaking which may significantly affect the employee's interests

but excluding representatives who are expected to receive information relevant only to a specific aspect of the terms and conditions or interests of the employee, such as health and safety or collective redundancies.

(3) Where sub-paragraph (1)(a) above applies, the election or appointment of members of the European Works Council shall be carried out by whatever method the UK employees' representatives decide.

(4) Where sub-paragraph (1)(b) applies, the UK members of the European Works Council are to be elected by a ballot of the UK employees in accordance with paragraphs 4 and 5.

4 Ballot arrangements

(1) The UK management must arrange for the holding of a ballot of employees referred to in paragraph 3(4), which satisfies the requirements specified in sub-paragraph (2).

(2) The requirements referred to in sub-paragraph (1) are that—

(a) the ballot of the UK employees must comprise a single ballot, but may instead, if the UK management so decides, comprise separate ballots of employees in such constituencies as the UK management may determine where—

(i) the number of UK members of the European Works Council to be elected is more than one, and

(ii) the UK management considers that if separate ballots were held for those constituencies, the UK members of the European Works Council to be elected would better reflect the interests of the UK employees as a whole than if a single ballot were held;

(b) a UK employee who is an employee of the Community-scale undertaking or the Community-scale group of undertakings on the day on which votes may be cast in the ballot or, if the votes may be cast on more than one day, on the first day of those days is entitled to vote in a ballot of the UK employees;

(c) any UK employee who is an employee of the Community-scale undertaking or Community-scale group of undertakings immediately before the latest time at which a person may become a candidate in the ballot, is entitled to stand in the ballot of the UK employees as a candidate for election as a UK member of the European Works Council;

(d) the UK management must, in accordance with sub-paragraph (6), appoint an independent ballot supervisor to supervise the conduct of the ballot of the UK employees but may instead, where there are to be separate ballots, appoint more than one independent ballot supervisor in accordance with that sub-paragraph, each of whom is to supervise such of the separate ballots as the UK management may determine, provided that each separate ballot is supervised by a supervisor;

(e) after the UK management has formulated proposals as to the arrangements for the ballot of the UK employees and before it has published the final arrangements under paragraph (f) it must, so far as reasonably practicable, consult with the UK employees' representatives on the proposed arrangements for the ballot of the UK employees;

(f) the UK management must publish the final arrangements for the ballot of the UK employees in such manner as to bring them to the attention of, so far as reasonably practicable, the UK employees and the UK employees' representatives.

(3) Any UK employee or UK employees' representative who believes that the arrangements for the ballot of the UK employees are defective may, within a period of 21 days beginning on the date the UK management published the final arrangements under paragraph (f), present a complaint to the CAC.

(4) Where the CAC finds the complaint well-founded it shall make a declaration to that effect and may make an order requiring the UK management to modify the arrangements it has made for the ballot of the UK employees or to satisfy the requirements in paragraph (e) or (f) of sub-paragraph (2).

(5) An order under sub-paragraph (4) shall specify the modifications to the arrangements which the UK management is required to make and the requirements which it must satisfy.

(6) A person is an independent ballot supervisor for the purposes of sub-paragraph (2)(d) if the UK management reasonably believes that he will carry out any functions conferred on him in relation to the ballot competently and has no reasonable grounds for believing that his independence in relation to the ballot might reasonably be called into question.

(7) For the purposes of sub-paragraph (3), the arrangements for the ballot of the UK employees are defective if—

(a) any of the requirements specified in paragraphs (b) to (f) of sub-paragraph (2) is not satisfied; or

(b) in a case where the ballot is to comprise separate ballots, the constituencies determined by the UK management do not reflect adequately the interests of the UK employees as a whole.

5 Conduct of ballot

(1) The UK management must—

(a) ensure that a ballot supervisor appointed under paragraph 4(2)(d) carries out his functions under this paragraph and that there is no interference with his carrying out of those functions from the UK management, or the central management (where it is not also the UK management); and

(b) comply with all reasonable requests made by a ballot supervisor for the purposes of, or in connection with, the carrying out of those functions.

(2) A ballot supervisor's appointment shall require that he—

(a) supervises the conduct of the ballot, or the separate ballots he is being appointed to supervise, in accordance with the arrangements for the ballot of the UK employees published by the UK management under paragraph 4(2)(f) or, where appropriate, in accordance with the arrangements as required to be modified by an order made as a result of a complaint presented under paragraph 4(3);

(b) does not conduct the ballot or any of the separate ballots before the UK management has satisfied the requirement specified in paragraph 4(2)(e) and—

(i) where no complaint has been presented under paragraph 4(3), before the expiry of a period of 21 days beginning on the date on which the UK management published its arrangements under paragraph 4(2)(f); or

(ii) where a complaint has been presented under paragraph 4(3), before the complaint has been determined and, where appropriate, the arrangements have been modified as required by an order made as a result of the complaint;

(c) conducts the ballot, or each separate ballot, so as to secure that—

(i) so far as reasonably practicable, those entitled to vote are given the opportunity to vote,

(ii) so far as reasonably practicable, those entitled to stand as candidates are given the opportunity to stand,

(iii) so far as is reasonably practicable, those voting are able to do so in secret, and

(iv) the votes given in the ballot are fairly and accurately counted.

(3) As soon as reasonably practicable after the holding of the ballot, or each separate ballot, the ballot supervisor must publish the results of the ballot in such manner as to make them available to the UK management and, so far as reasonably practicable, the UK employees entitled to vote in the ballot or who stood as candidates in the ballot.

(4) A ballot supervisor shall publish an ineffective ballot report where he considers (whether or not on the basis of representations made to him by another person) that—

(a) any of the requirements referred to in sub-paragraph (2) was not satisfied with the result that the outcome of the ballot would have been different; or

(b) there was interference with the carrying out of his functions or a failure by management to comply with all reasonable requests made by him with the result that he was unable to form a proper judgment as to whether each of the requirements referred to in sub-paragraph (2) was satisfied in relation to the ballot.

(5) Where a ballot supervisor publishes an ineffective ballot report the report must be published within a period of one month commencing on the date on which the ballot supervisor publishes the results of the ballot under sub-paragraph (3).

(6) A ballot supervisor shall publish an ineffective ballot report in such manner as to make it available to the UK management and, so far as reasonably practicable, the UK employees entitled to vote in the ballot or who stood as candidates in the ballot.

(7) Where a ballot supervisor publishes an ineffective ballot report then—

(a) if there has been a single ballot or an ineffective ballot report has been published in respect of every separate ballot, the outcome of the ballot or ballots shall have no effect and the UK management shall again be under the obligation in paragraph 4(1);

(b) if there have been separate ballots and paragraph (a) does not apply—

(i) the UK management shall arrange for the separate ballot or ballots in respect of which an ineffective ballot report was issued to be reheld in accordance with paragraph 4 and this paragraph, and

(ii) no such ballot shall have effect until it has been so reheld and no ineffective ballot report has been published in respect of it.

(8) All costs relating to the holding of a ballot, including payments made to a ballot supervisor for supervising the conduct of the ballot, shall be borne by the central management (whether or not an ineffective ballot report has been made).

6 Competence of the European Works Council

(1) The competence of the European Works Council shall be limited to information and consultation on the matters which concern the Community-scale undertaking or Community-scale group of undertakings as a whole or at least two of its establishments or group undertakings situated in different Member States.

(2) In the case of a Community-scale undertaking or Community-scale group of undertakings falling within regulation 5(1)(b) or 5(1)(c), the competence of the European Works Council shall be limited to those matters concerning all of its establishments or group undertakings situated within the Member States or concerning at least two of its establishments or group undertakings situated in different Member States.

7 Information and consultation meetings

(1) Subject to paragraph 8, the European Works Council shall have the right to meet with the central management once a year in an information and consultation meeting, to be informed and consulted, on the basis of a report drawn up by the central management, on the progress of the business of the Community-scale undertaking or Community-scale group of undertakings and its prospects.

(2) The central management shall inform the local managements accordingly.

(3) The information and consultation meeting shall relate in particular to the structure, economic and financial situation, the probable development of the business and of production and sales, the situation and probable trend of employment, investments, and substantial changes concerning organisation, introduction of new working methods or production processes, transfers of production, mergers, cut-backs or closures of undertakings, establishments or important parts thereof, and collective redundancies.

8 Exceptional information and consultation meetings

(1) Where there are exceptional circumstances affecting the employees' interests to a considerable extent, particularly in the event of relocations, the closure of establishments or undertakings or collective redundancies, the select committee or, where no such committee exists, the European Works Council shall have the right to be informed. It shall have the right to meet in an exceptional information and consultation meeting, at its request, the central

management, or any other more appropriate level of management within the Community-scale undertaking or group of undertakings having its own powers of decision, so as to be informed and consulted on measures significantly affecting employees' interests.

(2) Those members of the European Works Council who have been elected or appointed by the establishments or undertakings which are directly concerned by the measures in question shall also have the right to participate in an exceptional information and consultation meeting referred to in sub-paragraph (1) of this paragraph organised with the select committee elected under sub-paragraph (6) of paragraph 2.

(3) The exceptional information and consultation meeting referred to in sub-paragraph (1) of this paragraph shall take place as soon as possible on the basis of a report drawn up by the central management or any other appropriate level of management of the Community-scale undertaking or Community-scale group of undertakings, on which an opinion may be delivered at the end of the meeting or within a reasonable time.

(4) The exceptional information and consultation meeting referred to in sub-paragraph (1) of this paragraph shall not affect the prerogatives of the central management.

9 Procedures

(1) Before an information and consultation meeting or exceptional information and consultation meeting with the central management, the European Works Council or the select committee, where necessary enlarged in accordance with sub-paragraph (2) of paragraph 8, shall be entitled to meet without the management concerned being present.

(2) Subject to regulation 23, the members of the European Works Council shall inform—

- (a) the employees' representatives of the employees in the establishments of a Community-scale undertaking or in the undertakings of a Community-scale group of undertakings; or
- (b) to the extent that any employees are not represented by employees' representatives, the employees themselves

of the content and outcome of the information and consultation procedure carried out in accordance with the provisions of this Schedule.

(3) The European Works Council shall adopt its own rules of procedure.

(4) The European Works Council or the select committee may be assisted by experts of its choice, in so far as this is necessary for it to carry out its tasks.

(5) The operating expenses of the European Works Council shall be borne by the central management; but where the European Works Council is assisted by more than one expert the central management is not required to pay such expenses in respect of more than one of them.

(6) The central management shall provide the members of the European Works Council with such financial and material resources as enable them to perform their duties in an appropriate manner. In particular, the cost of organising meetings and arranging for interpretation facilities and the accommodation and travelling expenses of members of the European Works Council and its select committee shall be met by the central management unless the central management and European Works Council, or select committee, otherwise agree.

10 The continuing application of the subsidiary requirements

(1) Four years after the European Works Council is established it shall examine whether to open negotiations for the conclusion of an agreement referred to in regulation 17 or to continue to apply the subsidiary requirements adopted in accordance with the provisions of this Schedule.

(2) If the European Works Council decides to negotiate an agreement in accordance with regulation 17, it shall notify the central management in writing to that effect, and

- (a) such notification shall be treated as a valid request made under regulation 9; and
- (b) regulations 16, 17 and 18 shall apply in respect of the negotiations for an agreement as if references in those regulations to the special negotiating body were references to the European Works Council.

[2621]

DATA PROTECTION (PROCESSING OF SENSITIVE PERSONAL DATA) ORDER 2000

(SI 2000/417)

NOTES

Made: 17 February 2000.
Authority: Data Protection Act 1998, s 67(2), Sch 3, para 10.
Commencement: 1 March 2000.

1—(1) This Order may be cited as the Data Protection (Processing of Sensitive Personal Data) Order 2000 and shall come into force on 1st March 2000.

(2) In this Order, "the Act" means the Data Protection Act 1998.

[2622]

2 For the purposes of paragraph 10 of Schedule 3 to the Act, the circumstances specified in any of the paragraphs in the Schedule to this Order are circumstances in which sensitive personal data may be processed.

[2623]

SCHEDULE
CIRCUMSTANCES IN WHICH SENSITIVE PERSONAL DATA MAY BE PROCESSED

Article 2

1.—(1) The processing—
- (a) is in the substantial public interest;
- (b) is necessary for the purposes of the prevention or detection of any unlawful act; and
- (c) must necessarily be carried out without the explicit consent of the data subject being sought so as not to prejudice those purposes.

(2) In this paragraph, "act" includes a failure to act.

2. The processing—
- (a) is in the substantial public interest;
- (b) is necessary for the discharge of any function which is designed for protecting members of the public against—
  - (i) dishonesty, malpractice, or other seriously improper conduct by, or the unfitness or incompetence of, any person, or
  - (ii) mismanagement in the administration of, or failures in services provided by, any body or association; and
- (c) must necessarily be carried out without the explicit consent of the data subject being sought so as not to prejudice the discharge of that function.

3.—(1) The disclosure of personal data—
- (a) is in the substantial public interest;
- (b) is in connection with—
  - (i) the commission by any person of any unlawful act (whether alleged or established),
  - (ii) dishonesty, malpractice, or other seriously improper conduct by, or the unfitness or incompetence of, any person (whether alleged or established), or
  - (iii) mismanagement in the administration of, or failures in services provided by, any body or association (whether alleged or established);
- (c) is for the special purposes as defined in section 3 of the Act; and
- (d) is made with a view to the publication of those data by any person and the data controller reasonably believes that such publication would be in the public interest.

(2) In this paragraph, "act" includes a failure to act.

4. The processing—
- (a) is in the substantial public interest;

(b) is necessary for the discharge of any function which is designed for the provision of confidential counselling, advice, support or any other service; and
(c) is carried out without the explicit consent of the data subject because the processing—
(i) is necessary in a case where consent cannot be given by the data subject,
(ii) is necessary in a case where the data controller cannot reasonably be expected to obtain the explicit consent of the data subject, or
(iii) must necessarily be carried out without the explicit consent of the data subject being sought so as not to prejudice the provision of that counselling, advice, support or other service.

5.—(1) The processing—
(a) is necessary for the purpose of—
(i) carrying on insurance business, or
(ii) making determinations in connection with eligibility for, and benefits payable under, an occupational pension scheme as defined in section 1 of the Pension Schemes Act 1993;
(b) is of sensitive personal data consisting of information falling within section 2(e) of the Act relating to a data subject who is the parent, grandparent, great grandparent or sibling of—
(i) in the case of paragraph (a)(i), the insured person, or
(ii) in the case of paragraph (a)(ii), the member of the scheme;
(c) is necessary in a case where the data controller cannot reasonably be expected to obtain the explicit consent of that data subject and the data controller is not aware of the data subject withholding his consent; and
(d) does not support measures or decisions with respect to that data subject.

(2) In this paragraph—
[(a) insurance business" means business which consists of effecting or carrying out contracts of insurance of the following kind—
(i) life and annuity,
(ii) linked long term,
(iii) permanent health,
(iv) accident, or
(v) sickness; and]
(b) "insured" and "member" includes an individual who is seeking to become an insured person or member of the scheme respectively.

[(2A) The definition of "insurance business" in sub-paragraph (2) above must be read with—
(a) section 22 of the Financial Services and Markets Act 2000;
(b) any relevant order under that section; and
(c) Schedule 2 to that Act.]

6. The processing—
(a) is of sensitive personal data in relation to any particular data subject that are subject to processing which was already under way immediately before the coming into force of this Order;
(b) is necessary for the purpose of—
[(i) effecting or carrying out contracts of long-term insurance of the kind mentioned in sub-paragraph (2)(a)(i), (ii) or (iii) of paragraph 5 above;] or
(ii) establishing or administering an occupational pension scheme as defined in section 1 of the Pension Schemes Act 1993; and
(c) either—
(i) is necessary in a case where the data controller cannot reasonably be expected to obtain the explicit consent of the data subject and that data subject has not informed the data controller that he does not so consent, or
(ii) must necessarily be carried out even without the explicit consent of the data subject so as not to prejudice those purposes.

7.—(1) Subject to the provisions of sub-paragraph (2), the processing—
(a) is of sensitive personal data consisting of information falling within section 2(c) or (e) of the Act;
(b) is necessary for the purpose of identifying or keeping under review the existence or absence of equality of opportunity or treatment between persons—
(i) holding different beliefs as described in section 2(c) of the Act, or

(ii) of different states of physical or mental health or different physical or mental conditions as described in section 2(e) of the Act,

with a view to enabling such equality to be promoted or maintained;

(c) does not support measures or decisions with respect to any particular data subject otherwise than with the explicit consent of that data subject; and

(d) does not cause, nor is likely to cause, substantial damage or substantial distress to the data subject or any other person.

(2) Where any individual has given notice in writing to any data controller who is processing personal data under the provisions of sub-paragraph (1) requiring that data controller to cease processing personal data in respect of which that individual is the data subject at the end of such period as is reasonable in the circumstances, that data controller must have ceased processing those personal data at the end of that period.

8.—(1) Subject to the provisions of sub-paragraph (2), the processing—

(a) is of sensitive personal data consisting of information falling within section 2(b) of the Act;

(b) is carried out by any person or organisation included in the register maintained pursuant to section 1 of the Registration of Political Parties Act 1998 in the course of his or its legitimate political activities; and

(c) does not cause, nor is likely to cause, substantial damage or substantial distress to the data subject or any other person.

(2) Where any individual has given notice in writing to any data controller who is processing personal data under the provisions of sub-paragraph (1) requiring that data controller to cease processing personal data in respect of which that individual is the data subject at the end of such period as is reasonable in the circumstances, that data controller must have ceased processing those personal data at the end of that period.

9. The processing—

(a) is in the substantial public interest;

(b) is necessary for research purposes (which expression shall have the same meaning as in section 33 of the Act);

(c) does not support measures or decisions with respect to any particular data subject otherwise than with the explicit consent of that data subject; and

(d) does not cause, nor is likely to cause, substantial damage or substantial distress to the data subject or any other person.

10. The processing is necessary for the exercise of any functions conferred on a constable by any rule of law.

[2624]–[2627]

NOTES

Para 5: sub-para (2)(a) substituted, and sub-para (2A) inserted, by the Financial Services and Markets Act 2000 (Consequential Amendments and Repeals) Order 2001, SI 2001/3649, art 587(1)–(3).

Para 6: sub-para (b)(i) substituted by SI 2001/3649, art 587(1), (4).

TRADE UNION RECOGNITION (METHOD OF COLLECTIVE BARGAINING) ORDER 2000

(SI 2000/1300)

NOTES

Made: 11 May 2000.

Authority: Trade Union and Labour Relations (Consolidation) Act 1992, Sch A1, para 168(1).

Commencement: 6 June 2000.

See *Harvey* NI(7).

1 Citation and commencement

This Order may be cited as the Trade Union Recognition (Method of Collective Bargaining) Order 2000 and comes into force on 6th June 2000.

[2628]

2 Specification of method

The method specified for the purposes of paragraphs 31(3) and 63(2) of Schedule A1 to the Trade Union and Labour Relations (Consolidation) Act 1992 is the method set out under the heading "the specified method" in the Schedule to this Order.

[2629]

SCHEDULE

Article 2

PREAMBLE

The method specified below ("the specified method") is one by which collective bargaining might be conducted in the particular, and possibly rare, circumstances discussed in the following paragraph. The specified method is not designed to be applied as a model for voluntary procedural agreements between employers and unions. Because most voluntary agreements are not legally binding and are usually concluded in a climate of trust and co-operation, they do not need to be as prescriptive as the specified method. However, the Central Arbitration Committee ("CAC") must take the specified method into account when exercising its powers to impose a method of collective bargaining under paragraphs 31(3) and 63(2) of Schedule A1 to the Trade Union and Labour Relations (Consolidation) Act 1992. In exercising those powers the CAC may depart from the specified method to such extent as it thinks appropriate in the circumstances of individual cases.

Paragraph 31(3) provides for the CAC to impose a method of collective bargaining in cases where a union (or unions, where two or more unions act jointly) has been recognised by an employer by means of an award of the CAC under Part I of Schedule A1, but the employer and union(s) have been unable to agree a method of bargaining between themselves, or have failed to follow an agreed method. Paragraph 63(2) provides for the CAC to impose a bargaining method in cases where an employer and a union (or unions) have entered an agreement for recognition, as defined by paragraph 52 of Part II of Schedule A1, but cannot agree a method of bargaining, or have failed to follow the agreed method.

The bargaining method imposed by the CAC has effect as if it were a legally binding contract between the employer and the union(s). If one party believes the other is failing to respect the method, the first party may apply to the court for an order of specific performance, ordering the other party to comply with the method. Failure to comply with such an order could constitute contempt of court.

Once the CAC has imposed a bargaining method, the parties can vary it, including the fact that it is legally binding, by agreement provided that they do so in writing.

The fact that the CAC has imposed a method does not affect the rights of individual workers under either statute or their contracts of employment. For example, it does not prevent or limit the rights of individual workers to discuss, negotiate or agree with their employer terms of their contract of employment, which differ from the terms of any collective agreement into which the employer and the union may enter as a result of collective bargaining conducted by this method. Nor does the imposed method affect an individual's statutory entitlement to time off for trade union activities or duties.

In cases where the CAC imposes a bargaining method on the parties, the employer is separately obliged, in accordance with Section 70B of the Trade Union and Labour Relations (Consolidation) Act 1992 (as inserted by section 5 of the Employment Relations Act 1999), to consult union representatives periodically on his policy, actions and plans on training. The specified method does not discuss how such consultations should be organised.

The law confers certain entitlements on independent trade unions which are recognised for collective bargaining purposes. For example, employers must disclose, on request, certain types of information to the representatives of the recognised unions. The fact that the CAC has imposed a bargaining method does not affect these existing statutory entitlements.

THE SPECIFIED METHOD

The Parties

1. The method shall apply in each case to two parties, who are referred to here as the "employer" and the "union". Unless the text specifies otherwise, the term "union" should be read to mean "unions" in cases where two or more unions are jointly recognised.

The Purpose

2. The purpose is to specify a method by which the employer and the union conduct collective bargaining concerning the pay, hours and holidays of the workers comprising the bargaining unit.

3. The employer shall not grant the right to negotiate pay, hours and holidays to any other union in respect of the workers covered by this method.

The Joint Negotiating Body

4. The employer and the union shall establish a Joint Negotiating Body (JNB) to discuss and negotiate the pay, hours and holidays of the workers comprising the bargaining unit. No other body or group shall undertake collective bargaining on the pay, hours and holidays of these workers, unless the employer and the union so agree.

JNB Membership

5. The membership of the JNB shall usually comprise three employer representatives (who together shall constitute the Employer Side of the JNB) and three union representatives (who together shall constitute the Union Side of the JNB). Each union recognised by the employer in respect of the bargaining unit shall be entitled to one seat at least. To meet this requirement, the Union Side may need to be larger than three and in this eventuality the employer shall be entitled to increase his representation on the JNB by the same number, if he wishes.

6. The employer shall select those individuals who comprise the Employer Side. The individuals must either be those who take the final decisions within the employer's organisation in respect of the pay, hours and holidays of the workers in the bargaining unit or who are expressly authorised by the employer to make recommendations directly to those who take such final decisions. Unless it would be unreasonable to do so, the employer shall select as a representative the most senior person responsible for employment relations in the bargaining unit.

7. The union shall select those individuals who comprise the Union Side in accordance with its own rules and procedures. The representatives must either be individuals employed by the employer or individuals employed by the union who are officials of the union within the meaning of sections 1 and 119 of the Trade Union and Labour Relations (Consolidation) Act 1992 ("the 1992 Act").

8. The JNB shall determine their own rules in respect of the attendance at JNB meetings of observers and substitutes who deputise for JNB members.

Officers

9. The Employer Side shall select one of its members to act as its Chairman and one to act as its Secretary. The Union Side shall select one of its members to act as its Chairman and one to act as its Secretary. The same person may perform the roles of Chairman and Secretary of a Side.

10. For the twelve months from the date of the JNB's first meeting, meetings of the JNB shall be chaired by the Chairman of the Employer Side. The Chairman of the Union Side shall chair the JNB's meetings for the following twelve months. The chairmanship of JNB meetings will alternate in the same way thereafter at intervals of twelve months. In the absence of the person who should chair JNB meetings, a JNB meeting shall be chaired by another member of that person's Side.

11. The Secretary of the Employer Side shall act as Secretary to the JNB. He shall circulate documentation and agendas in advance of JNB meetings, arrange suitable accommodation for meetings, notify members of meetings and draft the written record of JNB meetings. The Secretary of the Employer Side shall work closely with the Secretary of the Union Side in the discharge of these duties, disclosing full information about his performance of these tasks.

JNB Organisation

12. Draft agendas shall be circulated at least three working days in advance of JNB meetings. The draft record of JNB meetings shall be circulated within ten working days of the

holding of meetings for approval at the next JNB meeting. The record does not need to be a verbatim account, but should fully describe the conclusions reached and the actions to be taken.

13. Subject to the timetable of meetings stipulated in paragraphs 15, 17, 20 and 28 below, the date, timing and location of meetings shall be arranged by the JNB's Secretary, in full consultation with the Secretary of the Union Side, to ensure maximum attendance at meetings. A meeting of the JNB shall be quorate if 50% or more of each Side's members (or, where applicable, their substitutes) are in attendance.

Bargaining Procedure

14 The union's proposals for adjustments to pay, hours and holidays shall be dealt with on an annual basis, unless the two Sides agree a different bargaining period.

15. The JNB shall conduct these negotiations for each bargaining round according to the following staged procedure.

Step 1—The union shall set out in writing, and send to the employer, its proposals (the "claim") to vary the pay, hours and holidays, specifying which aspects it wants to change. In its claim, the union shall set out the reasons for its proposals, together with the main supporting evidence at its disposal at the time. In cases where there is no established annual date when the employer reviews the pay, hours and holidays of all the workers in the bargaining unit, the union shall put forward its first claim within three months of this method being imposed (and by the same date in subsequent rounds). Where such a common review date is established, the union shall submit its first claim at least a month in advance of that date (and by the same date in subsequent rounds). In either case, the employer and the union may agree a different date by which the claim should be submitted each year. If the union fails to submit its claim by this date, then the procedure shall be ended for the bargaining round in question. Exceptionally, the union may submit a late claim without this penalty if its work on the claim was delayed while the Central Arbitration Committee considered a relevant complaint by the union of failure by the employer to disclose information for collective bargaining purposes.

Step 2—Within ten working days of the Employer Side's receipt of the union's letter, a quorate meeting of the JNB shall be held to discuss the claim. At this meeting, the Union Side shall explain its claim and answer any reasonable questions arising to the best of its ability.

Step 3—

(a) Within fifteen working days immediately following the Step 2 meeting, the employer shall either accept the claim in full or write to the union responding to its claim. If the Employer Side requests it, a quorate meeting of the JNB shall be held within the fifteen day period to enable the employer to present this written response directly to the Union Side. In explaining the basis of his response, the employer shall set out in this written communication all relevant information in his possession. In particular, the written communication shall contain information costing each element of the claim and describing the business consequences, particularly any staffing implications, unless the employer is not required to disclose such information for any of the reasons specified in section 182(1) of the 1992 Act. The basis of these estimated costs and effects, including the main assumptions that the employer has used, shall be set out in the communication. In determining what information is disclosed as relevant, the employer shall be under no greater obligation that he is under the general duty imposed on him by sections 181 and 182 of the 1992 Act to disclose information for the purposes of collective bargaining.

(b) If the response contains any counter-proposals, the written communication shall set out the reasons for making them, together with the supporting evidence. The letter shall provide information estimating the costs and staffing consequences of implementing each element of the counter-proposals, unless the employer is not required to disclose such information for any of the reasons specified in section 182(1) of the 1992 Act.

Step 4—Within ten working days of the Union Side's receipt of the employer's written communication, a further quorate meeting of the JNB shall be held to discuss the employer's response. At this meeting, the Employer Side shall explain its response and answer any reasonable questions arising to the best of its ability.

Step 5—If no agreement is reached at the Step 4 meeting (or the last of such meetings if more than one is held at that stage in the procedure), another quorate meeting of the JNB shall be held within ten working days. The union may bring to this meeting a maximum of two other individuals employed by the union who are officials within the meaning of the sections 1 and 119 of the 1992 Act. The employer may bring to the meeting a maximum of two other individuals who are employees or officials of an employer's organisation to which the employer belongs. These additional persons shall be allowed to contribute to the meeting, as if they were JNB members.

Step 6—If no agreement is reached at the Step 5 meeting (or the last of such meetings if more than one meeting is held at that stage in the procedure), within five working days the employer and the union shall consider, separately or jointly, consulting ACAS about the prospect of ACAS helping them to find a settlement of their differences through conciliation. In the event that both parties agree to invite ACAS to conciliate, both parties shall give such assistance to ACAS as is necessary to enable it to carry out the conciliation efficiently and effectively.

16. The parties shall set aside half a working day for each JNB meeting, unless the Employer Side Chairman and the Union Side Chairman agree a different length of time for the meeting. Unless it is essential to do otherwise, meetings shall be held during the normal working time of most union members of the JNB. Meetings may be adjourned, if both Sides agree. Additional meetings at any point in the procedure may be arranged, if both Sides agree. In addition, if the Employer Side requests it, a meeting of the JNB shall be held before the union has submitted its claim or before the employer is required to respond, enabling the Employer Side to explain the business context within which the employer shall assess the claim.

17. The employer shall not vary the contractual terms affecting the pay, hours or holidays of workers in the bargaining unit, unless he has first discussed his proposals with the union. Such proposals shall normally be made by the employer in the context of his consideration of the union's claim at Steps 3 or 4. If, however, the employer has not tabled his proposals during that process and he wishes to make proposals before the next bargaining round commences, he must write to the union setting out his proposals and the reasons for making them, together with the supporting evidence. The letter shall provide information estimating the costs and staffing consequences of implementing each element of the proposals, unless the employer is not required to disclose such information for any of the reasons specified in section 182(1) of the 1992 Act. A quorate meeting of the JNB shall be held within five working days of the Union Side's receipt of the letter. If there is a failure to resolve the issue at that meeting, then meetings shall be arranged, and steps shall be taken, in accordance with Steps 5 and 6 of the above procedure.

18. Paragraph 17 does not apply to terms in the contract of an individual worker where that worker has agreed that the terms may be altered only by direct negotiation between the worker and the employer.

Collective Agreements

19. Any agreements affecting the pay, hours and holidays of workers in the bargaining unit, which the employer and the union enter following negotiations, shall be set down in writing and signed by the Chairman of the Employer Side and by the Chairman of the Union Side or, in their absence, by another JNB member on their respective Sides.

20. If either the employer or union consider that there has been a failure to implement the agreement, then that party can request in writing a meeting of the JNB to discuss the alleged failure. A quorate meeting shall be held within five working days of the receipt of the request by the JNB Secretary. If there is a failure to resolve the issue at that meeting, then meetings shall be arranged, and steps shall be taken, in accordance with Steps 5 and 6 of the above procedure.

Facilities and Time Off

21. If they are employed by the employer, union members of the JNB:
- — shall be given paid time off by the employer to attend JNB meetings;
- — shall be given paid time off by the employer to attend a two hour pre-meeting of the Union Side before each JNB meeting; and
- — shall be given paid time off by the employer to hold a day-long meeting to prepare the claim at Step 1 in the bargaining procedure.

The union members of the JNB shall schedule such meetings at times which minimise the effect on production and services. In arranging these meetings, the union members of the JNB shall provide the employer and their line management with as much notice as possible and give details of the purpose of the time off, the intended location of the meeting and the timing and duration of the time off. The employer shall provide adequate heating and lighting for these meetings, and ensure that they are held in private.

22. If they are not employed by the employer, union members of the JNB or other union officials attending JNB meetings shall be given sufficient access to the employer's premises to allow them to attend Union Side pre-meetings, JNB meetings and meetings of the bargaining unit as specified in paragraph 23.

23. The employer shall agree to the union's reasonable request to hold meetings with members of the bargaining unit on company premises to discuss the Step 1 claim, the employer's offer or revisions to either. The request shall be made at least three working days in advance of the proposed meeting. However, the employer is not required to provide such facilities, if the employer does not possess available premises which can be used for meetings on the scale suggested by the union. The employer shall provide adequate heating and lighting for meetings, and ensure that the meeting is held in private. Where such meetings are held in working time, the employer is under no obligation to pay individuals for the time off. Where meetings take place outside normal working hours, they should be arranged at a time which is otherwise convenient for the workers.

24. Where resources permit, the employer shall make available to the Union Side of the JNB such typing, copying and word-processing facilities as it needs to conduct its business in private.

25. Where resources permit, the employer shall set aside a room for the exclusive use of the Union Side of the JNB. The room shall possess a secure cabinet and a telephone.

26. In respect of issues which are not otherwise specified in this method, the employer and the union shall have regard to the guidance issued in the ACAS Code of Practice on Time Off for Trade Union Duties and Activities and ensure that there is no unwarranted or unjustified failure to abide by it.

Disclosure of Information

27. The employer and the union shall have regard to the ACAS Code of Practice on the Disclosure of Information to Trade Unions for Collective Bargaining Purposes and ensure that there is no unwarranted or unjustified failure to abide by it in relation to the bargaining arrangements specified by this method.

Revision of the Method

28. The employer or the union may request in writing a meeting of the JNB to discuss revising any element of this method, including its status as a legally binding contract. A quorate meeting of the JNB shall be held within ten working days of the receipt of the request by the JNB Secretary. This meeting shall be held in accordance with the same arrangements for the holding of other JNB meetings.

General

29. The employer and the union shall take all reasonable steps to ensure that this method to conduct collective bargaining is applied efficiently and effectively.

30. The definition of a "working day" used in this method is any day other than a Saturday or a Sunday, Christmas Day or Good Friday, or a day which is a bank holiday.

31. All time limits mentioned in this method may be varied on any occasion, if both the employer and the union agree.

[2630]

RECOGNITION AND DERECOGNITION BALLOTS (QUALIFIED PERSONS) ORDER 2000

(SI 2000/1306)

NOTES

Made: 11 May 2000.
Authority: Trade Union and Labour Relations (Consolidation) Act 1992, Sch A1, paras 25(7)(a), 117(9)(a).
Commencement: 6 June 2000.

1 Citation, commencement and interpretation

(1) This Order may be cited as the Recognition and Derecognition Ballots (Qualified Persons) Order 2000 and shall come into force on 6th June 2000.

(2) In this Order "the relevant provisions" means paragraphs 25(7)(a) and 117(9)(a) of Schedule A1 to the Trade Union and Labour Relations (Consolidation) Act 1992.

[2631]

2 Qualifications

In relation to an individual, the condition specified for the purposes of the relevant provisions is that he—

(a) has in force a practising certificate issued by the Law Society of England and Wales or the Law Society of Scotland; or

(b) is eligible for appointment as a company auditor under section 25 of the Companies Act 1989.

[2632]

3 In relation to a partnership, the condition specified for the purposes of the relevant provisions is that every member of the partnership is an individual who satisfies the condition specified in Article 2.

[2633]

[4 Persons specified by name

The following persons are specified for the purposes of the relevant provisions—

The Association of Electoral Administrators;
Election.com Limited;
Electoral Reform (Ballot Services) Limited;
Involvement and Participation Association;
Popularis Limited; and
Twenty-First Century Press Limited.]

[2634]

NOTES

Commencement: 1 October 2002.
Substituted by the Recognition and Derecognition Ballots (Qualified Persons) Order 2000 (Amendment) Order 2002, SI 2002/2268, art 2, as from 1 October 2002.

EMPLOYMENT TRIBUNALS ACT 1996 (APPLICATION OF CONCILIATION PROVISIONS) ORDER 2000

(SI 2000/1337)

NOTES

Made: 16 May 2000.
Authority: Employment Tribunals Act 1996, s 18(8)(a), (b).
Commencement: 6 June 2000.

1 Citation and commencement

This Order may be cited as the Employment Tribunals Act 1996 (Application of Conciliation Provisions) Order 2000 and comes into force on 6th June 2000.

[2635]

2 (*Amends the Employment Tribunals Act 1996, s 18(1) at* **[975]**.)

3 The Secretary of State specifies section 70B of, and paragraph 156 of Schedule A1 to, the Trade Union and Labour Relations (Consolidation) Act 1992 as provisions to which section 18(1)(f) of the Employment Tribunals Act 1996 applies.

[2636]

PART-TIME WORKERS (PREVENTION OF LESS FAVOURABLE TREATMENT) REGULATIONS 2000

(SI 2000/1551)

NOTES

Made: 8 June 2000.

Authority: Employment Relations Act 1999, s 19.

Commencement: 1 July 2000.

These Regulations implement Council Directive 97/81/EC at **[3933]**, as extended to the United Kingdom by Council Directive 98/23/EC at **[3940]**.

Employment Appeal Tribunal: an appeal lies to the Employment Appeal Tribunal on any question of law arising from any decision of, or in any proceedings before, an employment tribunal under or by virtue of these Regulations; see the Employment Tribunals Act 1996, s 21(1)(j) at **[978]**.

Conciliation: employment tribunal proceedings and claims which could be the subject of employment tribunal proceedings arising out of a contravention, or alleged contravention, of reg 5(1) or reg 7(2) are proceedings to which the Employment Tribunals Act 1996, s 18 applies; see s 18(1)(h) of that Act at **[975]**. The standard conciliation period applies to such claims by virtue of the Employment Tribunals (Constitution and Rules of Procedure) Regulations 2004, SI 2004/1861, Sch 1, rule 22(1), (6).

See *Harvey* DII, J, R, T(A).

ARRANGEMENT OF REGULATIONS

PART I
GENERAL AND INTERPRETATION

PART II
RIGHTS AND REMEDIES

PART III
MISCELLANEOUS

PART IV
SPECIAL CLASSES OF PERSON

PART I
GENERAL AND INTERPRETATION

1 Citation, commencement and interpretation

(1) These Regulations may be cited as the Part-time Workers (Prevention of Less Favourable Treatment) Regulations 2000 and shall come into force on 1st July 2000.

(2) In these Regulations—

"the 1996 Act" means the Employment Rights Act 1996;

"contract of employment" means a contract of service or of apprenticeship, whether express or implied, and (if it is express) whether oral or in writing;

"employee" means an individual who has entered into or works under or (except where a provision of these Regulations otherwise requires) where the employment has ceased, worked under a contract of employment;

"employer", in relation to any employee or worker, means the person by whom the employee or worker is or (except where a provision of these Regulations otherwise requires) where the employment has ceased, was employed;

"pro rata principle" means that where a comparable full-time worker receives or is entitled to receive pay or any other benefit, a part-time worker is to receive or be entitled to receive not less than the proportion of that pay or other benefit that the number of his weekly hours bears to the number of weekly hours of the comparable full-time worker;

"worker" means an individual who has entered into or works under or (except where a provision of these Regulations otherwise requires) where the employment has ceased, worked under—

(a) a contract of employment; or

(b) any other contract, whether express or implied and (if it is express) whether oral or in writing, whereby the individual undertakes to do or perform personally any work or services for another party to the contract whose status is not by virtue of the contract that of a client or customer of any profession or business undertaking carried on by the individual.

(3) In the definition of the pro rata principle and in regulations 3 and 4 "weekly hours" means the number of hours a worker is required to work under his contract of employment in a week in which he has no absences from work and does not work any overtime or, where the number of such hours varies according to a cycle, the average number of such hours.

[2637]

2 Meaning of full-time worker, part-time worker and comparable full-time worker

(1) A worker is a full-time worker for the purpose of these Regulations if he is paid wholly or in part by reference to the time he works and, having regard to the custom and practice of the employer in relation to workers employed by the worker's employer under the same type of contract, is identifiable as a full-time worker.

(2) A worker is a part-time worker for the purpose of these Regulations if he is paid wholly or in part by reference to the time he works and, having regard to the custom and practice of the employer in relation to workers employed by the worker's employer under the same type of contract, is not identifiable as a full-time worker.

[(3) For the purposes of paragraphs (1), (2) and (4), the following shall be regarded as being employed under different types of contract—

(a) employees employed under a contract that is not a contract of apprenticeship;

(b) employees employed under a contract of apprenticeship;

(c) workers who are not employees;

(d) any other description of worker that it is reasonable for the employer to treat differently from other workers on the ground that workers of that description have a different type of contract.]

(4) A full-time worker is a comparable full-time worker in relation to a part-time worker if, at the time when the treatment that is alleged to be less favourable to the part-time worker takes place—

(a) both workers are—

(i) employed by the same employer under the same type of contract, and

(ii) engaged in the same or broadly similar work having regard, where relevant, to whether they have a similar level of qualification, skills and experience; and

(b) the full-time worker works or is based at the same establishment as the part-time worker or, where there is no full-time worker working or based at that establishment who satisfies the requirements of sub-paragraph (a), works or is based at a different establishment and satisfies those requirements.

[2638]

NOTES

Para (3): substituted by the Part-time Workers (Prevention of Less Favourable Treatment) Regulations 2000 (Amendment) Regulations 2002, SI 2002/2035, reg 2(a).

3 Workers becoming part-time

(1) This regulation applies to a worker who—

(a) was identifiable as a full-time worker in accordance with regulation 2(1); and

(b) following a termination or variation of his contract, continues to work under a new or varied contract, whether of the same type or not, that requires him to work for a number of weekly hours that is lower than the number he was required to work immediately before the termination or variation.

(2) Notwithstanding regulation 2(4), regulation 5 shall apply to a worker to whom this regulation applies as if he were a part-time worker and as if there were a comparable full-time worker employed under the terms that applied to him immediately before the variation or termination.

(3) The fact that this regulation applies to a worker does not affect any right he may have under these Regulations by virtue of regulation 2(4).

[2639]

4 Workers returning part-time after absence

(1) This regulation applies to a worker who—

(a) was identifiable as a full-time worker in accordance with regulation 2(1) immediately before a period of absence (whether the absence followed a termination of the worker's contract or not);

(b) returns to work for the same employer within a period of less than twelve months beginning with the day on which the period of absence started;

(c) returns to the same job or to a job at the same level under a contract, whether it is a different contract or a varied contract and regardless of whether it is of the same type, under which he is required to work for a number of weekly hours that is lower than the number he was required to work immediately before the period of absence.

(2) Notwithstanding regulation 2(4), regulation 5 shall apply to a worker to whom this regulation applies ("the returning worker") as if he were a part-time worker and as if there were a comparable full-time worker employed under—

(a) the contract under which the returning worker was employed immediately before the period of absence; or

(b) where it is shown that, had the returning worker continued to work under the contract mentioned in sub-paragraph (a) a variation would have been made to its term during the period of absence, the contract mentioned in that sub-paragraph including that variation.

(3) The fact that this regulation applies to a worker does not affect any right he may have under these Regulations by virtue of regulation 2(4).

[2640]

PART II
RIGHTS AND REMEDIES

5 Less favourable treatment of part-time workers

(1) A part-time worker has the right not to be treated by his employer less favourably than the employer treats a comparable full-time worker—

(a) as regards the terms of his contract; or

(b) by being subjected to any other detriment by any act, or deliberate failure to act, of his employer.

(2) The right conferred by paragraph (1) applies only if—

(a) the treatment is on the ground that the worker is a part-time worker, and

(b) the treatment is not justified on objective grounds.

(3) In determining whether a part-time worker has been treated less favourably than a comparable full-time worker the pro rata principle shall be applied unless it is inappropriate.

(4) A part-time worker paid at a lower rate for overtime worked by him in a period than a comparable full-time worker is or would be paid for overtime worked by him in the same period shall not, for that reason, be regarded as treated less favourably than the comparable full-time worker where, or to the extent that, the total number of hours worked by the part-time worker in the period, including overtime, does not exceed the number of hours the comparable full-time worker is required to work in the period, disregarding absences from work and overtime.

[2641]

NOTES

Conciliation: employment tribunal proceedings and claims which could be the subject of employment tribunal proceedings arising out of a contravention, or alleged contravention, of para (1) are proceedings to which the Employment Tribunals Act 1996, s 18 applies; see s 18(1)(h) of that Act at **[975]**. The standard conciliation period applies to such proceedings by virtue of the Employment Tribunals (Constitution and Rules of Procedure) Regulations 2004, SI 2004/1861, Sch 1, rule 22(1), (6).

6 Right to receive a written statement of reasons for less favourable treatment

(1) If a worker who considers that his employer may have treated him in a manner which infringes a right conferred on him by regulation 5 requests in writing from his employer a written statement giving particulars of the reasons for the treatment, the worker is entitled to be provided with such a statement within twenty-one days of his request.

(2) A written statement under this regulation is admissible as evidence in any proceedings under these Regulations.

(3) If it appears to the tribunal in any proceedings under these Regulations—

(a) that the employer deliberately, and without reasonable excuse, omitted to provide a written statement, or

(b) that the written statement is evasive or equivocal,

it may draw any inference which it considers it just and equitable to draw, including an inference that the employer has infringed the right in question.

(4) This regulation does not apply where the treatment in question consists of the dismissal of an employee, and the employee is entitled to a written statement of reasons for his dismissal under section 92 of the 1996 Act.

[2642]

7 Unfair dismissal and the right not to be subjected to detriment

(1) An employee who is dismissed shall be regarded as unfairly dismissed for the purposes of Part X of the 1996 Act if the reason (or, if more than one, the principal reason) for the dismissal is a reason specified in paragraph (3).

(2) A worker has the right not to be subjected to any detriment by any act, or any deliberate failure to act, by his employer done on a ground specified in paragraph (3).

(3) The reasons or, as the case may be, grounds are—

(a) that the worker has—

(i) brought proceedings against the employer under these Regulations;

(ii) requested from his employer a written statement of reasons under regulation 6;

(iii) given evidence or information in connection with such proceedings brought by any worker;

(iv) otherwise done anything under these Regulations in relation to the employer or any other person;

(v) alleged that the employer had infringed these Regulations; or

(vi) refused (or proposed to refuse) to forgo a right conferred on him by these Regulations, or

(b) that the employer believes or suspects that the worker has done or intends to do any of the things mentioned in sub-paragraph (a).

(4) Where the reason or principal reason for dismissal or, as the case may be, ground for subjection to any act or deliberate failure to act, is that mentioned in paragraph (3)(a)(v), or (b) so far as it relates thereto, neither paragraph (1) nor paragraph (2) applies if the allegation made by the worker is false and not made in good faith.

(5) Paragraph (2) does not apply where the detriment in question amounts to the dismissal of an employee within the meaning of Part X of the 1996 Act.

[2643]

NOTES

Conciliation: employment tribunal proceedings and claims which could be the subject of employment tribunal proceedings arising out of a contravention, or alleged contravention, of para (2) are proceedings to which the Employment Tribunals Act 1996, s 18 applies; see s 18(1)(h) of that Act at **[975]**. The standard conciliation period applies to such proceedings by virtue of the Employment Tribunals (Constitution and Rules of Procedure) Regulations 2004, SI 2004/1861, Sch 1, rule 22(1), (6).

8 Complaints to employment tribunals etc

(1) Subject to regulation 7(5), a worker may present a complaint to an employment tribunal that his employer has infringed a right conferred on him by regulation 5 or 7(2).

(2) Subject to paragraph (3), an employment tribunal shall not consider a complaint under this regulation unless it is presented before the end of the period of three months (or, in a case to which regulation 13 applies, six months) beginning with the date of the less favourable treatment or detriment to which the complaint relates or, where an act or failure to act is part of a series of similar acts or failures comprising the less favourable treatment or detriment, the last of them.

(3) A tribunal may consider any such complaint which is out of time if, in all the circumstances of the case, it considers that it is just and equitable to do so.

(4) For the purposes of calculating the date of the less favourable treatment or detriment under paragraph (2)—

(a) where a term in a contract is less favourable, that treatment shall be treated, subject to paragraph (b), as taking place on each day of the period during which the term is less favourable;

(b) where an application relies on regulation 3 or 4 the less favourable treatment shall be treated as occurring on, and only on, in the case of regulation 3, the first day on which the applicant worked under the new or varied contract and, in the case of regulation 4, the day on which the applicant returned; and

(c) a deliberate failure to act contrary to regulation 5 or 7(2) shall be treated as done when it was decided on.

(5) In the absence of evidence establishing the contrary, a person shall be taken for the purposes of paragraph (4)(c) to decide not to act—

(a) when he does an act inconsistent with doing the failed act; or

(b) if he has done no such inconsistent act, when the period expires within which he might reasonably have been expected to have done the failed act if it was to be done.

(6) Where a worker presents a complaint under this regulation it is for the employer to identify the ground for the less favourable treatment or detriment.

(7) Where an employment tribunal finds that a complaint presented to it under this regulation is well founded, it shall take such of the following steps as it considers just and equitable—

(a) making a declaration as to the rights of the complainant and the employer in relation to the matters to which the complaint relates;
(b) ordering the employer to pay compensation to the complainant;
(c) recommending that the employer take, within a specified period, action appearing to the tribunal to be reasonable, in all the circumstances of the case, for the purpose of obviating or reducing the adverse effect on the complainant of any matter to which the complaint relates.

(8) …

(9) Where a tribunal orders compensation under paragraph (7)(b), the amount of the compensation awarded shall be such as the tribunal considers just and equitable in all the circumstances … having regard to—
(a) the infringement to which the complaint relates, and
(b) any loss which is attributable to the infringement having regard, in the case of an infringement of the right conferred by regulation 5, to the pro rata principle except where it is inappropriate to do so.

(10) The loss shall be taken to include—
(a) any expenses reasonably incurred by the complainant in consequence of the infringement, and
(b) loss of any benefit which he might reasonably be expected to have had but for the infringement.

(11) Compensation in respect of treating a worker in a manner which infringes the right conferred on him by regulation 5 shall not include compensation for injury to feelings.

(12) In ascertaining the loss the tribunal shall apply the same rule concerning the duty of a person to mitigate his loss as applies to damages recoverable under the common law of England and Wales or (as the case may be) Scotland.

(13) Where the tribunal finds that the act, or failure to act, to which the complaint relates was to any extent caused or contributed to by action of the complainant, it shall reduce the amount of the compensation by such proportion as it considers just and equitable having regard to that finding.

(14) If the employer fails, without reasonable justification, to comply with a recommendation made by an employment tribunal under paragraph (7)(c) the tribunal may, if it thinks it just and equitable to do so—
(a) increase the amount of compensation required to be paid to the complainant in respect of the complaint, where an order was made under paragraph (7)(b); or
(b) make an order under paragraph (7)(b).

[2644]

NOTES

Para (8): revoked by the Part-time Workers (Prevention of Less Favourable Treatment) Regulations 2000 (Amendment) Regulations 2002, SI 2002/2035, reg 2(b)(i).
Para (9): words omitted revoked by SI 2002/2035, reg 2(b)(ii).

---

9 Restrictions on contracting out

Section 203 of the 1996 Act (restrictions on contracting out) shall apply in relation to these Regulations as if they were contained in that Act.

[2645]

PART III
MISCELLANEOUS

10 Amendments to primary legislation

The amendments in the Schedule to these Regulations shall have effect.

[2646]

11 Liability of employers and principals

(1) Anything done by a person in the course of his employment shall be treated for the purposes of these Regulations as also done by his employer, whether or not it was done with the employer's knowledge or approval.

(2) Anything done by a person as agent for the employer with the authority of the employer shall be treated for the purposes of these Regulations as also done by the employer.

(3) In proceedings under these Regulations against any person in respect of an act alleged to have been done by a worker of his, it shall be a defence for that person to prove that he took such steps as were reasonably practicable to prevent the worker from—

(a) doing that act; or

(b) doing, in the course of his employment, acts of that description.

[2647]

PART IV
SPECIAL CLASSES OF PERSON

12 Crown employment

(1) Subject to regulation 13, these Regulations have effect in relation to Crown employment and persons in Crown employment as they have effect in relation to other employment and other employees and workers.

(2) In paragraph (1) "Crown employment" means employment under or for the purposes of a government department or any officer or body exercising on behalf of the Crown functions conferred by a statutory provision.

(3) For the purposes of the application of the provisions of these Regulations in relation to Crown employment in accordance with paragraph (1)—

(a) references to an employee and references to a worker shall be construed as references to a person in Crown employment to whom the definition of employee or, as the case may be, worker is appropriate; and

(b) references to a contract in relation to an employee and references to a contract in relation to a worker shall be construed as references to the terms of employment of a person in Crown employment to whom the definition of employee or, as the case may be, worker is appropriate.

[2648]

13 Armed forces

(1) These Regulations, shall have effect in relation—

(a) subject to paragraphs (2) and (3) and apart from regulation 7(1), to service as a member of the armed forces, and

(b) to employment by an association established for the purposes of Part XI of the Reserve Forces Act 1996.

(2) These Regulations shall not have effect in relation to service as a member of the reserve forces in so far as that service consists in undertaking training obligations—

(a) under section 38, 40 or 41 of the Reserve Forces Act 1980,

(b) under section 22 of the Reserve Forces Act 1996,

(c) pursuant to regulations made under section 4 of the Reserve Forces Act 1996,

or consists in undertaking voluntary training or duties under section 27 of the Reserve Forces Act 1996.

(3) No complaint concerning the service of any person as a member of the armed forces may be presented to an employment tribunal under regulation 8 unless—

(a) that person has made a complaint in respect of the same matter to an officer under the service redress procedures, and

(b) that complaint has not been withdrawn.

(4) For the purposes of paragraph (3)(b), a person shall be treated as having withdrawn his complaint if, having made a complaint to an officer under the service redress procedures, he fails to submit the complaint to the Defence Council under those procedures.

(5) Where a complaint of the kind referred to in paragraph (3) is presented to an employment tribunal, the service redress procedures may continue after the complaint is presented.

(6) In this regulation, "the service redress procedures" means the procedures, excluding those which relate to the making of a report to Her Majesty, referred to in section 180 of the Army Act 1955, section 180 of the Air Force Act 1955 and section 130 of the Naval Discipline Act 1957.

[2649]

14 House of Lords staff

(1) These Regulations have effect in relation to employment as a relevant member of the House of Lords staff as they have effect in relation to other employment.

(2) In this regulation "relevant member of the House of Lords staff" means any person who is employed under a contract with the Corporate Officer of the House of Lords by virtue of which he is a worker.

[2650]

15 House of Commons staff

(1) These Regulations have effect in relation to employment as a relevant member of the House of Commons staff as they have effect in relation to other employment.

(2) In this regulation "relevant member of the House of Commons staff" means any person—

(a) who was appointed by the House of Commons Commission; or

(b) who is a member of the Speaker's personal staff.

[2651]

16 Police service

(1) For the purposes of these Regulations, the holding, otherwise than under a contract of employment, of the office of constable or an appointment as a police cadet shall be treated as employment, under a contract of employment, by the relevant officer.

[(1A) For the purposes of these Regulations, any constable who has been seconded to SOCA to serve as a member of its staff shall be treated as employed by SOCA, in respect of actions taken by, or on behalf of, SOCA.

(1B) For the purposes of regulation 11 (liability of employers and principals),—

(a) the secondment of any constable to SOCA to serve as a member of its staff shall be treated as employment by SOCA (and not as being employment by any other person); and

(b) anything done by a constable so seconded in the performance, or purported performance, of his functions shall be treated as done in the course of that employment.]

(2) In this regulation "the relevant officer" means—

(a) in relation to a member of a police force or a special constable or police cadet appointed for a police area, the chief officer of police (or, in Scotland, the chief constable);

(b) … ; and

(c) in relation to any other person holding the office of constable or an appointment as a police cadet, the person who has the direction and control of the body of constables or cadets in question.

[(4) For the purposes of these Regulations the relevant officer, as defined by paragraph (3), shall be treated as a corporation sole.

(5) In the application of this regulation to Scotland paragraph (4) shall have effect as if for the words "corporation sole" there were substituted "distinct juristic person (that is to say, as a juristic person distinct from the individual who for the time being is the office-holder).]

[(6) In this regulation "SOCA" means the Serious Organised Crime Agency.]

[2652]

NOTES

Paras (1A), (1B), (6): inserted and added respectively by the Serious Organised Crime and Police Act 2005 (Consequential and Supplementary Amendments to Secondary Legislation) Order 2006, SI 2006/594, art 2, Schedule, para 21(1), (2), (4), as from 1 April 2006.

Para (2): sub-para (b) revoked by SI 2006/594, art 2, Schedule, para 21(1), (3), as from 1 April 2006.

Paras (4), (5): added by the Part-time Workers (Prevention of Less Favourable Treatment) Regulations 2000 (Amendment) Order 2005, SI 2005/2240, art 2, as from 1 September 2005. Note that art 2 provides that these paragraphs should be inserted "after paragraph (3)"; this appears to be an error, as does the reference in para (4) to "paragraph (3)".

17 Holders of judicial offices

These Regulations do not apply to any individual in his capacity as the holder of a judicial office if he is remunerated on a daily fee-paid basis.

[2653]–[2654]

(*The Schedule amends the Employment Tribunals Act 1996, ss 18, 21 at* **[975]**, **[978]**, *the Employment Rights Act 1996, ss 105, 108 at* **[1149]**, **[1152]** *and amended s 109 of that Act* (*repealed*).)

TELECOMMUNICATIONS (LAWFUL BUSINESS PRACTICE) (INTERCEPTION OF COMMUNICATIONS) REGULATIONS 2000

(SI 2000/2699)

NOTES

Made: 2 October 2000.
Authority: Regulation of Investigatory Powers Act 2000, ss 4(2), 78(5).
Commencement: 24 October 2000.

1 Citation and commencement

These Regulations may be cited as the Telecommunications (Lawful Business Practice) (Interception of Communications) Regulations 2000 and shall come into force on 24th October 2000.

[2655]

2 Interpretation

In these Regulations—

(a) references to a business include references to activities of a government department, of any public authority or of any person or office holder on whom functions are conferred by or under any enactment;

(b) a reference to a communication as relevant to a business is a reference to—

(i) a communication—

(aa) by means of which a transaction is entered into in the course of that business, or

(bb) which otherwise relates to that business, or

(ii) a communication which otherwise takes place in the course of the carrying on of that business;

(c) "regulatory or self-regulatory practices or procedures" means practices or procedures—

(i) compliance with which is required or recommended by, under or by virtue of—

(aa) any provision of the law of a member state or other state within the European Economic Area, or

(bb) any standard or code of practice published by or on behalf of a body established in a member state or other state within the European Economic Area which includes amongst its objectives the publication of standards or codes of practice for the conduct of business, or

(ii) which are otherwise applied for the purpose of ensuring compliance with anything so required or recommended;

(d) "system controller" means, in relation to a particular telecommunication system, a person with a right to control its operation or use.

[2656]

3 Lawful interception of a communication

(1) For the purpose of section 1(5)(a) of the Act, conduct is authorised, subject to paragraphs (2) and (3) below, if it consists of interception of a communication, in the course

of its transmission by means of a telecommunication system, which is effected by or with the express or implied consent of the system controller for the purpose of—

(a) monitoring or keeping a record of communications—

(i) in order to—

(aa) establish the existence of facts, or

(bb) ascertain compliance with regulatory or self-regulatory practices or procedures which are—

applicable to the system controller in the carrying on of his business or

applicable to another person in the carrying on of his business where that person is supervised by the system controller in respect of those practices or procedures, or

(cc) ascertain or demonstrate the standards which are achieved or ought to be achieved by persons using the system in the course of their duties, or

(ii) in the interests of national security, or

(iii) for the purpose of preventing or detecting crime, or

(iv) for the purpose of investigating or detecting the unauthorised use of that or any other telecommunication system, or

(v) where that is undertaken—

(aa) in order to secure, or

(bb) as an inherent part of,

the effective operation of the system (including any monitoring or keeping of a record which would be authorised by section 3(3) of the Act if the conditions in paragraphs (a) and (b) thereof were satisfied); or

(b) monitoring communications for the purpose of determining whether they are communications relevant to the system controller's business which fall within regulation 2(b)(i) above; or

(c) monitoring communications made to a confidential voice-telephony counselling or support service which is free of charge (other than the cost, if any, of making a telephone call) and operated in such a way that users may remain anonymous if they so choose.

(2) Conduct is authorised by paragraph (1) of this regulation only if—

(a) the interception in question is effected solely for the purpose of monitoring or (where appropriate) keeping a record of communications relevant to the system controller's business;

(b) the telecommunication system in question is provided for use wholly or partly in connection with that business;

(c) the system controller has made all reasonable efforts to inform every person who may use the telecommunication system in question that communications transmitted by means thereof may be intercepted; and

(d) in a case falling within—

(i) paragraph (1)(a)(ii) above, the person by or on whose behalf the interception is effected is a person specified in section 6(2)(a) to (i) of the Act;

(ii) paragraph (1)(b) above, the communication is one which is intended to be received (whether or not it has been actually received) by a person using the telecommunication system in question.

[(3) Conduct falling within paragraph (1)(a)(i) above is authorised only to the extent that Article 5 of Directive 2002/58/EC of the European Parliament and of the Council of 12 July 2002 concerning the processing of personal data and the protection of privacy in the electronic communications sector so permits.]

[2657]

NOTES

Para (3): substituted by the Privacy and Electronic Communications (EC Directive) Regulations 2003, SI 2003/2426, reg 34, as from 11 December 2003.

EMPLOYMENT TRIBUNALS (CONSTITUTION AND RULES OF PROCEDURE) (SCOTLAND) REGULATIONS 2001 (NOTE)

(SI 2001/1170)

NOTES

These Regulations were revoked by the Employment Tribunals (Constitution and Rules of Procedure) Regulations 2004, SI 2004/1861, reg 1(3), as from 1 October 2004, subject to transitional provisions and savings contained in reg 20 of those Regulations at **[3170]**. The 2004 Regulations are at **[3151]** et seq.

[2658]–[2676]

EMPLOYMENT TRIBUNALS (CONSTITUTION AND RULES OF PROCEDURE) REGULATIONS 2001 (NOTE)

(SI 2001/1171)

NOTES

These Regulations were revoked by the Employment Tribunals (Constitution and Rules of Procedure) Regulations 2004, SI 2004/1861, reg 1(3), as from 1 October 2004, subject to transitional provisions and savings contained in reg 20 of those Regulations at **[3170]**. The 2004 Regulations are at **[3151]** et seq.

[2677]–[2699]

RIGHT TO TIME OFF FOR STUDY OR TRAINING REGULATIONS 2001 (NOTE)

(SI 2001/2801)

NOTES

These Regulations, which were reproduced in the fifteenth edition of this work, have been omitted for reasons of space.

[2700]–[2705]

RACE RELATIONS ACT 1976 (STATUTORY DUTIES) ORDER 2001

(SI 2001/3458)

NOTES

Made: 23 October 2001.

Authority: Race Relations Act 1976, s 71(2), (3).

Commencement: 3 December 2001.

See further, the Commission for Racial Equality's Code of Practice on the Duty to Promote Racial Equality (2002) at **[4632]** made under s 71C of the 1976 Act (and note that that section is prospectively repealed by the Equality Act 2006, ss 40, 91, Sch 3, paras 21, 30, Sch 4, as from a day to be appointed).

See also the Race Relations Act 1976 (Statutory Duties) (Scotland) Order 2002, SSI 2002/62 at **[2718]** and the note at the beginning of that Order. Note that although there is a separate Order applying to Scotland, this Order also applies to Scotland to the extent that bodies specified in any of the Schedules hereto have functions extending to Scotland.

See *Harvey* P.

ARRANGEMENT OF ARTICLES

SCHEDULES:

1 Citation, commencement and interpretation

(1) This Order may be cited as the Race Relations Act 1976 (Statutory Duties) Order 2001 and shall come into force on 3rd December 2001.

(2) In this Order—

"the Race Relations Act" means the Race Relations Act 1976;

"staff" includes any person treated as an employee for the purposes of Part II of the Race Relations Act (Discrimination in the Employment Field); and

references to "150 full-time staff" are references to such number of staff as would, if the hours they work were aggregated, amount to 150 staff working on a full-time basis.

[2706]

2 Race equality schemes

(1) A body or other person specified in Schedule 1 to this Order shall, before 31st May 2002, publish a Race Equality Scheme, that is a scheme showing how it intends to fulfil its duties under section 71(1) of the Race Relations Act and this Order.

(2) A Race Equality Scheme shall state, in particular—

(a) those of its functions and policies, or proposed policies, which that person has assessed as relevant to its performance of the duty imposed by section 71(1) of the Race Relations Act; and

(b) that person's arrangements for—

(i) assessing and consulting on the likely impact of its proposed policies on the promotion of race equality;

(ii) monitoring its policies for any adverse impact on the promotion of race equality;

(iii) publishing the results of such assessments and consultation as are mentioned in sub-paragraph (i) and of such monitoring as is mentioned in sub-paragraph (ii);

(iv) ensuring public access to information and services which it provides; and

(v) training staff in connection with the duties imposed by section 71(1) of the Race Relations Act and this Order.

(3) Such a person shall, within a period of three years from 31st May 2002, and within each further period of three years, review the assessment referred to in paragraph (2)(a).

[2707]

NOTES

Modifications: see the Equality Act 2006 (Dissolution of Commissions and Consequential and Transitional Provisions) Order 2007, SI 2007/2602, art 4 (at **[3473N]**) which provides that the Schedule to that Order has effect for the amendment and modification of subordinate legislation in consequence of the dissolution of the Commission for Racial Equality, the Disability Rights Commission and the Equal Opportunities Commission and the establishment of the Commission for Equality and Human Rights. Para 4 of the Schedule to that Order (as substituted by SI 2007/3555) provides that in the application of this Order to that Commission it shall have effect as if, for "31st May 2002" (in each place) there were substituted "1st April 2008".

See also the Offender Management Act 2007 (Consequential Amendments) Order 2008, SI 2008/912, art 3, Sch 2, para 4(3), (4), which provides as follows—

"(3) In its application to a probation trust, that Order shall have effect as if—

(a) in articles 2(1) and 5(1)(a), for "before 31st May 2002" there were substituted "within a period of one year from the date of the establishment of a probation trust under section 5(1) of the Offender Management Act 2007"; and

(b) in article 2(3), for "three years from 31st May 2002" there were substituted "three years from the date of publication of its Race Equality Scheme".

(4) In its application to a provider of probation services (other than the Secretary of State or a probation trust) that Order shall have effect, in relation to the performance of its statutory functions and

the carrying out by it of activities of a public nature in pursuance of arrangements made with it under section 3(2) of the Offender Management Act 2007, as if—

(a) in articles 2(1) and 5(1)(a), for "before 31st May 2002" there were substituted "within a period of one year from the date on which it first entered into arrangements under section 3(2) of the Offender Management Act 2007"; and

(b) in article 2(3), for "a period of three years from 31st May 2002" there were substituted "a period of three years from the date of publication of its Race Equality Scheme.".

3 Educational bodies

(1) A body specified in Part I or II of Schedule 2 to this Order shall, before 31st May 2002,

(a) prepare a written statement of its policy for promoting race equality (referred to in this article as its "race equality policy"), and

(b) have in place arrangements for fulfilling, as soon as is reasonably practicable, its duties under paragraph (3) or (4), as the case may be.

(2) Such a body shall,

(a) maintain a copy of the statement, and

(b) fulfil those duties in accordance with such arrangements.

(3) It shall be the duty of a body specified in Part I of Schedule 2 to this Order to—

(a) assess the impact of its policies, including its race equality policy, on pupils, staff and parents of different racial groups including, in particular, the impact on attainment levels of such pupils; and

(b) monitor, by reference to their impact on such pupils, staff and parents, the operation of such policies including, in particular, their impact on the attainment levels of such pupils.

(4) It shall be the duty of a body specified in Part II of Schedule 2 to this Order to—

(a) assess the impact of its policies, including its race equality policy, on students and staff of different racial groups;

(b) monitor, by reference to those racial groups, the admission and progress of students and the recruitment and career progress of staff; and

(c) include in its written statement of its race equality policy an indication of its arrangements for publishing that statement and the results of its assessment and monitoring under sub-paragraphs (a) and (b).

(5) Such a body shall take such steps as are reasonably practicable to publish annually the results of its monitoring under this article.

[2708]

NOTES

Modification (application to Commission for Equality and Human Rights): see the note to art 2 at **[2707]**.

4—(1) A body specified in Part III, IV or V of Schedule 2 to this Order shall, before 31st May 2002, have in place arrangements for fulfilling, as soon as is reasonably practicable, its duties under paragraph (2), (3) or (4), as the case may be, and shall fulfil those duties in accordance with such arrangements.

(2) It shall be the duty of a body specified in Part III of Schedule 2 to this Order to monitor, by reference to the racial groups to which they belong,

(a) the numbers at all maintained schools in its area of—

(i) staff in post, and

(ii) applicants for employment, training and promotion, from each such group, and

(b) in the case of all maintained schools in its area which have 150 or more full-time staff, the numbers of staff from each such group who—

(i) receive training;

(ii) benefit or suffer detriment as a result of its performance assessment procedures;

(iii) are involved in grievance procedures;

(iv) are the subject of disciplinary procedures; or

(v) cease employment with such schools.

(3) It shall be the duty of a body specified in Part IV of Schedule 2 to this Order to—

(a) monitor, by reference to the racial groups to which they belong, the numbers of teaching staff from each such group at all maintained schools in respect of which it exercises its functions; and

(b) take such steps as are reasonably practicable to use, for that purpose, data provided by Local Education Authorities.

(4) It shall be the duty of a body specified in Part V of Schedule 2 to this Order to monitor, by reference to the racial groups to which they belong, the numbers of teaching staff from each such group at all educational establishments in respect of which it exercises its functions.

(5) Such a body shall take such steps as are reasonably practicable to publish annually the results of its monitoring under this article.

(6) In this article references to "maintained schools" are references to such schools within the meaning given by section 20(7) of the School Standards and Framework Act 1998.

[2709]

NOTES

Modification (application to Commission for Equality and Human Rights): see the note to art 2 at **[2707]**.

5 Monitoring by Employers

(1) A person to which this article applies shall,

(a) before 31st May 2002, have in place arrangements for fulfilling, as soon as is reasonably practicable, its duties under paragraph (2); and

(b) fulfil those duties in accordance with such arrangements.

(2) It shall be the duty of such a person to monitor, by reference to the racial groups to which they belong,

(a) the numbers of—

(i) staff in post, and

(ii) applicants for employment, training and promotion, from each such group, and

(b) where that person has 150 or more full-time staff, the numbers of staff from each such group who—

(i) receive training;

(ii) benefit or suffer detriment as a result of its performance assessment procedures;

(iii) are involved in grievance procedures;

(iv) are the subject of disciplinary procedures; or

(v) cease employment with that person.

(3) Such a person shall publish annually the results of its monitoring under paragraph (2).

(4) Subject to paragraph (5), this article applies to a body or other person specified in Schedule 1A to the Race Relations Act.

(5) This article does not apply to—

(a) a body specified in Part I, II or III of Schedule 2;

(b) a person specified in Schedule 3;

(c) a Scottish public authority with mixed functions or no reserved functions, as referred to in section L2 of Part II of Schedule 5 to the Scotland Act 1998; or

(d) a cross-border public authority in relation to the exercise of its Scottish functions within the meaning given by that section.

(6) In paragraph (5) the reference to a "cross-border public authority" is a reference to such an authority within the meaning given by section 88(5) of the Scotland Act 1998.

[2710]

NOTES

Modification (application to Commission for Equality and Human Rights): see the note to art 2 at **[2707]**.

Modification (application to a probation trust and provider of probation services): see the note to art 2 at **[2707]**.

SCHEDULES

SCHEDULE 1
BODIES AND OTHER PERSONS REQUIRED TO PUBLISH RACE EQUALITY SCHEMES

Article 2

The Higher Education Funding Council for England.

A body corporate established pursuant to an order under section 67 of the Local Government Act 1985 (transfer of functions to successors of residuary bodies, etc).

[A fire and rescue authority constituted by a scheme under section 2 of the Fire and Rescue Services Act 2004 or a scheme to which section 4 of that Act applies.]

[A Strategic Health Authority established under section 8 of the National Health Service Act 1977.]

A Health Authority established under section 8 of the National Health Service Act 1977.

A housing action trust established under Part III of the Housing Act 1988.

A joint authority established under Part IV of the Local Government Act 1985 (fire services, civil defence and transport).

A joint authority established under section 21 of the Local Government Act 1992.

In England, a county council, a London borough council or a district council.

In Wales, a county council or a county borough council.

A local probation board established under section 4 of the Criminal Justice and Court Services Act 2000.

…

A Minister of the Crown or government department.

A National Health Service trust established under section 5 of the National Health Service and Community Care Act 1990.

A Passenger Transport Executive for a passenger transport area [in England and Wales] within the meaning of Part II of the Transport Act 1968.

A police authority established under section 3 of the Police Act 1996.

A primary care trust established under section 16A of the National Health Service Act 1977.

[A probation trust.]

[A provider of probation services (other than the Secretary of State or a probation trust), in respect of its statutory functions and the carrying out by it of activities of a public nature in pursuance of arrangements made with it under section 3(2) of the Offender Management Act 2007.]

A regional development agency established under the Regional Development Agencies Act 1998 (other than the London Development Agency).

A special health authority established under section 11 of the National Health Service Act 1977.

An Assembly subsidiary as defined by section 99(4) of the Government of Wales Act 1998.

Any of the naval, military or air forces of the Crown.

The Audit Commission for Local Authorities and the National Health Service in England and Wales.

The British Broadcasting Corporation, in respect of its public functions.

The British Transport Police.

…

The Channel Four Television Corporation, in respect of its public functions.

A chief constable of a police force maintained under section 2 of the Police Act 1996.

The Commissioner of Police of the Metropolis.

The Commissioner of Police for the City of London.

The Children and Family Court Advisory and Support Service.

…

[The Commission for Equality and Human Rights.]

…

English Partnerships.

…

…

The Health and Safety Executive.

The Higher Education Funding Council for Wales.

…

The Learning and Skills Council for England.

The Legal Services Commission.

…

The National Audit Office.

…

…

…

Sianel Pedwar Cymru (Welsh Fourth Channel Authority), in respect of its public functions.

The Strategic Rail Authority.

The Chief Constable for the Ministry of Defence Police appointed by the Secretary of State under section 1(3) of the Ministry of Defence Police Act 1987.

The Common Council of the City of London, in its capacity as a local authority or port health authority.

The Common Council of the City of London, in its capacity as a police authority.

The Council of the Isles of Scilly.

The Greater London Authority.

The Housing Corporation.

The London Development Agency.

The London Fire and Emergency Planning Authority.

The Metropolitan Police Authority established under section 5B of the Police Act 1996.

The National Assembly for Wales.

The Scottish Parliamentary Corporate Body.

[The Serious Organised Crime Agency.]

The Sub-Treasurer of the Inner Temple or the Under-Treasurer of the Middle Temple, in his capacity as a local authority.

Transport for London.

…

[2711]

NOTES

Entry relating to "A fire and rescue authority" substituted by the Race Relations Act 1976 (Statutory Duties) Order 2004, SI 2004/3125, art 4, as from 31 December 2004 (in relation to England), and by the Fire and Rescue Services Act 2004 (Consequential Amendments) (Wales) Order 2005, SI 2005/2929, art 62, as from 25 October 2005 (in relation to Wales).

Entry relating to "A Strategic Health Authority" inserted by the National Health Service Reform and Health Care Professions Act 2002 (Supplementary, Consequential etc Provisions) Regulations 2002, SI 2002/2469, reg 4, Sch 1, Pt 2, para 97, as from 1 October 2002.

Entry "The Commission for Health Improvement" (omitted) revoked by the Health and Social Care (Community Health and Standards) Act 2003 (Commission for Healthcare Audit and Inspection and Commission for Social Care Inspection) (Transitional and Consequential Provisions) Order 2004, SI 2004/664, art 2, Sch 1, para 6, as from 1 April 2004.

Entry relating to "A magistrates' courts committee" (omitted) revoked by the Courts Act 2003 (Consequential Provisions) (No 2) Order 2005, SI 2005/617, art 2, Schedule, para 193, as from 1 April 2005.

Entry "The National Council for Education and Training for Wales" (omitted) revoked by the National Council for Education and Training for Wales (Transfer of Functions to the National Assembly for Wales and Abolition) Order 2005, SI 2005/3238, art 9(2), Sch 2, para 22(1), as from 1 April 2006.

Words in square brackets in entry relating to "A Passenger Transport Executive" inserted, and entries "The Broadcasting Standards Commission", "The Independent Television Commission", "The Local Government Commission for England", "The Police Complaints Authority", and "The Radio Authority" (omitted) revoked, by the Race Relations Act 1976 (Statutory Duties) Order 2003, SI 2003/3006, art 5(a), as from 31 December 2003.

Entries "A probation trust" and "A provider of probation services" inserted by the Offender Management Act 2007 (Consequential Amendments) Order 2008, SI 2008/912, art 3, Sch 2, para 4(1), (2), as from 1 April 2008.

Entry "The Commission for Equality and Human Rights" substituted, for original entry "The Commission for Racial Equality", by the Equality Act 2006 (Dissolution of Commissions and Consequential and Transitional Provisions) Order 2007, SI 2007/2602, art 4(1), Schedule, para 5(a), as from 1 October 2007.

Entries "The Disability Rights Commission" and "The Equal Opportunities Commission" (omitted) revoked by SI 2007/2602, art 4(1), Schedule, para 5(b), as from 1 October 2007.

Entry "The Health and Safety Commission" (omitted) revoked by the Legislative Reform (Health and Safety Executive) Order 2008, SI 2008/960, art 22, Sch 3, as from 1 April 2008 (see further the note 'The Health and Safety Executive' at **[2038]**).

Entry "The Serious Organised Crime Agency" substituted, for original entries relating to "The Service Authority for the National Crime Squad" and "The Service Authority for the National Criminal Intelligence Authority", by the Serious Organised Crime and Police Act 2005 (Consequential and Supplementary Amendments to Secondary Legislation) Order 2006, SI 2006/594, art 2, Schedule, para 27, as from 1 April 2006.

Entry relating to "The Welsh Development Agency" (omitted) revoked by the Welsh Development Agency (Transfer of Functions to the National Assembly for Wales and Abolition) Order 2005, SI 2005/3226, art 7(1)(b), Sch 2, Pt 1, para 5, as from 1 April 2006.

Note also that the reference to the Audit Commission for Local Authorities and the National Health Service in England and Wales is to be construed as a reference to the Audit Commission for Local Authorities and the National Health Service in England (as from 1 April 2008); see the Local Government and Public Involvement in Health Act 2007, s 146(4).

SCHEDULE 2
EDUCATIONAL BODIES

Articles 3 and 4

PART I

The Governing body of an educational establishment maintained by a Local Education Authority.

The Governing body of a City Technology College, City College for Technology of the Arts or a City Academy.

[2712]

PART II

The Governing body of an institution within the further education sector within the meaning of section 91(3) of the Further and Higher Education Act 1992.

The Governing body of an institution within the higher education sector within the meaning of section 91(5) of the Act of 1992.

[2713]

PART III

A Local Education Authority.

[2714]

PART IV

[The Department for Children, Schools and Families].

[2715]

NOTES

Words in square brackets substituted by the Secretaries of State for Children, Schools and Families, for Innovation, Universities and Skills and for Business, Enterprise and Regulatory Reform Order 2007, SI 2007/3224, art 15, Schedule, Pt 2, para 29, as from 12 December 2007.

PART V

The Learning and Skills Council for England.

The Higher Education Funding Council for England.

The Higher Education funding Council for Wales.

[National Assembly for Wales.]

[2716]

NOTES

Entry "National Assembly for Wales" substituted, for original entry "The National Council for Education and Training for Wales", by the National Council for Education and Training for Wales (Transfer of Functions to the National Assembly for Wales and Abolition) Order 2005, SI 2005/3238, art 9(2), Sch 2, para 22(2), as from 1 April 2006.

SCHEDULE 3

BODIES AND OTHER PERSONS EXCEPTED BY ARTICLE 5(5)(B)

Article 5

A parish meeting constituted under section 13 of the Local Government Act 1972.

A Parish Council in England.

A community council in Wales.

The Administration of Radioactive Substances Advisory Committee, otherwise than in respect of its Scottish functions within the meaning given by section L2 of Part II of Schedule 5 to the Scotland Act 1998.

The Advisory Committee on Hazardous Substances, otherwise than in respect of its Scottish functions within the meaning given by section L2 of Part II of Schedule 5 to the Scotland Act 1998.

The Advisory Committee on Pesticides, otherwise than in respect of its Scottish functions within the meaning given by section L2 of Part II of Schedule 5 to the Scotland Act 1998.

The Advisory Committee on Releases to the Environment, otherwise than in respect of its Scottish functions within the meaning given by section L2 of Part II of Schedule 5 to the Scotland Act 1998.

The Advisory Council on Public Records.

The Advisory Council on the Misuse of Drugs, otherwise than in respect of its Scottish functions within the meaning given by section L2 of Part II of Schedule 5 to the Scotland Act 1998.

An Agricultural Dwelling House Advisory Committee, established under the Rent (Agriculture) Act 1976.

The Agricultural Wages Board for England and Wales.

An Agricultural Wages Committee.

…

The Animal Procedures Committee.

The Building Regulations Advisory Committee.

The Central Advisory Committee on War Pensions.

The Civil Justice Council.

The Civil Procedure Rule Committee.

The Commonwealth Scholarship Commission in the United Kingdom.

The Consumer Council for Postal Services [("Postwatch")].

The Council on Tribunals, otherwise than in respect of its Scottish functions within the meaning given by section L2 of Part II of Schedule 5 to the Scotland Act 1998.

The Crown Court Rule Committee.

The Disability Living Allowance Advisory Board.

The Disabled Persons Transport Advisory Committee, otherwise than in respect of its Scottish functions within the meaning given by section L2 of Part II of Schedule 5 to the Scotland Act 1998.

The Environment Agency Advisory Committee for Wales.

The Family Proceedings Rule Committee.

The Firearms Consultative Committee.

The Government Hospitality Advisory Committee for the Purchase of Wine.

The Hill Farming Advisory Sub-Committee for Wales.

…

The Honours Scrutiny Committee.

A Visiting Committee appointed under section 152 of the Immigration and Asylum Act 1999 for an immigration detention centre.

The Industrial Injuries Advisory Council.

The [Inland Waterways Advisory Council], otherwise than in respect of its Scottish functions within the meaning given by section L2 of Part II of Schedule 5 to the Scotland Act 1998.

The Insolvency Rules Committee.

The Joint Committee on Vaccination and Immunisation.

The Land Registration Rule Committee.

The Law Commission.

The Legal Services Consultative Panel.

The Local Government Boundary Commission for Wales.

The Low Pay Commission.

The Magistrates' Courts Rule Committee.

The Overseas Service Pensions Scheme Advisory Board.

The Police Negotiating Board, otherwise than in respect of its Scottish functions within the meaning given by section L2 of Part II of Schedule 5 to the Scotland Act 1998.

The Quality Assurance Agency for Higher Education.

A Regional Flood Defence Committee established under section 14 of the Environment Act 1995.

The School Teachers' Review Body.

The Sentencing Advisory Panel.

The Social Security Advisory Committee.

The Standing Dental Advisory Committee.

The Standing Medical Advisory Committee.

The Standing Nursing and Midwifery Advisory Committee.

The Standing Pharmaceutical Advisory Committee.

The Theatres Trust, otherwise than in respect of its Scottish functions within the meaning given by section L2 of Part II of Schedule 5 to the Scotland Act 1998.

The Treasure Valuation Committee.

The Unrelated Live Transplant Regulatory Authority, otherwise than in respect of its Scottish functions within the meaning given by section L2 of Part II of Schedule 5 to the Scotland Act 1998.

The Wales New Deal Advisory Task Force.

A War Pensions Committee.

The Welsh Committee for Professional Development of Pharmacy.

The Welsh Dental Committee.

The Welsh Industrial Development Advisory Board.

The Welsh Medical Committee.

The Welsh Nursing and Midwifery Committee.

The Welsh Optometric Committee.

The Welsh Pharmaceutical Committee.

The Welsh Scientific Advisory Committee.

The Wilton Park Academic Council.

[2717]

NOTES

Entry relating to "The Ancient Monuments Board for Wales" (omitted) revoked by the Ancient Monuments Board for Wales (Abolition) Order 2006, SI 2006/64, art 3(2)(a), as from 1 April 2006.

Word in square brackets in entry relating to "The Consumer Council for Postal Services" added, and entry "The Quality Assurance Agency for Higher Education" (omitted) revoked, by the Race Relations Act 1976 (Statutory Duties) Order 2003, SI 2003/3006, art 5(b), as from 31 December 2003.

In entry relating to "The Inland Waterways Advisory Council" words in square brackets substituted by the Natural Environment and Rural Communities Act 2006, s 105(1), Sch 11, Pt 2, para 175(1)(b), as from 1 April 2007.

Entry relating to "The Historic Buildings Council for Wales" (omitted) revoked by the Historic Buildings Council for Wales (Abolition) Order 2006, SI 2006/63, art 3(2)(a), as from 1 April 2006.

RACE RELATIONS ACT 1976 (STATUTORY DUTIES) (SCOTLAND) ORDER 2002

(SSI 2002/62)

NOTES

Made: 14 February 2002.
Authority: Race Relations Act 1976, s 71(2), (3).
Commencement: 13 March 2002.

This Order was made by the Scottish Parliament under its devolved powers and applies only within Scotland and to such bodies and persons as are specified in the Schedule. The equivalent Order, applying to non-devolved bodies within Scotland, as well as to England and Wales, is the Race Relations Act 1976 (Statutory Duties) Order 2001, SI 2001/3458 at **[2706]**.

ARRANGEMENT OF ARTICLES

SCHEDULES:

1 Citation, commencement and interpretation

(1) This Order may be cited as the Race Relations Act 1976 (Statutory Duties) (Scotland) Order 2001 and shall come into force on 13th March 2002.

(2) In this Order—

"cross-border public authority" and "Scottish public authority with mixed functions or no reserved functions" have the meaning given by the Scotland Act 1998;

"the Race Relations Act" means the Race Relations Act 1976;

"staff" includes any person treated as an employee for the purposes of Part II (Discrimination in the Employment Field) of the Race Relations Act;

references to "150 full-time staff" are references to such number of staff as would, if the hours they work were aggregated, amount to 150 staff working on a full-time basis;

"Scottish functions" has the meaning given by section L2 of Part II of Schedule 5 to the Scotland Act 1998;

"education authority" has the meaning given by section 135 of the Education (Scotland) Act 1980; and

"school" has the meaning given by section 135 of the Education (Scotland) Act 1980 but excluding independent schools and in addition includes a place, other than a school, at which an education authority provides school education for pupils who are under school age, other than such a place at which school education is being provided by a person with whom that authority has, by virtue of section 35 of the Standards in Scotland's Schools etc Act 2000, entered into arrangements for the provision of that education; where "independent school", "school education", "pupil" and "school age" have the meanings given by section 135 of the Education (Scotland) Act 1980.

[2718]

2 Race Equality Schemes

(1) [Subject to articles 2A and 2B,] this article applies to a body or person specified in Schedule 1 to this Order.

(2) A body or person to which this article applies shall, before 30th November 2002, publish a Race Equality Scheme, that is a scheme showing how it intends to fulfil its duties under section 71(1) of the Race Relations Act and this Order.

(3) A Race Equality Scheme shall state, in particular—

(a) those of its functions and policies, or proposed policies, which that body or person has assessed as relevant to its performance of the duty imposed by section 71(1) of the Race Relations Act; and

(b) that body or person's arrangements for—

(i) assessing and consulting on the likely impact of its proposed policies on the promotion of race equality;

(ii) monitoring its policies for any adverse impact on the promotion of race equality;

(iii) publishing the results of such assessments and consultation as are mentioned in paragraph (i) and of such monitoring as is mentioned in paragraph (ii);

(iv) ensuring public access to information and services which it provides; and

(v) training staff in connection with the duties imposed by section 71(1) of the Race Relations Act and this Order.

(4) Such a body or person shall, by no later than 30th November 2005 and at three yearly intervals thereafter, review the assessment referred to in paragraph (3)(a).

[2719]

NOTES

Para (1): words in square brackets substituted by the Race Relations Act 1976 (Statutory Duties) (Scotland) Amendment Order 2006, SSI 2006/467, arts 2, 3, as from 7 October 2006.

Modification: para (2) above is modified in relation to any Passenger Transport Executive within the meaning of the Transport Act 1968, Pt II for a passenger transport area within Scotland; see the Race Relations Act 1976 (Statutory Duties) (Scotland) Amendment Order 2003, SSI 2003/566 art 5(2).

[2A—(1) In the case of the bodies or persons specified in paragraph (2), article 2 shall apply subject to the modifications that—

(a) for "30th November 2002" in article 2(2) there is substituted "30th November 2005"; and

(b) for "30th November 2005" in article 2(4) there is substituted "30th November 2008".

(2) The specified bodies or persons are—

(a) The Law Society of Scotland, in respect of its public functions;

(b) The Scottish Commission for the Regulation of Care;

(c) The Scottish Qualifications Authority; and

(d) The Scottish Social Services Council.]

[2719A]

NOTES

Commencement: 31 December 2004.

Inserted by the Race Relations Act 1976 (Statutory Duties) (Scotland) Amendment Order 2004, SSI 2004/521, arts 2, 4, as from 31 December 2004.

[2B—(1) In the case of the bodies or persons specified in paragraph (2), article 2 shall apply subject to the modifications that—

(a) for "30th November 2002" in article 2(2) there is substituted "30th November 2007"; and

(b) for "30th November 2005" in article 2(4) there is substituted "30th November 2010".

(2) The specified bodies or persons are—

(a) Bòrd na Gàidhlig;

(b) The Board of Trustees for the National Galleries of Scotland established under section 3 of the National Galleries of Scotland Act 1906;

(c) The Board of Trustees of the National Museums of Scotland established under section 1 of the National Heritage (Scotland) Act 1985;

(d) The Cairngorms National Park Authority;

(e) A chief officer of a community justice authority appointed under section 4 of the Management of Offenders etc (Scotland) Act 2005;

(f) A Chief Officer of a relevant authority appointed under section 7 of the Fire (Scotland) Act 2005;

(g) The Commissioner for Children and Young People in Scotland;

(h) A community justice authority established under section 3 of the Management of Offenders etc (Scotland) Act 2005;

(i) A joint fire and rescue board constituted by a scheme under section 2(1) of the Fire (Scotland) Act 2005;

(k) The Loch Lomond and The Trossachs National Park Authority;

(l) The Scottish Arts Council;

(m) The Scottish Further and Higher Education Funding Council;

(n) Scottish Natural Heritage;

(o) Scottish Screen;

(p) The Scottish Sports Council;

(q) The Trustees of the National Library of Scotland, constituted under section 1 of the National Library of Scotland Act 1925.]

[2719B]

NOTES

Commencement: 7 October 2006.

Inserted by the Race Relations Act 1976 (Statutory Duties) (Scotland) Amendment Order 2006, SSI 2006/467, arts 2, 4, as from 7 October 2006.

3 Educational Bodies or Persons

(1) A body or person specified in Part I or II of Schedule 2 to this Order shall, before 30th November 2002—

(a) prepare a written statement of its policy for promoting race equality (referred to in this article as its "race equality policy"); and

(b) have in place arrangements for fulfilling, as soon as is reasonably practicable, its duties under paragraph (4) or (5), as the case may be.

(2) Such a body or person shall—

(a) maintain a copy of its race equality policy and in the case of an education authority ensure that each school under its management maintains such a copy; and

(b) fulfil those duties in accordance with such arrangements and in the case of an education authority ensure that each school under its management complies with the arrangements.

(3) A race equality policy prepared under paragraph (1)(a) and the arrangements put in place under paragraph (1)(b) by an education authority will apply to each school under its management.

(4) It shall be the duty of a body or person specified in Part I of Schedule 2 to this Order to make arrangements for each school under its management to—

(a) assess the impact of its policies, including its race equality policy, on pupils, staff and parents of different racial groups including, in particular, the impact on attainment levels of such pupils; and

(b) monitor, by reference to their impact on such pupils, staff and parents, the operation of such policies including, in particular, their impact on the attainment levels of such pupils.

(5) It shall be the duty of a body or person specified in Part II of Schedule 2 to this Order to—

(a) assess the impact of its policies, including its race equality policy, on students and staff of different racial groups;

(b) monitor, by reference to those racial groups, the admission and progress of students and the recruitment and career progress of staff; and

(c) include in its written statement of its race equality policy an indication of its arrangements for publishing that statement and the results of its assessment and monitoring under sub-paragraphs (a) and (b).

(6) Such a body or person shall take such steps as are reasonably practicable to publish annually the results of its monitoring under this article.

[2720]

4—(1) A body or person specified in Part I, III or IV of Schedule 2 to this Order shall, before 30th November 2002, have in place arrangements for fulfilling, as soon as is reasonably practicable, its duties under paragraph (2), (3) or (4), as the case may be, and shall fulfil those duties in accordance with such arrangements.

(2) It shall be the duty of a body or person specified in Part I of Schedule 2 to this Order to monitor, by reference to the racial groups to which they belong—

(a) the numbers at each school under its management of—

(i) staff in post; and

(ii) applicants for employment, training and promotion, from each such group; and

(b) in the case of bodies or persons specified in Part I of Schedule 2 to this Order which have 150 or more full-time staff in total in all schools under their management, the numbers of staff from each school and each such group who—

(i) receive training;

(ii) benefit or suffer detriment as a result of its performance assessment procedures;

(iii) are involved in grievance procedures;

(iv) are the subject of disciplinary procedures; or

(v) cease employment with such schools.

(3) It shall be the duty of a body or person specified in Part III of Schedule 2 to this Order to—

(a) monitor, by reference to the racial groups to which they belong, the numbers of teaching staff from each such group at all schools in respect of which it exercises its functions; and
(b) take such steps as are reasonably practicable to use, for that purpose, data provided by education authorities and schools.

(4) It shall be the duty of a body or person specified in Part IV of Schedule 2 to this Order to monitor, by reference to the racial groups to which they belong, the numbers of teaching staff from each such group at all educational establishments in respect of which it exercises its functions.

(5) Such a body or person shall take such steps as are reasonably practicable to publish annually the results of its monitoring under this article.

[(6) The Scottish Further and Higher Education Funding Council shall, before 31st May 2007, have in place arrangements for fulfilling, as soon as is reasonably practicable, the duty specified in paragraph (4), and shall fulfil that duty in accordance with such arrangements.

(7) The Scottish Further and Higher Education Funding Council shall take such steps as are reasonably practicable to publish annually commencing from 31st May 2007 the results of its monitoring under paragraph (6).]

[2721]

NOTES

Paras (6), (7): added by the Race Relations Act 1976 (Statutory Duties) (Scotland) Amendment Order 2006, SSI 2006/467, arts 2, 5, as from 7 October 2006.

5 Monitoring by Employers

(1) [Subject to [articles 5A, 5B and 5C,]] a body or person to which this article applies shall—
(a) before 30th November 2002, have in place arrangements for fulfilling, as soon as is reasonably practicable, its duties under paragraph (2); and
(b) fulfil those duties in accordance with such arrangements.

(2) It shall be the duty of such a body or person to monitor, by reference to the racial groups to which they belong—
(a) the numbers of—
(i) staff in post; and
(ii) applicants for employment, training and promotion, from each such group; and
(b) where that body or person has 150 or more full-time staff, the numbers of staff from each such group who—
(i) receive training;
(ii) benefit or suffer detriment as a result of its performance assessment procedures;
(iii) are involved in grievance procedures;
(iv) are the subject of disciplinary procedures; or
(v) cease employment with that person or other body.

(3) Such a body or person shall publish annually the results of its monitoring under paragraph (2).

(4) Except as provided for in paragraph (5), this article applies to a body or person specified in Schedule 1A to the Race Relations Act which is—
(a) a Scottish public authority with mixed functions or no reserved functions; or
(b) a cross-border public authority in relation to the exercise of its Scottish functions.

(5) This article does not apply to—
(a) education authorities but only in respect of staff employed at schools under their management;
(b) any other body or person specified in Part I or II of Schedule 2 to this Order;
(c) a body or person specified in Schedule 3 to this Order to the extent, if any, so specified.

[2722]

NOTES

Para (1): words in first (outer) pair of square brackets inserted by the Race Relations Act 1976 (Statutory Duties) (Scotland) Amendment Order 2003, SSI 2003/566, arts 2, 3, as from

31 December 2003; words in second (inner) pair of square brackets substituted by the Race Relations Act 1976 (Statutory Duties) (Scotland) Amendment Order 2006, SSI 2006/467, arts 2, 6, as from 7 October 2006.

[5A—(1) In the case of the bodies or persons specified in paragraph (2), article 5 shall apply subject to the modification that for "30th November 2002" in article 5(1)(a) there is substituted "31st May 2004".

(2) The specified bodies or persons are—

(a) The League for the Exchange of Commonwealth Teachers;

(b) a National Park authority established by a designation order made under section 6 of the National Parks (Scotland) Act 2000;

(c) The Royal College of Physicians of Edinburgh, in respect of its public functions;

(d) The Royal College of Physicians and Surgeons of Glasgow, in respect of its public functions;

(e) The Royal College of Surgeons of Edinburgh, in respect of its public functions;

(f) The Scottish Commission for the Regulation of Care;

(g) The Scottish Information Commissioner; and

(h) The Scottish Social Services Council.]

[2723]

NOTES

Commencement: 31 December 2003.

Inserted by the Race Relations Act 1976 (Statutory Duties) (Scotland) Amendment Order 2003, SSI 2003/566, arts 2, 4, as from 31 December 2003.

[5B In the case of Bòrd na Gàidhlig (Alba), article 5 shall apply subject to the modification that for "30th November 2002" in article 5(1)(a) there is substituted "31st May 2005".]

[2723A]

NOTES

Commencement: 31 December 2004.

Inserted by the Race Relations Act 1976 (Statutory Duties) (Scotland) Amendment Order 2004, SSI 2004/521, arts 2, 6, as from 31 December 2004.

[5C—(1) In the case of the bodies or persons specified in paragraph (2), article 5 shall apply subject to the modification that for "30th November 2002" in article 5(1)(a) there is substituted "31st May 2007".

(2) The specified bodies or persons are—

(a) Architecture and Design Scotland;

(b) Bòrd na Gàidhlig;

(c) The chief officer of a community justice authority appointed under section 4 of the Management of Offenders etc (Scotland) Act 2005;

(d) A Chief Officer of a relevant authority appointed under section 7 of the Fire (Scotland) Act 2005;

(e) The Commissioner for Children and Young People in Scotland;

(f) A community justice authority established under section 3 of the Management of Offenders etc (Scotland) Act 2005;

(g) A joint fire and rescue board constituted by a scheme under section 2(1) of the Fire (Scotland) Act 2005;

(h) The Risk Management Authority;

(i) The Scottish Further and Higher Education Funding Council;

(j) The Scottish Library and Information Council;

(k) The Scottish Museums Council;

(l) Scottish UfI Limited;

(m) Scottish UfI Trust Limited;

(n) A Transport Partnership created by virtue of an order under section 1 of the Transport (Scotland) Act 2005;

(o) The Water Industry Commission for Scotland established under section 1 of the Water Services etc (Scotland) Act 2005.]

[2723B]

NOTES

Commencement: 7 October 2006.

Inserted by the Race Relations Act 1976 (Statutory Duties) (Scotland) Amendment Order 2006, SSI 2006/467, arts 2, 7, as from 7 October 2006.

SCHEDULES

SCHEDULE 1
BODIES AND OTHER PERSONS REQUIRED TO PUBLISH RACE EQUALITY SCHEMES

Article 2

The Accounts Commission for Scotland

Audit Scotland

A Chief Constable of a police force maintained under s 1 of the Police (Scotland) Act 1967

The Common Services Agency for the NHS in Scotland

A council constituted under section 2 of the Local Government etc (Scotland) Act 1994

A Health Board constituted under section 2 of the National Health Service (Scotland) Act 1978

A joint board within the meaning of section 235(1) of the Local Government (Scotland) Act 1973

The Keeper of the Records of Scotland

The Keeper of the Registers of Scotland

A licensing board constituted under section 1 of the Licensing (Scotland) Act 1976

A National Health Service Trust established under section 12A of the National Health Service (Scotland) Act 1978

[A Passenger Transport Executive within the meaning of Part II of the Transport Act 1968 for a passenger transport area within Scotland]

A police authority established under section 2 of the Police (Scotland) Act 1967

The Registrar General of Births, Deaths and Marriages for Scotland

Scottish Enterprise and Highlands and Islands Enterprise established under the Enterprise and New Towns (Scotland) Act 1990

…

…

The Scottish Legal Aid Board

The Scottish Ministers

…

A Special Health Board constituted under section 2 of the National Health Service (Scotland) Act 1978

[Scottish Water]

[2724]

NOTES

Entry "A Passenger Transport Executive within the meaning of Part II of the Transport Act 1968 for a passenger transport area within Scotland" inserted by the Race Relations Act 1976 (Statutory Duties) (Scotland) Amendment Order 2003, SSI 2003/566, arts 2, 5(1), as from 31 December 2003.

Entries "The Scottish Further Education Funding Council" and "The Scottish Higher Education Funding Council" (omitted) revoked by the Race Relations Act 1976 (Statutory Duties) (Scotland) Amendment Order 2006, SSI 2006/467, arts 2, 8, as from 7 October 2006.

Entry "The Service Authority for the National Criminal Intelligence Service in respect of its Scottish functions" (omitted) revoked by the Serious Organised Crime and Police Act 2005 (Consequential and Supplementary Amendments) (Scotland) Order 2006, SSI 2006/129, art 2, Schedule, para 7, as from 1 April 2006.

Entry "Scottish Water" substituted for original entry "A water or sewerage authority constituted under section 62 of the Local Government etc (Scotland) Act 1994" by the Water Industry (Scotland) Act 2002 (Consequential Provisions) Order 2003, SSI 2003/331, art 2, Schedule, Pt II, para 14, as from 25 June 2003.

SCHEDULE 2
EDUCATIONAL BODIES OR PERSONS

Articles 3 and 4

PART I
EDUCATION AUTHORITIES

The managers of a grant-aided school (within the meaning of section 135 of the Education (Scotland) Act 1980)

The board of management of a self-governing school (within the meaning of the Self-Governing Schools etc (Scotland) Act 1989)

[2725]

PART II

The board of management of a college of further education (within the meaning of section 36(1) of the Further and Higher Education (Scotland) Act 1992)

A college of further education maintained by an education authority in the exercise of its further education functions in providing courses of further education within the meaning of section 1(5)(b)(ii) of the Education (Scotland) Act 1980

Newbattle Abbey College

Sabhal Mòr Ostaig College

The governing body of an institution within the higher education sector (within the meaning of Part II of the Further and Higher Education (Scotland) Act 1992) other than any institution whose activities are principally carried on outwith Scotland including the Open University

The managers of a central institution (within the meaning of section 135 of the Education (Scotland) Act 1980)

[2726]]

PART III

The Scottish Ministers within the meaning of section 44(2) of the Scotland Act 1998

[2727]–[2728]

(*Sch 2, Pt IV revoked by the Race Relations Act 1976 (Statutory Duties) (Scotland) Amendment Order 2006, SSI 2006/467, arts 2, 9, as from 7 October 2006.*)

SCHEDULE 3
BODIES OR PERSONS EXCEPTED BY ARTICLE 5(5)(B) OF THIS ORDER

Article 5

The Accounts Commission for Scotland

The Administration of Radioactive Substances Advisory Committee in respect of its Scottish functions

The Advisory Committee on Sites of Special Scientific Interest

The Advisory Committee on Hazardous Substances in respect of its Scottish functions

The Advisory Committee on Pesticides in respect of its Scottish functions

The Advisory Committee on Releases to the Environment in respect of its Scottish functions

The Advisory Council on the Misuse of Drugs in respect of its Scottish functions

…

The Building Standards Advisory Committee

A community council established under section 51 of the Local Government (Scotland) Act 1973

The Council on Tribunals in respect of its Scottish functions

The Disabled Persons Transport Advisory Committee in respect of its Scottish functions

The Fisheries (Electricity) Committee

The Hill Farming Advisory Committee for Scotland

[The Historic Environment Advisory Council for Scotland]

The [Inland Waterways Advisory Council] in respect of its Scottish functions

The Local Government Boundary Commission for Scotland

Members of the staff of the Scottish Administration within the meaning given by section 126(7)(b) of the Scotland Act 1998

[The Mobility and Access Committee for Scotland

An Office-holder in the Scottish Administration within the meaning given by section 126(7)(a) of the Scotland Act 1998 other than those listed in Schedule 1 to this Order

[The panel constituted under Schedule 4 of the Rent (Scotland) Act 1984]

The Police Negotiating Board in respect of its Scottish functions

…

[The Scottish Agricultural Wages Board]

The Scottish Dental Practice Board

The Scottish Hospital Endowments Research Trust

…

The Scottish Industrial Development Advisory Board

The Scottish Medical Practices Committee

The Scottish Records Advisory Council

The Theatres Trust in respect of its Scottish functions

The Unrelated Live Transplant Regulatory Authority in respect of its Scottish functions

[A Water Customer Consultation Panel established by order under section 2(1) of the Water Industry (Scotland) Act 2002]

[2729]

NOTES

Entry "The Ancient Monuments Board for Scotland" (omitted) revoked by the Race Relations Act 1976 (Statutory Duties) (Scotland) Amendment Order 2003, SSI 2003/566, arts 2, 6(a), as from 31 December 2003.

Entry "The Historic Environment Advisory Council for Scotland" substituted for original entry "The Historic Buildings Council for Scotland" by SSI 2003/566, arts 2, 6(c), as from 31 December 2003.

In entry "The Inland Waterways Advisory Council" words in square brackets substituted by the Natural Environment and Rural Communities Act 2006, s 105(1), Sch 11, Pt 2, para 175(1)(b), as from 1 April 2007.

Entries "The Mobility and Access Committee for Scotland" and "The panel constituted under Schedule 4 of the Rent (Scotland) Act 1984" inserted, and entry "The Royal Fine Art Commission for Scotland" (omitted) revoked, by the Race Relations Act 1976 (Statutory Duties) (Scotland) Amendment Order 2006, SSI 2006/467, arts 2, 10, as from 7 October 2006.

Entries "The Scottish Agricultural Wages Board" and "A Water Customer Consultation Panel established by Order under section 2(1) of the Water Industry (Scotland) Act 2002" inserted by SSI 2003/566, arts 2, 6(b), (d), as from 31 December 2003.

Entry "The Scottish Hospital Trust" (omitted) revoked by the Race Relations Act 1976 (Statutory Duties) (Scotland) Amendment Order 2004, SSI 2004/521, arts 2, 7, as from 31 December 2004.

FIXED-TERM EMPLOYEES (PREVENTION OF LESS FAVOURABLE TREATMENT) REGULATIONS 2002

(SI 2002/2034)

NOTES

Made: 30 July 2002.

Authority: Employment Act 2002, ss 45, 51(1).

Commencement: 1 October 2002.

These Regulations are the domestic implementation of Council Directive 99/70, and the framework agreement on fixed-term work embodied therein, at **[3968]**.

Conciliation: employment tribunal proceedings and claims which could be the subject of employment tribunal proceedings arising out of a contravention, or alleged contravention, of regs 3, 6(2), or under reg 9, are proceedings to which the Employment Tribunals Act 1996, s 18 applies; see s 18(1)(i), (j) of that Act at **[975]**. The standard conciliation period applies to such claims by virtue of the Employment Tribunals (Constitution and Rules of Procedure) Regulations 2004, SI 2004/1861, Sch 1, rule 22(1), (6).

Employment Appeal Tribunal: an appeal lies to the Employment Appeal Tribunal on any question of law arising from any decision of, or in any proceedings before, an employment tribunal under or by virtue of these Regulations; see the Employment Tribunals Act 1996, s 21(1)(k) at **[978]**.

ARRANGEMENT OF REGULATIONS

PART 1
GENERAL AND INTERPRETATION

PART 2
RIGHTS AND REMEDIES

PART 3
MISCELLANEOUS

PART 4
SPECIAL CLASSES OF PERSON

PART 5
EXCLUSIONS

SCHEDULES:

PART 1
GENERAL AND INTERPRETATION

1 Citation, commencement and interpretation

(1) These Regulations may be cited as the Fixed-term Employees (Prevention of Less Favourable Treatment) Regulations 2002 and shall come into force on 1st October 2002.

(2) In these Regulations—

"the 1996 Act" means the Employment Rights Act 1996;

"collective agreement" means a collective agreement within the meaning of section 178 of the Trade Union and Labour Relations (Consolidation) Act 1992; the trade union parties to which are independent trade unions within the meaning of section 5 of that Act;

"employer", in relation to any employee, means the person by whom the employee is (or, where the employment has ceased, was) employed;

"fixed-term contract" means a contract of employment that, under its provisions determining how it will terminate in the normal course, will terminate—

(a) on the expiry of a specific term,
(b) on the completion of a particular task, or
(c) on the occurrence or non-occurrence of any other specific event other than the attainment by the employee of any normal and bona fide retiring age in the establishment for an employee holding the position held by him,

and any reference to "fixed-term" shall be construed accordingly;

"fixed-term employee" means an employee who is employed under a fixed-term contract;

"permanent employee" means an employee who is not employed under a fixed-term contract, and any reference to "permanent employment" shall be construed accordingly;

"pro rata principle" means that where a comparable permanent employee receives or is entitled to pay or any other benefit, a fixed-term employee is to receive or be entitled to such proportion of that pay or other benefit as is reasonable in the circumstances having regard to the length of his contract of employment and to the terms on which the pay or other benefit is offered;

"renewal" includes extension and references to renewing a contract shall be construed accordingly;

"workforce agreement" means an agreement between an employer and his employees or their representatives in respect of which the conditions set out in Schedule 1 to these Regulations are satisfied.

[2730]

2 Comparable employees

(1) For the purposes of these Regulations, an employee is a comparable permanent employee in relation to a fixed-term employee if, at the time when the treatment that is alleged to be less favourable to the fixed-term employee takes place,

(a) both employees are—
  (i) employed by the same employer, and
  (ii) engaged in the same or broadly similar work having regard, where relevant, to whether they have a similar level of qualification and skills; and
(b) the permanent employee works or is based at the same establishment as the fixed-term employee or, where there is no comparable permanent employee working or based at that establishment who satisfies the requirements of sub-paragraph (a), works or is based at a different establishment and satisfies those requirements.

(2) For the purposes of paragraph (1), an employee is not a comparable permanent employee if his employment has ceased.

[2731]

PART 2
RIGHTS AND REMEDIES

3 Less favourable treatment of fixed-term employees

(1) A fixed-term employee has the right not to be treated by his employer less favourably than the employer treats a comparable permanent employee—

(a) as regards the terms of his contract; or

(b) by being subjected to any other detriment by any act, or deliberate failure to act, of his employer.

(2) Subject to paragraphs (3) and (4), the right conferred by paragraph (1) includes in particular the right of the fixed-term employee in question not to be treated less favourably than the employer treats a comparable permanent employee in relation to—

(a) any period of service qualification relating to any particular condition of service,

(b) the opportunity to receive training, or

(c) the opportunity to secure any permanent position in the establishment.

(3) The right conferred by paragraph (1) applies only if—

(a) the treatment is on the ground that the employee is a fixed-term employee, and

(b) the treatment is not justified on objective grounds.

(4) Paragraph (3)(b) is subject to regulation 4.

(5) In determining whether a fixed-term employee has been treated less favourably than a comparable permanent employee, the pro rata principle shall be applied unless it is inappropriate.

(6) In order to ensure that an employee is able to exercise the right conferred by paragraph (1) as described in paragraph (2)(c) the employee has the right to be informed by his employer of available vacancies in the establishment.

(7) For the purposes of paragraph (6) an employee is "informed by his employer" only if the vacancy is contained in an advertisement which the employee has a reasonable opportunity of reading in the course of his employment or the employee is given reasonable notification of the vacancy in some other way.

[2732]

NOTES

Conciliation: employment tribunal proceedings and claims which could be the subject of employment tribunal proceedings arising out of a contravention, or alleged contravention, of this regulation are proceedings to which the Employment Tribunals Act 1996, s 18 applies; see s 18(1)(i) of that Act at **[975]**. The standard conciliation period applies to such proceedings by virtue of the Employment Tribunals (Constitution and Rules of Procedure) Regulations 2004, SI 2004/1861, Sch 1, rule 22(1), (6).

4 Objective justification

(1) Where a fixed-term employee is treated by his employer less favourably than the employer treats a comparable permanent employee as regards any term of his contract, the treatment in question shall be regarded for the purposes of regulation 3(3)(b) as justified on objective grounds if the terms of the fixed-term employee's contract of employment, taken as a whole, are at least as favourable as the terms of the comparable permanent employee's contract of employment.

(2) Paragraph (1) is without prejudice to the generality of regulation 3(3)(b).

[2733]

5 Right to receive a written statement of reasons for less favourable treatment

(1) If an employee who considers that his employer may have treated him in a manner which infringes a right conferred on him by regulation 3 requests in writing from his employer a written statement giving particulars of the reasons for the treatment, the employee is entitled to be provided with such a statement within twenty-one days of his request.

(2) A written statement under this regulation is admissible as evidence in any proceedings under these Regulations.

(3) If it appears to the tribunal in any proceedings under these Regulations—

(a) that the employer deliberately, and without reasonable excuse, omitted to provide a written statement, or

(b) that the written statement is evasive or equivocal,

it may draw any inference which it considers it just and equitable to draw, including an inference that the employer has infringed the right in question.

(4) This regulation does not apply where the treatment in question consists of the dismissal of an employee, and the employee is entitled to a written statement of reasons for his dismissal under section 92 of the 1996 Act.

[2734]

6 Unfair dismissal and the right not to be subjected to detriment

(1) An employee who is dismissed shall be regarded as unfairly dismissed for the purposes of Part 10 of the 1996 Act if the reason (or, if more than one, the principal reason) for the dismissal is a reason specified in paragraph (3).

(2) An employee has the right not to be subjected to any detriment by any act, or any deliberate failure to act, of his employer done on a ground specified in paragraph (3).

(3) The reasons or, as the case may be, grounds are—

(a) that the employee—

(i) brought proceedings against the employer under these Regulations;

(ii) requested from his employer a written statement under regulation 5 or regulation 9;

(iii) gave evidence or information in connection with such proceedings brought by any employee;

(iv) otherwise did anything under these Regulations in relation to the employer or any other person;

(v) alleged that the employer had infringed these Regulations;

(vi) refused (or proposed to refuse) to forgo a right conferred on him by these Regulations;

(vii) declined to sign a workforce agreement for the purposes of these Regulations, or

(viii) being—

(aa) a representative of members of the workforce for the purposes of Schedule 1, or

(bb) a candidate in an election in which any person elected will, on being elected, become such a representative,

performed (or proposed to perform) any functions or activities as such a representative or candidate, or

(b) that the employer believes or suspects that the employee has done or intends to do any of the things mentioned in sub-paragraph (a).

(4) Where the reason or principal reason for dismissal or, as the case may be, ground for subjection to any act or deliberate failure to act, is that mentioned in paragraph (3)(a)(v), or (b) so far as it relates thereto, neither paragraph (1) nor paragraph (2) applies if the allegation made by the employee is false and not made in good faith.

(5) Paragraph (2) does not apply where the detriment in question amounts to dismissal within the meaning of Part 10 of the 1996 Act.

[2735]

7 Complaints to employment tribunals etc

(1) An employee may present a complaint to an employment tribunal that his employer has infringed a right conferred on him by regulation 3, or (subject to regulation 6(5)), regulation 6(2).

(2) Subject to paragraph (3), an employment tribunal shall not consider a complaint under this regulation unless it is presented before the end of the period of three months beginning—

(a) in the case of an alleged infringement of a right conferred by regulation 3(1) or 6(2), with the date of the less favourable treatment or detriment to which the complaint relates or, where an act or failure to act is part of a series of similar acts or failures comprising the less favourable treatment or detriment, the last of them;

(b) in the case of an alleged infringement of the right conferred by regulation 3(6), with the date, or if more than one the last date, on which other individuals, whether or not employees of the employer, were informed of the vacancy.

(3) A tribunal may consider any such complaint which is out of time if, in all the circumstances of the case, it considers that it is just and equitable to do so.

(4) For the purposes of calculating the date of the less favourable treatment or detriment under paragraph (2)(a)—

(a) where a term in a contract is less favourable, that treatment shall be treated, subject to paragraph (b), as taking place on each day of the period during which the term is less favourable;

(b) a deliberate failure to act contrary to regulation 3 or 6(2) shall be treated as done when it was decided on.

(5) In the absence of evidence establishing the contrary, a person shall be taken for the purposes of paragraph (4)(b) to decide not to act—

(a) when he does an act inconsistent with doing the failed act; or

(b) if he has done no such inconsistent act, when the period expires within which he might reasonably have been expected to have done the failed act if it was to be done.

(6) Where an employee presents a complaint under this regulation in relation to a right conferred on him by regulation 3 or 6(2) it is for the employer to identify the ground for the less favourable treatment or detriment.

(7) Where an employment tribunal finds that a complaint presented to it under this regulation is well founded, it shall take such of the following steps as it considers just and equitable—

(a) making a declaration as to the rights of the complainant and the employer in relation to the matters to which the complaint relates;

(b) ordering the employer to pay compensation to the complainant;

(c) recommending that the employer take, within a specified period, action appearing to the tribunal to be reasonable, in all the circumstances of the case, for the purpose of obviating or reducing the adverse effect on the complainant of any matter to which the complaint relates.

(8) Where a tribunal orders compensation under paragraph (7)(b), the amount of the compensation awarded shall be such as the tribunal considers just and equitable in all the circumstances having regard to—

(a) the infringement to which the complaint relates, and

(b) any loss which is attributable to the infringement.

(9) The loss shall be taken to include—

(a) any expenses reasonably incurred by the complainant in consequence of the infringement, and

(b) loss of any benefit which he might reasonably be expected to have had but for the infringement.

(10) Compensation in respect of treating an employee in a manner which infringes the right conferred on him by regulation 3 shall not include compensation for injury to feelings.

(11) In ascertaining the loss the tribunal shall apply the same rule concerning the duty of a person to mitigate his loss as applies to damages recoverable under the common law of England and Wales or (as the case may be) the law of Scotland.

(12) Where the tribunal finds that the act, or failure to act, to which the complaint relates was to any extent caused or contributed to by action of the complainant, it shall reduce the amount of the compensation by such proportion as it considers just and equitable having regard to that finding.

(13) If the employer fails, without reasonable justification, to comply with a recommendation made by an employment tribunal under paragraph (7)(c) the tribunal may, if it thinks it just and equitable to do so—

(a) increase the amount of compensation required to be paid to the complainant in respect of the complaint, where an order was made under paragraph (7)(b); or

(b) make an order under paragraph (7)(b).

[2736]

NOTES

Conciliation: employment tribunal proceedings and claims which could be the subject of employment tribunal proceedings arising out of a contravention, or alleged contravention, of reg 6(2) are proceedings to which the Employment Tribunals Act 1996, s 18 applies; see s 18(1)(i) of that Act at **[975]**. The standard conciliation period applies to such proceedings by virtue of the Employment Tribunals (Constitution and Rules of Procedure) Regulations 2004, SI 2004/1861, Sch 1, rule 22(1), (6).

8 Successive fixed-term contracts

(1) This regulation applies where—

(a) an employee is employed under a contract purporting to be a fixed-term contract, and

(b) the contract mentioned in sub-paragraph (a) has previously been renewed, or the employee has previously been employed on a fixed-term contract before the start of the contract mentioned in sub-paragraph (a).

(2) Where this regulation applies then, with effect from the date specified in paragraph (3), the provision of the contract mentioned in paragraph (1)(a) that restricts the duration of the contract shall be of no effect, and the employee shall be a permanent employee, if—

(a) the employee has been continuously employed under the contract mentioned in paragraph 1(a), or under that contract taken with a previous fixed-term contract, for a period of four years or more, and

(b) the employment of the employee under a fixed-term contract was not justified on objective grounds—

(i) where the contract mentioned in paragraph (1)(a) has been renewed, at the time when it was last renewed;

(ii) where that contract has not been renewed, at the time when it was entered into.

(3) The date referred to in paragraph (2) is whichever is the later of—

(a) the date on which the contract mentioned in paragraph (1)(a) was entered into or last renewed, and

(b) the date on which the employee acquired four years' continuous employment.

(4) For the purposes of this regulation Chapter 1 of Part 14 of the 1996 Act shall apply in determining whether an employee has been continuously employed, and any period of continuous employment falling before the 10th July 2002 shall be disregarded.

(5) A collective agreement or a workforce agreement may modify the application of paragraphs (1) to (3) of this regulation in relation to any employee or specified description of employees, by substituting for the provisions of paragraph (2) or paragraph (3), or for the provisions of both of those paragraphs, one or more different provisions which, in order to prevent abuse arising from the use of successive fixed-term contracts, specify one or more of the following—

(a) the maximum total period for which the employee or employees of that description may be continuously employed on a fixed-term contract or on successive fixed-term contracts;

(b) the maximum number of successive fixed-term contracts and renewals of such contracts under which the employee or employees of that description may be employed; or

(c) objective grounds justifying the renewal of fixed-term contracts, or the engagement of the employee or employees of that description under successive fixed-term contracts,

and those provisions shall have effect in relation to that employee or an employee of that description as if they were contained in paragraphs (2) and (3).

[2737]

9 Right to receive written statement of variation

(1) If an employee who considers that, by virtue of regulation 8, he is a permanent employee requests in writing from his employer a written statement confirming that his contract is no longer fixed-term or that he is now a permanent employee, he is entitled to be provided, within twenty-one days of his request, with either—

(a) such a statement, or

(b) a statement giving reasons why his contract remains fixed-term.

(2) If the reasons stated under paragraph (1)(b) include an assertion that there were objective grounds for the engagement of the employee under a fixed-term contract, or the renewal of such a contract, the statement shall include a statement of those grounds.

(3) A written statement under this regulation is admissible as evidence in any proceedings before a court, an employment tribunal and the Commissioners of the Inland Revenue.

(4) If it appears to the court or tribunal in any proceedings—

(a) that the employer deliberately, and without reasonable excuse, omitted to provide a written statement, or

(b) that the written statement is evasive or equivocal,

it may draw any inference which it considers it just and equitable to draw.

(5) An employee who considers that, by virtue of regulation 8, he is a permanent employee may present an application to an employment tribunal for a declaration to that effect.

(6) No application may be made under paragraph (5) unless—

(a) the employee in question has previously requested a statement under paragraph (1) and the employer has either failed to provide a statement or given a statement of reasons under paragraph (1)(b), and

(b) the employee is at the time the application is made employed by the employer.

[2738]

NOTES

Conciliation: employment tribunal proceedings and claims which could be the subject of employment tribunal proceedings under this regulation are proceedings to which the Employment Tribunals Act 1996, s 18 applies; see s 18(1)(j) of that Act at **[975]**. The standard conciliation period applies to such proceedings by virtue of the Employment Tribunals (Constitution and Rules of Procedure) Regulations 2004, SI 2004/1861, Sch 1, rule 22(1), (6).

Commissioners of Inland Revenue: a reference to the Commissioners of Inland Revenue is now to be taken as a reference to the Commissioners for Her Majesty's Revenue and Customs; see the Commissioners for Revenue and Customs Act 2005, s 50(1), (7).

PART 3
MISCELLANEOUS

10 Restrictions on contracting out

Section 203 of the 1996 Act (restrictions on contracting out) shall apply in relation to these Regulations as if they were contained in that Act.

[2739]

11 Amendments to primary legislation

The amendments in Part 1 of Schedule 2 to these Regulations shall have effect subject to the transitional provisions in Part 2 of the Schedule.

[2740]

12 Liability of employers and principals

(1) Anything done by a person in the course of his employment shall be treated for the purposes of these Regulations as also done by his employer, whether or not it was done with the employer's knowledge or approval.

(2) Anything done by a person as agent for the employer with the authority of the employer shall be treated for the purposes of these Regulations as also done by the employer.

(3) In proceedings under these Regulations against any person in respect of an act alleged to have been done by an employee of his, it shall be a defence for that person to prove that he took such steps as were reasonably practicable to prevent the employee from—

(a) doing that act, or

(b) doing, in the course of his employment, acts of that description.

[2741]

PART 4
SPECIAL CLASSES OF PERSON

13 Crown employment

(1) Subject to regulation 14, these Regulations have effect in relation to Crown employment and persons in Crown employment as they have effect in relation to other employment and other employees.

(2) For the purposes of paragraphs (1) and (3) a person is to be regarded as being in Crown employment only if—

(a) he is in employment under or for the purposes of a government department or any officer or body exercising on behalf of the Crown functions conferred by a statutory provision, and

(b) having regard to the terms and conditions under which he works, he would be an employee if he was not in Crown employment.

(3) For the purposes of the application of the provisions of these Regulations in relation to Crown employment and persons in Crown employment in accordance with paragraph (1)—

(a) references to an employee shall be construed as references to a person in Crown employment;

(b) references to a contract of employment shall be construed, in relation to a person in Crown employment, as references to the terms and conditions mentioned in paragraph (2)(b); and

(c) references to dismissal shall be construed as references to the termination of Crown employment.

[2742]

14 Armed forces

(1) These Regulations—

(a) do not apply to service as a member of the naval, military or air forces of the Crown, but

(b) do apply to employment by an association established for the purposes of Part 11 of the Reserve Forces Act 1996.

[2743]

NOTES

Note: this regulation is reproduced as it appears in the Queen's Printer's copy of these Regulations, ie, with no para (2).

15 House of Lords staff

(1) These Regulations have effect in relation to employment as a relevant member of the House of Lords staff as they have effect in relation to other employment.

(2) In this regulation "relevant member of the House of Lords staff" means any person who is employed under a contract with the Corporate Officer of the House of Lords by virtue of which he is an employee.

[2744]

16 House of Commons staff

(1) These Regulations have effect in relation to employment as a relevant member of the House of Commons staff as they have effect in relation to other employment.

(2) In this regulation "relevant member of the House of Commons staff" means any person—

(a) who was appointed by the House of Commons Commission; or

(b) who is a member of the Speaker's personal staff.

[2745]

17 Police service

(1) For the purposes of these Regulations, the holding, otherwise than under a contract of employment, of the office of constable or an appointment as a police cadet shall be treated as employment, under a contract of employment, by the relevant officer.

[(1A) For the purposes of these Regulations, any constable or other person who has been seconded to SOCA to serve as a member of its staff shall be treated as employed by SOCA, in respect of actions taken by, or on behalf of, SOCA.

(1B) For the purposes of regulation 12 (liability of employers and principals),—

(a) the secondment of any constable or other person to SOCA to serve as a member of its staff shall be treated as employment by SOCA (and not as being employment by any other person); and

(b) anything done by a person so seconded in the performance, or purported performance, of his functions shall be treated as done in the course of that employment.]

(2) In this regulation "the relevant officer" means—

(a) in relation to a member of a police force or a special constable or police cadet appointed for a police area, the chief officer of police (or, in Scotland, the chief constable);

(b) … ; and

(c) in relation to any other person holding the office of constable or an appointment as a police cadet, the person who has the direction and control of the body of constables or cadets in question.

[(3) In this regulation "SOCA" means the Serious Organised Crime Agency.]

[2746]

NOTES

Paras (1A), (1B), (4): inserted and added respectively by the Serious Organised Crime and Police Act 2005 (Consequential and Supplementary Amendments to Secondary Legislation) Order 2006, SI 2006/594, art 2, Schedule, para 30(1), (2), as from 1 April 2006.

Para (2): sub-para (b) revoked by SI 2006/594, art 2, Schedule, para 30(1), (3), as from 1 April 2006.

PART 5
EXCLUSIONS

18 Government training schemes etc

(1) These Regulations shall not have effect in relation to a fixed-term employee who is employed on a scheme, designed to provide him with training or work experience for the purpose of assisting him to seek or obtain work, which is either—

(a) provided to him under arrangements made by the Government, or

(b) funded in whole or part by an Institution of the European Community.

(2) These Regulations shall not have effect in relation to a fixed-term employee whose employment consists in attending a period of work experience not exceeding one year that he is required to attend as part of a higher education course.

(3) For the purpose of paragraph (2) "a higher education course" means—

(a) in England and Wales, a course of a description referred to in Schedule 6 to the Education Reform Act 1988;

(b) in Scotland, a course of a description falling within section 38 of the Further and Higher Education (Scotland) Act 1992; and

(c) in Northern Ireland, a course of a description referred to in Schedule 1 to the Further Education (Northern Ireland) Order 1997.

[2747]

19 Agency workers

(1) These Regulations shall not have effect in relation to employment under a fixed-term contract where the employee is an agency worker.

(2) In this regulation "agency worker" means any person who is supplied by an employment business to do work for another person under a contract or other arrangements made between the employment business and the other person.

(3) In this regulation "employment business" means the business (whether or not carried on with a view to profit and whether or not carried on in conjunction with any other business) of supplying persons in the employment of the person carrying on the business, to act for, and under the control of, other persons in any capacity.

[2748]

20 Apprentices

These Regulations shall not have effect in relation to employment under a fixed-term contract where the contract is a contract of apprenticeship.

[2749]

SCHEDULES

SCHEDULE 1
WORKFORCE AGREEMENTS

Regulations 1 and 8

1. An agreement is a workforce agreement for the purposes of these Regulations if the following conditions are satisfied—
   (a) the agreement is in writing;
   (b) it has effect for a specified period not exceeding five years;
   (c) it applies either—
      (i) to all of the relevant members of the workforce, or
      (ii) to all of the relevant members of the workforce who belong to a particular group;
   (d) the agreement is signed—
      (i) in the case of an agreement of the kind referred to in sub-paragraph (c)(i), by the representatives of the workforce, and in the case of an agreement of the kind referred to in sub-paragraph (c)(ii) by the representatives of the group to which the agreement applies (excluding, in either case, any representative not a relevant member of the workforce on the date on which the agreement was first made available for signature), or
      (ii) if the employer employed 20 or fewer employees on the date referred to in sub-paragraph (d)(i), either by the appropriate representatives in accordance with that sub-paragraph or by the majority of the employees employed by him;
   (e) before the agreement was made available for signature, the employer provided all the employees to whom it was intended to apply on the date on which it came into effect with copies of the text of the agreement and such guidance as those employees might reasonably require in order to understand it fully.

2. For the purposes of this Schedule—

"a particular group" is a group of the relevant members of a workforce who undertake a particular function, work at a particular workplace or belong to a particular department or unit within their employer's business;

"relevant members of the workforce" are all of the employees employed by a particular employer, excluding any employee whose terms and conditions of employment are provided for, wholly or in part, in a collective agreement;

"representatives of the workforce" are employees duly elected to represent the relevant members of the workforce, "representatives of the group" are employees duly elected to represent the members of a particular group, and representatives are "duly elected" if the election at which they were elected satisfied the requirements of paragraph 3 of this Schedule.

3. The requirements concerning elections referred to in paragraph 2 are that—
   (a) the number of representatives to be elected is determined by the employer;
   (b) the candidates for election as representatives of the workforce are relevant members of the workforce, and the candidates for election as representatives of a group are members of that group;
   (c) no employee who is eligible to be a candidate is unreasonably excluded from standing for election;
   (d) all the relevant members of the workforce are entitled to vote for representatives of the workforce, and all the members of a particular group are entitled to vote for representatives of the group;
   (e) the employees entitled to vote may vote for as many candidates as there are representatives to be elected;
   (f) the election is conducted so as to secure that—
      (i) so far as is reasonably practicable, those voting do so in secret, and
      (ii) the votes given at the election are fairly and accurately counted.

[2750]

SCHEDULE 2
Regulation 11

(*Sch 2, Pt 1 amends the Social Security Contributions and Benefits Act 1992, Sch 11 at* **[462]**, *the Employment Tribunals Act 1996, ss 18, 21 at* **[975]**, **[978]**, *the Employment Rights Act 1996, ss 29, 65, 86, 92, 95, 97, 105, 108, 136, 145, 199, 203, 235 at* **[1006]** *et seq, amended s 109 of that Act (repealed) and repeals s 197 of that Act.*)

PART 2
TRANSITIONAL PROVISIONS

4. Paragraph 1 of this Schedule applies where the relevant date (as defined in paragraph 3 of Schedule 11 to the Social Security Contributions and Benefits Act 1992) falls on or after 1st October 2002.

5.—(1) This paragraph applies to the dismissal of an employee employed under a contract for a fixed term of two years or more which consists of the expiry of the term without its being renewed, where the employee has agreed in accordance with section 197 of the 1996 Act to exclude any right to a redundancy payment in that event.

(2) The repeal of sections 197, 199(6) and 203(2)(d) of the 1996 Act provided for by paragraph 3(k) of this Schedule shall have effect in relation to a dismissal to which this paragraph applies where the relevant date (within the meaning of section 145 of the 1996 Act) falls on or after 1st October 2002, unless both the following conditions are satisfied—

(a) that, where there has been no renewal of the contract, the contract was entered into before 1st October 2002 or, where there have been one or more renewals, the only or most recent renewal was agreed before that date, and

(b) that the agreement to exclude any right to a redundancy payment was entered into and took effect before 1st October 2002.

[2751]

PATERNITY AND ADOPTION LEAVE REGULATIONS 2002

(SI 2002/2788)

NOTES

Made: 11 November 2002.

Authority: Employment Rights Act 1996, ss 47C(2), 75A(1)–(3), (6), (7), 75B(1), (2), (4), (8), 75C(1), (2), 75D(1), 80A(1), (2), (5), 80B(1), (2), (5), 80C(1), (6), 80D(1), 80E, 99(1).

Commencement: 8 December 2002; see reg 3 at **[2754]** for detailed provision as to the application of particular regulations.

Adoption from overseas: as to the application of these Regulations to adoptions from overseas, see the Paternity and Adoption Leave (Adoption from Overseas) Regulations 2003, SI 2003/921.

ARRANGEMENT OF REGULATIONS

PART 1
GENERAL

PART 2
PATERNITY LEAVE

PART 1
GENERAL

1 Citation and commencement

These Regulations may be cited as the Paternity and Adoption Leave Regulations 2002 and shall come into force on 8th December 2002.

[2752]

2 Interpretation

(1) In these Regulations—

"the 1996 Act" means the Employment Rights Act 1996;

"additional adoption leave" means leave under section 75B of the 1996 Act;

"additional maternity leave" means leave under section 73 of the 1996 Act;

"adopter", in relation to a child, means a person who has been matched with the child for adoption, or, in a case where two people have been matched jointly, whichever of them has elected to be the child's adopter for the purposes of these Regulations;

"adoption agency" has the meaning given, in relation to England and Wales, by section 1(4) of the Adoption Act 1976 and, in relation to Scotland, by section 1(4) of the Adoption (Scotland) Act 1978;

"adoption leave" means ordinary or additional adoption leave;

"child" means a person who is, or when placed with an adopter for adoption was, under the age of 18;

"contract of employment" means a contract of service or apprenticeship, whether express or implied, and (if it is express) whether oral or in writing;

"employee" means an individual who has entered into or works under (or, where the employment has ceased, worked under) a contract of employment;

"employer" means the person by whom an employee is (or, where the employment has ceased, was) employed;

"expected week", in relation to the birth of a child, means the week, beginning with midnight between Saturday and Sunday, in which it is expected that the child will be born;

"ordinary adoption leave" means leave under section 75A of the 1996 Act;

"parental leave" means leave under regulation 13(1) of the Maternity and Parental Leave etc Regulations 1999;

"partner", in relation to a child's mother or adopter, means a person (whether of a different sex or the same sex) who lives with the mother or adopter and the child in an enduring family relationship but is not a relative of the mother or adopter of a kind specified in paragraph (2);

"paternity leave" means leave under regulation 4 or regulation 8 of these Regulations;

["statutory adoption leave" means ordinary adoption leave and additional adoption leave;

"statutory adoption leave period" means the period during which the adopter is on statutory adoption leave;]

"statutory leave" means leave provided for in Part 8 of the 1996 Act.

(2) The relatives of a child's mother or adopter referred to in the definition of "partner" in paragraph (1) are the mother's or adopter's parent, grandparent, sister, brother, aunt or uncle.

(3) References to relationships in paragraph (2)—

(a) are to relationships of the full blood or half blood or, in the case of an adopted person, such of those relationships as would exist but for the adoption, and

(b) include the relationship of a child with his adoptive, or former adoptive, parents,

but do not include any other adoptive relationships.

(4) For the purposes of these Regulations—

(a) a person is matched with a child for adoption when an adoption agency decides that that person would be a suitable adoptive parent for the child, either individually or jointly with another person, and

(b) a person is notified of having been matched with a child on the date on which he receives notification of the agency's decision, under regulation 11(2) of the Adoption Agencies Regulations 1983 or regulation 12(3) of the Adoption Agencies (Scotland) Regulations 1996;

(c) a person elects to be a child's adopter, in a case where the child is matched with him and another person jointly, if he and that person agree, at the time at which they are matched, that he and not the other person will be the adopter.

(5) A reference in any provision of these Regulations to a period of continuous employment is to a period computed in accordance with Chapter 1 of Part 14 of the 1996 Act, as if that provision were a provision of that Act.

(6) For the purposes of these Regulations, any two employers shall be treated as associated if—

(a) one is a company of which the other (directly or indirectly) has control; or

(b) both are companies of which a third person (directly or indirectly) has control;

and "associated employer" shall be construed accordingly.

[2753]

NOTES

Para (1): definitions "statutory adoption leave" and "statutory adoption leave period" inserted by the Maternity and Parental Leave etc and the Paternity and Adoption Leave (Amendment) Regulations 2006, SI 2006/2014, regs 12, 13, as from 1 October 2006 (with effect only in relation to an employee with whom a child is expected to be placed for adoption, where the placement is expected to occur on or after 1 April 2007: see SI 2006/2014, reg 2(2) at **[3463A]**).

Adoption from overseas: as to the modification of this regulation in relation to adoptions from overseas, see the Paternity and Adoption Leave (Adoption from Overseas) Regulations 2003, SI 2003/921, reg 4. Note that the amendments made by SI 2006/2014 noted above, as applied to adoptions from overseas by virtue of, and as modified by, SI 2003/921, have effect only where the adopter's child enters Great Britain on or after 1 April 2007 (see SI 2006/2014, reg 2(3) at **[3463A]**).

---

3 Application

(1) The provisions relating to paternity leave under regulation 4 below have effect only in relation to children—

(a) born on or after 6th April 2003, or

(b) whose expected week of birth begins on or after that date.

(2) The provisions relating to paternity leave under regulation 8 and adoption leave under regulation 15 below have effect only in relation to children—

(a) matched with a person who is notified of having been matched on or after 6th April 2003, or

(b) placed for adoption on or after that date.

(3) Regulation 28 (protection from detriment) has effect only in relation to an act or failure to act which takes place on or after 8th December 2002.

(4) For the purposes of paragraph (3)—

(a) where an act extends over a period, the reference to the date of the act is a reference to the last day of that period, and

(b) a failure to act is to be treated as done when it was decided on.

(5) For the purposes of paragraph (4), in the absence of evidence establishing the contrary an employer shall be taken to decide on a failure to act—

(a) when he does an act inconsistent with doing the failed act, or

(b) if he has done no such inconsistent act, when the period expires within which he might reasonably have been expected to do the failed act if it was to be done.

(6) Regulation 29 (unfair dismissal) has effect only in relation to dismissals where the effective date of termination (within the meaning of section 97 of the 1996 Act) falls on or after 8th December 2002.

[2754]

NOTES

Adoption from overseas: as to the modification of this regulation in relation to adoptions from overseas, see the Paternity and Adoption Leave (Adoption from Overseas) Regulations 2003, SI 2003/921, reg 5.

PART 2
PATERNITY LEAVE

4 Entitlement to paternity leave: birth

(1) An employee is entitled to be absent from work for the purpose of caring for a child or supporting the child's mother if he—

(a) satisfies the conditions specified in paragraph (2), and

(b) has complied with the notice requirements in regulation 6 and, where applicable, the evidential requirements in that regulation.

(2) The conditions referred to in paragraph (1) are that the employee—

(a) has been continuously employed for a period of not less than 26 weeks ending with the week immediately preceding the 14th week before the expected week of the child's birth;

(b) is either—

(i) the father of the child or;

(ii) married to[, the civil partner] or the partner of the child's mother, but not the child's father;

(c) has, or expects to have—

(i) if he is the child's father, responsibility for the upbringing of the child;

(ii) if he is the mother's husband[, civil partner] or partner but not the child's father, the main responsibility (apart from any responsibility of the mother) for the upbringing of the child.

(3) An employee shall be treated as having satisfied the condition in paragraph (2)(a) on the date of the child's birth notwithstanding the fact that he has not then been continuously employed for a period of not less than 26 weeks, where—

(a) the date on which the child is born is earlier than the 14th week before the week in which its birth is expected, and

(b) the employee would have been continuously employed for such a period if his employment had continued until that 14th week.

(4) An employee shall be treated as having satisfied the condition in paragraph (2)(b)(ii) if he would have satisfied it but for the fact that the child's mother has died.

(5) An employee shall be treated as having satisfied the condition in paragraph (2)(c) if he would have satisfied it but for the fact that the child was stillborn after 24 weeks of pregnancy or has died.

(6) An employee's entitlement to leave under this regulation shall not be affected by the birth, or expected birth, of more than one child as a result of the same pregnancy.

[2755]

NOTES

Para (2): words in square brackets inserted by the Civil Partnership Act 2004 (Amendments to Subordinate Legislation) Order 2005, SI 2005/2114, art 2(17), Sch 17, para 1(1), (2), as from 5 December 2005.

Adoption from overseas: this regulation and regs 5–7 are disapplied in relation to adoptions from overseas, by the Paternity and Adoption Leave (Adoption from Overseas) Regulations 2003, SI 2003/921, reg 6.

5 Options in respect of leave under regulation 4

(1) An employee may choose to take either one week's leave or two consecutive weeks' leave in respect of a child under regulation 4.

(2) The leave may only be taken during the period which begins with the date on which the child is born and ends—

(a) except in the case referred to in sub-paragraph (b), 56 days after that date;

(b) in a case where the child is born before the first day of the expected week of its birth, 56 days after that day.

(3) Subject to paragraph (2) and, where applicable, paragraph (4), an employee may choose to begin his period of leave on—

(a) the date on which the child is born;

(b) the date falling such number of days after the date on which the child is born as the employee may specify in a notice under regulation 6, or

(c) a predetermined date, specified in a notice under that regulation, which is later than the first day of the expected week of the child's birth.

(4) In a case where the leave is in respect of a child whose expected week of birth begins before 6th April 2003, an employee may choose to begin a period of leave only on a predetermined date, specified in a notice under regulation 6, which is at least 28 days after the date on which that notice is given.

[2756]

NOTES

Adoption from overseas: disapplied as noted to reg 4 at **[2755]**.

6 Notice and evidential requirements for leave under regulation 4

(1) An employee must give his employer notice of his intention to take leave in respect of a child under regulation 4, specifying—

(a) the expected week of the child's birth;

(b) the length of the period of leave that, in accordance with regulation 5(1), the employee has chosen to take, and

(c) the date on which, in accordance with regulation 5(3) or (4), the employee has chosen that his period of leave should begin.

(2) The notice provided for in paragraph (1) must be given to the employer—

(a) in or before the 15th week before the expected week of the child's birth, or

(b) in a case where it was not reasonably practicable for the employee to give the notice in accordance with sub-paragraph (a), as soon as is reasonably practicable.

(3) Where the employer requests it, an employee must also give his employer a declaration, signed by the employee, to the effect that the purpose of his absence from work will be that specified in regulation 4(1) and that he satisfies the conditions of entitlement in regulation 4(2)(b) and (c).

(4) An employee who has given notice under paragraph (1) may vary the date he has chosen as the date on which his period of leave will begin, subject to paragraph (5) and provided that he gives his employer notice of the variation—

(a) where the variation is to provide for the employee's period of leave to begin on the date on which the child is born, at least 28 days before the first day of the expected week of the child's birth;
(b) where the variation is to provide for the employee's period of leave to begin on a date that is a specified number of days (or a different specified number of days) after the date on which the child is born, at least 28 days before the date falling that number of days after the first day of the expected week of the child's birth;
(c) where the variation is to provide for the employee's period of leave to begin on a predetermined date (or a different predetermined date), at least 28 days before that date,

or, if it is not reasonably practicable to give the notice at least 28 days before whichever day or date is relevant, as soon as is reasonably practicable.

(5) In a case where regulation 5(4) applies, an employee may only vary the date which he has chosen as the date on which his period of leave will begin by substituting a different predetermined date.

(6) In a case where—
(a) the employee has chosen to begin his period of leave on a particular predetermined date, and
(b) the child is not born on or before that date,

the employee must vary his choice of date, by substituting a later predetermined date or (except in a case where regulation 5(4) applies) exercising an alternative option under regulation 5(3), and give his employer notice of the variation as soon as is reasonably practicable.

(7) An employee must give his employer a further notice, as soon as is reasonably practicable after the child's birth, of the date on which the child was born.

(8) Notice under paragraph (1), (4), (6) or (7) shall be given in writing, if the employer so requests.

[2757]

NOTES

Adoption from overseas: disapplied as noted to reg 4 at **[2755]**.

7 Commencement of leave under regulation 4

(1) Except in the case referred to in paragraph (2), an employee's period of paternity leave under regulation 4 begins on the date specified in his notice under regulation 6(1), or, where he has varied his choice of date under regulation 6(4) or (6), on the date specified in his notice under that provision (or the last such notice if he has varied his choice more than once).

(2) In a case where—
(a) the employee has chosen to begin his period of leave on the date on which the child is born, and
(b) he is at work on that date,

the employee's period of leave begins on the day after that date.

[2758]

NOTES

Adoption from overseas: disapplied as noted to reg 4 at **[2755]**.

8 Entitlement to paternity leave: adoption

(1) An employee is entitled to be absent from work for the purpose of caring for a child or supporting the child's adopter if he—
(a) satisfies the conditions specified in paragraph (2), and
(b) has complied with the notice requirements in regulation 10 and, where applicable, the evidential requirements in that regulation.

(2) The conditions referred to in paragraph (1) are that the employee—
(a) has been continuously employed for a period of not less than 26 weeks ending with the week in which the child's adopter is notified of having been matched with the child;
(b) is either married to[, the civil partner] or the partner of the child's adopter, and

(c) has, or expects to have, the main responsibility (apart from the responsibility of the adopter) for the upbringing of the child.

(3) In paragraph (2)(a), "week" means the period of seven days beginning with Sunday.

(4) An employee shall be treated as having satisfied the condition in paragraph (2)(b) if he would have satisfied it but for the fact that the child's adopter died during the child's placement.

(5) An employee shall be treated as having satisfied the condition in paragraph (2)(c) if he would have satisfied it but for the fact that the child's placement with the adopter has ended.

(6) An employee's entitlement to leave under this regulation shall not be affected by the placement for adoption of more than one child as part of the same arrangement.

[2759]

NOTES

Para (2): words in square brackets in sub-para (b) inserted by the Civil Partnership Act 2004 (Amendments to Subordinate Legislation) Order 2005, SI 2005/2114, art 2(17), Sch 17, para 1(1), (3), as from 5 December 2005.

Adoption from overseas: as to the substitution of this regulation in relation to adoptions from overseas, see the Paternity and Adoption Leave (Adoption from Overseas) Regulations 2003, SI 2003/921, reg 7.

9 Options in respect of leave under regulation 8

(1) An employee may choose to take either one week's leave or two consecutive weeks' leave in respect of a child under regulation 8.

(2) The leave may only be taken during the period of 56 days beginning with the date on which the child is placed with the adopter.

(3) Subject to paragraph (2) and, where applicable, paragraph (4), an employee may choose to begin a period of leave under regulation 8 on—

(a) the date on which the child is placed with the adopter;

(b) the date falling such number of days after the date on which the child is placed with the adopter as the employee may specify in a notice under regulation 10, or

(c) a predetermined date, specified in a notice under that regulation, which is later than the date on which the child is expected to be placed with the adopter.

(4) In a case where the adopter was notified of having been matched with the child before 6th April 2003, the employee may choose to begin a period of leave only on a predetermined date, specified in a notice under regulation 10, which is at least 28 days after the date on which that notice is given.

[2760]

NOTES

Adoption from overseas: as to the substitution of this regulation in relation to adoptions from overseas, see the Paternity and Adoption Leave (Adoption from Overseas) Regulations 2003, SI 2003/921, reg 7.

10 Notice and evidential requirements for leave under regulation 8

(1) An employee must give his employer notice of his intention to take leave in respect of a child under regulation 8, specifying—

(a) the date on which the adopter was notified of having been matched with the child;

(b) the date on which the child is expected to be placed with the adopter;

(c) the length of the period of leave that, in accordance with regulation 9(1), the employee has chosen to take, and

(d) the date on which, in accordance with regulation 9(3) or (4), the employee has chosen that his period of leave should begin.

(2) The notice provided for in paragraph (1) must be given to the employer—

(a) no more than seven days after the date on which the adopter is notified of having been matched with the child, or

(b) in a case where it was not reasonably practicable for the employee to give notice in accordance with sub-paragraph (a), as soon as is reasonably practicable.

(3) Where the employer requests it, an employee must also give his employer a declaration, signed by the employee, to the effect that the purpose of his absence from work will be that specified in regulation 8(1) and that he satisfies the conditions of entitlement in regulation 8(2)(b) and (c).

(4) An employee who has given notice under paragraph (1) may vary the date he has chosen as the date on which his period of leave will begin, subject to paragraph (5) and provided that he gives his employer notice of the variation—

(a) where the variation is to provide for the employee's period of leave to begin on the date on which the child is placed with the adopter, at least 28 days before the date specified in the employee's notice under paragraph (1) as the date on which the child is expected to be placed with the adopter;

(b) where the variation is to provide for the employee's period of leave to begin on a date that is a specified number of days (or a different specified number of days) after the date on which the child is placed with the adopter, at least 28 days before the date falling that number of days after the date specified in the employee's notice under paragraph (1) as the date on which the child is expected to be placed with the adopter;

(c) where the variation is to provide for the employee's period of leave to begin on a predetermined date, at least 28 days before that date,

or, if it is not reasonably practicable to give the notice at least 28 days before whichever date is relevant, as soon as is reasonably practicable.

(5) In a case where regulation 9(4) applies, an employee may only vary the date which he has chosen as the date on which his period of leave will begin by substituting a different predetermined date.

(6) In a case where—

(a) the employee has chosen to begin his period of leave on a particular predetermined date, and

(b) the child is not placed with the adopter on or before that date,

the employee must vary his choice of date, by substituting a later predetermined date or (except in a case where regulation 9(4) applies) exercising an alternative option under regulation 9(3), and give his employer notice of the variation as soon as is reasonably practicable.

(7) An employee must give his employer a further notice, as soon as is reasonably practicable after the child's placement, of the date on which the child was placed.

(8) Notice under paragraph (1), (4), (6) or (7) shall be given in writing, if the employer so requests.

[2761]

NOTES

Adoption from overseas: as to the substitution of this regulation in relation to adoptions from overseas, see the Paternity and Adoption Leave (Adoption from Overseas) Regulations 2003, SI 2003/921, reg 7.

11 Commencement of leave under regulation 8

(1) Except in the case referred to in paragraph (2), an employee's period of paternity leave under regulation 8 begins on the date specified in his notice under regulation 10(1), or, where he has varied his choice of date under regulation 10(4) or (6), on the date specified in his notice under that provision (or the last such date if he has varied his choice more than once).

(2) In a case where—

(a) the employee has chosen to begin his period of leave on the date on which the child is placed with the adopter, and

(b) he is at work on that date,

the employee's period of leave begins on the day after that date.

[2762]

NOTES

Adoption from overseas: as to the modification of this regulation in relation to adoptions from overseas, see the Paternity and Adoption Leave (Adoption from Overseas) Regulations 2003, SI 2003/921, reg 8.

12 Application of terms and conditions during paternity leave

(1) An employee who takes paternity leave—

(a) is entitled, during the period of leave, to the benefit of all of the terms and conditions of employment which would have applied if he had not been absent, and

(b) is bound, during that period, by any obligations arising under those terms and conditions, subject only to the exception in section 80C(1)(b) of the 1996 Act.

(2) In paragraph (1)(a), "terms and conditions of employment" has the meaning given by section 80C(5) of the 1996 Act, and accordingly does not include terms and conditions about remuneration.

(3) For the purposes of section 80C of the 1996 Act, only sums payable to an employee by way of wages or salary are to be treated as remuneration.

[2763]

13 Right to return after paternity leave

(1) An employee who returns to work after a period of paternity leave which was—

(a) an isolated period of leave, or

(b) the last of two or more consecutive periods of statutory leave, which did not include any period of additional maternity leave or additional adoption leave or a period of parental leave of more than four weeks,

is entitled to return from leave to the job in which he was employed before his absence.

(2) An employee who returns to work after a period of paternity leave not falling within the description in paragraph (1)(a) or (b) above is entitled to return from leave to the job in which he was employed before his absence, or, if it is not reasonably practicable for the employer to permit him to return to that job, to another job which is both suitable for him and appropriate for him to do in the circumstances.

(3) The reference in paragraphs (1) and (2) to the job in which an employee was employed before his absence is a reference to the job in which he was employed—

(a) if his return is from an isolated period of paternity leave, immediately before that period began;

(b) if his return is from consecutive periods of statutory leave, immediately before the first such period.

[2764]

14 Incidents of the right to return after paternity leave

(1) An employee's right to return under regulation 13 is a right to return—

(a) with his seniority, pension rights and similar rights—

(i) in a case where the employee is returning from consecutive periods of statutory leave which included a period of additional adoption leave or additional maternity leave, as they would have been if the period or periods of his employment prior to the additional adoption leave or (as the case may be) additional maternity leave were continuous with the period of employment following it;

(ii) in any other case, as they would have been if he had not been absent, and

(b) on terms and conditions not less favourable than those which would have applied if he had not been absent.

(2) The provision in paragraph (1)(a)(i) concerning the treatment of periods of additional maternity leave or additional adoption leave is subject to the requirements of [paragraphs 5, 5B and 6 of Schedule 5 to the Social Security Act 1989 (equal treatment under pension schemes: maternity absence, adoption leave and family leave)].

(3) The provisions in paragraph (1)(a)(ii) and (b) for an employee to be treated as if he had not been absent refer to his absence—

(a) if his return is from an isolated period of paternity leave, since the beginning of that period;

(b) if his return is from consecutive periods of statutory leave, since the beginning of the first such period.

[2765]

NOTES

Para (2): words in square brackets substituted by the Pensions Act 2004 (Commencement No 2, Transitional Provisions and Consequential Amendments) Order 2005, SI 2005/275, art 5, as from 9 February 2005.

PART 3
ADOPTION LEAVE

15 Entitlement to ordinary adoption leave

(1) An employee is entitled to ordinary adoption leave in respect of a child if he—

(a) satisfies the conditions specified in paragraph (2), and

(b) has complied with the notice requirements in regulation 17 and, where applicable, the evidential requirements in that regulation.

(2) The conditions referred to in paragraph (1) are that the employee—

(a) is the child's adopter;

(b) has been continuously employed for a period of not less than 26 weeks ending with the week in which he was notified of having been matched with the child, and

(c) has notified the agency that he agrees that the child should be placed with him and on the date of placement.

(3) In paragraph (2)(b), "week" means the period of seven days beginning with Sunday.

(4) An employee's entitlement to leave under this regulation shall not be affected by the placement for adoption of more than one child as part of the same arrangement.

[2766]

NOTES

Adoption from overseas: as to the substitution of this regulation in relation to adoptions from overseas, see the Paternity and Adoption Leave (Adoption from Overseas) Regulations 2003, SI 2003/921, reg 9.

16 Options in respect of ordinary adoption leave

(1) Except in the case referred to in paragraph (2), an employee may choose to begin a period of ordinary adoption leave on—

(a) the date on which the child is placed with him for adoption, or

(b) a predetermined date, specified in a notice under regulation 17, which is no more than 14 days before the date on which the child is expected to be placed with the employee and no later than that date.

(2) In a case where the employee was notified of having been matched with the child before 6th April 2003, the employee may choose to begin a period of leave only on a predetermined date, specified in a notice under regulation 17, which is after 6th April 2003 and at least 28 days after the date on which that notice is given.

[2767]

NOTES

Adoption from overseas: as to the substitution of this regulation in relation to adoptions from overseas, see the Paternity and Adoption Leave (Adoption from Overseas) Regulations 2003, SI 2003/921, reg 9.

17 Notice and evidential requirements for ordinary adoption leave

(1) An employee must give his employer notice of his intention to take ordinary adoption leave in respect of a child, specifying—

(a) the date on which the child is expected to be placed with him for adoption, and

(b) the date on which, in accordance with regulation 16(1) or (2), the employee has chosen that his period of leave should begin.

(2) The notice provided for in paragraph (1) must be given to the employer—

(a) no more than seven days after the date on which the employee is notified of having been matched with the child for the purposes of adoption, or

(b) in a case where it was not reasonably practicable for the employee to give notice in accordance with sub-paragraph (a), as soon as is reasonably practicable.

(3) Where the employer requests it, an employee must also provide his employer with evidence, in the form of one or more documents issued by the adoption agency that matched the employee with the child, of—

(a) the name and address of the agency;

(b) …

(c) the date on which the employee was notified that he had been matched with the child, and

(d) the date on which the agency expects to place the child with the employee.

(4) An employee who has given notice under paragraph (1) may vary the date he has chosen as the date on which his period of leave will begin, subject to paragraph (5) and provided that he gives his employer notice of the variation—

(a) where the variation is to provide for the employee's period of leave to begin on the date on which the child is placed with him for adoption, at least 28 days before the date specified in his notice under paragraph (1) as the date on which the child is expected to be placed with him;

(b) where the variation is to provide for the employee's period of leave to begin on a predetermined date (or a different predetermined date), at least 28 days before that date,

or, if it is not reasonably practicable to give the notice 28 days before whichever date is relevant, as soon as is reasonably practicable.

(5) In a case where regulation 16(2) applies, an employee may only vary the date which he has chosen as the date on which his period of leave will begin by substituting a different predetermined date.

(6) Notice under paragraph (1) or (4) shall be given in writing, if the employer so requests.

(7) An employer who is given notice under paragraph (1) or (4) of the date on which an employee has chosen that his period of ordinary adoption leave should begin shall notify the employee, within 28 days of his receipt of the notice, of the date on which the period of additional adoption leave to which the employee will be entitled (if he satisfies the conditions in regulation 20(1)) after his period of ordinary adoption leave ends.

(8) The notification provided for in paragraph (7) shall be given to the employee—

(a) where the employer is given notice under paragraph (1), within 28 days of the date on which he received that notice;

(b) where the employer is given notice under paragraph (4), within 28 days of the date on which the employee's ordinary adoption leave period began.

[2768]

NOTES

Para (3): sub-para (b) revoked by the Paternity and Adoption Leave (Amendment) Regulations 2004, SI 2004/923, regs 2, 3, as from 6 April 2004.

Adoption from overseas: as to the substitution of this regulation in relation to adoptions from overseas, see the Paternity and Adoption Leave (Adoption from Overseas) Regulations 2003, SI 2003/921, reg 9.

18 Duration and commencement of ordinary adoption leave

(1) Subject to regulations 22 and 24, an employee's ordinary adoption leave period is a period of 26 weeks.

(2) Except in the case referred to in paragraph (3), an employee's ordinary adoption leave period begins on the date specified in his notice under regulation 17(1), or, where he has varied his choice of date under regulation 17(4), on the date specified in his notice under that provision (or the last such date if he has varied his choice more than once).

(3) In a case where—

(a) the employee has chosen to begin his period of leave on the date on which the child is placed with him, and

(b) he is at work on that date,

the employee's period of leave begins on the day after that date.

[2769]

NOTES

Adoption from overseas: as to the modification of this regulation in relation to adoptions from overseas, see the Paternity and Adoption Leave (Adoption from Overseas) Regulations 2003, SI 2003/921, reg 10.

19 Application of terms and conditions during ordinary adoption leave

(1) An employee who takes ordinary adoption leave—

(a) is entitled, during the period of leave, to the benefit of all of the terms and conditions of employment which would have applied if he had not been absent, and

(b) is bound, during that period, by any obligations arising under those terms and conditions, subject only to the exception in section 75A(3)(b) of the 1996 Act.

(2) In paragraph (1)(a), "terms and conditions of employment" has the meaning given by section 75A(4) of the 1996 Act, and accordingly does not include terms and conditions about remuneration.

(3) For the purposes of section 75A of the 1996 Act, only sums payable to an employee by way of wages or salary are to be treated as remuneration.

[2770]

20 Additional adoption leave: entitlement, duration and commencement

(1) An employee is entitled to additional adoption leave in respect of a child if—

(a) the child was placed with him for adoption,

(b) he took ordinary adoption leave in respect of the child, and

(c) his ordinary adoption leave period did not end prematurely under regulation 22(2)(a) or 24.

(2) Subject to regulations 22 and 24, an employee's additional adoption leave period is a period of 26 weeks beginning on the day after the last day of his ordinary adoption leave period.

[2771]

NOTES

Adoption from overseas: as to the modification of this regulation in relation to adoptions from overseas, see the Paternity and Adoption Leave (Adoption from Overseas) Regulations 2003, SI 2003/921, reg 11.

21 Application of terms and conditions during additional adoption leave

An employee who takes additional adoption leave—

(a) is entitled, during the period of leave, to the benefit of his employer's implied obligation to him of trust and confidence and of any terms and conditions of his employment relating to—

  (i) notice of the termination of the employment contract by his employer;

  (ii) compensation in the event of redundancy, or

  (iii) disciplinary or grievance procedures; and

(b) is bound, during that period, by his implied obligation to his employer of good faith and of any terms and conditions of his employment relating to—

  (i) notice of the termination of the employment contract by him,

  (ii) the disclosure of confidential information;

  (iii) the acceptance of gifts or other benefits, or

  (iv) the employee's participation in any other business.

[2772]

[21A Work during adoption leave period

(1) An employee may carry out up to 10 days' work for his employer during his statutory adoption leave period without bringing his statutory adoption leave to an end.

(2) For the purposes of this regulation, any work carried out on any day shall constitute a day's work.

(3) Subject to paragraph (4), for the purposes of this regulation, work means any work done under the contract of employment and may include training or any activity undertaken for the purposes of keeping in touch with the workplace.

(4) Reasonable contact from time to time between an employee and his employer which either party is entitled to make during an adoption leave period (for example to discuss an employee's return to work) shall not bring that period to an end.

(5) This regulation does not confer any right on an employer to require that any work be carried out during the statutory adoption leave period, nor any right on an employee to work during the statutory adoption leave period.

(6) Any days' work carried out under this regulation shall not have the effect of extending the total duration of the statutory adoption leave period.]

[2772A]

NOTES

Commencement: 1 October 2006 (with effect only in relation to an employee with whom a child is expected to be placed for adoption, where the placement is expected to occur on or after 1 April 2007).

Inserted by the Maternity and Parental Leave etc and the Paternity and Adoption Leave (Amendment) Regulations 2006, SI 2006/2014, regs 12, 14, as from 1 October 2006 (with effect only in relation to an employee with whom a child is expected to be placed for adoption, where the placement is expected to occur on or after 1 April 2007: see SI 2006/2014, reg 2(2) at **[3463A]**).

Adoptions from overseas: in relation to adoptions from overseas, this regulation has effect only where the adopter's child enters Great Britain on or after 1 April 2007 (see SI 2006/2014, reg 2(3) at **[3463A]**).

22 Disrupted placement in the course of adoption leave

(1) This regulation applies where—

- (a) an employee has begun a period of adoption leave in respect of a child before the placement of the child with him, and the employee is subsequently notified that the placement will not be made, or
- (b) during an employee's period of adoption leave in respect of a child placed with him—
  - (i) the child dies, or
  - (ii) the child is returned to the adoption agency under section 30(3) of the Adoption Act 1976 or section 30(3) of the Adoption (Scotland) Act 1978.

(2) Subject to regulation 24, in a case where this regulation applies—

- (a) except in the circumstances referred to in sub-paragraphs (b) and (c), the employee's adoption leave period ends eight weeks after the end of the relevant week specified in paragraph (3);
- (b) where the employee is taking ordinary adoption leave and the period of 26 weeks provided for in regulation 18 ends within eight weeks of the end of the relevant week—
  - (i) the employee's ordinary adoption leave period ends on the expiry of the 26-week period;
  - (ii) the employee is entitled to additional adoption leave, and
  - (iii) the employee's additional adoption leave period ends eight weeks after the end of the relevant week;
- (c) where the employee is taking additional adoption leave and the period of 26 weeks provided for in regulation 20 ends within eight weeks of the end of the relevant week, the employee's additional adoption leave period ends on the expiry of the 26-week period.

(3) The relevant week referred to in paragraph (2) is—

- (a) in a case falling within paragraph (1)(a), the week during which the person with whom the child was to be placed for adoption is notified that the placement will not be made;
- (b) in a case falling within paragraph (1)(b)(i), the week during which the child dies;
- (c) in a case falling within paragraph (1)(b)(ii), the week during which the child is returned.

(4) In paragraph (3), "week" means the period of seven days beginning with Sunday.

[2773]

NOTES

Adoption from overseas: as to the modification of this regulation in relation to adoptions from overseas, see the Paternity and Adoption Leave (Adoption from Overseas) Regulations 2003, SI 2003/921, reg 12.

23 Redundancy during adoption leave

(1) This regulation applies where, during an employee's ordinary or additional adoption leave period, it is not practicable by reason of redundancy for his employer to continue to employ him under his existing contract of employment.

(2) Where there is a suitable available vacancy, the employee is entitled to be offered (before the end of his employment under his existing contract) alternative employment with his employer or his employer's successor, or an associated employer, under a new contract of employment which complies with paragraph (3) and takes effect immediately on the ending of his employment under the previous contract.

(3) The new contract of employment must be such that—

(a) the work to be done under it is of a kind which is both suitable in relation to the employee and appropriate for him to do in the circumstances, and

(b) its provisions as to the capacity and place in which he is to be employed, and as to the other terms and conditions of his employment, are not substantially less favourable to him than if he had continued to be employed under the previous contract.

[2774]

24 Dismissal during adoption leave

Where an employee is dismissed after an ordinary or additional adoption leave period has begun but before the time when (apart from this regulation) that period would end, the period ends at the time of the dismissal.

[2775]

25 Requirement to notify intention to return during adoption leave period

(1) An employee who intends to return to work earlier than the end of his additional adoption leave period must give his employer at least [8 weeks'] notice of the date on which he intends to return.

(2) If an employee attempts to return to work earlier than the end of his additional adoption leave period without complying with paragraph (1), his employer is entitled to postpone his return to a date such as will secure, subject to paragraph (3), that he has at least [8 weeks'] notice of the employee's return.

[(2A) An employee who complies with his obligations in paragraph (1) or whose employer has postponed his return in the circumstances described in paragraph (2), and who then decides to return to work—

(a) earlier than the original return date, must give his employer not less than 8 weeks' notice of the date on which he now intends to return;

(b) later than the original return date, must give his employer not less than 8 weeks' notice ending with the original return date.

(2B) In paragraph (2A) the "original return date" means the date which the employee notified to his employer as the date of his return to work under paragraph (1), or the date to which his return was postponed by his employer under paragraph (2).]

(3) An employer is not entitled under paragraph (2) to postpone an employee's return to work to a date after the end of the employee's additional adoption leave period.

(4) If an employee whose return has been postponed under paragraph (2) has been notified that he is not to return to work before the date to which his return was postponed, the employer is under no contractual obligation to pay him remuneration until the date to which his return was postponed if he returns to work before that date.

(5) This regulation does not apply in a case where the employer did not notify the employee in accordance with regulation 17(7) and (8) of the date on which the employee's additional adoption leave period would end.

(6) In a case where an employee's adoption leave is curtailed because regulation 22 applies, the references in this regulation to the end of an employee's additional adoption leave period are references to the date on which that period would have ended had that regulation not applied, irrespective of whether it was the employee's ordinary adoption leave period or his additional adoption leave period that was curtailed.

[2776]

NOTES

Paras (1), (2): words in square brackets substituted by the Maternity and Parental Leave etc and the Paternity and Adoption Leave (Amendment) Regulations 2006, SI 2006/2014, regs 12, 15(a), (b), as from 1 October 2006 (with effect only in relation to an employee with whom a child is expected to be placed for adoption, where the placement is expected to occur on or after 1 April 2007: see SI 2006/2014, reg 2(2) at **[3463A]**).

Paras (2A), (2B):inserted by SI 2006/2014, regs 12, 15(c), as from 1 October 2006 (with effect only in relation to an employee with whom a child is expected to be placed for adoption, where the placement is expected to occur on or after 1 April 2007: see SI 2006/2014, reg 2(2) at **[3463A]**).

Adoption from overseas: note that the amendments made by SI 2006/2014 noted above, as applied to adoptions from overseas by virtue of, and as modified by, SI 2003/921, have effect only where the adopter's child enters Great Britain on or after 1 April 2007 (see SI 2006/2014, reg 2(3) at **[3463A]**).

26 Right to return after adoption leave

(1) An employee who returns to work after a period of ordinary adoption leave which was—

(a) an isolated period of leave, or

(b) the last of two or more consecutive periods of statutory leave, which did not include any period of additional maternity leave or additional adoption leave or a period of parental leave of more than four weeks,

is entitled to return from leave to the job in which he was employed before his absence.

(2) An employee who returns to work after—

(a) a period of additional adoption leave, whether or not preceded by another period of statutory leave, or

(b) a period of ordinary adoption leave not falling within the description in paragraph (1)(a) or (b) above,

is entitled to return from leave to the job in which he was employed before his absence, or, if it is not reasonably practicable for the employer to permit him to return to that job, to another job which is both suitable for him and appropriate for him to do in the circumstances.

(3) The reference in paragraphs (1) and (2) to the job in which an employee was employed before his absence is a reference to the job in which he was employed—

(a) if his return is from an isolated period of adoption leave, immediately before that period began;

(b) if his return is from consecutive periods of statutory leave, immediately before the first such period.

(4) This regulation does not apply where regulation 23 applies.

[2777]

27 Incidents of the right to return from adoption leave

(1) An employee's right to return under regulation 26 is to return—

(a) with his seniority, pension rights and similar rights—

(i) in a case where the employee is returning from additional adoption leave, or consecutive periods of statutory leave which included a period of additional adoption leave or additional maternity leave, as they would have been if the period or periods of his employment prior to his additional adoption leave or (as the case may be) additional maternity leave were continuous with the period of employment following it;

(ii) in any other case, as they would have been if he had not been absent, and

(b) on terms and conditions … not less favourable than those which would have been applied to him if he had not been absent.

(2) The provision in paragraph (1)(a)(i) concerning the treatment of periods of additional adoption leave or additional maternity leave is subject to the requirements of [paragraphs 5, 5B and 6 of Schedule 5 to the Social Security Act 1989 (equal treatment under pension schemes: maternity absence, adoption leave and family leave)].

(3) The provisions in paragraph (1)(a)(ii) and (b) for an employee to be treated as if he had not been absent refer to his absence—

(a) if his return is from an isolated period of ordinary adoption leave, since the beginning of that period;

(b) if his return is from consecutive periods of statutory leave, since the beginning of the first such period.

[2778]

NOTES

Para (1): words omitted from sub-para (b) revoked by the Paternity and Adoption Leave (Amendment) Regulations 2004, SI 2004/923, regs 2, 4, as from 6 April 2004.

Para (2): words in square brackets substituted by the Pensions Act 2004 (Commencement No 2, Transitional Provisions and Consequential Amendments) Order 2005, SI 2005/275, art 5, as from 9 February 2005.

PART 4
PROVISIONS APPLICABLE IN RELATION TO BOTH PATERNITY AND ADOPTION LEAVE

28 Protection from detriment

(1) An employee is entitled under section 47C of the 1996 Act not to be subjected to any detriment by any act, or any deliberate failure to act, by his employer because—

(a) the employee took or sought to take paternity leave or ordinary or additional adoption leave;

(b) the employer believed that the employee was likely to take ordinary or additional adoption leave, …

[(bb) the employee undertook, considered undertaking or refused to undertake work in accordance with regulation 21A; or]

(c) the employee failed to return after a period of additional adoption leave in a case where—

(i) the employer did not notify him, in accordance with regulation 17(7) and (8) or otherwise, of the date on which that period ended, and he reasonably believed that the period had not ended, or

(ii) the employer gave him less than 28 days' notice of the date on which the period would end, and it was not reasonably practicable for him to return on that date.

(2) Paragraph (1) does not apply where the detriment in question amounts to dismissal within the meaning of Part 10 of the 1996 Act.

[2779]

NOTES

Para (1): word omitted from sub-para (b) revoked, and sub-para (bb) inserted, by the Maternity and Parental Leave etc and the Paternity and Adoption Leave (Amendment) Regulations 2006, SI 2006/2014, regs 12, 16, as from 1 October 2006 (with effect only in relation to an employee with whom a child is expected to be placed for adoption, where the placement is expected to occur on or after 1 April 2007: see SI 2006/2014, reg 2(2) at **[3463A]**).

Adoption from overseas: note that the amendments made by SI 2006/2014 noted above, as applied to adoptions from overseas by virtue of, and as modified by, SI 2003/921, have effect only where the adopter's child enters Great Britain on or after 1 April 2007 (see SI 2006/2014, reg 2(3) at **[3463A]**).

29 Unfair dismissal

(1) An employee who is dismissed is entitled under section 99 of the 1996 Act to be regarded for the purpose of Part 10 of that Act as unfairly dismissed if—

(a) the reason or principal reason for the dismissal is of a kind specified in paragraph (3), or

(b) the reason or principal reason for the dismissal is that the employee is redundant, and regulation 23 has not been complied with.

(2) An employee who is dismissed shall also be regarded for the purposes of Part 10 of the 1996 Act as unfairly dismissed if—

(a) the reason (or, if more than one, the principal reason) for the dismissal is that the employee was redundant;

(b) it is shown that the circumstances constituting the redundancy applied equally to one or more employees in the same undertaking who had positions similar to that held by the employee and who have not been dismissed by the employer, and

(c) it is shown that the reason (or, if more than one, the principal reason) for which the employee was selected for dismissal was a reason of a kind specified in paragraph (3).

(3) The kinds of reason referred to in paragraph (1) and (2) are reasons connected with the fact that—

(a) the employee took, or sought to take, paternity or adoption leave;

(b) the employer believed that the employee was likely to take ordinary or additional adoption leave, …

[(bb) the employee undertook, considered undertaking or refused to undertake work in accordance with regulation 21A; or]

(c) the employee failed to return after a period of additional adoption leave in a case where—

(i) the employer did not notify him, in accordance with regulation 17(7) and (8) or otherwise, of the date on which that period would end, and he reasonably believed that the period had not ended, or

(ii) the employer gave him less than 28 days' notice of the date on which the period would end, and it was not reasonably practicable for him to return on that date.

(4) …

(5) Paragraph (1) does not apply in relation to an employee if—

(a) it is not reasonably practicable for a reason other than redundancy for the employer (who may be the same employer or a successor of his) to permit the employee to return to a job which is both suitable for the employee and appropriate for him to do in the circumstances;

(b) an associated employer offers the employee a job of that kind, and

(c) the employee accepts or unreasonably refuses that offer.

(6) Where, on a complaint of unfair dismissal, any question arises as to whether the operation of paragraph (1) is excluded by the provisions of paragraph … (5), it is for the employer to show that the provisions in question were satisfied in relation to the complainant.

[2780]

NOTES

Para (3): word omitted from sub-para (b) revoked, and sub-para (bb) inserted, by the Maternity and Parental Leave etc and the Paternity and Adoption Leave (Amendment) Regulations 2006, SI 2006/2014, regs 12, 17(a), as from 1 October 2006 (with effect only in relation to an employee with whom a child is expected to be placed for adoption, where the placement is expected to occur on or after 1 April 2007: see SI 2006/2014, reg 2(2) at **[3463A]**).

Para (4): revoked by SI 2006/2014, regs 12, 17(b), as from 1 October 2006 (with effect only in relation to an employee with whom a child is expected to be placed for adoption, where the placement is expected to occur on or after 1 April 2007: see SI 2006/2014, reg 2(2) at **[3463A]**).

Para (6): words omitted revoked by SI 2006/2014, regs 12, 17(c), as from 1 October 2006 (with effect only in relation to an employee with whom a child is expected to be placed for adoption, where the placement is expected to occur on or after 1 April 2007: see SI 2006/2014, reg 2(2) at **[3463A]**).

Adoption from overseas: note that the amendments made by SI 2006/2014 noted above, as applied to adoptions from overseas by virtue of, and as modified by, SI 2003/921, have effect only where the adopter's child enters Great Britain on or after 1 April 2007 (see SI 2006/2014, reg 2(3) at **[3463A]**).

30 Contractual rights to paternity or adoption leave

(1) This regulation applies where an employee is entitled to—

(a) paternity leave,

(b) ordinary adoption leave, or

(c) additional adoption leave,

(referred to in paragraph (2) as a "statutory right") and also to a right which corresponds to that right and which arises under the employee's contract of employment or otherwise.

(2) In a case where this regulation applies—

(a) the employee may not exercise the statutory right and the corresponding right separately but may, in taking the leave for which the two rights provide, take advantage of whichever right is, in any particular respect, the more favourable, and

(b) the provisions of the 1996 Act and of these Regulations relating to the statutory right apply, subject to any modifications necessary to give effect to any more favourable contractual terms, to the exercise of the composite right described in sub-paragraph (a) as they apply to the exercise of the statutory right.

[2781]

31 Calculation of a week's pay

Where—

(a) under Chapter 2 of Part 14 of the 1996 Act, the amount of a week's pay of an employee falls to be calculated by reference to the average rate of remuneration, or the average amount of remuneration, payable to the employee in respect of a period of twelve weeks ending on a particular date (referred to as "the calculation date");

(b) during a week in that period, the employee was absent from work on paternity leave or ordinary or additional adoption leave, and

(c) remuneration is payable to the employee in respect of that week under his contract of employment, but the amount payable is less than the amount that would be payable if he were working,

that week shall be disregarded for the purpose of the calculation and account shall be taken of remuneration in earlier weeks so as to bring up to twelve the number of weeks of which account is taken.

[2782]

STATUTORY PATERNITY PAY AND STATUTORY ADOPTION PAY (WEEKLY RATES) REGULATIONS 2002

(SI 2002/2818)

NOTES

Made: 11 November 2002.

Authority: Social Security Contributions and Benefits Act 1992, ss 171ZE(1), 171ZN(1); Social Security Administration Act 1992, s 5(1)(l).

Commencement: 8 December 2002.

Statutory paternity pay: the Work and Families Act 2006, s 11(2) at **[1697]** provides that any reference to statutory paternity pay in any instrument or document made before the commencement of paras 12 and 13 of Sch 1 to that Act is to be read, in relation to any time after that commencement, as a reference to ordinary statutory paternity pay. As of 6 April 2008, Sch 1, paras 12, 13 had not been brought into force.

1 Citation and commencement

These Regulations may be cited as the Statutory Paternity Pay and Statutory Adoption Pay (Weekly Rates) Regulations and shall come into force on 8th December 2002.

[2783]

[2 Weekly rate of payment of statutory paternity pay

The weekly rate of payment of statutory paternity pay shall be the smaller of the following two amounts—

(a) [£117.18];

(b) 90 per cent of the normal weekly earnings of the person claiming statutory paternity pay, determined in accordance with regulations 39 and 40 of the Statutory Paternity Pay and Statutory Adoption Pay (General) Regulations 2002.]

[2784]

NOTES

Commencement: 4 April 2004.

Substituted by the Statutory Paternity Pay and Statutory Adoption Pay (Weekly Rates) (Amendment) Regulations 2004, SI 2004/925, reg 2, as from 4 April 2004.

Sum in square brackets in para (a) substituted by the Social Security Benefits Up-rating Order 2008, SI 2008/632, art 11(a), as from 6 April 2008.

The previous amounts were: £100.00 (as from 8 December 2002, see the Social Security Benefits Up-rating Order 2004, SI 2004/552, art 11(a)); £102.80 (as from 4 April 2004, see SI 2004/552, art 11(a)); £106.00 (as from 3 April 2005, see the Social Security Benefits Up-rating Order 2005,

SI 2005/522, art 11(a)); £108.85 (as from 2 April 2006, see the Social Security Benefits Up-rating Order 2006, SI 2006/645, art 11(a)); £112.75 (as from 1 April 2007, see the Social Security Benefits Up-rating Order 2007, SI 2007/688, art 11(a)).

3 Weekly rate of payment of statutory adoption pay

The weekly rate of payment of statutory adoption pay shall be the smaller of the following two amounts—

(a) [£117.18];

(b) 90 per cent of the normal weekly earnings of the person claiming statutory adoption pay, determined in accordance with regulations 39 and 40 of the Statutory Paternity Pay and Statutory Adoption Pay (General) Regulations 2002.

[2785]

NOTES

Sum in square brackets in para (a) substituted by the Social Security Benefits Up-rating Order 2008, SI 2008/632, art 11(b), as from 6 April 2008.

The previous amounts were £100.00 (as from 8 December 2002, see the Social Security Benefits Up-rating Order 2004, SI 2004/552, art 11(b)); £102.80 (as from 4 April 2004, see SI 2004/552, art 11(b)); £106.00 (as from 3 April 2005, see the Social Security Benefits Up-rating Order 2005, SI 2005/522, art 11(b)); £108.85 (as from 2 April 2006, see the Social Security Benefits Up-rating Order 2006, SI 2006/645, art 11(b)); £112.75 (as from 1 April 2007, see the Social Security Benefits Up-rating Order 2007, SI 2007/688, art 11(b)).

[4 Rounding of fractional amounts

Where any payment of—

(a) statutory paternity pay is made on the basis of a calculation at—
- (i) the weekly rate specified in regulation 2(b); or
- (ii) the daily rate of one seventh of the weekly rate specified in regulation 2(a) or (b); or

(b) statutory adoption pay is made on the basis of a calculation at—
- (i) the weekly rate specified in regulation 3(b); or
- (ii) the daily rate of one-seventh of the weekly rate specified in regulation 3(a) or (b),

and that amount includes a fraction of a penny, the payment shall be rounded up to the next whole number of pence.]

[2786]

NOTES

Commencement: 1 October 2006.

Substituted by the Statutory Paternity Pay and Statutory Adoption Pay (General) and the Statutory Paternity Pay and Statutory Adoption Pay (Weekly Rates) (Amendment) Regulations 2006, SI 2006/2236, regs 6, 7, as from 1 October 2006 (see further the note below).

Note: the Statutory Paternity Pay and Statutory Adoption Pay (General) and the Statutory Paternity Pay and Statutory Adoption Pay (Weekly Rates) (Amendment) Regulations 2006, SI 2006/2236, reg 2 provides that this amendment applies in relation to an entitlement to (a) statutory paternity pay (birth) in respect of children whose expected week of birth begins on or after 1 April 2007; (b) statutory paternity pay (adoption) and statutory adoption pay in respect of children expected to be placed for adoption, where the placement is expected to occur on or after 1 April 2007. Note also that there is no equivalent modification of the commencement provisions in relation to adoptions from overseas to that made in relation to statutory adoption leave by SI 2006/2014, reg 2(3) at **[3463A]**.

STATUTORY PATERNITY PAY AND STATUTORY ADOPTION PAY (ADMINISTRATION) REGULATIONS 2002

(SI 2002/2820)

NOTES

Made: 13 November 2002.

Authority: Employment Act 2002, ss 7(1), (2)(a), (b), (4)(a)–(c), (5), 8(1), (2)(a)–(c), 10(1), (2), 51(1); Social Security Contributions (Transfer of Functions, etc) Act 1999, ss 8(1)(f), (ga), 25.

Commencement: 8 December 2002.

Statutory paternity pay: the Work and Families Act 2006, s 11(2) at **[1697]** provides that any reference to statutory paternity pay in any instrument or document made before the commencement of paras 12 and 13 of Sch 1 to that Act is to be read, in relation to any time after that commencement, as a reference to ordinary statutory paternity pay. As of 6 April 2008, Sch 1, paras 12, 13 had not been brought into force.

ARRANGEMENT OF REGULATIONS

1 Citation and commencement

These Regulations may be cited as the Statutory Paternity Pay and Statutory Adoption Pay (Administration) Regulations 2002 and shall come into force on 8th December 2002.

[2787]

2 Interpretation

(1) In these Regulations—

"adopter", in relation to a child, means a person with whom the child is matched for adoption;

"adoption leave" means leave under section 75A of the Employment Rights Act 1996;

"adoption pay period" means the period prescribed under section 171ZN(2) of the Contributions and Benefits Act as the period in respect of which statutory adoption pay is payable to a person;

"the Board" means the Commissioners of Inland Revenue;

"the Contributions and Benefits Act" means the Social Security Contributions and Benefits Act 1992;

"contributions payments" has the same meaning as in section 7 of the Employment Act;

"the Contributions Regulations" means the Social Security (Contributions) Regulations 2001;

"the Employment Act" means the Employment Act 2002;

"income tax month" means the period beginning on the 6th day of any calendar month and ending on the 5th day of the following calendar month;

"income tax quarter" means the period beginning on the 6th day of April and ending on the 5th day of July, the period beginning on the 6th day of July and ending on the 5th day of October, the period beginning on the 6th day of October and ending on the 5th day of January or the period beginning on the 6th day of January and ending on the 5th day of April;

"paternity leave" means leave under section 80A or section 80B of the Employment Rights Act 1996;

"paternity pay period" means the period determined in accordance with section 171ZE(2) of the Contributions and Benefits Act as the period in respect of which statutory paternity pay is payable to a person;

"statutory adoption pay" means any payment under section 171ZL of the Contributions and Benefits Act;

"statutory paternity pay" means any payment under section 171ZA or section 171ZB of the Contributions and Benefits Act;

"tax year" means the 12 months beginning with 6th April in any year;

"writing" includes writing delivered by means of electronic communications approved by directions issued by the Board pursuant to regulations under section 132 of the Finance Act 1999.

(2) Any reference in these Regulations to the employees of an employer includes former employees of his.

[2788]

NOTES

Adoption from overseas: as to the modification of this regulation in relation to adoptions from overseas, see the Statutory Paternity Pay (Adoption) and Statutory Adoption Pay (Adoptions from Overseas) (Administration) Regulations 2003, SI 2003/1192, reg 3(1)–(3).

Commissioners of Inland Revenue: a reference to the Commissioners of Inland Revenue is now to be taken as a reference to the Commissioners for Her Majesty's Revenue and Customs; see the Commissioners for Revenue and Customs Act 2005, s 50(1), (7).

3 Funding of employers' liabilities to make payments of statutory paternity or statutory adoption pay

(1) An employer who has made any payment of statutory paternity pay or statutory adoption pay shall be entitled—

(a) to an amount equal to 92 per cent of such payment; or

(b) if the payment qualifies for small employer's relief by virtue of section 7(3) of the Employment Act—

(i) to an amount equal to such payment; and

(ii) to an additional payment equal to the amount to which the employer would have been entitled under section 167(2)(b) of the Contributions and Benefits Act had the payment been a payment of statutory maternity pay.

(2) The employer shall be entitled in either case (a) or case (b) to apply for advance funding in respect of such payment in accordance with regulation 4, or to deduct it in accordance with regulation 5 from amounts otherwise payable by him.

[2789]

4 Application for funding from the Board

(1) If an employer is entitled to a payment determined in accordance with regulation 3 in respect of statutory paternity pay or statutory adoption pay which he is required to pay to an employee or employees for an income tax month or income tax quarter, and the payment exceeds the aggregate of—

(a) the total amount of tax which the employer is required to pay to the collector of taxes in respect of the deductions from the emoluments of his employees in accordance with the Income Tax (Employments) Regulations 1993 for the same income tax month or income tax quarter,

(b) the total amount of the deductions made by the employer from the emoluments of his employees for the same income tax month or income tax quarter in accordance with regulations under section 22(5) of the Teaching and Higher Education Act 1998 or section 73B of the Education (Scotland) Act 1980 or in accordance with article 3(5) of the Education (Student Support) (Northern Ireland) Order 1998,

(c) the total amount of contributions payments which the employer is required to pay to the collector of taxes in respect of the emoluments of his employees (whether by means of deduction or otherwise) in accordance with the Contributions Regulations for the same income tax month or income tax quarter, and

(d) the total amount of payments which the employer is required to pay to the collector of taxes in respect of the deductions made on account of tax from payments to sub-contractors in accordance with section 559 of the Income and Corporation Taxes Act 1988 for the same income tax month or income tax quarter,

the employer may apply to the Board in accordance with paragraph (2) for funds to pay the statutory paternity pay or statutory adoption pay (or so much of it as remains outstanding) to the employee or employees.

(2) Where—

(a) the condition in paragraph (1) is satisfied, or

(b) the employer considers that the condition in paragraph (1) will be satisfied on the date of any subsequent payment of emoluments to one or more employees who are entitled to payment of statutory paternity pay or statutory adoption pay,

the employer may apply to the Board for funding in a form approved for that purpose by the Board.

(3) An application by an employer under paragraph (2) shall be for an amount up to, but not exceeding, the amount of the payment to which the employer is entitled in accordance with regulation 3 in respect of statutory paternity pay and statutory adoption pay which he is required to pay to an employee or employees for the income tax month or income tax quarter to which the payment of emoluments relates.

[2790]

5 Deductions from payments to the Board

An employer who is entitled to a payment determined in accordance with regulation 3 may recover such payment by making one or more deductions from the aggregate of the amounts specified in sub-paragraphs (a) to (d) of regulation 4(1) except where and in so far as—

(a) those amounts relate to earnings paid before the beginning of the income tax month or income tax quarter in which the payment of statutory paternity pay or statutory adoption pay was made;

(b) those amounts are paid by him later than six years after the end of the tax year in which the payment of statutory paternity pay or statutory adoption pay was made;

(c) the employer has received payment from the Board under regulation 4; or

(d) the employer has made a request in writing under regulation 4 that the payment to which he is entitled in accordance with regulation 3 be paid to him and he has not received notification by the Board that the request is refused.

[2791]

6 Payments to employers by the Board

If the total amount which an employer is or would otherwise be entitled to deduct under regulation 5 is less than the payment to which the employer is entitled in accordance with regulation 3 in an income tax month or income tax quarter, and the Board are satisfied that this is so, then provided that the employer has in writing requested them to do so, the Board shall pay the employer such amount as the employer was unable to deduct.

[2792]

7 Date when certain contributions are to be treated as paid

Where an employer has made a deduction from a contributions payment under regulation 5, the date on which it is to be treated as having been paid for the purposes of section 7(5) of the Employment Act (when amount deducted from contributions payment to be treated as paid and received by the Board) is—

(a) in a case where the deduction did not extinguish the contributions payment, the date on which the remainder of the contributions payment or, as the case may be, the first date on which any part of the remainder of the contributions payment was paid; and

(b) in a case where the deduction extinguished the contributions payment, the 14th day after the end of the income tax month or income tax quarter during which there were paid the earnings in respect of which the contributions payment was payable.

[2793]

8 Overpayments

(1) This regulation applies where funds have been provided to the employer pursuant to regulation 4 in respect of one or more employees and it appears to an officer of the Board that the employer has not used the whole or part of those funds to pay statutory paternity pay or statutory adoption pay.

(2) An officer of the Board shall decide to the best of his judgement the amount of funds provided pursuant to regulation 4 and not used to pay statutory paternity pay or statutory adoption pay and shall serve notice in writing of his decision on the employer.

(3) A decision under this regulation may cover funds provided pursuant to regulation 4—

(a) for any one income tax month or income tax quarter, or more than one income tax month or income tax quarter, in a tax year, and

(b) in respect of a class or classes of employees specified in the decision notice (without naming the individual employees), or in respect of one or more employees named in the decision notice.

(4) Subject to the following provisions of this regulation, Part 6 of the Taxes Management Act 1970 (collection and recovery) shall apply with any necessary modifications to a decision under this regulation as if it were an assessment and as if the amount of funds determined were income tax charged on the employer.

(5) Where an amount of funds determined under this regulation relates to more than one employee, proceedings may be brought for the recovery of that amount without distinguishing the amounts making up that sum which the employer is liable to repay in respect of each employee and without specifying the employee in question, and the amount determined under this regulation shall be one cause of action or one matter of complaint for the purposes of proceedings under section 65, 66 or 67 of the Taxes Management Act 1970.

(6) Nothing in paragraph (5) prevents the bringing of separate proceedings for the recovery of any amount which the employer is liable to repay in respect of each employee.

[2794]

9 Records to be maintained by employers

Every employer shall maintain for three years after the end of a tax year in which he made payments of statutory paternity pay or statutory adoption pay to any employee of his a record of—

(a) if the employee's paternity pay period or adoption pay period began in that year—
  (i) the date on which that period began, and
  (ii) the evidence of entitlement to statutory paternity pay or statutory adoption pay provided by the employee pursuant to regulations made under section 171ZC(3)(c) or section 171ZL(8)(c) of the Contributions and Benefits Act;

(b) the weeks in that tax year in which statutory paternity pay or statutory adoption pay was paid to the employee and the amount paid in each week; and

(c) any week in that tax year which was within the employee's paternity pay period or adoption pay period but for which no payment of statutory paternity pay or statutory adoption pay was made to him and the reason no payment was made.

[2795]

10 Inspection of employers' records

(1) Every employer, whenever called upon to do so by any authorised officer of the Board, shall produce the documents and records specified in paragraph (2) to that officer for inspection, at such time as that officer may reasonably require, at the prescribed place.

(2) The documents and records specified in this paragraph are—

(a) all wages sheets, deductions working sheets, records kept in accordance with regulation 9 and other documents and records whatsoever relating to the calculation or payment of statutory paternity pay or statutory adoption pay to his employees in respect of the years specified by such officer; or

(b) such of those wages sheets, deductions working sheets, or other documents and records as may be specified by the authorised officer.

(3) The "prescribed place" mentioned in paragraph (1) means—

(a) such place in Great Britain as the employer and the authorised officer may agree upon; or

(b) in default of such agreement, the place in Great Britain at which the documents and records referred to in paragraph (2)(a) are normally kept; or

(c) in default of such agreement and if there is no such place as is referred to in sub-paragraph (b) above, the employer's principal place of business in Great Britain.

(4) The authorised officer may—

(a) take copies of, or make extracts from, any document or record produced to him for inspection in accordance with paragraph (1);

(b) remove any document or record so produced if it appears to him to be necessary to do so, at a reasonable time and for a reasonable period.

(5) Where any document or record is removed in accordance with paragraph (4)(b), the authorised officer shall provide—

(a) a receipt for the document or record so removed; and
(b) a copy of the document or record, free of charge, within seven days, to the person by whom it was produced or caused to be produced where the document or record is reasonably required for the proper conduct of a business.

(6) Where a lien is claimed on a document produced in accordance with paragraph (1), the removal of the document under paragraph (4)(b) shall not be regarded as breaking the lien.

(7) Where records are maintained by computer, the person required to make them available for inspection shall provide the authorised officer with all facilities necessary for obtaining information from them.

[2796]

11 Provision of information relating to entitlement to statutory paternity pay or statutory adoption pay

(1) Where an employer who has been given evidence of entitlement to statutory paternity pay or statutory adoption pay pursuant to regulations made under section 171ZC(3)(c) or section 171ZL(8)(c) of the Contributions and Benefits Act by a person who is or has been an employee decides that he has no liability to make payments of statutory paternity pay or statutory adoption pay to the employee, the employer shall furnish the employee with details of the decision and the reasons for it.

(2) Where an employer who has been given such evidence of entitlement to statutory adoption pay has made one or more payments of statutory adoption pay to the employee but decides, before the end of the adoption pay period, that he has no liability to make further payments to the employee because he has been detained in legal custody or sentenced to a term of imprisonment which was not suspended, the employer shall furnish the employee with—
(a) details of his decision and the reasons for it; and
(b) details of the last week in respect of which a liability to pay statutory adoption pay arose and the total number of weeks within the adoption pay period in which such a liability arose.

(3) The employer shall—
(a) return to the employee any evidence provided by him as referred to in paragraph (1) or (2); and
(b) comply with the requirements imposed by paragraph (1) within 28 days of—
(i) in the case of entitlement to statutory paternity pay under section 171ZA(1) of the Contributions and Benefits Act, the day the employee gave notice of his intended absence or the end of the fifteenth week before the expected week of birth, whichever is the later, or
(ii) in the case of entitlement to statutory paternity pay under section 171ZB(1) or of statutory adoption pay under section 171ZL(1) of the Contributions and Benefits Act, the end of the seven-day period that starts on the date on which the adopter is notified of having been matched with the child;
(c) comply with the requirements imposed by paragraph (2) within seven days of being notified of the employee's detention or sentence.

(4) For the purposes of paragraph (3)(b)(ii), an adopter is notified of having been matched with a child on the date on which he receives notification, under regulation 11(2) of the Adoption Agencies Regulations 1983 or regulation 12(3) of the Adoption Agencies (Scotland) Regulations 1996 that an adoption agency has decided that he would be a suitable adoptive parent for the child.

[2797]

NOTES

Adoption from overseas: as to the modification of this regulation in relation to adoptions from overseas, see the Statutory Paternity Pay (Adoption) and Statutory Adoption Pay (Adoptions from Overseas) (Administration) Regulations 2003, SI 2003/1192, reg 3(1), (4), (5).

12 Application for the determination of any issue arising as to, or in connection with, entitlement to statutory paternity pay or statutory adoption pay

(1) An application for the determination of any issue arising as to, or in connection with, entitlement to statutory paternity pay or statutory adoption pay may be submitted to an officer of the Board by the employee concerned.

(2) Such an issue shall be decided by an officer of the Board only on the basis of such an application or on his own initiative.

[2798]

13 Applications in connection with statutory paternity pay or statutory adoption pay

(1) An application for the determination of any issue referred to in regulation 12 shall be made in a form approved for the purpose by the Board.

(2) Where such an application is made by an employee, it shall—

(a) be made to an officer of the Board within six months of the earliest day in respect of which entitlement to statutory paternity pay or statutory adoption pay is in issue;

(b) state the period in respect of which entitlement to statutory paternity pay or statutory adoption pay is in issue; and

(c) state the grounds (if any) on which the applicant's employer had denied liability for statutory paternity pay or statutory adoption pay in respect of the period specified in the application.

[2799]

14 Provision of information

(1) Any person specified in paragraph (2) shall, where information or documents are reasonably required from him to ascertain whether statutory paternity pay or statutory adoption pay is or was payable, furnish that information or those documents within 30 days of receiving a notification from an officer of the Board requesting such information or documents.

(2) The requirement to provide such information or documents applies to—

(a) any person claiming to be entitled to statutory paternity pay or statutory adoption pay;

(b) any person who is, or has been, the spouse[, civil partner] or partner of such a person as is specified in paragraph (a);

(c) any person who is, or has been, an employer of such a person as is specified in paragraph (a);

(d) any person carrying on an agency or other business for the introduction or supply to persons requiring them of persons available to do work or to perform services; and

(e) any person who is a servant or agent of any such person as is specified in paragraphs (a) to (d).

[2800]

NOTES

Para (2): words in square brackets in sub-para (b) inserted by the Civil Partnership Act 2004 (Amendments to Subordinate Legislation) Order 2005, SI 2005/2114, art 2(17), Sch 17, para 2, as from 5 December 2005.

STATUTORY PATERNITY PAY AND STATUTORY ADOPTION PAY (GENERAL) REGULATIONS 2002

(SI 2002/2822)

NOTES

Made: 13 November 2002.

Authority: Social Security Contributions and Benefits Act 1992, ss 171ZA(2)(a), 171ZB(2)(a), 171ZC(3)(a), (c), (d), (f), (g), 171ZD(2), (3), 171ZE(2)(a), (b)(i), (3), (7), (8), 171ZG(3), 171ZJ(1), (3), (4), (7), (8), 171ZL(8)(b)–(d), (f), (g), 171ZM(2), (3), 171ZN(2), (5), (6), 171ZP(6), 171ZS(1), (3), (4), (7), (8), 175(4); Social Security Administration Act 1992, s 5(1)(g), (i), (p).

Commencement: 8 December 2002.

Statutory paternity pay: the Work and Families Act 2006, s 11(2) at **[1697]** provides that any reference to statutory paternity pay in any instrument or document made before the commencement of paras 12 and 13 of Sch 1 to that Act is to be read, in relation to any time after that commencement, as a reference to ordinary statutory paternity pay. As of 6 April 2008, Sch 1, paras 12, 13 had not been brought into force.

ARRANGEMENT OF REGULATIONS

PART 1
INTRODUCTION

PART 2
STATUTORY PATERNITY PAY (BIRTH)

PART 3
STATUTORY PATERNITY PAY (ADOPTION)

PART 4
STATUTORY PATERNITY PAY: PROVISIONS APPLICABLE TO BOTH STATUTORY PATERNITY PAY (BIRTH) AND STATUTORY PATERNITY PAY (ADOPTION)

PART 5
STATUTORY ADOPTION PAY

PART 6
STATUTORY PATERNITY PAY AND STATUTORY ADOPTION PAY: PROVISIONS APPLICABLE TO BOTH STATUTORY PATERNITY PAY AND STATUTORY ADOPTION PAY

PART 1
INTRODUCTION

1 Citation and commencement

These Regulations may be cited as the Statutory Paternity Pay and Statutory Adoption Pay (General) Regulations 2002 and shall come into force on 8th December 2002.

[2801]

2 Interpretation

(1) In these Regulations—

"the Act" means the Social Security Contributions and Benefits Act 1992;

"adopter", in relation to a child, means a person who has been matched with the child for adoption;

"adoption agency" has the meaning given, in relation to England and Wales, by section 1(4) of the Adoption Act 1976 and in relation to Scotland, by section 1(4) of the Adoption (Scotland) Act 1978;

"the Board" means the Commissioners of Inland Revenue;

"the Contributions Regulations" means the Social Security (Contributions) Regulations 2001;

"expected week", in relation to the birth of a child, means the week, beginning with midnight between Saturday and Sunday, in which it is expected that the child will be born;

"statutory paternity pay (adoption)" means statutory paternity pay payable in accordance with the provisions of Part 12ZA of the Act where the conditions specified in section 171ZB(2) of the Act are satisfied;

"statutory paternity pay (birth)" means statutory paternity pay payable in accordance with the provisions of Part 12ZA of the Act where the conditions specified in section 171ZA(2) of the Act are satisfied.

(2) For the purposes of these Regulations—

(a) a person is matched with a child for adoption when an adoption agency decides that that person would be a suitable adoptive parent for the child, either individually or jointly with another person, and

(b) a person is notified of having been matched with a child on the date on which he receives notification of the agency's decision, under regulation 11(2) of the Adoption Agencies Regulations 1983 or regulation 12(3) of the Adoption Agencies (Scotland) Regulations 1996.

[2802]

NOTES

Commissioners of Inland Revenue: a reference to the Commissioners of Inland Revenue is now to be taken as a reference to the Commissioners for Her Majesty's Revenue and Customs; see the Commissioners for Revenue and Customs Act 2005, s 50(1), (7).

3 Application

(1) Subject to the provisions of Part 12ZA of the Act (statutory paternity pay) and of these Regulations, there is entitlement to—

(a) statutory paternity pay (birth) in respect of children—

(i) born on or after 6th April 2003; or

(ii) whose expected week of birth begins on or after that date;

(b) statutory paternity pay (adoption) in respect of children—

(i) matched with a person who is notified of having been matched on or after 6th April 2003; or

(ii) placed for adoption on or after that date.

(2) Subject to the provisions of Part 12ZB of the Act (statutory adoption pay) and of these Regulations, there is entitlement to statutory adoption pay in respect of children—

(a) matched with a person who is notified of having been matched on or after 6th April 2003; or

(b) placed for adoption on or after that date.

[2803]

PART 2
STATUTORY PATERNITY PAY (BIRTH)

4 Conditions of entitlement to statutory paternity pay (birth): relationship with newborn child and child's mother

The conditions prescribed under section 171ZA(2)(a) of the Act are those prescribed in regulation 4(2)(b) and (c) of the Paternity and Adoption Leave Regulations 2002.

[2804]

5 Modification of entitlement conditions: early birth

Where a person does not meet the conditions specified in section 171ZA(2)(b) to (d) of the Act because the child's birth occurred earlier than the 14th week before the expected week of the birth, it shall have effect as if, for the conditions there set out, there were substituted the conditions that—

(a) the person would, but for the date on which the birth occurred, have been in employed earner's employment with an employer for a continuous period of at least 26 weeks ending with the week immediately preceding the 14th week before the expected week of the child's birth;

(b) his normal weekly earnings for the period of 8 weeks ending with the week immediately preceding the week in which the child is born are not less than the lower earnings limit in force under section 5(1)(a) of the Act immediately before the commencement of the week in which the child is born.

[2805]

6 Period of payment of statutory paternity pay (birth)

(1) Subject to paragraph (2) and regulation 8, a person entitled to statutory paternity pay (birth) may choose the statutory paternity pay period to begin on—

(a) the date on which the child is born or, where he is at work on that day, the following day;

(b) the date falling such number of days after the date on which the child is born as the person may specify;

(c) a predetermined date, specified by the person, which is later than the first day of the expected week of the child's birth.

(2) In a case where statutory paternity pay (birth) is payable in respect of a child whose expected week of birth begins before 6th April 2003, the statutory paternity pay period shall begin on a predetermined date, specified by the person entitled to such pay in a notice under section 171ZC(1) of the Act, which is at least 28 days after the date on which that notice was given, unless the person liable to pay statutory paternity pay (birth) agrees to the period beginning earlier.

(3) A person may choose for statutory paternity pay (birth) to be paid in respect of a period of a week.

(4) A choice made in accordance with paragraph (1) or (2) is not irrevocable, but where a person subsequently makes a different choice in relation to the beginning of the statutory pay period, section 171ZC(1) of the Act shall apply to it.

[2806]

7 Additional notice requirements for statutory paternity pay (birth)

(1) Where the choice made by a person in accordance with paragraph (1) of regulation 6 and notified in accordance with section 171ZC(1) of the Act is that mentioned in sub-paragraph (a) or (b) of that paragraph, the person shall give further notice to the person liable to pay him statutory paternity pay, as soon as is reasonably practicable after the child's birth, of the date the child was born.

(2) Where the choice made by a person in accordance with paragraph (1) of regulation 6 and notified in accordance with section 171ZC(1) of the Act is that specified in sub-paragraph (c) of that paragraph, and the date of the child's birth is later than the date so specified, the person shall, if he wishes to claim statutory paternity pay (birth), give notice to the person liable to pay it, as soon as is reasonably practicable, that the period in respect of which statutory paternity pay is to be paid shall begin on a date different from that originally chosen by him.

(3) That date may be any date chosen in accordance with paragraph (1) of regulation 6.

[2807]

8 Qualifying period for statutory paternity pay (birth)

The qualifying period for the purposes of section 171ZE(2) of the Act (period within which the statutory paternity pay period must occur) is a period which begins on the date of the child's birth and ends—

(a) except in the case referred to in paragraph (b), 56 days after that date;

(b) in a case where the child is born before the first day of the expected week of its birth, 56 days after that day.

[2808]

9 Evidence of entitlement to statutory paternity pay (birth)

(1) A person shall provide evidence of his entitlement to statutory paternity pay (birth) by providing in writing to the person who will be liable to pay him statutory paternity pay (birth)—

(a) the information specified in paragraph (2);

(b) a declaration that he meets the conditions prescribed under section 171ZA(2)(a) of the Act and that it is not the case that statutory paternity pay (birth) is not payable to him by virtue of the provisions of section 171ZE(4) of the Act.

(2) The information referred to in paragraph (1)(a) is as follows—

(a) the name of the person claiming statutory paternity pay (birth);

(b) the expected week of the child's birth and, where the birth has already occurred, the date of birth;

(c) the date from which it is expected that the liability to pay statutory paternity pay (birth) will begin;

(d) whether the period chosen in respect of which statutory paternity pay (birth) is to be payable is a week.

(3) The information and declaration referred to in paragraph (1) shall be provided at least 28 days before the date mentioned in sub-paragraph (c) of paragraph (2) or, if that is not reasonably practicable, as soon as is reasonably practicable thereafter.

(4) Where the person who will be liable to pay statutory paternity pay (birth) so requests, the person entitled to it shall inform him of the date of the child's birth within 28 days, or as soon as is reasonably practicable thereafter.

[2809]

10 Entitlement to statutory paternity pay (birth) where there is more than one employer

Statutory paternity pay (birth) shall be payable to a person in respect of a statutory pay week during any part of which he works only for an employer—

(a) who is not liable to pay him statutory paternity pay (birth); and

(b) for whom he has worked in the week immediately preceding the 14th week before the expected week of the child's birth.

[2810]

PART 3
STATUTORY PATERNITY PAY (ADOPTION)

11 Conditions of entitlement to statutory paternity pay (adoption): relationship with child and with person with whom the child is placed for adoption

(1) The conditions prescribed under section 171ZB(2)(a) of the Act are that a person—

(a) is married to[, the civil partner] or the partner of a child's adopter (or in a case where there are two adopters, married to[, the civil partner] or the partner of the other adopter), and

(b) has, or expects to have, the main responsibility (apart from the responsibility of the child's adopter, or in a case where there two adopters, together with the other adopter) for the upbringing of the child.

(2) For the purposes of paragraph (1), "partner" means a person (whether of a different sex or the same sex) who lives with the adopter and the child in an enduring family relationship but is not a relative of the adopter of a kind specified in paragraph [(2A)].

[(2A) The relatives of the adopter referred to in paragraph (2) are the adopter's parent, grandparent, sister, brother, aunt or uncle.]

(3) References to relationships in paragraph [(2A)]—

(a) are to relationships of the full blood or half blood, or, in the case of an adopted person, such of those relationships as would exist but for the adoption, and

(b) include the relationship of a child with his adoptive, or former adoptive parents but do not include any other adoptive relationships.

[2811]

NOTES

Para (1): words in square brackets in sub-para (a) inserted by the Civil Partnership Act 2004 (Amendments to Subordinate Legislation) Order 2005, SI 2005/2114, art 2(17), Sch 17, para 3, as from 5 December 2005.

Paras (2), (3): figures in square brackets substituted by the Statutory Paternity Pay and Statutory Adoption Pay (Amendment) Regulations 2004, SI 2004/488, reg 2(1), (2)(a), (c), as from 6 April 2004.

Para (2A): inserted by SI 2004/488, reg 2(1), (2)(b), as from 6 April 2004.

12 Period of payment of statutory paternity pay (adoption)

(1) Subject to paragraph (2) and regulation 14, a person entitled to statutory paternity pay (adoption) may choose the statutory paternity pay period to begin on—

(a) the date on which the child is placed with the adopter or, where the person is at work on that day, the following day;

(b) the date falling such number of days after the date on which the child is placed with the adopter as the person may specify;

(c) a predetermined date, specified by the person, which is later than the date on which the child is expected to be placed with the adopter.

(2) In a case where statutory paternity pay (adoption) is payable in respect of a child matched with an adopter who is notified of having been matched before 6th April 2003, the statutory paternity pay period shall begin on a predetermined date, specified by the person entitled to such pay in a notice under section 171ZC(1) of the Act, which is at least 28 days after the date on which that notice was given, unless the person liable to pay statutory paternity pay (birth) agrees to the period beginning earlier.

(3) A person may choose for statutory paternity pay (adoption) to be paid in respect of a period of a week.

(4) A choice made in accordance with paragraph (1) is not irrevocable, but where a person subsequently makes a different choice in relation to the beginning of the statutory paternity pay period, section 171ZC(1) of the Act shall apply to it.

[2812]

13 Additional notice requirements for statutory paternity pay (adoption)

(1) Where the choice made by a person in accordance with paragraph (1) of regulation 12 and notified in accordance with section 171ZC(1) of the Act is that mentioned in sub-paragraph (a) or (b) of that paragraph, the person shall give further notice to the person liable to pay him statutory paternity pay as soon as is reasonably practicable of the date on which the placement occurred.

(2) Where the choice made by a person in accordance with paragraph (1) of regulation 12 and notified in accordance with section 171ZC(1) of the Act is that mentioned in sub-paragraph (c) of that paragraph, or a date is specified under paragraph (2) of that regulation, and the child is placed for adoption later than the date so specified, the person shall, if he wishes to claim statutory paternity pay (adoption), give notice to the person liable to pay it, as soon as is reasonably practicable, that the period in respect of which statutory paternity pay is to be paid shall begin on a date different from that originally chosen by him.

(3) That date may be any date chosen in accordance with paragraph (1) of regulation 12.

[2813]

14 Qualifying period for statutory paternity pay (adoption)

The qualifying period for the purposes of section 171ZE(2) of the Act (period within which the statutory pay period must occur) is a period of 56 days beginning with the date of the child's placement for adoption.

[2814]

15 Evidence of entitlement for statutory paternity pay (adoption)

(1) A person shall provide evidence of his entitlement to statutory paternity pay (adoption) by providing in writing to the person who will be liable to pay him statutory paternity pay (adoption)—

- (a) the information specified in paragraph (2);
- (b) a declaration that he meets the conditions prescribed under section 171ZB(2)(a) of the Act and that it is not the case that statutory paternity pay (adoption) is not payable to him by virtue of the provisions of section 171ZE(4) of the Act;
- (c) a declaration that he has elected to receive statutory paternity pay (adoption), and not statutory adoption pay under Part 12ZB of the Act.

(2) The information referred to in paragraph (1) is as follows—

- (a) the name of the person claiming statutory paternity pay (adoption);
- (b) the date on which the child is expected to be placed for adoption or, where the child has already been placed for adoption, the date of placement of the child;
- (c) the date from which it is expected that the liability to pay statutory paternity pay (adoption) will begin;
- (d) whether the period chosen in respect of which statutory paternity pay (adoption) is to be payable is a week;
- (e) the date the adopter was notified he had been matched with the child for the purposes of adoption.

(3) The information and declarations referred to in paragraph (1) shall be provided to the person liable to pay statutory paternity pay at least 28 days before the date mentioned in sub-paragraph (c) of paragraph (2) or, if that is not reasonably practicable, as soon as is reasonably practicable thereafter.

(4) Where the person who will be liable to pay statutory paternity pay (adoption) so requests, the person entitled to it shall inform him of the date of the child's placement within 28 days, or as soon as is reasonably practicable thereafter.

[2815]

16 Entitlement to statutory paternity pay (adoption) where there is more than one employer

Statutory paternity pay (adoption) shall be payable to a person in respect of a statutory pay week during any part of which he works only for an employer—

- (a) who is not liable to pay him statutory paternity pay (adoption); and
- (b) for whom he has worked in the week in which the adopter is notified of being matched with the child.

[2816]

PART 4
STATUTORY PATERNITY PAY: PROVISIONS APPLICABLE TO BOTH STATUTORY PATERNITY PAY (BIRTH) AND STATUTORY PATERNITY PAY (ADOPTION)

17 Work during a statutory paternity pay period

(1) Where, in a case where statutory paternity pay is being paid to a person who works during the statutory paternity pay period for an employer who is not liable to pay him statutory paternity pay and who does not fall within paragraph (b) of regulation 10 or, as the case may be, paragraph (b) of regulation 16, there shall be no liability to pay statutory paternity pay in respect of any remaining part of the statutory paternity pay period.

(2) In a case falling within paragraph (1), the person shall notify the person liable to pay statutory paternity pay within 7 days of the first day during which he works during the statutory pay period.

(3) The notification mentioned in paragraph (2) shall be in writing, if the person who has been liable to pay statutory paternity pay so requests.

[2817]

18 Cases where there is no liability to pay statutory paternity pay

There shall be no liability to pay statutory paternity pay in respect of any week—

(a) during any part of which the person entitled to it is entitled to statutory sick pay under Part 11 of the Act;

(b) following that in which the person claiming it has died; or

(c) during any part of which the person entitled to it is detained in legal custody or sentenced to a term of imprisonment (except where the sentence is suspended), or which is a subsequent week within the same statutory paternity pay period.

[2818]

19 Statutory paternity pay and contractual remuneration

For the purposes of section 171ZG(1) and (2) of the Act, the payments which are to be treated as contractual remuneration are sums payable under a contract of service—

(a) by way of remuneration;

(b) for incapacity for work due to sickness or injury;

(c) by reason of the birth or adoption of a child.

[2819]

20 Avoidance of liability for statutory paternity pay

(1) A former employer shall be liable to make payments of statutory paternity pay to a former employee in any case where the employee had been employed for a continuous period of at least 8 weeks and his contract of service was brought to an end by the former employer solely, or mainly, for the purpose of avoiding liability for statutory paternity pay.

(2) In a case falling within paragraph (1)—

(a) the employee shall be treated as if he had been employed for a continuous period ending with the child's birth or, as the case may be, the placement of the child for adoption;

(b) his normal weekly earnings shall be calculated by reference to his normal weekly earnings for the period of 8 weeks ending with the last day in respect of which he was paid under his former contract of service.

[2820]

PART 5
STATUTORY ADOPTION PAY

21 Adoption pay period

(1) Subject to paragraph (2), a person entitled to statutory adoption pay may choose the adoption pay period to begin—

(a) on the date on which the child is placed with him for adoption or, where he is at work on that day, on the following day;

(b) subject to paragraph (2), on a predetermined date, specified by him, which is no more than 14 days before the date on which the child is expected to be placed with him and no later than that date.

(2) In a case where statutory adoption pay is payable in respect of a child matched with an adopter who is notified of having been matched before 6th April 2003, the statutory adoption pay period shall begin on a predetermined date which is—

(a) on or after 6th April 2003, and

(b) no more than 14 days before the date on which the child is expected to be placed with the adopter.

(3) Subject to paragraph (4), where the choice made is that mentioned in sub-paragraph (b) of paragraph (1) or in a case where paragraph (2) applies, the adoption pay period shall, unless the employer agrees to the adoption pay period beginning earlier, begin no earlier than 28 days after notice under section 171ZL(6) of the Act has been given.

(4) Where the beginning of the adoption pay period determined in accordance with paragraph (3) is later than the date of placement, it shall be the date of placement.

(5) Subject to regulation 22, the duration of any adoption pay period shall be a continuous period of [39] weeks.

(6) A choice made under paragraph (1), or a date specified under paragraph (2), is not irrevocable, but where a person subsequently makes a different choice, section 171ZL(6) of the Act shall apply to it.

[2821]

NOTES

Para (5): figure in square brackets substituted by the Statutory Paternity Pay and Statutory Adoption Pay (General) and the Statutory Paternity Pay and Statutory Adoption Pay (Weekly Rates) (Amendment) Regulations 2006, SI 2006/2236, regs 3, 4, as from 1 October 2006 (see further the note below).

Note: the Statutory Paternity Pay and Statutory Adoption Pay (General) and the Statutory Paternity Pay and Statutory Adoption Pay (Weekly Rates) (Amendment) Regulations 2006, SI 2006/2236, reg 2 provides that this amendment applies in relation to an entitlement to (a) statutory paternity pay (birth) in respect of children whose expected week of birth begins on or after 1 April 2007; (b) statutory paternity pay (adoption) and statutory adoption pay in respect of children expected to be placed for adoption, where the placement is expected to occur on or after 1 April 2007. Note also that there is no equivalent modification of the commencement provisions in relation to adoptions from overseas to that made in relation to statutory adoption leave by SI 2006/2014, reg 2(3) at **[3463A]**.

22 Adoption pay period in cases where adoption is disrupted

(1) Where—

(a) after a child has been placed for adoption—

(i) the child dies;

(ii) the child is returned to the adoption agency under section 30(3) of the Adoption Act 1976 or section 30(3) of the Adoption (Scotland) Act 1978, or

(b) the adoption pay period has begun prior to the date the child has been placed for adoption, but the placement does not take place,

the adoption pay period shall terminate in accordance with the provisions of paragraph (2).

(2) The adoption pay period shall, in a case falling within paragraph (1), terminate 8 weeks after the end of the week specified in paragraph (3).

(3) The week referred to in paragraph (2) is—

(a) in a case falling within paragraph (1)(a)(i), the week during which the child dies;

(b) in a case falling within paragraph (1)(a)(ii), the week during which the child is returned;

(c) in a case falling within paragraph (1)(b), the week during which the person with whom the child was to be placed for adoption is notified that the placement will not be made.

(4) For the purposes of paragraph (3), "week" means a period of seven days beginning with Sunday.

[2822]

23 Additional notice requirements for statutory adoption pay

(1) Where a person gives notice under section 171ZL(6) of the Act he shall at the same time give notice of the date on which the child is expected to be placed for adoption.

(2) Where the choice made in accordance with paragraph (1) of regulation 21 and notified in accordance with section 171ZL(6) of the Act is that mentioned in sub-paragraph (a) of that paragraph, the person shall give further notice to the person liable to pay him statutory adoption pay as soon as is reasonably practicable of the date the child is placed for adoption.

[2823]

24 Evidence of entitlement to statutory adoption pay

(1) A person shall provide evidence of his entitlement to statutory adoption pay by providing to the person who will be liable to pay it—

(a) the information specified in paragraph (2), in the form of one or more documents provided to him by an adoption agency, containing that information;

(b) a declaration that he has elected to receive statutory adoption pay, and not statutory paternity pay (adoption) under Part 12ZA of the Act.

(2) The information referred to in paragraph (1) is—

(a) the name and address of the adoption agency and of the person claiming payment of statutory adoption pay;

(b) the date on which the child is expected to be placed for adoption or, where the child has already been placed for adoption, the date of placement; and

(c) the date on which the person claiming payment of statutory adoption pay was informed by the adoption agency that the child would be placed for adoption with him.

(3) The information and declaration referred to in paragraph (1) shall be provided to the person liable to pay statutory adoption pay at least 28 days before the date chosen as the beginning of the adoption pay period in accordance with paragraph (1) of regulation 21, or, if that is not reasonably practicable, as soon as is reasonably practicable thereafter.

[2824]

25 Entitlement to statutory adoption pay where there is more than one employer

Statutory adoption pay shall be payable to a person in respect of a week during any part of which he works only for an employer—

(a) who is not liable to pay him statutory adoption pay; and

(b) for whom he has worked in the week in which he is notified of being matched with the child.

[2825]

26 Work during an adoption pay period

(1) Where, in a case where statutory adoption pay is being paid to a person who works during the adoption pay period for an employer who is not liable to pay him statutory adoption pay and who does not fall within paragraph (b) of regulation 25, there shall be no liability to pay statutory adoption pay in respect of any remaining part of the adoption pay period.

(2) In a case falling within paragraph (1), the person shall notify the person liable to pay statutory adoption pay within 7 days of the first day during which he works during the adoption pay period.

(3) The notification contained in paragraph (2) shall be in writing if the person who has been liable to pay statutory adoption pay so requests.

[2826]

27 Cases where there is no liability to pay statutory adoption pay

(1) There shall be no liability to pay statutory adoption pay in respect of any week—

(a) during any part of which the person entitled to it is entitled to statutory sick pay under Part 11 of the Act;

(b) following that in which the person claiming it has died; or

(c) subject to paragraph (2), during any part of which the person entitled to it is detained in legal custody or sentenced to a term of imprisonment (except where the sentence is suspended).

(2) There shall be liability to pay statutory adoption pay in respect of any week during any part of which the person entitled to it is detained in legal custody where that person—

(a) is released subsequently without charge;
(b) is subsequently found not guilty of any offence and is released; or
(c) is convicted of an offence but does not receive a custodial sentence.

[2827]

[27A Working for not more than 10 days during an adoption pay period

In the case where an employee does any work under a contract of service with his employer on any day for not more than 10 such days during his adoption pay period, whether consecutive or not, statutory adoption pay shall continue to be payable to the employee by the employer.]

[2827A]

NOTES

Commencement: 1 October 2006.

Inserted by the Statutory Paternity Pay and Statutory Adoption Pay (General) and the Statutory Paternity Pay and Statutory Adoption Pay (Weekly Rates) (Amendment) Regulations 2006, SI 2006/2236, regs 3, 5, as from 1 October 2006 (see further the note below).

Note: the Statutory Paternity Pay and Statutory Adoption Pay (General) and the Statutory Paternity Pay and Statutory Adoption Pay (Weekly Rates) (Amendment) Regulations 2006, SI 2006/2236, reg 2 provides that this amendment applies in relation to an entitlement to (a) statutory paternity pay (birth) in respect of children whose expected week of birth begins on or after 1 April 2007; (b) statutory paternity pay (adoption) and statutory adoption pay in respect of children expected to be placed for adoption, where the placement is expected to occur on or after 1 April 2007.

28 Statutory adoption pay and contractual remuneration

For the purposes of section 171ZP(4) and (5) of the Act, the payments which are to be treated as contractual remuneration are sums payable under a contract of service—

(a) by way of remuneration;
(b) for incapacity for work due to sickness or injury;
(c) by reason of the adoption of a child.

[2828]

29 Termination of employment before start of adoption pay period

(1) Where the employment of a person who satisfies the conditions of entitlement to statutory adoption pay terminates for whatever reason (including dismissal) before the adoption pay period chosen in accordance with regulation 21 has begun, the period shall begin 14 days before the expected date of placement or, where the termination occurs on, or within 14 days before, the expected date of placement, on the day immediately following the last day of his employment.

(2) In a case falling within paragraph (1), the notice requirements set out in section 171ZL(6) of the Act and these Regulations shall not apply.

[2829]

30 Avoidance of liability for statutory adoption pay

(1) A former employer shall be liable to make payments of statutory adoption pay to a former employee in any case where the employee had been employed for a continuous period of at least 8 weeks and his contract of service was brought to an end by the former employer solely, or mainly, for the purpose of avoiding liability for statutory adoption pay.

(2) In a case falling within paragraph (1)—

(a) the employee shall be treated as if he had been employed for a continuous period ending with the week in which he was notified of having been matched with the child for adoption; and
(b) his normal weekly earnings shall be calculated by reference to his normal weekly earnings for the period of 8 weeks ending with the last day in respect of which he was paid under his former contract of service.

[2830]

PART 6
STATUTORY PATERNITY PAY AND STATUTORY ADOPTION PAY: PROVISIONS APPLICABLE TO BOTH STATUTORY PATERNITY PAY AND STATUTORY ADOPTION PAY

31 Introductory

(1) Subject to paragraph (2), the provisions of regulations 32 to 47 below apply to statutory paternity pay payable under Part 12ZA of the Act and to statutory adoption pay payable under 12ZB of the Act.

(2) The provisions of regulation 44 only apply to statutory adoption pay.

[2831]

32 Treatment of persons as employees

(1) [Subject to paragraph (1A),] in a case where, and in so far as, a person … is treated as an employed earner by virtue of the Social Security (Categorisation of Earners) Regulations 1978 he shall be treated as an employee for the purposes of Parts 12ZA and 12ZB of the Act, and in a case where, and in so far as, such a person is treated otherwise than as an employed earner by virtue of those regulations, he shall not be treated as an employee for the purposes of Parts 12ZA and 12ZB of the Act.

[(1A) Paragraph (1) shall have effect in relation to a person who—
- (a) is under the age of 16; and
- (b) would or, as the case may be, would not have been treated as an employed earner by virtue of the Social Security (Categorisation of Earners) Regulations 1978 had he been over that age,

as it has effect in relation to a person who is or, as the case may be, is not so treated.]

(2) A person who is in employed earner's employment within the meaning of the Act under a contract of apprenticeship shall be treated as an employee for the purposes of Parts 12ZA and 12ZB of the Act.

(3) A person who is in employed earner's employment within the meaning of the Act but whose employer—
- (a) does not fulfil the conditions prescribed in regulation 145(1) of the Contributions Regulations in so far as that provision relates to residence or presence in Great Britain; or
- (b) is a person who, by reason of any international treaty to which the United Kingdom is a party or of any international convention binding the United Kingdom—
  - (i) is exempt from the provisions of the Act; or
  - (ii) is a person against whom the provisions of the Act are not enforceable,

shall not be treated as an employee for the purposes of Parts 12ZA and 12ZB of the Act.

[2832]

NOTES

Para (1): words in square brackets inserted, and words omitted revoked, by the Employment Equality (Age) Regulations 2006, SI 2006/1031, reg 49(1), Sch 8, Pt 2, paras 59, 60(1), (2), as from 1 October 2006.

Para (1A): inserted by SI 2006/1031, reg 49(1), Sch 8, Pt 2, paras 59, 60(1), (3), as from 1 October 2006; substituted by the Employment Equality (Age) (Consequential Amendments) Regulations 2007, SI 2007/825, reg 7, as from 6 April 2007.

33 Continuous employment

(1) Subject to the following provisions of this regulation, where in any week a person is, for the whole or part of the week—
- (a) incapable of work in consequence of sickness or injury;
- (b) absent from work on account of a temporary cessation of work;
- (c) absent from work in circumstances such that, by arrangement or custom, he is regarded as continuing in the employment of his employer for all or any purposes,

and returns to work for his employer after the incapacity for or absence from work, that week shall be treated for the purposes of sections 171ZA, 171ZB and 171ZL of the Act as part of a continuous period of employment with that employer, notwithstanding that no contract of service exists with that employer in respect of that week.

(2) Incapacity for work which lasts for more than 26 consecutive weeks shall not count for the purposes of paragraph (1)(a).

(3) Where a person—

(a) is an employee in an employed earner's employment in which the custom is for the employer—

(i) to offer work for a fixed period of not more than 26 consecutive weeks;

(ii) to offer work for such period on two or more occasions in a year for periods which do not overlap; and

(iii) to offer the work available to those persons who had worked for him during the last or a recent such period, but

(b) is absent from work because of incapacity arising from some specific disease or bodily or mental disablement,

then in that case paragraph (1) shall apply as if the words "and returns to work for his employer after the incapacity for or absence from work," were omitted and paragraph (4) shall not apply.

(4) Where a person is employed under a contract of service for part only of the relevant week within the meaning of subsection (3) of section 171ZL of the Act (entitlement to statutory adoption pay), the whole of that week shall count in computing a period of continuous employment for the purposes of that section.

[2833]

34 Continuous employment and unfair dismissal

(1) This regulation applies to a person in relation to whose dismissal an action is commenced which consists—

(a) of the presentation by him of a complaint under section 111(1) of the Employment Rights Act 1996;

(b) of his making a claim in accordance with a dismissals procedure agreement designated by an order under section 110 of that Act; ...

(c) of any action taken by a conciliation officer under section 18 of the Employment Tribunals Act 1996; [or

(d) of a decision arising out of the use of a statutory dispute resolution procedure contained in Schedule 2 to the Employment Act 2002 in a case where, in accordance with the Employment Act 2002 (Dispute Resolution) Regulations 2004, such a procedure applies].

(2) If, in consequence of an action of the kind specified in paragraph (1), a person is reinstated or re-engaged by his employer or by a successor or associated employer of that employer, the continuity of his employment shall be preserved for the purposes of Part 12ZA or, as the case may be, Part 12ZB of the Act, and any week which falls within the interval beginning with the effective date of termination and ending with the date of reinstatement or re-engagement, as the case may be, shall count in the computation of his period of continuous employment.

(3) In this regulation—

"successor" and "dismissal procedures agreement" have the same meanings as in section 235 of the Employment Rights Act 1996; and

"associated employer" shall be construed in accordance with section 231 of the Employment Rights Act 1996.

[2834]

NOTES

Para (1): word omitted from sub-para (b) revoked, and sub-para (d) and the word immediately preceding it inserted, by the Statutory Maternity Pay (General) and Statutory Paternity Pay and Statutory Adoption Pay (General) (Amendment) Regulations 2005, SI 2005/358, reg 4, as from 6 April 2005, in relation to a reinstatement or re-engagement of employment occurring on or after that date.

35 Continuous employment and stoppages of work

(1) Where, for any week or part of a week a person does not work because there is a stoppage of work due to a trade dispute within the meaning of section 35(1) of the Jobseekers Act 1995 at his place of employment, the continuity of his employment shall, subject to paragraph (2), be treated as continuing throughout the stoppage but, subject to paragraph (3), no such week shall count in the computation of his period of employment.

(2) Subject to paragraph (3), where during the stoppage of work a person is dismissed from his employment, the continuity of his employment shall not be treated in accordance with paragraph (1) as continuing beyond the commencement of the day he stopped work.

(3) The provisions of paragraph (1), to the extent that they provide that a week in which the stoppage of work occurred shall not count in the computation of a period of employment, and paragraph (2) shall not apply to a person who proves that at no time did he have a direct interest in the trade dispute in question.

[2835]

36 Change of employer

A person's employment shall, notwithstanding a change of employer, be treated as continuous employment with the second employer where—

(a) the employer's trade or business or an undertaking (whether or not it is an undertaking established by or under an Act of Parliament) is transferred from one person to another;

(b) by or under an Act of Parliament, whether public or local and whenever passed, a contract of employment between any body corporate and the person is modified and some other body corporate is substituted as his employer;

(c) on the death of his employer, the person is taken into employment of the personal representatives or trustees of the deceased;

(d) the person is employed by partners, personal representatives or trustees and there is a change in the partners, or, as the case may be, personal representatives or trustees;

(e) the person is taken into the employment of an employer who is, at the time he entered his employment, an associated employer of his previous employer, and for this purpose "associated employer" shall be construed in accordance with section 231 of the Employment Rights Act 1996;

(f) on the termination of his employment with an employer he is taken into the employment of another employer and those employers are governors of a school maintained by a local education authority and that authority.

[2836]

37 Reinstatement after service with the armed forces etc

If a person who is entitled to apply to his employer under the Reserve Forces (Safeguard of Employment) Act 1985 enters the employment of that employer within the 6-month period mentioned in section 1(4)(b) of that Act, his previous period of employment with that employer (or if there was more than one such period, the last of those periods) and the period of employment beginning in that 6 month period shall be treated as continuous.

[2837]

38 Treatment of two or more employers or two or more contracts of service as one

(1) In a case where the earnings paid to a person in respect of two or more employments are aggregated and treated as a single payment of earnings under regulation 15(1) of the Contributions Regulations, the employers of that person in respect of those employments shall be treated as one for the purposes of Part 12ZA or, as the case may be, Part 12ZB of the Act.

(2) Where two or more employers are treated as one under the provisions of paragraph (1), liability for statutory paternity pay or, as the case may be, statutory adoption pay, shall be apportioned between them in such proportions as they may agree or, in default of agreement, in the proportions which the person's earnings from each employment bear to the amount of the aggregated earnings.

(3) Where two or more contracts of service exist concurrently between one employer and one employee, they shall be treated as one for the purposes of Part 12ZA or, as the case may be, Part 12ZB of the Act, except where, by virtue of regulation 14 of the Contributions Regulations, the earnings from those contracts of service are not aggregated for the purposes of earnings-related contributions.

[2838]

39 Meaning of "earnings"

(1) For the purposes of section 171ZJ(6) (normal weekly earnings for the purposes of Part 12ZA of the Act) and of section 171ZS(6) of the Act (normal weekly earnings for the

purposes of Part 12ZB of the Act), the expression "earnings" shall be construed in accordance with the following provisions of this regulation.

(2) The expression "earnings" refers to gross earnings and includes any remuneration or profit derived from a person's employment except any payment or amount which is—

(a) excluded from the computation of a person's earnings under regulation 25 of and Schedule 3 to, and regulation 123 of, the Contributions Regulations (payments to be disregarded) and regulation 27 of those Regulations (payments to directors to be disregarded) [(or would have been so excluded had he not been under the age of 16)];

(b) a chargeable emolument under section 10A of the Act, except where, in consequence of such a chargeable emolument being excluded from earnings, a person would not be entitled to statutory paternity pay or, as the case may be, statutory adoption pay [(or where such a payment or amount would have been so excluded and in consequence he would not have been entitled to statutory paternity pay or, as the case may be, statutory adoption pay had he not been under the age of 16)].

(3) For the avoidance of doubt, "earnings" includes—

[(za) any amount retrospectively treated as earnings by regulations made by virtue of section 4B(2) of the Act;]

(a) any sum payable in respect of arrears of pay in pursuance of an order for reinstatement or re-engagement under the Employment Rights Act 1996;

(b) any sum payable by way of pay in pursuance of an order made under the Employment Rights Act 1996 for the continuation of a contract of employment;

(c) any sum payable by way of remuneration in pursuance of a protective award under section 189 of the Trade Union and Labour Relations (Consolidation) Act 1992;

(d) any sum payable by way of statutory sick pay, including sums payable in accordance with regulations made under section 151(6) of the Act;

(e) any sum payable by way of statutory maternity pay;

(f) any sum payable by way of statutory paternity pay;

(g) any sum payable by way of statutory adoption pay.

[2839]

NOTES

Para (2): words in square brackets inserted by the Employment Equality (Age) Regulations 2006, SI 2006/1031, reg 49(1), Sch 8, Pt 2, paras 59, 61, as from 1 October 2006.

Para (3): sub-para (za) inserted by the Social Security, Occupational Pension Schemes and Statutory Payments (Consequential Provisions) Regulations 2007, SI 2007/1154, reg 6(1), (2), as from 6 April 2007, with retrospective effect from 2 December 2004.

40 Normal weekly earnings

(1) For the purposes of Part 12ZA and Part 12ZB of the Act, a person's normal weekly earnings shall be calculated in accordance with the following provisions of this regulation.

(2) In this regulation—

"the appropriate date" means—

(a) in relation to statutory paternity pay (birth), the first day of the 14th week before the expected week of the child's birth or the first day in the week in which the child is born, whichever is the earlier;

(b) in relation to statutory paternity pay (adoption) and statutory adoption pay, the first day of the week after the week in which the adopter is notified of being matched with the child for the purposes of adoption;

"normal pay day" means a day on which the terms of a person's contract of service require him to be paid, or the practice in his employment is for him to be paid, if any payment is due to him; and

"day of payment" means a day on which the person was paid.

(3) Subject to paragraph (4), the relevant period for the purposes of section 171ZJ(6) and 171ZS(6) is the period between—

(a) the last normal pay day to fall before the appropriate date; and

(b) the last normal pay day to fall at least 8 weeks earlier than the normal pay day mentioned in sub-paragraph (a),

including the normal pay day mentioned in sub-paragraph (a) but excluding that first mentioned in sub-paragraph (b).

(4) In a case where a person has no identifiable normal pay day, paragraph (3) shall have effect as if the words "day of payment" were substituted for the words "normal pay day" in each place where they occur.

(5) In a case where a person has normal pay days at intervals of or approximating to one or more calendar months (including intervals of or approximating to a year) his normal weekly earnings shall be calculated by dividing his earnings in the relevant period by the number of calendar months in that period (or, if it is not a whole number, the nearest whole number), multiplying the result by 12 and dividing by 52.

(6) In a case to which paragraph (5) does not apply and the relevant period is not an exact number of weeks, the person's normal weekly earnings shall be calculated by dividing his earnings in the relevant period by the number of days in the relevant period and multiplying the result by 7.

(7) In any case where a person receives a back-dated pay increase which includes a sum in respect of a relevant period, normal weekly earnings shall be calculated as if such a sum was paid in that relevant period even though received after that period.

[2840]

41 Payment of statutory paternity pay and statutory adoption pay

Payments of statutory paternity pay and statutory adoption pay may be made in a like manner to payments of remuneration but shall not include payment in kind or by way of the provision of board or lodgings or of services or other facilities.

[2841]

42 Time when statutory paternity pay and statutory adoption pay are to be paid

(1) In this regulation, "pay day" means a day on which it has been agreed, or it is the normal practice between an employer or former employer and a person who is or was an employee of his, that payments by way of remuneration are to be made, or, where there is no such agreement or normal practice, the last day of a calendar month.

(2) In any case where—

(a) a decision has been made by an officer of the Board under section 8(1) of the Social Security Contributions (Transfer of Functions, etc) Act 1999 as a result of which a person is entitled to an amount of statutory paternity pay or statutory adoption pay; and

(b) the time for bringing an appeal against the decision has expired and either—

(i) no such appeal has been brought; or

(ii) such an appeal has been brought and has been finally disposed of,

that amount of statutory paternity pay or statutory adoption pay shall be paid within the time specified in paragraph (3).

(3) Subject to paragraphs (4) and (5), the employer or former employer shall pay the amount not later than the first pay day after—

(a) where an appeal has been brought, the day on which the employer or former employer receives notification that it has been finally disposed of;

(b) where leave to appeal has been refused and there remains no further opportunity to apply for leave, the day on which the employer or former employer receives notification of the refusal; and

(c) in any other case, the day on which the time for bringing an appeal expires.

(4) Subject to paragraph (5), where it is impracticable, in view of the employer's or former employer's methods of accounting for and paying remuneration, for the requirement of payment referred to in paragraph (3) to be met by the pay day referred to in that paragraph, it shall be met not later than the next following pay day.

(5) Where the employer or former employer would not have remunerated the employee for his work in the week in question as early as the pay day specified in paragraph (3) or (if it applies) paragraph (4), the requirement of payment shall be met on the first day on which the employee would have been remunerated for his work in that week.

[2842]

43 Liability of the Board to pay statutory paternity pay or statutory adoption pay

(1) Where—

(a) an officer of the Board has decided that an employer is liable to make payments of statutory paternity pay or, as the case may be, statutory adoption pay to a person;

(b) the time for appealing against the decision has expired; and

(c) no appeal against the decision has been lodged or leave to appeal against the decision is required and has been refused,

then for any week in respect of which the employer was liable to make payments of statutory paternity pay or, as the case may be, statutory adoption pay but did not do so, and for any subsequent weeks in the paternity pay period or, as the case may be, adoption pay period, the liability to make those payments shall, notwithstanding sections 171ZD and 171ZM of the Act, be that of the Board and not the employer.

(2) Liability to make payments of statutory paternity pay or, as the case may be, statutory adoption pay shall, notwithstanding sections 171ZD and 171ZM of the Act, be a liability of the Board and not the employer as from the week in which the employer first becomes insolvent until the end of the paternity pay or adoption pay period.

(3) For the purposes of paragraph (2) an employer shall be taken to be insolvent if, and only if—

(a) in England and Wales—

(i) he has been adjudged bankrupt or has made a composition or arrangement with his creditors;

(ii) he has died and his estate falls to be administered in accordance with an order made under section 421 of the Insolvency Act 1986; or

(iii) where an employer is a company or a limited liability partnership, a winding-up order … is made or a resolution for a voluntary winding-up is passed (or, in the case of a limited liability partnership, a determination for a voluntary winding-up has been made) with respect to it [or it enters administration], or a receiver or a manager of its undertaking is duly appointed, or possession is taken, by or on behalf of the holders of any debentures secured by a floating charge, of any property of the company or limited liability partnership comprised in or subject to the charge, or a voluntary arrangement proposed for the purposes of Part 1 of the Insolvency Act 1986 is approved under that Part of that Act;

(b) in Scotland—

(i) an award of sequestration is made on his estate or he executes a trust deed for his creditors or enters into a composition contract;

(ii) he has died and a judicial factor appointed under section 11A of the Judicial Factors (Scotland) Act 1889 is required by that section to divide his insolvent estate among his creditors; or

(iii) where the employer is a company or a limited liability partnership, a winding-up order … is made or a resolution for voluntary winding-up is passed (or, in the case of a limited liability partnership, a determination for a voluntary winding-up is made) with respect to it [or it enters administration], or a receiver of its undertaking is duly appointed, or a voluntary arrangement proposed for the purposes of Part 1 of the Insolvency Act 1986 is approved under that Part.

[2843]

NOTES

Para (3): words omitted revoked, and words in square brackets inserted, by the Enterprise Act 2002 (Insolvency) Order 2003, SI 2003/2096, art 5, Schedule, Pt 2, para 79, as from 15 September 2003, except in relation to any case where a petition for an administration order was presented before that date.

44 Liability of the Board to pay statutory adoption pay in cases of legal custody or imprisonment

Where—

(a) there is liability to pay statutory adoption pay in respect of a period which is subsequent to the last week falling within paragraph (1)(c) of regulation 27, or

(b) there is liability to pay statutory adoption pay during a period of detention in legal custody by virtue of the provisions of paragraph (2) of that regulation,

that liability shall, notwithstanding section 171ZM of the Act, be that of the Board and not the employer.

[2844]

45 Payments by the Board

Where the Board become liable in accordance with regulation 43 or 44 to make payments of statutory paternity pay or, as the case may be, statutory adoption pay to a person, the first payment shall be made as soon as reasonably practicable after they become so liable, and payments thereafter shall be made at weekly intervals, by means of an instrument of payment or by such other means as appears to the Board to be appropriate in the circumstance of any particular case.

[2845]

46 Persons unable to act

(1) Where in the case of any person—

(a) statutory paternity pay or, as the case may be, statutory adoption pay is payable to him or he is alleged to be entitled to it;

(b) he is unable for the time being to act; and

(c) either—

(i) no receiver has been appointed by the Court of Protection with power to receive statutory paternity pay or, as the case may be, statutory adoption pay on his behalf, or

(ii) in Scotland, his estate is not being administered by any tutor, curator or other guardian acting or appointed in terms of law,

the Board may, upon written application to them by a person who, if a natural person, is over the age of 18, appoint that person to exercise, on behalf of the person unable to act, any right to which he may be entitled under Part 12ZA or, as the case may be, Part 12ZB of the Act and to deal on his behalf with any sums payable to him.

(2) Where the Board have made an appointment under paragraph (1)—

(a) they may at any time in their absolute discretion revoke it;

(b) the person appointed may resign his office after having given one month's notice in writing to the Board of his intention to do so; and

(c) the appointment shall terminate when the Board are notified that a receiver or other person to whom paragraph (1)(c) applies has been appointed.

(3) Anything required by Part 12ZA or 12ZB of the Act to be done by or to any person who is unable to act may be done by or to the person appointed under this regulation to act on his behalf, and the receipt of the person so appointed shall be a good discharge to the person's employer or former employer for any sum paid.

[2846]

47 Service of notices by post

A notice given in accordance with the provisions of these Regulations in writing contained in an envelope which is properly addressed and sent by prepaid post shall be treated as having been given on the day on which it is posted.

[2847]–[2857]

FLEXIBLE WORKING (PROCEDURAL REQUIREMENTS) REGULATIONS 2002

(SI 2002/3207)

NOTES

Made: 20 December 2002.
Authority: Employment Rights Act 1996, s 80G(2), (3).
Commencement: 6 April 2003.

ARRANGEMENT OF REGULATIONS

1 Citation and commencement

These Regulations may be cited as the Flexible Working (Procedural Requirements) Regulations 2002 and shall come into force on 6th April 2003.

[2858]

2 Interpretation

(1) In these Regulations—

"the 1996 Act" means the Employment Rights Act 1996;

"application" means an application under section 80F of the 1996 Act (statutory right to request a contract variation);

"contract of employment" means a contract of service or apprenticeship, whether express or implied, and (if it is express) whether oral or in writing;

"contract variation" means a change in the terms and conditions of a contract of employment of a kind specified in section 80F(1)(a) of the 1996 Act;

"electronic communication" means an electronic communication within the meaning of section 15(1) of the Electronic Communications Act 2000;

"employee" means an individual who has entered into or works under (or, where the employment has ceased, worked under) a contract of employment;

"employer" means the person by whom an employee is (or, where the employment has ceased, was) employed;

"worker" means an individual who has entered into or works under (or, where the employment has ceased, worked under)—

(a) a contract of employment, or

(b) any other contract, whether express or implied and (if it is express) whether oral or in writing, whereby the individual undertakes to do or perform personally any work or services for another party to the contract whose status is not by virtue of the contract that of a client or customer of any profession or business undertaking carried on by the individual.

"writing" includes writing delivered by means of electronic communication.

(2) For the purposes of these Regulations, unless the contrary is proved, an application is taken as having been made on the day the application is received.

(3) The reference in paragraph (2) to the day on which an application is received is a reference—

(a) in relation to an application transmitted by electronic communication, to the day on which it is transmitted,

(b) in relation to an application sent by post, to the day on which the application would be delivered in the ordinary course of post.

(4) For the purpose of these Regulations, unless the contrary is proved, a notice is taken as being given—

(a) in relation to a notice transmitted by electronic communication, on the day on which it is transmitted,

(b) in relation to a notice sent by post, the day on which the notice would be delivered in the ordinary course of post.

[2859]

3 The meeting to discuss an application with an employee

(1) Subject to paragraph (2) and regulation 13, an employer to whom an application for a contract variation is made shall hold a meeting to discuss the application with the employee within 28 days after the date on which the application is made.

(2) Paragraph (1) does not apply where the employer agrees to the application and notifies the employee accordingly in writing within the period referred to in that paragraph.

(3) A notice under paragraph (2) shall specify—

(a) the contract variation agreed to, and
(b) the date from which the variation is to take effect.

[2860]

4 Where a meeting is held to discuss an application the employer shall give the employee notice of his decision on the application within 14 days after the date of the meeting.

[2861]

5 A notice under regulation 4 shall—
(a) be in writing,
(b)
(i) where the employer's decision is to agree to the application, specify the contract variation agreed to and state the date on which the variation is to take effect,
(ii) where the decision is to refuse the application, state which of the grounds for refusal specified in section 80G(1)(b) of the 1996 Act are considered by the employer to apply, contain a sufficient explanation as to why those grounds apply in relation to the application, and set out the appeal procedure, and
(c) be dated.

[2862]

6 Appeals

An employee is entitled to appeal against his employer's decision to refuse an application by giving notice in accordance with regulation 7 within 14 days after the date on which notice of the decision is given.

[2863]

7 A notice of appeal under regulation 6 shall—
(a) be in writing,
(b) set out the grounds of appeal, and
(c) be dated.

[2864]

8—(1) Subject to paragraph (2), the employer shall hold a meeting with the employee to discuss the appeal within 14 days after the employee's notice under regulation 6 is given.

(2) Paragraph (1) does not apply where, within 14 days after the date on which notice under regulation 6 is given, the employer—
(a) upholds the appeal, and
(b) notifies the employee in writing of his decision, specifying the contract variation agreed to and stating the date from which the contract variation is to take effect.

[2865]

9 Where a meeting is held to discuss the appeal, the employer shall notify the employee of his decision on the appeal within 14 days after the date of the meeting.

[2866]

10 Notice under regulation 9 shall—
(a) be in writing,
(b)
(i) where the employer upholds the appeal, specify the contract variation agreed to and state the date from which the variation is to take effect, or
(ii) where the employer dismisses the appeal, state the grounds for the decision and contain a sufficient explanation as to why those grounds apply, and
(c) be dated.

[2867]

11 The time and place of a meeting under regulation 3(1) or 8(1) shall be convenient to the employer and the employee.

[2868]

12 Extension of periods

(1) An employer and an employee may agree to an extension of any of the periods referred to in regulations 3, 4, 6, 8, 9 and 13.

(2) An agreement under paragraph (1) must be recorded in writing by the employer.

(3) The employer's record referred to in paragraph (2) must—

(a) specify what period the extension relates to,
(b) specify the date on which the extension is to end,
(c) be dated, and
(d) be sent to the employee.

[2869]

13 Where the individual who would ordinarily consider an application is absent from work on annual leave or on sick leave on the day on which the application is made, the period referred to in regulation 3(1) commences on the day the individual returns to work or 28 days after the application is made, whichever is the sooner.

[2870]

14 Right to be accompanied

(1) This regulation applies where—

(a) a meeting is held under regulation 3(1) or 8(1), and
(b) the employee reasonably requests to be accompanied at the meeting.

(2) Where this regulation applies the employer must permit the employee to be accompanied at the meeting by a single companion who—

(a) is chosen by the employee and is within paragraph (3),
(b) is to be permitted to address the meeting (but not to answer questions on behalf of the employee), and
(c) is to be permitted to confer with the employee during the meeting.

(3) A person comes within this paragraph if he is a worker employed by the same employer as the employee.

(4) If—

(a) an employee has a right under this regulation to be accompanied at a meeting,
(b) his chosen companion will not be available at the time proposed for the meeting by the employer, and
(c) the employee proposes an alternative time which satisfies paragraph (5),

the employer must postpone the meeting to the time proposed by the employee.

(5) An alternative time must—

(a) be convenient for employer, employee and companion, and
(b) fall before the end of the period of seven days beginning with the first day after the day proposed by the employer.

(6) An employer shall permit a worker to take time off during working hours for the purpose of accompanying an employee in accordance with a request under paragraph (1)(b).

(7) Sections 168(3) and (4), 169 and 171 to 173 of the Trade Union and Labour Relations (Consolidation) Act 1992 (time off for carrying out trade union duties) shall apply in relation to paragraph (6) above as they apply in relation to section 168(1) of that Act.

[2871]

15 Complaint to employment tribunal

(1) An employee may present a complaint to an employment tribunal that his employer has failed, or threatened to fail, to comply with regulation 14(2) or (4).

(2) A tribunal shall not consider a complaint under this regulation in relation to a failure or threat unless the complaint is presented—

(a) before the end of the period of three months beginning with the date of the failure or threat, or
(b) within such further period as the tribunal considers reasonable in a case where it is satisfied that it was not reasonably practicable for the complaint to be presented before the end of that period of three months.

(3) Where a tribunal finds that a complaint under this regulation is well-founded it shall order the employer to pay compensation to the worker of an amount not exceeding two weeks' pay.

(4) Chapter 2 of Part 14 of the 1996 Act (calculation of a week's pay) shall apply for the purposes of paragraph (3); and in applying that Chapter the calculation date shall be taken to be the date on which the relevant meeting took place (or was to have taken place).

(5) The limit in section 227(1) of the Employment Rights Act 1996 (maximum amount of a week's pay) shall apply for the purposes of paragraph (3) above.

[2872]

NOTES

There is no provision in ss 18 or 21 of the Employment Tribunals Act 1996 respectively for conciliation or complaints under this regulation, or for appeals to the EAT against any determination of an Employment Tribunal of such a complaint.

16 Detriment and dismissal

(1) A person has the right not to be subjected to any detriment by any act, or any deliberate failure to act, by his employer done on the ground that he—

(a) exercised or sought to exercise the right under regulation 14(2) or (4), or

(b) accompanied or sought to accompany an employee pursuant to a request under that regulation.

(2) Section 48 of the 1996 Act shall apply in relation to contraventions of paragraph (1) above as it applies in relation to contraventions of certain sections of that Act.

(3) A person who is dismissed shall be regarded for the purposes of Part 10 of the 1996 Act as unfairly dismissed if the reason (or, if more than one, the principle reason) for the dismissal is that he—

(a) exercised or sought to exercise his right under regulation 14(2) or (4), or

(b) accompanied or sought to accompany an employee pursuant to a request under that regulation.

(4) Sections 108 and 109 of the 1996 Act (qualifying period of employment and upper age limit) shall not apply in relation to paragraph (3) above.

(5) Sections 128 to 132 of the 1996 Act (interim relief) shall apply in relation to dismissal for the reason specified in paragraph 3(a) or (b) above as they apply in relation to dismissal for a reason specified in section 128(1)(b) of that Act.

(6) In the application of Chapter 2 of Part 10 of the 1996 Act in relation to paragraph (3) above, a reference to an employee shall be taken as a reference to a worker.

[2873]

NOTES

"Sections 108 and 109 of the 1996 Act": section 109 was repealed by the Employment Equality (Age) Regulations 2006, SI 2006/1031, reg 49(1), Sch 8, Pt 1, para 25, as from 1 October 2006, but there has been no corresponding amendment to para (4) above.

17 Withdrawal of application by the employee

(1) An employer shall treat an application as withdrawn where the employee has—

(a) notified to him whether orally or in writing that he is withdrawing the application,

(b) without reasonable cause, failed to attend a meeting under regulation 3(1) or 8(1) more than once, or

(c) without reasonable cause, refused to provide the employer with information the employer requires in order to assess whether the contract variation should be agreed to.

(2) An employer shall confirm the withdrawal of the application to the employee in writing unless the employee has provided him with written notice of the withdrawal under paragraph 1(a).

[2874]

FLEXIBLE WORKING (ELIGIBILITY, COMPLAINTS AND REMEDIES) REGULATIONS 2002

(SI 2002/3236)

NOTES

Made: 31 December 2002.
Authority: Employment Rights Act 1996, ss 80F(1)(b), (5), (8)(a), 80H(3)(b), 80I(3).
Commencement: 6 April 2003.

ARRANGEMENT OF REGULATIONS

1 Citation and commencement

These Regulations may be cited as the Flexible Working (Eligibility, Complaints and Remedies) Regulations 2002 and shall come into force on 6th April 2003.

[2875]

2 Interpretation

(1) In these Regulations—

"the 1996 Act" means the Employment Rights Act 1996;

"the Procedure Regulations" means the Flexible Working (Procedural Requirements) Regulations 2002;

["adopter", in relation to a child, means—

(a) a person with whom an adoption agency has decided the child should be placed for adoption, or

(b) a person who has given notice of his intention to apply for an adoption order as required by section 44 of the Adoption and Children Act 2002 or section 22 of the Adoption (Scotland) Act 1978;]

["adoption agency" means an adoption agency within the meaning of section 2 of the Adoption and Children Act 2002, Article 3(3) of the Adoption (Northern Ireland) Order 1987 or section 1(4) of the Adoption (Scotland) Act 1978;]

"application" means an application under section 80F of the 1996 Act (statutory right to request contract variation);

"contract of employment" means a contract of service or apprenticeship, whether express or implied, and (if it is express) whether oral or in writing;

"contract variation", means a change in the terms and conditions of a contract of employment of a kind specified in section 80F(1)(a) of the 1996 Act;

["disabled" means entitled to a disability living allowance within the meaning of section 71 of the Social Security Contributions and Benefits Act 1992;]

"electronic communication" means an electronic communication within the meaning of section 15(1) of the Electronic Communications Act 2000;

"employee" means an individual who has entered into or works under (or, where the employment has ceased, worked under) a contract of employment;

"employer" means the person by whom an employee is (or, where the employment has ceased, was) employed;

"foster parent" means a foster parent within the meaning of regulation 2(1) of the Fostering Services Regulations 2002 or a foster carer within the meaning of regulation 2(1) of the Fostering of Children (Scotland) Regulations 1996;

"guardian" means a person appointed as a guardian under section 5 of the Children Act 1989 or section 7 or 11 of the Children (Scotland) Act 1995;

["partner" means the other member of a couple consisting of—

(a) a man and a woman who are not married to each other but are living together as if they were husband and wife, or

(b) two people of the same sex who are not civil partners of each other but are living together as if they were civil partners;]

["private foster carer" means a person fostering a child privately within the meaning of section 66 of the Children Act 1989 or an individual other than a parent of the child who maintains the child as a foster child for the purposes of the Foster Children (Scotland) Act 1984, or otherwise looks after the child in circumstances in which that Act applies by virtue of section 17 of that Act;]

["relative" means a mother, father, adopter, guardian, special guardian, parent-in-law, step-parent, son, step-son, [son-in-law,] daughter, step-daughter, [daughter-in-law,] brother, step-brother, brother-in-law, sister, step-sister, sister-in-law, uncle, aunt or grandparent, and includes adoptive relationships and relationships of the full blood or half blood or, in the case of an adopted person, such of those relationships as would exist but for the adoption;

["residence order" means a residence order as defined by section 8(1) of the Children Act 1989 or section 11(2)(c) of the Children (Scotland) Act 1995;]

"special guardian", means a person appointed as a special guardian under section 14A of the Children Act 1989;]

"writing" includes writing delivered by means of electronic communication.

[(2) A reference in any provision of these Regulations to a period of continuous employment is to a period computed in accordance with Chapter 1 of Part 14 of the 1996 Act, as if the provision were a provision of that Act.]

(3) …

[2876]

NOTES

Para (1): definition "adopter" substituted, and definitions "adoption agency", "private foster carer" and "residence order" inserted, by the Flexible Working (Eligibility, Complaints and Remedies) (Amendment) (No 2) Regulations 2007, SI 2007/2286, regs 2, 3, as from 1 October 2007; definitions "disabled", "relative" and "special guardian" inserted, and definition "partner" substituted, by the Flexible Working (Eligibility, Complaints and Remedies) (Amendment) Regulations 2006, SI 2006/3314, regs 2, 3(1), (2), as from 6 April 2007; words in square brackets in definition "relative" inserted by the Flexible Working (Eligibility, Complaints and Remedies) (Amendment) Regulations 2007, SI 2007/1184, regs 2, 3, as from 3 May 2007.

Para (2): substituted by SI 2006/3314, regs 2, 3(1), (3), as from 6 April 2007.

Para (3): revoked by SI 2006/3314, regs 2, 3(1), (4), as from 6 April 2007.

3 Entitlement to request a contract variation [to take care for a child]

(1) An employee is entitled to make an application to his employer for a contract variation [to enable him, in accordance with section 80F(1)(b)(i) of the 1996 Act, to care for a child] if he—

(a) has been continuously employed for a period of not less than 26 weeks;

[(b) is either—

(i) the mother, father, adopter, guardian, special guardian, foster parent or private foster carer of, or a person in whose favour a residence order is in force in respect of, the child; or

(ii) married to, the civil partner of or the partner of—

(aa) the child's mother, father, adopter, guardian, special guardian, foster parent or private foster carer, or

(bb) a person in whose favour a residence order is in force in respect of the child;]

(c) has, or expects to have responsibility for the upbringing of the child.

(2) …

[2877]

NOTES

Regulation heading: words in square brackets inserted by the Flexible Working (Eligibility, Complaints and Remedies) (Amendment) Regulations 2006, SI 2006/3314, regs 2, 4(1), (2), as from 6 April 2007.

Para (1): first words in square brackets inserted by SI 2006/3314, regs 2, 4(1), (3), as from 6 April 2007; sub-para (b) substituted by the Flexible Working (Eligibility, Complaints and Remedies) (Amendment) (No 2) Regulations 2007, SI 2007/2286, regs 2, 4, as from 1 October 2007.

Para (2): revoked by SI 2006/3314, regs 2, 4(1), (5), as from 6 April 2007.

[3A Age of child

An application under regulation 3 must be made before the day on which the child concerned reaches the age of 6 or, if disabled, 18.]

[2877A]

NOTES

Commencement: 6 April 2007.

Inserted, together with reg 3B, by the Flexible Working (Eligibility, Complaints and Remedies) (Amendment) Regulations 2006, SI 2006/3314, regs 2, 5, as from 6 April 2007.

[3B Entitlement to request a contract variation to care for an adult

An employee is entitled to make an application to his employer for a contract variation to enable him, in accordance with section 80F(1)(b)(ii) of the 1996 Act, to care for a person aged 18 or over if the employee—

(a) has been continuously employed for a period of not less than 26 weeks;

(b) is or expects to be caring for a person in need of care who is either—

(i) married to or the partner or civil partner of the employee;

(ii) a relative of the employee; or

(iii) living at the same address as the employee.]

[2877B]

NOTES

Commencement: 6 April 2007.

Inserted as noted to reg 3A at **[2877A]**.

4 Form of the application

An application shall—

(a) be made in writing,

(b) state whether a previous application has been made by the employee to the employer and, if so, when, and

(c) be dated.

[2878]

5 Date when an application is taken as made

(1) Unless the contrary is proved, an application is taken as having been made on the day the application is received.

(2) The reference in paragraph (1) to the day on which an application is received is a reference—

(a) in relation to an application transmitted by electronic communication, to the day on which it is transmitted,

(b) in relation to an application sent by post, to the day on which the application would be delivered in the ordinary course of post.

[2879]

6 Breaches of the Procedure Regulations by the employer entitling an employee to make a complaint to an employment tribunal

The breaches of the Procedure Regulations which entitle an employee to make a complaint to an employment tribunal under section 80H of the 1996 Act notwithstanding the fact that his application has not been disposed of by agreement or withdrawn are—

(a) failure to hold a meeting in accordance with regulation 3(1) or 8(1),

(b) failure to notify a decision in accordance with regulation 4 or 9.

[2880]

7 Compensation

The maximum amount of compensation that an employment tribunal may award under section 80I of the 1996 Act where it finds a complaint by an employee under section 80H of the Act well-founded is 8 weeks' pay.

[2881]

REHABILITATION OF OFFENDERS ACT 1974 (EXCLUSIONS AND EXCEPTIONS) (SCOTLAND) ORDER 2003

(SSI 2003/231)

NOTES

Made: 28 March 2003.

Authority: Rehabilitation of Offenders Act 1974, ss 4(4), 7(4), 10(1).

Commencement: 29 March 2003.

This Order extends to Scotland only and, in so far as it extends beyond Scotland, it does so only as a matter of Scots law (see art 1 at **[2881A]**). The equivalent English and Welsh Order is at **[2009]**.

ARRANGEMENT OF ARTICLES

SCHEDULES:

1 Citation, commencement and extent

(1) This Order may be cited as the Rehabilitation of Offenders Act 1974 (Exclusions and Exceptions) (Scotland) Order 2003, and shall come into force the day after the day on which it is made.

(2) This Order extends to Scotland and, in so far as it extends beyond Scotland, it does so only as a matter of Scots law.

[2881A]

2 ((*Interpretation*) *outside the scope of this work*.)

3 Exclusion of section 4(1) of the Act

The application of section 4(1) (effect of rehabilitation generally and in proceedings before a judicial authority) of the Act is excluded in relation to—

(a) any proceedings specified in Schedule 1; and

(b) any proceedings with respect to a decision or a proposed decision specified in Part 1 of Schedule 2—

(i) to the extent that there falls to be determined in those proceedings any issue relating to a spent conviction for any relevant offence or to circumstances ancillary thereto; and

(ii) to the extent that section 4(1) renders inadmissible any evidence relating to such conviction or circumstances or removes the requirement to answer any question relating to the conviction or circumstances.

[2881B]

4 Exclusion of section 4(2)(a) and (b) of the Act

The provisions of section 4(2)(a) and (b) (questions seeking information with respect to previous convictions) of the Act are excluded in relation to questions put in the circumstances to which Schedule 3 applies.

[2881C]

5 Exceptions from section 4(3) of the Act

There is excepted from the provisions of section 4(3)(b) (effect of rehabilitation on grounds of dismissal or exclusion from an office, profession, occupation or employment) of the Act—

(a) any profession, office, employment or occupation specified in Schedule 4;

(b) any action taken for the purpose of safeguarding national security; and

(c) any decision or proposed decision taken by a person specified in Part 1 of Schedule 2 to do or to refuse to do anything specified in that Part.

[2881D]

6 (*Revokes* (*subject to the limited extent of this Order as set out in art 1*(2) *at* **[2881A]**) *the Rehabilitation of Offenders Act 1974* (*Exceptions*) *Order 1975, SI 1975/1023, the Rehabilitation of Offenders Act 1974* (*Exceptions*) (*Amendment*) *Order 1986, SI 1986/1249, and the Rehabilitation of Offenders Act 1974* (*Exceptions*) (*Amendment No 2*) *Order 1986, SI 1986/2268.*)

SCHEDULES

SCHEDULE 1
PROCEEDINGS

Article 3

1. Proceedings in respect of a person's admission to, or disciplinary proceedings against a member of, any profession specified in Part 1 of Schedule 4 to this Order.

2. Disciplinary proceedings against a constable.

3–24. (*Outside the scope of this work.*)

[2881E]

(*Sch 2* (*Financial services*) *outside the scope of this work.*)

SCHEDULE 3
EXCLUSION OF SECTION 4(2)(A) AND (B) OF THE ACT

Article 4

1 Application

Subject to paragraph 3, this Schedule applies, for the purposes of article 4, to questions put in the circumstances set out in paragraphs 4 to 9.

2 Interpretation

In this Schedule—

"adopt" includes any arrangements to adopt a child, including arrangements for adoption where the proposed adopter is a relative of the child, whether under section 12 or section 17 of the Adoption (Scotland) Act 1978 or in circumstances where the child is to be adopted outside of the United Kingdom;

["contracting authority" means a contracting authority within the meaning of Article 1(9) of Directive 2004/18/EC;

"contracting entity" means a contracting entity within the meaning of Article 2(2) of Directive 2004/17/EC;

"Directive 2004/17/EC" means Directive 2004/17/EC of the European Parliament and of the Council of 31st March 2004;

"Directive 2004/18/EC" means Directive 2004/18/EC of the European Parliament and of the Council of 31st March 2004;]

"foster" has the meaning given by regulation 2(1) of the Fostering of Children (Scotland) Regulations 1996;

"foster carer" means a person approved by a local authority in terms of regulation 7 of the Fostering of Children (Scotland) Regulations 1996; and

"private foster carer" means a person required to give notice to a local authority by virtue of section 5(1) or (2) of the Foster Children (Scotland) Act 1984.

3 Requirements to inform

(1) This Schedule applies only where the person questioned is informed at the time the question is asked that, by virtue of this Order, spent convictions are to be disclosed.

(2) In the case of questions put in the circumstances to which paragraph 7 applies, the person questioned is also to be informed at that time that spent convictions are to be disclosed in the interests of national security.

(3) In the case of questions put in the circumstances to which paragraph 8 applies, the person questioned is also to be informed at that time that the question relates only to spent convictions for a relevant offence.

4 Specified professions etc

(1) Any question asked in order to assess the suitability—

(a) of the person to whom the question relates for a profession specified in Part 1 of Schedule 4;

(b) of the person to whom the question relates for any office or employment specified in Part 2 of Schedule 4;

(c) of the person to whom the question relates or of any other person to pursue any occupation specified in Part 3 of Schedule 4 or to pursue it subject to a particular condition or restriction; and

(d) of the person to whom the question relates or of any other person to hold a licence, certificate or permit specified in sub-paragraph (3) or to hold it subject to a particular condition or restriction.

(2) For the avoidance of doubt, references in sub paragraph (1) to the suitability of a person for any profession or for any office, employment or occupation include the suitability of that person for training for such profession or, as the case may be, for training for such office, employment or occupation.

(3) The licences, certificates or permits referred to in [sub paragraph (1)(d)] are

(a) firearm certificates and shot gun certificates issued under the Firearms Act 1968, and permits issued under section 7(1), 9(2) or 13(1)(c) of that Act;

(b) licences issued under section 25 (Restrictions on persons under eighteen going abroad for the purpose of performing for profit) of the Children and Young Persons Act 1933; …

[(c) explosives certificates issued by a chief officer of police pursuant to regulation 4 of the Control of Explosives Regulations 1991 as to the fitness of a person to acquire or acquire and keep explosives; or

(d) licences granted under section 8 of the Private Security Industry Act 2001].

5–12. (*Outside the scope of this work.*)

[2881F]

NOTES

Para 2: definitions "contracting authority", "contracting entity", "Directive 2004/17/EC" and "Directive 2004/18/EC" inserted by the Rehabilitation of Offenders Act 1974 (Exclusions and Exceptions) (Scotland) Amendment Order 2007, SSI 2007/75, arts 2, 4(a), as from 14 February 2007.

Para 4: words in first pair of square brackets in sub-para (3) substituted, word omitted from sub-para (b) revoked, and sub-paras (c), (d) substituted for original sub-para (c), by SSI 2007/75, arts 2, 4(b), (c), as from 14 February 2007.

SCHEDULE 4
EXCEPTED PROFESSIONS, OFFICES, EMPLOYMENTS, AND OCCUPATIONS

Article 5, Sch 1, para 1 & Sch 3, para 4

PART 1
PROFESSIONS

1. Medical practitioner.

2. Advocate, solicitor.

3. Accountant.

[4. Dentist or any profession complementary to dentistry for which a title is specified in regulations under section 36A(2) of the Dentists Act 1984 (professions complementary to dentistry) by virtue of section 36A(3) of that Act.]

5. Veterinary surgeon.

[6. Nurse or midwife.]

7. Ophthalmic optician, dispensing optician.

[8. Registered pharmacist.]

9. Registered teacher.

[10. Any profession to which the Health Professions Order 2001 applies and which is undertaken following registration under that Order.]

11. Registered osteopath.

12. Registered chiropractor.

13. Chartered psychologist.

14. Actuary.

15. Registered European lawyer, registered foreign lawyer.

16. Social worker.

17. Social service worker.

[2881G]

NOTES

Para 4: substituted by the Rehabilitation of Offenders Act 1974 (Exclusions and Exceptions) (Scotland) Amendment Order 2007, SSI 2007/75, arts 2, 5(a), as from 14 February 2007.

Para 6: substituted by the Health Act 1999 (Consequential Amendments) (Nursing and Midwifery) Order 2004, SI 2004/1771, art 3, Schedule, Pt 2, para 17, as from 1 August 2004.

Para 8: substituted by the Pharmacists and Pharmacy Technicians Order 2007, SI 2007/289, art 67, Sch 1, Pt 2, para 31(a), as from 30 March 2007.

Para 10: substituted by the Health Professions Order 2001 (Consequential Amendments) Order 2003, SI 2003/1590, art 3, Schedule, Pt 2, para 7, as from 9 July 2003.

PART 2
OFFICES AND EMPLOYMENTS

1. Judicial appointments.

2. Prosecutors, officers assisting prosecutors, and officers assisting in the work of the Crown Office.

3. Signing justices, and their clerks and assistants.

4. Clerks (including depute and assistant clerks) and officers of the High Court of Justiciary, the Court of Session and the district court, sheriff clerks (including sheriff clerks depute) and their clerks and assistants.

5. Precognition agents.

6. Constables, police custody and security officers, persons appointed as police cadets to undergo training with a view to becoming constables and persons employed for the purposes of, or to assist the constables of, a police force established under any enactment, naval, military and air force police.

7. Any [office, employment or work] which is concerned with the administration of, or is otherwise normally carried out wholly or partly within the precincts of a prison, remand centre, young offenders institution, detention centre or removal centre, and members of visiting committees for prisons appointed under rules made under section 39 of the Prisons (Scotland) Act 1989 and members of visiting committees for remand centres and young offenders institutions appointed under section 19(3) of that Act.

8. Traffic wardens appointed under section 95 of the Road Traffic Regulation Act 1984 or section 9 of the Police (Scotland) Act 1967.

9. Any employment or work which is concerned with the provision of a care service.

10. Any employment or work which is concerned with the provision of health services and which is of such a kind as to enable the holder to have access to persons in receipt of such services in the course of that person's normal duties.

11. Any employment or work in a child care position.

12. Any person who provides a service, or who seeks to provide a service under Part 4 of the Adults with Incapacity (Scotland) Act 2000.

13. Any employment [or work] in the Scottish Society for the Prevention of Cruelty to Animals where the person employed or working, as part of his or her duties, may carry out the killing of animals.

14. Any office[, employment or work] in the Serious Fraud Office.

15. Any office[, employment or work] in the [Serious Organised Crime Agency].

16. Any office[, employment or work] in Her Majesty's [Revenue and Customs].

17. Any employment which is concerned with the monitoring, for the purposes of child protection, of communications by means of the internet.

18. Any office or employment in the Scottish Social Services Council.

[19. Her Majesty's Inspectors, or any person appointed by the Scottish Ministers for the purposes of section 66 of the Education (Scotland) Act 1980 or section 9 of the Standards in Scotland's Schools etc Act 2000, or members of any Management Board established to assist either Her Majesty's Inspectors or any such person, or any individual undertaking employment or work for Her Majesty's Inspectors or any such person in relation to the carrying out of inspections under section 66 of the Education (Scotland) Act 1980, section 9 of the Standards in Scotland's Schools etc Act 2000 or section 1 of the Joint Inspection of Children's Services and Inspection of Social Work Services (Scotland) Act 2006, or otherwise in regard to matters associated with such inspections.]

20. The Principal Reporter or officers appointed under section 128(5) of the Local Government etc (Scotland) Act 1994 to assist that officer.

21. Members of a panel established by virtue of section 101(1) of the Children (Scotland) Act 1995 (panels for curators ad litem, reporting officers and safeguarders).

[22. Any office or employment in the Risk Management Authority.

23. Any office or employment in the Scottish Criminal Cases Review Commission.

24. Members of the Mental Welfare Commission appointed under paragraph 3(1) of Part 1 of schedule 1 to the Mental Health (Care and Treatment) (Scotland) Act 2003.

25. Any office or employment in a relevant authority as defined in section 6 of the Fire (Scotland) Act 2005.

26. Social work inspectors appointed under section 4 of the Joint Inspection of Children's Services and Inspection of Social Work Services (Scotland) Act 2006, or members of any Management Board established to assist the social work inspectors, or any individual undertaking employment or work for the social work inspectors in relation to the carrying out of inspections, or otherwise in regard to matters associated with such inspections.

27. Any employment or work in a body concerned primarily with the provision of counselling or other support to individuals who are or appear to be victims of, or witnesses to, offences, and which involves having access to personal information about such individuals.]

[2881H]

NOTES

Paras 7, 14: words in square brackets substituted by the Rehabilitation of Offenders Act 1974 (Exclusions and Exceptions) (Scotland) Amendment Order 2007, SSI 2007/75, arts 2, 5(b)(i), (iii), as from 14 February 2007.

Para 13: words in square brackets inserted by SSI 2007/75, arts 2, 5(b)(ii), as from 14 February 2007.

Para 15: words in first pair of square brackets substituted by SSI 2007/75, arts 2, 5(b)(iv), as from 14 February 2007; words in second pair of square brackets substituted by the Rehabilitation of Offenders Act 1974 (Exclusions and Exceptions) (Amendment) (Scotland) Order 2006, SSI 2006/194, art 5(a), as from 1 April 2006.

Para 16: words in first pair of square brackets substituted by SSI 2007/75, arts 2, 5(b)(v), as from 14 February 2007; words in second pair of square brackets substituted by SSI 2006/194, art 5(b), as from 31 March 2006.

Para 19: substituted by SSI 2007/75, arts 2, 5(b)(vi), as from 14 February 2007.

Paras 22–27: inserted by SSI 2007/75, arts 2, 5(b)(vii), as from 14 February 2007.

PART 3
OCCUPATIONS

1. Firearms dealer.

2. Any occupation in respect of which an application to the [Gambling Commission] for a licence, certificate or registration is required by or under any enactment.

3. Any occupation which is concerned with the management of a place in respect of which the approval of the [Scottish Ministers] is required by section 1 of the Abortion Act 1967.

4. Any occupation in respect of which the holder[is required pursuant to regulation 4 of the Control of Explosives Regulations 1991 to obtain from the chief officer of police an explosives certificate certifying that person to be a fit person to acquire or acquire and keep explosives].

5. Taxi driver or private hire driver.

[6. Any occupation in respect of which an application to the Security Industry Authority for a licence is required by the Private Security Industry Act 2001.

7. Any occupation which is concerned with visiting persons detained in police stations, for the purposes of examining and reporting on the conditions under which they are held.]

[2881I]

NOTES

Paras 2, 4: words in square brackets substituted by the Rehabilitation of Offenders Act 1974 (Exclusions and Exceptions) (Scotland) Amendment Order 2007, SSI 2007/75, arts 2, 5(c)(i), (ii), as from 14 February 2007.

Para 3: words in square brackets substituted by the Rehabilitation of Offenders Act 1974 (Exclusions and Exceptions) (Amendment) (Scotland) Order 2006, SSI 2006/194, art 5(c), as from 31 March 2006.

Paras 6, 7: inserted by SSI 2007/75, arts 2, 5(c)(iii), as from 14 February 2007.

PART 4
INTERPRETATION

In this Schedule—

"actuary" means a member of the Institute of Actuaries or a member or student of the Faculty of Actuaries;

"accountant" means a member of—

(a) the Association of Certified Accountants;
(b) the Institute of Chartered Accountants in Scotland;
(c) the Institute of Chartered Accountants in England and Wales;
(d) the Chartered Institute of Public Finance Accountants; or
(e) the Chartered Institute of Management Accountants;

"chartered psychologist" means a psychologist included in the British Psychological Society's Register of Chartered Psychologists;

"child care position" has the meaning given by schedule 2 to the Protection of Children (Scotland) Act 2003;

"firearms dealer" has the meaning given by section 57(4) of the Firearms Act 1968;

"health services" means services provided under the National Health Service (Scotland) Act 1978 and similar services provided otherwise than under the National Health Service;

"Her Majesty's Inspectors" has the meaning given by section 135 of the Education (Scotland) Act 1980;

"judicial appointment" means an appointment to any office by virtue of which the holder has power (whether alone or with others) under any enactment or rule of law to determine any question affecting the rights, privileges, obligations or liabilities of any person;

["personal information" means any information which relates to a living individual who can be identified from that data, which is of a confidential nature and is not in the public domain, and it includes information in any form;]

"prosecutors" has the meaning given by section 307 of the Criminal Procedure (Scotland) Act 1995

"registered chiropractor" has the meaning given by section 43 of the Chiropractors Act 1994;

"registered foreign lawyer" and "registered European lawyer" have the meaning given by section 65 of the Solicitors (Scotland) Act 1980;

"registered osteopath" has the meaning given by section 41 of the Osteopaths Act 1993;

["registered pharmacist" means a person who is registered in the register maintained under article 10(1) of the Pharmacists and Pharmacy Technicians Order 2007;]

"registered teacher" means a teacher registered under the Teaching Council (Scotland) Act 1965;

"work" has the meaning given by section [18] of the Protection of Children (Scotland) Act 2003.

[2881J]

NOTES

Definition "personal information" inserted by the Rehabilitation of Offenders Act 1974 (Exclusions and Exceptions) (Scotland) Amendment Order 2007, SSI 2007/75, arts 2, 5(d), as from 14 February 2007.

Definition "registered pharmacist" inserted by the Pharmacists and Pharmacy Technicians Order 2007, SI 2007/289, art 67, Sch 1, Pt 2, para 31(b), as from 30 March 2007.

Figure in square brackets in definition "work" substituted by the Rehabilitation of Offenders Act 1974 (Exclusions and Exceptions) (Amendment) (Scotland) Order 2006, SSI 2006/194, art 5(d), as from 31 March 2006.

SOCIAL SECURITY CONTRIBUTIONS AND BENEFITS ACT 1992 (APPLICATION OF PARTS 12ZA AND 12ZB TO ADOPTIONS FROM OVERSEAS) REGULATIONS 2003 (NOTE)

(SI 2003/499)

NOTES

These Regulations, which were reproduced in the fifteenth edition of this work, have been omitted for reasons of space.

[2882]–[2886]

ACAS (FLEXIBLE WORKING) ARBITRATION SCHEME (ENGLAND AND WALES) ORDER 2003 (NOTE)

(SI 2003/694)

NOTES

This Order was revoked by the ACAS (Flexible Working) Arbitration Scheme (Great Britain) Order 2004, SI 2004/2333, art 3, as from 1 October 2004. Art 6 of the 2004 Order (at **[3223]**) provides that in a case where the appropriate date falls before 1 October 2004, the arbitration scheme set out in the Schedule to this Order continues to apply. The 2004 Order is at **[3218]** et seq.

[2887]–[2890]

DISABILITY DISCRIMINATION (BLIND AND PARTIALLY SIGHTED PERSONS) REGULATIONS 2003

(SI 2003/712)

NOTES

Made: 13 March 2003.
Authority: Disability Discrimination Act 1995, s 67(3), Sch 1, para 7(5).
Commencement: 14 April 2003.

1 Citation, commencement and extent

(1) These Regulations may be cited as the Disability Discrimination (Blind and Partially Sighted Persons) Regulations 2003 and shall come into force on 14th April 2003.

(2) These Regulations do not extend to Northern Ireland.

[2891]

NOTES

Commencement: 14 April 2003.

2 Interpretation

In these Regulations—

"certificate signed by a consultant ophthalmologist" means a certificate completed by a consultant ophthalmologist in accordance with the criteria laid down in the relevant guidance;

"consultant ophthalmologist" means a consultant or honorary consultant appointed in the medical specialty of ophthalmology, who is employed for the purposes of providing any service as part of the health service continued under section 1(1) of the National Health Service Act 1977, section 1(1) of the National Health Service (Scotland) Act 1978 or article 4(a) of the Health and Personal Social Services (Northern Ireland) Order 1972;

"local authority" means—

(a) in England and Wales, a council which is a local authority for the purposes of the Local Authority Social Services Act 1970, and

(b) in Scotland, a council constituted under section 2 of the Local Government (Scotland) Act 1994;

"registered person" means a person who is certified as blind or partially sighted by a consultant ophthalmologist and in consequence is registered as blind or partially sighted—

(a) in England and Wales, in a register maintained by or on behalf of a local authority under section 29(4)(g) of the National Assistance Act 1948 (welfare services), or

(b) in Scotland, in a register maintained by or on behalf of a local authority; and

"relevant guidance" means—

(a) in relation to a consultant ophthalmologist in England and Wales,

Department of Health Circular LASSL(90)1 entitled "Certification of Blind and Partially Sighted People: Revised Form BD8 and Procedures", and

(b) in relation to a consultant ophthalmologist in Scotland, Social Work Services Group Circular SWSG8/86, NHS 1998 (PCS) entitled "Registration of Blind and Partially Sighted People".

[2892]

NOTES

Commencement: 14 April 2003.

"Relevant guidance": the circulars referred to at available on the websites of the Department of Health (www.dh.gov.uk) and the Scottish government (www.scotland.gov.uk).

National Health Service Act 1977, s 1(1): repealed by the National Health Service (Consequential Provisions) Act 2006, s 6, Sch 4; the health service is now continued under the National Health Service Act 2006, s 1(1), (2) and the National Health Service (Wales) Act 2006, s 1(1), (2).

3 Persons deemed to have a disability

A person is deemed to have a disability, and hence to be a disabled person, for the purposes of the Disability Discrimination Act 1995 where—

(a) he is certified as blind or partially sighted by a consultant ophthalmologist in accordance with the relevant guidance; or

(b) he is a registered person.

[2893]

NOTES

Commencement: 14 April 2003.

4 Evidence

(1) For the purposes of regulation 3, the following shall be conclusive evidence of the matters certified in relation to the person with respect to whom it was issued—

(a) in the case of a person mentioned in paragraph (a) of that regulation, a certificate signed by a consultant ophthalmologist; and

(b) in the case of a person mentioned in paragraph (b) of that regulation, a certificate issued by or on behalf of a local authority stating that he is a registered person.

(2) Unless the contrary is shown, any document purporting to be a certificate for the purposes of paragraph (1) shall be taken to have been validly issued.

[2894]

NOTES

Commencement: 14 April 2003.

EQUAL PAY (QUESTIONS AND REPLIES) ORDER 2003

(SI 2003/722)

NOTES

Made: 13 March 2003.
Authority: Equal Pay Act 1970, s 7B.
Commencement: 6 April 2003.

ARRANGEMENT OF ARTICLES

SCHEDULES:

1 Citation, commencement and interpretation

(1) This Order may be cited as the Equal Pay (Questions and Replies) Order 2003 and shall come into force on 6th April 2003.

(2) In this Order—
"the Act" means the Equal Pay Act 1970;
"tribunal" means an employment tribunal.

[2895]

2 Forms for questions and replies

The forms set out in Schedules 1 and 2 to this Order or forms to the like effect are, respectively, hereby prescribed as forms by which—

(a) a complainant may question a respondent as mentioned in subsection (2)(a) of section 7B of the Act; and

(b) a respondent may if he so wishes reply to any questions.

[2896]

3 Period for service of questions

The period prescribed for the purposes of subsection (7)(a) of section 7B of the Act (period within which questions must be duly served in order to be admissible in proceedings before a tribunal under subsection (3) or (5) of section 7B) shall be—

(a) where a question was served before a complaint or reference had been presented or made to a tribunal, the period starting on 6th April 2003 and ending on the day before a complaint is presented to a tribunal; or

(b) where a question was served at or after the time when a complaint or reference had been presented or made to a tribunal—

(i) the period of twenty-one days beginning with the day on which the complaint or reference was presented or made; or

(ii) any longer period that the tribunal may on application allow.

[2897]

4 Period for service of reply

The period prescribed for the purpose of subsections (4)(a) and (6)(a) of section 7B (power of the tribunal to draw inferences from an employer's failure to reply to a question within such period) shall be—

(a) except where sub-paragraph (b) applies, the period of eight weeks starting on the day that a question was duly served; or

(b) where a question was asked before 6th April 2003, the period of eight weeks starting on 6th April 2003.

[2898]

5 Manner of service of questions and replies

Questions or, as the case may be, replies may be duly served—

(a) where the person to be served is the respondent, by delivering the question to him, or by sending it by post to him at his usual or last known residence or place of business; or

(b) where the person to be served is the complainant, by delivering the reply to her, or sending it by post to her at her address for reply as stated by her in the document containing the questions or, if no address is so stated, at her usual or last known residence; or

(c) where the person to be served is a body corporate or is a trade union or employers' association within the meaning of the Trade Union and Labour Relations (Consolidation) Act 1992, by delivering it to the secretary or clerk of the body, union or association at its registered or principal office or by sending it by post to the secretary or clerk at that office; or

(d) where the person to be served is acting by a solicitor, by delivering it at, or by sending it by post to, the solicitor's address for service.

[2899]

SCHEDULES

SCHEDULE 1
THE EQUAL PAY ACT 1970 S 7B(2)(A)

Article 2

QUESTION FORM (FOR COMPLAINANT)

To .... (*name of the person to be questioned* (*the respondent*))

of .... (*address*)

1. I .... (*name of complainant*)

of .... (*address*)

believe, for the following reasons, that I may not have received equal pay in accordance with the Equal Pay Act 1970. (*Give a short summary of the reason(s) that cause you to believe that you may not have received equal pay*).

2.—(a) I am claiming equal pay with the following comparator(s) .... (*Give the names or, if not known, the job titles, of the person or persons with whom equal pay is being claimed.*)

(b) Do you agree that I have received less pay than my comparator(s)?

(c) If you agree that I have received less pay, please explain the reasons for this difference.

(d) If you do not agree that I have received less pay, please explain why you disagree.

3. The Equal Pay Act requires equal pay between men and women where they are employed on equal work, which comprises like work, work rated as equivalent, or work of equal value.

(a) Do you agree that my work is equal to that of my comparator(s)?

(b) If you do not think that I am doing equal work, please give your reasons.

4. (*Any other relevant questions you may want to ask.*)

5. Please send your reply to the following address if different from my home address above

....

.... (*address*)

.... (*signature of complainant*)

.... (*date*)

By virtue of section 7B of the Act, this questionnaire and any reply are (subject to the provisions of the section) admissible in proceedings under the Act and a tribunal may draw any such inference as is just and equitable from a failure without reasonable excuse to reply within 8 weeks or from an evasive or equivocal reply, including an inference that the person questioned has discriminated unlawfully.

[2900]

SCHEDULE 2
THE EQUAL PAY ACT 1970 S 7B(2)(B)

Article 2

REPLY FORM (FOR RESPONDENT)

To .... (*name of questioner* (*the complainant*))

of .... (*address*)

1. I .... (*name of respondent*)

of .... (*address*)

acknowledge receipt of the questionnaire signed by you and dated .... (*date*) which was served on me on .... (*date*).

2. Set out below are the complainant's questions and my response to them.
   (a) Do you agree that the complainant has not received equal pay in accordance with the Equal Pay Act 1970? .... (yes/no*). (*If you do not agree with the complainant's statement, you should explain why you disagree.*)
   (b) Do you agree that the complainant has received less pay than his or her comparator(s)? .... (yes/no*). (*If you agree, you should explain the reasons for any difference in pay. If you do not agree, you should explain why you disagree.*)
   (c) Do you agree that the complainant is doing work equal to that of his or her comparator(s)? .... (yes/no*). (*If you do not agree, you should explain why you disagree.*)
   (d) (*Replies to the questions in paragraph 4 of the questionnaire.*)

3. I have deleted (in whole or in part) the paragraphs numbered .... above, since I am (unable/unwilling*) to reply to the corresponding questions of the questionnaire (........................ (*Give question numbers from questionnaire*)) for the following reasons .... (*Give reasons*).

.... (*signature of respondent*)

.... (*date*)

(*) delete as appropriate

[2901]

EMPLOYMENT RIGHTS ACT 1996 (APPLICATION OF SECTION 80B TO ADOPTIONS FROM OVERSEAS) REGULATIONS 2003 (NOTE)

(SI 2003/920)

NOTES

These Regulations, which were reproduced in the fifteenth edition of this work, have been omitted for reasons of space.

[2902]–[2904]

PATERNITY AND ADOPTION LEAVE (ADOPTION FROM OVERSEAS) REGULATIONS 2003 (NOTE)

(SI 2003/921)

NOTES

These Regulations, which were reproduced in the fifteenth edition of this work, have been omitted for reasons of space.

[2905]–[2916]

STATUTORY PATERNITY PAY (ADOPTION) AND STATUTORY ADOPTION PAY (ADOPTIONS FROM OVERSEAS) (ADMINISTRATION) REGULATIONS 2003 (NOTE)

(SI 2003/1192)

NOTES

These Regulations, which were reproduced in the fifteenth edition of this work, have been omitted for reasons of space.

[2917]–[2919]

STATUTORY PATERNITY PAY (ADOPTION) AND STATUTORY ADOPTION PAY (ADOPTIONS FROM OVERSEAS) (NO 2) REGULATIONS 2003 (NOTE)

(SI 2003/1194)

NOTES

These Regulations, which were reproduced in the fifteenth edition of this work, have been omitted for reasons of space.

[2920]–[2937]

RACE RELATIONS ACT 1976 (AMENDMENT) REGULATIONS 2003 (NOTE)

(SI 2003/1626)

NOTES

These Regulations, which were made under the European Communities Act 1972, s 2(2) and which came into force on 19 July 2003, implement (in Great Britain) Council Directive 2000/43/EC on the principle of equal treatment between persons irrespective of racial or ethnic origin at **[3975]**. The Regulations consist almost entirely of amendments to the Race Relations Act 1976 at **[207]** et seq. The 1976 Act is amended as noted to the provisions affected. Regulation 2 (transitional provisions) is as follows—

2 Transitional provisions

(1) Regulations 40 and 42 do not apply to proceedings commenced before 19th July 2003.

(2) Regulations 41 and 43 apply to proceedings commenced before 19th July 2003, as well as proceedings instituted on or after that date, but do not affect any case in which proceedings were determined before that date.

(3) The amendment made to section 65(2)(b) of the 1976 Act by regulation 47 shall not apply in the case of a question served on a respondent before 19th July 2003.

(4) In paragraph (3) "question" and "respondent" shall be construed in accordance with section 65 of the 1976 Act.

Note that regs 40 and 42 amend ss 54 and 57 of the 1976 Act at **[273]** and **[276]**. Regs 41 and 43 insert ss 54A and 57ZA of that Act at **[274]** and **[277]**.

[2938]

EQUAL PAY ACT 1970 (AMENDMENT) REGULATIONS 2003 (NOTE)

(SI 2003/1656)

NOTES

These Regulations were made under the European Communities Act 1972, s 2(2) and came into force on 19 July 2003 (subject to the transitional provisions in reg 2 *post*). The Regulations consist principally of amendments to the Equal Pay Act 1970 at **[5]** et seq. The 1970 Act is amended as follows: reg 3 amends s 2 at **[6]**; reg 4 inserts s 2ZA at **[7]**; reg 5 inserts ss 2ZB, 2ZC at **[8]**, **[9]**; reg 6 amends s 7A; reg 7 inserts s 7AA; reg 8 inserts ss 7AB, 7AC; reg 9 amends s 11 at **[18]**; reg 10 amends s 1 at **[5]**.

Regulation 2 provides as follows—

2 Application

(1) The following provisions—

(a) paragraph (2) of regulation 3, and

(b) regulation 4,

apply for the purpose of determining whether an employment tribunal may make a determination in proceedings instituted on or after the commencement date (subject to paragraph (2) below).

(2) Those provisions do not so apply if the last day on which the woman was employed in the employment falls more than six months before the commencement date.

(3) If those provisions do so apply so as to enable an employment tribunal to make a determination in proceedings in a stable employment case (within the meaning given by virtue of regulation 4), the determination may not relate to any non-qualifying contract of employment forming part of the stable employment relationship.

(4) For the purposes of paragraph (3) above a contract of employment is a non-qualifying contract of employment if it ended more than six months before the commencement date.

(5) The following provisions—
(a) paragraph (3) of regulation 3,
(b) regulation 5,
(c) paragraph (4) of regulation 6, and
(d) regulation 8,

apply in relation to proceedings instituted on or after the commencement date.

(6) The following provisions—
(a) paragraph (3) of regulation 6, and
(b) regulation 7,

apply for the purpose of determining whether an employment tribunal may make a determination on a complaint presented to it on or after the commencement date (subject to paragraph (7) below).

(7) Those provisions do not so apply if the last day of the woman's period of service falls more than nine months before the commencement date.

[2939]

SEX DISCRIMINATION ACT 1975 (AMENDMENT) REGULATIONS 2003 (NOTE)

(SI 2003/1657)

NOTES

These Regulations, which were made under the European Communities Act 1972, s 2(2) and which came into force on 19 July 2003, amend the Sex Discrimination Act 1975. Regulation 2 amends s 17 of the 1975 Act at **[119]**. Regulations 3 and 4 insert new ss 20A and 35C at **[123]** and **[145]** respectively. There are no transitional provisions.

[2940]

EMPLOYMENT EQUALITY (RELIGION OR BELIEF) REGULATIONS 2003

(SI 2003/1660)

NOTES

Made: 26 June 2003.

Authority: European Communities Act 1972, s 2(2).

Commencement: 2 December 2003.

Conciliation: employment tribunal proceedings and claims which could be the subject of employment tribunal proceedings under reg 28 are proceedings to which the Employment Tribunals Act 1996, s 18 applies; see s 18(1)(l) of that Act at **[975]**. There is no fixed conciliation period; see the Employment Tribunals (Constitution and Rules of Procedure) Regulations 2004, SI 2004/1861, Sch 1, rule 22(2).

Employment Appeal Tribunal: an appeal lies to the Employment Appeal Tribunal on any question of law arising from any decision of, or in any proceedings before, an employment tribunal under or by virtue of these Regulations; see the Employment Tribunals Act 1996, s 21(1)(m) at **[978]**.

As to the power of the Commission for Equality and Human Rights to issue a code of practice in connection with any matter addressed by Parts 2 and 3 of these Regulations, see the Equality Act 2006, s 14 at **[1657]**. As of 6 April 2008, no code has been issued under this power.

ARRANGEMENT OF REGULATIONS

PART 1
GENERAL

PART II
DISCRIMINATION IN EMPLOYMENT AND VOCATIONAL TRAINING

PART III
OTHER UNLAWFUL ACTS

PART IV
GENERAL EXCEPTIONS FROM PARTS II AND III

PART V
ENFORCEMENT

PART VI
SUPPLEMENTAL

SCHEDULES:

PART 1
GENERAL

1 Citation, commencement and extent

(1) These Regulations may be cited as the Employment Equality (Religion or Belief) Regulations 2003, and shall come into force on 2nd December 2003.

(2) These Regulations do not extend to Northern Ireland.

[2941]

NOTES

Commencement: 2 December 2003.

2 Interpretation

[(1) In these Regulations—
- (a) "religion" means any religion,
- (b) "belief" means any religious or philosophical belief,
- (c) a reference to religion includes a reference to lack of religion, and
- (d) a reference to belief includes a reference to lack of belief.]

(2) In these Regulations, references to discrimination are to any discrimination falling within regulation 3 (discrimination on grounds of religion or belief) or 4 (discrimination by way of victimisation) and related expressions shall be construed accordingly, and references to harassment shall be construed in accordance with regulation 5 (harassment on grounds of religion or belief).

(3) In these Regulations—

"act" includes a deliberate omission;

["benefits", except in regulation 9A (trustees and managers of occupational pension schemes), includes facilities and services;]

"detriment" does not include harassment within the meaning of regulation 5;

references to "employer", in their application to a person at any time seeking to employ another, include a person who has no employees at that time;

"employment" means employment under a contract of service or of apprenticeship or a contract personally to do any work, and related expressions shall be construed accordingly;

"Great Britain", except where the context otherwise requires in regulation 26 (protection of Sikhs from discrimination in connection with requirements as to wearing of safety helmets), includes such of the territorial waters of the United Kingdom as are adjacent to Great Britain;

"Minister of the Crown" includes the Treasury and the Defence Council; …

["proprietor", in relation to a school in England and Wales, has the meaning given by section 579 of the Education Act 1996, and, in relation to a school in Scotland, means the governing body, trustees, or other person or body of persons responsible for the management of the school; and]

"school", in England and Wales, has the meaning given by section 4 of the Education Act 1996, and, in Scotland, has the meaning given by section 135(1) of the Education (Scotland) Act 1980, and references to a school are to an institution in so far as it is engaged in the provision of education under those sections.

[2942]

NOTES

Commencement: 2 December 2003.

Para (1): substituted by the Equality Act 2006, s 77(1), as from 30 April 2007.

Para (3): definition "benefits" substituted by the Employment Equality (Religion or Belief) (Amendment) Regulations 2003, SI 2003/2828, reg 3(1), (2), as from 2 December 2003; word omitted from the definition "Minister of the Crown" revoked, and definition "proprietor" inserted, by the Employment Equality (Sexual Orientation) (Religion or Belief) (Amendment) Regulations 2007, SI 2007/2269, reg 4(1), (2), as from 14 September 2007.

3 Discrimination on grounds of religion or belief

(1) For the purposes of these Regulations, a person ("A") discriminates against another person ("B") if—

[(a) on the grounds of the religion or belief of B or of any other person except A (whether or not it is also A's religion or belief) A treats B less favourably than he treats or would treat other persons;]

(b) A applies to B a provision, criterion or practice which he applies or would apply equally to persons not of the same religion or belief as B, but—

(i) which puts or would put persons of the same religion or belief as B at a particular disadvantage when compared with other persons,

(ii) which puts B at that disadvantage, and

(iii) which A cannot show to be a proportionate means of achieving a legitimate aim.

(2) …

(3) A comparison of B's case with that of another person under paragraph (1) must be such that the relevant circumstances in the one case are the same, or not materially different, in the other.

[2943]

NOTES

Commencement: 2 December 2003.

Para (1): sub-para (a) substituted by the Equality Act 2006, s 77(2), as from 30 April 2007.

Para (2): revoked by the Equality Act 2006, s 77(3), as from 30 April 2007.

4 Discrimination by way of victimisation

(1) For the purposes of these Regulations, a person ("A") discriminates against another person ("B") if he treats B less favourably than he treats or would treat other persons in the same circumstances, and does so by reason that B has—

(a) brought proceedings against A or any other person under these Regulations;

(b) given evidence or information in connection with proceedings brought by any person against A or any other person under these Regulations;

(c) otherwise done anything under or by reference to these Regulations in relation to A or any other person; or

(d) alleged that A or any other person has committed an act which (whether or not the allegation so states) would amount to a contravention of these Regulations,

or by reason that A knows that B intends to do any of those things, or suspects that B has done or intends to do any of them.

(2) Paragraph (1) does not apply to treatment of B by reason of any allegation made by him, or evidence or information given by him, if the allegation, evidence or information was false and not made (or, as the case may be, given) in good faith.

[2944]

NOTES

Commencement: 2 December 2003.

5 Harassment on grounds of religion or belief

(1) For the purposes of these Regulations, a person ("A") subjects another person ("B") to harassment where, on grounds of religion or belief, A engages in unwanted conduct which has the purpose or effect of—

(a) violating B's dignity; or

(b) creating an intimidating, hostile, degrading, humiliating or offensive environment for B.

(2) Conduct shall be regarded as having the effect specified in paragraph (1)(a) or (b) only if, having regard to all the circumstances, including in particular the perception of B, it should reasonably be considered as having that effect.

[2945]

NOTES

Commencement: 2 December 2003.

PART II
DISCRIMINATION IN EMPLOYMENT AND VOCATIONAL TRAINING

6 Applicants and employees

(1) It is unlawful for an employer, in relation to employment by him at an establishment in Great Britain, to discriminate against a person—

(a) in the arrangements he makes for the purpose of determining to whom he should offer employment;

(b) in the terms on which he offers that person employment; or

(c) by refusing to offer, or deliberately not offering, him employment.

(2) It is unlawful for an employer, in relation to a person whom he employs at an establishment in Great Britain, to discriminate against that person—

(a) in the terms of employment which he affords him;

(b) in the opportunities which he affords him for promotion, a transfer, training, or receiving any other benefit;

(c) by refusing to afford him, or deliberately not affording him, any such opportunity; or

(d) by dismissing him, or subjecting him to any other detriment.

(3) It is unlawful for an employer, in relation to employment by him at an establishment in Great Britain, to subject to harassment a person whom he employs or who has applied to him for employment.

(4) Paragraph (2) does not apply to benefits of any description if the employer is concerned with the provision (for payment or not) of benefits of that description to the public, or to a section of the public which includes the employee in question, unless—

(a) that provision differs in a material respect from the provision of the benefits by the employer to his employees; or

(b) the provision of the benefits to the employee in question is regulated by his contract of employment; or

(c) the benefits relate to training.

(5) In paragraph (2)(d) reference to the dismissal of a person from employment includes reference—

(a) to the termination of that person's employment by the expiration of any period (including a period expiring by reference to an event or circumstance), not being a termination immediately after which the employment is renewed on the same terms; and

(b) to the termination of that person's employment by any act of his (including the giving of notice) in circumstances such that he is entitled to terminate it without notice by reason of the conduct of the employer.

[2946]

NOTES
Commencement: 2 December 2003.

7 Exception for genuine occupational requirement

(1) In relation to discrimination falling within regulation 3 (discrimination on grounds of religion or belief)—
- (a) regulation 6(1)(a) or (c) does not apply to any employment;
- (b) regulation 6(2)(b) or (c) does not apply to promotion or transfer to, or training for, any employment; and
- (c) regulation 6(2)(d) does not apply to dismissal from any employment,

where paragraph (2) or (3) applies.

(2) This paragraph applies where, having regard to the nature of the employment or the context in which it is carried out—
- (a) being of a particular religion or belief is a genuine and determining occupational requirement;
- (b) it is proportionate to apply that requirement in the particular case; and
- (c) either—
  - (i) the person to whom that requirement is applied does not meet it, or
  - (ii) the employer is not satisfied, and in all the circumstances it is reasonable for him not to be satisfied, that that person meets it,

and this paragraph applies whether or not the employer has an ethos based on religion or belief.

(3) This paragraph applies where an employer has an ethos based on religion or belief and, having regard to that ethos and to the nature of the employment or the context in which it is carried out—
- (a) being of a particular religion or belief is a genuine occupational requirement for the job;
- (b) it is proportionate to apply that requirement in the particular case; and
- (c) either—
  - (i) the person to whom that requirement is applied does not meet it, or
  - (ii) the employer is not satisfied, and in all the circumstances it is reasonable for him not to be satisfied, that that person meets it.

[2947]

NOTES
Commencement: 2 December 2003.

8 Contract workers

(1) It is unlawful for a principal, in relation to contract work at an establishment in Great Britain, to discriminate against a contract worker—
- (a) in the terms on which he allows him to do that work;
- (b) by not allowing him to do it or continue to do it;
- (c) in the way he affords him access to any benefits or by refusing or deliberately not affording him access to them; or
- (d) by subjecting him to any other detriment.

(2) It is unlawful for a principal, in relation to contract work at an establishment in Great Britain, to subject a contract worker to harassment.

(3) A principal does not contravene paragraph (1)(b) by doing any act in relation to a contract worker where, if the work were to be done by a person taken into the principal's employment, that act would be lawful by virtue of regulation 7 (exception for genuine occupational requirement).

(4) Paragraph (1) does not apply to benefits of any description if the principal is concerned with the provision (for payment or not) of benefits of that description to the public, or to a section of the public to which the contract worker in question belongs, unless that provision differs in a material respect from the provision of the benefits by the principal to his contract workers.

(5) In this regulation—

"principal" means a person ("A") who makes work available for doing by individuals who are employed by another person who supplies them under a contract made with A;

"contract work" means work so made available; and

"contract worker" means any individual who is supplied to the principal under such a contract.

[2948]

NOTES

Commencement: 2 December 2003.

9 Meaning of employment and contract work at establishment in Great Britain

(1) For the purposes of this Part ("the relevant purposes"), employment is to be regarded as being at an establishment in Great Britain if the employee—

(a) does his work wholly or partly in Great Britain; or

(b) does his work wholly outside Great Britain and paragraph (2) applies.

(2) This paragraph applies if—

(a) the employer has a place of business at an establishment in Great Britain;

(b) the work is for the purposes of the business carried on at that establishment; and

(c) the employee is ordinarily resident in Great Britain—

(i) at the time when he applies for or is offered the employment, or

(ii) at any time during the course of the employment.

(3) The reference to "employment" in paragraph (1) includes—

(a) employment on board a ship only if the ship is registered at a port of registry in Great Britain, and

(b) employment on an aircraft or hovercraft only if the aircraft or hovercraft is registered in the United Kingdom and operated by a person who has his principal place of business, or is ordinarily resident, in Great Britain.

(4) Subject to paragraph (5), for the purposes of determining if employment concerned with the exploration of the sea bed or sub-soil or the exploitation of their natural resources is outside Great Britain, this regulation has effect as if references to Great Britain included—

(a) any area designated under section 1(7) of the Continental Shelf Act 1964 except an area or part of an area in which the law of Northern Ireland applies; and

(b) in relation to employment concerned with the exploration or exploitation of the Frigg Gas Field, the part of the Norwegian sector of the Continental Shelf described in Schedule 1.

(5) Paragraph (4) shall not apply to employment which is concerned with the exploration or exploitation of the Frigg Gas Field unless the employer is—

(a) a company registered under the Companies Act 1985;

(b) an oversea company which has established a place of business within Great Britain from which it directs the exploration or exploitation in question; or

(c) any other person who has a place of business within Great Britain from which he directs the exploration or exploitation in question.

(6) In this regulation—

"the Frigg Gas Field" means the naturally occurring gas-bearing sand formations of the lower Eocene age located in the vicinity of the intersection of the line of latitude 59 degrees 53 minutes North and of the dividing line between the sectors of the Continental Shelf of the United Kingdom and the Kingdom of Norway and includes all other gas-bearing strata from which gas at the start of production is capable of flowing into the above-mentioned gas-bearing sand formations;

"oversea company" has the same meaning as in section 744 of the Companies Act 1985.

(7) This regulation applies in relation to contract work within the meaning of regulation 8 as it applies in relation to employment; and, in its application to contract work, references to "employee", "employer" and "employment" are references to (respectively) "contract worker", "principal" and "contract work" within the meaning of regulation 8.

[2949]

NOTES

Commencement: 2 December 2003.

[9A Trustees and managers of occupational pension schemes

(1) It is unlawful, except in relation to rights accrued or benefits payable in respect of periods of service prior to the coming into force of these Regulations, for the trustees or managers of an occupational pension scheme to discriminate against a member or prospective member of the scheme in carrying out any of their functions in relation to it (including in particular their functions relating to the admission of members to the scheme and the treatment of members of it).

(2) It is unlawful for the trustees or managers of an occupational pension scheme, in relation to the scheme, to subject to harassment a member or prospective member of it.

(3) Schedule 1A (occupational pension schemes) shall have effect for the purposes of—
- (a) defining terms used in this regulation and in that Schedule;
- (b) treating every occupational pension scheme as including a non-discrimination rule;
- (c) giving trustees or managers of an occupational pension scheme power to alter the scheme so as to secure conformity with the non-discrimination rule;
- (d) making provision in relation to the procedures, and remedies which may be granted, on certain complaints relating to occupational pension schemes presented to an employment tribunal under regulation 28 (jurisdiction of employment tribunals).]

[2950]

NOTES

Commencement: 2 December 2003.

Inserted by the Employment Equality (Religion or Belief) (Amendment) Regulations 2003, SI 2003/2828, reg 3(1), (3), as from 2 December 2003.

10 Office-holders etc

(1) It is unlawful for a relevant person, in relation to an appointment to an office or post to which this regulation applies, to discriminate against a person—
- (a) in the arrangements which he makes for the purpose of determining to whom the appointment should be offered;
- (b) in the terms on which he offers him the appointment; or
- (c) by refusing to offer him the appointment.

(2) It is unlawful, in relation to an appointment to an office or post to which this regulation applies and which is an office or post referred to in paragraph (8)(b), for a relevant person on whose recommendation (or subject to whose approval) appointments to the office or post are made, to discriminate against a person—
- (a) in the arrangements which he makes for the purpose of determining who should be recommended or approved in relation to the appointment; or
- (b) in making or refusing to make a recommendation, or giving or refusing to give an approval, in relation to the appointment.

(3) It is unlawful for a relevant person, in relation to a person who has been appointed to an office or post to which this regulation applies, to discriminate against him—
- (a) in the terms of the appointment;
- (b) in the opportunities which he affords him for promotion, a transfer, training or receiving any other benefit, or by refusing to afford him any such opportunity;
- (c) by terminating the appointment; or
- (d) by subjecting him to any other detriment in relation to the appointment.

(4) It is unlawful for a relevant person, in relation to an office or post to which this regulation applies, to subject to harassment a person—
- (a) who has been appointed to the office or post;
- (b) who is seeking or being considered for appointment to the office or post; or
- (c) who is seeking or being considered for a recommendation or approval in relation to an appointment to an office or post referred to in paragraph (8)(b).

(5) Paragraphs (1) and (3) do not apply to any act in relation to an office or post where, if the office or post constituted employment, that act would be lawful by virtue of regulation 7 (exception for genuine occupational requirement); and paragraph (2) does not apply to any act in relation to an office or post where, if the office or post constituted employment, it would be lawful by virtue of regulation 7 to refuse to offer the person such employment.

(6) Paragraph (3) does not apply to benefits of any description if the relevant person is concerned with the provision (for payment or not) of benefits of that description to the public, or a section of the public to which the person appointed belongs, unless—

(a) that provision differs in a material respect from the provision of the benefits by the relevant person to persons appointed to offices or posts which are the same as, or not materially different from, that which the person appointed holds; or

(b) the provision of the benefits to the person appointed is regulated by the terms and conditions of his appointment; or

(c) the benefits relate to training.

(7) In paragraph (3)(c) the reference to the termination of the appointment includes a reference—

(a) to the termination of the appointment by the expiration of any period (including a period expiring by reference to an event or circumstance), not being a termination immediately after which the appointment is renewed on the same terms and conditions; and

(b) to the termination of the appointment by any act of the person appointed (including the giving of notice) in circumstances such that he is entitled to terminate the appointment without notice by reason of the conduct of the relevant person.

(8) This regulation applies to—

(a) any office or post to which persons are appointed to discharge functions personally under the direction of another person, and in respect of which they are entitled to remuneration; and

(b) any office or post to which appointments are made by (or on the recommendation of or subject to the approval of) a Minister of the Crown, a government department, the [Welsh Ministers, the First Minister for Wales, the Counsel General to the Welsh Assembly Government] or any part of the Scottish Administration,

but not to a political office or a case where regulation 6 (applicants and employees), 8 (contract workers), 12 (barristers), 13 (advocates) or 14 (partnerships) applies, or would apply but for the operation of any other provision of these Regulations.

(9) For the purposes of paragraph (8)(a) the holder of an office or post—

(a) is to be regarded as discharging his functions under the direction of another person if that other person is entitled to direct him as to when and where he discharges those functions;

(b) is not to be regarded as entitled to remuneration merely because he is entitled to payments—

(i) in respect of expenses incurred by him in carrying out the functions of the office or post, or

(ii) by way of compensation for the loss of income or benefits he would or might have received from any person had he not been carrying out the functions of the office or post.

(10) In this regulation—

(a) appointment to an office or post does not include election to an office or post;

(b) "political office" means—

(i) any office of the House of Commons held by a member of it,

(ii) a life peerage within the meaning of the Life Peerages Act 1958, or any office of the House of Lords held by a member of it,

(iii) any office mentioned in Schedule 2 (Ministerial offices) to the House of Commons Disqualification Act 1975,

(iv) the offices of Leader of the Opposition, Chief Opposition Whip or Assistant Opposition Whip within the meaning of the Ministerial and other Salaries Act 1975,

(v) any office of the Scottish Parliament held by a member of it,

(vi) a member of the Scottish Executive within the meaning of section 44 of the Scotland Act 1998, or a junior Scottish Minister within the meaning of section 49 of that Act,

(vii) any office of the National Assembly for Wales held by a member of it,

[(viia) a member of the Welsh Assembly Government,]

(viii) in England, any office of a county council, a London borough council, a district council, or a parish council held by a member of it,

(ix) in Wales, any office of a county council, a county borough council, or a community council held by a member of it,

(x) in relation to a council constituted under section 2 of the Local Government etc (Scotland) Act 1994 or a community council established under section 51 of the Local Government (Scotland) Act 1973, any office of such a council held by a member of it,

(xi) any office of the Greater London Authority held by a member of it,

(xii) any office of the Common Council of the City of London held by a member of it,

(xiii) any office of the Council of the Isles of Scilly held by a member of it,

(xiv) any office of a political party;

(c) "relevant person", in relation to an office or post, means—

(i) any person with power to make or terminate appointments to the office or post, or to determine the terms of appointment,

(ii) any person with power to determine the working conditions of a person appointed to the office or post in relation to opportunities for promotion, a transfer, training or for receiving any other benefit, and

(iii) any person or body referred to in paragraph (8)(b) on whose recommendation or subject to whose approval appointments are made to the office or post;

(d) references to making a recommendation include references to making a negative recommendation; and

(e) references to refusal include references to deliberate omission.

[2951]

NOTES

Commencement: 2 December 2003.

Para (8): words in square brackets in sub-para (b) substituted by the Government of Wales Act 2006 (Consequential Modifications and Transitional Provisions) Order 2007, SI 2007/1388, art 3, Sch 1, para 150(a), as from 25 May 2007.

Para (10): sub-para (b)(viia) inserted by SI 2007/1388, art 3, Sch 1, para 150(b), as from 25 May 2007.

11 Police

(1) [Subject to regulation 11A,] for the purposes of this Part, the holding of the office of constable shall be treated as employment—

(a) by the chief officer of police as respects any act done by him in relation to a constable or that office;

(b) by the police authority as respects any act done by it in relation to a constable or that office.

(2) [Subject to regulation 11A,] for the purposes of regulation 22 (liability of employers and principals)—

(a) the holding of the office of constable shall be treated as employment by the chief officer of police (and as not being employment by any other person); and

(b) anything done by a person holding such an office in the performance, or purported performance, of his functions shall be treated as done in the course of that employment.

(3) There shall be paid out of the police fund—

(a) any compensation, costs or expenses awarded against a chief officer of police in any proceedings brought against him under these Regulations, and any costs or expenses incurred by him in any such proceedings so far as not recovered by him in the proceedings; and

(b) any sum required by a chief officer of police for the settlement of any claim made against him under these Regulations if the settlement is approved by the police authority.

(4) Any proceedings under these Regulations which, by virtue of paragraph (1), would lie against a chief officer of police shall be brought against the chief officer of police for the time being or, in the case of a vacancy in that office, against the person for the time being performing the functions of that office; and references in paragraph (3) to the chief officer of police shall be construed accordingly.

(5) A police authority may, in such cases and to such extent as appear to it to be appropriate, pay out of the police fund—

(a) any compensation, costs or expenses awarded in proceedings under these Regulations against a person under the direction and control of the chief officer of police;

(b) any costs or expenses incurred and not recovered by such a person in such proceedings; and

(c) any sum required in connection with the settlement of a claim that has or might have given rise to such proceedings.

(6) Paragraphs (1) and (2) apply to a police cadet and appointment as a police cadet as they apply to a constable and the office of constable.

(7) Subject to paragraph (8), in this regulation—

"chief officer of police"—

(a) in relation to a person appointed, or an appointment falling to be made, under a specified Act, has the same meaning as in the Police Act 1996,

(b) …

(c) in relation to a person appointed, or an appointment falling to be made, under the Police (Scotland) Act 1967, means the chief constable of the relevant police force,

(d) in relation to any other person or appointment means the officer or other person who has the direction and control of the body of constables or cadets in question;

"police authority"—

(a) in relation to a person appointed, or an appointment falling to be made, under a specified Act, has the same meaning as in the Police Act 1996,

(b) …

(c) in relation to a person appointed, or an appointment falling to be made, under the Police (Scotland) Act 1967, has the meaning given in that Act,

(d) in relation to any other person or appointment, means the authority by whom the person in question is or on appointment would be paid;

"police cadet" means any person appointed to undergo training with a view to becoming a constable;

"police fund"—

(a) in relation to a chief officer of police within sub-paragraph (a) of the above definition of that term, has the same meaning as in the Police Act 1996,

(b) …

(c) in any other case means money provided by the police authority; and

"specified Act" means the Metropolitan Police Act 1829, the City of London Police Act 1839 or the Police Act 1996.

(8) In relation to a constable of a force who is not under the direction and control of the chief officer of police for that force, references in this regulation to the chief officer of police are references to the chief officer of the force under whose direction and control he is, and references in this regulation to the police authority are references to the relevant police authority for that force.

[2952]

NOTES

Commencement: 2 December 2003.

Paras (1), (2): words in square brackets inserted by the Serious Organised Crime and Police Act 2005 (Consequential and Supplementary Amendments to Secondary Legislation) Order 2006, SI 2006/594, art 2, Schedule, para 36(1)–(3), as from 1 April 2006.

Para (7): para (b) of definitions "chief officer of police", "police authority", and "police fund" revoked by SI 2006/594, art 2, Schedule, para 36(1), (4), as from 1 April 2006.

[11A Serious Organised Crime Agency

(1) For the purposes of this Part, any constable or other person who has been seconded to SOCA to serve as a member of its staff shall be treated as employed by SOCA.

(2) For the purposes of regulation 22 (liability of employers and principals)—

(a) the secondment of any constable or other person to SOCA to serve as a member of its staff shall be treated as employment by SOCA (and not as being employment by any other person); and

(b) anything done by a person so seconded in the performance, or purported performance, of his functions shall be treated as done in the course of that employment.

(3) In this regulation "SOCA" means the Serious Organised Crime Agency.]

[2952A]

NOTES

Commencement: 1 April 2006.

Inserted by the Serious Organised Crime and Police Act 2005 (Consequential and Supplementary Amendments to Secondary Legislation) Order 2006, SI 2006/594, art 2, Schedule, para 36(1), (5), as from 1 April 2006.

12 Barristers

(1) It is unlawful for a barrister or barrister's clerk, in relation to any offer of a pupillage or tenancy, to discriminate against a person—

(a) in the arrangements which are made for the purpose of determining to whom the pupillage or tenancy should be offered;

(b) in respect of any terms on which it is offered; or

(c) by refusing, or deliberately not offering, it to him.

(2) It is unlawful for a barrister or barrister's clerk, in relation to a pupil or tenant in the set of chambers in question, to discriminate against him—

(a) in respect of any terms applicable to him as a pupil or tenant;

(b) in the opportunities for training, or gaining experience, which are afforded or denied to him;

(c) in the benefits which are afforded or denied to him; or

(d) by terminating his pupillage, or by subjecting him to any pressure to leave the chambers or other detriment.

(3) It is unlawful for a barrister or barrister's clerk, in relation to a pupillage or tenancy in the set of chambers in question, to subject to harassment a person who is, or has applied to be, a pupil or tenant.

(4) It is unlawful for any person, in relation to the giving, withholding or acceptance of instructions to a barrister, to discriminate against any person by subjecting him to a detriment, or to subject him to harassment.

(5) In this regulation—

"barrister's clerk" includes any person carrying out any of the functions of a barrister's clerk;

"pupil", "pupillage" and "set of chambers" have the meanings commonly associated with their use in the context of barristers practising in independent practice; and

"tenancy" and "tenant" have the meanings commonly associated with their use in the context of barristers practising in independent practice, but also include reference to any barrister permitted to work in a set of chambers who is not a tenant.

(6) This regulation extends to England and Wales only.

[2953]

NOTES

Commencement: 2 December 2003.

13 Advocates

(1) It is unlawful for an advocate, in relation to taking any person as his pupil, to discriminate against a person—

(a) in the arrangements which he makes for the purpose of determining whom he will take as his pupil;

(b) in respect of any terms on which he offers to take any person as his pupil; or

(c) by refusing to take, or deliberately not taking, a person as his pupil.

(2) It is unlawful for an advocate, in relation to a person who is his pupil, to discriminate against him—

(a) in respect of any terms applicable to him as a pupil;

(b) in the opportunities for training, or gaining experience, which are afforded or denied to him;
(c) in the benefits which are afforded or denied to him; or
(d) by terminating the relationship, or by subjecting him to any pressure to terminate the relationship or other detriment.

(3) It is unlawful for an advocate, in relation to a person who is his pupil or taking any person as his pupil, to subject such a person to harassment.

(4) It is unlawful for any person, in relation to the giving, withholding or acceptance of instructions to an advocate, to discriminate against any person by subjecting him to a detriment, or to subject him to harassment.

(5) In this regulation—
"advocate" means a member of the Faculty of Advocates practising as such; and
"pupil" has the meaning commonly associated with its use in the context of a person training to be an advocate.

(6) This regulation extends to Scotland only.

[2954]

NOTES
Commencement: 2 December 2003.

14 Partnerships

(1) It is unlawful for a firm, in relation to a position as partner in the firm, to discriminate against a person—
(a) in the arrangements they make for the purpose of determining to whom they should offer that position;
(b) in the terms on which they offer him that position;
(c) by refusing to offer, or deliberately not offering, him that position; or
(d) in a case where the person already holds that position—
(i) in the way they afford him access to any benefits or by refusing to afford, or deliberately not affording, him access to them, or
(ii) by expelling him from that position, or subjecting him to any other detriment.

(2) It is unlawful for a firm, in relation to a position as partner in the firm, to subject to harassment a person who holds or has applied for that position.

(3) Paragraphs (1)(a) to (c) and (2) apply in relation to persons proposing to form themselves into a partnership as they apply in relation to a firm.

(4) Paragraph (1) does not apply to any act in relation to a position as partner where, if the position were employment, that act would be lawful by virtue of regulation 7 (exception for genuine occupational requirement).

(5) In the case of a limited partnership references in this regulation to a partner shall be construed as references to a general partner as defined in section 3 of the Limited Partnerships Act 1907.

(6) This regulation applies to a limited liability partnership as it applies to a firm; and, in its application to a limited liability partnership, references to a partner in a firm are references to a member of the limited liability partnership.

(7) In this regulation, "firm" has the meaning given by section 4 of the Partnership Act 1890.

(8) In paragraph (1)(d) reference to the expulsion of a person from a position as partner includes reference—
(a) to the termination of that person's partnership by the expiration of any period (including a period expiring by reference to an event or circumstance), not being a termination immediately after which the partnership is renewed on the same terms; and
(b) to the termination of that person's partnership by any act of his (including the giving of notice) in circumstances such that he is entitled to terminate it without notice by reason of the conduct of the other partners.

[2955]

NOTES
Commencement: 2 December 2003.

15 Trade organisations

(1) It is unlawful for a trade organisation to discriminate against a person—

(a) in the terms on which it is prepared to admit him to membership of the organisation; or

(b) by refusing to accept, or deliberately not accepting, his application for membership.

(2) It is unlawful for a trade organisation, in relation to a member of the organisation, to discriminate against him—

(a) in the way it affords him access to any benefits or by refusing or deliberately omitting to afford him access to them;

(b) by depriving him of membership, or varying the terms on which he is a member; or

(c) by subjecting him to any other detriment.

(3) It is unlawful for a trade organisation, in relation to a person's membership or application for membership of that organisation, to subject that person to harassment.

(4) In this regulation—

"trade organisation" means an organisation of workers, an organisation of employers, or any other organisation whose members carry on a particular profession or trade for the purposes of which the organisation exists;

"profession" includes any vocation or occupation; and

"trade" includes any business.

[2956]

NOTES
Commencement: 2 December 2003.

16 Qualifications bodies

(1) It is unlawful for a qualifications body to discriminate against a person—

(a) in the terms on which it is prepared to confer a professional or trade qualification on him;

(b) by refusing or deliberately not granting any application by him for such a qualification; or

(c) by withdrawing such a qualification from him or varying the terms on which he holds it.

(2) It is unlawful for a qualifications body, in relation to a professional or trade qualification conferred by it, to subject to harassment a person who holds or applies for such a qualification.

(3) In this regulation—

"qualifications body" means any authority or body which can confer a professional or trade qualification, but it does not include—

(a) [a governing body of] an educational establishment to which regulation 20 (institutions of further and higher education) applies, or would apply but for the operation of any other provision of these Regulations, or

(b) [a proprietor of] a school;

"confer" includes renew or extend;

"professional or trade qualification" means any authorisation, qualification, recognition, registration, enrolment, approval or certification which is needed for, or facilitates engagement in, a particular profession or trade;

"profession" and "trade" have the same meaning as in regulation 15.

[2957]

NOTES
Commencement: 2 December 2003.

Para (3): words in square brackets in definition "qualifications body" inserted by the Employment Equality (Sexual Orientation) (Religion or Belief) (Amendment) Regulations 2007, SI 2007/2269, reg 4(1), (3), as from 14 September 2007.

17 [The provision of vocational training]

(1) It is unlawful, in relation to a person seeking or undergoing training which would help fit him for any employment, for any training provider to discriminate against him—

(a) in the terms on which the training provider affords him access to any training;

[(aa) in the arrangements he makes for the purpose of determining to whom he should offer training;]

(b) by refusing or deliberately not affording him such access;

(c) by terminating his training; or

(d) by subjecting him to any other detriment during his training.

(2) It is unlawful for a training provider, in relation to a person seeking or undergoing training which would help fit him for any employment, to subject him to harassment.

(3) Paragraph (1) does not apply if the discrimination only concerns training for employment which, by virtue of regulation 7 (exception for genuine occupational requirement), the employer could lawfully refuse to offer the person seeking training.

(4) In this regulation—

["registered pupil", in England and Wales, has the meaning given by section 434(5) of the Education Act 1996, and, in Scotland, means a pupil deemed to be attending or in attendance at a school in terms of section 135(1) of the Education (Scotland) Act 1980;]

["training" means—

(a) all types and all levels of training which would help fit a person for any employment;

(b) vocational guidance;

(c) facilities for training;

(d) practical work experience provided by an employer to a person whom he does not employ; and

(e) any assessment related to the award of any professional or trade qualification;]

"training provider" means any person who provides, or makes arrangements for the provision of, training which would help fit another person for any employment, but it does not include—

(a) an employer in relation to training for persons employed by him;

[(b) a governing body of an educational establishment to which regulation 20 (institutions of further and higher education) applies, or would apply but for the operation of any other provision of these Regulations, except in relation to a person who is undertaking practical work experience at the educational establishment and is not a student at, or employed by, that establishment; or]

[(c) a proprietor of a school in relation to a pupil registered at that or another school, except where that pupil is undertaking practical work experience provided by a school at which he is not registered and he is not employed by that school.]

[2958]

NOTES

Commencement: 2 December 2003.

Regulation heading: substituted by the Employment Equality (Sexual Orientation) (Religion or Belief) (Amendment) Regulations 2007, SI 2007/2269, reg 4(1), (4)(a), as from 14 September 2007.

Para (1): sub-para (aa) inserted by SI 2007/2269, reg 4(1), (4)(b), as from 14 September 2007.

Para (4): definition "registered pupil" inserted, definition "training" substituted, and in definition "training provider" paras (b), (c) substituted, by SI 2007/2269, reg 4(1), (4)(c), as from 14 September 2007.

18 Employment agencies, careers guidance etc

(1) It is unlawful for an employment agency to discriminate against a person—

(a) in the terms on which the agency offers to provide any of its services;

(b) by refusing or deliberately not providing any of its services; or

(c) in the way it provides any of its services.

(2) It is unlawful for an employment agency, in relation to a person to whom it provides its services, or who has requested it to provide its services, to subject that person to harassment.

(3) Paragraph (1) does not apply to discrimination if it only concerns employment which, by virtue of regulation 7 (exception for genuine occupational requirement), the employer could lawfully refuse to offer the person in question.

(4) An employment agency shall not be subject to any liability under this regulation if it proves that—

(a) it acted in reliance on a statement made to it by the employer to the effect that, by reason of the operation of paragraph (3), its action would not be unlawful, and

(b) it was reasonable for it to rely on the statement.

(5) A person who knowingly or recklessly makes a statement such as is referred to in paragraph (4)(a) which in a material respect is false or misleading commits an offence, and shall be liable on summary conviction to a fine not exceeding level 5 on the standard scale.

(6) For the purposes of this regulation—

(a) "employment agency" means a person who, for profit or not, provides services for the purpose of finding employment for workers or supplying employers with workers, but it does not include—

(i) [a governing body of] an educational establishment to which regulation 20 (institutions of further and higher education) applies, or would apply but for the operation of any other provision of these Regulations, or

(ii) [a proprietor of] a school; and

(b) references to the services of an employment agency include guidance on careers and any other services related to employment.

[2959]

NOTES

Commencement: 2 December 2003.

Para (6): words in square brackets inserted by the Employment Equality (Sexual Orientation) (Religion or Belief) (Amendment) Regulations 2007, SI 2007/2269, reg 4(1), (5), as from 14 September 2007.

19 Assisting persons to obtain employment etc

(1) It is unlawful for the Secretary of State to discriminate against any person by subjecting him to a detriment, or to subject a person to harassment, in the provision of facilities or services under section 2 of the Employment and Training Act 1973 (arrangements for assisting persons to obtain employment).

(2) It is unlawful for Scottish Enterprise or Highlands and Islands Enterprise to discriminate against any person by subjecting him to a detriment, or to subject a person to harassment, in the provision of facilities or services under such arrangements as are mentioned in section 2(3) of the Enterprise and New Towns (Scotland) Act 1990 (arrangements analogous to arrangements in pursuance of the said Act of 1973).

(3) This regulation does not apply in a case where—

(a) regulation 17 (providers of vocational training) applies, or would apply but for the operation of any other provision of these Regulations, or

(b) the Secretary of State is acting as an employment agency within the meaning of regulation 18.

[2960]

NOTES

Commencement: 2 December 2003.

20 Institutions of further and higher education

(1) It is unlawful, in relation to an educational establishment to which this regulation applies, for the governing body of that establishment to discriminate against a person—

(a) in the terms on which it offers to admit him to the establishment as a student;

(b) by refusing or deliberately not accepting an application for his admission to the establishment as a student; or

(c) where he is a student of the establishment—
  (i) in the way it affords him access to any benefits,
  (ii) by refusing or deliberately not affording him access to them, or
  (iii) by excluding him from the establishment or subjecting him to any other detriment.

(2) It is unlawful, in relation to an educational establishment to which this regulation applies, for the governing body of that establishment to subject to harassment a person who is a student at the establishment, or who has applied for admission to the establishment as a student.

(3) Paragraph (1) does not apply if the discrimination only concerns training which would help fit a person for employment which, by virtue of regulation 7 (exception for genuine occupational requirement), the employer could lawfully refuse to offer the person in question.

(4) [Subject to paragraph (4A),] this regulation applies to the following educational establishments in England and Wales, namely—
  (a) an institution within the further education sector (within the meaning of section 91(3) of the Further and Higher Education Act 1992);
  (b) a university;
  (c) an institution, other than a university, within the higher education sector (within the meaning of section 91(5) of the Further and Higher Education Act 1992).

[(4A) In relation to an institution specified in Schedule 1B, this regulation applies with the modification set out in that Schedule.]

(5) This regulation applies to the following educational establishments in Scotland, namely—
  (a) a college of further education within the meaning of section 36(1) of the Further and Higher Education (Scotland) Act 1992 under the management of a board of management within the meaning of Part I of that Act;
  (b) a college of further education maintained by an education authority in the exercise of its further education functions in providing courses of further education within the meaning of section 1(5)(b)(ii) of the Education (Scotland) Act 1980;
  (c) any other educational establishment (not being a school) which provides further education within the meaning of section 1 of the Further and Higher Education (Scotland) Act 1992;
  (d) an institution within the higher education sector (within the meaning of Part II of the Further and Higher Education (Scotland) Act 1992);
  (e) a central institution (within the meaning of section 135 of the Education (Scotland) Act 1980).

(6) In this regulation—

"education authority" has the meaning given by section 135(1) of the Education (Scotland) Act 1980;

"governing body" includes—
  (a) the board of management of a college referred to in paragraph (5)(a), and
  (b) the managers of a college or institution referred to in paragraph (5)(b) or (e);

"student" means any person who receives education at an educational establishment to which this regulation applies; and

"university" includes a university college and the college, school or hall of a university. **[2961]**

NOTES

Commencement: 2 December 2003.

Para (4): words in square brackets inserted by the Employment Equality (Religion or Belief) (Amendment) Regulations 2004, SI 2004/437, regs 2, 3(1), as from 1 April 2004.

Para (4A): inserted by SI 2004/437, regs 2, 3(2), as from 1 April 2004.

21 Relationships which have come to an end

(1) In this regulation a "relevant relationship" is a relationship during the course of which an act of discrimination against, or harassment of, one party to the relationship ("B") by the other party to it ("A") is unlawful by virtue of any preceding provision of this Part.

(2) Where a relevant relationship has come to an end, it is unlawful for A—

(a) to discriminate against B by subjecting him to a detriment; or

(b) to subject B to harassment,

where the discrimination or harassment arises out of and is closely connected to that relationship.

(3) In paragraph (1), reference to an act of discrimination or harassment which is unlawful includes, in the case of a relationship which has come to an end before the coming into force of these Regulations, reference to an act of discrimination or harassment which would, after the coming into force of these Regulations, be unlawful.

[2962]

NOTES

Commencement: 2 December 2003.

PART III
OTHER UNLAWFUL ACTS

22 Liability of employers and principals

(1) Anything done by a person in the course of his employment shall be treated for the purposes of these Regulations as done by his employer as well as by him, whether or not it was done with the employer's knowledge or approval.

(2) Anything done by a person as agent for another person with the authority (whether express or implied, and whether precedent or subsequent) of that other person shall be treated for the purposes of these Regulations as done by that other person as well as by him.

(3) In proceedings brought under these Regulations against any person in respect of an act alleged to have been done by an employee of his it shall be a defence for that person to prove that he took such steps as were reasonably practicable to prevent the employee from doing that act, or from doing in the course of his employment acts of that description.

[2963]

NOTES

Commencement: 2 December 2003.

23 Aiding unlawful acts

(1) A person who knowingly aids another person to do an act made unlawful by these Regulations shall be treated for the purpose of these Regulations as himself doing an unlawful act of the like description.

(2) For the purposes of paragraph (1) an employee or agent for whose act the employer or principal is liable under regulation 22 (or would be so liable but for regulation 22(3)) shall be deemed to aid the doing of the act by the employer or principal.

(3) A person does not under this regulation knowingly aid another to do an unlawful act if—

(a) he acts in reliance on a statement made to him by that other person that, by reason of any provision of these Regulations, the act which he aids would not be unlawful; and

(b) it is reasonable for him to rely on the statement.

(4) A person who knowingly or recklessly makes a statement such as is referred to in paragraph (3)(a) which in a material respect is false or misleading commits an offence, and shall be liable on summary conviction to a fine not exceeding level 5 on the standard scale.

[2964]

NOTES

Commencement: 2 December 2003.

PART IV
GENERAL EXCEPTIONS FROM PARTS II AND III

24 Exception for national security

Nothing in Part II or III shall render unlawful an act done for the purpose of safeguarding national security, if the doing of the act was justified by that purpose.

[2965]

NOTES

Commencement: 2 December 2003.

25 Exceptions for positive action

(1) Nothing in Part II or III shall render unlawful any act done in or in connection with—

(a) affording persons of a particular religion or belief access to facilities for training which would help fit them for particular work; or

(b) encouraging persons of a particular religion or belief to take advantage of opportunities for doing particular work,

where it reasonably appears to the person doing the act that it prevents or compensates for disadvantages linked to religion or belief suffered by persons of that religion or belief doing that work or likely to take up that work.

(2) Nothing in Part II or III shall render unlawful any act done by a trade organisation within the meaning of regulation 15 in or in connection with—

(a) affording only members of the organisation who are of a particular religion or belief access to facilities for training which would help fit them for holding a post of any kind in the organisation; or

(b) encouraging only members of the organisation who are of a particular religion or belief to take advantage of opportunities for holding such posts in the organisation,

where it reasonably appears to the organisation that the act prevents or compensates for disadvantages linked to religion or belief suffered by those of that religion or belief holding such posts or likely to hold such posts.

(3) Nothing in Part II or III shall render unlawful any act done by a trade organisation within the meaning of regulation 15 in or in connection with encouraging only persons of a particular religion or belief to become members of the organisation where it reasonably appears to the organisation that the act prevents or compensates for disadvantages linked to religion or belief suffered by persons of that religion or belief who are, or are eligible to become, members.

[2966]

NOTES

Commencement: 2 December 2003.

26 Protection of Sikhs from discrimination in connection with requirements as to wearing of safety helmets

(1) Where—

(a) any person applies to a Sikh any provision, criterion or practice relating to the wearing by him of a safety helmet while he is on a construction site; and

(b) at the time when he so applies the provision, criterion or practice that person has no reasonable grounds for believing that the Sikh would not wear a turban at all times when on such a site,

then, for the purposes of regulation 3(1)(b)(iii), the provision, criterion or practice shall be taken to be one which cannot be shown to be a proportionate means of achieving a legitimate aim.

(2) Any special treatment afforded to a Sikh in consequence of section 11(1) or (2) of the Employment Act 1989 (exemption of Sikhs from requirements as to wearing of safety helmets on construction sites) shall not be regarded as giving rise, in relation to any other person, to any discrimination falling within regulation 3.

(3) In this regulation—

"construction site" means any place in Great Britain where any building operations or works of engineering construction are being undertaken, but does not include any site within the territorial sea adjacent to Great Britain unless there are being undertaken on that site such operations or works as are activities falling within Article 8(a) of the Health and Safety at Work etc Act 1974 (Application outside Great Britain) Order 2001; and

"safety helmet" means any form of protective headgear.

(4) In this regulation—

(a) any reference to a Sikh is a reference to a follower of the Sikh religion; and

(b) any reference to a Sikh being on a construction site is a reference to his being there whether while at work or otherwise.

[2967]

NOTES

Commencement: 2 December 2003.

PART V

ENFORCEMENT

27 Restriction of proceedings for breach of Regulations

(1) Except as provided by these Regulations no proceedings, whether civil or criminal, shall lie against any person in respect of an act by reason that the act is unlawful by virtue of a provision of these Regulations.

(2) Paragraph (1) does not prevent the making of an application for judicial review [or the investigation or determination of any matter in accordance with Part X (investigations: the Pensions Ombudsman) of the Pension Schemes Act 1993 by the Pensions Ombudsman].

[2968]

NOTES

Commencement: 2 December 2003.

Para (2): words in square brackets added by the Employment Equality (Religion or Belief) (Amendment) Regulations 2003, SI 2003/2828, reg 3(1), (4), as from 2 December 2003.

28 Jurisdiction of employment tribunals

(1) A complaint by any person ("the complainant") that another person ("the respondent")—

(a) has committed against the complainant an act to which this regulation applies; or

(b) is by virtue of regulation 22 (liability of employers and principals) or 23 (aiding unlawful acts) to be treated as having committed against the complainant such an act,

may be presented to an employment tribunal.

(2) This regulation applies to any act of discrimination or harassment which is unlawful by virtue of any provision of Part II other than—

(a) where the act is one in respect of which an appeal or proceedings in the nature of an appeal may be brought under any enactment, regulation 16 (qualifications bodies);

(b) regulation 20 (institutions of further and higher education); or

(c) where the act arises out of and is closely connected to a relationship between the complainant and the respondent which has come to an end but during the course of which an act of discrimination against, or harassment of, the complainant by the respondent would have been unlawful by virtue of regulation 20, regulation 21 (relationships which have come to an end).

(3) In paragraph (2)(c), reference to an act of discrimination or harassment which would have been unlawful includes, in the case of a relationship which has come to an end before the coming into force of these Regulations, reference to an act of discrimination or harassment which would, after the coming into force of these Regulations, have been unlawful.

(4) In this regulation, "enactment" includes an enactment comprised in, or in an instrument made under, an Act of the Scottish Parliament.

[2969]

NOTES

Commencement: 2 December 2003.

Conciliation: employment tribunal proceedings and claims which could be the subject of employment tribunal proceedings under this regulation are proceedings to which the Employment Tribunals Act 1996, s 18 applies; see s 18(1)(l) of that Act at **[975]**. There is no fixed conciliation period for such proceedings: see the Employment Tribunals (Constitution and Rules of Procedure) Regulations 2004, SI 2004/1861, Sch 1, rule 22(1), (2).

Tribunal jurisdiction: the Employment Act 2002, ss 31, 32, 38, at **[1493]**, **[1494]**, **[1496]** apply to proceedings before the employment tribunal relating to a claim under this regulation; see ss 31(1), 32(1), 38(1) of, and Schs 3–5 to, the 2002 Act at **[1508]**–**[1510]**.

For the circumstances in which the normal time limit for presenting a complaint under this regulation is extended for a period of three months, see the Employment Act 2002 (Dispute Resolution) Regulations 2004, SI 2004/752, regs 15 and 18 at **[3096]** and **[3098]**, and reg 34 of these Regulations at **[2975]**.

29 Burden of proof: employment tribunals

(1) This regulation applies to any complaint presented under regulation 28 to an employment tribunal.

(2) Where, on the hearing of the complaint, the complainant proves facts from which the tribunal could, apart from this regulation, conclude in the absence of an adequate explanation that the respondent—

(a) has committed against the complainant an act to which regulation 28 applies; or

(b) is by virtue of regulation 22 (liability of employers and principals) or 23 (aiding unlawful acts) to be treated as having committed against the complainant such an act,

the tribunal shall uphold the complaint unless the respondent proves that he did not commit, or as the case may be, is not to be treated as having committed, that act.

[2970]

NOTES

Commencement: 2 December 2003.

30 Remedies on complaints in employment tribunals

(1) Where an employment tribunal finds that a complaint presented to it under regulation 28 is well-founded, the tribunal shall make such of the following as it considers just and equitable—

(a) an order declaring the rights of the complainant and the respondent in relation to the act to which the complaint relates;

(b) an order requiring the respondent to pay to the complainant compensation of an amount corresponding to any damages he could have been ordered by a county court or by a sheriff court to pay to the complainant if the complaint had fallen to be dealt with under regulation 31 (jurisdiction of county and sheriff courts);

(c) a recommendation that the respondent take within a specified period action appearing to the tribunal to be practicable for the purpose of obviating or reducing the adverse effect on the complainant of any act of discrimination or harassment to which the complaint relates.

(2) As respects an unlawful act of discrimination falling within regulation 3(1)(b), if the respondent proves that the provision, criterion or practice was not applied with the intention of treating the complainant unfavourably on grounds of religion or belief, an order may be made under paragraph (1)(b) only if the employment tribunal—

(a) makes such order under paragraph (1)(a) (if any) and such recommendation under paragraph (1)(c) (if any) as it would have made if it had no power to make an order under paragraph (1)(b); and

(b) (where it makes an order under paragraph (1)(a) or a recommendation under paragraph (1)(c) or both) considers that it is just and equitable to make an order under paragraph (1)(b) as well.

(3) If without reasonable justification the respondent to a complaint fails to comply with a recommendation made by an employment tribunal under paragraph (1)(c), then, if it thinks it just and equitable to do so—

(a) the tribunal may increase the amount of compensation required to be paid to the complainant in respect of the complaint by an order made under paragraph (1)(b); or

(b) if an order under paragraph (1)(b) was not made, the tribunal may make such an order.

(4) Where an amount of compensation falls to be awarded under paragraph (1)(b), the tribunal may include in the award interest on that amount subject to, and in accordance with, the provisions of the Employment Tribunals (Interest on Awards in Discrimination Cases) Regulations 1996.

[(5) This regulation has effect subject to paragraph 7 of Schedule 1A (occupational pension schemes).]

[2971]

NOTES

Commencement: 2 December 2003.

Para (5): added by the Employment Equality (Religion or Belief) (Amendment) Regulations 2003, SI 2003/2828, reg 3(1), (5), as from 2 December 2003.

Compensation for dismissal: as to the powers of an employment tribunal to award compensation where any act constitutes both unfair dismissal under the Employment Rights Act 1996, and discrimination under any one or more of the Sex Discrimination Act 1975, the Race Relations Act 1976, the Disability Discrimination Act 1995, the Employment Equality (Sexual Orientation) Regulations 2003, the Employment Equality (Religion or Belief) Regulations 2003, or the Employment Equality (Age) Regulations 2006, see s 126 of the 1996 Act at **[1170]**.

31 Jurisdiction of county and sheriff courts

(1) A claim by any person ("the claimant") that another person ("the respondent")—

(a) has committed against the claimant an act to which this regulation applies; or

(b) is by virtue of regulation 22 (liability of employers and principals) or 23 (aiding unlawful acts) to be treated as having committed against the claimant such an act,

may be made the subject of civil proceedings in like manner as any other claim in tort or (in Scotland) in reparation for breach of statutory duty.

(2) Proceedings brought under paragraph (1) shall—

(a) in England and Wales, be brought only in a county court; and

(b) in Scotland, be brought only in a sheriff court.

(3) For the avoidance of doubt it is hereby declared that damages in respect of an unlawful act to which this regulation applies may include compensation for injury to feelings whether or not they include compensation under any other head.

(4) This regulation applies to any act of discrimination or harassment which is unlawful by virtue of—

(a) regulation 20 (institutions of further and higher education); or

(b) where the act arises out of and is closely connected to a relationship between the claimant and the respondent which has come to an end but during the course of which an act of discrimination against, or harassment of, the claimant by the respondent would have been unlawful by virtue of regulation 20, regulation 21 (relationships which have come to an end).

(5) In paragraph (4)(b), reference to an act of discrimination or harassment which would have been unlawful includes, in the case of a relationship which has come to an end before the coming into force of these Regulations, reference to an act of discrimination or harassment which would, after the coming into force of these Regulations, have been unlawful.

[2972]

NOTES

Commencement: 2 December 2003.

Conciliation: for the powers of the Commission for Equality and Human Rights to make arrangements for the provision of conciliation services for disputes in respect of which proceedings have been, or could be, brought under this regulation, see the Equality Act 2006, s 27 at **[1670]**.

32 Burden of proof: county and sheriff courts

(1) This regulation applies to any claim brought under regulation 31 in a county court in England and Wales or a sheriff court in Scotland.

(2) Where, on the hearing of the claim, the claimant proves facts from which the court could, apart from this regulation, conclude in the absence of an adequate explanation that the respondent—

(a) has committed against the claimant an act to which regulation 31 applies; or

(b) is by virtue of regulation 22 (liability of employers and principals) or 23 (aiding unlawful acts) to be treated as having committed against the claimant such an act,

the court shall uphold the claim unless the respondent proves that he did not commit, or as the case may be, is not to be treated as having committed, that act.

[2973]

NOTES

Commencement: 2 December 2003.

33 Help for persons in obtaining information etc

(1) In accordance with this regulation, a person ("the person aggrieved") who considers he may have been discriminated against, or subjected to harassment, in contravention of these Regulations may serve on the respondent to a complaint presented under regulation 28 (jurisdiction of employment tribunals) or a claim brought under regulation 31 (jurisdiction of county and sheriff courts) questions in the form set out in Schedule 2 or forms to the like effect with such variation as the circumstances require; and the respondent may if he so wishes reply to such questions by way of the form set out in Schedule 3 or forms to the like effect with such variation as the circumstances require.

(2) Where the person aggrieved questions the respondent (whether in accordance with paragraph (1) or not)—

(a) the questions, and any reply by the respondent (whether in accordance with paragraph (1) or not) shall, subject to the following provisions of this regulation, be admissible as evidence in the proceedings;

(b) if it appears to the court or tribunal that the respondent deliberately, and without reasonable excuse, omitted to reply within eight weeks of service of the questions or that his reply is evasive or equivocal, the court or tribunal may draw any inference from that fact that it considers it just and equitable to draw, including an inference that he committed an unlawful act.

(3) In proceedings before a county court in England or Wales or a sheriff court in Scotland, a question shall only be admissible as evidence in pursuance of paragraph (2)(a)—

(a) where it was served before those proceedings had been instituted, if it was so served within the period of six months beginning when the act complained of was done;

(b) where it was served when those proceedings had been instituted, if it was served with the leave of, and within a period specified by, the court in question.

(4) In proceedings before an employment tribunal, a question shall only be admissible as evidence in pursuance of paragraph (2)(a)—

[(a) where it was served before a complaint had been presented to a tribunal, if it was so served—

(i) within the period of three months beginning when the act complained of was done; or

(ii) where paragraph (1A) of regulation 34 applies, within the extended period;]

(b) where it was served when a complaint had been presented to the tribunal, either—

(i) if it was so served within the period of twenty-one days beginning with the day on which the complaint was presented, or

(ii) if it was so served later with leave given, and within a period specified, by a direction of the tribunal.

(5) A question and any reply thereto may be served on the respondent or, as the case may be, on the person aggrieved—

(a) by delivering it to him;

(b) by sending it by post to him at his usual or last-known residence or place of business;

(c) where the person to be served is a body corporate or is a trade union or employers' association within the meaning of the Trade Union and Labour Relations (Consolidation) Act 1992, by delivering it to the secretary or clerk of the body, union or association at its registered or principal office or by sending it by post to the secretary or clerk at that office;

(d) where the person to be served is acting by a solicitor, by delivering it at, or by sending it by post to, the solicitor's address for service; or

(e) where the person to be served is the person aggrieved, by delivering the reply, or sending it by post, to him at his address for reply as stated by him in the document containing the questions.

(6) This regulation is without prejudice to any other enactment or rule of law regulating interlocutory and preliminary matters in proceedings before a county court, sheriff court or employment tribunal, and has effect subject to any enactment or rule of law regulating the admissibility of evidence in such proceedings.

(7) In this regulation "respondent" includes a prospective respondent.

[2974]

NOTES

Commencement: 2 December 2003.

Para (4): sub-para (a) substituted by the Employment Act 2002 (Dispute Resolution) Regulations 2004, SI 2004/752, reg 17(g)(i), as from 1 October 2004 (for transitional provisions and effect see reg 18 at **[3098]**).

34 Period within which proceedings to be brought

(1) An employment tribunal shall not consider a complaint under regulation 28 unless it is presented to the tribunal before the end of—

(a) the period of three months beginning when the act complained of was done; or

(b) in a case to which regulation 36(7) (armed forces) applies, the period of six months so beginning.

[(1A) Where the period within which a complaint must be presented in accordance with paragraph (1) is extended by regulation 15 of the Employment Act 2002 (Dispute Resolution) Regulations 2004, the period within which the complaint must be presented shall be the extended period rather than the period in paragraph (1).]

(2) A county court or a sheriff court shall not consider a claim brought under regulation 31 unless proceedings in respect of the claim are instituted before the end of the period of six months beginning when the act complained of was done.

(3) A court or tribunal may nevertheless consider any such complaint or claim which is out of time if, in all the circumstances of the case, it considers that it is just and equitable to do so.

(4) For the purposes of this regulation and regulation 33 (help for persons in obtaining information etc)—

(a) when the making of a contract is, by reason of the inclusion of any term, an unlawful act, that act shall be treated as extending throughout the duration of the contract; and

(b) any act extending over a period shall be treated as done at the end of that period; and

(c) a deliberate omission shall be treated as done when the person in question decided upon it,

and in the absence of evidence establishing the contrary a person shall be taken for the purposes of this regulation to decide upon an omission when he does an act inconsistent with doing the omitted act or, if he has done no such inconsistent act, when the period expires within which he might reasonably have been expected to do the omitted act if it was to be done.

[2975]

NOTES

Commencement: 2 December 2003.

Para (1A): inserted by the Employment Act 2002 (Dispute Resolution) Regulations 2004, SI 2004/752, reg 17(g)(ii), as from 1 October 2004 (for transitional provisions and effect see reg 18 at **[3098]**).

PART VI
SUPPLEMENTAL

35 Validity of contracts, collective agreements and rules of undertakings

Schedule 4 (validity of contracts, collective agreements and rules of undertakings) shall have effect.

[2976]

NOTES

Commencement: 2 December 2003.

---

36 Application to the Crown etc

(1) These Regulations apply—

(a) to an act done by or for purposes of a Minister of the Crown or government department; or

(b) to an act done on behalf of the Crown by a statutory body, or a person holding a statutory office,

as they apply to an act done by a private person.

(2) These Regulations apply to—

(a) service for purposes of a Minister of the Crown or government department, other than service of a person holding a statutory office;

(b) service on behalf of the Crown for purposes of a person holding a statutory office or purposes of a statutory body; or

(c) service in the armed forces,

as they apply to employment by a private person, and shall so apply as if references to a contract of employment included references to the terms of service.

(3) Paragraphs (1) and (2) have effect subject to regulation 11 (police).

(4) Regulation 9(3) (meaning of employment and contract work at establishment in Great Britain) shall have effect in relation to any ship, aircraft or hovercraft belonging to or possessed by Her Majesty in right of the government of the United Kingdom as it has effect in relation to a ship, aircraft or hovercraft specified in regulation 9(3)(a) or (b).

(5) The provisions of Parts II to IV of the Crown Proceedings Act 1947 shall apply to proceedings against the Crown under these Regulations as they apply to proceedings in England and Wales which by virtue of section 23 of that Act are treated for the purposes of Part II of that Act as civil proceedings by or against the Crown, except that in their application to proceedings under these Regulations section 20 of that Act (removal of proceedings from county court to High Court) shall not apply.

(6) The provisions of Part V of the Crown Proceedings Act 1947 shall apply to proceedings against the Crown under these Regulations as they apply to proceedings in Scotland which by virtue of the said Part are treated as civil proceedings by or against the Crown, except that in their application to proceedings under these Regulations the proviso to section 44 of that Act (removal of proceedings from the sheriff court to the Court of Session) shall not apply.

(7) This paragraph applies to any complaint by a person ("the complainant") that another person—

(a) has committed an act of discrimination or harassment against the complainant which is unlawful by virtue of regulation 6 (applicants and employees); or

(b) is by virtue of regulation 22 (liability of employers and principals) or 23 (aiding unlawful acts) to be treated as having committed such an act of discrimination or harassment against the complainant,

if at the time when the act complained of was done the complainant was serving in the armed forces and the discrimination or harassment in question relates to his service in those forces.

(8) A complainant may present a complaint to which paragraph (7) applies to an employment tribunal under regulation 28 only if—

(a) he has made a complaint in respect of the same matter to an officer under the service redress procedures applicable to him; and

(b) that complaint has not been withdrawn.

(9) For the purpose of paragraph (8)(b), a complainant shall be treated as having withdrawn his complaint if, having made a complaint to an officer under the service redress procedures applicable to him, he fails to submit that complaint to the Defence Council under those procedures.

(10) Where a complaint is presented to an employment tribunal under regulation 28 by virtue of paragraph (8), the service redress procedures may continue after the complaint is so presented.

(11) In this regulation—

"armed forces" means any of the naval, military or air forces of the Crown;

"service for purposes of a Minister of the Crown or government department" does not include service in any office mentioned in Schedule 2 (Ministerial offices) to the House of Commons Disqualification Act 1975;

"the service redress procedures" means the procedures, excluding those which relate to the making of a report on a complaint to Her Majesty, referred to in section 180 of the Army Act 1955, section 180 of the Air Force Act 1955 and section 130 of the Naval Discipline Act 1957; and

"statutory body" means a body set up by or in pursuance of an enactment, and "statutory office" means an office so set up.

[2977]

NOTES

Commencement: 2 December 2003.

37 Application to House of Commons staff

(1) These Regulations apply to an act done by an employer of a relevant member of the House of Commons staff, and to service as such a member, as they apply to an act done by and to service for purposes of a Minister of the Crown or government department, and accordingly apply as if references to a contract of employment included references to the terms of service of such a member.

(2) In this regulation "relevant member of the House of Commons staff" means any person—

(a) who was appointed by the House of Commons Commission; or

(b) who is a member of the Speaker's personal staff,

and subsections (6) to (12) of section 195 of the Employment Rights Act 1996 (person to be treated as employer of House of Commons staff) apply, with any necessary modifications, for the purposes of these Regulations.

[2978]

NOTES

Commencement: 2 December 2003.

38 Application to House of Lords staff

(1) These Regulations apply in relation to employment as a relevant member of the House of Lords staff as they apply in relation to other employment.

(2) In this regulation "relevant member of the House of Lords staff" means any person who is employed under a contract of employment with the Corporate Officer of the House of Lords, and section 194(7) of the Employment Rights Act 1996 (continuity of employment) applies for the purposes of this regulation.

[2979]

NOTES

Commencement: 2 December 2003.

39 Savings of, and amendments to, legislation

(1) These Regulations are without prejudice to—

(a) sections 58 to 60 [and 124A] of the School Standards and Framework Act 1998 (appointment and dismissal of teachers in schools with a religious character etc); and

(b) section 21 of the Education (Scotland) Act 1980 (management of denominational schools).

(2) Schedule 5 (amendments to legislation) shall have effect.

[2980]

NOTES

Commencement: 2 December 2003.

Para (1): words in square brackets in sub-para (a) inserted by the Independent Schools (Employment of Teachers in Schools with a Religious Character) Regulations 2003, SI 2003/2037, reg 6, as from 1 September 2003.

SCHEDULES

(*Sch 1* (*Norwegian part of the Frigg gas field*) *outside the scope of this work.*)

[SCHEDULE 1A
OCCUPATIONAL PENSION SCHEMES

Regulation 9A(3)

Interpretation

1.—(1) In this Schedule—

"active member", "deferred member", "managers", "pensioner member" and "trustees or managers", in relation to an occupational pension scheme, have the meanings given by section 124(1) of the Pensions Act 1995 … ;

"member", in relation to an occupational pension scheme, means any active member, deferred member or pensioner member;

"non-discrimination rule" means the rule in paragraph 2;

"occupational pension scheme" has the same meaning as in the Pension Schemes Act 1993 … ;

"prospective member", in relation to an occupational pension scheme, means any person who, under the terms of his employment or the rules of the scheme or both—

(a) is able, at his own option, to become a member of the scheme,

(b) shall become so able if he continues in the same employment for a sufficient period of time,

(c) shall be admitted to it automatically unless he makes an election not to become a member, or

(d) may be admitted to it subject to the consent of his employer.

(2) In paragraph 6 (procedure in employment tribunals), "employer", in relation to an occupational pension scheme, has the meaning given by section 124(1) of the Pensions Act 1995 …

(3) Any term used in regulation 9A (trustees and managers of occupational pension schemes) and in this Schedule shall have the same meaning in that regulation as it has in this Schedule.

Non-discrimination rule

2. Every occupational pension scheme shall be treated as including a provision ("the non-discrimination rule") containing a requirement that the trustees or managers of the scheme refrain from doing any act which is unlawful by virtue of regulation 9A.

3. The other provisions of the scheme are to have effect subject to the non-discrimination rule.

4. The trustees or managers of an occupational pension scheme may—

(a) if they do not (apart from this paragraph) have power to make such alterations to the scheme as may be required to secure conformity with the non-discrimination rule, or

(b) if they have such power but the procedure for doing so—

(i) is liable to be unduly complex or protracted, or

(ii) involves the obtaining of consents which cannot be obtained, or can only be obtained with undue delay or difficulty, by resolution make such alterations to the scheme.

5. Alterations made by a resolution such as is referred to in paragraph 4 may have effect in relation to a period before the alterations are made (but may not have effect in relation to any time before the coming into force of these Regulations).

Procedure in employment tribunals

6. Where under regulation 28 (jurisdiction of employment tribunals) a member or prospective member of an occupational pension scheme presents to an employment tribunal a complaint that the trustees or managers of the scheme—

(a) have committed against him an act which is unlawful by virtue of regulation 9A (trustees and managers of occupational pension schemes) or 21 (relationships which have come to an end); or

(b) are by virtue of regulation 22 (liability of employers and principals) or 23 (aiding unlawful acts) to be treated as having committed against him such an act,

the employer in relation to the scheme shall, for the purposes of the rules governing procedure, be treated as a party and be entitled to appear and be heard in accordance with those rules.

Remedies in employment tribunals

7.—(1) This paragraph applies where—

(a) under regulation 28 (jurisdiction of employment tribunals) a member or prospective member of an occupational pension scheme ("the complainant") presents to an employment tribunal a complaint against the trustees or managers of the scheme or an employer;

(b) the complainant is not a pensioner member of the scheme;

(c) the complaint relates to the terms on which persons become members of the scheme, or the terms on which members of the scheme are treated; and

(d) the tribunal finds the complaint to be well-founded.

(2) Where this paragraph applies, the employment tribunal may, without prejudice to the generality of its power under regulation 30(1)(a) (power to make order declaring rights of complainant and respondent), make an order declaring that the complainant has a right—

(a) where the complaint relates to the terms on which persons become members of the scheme, to be admitted to the scheme;

(b) where the complaint relates to the terms on which members of the scheme are treated, to membership of the scheme without discrimination.

(3) An order under sub-paragraph (2)—

(a) may be made in respect of such period as is specified in the order (but may not be made in respect of any time before the coming into force of these Regulations);

(b) may make such provision as the employment tribunal considers appropriate as to the terms on which, or the capacity in which, the complainant is to enjoy such admission or membership.

(4) Where this paragraph applies, the employment tribunal may not make an order for compensation under regulation 30(1)(b), whether in relation to arrears of benefits or otherwise, except—

(a) for injury to feelings;

(b) by virtue of regulation 30(3).]

[2981]

NOTES

Commencement: 2 December 2003.

Inserted by the Employment Equality (Religion or Belief) (Amendment) Regulations 2003, SI 2003/2828, reg 3(1), (6), as from 2 December 2003.

Para 1: words omitted revoked by the Employment Equality (Age) Regulations 2006, SI 2006/1031, reg 49(1), Sch 8, Pt 2, para 62, as from 1 October 2006.

[SCHEDULE 1B
INSTITUTIONS IN RELATION TO WHICH REGULATION 20 (INSTITUTIONS OF FURTHER AND HIGHER EDUCATION) IS MODIFIED

Regulation 20(4A)

1. This Schedule applies to the following institutions:—
   Aquinas Sixth Form College, Stockport
   Cardinal Newman College, Preston
   Carmel College, St Helens
   Christ The King Sixth Form College, Lewisham
   Holy Cross Sixth Form College, Bury
   Loreto College, Manchester
   Notre Dame Catholic Sixth Form College, Leeds
   St Brendan's Sixth Form College, Brislington, Bristol
   St Charles Catholic Sixth Form College, London W10
   St David's Catholic College/Coleg Catholig Dewi Sant, Cardiff
   St Dominic's Sixth Form College, Harrow on the Hill
   St Francis Xavier Sixth Form College, Clapham
   Saint John Rigby Catholic Sixth Form College, Orrell, Wigan
   St Mary's College, Blackburn
   St Mary's Sixth Form College, Middlesbrough
   Xaverian Sixth Form College, Manchester

2. Subject to paragraph 3, regulation 20(1)(b) shall not apply to the institutions specified in paragraph 1 in so far as it is necessary for an institution to give preference in its admissions to persons of a particular religion or belief in order to preserve that institution's religious ethos.

3. Paragraph 2 does not apply in relation to any admission to a course of vocational training.]

[2982]

NOTES

Commencement: 1 April 2004.
Inserted by the Employment Equality (Religion or Belief) (Amendment) Regulations 2004, SI 2004/437, regs 2, 3(3), as from 1 April 2004.

SCHEDULE 2
QUESTIONNAIRE OF PERSON AGGRIEVED

Regulation 33(1)

To .... (*name of person to be questioned*) of

.... (*address*)

1.—(1) I .... (*name of questioner*) of ....

.... (*address*)

consider that you may have discriminated against me [subjected me to harassment] contrary to the Employment Equality (Religion or Belief) Regulations 2003.

(2) (*Give date, approximate time and a factual description of the treatment received and of the circumstances leading up to the treatment.*)

(3) I consider that this treatment may have been unlawful [because ....

.... (*complete if you wish to give reasons, otherwise delete*)].

2. Do you agree that the statement in paragraph 1(2) above is an accurate description of what happened? If not, in what respect do you disagree or what is your version of what happened?

3. Do you accept that your treatment of me was unlawful discrimination [harassment]? If not—

(a) why not,
(b) for what reason did I receive the treatment accorded to me, and
(c) how far did considerations of religion or belief affect your treatment of me?

4. (*Any other questions you wish to ask.*)

5. My address for any reply you may wish to give to the questions raised above is [that set out in paragraph 1(1) above] [the following address ....

....].

.... (*signature of questioner*)

.... (*date*)

NB—By virtue of regulation 33 of the Employment Equality (Religion or Belief) Regulations 2003 this questionnaire and any reply are (subject to the provisions of that regulation) admissible in proceedings under the Regulations. A court or tribunal may draw any such inference as is just and equitable from a failure without reasonable excuse to reply within eight weeks of service of this questionnaire, or from an evasive or equivocal reply, including an inference that the person questioned has committed an unlawful act.

[2983]

NOTES

Commencement: 2 December 2003.

SCHEDULE 3
REPLY BY RESPONDENT

Regulation 33(1)

To .... (*name of questioner*) of

.... (*address*)

1. I .... (*name of person questioned*) of

.... (*address*)

hereby acknowledge receipt of the questionnaire signed by you and dated ....

which was served on me on .... (*date*).

2. [I agree that the statement in paragraph 1(2) of the questionnaire is an accurate description of what happened.]

[I disagree with the statement in paragraph 1(2) of the questionnaire in that ....

....]

3. I accept/dispute that my treatment of you was unlawful discrimination [harassment].

[My reasons for so disputing are ....

The reason why you received the treatment accorded to you and the answers to the other questions in paragraph 3 of the questionnaire are ....]

4. (*Replies to questions in paragraph 4 of the questionnaire.*)

[5. I have deleted (in whole or in part) the paragraph(s) numbered ....

above, since I am unable/unwilling to reply to the relevant questions in the correspondingly numbered paragraph(s) of the questionnaire for the following reasons ....

....]

.... (*signature of person questioned*)

.... (*date*)

[2984]

NOTES

Commencement: 2 December 2003.

SCHEDULE 4
VALIDITY OF CONTRACTS, COLLECTIVE AGREEMENT AND RULES OF UNDERTAKINGS

Regulation 35

PART 1
VALIDITY AND REVISION OF CONTRACTS

1.—(1) A term of a contract is void where—

(a) the making of the contract is, by reason of the inclusion of the term, unlawful by virtue of these Regulations;

(b) it is included in furtherance of an act which is unlawful by virtue of these Regulations; or

(c) it provides for the doing of an act which is unlawful by virtue of these Regulations.

(2) Sub-paragraph (1) does not apply to a term the inclusion of which constitutes, or is in furtherance of, or provides for, unlawful discrimination against, or harassment of, a party to the contract, but the term shall be unenforceable against that party.

(3) A term in a contract which purports to exclude or limit any provision of these Regulations is unenforceable by any person in whose favour the term would operate apart from this paragraph.

(4) Sub-paragraphs (1), (2) and (3) shall apply whether the contract was entered into before or after the date on which these Regulations come into force; but in the case of a contract made before that date, those sub-paragraphs do not apply in relation to any period before that date.

2.—(1) Paragraph 1(3) does not apply—

(a) to a contract settling a complaint to which regulation 28(1) (jurisdiction of employment tribunals) applies where the contract is made with the assistance of a conciliation officer within the meaning of section 211 of the Trade Union and Labour Relations (Consolidation) Act 1992;

(b) to a contract settling a complaint to which regulation 28(1) applies if the conditions regulating compromise contracts under this Schedule are satisfied in relation to the contract; or

(c) to a contract settling a claim to which regulation 31 (jurisdiction of county or sheriff courts) applies.

(2) The conditions regulating compromise contracts under this Schedule are that—

(a) the contract must be in writing;

(b) the contract must relate to the particular complaint;

(c) the complainant must have received advice from a relevant independent adviser as to the terms and effect of the proposed contract and in particular its effect on his ability to pursue a complaint before an employment tribunal;

(d) there must be in force, when the adviser gives the advice, a contract of insurance, or an indemnity provided for members of a profession or professional body, covering the risk of a claim by the complainant in respect of loss arising in consequence of the advice;

(e) the contract must identify the adviser; and

(f) the contract must state that the conditions regulating compromise contracts under this Schedule are satisfied.

(3) A person is a relevant independent adviser for the purposes of sub-paragraph (2)(c)—

(a) if he is a qualified lawyer;

(b) if he is an officer, official, employee or member of an independent trade union who has been certified in writing by the trade union as competent to give advice and as authorised to do so on behalf of the trade union; or

(c) if he works at an advice centre (whether as an employee or a volunteer) and has been certified in writing by the centre as competent to give advice and as authorised to do so on behalf of the centre.

(4) But a person is not a relevant independent adviser for the purposes of sub-paragraph (2)(c) in relation to the complainant—

(a) if he is, is employed by or is acting in the matter for the other party or a person who is connected with the other party;

(b) in the case of a person within sub-paragraph (3)(b) or (c), if the trade union or advice centre is the other party or a person who is connected with the other party; or
(c) in the case of a person within sub-paragraph (3)(c), if the complainant makes a payment for the advice received from him.

(5) In sub-paragraph (3)(a) "qualified lawyer" means—
(a) as respects England and Wales, a barrister (whether in practice as such or employed to give legal advice), a solicitor who holds a practising certificate, or a person other than a barrister or solicitor who is an authorised advocate or authorised litigator (within the meaning of the Courts and Legal Services Act 1990); and
(b) as respects Scotland, an advocate (whether in practice as such or employed to give legal advice), or a solicitor who holds a practising certificate.

[(5A) A person shall be treated as being a qualified lawyer within sub-paragraph (5)(a) if he is a Fellow of the Institute of Legal Executives employed by a solicitors' practice.]

(6) In sub-paragraph (3)(b) "independent trade union" has the same meaning as in the Trade Union and Labour Relations (Consolidation) Act 1992.

(7) For the purposes of sub-paragraph (4)(a) any two persons are to be treated as connected—
(a) if one is a company of which the other (directly or indirectly) has control; or
(b) if both are companies of which a third person (directly or indirectly) has control.

(8) An agreement under which the parties agree to submit a dispute to arbitration—
(a) shall be regarded for the purposes of sub-paragraph (1)(a) and (b) as being a contract settling a complaint if—
(i) the dispute is covered by a scheme having effect by virtue of an order under section 212A of the Trade Union and Labour Relations (Consolidation) Act 1992, and
(ii) the agreement is to submit it to arbitration in accordance with the scheme, but
(b) shall be regarded as neither being nor including such a contract in any other case.

3.—(1) On the application of a person interested in a contract to which paragraph 1(1) or (2) applies, a county court or a sheriff court may make such order as it thinks fit for—
(a) removing or modifying any term rendered void by paragraph 1(1), or
(b) removing or modifying any term made unenforceable by paragraph 1(2);
but such an order shall not be made unless all persons affected have been given notice in writing of the application (except where under rules of court notice may be dispensed with) and have been afforded an opportunity to make representations to the court.

(2) An order under sub-paragraph (1) may include provision as respects any period before the making of the order (but after the coming into force of these Regulations).

[2985]

NOTES

Commencement: 2 December 2003.

Para 2: sub-para (5A) inserted by the Employment Equality (Religion or Belief) Regulations 2003 (Amendment) (No 2) Regulations 2004, SI 2004/2520, reg 2, as from 1 October 2004.

PART 2
COLLECTIVE AGREEMENTS AND RULES OF UNDERTAKINGS

4.—(1) This Part of this Schedule applies to—
(a) any term of a collective agreement, including an agreement which was not intended, or is presumed not to have been intended, to be a legally enforceable contract;
(b) any rule made by an employer for application to all or any of the persons who are employed by him or who apply to be, or are, considered by him for employment;
(c) any rule made by a trade organisation (within the meaning of regulation 15) or a qualifications body (within the meaning of regulation 16) for application to—
(i) all or any of its members or prospective members; or
(ii) all or any of the persons on whom it has conferred professional or trade

qualifications (within the meaning of regulation 16) or who are seeking the professional or trade qualifications which it has power to confer.

(2) Any term or rule to which this Part of this Schedule applies is void where—

(a) the making of the collective agreement is, by reason of the inclusion of the term, unlawful by virtue of these Regulations;

(b) the term or rule is included or made in furtherance of an act which is unlawful by virtue of these Regulations; or

(c) the term or rule provides for the doing of an act which is unlawful by virtue of these Regulations.

(3) Sub-paragraph (2) shall apply whether the agreement was entered into, or the rule made, before or after the date on which these Regulations come into force; but in the case of an agreement entered into, or a rule made, before the date on which these Regulations come into force, that sub-paragraph does not apply in relation to any period before that date.

5. A person to whom this paragraph applies may present a complaint to an employment tribunal that a term or rule is void by virtue of paragraph 4 if he has reason to believe—

(a) that the term or rule may at some future time have effect in relation to him; and

(b) where he alleges that it is void by virtue of paragraph 4(2)(c), that—

(i) an act for the doing of which it provides, may at some such time be done in relation to him, and

(ii) the act would be unlawful by virtue of these Regulations if done in relation to him in present circumstances.

6. In the case of a complaint about—

(a) a term of a collective agreement made by or on behalf of—

(i) an employer,

(ii) an organisation of employers of which an employer is a member, or

(iii) an association of such organisations of one of which an employer is a member, or

(b) a rule made by an employer within the meaning of paragraph 4(1)(b),

paragraph 5 applies to any person who is, or is genuinely and actively seeking to become, one of his employees.

7. In the case of a complaint about a rule made by an organisation or body to which paragraph 4(1)(c) applies, paragraph 5 applies to any person—

(a) who is, or is genuinely and actively seeking to become, a member of the organisation or body;

(b) on whom the organisation or body has conferred a professional or trade qualification (within the meaning of regulation 16); or

(c) who is genuinely and actively seeking such a professional or trade qualification which the organisation or body has power to confer.

8.—(1) When an employment tribunal finds that a complaint presented to it under paragraph 5 is well-founded the tribunal shall make an order declaring that the term or rule is void.

(2) An order under sub-paragraph (1) may include provision as respects any period before the making of the order (but after the coming into force of these Regulations).

9. The avoidance by virtue of paragraph 4(2) of any term or rule which provides for any person to be discriminated against shall be without prejudice to the following rights (except in so far as they enable any person to require another person to be treated less favourably than himself), namely—

(a) such of the rights of the person to be discriminated against; and

(b) such of the rights of any person who will be treated more favourably in direct or indirect consequence of the discrimination,

as are conferred by or in respect of a contract made or modified wholly or partly in pursuance of, or by reference to, that term or rule.

10. In this Schedule "collective agreement" means any agreement relating to one or more of the matters mentioned in section 178(2) of the Trade Union and Labour Relations (Consolidation) Act 1992 (meaning of trade dispute), being an agreement made by or on

behalf of one or more employers or one or more organisations of employers or associations of such organisations with one or more organisations of workers or associations of such organisations.

[2986]

NOTES

Commencement: 2 December 2003.

(*Sch 5 amends the Employment Tribunals Act 1996, ss 18, 21 at* **[975]**, **[978]**, *the Employment Rights Act 1996, s 126 at* **[1170]**, *the Employment Tribunals (Interest on Awards in Discrimination Cases) Regulations 1996, SI 1996/2803, reg 1 at* **[2390]**, *and the Employment Act 2002, Schs 3–5 at* **[1508]**–**[1510]**.)

EMPLOYMENT EQUALITY (SEXUAL ORIENTATION) REGULATIONS 2003

(SI 2003/1661)

NOTES

Made: 26 June 2003.

Authority: European Communities Act 1972, s 2(2).

Commencement: 1 December 2003.

Conciliation: employment tribunal proceedings and claims which could be the subject of employment tribunal proceedings under reg 28 are proceedings to which the Employment Tribunals Act 1996, s 18 applies; see s 18(1)(k) of that Act at **[975]**. There is no fixed conciliation period; see the Employment Tribunals (Constitution and Rules of Procedure) Regulations 2004, SI 2004/1861, Sch 1, rule 22(2).

Employment Appeal Tribunal: an appeal lies to the Employment Appeal Tribunal on any question of law arising from any decision of, or in any proceedings before, an employment tribunal under or by virtue of these Regulations; see the Employment Tribunals Act 1996, s 21(1)(l) at **[978]**.

As to the power of the Commission for Equality and Human Rights to issue a code of practice in connection with any matter addressed by Parts 2 and 3 of these Regulations, see the Equality Act 2006, s 14 at **[1657]**. As of 6 April 2008, no code has been issued under this power.

ARRANGEMENT OF REGULATIONS

PART I
GENERAL

PART II
DISCRIMINATION IN EMPLOYMENT AND VOCATIONAL TRAINING

PART III
OTHER UNLAWFUL ACTS

PART IV
GENERAL EXCEPTIONS FROM PARTS II AND III

PART V
ENFORCEMENT

PART VI
SUPPLEMENTAL

SCHEDULES:

PART I
GENERAL

1 Citation, commencement and extent

(1) These Regulations may be cited as the Employment Equality (Sexual Orientation) Regulations 2003, and shall come into force on 1st December 2003.

(2) These Regulations do not extend to Northern Ireland.

[2987]

NOTES

Commencement: 1 December 2003.

2 Interpretation

(1) In these Regulations, "sexual orientation" means a sexual orientation towards—
(a) persons of the same sex;
(b) persons of the opposite sex; or
(c) persons of the same sex and of the opposite sex.

(2) In these Regulations, references to discrimination are to any discrimination falling within regulation 3 (discrimination on grounds of sexual orientation) or 4 (discrimination by way of victimisation) and related expressions shall be construed accordingly, and references to harassment shall be construed in accordance with regulation 5 (harassment on grounds of sexual orientation).

(3) In these Regulations—
"act" includes a deliberate omission;
["benefits", except in regulation 9A (trustees and managers of occupational pension schemes), includes facilities and services;]
"detriment" does not include harassment within the meaning of regulation 5;
references to "employer", in their application to a person at any time seeking to employ another, include a person who has no employees at that time;
"employment" means employment under a contract of service or of apprenticeship or a contract personally to do any work, and related expressions shall be construed accordingly;
"Great Britain" includes such of the territorial waters of the United Kingdom as are adjacent to Great Britain;
"Minister of the Crown" includes the Treasury and the Defence Council; …
["proprietor", in relation to a school in England and Wales, has the meaning given by section 579 of the Education Act 1996, and, in relation to a school in Scotland, means the governing body, trustees, or other person or body of persons responsible for the management of the school; and]
"school", in England and Wales, has the meaning given by section 4 of the Education Act 1996, and, in Scotland, has the meaning given by section 135(1) of the Education (Scotland) Act 1980, and references to a school are to an institution in so far as it is engaged in the provision of education under those sections.

[2988]

NOTES

Commencement: 1 December 2003.

Para (3): definition "benefits" substituted by the Employment Equality (Sexual Orientation) (Amendment) Regulations 2003, SI 2003/2827, reg 3(1), (2), as from 1 December 2003; definition "proprietor" inserted, and word omitted from the definition "Minister of the Crown" revoked, by the Employment Equality (Sexual Orientation) (Religion or Belief) (Amendment) Regulations 2007, SI 2007/2269, reg 3(1), (2), as from 14 September 2007.

3 Discrimination on grounds of sexual orientation

(1) For the purposes of these Regulations, a person ("A") discriminates against another person ("B") if—
(a) on grounds of sexual orientation, A treats B less favourably than he treats or would treat other persons; or
(b) A applies to B a provision, criterion or practice which he applies or would apply equally to persons not of the same sexual orientation as B, but—
(i) which puts or would put persons of the same sexual orientation as B at a particular disadvantage when compared with other persons,
(ii) which puts B at that disadvantage, and
(iii) which A cannot show to be a proportionate means of achieving a legitimate aim.

(2) A comparison of B's case with that of another person under paragraph (1) must be such that the relevant circumstances in the one case are the same, or not materially different, in the other.

[(3) For the purposes of paragraph (2), in a comparison of B's case with that of another person the fact that one of the persons (whether or not B) is a civil partner while the other is married shall not be treated as a material difference between their respective circumstances.]

[2989]

NOTES

Commencement: 1 December 2003.

Para (3): added by the Civil Partnership Act 2004 (Amendments to Subordinate Legislation) Order 2005, SI 2005/2114, art 2(17), Sch 17, para 7(1), (2), as from 5 December 2005.

4 Discrimination by way of victimisation

(1) For the purposes of these Regulations, a person ("A") discriminates against another person ("B") if he treats B less favourably than he treats or would treat other persons in the same circumstances, and does so by reason that B has—

- (a) brought proceedings against A or any other person under these Regulations;
- (b) given evidence or information in connection with proceedings brought by any person against A or any other person under these Regulations;
- (c) otherwise done anything under or by reference to these Regulations in relation to A or any other person; or
- (d) alleged that A or any other person has committed an act which (whether or not the allegation so states) would amount to a contravention of these Regulations,

or by reason that A knows that B intends to do any of those things, or suspects that B has done or intends to do any of them.

(2) Paragraph (1) does not apply to treatment of B by reason of any allegation made by him, or evidence or information given by him, if the allegation, evidence or information was false and not made (or, as the case may be, given) in good faith.

[2990]

NOTES

Commencement: 1 December 2003.

5 Harassment on grounds of sexual orientation

(1) For the purposes of these Regulations, a person ("A") subjects another person ("B") to harassment where, on grounds of sexual orientation, A engages in unwanted conduct which has the purpose or effect of—

- (a) violating B's dignity; or
- (b) creating an intimidating, hostile, degrading, humiliating or offensive environment for B.

(2) Conduct shall be regarded as having the effect specified in paragraph (1)(a) or (b) only if, having regard to all the circumstances, including in particular the perception of B, it should reasonably be considered as having that effect.

[2991]

NOTES

Commencement: 1 December 2003.

PART II
DISCRIMINATION IN EMPLOYMENT AND VOCATIONAL TRAINING

6 Applicants and employees

(1) It is unlawful for an employer, in relation to employment by him at an establishment in Great Britain, to discriminate against a person—

- (a) in the arrangements he makes for the purpose of determining to whom he should offer employment;
- (b) in the terms on which he offers that person employment; or
- (c) by refusing to offer, or deliberately not offering, him employment.

(2) It is unlawful for an employer, in relation to a person whom he employs at an establishment in Great Britain, to discriminate against that person—

- (a) in the terms of employment which he affords him;
- (b) in the opportunities which he affords him for promotion, a transfer, training, or receiving any other benefit;

(c) by refusing to afford him, or deliberately not affording him, any such opportunity; or

(d) by dismissing him, or subjecting him to any other detriment.

(3) It is unlawful for an employer, in relation to employment by him at an establishment in Great Britain, to subject to harassment a person whom he employs or who has applied to him for employment.

(4) Paragraph (2) does not apply to benefits of any description if the employer is concerned with the provision (for payment or not) of benefits of that description to the public, or to a section of the public which includes the employee in question, unless—

(a) that provision differs in a material respect from the provision of the benefits by the employer to his employees; or

(b) the provision of the benefits to the employee in question is regulated by his contract of employment; or

(c) the benefits relate to training.

(5) In paragraph (2)(d) reference to the dismissal of a person from employment includes reference—

(a) to the termination of that person's employment by the expiration of any period (including a period expiring by reference to an event or circumstance), not being a termination immediately after which the employment is renewed on the same terms; and

(b) to the termination of that person's employment by any act of his (including the giving of notice) in circumstances such that he is entitled to terminate it without notice by reason of the conduct of the employer.

[2992]

NOTES

Commencement: 1 December 2003.

---

7 Exception for genuine occupational requirement etc

(1) In relation to discrimination falling within regulation 3 (discrimination on grounds of sexual orientation)—

(a) regulation 6(1)(a) or (c) does not apply to any employment;

(b) regulation 6(2)(b) or (c) does not apply to promotion or transfer to, or training for, any employment; and

(c) regulation 6(2)(d) does not apply to dismissal from any employment,

where paragraph (2) or (3) applies.

(2) This paragraph applies where, having regard to the nature of the employment or the context in which it is carried out—

(a) being of a particular sexual orientation is a genuine and determining occupational requirement;

(b) it is proportionate to apply that requirement in the particular case; and

(c) either—

(i) the person to whom that requirement is applied does not meet it, or

(ii) the employer is not satisfied, and in all the circumstances it is reasonable for him not to be satisfied, that that person meets it,

and this paragraph applies whether or not the employment is for purposes of an organised religion.

(3) This paragraph applies where—

(a) the employment is for purposes of an organised religion;

(b) the employer applies a requirement related to sexual orientation—

(i) so as to comply with the doctrines of the religion, or

(ii) because of the nature of the employment and the context in which it is carried out, so as to avoid conflicting with the strongly held religious convictions of a significant number of the religion's followers; and

(c) either—

(i) the person to whom that requirement is applied does not meet it, or

(ii) the employer is not satisfied, and in all the circumstances it is reasonable for him not to be satisfied, that that person meets it.

[2993]

NOTES
Commencement: 1 December 2003.

8 Contract workers

(1) It is unlawful for a principal, in relation to contract work at an establishment in Great Britain, to discriminate against a contract worker—

(a) in the terms on which he allows him to do that work;
(b) by not allowing him to do it or continue to do it;
(c) in the way he affords him access to any benefits or by refusing or deliberately not affording him access to them; or
(d) by subjecting him to any other detriment.

(2) It is unlawful for a principal, in relation to contract work at an establishment in Great Britain, to subject a contract worker to harassment.

(3) A principal does not contravene paragraph (1)(b) by doing any act in relation to a contract worker where, if the work were to be done by a person taken into the principal's employment, that act would be lawful by virtue of regulation 7 (exception for genuine occupational requirement etc).

(4) Paragraph (1) does not apply to benefits of any description if the principal is concerned with the provision (for payment or not) of benefits of that description to the public, or to a section of the public to which the contract worker in question belongs, unless that provision differs in a material respect from the provision of the benefits by the principal to his contract workers.

(5) In this regulation—

"principal" means a person ("A") who makes work available for doing by individuals who are employed by another person who supplies them under a contract made with A;

"contract work" means work so made available; and

"contract worker" means any individual who is supplied to the principal under such a contract.

[2994]

NOTES
Commencement: 1 December 2003.

9 Meaning of employment and contract work at establishment in Great Britain

(1) For the purposes of this Part ("the relevant purposes"), employment is to be regarded as being at an establishment in Great Britain if the employee—

(a) does his work wholly or partly in Great Britain; or
(b) does his work wholly outside Great Britain and paragraph (2) applies.

(2) This paragraph applies if—

(a) the employer has a place of business at an establishment in Great Britain;
(b) the work is for the purposes of the business carried on at that establishment; and
(c) the employee is ordinarily resident in Great Britain—
 (i) at the time when he applies for or is offered the employment, or
 (ii) at any time during the course of the employment.

(3) The reference to "employment" in paragraph (1) includes—

(a) employment on board a ship only if the ship is registered at a port of registry in Great Britain, and
(b) employment on an aircraft or hovercraft only if the aircraft or hovercraft is registered in the United Kingdom and operated by a person who has his principal place of business, or is ordinarily resident, in Great Britain.

(4) Subject to paragraph (5), for the purposes of determining if employment concerned with the exploration of the sea bed or sub-soil or the exploitation of their natural resources is outside Great Britain, this regulation has effect as if references to Great Britain included—

(a) any area designated under section 1(7) of the Continental Shelf Act 1964 except an area or part of an area in which the law of Northern Ireland applies; and

(b) in relation to employment concerned with the exploration or exploitation of the Frigg Gas Field, the part of the Norwegian sector of the Continental Shelf described in Schedule 1.

(5) Paragraph (4) shall not apply to employment which is concerned with the exploration or exploitation of the Frigg Gas Field unless the employer is—

(a) a company registered under the Companies Act 1985;

(b) an oversea company which has established a place of business within Great Britain from which it directs the exploration or exploitation in question; or

(c) any other person who has a place of business within Great Britain from which he directs the exploration or exploitation in question.

(6) In this regulation—

"the Frigg Gas Field" means the naturally occurring gas-bearing sand formations of the lower Eocene age located in the vicinity of the intersection of the line of latitude 59 degrees 53 minutes North and of the dividing line between the sectors of the Continental Shelf of the United Kingdom and the Kingdom of Norway and includes all other gas-bearing strata from which gas at the start of production is capable of flowing into the above-mentioned gas-bearing sand formations;

"oversea company" has the same meaning as in section 744 of the Companies Act 1985.

(7) This regulation applies in relation to contract work within the meaning of regulation 8 as it applies in relation to employment; and, in its application to contract work, references to "employee", "employer" and "employment" are references to (respectively) "contract worker", "principal" and "contract work" within the meaning of regulation 8.

[2995]

NOTES

Commencement: 1 December 2003.

[9A Trustees and managers of occupational pension schemes

(1) It is unlawful, except in relation to rights accrued or benefits payable in respect of periods of service prior to the coming into force of these Regulations, for the trustees or managers of an occupational pension scheme to discriminate against a member or prospective member of the scheme in carrying out any of their functions in relation to it (including in particular their functions relating to the admission of members to the scheme and the treatment of members of it).

(2) It is unlawful for the trustees or managers of an occupational pension scheme, in relation to the scheme, to subject to harassment a member or prospective member of it.

(3) Schedule 1A (occupational pension schemes) shall have effect for the purposes of—

(a) defining terms used in this regulation and in that Schedule;

(b) treating every occupational pension scheme as including a non-discrimination rule;

(c) giving trustees or managers of an occupational pension scheme power to alter the scheme so as to secure conformity with the non-discrimination rule;

(d) making provision in relation to the procedures, and remedies which may be granted, on certain complaints relating to occupational pension schemes presented to an employment tribunal under regulation 28 (jurisdiction of employment tribunals).]

[2996]

NOTES

Commencement: 1 December 2003.

Inserted by the Employment Equality (Sexual Orientation) (Amendment) Regulations 2003, SI 2003/2827, reg 3(1), (3), as from 1 December 2003.

10 Office-holders etc

(1) It is unlawful for a relevant person, in relation to an appointment to an office or post to which this regulation applies, to discriminate against a person—

(a) in the arrangements which he makes for the purpose of determining to whom the appointment should be offered;

(b) in the terms on which he offers him the appointment; or

(c) by refusing to offer him the appointment.

(2) It is unlawful, in relation to an appointment to an office or post to which this regulation applies and which is an office or post referred to in paragraph (8)(b), for a relevant person on whose recommendation (or subject to whose approval) appointments to the office or post are made, to discriminate against a person—

(a) in the arrangements which he makes for the purpose of determining who should be recommended or approved in relation to the appointment; or

(b) in making or refusing to make a recommendation, or giving or refusing to give an approval, in relation to the appointment.

(3) It is unlawful for a relevant person, in relation to a person who has been appointed to an office or post to which this regulation applies, to discriminate against him—

(a) in the terms of the appointment;

(b) in the opportunities which he affords him for promotion, a transfer, training or receiving any other benefit, or by refusing to afford him any such opportunity;

(c) by terminating the appointment; or

(d) by subjecting him to any other detriment in relation to the appointment.

(4) It is unlawful for a relevant person, in relation to an office or post to which this regulation applies, to subject to harassment a person—

(a) who has been appointed to the office or post;

(b) who is seeking or being considered for appointment to the office or post; or

(c) who is seeking or being considered for a recommendation or approval in relation to an appointment to an office or post referred to in paragraph (8)(b).

(5) Paragraphs (1) and (3) do not apply to any act in relation to an office or post where, if the office or post constituted employment, that act would be lawful by virtue of regulation 7 (exception for genuine occupational requirement etc); and paragraph (2) does not apply to any act in relation to an office or post where, if the office or post constituted employment, it would be lawful by virtue of regulation 7 to refuse to offer the person such employment.

(6) Paragraph (3) does not apply to benefits of any description if the relevant person is concerned with the provision (for payment or not) of benefits of that description to the public, or a section of the public to which the person appointed belongs, unless—

(a) that provision differs in a material respect from the provision of the benefits by the relevant person to persons appointed to offices or posts which are the same as, or not materially different from, that which the person appointed holds; or

(b) the provision of the benefits to the person appointed is regulated by the terms and conditions of his appointment; or

(c) the benefits relate to training.

(7) In paragraph (3)(c) the reference to the termination of the appointment includes a reference—

(a) to the termination of the appointment by the expiration of any period (including a period expiring by reference to an event or circumstance), not being a termination immediately after which the appointment is renewed on the same terms and conditions; and

(b) to the termination of the appointment by any act of the person appointed (including the giving of notice) in circumstances such that he is entitled to terminate the appointment without notice by reason of the conduct of the relevant person.

(8) This regulation applies to—

(a) any office or post to which persons are appointed to discharge functions personally under the direction of another person, and in respect of which they are entitled to remuneration; and

(b) any office or post to which appointments are made by (or on the recommendation of or subject to the approval of) a Minister of the Crown, a government department, the [Welsh Ministers, the First Minister for Wales, the Counsel General to the Welsh Assembly Government] or any part of the Scottish Administration,

but not to a political office or a case where regulation 6 (applicants and employees), 8 (contract workers), 12 (barristers), 13 (advocates) or 14 (partnerships) applies, or would apply but for the operation of any other provision of these Regulations.

(9) For the purposes of paragraph (8)(a) the holder of an office or post—

(a) is to be regarded as discharging his functions under the direction of another person if that other person is entitled to direct him as to when and where he discharges those functions;
(b) is not to be regarded as entitled to remuneration merely because he is entitled to payments—
(i) in respect of expenses incurred by him in carrying out the functions of the office or post, or
(ii) by way of compensation for the loss of income or benefits he would or might have received from any person had he not been carrying out the functions of the office or post.

(10) In this regulation—
(a) appointment to an office or post does not include election to an office or post;
(b) "political office" means—
(i) any office of the House of Commons held by a member of it,
(ii) a life peerage within the meaning of the Life Peerages Act 1958, or any office of the House of Lords held by a member of it,
(iii) any office mentioned in Schedule 2 (Ministerial offices) to the House of Commons Disqualification Act 1975,
(iv) the offices of Leader of the Opposition, Chief Opposition Whip or Assistant Opposition Whip within the meaning of the Ministerial and other Salaries Act 1975,
(v) any office of the Scottish Parliament held by a member of it,
(vi) a member of the Scottish Executive within the meaning of section 44 of the Scotland Act 1998, or a junior Scottish Minister within the meaning of section 49 of that Act,
(vii) any office of the National Assembly for Wales held by a member of it,
[(viia) a member of the Welsh Assembly Government,]
(viii) in England, any office of a county council, a London borough council, a district council, or a parish council held by a member of it,
(ix) in Wales, any office of a county council, a county borough council, or a community council held by a member of it,
(x) in relation to a council constituted under section 2 of the Local Government etc (Scotland) Act 1994 or a community council established under section 51 of the Local Government (Scotland) Act 1973, any office of such a council held by a member of it,
(xi) any office of the Greater London Authority held by a member of it,
(xii) any office of the Common Council of the City of London held by a member of it,
(xiii) any office of the Council of the Isles of Scilly held by a member of it,
(xiv) any office of a political party;
(c) "relevant person", in relation to an office or post, means—
(i) any person with power to make or terminate appointments to the office or post, or to determine the terms of appointment,
(ii) any person with power to determine the working conditions of a person appointed to the office or post in relation to opportunities for promotion, a transfer, training or for receiving any other benefit, and
(iii) any person or body referred to in paragraph (8)(b) on whose recommendation or subject to whose approval appointments are made to the office or post;
(d) references to making a recommendation include references to making a negative recommendation; and
(e) references to refusal include references to deliberate omission.

[2997]

NOTES

Commencement: 1 December 2003.

Para (8): words in square brackets substituted by the Government of Wales Act 2006 (Consequential Modifications and Transitional Provisions) Order 2007, SI 2007/1388, art 3, Sch 1, para 151(a), as from 25 May 2007.

Para (10): sub-para (b)(viia) inserted by SI 2007/1388, art 3, Sch 1, para 151(b), as from 25 May 2007.

11 Police

(1) [Subject to regulation 11A,] for the purposes of this Part, the holding of the office of constable shall be treated as employment—

(a) by the chief officer of police as respects any act done by him in relation to a constable or that office;
(b) by the police authority as respects any act done by it in relation to a constable or that office.

(2) [Subject to regulation 11A,] for the purposes of regulation 22 (liability of employers and principals)—
(a) the holding of the office of constable shall be treated as employment by the chief officer of police (and as not being employment by any other person); and
(b) anything done by a person holding such an office in the performance, or purported performance, of his functions shall be treated as done in the course of that employment.

(3) There shall be paid out of the police fund—
(a) any compensation, costs or expenses awarded against a chief officer of police in any proceedings brought against him under these Regulations, and any costs or expenses incurred by him in any such proceedings so far as not recovered by him in the proceedings; and
(b) any sum required by a chief officer of police for the settlement of any claim made against him under these Regulations if the settlement is approved by the police authority.

(4) Any proceedings under these Regulations which, by virtue of paragraph (1), would lie against a chief officer of police shall be brought against the chief officer of police for the time being or, in the case of a vacancy in that office, against the person for the time being performing the functions of that office; and references in paragraph (3) to the chief officer of police shall be construed accordingly.

(5) A police authority may, in such cases and to such extent as appear to it to be appropriate, pay out of the police fund—
(a) any compensation, costs or expenses awarded in proceedings under these Regulations against a person under the direction and control of the chief officer of police;
(b) any costs or expenses incurred and not recovered by such a person in such proceedings; and
(c) any sum required in connection with the settlement of a claim that has or might have given rise to such proceedings.

(6) Paragraphs (1) and (2) apply to a police cadet and appointment as a police cadet as they apply to a constable and the office of constable.

(7) Subject to paragraph (8), in this regulation—

"chief officer of police"—
(a) in relation to a person appointed, or an appointment falling to be made, under a specified Act, has the same meaning as in the Police Act 1996,
(b) . . .
(c) in relation to a person appointed, or an appointment falling to be made, under the Police (Scotland) Act 1967, means the chief constable of the relevant police force,
(d) in relation to any other person or appointment means the officer or other person who has the direction and control of the body of constables or cadets in question;

"police authority"—
(a) in relation to a person appointed, or an appointment falling to be made, under a specified Act, has the same meaning as in the Police Act 1996,
(b) . . .
(c) in relation to a person appointed, or an appointment falling to be made, under the Police (Scotland) Act 1967, has the meaning given in that Act,
(d) in relation to any other person or appointment, means the authority by whom the person in question is or on appointment would be paid;

"police cadet" means any person appointed to undergo training with a view to becoming a constable;

"police fund"—
(a) in relation to a chief officer of police within sub-paragraph (a) of the above definition of that term, has the same meaning as in the Police Act 1996,
(b) . . .
(c) in any other case means money provided by the police authority; and

"specified Act" means the Metropolitan Police Act 1829, the City of London Police Act 1839 or the Police Act 1996.

(8) In relation to a constable of a force who is not under the direction and control of the chief officer of police for that force, references in this regulation to the chief officer of police are references to the chief officer of the force under whose direction and control he is, and references in this regulation to the police authority are references to the relevant police authority for that force.

[2998]

NOTES

Commencement: 1 December 2003.

Paras (1), (2): words in square brackets inserted by the Serious Organised Crime and Police Act 2005 (Consequential and Supplementary Amendments to Secondary Legislation) Order 2006, SI 2006/594, art 2, Schedule, para 37(1)–(3), as from 1 April 2006.

Para (7): para (b) of definitions "chief officer of police", "police authority", and "police fund" revoked by SI 2006/594, art 2, Schedule, para 37(1), (4), as from 1 April 2006.

[11A Serious Organised Crime Agency

(1) For the purposes of this Part, any constable or other person who has been seconded to SOCA to serve as a member of its staff shall be treated as employed by SOCA.

(2) For the purposes of regulation 22 (liability of employers and principals)—

(a) the secondment of any constable or other person to SOCA to serve as a member of its staff shall be treated as employment by SOCA (and not as being employment by any other person); and

(b) anything done by a person so seconded in the performance, or purported performance, of his functions shall be treated as done in the course of that employment.

(3) In this regulation "SOCA" means the Serious Organised Crime Agency.]

[2998A]

NOTES

Commencement: 1 April 2006.

Inserted by the Serious Organised Crime and Police Act 2005 (Consequential and Supplementary Amendments to Secondary Legislation) Order 2006, SI 2006/594, art 2, Schedule, para 37(1), (5), as from 1 April 2006.

12 Barristers

(1) It is unlawful for a barrister or barrister's clerk, in relation to any offer of a pupillage or tenancy, to discriminate against a person—

(a) in the arrangements which are made for the purpose of determining to whom the pupillage or tenancy should be offered;

(b) in respect of any terms on which it is offered; or

(c) by refusing, or deliberately not offering, it to him.

(2) It is unlawful for a barrister or barrister's clerk, in relation to a pupil or tenant in the set of chambers in question, to discriminate against him—

(a) in respect of any terms applicable to him as a pupil or tenant;

(b) in the opportunities for training, or gaining experience, which are afforded or denied to him;

(c) in the benefits which are afforded or denied to him; or

(d) by terminating his pupillage, or by subjecting him to any pressure to leave the chambers or other detriment.

(3) It is unlawful for a barrister or barrister's clerk, in relation to a pupillage or tenancy in the set of chambers in question, to subject to harassment a person who is, or has applied to be, a pupil or tenant.

(4) It is unlawful for any person, in relation to the giving, withholding or acceptance of instructions to a barrister, to discriminate against any person by subjecting him to a detriment, or to subject him to harassment.

(5) In this regulation—

"barrister's clerk" includes any person carrying out any of the functions of a barrister's clerk;

"pupil", "pupillage" and "set of chambers" have the meanings commonly associated with their use in the context of barristers practising in independent practice; and

"tenancy" and "tenant" have the meanings commonly associated with their use in the context of barristers practising in independent practice, but also include reference to any barrister permitted to work in a set of chambers who is not a tenant.

(6) This regulation extends to England and Wales only.

[2999]

NOTES

Commencement: 1 December 2003.

13 Advocates

(1) It is unlawful for an advocate, in relation to taking any person as his pupil, to discriminate against a person—

(a) in the arrangements which he makes for the purpose of determining whom he will take as his pupil;

(b) in respect of any terms on which he offers to take any person as his pupil; or

(c) by refusing to take, or deliberately not taking, a person as his pupil.

(2) It is unlawful for an advocate, in relation to a person who is his pupil, to discriminate against him—

(a) in respect of any terms applicable to him as a pupil;

(b) in the opportunities for training, or gaining experience, which are afforded or denied to him;

(c) in the benefits which are afforded or denied to him; or

(d) by terminating the relationship, or by subjecting him to any pressure to terminate the relationship or other detriment.

(3) It is unlawful for an advocate, in relation to a person who is his pupil or taking any person as his pupil, to subject such a person to harassment.

(4) It is unlawful for any person, in relation to the giving, withholding or acceptance of instructions to an advocate, to discriminate against any person by subjecting him to a detriment, or to subject him to harassment.

(5) In this regulation—

"advocate" means a member of the Faculty of Advocates practising as such; and

"pupil" has the meaning commonly associated with its use in the context of a person training to be an advocate.

(6) This regulation extends to Scotland only.

[3000]

NOTES

Commencement: 1 December 2003.

14 Partnerships

(1) It is unlawful for a firm, in relation to a position as partner in the firm, to discriminate against a person—

(a) in the arrangements they make for the purpose of determining to whom they should offer that position;

(b) in the terms on which they offer him that position;

(c) by refusing to offer, or deliberately not offering, him that position; or

(d) in a case where the person already holds that position—

(i) in the way they afford him access to any benefits or by refusing to afford, or deliberately not affording, him access to them, or

(ii) by expelling him from that position, or subjecting him to any other detriment.

(2) It is unlawful for a firm, in relation to a position as partner in the firm, to subject to harassment a person who holds or has applied for that position.

(3) Paragraphs (1)(a) to (c) and (2) apply in relation to persons proposing to form themselves into a partnership as they apply in relation to a firm.

(4) Paragraph (1) does not apply to any act in relation to a position as partner where, if the position were employment, that act would be lawful by virtue of regulation 7 (exception for genuine occupational requirement etc).

(5) In the case of a limited partnership references in this regulation to a partner shall be construed as references to a general partner as defined in section 3 of the Limited Partnerships Act 1907.

(6) This regulation applies to a limited liability partnership as it applies to a firm; and, in its application to a limited liability partnership, references to a partner in a firm are references to a member of the limited liability partnership.

(7) In this regulation, "firm" has the meaning given by section 4 of the Partnership Act 1890.

(8) In paragraph (1)(d) reference to the expulsion of a person from a position as partner includes reference—

(a) to the termination of that person's partnership by the expiration of any period (including a period expiring by reference to an event or circumstance), not being a termination immediately after which the partnership is renewed on the same terms; and

(b) to the termination of that person's partnership by any act of his (including the giving of notice) in circumstances such that he is entitled to terminate it without notice by reason of the conduct of the other partners.

[3001]

NOTES

Commencement: 1 December 2003.

15 Trade organisations

(1) It is unlawful for a trade organisation to discriminate against a person—

(a) in the terms on which it is prepared to admit him to membership of the organisation; or

(b) by refusing to accept, or deliberately not accepting, his application for membership.

(2) It is unlawful for a trade organisation, in relation to a member of the organisation, to discriminate against him—

(a) in the way it affords him access to any benefits or by refusing or deliberately omitting to afford him access to them;

(b) by depriving him of membership, or varying the terms on which he is a member; or

(c) by subjecting him to any other detriment.

(3) It is unlawful for a trade organisation, in relation to a person's membership or application for membership of that organisation, to subject that person to harassment.

(4) In this regulation—

"trade organisation" means an organisation of workers, an organisation of employers, or any other organisation whose members carry on a particular profession or trade for the purposes of which the organisation exists;

"profession" includes any vocation or occupation; and

"trade" includes any business.

[3002]

NOTES

Commencement: 1 December 2003.

16 Qualifications bodies

(1) It is unlawful for a qualifications body to discriminate against a person—

(a) in the terms on which it is prepared to confer a professional or trade qualification on him;

(b) by refusing or deliberately not granting any application by him for such a qualification; or

(c) by withdrawing such a qualification from him or varying the terms on which he holds it.

(2) It is unlawful for a qualifications body, in relation to a professional or trade qualification conferred by it, to subject to harassment a person who holds or applies for such a qualification.

(3) Paragraph (1) does not apply to a professional or trade qualification for purposes of an organised religion where a requirement related to sexual orientation is applied to the qualification so as to comply with the doctrines of the religion or avoid conflicting with the strongly held religious convictions of a significant number of the religion's followers.

(4) In this regulation—

"qualifications body" means any authority or body which can confer a professional or trade qualification, but it does not include—

(a) [a governing body of] an educational establishment to which regulation 20 (institutions of further and higher education) applies, or would apply but for the operation of any other provision of these Regulations, or

(b) [a proprietor of] a school;

"confer" includes renew or extend;

"professional or trade qualification" means any authorisation, qualification, recognition, registration, enrolment, approval or certification which is needed for, or facilitates engagement in, a particular profession or trade;

"profession" and "trade" have the same meaning as in regulation 15.

[3003]

NOTES

Commencement: 1 December 2003.

Para (4): words in square brackets in definition "qualifications body" inserted by the Employment Equality (Sexual Orientation) (Religion or Belief) (Amendment) Regulations 2007, SI 2007/2269, reg 3(1), (3), as from 14 September 2007.

17 [The provision of vocational training]

(1) It is unlawful, in relation to a person seeking or undergoing training which would help fit him for any employment, for any training provider to discriminate against him—

[(aa) in the arrangements he makes for the purpose of determining to whom he should offer training;]

(a) in the terms on which the training provider affords him access to any training;

(b) by refusing or deliberately not affording him such access;

(c) by terminating his training; or

(d) by subjecting him to any other detriment during his training.

(2) It is unlawful for a training provider, in relation to a person seeking or undergoing training which would help fit him for any employment, to subject him to harassment.

(3) Paragraph (1) does not apply if the discrimination only concerns training for employment which, by virtue of regulation 7 (exception for genuine occupational requirement etc), the employer could lawfully refuse to offer the person seeking training.

(4) In this regulation—

["registered pupil", in England and Wales, has the meaning given by section 434(5) of the Education Act 1996, and, in Scotland, means a pupil deemed to be attending or in attendance at a school in terms of section 135(1) of the Education (Scotland) Act 1980;]

["training" means—

(a) all types and all levels of training which would help fit a person for any employment;

(b) vocational guidance;

(c) facilities for training;

(d) practical work experience provided by an employer to a person whom he does not employ; and

(e) any assessment related to the award of any professional or trade qualification;]

"training provider" means any person who provides, or makes arrangements for the provision of, training which would help fit another person for any employment, but it does not include—

(a) an employer in relation to training for persons employed by him;

[(b) a governing body of an educational establishment to which regulation 20 (institutions of further and higher education) applies, or would apply but for the operation of any other provision of these Regulations, except in relation to a person who is undertaking practical work experience at the educational establishment and is not a student at, or employed by, that establishment; or]

[(c) a proprietor of a school in relation to a pupil registered at that or another school, except where that pupil is undertaking practical work experience provided by a school at which he is not registered and he is not employed by that school].

[3004]

NOTES

Commencement: 1 December 2003.

Section heading: substituted by the Employment Equality (Sexual Orientation) (Religion or Belief) (Amendment) Regulations 2007, SI 2007/2269, reg 3(1), (4)(a), as from 14 September 2007.

Para (1): sub-para (aa) inserted by SI 2007/2269, reg 3(1), (4)(b), as from 14 September 2007.

Para (4): definition "registered pupil" inserted, definition "training" substituted, and in definition "training provider" paras (b), (c) substituted, by SI 2007/2269, reg 3(1), (4)(c), as from 14 September 2007.

18 Employment agencies, careers guidance etc

(1) It is unlawful for an employment agency to discriminate against a person—

(a) in the terms on which the agency offers to provide any of its services;

(b) by refusing or deliberately not providing any of its services; or

(c) in the way it provides any of its services.

(2) It is unlawful for an employment agency, in relation to a person to whom it provides its services, or who has requested it to provide its services, to subject that person to harassment.

(3) Paragraph (1) does not apply to discrimination if it only concerns employment which, by virtue of regulation 7 (exception for genuine occupational requirement etc), the employer could lawfully refuse to offer the person in question.

(4) An employment agency shall not be subject to any liability under this regulation if it proves that—

(a) it acted in reliance on a statement made to it by the employer to the effect that, by reason of the operation of paragraph (3), its action would not be unlawful, and

(b) it was reasonable for it to rely on the statement.

(5) A person who knowingly or recklessly makes a statement such as is referred to in paragraph (4)(a) which in a material respect is false or misleading commits an offence, and shall be liable on summary conviction to a fine not exceeding level 5 on the standard scale.

(6) For the purposes of this regulation—

(a) "employment agency" means a person who, for profit or not, provides services for the purpose of finding employment for workers or supplying employers with workers, but it does not include—

(i) [a governing body of] an educational establishment to which regulation 20 (institutions of further and higher education) applies, or would apply but for the operation of any other provision of these Regulations, or

(ii) [a proprietor of] a school; and

(b) references to the services of an employment agency include guidance on careers and any other services related to employment.

[3005]

NOTES

Commencement: 1 December 2003.

Para (6): words in square brackets inserted by the Employment Equality (Sexual Orientation) (Religion or Belief) (Amendment) Regulations 2007, SI 2007/2269, reg 3(1), (5), as from 14 September 2007.

19 Assisting persons to obtain employment etc

(1) It is unlawful for the Secretary of State to discriminate against any person by subjecting him to a detriment, or to subject a person to harassment, in the provision of facilities or services under section 2 of the Employment and Training Act 1973 (arrangements for assisting persons to obtain employment).

(2) It is unlawful for Scottish Enterprise or Highlands and Islands Enterprise to discriminate against any person by subjecting him to a detriment, or to subject a person to harassment, in the provision of facilities or services under such arrangements as are mentioned in section 2(3) of the Enterprise and New Towns (Scotland) Act 1990 (arrangements analogous to arrangements in pursuance of the said Act of 1973).

(3) This regulation does not apply in a case where—

- (a) regulation 17 (providers of vocational training) applies, or would apply but for the operation of any other provision of these Regulations, or
- (b) the Secretary of State is acting as an employment agency within the meaning of regulation 18.

[3006]

NOTES

Commencement: 1 December 2003.

20 Institutions of further and higher education

(1) It is unlawful, in relation to an educational establishment to which this regulation applies, for the governing body of that establishment to discriminate against a person—

- (a) in the terms on which it offers to admit him to the establishment as a student;
- (b) by refusing or deliberately not accepting an application for his admission to the establishment as a student; or
- (c) where he is a student of the establishment—
  - (i) in the way it affords him access to any benefits,
  - (ii) by refusing or deliberately not affording him access to them, or
  - (iii) by excluding him from the establishment or subjecting him to any other detriment.

(2) It is unlawful, in relation to an educational establishment to which this regulation applies, for the governing body of that establishment to subject to harassment a person who is a student at the establishment, or who has applied for admission to the establishment as a student.

(3) Paragraph (1) does not apply if the discrimination only concerns training which would help fit a person for employment which, by virtue of regulation 7 (exception for genuine occupational requirement etc), the employer could lawfully refuse to offer the person in question.

(4) This regulation applies to the following educational establishments in England and Wales, namely—

- (a) an institution within the further education sector (within the meaning of section 91(3) of the Further and Higher Education Act 1992);
- (b) a university;
- (c) an institution, other than a university, within the higher education sector (within the meaning of section 91(5) of the Further and Higher Education Act 1992).

(5) This regulation applies to the following educational establishments in Scotland, namely—

- (a) a college of further education within the meaning of section 36(1) of the Further and Higher Education (Scotland) Act 1992 under the management of a board of management within the meaning of Part I of that Act;
- (b) a college of further education maintained by an education authority in the exercise of its further education functions in providing courses of further education within the meaning of section 1(5)(b)(ii) of the Education (Scotland) Act 1980;
- (c) any other educational establishment (not being a school) which provides further education within the meaning of section 1 of the Further and Higher Education (Scotland) Act 1992;
- (d) an institution within the higher education sector (within the meaning of Part II of the Further and Higher Education (Scotland) Act 1992);

(e) a central institution (within the meaning of section 135 of the Education (Scotland) Act 1980).

(6) In this regulation—

"education authority" has the meaning given by section 135(1) of the Education (Scotland) Act 1980;

"governing body" includes—

(a) the board of management of a college referred to in paragraph (5)(a), and

(b) the managers of a college or institution referred to in paragraph (5)(b) or (e);

"student" means any person who receives education at an educational establishment to which this regulation applies; and

"university" includes a university college and the college, school or hall of a university.

[3007]

NOTES

Commencement: 1 December 2003.

21 Relationships which have come to an end

(1) In this regulation a "relevant relationship" is a relationship during the course of which an act of discrimination against, or harassment of, one party to the relationship ("B") by the other party to it ("A") is unlawful by virtue of any preceding provision of this Part.

(2) Where a relevant relationship has come to an end, it is unlawful for A—

(a) to discriminate against B by subjecting him to a detriment; or

(b) to subject B to harassment,

where the discrimination or harassment arises out of and is closely connected to that relationship.

(3) In paragraph (1), reference to an act of discrimination or harassment which is unlawful includes, in the case of a relationship which has come to an end before the coming into force of these Regulations, reference to an act of discrimination or harassment which would, after the coming into force of these Regulations, be unlawful.

[3008]

NOTES

Commencement: 1 December 2003.

PART III
OTHER UNLAWFUL ACTS

22 Liability of employers and principals

(1) Anything done by a person in the course of his employment shall be treated for the purposes of these Regulations as done by his employer as well as by him, whether or not it was done with the employer's knowledge or approval.

(2) Anything done by a person as agent for another person with the authority (whether express or implied, and whether precedent or subsequent) of that other person shall be treated for the purposes of these Regulations as done by that other person as well as by him.

(3) In proceedings brought under these Regulations against any person in respect of an act alleged to have been done by an employee of his it shall be a defence for that person to prove that he took such steps as were reasonably practicable to prevent the employee from doing that act, or from doing in the course of his employment acts of that description.

[3009]

NOTES

Commencement: 1 December 2003.

23 Aiding unlawful acts

(1) A person who knowingly aids another person to do an act made unlawful by these Regulations shall be treated for the purpose of these Regulations as himself doing an unlawful act of the like description.

(2) For the purposes of paragraph (1) an employee or agent for whose act the employer or principal is liable under regulation 22 (or would be so liable but for regulation 22(3)) shall be deemed to aid the doing of the act by the employer or principal.

(3) A person does not under this regulation knowingly aid another to do an unlawful act if—

(a) he acts in reliance on a statement made to him by that other person that, by reason of any provision of these Regulations, the act which he aids would not be unlawful; and

(b) it is reasonable for him to rely on the statement.

(4) A person who knowingly or recklessly makes a statement such as is referred to in paragraph (3)(a) which in a material respect is false or misleading commits an offence, and shall be liable on summary conviction to a fine not exceeding level 5 on the standard scale.

[3010]

NOTES

Commencement: 1 December 2003.

PART IV
GENERAL EXCEPTIONS FROM PARTS II AND III

24 Exception for national security

Nothing in Part II or III shall render unlawful an act done for the purpose of safeguarding national security, if the doing of the act was justified by that purpose.

[3011]

NOTES

Commencement: 1 December 2003.

[25 Exception for benefits dependent on a person's status

Nothing in Part II or III shall render unlawful—

(a) anything which prevents or restricts access to a benefit by reference to marital status where the right to the benefit accrued or the benefit is payable in respect of periods of service prior to the coming into force of the Civil Partnership Act 2004;

(b) the conferring of a benefit on married persons and civil partners to the exclusion of all other persons.]

[3012]

NOTES

Commencement: 5 December 2005.

Substituted by the Civil Partnership Act 2004 (Amendments to Subordinate Legislation) Order 2005, SI 2005/2114, art 2(17), Sch 17, para 7(1), (3), as from 5 December 2005.

26 Exceptions for positive action

(1) Nothing in Part II or III shall render unlawful any act done in or in connection with—

(a) affording persons of a particular sexual orientation access to facilities for training which would help fit them for particular work; or

(b) encouraging persons of a particular sexual orientation to take advantage of opportunities for doing particular work,

where it reasonably appears to the person doing the act that it prevents or compensates for disadvantages linked to sexual orientation suffered by persons of that sexual orientation doing that work or likely to take up that work.

(2) Nothing in Part II or III shall render unlawful any act done by a trade organisation within the meaning of regulation 15 in or in connection with—

(a) affording only members of the organisation who are of a particular sexual orientation access to facilities for training which would help fit them for holding a post of any kind in the organisation; or

(b) encouraging only members of the organisation who are of a particular sexual orientation to take advantage of opportunities for holding such posts in the organisation, where it reasonably appears to the organisation that the act prevents or compensates for disadvantages linked to sexual orientation suffered by those of that sexual orientation holding such posts or likely to hold such posts.

(3) Nothing in Part II or III shall render unlawful any act done by a trade organisation within the meaning of regulation 15 in or in connection with encouraging only persons of a particular sexual orientation to become members of the organisation where it reasonably appears to the organisation that the act prevents or compensates for disadvantages linked to sexual orientation suffered by persons of that sexual orientation who are, or are eligible to become, members.

[3013]

NOTES

Commencement: 1 December 2003.

PART V
ENFORCEMENT

27 Restriction of proceedings for breach of Regulations

(1) Except as provided by these Regulations no proceedings, whether civil or criminal, shall lie against any person in respect of an act by reason that the act is unlawful by virtue of a provision of these Regulations.

(2) Paragraph (1) does not prevent the making of an application for judicial review [or the investigation or determination of any matter in accordance with Part X (investigations: the Pensions Ombudsman) of the Pension Schemes Act 1993 by the Pensions Ombudsman].

[3014]

NOTES

Commencement: 1 December 2003.

Para (2): words in square brackets inserted by the Employment Equality (Sexual Orientation) (Amendment) Regulations 2003, SI 2003/2827, reg 3(1), (4), as from 1 December 2003.

28 Jurisdiction of employment tribunals

(1) A complaint by any person ("the complainant") that another person ("the respondent")—

(a) has committed against the complainant an act to which this regulation applies; or

(b) is by virtue of regulation 22 (liability of employers and principals) or 23 (aiding unlawful acts) to be treated as having committed against the complainant such an act,

may be presented to an employment tribunal.

(2) This regulation applies to any act of discrimination or harassment which is unlawful by virtue of any provision of Part II other than—

(a) where the act is one in respect of which an appeal or proceedings in the nature of an appeal may be brought under any enactment, regulation 16 (qualifications bodies);

(b) regulation 20 (institutions of further and higher education); or

(c) where the act arises out of and is closely connected to a relationship between the complainant and the respondent which has come to an end but during the course of which an act of discrimination against, or harassment of, the complainant by the respondent would have been unlawful by virtue of regulation 20, regulation 21 (relationships which have come to an end).

(3) In paragraph (2)(c), reference to an act of discrimination or harassment which would have been unlawful includes, in the case of a relationship which has come to an end before the coming into force of these Regulations, reference to an act of discrimination or harassment which would, after the coming into force of these Regulations, have been unlawful.

(4) In this regulation, "enactment" includes an enactment comprised in, or in an instrument made under, an Act of the Scottish Parliament.

[3015]

NOTES

Commencement: 1 December 2003.

Conciliation: employment tribunal proceedings and claims which could be the subject of employment tribunal proceedings under this regulation are proceedings to which the Employment Tribunals Act 1996, s 18 applies; see s 18(1)(k) of that Act at **[975]**. There is no fixed conciliation period for such proceedings: see the Employment Tribunals (Constitution and Rules of Procedure) Regulations 2004, SI 2004/1861, Sch 1, rule 22(1), (2) at **[3171]**.

Tribunal jurisdiction: the Employment Act 2002, ss 31, 32, 38, at **[1493]**, **[1494]**, **[1496]** apply to proceedings before the employment tribunal relating to a claim under this regulation; see ss 31(1), 32(1), 38(1) of, and Schs 3–5 to, the 2002 Act at **[1508]–[1510]**.

For the circumstances in which the normal time limit for presenting a complaint under this regulation is extended for a period of three months, see the Employment Act 2002 (Dispute Resolution) Regulations 2004, SI 2004/752, regs 15 and 18 at **[3096]** and **[3098]**, and reg 34 of these Regulations at **[3021]**.

29 Burden of proof: employment tribunals

(1) This regulation applies to any complaint presented under regulation 28 to an employment tribunal.

(2) Where, on the hearing of the complaint, the complainant proves facts from which the tribunal could, apart from this regulation, conclude in the absence of an adequate explanation that the respondent—

(a) has committed against the complainant an act to which regulation 28 applies; or

(b) is by virtue of regulation 22 (liability of employers and principals) or 23 (aiding unlawful acts) to be treated as having committed against the complainant such an act,

the tribunal shall uphold the complaint unless the respondent proves that he did not commit, or as the case may be, is not to be treated as having committed, that act.

[3016]

NOTES

Commencement: 1 December 2003.

30 Remedies on complaints in employment tribunals

(1) Where an employment tribunal finds that a complaint presented to it under regulation 28 is well-founded, the tribunal shall make such of the following as it considers just and equitable—

(a) an order declaring the rights of the complainant and the respondent in relation to the act to which the complaint relates;

(b) an order requiring the respondent to pay to the complainant compensation of an amount corresponding to any damages he could have been ordered by a county court or by a sheriff court to pay to the complainant if the complaint had fallen to be dealt with under regulation 31 (jurisdiction of county and sheriff courts);

(c) a recommendation that the respondent take within a specified period action appearing to the tribunal to be practicable for the purpose of obviating or reducing the adverse effect on the complainant of any act of discrimination or harassment to which the complaint relates.

(2) As respects an unlawful act of discrimination falling within regulation 3(1)(b), if the respondent proves that the provision, criterion or practice was not applied with the intention of treating the complainant unfavourably on grounds of sexual orientation, an order may be made under paragraph (1)(b) only if the employment tribunal—

(a) makes such order under paragraph (1)(a) (if any) and such recommendation under paragraph (1)(c) (if any) as it would have made if it had no power to make an order under paragraph (1)(b); and

(b) (where it makes an order under paragraph (1)(a) or a recommendation under paragraph (1)(c) or both) considers that it is just and equitable to make an order under paragraph (1)(b) as well.

(3) If without reasonable justification the respondent to a complaint fails to comply with a recommendation made by an employment tribunal under paragraph (1)(c), then, if it thinks it just and equitable to do so—

(a) the tribunal may increase the amount of compensation required to be paid to the complainant in respect of the complaint by an order made under paragraph (1)(b); or

(b) if an order under paragraph (1)(b) was not made, the tribunal may make such an order.

(4) Where an amount of compensation falls to be awarded under paragraph (1)(b), the tribunal may include in the award interest on that amount subject to, and in accordance with, the provisions of the Employment Tribunals (Interest on Awards in Discrimination Cases) Regulations 1996.

[(5) This regulation has effect subject to paragraph 7 of Schedule 1A (occupational pension schemes).]

[3017]

NOTES

Commencement: 1 December 2003.

Para (5): added by the Employment Equality (Sexual Orientation) (Amendment) Regulations 2003, SI 2003/2827, reg 3(1), (5), as from 1 December 2003.

Compensation for dismissal: as to the powers of an employment tribunal to award compensation where any act constitutes both unfair dismissal under the Employment Rights Act 1996, and discrimination under any one or more of the Sex Discrimination Act 1975, the Race Relations Act 1976, the Disability Discrimination Act 1995, the Employment Equality (Sexual Orientation) Regulations 2003, the Employment Equality (Religion or Belief) Regulations 2003, or the Employment Equality (Age) Regulations 2006, see s 126 of the 1996 Act at **[1170]**.

31 Jurisdiction of county and sheriff courts

(1) A claim by any person ("the claimant") that another person ("the respondent")—

(a) has committed against the claimant an act to which this regulation applies; or

(b) is by virtue of regulation 22 (liability of employers and principals) or 23 (aiding unlawful acts) to be treated as having committed against the claimant such an act,

may be made the subject of civil proceedings in like manner as any other claim in tort or (in Scotland) in reparation for breach of statutory duty.

(2) Proceedings brought under paragraph (1) shall—

(a) in England and Wales, be brought only in a county court; and

(b) in Scotland, be brought only in a sheriff court.

(3) For the avoidance of doubt it is hereby declared that damages in respect of an unlawful act to which this regulation applies may include compensation for injury to feelings whether or not they include compensation under any other head.

(4) This regulation applies to any act of discrimination or harassment which is unlawful by virtue of—

(a) regulation 20 (institutions of further and higher education); or

(b) where the act arises out of and is closely connected to a relationship between the claimant and the respondent which has come to an end but during the course of which an act of discrimination against, or harassment of, the claimant by the respondent would have been unlawful by virtue of regulation 20, regulation 21 (relationships which have come to an end).

(5) In paragraph (4)(b), reference to an act of discrimination or harassment which would have been unlawful includes, in the case of a relationship which has come to an end before the coming into force of these Regulations, reference to an act of discrimination or harassment which would, after the coming into force of these Regulations, have been unlawful.

[3018]

NOTES

Commencement: 1 December 2003.

Conciliation: the Commission for Equality and Human Rights may make arrangements for the provision of conciliation services for disputes in respect of which proceedings have been, or could be, brought under this regulation; see the Equality Act 2006, s 27 at **[1670]**.

32 Burden of proof: county and sheriff courts

(1) This regulation applies to any claim brought under regulation 31 in a county court in England and Wales or a sheriff court in Scotland.

(2) Where, on the hearing of the claim, the claimant proves facts from which the court could, apart from this regulation, conclude in the absence of an adequate explanation that the respondent—

(a) has committed against the claimant an act to which regulation 31 applies; or

(b) is by virtue of regulation 22 (liability of employers and principals) or 23 (aiding unlawful acts) to be treated as having committed against the claimant such an act,

the court shall uphold the claim unless the respondent proves that he did not commit, or as the case may be, is not to be treated as having committed, that act.

[3019]

NOTES

Commencement: 1 December 2003.

33 Help for persons in obtaining information etc

(1) In accordance with this regulation, a person ("the person aggrieved") who considers he may have been discriminated against, or subjected to harassment, in contravention of these Regulations may serve on the respondent to a complaint presented under regulation 28 (jurisdiction of employment tribunals) or a claim brought under regulation 31 (jurisdiction of county and sheriff courts) questions in the form set out in Schedule 2 or forms to the like effect with such variation as the circumstances require; and the respondent may if he so wishes reply to such questions by way of the form set out in Schedule 3 or forms to the like effect with such variation as the circumstances require.

(2) Where the person aggrieved questions the respondent (whether in accordance with paragraph (1) or not)—

(a) the questions, and any reply by the respondent (whether in accordance with paragraph (1) or not) shall, subject to the following provisions of this regulation, be admissible as evidence in the proceedings;

(b) if it appears to the court or tribunal that the respondent deliberately, and without reasonable excuse, omitted to reply within eight weeks of service of the questions or that his reply is evasive or equivocal, the court or tribunal may draw any inference from that fact that it considers it just and equitable to draw, including an inference that he committed an unlawful act.

(3) In proceedings before a county court in England or Wales or a sheriff court in Scotland, a question shall only be admissible as evidence in pursuance of paragraph (2)(a)—

(a) where it was served before those proceedings had been instituted, if it was so served within the period of six months beginning when the act complained of was done;

(b) where it was served when those proceedings had been instituted, if it was served with the leave of, and within a period specified by, the court in question.

(4) In proceedings before an employment tribunal, a question shall only be admissible as evidence in pursuance of paragraph (2)(a)—

[(a) where it was served before a complaint had been presented to a tribunal, if it was so served—

(i) within the period of three months beginning when the act complained of was done; or

(ii) where paragraph (1A) of regulation 34 applies, within the extended period;]

(b) where it was served when a complaint had been presented to the tribunal, either—

(i) if it was so served within the period of twenty-one days beginning with the day on which the complaint was presented, or

(ii) if it was so served later with leave given, and within a period specified, by a direction of the tribunal.

(5) A question and any reply thereto may be served on the respondent or, as the case may be, on the person aggrieved—

(a) by delivering it to him;

(b) by sending it by post to him at his usual or last-known residence or place of business;

(c) where the person to be served is a body corporate or is a trade union or employers' association within the meaning of the Trade Union and Labour Relations (Consolidation) Act 1992, by delivering it to the secretary or clerk of the body, union or association at its registered or principal office or by sending it by post to the secretary or clerk at that office;

(d) where the person to be served is acting by a solicitor, by delivering it at, or by sending it by post to, the solicitor's address for service; or

(e) where the person to be served is the person aggrieved, by delivering the reply, or sending it by post, to him at his address for reply as stated by him in the document containing the questions.

(6) This regulation is without prejudice to any other enactment or rule of law regulating interlocutory and preliminary matters in proceedings before a county court, sheriff court or employment tribunal, and has effect subject to any enactment or rule of law regulating the admissibility of evidence in such proceedings.

(7) In this regulation "respondent" includes a prospective respondent.

[3020]

NOTES

Commencement: 1 December 2003.

Para (4): sub-para (a) substituted by the Employment Act 2002 (Dispute Resolution) Regulations 2004, SI 2004/752, reg 17(h)(i), as from 1 October 2004 (for transitional provisions and effect see reg 18 of those Regulations at **[3098]**).

34 Period within which proceedings to be brought

(1) An employment tribunal shall not consider a complaint under regulation 28 unless it is presented to the tribunal before the end of—

(a) the period of three months beginning when the act complained of was done; or

(b) in a case to which regulation 36(7) (armed forces) applies, the period of six months so beginning.

[(1A) Where the period within which a complaint must be presented in accordance with paragraph (1) is extended by regulation 15 of the Employment Act 2002 (Dispute Resolution) Regulations 2004, the period within which the complaint must be presented shall be the extended period rather than the period in paragraph (1).]

(2) A county court or a sheriff court shall not consider a claim brought under regulation 31 unless proceedings in respect of the claim are instituted before the end of the period of six months beginning when the act complained of was done.

(3) A court or tribunal may nevertheless consider any such complaint or claim which is out of time if, in all the circumstances of the case, it considers that it is just and equitable to do so.

(4) For the purposes of this regulation and regulation 33 (help for persons in obtaining information etc)—

(a) when the making of a contract is, by reason of the inclusion of any term, an unlawful act, that act shall be treated as extending throughout the duration of the contract; and

(b) any act extending over a period shall be treated as done at the end of that period; and

(c) a deliberate omission shall be treated as done when the person in question decided upon it,

and in the absence of evidence establishing the contrary a person shall be taken for the purposes of this regulation to decide upon an omission when he does an act inconsistent with doing the omitted act or, if he has done no such inconsistent act, when the period expires within which he might reasonably have been expected to do the omitted act if it was to be done.

[3021]

NOTES

Commencement: 1 December 2003.

Para (1A): inserted by the Employment Act 2002 (Dispute Resolution) Regulations 2004, SI 2004/752, reg 17(h)(ii), as from 1 October 2004 (for transitional provisions and effect see reg 18 of those Regulations at **[3098]**).

PART VI
SUPPLEMENTAL

35 Validity of contracts, collective agreements and rules of undertakings

Schedule 4 (validity of contracts, collective agreements and rules of undertakings) shall have effect.

[3022]

NOTES

Commencement: 1 December 2003.

36 Application to the Crown etc

(1) These Regulations apply—

(a) to an act done by or for purposes of a Minister of the Crown or government department; or

(b) to an act done on behalf of the Crown by a statutory body, or a person holding a statutory office,

as they apply to an act done by a private person.

(2) These Regulations apply to—

(a) service for purposes of a Minister of the Crown or government department, other than service of a person holding a statutory office;

(b) service on behalf of the Crown for purposes of a person holding a statutory office or purposes of a statutory body; or

(c) service in the armed forces,

as they apply to employment by a private person, and shall so apply as if references to a contract of employment included references to the terms of service.

(3) Paragraphs (1) and (2) have effect subject to regulation 11 (police).

(4) Regulation 9(3) (meaning of employment and contract work at establishment in Great Britain) shall have effect in relation to any ship, aircraft or hovercraft belonging to or possessed by Her Majesty in right of the government of the United Kingdom as it has effect in relation to a ship, aircraft or hovercraft specified in regulation 9(3)(a) or (b).

(5) The provisions of Parts II to IV of the Crown Proceedings Act 1947 shall apply to proceedings against the Crown under these Regulations as they apply to proceedings in England and Wales which by virtue of section 23 of that Act are treated for the purposes of Part II of that Act as civil proceedings by or against the Crown, except that in their application to proceedings under these Regulations section 20 of that Act (removal of proceedings from county court to High Court) shall not apply.

(6) The provisions of Part V of the Crown Proceedings Act 1947 shall apply to proceedings against the Crown under these Regulations as they apply to proceedings in Scotland which by virtue of the said Part are treated as civil proceedings by or against the Crown, except that in their application to proceedings under these Regulations the proviso to section 44 of that Act (removal of proceedings from the sheriff court to the Court of Session) shall not apply.

(7) This paragraph applies to any complaint by a person ("the complainant") that another person—

(a) has committed an act of discrimination or harassment against the complainant which is unlawful by virtue of regulation 6 (applicants and employees); or

(b) is by virtue of regulation 22 (liability of employers and principals) or 23 (aiding unlawful acts) to be treated as having committed such an act of discrimination or harassment against the complainant,

if at the time when the act complained of was done the complainant was serving in the armed forces and the discrimination or harassment in question relates to his service in those forces.

(8) A complainant may present a complaint to which paragraph (7) applies to an employment tribunal under regulation 28 only if—

(a) he has made a complaint in respect of the same matter to an officer under the service redress procedures applicable to him; and

(b) that complaint has not been withdrawn.

(9) For the purpose of paragraph (8)(b), a complainant shall be treated as having withdrawn his complaint if, having made a complaint to an officer under the service redress procedures applicable to him, he fails to submit that complaint to the Defence Council under those procedures.

(10) Where a complaint is presented to an employment tribunal under regulation 28 by virtue of paragraph (8), the service redress procedures may continue after the complaint is so presented.

(11) In this regulation—

"armed forces" means any of the naval, military or air forces of the Crown;

"service for purposes of a Minister of the Crown or government department" does not include service in any office mentioned in Schedule 2 (Ministerial offices) to the House of Commons Disqualification Act 1975;

"the service redress procedures" means the procedures, excluding those which relate to the making of a report on a complaint to Her Majesty, referred to in section 180 of the Army Act 1955, section 180 of the Air Force Act 1955 and section 130 of the Naval Discipline Act 1957; and

"statutory body" means a body set up by or in pursuance of an enactment, and "statutory office" means an office so set up.

[3023]

NOTES

Commencement: 1 December 2003.

37 Application to House of Commons staff

(1) These Regulations apply to an act done by an employer of a relevant member of the House of Commons staff, and to service as such a member, as they apply to an act done by and to service for purposes of a Minister of the Crown or government department, and accordingly apply as if references to a contract of employment included references to the terms of service of such a member.

(2) In this regulation "relevant member of the House of Commons staff" means any person—

(a) who was appointed by the House of Commons Commission; or

(b) who is a member of the Speaker's personal staff,

and subsections (6) to (12) of section 195 of the Employment Rights Act 1996 (person to be treated as employer of House of Commons staff) apply, with any necessary modifications, for the purposes of these Regulations.

[3024]

NOTES

Commencement: 1 December 2003.

38 Application to House of Lords staff

(1) These Regulations apply in relation to employment as a relevant member of the House of Lords staff as they apply in relation to other employment.

(2) In this regulation "relevant member of the House of Lords staff" means any person who is employed under a contract of employment with the Corporate Officer of the House of Lords, and section 194(7) of the Employment Rights Act 1996 (continuity of employment) applies for the purposes of this regulation.

[3025]

NOTES

Commencement: 1 December 2003.

39 Amendments to legislation

Schedule 5 (amendments to legislation) shall have effect.

[3026]

NOTES

Commencement: 1 December 2003.

SCHEDULES

(*Sch 1 (Norwegian part of the Frigg gas field) outside the scope of this work.*)

[SCHEDULE 1A
OCCUPATIONAL PENSION SCHEMES

Regulation 9A(3)

Interpretation

1.—(1) In this Schedule—

"active member", "deferred member", "managers", "pensioner member" and "trustees or managers", in relation to an occupational pension scheme, have the meanings given by section 124(1) of the Pensions Act 1995 … ;

"member", in relation to an occupational pension scheme, means any active member, deferred member or pensioner member;

"non-discrimination rule" means the rule in paragraph 2;

"occupational pension scheme" has the same meaning as in the Pension Schemes Act 1993 … ;

"prospective member", in relation to an occupational pension scheme, means any person who, under the terms of his employment or the rules of the scheme or both—

(a) is able, at his own option, to become a member of the scheme,

(b) shall become so able if he continues in the same employment for a sufficient period of time,

(c) shall be admitted to it automatically unless he makes an election not to become a member, or

(d) may be admitted to it subject to the consent of his employer.

(2) In paragraph 6 (procedure in employment tribunals), "employer", in relation to an occupational pension scheme, has the meaning given by section 124(1) of the Pensions Act 1995 …

(3) Any term used in regulation 9A (trustees and managers of occupational pension schemes) and in this Schedule shall have the same meaning in that regulation as it has in this Schedule.

Non-discrimination rule

2. Every occupational pension scheme shall be treated as including a provision ("the non-discrimination rule") containing a requirement that the trustees or managers of the scheme refrain from doing any act which is unlawful by virtue of regulation 9A.

3. The other provisions of the scheme are to have effect subject to the non-discrimination rule.

4. The trustees or managers of an occupational pension scheme may—

(a) if they do not (apart from this paragraph) have power to make such alterations to the scheme as may be required to secure conformity with the non-discrimination rule, or

(b) if they have such power but the procedure for doing so—

(i) is liable to be unduly complex or protracted, or

(ii) involves the obtaining of consents which cannot be obtained, or can only be obtained with undue delay or difficulty,

by resolution make such alterations to the scheme.

5. Alterations made by a resolution such as is referred to in paragraph 4 may have effect in relation to a period before the alterations are made (but may not have effect in relation to any time before the coming into force of these Regulations).

Procedure in employment tribunals

6. Where under regulation 28 (jurisdiction of employment tribunals) a member or prospective member of an occupational pension scheme presents to an employment tribunal a complaint that the trustees or managers of the scheme—

(a) have committed against him an act which is unlawful by virtue of regulation 9A (trustees and managers of occupational pension schemes) or 21 (relationships which have come to an end); or

(b) are by virtue of regulation 22 (liability of employers and principals) or 23 (aiding unlawful acts) to be treated as having committed against him such an act,

the employer in relation to the scheme shall, for the purposes of the rules governing procedure, be treated as a party and be entitled to appear and be heard in accordance with those rules.

Remedies in employment tribunals

7.—(1) This paragraph applies where—

(a) under regulation 28 (jurisdiction of employment tribunals) a member or prospective member of an occupational pension scheme ("the complainant") presents to an employment tribunal a complaint against the trustees or managers of the scheme or an employer;

(b) the complainant is not a pensioner member of the scheme;

(c) the complaint relates to the terms on which persons become members of the scheme, or the terms on which members of the scheme are treated; and

(d) the tribunal finds the complaint to be well-founded.

(2) Where this paragraph applies, the employment tribunal may, without prejudice to the generality of its power under regulation 30(1)(a) (power to make order declaring rights of complainant and respondent), make an order declaring that the complainant has a right—

(a) where the complaint relates to the terms on which persons become members of the scheme, to be admitted to the scheme;

(b) where the complaint relates to the terms on which members of the scheme are treated, to membership of the scheme without discrimination.

(3) An order under sub-paragraph (2)—

(a) may be made in respect of such period as is specified in the order (but may not be made in respect of any time before the coming into force of these Regulations);

(b) may make such provision as the employment tribunal considers appropriate as to the terms on which, or the capacity in which, the complainant is to enjoy such admission or membership.

(4) Where this paragraph applies, the employment tribunal may not make an order for compensation under regulation 30(1)(b), whether in relation to arrears of benefits or otherwise, except—

(a) for injury to feelings;

(b) by virtue of regulation 30(3).]

[3027]

NOTES

Commencement: 1 December 2003.

Inserted by the Employment Equality (Sexual Orientation) (Amendment) Regulations 2003, SI 2003/2827, reg 3(1), (6), as from 1 December 2003.

Para 1: words omitted revoked by the Employment Equality (Age) Regulations 2006, SI 2006/1031, reg 49(1), Sch 8, Pt 2, para 63, as from 1 October 2006.

SCHEDULE 2
QUESTIONNAIRE OF PERSON AGGRIEVED

Regulation 33(1)

To .... (*name of person to be questioned*) of

.... (*address*)

1.—(1) I .... (*name of questioner*) of ....

.... (*address*)

consider that you may have discriminated against me [subjected me to harassment] contrary to the Employment Equality (Sexual Orientation) Regulations 2003.

(2) (*Give date, approximate time and a factual description of the treatment received and of the circumstances leading up to the treatment.*)

(3) I consider that this treatment may have been unlawful [because ....

.... (*complete if you wish to give reasons, otherwise delete*)].

2. Do you agree that the statement in paragraph 1(2) above is an accurate description of what happened? If not, in what respect do you disagree or what is your version of what happened?

3. Do you accept that your treatment of me was unlawful discrimination [harassment]?

If not—

(a) why not,
(b) for what reason did I receive the treatment accorded to me, and
(c) how far did considerations of sexual orientation affect your treatment of me?

4. (*Any other questions you wish to ask.*)

5. My address for any reply you may wish to give to the questions raised above is [that set out in paragraph 1(1) above] [the following address ....

....].

.... (*signature of questioner*)

.... (*date*)

NB—By virtue of regulation 33 of the Employment Equality (Sexual Orientation) Regulations 2003 this questionnaire and any reply are (subject to the provisions of that regulation) admissible in proceedings under the Regulations. A court or tribunal may draw any such inference as is just and equitable from a failure without reasonable excuse to reply within eight weeks of service of this questionnaire, or from an evasive or equivocal reply, including an inference that the person questioned has committed an unlawful act.

[3028]

NOTES

Commencement: 1 December 2003.

SCHEDULE 3
REPLY BY RESPONDENT

Regulation 33(1)

To .... (*name of questioner*) of

.... (*address*)

1. I .... (*name of person questioned*) of

.... (*address*)

hereby acknowledge receipt of the questionnaire signed by you and dated ....

which was served on me on .... (*date*).

2. [I agree that the statement in paragraph 1(2) of the questionnaire is an accurate description of what happened.]

[I disagree with the statement in paragraph 1(2) of the questionnaire in that ....

....]

3. I accept/dispute that my treatment of you was unlawful discrimination [harassment].

[My reasons for so disputing are ....

The reason why you received the treatment accorded to you and the answers to the other questions in paragraph 3 of the questionnaire are ....]

4. (*Replies to questions in paragraph 4 of the questionnaire.*)

[5. I have deleted (in whole or in part) the paragraph(s) numbered ....

above, since I am unable/unwilling to reply to the relevant questions in the correspondingly numbered paragraph(s) of the questionnaire for the following reasons ....

....]

.... (*signature of person questioned*)

.... (*date*)

[3029]

NOTES

Commencement: 1 December 2003.

SCHEDULE 4
VALIDITY OF CONTRACTS, COLLECTIVE AGREEMENTS AND RULES OF UNDERTAKINGS

Regulation 35

PART 1
VALIDITY AND REVISION OF CONTRACTS

1.—(1) A term of a contract is void where—

(a) the making of the contract is, by reason of the inclusion of the term, unlawful by virtue of these Regulations;

(b) it is included in furtherance of an act which is unlawful by virtue of these Regulations; or

(c) it provides for the doing of an act which is unlawful by virtue of these Regulations.

(2) Sub-paragraph (1) does not apply to a term the inclusion of which constitutes, or is in furtherance of, or provides for, unlawful discrimination against, or harassment of, a party to the contract, but the term shall be unenforceable against that party.

(3) A term in a contract which purports to exclude or limit any provision of these Regulations is unenforceable by any person in whose favour the term would operate apart from this paragraph.

(4) Sub-paragraphs (1), (2) and (3) shall apply whether the contract was entered into before or after the date on which these Regulations come into force; but in the case of a contract made before that date, those sub-paragraphs do not apply in relation to any period before that date.

2.—(1) Paragraph 1(3) does not apply—

(a) to a contract settling a complaint to which regulation 28(1) (jurisdiction of employment tribunals) applies where the contract is made with the assistance of a conciliation officer within the meaning of section 211 of the Trade Union and Labour Relations (Consolidation) Act 1992;

(b) to a contract settling a complaint to which regulation 28(1) applies if the conditions regulating compromise contracts under this Schedule are satisfied in relation to the contract; or

(c) to a contract settling a claim to which regulation 31 (jurisdiction of county or sheriff courts) applies.

(2) The conditions regulating compromise contracts under this Schedule are that—

(a) the contract must be in writing;

(b) the contract must relate to the particular complaint;

(c) the complainant must have received advice from a relevant independent adviser as to the terms and effect of the proposed contract and in particular its effect on his ability to pursue a complaint before an employment tribunal;

(d) there must be in force, when the adviser gives the advice, a contract of insurance, or an indemnity provided for members of a profession or professional body, covering the risk of a claim by the complainant in respect of loss arising in consequence of the advice;

(e) the contract must identify the adviser; and

(f) the contract must state that the conditions regulating compromise contracts under this Schedule are satisfied.

(3) A person is a relevant independent adviser for the purposes of sub-paragraph (2)(c)—

(a) if he is a qualified lawyer;

(b) if he is an officer, official, employee or member of an independent trade union who has been certified in writing by the trade union as competent to give advice and as authorised to do so on behalf of the trade union; or

(c) if he works at an advice centre (whether as an employee or a volunteer) and has been certified in writing by the centre as competent to give advice and as authorised to do so on behalf of the centre.

(4) But a person is not a relevant independent adviser for the purposes of sub-paragraph (2)(c) in relation to the complainant—

(a) if he is, is employed by or is acting in the matter for the other party or a person who is connected with the other party;

(b) in the case of a person within sub-paragraph (3)(b) or (c), if the trade union or advice centre is the other party or a person who is connected with the other party; or

(c) in the case of a person within sub-paragraph (3)(c), if the complainant makes a payment for the advice received from him.

(5) In sub-paragraph (3)(a) "qualified lawyer" means—

(a) as respects England and Wales, a barrister (whether in practice as such or employed to give legal advice), a solicitor who holds a practising certificate, or a person other than a barrister or solicitor who is an authorised advocate or authorised litigator (within the meaning of the Courts and Legal Services Act 1990); and

(b) as respects Scotland, an advocate (whether in practice as such or employed to give legal advice), or a solicitor who holds a practising certificate.

[(5A) A person shall be treated as being a qualified lawyer within sub-paragraph (5)(a) if he is a Fellow of the Institute of Legal Executives employed by a solicitors' practice.]

(6) In sub-paragraph (3)(b) "independent trade union" has the same meaning as in the Trade Union and Labour Relations (Consolidation) Act 1992.

(7) For the purposes of sub-paragraph (4)(a) any two persons are to be treated as connected—

(a) if one is a company of which the other (directly or indirectly) has control; or

(b) if both are companies of which a third person (directly or indirectly) has control.

(8) An agreement under which the parties agree to submit a dispute to arbitration—

(a) shall be regarded for the purposes of sub-paragraph (1)(a) and (b) as being a contract settling a complaint if—

  (i) the dispute is covered by a scheme having effect by virtue of an order under section 212A of the Trade Union and Labour Relations (Consolidation) Act 1992, and

  (ii) the agreement is to submit it to arbitration in accordance with the scheme, but

(b) shall be regarded as neither being nor including such a contract in any other case.

3.—(1) On the application of a person interested in a contract to which paragraph 1(1) or (2) applies, a county court or a sheriff court may make such order as it thinks fit for—

(a) removing or modifying any term rendered void by paragraph 1(1), or

(b) removing or modifying any term made unenforceable by paragraph 1(2);

but such an order shall not be made unless all persons affected have been given notice in writing of the application (except where under rules of court notice may be dispensed with) and have been afforded an opportunity to make representations to the court.

(2) An order under sub-paragraph (1) may include provision as respects any period before the making of the order (but after the coming into force of these Regulations).

[3030]

NOTES

Commencement: 1 December 2003.

Para 2: sub-para (5A) inserted by the Employment Equality (Sexual Orientation) Regulations 2003 (Amendment) Regulations 2004, SI 2004/2519, reg 2, as from 1 October 2004.

PART 2
COLLECTIVE AGREEMENTS AND RULES OF UNDERTAKINGS

4.—(1) This Part of this Schedule applies to—

(a) any term of a collective agreement, including an agreement which was not intended, or is presumed not to have been intended, to be a legally enforceable contract;

(b) any rule made by an employer for application to all or any of the persons who are employed by him or who apply to be, or are, considered by him for employment;

(c) any rule made by a trade organisation (within the meaning of regulation 15) or a qualifications body (within the meaning of regulation 16) for application to—

(i) all or any of its members or prospective members; or

(ii) all or any of the persons on whom it has conferred professional or trade qualifications (within the meaning of regulation 16) or who are seeking the professional or trade qualifications which it has power to confer.

(2) Any term or rule to which this Part of this Schedule applies is void where—

(a) the making of the collective agreement is, by reason of the inclusion of the term, unlawful by virtue of these Regulations;

(b) the term or rule is included or made in furtherance of an act which is unlawful by virtue of these Regulations; or

(c) the term or rule provides for the doing of an act which is unlawful by virtue of these Regulations.

(3) Sub-paragraph (2) shall apply whether the agreement was entered into, or the rule made, before or after the date on which these Regulations come into force; but in the case of an agreement entered into, or a rule made, before the date on which these Regulations come into force, that sub-paragraph does not apply in relation to any period before that date.

5. A person to whom this paragraph applies may present a complaint to an employment tribunal that a term or rule is void by virtue of paragraph 4 if he has reason to believe—

(a) that the term or rule may at some future time have effect in relation to him; and

(b) where he alleges that it is void by virtue of paragraph 4(2)(c), that—

(i) an act for the doing of which it provides, may at some such time be done in relation to him, and

(ii) the act would be unlawful by virtue of these Regulations if done in relation to him in present circumstances.

6. In the case of a complaint about—

(a) a term of a collective agreement made by or on behalf of—

(i) an employer,

(ii) an organisation of employers of which an employer is a member, or

(iii) an association of such organisations of one of which an employer is a member, or

(b) a rule made by an employer within the meaning of paragraph 4(1)(b),

paragraph 5 applies to any person who is, or is genuinely and actively seeking to become, one of his employees.

7. In the case of a complaint about a rule made by an organisation or body to which paragraph 4(1)(c) applies, paragraph 5 applies to any person—

(a) who is, or is genuinely and actively seeking to become, a member of the organisation or body;

(b) on whom the organisation or body has conferred a professional or trade qualification (within the meaning of regulation 16); or

(c) who is genuinely and actively seeking such a professional or trade qualification which the organisation or body has power to confer.

8.—(1) When an employment tribunal finds that a complaint presented to it under paragraph 5 is well-founded the tribunal shall make an order declaring that the term or rule is void.

(2) An order under sub-paragraph (1) may include provision as respects any period before the making of the order (but after the coming into force of these Regulations).

9. The avoidance by virtue of paragraph 4(2) of any term or rule which provides for any person to be discriminated against shall be without prejudice to the following rights (except in so far as they enable any person to require another person to be treated less favourably than himself), namely—

(a) such of the rights of the person to be discriminated against; and
(b) such of the rights of any person who will be treated more favourably in direct or indirect consequence of the discrimination,

as are conferred by or in respect of a contract made or modified wholly or partly in pursuance of, or by reference to, that term or rule.

10. In this Schedule "collective agreement" means any agreement relating to one or more of the matters mentioned in section 178(2) of the Trade Union and Labour Relations (Consolidation) Act 1992 (meaning of trade dispute), being an agreement made by or on behalf of one or more employers or one or more organisations of employers or associations of such organisations with one or more organisations of workers or associations of such organisations.

[3031]

NOTES

Commencement: 1 December 2003.

(*Sch 5 amends the Employment Tribunals Act 1996, ss 18, 21 at* **[975]**, **[978]**, *the Employment Rights Act 1996, s 126 at* **[1170]**, *the Employment Tribunals (Interest on Awards in Discrimination Cases) Regulations 1996, SI 1996/2803, reg 1 at* **[2390]**, *and the Employment Act 2002, Schs 3–5 at* **[1508]**–**[1510]**.)

DISABILITY DISCRIMINATION ACT 1995 (AMENDMENT) REGULATIONS 2003

(SI 2003/1673)

NOTES

Made: 26 June 2003.

Authority: European Communities Act 1972, s 2(2).

Commencement: 3 July 2003 (in so far as enabling anything to be done for the purposes of preparing and bringing into force on or after 1 October 2004 a code of practice under the Disability Discrimination Act 1995, s 53A (repealed by the Equality Act 2006, ss 40, 91, Sch 3, paras 41, 52, Sch 4, as from 1 October 2007)); 1 October 2004 (otherwise).

These Regulations are the principal domestic implementation, in relation to disability, of the EU Equality Directive (Council Directive 2000/78/EC establishing a general framework for equal treatment in employment and occupation at **[3994]**). They make extensive amendments to the Disability Discrimination Act 1995 (albeit more of form and structure than of substance) and the 1995 Act is printed with the amendments incorporated and annotated. For that reason, only the introductory provisions of these Regulations are printed here.

PART 1
INTRODUCTORY

1 Citation, commencement, extent and interpretation

(1) These Regulations may be cited as the Disability Discrimination Act 1995 (Amendment) Regulations 2003.

(2) These Regulations shall come into force on the day after that on which they are made so far as enabling anything to be done for the purposes of preparing and bringing into force on

or after 1st October 2004 a code of practice under section 53A of the 1995 Act concerning any provision of that Act as it will have effect on or after that date by virtue of these Regulations.

(3) Except as provided by paragraph (2), these Regulations shall come into force on 1st October 2004.

(4) These Regulations shall not extend to Northern Ireland.

(5) In these Regulations—

"the 1995 Act" means the Disability Discrimination Act 1995; and

"the 1999 Act" means the Disability Rights Commission Act 1999.

[3032]

NOTES

Commencement: 3 July 2003 (in so far as enabling anything to be done for the purposes of preparing and bringing into force on or after 1 October 2004 a code of practice under the Disability Discrimination Act 1995, s 53A (repealed by the Equality Act 2006, ss 40, 91, Sch 3, paras 41, 52, Sch 4, as from 1 October 2007)); 1 October 2004 (otherwise).

2 Transitional provisions

(1) Subsection (1C) of section 17A of the 1995 Act (as inserted by regulation 9(2)(c)) applies in relation to a complaint presented to an employment tribunal before the commencement date, as well as one presented on or after that date; but it does not affect any case in which a complaint was determined by an employment tribunal before the commencement date.

(2) …

(3) In paragraph (2), "question" and "respondent" shall be construed in accordance with section 56 of the 1995 Act.

(4) In this regulation, "the commencement date" means 1st October 2004.

[3033]

NOTES

Commencement: 3 July 2003 (in so far as enabling anything to be done for the purposes of preparing and bringing into force on or after 1 October 2004 a code of practice under the Disability Discrimination Act 1995, s 53A (repealed by the Equality Act 2006, ss 40, 91, Sch 3, paras 41, 52, Sch 4, as from 1 October 2007)); 1 October 2004 (otherwise).

Para (2): contained transitional provisions with regard to the amendment made to s 56 of the 1995 Act and is now spent following the substitution of that section by the Disability Discrimination Act 2005, s 17 (with effect from 4 December 2006).

3 Amendment of the 1995 Act and other legislation

(1) The amendments to the 1995 Act set out in Part 2 of these Regulations shall have effect.

(2) The amendments set out in Part 3 of these Regulations (in relation to the 1999 Act and other legislation) shall have effect.

[3034]

NOTES

Commencement: 3 July 2003 (in so far as enabling anything to be done for the purposes of preparing and bringing into force on or after 1 October 2004 a code of practice under the Disability Discrimination Act 1995, s 53A (repealed by the Equality Act 2006, ss 40, 91, Sch 3, paras 41, 52, Sch 4, as from 1 October 2007)); 1 October 2004 (otherwise).

4–31 (*Regs 4–29 amend, insert or substitute various provisions in the Disability Discrimination Act 1995 at* **[900]** ***et seq*** (*see the final note at the beginning of these Regulations*)*; regs 30, 31 amend the Disability Rights Commission Act 1999* (*repealed subject to savings*)*, the Local Government and Housing Act 1989, s 7, the Employment Tribunals Act 1996, ss 12, 18 at* **[968]**, **[975]**, *the Employment Act 2002, Schs 3–5, at* **[1508]–[1510]**, *the Employment Tribunals* (*Constitution and Rules of Procedure*) (*Scotland*) *Regulations 2001, SI 2001/1170, Sch 1* (*revoked subject to savings*)*, and the Employment Tribunals* (*Constitution and Rules of Procedure*) *Regulations 2001, SI 2001/1171, Sch 1* (*revoked subject to savings*).)

(*Schedule sets out the Disability Discrimination Act 1995, Sch 3A at* **[949]–[951]**.)

WORKING TIME (AMENDMENT) REGULATIONS 2003 (NOTE)

(SI 2003/1684)

NOTES

These Regulations were made under the European Communities Act 1972, s 2(2) and came into force on 1 August 2003 (with the exception of reg 7 which came into force on 1 August 2004). They implement Council Directive 2000/34/EC. That Directive extends Council Directive 93/104/EC concerning certain aspects of the organisation of working time, to sectors and activities which were previously excluded from the scope of the 1993 Directive. Both Directives were subsequently consolidated in European Parliament and Council Directive 2003/88/EC concerning certain aspects of the organisation of working time (at **[4090]**). Council Directive 93/104/EC was implemented by the Working Time Regulations 1998 (SI 1998/1833) and these Regulations amend the 1998 Regulations at **[2411]** et seq. Since these Regulations consist entirely of amendments they are not printed for reasons of space. The 1998 Regulations are printed as amended by these Regulations.

[3034A]

SCHOOL STAFFING (ENGLAND) REGULATIONS 2003

(SI 2003/1963)

NOTES

Made: 5 August 2003.

Authority: School Standards and Framework Act 1998, ss 72, 138(7); Education Act 2002, ss 19(3), 26, 34(5), 35(4), (5), 36(4), (5), 210(7).

Commencement: 1 September 2003.

Staffing of federations: as to the application of these Regulations to the staffing of federations, see the School Governance (Federations) (England) Regulations 2007, SI 2007/960, reg 32, Sch 9.

Pupil referral units: as to the application of these Regulations to pupil referral units, see the Education (Pupil Referral Units) (Application of Enactments) (England) Regulations 2007, SI 2007/2979, reg 3, Sch 1, Pt 1, para 26.

These Regulations apply only to England. The equivalent Regulations applying to Wales (not reproduced for reasons of space) are the Staffing of Maintained Schools (Wales) Regulations 2006, SI 2006/873. There are no directly equivalent Regulations for Scotland.

ARRANGEMENT OF REGULATIONS

PART 1
GENERAL

PART 2
PROVISIONS RELATING TO COMMUNITY, VOLUNTARY CONTROLLED, COMMUNITY SPECIAL AND MAINTAINED NURSERY SCHOOLS

PART 1
GENERAL

1 Citation, commencement and application

(1) These Regulations may be cited as the School Staffing (England) Regulations 2003.

(2) These Regulations come into force on 1st September 2003.

(3) These Regulations apply only in relation to England.

[3034B]

NOTES

Commencement: 1 September 2003.

2 (*Revokes the Education* (*School Meals Staff*) (*England*) *Regulations 1999, SI 1999/2258, and the Education* (*New Schools*) (*England*) *Regulations 1999, SI 1999/2262, regs 45–52.*)

3 Interpretation

(1) In these Regulations—

"the 1998 Act" means the School Standards and Framework Act 1998;

"the 2002 Act" means the Education Act 2002;

"authority" means the local education authority by which a maintained school is, or a proposed school is to be, maintained;

["children's suitability statement" has the meaning given by section 113C(2) of the Police Act 1997;]

"dismissal" is to be interpreted in accordance with sections 95 and 136 of the Employment Rights Act 1996;

["employment business" has the meaning given by section 13(3) of the Employment Agencies Act 1973 and includes a local authority and a person carrying on an employment business;]

"support staff" means any member of a school's staff other than a teacher;

"teacher" means a person who is a school teacher for the purposes of section 122 of the 2002 Act and includes a person who would be regarded as a teacher but for the fact the other party to the contract is not an authority or a governing body of a school falling within Part 3 of these Regulations.

(2) References to a vacancy in any post include a prospective vacancy in the post.

(3) A person is to be treated as meeting any staff qualification requirements if he—

(a) fulfils any requirements with respect to qualifications or registration which apply to him as a result of regulations made under sections 132 to 135 of the 2002 Act and regulations made under section 19 of the Teaching and Higher Education Act 1998,

(b) meets any conditions with respect to health and physical capacity which apply to him as a result of Part 3 of the Education (Teachers' Qualifications and Health Standards) (England) Regulations 1999 or regulations made under section 141 of the 2002 Act, and

(c) is not subject to any direction made under section 142 of the 2002 Act, that he may not carry out work to which that section applies.

(4) References to support staff include support staff employed, or engaged otherwise than under a contract of employment, to provide community facilities and services under section 27 of the 2002 Act.

[(5) For the purposes of these Regulations a person applies for an enhanced criminal record certificate if he countersigns an application for the certificate as a registered person (within the meaning of section 120 of the Police Act 1997) or if an application is countersigned on his behalf, and the application is submitted to the Secretary of State in accordance with Part V of that Act.]

[3034C]

NOTES

Commencement: 1 September 2003.

Para (1): definitions "children's suitability statement" and "employment business" inserted by the School Staffing (England) (Amendment) (No 2) Regulations 2006, SI 2006/3197, reg 3(1), (2), as from 1 January 2007.

Para (5): added by SI 2006/3197, reg 3(1), (3), as from 1 January 2007.

Police Act 1997, s 113C(2): repealed by the Safeguarding Vulnerable Groups Act 2006, s 63(2), Sch 10, the Protection of Vulnerable Groups (Scotland) Act 2007, s 88, Sch 4, paras 27, 30 and the Safeguarding Vulnerable Groups (Northern Ireland) Order 2007, SI 2007/1351, art 60(2), Sch 8 (as from a day to be appointed).

Education (Teachers' Qualifications and Health Standards) (England) Regulations 1999, SI 1999/2166, Pt 3, revoked and replaced by SI 2003/3139.

Education Act 2002, s 142: repealed by the Safeguarding Vulnerable Groups Act 2006, s 63(2), Sch 10 (as from a day to be appointed).

4 Delegation of authority

(1) The governing body may delegate—

(a) its functions under regulations 14, 15, 17, 23 and 24, and

(b) its power to appoint or dismiss any member of staff at a school to which Part 3 applies.

(2) Subject to paragraph (4), any such delegation may be to—

(a) the head teacher,

(b) one or more governors, or

(c) one or more governors and the head teacher.

(3) Where the governing body has made any such delegation to one or more governors, the head teacher may attend and offer advice at all relevant proceedings. Such advice must be considered by the governor or governors to whom the delegation has been made.

(4) The governing body may delegate any decision whether or not to make a determination that the head teacher should cease to work at the school, or to dismiss the head teacher, to one or more governors.

[3034D]

NOTES

Commencement: 1 September 2003.

5 Performance of the head teacher

Where the authority has any serious concerns about the performance of the head teacher of a school—

(a) it must make a written report of its concerns to the chair of the governing body of the school, at the same time sending a copy to the head teacher; and

(b) the chair of the governing body must notify the authority in writing of the action he proposes to take in the light of the report.

[3034E]

NOTES
Commencement: 1 September 2003.

6 Conduct and discipline of staff

(1) The governing body must establish procedures—
(a) for the regulation of the conduct and discipline of staff at the school; and
(b) by which staff may seek redress for any grievance relating to their work at the school.

(2) Where the implementation of any determination made by the governing body in operation of the procedures requires any action which—
(a) is not within the functions exercisable by the governing body by or under the 2002 Act, but
(b) is within the power of the authority,

the authority must take that action at the request of the governing body.

[3034F]

NOTES
Commencement: 1 September 2003.

7 Capability of staff

The governing body must establish procedures for dealing with lack of capability on the part of staff at the school.

[3034G]

NOTES
Commencement: 1 September 2003.

8 (*Amends the School Governance (Procedures) (England) Regulations 2003, SI 2003/1377, reg 16.*)

9 Transitional provisions

The Schedule to these Regulations has effect for the purpose of making transitional provisions.

[3034H]

NOTES
Commencement: 1 September 2003.

PART 2
PROVISIONS RELATING TO COMMUNITY, VOLUNTARY CONTROLLED, COMMUNITY SPECIAL AND MAINTAINED NURSERY SCHOOLS

10 Interpretation of Part 2

This Part applies to community, voluntary controlled, community special and maintained nursery schools.

[3034I]

NOTES
Commencement: 1 September 2003.

11 Manner of appointment

(1) Where a governing body approves, identifies, selects or recommends a person for appointment under regulations 13(5), 13(7), 14(3) or 15(1), it is for the governing body to determine whether that person is appointed—

(a) under a contract of employment with the authority,
(b) by the authority otherwise than under a contract of employment, or
(c) by the governing body otherwise than under a contract of employment.

[(2) The identity of any such person must be checked, he must meet all relevant staff qualification requirements and a check must be made of his right to work in the United Kingdom.

(3) An enhanced criminal record certificate issued pursuant to Part V of the Police Act 1997 must be obtained in respect of any such person before or as soon as practicable after his appointment, and the application for such a certificate must be accompanied by a children's suitability statement.

(4) In the case of any such person for whom, by reason of his having lived outside the United Kingdom, obtaining such a certificate is not sufficient to establish his suitability to work in a school, such further checks as the authority considers appropriate, having regard to any guidance issued by the Secretary of State, must be made.

(5) The checks referred to in paragraphs (2) and (4) must be completed before a person's appointment.

(6) Paragraphs (3) and (4) do not apply to a person who has worked in—
(a) a school in England in a post—
(i) which brought him regularly into contact with children or young persons, or
(ii) to which he was appointed on or after 12th May 2006 and which did not bring him regularly into contact with children or young persons; or
(b) an institution within the further education sector in England in which his post involved the provision of education which brought him regularly into contact with children or young persons,

during a period which ended not more than three months before his appointment.

(7) A register must be kept which meets the requirements mentioned in paragraphs (8) to (12).

(8) In relation to each member of staff appointed on or after 1st January 2007, the register must show whether—
(a) his identity was checked;
(b) a check was made to establish whether he is subject to any direction made under section 142 of the Education Act 2002 or any prohibition, restriction or order having effect as such a direction;
(c) checks were undertaken to ensure that he met the requirements with respect to qualifications or registration mentioned in regulation 3(3)(a);
(d) an enhanced criminal record certificate was obtained in respect of him;
(e) checks were made pursuant to paragraph (4); and
(f) a check of his right to work in the United Kingdom was made,

and the register must include the date on which each such check was completed or the certificate obtained.

(9) In relation to each member of staff in post on 1st April 2007 who was appointed at any time before 1st January 2007, the register must show whether each check referred to in paragraph (8) was made and whether an enhanced criminal record certificate was obtained, together with the date on which any check was completed or certificate obtained.

(10) Paragraph (9) applies, in the case of a member of staff appointed before 12th May 2006, only if the work of his post brings him regularly into contact with children or young persons.

(11) In relation to any person supplied by an employment business to work at the school, the register must show whether written notification has been received from the employment business that—
(a) it has made checks corresponding to those which paragraph (8)(a) to (c), (e) and (f) requires to be recorded in relation to a member of staff of a school;
(b) it or another employment business has applied, with a children's suitability statement, for an enhanced criminal record certificate; and
(c) it has obtained such a certificate in response to an application made by that or another employment business;

together with the date the notification was received.

(12) Where written notification has been received from the employment business in accordance with a contract or other arrangements made pursuant to regulation 15A(5) that it has obtained an enhanced criminal record certificate which disclosed any matter or information, or that information was provided to it in accordance with section 113B(6) of the Police Act 1997, the register must also show whether the employment business supplied a copy of the certificate to the school.

(13) It is immaterial for the purposes of paragraphs (8) and (9) whether the check was made or certificate obtained pursuant to a legal obligation.

(14) The register required to be kept pursuant to this regulation may be kept in electronic form, provided that the information so recorded is capable of being reproduced in legible form.]

[3034J]

NOTES

Commencement: 1 September 2003.

Paras (2)–(14): substituted, for original paras (2)–(5), by the School Staffing (England) (Amendment) (No 2) Regulations 2006, SI 2006/3197, reg 3(1), (4), as from 1 January 2007.

Education Act 2002, s 142: repealed by the Safeguarding Vulnerable Groups Act 2006, s 63(2), Sch 10 (as from a day to be appointed).

[11A

Regulation 11(2) to (6), (7) (insofar as it relates to paragraphs (8) to (10) of that regulation), (8) to (10), (13) and (14) also applies in relation to—

(a) any person appointed by a local education authority for the purpose of working at a school to which this Part or Part 3 applies in the temporary absence of a member of staff of the school; and

(b) any person appointed by a local education authority to work at a school as a member of the school meals staff.]

[3034K]

NOTES

Commencement: 1 January 2007.

Inserted by the School Staffing (England) (Amendment) Regulations 2006, SI 2006/1067, reg 3(1), (3), as from 12 May 2006.

Substituted by the School Staffing (England) (Amendment) (No 2) Regulations 2006, SI 2006/3197, reg 3(1), (5), as from 1 January 2007.

12 Authority's entitlement to offer advice

(1) A representative of the authority may attend and offer advice at all proceedings relating to the selection or dismissal of any teacher.

(2) Such advice must be considered by the governing body or any person or persons to whom such functions have been delegated when reaching any such decision.

[3034L]

NOTES

Commencement: 1 September 2003.

13 Appointment of head teacher and deputy head teacher

(1) The governing body must notify the authority of—

(a) any vacancy for the head teacher, and

(b) where it identifies the post of deputy head teacher as one to be filled, that post.

(2) The governing body must advertise any such vacancy or post in such manner as it considers appropriate.

(3) The governing body must appoint a selection panel consisting of at least three of its members, to—

(a) select for interview such applicants for the post as it thinks fit and, where the post is that of head teacher, notify the authority in writing of the names of the applicants so selected,

(b) interview such of those applicants as attend for the purpose, and
(c) where they consider it appropriate, recommend to the governing body for approval one of the applicants interviewed by them.

(4) If within a period of seven days beginning with the date when it receives notification under paragraph (3)(a), the authority makes written representations to the selection panel that any applicant is not a suitable person for the appointment, the selection panel must—
(a) consider those representations, and
(b) where it decides to recommend for appointment any person about whom representations have been made, notify the governing body and authority in writing of its reasons.

(5) Subject to regulation 11(2), where the person recommended by the selection panel is approved by the governing body for appointment, the authority must appoint the person, unless regulation 11(1)(c) applies.

(6) If—
(a) the selection panel do not recommend a person to the governing body, or
(b) the governing body declines to approve the person recommended by the selection panel, or
(c) the authority declines to appoint the person that the governing body approves,

the selection panel may select another person in accordance with this regulation (but this does not prevent the selection of an existing applicant).

(7) Subject to regulation 11(2), if the governing body has good reason not to advertise and conduct a selection process to fill the vacancy or post in accordance with paragraphs (2) to (4), the authority must appoint the person identified by the governing body to fill the vacancy or post, unless regulation 11(1)(c) applies.

[3034M]

NOTES

Commencement: 1 September 2003.

14 Appointment of other teachers

(1) This regulation applies to any post of teacher, other than a post of head teacher or deputy head teacher . . .

(2) Where the governing body identifies any such post to be filled [for a period of more than four months], it must send a specification for the post to the authority.

(3) Subject to regulation 11(2), where a person is selected by the governing body for appointment, the authority must appoint the person, unless regulation 11(1)(c) applies.

(4) If the authority declines to appoint a person that the governing body selects, the governing body may select another person for appointment in accordance with this regulation (but this does not prevent the selection of an existing applicant).

[3034N]

NOTES

Commencement: 1 September 2003.

Para (1): words omitted revoked by the School Staffing (England) (Amendment) (No 2) Regulations 2006, SI 2006/3197, reg 3(1), (6)(a), as from 1 January 2007.

Para (2): words in square brackets inserted by SI 2006/3197, reg 3(1), (6)(b), as from 1 January 2007.

15 Appointment of support staff

(1) Subject to regulation 18, where the governing body identifies a support staff post to be filled, it may recommend a person to the authority for appointment.

(2) Any such recommendation must be sent to the authority with a job specification for the post. The job specification must include the governing body's recommendations as to—
(a) the duties to be performed,
(b) the hours of work (where the post is part-time),
(c) the duration of appointment,
(d) the grade, and
(e) the remuneration.

(3) The grade must be on the scale of grades applicable in relation to employment with the authority, and such as the governing body considers appropriate.

(4) Where the authority has discretion with respect to remuneration, it must exercise that discretion in accordance with the governing body's recommendation. The authority may be regarded as having discretion if any provisions regulating the rates of remuneration or allowances payable to persons in the authority's employment either—

(a) do not apply in relation to that appointment, or

(b) leave to the authority any degree of discretion as to the rate of remuneration.

(5) If within a period of seven days after receiving the job specification the authority makes written representations to the governing body relating to the grade or remuneration to be paid, the governing body must—

(a) consider those representations, and

(b) where it decides not to change the grade or remuneration to be paid, notify the authority in writing of its reasons.

(6) Subject to regulation 11(2), the authority must appoint a person recommended to the post by the governing body, unless regulation 11(1)(c) applies.

[3034O]

NOTES

Commencement: 1 September 2003.

[15A Supply staff

(1) No person supplied by an employment business to a school may begin work as a teacher or member of support staff at the school unless the authority or (as the case may be) the governing body have received—

(a) written notification from the employment business in relation to that person—

(i) that the checks referred to in regulation 11(11)(a) have been made, and

(ii) that an application for an enhanced criminal record certificate accompanied by a children's suitability statement has been made, or such a certificate has been obtained in response to an application made by that or another employment business; and

(iii) whether, if the employment business has obtained such a certificate before the person is due to begin work at the school, it disclosed any matter or information, or any information was supplied to the employment business in accordance with section 113B(6) of the Police Act 1997; and

(b) where the employment business has obtained an enhanced criminal record certificate before the person is due to begin work at the school, and it discloses any matter or information, or any information was provided to the employment business in accordance with section 113B(6) of the Police Act 1997, a copy of the certificate.

(2) Except in the case of a person to whom paragraph (3) applies the certificate referred to in paragraph (1)(a)(ii) must have been obtained not less than three months before the date on which the person is due to begin work at the school.

(3) This paragraph applies to a person who has worked in—

(a) a school in England in a post—

(i) which brought him regularly into contact with children or young persons, or

(ii) to which he was appointed on or after 12th May 2006 and which did not bring him regularly into contact with children or young persons; or

(b) an institution within the further education sector in England in which his post involved the provision of education which brought him regularly into contact with children or young persons,

during a period which ended not more than three months before the date on which he is due to begin work at the school.

(4) Before a person offered for supply by an employment business may begin work at the school his identity must be checked by the governing body at the school (irrespective of any such check carried out by the employment business before the person was offered for supply).

(5) The authority or (as the case may be) the governing body shall in the contract or other arrangements which they make with any employment business require it, in respect of any person whom the employment business supplies to the school—

(a) to provide the notification referred to in paragraph (1), and

(b) if any enhanced criminal record certificate which the employment business obtains contains any matter or information, or if any information was supplied to the employment business in accordance with section 113B(6) of the Police Act 1997, to provide a copy of the certificate.]

[3034P]

NOTES

Commencement: 1 January 2007.

Inserted by the School Staffing (England) (Amendment) (No 2) Regulations 2006, SI 2006/3197, reg 3(1), (7), as from 1 January 2007.

16 Suspension of staff

(1) Subject to regulation 18, both the governing body and the head teacher have power to suspend any person employed or engaged otherwise than under a contract of employment to work at the school where, in the opinion of the governing body or (as the case may be) the head teacher, his suspension is required.

(2) The governing body or head teacher must, when exercising that power, immediately inform the authority and the head teacher or (as the case may be) governing body.

(3) A suspension under this regulation may only be ended by the governing body.

(4) The governing body must, on ending such a suspension, immediately inform the authority and the head teacher.

(5) In this regulation "suspend" means suspend without loss of emoluments.

[3034Q]

NOTES

Commencement: 1 September 2003.

17 Dismissal of staff

(1) Subject to regulation 18, where the governing body determines that any person employed or engaged by the authority to work at the school should cease to work there, it must notify the authority in writing of its determination and the reasons for it.

(2) If the person concerned is employed or engaged to work solely at the school (and does not resign), the authority must, before the end of the period of fourteen days beginning with the date on which the notification under paragraph (1) is given, either—

(a) give him such notice terminating his contract with the authority as is required under that contract, or

(b) terminate that contract without notice if the circumstances are such that it is entitled to do so by reason of his conduct.

(3) If the person concerned is not employed or engaged by the authority to work solely at the school, the authority must require him to cease to work at the school.

[3034R]

NOTES

Commencement: 1 September 2003.

18 School meals staff

(1) Subject to paragraphs (2) to (4), the authority is responsible for the appointment, discipline, suspension and dismissal of school meals staff who work or are to work at a school. Before exercising any such function the authority must consult the school's governing body to such extent as the authority thinks fit.

(2) Where an order is in force under section 512A(1) of the Education Act 1996 imposing on the governing body of a school a duty corresponding to a duty of the authority mentioned in section 512(3) and (4) of that Act (duty to provide school lunches) or section 512ZB(1) of that Act (duty to provide school lunches free of charge), paragraph (3) or (4) applies as appropriate.

(3) Where the governing body has entered into an agreement with the authority that the authority should provide lunches at the school, then where the governing body determines that any school meals staff member should cease to work at the school it must notify the authority in writing of its determination and the reason for it, and the authority must then require the person to cease to work at the school.

(4) Where no such agreement has been entered into, then regulations 6 and 15 to 17 apply to such staff members.

[3034S]

NOTES

Commencement: 1 September 2003.

[18A Checks on change of post

Where a member of the school staff who was appointed before 12th May 2006 moves from a post which did not bring him regularly into contact with children or young persons to a post which does, an enhanced criminal record certificate must be obtained in respect of him before or as soon as practicable after he moves to his new post, and the application for such a certificate must be accompanied by a children's suitability certificate.]

[3034T]

NOTES

Commencement: 1 January 2007.
Inserted by the School Staffing (England) (Amendment) (No 2) Regulations 2006, SI 2006/3197, reg 3(1), (8), as from 1 January 2007.

PART 3
PROVISIONS RELATING TO FOUNDATION, VOLUNTARY AIDED AND FOUNDATION SPECIAL SCHOOLS

19 Interpretation of Part 3

This Part applies to foundation, voluntary aided and foundation special schools.

[3034U]

NOTES

Commencement: 1 September 2003.

20 Manner of appointment

(1) Where the governing body has selected a person for appointment he may be appointed either—

(a) under a contract of employment, or
(b) otherwise than under a contract of employment.

[(2) The identity of any such person must be checked, he must meet all relevant staff qualification requirements and a check must be made of his right to work in the United Kingdom.

(3) An enhanced criminal record certificate issued pursuant to Part V of the Police Act 1997 must be obtained in respect of any such person so before or as soon as practicable after his appointment, and the application for such a certificate must be accompanied by a children's suitability statement.

(4) In the case of any such person for whom, by reason of his having lived outside the United Kingdom, obtaining such a certificate is not sufficient to establish his suitability to work in a school, such further checks as the governing body consider appropriate, having regard to any guidance issued by the Secretary of State, must be made.

(5) The checks referred to in paragraphs (2) and (4) must be completed prior to a person's appointment.

(6) Paragraphs (3) and (4) do not apply to a person who has worked in—

(a) a school in England in a post—

(i) which brought him regularly into contact with children or young persons, or

(ii) to which he was appointed on or after 12th May 2006 and which did not bring him regularly into contact with children or young persons; or

(b) an institution within the further education sector in England in which his post involved the provision of education which brought him regularly into contact with children or young persons,

during a period which ended not more than three months before his appointment.

(7) A separate register must be kept which meets the requirements mentioned in paragraphs (8) to (12).

(8) In relation to each member of staff appointed on or after 1st January 2007, the register must show whether—

(a) his identity was checked;

(b) a check was made to establish whether he is subject to any direction made under section 142 of the Education Act 2002 or any prohibition, restriction or order having effect as such a direction;

(c) checks were undertaken to ensure that he met the requirements with respect to qualifications or registration mentioned in regulation 3(3)(a);

(d) an enhanced criminal record certificate was obtained in respect of him;

(e) checks were made pursuant to paragraph (4); and

(f) a check of his right to work in the United Kingdom was made,

and the register must include the date on which each such check was completed or the certificate obtained.

(9) In relation to each member of staff in post on 1st April 2007 who was appointed at any time before 1st January 2007, the register must show whether each check referred to in paragraph (8) was made and whether an enhanced criminal record certificate was obtained, together with the date on which any such check was completed or certificate obtained.

(10) Paragraph (9) applies, in the case of a member of staff appointed before 12th May 2006, only if the work of his post brings him regularly into contact with children or young persons.

(11) In relation to any person supplied by an employment business to work at the school, the register must show whether written notification has been received from the employment business that—

(a) it has made checks corresponding to those which paragraph (8)(a) to (c), (e) and (f) requires to be recorded in relation to a member of staff of a school;

(b) it or another employment business has applied, with a children's suitability statement, for an enhanced criminal record certificate; and

(c) it has obtained such a certificate in response to an application made by that or another employment business;

together with the date the notification was received.

(12) Where written notification has been received from the employment business in accordance with a contract or other arrangements made under regulation 24A(5) that it has obtained an enhanced criminal record certificate which disclosed any matter or information, or that information was provided to it in accordance with section 113B(6) of the Police Act 1997, the register must also show whether the employment business supplied a copy of the certificate to the school.

(13) It is immaterial for the purposes of paragraphs (8) and (9) whether the check was made or certificate obtained pursuant to a legal obligation.

(14) The register required to be kept pursuant to this regulation may be kept in electronic form, provided that the information so recorded is capable of being reproduced in legible form.]

[3034V]

NOTES

Commencement: 1 September 2003.

Paras (2)–(14): substituted, for original paras (2)–(5), by the School Staffing (England) (Amendment) (No 2) Regulations 2006, SI 2006/3197, reg 3(1), (9), as from 1 January 2007.

21 Authority's entitlement to offer advice

(1) The authority is entitled to advise the governing body in relation to the exercise of any of the governing body's functions of appointment, engagement and dismissal of any teacher, to the extent provided by, and subject to, any relevant agreement.

(2) A "relevant agreement" is an agreement in writing between the authority and the governing body which gives the authority an entitlement to advise the governing body in relation to the exercise of some or all of those functions, and which has not been terminated by notice in writing given by the governing body to the authority.

(3) In the absence of a relevant agreement, it is for the Secretary of State to determine the extent to which the authority is entitled to advise the governing body in relation to the exercise of any of those functions.

(4) The governing body, or any other person to whom the functions in question have been delegated, must consider any advice given by the authority pursuant to an entitlement under paragraphs (1) to (3).

(5) The Secretary of State may at any time withdraw a determination.

[3034W]

NOTES

Commencement: 1 September 2003.

22 Appointment of head teacher and deputy head teacher

(1) The governing body must notify the authority of—
- (a) any vacancy for the head teacher, and
- (b) where it identifies a post of deputy head teacher as one to be filled, that post.

(2) The governing body must advertise any such vacancy or post in such manner as it considers appropriate.

(3) The governing body must appoint a selection panel consisting of at least three of its members, to—
- (a) select for interview such applicants for the post as they think fit and, where the post is that of head teacher, notify the authority in writing of the names of the applicants so selected,
- (b) interview such of those applicants as attend for the purpose, and
- (c) where they consider it appropriate to do so, recommend to the governing body for appointment one of the applicants interviewed by them.

(4) If within a period of seven days beginning with the date when it receives notification under paragraph (3)(a), the authority makes written representations to the selection panel that any of the applicants is not a suitable person for the appointment, the selection panel must—
- (a) consider those representations, and
- (b) where they decide to recommend for appointment the person about whom the representations have been made, notify the authority in writing of their reasons.

(5) Subject to regulation 20(2), the governing body may appoint the person recommended by the selection panel to the vacancy or the post to be filled.

(6) If—
- (a) the selection panel do not recommend a person to the governing body, or
- (b) the governing body declines to appoint the person selected by the selection panel,

the selection panel may select another person for appointment in accordance with this regulation (but this does not prevent the selection of an existing applicant).

(7) Subject to regulation 20(2), if the governing body has good reason not to advertise and conduct a selection process to fill the vacancy or post in accordance with paragraphs (2) to (4), the governing body may appoint such other person it has identified to the vacancy or post to be filled.

(8) Paragraphs (2) to (7) are subject to regulation 27.

[3034X]

NOTES

Commencement: 1 September 2003.

23 Appointment of other teachers

Where the governing body identifies any post of teacher (other than head teacher or deputy head teacher) which is to be filled for a period of more than four months, it must send a specification for the post to the authority.

[3034Y]

NOTES

Commencement: 1 September 2003.

24 Appointment of support staff

Any appointment of support staff must be made by the governing body unless the governing body and the authority agree that the appointment should be made by the authority.

[3034Z]

NOTES

Commencement: 1 September 2003.

[24A Supply staff

(1) No person supplied by an employment business to a school may begin work as a teacher or member of support staff at the school unless the governing body have received—

(a) written notification from the employment business in relation to that person—

(i) that the checks referred to in regulation 20(11)(a) have been made, and

(ii) that an application for an enhanced criminal record certificate accompanied by a children's suitability statement has been made, or such a certificate has been obtained in response to an application by that or another employment business; and

(iii) whether, if the employment business has obtained such a certificate before the person is due to begin work at the school, it disclosed any matter or information, or any information was supplied to the employment business in accordance with section 113B(6) of the Police Act 1997; and

(b) where the employment business has obtained such a certificate before the person is due to begin work at the school, and it discloses any matter or information, or any information was provided to the employment business in accordance with section 113B(6) of the Police Act 1997, a copy of the certificate.

(2) Except in the case of a person to whom paragraph (3) applies the certificate referred to in paragraph (1)(a)(ii) must have been obtained not less than three months before the date on which the person is due to begin work at the school.

(3) This paragraph applies to a person who has worked in—

(a) a school in England in a post—

(i) which brought him regularly into contact with children or young persons, or

(ii) to which he was appointed on or after 12th May 2006 and which did not bring him regularly into contact with children or young persons; or

(b) an institution within the further education sector in England in which his post involved the provision of education which brought him regularly into contact with children or young persons,

during a period which ended not more than three months before the date on which he is due to begin work at the school.

(4) Before a person offered for supply by an employment business may begin work at the school his identity must be checked by the governing body at the school (irrespective of any such check carried out by the employment business before the person was offered for supply).

(5) The governing body shall in the contract or other arrangements which they make with any employment business require it, in respect of any person whom the employment business supplies to the school—

(a) to provide the notification referred to in paragraph (1), and

(b) if any enhanced criminal record certificate which the employment business obtains contains any matter or information, or if any information was supplied to the employment business in accordance with section 113B(6) of the Police Act 1997, to provide a copy of the certificate.]

[3034ZA]

NOTES

Commencement: 1 January 2007.

Inserted by the School Staffing (England) (Amendment) (No 2) Regulations 2006, SI 2006/3197, reg 3(1), (10), as from 1 January 2007.

25 Suspension of staff

(1) Both the governing body and the head teacher have power to suspend any person employed or engaged otherwise than under a contract of employment to work at the school where in the opinion of the governing body or (as the case may be) the head teacher, his suspension from the school is required.

(2) The governing body or head teacher must in exercising that power, immediately inform the head teacher or (as the case may be) the governing body.

(3) A suspension under this regulation may only be ended by the governing body.

(4) The governing body must, on ending such a suspension, inform the head teacher.

(5) In this regulation "suspend" means suspend without loss of emoluments.

[3034ZB]

NOTES

Commencement: 1 September 2003.

26 Suspension and dismissal of authority staff

In the case of staff employed, or engaged otherwise than under a contract of employment, by the authority under regulation 24, regulation 16 (in place of regulation 25) and regulation 17 apply as they apply to schools referred to in regulation 10.

[3034ZC]

NOTES

Commencement: 1 September 2003.

[26A Checks on change of post

Where a member of the school staff who was appointed before 12th May 2006 moves from a post which did not bring him regularly into contact with children or young persons to a post which does, an enhanced criminal record certificate must be obtained in respect of him before or as soon as practicable after he moves to his new post, and the application for such a certificate must be accompanied by a children's suitability certificate.]

[3034ZD]

NOTES

Commencement: 1 January 2007.

Inserted by the School Staffing (England) (Amendment) (No 2) Regulations 2006, SI 2006/3197, reg 3(1), (11), as from 1 January 2007.

27 Appointment of head teachers for schools of Roman Catholic religious orders

(1) This regulation applies to a voluntary aided school if the trustees under a trust deed relating to the school are also trustees of a Roman Catholic religious order ("the order").

(2) Subject to paragraph (5), paragraphs (3) and (4) have effect in relation to the filling of a vacancy in the post of head teacher of the school, in place of regulation 22(2) to (7).

(3) The governing body must notify the Major Superior of the vacancy in writing.

(4) The governing body must—

- (a) interview such persons who are members of the order as are proposed as candidates for appointment to the post by the Major Superior, and
- (b) appoint to the post one of the persons so interviewed unless, by virtue of regulation 20(2) or otherwise, the governing body has good reason for not making any such appointment.

(5) If no appointment is made by the governing body under paragraph (4)(b), regulation 22(2) to (7), have effect in relation to the filling of the vacancy.

(6) In this regulation—

"the Major Superior" means the Major Superior of the order;

"Roman Catholic religious order" means a Roman Catholic religious institute or society of apostolic life.

[3034ZE]–[3035]

NOTES

Commencement: 1 September 2003.

28–37, Schedule (*Pt 4* (*Collaboration between schools*) *and Pt 5* (*Staffing of new schools*) *outside the scope of this work; Schedule* (*Transitional dismissal and disciplinary procedures*) *spent.*)

EDUCATION (MODIFICATION OF ENACTMENTS RELATING TO EMPLOYMENT) (ENGLAND) ORDER 2003

(SI 2003/1964)

NOTES

Made: 5 August 2003.

Authority: School Standards and Framework Act 1998, ss 81, 138(7).

Commencement: 1 September 2003.

Extent: this Order applies to England. The equivalent provisions for Wales are in the Education (Modification of Enactments Relating to Employment) (Wales) Order 2006, SI 2006/1073 at **[3461]**.

ARRANGEMENT OF ARTICLES

1 Citation, commencement, application and revocation

(1) This Order may be cited as the Education (Modification of Enactments Relating to Employment) (England) Order 2003 and shall come into force on 1st September 2003.

(2) These Regulations apply only in relation to England.

(3) The Education (Modification of Enactments Relating to Employment) Order 1999 is revoked, in relation to England.

[3035A]

NOTES

Commencement: 1 September 2003.

2 Interpretation

(1) In this Order—

"the 1996 Act" means the Employment Rights Act 1996;

"the 1998 Act" means the School Standards and Framework Act 1998;

"the 2003 Regulations" mean the School Staffing (England) Regulations 2003;

"authority" means the local education authority by which a maintained school is, or a proposed school is to be, maintained;

"governing body" means the governing body of a school which is maintained by an authority;

"governing body having a right to a delegated budget" and "school having a delegated budget" have the same meaning as in Part 2 of the 1998 Act.

(2) In this Order references to employment powers are references to the powers of appointment, suspension, conduct and discipline, capability and dismissal of staff conferred by the 2003 Regulations.

[3035B]

NOTES

Commencement: 1 September 2003.

3 General modifications of employment enactments

(1) In their application to a governing body having a right to a delegated budget, the enactments set out in the Schedule have effect as if—

(a) any reference to an employer (however expressed) included a reference to the governing body acting in the exercise of its employment powers and as if that governing body had at all material times been such an employer;

(b) in relation to the exercise of the governing body's employment powers, employment by the authority at a school were employment by the governing body of the school;

(c) references to employees were references to employees at the school in question;

(d) references to dismissal by an employer included references to dismissal by the authority following notification of a determination by a governing body under regulation 18(1) of the 2003 Regulations; and

(e) references to trade unions recognised by an employer were references to trade unions recognised by the authority or the governing body.

(2) Paragraph (1) does not cause the exemption in respect of an employer with fewer employees than is specified in section 7(1) of the Disability Discrimination Act 1995 to apply (without prejudice to whether it applies irrespective of that paragraph).

[3035C]

NOTES

Commencement: 1 September 2003.

4 Without prejudice to the generality of article 3, where an employee employed at a school having a delegated budget is dismissed by the authority following notification of such a determination as is mentioned in article 3(1)(d)—

(a) section 92 of the 1996 Act has effect as if the governing body had dismissed him and as if references to the employer's reasons for dismissing the employee were references to the reasons for which the governing body made its determination; and

(b) Part X of the 1996 Act has effect in relation to the dismissal as if the governing body had dismissed him, and the reason or principal reason for which the governing body did so had been the reason or principal reason for which it made its determination.

[3035D]

NOTES

Commencement: 1 September 2003.

5 Trade disputes

(1) Subject to paragraph (2), a dispute between staff employed to work at a school having a delegated budget and the school's governing body, which relates wholly or mainly to one of the matters set out in section 244(1) of the Trade Union and Labour Relations (Consolidation) Act 1992 is a trade dispute within the meaning of that Act.

(2) In any case where there is a trade dispute only by virtue of this article, nothing in section 219 of that Act prevents an act from being actionable in tort where the inducement, interference or threat mentioned in that section relates to a contract the performance of which does not affect directly or indirectly the school over which the governing body in question exercises its functions.

[3035E]

NOTES

Commencement: 1 September 2003.

6 Applications to Employment Tribunals

(1) Without prejudice to articles 3 and 4, and notwithstanding any provision in the Employment Tribunals Act 1996 and any regulations made under section 1(1) of that Act, this article applies in respect of any application to an employment tribunal, and any proceedings pursuant to such an application, in relation to which by virtue of article 3 or 4 a governing body is to be treated as if it were an employer (however expressed).

(2) The application must be made, and the proceedings must be carried on, against that governing body.

(3) Notwithstanding paragraph (2), any decision, declaration, order, recommendation or award made in the course of such proceedings except in so far as it requires reinstatement or re-engagement has effect as if made against the authority.

(4) Where any application is made against a governing body under paragraph (2)—

(a) the governing body must notify the authority within 14 days of receiving notification; and

(b) the authority, on written application to the employment tribunal, is entitled to be made an additional party to the proceedings and to take part in the proceedings accordingly.

[3035F]

NOTES

Commencement: 1 September 2003.

SCHEDULE

Article 3

Sex Discrimination Act 1975
sections 6, 7, 9, 41 and 82(1A)

Race Relations Act 1976
sections 4, 5, 7 and 32

Trade Union and Labour Relations (Consolidation) Act 1992
sections 146, 147, 152–154 and 181–185

Disability Discrimination Act 1995
sections 4–6, 11, 12, 16, 55, 57 and 58

Employment Rights Act 1996
sections 66–68, 70, 71, 92, 93 and Part X

[Employment Act 2002
sections 29–32 and Schedules 2–4].

[3035G]

NOTES

Commencement: 1 September 2003.

Entry relating to the "Employment Act 2002" inserted by the Education (Modification of Enactments Relating to Employment) (England) (Amendment) Order 2004, SI 2004/2325, art 2, as from 1 October 2004.

DISABILITY DISCRIMINATION ACT 1995 (PENSIONS) REGULATIONS 2003 (NOTE)

(SI 2003/2770)

NOTES

These Regulations were made under the European Communities Act 1972, s 2(2). They come into force on 1 December 2003 in so far as enabling anything to be done for the purposes of preparing and bringing into force, on or after 1 October 2004, a code of practice under s 53A of the Disability Discrimination Act 1995 concerning any provision of that Act as it will have effect on or after that date by virtue of these Regulations, and on 1 October 2004 (otherwise). Note that s 53A of the 1995 Act was repealed by the Equality Act 2006, ss 40, 91, Sch 3, paras 41, 52, Sch 4, as from 1 October 2007. The Regulations are a further implementation domestically of the EU Equality Directive (Council Directive 2000/78/EC establishing a general framework for equal treatment in employment and occupation at **[3994]**) so far as it relates to disability discrimination by trustees or managers of occupational pension schemes. The Regulations insert ss 4G–4K of the 1995 Act, repeal s 17 of that Act, and amend ss 18D and 55 of, and Schs 2 and 3 to, that Act. The 1995 Act is printed as so amended at **[900]** et seq.

[3036]

RACE RELATIONS ACT 1976 (STATUTORY DUTIES) ORDER 2003

(SI 2003/3006)

NOTES

Made: 24 November 2003.
Authority: Race Relations Act 1976, s 71(2), (3).
Commencement: 31 December 2003.

ARRANGEMENT OF ARTICLES

1 Citation, commencement and interpretation

(1) This Order may be cited as the Race Relations Act 1976 (Statutory Duties) Order 2003 and shall come into force on 31st December 2003.

(2) In this Order—

"the Assembly" means the National Assembly for Wales;

"the Race Relations Act" means the Race Relations Act 1976;

"staff" includes any person treated as an employee for the purposes of Part II of the Race Relations Act (discrimination in the employment field);

"the 2001 Order" means the Race Relations Act 1976 (Statutory Duties) Order 2001, and

references to "150 full-time staff" are references to such number of staff as would, if the hours they work were aggregated, amount to 150 staff working on a full-time basis.

[3037]

NOTES

Commencement: 31 December 2003.

2 Race equality schemes

(1) A body or other person specified in Schedule 1 to this Order shall, before 31st May 2004, publish a Race Equality Scheme, that is a scheme showing how it intends to fulfil its duties under section 71(1) of the Race Relations Act and this Order.

(2) A Race Equality Scheme shall state, in particular—

(a) those of its functions and policies, or proposed policies, which that person has assessed as relevant to its performance of the duty imposed by section 71(1) of the Race Relations Act; and

(b) that person's arrangements for—

(i) assessing and consulting on the likely impact of its proposed policies on the promotion of race equality;

(ii) monitoring its policies for any adverse impact on the promotion of race equality;

(iii) publishing the results of such assessments and consultation as are mentioned in sub-paragraph (i) and of such monitoring as is mentioned in sub-paragraph (ii);

(iv) ensuring public access to information and services which it provides; and

(v) training staff in connection with the duties imposed by section 71(1) of the Race Relations Act and this Order.

(3) Such a person shall, within a period of three years from 31st May 2004, and within each further period of three years, review the assessment referred to in paragraph (2)(a).

[3038]

NOTES

Commencement: 31 December 2003.

3 Education

(1) The Assembly shall, before 31st May 2004, have in place arrangements for fulfilling, as soon as is reasonably practicable, its duties under paragraph (2) and shall fulfil those duties in accordance with such arrangements.

(2) It shall be the duty of the Assembly to—

(a) monitor, by reference to the racial groups to which they belong, the numbers of teaching staff from each such group at all maintained schools in respect of which it exercises its functions; and

(b) take such steps as are reasonably practicable to use, for that purpose, data provided by Local Education Authorities.

(3) The Assembly shall take such steps as are reasonably practicable to publish annually the results of its monitoring under paragraph (2).

(4) In paragraph (2) the reference to "maintained schools" is a reference to such schools within the meaning given by section 20 (7) of the School Standards and Framework Act 1998.

[3039]

NOTES

Commencement: 31 December 2003.

4 Monitoring by employers

(1) A person to which this article applies shall,

(a) before 31st May 2004 have in place arrangements for fulfilling, as soon as is reasonably practicable, its duties under paragraph (2); and

(b) fulfil those duties in accordance with such arrangements.

(2) It shall be the duty of such a person to monitor, by reference to the racial groups to which they belong,

(a) the numbers of—

(i) staff in post, and

(ii) applicants for employment, training and promotion, from each such group, and

(b) where that person has 150 or more full-time staff, the numbers of staff from each such group who—

(i) receive training;

(ii) benefit or suffer detriment as a result of its performance assessment procedures;

(iii) are involved in grievance procedures;

(iv) are the subject of disciplinary procedures; or

(v) cease employment with that person.

(3) Such a person shall publish annually the results of its monitoring under paragraph (2).

(4) Subject to paragraph (5), this article applies to a body or other person specified in Part III of Schedule 1A to the Race Relations Act.

(5) This article does not apply to—
- (a) a person specified in Schedule 2 to this Order;
- (b) a Scottish public authority with mixed functions or no reserved functions, as referred to in section L.2 of Part II of Schedule 5 to the Scotland Act 1998; or
- (c) a cross-border public authority in relation to the exercise of its Scottish functions within the meaning given by that section.

(6) In paragraph (5) the reference to a "cross-border public authority" is a reference to such an authority within the meaning given by section 88(5) of the Scotland Act 1998.

[3040]

NOTES

Commencement: 31 December 2003.

5 (*Amends the Race Relations Act 1976 (Statutory Duties) Order 2001, SI 2001/3458, Schs 1, 3 at* **[2711]**, **[2717]**.)

SCHEDULES

SCHEDULE 1
BODIES AND OTHER PERSONS REQUIRED TO PUBLISH RACE EQUALITY SCHEMES BY 31ST MAY 2004

The Commission for Patient and Public Involvement in Health.

The Central Police Training and Development Authority (CENTREX).

The Electoral Commission.

The Director-General of the National Crime Squad.

The General Teaching Council for England.

The Security Industry Authority.

A Strategic Health Authority.

[3041]

NOTES

Commencement: 31 December 2003.

Entry "The Commission for Patient and Public Involvement in Health" revoked by the Local Government and Public Involvement in Health Act 2007 Consequential Provisions Order 2008, SI 2008/526, art 2 as from 30 June 2008.

National Crime Squad: this ceased to exist on 1 April 2006; see the NCIS and NCS (Abolition) Order 2006, SI 2006/540 (made under the Serious Organised Crime and Police Act 2005, s 1).

SCHEDULE 2
BODIES AND OTHER PERSONS EXCEPTED BY ARTICLE 4(5)(A)

The Council for the Regulation of Health Care Professionals.

The Criminal Injuries Compensation Authority.

The Financial Reporting Review Panel.

…

A Port Police established under an order made under section 14 of the Harbour Act 1964.

A Port Police Force established under Part X of the Port of London Act 1968.

A Port Police Force established under section 79 of the Harbours, Docks and Piers Clauses Act 1847.

The Royal College of Veterinary Surgeons.

The Royal Commission on Environmental Pollution.

SITPRO Ltd.

[3042]–[3047]

NOTES

Commencement: 31 December 2003.

Entry "The Pensions Compensation Board" revoked by the Race Relations Act 1976 (Statutory Duties) Order 2006, SI 2006/2471, art 4, as from 3 October 2006.

CONDUCT OF EMPLOYMENT AGENCIES AND EMPLOYMENT BUSINESSES REGULATIONS 2003

(SI 2003/3319)

NOTES

Made: 17 December 2003.

Authority: Employment Agencies Act 1973, ss 5(1), 6(1), 12(3).

Commencement: 6 April 2004 (all except regs 26(7), 32); 6 July 2004 (regs 26(7), 32).

Only those provisions of most relevance to this work have been included.

ARRANGEMENT OF REGULATIONS

PART I
GENERAL AND INTERPRETATION

PART II
GENERAL OBLIGATIONS

PART III
REQUIREMENTS TO BE SATISFIED BEFORE SERVICES ARE PROVIDED

PART IV
REQUIREMENTS TO BE SATISFIED IN RELATION TO THE INTRODUCTION OR SUPPLY OF A WORK-SEEKER TO A HIRER

PART I
GENERAL AND INTERPRETATION

1 Citation and commencement

(1) These Regulations may be cited as the Conduct of Employment Agencies and Employment Businesses Regulations 2003.

(2) With the exception of regulations 26(7) and 32, the Regulations shall come into force on 6th April 2004.

(3) Regulations 26(7) and 32 shall come into force on 6th July 2004.

[3048]

NOTES

Commencement: 6 April 2004.

2 Interpretation

In these Regulations, unless the context otherwise requires—

"the Act" means the Employment Agencies Act 1973;

"advertisement" includes every form of advertising by whatever means;

"agency" means an employment agency as defined in section 13(1) and (2) of the Act and includes a person carrying on an agency, and in the case of a person who carries on both an agency and an employment business means such a person in his capacity in carrying on the agency;

"business day" means a day other than a Saturday or a Sunday, Christmas Day or Good Friday, or a day which is a bank holiday under or by virtue of the Banking and Financial Dealings Act 1971 in that part of Great Britain;

"company" includes any body corporate (whether incorporated in Great Britain or elsewhere) and references to directors and other officers of a company and to voting power at any general meeting of a company have effect in the case of a company incorporated outside Great Britain with any necessary modifications;

"employment business" means an employment business as defined in section 13(1) and (3) of the Act and includes a person carrying on an employment business, and in the case of a person who carries on both an employment business and an agency means such a person in his capacity in carrying on the employment business;

"hirer" means a person (including an employment business) to whom an agency or employment business introduces or supplies or holds itself out as being capable of introducing or supplying a work-seeker;

"publication" means any publication whether in paper or electronic form other than a programme service within the meaning of the Broadcasting Act 1990;

"work-finding services" means services (whether by the provision of information or otherwise) provided—

(a) by an agency to a person for the purpose of finding that person employment or seeking to find that person employment;

(b) by an employment business to an employee of the employment business for the purpose of finding or seeking to find another person, with a view to the employee acting for and under the control of that other person;

(c) by an employment business to a person (the "first person") for the purpose of finding or seeking to find another person (the "second person"), with a view to the first person becoming employed by the employment business and acting for and under the control of the second person;

"work-seeker" means a person to whom an agency or employment business provides or holds itself out as being capable of providing work-finding services.

[3049]

NOTES

Commencement: 6 April 2004.

3 The meaning of "connected"

(1) For the purposes of these Regulations a person is connected with—

(a) his spouse [or civil partner] or minor child or stepchild;

(b) any individual who employs him or is his employee;

(c) any person who is in partnership with him;

(d) any company of which he is a director or other officer and any company connected with that company;

(e) in the case of a company—

(i) any person who is a director or other officer of that company;

(ii) any subsidiary or holding company, both as defined in section 736 of the Companies Act 1985, of that company and any person who is a director or other officer, or an employee of any such subsidiary or holding company;

(iii) any company of which the same person or persons have control; and

(f) in the case of a trustee of a trust, a beneficiary of the trust, and any person to whom the terms of the trust confer a power that may be exercised for that person's benefit.

(2) For the purposes of paragraph (1)(e)(iii) a person is to be taken as having control of a company if—

(a) he or any person with whom he is connected is a director of that company or of another company which has control of it;

(b) the directors of that company or another company which has control of it (or any of them) are accustomed to act in accordance with his directions or instructions; or

(c) he is entitled to exercise, or control the exercise of, one third or more of the voting power at any general meeting of the company or of another company which has control of it.

[3050]

NOTES

Commencement: 6 April 2004.

Para (1): words in square brackets in sub-para (a) inserted by the Civil Partnership Act 2004 (Amendments to Subordinate Legislation) Order 2005, SI 2005/2114, art 2(17), Sch 17, para 8, as from 5 December 2005.

Stepchild: as to the interpretation of the word "stepchild" in reg 3(1)(a), see the Civil Partnership Act 2004, s 246 and the Civil Partnership Act 2004 (Relationships Arising Through Civil Partnership) Order 2005, SI 2005/3137, art 3(1), Schedule, para 129.

Companies Act 1985, s 736: prospectively repealed and replaced by the Companies Act 2006, s 1295, Sch 16. The relevant section of the 2006 Act is s 1159. There has been no amendment to this section to reflect the change.

4 Transitional and Saving Provisions and Revocation

(1) The transitional and saving provisions in Schedule 1 shall apply.

(2) Subject to the provisions of Schedule 1, the following statutory instruments are hereby revoked—

(a) the Conduct of Employment Agencies and Employment Businesses Regulations 1976;

(b) the Employment Agencies Act 1973 (Charging Fees to Workers) Regulations 1976; and

(c) the Employment Agencies Act 1973 (Charging Fees to Au Pairs) Regulations 1981.

[3051]

NOTES

Commencement: 6 April 2004.

PART II
GENERAL OBLIGATIONS

5 [Restriction on use of additional services]

[(1)] Neither an agency nor an employment business may make the provision to a work-seeker of work-finding services conditional upon the work-seeker—

(a) using other services for which the Act does not prohibit the charging of a fee, or

(b) hiring or purchasing goods,

whether provided by the agency or the employment business or by any person with whom the agency or employment business is connected.

[(2) Where the work-seeker uses services for which the Act does not prohibit the charging of a fee, an agency or employment business providing or making provision for such services shall ensure that the work-seeker is able to cancel or withdraw from those services at any time without incurring any detriment or penalty, subject to the work-seeker giving to the provider of those services in paper form or by electronic means notice of five business days or, for services relating to the provision of living accommodation, notice of ten business days.]

[3052]

NOTES

Commencement: 6 April 2004.

Regulation heading substituted, para (1) numbered as such, and para (2) added, by the Conduct of Employment Agencies and Employment Businesses (Amendment) Regulations 2007, SI 2007/3575, regs 2, 3, as from 6 April 2008.

6 Restriction on detrimental action relating to work-seekers working elsewhere

(1) Neither an agency nor an employment business may (whether by the inclusion of a term in a contract with a relevant work-seeker or otherwise)—

(a) subject or threaten to subject a relevant work-seeker to any detriment on the ground that—

(i) the relevant work-seeker has terminated or given notice to terminate any contract between the work-seeker and the agency or employment business, or

(ii) in the case of an employment business, the relevant work-seeker has taken up or proposes to take up employment with any other person; or

(b) require the relevant work-seeker to notify the agency or the employment business, or any person with whom it is connected, of the identity of any future employer of the relevant work-seeker.

(2) For the avoidance of doubt, the following shall not constitute a detriment within the meaning of paragraph (1)(a)—

(a) the loss of any benefits to which the relevant work-seeker might have become entitled had he not terminated the contract;

(b) the recovery of losses incurred by an agency or employment business as a result of the failure of the relevant work-seeker to perform work he has agreed to perform; or

(c) a requirement in a contract with the agency or employment business for the work-seeker to give a period of notice which is reasonable to terminate the contract.

(3) In this regulation, "relevant work-seeker" means any work-seeker other than, in the case of an employment business, a work-seeker who is or will be employed by the employment business under a contract of service or apprenticeship.

[3053]

NOTES

Commencement: 6 April 2004.

7 Restriction on providing work-seekers in industrial disputes

(1) Subject to paragraph (2) an employment business shall not introduce or supply a work-seeker to a hirer to perform—

(a) the duties normally performed by a worker who is taking part in a strike or other industrial action ("the first worker"), or

(b) the duties normally performed by any other worker employed by the hirer and who is assigned by the hirer to perform the duties normally performed by the first worker,

unless in either case the employment business does not know, and has no reasonable grounds for knowing, that the first worker is taking part in a strike or other industrial action.

(2) Paragraph (1) shall not apply if, in relation to the first worker, the strike or other industrial action in question is an unofficial strike or other unofficial industrial action for the purposes of section 237 of the Trade Union and Labour Relations (Consolidation) Act 1992.

[3054]

NOTES

Commencement: 6 April 2004.

8 Restriction on paying work-seekers' remuneration

(1) Subject to paragraph (2), an agency shall not, in respect of a work-seeker whom the agency has introduced or supplied to a hirer—

(a) pay to;

(b) make arrangements for the payment to; or

(c) introduce or refer the hirer to any person with whom the agency is connected with a view to that person paying to, or making arrangements for the payment to,

the work-seeker, his remuneration arising from the employment with the hirer.

(2) Paragraph (1) shall not apply in the case of an introduction or supply of a work-seeker to a hirer where—

(a)

(i) the agency is permitted by regulation 26(1) to charge a fee to that work-seeker in respect of that introduction or supply; and

(ii) the agency complies with the provisions of regulation 25 and Schedule 2; or

(b) the hirer and the agency are connected.

[3055]

NOTES

Commencement: 6 April 2004.

9 Restriction on agencies and employment businesses purporting to act on a different basis

(1) Neither an agency nor an employment business may, in relation to the introduction or supply of a work-seeker to a hirer, purport to the work-seeker to be acting as an agency and purport to the hirer to be acting as an employment business.

(2) Neither an agency nor an employment business may, in relation to the introduction or supply of a work-seeker to a hirer, purport to the work-seeker to be acting as an employment business and purport to the hirer to be acting as an agency.

[3056]

NOTES

Commencement: 6 April 2004.

10 Restriction on charges to hirers

(1) Any term of a contract between an employment business and a hirer which is contingent on a work-seeker taking up employment with the hirer or working for the hirer pursuant to being supplied by another employment business is unenforceable by the employment business in relation to that work-seeker unless the contract provides that instead of a transfer fee the hirer may by notice to the employment business elect for a hire period of such length as is specified in the contract during which the work-seeker will be supplied to the hirer—

(a) in a case where there has been no supply, on the terms specified in the contract; or
(b) in any other case, on terms no less favourable to the hirer than those which applied immediately before the employment business received the notice.

(2) In paragraph (1), "transfer fee" means any payment in connection with the work-seeker taking up employment with the hirer or in connection with the work-seeker working for the hirer pursuant to being supplied by another employment business.

(3) Any term as mentioned in paragraph (1) is unenforceable where the employment business does not supply the work-seeker to the hirer, in accordance with the contract, for the duration of the hire period referred to in paragraph (1) unless the employment business is in no way at fault.

(4) Any term of a contract between an employment business and a hirer which is contingent on any of the following events, namely a work-seeker—

(a) taking up employment with the hirer;
(b) taking up employment with any person (other than the hirer) to whom the hirer has introduced him; or
(c) working for the hirer pursuant to being supplied by another employment business,

is unenforceable by the employment business in relation to the event concerned where the work-seeker begins such employment or begins working for the hirer pursuant to being supplied by another employment business, as the case may be, after the end of the relevant period.

(5) In paragraph (4), "the relevant period" means whichever of the following periods ends later, namely—

(a) the period of 8 weeks commencing on the day after the day on which the work-seeker last worked for the hirer pursuant to being supplied by the employment business; or
(b) subject to paragraph (6), the period of 14 weeks commencing on the first day on which the work-seeker worked for the hirer pursuant to the supply of that work-seeker to that hirer by the employment business.

(6) In determining for the purposes of paragraph (5)(b) the first day on which the work-seeker worked for the hirer pursuant to the supply of that work-seeker to that hirer by the employment business, no account shall be taken of any supply that occurred prior to a period of more than 42 days during which that work-seeker did not work for that hirer pursuant to being supplied by that employment business.

(7) An employment business shall not—

(a) seek to enforce against the hirer, or otherwise seek to give effect to, any term of a contract which is unenforceable by virtue of paragraph (1), (3) or (4); or
(b) otherwise directly or indirectly request a payment to which by virtue of this regulation the employment business is not entitled.

[3057]

NOTES

Commencement: 6 April 2004.

11 Entering into a contract on behalf of a client

(1) An employment business shall not enter into, nor purport to enter into, a contract—

(a) on behalf of a work-seeker, with a hirer; or
(b) on behalf of a hirer, with a work-seeker.

(2) An agency shall not enter into, nor purport to enter into, a contract—

(a) on behalf of a work-seeker, with a hirer; or
(b) on behalf of a hirer, with a work-seeker,

unless the requirements in paragraph (3) are satisfied.

(3) The requirements referred to in paragraph (2) are that—

(a) the person for whom the agency acts has appointed the agency as his agent with authority to enter into the contract on his behalf; and

(b) where the agency acts for the work-seeker, it is permitted by regulation 26(1) to charge a fee in relation to the introduction or supply to which the contract relates.

(4) Where an agency enters into a contract on behalf of a work-seeker with a hirer, or on behalf of a hirer with a work-seeker, the agency shall ensure that the terms of the contract are notified to the party on whose behalf the agency entered into the contract, as soon as is reasonably practicable and in any event no later than the end of the fifth business day following the day on which the agency entered into the contract.

(5) Where an agency enters into a contract on behalf of a work-seeker with a hirer, or on behalf of a hirer with a work-seeker, the agency shall ensure that the terms of the contract are notified to the party or parties to the contract other than the party on whose behalf the contract was entered into, as soon as is reasonably practicable and in any event no later than the end of the fifth business day following the day on which the agency entered into the contract.

(6) An agency shall not enter into a contract between a work-seeker and a hirer on behalf of both the work-seeker and the hirer.

[3058]

NOTES

Commencement: 6 April 2004.

12 Prohibition on employment businesses withholding payment to work-seekers on certain grounds

An employment business shall not, in respect of a work-seeker whom it supplies to a hirer, withhold or threaten to withhold from the work-seeker (whether by means of the inclusion of a term in a contract with the work-seeker or otherwise) the whole or any part of any payment in respect of any work done by the work-seeker on any of the following grounds—

(a) non-receipt of payment from the hirer in respect of the supply of any service provided by the employment business to the hirer;

(b) the work-seeker's failure to produce documentary evidence authenticated by the hirer of the fact that the work-seeker has worked during a particular period of time, provided that this provision shall not prevent the employment business from satisfying itself by other means that the work-seeker worked for the particular period in question;

(c) the work-seeker not having worked during any period other than that to which the payment relates; or

(d) any matter within the control of the employment business.

[3059]

NOTES

Commencement: 6 April 2004.

PART III
REQUIREMENTS TO BE SATISFIED BEFORE SERVICES ARE PROVIDED

13 Notification of charges and the terms of offers

(1) Subject to paragraph (2), on the first occasion that an agency or employment business offers to provide or arrange the provision of a service to a work-seeker, the agency or employment business shall give notice to the work-seeker stating—

(a) whether that service is a work-finding service for which the Act prohibits the agency or employment business from charging a fee; and

(b) whether any other services or goods which may be provided by the agency or employment business or any other person are services or goods for which the agency or employment business or other person providing them will or may charge a fee, together with details of any such fee including—

(i) the amount or method of calculation of the fee;

(ii) the identity of the person to whom the fee is or will be payable;
(iii) a description of the services or goods to which the fee relates [and a statement of the work-seeker's right to cancel or withdraw from the service and the notice period required]; and
(iv) the circumstances, if any, in which refunds or rebates are payable to the work-seeker, the scale of such refunds or rebates, and if no refunds or rebates are payable, a statement to that effect.

(2) Paragraph (1) shall apply only where one or more services or goods referred to in paragraph (1)(b) for which the work-seeker will or may be charged a fee may be provided to the work-seeker.

(3) An agency or employment business shall give a further notice to a work-seeker stating the matters referred to in paragraph (1)(b) where, subsequent to the first occasion that it offers to provide or arrange the provision of a service to the work-seeker, the agency or employment business or the person providing to the work-seeker any services or goods referred to in paragraph 1(b), introduces or varies any fees in relation to any services or goods referred to in paragraph 1(b).

(4) Where an agency or employment business offers any gift or makes an offer of any benefit to a work-seeker, in order to induce him to engage the agency or employment business to provide him with services, the agency or employment business shall notify the work-seeker of the terms on which the gift or benefit is offered before the offer is open for acceptance by the work-seeker.

[3060]

NOTES

Commencement: 6 April 2004.

Para (1): words in square brackets in sub-para (b)(iii) inserted by the Conduct of Employment Agencies and Employment Businesses (Amendment) Regulations 2007, SI 2007/3575, regs 2, 4, as from 6 April 2008.

14 Requirement to obtain agreement to terms with work-seekers

(1) Subject to paragraph (7), before first providing any work-finding services to a work-seeker, an agency or employment business shall obtain the agreement of the work-seeker to the terms which apply or will apply as between the agency or employment business and the work-seeker including—

(a) whether the agency or employment business will operate as an employment agency or an employment business in relation to the work-seeker;

(b) the type of work the agency or employment business will find or seek to find for the work-seeker; and

(c) in the case of an employment business, the terms referred to in regulation 15, and in the case of an agency which is to provide any work-finding services mentioned in regulation 16, the terms referred to in that regulation.

(2) Subject to paragraph (3), an agency or employment business shall ensure that—

(a) all terms in respect of which the agency or employment business has obtained a work-seeker's agreement are recorded in a single document, or where this is not possible, in more than one document; and

(b) copies of all such documents are given at the same time as each other by the agency or employment business to the work-seeker with whom they are agreed before the agency or employment business provides any services to the work-seeker to which the terms contained in such documents relate.

(3) Paragraph (2) shall not apply in the case of an employment business where the work-seeker has been given a written statement of particulars of employment in accordance with Part I of the Employment Rights Act 1996.

(4) Neither an agency nor an employment business may vary any terms set out in a document issued in accordance with paragraph (2), unless the work-seeker to whom they relate agrees to the variation.

(5) If the agency or employment business and the work-seeker agree to any variation in the terms set out in the documents referred to in paragraph (2), the agency or employment business shall as soon as possible and in any event no later than the end of the fifth business day following the day on which the agency or employment business and the work-seeker

agree to the variation give to the work-seeker a single document containing details of the terms as agreed to be varied and stating the date on or after which it is agreed that the varied terms are to take effect.

(6) Neither an agency nor an employment business may make the continued provision of any services by it to a work-seeker conditional on the agreement by the work-seeker to any such variation.

(7) This regulation shall not apply in the case of an agency where the only service provided by the agency to the work-seeker concerned is the provision of information to him in the form of a publication.

[3061]

NOTES

Commencement: 6 April 2004.

15 Content of terms with work-seekers: Employment businesses

In the case of an employment business, the terms to be agreed in accordance with regulation 14 shall include—

(a) whether the work-seeker is or will be employed by the employment business under a contract of service or apprenticeship, or a contract for services, and in either case, the terms and conditions of employment of the work-seeker which apply, or will apply;

(b) an undertaking that the employment business will pay the work-seeker in respect of work done by him, whether or not it is paid by the hirer in respect of that work;

(c) the length of notice of termination which the work-seeker will be required to give the employment business, and which he will be entitled to receive from the employment business, in respect of particular assignments with hirers;

(d) either—

(i) the rate of remuneration payable to the work-seeker; or

(ii) the minimum rate of remuneration the employment business reasonably expects to achieve for the work-seeker;

(e) details of the intervals at which remuneration will be paid; and

(f) details of any entitlement to annual holidays and to payment in respect of such holidays.

[3062]

NOTES

Commencement: 6 April 2004.

16 Content of terms with work-seekers: Agencies

In the case of an agency which is to provide the work-seeker with work-finding services for which it is permitted by regulation 26(1) to charge a fee, the terms to be agreed in accordance with regulation 14 shall include—

(a) details of the work-finding services to be provided by the agency;

(b) details of the agency's authority, if any, to act on behalf of the work-seeker, including whether, and if so, upon what terms it is (in accordance with regulation 11) authorised to enter into contracts with hirers on behalf of the work-seeker;

(c) a statement as to whether the agency is authorised to receive money on behalf of the work-seeker;

(d) details of any fee which may be payable by the work-seeker to the agency for work-finding services including—

(i) the amount or method of calculation of the fee;

(ii) a description of the particular work-finding service to which the fee relates;

(iii) the circumstances, if any, in which refunds or rebates are payable to the work-seeker, the scale of such refunds or rebates, and if no refunds or rebates are payable, a statement to that effect; and

(iv) the method of payment of the fee and, if the fee is to be deducted from the work-seeker's earnings received by the agency, the circumstances in which it is to be so deducted;

(e) a statement as to whether the work-seeker is required to give notice to terminate the contract between the work-seeker and the agency and, if so, a statement as to the length of the notice required; and

(f) a statement as to whether the work-seeker is entitled to receive notice of termination of the contract between the work-seeker and the agency and, if so, a statement of the length of the notice.

[3063]

NOTES

Commencement: 6 April 2004.

17 Requirement to obtain agreement to terms with hirers

(1) Before first providing services (other than the provision of information in the form of a publication) to a hirer, an agency or employment business shall agree with the hirer the terms which apply or will apply between the agency or employment business and the hirer, including—

(a) a statement as to whether the agency or employment business will operate as an employment agency or an employment business in relation to the hirer;

(b) details of any fee which may be payable by the hirer to the agency or employment business including—

(i) the amount or method of calculation of such fee; and

(ii) the circumstances, if any, in which refunds or rebates are payable to the hirer, the scale of such refunds or rebates, and if no refunds or rebates are payable, a statement to that effect;

(c) in the case of an employment business, details of the procedure to be followed if a work-seeker introduced or supplied to the hirer proves unsatisfactory; and

(d) in the case of an agency, details of the agency's authority, if any, to act for the hirer, including whether, and if so upon what terms, it is (in accordance with regulation 11) authorised to enter into contracts with work-seekers on behalf of the hirer.

(2) The agency or employment business shall ensure that all of the terms are recorded in a single document and that, unless the hirer has a copy thereof, a copy is sent to the hirer as soon as is reasonably practicable.

(3) If the agency or employment business and the hirer agree to any variation in the terms set out in the document referred to in paragraph (2), the agency or employment business shall, unless the hirer has a copy thereof, as soon as is reasonably practicable, give to the hirer a document containing details of the variation and stating the date on or after which it is agreed that the varied terms are to take effect.

[3064]

NOTES

Commencement: 6 April 2004.

PART IV
REQUIREMENTS TO BE SATISFIED IN RELATION TO THE INTRODUCTION OR SUPPLY OF A WORK-SEEKER TO A HIRER

18 Information to be obtained from a hirer

Neither an agency nor an employment business may introduce or supply a work-seeker to a hirer unless the agency or employment business has obtained sufficient information from the hirer to select a suitable work-seeker for the position which the hirer seeks to fill, including the following information—

(a) the identity of the hirer and, if applicable, the nature of the hirer's business;

(b) the date on which the hirer requires a work-seeker to commence work and the duration, or likely duration, of the work;

(c) the position which the hirer seeks to fill, including the type of work a work-seeker in that position would be required to do, the location at which and the hours during which he would be required to work and any risks to health or safety known to the hirer and what steps the hirer has taken to prevent or control such risks;

(d) the experience, training, qualifications and any authorisation which the hirer considers are necessary, or which are required by law, or by any professional body, for a work-seeker to possess in order to work in the position;
(e) any expenses payable by or to the work-seeker; and
(f) in the case of an agency—
  (i) the minimum rate of remuneration and any other benefits which the hirer would offer to a person in the position which it seeks to fill, and the intervals at which the person would be paid; and
  (ii) where applicable, the length of notice which a work-seeker in such a position would be required to give, and entitled to receive, to terminate the employment with the hirer.

[3065]

NOTES

Commencement: 6 April 2004.

19 Confirmation to be obtained about a work-seeker

Neither an agency nor an employment business may introduce or supply a work-seeker to a hirer unless it has obtained confirmation—
(a) of the identity of the work-seeker;
(b) that the work-seeker has the experience, training, qualifications and any authorisation which the hirer considers are necessary, or which are required by law or by any professional body, to work in the position which the hirer seeks to fill; and
(c) that the work-seeker is willing to work in the position which the hirer seeks to fill.

[3066]

NOTES

Commencement: 6 April 2004.

20 Steps to be taken for the protection of the work-seeker and the hirer

(1) Neither an agency nor an employment business may introduce or supply a work-seeker to a hirer unless the agency or employment business has—
(a) taken all such steps, as are reasonably practicable, to ensure that the work-seeker and the hirer are each aware of any requirements imposed by law, or by any professional body, which must be satisfied by the hirer or the work-seeker to enable the work-seeker to work for the hirer in the position which the hirer seeks to fill; and
(b) without prejudice to any of its duties under any enactment or rule of law in relation to health and safety at work, made all such enquiries, as are reasonably practicable, to ensure that it would not be detrimental to the interests of the work-seeker or the hirer for the work-seeker to work for the hirer in the position which the hirer seeks to fill.

(2) Where an employment business receives or obtains information, which gives it reasonable grounds to believe that a work-seeker is unsuitable for the position with a hirer for which the work-seeker is being supplied, it shall, without delay—
(a) inform the hirer of that information; and
(b) end the supply of that work-seeker to the hirer.

(3) Where an employment business receives or obtains information which indicates that a work-seeker may be unsuitable for the position with a hirer for which the work-seeker is being supplied, but where that information does not give it reasonable grounds to believe that the work-seeker is unsuitable, it shall, without delay—
(a) inform the hirer of that information; and
(b) commence making such further enquiries as are reasonably practicable as to the suitability of the work-seeker for the position concerned, and inform the hirer of the enquiries made and any further information it receives or obtains.

(4) Where, as a result of the enquiries made under paragraph (3) an employment business has reasonable grounds to believe that the work-seeker is unsuitable for the position concerned, it shall, without delay—
(a) inform the hirer of that information; and

(b) end the supply of that work-seeker to the hirer.

(5) Where an agency, having introduced a work-seeker to a hirer, receives or obtains information, which indicates that the work-seeker is or may be unsuitable for the position in which the work-seeker has been employed with that hirer, it shall inform the hirer of that information without delay.

(6) Paragraph (5) shall apply for a period of 3 months from the date of introduction of a work-seeker by an agency to a hirer.

(7) In this regulation, "without delay" means on the same day, or where that is not reasonably practicable, on the next business day.

[3067]

NOTES

Commencement: 6 April 2004.

21 Provision of information to work-seekers and hirers

(1) Subject to [paragraphs (3), (4) and (5)], an agency or employment business shall ensure that at the same time as—

(a) it proposes a particular work-seeker to a hirer—

(i) it gives to the hirer (whether orally or otherwise) all information it has been provided with about the matters referred to in regulation 19; and

(ii) in the case of an employment business, the information it gives to the hirer (whether orally or otherwise) includes whether the work-seeker to be supplied will be employed by it under a contract of service or apprenticeship or a contract for services;

(b) it offers a work-seeker a position with a hirer—

(i) it gives to the work-seeker (whether orally or otherwise) all information it has been provided with about the matters referred to in paragraphs (a) to (e) and, where applicable, paragraph (f) of regulation 18; and

(ii) in the case of an employment business that has not agreed a rate of remuneration in accordance with regulation 15(d)(i), it informs the work-seeker (whether orally or otherwise) of the rate of remuneration it will pay him to work in that position.

(2) Where any of the information referred to in paragraph (1) is not given to the work-seeker or hirer, as the case may be, in paper form or by electronic means at the time referred to in paragraph (1), the agency or employment business shall confirm such information in paper form or by electronic means to the work-seeker or hirer, as the case may be, as soon as possible and in any event no later than the end of the third business day following the day on which it was given to the work-seeker or hirer in accordance with paragraph (1).

(3) Paragraph (1) shall not apply where—

(a) an agency or employment business intends to introduce or supply a work-seeker to a hirer to work in the same position with that hirer as he has worked within the previous five business days; and

(b) the information which that agency or employment business would be required to give the work-seeker and hirer by virtue of this regulation (other than that required by regulation 18(b)), would be the same as the information which the work-seeker and hirer have already received,

unless the work-seeker or hirer requests otherwise.

[(4) Subject to paragraphs (3) and (5), where an employment business intends to introduce or supply a work-seeker to a hirer for an assignment of five consecutive business days' duration or less—

(a) paragraph (1)(a)(i) may be satisfied by the employment business giving to the hirer (whether orally or otherwise) the name of the work-seeker to be supplied and a written confirmation by the employment business that it has complied with regulation 19; and

(b) paragraph (1)(b) may be satisfied, where the employment business has previously provided the work-seeker with the information referred to under that paragraph and that information remains unchanged, by the employment business giving to the work-seeker in paper form or by electronic means the information referred to in regulation 18(a) and (b).

(5) Where, after it has started, an assignment to which paragraph (4) applies is extended beyond a duration of five business days, the information referred to in paragraph (1) which has not already been provided shall be provided in paper form or by electronic means by the end of the eighth business day of the assignment, or by the end of the assignment if sooner.]

[3068]

NOTES

Commencement: 6 April 2004.

Para (1): words in square brackets substituted by the Conduct of Employment Agencies and Employment Businesses (Amendment) Regulations 2007, SI 2007/3575, regs 2, 5(a), as from 6 April 2008.

Paras (4), (5): added by SI 2007/3575, regs 2, 5(b), as from 6 April 2008.

22 Additional requirements where professional qualifications are required or where work-seekers are to work with vulnerable persons

(1) Where the work-seeker is—

(a) required by law, or any professional body, to have any qualifications or authorisation to work in a position for which he is to be supplied or introduced to a hirer;

(b) to be supplied or introduced to a hirer with a view to taking up a position which involves working with or caring for or attending any one or more persons under the age of eighteen; or

(c) to be supplied or introduced to a hirer with a view to taking up a position which involves caring for or attending any person who by reason of age, infirmity, or any other circumstances is in need of care or attention,

neither an agency nor an employment business may introduce or supply him to a hirer unless, in addition to the requirements in regulations 18 to 21, the requirements in paragraph (2) are satisfied.

(2) The requirements referred to in paragraph (1) are that the agency or employment business has—

(a) subject to paragraph (3) obtained copies of any relevant qualifications or authorisations of the work-seeker, and offered to provide copies thereof to the hirer;

(b) subject to paragraph (3), obtained two references from persons who are not relatives of the work-seeker and who have agreed that the reference they provide may be disclosed to the hirer, and offered to provide copies thereof to the hirer; and

(c) in a case falling within paragraph (1)(b) or (c), taken all other reasonably practicable steps to confirm that the work-seeker is not unsuitable for the position concerned.

(3) Where the agency or employment business has taken all reasonably practicable steps to comply with the requirements in [paragraph (2)(a) and (b)] and has been unable to do so fully, it may instead—

(a) comply with those requirements to the extent that it is able to do so;

(b) inform the hirer that it has taken all reasonably practicable steps to comply fully with those requirements and has been unable to do so; and

(c) inform the hirer of the details of the steps that it has taken in order to try and comply fully with those requirements.

(4) In this regulation "relative" has the same meaning as it is given in section 63 of the Family Law Act 1996.

[3069]

NOTES

Commencement: 6 April 2004.

Para (3): words in square brackets substituted by the Conduct of Employment Agencies and Employment Businesses (Amendment) Regulations 2007, SI 2007/3575, regs 2, 6, as from 6 April 2008.

23, 24 ((*Pt V Special situations*) *outside the scope of this work.*)

PART VI
CLIENT ACCOUNTS AND CHARGES TO WORK-SEEKERS

25 ((*Client accounts*) *outside the scope of this work.*)

26 Circumstances in which fees may be charged to work-seekers

(1) Subject to paragraphs (3) and (4), the restriction on charging fees to work-seekers contained in section 6(1)(a) of the Act shall not apply in respect of a fee charged by an agency for the service provided by it of finding or seeking to find a work-seeker employment in any of the occupations listed in Schedule 3.

(2) Where paragraph (1) applies, subject to paragraph (5), any fee charged by the agency may consist only of a charge or commission payable out of the work-seeker's earnings in any such employment which the agency has found for him.

(3) Paragraphs (1) and (7) shall not apply where the agency, or any person connected with it, charges a fee to the hirer in respect of the service of supplying or introducing that work-seeker to him.

(4) In any case in which the agency is connected with the hirer, paragraphs (1) and (7) only apply if, prior to the provision of the service in respect of which the fee is to be charged, the agency informs the work-seeker of the fact that it is connected with the hirer.

(5) Paragraph (2) shall not apply to any fee charged to a work-seeker by an agency in respect of the inclusion of information about the work-seeker in a publication provided that—

- (a) the publication is wholly for one or both of the following purposes, namely the purpose of finding work-seekers employment in, or providing hirers with information about work-seekers in relation to, any of the occupations listed in Schedule 3; and
- (b) either—
  - (i) the only work-finding service provided by the agency or any person connected with it to the work-seeker is the service described in this paragraph; or
  - (ii) the fee charged to the work-seeker amounts to no more than a reasonable estimate of the cost of production and circulation of the publication attributable to the inclusion of information about that work-seeker in the publication; and
- (c) in addition to the requirements in regulations 13, 14 and 16, in so far as they are applicable, the agency has, before it entered into the contract with the work-seeker by reference to which the fee is to be charged, made available to him a copy of a current edition of the publication (or, where the publication exists only in electronic form, given him access to a current edition of the publication) in which it is offering to include information about him[; and]
- [(d) where an agency proposes to include information about a work-seeker in a publication, for 7 days from the date of the agency and the work-seeker entering into any contract, whether written or oral and whether or not expressly mentioning fees permitted under this paragraph—
  - (i) no fee permitted under this paragraph shall be payable by the work-seeker;
  - (ii) the work-seeker shall be entitled without detriment or penalty to cancel or withdraw from any such contract with immediate effect by informing the agency of such cancellation or withdrawal; and
  - (iii) the agency shall not include the information in the publication.]

(6) The restrictions on charging fees to work-seekers contained in section 6(1)(a) of the Act shall not apply to any fee consisting of a charge to a work-seeker in respect of the purchase of or subscription for a publication containing information about employers provided that—

- (a) this is the only work-finding service provided by the agency or any person connected with it to the work-seeker; and
- (b) the agency has made available to the work-seeker a copy of a current edition of the publication (or, where the publication exists only in electronic form, given him access to a current edition of the publication) in advance of the work-seeker purchasing or subscribing for it.

(7) The restriction on charging fees to work-seekers contained in section 6(1)(a) of the Act shall not apply in respect of a fee charged by an agency for the service provided by it of finding or seeking to find a work-seeker employment where—

(a) the work-seeker in question is a company; and
(b) the employment is in an occupation other than any of those occupations listed in Schedule 3.

[3070]

NOTES

Commencement: 6 April 2004 (sub-ss (1)–(6)); 6 July 2004 (otherwise).

Para (5): word in square brackets at the end of sub-para (c) substituted, and sub-para (d) added, by the Conduct of Employment Agencies and Employment Businesses (Amendment) Regulations 2007, SI 2007/3575, regs 2, 7, as from 6 April 2008.

PART VII
MISCELLANEOUS

27–29 (*Reg 27* (*advertisements*), *reg 28* (*confidentiality*), *and reg 29* (*records*) *outside the scope of this work.*)

30 Civil liability

(1) Without prejudice to—
(a) any right of action; and
(b) any defence,

which exists or may be available apart from the provisions of the Act and these Regulations, contravention of, or failure to comply with, any of the provisions of the Act or of these Regulations by an agency or employment business shall, so far as it causes damage, be actionable.

(2) In this regulation, "damage" includes the death of, or injury to, any person (including any disease and any impairment of that person's physical or mental condition).

[3071]

NOTES

Commencement: 6 April 2004.

31 Effect of prohibited or unenforceable terms and recoverability of monies

(1) Where any term of a contract is prohibited or made unenforceable by these Regulations, the contract shall continue to bind the parties to it if it is capable of continuing in existence without that term.

(2) Where a hirer pays any money pursuant to a contractual term which is unenforceable by virtue of regulation 10, the hirer is entitled to recover that money.

[3072]

NOTES

Commencement: 6 April 2004.

32, 33 (*Reg 32* (*application of the Regulations to work-seekers which are incorporated*), *and reg 33* (*electronic and other communications*) *outside the scope of this work.*)

SCHEDULES

(*Sch 1* (*transitional and saving provisions*), *and Sch 2* (*client accounts*) *outside the scope of this work.*)

SCHEDULE 3
OCCUPATIONS IN RESPECT OF WHICH EMPLOYMENT AGENCIES MAY CHARGE FEES TO WORK-SEEKERS

Regulation 26

Actor, musician, singer, dancer, or other performer;

Composer, writer, artist, director, production manager, lighting cameraman, camera operator, make up artist, [clothes, hair or make up stylist,] film editor, action arranger or co-ordinator, stunt arranger, costume or production designer, recording engineer, property master, film continuity person, sound mixer, photographer, stage manager, producer, choreographer, theatre designer;

Photographic or fashion model;

Professional sports person.

[3073]

NOTES

Commencement: 6 April 2004.

Words in square brackets inserted by the Conduct of Employment Agencies and Employment Businesses (Amendment) Regulations 2007, SI 2007/3575, regs 2, 10, as from 6 April 2008.

(Sch 4 (particulars to be included in an agency's or employment business's records relating to work-seekers), Sch 5 (particulars to be included in an agency's or employment business's records relating to hirers), and Sch 6 (particulars to be included in an agency's or employment business's records relating to other agencies or employment businesses) outside the scope of this work.)

DISABILITY DISCRIMINATION (EMPLOYMENT FIELD) (LEASEHOLD PREMISES) REGULATIONS 2004

(SI 2004/153)

NOTES

Made: 26 January 2004.

Authority: originally made under the Disability Discrimination Act 1995, s 5(6), (7), 6(8), (10), 12(3), 16(3), 67(3), Sch 4, paras 3, 4. Following the amendment of that Act by the Disability Discrimination Act 1995 (Amendment) Regulations 2003, SI 2003/1673, these Regulations now have effect as if made under ss 18A, 67(3) of, and Sch 4, paras 3, 4 to, the 1995 Act.

Commencement: 1 October 2004.

ARRANGEMENT OF REGULATIONS

1 Citation, commencement and extent

(1) These Regulations may be cited as the Disability Discrimination (Employment Field) (Leasehold Premises) Regulations 2004 and shall come into force on 1st October 2004.

(2) These Regulations shall not extend to Northern Ireland.

[3074]

NOTES

Commencement: 1 October 2004.

2 Interpretation

In these Regulations—

"the Act" means the Disability Discrimination Act 1995; and

"binding obligation" means a legally binding obligation (not contained in a lease) in relation to the premises whether arising from an agreement or otherwise.

[3075]

NOTES

Commencement: 1 October 2004.

3 (*Revokes the Disability Discrimination (Employment) Regulations 1996, SI 1996/1456, and the Disability Discrimination (Sub-leases and Sub-tenancies) Regulations 1996, SI 1996/1333.*)

4 Lessor withholding consent

(1) For the purposes of section 18A of and Part I of Schedule 4 to the Act, a lessor is to be taken to have withheld his consent to an alteration where he has received a written application by or on behalf of the occupier for consent to make the alteration and has failed to meet the requirements specified in paragraph (2).

(2) The requirements are that the lessor within a period of 21 days (beginning with the day on which he receives the application referred to in paragraph (1)) or such longer period as is reasonable—

(a) replies consenting to or refusing the application, or

(b)

(i) replies consenting to the application subject to obtaining the consent of another person required under a superior lease or pursuant to a binding obligation, and

(ii) seeks that consent.

(3) A lessor who fails to meet the requirements in paragraph (2) but who subsequently meets those requirements (except as to time)—

(a) shall be taken to have withheld his consent from the date of such failure, and

(b) shall be taken not to have withheld his consent from the time he met those requirements (except as to time).

(4) For the purposes of this regulation, a lessor is to be treated as not having sought another person's consent unless he has applied in writing to that person indicating—

(a) that the lessor's consent to the alteration has been applied for in order to comply with a duty to make reasonable adjustments, and

(b) that he has given his consent conditionally upon obtaining the other person's consent.

[3076]

NOTES

Commencement: 1 October 2004.

5 Lessor withholding consent unreasonably

(1) For the purposes of section 18A of and Part I of Schedule 4 to the Act, a lessor is to be taken to have withheld his consent unreasonably where paragraph (2), (3) or (4) applies.

(2) This paragraph applies where—

(a) the lease provides that consent shall or will be given to an alteration of the kind in question; and

(b) the lessor withholds his consent to the alteration.

(3) This paragraph applies where—

(a) the lease provides that consent shall or will be given to an alteration of the kind in question if it is sought in a particular way;

(b) it is sought in that way; and

(c) the lessor withholds his consent to the alteration.

(4) This paragraph applies where the lessor is taken to have withheld his consent by virtue of regulation 4.

[3077]

NOTES

Commencement: 1 October 2004.

6 Lessor withholding consent reasonably

(1) For the purposes of section 18A of and Part I of Schedule 4 to the Act, a lessor is to be taken to have acted reasonably in withholding his consent where—

(a) there is a binding obligation requiring the consent of any person to the alteration;
(b) he has taken steps to seek that consent; and
(c) that consent has not been given or has been given subject to a condition making it reasonable for him to withhold his consent.

(2) For the purposes of section 18A of and Part I of Schedule 4 to the Act, a lessor is to be taken to have acted reasonably in withholding his consent where—

(a) he is bound by an agreement which allows him to consent to the alteration in question subject to a condition that he makes a payment, and
(b) that condition does not permit the lessor to make his own consent subject to a condition that the occupier reimburse him the payment.

[3078]

NOTES

Commencement: 1 October 2004.

7 Lessor's consent subject to conditions

(1) For the purposes of section 18A of and Part I of Schedule 4 to the Act, a condition subject to which a lessor has given his consent is to be taken to be reasonable if it is any of the following (or a condition to similar effect)—

(a) that the occupier must obtain any necessary planning permission and any other consent or permission required by or under any enactment;
(b) that the occupier must submit any plans or specifications for the alteration to the lessor for approval (provided that the condition binds the lessor not to withhold approval unreasonably) and that the work is carried out in accordance with such plans or specifications;
(c) that the lessor must be permitted a reasonable opportunity to inspect the work when completed; and
(d) that the occupier must repay to the lessor the costs reasonably incurred in connection with the giving of his consent.

(2) For the purposes of section 18A of and Part I of Schedule 4 to the Act, in a case where it would be reasonable for the lessor to withhold consent, a condition that upon expiry of the lease the occupier (or any assignee or successor) must reinstate any relevant part of the premises which is to be altered to its state before the alteration was made is to be taken to be reasonable.

[3079]

NOTES

Commencement: 1 October 2004.

8 Definition of sub-lease and sub-tenancy

For the purposes of section 18A of the Act—

"sub-lease" means any sub-term created out of, or deriving from, a leasehold interest; and

"sub-tenancy" means any tenancy created out of, or deriving from, a superior tenancy.

[3080]

NOTES

Commencement: 1 October 2004.

9 Modification of section 18A and Part I of Schedule 4

In relation to any case where the occupier occupies premises under a sub-lease or sub-tenancy, the provisions of section 18A of and Part I of Schedule 4 to the Act shall have effect as if they contained the following modifications—

(a) in section 18A, for "the lessor" substitute "his immediate landlord" where it occurs in subsection (2)(a) and (b), and "the immediate landlord" where it occurs in subsection (2)(c) and (d) and subsection (4);

(b) after section 18A(2) insert—

"(2A) Except to the extent to which it expressly so provides, any superior lease under which the premises are held shall have effect in relation to the lessor and lessee who are parties to that superior lease as if it provided—

(a) for the lessee to have to make a written application to the lessor for consent to the alteration;

(b) if such an application is made, for the lessor not to withhold his consent unreasonably; and

(c) for the lessor to be entitled to make his consent subject to reasonable conditions.";

(c) in paragraph 2 of Schedule 4, at the end insert—

"(10) In this paragraph and paragraph 3, references to a lessor include any superior landlord.".

[3081]

NOTES

Commencement: 1 October 2004.

EMPLOYMENT ACT 2002 (DISPUTE RESOLUTION) REGULATIONS 2004

(SI 2004/752)

NOTES

Made: 12 March 2004.
Authority: Employment Act 2002, ss 31(6), 32(7), 33, 51(1)(a), (b).
Commencement: 1 October 2004 (for transitional provisions see reg 18 at **[3098]**).

ARRANGEMENT OF REGULATIONS

1 Citation and Commencement

These Regulations may be cited as the Employment Act 2002 (Dispute Resolution) Regulations 2004 and shall come into force on 1st October 2004.

[3082]

NOTES

Commencement: 1 October 2004.

2 Interpretation

(1) In these Regulations—

"the 1992 Act" means the Trade Union and Labour Relations (Consolidation) Act 1992;

"the 1996 Act" means the Employment Rights Act 1996;
"the 1999 Act" means the Employment Relations Act 1999;
"the 2002 Act" means the Employment Act 2002;
"action" means any act or omission;
"applicable statutory procedure" means the statutory procedure that applies in relation to a particular case by virtue of these Regulations;
"collective agreement" has the meaning given to it by section 178(1) of the 1992 Act;
"dismissal and disciplinary procedures" means the statutory procedures set out in Part 1 of Schedule 2;
"dismissed" has the meaning given to it in section 95(1)(a) and (b) of the 1996 Act;
"employers' association" has the meaning given to it by section 122 of the 1992 Act;
"grievance" means a complaint by an employee about action which his employer has taken or is contemplating taking in relation to him;
"grievance procedures" means the statutory procedures set out in Part 2 of Schedule 2;
"independent trade union" has the meaning given to it by section 5 of the 1992 Act;
"modified dismissal procedure" means the procedure set out in Chapter 2 of Part 1 of Schedule 2;
"modified grievance procedure" means the procedure set out in Chapter 2 of Part 2 of Schedule 2;
"non-completion" of a statutory procedure includes non-commencement of such a procedure except where the term is used in relation to the non-completion of an identified requirement of a procedure or to circumstances where a procedure has already been commenced;
"party" means the employer or the employee;
"relevant disciplinary action" means action, short of dismissal, which the employer asserts to be based wholly or mainly on the employee's conduct or capability, other than suspension on full pay or the issuing of warnings (whether oral or written);
"standard dismissal and disciplinary procedure" means the procedure set out in Chapter 1 of Part 1 of Schedule 2;
"standard grievance procedure" means the procedure set out in Chapter 1 of Part 2 of Schedule 2;

and a reference to a Schedule is a reference to a Schedule to the 2002 Act.

(2) In determining whether a meeting or written communication fulfils a requirement of Schedule 2, it is irrelevant whether the meeting or communication deals with any other matter (including a different matter required to be dealt with in a meeting or communication intended to fulfil a requirement of Schedule 2).

[3083]

NOTES

Commencement: 1 October 2004.

3 Application of dismissal and disciplinary procedures

(1) Subject to paragraph (2) and regulation 4, the standard dismissal and disciplinary procedure applies when an employer contemplates dismissing or taking relevant disciplinary action against an employee.

(2) Subject to regulation 4, the modified dismissal procedure applies in relation to a dismissal where—

(a) the employer dismissed the employee by reason of his conduct without notice,
(b) the dismissal occurred at the time the employer became aware of the conduct or immediately thereafter,
(c) the employer was entitled, in the circumstances, to dismiss the employee by reason of his conduct without notice or any payment in lieu of notice, and
(d) it was reasonable for the employer, in the circumstances, to dismiss the employee before enquiring into the circumstances in which the conduct took place,

but neither of the dismissal and disciplinary procedures applies in relation to such a dismissal where the employee presents a complaint relating to the dismissal to an employment tribunal at a time when the employer has not complied with paragraph 4 of Schedule 2.

[3084]

NOTES

Commencement: 1 October 2004.

4 Dismissals to which the dismissal and disciplinary procedures do not apply

(1) Neither of the dismissal and disciplinary procedures applies in relation to the dismissal of an employee where—

(a) all the employees of a description or in a category to which the employee belongs are dismissed, provided that the employer offers to re-engage all the employees so dismissed either before or upon the termination of their contracts;

(b) the dismissal is one of a number of dismissals in respect of which the duty in section 188 of the 1992 Act (duty of employer to consult representatives when proposing to dismiss as redundant a certain number of employees) applies;

(c) at the time of the employee's dismissal he is taking part in—

(i) an unofficial strike or other unofficial industrial action, or

(ii) a strike or other industrial action (being neither unofficial industrial action nor protected industrial action), unless the circumstances of the dismissal are such that, by virtue of section 238(2) of the 1992 Act, an employment tribunal is entitled to determine whether the dismissal was fair or unfair;

(d) the reason (or, if more than one, the principal reason) for the dismissal is that the employee took protected industrial action and the dismissal would be regarded, by virtue of section 238A(2) of the 1992 Act, as unfair for the purposes of Part 10 of the 1996 Act;

(e) the employer's business suddenly ceases to function, because of an event unforeseen by the employer, with the result that it is impractical for him to employ any employees;

(f) the reason (or, if more than one principal reason) for the dismissal is that the employee could not continue to work in the position which he held without contravention (either on his part or on that of his employer) of a duty or restriction imposed by or under any enactment; …

(g) the employee is one to whom a dismissal procedures agreement designated by an order under section 110 of the 1996 Act applies at the date of dismissal[; or

(h) the reason (or, if more than one, the principal reason) for the dismissal is retirement of the employee (to be determined in accordance with section 98ZA to 98ZF of the 1996 Act)].

(2) For the purposes of paragraph (1)—

"unofficial" shall be construed in accordance with subsections (2) to (4) of section 237 of the 1992 Act;

"strike" has the meaning given to it by section 246 of the 1992 Act;

"protected industrial action" shall be construed in accordance with section 238A(1) of the 1992 Act;

and an employer shall be regarded as offering to re-engage an employee if that employer, a successor of that employer or an associated employer of that employer offers to re-engage the employee, either in the job which he held immediately before the date of dismissal or in a different job which would be suitable in his case.

[3085]

NOTES

Commencement: 1 October 2004.

Para (1): word omitted from sub-para (f) revoked, and sub-para (h) and the word immediately preceding it added, by the Employment Equality (Age) Regulations 2006, SI 2006/1031, reg 49(1), Sch 8, Pt 2, para 64, as from 1 October 2006.

Note: it should be noted that para (1)(d) above provides "the reason (or, if more than one, the principal reason) for the dismissal …", whereas para (1)(f) uses different wording and provides "the reason (or, if more than one principal reason) for the dismissal …". It has been confirmed by the DTI (now BERR) that the wording in para (1)(f) is a drafting error.

5 Circumstances in which parties are treated as complying with the dismissal and disciplinary procedures

(1) Where—

(a) either of the dismissal and disciplinary procedures is the applicable statutory procedure in relation to a dismissal,

(b) the employee presents an application for interim relief to an employment tribunal pursuant to section 128 of the 1996 Act (interim relief pending determination of complaint) in relation to his dismissal, and

(c) at the time the application is presented, the requirements of paragraphs 1 and 2 or, as the case may be, paragraph 4 of Schedule 2 have been complied with but the requirements of paragraph 3 or 5 of Schedule 2 have not,

the parties shall be treated as having complied with the requirements of paragraph 3 or 5 of Schedule 2.

(2) Where either of the dismissal and disciplinary procedures is the applicable statutory procedure in relation to the dismissal of an employee or to relevant disciplinary action taken against an employee but—

(a) at the time of the dismissal or the taking of the action an appropriate procedure exists,

(b) the employee is entitled to appeal under that procedure against his dismissal or the relevant disciplinary action taken against him instead of appealing to his employer, and

(c) the employee has appealed under that procedure,

the parties shall be treated as having complied with the requirements of paragraph 3 or 5 of Schedule 2.

(3) For the purposes of paragraph (2) a procedure is appropriate if it—

(a) gives the employee an effective right of appeal against dismissal or disciplinary action taken against him, and

(b) operates by virtue of a collective agreement made between two or more employers or an employers' association and one or more independent trade unions.

[3086]

NOTES

Commencement: 1 October 2004.

6 Application of the grievance procedures

(1) The grievance procedures apply, in accordance with the paragraphs (2) to (7) of this regulation, in relation to any grievance about action by the employer that could form the basis of a complaint by an employee to an employment tribunal under a jurisdiction listed in Schedule 3 or 4, or could do so if the action took place.

(2) Subject to paragraphs (3) to (7), the standard grievance procedure applies in relation to any such grievance.

(3) Subject to paragraphs (4) to (7), the modified grievance procedure applies in relation to a grievance where—

(a) the employee has ceased to be employed by the employer;

(b) the employer—

  (i) was unaware of the grievance before the employment ceased, or

  (ii) was so aware but the standard grievance procedure was not commenced or was not completed before the last day of the employee's employment; and

(c) the parties have agreed in writing in relation to the grievance, whether before, on or after that day, but after the employer became aware of the grievance, that the modified procedure should apply.

(4) Neither of the grievance procedures applies where—

(a) the employee has ceased to be employed by the employer;

(b) neither procedure has been commenced; and

(c) since the employee ceased to be employed it has ceased to be reasonably practicable for him to comply with paragraph 6 or 9 of Schedule 2.

(5) Neither of the grievance procedures applies where the grievance is that the employer has dismissed or is contemplating dismissing the employee.

(6) Neither of the grievance procedures applies where the grievance is that the employer has taken or is contemplating taking relevant disciplinary action against the employee unless one of the reasons for the grievance is a reason mentioned in regulation 7(1).

(7) Neither of the grievance procedures applies where regulation 11(1) applies.

[3087]

NOTES

Commencement: 1 October 2004.

7 Circumstances in which parties are treated as complying with the grievance procedures

(1) Where the grievance is that the employer has taken or is contemplating taking relevant disciplinary action against the employee and one of the reasons for the grievance is—

(a) that the relevant disciplinary action amounted to or, if it took place, would amount to unlawful discrimination, or

(b) that the grounds on which the employer took the action or is contemplating taking it were or are unrelated to the grounds on which he asserted that he took the action or is asserting that he is contemplating taking it,

the standard grievance procedure or, as the case may be, modified grievance procedure shall apply but the parties shall be treated as having complied with the applicable procedure if the employee complies with the requirement in paragraph (2).

(2) The requirement is that the employee must set out the grievance in a written statement and send the statement or a copy of it to the employer—

(a) where either of the dismissal and disciplinary procedures is being followed, before the meeting referred to in paragraph 3 or 5 (appeals under the dismissal and disciplinary procedures) of Schedule 2, or

(b) where neither of those procedures is being followed, before presenting any complaint arising out of the grievance to an employment tribunal.

(3) In paragraph (1)(a) "unlawful discrimination" means an act or omission in respect of which a right of complaint lies to an employment tribunal under any of the following tribunal jurisdictions (specified in Schedules 3 and 4)—

section 2 of the Equal Pay Act 1970;
section 63 of the Sex Discrimination Act 1975;
section 54 of the Race Relations Act 1976;
section 17A of the Disability Discrimination Act 1995;
regulation 28 of the Employment Equality (Religion or Belief) Regulations 2003,
regulation 28 of the Employment Equality (Sexual Orientation) Regulations 2003[;
regulation 36 of the Employment Equality (Age) Regulations 2006].

[3088]

NOTES

Commencement: 1 October 2004.

Para (3): words in square brackets added by the Employment Equality (Age) (Consequential Amendments) Regulations 2007, SI 2007/825, reg 8(1), (2), as from 6 April 2007.

8—(1) Where—

(a) the standard grievance procedure is the applicable statutory procedure,

(b) the employee has ceased to be employed by the employer,

(c) paragraph 6 of Schedule 2 has been complied with (whether before or after the end of his employment); and

(d) since the end of his employment it has ceased to be reasonably practicable for the employee, or his employer, to comply with the requirements of paragraph 7 or 8 of Schedule 2,

the parties shall be treated, subject to paragraph (2), as having complied with such of those paragraphs of Schedule 2 as have not been complied with.

(2) In a case where paragraph (1) applies and the requirements of paragraphs 7(1) to (3) of Schedule 2 have been complied with but the requirement in paragraph 7(4) of Schedule 2 has not, the employer shall be treated as having failed to comply with paragraph 7(4) unless he informs the employee in writing of his decision as to his response to the grievance.

[3089]

NOTES

Commencement: 1 October 2004.

9—(1) Where either of the grievance procedures is the applicable statutory procedure, the parties shall be treated as having complied with the requirements of the procedure if a person who is an appropriate representative of the employee having the grievance has—

(a) written to the employer setting out the grievance; and

(b) specified in writing to the employer (whether in setting out the grievance or otherwise) the names of at least two employees, of whom one is the employee having the grievance, as being the employees on behalf of whom he is raising the grievance.

(2) For the purposes of paragraph (1), a person is an appropriate representative if, at the time he writes to the employer setting out the grievance, he is—

(a) an official of an independent trade union recognised by the employer for the purposes of collective bargaining in respect of a description of employees that includes the employee having the grievance, or

(b) an employee of the employer who is an employee representative elected or appointed by employees consisting of or including employees of the same description as the employee having the grievance and who, having regard to the purposes for which and method by which he was elected or appointed, has the authority to represent employees of that description under an established procedure for resolving grievances agreed between employee representatives and the employer.

(3) For the purposes of paragraph (2)(a) the terms "official", "recognised" and "collective bargaining" have the meanings given to them by, respectively, sections 119, 178(3) and 178(1) of the 1992 Act.

[3090]

NOTES

Commencement: 1 October 2004.

10 Where either of the grievance procedures is the applicable statutory procedure but—

(a) at the time the employee raises his grievance there is a procedure in operation, under a collective agreement made between two or more employers or an employers' association and one or more independent trade unions, that provides for employees of the employer to raise grievances about the behaviour of the employer and have them considered, and

(b) the employee is entitled to raise his grievance under that procedure and does so,

the parties shall be treated as having complied with the applicable statutory procedure.

[3091]

NOTES

Commencement: 1 October 2004.

11 General circumstances in which the statutory procedures do not apply or are treated as being complied with

(1) Where the circumstances specified in paragraph (3) apply and in consequence the employer or employee does not commence the procedure that would otherwise be the applicable statutory procedure (by complying with paragraph 1, 4, 6 or 9 of Schedule 2), the procedure does not apply.

(2) Where the applicable statutory procedure has been commenced, but the circumstances specified in paragraph (3) apply and in consequence a party does not comply with a subsequent requirement of the procedure, the parties shall be treated as having complied with the procedure.

(3) The circumstances referred to in paragraphs (1) and (2) are that—

(a) the party has reasonable grounds to believe that commencing the procedure or complying with the subsequent requirement would result in a significant threat to himself, his property, any other person or the property of any other person;

(b) the party has been subjected to harassment and has reasonable grounds to believe that commencing the procedure or complying with the subsequent requirement would result in his being subjected to further harassment; or

(c) it is not practicable for the party to commence the procedure or comply with the subsequent requirement within a reasonable period.

(4) In paragraph (3)(b), "harassment" means conduct which has the purpose or effect of—

(a) violating the person's dignity, or

(b) creating an intimidating, hostile, degrading, humiliating or offensive environment for him,

but conduct shall only be regarded as having that purpose or effect if, having regard to all the circumstances, including in particular the perception of the person who was the subject of the conduct, it should reasonably be considered as having that purpose or effect.

[3092]

NOTES

Commencement: 1 October 2004.

12 Failure to comply with the statutory procedures

(1) If either party fails to comply with a requirement of an applicable statutory procedure, including a general requirement contained in Part 3 of Schedule 2, then, subject to paragraph (2), the non-completion of the procedure shall be attributable to that party and neither party shall be under any obligation to comply with any further requirement of the procedure.

(2) Except as mentioned in paragraph (4), where the parties are to be treated as complying with the applicable statutory procedure, or any requirement of it, there is no failure to comply with the procedure or requirement.

(3) Notwithstanding that if regulation 11(1) applies the procedure that would otherwise be the applicable statutory procedure does not apply, where that regulation applies because the circumstances in sub-paragraph (a) or (b) of regulation 11(3) apply and it was the behaviour of one of the parties that resulted in those circumstances applying, that party shall be treated as if—

(a) the procedure had applied, and

(b) there had been a failure to comply with a requirement of the procedure that was attributable to him.

(4) In a case where regulation 11(2) applies in relation to a requirement of the applicable statutory procedure because the circumstances in sub-paragraph (a) or (b) of regulation 11(3) apply, and it was the behaviour of one of the parties that resulted in those circumstances applying, the fact that the requirement was not complied with shall be treated as being a failure, attributable to that party, to comply with a requirement of the procedure.

[3093]

NOTES

Commencement: 1 October 2004.

13 Failure to attend a meeting

(1) Without prejudice to regulation 11(2) and (3)(c), if it is not reasonably practicable for—

(a) the employee, or, if he is exercising his right under section 10 of the 1999 Act (right to be accompanied), his companion; or

(b) the employer,

to attend a meeting organised in accordance with the applicable statutory procedure for a reason which was not foreseeable when the meeting was arranged, the employee or, as the case may be, employer shall not be treated as having failed to comply with that requirement of the procedure.

(2) In the circumstances set out in paragraph (1), the employer shall continue to be under the duty in the applicable statutory procedure to invite the employee to attend a meeting and, where the employee is exercising his rights under section 10 of the 1999 Act and the employee proposes an alternative time under subsection (4) of that section, the employer shall be under a duty to invite the employee to attend a meeting at that time.

(3) The duty to invite the employee to attend a meeting referred to in paragraph (2) shall cease if the employer has invited the employee to attend two meetings and paragraph (1) applied in relation to each of them.

(4) Where the duty in paragraph (2) has ceased as a result of paragraph (3), the parties shall be treated as having complied with the applicable statutory procedure.

[3094]

NOTES

Commencement: 1 October 2004.

14 Questions to obtain information not to constitute statement of grievance

(1) Where a person aggrieved questions a respondent under any of the provisions set out in paragraph (2), those questions shall not constitute a statement of grievance under paragraph 6 or 9 of Schedule 2.

(2) The provisions referred to in paragraph (1) are—
section 7B of the Equal Pay Act 1970;
section 74 of the Sex Discrimination Act 1975;
section 65 of the Race Relations Act 1976;
section 56 of the Disability Discrimination Act 1995;
regulation 33 of the Employment Equality (Religion or Belief) Regulations 2003;
regulation 33 of the Employment Equality (Sexual Orientation) Regulations 2003[;
regulation 41 of the Employment Equality (Age) Regulations 2006].

[3095]

NOTES

Commencement: 1 October 2004.
Para (2): words in square brackets added by the Employment Equality (Age) (Consequential Amendments) Regulations 2007, SI 2007/825, reg 8(1), (3), as from 6 April 2007.

15 Extension of time limits

(1) Where a complaint is presented to an employment tribunal under a jurisdiction listed in Schedule 3 or 4 and—

(a) either of the dismissal and disciplinary procedures is the applicable statutory procedure and the circumstances specified in paragraph (2) apply; or

(b) either of the grievance procedures is the applicable statutory procedure and the circumstances specified in paragraph (3) apply;

the normal time limit for presenting the complaint is extended for a period of three months beginning with the day after the day on which it would otherwise have expired.

(2) The circumstances referred to in paragraph (1)(a) are that the employee presents a complaint to the tribunal after the expiry of the normal time limit for presenting the complaint but had reasonable grounds for believing, when that time limit expired, that a dismissal or disciplinary procedure, whether statutory or otherwise (including an appropriate procedure for the purposes of regulation 5(2)), was being followed in respect of matters that consisted of or included the substance of the tribunal complaint.

(3) The circumstances referred to in paragraph (1)(b) are that the employee presents a complaint to the tribunal—

(a) within the normal time limit for presenting the complaint but in circumstances in which section 32(2) or (3) of the 2002 Act does not permit him to do so; or

(b) after the expiry of the normal time limit for presenting the complaint, having complied with paragraph 6 or 9 of Schedule 2 in relation to his grievance within that normal time limit.

(4) For the purposes of paragraph (3) and section 32 of the 2002 Act the following acts shall be treated, in a case to which the specified regulation applies, as constituting compliance with paragraph 6 or 9 of Schedule 2—

(a) in a case to which regulation 7(1) applies, compliance by the employee with the requirement in regulation 7(2);

(b) in a case to which regulation 9(1) applies, compliance by the appropriate representative with the requirement in sub-paragraph (a) or (b) of that regulation, whichever is the later; and

(c) in a case to which regulation 10 applies, the raising of his grievance by the employee in accordance with the procedure referred to in that regulation.

(5) In this regulation "the normal time limit" means—

(a) subject to sub-paragraph (b), the period within which a complaint under the relevant jurisdiction must be presented if there is to be no need for the tribunal, in order to be entitled to consider it to—

(i) exercise any discretion, or
(ii) make any determination as to whether it is required to consider the complaint,

that the tribunal would have to exercise or make in order to consider a complaint presented outside that period; and

(b) in relation to claims brought under the Equal Pay Act 1970, the period ending on the date on or before which proceedings must be instituted in accordance with section 2(4) of that Act.

[3096]

NOTES

Commencement: 1 October 2004.

Note: the text of this provision has been changed following the comments of Underhill J in *HM Prison Service v Barua* [2007] IRLR 4. In setting out this regulation in the text of his judgment, Underhill J commented—

"I should say that in reproducing the text of the regulation I have altered the lineation in para (5)(a) from what appears in the "Queen's Printer's copy" (and which is faithfully reproduced in the versions on the official OPSI website and in Butterworths Employment Law Handbook). Counsel submitted, and I agree, that the words "that the tribunal would have … etc." must be intended to govern both sub-para (i) and sub-para (ii), rather than only sub-para (ii) as suggested by the lineation as printed: that appears not just from the overall sense but from the phrase "would have to exercise or make", where "exercise" plainly goes with "discretion" in sub-para (i) and "make" plainly goes with "determination" in sub-para (ii)".

Accordingly, the words "that the tribunal would have to exercise or make in order to consider a complaint presented outside that period; and" have been moved so that they no longer form part of sub-para (ii) as they did in the fourteenth edition of this work.

16 National security

Where it would not be possible to comply with an applicable statutory procedure without disclosing information the disclosure of which would be contrary to the interests of national security, nothing in these Regulations requires either party to comply with that procedure.

[3097]

NOTES

Commencement: 1 October 2004.

17 (*Amends the Sex Discrimination (Questions and Replies) Order 1975, SI 1975/2048, art 5 at* **[2030]**, *the Race Relations (Questions and Replies) Order 1977, SI 1977/842, art 5 at* **[2061]**, *the Employment Tribunals Extension of Jurisdiction (England and Wales) Order 1994, SI 1994/1623, art 7 at* **[2258]**, *the Employment Tribunals Extension of Jurisdiction (Scotland) Order 1994, SI 1994/1624, art 7 at* **[2268]**, *the Employment Protection (Continuity of Employment) Regulations 1996, SI 1996/3147, reg 2 at* **[2399]**, *the Working Time Regulations 1998, SI 1998/1833, reg 30 at* **[2451]**, *the Employment Equality (Religion or Belief) Regulations 2003, SI 2003/1660, regs 33, 34 at* **[2974]**, **[2975]**, *and the Employment Equality (Sexual Orientation) Regulations 2003, SI 2003/1661, regs 33, 34 at* **[3020]**, **[3021]**.)

18 Transitional Provisions

These Regulations shall apply—

(a) in relation to dismissal and relevant disciplinary action, where the employer first contemplates dismissing or taking such action against the employee after these Regulations come into force; and

(b) in relation to grievances, where the action about which the employee complains occurs or continues after these Regulations come into force,

but shall not apply in relation to a grievance where the action continues after these Regulations come into force if the employee has raised a grievance about the action with the employer before they come into force.

[3098]

NOTES

Commencement: 1 October 2004.

ACAS ARBITRATION SCHEME (GREAT BRITAIN) ORDER 2004

(SI 2004/753)

NOTES

Made: 9 March 2004.

Authority: Trade Union and Labour Relations (Consolidation) Act 1992, s 212A(1), (3), (6), (7), (8), (9).

Commencement: 6 April 2004.

ARRANGEMENT OF ARTICLES

1 Citation, commencement, interpretation and extent

(1) This Order may be cited as the ACAS Arbitration Scheme (Great Britain) Order 2004 and shall come into force on 6th April 2004.

(2) In this Order—

"the 1996 Act" means the Employment Rights Act 1996;

"basic amount" means such part of an award of compensation made by an arbitrator as comprises the basic amount, determined in accordance with paragraphs 139 to 146 of the Scheme;

"English/Welsh arbitration" means an arbitration under the Scheme, which the parties have agreed shall be determined under the laws of England and Wales;

"the Scheme" means the arbitration scheme set out in the Schedule with the exception of paragraphs 52EW, 110EW, 183EW, 187EW, 194EW, 200EW, 205EW, 209EW, 212EW, 217EW, 223EW and 224EW thereof;

"Scottish arbitration" means an arbitration under the Scheme, which the parties have agreed shall be determined according to the laws of Scotland.

(3) This Order extends to Great Britain.

(4) Paragraphs in the Schedule marked "EW" apply only to English/Welsh arbitrations.

(5) Paragraphs in the Schedule marked "S" apply only to Scottish arbitrations.

(6) Paragraphs in the Schedule not marked "EW" or "S" apply to both English/Welsh arbitrations and Scottish arbitrations.

[3099]

NOTES

Commencement: 6 April 2004.

2 Commencement of the Scheme

The Scheme shall come into effect on 6th April 2004.

[3100]

NOTES

Commencement: 6 April 2004.

3 Revocation

Subject to article 8, the ACAS Arbitration Scheme (England and Wales) Order 2001 is revoked.

[3101]

NOTES

Commencement: 6 April 2004.

4 Application of Part I of the Arbitration Act 1996

The provisions of Part I of the Arbitration Act 1996 referred to in the Schedule at paragraphs 52EW, 110EW, 183EW, 187EW, 194EW, 200EW, 205EW, 209EW, 212EW, 217EW, 223EW and 224EW and shown in italics shall, as modified in those paragraphs, apply to English/Welsh arbitrations conducted in accordance with the Scheme.

[3102]

NOTES

Commencement: 6 April 2004.

5—(1) Section 46(1)(b) of the Arbitration Act 1996 shall apply to English/Welsh arbitrations conducted in accordance with the Scheme, subject to the following modification.

(2) For "such other considerations as are agreed by them or determined by the tribunal" in section 46(1)(b) substitute "the Terms of Reference in paragraph 17 of the arbitration scheme set out in the Schedule to the ACAS Arbitration Scheme (Great Britain) Order 2004".

[3103]

NOTES

Commencement: 6 April 2004.

6 Enforcement of re-employment orders

(1) Employment tribunals shall enforce re-employment orders made in arbitrations conducted in accordance with the Scheme in accordance with section 117 of the 1996 Act (enforcement by award of compensation), modified as follows.

(2) In subsection (1)(a), subsection (3) and subsection (8), for the words "section 113" substitute in each case "paragraph 123(i) of the Scheme".

(3) In subsection (2) for "section 124" substitute "section 124(1) and (5) and subsections (9) and (10)".

(4) In subsection (3)(a) for the words "sections 118 to 127A" substitute the words "sections 118 to 123, section 124(1) and (5), sections 126 and 127A and subsections (9) and (11)".

(5) After subsection (8) insert—

"(9) Section 124(1) shall not apply to compensation awarded, or to a compensatory award made, to a person in a case where the arbitrator finds the reason (or, if more than one, the principal reason) for the dismissal (or, in a redundancy case, for which the employee was selected for dismissal) to be a reason specified in any of the enactments mentioned in section 124(1)A.

(10) In the case of compensation awarded to a person under section 117(1) and (2), the limit imposed by section 124(1) may be exceeded to the extent necessary to enable the award fully to reflect the amount specified as payable under the arbitrator's award in accordance with paragraphs 131(i) or 134(iv) of the Scheme.

(11) Where—

(a) a compensatory award is an award under subsection (3)(a) of section 117, and

(b) an additional award falls to be made under subsection (3)(b) of that section, the limit imposed by section 124(1) on the compensatory award may be exceeded to the extent necessary to enable the aggregate of the compensatory award and additional awards fully to reflect the amount specified as payable under the arbitrator's award in accordance with paragraphs 131(i) or 134(iv) of the Scheme.

(12) In this section "the Scheme" means the arbitration scheme set out in the Schedule to the ACAS Arbitration Scheme (Great Britain) Order 2004.".

[3104]

NOTES

Commencement: 6 April 2004.

7 Awards of compensation

An award of a basic amount shall be treated as a basic award of compensation for unfair dismissal for the purposes of section 184(1)(d) of the 1996 Act (which specifies such an award as a debt which the Secretary of State must satisfy if the employer has become insolvent).

[3105]

NOTES

Commencement: 6 April 2004.

8 Transitional provision

(1) The Scheme has effect in any case where the appropriate date falls on or after 6th April 2004.

(2) In a case where the appropriate date falls before 6th April 2004, the arbitration scheme set out in the Schedule to the ACAS Arbitration Scheme (England and Wales) Order 2001 continues to apply.

(3) In this article, the "appropriate date" means the date of the Arbitration Agreement. Where the parties sign the Arbitration Agreement on different dates, the appropriate date is the date of the first signature.

(4) In this article, "Arbitration Agreement" means an agreement to submit the dispute to arbitration, as defined in paragraph 26 of the Scheme.

[3106]–[3137]

NOTES

Commencement: 6 April 2004.

(The Schedule (omitted for reasons of space) sets out the scheme, submitted to the Secretary of State by ACAS pursuant to the Trade Union and Labour Relations (Consolidation) Act 1992, s 212A, providing for arbitration in the case of disputes involving proceedings, or claims which could be the subject of proceedings, before an employment tribunal arising out of a contravention, or alleged contravention, of the Employment Rights Act 1996, Pt X (unfair dismissal). The Scheme does not extend to other kinds of claim related to, or raised at the same time as, a claim of unfair dismissal, for example, sex discrimination cases, and claims for unpaid wages. The Scheme provides a voluntary alternative to the employment tribunal for the resolution by arbitration of such claims where both parties agree. The full text of the scheme is included in the fifteenth edition of this Handbook.)

COMPROMISE AGREEMENTS (DESCRIPTION OF PERSON) ORDER 2004

(SI 2004/754)

NOTES

Made: 12 March 2004.

Authority: Sex Discrimination Act 1975, s 77(4B)(d); Race Relations Act 1976, s 72(4B)(d); Trade Union and Labour Relations (Consolidation) Act 1992, s 288(4)(d); Disability Discrimination Act 1995, s 9(4)(d); Employment Rights Act 1996, s 203(3A)(d); National Minimum Wage Act 1998, s 49(5)(d).

Note: the Disability Discrimination Act 1995, s 9 was repealed by the Disability Discrimination Act 1995 (Amendment) Regulations 2003, SI 2003/1673, as from 1 October 2004. That provision was replaced by a new Sch 3A, Pt 1 to that Act as added by the 2003 Regulations. However, the new Part does not contain a provision similar to the one formerly in s 9(4)(d), ie, a person is a relevant independent adviser for the purposes of that section if he is a person of a description specified in an Order made by the Secretary of State. It was therefore not clear whether this Order (or the amending SI 2004/2515 which was also partly made under that section) continued to have effect in so far as made under the 1995 Act.

The situation was clarified by the Compromise Agreements (Description of Person) Order 2005, SI 2005/2364 (made under s 67 of, and Sch 3A, para 2(3)(d) to, the 1995 Act) which provides that a Fellow of the Institute of Legal Executives employed by a solicitors' practice is specified for the purposes of para 2(3)(d). Accordingly, this Order (and the amending SI 2004/2515) has lapsed in so far as made under the 1995 Act.

Commencement: 6 April 2004.

1 Citation, commencement and interpretation

(1) This Order may be cited as The Compromise Agreements (Description of Person) Order 2004 and shall come into force on 6th April 2004.

(2) In this Order—

(a) "the 1975 Act" means the Sex Discrimination Act 1975;
(b) "the 1976 Act" means the Race Relations Act 1976;
(c) "the 1992 Act" means the Trade Union and Labour Relations (Consolidation) Act 1992;
(d) "the 1995 Act" means the Disability Discrimination Act 1995;
(e) "the 1996 Act" means the Employment Rights Act 1996; and
(f) "the 1998 Act" means the National Minimum Wage Act 1998.

[3138]

NOTES

Commencement: 6 April 2004.

2 Person specified

For the purposes of section 77(4B)(d) of the 1975 Act, section 72(4B)(d) of the 1976 Act, section 288(4)(d) of the 1992 Act, section 9(4)(d) of the 1995 Act, section 203(3A)(d) of the 1996 Act and section 49(5)(d) of the 1998 Act, a Fellow of the Institute of Legal Executives employed by a solicitors' practice is specified.

[3139]–[3140]

NOTES

Commencement: 6 April 2004.

3 (*Revoked by the Compromise Agreements (Description of Person) Order 2004 (Amendment) Order 2004, SI 2004/2515, art 2, as from 1 October 2004.*)

DISABILITY DISCRIMINATION (QUESTIONS AND REPLIES) ORDER 2004

(SI 2004/1168)

NOTES

Made: 20 April 2004.
Authority: Disability Discrimination Act 1995, ss 56(2), (4), 67(3).
Commencement: 1 October 2004.

ARRANGEMENT OF ARTICLES

SCHEDULES:

1 Citation, commencement and interpretation

(1) This Order may be cited as the Disability Discrimination (Questions and Replies) Order 2004 and shall come into force on 1st October 2004.

(2) This Order does not extend to Northern Ireland.

(3) In this Order—
"the Act" means the Disability Discrimination Act 1995;
"tribunal" means an employment tribunal.

[3141]

NOTES

Commencement: 1 October 2004.

2 Revocation

The Disability Discrimination (Questions and Replies) Order 1996 is hereby revoked.

[3142]

NOTES

Commencement: 1 October 2004.

3 Forms for questions and replies

The forms respectively set out in Schedules 1 and 2 to this Order or forms to the like effect with such variation as the circumstances may require are, respectively, hereby prescribed for the purposes of section 56 of the Act [for cases falling within Part 2 of the Act (the employment field and members of locally-electable authorities) and, in relation to Part 3 of the Act (discrimination in other areas), for cases falling within section 21A (employment services) and sections 19 to 21 of the Act (discrimination in relation to services and duty to make adjustments) in so far as sections 19 to 21 relate to a group insurance arrangement] as forms—

(a) by which a [person aggrieved] may question a respondent on his reasons for doing any relevant act, or any other matter which is or may be relevant; and

(b) by which the respondent may if he wishes reply to any questions.

[3143]

NOTES

Commencement: 1 October 2004.

Words in first pair of square brackets inserted, and words in second pair of square brackets substituted, by the Disability Discrimination (Questions and Replies) Order 2005, SI 2005/2703, art 5(1), (2), as from 5 December 2005.

4 Period for service of questions

In proceedings before a tribunal, a question shall only be admissible as evidence in pursuance of section 56(3) of the Act—

(a) where it was served before a complaint had been presented to a tribunal, if it was so served—

(i) within the period of three months beginning when the act complained of was done; or

(ii) where the period under paragraph 3 of Schedule 3 to the Act within which proceedings must be brought is extended by regulation 15 of the Employment Act 2002 (Dispute Resolution) Regulations 2004, within that extended period;

(b) where it was served after a complaint had been presented to a tribunal—

(i) if it was served within the period of twenty eight days beginning with the day on which the complaint was presented, or

(ii) if it was served with the leave of a tribunal, within the period specified by that tribunal.

[3144]

NOTES

Commencement: 1 October 2004.

5 Manner of service of questions and replies

A question, or as the case may be, a reply may be duly served—

(a) where the person to be served is the respondent, by delivering the question to him, or by sending it by post to him at his usual or last known residence or place of business; or

(b) where the person to be served is the [person aggrieved], by delivering the reply to him, or sending it by post to him at his address for reply as stated by him in the document containing the questions or, if no address is so stated, at his usual or last known residence; or

(c) where the person to be served is a body corporate or is a trade union or employers' association within the meaning of the Trade Union and Labour Relations (Consolidation) Act 1992, by delivering it to the secretary or clerk of the body, union, or association at its registered or principal office or by sending it by post to the secretary or clerk at that office; or

(d) where the person to be served is acting by a solicitor, by delivering it at, or by sending it by post to, the solicitor's address for service.

[3145]

NOTES

Commencement: 1 October 2004.

Words in square brackets in para (b) substituted by the Disability Discrimination (Questions and Replies) Order 2005, SI 2005/2703, art 5(1), (3), as from 5 December 2005.

SCHEDULES

SCHEDULE 1
THE DISABILITY DISCRIMINATION ACT 1995 S 56(2)(A)

Article 2

Questionnaire of [person aggrieved]

To ....

(*name of person to be questioned* (*the respondent*))

of ....

(*address*)

1. I ....

(*name of [person aggrieved]*)

of ....

(*address*)

* consider that you may have discriminated against me contrary to [Part 2 of the Disability Discrimination Act 1995 ("the Act") or Part 3 of that Act so far as it relates to employment services or a group insurance arrangement by]

* (a)—(i) directly discriminating against me [(not applicable in a group insurance case)], or

(ii) otherwise treating me less favourably for a reason relating to my disability in circumstances in which that treatment cannot be justified,

* (b) failing to comply with a duty to make a reasonable adjustment which applied to you in my case,

* (c) victimising me

* and/or

* consider that you may have subjected me to harassment contrary to the Act [(not applicable in a group insurance case)].

2. (*Give details, including a factual description of the treatment received, the effect of the treatment received* (*if the complaint relates to harassment*)*, or the failure complained of. Describe any relevant circumstances leading up to this and include any relevant dates or approximate dates*).

3. I consider this treatment or failure on your part may have been unlawful (because ....
(*complete if you wish to give reasons, otherwise delete*)).

4. Do you agree that the statement in paragraph 2 above is an accurate description of what happened? If not, in what respect do you disagree or what is your version of what happened?

5. Do you accept that your treatment of me or any failure complained of was unlawful? If not, why not?

6. (*Any other questions you wish to ask.*)

7. Please send your reply to *(the above address) *(the following address)

(*address*) ....

....

(*signature of [person aggrieved]*) ....

(*date*) ....

* delete as appropriate

Notes

[(1) Under section 56(3) of the Act (as substituted by the Disability Discrimination Act 2005), this questionnaire and any reply are admissible in evidence in employment tribunal proceedings brought under Part 2 of the Act or under section 21A (employment services) and sections 19 to 21 (discrimination in relation to services and duty to make adjustments) in so far as sections 19 to 21 relate to a group insurance arrangement, of Part 3 of the Act.]

(2) Section 56(3)(b) allows a tribunal to draw any inference it considers is just and equitable from

— [a deliberate failure,] without reasonable excuse, to reply to the questions within eight weeks, or
— an evasive or equivocal reply.

This could include an inference that the person questioned has discriminated against the [person aggrieved] or subjected the [person aggrieved] to harassment in a way which is unlawful under Part 2 of the Act or under [the provisions of Part 3 mentioned in paragraph (1)].

[3146]

NOTES

Commencement: 1 October 2004.

Words in square brackets substituted or inserted by the Disability Discrimination (Questions and Replies) Order 2005, SI 2005/2703, art 5(1), (4), as from 5 December 2005.

SCHEDULE 2
THE DISABILITY DISCRIMINATION ACT 1995 S 56(2)(B)

Article 2

Reply by the respondent

To ....

[(*name of person aggrieved*)]

of ....

(*address*)

1. I ....

(*name of respondent*)

of ....

(*address*)

hereby acknowledge receipt of the questionnaire signed by you and dated

which was served on me on ....(*date*).

2. * I agree that the statement in paragraph 2 of the questionnaire is an accurate description of what happened.

* I disagree with the statement in paragraph 2 of the questionnaire in that ....

....

(*State which parts of the statement in paragraph 2 you disagree with and why*)

3. * I accept

* I dispute

that my treatment of you or any failure on my part to comply with a duty to make a reasonable adjustment was unlawful.

* My reasons for disputing this are ....

....

[(*Include any reasons which in your view explain or justify your treatment of the person aggrieved or which explain, or in a group insurance case justify, any failure on your part to comply with a duty to make a reasonable adjustment*).]

4. (*Replies to questions in paragraph 6 of the questionnaire*).

5. * I have deleted (in whole or in part) the paragraph(s) numbered ....

above, since I am unable/unwilling to reply to the relevant questions for the following reasons:

....

....

(*signature of the respondent*) ....

(*date*) ....

* delete as appropriate

[3147]–[3150]

NOTES

Commencement: 1 October 2004.

Words in square brackets substituted by the Disability Discrimination (Questions and Replies) Order 2005, SI 2005/2703, art 5(1), (5), as from 5 December 2005.

EMPLOYMENT TRIBUNALS (CONSTITUTION AND RULES OF PROCEDURE) REGULATIONS 2004

(SI 2004/1861)

NOTES

Made: 19 July 2004.

Authority: Health and Safety at Work etc Act 1974, s 24(2); Employment Tribunals Act 1996, ss 1(1), 4(6), (6A), 7(1), (3), (3ZA), (3A), (5), 7A(1), (2), 9(1), (2), (4), 10(2), (5), (6), (7), 10A(1), 11(1), 12(2), 13, 13A(1), (2), 19, 41(4); Government of Wales Act 1998, Sch 8, para 36 (repealed by the Government of Wales Act 2006, s 163, Sch 12, as from 25 May 2007; by virtue of the Interpretation Act 1978, s 17(2)(b), in so far as these regulations were made under the 1998 Act, they now have effect as if made under the Government of Wales Act 2006, Sch 9, para 32); Scotland Act 1998, Sch 6, para 37.

Commencement: 1 October 2004. These Regulations and the Rules contained in Schs 1–6 apply as from that date in relation to all proceedings, whenever commenced, except to the extent provided for by transitional provisions contained in reg 20 at **[3170]**. The Regulations and Rules apply equally to England and Wales, and to Scotland with such modifications as indicated).

Employment Judges: a person who is a member of a panel of chairmen of employment tribunals which is appointed in accordance with regulations under the Employment Tribunals Act 1996, s 1(1) may be referred to as an Employment Judge; see s 3A of the 1996 Act at **[956A]** (as inserted by the Tribunals, Courts and Enforcement Act 2007, s 48(1), Sch 8, paras 35, 36, as from 1 December 2007). However, no corresponding amendments have been made (as at 6 April 2008) to these Regulations, or the Rules of Procedure in Schs 1–6, to reflect this change.

ARRANGEMENT OF REGULATIONS

SCHEDULES:

1 Citation, commencement and revocation

[(1) These Regulations may be cited as the Employment Tribunals (Constitution and Rules of Procedure) Regulations 2004 and the Rules of Procedure contained in Schedules 1, 2, 3, 4, 5 and 6 to these Regulations may be referred to, respectively, as—

(a) the Employment Tribunals Rules of Procedure [2004];
(b) the Employment Tribunals (National Security) Rules of Procedure [2004];
(c) the Employment Tribunals (Levy Appeals) Rules of Procedure [2004];
(d) the Employment Tribunals (Health and Safety – Appeals against Improvement and Prohibition Notices) Rules of Procedure [2004];
(e) the Employment Tribunals (Non-Discrimination Notices Appeals) Rules of Procedure [2004]; and
(f) the Employment Tribunals (Equal Value) Rules of Procedure [2004].]

(2) These Regulations shall come into force on 1 October 2004.

(3) Subject to the savings in regulation 20, the Employment Tribunals (Constitution and Rules of Procedure) Regulations 2001 and the Employment Tribunals (Constitution and Rules of Procedure) (Scotland) Regulations 2001 are revoked.

[3151]

NOTES

Commencement: 1 October 2004.

Para (1): substituted by the Employment Tribunals (Constitution and Rules of Procedure) (Amendment) Regulations 2004, SI 2004/2351, reg 2(1), (2), as from 1 October 2004; date in square brackets in sub-paras (a)–(f) inserted by the Employment Tribunals (Constitution and Rules of Procedure) (Amendment) (No 2) Regulations 2005, SI 2005/1865, reg 2(1), (2), as from 1 October 2005.

2 Interpretation

[(1)] [In these Regulations and in Schedules 1, 2, 3, 4, 5 and 6—]

"ACAS" means the Advisory, Conciliation and Arbitration Service referred to in section 247 of TULR(C)A;

"appointing office holder" means, in England and Wales, the Lord Chancellor, and in Scotland, the Lord President;

"chairman" means the President or a member of the panel of chairmen appointed in accordance with regulation 8(3)(a), or, for the purposes of national security proceedings, a member of the panel referred to in regulation 10 selected in accordance with regulation 11(a), and in relation to particular proceedings it means the chairman to whom the proceedings have been referred by the President, Vice President or a Regional Chairman;

"compromise agreement" means an agreement to refrain from continuing proceedings where the agreement meets the conditions in section 203(3) of the Employment Rights Act;

"constructive dismissal" has the meaning set out in section 95(1)(c) of the Employment Rights Act;

"Disability Discrimination Act" means the Disability Discrimination Act 1995;

"electronic communication" has the meaning given to it by section 15(1) of the Electronic Communications Act 2000;

"Employment Act" means the Employment Act 2002;

"Employment Rights Act" means the Employment Rights Act 1996;

"Employment Tribunals Act" means the Employment Tribunals Act 1996;

"Employment Tribunal Office" means any office which has been established for any area in either England & Wales or Scotland specified by the President and which carries out administrative functions in support of functions being carried out by a tribunal or chairman, and in relation to particular proceedings it is the office notified to the parties in accordance with rule 61(3) of Schedule 1;

"enactment" includes an enactment comprised in, or in an instrument made under, an Act of the Scottish Parliament;

"Equal Pay Act" means the Equal Pay Act 1970;

"excluded person" means, in relation to any proceedings, a person who has been excluded from all or part of the proceedings by virtue of—

(a) a direction of a Minister of the Crown under rule 54(1)(b) or (c) of Schedule 1, or

(b) an order of the tribunal under rule 54(2)(a) read with 54(1)(b) or (c) of Schedule 1;

"hearing" means a case management discussion, pre-hearing review, review hearing or Hearing (as those terms are defined in Schedule 1) or a sitting of a chairman or a tribunal duly constituted for the purpose of receiving evidence, hearing addresses and witnesses or doing anything lawful to enable the chairman or tribunal to reach a decision on any question;

"legally represented" has the meaning set out in rule 38(5) of Schedule 1;

"Lord President" means the Lord President of the Court of Session;

"misconceived" includes having no reasonable prospect of success;

"national security proceedings" means proceedings in relation to which a direction is given under rule 54(1) of Schedule 1, or an order is made under rule 54(2) of that Schedule;

"old (England & Wales) regulations" means the Employment Tribunals (Constitution and Rules of Procedure) … Regulations 2001;

"old (Scotland) regulations" means the Employment Tribunals (Constitution and Rules of Procedure) [(Scotland)] Regulations 2001;

"panel of chairmen" means a panel referred to in regulation 8(3)(a);

"President" means, in England and Wales, the person [appointed by the Lord Chancellor or nominated by the Lord Chief Justice] to discharge for the time being the functions of the President of Employment Tribunals (England and Wales), and, in Scotland, the person appointed or nominated by the Lord President to discharge for the time being the functions of the President of Employment Tribunals (Scotland);

"Race Relations Act" means the Race Relations Act 1976;

"Regional Chairman" means a member of the panel of chairmen who has been appointed to the position of Regional Chairman in accordance with regulation 6 or who has been nominated to discharge the functions of a Regional Chairman in accordance with regulation 6;

"Register" means the Register of judgments and written reasons kept in accordance with regulation 17;

"Secretary" means a person for the time being appointed to act as the Secretary of employment tribunals either in England and Wales or in Scotland;

"Sex Discrimination Act" means the Sex Discrimination Act 1975;

"special advocate" means a person appointed in accordance with rule 8 of Schedule 2;

"tribunal" means an employment tribunal established in accordance with regulation 5, and in relation to any proceedings means the tribunal to which the proceedings have been referred by the President, Vice President or a Regional Chairman;

"TULR(C)A" means the Trade Union and Labour Relations (Consolidation) Act 1992;

"Vice President" means a person who has been appointed to the position of Vice President in accordance with regulation 7 or who has been nominated to discharge the functions of the Vice President in accordance with that regulation;

"writing" includes writing delivered by means of electronic communication.

[(2) The Lord Chief Justice may nominate a judicial office holder (as defined in section 109(4) of the Constitutional Reform Act 2005) to exercise his functions under this regulation.]

[3152]

NOTES

Commencement: 1 October 2004.

Para (1): numbered as such, and words in square brackets in definition "President" substituted, by the Lord Chancellor (Transfer of Functions and Supplementary Provisions) Order 2006, SI 2006/680, art 2, Sch 1, paras 73, 74(1)–(3), as from 3 April 2006; words in first pair of square brackets substituted by the Employment Tribunals (Constitution and Rules of Procedure) (Amendment) Regulations 2004, SI 2004/2351, reg 2(1), (3), as from 1 October 2004; word omitted from definition "old (England & Wales) regulations" revoked, and word in square brackets in definition "old (Scotland) regulations" inserted, by the Employment Tribunals (Constitution and Rules of Procedure) (Amendment) (No 2) Regulations 2005, SI 2005/1865, reg 2(1), (3)(b), as from 1 October 2005.

Para (2): added by SI 2006/680, art 2, Sch 1, paras 73, 74(1), (4), as from 3 April 2006.

3 Overriding objective

[(1) The overriding objective of these Regulations and the rules in Schedules 1, 2, 3, 4, 5 and 6 is to enable tribunals and chairmen to deal with cases justly.]

(2) Dealing with a case justly includes, so far as practicable—

(a) ensuring that the parties are on an equal footing;

(b) dealing with the case in ways which are proportionate to the complexity or importance of the issues;

(c) ensuring that it is dealt with expeditiously and fairly; and

(d) saving expense.

[(3) A tribunal or chairman shall seek to give effect to the overriding objective when it or he:

(a) exercises any power given to it or him by these Regulations or the rules in Schedules 1, 2, 3, 4, 5 and 6; or

(b) interprets these Regulations or any rule in Schedules 1, 2, 3, 4, 5 and 6.]

(4) The parties shall assist the tribunal or the chairman to further the overriding objective.

[3153]

NOTES

Commencement: 1 October 2004.

Paras (1), (3): substituted by the Employment Tribunals (Constitution and Rules of Procedure) (Amendment) Regulations 2004, SI 2004/2351, reg 2(1), (4), (5), as from 1 October 2004.

4 President of Employment Tribunals

(1) There shall be a President of Employment Tribunals (England and Wales), responsible for the administration of justice by tribunals and chairmen in England and Wales, who shall be appointed by the Lord Chancellor and shall be a person described in paragraph (3).

(2) There shall be a President of Employment Tribunals (Scotland), responsible for the administration of justice by tribunals and chairmen in Scotland, who shall be appointed by the Lord President and shall be a person described in paragraph (3).

(3) A President shall be a person—

(a) having a seven year general qualification within the meaning of section 71 of the Courts and Legal Services Act 1990;

(b) being an advocate or solicitor admitted in Scotland of at least seven years standing; or

(c) being a member of the Bar of Northern Ireland or *solicitor of the Supreme Court of Northern Ireland* of at least seven years standing.

(4) A President may resign his office by notice in writing to the appointing office holder.

(5) If the appointing office holder is satisfied that the President is incapacitated by infirmity of mind or body from discharging the duties of his office, or the President is adjudged to be bankrupt or makes a composition or arrangement with his creditors, the appointing office holder may revoke his appointment.

[(5A) Where the Lord Chancellor is the appointing office holder, he may revoke an appointment in accordance with paragraph (5) only with the concurrence of the Lord Chief Justice.]

(6) The functions of President under these Regulations may, if he is for any reason unable to act or during any vacancy in his office, be discharged by a person nominated for that purpose by the appointing office holder [where that is the Lord President, or, where the appointing office holder is the Lord Chancellor, by the Lord Chief Justice after consulting the Lord Chancellor].

[(7) The Lord Chief Justice may nominate a judicial office holder (as defined in section 109(4) of the Constitutional Reform Act 2005) to exercise his functions under this regulation.]

[3154]

NOTES

Commencement: 1 October 2004.

Para (3): for the words in italics in sub-para (c) there are substituted the words "solicitor of the Court of Judicature of Northern Ireland" by the Constitutional Reform Act 2005, s 59(5), Sch 11, Pt 3, para 5, as from a day to be appointed.

Para (5A): inserted by the Constitutional Reform Act 2005, s 15(1), Sch 4, Pt 1, para 360, as from 3 April 2006.

Para (6): words in square brackets inserted by the Lord Chancellor (Transfer of Functions and Supplementary Provisions) Order 2006, SI 2006/680, art 2, Sch 1, paras 73, 75(1), (2), as from 3 April 2006.

Para (7): added by SI 2006/680, art 2, Sch 1, paras 73, 75(1), (3), as from 3 April 2006.

5 Establishment of employment tribunals

(1) Each President shall, in relation to that part of Great Britain for which he has responsibility, from time to time determine the number of tribunals to be established for the purposes of determining proceedings.

(2) The President, a Regional Chairman or the Vice President shall determine, in relation to the area specified in relation to him, at what times and in what places in that area tribunals and chairmen shall sit.

[3155]

NOTES

Commencement: 1 October 2004.

6 Regional Chairmen

(1) The Lord Chancellor may from time to time appoint Regional Chairmen from the panel of full-time chairmen and each Regional Chairman shall be responsible to the President (England and Wales) for the administration of justice by tribunals and chairmen in the area specified by the President (England and Wales) in relation to him.

(2) The President (England and Wales) or the Regional Chairman for an area may from time to time nominate a member of the panel of full time chairmen to discharge for the time being the functions of the Regional Chairman for that area.

[3156]

NOTES

Commencement: 1 October 2004.

7 Vice President

(1) The Lord President may from time to time appoint a Vice President from the panel of full time chairmen and the Vice President shall be responsible to the President (Scotland) for the administration of justice by tribunals and chairmen in Scotland.

(2) The President (Scotland) or the Vice President may from time to time nominate a member of the panel of full time chairmen to discharge for the time being the functions of the Vice President.

[3157]

NOTES

Commencement: 1 October 2004.

8 Panels of members of tribunals—general

(1) There shall be three panels of members of Employment Tribunals (England and Wales), as set out in paragraph (3).

(2) There shall be three panels of members of Employment Tribunals (Scotland), as set out in paragraph (3).

(3) The panels referred to in paragraphs (1) and (2) are—

(a) a panel of full-time and part-time chairmen appointed by the appointing office holder consisting of persons—

(i) having a seven year general qualification within the meaning of section 71 of the Courts and Legal Services Act 1990;

(ii) being an advocate or solicitor admitted in Scotland of at least seven years standing; or

(iii) being a member of the Bar of Northern Ireland or *solicitor of the Supreme Court of Northern Ireland* of at least seven years standing;

(b) a panel of persons appointed by the Secretary of State after consultation with such organisations or associations of organisations representative of employees as she sees fit; and

(c) a panel of persons appointed by the Secretary of State after consultation with such organisations or associations of organisations representative of employers as she sees fit.

(4) Members of the panels constituted under these Regulations shall hold and vacate office under the terms of the instrument under which they are appointed but may resign their office by notice in writing, in the case of a member of the panel of chairmen, to the appointing office holder and, in any other case, to the Secretary of State; and any such member who ceases to hold office shall be eligible for reappointment.

(5) The President may establish further specialist panels of chairmen and persons referred to in paragraphs (3)(b) and (c) and may select persons from such specialist panels in order to deal with proceedings in which particular specialist knowledge would be beneficial.

[3158]

NOTES

Commencement: 1 October 2004.

Para (3): for the words in italics in sub-para (a)(iii) there are substituted the words "solicitor of the Court of Judicature of Northern Ireland" by the Constitutional Reform Act 2005, s 59(5), Sch 11, Pt 3, para 5, as from a day to be appointed.

9 Composition of tribunals—general

(1) For each hearing, the President, Vice President or the Regional Chairman shall select a chairman, who shall, subject to regulation 11, be a member of the panel of chairmen, and the President, Vice President or the Regional Chairman may select himself.

(2) In any proceedings which are to be determined by a tribunal comprising a chairman and two other members, the President, Regional Chairman or Vice President shall, subject to regulation 11, select one of those other members from the panel of persons appointed by the Secretary of State under regulation 8(3)(b) and the other from the panel of persons appointed under regulation 8(3)(c).

(3) In any proceedings which are to be determined by a tribunal whose composition is described in paragraph (2) or, as the case may be, regulation 11(b), those proceedings may, with the consent of the parties, be heard and determined in the absence of any one member other than the chairman.

(4) The President, Vice President, or a Regional Chairman may at any time select from the appropriate panel another person in substitution for the chairman or other member of the tribunal previously selected to hear any proceedings before a tribunal or chairman.

[3159]

NOTES

Commencement: 1 October 2004.

10 Panels of members of tribunals—national security proceedings

In relation to national security proceedings, the President shall—

(a) select a panel of persons from the panel of chairmen to act as chairmen in such cases; and
(b) select—
  (i) a panel of persons from the panel referred to in regulation 8(3)(b) as persons suitable to act as members in such cases; and
  (ii) a panel of persons from the panel referred to in regulation 8(3)(c) as persons suitable to act as members in such cases.

[3160]

NOTES

Commencement: 1 October 2004.

11 Composition of tribunals—national security proceedings

In relation to national security proceedings—

(a) the President, the Regional Chairman or the Vice President shall select a chairman, who shall be a member of the panel selected in accordance with regulation 10(a), and the President, Regional Chairman or Vice President may select himself; and
(b) in any such proceedings which are to be determined by a tribunal comprising a chairman and two other members, the President, Regional Chairman or Vice President shall select one of those other members from the panel selected in accordance with regulation 10(b)(i) and the other from the panel selected in accordance with regulation 10(b)(ii).

[3161]

NOTES

Commencement: 1 October 2004.

12 Modification of section 4 of the Employment Tribunals Act (national security proceedings)

(1) For the purposes of national security proceedings section 4 of the Employment Tribunals Act shall be modified as follows.

(2) In section 4(1)(a), for the words "in accordance with regulations made under section 1(1)" substitute the words "in accordance with regulation 11(a) of the Employment Tribunals (Constitution and Rules of Procedure) Regulations 2004".

(3) In section 4(1)(b), for the words "in accordance with regulations so made" substitute the words "in accordance with regulation 11(b) of those Regulations".

(4) In section 4(5), for the words "in accordance with Regulations made under section 1(1)" substitute the words "in accordance with regulation 10(a) of the Employment Tribunals (Constitution and Rules of Procedure) Regulations 2004".

[3162]

NOTES

Commencement: 1 October 2004.

13 Practice directions

(1) The President may make practice directions about the procedure of employment tribunals in the area for which he is responsible, including practice directions about the exercise by tribunals or chairmen of powers under these Regulations or the Schedules to them.

(2) The power of the President to make practice directions under paragraph (1) includes power—

(a) to vary or revoke practice directions;

(b) to make different provision for different cases or different areas, including different provision for specific types of proceedings.

(3) The President shall publish a practice direction made under paragraph (1), and any revocation or variation of it, in such manner as he considers appropriate for bringing it to the attention of the persons to whom it is addressed.

[3163]

NOTES

Commencement: 1 October 2004.

14 Power to prescribe

(1) The Secretary of State may prescribe—

(a) one or more versions of a form, one of which shall be used by all claimants for the purpose of commencing proceedings in an employment tribunal ("claim form") except any claim or proceedings listed in paragraph (3);

(b) one or more versions of a form, one of which shall be used by all respondents to a claim for the purpose of responding to a claim before an employment tribunal ("response form") except respondents to a claim or proceedings listed in paragraph (3); and

(c) that the provision of certain information and answering of certain questions in a claim form or in a response form is mandatory in all proceedings save those listed in paragraph (3).

(2) The Secretary of State shall publish the forms and matters prescribed pursuant to paragraph (1) in such manner as she considers appropriate in order to bring them to the attention of potential claimants, respondents and their advisers.

(3) The proceedings referred to in paragraph (1) are—

(a) those referred to an employment tribunal by a court;

(b) proceedings to which any of Schedules 3 to 5 apply; or

(c) proceedings brought under any of the following enactments—

(i) sections 19, 20 or 22 of the National Minimum Wage Act 1998;

(ii) section 11 of the Employment Rights Act where the proceedings are brought by the employer.

[3164]

NOTES

Commencement: 1 October 2004.

The claim and response forms prescribed under this regulation are at **[5033]** and **[5034]** respectively.

15 Calculation of time limits

[(1) Any period of time for doing any act required or permitted to be done under any of the rules in Schedules 1, 2, 3, 4, 5 and 6, or under any decision, order or judgment of a tribunal or a chairman, shall be calculated in accordance with paragraphs (2) to (6).]

(2) Where any act must or may be done within a certain number of days of or from an event, the date of that event shall not be included in the calculation. For example, a respondent is sent a copy of a claim on 1st October. He must present a response to the Employment Tribunal Office within 28 days of the date on which he was sent the copy. The last day for presentation of the response is 29th October.

(3) Where any act must or may be done not less than a certain number of days before or after an event, the date of that event shall not be included in the calculation. For example, if a party wishes to submit representations in writing for consideration by a tribunal at a hearing, he must submit them not less than 7 days before the hearing. If the hearing is fixed for 8th October, the representations must be submitted no later than 1st October.

(4) Where the tribunal or a chairman gives any decision, order or judgment which imposes a time limit for doing any act, the last date for compliance shall, wherever practicable, be expressed as a calendar date.

(5) In rule 14(4) of Schedule 1 the requirement to send the notice of hearing to the parties not less than 14 days before the date fixed for the hearing shall not be construed as a requirement for service of the notice to have been effected not less than 14 days before the hearing date, but as a requirement for the notice to have been placed in the post not less than 14 days before that date. For example, a hearing is fixed for 15th October. The last day on which the notice may be placed in the post is 1st October.

(6) Where any act must or may have been done within a certain number of days of a document being sent to a person by the Secretary, the date when the document was sent shall, unless the contrary is proved, be regarded as the date on the letter from the Secretary which accompanied the document. For example, a respondent must present his response to a claim to the Employment Tribunal Office [within 28 days of the date on which] he was sent a copy of the claim. If the letter from the Secretary sending him a copy of the claim is dated 1st October, the last day for presentation of the response is 29th October.

[3165]

NOTES

Commencement: 1 October 2004.

Para (1): substituted by the Employment Tribunals (Constitution and Rules of Procedure) (Amendment) Regulations 2004, SI 2004/2351, reg 2(1), (6)(a), as from 1 October 2004.

Para (6): words in square brackets substituted by SI 2004/2351, reg 2(1), (6)(b), as from 1 October 2004.

16 Application of Schedules 1–5 to proceedings

(1) [Subject to paragraphs (2), (3) and (4)], the rules in Schedule 1 shall apply in relation to all proceedings before an employment tribunal except where separate rules of procedure made under the provisions of any enactment are applicable.

(2) In proceedings to which the rules in Schedule 1 apply and in which any power conferred on the Minister, the tribunal or a chairman by rule 54 (national security proceedings) of Schedule 1 is exercised, Schedule 1 shall be modified in accordance with Schedule 2.

(3) The rules in Schedules 3, 4 and 5 shall apply to modify the rules in Schedule 1 in relation to proceedings which consist, respectively, in—

(a) an appeal by a person assessed to levy imposed under a levy order made under section 12 of the Industrial Training Act 1982;

(b) an appeal against an improvement or prohibition notice under section 24 of the Health and Safety at Work etc Act 1974; and

[(c) an appeal against an unlawful act notice under section 21 of the Equality Act 2006].

[(4) In proceedings which involve an equal value claim (as defined in rule 2 of Schedule 6), Schedule 1 shall be modified in accordance with Schedule 6.]

[3166]

NOTES

Commencement: 1 October 2004.

Para (1): words in square brackets substituted by the Employment Tribunals (Constitution and Rules of Procedure) (Amendment) Regulations 2004, SI 2004/2351, reg 2(1), (7)(a), as from 1 October 2004.

Para (3): sub-para (c) substituted by the Equality Act 2006 (Dissolution of Commissions and Consequential and Transitional Provisions) Order 2007, SI 2007/2602, art 4(1), Schedule, para 7(a), as from 1 October 2007.

Para (4): added by SI 2004/2351, reg 2(1), (7)(b), as from 1 October 2004.

17 Register

(1) The Secretary shall maintain a Register which shall be open to the inspection of any person without charge at all reasonable hours.

(2) The Register shall contain a copy of all judgments and any written reasons issued by any tribunal or chairman which are required to be entered in the Register in accordance with the rules in Schedules 1 to 5.

(3) The Register, or any part of it, may be kept by means of a computer.

[3167]

NOTES

Commencement: 1 October 2004.

18 Proof of decisions of tribunals

The production in any proceedings in any court of a document purporting to be certified by the Secretary to be a true copy of an entry of a judgment in the Register shall, unless the contrary is proved, be sufficient evidence of the document and of the facts stated therein.

[3168]

NOTES

Commencement: 1 October 2004.

19 Jurisdiction of tribunals in Scotland and in England & Wales

(1) An employment tribunal in England or Wales shall only have jurisdiction to deal with proceedings (referred to as "English and Welsh proceedings") where—

- (a) the respondent or one of the respondents resides or carries on business in England and Wales;
- (b) had the remedy been by way of action in the county court, the cause of action would have arisen wholly or partly in England and Wales;
- (c) the proceedings are to determine a question which has been referred to the tribunal by a court in England and Wales; or
- (d) in the case of proceedings to which Schedule 3, 4 or 5 applies, the proceedings relate to matters arising in England and Wales.

(2) An employment tribunal in Scotland shall only have jurisdiction to deal with proceedings (referred to as "Scottish proceedings") where—

- (a) the respondent or one of the respondents resides or carries on business in Scotland;
- (b) the proceedings relate to a contract of employment the place of execution or performance of which is in Scotland;
- (c) the proceedings are to determine a question which has been referred to the tribunal by a sheriff in Scotland; or
- (d) in the case of proceedings to which Schedule 3, 4 or 5 applies, the proceedings relate to matters arising in Scotland.

[3169]

NOTES

Commencement: 1 October 2004.

20 Transitional provisions

(1) [These Regulations and Schedules 1 to 6] to them shall apply in relation to all proceedings to which they relate where those proceedings were commenced on or after 1 October 2004.

(2) These Regulations and Schedules 1 and 2 to them (with the exception of rules 1 to 3 and 38 to 48 of Schedule 1) shall apply to proceedings—

(a) which were commenced prior to 1 October 2004; and

(b) to which Schedule 1 to either the old (England & Wales) regulations or the old (Scotland) regulations applied;

provided that a copy of the originating application was not sent to the respondent prior to 1 October 2004.

(3) In relation to the proceedings described in paragraph (2), the following provisions of Schedule 1 to the old (England & Wales) regulations or the old (Scotland) regulations (as the case may be) shall continue to apply—

(a) rule 1 (originating application);

(b) rule 2 (action upon receipt of originating application) with the exception of paragraphs (2), (4) and (5) of that rule; and

(c) rule 14 (costs).

(4) In relation to proceedings described in paragraph (2) but where a copy of the originating application was sent to the respondent prior to 1 October 2004, Schedules 1 and 2 to these Regulations shall apply with the exception of rules 1 to 9, 21 to 24, 33 and 38 to 48 of Schedule 1 and rules 2, 3 and 4 of Schedule 2.

(5) In relation to proceedings described in paragraph (4), the following provisions of the old (England & Wales) regulations or the old (Scotland) regulations (as the case may be) shall continue to apply—

(a) in Schedule 1—

(i) rule 1 (originating application);

(ii) rule 2 (action upon receipt of originating application) with the exception of paragraphs (2), (4) and (5) of that rule;

(iii) rule 3 (appearance by respondent);

(iv) rule 8 (national security);

(v) rule 14 (costs); and

(b) rule 1 of Schedule 2.

(6) In relation to proceedings commenced prior to 1 October 2004 and to which Schedule 4, 5 or 6 to the old (England & Wales) regulations or the old (Scotland) regulations (as the case may be) applied, the provisions of those schedules shall continue to apply to such proceedings.

[(7) In relation to proceedings—

(i) which were commenced prior to 1 October 2004;

(ii) to which Schedule 3 to either the old (England & Wales) regulations or the old (Scotland) regulations applied; and

(iii) in which the tribunal has not, prior to 1 October 2004, required a member of the panel of independent experts to prepare a report under section 2A(1)(b) of the Equal Pay Act;

these Regulations and rules 1 to 13 of Schedule 6, with the exception of rule 4(3)(a), shall apply.

(8) In relation to proceedings—

(i) which were commenced prior to 1 October 2004;

(ii) to which Schedule 3 to either the old (England & Wales) regulations or the old (Scotland) regulations applied; and

(iii) in which the tribunal has, prior to 1 October 2004, required a member of the panel of independent experts to prepare a report under section 2A(1)(b) of the Equal Pay Act;

Schedule 3 to either the old (England & Wales) regulations or the old (Scotland) regulations (as the case may be) shall continue to apply.

(9) In relation to proceedings described in paragraph (8), the following rules of Schedule 6 shall also apply and shall take precedence over any conflicting provision in Schedule 3 to either the old (England & Wales) regulations or the old (Scotland) regulations, namely:

— rules 3, 11(2), 11(4), 12, 13(1) and 13(3).

(10) Rule 14 of Schedule 6 shall apply to all proceedings to which, in accordance with this regulation, rule 10 of Schedule 2 applies.]

[3170]

NOTES

Commencement: 1 October 2004.

Para (1): words in square brackets substituted by the Employment Tribunals (Constitution and Rules of Procedure) (Amendment) Regulations 2004, SI 2004/2351, reg 2(1), (8)(a), as from 1 October 2004.

Paras (7)–(10): added by SI 2004/2351, reg 2(1), (8)(b), as from 1 October 2004.

SCHEDULES

SCHEDULE 1
THE EMPLOYMENT TRIBUNALS RULES OF PROCEDURE

Regulation 16

How to bring a claim

1 Starting a claim

(1) A claim shall be brought before an employment tribunal by the claimant presenting to an Employment Tribunal Office the details of the claim in writing. Those details must include all the relevant required information (subject to paragraph (5) of this rule and to rule 53 (Employment Agencies Act 1973)).

(2) The claim may only be presented to an Employment Tribunal Office in England and Wales if it relates to English and Welsh proceedings (defined in regulation 19(1)). The claim may only be presented to an Employment Tribunal Office in Scotland if it relates to Scottish proceedings (defined in regulation 19(2)).

(3) Unless it is a claim in proceedings described in regulation 14(3), a claim which is presented on or after [1st October 2005] must be presented on a claim form which has been prescribed by the Secretary of State in accordance with regulation 14.

(4) Subject to paragraph (5) and to rule 53, the required information in relation to the claim is—

(a) each claimant's name;

(b) each claimant's address;

(c) the name of each person against whom the claim is made ("the respondent");

(d) each respondent's address;

(e) details of the claim;

(f) whether or not the claimant is or was an employee of the respondent;

(g) whether or not the claim includes a complaint that the respondent has dismissed the claimant or has contemplated doing so;

(h) whether or not the claimant has raised the subject matter of the claim with the respondent in writing at least 28 days prior to presenting the claim to an Employment Tribunal Office;

(i) if the claimant has not done as described in (h), why he has not done so.

(5) In the following circumstances the required information identified below is not required to be provided in relation to that claim—

(a) if the claimant is not or was not an employee of the respondent, the information in paragraphs (4)(g) to (i) is not required;

(b) if the claimant was an employee of the respondent and the claim consists only of a complaint that the respondent has dismissed the claimant or has contemplated doing so, the information in paragraphs (4)(h) and (i) is not required;

(c) if the claimant was an employee of the respondent and the claim does not relate to the claimant being dismissed or a contemplated dismissal by the respondent, and the claimant has raised the subject matter of the claim with the respondent as described in paragraph (4)(h), the information in paragraph (4)(i) is not required.

(6) References in this rule to being dismissed or a dismissal by the respondent do not include references to constructive dismissal.

(7) Two or more claimants may present their claims in the same document if their claims arise out of the same set of facts.

(8) When section 32 of the Employment Act applies to the claim or part of one and a chairman considers in accordance with subsection (6) of section 32 that there has been a breach of subsections (2) to (4) of that section, neither a chairman nor a tribunal shall consider

the substance of the claim (or the relevant part of it) until such time as those subsections have been complied with in relation to the claim or the relevant part of it.

Acceptance of claim procedure

2 What the tribunal does after receiving the claim

(1) On receiving the claim the Secretary shall consider whether the claim or part of it should be accepted in accordance with rule 3. If a claim or part of one is not accepted the tribunal shall not proceed to deal with any part which has not been accepted (unless it is accepted at a later date). If no part of a claim is accepted the claim shall not be copied to the respondent.

(2) If the Secretary accepts the claim or part of it, he shall—

(a) send a copy of the claim to each respondent and record in writing the date on which it was sent;

(b) inform the parties in writing of the case number of the claim (which must from then on be referred to in all correspondence relating to the claim) and the address to which notices and other communications to the Employment Tribunal Office must be sent;

(c) inform the respondent in writing about how to present a response to the claim, the time limit for doing so, what may happen if a response is not entered within the time limit and that the respondent has a right to receive a copy of any judgment disposing of the claim;

(d) when any enactment relevant to the claim provides for conciliation, notify the parties that the services of a conciliation officer are available to them;

(e) when rule 22 (fixed period for conciliation) applies, notify the parties of the date on which the conciliation officer's duty to conciliate ends and that after that date the services of a conciliation officer shall be available to them only in limited circumstances; and

(f) if only part of the claim has been accepted, inform the claimant and any respondent which parts of the claim have not been accepted and that the tribunal shall not proceed to deal with those parts unless they are accepted at a later date.

3 When the claim will not be accepted by the Secretary

(1) When a claim is required by rule 1(3) to be presented using a prescribed form, but the prescribed form has not been used, the Secretary shall not accept the claim and shall return it to the claimant with an explanation of why the claim has been rejected and provide a prescribed claim form.

(2) The Secretary shall not accept the claim (or a relevant part of one) if it is clear to him that one or more of the following circumstances applies—

(a) the claim does not include all the relevant required information;

(b) the tribunal does not have power to consider the claim (or that relevant part of it); or

(c) section 32 of the Employment Act (complaints about grievances) applies to the claim or part of it and the claim has been presented to the tribunal in breach of subsections (2) to (4) of section 32.

(3) If the Secretary decides not to accept a claim or part of one for any of the reasons in paragraph (2), he shall refer the claim together with a statement of his reasons for not accepting it to a chairman. The chairman shall decide in accordance with the criteria in paragraph (2) whether the claim or part of it should be accepted and allowed to proceed.

(4) If the chairman decides that the claim or part of one should be accepted he shall inform the Secretary in writing and the Secretary shall accept the relevant part of the claim and then proceed to deal with it in accordance with rule 2(2).

(5) If the chairman decides that the claim or part of it should not be accepted he shall record his decision together with the reasons for it in writing in a document signed by him. The Secretary shall as soon as is reasonably practicable inform the claimant of that decision and the reasons for it in writing together with information on how that decision may be reviewed or appealed.

(6) Where a claim or part of one has been presented to the tribunal in breach of subsections (2) to (4) of section 32 of the Employment Act, the Secretary shall notify the claimant of the time limit which applies to the claim or the part of it concerned and shall inform the claimant of the consequences of not complying with section 32 of that Act.

(7) Except for the purposes of paragraph (6) and (8) or any appeal to the Employment Appeal Tribunal, where a chairman has decided that a claim or part of one should not be accepted such a claim (or the relevant part of it) is to be treated as if it had not been received by the Secretary on that occasion.

(8) Any decision by a chairman not to accept a claim or part of one may be reviewed in accordance with rules 34 to 36. If the result of such review is that any parts of the claim should have been accepted, then paragraph (7) shall not apply to the relevant parts of that claim and the Secretary shall then accept such parts and proceed to deal with it as described in rule 2(2).

(9) A decision to accept or not to accept a claim or part of one shall not bind any future tribunal or chairman where any of the issues listed in paragraph (2) fall to be determined later in the proceedings.

(10) Except in rule 34 (review of other judgments and decisions), all references to a claim in the remainder of these rules are to be read as references to only the part of the claim which has been accepted.

Response

4 Responding to the claim

(1) If the respondent wishes to respond to the claim made against him he must present his response to the Employment Tribunal Office within 28 days of the date on which he was sent a copy of the claim. The response must include all the relevant required information. The time limit for the respondent to present his response may be extended in accordance with paragraph (4).

(2) Unless it is a response in proceedings described in regulation 14(3), any response presented on or after [1st October 2005] must be on a response form prescribed by the Secretary of State pursuant to regulation 14.

(3) The required information in relation to the response is—

(a) the respondent's full name;
(b) the respondent's address;
(c) whether or not the respondent wishes to resist the claim in whole or in part; and
(d) if the respondent wishes to so resist, on what grounds.

(4) The respondent may apply under rule 11 for an extension of the time limit within which he is to present his response. The application must be presented to the Employment Tribunal Office within 28 days of the date on which the respondent was sent a copy of the claim (unless the application is made under rule 33(1)) and must explain why the respondent cannot comply with the time limit. Subject to rule 33, the chairman shall only extend the time within which a response may be presented if he is satisfied that it is just and equitable to do so.

(5) A single document may include the response to more than one claim if the relief claimed arises out of the same set of facts, provided that in respect of each of the claims to which the single response relates—

(a) the respondent intends to resist all the claims and the grounds for doing so are the same in relation to each claim; or
(b) the respondent does not intend to resist any of the claims.

(6) A single document may include the response of more than one respondent to a single claim provided that—

(a) each respondent intends to resist the claim and the grounds for doing so are the same for each respondent; or
(b) none of the respondents intends to resist the claim.

Acceptance of response procedure

5 What the tribunal does after receiving the response

(1) On receiving the response the Secretary shall consider whether the response should be accepted in accordance with rule 6. If the response is not accepted it shall be returned to the respondent and (subject to paragraphs (5) and (6) of rule 6) the claim shall be dealt with as if no response to the claim had been presented.

(2) If the Secretary accepts the response he shall send a copy of it to all other parties and record in writing the date on which he does so.

6 When the response will not be accepted by the Secretary

(1) Where a response is required to be presented using a prescribed form by rule 4(2), but the prescribed form has not been used, the Secretary shall not accept the response and shall return it to the respondent with an explanation of why the response has been rejected and provide a prescribed response form.

(2) The Secretary shall not accept the response if it is clear to him that any of the following circumstances apply—

(a) the response does not include all the required information (defined in rule 4(3));
(b) the response has not been presented within the relevant time limit.

(3) If the Secretary decides not to accept a response for either of the reasons in paragraph (2), he shall refer the response together with a statement of his reasons for not accepting the response to a chairman. The chairman shall decide in accordance with the criteria in paragraph (2) whether the response should be accepted.

(4) If the chairman decides that the response should be accepted he shall inform the Secretary in writing and the Secretary shall accept the response and then deal with it in accordance with rule 5(2).

(5) If the chairman decides that the response should not be accepted he shall record his decision together with the reasons for it in writing in a document signed by him. The Secretary shall inform both the claimant and the respondent of that decision and the reasons for it. The Secretary shall also inform the respondent of the consequences for the respondent of that decision and how it may be reviewed or appealed.

(6) Any decision by a chairman not to accept a response may be reviewed in accordance with rules 34 to 36. If the result of such a review is that the response should have been accepted, then the Secretary shall accept the response and proceed to deal with the response as described in rule 5(2).

7 Counterclaims

(1) When a respondent wishes to present a claim against the claimant ("a counterclaim") in accordance with article 4 of the Employment Tribunals Extension of Jurisdiction (England and Wales) Order 1994, or as the case may be, article 4 of the Employment Tribunals Extension of Jurisdiction (Scotland) Order 1994, he must present the details of his counterclaim to the Employment Tribunal Office in writing. Those details must include—

(a) the respondent's name;
(b) the respondent's address;
(c) the name of each claimant whom the counterclaim is made against;
(d) the claimant's address;
(e) details of the counterclaim.

(2) A chairman may in relation to particular proceedings by order made under rule 10(1) establish the procedure which shall be followed by the respondent making the counterclaim and any claimant responding to the counterclaim.

(3) The President may by a practice direction made under regulation 13 make provision for the procedure which is to apply to counterclaims generally.

Consequences of a response not being presented or accepted

8 Default judgments

(1) In any proceedings if the relevant time limit for presenting a response has passed, a chairman may, in the circumstances listed in paragraph (2), issue a default judgment to determine the claim without a hearing if he considers it appropriate to do so.

[(2) Those circumstances are when either—

(a) no response in those proceedings has been presented to the Employment Tribunal Office within the relevant time limit;
(b) a response has been so presented, but a decision has been made not to accept the

response either by the Secretary under rule 6(1) or by a chairman under rule 6(3), and the Employment Tribunal Office has not received an application under rule 34 to have that decision reviewed; or

(c) a response has been accepted in those proceedings, but the respondent has stated in the response that he does not intend to resist the claim.]

(3) A default judgment may determine liability only or it may determine liability and remedy. If a default judgment determines remedy it shall be such remedy as it appears to the chairman that the claimant is entitled to on the basis of the information before him.

(4) Any default judgment issued by a chairman under this rule shall be recorded in writing and shall be signed by him. The Secretary shall send a copy of that judgment to the parties, to ACAS, and, if the proceedings were referred to the tribunal by a court, to that court. The Secretary shall also inform the parties of their right to have the default judgment reviewed under rule 33. The Secretary shall put a copy of the default judgment on the Register (subject to rule 49 (sexual offences and the Register)).

(5) The claimant or respondent may apply to have the default judgment reviewed in accordance with rule 33.

(6) If the parties settle the proceedings (either by means of a compromise agreement (as defined in rule 23(2)) or through ACAS) before or on the date on which a default judgment in those proceedings is issued, the default judgment shall have no effect.

(7) When paragraph (6) applies, either party may apply under rule 33 to have the default judgment revoked.

9 Taking no further part in the proceedings

A respondent who has not presented a response to a claim or whose response has not been accepted shall not be entitled to take any part in the proceedings except to—

(a) make an application under rule 33 (review of default judgments);

(b) make an application under rule 35 (preliminary consideration of application for review) in respect of rule [rule 34(3)(a), (b) or (e)];

(c) be called as a witness by another person; or

(d) be sent a copy of a document or corrected entry in accordance with rule 8(4), 29(2) or 37;

and in these rules the word "party" or "respondent" includes a respondent only in relation to his entitlement to take such a part in the proceedings, and in relation to any such part which he takes.

Case management

10 General power to manage proceedings

(1) Subject to the following rules, the chairman may at any time either on the application of a party or on his own initiative make an order in relation to any matter which appears to him to be appropriate. Such orders may be any of those listed in paragraph (2) or such other orders as he thinks fit. Subject to the following rules, orders may be issued as a result of a chairman considering the papers before him in the absence of the parties, or at a hearing (see regulation 2 for the definition of "hearing").

(2) Examples of orders which may be made under paragraph (1) are orders—

(a) as to the manner in which the proceedings are to be conducted, including any time limit to be observed;

(b) that a party provide additional information;

(c) requiring the attendance of any person in Great Britain either to give evidence or to produce documents or information;

(d) requiring any person in Great Britain to disclose documents or information to a party to allow a party to inspect such material as might be ordered by a County Court (or in Scotland, by a sheriff);

(e) extending any time limit, whether or not expired (subject to rules 4(4), 11(2), 25(5), 30(5), 33(1), 35(1), 38(7) and 42(5) of this Schedule, and to rule 3(4) of Schedule 2);

(f) requiring the provision of written answers to questions put by the tribunal or chairman;

(g) that, subject to rule 22(8), a short conciliation period be extended into a standard conciliation period;

(h) staying (in Scotland, sisting) the whole or part of any proceedings;
(i) that part of the proceedings be dealt with separately;
(j) that different claims be considered together;
(k) that any person who the chairman or tribunal considers may be liable for the remedy claimed should be made a respondent in the proceedings;
(l) dismissing the claim against a respondent who is no longer directly interested in the claim;
(m) postponing or adjourning any hearing;
(n) varying or revoking other orders;
(o) giving notice to the parties of a pre-hearing review or the Hearing;
(p) giving notice under rule 19;
(q) giving leave to amend a claim or response;
(r) that any person who the chairman or tribunal considers has an interest in the outcome of the proceedings may be joined as a party to the proceedings;
(s) that a witness statement be prepared or exchanged; or
(t) as to the use of experts or interpreters in the proceedings.

(3) An order may specify the time at or within which and the place at which any act is required to be done. An order may also impose conditions and it shall inform the parties of the potential consequences of non-compliance set out in rule 13.

(4) When a requirement has been imposed under paragraph (1) the person subject to the requirement may make an application under rule 11 (applications in proceedings) for the order to be varied or revoked.

(5) An order described in … paragraph (2)(d) which requires a person other than a party to grant disclosure or inspection of material may be made only when the disclosure sought is necessary in order to dispose fairly of the claim or to save expense.

(6) Any order containing a requirement described in either sub-paragraph (2)(c) or (d) shall state that under section 7(4) of the Employment Tribunals Act, any person who without reasonable excuse fails to comply with the requirement shall be liable on summary conviction to a fine, and the document shall also state the amount of the maximum fine.

(7) An order as described in paragraph (2)(j) may be made only if all relevant parties have been given notice that such an order may be made and they have been given the opportunity to make oral or written representations as to why such an order should or should not be made.

(8) Any order made under this rule shall be recorded in writing and signed by the chairman and the Secretary shall inform all parties to the proceedings of any order made as soon as is reasonably practicable.

11 Applications in proceedings

(1) At any stage of the proceedings a party may apply for an order to be issued, varied or revoked or for a case management discussion or pre-hearing review to be held.

(2) An application for an order must be made not less than 10 days before the date of the hearing at which it is to be considered (if any) unless it is not reasonably practicable to do so, or the chairman or tribunal considers it in the interests of justice that shorter notice be allowed. The application must (unless a chairman orders otherwise) be in writing to the Employment Tribunal Office and include the case number for the proceedings and the reasons for the request. If the application is for a case management discussion or a pre-hearing review to be held, it must identify any orders sought.

(3) An application for an order must include an explanation of how the order would assist the tribunal or chairman in dealing with the proceedings efficiently and fairly.

(4) When a party is legally represented in relation to the application (except where the application is for a witness order described in rule 10(2)(c) only), that party or his representative must, at the same time as the application is sent to the Employment Tribunal Office, provide all other parties with the following information in writing—

(a) details of the application and the reasons why it is sought;
(b) notification that any objection to the application must be sent to the Employment Tribunal Office within 7 days of receiving the application, or before the date of the hearing (whichever date is the earlier);
(c) that any objection to the application must be copied to both the Employment Tribunal Office and all other parties;

and the party or his representative must confirm in writing to the Employment Tribunal Office that this rule has been complied with.

(5) Where a party is not legally represented in relation to the application, the Secretary shall inform all other parties of the matters listed in paragraphs (4)(a) to (c).

(6) A chairman may refuse a party's application and if he does so the Secretary shall inform the parties in writing of such refusal unless the application is refused at a hearing.

12 Chairman acting on his own initiative

(1) Subject to paragraph (2) and to rules 10(7) and 18(7), a chairman may make an order on his own initiative with or without hearing the parties or giving them an opportunity to make written or oral representations. He may also decide to hold a case management discussion or pre-hearing review on his own initiative.

(2) Where a chairman makes an order without giving the parties the opportunity to make representations—

(a) the Secretary must send to the party affected by such order a copy of the order and a statement explaining the right to make an application under paragraph (2)(b); and

(b) a party affected by the order may apply to have it varied or revoked.

(3) An application under paragraph (2)(b) must (subject to rule 10(2)(e)) be made before the time at which, or the expiry of the period within which, the order was to be complied with. Such an application must (unless a chairman orders otherwise) be made in writing to an Employment Tribunal Office and it must include the reasons for the application. Paragraphs (4) and (5) of rule 11 apply in relation to informing the other parties of the application.

13 Compliance with orders and practice directions

(1) If a party does not comply with an order made under these rules, under rule 8 of Schedule 3, rule 7 of Schedule 4 or a practice direction, a chairman or tribunal—

(a) may make an order in respect of costs or preparation time under rules 38 to 46; or

(b) may (subject to paragraph (2) and rule 19) at a pre-hearing review or a Hearing make an order to strike out the whole or part of the claim or, as the case may be, the response and, where appropriate, order that a respondent be debarred from responding to the claim altogether.

(2) An order may also provide that unless the order is complied with, the claim or, as the case may be, the response shall be struck out on the date of non-compliance without further consideration of the proceedings or the need to give notice under rule 19 or hold a pre-hearing review or Hearing.

(3) Chairmen and tribunals shall comply with any practice directions issued under regulation 13.

Different types of hearing

14 Hearings—general

(1) A chairman or a tribunal (depending on the relevant rule) may hold the following types of hearing—

(a) a case management discussion under rule 17;

(b) a pre-hearing review under rule 18;

(c) a Hearing under rule 26; or

(d) a review hearing under rule 33 or 36.

(2) So far as it appears appropriate to do so, the chairman or tribunal shall seek to avoid formality in his or its proceedings and shall not be bound by any enactment or rule of law relating to the admissibility of evidence in proceedings before the courts.

(3) The chairman or tribunal (as the case may be) shall make such enquiries of persons appearing before him or it and of witnesses as he or it considers appropriate and shall otherwise conduct the hearing in such manner as he or it considers most appropriate for the clarification of the issues and generally for the just handling of the proceedings.

(4) Unless the parties agree to shorter notice, the Secretary shall send notice of any hearing (other than a case management discussion) to every party not less than 14 days before

the date fixed for the hearing and shall inform them that they have the opportunity to submit written representations and to advance oral argument. The Secretary shall give the parties reasonable notice before a case management discussion is held.

(5) If a party wishes to submit written representations for consideration at a hearing (other than a case management discussion) he shall present them to the Employment Tribunal Office not less than 7 days before the hearing and shall at the same time send a copy to all other parties.

(6) The tribunal or chairman may, if it or he considers it appropriate, consider representations in writing which have been submitted otherwise than in accordance with paragraph (5).

15 Use of electronic communications

(1) A hearing (other than those mentioned in sub-paragraphs (c) and (d) of rule 14(1)) may be conducted by use of electronic communications provided that the chairman or tribunal conducting the hearing considers it just and equitable to do so.

(2) Where a hearing is required by these rules to be held in public and it is to be conducted by use of electronic communications in accordance with this rule then, subject to rule 16, it must be held in a place to which the public has access and using equipment so that the public is able to hear all parties to the communication.

16 Hearings which may be held in private

(1) A hearing or part of one may be conducted in private for the purpose of hearing from any person evidence or representations which in the opinion of the tribunal or chairman is likely to consist of information—

- (a) which he could not disclose without contravening a prohibition imposed by or by virtue of any enactment;
- (b) which has been communicated to him in confidence, or which he has otherwise obtained in consequence of the confidence placed in him by another person; or
- (c) the disclosure of which would, for reasons other than its effect on negotiations with respect to any of the matters mentioned in section 178(2) of TULR(C)A, cause substantial injury to any undertaking of his or any undertaking in which he works.

(2) Where a tribunal or chairman decides to hold a hearing or part of one in private, it or he shall give reasons for doing so. A member of the Council on Tribunals (in Scotland, a member of the Council on Tribunals or its Scottish Committee) shall be entitled to attend any Hearing or pre-hearing review taking place in private in his capacity as a member.

Case management discussions

17 Conduct of case management discussions

(1) Case management discussions are interim hearings and may deal with matters of procedure and management of the proceedings and they [shall be held in private]. Case management discussions shall be conducted by a chairman.

(2) Any determination of a person's civil rights or obligations shall not be dealt with in a case management discussion. The matters listed in rule 10(2) are examples of matters which may be dealt with at case management discussions. Orders and judgments listed in rule 18(7) may not be made at a case management discussion.

Pre-hearing reviews

18 Conduct of pre-hearing reviews

(1) Pre-hearing reviews are interim hearings and shall be conducted by a chairman unless the circumstances in paragraph (3) are applicable. Subject to rule 16, they shall take place in public.

(2) At a pre-hearing review the chairman may carry out a preliminary consideration of the proceedings and he may—

- (a) determine any interim or preliminary matter relating to the proceedings;

(b) issue any order in accordance with rule 10 or do anything else which may be done at a case management discussion;
(c) order that a deposit be paid in accordance with rule 20 without hearing evidence;
(d) consider any oral or written representations or evidence;
(e) deal with an application for interim relief made under section 161 of TULR(C)A or section 128 of the Employment Rights Act.

(3) Pre-hearing reviews shall be conducted by a tribunal composed in accordance with section 4(1) and (2) of the Employment Tribunals Act if—
(a) a party has made a request in writing not less than 10 days before the date on which the pre-hearing review is due to take place that the pre-hearing review be conducted by a tribunal instead of a chairman; and
(b) a chairman considers that one or more substantive issues of fact are likely to be determined at the pre-hearing review, that it would be desirable for the pre-hearing review to be conducted by a tribunal and he has issued an order that the pre-hearing review be conducted by a tribunal.

(4) If an order is made under paragraph (3), any reference to a chairman in relation to a pre-hearing review shall be read as a reference to a tribunal.

(5) Notwithstanding the preliminary or interim nature of a pre-hearing review, at a pre-hearing review the chairman may give judgment on any preliminary issue of substance relating to the proceedings. Judgments or orders made at a pre-hearing review may result in the proceedings being struck out or dismissed or otherwise determined with the result that a Hearing is no longer necessary in those proceedings.

(6) Before a judgment or order listed in paragraph (7) is made, notice must be given in accordance with rule 19. The judgments or [orders] listed in paragraph (7) must be made at a pre-hearing review or a Hearing if one of the parties has so requested. If no such request has been made such judgments or [orders] may be made in the absence of the parties.

(7) Subject to paragraph (6), a chairman or tribunal may make a judgment or order—
(a) as to the entitlement of any party to bring or contest particular proceedings;
(b) striking out or amending all or part of any claim or response on the grounds that it is scandalous, or vexatious or has no reasonable prospect of success;
(c) striking out any claim or response (or part of one) on the grounds that the manner in which the proceedings have been conducted by or on behalf of the claimant or the respondent (as the case may be) has been scandalous, unreasonable or vexatious;
(d) striking out a claim which has not been actively pursued;
(e) striking out a claim or response (or part of one) for non-compliance with an order or practice direction;
(f) striking out a claim where the chairman or tribunal considers that it is no longer possible to have a fair Hearing in those proceedings;
(g) making a restricted reporting order (subject to rule 50).

(8) A claim or response or any part of one may be struck out under these rules only on the grounds stated in sub-paragraphs (7)(b) to (f).

(9) If at a pre-hearing review a requirement to pay a deposit under rule 20 has been considered, the chairman who conducted that pre-hearing review shall not be a member of the tribunal at the Hearing in relation to those proceedings.

19 Notice requirements

(1) Before a chairman or a tribunal makes a judgment or order described in rule 18(7), except where the order is one described in rule 13(2) or it is a temporary restricted reporting order made in accordance with rule 50, the Secretary shall send notice to the party against whom it is proposed that the order or judgment should be made. The notice shall inform him of the order or judgment to be considered and give him the opportunity to give reasons why the order or judgment should not be made. This paragraph shall not be taken to require the Secretary to send such notice to that party if that party has been given an opportunity to give reasons orally to the chairman or the tribunal as to why the order should not be made.

(2) Where a notice required by paragraph (1) is sent in relation to an order to strike out a claim which has not been actively pursued, unless the contrary is proved, the notice shall be treated as if it were received by the addressee if it has been sent to the address specified in the claim as the address to which notices are to be sent (or to any subsequent replacement for that address which has been notified to the Employment Tribunal Office).

Payment of a deposit

20 Requirement to pay a deposit in order to continue with proceedings

(1) At a pre-hearing review if a chairman considers that the contentions put forward by any party in relation to a matter required to be determined by a tribunal have little reasonable prospect of success, the chairman may make an order against that party requiring the party to pay a deposit of an amount not exceeding £500 as a condition of being permitted to continue to take part in the proceedings relating to that matter.

(2) No order shall be made under this rule unless the chairman has taken reasonable steps to ascertain the ability of the party against whom it is proposed to make the order to comply with such an order, and has taken account of any information so ascertained in determining the amount of the deposit.

(3) An order made under this rule, and the chairman's grounds for making such an order, shall be recorded in a document signed by the chairman. A copy of that document shall be sent to each of the parties and shall be accompanied by a note explaining that if the party against whom the order is made persists in making those contentions relating to the matter to which the order relates, he may have an award of costs or preparation time made against him and could lose his deposit.

(4) If a party against whom an order has been made does not pay the amount specified in the order to the Secretary either—

(a) within the period of 21 days of the day on which the document recording the making of the order is sent to him; or

(b) within such further period, not exceeding 14 days, as the chairman may allow in the light of representations made by that party within the period of 21 days;

a chairman shall strike out the claim or response of that party or, as the case may be, the part of it to which the order relates.

(5) The deposit paid by a party under an order made under this rule shall be refunded to him in full except where rule 47 applies.

Conciliation

21 Documents to be sent to conciliators

In proceedings brought under the provisions of any enactment providing for conciliation, the Secretary shall send copies of all documents, orders, judgments, written reasons and notices to an ACAS conciliation officer except where the Secretary and ACAS have agreed otherwise.

22 Fixed period for conciliation

(1) This rule and rules 23 and 24 apply to all proceedings before a tribunal which are brought under any enactment which provides for conciliation except national security proceedings and proceedings which include a claim made under one or more of the following enactments—

(a) the Equal Pay Act, section 2(1);
(b) the Sex Discrimination Act, Part II, section 63;
(c) the Race Relations Act, Part II, section 54;
(d) the Disability Discrimination Act, Part II, section 17A or 25(8);
(e) the Employment Equality (Sexual Orientation) Regulations 2003;
(f) the Employment Equality (Religion or Belief) Regulations 2003; …
(g) Employment Rights Act, sections 47B, 103A and 105(6A)[; and
(h) the Employment Equality (Age) Regulations 2006].

(2) In all proceedings to which this rule applies there shall be a conciliation period to give a time limited opportunity for the parties to reach an ACAS conciliated settlement (the "conciliation period"). In proceedings in which there is more than one respondent there shall be a conciliation period in relation to each respondent.

(3) In any proceedings to which this rule applies a Hearing shall not take place during a conciliation period and where the time and place of a Hearing has been fixed to take place during a conciliation period, such Hearing shall be postponed until after the end of any conciliation period. The fixing of the time and place for the Hearing may take place during a conciliation period. Pre-hearing reviews and case management discussions may take place during a conciliation period.

(4) In relation to each respondent the conciliation period commences on [the day following] the date on which the Secretary sends a copy of the claim to that respondent. The duration of the conciliation period shall be determined in accordance with the following paragraphs and rule 23.

(5) In any proceedings which consist of claims under any of the following enactments (but no other enactments) the conciliation period is seven weeks (the "short conciliation period")—

- (a) Employment Tribunals Act, section 3 (breach of contract);
- (b) the following provisions of the Employment Rights Act—
  - (i) sections 13 to 27 (failure to pay wages or an unauthorised deduction of wages);
  - (ii) section 28 (right to a guarantee payment);
  - (iii) section 50 (right to time off for public duties);
  - (iv) section 52 (right to time off to look for work or arrange training);
  - (v) section 53 (right to remuneration for time off under section 52);
  - (vi) section 55 (right to time off for ante-natal care);
  - (vii) section 56 (right to remuneration for time off under section 55);
  - (viii) section 64 (failure to pay remuneration whilst suspended for medical reasons);
  - (ix) section 68 (right to remuneration whilst suspended on maternity grounds);
  - (x) sections 163 or 164 (failure to pay a redundancy payment);
- (c) the following provisions of TULR(C)A—
  - (i) section 68 (right not to suffer deduction of unauthorised subscriptions)
  - (ii) section 168 (time off for carrying out trade union duties);
  - (iii) section 169 (payment for time off under section 168);
  - (iv) section 170 (time off for trade union activities);
  - (v) section 192 (failure to pay remuneration under a protective award);
- (d) [regulation 15(10) of the Transfer of Undertakings (Protection of Employment) Regulations 2006] (failure to pay compensation following failure to inform or consult);
- [(e) regulations 13, 14(2) or 16(1) of the Working Time Regulations 1998 (right to paid annual leave)].

(6) In all other proceedings to which this rule applies the conciliation period is thirteen weeks (the "standard conciliation period").

(7) In proceedings to which the standard conciliation period applies, that period shall be extended by a period of a further two weeks if ACAS notifies the Secretary in writing that all of the following circumstances apply before the expiry of the standard conciliation period—

- (a) all parties to the proceedings agree to the extension of any relevant conciliation period;
- (b) a proposal for settling the proceedings has been made by a party and is under consideration by the other parties to the proceedings; and
- (c) ACAS considers it probable that the proceedings will be settled during the further extended conciliation period.

(8) A short conciliation period in any proceedings may, if that period has not already ended, be extended into a standard conciliation period if a chairman considers on the basis of the complexity of the proceedings that a standard conciliation period would be more appropriate. Where a chairman makes an order extending the conciliation period in such circumstances, the Secretary shall inform the parties to the proceedings and ACAS in writing as soon as is reasonably practicable.

23 Early termination of conciliation period

(1) Should one of the following circumstances arise during a conciliation period (be it short or standard) which relates to a particular respondent (referred to in this rule as the relevant respondent), that conciliation period shall terminate early on the relevant date specified (and if more than one circumstance or date listed below is applicable to any conciliation period, that conciliation period shall terminate on the earliest of those dates)—

- (a) where a default judgment is issued against the relevant respondent which determines both liability and remedy, the date on which the default judgment is signed;
- (b) where a default judgment is issued against the relevant respondent which determines liability only, the date which is 14 days after the date on which the default judgment is signed;

(c) where either the claim or the response entered by the relevant respondent is struck out, the date on which the judgment to strike out is signed;

(d) where the claim is withdrawn, the date of receipt by the Employment Tribunal Office of the notice of withdrawal;

(e) where the claimant or the relevant respondent has informed ACAS in writing that they do not wish to proceed with attempting to conciliate in relation to those proceedings, the date on which ACAS sends notice of such circumstances to the parties and to the Employment Tribunal Office;

(f) where the claimant and the relevant respondent have reached a settlement by way of a compromise agreement (including a compromise agreement to refer proceedings to arbitration), the date on which the Employment Tribunal Office receives notice from both of those parties to that effect;

(g) where the claimant and the relevant respondent have reached a settlement through a conciliation officer (including a settlement to refer the proceedings to arbitration), the date of the settlement;

(h) where no response presented by the relevant respondent has been accepted in the proceedings and no default judgment has been issued against that respondent, the date which is 14 days after the expiry of the time limit for presenting the response to the Secretary.

(2) Where a chairman or tribunal makes an order which re-establishes the relevant respondent's right to respond to the claim (for example, revoking a default judgment) and when that order is made, the conciliation period in relation to that respondent has terminated early under paragraph (1) or has otherwise expired, the chairman or tribunal may order that a further conciliation period shall apply in relation to that respondent if they consider it appropriate to do so.

(3) When an order is made under paragraph (2), the further conciliation period commences on the date of that order and the duration of that period shall be determined in accordance with paragraphs (5) to (8) of rule 22 and paragraph (1) of this rule as if the earlier conciliation period in relation to that respondent had not taken place.

24 Effect of staying or sisting proceedings on the conciliation period

Where during a conciliation period an order is made to stay (or in Scotland, sist) the proceedings, that order has the effect of suspending any conciliation period in those proceedings. Any unexpired portion of a conciliation period takes effect from the date on which the stay comes to an end (or in Scotland, the sist is recalled) and continues for the duration of the unexpired portion of that conciliation period or two weeks (whichever is the greater).

Withdrawal of proceedings

25 Right to withdraw proceedings

(1) A claimant may withdraw all or part of his claim at any time – this may be done either orally at a hearing or in writing in accordance with paragraph (2).

(2) To withdraw a claim or part of one in writing the claimant must inform the Employment Tribunal Office of the claim or the parts of it which are to be withdrawn. Where there is more than one respondent the notification must specify against which respondents the claim is being withdrawn.

(3) The Secretary shall inform all other parties of the withdrawal. Withdrawal takes effect on the date on which the Employment Tribunal Office (in the case of written notifications) or the tribunal (in the case of oral notification) receives notice of it and where the whole claim is withdrawn, subject to paragraph (4), proceedings are brought to an end against the relevant respondent on that date. Withdrawal does not affect proceedings as to costs, preparation time or wasted costs.

(4) Where a claim has been withdrawn, a respondent may make an application to have the proceedings against him dismissed. Such an application must be made by the respondent in writing to the Employment Tribunal Office within 28 days of the notice of the withdrawal being sent to the respondent. If the respondent's application is granted and the proceedings are dismissed those proceedings cannot be continued by the claimant (unless the decision to dismiss is successfully reviewed or appealed).

(5) The time limit in paragraph (4) may be extended by a chairman if he considers it just and equitable to do so.

The hearing

26 Hearings

(1) A Hearing is held for the purpose of determining outstanding procedural or substantive issues or disposing of the proceedings. In any proceedings there may be more than one Hearing and there may be different categories of Hearing, such as a Hearing on liability, remedies, costs (in Scotland, expenses) or preparation time.

(2) Any Hearing of a claim shall be heard by a tribunal composed in accordance with section 4(1) and (2) of the Employment Tribunals Act.

(3) Any Hearing of a claim shall take place in public, subject to rule 16.

27 What happens at the Hearing

(1) The President, Vice President or a Regional Chairman shall fix the date, time and place of the Hearing and the Secretary shall send to each party a notice of the Hearing together with information and guidance as to procedure at the Hearing.

(2) Subject to rule 14(3), at the Hearing a party shall be entitled to give evidence, to call witnesses, to question witnesses and to address the tribunal.

(3) The tribunal shall require parties and witnesses who attend the Hearing to give their evidence on oath or affirmation.

(4) The tribunal may exclude from the Hearing any person who is to appear as a witness in the proceedings until such time as they give evidence if it considers it in the interests of justice to do so.

(5) If a party fails to attend or to be represented (for the purpose of conducting the party's case at the Hearing) at the time and place fixed for the Hearing, the tribunal may dismiss or dispose of the proceedings in the absence of that party or may adjourn the Hearing to a later date.

(6) If the tribunal wishes to dismiss or dispose of proceedings in the circumstances described in paragraph (5), it shall first consider any information in its possession which has been made available to it by the parties.

(7) At a Hearing a tribunal may exercise any powers which may be exercised by a chairman under these rules.

Orders, judgments and reasons

28 Orders and judgments

(1) Chairmen or tribunals may issue the following—

(a) a "judgment", which is a final determination of the proceedings or of a particular issue in those proceedings; it may include an award of compensation, a declaration or recommendation and it may also include orders for costs, preparation time or wasted costs;

(b) an "order", which may be issued in relation to interim matters and it will require a person to do or not to do something.

(2) If the parties agree in writing upon the terms of any order or judgment a chairman or tribunal may, if he or it thinks fit, make such order or judgment.

(3) At the end of a hearing the chairman (or, as the case may be, the tribunal) shall either issue any order or judgment orally or shall reserve the judgment or order to be given in writing at a later date.

(4) Where a tribunal is composed of three persons any order or judgment may be made or issued by a majority; and if a tribunal is composed of two persons only, the chairman has a second or casting vote.

29 Form and content of judgments

(1) When judgment is reserved a written judgment shall be sent to the parties as soon as practicable. All judgments (whether issued orally or in writing) shall be recorded in writing and signed by the chairman.

(2) The Secretary shall provide a copy of the judgment to each of the parties and, where the proceedings were referred to the tribunal by a court, to that court. The Secretary shall include guidance to the parties on how the judgment may be reviewed or appealed.

(3) Where the judgment includes an award of compensation or a determination that one party is required to pay a sum to another (excluding an order for costs, expenses, allowances, preparation time or wasted costs), the document shall also contain a statement of the amount of compensation awarded, or of the sum required to be paid.

30 Reasons

(1) A tribunal or chairman must give reasons (either oral or written) for any—

(a) judgment; or

(b) order, if a request for reasons is made before or at the hearing at which the order is made.

(2) Reasons may be given orally at the time of issuing the judgment or order or they may be reserved to be given in writing at a later date. If reasons are reserved, they shall be signed by the chairman and sent to the parties by the Secretary.

(3) [Subject to paragraph (1), written reasons shall only be provided]—

(a) in relation to judgments if requested by one of the parties within the time limit set out in paragraph (5); or

(b) in relation to any judgment or order if requested by the Employment Appeal Tribunal at any time.

(4) When written reasons are provided, the Secretary shall send a copy of the reasons to all parties to the proceedings and record the date on which the reasons were sent. Written reasons shall be signed by the chairman.

(5) A request for written reasons for a judgment must be made by a party either orally at the hearing (if the judgment is issued at a hearing), or in writing within 14 days of the date on which the judgment was sent to the parties. This time limit may be extended by a chairman where he considers it just and equitable to do so.

(6) Written reasons for a judgment shall include the following information—

(a) the issues which the tribunal or chairman has identified as being relevant to the claim;

(b) if some identified issues were not determined, what those issues were and why they were not determined;

(c) findings of fact relevant to the issues which have been determined;

(d) a concise statement of the applicable law;

(e) how the relevant findings of fact and applicable law have been applied in order to determine the issues; and

(f) where the judgment includes an award of compensation or a determination that one party make a payment to the other, a table showing how the amount or sum has been calculated or a description of the manner in which it has been calculated.

31 Absence of chairman

Where it is not possible for a judgment, order or reasons to be signed by the chairman due to death, incapacity or absence—

(a) if the chairman has dealt with the proceedings alone the document shall be signed by the Regional Chairman, Vice President or President when it is practicable for him to do so; and

(b) if the proceedings have been dealt with by a tribunal composed of two or three persons, the document shall be signed by the other person or persons;

and any person who signs the document shall certify that the chairman is unable to sign.

32 The Register

(1) Subject to rule 49, the Secretary shall enter a copy of the following documents in the Register—

(a) any judgment (including any costs, expenses, preparation time or wasted costs order); and

(b) any written reasons provided in accordance with rule 30 in relation to any judgment.

(2) Written reasons for judgments shall be omitted from the Register in any case in which evidence has been heard in private and the tribunal or chairman so orders. In such a

case the Secretary shall send the reasons to each of the parties and where there are proceedings before a superior court relating to the judgment in question, he shall send the reasons to that court, together with a copy of the entry in the Register of the judgment to which the reasons relate.

Power to review judgments and decisions

33 Review of default judgments

(1) A party may apply to have a default judgment against or in favour of him reviewed. An application must be made in writing and presented to the Employment Tribunal Office within 14 days of the date on which the default judgment was sent to the parties. The 14 day time limit may be extended by a chairman if he considers that it is just and equitable to do so.

(2) The application must state the reasons why the default judgment should be varied or revoked. When it is the respondent applying to have the default judgment reviewed, the application must include with it the respondent's proposed response to the claim, an application for an extension of the time limit for presenting the response and an explanation of why rules 4(1) and (4) were not complied with.

(3) A review of a default judgment shall be conducted by a chairman in public. Notice of the hearing and a copy of the application shall be sent by the Secretary to all other parties.

(4) The chairman may—

(a) refuse the application for a review;
(b) vary the default judgment;
(c) revoke all or part of the default judgment;
(d) confirm the default judgment;

and all parties to the proceedings shall be informed by the Secretary in writing of the chairman's judgment on the application.

(5) A default judgment must be revoked if the whole of the claim was satisfied before the judgment was issued or if rule 8(6) applies. A chairman may revoke or vary all or part of a default judgment if the respondent has a reasonable prospect of successfully responding to the claim or part of it.

(6) In considering the application for a review of a default judgment the chairman must have regard to whether there was good reason for the response not having been presented within the applicable time limit.

(7) If the chairman decides that the default judgment should be varied or revoked and that the respondent should be allowed to respond to the claim the Secretary shall accept the response and proceed in accordance with rule 5(2).

34 Review of other judgments and decisions

(1) Parties may apply to have certain judgments and decisions made by a tribunal or a chairman reviewed under rules 34 to 36. Those judgments and decisions are—

(a) a decision not to accept a claim, response or counterclaim;
(b) a judgment (other than a default judgment but including an order for costs, expenses, preparation time or wasted costs); and
(c) a decision made under rule 6(3) of Schedule 4;

and references to "decision" in rules 34 to 37 are references to the above judgments and decisions only. Other decisions or orders may not be reviewed under these rules.

(2) In relation to a decision not to accept a claim or response, only the party against whom the decision is made may apply to have the decision reviewed.

(3) Subject to paragraph (4), decisions may be reviewed on the following grounds only—

(a) the decision was wrongly made as a result of an administrative error;
(b) a party did not receive notice of the proceedings leading to the decision;
(c) the decision was made in the absence of a party;
(d) new evidence has become available since the conclusion of the hearing to which the decision relates, provided that its existence could not have been reasonably known of or foreseen at that time; or
(e) the interests of justice require such a review.

(4) A decision not to accept a claim or response may only be reviewed on the grounds listed in paragraphs (3)(a) and (e).

(5) A tribunal or chairman may on its or his own initiative review a decision made by it or him on the grounds listed in paragraphs (3) or (4).

35 Preliminary consideration of application for review

(1) An application under rule 34 to have a decision reviewed must be made to the Employment Tribunal Office within 14 days of the date on which the decision was sent to the parties. The 14 day time limit may be extended by a chairman if he considers that it is just and equitable to do so.

(2) The application must be in writing and must identify the grounds of the application in accordance with rule 34(3), but if the decision to be reviewed was made at a hearing, an application may be made orally at that hearing.

(3) The application to have a decision reviewed shall be considered (without the need to hold a hearing) by the chairman of the tribunal which made the decision or, if that is not practicable, by—

(a) a Regional Chairman or the Vice President;
(b) any chairman nominated by a Regional Chairman or the Vice President; or
(c) the President;

and that person shall refuse the application if he considers that there are no grounds for the decision to be reviewed under rule 34(3) or there is no reasonable prospect of the decision being varied or revoked.

(4) If an application for a review is refused after such preliminary consideration the Secretary shall inform the party making the application in writing of the chairman's decision and his reasons for it. If the application for a review is not refused the decision shall be reviewed under rule 36.

36 The review

(1) When a party has applied for a review and the application has not been refused after the preliminary consideration above, the decision shall be reviewed by the chairman or tribunal who made the original decision. If that is not practicable a different chairman or tribunal (as the case may be) shall be appointed by a Regional Chairman, the Vice President or the President.

(2) Where no application has been made by a party and the decision is being reviewed on the initiative of the tribunal or chairman, the review must be carried out by the same tribunal or chairman who made the original decision and—

(a) a notice must be sent to each of the parties explaining in summary the grounds upon which it is proposed to review the decision and giving them an opportunity to give reasons why there should be no review; and
(b) such notice must be sent before the expiry of 14 days from the date on which the original decision was sent to the parties.

(3) A tribunal or chairman who reviews a decision under paragraph (1) or (2) may confirm, vary or revoke the decision. If the decision is revoked, the tribunal or chairman must order the decision to be taken again. When an order is made that the original decision be taken again, if the original decision was taken by a chairman without a hearing, the new decision may be taken without hearing the parties and if the original decision was taken at a hearing, a new hearing must be held.

37 Correction of judgments, decisions or reasons

(1) Clerical mistakes in any order, judgment, decision or reasons, or errors arising in those documents from an accidental slip or omission, may at any time be corrected by certificate by the chairman, Regional Chairman, Vice President or President.

(2) If a document is corrected by certificate under paragraph (1), or if a decision is revoked or varied under rules 33 or 36 or altered in any way by order of a superior court, the Secretary shall alter any entry in the Register which is so affected to conform with the certificate or order and send a copy of any entry so altered to each of the parties and, if the proceedings have been referred to the tribunal by a court, to that court.

(3) Where a document omitted from the Register under rules 32 or 49 is corrected by certificate under this rule, the Secretary shall send a copy of the corrected document to the parties; and where there are proceedings before any superior court relating to the decision or

reasons in question, he shall send a copy to that court together with a copy of the entry in the Register of the decision, if it has been altered under this rule.

(4) In Scotland, the references in paragraphs (2) and (3) to superior courts shall be read as referring to appellate courts.

Costs orders and orders for expenses

38 General power to make costs and expenses orders

(1) Subject to paragraph (2) and in the circumstances listed in rules 39, 40 and 47 a tribunal or chairman may make an order ("a costs order") that—

(a) a party ("the paying party") make a payment in respect of the costs incurred by another party ("the receiving party");

(b) the paying party pay to the Secretary of State, in whole or in part, any allowances (other than allowances paid to members of tribunals) paid by the Secretary of State under section 5(2) or (3) of the Employment Tribunals Act to any person for the purposes of, or in connection with, that person's attendance at the tribunal.

(2) A costs order may be made under rules 39, 40 and 47 only where the receiving party has been legally represented at the Hearing or, in proceedings which are determined without a Hearing, if the receiving party is legally represented when the proceedings are determined. If the receiving party has not been so legally represented a tribunal [or chairman] may make a preparation time order (subject to rules 42 to 45). (See rule 46 on the restriction on making a costs order and a preparation time order in the same proceedings.)

(3) For the purposes of these rules "costs" shall mean fees, charges, disbursements or expenses incurred by or on behalf of a party, in relation to the proceedings. In Scotland all references to costs (except when used in the expression "wasted costs") or costs orders shall be read as references to expenses or orders for expenses.

(4) A costs order may be made against or in favour of a respondent who has not had a response accepted in the proceedings in relation to the conduct of any part which he has taken in the proceedings.

(5) In these rules legally represented means having the assistance of a person (including where that person is the receiving party's employee) who—

(a) has a general qualification within the meaning of section 71 of the Courts and Legal Services Act 1990;

(b) is an advocate or solicitor in Scotland; or

(c) is a member of the Bar of Northern Ireland or a *solicitor of the Supreme Court of Northern Ireland*.

(6) Any costs order made under rules 39, 40 or 47 shall be payable by the paying party and not his representative.

(7) A party may apply for a costs order to be made at any time during the proceedings. An application may be made at the end of a hearing, or in writing to the Employment Tribunal Office. An application for costs which is received by the Employment Tribunal Office later than 28 days from the issuing of the judgment determining the claim shall not be accepted or considered by a tribunal or chairman unless it or he considers that it is in the interests of justice to do so.

(8) In paragraph (7), the date of issuing of the judgment determining the claim shall be either—

(a) the date of the Hearing if the judgment was issued orally; or

(b) if the judgment was reserved, the date on which the written judgment was sent to the parties.

(9) No costs order shall be made unless the Secretary has sent notice to the party against whom the order may be made giving him the opportunity to give reasons why the order should not be made. This paragraph shall not be taken to require the Secretary to send notice to that party if the party has been given an opportunity to give reasons orally to the chairman or tribunal as to why the order should not be made.

(10) Where a tribunal or chairman makes a costs order it or he shall provide written reasons for doing so if a request for written reasons is made within 14 days of the date of the costs order. The Secretary shall send a copy of the written reasons to all parties to the proceedings.

39 When a costs or expenses order must be made

(1) Subject to rule 38(2), a tribunal [or chairman] must make a costs order against a respondent where in proceedings for unfair dismissal a Hearing has been postponed or adjourned and—

(a) the claimant has expressed a wish to be reinstated or re-engaged which has been communicated to the respondent not less than 7 days before the Hearing; and

(b) the postponement or adjournment of that Hearing has been caused by the respondent's failure, without a special reason, to adduce reasonable evidence as to the availability of the job from which the claimant was dismissed, or of comparable or suitable employment.

(2) A costs order made under paragraph (1) shall relate to any costs incurred as a result of the postponement or adjournment of the Hearing.

40 When a costs or expenses order may be made

(1) A tribunal or chairman may make a costs order when on the application of a party it has postponed the day or time fixed for or adjourned a Hearing or pre-hearing review. The costs order may be against or, as the case may require, in favour of that party as respects any costs incurred or any allowances paid as a result of the postponement or adjournment.

(2) A tribunal or chairman shall consider making a costs order against a paying party where, in the opinion of the tribunal or chairman (as the case may be), any of the circumstances in paragraph (3) apply. Having so considered, the tribunal or chairman may make a costs order against the paying party if it or he considers it appropriate to do so.

(3) The circumstances referred to in paragraph (2) are where the paying party has in bringing the proceedings, or he or his representative has in conducting the proceedings, acted vexatiously, abusively, disruptively or otherwise unreasonably, or the bringing or conducting of the proceedings by the paying party has been misconceived.

(4) A tribunal or chairman may make a costs order against a party who has not complied with an order or practice direction.

41 The amount of a costs or expenses order

(1) The amount of a costs order against the paying party shall be determined in any of the following ways—

(a) the tribunal may specify the sum which the paying party must pay to the receiving party, provided that sum does not exceed £10,000;

(b) the parties may agree on a sum to be paid by the paying party to the receiving party and if they do so the costs order shall be for the sum so agreed;

(c) the tribunal may order the paying party to pay the receiving party the whole or a specified part of the costs of the receiving party with the amount to be paid being determined by way of detailed assessment in a County Court in accordance with the Civil Procedure Rules 1998 or, in Scotland, as taxed according to such part of the table of fees prescribed for proceedings in the sheriff court as shall be directed by the order.

(2) The tribunal or chairman may have regard to the paying party's ability to pay when considering whether it or he shall make a costs order or how much that order should be.

(3) For the avoidance of doubt, the amount of a costs order made under paragraphs (1)(b) or (c) may exceed £10,000.

Preparation time orders

42 General power to make preparation time orders

(1) Subject to paragraph (2) and in the circumstances described in rules 43, 44 and 47 a tribunal or chairman may make an order ("a preparation time order") that a party ("the paying party") make a payment in respect of the preparation time of another party ("the receiving party").

(2) A preparation time order may be made under rules 43, 44 or 47 only where the receiving party has not been legally represented at a Hearing or, in proceedings which are determined without a Hearing, if the receiving party has not been legally represented when the proceedings are determined. (See: rules 38 to 41 on when a costs order may be made;

rule 38(5) for the definition of legally represented; and rule 46 on the restriction on making a costs order and a preparation time order in the same proceedings).

(3) For the purposes of these rules preparation time shall mean time spent by—

(a) the receiving party or his employees carrying out preparatory work directly relating to the proceedings; and

(b) the receiving party's legal or other advisers relating to the conduct of the proceedings;

up to but not including time spent at any Hearing.

(4) A preparation time order may be made against a respondent who has not had a response accepted in the proceedings in relation to the conduct of any part which he has taken in the proceedings.

(5) A party may apply to the tribunal for a preparation time order to be made at any time during the proceedings. An application may be made at the end of a hearing or in writing to the Secretary. An application for preparation time which is received by the Employment Tribunal Office later than 28 days from the issuing of the judgment determining the claim shall not be accepted or considered by a tribunal or chairman unless they consider that it is in the interests of justice to do so.

(6) In paragraph (5) the date of issuing of the judgment determining the claim shall be either—

(a) the date of the Hearing if the judgment was issued orally; or,

(b) if the judgment was reserved, the date on which the written judgment was sent to the parties.

(7) No preparation time order shall be made unless the Secretary has sent notice to the party against whom the order may be made giving him the opportunity to give reasons why the order should not be made. This paragraph shall not be taken to require the Secretary to send notice to that party if the party has been given an opportunity to give reasons orally to the chairman or tribunal as to why the order should not be made.

(8) Where a tribunal or chairman makes a preparation time order it or he shall provide written reasons for doing so if a request for written reasons is made within 14 days of the date of the preparation time order. The Secretary shall send a copy of the written reasons to all parties to the proceedings.

43 When a preparation time order must be made

(1) Subject to rule 42(2), a tribunal [or chairman] must make a preparation time order against a respondent where in proceedings for unfair dismissal a Hearing has been postponed or adjourned and—

(a) the claimant has expressed a wish to be reinstated or re-engaged which has been communicated to the respondent not less than 7 days before the Hearing; and

(b) the postponement or adjournment of that Hearing has been caused by the respondent's failure, without a special reason, to adduce reasonable evidence as to the availability of the job from which the claimant was dismissed, or of comparable or suitable employment.

(2) A preparation time order made under paragraph (1) shall relate to any preparation time spent as a result of the postponement or adjournment of the Hearing.

44 When a preparation time order may be made

(1) A tribunal or chairman may make a preparation time order when on the application of a party it has postponed the day or time fixed for or adjourned a Hearing or a pre-hearing review. The preparation time order may be against or, as the case may require, in favour of that party as respects any preparation time spent as a result of the postponement or adjournment.

(2) A tribunal or chairman shall consider making a preparation time order against a party (the paying party) where, in the opinion of the tribunal or the chairman (as the case may be), any of the circumstances in paragraph (3) apply. Having so considered the tribunal or chairman may make a preparation time order against that party if it considers it appropriate to do so.

(3) The circumstances described in paragraph (2) are where the paying party has in bringing the proceedings, or he or his representative has in conducting the proceedings, acted

vexatiously, abusively, disruptively or otherwise unreasonably, or the bringing or conducting of the proceedings by the paying party has been misconceived.

(4) A tribunal or chairman may make a preparation time order against a party who has not complied with an order or practice direction.

45 Calculation of a preparation time order

(1) In order to calculate the amount of preparation time the tribunal or chairman shall make an assessment of the number of hours spent on preparation time on the basis of—

(a) information on time spent provided by the receiving party; and

(b) the tribunal or chairman's own assessment of what it or he considers to be a reasonable and proportionate amount of time to spend on such preparatory work and with reference to, for example, matters such as the complexity of the proceedings, the number of witnesses and documentation required.

(2) Once the tribunal or chairman has assessed the number of hours spent on preparation time in accordance with paragraph (1), it or he shall calculate the amount of the award to be paid to the receiving party by applying an hourly rate of £25.00 to that figure (or such other figure calculated in accordance with paragraph (4)). No preparation time order made under these rules may exceed the sum of £10,000.

(3) The tribunal or chairman may have regard to the paying party's ability to pay when considering whether it or he shall make a preparation time order or how much that order should be.

(4) For the year commencing on 6th April 2006, the hourly rate of £25 shall be increased by the sum of £1.00 and for each subsequent year commencing on 6 April, the hourly rate for the previous year shall also be increased by the sum of £1.00.

46 Restriction on making costs or expenses orders and preparation time orders

(1) A tribunal or chairman may not make a preparation time order and a costs order in favour of the same party in the same proceedings. However where a preparation time order is made in favour of a party in proceedings, the tribunal or chairman may make a costs order in favour of another party or in favour of the Secretary of State under rule 38(1)(b) in the same proceedings.

(2) If a tribunal or a chairman wishes to make either a costs order or a preparation time order in proceedings, before the claim has been determined, it or he may make an order that either costs or preparation time be awarded to the receiving party. In such circumstances a tribunal or chairman may decide whether the award should be for costs or preparation time after the proceedings have been determined.

47 Costs, expenses or preparation time orders when a deposit has been taken

(1) When—

(a) a party has been ordered under rule 20 to pay a deposit as a condition of being permitted to continue to participate in proceedings relating to a matter;

(b) in respect of that matter, the tribunal or chairman has found against that party in its or his judgment; and

(c) no award of costs or preparation time has been made against that party arising out of the proceedings on the matter;

the tribunal or chairman shall consider whether to make a costs or preparation time order against that party on the ground that he conducted the proceedings relating to the matter unreasonably in persisting in having the matter determined; but the tribunal or chairman shall not make a costs or preparation time order on that ground unless it has considered the document recording the order under rule 20 and is of the opinion that the grounds which caused the tribunal or chairman to find against the party in its judgment were substantially the same as the grounds recorded in that document for considering that the contentions of the party had little reasonable prospect of success.

(2) When a costs or preparation time order is made against a party who has had an order under rule 20 made against him (whether the award arises out of the proceedings relating to the matter in respect of which the order was made or out of proceedings relating to any other matter considered with that matter), his deposit shall be paid in part or full settlement of the costs or preparation time order—

(a) when an order is made in favour of one party, to that party; and

(b) when orders are made in favour of more than one party, to all of them or any one or more of them as the tribunal or chairman thinks fit, and if to all or more than one, in such proportions as the tribunal or chairman considers appropriate;

and if the amount of the deposit exceeds the amount of the costs or preparation time order, the balance shall be refunded to the party who paid it.

Wasted costs orders against representatives

48 Personal liability of representatives for costs

(1) A tribunal or chairman may make a wasted costs order against a party's representative.

(2) In a wasted costs order the tribunal or chairman may—

(a) disallow, or order the representative of a party to meet the whole or part of any wasted costs of any party, including an order that the representative repay to his client any costs which have already been paid; and

(b) order the representative to pay to the Secretary of State, in whole or in part, any allowances (other than allowances paid to members of tribunals) paid by the Secretary of State under section 5(2) or (3) of the Employment Tribunals Act to any person for the purposes of, or in connection with, that person's attendance at the tribunal by reason of the representative's conduct of the proceedings.

(3) "Wasted costs" means any costs incurred by a party—

(a) as a result of any improper, unreasonable or negligent act or omission on the part of any representative; or

(b) which, in the light of any such act or omission occurring after they were incurred, the tribunal considers it unreasonable to expect that party to pay.

(4) In this rule "representative" means a party's legal or other representative or any employee of such representative, but it does not include a representative who is not acting in pursuit of profit with regard to those proceedings. A person is considered to be acting in pursuit of profit if he is acting on a conditional fee arrangement.

(5) A wasted costs order may be made in favour of a party whether or not that party is legally represented and such an order may also be made in favour of a representative's own client. A wasted costs order may not be made against a representative where that representative is an employee of a party.

(6) Before making a wasted costs order, the tribunal or chairman shall give the representative a reasonable opportunity to make oral or written representations as to reasons why such an order should not be made. [The tribunal or chairman may also have regard to the representative's ability to pay] when considering whether it shall make a wasted costs order or how much that order should be.

(7) When a tribunal or chairman makes a wasted costs order, it must specify in the order the amount to be disallowed or paid.

(8) The Secretary shall inform the representative's client in writing—

(a) of any proceedings under this rule; or

(b) of any order made under this rule against the party's representative.

(9) Where a tribunal or chairman makes a wasted costs order it or he shall provide written reasons for doing so if a request is made for written reasons within 14 days of the date of the wasted costs order. This 14 day time limit may not be extended under rule 10. The Secretary shall send a copy of the written reasons to all parties to the proceedings.

Powers in relation to specific types of proceedings

49 Sexual offences and the Register

In any proceedings appearing to involve allegations of the commission of a sexual offence the tribunal, the chairman or the Secretary shall omit from the Register, or delete from the Register or any judgment, document or record of the proceedings, which is available to the public, any identifying matter which is likely to lead members of the public to identify any person affected by or making such an allegation.

50 Restricted reporting orders

(1) A restricted reporting order may be made in the following types of proceedings—

(a) any case which involves allegations of sexual misconduct;
(b) a complaint under section 17A or 25(8) of the Disability Discrimination Act in which evidence of a personal nature is likely to be heard by the tribunal or a chairman.

(2) A party (or where a complaint is made under the Disability Discrimination Act, the complainant) may apply for a restricted reporting order (either temporary or full) in writing to the Employment Tribunal Office, or orally at a hearing, or the tribunal or chairman may make the order on its or his own initiative without any application having been made.

(3) A chairman or tribunal may make a temporary restricted reporting order without holding a hearing or sending a copy of the application to other parties.

(4) Where a temporary restricted reporting order has been made the Secretary shall inform all parties to the proceedings in writing as soon as possible of—
(a) the fact that the order has been made; and
(b) their right to apply to have the temporary restricted reporting order revoked or converted into a full restricted reporting order within 14 days of the temporary order having been made.

(5) If no application under paragraph (4)(b) is made within the 14 days, the temporary restricted reporting order shall lapse and cease to have any effect on the fifteenth day after the order was made. If such an application is made the temporary restricted reporting order shall continue to have effect until the pre-hearing review or Hearing at which the application is considered.

(6) All parties must be given an opportunity to advance oral argument at a pre-hearing review or a Hearing before a tribunal or chairman decides whether or not to make a full restricted reporting order (whether or not there was previously a temporary restricted reporting order in the proceedings).

(7) Any person may make an application to the chairman or tribunal to have a right to make representations before a full restricted reporting order is made. The chairman or tribunal shall allow such representations to be made where he or it considers that the applicant has a legitimate interest in whether or not the order is made.

(8) Where a tribunal or chairman makes a restricted reporting order—
(a) it shall specify in the order the persons who may not be identified;
(b) a full order shall remain in force until both liability and remedy have been determined in the proceedings unless it is revoked earlier; and
(c) the Secretary shall ensure that a notice of the fact that a restricted reporting order has been made in relation to those proceedings is displayed on the notice board of the employment tribunal with any list of the proceedings taking place before the employment tribunal, and on the door of the room in which the proceedings affected by the order are taking place.

(9) Where a restricted reporting order has been made under this rule and that complaint is being dealt with together with any other proceedings, the tribunal or chairman may order that the restricted reporting order applies also in relation to those other proceedings or a part of them.

(10) A tribunal or chairman may revoke a restricted reporting order at any time.

(11) For the purposes of this rule liability and remedy are determined in the proceedings on the date recorded as being the date on which the judgment disposing of the claim was sent to the parties, and references to a restricted reporting order include references to both a temporary and a full restricted reporting order.

51 Proceedings involving the National Insurance Fund

The Secretary of State shall be entitled to appear as if she were a party and be heard at any hearing in relation to proceedings which may involve a payment out of the National Insurance Fund, and in that event she shall be treated for the purposes of these rules as if she were a party.

52 Collective agreements

Where a claim includes a complaint under section 6(4A) of the Sex Discrimination Act 1986 relating to a term of a collective agreement, the following persons, whether or not identified in the claim, shall be regarded as the persons against whom a remedy is claimed and shall be treated as respondents for the purposes of these rules, that is to say—

(a) the claimant's employer (or prospective employer); and
(b) every organisation of employers and organisation of workers, and every association of or representative of such organisations, which, if the terms were to be varied voluntarily, would be likely, in the opinion of a chairman, to negotiate the variation;

provided that such an organisation or association shall not be treated as a respondent if the chairman, having made such enquiries of the claimant and such other enquiries as he thinks fit, is of the opinion that it is not reasonably practicable to identify the organisation or association.

53 Employment Agencies Act 1973

In relation to any claim in respect of an application under section 3C of the Employment Agencies Act 1973 for the variation or revocation of a prohibition order, the Secretary of State shall be treated as the respondent in such proceedings for the purposes of these rules. In relation to such an application the claim does not need to include the name and address of the persons against whom the claim is being made.

54 National security proceedings

(1) A Minister of the Crown (whether or not he is a party to the proceedings) may, if he considers it expedient in the interests of national security, direct a tribunal or chairman by notice to the Secretary to—
(a) conduct proceedings in private for all or part of particular Crown employment proceedings;
(b) exclude the claimant from all or part of particular Crown employment proceedings;
(c) exclude the claimant's representative from all or part of particular Crown employment proceedings;
(d) take steps to conceal the identity of a particular witness in particular Crown employment proceedings.

(2) A tribunal or chairman may, if it or he considers it expedient in the interests of national security, by order—
(a) do [in relation to particular proceedings before it] anything which can be required by direction to be done [in relation to particular Crown employment proceedings] under paragraph (1);
(b) order any person to whom any document (including any judgment or record of the proceedings) has been provided for the purposes of the proceedings not to disclose any such document or the content thereof—
  (i) to any excluded person;
  (ii) in any case in which a direction has been given under paragraph (1)(a) or an order has been made under paragraph (2)(a) read with paragraph (1)(a), to any person excluded from all or part of the proceedings by virtue of such direction or order; or
  (iii) in any case in which a Minister of the Crown has informed the Secretary in accordance with paragraph (3) that he wishes to address the tribunal or chairman with a view to an order being made under paragraph (2)(a) read with paragraph (1)(b) or (c), to any person who may be excluded from all or part of the proceedings by virtue of such an order, if an order is made, at any time before the tribunal or chairman decides whether or not to make such an order;
(c) take steps to keep secret all or part of the reasons for its judgment.

The tribunal or chairman (as the case may be) shall keep under review any order it or he has made under this paragraph.

(3) In any proceedings in which a Minister of the Crown considers that it would be appropriate for a tribunal or chairman to make an order as referred to in paragraph (2), he shall (whether or not he is a party to the proceedings) be entitled to appear before and to address the tribunal or chairman thereon. The Minister shall inform the Secretary by notice that he wishes to address the tribunal or chairman and the Secretary shall copy the notice to the parties.

(4) When exercising its or his functions, a tribunal or chairman shall ensure that information is not disclosed contrary to the interests of national security.

55 Dismissals in connection with industrial action

(1) In relation to a complaint under section 111 of the Employment Rights Act 1996 (unfair dismissal: complaints to employment tribunal) that a dismissal is unfair by virtue of section 238A of TULR(C)A (participation in official industrial action) a tribunal or chairman may adjourn the proceedings where civil proceedings have been brought until such time as interim proceedings arising out of the civil proceedings have been concluded.

(2) In this rule—

(a) "civil proceedings" means legal proceedings brought by any person against another person in which it is to be determined whether an act of that other person, which induced the claimant to commit an act, or each of a series of acts, is by virtue of section 219 of TULR(C)A not actionable in tort or in delict; and

(b) the interim proceedings shall not be regarded as having concluded until all rights of appeal have been exhausted or the time for presenting any appeal in the course of the interim proceedings has expired.

56 Devolution issues

(1) In any proceedings in which a devolution issue within the definition of the term in paragraph 1 of Schedule 6 to the Scotland Act 1998 arises, the Secretary shall as soon as reasonably practicable by notice inform the Advocate General for Scotland and the Lord Advocate thereof (unless they are a party to the proceedings) and shall at the same time—

(a) send a copy of the notice to the parties to the proceedings; and

(b) send the Advocate General for Scotland and the Lord Advocate a copy of the claim and the response.

(2) In any proceedings in which a devolution issue within the definition of the term in paragraph 1 of [Schedule 9 to the Government of Wales Act 2006] arises, the Secretary shall as soon as reasonably practicable by notice inform the Attorney General and the [Counsel General to the Welsh Assembly Government] thereof (unless they are a party to the proceedings) and shall at the same time—

(a) send a copy of the notice to the parties to the proceedings; and

(b) send the Attorney General and the [Counsel General to the Welsh Assembly Government] a copy of the claim and the response.

(3) A person to whom notice is given in pursuance of paragraph (1) or (2) may within 14 days of receiving it, by notice to the Secretary, take part as a party in the proceedings, so far as they relate to the devolution issue. The Secretary shall send a copy of the notice to the other parties to the proceedings.

57 Transfer of proceedings between Scotland and England & Wales

(1) The President (England and Wales) or a Regional Chairman may at any time, with the consent of the President (Scotland), order any proceedings in England and Wales to be transferred to an Employment Tribunal Office in Scotland if it appears to him that the proceedings could be (in accordance with regulation 19), and would more conveniently be, determined in an employment tribunal located in Scotland.

(2) The President (Scotland) or the Vice President may at any time, with the consent of the President (England and Wales), order any proceedings in Scotland to be transferred to an Employment Tribunal Office in England and Wales if it appears to him that the proceedings could be (in accordance with regulation 19), and would more conveniently be, determined in an employment tribunal located in England or Wales.

(3) An order under paragraph (1) or (2) may be made by the President, Vice President or Regional Chairman without any application having been made by a party. A party may apply for an order under paragraph (1) or (2) in accordance with rule 11.

(4) Where proceedings have been transferred under this rule, they shall be treated as if in all respects they had been presented to the Secretary by the claimant.

58 References to the European Court of Justice

Where a tribunal or chairman makes an order referring a question to the European Court of Justice for a preliminary ruling under Article 234 of the Treaty establishing the European Community, the Secretary shall send a copy of the order to the Registrar of that Court.

59 Transfer of proceedings from a court

Where proceedings are referred to a tribunal by a court, these rules shall apply to them as if the proceedings had been sent to the Secretary by the claimant.

General provisions

60 Powers

(1) Subject to the provisions of these rules and any practice directions, a tribunal or chairman may regulate its or his own procedure.

(2) At a Hearing, or a pre-hearing review held in accordance with rule 18(3), a tribunal may make any order which a chairman has power to make under these rules, subject to compliance with any relevant notice or other procedural requirements.

(3) Any function of the Secretary may be performed by a person acting with the authority of the Secretary.

61 Notices, etc

(1) Any notice given or document sent under these rules shall (unless a chairman or tribunal orders otherwise) be in writing and may be given or sent—

(a) by post;
(b) by fax or other means of electronic communication; or
(c) by personal delivery.

(2) Where a notice or document has been given or sent in accordance with paragraph (1), that notice or document shall, unless the contrary is proved, be taken to have been received by the party to whom it is addressed—

(a) in the case of a notice or document given or sent by post, on the day on which the notice or document would be delivered in the ordinary course of post;
(b) in the case of a notice or document transmitted by fax or other means of electronic communication, on the day on which the notice or document is transmitted;
(c) in the case of a notice or document delivered in person, on the day on which the notice or document is delivered.

(3) All notices and documents required by these rules to be presented to the Secretary or an Employment Tribunal Office, other than a claim, shall be presented at the Employment Tribunal Office as notified by the Secretary to the parties.

(4) All notices and documents required or authorised by these rules to be sent or given to any person listed below may be sent to or delivered at—

(a) in the case of a notice or document directed to the Secretary of State in proceedings to which she is not a party and which are brought under section 170 of the Employment Rights Act, the offices of the Redundancy Payments Directorate of the Insolvency Service at PO Box 203, 21 Bloomsbury Street, London WC1B 3QW, or such other office as may be notified by the Secretary of State;
(b) in the case of any other notice or document directed to the Secretary of State in proceedings to which she is not a party (or in respect of which she is treated as a party for the purposes of these rules by rule 51), the offices of [the Department for Business, Enterprise and Regulatory Reform] (Employment Relations Directorate) at 1 Victoria Street, London, SW1H 0ET, or such other office as be notified by the Secretary of State;
(c) in the case of a notice or document directed to the Attorney General under rule 56, the Attorney General's Chambers, 9 Buckingham Gate, London, SW1E 7JP;
(d) in the case of a notice or document directed to the [Counsel General to the Welsh Assembly Government] under rule 56, the [Counsel General to the Welsh Assembly Government], Crown Buildings, Cathays Park, Cardiff, CF10 3NQ;
(e) in the case of a notice or document directed to the Advocate General for Scotland under rule 56, the Office of the Solicitor to the Advocate General for Scotland, Victoria Quay, Edinburgh, EH6 6QQ;
(f) in the case of a notice or document directed to the Lord Advocate under rule 56, the Legal Secretariat to the Lord Advocate, 25 Chambers Street, Edinburgh, EH1 1LA;
(g) in the case of a notice or document directed to a court, the office of the clerk of the court;

(h) in the case of a notice or document directed to a party—
  (i) the address specified in the claim or response to which notices and documents are to be sent, or in a notice under paragraph (5); or
  (ii) if no such address has been specified, or if a notice sent to such an address has been returned, to any other known address or place of business in the United Kingdom or, if the party is a corporate body, the body's registered or principal office in the United Kingdom, or, in any case, such address or place outside the United Kingdom as the President, Vice President or a Regional Chairman may allow;

(i) in the case of a notice or document directed to any person (other than a person specified in the foregoing provisions of this paragraph), his address or place of business in the United Kingdom or, if the person is a corporate body, the body's registered or principal office in the United Kingdom;

and a notice or document sent or given to the authorised representative of a party shall be taken to have been sent or given to that party.

(5) A party may at any time by notice to the Employment Tribunal Office and to the other party or parties (and, where appropriate, to the appropriate conciliation officer) change the address to which notices and documents are to be sent or transmitted.

(6) The President, Vice President or a Regional Chairman may order that there shall be substituted service in such manner as he may deem fit in any case he considers appropriate.

(7) In proceedings which may involve a payment out of the National Insurance Fund, the Secretary shall, where appropriate, send copies of all documents and notices to the Secretary of State whether or not she is a party.

[(8) In proceedings under the Equal Pay Act, the Sex Discrimination Act, the Sex Discrimination Act 1986, the Race Relations Act or the Disability Discrimination Act, copies of every document sent to the parties under rules 29, 30 or 32 shall be sent by the Secretary to the Commission for Equality and Human Rights.]

[3171]

NOTES

Commencement: 1 October 2004.

Rules 1, 4: words in square brackets substituted by the Employment Tribunals (Constitution and Rules of Procedure) (Amendment) Regulations 2005, SI 2005/435, reg 2, as from 5 April 2005.

Rule 8: para (2) substituted by the Employment Tribunals (Constitution and Rules of Procedure) (Amendment) Regulations 2004, SI 2004/2351, reg 2(1), (9)(a), as from 1 October 2004.

Rules 9, 17, 18, 39, 41: words in square brackets substituted by the Employment Tribunals (Constitution and Rules of Procedure) (Amendment) (No 2) Regulations 2005, SI 2005/1865, reg 2(1), (4)(a), (c), (d), (i), as from 1 October 2005.

Rule 10: word omitted from para (5) revoked by SI 2005/1865, reg 2(1), (4)(b), as from 1 October 2005.

Rule 22: word omitted from para (1)(f) revoked, and para (1)(h) and the word immediately preceding it added, by the Employment Equality (Age) (Consequential Amendments) Regulations 2007, SI 2007/825, reg 9, as from 6 April 2007; words in square brackets in para (4), and para (5)(e), inserted by SI 2005/1865, reg 2(1), (4)(e), (f), as from 1 October 2005; words in square brackets in para (5)(d) substituted by the Transfer of Undertakings (Protection of Employment) (Consequential Amendments) Regulations 2006, SI 2006/2405, reg 3, as from 1 October 2006 (subject to savings in cases where the 1981 Regulations continue to apply by virtue of reg 21 of the Transfer of Undertakings (Protection of Employment) Regulations 2006, SI 2006/246 at **[3395]**).

Rule 30: words in first (outer) pair of square brackets in para (3) substituted by SI 2004/2351, reg 2(1), (9)(c), as from 1 October 2004; words in second (inner) pair of square brackets substituted by SI 2005/1865, reg 2(1), (4)(h), as from 1 October 2005.

Rule 38: words in square brackets in para (2) inserted by SI 2005/1865, reg 2(1), (4)(i), as from 1 October 2005; for the words in italics in para (5)(c) there are substituted the words "solicitor of the Court of Judicature of Northern Ireland" by the Constitutional Reform Act 2005, s 59(5), Sch 11, Pt 3, para 5, as from a day to be appointed.

Rule 48: words in square brackets in para (6) substituted by SI 2004/2351, reg 2(1), (9)(d), as from 1 October 2004.

Rule 54: words in square brackets in para (2)(a) inserted by SI 2005/1865, reg 2(1), (4)(j), as from 1 October 2005.

Rule 56: words in square brackets in para (2) substituted by the National Assembly for Wales (Diversion of Functions) (No 2) Order 2007, SI 2007/2142, art 4(1), (2), as from 26 July 2007.

Rule 61: words in square brackets in para (4)(b) substituted by the Secretaries of State for Children, Schools and Families, for Innovation, Universities and Skills and for Business, Enterprise and Regulatory Reform Order 2007, SI 2007/3224, art 15, Schedule, Pt 2, para 45, as from 12 December 2007; words in square brackets in para (4)(d) substituted by the National Assembly for Wales (Diversion of Functions) (No 2) Order 2007, SI 2007/2142, art 4(1), (3), as from 26 July 2007; para (8) substituted by the Equality

Act 2006 (Dissolution of Commissions and Consequential and Transitional Provisions) Order 2007, SI 2007/2602, art 4(1), Schedule, para 7(b), as from 1 October 2007.

SCHEDULE 2
THE EMPLOYMENT TRIBUNALS (NATIONAL SECURITY) RULES OF PROCEDURE

Regulation 16(2)

1 Application of Schedule 2

(1) The rules in this Schedule only apply to national security proceedings or proceedings where the right in rule 54(3) of Schedule 1 has been exercised.

(2) The rules in this Schedule modify the rules in Schedule 1 in relation to such proceedings. If there is conflict between the rules contained in this Schedule and those in any other Schedule to these Regulations, the rules in this Schedule shall prevail.

(3) Any reference in this Schedule to rule 54 is a reference to rule 54 in Schedule 1.

2 Notification of national security proceedings

When proceedings before an employment tribunal become national security proceedings the Secretary shall inform the parties of that fact in writing as soon as practicable.

3 Responding to a claim

(1) If before the expiry of the period for entering the response—

(a) a direction of a Minister of the Crown under rule 54(1)(b) (exclusion of claimant) applicable to this stage of the proceedings is given; or

(b) a Minister of the Crown has informed the Secretary in accordance with rule 54(3) that he wishes to address the tribunal or chairman with a view to the tribunal or chairman making an order under rule 54(2) applicable to this stage of the proceedings to exclude the claimant;

rule 4(3)(d) (grounds for the response) of Schedule 1 shall not apply and paragraphs (2) and (3) of this rule shall apply instead.

(2) In a case falling within paragraph (1)(b), if the tribunal or chairman decides not to make an order under rule 54(2), the respondent shall within 28 days of the decision present to the Employment Tribunal Office the written grounds on which he resists the claim. On receiving the written grounds the Secretary shall send a copy of them to all other parties and they shall be treated as part of the response.

(3) In a case falling within paragraph (1)(b) where the tribunal or chairman makes the order, or in a case falling within paragraph (1)(a), the respondent shall with 44 days of the direction or order being made, present to the Employment Tribunal Office (and, where applicable, to the special advocate) the written grounds on which he resists the claim and they shall be treated as part of the response.

(4) The time limits in paragraphs (2) and (3) may be extended if it is just and equitable to do so and if an application is presented to the Employment Tribunal Office before the expiry of the relevant time limit. The application must explain why the respondent cannot comply with the time limit.

4 Serving of documents by the Secretary

(1) The Secretary shall not send a copy of the response or grounds for the response to any person excluded from all or part of the proceedings by virtue of a direction or order given or made under rule 54.

(2) Where a Minister of the Crown has informed the Secretary in accordance with rule 54(3) that he wishes to address the tribunal or chairman with a view to an order being made under rule 54(2)(a) to exclude the claimant's representative from all or part of the proceedings, the Secretary shall not at any time before the tribunal or chairman has considered the Minister's representations, send a copy of the response or the grounds for the response to any person who may be excluded from all or part of the proceedings by such an order if it were made.

5 Default judgment

Rule 8(1) (default judgments) of Schedule 1 shall apply in relation to the time limit for presenting a response, but it shall not apply in relation to the time limits in paragraphs (2) and (3) of rule 3 in this Schedule.

6 Witness orders and disclosure of documents

(1) Where—

(a) a Minister has issued a direction or the tribunal or a chairman has made an order under rule 54 to exclude a claimant or his representative from all or part of the proceedings; and

(b) a chairman or the tribunal is considering whether to make, or has made, an order described in rule 10(2)(c) or (d) of Schedule 1 (requiring a person to attend and give evidence or to produce documents) or under rule 8 of Schedule 3 or rule 7 of Schedule 4;

a Minister of the Crown (whether or not he is a party to the proceedings) may make an application to the tribunal or chairman objecting to the imposition of a requirement described in rule 10(2)(c) or (d) of Schedule 1 or under Schedules 3 or 4. If such an order has been made the Minister may make an application to vary or set aside the order.

(2) The tribunal or chairman shall hear and determine the Minister's application in private and the Minister shall be entitled to address the tribunal or chairman. The application shall be made by notice to the Secretary and the Secretary shall give notice of the application to all parties.

7 Case management discussions and pre-hearing reviews

(1) Rule 14(4) (hearings – general) of Schedule 1 shall be modified in accordance with paragraph (2).

(2) In proceedings in which a special advocate has been appointed in respect of the claimant, if the claimant has been excluded from a case management discussion or a pre-hearing review, at such a hearing the claimant shall not have the right to advance oral argument, but oral argument may be advanced on the claimant's behalf by the special advocate.

8 Special advocate

(1) In any proceedings in which there is an excluded person the tribunal or chairman shall inform the Attorney General (or in Scotland, the Advocate General) of the proceedings before it with a view to the Attorney General (or the Advocate General, in Scotland), if he thinks it fit to do so, appointing a special advocate to represent the interests of the claimant in respect of those parts of the proceedings from which—

(a) any representative of his is excluded;

(b) both he and his representative are excluded; or

(c) he is excluded, where he does not have a representative.

(2) A special advocate shall have a general qualification for the purposes of section 71 of the Courts and Legal Services Act 1990 or shall be an advocate or a solicitor admitted in Scotland.

(3) Where the excluded person is the claimant, he shall be permitted to make a statement to the tribunal or chairman before the commencement of the proceedings, or the part of the proceedings, from which he is excluded.

(4) Except in accordance with paragraphs (5) to (7), the special advocate may not communicate directly or indirectly with any person (including an excluded person)—

(a) (except in the case of the tribunal, chairman and the respondent) on any matter contained in the grounds for the response referred to in rule 3(3);

(b) (except in the case of a person who was present) on any matter discussed or referred to during any part of the proceedings in which the tribunal or chairman sat in private in accordance with a direction or an order given or made under rule 54.

(5) The special advocate may apply for orders from the tribunal or chairman authorising him to seek instructions from, or otherwise to communicate with, an excluded person—

(a) on any matter contained in the grounds for the response referred to in rule 3(3); or

(b) on any matter discussed or referred to during any part of the proceedings in which the tribunal or chairman sat in private in accordance with a direction or an order given or made under rule 54.

(6) An application under paragraph (5) shall be made in writing to the Employment Tribunal Office and shall include the title of the proceedings and the grounds for the application.

(7) The Secretary shall notify the Minister of an application under paragraph (5) and the Minister shall be entitled to address the tribunal or chairman on the application.

(8) In these rules and those in Schedule 1, in any case in which a special advocate has been appointed to represent the interests of the claimant in accordance with paragraph (1), any reference to a party shall (save in those references specified in paragraph (9)) include the special advocate.

(9) The following references to "party" or "parties" shall not include the special advocate—

(a) regulation 9(3);

(b) in Schedule 1, rule 2(2)(b), 9, 10(2)(r), 10(3), the first two references in rule 11(4), 11(5), 18(7), 20, 22, 23, 27(3), 27(5), 29(3), 30(6)(f), 33(1), 34(2), all references in rule 38 save that in 38(10), 39, 40, 41, all references in rule 42 save that in rule 42(8), 44 to 48, 51, 54(1), the first reference in rule 54(3), 56(3), 61(3), 61(4)(a) and (b), and 61(7);

(c) in Schedule 4, rule 5(b), 6(5) and 10; and

(d) in Schedule 5, rule 4(b).

9 Hearings

(1) Any hearing of or in connection with a claim shall, subject to any direction of a Minister of the Crown or order of a tribunal or chairman under rule 54 that all or part of the proceedings are to take place in private and subject to rule 16 of Schedule 1, take place in public.

(2) A member of the Council on Tribunals shall not be entitled to attend any hearing taking place in private in his capacity as member where the hearing is taking place in private under a direction of a Minister of the Crown or an order of a tribunal or chairman under rule 54.

(3) Subject to any direction of a Minister of the Crown or order of a tribunal or chairman under rule 54, a party shall be entitled to give evidence, to call witnesses, to question any witnesses and to address the tribunal at a Hearing.

10 Reasons in national security proceedings

(1) This rule applies to written reasons given under rule 30 of Schedule 1 for a judgment or order made by the tribunal or chairman in national security proceedings.

(2) Before the Secretary sends a copy of the written reasons ("the full written reasons") to any party, or enters them in the Register under rule 32 of Schedule 1, he shall send a copy of the full written reasons to the Minister.

(3) If the Minister considers it expedient in the interests of national security and he has given a direction or the tribunal or a chairman has made an order under rule 54 in those proceedings, the Minister may—

(a) direct the tribunal or chairman that the full written reasons shall not be disclosed to persons specified in the direction, and to prepare a further document ("the edited reasons") setting out the reasons for the judgment or order, but with the omission of such of the information as is specified in the direction;

(b) direct the tribunal or chairman that the full written reasons shall not be disclosed to persons specified in the direction, but that no further document setting out the tribunal or chairman's reasons should be prepared.

(4) Where the Minister has directed the tribunal or chairman in accordance with paragraph 3(a), the edited reasons shall be signed by the chairman and initialled in each place where an omission has been made.

(5) Where a direction has been made under paragraph (3)(a), the Secretary shall—

(a) send a copy of the edited reasons referred to in paragraph (3)(a) to any person specified in the direction and to the persons listed in paragraph (7);

(b) enter the edited reasons in the Register, but omit from the Register the full written reasons; and

(c) send a copy of the full written reasons to the persons listed in paragraph (7).

(6) Where a direction has been made under paragraph (3)(b), the Secretary shall send a copy of the full written reasons to the persons listed in paragraph (7), but he shall not enter the full written reasons in the Register.

(7) The persons to whom full written reasons should be sent in accordance with paragraph (5) or (6) are—

(a) the respondent;

(b) the claimant or the claimant's representative if they were not specified in the direction made under paragraph (3);

(c) if applicable, the special advocate;

(d) where the proceedings were referred to the tribunal by a court, to that court; and

(e) where there are proceedings before a superior court (or in Scotland, an appellate court) relating to the decision in question, to that court.

11 Correction of written reasons

Where written reasons (whether "full" or "edited") have been omitted from the Register in accordance with rule 10 and they are corrected by certificate under rule 37 of Schedule 1, the Secretary shall send a copy of the corrected reasons to the same persons who had been sent the reasons in accordance with rule 10.

12 Review of judgments or decisions

In rule 34(3) of Schedule 1 (review of other judgments and decisions), the reference in sub-paragraph (c) to decisions being made in the absence of a party does not include reference to decisions being made in the absence of a party where this is done in accordance with a direction given or an order made under rule 54.

[3172]

NOTES

Commencement: 1 October 2004.

SCHEDULE 3

THE EMPLOYMENT TRIBUNALS (LEVY APPEALS) RULES OF PROCEDURE

Regulation 16(3)(a)

For use only in proceedings on levy appeals

1 Application of Schedule 1

Subject to rules 9 and 10 of this Schedule, Schedule 1 shall apply to levy appeals. The rules in this Schedule modify the rules in Schedule 1 in relation to levy appeals. If there is conflict between the rules contained in this Schedule and those in Schedule 1, the rules in this Schedule shall prevail.

2 Definitions

In this Schedule and in relation to proceedings to which this Schedule applies—

"Board" means in relation to an appeal the respondent industrial training board;

"Industrial Training Act" means the Industrial Training Act 1982;

"levy" means a levy imposed under section 11 of the Industrial Training Act;

"levy appeal" means an appeal against an assessment to a levy;

"respondent" means the Board.

3 Notice of Appeal

A person wishing to appeal an assessment to a levy (the appellant) shall do so by sending to the Board two copies of a notice of appeal which must be substantially in accordance with Form 1 in the Annex to this Schedule, and they must include the grounds of their appeal.

4 Action on receipt of appeal

(1) Subject to rules 5 and 6, the Board shall, within 21 days of receiving the notice of appeal send the following documents to the Employment Tribunal Office—

(a) one copy of the notice of appeal;

(b) a copy of the assessment notice and of any notice by the Board allowing further time for appealing;

(c) a notice giving the Board's address for service under these rules where that address is different from the address specified in the assessment notice as the address for service of a notice of appeal; and

(d) any representations in writing relating to the appeal that the Board wishes to submit to the tribunal.

(2) Failure to comply with any provision of this rule or rule 5 shall not make the appeal invalid.

5 Requests for further information

(1) Subject to rule 6, this rule applies when, on receiving the notice of appeal, the Board considers that it requires further information on the appellant's grounds for the appeal and of any facts relevant to those grounds.

(2) The Board shall send the appellant a notice specifying the further information required by the Board within 21 days of receiving the notice of appeal.

(3) The appellant shall send the Board two copies of the further information within 21 days of receiving the notice requesting the information, or within such further period as the Board may allow.

(4) Subject to paragraph (5), within 21 days of receiving the further information the Board shall send the following documents to the Employment Tribunal Office—

(a) the documents listed in rule 4(1);

(b) a copy of the notice requesting further information;

(c) any further information which has been provided to the Board; and

(d) any representations in writing regarding such information which the Board wishes to submit to the tribunal.

(5) If further information is not received by the Board within the time limit, the documents listed in sub-paragraphs (a) and (b) of paragraph (4) shall be sent by the Board to the Employment Tribunal Office—

(a) within 50 days of the receipt of the notice of appeal by the Board; or

(b) if the Board has allowed a further period of time for delivery of further particulars under paragraph (3), within 7 days of the end of that period.

6 Withdrawal of appeal or assessment

(1) The appellant may withdraw the notice of appeal by notice given to the Board at any time and in that event no further action shall be taken in relation to the appeal.

(2) When an assessment is withdrawn by the Board, it shall notify the Employment Tribunal Office and no further action shall be taken in relation to the appeal.

7 Entry of appeal

(1) The Secretary shall as soon as reasonably practicable after receiving from the Board the relevant documents in accordance with rule 4(1), 5(4) or 5(5)—

(a) give notice to the appellant and to the Board of the case number of the appeal (which must from then on be referred to in all correspondence relating to the appeal) and of the address to which notices and other communications to the Employment Tribunal Office shall be sent;

(b) give notice to the appellant of the Board's address for service; and

(c) send to the appellant a copy of any representations in writing that the Board has submitted to the tribunal under rule 4 or 5.

8 Order for further information

(1) In any case in which the appellant has not sent to the Board further information which has been requested by the Board in accordance with rule 5, a chairman or tribunal may, on the application of the Board, by notice order the appellant to supply such further information as may be specified in the notice, and the appellant shall send two copies of such information to the Employment Tribunal Office within such time as the chairman or tribunal may direct.

(2) As soon as is reasonably practicable after receiving the further information from the appellant, the Secretary shall send a copy of the information to the Board.

(3) An order made under paragraph (1) shall be treated as an order made under rule 10 of Schedule 1 for the purposes of rule 13 of Schedule 1 (compliance with orders and practice directions).

9 Provisions of Schedule 1 which do not apply to levy appeals

The following rules in Schedule 1 shall not apply in relation to levy appeals: rules 1 to 9, 16(1)(c), 18(2)(c) and (e), 20 to 25, 33, 34(1)(a), 34(2), 34(4), 38(4), 39, 42(4), 43, 47, 49 to 53, 55, and paragraphs (4)(a), (7) and (8) of rule 61. All references in Schedule 1 to the rules listed in this rule shall have no effect in relation to a levy appeal.

10 Modification of Schedule 1

Schedule 1 shall be further modified in relation to levy appeals as follows—

(a) all references in Schedule 1 to a claim or claimant shall be read as references to a levy appeal or to an appellant in a levy appeal respectively and as the context may require; and

(b) in rule 61 (Notices, etc) after paragraph 4(i) insert—

"(j) in the case of a notice of an appeal brought under the Industrial Training Act, the Board's address for service specified in the assessment notice;

(k) in the case of any other document directed to the Board, the Board's address for service;".

ANNEX

FORM 1
INDUSTRIAL TRAINING ACT 1982
NOTICE OF APPEAL AGAINST AN ASSESSMENT

TO

*INDUSTRIAL TRAINING BOARD

... [ ] ....

....

....

....

AND TO

The Secretary of Tribunals (England and Wales) + (Scotland)

I/We + ...of

... # ....

....

hereby give notice that I/we + appeal to an employment tribunal under the Industrial Training Act 1982, section 12, against the assessment to the levy made by the above-mentioned industry training board on .... 20 .... being the assessment numbered ....

Grounds of appeal

The grounds of my/our + appeal are as follows—

Address for service

All communications regarding the appeal should be addressed to me/us + at

.... # ....

....

to my/our + Solicitor(s)Agent(s)~,

.... at .... # ....

Date .... 2 ....

Signed ....

* Insert name of the Board.

[ ] Insert the address of the Board.

+ Delete as relevant.

Insert address applicable.

~ If the notice is signed on behalf of the appellant, the signatory must state in what capacity or what authority he signs.

[3173]

NOTES

Commencement: 1 October 2004.

SCHEDULE 4

THE EMPLOYMENT TRIBUNALS (HEALTH AND SAFETY—APPEALS AGAINST IMPROVEMENT AND PROHIBITION NOTICES) RULES OF PROCEDURE

Regulation 16(3)(b)

For use only in proceedings in an appeal against an improvement or prohibition notice

1 Application of Schedule 1

Subject to rules 11 and 12 of this Schedule, Schedule 1 shall apply to appeals against an improvement notice or a prohibition notice. The rules in this Schedule modify the rules in Schedule 1 in relation to such appeals. If there is conflict between the rules contained in this Schedule and those in Schedule 1, the rules in this Schedule shall prevail.

2 Definitions

In this Schedule and in relation to proceedings to which this Schedule applies—

"Health and Safety Act" means the Health and Safety at Work etc Act 1974;

"improvement notice" means a notice under section 21 of the Health and Safety Act;

"inspector" means a person appointed under section 19(1) of the Health and Safety Act;

"prohibition notice" means a notice under section 22 of the Health and Safety Act; and

"respondent" means the inspector who issued the improvement notice or prohibition notice which is the subject of the appeal.

3 Notice of appeal

A person wishing to appeal an improvement notice or a prohibition notice (the appellant) shall do so by sending to the Employment Tribunal Office … a notice of appeal which must include the following—

(a) the name and address of the appellant and, if different, an address to which he requires notices and documents relating to the appeal to be sent;

(b) the date of the improvement notice or prohibition notice appealed against and the address of the premises or the place concerned;

(c) the name and address of the respondent;

(d) details of the requirements or directions which are being appealed; and

(e) the grounds for the appeal.

4 Time limit for bringing appeal

(1) Subject to paragraph (2), the notice of appeal must be sent to the Employment Tribunal Office within 21 days from the date of the service on the appellant of the notice appealed against.

(2) A tribunal may extend the time mentioned above where it is satisfied, on an application made in writing to the Secretary either before or after the expiration of that time, that it is or was not reasonably practicable for an appeal to be brought within that time.

5 Action on receipt of appeal

On receiving the notice of appeal the Secretary shall—

(a) send a copy of the notice of appeal to the respondent; and

(b) inform the parties in writing of the case number of the appeal (which must from then on be referred to in all correspondence relating to the appeal) and of the address to which notices and other communications to the Employment Tribunal Office shall be sent.

6 Application for a direction suspending the operation of a prohibition notice

(1) When an appeal is brought against a prohibition notice, an application may be made by the appellant under section 24(3)(b) of the Health and Safety Act for a direction

suspending the operation of the prohibition notice until the appeal is determined or withdrawn. The application must be presented to the Employment Tribunal Office in writing and shall include—

(a) the case number of the appeal, or if there is no case number sufficient details to identify the appeal; and
(b) the grounds on which the application is made.

(2) The Secretary shall send a copy of the application to the respondent as soon as practicable after it has been received and shall inform the respondent that he has the opportunity to submit representations in writing if he so wishes, within a specified time but not less than 7 days.

(3) The chairman shall consider the application and any representations submitted by the respondent, and may—

(a) order that the application should not be determined separately from the full hearing of the appeal;
(b) order that the operation of the prohibition notice be suspended until the appeal is determined or withdrawn;
(c) dismiss the appellant's application; or
(d) order that the application be determined at a Hearing (held in accordance with rule 26 of Schedule 1).

(4) The chairman must give reasons for any decision made under paragraph (3) or made following a Hearing ordered under paragraph (3)(d).

(5) A decision made under paragraph (3) or made following a Hearing ordered under paragraph (3)(d) shall be treated as a decision which may be reviewed upon the application of a party under rule 34 of Schedule 1.

7 General power to manage proceedings

(1) The chairman may at any time on the application of a party, make an order in relation to any matter which appears to him to be appropriate. Such orders may be those listed in rule 10(2) of Schedule 1 (subject to rule 11 below) or such other orders as he thinks fit. Subject to the case management rules in Schedule 1, orders may be issued as a result of a chairman considering the papers before him in the absence of the parties, or at a hearing (see regulation 2 for the definition of "hearing").

(2) If the parties agree in writing upon the terms of any decision to be made by the tribunal or chairman, the chairman may, if he thinks fit, decide accordingly.

8 Appointment of an assessor

The President, Vice President or a Regional Chairman may, if he thinks fit, appoint in accordance with section 24(4) of the Health and Safety Act a person having special knowledge or experience in relation to the subject matter of the appeal to sit with the tribunal or chairman as an assessor.

9 Right to withdraw proceedings

(1) An appellant may withdraw all or part of the appeal at any time. This may be done either orally at a hearing or in writing in accordance with paragraph (2).

(2) To withdraw an appeal or part of one in writing the appellant must inform the Employment Tribunal Office in writing of the appeal or the parts of it which are to be withdrawn.

(3) The Secretary shall inform all other parties of the withdrawal. Withdrawal takes effect on the date on which the Employment Tribunal Office (in the case of written notifications) or the tribunal or chairman receives notice of it and where the whole appeal is withdrawn proceedings are brought to an end against the respondent on that date and the tribunal or chairman shall dismiss the appeal.

10 Costs and expenses

(1) A tribunal or chairman may make an order ("a costs order") that a party ("the paying party") make a payment in respect of the costs incurred by another party ("the receiving party").

(2) For the purposes of paragraph (1) "costs" shall mean fees, charges, disbursements [or expenses] incurred by or on behalf of a party in relation to the proceedings. In Scotland all references in this Schedule to costs or costs orders shall be read as references to expenses or orders for expenses.

(3) The amount of a costs order against the paying party can be determined in the following ways—

(a) the tribunal may specify the sum which the party must pay to the receiving party, provided that sum does not exceed £10,000;

(b) the parties may agree on a sum to be paid by the paying party to the receiving party and if they do so the costs order shall be for the sum so agreed;

(c) the tribunal may order the paying party to pay the receiving party the whole or a specified part of the costs of the second party with the amount to be paid being determined by way of detailed assessment in a County Court in accordance with the Civil Procedure Rules or, in Scotland, as taxed according to such part of the table of fees prescribed for proceedings in the sheriff court as shall be directed by the order.

(4) The tribunal or chairman shall have regard to the paying party's ability to pay when considering whether it or he shall make a costs order or how much that order should be.

(5) For the avoidance of doubt, the amount of a costs order made under either paragraph (4)(b) or (c) may exceed £10,000.

11 Provisions of Schedule 1 which do not apply to appeals against improvement notices or prohibition notices

The following rules in Schedule 1 shall not apply in relation to appeals against improvement and prohibition notices: rules 1 to 9, 10(1), 10(2)(g), (i), (k), (l) and (r), 12, 13, 16(1)(c), 18(2)(c) and (e), 18(8), 20 to 25, 29(3), 33, 34(1)(a), 34(2), 38 to 47, 49 to 53, 55, and 61(4)(a), (7) and (8). All references in Schedule 1 to the rules listed in this rule shall have no effect in relation to an appeal against an improvement notice or a prohibition notice.

12 Modification of Schedule 1

Schedule 1 shall be further modified so that all references in Schedule 1 to a claim shall be read as references to a notice of appeal or to an appeal against an improvement notice or a prohibition notice, as the context may require, and all references to the claimant shall be read as references to the appellant in such an appeal.

[3174]

NOTES

Commencement: 1 October 2004.

Rule 3: words omitted revoked by the Employment Tribunals (Constitution and Rules of Procedure) (Amendment) Regulations 2004, SI 2004/2351, reg 2(1), (10), as from 1 October 2004.

Rule 10: words in square brackets in para (2) substituted by the Employment Tribunals (Constitution and Rules of Procedure) (Amendment) (No 2) Regulations 2005, SI 2005/1865, reg 2(1), (5), as from 1 October 2005.

SCHEDULE 5
THE EMPLOYMENT TRIBUNALS ([UNLAWFUL ACT NOTICE] APPEALS) RULES OF PROCEDURE

Regulation 16(3)(c)

For use only in proceedings in an appeal against [an unlawful act notice]

1 Application of Schedule 1

Subject to rules 5 and 6 of this Schedule, Schedule 1 shall apply to appeals against [an unlawful act notice]. The rules in this Schedule modify the rules in Schedule 1 in relation to such appeals. If there is conflict between the rules contained in this Schedule and those in Schedule 1, the rules in this Schedule shall prevail.

[2 Definitions

In this Schedule and in relation to proceedings to which this Schedule applies—

"appeal", unless the context requires otherwise, means an appeal referred to in section 21 of the Equality Act 2006;

"unlawful act notice" means a notice under that section; and
"respondent" means the Commission for Equality and Human Rights established under section 1 of the Equality Act 2006.]

3 Notice of Appeal

A person wishing to appeal [an unlawful act notice] (the appellant) shall do so by sending to the Employment Tribunal Office … a notice of appeal which must be in writing and must include the following—

(a) the name and address of the appellant and, if different, an address to which he requires notices and documents relating to the appeal to be sent;
(b) the date of [the unlawful act notice] appealed against;
(c) the name and address of the respondent;
(d) details of the requirements which are being appealed; and
(e) the grounds for the appeal.

4 Action on receipt of appeal

On receiving the notice of appeal the Secretary shall—

(a) send a copy of the notice of appeal to the respondent; and
(b) inform the parties in writing of the case number of the appeal (which must from then on be referred to in all correspondence relating to the appeal) and of the address to which notices and other communications to the Employment Tribunal Office shall be sent.

5 Provisions of Schedule 1 which do not apply to appeals against [unlawful act notices]

The following rules in Schedule 1 shall not apply in relation to appeals against [an unlawful act notice]: rules 1 to 9, 16(1)(c), 18(2)(c) and (e), 20 to 24, 33, 34(1)(a), 34(2), 34(4), 38(4), 39, 42(4), 43, 47,49 to 53, 55, and paragraphs (4)(a), (7) and (8) of rule 61. All references in Schedule 1 to the rules listed in this rule shall have no effect in relation to an appeal against [an unlawful act notice].

6 Modification of Schedule 1

Schedule 1 shall be further modified so that all references in Schedule 1 to a claim shall be read as references to a notice of appeal or to an appeal against [an unlawful act notice], as the context may require, and all references to the claimant shall be read as references to the appellant in such an appeal.

[3175]

NOTES

Commencement: 1 October 2004.

Headings and rules 1, 3, 5, 6: words in square brackets substituted by the Equality Act 2006 (Dissolution of Commissions and Consequential and Transitional Provisions) Order 2007, SI 2007/2602, art 4(1), Schedule, para 7(c)(i)–(iii), as from 1 October 2007.

Rule 2: substituted by SI 2007/2602, art 4(1), Schedule, para 7(c)(iv), as from 1 October 2007.

Rule 3: words omitted revoked by the Employment Tribunals (Constitution and Rules of Procedure) (Amendment) Regulations 2004, SI 2004/2351, reg 2(1), (10), as from 1 October 2004.

[SCHEDULE 6
THE EMPLOYMENT TRIBUNALS (EQUAL VALUE) RULES OF PROCEDURE

Regulation 16(4)

1 General

The rules in this Schedule shall only apply in proceedings involving an equal value claim and they modify and supplement the rules in Schedule 1. If there is conflict between Schedule 1 and this Schedule, the provisions of this Schedule shall prevail.

2 Interpretation

(1) In this Schedule and in relation to proceedings to which this Schedule applies:

"comparator" means the person of the opposite sex to the claimant in relation to whom the claimant claims that his work is of equal value as described in section 1(2)(c) of the Equal Pay Act;

"Equal Pay Act" means the Equal Pay Act 1970;

"equal value claim" means a claim by a claimant which rests upon entitlement to the benefit of an equality clause by virtue of the operation of section 1(2)(c) of the Equal Pay Act;

"the facts relating to the question" has the meaning in rule 7(3);

"independent expert" means a member of the panel of independent experts mentioned in section 2A(4) of the Equal Pay Act;

"indicative timetable" means the indicative timetable set out in the Annex to this Schedule;

"the question" means whether the claimant's work is of equal value to that of the comparator as described in section 1(2)(c) of the Equal Pay Act; and

"report" means a report required by a tribunal to be prepared by an independent expert, in accordance with section 2A(1)(b) of the Equal Pay Act.

(2) A reference in this Schedule to a rule, is a reference to a rule in this Schedule unless otherwise provided.

(3) A reference in this Schedule to "these rules" is a reference to the rules in Schedules 1 and 6 unless otherwise provided.

3 General power to manage proceedings

(1) In addition to the power to make orders described in rule 10 of Schedule 1, the tribunal or chairman shall have power (subject to rules 4(3) and 7(4)) to make the following orders:

(a) the standard orders set out in rules 5 or 8, with such addition to, omission or variation of those orders (including specifically variations as to the periods within which actions are to be taken by the parties) as the chairman or tribunal considers is appropriate;

(b) that no new facts shall be admitted in evidence by the tribunal unless they have been disclosed to all other parties in writing before a date specified by the tribunal (unless it was not reasonably practicable for a party to have done so);

(c) that the parties may be required to send copies of documents or provide information to the other parties and to the independent expert;

(d) that the respondent is required to grant the independent expert access to his premises during a period specified by the tribunal or chairman in order for the independent expert to conduct interviews with persons identified as relevant by the independent expert;

(e) when more than one expert is to give evidence in the proceedings, that those experts present to the tribunal a joint statement of matters which are agreed between them and those matters on which they disagree;

(f) where proceedings have been joined, that lead claimants be identified.

(2) Any reference in Schedule 1 or 2 to an order made under rule 10 of Schedule 1 shall include reference to an order made in accordance with this Schedule.

4 Conduct of stage 1 equal value hearing

(1) When in an equal value claim there is a dispute as to whether any work is of equal value as mentioned in section 1(2)(c) of the Equal Pay Act, the tribunal shall conduct a "stage 1 equal value hearing" in accordance with both this rule and the rules applicable to pre-hearing reviews in Schedule 1.

(2) Notwithstanding rule 18(1) and (3) of Schedule 1, a stage 1 equal value hearing shall be conducted by a tribunal composed in accordance with section 4(1) of the Employment Tribunals Act.

(3) At the stage 1 equal value hearing the tribunal shall:

(a) where section 2A(2) of the Equal Pay Act applies, strike out the claim (or the relevant part of it) if, in accordance with section 2A(2A) of that Act, the tribunal must determine that the work of the claimant and the comparator are not of equal value;

(b) decide, in accordance with section 2A(1) of the Equal Pay Act, either that:

(i) the tribunal shall determine the question; or

(ii) it shall require a member of the panel of independent experts to prepare a report with respect to the question;

(c) subject to rule 5 and with regard to the indicative timetable, make the standard orders for the stage 1 equal value hearing as set out in rule 5;

(d) if the tribunal has decided to require an independent expert to prepare a report on the question, require the parties to copy to the independent expert all information which they are required by an order to disclose or agree between each other;

(e) if the tribunal has decided to require an independent expert to prepare a report on the question, fix a date for the stage 2 equal value hearing, having regard to the indicative timetable;

(f) if the tribunal has not decided to require an independent expert to prepare a report on the question, fix a date for the Hearing, having regard to the indicative timetable;

(g) consider whether any further orders are appropriate.

(4) Before a claim or part of one is struck out under paragraph (3)(a), the Secretary shall send notice to the claimant giving him the opportunity to make representations to the tribunal as to whether the evaluation contained in the study in question falls within paragraph (a) or (b) of section 2A(2A) of the Equal Pay Act. The Secretary shall not be required to send a notice under this paragraph if the claimant has been given an opportunity to make such representations orally to the tribunal as to why such a judgment should not be issued.

(5) The tribunal may, on the application of a party, hear evidence upon and permit the parties to address it upon the issue contained in section 1(3) of the Equal Pay Act (defence of a genuine material factor) before determining whether to require an independent expert to prepare a report under paragraph (3)(b)(ii).

(6) When the Secretary gives notice to the parties of the stage 1 equal value hearing under rule 14(4) of Schedule 1, he shall also give the parties notice of the matters which the tribunal may and shall consider at that hearing which are described in paragraphs (3) and (5) of this rule and he shall give the parties notice of the standard orders in rule 5.

(7) The tribunal's power to strike out the claim or part of it under paragraph (3)(a) is in addition to powers to strike out a claim under rule 18(7) of Schedule 1.

5 Standard orders for stage 1 equal value hearing

(1) At a stage 1 equal value hearing a tribunal shall, unless it considers it inappropriate to do so and subject to paragraph (2), order that—

(a) before the end of the period of 14 days after the date of the stage 1 equal value hearing the claimant shall:

(i) disclose in writing to the respondent the name of any comparator, or, if the claimant is not able to name the comparator he shall instead disclose such information as enables the comparator to be identified by the respondent; and

(ii) identify to the respondent in writing the period in relation to which he considers that the claimant's work and that of the comparator are to be compared;

(b) before the end of the period of 28 days after the date of the stage 1 equal value hearing:

(i) where the claimant has not disclosed the name of the comparator to the respondent under sub-paragraph (a), if the respondent has been provided with sufficient detail to be able to identify the comparator, he shall disclose in writing the name of the comparator to the claimant;

(ii) the parties shall provide each other with written job descriptions for the claimant and any comparator;

(iii) the parties shall identify to each other in writing the facts which they consider to be relevant to the question;

(c) the respondent is required to grant access to the claimant and his representative (if any) to his premises during a period specified by the tribunal or chairman in order for him or them to interview any comparator;

(d) the parties shall before the end of the period of 56 days after the date of the stage 1 equal value hearing present to the tribunal a joint agreed statement in writing of the following matters:

(i) job descriptions for the claimant and any comparator;

(ii) facts which both parties consider are relevant to the question;

(iii) facts on which the parties disagree (as to the fact or as to the relevance to the question) and a summary of their reasons for disagreeing;

(e) the parties shall, at least 56 days prior to the Hearing, disclose to each other, to any independent or other expert and to the tribunal written statements of any facts on which they intend to rely in evidence at the Hearing; and

(f) the parties shall, at least 28 days prior to the Hearing, present to the tribunal a statement of facts and issues on which the parties are in agreement, a statement of facts and issues on which the parties disagree and a summary of their reasons for disagreeing.

(2) Any of the standard orders for the stage 1 equal value hearing may be added to, varied or omitted as the tribunal considers appropriate.

6 Involvement of independent expert in fact finding

(1) This rule applies only to proceedings in relation to which the tribunal has decided to require an independent expert to prepare a report on the question.

(2) In proceedings to which this rule applies a tribunal or chairman may if it or he considers it appropriate at any stage of the proceedings order an independent expert to assist the tribunal in establishing the facts on which the independent expert may rely in preparing his report.

(3) Examples of the circumstances in which the tribunal or chairman may make an order described in paragraph (2) may include:

(a) a party not being legally represented;

(b) the parties are unable to reach agreement as required by an order of the tribunal or chairman;

(c) the tribunal or chairman considers that insufficient information may have been disclosed by a party and this may impair the ability of the independent expert to prepare a report on the question;

(d) the tribunal or chairman considers that the involvement of the independent expert may promote fuller compliance with orders made by the tribunal or a chairman.

(4) A party to proceedings to which this rule applies may make an application under rule 11 of Schedule 1 for an order under paragraph (2).

7 Conduct of stage 2 equal value hearing

(1) This rule applies only to proceedings in relation to which the tribunal has decided to require an independent expert to prepare a report on the question. In such proceedings the tribunal shall conduct a "stage 2 equal value hearing" in accordance with both this rule and the rules applicable to pre-hearing reviews in Schedule 1.

(2) Notwithstanding rule 18(1) and (3) of Schedule 1, a stage 2 equal value hearing shall be [conducted by a tribunal] composed in accordance with section 4(1) of the Employment Tribunals Act.

(3) At the stage 2 equal value hearing the tribunal shall make a determination of facts on which the parties cannot agree which relate to the question and shall require the independent expert to prepare his report on the basis of facts which have (at any stage of the proceedings) either been agreed between the parties or determined by the tribunal (referred to as "the facts relating to the question").

(4) At the stage 2 equal value hearing the tribunal shall:

(a) [subject] to rule 8 and having regard to the indicative timetable, make the standard orders for the stage 2 equal value hearing as set out in rule 8;

(b) make any orders which it considers appropriate;

(c) fix a date for the Hearing, having regard to the indicative timetable.

(5) Subject to paragraph (6), the facts relating to the question shall, in relation to the question, be the only facts on which the tribunal shall rely at the Hearing.

(6) At any stage of the proceedings the independent expert may make an application to the tribunal for ... some or all of the facts relating to the question to be amended, supplemented or omitted.

(7) When the Secretary gives notice to the parties and to the independent expert of the stage 2 equal value hearing under rule 14(4) of Schedule 1, he shall also give the parties notice of the standard orders in rule 8 and draw the attention of the parties to paragraphs (4) and (5) of this rule.

8 Standard orders for stage 2 equal value hearing

(1) At a stage 2 equal value hearing a tribunal shall, unless it considers it inappropriate to do so and subject to paragraph (2), order that—

(a) by a date specified by the tribunal (with regard to the indicative timetable) the independent expert shall prepare his report on the question and shall (subject to rule 14) have sent copies of it to the parties and to the tribunal; and

(b) the independent expert shall prepare his report on the question on the basis of the facts relating to the question and no other facts which may or may not relate to the question.

(2) Any of the standard orders for the stage 2 equal value hearing may be added to, varied or omitted as the tribunal considers appropriate.

9 The Hearing

(1) In proceedings in relation to which an independent expert has prepared a report, unless the tribunal determines that the report is not based on the facts relating to the question, the report of the independent expert shall be admitted in evidence in those proceedings.

(2) If the tribunal does not admit the report of an independent expert in accordance with paragraph (1), it may determine the question itself or require another independent expert to prepare a report on the question.

(3) The tribunal may refuse to admit evidence of facts or hear argument as to issues which have not been disclosed to the other party as required by these rules or any order made under them, unless it was not reasonably practicable for the party to have so complied.

10 Duties and powers of the independent expert

(1) When a tribunal requires an independent expert to prepare a report with respect to the question or an order is made under rule 6(2), the Secretary shall inform that independent expert of the duties and powers he has under this rule.

(2) The independent expert shall have a duty to the tribunal to:

(a) assist it in furthering the overriding objective in regulation 3;

(b) comply with the requirements of these rules and any orders made by the tribunal or a chairman in relation to the proceedings;

(c) keep the tribunal informed of any delay in complying with any order in the proceedings with the exception of minor or insignificant delays in compliance;

(d) comply with any timetable imposed by the tribunal or chairman in so far as this is reasonably practicable;

(e) inform the tribunal or a chairman on request by it or him of progress in the preparation of the independent expert's report;

(f) prepare a report on the question based on the facts relating to the question and (subject to rule 14) send it to the tribunal and the parties;

(g) make himself available to attend hearings in the proceedings.

(3) The independent expert may make an application for any order or for a hearing to be held as if he were a party to the proceedings.

(4) At any stage of the proceedings the tribunal may, after giving the independent expert the opportunity to make representations, withdraw the requirement on the independent expert to prepare a report. If it does so, the tribunal may itself determine the question, or it may determine that a different independent expert should be required to prepare the report.

(5) When paragraph (4) applies the independent expert who is no longer required to prepare the report shall provide the tribunal with all documentation and work in progress relating to the proceedings by a date specified by the tribunal. Such documentation and work in progress must be in a form which the tribunal is able to use. Such documentation and work in progress may be used in relation to those proceedings by the tribunal or by another independent expert.

(6) When an independent expert has been required to prepare a report in proceedings the Secretary shall give the independent expert notice of all hearings, orders or judgments in those proceedings as if the independent expert were a party to those proceedings and when these rules require a party to provide information to another party, such information shall also be provided to the independent expert.

11 Use of expert evidence

(1) Expert evidence shall be restricted to that which, in the opinion of the tribunal, is reasonably required to resolve the proceedings.

(2) An expert shall have a duty to assist the tribunal on matters within his expertise. This duty overrides any obligation to the person from whom he has received instructions or by whom he is paid.

(3) No party may call an expert or put in evidence an expert's report without the permission of the tribunal. No expert report shall be put in evidence unless it has been disclosed to all other parties and any independent expert at least 28 days prior to the Hearing.

(4) In proceedings in which an independent expert has been required to prepare a report on the question, the tribunal shall not admit evidence of another expert on the question unless such evidence is based on the facts relating to the question. Unless the tribunal considers it inappropriate to do so, any such expert report shall be disclosed to all parties and to the tribunal on the same date on which the independent expert is required to send his report to the parties and to the tribunal.

(5) If an expert (other than an independent expert) does not comply with these rules or an order made by the tribunal or a chairman, the tribunal may order that the evidence of that expert shall not be admitted.

(6) Where two or more parties wish to submit expert evidence on a particular issue, the tribunal may order that the evidence on that issue is to be given by one joint expert only. When such an order has been made, if the parties wishing to instruct the joint expert cannot agree who should be the expert, the tribunal may select the expert.

12 Written questions to experts

(1) When any expert (including an independent expert) has prepared a report, a party or any other expert (including an independent expert) involved in the proceedings may put written questions about the report to the expert who has prepared the report.

(2) Unless the tribunal or chairman agrees otherwise, written questions under paragraph (1):

(a) may be put once only;
(b) must be put within 28 days of the date on which the parties were sent the report;
(c) must be for the purpose only of clarifying the factual basis of the report;
(d) must be copied to all other parties and experts involved in the proceedings at the same time as they are sent to the expert who prepared the report.

(3) When written questions have been put to an expert in accordance with paragraph (2) he shall answer those questions within 28 days of receiving them.

(4) An expert's answers to questions put in accordance with paragraph (2) shall be treated as part of the expert's report.

(5) Where a party has put a written question in accordance with this rule to an expert instructed by another party and the expert does not answer that question, or does not do so within 28 days, the tribunal may order that the party instructing the expert may not rely on the evidence of that expert.

13 Procedural matters

(1) In proceedings in which an independent expert has been required to prepare a report, the Secretary shall send him notices and inform him of any hearing, application, order or judgment in those proceedings as if he were a party to those proceedings.

(2) For the avoidance of doubt, any requirement in this Schedule to hold a stage 1 or a stage 2 equal value hearing does not preclude holding more than one of each of those types of hearing or other hearings from being held in accordance with Schedule 1.

(3) Any power conferred on a chairman in Schedule 1 may (subject to the provisions of this Schedule) be carried out by a tribunal or a chairman in relation to proceedings to which this Schedule applies.

14 National security proceedings

(1) In equal value cases which are also national security proceedings, if a tribunal has required an independent expert to prepare a report on the question, the independent expert shall send a copy of the report to the tribunal and shall not send it to the parties. In such proceedings if written questions have been put to the independent expert under rule 12, the independent expert shall send any answers to those questions to the tribunal and not to the parties.

(2) Before the Secretary sends to the parties a copy of a report or answers which have been sent to him by the independent expert under paragraph (1), he shall follow the procedure set out in rule 10 of Schedule 2 as if that rule referred to the independent expert's report or answers (as the case may be) instead of written reasons, except that the independent expert's report or answers shall not be entered on the Register.

(3) If the Minister does not give a direction under rule 10(3) of Schedule 2 within the period of 28 days from the date on which the Minister was sent the report or answers to written questions the Secretary shall send a copy of the independent expert's report or answers to written questions (as the case may be) to the parties.

ANNEX

The indicative timetable

Claims *not* involving an independent expert	Claims involving an independent expert
Claim	Claim
↓	↓
28 days	28 days
↓	↓
Response	Response
	↓
3 weeks	3 weeks
↓	↓
Stage 1 equal value hearing	Stage 1 equal value hearing
↓	↓
↓	10 weeks
↓	↓
↓	Stage 2 equal value hearing
↓	↓
↓	[8 weeks]
↓	↓
↓	Independent expert's report
18 weeks	↓
↓	4 weeks
↓	↓
↓	written questions
↓	↓
↓	8 weeks
↓	↓
Hearing	Hearing
Total 25 weeks	Total 37 weeks.]

[3176]

NOTES

Commencement: 1 October 2004.

Added by the Employment Tribunals (Constitution and Rules of Procedure) (Amendment) Regulations 2004, SI 2004/2351, reg 2(1), (11), as from 1 October 2004.

Rule 7: words in square brackets in para (2) inserted, word in square brackets in para (4)(a) substituted, and words omitted from para (6) revoked, by the Employment Tribunals (Constitution and Rules of Procedure) (Amendment) (No 2) Regulations 2005, SI 2005/1865, reg 2(1), (6)(a)–(c), as from 1 October 2005.

Annex: words in square brackets inserted by SI 2005/1865, reg 2(1), (6)(d), as from 1 October 2005.

EUROPEAN PUBLIC LIMITED-LIABILITY COMPANY REGULATIONS 2004

(SI 2004/2326)

NOTES

Made: 6 September 2004.

Authority: European Communities Act 1972, s 2(2).

Commencement: 8 October 2004.

These Regulations are, in part, the domestic implementation of Council Directive 2001/86/EC supplementing the Statute for a European company with regard to the involvement of employees at **[4032]**; they also implement the Statute itself (Council Regulation 2157/2001/EC). Only those regulations relevant to employment law are reproduced.

Conciliation: employment tribunal proceedings and claims which could be the subject of employment tribunal proceedings under regs 41, 45 are proceedings to which the Employment Tribunals Act 1996, s 18 applies; see s 18(1)(n) of that Act at **[975]**. The standard conciliation period applies to such claims by virtue of the Employment Tribunals (Constitution and Rules of Procedure) Regulations 2004, SI 2004/1861, Sch 1, rule 22(1), (6).

Employment Appeal Tribunal: an appeal lies to the Employment Appeal Tribunal on any question of law arising from any decision of, or in any proceedings before, an employment tribunal under or by virtue of these Regulations; see the Employment Tribunals Act 1996, s 21(1)(o) at **[978]**.

ARRANGEMENT OF REGULATIONS

PART 1
GENERAL

PART 3
EMPLOYEE INVOLVEMENT

CHAPTER 1
INTERPRETATION OF PART 3

CHAPTER 2
PARTICIPATING COMPANIES AND THE SPECIAL NEGOTIATING BODY

CHAPTER 3
ELECTION OR APPOINTMENT OF UK MEMBERS OF THE SPECIAL NEGOTIATING BODY

CHAPTER 4
NEGOTIATION OF THE EMPLOYEE INVOLVEMENT AGREEMENT

CHAPTER 5
STANDARD RULES ON EMPLOYEE INVOLVEMENT

CHAPTER 6
COMPLIANCE AND ENFORCEMENT

CHAPTER 7
CONFIDENTIAL INFORMATION

CHAPTER 8
PROTECTION FOR MEMBERS OF SPECIAL NEGOTIATING BODY, ETC

CHAPTER 9
MISCELLANEOUS

SCHEDULES:

PART 1
GENERAL

1 Citation, commencement and extent

(1) These Regulations may be cited as the European Public Limited-Liability Company Regulations 2004.

(2) These Regulations come into force on 8th October 2004.

(3) These Regulations extend to Great Britain.

[3177]

NOTES

Commencement: 8 October 2004.

Note that despite para (3) above, the enactments in force in Great Britain relating to SEs extend to Northern Ireland; see the Companies Act 2006, s 1285(1).

2 EC Directive and EC Regulation

In these Regulations—

"the EC Directive" means Council Directive 2001/86/EC of 8 October 2001 supplementing the Statute for a European Company with regard to the involvement of employees;

"the EC Regulation" means Council Regulation 2157/2001/EC of 8 October 2001 on the Statute for a European Company;

and references to numbered Articles are, unless otherwise specified, references to Articles in the EC Regulation.

[3178]

NOTES

Commencement: 8 October 2004.

3 Interpretation

(1) In these Regulations—

the "1985 Act" mean the Companies Act 1985;

the "1996 Act" means the Employment Rights Act 1996;

["the Companies Acts" has the meaning given by section 2 of the Companies Act 2006;]

"SE" means a European Public Limited-Liability Company (or Societas Europaea) within the meaning of the EC Regulation and, except as provided in these Regulations, means an SE which is to be, or is, registered in Great Britain.

(2) Except as otherwise provided in these Regulations, words and expressions [defined for the purposes of the Companies Acts have the same meaning in these Regulations].

(3) Except as otherwise provided in these Regulations, words and expressions which are used in the EC Regulation or the EC Directive have the same meaning as they have in that Regulation or Directive.

(4) Where a word or expression is both [defined as mentioned] in paragraph (2) and used in the EC Regulation or the EC Directive, it has the meaning it has in that Regulation or Directive except as otherwise provided in these Regulations.

[3179]

NOTES

Commencement: 8 October 2004.

Para (1): definition "the Companies Acts" inserted by the Companies Act 2006 (Consequential Amendments etc) Order 2008, SI 2008/948, art 3(1)(b), Sch 1, Pt 2, para 235(1), (2)(a), as from 6 April 2008.

Paras (2), (4): words in square brackets substituted by SI 2008/948, art 3(1)(b), Sch 1, Pt 2, para 235(1), (2)(b), (c), as from 6 April 2008.

4–15 ((*Pt 2: Registration of SEs and the Registrar etc*) *outside the scope of this work.*)

PART 3
EMPLOYEE INVOLVEMENT

CHAPTER 1
INTERPRETATION OF PART 3

16 Interpretation of Part 3

(1) In this Part—

"absolute majority vote" means a vote passed by a majority of the total membership of the special negotiating body where the members voting with that majority represent the majority of the employees of the participating companies and their concerned subsidiaries and establishments employed in the Member States;

"Appeal Tribunal" means the Employment Appeal Tribunal;

"CAC" means the Central Arbitration Committee;

"dismissed" and "dismissal", in relation to an employee, shall be construed in accordance with Part 10 of the 1996 Act;

"EEA state" means a Member State, Norway, Iceland and Lichtenstein;

"employee" means an individual who has entered into or works under a contract of employment and includes, where the employment has ceased, an individual who worked under a contract of employment;

"employee involvement agreement" means an agreement reached between the special negotiating body and the competent organs of the participating companies governing the arrangements for the involvement of employees within the SE;

"employees' representatives" means—

(a) if the employees are of a description in respect of which an independent trade union is recognised by their employer for the purpose of collective bargaining, representatives of the trade union who normally take part as negotiators in the collective bargaining process, and

(b) any other employees of their employer who are elected or appointed as employee representatives to positions in which they are expected to receive, on behalf of the employees, information—

(i) which is relevant to the terms and conditions of employment of the employees, or

(ii) about the activities of the undertaking which may significantly affect the interests of the employees,

but excluding representatives who are expected to receive information relevant only to a specific aspect of the terms and conditions or interests of the employees, such as health and safety or collective redundancies;

"information and consultation representative" has the meaning given to it in regulation 27(5);

"participation" means the influence of the representative body and the employees' representatives in the SE or a participating company by way of the right to—

(a) elect or appoint some of the members of the SE's or the participating company's supervisory or administrative organ; or

(b) recommend and/or oppose the appointment of some or all of the members of the SE's or the participating company's supervisory or administrative organ;

"representative body" means the persons elected or appointed under the employee involvement agreement or under the standard rules on employee involvement;

"SE established by merger" means an SE established in accordance with Article 2(1);

"SE established by formation of a holding company or subsidiary company" means an SE established in accordance with Article 2(2) or 2(3), as the case may be;

"SE established by transformation" means an SE established in accordance with Article 2(4);

"standard rules on employee involvement" means the rules in Schedule 3;

"two thirds majority vote" means a vote passed by a majority of at least two thirds of the total membership of the special negotiating body where the members voting with that majority—

(a) represent at least two thirds of the employees of the participating companies and their concerned subsidiaries and establishments employed in the Member States; and

(b) include members representing employees employed in at least two Member States;

"UK employee" means an employee employed to work in the United Kingdom; and

"UK members of the special negotiating body" means members of the special negotiating body elected or appointed by UK employees.

(2) In this Part, the following terms have the meaning given by Article 2 of the EC Directive—

"participating companies"
"subsidiary"
"special negotiating body"
"involvement of employees"
"information"
"consultation"

and references to a "concerned subsidiary" or a "concerned establishment" shall be construed in accordance with the definition of "concerned subsidiary or establishment" in the EC Directive.

[3180]

NOTES

Commencement: 8 October 2004.

CHAPTER 2
PARTICIPATING COMPANIES AND THE SPECIAL NEGOTIATING BODY

17 Circumstances in which certain provisions of Part 3 apply

(1) Subject to paragraphs (2) and (3), this Part shall apply where—

(a) a participating company intends to establish an SE whose registered office is to be in Great Britain; or
(b) an SE has its registered office in Great Britain.

(2) Where there are UK employees, Chapter 2 (election or appointment of members of special negotiating body and representation of employees) shall apply, regardless of where the registered office is to be situated, in relation to the election or appointment of UK members of the special negotiating body unless the majority of those employees is employed to work in Northern Ireland.

(3) Chapters 6 to 9 shall apply, regardless of where the registered office of the SE is, or is intended to be situated, where—

(a) a participating company, its concerned subsidiaries or establishments;
(b) a subsidiary of an SE;
(c) an establishment of an SE; or
(d) an employee or an employees' representative,

is registered or situated, as the case may be, in Great Britain.

[3181]

NOTES

Commencement: 8 October 2004.

18 Duty on participating company to provide information

(1) When the competent organ of a participating company decides to form an SE, that organ shall, as soon as possible after—

(a) publishing the draft terms of merger,
(b) creating a holding company, or
(c) agreeing a plan to form a subsidiary or to transform into an SE,

provide information to the employees' representatives of the participating company, its concerned subsidiaries and establishments or, if no such representatives exist, the employees themselves.

(2) The information referred to in paragraph (1) must include, as a minimum, information—

(a) identifying the participating companies, concerned subsidiaries and establishments,
(b) giving the number of employees employed by each participating company and concerned subsidiary and at each concerned establishment, and
(c) giving the number of employees employed to work in each EEA State.

(3) When a special negotiating body has been formed in accordance with regulation 20, the competent organs of each participating company must provide that body with such information as is necessary to keep it informed of the plan and progress of establishing the SE up to the time the SE has been registered.

[3182]

NOTES

Commencement: 8 October 2004.

19 Complaint of failure to provide information

(1) An employees' representative or, where there is no such representative for an employee, the employee may present a complaint to the CAC that—

(a) the competent organ of a participating company has failed to provide the information referred to in regulation 18; or

(b) the information provided by the competent organ of a participating company for the purpose of complying with regulation 18 is false or incomplete in a material particular.

(2) Where the CAC finds the complaint well-founded it shall make an order requiring the competent organ to disclose information to the complainant which order shall specify—

(a) the information in respect of which the CAC finds that the complaint is well-founded and which is to be disclosed to the complainant; and

(b) a date (not being less than one week from the date of the order) by which the competent organ must disclose the information specified in the order.

[3183]

NOTES

Commencement: 8 October 2004.

20 Function of the special negotiating body

The special negotiating body and the competent organs of the participating companies shall have the task of reaching an employee involvement agreement.

[3184]

NOTES

Commencement: 8 October 2004.

21 Composition of the special negotiating body

(1) The competent organs of the participating companies shall make arrangements for the establishment of a special negotiating body which shall be constituted in accordance with paragraphs (2) to (7) below.

(2) In each EEA state in which employees of a participating company or concerned subsidiary are employed to work, those employees shall be given an entitlement to elect or appoint one member of the special negotiating body for each 10% or fraction thereof which those employees represent of the total workforce. These members shall be the 'ordinary members'.

(3) If, in the case of an SE to be established by merger, following an election or appointment under paragraph (2), the members elected or appointed to the special negotiating body do not include at least one eligible member in respect of each relevant company the employees of any relevant company in respect of which there is no eligible member shall be given an entitlement, subject to paragraph (4), to elect or appoint an additional member to the special negotiating body.

(4) The number of additional members which the employees are entitled to elect or appoint under paragraph (3) shall not exceed 20% of the number of ordinary members elected or appointed under paragraph (2) and if the number of additional members under paragraph (3) would exceed that percentage the employees who are entitled to appoint or elect the additional members shall be:

(a) if one additional member is to be appointed or elected, those employed by the company not represented under paragraph (3) having the highest number of employees; and

(b) if more than one additional member is to be appointed or elected, those employed by the companies in each EEA state that are not represented under paragraph (3) having the highest number of employees in descending order, starting with the company with the highest number, followed by those employed by the companies in each EEA state that are not so represented having the second highest number of employees in descending order, starting with the company (among those companies) with the highest number.

(5) The competent organs of the participating companies shall, as soon as reasonably practicable and in any event no later than one month after the establishment of the special negotiating body, inform their employees and those of their concerned subsidiaries of the identity of the members of the special negotiating body.

(6) If, following the appointment or election of members to the special negotiating body in accordance with this regulation,

(a) changes to the participating companies, concerned subsidiaries or concerned establishments result in the number of ordinary or additional members which employees would be entitled to elect or appoint under this regulation either increasing or decreasing, the original appointment or election of members of the special negotiating body shall cease to have effect and those employees shall be entitled to elect or appoint the new number of members in accordance with the provisions of these Regulations; and

(b) a member of the special negotiating body is no longer willing or able to continue serving as such a member, the employees whom he represents shall be entitled to elect or appoint a new member in his place.

(7) In this regulation—

(a) "eligible member" means a person who is—

(i) in the case of a relevant company registered in a EEA state whose legislation allows representatives of trade unions who are not employees to be elected to the special negotiating body, an employee of the relevant company or a trade union representative; and

(ii) in the case of a relevant company not registered in such a EEA state, an employee of the relevant company.

(b) "relevant company" means a participating company which has employees in the EEA state in which it is registered and which it is proposed will cease to exist on or following the registration of the SE; and

(c) "the total workforce" means the total number of employees employed by all participating companies and concerned subsidiaries throughout all EEA states.

[3185]

NOTES

Commencement: 8 October 2004.

22 Complaint about establishment of special negotiating body

(1) An application may be presented to the CAC for a declaration that the special negotiating body has not been established at all or has not been established properly in accordance with regulation 21.

(2) An application may be presented under this regulation by—

(a) a person elected or appointed to be a member of the special negotiating body;

(b) an employees' representative or, where no such representative exists in respect of a participating company or concerned subsidiary, an employee of that participating company or concerned subsidiary; or

(c) the competent organ of a participating company or concerned subsidiary.

(3) The CAC shall only consider an application made under paragraph (1) if it is made within a period of one month from the date or, if more than one, the last date on which the participating companies complied or should have complied with the obligation to inform their employees under regulation 21(5).

(4) Where the CAC finds the application well-founded it shall make a declaration that the special negotiating body has not been established at all or has not been established properly and the competent organs of the participating companies continue to be under the obligation in regulation 21(1).

[3186]

NOTES

Commencement: 8 October 2004.

CHAPTER 3
ELECTION OR APPOINTMENT OF UK MEMBERS OF THE SPECIAL NEGOTIATING BODY

23 Ballot arrangements

(1) Subject to regulation 24, the UK members of the special negotiating body shall be elected by balloting the UK employees.

(2) The management of the participating companies that employ UK employees ("the management") must arrange for the holding of a ballot or ballots of those employees in accordance with the requirements of paragraph (3).

(3) The requirements referred to in paragraph (2) are—

(a) in relation to the election of ordinary members under regulation 21(2), that—

(i) if the number of members which UK employees are entitled to elect to the special negotiating body is equal to the number of participating companies which have UK employees, there shall be separate ballots of the UK employees in each participating company;

(ii) if the number of members which the UK employees are entitled to elect to the special negotiating body is greater than the number of participating companies which have UK employees, there shall be separate ballots of the UK employees in each participating company and the management shall ensure, as far as practicable, that at least one member representing each such participating company is elected to the special negotiating body and that the number of members representing each company is proportionate to the number of employees in that company;

(iii) if the number of members which the UK employees are entitled to elect to the special negotiating body is smaller than the number of participating companies which have employees in the UK,—

(aa) the number of ballots held shall be equivalent to the number of members to be elected;

(bb) a separate ballot shall be held in respect of each of the participating companies with the higher or highest number of employees; and

(cc) it shall be ensured that any employees of a participating company in respect of which a ballot does not have to be held are entitled to vote in a ballot held in respect of one of the other participating companies; and

(iv) if there are any UK employees employed by a concerned subsidiary or establishment of non-UK participating companies, the management shall ensure that those employees are entitled to vote in a ballot held pursuant to this regulation.

(b) that in relation to the ballot of additional members under regulation 21(3) the management shall hold a separate ballot in respect of each participating company entitled to elect an additional member.

(c) that in a ballot in respect of a particular participating company, all UK employees employed by that participating company or by its concerned subsidiaries or at its concerned establishments are entitled to vote;

(d) that in a ballot in respect of a particular participating company, any person who is immediately before the latest time at which a person may become a candidate—

(i) a UK employee employed by that participating company, by any of its concerned subsidiaries or at any of its concerned establishments; or

(ii) if the management of that participating company so permits, a representative of a trade union who is not an employee of that participating company or any of its concerned subsidiaries, is entitled to stand as a candidate for election as a member of the special negotiating body in that ballot.

(e) that the management must, in accordance with paragraph (7), appoint an independent ballot supervisor to supervise the conduct of the ballot of UK employees but may instead, where there is to be more than one ballot, appoint more than one independent ballot supervisor in accordance with that paragraph, each of whom is to supervise such of the separate ballots as the management may determine, provided that each separate ballot is supervised by a supervisor;

(f) that after the management has formulated proposals as to the arrangements for the ballot of UK employees and before it has published the final arrangements under sub-paragraph (g) it must, so far as reasonably practicable, consult with the UK employees' representatives on the proposed arrangements for the ballot of UK employees; and

(g) that the management must publish the final arrangements for the ballot of UK employees in such manner as to bring them to the attention of, so far as reasonably practicable, all UK employees and the UK employees' representatives.

(4) Any UK employee or UK employees' representative who believes that the arrangements for the ballot of the UK employees do not comply with the requirements of paragraph (3) may, within a period of 21 days beginning on the date on which the management published the final arrangements under sub-paragraph (g), present a complaint to the CAC.

(5) Where the CAC finds the complaint well-founded it shall make a declaration to that effect and may make an order requiring the management to modify the arrangements it has made for the ballot of UK employees or to satisfy the requirements in sub-paragraph (f) or (g) of paragraph (3).

(6) An order under paragraph (5) shall specify the modifications to the arrangements which the management is required to make and the requirements it must satisfy.

(7) A person is an independent ballot supervisor for the purposes of paragraph (3)(e) if the management reasonably believes that he will carry out any functions conferred on him in relation to the ballot competently and has no reasonable grounds for believing that his independence in relation to the ballot might reasonably be called into question.

[3187]

NOTES

Commencement: 8 October 2004.

24 Conduct of the ballot

(1) The management must—

(a) ensure that a ballot supervisor appointed under regulation 23(3)(e) carries out his functions under this regulation and that there is no interference with his carrying out of those functions from the management; and

(b) comply with all reasonable requests made by a ballot supervisor for the purposes of, or in connection with, the carrying out of those functions.

(2) A ballot supervisor's appointment shall require that he—

(a) supervises the conduct of the ballot, or the separate ballots he is being appointed to supervise, in accordance with the arrangements for the ballot of UK employees published by the management under regulation 23(3)(g) or, where appropriate, in accordance with the arrangements as required to be modified by an order made as a result of a complaint presented under regulation 23(4);

(b) does not conduct the ballot or any of the separate ballots before the UK management has satisfied the requirement specified in regulation 23(3)(g) and—

(i) where no complaint has been presented under regulation 23(4), before the expiry of a period of 21 days beginning on the date on which the management published its arrangements under regulation 23(3)(g); or

(ii) where a complaint has been presented under regulation 23(4), before the complaint has been determined and, where appropriate, the arrangements have been modified as required by an order made as a result of that complaint;

(c) conducts the ballot, or each separate ballot so as to secure that—

(i) so far as reasonably practicable, those entitled to vote are given the opportunity to vote;

(ii) so far as reasonably practicable, those entitled to stand as candidates are given the opportunity to stand;

(iii) so far as reasonably practicable, those voting are able to do so in secret, and

(iv) the votes given in the ballot are fairly and accurately counted.

(3) As soon as reasonably practicable after the holding of the ballot, the ballot supervisor must publish the results of the ballot in such manner as to make them available to the management and, so far as reasonably practicable, the UK employees entitled to vote in the ballot and the persons who stood as candidates.

(4) A ballot supervisor shall publish a report ("an ineffective ballot report") where he considers (whether on the basis of representations made to him by another person or otherwise) that—

(a) any of the requirements referred to in paragraph (2) was not satisfied with the result that the outcome of the ballot would have been different; or

(b) there was an interference with the carrying out of his functions or a failure by management to comply with all reasonable requests made by him with the result that he was unable to form a proper judgement as to whether each of the requirements referred to in paragraph (2) was satisfied in the ballot.

(5) Where a ballot supervisor publishes an ineffective ballot report the report must be published within a period of one month commencing on the date on which the ballot supervisor publishes the results of the ballot under paragraph (3).

(6) A ballot supervisor shall publish an ineffective ballot report in such manner as to make it available to the management and, so far as reasonably practicable, the UK employees entitled to vote in the ballot and the persons who stood as candidates in the ballot.

(7) Where a ballot supervisor publishes an ineffective ballot report then—

(a) if there has been a single ballot or an ineffective ballot report has been published in respect of every separate ballot, the outcome of the ballot or ballots shall have no effect and the UK management shall again be under the obligation in regulation 23(2).

(b) If there have been separate ballots and sub-paragraph (a) does not apply—

(i) the management shall arrange for the separate ballot or ballots in respect of which an ineffective ballot report was published to be re-held in accordance with regulation 23 and this regulation; and

(ii) no such ballot shall have effect until it has been re-held and no ineffective ballot report has been published in respect of it.

(8) All costs relating to the holding of a ballot, including payments made to a ballot supervisor for supervising the conduct of the ballot, shall be borne by the management (whether or not an ineffective ballot report has been published).

[3188]

NOTES

Commencement: 8 October 2004.

---

25 Appointment of UK members by a consultative committee

(1) This regulation applies where—

(a) regulation 23(3)(a)(i) or (ii) or (b) would require a ballot to be held; and

(b) there exists in the participating company in respect of which a ballot would be held under regulation 23, a consultative committee.

(2)

(a) Where this regulation applies, the election provided for in regulation 23 shall not take place but the consultative committee shall be entitled to appoint the UK member or members of the special negotiating body who would otherwise be elected pursuant to regulation 22 provided that the consultative committee's appointment complied with sub-paragraph (b).

(b) The consultative committee is entitled to appoint as a member of the special negotiating body:

(i) one of their number; or

(ii) if the management of the participating company in respect of which the consultative committee exists so permits, a trade union representative who is not an employee of that company.

(3) In this regulation, "a consultative committee" means a body of persons—

(a) whose normal functions include or comprise the carrying out of an information and consultation function;

(b) which is able to carry out its information and consultation function without interference from the management of the participating company;

(c) which, in carrying out its information and consultation function, represents all the employees of the participating company; and

(d) which consists wholly of persons who are employees of the participating company or its concerned subsidiaries.

(4) In paragraph (3) "information and consultation function" means the function of—

(a) receiving, on behalf of all the employees of the participating company, information which may significantly affect the interests of the employees of that company, but excluding information which is relevant only to a specific aspect of the interests of the employees, such as health and safety or collective redundancies; and

(b) being consulted by the management of the participating company on the information referred to in sub-paragraph (a) above.

(5) The consultative committee must publish the names of the persons whom it has appointed to be members of the special negotiating body in such a manner as to bring them to the attention of the management of the participating company and, so far as reasonably practicable, the employees and the employees' representatives of that company and its concerned subsidiaries.

(6) Where the management of the participating company, an employee or an employees' representative believes that—

(a) the consultative committee does not satisfy the requirements in paragraph (3) above; or

(b) any of the persons appointed by the consultative committee is not entitled to be appointed,

it, or as the case may be, he may, within a period of 21 days beginning on the date on which the consultative committee published under paragraph (5) the names of the persons appointed, present a complaint to the CAC.

(7) Where the CAC finds the complaint well-founded it shall make a declaration to that effect.

(8) Where the CAC has made a declaration under paragraph (7)—

(a) no appointment made by the consultative committee shall have effect; and

(b) the members of the special negotiating body shall be elected by a ballot of the employees in accordance with regulation 23.

(9) Where the consultative committee appoints any person to be a member of the special negotiating body, that appointment shall have effect—

(a) where no complaint has been presented under paragraph (6), after the expiry of a period of 21 days beginning on the date on which the consultative committee published under paragraph (5) the names of the persons nominated; or

(b) where a complaint has been presented under paragraph (6), as from the day on which the complaint has been determined without a declaration under paragraph (7) being made.

[3189]

NOTES

Commencement: 8 October 2004.

26 Representation of employees

(1) Subject to paragraphs (2) and (3) below, a member elected in a ballot in accordance with regulation 21(2), shall be treated as representing the employees for the time being of the participating company and of any concerned subsidiary or establishment whose employees were entitled to vote in the ballot in which he was elected.

(2) If an additional member is elected in accordance with regulation 21(3) and (4), he, and not any member elected in accordance with regulation 21(2), shall be treated as representing the employees for the time being of the participating company and of any concerned subsidiary or establishment whose employees were entitled to vote in the ballot in which he was elected.

(3) When a member of the special negotiating body is appointed by a consultative committee in accordance with regulation 25, the employees whom the consultative committee represents and the employees of any concerned subsidiary shall be treated as being represented by the member so appointed.

[3190]

NOTES

Commencement: 8 October 2004.

CHAPTER 4
NEGOTIATION OF THE EMPLOYEE INVOLVEMENT AGREEMENT

27 Negotiations to reach an employee involvement agreement

(1) In this regulation and in regulation 28 the competent organs of the participating companies and the special negotiating body are referred to as "the parties".

(2) The parties are under a duty to negotiate in a spirit of cooperation with a view to reaching an employee involvement agreement.

(3) The duty referred to in paragraph (2) commences one month after the date or, if more than one, the last date on which the members of the special negotiating body were elected or appointed and applies—

(a) for the period of six months starting with the day on which the duty commenced or, where an employee involvement agreement is successfully negotiated within that period, until the completion of the negotiations;

(b) where the parties agree before the end of that six month period that it is to be extended, for the period of twelve months starting with the day on which the duty commenced or, where an employee involvement agreement is successfully negotiated within the twelve month period, until the completion of the negotiations.

[3191]

NOTES

Commencement: 8 October 2004.

28 The employee involvement agreement

(1) The employee involvement agreement must be in writing.

(2) Without prejudice to the autonomy of the parties and subject to paragraph (4), the employee involvement agreement shall specify:

(a) the scope of the agreement;

(b) the composition, number of members and allocation of seats on the representative body;

(c) the functions and the procedure for the information and consultation of the representative body;

(d) the frequency of meetings of the representative body;

(e) the financial and material resources to be allocated to the representative body;

(f) if, during negotiations, the parties decide to establish one or more information and consultation procedures instead of a representative body, the arrangements for implementing those procedures;

(g) if, during negotiations, the parties decide to establish arrangements for participation, the substance of those arrangements including (if applicable) the number of members in the SE's administrative or supervisory body which the employees will be entitled to elect, appoint, recommend or oppose, the procedures as to how these members may be elected, appointed, recommended or opposed by the employees, and their rights; and

(h) the date of entry into force of the agreement and its duration, the circumstances, if any in which the agreement is required to be re-negotiated and the procedure for its re-negotiation.

(3) The employee involvement agreement shall not be subject to the standard rules on employee involvement, unless it contains a provision to the contrary.

(4) In relation to an SE to be established by way of transformation, the employee involvement agreement shall provide for the elements of employee involvement at all levels to be at least as favourable as those which exist in the company to be transformed into an SE.

(5) If the parties decide, in accordance with paragraph (2)(f), to establish one or more information and consultation procedures instead of a representative body and if those procedures include a provision for representatives to be elected or appointed to act in relation to information and consultation, those representatives shall be "information and consultation representatives".

[3192]

NOTES

Commencement: 8 October 2004.

29 Decisions of the special negotiating body

(1) Each member of the special negotiating body shall have one vote.

(2) Subject to paragraph (3) and regulation 30, the special negotiating body shall take decisions by an absolute majority vote.

(3) In the following circumstances any decision which would result in a reduction of participation rights must be taken by a two thirds majority vote:

(a) where an SE is to be established by merger and at least 25% of the employees employed to work in the EEA states by the participating companies which are due to merge have participation rights; and

(b) where an SE is to be established by formation of a holding company or of a subsidiary company and at least 50% of the total number of employees employed to work in the EEA states by the participating companies have participation rights, and

in this paragraph, reduction of participation rights means that the body representative of the employees has participation rights in relation to a smaller proportion of members of the supervisory or administrative organs of the SE than the employees' representatives had in the participating company which gave participation rights in relation to the highest proportion of such members in that company.

(4) The special negotiating body must publish the details of any decision taken under this regulation or under regulation 30 in such a manner as to bring the decision, so far as reasonably practicable, to the attention of the employees whom they represent and such publication shall take place as soon as reasonably practicable and, in any event no later than 14 days after the decision has been taken.

(5) For the purpose of negotiations, the special negotiating body may be assisted by experts of its choice.

(6) The participating company or companies shall pay for any reasonable expenses of the functioning of the special negotiating body and any reasonable expenses relating to the negotiations that are necessary to enable the special negotiating body to carry out its functions in an appropriate manner; but where the special negotiating body is assisted by more than one expert the participating company is not required to pay such expenses in respect of more than one of them.

[3193]

NOTES

Commencement: 8 October 2004.

30 Decision not to open or to terminate negotiations

(1) Subject to paragraph (2), the special negotiating body may decide, by a two thirds majority vote, not to open negotiations with the competent organs of the participating companies or to terminate any such negotiations.

(2) The special negotiating body cannot take the decision referred to in paragraph (1) in relation to an SE to be established by transformation if any employees of the company to be transformed have participation rights.

(3) Any decision made under paragraph (1) shall have the following effects—

(a) the duty in regulation 27(2) to negotiate with a view to reaching an employee involvement agreement shall cease as from the date of the decision;

(b) any rules relating to the information and consultation of employees in a EEA state in which employees of the SE are employed shall apply to the employees of the SE in that EEA state; and

(c) the special negotiating body shall be reconvened only if a valid request in accordance with paragraph (4) is made by employees or employees' representatives.

(4) To amount to a valid request, the request referred to in paragraph (3)(c) must—

(a) be in writing;

(b) be made by at least 10% of the employees of, or by employees' representatives representing at least 10% of the total number of employees employed by—

(i) the participating companies and its concerned subsidiaries, or

(ii) where the SE has been registered, the SE and it subsidiaries; and

(c) be made no earlier than two years after the decision made under paragraph (1) was or should have been published in accordance with regulation 29(4) unless the special negotiating body and the competent organs of every participating company or, where the SE has been registered, the SE agree to the special negotiating body being reconvened earlier.

[3194]

NOTES

Commencement: 8 October 2004.

31 Complaint about decisions of special negotiating body

(1) If a member of the special negotiating body, an employees' representative, or where there is no such representative in respect of an employee, that employee believes that the special negotiating body has taken a decision referred to in regulation 29 or 30 and—

(a) that the decision was not taken by the majority required by regulation 29 or 30, as the case may be; or

(b) the special negotiating body failed to publish the decision in accordance with regulation 29(4),

he may present a complaint to the CAC within 21 days of the date the special negotiating body did or should have published their decision in accordance with regulation 29(4).

(2) Where the CAC finds the complaint well-founded it shall make a declaration that the decision was not taken properly and that it shall have no effect.

[3195]

NOTES

Commencement: 8 October 2004.

CHAPTER 5
STANDARD RULES ON EMPLOYEE INVOLVEMENT

32 Standard rules on employee involvement

(1) Without prejudice to paragraph (3), where this regulation applies, the competent organ of the SE and its subsidiaries and establishments shall make arrangements for the involvement of employees of the SE and its subsidiaries and establishments in accordance with the standard rules on employee involvement.

(2) This regulation applies in the following circumstances:

(a) where the parties agree that the standard rules on employee involvement shall apply; or

(b) where the period specified in regulation 27(3)(a) or, where applicable, (b) has expired without the parties reaching an employee involvement agreement and—

(i) the competent organs of each of the participating companies agree that the standard rules on employee involvement shall apply and so continue with the registration of the SE; and

(ii) the special negotiating body has not taken any decision under regulation 30(1) either not to open or to terminate the negotiations referred to in that regulation.

PART 2

(3) The standard rules set out in Part 3 of Schedule 3 to these Regulations (standard rules on participation) only apply in the following circumstances—

(a) in the case of an SE established by merger if, before registration of the SE, one or more forms of participation existed in at least one of the participating companies and either—

(i) that participation applied to at least 25% of the total number of employees of the participating companies employed in the EEA states, or

(ii) that participation applied to less than 25% of the total number of employees of the participating companies employed in the EEA states but the special negotiating body has decided that the standard rules of participation will apply to the employees of the SE; or

(b) in the case of an SE established by formation of a holding company or subsidiary company if, before registration of the SE, one or more forms of employee participation existed in at least one of the participating companies and either:

(i) that participation applied to at least 50% of the total number of employees of the participating companies employed in the EEA states; or

(ii) that participation applied to less than 50% of the total number of employees of the participating companies employed in the EEA states but the special negotiating body has decided that the standard rules of participation will apply to the employees of the SE.

(4) Where the standard rules on participation apply and more than one form of employee participation exist in the participating companies, the special negotiating body shall decide which of the existing forms of participation shall exist in the SE and shall inform the competent organs of the participating companies accordingly.

[3196]

NOTES

Commencement: 8 October 2004.

CHAPTER 6
COMPLIANCE AND ENFORCEMENT

33 Disputes about operation of an employee involvement agreement or the standard rules on employee involvement

(1) Where—

(a) an employee involvement agreement has been agreed; or

(b) the standard rules on employee involvement apply,

a complaint may be presented to the CAC by a relevant applicant who considers that the competent organ of a participating company or of the SE has failed to comply with the terms of the employee involvement agreement or, as the case may be, one or more of the standard information and consultation provisions.

(2) A complaint brought under paragraph (1) must be brought within a period of 3 months commencing with the date of the alleged failure or where the failure takes place over a period, the last day of that period.

(3) In this regulation—

"failure" means an act or omission,

"relevant applicant" means—

(a) in a case where a representative body has been appointed or elected, a member of that body; or

(b) in a case where no representative body has been elected or appointed, an information and consultation representative or an employee of the SE.

(4) Where the CAC finds the complaint well-founded it shall make a declaration to that effect and may make an order requiring the SE to take such steps as are necessary to comply with the terms of the employee involvement agreement or, as the case may be, the standard rules on employee involvement.

(5) An order made under paragraph (4) shall specify—

(a) the steps which the SE is required to take;

(b) the date of the failure; and

(c) the period within which the order must be complied with.

(6) If the CAC makes a declaration under paragraph (4), the relevant applicant may, within the period of three months beginning with the day on which the decision is made, make an application to the Appeal Tribunal for a penalty notice to be issued.

(7) Where such an application is made, the Appeal Tribunal shall issue a written penalty notice to the SE requiring it to pay a penalty to the Secretary of State in respect of the failure unless satisfied, on hearing representations from the SE, that the failure resulted from a reason beyond the its control or that he has some other reasonable excuse for its failure.

(8) Regulation 33 shall apply in respect of a penalty notice issued under this regulation.

(9) No order of the CAC under this regulation shall have the effect of suspending or altering the effect of any act done or of any agreement made by the participating company of the SE.

[3197]

NOTES

Commencement: 8 October 2004.

34 Penalties

(1) A penalty notice issued under regulation 33 shall specify—

(a) the amount of the penalty which is payable;

(b) the date before which the penalty must be paid; and

(c) the failure and period to which the penalty relates.

(2) No penalty set by the Appeal Tribunal under this regulation may exceed £75,000.

(3) When setting the amount of the penalty, the Appeal Tribunal shall take into account—

(a) the gravity of the failure;

(b) the period of time over which the failure occurred;

(c) the reason for the failure;

(d) the number of employees affected by the failure; and

(e) the number of employees employed by the undertaking.

(4) The date specified under paragraph (1)(b) above must not be earlier than the end of the period within which an appeal against a decision or order made by the CAC under regulation 33 may be made.

(5) If the specified date in a penalty notice has passed and—

(a) the period during which an appeal may be made has expired without an appeal having been made; or

(b) such an appeal has been made and determined,

the Secretary of State may recover from the SE, as a civil debt due to him, any amount payable under the penalty notice which remains outstanding.

(6) The making of an appeal suspends the effect of the penalty notice.

(7) Any sums received by the Secretary of State under regulation 33 or this regulation shall be paid into the Consolidated Fund.

[3198]

NOTES

Commencement: 8 October 2004.

35 Misuse of procedures

(1) If an employees' representative or where there is no such representative in relation to an employee, the employee, believes that a participating company or an SE is misusing or intending to misuse the SE or the powers in these Regulations for the purpose of—

(a) depriving the employees of that participating company or of any of its concerned subsidiaries or, as the case may be, of the SE or of its subsidiaries of their rights to employee involvement; or

(b) withholding rights from any of the people referred to in sub-paragraph (a),

he may make present a complaint to the CAC

(2) Where a complaint is made to the CAC under paragraph (1) before registration or within a period of 12 months of the date of the registration of the SE, the CAC shall uphold the complaint unless the respondent proves that it did not misuse or intend to misuse the SE or the powers in these Regulations for either of the purposes set out in sub-paragraphs (a) or (b) of paragraph (1).

(3) If the CAC finds the complaint to be well founded—

(a) it shall make a declaration to that effect and may make an order requiring the participating company or of the SE, as the case may be, to take such action as is specified in the order to ensure that the employees referred to in paragraph (1)(a) are not deprived of their rights to employee involvement or that such rights are not withheld from them; and

(b) the provisions in regulations 33(6) to (9) and 34 shall apply to the complaint.

[3199]

NOTES

Commencement: 8 October 2004.

36 Exclusivity of remedy

The remedy for infringement of the rights conferred by these Regulations is by way of complaint to the CAC in accordance with Chapters 1 to 5 of this Part and not otherwise.

[3200]

NOTES

Commencement: 8 October 2004.

CHAPTER 7
CONFIDENTIAL INFORMATION

37 Breach of statutory duty

(1) Where an SE, a subsidiary of an SE, a participating company or any concerned subsidiary entrusts a person, pursuant to the provisions of this Part of these Regulations, with any information or document on terms requiring it to be held in confidence, the person shall not disclose that information or document except in accordance with the terms on which it was disclosed to him.

(2) In this regulation a person referred to in paragraph (1) to whom information or a document is entrusted is referred to as a "recipient".

(3) The obligation to comply with paragraph (1) is a duty owed to the company that disclosed the information to the person and a breach of the duty is actionable accordingly (subject to the defences and other incidents applying to actions for breach of statutory duty).

(4) Paragraph (3) does not affect any legal liability which any person may incur by disclosing the information, or any right which any person may have in relation to such disclosure otherwise than under this Regulation.

(5) No action shall lie under paragraph (3) where the recipient reasonably believed the disclosure to be a "protected disclosure" within the meaning given to that expression by section 43A of the 1996 Act.

(6) A recipient to whom a company has entrusted any information or document on terms requiring it to be held in confidence may apply to the CAC for a declaration as to whether it was reasonable for the company to require the recipient to hold the information or document in confidence.

(7) If the CAC considers that the disclosure of the information or the document by the recipient would not, or would not be likely to, harm the legitimate interests of the undertaking, it shall make a declaration that it was not reasonable for the competent organ to require the recipient to hold the information or document in confidence.

(8) If a declaration is made under paragraph (7), the information or document shall not at any time thereafter be regarded as having been entrusted to the recipient who made the application under paragraph (6), or to any other recipient, on terms requiring it to be held in confidence.

[3201]

NOTES

Commencement: 8 October 2004.

38 Withholding of information by the competent organ

(1) Neither an SE registered in Great Britain nor a participating company registered in Great Britain is required to disclose any information or document to a person for the purposes of this Part of these Regulations where the nature of the information or document is such that, according to objective criteria, the disclosure of the information or document would seriously harm the functioning of, or would be prejudicial to the SE or any subsidiary or establishment of the SE or, as the case may be, to the participating company or any subsidiary or establishment of the participating company.

(2) Where there is a dispute between the SE or participating company and—

(a) where a representative body has been appointed or elected, a member of that body; or

(b) where no representative body has been elected or appointed, an information and consultation representative or an employee,

as to whether the nature of the information or document which the SE or the participating company has failed to provide is such as is described in paragraph (1), the SE or participating company or a person referred to in sub-paragraph (a) or (b) may apply to the CAC for a declaration as to whether the information or document is of such a nature.

(3) If the CAC makes a declaration that the disclosure of the information or document in question would not, according to objective criteria, be seriously harmful or prejudicial as mentioned in paragraph (1), the CAC shall order the competent organ to disclose the information or document.

(4) An order under paragraph (3) shall specify—

(a) the information or document to be disclosed;

(b) the person or persons to whom the information or document is to be disclosed;

(c) any terms on which the information or document is to be disclosed; and

(d) the date before which the information or document is to be disclosed.

[3202]

NOTES

Commencement: 8 October 2004.

CHAPTER 8
PROTECTION FOR MEMBERS OF SPECIAL NEGOTIATING BODY, ETC

39 Right to time off for members of special negotiating body, etc

(1) An employee who is—

(a) a member of a special negotiating body;

(b) a member of a representative body;

(c) an information and consultation representative;

(d) an employee member on a supervisory or administrative organ; or

(e) a candidate in an election in which any person elected will, on being elected, be such a member or a representative,

is entitled to be permitted by his employer to take reasonable time off during the employee's working hours in order to perform his functions as such a member, representative or candidate.

(2) For the purpose of this regulation the working hours of an employee shall be taken to be any time when, in accordance with his contract of employment, the employee is required to be at work.

[3203]

NOTES

Commencement: 8 October 2004.

40 Right to remuneration for time off under regulation 39

(1) An employee who is permitted to take time off under regulation 39 is entitled to be paid remuneration by his employer for the time taken off at the appropriate hourly rate.

(2) Chapter II of Part XIV of the 1996 Act (a week's pay) shall apply in relation to this regulation as it applies in relation to section 62 of the 1996 Act.

(3) The appropriate hourly rate, in relation to an employee, is the amount of one week's pay divided by the number of normal working hours in a week for that employee when employed under the contract of employment in force on the day when the time is taken.

(4) But where the number of normal working hours differs from week to week or over a longer period, the amount of one week's pay shall be divided instead by—

(a) the average number of normal working hours calculated by dividing by twelve the total number of the employee's normal working hours during the period of twelve weeks ending with the last complete week before the day on which the time off is taken; or

(b) where the employee has not been employed for a sufficient period to enable the calculation to be made under sub-paragraph (a), a number which fairly represents the number of normal working hours in a week having regard to such of the considerations specified in paragraph (5) as are appropriate in the circumstances.

(5) The considerations referred to in paragraph (4)(b) are—

(a) the average number of normal working hours in a week which the employee could expect in accordance with the terms of his contract; and

(b) the average number of normal working hours of other employees engaged in relevant comparable employment with the same employer.

(6) A right to any amount under paragraph (1) does not affect any right of an employee in relation to remuneration under his contract of employment.

(7) Any contractual remuneration paid to an employee in respect of a period of time off under regulation 39 goes towards discharging any liability of the employer to pay remuneration under paragraph (1) in respect of that period, and conversely, any payment of remuneration under paragraph (1) in respect of a period goes towards discharging any liability of the employer to pay contractual remuneration in respect of that period.

[3204]

NOTES

Commencement: 8 October 2004.

41 Right to time off: complaints to tribunals

(1) An employee may present a complaint to an employment tribunal that his employer—

(a) has unreasonably refused to permit him to take time off as required under regulation 39; or

(b) has failed to pay the whole or any part of any amount to which the employee is entitled under regulation 40.

(2) A tribunal shall not consider a complaint under this regulation unless it is presented—

(a) before the end of the period of three months beginning with the day on which the time off was taken or on which it is alleged the time off should have been permitted; or

(b) within such further period as the tribunal considers reasonable in a case where it is satisfied that it was not reasonably practicable for the complaint to be presented before the end of that period of three months.

(3) Where a tribunal finds a complaint under this regulation well-founded, the tribunal shall make a declaration to that effect.

(4) If the complaint is that the employer has unreasonably refused to permit the employee to take time off, the tribunal shall also order the employer to pay to the employee an amount equal to the remuneration to which he would have been entitled under regulation 40 if the employer had not refused.

(5) If the complaint is that the employer has failed to pay the employee the whole or part of any amount to which he is entitled under regulation 40, the tribunal shall also order him to pay to the employee the amount which it finds is due to him.

[3205]

NOTES

Commencement: 8 October 2004.

Conciliation: employment tribunal proceedings and claims which could be the subject of employment tribunal proceedings under this regulation are proceedings to which the Employment Tribunals Act 1996, s 18 applies; see s 18(1)(n) of that Act at **[975]**. The standard conciliation period applies to such proceedings by virtue of the Employment Tribunals (Constitution and Rules of Procedure) Regulations 2004, SI 2004/1861, Sch 1, rule 22(1), (6) at **[3171]**.

42 Unfair dismissal

(1) An employee who is dismissed and to whom paragraph (2) or (5) applies shall be regarded, if the reason (or, if more than one, the principal reason) for the dismissal is a reason specified in, respectively, paragraph (3) or (6), as unfairly dismissed for the purposes of Part 10 of the 1996 Act.

(2) This paragraph applies to an employee who is—
- (a) a member of a special negotiating body;
- (b) a member of a representative body;
- (c) an information and consultation representative;
- (d) an employee member in a supervisory or administrative organ; or
- (e) a candidate in an election in which any person elected will, on being elected, be such a member or a representative.

(3) The reason is that—
- (a) the employee performed or proposed to perform any functions or activities as such a member, representative or candidate; or
- (b) the employee or a person acting on his behalf made or proposed to make a request to exercise an entitlement conferred on the employee by regulation 39 or 40.

(4) Paragraph (1) does not apply in the circumstances set out in paragraph (3)(a) where the reason (or principal reason) for the dismissal is that in the performance, or purported performance, of the employee's functions or activities he has disclosed any information or document in breach of the duty in regulation 37, unless the employee reasonably believed the disclosure to be a 'protected disclosure' within the meaning given to that expression by section 43A of the 1996 Act.

(5) This paragraph applies to any employee whether or not he is an employee to whom paragraph (2) applies.

(6) The reasons are that the employee—
- (a) took, or proposed to take, any proceedings before an employment tribunal to enforce any right conferred on him by these Regulations;
- (b) exercised, or proposed to exercise, any entitlement to apply or complain to the CAC or the Appeal Tribunal conferred by these Regulations or to exercise the right to appeal in connection with any rights conferred by these Regulations;
- (c) acted with a view to securing that a special negotiating body, a representative body or an information and consultation procedure did or did not come into existence;
- (d) indicated that he did or did not support the coming into existence of a special negotiating body, a representative body or an information and consultation procedure;
- (e) stood as a candidate in an election in which any person elected would, on being elected, be a member of a special negotiating body, a representative body, an employee member on a supervisory or administrative organ or be an information and consultation representative;
- (f) influenced or sought to influence by lawful means the way in which votes were to be cast by other employees in a ballot arranged under these Regulations;
- (g) voted in such a ballot;
- (h) expressed doubts, whether to a ballot supervisor or otherwise, as to whether such a ballot had been properly conducted; or
- (i) proposed to do, failed to do, or proposed to decline to do, any of the things mentioned in sub-paragraphs (d) to (h).

PART 2

(7) It is immaterial for the purposes of paragraph (6)(a)—

(a) whether or not the employee has the right or entitlement; or

(b) whether or not the right has been infringed,

but for that sub-paragraph to apply, the claim to the right and, if applicable, the claim that it has been infringed must be made in good faith.

[3206]

NOTES

Commencement: 8 October 2004.

43 (*Amends the Employment Rights Act 1996, ss 105, 108 at* **[1149]**, **[1152]**, *and amended s 109* (*repealed*).)

44 Detriment

(1) An employee to whom paragraph (2) or (5) applies has the right not to be subjected to any detriment by any act, or deliberate failure to act, by his employer, done on a ground specified in, respectively, paragraph (3) or (6).

(2) This paragraph applies to an employee who is—

(a) a member of a special negotiating body;

(b) a member of a representative body;

(c) an information and consultation representative;

(d) an employee member on a supervisory or administrative organ; or

(e) a candidate in an election in which any person elected will, on being elected, be such a member or a representative.

(3) The ground is that—

(a) the employee performed or proposed to perform any functions or activities as such a member, representative or candidate; or

(b) the employee or person acting on his behalf made or proposed to make a request to exercise an entitlement conferred on the employee by regulation 39 or 40.

(4) Paragraph (1) does not apply in the circumstances set out in paragraph (3)(a) where the ground for the subjection to detriment is that in the performance, or purported performance, of the employee's functions or activities he has disclosed any information or document in breach of the duty in regulation 37, unless the employee reasonably believed the disclosure to be a "protected disclosure" within the meaning given to that expression by section 43A of the 1996 Act.

(5) This paragraph applies to any employee, whether or not he is an employee to whom paragraph (2) applies.

(6) The grounds are that the employee—

(a) took, or proposed to take, any proceedings before an employment tribunal to enforce any right conferred on him by these Regulations;

(b) exercised, or proposed to exercise, any entitlement to apply or complain to the CAC or the Appeal Tribunal conferred by these Regulations or to exercise the right to appeal in connection with any rights conferred by these Regulations;

(c) acted with a view to securing that a special negotiating body, a representative body or an information and consultation procedure did or did not come into existence;

(d) indicated that he did or did not support the coming into existence of a special negotiating body, a representative body or an information and consultation procedure;

(e) stood as a candidate in an election in which any person elected would, on being elected, be a member of a special negotiating body, a representative body, an employee member on a supervisory or administrative organ or be an information and consultation representative;

(f) influenced or sought to influence by lawful means the way in which votes were to be cast by other employees in a ballot arranged under these Regulations;

(g) voted in such a ballot;

(h) expressed doubts, whether to a ballot supervisor or otherwise, as to whether such a ballot had been properly conducted; or

(i) proposed to do, failed to do, or proposed to decline to do, any of the things mentioned in sub-paragraphs (d) to (h).

(7) It is immaterial for the purposes of paragraph (6)(a)—

(a) whether or not the employee has the right or entitlement; or

(b) whether or not the right has been infringed,

but for that sub-paragraph to apply, the claim to the right and, if applicable, the claim that has been infringed must be made in good faith.

(8) This regulation does not apply where the detriment in question amounts to dismissal.

[3207]

NOTES

Commencement: 8 October 2004.

45 Detriment: enforcement and subsidiary provisions

(1) An employee may present a complaint to an employment tribunal that he has been subjected to a detriment in contravention of regulation 44.

(2) The provisions of sections 48(2) to (4) of the 1996 Act (complaints to employment tribunals and remedies) shall apply in relation to a complaint under this regulation as they apply in relation to a complaint under section 48 of that Act but taking references in those provisions to the employer as references to the employer within the meaning of regulation 44(1) above.

(3) The provisions of section 49(1) to (5) of the 1996 Act shall apply in relation to a complaint under this regulation.

[3208]

NOTES

Commencement: 8 October 2004.

Conciliation: employment tribunal proceedings and claims which could be the subject of employment tribunal proceedings under this regulation are proceedings to which the Employment Tribunals Act 1996, s 18 applies; see s 18(1)(n) of that Act at **[975]**. The standard conciliation period applies to such proceedings by virtue of the Employment Tribunals (Constitution and Rules of Procedure) Regulations 2004, SI 2004/1861, Sch 1, rule 22(1), (6) at **[3171]**.

Tribunal jurisdiction: the Employment Act 2002, ss 31, 32, 38, at **[1493]**, **[1494]**, **[1496]** apply to proceedings before the employment tribunal relating to a claim under this regulation; see ss 31(1), 32(1), 38(1) of, and Schs 3–5 to, the 2002 Act at **[1508]**–**[1510]**.

For the circumstances in which the normal time limit for presenting a complaint under this regulation is extended for a period of three months, see the Employment Act 2002 (Dispute Resolution) Regulations 2004, SI 2004/752, regs 15 and 18 at **[3096]** and **[3098]**.

46 (*Amends the Employment Tribunals Act 1996, s 18 at* **[975]**.)

CHAPTER 9
MISCELLANEOUS

47 CAC proceedings

(1) Where under these Regulations a person presents a complaint or makes an application to the CAC the complaint or application must be in writing and in such form as the CAC may require.

(2) In its consideration of a complaint or application under these Regulations, the CAC shall make such enquiries as it sees fit and give any person whom it considers has a proper interest in the complaint or application an opportunity to be heard.

(3) Where the participating company, concerned subsidiary or establishment or the SE has its registered office in England and Wales—

(a) a declaration made by the CAC under these Regulations may be relied on as if it were a declaration or order made by the High Court in England and Wales; and

(b) an order made by the CAC under these Regulations may be enforced in the same way as an order of the High Court in England and Wales.

(4) Where a participating company or concerned subsidiary or an SE has its registered office in Scotland—

(a) a declaration or order made by the CAC under these Regulations may be relied on as if it were a declaration or order made by the Court of Session; and

PART 2

(b) an order made by the CAC under these Regulations may be enforced in the same way as an order of the Court of Session.

(5) A declaration or order made by the CAC under these Regulations must be in writing and state the reasons for the CAC's findings.

(6) An appeal lies to the Appeal Tribunal on any question of law arising from any declaration or order of, or arising in any proceedings before, the CAC under these Regulations.

[3209]

NOTES

Commencement: 8 October 2004.

48 Appeal Tribunal: location of certain proceedings under these Regulations

(1) Any proceedings before the Appeal Tribunal under these Regulations, other than appeals under paragraph (o) of section 21(1) of the Employment Tribunals Act 1996 (appeals from employment tribunals on questions of law), shall—

(a) where the registered office of the participating company, concerned subsidiary or the SE is situated in England and Wales, be held in England and Wales; and

(b) where the registered office of the participating company, concerned subsidiary or the SE is situated in Scotland, be held in Scotland.

(2) …

[3210]

NOTES

Commencement: 8 October 2004.
Para (2): amends the Employment Tribunals Act 1996, s 20 at **[977]**.

49 (*Amends the Employment Tribunals Act 1996, s 21 at* **[978]**.)

50 ACAS

(1) If on receipt of an application or complaint under these Regulations the CAC is of the opinion that it is reasonably likely to be settled by conciliation, it shall refer the application or complaint to the Advisory, Conciliation and Arbitration Service ("ACAS") and shall notify the applicant or complainant and any persons whom it considers have a proper interest in the application or complaint accordingly, whereupon ACAS shall seek to promote a settlement of the matter.

(2) If an application or complaint so referred is not settled or withdrawn and ACAS is of the opinion that further attempts at conciliation are unlikely to result in a settlement, it shall inform the CAC of its opinion.

(3) If the application or complaint is not referred to ACAS or if it is so referred, on ACAS informing the CAC of its opinion that further attempts at conciliation are unlikely to result in a settlement, the CAC shall proceed to hear and determine the application or complaint.

[3211]

NOTES

Commencement: 8 October 2004.

51 Restrictions on contracting out: general

(1) Any provision in any agreement (whether an employee's contract or not) is void in so far as it purports—

(a) to exclude or limit the operation of any provision of this Part of these Regulations other than a provision of Chapter 8 of this Part; or

(b) to preclude a person from bringing any proceedings before the CAC, under any provision of this Part of these Regulations other than a provision of that Chapter.

(2) Paragraph (1) does not apply to any agreement to refrain from continuing any proceedings referred to in sub-paragraph (b) of that paragraph made after the proceedings have been instituted.

[3212]

NOTES

Commencement: 8 October 2004.

52 Restrictions on contracting out: Chapter 8 of this Part

(1) Any provision in any agreement (whether an employee's contract or not) is void in so far as it purports—

(a) to exclude or limit the operation of any provision of Chapter 8 of this Part of these Regulations; or

(b) to preclude a person from bringing any proceedings before an employment tribunal under that Chapter.

(2) Paragraph (1) does not apply to any agreement to refrain from instituting or continuing proceedings before an employment tribunal where a conciliation officer has taken action under section 18 of the Employment Tribunals Act 1996 (conciliation).

(3) Paragraph (1) does not apply to any agreement to refrain from instituting or continuing before an employment tribunal proceedings within section 18(1)(k) of the Employment Tribunals Act 1996 (proceedings under these Regulations where conciliation is available) if the conditions regulating compromise agreements under these Regulations are satisfied in relation to the agreement.

(4) For the purposes of paragraph (3) the conditions regulating compromise agreements are that—

(a) the agreement must be in writing;

(b) the agreement must relate to the particular proceedings;

(c) the employee must have received advice from a relevant independent adviser as to the terms and effect of the proposed agreement and, in particular, its effect on his ability to pursue his rights before an employment tribunal;

(d) there must be in force, when the adviser gives the advice, a contract of insurance, or an indemnity provided for members of a profession or professional body, covering the risk of a claim by the employee in respect of loss arising in consequence of the advice;

(e) the agreement must identify the adviser; and

(f) the agreement must state that the conditions in sub-paragraphs (a) to (e) are satisfied.

(5) A person is a relevant independent adviser for the purposes of paragraph (4)(c)—

(a) if he is a qualified lawyer;

(b) if he is an officer, official, employee or member of an independent trade union who has been certified in writing by the trade union as competent to give advice and authorised to do so on behalf of the trade union; or

(c) if he works at an advice centre (whether as an employee or as a volunteer) and has been certified in writing by the centre as competent to give advice and authorised to do so on behalf of the centre.

(6) But a person is not a relevant independent adviser for the purposes of paragraph (4)(c) in relation to the employee—

(a) if he is, is employed by or is acting in the matter for the employer or an associated employer;

(b) in the case of a person within paragraph (5)(b) or (c), if the trade union or advice centre is the employer or an associated employer; or

(c) in the case of a person within paragraph (5)(c), if the employee makes a payment for the advice received by him.

(7) In paragraph (5)(a), a "qualified lawyer" means—

(a) as respects England and Wales, a barrister (whether in practice as such or employed to give legal advice), a solicitor who holds a practicing certificate, or a person other than a barrister or solicitor who is an authorised advocate or authorised litigator (within the meaning of the Courts and Legal Services Act 1990); and

(b) as respects Scotland, an advocate (whether in practice as such or employed to give legal advice) or a solicitor who holds a practising certificate.

(8) For the purposes of paragraph (6) any two employers shall be treated as associated if—

(a) one is a company of which the other (directly or indirectly) has control; or

(b) both are companies of which a third person (directly or indirectly) has control;

and "associated employer" shall be construed accordingly.

[3213]

NOTES

Commencement: 8 October 2004.

53 (*Inserts the Transnational Information and Consultation of Employees Regulations 1999, SI 1999/3323, reg 46A at* **[2618A]**.)

54 Existing employee involvement rights

(1) Subject to paragraph (2), nothing in these Regulations shall affect involvement rights of employees of an SE, its subsidiaries or establishments provided for by law or practice in the EEA state in which they were employed immediately prior to the registration of the SE.

(2) Paragraph (1) does not apply to rights to participation.

[3214]

NOTES

Commencement: 8 October 2004.

55–89 (*Pt 4 (Exercise of Member States Options' under the EC Regulation), Pt 5 (Provisions Required by the EC Regulation), Pt 6 (Provisions Relating to the Effective Application of the EC Regulation), Pt 7 (Provisions Relating to the Conversion of an SE to a Public Company in Accordance with Article 66 of the EC Regulation) outside the scope of this work.*)

SCHEDULES

(*Schs 1, 2 (Forms and application of the Companies Act 1985 to the registration of SEs) outside the scope of this work.*)

SCHEDULE 3
STANDARD RULES ON EMPLOYEE INVOLVEMENT

Regulation 32

PART 1
COMPOSITION OF THE REPRESENTATIVE BODY

1.—(1) The management of the SE shall arrange for the establishment of a representative body in accordance with the following provisions-

(a) the representative body shall be composed of employees of the SE and its subsidiaries and establishments;

(b) the representative body shall be composed of one member for each 10% of fraction thereof of employees of the SE, its subsidiaries and establishments employed for the time being in each Member State;

(c) the members of the representative body shall be elected or appointed by the members of the special negotiating body; and

(d) the election or appointment shall be carried out by whatever method the special negotiating body decides.

2. Where its size so warrants, the representative body shall elect a select committee from among its members comprising at most three members.

3. The representative body shall adopt rules of procedure.

4. The representative body shall inform the competent organ of the SE of the composition of the representative body and any changes in its composition.

5.—(1) Four years after its establishment, the representative body shall decide whether to open negotiations with the competent organ of the SE to reach an employee involvement agreement or whether the standard rules in Part 2 and, where applicable, Part 3 of this Schedule shall continue to apply.

(2) Where a decision is taken under sub-paragraph (1) to open negotiations, regulations 27 to 29 and 31 shall apply to the representative body as they apply to the special negotiating body.

[3215]

NOTES

Commencement: 8 October 2004.

PART 2

STANDARD RULES FOR INFORMATION AND CONSULTATION

6.—(1) The competence of the representative body shall be limited to questions which concern the SE itself and any of its subsidiaries or establishments in another Member State or which exceed the powers of the decision-making organ in a single Member State.

(2) For the purpose of informing and consulting under sub-paragraph (1) the competent organ of the SE shall:

(a) prepare and provide to the representative body regular reports on the progress of the business of the SE and the SE's prospects;

(b) provide the representative body with the agenda for meetings of the administrative or, where appropriate, the management or supervisory organs and copies of all documents submitted to the general meeting of its shareholders.

(c) inform the representative body when there are exceptional circumstances affecting the employees' interests to a considerable extent, particularly in the event of relocations, transfers, the closure of establishments or undertakings or collective redundancies.

(3)

(a) The competent organ shall, if the representative body so desires, meet with that body, without prejudice to sub-paragraph (b) below, at least once a year to discuss the reports referred to in sub-paragraph (2)(a). The meetings shall relate in particular to the structure, economic and financial situation, the probable development of business and of production and sales, the situation and probable trend of employment, investments and substantial changes concerning organisation, introduction of new working methods or production processes, transfers of production, mergers, cut-backs or closures of undertakings, establishments or important parts thereof and collective redundancies;

(b) in the circumstances set out in sub-paragraph (2)(c), the representative body may decide, for reasons of urgency, to allow the select committee to meet the competent organ and it shall have the right to meet a more appropriate level of management within the SE rather than the competent organ itself;

(c) in the event of the competent organ not acting in accordance with the opinion expressed by the representative body, the two bodies shall meet again to seek an agreement, if the representative body so wishes.

(4) In the circumstances set out in (3)(b) above, if the select committee attends the meeting, any other members of the representative body who represent employees who are directly concerned by the measures being discussed also have the right to participate in the meeting.

(5) Before any meeting referred to in paragraph (3), the members of the representative body or the select committee, as the case may be shall be entitled to meet without the representatives of the competent organ being present.

(6) Without prejudice to regulations 37 and 38, the members of the representative body shall inform the employees' representatives or, if no such representatives exist, the employees of the SE and its subsidiaries and establishments, of the content and outcome of the information and consultation procedures.

(7) The representative body and the select committee may be assisted by experts of its choice.

(8) The costs of the representative body shall be borne by the SE which shall provide the members of that body with financial and material resources needed to enable them to perform their duties in an appropriate manner, including (unless agreed otherwise) the cost of organising meetings, providing interpretation facilities and accommodation and travelling expenses. However, where the representative body or the select committee is assisted by more than one expert the SE is not required to pay the expenses of more than one of them. **[3216]**

NOTES

Commencement: 8 October 2004.

PART 3
STANDARD RULES FOR PARTICIPATION

7.—(1) In the case of an SE established by transformation, if the rules of a Member State relating to employee participation in the administrative or supervisory body applied before registration, all aspects of employee participation shall continue to apply to the SE. Sub-paragraph (2) shall apply *mutatis mutandis* to that end.

(2) In the case where an SE is established other than by transformation and where the employees or their representatives of at least one of the participating companies had participation rights, the representative body shall have the right to elect, appoint, recommend or oppose the appointment of a number of members of the administrative or supervisory body of the SE, such number shall be equal to the highest proportion in force in the participating companies concerned before the registration of the SE.

(3)

(a) Subject to sub-paragraph (b), the representative body shall, taking into account the proportion of employees of the SE employed in each Member State, decide on the allocation of seats within the administrative or supervisory body.

(b) In making the decision set out in sub-paragraph (a), if the employees of one or more Member State is not covered by the proportional criterion set out in (a), the representative body shall appoint a member from one of those Member States including one from the Member State in which the SE is registered, if appropriate.

(c) Every member of the administrative body or, where appropriate, the supervisory body of the SE who has been elected, appointed or recommended by the representative body or the employees shall be a full member with the same rights and obligations as the members representing shareholders, including the right to vote. **[3217]**

NOTES

Commencement: 8 October 2004.

(*Sch 4 (Modification of the Companies Acts and Insolvency Act 1986) outside the scope of this work.*)

ACAS (FLEXIBLE WORKING) ARBITRATION SCHEME (GREAT BRITAIN) ORDER 2004

(SI 2004/2333)

NOTES

Made: 6 September 2004.
Authority: Trade Union and Labour Relations (Consolidation) Act 1992, s 212A(3), (6), (7).
Commencement: 1 October 2004.

1 Citation, commencement, interpretation and extent

(1) This Order may be cited as the ACAS (Flexible Working) Arbitration Scheme (Great Britain) Order 2004 and shall come into force on 1st October 2004.

(2) In this Order—

"the 1996 Act" means the Employment Rights Act 1996;

"English/Welsh arbitration" means an arbitration under the Scheme which the parties have agreed shall be determined under the laws of England and Wales;

"the Scheme" means the arbitration scheme set out in the Schedule to this Order, with the exception of paragraphs 52EW, 108EW, 135EW, 138EW, 145EW, 151EW, 156EW, 160EW, 163EW, 174EW and 175EW thereof;

"Scottish arbitration" means and arbitration under the Scheme which the parties have agreed shall be determined under the laws of Scotland.

(3) This Order extends to Great Britain.

(4) Paragraphs in the Schedule marked "EW" apply only to English/Welsh arbitrations.

(5) Paragraphs in the Schedule marked "S" apply only to Scottish arbitrations.

(6) Paragraphs in the Schedule not marked "EW" or "S" apply to both English/Welsh arbitrations and Scottish arbitrations.

[3218]

NOTES

Commencement: 1 October 2004.

2 Commencement of the Scheme

The Scheme shall come into effect on 1st October 2004.

[3219]

NOTES

Commencement: 1 October 2004.

3 Revocation

Subject to article 6, the ACAS (Flexible Working) Arbitration Scheme (England and Wales) Order 2003 is revoked.

[3220]

NOTES

Commencement: 1 October 2004.

4 Application of Part I of the Arbitration Act 1996

The provisions of Part I of the Arbitration Act 1996 referred to in paragraphs 52EW, 108EW, 135EW, 138EW, 145EW, 151EW, 156EW, 160EW, 163EW, 174EW and 175EW of the Schedule and shown in italics shall, as modified in those paragraphs, apply to English/Welsh arbitrations conducted in accordance with the Scheme.

[3221]

NOTES

Commencement: 1 October 2004.

5—(1) Section 46(1)(b) of the Arbitration Act 1996 shall apply to English/Welsh arbitrations conducted in accordance with the Scheme, subject to the following modification.

(2) For "such other considerations as are agreed by them or determined by the tribunal" in section 46(1)(b) substitute "the Terms of Reference in paragraph 18 of the arbitration scheme set out in the Schedule to the ACAS (Flexible Working) Arbitration Scheme (Great Britain) Order 2004".

[3222]

NOTES
Commencement: 1 October 2004.

6 Transitional provision

(1) The Scheme has effect in any case where the appropriate date falls on or after 1st October 2004.

(2) In a case where the appropriate date falls before 1st October 2004, the arbitration scheme set out in the Schedule to the ACAS (Flexible Working) Arbitration Scheme (England and Wales) Order 2003 continues to apply.

(3) In this article — the

"appropriate date" means the date of signature of the Arbitration Agreement. Where the parties sign the Arbitration Agreement on different dates, the appropriate date is the date of the first signature.

"Arbitration Agreement" means an agreement to submit the dispute to arbitration, as defined in paragraph 26 of the Scheme.

[3223]–[3253]

NOTES
Commencement: 1 October 2004.

(The Schedule (omitted for reasons of space) sets out the scheme, submitted to the Secretary of State by ACAS pursuant to the Trade Union and Labour Relations (Consolidation) Act 1992, s 212A, providing for arbitration in the case of disputes involving proceedings, or claims which could be the subject of proceedings, before an employment tribunal arising out of a contravention, or alleged contravention, of the Employment Rights Act 1996, ss 80G(1) or 80H(1)(b) (flexible working). The Scheme provides a voluntary alternative to the employment tribunal for the resolution by arbitration of claims arising out of an application for flexible working made under s 80F(1) of the 1996 Act where both parties agree.)

INFORMATION AND CONSULTATION OF EMPLOYEES REGULATIONS 2004

(SI 2004/3426)

NOTES
Made: 21 December 2004.
Authority: Employment Relations Act 2004, s 42.
Commencement: 6 April 2005 (subject to transitional provisions in Sch 1 at **[3293]**).
These Regulations are the domestic implementation of European Parliament and Council Directive 2002/14/EC establishing a general framework for informing and consulting employees in the European Community at **[4052]**.
Conciliation: employment tribunal proceedings and claims which could be the subject of employment tribunal proceedings under regs 29, 33 are proceedings to which the Employment Tribunals Act 1996, s 18 applies; see s 18(1)(p) of that Act at **[975]**. The standard conciliation period applies to such claims by virtue of the Employment Tribunals (Constitution and Rules of Procedure) Regulations 2004, SI 2004/1861, Sch 1, rule 22(1), (6).
Employment Appeal Tribunal: an appeal lies to the Employment Appeal Tribunal on any question of law arising from any decision of, or in any proceedings before, an employment tribunal under or by virtue of these Regulations; see the Employment Tribunals Act 1996, s 21(1)(q) at **[978]**.
As to the application of these Regulations to undertakings with fewer than 150 employees, see regs 3, 4 at **[3256]**, **[3257]** and Sch 1 at **[3293]**.

ARRANGEMENT OF REGULATIONS

PART 1
GENERAL

PART II
EMPLOYEE NUMBERS AND ENTITLEMENT TO DATA

PART III
NEGOTIATED AGREEMENTS

PART IV
STANDARD INFORMATION AND CONSULTATION PROVISIONS

PART V
DUTY OF CO-OPERATION

PART VI
COMPLIANCE AND ENFORCEMENT

PART VII
CONFIDENTIAL INFORMATION

PART VIII
PROTECTIONS FOR INFORMATION AND CONSULTATION REPRESENTATIVES, ETC

PART 1
GENERAL

1 Citation, commencement and extent

(1) These Regulations may be cited as the Information and Consultation of Employees Regulations 2004 and shall come into force on 6th April 2005.

(2) These Regulations extend to Great Britain.

[3254]

NOTES

Commencement: 6 April 2005.

2 Interpretation

In these Regulations—

"the 1996 Act" means the Employment Rights Act 1996;

"Appeal Tribunal" means the Employment Appeal Tribunal;

"CAC" means the Central Arbitration Committee;

"consultation" means the exchange of views and establishment of a dialogue between—

(a) information and consultation representatives and the employer; or

(b) in the case of a negotiated agreement which provides as mentioned in regulation 16(1)(f)(ii), the employees and the employer;

"contract of employment" means a contract of service or apprenticeship, whether express or implied, and (if it is express) whether oral or in writing;

"date of the ballot" means the day or last day on which voting may take place and, where voting in different parts of the ballot is arranged to take place on different days or during periods ending on different days, the last of those days;

"employee" means an individual who has entered into or works under a contract of employment and in Part VIII and regulation 40 includes, where the employment has ceased, an individual who worked under a contract of employment;

"employee request" means a request by employees under regulation 7 for the employer to initiate negotiations to reach an agreement under these Regulations;

"employer notification" means a notification by an employer under regulation 11 that he wishes to initiate negotiations to reach an agreement under these Regulations;

"information" means data transmitted by the employer—

(a) to the information and consultation representatives; or

(b) in the case of a negotiated agreement which provides as mentioned in regulation 16(1)(f)(ii), directly to the employees,

in order to enable those representatives or those employees to examine and to acquaint themselves with the subject matter of the data;

"Information and Consultation Directive" means European Parliament and Council Directive 2002/14/EC of 11 March 2002 establishing a general framework for informing and consulting employees in the European Community;

"information and consultation representative" means—

(a) in the case of a negotiated agreement which provides as mentioned in regulation 16(1)(f)(i), a person appointed or elected in accordance with that agreement; or

(b) a person elected in accordance with regulation 19(1);

"negotiated agreement" means—

(a) an agreement between the employer and the negotiating representatives reached through negotiations as provided for in regulation 14 which satisfies the requirements of regulation 16(1); or

(b) an agreement between the employer and the information and consultation representatives referred to in regulation 18(2);

"negotiating representative" means a person elected or appointed pursuant to regulation 14(1)(a);

"parties" means the employer and the negotiating representatives or the information and consultation representatives, as the case may be;

["Pension Schemes Regulations" means the Occupational and Personal Pension Schemes (Consultation by Employers and Miscellaneous Amendment) Regulations 2006;]

"pre-existing agreement" means an agreement between an employer and his employees or their representatives which—

(a) is made prior to the making of an employee request; and

(b) satisfies the conditions set out in regulation 8(1)(a) to (d),

but does not include an agreement concluded in accordance with regulations 17 or 42 to 45 of the Transnational Information and Consultation of Employees Regulations 1999 or a negotiated agreement;

"standard information and consultation provisions" means the provisions set out in regulation 20;

"undertaking" means a public or private undertaking carrying out an economic activity, whether or not operating for gain;

"valid employee request" means an employee request made to their employer by the employees of an undertaking to which these Regulations apply (under regulation 3) that satisfies the requirements of regulation 7 and is not prevented from being valid by regulation 12.

[3255]

NOTES

Commencement: 6 April 2005.

Definition "Pension Schemes Regulations" inserted by the Information and Consultation of Employees (Amendment) Regulations 2006, SI 2006/514, regs 2, 3, as from 6 April 2006.

3 Application

(1) These Regulations apply to undertakings—

(a) employing in the United Kingdom, in accordance with the calculation in regulation 4, at least the number of employees in column 1 of the table in Schedule 1 to these Regulations on or after the corresponding date in column 2 of that table; and

(b) subject to paragraph (2), whose registered office, head office or principal place of business is situated in Great Britain.

(2) Where the registered office is situated in Great Britain and the head office or principal place of business is situated in Northern Ireland or vice versa, these Regulations shall only apply where the majority of employees are employed to work in Great Britain.

(3) In these Regulations, an undertaking to which these Regulations apply is referred to, in relation to its employees, as "the employer".

[3256]

NOTES

Commencement: 6 April 2005.

PART II
EMPLOYEE NUMBERS AND ENTITLEMENT TO DATA

4 Calculation of number of employees

(1) Subject to paragraph (4), the number of employees for the purposes of regulation 3(1) shall be determined by ascertaining the average number of employees employed in the previous twelve months, calculated in accordance with paragraph (2).

(2) Subject to paragraph (3), the average number of employees is to be ascertained by determining the number of employees employed in each month in the previous twelve months (whether they were employed throughout the month or not), adding together those monthly figures and dividing the number by 12.

(3) For the purposes of the calculation in paragraph (2) if, for the whole of a month within the twelve month period, an employee works under a contract by virtue of which he would have worked for 75 hours or less in that month—

(i) were the month to have contained 21 working days;
(ii) were the employee to have had no absences from work; and
(iii) were the employee to have worked no overtime,

the employee may be counted as representing half of a full-time employee for the month in question, if the employer so decides.

(4) If the undertaking has been in existence for less than twelve months, the references to twelve months in paragraphs (1), (2) and (3), and the divisor of 12 referred to in paragraph (2), shall be replaced by the number of months the undertaking has been in existence.

[3257]

NOTES

Commencement: 6 April 2005.

5 Entitlement to data

(1) An employee or an employees' representative may request data from the employer for the purpose of determining the number of people employed by the employer's undertaking in the United Kingdom.

(2) Any request for data made under paragraph (1) must be in writing and be dated.

(3) The employer must provide the employee or the employees' representative who made the request with data to enable him to—

(a) make the calculation of the numbers of employees referred to in regulation 4, and
(b) determine, for the purpose of regulation 7(2), what number of employees constitutes 10% of the employees in the undertaking.

[3258]

NOTES

Commencement: 6 April 2005.

6 Complaint of failure to provide data

(1) An employee or an employees' representative who has requested data under regulation 5 may present a complaint to the CAC that—

(a) the employer has failed to provide the data referred to in regulation 5(3); or
(b) the data which has been provided by the employer is false or incomplete in a material particular.

(2) Where the CAC finds the complaint to be well-founded it shall make an order requiring the employer to disclose data to the complainant which order shall specify—

(a) the data in respect of which the CAC finds that the complaint is well-founded and which is to be disclosed to the complainant;
(b) the date (or if more than one, the earliest date) on which the employer refused or failed to disclose data, or disclosed false or incomplete information;
(c) a date, not being less than one week from the date of the order, by which the employer must disclose the data specified in the order.

(3) The CAC shall not consider a complaint presented under this regulation unless it is made after the expiry of a period of one month beginning on the date on which the complainant made his request for data under regulation 5.

[3259]

NOTES

Commencement: 6 April 2005.

PART III
NEGOTIATED AGREEMENTS

7 Employee request to negotiate an agreement in respect of information and consultation

(1) On receipt of a valid employee request, the employer shall, subject to paragraphs (8) and (9), initiate negotiations by taking the steps set out in regulation 14(1).

(2) Subject to paragraph (3), an employee request is not a valid employee request unless it consists of—

(a) a single request made by at least 10% of the employees in the undertaking; or

(b) a number of separate requests made on the same or different days by employees which when taken together mean that at least 10% of the employees in that undertaking have made requests, provided that the requests are made within a period of six months.

(3) Where the figure of 10% in paragraph (2) would result in less than 15 or more than 2,500 employees being required in order for a valid employee request to be made, that paragraph shall have effect as if, for the figure of 10%, there were substituted the figure of 15, or as the case may be, 2,500.

(4) An employee request is not a valid employee request unless the single request referred to in paragraph (2)(a) or each separate request referred to in paragraph (2)(b)—

(a) is in writing;

(b) is sent to—

(i) the registered office, head office or principal place of business of the employer; or

(ii) the CAC; and

(c) specifies the names of the employees making it and the date on which it is sent.

(5) Where a request is sent to the CAC under paragraph (4)(b)(ii), the CAC shall—

(a) notify the employer that the request has been made as soon as reasonably practicable;

(b) request from the employer such information as it needs to verify the number and names of the employees who have made the request; and

(c) inform the employer and the employees who have made the request how many employees have made the request on the basis of the information provided by the employees and the employer.

(6) Where the CAC requests information from the employer under paragraph (5)(b), the employer shall provide the information requested as soon as reasonably practicable.

(7) The date on which an employee request is made is—

(a) where the request consists of a single request satisfying paragraph (2)(a) or of separate requests made on the same day satisfying paragraph (2)(b), the date on which the request is or requests are sent to the employer by the employees or the date on which the CAC informs the employer and the employees in accordance with paragraph (5)(c) of how many employees have made the request; and

(b) where the request consists of separate requests made on different days, the date on which—

(i) the request which results in paragraph (2)(b) being satisfied is sent to the employer by the employees; or

(ii) the CAC informs the employer and the employees in accordance with paragraph (5)(c) of how many employees have made the request where that request results in paragraph (2)(b) being satisfied.

(8) If the employer decides to hold a ballot under regulation 8 or 9, the employer shall not be required to initiate negotiations unless and until the outcome of the ballot is that in regulation 8(5)(b).

(9) If an application is made to the CAC under regulation 13, the employer shall not be required to initiate negotiations unless and until if the CAC declares that there was a valid employee request or that the employer's notification was valid.

[3260]

NOTES

Commencement: 6 April 2005.

---

8 Pre-existing agreements: ballot for endorsement of employee request

(1) Subject to regulation 9, this regulation applies where a valid employee request has been made under regulation 7 by fewer than 40% of employees employed in the undertaking on the date that request was made and where there exists one or more pre-existing agreements which—

(a) are in writing;
(b) cover all the employees of the undertaking;
(c) have been approved by the employees; and
(d) set out how the employer is to give information to the employees or their representatives and seek their views on such information.

(2) Where this regulation applies, the employer may, instead of initiating negotiations in accordance with regulation 7(1), hold a ballot to seek the endorsement of the employees of the undertaking for the employee request in accordance with paragraphs (3) and (4).

(3) The employer must—

(a) inform the employees in writing within one month of the date of the employee request that he intends to hold a ballot under this regulation; and
(b) arrange for the ballot to be held as soon as reasonably practicable thereafter, provided that the ballot does not take place before a period of 21 days has passed since the employer informed the employees under sub-paragraph (a).

(4) A ballot must satisfy the following requirements—

(a) the employer must make such arrangements as are reasonably practicable to ensure that the ballot is fair;
(b) all employees of the undertaking on the day on which the votes may be cast in the ballot, or if the votes may be cast on more than one day, on the first day of those days, must be given an entitlement to vote in the ballot;
(c) the ballot must be conducted so as to secure that—
  (i) so far as is reasonably practicable, those voting do so in secret; and
  (ii) the votes given in the ballot are accurately counted.

(5) Where the employer holds a ballot under this regulation—

(a) he must, as soon as reasonably practicable after the date of the ballot, inform the employees of the result; and
(b) if the employees endorse the employee request, the employer is under the obligation in regulation 7(1) to initiate negotiations; and
(c) if the employees do not endorse the employee request, the employer is no longer under the obligation in regulation 7(1) to initiate negotiations.

(6) For the purposes of paragraph (5), the employees are to be regarded as having endorsed the employee request if—

(a) at least 40% of the employees employed in the undertaking; and
(b) the majority of the employees who vote in the ballot,

have voted in favour of endorsing the request.

(7) An employee or an employees' representative who believes that an employer has not, pursuant to paragraph (3)(a), informed his employees that he intends to hold a ballot within the period specified in that paragraph may apply to the CAC for a declaration that the employer is under the duty in regulation 7(1) to initiate negotiations.

(8) Where an employer, acting pursuant to paragraph (3)(a), has informed the employees that he intends to hold a ballot, any employee or employees' representative who believes that the employer has not complied with paragraph (3)(b) may present a complaint to the CAC

(9) Where the CAC finds a complaint under paragraph (8) well-founded it shall make an order requiring the employer to hold the ballot within such period as the order may specify.

[3261]

NOTES

Commencement: 6 April 2005.

9 Pre-existing agreements covering groups of undertakings

(1) This regulation applies where—

(a) the requirements of regulation 8(1) are satisfied in relation to an undertaking;

(b) the pre-existing agreement or one of the pre-existing agreements covers employees in one or more undertakings other than the undertaking mentioned in sub-paragraph (a); and

(c) the other undertaking or each of the other undertakings mentioned in sub-paragraph (b) is one in respect of which there is an agreement that satisfied, or are agreements that taken together satisfied, the requirements in sub-paragraphs (a) to (d) of regulation 8(1) on the date on which the valid employee request was made in respect of the undertaking mentioned in sub-paragraph (a); and

(d) the valid employee request in relation to the undertaking mentioned in sub-paragraph (a) either—

(i) alone, or

(ii) aggregated with any requests made by employees in the undertakings mentioned in sub-paragraph (b) within the period of six months preceding the date of the valid employee request mentioned in regulation 8(1),

is made by fewer than 40% of the employees in the undertakings mentioned in paragraph (1)(a) and (b).

(2) Where this regulation applies the employers may hold a combined ballot for endorsement of the employee request in accordance with this regulation and in that event regulation 8 shall apply to the ballot with the modification that references to employees shall be treated as referring to the employees employed in all of the undertakings referred to in paragraph (1)(a) and (b).

(3) Notwithstanding paragraph (2), the undertaking mentioned in paragraph (1)(a) may choose to hold the ballot for endorsement of the employee request in accordance with regulation 8 rather than under this regulation.

[3262]

NOTES

Commencement: 6 April 2005.

10 Complaint about ballot for endorsement of employee request

(1) Any employee in the undertaking referred to in regulation 8(1) or employee in one of the undertakings referred to in regulation 9(1), or representative of such employees, who believes that a requirement has not been satisfied that has to be satisfied in order to entitle either the employer, in accordance with regulation 8(2), to hold a ballot, or the employers, in accordance with regulation 9(2), to hold a combined ballot may, within 21 days of the employer informing the employees of the relevant undertaking under regulation 8(3)(a), present a complaint to the CAC

(2) Any employee or employees' representative who believes that the arrangements for a ballot held under regulation 8 or 9, as the case may be, did not satisfy one or more of the requirements set out in regulation 8(4) may, within 21 days of the date of the ballot, present a complaint to the CAC

(3) Where the CAC finds a complaint under paragraph (1) or (2) well-founded it shall—

(a) in the case of a finding on a complaint under paragraph (1) that any requirement set out in sub-paragraphs (a) to (d) of regulation 8(1) was not satisfied in relation to the undertaking referred to in regulation 8(1) or 9(1)(a), make an order requiring the employer to whom regulation 8(1) or 9(1)(a) relates to initiate negotiations in accordance with regulation 7(1);

(b) in the case of a finding on a complaint under paragraph (1) that any requirement set out in sub-paragraphs (b) to (d) of regulation 9(1) has not been satisfied, make an order that no combined ballot shall take place and requiring the employer to whom regulation 9(1)(a) relates, according to the preference he has expressed, to initiate negotiations in accordance with regulation 7(1) or, within such period as the order may specify, to conduct a ballot under regulation 8; and

(c) in the case of a complaint under paragraph (2)—

(i) where prior to the order being made, the employer referred to in regulation 8(1) or 9(1)(a) makes representations to the CAC that he would prefer to initiate negotiations under regulation 7, make an order requiring that employer to do so; or

(ii) in the absence of such representations, order the employer or employers to hold the ballot under regulation 8 or 9, as the case may be, again within such period as the order may specify.

[3263]

NOTES

Commencement: 6 April 2005.

11 Employer notification of decision to initiate negotiations

(1) The employer may start the negotiation process set out in regulation 14(1) on his own initiative by issuing a written notification satisfying the requirements of paragraph (2), and where the employer issues such a notification regulations 14 to 17 shall apply.

(2) The notification referred to in paragraph (1) must—

(a) state that the employer intends to start the negotiating process and that the notification is given for the purpose of these Regulations;

(b) state the date on which it is issued; and

(c) be published in such a manner as to bring it to the attention of, so far as reasonably practicable, all the employees of the undertaking.

[3264]

NOTES

Commencement: 6 April 2005.

12 Restrictions on employee request and employer notification

(1) Subject to paragraph (2), no employee request or employer notification is valid if it is made or issued, as the case may be,—

(a) where a negotiated agreement applies, within a period of three years from the date of the agreement or, where the agreement is terminated within that period, before the date on which the termination takes effect;

(b) where the standard information and consultation provisions apply within a period of three years from the date on which they started to apply; and

(c) where the employer has held a ballot under regulation 8, or was one of the employers who held a ballot under regulation 9 and the result was that the employees did not endorse the valid employee request referred to in regulation 8(1), within a period of three years from the date of that request.

(2) Paragraph (1) does not apply where there are material changes in the undertaking during the applicable period having the result—

(a) where a ballot held under regulation 8 or 9 had the result that the employees did not endorse the valid employee request, that there is no longer a pre-existing agreement which satisfies paragraph (1)(b) and (c) of regulation 8 or in the case of a ballot held under regulation 9, that there is no longer an agreement satisfying paragraph (1)(b) of that regulation; or

(b) where a negotiated agreement exists, that the agreement no longer complies with the requirement in regulation 16(1) that it must cover all the employees of the undertaking.

[3265]

NOTES

Commencement: 6 April 2005.

13 Dispute about employee request, employer notification or whether obligation in regulation 7(1) applies

(1) If the employer considers that there was no valid employee request—

(a) because the employee request did not satisfy any requirement of regulation 7(2) to (4) or was prevented from being valid by regulation 12, or

(b) because the undertaking was not one to which these Regulations applied (under Regulation 3) on the date on which the employee request was made,

the employer may apply to the CAC for a declaration as to whether there was a valid employee request.

(2) If an employee or an employees' representative considers that an employer notification was not valid because it did not comply with one or more of the requirements in regulation 11(2) or was prevented from being valid by regulation 12, he may apply to the CAC for a declaration as to whether the notification was valid.

(3) The CAC shall only consider an application for a declaration made under paragraph (1) or (2) if the application is made within a one month period beginning on the date of the employee request or the date on which the employer notification is made.

[3266]

NOTES

Commencement: 6 April 2005.

14 Negotiations to reach an agreement

(1) In order to initiate negotiations to reach an agreement under these Regulations the employer must as soon as reasonably practicable—

(a) make arrangements, satisfying the requirements of paragraph (2), for the employees of the undertaking to elect or appoint negotiating representatives; and thereafter

(b) inform the employees in writing of the identity of the negotiating representatives; and

(c) invite the negotiating representatives to enter into negotiations to reach a negotiated agreement.

(2) The requirements for the election or appointment of negotiating representatives under paragraph (1)(a) are that—

(a) the election or appointment of the representatives must be arranged in such a way that, following their election or appointment, all employees of the undertaking are represented by one or more representatives; and

(b) all employees of the undertaking must be entitled to take part in the election or appointment of the representatives and, where there is an election, all employees of the undertaking on the day on which the votes may be cast in the ballot, or if the votes may be cast on more than one day, on the first day of those days, must be given an entitlement to vote in the ballot.

(3) The negotiations referred to in paragraph (1)(c) shall last for a period not exceeding six months commencing at the end of the period of three months beginning with the date on which the valid employee request was made or the valid employer notification was issued; but the following periods shall not count towards the three month period—

(a) where the employer holds a ballot pursuant to regulation 8 or 9, the period between the employer notifying the employees of his decision to hold such a ballot and whichever of the following dates is applicable—

(i) where there is no complaint to the CAC under regulation 10, the date of the ballot;

(ii) where there is a complaint to the CAC under regulation 10 and the complaint is dismissed by the CAC or on appeal, the date on which it is finally dismissed;

(iii) where there is a complaint to the CAC and the outcome, whether of the complaint or of any appeal from it, is an order to hold the ballot under regulation 8 or 9 again, the date of the ballot that most recently took place;

(iv) where there is a complaint to the CAC under regulation 10 and the outcome, whether of the complaint or of any appeal from it, is an order requiring the employer to initiate negotiations in accordance with regulation 7(1), the date on which the order is made;

(b) where an application for a declaration is made to the CAC pursuant to regulation 13, the period between the date of that application and the final decision of the CAC or any appeal from that decision; and

(c) where a complaint about the election or appointment of negotiating representatives is presented pursuant to regulation 15, the time between the date of the complaint and the determination of the complaint, including any appeal and, where the complaint is upheld, the further period until the negotiating representatives are re-elected or re-appointed.

(4) Where a complaint about the ballot for employee approval of a negotiated agreement is presented pursuant to regulation 17, the time between the date the complaint is presented to the CAC and the determination of the complaint (including any appeal and, where the complaint is upheld, the further period until the re-holding of the ballot) shall not count towards the six month period mentioned in paragraph (3).

(5) If, before the end of the six month period referred to in paragraph (3), the employer and a majority of the negotiating representatives agree that that period should be extended, it may be extended by such period as the parties agree and thereafter may be further extended by such period or periods as the parties agree.

(6) Where one or more employers wish to initiate negotiations to reach an agreement to cover employees in more than one undertaking, any employer whose employees have not made a valid employee request and who has not issued a valid employer notification, shall issue such a notification.

(7) Where paragraph (6) applies, the provisions of paragraphs (1) to (5) of this regulation and regulations 15 and 16 apply with the following modifications—

(a) the references to the employees of the undertaking refer to the employees of all the undertakings to be covered by any agreement negotiated; and

(b) references to employees refer to employees of all the undertakings to be covered by any agreement negotiated.

[3267]

NOTES

Commencement: 6 April 2005.

15 Complaints about election or appointment of negotiating representatives

(1) If an employee or an employees' representative considers that one or both of the requirements for the appointment or election of negotiating representatives set out in regulation 14(2) have not been complied with, he may, within 21 days of the election or appointment, present a complaint to the CAC.

(2) Where the CAC finds the complaint well-founded it shall make an order requiring the employer to arrange for the process of election or appointment of negotiating representatives referred to in regulation 14 to take place again within such period as the order shall specify.

[3268]

NOTES

Commencement: 6 April 2005.

16 Negotiated agreements

(1) A negotiated agreement must cover all employees of the undertaking and may consist either of a single agreement or of different parts (each being approved in accordance with paragraph (4)) which, taken together, cover all the employees of the undertaking. The single agreement or each part must—

(a) set out the circumstances in which the employer must inform and consult the employees to which it relates;

(b) be in writing;

(c) be dated;

(d) be approved in accordance with paragraphs (3) to (5);

(e) be signed by or on behalf of the employer; and

(f) either—

(i) provide for the appointment or election of information and consultation representatives to whom the employer must provide the information and whom the employer must consult in the circumstances referred to in sub-paragraph (a); or

(ii) provide that the employer must provide information directly to the employees to which it relates and consult those employees directly in the circumstances referred to in sub-paragraph (a).

(2) Where a negotiated agreement consist of different parts they may provide differently in relation to the matters referred to in paragraph (1)(a) and (f).

(3) A negotiated agreement consisting of a single agreement shall be treated as being approved for the purpose of paragraph (1)(d) if—

(a) it has been signed by all the negotiating representatives; or

(b) it has been signed by a majority of negotiating representatives and either—

(i) approved in writing by at least 50% of employees employed in the undertaking, or

(ii) approved by a ballot of those employees, the arrangements for which satisfied the requirements set out in paragraph (5), in which at least 50% of the employees voting, voted in favour of approval.

(4) A part shall be treated as being approved for the purpose of paragraph (1)(d) if the part—

(a) has been signed by all the negotiating representatives involved in negotiating the part; or

(b) has been signed by a majority of those negotiating representatives and either—

(i) approved in writing by at least 50% of employees (employed in the undertaking) to which the part relates, or

(ii) approved by a ballot of those employees, the arrangements for which satisfied the requirements set out in paragraph (5), in which at least 50% of the employees voting, voted in favour of approving the part.

(5) The ballots referred to in paragraphs (3) and (4) must satisfy the following requirements—

(a) the employer must make such arrangements as are reasonably practicable to ensure that the ballot is fair;

(b) all employees of the undertaking or, as the case may be, to whom the part of the agreement relates, on the day on which the votes may be cast in the ballot, or if the votes may be cast on more than one day, on the first day of those days, must be given an entitlement to vote in the ballot; and

(c) the ballot must be conducted so as to secure that—

(i) so far as is reasonably practicable, those voting do so in secret; and

(ii) the votes given in the ballot are accurately counted.

(6) Where the employer holds a ballot under this regulation he must, as soon as reasonably practicable after the date of the ballot, inform the employees entitled to vote of the result.

[3269]

NOTES

Commencement: 6 April 2005.

17 Complaints about ballot for employee approval of negotiated agreement

(1) Any negotiating representative who believes that the arrangements for a ballot held under regulation 16 did not satisfy one or more of the requirements set out in paragraph (5) of that regulation, may, within 21 days of the date of the ballot, present a complaint to the CAC.

(2) Where the CAC finds the complaint well-founded it shall make an order requiring the employer to hold the ballot referred to in regulation 16 again within such period as the order may specify.

[3270]

NOTES

Commencement: 6 April 2005.

[17A Negotiated agreements and listed changes to pension schemes

(1) A requirement in any negotiated agreement or any part of such an agreement made before 6th April 2006 to inform and consult employees or their representatives about a listed change shall cease to apply once—

(a) the employer is under a duty under any of regulations 7(3) and 11 to 13 of the Pension Schemes Regulations; and

(b) he has notified the information and consultation representatives or, where he must consult employees directly, the employees in writing that he will be complying with his duty under the provisions of the Pension Schemes Regulations referred to in sub-paragraph (a), instead of his obligations under the negotiated agreement, provided that the notification is given on each occasion on which the employer has become or is about to become subject to the duty.

(2) For the purposes of this regulation "listed change" has the meaning given by regulation 6(2) of the Pension Schemes Regulations.]

[3270A]

NOTES

Commencement: 6 April 2006.

Inserted by the Information and Consultation of Employees (Amendment) Regulations 2006, SI 2006/514, regs 2, 4, as from 6 April 2006.

PART IV
STANDARD INFORMATION AND CONSULTATION PROVISIONS

18 Application of standard information and consultation provisions

(1) Subject to paragraph (2)—

(a) where the employer is under a duty, following the making of a valid employee request or issue of a valid employer notification, to initiate negotiations in accordance with regulation 14 but does not do so, the standard information and consultation provisions shall apply from the date—

(i) which is six months from the date on which the valid employee request was made or the valid employer notification was issued, or

(ii) information and consultation representatives are elected under regulation 19,

whichever is the sooner; and

(b) if the parties do not reach a negotiated agreement within the time limit referred to in regulation 14(3) (or that period as extended by agreement under paragraph (5) of that regulation) the standard information and consultation provisions shall apply from the date—

(i) which is six months from the date on which that time limit expires; or

(ii) information and consultation representatives are elected under regulation 19,

whichever is the sooner.

(2) Where the standard information and consultation provisions apply, the employer and the information and consultation representatives elected pursuant to regulation 19 may, at any time, reach an agreement that provisions other than the standard information and consultation provisions shall apply.

(3) An agreement referred to in paragraph (2) shall only have effect if it covers all the employees of the undertaking, complies with the requirements listed in regulation 16(1)(a) to (c), (e) and (f), and is signed by a majority of the information and consultation representatives.

[3271]

NOTES

Commencement: 6 April 2005.

19 Election of information and consultation representatives

(1) Where the standard information and consultation provisions are to apply, the employer shall, before the standard information and consultation provisions start to apply, arrange for the holding of a ballot of its employees to elect the relevant number of information and consultation representatives.

(2) The provisions in Schedule 2 to these Regulations apply in relation to the arrangements for and conduct of any such ballot.

(3) In this regulation the "relevant number of information and consultation representatives" means one representative per fifty employees or part thereof, provided that that number is at least 2 and does not exceed 25.

(4) An employee or an employee's representative may complain to the CAC that the employer has not arranged for the holding of a ballot in accordance with paragraph (1).

(5) Where the CAC finds the complaint well-founded, it shall make an order requiring the employer to arrange, or re-arrange, and hold the ballot.

(6) Where the CAC finds a complaint under paragraph (4) well-founded, the employee or the employee's representative may make an application to the Appeal Tribunal under regulation 22(6) and paragraphs (7) and (8) of that regulation shall apply to any such application.

[3272]

NOTES

Commencement: 6 April 2005.

20 Standard information and consultation provisions

(1) Where the standard information and consultation provisions apply pursuant to regulation 18, the employer must provide the information and consultation representatives with information on—

(a) the recent and probable development of the undertaking's activities and economic situation;

(b) the situation, structure and probable development of employment within the undertaking and on any anticipatory measures envisaged, in particular, where there is a threat to employment within the undertaking; and

(c) subject to paragraph (5), decisions likely to lead to substantial changes in work organisation or in contractual relations, including those referred to in—

(i) sections 188 to 192 of the Trade Union and Labour Relations (Consolidation) Act 1992; and

[(ii) regulations 13 to 16 of the Transfer of Undertakings (Protection of Employment) Regulations 2006].

(2) The information referred to in paragraph (1) must be given at such time, in such fashion and with such content as are appropriate to enable, in particular, the information and consultation representatives to conduct an adequate study and, where necessary, to prepare for consultation.

(3) The employer must consult the information and consultation representatives on the matters referred to in paragraph (1)(b) and (c).

(4) The employer must ensure that the consultation referred to in paragraph (3) is conducted—

(a) in such a way as to ensure that the timing, method and content of the consultation are appropriate;

(b) on the basis of the information supplied by the employer to the information and consultation representatives and of any opinion which those representatives express to the employer;

(c) in such a way as to enable the information and consultation representatives to meet the employer at the relevant level of management depending on the subject under discussion and to obtain a reasoned response from the employer to any such opinion; and

(d) in relation to matters falling within paragraph (1)(c), with a view to reaching agreement on decisions within the scope of the employer's powers.

(5) The duties in this regulation to inform and consult the information and consultation representatives on decisions falling within paragraph (1)(c) cease to apply once the employer is under a duty under—

(a) section 188 of the Act referred to in paragraph (1)(c)(i) (duty of employer to consult representatives); …

(b) [regulation 13] of the Regulations referred to in paragraph (1)(c)(ii) (duty to inform and consult representatives), [or

(c) any of regulations 11 to 13 of the Pension Schemes Regulations,]

and he has notified the information and consultation representatives in writing that he will be complying with his duty under the legislation referred to in [sub-paragraph (a), (b) or (c)], as the case may be, instead of under these Regulations, provided that the notification is given on each occasion on which the employer has become or is about to become subject to the duty.

(6) Where there is an obligation in these Regulations on the employer to inform and consult his employees, a failure on the part of a person who controls the employer (either directly or indirectly) to provide information to the employer shall not constitute a valid reason for the employer failing to inform and consult.

[3273]

NOTES

Commencement: 6 April 2005.

Para (1): sub-para (c)(ii) substituted by the Transfer of Undertakings (Protection of Employment) (Consequential Amendments) Regulations 2006, SI 2006/2405, reg 2, as from 1 October 2006.

Para (5): word omitted from sub-para (a) revoked, sub-para (c) and the word immediately preceding it inserted, and final words in square brackets substituted, by the Information and Consultation of Employees (Amendment) Regulations 2006, SI 2006/514, regs 2, 5(a), as from 6 April 2006; words in square brackets in sub-para (b) substituted by SI 2006/2405, reg 2, as from 1 October 2006.

PART V
DUTY OF CO-OPERATION

21 Co-operation

The parties are under a duty, when negotiating or implementing a negotiated agreement or when implementing the standard information and consultation provisions, to work in a spirit of co-operation and with due regard for their reciprocal rights and obligations, taking into account the interests of both the undertaking and the employees.

[3274]

NOTES

Commencement: 6 April 2005.

PART VI
COMPLIANCE AND ENFORCEMENT

22 Disputes about operation of a negotiated agreement or the standard information and consultation provisions

(1) Where—

(a) a negotiated agreement has been agreed; or

(b) the standard information and consultation provisions apply,

a complaint may be presented to the CAC by a relevant applicant who considers that the employer has failed to comply with the terms of the negotiated agreement or, as the case may be, one or more of the standard information and consultation provisions.

(2) A complaint brought under paragraph (1) must be brought within a period of three months commencing with the date of the alleged failure.

(3) In this regulation—

"failure" means an act or omission; and

"relevant applicant" means—

(a) in a case where information and consultation representatives have been elected or appointed, an information and consultation representative, or

(b) in a case where no information and consultation representatives have been elected or appointed, an employee or an employees' representative.

(4) Where the CAC finds the complaint well-founded it shall make a declaration to that effect and may make an order requiring the employer to take such steps as are necessary to comply with the terms of the negotiated agreement or, as the case may be, the standard information and consultation provisions.

(5) An order made under paragraph (4) shall specify—

(a) the steps which the employer is required to take; and

(b) the period within which the order must be complied with.

(6) If the CAC makes a declaration under paragraph (4) the relevant applicant may, within the period of three months beginning with the date on which the declaration is made, make an application to the Appeal Tribunal for a penalty notice to be issued.

(7) Where such an application is made, the Appeal Tribunal shall issue a written penalty notice to the employer requiring him to pay a penalty to the Secretary of State in respect of the failure unless satisfied, on hearing representations from the employer, that the failure resulted from a reason beyond the employer's control or that he has some other reasonable excuse for his failure.

(8) Regulation 23 shall apply in respect of a penalty notice issued under this regulation.

(9) No order of the CAC under this regulation shall have the effect of suspending or altering the effect of any act done or of any agreement made by the employer or of preventing or delaying any act or agreement which the employer proposes to do or to make.

[3275]

NOTES

Commencement: 6 April 2005.

23 Penalties

(1) A penalty notice issued under regulation 22 shall specify—

(a) the amount of the penalty which is payable;

(b) the date before which the penalty must be paid; and

(c) the failure and period to which the penalty relates.

(2) No penalty set by the Appeal Tribunal under this regulation may exceed £75,000.

(3) Matters to be taken into account by the Appeal Tribunal when setting the amount of the penalty shall include—

(a) the gravity of the failure;

(b) the period of time over which the failure occurred;

(c) the reason for the failure;

(d) the number of employees affected by the failure; and

(e) the number of employees employed by the undertaking or, where a negotiated agreement covers employees in more than one undertaking, the number of employees employed by both or all of the undertakings.

(4) The date specified under paragraph (1)(b) must not be earlier than the end of the period within which an appeal against a declaration or order made by the CAC under regulation 22 may be made.

(5) If the specified date in a penalty notice has passed and—

(a) the period during which an appeal may be made has expired without an appeal having been made; or

(b) such an appeal has been made and determined,

the Secretary of State may recover from the employer, as a civil debt due to him, any amount payable under the penalty notice which remains outstanding.

(6) The making of an appeal suspends the effect of a penalty notice.

(7) Any sums received by the Secretary of State under regulation 22 or this regulation shall be paid into the Consolidated Fund.

[3276]

NOTES

Commencement: 6 April 2005.

24 Exclusivity of remedy

The remedy for infringement of the rights conferred by Parts I to VI of these Regulations is by way of complaint to the CAC, and not otherwise.

[3277]

NOTES

Commencement: 6 April 2005.

PART VII
CONFIDENTIAL INFORMATION

25 Breach of statutory duty

(1) A person to whom the employer, pursuant to his obligations under these Regulations, entrusts any information or document on terms requiring it to be held in confidence shall not disclose that information or document except, where the terms permit him to do so, in accordance with those terms.

(2) In this regulation a person referred to in paragraph (1) to whom information or a document is entrusted is referred to as a "recipient".

(3) The obligation to comply with paragraph (1) is a duty owed to the employer, and a breach of the duty is actionable accordingly (subject to the defences and other incidents applying to actions for breaches of statutory duty).

(4) Paragraph (3) shall not affect any legal liability which any person may incur by disclosing the information or document, or any right which any person may have in relation to such disclosure otherwise than under this regulation.

(5) No action shall lie under paragraph (3) where the recipient reasonably believed the disclosure to be a "protected disclosure" within the meaning given to that expression by section 43A of the 1996 Act.

(6) A recipient to whom the employer has entrusted any information or document on terms requiring it to be held in confidence may apply to the CAC for a declaration as to whether it was reasonable for the employer to require the recipient to hold the information or document in confidence.

(7) If the CAC considers, on an application under paragraph (6), that the disclosure of the information or document by the recipient would not, or would not be likely to, harm the legitimate interests of the undertaking, it shall make a declaration that it was not reasonable for the employer to require the recipient to hold the information or document in confidence.

(8) If a declaration is made under paragraph (7), the information or document shall not at any time thereafter be regarded as having been entrusted to the recipient who made the application under paragraph (6), or to any other recipient, on terms requiring it to be held in confidence.

[3278]

NOTES

Commencement: 6 April 2005.

26 Withholding of information by the employer

(1) The employer is not required to disclose any information or document to a person for the purposes of these Regulations where the nature of the information or document is such that, according to objective criteria, the disclosure of the information or document would seriously harm the functioning of, or would be prejudicial to, the undertaking.

(2) If there is a dispute between the employer and—

(a) where information and consultation representatives have been elected or appointed, such a representative; or

(b) where no information and consultation representatives have been elected or appointed, an employee or an employees' representative,

as to whether the nature of the information or document which the employer has failed to provide is such as is described in paragraph (1), the employer or a person referred to in sub-paragraph (a) or (b) may apply to the CAC for a declaration as to whether the information or document is of such a nature.

(3) If the CAC makes a declaration that the disclosure of the information or document in question would not, according to objective criteria, be seriously harmful or prejudicial as mentioned in paragraph (1), the CAC shall order the employer to disclose the information or document.

(4) An order under paragraph (3) shall specify—

(a) the information or document to be disclosed;
(b) the person or persons to whom the information or document is to be disclosed;
(c) any terms on which the information or document is to be disclosed; and
(d) the date before which the information or document is to be disclosed.

[3279]

NOTES

Commencement: 6 April 2005.

PART VIII
PROTECTIONS FOR INFORMATION AND CONSULTATION REPRESENTATIVES, ETC

27 Right to time off for information and consultation representatives, etc

(1) An employee who is—

(a) a negotiating representative; or
(b) an information and consultation representative,

is entitled to be permitted by his employer to take reasonable time off during the employee's working hours in order to perform his functions as such a representative.

(2) For the purposes of this regulation, the working hours of an employee shall be taken to be any time when, in accordance with his contract of employment, the employee is required to be at work.

[3280]

NOTES

Commencement: 6 April 2005.

28 Right to remuneration for time off under regulation 27

(1) An employee who is permitted to take time off under regulation 27 is entitled to be paid remuneration by his employer for the time taken off at the appropriate hourly rate.

(2) Chapter II of Part XIV of the 1996 Act (a week's pay) shall apply in relation to this regulation as it applies in relation to section 62 of the 1996 Act.

(3) The appropriate hourly rate, in relation to an employee, is the amount of one week's pay divided by the number of normal working hours in a week for that employee when employed under the contract of employment in force on the day when time is taken.

(4) But where the number of normal working hours differs from week to week or over a longer period, the amount of one week's pay shall be divided instead by—

(a) the average number of normal working hours calculated by dividing by twelve the total number of the employee's normal working hours during the period of twelve weeks ending with the last complete week before the day on which the time is taken off; or
(b) where the employee has not been employed for a sufficient period to enable the calculations to be made under sub-paragraph (a), a number which fairly represents the number of normal working hours in a week having regard to such of the considerations specified in paragraph (5) as are appropriate in the circumstances.

(5) The considerations referred to in paragraph (4)(b) are—

(a) the average number of normal working hours in a week which the employee could expect in accordance with the terms of his contract; and

(b) the average number of normal working hours of other employees engaged in relevant comparable employment with the same employer.

(6) A right to any amount under paragraph (1) does not affect any right of an employee in relation to remuneration under his contract of employment ("contractual remuneration").

(7) Any contractual remuneration paid to an employee in respect of a period of time off under regulation 27 goes towards discharging any liability of the employer to pay remuneration under paragraph (1) in respect of that period, and, conversely, any payment of remuneration under paragraph (1) in respect of a period goes towards discharging any liability of the employer to pay contractual remuneration in respect of that period.

[3281]

NOTES

Commencement: 6 April 2005.

29 Right to time off: complaint to tribunals

(1) An employee may present a complaint to an employment tribunal that his employer—

(a) has unreasonably refused to permit him to take time off as required by regulation 27; or

(b) has failed to pay the whole or part of any amount to which the employee is entitled under regulation 28.

(2) A tribunal shall not consider a complaint under this regulation unless it is presented—

(a) before the end of the period of three months beginning with the day on which the time off was taken or on which it is alleged the time off should have been permitted; or

(b) within such further period as the tribunal considers reasonable in a case where it is satisfied that it was not reasonably practicable for the complaint to be presented before the end of that period of three months.

(3) Where a tribunal finds a complaint under this regulation well-founded, the tribunal shall make a declaration to that effect.

(4) If the complaint is that the employer has unreasonably refused to permit the employee to take time off, the tribunal shall also order the employer to pay to the employee an amount equal to the remuneration to which he would have been entitled under regulation 28 if the employer had not refused.

(5) If the complaint is that the employer has failed to pay the employee the whole or part of any amount to which he is entitled under regulation 28, the tribunal shall also order the employer to pay to the employee the amount it finds due to him.

[3282]

NOTES

Commencement: 6 April 2005.

Conciliation: employment tribunal proceedings and claims which could be the subject of employment tribunal proceedings under this regulation are proceedings to which the Employment Tribunals Act 1996, s 18 applies; see s 18(1)(p) of that Act at **[975]**. The standard conciliation period applies to such proceedings by virtue of the Employment Tribunals (Constitution and Rules of Procedure) Regulations 2004, SI 2004/1861, Sch 1, rule 22(1), (6) at **[3171]**.

30 Unfair dismissal

(1) An employee who is dismissed and to whom paragraph (2) or (5) applies shall be regarded, if the reason (or, if more than one, the principal reason) for the dismissal is a reason specified in, respectively, paragraph (3) or (6), as unfairly dismissed for the purposes of Part 10 of the 1996 Act.

(2) This paragraph applies to an employee who is—

(a) an employees' representative;

(b) a negotiating representative;

(c) an information and consultation representative; or
(d) a candidate in an election in which any person elected will, on being elected, be such a representative.

(3) The reasons are that—

(a) the employee performed or proposed to perform any functions or activities as such a representative or candidate;
(b) the employee exercised or proposed to exercise an entitlement conferred on the employee by regulation 27 or 28; or
(c) the employee (or a person acting on his behalf) made or proposed to make a request to exercise such an entitlement.

(4) Paragraph (1) does not apply in the circumstances set out in paragraph (3)(a) where the reason (or principal reason) for the dismissal is that in the performance, or purported performance, of the employee's functions or activities he has disclosed any information or document in breach of the duty in regulation 25, unless the employee reasonably believed the disclosure to be a "protected disclosure" within the meaning given to that expression by section 43A of the 1996 Act.

(5) This paragraph applies to any employee whether or not he is an employee to whom paragraph (2) applies.

(6) The reasons are that the employee—

(a) took, or proposed to take, any proceedings before an employment tribunal to enforce a right or secure an entitlement conferred on him by these Regulations;
(b) exercised, or proposed to exercise, any entitlement to apply or complain to the CAC or the Appeal Tribunal conferred by these Regulations or to exercise the right to appeal in connection with any rights conferred by these Regulations;
(c) requested, or proposed to request, data in accordance with regulation 5;
(d) acted with a view to securing that an agreement was or was not negotiated or that the standard information and consultation provisions did or did not become applicable;
(e) indicated that he supported or did not support the coming into existence of a negotiated agreement or the application of the standard information and consultation provisions;
(f) stood as a candidate in an election in which any person elected would, on being elected, be a negotiating representative or an information and consultation representative;
(g) influenced or sought to influence by lawful means the way in which votes were to be cast by other employees in a ballot arranged under these Regulations;
(h) voted in such a ballot;
(i) expressed doubts, whether to a ballot supervisor or otherwise, as to whether such a ballot had been properly conducted; or
(j) proposed to do, failed to do, or proposed to decline to do, any of the things mentioned in sub-paragraphs (d) to (i).

(7) It is immaterial for the purpose of paragraph (6)(a)—

(a) whether or not the employee has the right or entitlement; or
(b) whether or not the right has been infringed;

but for that sub-paragraph to apply, the claim to the right and, if applicable, the claim that it has been infringed must be made in good faith.

[3283]

NOTES

Commencement: 6 April 2005.

---

31 (*Amends the Employment Rights Act 1996, ss 105, 108 at* **[1149]**, **[1152]**, *and amended s 109* (*repealed*).)

32 Detriment

(1) An employee to whom paragraph (2) or (5) applies has the right not to be subjected to any detriment by any act, or deliberate failure to act, by his employer, done on a ground specified in, respectively, paragraph (3) or (6).

(2) This paragraph applies to an employee who is—

(a) an employees' representative;
(b) a negotiating representative;
(c) an information and consultation representative; or
(d) a candidate in an election in which any person elected will, on being elected, be such a representative.

(3) The ground is that—
(a) the employee performed or proposed to perform any functions or activities as such a representative or candidate;
(b) the employee exercised or proposed to exercise an entitlement conferred on the employee by regulation 27 or 28; or
(c) the employee (or a person acting on his behalf) made or proposed to make a request to exercise such an entitlement.

(4) Paragraph (1) does not apply in the circumstances set out in paragraph (3)(a) where the ground (or principal ground) for the subjection to detriment is that in the performance, or purported performance, of the employee's functions or activities he has disclosed any information or document in breach of the duty in regulation 25, unless the employee reasonably believed the disclosure to be a "protected disclosure" within the meaning given to that expression by section 43A of the 1996 Act.

(5) This paragraph applies to any employee whether or not he is an employee to whom paragraph (2) applies.

(6) The grounds are that the employee—
(a) took, or proposed to take, any proceedings before an employment tribunal to enforce a right or secure an entitlement conferred on him by these Regulations;
(b) exercised, or proposed to exercise, any entitlement to apply or complain to the CAC or the Appeal Tribunal conferred by these Regulations or to exercise the right to appeal in connection with any rights conferred by these Regulations;
(c) requested, or proposed to request, data in accordance with regulation 5;
(d) acted with a view to securing that an agreement was or was not negotiated or that the standard information and consultation provisions did or did not become applicable;
(e) indicated that he supported or did not support the coming into existence of a negotiated agreement or the application of the standard information and consultation provisions;
(f) stood as a candidate in an election in which any person elected would, on being elected, be a negotiating representative or an information and consultation representative;
(g) influenced or sought to influence by lawful means the way in which votes were to be cast by other employees in a ballot arranged under these Regulations;
(h) voted in such a ballot;
(i) expressed doubts, whether to a ballot supervisor or otherwise, as to whether such a ballot had been properly conducted; or
(j) proposed to do, failed to do, or proposed to decline to do, any of the things mentioned in sub-paragraphs (d) to (i).

(7) It is immaterial for the purpose of paragraph (6)(a)—
(a) whether or not the employee has the right or entitlement; or
(b) whether or not the right has been infringed,

but for that sub-paragraph to apply, the claim to the right and, if applicable, the claim that it has been infringed must be made in good faith.

(8) This regulation does not apply where the detriment in question amounts to dismissal. **[3284]**

NOTES

Commencement: 6 April 2005.

33 Detriment: enforcement and subsidiary provisions

(1) An employee may present a complaint to an employment tribunal that he has been subjected to a detriment in contravention of regulation 32.

(2) The provisions of sections 48(2) to (4) and 49(1) to (5) of the 1996 Act (complaints to employment tribunals and remedies) shall apply in relation to a complaint under this

regulation as they apply in relation to a complaint under section 48 of the Act but taking references to the employer as references to the employer within the meaning of regulation 32(1) above.

[3285]

NOTES

Commencement: 6 April 2005.

Conciliation: employment tribunal proceedings and claims which could be the subject of employment tribunal proceedings under this regulation are proceedings to which the Employment Tribunals Act 1996, s 18 applies; see s 18(1)(p) of that Act at **[975]**. The standard conciliation period applies to such proceedings by virtue of the Employment Tribunals (Constitution and Rules of Procedure) Regulations 2004, SI 2004/1861, Sch 1, rule 22(1), (6) at **[3171]**.

Tribunal jurisdiction: the Employment Act 2002, ss 31, 32, 38, at **[1493]**, **[1494]**, **[1496]** apply to proceedings before the employment tribunal relating to a claim under this regulation; see ss 31(1), 32(1), 38(1) of, and Schs 3–5 to, the 2002 Act at **[1508]**–**[1510]**.

For the circumstances in which the normal time limit for presenting a complaint under this regulation is extended for a period of three months, see the Employment Act 2002 (Dispute Resolution) Regulations 2004, SI 2004/752, regs 15 and 18 at **[3096]** and **[3098]**.

34 (*Amends the Employment Tribunals Act 1996, s 18 at* **[975]**.)

PART IX
MISCELLANEOUS

35 CAC proceedings

(1) Where under these Regulations a person presents a complaint or makes an application to the CAC the complaint or application must be in writing and in such form as the CAC may require.

(2) In its consideration of a complaint or application under these Regulations, the CAC shall make such enquiries as it sees fit and so far as reasonably practicable give any person whom it considers has a proper interest in the complaint or application an opportunity to be heard.

(3) The CAC may draw an adverse inference from a party's failure to comply with any reasonable request to provide information or documents relevant to a complaint presented to it or an application made to it.

(4) A declaration or order made by the CAC under these Regulations may be relied on—

(a) in relation to an employer whose registered office, head office or principal place of business is in England or Wales, as if it were a declaration or order made by the High Court, and

(b) in relation to an employer whose registered office, head office or principal place of business is in Scotland as if it were a declaration or order made by the Court of Session.

(5) A declaration or order made by the CAC under these Regulations must be in writing and state the reasons for the CAC's findings.

(6) An appeal lies to the Appeal Tribunal on any question of law arising from any declaration or order of, or arising in any proceedings before, the CAC under these Regulations.

[3286]

NOTES

Commencement: 6 April 2005.

36 Appeal Tribunal: location of certain proceedings under these Regulations

(1) Any proceedings before the Appeal Tribunal arising under these Regulations, other than appeals under paragraph (n) of section 21(1) of the Employment Tribunals Act 1996 (appeals from employment tribunals on questions of law), shall—

(a) where the registered office or, where there is no registered office, the head office or principal place of business is situated in England and Wales, be held in England and Wales; and

(b) where the registered office or, where there is no registered office, the head office or principal place of business is situated in Scotland, be held in Scotland.

(2) …

[3287]

NOTES

Commencement: 6 April 2005.

Para (2) amends the Employment Tribunals Act 1996, s 20 at **[977]**.

37 (*Amends the Employment Tribunals Act 1996, s 21 at* **[978]**.)

38 ACAS

(1) If on receipt of an application or complaint under these Regulations the CAC is of the opinion that it is reasonably likely to be settled by conciliation or other assistance provided by the Advisory, Conciliation and Arbitration Service ('ACAS') in accordance with paragraph (2), it shall refer the application or complaint to ACAS and shall notify the applicant or complainant and any persons whom it considers have a proper interest in the application or complaint accordingly.

(2) Where the CAC refers an application or complaint to ACAS under paragraph (1), section 210 of the Trade Union and Labour Relations (Consolidation) Act 1992 (power of ACAS to offer assistance to settle disputes) shall apply, and ACAS may offer the parties to the application or complaint its assistance under that section with a view to bringing about a settlement, as if—

(a) the dispute or difference between the parties amounted to a trade dispute as defined in section 218 of that Act; and

(b) the parties to the application or complaint had requested the assistance of ACAS under section 210.

(3) If ACAS does not consider it appropriate to offer its assistance in accordance with paragraph (2) it shall inform the CAC.

(4) If ACAS has offered the parties its assistance in accordance with paragraph (2), the application or complaint referred has not thereafter been settled or withdrawn, and ACAS is of the opinion that no provision or further provision of its assistance is likely to result in a settlement or withdrawal, it shall inform the CAC of its opinion.

(5) If—

(a) an application or complaint is not referred to ACAS, or

(b) it is so referred, but ACAS informs the CAC as mentioned in paragraph (3) or (4),

the CAC shall proceed to hear and determine the application or complaint.

[3288]

NOTES

Commencement: 6 April 2005.

39 Restrictions on contracting out: general

(1) Any provision in any agreement (whether an employee's contract or not) is void in so far as it purports—

(a) to exclude or limit the operation of any provision of these Regulations other than a provision of Part VIII; or

(b) to preclude a person from bringing any proceedings before the CAC or the Appeal Tribunal under any provision of these Regulations other than a provision of Part VIII.

(2) Paragraph (1) does not apply to any agreement to refrain from continuing any proceedings referred to in sub-paragraph (b) of that paragraph made after the proceedings have been instituted.

[3289]

NOTES

Commencement: 6 April 2005.

40 Restrictions on contracting out: Part VIII

(1) Any provision in any agreement (whether an employee's contract or not) is void in so far as it purports—

(a) to exclude or limit the operation of any provision of Part VIII; or

(b) to preclude a person from bringing any proceedings before an employment tribunal under that Part.

(2) Paragraph (1) does not apply to any agreement to refrain from instituting or continuing proceedings before an employment tribunal where a conciliation officer has taken action under section 18 of the Employment Tribunals Act 1996 (conciliation).

(3) Paragraph (1) does not apply to any agreement to refrain from instituting or continuing before an employment tribunal proceedings within section 18(1) of the Employment Tribunals Act 1996 (proceedings under these Regulations where conciliation is available) if the conditions regulating compromise agreements under these Regulations are satisfied in relation to the agreement.

(4) For the purposes of paragraph (3) the conditions regulating compromise agreements are that—

(a) the agreement must be in writing;

(b) the agreement must relate to the particular proceedings;

(c) the employee must have received advice from a relevant independent adviser as to the terms and effect of the proposed agreement and, in particular, its effect on his ability to pursue his rights before an employment tribunal;

(d) there must be in force, when the adviser gives the advice, a contract of insurance, or an indemnity provided for members of a profession or a professional body, covering the risk of a claim by the employee in respect of loss arising in consequence of the advice;

(e) the agreement must identify the adviser; and

(f) the agreement must state that the conditions in sub-paragraphs (a) to (e) are satisfied.

(5) A person is a relevant independent adviser for the purposes of paragraph (4)(c)—

(a) if he is a qualified lawyer;

(b) if he is an officer, official, employee or member of an independent trade union who has been certified in writing by the trade union as competent to give advice and as authorised to do so on behalf of the trade union; or

(c) if he works at an advice centre (whether as an employee or as a volunteer) and has been certified in writing by the centre as competent to give advice and as authorised to do so on behalf of the centre.

(6) But a person is not a relevant independent adviser for the purposes of paragraph (4)(c)—

(a) if he is, is employed by or is acting in the matter for the employer or an associated employer;

(b) in the case of a person within paragraph (5)(b) or (c), if the trade union or advice centre is the employer or an associated employer; or

(c) in the case of a person within (5)(c), if the employee makes a payment for the advice received from him.

(7) In paragraph (5)(a), "qualified lawyer" means—

(a) as respects England and Wales, a barrister (whether in practice as such or employed to give legal advice), a solicitor who holds a practising certificate, or a person other than a barrister or a solicitor who is an authorised advocate or authorised litigator (within the meaning of the Courts and Legal Services Act 1990); and

(b) as respects Scotland, an advocate (whether in practice as such or employed to give legal advice) or a solicitor who holds a practising certificate.

(8) A person shall be treated as being a qualified lawyer within the meaning of paragraph (7)(a) if he is a Fellow of the Institute of Legal Executives employed by a solicitors' practice.

(9) For the purposes of paragraph (6) any two employers shall be treated as associated if—

(a) one is a company of which the other (directly or indirectly) has control; or

(b) both are companies of which a third person (directly or indirectly) has control;

and "associated employer" shall be construed accordingly.

[3290]

NOTES

Commencement: 6 April 2005.

41 (*Amends the Employment Appeal Tribunal Rules 1993, SI 1993/2854, rr 2–5, 7, 16AA, 26, 31, Schedule at* **[2189]–[2192]**, **[2194]**, **[2204A]**, **[2218]**, **[2224]**, **[2235]** *et seq.*)

42 Crown employment

(1) These Regulations have effect in relation to Crown employment and persons in Crown employment as they have effect in relation to other employment and other employees.

(2) In these Regulations "Crown employment" means employment in an undertaking to which these Regulations apply and which is under or for the purposes of a government department or any officer or body exercising on behalf of the Crown functions conferred by a statutory provision.

(3) For the purposes of the application of these Regulations in relation to Crown employment in accordance with paragraph (1)—

(a) references to an employee shall be construed as references to a person in Crown employment; and

(b) references to a contract of employment shall be construed as references to the terms of employment of a person in Crown employment.

[3291]

NOTES

Commencement: 6 April 2005.

43 Exception for merchant navy

(1) Subject to paragraph (3), no long haul crew member shall be—

(a) a negotiating representative; or

(b) an information and consultation representative.

(2) In paragraph (1), a "long haul crew member" means a person who is a member of a merchant navy crew other than—

(a) a ferry worker; or

(b) a person who normally works on voyages the duration of which is less than 48 hours.

(3) Paragraph (1) does not apply where the employer decides that the long haul crew member in question shall be permitted to be, as the case may be, a negotiating representative or an information and consultation representative.

(4) Where paragraph (1) applies, no long haul crew member shall—

(a) stand as a candidate for election as a negotiating representative or an information and consultation representative; or

(b) be appointed or elected to be a negotiating representative or an information and consultation representative.

[3292]

NOTES

Commencement: 6 April 2005.

SCHEDULES

SCHEDULE 1
APPLICATION OF REGULATIONS

Regulation 3

Number of employees	**Date Regulations apply**
At least 150	6 April 2005
At least 100	6 April 2007
At least 50	6 April 2008

[3293]

NOTES

Commencement: 6 April 2005.

SCHEDULE 2
REQUIREMENTS FOR BALLOTS HELD UNDER REGULATION 19

Regulation 19

Ballot Arrangements

1. Ballots held under regulation 19 must comply with the requirements specified in paragraph 2.

2. The requirements referred to in paragraph 1 are that—
   (a) the ballot must comprise a single ballot but may instead, if the employer so decides, comprise separate ballots of employees in such constituencies as the employer may decide where the employer considers that if separate ballots were to be held for those constituencies, the information and consultation representatives to be elected would better reflect the interests of the employees as a whole than if a single ballot were held;
   (b) if, at any point, it becomes clear that the number of people standing as candidates in the ballot is equal to or fewer than the relevant number of information and consultation representatives (as defined in regulation 19(3)), the obligation on the employer to hold the ballot in regulation 19 will cease and the candidates referred to above will become the information and consultation representatives;
   (c) all employees of the undertaking on the day on which the votes may be cast in the ballot, or if the votes may be cast on more than one day, on the first day of those days, must be given an entitlement to vote in the ballot;
   (d) any employee who is an employee of the undertaking at the latest time at which a person may become a candidate in the ballot is entitled to stand in the ballot as a candidate as an information and consultation representative;
   (e) the employer must, in accordance with paragraph 6, appoint an independent ballot supervisor to supervise the conduct of the ballot;
   (f) after the employer has formulated proposals as to the arrangements for the ballot and before he has published the final arrangements under sub-paragraph (g) he must, so far as reasonably practicable, consult with employees' representatives or, if no such representatives exist, the employees, on the proposed arrangements for the ballot; and
   (g) the employer must publish the final arrangements for the ballot in such manner as to bring them to the attention of, so far as reasonably practicable, his employees and, where they exist, the employees' representatives.

3. Any employee or an employees' representative who believes that the arrangements for the ballot are defective may, within a period of 21 days beginning on the date on which the employer published the final arrangements under paragraph 2(g), present a complaint to the CAC.

4. Where the CAC finds the complaint well-founded it shall make a declaration to that effect and may make an order requiring the employer to modify the arrangements he has made for the ballot or to satisfy the requirements in sub-paragraphs (a) to (f) of paragraph 2.

5. An order under paragraph 4 shall specify the modifications to the arrangements which the employer is required to make and the requirements he must satisfy.

6. A person is an independent ballot supervisor for the purposes of paragraph 2(e) if the employer reasonably believes that he will carry out any functions conferred on him in relation to the ballot competently and has no reasonable grounds for believing that his independence might reasonably be called into question.

7. For the purposes of paragraph 3 the arrangements for the ballot are defective if any of the requirements specified in sub-paragraphs (a) to (f) of paragraph 2 is not satisfied.

Conduct of the Ballot

8. The employer must—
   (a) ensure that a ballot supervisor appointed under paragraph 2(e) carries out his functions under this Schedule and that there is no interference with his carrying out of those functions; and
   (b) comply with all reasonable requests made by a ballot supervisor for the purposes of or in connection with the carrying out of those functions.

9. A ballot supervisor's appointment shall require that he—
   (a) supervises the conduct of the ballot he is being appointed to supervise, in accordance with the arrangements for the ballot published by the employer under paragraph 2(g) or, where appropriate, in accordance with the arrangements as required to be modified by an order made under paragraph 4;
   (b) does not conduct the ballot before the employer has satisfied the requirement specified in paragraph 2(g) and—
      (i) where no complaint has been presented under paragraph 3, before the expiry of 21 days beginning with the date on which the employer published his arrangements under paragraph 2(g); or
      (ii) where a complaint has been presented under paragraph 3, before the complaint has been determined and, where appropriate, the arrangements have been modified as required by an order made as a result of the complaint;
   (c) conducts the ballot so as to secure that—
      (i) so far as reasonably practicable, those entitled to vote are given the opportunity to do so;
      (ii) so far as reasonably practicable, those entitled to stand as candidates are given the opportunity to stand;
      (iii) so far as reasonably practicable, those voting are able to do so in secret; and
      (iv) the votes given in the ballot are fairly and accurately counted.

10. As soon as reasonably practicable after the date of the ballot, the ballot supervisor must publish the results of the ballot in such manner as to make them available to the employer and, so far as reasonably practicable, the employees entitled to vote in the ballot and the persons who stood as candidates in the ballot.

11. A ballot supervisor shall publish a report ("an ineffective ballot report") where he considers (whether or not on the basis of representations made to him by another person) that—
   (a) any of the requirements referred to in paragraph 2 was not satisfied with the result that the outcome of the ballot would have been different; or
   (b) there was interference with the carrying out of his functions or a failure by the employer to comply with all reasonable requests made by him with the result that he was unable to form a proper judgement as to whether each of the requirements referred to in paragraph 2 was satisfied in the ballot.

12. Where a ballot supervisor publishes an ineffective ballot report the report must be published within a period of one month commencing on the date on which the ballot supervisor publishes the results of the ballot under paragraph 10.

13 A ballot supervisor must publish an ineffective ballot report in such manner as to make it available to the employer and, so far as reasonably practicable, the employees entitled to vote in the ballot and the persons who stood as candidates in the ballot.

14. Where a ballot supervisor publishes an ineffective ballot report, the outcome of the ballot shall be of no effect and—

(a) if there has been a single ballot or an ineffective ballot report has been published in respect of every separate ballot, the outcome of the ballot or ballots shall be of no effect and the employer shall again be under the obligation in regulation 19;

(b) if there have been separate ballots and sub-paragraph (a) does not apply—

(i) the employer shall arrange for the separate ballot or ballots in respect of which an ineffective ballot report has been issued to be reheld in accordance with regulation 19, and

(ii) no such ballot shall have effect until it has been reheld and no ineffective ballot report has been published in respect of it.

15. All costs relating to the holding of the ballot, including payments made to a ballot supervisor for supervising the conduct of the ballot, shall be borne by the employer (whether or not an ineffective ballot report has been made).

[3294]

NOTES

Commencement: 6 April 2005.

ROAD TRANSPORT (WORKING TIME) REGULATIONS 2005

(SI 2005/639)

NOTES

Made: 10 March 2005.

Authority: European Communities Act 1972, s 2(2).

Commencement: 4 April 2005.

These Regulations are the domestic implementation of European Parliament and Council Directive 2002/15/EC on the organisation of working time of persons performing mobile transport activities at **[4065A]**.

Regulatory functions: the regulatory functions conferred by these Regulations are subject to the Legislative and Regulatory Reform Act 2006, ss 21, 22 at **[1783]**, **[1784]**; see the Legislative and Regulatory Reform (Regulatory Functions) Order 2007, SI 2007/3544 (made under s 24(2) of the 2006 Act) for details.

ARRANGEMENT OF REGULATIONS

SCHEDULES:

1 Citation, commencement and extent

(1) These Regulations may be cited as the Road Transport (Working Time) Regulations 2005 and shall come into force on 4th April 2005.

(2) These Regulations extend to Great Britain only.

[3294A]

NOTES

Commencement: 4 April 2005.

2 Interpretation

In these Regulations—

"AETR" means the European agreement concerning the work of crews of vehicles engaged in international road transport of 1st July 1970;

"collective agreement" means a collective agreement within the meaning of section 178 of the Trade Union and Labour Relations (Consolidation) Act 1992, the trade union parties to which are independent trade unions within the meaning of section 5 of that Act;

["the Community Drivers' Hours Regulation" means Regulation (EC) No 561/2006 of the European Parliament and of the Council of 15 March 2006 on the harmonisation of certain social legislation relating to road transport (and amending and repealing certain Council Regulations);]

"employer" in relation to a worker, means the person by whom the worker is (or, where the employment has ceased, was) employed;

"employment" in relation to a worker, means employment under his contract, and "employed" shall be construed accordingly;

"goods" includes goods or burden of any description;

"goods vehicle" means a motor vehicle constructed or adapted for use for the carriage of goods, or a trailer so constructed or adapted;

"inspector" means a person appointed under paragraph 1 of Schedule 2;

"mobile worker" means any worker forming part of the travelling staff, including trainees and apprentices, who is in the service of an undertaking which operates transport services for passengers or goods by road for hire or reward or on its own account;

"night time" means in respect of goods vehicles the period between midnight and 4am and in respect of passenger vehicles the period between 1am and 5am;

"motor vehicle" means a mechanically propelled vehicle intended or adapted for use on roads;

"night work" means any work performed during night time;

"passenger vehicle" means a motor vehicle which is constructed or adapted to carry more than eight seated passengers in addition to the driver;

"period of availability" means a period during which the mobile worker is not required to remain at his workstation, but is required to be available to answer any calls to start or resume driving or to carry out other work , including periods during which the mobile worker is accompanying a vehicle being transported by a ferry or by a train as well as periods of waiting at frontiers and those due to traffic prohibitions;

"reference period" means the period for calculation of the average maximum weekly working time;

"relevant requirements" means regulations 4(8), 7(5), 8(2), 9(4), 10, 11 and 12;

"self-employed driver" means anyone whose main occupation is to transport passengers or goods by road for hire or reward within the meaning of Community legislation under cover of a Community licence or any other professional authorisation to carry out such transport, who is entitled to work for himself and who is not tied to an employer by an employment contract or by any other type of working hierarchical relationship, who is free to organise the relevant working activities, whose income depends directly on the profits made and who has the freedom, individually or through a co-operation between self-employed drivers, to have commercial relations with several customers;

"vehicle" means a goods vehicle or a passenger vehicle;

"week" means a period of seven days beginning at midnight between Sunday and Monday;

"worker" means an individual who has entered into or works under (or, where employment has ceased, worked under)—

(a) a contract of employment; or
(b) any other contract, whether express or implied and (if it is express) whether oral or in writing, whereby the individual undertakes to do or perform personally any work or services for another party to the contract;

and any reference to a worker's contract shall be construed accordingly;

"workforce agreement" means an agreement between an employer and mobile workers employed by him or their representatives in respect of which the conditions set out in Schedule 1 to these Regulations are satisfied;

"working time" means the time from the beginning to the end of work during which the mobile worker is at his workstation, at the disposal of his employer and exercising his functions or activities, being

(a) time devoted to all road transport activities, including, in particular—
  (i) driving;
  (ii) loading and unloading;
  (iii) assisting passengers boarding and disembarking from the vehicle;
  (iv) cleaning and technical maintenance;
  (v) all other work intended to ensure the safety of the vehicle, its cargo and passengers or to fulfil the legal or regulatory obligations directly linked to the specific transport operation under way, including monitoring of loading and unloading and dealing with administrative formalities with police, customs, immigration officers and others; or
(b) time during which the mobile worker cannot dispose freely of his time and is required to be at his workstation, ready to take up normal work, with certain tasks associated with being on duty, in particular during periods awaiting loading or unloading where their foreseeable duration is not known in advance, that is to say either before departure or just before the actual start of the period in question, or under collective agreements or workforce agreements;

"workstation" means

(a) the location of the main place of business of the undertaking for which the person performing mobile transport activities carries out duties, together with its various subsidiary places of business, regardless of whether they are located in the same place as its head office or its main place of business;
(b) the vehicle which the person performing mobile road transport activities uses when he carries out duties; or
(c) any other place in which activities connected with transport are carried out.

[3294B]

NOTES

Commencement: 4 April 2005.

Definition "the Community Drivers' Hours Regulation" substituted by the Road Transport (Working Time) (Amendment) Regulations 2007, SI 2007/853, reg 2(1), (2), as from 11 April 2007.

3 Application

(1) These Regulations apply to mobile workers who are employed by, or who do work for, undertakings established in a Member State of the European Union, and to whom paragraph (2) or paragraph (3) applies.

[(2) This paragraph applies to mobile workers who, in the course of that employment or work, drive or travel in or on vehicles—

(a) which are vehicles within the meaning of Article 4(b) of the Community Drivers' Hours Regulation,
(b) which are not vehicles described in Article 3 of that Regulation, and
(c) which are not vehicles exempted from the provisions of that Regulation under regulation 2 of the Community Drivers' Hours and Recording Equipment (Exemptions and Supplementary Provisions) Regulations 1986.]

(3) This paragraph applies to mobile workers, to whom paragraph (2) does not apply, who in the course of that employment or work drive, or travel in, vehicles

(a) which fall within the meaning of a "vehicle" in Article 1 of the AETR;
(b) which are not referred to in Article 2(2)(b) of the AETR; and
(c) which are performing international transport.

(4) These Regulations do not apply to—

(a) self-employed drivers, or

(b) any worker who does work which is included in the calculation of working time—
   (i) where the reference period is shorter than 26 weeks, on fewer than 11 days in a reference period applicable to that worker, or
   (ii) in any other case on fewer than 16 days in a reference period applicable to that worker.

[3294C]

NOTES

Commencement: 4 April 2005.
Para (2): substituted by the Road Transport (Working Time) (Amendment) Regulations 2007, SI 2007/853, reg 2(1), (3), as from 11 April 2007.

4 Working time

(1) Subject to paragraph (2) below, the working time, including overtime, of a mobile worker shall not exceed 60 hours in a week.

(2) In any reference period which is applicable to his case, a mobile worker's working time shall not exceed an average of 48 hours for each week.

(3) The reference periods which apply in the case of a mobile worker shall be—
(a) where a collective agreement or a workforce agreement provides for the application of this regulation in relation to successive periods of 17 weeks, each such period,
(b) in a case where—
   (i) there is no such provision, and
   (ii) the employer gives written notice to the mobile worker in writing that he intends to apply this subparagraph,

any period of 17 weeks in the course of the worker's employment, or
(c) in any other case, the period ending at midnight between Sunday 31st July 2005 and Monday 1st August 2005 and thereafter, in each year, the successive periods beginning at midnight at the beginning of the Monday which falls on, or is the first Monday after, a date in column 1 below and ending at midnight at the beginning of the Monday which falls on, or is the first Monday after, the date on the same line in column 2 below.

Column 1 (beginning)	Column 2 (end)
1st December	1st April
1st April	1st August
1st August	1st December

(4) The reference period may be extended in relation to particular mobile workers or groups of mobile workers for objective or technical reasons or reasons concerning the organisation of work, by a collective agreement or a workforce agreement, by the substitution for 17 weeks of a period not exceeding 26 weeks in the application of paragraphs (2) and (3)(a) above.

(5) A mobile worker's average weekly working time during a reference period shall be determined according to the formula—

(A + B) / C

where—

A is the aggregate number of hours comprised in the mobile worker's working time during the course of the reference period;

B is the number of excluded hours during the reference period; and

C is the number of weeks in the reference period.

(6) In paragraph (5), "excluded hours" means hours comprised in—
(a) any period of annual leave taken by the mobile worker in exercise of entitlement under regulation 13 of the Working Time Regulations 1998;

(b) any period of sick leave taken by the mobile worker;

(c) any period of maternity, paternity, adoption or parental leave taken by the mobile worker;

(7) For the purposes of paragraph (5), the number of hours in a whole day shall be eight and the number of hours in a whole week shall be forty-eight.

(8) An employer shall take all reasonable steps, in keeping with the need to protect the health and safety of the mobile worker, to ensure that the limits specified above are complied with in the case of each mobile worker employed by him.

[3294D]

NOTES

Commencement: 4 April 2005.

5 The times of breaks, rests and periods of availability shall not be included in the calculation of working time.

[3294E]

NOTES

Commencement: 4 April 2005.

6 Periods of availability

(1) A period shall not be treated as a period of availability unless the mobile worker knows before the start of the relevant period about that period of availability and its reasonably foreseeable duration.

(2) The time spent by a mobile worker, who is working as part of a team, travelling in, but not driving, a moving vehicle as part of that team shall be a period of availability for that mobile worker.

(3) Subject to paragraph (4) a period of availability shall not include a period of rest or a break.

(4) A period of availability may include a break taken by a mobile worker during waiting time or time which is not devoted to driving by the mobile worker and is spent in a moving vehicle, a ferry or a train.

[3294F]

NOTES

Commencement: 4 April 2005.

7 Breaks

(1) No mobile worker shall work for more than six hours without a break.

(2) Where a mobile worker's working time exceeds six hours but does not exceed nine hours, the worker shall be entitled to a break lasting at least 30 minutes and interrupting that time.

(3) Where a mobile worker's working time exceeds nine hours, the worker shall be entitled to a break lasting at least 45 minutes and interrupting that period.

(4) Each break may be made up of separate periods of not less than 15 minutes each.

(5) An employer shall take all reasonable steps, in keeping with the need to protect the health and safety of the mobile worker, to ensure that the limits specified above are complied with in the case of each mobile worker employed by him.

[3294G]

NOTES

Commencement: 4 April 2005.

8 Rest periods

(1) In the application of these Regulations, the provisions of the Community Drivers' Hours Regulation relating to daily and weekly rest shall apply to all mobile workers to whom they do not apply under that Regulation as they apply to other mobile workers under that Regulation.

(2) An employer shall take all reasonable steps, in keeping with the need to protect the health and safety of the mobile worker, to ensure that those provisions are complied with in the case of each mobile worker employed by him, to whom they are applied by paragraph (1).

[3294H]

NOTES

Commencement: 4 April 2005.

9 Night work

(1) The working time of a mobile worker, who performs night work in any period of 24 hours, shall not exceed 10 hours during that period.

(2) The period of 10 hours may be extended in relation to particular mobile workers or groups of mobile workers for objective or technical reasons or reasons concerning the organisation of work, by a collective agreement or a workforce agreement.

(3) Compensation for night work shall not be given to a mobile worker in any manner which is liable to endanger road safety.

(4) An employer shall take all reasonable steps in keeping with the need to protect the health and safety of mobile workers to ensure that the limit specified in paragraph (1), or extended in accordance with paragraph (2), is complied with in the case of each mobile worker employed by him.

[3294I]

NOTES

Commencement: 4 April 2005.

10 Information and records

An employer of mobile workers shall notify each worker of the provisions of these Regulations and the provisions of any collective or workforce agreement which is capable of application to that worker.

[3294J]

NOTES

Commencement: 4 April 2005.

11 An employer of a mobile worker shall

(a) request from each mobile worker details of any time worked by that worker for another employer;

(b) include time worked for another employer in the calculation of the mobile worker's working time;

(c) keep records which are adequate to show whether the requirements of these Regulations are being complied with in the case of each mobile worker employed by him to whom they apply;

(d) retain such records for at least two years after the end of the period covered by those records;

(e) provide, at the request of a mobile worker, a copy of the record of hours worked by that worker;

(f) provide to an enforcement officer copies of such records relating to mobile workers as the officer may require;

(g) provide to a mobile worker or enforcement officer copies of such documentary evidence in the employer's possession as may be requested by the worker or officer in relation to records provided to him in accordance with paragraph (e) or (f) above.

[3294K]

NOTES

Commencement: 4 April 2005.

12 A mobile worker shall, at the request of his employer under regulation 11(a), notify his employer in writing of time worked by the worker for another employer for inclusion in the calculation of the mobile worker's working time.

[3294L]

NOTES

Commencement: 4 April 2005.

13—(1) The Secretary of State shall arrange for the publication, in such form and manner as he considers appropriate, of information and advice concerning the operation of these Regulations.

(2) The information and advice shall be such as appear to him best calculated to enable employers and workers affected by these Regulations to understand their respective rights and obligations.

[3294M]

NOTES

Commencement: 4 April 2005.

14 Agency workers not otherwise mobile workers

(1) This regulation applies in any case where an individual ("the agency worker")—

(a) is supplied by a person ("the agent") to do the work of a mobile worker for another ("the principal") under a contract or other arrangements made between the agent and the principal; but

(b) is not, as respects that work, a worker, because of the absence of a worker's contract between the individual and the agent or the principal; and

(c) is not a party to a contract under which he undertakes to do the work for another party to the contract whose status is, by virtue of the contract, that of a client or customer or any profession or business undertaking carried on by the individual.

(2) In a case where this regulation applies, the other provisions of these Regulations shall have effect as if there were a contract for the doing of the work by the agency worker made between the agency worker and—

(a) whichever of the agent and the principal is responsible for paying the agency worker in respect of the work; or

(b) if neither the agent nor the principal is so responsible, whichever of them pays the agency worker in respect of the work,

(c) and as if that person were the agency worker's employer.

[3294N]

NOTES

Commencement: 4 April 2005.

[15 Individual carrying on trade or business

(1) This regulation applies to an individual who—

(a) for the purpose of a trade or business carried on by him, drives a vehicle described in paragraph (2) or (3) of regulation 3, and

(b) is neither—

(i) a self-employed driver, nor

(ii) an agency worker within the meaning of regulation 14.

(2) Where this regulation applies, these Regulations shall have effect as if—

(a) the individual were both a mobile worker and the employer of that mobile worker, and

(b) regulations 10, 11(a) and (e) and 12 were omitted.]

[3294O]

NOTES

Commencement: 11 April 2007.

Substituted by the Road Transport (Working Time) (Amendment) Regulations 2007, SI 2007/853, reg 2(1), (4), as from 11 April 2007.

16 Enforcement

(1) It shall be the duty of the Secretary of State to enforce the requirements of these Regulations.

(2) Schedule 2 shall apply in relation to the enforcement of the relevant requirements.

[3294P]

NOTES

Commencement: 4 April 2005.

17—(1) Any person who fails to comply with any of the relevant requirements shall be guilty of an offence.

(2) The provisions of paragraph (3) shall apply where an inspector is exercising or has exercised any power conferred by Schedule 2.

(3) It is an offence for a person—

- (a) to contravene any requirement imposed by an inspector under paragraph 2 of Schedule 2;
- (b) to prevent or attempt to prevent any other person from appearing before an inspector or from answering any question to which an inspector may by virtue of paragraph 2(2)(e) of Schedule 2 require an answer;
- (c) to contravene any requirement or prohibition imposed by an improvement notice or a prohibition notice referred to in paragraphs 3 and 4 of Schedule 2 (including any such notice as is modified on appeal);
- (d) intentionally to obstruct an inspector in the exercise or performance of his powers;
- (e) to use or disclose any information in contravention of paragraph 7 of Schedule 2;
- (f) to make a statement which he knows to be false or recklessly to make a statement which is false where the statement is made in purported compliance with a requirement to furnish any information imposed by or under these Regulations.

(4) Any person guilty of an offence under paragraph (1) shall be liable—

- (a) on summary conviction, to a fine not exceeding the statutory maximum;
- (b) on conviction on indictment, to a fine.

(5) A person guilty of an offence under paragraph (3)(b) or (d) shall be liable on summary conviction to a fine not exceeding level 5 on the standard scale.

(6) A person guilty of an offence under paragraph (3)(c) shall be liable—

- (a) on summary conviction, to imprisonment for a term not exceeding three months, or a fine not exceeding the statutory maximum;
- (b) on conviction on indictment, to imprisonment for a term not exceeding two years, or a fine or both.

(7) A person guilty of an offence under paragraph (3)(a), (e) or (f) shall be liable—

- (a) on summary conviction, to a fine not exceeding the statutory maximum;
- (b) on conviction on indictment—
  - (i) if the offence is under paragraph (3)(e), to imprisonment for a term not exceeding two years or a fine or both,
  - (ii) if the offence is under paragraph (3)(a) or (f), to a fine.

(8) The provisions set out in regulations 18 to 22 shall apply in relation to the offences provided for in paragraphs (1) and (3).

[3294Q]

NOTES

Commencement: 4 April 2005.

18 Offences due to fault of other person

Where the commission by any person of an offence is due to the act or default of some other person, that other person shall be guilty of the offence, and a person may be charged with the conviction of the offence by virtue of this regulation whether or not proceedings are taken against the first-mentioned person.

[3294R]

NOTES

Commencement: 4 April 2005.

19 Offences by bodies corporate

(1) Where an offence committed by a body corporate is proved to have been committed with the consent or connivance of, or to have been attributable to any neglect on the part of, any director, manager, secretary or other similar officer of the body corporate or a person who was purporting to act in any such capacity, he as well as the body corporate shall be guilty of that offence and shall be liable to be proceeded against and punished accordingly.

(2) Where the affairs of a body corporate are managed by its members, the preceding paragraph shall apply in relation to the acts and defaults of a member in connection with his functions of management as if he were a director of the body corporate.

[3294S]

NOTES

Commencement: 4 April 2005.

20 Restriction on institution of proceedings in England and Wales

Proceedings for an offence shall not be instituted in England or Wales except by an inspector or by, or with the consent of, the Director of Public Prosecutions.

[3294T]

NOTES

Commencement: 4 April 2005.

21 Prosecution by inspectors

(1) If authorised in that behalf by the Secretary of State an inspector may prosecute proceedings for an offence before a magistrates court even though the inspector is not of counsel or a solicitor.

(2) This regulation shall not apply in Scotland.

[3294U]

NOTES

Commencement: 4 April 2005.

22 Power of court to order cause of offence to be remedied

(1) This regulation applies where a person is convicted of an offence in respect of any matter which appears to the court to be a matter which it is in his power to remedy.

(2) In addition to or instead of imposing any punishment, the court may order the person in question to take such steps as may be specified in the order for remedying the said matters within such time as may be fixed by the order.

(3) The time fixed by an order under paragraph (2) may be extended or further extended by order of the court on an application made before the end of that time as originally fixed or as extended under this paragraph, as the case may be.

(4) Where a person is ordered under paragraph (2) to remedy any matters, that person shall not be liable under these Regulations in respect of that matter in so far as it continues during the time fixed by the order or any further time allowed under paragraph (3).

[3294V]

NOTES
Commencement: 4 April 2005.

SCHEDULES

SCHEDULE 1
WORKFORCE AGREEMENTS

Regulation 2

1. An agreement is a workforce agreement for the purposes of these Regulations if the following conditions are satisfied—
   (a) the agreement is in writing;
   (b) it has effect for a specified period not exceeding five years;
   (c) it applies either—
      (i) to all of the relevant members of the workforce, or
      (ii) to all of the relevant members of the workforce who belong to a particular group;
   (d) the agreement is signed—
      (i) in the case of an agreement of the kind referred to in sub-paragraph (c)(i), by the representatives of the workforce, and in the case of an agreement of the kind referred to in sub-paragraph (c)(ii), by the representatives of the group to which the agreement applies (excluding, in either case, any representative not a relevant member of the workforce on the date on which the agreement was first made available for signature), or
      (ii) if the employer employed 20 or fewer workers on the date referred to in sub-paragraph (d)(i), either by the appropriate representatives in accordance with that sub-paragraph or by the majority of the workers employed by him; and
   (e) before the agreement was made available for signature, the employer provided all the workers to whom it was intended to apply on the date on which it came into effect with copies of the text of the agreement and such guidance as those employees might reasonably require in order to understand it in full.

2. For the purposes of this Schedule—
   "a particular group" is a group of the relevant members of a workforce who undertake a particular function, work at a particular workplace or belong to a particular department or unit within their employer's business;
   "relevant members of the workforce" are all of the workers employed by a particular employer, excluding any worker whose terms and conditions of employment are provided for, wholly or in part, in a collective agreement;
   "representatives of the group" are workers duly elected to represent the members of a particular group;
   "representatives of the workforce" are workers duly elected to represent the relevant members of the workforce;
   and representatives are "duly elected" if the election at which they were elected satisfied the requirements of paragraph 3.

3. The requirements concerning elections referred to in paragraph 2 are that—
   (a) the number of representatives to be elected is determined by the employer;
   (b) the candidates for election as representatives of the workforce are relevant members of the workforce, and candidates for election as representatives of the group are members of the group;
   (c) no worker who is eligible to be a candidate is unreasonably excluded from standing for election;
   (d) all the relevant members of the workforce are entitled to vote for representatives of the workforce, and all the members of a particular group are entitled to vote for representatives of the group;
   (e) the workers entitled to vote may vote for as many candidates as there are representatives to be elected; and
   (f) the election is conducted so as to secure that—
      (i) so far as is reasonably practicable, those voting do so in secret, and
      (ii) the votes given at the election are fairly and accurately counted.

[3294W]

NOTES

Commencement: 4 April 2005.

SCHEDULE 2
ENFORCEMENT

Regulation 16(2)

1 Appointment of inspectors

(1) The Secretary of State may appoint as inspectors (under whatever title he may from time to time determine) such persons having suitable qualifications as he thinks necessary for carrying into effect these Regulations, and may terminate any appointment made under this paragraph.

(2) Every appointment of a person as an inspector under this paragraph shall be made by an instrument in writing specifying which of the powers conferred on inspectors by these Regulations are to be exercisable by the person appointed; and an inspector shall in right of his appointment under this paragraph be entitled to exercise only such of those powers as are so specified.

(3) So much of an inspector's instrument of appointment as specifies the powers which he is entitled to exercise may be varied by the Secretary of State.

(4) An inspector shall, if so required when exercising or seeking to exercise any power conferred on him by these Regulations, produce his instrument of appointment or a duly authenticated copy thereof.

2 Powers of inspectors

(1) Subject to the provisions of paragraph 1 and this paragraph, an inspector may for the purpose of carrying into effect these Regulations exercise the powers set out in sub-paragraph (2).

(2) The powers of an inspector are the following, namely—

(a) at any reasonable time (or in a situation which in his opinion may be dangerous, at any time) to enter any premises which he has reason to believe it is necessary for him to enter for the purposes mentioned in sub-paragraph (1);

(b) to take with him a constable if he has reasonable cause to apprehend any serious obstruction in the execution of his duty;

(c) without prejudice to paragraph (b), on entering any premises by virtue of paragraph (a) to take with him—

- (i) any other person duly authorised by the Secretary of State; and
- (ii) any equipment or material required for any purpose for which the power of entry is being exercised;

(d) to make such examination and investigation as may in any circumstances be necessary for the purpose mentioned in sub-paragraph (1);

(e) to require any person whom he has reasonable cause to believe to be able to give any information relevant to any examination or investigation under paragraph (d) to answer (in the absence of persons other than a person nominated by him to be present and any persons whom the inspector may allow to be present) such questions as the inspector thinks fit to ask and to sign a declaration of the truth of his answers;

(f) to require the production of, inspect, and take copies of, or of any entry in—

- (i) any records which by virtue of these Regulations are required to be kept, and
- (ii) any other books, records or documents which it is necessary for him to see for the purposes of any examination or investigation under paragraph (d);

(g) to require any person to afford him such facilities and assistance with respect to any matters or things within that person's control or in relation to which that person has responsibilities as are necessary to enable the inspector to exercise any of the powers conferred on him by this sub-paragraph;

(h) any other power which is necessary for the purpose mentioned in sub-paragraph (1).

(3) No answer given by a person in pursuance of a requirement imposed under sub-paragraph (2)(e) shall be admissible in evidence against that person or the husband or wife of that person in any proceedings.

(4) Nothing in this paragraph shall be taken to compel the production by any person of a document of which he would on grounds of legal professional privilege be entitled to withhold production on an order for discovery in an action in the High Court or, as the case may be, an order for the production of documents in an action in the Court of Session.

3 Improvement notices

If an inspector is of the opinion that a person—

(a) is contravening one or more of these Regulations; or

(b) has contravened one or more of these Regulations in circumstances that make it likely that the contravention will continue or be repeated,

he may serve on him a notice (in this Schedule referred to as "an improvement notice") stating that he is of that opinion, specifying the provision or provisions as to which he is of that opinion, giving particulars of the reasons why he is of that opinion, and requiring that person to remedy the contravention or, as the case may be, the matter occasioning it within such period (ending not earlier than the period within which an appeal against the notice can be brought under paragraph (6)) as may be specified in the notice.

4 Prohibition notices

(1) This paragraph applies to any activities which are being, or are likely to be, carried on by or under the control of any person, being activities to or in relation to which any of these Regulations apply or will, if the activities are so carried on, apply.

(2) If as regards any activities to which this paragraph applies an inspector is of the opinion that, as carried on by or under the control of the person in question, the activities involve or, as the case may be, will involve a risk of serious personal injury, the inspector may serve on that person a notice (in this Schedule referred to as "a prohibition notice").

(3) A prohibition notice shall—

(a) state that the inspector is of the said opinion;

(b) specify the matters which in his opinion give or, as the case may be, will give rise to the said risk;

(c) where in his opinion any of those matters involves or, as the case may be, will involve a contravention of any of these Regulations, state that he is of that opinion, specify the regulation or regulations as to which he is of that opinion, and give particulars of the reasons why he is of that opinion; and

(d) direct that the activities to which the notice relates shall not be carried on by or under the control of the person on whom the notice is served unless the matters specified in the notice in pursuance of paragraph (b) and any associated contraventions of provisions so specified in pursuance of paragraph (c) have been remedied.

(4) A direction contained in a prohibition notice in pursuance of sub-paragraph (3)(d) shall take effect—

(a) at the end of the period specified in the notice; or

(b) if the notice so declares, immediately.

5 Provisions supplementary to paragraphs 3 and 4

(1) In this paragraph "a notice" means an improvement notice or a prohibition notice.

(2) A notice may (but need not) include directions as to the measures to be taken to remedy any contravention or matter to which the notice relates; and any such directions—

(a) may be framed to any extent by reference to any approved code of practice; and

(b) may be framed so as to afford the person on whom the notice is served a choice between different ways of remedying the contravention or matter.

(3) Where an improvement notice or prohibition notice which is not to take immediate effect has been served—

(a) the notice may be withdrawn by an inspector at any time before the end of the period specified therein in pursuance of paragraph 3 or paragraph 4(4) as the case may be; and

(b) the period so specified may be extended or further extended by an inspector at any time when an appeal against the notice is not pending.

6 Appeal against improvement or prohibition notice

(1) In this paragraph "a notice" means an improvement or prohibition notice.

(2) A person on whom a notice is served may within 21 days from the date of its service appeal to an employment tribunal; and on such an appeal the tribunal may either cancel or affirm the notice and, if it affirms it, may do so either in its original form or with such modifications as the tribunal may in the circumstances think fit.

(3) Where an appeal under this paragraph is brought against a notice within the period allowed under the preceding sub-paragraph, then—

(a) in the case of an improvement notice, the bringing of the appeal shall have the effect of suspending the operation of the notice until the appeal is finally disposed of or, if the appeal is withdrawn, until the withdrawal of the appeal;

(b) in the case of a prohibition notice, the bringing of the appeal shall have the like effect if, but only if, on the application of the appellant the tribunal so directs (and then only from the giving of the direction).

(4) One or more assessors may be appointed for the purposes of any proceedings brought before an employment tribunal under this paragraph.

7 Restrictions on disclosure of information

(1) In this paragraph—

"relevant information" means information obtained by an inspector in pursuance of a requirement imposed under paragraph 2;

"relevant statutory provisions" means the provisions of Part 6 of the Transport Act 1968 and of any orders or regulations made under powers contained in that Part; and

"the recipient", in relation to any relevant information, means the person by whom that information was so obtained or to whom that information was so furnished, as the case may be.

(2) Subject to the following sub-paragraph, no relevant information shall be disclosed without the consent of the person by whom it was furnished.

(3) The preceding sub-paragraph shall not apply to—

(a) disclosure of information to a government department;

(b) without prejudice to paragraph (a), disclosure by the recipient of information to any person for the purpose of any function conferred on the recipient by or under any of the relevant statutory provisions or under these Regulations;

(c) without prejudice to paragraph (a), disclosure by the recipient of information to—

(i) an officer of a local authority who is authorised by that authority to receive it: or

(ii) a constable authorised by a chief officer of police to receive it; or

(d) disclosure by the recipient of information in a form calculated to prevent it from being identified as relating to a particular person or case.

(4) A person to whom information is disclosed in pursuance of sub-paragraph (3) shall not use the information for a purpose other than—

(a) in a case falling within sub-paragraph (3)(a), a purpose of a government department or local authority in connection with these Regulations or with the relevant statutory provisions, or any enactment whatsoever relating to working time;

(b) in the case of information given to a constable, the purposes of the police in connection with these Regulations, the relevant statutory provisions or any enactment relating to working time.

(5) A person shall not disclose any information obtained by him as a result of the exercise of any power conferred by paragraph 2 (including in particular any information with respect to any trade secret obtained by him in any premises entered by him by virtue of any such power) except—

(a) for the purposes of his functions; or

(b) for the purposes of any legal proceedings; or

(c) with the relevant consent.

In this sub-paragraph "the relevant consent" means, in the case of information furnished in pursuance of a requirement imposed under paragraph 2, the consent of the person who furnished it, and, in any other case, the consent of a person having responsibilities in relation to the premises where the information was obtained.

(6) Notwithstanding anything in sub-paragraph (5) an inspector shall, in circumstances in which it is necessary to do so for the purpose of assisting in keeping persons (or the

representatives of persons) adequately informed about matters affecting their health, safety and welfare or working time, give to such persons or their representatives the following descriptions of information, that is to say—

(a) factual information obtained by him as mentioned in that sub-paragraph which relates to their working environment; and

(b) information with respect to any action which he has taken or proposes to take in or in connection with the performance of his functions in relation to their working environment;

and, where an inspector does as aforesaid, he shall give the like information to the employer of the first-mentioned persons.

(7) Notwithstanding anything in sub-paragraph (5), a person who has obtained such information as is referred to in that sub-paragraph may furnish to a person who appears to him to be likely to be a party to any civil proceedings arising out of any accident, occurrence, situation or other matter, a written statement of the relevant facts observed by him in the course of exercising any of the powers referred to in that sub-paragraph.

[3294X]

NOTES

Commencement: 4 April 2005.

TRANSFER OF EMPLOYMENT (PENSION PROTECTION) REGULATIONS 2005

(SI 2005/649)

NOTES

Made: 10 March 2005.
Authority: Pensions Act 2004, ss 258(2)(c)(ii), (7), 315(2), 318(1).
Commencement: 6 April 2005.

1 Citation, commencement, application and interpretation

(1) These Regulations may be cited as the Transfer of Employment (Pension Protection) Regulations 2005 and shall come into force on 6th April 2005.

(2) These Regulations apply in the case of a person ("the employee") in relation to whom section 257 of the Act (conditions for pension protection) applies, that is to say a person who, in the circumstances described in subsection (1) of that section, ceases to be employed by the transferor of an undertaking or part of an undertaking and becomes employed by the transferee.

(3) In these Regulations "the Act" means the Pensions Act 2004.

[3295]

NOTES

Commencement: 6 April 2005.

2 Requirements concerning a transferee's pension scheme

(1) In a case where these Regulations apply, and the transferee is the employer in relation to a pension scheme which is not a money purchase scheme, that scheme complies with section 258(2)(c)(ii) of the Act (alternative standard for a scheme which is not a money purchase scheme) if it provides either—

(a) for members to be entitled to benefits the value of which equals or exceeds 6 per cent of pensionable pay for each year of employment together with the total amount of any contributions made by them, and, where members are required to make contributions to the scheme, for them to contribute at a rate which does not exceed 6 per cent of their pensionable pay; or

(b) for the transferee to make relevant contributions to the scheme on behalf of each employee of his who is an active member of it.

(2) In this regulation—

"pensionable pay" means that part of the remuneration payable to a member of a scheme by reference to which the amount of contributions and benefits are determined under the rules of the scheme.

[3296]

NOTES

Commencement: 6 April 2005.

3 Requirements concerning a transferee's pension contributions

(1) In a case where these Regulations apply, the transferee's pension contributions are relevant contributions for the purposes of section 258(2)(b) of the Act in the case of a money purchase scheme, section 258(3) to (5) of the Act in the case of a stakeholder pension scheme, and regulation 2(1)(b) above in the case of a scheme which is not a money purchase scheme, if—

(a) the contributions are made in respect of each period for which the employee is paid remuneration, provided that the employee also contributes to the scheme in respect of that period, and

(b) the amount contributed in respect of each such period is—

(i) in a case where the employee's contribution in respect of that period is less than 6 per cent of the remuneration paid to him, an amount at least equal to the amount of the employee's contribution;

(ii) in a case where the employee's contribution in respect of that period equals or exceeds 6 per cent of the remuneration paid to him, an amount at least equal to 6 per cent of that remuneration.

(2) In calculating the amount of an employee's remuneration for the purposes of paragraph (1)—

(a) only payments made in respect of basic pay shall be taken into account, and bonus, commission, overtime and similar payments shall be disregarded, and

(b) no account shall be taken of any deductions which are made in respect of tax, national insurance or pension contributions.

(3) In calculating the amount of a transferee's pension contributions for the purposes of paragraph (1) in the case of a scheme which is contracted-out by virtue of section 9 of the Pension Schemes Act 1993, minimum payments within the meaning of that Act shall be disregarded.

[3297]–[3319]

NOTES

Commencement: 6 April 2005.

OCCUPATIONAL PENSION SCHEMES (EQUAL TREATMENT) (AMENDMENT) REGULATIONS 2005

(SI 2005/1923)

NOTES

Made: 14 July 2005.

Authority: European Communities Act 1972, s 2(2); Pensions Act 1995, ss 63(5), 66(4), 124(1), 174(2), (3).

Commencement: 10 August 2005.

Part 3 (Equal Treatment Rule: Armed Forces Schemes (regs 7–11)) and Part 4 (Equality Clause: Service in Armed Forces (regs 12–15)) of these Regulations were reproduced in previous Editions of this work. They have been omitted from this Edition as they modify sections of the Equal Pay Act 1970 that are outside the scope of this work.

PART 1
GENERAL

1 Citation, commencement and interpretation

(1) These Regulations may be cited as the Occupational Pension Schemes (Equal Treatment) (Amendment) Regulations 2005.

(2) These Regulations shall come into force on 10th August 2005.

(3) In these Regulations—

"armed forces" means the naval, military or air forces of the Crown;

"armed forces scheme" means any occupational pension scheme—

(a) made under section 3 of the Naval and Marine Pay and Pensions Act 1865 (payment of naval and marine pay and pensions according to Order in Council),

(b) set out in the Army Pensions Warrant 1977,

(c) made under section 2 of the Air Force (Constitution) Act 1917 (government, discipline and pay of Air Force),

(d) made under sections 4 and 8 of the Reserve Forces Act 1996 (orders and regulations concerning the reserve forces), or

(e) made under section 1 of the Armed Forces (Pensions and Compensation) Act 2004 (pension and compensation schemes: armed and reserve forces);

"commencement date" means the date specified in paragraph (2);

"Equal Pay Act" means the Equal Pay Act 1970;

"equality clause" shall be construed in accordance with section 1(2) of the Equal Pay Act;

"occupational pension scheme" has the meaning given by section 1 of the Pension Schemes Act 1993 (categories of pension scheme);

"pension-related term of service" has the meaning given by regulation 12(2); and

"pensioner member" includes a person who is entitled to the present payment of pension or other benefits derived through a member.

[3320]

NOTES
Commencement: 10 August 2005.

PART 2
EQUAL TREATMENT: AMENDMENTS

2 Application of Part 2

(1) The modifications contained in amendments made by this Part of these Regulations apply to proceedings in respect of the terms of an occupational pension scheme if the proceedings are instituted on or after the commencement date (subject to paragraph (2)).

(2) Those modifications do not so apply if the last day on which the woman was employed in the employment to which the occupational pension scheme relates falls more than six months before the commencement date.

[3321]–[3337]

NOTES
Commencement: 10 August 2005.

3–6 (*Reg 3 amends the Pensions Act 1995, s 63 at* **[891]***; regs 4–6 amend the Occupational Pension Schemes* (*Equal Treatment*) *Regulations 1995, SI 1995/3183, reg 2 at* **[2306]***, and substitute regs 5, 7, 10 at* **[2309]**, **[2311]**, **[2314]**.)

EMPLOYMENT EQUALITY (SEX DISCRIMINATION) REGULATIONS 2005

(SI 2005/2467)

NOTES

Made: 5 September 2005.
Authority: European Communities Act 1972, s 2(2).
Commencement: 1 October 2005.

1 Citation, commencement, extent and interpretation

(1) These Regulations may be cited as the Employment Equality (Sex Discrimination) Regulations 2005 and shall come into force on 1st October 2005.

(2) These Regulations do not extend to Northern Ireland.

(3) The repeal made by regulation 20(2) does not extend to the Isle of Man or the Channel Islands.

(4) In these Regulations "the 1975 Act" means the Sex Discrimination Act 1975 and "the 1970 Act" means the Equal Pay Act 1970.

[3338]

NOTES

Commencement: 1 October 2005.

2 Transitional provisions

(1) The amendments made by regulations 28(3), 29(3), 30(3) and 31(2) do not apply in relation to proceedings where the act complained of took place before 1st October 2005.

(2) The amendment made to section 74 of the 1975 Act by regulation 32 shall not apply in the case of a question served on a respondent before 1st October 2005.

(3) In paragraph (2) "question" and "respondent" shall be construed in accordance with section 74 of the 1975 Act.

[3339]

NOTES

Commencement: 1 October 2005.
Note: the amendments referred to in para (1) are respectively to ss 63, 63A, 66 and 66A of the Sex Discrimination Act 1975.

3–36 (*Reg 3 amends the Sex Discrimination Act 1975, ss 1, 3 at* **[100]**, **[103]**; *regs 4, 5 insert ss 3A, 4A of the 1975 Act at* **[103A]**, **[104A]**; *regs 6, 7 amend ss 5, 6 of the 1975 Act at* **[105]**, **[106]**; *reg 8 inserts s 6A of the 1975 Act at* **[106A]**; *regs 9–11 amend ss 7B, 9, 10 of the 1975 Act at* **[109]**, **[111]**, **[112]**; *reg 12 amends the Sex Discrimination and Equal Pay (Offshore Employment) Order 1987, SI 1987/930, art 2; reg 13 inserts ss 10A, 10B of the 1975 Act at* **[112A]**, **[112B]**, *and repeals s 86 of that Act; reg 14 amends s 11 of the 1975 Act at* **[113]**, *and amends the Sex Discrimination Act 1986, s 2; regs 15–19 amend ss 12–16, 52A of the 1975 Act at* **[114]–[118]**, **[165]**; *reg 20 substitutes s 19 of the 1975 Act at* **[121]**, *repeals the Priests (Ordination of Women) Measure 1993, s 6, and revokes the Sex Discrimination (Gender Reassignment) Regulations 1999, SI 1999/1102, reg 5; regs 21, 22 amend ss 20A, 22, 26, 27 of the 1975 Act at* **[123]**, **[124]**, **[133]**, **[134]**; *reg 23 amends s 35 of the 1975 Act at* **[142]**, *and repeals s 28 of that Act, the Learning and Skills Act 2000, Sch 9, para 8, and the Education Reform Act 1988, Sch 12, para 75; regs 24–34 amend ss 35A–35C, 63, 63A, 66, 66A, 74, 82, 85 of the 1975 Act at* **[143]–[145]**, **[177]**, **[178]**, **[180]**, **[180A]**, **[188]**, **[196]**, **[199]** (*and amended ss 54, 56A, 59 (repealed)*) *regs 35, 36 amend the Equal pay Act 1970, s 1, 2, 6 at* **[5]**, **[6]**, **[11]** (*and s 7A outside the scope of this work*), *and insert s 1A of that Act at* **[5A]**).

DISABILITY DISCRIMINATION (QUESTIONS AND REPLIES) ORDER 2005 (NOTE)

(SI 2005/2703)

NOTES

This Order, which was reproduced in the fifteenth edition of this work, has been omitted for reasons of space. See also the Disability Discrimination (Questions and Replies) Order 2004, SI 2004/1168 (at **[3141]**) which is the relevant Order for claims and potential claims under Part 2 of the Disability Discrimination Act 1995.

[3340]–[3345]

DISABILITY DISCRIMINATION (PUBLIC AUTHORITIES) (STATUTORY DUTIES) REGULATIONS 2005

(SI 2005/2966)

NOTES

Made: 21 October 2005.

Authority: Disability Discrimination Act 1995, ss 49D(1), (2), 67(2), (3).

Commencement: 5 December 2005.

These Regulations apply to England and Wales and, to the extent that the functions of bodies to which they apply extend to Scotland, also to Scotland. The equivalent Regulations relating to Scotland (and applying to bodies accountable to the Scottish Parliament) are the Disability Discrimination (Public Authorities) (Statutory Duties) (Scotland) Regulations 2005, SSI 2005/565 at **[3356]**.

ARRANGEMENT OF REGULATIONS

SCHEDULES:

1 Citation, commencement and interpretation

(1) These Regulations may be cited as the Disability Discrimination (Public Authorities) (Statutory Duties) Regulations 2005 and shall come into force on 5th December 2005.

(2) In these Regulations—

"section 49A(1) duty", in relation to a public authority, means its duty under section 49A(1) of the Disability Discrimination Act 1995; and

"school" means a school maintained by a local education authority.

[3346]

NOTES

Commencement: 5 December 2005.

2 Preparation and publication of a Disability Equality Scheme

(1) A public authority listed in Schedule 1 shall, on or before the relevant publication date, publish a Disability Equality Scheme ("Scheme"), that is, a scheme showing how it intends to fulfil its section 49A(1) duty and its duties under these Regulations.

(2) Such an authority shall involve in the development of the Scheme disabled people who appear to that authority to have an interest in the way it carries out its functions.

(3) A Scheme shall include a statement of—

(a) the ways in which such disabled people have been involved in its development;

(b) that authority's methods for assessing the impact of its policies and practices, or the likely impact of its proposed policies and practices, on equality for disabled persons;

(c) the steps which that authority proposes to take towards the fulfilment of its section 49A(1) duty;

(d) that authority's arrangements for gathering information on the effect of its policies and practices on disabled persons and in particular its arrangements for gathering information on—

(i) their effect on the recruitment, development and retention of its disabled employees,

(ii) their effect, in the case of an authority specified in Part II, III or IV of Schedule 1, on the educational opportunities available to, and on the achievements of, disabled pupils and students, and

(iii) the extent to which, in the case of an authority specified in [Part I, V or VI of Schedule 1], the services it provides and those other functions it performs take account of the needs of disabled persons; and

(e) that authority's arrangements for making use of such information to assist it in the performance of its section 49A(1) duty and, in particular, its arrangements for—

(i) reviewing on a regular basis the effectiveness of the steps referred to in sub-paragraph (c), and

(ii) preparing subsequent Schemes.

(4) Such an authority shall review its Scheme and publish a revised Scheme—

(a) not later than the end of the period of three years beginning with the date of publication of its first Scheme; and

(b) subsequently at intervals of not more than three years beginning with the date of publication of the last revision of the Scheme.

(5) Such an authority may comply with the duty to publish under paragraph (1) or (4) by setting out its Scheme as part of another published document or within a number of other published documents.

(6) [Subject to paragraphs (7) to (9),] in this regulation, "the relevant publication date" means—

(a) in the case of a public authority listed in Part I or II of Schedule 1, 4th December 2006;

(b) in the case of a public authority listed in Part III of Schedule 1, 3rd December 2007;

(c) in the case of a public authority listed in Part IV of Schedule 1, 1st April 2007;

[(d) in the case of a public authority listed in Part V of Schedule 1, 3rd December 2007];

[(e) in the case of a public authority listed in Part VI of Schedule 1, 1st December 2008].

[(7) In the case of a public authority listed in Parts I or II of Schedule 1 which was established on or after 4th December 2006 and before 3rd December 2007, the relevant publication date is 1st December 2008.

(8) In the case of a public authority listed in Parts I or II of Schedule 1 which is established on or after 3rd December 2007, the relevant publication date is the date falling twelve months after its establishment.

(9) In the case of a public authority listed in Parts III to V of Schedule 1 which is established on or after the relevant publication date which would have applied to it had the public authority been established before that date, the relevant publication date is the date falling twelve months after the establishment of the public authority.]

[3347]

NOTES

Commencement: 5 December 2005.

Para (3): words in square brackets in sub-para (d)(iii) substituted by the Disability Discrimination (Public Authorities) (Statutory Duties) (Amendment) Regulations 2008, SI 2008/641, reg 2(a), as from 6 April 2008.

Para (6): words in first pair of square brackets inserted, and sub-para (e) added by SI 2008/641, reg 2(b), (c), as from 6 April 2008; sub-para (d) added by the Disability Discrimination (Public Authorities) (Statutory Duties) (Amendment) Regulations 2007, SI 2007/618, reg 2(b), as from 6 April 2007.

Paras (7)–(9): added by SI 2008/641, reg 2(d), as from 6 April 2008.

Modification: see the Equality Act 2006 (Dissolution of Commissions and Consequential and Transitional Provisions) Order 2007, SI 2007/2602, art 4 (at **[3473N]**) which provides that the Schedule to that Order has effect for the amendment and modification of subordinate legislation in consequence of the dissolution of the Commission for Racial Equality, the Disability Rights Commission and the Equal Opportunities Commission and the establishment of the Commission for Equality and Human Rights. Para 9 of the Schedule to that Order (as substituted by SI 2007/3555) provides as follows—

"In the application of the Disability Discrimination (Public Authorities) (Statutory Duties) Regulations 2005 to the Commission, regulation 2(6) shall have effect as if, after paragraph (d), there were inserted—

"(e) in the case of the Commission for Equality and Human Rights, 1st April 2008."".

3 Implementation of the Disability Equality Scheme

(1) A public authority listed in Schedule 1 shall within the period of three years beginning with the date when a Scheme prepared for the purposes of regulation 2 is published—

(a) take the steps which it has been required to set out in the Scheme by virtue of regulation 2(3)(c); and

(b) put into effect its arrangements, which it has been required to set out in the Scheme by virtue of regulations 2(3)(d) and (e), for—

(i) gathering information, and

(ii) making use of such information.

(2) Nothing in this regulation imposes any duty on an authority where, in all the circumstances, it would be unreasonable or impracticable for it to perform the duty.

[3348]

NOTES

Commencement: 5 December 2005.

4 Annual reporting

(1) A public authority listed in Schedule 1 shall publish a report—

(a) not later than the end of the period of one year beginning with the date of publication of its first Scheme; and

(b) subsequently at intervals of not more than one year beginning with the date of publication of the last report.

(2) The report shall contain a summary of—

(a) the steps the authority has taken for the purposes of regulation 3(1)(a);

(b) the results of the information-gathering it has carried out for the purposes of regulation 3(1)(b)(i); and

(c) the use it has made of such information it has gathered for the purposes of regulation 3(1)(b)(ii).

(3) Such an authority may comply with the duty to publish under paragraph (1) by setting out its report within another published document.

[3349]

NOTES

Commencement: 5 December 2005.

5 Duty on public authorities listed in Schedule 2

(1) A reporting authority shall, in respect of its policy sector, publish a report—

(a) not later than 1st December 2008; and
(b) subsequently not later than the end of each successive period of three years beginning with 1st December 2008.

(2) The report shall—
(a) give an overview of progress towards equality of opportunity between disabled persons and other persons made by public authorities operating in the policy sector; and
(b) set out the reporting authority's proposals for the coordination of action by public authorities operating in that sector so as to bring about further progress towards equality of opportunity between disabled persons and other persons.

(3) In paragraph (1)—
"reporting authority" means a person specified in Schedule 2;
"policy sector" means the sector of public activity in which the reporting authority carries out public functions.

[3350]

NOTES
Commencement: 5 December 2005.

SCHEDULES

SCHEDULE 1

Regulation 2

PART I

...

The Advisory, Conciliation and Arbitration Service

Any of the naval, military or air forces of the Crown (except in relation to employment in the armed forces)

The Arts Council of England

The Arts Council of Wales

The Audit Commission for Local Authorities and the National Health Service in England and Wales

The Arts and Humanities Research Council

An Assembly subsidiary as defined by section 99(4) of the Government of Wales Act 1998

The Big Lottery Fund

The Biotechnology & Biological Sciences Research Council

A body corporate established pursuant to an order under section 67 of the Local Government Act 1985 (transfer of functions to successors of residuary bodies, etc)

The British Broadcasting Corporation, in respect of its public functions

The British Council

The British Educational Communications and Technology Agency (BECTA)

The British Library

The British Museum

...

The British Transport Police

The British Waterways Board

...

The Channel Four Television Corporation, in respect of its public functions

The Chief Constable for the Ministry of Defence Police appointed by the Secretary of State under section 1(3) of the Ministry of Defence Police Act 1987

A chief constable of a police force maintained under section 2 of the Police Act 1996

The Children and Family Court Advisory and Support Service

The Children's Commissioner for Wales

[The Commission for Equality and Human Rights]

The Commission for Healthcare Audit and Inspection

The Commission for Patient and Public Involvement in Health

…

The Commission for Social Care Inspection

The Commissioner of Police for the City of London

The Commissioner of Police of the Metropolis

The Common Council of the City of London, in its capacity as a local authority or port health authority

The Common Council of the City of London, in its capacity as a police authority

In England, a county council, a London borough council or a district council

In Wales, a county council or a county borough council

The Council of the Isles of Scilly

…

The Countryside Council for Wales

The Criminal Injuries Compensation Authority

…

…

The Economic & Social Research Council

The Electoral Commission

English Heritage

English Nature

English Partnerships

The Engineering & Physical Sciences Research Council

The Environment Agency

…

Estyn

The Financial Services Authority

A fire authority constituted by a combination scheme under section 5 or 6 of the Fire Services Act 1947

The General Dental Council

The General Medical Council

The General Social Care Council

The General Teaching Council for England

The Greater London Authority

A Health Authority established under section 8 of the National Health Service Act 1977

…

The Health and Safety Executive

The Heritage Lottery Fund

The Higher Education Funding Council for England

The Higher Education Funding Council for Wales

The Historic Royal Palaces Trust

The Horniman Museum

A housing action trust established under Part 3 of the Housing Act 1988

The Housing Corporation

The Human Fertilisation and Embryology Authority

The Imperial War Museum

The Independent Police Complaints Commission

[the Independent Regulator of NHS Foundation Trusts]

The Independent Review Service

The Information Commissioner

A joint authority established under Part 4 of the Local Government Act 1985 (police, fire services, civil defence and transport)

A joint authority established under section 21 of the Local Government Act 1992

The Law Society of England and Wales

The Learning and Skills Council for England

The Legal Services Commission

A Local Health Board established under section 16BA of the National Health Service Act 1977

A local probation board established under section 4 of the Criminal Justice and Court Services Act 2000

The London Development Agency

The London Fire and Emergency Planning Authority

The Medical Research Council

The Metropolitan Police Authority established under section 5B of the Police Act 1996

A Minister of the Crown or government department

The Museum of London

The Museum of Science and Industry in Manchester

The Museums, Libraries and Archives Council

The National Assembly for Wales

The National Audit Office

The National College for School Leadership

The National Consumer Council

The National Forest Company

The National Gallery

A National Health Service trust established under section 5 of the National Health Service and Community Care Act 1990

The National Library of Wales

The National Lottery Commission

The National Maritime Museum

The National Museum for Science and Industry

A National Park Authority established by an order under s 63 of the Environment Act 1995

PART 2

[The National Policing Improvement Agency]

The National Portrait Gallery

The Natural Environment Research Council

The Natural History Museum

The Nursing and Midwifery Council

Ofcom

…

A Passenger Transport Executive for a passenger transport area in England and Wales within the meaning of Part 2 of the Transport Act 1968

A police authority established under section 3 of the Police Act 1996

A primary care trust established under section 16A of the National Health Service Act 1977

The Qualifications and Curriculum Authority (QCA)

A regional development agency established under the Regional Development Agencies Act 1998 (other than the London Development Agency)

Remploy Limited

…

[The Science and Technology Facilities Council]

The Science Museum

The Scottish Parliamentary Corporate Body

The Security Industry Authority

[The Serious Organised Crime Agency]

Sianel Pedwar Cymru (Welsh Fourth Channel Authority), in respect of its public functions

Sir John Soanes's Museum

The Social Fund Commissioner of the Independent Review Service

A special health authority established under section 11 of the National Health Service Act 1977

The Sports Council for Wales

Sport England

The Standards Board for England

A Strategic Health Authority established under section 8 of the National Health Service Act 1977

Student Loans Company Ltd

The Sub-Treasurer of the Inner Temple or the Under-Treasurer of the Middle Temple, in his capacity as a local authority

The Tate Gallery

The Training and Development Agency for Schools

Transport for London

UK Film Council

UK Sport

The UK Sports Council

The Victoria and Albert Museum

[Visit Britain]

The Wallace Collection

[3351]

NOTES

Commencement: 5 December 2005.

Entry "The Adult Learning Inspectorate" (omitted) revoked by the Disability Discrimination (Public Authorities) (Statutory Duties) (Amendment) Regulations 2008, SI 2008/641, reg 3(1)(d), as from 6 April 2008.

Entry "The British Tourist Authority" (omitted) revoked by SI 2008/641, reg 3(1)(a), as from 6 April 2008.

Entry "The Central Police Training and Development Authority (CENTREX)" (omitted) revoked by SI 2008/641, reg 3(1)(b), as from 6 April 2008.

Entry "The Commission for Equality and Human Rights" inserted by the Equality Act 2006 (Dissolution of Commissions and Consequential and Transitional Provisions) Order 2007, SI 2007/2602, art 4(1), Schedule, para 10(b), as from 1 October 2007.

Entry "The Commission for Patient and Public Involvement in Health" revoked by the Local Government and Public Involvement in Health Act 2007 Consequential Provisions Order 2008, SI 2008/526, art 3, as from 30 June 2008.

Entry "The Commission for Racial Equality" (omitted) revoked by SI 2007/2602, art 4(1), Schedule, para 10(a)(i), as from 1 October 2007.

Entry "The Council for the Central Laboratory of the Research Councils" (omitted) revoked by SI 2008/641, reg 3(1)(c), as from 6 April 2008.

Entry "The Director-General of the National Crime Squad" (omitted) revoked by the Serious Organised Crime and Police Act 2005 (Consequential and Supplementary Amendments to Secondary Legislation) Order 2006, SI 2006/594, art 2, Schedule, para 47(a), as from 1 April 2006.

Entry "The Disability Rights Commission" (omitted) revoked by SI 2007/2602, art 4(1), Schedule, para 10(a)(ii), as from 1 October 2007.

Entry "The Equal Opportunities Commission" (omitted) revoked by SI 2007/2602, art 4(1), Schedule, para 10(a)(iii), as from 1 October 2007.

Entry "The Health and Safety Commission" (omitted) revoked by the Legislative Reform (Health and Safety Executive) Order 2008, SI 2008/960, art 22, Sch 3, as from 1 April 2008 (see further the note 'The Health and Safety Executive' at **[2038]**).

Entry "the Independent Regulator of NHS Foundation Trusts" substituted by the Disability Discrimination (Public Authorities) (Statutory Duties) (Amendment) Regulations 2007, SI 2007/618, reg 3(a), as from 6 April 2007.

Entry "The National Policing Improvement Agency" inserted by SI 2008/641, reg 3(1)(b), as from 6 April 2008.

Entry "The Particle Physics & Astronomy Research Council" (omitted) revoked by SI 2008/641, reg 3(1)(c), as from 6 April 2008.

Entry "Royal Mail Group" (omitted) revoked by SI 2007/618, reg 3(b), as from 6 April 2007.

Entry "The Science and Technology Facilities Council" inserted by SI 2008/641, reg 3(1)(c), as from 6 April 2008.

Entry "The Serious Organised Crime Agency" substituted for original entries relating to "the Service Authority for the National Crime Squad" and "the National Criminal Intelligence Service", by SI 2006/594, art 2, Schedule, para 47, as from 1 April 2006.

Entry "Visit Britain" inserted by SI 2008/641, reg 3(1)(a), as from 6 April 2008.

Note also that the reference to the Audit Commission for Local Authorities and the National Health Service in England and Wales is to be construed as a reference to the Audit Commission for Local Authorities and the National Health Service in England (as from 1 April 2008); see the Local Government and Public Involvement in Health Act 2007, s 146(4).

PART II

The governing body of a secondary school, in England, within the meaning of section 5(2) of the Education Act 1996, and any such school as may be determined by the Secretary of State to be treated as a secondary school under section 5(4) of that Act

The proprietor of a City Technology College, City College for Technology of the Arts, or an Academy

The governing body of an institution within the further education sector within the meaning of section 91(3) of the Further and Higher Education Act 1992

The governing body of an institution within the higher education sector within the meaning of section 91(5) of the Further and Higher Education Act 1992

A local education authority

[3352]

NOTES

Commencement: 5 December 2005.

PART III

The governing body of a primary school, in England, within the meaning of section 5(1) of the Education Act 1996, and any such school as may be determined by the Secretary of State to be treated as a primary school under section 5(4) of that Act

The governing body of a community special school or a foundation special school, in England, within the meaning of section 20 of the School Standards and Framework Act 1998

A local authority with respect to the pupil referral units it establishes and maintains, by virtue of section 19 of the Education Act 1996

[3353]

NOTES

Commencement: 5 December 2005.

PART IV

The governing body of an educational establishment maintained by a local education authority, in Wales

[3354]

NOTES

Commencement: 5 December 2005.

[PART V
(AUTHORITIES ADDED ON 6TH APRIL 2007)

Archwilydd Cyffredinol Cymru (The Auditor General for Wales)

The Board of the Pension Protection Fund

The Board of Trustees of the Armouries

The British Transport Police Authority

Bwrdd yr Iaith Gymraeg (The Welsh Language Board)

The Children's Commissioner for England [and 11 MILLION]

The Construction Industry Training Board

The Council for Healthcare Regulatory Excellence

Cyngor Addysgu Cyffredinol Cymru (The General Teaching Council for Wales)

The Gambling Commission

The General Chiropractic Council

The General Council of the Bar

The General Optical Council

The Health Protection Agency

The Judicial Appointments Commission

The Judicial Studies Board

The London Organising Committee of the Olympic Games and Paralympic Games

An NHS foundation trust

The National Museums and Galleries on Merseyside

The Olympic Delivery Authority

Passenger Focus (the operating name of the Rail Passengers' Council established under the Railways Act 2005)

The Pensions Ombudsman

The Pensions Regulator

The Postgraduate Medical Education and Training Board

The Quality Improvement Agency

The Sector Skills Development Agency

University for Industry

The Youth Justice Board for England and Wales.]

[3354A]

NOTES

Commencement: 6 April 2007.

Inserted by the Disability Discrimination (Public Authorities) (Statutory Duties) (Amendment) Regulations 2007, SI 2007/618, reg 4, as from 6 April 2007.

Words in square brackets in the entry "The Children's Commissioner for England" inserted by the Disability Discrimination (Public Authorities) (Statutory Duties) (Amendment) Regulations 2008, SI 2008/641, reg 3(2), as from 6 April 2008.

[PART VI
(AUTHORITIES ADDED ON 6TH APRIL 2008)

Amgueddfa Genedlaethol Cymru (The National Museum of Wales)

The Appointments Commission

The Bank of England

The Civil Aviation Authority

The Commission for Architecture and the Built Environment (CABE)

The Community Development Foundation

The Competition Commission

The Consumer Council for Water

The Council for Licensed Conveyancers

The Criminal Cases Review Commission

Cyngor Gofal Cymru (The Care Council for Wales)

The Design Council

The Engineering Construction Industry Training Board (ECITB)

The General Osteopathic Council

The Independent Living Funds

The Institute of Legal Executives

Investors in People UK

The National Army Museum

The National Endowment for Science, Technology and the Arts (NESTA)

The Nuclear Decommissioning Authority

The Office of the Immigration Services Commissioner

The Parole Board

Partnerships for Schools

The Personal Accounts Delivery Authority

The Royal Air Force Museum

Royal Botanic Gardens, Kew

The United Kingdom Atomic Energy Authority

The Valuation Tribunal Service.]

[3354B]

NOTES

Commencement: 6 April 2008.

Inserted by the Disability Discrimination (Public Authorities) (Statutory Duties) (Amendment) Regulations 2008, SI 2008/641, reg 4, as from 6 April 2008.

SCHEDULE 2

Regulation 5

The National Assembly for Wales

...

[The Secretary of State for Business, Enterprise and Regulatory Reform]

[The Secretary of State for Children, Schools and Families]

[The Secretary of State for Communities and Local Government]

...

The Secretary of State for Culture, Media and Sport

...

The Secretary of State for Environment, Food and Rural Affairs

The Secretary of State for Health

The Secretary of State for the Home Department

[The Secretary of State for Innovation, Universities and Skills]

[The Secretary of State for Justice]

The Secretary of State for Trade and Industry

The Secretary of State for Transport

The Secretary of State for Work and Pensions

[3355]

NOTES

Commencement: 5 December 2005.

Entry "The First Secretary of State" (omitted) revoked, and entry "The Secretary of State for Communities and Local Government" inserted, by the Secretary of State for Communities and Local Government Order 2006, SI 2006/1926, art 9, Schedule, para 9, as from 21 August 2006.

Entries "The Secretary of State for Business, Enterprise and Regulatory Reform", "The Secretary of State for Children, Schools and Families", and "The Secretary of State for Innovation, Universities and Skills" inserted, and entries "The Secretary of State for Education and Skills" and "The Secretary of State for Trade and Industry" (omitted) revoked, by the Secretaries of State for Children, Schools and Families, for Innovation, Universities and Skills and for Business, Enterprise and Regulatory Reform Order 2007, SI 2007/3224, art 15, Schedule, Pt 2, para 57, as from 12 December 2007.

Entry "The Secretary of State for Constitutional Affairs" (omitted) revoked, and entry "The Secretary of State for Justice" inserted, by the Secretary of State for Justice Order 2007, SI 2007/2128, art 8, Schedule, Pt 2, para 22, as from 22 August 2007.

DISABILITY DISCRIMINATION (PUBLIC AUTHORITIES) (STATUTORY DUTIES) (SCOTLAND) REGULATIONS 2005

(SSI 2005/565)

NOTES

Made: 9 November 2005.

Authority: Disability Discrimination Act 1995, s 49D(3), (4).

Commencement: 5 December 2005.

These Regulations apply to the bodies listed in the Schedule which are within the jurisdiction of the Scottish Parliament. The equivalent Regulations for other bodies are the Disability Discrimination (Public Authorities) (Statutory Duties) Regulations 2005, SI 2005/2966 at **[3346]**.

ARRANGEMENT OF REGULATIONS

SCHEDULES:

1 Citation, commencement and interpretation

(1) These Regulations may be cited as the Disability Discrimination (Public Authorities) (Statutory Duties) (Scotland) Regulations 2005 and shall come into force on 5th December 2005.

(2) In these Regulations—

"section 49A(1) duty", in relation to a public authority, means its duty under section 49A(1) of the Disability Discrimination Act 1995;

"school" has the meaning given by section 135 of the Education (Scotland) Act 1980 but excluding independent schools and in addition includes a place, other than a school, at which an education authority provides school education for pupils who are under school age, other than such a place at which school education is being provided by a person with whom that authority has, by virtue of section 35 of the Standards in Scotland's Schools etc Act 2000, entered into arrangements for the provision of that education; where "independent school", "school education", "pupil" and "school age" have the meanings given by section 135 of the Education (Scotland) Act 1980.

[3356]

NOTES

Commencement: 5 December 2005.

2 Preparation and Publication of a Disability Equality Scheme

(1) A public authority specified in Parts I to III of the Schedule to these Regulations shall, on or before the relevant publication date, publish a Disability Equality Scheme ("Scheme"), that is, a scheme showing how it intends to fulfil its section 49A(1) duty and its duties under these Regulations.

(2) Such an authority shall involve in the development of the Scheme those disabled persons who appear to that authority to have an interest in the way it carries out its functions.

(3) The Scheme shall include a statement of—

(a) the ways in which such disabled persons have been involved in its development;

(b) that authority's methods for assessing the impact of its policies and practices, or the likely impact of its proposed policies and practices, on equality for disabled persons;

(c) the steps which that authority proposes to take towards the fulfilment of its section 49A(1) duty;

(d) that authority's arrangements for gathering information on the effect of its policies and practices on disabled persons and in particular its arrangements for gathering information on—

PART 2

(i) their effect on the recruitment, development and retention of its disabled employees,
(ii) their effect, in the case of an authority specified in Parts II or III of the Schedule, on the educational opportunities available to, and on the achievements of, disabled pupils and students; and
(iii) the extent to which, in the case of an authority other than one specified in Parts II or III of the Schedule, the services it provides and those other functions it performs take account of the needs of disabled persons; and

(e) that authority's arrangements for making use of such information to assist it in the performance of its section 49A(1) duty and, in particular, its arrangements for—
(i) reviewing on a regular basis the effectiveness of the steps referred to in sub paragraph (c), and
(ii) preparing subsequent Schemes.

(4) Such an authority shall review its Scheme and publish a revised Scheme—

(a) no later than the end of the period of three years beginning with the date of publication of its first Scheme; and

(b) subsequently at intervals of not more than three years beginning with the date of publication of the last revision of the Scheme.

(5) Such an authority may comply with the duty to publish under paragraph (1) or (4) by setting out its Scheme as part of another published document or within a number of other published documents.

(6) In this regulation, "the relevant publication date" means 4th December 2006.

[3357]

NOTES

Commencement: 5 December 2005.

Relevant publication date: in the case of the authorities inserted in Part I of Schedule 1 to these Regulations by the Disability Discrimination (Public Authorities) (Statutory Duties) (Scotland) Amendment Regulations 2007, SSI 2007/195, reg 2, "the relevant publication date" is to be read as a reference to 3 December 2007; see reg 3 of the 2007 Regulations.

3 Education bodies or persons

It shall be the duty of a body or person specified in Part II of the Schedule to make arrangements for each school under its management to—

(a) assess the impact of its policies and practices, or the likely impact of its proposed policies and practices, on equality for disabled pupils;

(b) gather information on the effects of its policies and practices and the educational opportunities available to, and on the achievements of, disabled pupils;

(c) provide such a body or person with an annual report in respect of the matters contained in paragraphs (a) and (b);

(d) carry out such steps which that body or person proposes to take towards the fulfilment of its section 49A(1) duty; and

(e) maintain a copy of the Scheme.

[3358]

NOTES

Commencement: 5 December 2005.

4 Implementation of the Disability Equality Scheme

(1) A public authority specified in Parts I to III of the Schedule shall within the period of three years beginning with the date when a Scheme prepared for the purposes of regulation 2 is published—

(a) take the steps which it is required to as set out in the Scheme by virtue of regulation 2(3)(c);

(b) put into effect its arrangements, which it has been required to set out in the Scheme by virtue of regulations 2(3)(d) and (e), for—
(i) gathering information, and
(ii) making use of such information.

(2) Nothing in this regulation imposes any duty on an authority where, in all the circumstances of the case, it would be unreasonable and impracticable for it to perform the duty.

[3359]

NOTES

Commencement: 5 December 2005.

5 Annual Reporting

(1) A public authority specified in Parts I to III of the Schedule shall publish a report—

(a) not later than the end of the period of one year beginning with the date of publication of its first Scheme: and

(b) subsequently at intervals of not more than one year beginning with the date of publication of the last report.

(2) The report shall contain a summary of—

(a) the steps it has taken for the purposes of regulation 4(1)(a);

(b) the results of the information-gathering it has carried out for the purposes of regulation 4(1)(b)(i); and

(c) the use it has made of the information it has gathered for the purposes of regulation 4(1)(b)(ii).

(3) Such an authority may comply with the duty to publish under paragraph (1) by setting out its report within another published document.

[3360]

NOTES

Commencement: 5 December 2005.

6 Duty on Scottish Ministers

(1) The Scottish Ministers shall publish reports—

(a) not later than 1st December 2008; and

(b) subsequently not later than the end of each successive period of three years beginning with 1st December 2008.

(2) The reports shall—

(a) give an overview of progress towards equality of opportunity between disabled persons and other persons made by public authorities; and

(b) set out the Scottish Ministers proposals for the coordination of action by public authorities so as to bring about further progress towards equality of opportunity between disabled persons and other persons.

[3361]

NOTES

Commencement: 5 December 2005.

SCHEDULE 1

PART I

The Accounts Commission for Scotland

Audit Scotland

Bord na Gaidhlig (Alba)

[the British Waterways Board in respect of its Scottish functions]

The Cairngorms National Park Authority established under section 6 of the National Parks (Scotland) Act 2000

[A Chief Officer of a relevant authority appointed under section 7 of the Fire (Scotland) Act 2005]

[The Commissioner for Children and Young People in Scotland]

[The Construction Industry Training Board in respect of its Scottish functions]

The Criminal Injuries Compensation Authority in respect of its Scottish functions

A Chief Constable of a police force maintained under s 1 of the Police (Scotland) Act 1967

NHS National Services Scotland

A council constituted under section 2 of the Local Government etc (Scotland) Act 1994

A Health Board constituted under section 2 of the National Health Service (Scotland) Act 1978

A joint board within the meaning of section 235(1) of the Local Government (Scotland) Act 1973

A joint fire and rescue board constituted by a scheme under section 2(1) of the Fire (Scotland) Act 2005

The Keeper of the Records of Scotland

The Keeper of the Registers of Scotland

The Law Society of Scotland, in respect of its public functions

[Learning and Teaching Scotland]

The Loch Lomond and the Trossachs National Park Authority established under section 6 of the National Parks (Scotland) Act 2000

A licensing board constituted under section 1 of the Licensing (Scotland) Act 1976

[The Mental Welfare Commission for Scotland]

The Board of Trustees for the National Galleries of Scotland established under section 3 of the National Galleries of Scotland Act 1906

The Trustees of the National Library of Scotland, constituted under section 1 of the National Library of Scotland Act 1925

The Board of Trustees of the National Museums of Scotland established by the National Heritage (Scotland) Act 1985

A Passenger Transport Executive within the meaning of Part II of the Transport Act 1968 for a passenger transport area within Scotland

A police authority established under section 2 of the Police (Scotland) Act 1967

The Registrar General of Births, Deaths and Marriages for Scotland

The Scottish Arts Council

Scottish Natural Heritage

Scottish Screen

Sportscotland

Scottish Water

The Scottish Commission for the Regulation of Care

Scottish Enterprise and Highlands and Islands Enterprise established under the Enterprise and New Towns (Scotland) Act 1990

The Scottish Further and Higher Education Funding Council

The Scottish Legal Aid Board

The Scottish Ministers

…

The Scottish Qualifications Authority

The Scottish Social Services Council

A Special Health Board constituted under section 2 of the National Health Service (Scotland) Act 1978

[A Transport Partnership created by an order under section 1(1) of the Transport (Scotland) Act 2005]

Visitscotland

[3362]

NOTES

Commencement: 5 December 2005.

Entries "the British Waterways Board in respect of its Scottish functions", "A Chief Officer of a relevant authority appointed under section 7 of the Fire (Scotland) Act 2005", "The Commissioner for Children and Young People in Scotland", "The Construction Industry Training Board in respect of its Scottish functions", "Learning and Teaching Scotland", "The Mental Welfare Commission for Scotland", and "A Transport Partnership created by an order under section 1(1) of the Transport (Scotland) Act 2005" inserted by the Disability Discrimination (Public Authorities) (Statutory Duties) (Scotland) Amendment Regulations 2007, SSI 2007/195, reg 2, as from 1 April 2007.

Entry "The Service Authority for the National Criminal Intelligence Service in respect of its Scottish functions" revoked by the Serious Organised Crime and Police Act 2005 (Consequential and Supplementary Amendments) (Scotland) Order 2006, SSI 2006/129, art 2, Schedule, para 10, as from 1 April 2006.

PART II

Education authorities

The managers of a grant-aided school (within the meaning of section 135 of the Education (Scotland) Act 1980)

[3363]

NOTES

Commencement: 5 December 2005.

PART III

Fundable Bodies as defined in Schedule 2 of the Further and Higher Education (Scotland) Act 2005

The managers of a central institution (within the meaning of section 135 of the Education (Scotland) Act 1980)

[3364]–[3369]

NOTES

Commencement: 5 December 2005.

(*Note: there is no Schedule 2 to these Regulations.*)

PROHIBITION OF SMOKING IN CERTAIN PREMISES (SCOTLAND) REGULATIONS 2006

(SSI 2006/90)

NOTES

Made: 28 February 2006.

Authority: Smoking, Health and Social Care (Scotland) Act 2005, ss 3(3), 4(2), 4(3), 4(6), 4(7), 40(1)(b), Sch 1, paras 2, 4(1), 5(2), 12.

Commencement: 26 March 2006 (at 0600 hours).

ARRANGEMENT OF REGULATIONS

SCHEDULES:

1 Citation, interpretation and commencement

(1) These Regulations may be cited as the Prohibition of Smoking in Certain Premises (Scotland) Regulations 2006.

(2) In these Regulations—

"the Act" means the Smoking, Health and Social Care (Scotland) Act 2005;

"adult" means a person aged 16 years or over;

"adult care home" means an establishment providing a care home service exclusively for adults;

"adult hospice" means a hospice providing care exclusively for adults;

"bar" means any premises exclusively or mainly used for the sale and consumption of beverages, whether alcoholic or not;

"car" means a mechanically propelled road vehicle which is not—

(a) a goods vehicle;
(b) a motor cycle; or
(c) a vehicle of a type not commonly used as a private vehicle and unsuitable to be so used;

"care home service" means a care home service within the meaning of section 2(3) of the Regulation of Care (Scotland) Act 2001;

"club premises" means any premises which are used by and for the purposes of a club or other unincorporated association, whether for profit or not;

"council" means a council constituted under section 2 of the Local Government etc (Scotland) Act 1994;

"designated hotel bedroom" means a room in a hotel which—

(a) is set apart exclusively for the sleeping accommodation of travellers;
(b) has been designated by the person having the management or control of the hotel as being a room in which smoking is permitted;
(c) has a ceiling and, except for doors and windows, is completely enclosed on all sides by solid floor to ceiling walls;
(d) has a ventilation system that does not ventilate into any other part of the hotel (except any other designated hotel bedrooms); and
(e) is clearly marked as a bedroom in which smoking is permitted;

"designated laboratory room" means a room in a laboratory, the recognised activities of which laboratory consist of, or include, the conduct of scientific education or research into smoking, which—

(a) is set apart exclusively for the testing of smoke;
(b) has been designated by the person having the management or control of the laboratory as being a room in which smoking is only permitted for scientific purposes;
(c) has a ceiling and, except for doors and windows, is completely enclosed on all sides by solid floor to ceiling walls;
(d) has a ventilation system that does not ventilate into any other part of the laboratory (except any other designated laboratory rooms); and
(e) is clearly marked as a room in which smoking is only permitted for scientific purposes;

"designated room" means a room which—

(a) has been designated by the person having the management or control of the no smoking premises in question as being a room in which smoking is permitted;
(b) has a ceiling and, except for doors and windows, is completely enclosed on all sides by solid floor to ceiling walls;
(c) has a ventilation system that does not ventilate into any other part of the no smoking premises in question (except any other designated rooms); and
(d) is clearly marked as a room in which smoking is permitted;

"detention or interview room" means a room—

(a) within a police station which is used for the purposes of interviewing or detaining persons;
(b) within a police station which is used for the purposes of cell accommodation;
(c) which is a legalised police cell; or
(d) within premises used by a person appointed as an officer of Revenue and Customs under section 2(1) of the Commissioners for Revenue and Customs Act 2005 for the purposes of interviewing or detaining persons;

"domestic premises" means premises occupied as a private dwelling (including any garage, outhouse, or other appurtenance of such premises which is not used in common by the occupants of more than one such dwelling), and "non-domestic premises" shall be construed accordingly;

"educational institution" means—
(a) a school within the meaning of section 135(1) of the Education (Scotland) Act 1980;
(b) a school care accommodation service within the meaning of section 2(4) of the Regulation of Care (Scotland) Act 2001;
(c) a college or other institution providing further education within the meaning of section 1 of the Further and Higher Education (Scotland) Act 1992 and section 1(5)(b) of the Education (Scotland) Act 1980;
(d) a university or other institution providing higher education within the meaning of section 38 of the Further and Higher Education (Scotland) Act 1992; and
(e) any other educational and vocational institution;

"health care premises" means any premises provided by the Scottish Ministers in accordance with the provisions of section 36(1)(b) of the National Health Service (Scotland) Act 1978 and any other premises which are not a hospital and which are used for the purpose of providing medical, dental, pharmaceutical, ophthalmic or chiropody services to non-resident persons;

"hospice" means an establishment the whole or main purpose of which is to provide palliative care for persons resident there who are suffering from a progressive disease in its final stages;

"hospital" means—
(a) any institution for the reception and treatment of persons suffering from illness;
(b) any maternity home; and
(c) any institution for the reception and treatment of persons during convalescence or persons requiring medical rehabilitation, and any institution for providing dental treatment maintained in connection with a dental school,

and includes clinics, dispensaries and out-patient departments which are not health care premises which are maintained in connection with any such home or institution;

"hospital unit" means any part of a hospital which is treated as a separate unit;

"hotel" means a hotel, boarding house, guest house, inn or hostel containing at least two rooms or apartments set apart exclusively for the sleeping accommodation of travellers;

"illness" includes mental disorder within the meaning of section 328 of the Mental Health (Care and Treatment) (Scotland) Act 2003 and any injury or disability requiring medical or dental treatment or nursing;

"legalised police cell" means a police cell within the meaning of section 14(1) of the Prisons (Scotland) Act 1989;

"no smoking notice" means a notice displayed in accordance with section 3(1) of the Act;

"offender accommodation service" means an offender accommodation service within the meaning of section 2(10) of the Regulation of Care (Scotland) Act 2001;

"offshore installation" means any offshore installation within the meaning of regulation 3 of the Offshore Installations and Pipeline Works (Management and Administration) Regulations 1995;

"premises" includes—
(a) any building or part of a building;
(b) any structure or part of a structure, whether moveable or otherwise;
(c) any installation on land (including the foreshore and other land intermittently covered by water), any offshore installation, and any other installation (whether floating, or resting on the seabed or the subsoil thereof, or resting on other land covered with water or the subsoil thereof);

(d) any tent, marquee or stall; and
(e) any vehicle;

"private hire car" means a hire car other than a taxi within the meaning of section 23(1) of the Civic Government (Scotland) Act 1982;

"private vehicle" means—

(a) any car which is not a public transportation vehicle; and
(b) any other vehicle which is used primarily for the private purposes of the person who owns it or of a person having the right to use it, provided always that such right to use a vehicle does not, in relation to that vehicle, include a reference to a person whose right to use the vehicle derives only from having paid, or undertaken to pay, for the use of the vehicle and its driver for a particular journey nor does it include a reference to any public transportation vehicle;

"psychiatric hospital" means a hospital the whole or main purpose of which is to treat persons with a mental disorder within the meaning of section 328 of the Mental Health (Care and Treatment) (Scotland) Act 2003, and includes a state hospital;

"psychiatric unit" means a hospital unit the whole or main purpose of which is to treat persons with a mental disorder within the meaning of section 328 of the Mental Health (Care and Treatment) (Scotland) Act 2003;

"public house" includes an inn, ale house, victualling house or other premises in which alcoholic drink is sold by retail for consumption either on or off the premises;

"public transportation facilities" includes train stations, bus stations, bus shelters, waiting rooms, ticket offices and terminal buildings provided in connection with any public transportation vehicle;

"public transportation vehicle" means any vehicle available to the public as a means of transportation and includes a taxi and a private hire car;

"residential accommodation" means so much of any premises as is for the time being occupied or used by any person for residential purposes, but does not include so much of any such premises as constitutes a common area to which the person has or is allowed access in connection with the person's use or occupation of that accommodation, nor does it include an adult care home, an adult hospice, a psychiatric hospital, a psychiatric unit or premises providing a secure accommodation service;

"restaurant" means—

(a) a café, coffee shop, bistro, fast food establishment or snack bar; and
(b) any other premises exclusively or mainly used for the sale and consumption of food;

"secure accommodation service" means a secure accommodation service within the same meaning of section 2(9) of the Regulation of Care (Scotland) Act 2001;

"sports centre" means any gymnasium, health spa, swimming pool, roller or ice rink, bowling alley and other similar premises used to engage in sports, athletics or recreational activities or to witness sports, athletics, recreational or similar activities;

"state hospital" means a state hospital provided under section 102(1) of the National Health Service (Scotland) Act 1978;

"taxi" means a hire car within the meaning of section 23(1) of the Civic Government (Scotland) Act 1982; and

"vehicle" includes any train, bus, car and any vessel (whether navigable or not), boat or hovercraft.

(3) A reference to premises includes any premises within premises.

(4) These Regulations shall come into force at 0600 hours on 26th March 2006.

[3370]

NOTES

Commencement: 26 March 2006 (at 0600 hours).

"Vehicle": by virtue of the Prohibition of Smoking in Certain Premises (Scotland) Regulations 2006 (Consequential Provisions) (Scotland) Order 2006, SI 2006/1115, art 3(2), the definition of "vehicle" in para (2) above has effect as if it includes a reference to a relevant ship within the meaning of art 3(1) of that Order. See also art 3(3) of the 2006 Order as to which provisions of the Act apply in such circumstances.

2 Display of no-smoking notices

(1) At least one no smoking notice displayed in no-smoking premises that are not a vehicle shall—

(a) be a minimum size of 230mm by 160mm;
(b) display the international "no smoking" symbol, consisting of a graphic representation of a burning cigarette enclosed in a red circle with a red bar across it, at least 85mm in diameter; and
(c) display the name of the person to whom a complaint may be made by any person who observes another person smoke in the no-smoking premises in question and state that a complaint may be so made.

(2) The remainder of no-smoking notices displayed in no-smoking premises that are not a vehicle and any no smoking notices displayed on or near no-smoking premises that are not a vehicle shall display the international "no smoking" symbol, consisting of a graphic representation of a burning cigarette enclosed in a red circle with a red bar across it, at least 85mm in diameter.

(3) A no smoking notice displayed in no-smoking premises that are a vehicle shall—
(a) display the international "no smoking" symbol, consisting of a graphic representation of a burning cigarette enclosed in a red circle with a red bar across it; and
(b) display the holder of a particular post to whom a complaint may be made by any person who observes another person smoke in the no smoking premises in question and state that a complaint may be so made.

(4) A no smoking notice shall be displayed by the person having the management or control of the no smoking premises in such a manner that it is protected from tampering, damage, removal or concealment.

(5) The requirements in paragraphs (1) to (4) as to the manner of display, form and content of no smoking notices are to be treated for the purposes of section 3(1) of the Act as if incorporated in it.

[3371]

NOTES

Commencement: 26 March 2006 (at 0600 hours).

3 "No-smoking premises"

(1) The premises or classes of premises prescribed under section 4(2) of the Act as being "no smoking premises" for the purposes of Part 1 of the Act are the premises or classes of premises specified in Schedule 1 to these Regulations, being premises or classes of premises which are wholly or substantially enclosed.

(2) The premises or parts of premises or classes of premises or parts of premises prescribed under section 4(2) of the Act which are excluded from the definition of "no smoking premises" are the premises or parts of premises or classes of premises or parts of premises specified in Schedule 2 to these Regulations.

(3) For the purposes of section 4(2) of the Act—
(a) "premises" includes—
(i) any building or part of a building;
(ii) any structure or part of a structure, whether moveable or otherwise;
(iii) any installation on land (including the foreshore and other land intermittently covered by water), any offshore installation, and any other installation (whether floating, or resting on the seabed or the subsoil thereof, or resting on other land covered with water or the subsoil thereof);
(iv) any tent, marquee or stall; and
(v) any vehicle.
(b) "wholly enclosed" means—
(i) for premises other than a vehicle or part of a vehicle, having a ceiling or roof and, except for doors, windows and passageways, wholly enclosed, whether permanently or temporarily; or
(ii) for premises that are a vehicle, or part of a vehicle, having a top or roof and, except for doors, windows or exits, wholly enclosed, whether permanently or temporarily;
(c) "substantially enclosed" means—
(i) for premises other than a vehicle or part of a vehicle, having a ceiling or roof and, except for doors, windows and passageways, substantially enclosed, whether permanently or temporarily; or

(ii) for premises that are a vehicle, or part of a vehicle, having a top or roof and, except for doors, windows or exits, substantially enclosed, whether permanently or temporarily,

and in determining whether premises are "substantially enclosed", no account is to be taken of openings in which there are doors, windows or other fittings that can be opened or shut;

(d) premises shall be taken to be "substantially enclosed" if—

(i) the opening in the premises has an area; or

(ii) if there is more than one, both or all those openings have an aggregate area,

which is less than half of the area of the walls, including any other structures serving the purpose of walls, which constitute the perimeter of the premises;

(e) where an opening is in, or consists of the absence of, such walls or other structures or a part of them, their area shall be measured for the purposes of paragraph (d) as if it included the area of the opening; and

(f) "has access" means has access whether on payment or otherwise, and whether as of right or by virtue of express or implied permission.

[3372]

NOTES

Commencement: 26 March 2006 (at 0600 hours).

4 Fixed penalty time limits, amounts and payments

(1) The time limit prescribed under paragraph 2 of schedule 1 to the Act relating to the offence after which a fixed penalty notice may not be given shall be 7 days.

(2) The amount of the fixed penalty prescribed under paragraph 4(1) of schedule 1 to the Act is—

(a) £200 for an offence under section 1 of the Act;

(b) £50 for an offence under section 2 of the Act; and

(c) £200 for an offence under section 3 of the Act.

(3) The discounted amount prescribed under paragraph 5(2) of schedule 1 to the Act for a fixed penalty is—

(a) £150 for an offence under section 1 of the Act;

(b) £30 for an offence under section 2 of the Act; and

(c) £150 for an offence under section 3 of the Act.

[3373]

NOTES

Commencement: 26 March 2006 (at 0600 hours).

5 (*(Application by councils of fixed penalty notices and account keeping) outside the scope of this work.*)

SCHEDULES

SCHEDULE 1
NO-SMOKING PREMISES

Regulation 3(1)

1. Restaurants.

2. Bars and public houses.

3. Shops and shopping centres.

4. Hotels.

5. Libraries, archives, museums and galleries.

6. Cinemas, concert halls, theatres, bingo halls, gaming and amusement arcades, casinos, dance halls, discotheques and other premises used for the entertainment of members of the public.

7. Premises used as a broadcasting studio or film studio or for the recording of a performance with a view to its use in a programme service or in a film intended for public exhibition.

8. Halls and any other premises used for the assembly of members of the public for social or recreational purposes.

9. Conference centres, public halls and exhibition halls.

10. Public toilets.

11. Club premises.

12. Offices, factories and other premises that are non-domestic premises in which one or more persons work.

13. Offshore installations.

14. Educational institution premises.

15. Premises providing care home services, sheltered housing or secure accommodation services and premises that are non-domestic premises which provide offender accommodation services.

16. Hospitals, hospices, psychiatric hospitals, psychiatric units and health care premises.

17. Crèches, day nurseries, day centres and other premises used for the day care of children or adults.

18. Premises used for, or in connection with, public worship or religious instruction, or the social or recreational activities of a religious body.

19. Sports centres.

20. Airport passenger terminals and any other public transportation facilities.

21. Public transportation vehicles.

22. Vehicles which one or more persons use for work.

23. Public telephone kiosks.

[3374]

NOTES

Commencement: 26 March 2006 (at 0600 hours).

SCHEDULE 2
EXEMPTIONS

Regulation 3(2)

1. Residential accommodation.

2. Designated rooms in adult care homes.

3. Adult hospices.

4. Designated rooms in psychiatric hospitals and psychiatric units.

5. Designated hotel bedrooms.

6. Detention or interview rooms which are designated rooms.

7. Designated rooms in offshore installations.

8. Private vehicles

9. Designated laboratory rooms.

10. HM Submarines and ships of the Royal Fleet Auxiliary.

[3375]

NOTES

Commencement: 26 March 2006 (at 0600 hours).

TRANSFER OF UNDERTAKINGS (PROTECTION OF EMPLOYMENT) REGULATIONS 2006

(SI 2006/246)

NOTES

Made: 6 February 2006.

Authority: European Communities Act 1972, s 2(2); Employment Relations Act 1999, s 38.

Commencement: 6 April 2006 (subject to the transitional provisions in reg 21 at **[3395]**).

These Regulations represent the current domestic implementation of Council Directive 2001/23/EC at **[4015]**, re-enacting the original Directive 77/187/EEC together with later amendments. They revoke and replace the Transfer of Undertakings (Protection of Employment) Regulations 1981, SI 1981/1794, subject to transitional provisions and savings in reg 21 *post*.

Employment Appeal Tribunal: an appeal lies to the Employment Appeal Tribunal on a question of law arising from any decision of, or arising in any proceedings before, an employment tribunal under or by virtue of these Regulations; see reg 16(2) of these Regulations at **[3391]**.

Conciliation: employment tribunal proceedings and claims which could be the subject of employment tribunal proceedings under regulation 15 are proceedings to which the Employment Tribunals Act 1996, s 18 applies; see reg 16(1) of these Regulations at **[3391]**.

Modifications: these Regulations are applied and modified by:

(a) the Industrial Training Act 1982, s 3B (as amended by Sch 2 to these Regulations), so as to apply them to the transfer of the activities of an industrial training board;

(b) the Ordnance Factories and Military Services Act 1984, s 4, Sch 2, para 2 (as amended by Sch 2 to these Regulations), so as to apply them with modifications to personnel transferred as a result of a transfer scheme made under s 1(1) of that Act;

(c) the Dockyard Services Act 1986, s 1(4)–(9) (as amended by Sch 2 to these Regulations), in their application to transfers of dockyard undertakings under that Act;

(d) the Dartford-Thurrock Crossing Act 1988, Sch 5 (as amended by Sch 2 to these Regulations), to any transfer of an undertaking effected, or treated as effected, by s 14 of that Act (termination of appointment of person appointed to levy tolls);

(e) the Atomic Weapons Establishment Act 1991, s 2 (as amended by Sch 2 to these Regulations), so as to apply them to the transfer of certain staff employed in the Atomic Weapons Establishment and provide that, upon such a transfer, civil service redundancy procedures shall not apply to former civil service employees in cases where designated activities (as defined in the 1991 Act, s 1(2)) are carried on;

(f) the Export and Investment Guarantees Act 1991, s 9 (as amended by Sch 2 to these Regulations), so as to provide that where, on the transfer of property, rights or liabilities under a scheme under the 1991 Act, s 8, a person ceases to be employed in the civil service and becomes employed by a transferee, he shall not on so ceasing be treated for the purposes of any scheme under the Superannuation Act 1972, s 1, as having retired on redundancy and his ceasing to be employed in that service shall not be regarded as an occasion of redundancy for the purposes of the agreed redundancy procedures applicable to persons employed in that service;

(g) the Ports Act 1991, Sch 1, para 5 (as amended by Sch 2 to these Regulations), so as to apply them to certain transfers of port undertakings made under s 2 of that Act;

(h) the Coal Industry Act 1994, s 12(8), Sch 2, para 7, so as to apply these Regulations with modifications to any transfer of any undertaking or part of an undertaking in accordance with a restructuring scheme under s 12 of, and Sch 2 to, that Act or a modification agreement under Sch 2, para 6 thereto (note that the reference to the 1981 Regulations in the 1994 Act was not amended by Sch 2 to these Regulations);

(i) the Energy Act 2004, s 38(8), Sch 5, para 10 (as amended by Sch 2 to these Regulations), so as to apply them with modifications to a transfer of an undertaking or part of an undertaking in accordance with a nuclear transfer scheme or a modification agreement under that Act.

(j) the Criminal Proceedings etc (Reform) (Scotland) Act 2007, s 65(4), so as to apply them to a scheme for the transfer of the employment of the Scottish Administration of clerks, assessors and other staff of the district court to which an order under s 64(1) of that Act applies.

ARRANGEMENT OF REGULATIONS

1 Citation, commencement and extent

(1) These Regulations may be cited as the Transfer of Undertakings (Protection of Employment) Regulations 2006.

(2) These Regulations shall come into force on 6 April 2006.

(3) These Regulations shall extend to Northern Ireland, except where otherwise provided.

[3376]

NOTES

Commencement: 6 April 2006.

2 Interpretation

(1) In these Regulations—

"assigned" means assigned other than on a temporary basis;

"collective agreement", "collective bargaining" and "trade union" have the same meanings respectively as in the 1992 Act;

"contract of employment" means any agreement between an employee and his employer determining the terms and conditions of his employment;

references to "contractor" in regulation 3 shall include a sub-contractor;

"employee" means any individual who works for another person whether under a contract of service or apprenticeship or otherwise but does not include anyone who provides services under a contract for services and references to a person's employer shall be construed accordingly;

"insolvency practitioner" has the meaning given to the expression by Part XIII of the Insolvency Act 1986;

references to "organised grouping of employees" shall include a single employee;

"recognised" has the meaning given to the expression by section 178(3) of the 1992 Act;

"relevant transfer" means a transfer or a service provision change to which these Regulations apply in accordance with regulation 3 and "transferor" and "transferee" shall be construed accordingly and in the case of a service provision change falling within regulation 3(1)(b), "the transferor" means the person who carried out the activities prior to the service provision change and "the transferee" means the person who carries out the activities as a result of the service provision change;

"the 1992 Act" means the Trade Union and Labour Relations (Consolidation) Act 1992;

"the 1996 Act" means the Employment Rights Act 1996;

"the 1996 Tribunals Act" means the Employment Tribunals Act 1996;

"the 1981 Regulations" means the Transfer of Undertakings (Protection of Employment) Regulations 1981.

(2) For the purposes of these Regulations the representative of a trade union recognised by an employer is an official or other person authorised to carry on collective bargaining with that employer by that trade union.

(3) In the application of these Regulations to Northern Ireland the Regulations shall have effect as set out in Schedule 1.

[3377]

NOTES

Commencement: 6 April 2006.

3 A relevant transfer

(1) These Regulations apply to—

(a) a transfer of an undertaking, business or part of an undertaking or business situated immediately before the transfer in the United Kingdom to another person where there is a transfer of an economic entity which retains its identity;

(b) a service provision change, that is a situation in which—

(i) activities cease to be carried out by a person ("a client") on his own behalf and are carried out instead by another person on the client's behalf ("a contractor");

(ii) activities cease to be carried out by a contractor on a client's behalf (whether or not those activities had previously been carried out by the client on his own behalf) and are carried out instead by another person ("a subsequent contractor") on the client's behalf; or

(iii) activities cease to be carried out by a contractor or a subsequent contractor on a client's behalf (whether or not those activities had previously been carried out by the client on his own behalf) and are carried out instead by the client on his own behalf,

and in which the conditions set out in paragraph (3) are satisfied.

(2) In this regulation "economic entity" means an organised grouping of resources which has the objective of pursuing an economic activity, whether or not that activity is central or ancillary.

(3) The conditions referred to in paragraph (1)(b) are that—

(a) immediately before the service provision change—

(i) there is an organised grouping of employees situated in Great Britain which has as its principal purpose the carrying out of the activities concerned on behalf of the client;

(ii) the client intends that the activities will, following the service provision change, be carried out by the transferee other than in connection with a single specific event or task of short-term duration; and

(b) the activities concerned do not consist wholly or mainly of the supply of goods for the client's use.

(4) Subject to paragraph (1), these Regulations apply to—

(a) public and private undertakings engaged in economic activities whether or not they are operating for gain;

(b) a transfer or service provision change howsoever effected notwithstanding—

(i) that the transfer of an undertaking, business or part of an undertaking or business is governed or effected by the law of a country or territory outside the United Kingdom or that the service provision change is governed or effected by the law of a country or territory outside Great Britain;

(ii) that the employment of persons employed in the undertaking, business or part transferred or, in the case of a service provision change, persons employed in the organised grouping of employees, is governed by any such law;

(c) a transfer of an undertaking, business or part of an undertaking or business (which may also be a service provision change) where persons employed in the undertaking, business or part transferred ordinarily work outside the United Kingdom.

(5) An administrative reorganisation of public administrative authorities or the transfer of administrative functions between public administrative authorities is not a relevant transfer.

(6) A relevant transfer—

(a) may be effected by a series of two or more transactions; and
(b) may take place whether or not any property is transferred to the transferee by the transferor.

(7) Where, in consequence (whether directly or indirectly) of the transfer of an undertaking, business or part of an undertaking or business which was situated immediately before the transfer in the United Kingdom, a ship within the meaning of the Merchant Shipping Act 1995 registered in the United Kingdom ceases to be so registered, these Regulations shall not affect the right conferred by section 29 of that Act (right of seamen to be discharged when ship ceases to be registered in the United Kingdom) on a seaman employed in the ship.

[3378]

NOTES

Commencement: 6 April 2006.

4 Effect of relevant transfer on contracts of employment

(1) Except where objection is made under paragraph (7), a relevant transfer shall not operate so as to terminate the contract of employment of any person employed by the transferor and assigned to the organised grouping of resources or employees that is subject to the relevant transfer, which would otherwise be terminated by the transfer, but any such contract shall have effect after the transfer as if originally made between the person so employed and the transferee.

(2) Without prejudice to paragraph (1), but subject to paragraph (6), and regulations 8 and 15(9), on the completion of a relevant transfer—
(a) all the transferor's rights, powers, duties and liabilities under or in connection with any such contract shall be transferred by virtue of this regulation to the transferee; and
(b) any act or omission before the transfer is completed, of or in relation to the transferor in respect of that contract or a person assigned to that organised grouping of resources or employees, shall be deemed to have been an act or omission of or in relation to the transferee.

(3) Any reference in paragraph (1) to a person employed by the transferor and assigned to the organised grouping of resources or employees that is subject to a relevant transfer, is a reference to a person so employed immediately before the transfer, or who would have been so employed if he had not been dismissed in the circumstances described in regulation 7(1), including, where the transfer is effected by a series of two or more transactions, a person so employed and assigned or who would have been so employed and assigned immediately before any of those transactions.

(4) Subject to regulation 9, in respect of a contract of employment that is, or will be, transferred by paragraph (1), any purported variation of the contract shall be void if the sole or principal reason for the variation is—
(a) the transfer itself; or
(b) a reason connected with the transfer that is not an economic, technical or organisational reason entailing changes in the workforce.

(5) Paragraph (4) shall not prevent the employer and his employee, whose contract of employment is, or will be, transferred by paragraph (1), from agreeing a variation of that contract if the sole or principal reason for the variation is—
(a) a reason connected with the transfer that is an economic, technical or organisational reason entailing changes in the workforce; or
(b) a reason unconnected with the transfer.

(6) Paragraph (2) shall not transfer or otherwise affect the liability of any person to be prosecuted for, convicted of and sentenced for any offence.

(7) Paragraphs (1) and (2) shall not operate to transfer the contract of employment and the rights, powers, duties and liabilities under or in connection with it of an employee who informs the transferor or the transferee that he objects to becoming employed by the transferee.

(8) Subject to paragraphs (9) and (11), where an employee so objects, the relevant transfer shall operate so as to terminate his contract of employment with the transferor but he shall not be treated, for any purpose, as having been dismissed by the transferor.

(9) Subject to regulation 9, where a relevant transfer involves or would involve a substantial change in working conditions to the material detriment of a person whose contract of employment is or would be transferred under paragraph (1), such an employee may treat the contract of employment as having been terminated, and the employee shall be treated for any purpose as having been dismissed by the employer.

(10) No damages shall be payable by an employer as a result of a dismissal falling within paragraph (9) in respect of any failure by the employer to pay wages to an employee in respect of a notice period which the employee has failed to work.

(11) Paragraphs (1), (7), (8) and (9) are without prejudice to any right of an employee arising apart from these Regulations to terminate his contract of employment without notice in acceptance of a repudiatory breach of contract by his employer.

[3379]

NOTES

Commencement: 6 April 2006.

5 Effect of relevant transfer on collective agreements

Where at the time of a relevant transfer there exists a collective agreement made by or on behalf of the transferor with a trade union recognised by the transferor in respect of any employee whose contract of employment is preserved by regulation 4(1) above, then—

(a) without prejudice to sections 179 and 180 of the 1992 Act (collective agreements presumed to be unenforceable in specified circumstances) that agreement, in its application in relation to the employee, shall, after the transfer, have effect as if made by or on behalf of the transferee with that trade union, and accordingly anything done under or in connection with it, in its application in relation to the employee, by or in relation to the transferor before the transfer, shall, after the transfer, be deemed to have been done by or in relation to the transferee; and

(b) any order made in respect of that agreement, in its application in relation to the employee, shall, after the transfer, have effect as if the transferee were a party to the agreement.

[3380]

NOTES

Commencement: 6 April 2006.

6 Effect of relevant transfer on trade union recognition

(1) This regulation applies where after a relevant transfer the transferred organised grouping of resources or employees maintains an identity distinct from the remainder of the transferee's undertaking.

(2) Where before such a transfer an independent trade union is recognised to any extent by the transferor in respect of employees of any description who in consequence of the transfer become employees of the transferee, then, after the transfer—

(a) the trade union shall be deemed to have been recognised by the transferee to the same extent in respect of employees of that description so employed; and

(b) any agreement for recognition may be varied or rescinded accordingly.

[3381]

NOTES

Commencement: 6 April 2006.

7 Dismissal of employee because of relevant transfer

(1) Where either before or after a relevant transfer, any employee of the transferor or transferee is dismissed, that employee shall be treated for the purposes of Part X of the 1996 Act (unfair dismissal) as unfairly dismissed if the sole or principal reason for his dismissal is—

(a) the transfer itself; or

(b) a reason connected with the transfer that is not an economic, technical or organisational reason entailing changes in the workforce.

(2) This paragraph applies where the sole or principal reason for the dismissal is a reason connected with the transfer that is an economic, technical or organisational reason entailing changes in the workforce of either the transferor or the transferee before or after a relevant transfer.

(3) Where paragraph (2) applies—

(a) paragraph (1) shall not apply;

(b) without prejudice to the application of section 98(4) of the 1996 Act (test of fair dismissal), the dismissal shall, for the purposes of sections 98(1) and 135 of that Act (reason for dismissal), be regarded as having been for redundancy where section 98(2)(c) of that Act applies, or otherwise for a substantial reason of a kind such as to justify the dismissal of an employee holding the position which that employee held.

(4) The provisions of this regulation apply irrespective of whether the employee in question is assigned to the organised grouping of resources or employees that is, or will be, transferred.

(5) Paragraph (1) shall not apply in relation to the dismissal of any employee which was required by reason of the application of section 5 of the Aliens Restriction (Amendment) Act 1919 to his employment.

(6) Paragraph (1) shall not apply in relation to a dismissal of an employee if the application of section 94 of the 1996 Act to the dismissal of the employee is excluded by or under any provision of the 1996 Act, the 1996 Tribunals Act or the 1992 Act.

[3382]

NOTES

Commencement: 6 April 2006.

8 Insolvency

(1) If at the time of a relevant transfer the transferor is subject to relevant insolvency proceedings paragraphs (2) to (6) apply.

(2) In this regulation "relevant employee" means an employee of the transferor—

(a) whose contract of employment transfers to the transferee by virtue of the operation of these Regulations; or

(b) whose employment with the transferor is terminated before the time of the relevant transfer in the circumstances described in regulation 7(1).

(3) The relevant statutory scheme specified in paragraph (4)(b) (including that sub-paragraph as applied by paragraph 5 of Schedule 1) shall apply in the case of a relevant employee irrespective of the fact that the qualifying requirement that the employee's employment has been terminated is not met and for those purposes the date of the transfer shall be treated as the date of the termination and the transferor shall be treated as the employer.

(4) In this regulation the "relevant statutory schemes" are—

(a) Chapter VI of Part XI of the 1996 Act;

(b) Part XII of the 1996 Act.

(5) Regulation 4 shall not operate to transfer liability for the sums payable to the relevant employee under the relevant statutory schemes.

(6) In this regulation "relevant insolvency proceedings" means insolvency proceedings which have been opened in relation to the transferor not with a view to the liquidation of the assets of the transferor and which are under the supervision of an insolvency practitioner.

(7) Regulations 4 and 7 do not apply to any relevant transfer where the transferor is the subject of bankruptcy proceedings or any analogous insolvency proceedings which have been instituted with a view to the liquidation of the assets of the transferor and are under the supervision of an insolvency practitioner.

[3383]

NOTES

Commencement: 6 April 2006.

9 Variations of contract where transferors are subject to relevant insolvency proceedings

(1) If at the time of a relevant transfer the transferor is subject to relevant insolvency proceedings these Regulations shall not prevent the transferor or transferee (or an insolvency practitioner) and appropriate representatives of assigned employees agreeing to permitted variations.

(2) For the purposes of this regulation "appropriate representatives" are—

(a) if the employees are of a description in respect of which an independent trade union is recognised by their employer, representatives of the trade union; or

(b) in any other case, whichever of the following employee representatives the employer chooses—

(i) employee representatives appointed or elected by the assigned employees (whether they make the appointment or election alone or with others) otherwise than for the purposes of this regulation, who (having regard to the purposes for, and the method by which they were appointed or elected) have authority from those employees to agree permitted variations to contracts of employment on their behalf;

(ii) employee representatives elected by assigned employees (whether they make the appointment or election alone or with others) for these particular purposes, in an election satisfying requirements identical to those contained in regulation 14 except those in regulation 14(1)(d).

(3) An individual may be an appropriate representative for the purposes of both this regulation and regulation 13 provided that where the representative is not a trade union representative he is either elected by or has authority from assigned employees (within the meaning of this regulation) and affected employees (as described in regulation 13(1)).

(4) …

(5) Where assigned employees are represented by non-trade union representatives—

(a) the agreement recording a permitted variation must be in writing and signed by each of the representatives who have made it or, where that is not reasonably practicable, by a duly authorised agent of that representative; and

(b) the employer must, before the agreement is made available for signature, provide all employees to whom it is intended to apply on the date on which it is to come into effect with copies of the text of the agreement and such guidance as those employees might reasonably require in order to understand it fully.

(6) A permitted variation shall take effect as a term or condition of the assigned employee's contract of employment in place, where relevant, of any term or condition which it varies.

(7) In this regulation—

"assigned employees" means those employees assigned to the organised grouping of resources or employees that is the subject of a relevant transfer;

"permitted variation" is a variation to the contract of employment of an assigned employee where—

(a) the sole or principal reason for it is the transfer itself or a reason connected with the transfer that is not an economic, technical or organisational reason entailing changes in the workforce; and

(b) it is designed to safeguard employment opportunities by ensuring the survival of the undertaking, business or part of the undertaking or business that is the subject of the relevant transfer;

"relevant insolvency proceedings" has the meaning given to the expression by regulation 8(6).

[3384]

NOTES

Commencement: 6 April 2006.

Sub-s (4): amends the Trade Union and Labour Relations (Consolidation) Act 1992, s 168 at **[651]**.

10 Pensions

(1) Regulations 4 and 5 shall not apply—

(a) to so much of a contract of employment or collective agreement as relates to an occupational pension scheme within the meaning of the Pension Schemes Act 1993; or

(b) to any rights, powers, duties or liabilities under or in connection with any such contract or subsisting by virtue of any such agreement and relating to such a scheme or otherwise arising in connection with that person's employment and relating to such a scheme.

(2) For the purposes of paragraphs (1) and (3), any provisions of an occupational pension scheme which do not relate to benefits for old age, invalidity or survivors shall not be treated as being part of the scheme.

(3) An employee whose contract of employment is transferred in the circumstances described in regulation 4(1) shall not be entitled to bring a claim against the transferor for—

(a) breach of contract; or

(b) constructive unfair dismissal under section 95(1)(c) of the 1996 Act,

arising out of a loss or reduction in his rights under an occupational pension scheme in consequence of the transfer, save insofar as the alleged breach of contract or dismissal (as the case may be) occurred prior to the date on which these Regulations took effect.

[3385]

NOTES

Commencement: 6 April 2006.

11 Notification of Employee Liability Information

(1) The transferor shall notify to the transferee the employee liability information of any person employed by him who is assigned to the organised grouping of resources or employees that is the subject of a relevant transfer—

(a) in writing; or

(b) by making it available to him in a readily accessible form.

(2) In this regulation and in regulation 12 "employee liability information" means—

(a) the identity and age of the employee;

(b) those particulars of employment that an employer is obliged to give to an employee pursuant to section 1 of the 1996 Act;

(c) information of any—

(i) disciplinary procedure taken against an employee;

(ii) grievance procedure taken by an employee,

within the previous two years, in circumstances where the Employment Act 2002 (Dispute Resolution) Regulations 2004 apply;

(d) information of any court or tribunal case, claim or action—

(i) brought by an employee against the transferor, within the previous two years;

(ii) that the transferor has reasonable grounds to believe that an employee may bring against the transferee, arising out of the employee's employment with the transferor; and

(e) information of any collective agreement which will have effect after the transfer, in its application in relation to the employee, pursuant to regulation 5(a).

(3) Employee liability information shall contain information as at a specified date not more than fourteen days before the date on which the information is notified to the transferee.

(4) The duty to provide employee liability information in paragraph (1) shall include a duty to provide employee liability information of any person who would have been employed by the transferor and assigned to the organised grouping of resources or employees that is the subject of a relevant transfer immediately before the transfer if he had not been dismissed in the circumstances described in regulation 7(1), including, where the transfer is effected by a series of two or more transactions, a person so employed and assigned or who would have been so employed and assigned immediately before any of those transactions.

(5) Following notification of the employee liability information in accordance with this regulation, the transferor shall notify the transferee in writing of any change in the employee liability information.

(6) A notification under this regulation shall be given not less than fourteen days before the relevant transfer or, if special circumstances make this not reasonably practicable, as soon as reasonably practicable thereafter.

(7) A notification under this regulation may be given—

(a) in more than one instalment;

(b) indirectly, through a third party.

[3386]

NOTES

Commencement: 6 April 2006 (subject to reg 21(4) at **[3395]**).

12 Remedy for failure to notify employee liability information

(1) On or after a relevant transfer, the transferee may present a complaint to an employment tribunal that the transferor has failed to comply with any provision of regulation 11.

(2) An employment tribunal shall not consider a complaint under this regulation unless it is presented—

(a) before the end of the period of three months beginning with the date of the relevant transfer;

(b) within such further period as the tribunal considers reasonable in a case where it is satisfied that it was not reasonably practicable for the complaint to be presented before the end of that period of three months.

(3) Where an employment tribunal finds a complaint under paragraph (1) well-founded, the tribunal—

(a) shall make a declaration to that effect; and

(b) may make an award of compensation to be paid by the transferor to the transferee.

(4) The amount of the compensation shall be such as the tribunal considers just and equitable in all the circumstances, subject to paragraph (5), having particular regard to—

(a) any loss sustained by the transferee which is attributable to the matters complained of; and

(b) the terms of any contract between the transferor and the transferee relating to the transfer under which the transferor may be liable to pay any sum to the transferee in respect of a failure to notify the transferee of employee liability information.

(5) Subject to paragraph (6), the amount of compensation awarded under paragraph (3) shall be not less than £500 per employee in respect of whom the transferor has failed to comply with a provision of regulation 11, unless the tribunal considers it just and equitable, in all the circumstances, to award a lesser sum.

(6) In ascertaining the loss referred to in paragraph (4)(a) the tribunal shall apply the same rule concerning the duty of a person to mitigate his loss as applies to any damages recoverable under the common law of England and Wales, Northern Ireland or Scotland, as applicable.

(7) Section 18 of the 1996 Tribunals Act (conciliation) shall apply to the right conferred by this regulation and to proceedings under this regulation as it applies to the rights conferred by that Act and the employment tribunal proceedings mentioned in that Act.

[3387]

NOTES

Commencement: 6 April 2006.

13 Duty to inform and consult representatives

(1) In this regulation and regulations 14 and 15 references to affected employees, in relation to a relevant transfer, are to any employees of the transferor or the transferee (whether or not assigned to the organised grouping of resources or employees that is the subject of a relevant transfer) who may be affected by the transfer or may be affected by measures taken in connection with it; and references to the employer shall be construed accordingly.

(2) Long enough before a relevant transfer to enable the employer of any affected employees to consult the appropriate representatives of any affected employees, the employer shall inform those representatives of—

(a) the fact that the transfer is to take place, the date or proposed date of the transfer and the reasons for it;

(b) the legal, economic and social implications of the transfer for any affected employees;

(c) the measures which he envisages he will, in connection with the transfer, take in relation to any affected employees or, if he envisages that no measures will be so taken, that fact; and

(d) if the employer is the transferor, the measures, in connection with the transfer, which he envisages the transferee will take in relation to any affected employees who will become employees of the transferee after the transfer by virtue of regulation 4 or, if he envisages that no measures will be so taken, that fact.

(3) For the purposes of this regulation the appropriate representatives of any affected employees are—

(a) if the employees are of a description in respect of which an independent trade union is recognised by their employer, representatives of the trade union; or

(b) in any other case, whichever of the following employee representatives the employer chooses—

(i) employee representatives appointed or elected by the affected employees otherwise than for the purposes of this regulation, who (having regard to the purposes for, and the method by which they were appointed or elected) have authority from those employees to receive information and to be consulted about the transfer on their behalf;

(ii) employee representatives elected by any affected employees, for the purposes of this regulation, in an election satisfying the requirements of regulation 14(1).

(4) The transferee shall give the transferor such information at such a time as will enable the transferor to perform the duty imposed on him by virtue of paragraph (2)(d).

(5) The information which is to be given to the appropriate representatives shall be given to each of them by being delivered to them, or sent by post to an address notified by them to the employer, or (in the case of representatives of a trade union) sent by post to the trade union at the address of its head or main office.

(6) An employer of an affected employee who envisages that he will take measures in relation to an affected employee, in connection with the relevant transfer, shall consult the appropriate representatives of that employee with a view to seeking their agreement to the intended measures.

(7) In the course of those consultations the employer shall—

(a) consider any representations made by the appropriate representatives; and

(b) reply to those representations and, if he rejects any of those representations, state his reasons.

(8) The employer shall allow the appropriate representatives access to any affected employees and shall afford to those representatives such accommodation and other facilities as may be appropriate.

(9) If in any case there are special circumstances which render it not reasonably practicable for an employer to perform a duty imposed on him by any of paragraphs (2) to (7), he shall take all such steps towards performing that duty as are reasonably practicable in the circumstances.

(10) Where—

(a) the employer has invited any of the affected employee to elect employee representatives; and

(b) the invitation was issued long enough before the time when the employer is required to give information under paragraph (2) to allow them to elect representatives by that time,

the employer shall be treated as complying with the requirements of this regulation in relation to those employees if he complies with those requirements as soon as is reasonably practicable after the election of the representatives.

(11) If, after the employer has invited any affected employees to elect representatives, they fail to do so within a reasonable time, he shall give to any affected employees the information set out in paragraph (2).

(12) The duties imposed on an employer by this regulation shall apply irrespective of whether the decision resulting in the relevant transfer is taken by the employer or a person controlling the employer.

[3388]

NOTES

Commencement: 6 April 2006 (see further as to the commencement of this regulation, and regs 14–16, the transitional provisions in reg 21(5) at **[3395]**).

14 Election of employee representatives

(1) The requirements for the election of employee representatives under regulation 13(3) are that—

(a) the employer shall make such arrangements as are reasonably practicable to ensure that the election is fair;

(b) the employer shall determine the number of representatives to be elected so that there are sufficient representatives to represent the interests of all affected employees having regard to the number and classes of those employees;

(c) the employer shall determine whether the affected employees should be represented either by representatives of all the affected employees or by representatives of particular classes of those employees;

(d) before the election the employer shall determine the term of office as employee representatives so that it is of sufficient length to enable information to be given and consultations under regulation 13 to be completed;

(e) the candidates for election as employee representatives are affected employees on the date of the election;

(f) no affected employee is unreasonably excluded from standing for election;

(g) all affected employees on the date of the election are entitled to vote for employee representatives;

(h) the employees entitled to vote may vote for as many candidates as there are representatives to be elected to represent them or, if there are to be representatives for particular classes of employees, may vote for as many candidates as there are representatives to be elected to represent their particular class of employee;

(i) the election is conducted so as to secure that—

(i) so far as is reasonably practicable, those voting do so in secret; and

(ii) the votes given at the election are accurately counted.

(2) Where, after an election of employee representatives satisfying the requirements of paragraph (1) has been held, one of those elected ceases to act as an employee representative and as a result any affected employees are no longer represented, those employees shall elect another representative by an election satisfying the requirements of paragraph (1)(a), (e), (f) and (i).

[3389]

NOTES

Commencement: 6 April 2006 (see further the note to reg 13 at **[3388]**).

15 Failure to inform or consult

(1) Where an employer has failed to comply with a requirement of regulation 13 or regulation 14, a complaint may be presented to an employment tribunal on that ground—

(a) in the case of a failure relating to the election of employee representatives, by any of his employees who are affected employees;

(b) in the case of any other failure relating to employee representatives, by any of the employee representatives to whom the failure related;

(c) in the case of failure relating to representatives of a trade union, by the trade union; and

(d) in any other case, by any of his employees who are affected employees.

(2) If on a complaint under paragraph (1) a question arises whether or not it was reasonably practicable for an employer to perform a particular duty or as to what steps he took towards performing it, it shall be for him to show—

(a) that there were special circumstances which rendered it not reasonably practicable for him to perform the duty; and

(b) that he took all such steps towards its performance as were reasonably practicable in those circumstances.

(3) If on a complaint under paragraph (1) a question arises as to whether or not an employee representative was an appropriate representative for the purposes of regulation 13, it shall be for the employer to show that the employee representative had the necessary authority to represent the affected employees.

(4) On a complaint under paragraph (1)(a) it shall be for the employer to show that the requirements in regulation 14 have been satisfied.

(5) On a complaint against a transferor that he had failed to perform the duty imposed upon him by virtue of regulation 13(2)(d) or, so far as relating thereto, regulation 13(9), he may not show that it was not reasonably practicable for him to perform the duty in question for the reason that the transferee had failed to give him the requisite information at the requisite time in accordance with regulation 13(4) unless he gives the transferee notice of his intention to show that fact; and the giving of the notice shall make the transferee a party to the proceedings.

(6) In relation to any complaint under paragraph (1), a failure on the part of a person controlling (directly or indirectly) the employer to provide information to the employer shall not constitute special circumstances rendering it not reasonably practicable for the employer to comply with such a requirement.

(7) Where the tribunal finds a complaint against a transferee under paragraph (1) well-founded it shall make a declaration to that effect and may order the transferee to pay appropriate compensation to such descriptions of affected employees as may be specified in the award.

(8) Where the tribunal finds a complaint against a transferor under paragraph (1) well-founded it shall make a declaration to that effect and may—

(a) order the transferor, subject to paragraph (9), to pay appropriate compensation to such descriptions of affected employees as may be specified in the award; or

(b) if the complaint is that the transferor did not perform the duty mentioned in paragraph (5) and the transferor (after giving due notice) shows the facts so mentioned, order the transferee to pay appropriate compensation to such descriptions of affected employees as may be specified in the award.

(9) The transferee shall be jointly and severally liable with the transferor in respect of compensation payable under sub-paragraph (8)(a) or paragraph (11).

(10) An employee may present a complaint to an employment tribunal on the ground that he is an employee of a description to which an order under paragraph (7) or (8) relates and that—

(a) in respect of an order under paragraph (7), the transferee has failed, wholly or in part, to pay him compensation in pursuance of the order;

(b) in respect of an order under paragraph (8), the transferor or transferee, as applicable, has failed, wholly or in part, to pay him compensation in pursuance of the order.

(11) Where the tribunal finds a complaint under paragraph (10) well-founded it shall order the transferor or transferee as applicable to pay the complainant the amount of compensation which it finds is due to him.

(12) An employment tribunal shall not consider a complaint under paragraph (1) or (10) unless it is presented to the tribunal before the end of the period of three months beginning with—

(a) in respect of a complaint under paragraph (1), the date on which the relevant transfer is completed; or

(b) in respect of a complaint under paragraph (10), the date of the tribunal's order under paragraph (7) or (8),

or within such further period as the tribunal considers reasonable in a case where it is satisfied that it was not reasonably practicable for the complaint to be presented before the end of the period of three months.

[3390]

NOTES

Commencement: 6 April 2006 (see further the note to reg 13 at **[3388]**).

Conciliation: employment tribunal proceedings and claims which could be the subject of employment tribunal proceedings under this regulation are proceedings to which the Employment Tribunals Act 1996, s 18 applies; see reg 16 of these Regulations at **[3391]**. The short conciliation period applies to claims under paragraph (10), but not paragraph (1), by virtue of the Employment Tribunals (Constitution and Rules of Procedure) Regulations 2004, SI 2004/1861, Sch 1, rule 22(5)(e). The standard conciliation period applies to claims under paragraph (1) by virtue of SI 2004/1861, Sch 1, rule 22(1), (6)).

16 Failure to inform or consult: supplemental

(1) Section 205(1) of the 1996 Act (complaint to be sole remedy for breach of relevant rights) and section 18 of the 1996 Tribunals Act (conciliation) shall apply to the rights conferred by regulation 15 and to proceedings under this regulation as they apply to the rights conferred by those Acts and the employment tribunal proceedings mentioned in those Acts.

(2) An appeal shall lie and shall lie only to the Employment Appeal Tribunal on a question of law arising from any decision of, or arising in any proceedings before, an employment tribunal under or by virtue of these Regulations; and section 11(1) of the Tribunals and Inquiries Act 1992 (appeals from certain tribunals to the High Court) shall not apply in relation to any such proceedings.

(3) "Appropriate compensation" in regulation 15 means such sum not exceeding thirteen weeks' pay for the employee in question as the tribunal considers just and equitable having regard to the seriousness of the failure of the employer to comply with his duty.

(4) Sections 220 to 228 of the 1996 Act shall apply for calculating the amount of a week's pay for any employee for the purposes of paragraph (3) and, for the purposes of that calculation, the calculation date shall be—

(a) in the case of an employee who is dismissed by reason of redundancy (within the meaning of sections 139 and 155 of the 1996 Act) the date which is the calculation date for the purposes of any entitlement of his to a redundancy payment (within the meaning of those sections) or which would be that calculation date if he were so entitled;

(b) in the case of an employee who is dismissed for any other reason, the effective date of termination (within the meaning of sections 95(1) and (2) and 97 of the 1996 Act) of his contract of employment;

(c) in any other case, the date of the relevant transfer.

[3391]

NOTES

Commencement: 6 April 2006 (see further the note to reg 13 at **[3388]**).
Conciliation: see the note to reg 15 at **[3390]**.

17 Employers' Liability Compulsory Insurance

(1) Paragraph (2) applies where—

(a) by virtue of section 3(1)(a) or (b) of the Employers' Liability (Compulsory Insurance) Act 1969 ("the 1969 Act"), the transferor is not required by that Act to effect any insurance; or

(b) by virtue of section 3(1)(c) of the 1969 Act, the transferor is exempted from the requirement of that Act to effect insurance.

(2) Where this paragraph applies, on completion of a relevant transfer the transferor and the transferee shall be jointly and severally liable in respect of any liability referred to in section 1(1) of the 1969 Act, in so far as such liability relates to the employee's employment with the transferor.

[3392]

NOTES

Commencement: 6 April 2006.

18 Restriction on contracting out

Section 203 of the 1996 Act (restrictions on contracting out) shall apply in relation to these Regulations as if they were contained in that Act, save for that section shall not apply in so far as these Regulations provide for an agreement (whether a contract of employment or not) to exclude or limit the operation of these Regulations.

[3393]

NOTES

Commencement: 6 April 2006.

19 (*Amends the Employment Rights Act 1996, s 104 at* **[1145]**.)

20 Repeals, revocations and amendments

(1) Subject to regulation 21, the 1981 Regulations are revoked.

(2) Section 33 of, and paragraph 4 of Schedule 9 to, the Trade Union Reform and Employment Rights Act 1993 are repealed.

(3) Schedule 2 (consequential amendments) shall have effect.

[3394]

NOTES

Commencement: 6 April 2006.

21 Transitional provisions and savings

(1) These Regulations shall apply in relation to—

(a) a relevant transfer that takes place on or after 6 April 2006;

(b) a transfer or service provision change, not falling within sub-paragraph (a), that takes place on or after 6 April 2006 and is regarded by virtue of any enactment as a relevant transfer.

(2) The 1981 Regulations shall continue to apply in relation to—

(a) a relevant transfer (within the meaning of the 1981 Regulations) that took place before 6 April 2006;

(b) a transfer, not falling within sub-paragraph (a), that took place before 6 April 2006 and is regarded by virtue of any enactment as a relevant transfer (within the meaning of the 1981 Regulations).

(3) In respect of a relevant transfer that takes place on or after 6 April 2006, any action taken by a transferor or transferee to discharge a duty that applied to them under regulation 10 or 10A of the 1981 Regulations shall be deemed to satisfy the corresponding obligation imposed by regulations 13 and 14 of these Regulations, insofar as that action would have discharged those obligations had the action taken place on or after 6 April 2006.

(4) The duty on a transferor to provide a transferee with employee liability information shall not apply in the case of a relevant transfer that takes place on or before 19 April 2006.

(5) Regulations 13, 14, 15 and 16 shall not apply in the case of a service provision change that is not also a transfer of an undertaking, business or part of an undertaking or business that takes place on or before 4 May 2006.

(6) The repeal of paragraph 4 of Schedule 9 to the Trade Union Reform and Employment Rights Act 1993 does not affect the continued operation of that paragraph so far as it remains capable of having effect.

[3395]

NOTES

Commencement: 6 April 2006.

(*Sch 1* (*Application of the Regulations to Northern Ireland*) *outside the scope of this work; Sch 2 contains consequential amendments only and, in so far as relevant to this work, these have been incorporated at the appropriate place.*)

OCCUPATIONAL AND PERSONAL PENSION SCHEMES (CONSULTATION BY EMPLOYERS AND MISCELLANEOUS AMENDMENT) REGULATIONS 2006

(SI 2006/349)

NOTES

Made: 15 February 2006.

Authority: Pensions Act 2004, ss 10(5)(a), 259(1), (2), 260(1), 261(2), (4), 286(1), (3)(g), 315(2), (3), (5), 318(1), (4)(a), (5).

Commencement: 6 February 2006 (reg 22); 6 April 2006 (otherwise).

Conciliation: employment tribunal proceedings and claims which could be the subject of employment tribunal proceedings under paras 4 or 8 of the Schedule to these Regulations are proceedings to which the Employment Tribunals Act 1996, s 18 applies; see s 18(1)(q) of that Act at **[975]**. The standard conciliation period applies by virtue of the Employment Tribunals (Constitution and Rules of Procedure) Regulations 2004, SI 2004/1861, Sch 1, rule 22(1), (6).

Employment Appeal Tribunal: an appeal lies to the Employment Appeal Tribunal on any question of law arising from any decision of, or in any proceedings before, an employment tribunal under or by virtue of the Schedule to these Regulations; see the Employment Tribunals Act 1996, s 21(1)(r) at **[978]**.

ARRANGEMENT OF REGULATIONS

Introductory

1 Citation, commencement and extent

(1) These Regulations may be cited as the Occupational and Personal Pension Schemes (Consultation by Employers and Miscellaneous Amendment) Regulations 2006.

(2) Subject to paragraph (3), these Regulations shall come into force on 6th April 2006.

(3) Regulation 22 shall come into force on the day after the day on which these Regulations are made.

(4) Regulation 22 extends to Northern Ireland.

[3395A]

NOTES

Commencement: 6 February 2006 (for the purposes of reg 22); 6 April 2006 (otherwise).

2 Interpretation

In these Regulations—

"active member"—

(a) in relation to an occupational pension scheme, has the meaning given by section 124 of the Pensions Act 1995 (interpretation), and

(b) in relation to a personal pension scheme, means any member in respect of whom employer contributions fall to be paid;

"affected members" has the meaning given by regulation 7(4);

"employer contributions", in relation to an occupational or personal pension scheme, means contributions payable by or on behalf of the employer in relation to the scheme on his own account (but in respect of one or more employees);

"member contributions", in relation to an occupational or personal pension scheme, means contributions, other than voluntary contributions, by or on behalf of active members of the scheme which are payable out of deductions from the member's earnings;

"listed change" has the meaning given by regulation 6(2);

"multi-employer scheme" has the meaning given by section 307 of the Pensions Act 2004 (modification of Act in relation to certain categories of schemes);

"personal pension scheme" has the meaning given by regulation 3(3);

"prospective member"—

(a) in relation to an occupational pension scheme, means any person who, under the terms of his contract of service or the rules of the scheme—

(i) is able, at his own option, to become a member of the scheme,

(ii) will become so able if he continues in the same employment for a sufficiently long period,

(iii) will be admitted to the scheme automatically unless he makes an election not to become a member, or

(iv) may be admitted to it subject to the consent of his employer;

(b) in relation to a personal pension scheme, means any person who, under the terms of his contract of service, is eligible if he becomes a member of the scheme for employer contributions to be paid in respect of him;

"the Regulator" means the Pensions Regulator established under section 1 of the Pensions Act 2004 (the Pensions Regulator); and

"relevant employer" has the meaning given by regulation 3(2).

[3395B]

NOTES

Commencement: 6 April 2006.

Application of Regulations

3 Application

(1) These Regulations apply to—

(a) in the case of an occupational pension scheme which is not a multi-employer scheme—

(i) any relevant employer, and

(ii) if there is a relevant employer, the trustees or managers of the scheme;

(b) in the case of a multi-employer scheme in relation to which there are one or more relevant employers—

(i) each relevant employer,

(ii) the trustees or managers of the scheme, and
(iii) any other person who, under the rules of the scheme, has the power to make a listed change affecting the scheme; and

(c) in the case of a personal pension scheme where direct payment arrangements exist in respect of one or more members of the scheme who are his employees, a relevant employer.

[(2) For the purposes of these Regulations "relevant employer" means—

(a) an employer employing in Great Britain at least the number of employees specified in paragraph (2A); and

(b) in the case of—

(i) an occupational pension scheme, an employer in relation to the scheme other than one who is excluded by regulation 4, and
(ii) a personal pension scheme, an employer in relation to the scheme other than one who is excluded by regulation 5.

(2A) The number of employees referred to in paragraph (2)(a) is—

(a) 150 from 6th April 2006 to 5th April 2007,
(b) 100 from 6th April 2007 to 5th April 2008, and
(c) 50 from 6th April 2008 onwards.

(2B) For the purposes of paragraph (2)(a)—

(a) the number of people employed by an employer is to be determined using the same method of calculation as is set out in regulation 4 of the Information and Consultation of Employees Regulations 2004 (calculation of number of employees), but
(b) references in that regulation to the previous twelve months are to be taken as references to the period of twelve months ending with the date of the proposal to make a listed change to which regulation 6 of these Regulations applies.]

(3) In these Regulations references to a personal pension scheme are to a personal pension scheme falling within paragraph (1)(c).

[3395C]

NOTES

Commencement: 6 April 2006.

Paras (2), (2A), (2B): substituted, for original para (2), by the Occupational and Personal Pension Schemes (Miscellaneous Amendments) Regulations 2006, SI 2006/778, reg 10(1), (2), as from 6 April 2006.

4 Excluded employers: occupational pension schemes

(1) This regulation excludes—

(a) any employer in relation to a public service pension scheme;
(b) any employer in relation to a small occupational pension scheme;
(c) any employer in relation to an occupational pension scheme with fewer than two members;
(d) any employer in relation to an occupational pension scheme which is an employer-financed retirement benefits scheme;
(e) any employer in relation to an unregistered occupational pension scheme which has its main administration outside the [EEA states]; and
(f) …

(2), (3) …

(4) In this regulation—

"employer-financed retirement benefits scheme" has the meaning given by section 393A of the Income Tax (Earnings and Pensions) Act 2003 (employer-financed retirement benefits scheme);

"public service pension scheme" has the meaning given by section 1(1) of the Pension Schemes Act 1993;

"small occupational pension scheme" means—

(a) a scheme with fewer than twelve members where all of the members are trustees of the scheme and either—

(i) the provisions of the scheme provide that [any decision made by the trustees is made by the unanimous agreement of] the trustees who are members of the scheme, or

(ii) the scheme has a trustee who is independent in relation to the scheme for the purposes of section 23 of the Pensions Act 1995 (power to appoint independent trustees) and is registered in the register maintained by the Regulator in accordance with regulations made under subsection (4) of that section;

(b) a scheme with fewer than twelve members [where a company is the sole trustee] of the scheme, and all the members of the scheme are directors of the company and either—

(i) the provisions of the scheme provide that any decision made by the company in its capacity as trustee [is made by the unanimous agreement of the directors] who are members of the scheme, or

(ii) [one of the directors of the company] is independent in relation to the scheme for the purposes of section 23 of the Pensions Act 1995 and is registered in the register maintained by the Regulator in accordance with regulations made under subsection (4) of that section; and

"unregistered occupational pension scheme" means an occupational pension scheme which is not registered under section 153 of the Finance Act 2004 (registration of pension schemes).

[3395D]

NOTES

Commencement: 6 April 2006.

Para (1): words in square brackets in sub-para (e) substituted by the Occupational Pension Schemes (EEA States) Regulations 2007, SI 2007/3014, reg 2(b), Schedule, para 9, as from 26 November 2007; sub-para (f) revoked by the Occupational and Personal Pension Schemes (Miscellaneous Amendments) Regulations 2006, SI 2006/778, reg 10(1), (3), as from 6 April 2006.

Paras (2), (3): revoked by SI 2006/778, reg 10(3), as from 6 April 2006.

Para (4): words in square brackets in definition "small occupational pension scheme" substituted by the Occupational and Personal Pension Schemes (Miscellaneous Amendments) Regulations 2007, SI 2007/814, reg 19, as from 6 April 2007.

[5 Excluded employers: personal pension schemes

This regulation excludes any employer in relation to a personal pension scheme where no employer contributions fall to be paid towards the scheme.]

[3395E]

NOTES

Commencement: 6 April 2006.

Substituted by the Occupational and Personal Pension Schemes (Miscellaneous Amendments) Regulations 2006, SI 2006/778, reg 10(1), (4), as from 6 April 2006.

Restriction on Decision-Making Pending Completion of Consultation

6 Consultation required before decisions to make listed changes affecting schemes

(1) No person falling within regulation 3(1) may decide to make a listed change that affects an occupational or personal pension scheme unless such consultation as is required by regulation 7(3) has been carried out.

(2) For the purposes of these Regulations, a change affecting an occupational or personal pension scheme is a "listed change" if—

(a) in relation to an occupational pension scheme, it is listed in regulation 8, or

(b) in relation to a personal pension scheme, it is listed in regulation 9,

and it is not excluded by virtue of regulation 10.

(3) Paragraph (1) does not require consultation to be carried out in any of the four cases described in paragraphs (4) to (7).

(4) The first case is where the active or prospective members of the scheme to whom the listed change relates were notified before 6th April 2006 of the proposal to make that change.

(5) The second case is where, in relation to an occupational pension scheme—

(a) consultation has already been carried out under these Regulations in respect of a proposal to prevent the future accrual of benefits, as described in regulation 8(1)(c), and

(b) there is a further proposal as a result of that consultation to make a decision to reduce the rate of such accrual, as described in regulation 8(3)(d).

(6) The third case is where, in relation to an occupational pension scheme—

(a) consultation has already been carried out under these Regulations in respect of a proposal to remove the liability to make employer contributions, as described in regulation 8(1)(d), and

(b) there is a further proposal as a result of that consultation to make a decision to reduce such contributions, as described in regulation 8(2).

(7) The fourth case is where, in relation to a personal pension scheme—

(a) consultation has already been carried out under these Regulations in respect of a proposal to cease employer contributions, as described in regulation 9(a), and

(b) there is a further proposal as a result of that consultation to make a decision to reduce such contributions, as described in regulation 9(b).

[3395F]

NOTES

Commencement: 6 April 2006.

7 Notifications to employers and duty to consult

(1) Any person falling within regulation 3(1) who proposes to make a listed change affecting an occupational or personal pension scheme must give written notice of that change to each employer in relation to the scheme.

(2) Paragraph (1) does not apply—

(a) in any of the four cases described in regulation 6(4) to (7), or

(b) where the person proposing the change is a relevant employer in relation to—

(i) an occupational pension scheme which is not a multi-employer scheme, or

(ii) a personal pension scheme.

(3) If his employees appear to him to include affected members—

(a) any employer notified under paragraph (1) who is a relevant employer, and

(b) any relevant employer falling within paragraph (2)(b),

must consult about the listed change in accordance with regulations 11 to 16.

(4) For the purposes of these Regulations "affected members", in relation to a proposal to make a listed change affecting an occupational or personal pension scheme, means the active or prospective members of the scheme to whom the listed change relates.

[3395G]

NOTES

Commencement: 6 April 2006.

8 Listed changes: occupational pension schemes

(1) Listed changes that affect occupational pension schemes are—

(a) to increase the normal pension age specified in the scheme rules for members or members of a particular description;

(b) to prevent new members, or new members of a particular description, from being admitted to the scheme;

(c) to prevent the future accrual of benefits under the scheme for or in respect of members or members of a particular description;

(d) to remove the liability to make employer contributions towards the scheme in respect of members or members of a particular description;

(e) to introduce member contributions in any circumstances in which no such contributions were previously payable;

(f) to make any increase in member contributions by or on behalf of members or members of a particular description;

(g) to make any change specified in paragraph (2) or (3).

(2) A listed change affecting only money purchase benefits is to make any reduction in the amount of employer contributions towards the scheme in respect of members or members of a particular description.

(3) Listed changes affecting only benefits which are not money purchase benefits are—

(a) to change to money purchase benefits some or all of the benefits that may be provided under the scheme to or in respect of members or members of a particular description;

(b) to change, in whole or in part, the basis for determining the rate of future accrual of benefits under the scheme for or in respect of members or members of a particular description;

(c) to modify the scheme under section 229(2) of the Pensions Act 2004 (matters requiring agreement of the employer) so as to reduce the rate of future accrual of benefits under the scheme for or in respect of members or members of a particular description;

(d) to make any other reduction in the rate of future accrual of benefit under the scheme for or in respect of members or members of a particular description.

(4) "Normal pension age" has the meaning given by section 180 of the Pension Schemes Act 1993 (normal pension age).

[3395H]

NOTES

Commencement: 6 April 2006.

9 Listed changes: personal pension schemes

Listed changes that affect personal pension schemes are—

(a) to cease employer contributions towards the scheme in respect of members or members of a particular description;

(b) to make any reduction in the amount of employer contributions towards the scheme in respect of members or members of a particular description;

(c) to make any increase in member contributions by or on behalf of members or members of a particular description.

[3395I]

NOTES

Commencement: 6 April 2006.

10 Listed changes: exclusions

(1) For the purposes of regulations 8 and 9, no account is to be taken of any change which—

(a) is made for the purposes of complying with a statutory provision,

(b) is made for the purposes of complying with a determination made by the Regulator, or

(c) has no lasting effect on a person's rights to be admitted to a scheme or on the benefits that may be provided under it.

(2) No change which is—

(a) a regulated modification within the meaning of the subsisting rights provisions, and

(b) subject to the requirements of those provisions,

falls within regulation 8.

(3) "Statutory provision" means a provision comprised in—

(a) an Act of Parliament or subordinate legislation made under such an Act, whenever passed or made,

(b) an Act of the Scottish Parliament or subordinate legislation made under such an Act, whenever passed or made.

(4) "Subsisting rights provisions" has the meaning given by section 67 of the Pensions Act 1995 (the subsisting rights provisions).

[3395J]

NOTES

Commencement: 6 April 2006.

Information Provision and Consultation

11 Requirement to provide information

(1) In relation to a proposal to make a listed change affecting an occupational or personal pension scheme, each relevant employer to whom regulation 7(3) applies must provide information about the proposal to—

(a) such of his employees as appear to him to be affected members of the scheme, and

(b) any representatives of such members who are to be consulted under regulation 12(2)(a) or (3) or 13(2).

(2) The information provided under paragraph (1) must—

(a) be in writing,

(b) be provided before the start of consultation under regulation 12 or 13,

(c) describe the listed change and state what effects it would (or would be likely to) have on the scheme and its members,

(d) be accompanied by any relevant background information,

(e) indicate the timescale on which measures giving effect to the change are proposed to be introduced, and

(f) be given in such fashion and with such content as are appropriate to enable, in particular, representatives of affected members to consider, conduct a study of, and give their views to the employer on, the impact of the listed change on such members.

[3395K]

NOTES

Commencement: 6 April 2006.

12 Consultation under existing arrangements

(1) If arrangements specified in paragraph (2) or (3) exist in relation to his employees, each relevant employer to whom regulation 7(3) applies must consult about a listed change in accordance with such one or more of those arrangements as he may choose.

(2) The specified arrangements are arrangements under which employees appearing to the employer to be affected members—

(a) are represented by—

(i) in the case of employees of a description in respect of which an independent trade union is recognised by the employer, the representatives of the trade union,

(ii) in the case of employees of a description which has elected or appointed information and consultation representatives, those representatives, or

(iii) where there exists one or more pre-existing agreements which apply to any of the employees, any representatives identified in accordance with such agreement or agreements; or

(b) are to be consulted directly in accordance with the terms of a negotiated agreement or a pre-existing agreement.

(3) In any case where—

(a) an election of representatives as described in regulation 13(2) has taken place before any arrangements referred to in paragraph (2) are made, and

(b) the interests of affected members are represented by such representatives,

the specified arrangements also include arrangements for consultation of those representatives.

(4) "Independent trade union" and "recognised", in relation to an independent trade union, have the same meaning as in the Trade Union and Labour Relations (Consolidation) Act 1992.

(5) "Information and consultation representatives" and "negotiated agreement" have the same meaning as in the Information and Consultation of Employees Regulations 2004.

(6) "Pre-existing agreement"—

(a) means an agreement between an employer and his employees or their representatives which satisfies the conditions set out in regulation 8(1)(a) to (d) of the Information and Consultation of Employees Regulations 2004 and which has not been superseded, but

(b) does not include an agreement concluded in accordance with regulations 17 or 42 to 45 of the Transnational Information and Consultation of Employees Regulations 1999 or a negotiated agreement.

[3395L]

NOTES

Commencement: 6 April 2006.

13 Consultation in cases not covered by regulation 12

(1) This regulation applies to a relevant employer to whom regulation 7(3) applies if (and only if) any of the employees who appear to the employer to be affected members are not covered by consultation arrangements referred to in regulation 12.

(2) Where, for the purposes of engaging in consultations under these Regulations, representatives of any affected members have been elected in an election which satisfies the requirements of regulation 14(1), the relevant employer must consult with those representatives about a listed change.

(3) If the interests of any affected members are not represented by representatives who are consulted under paragraph (2), the relevant employer must also consult directly with those members.

(4) If no representatives have been elected as described in paragraph (2), the relevant employer must consult directly with the affected members about a listed change.

(5) Consultation under this regulation—

(a) is required only in relation to the affected members falling within paragraph (1), and

(b) is additional to any consultation in relation to other affected members which is required by regulation 12.

[3395M]

NOTES

Commencement: 6 April 2006.

14 Election of representatives

(1) The requirements of this paragraph are that—

(a) the employer must make such arrangements as are reasonably practical to ensure that the election is fair;

(b) the employer must determine the number of representatives to be elected so that there are sufficient representatives to represent the interests of active members and the interests of prospective members;

(c) the employer must determine whether the active and prospective members should be represented by representatives of all such members or by representatives of particular descriptions of such members;

(d) before the election the employer must determine the term of office as representative of active and prospective members;

(e) the candidates for election must be active or prospective members of the scheme on the date of the election;

(f) no active or prospective member may unreasonably be excluded from standing for election;

(g) all active or prospective members on the date of the election are entitled to vote for member representatives;

(h) the members entitled to vote may vote for as many candidates as there are representatives to be elected to represent them or, if there are to be classes of representative for particular descriptions of member, may vote for as many candidates as there are representatives to be elected to represent their particular description of member;

(i) the election is conducted so as to secure that—

(i) so far as is reasonably practicable, those voting do so in secret, and

(ii) the votes given at the election are accurately counted.

(2) Where, after an election of representatives satisfying the requirements of paragraph (1) has been held—

(a) one of those elected ceases to act as a representative, and

(b) the active or prospective members (or any description of them) are no longer represented,

those members must elect another representative by an election satisfying the requirements of paragraph (1)(a), (e), (f) and (i).

(3) The relevant employer must from time to time review the number of representatives determined under paragraph (1)(b) and the number of representatives elected must be adjusted accordingly (whether by members electing one or more other representatives by an election satisfying the requirements of paragraph (1)(a), (e), (f) and (i), by not holding an election under paragraph (2) or otherwise).

[3395N]

NOTES

Commencement: 6 April 2006.

15 Conduct of consultation

(1) Each relevant employer who carries out a consultation must make such arrangements with respect to the persons to be consulted as appear to him to secure that, so far as is reasonably practicable, the consultation covers all affected members.

(2) In the course of consultation, the relevant employer and any person consulted are under a duty to work in a spirit of co-operation, taking into account the interests of both sides.

(3) At the start of any consultation required by these Regulations, the relevant employer must notify the persons to be consulted of any date set for the end of the consultation or for the submission of written comments.

(4) An appropriate period must be allowed for carrying out the consultation which in any event must not be less than 60 days.

(5) If no responses to the consultation are received before the end of the period allowed for the consultation in accordance with paragraphs (3) and (4), the consultation is to be regarded as complete.

[3395O]

NOTES

Commencement: 6 April 2006.

16 End of consultation

(1) Where the relevant employer who carries out a consultation is not the person who proposed the listed change ("P"), the relevant employer must, as soon as reasonably practicable after the consultation is complete—

(a) report to P on the views (if any) which were expressed to the relevant employer otherwise than in writing,

(b) where the responses include written comments, forward those comments to P, and

(c) in any case where no responses were received, notify P accordingly.

(2) In a case falling within paragraph (1), P must take reasonable steps to satisfy himself that each consultation required by these Regulations in relation to the scheme was carried out in accordance with regulations 11 to 15.

(3) After the end of the period allowed for the consultation, the person who proposed the listed change must consider the responses (if any) received in the course of consultation before making his decision as to whether or not to make a listed change.

[3395P]

NOTES

Commencement: 6 April 2006.

Miscellaneous

17 Employment rights and protections in connection with consultation

The Schedule to these Regulations contains provision as to employment rights and protections which, in connection with consultation under these Regulations, apply to the employees of an employer in relation to an occupational or personal pension scheme.

[3395Q]

NOTES

Commencement: 6 April 2006.

18 Exclusivity of remedy

(1) The remedy for a failure to comply with any obligations under regulations 6 to 16 in respect of any proposal or decision to make a listed change is by way of complaint to the Regulator.

(2) A complaint may be made by—

(a) any representative of affected members who falls within regulation 12(2)(a) or (3) or 13(2) (including any such representative who is not consulted), and

(b) any active or prospective member of an occupational or personal pension scheme who considers that he is or may be an affected member.

[3395R]

NOTES

Commencement: 6 April 2006.

19 Powers of the Regulator to waive or relax requirements

(1) The Regulator may by order waive or relax any of the requirements of regulations 6 to 16.

(2) The power under paragraph (1) may be exercised only if the Regulator is satisfied that it is necessary to do so in order to protect the interests of the generality of the members of the scheme.

[3395S]

NOTES

Commencement: 6 April 2006.

20 (*Adds the Pensions Act 2004, Sch 2, Pt 5.*)

21 Waiver or relaxation of requirements: prescribed regulatory function

The Regulator's power to make an order under regulation 19 to waive or relax any of the requirements of regulations 6 to 16 is prescribed for the purposes of section 97(5)(u) of the Pensions Act 2004 (special procedure: applicable cases).

[3395T]

NOTES

Commencement: 6 April 2006.

22 (*Amends the Financial Assistance Scheme (Internal Review) Regulations 2005, SI 2005/1994, reg 5.*)

SCHEDULE
EMPLOYMENT RIGHTS AND PROTECTIONS IN CONNECTION WITH CONSULTATION

Regulation 17

1. In this Schedule—

"the 1996 Act" means the Employment Rights Act 1996;

"consulted representative" has the meaning given by paragraph 2(2);

"contract of employment" means a contract of service or apprenticeship whether express or implied and (if it is express) whether oral or in writing;

"employee" means an individual who has entered into or works under a contract of employment and includes, where the employment has ceased, an individual who worked under a contract of employment;

"employment", in relation to an employee, means employment under a contract of employment (and "employed" has a corresponding meaning);

"employer", in relation to an employee, means the person by whom the employee is (or where employment has ceased, was) employed.

Right to time off and Remuneration

2.—(1) An employee who—

(a) is a representative falling within regulation 12(2)(a) or (3) or 13(2), and

(b) is consulted under these Regulations about a listed change by a relevant employer,

is entitled to be permitted by his employer to take reasonable time off during the employee's working hours in order to perform his functions as such a representative.

(2) In this Schedule "consulted representative" means an employee who satisfies the conditions specified in sub-paragraph (1)(a) and (b).

(3) For the purposes of this paragraph, the working hours of an employee shall be taken to be any time when, in accordance with his contract of employment, the employee is required to be at work.

3.—(1) An employee who is permitted to take time off under paragraph 2 is entitled to be paid remuneration by his employer for the time taken off at the appropriate hourly rate.

(2) Chapter 2 of Part 14 of the 1996 Act (a week's pay) shall apply in relation to this paragraph as it applies in relation to section 62 of the 1996 Act (right to remuneration of certain representatives).

(3) The appropriate hourly rate, in relation to an employee, is the amount of one week's pay divided by the number of normal working hours in a week for that employee when employed under the contract of employment in force on the day when the time is taken off.

(4) But where the number of normal working hours differs from week to week or over a longer period, the amount of one week's pay shall be divided instead by—

(a) the average number of normal working hours calculated by dividing by twelve the total number of the employee's normal working hours during the period of twelve weeks ending with the last complete week before the day when the time is taken off, or

(b) where the employee has not been employed for a sufficient period to enable the calculations to be made under paragraph (a), a number which fairly represents the number of normal working hours in a week having regard to such of the considerations specified in sub-paragraph (5) as are appropriate in the circumstances.

(5) The considerations referred to in sub-paragraph (4)(b) are—

(a) the average number of normal working hours in a week which the employee could expect in accordance with the terms of his contract, and

(b) the average number of normal working hours of other employees engaged in relevant comparable employment with the same employer.

(6) A right to any amount under sub-paragraph (1) does not affect any right of an employee in relation to remuneration under his contract of employment ("contractual remuneration").

(7) Any contractual remuneration paid to an employee in respect of a period of time off under paragraph 2 goes towards discharging any liability of the employer to pay remuneration under sub-paragraph (1) in respect of that period, and, conversely, any payment of remuneration under sub-paragraph (1) in respect of a period goes towards discharging any liability of the employer to pay contractual remuneration in respect of that period.

4.—(1) An employee may present a complaint to an employment tribunal that his employer—

(a) has unreasonably refused to permit him to take time off as required by paragraph 2, or

(b) has failed to pay the whole or part of any amount to which the employee is entitled under paragraph 3.

(2) A tribunal shall not consider a complaint under this paragraph unless it is presented—

(a) before the end of the period of three months beginning with the day on which the time off was taken or on which it is alleged the time off should have been permitted, or

(b) within such further period as the tribunal considers reasonable in a case where it is satisfied that it was not reasonably practicable for the complaint to be presented before the end of that period of three months.

(3) Where a tribunal finds a complaint under this paragraph well-founded, the tribunal shall make a declaration to that effect.

(4) If the complaint is that the employer has unreasonably refused to permit the employee to take time off, the tribunal shall also order the employer to pay to the employee an amount equal to the remuneration to which he would have been entitled under paragraph 3 if the employer had not refused.

(5) If the complaint is that the employer has failed to pay the employee the whole or part of any amount to which he is entitled under paragraph 3, the tribunal shall also order the employer to pay to the employee the amount it finds due to him.

Protections against Unfair Dismissal

5.—(1) An employee who is dismissed and to whom sub-paragraph (2) or (4) applies shall be regarded, if the reason (or if more than one, the principal reason) for the dismissal is a reason specified in, respectively, sub-paragraph (3) or (5), as unfairly dismissed for the purposes of Part 10 of the 1996 Act (which makes provision as to rights and remedies relating to unfair dismissal).

(2) This sub-paragraph applies to an employee who is—

(a) a consulted representative, or

(b) a candidate in an election in which any person elected will, on being elected, be a representative of such description as is referred to in regulation 13(2).

(3) The reasons are that—

(a) the employee performed or proposed to perform any functions or activities under these Regulations in his capacity as such a representative or candidate,

(b) the employee exercised or proposed to exercise an entitlement conferred on the employee by paragraph 2 or 3, or

(c) the employee (or a person acting on his behalf) made or proposed to make a request to exercise such an entitlement.

(4) This sub-paragraph applies to any employee who is an active or prospective member of an occupational or personal pension scheme, whether or not he is an employee to whom sub-paragraph (2) applies.

(5) The reasons are that the employee—

(a) took, or proposed to take, any proceedings before an employment tribunal to enforce a right or secure an entitlement conferred on him by this Schedule,

(b) complained or proposed to complain to the Regulator that any person falling within regulation 3(1)—

(i) has decided to make a listed change affecting an occupational or personal pension scheme in contravention of regulation 6(1), or

(ii) has failed to comply with the requirements of regulation 16(2) or (3),

(c) complained or proposed to complain to the Regulator that any consultation required by these Regulations was not carried out in accordance with the requirements of these Regulations,

(d) stood as a candidate in an election in which any person elected would, on being elected, be a representative of such description as is referred to in regulation 13(2),

(e) influenced or sought to influence by lawful means the way in which votes were to be cast by other employees in an election arranged under regulation 14,

(f) voted in such an election,

(g) expressed doubts, whether to an election supervisor or otherwise, as to whether such an election had been properly conducted, or

(h) proposed to do, failed to do, or proposed to decline to do any of the things mentioned in paragraphs (d) to (g).

(6) It is immaterial for the purpose of sub-paragraph (5)(a)—

(a) whether or not the employee has the right or entitlement, or

(b) whether or not the right has been infringed,

but for that provision to apply, the claim to the right and, if applicable, the claim that it has been infringed must be made in good faith.

6. …

Protections from Suffering other Detriment in Employment

7.—(1) An employee to whom sub-paragraph (2) or (4) applies has the right not to be subjected to any detriment by any act, or deliberate failure to act, by his employer done on a ground specified in, respectively, sub-paragraph (3) or (5).

(2) This sub-paragraph applies to an employee who is—

(a) a consulted representative, or

(b) a candidate in an election in which any person elected will, on being elected, be a representative of such description as is referred to in regulation 13(2).

(3) The grounds are that—

(a) the employee performed or proposed to perform any functions or activities under these Regulations in his capacity as such a representative or candidate,

(b) the employee exercised or proposed to exercise an entitlement conferred on the employee by paragraph 2 or 3, or

(c) the employee (or a person acting on his behalf) made or proposed to make a request to exercise such an entitlement.

(4) This sub-paragraph applies to any employee who is an active or prospective member of an occupational or personal pension scheme, whether or not he is an employee to whom sub-paragraph (2) applies.

(5) The grounds are that the employee—

(a) took, or proposed to take, any proceedings before an employment tribunal to enforce a right or secure an entitlement conferred on him by this Schedule,

(b) complained or proposed to complain to the Regulator that any person falling within regulation 3(1)—

(i) has decided to make a listed change affecting an occupational or personal pension scheme in contravention of regulation 6(1), or

(ii) has failed to comply with the requirements of regulation 16(2) or (3),

(c) complained or proposed to complain to the Regulator that any consultation required by these Regulations was not carried out in accordance with the requirements of these Regulations,

(d) stood as a candidate in an election in which any person elected would, on being elected, be a representative of such description as is referred to in regulation 13(2),

(e) influenced or sought to influence by lawful means the way in which votes were to be cast by other employees in an election arranged under regulation 14,

(f) voted in such a election,

(g) expressed doubts, whether to an election supervisor or otherwise, as to whether such an election had been properly conducted, or

(h) proposed to do, failed to do, or proposed to decline to do any of the things mentioned in paragraphs (d) to (g).

(6) It is immaterial for the purpose of sub-paragraph (5)(a)—

(a) whether or not the employee has the right or entitlement, or

(b) whether or not the right has been infringed,

but for that provision to apply, the claim to the right and, if applicable, the claim that it has been infringed must be made in good faith.

(7) This paragraph does not apply where the detriment in question amounts to dismissal.

8.—(1) An employee may present a complaint to an employment tribunal that he has been subjected to a detriment in contravention of paragraph 7.

(2) The provisions of sections 48(2) to (4) and 49(1) to (5) of the 1996 Act (complaints to employment tribunals and remedies) shall apply in relation to a complaint under this paragraph as they apply in relation to a complaint under section 48 of that Act.

Conciliation and Appeals

9, 10. …

Miscellaneous

11. Any provision in any agreement (whether an employee's contract or not) is void in so far as it purports to exclude or limit the operation of any provision of regulations 6 to 16.

12.—(1) Any provision in any agreement (whether an employee's contract or not) is void in so far as it purports—

(a) to exclude or limit the operation of any provision of this Schedule, or
(b) to preclude a person from bringing any proceedings before an employment tribunal under this Schedule.

(2) Sub-paragraph (1) does not apply to any agreement to refrain from instituting or continuing proceedings before an employment tribunal where a conciliation officer has taken action under section 18 of the Employment Tribunals Act 1996 (conciliation).

(3) Sub-paragraph (1) does not apply to any agreement to refrain from instituting or continuing before an employment tribunal proceedings within section 18(1) of the Employment Tribunals Act 1996 (which specifies proceedings under these Regulations as being proceedings where conciliation is available) if the conditions specified in paragraph 13 regulating compromise agreements are satisfied in relation to the agreement.

13.—(1) For the purposes of paragraph 12(3) the conditions regulating compromise agreements are that—

(a) the agreement must be in writing,
(b) the agreement must relate to the particular proceedings,
(c) the employee must have received advice from a relevant independent adviser as to the terms and effect of the proposed agreement and, in particular, its effect on his ability to pursue his rights before an employment tribunal,
(d) there must be in force, when the adviser gives the advice, a contract of insurance, or an indemnity provided for members of a profession or a professional body, covering the risk of a claim by the employee in respect of loss arising in consequence of the advice,
(e) the agreement must identify the adviser, and
(f) the agreement must state that the conditions in paragraphs (a) to (e) are satisfied.

(2) A person is a relevant independent adviser for the purposes of sub-paragraph (1)(c)—

(a) if he is a qualified lawyer,
(b) if he is an officer, official, employee or member of an independent trade union who has been certified in writing by the trade union as competent to give advice and as authorised to do so on behalf of the trade union, or
(c) if he works at an advice centre (whether as an employee or as a volunteer) and has been certified in writing by the centre as competent to give advice and as authorised to do so on behalf of the centre.

(3) But a person is not a relevant independent adviser for the purposes of sub-paragraph (1)(c)—

(a) if he is, is employed by or is acting in the matter for the employer or an associated employer,
(b) in the case of a person within sub-paragraph (2)(b) or (c), if the trade union or advice centre is the employer or an associated employer, or
(c) in the case of a person within sub-paragraph (2)(c), if the employee makes a payment for the advice received from him.

(4) In sub-paragraph (2)(a) "qualified lawyer" means—

(a) as respects England and Wales, a barrister (whether in practice as such or employed to give legal advice), a solicitor who holds a practising certificate, or a person other than a barrister or a solicitor who is an authorised advocate or authorised litigator (within the meaning of the Courts and Legal Services Act 1990);

(b) as respects Scotland, an advocate (whether in practice as such or employed to give legal advice) or a solicitor who holds a practising certificate.

(5) A person shall be treated as being a qualified lawyer within the meaning of sub-paragraph (4)(a) if he is a Fellow of the Institute of Legal Executives employed by a solicitors' practice.

(6) In this paragraph—

(a) "independent trade union" has the same meaning as in the Trade Union and Labour Relations (Consolidation) Act 1992; and

(b) for the purposes of sub-paragraph (3) any two employers shall be treated as associated if—

(i) one is a company of which the other (directly or indirectly) has control, or

(ii) both are companies of which a third person (directly or indirectly) has control,

and "associated employer" shall be construed accordingly.

[3395U]

NOTES

Commencement: 6 April 2006.

Para 6: amends the Employment Rights Act 1996, ss 105, 108 at **[1149]**, **[1152]**, and amended s 109 (repealed).

Paras 9, 10: amend the Employment Tribunals Act 1996, ss 18, 21 at **[975]**, **[978]**.

Conciliation: employment tribunal proceedings and claims which could be the subject of employment tribunal proceedings under paras 4 or 8 of this Schedule are proceedings to which the Employment Tribunals Act 1996, s 18 applies; see s 18(1)(q) of that Act at **[975]**. The standard conciliation period applies to such proceedings by virtue of the Employment Tribunals (Constitution and Rules of Procedure) Regulations 2004, SI 2004/1861, Sch 1, rule 22(1), (6).

Tribunal jurisdiction: the Employment Act 2002, ss 31, 32, 38, at **[1493]**, **[1494]**, **[1496]** apply to proceedings before the employment tribunal relating to a claim under para 8 of this Schedule; see ss 31(1), 32(1), 38(1) of, and Schs 3–5 to, the 2002 Act at **[1508]–[1510]**.

For the circumstances in which the normal time limit for presenting a complaint under para 8 of this Schedule is extended for a period of three months, see the Employment Act 2002 (Dispute Resolution) Regulations 2004, SI 2004/752, regs 15 and 18 at **[3096]** and **[3098]**, and reg 34 of these Regulations at **[3021]**.

Employment Appeal Tribunal: see the introductory notes to these Regulations.

OCCUPATIONAL PENSION SCHEMES (MEMBER-NOMINATED TRUSTEES AND DIRECTORS) REGULATIONS 2006

(SI 2006/714)

NOTES

Made: 13 March 2006.

Authority: Pensions Act 2004, ss 241(8)(c), 242(10), 243(2), 315(2), (4), (5), 318(1).

Commencement: 6 April 2006 (see further reg 1(1) at **[3396]**).

1 Citation, commencement and interpretation

(1) These Regulations may be cited as the Occupational Pension Schemes (Member-nominated Trustees and Directors) Regulations 2006 and shall come into force on 6th April 2006, immediately prior to the coming into force of Article 2(6) of the Pensions Act 2004 (Commencement No 8) Order.

(2) In these Regulations—

"the Act" means the Pensions Act 2004;

"the 1995 Act" means the Pensions Act 1995;

"associated" shall be construed in accordance with paragraph (4);

"church legislation" means—

(a) any Measure of the Church Assembly or of the General Synod of the Church of England; or

(b) any order, regulation or other instrument made under, or by virtue of such a Measure;

"connected" shall be construed in accordance with paragraph (4);

"direct payment paid-up insurance scheme" means a scheme under which—

(a) no further contributions are payable;

(b) the benefits that may be provided in respect of an individual are determined by reference to the value of the whole or a specified part of the rights under a contract of insurance; and

(c) the benefits in respect of any member are, in accordance with an agreement made between the insurer and the trustees of the scheme (or a subsequent agreement made with any person for the provision of those benefits in respect of the member, by that person), to be paid by the insurer (or that person) directly to the member or to a person entitled to benefits in respect of that member;

"former old code scheme" means a registered pension scheme which was formerly approved under section 208 of the Income and Corporation Taxes Act 1970 (approved superannuation funds) and under the provisions of which—

(a) no further contributions are payable; and

(b) the entitlement in respect of each member is to a benefit consisting of a specified fixed amount which may not be altered unless—

(i) the member retires otherwise than at his normal pension age; or

(ii) another person becomes entitled to a benefit in respect of him;

"independently selected" in relation to a trustee of a scheme or a director of a company which is a trustee of a scheme, means selected as a trustee (or, as the case may, be a director)—

(a) by some or all of the members of the scheme (otherwise than wholly or mainly by members who are directors of companies which are employers in relation to the scheme); or

(b) by an organisation which represents some or all of the members of the scheme (other than wholly or mainly members who are such directors);

"insurer" (subject to paragraph (5), means—

(a) a person who has permission under Part 4 of the Financial Services and Markets Act 2000 (permission to carry on regulated activities) to effect or carry out contracts of long-term insurance; or

(b) an EEA firm of the kind mentioned in paragraph 5(d) of Schedule 3 to that Act (EEA passport rights), which has permission under paragraph 15 of that Schedule (grant of permission) (as a result of qualifying for authorisation under paragraph 12 of that Schedule) to effect or carry out contracts of long-term insurance;

"registered pension scheme" has the meaning given in section 150(2) of the Finance Act 2004 (meaning of pension scheme);

"relevant centralised scheme" means a scheme in which—

(a) membership is open to employees of more than one employer under a single scheme;

(b) at least two of the employers are not associated or connected; and

(c) in the case of a scheme which has one or more trustee and in which each trustee is a company—

(i) the scheme rules do not provide that the power to appoint or remove all the directors is exercisable solely by one employer; and

(ii) at least one-third of the directors of the company or each of those companies are independent or independently selected; or

(d) in the case of a scheme where at least one of the trustees is not a company, either—

(i) the scheme rules do not provide that the power to appoint or remove all the trustees is exercisable solely by one employer; or

(ii) at least one-third of the trustees are persons who—

(aa) have no legal or beneficial interest in the assets of any of the employers or of the scheme (otherwise than as trustees) and are neither connected nor associated with, any of the employers; and

(bb) have been independently selected;

"relevant executive pension scheme" means a scheme—

(a) in relation to which the company is the only employer and the sole trustee; and

(b) the members of which are either current or former directors of the company and which includes at least one-third of the current directors;

["relevant small occupational pension scheme" means a scheme with fewer than twelve members, where—

(a) all the members are trustees of the scheme and either—

(i) the provisions of the scheme provide that any decision made by the trustees is made by the unanimous agreement of the trustees who are members of the scheme, or

(ii) the scheme has a trustee who is independent in relation to the scheme for the purposes of section 23 of the 1995 Act (power to appoint independent trustees), and is registered in the register maintained by the Authority in accordance with regulations made under subsection (4) of that section; or

(b) all the members are directors of a company which is the sole trustee of the scheme, and either—

(i) the provisions of the scheme provide that any decision made by the company in its capacity as trustee are made by the unanimous agreement of the directors who are members of the scheme, or

(ii) one of the directors of the company is independent in relation to the scheme for the purposes of section 23 of the 1995 Act, and is registered in the register maintained by the Authority in accordance with regulations made under subsection (4) of that section;]

"relevant wholly insured scheme" means a scheme under which there is a sole trustee and all the benefits are secured by contracts of insurance or annuity contracts, some or all of which are with an insurer who—

(a) is, or is connected, with the sole trustee of the scheme; but

(b) is not, and is not connected, with the employer;

"section 615(6) scheme" means a scheme with such a superannuation fund as is mentioned in section 615(6) of the Income and Corporation Taxes Act 1988 (exemption from tax in respect of certain pensions);

"small insured scheme" means a scheme—

(a) with fewer than twelve members; and

(b) in which all the scheme benefits are secured with an insurer under a contract of insurance or annuity contract.

(3) For the purposes of paragraph (2), a director is independent in relation to a scheme only if he—

(a) has no direct legal or beneficial interest in the assets of any of the employers or of the scheme; and

(b) is neither connected, nor associated with, any of the employers.

(4) For the purposes of these Regulations—

(a) sections 249 and 435 of the Insolvency Act 1986 (connected and associated persons) shall apply as they apply for the purposes of that Act; and

(b) section 74 of the Bankruptcy (Scotland) Act 1985 (associated persons) shall apply as it applies for the purposes of that Act.

(5) The definition of insurer in paragraph (2) must be read with—

(a) section 22 of the Financial Services and Markets Act 2000 (the classes of activity and categories of investment); and

(b) any relevant order under that section; or

(c) Schedule 2 to that Act (regulated activities).

(6) References to "employer" and "employers" in paragraphs (c)(i) and (d) of the definition in paragraph (2) of "relevant centralised scheme" and in paragraph (3) do not include companies which carry on the business of acting as trustee of, or providing administrative services to, the scheme and no other business.

[3396]

NOTES

Commencement: 6 April 2006 (see further para (1) above).

Para (2): definition "relevant small occupational pension scheme" substituted by the Occupational and Personal Pension Schemes (Miscellaneous Amendments) Regulations 2007, SI 2007/814, reg 21(1), (2), as from 6 April 2007.

2 Exemptions from requirement to have member-nominated trustees

For the purposes of section 241(8)(c) of the Act (requirement for member-nominated trustees) a scheme is of a prescribed description, if the scheme—

(a) has fewer than two members;
(b) is a scheme to which section 22 of the 1995 Act (independent trustees – circumstances in which following provisions apply) applies;
(c) is an occupational pension scheme within the meaning given by section 1 of the Pension Schemes Act 1993 (categories of pension schemes), but if it is not a registered pension scheme;
(d) is a relevant small occupational pension scheme;
(e) is a relevant centralised scheme;
(f) is a direct payment, paid-up insurance scheme;
(g) is a former old code scheme;
(h) is a section 615(6) scheme;
(i) is set up under section 2 of the Parliamentary and other Pensions Act 1987 (power to provide for pensions for Members of the House of Commons etc);
(j) has been modified under Schedule 5 to the Coal Industry Act 1994 (pension provision in connection with restructuring);
(k) is a scheme where the sole trustee, or all the trustees are independent within the meaning given by section 23(3) of the 1995 Act;
(l) is a stakeholder pension scheme within the meaning of section 1 of the Welfare Reform and Pensions Act 1999 (meaning of "stakeholder pension scheme");
(m) is a small insured scheme;
(n) is independent of the employer by virtue of the employer having been dissolved or liquidated prior to 6th April 2005; …
(o) is a scheme where the trustee is a body governed by church legislation;
[(p) is set up under section 18 of the Government of Wales Act 1998;
(q) is designated as an existing scheme by virtue of article 15 of the Railway Pensions (Protection and Designation of Schemes) Order 1994 (designation of existing schemes)].

[3397]

NOTES

Commencement: 6 April 2006 (see further reg 1(1) at **[3396]**).

Word omitted from para (n) revoked, and paras (p), (q) added, by the Occupational and Personal Pension Schemes (Miscellaneous Amendments) Regulations 2007, SI 2007/814, reg 21(1), (3), as from 6 April 2007.

3 Prescribed exemptions from requirement to have member-nominated directors of corporate trustees

For the purposes of section 242(10) of the Act (requirement for member-nominated directors of corporate trustees) a scheme is of a prescribed description if the scheme—

(a) has fewer than two members;
(b) is a scheme to which section 22 of the 1995 Act applies;
(c) is an occupational pension scheme within the meaning given by section 1 of the Pension Schemes Act 1993, but if it is not a registered pension scheme;
(d) is a relevant small occupational pension scheme;
(e) is a relevant centralised scheme;
(f) is a direct payment, paid-up insurance scheme;
(g) is a former old code scheme;
(h) is a section 615(6) scheme;
(i) is set up under section 2 of the Parliamentary and other Pensions Act 1987;
(j) has been modified under Schedule 5 to the Coal Industry Act 1994;
(k) is a stakeholder pension scheme within the meaning of section 1 of the Welfare Reform and Pensions Act 1999;
(l) is a scheme which is a relevant executive pension scheme in relation to the company;
(m) is a scheme where the sole director, or all the directors are independent within the meaning given by section 23(3) of the 1995 Act;
(n) is a small insured scheme;
(o) is independent of the employer by virtue of the employer having been dissolved or liquidated prior to 6th April 2005;
(p) is a scheme which is a relevant wholly insured scheme; …

(q) is a scheme where the trustee is a body governed by church legislation;
[(r) is set up under section 18 of the Government of Wales Act 1998;
(s) is designated as an existing scheme by virtue of article 15 of the Railway Pensions (Protection and Designation of Schemes) Order 1994].

[3398]

NOTES

Commencement: 6 April 2006 (see further reg 1(1) at **[3396]**).

Word omitted from para (p) revoked, and paras (r), (s) added, by the Occupational and Personal Pension Schemes (Miscellaneous Amendments) Regulations 2007, SI 2007/814, reg 21(1), (4), as from 6 April 2007.

4 Transitional

In relation to a scheme which has alternative arrangements for the appointment of trustees or directors approved under section 17(1) (exceptions), or 19(1) (corporate trustees: exceptions) of the 1995 Act immediately prior to the date those sections were repealed, the approval of such arrangements shall cease to have effect—

(a) on the date the approval under regulation 20 of the Occupational Pension Schemes (Member-nominated Trustees and Directors) Regulations 1996 (cessation of approval of appropriate rules and alternative arrangements) would cease to have effect but for the revocation of those Regulations; or
(b) on 31st October 2007,

whichever is the earlier.

[3399]

NOTES

Commencement: 6 April 2006 (see further reg 1(1) at **[3396]**).

5 Modifications of sections 241 and 242 of the Act

(1) Sections 241 (requirement for member-nominated trustees) and 242 (requirement for member-nominated directors of corporate trustees) of the Act are modified in their application to the cases prescribed in paragraphs (2) to (6).

(2) In relation to a scheme where the scheme rules contain provisions requiring that there be more than one-third member-nominated trustees or directors as the case may be, sections 241 and 242 of the Act are modified as if—

(a) in section 241(1)(a) for "at least one-third of the total number of trustees" there were substituted "the nomination and selection of member-nominated trustees at least in a proportion not less than that proportion set out in the scheme rules";
(b) section 241(4) were omitted;
(c) in section 242(1)(a) for "at least one-third of the total number of directors of the company" there were substituted "the nomination and selection of member-nominated directors at least in a proportion not less than that proportion set out in the scheme rules"; and
(d) section 242(4) were omitted.

(3) In relation to a scheme where the scheme rules provide that trustees of the scheme may be removed by a vote of the membership, then in relation to any application of that scheme rule, section 241 shall be modified as if subsection (6) were omitted.

(4) In relation to a scheme which has member-nominated trustees or, as the case may be, directors appointed under section 16(1) (requirement for member-nominated trustees) or section 18(1) of the 1995 Act (corporate trustees: member-nominated directors) immediately prior to the date those sections are repealed, sections 241 and 242 of the Act are modified as if—

(a) in section 241 after subsection (2) there were inserted—

"(2A) In the case of a scheme which has member-nominated trustees appointed under section 16(1) of the Pensions Act 1995 immediately prior to the date that section was revoked, "member-nominated trustees" includes any member-nominated trustees appointed under that section for the remainder of their term of office under section 16(5)."; and

(b) in section 242 after subsection (2) there were inserted—

"(2A) In the case of a scheme which has member-nominated directors appointed under section 18(1) of the Pensions Act 1995 immediately prior to the date that section was revoked, "member-nominated directors" includes any member-nominated directors appointed under that section for the remainder of their term of office under section 18(5).".

(5) In relation to a scheme which has arrangements for the appointment of member-nominated trustees or directors approved under sections 17(1) or 19(1) of the 1995 Act, immediately prior to the date those sections are repealed, sections 241 and 242 of the Act are modified as if—

(a) in section 241 for subsection (3)(a) and (b) there were substituted—

"(a) the date the approval under regulation 20 of the Occupational Pension Schemes (Member-nominated Trustees and Directors) Regulations 1996 (cessation of approval of appropriate rules and alternative arrangements) would cease to have effect but for the revocation of those Regulations; or

(b) 31st October 2007,

whichever is the earlier."; and

(b) in section 242 for subsection (3)(a) and (b) there were substituted—

"(a) the date the approval under regulation 20 of the Occupational Pension Schemes (Member-nominated Trustees and Directors) Regulations 1996 (cessation of approval of appropriate rules and alternative arrangements) would cease to have effect but for the revocation of those Regulations; or

(b) 31st October 2007;

whichever is the earlier.".

(6) In relation to a scheme which has no active or pensioner members section 241 and 242 of the Act are modified as if for subsection (2)(a) in both sections, there were substituted—

"(a) are nominated as the result of a process in which at least such deferred members as the trustees determine are eligible to participate, and".

[3400]–[3402]

NOTES

Commencement: 6 April 2006 (see further reg 1(1) at **[3396]**).

6, Schedule (*Reg 6 introduces the Schedule to these Regulations* (*revocations*)*, all of which are outside the scope of this work.*)

EMPLOYMENT EQUALITY (AGE) REGULATIONS 2006

(SI 2006/1031)

NOTES

Made: 3 April 2006.

Authority: European Communities Act 1972, s 2(2).

Commencement: 1 October 2006 (certain purposes); 1 December 2006 (otherwise); see reg 1 at **[3403]**.

These Regulations are the final stage of domestic implementation in the UK of the EU Equality Directive 2000/78/EC at **[3994]**.

Conciliation: employment tribunal proceedings and claims which could be the subject of employment tribunal proceedings under reg 36 of these Regulations (but not Sch 6, paras 11 or 12) are proceedings to which the Employment Tribunals Act 1996, s 18 applies; see s 18(1)(r) of that Act at **[975]**.

Employment Appeal Tribunal: an appeal lies to the Employment Appeal Tribunal on any question of law arising from any decision of, or in any proceedings before, an employment tribunal under or by virtue of these Regulations; see the Employment Tribunals Act 1996, s 21(1)(s) at **[978]**.

ARRANGEMENT OF REGULATIONS

PART 1
GENERAL

PART 2
DISCRIMINATION IN EMPLOYMENT AND VOCATIONAL TRAINING

PART 3
OTHER UNLAWFUL ACTS

PART 4
GENERAL EXCEPTIONS FROM PARTS 2 AND 3

PART 5
ENFORCEMENT

PART 6
SUPPLEMENTAL

SCHEDULES:

PART 1
GENERAL

1 Citation, commencement and extent

(1) These Regulations may be cited as the Employment Equality (Age) Regulations 2006, and shall come into force[—

(a) subject to sub-paragraphs (b) and (c), on 1st October 2006;

(b) for the purposes of regulation 7 (Applicants and Employees) and regulation 24 (Relationships which have come to an end), in so far as either regulation relates to arrangements for—

(i) the payment of pension contributions;

(ii) admission to a pension scheme; and

(iii) the provision of any benefits relating to pensions,

on 1st December 2006, and

(c) for the purposes of regulation 11 (Pension Schemes) and Schedule 2 (Pension Schemes), on 1st December 2006].

(2) Any amendment, repeal or revocation made by these Regulations has the same extent as the provision to which it relates.

(3) Subject to that, these Regulations do not extend to Northern Ireland.

[3403]

NOTES

Commencement: 1 October 2006.

Para (1): words in square brackets substituted by the Employment Equality (Age) (Amendment) Regulations 2006, SI 2006/2408, reg 2(1), (2), as from 30 September 2006 (see further the note below).

Note: as originally enacted, para (1) above provided that the whole of these Regulations come into force on 1 October 2006. However, on the day before they were due to come into force the commencement of regs 7, 11, 24 and Sch 2 was changed by the amending Regulations noted above.

2 Interpretation

(1) In these Regulations, references to discrimination are to any discrimination falling within regulation 3 (discrimination on grounds of age), regulation 4 (discrimination by way of

victimisation) or regulation 5 (instructions to discriminate) and related expressions shall be construed accordingly, and references to harassment shall be construed in accordance with regulation 6 (harassment on grounds of age).

(2) In these Regulations—

"1996 Act" means the Employment Rights Act 1996;

"act" includes a deliberate omission;

"benefit", except in regulation 11 and Schedule 2 (pension schemes), includes facilities and services;

"commencement date" means 1st October 2006;

"Crown employment" means—

(a) service for purposes of a Minister of the Crown or government department, other than service of a person holding a statutory office; or

(b) service on behalf of the Crown for purposes of a person holding a statutory office or purposes of a statutory body;

"detriment" does not include harassment within the meaning of regulation 6;

"employment" means employment under a contract of service or of apprenticeship or a contract personally to do any work, and related expressions (such as "employee" and "employer") shall be construed accordingly, but this definition does not apply in relation to regulation 30 (exception for retirement) or to Schedules 2, 6, 7 and 8;

"Great Britain" includes such of the territorial waters of the United Kingdom as are adjacent to Great Britain;

"Minister of the Crown" includes the Treasury and the Defence Council;

"proprietor", in relation to a school, has the meaning given by section 579 of the Education Act 1996;

"relevant member of the House of Commons staff" means any person who was appointed by the House of Commons Commission or who is a member of the Speaker's personal staff;

"relevant member of the House of Lords staff" means any person who is employed under a contract of employment with the Corporate Officer of the House of Lords;

"school", in England and Wales, has the meaning given by section 4 of the Education Act 1996, and, in Scotland, has the meaning given by section 135(1) of the Education (Scotland) Act 1980, and references to a school are to an institution in so far as it is engaged in the provision of education under those sections;

"service for purposes of a Minister of the Crown or government department" does not include service in any office mentioned in Schedule 2 (Ministerial offices) to the House of Commons Disqualification Act 1975;

"statutory body" means a body set up by or in pursuance of an enactment, and "statutory office" means an office so set up; and

"worker" in relation to regulations 32 and 34 and to Schedule 2, means, as the case may be—

(a) an employee;

(b) a person holding an office or post to which regulation 12 (office-holders etc) applies;

(c) a person holding the office of constable;

(d) a partner within the meaning of regulation 17 (partnerships);

(e) a member of a limited liability partnership within the meaning of that regulation;

(f) a person in Crown employment;

(g) a relevant member of the House of Commons staff;

(h) a relevant member of the House of Lords staff.

(3) In these Regulations references to "employer", in their application to a person at any time seeking to employ another, include a person who has no employees at that time.

[3404]

NOTES

Commencement: 1 October 2006.

3 Discrimination on grounds of age

(1) For the purposes of these Regulations, a person ("A") discriminates against another person ("B") if—

(a) on grounds of B's age, A treats B less favourably than he treats or would treat other persons, or

(b) A applies to B a provision, criterion or practice which he applies or would apply equally to persons not of the same age group as B, but—
   (i) which puts or would put persons of the same age group as B at a particular disadvantage when compared with other persons, and
   (ii) which puts B at that disadvantage,

and A cannot show the treatment or, as the case may be, provision, criterion or practice to be a proportionate means of achieving a legitimate aim.

(2) A comparison of B's case with that of another person under paragraph (1) must be such that the relevant circumstances in the one case are the same, or not materially different, in the other.

(3) In this regulation—

(a) "age group" means a group of persons defined by reference to age, whether by reference to a particular age or a range of ages; and

(b) the reference in paragraph (1)(a) to B's age includes B's apparent age.

[3405]

NOTES

Commencement: 1 October 2006.

4 Discrimination by way of victimisation

(1) For the purposes of these Regulations, a person ("A") discriminates against another person ("B") if he treats B less favourably than he treats or would treat other persons in the same circumstances, and does so by reason that B has—

(a) brought proceedings against A or any other person under or by virtue of these Regulations;

(b) given evidence or information in connection with proceedings brought by any person against A or any other person under or by virtue of these Regulations;

(c) otherwise done anything under or by reference to these Regulations in relation to A or any other person; or

(d) alleged that A or any other person has committed an act which (whether or not the allegation so states) would amount to a contravention of these Regulations,

or by reason that A knows that B intends to do any of those things, or suspects that B has done or intends to do any of them.

(2) Paragraph (1) does not apply to treatment of B by reason of any allegation made by him, or evidence or information given by him, if the allegation, evidence or information was false and not made (or, as the case may be, given) in good faith.

[3406]

NOTES

Commencement: 1 October 2006.

5 Instructions to discriminate

For the purposes of these Regulations, a person ("A") discriminates against another person ("B") if he treats B less favourably than he treats or would treat other persons in the same circumstances, and does so by reason that—

(a) B has not carried out (in whole or in part) an instruction to do an act which is unlawful by virtue of these Regulations, or

(b) B, having been given an instruction to do such an act, complains to A or to any other person about that instruction.

[3407]

NOTES

Commencement: 1 October 2006.

6 Harassment on grounds of age

(1) For the purposes of these Regulations, a person ("A") subjects another person ("B") to harassment where, on grounds of age, A engages in unwanted conduct which has the purpose or effect of—

(a) violating B's dignity; or

(b) creating an intimidating, hostile, degrading, humiliating or offensive environment for B.

(2) Conduct shall be regarded as having the effect specified in paragraph (1)(a) or (b) only if, having regard to all the circumstances, including in particular the perception of B, it should reasonably be considered as having that effect.

[3408]

NOTES

Commencement: 1 October 2006.

PART 2
DISCRIMINATION IN EMPLOYMENT AND VOCATIONAL TRAINING

7 Applicants and employees

(1) It is unlawful for an employer, in relation to employment by him at an establishment in Great Britain, to discriminate against a person—

(a) in the arrangements he makes for the purpose of determining to whom he should offer employment;

(b) in the terms on which he offers that person employment; or

(c) by refusing to offer, or deliberately not offering, him employment.

(2) It is unlawful for an employer, in relation to a person whom he employs at an establishment in Great Britain, to discriminate against that person—

(a) in the terms of employment which he affords him;

(b) in the opportunities which he affords him for promotion, a transfer, training, or receiving any other benefit;

(c) by refusing to afford him, or deliberately not affording him, any such opportunity; or

(d) by dismissing him, or subjecting him to any other detriment.

(3) It is unlawful for an employer, in relation to employment by him at an establishment in Great Britain, to subject to harassment a person whom he employs or who has applied to him for employment.

(4) Subject to paragraph (5), paragraph (1)(a) and (c) does not apply in relation to a person—

(a) whose age is greater than the employer's normal retirement age or, if the employer does not have a normal retirement age, the age of 65; or

(b) who would, within a period of six months from the date of his application to the employer, reach the employer's normal retirement age or, if the employer does not have a normal retirement age, the age of 65.

(5) Paragraph (4) only applies to a person to whom, if he was recruited by the employer, regulation 30 (exception for retirement) could apply.

(6) Paragraph (2) does not apply to benefits of any description if the employer is concerned with the provision (for payment or not) of benefits of that description to the public, or to a section of the public which includes the employee in question, unless—

(a) that provision differs in a material respect from the provision of the benefits by the employer to his employees; or

(b) the provision of the benefits to the employee in question is regulated by his contract of employment; or

(c) the benefits relate to training.

(7) In paragraph (2)(d) reference to the dismissal of a person from employment includes reference—

(a) to the termination of that person's employment by the expiration of any period (including a period expiring by reference to an event or circumstance), not being a termination immediately after which the employment is renewed on the same terms; and

(b) to the termination of that person's employment by any act of his (including the giving of notice) in circumstances such that he is entitled to terminate it without notice by reason of the conduct of the employer.

(8) In paragraph (4) "normal retirement age" is an age of 65 or more which meets the requirements of section 98ZH of the 1996 Act.

[3409]

NOTES

Commencement: 1 October 2006 (certain purposes); 1 December 2006 (otherwise); see reg 1 at **[3403]**.

8 Exception for genuine occupational requirement etc

(1) In relation to discrimination falling within regulation 3 (discrimination on grounds of age)—

(a) regulation 7(1)(a) or (c) does not apply to any employment;

(b) regulation 7(2)(b) or (c) does not apply to promotion or transfer to, or training for, any employment; and

(c) regulation 7(2)(d) does not apply to dismissal from any employment,

where paragraph (2) applies.

(2) This paragraph applies where, having regard to the nature of the employment or the context in which it is carried out—

(a) possessing a characteristic related to age is a genuine and determining occupational requirement;

(b) it is proportionate to apply that requirement in the particular case; and

(c) either—

(i) the person to whom that requirement is applied does not meet it, or

(ii) the employer is not satisfied, and in all the circumstances it is reasonable for him not to be satisfied, that that person meets it.

[3410]

NOTES

Commencement: 1 October 2006.

9 Contract workers

(1) It is unlawful for a principal, in relation to contract work at an establishment in Great Britain, to discriminate against a contract worker—

(a) in the terms on which he allows him to do that work;

(b) by not allowing him to do it or continue to do it;

(c) in the way he affords him access to any benefits or by refusing or deliberately not affording him access to them; or

(d) by subjecting him to any other detriment.

(2) It is unlawful for a principal, in relation to contract work at an establishment in Great Britain, to subject a contract worker to harassment.

(3) A principal does not contravene paragraph (1)(b) by doing any act in relation to a contract worker where, if the work were to be done by a person taken into the principal's employment, that act would be lawful by virtue of regulation 8 (exception for genuine occupational requirement etc).

(4) Paragraph (1) does not apply to benefits of any description if the principal is concerned with the provision (for payment or not) of benefits of that description to the public, or to a section of the public to which the contract worker in question belongs, unless that provision differs in a material respect from the provision of the benefits by the principal to his contract workers.

(5) In this regulation—

"principal" means a person ("A") who makes work available for doing by individuals who are employed by another person who supplies them under a contract made with A;

"contract work" means work so made available; and

"contract worker" means any individual who is supplied to the principal under such a contract.

[3411]

NOTES
Commencement: 1 October 2006.

10 Meaning of employment and contract work at establishment in Great Britain

(1) For the purposes of this Part ("the relevant purposes"), employment is to be regarded as being at an establishment in Great Britain if the employee—
(a) does his work wholly or partly in Great Britain; or
(b) does his work wholly outside Great Britain and paragraph (2) applies.

(2) This paragraph applies if—
(a) the employer has a place of business at an establishment in Great Britain;
(b) the work is for the purposes of the business carried on at that establishment; and
(c) the employee is ordinarily resident in Great Britain—
(i) at the time when he applies for or is offered the employment, or
(ii) at any time during the course of the employment.

(3) The reference to "employment" in paragraph (1) includes—
(a) employment on board a ship only if the ship is registered at a port of registry in Great Britain, and
(b) employment on an aircraft or hovercraft only if the aircraft or hovercraft is registered in the United Kingdom and operated by a person who has his principal place of business, or is ordinarily resident, in Great Britain.

(4) Subject to paragraph (5), for the purposes of determining if employment concerned with the exploration of the sea bed or sub-soil or the exploitation of their natural resources is outside Great Britain, this regulation has effect as if references to Great Britain included—
(a) any area designated under section 1(7) of the Continental Shelf Act 1964 except an area or part of an area in which the law of Northern Ireland applies; and
(b) in relation to employment concerned with the exploration or exploitation of the Frigg Gas Field, the part of the Norwegian sector of the Continental Shelf described in Schedule 1.

(5) Paragraph (4) shall not apply to employment which is concerned with the exploration or exploitation of the Frigg Gas Field unless the employer is—
(a) a company registered under the Companies Act 1985;
(b) an oversea company which has established a place of business within Great Britain from which it directs the exploration or exploitation in question; or
(c) any other person who has a place of business within Great Britain from which he directs the exploration or exploitation in question.

(6) In this regulation—
"the Frigg Gas Field" means the naturally occurring gas-bearing sand formations of the lower Eocene age located in the vicinity of the intersection of the line of latitude 59 degrees 53 minutes North and of the dividing line between the sectors of the Continental Shelf of the United Kingdom and the Kingdom of Norway and includes all other gas-bearing strata from which gas at the start of production is capable of flowing into the above-mentioned gas-bearing sand formations;
"oversea company" has the same meaning as in section 744 of the Companies Act 1985.

(7) This regulation applies in relation to contract work within the meaning of regulation 9 as it applies in relation to employment; and, in its application to contract work, references to "employee", "employer" and "employment" are references to (respectively) "contract worker", "principal" and "contract work" within the meaning of regulation 9.
[3412]

NOTES
Commencement: 1 October 2006.

11 Pension schemes

(1) It is unlawful, except in relation to rights accrued or benefits payable in respect of periods of [pensionable service] prior to the coming into force of [this Regulation], for the trustees or managers of[, or any employer in relation to,] an occupational pension scheme to discriminate against a member or prospective member of the scheme in carrying out any of

their functions in relation to it (including in particular their functions relating to the admission of members to the scheme and the treatment of members of it).

(2) It is unlawful for the trustees or managers of[, or any employer in relation to,] an occupational pension scheme, in relation to the scheme, to subject to harassment a member or prospective member of it.

(3) Schedule 2 (pension schemes) shall have effect for the purposes of—

(a) defining terms used in this regulation and in that Schedule;

(b) exempting certain rules and practices in or relating to pension schemes from Parts 2 and 3 of these Regulations;

(c) treating every occupational pension scheme as including a non-discrimination rule;

(d) giving trustees or managers of an occupational pension scheme power to alter the scheme so as to secure conformity with the non-discrimination rule;

(e) making provision in relation to the procedures, and remedies which may be granted, on certain complaints relating to occupational pension schemes presented to an employment tribunal under regulation 36 (jurisdiction of employment tribunals).

[3413]

NOTES

Commencement: 1 December 2006.

Para (1): words in first pair of square brackets substituted, and words in third pair of square brackets inserted, by the Employment Equality (Age) (Amendment No 2) Regulations 2006, SI 2006/2931, regs 2, 3, as from 1 December 2006; words in second pair of square brackets substituted by the Employment Equality (Age) (Amendment) Regulations 2006, SI 2006/2408, reg 2(1), (3), as from 30 September 2006.

Para (2): words in square brackets inserted by SI 2006/2931, regs 2, 3(a), as from 1 December 2006.

12 Office-holders etc

(1) It is unlawful for a relevant person, in relation to an appointment to an office or post to which this regulation applies, to discriminate against a person—

(a) in the arrangements which he makes for the purpose of determining to whom the appointment should be offered;

(b) in the terms on which he offers him the appointment; or

(c) by refusing to offer him the appointment.

(2) It is unlawful, in relation to an appointment to an office or post to which this regulation applies and which is an office or post referred to in paragraph (8)(b), for a relevant person on whose recommendation (or subject to whose approval) appointments to the office or post are made, to discriminate against a person—

(a) in the arrangements which he makes for the purpose of determining who should be recommended or approved in relation to the appointment; or

(b) in making or refusing to make a recommendation, or giving or refusing to give an approval, in relation to the appointment.

(3) It is unlawful for a relevant person, in relation to a person who has been appointed to an office or post to which this regulation applies, to discriminate against him—

(a) in the terms of the appointment;

(b) in the opportunities which he affords him for promotion, a transfer, training or receiving any other benefit, or by refusing to afford him any such opportunity;

(c) by terminating the appointment; or

(d) by subjecting him to any other detriment in relation to the appointment.

(4) It is unlawful for a relevant person, in relation to an office or post to which this regulation applies, to subject to harassment a person—

(a) who has been appointed to the office or post;

(b) who is seeking or being considered for appointment to the office or post; or

(c) who is seeking or being considered for a recommendation or approval in relation to an appointment to an office or post referred to in paragraph (8)(b).

(5) Paragraphs (1) and (3) do not apply to any act in relation to an office or post where, if the office or post constituted employment, that act would be lawful by virtue of regulation 8 (exception for genuine occupational requirement etc); and paragraph (2) does not apply to any act in relation to an office or post where, if the office or post constituted employment, it would be lawful by virtue of regulation 8 to refuse to offer the person such employment.

(6) Paragraph (3) does not apply to benefits of any description if the relevant person is concerned with the provision (for payment or not) of benefits of that description to the public, or a section of the public to which the person appointed belongs, unless—

(a) that provision differs in a material respect from the provision of the benefits by the relevant person to persons appointed to offices or posts which are the same as, or not materially different from, that which the person appointed holds; or

(b) the provision of the benefits to the person appointed is regulated by the terms and conditions of his appointment; or

(c) the benefits relate to training.

(7) In paragraph (3)(c) the reference to the termination of the appointment includes a reference—

(a) to the termination of the appointment by the expiration of any period (including a period expiring by reference to an event or circumstance), not being a termination immediately after which the appointment is renewed on the same terms and conditions; and

(b) to the termination of the appointment by any act of the person appointed (including the giving of notice) in circumstances such that he is entitled to terminate the appointment without notice by reason of the conduct of the relevant person.

(8) This regulation applies to—

(a) any office or post to which persons are appointed to discharge functions personally under the direction of another person, and in respect of which they are entitled to remuneration; and

(b) any office or post to which appointments are made by (or on the recommendation of or subject to the approval of) a Minister of the Crown, a government department, the [Welsh Ministers, the First Minister for Wales, the Counsel General to the Welsh Assembly Government] or any part of the Scottish Administration,

but not to a political office or a case where regulation 7 (applicants and employees), 9 (contract workers), 15 (barristers), 16 (advocates) or 17 (partnerships) applies, or would apply but for the operation of any other provision of these Regulations.

(9) For the purposes of paragraph (8)(a) the holder of an office or post—

(a) is to be regarded as discharging his functions under the direction of another person if that other person is entitled to direct him as to when and where he discharges those functions;

(b) is not to be regarded as entitled to remuneration merely because he is entitled to payments—

(i) in respect of expenses incurred by him in carrying out the function of the office or post; or

(ii) by way of compensation for the loss of income or benefits he would or might have received from any person had he not been carrying out the functions of the office or post.

(10) In this regulation—

(a) appointment to an office or post does not include election to an office or post;

(b) "political office" means—

(i) any office of the House of Commons held by a member of it;

(ii) a life peerage within the meaning of the Life Peerages Act 1958, or any office of the House of Lords held by a member of it;

(iii) any office mentioned in Schedule 2 (Ministerial offices) to the House of Commons Disqualification Act 1975;

(iv) the offices of Leader of the Opposition, Chief Opposition Whip or Assistant Opposition Whip within the meaning of the Ministerial and other Salaries Act 1975;

(v) any office of the Scottish Parliament held by a member of it;

(vi) a member of the Scottish Executive within the meaning of section 44 of the Scotland Act 1998, or a junior Scottish Minister within the meaning of section 49 of that Act;

(vii) any office of the National Assembly for Wales held by a member of it;

[(viia) a member of the Welsh Assembly Government,]

(viii) in England, any office of a county council, a London borough council, a district council, or a parish council held by a member of it;

(ix) in Wales, any office of a county council, a county borough council, or a community council held by a member of it;

(x) in relation to a council constituted under section 2 of the Local Government etc (Scotland) Act 1994 or a community council established under section 51 of the Local Government (Scotland) Act 1973, any office of such a council held by a member of it;

(xi) any office of the Greater London Authority held by a member of it;

(xii) any office of the Common Council of the City of London held by a member of it;

(xiii) any office of the Council of the Isles of Scilly held by a member of it;

(xiv) any office of a political party;

(c) "relevant person", in relation to an office or post, means—

(i) any person with power to make or terminate appointments to the office or post, or to determine the terms of appointment,

(ii) any person with power to determine the working conditions of a person appointed to the office or post in relation to opportunities for promotion, a transfer, training or for receiving any other benefit, and

(iii) any person or body referred to in paragraph (8)(b) on whose recommendation or subject to whose approval appointments are made to the office or post;

(d) references to making a recommendation include references to making a negative recommendation; and

(e) references to refusal include references to deliberate omission.

[3414]

NOTES

Commencement: 1 October 2006.

Para (8): words in square brackets in sub-para (b) substituted by the Government of Wales Act 2006 (Consequential Modifications and Transitional Provisions) Order 2007, SI 2007/1388, art 3, Sch 1, paras 153, 154(1), (2), as from 25 May 2007.

Para (10): sub-para (viia) inserted by SI 2007/1388, art 3, Sch 1, paras 153, 154(1), (3), as from 25 May 2007.

13 Police

(1) For the purposes of this Part, the holding of the office of constable shall be treated as employment—

(a) by the chief officer of police as respects any act done by him in relation to a constable or that office;

(b) by the police authority as respects any act done by it in relation to a constable or that office.

(2) For the purposes of regulation 25 (liability of employers and principals)—

(a) the holding of the office of constable shall be treated as employment by the chief officer of police (and as not being employment by any other person); and

(b) anything done by a person holding such an office in the performance, or purported performance, of his functions shall be treated as done in the course of that employment.

(3) There shall be paid out of the police fund—

(a) any compensation, costs or expenses awarded against a chief officer of police in any proceedings brought against him under these Regulations, and any costs or expenses incurred by him in any such proceedings so far as not recovered by him in the proceedings; and

(b) any sum required by a chief officer of police for the settlement of any claim made against him under these Regulations if the settlement is approved by the police authority.

(4) Any proceedings under these Regulations which, by virtue of paragraph (1), would lie against a chief officer of police shall be brought against the chief officer of police for the time being or in the case of a vacancy in that office, against the person for the time being performing the functions of that office; and references in paragraph (3) to the chief officer of police shall be construed accordingly.

(5) A police authority may, in such cases and to such extent as appear to it to be appropriate, pay out of the police fund—

(a) any compensation, costs or expenses awarded in proceedings under these Regulations against a person under the direction and control of the chief officer of police;

(b) any costs or expenses incurred and not recovered by such a person in such proceedings; and

(c) any sum required in connection with the settlement of a claim that has or might have given rise to such proceedings.

(6) Paragraphs (1) and (2) apply to a police cadet and appointment as a police cadet as they apply to a constable and the office of constable.

(7) Subject to paragraph (8), in this regulation—

"chief officer of police"—

(a) in relation to a person appointed, or an appointment falling to be made, under a specified Act, has the same meaning as in the Police Act 1996;

(b) in relation to a person appointed, or an appointment falling to be made, under the Police (Scotland) Act 1967, means the chief constable of the relevant police force;

(c) in relation to any other person or appointment means the officer or other person who has the direction and control of the body of constables or cadets in question;

"police authority"—

(a) in relation to a person appointed, or an appointment falling to be made, under a specified Act, has the same meaning as in the Police Act 1996;

(b) in relation to a person appointed, or an appointment falling to be made, under the Police (Scotland) Act 1967, has the meaning given in that Act;

(c) in relation to any other person or appointment, means the authority by whom the person in question is or on appointment would be paid;

"police cadet" means any person appointed to undergo training with a view to becoming a constable;

"police fund"—

(a) in relation to a chief officer of police within sub-paragraph (a) of the above definition of that term, has the same meaning as in the Police Act 1996;

(b) in any other case means money provided by the police authority; and

"specified Act" means the Metropolitan Police Act 1829, the City of London Police Act 1839 or the Police Act 1996.

(8) In relation to a constable of a force who is not under the direction and control of the chief officer of police for that force, references in this regulation to the chief officer of police are references to the chief officer of the force under whose direction and control he is, and references in this regulation to the police authority are references to the relevant police authority for that force.

(9) This regulation is subject to regulation 14.

[3415]

NOTES

Commencement: 1 October 2006.

14 Serious Organised Crime Agency

(1) For the purposes of this Part, any constable or other person who has been seconded to SOCA to serve as a member of its staff shall be treated as employed by SOCA.

(2) For the purposes of regulation 25 (liability of employers and principals)—

(a) the secondment of any constable or other person to SOCA to serve as a member of its staff shall be treated as employment by SOCA (and not as employment by any other person); and

(b) anything done by a person so seconded in the performance, or purported performance, of his functions shall be treated as done in the course of that employment.

(3) In this regulation "SOCA" means the Serious Organised Crime Agency established under section 1 of, and Schedule 1 to, the Serious Organised Crime and Police Act 2005.

[3416]

NOTES

Commencement: 1 October 2006.

15 Barristers

(1) It is unlawful for a barrister or barrister's clerk, in relation to any offer of a pupillage or tenancy, to discriminate against a person—

(a) in the arrangements which are made for the purpose of determining to whom the pupillage or tenancy should be offered;

(b) in respect of any terms on which it is offered; or

(c) by refusing, or deliberately not offering, it to him.

(2) It is unlawful for a barrister or barrister's clerk, in relation to a pupil or tenant in the set of chambers in question, to discriminate against him—

(a) in respect of any terms applicable to him as a pupil or tenant;

(b) in the opportunities for training, or gaining experience, which are afforded or denied to him;

(c) in the benefits which are afforded or denied to him; or

(d) by terminating his pupillage, or by subjecting him to any pressure to leave the chambers or other detriment.

(3) It is unlawful for a barrister or barrister's clerk, in relation to a pupillage or tenancy in the set of chambers in question, to subject to harassment a person who is, or has applied to be, a pupil or tenant.

(4) It is unlawful for any person, in relation to the giving, withholding or acceptance of instructions to a barrister, to discriminate against any person by subjecting him to a detriment, or to subject him to harassment.

(5) In this regulation—

"barrister's clerk" includes any person carrying out any of the functions of a barrister's clerk;

"pupil", "pupillage" and "set of chambers" have the meanings commonly associated with their use in the context of barristers practising in independent practice; and

"tenancy" and "tenant" have the meanings commonly associated with their use in the context of barristers practising in independent practice, but also include reference to any barrister permitted to work in a set of chambers who is not a tenant.

(6) This regulation extends to England and Wales only.

[3417]

NOTES

Commencement: 1 October 2006.

16 Advocates

(1) It is unlawful for an advocate, in relation to taking any person as his pupil, to discriminate against a person—

(a) in the arrangements which he makes for the purpose of determining whom he will take as his pupil;

(b) in respect of any terms on which he offers to take any person as his pupil; or

(c) by refusing to take, or deliberately not taking, a person as his pupil.

(2) It is unlawful for an advocate, in relation to a person who is his pupil, to discriminate against him—

(a) in respect of any terms applicable to him as a pupil;

(b) in the opportunities for training, or gaining experience, which are afforded or denied to him;

(c) in the benefits which are afforded or denied to him; or

(d) by terminating the relationship, or by subjecting him to any pressure to terminate the relationship or other detriment.

(3) It is unlawful for an advocate, in relation to a person who is his pupil or taking any person as his pupil, to subject such a person to harassment.

PART 2

(4) It is unlawful for any person, in relation to the giving, withholding or acceptance of instructions to an advocate, to discriminate against any person by subjecting him to a detriment, or to subject him to harassment.

(5) In this regulation—
"advocate" means a member of the Faculty of Advocates practising as such; and
"pupil" has the meaning commonly associated with its use in the context of a person training to be an advocate.

(6) This regulation extends to Scotland only.

[3418]

NOTES

Commencement: 1 October 2006.

17 Partnerships

(1) It is unlawful for a firm, in relation to a position as partner in the firm, to discriminate against a person—

- (a) in the arrangements they make for the purpose of determining to whom they should offer that position;
- (b) in the terms on which they offer him that position;
- (c) by refusing to offer, or deliberately not offering, him that position; or
- (d) in a case where the person already holds that position—
  - (i) in the way they afford him access to any benefits or by refusing to afford, or deliberately not affording, him access to them; or
  - (ii) by expelling him from that position, or subjecting him to any other detriment.

(2) It is unlawful for a firm, in relation to a position as partner in the firm, to subject to harassment a person who holds or has applied for that position.

(3) Paragraphs (1)(a) to (c) and (2) apply in relation to persons proposing to form themselves into a partnership as they apply in relation to a firm.

(4) Paragraph (1) does not apply to any act in relation to a position as partner where, if the position were employment, that act would be lawful by virtue of regulation 8 (exception for genuine occupational requirement etc).

(5) In the case of a limited partnership references in this regulation to a partner shall be construed as references to a general partner as defined in section 3 of the Limited Partnerships Act 1907.

(6) This regulation applies to a limited liability partnership as it applies to a firm; and, in its application to a limited liability partnership, references to a partner in a firm are references to a member of the limited liability partnership.

(7) In this regulation, "firm" has the meaning given by section 4 of the Partnership Act 1890.

(8) In paragraph (1)(d) reference to the expulsion of a person from a position as partner includes reference—

- (a) to the termination of that person's partnership by the expiration of any period (including a period expiring by reference to an event or circumstance), not being a termination immediately after which the partnership is renewed on the same terms; and
- (b) to the termination of that person's partnership by any act of his (including the giving of notice) in circumstances such that he is entitled to terminate it without notice by reason of the conduct of the other partners.

[3419]

NOTES

Commencement: 1 October 2006.

18 Trade organisations

(1) It is unlawful for a trade organisation to discriminate against a person—

(a) in the terms on which it is prepared to admit him to membership of the organisation; or

(b) by refusing to accept, or deliberately not accepting, his application for membership.

(2) It is unlawful for a trade organisation, in relation to a member of the organisation, to discriminate against him—

(a) in the way it affords him access to any benefits or by refusing or deliberately omitting to afford him access to them;

(b) by depriving him of membership, or varying the terms on which he is a member; or

(c) by subjecting him to any other detriment.

(3) It is unlawful for a trade organisation, in relation to a person's membership or application for membership of that organisation, to subject that person to harassment.

(4) In this regulation—

"trade organisation" means an organisation of workers, an organisation of employers, or any other organisation whose members carry on a particular profession or trade for the purposes of which the organisation exists;

"profession" includes any vocation or occupation; and

"trade" includes any business.

[3420]

NOTES

Commencement: 1 October 2006.

19 Qualifications bodies

(1) It is unlawful for a qualifications body to discriminate against a person—

(a) in the terms on which it is prepared to confer a professional or trade qualification on him;

(b) by refusing or deliberately not granting any application by him for such a qualification; or

(c) by withdrawing such a qualification from him or varying the terms on which he holds it.

(2) It is unlawful for a qualifications body, in relation to a professional or trade qualification conferred by it, to subject to harassment a person who holds or applies for such a qualification.

(3) In this regulation—

"qualifications body" means any authority or body which can confer a professional or trade qualification, but it does not include—

(a) a governing body of an educational establishment to which regulation 23 (institutions of further and higher education) applies, or would apply but for the operation of any other provision of these Regulations, or

(b) a proprietor of a school;

"confer" includes renew or extend;

"professional or trade qualification" means any authorisation, qualification, recognition, registration, enrolment, approval or certification which is needed for, or facilitates engagement in, a particular profession or trade;

"profession" and "trade" have the same meaning as in regulation 18.

[3421]

NOTES

Commencement: 1 October 2006.

20 The provision of vocational training

(1) It is unlawful, in relation to a person seeking or undergoing training, for any training provider to discriminate against him—

(a) in the arrangements he makes for the purpose of determining to whom he should offer training;

(b) in the terms on which the training provider affords him access to any training;

(c) by refusing or deliberately not affording him such access;

(d) by terminating his training; or
(e) by subjecting him to any other detriment during his training.

(2) It is unlawful for a training provider, in relation to a person seeking or undergoing training, to subject him to harassment.

(3) Paragraph (1) does not apply if the discrimination concerns training that would only fit a person for employment which, by virtue of regulation 8 (exception for genuine occupational requirement etc), the employer could lawfully refuse to offer the person seeking training.

(4) In this regulation—
"professional or trade qualification" has the same meaning as in regulation 19;
"registered pupil" has the meaning given by section 434 of the Education Act 1996;
"training" means—
(a) all types and all levels of training which would help fit a person for any employment;
(b) vocational guidance;
(c) facilities for training;
(d) practical work experience provided by an employer to a person whom he does not employ; and
(e) any assessment related to the award of any professional or trade qualification;

"training provider" means any person who provides, or makes arrangements for the provision of, training, but it does not include—
(a) an employer in relation to training for persons employed by him;
(b) a governing body of an educational establishment to which regulation 23 (institutions of further and higher education) applies, or would apply but for the operation of any other provision of these Regulations; or
(c) a proprietor of a school in relation to any registered pupil.

[3422]

NOTES
Commencement: 1 October 2006.

21 Employment agencies, careers guidance etc

(1) It is unlawful for an employment agency to discriminate against a person—
(a) in the terms on which the agency offers to provide any of its services;
(b) by refusing or deliberately not providing any of its services; or
(c) in the way it provides any of its services.

(2) It is unlawful for an employment agency, in relation to a person to whom it provides its services, or who has requested it to provide its services, to subject that person to harassment.

(3) Paragraph (1) does not apply to discrimination if it only concerns employment which, by virtue of regulation 8 (exception for genuine occupational requirement etc), the employer could lawfully refuse to offer the person in question.

(4) An employment agency shall not be subject to any liability under this regulation if it proves that—
(a) it acted in reliance on a statement made to it by the employer to the effect that, by reason of the operation of paragraph (3), its action would not be unlawful; and
(b) it was reasonable for it to rely on the statement.

(5) A person who knowingly or recklessly makes a statement such as is referred to in paragraph (4)(a) which in a material respect is false or misleading commits an offence, and shall be liable on summary conviction to a fine not exceeding level 5 on the standard scale.

(6) For the purposes of this regulation—
(a) "employment agency" means a person who, for profit or not, provides services for the purpose of finding employment for workers or supplying employers with workers, but it does not include—
(i) a governing body of an educational establishment to which regulation 23 (institutions of further and higher education) applies, or would apply but for the operation of any other provision of these Regulations; or
(ii) a proprietor of a school; and

(b) references to the services of an employment agency include guidance on careers and any other services related to employment.

[3423]

NOTES

Commencement: 1 October 2006.

22 Assisting persons to obtain employment etc

(1) It is unlawful for the Secretary of State to discriminate against any person by subjecting him to a detriment, or to subject a person to harassment, in the provision of facilities or services under section 2 of the Employment and Training Act 1973 (arrangements for assisting persons to obtain employment).

(2) It is unlawful for Scottish Enterprise or Highlands and Islands Enterprise to discriminate against any person by subjecting him to a detriment, or to subject a person to harassment, in the provision of facilities or services under such arrangements as are mentioned in section 2(3) of the Enterprise and New Towns (Scotland) Act 1990 (arrangements analogous to arrangements in pursuance of the said Act of 1973).

(3) This regulation does not apply in a case where—

(a) regulation 20 (the provision of vocational training) applies or would apply but for the operation of any other provision of these Regulations, or

(b) the Secretary of State is acting as an employment agency within the meaning of regulation 21 (employment agencies, careers guidance etc).

[3424]

NOTES

Commencement: 1 October 2006.

23 Institutions of further and higher education

(1) It is unlawful, in relation to an educational establishment to which this regulation applies, for the governing body of that establishment to discriminate against a person—

(a) in the terms on which it offers to admit him to the establishment as a student;

(b) by refusing or deliberately not accepting an application for his admission to the establishment as a student; or

(c) where he is a student of the establishment—

(i) in the way it affords him access to any benefits,

(ii) by refusing or deliberately not affording him access to them, or

(iii) by excluding him from the establishment or subjecting him to any other detriment.

(2) It is unlawful, in relation to an educational establishment to which this regulation applies, for the governing body of that establishment to subject to harassment a person who is a student at the establishment, or who has applied for admission to the establishment as a student.

(3) Paragraph (1) does not apply if the discrimination concerns training that would only fit a person for employment which, by virtue of regulation 8 (exception for genuine occupational requirement etc), the employer could lawfully refuse to offer the person in question.

(4) This regulation applies to the following educational establishments in England and Wales, namely—

(a) an institution within the further education sector (within the meaning of section 91(3) of the Further and Higher Education Act 1992);

(b) a university;

(c) an institution, other than a university, within the higher education sector (within the meaning of section 91(5) of the Further and Higher Education Act 1992).

(5) This regulation applies to the following educational establishments in Scotland, namely—

(a) a college of further education within the meaning of section 36(1) of the Further and Higher Education (Scotland) Act 1992 under the management of a board of management within the meaning of Part I of that Act;

(b) a college of further education maintained by an education authority in the exercise of its further education functions in providing courses of further education within the meaning of section 1(5)(b)(ii) of the Education (Scotland) Act 1980;

(c) any other educational establishment (not being a school) which provides further education within the meaning of section 1 of the Further and Higher Education (Scotland) Act 1992;

(d) an institution within the higher education sector (within the meaning of Part 2 of the Further and Higher Education (Scotland) Act 1992);

(e) a central institution (within the meaning of section 135 of the Education (Scotland) Act 1980).

(6) In this regulation—

"education authority" has the meaning given by section 135(1) of the Education (Scotland) Act 1980;

"governing body" includes—

(a) the board of management of a college referred to in paragraph (5)(a), and

(b) the managers of a college or institution referred to in paragraph (5)(b) or (e);

"student" means any person who receives education at an educational establishment to which this regulation applies; and

"university" includes a university college and the college, school or hall of a university.

[3425]

NOTES

Commencement: 1 October 2006.

24 Relationships which have come to an end

(1) In this regulation a "relevant relationship" is a relationship during the course of which an act of discrimination against, or harassment of, one party to the relationship ("B") by the other party to it ("A") is unlawful by virtue of any preceding provision of this Part.

(2) Where a relevant relationship has come to an end, it is unlawful for A—

(a) to discriminate against B by subjecting him to a detriment; or

(b) to subject B to harassment;

where the discrimination or harassment arises out of and is closely connected to that relationship.

(3) In paragraph (1), reference to an act of discrimination or harassment which is unlawful includes, in the case of a relationship which has come to an end before [the date on which the act of discrimination or harassment became unlawful by virtue of these Regulations], reference to an act of discrimination or harassment which would, after [that date], be unlawful.

[3426]

NOTES

Commencement: 1 October 2006 (certain purposes); 1 December 2006 (otherwise); see reg 1 at **[3403]**.

Para (3): words in square brackets substituted by the Employment Equality (Age) (Amendment) Regulations 2006, SI 2006/2408, reg 2(1), (4), as from 30 September 2006.

PART 3
OTHER UNLAWFUL ACTS

25 Liability of employers and principals

(1) Anything done by a person in the course of his employment shall be treated for the purposes of these Regulations as done by his employer as well as by him, whether or not it was done with the employer's knowledge or approval.

(2) Anything done by a person as agent for another person with the authority (whether express or implied, and whether precedent or subsequent) of that other person shall be treated for the purposes of these Regulations as done by that other person as well as by him.

(3) In proceedings brought under these Regulations against any person in respect of an act alleged to have been done by an employee of his it shall be a defence for that person to

prove that he took such steps as were reasonably practicable to prevent the employee from doing that act, or from doing in the course of his employment acts of that description.

[3427]

NOTES

Commencement: 1 October 2006.

26 Aiding unlawful acts

(1) A person who knowingly aids another person to do an act made unlawful by these Regulations shall be treated for the purpose of these Regulations as himself doing an unlawful act of the like description.

(2) For the purposes of paragraph (1) an employee or agent for whose act the employer or principal is liable under regulation 25 (or would be so liable but for regulation 25(3)) shall be deemed to aid the doing of the act by the employer or principal.

(3) A person does not under this regulation knowingly aid another to do an unlawful act if—

(a) he acts in reliance on a statement made to him by that other person that, by reason of any provision of these Regulations, the act which he aids would not be unlawful; and

(b) it is reasonable for him to rely on the statement.

(4) A person who knowingly or recklessly makes a statement such as is referred to in paragraph (3)(a) which in a material respect is false or misleading commits an offence, and shall be liable on summary conviction to a fine not exceeding level 5 on the standard scale.

[3428]

NOTES

Commencement: 1 October 2006.

PART 4
GENERAL EXCEPTIONS FROM PARTS 2 AND 3

27 Exception for statutory authority

(1) Nothing in Part 2 or 3 shall render unlawful any act done in order to comply with a requirement of any statutory provision.

(2) In this regulation "statutory provision" means any provision (whenever enacted) of—

(a) an Act or an Act of the Scottish Parliament;

[(aa) a Measure or Act of the National Assembly for Wales;]

(b) an instrument made by a Minister of the Crown under an Act;

(c) an instrument made under an Act or an Act of the Scottish Parliament by the Scottish Ministers or a member of the Scottish Executive;

[(d) an instrument made after the end of the initial period under an Act, or under a Measure or Act of the National Assembly for Wales, by the Welsh Ministers, the First Minister for Wales or the Counsel General to the Welsh Assembly Government].

[(3) In paragraph (2)(d) "the initial period" has the same meaning as in the Government of Wales Act 2006 (*see* section 161(6) of that Act).]

[3429]

NOTES

Commencement: 1 October 2006.

Para (2): sub-paras (aa), (d) inserted and added respectively by the Government of Wales Act 2006 (Consequential Modifications and Transitional Provisions) Order 2007, SI 2007/1388, art 3, Sch 1, paras 153, 155(1)–(3), as from 25 May 2007.

Para (3): added by SI 2007/1388, art 3, Sch 1, paras 153, 155(1), (3), as from 25 May 2007.

28 Exception for national security

Nothing in Part 2 or 3 shall render unlawful an act done for the purpose of safeguarding national security, if the doing of the act was justified by that purpose.

[3430]

NOTES

Commencement: 1 October 2006.

29 Exceptions for positive action

(1) Nothing in Part 2 or 3 shall render unlawful any act done in or in connection with—

(a) affording persons of a particular age or age group access to facilities for training which would help fit them for particular work; or

(b) encouraging persons of a particular age or age group to take advantage of opportunities for doing particular work;

where it reasonably appears to the person doing the act that it prevents or compensates for disadvantages linked to age suffered by persons of that age or age group doing that work or likely to take up that work.

(2) Nothing in Part 2 or 3 shall render unlawful any act done by a trade organisation within the meaning of regulation 18 in or in connection with—

(a) affording only members of the organisation who are of a particular age or age group access to facilities for training which would help fit them for holding a post of any kind in the organisation; or

(b) encouraging only members of the organisation who are of a particular age or age group to take advantage of opportunities for holding such posts in the organisation,

where it reasonably appears to the organisation that the act prevents or compensates for disadvantages linked to age suffered by those of that age or age group holding such posts or likely to hold such posts.

(3) Nothing in Part 2 or 3 shall render unlawful any act done by a trade organisation within the meaning of regulation 18 in or in connection with encouraging only persons of a particular age or age group to become members of the organisation where it reasonably appears to the organisation that the act prevents or compensates for disadvantages linked to age suffered by persons of that age or age group who are, or are eligible to become, members.

[3431]

NOTES

Commencement: 1 October 2006.

30 Exception for retirement

(1) This regulation applies in relation to an employee within the meaning of section 230(1) of the 1996 Act, a person in Crown employment, a relevant member of the House of Commons staff, and a relevant member of the House of Lords staff.

(2) Nothing in Part 2 or 3 shall render unlawful the dismissal of a person to whom this regulation applies at or over the age of 65 where the reason for the dismissal is retirement.

(3) For the purposes of this regulation, whether or not the reason for a dismissal is retirement shall be determined in accordance with sections 98ZA to 98ZF of the 1996 Act.

[3432]

NOTES

Commencement: 1 October 2006.

31 Exception for the national minimum wage

(1) Nothing in Part 2 or 3 shall render it unlawful for a relevant person ("A") to be remunerated in respect of his work at a rate which is lower than the rate at which another such person ("B") is remunerated for his work where—

(a) the hourly rate of the national minimum wage for a person of A's age is lower than that for a person of B's age, and

(b) the rate at which A is remunerated is below the single hourly rate for the national minimum wage prescribed by the Secretary of State under section 1(3) of the National Minimum Wage Act 1998.

(2) Nothing in Part 2 or 3 shall render it unlawful for an apprentice who is not a relevant person to be remunerated in respect of his work at a rate which is lower than the rate at which an apprentice who is a relevant person is remunerated for his work.

(3) In this regulation—

"apprentice" means a person who is employed under a contract of apprenticeship or, in accordance with regulation 12(3) of the National Minimum Wage Regulations 1999, is to be treated as employed under such a contract;

"relevant person" means a person who qualifies for the national minimum wage (whether at the single hourly rate for the national minimum wage prescribed by the Secretary of State under section 1(3) of the National Minimum Wage Act 1998 or at a different rate).

[3433]

NOTES

Commencement: 1 October 2006.

32 Exception for provision of certain benefits based on length of service

(1) Subject to paragraph (2), nothing in Part 2 or 3 shall render it unlawful for a person ("A"), in relation to the award of any benefit by him, to put a worker ("B") at a disadvantage when compared with another worker ("C"), if and to the extent that the disadvantage suffered by B is because B's length of service is less than that of C.

(2) Where B's length of service exceeds 5 years, it must reasonably appear to A that the way in which he uses the criterion of length of service, in relation to the award in respect of which B is put at a disadvantage, fulfils a business need of his undertaking (for example, by encouraging the loyalty or motivation, or rewarding the experience, of some or all of his workers).

(3) In calculating a worker's length of service for these purposes, A shall calculate—

(a) the length of time the worker has been working for him doing work which he reasonably considers to be at or above a particular level (assessed by reference to the demands made on the worker, for example, in terms of effort, skills and decision making); or

(b) the length of time the worker has been working for him in total;

and on each occasion on which he decides to use the criterion of length of service in relation to the award of a benefit to workers, it is for him to decide which of these definitions to use to calculate their lengths of service.

(4) For the purposes of paragraph (3), in calculating the length of time a worker has been working for him—

(a) A shall calculate the length of time in terms of the number of weeks during the whole or part of which the worker was working for him;

(b) A may discount any period during which the worker was absent from work (including any period of absence which at the time it occurred was thought by A or the worker to be permanent) unless in all the circumstances (including the way in which other workers' absences occurring in similar circumstances are treated by A in calculating their lengths of service) it would not be reasonable for him to do so;

(c) A may discount any period of time during which the worker was present at work ("the relevant period") where—

(i) the relevant period preceded a period during which the worker was absent from work, and

(ii) in all the circumstances (including the length of the worker's absence, the reason for his absence, the effect his absence has had on his ability to discharge the duties of his work, and the way in which other workers are treated by A in similar circumstances) it is reasonable for A to discount the relevant period.

(5) For the purposes of paragraph (3)(b), a worker shall be treated as having worked for A during any period during which he worked for another if—

(a) that period is treated as a period of employment with A for the purposes of the 1996 Act by virtue of the operation of section 218 of that Act; …

(b) were the worker to be made redundant by A, that period and the period he has worked for A would amount to "relevant service" within the meaning of section 155 of that Act[; or

(c) in any case to which sub-paragraph (a) or (b) does not apply, that period is treated as a period of employment with A by or under an enactment pursuant to which his employment was transferred to A].

(6) In paragraph (5)—

(a) the reference to being made redundant is a reference to being dismissed by reason of redundancy for the purposes of the 1996 Act;

(b) the reference to section 155 of that Act is a reference to that section as modified by the Redundancy Payments (Continuity of Employment in Local Government, etc.) (Modification) Order 1999.

(7) In this regulation—

"benefit" does not include any benefit awarded to a worker by virtue of his ceasing to work for A;

["enactment" includes an enactment comprised in, or in an instrument made under, an Act of the Scottish Parliament;] and

"year" means a year of 12 calendar months.

[3434]

NOTES

Commencement: 1 October 2006.

Para (5): word omitted from sub-para (a) revoked, and sub-para (c) (and the word immediately preceding it) added by the Employment Equality (Age) Regulations 2006 (Amendment) Regulations 2008, SI 2008/573, regs 2, 3(a), (b), as from 6 April 2008.

Para (7): definition "enactment" inserted by SI 2008/573, regs 2, 3(c), as from 6 April 2008.

33 Exception for provision of enhanced redundancy payments to employees

(1) Nothing in Part 2 or 3 shall render it unlawful for an employer—

(a) to give a qualifying employee an enhanced redundancy payment which is less in amount than the enhanced redundancy payment which he gives to another such employee if both amounts are calculated in the same way;

(b) to give enhanced redundancy payments only to those who are qualifying employees by virtue of sub-paragraph (a) or (c)(i) of the definition of qualifying employee below.

(2) In this regulation—

"the appropriate amount", "a redundancy payment" and "a week's pay" have the same meaning as they have in section 162 of the 1996 Act;

"enhanced redundancy payment" means a payment of an amount calculated in accordance with paragraph (3) or (4);

"qualifying employee" means—

(a) an employee who is entitled to a redundancy payment by virtue of section 135 of the 1996 Act;

(b) an employee who would have been so entitled but for the operation of section 155 of that Act;

(c) an employee who agrees to the termination of his employment in circumstances where, had he been dismissed—

(i) he would have been a qualifying employee by virtue of sub-paragraph (a) of this definition; or

(ii) he would have been a qualifying employee by virtue of sub-paragraph (b).

(3) For an amount to be calculated in accordance with this paragraph it must be calculated in accordance with section 162(1) to (3) of the 1996 Act.

(4) For an amount to be calculated in accordance with this paragraph—

(a) it must be calculated as in paragraph (3);

(b) however, in making that calculation, the employer may do one or both of the following things—

(i) he may treat a week's pay as not being subject to a maximum amount or as being subject to a maximum amount above the amount laid down in section 227 of the 1996 Act;

(ii) he may multiply the appropriate amount allowed for each year of employment by a figure of more than one;

(c) having made the calculation as in paragraph (3) (whether or not in making that calculation he has done anything mentioned in sub-paragraph (b)) the employer may increase the amount thus calculated by multiplying it by a figure of more than one.

(5) For the purposes of paragraphs (3) and (4), the reference to "the relevant date" in section 162(1)(a) of the 1996 Act is to be read, in the case of a qualifying employee who agrees to the termination of his employment, as a reference to the date on which that termination takes effect.

[3435]

NOTES

Commencement: 1 October 2006.

34 Exception for provision of life assurance cover to retired workers

(1) Where a person ("A") arranges for workers to be provided with life assurance cover after their early retirement on grounds of ill health, nothing in Part 2 or 3 shall render it unlawful—

(a) where a normal retirement age applied in relation to any such workers at the time they took early retirement, for A to arrange for such cover to cease when such workers reach that age;

(b) in relation to any other workers, for A to arrange for such cover to cease when the workers reach the age of 65.

(2) In this regulation, "normal retirement age", in relation to a worker who has taken early retirement, means the age at which workers in A's undertaking who held the same kind of position as the worker held at the time of his retirement were normally required to retire.

[3436]

NOTES

Commencement: 1 October 2006.

PART 5
ENFORCEMENT

35 Restriction of proceedings for breach of Regulations

(1) Except as provided by these Regulations no proceedings, whether civil or criminal, shall lie against any person in respect of an act by reason that the act is unlawful by virtue of a provision of these Regulations.

(2) Paragraph (1) does not prevent the making of an application for judicial review or the investigation or determination of any matter in accordance with Part 10 (investigations: the Pensions Ombudsman) of the Pension Schemes Act 1993 by the Pensions Ombudsman.

[3437]

NOTES

Commencement: 1 October 2006.

36 Jurisdiction of employment tribunals

(1) A complaint by any person ("the complainant") that another person ("the respondent")—

(a) has committed against the complainant an act to which this regulation applies; or

(b) is by virtue of regulation 25 (liability of employers and principals) or 26 (aiding unlawful acts) to be treated as having committed against the complainant such an act;

may be presented to an employment tribunal.

(2) This regulation applies to any act of discrimination or harassment which is unlawful by virtue of any provision of Part 2 other than—

(a) where the act is one in respect of which an appeal or proceedings in the nature of an appeal may be brought under any enactment, regulation 19 (qualifications bodies);

(b) regulation 23 (institutions of further and higher education); or

(c) where the act arises out of and is closely connected to a relationship between the complainant and the respondent which has come to an end but during the course of which an act of discrimination against, or harassment of, the complainant by the respondent would have been unlawful by virtue of regulation 23, regulation 24 (relationships which have come to an end).

(3) In paragraph (2)(c), reference to an act of discrimination or harassment which would have been unlawful includes, in the case of a relationship which has come to an end before [the date on which the act of discrimination or harassment became unlawful by virtue of these Regulations], reference to an act of discrimination or harassment which would, after [that date], have been unlawful.

(4) In this regulation, "enactment" includes an enactment comprised in, or in an instrument made under, an Act of the Scottish Parliament.

[3438]

NOTES

Commencement: 1 October 2006.

Para (3): words in square brackets substituted by the Employment Equality (Age) (Amendment) Regulations 2006, SI 2006/2408, reg 2(1), (4), as from 30 September 2006.

Conciliation: employment tribunal proceedings and claims which could be the subject of employment tribunal proceedings under this regulation are proceedings to which the Employment Tribunals Act 1996, s 18 applies; see s 18(1)(r) of that Act at **[975]**. There is no fixed conciliation period for such proceedings: see the Employment Tribunals (Constitution and Rules of Procedure) Regulations 2004, SI 2004/1861, Sch 1, rule 22(1), (2).

Tribunal jurisdiction: the Employment Act 2002, ss 31, 32, 38, at **[1493]**, **[1494]**, **[1496]** apply to proceedings before the employment tribunal relating to a claim under this regulation; see ss 31(1), 32(1), 38(1) of, and Schs 3–5 to, the 2002 Act at **[1508]–[1510]**.

For the circumstances in which the normal time limit for presenting a complaint under this regulation is extended for a period of three months, see the Employment Act 2002 (Dispute Resolution) Regulations 2004, SI 2004/752, regs 15 and 18 at **[3096]** and **[3098]**.

37 Burden of proof: employment tribunals

(1) This regulation applies to any complaint presented under regulation 36 to an employment tribunal.

(2) Where, on the hearing of the complaint, the complainant proves facts from which the tribunal could, apart from this regulation, conclude in the absence of an adequate explanation that the respondent—

(a) has committed against the complainant an act to which regulation 36 applies; or

(b) is by virtue of regulation 25 (liability of employers and principals) or 26 (aiding unlawful acts) to be treated as having committed against the complainant such an act,

the tribunal shall uphold the complaint unless the respondent proves that he did not commit, or as the case may be, is not to be treated as having committed, that act.

[3439]

NOTES

Commencement: 1 October 2006.

38 Remedies on complaints in employment tribunals

(1) Where an employment tribunal finds that a complaint presented to it under regulation 36 is well-founded, the tribunal shall make such of the following as it considers just and equitable—

(a) an order declaring the rights of the complainant and the respondent in relation to the act to which the complaint relates;

(b) an order requiring the respondent to pay to the complainant compensation of an amount corresponding to any damages he could have been ordered by a county court or by a sheriff court to pay to the complainant if the complaint had fallen to be dealt with under regulation 39 (jurisdiction of county and sheriff courts);

(c) a recommendation that the respondent take within a specified period action appearing to the tribunal to be practicable for the purpose of obviating or reducing the adverse effect on the complainant of any act of discrimination or harassment to which the complaint relates.

(2) As respects an unlawful act of discrimination falling within regulation 3(1)(b) (discrimination on the grounds of age), if the respondent proves that the provision, criterion or practice was not applied with the intention of treating the complainant unfavourably on grounds of age, an order may be made under paragraph (1)(b) only if the employment tribunal—

(a) makes such order under paragraph (1)(a) (if any) and such recommendation under paragraph (1)(c) (if any) as it would have made if it had no power to make an order under paragraph (1)(b); and

(b) (where it makes an order under paragraph (1)(a) or a recommendation under paragraph (1)(c) or both) considers that it is just and equitable to make an order under paragraph (1)(b) as well.

(3) If without reasonable justification the respondent to a complaint fails to comply with a recommendation made by an employment tribunal under paragraph (1)(c), then, if it thinks it just and equitable to do so—

(a) the tribunal may increase the amount of compensation required to be paid to the complainant in respect of the complaint by an order made under paragraph (1)(b); or

(b) if an order under paragraph (1)(b) was not made, the tribunal may make such an order.

(4) Where an amount of compensation falls to be awarded under paragraph (1)(b), the tribunal may include in the award interest on that amount subject to, and in accordance with, the provisions of the Employment Tribunals (Interest on Awards in Discrimination Cases) Regulations 1996.

(5) This regulation has effect subject to paragraph 6 of Schedule 2 (pension schemes).

[3440]

NOTES

Commencement: 1 October 2006.

39 Jurisdiction of county and sheriff courts

(1) A claim by any person ("the claimant") that another person ("the respondent")—

(a) has committed against the claimant an act to which this regulation applies; or

(b) is by virtue of regulation 25 (liability of employers and principals) or 26 (aiding unlawful acts) to be treated as having committed against the claimant such an act,

may be made the subject of civil proceedings in like manner as any other claim in tort or (in Scotland) in reparation for breach of statutory duty.

(2) Proceedings brought under paragraph (1) shall—

(a) in England and Wales, be brought only in a county court; and

(b) in Scotland, be brought only in a sheriff court.

(3) For the avoidance of doubt it is hereby declared that damages in respect of an unlawful act to which this regulation applies may include compensation for injury to feelings whether or not they include compensation under any other head.

(4) This regulation applies to any act of discrimination or harassment which is unlawful by virtue of—

(a) regulation 23 (institutions of further and higher education); or

(b) where the act arises out of and is closely connected to a relationship between the claimant and the respondent which has come to an end but during the course of which an act of discrimination against, or harassment of, the claimant by the respondent would have been unlawful by virtue of regulation 23, regulation 24 (relationships which have come to an end).

(5) In paragraph (4)(b), reference to an act of discrimination or harassment which would have been unlawful includes, in the case of a relationship which has come to an end before [the date on which the act of discrimination or harassment became unlawful by virtue of these Regulations], reference to an act of discrimination or harassment which would, after [that date], have been unlawful.

[3441]

NOTES

Commencement: 1 October 2006.

Para (5): words in square brackets substituted by the Employment Equality (Age) (Amendment) Regulations 2006, SI 2006/2408, reg 2(1), (4), as from 30 September 2006.

Conciliation: for the powers of the Commission for Equality and Human Rights to make arrangements for the provision of conciliation services for disputes in respect of which proceedings have been, or could be, brought under this regulation, see the Equality Act 2006, s 27 at **[1670]**.

40 Burden of proof: county and sheriff courts

(1) This regulation applies to any claim brought under regulation 39 in a county court in England and Wales or a sheriff court in Scotland.

(2) Where, on the hearing of the claim, the claimant proves facts from which the court could, apart from this regulation, conclude in the absence of an adequate explanation that the respondent—

(a) has committed against the claimant an act to which regulation 39 applies; or

(b) is by virtue of regulation 25 (liability of employers and principals) or 26 (aiding unlawful acts) to be treated as having committed against the claimant such an act,

the court shall uphold the claim unless the respondent proves that he did not commit, or as the case may be, is not to be treated as having committed, that act.

[3442]

NOTES

Commencement: 1 October 2006.

41 Help for persons in obtaining information etc

(1) In accordance with this regulation, a person ("the person aggrieved") who considers he may have been discriminated against, or subjected to harassment, in contravention of these Regulations may serve on the respondent to a complaint presented under regulation 36 (jurisdiction of employment tribunals) or a claim brought under regulation 39 (jurisdiction of county and sheriff courts) questions in the form set out in Schedule 3 or forms to the like effect with such variation as the circumstances require; and the respondent may if he so wishes reply to such questions by way of the form set out in Schedule 4 or forms to the like effect with such variation as the circumstances require.

(2) Where the person aggrieved questions the respondent (whether in accordance with paragraph (1) or not)—

(a) the questions, and any reply by the respondent (whether in accordance with paragraph (1) or not) shall, subject to the following provisions of this regulation, be admissible as evidence in the proceedings;

(b) if it appears to the court or tribunal that the respondent deliberately, and without reasonable excuse, omitted to reply within eight weeks of service of the questions or that his reply is evasive or equivocal, the court or tribunal may draw any inference from that fact that it considers it just and equitable to draw, including an inference that he committed an unlawful act.

(3) In proceedings before a county court in England or Wales or a sheriff court in Scotland, a question shall only be admissible as evidence in pursuance of paragraph (2)(a)—

(a) where it was served before those proceedings had been instituted, if it was so served within the period of six months beginning when the act complained of was done;

(b) where it was served when those proceedings had been instituted, if it was served with the leave of, and within a period specified by, the court in question.

(4) In proceedings before an employment tribunal, a question shall only be admissible as evidence in pursuance of paragraph (2)(a)—

[(a) where it was served before a complaint had been presented to a tribunal, if it was so served—

(i) within the period of three months beginning when the act complained of was done; or

(ii) where regulation 42(1A) applies, within the extended period;]

(b) where it was so served when a complaint had been presented to the tribunal, either—

(i) if it was served within the period of twenty-one days beginning with the day on which the complaint was presented, or

(ii) if it was so served later with leave given, and within a period specified, by a direction of the tribunal.

(5) A question and any reply thereto may be served on the respondent or, as the case may be, on the person aggrieved—

(a) by delivering it to him;

(b) by sending it by post to him at his usual or last-known residence or place of business;

(c) where the person to be served is a body corporate or is a trade union or employers' association within the meaning of the Trade Union and Labour Relations (Consolidation) Act 1992, by delivering it to the secretary or clerk of the body, union or association at its registered or principal office or by sending it by post to the secretary or clerk at that office;

(d) where the person to be served is acting by a solicitor, by delivering it at, or by sending it by post to, the solicitor's address for service; or

(e) where the person to be served is the person aggrieved, by delivering the reply, or sending it by post, to him at his address for reply as stated by him in the document containing the questions.

(6) This regulation is without prejudice to any other enactment or rule of law regulating interlocutory and preliminary matters in proceedings before a county court, sheriff court or employment tribunal, and has effect subject to any enactment or rule of law regulating the admissibility of evidence in such proceedings.

(7) In this regulation "respondent" includes a prospective respondent.

[3443]

NOTES

Commencement: 1 October 2006.

Para (4): sub-para (a) substituted by the Employment Equality (Age) Regulations 2006 (Amendment) Regulations 2008, SI 2008/573, regs 2, 4, as from 6 April 2008.

42 Period within which proceedings to be brought

(1) An employment tribunal shall not consider a complaint under regulation 36 unless it is presented to the tribunal before the end of the period of three months beginning when the act complained of was done.

[(1A) Where the period within which a complaint must be presented in accordance with paragraph (1) is extended by regulation 15 of the Employment Act 2002 (Dispute Resolution) Regulations 2004, the period within which the complaint must be presented shall be the extended period rather than the period in paragraph (1).]

(2) A county court or a sheriff court shall not consider a claim brought under regulation 39 unless proceedings in respect of the claim are instituted before the end of the period of six months beginning when the act complained of was done.

(3) A court or tribunal may nevertheless consider any such complaint or claim which is out of time if, in all the circumstances of the case, it considers that it is just and equitable to do so.

(4) For the purposes of this regulation and regulation 41 (help for persons in obtaining information etc)—

(a) when the making of a contract is, by reason of the inclusion of any term, an unlawful act, that act shall be treated as extending throughout the duration of the contract; and

(b) any act extending over a period shall be treated as done at the end of that period; and

(c) a deliberate omission shall be treated as done when the person in question decided upon it,

and in the absence of evidence establishing the contrary a person shall be taken for the purposes of this regulation to decide upon an omission when he does an act inconsistent with doing the omitted act or, if he has done no such inconsistent act, when the period expires within which he might reasonably have been expected to do the omitted act if it was to be done.

[3444]

NOTES

Commencement: 1 October 2006.

Para (1A): inserted by the Employment Equality (Age) Regulations 2006 (Amendment) Regulations 2008, SI 2008/573, regs 2, 5, as from 6 April 2008.

PART 6
SUPPLEMENTAL

43 Validity of contracts, collective agreements and rules of undertakings

Schedule 5 (validity of contracts, collective agreements and rules of undertakings) shall have effect.

[3445]

NOTES

Commencement: 1 October 2006.

44 Application to the Crown etc

(1) These Regulations apply—

(a) to an act done by or for purposes of a Minister of the Crown or government department; or

(b) to an act done on behalf of the Crown by a statutory body, or a person holding a statutory office,

as they apply to an act done by a private person.

(2) These Regulations apply to Crown employment as they apply to employment by a private person, and shall so apply as if references to a contract of employment included references to the terms of service and references to dismissal included references to termination of Crown employment.

(3) Paragraphs (1) and (2) have effect subject to paragraph (4) and regulations 13 (police) and 14 (Serious Organised Crime Agency).

(4) These regulations do not apply to service in any of the naval, military or air forces of the Crown.

(5) Regulation 10(3) (meaning of employment and contract work at establishment in Great Britain) shall have effect in relation to any ship, aircraft or hovercraft belonging to or possessed by Her Majesty in right of the government of the United Kingdom as it has effect in relation to a ship, aircraft or hovercraft specified in regulation 10(3)(a) or (b).

(6) The provisions of Parts 2 to 4 of the Crown Proceedings Act 1947 shall apply to proceedings against the Crown under these Regulations as they apply to proceedings in England and Wales which by virtue of section 23 of that Act are treated for the purposes of Part 2 of that Act as civil proceedings by or against the Crown, except that in their application to proceedings under these Regulations section 20 of that Act (removal and transfer of proceedings) shall not apply.

(7) The provisions of Part 5 of the Crown Proceedings Act 1947 shall apply to proceedings against the Crown under these Regulations as they apply to proceedings in Scotland which by virtue of the said Part are treated as civil proceedings by or against the Crown, except that in their application to proceedings under these Regulations the proviso to section 44 of that Act (proceedings against the Crown in the Sheriff Court) shall not apply.

[3446]

NOTES

Commencement: 1 October 2006.

45 Application to House of Commons staff

(1) Subject to paragraphs (2) and (3), these Regulations apply in relation to employment as a relevant member of the House of Commons staff as they apply in relation to other employment.

(2) These Regulations apply to employment as such a member as they apply to employment by a private person, and shall so apply as if references to a contract of employment included references to the terms of employment of such a member and references to dismissal included references to termination of such employment.

(3) In relation to employment as such a member, subsections (6) to (12) of section 195 of the 1996 Act (person to be treated as employer of House of Commons staff) apply, with any necessary modifications, for the purposes of these Regulations.

[3447]

NOTES

Commencement: 1 October 2006.

46 Application to House of Lords staff

(1) These Regulations apply in relation to employment as a relevant member of the House of Lords staff as they apply in relation to other employment.

(2) Section 194(7) of the 1996 Act (continuity of employment) applies for the purposes of this regulation.

[3448]

NOTES

Commencement: 1 October 2006.

47 Duty to consider working beyond retirement

Schedule 6, which sets out the procedure to be followed if an employee (within the meaning of that Schedule) is to be retired, shall have effect.

[3449]

NOTES

Commencement: 1 October 2006.

48 Duty to consider working beyond retirement – transitional provisions

Schedule 7, which sets out transitional provisions in relation to the duty to consider working beyond retirement, shall have effect.

[3450]

NOTES

Commencement: 1 October 2006.

49 Amendments, transitionals, repeals and revocations

(1) Schedule 8, which contains amendments to and repeals of legislation and related transitional provisions, shall have effect.

(2) Schedule 9, which contains repeals and revocations, shall have effect.

[3451]

NOTES

Commencement: 1 October 2006.

SCHEDULES

(Sch 1 (Norwegian part of the Frigg gas field) outside the scope of this work.)

SCHEDULE 2
PENSION SCHEMES

Regulation 11(3)

PART 1
PENSION SCHEMES – GENERAL

1 Interpretation

(1) In this Schedule, subject to sub-paragraphs (2) and (3), "occupational pension scheme" means an occupational pension scheme within the meaning of section 1(1) of the Pension Schemes Act 1993.

(2) In relation to rules, practices, actions and decisions identified at paragraph 7(a), "occupational pension scheme" means an occupational pension scheme within the meaning of section 1(1) of the Pension Schemes Act 1993 under which only retirement-benefit activities within the meaning of section 255(4) of the Pensions Act 2004 are carried out.

(3) In relation to rules, practices, actions and decisions identified at [paragraphs 3A, 7(b), 9, 15A, 17 to 21, 23, 24, 25, 25A and 30], "occupational pension scheme" means an occupational pension scheme within the meaning of either section 1(1) of the Pension Schemes Act 1993 or section 150(5) of the Finance Act 2004.

(4) In this Schedule, "scheme" means an occupational pension scheme, construed in accordance with sub-paragraphs (1) to (3).

(5) In this Schedule, in relation to a scheme—

"active member" has the meaning given by section 124(1) of the Pensions Act 1995, but in paragraph 13 also includes an active member within the meaning of section 151(2) of the Finance Act 2004;

["additional state retirement pension" means the additional pension in the Category A retirement pension within the meaning of sections 44 and 45 of the Social Security Contributions and Benefits Act 1992;]

"age related benefit" means benefit provided from a scheme to a member—
(a) on or following his retirement (including early retirement on grounds of ill health or otherwise),
(b) on his reaching a particular age, or
(c) on termination of his service in an employment;

["basic state retirement pension" means the basic pension in the Category A retirement pension within the meaning of section 44 of the Social Security Contributions and Benefits Act 1992;]

["block transfer" means a transfer in a single transaction or a series of transactions from a scheme of all the sums and assets held for the purposes of, or representing, or derived from—
(i) all accrued rights under a scheme,
(ii) contracted-out rights, or
(iii) rights which are not contracted-out rights,

relating to a period of continuous pensionable service (or pensionable service which is treated as continuous) or one or more of a number of separate periods of such pensionable service which relate to a member and at least one other member;]

["contracted-out rights" are such rights, under or derived from an occupational pension scheme or an appropriate personal pension scheme as fall within the following categories—
(a) entitlement to payment of, or accrued rights to, guaranteed minimum pensions;
(b) protected rights; or
(c) section 9(2B) rights,

but not safeguarded rights (within the meaning of section 68A of the Pension Schemes Act 1993);]

"death benefit" means benefit payable from a [scheme], in respect of a member, in consequence of his death;

"deferred member" has the meaning given by section 124(1) of the Pensions Act 1995;

"defined benefits arrangement" has the meaning given by section 152(6) of the Finance Act 2004, but the reference in that section to an arrangement shall be read as referring to an arrangement in respect of a member under a scheme as defined in section 1(1) of the Pension Schemes Act 1993 rather than in respect of a member under a pension scheme as defined in section 150(1) of the Finance Act 2004;

"dependant" means [a widow, widower or surviving civil partner or a] dependant as defined in the scheme rules;

["early retirement pivot age" means, in relation to age related benefit provided under a scheme, an age specified in the scheme rules (or otherwise determined) as the earliest age at which entitlement arises—

(a) without consent (whether of an employer, the trustees or managers of the scheme or otherwise), and

(b) without an actuarial reduction,

but disregarding any special provision as to early payment on grounds of ill health or otherwise;]

"employer" has the meaning given by section 318(1) of the Pensions Act 2004;

…

"employment" includes any trade, business, profession, office or vocation, whether or not a person is employed in it under a contract of employment or is self employed;

["guaranteed minimum pension" has the meaning given in section 8(2) of the Pension Schemes Act 1993;]

"late retirement pivot age" means an age specified in the scheme rules [(or otherwise determined)] above which benefit becomes payable with actuarial enhancement;

["lower earnings limit" means the amount specified for the tax year in question in regulations made under section 5(1)(a)(i) of the Social Security Contributions and Benefits Act 1992 (earnings limits and thresholds for Class 1 contributions);]

"managers" has the meaning given by section 124(1) of the Pensions Act 1995;

"member" means any active member, deferred member or pensioner member, but in paragraph 12 includes any active, deferred or pensioner member within the meaning of section 151(2) to (4) of the Finance Act 2004;

…

"money purchase arrangement" has the meaning given by section 152(2) of the Finance Act 2004, but the reference in that section to an arrangement shall be read as referring to an arrangement in respect of a member under a scheme as defined in section 1(1) of the Pension Schemes Act 1993 rather than in respect of a member under a pension scheme as defined in section 150(1) of the Finance Act 2004;

"non-discrimination rule" means the rule in paragraph 2(1);

"normal pension age" has the meaning given by section 180 of the Pension Schemes Act 1993;

"normal retirement age", in relation to a member, means the age at which workers in the undertaking for which the member worked at the time of his retirement, and who held the same kind of position as the member held at his retirement, were normally required to retire;

…

"pensionable pay" means that part of a member's pay which counts as pensionable pay under the scheme rules;

"pensionable service" has the meaning given by section 124(1) of the Pensions Act 1995;

"pensioner member" has the meaning given by section 124(1) of the Pensions Act 1995; and

"prospective member" means any person who, under the terms of his employment or the scheme rules or both—

(a) is able, at his own option, to become a member of the scheme,

(b) shall become so able if he continues in the same employment for a sufficient period of time,

(c) shall be so admitted to it automatically unless he makes an election not to become a member, or

(d) may be admitted to it subject to the consent of any person;

["protected rights" has the meaning given in section 10 of the Pension Schemes Act 1993;]

["redundancy" means being dismissed by reason of redundancy for the purposes of the Employment Rights Act 1996;]

["relevant transfer" has the meaning given in—

(a) regulation 2(1) of the Transfer of Undertakings (Protection of Employment) Regulations 1981 (a relevant transfer), or as the case may be,

(b) regulation 2(1) of the Transfer of Undertakings (Protection of Employment) Regulations 2006 (a relevant transfer);]

["section 9(2B) rights" are—

(a) rights to the payment of pensions and accrued rights to pensions (other than rights attributable to voluntary contributions) under a scheme contracted-out by virtue of section 9(2B) of the Pension Schemes Act 1993, so far as attributable to an earner's service in contracted-out employment on or after 6th April 1997; and

(b) where a transfer payment has been made to such a scheme, any rights arising under the scheme as a consequence of that payment which are derived directly or indirectly from—

(i) such rights as are referred to in sub-paragraph (a) under another scheme contracted-out by virtue of section 9(2B) of that Act; or

(ii) protected rights under another occupational pension scheme or under a personal pension scheme attributable to payments or contributions in respect of employment on or after 6th April 1997;]

["upper earnings limit" means the amount specified for the tax year in question in regulations made under section 5(1)(a)(iii) of the Social Security Contributions and Benefits Act 1992 (earnings limits and thresholds for Class 1 contributions)].

(6) …

(7) In this Schedule—

"personal pension scheme" has the meaning given by section 1(1) of the Pension Schemes Act 1993;

"registered pension scheme" has the meaning given by section 150(2) of the Finance Act 2004; and

references to contributions under a money purchase arrangement shall be construed as including amounts credited to a member's account whether or not they reflect payments actually made under the scheme.

(8) Any term used in regulation 11 (pension schemes) shall have the same meaning in that regulation as it has in this Schedule [and "occupational pension scheme" shall mean an occupational pension scheme within the meaning of either section 1(1) of the Pension Schemes Act 1993 or section 150(5) of the Finance Act 2004].

2 Non-discrimination rule

(1) Every scheme shall be treated as including a provision ("the non-discrimination rule") containing a requirement that the trustees or managers of the scheme refrain from doing any act which is unlawful by virtue of regulation 11.

(2) The other provisions of the scheme are to have effect subject to the non-discrimination rule.

(3) The trustees or managers of a scheme may—

(a) if they do not (apart from this sub-paragraph) have power to make such alterations to the scheme as may be required to secure conformity with the non-discrimination rule, or

(b) if they have such power but the procedure for doing so—

(i) is liable to be unduly complex or protracted, or

(ii) involves the obtaining of consents which cannot be obtained, or can only be obtained with undue delay or difficulty,

by resolution make such alterations to the scheme.

(4) Alterations made by a resolution such as is referred to in sub-paragraph (3)—

(a) may have effect in relation to a period before the alterations are made (but may not have effect in relation to any time before [1st December 2006]), and

(b) shall be subject to the consent of any employer in relation to the scheme whose consent would be required for such a modification if it were to be made under the scheme rules.

3 Exception for rules, practices, actions and decisions relating to occupational pension schemes

Nothing in Part 2 or 3 of these Regulations shall render it unlawful for an employer, or for trustees or managers, to maintain or use, in relation to a scheme, any of the rules, practices, actions or decisions set out in Part 2 of this Schedule.

[3A Length of service exemptions

(1) Subject to sub-paragraph (2), nothing in Part 2 or 3 of these Regulations shall render it unlawful for—

(a) any rule, practice, action or decision of the trustees or managers ("A") of a scheme regarding—
(i) admission to the scheme ("admission terms"); or
(ii) the accrual of, or eligibility for, any benefit under the scheme ("benefit terms"),

where the admission terms or the benefit terms put a member ("B") of the scheme at a disadvantage when compared with another member ("C") if and to the extent that the disadvantage suffered by B is because B's length of service with an employer ("D") in relation to the scheme is less than that of C;

(b) any rule, practice, action or decision of an employer ("E") in relation to a scheme regarding the admission terms or benefit terms where it puts a member ("F") of the scheme at a disadvantage when compared with another member ("G") if and to the extent that the disadvantage suffered by F is because F's length of service with E is less than that of G; or

(c) any rule, practice, action or decision of an employer ("H") regarding payment of contributions in respect of a worker ("I") to a personal pension scheme or to a money purchase arrangement ("contribution terms") where it puts I at a disadvantage when compared with another worker ("J") if and to the extent that the disadvantage suffered by I is because I's length of service with H is less than that of J.

(2) Where B's, or as the case may be, F's or I's length of service exceeds 5 years and a length of service criterion in the admission terms or as the case may be, the benefit terms or contribution terms puts B or F or I at a disadvantage—

(a) where sub-paragraph (1)(a) applies, A—
(i) must ask D to confirm whether the length of service criterion reasonably appears to D to fulfil a business need of D's undertaking (for example by encouraging the loyalty or motivation, or rewarding the experience, of some or all of his workers), and
(ii) may rely on D's confirmation;

(b) for the purposes of paragraph (a)(i), D must—
(i) calculate B's length of service;
(ii) provide A with details of B's length of service; and
(iii) respond to A's request within a reasonable time;

(c) where sub-paragraph (1)(a) or (b) or (c) applies, it must reasonably appear to D or, as the case may be, E or H that the length of service criterion applies in such a way that it fulfils a business need of his undertaking (for example by encouraging the loyalty or motivation, or rewarding the experience, of some or all of his workers).

(3) When calculating B's or, as the case may be, F's or I's length of service D or, as the case may be, E or H shall calculate—

(a) the length of time the member or worker has been working for him doing work which he reasonably considers to be at or above a particular level (assessed by reference to the demands made on the member or worker, for example, in terms of effort, skills and decision making), or

(b) the length of time the member or worker has been working for him in total,

and it is for D or, as the case may be, E or H to decide which of paragraphs (a) or (b) to use.

(4) For the purposes of sub-paragraph (3), D or, as the case may be, E or H shall calculate the length of time a member or worker has been working for him in accordance with paragraphs (4) to (7) of regulation 32 (exception for provision of certain benefits based on length of service) and any reference in those paragraphs to—

(a) "A" shall be read as if it were a reference to "D" or, as the case may be, "E" or "H"; and

(b) "worker" shall, where sub-paragraph (1)(a) or (b) applies, be read as if it were a reference to "member".

(5) For the purposes of this paragraph, a "member" shall include a "prospective member".]

4 Exception for rules, practices, actions and decisions relating to contributions by employers to personal pension schemes

Nothing in Part 2 or 3 of these Regulations shall render it unlawful for an employer, in relation to the payment of contributions to any personal pension scheme in respect of a worker, to maintain or use any of the rules, practices, actions or decisions set out in Part 3 of this Schedule.

[4A Unlawfulness of rules, practices, actions or decisions relating to Part 2 or Part 3 of Schedule 2

(1) The inclusion of a rule, practice, action or decision in Part 2 of this Schedule (excepted rules, practices, actions and decisions relating to occupational pension schemes) shall not be taken to mean that, but for the exemption in Part 2, the use or maintenance by an employer, trustees or managers of a scheme of the rule, practice, action or decision in relation to the scheme, would be unlawful.

(2) The inclusion of a rule, practice, action or decision in Part 3 of this Schedule (excepted rules, practices, actions and decisions relating to contributions by employers to personal pension schemes) shall not be taken to mean that, but for the exemption in Part 3, the use or maintenance by an employer of the rule, practice, action or decision in relation to the payment of contributions to a personal pension scheme in respect of a worker, would be unlawful.]

5 Procedure in employment tribunals

Where under regulation 36 (jurisdiction of employment tribunals) a member or prospective member of a scheme presents to an employment tribunal a complaint that the trustees or managers of the scheme—

(a) have committed against him an act which is unlawful by virtue of regulation 11 (pension schemes) or 24 (relationships which have come to an end); or

(b) are by virtue of regulation 25 (liability of employers and principals) or 26 (aiding unlawful acts) to be treated as having committed against him such an act,

the employer in relation to the scheme shall, for the purposes of the rules governing procedure, be treated as a party and be entitled to appear and be heard in accordance with those rules.

6 Remedies in employment tribunals

(1) This paragraph applies where—

(a) under regulation 36 (jurisdiction of employment tribunals) a member or prospective member of a scheme ("the complainant") presents to an employment tribunal a complaint against the trustees or managers of the scheme or an employer;

(b) the complainant is not a pensioner member of the scheme;

(c) the complaint relates to the terms on which persons become members of the scheme, or the terms on which members of the scheme are treated; and

(d) the tribunal finds the complaint to be well-founded.

(2) Where this paragraph applies, the employment tribunal may, without prejudice to the generality of its power under regulation 38(1)(a) (power to make order declaring rights of complainant and respondent), make an order declaring that the complainant has a right—

(a) where the complaint relates to the terms on which persons become members of the scheme, to be admitted to the scheme;

(b) where the complaint relates to the terms on which members of the scheme are treated, to membership of the scheme without discrimination.

(3) An order under sub-paragraph (2)—

(a) may be made in respect of such period as is specified in the order (but may not be made in respect of any time before [1st December 2006]);

(b) may make such provision as the employment tribunal considers appropriate as to the terms on which, or the capacity in which, the complainant is to enjoy such admission or membership.

(4) Where this paragraph applies, the employment tribunal may not make an order for compensation under regulation 38(1)(b), whether in relation to arrears of benefits or otherwise, except—

(a) for injury to feelings;

(b) by virtue of regulation 38(3).

[3452]

NOTES

Commencement: 1 December 2006.

Para 1: all amendments to this paragraph were made by the Employment Equality (Age) (Amendment No 2) Regulations 2006, SI 2006/2931, regs 2, 4, as from 1 December 2006.

Paras 2, 6: words in square brackets substituted by the Employment Equality (Age) (Amendment) Regulations 2006, SI 2006/2408, reg 2(1), (5), as from 30 September 2006.

Paras 3A, 4A: inserted by SI 2006/2931, regs 2, 5, 6, as from 1 December 2006.

PART 2
EXCEPTED RULES, PRACTICES, ACTIONS AND DECISIONS RELATING TO OCCUPATIONAL PENSION SCHEMES

7 Admission to schemes

In relation to admission to a scheme—

(a) a minimum or maximum age for admission, including different ages for admission for different groups or categories of worker;

[(b) a minimum level of pensionable pay for admission where that minimum—

(i) does not exceed one and a half times the lower earnings limit;

(ii) does not exceed an amount calculated by reference to the lower earnings limit where the aim is more or less to reflect the amount of the basic state retirement pension; or

(iii) does not exceed an amount calculated more or less to reflect the amount of the basic state retirement pension plus the additional state retirement pension].

8 The use of age criteria in actuarial calculations

The use of age criteria in actuarial calculations [in a scheme], for example in the actuarial calculation of—

(a) any age related benefit commencing before any early retirement pivot age or enhancement of such benefit commencing after any late retirement pivot age;

(b) member or employer contributions [by or in respect of a member] to a scheme; or

(c) any age related benefit commuted in exchange for the payment of any lump sum.

9 Contributions

Any difference in the rate of member or employer contributions[, to a scheme,] by or in respect of different members to the extent that this is attributable to any differences in the pensionable pay [or, where paragraph 19A applies, different accrual rates] of those members.

10 Contributions under money purchase arrangements

Under a money purchase arrangement—

(a) different rates of member or employer contributions according to the age of the members by or in respect of whom contributions are made where the aim in setting the different rates is—

(i) to equalise the [amount of age related benefit in respect of comparable aggregate periods of pensionable service] to which members of different ages who are otherwise in a comparable situation will become entitled under the arrangement, or

[(ii) to make more nearly equal the amount of the age related benefit, in respect of comparable aggregate periods of pensionable service, to which members of different ages who are otherwise in a comparable situation will become entitled under the arrangement];

(b) equal rates of member or employer contributions irrespective of the age of the members by or in respect of whom contributions are made;

[(c) any limitation on any employer contributions in respect of a member or member contributions by reference to a maximum level of pensionable pay].

11 Contributions under defined benefits arrangements

Under a defined benefits arrangement, different rates of member or employer contributions according to the age of the members by or in respect of whom contributions are made, to the extent that—

(a) each year of pensionable service entitles members in a comparable situation to accrue a right to defined benefits based on the same fraction of pensionable pay, and

(b) the aim in setting the different rates is to reflect the increasing cost of providing the defined benefits in respect of members as they get older.

[11A. Any limitation on employer contributions in respect of a member or member contributions to a defined benefit arrangement by reference to a maximum level of pensionable pay.]

[12 Age related rules, practices, actions and decisions relating to benefit

(1) Subject to sub-paragraph (4), a minimum age for any member of a scheme to be entitled to a particular age related benefit that is paid in accordance with sub-paragraph (2) and is paid—

(a) either with or without consent (whether of an employer, the trustees or managers of the scheme or otherwise), and

(b) before the early retirement pivot age relevant to that age related benefit.

(2) The age related benefit must—

(a) be actuarially reduced on the basis that the aim is to reflect that it is paid on a date before the applicable early retirement pivot age; and

(b) not be enhanced by crediting the member with any additional periods of pensionable service or additional benefits.

(3) Sub-paragraph (1) shall also apply to different minimum ages for different groups or categories of members.

(4) Sub-paragraph (1) shall not apply to any member who retires on the grounds to which paragraph 13, 13A or 15 apply.]

[13.—(1) A minimum age for any active or prospective members of a scheme for payment of or entitlement to a particular age related benefit before the early retirement pivot age relevant to that age related benefit where—

(a) the entitlement to the age related benefit at a minimum age applies to a member who is an active or prospective member of the scheme on 1st December 2006;

(b) the age related benefit may be paid, at a minimum age, to the active or prospective member either with or without consent (whether of an employer, the trustees or managers of the scheme or otherwise); and

(c) the age related benefit is enhanced in one or more of the ways specified in sub-paragraph (2).

(2) For the purposes of sub-paragraph (1)(c) the specified ways are the enhancement of any age related benefit payable to or in respect of the member calculated in one or more of the following ways—

(a) by reference to some or all of the years of prospective pensionable service a member would have completed if he had remained in pensionable service until normal pension age;

(b) by reference to a fixed number of years of prospective pensionable service;

(c) by making an actuarial reduction which is smaller than if early retirement had been on grounds to which paragraph 12 applies; or

(d) by not making any actuarial reduction for early retirement.

(3) Sub-paragraph (1) shall also apply to different minimum ages for different groups or categories of active or prospective members.

13A. Paragraph 13 shall continue to apply to any member who after 1st December 2006—

(a) joins a scheme as a result of a block transfer or relevant transfer;

(b) joins a scheme as a result of a block transfer or relevant transfer from a scheme to which paragraph (a) applied; or

(c) joins a scheme on the basis that it will provide the same benefits as those provided by the scheme to which paragraph 13 applied.

13B.—(1) A minimum age for any member of a scheme for payment of or entitlement to a particular age related benefit on the grounds of redundancy where it is enhanced in accordance with sub-paragraph (2) and paid either with or without consent (whether of an employer, the trustees or managers of the scheme or otherwise).

(2) The enhancement of any age related benefit payable to or in respect of a member on the grounds of redundancy where the enhancement is calculated in one or more of the following ways—

(a) by reference to the years of prospective pensionable service a member would have completed if he had remained in pensionable service until normal pension age;

(b) by reference to a fixed number of years of prospective pensionable service;

(c) by making an actuarial reduction which is smaller than if early retirement had been on grounds to which paragraph 12 applied; or

(d) by not making any actuarial reduction for early retirement.

(3) Sub-paragraph (1) shall also apply to different minimum ages for different groups or categories of members.]

[14. An early retirement pivot age or a late retirement pivot age including—

(a) different such ages for different groups or categories of member, and

(b) any early retirement pivot age or late retirement pivot age for deferred members which is different than for active members.]

[15.—(1) A minimum age for any member of a scheme for payment of or entitlement to a particular age related benefit on the grounds of ill health where the age related benefit is enhanced in accordance with sub-paragraph (2) and paid either with or without consent (whether of an employer, the trustees or managers of the scheme or otherwise).

(2) The enhancement of any age related benefit payable to or in respect of a member on the grounds of ill health where the enhancement is calculated in one or more of the following ways—

(a) by reference to some or all of the years of prospective pensionable service a member would have completed if he had remained in pensionable service until normal pension age;

(b) by reference to a fixed number of years of prospective pensionable service;

(c) by making an actuarial reduction which is smaller than if early retirement had been on the grounds to which paragraph 12 applied; or

(d) by not making any actuarial reduction for early retirement.

(3) Sub-paragraph (1) shall also apply to different minimum ages for different groups or categories of members.

15A.—(1) The calculation of any death benefit payable in respect of a member—

(a) by reference to some or all of the years of prospective pensionable service a member would have completed if he had remained in service until normal pension age; or

(b) by reference to a fixed number of years of prospective pensionable service.

(2) Payment after a member's death of a death benefit calculated by reference to the period remaining in a pension guarantee period.

(3) For the purposes of sub-paragraph (2), a pension guarantee period means a fixed period specified in or permitted by the scheme rules beginning on—

(a) the date on which the payment of pension to or in respect of the member began, or

(b) if specified in the scheme rules, the date of the member's death on or after normal pension age where payment of pension to or in respect of him had not begun.

(4) Any difference between the death benefits payable in respect of deferred members who die before normal pension age and the death benefits payable in respect of deferred members who die on or after normal pension age.]

[16.—(1) Any rule, practice, action or decision where—

(a) the rate of pension to which a pensioner member is entitled is reduced at any time between age 60 and 65 ("the reduction date"), by either—

(i) an amount not exceeding the relevant state retirement pension rate at the reduction date, or

(ii) the rate of the pension in payment where on the reduction date the relevant state retirement pension rate is greater than the rate of that pension;

(b) from the date a member is entitled to present payment of a pension from a scheme he is entitled to an additional amount of pension which does not exceed the amount of the basic state retirement pension plus the additional state retirement pension that would be payable at state pension age; or

(c) a member who reaches his state pension age is not entitled to, or no longer entitled to, an additional amount of pension which does not exceed the amount of the basic state retirement pension plus the additional state retirement pension that would be payable at state pension age.

(2) For the purposes of paragraph (1)—

"relevant state retirement pension rate" has the same meaning as in paragraph 2(5) of Schedule 28 to the Finance Act 2004;

"state pension age" means the pensionable age specified in the rules in paragraph 1 of Schedule 4 to the Pensions Act 1995.]

17. The [actuarial] reduction of any pension payable [from a scheme] in consequence of a member's death to any dependant of the member where that dependant is more than a specified number of years younger than the member.

18. In relation to pensioner members who have retired [from a scheme] on ill health grounds … , discontinuation of any life assurance cover once any such members reach the normal retirement age which applied to them at the time they retired, or in relation to members to whom no such normal retirement age applied, once such members reach the age of 65.

19 Other rules, practices, actions and decisions relating to benefit

Any difference in the amount of any age related benefit or death benefit payable under a [scheme] to or in respect of members with different lengths of pensionable service to the extent that the difference in amount is attributable to their differing lengths of service, provided that, for each year of pensionable service, members in a comparable situation are entitled to accrue a right to benefit based upon the same fraction of pensionable pay.

[19A.—(1) Any differences in—

(a) the fraction of pensionable pay at which any age related benefit accrues, or

(b) the amount of death benefit,

to or in respect of active or prospective members of a scheme where the differences are attributable to the aim specified in sub-paragraph (2).

(2) The aim referred to in sub-paragraph (1) is that members in a comparable situation will have the right to age related benefit or death benefit equal to the same fraction, proportion or multiple of pensionable pay—

(a) without regard to each member's length of pensionable service under the scheme, and

(b) provided that each member continues in pensionable service under the scheme until normal pension age.

(3) Any differences in age related benefits which accrue, or entitlement to any death benefits which arises, to or in respect of active or prospective members of a scheme who are in a comparable situation where—

(a) those differences are attributable to the aim specified in sub-paragraph (2), and

(b) the member's pensionable service under the arrangement ceases before normal pension age.

(4) Where sub-paragraph (1) applies, any limitation on the amount of any age related benefit or death benefit payable from a scheme where the limitation arises from imposing one or both of the following—

(a) a maximum amount on the age related benefit or death benefit which is equal to a fraction, proportion or multiple of the member's pensionable pay, or

(b) a minimum period of pensionable service.

19B. Where paragraph 19A applies, different rates of member or employer contributions according to the age of the members by, or in respect of whom, contributions are made, where for each year of pensionable service members in comparable situations accrue different fractions of pensionable pay.]

20. Any difference in the amount of any age related benefit or death benefit payable from a scheme to or in respect of different members to the extent that the difference in amount is attributable to differences over time in the pensionable pay of those members.

[21.—(1) Any limitation on the amount of any age related benefit or death benefit payable from a scheme where either or both sub-paragraphs (2) and (3) apply.

(2) The limitation results from imposing a maximum number of years of pensionable service by reference to which the age related benefit or death benefit may be calculated.

(3) The limitation arises from imposing a maximum amount on the age related benefit or death benefit which is equal to a fraction, proportion or multiple of a member's pensionable pay.]

[22. Any rule, practice, action or decision where any age related benefit or death benefit is only payable from a scheme where a member is entitled to short service benefit under section 71 of the Pension Schemes Act 1993 (basic principles as to short service benefit).]

[23. When determining a member's pensionable pay by reference to which any age related benefit or death benefit payable to or in respect of a member is calculated, to exclude from the member's remuneration an amount which—

- (a) does not exceed one and a half times the lower earnings limit;
- (b) does not exceed an amount calculated by reference to the lower earnings limit where the aim is more or less to reflect the amount of the basic state retirement pension; or
- (c) does not exceed an amount calculated more or less to reflect the amount of the basic state retirement pension plus the additional state retirement pension.]

[23A. Any difference in the amount of age related benefit or death benefit payable under a scheme to or in respect of members where the difference is attributable to accrual of age related benefit at a higher fraction of pensionable pay for pensionable pay over the upper earnings limit (and a lower fraction of pensionable pay for pensionable pay under the upper earnings limit) where the aim is to reflect the additional state retirement pension.]

[24. Any limitation on the amount of any age related benefit or death benefit payable from a scheme where the limitation—

- (a) relates to—
  - (i) all members who joined, or who became eligible to join the scheme on, after or before a particular date; or
  - (ii) any group or category of members who joined, or who became eligible to join the scheme on, after or before a particular date; and
- (b) results from imposing a maximum level of pensionable pay by reference to which the age related benefit or death benefit may be calculated.]

25 Closure of schemes

The closure of a scheme, from a particular date, to workers who have not already joined it.

[25A Closure of sections of schemes

(1) The closure of any section of a scheme, from a particular date, to workers who have not already joined it.

(2) For the purposes of paragraph (1)—

- (a) a scheme may be divided into two or more sections, and
- (b) a section of a scheme shall mean any of the groups in sub-paragraph (3).

(3) A section of a scheme shall mean any of the following—

- (a) any group of members who became eligible to join, or who joined, the scheme on, after or before a particular date on the basis that particular benefits will be provided to or in respect of those members or that a particular level of contributions will be paid in respect of those members; or
- (b) any group of members who became eligible to join, or who joined, the scheme as a result of a block transfer or relevant transfer.]

26 Other rules, practices, actions and decisions

Increases of pensions in payment which are made to members over 55 but not to members below that age.

27. Any difference in the rate of increase of pensions in payment for members of different ages to the extent that the aim in setting the different rates is to maintain [or more nearly maintain] the relative value of members' pensions.

28. Any difference in the rate of increase of pensions in payment for members whose pensions have been in payment for different lengths of time to the extent that the aim in setting the different rates is to maintain [or more nearly maintain] the relative value of members' pensions.

29. The application of an age limit for transfer of the value of a member's accrued rights into or out of a scheme, provided that any such age limit is not more than one year before the member's normal pension age.

30 Registered pension schemes

(1) … Any rules, practices, actions or decisions relating to entitlement to or payment of benefits under a [scheme which is a] registered pension scheme insofar as compliance is necessary to secure any tax relief or exemption available under Part 4 of the Finance Act 2004 or to prevent any charge to tax arising under that Part of that Act, whoever is liable in relation to such charge.

(2) … **[3453]**

NOTES

Commencement: 1 December 2006.

Paras 7, 19: words in square brackets substituted by the Employment Equality (Age) (Amendment No 2) Regulations 2006, SI 2006/2931, regs 2, 7(1), 17, as from 1 December 2006.

Paras 8, 9, 17, 27, 28: words in square brackets inserted by SI 2006/2931, regs 2, 8, 15, 23, as from 1 December 2006.

Para 10: words in square brackets in sub-para (a)(i) and the whole of sub-para (a)(ii) substituted, and sub-para (c) added, by SI 2006/2931, regs 2, 9, as from 1 December 2006.

Para 11A, 19A, 19B, 23A, 25A: inserted by SI 2006/2931, regs 2, 7(3), 10, 18, 22, as from 1 December 2006.

Paras 12, 14, 16, 21–23, 24: substituted by SI 2006/2931, regs 2, 7(2), 11(1), 12, 14, 19–21, as from 1 December 2006.

Paras 13, 13A, 13B: substituted, for original para 13, by SI 2006/2931, regs 2, 11(2), as from 1 December 2006.

Para 15, 15A: substituted, for original para 15, by SI 2006/2931, regs 2, 13(1), as from 1 December 2006.

Paras 18, 30: words in square brackets inserted, and words omitted revoked, by SI 2006/2931, regs 2, 16, 24, as from 1 December 2006.

PART 3
EXCEPTED RULES, PRACTICES, ACTIONS AND DECISIONS RELATING TO CONTRIBUTIONS BY EMPLOYERS TO PERSONAL PENSION SCHEMES

31 Contributions by employers

Different rates of contributions by an employer [to a personal pension scheme] according to the age of the workers in respect of whom the contributions are made where the aim in setting the different rates is—

(a) to equalise the [amount of age related benefit, derived from contributions made each year by the employer,] to which workers of different ages who are otherwise in a comparable situation will become entitled under their personal pension schemes, or

[(b) to make more nearly equal the amount of the age related benefit, derived from contributions made each year by the employer, to which workers of different ages who are otherwise in a comparable situation will become entitled under their personal pension schemes].

32. Any difference in the rate of contributions by an employer [to a personal pension scheme] in respect of different workers to the extent that this is attributable to any differences in remuneration payable to those workers.

[33. Any limitation on any contributions by an employer, to a personal pension scheme, by reference to a maximum level of remuneration.

34. A minimum age for commencement of payment of contributions by an employer to a personal pension scheme in respect of a worker.

35. Different minimum ages for commencement of payment of contributions by an employer to a personal pension scheme in respect of different groups or categories of workers.

36. Equal rates of contributions by an employer to a personal pension scheme irrespective of the age of the workers in respect of whom contributions are made.]

[3454]

NOTES

Commencement: 1 December 2006.

Para 31: words in first pair of square brackets inserted, and words in second and third pairs of square brackets substituted, by the Employment Equality (Age) (Amendment No 2) Regulations 2006, SI 2006/2931, regs 2, 25, as from 1 December 2006.

Para 32: words in square brackets inserted by SI 2006/2931, regs 2, 25, as from 1 December 2006.

Paras 33–36: added by SI 2006/2931, regs 2, 27, as from 1 December 2006.

SCHEDULE 3

Regulation 41(1)

Questionnaire of Person Aggrieved

To ....

(*name of person to be questioned*)

of ....

(*address*)

1.—(1) I ....

(*name of questioner*)

of ....

(*address*)

consider that you may have discriminated against me [subjected me to harassment] contrary to the Employment Equality (Age) Regulations 2006.

(2) (*Give date, approximate time and a factual description of the treatment received and of the circumstances leading up to the treatment.*)

(3) I consider that this treatment may have been unlawful because

....

(*complete if you wish to give reasons, otherwise delete*)

2. Do you agree that the statement in paragraph 1(2) above is an accurate description of what happened? If not, in what respect do you disagree or what is your version of what happened?

3. Do you accept that your treatment of me was unlawful discrimination [harassment]?

If not—

(a) why not,

(b) for what reason did I receive the treatment accorded to me, and

(c) how far did considerations of age affect your treatment of me?

4. (*Any other questions you wish to ask.*)

5. My address for any reply you may wish to give to the questions raised above is [that set out in paragraph 1(1) above] [the following address

....]

.... (*signature of questioner*)

.... (*date*)

N.B.—By virtue of regulation 41 of the Employment Equality (Age) Regulations 2006 this questionnaire and any reply are (subject to the provisions of that regulation) admissible in proceedings under the Regulations. A court or tribunal may draw any such inference as is just and equitable from a failure without reasonable excuse to reply within eight weeks of service of this questionnaire, or from an evasive or equivocal reply, including an inference that the person questioned has committed an unlawful act.

[3455]

NOTES

Commencement: 1 October 2006.

SCHEDULE 4

Regulation 41(1)

Reply by the Respondent

To ....

(*name of questioner*)

of ....

(*address*)

1. I ....

(*name of person questioned*)

of ....

(*address*)

hereby acknowledge receipt of the questionnaire signed by you and dated ....

which was served on me on ....(*date*).

2. [I agree that the statement in paragraph 1(2) of the questionnaire is an accurate description of what happened.]

[I disagree with the statement in paragraph 1(2) of the questionnaire in that ....

....]

3. I accept/dispute that my treatment of you was unlawful discrimination [harassment].

[My reasons for so disputing are ....

....

The reason why you received the treatment accorded to you and the answers to the other questions in paragraph 3 of the questionnaire are ....

....

4. (*Replies to questions in paragraph 4 of the questionnaire.*)

5. [I have deleted (in whole or in part) the paragraph(s) numbered ....

above, since I am unable/unwilling to reply to the relevant questions in the correspondingly numbered paragraph(s) of the questionnaire for the following reasons ....

....

.... (*signature of person questioned*)

.... (*date*)

[3456]

NOTES

Commencement: 1 October 2006.

SCHEDULE 5
VALIDITY OF CONTRACTS, COLLECTIVE AGREEMENTS AND RULES OF UNDERTAKINGS

Regulation 43

PART 1
VALIDITY AND REVISION OF CONTRACTS

1.—(1) A term of a contract is void where—

(a) the making of the contract is, by reason of the inclusion of the term, unlawful by virtue of these Regulations;

(b) it is included in furtherance of an act which is unlawful by virtue of these Regulations; or

(c) it provides for the doing of an act which is unlawful by virtue of these Regulations.

(2) Sub-paragraph (1) does not apply to a term the inclusion of which constitutes, or is in furtherance of, or provides for, unlawful discrimination against, or harassment of, a party to the contract, but the term shall be unenforceable against that party.

(3) A term in a contract which purports to exclude or limit any provision of these Regulations is unenforceable by any person in whose favour the term would operate apart from this paragraph.

[(4) Sub-paragraphs (1), (2) and (3) shall apply whether the contract was entered into before or after the date on which any term of the contract became unlawful by virtue of these Regulations, but in the case of a contract made before the date on which a term became unlawful, those sub-paragraphs do not apply to that term in relation to any period before that date.]

2.—(1) Paragraph 1(3) does not apply—

(a) to a contract settling a complaint to which regulation 36(1) (jurisdiction of employment tribunals) applies where the contract is made with the assistance of a conciliation officer within the meaning of section 211 of the Trade Union and Labour Relations (Consolidation) Act 1992;

(b) to a contract settling a complaint to which regulation 36(1) applies if the conditions regulating compromise contracts under this Schedule are satisfied in relation to the contract; or

(c) to a contract settling a claim to which regulation 39 (jurisdiction of county or sheriff courts) applies.

(2) The conditions regulating compromise contracts under this Schedule are that—

(a) the contract must be in writing;

(b) the contract must relate to the particular complaint;

(c) the complainant must have received advice from a relevant independent adviser as to the terms and effect of the proposed contract and in particular its effect on his ability to pursue a complaint before an employment tribunal;

(d) there must be in force, when the adviser gives the advice, a contract of insurance, or an indemnity provided for members of a profession or professional body, covering the risk of a claim by the complainant in respect of loss arising in consequence of the advice;

(e) the contract must identify the adviser; and

(f) the contract must state that the conditions regulating compromise contracts under this Schedule are satisfied.

(3) A person is a relevant independent adviser for the purposes of sub-paragraph (2)(c)—

(a) if he is a qualified lawyer;

(b) if he is an officer, official, employee or member of an independent trade union who has been certified in writing by the trade union as competent to give advice and as authorised to do so on behalf of the trade union; or

(c) if he works at an advice centre (whether as an employee or a volunteer) and has been certified in writing by the centre as competent to give advice and as authorised to do so on behalf of the centre.

(4) But a person is not a relevant independent adviser for the purposes of sub-paragraph (2)(c) in relation to the complainant—

(a) if he is employed by, or is acting in the matter for the other party, or is a person who is connected with the other party;

(b) in the case of a person within sub-paragraph (3)(b) or (c), if the trade union or advice centre is the other party or a person who is connected with the other party; or

(c) in the case of a person within sub-paragraph (3)(c), if the complainant makes a payment for the advice received from him.

(5) In sub-paragraph (3)(a) "qualified lawyer" means—

(a) as respects England and Wales, a barrister (whether in practice as such or employed to give legal advice), a solicitor who holds a practising certificate, or a person other than a barrister or solicitor who is an authorised advocate or authorised litigator (within the meaning of the Courts and Legal Services Act 1990; and

(b) as respects Scotland, an advocate (whether in practice as such or employed to give legal advice), or a solicitor who holds a practising certificate.

(6) A person shall be treated as being a qualified lawyer within sub-paragraph (5)(a) if he is a Fellow of the Institute of Legal Executives employed by a solicitors' practice.

(7) In sub-paragraph (3)(b) "independent trade union" has the same meaning as in the Trade Union and Labour Relations (Consolidation) Act 1992.

(8) For the purposes of sub-paragraph (4)(a) any two persons are to be treated as connected—

(a) if one is a company of which the other (directly or indirectly) has control; or

(b) if both are companies of which a third person (directly or indirectly) has control.

(9) An agreement under which the parties agree to submit a dispute to arbitration—

(a) shall be regarded for the purposes of sub-paragraphs (1)(a) and (b) as being a contract settling a complaint if—

(i) the dispute is covered by a scheme having effect by virtue of an order under section 212A of the Trade Union and Labour Relations (Consolidation) Act 1992, and

(ii) the agreement is to submit it to arbitration in accordance with the scheme, but

(b) shall be regarded as neither being nor including such a contract in any other case.

3.—(1) On the application of a person interested in a contract to which paragraph 1(1) or (2) applies, a county court or a sheriff court may make such order as it thinks fit for—

(a) removing or modifying any term rendered void by paragraph 1(1), or

(b) removing or modifying any term made unenforceable by paragraph 1(2);

but such an order shall not be made unless all persons affected have been given notice in writing of the application (except where under rules of court notice may be dispensed with) and have been afforded an opportunity to make representations to the court.

An order under sub-paragraph (1) may include provision as respects any period before the making of the order (but after [the date on which the inclusion of any term which is the subject of the order becomes unlawful by virtue of these Regulations]).

[3457]

NOTES

Commencement: 1 October 2006.

Para 1: sub-para (4) substituted by the Employment Equality (Age) (Amendment) Regulations 2006, SI 2006/2408, reg 2(1), (6)(a), as from 30 September 2006.

Para 3: words in square brackets in sub-para (2) substituted by SI 2006/2408, reg 2(1), (6)(b), as from 30 September 2006.

PART 2
COLLECTIVE AGREEMENTS AND RULES OF UNDERTAKINGS

4.—(1) This Part of this Schedule applies to—

(a) any term of a collective agreement, including an agreement which was not intended, or is presumed not to have been intended, to be a legally enforceable contract;

(b) any rule made by an employer for application to all or any of the persons who are employed by him or who apply to be, or are, considered by him for employment;

(c) any rule made by a trade organisation (within the meaning of regulation 18) or a qualifications body (within the meaning of regulation 19) for application to—
   (i) all or any of its members or prospective members; or
   (ii) all or any of the persons on whom it has conferred professional or trade qualifications (within the meaning of regulation 19) or who are seeking the professional or trade qualifications which it has power to confer.

(2) Any term or rule to which this Part of this Schedule applies is void where—
(a) the making of the collective agreement is, by reason of the inclusion of the term, unlawful by virtue of these Regulations;
(b) the term or rule is included or made in furtherance of an act which is unlawful by virtue of these Regulations; or
(c) the term or rule provides for the doing of an act which is unlawful by virtue of these Regulations.

[(3) Sub-paragraph (2) shall apply whether the agreement was entered into, or the rule made, before or after the date on which any term of the agreement or rule became unlawful by virtue of these Regulations; but in the case of an agreement entered into, or a rule made, before the date on which a term, or rule, became unlawful, that sub-paragraph does not apply to that term or rule in relation to any period before that date.]

5. A person to whom this paragraph applies may present a complaint to an employment tribunal that a term or rule is void by virtue of paragraph 4 if he has reason to believe—
(a) that the term or rule may at some future time have effect in relation to him; and
(b) where he alleges that it is void by virtue of paragraph 4(2)(c), that—
   (i) an act for the doing of which it provides, may at some such time be done in relation to him, and
   (ii) the act would be unlawful by virtue of these Regulations if done in relation to him in present circumstances.

6. In the case of a complaint about—
(a) a term of a collective agreement made by or on behalf of—
   (i) an employer,
   (ii) an organisation of employers of which an employer is a member, or
   (iii) an association of such organisations of one of which an employer is a member, or
(b) a rule made by an employer within the meaning of paragraph 4(1)(b),

paragraph 5 applies to any person who is, or is genuinely and actively seeking to become, one of his employees.

7. In the case of a complaint about a rule made by an organisation or body to which paragraph 4(1)(c) applies, paragraph 5 applies to any person—
(a) who is, or is genuinely and actively seeking to become, a member of the organisation or body;
(b) on whom the organisation or body has conferred a professional or trade qualification (within the meaning of regulation 19) which the organisation or body has power to confer; or
(c) who is genuinely and actively seeking such a professional or trade qualification which the organisation or body has power to confer.

8.—(1) When an employment tribunal finds that a complaint presented to it under paragraph 5 is well-founded the tribunal shall make an order declaring that the term or rule is void.

(2) An order under sub-paragraph (1) may include provision as respects any period before the making of the order (but after [the date on which the inclusion of the term or rule became unlawful by virtue of these Regulations]).

9. The avoidance by virtue of paragraph 4(2) of any term or rule which provides for any person to be discriminated against shall be without prejudice to the following rights (except in so far as they enable any person to require another person to be treated less favourably than himself), namely—
(a) such of the rights of the person to be discriminated against; and
(b) such of the rights of any person who will be treated more favourably in direct or indirect consequence of the discrimination,

as are conferred by or in respect of a contract made or modified wholly or partly in pursuance of, or by reference to, that term or rule.

10. In this Schedule "collective agreement" means any agreement relating to one or more of the matters mentioned in section 178(2) of the Trade Union and Labour Relations (Consolidation) Act 1992 (collective agreements and collective bargaining), being an agreement made by or on behalf of one or more employers or one or more organisations of employers or associations of such organisations with one or more organisations of workers or associations of such organisations.

[3458]

NOTES

Commencement: 1 October 2006.

Para 4: sub-para (3) substituted by the Employment Equality (Age) (Amendment) Regulations 2006, SI 2006/2408, reg 2(1), (6)(c), as from 30 September 2006.

Para 8: words in square brackets in sub-para (2) substituted by SI 2006/2408, reg 2(1), (6)(d), as from 30 September 2006.

SCHEDULE 6
DUTY TO CONSIDER WORKING BEYOND RETIREMENT

Regulation 47

1 Interpretation

(1) In this Schedule—

"dismissal" means a dismissal within the meaning of section 95 of the 1996 Act;

"employee" means a person to whom regulation 30 (exception for retirement) applies and references to "employer" shall be construed accordingly;

"intended date of retirement" has the meaning given by sub-paragraph (2);

"operative date of termination" means (subject to paragraph 10(3))—

(a) where the employer terminates the employee's contract of employment by notice, the date on which the notice expires, or

(b) where the employer terminates the contract of employment without notice, the date on which the termination takes effect;

"request" means a request made under paragraph 5; and

"worker" has the same meaning as in section 230(3) of the 1996 Act.

(2) In this Schedule "intended date of retirement" means—

(a) where the employer notifies a date in accordance with paragraph 2, that date;

(b) where the employer notifies a date in accordance with paragraph 4 and either no request is made or a request is made after the notification, that date;

(c) where,

(i) the employer has not notified a date in accordance with paragraph 2,

(ii) a request is made before the employer has notified a date in accordance with paragraph 4 (including where no notification in accordance with that paragraph is given),

(iii) the request is made by an employee who has reasonable grounds for believing that the employer intends to retire him on a certain date, and,

(iv) the request identifies that date,

the date so identified;

(d) in a case to which paragraph 3 has applied, any earlier or later date that has superseded the date mentioned in paragraph (a), (b) or (c) as the intended date of retirement by virtue of paragraph 3(3);

(e) in a case to which paragraph 10 has applied, the later date that has superseded the date mentioned in paragraph (a), (b) or (c) as the intended date of retirement by virtue of paragraph 10(3)(b).

2 Duty of employer to inform employee

(1) An employer who intends to retire an employee has a duty to notify the employee in writing of—

(a) the employee's right to make a request; and

(b) the date on which he intends the employee to retire,

not more than one year and not less than six months before that date.

(2) The duty to notify applies regardless of—

(a) whether there is any term in the employee's contract of employment indicating when his retirement is expected to take place,

(b) any other notification of, or information about, the employee's date of retirement given to him by the employer at any time, and

(c) any other information about the employee's right to make a request given to him by the employer at any time.

3.—(1) This paragraph applies if the employer has notified the employee in accordance with paragraph 2 or 4 or the employee has made a request before being notified in accordance with paragraph 4 (including where no notification in accordance with that paragraph is given), and—

(a) the employer and employee agree, in accordance with paragraph 7(3)(b) or 8(5)(b), that the dismissal is to take effect on a date later than the relevant date;

(b) the employer gives notice to the employee, in accordance with paragraph 7(7)(a)(ii) or, where the employee appeals, paragraph 8(9)(a)(ii), that the dismissal is to take effect on a date later than the relevant date; or

(c) the employer and employee agree that the dismissal is to take effect on a date earlier than the relevant date.

(2) This Schedule does not require the employer to give the employee a further notification in respect of dismissal taking effect on a date—

(a) agreed as mentioned in sub-paragraph (1)(a) or notified as mentioned in sub-paragraph (1)(b) that is later than the relevant date and falls six months or less after the relevant date; or

(b) agreed as mentioned in sub-paragraph (1)(c) that is earlier than the relevant date.

(3) If—

(a) a date later than the relevant date is agreed as mentioned in sub-paragraph (1)(a) or notified as mentioned in sub-paragraph (1)(b) and falls six months or less after the relevant date, or

(b) a date earlier than the relevant date is agreed as mentioned in sub-paragraph (1)(c),

the earlier or later date shall supersede the relevant date as the intended date of retirement.

(4) In this paragraph, "the relevant date" means the date that is defined as the intended date of retirement in paragraph (a), (b) or (c) of paragraph 1(2).

4 Continuing duty to inform employee

Where the employer has failed to comply with paragraph 2, he has a continuing duty to notify the employee in writing as described in paragraph 2(1) until the fourteenth day before the operative date of termination.

5 Statutory right to request not to retire

(1) An employee may make a request to his employer not to retire on the intended date of retirement.

(2) In his request the employee must propose that his employment should continue, following the intended date of retirement—

(a) indefinitely,

(b) for a stated period, or

(c) until a stated date;

and, if the request is made at a time when it is no longer possible for the employer to notify in accordance with paragraph 2 and the employer has not yet notified in accordance with paragraph 4, must identify the date on which he believes that the employer intends to retire him.

(3) A request must be in writing and state that it is made under this paragraph.

(4) An employee may only make one request under this paragraph in relation to any one intended date of retirement and may not make a request in relation to a date that supersedes a different date as the intended date of retirement by virtue of paragraph 3(3) or 10(3)(b).

(5) A request is only a request made under this paragraph if it is made—

(a) in a case where the employer has complied with paragraph 2, more than three months but not more than six months before the intended date of retirement, or

(b) in a case where the employer has not complied with paragraph 2, before, but not more than six months before, the intended date of retirement.

6 An employer's duty to consider a request

An employer to whom a request is made is under a duty to consider the request in accordance with paragraphs 7 to 9.

7 Meeting to consider request

(1) An employer having a duty under paragraph 6 to consider a request shall hold a meeting to discuss the request with the employee within a reasonable period after receiving it.

(2) The employer and employee must take all reasonable steps to attend the meeting.

(3) The duty to hold a meeting does not apply if, before the end of the period that is reasonable—

(a) the employer and employee agree that the employee's employment will continue indefinitely and the employer gives notice to the employee to that effect; or

(b) the employer and employee agree that the employee's employment will continue for an agreed period and the employer gives notice to the employee of the length of that period or of the date on which it will end.

(4) The duty to hold a meeting does not apply if—

(a) it is not practicable to hold a meeting within the period that is reasonable, and

(b) the employer complies with sub-paragraph (5).

(5) Where sub-paragraph (4)(a) applies, the employer may consider the request without holding a meeting provided he considers any representations made by the employee.

(6) The employer shall give the employee notice of his decision on the request as soon as is reasonably practicable after the date of the meeting or, if sub-paragraphs (4) and (5) apply, his consideration of the request.

(7) A notice given under sub-paragraph (6) shall—

(a) where the decision is to accept the request, state that it is accepted and—

(i) where the decision is that the employee's employment will continue indefinitely, state that fact, or

(ii) where the decision is that the employee's employment will continue for a further period, state that fact and specify the length of the period or the date on which it will end,

(b) where the decision is to refuse the request, confirm that the employer wishes to retire the employee and the date on which the dismissal is to take effect,

and, in the case of a notice falling within paragraph (b), and of a notice referred to in paragraph (a) that specifies a period shorter than the period proposed by the employee in the request, shall inform the employee of his right to appeal.

(8) All notices given under this paragraph shall be in writing and be dated.

8 Appeals

(1) An employee is entitled to appeal against—

(a) a decision of his employer to refuse the request, or

(b) a decision of his employer to accept the request where the notice given under paragraph 7(6) states as mentioned in paragraph 7(7)(a)(ii) and specifies a period shorter than the period proposed by the employee in the request,

by giving notice in accordance with sub-paragraph (2) as soon as is reasonably practicable after the date of the notice given under paragraph 7(6).

(2) A notice of appeal under sub-paragraph (1) shall set out the grounds of appeal.

(3) The employer shall hold a meeting with the employee to discuss an appeal within a reasonable period after the date of the notice of appeal.

(4) The employer and employee must take all reasonable steps to attend the meeting.

(5) The duty to hold a meeting does not apply if, before the end of the period that is reasonable—

(a) the employer and employee agree that the employee's employment will continue indefinitely and the employer gives notice to the employee to that effect; or

(b) the employer and employee agree that the employee's employment will continue for an agreed period and the employer gives notice to the employee of the length of that period or of the date on which it will end.

(6) The duty to hold a meeting does not apply if—

(a) it is not practicable to hold a meeting within the period that is reasonable, and
(b) the employer complies with sub-paragraph (7).

(7) Where sub-paragraph (6)(a) applies, the employer may consider the appeal without holding a meeting provided he considers any representations made by the employee.

(8) The employer shall give the employee notice of his decision on the appeal as soon as is reasonably practicable after the date of the meeting or, if sub-paragraphs (6) and (7) apply, his consideration of the appeal.

(9) A notice under sub-paragraph (8) shall—
(a) where the decision is to accept the appeal, state that it is accepted and—
(i) where the decision is that the employee's employment will continue indefinitely, state that fact, or
(ii) where the decision is that the employee's employment will continue for a further period, state that fact and specify the length of the period or the date on which it will end,
(b) where the decision is to refuse the appeal, confirm that the employer wishes to retire the employee and the date on which the dismissal is to take effect.

(10) All notices given under this paragraph shall be in writing and be dated.

9 Right to be accompanied

(1) This paragraph applies where—
(a) a meeting is held under paragraph 7 or 8, and
(b) the employee reasonably requests to be accompanied at the meeting.

(2) Where this paragraph applies the employer must permit the employee to be accompanied at the meeting by one companion who—
(a) is chosen by the employee;
(b) is a worker employed by the same employer as the employee;
(c) is to be permitted to address the meeting (but not to answer questions on behalf of the employee); and
(d) is to be permitted to confer with the employee during the meeting.

(3) If—
(a) an employee has a right under this paragraph to be accompanied at a meeting,
(b) his chosen companion will not be available at the time proposed for the meeting by the employer, and
(c) the employee proposes an alternative time which satisfies sub-paragraph (4),

the employer must postpone the meeting to the time proposed by the employee.

(4) An alternative time must—
(a) be convenient for employer, employee and companion, and
(b) fall before the end of the period of seven days beginning with the first day after the day proposed by the employer.

(5) An employer shall permit a worker to take time off during working hours for the purpose of accompanying an employee in accordance with a request under sub-paragraph (1)(b).

(6) Sections 168(3) and (4), 169 and 171 to 173 of the Trade Union and Labour Relations (Consolidation) Act 1992 (time off for carrying out trade union duties) shall apply in relation to sub-paragraph (5) above as they apply in relation to section 168(1) of that Act.

10 Dismissal before request considered

(1) This paragraph applies where—
(a) by virtue of paragraph 6 an employer is under a duty to consider a request;
(b) the employer dismisses the employee;
(c) that dismissal is the contemplated dismissal to which the request relates; and
(d) the operative date of termination would, but for sub-paragraph (3), fall on or before the day on which the employer gives notice in accordance with paragraph 7(6).

(2) Subject to paragraph (4), the contract of employment shall continue in force for all purposes, including the purpose of determining for any purpose the period for which the employee has been continuously employed, until the day following that on which the notice under paragraph 7(6) is given.

(3) The day following the day on which that notice is given shall supersede—

(a) the date mentioned in sub-paragraph (1)(d) as the operative date of termination; and

(b) the date defined as the intended date of retirement in paragraph (a), (b) or (c) of paragraph 1(2) as the intended date of retirement.

(4) Any continuation of the contract of employment under sub-paragraph (2) shall be disregarded when determining the operative date of termination for the purposes of sections 98ZA to 98ZH of the 1996 Act.

11 Complaint to employment tribunal: failure to comply with paragraph 2

(1) An employee may present a complaint to an employment tribunal that his employer has failed to comply with the duty to notify him in paragraph 2.

(2) A tribunal shall not consider a complaint under this paragraph unless the complaint is presented—

(a) before the end of the period of three months beginning with—

(i) the last day permitted to the employer by paragraph 2 for complying with the duty to notify, or

(ii) if the employee did not then know the date that would be the intended date of retirement, the first day on which he knew or should have known that date; or

(b) within such further period as the tribunal considers reasonable in a case where it is satisfied that it was not reasonably practicable for the complaint to be presented before the end of that period of three months.

(3) Where a tribunal finds that a complaint under this paragraph is well-founded it shall order the employer to pay compensation to the employee of such amount, not exceeding 8 weeks' pay, as the tribunal considers just and equitable in all the circumstances.

(4) Chapter 2 of Part 14 of the 1996 Act (calculation of a week's pay) shall apply for the purposes of sub-paragraph (3); and in applying that Chapter the calculation date shall be taken to be the date on which the complaint was presented or, if earlier, the operative date of termination.

(5) The limit in section 227(1) of the 1996 Act (maximum amount of a week's pay) shall apply for the purposes of sub-paragraph (3).

12 Complaint to employment tribunal: denial of right to be accompanied

(1) An employee may present a complaint to an employment tribunal that his employer has failed, or threatened to fail, to comply with paragraph 9(2) or (3).

(2) A tribunal shall not consider a complaint under this paragraph in relation to a failure or threat unless the complaint is presented—

(a) before the end of the period of three months beginning with the date of the failure or threat; or

(b) within such further period as the tribunal considers reasonable in a case where it is satisfied that it was not reasonably practicable for the complaint to be presented before the end of that period of three months.

(3) Where a tribunal finds that a complaint under this paragraph is well-founded it shall order the employer to pay compensation to the worker of an amount not exceeding two weeks' pay.

(4) Chapter 2 of Part 14 of the 1996 Act (calculation of a week's pay) shall apply for the purposes of sub-paragraph (3); and in applying that Chapter the calculation date shall be taken to be the date on which the relevant meeting took place (or was to have taken place).

(5) The limit in section 227(1) of the 1996 Act (maximum amount of a week's pay) shall apply for the purposes of sub-paragraph (3).

13 Detriment and dismissal

(1) An employee has the right not to be subjected to any detriment by any act by his employer done on the ground that he exercised or sought to exercise his right to be accompanied in accordance with paragraph 9.

(2) A worker has the right not to be subjected to any detriment by any act, or any deliberate failure to act, by his employer done on the ground that he accompanied or sought to accompany an employee pursuant to a request under paragraph 9.

(3) Section 48 of the 1996 Act shall apply in relation to contraventions of sub-paragraph (1) or (2) above as it applies in relation to contraventions of certain sections of that Act.

(4) Sub-paragraph (2) does not apply where the worker is an employee and the detriment in question amounts to dismissal (within the meaning of Part 10 of the 1996 Act).

(5) An employee who is dismissed shall be regarded for the purposes of Part 10 of the 1996 Act as unfairly dismissed if the reason (or, if more than one, the principal reason) for the dismissal is that he—

(a) exercised or sought to exercise his right to be accompanied in accordance with paragraph 9, or

(b) accompanied or sought to accompany an employee pursuant to a request under that paragraph.

(6) Sections 128 to 132 of the 1996 Act (interim relief) shall apply in relation to dismissal for the reason specified in sub-paragraph (5)(a) or (b) above as they apply in relation to dismissal for a reason specified in section 128(1)(b) of that Act.

[3459]

NOTES

Commencement: 1 October 2006.

Note that there is no provision in the Employment Tribunals Act 1996, s 18 applying the conciliation provisions of that section in respect of complaints under para 11 or 12 of this Schedule.

SCHEDULE 7
DUTY TO CONSIDER WORKING BEYOND RETIREMENT – TRANSITIONAL PROVISIONS

Regulation 48

1. In paragraphs 2 to 6—

(a) "the expiry date" means the date on which notice of dismissal given by an employer expires; and

(b) words and expressions shall have the same meanings as they do in Schedule 6.

2.—(1) This paragraph applies in a case where—

(a) an employer has given notice of dismissal to the employee before the commencement date of—

(i) at least the period required by the contract of employment; or

(ii) where the period required by the contract exceeds four weeks, at least four weeks;

(b) the expiry date falls before 1st April 2007; and

(c) the employer has made the employee aware, before the commencement date, that the employer considers that the employee is being retired on the expiry date.

(2) Where this paragraph applies and the employer on or as soon as is practicable after the commencement date notifies the employee in writing of the employee's right to make a request under paragraph 5 of Schedule 6—

(a) the employer shall be treated as complying with the duty in paragraph 2 of Schedule 6;

(b) a request shall be treated as being a request made under paragraph 5 of Schedule 6 provided it—

(i) is made after the employer notified the employee of his right to make a request;

(ii) satisfies the requirements of sub-paragraphs (2) and (3) of paragraph 5 of Schedule 6; and

(iii) is made—

(aa) where practicable, at least four weeks before the expiry date; or

(bb) where that is not practicable, as soon as reasonably practicable (whether before or after the expiry date) after the employer notified the employee of his right to make a request, but not more than four weeks after the expiry date.

(3) Where this paragraph applies and the employer does not, on or as soon as is practicable after the commencement date, notify the employee in writing of the employee's right to make a request under paragraph 5 of Schedule 6—

(a) the duty to notify in accordance with paragraph 2 of Schedule 6 does not apply;

(b) the duty to notify in accordance with paragraph 4 of Schedule 6 applies as if—
(i) the employer had failed to notify in accordance with paragraph 2 of that Schedule; and
(ii) the duty was one to notify at any time before the expiry date;
(c) a request shall be treated as being a request made under paragraph 5 of Schedule 6 if it satisfies the requirements of sub-paragraphs (2) and (3) of that paragraph and is made—
(i) before any notification given in accordance with paragraph 4 of Schedule 6; or
(ii) after such notification and—
(aa) where practicable, at least four weeks before the expiry date; or
(bb) where that is not practicable, as soon as reasonably practicable (whether before or after the expiry date) after the employer notified the employee of his right to make a request, but not more than four weeks after the expiry date.

3.—(1) This paragraph applies in a case where the employer has given notice of dismissal to the employee before the commencement date and—
(a) the expiry date falls before 1st April 2007, but
(b) the period of notice given is shorter than the minimum period of notice required by paragraph 2(1)(a) or the employer has not complied with paragraph 2(1)(c).

(2) Where this paragraph applies—
(a) the duty to notify in accordance with paragraph 2 of Schedule 6 does not apply;
(b) the duty to notify in accordance with paragraph 4 of Schedule 6 applies as if—
(i) the employer had failed to notify in accordance with paragraph 2 of that Schedule; and
(ii) the duty was one to notify at any time before the expiry date;
(c) a request shall be treated as being a request made under paragraph 5 of Schedule 6 if it satisfies the requirements of sub-paragraphs (2) and (3) of that paragraph and is made—
(i) before any notification given in accordance with paragraph 4 of Schedule 6; or
(ii) after such notification and—
(aa) where practicable, at least four weeks before the expiry date; or
(bb) where that is not practicable, as soon as reasonably practicable (whether before or after the expiry date) after the employer notified the employee of his right to make a request, but not more than four weeks after the expiry date.

4.—(1) This paragraph applies in a case where—
(a) notice of dismissal is given on or after the commencement date of at least—
(i) the period required by the contract of employment; or
(ii) if longer, the period required by section 86 of the 1996 Act; and
(b) the expiry date falls before 1st April 2007.

(2) Where this paragraph applies and the employer notifies the employee in writing of the employee's right to make a request under paragraph 5 of Schedule 6 before, or on the same day as, the day on which notice of dismissal is given—
(a) the employer shall be treated as complying with the duty in paragraph 2 of Schedule 6;
(b) a request shall be treated as being a request made under paragraph 5 of Schedule 6 provided it—
(i) is made after the employer notified the employee of his right to make a request;
(ii) satisfies the requirements of sub-paragraphs (2) and (3) of paragraph 5 of Schedule 6; and
(iii) is made—
(aa) where practicable, at least four weeks before the expiry date; or
(bb) where that is not practicable, as soon as reasonably practicable (whether before or after the expiry date) after the employer notified the employee of his right to make a request, but not more than four weeks after the expiry date.

(3) Where this paragraph applies but the employer does not notify the employee in writing of the employee's right to make a request under paragraph 5 of Schedule 6 before, or on the same day as, the day on which notice of dismissal is given—

(a) the duty to notify in accordance with paragraph 2 of Schedule 6 does not apply;
(b) the duty to notify in accordance with paragraph 4 of Schedule 6 applies as if—
  (i) the employer had failed to notify in accordance with paragraph 2 of that Schedule; and
  (ii) the duty was one to notify at any time before the expiry date;
(c) a request shall be treated as being a request made under paragraph 5 of Schedule 6 if it satisfies the requirements of sub-paragraphs (2) and (3) of that paragraph and is made—
  (i) before any notification given in accordance with paragraph 4 of Schedule 6; or
  (ii) after such notification and—
    (aa) where practicable, at least four weeks before the expiry date; or
    (bb) where that is not practicable, as soon as reasonably practicable (whether before or after the expiry date) after the employer notified the employee of his right to make a request, but not more than four weeks after the expiry date.

5.—(1) This paragraph applies in a case where—
(a) notice of dismissal is given on or after the commencement date and is for a period shorter than—
  (i) the period required by the contract of employment; or
  (ii) if longer, the period required by section 86 of the 1996 Act; and
(b) the period of notice expires on a date falling before 1st April 2007.

(2) Where this paragraph applies—
(a) the duty to notify in accordance with paragraph 2 of Schedule 6 does not apply;
(b) the duty to notify in accordance with paragraph 4 of Schedule 6 applies as if—
  (i) the employer had failed to notify in accordance with paragraph 2 of that Schedule; and
  (ii) the duty was one to notify at any time before the expiry date;
(c) a request shall be treated as being a request made under paragraph 5 of Schedule 6 if it satisfies the requirements of sub-paragraphs (2) and (3) of that paragraph and is made—
  (i) before any notification given in accordance with paragraph 4 of Schedule 6; or
  (ii) after such notification and—
    (aa) where practicable, at least four weeks before the expiry date; or
    (bb) where that is not practicable, as soon as reasonably practicable (whether before or after the expiry date) after the employer notified the employee of his right to make a request, but not more than four weeks after the expiry date.

6. In every case to which paragraph 2, 3, 4 or 5 applies—
(a) paragraph 10 of Schedule 6 does not apply; and
(b) the employer is under a duty to consider any request which complies with the requirements of paragraph 2(2)(b), 2(3)(c), 3(2)(c), 4(2)(b), 4(3)(c) or 5(2)(c) in accordance with paragraphs 7 to 9 of Schedule 6.

[3460]

NOTES

Commencement: 1 October 2006.

(*Sch 8 contains amendments to various Acts and Regulations and, in so far as relevant to this work, these have been incorporated at the appropriate place; Sch 9* (*Repeals and revocations*) *contains no repeals or revocations to any provisions in this Handbook.*)

EDUCATION (MODIFICATION OF ENACTMENTS RELATING TO EMPLOYMENT) (WALES) ORDER 2006

(SI 2006/1073)

NOTES

Made: 5 April 2006.
Authority: School Standards and Framework Act 1998, ss 81(1), 138(7).
Commencement: 12 May 2006.
Extent: this Order applies to Wales; the equivalent provisions for England are in SI 2003/1964 at **[3035A]**.

ARRANGEMENT OF ARTICLES

1 Citation, commencement, application and revocation

(1) This Order may be cited as the Education (Modification of Enactments Relating to Employment) (Wales) Order 2006 and shall come into force on 12th May 2006.

(2) This Order applies in relation to Wales.

(3) The Education (Modification of Enactments Relating to Employment) Order 1999 is revoked.

[3461]

NOTES

Commencement: 12 May 2006.

2 Interpretation

(1) In this Order—

"the 1996 Act" means the Employment Rights Act 1996;

"the 1998 Act" means the School Standards and Framework Act 1998;

"the 2006 Regulations" mean the Staffing of Maintained Schools (Wales) Regulations 2006;

"authority" means the local education authority by which a maintained school is, or a proposed school is to be, maintained;

"governing body" means the governing body of a school which is maintained by a local education authority;

"governing body having a right to a delegated budget" and "school having a delegated budget" have the same meaning as in Part 2 of the 1998 Act.

(2) In this Order references to employment powers are references to the powers of appointment, suspension, conduct and discipline, capability and dismissal of staff conferred by the 2006 Regulations.

[3462]

NOTES

Commencement: 12 May 2006.

3 General modifications of employment enactments

(1) In their application to a governing body having a right to a delegated budget, the enactments set out in the Schedule have effect as if—

(a) any reference to an employer (however expressed) included a reference to the governing body acting in the exercise of its employment powers and as if that governing body had at all material times been such an employer;

(b) in relation to the exercise of the governing body's employment powers, employment by the authority at a school were employment by the governing body of the school;

(c) references to employees were references to employees at the school in question;

(d) references to dismissal by an employer included references to dismissal by the authority following notification of a determination by a governing body under regulation 17(1) of the 2006 Regulations; and

(e) references to trade unions recognised by an employer were references to trade unions recognised by the authority or the governing body.

(2) Paragraph (1) does not cause the exemption in respect of an employer with fewer employees than is specified in section 7(1) of the Disability Discrimination Act 1995 to apply (without prejudice to whether it applies irrespective of that paragraph).

[3462A]

NOTES

Commencement: 12 May 2006.

4 Without prejudice to the generality of article 3, where an employee employed at a school having a delegated budget is dismissed by the authority following notification of such a determination as is mentioned in article 3(1)(d)—

(a) section 92 of the 1996 Act has effect as if the governing body had dismissed him and as if references to the employer's reasons for dismissing the employee were references to the reasons for which the governing body made its determination; and

(b) Part X of the 1996 Act has effect in relation to the dismissal as if the governing body had dismissed him, and the reason or principal reason for which the governing body did so had been the reason or principal reason for which it made its determination.

[3462B]

NOTES

Commencement: 12 May 2006.

5 Trade disputes

(1) Subject to paragraph (2), a dispute between staff employed to work at a school having a delegated budget and the school's governing body, which relates wholly or mainly to one of the matters set out in section 244(1) of the Trade Union and Labour Relations (Consolidation) Act 1992 is a trade dispute within the meaning of that Act.

(2) In any case where there is a trade dispute only by virtue of this article, nothing in section 219 of that Act prevents an act from being actionable in tort where the inducement, interference or threat mentioned in that section relates to a contract the performance of which does not affect directly or indirectly the school over which the governing body in question exercises its functions.

[3462C]

NOTES

Commencement: 12 May 2006.

6 Applications to Employment Tribunals

(1) Without prejudice to articles 3 and 4, and despite any provision in the Employment Tribunals Act 1996 and any regulations made under section 1(1) of that Act, this article applies in respect of any application to an employment tribunal, and any proceedings pursuant to such an application, in relation to which by virtue of article 3 or 4 a governing body is to be treated as if it were an employer (however expressed).

(2) The application must be made, and the proceedings must be carried on, against that governing body.

(3) Despite paragraph (2), any decision, declaration, order, recommendation or award made in the course of such proceedings except in so far as it requires reinstatement or re-engagement has effect as if made against the authority.

(4) Where any application is made against a governing body under paragraph (2)—

(a) the governing body must notify the authority within 14 days of receiving notification; and

(b) the authority, on written application to the employment tribunal, is entitled to be made an additional party to the proceedings and to take part in the proceedings accordingly.

[3462D]

NOTES

Commencement: 12 May 2006.

SCHEDULE

Article 3

Sex Discrimination Act 1975

sections 6, 7, 9, 41 and 82(1A)

Race Relations Act 1976

sections 4, 5, 7 and 32

Trade Union and Labour Relations (Consolidation) Act 1992

sections 146, 147, 152–154 and 181–185

Disability Discrimination Act 1995

sections 4–6, 11, 12, 16, 55, 57 and 58

Employment Rights Act 1996

sections 66–68, 70, 71, 92, 93 and Part X

Employment Act 2002

sections 29–32 and Schedules 2–4

[3462E]

NOTES

Commencement: 12 May 2006.

MATERNITY AND PARENTAL LEAVE ETC AND THE PATERNITY AND ADOPTION LEAVE (AMENDMENT) REGULATIONS 2006

(SI 2006/2014)

NOTES

Made: 23 July 2006.

Authority: Employment Rights Act 1996, ss 47C(2), 71(3), 73(2), (3), 74(2), (3), (4), 75(1), (2), 75A(2), (2A), 75B(2), (3), 75C, 75D(1), 99(1).

Commencement: 1 October 2006.

1 Citation and commencement

These Regulations may be cited as the Maternity and Parental Leave etc and the Paternity and Adoption Leave (Amendment) Regulations 2006 and shall come into force on 1st October 2006.

[3463]

NOTES

Commencement: 1 October 2006.

2 Application

(1) The amendments to the Maternity and Parental Leave etc Regulations 1999 provided for in these Regulations have effect only in relation to employees whose expected week of childbirth begins on or after 1st April 2007.

(2) The amendments to the Paternity and Adoption Leave Regulations 2002 provided for in these Regulations have effect only in relation to an employee with whom a child is expected to be placed for adoption, where the placement is expected to occur on or after 1st April 2007. For the purposes of this paragraph, the date on which the child is actually placed for adoption is immaterial.

(3) The amendments to the Paternity and Adoption Leave Regulations 2002 applied to adoption from overseas by virtue of and as modified by the Paternity and Adoption Leave (Adoption from Overseas) Regulations 2003 have effect only where the adopter's child enters Great Britain on or after 1st April 2007.

(4) For the purposes of paragraph (3)—

"adopter", in relation to a child, means a person by whom the child has been or is to be adopted or, in a case where the child has been or is to be adopted by two people jointly, whichever of them has elected to take adoption leave in respect of the child;

"adoption from overseas" means the adoption of a child who enters Great Britain from outside the United Kingdom in connection with or for the purposes of adoption which does not involve the placement of the child for adoption under the law of any part of the United Kingdom;

"enters Great Britain" means enters Great Britain from outside the United Kingdom in connection with or for the purposes of adoption.

[3463A]

NOTES

Commencement: 1 October 2006

3–17 (*Regs 3–11 amend the Maternity and Parental Leave etc Regulations 1999, SI 1999/3312, regs 2, 4, 7, 11, 19, 20, revoke reg 5 of those Regulations, and insert reg 12A* (*see* **[2553]** *et seq*)*; regs 12–17 amend the Paternity and Adoption Leave Regulations 2002, SI 2002/2788, regs 2, 25, 28, 29, and insert reg 21A of those Regulations* (*see* **[2752]** *et seq*).)

EUROPEAN COOPERATIVE SOCIETY (INVOLVEMENT OF EMPLOYEES) REGULATIONS 2006

(SI 2006/2059)

NOTES

Made: 25 July 2006.

Authority: European Communities Act 1972, s 2(2).

Commencement: 18 August 2006.

Conciliation: employment tribunal proceedings and claims which could be the subject of employment tribunal proceedings under regs 30 and 34 are proceedings to which the Employment Tribunals Act 1996, s 18 applies; see s 18(1)(s) of that Act at **[975]**. The standard conciliation period applies to such claims by virtue of the Employment Tribunals (Constitution and Rules of Procedure) Regulations 2004, SI 2004/1861, Sch 1, rule 22(1), (6).

Employment Appeal Tribunal: an appeal lies to the Employment Appeal Tribunal on any question of law arising from any decision of, or in any proceedings before, an employment tribunal under or by virtue of these Regulations; see the Employment Tribunals Act 1996, s 21(1)(t) at **[978]**.

/754

ARRANGEMENT OF REGULATIONS

PART 1
GENERAL

PART 2
PARTICIPATING INDIVIDUALS AND LEGAL ENTITIES AND THE SPECIAL NEGOTIATING BODY

PART 3
ELECTION OR APPOINTMENT OF UK MEMBERS OF THE SPECIAL NEGOTIATING BODY

PART 4
NEGOTIATION OF THE EMPLOYEE INVOLVEMENT AGREEMENT

PART 5
STANDARD RULES ON EMPLOYEE INVOLVEMENT

PART 6
COMPLIANCE AND ENFORCEMENT

PART 7
CONFIDENTIAL INFORMATION

PART 8
PROTECTION FOR MEMBERS OF SPECIAL NEGOTIATING BODY, ETC

PART 9
MISCELLANEOUS

SCHEDULES:

PART 1
GENERAL

1 Citation and commencement

(1) These Regulations may be cited as the European Cooperative Society (Involvement of Employees) Regulations 2006.

(2) These Regulations come into force on 18th August 2006.

[3463B]

NOTES

Commencement: 18 August 2006.

2 Extent and application

(1) These Regulations extend to Northern Ireland.

(2) These Regulations, in their application in relation to Northern Ireland, shall have effect subject to the modifications set out in Schedule 3.

[3463C]

NOTES

Commencement: 18 August 2006.

3 Interpretation

(1) In these Regulations—

"the 1996 Act" means the Employment Rights Act 1996;

"absolute majority vote" means a vote passed by a majority of the total membership of the special negotiating body where the members voting with that majority represent the majority of the employees of—

(a) the participating individuals, participating legal entities and such participating legal entities' concerned subsidiaries employed in the EEA States; or

(b) in relation to an SCE to which regulation 6(1) applies, the SCE and its subsidiaries employed in the EEA States;

"Appeal Tribunal" means the Employment Appeal Tribunal;

"CAC" means the Central Arbitration Committee;

"contract of employment" means a contract of service or apprenticeship whether express or implied, and (if it is express), whether oral or in writing;

"dismissed" and "dismissal", in relation to an employee, shall be construed in accordance with Part 10 of the 1996 Act;

"the EC Directive" means Council Directive 2003/72/EC of 22 July 2003 supplementing the Statute for a European Cooperative Society with regard to the involvement of employees;

"the EC Regulation" means Council Regulation 1435/2003/EC of 22 July 2003 on the Statute for a European Cooperative Society;

"EEA State" means a Member State, Norway, Iceland or Liechtenstein;

"employee" means an individual who has entered into or works under a contract of employment and, in Part 8 and regulation 41, includes, where the employment has ceased, an individual who worked under a contract of employment;

"employee involvement agreement" means an agreement reached—

(a) between the special negotiating body on the one hand and the participating individuals and competent organs of the participating legal entities on the other governing the arrangements for the involvement of employees within the SCE; or

(b) in relation to an SCE to which regulation 6(1) applies, between the special negotiating body on the one hand and the competent organ of the SCE on the other governing the arrangements for the involvement of employees within the SCE;

"employees' representatives" means—

(a) if the employees are of a description in respect of which an independent trade union is recognised by their employer for the purpose of collective bargaining, representatives of the trade union who normally take part as negotiators in the collective bargaining process, and

(b) any other employees of their employer who are elected or appointed as employee representatives to positions in which they are expected to receive, on behalf of the employees, information—

(i) which is relevant to the terms and conditions of employment of the employees, or

(ii) about the activities of the undertaking which may significantly affect the interests of the employees,

but excluding representatives who are expected to receive information relevant only to a specific aspect of the terms and conditions or interests of the employees, such as health and safety, collective redundancies, or pension schemes;

"information and consultation representative" has the meaning given to it in regulation 17(5) or, in relation to an SCE to which regulation 6(1) applies, under paragraph 11(4) of Schedule 1;

"participating individual" means a natural person directly participating in the establishing of an SCE;

"participation" means the influence of the representative body and the employees' representatives in the SCE or a participating legal entity by way of the right to—

(a) elect or appoint some of the members of the SCE's or the participating legal entity's supervisory or administrative organ; or

(b) recommend or oppose the appointment of some or all of the members of the SCE's or the participating legal entity's supervisory or administrative organ;

"participating cooperative" means a participating legal entity which is a cooperative;

"relevant time" means the happening of an event referred to in paragraphs (a) to (c) of regulation 7(1);

"representative body" means the persons elected or appointed under the employee involvement agreement or under the standard rules on employee involvement;

"SCE" means a European Cooperative Society within the meaning of the EC Regulation and, except as provided in these Regulations, means an SCE which is to be, or is, registered in the UK;

"SCE to be formed by merger" means an SCE to be formed in accordance with the penultimate paragraph of Article 2(1) of the EC Regulation;

"SCE to be formed by conversion" means an SCE to be formed in accordance with the final paragraph of Article 2(1) of the EC Regulation and "SCE formed by conversion" shall be construed accordingly;

"standard rules on employee involvement" means the rules in Schedule 2;

"total workforce" means the total number of employees employed by—

(a) all participating individuals, participating legal entities and concerned subsidiaries throughout all EEA States; or

(b) in relation to an SCE to which regulation 6(1) applies, employed by the SCE and its subsidiaries throughout all EEA States;

"two thirds majority vote" means a vote passed by a majority of at least two thirds of the total membership of the special negotiating body where the members voting with that majority—

(a) represent at least two thirds of the employees of the participating individuals, participating legal entities and their concerned subsidiaries employed in the EEA States; or

(b) in relation to an SCE to which regulation 6(1) applies, represent at least two thirds of the employees of the SCE and its subsidiaries employed in the EEA States, and

in either case include members representing employees employed in at least two EEA States;

"UK employee" means an employee employed to work in the United Kingdom; and

"UK members of the special negotiating body" means members of the special negotiating body elected or appointed by UK employees.

(2) The following terms have the same meaning in these Regulations as that given by Article 2 of the EC Directive—

"participating legal entities"
"subsidiary"
"involvement of employees"
"information"
"consultation"

and references to a "concerned subsidiary" or a "concerned establishment" shall be construed in accordance with the definition of "concerned subsidiary or establishment" in the EC Directive, except that the references in such definition to an "establishment of a participating legal entity" shall be taken to include an establishment of a participating individual.

(3) In these Regulations, "special negotiating body" means—

(a) the body established pursuant to regulation 10 to negotiate with the participating individuals and the competent organs of the participating legal entities, or

(b) in relation to an SCE to which regulation 6(1) applies, the body established pursuant to paragraph 4 of Schedule 1 to negotiate with the competent organ of the SCE,

in either case, as to the establishment of arrangements for the involvement of employees within the SCE.

(4) Except as otherwise provided in these Regulations, words and expressions which are used in the EC Regulation or the EC Directive have the same meaning as they have in that Regulation or Directive.

[3463D]

NOTES

Commencement: 18 August 2006.

PART 2
PARTICIPATING INDIVIDUALS AND LEGAL ENTITIES AND THE SPECIAL NEGOTIATING BODY

4 Circumstances in which different regulations apply

(1) This regulation is subject to regulation 5.

(2) These Regulations shall apply where—

(a) a participating individual or a participating legal entity intends to form an SCE whose registered office is to be in the UK; or

(b) an SCE has its registered office in the UK.

(3) Where there are UK employees, without prejudice to paragraph (2), Part 3 (or, in relation to an SCE to which regulation 6(1) applies, Part 2 of Schedule 1) shall apply (election or appointment of UK members of the special negotiating body and representation of employees), regardless of where the registered office is, or is intended to be, situated, in relation to the election or appointment of UK members of the special negotiating body.

(4) Parts 6 to 9 shall apply, without prejudice to paragraph (2) regardless of where the registered office of the SCE is, or is intended to be situated, where—

(a) a participating individual;

(b) a participating legal entity, its concerned subsidiaries or concerned establishments;

(c) a subsidiary of an SCE;
(d) an establishment of an SCE; or
(e) an employee or an employees' representative,

is resident, registered, or situated, as the case may be, in the UK.

[3463E]

NOTES

Commencement: 18 August 2006.

5 Exempt formations and SCEs

(1) These Regulations shall not apply where a participating individual intends to form an SCE and at the relevant time—

(a) all or all but one of the other parties to its formation are participating individuals; and

(b) the total workforce at the relevant time comprises employees employed to work in one EEA State only or numbers less than 50.

(2) These Regulations shall not apply where a participating legal entity intends to form an SCE where—

(a) all of the other parties to its formation are participating individuals, and
(b) the total workforce at the relevant time comprises employees employed to work in one EEA State only or numbers less than 50.

(3) Subject to regulation 6, these Regulations shall not apply where an SCE has been registered and at the relevant time the circumstances in regulation 5(1) or 5(2) applied.

(4) Notwithstanding paragraphs (1) to (3), in the case of transfer from another EEA state to the UK of the registered office of an SCE governed by participation, at least the same level of employee participation rights shall continue to apply after that transfer.

[3463F]

NOTES

Commencement: 18 August 2006.

6 Subsequent application of Regulations to a formerly exempt SCE

(1) If a relevant condition is satisfied in respect of an SCE referred to in regulation 5(3), these Regulations, subject to paragraph (2), shall apply.

(2) The provisions in Schedule 1 shall have effect in substitution for regulations 7 to 21.

(3) In this regulation, "relevant condition" means—

(a) the total workforce is 50 or more and includes employees employed to work in at least two different EEA States; or

(b) a valid request is made to the effect that these Regulations be applied.

(4) A request pursuant to paragraph 3(b) is not a valid request unless

(a) it consists of—
  (i) a single request made by at least one third of the total workforce; or
  (ii) a series of separate requests made within a period of six months which when taken together mean that it is made by at least one third of the total workforce;

(b) the employees comprising such third include employees employed to work in at least two different EEA States; and

(c) the single request, or each separate request, of which it consists—
  (i) is in writing;
  (ii) is sent to the registered office, head office or principal place of business of the SCE or any subsidiary; and
  (iii) specifies the names of the employees making it and the date on which it is made.

(5) If a relevant condition is satisfied but subsequently ceases to be satisfied, these Regulations (as modified by virtue of paragraph (2)), shall continue to apply.

[3463G]

NOTES

Commencement: 18 August 2006.

7 Duty on participating individual and participating legal entity to provide information

(1) When a participating individual or the competent organ of a participating legal entity decides to form an SCE, that individual or organ shall, as soon as possible after—

(a) in the case of an SCE to be formed by merger, publishing the draft terms of merger,

(b) in the case of an SCE to be formed by conversion, publishing the draft terms of conversion, or

(c) in the case of an SCE to be formed in any other way, agreeing a plan to form an SCE,

provide information to the employees' representatives of the participating individual or the participating legal entity, any concerned subsidiaries and concerned establishments or, if no such representatives exist, the employees themselves.

(2) The information referred to in paragraph (1) must include, as a minimum, information—

(a) identifying the participating individuals, participating legal entities, subsidiaries and establishments,

(b) identifying the concerned subsidiaries and concerned establishments,

(c) giving the number of employees employed by each participating individual, participating legal entity, subsidiary and at each establishment, and

(d) giving the number of employees employed to work in each EEA State.

(3) When a special negotiating body has been formed in accordance with regulation 10, each participating individual and the competent organs of each participating legal entity must provide that body with such information as is necessary to keep it informed of the plan to establish and the progress of establishing the SCE up to the time the SCE has been registered.

[3463H]

NOTES

Commencement: 18 August 2006.

8 Complaint of failure to provide information

(1) An employees' representative or, where there is no such representative for an employee, the employee, may present a complaint to the CAC that—

(a) a participating individual or the competent organ of a participating legal entity has failed to provide the information referred to in regulation 7; or

(b) the information provided by the participating individual or the competent organ of a participating legal entity for the purpose of complying with regulation 7 is false or incomplete in a material particular.

(2) Where the CAC finds the complaint well-founded it shall make an order requiring the participating individual or the competent organ to disclose information to the complainant which order shall specify—

(a) the information in respect of which the CAC finds that the complaint is well-founded and which is to be disclosed to the complainant; and

(b) a date (not being less than one week from the date of the order) by which the participating individual or the competent organ must disclose the information specified in the order.

[3463I]

NOTES

Commencement: 18 August 2006.

9 Function of the special negotiating body

The special negotiating body and the participating individuals and competent organs of the participating legal entities shall have the task of reaching an employee involvement agreement.

[3463J]

NOTES

Commencement: 18 August 2006.

10 Composition of the special negotiating body

(1) The participating individuals and the competent organs of the participating legal entities shall make arrangements for the establishment of a special negotiating body, which body shall be constituted as soon as possible after the relevant time and in accordance with paragraphs (2) to (7) below. The method used to elect or appoint employee representatives to the special negotiating body should seek to promote gender balance.

(2) The total number of employees employed to work in each EEA State of the participating individuals, participating legal entities and concerned subsidiaries shall be given an entitlement to elect or appoint one member of the special negotiating body for each 10% or fraction thereof which those employees represent of the total workforce. These members shall be the "ordinary members".

(3) If, in the case of an SCE to be formed by merger, following an election or appointment under paragraph (2), the members elected or appointed to the special negotiating body do not include at least one eligible member in respect of each relevant cooperative, the employees of any relevant cooperative in respect of which there is no eligible member shall be given an entitlement, subject to paragraph (4), to elect or appoint an additional member to the special negotiating body.

(4) The number of additional members which the employees are entitled to elect or appoint under paragraph (3) shall not exceed 20% of the number of ordinary members elected or appointed under paragraph (2) and if the number of additional members under paragraph (3) would exceed that percentage the employees who are entitled to appoint or elect the additional members shall be:

(a) if one additional member is to be appointed or elected, those employed by the relevant cooperative not represented under paragraph (3) having the highest number of employees; and

(b) if more than one additional member is to be appointed or elected, those employed by the relevant cooperatives in each EEA State that are not represented under paragraph (3) having the highest number of employees in descending order, starting with the relevant cooperative with the highest number, followed by those employed by the relevant cooperative in each EEA State that are not so represented having the second highest number of employees in descending order, starting with the relevant cooperative (among those relevant cooperatives) with the highest number.

(5) The participating individuals and the competent organs of the participating legal entities shall, as soon as reasonably practicable and in any event no later than one month after the establishment of the special negotiating body, inform their employees and those of any concerned subsidiaries of the identity of the members of the special negotiating body.

(6) If, following the appointment or election of members to the special negotiating body in accordance with this regulation,

(a) changes to the participating individuals, participating legal entities, concerned subsidiaries or concerned establishments result in the number of ordinary or additional members which employees would be entitled to elect or appoint under this regulation either materially increasing or decreasing, the original appointment or election of members of the special negotiating body shall cease to have effect and those employees shall be entitled to elect or appoint the new number of members in accordance with the provisions of these Regulations; and

(b) a member of the special negotiating body is no longer willing or able to continue serving as such a member, the employees whom he represents shall be entitled to elect or appoint a new member in his place.

(7) In this regulation—

(a) "eligible member" means a person who is—

(i) in the case of a relevant cooperative formed under the law of an EEA State whose legislation allows representatives of trade unions who are not employees to be elected to the special negotiating body, an employee of the relevant cooperative or a trade union representative; and

(ii) in the case of a relevant cooperative not formed under the law of such an EEA State, an employee of the relevant cooperative; and

(b) "relevant cooperative" means a participating legal entity which has employees in the EEA State under whose law it is formed and which it is proposed will cease to exist on or following the registration of the SCE.

[3463K]

NOTES

Commencement: 18 August 2006.

11 Complaint about establishment of special negotiating body

(1) An application may be presented to the CAC for a declaration that the special negotiating body has not been established at all or has not been established properly in accordance with regulation 10.

(2) An application may be presented under this regulation by—

(a) a person elected or appointed to be a member of the special negotiating body;

(b) an employees' representative or, where no such representative exists in respect of a participating individual, participating legal entity or concerned subsidiary, an employee of that participating individual, participating legal entity or concerned subsidiary; or

(c) a participating individual or the competent organ of a participating legal entity or concerned subsidiary.

(3) The CAC shall only consider an application made under paragraph (1) that a special negotiating body has not been properly constituted if it is made within a period of one month from the date or, if more than one, the last date on which the participating individuals and participating legal entities complied or should have complied with the obligation to inform the employees under regulation 10(5).

(4) Where the CAC finds the application well-founded it shall make a declaration that the special negotiating body has not been established at all or has not been established properly and the participating individuals and the competent organs of the participating legal entities continue to be under the obligation in regulation 10(1).

[3463L]

NOTES

Commencement: 18 August 2006.

PART 3
ELECTION OR APPOINTMENT OF UK MEMBERS OF THE SPECIAL NEGOTIATING BODY

12 Ballot arrangements

(1) Subject to regulation 14, the UK members of the special negotiating body shall be elected by balloting the UK employees.

(2) The participating individuals and the participating legal entities that employ UK employees ("the relevant employers") must arrange for the holding of a ballot or ballots of those employees in accordance with the requirements of paragraph (3), and having regard to the fact that the methods of election should seek to promote gender balance.

(3) The requirements referred to in paragraph (2) are—

(a) in relation to the election of ordinary members under regulation 10(2), that—

(i) if the number of members which UK employees are entitled to elect to the special negotiating body is equal to the number of relevant employers, there shall be separate ballots of the UK employees of each relevant employer;

(ii) if the number of members which the UK employees are entitled to elect to the special negotiating body is greater than the number of relevant employers, there shall be separate ballots of the UK employees of each relevant employer and the relevant employers shall ensure, as far as practicable, that at least one member representing the UK employees of each such relevant employer is elected to the special negotiating body and that the number of members representing the UK employees of that employer is proportionate to the number of employees of that employer;

(iii) if the number of members which the UK employees are entitled to elect to the special negotiating body is smaller than the number of relevant employers—

(aa) the number of ballots held shall be equivalent to the number of members to be elected;

(bb) a separate ballot shall be held in respect of each of the relevant employers with the higher or highest number of employees; and

(cc) it shall be ensured that any employees of a relevant employer in respect of which a ballot does not have to be held are entitled to vote in a ballot held in respect of one of the other relevant employers; and

(iv) if there are any UK employees employed by a concerned subsidiary or at a concerned establishment of non-UK participating legal entities, or non-UK participating individuals, the relevant employers shall ensure that those employees are entitled to vote in a ballot held pursuant to this regulation;

(b) that in relation to the ballot of additional members under regulation 10(3), that a separate ballot is held in respect of the employees of each relevant employer entitled to elect an additional member.

(c) that in a ballot in respect of the employees of a particular relevant employer, all UK employees employed by that employer or by such employer's concerned subsidiaries or at its concerned establishments are entitled to vote;

(d) that in a ballot in respect of the employees of a particular relevant employer, any person who is immediately before the latest time at which a person may become a candidate—

(i) a UK employee employed by that employer or by any of such employer's concerned subsidiaries or at any of its concerned establishments; or

(ii) if the relevant employer so permits, a representative of a trade union who is not an employee of that employer or any of such employer's concerned subsidiaries,

is entitled to stand as a candidate for election as a member of the special negotiating body in that ballot;

(e) that the relevant employers appoint an independent ballot supervisor to supervise the conduct of the ballot of UK employees except that, where there is to be more than one ballot, the relevant employers may appoint more than one independent ballot supervisor, each of whom is to supervise such of the separate ballots as the relevant employers may determine, provided that each separate ballot is supervised by a supervisor;

(f) that after the relevant employers have formulated proposals as to the arrangements for the ballot of UK employees and before they have published the final arrangements under sub-paragraph (g) they must, so far as reasonably practicable, consult with the UK employees' representatives on the proposed arrangements for the ballot of UK employees; and

(g) that the relevant employers must publish the final arrangements for the ballot of UK employees in such manner as to bring them to the attention of, so far as reasonably practicable, all UK employees and the UK employees' representatives.

(4) Any UK employee or UK employees' representative who believes that the arrangements for the ballot of the UK employees do not comply with the requirements of paragraph (3) may, within a period of 21 days beginning on the date on which the final arrangements were published under sub-paragraph (g), present a complaint to the CAC

(5) Where the CAC finds the complaint well-founded it shall make a declaration to that effect and may make an order requiring the relevant employers to modify the arrangements they have made for the ballot of UK employees or to satisfy the requirements in sub-paragraph (f) or (g) of paragraph (3).

(6) An order under paragraph (5) shall specify the modifications to the arrangements which the relevant employers are required to make and the requirements they must satisfy.

(7) A person is an independent ballot supervisor for the purposes of paragraph (3)(e) if the relevant employers reasonably believe that he will carry out any functions conferred on him in relation to the ballot competently and have no reasonable grounds for believing that his independence in relation to the ballot might reasonably be called into question.

[3463M]

NOTES

Commencement: 18 August 2006.

13 Conduct of the ballot

(1) The relevant employers must—

(a) ensure that a ballot supervisor appointed under regulation 12(3)(e) carries out his functions under this regulation and that there is no interference with his carrying out of those functions from the relevant employers; and

(b) comply with all reasonable requests made by a ballot supervisor for the purposes of, or in connection with, the carrying out of those functions.

(2) A ballot supervisor's appointment shall require that he—

(a) supervises the conduct of the ballot, or the separate ballots he is being appointed to supervise, in accordance with the arrangements for the ballot of UK employees published by the relevant employers under regulation 12(3)(g) or, where appropriate, in accordance with the arrangements as required to be modified by an order made as a result of a complaint presented under regulation 12(4);

(b) does not conduct the ballot or any of the separate ballots before the relevant employers have satisfied the requirement specified in regulation 12(3)(g) and—

(i) where no complaint has been presented under regulation 12(4), before the expiry of a period of 21 days beginning on the date on which the relevant employers published their arrangements under regulation 12(3)(g); or

(ii) where a complaint has been presented under regulation 12(4), before the complaint has been determined and, where appropriate, the arrangements have been modified as required by an order made as a result of that complaint;

(c) conducts the ballot, or each separate ballot, so as to secure that—

(i) so far as reasonably practicable, those entitled to vote are given the opportunity to vote;

(ii) so far as reasonably practicable, those entitled to stand as candidates are given the opportunity to stand;

(iii) so far as reasonably practicable, those voting are able to do so in secret; and

(iv) the votes given in the ballot are fairly and accurately counted.

(3) As soon as reasonably practicable after the holding of the ballot, the ballot supervisor must publish the results of the ballot in such manner as to make them available to the relevant employers and, so far as reasonably practicable, the UK employees entitled to vote in the ballot and the persons who stood as candidates.

(4) A ballot supervisor shall publish a report ("an ineffective ballot report") where he considers (whether on the basis of representations made to him by another person or otherwise) that—

(a) any of the requirements referred to in paragraph (2) was not satisfied with the result that the outcome of the ballot would have been different; or

(b) there was an interference with the carrying out of his functions or a failure by the relevant employers to comply with all reasonable requests made by him with the result that he was unable to form a proper judgement as to whether each of the requirements referred to in paragraph (2) was satisfied in the ballot.

(5) Where a ballot supervisor publishes an ineffective ballot report the report must be published within a period of one month commencing on the date on which the ballot supervisor publishes the results of the ballot under paragraph (3).

(6) A ballot supervisor shall publish an ineffective ballot report in such manner as to make it available to the relevant employers and, so far as reasonably practicable, the UK employees entitled to vote in the ballot and the persons who stood as candidates in the ballot.

(7) Where a ballot supervisor publishes an ineffective ballot report then—

(a) if there has been a single ballot or an ineffective ballot report has been published in respect of every separate ballot, the outcome of the ballot or ballots shall have no effect and the relevant employers shall again be under the obligation in regulation 12(2).

(b) If there have been separate ballots and sub-paragraph (a) does not apply—

(i) the relevant employers shall arrange for the separate ballot or ballots in respect of which an ineffective ballot report was published to be re-held in accordance with regulation 12 and this regulation; and

(ii) no such ballot shall have effect until it has been re-held and no ineffective ballot report has been published in respect of it within the period specified in paragraph 5.

(8) All costs relating to the holding of a ballot, including payments made to a ballot supervisor for supervising the conduct of the ballot, shall be borne by the relevant employers (whether or not an ineffective ballot report has been published).

[3463N]

NOTES

Commencement: 18 August 2006.

14 Appointment of UK members by a consultative committee

(1) This regulation applies where—

(a) regulation 12(3)(a)(i) or (ii) or (b) would require a ballot to be held; and

(b) there exists in relation to the participating individual or the participating legal entity whose employees would otherwise need to be balloted under regulation 12, a consultative committee.

(2)

(a) Where this regulation applies, the election provided for in regulation 12 shall not take place but the consultative committee shall be entitled to appoint the UK member or members of the special negotiating body who would otherwise be elected pursuant to regulation 12, where appropriate having regard to the fact that the method used should seek to promote gender balance.

(b) The consultative committee is entitled to appoint as a member of the special negotiating body:

(i) one of their number; or

(ii) if the participating individual or the participating legal entity in respect of which the consultative committee exists so permits, a trade union representative who is not an employee of that participating individual or that participating legal entity.

(3) In this regulation, "a consultative committee" means a body of persons—

(a) whose normal functions include or comprise the carrying out of an information and consultation function;

(b) which is able to carry out its information and consultation function without interference from the participating individual or the participating legal entity;

(c) which, in carrying out its information and consultation function, represents all the employees of the participating individual or the participating legal entity; and

(d) which consists wholly of persons who are employees of the participating individual or the participating legal entity or such participating legal entity's concerned subsidiaries.

(4) In paragraph (3) "information and consultation function" means the function of—

(a) receiving, on behalf of all the employees of the participating individual or the participating legal entity, information which may significantly affect the interests of the employees of that participating individual or participating legal entity, but excluding information which is relevant only to a specific aspect of the interests of the employees, such as health and safety, collective redundancies or pension schemes; and

(b) being consulted by the participating individual or the participating legal entity on the information referred to in sub-paragraph (a) above.

(5) The consultative committee must publish the names of the persons whom it has appointed to be members of the special negotiating body in such a manner as to bring them to the attention of the participating individual or the participating legal entity and, so far as reasonably practicable, the employees and the employees' representatives of that participating individual or participating legal entity and such participating entity's concerned subsidiaries.

(6) Where the participating individual, the participating legal entity, an employee or an employees' representative believes that—

(a) the consultative committee does not satisfy the requirements in paragraph (3) above; or

(b) any of the persons appointed by the consultative committee is not entitled to be appointed,

he, or as the case may be, it, may, within a period of 21 days beginning on the date on which the consultative committee published under paragraph (5) the names of the persons appointed, present a complaint to the CAC

(7) Where the CAC finds the complaint well-founded it shall make a declaration to that effect.

(8) Where the CAC has made a declaration under paragraph (7)—

(a) no appointment made by the consultative committee shall have effect; and

(b) the members of the special negotiating body shall be elected by a ballot of the employees in accordance with regulation 12.

(9) Where the consultative committee appoints any person to be a member of the special negotiating body, that appointment shall have effect—

(a) where no complaint has been presented under paragraph (6), after the expiry of a period of 21 days beginning on the date on which the consultative committee published under paragraph (5) the names of the persons nominated; or

(b) where a complaint has been presented under paragraph (6), as from the day on which the complaint has been determined without a declaration under paragraph (7) being made.

[3463O]

NOTES

Commencement: 18 August 2006.

15 Representation of employees

(1) Subject to paragraphs (2) and (3) below, a member elected in a ballot in accordance with regulation 10(2), shall be treated as representing the employees for the time being of the participating individual or of the participating legal entity, and of any concerned subsidiary or concerned establishment, whose employees were entitled to vote in the ballot in which he was elected.

(2) If an additional member is elected in accordance with regulation 10(3) and (4), he, and not any member elected in accordance with regulation 10(2), shall be treated as representing the employees for the time being of the participating individual or the participating legal entity, and of any concerned subsidiary or concerned establishment, whose employees were entitled to vote in the ballot in which he was elected.

(3) When a member of the special negotiating body is appointed by a consultative committee in accordance with regulation 14, the employees whom the consultative committee represents and the UK employees of any concerned subsidiary shall be treated as being represented by the member so appointed.

[3463P]

NOTES

Commencement: 18 August 2006.

PART 4
NEGOTIATION OF THE EMPLOYEE INVOLVEMENT AGREEMENT

16 Negotiations to reach an employee involvement agreement

(1) In this regulation and in regulation 17 the participating individuals and competent organs of the participating legal entities on the one hand and the special negotiating body on the other are referred to as "the parties".

(2) The parties are under a duty to negotiate in a spirit of cooperation with a view to reaching an employee involvement agreement.

(3) The duty referred to in paragraph (2) commences one month after the date or, if more than one, the last date on which the members of the special negotiating body were elected or appointed and applies—

(a) for the period of 6 months starting with the day on which the duty commenced or, where an employee involvement agreement is successfully negotiated within that period, until the completion of the negotiations; or

(b) where the parties agree before the end of that 6 month period that it is to be extended, for the period of 12 months starting with the day on which the duty commenced or, where an employee involvement agreement is successfully negotiated within the 12 month period, until the completion of the negotiations.

[3463Q]

NOTES

Commencement: 18 August 2006.

17 The employee involvement agreement

(1) The employee involvement agreement must be in writing.

(2) Without prejudice to the autonomy of the parties and subject to paragraph (4), the employee involvement agreement shall specify:

(a) the scope of the agreement;

(b) the composition, number of members and allocation of seats on the representative body;

(c) the functions and the procedure for the information and consultation of the representative body;

(d) the frequency of meetings of the representative body;

(e) the financial and material resources to be allocated to the representative body;

(f) if, during negotiations, the parties decide to establish one or more information and consultation procedures instead of a representative body, the arrangements for implementing those procedures;

(g) if, during negotiations, the parties decide to establish arrangements for participation, the substance of those arrangements including (if applicable) the number of members in the SCE's administrative or supervisory organ which the employees will be entitled to elect, appoint, recommend or oppose, the procedures as to how these members may be elected, appointed, recommended or opposed by the employees, and their rights; and

(h) if, where the statute of the SCE so provides, during negotiations the parties decide to establish arrangements for employees or their representatives to participate in and vote in the general meeting or any section or sectorial meetings of the SCE, the substance of those arrangements, including (where appropriate) the number of employees or representatives who will be entitled to participate, the procedure as to how they are to be elected, appointed, recommended or opposed, and their rights; and

(i) the date of entry into force of the agreement, its duration, the circumstances, if any, in which the agreement is required to be re-negotiated including (where appropriate), in the event of changes in the structure of the SCE or its subsidiaries or establishments, and the procedure for its re-negotiation.

(3) The employee involvement agreement shall not be subject to the standard rules on employee involvement, unless it contains a provision to the contrary.

(4) In relation to an SCE to be formed by conversion, the employee involvement agreement shall provide for the elements of employee involvement at all levels to be at least as favourable as those which exist in the cooperative to be converted into an SCE.

(5) If the parties decide, in accordance with paragraph (2)(f), to establish one or more information and consultation procedures instead of a representative body and if those procedures include a provision for representatives to be elected or appointed to act in relation to information and consultation, those representatives shall be "information and consultation representatives".

[3463R]

NOTES

Commencement: 18 August 2006.

18 Decisions of the special negotiating body

(1) Each member of the special negotiating body shall have one vote.

(2) Subject to paragraph (3) and regulation 19, the special negotiating body shall take decisions by an absolute majority vote.

(3) In the following circumstances any decision which would result in a reduction of participation must be taken by a two thirds majority vote:

(a) where an SCE is to be formed by merger and at least 25% of the employees employed to work in the EEA States by the participating cooperatives which are due to merge have participation; and

(b) where an SCE is to be formed in any other way and at least 50% of the total number of employees employed to work in the EEA States by the participating individuals and participating legal entities have participation.

In this paragraph, reduction of participation means that the proportion of members of the supervisory or administrative organ of the SCE who may be elected or appointed (or whose appointment may be recommended or opposed) by virtue of participation is lower than the proportion of such members in the participating legal entity which had the highest proportion of such members.

(4) The special negotiating body must publish the details of any decision taken under this regulation or under regulation 19 in such a manner as to bring the decision, so far as reasonably practicable, to the attention of the employees whom they represent and such publication shall take place as soon as reasonably practicable and, in any event no later than 14 days after the decision has been taken.

(5) For the purpose of negotiations, the special negotiating body may be assisted by experts of its choice.

(6) The participating individuals and participating legal entities shall pay for any reasonable expenses of the functioning of the special negotiating body and any reasonable expenses relating to the negotiations that are necessary to enable the special negotiating body to carry out its functions in an appropriate manner; but where the special negotiating body is assisted by more than one expert the participating individuals and participating legal entities are not required to pay such expenses in respect of more than one of them.

[3463S]

NOTES

Commencement: 18 August 2006.

19 Decision not to open or to terminate negotiations

(1) Subject to paragraph (2), the special negotiating body may decide, by a two thirds majority vote, not to open negotiations with the participating individuals and the competent organs of the participating legal entities or to terminate any such negotiations.

(2) The special negotiating body cannot take the decision referred to in paragraph (1) in relation to an SCE to be formed by conversion if any employees of the cooperative to be converted have participation.

(3) Any decision made under paragraph (1) shall have the following effects—

(a) the duty in regulation 16(2) to negotiate with a view to reaching an employee involvement agreement shall cease as from the date of the decision;

(b) any rules relating to the information and consultation of employees in an EEA State in which employees of the SCE are employed shall apply to the employees of the SCE in that EEA State; and

(c) the special negotiating body shall be reconvened only if a valid request in accordance with paragraph (4) is made by employees or employees' representatives.

(4) To amount to a valid request, the request referred to in paragraph (3)(c) must—

(a) be in writing;

(b) be made by at least 10% of the employees of, or by employees' representatives representing at least 10% of, the total number of employees employed by—

(i) the participating individuals, the participating legal entities and such participating legal entities' concerned subsidiaries, or

(ii) where the SCE has been registered, the SCE and it subsidiaries; and

(c) be made no earlier than two years after the decision made under paragraph (1) was or should have been published in accordance with regulation 18(4) unless the special negotiating body and every participating individual and the competent organs of every participating legal entity or, where the SCE has been registered, the SCE agree to the special negotiating body being reconvened earlier.

[3463T]

NOTES

Commencement: 18 August 2006.

20 Complaint about decisions of the special negotiating body

(1) If a member of the special negotiating body, an employees' representative, or where there is no such representative in respect of an employee, that employee believes that the special negotiating body has taken a decision referred to in regulation 18 or 19 and—

(a) that the decision was not taken by the majority required by regulation 18 or 19, as the case may be; or

(b) the special negotiating body failed to publish the decision in accordance with regulation 18(4),

he may present a complaint to the CAC within 21 days of the date the special negotiating body did or should have published their decision in accordance with regulation 18(4).

(2) Where the CAC finds the complaint well-founded it shall make a declaration that the decision was not taken properly and that it shall have no effect.

[3463U]

NOTES

Commencement: 18 August 2006.

PART 5

STANDARD RULES ON EMPLOYEE INVOLVEMENT

21 Standard rules on employee involvement

(1) Without prejudice to paragraphs (3) and (5), where this regulation applies, the competent organ of the SCE and its subsidiaries and establishments shall make arrangements for the involvement of employees of the SCE and its subsidiaries and establishments in accordance with the standard rules on employee involvement.

(2) This regulation, save for paragraph 5, applies in the following circumstances:

(a) where it is agreed that the standard rules on employee involvement shall apply; or

(b) where the period specified in regulation 16(3)(a) or, where applicable, (b) has expired without an employee involvement agreement having been reached and—

(i) each participating individual and the competent organs of each of the participating legal entities agree that the standard rules on employee involvement shall apply and so continue with the registration of the SCE; and

(ii) the special negotiating body has not taken any decision under regulation 19(1) either not to open or to terminate the negotiations referred to in that regulation.

(3) The standard rules set out in Part 3 of Schedule 2 to these Regulations (standard rules on participation) only apply in the following circumstances—

(a) in the case of an SCE to be formed by merger if, before registration of the SCE, one or more forms of participation existed in at least one of the participating legal entities and either—

(i) that participation applied to at least 25% of the total number of employees of the participating legal entities employed in the EEA States, or

(ii) that participation applied to less than 25% of the total number of employees of the participating legal entities employed in the EEA States but the special negotiating body has decided that the standard rules of participation will apply to the employees of the SCE; or

(b) in the case of an SCE to be formed in any other way if, before registration of the SCE, one or more forms of employee participation existed in at least one of the participating legal entities and either:

(i) that participation applied to at least 50% of the total number of employees of the participating individuals and participating legal entities employed in the EEA States; or

(ii) that participation applied to less than 50% of the total number of employees of the participating individuals and participating legal entities employed in the EEA States but the special negotiating body has decided that the standard rules of participation will apply to the employees of the SCE.

(4) Where the standard rules on participation apply and more than one form of employee participation exists in the participating legal entities, the special negotiating body shall decide which of the existing forms of participation shall exist in the SCE and shall inform the competent organs of the participating legal entities accordingly.

(5) The standard rule set out in paragraph 7(4) of Schedule 2 to these Regulations shall apply only in the following circumstances—

(a) the SCE is established by means other than conversion;

(b) there is a participating cooperative which is governed by a system whereby employees or employee representatives may participate in general meetings or section or sectorial meetings, and that participating cooperative has the highest proportion of participation, within the meaning of regulation 3, in force in the participating cooperatives concerned before registration of the SCE;

(c) the period specified in regulation 16(3)(a) or, where applicable, (b) has expired without an employee involvement agreement having been reached;

(d) each participating individual and the competent organs of each of the participating legal entities agree that the standard rules on employee involvement shall apply and so continue with the registration of the SCE; and

(e) the special negotiating body has not taken any decision under regulation 19(1) either not to open or to terminate the negotiations referred to in that regulation.

[3463V]

NOTES

Commencement: 18 August 2006.

PART 6
COMPLIANCE AND ENFORCEMENT

22 Disputes about operation of an employee involvement agreement or the standard rules on employee involvement

(1) Where—

(a) an employee involvement agreement has been agreed; or

(b) the standard rules on employee involvement apply,

a complaint may be presented to the CAC by a relevant applicant who considers that a participating individual or the competent organ of a participating legal entity or of the SCE has failed to comply with the terms of the employee involvement agreement or, as the case may be, one or more of the standard information and consultation provisions.

(2) A complaint brought under paragraph (1) must be brought within a period of three months commencing with the date of the alleged failure or, where the failure takes place over a period, the last day of that period.

(3) In this regulation—

"failure" means an act or omission,

"relevant applicant" means—

(a) in a case where a representative body has been elected or appointed, a member of that body; or

(b) in a case where no representative body has been elected or appointed, an information and consultation representative or an employee of the SCE.

(4) Where the CAC finds the complaint well-founded it shall make a declaration to that effect and may make an order requiring, as appropriate, the participating individual, participating legal entity or SCE to take such steps as are necessary to comply with the terms of the employee involvement agreement or, as the case may be, the standard rules on employee involvement.

(5) An order made under paragraph (4) shall specify—

(a) the steps which, as appropriate, the participating individual, participating legal entity or SCE is required to take;

(b) the date of the failure; and

(c) the period within which the order must be complied with.

(6) If the CAC makes a declaration under paragraph (4), the relevant applicant may, within the period of three months beginning with the day on which the decision is made, make an application to the Appeal Tribunal for a penalty notice to be issued.

(7) Where such an application is made, the Appeal Tribunal shall issue a written penalty notice to, as appropriate, the participating individual, participating legal entity or SCE requiring it to pay a penalty to the Secretary of State in respect of the failure unless satisfied, on hearing representations, that the failure resulted from a reason beyond the its control or that it has some other reasonable excuse for its failure.

(8) Regulation 23 shall apply in respect of a penalty notice issued under this regulation.

(9) No order of the CAC under this regulation shall have the effect of suspending or altering the effect of any act done or of any agreement made by the participating individual, participating legal entity or by the SCE.

[3463W]

NOTES

Commencement: 18 August 2006.

23 Penalties

(1) A penalty notice issued under regulation 22 shall specify—

(a) the amount of the penalty which is payable;
(b) the date before which the penalty must be paid; and
(c) the failure and period to which the penalty relates.

(2) No penalty set by the Appeal Tribunal under this regulation may exceed £75,000.

(3) When setting the amount of the penalty, the Appeal Tribunal shall take into account—

(a) the gravity of the failure;
(b) the period of time over which the failure occurred;
(c) the reason for the failure;
(d) the number of employees affected by the failure; and
(e) the number of employees employed by the SCE.

(4) The date specified under paragraph (1)(b) above must not be earlier than the end of the period within which an appeal against a decision or order made by the CAC under regulation 22 may be made.

(5) If the specified date in a penalty notice has passed and—

(a) the period during which an appeal may be made has expired without an appeal having been made; or
(b) such an appeal has been made and determined,

the Secretary of State may recover from, as appropriate, the participating individual, participating legal entity or SCE, as a civil debt due to him, any amount payable under the penalty notice which remains outstanding.

(6) The making of an appeal suspends the effect of the penalty notice.

(7) Any sums received by the Secretary of State under regulation 22 or this regulation shall be paid into the Consolidated Fund.

[3463X]

NOTES

Commencement: 18 August 2006.

24 Misuse of procedures

(1) If an employees' representative or where there is no such representative in relation to an employee, the employee, believes that a participating individual, a participating legal entity or an SCE is misusing or intending to misuse the SCE or the powers in these Regulations for the purpose of—

(a) depriving the employees of, as appropriate, that participating individual, that participating legal entity or of any of its concerned subsidiaries, or that SCE or of its subsidiaries of their rights to employee involvement; or

(b) withholding rights to employee involvement from any of the people referred to in sub-paragraph (a),

he may make present a complaint to the CAC

(2) Where a complaint is made to the CAC under paragraph (1) before registration or within a period of 12 months of the date of the registration of the SCE, the CAC shall uphold the complaint unless the respondent proves that it did not misuse or intend to misuse the SCE or the powers in these Regulations for either of the purposes set out in sub-paragraphs (a) or (b) of paragraph (1).

(3) If the CAC finds the complaint to be well founded—

(a) it shall make a declaration to that effect and may make an order requiring, as appropriate, the participating individual, participating legal entity or SCE, to take such action as is specified in the order to ensure that the employees referred to in paragraph (1)(a) are not deprived of their rights to employee involvement or that such rights are not withheld from them; and

(b) the provisions in regulations 22(6) to (9) and 23 shall apply to the complaint.

[3463Y]

NOTES

Commencement: 18 August 2006.

25 Exclusivity of remedy

Where Parts 2 to 6 of, and Schedule 1 to, these Regulations provide for a remedy of infringement of any right by way of application or complaint to the CAC, and provide for no other remedy, no other remedy is available for infringement of that right.

[3463Z]

NOTES

Commencement: 18 August 2006.

PART 7
CONFIDENTIAL INFORMATION

26 Breach of statutory duty

(1) Where an SCE, a subsidiary of an SCE, a participating legal entity, any concerned subsidiary, or a participating individual entrusts a person, pursuant to these Regulations, with any information or document on terms requiring it to be held in confidence, the person shall not disclose that information or document except in accordance with the terms on which it was disclosed to him.

(2) In this regulation a person referred to in paragraph (1) to whom information or a document is entrusted is referred to as a "recipient".

(3) The obligation to comply with paragraph (1) is a duty owed to the SCE, subsidiary of an SCE, participating legal entity, concerned subsidiary, or participating individual that disclosed the information to the person and a breach of the duty is actionable accordingly (subject to the defences and other incidents applying to actions for breach of statutory duty).

(4) Paragraph (3) does not affect any legal liability which any person may incur by disclosing the information, or any right which any person may have in relation to such disclosure otherwise than under this Regulation.

(5) No action shall lie under paragraph (3) where the recipient reasonably believed the disclosure to be a "protected disclosure" within the meaning given to that expression by section 43A of the 1996 Act.

(6) A recipient to whom an SCE, subsidiary of an SCE, participating legal entity, concerned subsidiary or participating individual has entrusted any information or document on terms requiring it to be held in confidence, may apply to the CAC for a declaration as to whether it was reasonable to have required him to hold the information or document in confidence.

(7) If the CAC considers that the disclosure of the information or the document by the recipient would not, or would not be likely to, harm the legitimate interests of the SCE, subsidiary of an SCE, participating legal entity, concerned subsidiary or participating individual, as the case may be, it shall make a declaration that it was not reasonable to have required the recipient to hold the information or document in confidence.

(8) If a declaration is made under paragraph (7), the information or document shall not at any time thereafter be regarded as having been entrusted to the recipient who made the application under paragraph (6), or to any other recipient, on terms requiring it to be held in confidence.

[3463ZA]

NOTES

Commencement: 18 August 2006.

27 Withholding of information

(1) An SCE, participating legal entity, or participating individual may refuse to disclose any information or document to a person for the purposes of these Regulations where the nature of the information or document is such that, according to objective criteria, the disclosure of the information or document would seriously harm the functioning of, or would be prejudicial to, as appropriate, the SCE or any subsidiary or establishment of the SCE, the participating legal entity or any subsidiary or establishment of the participating legal entity, the participating individual or any establishment of the participating individual.

(2) Where there is a dispute between the SCE, participating legal entity or participating individual and—

(a) where a representative body has been appointed or elected, a member of that body; or

(b) where no representative body has been elected or appointed, an information and consultation representative or an employee,

as to whether the nature of the information or document which the SCE, the participating legal entity or participating individual has failed to provide is such as is described in paragraph (1), the SCE, participating legal entity, participating individual or a person referred to in sub-paragraph (a) or (b) may apply to the CAC for a declaration as to whether the information or document is of such a nature.

(3) If the CAC makes a declaration that the disclosure of the information or document in question would not, according to objective criteria, be seriously harmful or prejudicial as mentioned in paragraph (1), the CAC shall order the SCE, participating legal entity or participating individual, as the case may be, to disclose the information or document.

(4) An order under paragraph (3) shall specify—

(a) the information or document to be disclosed;

(b) the person or persons to whom the information or document is to be disclosed;

(c) any terms on which the information or document is to be disclosed; and

(d) the date before which the information or document is to be disclosed.

[3463ZB]

NOTES

Commencement: 18 August 2006.

PART 8
PROTECTION FOR MEMBERS OF SPECIAL NEGOTIATING BODY, ETC

28 Right to time off for members of special negotiating body, etc

(1) An employee who is—

(a) a member of a special negotiating body;

(b) a member of a representative body;

(c) an information and consultation representative;

(d) an employee member of a supervisory or administrative organ;

(e) a candidate in an election in which any person elected will, on being elected, be such a member or a representative; or

(f) a participant in general meetings or section or sectorial meetings of the SCE as provided for in regulation 17(2)(h) or paragraph 11(2)(h) of Schedule 1 or paragraph 7(4) of Schedule 2,

is entitled to be permitted by his employer to take reasonable time off during the employee's working hours in order to perform his functions as such a member, representative, candidate or participant.

(2) For the purpose of this regulation the working hours of an employee shall be taken to be any time when, in accordance with his contract of employment, the employee is required to be at work.

[3463ZC]

NOTES

Commencement: 18 August 2006.

29 Right to remuneration for time off under regulation 28

(1) An employee who is permitted to take time off under regulation 28 is entitled to be paid remuneration by his employer for the time taken off at the appropriate hourly rate.

(2) Chapter 2 of Part 14 of the 1996 Act (a week's pay) shall apply in relation to this regulation as it applies in relation to section 62 of the 1996 Act.

(3) The appropriate hourly rate, in relation to an employee, is the amount of one week's pay divided by the number of normal working hours in a week for that employee when employed under the contract of employment in force on the day when the time is taken.

(4) But where the number of normal working hours differs from week to week or over a longer period, the amount of one week's pay shall be divided instead by—

(a) the average number of normal working hours calculated by dividing by twelve the total number of the employee's normal working hours during the period of twelve weeks ending with the last complete week before the day on which the time off is taken; or

(b) where the employee has not been employed for a sufficient period to enable the calculation to be made under sub-paragraph (a), a number which fairly represents the number of normal working hours in a week having regard to such of the considerations specified in paragraph (5) as are appropriate in the circumstances.

(5) The considerations referred to in paragraph (4)(b) are—

(a) the average number of normal working hours in a week which the employee could expect in accordance with the terms of his contract; and

(b) the average number of normal working hours of other employees engaged in relevant comparable employment with the same employer.

(6) A right to any amount under paragraph (1) does not affect any right of an employee in relation to remuneration under his contract of employment.

(7) Any contractual remuneration paid to an employee in respect of a period of time off under regulation 28 goes towards discharging any liability of the employer to pay remuneration under paragraph (1) in respect of that period, and conversely, any payment of remuneration under paragraph (1) in respect of a period goes towards discharging any liability of the employer to pay contractual remuneration in respect of that period.

[3463ZD]

NOTES

Commencement: 18 August 2006.

30 Right to time off: complaints to tribunals

(1) An employee may present a complaint to an employment tribunal that his employer—

(a) has unreasonably refused to permit him to take time off as required under regulation 28; or

(b) has failed to pay the whole or any part of any amount to which the employee is entitled under regulation 29.

(2) A tribunal shall not consider a complaint under this regulation unless it is presented—

(a) before the end of the period of three months beginning with the day on which the time off was taken or on which it is alleged the time off should have been permitted; or

(b) within such further period as the tribunal considers reasonable in a case where it is satisfied that it was not reasonably practicable for the complaint to be presented before the end of that period of three months.

(3) Where a tribunal finds a complaint under this regulation well-founded, the tribunal shall make a declaration to that effect.

(4) If the complaint is that the employer has unreasonably refused to permit the employee to take time off, the tribunal shall also order the employer to pay to the employee an amount equal to the remuneration to which he would have been entitled under regulation 29 if the employer had not refused.

(5) If the complaint is that the employer has failed to pay the employee the whole or part of any amount to which he is entitled under regulation 29, the tribunal shall also order him to pay to the employee the amount which it finds is due to him.

[3463ZE]

NOTES

Commencement: 18 August 2006.

Conciliation: employment tribunal proceedings and claims which could be the subject of employment tribunal proceedings under this regulation are proceedings to which the Employment Tribunals Act 1996, s 18 applies; see s 18(1)(s) of that Act at **[975]**. The standard conciliation period applies to such claims by virtue of the Employment Tribunals (Constitution and Rules of Procedure) Regulations 2004, SI 2004/1861, Sch 1, rule 22(1), (6).

31 Unfair dismissal

(1) An employee who is dismissed and to whom paragraph (2) or (5) applies shall be regarded, if the reason (or, if more than one, the principal reason) for the dismissal is a reason specified in, respectively, paragraph (3) or (6), as unfairly dismissed for the purposes of Part 10 of the 1996 Act.

(2) This paragraph applies to an employee who is—

(a) a member of a special negotiating body;

(b) a member of a representative body;

(c) an information and consultation representative;

(d) an employee member of a supervisory or administrative organ; or

(e) a candidate in an election in which any person elected will, on being elected, be such a member or a representative; or

(f) a participant in general meetings or section or sectorial meetings of the SCE as provided for in regulation 17(2)(h) or paragraph 11(2)(h) of Schedule 1, or paragraph 7(4) of Schedule 2.

(3) The reason is that—

(a) the employee performed or proposed to perform any functions or activities as such a member, representative, candidate or participant; or

(b) the employee or a person acting on his behalf made or proposed to make a request to exercise an entitlement conferred on the employee by regulation 28 or 29.

(4) Paragraph (1) does not apply in the circumstances set out in paragraph (3)(a) where the reason (or principal reason) for the dismissal is that in the performance, or purported performance, of the employee's functions or activities he has disclosed any information or document in breach of the duty in regulation 26, unless the employee reasonably believed the disclosure to be a "protected disclosure" within the meaning given to that expression by section 43A of the 1996 Act.

(5) This paragraph applies to any employee whether or not he is an employee to whom paragraph (2) applies.

(6) The reasons are that the employee—

(a) took, or proposed to take, any proceedings before an employment tribunal to enforce any right conferred on him by these Regulations;

(b) exercised, or proposed to exercise, any entitlement to apply or complain to the CAC or the Appeal Tribunal conferred by these Regulations or to exercise the right to appeal in connection with any rights conferred by these Regulations;

(c) acted with a view to securing that a special negotiating body, a representative body or an information and consultation procedure did or did not come into existence;
(d) indicated that he did or did not support the coming into existence of a special negotiating body, a representative body or an information and consultation procedure;
(e) stood as a candidate in an election in which any person elected would, on being elected, be a member of a special negotiating body, a representative body, an employee member of a supervisory or administrative organ, a participant in general or section or sectorial meetings or an information and consultation representative;
(f) influenced or sought to influence by lawful means the way in which votes were to be cast by other employees in a ballot arranged under these Regulations;
(g) voted in such a ballot;
(h) expressed doubts, whether to a ballot supervisor or otherwise, as to whether such a ballot had been properly conducted; or
(i) proposed to do, failed to do, or proposed to decline to do, any of the things mentioned in sub-paragraphs (d) to (h).

(7) It is immaterial for the purposes of sub-paragraph (a) of paragraph (6)—
(a) whether or not the employee has the right, or
(b) whether or not the right has been infringed,
but for that sub-paragraph to apply, the claim to the right and, if applicable, the claim that it has been infringed must be made in good faith.

[3463ZF]

NOTES

Commencement: 18 August 2006.

32 (*Amends the Employment Rights Act 1996, ss 105, 108 at* **[1149]**, **[1152]**, *and amended s 109 of that Act* (*repealed*).)

33 Detriment

(1) An employee to whom paragraph (2) or (5) applies has the right not to be subjected to any detriment by any act, or deliberate failure to act, by his employer, done on a ground specified in, respectively, paragraph (3) or (6).

(2) This paragraph applies to an employee who is—
(a) a member of a special negotiating body;
(b) a member of a representative body;
(c) an information and consultation representative;
(d) an employee member of a supervisory or administrative organ;
(e) a candidate in an election in which any person elected will, on being elected, be such a member or a representative; or
(f) a participant in general meetings or section or sectorial meetings of the SCE as provided for in regulation 17(2)(h) or paragraph 11(2)(h) of Schedule 1, or paragraph 7(4) of Schedule 2.

(3) The ground is that—
(a) the employee performed or proposed to perform any functions or activities as such a member, representative, candidate or participant; or
(b) the employee or person acting on his behalf made or proposed to make a request to exercise an entitlement conferred on the employee by regulation 28 or 29.

(4) Paragraph (1) does not apply in the circumstances set out in paragraph (3)(a) where the ground for the subjection to detriment is that in the performance, or purported performance, of the employee's functions or activities he has disclosed any information or document in breach of the duty in regulation 26, unless the employee reasonably believed the disclosure to be a "protected disclosure" within the meaning given to that expression by section 43A of the 1996 Act.

(5) This paragraph applies to any employee, whether or not he is an employee to whom paragraph (2) applies.

(6) The grounds are that the employee—

(a) took, or proposed to take, any proceedings before an employment tribunal to enforce any right conferred on him by these Regulations;

(b) exercised, or proposed to exercise, any entitlement to apply or complain to the CAC or the Appeal Tribunal conferred by these Regulations or to exercise the right to appeal in connection with any rights conferred by these Regulations;

(c) acted with a view to securing that a special negotiating body, a representative body or an information and consultation procedure did or did not come into existence;

(d) indicated that he did or did not support the coming into existence of a special negotiating body, a representative body or an information and consultation procedure;

(e) stood as a candidate in an election in which any person elected would, on being elected, be a member of a special negotiating body, a representative body, an employee member of a supervisory or administrative organ, a participant in general or section or sectorial meetings or be an information and consultation representative;

(f) influenced or sought to influence by lawful means the way in which votes were to be cast by other employees in a ballot arranged under these Regulations;

(g) voted in such a ballot;

(h) expressed doubts, whether to a ballot supervisor or otherwise, as to whether such a ballot had been properly conducted; or

(i) proposed to do, failed to do, or proposed to decline to do, any of the things mentioned in sub-paragraphs (d) to (h).

(7) It is immaterial for the purposes of paragraph (6)(a)—

(a) whether or not the employee has the right or entitlement; or

(b) whether or not the right has been infringed,

but for that sub-paragraph to apply, the claim to the right and, if applicable, the claim that has been infringed must be made in good faith.

(8) This regulation does not apply where the detriment in question amounts to dismissal.

[3463ZG]

NOTES

Commencement: 18 August 2006.

34 Detriment: enforcement and subsidiary provisions

(1) An employee may present a complaint to an employment tribunal that he has been subjected to a detriment in contravention of regulation 33.

(2) The provisions of sections 48(2) to (4) of the 1996 Act (complaints to employment tribunals) shall apply in relation to a complaint under this regulation as they apply in relation to a complaint under section 48 of that Act.

(3) The provisions of section 49(1) to (5) of the 1996 Act shall apply in relation to a complaint under this regulation.

(4) (*Amends the Employment Act 2002, Schs 3–5 at* **[1508]–[1510]**.)

[3463ZH]

NOTES

Commencement: 18 August 2006.

Conciliation: employment tribunal proceedings and claims which could be the subject of employment tribunal proceedings under this regulation are proceedings to which the Employment Tribunals Act 1996, s 18 applies; see s 18(1)(s) of that Act at **[975]**. The standard conciliation period applies to such claims by virtue of the Employment Tribunals (Constitution and Rules of Procedure) Regulations 2004, SI 2004/1861, Sch 1, rule 22(1), (6).

Tribunal jurisdiction: the Employment Act 2002, ss 31, 32, 38, at **[1493]**, **[1494]**, **[1496]** apply to proceedings before the employment tribunal relating to a claim under this regulation; see ss 31(1), 32(1), 38(1) of, and Schs 3–5 to, the 2002 Act at **[1508]–[1510]**.

For the circumstances in which the normal time limit for presenting a complaint under this regulation is extended for a period of three months, see the Employment Act 2002 (Dispute Resolution) Regulations 2004, SI 2004/752, regs 15 and 18 at **[3096]** and **[3098]**.

35 (*Amends the Employment Tribunals Act 1996, s 18 at* **[975]**.)

PART 9
MISCELLANEOUS

36 CAC proceedings

(1) Where under these Regulations a person presents a complaint or makes an application to the CAC the complaint or application must be in writing and in such form as the CAC may require.

(2) In its consideration of a complaint or application under these Regulations, the CAC shall make such enquiries as it sees fit and give any person whom it considers has a proper interest in the complaint or application an opportunity to be heard.

(3) In the case of a participating individual resident in England and Wales, an SCE with its registered office in England and Wales, or a participating legal entity or concerned subsidiary with its registered office (or principal place of business if not a body corporate), in England and Wales—

(a) a declaration made by the CAC under these Regulations may be relied on as if it were a declaration or order made by the High Court in England and Wales; and

(b) an order made by the CAC under these Regulations may be enforced in the same way as an order of the High Court in England and Wales.

(4) In the case of a participating individual resident in Scotland, an SCE with its registered office in Scotland, or a participating legal entity or concerned subsidiary with its registered office (or principal place of business if not a body corporate), in Scotland—

(a) a declaration or order made by the CAC under these Regulations may be relied on as if it were a declaration or order made by the Court of Session; and

(b) an order made by the CAC under these Regulations may be enforced in the same way as an order of the Court of Session.

(5) A declaration or order made by the CAC under these Regulations must be in writing and state the reasons for the CAC's findings.

(6) An appeal lies to the Appeal Tribunal on any question of law arising from any declaration or order of, or arising in any proceedings before, the CAC under these Regulations.

[3463ZI]

NOTES

Commencement: 18 August 2006.

37 Appeal Tribunal: location of certain proceedings under these Regulations

(1) Any proceedings before the Appeal Tribunal under these Regulations, other than appeals under paragraph (r) of section 21(1) of the Employment Tribunals Act 1996 (appeals from employment tribunals on questions of law), shall—

(a) in the case of a participating individual resident in England and Wales, an SCE with its registered office in England and Wales, or a participating legal entity or concerned subsidiary with its registered office (or principal place of business, if not a body corporate) in England and Wales, be held in England and Wales;

(b) in the case of a participating individual resident in Scotland, an SCE with its registered office in Scotland, or a participating legal entity or concerned subsidiary with its registered office (or principal place of business, if not a body corporate) in Scotland, be held in Scotland.

(2) (*Amends the Employment Tribunals Act 1996, s 20 at* **[977]**.)

[3463ZJ]

NOTES

Commencement: 18 August 2006.

38 (*Amends the Employment Tribunals Act 1996, s 21 at* **[978]**.)

39 ACAS

(1) If on receipt of an application or complaint under these Regulations the CAC is of the opinion that it is reasonably likely to be settled by conciliation or other assistance provided by

PART 2

the Advisory, Conciliation and Arbitration Service ("ACAS") in accordance with paragraph (2), it shall refer the application or complaint to ACAS and notify the applicant or complainant and any persons whom it considers have a proper interest in the application or complaint accordingly.

(2) Where the CAC refers an application or complaint to ACAS under paragraph (1), section 210 of the Trade Union and Labour Relations (Consolidation) Act 1992 (power of ACAS to offer assistance to settle disputes) shall apply, and ACAS may offer the parties to the application or complaint its assistance under that section with a view to bringing about a settlement, as if the dispute or difference between the parties amounted to a trade dispute as defined in section 218 of that Act.

(3) If ACAS does not consider it appropriate to offer its assistance in accordance with paragraph (2) it shall inform the CAC

(4) If ACAS has offered the parties its assistance in accordance with paragraph (2), the application or complaint referred has not thereafter been settled or withdrawn, and ACAS is of the opinion that no provision or further provision of its assistance is likely to result in a settlement or withdrawal, it shall inform the CAC of its opinion.

(5) If—

(a) an application or complaint is not referred to ACAS, or

(b) it is so referred, but ACAS informs the CAC as mentioned in paragraph (3) or (4),

the CAC shall proceed to hear and determine the application or complaint.

[3463ZK]

NOTES

Commencement: 18 August 2006.

40 Restrictions on contracting out: general

(1) Any provision in any agreement (whether a contract of employment or not) is void in so far as it purports—

(a) to exclude or limit the operation of any provision of these Regulations other than a provision of Part 8; or

(b) to preclude a person from bringing any proceedings before the CAC under these Regulations other than under a provision of Part 8.

(2) Paragraph (1) does not apply to any agreement to refrain from continuing any proceedings referred to in sub-paragraph (b) of that paragraph made after the proceedings have been instituted.

[3463ZL]

NOTES

Commencement: 18 August 2006.

41 Restrictions on contracting out: Part 8

(1) Any provision in any agreement (whether a contract of employment or not) is void in so far as it purports—

(a) to exclude or limit the operation of any provision of Part 8 of these Regulations; or

(b) to preclude a person from bringing any proceedings before an employment tribunal under that Part.

(2) Paragraph (1) does not apply to any agreement to refrain from instituting or continuing proceedings before an employment tribunal where a conciliation officer has taken action under section 18 of the Employment Tribunals Act 1996 (conciliation).

(3) Paragraph (1) does not apply to any agreement to refrain from instituting or continuing before an employment tribunal proceedings within section 18(1)(s) of the Employment Tribunals Act 1996 (proceedings under these Regulations where conciliation is available) if the conditions regulating compromise agreements under these Regulations are satisfied in relation to the agreement.

(4) For the purposes of paragraph (3) the conditions regulating compromise agreements are that—

(a) the agreement must be in writing;

(b) the agreement must relate to the particular proceedings;

(c) the employee must have received advice from a relevant independent adviser as to the terms and effect of the proposed agreement and, in particular, its effect on his ability to pursue his rights before an employment tribunal;

(d) there must be in force, when the adviser gives the advice, a contract of insurance, or an indemnity provided for members of a profession or professional body, covering the risk of a claim by the employee in respect of loss arising in consequence of the advice;

(e) the agreement must identify the adviser; and

(f) the agreement must state that the conditions in sub-paragraphs (a) to (e) are satisfied.

(5) A person is a relevant independent adviser for the purposes of paragraph (4)(c)—

(a) if he is a qualified lawyer;

(b) if he is an officer, official, employee or member of an independent trade union who has been certified in writing by the trade union as competent to give advice and authorised to do so on behalf of the trade union; or

(c) if he works at an advice centre (whether as an employee or as a volunteer) and has been certified in writing by the centre as competent to give advice and authorised to do so on behalf of the centre.

(6) But a person is not a relevant independent adviser for the purposes of paragraph (4)(c) in relation to the employee—

(a) if he is, is employed by or is acting in the matter for the employer or an associated employer;

(b) in the case of a person within paragraph (5)(b) or (c), if the trade union or advice centre is the employer or an associated employer; or

(c) in the case of a person within paragraph (5)(c), if the employee makes a payment for the advice received by him.

(7) In paragraph (5)(a), a "qualified lawyer" means—

(a) as respects England and Wales, a barrister (whether in practice as such or employed to give legal advice), a solicitor who holds a practising certificate, or a person other than a barrister or solicitor who is an authorised advocate or authorised litigator (within the meaning of the Courts and Legal Services Act 1990); and

(b) as respects Scotland, an advocate (whether in practice as such or employed to give legal advice) or a solicitor who holds a practising certificate.

(8) A person shall be treated as being a qualified lawyer within sub-paragraph (7)(a) if he is a Fellow of the Institute of Legal Executives employed by a solicitors' practice.

(9) For the purposes of paragraph (6) any two employers shall be treated as associated if—

(a) one is a company of which the other (directly or indirectly) has control; or

(b) both are companies of which a third person (directly or indirectly) has control;

and "associated employer" shall be construed accordingly.

[3463ZM]

NOTES

Commencement: 18 August 2006.

42 (*Inserts the Transnational Information and Consultation of Employees Regulations 1999, SI 1999/3323, reg 46A at* **[2618A]**.)

43 Existing employee involvement rights

(1) Subject to paragraph (2), nothing in these Regulations shall prejudice involvement rights of employees of an SCE, its subsidiaries or establishments provided for by law or practice in the EEA State in which they were employed immediately prior to the registration of the SCE.

(2) Paragraph (1) does not apply to rights to participation.

[3463ZN]

NOTES

Commencement: 18 August 2006.

SCHEDULES

SCHEDULE 1

Regulation 6(2)

PART 1

PROVISION OF INFORMATION AND THE SPECIAL NEGOTIATING BODY

1 Duty on SCE to provide information

(1) The competent organ of the SCE shall, as soon as possible after the satisfaction of a relevant condition (within the meaning given in regulation 6(3)), provide information to the employees' representatives of the SCE and of any subsidiaries and establishments or, if no such representatives exist, the employees themselves.

(2) The information referred to in paragraph (1) must include, as a minimum, information—

(a) identifying the SCE and any subsidiaries and establishments,

(b) giving the number of employees employed by the SCE, any subsidiary and at any establishment, and

(c) giving the number of employees employed to work in each EEA State.

2 Complaint of failure to provide information

(1) An employees' representative or, where there is no such representative for an employee, the employee, may present a complaint to the CAC that—

(a) the competent organ of the SCE has failed to provide the information to paragraph 1; or

(b) the information provided by such competent organ for the purpose of complying with paragraph 1 is false or incomplete in a material particular.

(2) Where the CAC finds the complaint well-founded it shall make an order requiring the competent organ to disclose information to the complainant which order shall specify—

(a) the information in respect of which the CAC finds that the complaint is well-founded and which is to be disclosed to the complainant; and

(b) a date, (not being less than one week from the date of the order) by which the competent organ must disclose the information specified in the order.

3 Function of the special negotiating body

The special negotiating body and the competent organ of the SCE shall have the task of reaching an employee involvement agreement.

4 Composition of the special negotiating body

(1) The competent organ of the SCE shall make arrangements for the establishment of a special negotiating body, which body shall be constituted as soon as possible and in accordance with sub-paragraphs (2) to (4) below. The methods used to elect or appoint employee representatives to the special negotiating body should seek to promote gender balance.

(2) The total number of employees employed to work in each EEA State of the SCE and its subsidiaries shall be given an entitlement to elect or appoint one member of the special negotiating body for each 10% or fraction thereof which those employees represent of the total workforce.

(3) The competent organ of the SCE shall, as soon as reasonably practicable and in any event no later than one month after the establishment of the special negotiating body, inform its employees and those of its subsidiaries of the identity of the members of the special negotiating body.

(4) If, following the appointment or election of members to the special negotiating body in accordance with this paragraph,

(a) changes to the SCE, its subsidiaries or establishments result in the number of members which employees would be entitled to elect or appoint under this paragraph either materially increasing or decreasing, the original appointment or election of members of the special negotiating body shall cease to have effect and those employees shall be entitled to elect or appoint the new number of members in accordance with the provisions of this Schedule; and

(b) a member of the special negotiating body is no longer willing or able to continue serving as such a member, the employees whom he represents shall be entitled to elect or appoint a new member in his place.

5 Complaint about establishment of the special negotiating body

(1) An application may be presented to the CAC for a declaration that the special negotiating body has not been established at all or has not been established properly in accordance with paragraph 4.

(2) An application may be presented under this paragraph by—

(a) a person elected or appointed to be a member of the special negotiating body;

(b) an employees' representative or, where no such representative exists in respect of an SCE or subsidiary, an employee of the SCE or subsidiary; or

(c) the competent organ of an SCE or subsidiary.

(3) The CAC shall only consider an application made under sub-paragraph (1) that a special negotiating body had not been properly constituted if it is made within a period of one month from the date on which the competent organ of the SCE complied or should have complied with the obligation to inform the employees under paragraph 4(3).

(4) Where the CAC finds the application well-founded it shall make a declaration that the special negotiating body has not been established at all or has not been established properly and the competent organ of the SCE continues to be under the obligation in paragraph 4(1).

[3463ZO]

NOTES

Commencement: 18 August 2006.

PART 2
ELECTION OR APPOINTMENT OF UK MEMBERS OF THE SPECIAL NEGOTIATING BODY

6 Ballot arrangements

(1) Subject to paragraph 8, the UK members of the special negotiating body shall be elected by balloting the UK employees.

(2) An SCE and its subsidiaries employing UK employees ("the relevant employers") must arrange for the holding of a ballot or ballots of those employees in accordance with the requirements of sub-paragraph (3), and having regard to the fact that the methods of election should seek to promote gender balance.

(3) The requirements referred to in sub-paragraph (2) are—

(a) in relation to the election of members under paragraph 4(2), that—

(i) if the number of members which UK employees are entitled to elect to the special negotiating body is equal to the number of relevant employers, there shall be separate ballots of the UK employees of each relevant employer;

(ii) if the number of members which the UK employees are entitled to elect to the special negotiating body is greater than the number of relevant employers there shall be separate ballots of the UK employees of each relevant employer and the relevant employers shall ensure, as far as practicable, that at least one member representing the UK employees of each such employer is elected to the special negotiating body and that the number of members representing the UK employees of that employer is proportionate to the number of employees of that employer;

(iii) if the number of members which the UK employees are entitled to elect to the special negotiating body is smaller than the number of relevant employers,—

(aa) the number of ballots held shall be equivalent to the number of members to be elected;

(bb) a separate ballot shall be held in respect of each of the relevant employers with the higher or highest number of employees; and

(cc) it shall be ensured that any employees of a relevant employer in respect of which a ballot does not have to be held are entitled to vote in a ballot held in respect of one of the other relevant employers; and

(iv) if there are any UK employees employed by a non-UK SCE or by a subsidiary or at an establishment of an non-UK SCE, the relevant employers shall ensure that those employees are entitled to vote in a ballot held pursuant to this paragraph;

(b) that in a ballot in respect of a particular relevant employer all UK employees employed by that employer at its establishments are entitled to vote;

(c) that in a ballot in respect of a particular relevant employer any person who is immediately before the latest time at which a person may become a candidate—

(i) a UK employee employed by that employer or at any of its establishments; or

(ii) if the employer so permits, a representative of a trade union who is not an employee of that employer,

is entitled to stand as a candidate for election as a member of the special negotiating body in that ballot;

(d) that the relevant employers appoint an independent ballot supervisor to supervise the conduct of the ballot of UK employees except that, where there is to be more than one ballot, the relevant employers may appoint more than one independent ballot supervisor, each of whom is to supervise such of the separate ballots as the relevant employers may determine, provided that each separate ballot is supervised by a supervisor;

(e) that after the relevant employers have formulated proposals as to the arrangements for the ballot of UK employees and before they have published the final arrangements under paragraph (f) they must, so far as reasonably practicable, consult with the UK employees' representatives on the proposed arrangements for the ballot of UK employees; and

(f) that the relevant employers must publish the final arrangements for the ballot of UK employees in such manner as to bring them to the attention of, so far as reasonably practicable, all UK employees and the UK employees' representatives.

(4) Any UK employee or UK employees' representative who believes that the arrangements for the ballot of the UK employees do not comply with the requirements of sub-paragraph (3) may, within a period of 21 days beginning on the date on which the management published the final arrangements under paragraph (f), present a complaint to the CAC.

(5) Where the CAC finds the complaint well-founded it shall make a declaration to that effect and may make an order requiring the relevant employers to modify the arrangements they have made for the ballot of UK employees or to satisfy the requirements in paragraph (e) or (f) of sub-paragraph (3).

(6) An order under sub-paragraph (5) shall specify the modifications to the arrangements which the relevant employers are required to make and the requirements they must satisfy.

(7) A person is an independent ballot supervisor for the purposes of sub-paragraph (3)(d) if the relevant employers reasonably believe that he will carry out any functions conferred on him in relation to the ballot competently and have no reasonable grounds for believing that his independence in relation to the ballot might reasonably be called into question.

7 Conduct of the ballot

(1) The relevant employers must—

(a) ensure that a ballot supervisor appointed under paragraph 6(3)(d) carries out his functions under this paragraph and that there is no interference with his carrying out of those functions from the relevant employers; and

(b) comply with all reasonable requests made by a ballot supervisor for the purposes of, or in connection with, the carrying out of those functions.

(2) A ballot supervisor's appointment shall require that he—

(a) supervises the conduct of the ballot, or the separate ballots he is being appointed to supervise, in accordance with the arrangements for the ballot of UK employees published by the relevant employers under paragraph 6(3)(f) or, where appropriate, in accordance with the arrangements as required to be modified by an order made as a result of a complaint presented under paragraph 6(4);

(b) does not conduct the ballot or any of the separate ballots before the relevant employers have satisfied the requirement specified in paragraph 6(3)(f) and—
   (i) where no complaint has been presented under paragraph 6(4), before the expiry of a period of 21 days beginning on the date on which the relevant employers published their arrangements under paragraph 6(3)(f); or
   (ii) where a complaint has been presented under paragraph 6(4), before the complaint has been determined and, where appropriate, the arrangements have been modified as required by an order made as a result of that complaint;

(c) conducts the ballot, or each separate ballot so as to secure that—
   (i) so far as reasonably practicable, those entitled to vote are given the opportunity to vote;
   (ii) so far as reasonably practicable, those entitled to stand as candidates are given the opportunity to stand;
   (iii) so far as reasonably practicable, those voting are able to do so in secret; and
   (iv) the votes given in the ballot are fairly and accurately counted.

(3) As soon as reasonably practicable after the holding of the ballot, the ballot supervisor must publish the results of the ballot in such manner as to make them available to the relevant employers and, so far as reasonably practicable, the UK employees entitled to vote in the ballot and the persons who stood as candidates.

(4) A ballot supervisor shall publish a report ("an ineffective ballot report") where he considers (whether on the basis of representations made to him by another person or otherwise) that—

(a) any of the requirements referred to in sub-paragraph (2) was not satisfied with the result that the outcome of the ballot would have been different; or

(b) there was an interference with the carrying out of his functions or a failure by the relevant employers to comply with all reasonable requests made by him with the result that he was unable to form a proper judgement as to whether each of the requirements referred to in sub paragraph (2) was satisfied in the ballot.

(5) Where a ballot supervisor publishes an ineffective ballot report the report must be published within a period of one month commencing on the date on which the ballot supervisor publishes the results of the ballot under sub-paragraph (3).

(6) A ballot supervisor shall publish an ineffective ballot report in such manner as to make it available to the relevant employers and, so far as reasonably practicable, the UK employees entitled to vote in the ballot and the persons who stood as candidates in the ballot.

(7) Where a ballot supervisor publishes an ineffective ballot report then—

(a) if there has been a single ballot or an ineffective ballot report has been published in respect of every separate ballot, the outcome of the ballot or ballots shall have no effect and the relevant employers shall again be under the obligation in paragraph 6(2).

(b) If there have been separate ballots and paragraph (a) does not apply—
   (i) the relevant employers shall arrange for the separate ballot or ballots in respect of which an ineffective ballot report was published to be re-held in accordance with paragraph 6 and this paragraph; and
   (ii) no such ballot shall have effect until it has been re-held and no ineffective ballot report has been published in respect of it within the period specified in sub-paragraph (5).

(8) All costs relating to the holding of a ballot, including payments made to a ballot supervisor for supervising the conduct of the ballot, shall be borne by the relevant employers (whether or not an ineffective ballot report has been published).

8 Appointment of UK members by a consultative committee

(1) This paragraph applies where—

(a) paragraph 6(3)(i) or (ii) would require a ballot to be held; and

(b) there exists in relation to the SCE whose employees would otherwise need to be balloted under paragraph 6, a consultative committee.

(2)

(a) Where this paragraph applies, the election provided for in paragraph 4 shall not take place but the consultative committee shall be entitled to appoint the UK member or members of the special negotiating body who would otherwise be elected pursuant to paragraph 6, where appropriate having regard to the fact that the method used should seek to promote gender balance.

(b) The consultative committee is entitled to appoint as a member of the special negotiating body:
  (i) one of their number; or
  (ii) if the SCE in respect of which the consultative committee exists so permits, a trade union representative who is not an employee of that SCE.

(3) In this regulation, "a consultative committee" means a body of persons—
(a) whose normal functions include or comprise the carrying out of an information and consultation function;
(b) which is able to carry out its information and consultation function without interference from the SCE;
(c) which, in carrying out its information and consultation function, represents all the employees of the SCE; and
(d) which consists wholly of persons who are employees of the SCE or such SCE's subsidiaries.

(4) In sub-paragraph (3) "information and consultation function" means the function of—
(a) receiving, on behalf of all of the employees of the SCE, information which may significantly affect the interests of the employees of that SCE, but excluding information which is relevant only to a specific aspect of the interests of the employees, such as health and safety, collective redundancies or pension schemes; and
(b) being consulted by the SCE on the information referred to in paragraph (a) above.

(5) The consultative committee must publish the names of the persons whom it has appointed to be members of the special negotiating body in such a manner as to bring them to the attention of the SCE and, so far as reasonably practicable, the employees and the employees' representatives of the SCE and such SCE's subsidiaries.

(6) Where the SCE, an employee or an employees' representative believes that—
(a) the consultative committee does not satisfy the requirements in sub-paragraph (3) above; or
(b) any of the persons appointed by the consultative committee is not entitled to be appointed,

he, or as the case may be, it may, within a period of 21 days beginning on the date on which the consultative committee published under sub-paragraph (5) the names of the persons appointed, present a complaint to the CAC

(7) Where the CAC finds the complaint well-founded it shall make a declaration to that effect.

(8) Where the CAC has made a declaration under sub-paragraph (7)—
(a) no appointment made by the consultative committee shall have effect; and
(b) the members of the special negotiating body shall be elected by a ballot of the employees in accordance with paragraph 6.

(9) Where the consultative committee appoints any person to be a member of the special negotiating body, that appointment shall have effect—
(a) where no complaint has been presented under sub-paragraph (6), after the expiry of a period of 21 days beginning on the date on which the consultative committee published under sub-paragraph (5) the names of the persons nominated; or
(b) where a complaint has been presented under sub-paragraph (6), as from the day on which the complaint has been determined without a declaration under sub-paragraph (7) being made.

9 Representation of employees

(1) Subject to sub-paragraph (2) below, a member elected in a ballot in accordance with paragraph 6(2), shall be treated as representing the employees for the time being of the SCE and of any such SCE's subsidiary or establishment whose employees were entitled to vote in the ballot in which he was elected.

(2) When a member of the special negotiating body is appointed by a consultative committee in accordance with paragraph 8, the employees whom the consultative committee represents and the UK employees of any subsidiary of the SCE or establishment shall be treated as being represented by the member so appointed.

[3463ZP]

NOTES

Commencement: 18 August 2006.

PART 3
NEGOTIATION OF THE EMPLOYEE INVOLVEMENT AGREEMENT

10 Negotiations to reach an employee involvement agreement

(1) In this paragraph and in paragraph 11 the competent organ of the SCE and the special negotiating body are referred to as "the parties".

(2) The parties are under a duty to negotiate in a spirit of cooperation with a view to reaching an employee involvement agreement.

(3) The duty referred to in paragraph (2) commences one month after the date or, if more than one, the last date on which the members of the special negotiating body were elected or appointed and applies—

(a) for the period of 6 months starting with the day on which the duty commenced or, where an employee involvement agreement is successfully negotiated within that period, until the completion of the negotiations; or

(b) where the parties agree before the end of that 6 month period that it is to be extended, for the period of 12 months starting with the day on which the duty commenced or, where an employee involvement agreement is successfully negotiated within the 12 month period, until the completion of the negotiations.

11 The employee involvement agreement

(1) The employee involvement agreement must be in writing.

(2) Without prejudice to the autonomy of the parties, the employee involvement agreement shall specify:

(a) the scope of the agreement;

(b) the composition, number of members and allocation of seats on the representative body;

(c) the functions and the procedure for the information and consultation of the representative body;

(d) the frequency of meetings of the representative body;

(e) the financial and material resources to be allocated to the representative body;

(f) if, during negotiations, the parties decide to establish one or more information and consultation procedures instead of a representative body, the arrangements for implementing those procedures;

(g) if, during negotiations, the parties decide to establish arrangements for participation, the substance of those arrangements including (if applicable) the number of members of the SCE's administrative or supervisory organ which the employees will be entitled to elect, appoint, recommend or oppose, the procedures as to how these members may be elected, appointed, recommended or opposed by the employees, and their rights;

(h) if, where the statute of the SCE so provides, during negotiations the parties decide to establish arrangements for employees or their representatives to participate in and vote in the general meeting or any section or sectorial meetings of the SCE, the substance of those arrangements including (if applicable) the number of employees or representatives who will be entitled to participate, the procedure as to how they are to be elected, appointed, recommended or opposed, and their rights; and

(i) the date of entry into force of the agreement, its duration, the circumstances, if any, in which the agreement is required to be re-negotiated including (where appropriate) in the event of changes in the structure of the SCE or its subsidiaries or establishments, and the procedure for its re-negotiation.

(3) The employee involvement agreement shall not be subject to the standard rules on employee involvement, unless it contains a provision to the contrary.

(4) If the parties decide, in accordance with paragraph (2)(f), to establish one or more information and consultation procedures instead of a representative body and if those

procedures include a provision for representatives to be elected or appointed to act in relation to information and consultation, those representatives shall be "information and consultation representatives".

12 Decisions of the special negotiating body

(1) Each member of the special negotiating body shall have one vote.

(2) Subject to paragraph 13, the special negotiating body shall take decisions by an absolute majority vote.

(3) The special negotiating body must publish the details of any decision taken under this paragraph or under paragraph 13 in such a manner as to bring the decision, so far as reasonably practicable, to the attention of the employees whom it represents and such publication shall take place as soon as reasonably practicable and, in any event no later than 14 days after the decision has been taken.

(4) For the purpose of negotiations, the special negotiating body may be assisted by experts of its choice.

(5) The SCE shall pay for any reasonable expenses of the functioning of the special negotiating body and any reasonable expenses relating to the negotiations that are necessary to enable the special negotiating body to carry out its functions in an appropriate manner but where the special negotiating body is assisted by more than one expert the SCE is not required to pay such expenses in respect of more than one of them.

13 Decision not to open or to terminate negotiations

(1) The special negotiating body may decide, by a two thirds majority vote, not to open negotiations with the competent organ of the SCE or to terminate any such negotiations.

(2) Any decision made under sub-paragraph (1) shall have the following effects—
- (a) the duty in paragraph 10(2) to negotiate with a view to reaching an employee involvement agreement shall cease as from the date of the decision;
- (b) any rules relating to the information and consultation of employees in an EEA State in which employees of the SCE are employed shall apply to the employees of the SCE in that EEA State; and
- (c) the special negotiating body shall be reconvened only if a valid request in accordance with sub-paragraph (3) is made by employees or employees' representatives.

(3) To amount to a valid request, the request referred to in sub-paragraph (2)(c) must—
- (a) be in writing;
- (b) be made by at least 10% of the employees of, or by employees' representatives representing at least 10% of, the total number of employees employed by the SCE and it subsidiaries; and
- (c) be made no earlier than two years after the decision made under sub-paragraph (1) was or should have been published in accordance with paragraph 12(3) unless the special negotiating body and the SCE agrees to the special negotiating body being reconvened earlier.

14 Complaint about decisions of the special negotiating body

(1) If a member of the special negotiating body, an employees' representative, or where there is no such representative in respect of an employee, that employee believes that the special negotiating body has taken a decision referred to in paragraph 12 or 13 and—
- (a) that the decision was not taken by the majority required by paragraph 12 or 13, as the case may be; or
- (b) the special negotiating body failed to publish the decision in accordance with paragraph 12(3),

he may present a complaint to the CAC within 21 days of the date the special negotiating body did or should have published its decision in accordance with paragraph 12(3).

(2) Where the CAC finds the complaint well-founded it shall make a declaration that the decision was not taken properly and that it shall have no effect.

[3463ZQ]

NOTES

Commencement: 18 August 2006.

PART 4
STANDARD RULES ON EMPLOYEE INVOLVEMENT

15 Standard rules on employee involvement

(1) Without prejudice to sub-paragraphs (3) and (4), where this paragraph applies, the competent organ of the SCE and its subsidiaries and establishments shall make arrangements for the involvement of employees of the SCE and its subsidiaries and establishments in accordance with the standard rules on employee involvement.

(2) This paragraph save for sub-paragraph 4, applies in the following circumstances:
(a) where it is agreed that the standard rules on employee involvement shall apply; or
(b) where the period specified in paragraph 10(3)(a) or, where applicable, (b) has expired without an employee involvement agreement having been reached and the special negotiating body has not taken any decision under paragraph 13(1) either not to open or to terminate the negotiations referred to in that regulation.

(3) Paragraph 7(1) of Part 3 of Schedule 2 to these Regulations (standard rules for participation) does not apply and the remaining provisions of that Part only apply if:
(a) a participating legal entity was a party to the formation of the SCE and, before its registration, one or more forms of employee participation existed in the participating legal entity, and,
(b) the special negotiating body has decided that the standard rules for participation will apply to the employees of the SCE.

(4) The standard rule set out in paragraph 7(4) of Part 3 of Schedule 2 to these Regulations shall apply only in the following circumstances—
(a) the SCE is established by means other than conversion;
(b) there is a participating cooperative which, immediately prior to the establishment of the SCE, was governed by a system whereby employees or employee representatives may participate in general meetings or section or sectorial meetings, and that participating cooperative had the highest proportion of participation, within the meaning of regulation 3, in force in the participating cooperatives concerned before registration of the SCE; and
(c) the period specified in paragraph 10(3)(a) or, where applicable, (b) has expired without an employee involvement agreement having been reached, and the special negotiating body has not taken any decision under paragraph 13(1) either not to open or to terminate the negotiations referred to in that paragraph.

[3463ZR]

NOTES

Commencement: 18 August 2006.

SCHEDULE 2
STANDARD RULES ON EMPLOYEE INVOLVEMENT
Regulation 21 and paragraph 15 of Schedule 1

PART 1
COMPOSITION OF THE REPRESENTATIVE BODY

1.—(1) The management of the SCE shall arrange for the establishment of a representative body in accordance with the following provisions—
(a) the representative body shall be composed of employees of the SCE and its subsidiaries and establishments;
(b) the representative body shall be composed of one member for each 10% or fraction thereof of employees of the SCE, its subsidiaries and establishments employed for the time being in each EEA State;
(c) the members of the representative body shall be elected or appointed by the members of the special negotiating body or, in the absence thereof, by the employees; and
(d) the election or appointment shall be carried out by whatever method the special negotiating body decides which should seek to promote gender balance.

2. Where its size so warrants, the representative body shall elect a select committee from among its members comprising at most three members.

3. The representative body shall adopt rules of procedure.

4. The representative body shall inform the competent organ of the SCE of the composition of the representative body and any changes in its composition.

5.—(1) Not later than four years after its establishment, the representative body shall decide whether to open negotiations with the competent organ of the SCE to reach an employee involvement agreement or whether the standard rules in Part 2 and, where applicable, Part 3 of this Schedule shall continue to apply.

(2) Where a decision is taken under sub-paragraph (1) to open negotiations, paragraphs 10 to 12 and paragraph 14 of Schedule 1 shall apply to the representative body as they apply to the special negotiating body.

[3463ZS]

NOTES

Commencement: 18 August 2006.

PART 2

STANDARD RULES FOR INFORMATION AND CONSULTATION

6.—(1) The competence of the representative body shall be limited to questions which concern the SCE itself and any of its subsidiaries or establishments in another EEA State or which exceed the powers of the decision-making organ in a single EEA State.

(2) For information and consultation purposes, the competent organ of the SCE shall—

(a) prepare and provide to the representative body regular reports on the progress of the business of the SCE and the SCE's prospects;

(b) provide the representative body with the agenda for meetings of the administrative or, where appropriate, the management or supervisory organs and copies of all documents submitted to the general meeting of its members; and

(c) inform the representative body when there are exceptional circumstances affecting the employees' interests to a considerable extent, particularly in the event of relocations, transfers, the closure of establishments or undertakings or collective redundancies.

(3) The following provisions shall apply to the relationship between the competent organ and the representative body—

(a) The competent organ shall, if the representative body so desires, meet with that body, without prejudice to paragraph (b) below, at least once a year to discuss the reports referred to in sub-paragraph (2)(a). The meetings shall relate in particular to the structure, economic and financial situation, the probable development of business and of production and sales, the situation and probable trend of employment, investments and substantial changes concerning organisation, introduction of new working methods or production processes, transfers of production, mergers, cut-backs or closures of undertakings, establishments or important parts thereof; collective redundancies; and initiatives with regard to corporate social responsibility;

(b) in the circumstances set out in sub-paragraph (2)(c), the representative body or, where it so decides (in particular, for reasons of urgency), any select committee, is entitled to meet the competent organ of the SCE or any more appropriate level of management within the SCE on request; and

(c) in the event of the competent organ not acting in accordance with the opinion expressed by the representative body, the two bodies shall meet again to seek agreement, if the representative body so wishes.

(4) In the circumstances set out in sub-paragraph (3)(b) above, if the select committee attends the meeting, any other members of the representative body who represent employees who are directly concerned by the measures being discussed also have the right to participate in the meeting.

(5) Before any meeting referred to in sub-paragraph (3), the members of the representative body or the select committee, as the case may be, shall be entitled to meet without the representatives of the competent organ being present.

(6) Without prejudice to regulations 26 and 27, the members of the representative body shall inform the employees' representatives or, if no such representatives exist, the employees of the SCE and its subsidiaries and establishments, of the content and outcome of the information and consultation procedures.

(7) The representative body and any select committee may be assisted by experts of its choice.

(8) The costs of the representative body shall be borne by the SCE which shall provide the members of that body with financial and material resources needed to enable them to perform their duties in an appropriate manner, including (unless agreed otherwise) the cost of organising meetings, providing interpretation facilities and accommodation and travelling expenses. However, where the representative body or the select committee is assisted by more than one expert the SCE is not required to pay the expenses of more than one of them.

[3463ZT]

NOTES

Commencement: 18 August 2006.

PART 3
STANDARD RULES FOR PARTICIPATION

7.—(1) In the case of an SCE formed by conversion, if the rules of an EEA State relating to employee participation in the administrative or supervisory body applied before registration, all aspects of employee participation shall continue to apply to the SCE. Sub-paragraph (3) shall apply with any necessary modifications to that end.

(2) In the case where an SCE is formed other than by conversion and where the employees or the representatives of the employees of at least one of the participating legal entities had participation, the representative body shall have the right to elect, appoint, recommend or oppose the appointment of a number of members of the administrative or supervisory body of the SCE, such number to be equal to the number in the participating legal entity which had the highest proportion of such members.

(3) The following provisions shall apply to the allocation of seats within and membership of the administration or supervisory body—

- (a) subject to paragraph (b), the representative body shall, taking into account the proportion of employees of the SCE employed in each EEA State, decide on the allocation of seats within the administrative or supervisory body, or on the means by which the SCE's employees may recommend or oppose the appointment of the members of these bodies;
- (b) in making the decision set out in paragraph (a), if the employees of one or more EEA State are not included by virtue of the proportional criterion set out in that paragraph, the representative body shall appoint a member from one of those EEA States including one from the EEA State in which the SCE is registered, if appropriate;
- (c) every member of the administrative body or, where appropriate, the supervisory body of the SCE who has been elected, appointed or recommended by the representative body or the employees shall be a full member with the same rights and obligations as the members representing the members of the SCE including the right to vote.

(4) In the case where regulation 21(5) or paragraph 15(4) of Schedule 1 applies, the rules for employees or employees' representatives participating in general meetings or, if applicable, section or sectorial meeting, shall be determined—

- (a) by agreement between the representative body and the competent organ of the SCE; or
- (b) if no such agreement is reached, by the rules applicable to the participating cooperative governed by such a system which has the highest proportion of participation, within the meaning of regulation 3, in force in the participating cooperatives concerned before registration of the SCE.

[3463ZU]

NOTES

Commencement: 18 August 2006.

(*Sch 3* (*Application of the Regulations in relation to Northern Ireland* (*outside the scope of this work*))

STATUTORY PATERNITY PAY AND STATUTORY ADOPTION PAY (GENERAL) AND THE STATUTORY PATERNITY PAY AND STATUTORY ADOPTION PAY (WEEKLY RATES) (AMENDMENT) REGULATIONS 2006 (NOTE)

(SI 2006/2236)

NOTES

These Regulations, which were reproduced in the fifteenth edition of this work, have been omitted for reasons of space.

[3464]–[3464A]

RACE RELATIONS ACT 1976 (STATUTORY DUTIES) ORDER 2006

(SI 2006/2471)

NOTES

Made: 11 September 2006.
Authority: Race Relations Act 1976, s 71(2), (3).
Commencement: 3 October 2006.

1 Citation, commencement and interpretation

(1) This Order may be cited as the Race Relations Act 1976 (Statutory Duties) Order 2006 and shall come into force on 3rd October 2006 immediately after the Race Relations Act 1976 (General Statutory Duty) Order 2006 comes into force.

(2) In this Order—

"the Race Relations Act" means the Race Relations Act 1976; and

"staff" includes any person treated as an employee for the purposes of Part 2 of the Race Relations Act (discrimination in the employment field).

[3465]

NOTES

Commencement: 3 October 2006.

2 Race Equality Schemes

(1) A body or other person specified in the Schedule to this Order shall, before 2nd March 2007, publish a Race Equality Scheme, that is a scheme showing how it intends to fulfil its duties under section 71(1) of the Race Relations Act and this Order.

(2) A Race Equality Scheme shall state, in particular—

(a) those of its functions and policies, or proposed policies, which that person has assessed as relevant to its performance of the duty imposed by section 71(1) of the Race Relations Act; and

(b) that person's arrangements for—

(i) assessing and consulting on the likely impact of its proposed policies on the promotion of race equality;

(ii) monitoring its policies for any adverse impact on the promotion of race equality;

(iii) publishing the results of such assessments and consultation as are mentioned in paragraph (i) and of such monitoring as is mentioned in paragraph (ii);

(iv) ensuring public access to information and services which it provides; and

(v) training staff in connection with the duties imposed by section 71(1) of the Race Relations Act and this Order.

(3) Such a person shall, within a period of three years from 2nd March 2007, and within each further period of three years, review the assessment referred to in paragraph (2)(a).

[3465A]

NOTES

Commencement: 3 October 2006.

3 Monitoring by employers

(1) A person to which this article applies shall,

(a) before 2nd March 2007 have in place arrangements for fulfilling, as soon as is reasonably practicable, its duties under paragraph (2); and

(b) fulfil those duties in accordance with such arrangements.

(2) It shall be the duty of such a person to monitor, by reference to the racial groups to which they belong—

(a) the numbers of—

(i) staff in post, and

(ii) applicants for employment, training and promotion, from each such group, and

(b) where that person has 150 or more full-time staff, the number of staff from each such group who—

(i) receive training;

(ii) benefit or suffer detriment as a result of its performance assessment procedures;

(iii) are involved in grievance procedures;

(iv) are the subject of disciplinary procedures; or

(v) cease employment with that person.

(3) Such a person shall publish annually the results of its monitoring under paragraph (2).

(4) Subject to paragraph (5), this article applies to a body or other person specified in Part 5 of Schedule 1A to the Race Relations Act.

(5) This article does not apply to—

(a) The Office for Fair Access; and

(b) a Scottish public authority with mixed functions or no reserved functions, as referred to section L2 of Part 2 of Schedule 5 to the Scotland Act 1998.

(6) In paragraph (2)(b), the reference to 150 full-time staff is a reference to such number of staff as would, if the hours they work were aggregated, amount to 150 staff working on a full-time basis.

[3465B]

NOTES

Commencement: 3 October 2006.

4 (*Amends the Race Relations Act 1976 (Statutory Duties) Order 2003, SI 2003/3006, Sch 2 at* **[3042]**.)

SCHEDULE

BODIES AND OTHER PERSONS REQUIRED TO PUBLISH RACE EQUALITY SCHEMES BY 2ND MARCH 2007

Article 2(1)

The British Transport Police Authority

The General Medical Council

The Olympic Delivery Authority

The Board of the Pension Protection Fund

The Serious Organised Crime Agency

The Training and Development Agency for Schools.

[3465C]

NOTES

Commencement: 3 October 2006.

LOCAL GOVERNMENT (EARLY TERMINATION OF EMPLOYMENT) (DISCRETIONARY COMPENSATION) (ENGLAND AND WALES) REGULATIONS 2006

(SI 2006/2914)

NOTES

Made: 6 November 2006.
Authority: Superannuation Act 1972, s 24.
Commencement: 29 November 2006 (with effect from 1 October 2006).

ARRANGEMENT OF REGULATIONS

1 Citation, commencement and extent

(1) These Regulations may be cited as the Local Government (Early Termination of Employment) (Discretionary Compensation) (England and Wales) Regulations 2006.

(2) They shall come into force on 29th November 2006 but shall have effect from 1st October 2006 and extend to England and Wales.

[3466]

NOTES

Commencement: 29 November 2006 (with effect from 1 October 2006).

2 Interpretation

(1) In these Regulations—

"the 1996 Act" means the Employment Rights Act 1996;

"the 2000 Regulations" means the Local Government (Early Termination of Employment) (Discretionary Compensation) (England and Wales) Regulations 2000

"employing authority", in relation to a person, means—

(a) a body listed in Schedule 2 (Scheme employers) to the Pension Regulations by whom he is employed immediately before the termination date;

(b) a body listed in regulation 4(6) (resolution bodies) of those Regulations—

(i) by whom he is employed immediately before the termination date; and

(ii) which has passed a relevant resolution, within the meaning of regulation 4(5) of those Regulations, which covers him; or

(c) in the case of a person who is eligible to be a Scheme member under regulation 127(1)(a) or (aa) of the Pension Regulations, the local education authority by whom he is deemed to be employed under regulation 128 of the Pension Regulations.

"employment" includes office but does not include a period as—

(a) the Mayor of London,

(b) a member of the London Assembly, or

(c) a councillor member;

"Pension Regulations" means the Local Government Pension Scheme Regulations 1997;

"Scheme member" means a member of the Local Government Pension Scheme constituted by the Pension Regulations;

"termination date" in relation to a person means the final day of his employment.

(2) Expressions not defined in paragraph (1) but used in these Regulations and in the Pension Regulations have the same meaning as in those Regulations.

[3466A]

NOTES

Commencement: 29 November 2006 (with effect from 1 October 2006).

3 Application to the Isles of Scilly

These Regulations apply to the Isles of Scilly as if they were a district in the county of Cornwall and the Council of the Isles of Scilly were a council of that district.

[3466B]

NOTES

Commencement: 29 November 2006 (with effect from 1 October 2006).

4 Application of the Regulations

(1) Subject to regulation 11(2), these Regulations apply in relation to a person—

(a) whose employment is terminated—

(i) by reason of redundancy,

(ii) in the interests of the efficient exercise of the employing authority's functions, or

(iii) in the case of a joint appointment, because the other holder of the appointment has left it;

(b) who, on the termination date, is—

(i) employed by an employing authority, and

(ii) eligible to be a Scheme member (whether or not he is such a member) or would be so eligible but for the giving of a notification under regulation 8 of the Pension Regulations; and

(c) whose termination date is on or after 1st October 2006,

and in the following provisions of these Regulations, "person" shall be construed accordingly, unless the context indicates that it has a different meaning.

(2) Where an additional requirement is specified in any provision of regulations 5 and 6 in relation to a person, that provision does not apply in relation to him unless he satisfies that additional requirement.

[3466C]

NOTES

Commencement: 29 November 2006 (with effect from 1 October 2006).

5 Power to increase statutory redundancy payments

(1) Compensation may be paid in accordance with this regulation to a person who is entitled to a redundancy payment under the 1996 Act on the termination of his employment.

(2) The amount which may be paid must not be more than the difference between—

(a) the redundancy payment to which he is entitled under Part 11 of the 1996 Act; and

(b) the payment to which he would have been entitled if there had been no limit on the amount of a week's pay used in the calculation of his redundancy payment.

(3) The power to pay compensation is exercisable by the employing authority.

[3466D]

NOTES

Commencement: 29 November 2006 (with effect from 1 October 2006).

6 Discretionary compensation

(1) This regulation applies where a person—

(a) ceases to hold his employment with an employing authority, and

(b) in respect of that cessation may not count an additional period of membership under regulation 52 (power of employing authority to increase total membership of members) of the Pension Regulations.

(2) Where this regulation applies, the employing authority may, not later than six months after the termination date, decide to pay compensation under this regulation and in that event shall, as soon as reasonably practicable after the decision, notify the person in whose favour it has been made, giving details of the amount of the compensation.

(3) The amount of compensation must not exceed 104 weeks' pay.

(4) Chapter 2 (a week's pay) of Part 14 (Interpretation) of the 1996 Act shall apply for the purpose of calculating a person's week's pay as it applies for the purpose of calculating redundancy payments but—

(a) with the substitution for references to the calculation date of references to the termination date; and

(b) without the limit on a week's pay imposed by section 227 of that Act.

(5) If the person in whose favour a decision under paragraph (2) has been made receives a redundancy payment under Part 11 of the 1996 Act or compensation under regulation 5 of these Regulations, the equivalent amount shall be deducted from the compensation otherwise payable to him under this regulation.

(6) Compensation under this regulation shall be paid by the employing authority as soon as practicable after the decision under paragraph (2).

(7) The compensation shall be payable in the form of a lump sum.

[3466E]

NOTES

Commencement: 29 November 2006 (with effect from 1 October 2006).

7 Policy Statements

(1) Each employing authority must formulate, publish and keep under review the policy that they apply in the exercise of their discretionary powers under regulations 5 and 6.

(2) If the authority decide to change their policy, they must publish a statement of the amended policy and may not give effect to any policy change until one month after the date of publication.

(3) In formulating and reviewing their policy the authority must—

(a) have regard to the extent to which the exercise of their discretionary powers (in accordance with the policy), unless properly limited, could lead to a serious loss of confidence in the public service; and

(b) be satisfied that the policy is workable, affordable and reasonable having regard to the foreseeable costs.

[3466F]

NOTES

Commencement: 29 November 2006 (with effect from 1 October 2006).

8 Payments and repayments

(1) Any compensation payable under these Regulations is payable to or in trust for the person entitled to receive it.

(2) Where any compensation is paid in error to any person—

- (a) the employing authority must, as soon as possible after the discovery of the error—
  - (i) inform the person concerned, by notice in writing, giving details of the relevant calculation,
  - (ii) where there has been an underpayment, make a further payment,
  - (iii) where there has been an overpayment, specify a reasonable period for repayment;
- (b) a person who has received a notice under sub-paragraph (a) must repay any overpayment within the specified period; and
- (c) the employing authority may take such steps as they consider appropriate to recover from the person to whom it was paid any overpayment which has not been repaid within the specified period.

(3) The employing authority shall take into account the person's circumstances (so far as known or reasonably ascertainable) before taking steps under paragraph (2)(c).

[3466G]

NOTES

Commencement: 29 November 2006 (with effect from 1 October 2006).

9 Finance

The cost of any payment to be made under these Regulations must not be met out of any pension fund maintained under the Pension Regulations.

[3466H]

NOTES

Commencement: 29 November 2006 (with effect from 1 October 2006).

10 Consequential amendments

Schedule 1 shall have effect for the purpose of making amendments which are consequential on the making of these Regulations.

[3466I]

NOTES

Commencement: 29 November 2006 (with effect from 1 October 2006).

11 Revocation of Regulations, transitional provisions and savings

(1) The following are revoked but subject to the transitional provision in paragraph (2) and the savings in Schedule 2—

- (a) the 2000 Regulations,
- (b) regulation 598 of the Financial Services and Markets Act 2000 (Consequential Amendments and Repeals) Order 2001,
- (c) the Local Government (Early Termination of Employment) (Discretionary Compensation) (England and Wales) (Miscellaneous) Regulations 2002,
- (d) regulation 9(2) of the Local Government Pension Scheme and Discretionary Compensation (Local Authority Members in England) Regulations 2003, and
- (e) regulation 5 of the Local Government Pension Scheme (Civil Partnership) (Amendment) (England and Wales) Regulations 2005

(2) An employing authority may decide to pay compensation under the 2000 Regulations to a person whose employment with them commenced before 1st October 2006 and whose termination date is after 30th September 2006 and before 1st April 2007.

(3) An employing authority may decide to pay compensation under regulation 6 of these Regulations to a person—

- (a) whose employment with them terminated after 30th September 2006 and before the date on which these Regulations come into force, and

(b) in respect of whom a decision to pay lump sum compensation has been made and notified under Part 3 of the 2000 Regulations before the date on which these Regulations come into force ("the 2000 lump sum").

(4) The amount that an employing authority may decide to pay under paragraph (3) may not exceed the difference between—

(a) 104 weeks' pay, and

(b) the 2000 lump sum

but if the person in whose favour a decision under paragraph (3) has been made receives a redundancy payment under Part 11 of the 1996 Act or compensation under regulation 5 of the 2000 Regulations or regulation 5 of these Regulations, the equivalent amount shall be deducted from the compensation otherwise payable to him under paragraph (3) if no such adjustment has already been made.

(5) Nothing in these Regulations shall place any individual who is eligible to participate in the benefits for which the 2000 Regulations provide in a worse position than he would have been in if all the provisions of these Regulations had been framed so as to have effect only from the date of their making.

[3466J]

NOTES

Commencement: 29 November 2006 (with effect from 1 October 2006).

SCHEDULES

(Sch 1 amends the Local Government Reorganisation (Compensation for Loss of Remuneration) Regulations 1995, SI 1995/2837, the Local Government Changes for England (Miscellaneous Provision) Regulations 1996, SI 1996/330, the Local Authorities (Capital Finance and Accounting) (Wales) Regulations 2003, SI 2003/3239, and the Accounts and Audit Regulations 2003, SI 2003/533.)

SCHEDULE 2
SAVINGS

Regulation 11

1. The revocation of the 2000 Regulations does not affect—

(a) any person whose termination date is before 1st October 2006 and who is eligible for compensation under the provisions of those Regulations,

(b) any person to whom an employing authority have decided that compensation shall be paid under those Regulations in accordance with regulation 11(2) of these Regulations, or

(c) the rights of any person who is entitled to benefits under those Regulations in consequence of the death of such a person

and in relation to such persons those Regulations shall continue to apply.

2. Where—

(a) any provision continues to have effect in relation to any person by virtue of paragraph 1, and

(b) immediately before 1st October 2006 it has effect in relation to him subject to any saving, transitional provision or modification

nothing in these Regulations affects the operation of that saving, transitional provision or modification.

3. The revocation by these Regulations of any provision which previously revoked any provision subject to savings does not affect the continued operation of those savings, in so far as they remain capable of having effect.

[3466K]

NOTES

Commencement: 29 November 2006 (with effect from 1 October 2006).

SEX DISCRIMINATION ACT 1975 (PUBLIC AUTHORITIES) (STATUTORY DUTIES) ORDER 2006

(SI 2006/2930)

NOTES

Made: 7 November 2006.

Authority: Sex Discrimination Act 1975, ss 76B(1), 76C(2).

Commencement: 6 April 2007.

This Order applies to England and Wales, and to Scotland to the extent that the functions of the bodies listed in the Schedule extend to Scotland. For the equivalent Scottish Order, applying to bodies subject to the jurisdiction of the Scottish Parliament, see the Sex Discrimination (Public Authorities) (Statutory Duties) (Scotland) Order 2007, SSI 2007/32 at **[3472]**.

ARRANGEMENT OF ARTICLES

1 Citation, commencement and interpretation

(1) This Order may be cited as the Sex Discrimination Act 1975 (Public Authorities) (Statutory Duties) Order 2006 and shall come into force on 6th April 2007 immediately after section 76A of the Sex Discrimination Act 1975.

(2) In this Order—

"listed authority" means a public authority listed in the Schedule to this Order;

"section 76A(1) duty" means the duty of a public authority, under section 76A(1) of the Sex Discrimination Act 1975, in carrying out its functions, to have due regard to the need to eliminate unlawful discrimination and harassment and to promote equality of opportunity between men and women; and

"staff" includes any person treated as an employee for the purposes of Part 2 of the Sex Discrimination Act 1975 (Employment Field).

[3467]

NOTES

Commencement: 6 April 2007.

2 Preparation and publication of a Gender Equality Scheme

(1) A listed authority shall by 30th April 2007 prepare and publish a Gender Equality Scheme (a "Scheme"), that is a scheme showing how it intends to fulfil its section 76A(1) duty and its duties under this Order.

(2) In preparing a Scheme, a listed authority shall consult its employees, service users and others (including trade unions) who appear to it to have an interest in the way it carries out its functions.

(3) In preparing a Scheme, a listed authority shall take into account any information it has gathered of the kind described in paragraph (6)(a) and any other information it considers to be relevant to the performance of its section 76A(1) duty and its duties under this Order.

(4) A listed authority shall ensure that its Scheme sets out the overall objectives which it has identified as being necessary for it to perform its section 76A(1) duty and its duties under this Order.

(5) A listed authority shall, when formulating its objectives for the purposes of paragraph (4), consider the need to have objectives that address the causes of any differences between the pay of men and women that are related to their sex.

(6) A listed authority shall ensure that its Scheme sets out the actions which it has taken or intends to take to—

(a) gather information on the effect of its policies and practices on men and women and in particular—
  (i) the extent to which they promote equality between its male and female staff, and
  (ii) the extent to which the services it provides and the functions it performs take account of the needs of men and women;
(b) make use of such information and any other information the authority considers to be relevant, to assist it in the performance of its section 76A(1) duty, its duties under this Order and in particular its regular review of—
  (i) the effectiveness of the actions identified for the purposes of sub-paragraph (e), and
  (ii) its arrangements for the preparation of subsequent Schemes;
(c) assess the impact of its policies and practices, or the likely impact of its proposed policies and practices, on equality between women and men;
(d) consult relevant employees, service users and others (including trade unions); and
(e) achieve the fulfilment of the objectives set out for the purposes of paragraph (4).

[3467A]

NOTES

Commencement: 6 April 2007.

Modifications: see the Equality Act 2006 (Dissolution of Commissions and Consequential and Transitional Provisions) Order 2007, SI 2007/2602, art 4 (at **[3473N]**) which provides that the Schedule to that Order has effect for the amendment and modification of subordinate legislation in consequence of the dissolution of the Commission for Racial Equality, the Disability Rights Commission and the Equal Opportunities Commission and the establishment of the Commission for Equality and Human Rights. Para 11 of the Schedule to that Order (as substituted by SI 2007/3555) provides that in the application of this Order to the Commission art 2(1) shall have effect as if, for "30th April 2007", there were substituted "1st April 2008".

See also the Offender Management Act 2007 (Consequential Amendments) Order 2008, SI 2008/912, art 3, Sch 2, para 14(3), (4), which provides as follows—

"(3) In its application to a probation trust, article 2(1) shall have effect as if for "by 30th April 2007" there were substituted "within one year from the date of the establishment of a probation trust under section 5(1) of the Offender Management Act 2007".

(4) In its application to a provider of probation services (other than the Secretary of State or a probation trust), in relation to the performance of its statutory functions and the carrying out by it of activities of a public nature in pursuance of arrangements made with it under section 3(2) of the Offender Management Act 2007, article 2(1) shall have effect as if for "by 30th April 2007" there were substituted "within one year from the date on which the provider first entered into arrangements under section 3(2) of the Offender Management Act 2007".".

3 Implementation of the Gender Equality Scheme

(1) A listed authority shall, within the period of three years beginning with the date when a Scheme or a revised Scheme is prepared and published under article 2 or 4, put into effect the actions identified for the purposes of—
(a) article 2(6)(a);
(b) article 2(6)(b); and
(c) article 2(6)(e).

(2) Nothing in this article imposes any requirement on a listed authority where, in all the circumstances, it would be unreasonable or impracticable for it to perform the requirement.

[3467B]

NOTES

Commencement: 6 April 2007.

4 Review of a Gender Equality Scheme

A listed authority shall review its Scheme and prepare and publish a revised Scheme—
(a) not later than the end of the period of three years beginning with the date of publication of its first Scheme; and
(b) subsequently at intervals of not more than three years beginning with the date of publication of the last revision of a Scheme.

[3467C]

NOTES

Commencement: 6 April 2007.

5 Publication of a Gender Equality Scheme as part of another document

A listed authority may comply with the duty to publish under article 2 or 4 by setting out its Scheme as part of another published document or within a number of other published documents.

[3467D]

NOTES

Commencement: 6 April 2007.

6 Annual reporting

(1) A listed authority shall take such steps as are reasonably practicable to publish annually a report summarising the actions that the authority has taken towards the achievement of the objectives identified for the purposes of article 2(4).

(2) Such an authority may comply with the duty to publish under paragraph (1) by setting out its report within another published document.

[3467E]

NOTES

Commencement: 6 April 2007.

SCHEDULE

Article 1(2)

The Advisory, Conciliation and Arbitration Service

Any of the naval, military or air forces of the Crown

The Arts and Humanities Research Council

The Arts Council of England

The Audit Commission for Local Authorities and the National Health Service in England and Wales

The Biotechnology & Biological Sciences Research Council

A body corporate established pursuant to an order under section 67 of the Local Government Act 1985 (transfer of functions to successors of residuary bodies etc)

The British Broadcasting Corporation, in respect of its public functions

The British Council

The British Library

The British Museum

The British Transport Police Authority

The British Waterways Board

The Central Police Training and Development Authority (CENTREX)

The Channel Four Television Corporation, in respect of its public functions

The chief constable for the Ministry of Defence Police appointed by the Secretary of State under section 1(3) of the Ministry of Defence Police Act 1987

A chief constable of a police force maintained under section 2 of the Police Act 1996 for a police area in England

The Children and Family Court Advisory and Support Service

The Children's Commissioner for England

[The Commission for Equality and Human Rights]

The Commission for Healthcare Audit and Inspection

...

The Commission for Social Care Inspection

The Commissioner of Police for the City of London

The Commissioner of Police for the Metropolis

The Common Council of the City of London, in its capacity as a local authority, a police authority or a port health authority

The Construction Industry Training Board

Council for Healthcare Regulatory Excellence

Council for Licensed Conveyancers

In England, a county council, a London borough council or a district council

The Council of the Isles of Scilly

The Council for the Central Laboratory of the Research Councils

The Court of Faculties

...

The Economic & Social Research Council

The Electoral Commission

English Partnerships

The Engineering Construction Industry Training Board

The Engineering & Physical Sciences Research Council

...

The Financial Services Authority

A fire and rescue authority in England constituted by a scheme under section 2 of the Fire and Rescue Services Act 2004 or by a scheme to which section 4 of that Act applies

The General Chiropractic Council

The General Council of the Bar

The General Dental Council

The General Medical Council

The General Optical Council

The General Osteopathic Council

The General Social Care Council

The General Teaching Council for England

The governing body of an educational establishment maintained by a local education authority, in England

The governing body of an institution within the further education sector in England, within the meaning of section 91(3) of the Further and Higher Education Act 1992

The governing body of an institution within the higher education sector in England, within the meaning of section 91(5) of the Further and Higher Education Act 1992

The Greater London Authority

A Health Authority established under section 8 of the National Health Service Act 1977

The Health Protection Agency

...

The Health and Safety Executive

The Higher Education Funding Council for England

The Historic Royal Palaces Trust

The Horniman Museum

A housing action trust for an area of land in England established under Part 3 of the Housing Act 1988

The Housing Corporation

The Human Fertilisation and Embryology Authority

The Imperial War Museum

The Independent Police Complaints Commission

The Institute of Legal Executives

The Institute of Trademark Attorneys

A joint authority in England established under Part 4 of the Local Government Act 1985 (police, fire services, civil defence and transport)

A joint authority in England established under section 21 of the Local Government Act 1992

The Judicial Appointments Commission

The Law Society of England and Wales

The Learning and Skills Council for England

The Legal Services Commission

A local authority with respect to the pupil referral units it establishes and maintains in England by virtue of section 19 of the Education Act 1996

A local education authority in England

A local probation board for an area in England established under section 4 of the Criminal Justice and Court Services Act 2000

The London Development Agency

The London Fire and Emergency Planning Authority

The Medical Research Council

Her Majesty's Inspectorate of Court Administration

The Metropolitan Police Authority established under section 5B of the Police Act 1996

A Minister of the Crown or government department

The Museums Libraries and Archives Council

The Museum of London

The Museum of Science and Industry in Manchester

The National Audit Office

The National College for School Leadership

The National Gallery

A National Health Service trust in England established under section 5 of the National Health Service and Community Care Act 1990

A National Health Service foundation trust established by the Health and Community Care (Community Health and Standards) Act 2003

The National Lottery Commission

The National Maritime Museum

The National Museum for Science and Industry

A National Park Authority for a National Park in England established by an order under section 63 of the Environment Act 1995

The National Portrait Gallery

Natural England

The Natural Environment Research Council

The Natural History Museum

The Nursing and Midwifery Council

Ofcom

The Olympic Delivery Authority

The Particle Physics and Astronomy Research Council

A Passenger Transport Executive for a passenger transport area in England and Wales within the meaning of Part 2 of the Transport Act 1968

A police authority established in England under section 3 of the Police Act 1996

The Postgraduate Medical Education and Training Board

A primary care trust established under section 16A of the National Health Service Act 1977

[A probation trust]

The proprietor of a City Technology College, a City College for Technology of the Arts or an Academy

[A provider of probation services (other than the Secretary of State or a probation trust), in respect of its statutory functions and the carrying out by it of activities of a public nature in pursuance of arrangements made with it under section 3(2) of the Offender Management Act 2007]

The Qualifications and Curriculum Authority (QCA)

The Quality Improvement Agency

A regional development agency established under the Regional Development Agencies Act 1998 (other than the London Development Agency)

Remploy Limited

The Sector Skills Development Agency

The Security Industry Authority

The Serious Organised Crime Agency

Sir John Soane's Museum

The Standards Board for England

Student Loans Company Ltd

The Sub-Treasurer of the Inner Temple or the Under-Treasurer of the Middle Temple, in his capacity as a local authority

The Tate Gallery

The Training and Development Agency for Schools

Transport for London

The UK Film Council

UK Sport

The Victoria and Albert Museum

VisitBritain

The Wallace Collection

[3467F]–[3468D]

NOTES

Commencement: 6 April 2007.

Entry "The Commission for Equality and Human Rights" inserted, and entries "The Commission for Racial Equality", "The Disability Rights Commission", and "The Equal Opportunities Commission" (omitted) revoked, by the Equality Act 2006 (Dissolution of Commissions and Consequential and Transitional Provisions) Order 2007, SI 2007/2602, art 4(1), Schedule, para 12, as from 1 October 2007.

Entry "The Health and Safety Commission" (omitted) revoked by the Legislative Reform (Health and Safety Executive) Order 2008, SI 2008/960, art 22, Sch 3, as from 1 April 2008 (see further the note 'The Health and Safety Executive' at **[2038]**).

Entries "A probation trust" and "A provider of probation services" inserted by the Offender Management Act 2007 (Consequential Amendments) Order 2008, SI 2008/912, art 3, Sch 2, para 14(1), (2), as from 1 April 2008.

Note also that the reference to the Audit Commission for Local Authorities and the National Health Service in England and Wales is to be construed as a reference to the Audit Commission for Local Authorities and the National Health Service in England (as from 1 April 2008); see the Local Government and Public Involvement in Health Act 2007, s 146(4).

COMPENSATION (REGULATED CLAIMS MANAGEMENT SERVICES) ORDER 2006

(SI 2006/3319)

NOTES

Made: 12 December 2006.
Authority: Compensation Act 2006, ss 4(2)(e), 15(1).
Commencement: 13 December 2006.

1 Citation

This Order may be cited as the Compensation (Regulated Claims Management Services) Order 2006.

[3469]

NOTES

Commencement: 13 December 2006.

2 Commencement

This Order comes into force on the day after the day on which it is made.

[3469A]

NOTES

Commencement: 13 December 2006.

3 Definition—"the Act"

In this Order, "the Act" means the Compensation Act 2006.

[3469B]

NOTES

Commencement: 13 December 2006.

4 Regulated services

(1) For the purposes of Part 2 of the Act, services of a kind specified in paragraph (2) are prescribed if rendered in relation to the making of a claim of a kind described in paragraph (3), or in relation to a cause of action that may give rise to such a claim.

(2) The kinds of service are the following—

(a) advertising for, or otherwise seeking out (for example, by canvassing or direct marketing), persons who may have a cause of action;

(b) advising a claimant or potential claimant in relation to his claim or cause of action;

(c) subject to paragraph (4), referring details of a claim or claimant, or a cause of action or potential claimant, to another person, including a person having the right to conduct litigation;

(d) investigating, or commissioning the investigation of, the circumstances, merits or foundation of a claim, with a view to the use of the results in pursuing the claim;

(e) representation of a claimant (whether in writing or orally, and regardless of the tribunal, body or person to or before which or whom the representation is made).

(3) The kinds of claim are the following—

(a) claims for personal injuries, within the meaning in the Civil Procedure Rules 1998;

(b) claims under the Criminal Injuries Compensation Scheme established under the Criminal Injuries Compensation Act 1995;

(c) claims for a benefit specified or referred to in article 3 of the Compensation (Specification of Benefits) Order 2006;

(d) claims in relation to employment (including claims in relation to wages and salaries and other employment-related payments, and claims in relation to wrongful or unfair dismissal, redundancy, discrimination and harassment);

(e) claims for housing disrepair (that is, claims under section 11 of the Landlord and Tenant Act 1985 or section 4 of the Defective Premises Act 1972, claims in relation to the disrepair of premises under a term of a tenancy agreement or lease or under the common law relating to nuisance or negligence, but not claims for statutory nuisance under section 82 of the Environmental Protection Act 1990);

(f) claims in relation to financial products or services.

(4) In spite of paragraph (2)(c), the service of referring a claim's or a claimant's details to another person is not a regulated claims management service if it is not undertaken for or in expectation of a fee, gain or reward.

[3469C]

NOTES

Commencement: 13 December 2006.

EMPLOYMENT ACT 2002 (AMENDMENT OF SCHEDULES 3, 4 AND 5) ORDER 2007

(SI 2007/30)

NOTES

Made: 9 January 2007.
Authority: Employment Act 2002, ss 31(7), 32(8), 38(8), 51(1)(a), (b).
Commencement: 6 April 2007.

1 Citation and Commencement

This Order may be cited as the Employment Act 2002 (Amendment of Schedules 3, 4 and 5) Order 2007 and shall come into force on 6th April 2007.

[3470]

NOTES

Commencement: 6 April 2007.

2 (*Amends the Employment Act 2002, Schs 3–5 at* **[1508]–[1510]**.)

3 Transitional Provisions

This Order shall apply—

(a) in relation to dismissal and disciplinary action, where the employer first contemplates dismissing or taking disciplinary action against the employee after this Order comes into force; and

(b) in relation to grievances, where the action about which the employee complains occurs or continues after this Order comes into force,

but shall not apply in relation to a grievance where the action continues after this Order comes into force if the employee has raised a grievance about the action with the employer or has presented a complaint to the employment tribunal about the grievance before it came into force.

[3470A]

NOTES
Commencement: 6 April 2007.

COMPENSATION (EXEMPTIONS) ORDER 2007

(SI 2007/209)

NOTES
Made: 30 January 2007.
Authority: Compensation Act 2006, s 6.
Commencement: 31 January 2007.

ARRANGEMENT OF ARTICLES

1 Citation

This Order may be cited as the Compensation (Exemptions) Order 2007.

[3471]

NOTES
Commencement: 31 January 2007.

2 Commencement

This Order comes into force on the day after the day on which it is made.

[3471A]

NOTES
Commencement: 31 January 2007.

3 Definition "the Act"

In this Order, "the Act" means the Compensation Act 2006.

[3471B]

NOTES
Commencement: 31 January 2007.

4 Legal practitioners

(1) Section 4(1) of the Act does not prevent the provision of a regulated claims management service in the circumstances that—

(a) the service is provided—

(i) by a legal practitioner;

(ii) by a firm, organisation or body corporate that provides the service through a legal practitioner; or

(iii) by an individual who provides the service at the direction, and under the supervision, of a legal practitioner who is—

(aa) his employer or fellow employee; or

(bb) a director of a company, or a member of a limited liability partnership, that provides the service and is his employer; and

(b) the legal practitioner acts in the normal course of practice in a way permitted by the professional rules to which he is subject.

(2) In paragraph (1), "legal practitioner" means—

(a) a solicitor, barrister or advocate of any part of the United Kingdom;

(b) a Fellow of the Institute of Legal Executives;

(c) a European lawyer, as defined in the European Communities (Services of Lawyers) Order 1978;

(d) a registered foreign lawyer, as defined in section 89(9) of the Courts and Legal Services Act 1990; or

(e) any other member of a legal profession, of a jurisdiction other than England and Wales, that is recognised by the Law Society or the General Council of the Bar as a regulated legal profession.

[3471C]

NOTES

Commencement: 31 January 2007.

5 Persons providing services regulated under the Financial Services and Markets Act 2000

(1) Section 4(1) of the Act does not prevent the provision of a regulated claims management service by a person if in providing that service, he is carrying on a regulated activity for the purposes of section 19 of the Financial Services and Markets Act 2000 ("FSMA"), or would be doing so except that—

(a) he is an exempt person (that is, a person who is exempt from the general prohibition under FSMA), or

(b) he has the benefit of an exclusion under the Financial Services and Markets Act 2000 (Regulated Activities) Order 2001.

(2) In paragraph (1)(a),"general prohibition" has the meaning given by FSMA.

(3) References in paragraph (1) to a regulated activity carried on by a person must be read with—

(a) section 22 of FSMA;

(b) any relevant order under that section; and

(c) Schedule 2 to FSMA.

[3471D]

NOTES

Commencement: 31 January 2007.

6 Charities and not-for-profit advice agencies

(1) Section 4(1) of the Act does not prevent the provision of a regulated claims management service by a not for profit body, that is, a body that, by or under its constitution—

(a) is required to apply the whole of its net income, and any expendable capital, after payment of outgoings for charitable or public purposes; and

(b) subject to paragraph (2), is prohibited from distributing, directly or indirectly, any part of its net income by way of profits, or its assets, among any of its members.

(2) A body is not prevented from being a not-for-profit body for the purposes of paragraph (1) if its constitution permits:

(a) the payment, out of the body's funds, of reasonable and proper remuneration for goods or services supplied to the body by a member;

(b) in the case of a not-for-profit body that is a charity, the payment to a member of a benefit to which he is entitled because he is a beneficiary of the charity; or

(c) the purchase, out of the body's funds, of indemnity insurance for trustees of the body.

[3471E]

NOTES

Commencement: 31 January 2007.

7 Independent Complaints Reviewers

Section 4(1) of the Act does not prevent the provision of a regulated claims management service by a person appointed from time to time by a statutory or other public body as an Independent Complaints Reviewer or Independent Case Examiner in the course of carrying out her duties under the appointment.

[3471F]

NOTES

Commencement: 31 January 2007.

8 Motor Insurers Bureau

Section 4(1) of the Act does not prevent the provision of a regulated claims management service by the Motor Insurers Bureau (being the company limited by guarantee mentioned in section 95(2) of the Road Traffic Act 1988).

[3471G]

NOTES

Commencement: 31 January 2007.

9 Medical Protection Society and medical defence unions

Section 4(1) of the Act does not prevent the provision of a regulated claims management service—

(a) by the Medical Protection Society Limited to its members;
(b) by The Medical Defence Union Ltd to its members; or
(c) by The Medical and Dental Defence Union of Scotland Limited to its members.

[3471H]

NOTES

Commencement: 31 January 2007.

10 Independent trade unions

(1) Section 4(1) of the Act does not prevent the provision of a regulated claims management service by an independent trade union to—

(a) a member (including a retired member or a student member) of the trade union;
(b) a member of the family of a member referred to in sub-paragraph (a); or
(c) a former member of the trade union to whom the trade union may, under its rules, provide claims management services, or a member of the family of such a former member.

(2) In paragraph (1), "independent trade union" has the same meaning as in the Trade Union and Labour Relations (Consolidation) Act 1992.

(3) For the purposes of paragraph (1)—

(a) subject to sub-paragraph (b), whether a person is or has been a member (including a retired member or a student member) of a trade union is to be decided in accordance with the rules of the trade union;
(b) "member" of a trade union does not include a person who, under those rules, is a member only for the purpose of pursuing a claim or claims; and
(c) whether a person is a member of the family of a member of a trade union is to be decided in accordance with the rules of the trade union.

(4) An exemption of a trade union under this article is subject to compliance by the trade union with the condition that the trade union, in providing regulated claims management

services, must act in accordance with the code of practice for the provision of regulated claims management services by trade unions issued by the Secretary of State on 28th November 2006.

[3471I]

NOTES

Commencement: 31 January 2007.

11 Students' unions

Section 4(1) of the Act does not prevent the provision of a regulated claims management service by a students' union (as defined in section 20 of the Education Act 1994) to a member of the students' union or (in the case of a students' union referred to in section 20(3) of that Act) a member of a constituent or affiliated association or body.

[3471J]

NOTES

Commencement: 31 January 2007.

12 Certain providers of referrals

(1) In this article, "legal practitioner" has the meaning given by article 4(2).

(2) Section 4(1) of the Act does not prevent the provision of the regulated claims management service of referring details of potential claims or potential claimants to another person if—

- (a) the person who refers those details ("the introducer") provides no other regulated claims management service;
- (b) the provision of the service is incidental to the introducer's main business;
- (c) the details are referred to authorised persons or legal practitioners or firms of legal practitioners;
- (d) the introducer refers such details only to persons of those kinds;
- (e) of the cases that the introducer refers to such persons, he is paid, in money or money's worth, for no more than 25 cases per calendar quarter; and
- (f) subject to paragraph (3), the persons to which the details are referred must be satisfied that the introducer obtains those details in a way consistent with the rules prescribed by the Regulator under paragraph 8 of the Schedule to the Act.

(3) Paragraph (2)(f) does not apply in the case of a referral to a legal practitioner or firm of legal practitioners.

[3471K]

NOTES

Commencement: 31 January 2007.

[13 Exemption for claims in certain circumstances

Section 4(1) of the Act does not prevent the provision of a regulated claims management service in the circumstances that—

- (a) a claim has been made by a person ("the claimant") against another person ("the defendant"); and
- (b) the service is provided to the defendant in connection with—
  - (i) the making of a counterclaim against the claimant arising out of the same set of facts as the claim referred to in sub-paragraph (a); or
  - (ii) the making of a claim against a third party (whether for contribution, as a subrogated claim, or otherwise) which is incidental to, or consequent on, the claim referred to in sub-paragraph (a).]

[3471L]

NOTES

Commencement: 23 April 2007.

Added by the Compensation (Exemptions) (Amendment) (No 1) Order 2007, SI 2007/1090, art 3, as from 23 April 2007.

SEX DISCRIMINATION (PUBLIC AUTHORITIES) (STATUTORY DUTIES) (SCOTLAND) ORDER 2007

(SSI 2007/32)

NOTES

Made: 30 January 2007.
Authority: Sex Discrimination Act 1975, ss 76C(3), 81(4).
Commencement: 9 April 2007.
This Order applies only to the bodies specified in the Schedule; for the corresponding Order covering bodies outside of the jurisdiction of the Scottish Parliament, see the Sex Discrimination Act 1975 (Public Authorities) (Statutory Duties) Order 2006, SI 2006/2930 at **[3467]**.

ARRANGEMENT OF ARTICLES

1 Citation, commencement and interpretation

(1) This Order may be cited as the Sex Discrimination (Public Authorities) (Statutory Duties) (Scotland) Order 2007 and shall come into force on 9th April 2007.

(2) In this Order—

"education authority", "grant-aided school", "independent school", "pupil", "school age" and "school education" have the meanings respectively given by section 135 of the Education (Scotland) Act 1980;

"listed authority" means a public authority listed in either of Parts I or II of the Schedule to this Order;

references to "150 full-time staff" are references to such number of staff as would, if the hours they work were aggregated, amount to 150 staff working on a full-time basis;

"relevant Scottish authority" has the meaning contained in section 76C(9) of the Sex Discrimination Act 1975;

"Scheme" means a gender equality scheme prepared in accordance with article 2;

"school" has the meaning given by section 135 of the Education (Scotland) Act 1980, and includes a place (other than a school as so defined) at which an education authority provides school education for pupils who are under school age, but excluding—

(a) any independent school; and

(b) such a place (other than a school as so defined) at which school education is being provided by a person with whom that authority has, by virtue of section 35 of the Standards in Scotland's Schools etc Act 2000 entered into arrangements for the provision of that education; and

"section 76A(1) duty", in relation to a public authority, means its duty under section 76A(1) of the Sex Discrimination Act 1975 (public authorities: general statutory duty);

"staff" includes any person treated as an employee for the purposes of Part 2 of the Sex Discrimination Act 1975 (Employment Field).

[3472]

NOTES

Commencement: 9 April 2007.

2 Preparation and publication of a gender equality scheme

(1) A listed authority shall, on or before 29th June 2007, prepare and publish a Scheme which shows how it intends to fulfil its section 76A(1) duty and its duties under this Order.

(2) In preparing a Scheme, a listed authority shall consult staff, service users and others (including trade unions), who appear to that authority to have an interest in the way the authority carries out its functions.

(3) In preparing a Scheme, a listed authority shall take into account any information it has gathered of the kind described in paragraph (6)(a) and any other information the authority considers to be relevant to the performance of its section 76A(1) duty and its duties under this Order.

(4) A listed authority shall ensure that its Scheme sets out the overall objectives which that authority has identified as being necessary for it to perform its section 76A(1) duty and its duties under this Order.

(5) A listed authority shall, when formulating its objectives for the purposes of paragraph (4), consider the need to have objectives that address the causes of any differences between the pay of men and women that are related to their sex.

(6) A listed authority shall ensure that its Scheme sets out the actions which that authority has taken or intends to take to—

- (a) gather information on the effect of its policies and practices on men and women and in particular—
  - (i) the extent to which they promote equality between male and female staff, and
  - (ii) the extent to which the services it provides and the functions it performs take account of the needs of men and women;
- (b) make use of such information, and any other information the authority considers to be relevant, to assist it in the performance of its section 76A(1) duty, its duties under this Order and in particular its regular review of—
  - (i) the effectiveness of the actions identified for the purposes of sub-paragraph (e), and
  - (ii) its arrangements for the preparation of subsequent Schemes;
- (c) assess the impact of its policies and practices, or the likely impact of its proposed policies and practices, on equality between women and men and (so far as reasonable and practicable to do so) to have due regard to the results of such assessments of impact;
- (d) consult relevant staff, service users and others (including trade unions); and
- (e) achieve the fulfilment of the objectives set out for the purposes of paragraph (4).

[3472A]

NOTES

Commencement: 9 April 2007.

3 Implementation of the gender equality scheme

(1) A listed authority shall within the period of three years beginning with the date when a Scheme or a revised Scheme is prepared and published for the purposes of articles 2 or 4 put into effect the actions identified for the purposes of article 2(6)(a), (b) and (e).

(2) Nothing in this article imposes any requirement on a listed authority where, in all the circumstances, it would be unreasonable or impracticable for it to perform the requirement.

[3472B]

NOTES

Commencement: 9 April 2007.

4 Review of a gender equality scheme

A listed authority shall review its Scheme and prepare and publish a revised Scheme—

- (a) not later than the end of the period of three years beginning with the date of publication of its first Scheme; and
- (b) subsequently at intervals of not more than three years beginning with the date of publication of the last revision of a Scheme.

[3472C]

NOTES
Commencement: 9 April 2007.

5 Annual reporting

(1) A listed authority shall publish reports summarising the actions that the authority has taken towards the achievement of the objectives identified for the purposes of article 2(4)—

(a) not later than the end of the period of one year beginning with the date of publication of its first Scheme; and

(b) subsequently at intervals of not more than one year beginning with the date of publication of the last report.

(2) Such an authority may comply with the duty to publish under paragraph (1) by setting out its report within another published document.

[3472D]

NOTES
Commencement: 9 April 2007.

6 Preparation and publication of an equal pay statement

A listed authority which has at least 150 full time staff in total shall, on or before 28th September 2007, prepare and publish an equal pay statement which states that authority's policy on equal pay between men and women.

[3472E]

NOTES
Commencement: 9 April 2007.

7 Review of an equal pay statement

Where a listed authority is required to publish an equal pay statement in terms of article 6, the authority shall review its equal pay statement and publish a report on its equal pay policy—

(a) not later than the end of the period of 3 years beginning with the date of publication of its first equal pay statement; and

(b) subsequently at intervals of not more than 3 years beginning with the date of publication of the last revision of the equal pay statement.

[3472F]

NOTES
Commencement: 9 April 2007.

8 Publication of a gender equality scheme and equal pay statement

A listed authority may comply with the duties to publish under articles 2, 4, 6 and 7 by setting out its Scheme or equal pay statement as part of another published document or within a number of other published documents.

[3472G]

NOTES
Commencement: 9 April 2007.

9 Duty on the Scottish Ministers

(1) The Scottish Ministers shall publish reports—

(a) not later than 1st July 2010; and

(b) subsequently not later than the end of each successive period of 3 years beginning with 1st July 2010.

(2) These reports shall—

(a) set out the priority areas across the functions and activities of relevant Scottish authorities that the Scottish Ministers have identified for the advancement of equality of opportunity between men and women in Scotland; and

(b) provide an overview of progress in those priority areas toward equality of opportunity between men and women.

[3472H]

NOTES

Commencement: 9 April 2007.

10 School education bodies and persons

A body or person specified in Part II of the Schedule shall make arrangements for each school under its management to—

(a) gather information on the effect of its policies and practices in relation to the extent to which they promote equality between male and female pupils;

(b) assess the impact of its policies and practices, or the likely impact of its proposed policies and practices, on equality between male and female pupils;

(c) provide such a body or person with an annual report in respect of the matters contained in paragraphs (a) and (b);

(d) carry out such steps which that body or person proposes to take toward the fulfilment of its section 76A(1) duty; and

(e) maintain a copy of the Scheme.

[3472I]

NOTES

Commencement: 9 April 2007.

SCHEDULE

PART I

The Accounts Commission for Scotland

Audit Scotland

The Board of Trustees for the National Galleries of Scotland established under section 3 of the National Galleries of Scotland Act 1906

The Board of Trustees of the National Museums of Scotland established by the National Heritage (Scotland) Act 1985

Bòrd na Gàidhlig

The Cairngorms National Park Authority established under section 6 of the National Parks (Scotland) Act 2000

A Chief Constable of a police force maintained under section 1 of the Police (Scotland) Act 1967

A Chief Officer of a relevant authority appointed under section 7 of the Fire (Scotland) Act 2005;

A council constituted under section 2 of the Local Government etc (Scotland) Act 1994

Fundable Bodies as specified in schedule 2 to the Further and Higher Education (Scotland) Act 2005

A Health Board constituted under section 2 of the National Health Service (Scotland) Act 1978

A joint board within the meaning of section 235(1) of the Local Government (Scotland) Act 1973

A joint fire and rescue board constituted by a scheme under section 2(1) of the Fire (Scotland) Act 2005

The Keeper of the Records of Scotland

The Keeper of the Registers of Scotland

The Law Society of Scotland, in respect of its public functions

Learning and Teaching Scotland

A licensing board constituted under section 1 of the Licensing (Scotland) Act 1976

The Loch Lomond and the Trossachs National Park Authority established under section 6 of the National Parks (Scotland) Act 2000

The managers of a central institution within the meaning of section 135 of the Education (Scotland) Act 1980

The Mental Welfare Commission for Scotland

NHS National Services Scotland

A police authority established under section 2 of the Police (Scotland) Act 1967

The Registrar General of Births, Deaths and Marriages for Scotland

The Scottish Arts Council

The Scottish Commission for the Regulation of Care

Scottish Enterprise and Highlands and Islands Enterprise established under the Enterprise and New Towns (Scotland) Act 1990

The Scottish Further and Higher Education Funding Council

The Scottish Legal Aid Board

The Scottish Ministers

Scottish Natural Heritage

The Scottish Qualifications Authority

Scottish Screen

The Scottish Social Services Council

The Scottish Sports Council

The Scottish Tourist Board

Scottish Water

A Special Health Board constituted under section 2 of the National Health Service (Scotland) Act 1978

Transport Partnerships established under section 1 of the Transport (Scotland) Act 2005

The Trustees of the National Library of Scotland, constituted under section 1 of the National Library of Scotland Act 1925

[3472J]

NOTES

Commencement: 9 April 2007.

PART II

Education authorities

The managers of a grant-aided school

[3472K]

NOTES

Commencement: 9 April 2007.

SMOKE-FREE (EXEMPTIONS AND VEHICLES) REGULATIONS 2007

(SI 2007/765)

NOTES

Made: 7 March 2007.
Authority: Health Act 2006, ss 3, 5, 79(3).

Commencement: 1 July 2007.

These Regulations apply only in relation to England (see reg 1(2)). See also the Smoke-free Premises etc (Wales) Regulations 2007, SI 2007/787, which came into force on 2 April 2007 (omitted for reasons of space). As to the equivalent provisions for Scotland, see the Prohibition of Smoking in Certain Premises (Scotland) Regulations 2006, SSI 2006/90 at **[3370]**.

ARRANGEMENT OF REGULATIONS

PART 1
GENERAL

PART 2
EXEMPTIONS

PART 3
VEHICLES

PART 1
GENERAL

1 Citation, commencement and application

(1) These Regulations which may be cited as the Smoke-free (Exemptions and Vehicles) Regulations 2007 shall come into force on 1st July 2007.

(2) These Regulations apply in relation to England.

[3473]

NOTES

Commencement: 1 July 2007.

PART 2
EXEMPTIONS

2 Application of Part 2

The exemptions in this Part apply only to premises that would be smoke-free under section 2 of the Health Act 2006 if those exemptions had not been made.

[3473A]

NOTES

Commencement: 1 July 2007.

3 Private accommodation

(1) A private dwelling is not smoke-free except for any part of it which is—

(a) used in common in relation to more than one set of premises (including premises so used in relation to any other private dwelling or dwellings); or

(b) used solely as a place of work (other than work that is excluded by paragraph (2)) by—

(i) more than one person who does not live in the dwelling;

(ii) a person who does not live in the dwelling and any person who does live in the dwelling; or

(iii) a person (whether he lives in the dwelling or not) who in the course of his work invites persons who do not live or work in the dwelling to attend the part of it which is used solely for work.

(2) There is excluded from paragraph (1)(b) all work that is undertaken solely—

(a) to provide personal care for a person living in the dwelling;

(b) to assist with the domestic work of the household in the dwelling;

(c) to maintain the structure or fabric of the dwelling; or

(d) to install, maintain or remove any service provided to the dwelling for the benefit of persons living in it.

(3) In this regulation, "private dwelling" includes self-contained residential accommodation for temporary or holiday use and any garage, outhouse or other structure for the exclusive use of persons living in the dwelling.

[3473B]

NOTES

Commencement: 1 July 2007.

4 Accommodation for guests and club members

(1) A designated bedroom in a hotel, guest house, inn, hostel or members' club is not smoke-free.

(2) In this regulation "a designated bedroom" means a room which—

(a) is set apart exclusively for sleeping accommodation;

(b) has been designated in writing by the person having the charge of the premises in which the room is situated as being a room in which smoking is permitted;

(c) has a ceiling and, except for doors and windows, is completely enclosed on all sides by solid, floor-to-ceiling walls;

(d) does not have a ventilation system that ventilates into any other part of the premises (except any other designated bedrooms);

(e) does not have any door that opens onto smoke-free premises which is not mechanically closed immediately after use; and

(f) is clearly marked as a bedroom in which smoking is permitted.

(3) In this regulation "bedroom" does not include any dormitory or other room that a person in charge of premises makes available under separate arrangements for persons to share at the same time.

[3473C]

NOTES

Commencement: 1 July 2007.

5 Other residential accommodation

(1) A designated room that is used as accommodation for persons aged 18 years or over in the premises specified in paragraph (2) is not smoke-free.

(2) The specified premises are—

(a) care homes as defined in section 3 (care homes) of the Care Standards Act 2000;

(b) hospices which as their whole or main purpose provide palliative care for persons resident there who are suffering from progressive disease in its final stages; and

(c) prisons.

(3) In this regulation "designated room" means a bedroom or a room used only for smoking which—

(a) has been designated in writing by the person having charge of the premises in which the room is situated as being a room in which smoking is permitted;

(b) has a ceiling and, except for doors and windows, is completely enclosed on all sides by solid, floor-to-ceiling walls;
(c) does not have a ventilation system that ventilates into any other part of the premises (except any other designated rooms);
(d) is clearly marked as a room in which smoking is permitted; and
(e) except where the room is in a prison, does not have any door that opens onto smoke-free premises which is not mechanically closed immediately after use.

[3473D]

NOTES

Commencement: 1 July 2007.

6 Performers

Where the artistic integrity of a performance makes it appropriate for a person who is taking part in that performance to smoke, the part of the premises in which that person performs is not smoke-free in relation to that person during his performance.

[3473E]

NOTES

Commencement: 1 July 2007.

7 Specialist tobacconists

(1) The shop of a specialist tobacconist that is being used by persons who are sampling cigars and pipe tobacco is not smoke-free for the duration of that sampling if it—
(a) has a ceiling and, except for doors and windows, is completely enclosed on all sides by solid, floor-to-ceiling walls;
(b) does not have a ventilation system that ventilates into any smoke-free premises;
(c) does not have any door that opens onto smoke-free premises which is not mechanically closed immediately after use; and
(d) is clearly marked as premises in which smoking is permitted.

(2) In this regulation "cigar" has the same meaning as in the Tobacco Products (Descriptions of Products) Order 2003 and "specialist tobacconist" has the same meaning as in section 6(2) of the Tobacco Advertising and Promotion Act 2002.

[3473F]

NOTES

Commencement: 1 July 2007.

8 Offshore installations

(1) A designated room in an offshore installation is not smoke-free.

(2) In this regulation a "designated room" means a room used only for smoking which—
(a) has been designated in writing by the person in charge of the installation in which the room is situated as being a room in which smoking is permitted;
(b) has a ceiling and, except for doors and windows, is completely enclosed on all sides by solid, floor-to-ceiling walls;
(c) does not have a ventilation system that ventilates into any other part of the premises (except any other designated rooms);
(d) does not have any door that opens onto smoke-free premises which is not mechanically closed immediately after use; and
(e) is clearly marked as a room in which smoking is permitted.

[3473G]

NOTES

Commencement: 1 July 2007.

9 Research and testing facilities

(1) A designated room in a research or testing facility is not smoke-free whilst it is being used for any research or tests specified in paragraph (2).

(2) The research or tests that are specified are those that relate to—

(a) emissions from tobacco and other products used for smoking;

(b) development of products for smoking with lower fire hazards;

(c) the fire safety testing of materials involving products for smoking;

(d) development of smoking or pharmaceutical products that could result in the manufacture of less dangerous products for smoking; or

(e) smoking cessation programmes.

(3) In this regulation a "designated room" means a room which—

(a) has been designated in writing by the person in charge of the research or testing facility in which the room is situated as being a room in which smoking is permitted for research or tests specified in paragraph (2) and is a room for the use only of the persons who are required to supervise or participate in the research or tests;

(b) has a ceiling and, except for doors and windows, is completely enclosed on all sides by solid, floor-to-ceiling walls;

(c) does not have a ventilation system that ventilates into any other part of the premises or other premises (except any other designated rooms);

(d) does not have any door that opens onto smoke-free premises which is not mechanically closed immediately after use; and

(e) is clearly marked as a room in which smoking is permitted.

[3473H]

NOTES

Commencement: 1 July 2007.

10 Temporary exemption for mental health units

(1) A designated room for the use of patients aged 18 years or over in residential accommodation in a mental health unit is not smoke-free.

(2) In this regulation—

"designated room" means a bedroom or a room used only for smoking which—

(a) has been designated in writing by the person in charge of the mental health unit as being a room in which smoking is permitted;

(b) has a ceiling and, except for doors and windows, is completely enclosed on all sides by solid, floor-to-ceiling walls;

(c) does not have a ventilation system that ventilates into any other part of the premises (except any other designated room);

(d) is clearly marked as a room in which smoking is permitted; and

(e) does not have any door that opens on to smoke-free premises which is not mechanically closed immediately after use; and

"mental health unit" means any establishment (or part of an establishment) maintained wholly or mainly for the reception and treatment of persons suffering from any form of mental disorder as defined in section 1(2) of the Mental Health Act 1983.

(3) Paragraphs (1) and (2) shall cease to have effect on 1st July 2008.

[3473I]

NOTES

Commencement: 1 July 2007.

PART 3
VEHICLES

11 Enclosed vehicles

(1) Subject to the following paragraphs of this regulation, an enclosed vehicle and any enclosed part of a vehicle is smoke-free if it is used—

(a) by members of the public or a section of the public (whether or not for reward or hire); or

(b) in the course of paid or voluntary work by more than one person (even if those persons use the vehicle at different times, or only intermittently).

(2) A vehicle or part of a vehicle is enclosed for the purposes of paragraph (1) where it is enclosed wholly or partly by a roof and by any door or window that may be opened.

(3) Except where paragraph (4) applies, "roof" in paragraph (2) includes any fixed or moveable structure or device which is capable of covering all or part of the vehicle, including any canvas, fabric or other covering.

(4) In relation to a vehicle that is engaged in conveying persons, "roof" does not include any fixed or moveable structure or device which is completely stowed away so that it does not cover all or any part of the vehicle.

(5) A vehicle is not used in the course of paid or voluntary work for the purposes of paragraph (1)(b) where it is used primarily for the private purposes of a person who—
- (a) owns it; or
- (b) has a right to use it which is not restricted to a particular journey.

(6) This regulation applies to all vehicles other than—
- (a) aircraft; or
- (b) ships or hovercraft in respect of which regulations could be made under section 85 of the Merchant Shipping Act 1995 (safety and health on ships), including that section as applied by any Order in Council under section 1(1)(h) of the Hovercraft Act 1968 or to persons on any such ships or hovercraft.

[3473J]

NOTES
Commencement: 1 July 2007.

EQUALITY ACT 2006 (DISSOLUTION OF COMMISSIONS AND CONSEQUENTIAL AND TRANSITIONAL PROVISIONS) ORDER 2007

(SI 2007/2602)

NOTES
Made: 7 September 2007.
Authority: Equality Act 2006, ss 36(1)(a), 39(2)(c), 42(1)(b).
Commencement: 1 October 2007.

1 Citation, commencement and extent

(1) This Order may be cited as the Equality Act 2006 (Dissolution of Commissions and Consequential and Transitional Provisions) Order 2007 and shall come into force on 1st October 2007.

(2) This Order does not extend to Northern Ireland.

[3473K]

NOTES
Commencement: 1 October 2007.

2 Interpretation

In this Order—

"the 1975 Act" means the Sex Discrimination Act 1975;
"the 1976 Act" means the Race Relations Act 1976;
"the 1999 Act" means the Disability Rights Commission Act 1999;
"the 2006 Act" means the Equality Act 2006;
except in paragraph (2) of article 4 "the Commission" means the Commission for Equality and Human Rights; and
"the former Commissions" means the Commission for Racial Equality, the Disability Rights Commission and the Equal Opportunities Commission.

[3473L]

NOTES
Commencement: 1 October 2007.

3 Dissolution of former Commissions

The former Commissions shall cease to exist.

[3473M]

NOTES

Commencement: 1 October 2007.

4 Consequential amendments and modifications

(1) The Schedule to this Order shall have effect for the amendment and modification of subordinate legislation in consequence of the dissolution of the former Commissions and the establishment of the Commission.

(2) Section 61 of the 1975 Act (restriction on disclosure of information), section 52 of the 1976 Act (restriction on disclosure of information) and paragraph 22 of Schedule 3 to the 1999 Act (restriction on disclosure of information) shall apply in relation to the Commission for Equality and Human Rights as if—

(a) references to the Commission include the Commission for Equality and Human Rights;

(b) references to Commissioner include commissioners of the Commission for Equality and Human Rights;

(c) references to additional Commissioners include Investigating Commissioners under paragraph 9 of Schedule 1 to the 2006 Act; and

(d) references to employees of the Commission include employees of the Commission for Equality and Human Rights.

[3473N]

NOTES

Commencement: 1 October 2007.

5 Transitional provisions: the Commission and the functions of the former Commissions

(1) The Commission shall discharge the functions of the former Commissions—

(a) in relation to section 56 of the 1975 Act (annual reports), in so far as those functions relate to the calendar year ending 31st December 2007 and have not been discharged before 1st October 2007, until the Secretary of State has laid a copy of the annual report before Parliament and caused it to be published;

(b) in relation to paragraph 16 of Schedule 1 to the 1999 Act (annual reports), in so far as those functions relate to the financial year beginning 1st April 2007 and have not been discharged before 1st October 2007, until the Secretary of State has laid a copy of the annual report before Parliament and caused it to be published;

(c) in relation to paragraph 15 of Schedule 3 to the 1975 Act (accounts) and paragraph 15 of Schedule 1 to the 1999 Act (accounts), in so far as those functions relate to the financial year beginning 1st April 2007 and have not been discharged before 1st October 2007, until the Comptroller and Auditor General has laid a copy of the statement of accounts and his report on it before Parliament;

(d) in relation to section 46 of the 1976 Act (annual reports), in so far as those functions relate to the calendar years ending 31st December 2006 or 31st December 2007 and have not been discharged before 1st October 2007, until the Secretary of State has laid a copy of the annual report before Parliament and caused it to be published;

(e) in relation to paragraph 17 of Schedule 1 to the 1976 Act (accounts), in so far as those functions relate to the financial years beginning 1st April 2006 or 1st April 2007 and have not been discharged before 1st October 2007, until the Comptroller and Auditor General has laid a copy of the statement of accounts and his report on it before Parliament;

(f) in relation to sections 57 to 60 of the 1975 Act (investigations) and sections 48 to 51 of the 1976 Act (investigations), in so far as those functions relate to any investigation that has been commenced but not concluded before 1st October 2007, until the Commission delivers its report to the Secretary of State, if required, or the Commission publishes the report or otherwise makes it available for inspection; and

(g) in relation to section 70 of the 1975 Act (register of non-discrimination notices) and section 61 of the 1976 Act (register of non-discrimination notices), until 1st October 2013.

(2) In its application to any investigation to which paragraph (1)(f) applies, paragraph 9(3)(b) of Schedule 1 to the 2006 Act shall have effect as if, after "section 20", there were inserted "of this Act, section 57 of the Sex Discrimination Act 1975 or section 48 of the Race Relations Act 1976".

(3) Section 21(1)(a) of the 2006 Act shall apply in relation to an investigation under section 57 of the 1975 Act or section 48 of the 1976 Act as if, after "section 20(1)(a)", there were inserted "of this Act, section 57 of the Sex Discrimination Act 1975 or section 48 of the Race Relations Act 1976".

(4) Section 32(8) of the 2006 Act shall apply in relation to notices issued under section 76D of the 1975 Act (specific duties: enforcement) or section 71D of the 1976 Act (general statutory duty: compliance notices) as if, after "this section", there were inserted ", section 76D of the Sex Discrimination Act 1975 or section 71D of the Race Relations Act 1976".

[3473O]

NOTES

Commencement: 1 October 2007.

(The Schedule to this Order (as amended) contains amendments and modifications in consequence of the dissolution of the Commission for Racial Equality, the Disability Rights Commission and the Equal Opportunities Commission and the establishment of the Commission for Equality and Human Rights. Where relevant to this work they have been noted in the appropriate place.)

EQUALITY ACT 2006 (COMMENCEMENT NO 3 AND SAVINGS) ORDER 2007

(SI 2007/2603)

NOTES

Made: 7 September 2007.
Authority: Equality Act 2006, s 93.

1 Citation and interpretation

(1) This Order may be cited as the Equality Act 2006 (Commencement No 3 and Savings) Order 2007.

(2) In this Order—

"the 1975 Act" means the Sex Discrimination Act 1975;
"the 1976 Act" means the Race Relations Act 1976;
"the 1999 Act" means the Disability Rights Commission Act 1999;
"the 2006 Act" means the Equality Act 2006; and
"the Commission" means the Commission for Equality and Human Rights.

[3473P]

2 Provisions coming into force

Subject to article 3, the following provisions of the 2006 Act shall come into force on 1st October 2007—

(a) sections 6 to 32;
(b) section 40 (in so far as it is not yet in force);
(c) section 91; and
(d) Schedules 2 to 4.

[3473Q]

3 Savings

The consequential amendments in paragraphs 11, 12 (in so far as it applies to section 70 of the 1975 Act), 26, 27 (in so far as it applies to section 61 of the 1976 Act) and 59 of Schedule 3 to the 2006 Act and the repeals in Schedule 4 to that Act of Part VI and section 70 of the 1975 Act, Part VII and section 61 of the 1976 Act and the 1999 Act shall not have effect in relation to—

(a) the discharge by the Commission of the functions specified in article 5(1) of the Equality Act 2006 (Dissolution of Commissions and Consequential and Transitional Provisions) Order 2007 (discharge by the Commission of certain functions of the Commission for Racial Equality, the Disability Rights Commission and the Equal Opportunities Commission), or

(b) section 61 of the 1975 Act (restriction on disclosure of information), section 52 of the 1976 Act (restriction on disclosure of information) and paragraph 22 of Schedule 3 to the 1999 Act (restriction on disclosure of information).

[3473R]

IMMIGRATION (RESTRICTIONS ON EMPLOYMENT) ORDER 2007

(SI 2007/3290)

NOTES

Made: 15 November 2007.
Authority: Immigration, Asylum and Nationality Act 2006, ss 15(3), (7), 16(3), (5), 19(2), 23(3), 25(d).
Commencement: 29 February 2008.

ARRANGEMENT OF ARTICLES

Citation, commencement and interpretation

1 This order may be cited as the Immigration (Restrictions on Employment) Order 2007 and shall come into force on 29 February 2008.

[3473S]

NOTES

Commencement: 29 February 2008.

2 In this order—

"the 2006 Act" means the Immigration, Asylum and Nationality Act 2006; and

"document" means an original document.

[3473T]

NOTES

Commencement: 29 February 2008.

Excuse from paying civil penalty

3—(1) To the extent provided for by paragraph (2) an employer is excused from paying a penalty under section 15 of the 2006 Act if—

(a) the employee or prospective employee produces to the employer any of the documents or combinations of documents described in list A in the Schedule to this Order; and

(b) the employer complies with the requirements set out in article 6 of this order.

(2) An employer will be excused under this article from paying a penalty under section 15 of the 2006 Act—

(a) for the duration of the employment, if the document or combination of documents is produced prior to the commencement of employment; or

(b) subject to article 5, for the remainder of the employment, if the document or combination of documents is produced after the employment has commenced.

[3473U]

NOTES

Commencement: 29 February 2008.

4—(1) To the extent provided for by paragraph (2) an employer is excused from paying a penalty under section 15 of the 2006 Act if—

(a) the employee or prospective employee produces to the employer any of the documents or combination of documents described in list B in the Schedule to this Order; and

(b) the employer complies with the requirements set out in article 6 of this Order.

(2) Subject to article 5 an employer will be excused under this article from paying a penalty under section 15 of the 2006 Act for a period of twelve months, beginning with the date on which the employee produced the document or combination of documents.

[3473V]

NOTES

Commencement: 29 February 2008.

5 An employer is excused from paying a penalty under section 15 of the 2006 Act by virtue of article 3(2)(b) and article 4(2) only if prior to the commencement of employment the employee produced to the employer any of the documents or combination of documents described in the Schedule to this Order.

[3473W]

NOTES

Commencement: 29 February 2008.

6 The requirements in relation to any documents or combinations of documents produced by an employee pursuant to articles 3 or 4 of this order are that—

(a) the employer takes all reasonable steps to check the validity of the document;

(b) the copy or copies are retained securely by the employer for a period of not less than two years after the employment has come to an end;

(c) if a document contains a photograph, the employer has satisfied himself that the photograph is of the prospective employee or employee;

(d) if a document contains a date of birth, the employer has satisfied himself that the date of birth is consistent with the appearance of the prospective employee or employee;

(e) the employer takes all other reasonable steps to check that the prospective employee or employee is the rightful owner of the document;

(f) if the document is not a passport or other travel document the employer retains a copy of whole of the document in a format which cannot be subsequently altered; and

(g) if the document is a passport or other travel document, the following pages of that document are copied in a format which cannot be subsequently altered—

(i) the front cover;

(ii) any page containing the holder's personal details including nationality;

(iii) any page containing the holder's photograph;

(iv) any page containing the holder's signature;

(v) any page containing the date of expiry; and

(vi) any page containing information indicating the holder has an entitlement to enter or remain in the UK and undertake the work in question.

[3473X]

NOTES

Commencement: 29 February 2008.

7 Nothing in this Order permits employers to retain documents produced by an employee for the purposes of articles 3 or 4 for any period longer than is necessary for the purposes of ensuring compliance with article 6.

[3473Y]

NOTES

Commencement: 29 February 2008.

Objections

8 The manner prescribed in which the notice of objection must be given is that it must contain—

(a) the reference number of the notice given under section 15(2) of the 2006 Act;

(b) the name and contact address of the employer;

(c) the name and contact address of the employee in respect of whom the penalty was issued;

(d) the full grounds of objection;

(e) where the employer requests permission to pay by instalments, full details of the employer's ability to pay the penalty;

(f) confirmation and details of any appeal made by the employer to a County Court or Sheriff Court on the basis that the employer is not liable to the penalty, he is excused payment by virtue of section 15(3) of the 2006 Act, or that the amount of the penalty is too high; and

(g) any documents to be relied upon in support of the objection.

[3473Z]

NOTES

Commencement: 29 February 2008.

9 The prescribed period within which a notice of objection must be given for the purposes of section 16(3)(d) of the 2006 Act is 28 days, beginning with the date specified in the penalty notice as the date upon which it is given.

[3474]

NOTES

Commencement: 29 February 2008.

10 The period prescribed for the purposes of section 16(5)(b) of the 2006 Act within which the Secretary of State must inform the objector of his decision is 28 days, beginning with the date on which the notice of objection was given to the Secretary of State.

[3474A]

NOTES

Commencement: 29 February 2008.

Codes of Practice

11 The code of practice entitled "Civil Penalties for Employers", issued by the Secretary of State under section 19(1) of the 2006 Act shall come into force on 29 February 2008.

[3474B]

NOTES

Commencement: 29 February 2008.
The code of practice is reproduced at **[4766]**.

12 The code of practice entitled "Guidance for Employers on the Avoidance of Unlawful Discrimination in Employment Practice While Seeking to Prevent Illegal Working", issued by the Secretary of State under section 23(1) of the 2006 Act shall come into force on 29 February 2008.

[3474C]

NOTES

Commencement: 29 February 2008.
The code of practice is reproduced at **[4772]**.

SCHEDULE

Articles 3 and 4

List A

1. A passport showing that the holder, or a person named in the passport as the child of the holder, is a British citizen or a citizen of the United Kingdom and Colonies having the right of abode in the United Kingdom.

2. A passport or national identity card showing that the holder, or a person named in the passport as the child of the holder, is a national of the European Economic Area or Switzerland.

3. A residence permit, registration certificate or document certifying or indicating permanent residence issued by the Home Office or the Border and Immigration Agency to a national of a European Economic Area country or Switzerland.

4. A permanent residence card issued by the Home Office or the Border and Immigration Agency to the family member of a national of a European Economic Area country or Switzerland.

5. A Biometric Immigration Document issued by the Border and Immigration Agency to the holder which indicates that the person named in it is allowed to stay indefinitely in the United Kingdom, or has no time limit on their stay in the United Kingdom.

6. A passport or other travel document endorsed to show that the holder is exempt from immigration control, is allowed to stay indefinitely in the United Kingdom, has the right of abode in the United Kingdom, or has no time limit on their stay in the United Kingdom.

7. An Immigration Status Document issued by the Home Office or the Border and Immigration Agency to the holder with an endorsement indicating that the person named in it is allowed to stay indefinitely in the United Kingdom or has no time limit on their stay in the United Kingdom, when produced in combination with an official document giving the person's permanent National Insurance Number and their name issued by a Government agency or a previous employer.

8. A full birth certificate issued in the United Kingdom which includes the name(s) of at least one of the holder's parents, when produced in combination with an official document giving the person's permanent National Insurance Number and their name issued by a Government agency or a previous employer.

9. A full adoption certificate issued in the United Kingdom which includes the name(s) of at least one of the holder's adoptive parents when produced in combination with an official document giving the person's permanent National Insurance Number and their name issued by a Government agency or a previous employer.

10. A birth certificate issued in the Channel Islands, the Isle of Man or Ireland, when produced in combination with an official document giving the person's permanent National Insurance Number and their name issued by a Government agency or a previous employer.

11. An adoption certificate issued in the Channel Islands, the Isle of Man or Ireland, when produced in combination with an official document giving the person's permanent National Insurance Number and their name issued by a Government agency or a previous employer.

12. A certificate of registration or naturalisation as a British citizen, when produced in combination with an official document giving the person's permanent National Insurance Number and their name issued by a Government agency or a previous employer.

13. A letter issued by the Home Office or the Border and Immigration Agency to the holder which indicates that the person named in it is allowed to stay indefinitely in the United Kingdom when produced in combination with an official document giving the person's permanent National Insurance Number and their name issued by a Government agency or a previous employer.

List B

1. A passport or travel document endorsed to show that the holder is allowed to stay in the United Kingdom and is allowed to do the type of work in question, provided that it does not require the issue of a work permit.

2. A Biometric Immigration Document issued by the Border and Immigration Agency to the holder which indicates that the person named in it can stay in the United Kingdom and is allowed to do the work in question.

3. A work permit or other approval to take employment issued by the Home Office or the Border and Immigration Agency when produced in combination with either a passport or another travel document endorsed to show the holder is allowed to stay in the United Kingdom and is allowed to do the work in question, or a letter issued by the Home Office or the Border and Immigration Agency to the holder or the employer or prospective employer confirming the same.

4. A certificate of application issued by the Home Office or the Border and Immigration Agency to or for a family member of a national of a European Economic Area country or Switzerland stating that the holder is permitted to take employment which is less than 6 months old when produced in combination with evidence of verification by the Border and Immigration Agency Employer Checking Service.

5. A residence card or document issued by the Home Office or the Border and Immigration Agency to a family member of a national of a European Economic Area country or Switzerland.

6. An Application Registration Card issued by the Home Office or the Border and Immigration Agency stating that the holder is permitted to take employment, when produced in combination with evidence of verification by the Border and Immigration Agency Employer Checking Service.

7. An Immigration Status Document issued by the Home Office or the Border and Immigration Agency to the holder with an endorsement indicating that the person named in it can stay in the United Kingdom, and is allowed to do the type of work in question, when produced in combination with an official document giving the person's permanent National Insurance Number and their name issued by a Government agency or a previous employer.

8. A letter issued by the Home Office or the Border and Immigration Agency to the holder or the employer or prospective employer, which indicates that the person named in it can stay in the United Kingdom and is allowed to do the work in question when produced in combination with an official document giving the person's permanent National Insurance Number and their name issued by a Government agency or a previous employer.

[3474D]

NOTES

Commencement: 29 February 2008.

EMPLOYMENT RIGHTS (INCREASE OF LIMITS) ORDER 2007

(SI 2007/3570)

NOTES

Made: 18 December 2007.
Authority: Employment Relations Act 1999, s 34.
Commencement: 1 February 2008.

1 Citation, commencement and interpretation

(1) This Order may be cited as the Employment Rights (Increase of Limits) Order 2007 and shall come into force on 1st February 2008.

(2) In this Order—

(a) "the 1992 Act" means the Trade Union and Labour Relations (Consolidation) Act 1992; and

(b) "the 1996 Act" means the Employment Rights Act 1996.

[3474E]

NOTES

Commencement: 1 February 2008.

2 Revocation

The Employment Rights (Increase of Limits) Order 2006 is revoked.

[3474F]

NOTES

Commencement: 1 February 2008.

3 Increase of limits

In the provisions set out in column 1 of the Schedule to this Order (generally described in column 2), for the sums specified in column 3 substitute the sums specified in column 4.

[3474G]

NOTES

Commencement: 1 February 2008.

4 Transitional provisions

(1) The revocation in article 2 and the substitutions made by article 3 do not have effect in relation to a case where the appropriate date falls before 1st February 2008.

(2) In this article "the appropriate date" means—

(a) in the case of an application made under section 67(1) of the 1992 Act (compensation for unjustifiable discipline by a trade union), the date of the determination infringing the applicant's right;

(b) in the case of a complaint presented under section 70C(1) of the 1992 Act (failure by an employer to consult with a trade union on training matters), the date of the failure;

(c) in the case of a complaint presented under section 137(2) of the 1992 Act (refusal of employment on grounds related to union membership) or section 138(2) of that Act (refusal of service of employment agency on grounds related to union membership), the date of the conduct to which the complaint relates, as determined under section 139 of that Act;

(d) in the case of an award under section 145E(2)(b) of the 1992 Act (award to worker in respect of offer made by employer in contravention of section 145A or 145B of that Act), the date of the offer;

(e) in the case of an application made under section 176(2) of the 1992 Act (compensation for exclusion or expulsion from a trade union), the date of the exclusion or expulsion from the union;

(f) in the case of an award under paragraph 159(1) of Schedule A1 to the 1992 Act, where a worker has suffered a detriment that is the termination of the worker's contract, the date of the termination;

(g) in the case of a guarantee payment to which an employee is entitled under section 28(1) of the 1996 Act, the day in respect of which the payment is due;

(h) in the case of an award of compensation under section 49(1)(b) of the 1996 Act by virtue of section 24(2) of the National Minimum Wage Act 1998, where a worker has suffered a detriment that is the termination of the worker's contract, the date of the termination;

(i) in the case of an award under section 80I of the 1996 Act (award of compensation relating to an application for contract variation), the date of the failure in relation to the application or of the decision to reject the application;

(j) in the case of an award under section 112(4) or (5) of the 1996 Act (award in relation to unfair dismissal) the effective date of termination as defined by section 97 of that Act;

(k) in the case of an award under section 117(1) or (3) of the 1996 Act, where an employer has failed to comply fully with the terms of an order for reinstatement or re-engagement or has failed to reinstate or re-engage the complainant in accordance with such an order, the date by which the order for reinstatement (specified under section 114(2)(c) of that Act) or, as the case may be, re-engagement (specified under section 115(2)(f) of that Act), should have been complied with;

(l) in the case of entitlement to a redundancy payment by virtue of section 135(1)(a) of the 1996 Act (dismissal by reason of redundancy), the relevant date as defined by section 145 of that Act;

(m) in the case of entitlement to a redundancy payment by virtue of section 135(1)(b) of the 1996 Act (lay-off or short-time), the relevant date as defined by section 153 of that Act;

(n) in the case of entitlement to a payment under section 182 of the 1996 Act (payments by the Secretary of State), the appropriate date as defined by section 185 of that Act;

(o) in the case of a complaint presented under section 11(1) of the Employment Relations Act 1999 (failure or threatened failure to allow the worker to be accompanied at the disciplinary or grievance hearing, to allow the companion to address the hearing or confer with the worker, or to postpone the hearing), the date of the failure or threat;

(p) in the case of an award made under section 38(2) of the Employment Act 2002 (duty to give a written statement of initial employment particulars or of particulars of change), the date the proceedings to which that section applies were begun;

(q) in the case of an increase in an award in pursuance of section 38(3) of the Employment Act 2002, the date the proceedings to which that section applies were begun;

(r) in the case of a complaint presented under regulation 15 of the Flexible Working (Procedural Requirements) Regulations 2002 (failure or threatened failure to allow an employee to be accompanied at a meeting or to postpone the meeting), the date of the failure or threat;

(s) in the case of a complaint presented under paragraph 11(1) of Schedule 6 to the Employment Equality (Age) Regulations 2006 (failure of employer to comply with duty to notify employee of date on which he intends employee to retire or of right to make request not to retire on the intended date), the date of the failure; and

(t) in the case of a complaint presented under paragraph 12(1) of Schedule 6 to the Employment Equality (Age) Regulations 2006 (failure or threatened failure to allow an employee to be accompanied at a meeting, to allow the companion to address the meeting or confer with the employee, or to postpone the meeting), the date of the failure or threat.

[3474H]

NOTES

Commencement: 1 February 2008.

SCHEDULE

Article 3

Column 1 *Relevant statutory provision*	*Column 2* *Subject of provision*	*Column 3* *Old limits*	*Column 4* *New limits*
1. Section 145E(3) of the 1992 Act	Amount of award for unlawful inducement relating to trade union membership or activities, or for unlawful inducement relating to collective bargaining.	£2,700	£2,900
2. Section 156(1) of the 1992 Act	Minimum amount of basic award of compensation where dismissal is unfair by virtue of section 152(1) or 153 of the 1992 Act.	£4,200	£4,400
3. Section 176(6A) of the 1992 Act	Minimum amount of compensation where individual excluded or expelled from union in contravention of section 174 of the 1992 Act and not admitted or re-admitted by date of tribunal application.	£6,600	£6,900
4. Section 31(1) of the 1996 Act	Limit on amount of guarantee payment payable to an employee in respect of any day.	£19.60	£20.40
5. Section 120(1) of the 1996 Act	Minimum amount of basic award of compensation where dismissal is unfair by virtue of section 100(1)(a) and (b), 101A(d), 102(1) or 103 of the 1996 Act.	£4,200	£4,400
6. Section 124(1) of the 1996 Act	Limit on amount of compensatory award for unfair dismissal.	£60,600	£63,000
7. Paragraphs (a) and (b) of section 186(1) of the 1996 Act	Limit on amount in respect of any one week payable to an employee in respect of a debt to which Part XII of the 1996 Act applies and which is referable to a period of time.	£310	£330
8. Section 227(1) of the 1996 Act	Maximum amount of "a week's pay" for the purpose of calculating a redundancy payment or for various awards including the basic or additional award of compensation for unfair dismissal.	£310	£330

[3474I]

NOTES

Commencement: 1 February 2008.

IMMIGRATION (EMPLOYMENT OF ADULTS SUBJECT TO IMMIGRATION CONTROL) (MAXIMUM PENALTY) ORDER 2008

(SI 2008/132)

NOTES

Made: 22 January 2008.
Authority: Immigration, Asylum and Nationality Act 2006, s 15(2).
Commencement: 29 February 2008.

1 Citation and Commencement

This Order may be cited as the Immigration (Employment of Adults Subject to Immigration Control) (Maximum Penalty) Order 2008 and shall come into force on 29th February 2008.

[3474J]

NOTES

Commencement: 29 February 2008.

2 Maximum Penalty

For the purposes of section 15(2) of the Immigration, Asylum and Nationality Act 2006 (employment of adults subject to immigration control: penalty notice) the prescribed maximum is £10,000.

[3474K]

NOTES

Commencement: 29 February 2008.

OCCUPATIONAL PENSION SCHEMES (INTERNAL DISPUTE RESOLUTION PROCEDURES CONSEQUENTIAL AND MISCELLANEOUS AMENDMENTS) REGULATIONS 2008

(SI 2008/649)

NOTES

Made: 5 March 2008.
Authority: Pension Schemes Act 1993, ss 113(1)(d), 181(1), 182(2), (3); Pensions Act 1995, ss 50(8)(c), (9)(c), 124(1), 174(2), (3).
Commencement: 6 April 2008.

1 Citation, commencement and interpretation

(1) These Regulations may be cited as the Occupational Pension Schemes (Internal Dispute Resolution Procedures Consequential and Miscellaneous Amendments) Regulations 2008 and shall come into force on 6th April 2008.

(2) In these Regulations "the Act" means the Pensions Act 1995.

[3474KA]

NOTES

Commencement: 6 April 2008.

2 Information requirements

(1) When the trustees or managers of an occupational pension scheme receive (or, as the case may be, the specified person receives) an application under the relevant procedure, they must as soon as is reasonably practicable—

(a) inform the applicant that TPAS (the Pensions Advisory Service) is available to assist members and beneficiaries of the scheme in connection with any difficulty with the scheme, and

(b) give the applicant the contact details for TPAS.

(2) For the purposes of paragraph (1), the relevant procedure is a procedure for the application for the resolution of a pension dispute under section 50(4) of the Act (procedure for resolution of a pensions dispute).

(3) For the purposes of paragraph (1), "member" has the meaning given to it in section 124(1) and 125(4) of the Act (interpretation of Part 1 and supplementary), and "members" is to be construed accordingly.

(4) When the trustees or managers of an occupational pension scheme notify the applicant of their decision on the matters in dispute in accordance with section 50(5)(b) of the Act (dispute resolution arrangements—duties of trustees or managers), the notification shall include—

(a) a statement that the Pensions Ombudsman appointed under section 145(2) of the Pension Schemes Act 1993 may investigate and determine any complaint or dispute of fact or law, in relation to a scheme, made or referred in accordance with that Act, and

(b) the Pensions Ombudsman's contact details.

[3474KB]

NOTES

Commencement: 6 April 2008.

3 Exempted schemes

An occupational pension scheme of a description prescribed for the purposes of section 50(8)(c) of the Act (schemes to which section 50 does not apply) is a scheme in relation to which the sole trustee of the scheme is a company and all members of the scheme are directors of that company.

[3474KC]

NOTES

Commencement: 6 April 2008.

4 Exempted disputes

A dispute of a description prescribed for the purposes of section 50(9)(c) of the Act (exempted disputes) is a dispute in respect of which a notice of appeal has been issued by the complainant in accordance with—

(a) regulation H2 of the Police Pensions Regulations 1987 (appeal to board of medical referees);

(b) rule H2 of Schedule 2 to the Firemen's Pension Scheme Order 1992 (appeal against opinion on a medical issue);

(c) rule 2 of Part 6 of Schedule 1 to the Firefighters' Compensation Scheme (Scotland) Order 2006 (appeal to medical referee);

(d) regulation 31 of the Police (Injury Benefit) Regulations 2006 (appeal to board of medical referees);

(e) rule 2 of Part 6 of Schedule 1 to the Firefighters' Compensation Scheme (England) Order 2006 (appeal to medical referee);

(f) regulation 72 of the Police Pensions Regulations 2006 (appeal to board of medical referees);

(g) rule 4 of Part 8 of Schedule 1 to the Firefighters' Pension Scheme (England) Order 2006 (appeals against decisions based on medical advice);

(h) regulation 31 of the Police (Injury Benefit) (Scotland) Regulations 2007 (appeal to board of medical referees);

(i) rule 4 of Part 8 of Schedule 1 to the Firefighters' Pension Scheme (Scotland) Order 2007 (appeals against decisions based on medical advice);

(j) regulation 72 of Part 7 of the Police Pensions (Scotland) Regulations 2007 (appeal to board of medical referees);

(k) rule 4 of Part 8 of Schedule 1 to the Firefighters' Pension Scheme (Wales) Order 2007 (appeals against decisions based on medical advice); or

(l) rule 2 of Part 6 of Schedule 1 to the Firefighters' Compensation Scheme (Wales) Order 2007 (appeal to medical referee).

[3474KD]

NOTES

Commencement: 6 April 2008.

5 Transitional provisions

(1) Any disagreement which was ongoing before 6th April 2008 under arrangements made and implemented under section 50(1) of the Act shall continue until the procedure under those arrangements comes to an end, as if the relevant legislative provisions governing those arrangements were still in force.

(2) For the purposes of paragraph (1), the relevant legislative provisions are—

(a) section 50 of the Act as it was in force immediately before 6th April 2008; and

(b) the Occupational Pension Schemes (Internal Dispute Resolution Procedures) Regulations 1996.

(3) In the case of any relevant application, regulation 3 of the Personal and Occupational Pension Schemes (Pensions Ombudsman) Regulations 1996 shall apply as it had effect before 6th April 2008.

(4) For the purposes of paragraph (3), "relevant application" means an application concerning a complaint or dispute made—

(a) to an occupational pension scheme under the arrangements required by section 50 of the Act; and

(b) before 6th April 2008.

[3474KE]

NOTES

Commencement: 6 April 2008.

6, 7 (*Reg 6* (*Consequential and miscellaneous amendments*) *amends the Personal and Occupational Pension Schemes* (*Pensions Ombudsman*) *Regulations 1996 SI 1996/2475, reg 3 at* **[2378]**, *and contains other amendments to legislation that is outside the scope of this work; reg 7 revokes the Occupational Pension Schemes* (*Internal Dispute Resolution Procedures*) *Regulations 1996, SI 1996/1270.*)

LEGISLATIVE REFORM (HEALTH AND SAFETY EXECUTIVE) ORDER 2008

(SI 2008/960)

NOTES

Made: 31 March 2008.
Authority: Legislative and Regulatory Reform Act 2006, s 2.
Commencement: 1 April 2008.

1 Citation and Commencement

This Order may be cited as the Legislative Reform (Health and Safety Executive) Order 2008 and shall come into force on the day after it is made.

[3474L]

NOTES

Commencement: 1 April 2008.

2 Abolition of the Health and Safety Commission and Executive

The Health and Safety Commission and the Health and Safety Executive, as established under section 10 of the Health and Safety at Work etc Act 1974, are abolished.

[3474M]

NOTES

Commencement: 1 April 2008.

3–20 (*Contain various amendments to the Health and Safety at Work etc Act 1974* (*at* **[30]** *et seq*) *in consequence of the abolition of the Health and Safety Commission and the Health and Safety Executive, and their replacement with a single Health and Safety Executive.*)

21 Transitional provisions

(1) Any reference to the Health and Safety Executive in any enactment passed or made before the day on which this Order comes into force shall have effect on and after that day as a reference to the Health and Safety Executive as established by this Order.

(2) Schedule 2 has effect.

[3474N]

NOTES

Commencement: 1 April 2008.

22 (*Introduces Sch 3* (*Consequential Amendments*).)

SCHEDULES

(*Sch 1 substitutes the Health and Safety at Work etc Act 1974, Sch 2 at* **[89]**.)

SCHEDULE 2
TRANSITIONAL PROVISIONS

Article 21

1. In this Schedule—

"the Act" means the Health and Safety at Work etc Act 1974 as amended by this Order;

"the appointed day" means the day on which this Order comes into force;

"the Chairman" means the chairman of the Commission;

"Commission" means the Health and Safety Commission abolished by article 2 of this Order;

"Commissioner" means a member of the Commission;

"the existing Act" means the Health and Safety at Work etc Act 1974 before the appointed day;

"the former Executive" means the Health and Safety Executive abolished by article 2 of this Order;

"instrument of appointment" means the letter of appointment and terms and conditions of appointment under which a Commissioner or the Chairman, or the director or other members of the former Executive were appointed;

"the new Executive" means the Health and Safety Executive as established under section 10 of the Act;

"relevant statutory provisions" has the meaning given by section 53(1) of the Act;

"servant of the former Executive" means a civil servant on the staff of the former Executive.

Transfer of Chairman and members of the Commission

2.—(1) The person who immediately before the appointed day was the Chairman shall on the appointed day become the Chair of the new Executive as if duly appointed under paragraph 2 of Schedule 2 to the Act.

(2) Any other person who before the appointed day was a Commissioner shall on the appointed day become a member of the new Executive as if duly appointed under paragraph 2 of that Schedule.

(3) While a person holds office as the Chair or other member of the new Executive by virtue of this paragraph, he shall hold that office on the terms on which he held office as the Chairman or as a Commissioner immediately before the appointed day.

(4) Sub-paragraph (3) is subject to—
  (a) sub-paragraph (5), and
  (b) any necessary modifications to the terms in question.

(5) A person's term of office as a member of the new Executive shall expire on the date set out in the instrument under which he was appointed as the Chairman or as a Commissioner for the expiry of his term of office as a member of the Commission.

(6) No compensation shall be paid to either the Chairman or a Commissioner as a result of the operation of this paragraph .

Transfer of officers and staff

3.—(1) Where immediately before the appointed day a person holds appointment under paragraph 11 of Schedule 2 to the existing Act as a servant of the former Executive, his appointment shall continue in effect on and after the appointed day in the service of the new Executive as if made by the new Executive under paragraph 8(2) of Schedule 2 to the Act.

(2) The person who immediately before the appointed day was the director of the former Executive shall on the appointed day become the Chief Executive of the new Executive as if appointed by the new Executive under paragraph 8(1) of Schedule 2 to the Act.

(3) Where immediately before the appointed day a person holds appointment as a member (but not as the director) of the former Executive under section 10(5) of the existing Act, his appointment shall continue to have effect on and after the appointed day, but as a member of staff of the new Executive as if made by the new Executive under paragraph 8(2) of Schedule 2 to the Act.

(4) A person referred to in sub-paragraph (3) shall not be paid any compensation as a result of the operation of this paragraph.

First annual report and statement of accounts of the new Executive

4.—(1) This paragraph applies if there is a period of one or more days which—
  (a) began on the day after the end of the last year for which the Commission made a report under paragraph 15 of Schedule 2 to the existing Act, and
  (b) ended on the day before the appointed day.

(2) The first report published by the new Executive under paragraph 10 of Schedule 2 to the Act shall also be a report on the operations of the Commission and the former Executive during the period mentioned in sub-paragraph (1).

(3) The first statement of accounts prepared by the Chief Executive under paragraph 10 of Schedule 2 to the Act shall also contain statements of accounts for the Commission and for the former Executive for the period mentioned in sub-paragraph (1).

Investigations and special reports

5.—(1) This paragraph applies where, before the appointed day, the Commission authorised a person to investigate and make a special report under section 14(2) of the existing Act.

(2) For the purposes of carrying out or continuing the investigation and the making of a special report on or after the appointed day, the authorisation shall be treated as an authorisation by the new Executive.

(3) If—
  (a) the person to whom the Commission gave the authorisation has made a special report to the Commission, but
  (b) the Commission has not yet caused the report, or a part of it, to be made public under section 14(5) of the existing Act,

the report shall be treated as if it had been made to the new Executive under section 14(2) of the Act.

(4) If the person to whom the Commission gave the authorisation has not yet made a special report to the Commission, the new Executive may direct that person to—
  (a) abandon the investigation without making a special report, or

(b) continue the investigation in such manner as the new Executive may direct.

(5) Where the Commission agreed before the appointed day to exercise its power under section 14(6)(a) or (c) of the existing Act to pay remuneration or expenses to any person in respect of the investigation and special report, or to defray costs of the investigation and report, the new Executive shall pay such remuneration or expenses or defray the costs of the investigation and report as agreed.

(6) Sub-paragraph (5) does not affect the new Executive's power under section 14(6) of the Act to make other payments of remuneration or expenses or to defray costs.

Inquiries

6.—(1) This paragraph applies where, before the appointed day, the Commission directed an inquiry to be held under section 14(2) of the existing Act.

(2) Section 14 of the Act shall continue to apply in relation to that inquiry on or after the appointed day but as if all things done or required to be done by or in relation to the Commission under that section were done or required to be done by or in relation to the new Executive.

(3) Where the Commission agreed before the appointed day to exercise its power under section 14(6)(b) or (c) of the existing Act to pay remuneration or expenses to any person in respect of the inquiry or to defray costs of the inquiry, the new Executive shall pay such remuneration or expenses or defray the costs of the inquiry as agreed.

(4) Sub-paragraph (3) does not affect the new Executive's power under section 14(6) of the Act to make other payments of remuneration or expenses or to defray costs.

Agreements entered into with other public bodies

7.—(1) This paragraph applies where, before the appointed day, the Commission either—

(a) entered into an agreement under section 13(1)(a) of the existing Act with any government department or person for that department or other person to perform any of the Commission's functions; or

(b) entered into an agreement under section 13(1)(b) of the existing Act with any Minister of the Crown, government department or other public authority to perform their functions.

(2) Any agreement to which this paragraph applies shall continue to have effect on and after the appointed day as if it had been duly entered into between that Minister of the Crown, government department, person or public authority concerned and the new Executive.

Approval of Codes of Practice

8.—(1) This paragraph applies where, before the appointed day, the Commission—

(a) approved or issued a code of practice under section 16(1) of the existing Act; or

(b) revised, or approved a revision (or proposed revision) of, a code of practice or part of a code of practice, under section 16(4) of the existing Act.

(2) On and after the appointed day—

(a) any code of practice to which this paragraph applies shall have effect as if the code, and any revision of the code, had been approved or issued by the new Executive;

(b) any withdrawal under section 16(5) of the existing Act of the Commission's approval of any code of practice to which this paragraph applies shall have effect as if it had been done by the new Executive; and

(c) any notices issued by the Commission under section 16(3) or (6) shall have effect as if they had been issued by the new Executive.

Information

9.—(1) This paragraph applies where, before the appointed day, the Commission served a notice under section 27(1) of the Act requiring any person to furnish information to the Commission.

(2) Any notice to which this paragraph applies shall have effect on and after the appointed day as if requiring such information to be furnished to the new Executive.

(3) Information obtained by a notice to which this paragraph applies shall on the appointed day be transferred to the new Executive, and shall be treated for the purposes of section 28 to the Act as if it had been obtained by or as the case may be, furnished or disclosed to the new Executive.

Other provisions

10. Subject to paragraphs 5 to 9, anything done by, on behalf of or in relation to the Commission or the former Executive, in particular but not limited to—

(a) any proposals submitted under section 11(2)(d) of the existing Act;

(b) any direction given by the Secretary of State under section 12(b) of the existing Act;

(c) any guidance given under section 18(4)(b) of the existing Act;

(d) any appointment of inspectors made under section 19 of the existing Act;

(e) any consultation undertaken under section 50(3) of the existing Act; or

(f) any exercise of powers conferred on them by the relevant statutory provisions,

which is in effect immediately before the appointed day shall, so far as is necessary for continuing its effect after that day, have effect on and after the appointed day as if duly done by, on behalf of or in relation to the new Executive.

General transfer

11.—(1) By virtue of this paragraph, the property, rights and liabilities to which the Commission or the former Executive was entitled or subject immediately before the appointed day, shall become on that day the property, rights and liabilities of the new Executive.

(2) Sub-paragraph (1) has effect in relation to property, rights and liabilities—

(a) despite any provision (of whatever nature) which would otherwise prevent, penalise or restrict their transfer by the Commission or by the former Executive; and

(b) without any instrument or other formality being required.

(3) So far as is necessary or appropriate in consequence of sub-paragraph (1), on or after the appointed day a reference to the Commission or to the former Executive in an instrument or other document shall be treated as a reference to the new Executive.

(4) Anything (including any legal proceedings) which—

(a) relates to anything transferred by sub-paragraph (1); and

(b) is in the process of being done by, on behalf of or in relation to the Commission or the former Executive,

may be continued on and after the appointed day by, on behalf of or in relation to the new Executive.

(5) Nothing in this paragraph affects the validity of anything done by the new Executive.
[3474O]

NOTES

Commencement: 1 April 2008.

(Sch 3 contains consequential amendments to the Sex Discrimination Act 1975, the Race Relations Act 1976, the Safety Representatives and Safety Committees Regulations 1977 SI 1977/500, the Working Time Regulations 1998 SI 1998/1833, the Race Relations Act 1976 (Statutory Duties) Order 2001, SI 2001/3458, the Disability Discrimination (Public Authorities) (Statutory Duties) Regulations 2005, SI 2005/2966, the Sex Discrimination Act 1975 (Public Authorities) (Statutory Duties) Order 2006, SI 2006/2930, and various other enactments that are outside the scope of this work. In so far as relevant, these have been incorporated at the appropriate place.)

SEX DISCRIMINATION (AMENDMENT OF LEGISLATION) REGULATIONS 2008

(SI 2008/963)

NOTES

Made: 1 April 2008.
Authority: European Communities Act 1972, s 2(2).
Commencement: 6 April 2008.

1 Citation, commencement, extent and interpretation

(1) These Regulations may be cited as the Sex Discrimination (Amendment of Legislation) Regulations 2008 and come into force on the fifth day after the day on which they are made, or on 6th April 2008, whichever is the later.

(2) Regulations 2(1) and 4 extend to Great Britain only.

(3) Regulations 1(7), 2(2) and 5 extend to Northern Ireland only.

(4) Regulation 3 extends to England and Wales only.

(5) The remainder of these Regulations extend to the whole of the United Kingdom.

(6) In these Regulations—
"the 1975 Act" means the Sex Discrimination Act 1975 and;
"the 1976 Order" means the Sex Discrimination (Northern Ireland) Order 1976.

(7) The Interpretation Act (Northern Ireland) 1954 shall apply to regulations 1(3), 2(2) and 5 and Schedule 2 as it applies to an Act of the Northern Ireland Assembly.

[3474P]

NOTES

Commencement: 6 April 2008.

2 Amendment of the 1975 Act and the 1976 Order

(1) The 1975 Act shall be amended in accordance with Schedule 1.

(2) The 1976 Order shall be amended in accordance with Schedule 2.

[3474Q]

NOTES

Commencement: 6 April 2008.

3 (*Amends the Public Health Act 1936, s 87* (*outside the scope of this work*).)

4 Transitional provisions in respect of the 1975 Act

(1) The amendment made by paragraph 17 of Schedule 1 (burden of proof) shall not apply in relation to proceedings where the act complained of took place before the date on which these Regulations come into force.

(2) The amendment made by paragraph 18 of Schedule 1 (time for answering questions from aggrieved persons) shall not apply in the case of a question served on a respondent before the date on which these Regulations come into force.

(3) Section 45(3)(a)(iv) of the 1975 Act, inserted by paragraph 13 of Schedule 1 (insurance) shall not apply to contracts entered into before 22nd December 2008.

[3474R]–[3500]

NOTES

Commencement: 6 April 2008.

5 (*Transitional provisions in respect of the Sex Discrimination* (*Northern Ireland*) *Order 1976* (*outside the scope of this work*).)

(*Sch 1 amends the Sex Discrimination Act 1975 at* **[100]** *et seq; Sch 2 amends the Sex Discrimination* (*Northern Ireland*) *Order 1976* (*outside the scope of this work*).)

PART 3
EC MATERIALS

A. CONSTITUTIONAL MATERIALS

CONSOLIDATED VERSION OF THE TREATY ESTABLISHING THE EUROPEAN COMMUNITY (THE TREATY OF ROME)

NOTES

Only those Articles of particular relevance to employment law are printed here. These include those relating to the free movement of persons and the right of establishment; social policy; the legislative powers of the Community and the powers of the Court of Justice.

The Treaty is set out as consolidated by the Treaty of Amsterdam amending the Treaty on European Union, the Treaties establishing the European Communities and certain related acts, signed at Amsterdam, 2 October 1997 (OJ C340, 10.11.97, p 1), and as subsequently amended by the Treaty of Nice in 2001 (OJ C80, 10.03.2001, p 1; these amendments came into force on 1 December 2002). The Treaty of Amsterdam and its consequential renumbering of, and amendments to, these provisions, came into force on 1 May 1999. The Treaty will be further extensively amended if the Treaty of Lisbon comes into effect. As this is dependent on ratification by all 27 member states, and in the interests of space, the amendments have not been included in this edition; they will be included (subject to ratification of the Treaty) in the next edition.

PART ONE
PRINCIPLES

Article 1

(ex Article 1)

By this Treaty, the HIGH CONTRACTING PARTIES establish among themselves a EUROPEAN COMMUNITY.

[3501]

Article 2

(ex Article 2)

The Community shall have as its task, by establishing a common market and an economic and monetary union and by implementing common policies or activities referred to in Articles 3 and 4, to promote throughout the Community a harmonious, balanced and sustainable development of economic activities, a high level of employment and of social protection, equality between men and women, sustainable and non-inflationary growth, a high degree of competitiveness and convergence of economic performance, a high level of protection and improvement of the quality of the environment, the raising of the standard of living and quality of life, and economic and social cohesion and solidarity among Member States.

[3502]

Article 3

(ex Article 3)

1. For the purposes set out in Article 2, the activities of the Community shall include, as provided in this Treaty and in accordance with the timetable set out therein:

(a) the prohibition, as between Member States, of customs duties and quantitative restrictions on the import and export of goods, and of all other measures having equivalent effect;
(b) a common commercial policy;
(c) an internal market characterised by the abolition, as between Member States, of obstacles to the free movement of goods, persons, services and capital;
(d) measures concerning the entry and movement of persons as provided for in Title IV;
(e) a common policy in the sphere of agriculture and fisheries;
(f) a common policy in the sphere of transport;
(g) a system ensuring that competition in the internal market is not distorted;
(h) the approximation of the laws of Member States to the extent required for the functioning of the common market;

(i) the promotion of co-ordination between employment policies of the Member States with a view to enhancing their effectiveness by developing a co-ordinated strategy for employment;
(j) a policy in the social sphere comprising a European Social Fund;
(k) the strengthening of economic and social cohesion;
(l) a policy in the sphere of the environment;
(m) the strengthening of the competitiveness of Community industry;
(n) the promotion of research and technological development;
(o) encouragement for the establishment and development of trans-European networks;
(p) a contribution to the attainment of a high level of health protection;
(q) a contribution to education and training of quality and to the flowering of the cultures of the Member States;
(r) a policy in the sphere of development co-operation;
(s) the association of the overseas countries and territories in order to increase trade and promote jointly economic and social development;
(t) a contribution to the strengthening of consumer protection;
(u) measures in the spheres of energy, civil protection and tourism.

2. In all the activities referred to in this Article, the Community shall aim to eliminate inequalities, and to promote equality, between men and women.

[3503]

Article 12

(ex Article 6)

Within the scope of application of this Treaty, and without prejudice to any special provisions contained therein, any discrimination on grounds of nationality shall be prohibited.

The Council, acting in accordance with the procedure referred to in Article 251, may adopt rules designed to prohibit such discrimination.

[3504]

Article 13

(ex Article 6a)

[1.] Without prejudice to the other provisions of this Treaty and within the limits of the powers conferred by it upon the Community, the Council, acting unanimously on a proposal from the Commission and after consulting the European Parliament, may take appropriate action to combat discrimination based on sex, racial or ethnic origin, religion or belief, disability, age or sexual orientation.

[2. By way of derogation from paragraph 1, when the Council adopts Community incentive measures, excluding any harmonisation of the laws and regulations of the Member States, to support action taken by the Member States in order to contribute to the achievement of the objectives referred to in paragraph 1, it shall act in accordance with the procedure referred to in Article 251.]

[3505]

NOTES

Para 1 numbered as such and para 2 added by the Treaty of Nice, Art 2(2).

PART THREE
COMMUNITY POLICIES

TITLE III
FREE MOVEMENT OF PERSONS, SERVICES AND CAPITAL

CHAPTER 1
WORKERS

Article 39

(ex Article 48)

1. Freedom of movement for workers shall be secured within the Community.

2. Such freedom of movement shall entail the abolition of any discrimination based on nationality between workers of the Member States as regards employment, remuneration and other conditions of work and employment.

3. It shall entail the right, subject to limitations justified on grounds of public policy, public security or public health:
- (a) to accept offers of employment actually made;
- (b) to move freely within the territory of Member States for this purpose;
- (c) to stay in a Member State for the purpose of employment in accordance with the provisions governing the employment of nationals of that State laid down by law, regulation or administrative action;
- (d) to remain in the territory of a Member State after having been employed in that State, subject to conditions which shall be embodied in implementing regulations to be drawn up by the Commission.

4. The provisions of this Article shall not apply to employment in the public service.

[3506]

Article 40

(ex Article 49)

The Council shall, acting in accordance with the procedure referred to in Article 251 and after consulting the Economic and Social Committee, issue directives or make regulations setting out the measures required to bring about freedom of movement for workers, as defined in Article 39, in particular:
- (a) by ensuring close co-operation between national employment services;
- (b) by abolishing those administrative procedures and practices and those qualifying periods in respect of eligibility for available employment, whether resulting from national legislation or from agreements previously concluded between Member States, the maintenance of which would form an obstacle to liberalisation of the movement of workers;
- (c) by abolishing all such qualifying periods and other restrictions provided for either under national legislation or under agreements previously concluded between Member States as imposed on workers of other Member States conditions regarding the free choice of employment other than those imposed on workers of the State concerned;
- (d) by setting up appropriate machinery to bring offers of employment into touch with applications for employment and to facilitate the achievement of a balance between supply and demand in the employment market in such a way as to avoid serious threats to the standard of living and level of employment in the various regions and industries.

[3507]

Article 41

(ex Article 50)

Member States shall, within the framework of a joint programme, encourage the exchange of young workers.

[3508]

Article 42

(ex Article 51)

The Council shall, acting in accordance with the procedure referred to in Article 251, adopt such measures in the field of social security as are necessary to provide freedom of movement for workers; to this end, it shall make arrangements to secure for migrant workers and their dependants:
- (a) aggregation, for the purpose of acquiring and retaining the right to benefit and of calculating the amount of benefit, of all periods taken into account under the laws of the several countries;
- (b) payment of benefits to persons resident in the territories of Member States.

The Council shall act unanimously throughout the procedure referred to in Article 251.

[3509]

PART 3

CHAPTER 3
SERVICES

Article 49

(ex Article 59)

Within the framework of the provisions set out below, restrictions on freedom to provide services within the Community shall be prohibited in respect of nationals of Member States who are established in a State of the Community other than that of the person for whom the services are intended.

The Council may, acting by a qualified majority on a proposal from the Commission, extend the provisions of the Chapter to nationals of a third country who provide services and who are established within the Community.

[3510]

Article 50

(ex Article 60)

Services shall be considered to be 'services' within the meaning of this Treaty where they are normally provided for remuneration, insofar as they are not governed by the provisions relating to freedom of movement for goods, capital and persons.

'Services' shall in particular include—

(a) activities of an industrial character;
(b) activities of a commercial character;
(c) activities of craftsmen;
(d) activities of the professions.

Without prejudice to the provisions of the Chapter relating to the right of establishment, the person providing a service may, in order to do so, temporarily pursue his activity in the State where the service is provided, under the same conditions as are imposed by that State on its own nationals.

[3511]

Article 54

(ex Article 65)

As long as restrictions on freedom to provide services have not been abolished, each Member State shall apply such restrictions without distinction on grounds of nationality or residence to all persons providing services within the meaning of the first paragraph of Article 49.

[3512]

TITLE VI
COMMON RULES ON COMPETITION, TAXATION AND APPROXIMATION OF LAWS

CHAPTER III
APPROXIMATION OF LAWS

Article 94

(ex Article 100)

The Council shall, acting unanimously on a proposal from the Commission and after consulting the European Parliament and the Economic and Social Committee, issue directives for the approximation of such laws, regulations or administrative provisions of the Member States as directly affect the establishment or functioning of the common market.

[3513]

Article 95

(ex Article 100a)

1. By way of derogation from Article 94 and save where otherwise provided in this Treaty, the following provisions shall apply for the achievement of the objectives set out in

Article 14. The Council shall, acting in accordance with the procedure referred to in Article 251 and after consulting the Economic and Social Committee, adopt the measures for the approximation of the provisions laid down by law, regulation or administrative action in Member States which have as their object the establishment and functioning of the internal market.

2. Paragraph 1 shall not apply to fiscal provisions, to those relating to the free movement of persons nor to those relating to the rights and interests of employed persons.

3. The Commission, in its proposals envisaged in paragraph 1 concerning health, safety, environmental protection and consumer protection, will take as a base a high level of protection, taking account in particular of any new development based on scientific facts. Within their respective powers, the European Parliament and the Council will also seek to achieve this objective.

4. If, after the adoption by the Council or by the Commission of a harmonisation measure, a Member State deems it necessary to maintain national provisions on grounds of major needs referred to in Article 30, or relating to the protection of the environment or the working environment, it shall notify the Commission of these provisions as well as the grounds for maintaining them.

5. Moreover, without prejudice to paragraph 4, if, after the adoption by the Council or by the Commission of a harmonisation measure, a Member State deems it necessary to introduce national provisions based on new scientific evidence relating to the protection of the environment or the working environment on grounds of a problem specific to that Member State arising after the adoption of the harmonisation measure, it shall notify the Commission of the envisaged provisions as well as the grounds for introducing them.

6. The Commission shall, within six months of the notifications as referred to in paragraphs 4 and 5, approve or reject the national provisions involved after having verified whether or not they are a means of arbitrary discrimination or a disguised restriction on trade between Member States and whether or not they shall constitute an obstacle to the functioning of the internal market.

In the absence of a decision by the Commission within this period the national provisions referred to in paragraphs 4 and 5 shall be deemed to have been approved.

When justified by the complexity of the matter and in the absence of danger for human health, the Commission may notify the Member State concerned that the period referred to in this paragraph may be extended for a further period of up to six months.

7. When, pursuant to paragraph 6, a Member State is authorised to maintain or introduce national provisions derogating from a harmonisation measure, the Commission shall immediately examine whether to propose an adaptation to that measure.

8. When a Member State raises a specific problem on public health in a field which has been the subject of prior harmonisation measures, it shall bring it to the attention of the Commission which shall immediately examine whether to propose appropriate measures to the Council.

9. By way of derogation from the procedure laid down in Articles 226 and 227, the Commission and any Member State may bring the matter directly before the Court of Justice if it considers that another Member State is making improper use of the powers provided for in this Article.

10. The harmonisation measures referred to above shall, in appropriate cases, include a safeguard clause authorising the Member States to take, for one or more of the non-economic reasons referred to in Article 30, provisional measures subject to a Community control procedure.

[3514]

TITLE VIII
EMPLOYMENT

Article 125

(ex Article 109n)

Member States and the Community shall, in accordance with this Title, work towards developing a co-ordinated strategy for employment and particularly for promoting a skilled, trained and adaptable workforce and labour markets responsive to economic change with a view to achieving the objectives defined in Article 2 of the Treaty on European Union and in Article 2 of this Treaty.

[3515]

Article 126

(ex Article 109o)

1. Member States, through their employment policies, shall contribute to the achievement of the objectives referred to in Article 125 in a way consistent with the broad guidelines of the economic policies of the Member States and of the Community adopted pursuant to Article 99(2).

2. Member States, having regard to national practices related to the responsibilities of management and labour, shall regard promoting employment as a matter of common concern and shall co-ordinate their action in this respect within the Council, in accordance with the provisions of Article 128.

[3516]

Article 127

(ex Article 109p)

1. The Community shall contribute to a high level of employment by encouraging co-operation between Member States and by supporting and, if necessary, complementing their action. In doing so, the competences of the Member States shall be respected.

2. The objective of a high level of employment shall be taken into consideration in the formulation and implementation of Community policies and activities.

[3517]

Article 128

(ex Article 109q)

1. The European Council shall each year consider the employment situation in the Community and adopt conclusions thereon, on the basis of a joint annual report by the Council and the Commission.

2. On the basis of the conclusions of the European Council, the Council, acting by a qualified majority on a proposal from the Commission and after consulting the European Parliament, the Economic and Social Committee, the Committee of the Regions and the Employment Committee referred to in Article 130, shall each year draw up guidelines which the Member States shall take into account in their employment policies. These guidelines shall be consistent with the broad guidelines adopted pursuant to Article 99(2).

3. Each Member State shall provide the Council and the Commission with an annual report on the principal measures taken to implement its employment policy in the light of the guidelines for employment as referred to in paragraph 2.

4. The Council, on the basis of the reports referred to in paragraph 3 and having received the views of the Employment Committee, shall each year carry out an examination of the implementation of the employment policies of the Member States in the light of the guidelines for employment. The Council, acting by a qualified majority on a recommendation from the Commission, may, if it considers it appropriate in the light of that examination, make recommendations to Member States.

5. On the basis of the results of that examination, the Council and the Commission shall make a joint annual report to the European Council on the employment situation in the Community and on the implementation of the guidelines for employment.

[3518]

Article 129

(ex Article 109r)

The Council, acting in accordance with the procedure referred to in Article 251 and after consulting the Economic and Social Committee and the Committee of the Regions, may adopt incentive measures designed to encourage co-operation between Member States and to support their action in the field of employment through initiatives aimed at developing exchanges of information and best practices, providing comparative analysis and advice as well as promoting innovative approaches and evaluating experiences, in particular by recourse to pilot projects.

Those measures shall not include harmonisation of the laws and regulations of the Member States.

[3519]

TITLE XI
SOCIAL POLICY, EDUCATION, VOCATIONAL TRAINING AND YOUTH

CHAPTER 1
SOCIAL PROVISIONS

Article 136

(ex Article 117)

The Community and the Member States, having in mind fundamental social rights such as those set out in the European Social Charter signed at Turin on 18 October 1961 and in the 1989 Community Charter of the Fundamental Social Rights of Workers, shall have as their objectives the promotion of employment, improved living and working conditions, so as to make possible their harmonisation while the improvement is being maintained, proper social protection, dialogue between management and labour, the development of human resources with a view to lasting high employment and the combating of exclusion.

To this end the Community and the Member States shall implement measures which take account of the diverse forms of national practices, in particular in the field of contractual relations, and the need to maintain the competitiveness of the Community economy.

They believe that such a development will ensue not only from the functioning of the common market, which will favour the harmonisation of social systems, but also from the procedures provided for in this Treaty and from the approximation of provisions laid down by law, regulation or administrative action.

[3520]

[Article 137

(ex Article 118)

1. With a view to achieving the objectives of Article 136, the Community shall support and complement the activities of the Member States in the following fields—
   (a) improvement in particular of the working environment to protect workers' health and safety;
   (b) working conditions;
   (c) social security and social protection of workers;
   (d) protection of workers where their employment contract is terminated;
   (e) the information and consultation of workers;
   (f) representation and collective defence of the interests of workers and employers, including co-determination, subject to paragraph 5;
   (g) conditions of employment for third-country nationals legally residing in Community territory;
   (h) the integration of persons excluded from the labour market, without prejudice to Article 150;
   (i) equality between men and women with regard to labour market opportunities and treatment at work;
   (j) the combating of social exclusion;
   (k) the modernisation of social protection systems without prejudice to point (c).

2. To this end, the Council:
   (a) may adopt measures designed to encourage cooperation between Member States through initiatives aimed at improving knowledge, developing exchanges of information and best practices, promoting innovative approaches and evaluating experiences, excluding any harmonisation of the laws and regulations of the Member States;
   (b) may adopt, in the fields referred to in paragraph 1(a) to (i), by means of directives, minimum requirements for gradual implementation, having regard to the

PART 3

conditions and technical rules obtaining in each of the Member States. Such directives shall avoid imposing administrative, financial and legal constraints in a way which would hold back the creation and development of small and medium-sized undertakings.

The Council shall act in accordance with the procedure referred to in Article 251 after consulting the Economic and Social Committee and the Committee of the Regions, except in the fields referred to in paragraph 1(c), (d), (f) and (g) of this Article, where the Council shall act unanimously on a proposal from the Commission, after consulting the European Parliament and the said Committees. The Council, acting unanimously on a proposal from the Commission, after consulting the European Parliament, may decide to render the procedure referred to in Article 251 applicable to paragraph 1(d), (f) and (g) of this Article.

3. A Member State may entrust management and labour, at their joint request, with the implementation of directives adopted pursuant to paragraph 2.

In this case, it shall ensure that, no later than the date on which a directive must be transposed in accordance with Article 249, management and labour have introduced the necessary measures by agreement, the Member State concerned being required to take any necessary measure enabling it at any time to be in a position to guarantee the results imposed by that directive.

4. The provisions adopted pursuant to this Article:
- shall not affect the right of Member States to define the fundamental principles of their social security systems and must not significantly affect the financial equilibrium thereof;
- shall not prevent any Member State from maintaining or introducing more stringent protective measures compatible with this Treaty.

5. The provisions of this Article shall not apply to pay, the right of association, the right to strike or the right to impose lock-outs.]

[3521]

NOTES

Substituted by the Treaty of Nice, Art 2(9).

Article 138

(ex Article 118a)

1. The Commission shall have the task of promoting the consultation of management and labour at Community level and shall take any relevant measure to facilitate their dialogue by ensuring balanced support for the parties.

2. To this end, before submitting proposals in the social policy field, the Commission shall consult management and labour on the possible direction of Community action.

3. If, after such consultation, the Commission considers Community action advisable, it shall consult management and labour on the content of the envisaged proposal. Management and labour shall forward to the Commission an opinion or, where appropriate, a recommendation.

4. On the occasion of such consultation, management and labour may inform the Commission of their wish to initiate the process provided for in Article 139. The duration of the procedure shall not exceed nine months, unless the management and labour concerned and the Commission decide jointly to extend it.

[3522]

Article 139

(ex Article 118b)

1. Should management and labour so desire, the dialogue between them at Community level may lead to contractual relations, including agreements.

2. Agreements concluded at Community level shall be implemented either in accordance with the procedures and practices specific to management and labour and the Member States or, in matters covered by Article 137, at the joint request of the signatory parties, by a Council decision on a proposal from the Commission.

[The Council shall act by a qualified majority, except where the agreement in question contains one or more provisions relating to one of the areas for which unanimity is required pursuant to Article 137(2). In that case, it shall act unanimously.]

[3523]

NOTES

Para 2: words in square brackets substituted by The Treaty of Nice, Art 2(10).

Article 140

(ex Article 118c)

With a view to achieving the objectives of Article 136 and without prejudice to the other provisions of this Treaty, the Commission shall encourage co-operation between the Member States and facilitate the co-ordination of their action in all social policy fields under this chapter, particularly in matters relating to—

— employment;
— labour law and working conditions;
— basic and advanced vocational training;
— social security;
— prevention of occupational accidents and diseases;
— occupational hygiene;
— the right of association and collective bargaining between employers and workers.

To this end, the Commission shall act in close contact with Member States by making studies, delivering opinions and arranging consultations both on problems arising at national level and on those of concern to international organisations.

Before delivering the opinions provided for in this Article, the Commission shall consult the Economic and Social Committee.

[3524]

Article 141

(ex Article 119)

1. Each Member State shall ensure that the principle of equal pay for male and female workers for equal work or work of equal value is applied.

2. For the purpose of this Article, 'pay' means the ordinary basic or minimum wage or salary and any other consideration, whether in cash or in kind, which the worker receives directly or indirectly, in respect of his employment, from his employer.

Equal pay without discrimination based on sex means—

(a) that pay for the same work at piece rates shall be calculated on the basis of the same unit of measurement;
(b) that pay for work at time rates shall be the same for the same job.

3. The Council, acting in accordance with the procedure referred to in Article 251, and after consulting the Economic and Social Committee, shall adopt measures to ensure the application of the principle of equal opportunities and equal treatment of men and women in matters of employment and occupation, including the principle of equal pay for equal work or work of equal value.

4. With a view to ensuring full equality in practice between men and women in working life, the principle of equal treatment shall not prevent any Member State from maintaining or adopting measures providing for specific advantages in order to make it easier for the under-represented sex to pursue a vocational activity or to prevent or compensate for disadvantages in professional careers.

[3525]

Article 142

(ex Article 119a)

Member States shall endeavour to maintain the existing equivalence between paid holiday schemes.

[3526]

PART 3

Article 143

(ex Article 120)

The Commission shall draw up a report each year on progress in achieving the objectives of Article 136, including the demographic situation in the Community. It shall forward the report to the European Parliament, the Council and the Economic and Social Committee.

The European Parliament may invite the Commission to draw up reports on particular problems concerning the social situation.

[3527]

[Article 144

(ex Article 121)

The Council, after consulting the European Parliament, shall establish a Social Protection Committee with advisory status to promote cooperation on social protection policies between Member States and with the Commission. The tasks of the Committee shall be:

— to monitor the social situation and the development of social protection policies in the Member States and the Community;
— to promote exchanges of information, experience and good practice between Member States and with the Commission;
— without prejudice to Article 207, to prepare reports, formulate opinions or undertake other work within its fields of competence, at the request of either the Council or the Commission or on its own initiative.

In fulfilling its mandate, the Committee shall establish appropriate contacts with management and labour.

Each Member State and the Commission shall appoint two members of the Committee.]

[3528]

NOTES

Substituted by the Treaty of Nice, Art 2(11).

Article 145

(ex Article 122)

The Commission shall include a separate chapter on social developments within the Community in its annual report to the European Parliament.

The European Parliament may invite the Commission to draw up reports on any particular problems concerning social conditions.

[3529]

PART FIVE
INSTITUTIONS OF THE COMMUNITY

TITLE I
PROVISIONS GOVERNING THE INSTITUTIONS

CHAPTER 1
THE INSTITUTIONS

SECTION 4
THE COURT OF JUSTICE

[Article 220

(ex Article 164)

The Court of Justice and the Court of First Instance, each within its jurisdiction, shall ensure that in the interpretation and application of this Treaty the law is observed.

In addition, judicial panels may be attached to the Court of First Instance under the conditions laid down in Article 225a in order to exercise, in certain specific areas, the judicial competence laid down in this Treaty.]

[3530]

NOTES

Substituted by the Treaty of Nice, Art 2(26).

[Article 221

(ex Article 165)

The Court of Justice shall consist of one judge per Member State.

The Court of Justice shall sit in chambers or in a Grand Chamber, in accordance with the rules laid down for that purpose in the Statute of the Court of Justice.

When provided for in the Statute, the Court of Justice may also sit as a full Court.]

[3531]

NOTES

Substituted by the Treaty of Nice, Art 2(27).

[Article 222

(ex Article 166)

The Court of Justice shall be assisted by eight Advocates-General. Should the Court of Justice so request, the Council, acting unanimously, may increase the number of Advocates-General.

It shall be the duty of the Advocate-General, acting with complete impartiality and independence, to make, in open court, reasoned submissions on cases which, in accordance with the Statute of the Court of Justice, require his involvement.]

[3532]

NOTES

Substituted by the Treaty of Nice, Art 2(28).

[Article 223

(ex Article 167)

The Judges and Advocates-General of the Court of Justice shall be chosen from persons whose independence is beyond doubt and who possess the qualifications required for appointment to the highest judicial offices in their respective countries or who are jurisconsults of recognised competence; they shall be appointed by common accord of the governments of the Member States for a term of six years.

Every three years there shall be a partial replacement of the Judges and Advocates-General, in accordance with the conditions laid down in the Statute of the Court of Justice.

The Judges shall elect the President of the Court of Justice from among their number for a term of three years. He may be re-elected.

Retiring Judges and Advocates-General may be reappointed.

The Court of Justice shall appoint its Registrar and lay down the rules governing his service.

The Court of Justice shall establish its Rules of Procedure. Those Rules shall require the approval of the Council, acting by a qualified majority.]

[3533]

NOTES

Substituted by the Treaty of Nice, Art 2(29).

Article 226

(ex Article 169)

If the Commission considers that a Member State has failed to fulfil an obligation under this Treaty, it shall deliver a reasoned opinion on the matter after giving the State concerned the opportunity to submit its observations.

If the State concerned does not comply with the opinion within the period laid down by the Commission, the latter may bring the matter before the Court of Justice.

[3534]

Article 227

(ex Article 170)

A Member State which considers that another Member State has failed to fulfil an obligation under this Treaty may bring the matter before the Court of Justice.

Before a Member State brings an action against another Member State for an alleged infringement of an obligation under this Treaty, it shall bring the matter before the Commission.

The Commission shall deliver a reasoned opinion after each of the States concerned has been given the opportunity to submit its own case and its observations on the other party's case both orally and in writing.

If the Commission has not delivered an opinion within three months of the date on which the matter was brought before it, the absence of such opinion shall not prevent the matter from being brought before the Court of Justice.

[3535]

Article 228

(ex Article 171)

1. If the Court of Justice finds that a Member State has failed to fulfil an obligation under this Treaty, the State shall be required to take the necessary measures to comply with the judgment of the Court of Justice.

2. If the Commission considers that the Member State concerned has not taken such measures it shall, after giving that State the opportunity to submit its observations, issue a reasoned opinion specifying the points on which the Member State concerned has not complied with the judgment of the Court of Justice.

If the Member State concerned fails to take the necessary measures to comply with the Court's judgment within the time-limit laid down by the Commission, the latter may bring the case before the Court of Justice. In so doing it shall specify the amount of the lump sum or penalty payment to be paid by the Member State concerned which it considers appropriate in the circumstances.

If the Court of Justice finds that the Member State concerned has not complied with its judgment it may impose a lump sum or penalty payment on it.

This procedure shall be without prejudice to Article 227.

[3536]

Article 229

(ex Article 172)

Regulations adopted jointly by the European Parliament and the Council, and by the Council, pursuant to the provisions of this Treaty, may give the Court of Justice unlimited jurisdiction with regard to the penalties provided for in such regulations.

[3537]

[Article 229a

Without prejudice to the other provisions of this Treaty, the Council, acting unanimously on a proposal from the Commission and after consulting the European Parliament, may adopt provisions to confer jurisdiction, to the extent that it shall determine, on the Court of Justice in disputes relating to the application of acts adopted on the basis of this Treaty which create Community industrial property rights. The Council shall recommend those provisions to the Member States for adoption in accordance with their respective constitutional requirements.]

[3538]

NOTES

Inserted by the Treaty of Nice, Art 2(33).

Article 230

(ex Article 173)

The Court of Justice shall review the legality of acts adopted jointly by the European Parliament and the Council, of acts of the Council, of the Commission and of the ECB, other than recommendations and opinions, and of acts of the European Parliament intended to produce legal effects vis-à-vis third parties.

[It shall for this purpose have jurisdiction in actions brought by a Member State, the European Parliament, the Council or the Commission on grounds of lack of competence, infringement of an essential procedural requirement, infringement of this Treaty or of any rule of law relating to its application, or misuse of powers.

The Court of Justice shall have jurisdiction under the same conditions in actions brought by the Court of Auditors and by the ECB for the purpose of protecting their prerogatives.]

Any natural or legal person may, under the same conditions, institute proceedings against a decision addressed to that person or against a decision which, although in the form of a regulation or a decision addressed to another person, is of direct and individual concern to the former.

The proceedings provided for in this Article shall be instituted within two months of the publication of the measure, or of its notification to the plaintiff, or, in the absence thereof, of the day on which it came to the knowledge of the latter, as the case may be.

[3539]

NOTES

Words in square brackets substituted by the Treaty of Nice, Art 2(34).

Article 231

(ex Article 174)

If the action is well founded, the Court of Justice shall declare the act concerned to be void.

In the case of a regulation, however, the Court of Justice shall, if it considers this necessary, state which of the effects of the regulation which it has declared void shall be considered as definitive.

[3540]

Article 234

(ex Article 177)

The Court of Justice shall have jurisdiction to give preliminary rulings concerning:

(a) the interpretation of this Treaty;

(b) the validity and interpretation of acts of the institutions of the Community and of the ECB;

(c) the interpretation of the statutes of bodies established by an act of the Council, where those statutes so provide.

Where such a question is raised before any court or tribunal of a Member State, that court or tribunal may, if it considers that a decision on the question is necessary to enable it to give judgment, request the Court of Justice to give a ruling thereon.

Where any such question is raised in a case pending before a court or tribunal of a Member State against whose decisions there is no judicial remedy under national law, that court or tribunal shall bring the matter before the Court of Justice.

[3541]

Article 236

(ex Article 179)

The Court of Justice shall have jurisdiction in any dispute between the Community and its servants within the limits and under the conditions laid down in the Staff Regulations or the Conditions of Employment.

[3542]

CHAPTER 2
PROVISIONS COMMON TO SEVERAL INSTITUTIONS

Article 249

(ex Article 189)

In order to carry out their task and in accordance with the provisions of this Treaty, the European Parliament acting jointly with the Council, the Council and the Commission shall make regulations and issue directives, take decisions, make recommendations or deliver opinions.

A regulation shall have general application. It shall be binding in its entirety and directly applicable in all Member States.

A directive shall be binding, as to the result to be achieved, upon each Member State to which it is addressed, but shall leave to the national authorities the choice of form and methods.

A decision shall be binding in its entirety upon those to whom it is addressed.

Recommendations and opinions shall have no binding force.

[3543]

Article 250

(ex Article 189a)

1. Where, in pursuance of this Treaty, the Council acts on a proposal from the Commission, unanimity shall be required for an act constituting an amendment to that proposal, subject to Article 251(4) and (5).

2. As long as the Council has not acted, the Commission may alter its proposal at any time during the procedures leading to the adoption of a Community act.

[3544]

Article 251

(ex Article 189b)

1. Where reference is made in this Treaty to this Article for the adoption of an act, the following procedure shall apply.

2. The Commission shall submit a proposal to the European Parliament and the Council.

The Council, acting by a qualified majority after obtaining the opinion of the European Parliament,

— if it approves all the amendments contained in the European Parliament's opinion, may adopt the proposed act thus amended;
— if the European Parliament does not propose any amendments, may adopt the proposed act;
— shall otherwise adopt a common position and communicate it to the European Parliament. The Council shall inform the European Parliament fully of the reasons which led it to adopt its common position. The Commission shall inform the European Parliament fully of its position.

If, within three months of such communication, the European Parliament:

(a) approves the common position or has not taken a decision, the act in question shall be deemed to have been adopted in accordance with that common position;
(b) rejects, by an absolute majority of its component members, the common position, the proposed act shall be deemed not to have been adopted;
(c) proposes amendments to the common position by an absolute majority of its component members, the amended text shall be forwarded to the Council and to the Commission, which shall deliver an opinion on those amendments.

3. If, within three months of the matter being referred to it, the Council, acting by a qualified majority, approves all the amendments of the European Parliament, the act in question shall be deemed to have been adopted in the form of the common position thus amended; however, the Council shall act unanimously on the amendments on which the Commission has delivered a negative opinion. If the Council does not approve all the

amendments, the President of the Council, in agreement with the President of the European Parliament, shall within six weeks convene a meeting of the Conciliation Committee.

4. The Conciliation Committee, which shall be composed of the members of the Council or their representatives and an equal number of representatives of the European Parliament, shall have the task of reaching agreement on a joint text, by a qualified majority of the members of the Council or their representatives and by a majority of the representatives of the European Parliament. The Commission shall take part in the Conciliation Committee's proceedings and shall take all the necessary initiatives with a view to reconciling the positions of the European Parliament and the Council. In fulfilling this task, the Conciliation Committee shall address the common position on the basis of the amendments proposed by the European Parliament.

5. If, within six weeks of its being convened, the Conciliation Committee approves a joint text, the European Parliament, acting by an absolute majority of the votes cast, and the Council, acting by a qualified majority, shall each have a period of six weeks from that approval in which to adopt the act in question in accordance with the joint text. If either of the two institutions fails to approve the proposed act within that period, it shall be deemed not to have been adopted.

6. Where the Conciliation Committee does not approve a joint text, the proposed act shall be deemed not to have been adopted.

7. The periods of three months and six weeks referred to in this Article shall be extended by a maximum of one month and two weeks respectively at the initiative of the European Parliament or the Council.

[3545]

Article 252

(ex Article 189c)

Where reference is made in this Treaty to this Article for the adoption of an act, the following procedure shall apply—

(a) The Council, acting by a qualified majority on a proposal from the Commission and after obtaining the opinion of the European Parliament, shall adopt a common position.

(b) The Council's common position shall be communicated to the European Parliament. The Council and the Commission shall inform the European Parliament fully of the reasons which led the Council to adopt its common position and also of the Commission's position.
If, within three months of such communication, the European Parliament approves this common position or has not taken a decision within that period, the Council shall definitively adopt the act in question in accordance with the common position.

(c) The European Parliament may, within the period of three months referred to in point (b), by an absolute majority of its component Members, propose amendments to the Council's common position. The European Parliament may also, by the same majority, reject the Council's common position. The result of the proceedings shall be transmitted to the Council and the Commission.
If the European Parliament has rejected the Council's common position, unanimity shall be required for the Council to act on a second reading.

(d) The Commission shall, within a period of one month, re-examine the proposal on the basis of which the Council adopted its common position, by taking into account the amendments proposed by the European Parliament.
The Commission shall forward to the Council, at the same time as its re-examined proposal, the amendments of the European Parliament which it has not accepted, and shall express its opinion on them. The Council may adopt these amendments unanimously.

(e) The Council, acting by a qualified majority, shall adopt the proposal as re-examined by the Commission.
Unanimity shall be required for the Council to amend the proposal as re-examined by the Commission.

(f) In the cases referred to in points (c), (d) and (e), the Council shall be required to act within a period of three months. If no decision is taken within this period, the Commission proposal shall be deemed not to have been adopted.

(g) The periods referred to in points (b) and (f) may be extended by a maximum of one month by common accord between the Council and the European Parliament.

[3546]

Article 253

(ex Article 190)

Regulations, directives and decisions adopted jointly by the European Parliament and the Council, and such acts adopted by the Council or the Commission, shall state the reasons on which they are based and shall refer to any proposals or opinions which were required to be obtained pursuant to this Treaty.

[3547]

PART SIX
GENERAL AND FINAL PROVISIONS

Article 308

(ex Article 235)

If action by the Community should prove necessary to attain, in the course of the operation of the common market, one of the objectives of the Community and this Treaty has not provided the necessary powers, the Council shall, acting unanimously on a proposal from the Commission and after consulting the European Parliament, take the appropriate measures.

[3548]

COMMUNITY CHARTER OF THE FUNDAMENTAL SOCIAL RIGHTS OF WORKERS

[10 December 1989]

NOTES

This "Social Charter" was adopted by the Heads of Government of all member states of the Community except the United Kingdom. It was subsequently adopted by the United Kingdom in 1998. There is no express legal provision for such a charter in the Treaty and it does not have any direct legal status except as instructions to the Commission to prepare a programme of measures to implement its objectives. It is included for its general interest and because of the importance of the Community instruments it may generate and has generated, including the Protocol to the Maastricht Treaty on Social Policy 1992, and because of its relevance to issues arising on the legality or interpretation of EU measures before the Court.

THE HEADS OF STATE AND GOVERNMENT OF THE MEMBER STATES OF THE EUROPEAN COMMUNITY MEETING AT STRASBOURG ON 10 DECEMBER 1989

Whereas, under the terms of Article 117 of the EEC Treaty, the Member States have agreed on the need to promote improved living and working conditions for workers so as to make possible their harmonisation while the improvement is being maintained;

Whereas following on from the conclusions of the European Councils of Hanover and Rhodes the European Council of Madrid considered that, in the context of the establishment of the single European market, the same importance must be attached to the social aspects as to the economic aspects and whereas, therefore, they must be developed in a balanced manner;

Having regard to the Resolutions of the European Parliament of 15 March 1989 and 14 September 1989 and to the Opinion of the Economic and Social Committee of 22 February 1989;

Whereas the completion of the internal market is the most effective means of creating employment and ensuring maximum well-being in the Community; whereas employment development and creation must be given first priority in the completion of the internal market; whereas it is for the Community to take up the challenges of the future with regard to economic competitiveness, taking into account, in particular, regional imbalances;

Whereas the social consensus contributes to the strengthening of the competitiveness of undertakings and of the economy as a whole and to the creation of employment; whereas in this respect it is an essential condition for ensuring sustained economic development;

Whereas the completion of the internal market must favour the approximation of improvements in living and working conditions, as well as economic and social cohesion within the European Community, while avoiding distortions of competition;

Whereas the completion of the internal market must offer improvements in the social field for workers of the European Community, especially in terms of freedom of movement, living and working conditions, health and safety at work, social protection, education and training;

Whereas, in order to ensure equal treatment, it is important to combat every form of discrimination, including discrimination on grounds of sex, colour, race, opinion and beliefs, and whereas, in a spirit of solidarity, it is important to combat social exclusion;

Whereas it is for Member States to guarantee that workers from non-member countries and members of their families who are legally resident in a Member State of the European Community are able to enjoy, as regards their living and working conditions, treatment comparable to that enjoyed by workers who are nationals of the Member State concerned;

Whereas inspiration should be drawn from the Conventions of the International Labour Organisation and from the European Social Charter of the Council of Europe;

Whereas the Treaty, as amended by the Single European Act, contains provisions laying down the powers of the Community relating, inter alia, to the freedom of movement of workers (Articles 7, 48–51), to the right of establishment (Articles 52–58), to the social field under the conditions laid down in Articles 117–122—in particular as regards the improvement of health and safety in the working environment (Article 118a), the development of the dialogue between management and labour at European level (Article 118b), equal pay for men and women for equal work (Article 119)—to the general principles for implementing a common vocational training policy (Article 128), to economic and social cohesion (Article 130a to 130e) and, more generally, to the approximation of legislation (Articles 100, 100a and 235); whereas the implementation of the Charter must not entail an extension of the Community's powers as defined by the Treaties;

Whereas the aim of the present Charter is on the one hand to consolidate the progress made in the social field, through action by the Member States, the two sides of industry and the Community;

Whereas its aim is on the other hand to declare solemnly that the implementation of the Single European Act must take full account of the social dimension of the Community and that it is necessary in this context to ensure at appropriate levels the development of the social rights of workers of the European Community, especially employed workers and self-employed persons;

Whereas, in accordance with the conclusions of the Madrid European Council, the respective roles of Community rules, national legislation and collective agreements must be clearly established;

Whereas, by virtue of the principle of subsidiarity, responsibility for the initiatives to be taken with regard to the implementation of these social rights lies with the Member States or their constituent parts and, within the limits of its powers, with the European Community; whereas such implementation may take the form of laws, collective agreements or existing practices at the various appropriate levels and whereas it requires in many spheres the active involvement of the two sides of industry;

Whereas the solemn proclamation of fundamental social rights at European Community level may not, when implemented, provide grounds for any retrogression compared with the situation currently existing in each Member State.

HAVE ADOPTED THE FOLLOWING DECLARATION CONSTITUTING THE "COMMUNITY CHARTER OF THE FUNDAMENTAL SOCIAL RIGHTS OF WORKERS"—

TITLE I
FUNDAMENTAL SOCIAL RIGHTS OF WORKERS

FREEDOM OF MOVEMENT

1. Every worker of the European Community shall have the right to freedom of movement throughout the territory of the Community, subject to restrictions justified on grounds of public order, public safety or public health.

2. The right to freedom of movement shall enable any worker to engage in any occupation or profession in the Community in accordance with the principles of equal treatment as regards access to employment, working conditions and social protection in the host country.

3. The right of freedom of movement shall also imply—

— harmonisation of conditions of residence in all Member States, particularly those concerning qualifications;

— elimination of obstacles arising from the non-recognition of diplomas or equivalent occupational qualifications;
— improvement of the living and working conditions of frontier workers.

[3549]

EMPLOYMENT AND REMUNERATION

4. Every individual shall be free to choose and engage in an occupation according to the regulations governing each occupation.

5. All employment shall be fairly remunerated.

To this effect, in accordance with arrangements applying in each country—
— workers shall be assured of an equitable wage, i e a wage sufficient to enable them to have a decent standard of living;
— workers subject to terms of employment other than an open-ended full time contract shall receive an equitable reference wage;
— wages may be withheld, seized or transferred only in accordance with the provisions of national law; such provisions should entail measures enabling the worker concerned to continue to enjoy the necessary means of subsistence for himself and his family.

6. Every individual must be able to have access to public placement services free of charge.

[3550]

IMPROVEMENT OF LIVING AND WORKING CONDITIONS

7. The completion of the internal market must lead to an improvement in the living and working conditions of workers in the European Community. This process must result from an approximation of these conditions while the improvement is being maintained, as regards in particular the duration and organisation of working time and forms of employment other than open-ended contracts, such as fixed-term contracts, part-time working, temporary work and seasonal work.

The improvement must cover, where necessary, the development of certain aspects of employment regulations such as procedures for collective redundancies and those regarding bankruptcies.

8. Every worker of the European Community shall have a right to a weekly rest period and to annual paid leave, the duration of which must be harmonised in accordance with national practices while the improvement is being maintained.

9. The conditions of employment of every worker of the European Community shall be stipulated in laws, in a collective agreement or in a contract of employment, according to arrangements applying in each country.

[3551]

SOCIAL PROTECTION

According to the arrangements applying in each country—

10. Every worker of the European Community shall have a right to adequate social protection and shall, whatever his status and whatever the size of the undertaking in which he is employed, enjoy an adequate level of social security benefits.

Persons who have been unable either to enter or re-enter the labour market and have no means of subsistence must be able to receive sufficient resources and social assistance in keeping with their particular situation.

[3552]

FREEDOM OF ASSOCIATION AND COLLECTIVE BARGAINING

11. Employers and workers of the European Community shall have the right of association in order to constitute professional organisations or trade unions of their choice for the defence of their economic and social interests.

Every employer and every worker shall have the freedom to join or not to join such organisations without any personal or occupational damage being thereby suffered by him.

12. Employers or employers' organisations, on the one hand, and workers' organisations, on the other, shall have the right to negotiate and conclude collective agreements under the conditions laid down by national legislation and practice.

The dialogue between the two sides of industry at European level which must be developed, may, if the parties deem it desirable, result in contractual relations, in particular at inter-occupational and sectoral level.

13. The right to resort to collective action in the event of a conflict of interests shall include the right to strike, subject to the obligations arising under national regulations and collective agreements.

In order to facilitate the settlement of industrial disputes the establishment and utilisation at the appropriate levels of conciliation, mediation and arbitration procedures should be encouraged in accordance with national practice.

14. The internal legal order of the Member States shall determine under which conditions and to what extent the rights provided for in Articles 11 to 13 apply to the armed forces, the police and the civil service.

[3553]

VOCATIONAL TRAINING

15. Every worker of the European Community must be able to have access to vocational training and to receive such training throughout his working life. In the conditions governing access to such training there may be no discrimination on grounds of nationality.

The competent public authorities, undertakings or the two sides of industry each within their own sphere of competence, should set up continuing and permanent training systems enabling every person to undergo retraining more especially through leave for training purposes, to improve his skills or to acquire new skills, particularly in the light of technical developments.

[3554]

EQUAL TREATMENT FOR MEN AND WOMEN

16. Equal treatment for men and women must be assured. Equal opportunities for men and women must be developed.

To this end, action should be intensified wherever necessary to ensure the implementation of the principle of equality between men and women as regards in particular access to employment, remuneration, working conditions, social protection, education, vocational training and career development.

Measures should also be developed enabling men and women to reconcile their occupational and family obligations.

[3555]

INFORMATION, CONSULTATION AND PARTICIPATION FOR WORKERS

17. Information, consultation and participation for workers must be developed along appropriate lines, taking account of the practice in force in the various Member States.

This shall apply especially in companies or groups of companies having establishments or companies in several Member States of the European Community.

18. Such information, consultation and participation must be implemented in due time, particularly in the following cases—

- when technological changes which, from the point of view of working conditions and work organisation, have major implications for the work force are introduced into undertakings;
- in connection with restructuring operations in undertakings or in cases of mergers having an impact on the employment of workers;
- in cases of collective redundancy procedures;
- when transfrontier workers in particular are affected by employment policies pursued by the undertaking where they are employed.

[3556]

HEALTH PROTECTION AND SAFETY AT THE WORKPLACE

19. Every worker must enjoy satisfactory health and safety conditions in his working environment. Appropriate measures must be taken in order to achieve further harmonisation of conditions in this area while maintaining the improvements made.

These measures shall take account, in particular, of the need for the training, information, consultation and balanced participation of workers as regards the risks incurred and the steps taken to eliminate or reduce them.

The provisions regarding implementation of the internal market shall help to ensure such protection.

[3557]

PROTECTION OF CHILDREN AND ADOLESCENTS

20. Without prejudice to such rules as may be more favourable to young people, in particular those ensuring their preparation for work through vocational training, and subject to derogations limited to certain light work, the minimum employment age must not be lower than the minimum school-leaving age and, in any case, not lower than 15 years.

21. Young people who are in gainful employment must receive equitable remuneration in accordance with national practice.

22. Appropriate measures must be taken to adjust labour regulations applicable to young workers so that their specific needs regarding development, vocational training and access to employment are met.

The duration of work must, in particular, be limited—without it being possible to circumvent this limitation through recourse to overtime—and night work prohibited in the case of workers of under eighteen years of age, save in the case of certain jobs laid down in national legislation or regulations.

23. Following the end of compulsory education, young people must be entitled to receive initial vocational training of a sufficient duration to enable them to adapt to the requirements of their future working life; for young workers, such training should take place during working hours.

[3558]

ELDERLY PERSONS

According to the arrangements applying in each country—

24. Every worker of the European Community must, at the time of retirement, be able to enjoy resources affording him or her a decent standard of living.

25. Every person who has reached retirement age but who is not entitled to a pension or who does not have other means of subsistence, must be entitled to sufficient resources and to medical and social assistance specifically suited to his needs.

[3559]

DISABLED PERSONS

26. All disabled persons, whatever the origin and nature of their disablement, must be entitled to additional concrete measures aimed at improving their social and professional integration.

These measures must concern, in particular, according to the capacities of the beneficiaries, vocational training, ergonomics, accessibility, mobility, means of transport and housing.

[3560]

TITLE II
IMPLEMENTATION OF THE CHARTER

27. It is more particularly the responsibility of the Member States, in accordance with the national practices, notably through legislative measures or collective agreements, to guarantee the fundamental social rights in this Charter and to implement the social measures indispensable to the smooth operation of the internal market as part of a strategy of economic and social cohesion.

28. The European Council invites the Commission to submit as soon as possible initiatives which fall within its powers, as provided for in the Treaties, with a view to the adoption of legal instruments for the effective implementation, as and when the internal market is completed, of those rights which come within the Community's area of competence.

29. The Commission shall establish each year, during the last three months, a report on the application of the Charter by the Member States and by the European Community.

30. The report of the Commission shall be forwarded to the European Council, the European Parliament and the Economic and Social Committee.

[3561]–[3700]

AGREEMENT ON SOCIAL POLICY CONCLUDED BETWEEN THE MEMBER STATES OF THE EUROPEAN COMMUNITY WITH THE EXCEPTION OF THE UNITED KINGDOM OF GREAT BRITAIN AND NORTHERN IRELAND 1992 (NOTE)

NOTES

This Agreement, which was incorporated into the (Maastricht) Treaty on European Union 1992 via the Protocol on Social Policy, has been substantively incorporated into the Consolidated Treaty Establishing the European Community enacted by the Treaty of Amsterdam (see in particular Arts 138–141 at **[3522]**–**[3525]**), and therefore lapsed on the coming into force of the Treaty of Amsterdam on 1 May 1999.

[3701]

B. REGULATIONS, DIRECTIVES AND RECOMMENDATIONS

COUNCIL DIRECTIVE

of 10 February 1975

on the approximation of the laws of the Member States relating to the application of the principle of equal pay for men and women

(75/117/EEC)

NOTES

Date of publication in OJ: OJ L45, 19.2.75, p 19.

This Directive is repealed, with effect from 15 August 2009, by the Directive of the European Parliament and of the Council on the implementation of the principle of equal opportunities and equal treatment of men and women in matters of employment and occupation (recast) (Directive 2006/54/EC at **[4122]** et seq). The 2006 Directive consolidates and updates the four major Directives on gender equality; ie, this Directive, the Equal Treatment Directive (76/207/EEC), the Directive on Equal Treatment in Occupational Social Security Schemes (86/378/EEC), and the Burden of Proof Directive (97/80/EC). These Directives are repealed by Art 34 of, and Annex I, Pt A to, the 2006 Directive, with effect from 15 August 2009 (see **[4155]** and **[4158]**).

For the domestic legislation treated as implementing this Directive see the Equal Pay Act 1970, at **[5]**.

THE COUNCIL OF THE EUROPEAN COMMUNITIES,

Having regard to the Treaty establishing the European Economic Community, and in particular Article 100 thereof:

Having regard to the proposal from the Commission;

Having regard to the Opinion of the European Parliament;[1] *Having regard to the Opinion of the Economic and Social Committee;*[2]

Whereas implementation of the principle that men and women should receive equal pay contained in Article 119 of the Treaty is an integral part of the establishment and functioning of the common market;

Whereas it is primarily the responsibility of the Member States to ensure the application of this principle by means of appropriate laws, regulations and administrative provisions;

Whereas the Council resolution of January 21, 1974[3] *concerning a social action programme, aimed at making it possible to harmonise living and working conditions while the improvement is being maintained and at achieving a balanced social and economic development of the Community, recognised that priority should be given to action taken on behalf of women as regards access to employment and vocational training and advancement, and as regards working conditions, including pay;*

Whereas it is desirable to reinforce the basic laws by standards aimed at facilitating the practical application of the principle of equality in such a way that all employees in the Community can be protected in these matters;

Whereas differences continue to exist in the various Member States despite the efforts made to apply the resolution of the conference of the Member States of December 30, 1961 on equal pay for men and women and whereas, therefore, the national provisions should be approximated as regards application of the principle of equal pay.

NOTES

Repealed as noted at the beginning of this Directive.

1 OJ C55, 13.5.74, p 43.
2 OJ C88, 26.7.74, p 7.
3 OJ C13, 12.2.74, p 1.

HAS ADOPTED THIS DIRECTIVE—

Article 1

The principle of equal pay for men and women outlined in Article 119 of the Treaty, hereinafter called "principle of equal pay", means, for the same work or for work to which equal value is attributed, the elimination of all discrimination on grounds of sex with regard to all aspects and conditions of remuneration.

In particular, where a job classification system is used for determining pay, it must be based on the same criteria for both men and women and so drawn up as to exclude any discrimination on grounds of sex.

[3702]

NOTES

Repealed as noted at the beginning of this Directive.

Article 2

Member States shall introduce into their national legal systems such measures as are necessary to enable all employees who consider themselves wronged by failure to apply the principle of equal pay to pursue their claims by judicial process after possible recourse to other competent authorities.

[3703]

NOTES

Repealed as noted at the beginning of this Directive.

Article 3

Member States shall abolish all discrimination between men and women arising from laws, regulations or administrative provisions which is contrary to the principle of equal pay.

[3704]

NOTES

Repealed as noted at the beginning of this Directive.

Article 4

Member States shall take the necessary measures to ensure that provisions appearing in collective agreements, wage scales, wage agreements or individual contracts of employment which are contrary to the principle of equal pay shall be, or may be declared, null and void or may be amended.

[3705]

NOTES

Repealed as noted at the beginning of this Directive.

Article 5

Member States shall take the necessary measures to protect employees against dismissal by the employer as a reaction to a complaint within the undertaking or to any legal proceedings aimed at enforcing compliance with the principle of equal pay.

[3706]

NOTES

Repealed as noted at the beginning of this Directive.

Article 6

Member States shall, in accordance with their national circumstances and legal systems, take the measures necessary to ensure that the principle of equal pay is applied. They shall see that effective means are available to take care that this principle is observed.

[3707]

NOTES

Repealed as noted at the beginning of this Directive.

Article 7

Member States shall take care that the provisions adopted pursuant to this Directive together with the relevant provisions already in force, are brought to the attention of employees by all appropriate means, for example at their place of employment.

[3708]

NOTES

Repealed as noted at the beginning of this Directive.

Article 8

1. Member States shall put into force the laws, regulations and administrative provisions necessary in order to comply with this Directive within one year of its notification and shall immediately inform the Commission thereof.

2. Member States shall communicate to the Commission the texts of the laws, regulations and administrative provisions which they adopt in the field covered by this Directive.

[3709]

NOTES

Repealed as noted at the beginning of this Directive.

Article 9

Within two years of the expiry of the one-year period referred to in Article 8, Member States shall forward all necessary information to the Commission to enable it to draw up a report on the application of this Directive for submission to the Council.

[3710]

NOTES

Repealed as noted at the beginning of this Directive.

Article 10

This Directive is addressed to the Member States.

[3711]

NOTES

Repealed as noted at the beginning of this Directive.

COUNCIL DIRECTIVE

of 17 February 1975

on the approximation of the laws of the Member States relating to collective redundancies (Note)

(75/129/EEC)

NOTES

Date of publication in OJ: OJ L39, 14.2.76, p 40.

This Directive (as amended by Council Directive 92/56/EC) has been repealed and replaced by Council Directive 98/59/EC (OJ L225, 12.8.98, p 16) at **[3955]**.

[3712]

COUNCIL DIRECTIVE

of 9 February 1976

on the implementation of the principle of equal treatment for men and women as regards access to employment, vocational training and promotion, and working conditions

(76/207/EEC)

NOTES

Date of publication in OJ: OJ L39, 14.2.76, p 40.

This Directive is repealed, with effect from 15 August 2009, by the Directive of the European Parliament and of the Council on the implementation of the principle of equal opportunities and equal treatment of men and women in matters of employment and occupation (recast) (Directive 2006/54/EC at **[4122]** et seq). The 2006 Directive consolidates and updates the four major Directives on gender equality; ie, this Directive, the Equal Pay Directive (75/117/EEC), the Directive on Equal Treatment in Occupational Social Security Schemes (86/378/EEC), and the Burden of Proof Directive (97/80/EC). These Directives are repealed by Art 34 of, and Annex I, Pt A to, the 2006 Directive, with effect from 15 August 2009 (see **[4155]** and **[4158]**).

This Directive is printed as amended by European Parliament and Council Directive 2002/73, Art 1, which had a transposition date of 5 October 2005 (see Art 2 of the 2002 Directive at **[4066]**).

For the principal domestic legislation treated as implementing this Directive, see the Sex Discrimination Act 1975 at **[100]** et seq, as amended, inter alia, by the Employment Equality (Sex Discrimination) Regulations 2005, SI 2005/2467, to give effect to the amending Directive referred to above.

THE COUNCIL OF THE EUROPEAN COMMUNITIES,

Having regard to the Treaty establishing the European Economic Community, and in particular Article 235 thereof;

Having regard to the proposal from the Commission;

Having regard to the opinion of the European Parliament;[1]

Having regard to the opinion of the Economic and Social Committee;[2]

Whereas the Council, in its resolution of 21 January 1974 concerning a social action programme[3] *included among the priorities action for the purpose of achieving equality between men and women as regards access to employment and vocational training and promotion and as regards working conditions, including pay;*

Whereas, with regard to pay, the Council adopted on 10 February 1975 Directive 75/117/EEC on the approximation of the laws of the Member States relating to the application of the principle of equal pay for men and women;[4]

Whereas Community action to achieve the principle of equal treatment for men and women in respect of access to employment and vocational training and promotion and in respect of other working conditions also appears to be necessary; whereas, equal treatment for male and female workers constitutes one of the objectives of the Community, in so far as the harmonization of living and working conditions while maintaining their improvement are inter alia to be furthered; whereas the Treaty does not confer the necessary specific powers for this purpose;

Whereas the definition and progressive implementation of the principle of equal treatment in matters of social security should be ensured by means of subsequent instruments,

NOTES

Repealed as noted at the beginning of this Directive.

1 OJ C111, 20.5.75, p 14.
2 OJ C286, 15.12.75, p 8.
3 OJ C13, 12.2.74, p 1.
4 OJ L45, 19.2.75, p 19.

HAS ADOPTED THIS DIRECTIVE—

Article 1

1. The purpose of this Directive is to put into effect in the Member States the principle of equal treatment for men and women as regards access to employment, including promotion, and to vocational training and as regards working conditions and, on the conditions referred to in paragraph 2, social security. This principle is hereinafter referred to as "the principle of equal treatment".

[1a. Member States shall actively take into account the objective of equality between men and women when formulating and implementing laws, regulations, administrative provisions, policies and activities in the areas referred to in paragraph 1.]

2. With a view to ensuring the progressive implementation of the principle of equal treatment in matters of social security, the Council, acting on a proposal from the Commission, will adopt provisions defining its substance, its scope and the arrangements for its application.

[3713]

NOTES

Repealed as noted at the beginning of this Directive.

Para 1a: inserted by European Parliament and Council Directive 2002/73, Art 1(2).

[Article 2

1. For the purposes of the following provisions, the principle of equal treatment shall mean that there shall be no discrimination whatsoever on grounds of sex either directly or indirectly by reference in particular to marital or family status.

2. For the purposes of this Directive, the following definitions shall apply—

— *direct discrimination: where one person is treated less favourably on grounds of sex than another is, has been or would be treated in a comparable situation,*

— *indirect discrimination: where an apparently neutral provision, criterion or practice would put persons of one sex at a particular disadvantage compared with persons of the other sex, unless that provision, criterion or practice is objectively justified by a legitimate aim, and the means of achieving that aim are appropriate and necessary,*

— *harassment: where an unwanted conduct related to the sex of a person occurs with the purpose or effect of violating the dignity of a person, and of creating an intimidating, hostile, degrading, humiliating or offensive environment,*

— *sexual harassment: where any form of unwanted verbal, non-verbal or physical conduct of a sexual nature occurs, with the purpose or effect of violating the dignity of a person, in particular when creating an intimidating, hostile, degrading, humiliating or offensive environment.*

3. Harassment and sexual harassment within the meaning of this Directive shall be deemed to be discrimination on the grounds of sex and therefore prohibited.

A person's rejection of, or submission to, such conduct may not be used as a basis for a decision affecting that person.

4. An instruction to discriminate against persons on grounds of sex shall be deemed to be discrimination within the meaning of this Directive.

5. Member States shall encourage, in accordance with national law, collective agreements or practice, employers and those responsible for access to vocational training to take measures to prevent all forms of discrimination on grounds of sex, in particular harassment and sexual harassment at the workplace.

6. Member States may provide, as regards access to employment including the training leading thereto, that a difference of treatment which is based on a characteristic related to sex shall not constitute discrimination where, by reason of the nature of the particular occupational activities concerned or of the context in which they are carried out, such a characteristic constitutes a genuine and determining occupational requirement, provided that the objective is legitimate and the requirement is proportionate.

7. This Directive shall be without prejudice to provisions concerning the protection of women, particularly as regards pregnancy and maternity.

A woman on maternity leave shall be entitled, after the end of her period of maternity leave, to return to her job or to an equivalent post on terms and conditions which are no less favourable to her and to benefit from any improvement in working conditions to which she would be entitled during her absence.

Less favourable treatment of a woman related to pregnancy or maternity leave within the meaning of Directive 92/85/EEC shall constitute discrimination within the meaning of this Directive.

This Directive shall also be without prejudice to the provisions of Council Directive 96/34/EC of 3 June 1996 on the framework agreement on parental leave concluded by UNICE, CEEP and the ETUC[1] *and of Council Directive 92/85/EEC of 19 October 1992 on the introduction of measures to encourage improvements in the safety and health at work of pregnant workers and workers who have recently given birth or are breastfeeding (tenth individual Directive within the meaning of Article 16(1) of Directive 89/391/EEC).*[2] *It is also without prejudice to the right of Member States to recognise distinct rights to paternity and/or adoption leave. Those Member States which recognise such rights shall take the necessary measures to protect working men and women against dismissal due to exercising those rights and ensure that, at the end of such leave, they shall be entitled to return to their jobs or to equivalent posts on terms and conditions which are no less favourable to them, and to benefit from any improvement in working conditions to which they would have been entitled during their absence.*

8. Member States may maintain or adopt measures within the meaning of Article 141(4) of the Treaty with a view to ensuring full equality in practice between men and women.]

[3714]

NOTES

Substituted by European Parliament and Council Directive 2002/73, Art 1(2).
Repealed as noted at the beginning of this Directive.

1 OJ L145, 19.6.1996, p 4.
2 OJ L348, 28.11.1992, p 1.

[Article 3

1. Application of the principle of equal treatment means that there shall be no direct or indirect discrimination on the grounds of sex in the public or private sectors, including public bodies, in relation to—

(*a*) *conditions for access to employment, to self-employment or to occupation, including selection criteria and recruitment conditions, whatever the branch of activity and at all levels of the professional hierarchy, including promotion;*
(*b*) *access to all types and to all levels of vocational guidance, vocational training, advanced vocational training and retraining, including practical work experience;*
(*c*) *employment and working conditions, including dismissals, as well as pay as provided for in Directive 75/117/EEC;*
(*d*) *membership of, and involvement in, an organisation of workers or employers, or any organisation whose members carry on a particular profession, including the benefits provided for by such organisations.*

2. To that end, Member States shall take the necessary measures to ensure that—

(*a*) *any laws, regulations and administrative provisions contrary to the principle of equal treatment are abolished;*
(*b*) *any provisions contrary to the principle of equal treatment which are included in contracts or collective agreements, internal rules of undertakings or rules governing the independent occupations and professions and workers' and employers' organisations shall be, or may be declared, null and void or are amended.]*

[3715]–[3717]

NOTES

Substituted by European Parliament and Council Directive 2002/73, Art 1(3).
Repealed as noted at the beginning of this Directive.

Articles 4, 5

(*Repealed by European Parliament and Council Directive 2002/73, Art 1(4).*)

[Article 6

1. Member States shall ensure that judicial and/or administrative procedures, including where they deem it appropriate conciliation procedures, for the enforcement of obligations under this Directive are available to all persons who consider themselves wronged by failure to apply the principle of equal treatment to them, even after the relationship in which the discrimination is alleged to have occurred has ended.

2. Member States shall introduce into their national legal systems such measures as are necessary to ensure real and effective compensation or reparation as the Member States so determine for the loss and damage sustained by a person injured as a result of discrimination contrary to Article 3, in a way which is dissuasive and proportionate to the damage suffered; such compensation or reparation may not be restricted by the fixing of a prior upper limit, except in cases where the employer can prove that the only damage suffered by an applicant as a result of discrimination within the meaning of this Directive is the refusal to take his/her job application into consideration.

3. Member States shall ensure that associations, organisations or other legal entities which have, in accordance with the criteria laid down by their national law, a legitimate interest in ensuring that the provisions of this Directive are complied with, may engage, either on behalf or in support of the complainants, with his or her approval, in any judicial and/or administrative procedure provided for the enforcement of obligations under this Directive.

4. Paragraphs 1 and 3 are without prejudice to national rules relating to time limits for bringing actions as regards the principle of equal treatment.]

[3718]

NOTES

Substituted by European Parliament and Council Directive 2002/73, Art 1(5).
Repealed as noted at the beginning of this Directive.

[Article 7

Member States shall introduce into their national legal systems such measures as are necessary to protect employees, including those who are employees' representatives provided for by national laws and/or practices, against dismissal or other adverse treatment by the employer as a reaction to a complaint within the undertaking or to any legal proceedings aimed at enforcing compliance with the principle of equal treatment.]

[3719]

NOTES

Substituted by European Parliament and Council Directive 2002/73, Art 1(6).
Repealed as noted at the beginning of this Directive.

Article 8

Member States shall take care that the provisions adopted pursuant to this Directive, together with the relevant provisions already in force, are brought to the attention of employees by all appropriate means, for example at their place of employment.

[3720]

NOTES

Repealed as noted at the beginning of this Directive.

[Article 8a

1. Member States shall designate and make the necessary arrangements for a body or bodies for the promotion, analysis, monitoring and support of equal treatment of all persons without discrimination on the grounds of sex. These bodies may form part of agencies charged at national level with the defence of human rights or the safeguard of individuals' rights.

2. Member States shall ensure that the competences of these bodies include:

(*a*) *without prejudice to the right of victims and of associations, organisations or other legal entities referred to in Article 6(3), providing independent assistance to victims of discrimination in pursuing their complaints about discrimination;*
(*b*) *conducting independent surveys concerning discrimination;*
(*c*) *publishing independent reports and making recommendations on any issue relating to such discrimination.]*

[3721]

NOTES

Inserted by European Parliament and Council Directive 2002/73, Art 1(7).
Repealed as noted at the beginning of this Directive.

[Article 8b

1. Member States shall, in accordance with national traditions and practice, take adequate measures to promote social dialogue between the social partners with a view to fostering equal treatment, including through the monitoring of workplace practices, collective agreements, codes of conduct, research or exchange of experiences and good practices.

2. Where consistent with national traditions and practice, Member States shall encourage the social partners, without prejudice to their autonomy, to promote equality between women and men and to conclude, at the appropriate level, agreements laying down anti-discrimination rules in the fields referred to in Article 1 which fall within the scope of collective bargaining. These agreements shall respect the minimum requirements laid down by this Directive and the relevant national implementing measures.

3. Member States shall, in accordance with national law, collective agreements or practice, encourage employers to promote equal treatment for men and women in the workplace in a planned and systematic way.

4. To this end, employers should be encouraged to provide at appropriate regular intervals employees and/or their representatives with appropriate information on equal treatment for men and women in the undertaking.

Such information may include statistics on proportions of men and women at different levels of the organisation and possible measures to improve the situation in cooperation with employees' representatives.]

[3722]

NOTES

Inserted by European Parliament and Council Directive 2002/73, Art 1(7).
Repealed as noted at the beginning of this Directive.

[Article 8c

Member States shall encourage dialogue with appropriate non-governmental organisations which have, in accordance with their national law and practice, a legitimate interest in contributing to the fight against discrimination on grounds of sex with a view to promoting the principle of equal treatment.]

[3723]

NOTES

Inserted by European Parliament and Council Directive 2002/73, Art 1(7).
Repealed as noted at the beginning of this Directive.

[Article 8d

Member States shall lay down the rules on sanctions applicable to infringements of the national provisions adopted pursuant to this Directive, and shall take all measures necessary to ensure that they are applied.

The sanctions, which may comprise the payment of compensation to the victim, must be effective, proportionate and dissuasive. The Member States shall notify those provisions to the Commission by 5 October 2005 at the latest and shall notify it without delay of any subsequent amendment affecting them.]

[3724]

NOTES

Inserted by European Parliament and Council Directive 2002/73, Art 1(7).
Repealed as noted at the beginning of this Directive.

[Article 8e

1. Member States may introduce or maintain provisions which are more favourable to the protection of the principle of equal treatment than those laid down in this Directive.

2. The implementation of this Directive shall under no circumstances constitute grounds for a reduction in the level of protection against discrimination already afforded by Member States in the fields covered by this Directive.]

[3725]

NOTES

Inserted by European Parliament and Council Directive 2002/73, Art 1(7).
Repealed as noted at the beginning of this Directive.

Article 9

1. Member States shall put into force the laws, regulations and administrative provisions necessary in order to comply with this Directive within 30 months of its notification and shall immediately inform the Commission thereof.

However, as regards the first part of Article 3(2)(c) and the first part of Article 5(2)(c), Member States shall carry out a first examination and if necessary a first revision of the laws, regulations and administrative provisions referred to therein within four years of notification of this Directive.

2. Member States shall periodically assess the occupational activities referred to in Article 2(2) in order to decide, in the light of social developments, whether there is justification for maintaining the exclusions concerned. They shall notify the Commission of the results of this assessment.

3. Member States shall also communicate to the Commission the texts of laws, regulations and administrative provisions which they adopt in the field covered by this Directive.

[3726]

NOTES

Repealed as noted at the beginning of this Directive.

Article 10

Within two years following expiry of the 30-month period laid down in the first subparagraph of Article 9(1), Member States shall forward all necessary information to the Commission to enable it to draw up a report on the application of this Directive for submission to the Council.

[3727]

NOTES

Repealed as noted at the beginning of this Directive.

Article 11

This Directive is addressed to the Member States.

[3728]

NOTES

Repealed as noted at the beginning of this Directive.

COUNCIL DIRECTIVE

of 14 February 1977

on the approximation of the laws of the Member States relating to the safeguarding of employees' rights in the event of transfers of undertakings, businesses or parts of undertakings or businesses (Note)

(77/187/EEC)

NOTES

Date of publication in OJ: OJ L61, 5.3.77, p 26.
Repealed and replaced by Council Directive 2001/23/EC at **[4015]**.

[3729]

COUNCIL DIRECTIVE

of 19 December 1978

on the progressive implementation of the principle of equal treatment for men and women in matters of social security

(79/7/EEC)

NOTES

Date of publication in OJ: OJ L6, 10.1.79, p 24.

THE COUNCIL OF THE EUROPEAN COMMUNITIES,

Having regard to the Treaty establishing the European Economic Community, and in particular Article 235 thereof;

Having regard to the proposal from the Commission;[1]

Having regard to the opinion of the European Parliament;[2]

Having regard to the opinion of the Economic and Social Committee;[3]

Whereas Article 1(2) of Council Directive 76/207/EEC of 9 February 1976 on the implementation of the principle of equal treatment for men and women as regards access to employment, vocational training and promotion, and working conditions[4] provides that, with a view to ensuring the progressive implementation of the principle of equal treatment in matters of social security, the Council, acting on a proposal from the Commission, will adopt provisions defining its substance, its scope and the arrangements for its application; whereas the Treaty does not confer the specific powers required for this purpose;

Whereas the principle of equal treatment in matters of social security should be implemented in the first place in the statutory schemes which provide protection against the risks of sickness, invalidity, old age, accidents at work, occupational diseases and unemployment, and in social assistance in so far as it is intended to supplement or replace the abovementioned schemes;

Whereas the implementation of the principle of equal treatment in matters of social security does not prejudice the provisions relating to the protection of women on the ground of maternity; whereas, in this respect, Member States may adopt specific provisions for women to remove existing instances of unequal treatment,

NOTES

1. OJ C34, 11.2.77, p 3.
2. OJ C299, 12.12.77, p 13.
3. OJ C180, 28.7.77, p 36.
4. OJ L39, 14.2.76, p 40.

HAS ADOPTED THIS DIRECTIVE—

Article 1

The purpose of this Directive is the progressive implementation, in the field of social security and other elements of social protection provided for in Article 3, of the principle of equal treatment for men and women in matters of social security, hereinafter referred to as 'the principle of equal treatment'.

[3730]

Article 2

This Directive shall apply to the working population—including self-employed persons, workers and self-employed persons whose activity is interrupted by illness, accident or involuntary unemployment and persons seeking employment—and to retired or invalided workers and self-employed persons.

[3731]

Article 3

1. This Directive shall apply to—

(a) statutory schemes which provide protection against the following risks—
— sickness,
— invalidity,
— old age,
— accidents at work and occupational diseases,
— unemployment;

(b) social assistance, in so far as it is intended to supplement or replace the schemes referred to in (a).

2. This Directive shall not apply to the provisions concerning survivors' benefits nor to those concerning family benefits, except in the case of family benefits granted by way of increases of benefits due in respect of the risks referred to in paragraph 1(a).

3. With a view to ensuring implementation of the principle of equal treatment in occupational schemes, the Council, acting on a proposal from the Commission, will adopt provisions defining its substance, its scope and the arrangements for its application.

[3732]

Article 4

1. The principle of equal treatment means that there shall be no discrimination whatsoever on ground of sex either directly, or indirectly by reference in particular to marital or family status, in particular as concerns—

— the scope of the schemes and the conditions of access thereto,
— the obligation to contribute and the calculation of contributions,
— the calculation of benefits including increases due in respect of a spouse and for dependants and the conditions governing the duration and retention of entitlement to benefits.

2. The principle of equal treatment shall be without prejudice to the provisions relating to the protection of women on the grounds of maternity.

[3733]

Article 5

Member States shall take the measures necessary to ensure that any laws, regulations and administrative provisions contrary to the principle of equal treatment are abolished.

[3734]

Article 6

Member States shall introduce into their national legal systems such measures as are necessary to enable all persons who consider themselves wronged by failure to apply the principle of equal treatment to pursue their claims by judicial process, possibly after recourse to other competent authorities.

[3735]

Article 7

1. This Directive shall be without prejudice to the right of Member States to exclude from its scope—

(a) the determination of pensionable age for the purposes of granting old-age and retirement pensions and the possible consequences thereof for other benefits;

(b) advantages in respect of old-age pension schemes granted to persons who have brought up children; the acquisition of benefit entitlements following periods of interruption of employment due to the bringing up of children;

(c) the granting of old-age or invalidity benefit entitlements by virtue of the derived entitlements of a wife;

(d) the granting of increases of long-term invalidity, old-age, accidents at work and occupational disease benefits for a dependent wife;

(e) the consequences of the exercise, before the adoption of this Directive, of a right of option not to acquire rights to incur obligations under a statutory scheme.

2. Member States shall periodically examine matters excluded under paragraph 1 in order to ascertain, in the light of social developments in the matter concerned, whether there is justification for maintaining the exclusions concerned.

[3736]

Article 8

1. Member States shall bring into force the laws, regulations and administrative provisions necessary to comply with this Directive within six years of its notification. They shall immediately inform the Commission thereof.

2. Member States shall communicate to the Commission the text of laws, regulations and administrative provisions which they adopt in the field covered by this Directive, including measures adopted pursuant to Article 7(2).

They shall inform the Commission of their reasons for maintaining any existing provisions on the matters referred to in Article 7(1) and of the possibilities for reviewing them at a later date.

[3737]

Article 9

Within seven years of notification of this Directive, Member States shall forward all information necessary to the Commission to enable it to draw up a report on the application of this Directive for submission to the Council and to propose such further measures as may be required for the implementation of the principle of equal treatment.

[3738]

Article 10

This Directive is addressed to the Member States.

[3739]

[COUNCIL DIRECTIVE

of 20 October 1980

on the protection of employees in the event of the insolvency of their employer

(80/987/EEC)]

NOTES

Date of publication in OJ: OJ L283, 28.10.80, p 23.

This Directive is printed as amended by European Parliament and Council Directive 2002/74, Art 1, which had a transposition date of 8 October 2005 (see Art 2 of the 2002 Directive at **[4069]**).

Title: substituted by European Parliament and Council Directive 2002/74, Art 1(1). The original title was "Council Directive of 20 October 1980 on the approximation of the laws of the Member States relating to the protection of employees in the event of the insolvency of their employer".

For the domestic implementation of this Directive, see now the Employment Rights Act 1996, Pt XII at **[1226]–[1234]**.

THE COUNCIL OF THE EUROPEAN COMMUNITIES,

Having regard to the Treaty establishing the European Economic Community, and in particular Article 100 thereof,

Having regard to the proposal from the Commission,[1]

Having regard to the opinion of the European Parliament,[2]

Having regard to the opinion of the Economic and Social Committee,[3]

Whereas it is necessary to provide for the protection of employees in the event of the insolvency of their employer, in particular in order to guarantee payment of their outstanding claims, while taking account of the need for balanced economic and social development in the Community;

Whereas differences still remain between the Member States as regards the extent of the protection of employees in this respect; whereas efforts would be directed towards reducing these differences, which can have a direct effect on the functioning of the common market;

Whereas the approximation of laws in this field should, therefore, be promoted while the improvement within the meaning of Article 117 of the Treaty is maintained;

Whereas as a result of the geographical situation and the present job structures in that area, the labour market in Greenland is fundamentally different from that of the other areas of the Community;

Whereas to the extent that the Hellenic Republic is to become a member of the European Economic Community on 1 January 1981 in accordance with the Act concerning the Conditions of Accession of the Hellenic Republic and the Adjustments to the Treaties, it is appropriate to stipulate in the Annex to the Directive under the heading "Greece", those categories of employees whose claims may be excluded in accordance with Article 1(2) of the Directive,

NOTES

1 OJ C135, 9.6.79, p 2.
2 OJ C39, 12.2.79, p 26.
3 OJ C105, 26.4.79, p 15.

HAS ADOPTED THIS DIRECTIVE—

[SECTION I
SCOPE AND DEFINITIONS

Article 1

1. This Directive shall apply to employees' claims arising from contracts of employment or employment relationships and existing against employers who are in a state of insolvency within the meaning of Article 2(1).

2. Member States may, by way of exception, exclude claims by certain categories of employee from the scope of this Directive, by virtue of the existence of other forms of guarantee if it is established that these offer the persons concerned a degree of protection equivalent to that resulting from this Directive.

3. Where such provision already applies in their national legislation, Member States may continue to exclude from the scope of this Directive—

(a) domestic servants employed by a natural person;
(b) share-fishermen.]

[3740]

NOTES

Section I (Arts 1 and 2 and the preceding heading) substituted by European Parliament and Council Directive 2002/74, Art 1(2).

[Article 2

1. For the purposes of this Directive, an employer shall be deemed to be in a state of insolvency where a request has been made for the opening of collective proceedings based on insolvency of the employer, as provided for under the laws, regulations and administrative provisions of a Member State, and involving the partial or total divestment of the employer's assets and the appointment of a liquidator or a person performing a similar task, and the authority which is competent pursuant to the said provisions has—

(a) either decided to open the proceedings, or

(b) established that the employer's undertaking or business has been definitively closed down and that the available assets are insufficient to warrant the opening of the proceedings.

2. This Directive is without prejudice to national law as regards the definition of the terms 'employee', 'employer', 'pay', 'right conferring immediate entitlement' and 'right conferring prospective entitlement'.

However, the Member States may not exclude from the scope of this Directive—

(a) part-time employees within the meaning of Directive 97/81/EC;
(b) workers with a fixed-term contract within the meaning of Directive 1999/70/EC;
(c) workers with a temporary employment relationship within the meaning of Article 1(2) of Directive 91/383/EEC.

3. Member States may not set a minimum duration for the contract of employment or the employment relationship in order for workers to qualify for claims under this Directive.

4. This Directive does not prevent Member States from extending workers' protection to other situations of insolvency, for example where payments have been de facto stopped on a permanent basis, established by proceedings different from those mentioned in paragraph 1 as provided for under national law.

Such procedures shall not however create a guarantee obligation for the institutions of the other Member States in the cases referred to in Section IIIa.]

[3741]

NOTES

Substituted as noted to Art 1 at **[3740]**.

SECTION II
PROVISIONS CONCERNING GUARANTEE INSTITUTIONS

[Article 3

Member States shall take the measures necessary to ensure that guarantee institutions guarantee, subject to Article 4, payment of employees' outstanding claims resulting from contracts of employment or employment relationships, including, where provided for by national law, severance pay on termination of employment relationships.

The claims taken over by the guarantee institution shall be the outstanding pay claims relating to a period prior to and/or, as applicable, after a given date determined by the Member States.]

[3742]

NOTES

Substituted, together with Art 4, by European Parliament and Council Directive 2002/74, Art 1(3).

[Article 4

1. Member States shall have the option to limit the liability of the guarantee institutions referred to in Article 3.

2. When Member States exercise the option referred to in paragraph 1, they shall specify the length of the period for which outstanding claims are to be met by the guarantee institution. However, this may not be shorter than a period covering the remuneration of the last three months of the employment relationship prior to and/or after the date referred to in Article 3. Member States may include this minimum period of three months in a reference period with a duration of not less than six months.

Member States having a reference period of not less than 18 months may limit the period for which outstanding claims are met by the guarantee institution to eight weeks. In this case, those periods which are most favourable to the employee are used for the calculation of the minimum period.

3. Furthermore, Member States may set ceilings on the payments made by the guarantee institution. These ceilings must not fall below a level which is socially compatible with the social objective of this Directive.

When Member States exercise this option, they shall inform the Commission of the methods used to set the ceiling.]

[3743]

NOTES

Substituted as noted to Art 3 at **[3742]**.

Article 5

Member States shall lay down detailed rules for the organization, financing and operation of the guarantee institutions, complying with the following principles in particular—

(a) the assets of the institutions shall be independent of the employers' operating capital and be inaccessible to proceedings for insolvency;
(b) employers shall contribute to financing, unless it is fully covered by the public authorities;
(c) the institutions' liabilities shall not depend on whether or not obligations to contribute to financing have been fulfilled.

[3744]

SECTION III
PROVISIONS CONCERNING SOCIAL SECURITY

Article 6

Member States may stipulate that Articles 3, 4 and 5 shall not apply to contributions due under national statutory social security schemes or under supplementary company or inter-company pension schemes outside the national statutory social security schemes.

[3745]

Article 7

Member States shall take the measures necessary to ensure that non-payment of compulsory contributions due from the employer, before the onset of his insolvency, to their insurance institutions under national statutory social security schemes does not adversely affect employees' benefit entitlement in respect of these insurance institutions inasmuch as the employees' contributions were deducted at source from the remuneration paid.

[3746]

Article 8

Member States shall ensure that the necessary measures are taken to protect the interests of employees and of persons having already left the employer's undertaking or business at the date of the onset of the employer's insolvency in respect of rights conferring on them immediate or prospective entitlement to old-age benefits, including survivors' benefits, under supplementary company or inter-company pension schemes outside the national statutory social security schemes.

[3747]

[SECTION IIIA
PROVISIONS CONCERNING TRANSNATIONAL SITUATIONS

Article 8a

1. When an undertaking with activities in the territories of at least two Member States is in a state of insolvency within the meaning of Article 2(l), the institution responsible for meeting employees' outstanding claims shall be that in the Member State in whose territory they work or habitually work.

2. The extent of employees' rights shall be determined by the law governing the competent guarantee institution.

3. Member States shall take the measures necessary to ensure that, in the cases referred to in paragraph 1, decisions taken in the context of insolvency proceedings referred to in Article 2(1), which have been requested in another Member State, are taken into account when determining the employer's state of insolvency within the meaning of this Directive.]

[3748]

NOTES

Inserted, together with the preceding heading and Art 8b, by European Parliament and Council Directive 2002/74, Art 1(4).

[Article 8b

1. For the purposes of implementing Article 8a, Member States shall make provision for the sharing of relevant information between their competent administrative authorities and/or the guarantee institutions mentioned in Article 3, making it possible in particular to inform the guarantee institution responsible for meeting the employees' outstanding claims.

2. Member States shall notify the Commission and the other Member States of the contact details of their competent administrative authorities and/or guarantee institutions. The Commission shall make these communications publicly accessible.]

[3749]

NOTES

Inserted as noted to Art 8a at **[3748]**.

SECTION IV
GENERAL AND FINAL PROVISIONS

Article 9

This Directive shall not affect the option of Member States to apply or introduce laws, regulations or administrative provisions which are more favourable to employees.

[Implementation of this Directive shall not under any circumstances be sufficient grounds for a regression in relation to the current situation in the Member States and in relation to the general level of protection of workers in the area covered by it.]

[3750]

NOTES

Second paragraph added by European Parliament and Council Directive 2002/74, Art 1(5).

Article 10

This Directive shall not affect the option of Member States—

(a) to take the measures necessary to avoid abuses;

(b) to refuse or reduce the liability referred to in Article 3 or the guarantee obligation referred to in Article 7 if it appears that fulfilment of the obligation is unjustifiable because of the existence of special links between the employee and the employer and of common interests resulting in collusion between them;

[(c) to refuse or reduce the liability referred to in Article 3 or the guarantee obligation referred to in Article 7 in cases where the employee, on his or her own or together with his or her close relatives, was the owner of an essential part of the employer's undertaking or business and had a considerable influence on its activities.]

[3751]

NOTES

Para (c) added by European Parliament and Council Directive 2002/74, Art 1(6).

[Article 10a

Member States shall notify the Commission and the other Member States of the types of national insolvency proceedings falling within the scope of this Directive, and of any amendments relating thereto. The Commission shall publish these communications in the Official Journal of the European Communities.]

[3752]

NOTES

Inserted by European Parliament and Council Directive 2002/74, Art 1(7).

Article 11

1. Member States shall bring into force the laws, regulations and administrative provisions necessary to comply with this Directive within 36 months of its notification. They shall forthwith inform the Commission thereof.

2. Member States shall communicate to the Commission the texts of the laws, regulations and administrative provisions which they adopt in the field governed by this Directive.

[3753]

Article 12

Within 18 months of the expiry of the period of 36 months laid down in Article 11(1), Member States shall forward all relevant information to the Commission in order to enable it to draw up a report on the application of this Directive for submission to the Council.

[3754]

Article 13

This Directive is addressed to the Member States.

[3755]–[3757]

(*Annex: repealed by European Parliament and Council Directive 2002/74, Art 1*(*8*).)

COUNCIL DIRECTIVE

of 24 July 1986

on the implementation of the principle of equal treatment for men and women in occupational social security schemes

(86/378/EEC)

NOTES

Date of publication in OJ: OJ L225, 12.8.86, p 40.

This Directive is repealed, with effect from 15 August 2009, by the Directive of the European Parliament and of the Council on the implementation of the principle of equal opportunities and equal treatment of men and women in matters of employment and occupation (recast) (Directive 2006/54/EC at **[4122]** et seq). The 2006 Directive consolidates and updates the four major Directives on gender equality; ie, this Directive, the Equal Pay Directive (75/117/EEC), the Equal Treatment Directive (76/207/EEC), and the Burden of Proof Directive (97/80/EC). These Directives are repealed by Art 34 of, and Annex I, Pt A to, the 2006 Directive, with effect from 15 August 2009 (see **[4155]** and **[4158]**).

For the domestic implementation of this Directive, see (inter alia) the Social Security Act 1989, Sch 5 at **[401]**, and the Pensions Act 1995, ss 62–66 at **[890]–[894]**.

THE COUNCIL OF THE EUROPEAN COMMUNITIES,

Having regard to the Treaty establishing the European Economic Community, and in particular Articles 100 and 235 thereof,

Having regard to the proposal from the Commission,[1]

Having regard to the opinion of the European Parliament,[2]

Having regard to the opinion of the Economic and Social Committee,[3]

Whereas the Treaty provides that each Member State shall ensure the application of the principle that men and women should receive equal pay for equal work; whereas "pay" should be taken to mean the ordinary basic or minimum wage or salary and any other consideration, whether in cash or in kind, which the worker receives, directly or indirectly, from his employer in respect of his employment;

Whereas, although the principle of equal pay does indeed apply directly in cases where discrimination can be determined solely on the basis of the criteria of equal treatment and equal pay, there are also situations in which implementation of this principle implies the adoption of additional measures which more clearly define its scope;

Whereas Article 1(2) of Council Directive 76/207/EEC of 9 February 1976 on the implementation of the principle of equal treatment for men and women as regards access to employment, vocational training and promotion, and working conditions[4] *provides that, with a view to ensuring the progressive implementation of the principle of equal treatment in matters of social security, the Council, acting on a proposal from the Commission, will adopt provisions defining its substance, its scope and the arrangements for its application; whereas the Council adopted to this end Directive 79/7/EEC of 19 December 1978 on the progressive implementation of the principle of equal treatment for men and women in matters of social security;*[5]

Whereas Article 3(3) of Directive 79/7/EEC provides that, with a view to ensuring implementation of the principle of equal treatment in occupational schemes, the Council, acting on a proposal from the Commission, will adopt provisions defining its substance, its scope and the arrangements for its application;

Whereas the principle of equal treatment should be implemented in occupational social security schemes which provide protection against the risks specified in Article 3(1) of Directive 79/7/EEC as well as those which provide employees with any other consideration in cash or in kind within the meaning of the Treaty;

Whereas implementation of the principle of equal treatment does not prejudice the provisions relating to the protection of women by reason of maternity,

NOTES

Repealed as noted at the beginning of this Directive.

1 OJ C134, 21.5.83, p 7.
2 OJ C117, 30.4.84, p 169.
3 OJ C35, 9.2.84, p 7.
4 OJ L39, 14.2.76, p 40.
5 OJ L6, 10.1.79, p 24.

HAS ADOPTED THIS DIRECTIVE—

Article 1

The object of this Directive is to implement, in occupational social security schemes, the principle of equal treatment for men and women, hereinafter referred to as "the principle of equal treatment".

[3758]

NOTES

Repealed as noted at the beginning of this Directive.

[Article 2

1. "Occupational social security schemes" means schemes not governed by Directive 79/7/EEC whose purpose is to provide workers, whether employees or self-employed, in an undertaking or group of undertakings, area of economic activity, occupational sector or group of sectors with benefits intended to supplement the benefits provided by statutory social security schemes or to replace them, whether membership of such schemes is compulsory or optional.

2. This Directive does not apply to—

(*a*) *individual contracts for self-employed workers;*
(*b*) *schemes for self-employed workers having only one member;*
(*c*) *insurance contracts to which the employer is not a party, in the case of salaried workers;*
(*d*) *optional provisions of occupational schemes offered to participants individually to guarantee them—*
  — *either additional benefits, or*
  — *a choice of date on which the normal benefits for self-employed workers will start, or a choice between several benefits;*
(*e*) *occupational schemes in so far as benefits are financed by contributions paid by workers on a voluntary basis.*

3. This Directive does not preclude an employer granting to persons who have already reached the retirement age for the purposes of granting a pension by virtue of an occupational scheme, but who have not yet reached the retirement age for the purposes of granting a statutory retirement pension, a pension supplement, the aim of which is to make equal or more nearly equal the overall amount of benefit paid to these persons in relation to the amount paid to persons of the other sex in the same situation who have already reached the statutory retirement age, until the persons benefiting from the supplement reach the statutory retirement age.]

[3759]

NOTES
Substituted by Council Directive 96/97/EC, Art 1.
Repealed as noted at the beginning of this Directive.

[Article 3

This Directive shall apply to members of the working population, including self-employed persons, persons whose activity is interrupted by illness, maternity, accident or involuntary unemployment and persons seeking employment, to retired and disabled workers and to those claiming under them, in accordance with national law and/or practice.]

[3760]

NOTES
Substituted by Council Directive 96/97/EC, Art 2.
Repealed as noted at the beginning of this Directive.

Article 4

This Directive shall apply to—

(*a*) *occupational schemes which provide protection against the following risks—*
- *sickness,*
- *invalidity,*
- *old age, including early retirement,*
- *industrial accidents and occupational diseases,*
- *unemployment;*

(*b*) *occupational schemes which provide for other social benefits, in cash or in kind, and in particular survivors' benefits and family allowances, if such benefits are accorded to employed persons and thus constitute a consideration paid by the employer to the worker by reason of the latter's employment.*

[3761]

NOTES
Repealed as noted at the beginning of this Directive.

Article 5

1. Under the conditions laid down in the following provisions, the principle of equal treatment implies that there shall be no discrimination on the basis of sex, either directly or indirectly, by reference in particular to marital or family status, especially as regards—
- *the scope of the schemes and the conditions of access to them;*
- *the obligation to contribute and the calculation of contributions;*
- *the calculation of benefits, including supplementary benefits due in respect of a spouse or dependants, and the conditions governing the duration and retention of entitlement to benefits.*

2. The principle of equal treatment shall not prejudice the provisions relating to the protection of women by reason of maternity.

[3762]

NOTES
Repealed as noted at the beginning of this Directive.

[Article 6

1. Provisions contrary to the principle of equal treatment shall include those based on sex, either directly or indirectly, in particular by reference to marital or family status, for—

(*a*) *determining the persons who may participate in an occupational scheme;*
(*b*) *fixing the compulsory or optional nature of participation in an occupational scheme;*
(*c*) *laying down different rules as regards the age of entry into the scheme or the minimum period of employment or membership of the scheme required to obtain the benefits thereof;*
(*d*) *laying down different rules, except as provided for in points* (*h*) *and* (*i*), *for the*

reimbursement of contributions where a worker leaves a scheme without having fulfilled the conditions guaranteeing a deferred right to long-term benefits;

(*e*) *setting different conditions for the granting of benefits or restricting such benefits to workers of one or other of the sexes;*

(*f*) *fixing different retirement ages;*

(*g*) *suspending the retention or acquisition of rights during periods of maternity leave or leave for family reasons which are granted by law or agreement and are paid by the employer;*

(*h*) *setting different levels of benefit, except in so far as may be necessary to take account of actuarial calculation factors which differ according to sex in the case of defined-contribution schemes.*

In the case of funded defined-benefit schemes, certain elements (examples of which are annexed) may be unequal where the unequality of the amounts results from the effects of the use of actuarial factors differing according to sex at the time when the scheme's funding is implemented;

(*i*) *setting different levels for workers' contributions;*
setting different levels for employers' contributions, except—

— *in the case of defined-contribution schemes if the aim is to equalize the amount of the final benefits or to make them more nearly equal for both sexes,*

— *in the case of funded defined-benefit schemes where the employer's contributions are intended to ensure the adequacy of the funds necessary to cover the cost of the benefits defined,*

(*j*) *laying down different standards or standards applicable only to workers of a specified sex, except as provided for in points (h) and (i), as regards the guarantee or retention of entitlement to deferred benefits when a worker leaves a scheme.*

2. *Where the granting of benefits within the scope of this Directive is left to the discretion of the scheme's management bodies, the latter must comply with the principle of equal treatment.]*

[3763]

NOTES

Substituted by Council Directive 96/97/EC, Art 3.
Repealed as noted at the beginning of this Directive.

Article 7

Member States shall take all necessary steps to ensure that—

(*a*) *provisions contrary to the principle of equal treatment in legally compulsory collective agreements, staff rules of undertakings or any other arrangements relating to occupational schemes are null and void, or may be declared null and void or amended;*

(*b*) *schemes containing such provisions may not be approved or extended by administrative measures.*

[3764]

NOTES

Repealed as noted at the beginning of this Directive.

[Article 8

1. *Member States shall take the necessary steps to ensure that the provisions of occupational schemes for self-employed workers contrary to the principle of equal treatment are revised with effect from 1 January 1993 at the latest.*

2. *This Directive shall not preclude rights and obligations relating to a period of membership of an occupational scheme prior to revision of that scheme from remaining subject to the provisions of the scheme in force during that period.]*

[3765]

NOTES

Substituted by Council Directive 96/97/EC, Art 4.
Repealed as noted at the beginning of this Directive.

[Article 9

As regards schemes for self-employed workers, Member States may defer compulsory application of the principle of equal treatment with regard to—

(*a*) *determination of pensionable age for the granting of old-age or retirement pensions, and the possible implications for other benefits—*

— *either until the date on which such equality is achieved in statutory schemes,*

— *or, at the latest, until such equality is prescribed by a directive;*

(*b*) *survivors' pensions until Community law establishes the principle of equal treatment in statutory social security schemes in that regard;*

(*c*) *the application of the first subparagraph of point (i) of Article 6(1) to take account of the different actuarial calculation factors, at the latest until 1 January 1999.]*

[3766]

NOTES

Substituted by Council Directive 96/97/EC, Art 5.
Repealed as noted at the beginning of this Directive.

[Article 9a

Where men and women may claim a flexible pensionable age under the same conditions, this shall not be deemed to be incompatible with this Directive.]

[3767]

NOTES

Inserted by Council Directive 96/97/EC, Art 6.
Repealed as noted at the beginning of this Directive.

Article 10

Member States shall introduce into their national legal systems such measures as are necessary to enable all persons who consider themselves injured by failure to apply the principle of equal treatment to pursue their claims before the courts, possibly after bringing the matters before other competent authorities.

[3768]

NOTES

Repealed as noted at the beginning of this Directive.

Article 11

Member States shall take all the necessary steps to protect worker against dismissal where this constitutes a response on the part of the employer to a complaint made at undertaking level or to the institution of legal proceedings aimed at enforcing compliance with the principle of equal treatment.

[3769]

NOTES

Repealed as noted at the beginning of this Directive.

Article 12

1. *Member States shall bring into force such laws, regulations and administrative provisions as are necessary in order to comply with this Directive at the latest three years after notification thereof. They shall immediately inform the Commission thereof.*

2. *Member States shall communicate to the Commission at the latest five years after notification of this Directive all information necessary to enable the Commission to draw up a report on the application of this Directive for submission to the Council.*

[3770]

NOTES

Repealed as noted at the beginning of this Directive.
This Directive was notified to the Member States on 30 July 1986.

Article 13

This Directive is addressed to the Member States.

[3771]

NOTES

Repealed as noted at the beginning of this Directive.

[ANNEX

Examples of elements which may be unequal, in respect of funded defined-benefit schemes, as referred to in Article 6(h)—

— *conversion into a capital sum of part of a periodic pension,*

— *transfer of pension rights,*

— *a reversionary pension payable to a dependant in return for the surrender of part of a pension,*

— *a reduced pension where the worker opts to take early retirement.]*

[3772]

NOTES

Added by Council Directive 96/97/EC, Art 7.

Repealed as noted at the beginning of this Directive.

COUNCIL DIRECTIVE

of 12 June 1989

on the introduction of measures to encourage improvements in the safety and health of workers at work

(89/391/EEC)

NOTES

Date of publication in OJ: OJ L183, 29.6.89, p 1.

For the domestic implementation of this Directive see in particular the Management of Health and Safety at Work Regulations 1999, SI 1999/3242 at **[2526]**, the Employment Rights Act 1996, ss 44, 100 at **[1063]**, **[1139]**, and the Health and Safety (Consultation with Employees) Regulations 1996, SI 1996/1513 at **[2351]** et seq.

THE COUNCIL OF THE EUROPEAN COMMUNITIES,

Having regard to the Treaty establishing the European Economic Community, and in particular Article 118a thereof,

Having regard to the proposal from the Commission,[1] drawn up after consultation with the Advisory Committee on Safety, Hygiene and Health Protection at Work,

In cooperation with the European Parliament,[2]

Having regard to the opinion of the Economic and Social Committtee,[3]

Whereas Article 118a of the Treaty provides that the Council shall adopt, by means of Directives, minimum requirements for encouraging improvements, especially in the working environment, to guarantee a better level of protection of the safety and health of workers;

Whereas this Directive does not justify any reduction in levels of protection already achieved in individual Member States, the Member State being committed, under the Treaty, to encouraging improvements in conditions in this area and to harmonising conditions while maintaining the improvements made;

Whereas it is known that workers can be exposed to the effects of dangerous environmental factors at the work place during the course of their working life;

Whereas, pursuant to Article 118a of the Treaty, such Directives must avoid imposing administrative, financial and legal constraints which would hold back the creation and development of small and medium-sized undertakings;

Whereas the communication from the Commission on its programme concerning safety, hygiene and health at work[4] provides for the adoption of Directives designed to guarantee the safety and health of workers;

Whereas the Council, in its resolution of 21 December 1987 on safety, hygiene and health at work,[5] took note of the Commission's intention to submit to the Council in the near future a Directive on the organisation of the safety and health of workers at the work place;

Whereas in February 1988 the European Parliament adopted four resolutions following the debate on the internal market and worker protection; whereas these resolutions specifically invited the Commission to draw up a framework Directive to serve as a basis for more specific Directives covering all the risks connected with safety and health at the work place;

Whereas Member States have a responsibility to encourage improvements in the safety and health of workers on their territory; whereas taking measures to protect the health and safety of workers at work also helps, in certain cases, to preserve the health and possibly the safety of persons residing with them;

Whereas Member States' legislative systems covering safety and health at the work place differ widely and need to be improved; whereas national provisions on the subject, which often include technical specifications and/or self-regulatory standards, may result in different levels of safety and health protection and allow competition at the expense of safety and health;

Whereas the incidence of accidents at work and occupational diseases is still too high; whereas preventive measures must be introduced or improved without delay in order to safeguard the safety and health of workers and ensure a higher degree of protection;

Whereas, in order to ensure an improved degree of protection, workers and/or their representatives must be informed of the risks to their safety and health and of the measures required to reduce or eliminate these risks; whereas they must also be in a position to contribute, by means of balanced participation in accordance with national laws and/or practices, to seeing that the necessary protective measures are taken;

Whereas information, dialogue and balanced participation on safety and health at work must be developed between employers and workers and/or their representatives by means of appropriate procedures and instruments, in accordance with national laws and/or practices;

Whereas the improvement of workers' safety, hygiene and health at work is an objective which should not be subordinated to purely economic considerations;

Whereas employers shall be obliged to keep themselves informed of the latest advances in technology and scientific findings concerning work-place design, account being taken of the inherent dangers in their undertaking, and to inform accordingly the workers' representatives exercising participation rights under this Directive, so as to be able to guarantee a better level of protection of workers' health and safety;

Whereas the provisions of this Directive apply, without prejudice to more stringent present or future Community provisions, to all risks, and in particular to those arising from the use at work of chemical, physical and biological agents covered by Directive 80/1107/EEC,[6] as last amended by Directive 88/642/EEC;[7]

Whereas, pursuant to Decision 74/325/EEC,[8] the Advisory Committee on Safety, Hygiene and Health Protection at Work is consulted by the Commission on the drafting of proposals in this field;

Whereas a Committee composed of members nominated by the Member States needs to be set up to assist the Commission in making the technical adaptations to the individual Directives provided for in this Directive.

NOTES

1 OJ C141, 30.5.88, p 1.
2 OJ C326, 19.12.88, p 102 and OJ C158, 26.6.89.
3 OJ C175, 4.7.88, p 22.
4 OJ C28, 3.2.88, p 3.
5 OJ C28, 3.2.88, p 1.
6 OJ L327, 3.12.80, p 8.
7 OJ L356, 24.12.88, p 74.
8 OJ L185, 9.7.74, p 15.

HAS ADOPTED THIS DIRECTIVE—

SECTION I
GENERAL PROVISIONS

Article 1

Object

1. The object of this Directive is to introduce measures to encourage improvements in the safety and health of workers at work.

2. To that end it contains general principles concerning the prevention of occupational risks, the protection of safety and health, the elimination of risk and accident factors, the informing, consultation, balanced participation in accordance with national laws and/or practices and training of workers and their representatives, as well as general guidelines for the implementation of the said principles.

3. This Directive shall be without prejudice to existing or future national and Community provisions which are more favourable to protection of the safety and health of workers at work.

[3773]

Article 2

Scope

1. This Directive shall apply to all sectors of activity, both public and private (industrial, agricultural, commercial, administrative, service, educational, cultural, leisure, etc).

2. This Directive shall not be applicable where characteristics peculiar to certain specific service activities, such as the armed forces or the police, or to certain specific activities in the civil protection services inevitably conflict with it.

In that event, the safety and health of workers must be ensured as far as possible in the light of the objectives of this Directive.

[3774]

Article 3

Definitions

For the purposes of this Directive, the following terms shall have the following meanings—

(a) worker: any person employed by an employer, including trainees and apprentices but excluding domestic servants;

(b) employer: any natural or legal person who has an employment relationship with the worker and has responsibility for the undertaking and/or establishment;

(c) workers' representative with specific responsibility for the safety and health of workers: any person elected, chosen or designated in accordance with national laws and/or practices to represent workers where problems arise relating to the safety and health protection of workers at work;

(d) prevention: all the steps or measures taken or planned at all stages of work in the undertaking to prevent or reduce occupational risks.

[3775]

Article 4

1. Member States shall take the necessary steps to ensure that employers, workers and workers' representatives are subject to the legal provisions necessary for the implementation of this Directive.

2. In particular, Member States shall ensure adequate controls and supervision.

[3776]

SECTION II
EMPLOYERS' OBLIGATIONS

Article 5

General provision

1. The employer shall have a duty to ensure the safety and health of workers in every aspect related to the work.

2. Where, pursuant to Article 7(3), an employer enlists competent external services or persons, this shall not discharge him from his responsibilities in this area.

3. The workers' obligations in the field of safety and health at work shall not affect the principle of the responsibility of the employer.

4. This Directive shall not restrict the option of Member States to provide for the exclusion or the limitation of employers' responsibility where occurrences are due to unusual

and unforeseeable circumstances, beyond the employers' control, or to exceptional events, the consequences of which could not have been avoided despite the exercise of all due care.

Member States need not exercise the option referred to in the first sub-paragraph.

[3777]

Article 6

General obligations on employers

1. Within the context of his responsibilities, the employer shall take the measures necessary for the safety and health protection of workers, including prevention of occupational risks and provision of information and training, as well as provision of the necessary organisation and means.

The employer shall be alert to the need to adjust these measures to take account of changing circumstances and aim to improve existing situations.

2. The employer shall implement the measures referred to in the first subparagraph of paragraph 1 on the basis of the following general principles of prevention—

(a) avoiding risks;
(b) evaluating the risks which cannot be avoided;
(c) combating the risk at source;
(d) adapting the work to the individual, especially as regards the design of work places, the choice of work equipment and the choice of working and production methods, with a view, in particular, to alleviating monotonous work and work at a predetermined work-rate and to reducing their effect on health;
(e) adapting to technical progress;
(f) replacing the dangerous by the non-dangerous or the less dangerous;
(g) developing a coherent overall prevention policy which covers technology, organisation of work, working conditions, social relationships and the influence of factors related to the working environment;
(h) giving collective protective measures priority over individual protective measures;
(i) giving appropriate instructions to the workers.

3. Without prejudice to the other provisions of this Directive, the employers shall, taking into account the nature of the activities of the enterprise and/or establishment—

(a) evaluate the risks to the safety and health of workers, *inter alia* in the choice of work equipment, the chemical substances or preparations used, and the fitting-out of work places.
Subsequent to this evaluation and as necessary, the preventive measures and the working and production methods implemented by the employer must—
— assure an improvement in the level of protection afforded to workers with regard to safety and health,
— be integrated into all the activities of the undertaking and/or establishment and at all hierarchical levels;
(b) where he entrusts tasks to a worker, take into consideration the worker's capabilities as regards health and safety;
(c) ensure that the planning and introduction of new technologies are the subject of consultation with the workers and/or their representatives, as regards the consequences of the choice of equipment, the working conditions and the working environment for the safety and health of workers;
(d) take appropriate steps to ensure that only workers who have received adequate instructions may have access to areas where there is serious and specific danger.

4. Without prejudice to the other provisions of this Directive, where several undertakings share a work place, the employers shall co-operate in implementing the safety, health and occupational hygiene provisions and, taking into account the nature of the activities, shall coordinate their actions in matters of the protection and prevention of occupational risks, and shall inform one another and their respective workers and/or workers' representatives of these risks.

5. Measures related to safety, hygiene and health at work may in no circumstances involve the workers in financial cost.

[3778]

Article 7

Protective and preventive services

1. Without prejudice to the obligations referred to in Articles 5 and 6, the employer shall designate one or more workers to carry out activities related to the protection and prevention of occupational risks for the undertaking and/or establishment.

2. Designated workers may not be placed at any disadvantage because of their activities related to the protection and prevention of occupational risks.

Designated workers shall be allowed adequate time to enable them to fulfil their obligations arising from this Directive.

3. If such protective and preventive measures cannot be organised for lack of competent personnel in the undertaking and/or establishment, the employer shall enlist competent external services or persons.

4. Where the employer enlists such services or persons, he shall inform them of the factors known to affect, or suspected of affecting, the safety and health of the workers and they must have access to the information referred to in Article 10(2).

5. In all cases—

— the workers designated must have the necessary capabilities and the necessary means,

— the external services or persons consulted must have the necessary aptitudes and the necessary personal and professional means, and

— the workers designated and the external services or persons consulted must be sufficient in number

to deal with the organisation of protective and preventive measures, taking into account the size of the undertaking and/or establishment and/or the hazards to which the workers are exposed and their distribution throughout the entire undertaking and/or establishment.

6. The protection from, and prevention of, the health and safety risks which form the subject of this Article shall be the responsibility of one or more workers, of one service or of separate services whether from inside or outside the undertaking and/or establishment.

The worker(s) and/or agency(ies) must work together whenever necessary.

7. Member States may define, in the light of the nature of the activities and size of the undertakings, the categories or undertakings in which the employer, provided he is competent, may himself take responsibility for the measures referred to in paragraph 1.

8. Member States shall define the necessary capabilities and aptitudes referred to in paragraph 5.

They may determine the sufficient number referred to in paragraph 5.

[3779]

Article 8

First aid, fire-fighting and evacuation of workers, serious and imminent danger

1. The employer shall—

— take the necessary measures for first aid, fire-fighting and evacuation of workers, adapted to the nature of the activities and the size of the undertaking and/or establishment and taking into account other persons present;

— arrange any necessary contacts with external services, particularly as regards first aid, emergency medical care, rescue work and fire-fighting.

2. Pursuant to paragraph 1, the employer shall, *inter alia*, for first aid, fire-fighting and the evacuation of workers, designate the workers required to implement such measures.

The number of such workers, their training and the equipment available to them shall be adequate, taking account of the size and/or specific hazards of the undertaking and/or establishment.

3. The employer shall—

(a) as soon as possible, inform all workers who are, or may be, exposed to serious and imminent danger of the risk involved and of the steps taken or to be taken as regards protection;

(b) take action and give instructions to enable workers in the event of serious, imminent and unavoidable danger to stop work and/or immediately to leave the work place and proceed to a place of safety;

(c) save in exceptional cases for reasons duly substantiated, refrain from asking workers to resume work in a working situation where there is still a serious and imminent danger.

4. Workers who, in the event of serious, imminent and unavoidable danger, leave their workstation and/or a dangerous area may not be placed at any disadvantage because of their action and must be protected against any harmful and unjustified consequences, in accordance with national laws and/or practices.

5. The employer shall ensure that all workers are able, in the event of serious and imminent danger to their own safety and/or that of other persons, and where the immediate superior responsible cannot be contacted, to take the appropriate steps in the light of their knowledge and the technical means at their disposal, to avoid the consequences of such danger.

Their actions shall not place them at any disadvantage, unless they acted carelessly or there was negligence on their part.

[3780]

Article 9

Various obligations on employers

1. The employer shall—
   (a) be in possession of an assessment of the risks to safety and health at work, including those facing groups of workers exposed to particular risks;
   (b) decide on the protective measures to be taken and, if necessary, the protective equipment to be used;
   (c) keep a list of occupational accidents resulting in a worker being unfit for work for more than three working days;
   (d) draw up, for the responsible authorities and in accordance with national laws and/or practices, reports on occupational accidents suffered by his workers.

2. Member States shall define, in the light of the nature of the activities and size of the undertaking, the obligations to be met by the different categories of undertakings in respect of the drawing-up of the documents provided for in paragraph 1(a) and (b) and when preparing the documents provided for in paragraph 1(c) and (d).

[3781]

Article 10

Worker information

1. The employer shall take appropriate measures so that workers and/or their representatives in the undertaking and/or establishment receive in accordance with national laws and/or practices which may take account, *inter alia*, of the size of the undertaking and/or establishment, all the necessary information concerning—
   (a) the safety and health risks and protective and preventive measures and activities in respect of both the undertaking and/or establishment in general and each type of workstation and/or job;
   (b) the measures taken pursuant to Article 8(2).

2. The employer shall take appropriate measures so that employers of workers from any outside undertakings and/or establishments engaged in work in his undertaking and/or establishment receive, in accordance with national laws and/or practices, adequate information concerning the points referred to in paragraph 1(a) and (b) which is to be provided to the workers in question.

3. The employer shall take appropriate measures so that workers with specific functions in protecting the safety and health of workers, or workers' representatives with specific responsibility for the safety and health of workers shall have access, to carry out their functions and in accordance with national laws and/or practices, to—
   (a) the risk assessment and protective measures referred to in Article 9(1)(a) and (b);
   (b) the list and reports referred to in Article 9(1)(c) and (d);
   (c) the information yielded by protective and preventive measures, inspection agencies and bodies responsible for safety and health.

[3782]

Article 11

Consultation and participation of workers

1. Employers shall consult workers and/or their representatives and allow them to take part in discussions on all questions relating to safety and health at work.

This presupposes—
- the consultation of workers,
- the right of workers and/or their representatives to make proposals,

— balanced participation in accordance with national laws and/or practices.

2. Workers or workers' representatives with specific responsibility for the safety and health of workers shall take part in a balanced way, in accordance with national laws and/or practices, or shall be consulted in advance and in good time by the employer with regard to—

(a) any measure which may substantially affect safety and health;

(b) the designation of workers referred to in Articles 7(1) and 8(2) and the activities referred to in Article 7(1);

(c) the information referred to in Articles 9(1) and 10;

(d) the enlistment, where appropriate, of the competent services or persons outside the undertaking and/or establishment, as referred to in Article 7(3);

(e) the planning and organisation of the training referred to in Article 12.

3. Workers' representatives with specific responsibility for the safety and health of workers shall have the right to ask the employer to take appropriate measures and to submit proposals to him to that end to mitigate hazards for workers and/or to remove sources of danger.

4. The workers referred to in paragraph 2 and the workers' representatives referred to in paragraphs 2 and 3 may not be placed at a disadvantage because of their respective activities referred to in paragraphs 2 and 3.

5. Employers must allow workers' representatives with specific responsibility for the safety and health of workers adequate time off work, without loss of pay, and provide them with the necessary means to enable such representatives to exercise their rights and functions deriving from this Directive.

6. Workers and/or their representatives are entitled to appeal, in accordance with national law and/or practice, to the authority responsible for safety and health protection at work if they consider that the measures taken and the means employed by the employer are inadequate for the purposes of ensuring safety and health at work.

Workers' representatives must be given the opportunity to submit their observations during inspection visits by the competent authority.

[3783]

Article 12

Training of workers

1. The employer shall ensure that each worker receives adequate safety and health training, in particular in the form of information and instructions specific to his workstation or job—

— on recruitment,
— in the event of a transfer or a change of job,
— in the event of the introduction of new work equipment or a change in equipment,
— in the event of the introduction of any new technology.

The training shall be—

— adapted to take account of new or changed risks, and
— repeated periodically if necessary.

2. The employer shall ensure that workers from outside undertakings and/or establishments engaged in work in his undertaking and/or establishment have in fact received appropriate instructions regarding health and safety risks during their activities in his undertaking and/or establishment.

3. Workers' representatives with a specific role in protecting the safety and health of workers shall be entitled to appropriate training.

4. The training referred to in paragraphs 1 and 3 may not be at the workers' expense or at that of the workers' representatives.

The training referred to in paragraph 1 must take place during working hours.

The training referred to in paragraph 3 must take place during working hours or in accordance with national practice either within or outside the undertaking and/or the establishment.

[3784]

SECTION III
WORKERS' OBLIGATIONS

Article 13

1. It shall be the responsibility of each worker to take care as far as possible of his own safety and health and that of other persons affected by his acts or omissions at work in accordance with his training and the instructions given by his employer.

2. To this end, workers must in particular, in accordance with their training and the instructions given by their employer—

(a) make correct use of machinery, apparatus, tools, dangerous substances, transport equipment and other means of production;

(b) make correct use of the personal protective equipment supplied to them and, after use, return it to its proper place;

(c) refrain from disconnecting, changing or removing arbitrarily safety devices fitted, e g to machinery, apparatus, tools, plant and buildings, and use such safety devices correctly;

(d) immediately inform the employer and/or the workers with specific responsibility for the safety and health of workers of any work situation they have reasonable grounds for considering represents a serious and immediate danger to safety and health and of any shortcomings in the protection arrangements;

(e) co-operate, in accordance with national practice, with the employer and/or workers with specific responsibility for the safety and health of workers, for as long as may be necessary to enable any tasks or requirements imposed by the competent authority to protect the safety and health of workers at work to be carried out;

(f) co-operate, in accordance with national practice, with the employer and/or workers with specific responsibility for the safety and health of workers, for as long as may be necessary to enable the employer to ensure that the working environment and working conditions are safe and pose no risk to safety and health within their field of activity.

[3785]

SECTION IV
MISCELLANEOUS PROVISIONS

Article 14

Health surveillance

1. To ensure that workers receive health surveillance appropriate to the health and safety risks they incur at work, measures shall be introduced in accordance with national law and/or practices.

2. The measures referred to in paragraph 1 shall be such that each worker, if he so wishes, may receive health surveillance at regular intervals.

3. Health surveillance may be provided as part of a national health system.

[3786]

Article 15

Risk groups

Particularly sensitive risk groups must be protected against the dangers which specifically affect them.

[3787]

Article 16

Individual Directives—Amendments—General scope of this Directive

1. The Council, acting on a proposal from the Commission based on Article 118a of the Treaty, shall adopt individual Directives, *inter alia*, in the areas listed in the Annex.

2. This Directive and, without prejudice to the procedure referred to in Article 17 concerning technical adjustments, the individual Directives may be amended in accordance with the procedure provided for in Article 118a of the Treaty.

3. The provisions of this Directive shall apply in full to all the areas covered by the individual Directives, without prejudice to more stringent and/or specific provisions contained in these individual Directives.

[3788]

NOTES

Article 118a: see now Art 138 at **[3522]**.

[Article 17

Committee

1. For the purely technical adjustments to the individual Directives provided for in Article 16(1) to take account of:

— the adoption of Directives in the field of technical harmonisation and standardisation, and/or

— technical progress, changes in international regulations or specifications, and new findings,

the Commission shall be assisted by a committee.

2. Articles 5 and 7 of Decision 1999/468/EC(42) shall apply, having regard to the provisions of Article 8 thereof.

The period laid down in Article 5(6) of Decision 1999/468/EC shall be set at three months.

3. The Committee shall adopt its rules of procedure.]

[3789]

NOTES

Substituted by European Parliament and Council Regulation 1882/2003/EC, Art 3, Annex III, para 17, as from 20 November 2003.

[Article 17a

Implementation reports

1. Every five years, the Member States shall submit a single report to the Commission on the practical implementation of this Directive and individual Directives within the meaning of Article 16(1), indicating the points of view of the social partners. The report shall assess the various points related to the practical implementation of the different Directives and, where appropriate and available, provide data disaggregated by gender.

2. The structure of the report, together with a questionnaire specifying its content, shall be defined by the Commission, in cooperation with the Advisory Committee on Safety and Health at Work.

The report shall include a general part on the provisions of this Directive relating to the common principles and points applicable to all of the Directives referred to in paragraph 1.

To complement the general part, specific chapters shall deal with implementation of the particular aspects of each Directive, including specific indicators, where available.

3. The Commission shall submit the structure of the report, together with the above-mentioned questionnaire specifying its content, to the Member States at least six months before the end of the period covered by the report. The report shall be transmitted to the Commission within 12 months of the end of the five-year period that it covers.

4. Using these reports as a basis, the Commission shall evaluate the implementation of the Directives concerned in terms of their relevance, of research and of new scientific knowledge in the various fields in question. It shall, within 36 months of the end of the five-year period, inform the European Parliament, the Council, the European Economic and Social Committee and the Advisory Committee on Safety and Health at Work of the results of this evaluation and, if necessary, of any initiatives to improve the operation of the regulatory framework.

5. The first report shall cover the period 2007 to 2012.]

[3789A]

NOTES

Inserted by European Parliament and Council Directive 2007/30/EC, Art 1, as from 28 June 2007. Note that the 2007 Directive has a transposition date of 31 December 2012.

Article 18

Final provisions

1. Member States shall bring into force the laws, regulations and administrative provisions necessary to comply with this Directive by 31 December 1992.

They shall forthwith inform the Commission thereof.

2. Member States shall communicate to the Commission the texts of the provisions of rational law which they have already adopted or adopt in the field covered by this Directive.

3, 4. …

[3790]

NOTES

Paras 3, 4: repealed by European Parliament and Council Directive 2007/30/EC, Art 3(1), as from 27 June 2007. Note that the 2007 Directive has a transposition date of 31 December 2012, and paras 3, 4 originally read as follows:

"3. Member States shall report to the Commission every five years on the practical implementation of the provisions of this Directive, indicating the points of view of employers and workers.

The Commission shall inform the European Parliament, the Council, the Economic and Social Committee and the Advisory Committee on Safety, Hygiene and Health Protection at Work.

4. The Commission shall submit periodically to the European Parliament, the Council and the Economic and Social Committee a report on the implementation of this Directive, taking into account paragraphs 1 to 3.".

Article 19

This Directive is addressed to the Member States.

[3791]

ANNEX

LIST OF AREAS REFERRED TO IN ARTICLE 16(1)

— Work places

— Work equipment

— Personal protective equipment

— Work with visual display units

— Handling of heavy loads involving risk of back injury

— Temporary or mobile work sites

— Fisheries and agriculture.

[3792]

COUNCIL DIRECTIVE

of 14 October 1991

on an employer's obligation to inform employees of the conditions applicable to the contract or employment relationship

(91/533/EEC)

NOTES

Date of publication in OJ: OJ L288, 18.10.91, p 32.

There is no specific domestic legislation introduced to implement this Directive as its provisions were already reflected in what is now Part I of the Employment Rights Act 1996 (qv, at **[1006]**–**[1019]**).

THE COUNCIL OF THE EUROPEAN COMMUNITIES,

Having regard to the Treaty establishing the European Economic Community, and in particular Article 100 thereof,

Having regard to the proposal from the Commission,[1]

Having regard to the opinion of the European Parliament,[2]

Having regard to the opinion of the Economic and Social Committee,[3]

Whereas the development, in the Member States, of new forms of work has led to an increase in the number of types of employment relationship;

Whereas, faced with this development, certain Member States have considered it necessary to subject employment relationships to formal requirements; whereas these provisions are designed to provide employees with improved protection against possible infringements of their rights and to create greater transparency on the labour market;

Whereas the relevant legislation of the Member States differs considerably on such fundamental points as the requirement to inform employees in writing of the main terms of the contract or employment relationship;

Whereas differences in the legislation of Member States may have a direct effect on the operation of the common market;

Whereas Article 117 of the Treaty provides for the Member States to agree upon the need to promote improved working conditions and an improved standard of living for workers, so as to make possible their harmonisation while the improvement is being maintained;

Whereas point 9 of the Community Charter of Fundamental Social Rights for Workers, adopted at the Strasbourg European Council on 9 December 1989 by the Heads of State and Government of 11 Member States, states—

'The conditions of employment of every worker of the European Community shall be stipulated in laws, a collective agreement or a contract of employment, according to arrangements applying in each country.';

Whereas it is necessary to establish at Community level the general requirement that every employee must be provided with a document containing information on the essential elements of his contract or employment relationship;

Whereas, in view of the need to maintain a certain degree of flexibility in employment relationships, Member States should be able to exclude certain limited cases of employment relationship from this Directive's scope of application;

Whereas the obligation to provide information may be met by means of a written contract, a letter of appointment or one or more other documents or, if they are lacking, a written statement signed by the employer;

Whereas, in the case of expatriation of the employee, the latter must, in addition to the main terms of this contract or employment relationship, be supplied with relevant information connected with his secondment;

Whereas, in order to protect the interests of employees with regard to obtaining a document, any change in the main terms of the contract or employment relationship must be communicated to them in writing;

Whereas it is necessary for Member States to guarantee that employees can claim the rights conferred on them by this Directive;

Whereas Member States are to adopt the laws, regulations and legislative provisions necessary to comply with this Directive or are to ensure that both sides of industry set up the necessary provisions by agreement, with Member States being obliged to take the necessary steps enabling them at all times to guarantee the results imposed by this Directive,

NOTES

1 OJ C24, 31.1.1991, p 3.

2 OJ C240, 16.9.1991, p 21.

3 OJ C159, 17.6.1991, p 32.

HAS ADOPTED THIS DIRECTIVE—

Article 1

Scope

1. This Directive shall apply to every paid employee having a contract or employment relationship defined by the law in force in a Member State and/or governed by the law in force in a Member State.

2. Member States may provide that this Directive shall not apply to employees having a contract or employment relationship—

(a) with a total duration not exceeding one month, and/or with a working week not exceeding eight hours; or

(b) of a casual and/or specific nature provided, in these cases, that its non-application is justified by objective considerations.

[3793]

Article 2

Obligation to provide information

1. An employer shall be obliged to notify an employee to whom this Directive applies, hereinafter referred to as 'the employee', of the essential aspects of the contract or employment relationship.

2. The information referred to in paragraph 1 shall cover at least the following—

(a) the identities of the parties;

(b) the place of work; where there is no fixed or main place of work, the principle that the employee is employed at various places and the registered place of business or, where appropriate, the domicile of the employer;

(c)

(i) the title, grade, nature or category of the work for which the employee is employed; or

(ii) a brief specification or description of the work;

(d) the date of commencement of the contract or employment relationship;

(e) in the case of a temporary contract or employment relationship, the expected duration thereof;

(f) the amount of paid leave to which the employee is entitled or, where this cannot be indicated when the information is given, the procedures for allocating and determining such leave;

(g) the length of the periods of notice to be observed by the employer and the employee should their contract or employment relationship be terminated or, where this cannot be indicated when the information is given, the method for determining such periods of notice;

(h) the initial basic amount, the other component elements and the frequency of payment of the remuneration to which the employee is entitled;

(i) the length of the employee's normal working day or week;

(j) where appropriate—

(i) the collective agreements governing the employee's conditions of work; or

(ii) in the case of collective agreements concluded outside the business by special joint bodies or institutions, the name of the competent body or joint institution within which the agreements were concluded.

3. The information referred to in paragraph 2(f), (g), (h) and (i) may, where appropriate, be given in the form of a reference to the laws, regulations and administrative or statutory provisions or collective agreements governing those particular points.

[3794]

Article 3

Means of information

1. The information referred to in Article 2(2) may be given to the employee, not later than two months after the commencement of employment, in the form of—

(a) a written contract of employment; and/or

(b) a letter of engagement; and/or

(c) one or more other written documents, where one of these documents contains at least all the information referred to in Article 2(2)(a), (b), (c), (d), (h) and (i).

2. Where none of the documents referred to in paragraph 1 is handed over to the employee within the prescribed period, the employer shall be obliged to give the employee, not later than two months after the commencement of employment, a written declaration signed by the employer and containing at least the information referred to in Article 2(2).

Where the document(s) referred to in paragraph 1 contain only part of the information required, the written declaration provided for in the first subparagraph of this paragraph shall cover the remaining information.

3. Where the contract or employment relationship comes to an end before expiry of a period of two months as from the date of the start of work, the information provided for in Article 2 and in this Article must be made available to the employee by the end of this period at the latest.

[3795]

Article 4

Expatriate employees

1. Where an employee is required to work in a country or countries other than the Member State whose law and/or practice governs the contract or employment relationship, the document(s) referred to in Article 3 must be in his/ her possession before his/her departure and must include at least the following additional information—

(a) the duration of the employment abroad;
(b) the currency to be used for the payment of remuneration;
(c) where appropriate, the benefits in cash or kind attendant on the employment abroad;
(d) where appropriate, the conditions governing the employee's repatriation.

2. The information referred to in paragraph 1(b) and (c) may, where appropriate, be given in the form of a reference to the laws, regulations and administrative or statutory provisions or collective agreements governing those particular points.

3. Paragraphs 1 and 2 shall not apply if the duration of the employment outside the country whose law and/or practice governs the contract or employment relationship is one month or less.

[3796]

Article 5

Modification of aspects of the contract or employment relationship

1. Any change in the details referred to in Articles 2(2) and 4(1) must be the subject of a written document to be given by the employer to the employee at the earliest opportunity and not later than one month after the date of entry into effect of the change in question.

2. The written document referred to in paragraph 1 shall not be compulsory in the event of a change in the laws, regulations and administrative or statutory provisions or collective agreements cited in the documents referred to in Article 3, supplemented, where appropriate, pursuant to Article 4(1).

[3797]

Article 6

Form and proof of the existence of a contract or employment relationship and procedural rules

This Directive shall be without prejudice to national law and practice concerning—

— the form of the contract or employment relationship,
— proof as regards the existence and content of a contract or employment relationship,
— the relevant procedural rules.

[3798]

Article 7

More favourable provisions

This Directive shall not affect Member States' prerogative to apply or to introduce laws, regulations or administrative provisions which are more favourable to employees or to encourage or permit the application of agreements which are more favourable to employees.

[3799]

Article 8

Defence of rights

1. Member States shall introduce into their national legal systems such measures as are necessary to enable all employees who consider themselves wronged by failure to comply with the obligations arising from this Directive to pursue their claims by judicial process after possible recourse to other competent authorities.

2. Member States may provide that access to the means of redress referred to in paragraph 1 are subject to the notification of the employer by the employee and the failure by the employer to reply within 15 days of notification.

However, the formality of prior notification may in no case be required in the cases referred to in Article 4, neither for workers with a temporary contract or employment relationship, nor for employees not covered by a collective agreement or by collective agreements relating to the employment relationship.

[3800]

Article 9

Final provisions

1. Member States shall adopt the laws, regulations and administrative provisions necessary to comply with this Directive no later than 30 June 1993 or shall ensure by that date that the employers' and workers' representatives introduce the required provisions by way of agreement, the Member States being obliged to take the necessary steps enabling them at all times to guarantee the results imposed by this Directive.

They shall forthwith inform the Commission thereof.

2. Member States shall take the necessary measures to ensure that, in the case of employment relationships in existence upon entry into force of the provisions that they adopt, the employer gives the employee, on request, within two months of receiving that request; any of the documents referred to in Article 3, supplemented, where appropriate, pursuant to Article 4(1).

3. When Member States adopt the measures referred to in paragraph 1, such measures shall contain a reference to this Directive or shall be accompanied by such reference on the occasion of their official publication. The methods of making such a reference shall be laid down by the Member States.

4. Member States shall forthwith inform the Commission of the measures they take to implement this Directive.

[3801]

Article 10

This Directive is addressed to the Member States.

[3802]

COMMISSION RECOMMENDATION

of 27 November 1991

on the protection of the dignity of women and men at work

(92/131/EEC)

NOTES

Date of publication in OJ: OJ L49, 24.2.92, p 1.

THE COMMISSION OF THE EUROPEAN COMMUNITIES

Having regard to the Treaty establishing the European Economic Community and the second indent of Article 155 thereof;

Whereas unwanted conduct of a sexual nature, or other conduct based on sex affecting the dignity of women and men at work, including the conduct of superiors and colleagues, is unacceptable and may, in certain circumstances, be contrary to the principle of equal treatment within the meaning of Articles 3, 4 and 5 of Council Directive 76/207/EEC of 9 February 1976 on the implementation of the principle of equal treatment for men and women as regards access to employment, vocational training and promotion and working conditions,[1] a view supported by case law in some Member States;

Whereas, in accordance with the Council Recommendation of 13 December 1984 on the promotion of positive action for women,[2] many Member States have carried out a variety of positive action measures and actions having a bearing, inter alia, on respect for the dignity of women at the workplace;

Whereas the European Parliament, in its resolution of 11 June 1986 on violence against women,[3] has called upon national governments, equal opportunities committees and trade unions to carry out concerted information campaigns to create a proper awareness of the individual rights of all members of the labour force;

Whereas the Advisory Committee on Equal Opportunities for Women and Men, in its opinion of 20 June 1988, has unanimously recommended that there should be a Recommendation and code of conduct on sexual harassment in the workplace covering harassment of both sexes;

Whereas the Commission in its action programme relating to the implementation of the Community Charter of Basic Social Rights for workers undertook to examine the protection of workers and their dignity at work, having regard to the reports and recommendations prepared on various aspect of implementation of Community law;[4]

Whereas the Council, in its resolution of 29 May 1990 on the protection of the dignity of women and men at work , affirms that conduct based on sex affecting the dignity of women and men at work,[5] including conduct of superiors and colleagues, constitutes an intolerable violation of the dignity of workers or trainees, and calls on the Member States and the institutions and organs of the European Communities to develop positive measures designed to create a climate at work in which women and men respect one another's human integrity;

Whereas the Commission, in its third action programme on equal opportunities for women and men, 1991–1995 and pursuant to paragraph 3.2 of the said Council Resolution of 29 May 1990, resolved to draw up a code of conduct on the protection of the dignity of women and men at work,[6] based on experience and best practice in the Member States, to provide guidance on initiating and pursuing positive measures designed to create a climate at work in which women and men respect one another's human integrity;

Whereas the European Parliament, on 22 October 1991, adopted a Resolution on the protection of the dignity of women and men at work;[7]

Whereas the Economic and Social Committee, on 30 October 1991, adopted an Opinion on the protection of the dignity of women and men at work,[8]

NOTES

1 OJ L39, 14.2.76, p 40.
2 OJ L331, 19.12.84, p 34.
3 OJ C176, 14.7.86, p 79.
4 COM(89) final, 29.11.1989. For example, "The dignity of women at work: A report on the problem of sexual harassment in the Member States of the European Communities", October 1987, by Michael Rubenstein (ISBN 92-825-8764-9).
5 OJ C157, 27.6.90, p 3.
6 COM(90) 449 final, 6.11.90.
7 OJ C305, 25.11.91.
8 OJ C14, 20.1.92.

RECOMMENDS AS FOLLOWS—

Article 1

It is recommended that the Member State take action to promote awareness that conduct of a sexual nature, or other conduct based on sex affecting the dignity of women and men at work, including conduct of superiors and colleagues, is unacceptable if—

(a) such conduct is unwanted, unreasonable and offensive to the recipient;

(b) a person's rejection of or submission to such conduct on the part of employers or workers (including superiors or colleagues) is used explicitly or implicitly as a basis for a decision which affects that person's access to vocational training, access to employment, continued employment, promotion, salary or other employment decisions; and/or

(c) such conduct creates an intimidating, hostile or humiliating work environment for the recipient;

and that such conduct may, in certain circumstances, be contrary to the principle of equal treatment within the meaning of Articles 3, 4 and 5 of Directive 76/207/EEC.

[3803]

Article 2

It is recommended that Member States should take action, in the public sector, to implement the Commission's Code of Practice on the protection of the dignity of women and men at work, annexed hereto. The action of the Member States, in thus initiating and pursuing positive measures designed to create a climate at work in which women and men respect one another's human integrity, should serve as an example to the private sector.

[3804]

Article 3

It is recommended that Member States encourage employers and employee representatives to develop measures to implement the Commission's Code of Practice on the protection of the dignity of women and men at work.

[3805]

Article 4

The Member States shall inform the Commission within three years of the date of this Recommendation of the measures taken to give effect to it, in order to allow the Commission to draw up a report on all such measures. The Commission shall, within this period, ensure the widest possible circulation of the Code of Practice. The report should examine the degree of awareness of the Code, its perceived effectiveness, its degree of application and the extent of its use in collective bargaining between the social partners.

[3806]

Article 5

This Recommendation is addressed to the Member States.

[3807]

COMMISSION CODE OF PRACTICE ON PROTECTING THE DIGNITY OF WOMEN AND MEN AT WORK

A CODE OF PRACTICE ON MEASURES TO COMBAT SEXUAL HARASSMENT

1. Introduction

This code of practice is issued in accordance with the resolution of the Council of Ministers on the protection of the dignity of women and men at work,[1] and to accompany the Commission's Recommendations on this issue.

Its purpose is to give practical guidance to employers, trade unions, and employees on the protection of the dignity of women and men at work. The Code is intended to be applicable in both the public and the private sector and employers are encouraged to follow the recommendations contained in the Code in a way which is appropriate to the size and structure of their organisation. It may be particularly relevant for small and medium-sized enterprises to adapt some of the practical steps to their specific needs.

The aim is to ensure that sexual harassment does not occur and, if it does occur, to ensure that adequate procedures are readily available to deal with the problem and prevent its recurrence. The Code thus seeks to encourage the development and implementation of policies and practices which establish working environments free of sexual harassment and in which women and men respect one another's human integrity.

The expert report carried out on behalf of the Commission found that sexual harassment is a serious problem for many working women in the European Community[2] and research in Member States has proven beyond doubt that sexual harassment at work is not an isolated phenomenon. On the contrary, it is clear that for millions of women in the European Community, sexual harassment is an unpleasant and unavoidable part of their working lives. Men too may suffer sexual harassment and should, of course, have the same rights as women to the protection of their dignity.

Some specific groups are particularly vulnerable to sexual harassment. Research in several Member States, which documents the link between the risk of sexual harassment and the recipient's perceived vulnerability, suggests that divorced and separated women, young women and new entrants to the labour market and those with irregular or precarious employment contracts, women in non-traditional jobs, women with disabilities, lesbians and women from racial minorities are disproportionately at risk. Gay men and young men are also vulnerable to harassment. It is undeniable that harassment on grounds of sexual orientation undermines the dignity at work of those affected and it is impossible to regard such harassment as appropriate workplace behaviour.

Sexual harassment pollutes the working environment and can have a devastating effect upon the health, confidence, morale and performance of those affected by it. The anxiety and stress produced by sexual harassment commonly leads to those subjected to it taking time off work due to sickness, being less efficient at work, or leaving their job to seek work elsewhere. Employees often suffer the adverse consequences of the harassment itself and short- and long-term damage to their employment prospects if they are forced to change jobs. Sexual harassment may also have a damaging impact on employees not themselves the object of unwanted behaviour but who are witness to it or have a knowledge of the unwanted behaviour.

There are also adverse consequences arising from sexual harassment for employers. It has a direct impact on the profitability of the enterprise where staff take sick leave or resign their posts because of sexual harassment, and on the economic efficiency of the enterprise where employees' productivity is reduced by having to work in a climate in which individuals' integrity is not respected.

In general terms, sexual harassment is an obstacle to the proper integration of women into the labour market and the Commission is committed to encouraging the development of comprehensive measures to improve such integration.[3]

[3808]

NOTES

1 OJ C157, 27.6.90, p 3.

2 "The dignity of women at work: A report on the problem of sexual harassment in the Member States of the European Communities", October 1987, by Michael Rubenstein (ISBN 92-825-8764-9).

3 Third action programme on equal opportunities for women and men, 1991 to 1995, COM(90) 449, 6.11.1990.

2. Definition

Sexual harassment means "unwanted conduct of a sexual nature, or other conduct based on sex affecting the dignity of women and men at work".[1] This can include unwelcome physical, verbal or non-verbal conduct.

Thus, a range of behaviour may be considered to constitute sexual harassment. It is unacceptable if such conduct is unwanted, unreasonable and offensive to the recipient; a person's rejection of or submission to such conduct on the part of employers or workers (including superiors or colleagues) is used explicitly or implicitly as a basis for a decision which affects that person's access to vocational training or to employment, continued employment, promotion, salary or any other employment decisions; and/or such conduct creates an intimidating, hostile or humiliating working environment for the recipient.

The essential characteristic of sexual harassment is that it is unwanted by the recipient, that it is for each individual to determine what behaviour is acceptable to them and what they regard as offensive. Sexual attention becomes sexual harassment if it is persisted in once it has been made clear that it is regarded by the recipient as offensive, although one incident of harassment may constitute sexual harassment if sufficiently serious. It is the unwanted nature of the conduct which distinguishes sexual harassment from friendly behaviour, which is welcome and mutual.

[3809]

NOTES

1 Council resolution on the protection of the dignity of men and women at work (OJ C157, 27.6.90, point 1.)

3. The law and employers' responsibilities

Conduct of a sexual nature or other conduct based on sex affecting the dignity of women and men at work may be contrary to the principle of equal treatment within the meaning of Articles 3, 4 and 5 of Council Directive 76/207/EEC of 9 February 1976 on the implementation of the principle of equal treatment for men and women as regards access to employment, vocational training and promotion and working conditions.[1] This principle means that there shall be no discrimination whatsoever on grounds of sex either directly or indirectly by reference in particular to marital or family status.

In certain circumstances, and depending upon national law, sexual harassment may also be a criminal offence or may contravene other obligations imposed by the law, such as health and safety duties, or a duty, contractual or otherwise, to be a good employer. Since sexual harassment is a form of employee misconduct, employers have a responsibility to deal with it as they do with any other form of employee misconduct as well as to refrain from harassing employees themselves. Since sexual harassment is a risk to health and safety, employers have a responsibility to take steps to minimise the risk as they do with other hazards. Since sexual harassment often entails an abuse of power, employers may have a responsibility for the misuse of the authority they delegate.

This Code, however, focuses on sexual harassment as a problem of sex discrimination. Sexual harassment is sex discrimination because the gender of the recipient is the determining factor in who is harassed. Conduct of a sexual nature or other conduct based on sex affecting the dignity of women and men at work in some Member States already has been found to contravene national equal treatment laws and employers have a responsibility to seek to ensure that the work environment is free from such conduct.[2]

As sexual harassment is often a function of women's status in the employment hierarchy, policies to deal with sexual harassment are likely to be most effective where they are linked to a broader policy to promote equal opportunities and to improve the position of women. Advice on steps which can be taken generally to implement an equal opportunities policy is set out in the Commission's guide to positive action.[3]

Similarly, a procedure to deal with complaints of sexual harassment should be regarded as only one component of a strategy to deal with the problem. The prime objective should be to change behaviour and attitudes, to seek to ensure the prevention of sexual harassment.

[3810]

NOTES

1 OJ L39, 14.2.76, p 40.

2 Third action programme on equal opportunities for women and men, 1991 to 1995, COM(90) 449, 6.11.1990.

3 Positive action: Equal opportunities for women in employment—a guide, Office for Official Publications of the European Communities, 1988.

4. Collective bargaining

The majority of the recommendations contained in this Code are for action by employers, since employers have clear responsibilities to ensure the protection of the dignity of women and men at work.

Trade unions also have responsibilities to their members and they can and should play an important role in the prevention of sexual harassment in the workplace. It is recommended that the question of including appropriate clauses in agreements is examined in the context of the collective bargaining process, with the aim of achieving a work environment free from unwanted conduct of a sexual nature or other conduct based on sex affecting the dignity of women and men at work and free from victimisation of a complainant or of a person wishing to give, or giving, evidence in the event of a complaint.

[3811]

5. Recommendations to employers

The policies and procedures recommended below should be adopted, where appropriate, after consultation or negotiation with trade unions or employee representatives. Experience suggests that strategies to create and maintain a working environment in which the dignity of employees is respected are most likely to be effective where they are jointly agreed.

It should be emphasised that a distinguishing characteristic of sexual harassment is that employees subjected to it often will be reluctant to complain. An absence of complaints about sexual harassment in a particular organisation, therefore, does not necessarily mean an absence of sexual harassment. It may mean that the recipients of sexual harassment think that there is no point in complaining because nothing will be done about it, or because it will be trivialised or the complainant subjected to ridicule, or because they fear reprisals. Implementing the preventative and procedural recommendations outlined below should facilitate the creation of a climate at work in which such concerns have no place.

[3812]

A Prevention

(i) Policy statements

As a first step in showing senior management's concern and their commitment to dealing with the problem of sexual harassment, employers should issue a policy statement which expressly states that all employees have a right to be treated with dignity, that sexual harassment at work will not be permitted or condoned and that employees have a right to complain about it should it occur.

It is recommended that the policy statement makes clear what is considered inappropriate behaviour at work, and explain that such behaviour, in certain circumstances, may be unlawful. It is advisable for the statement to set out a positive duty on managers and supervisors to implement the policy and to take corrective action to ensure compliance with it. It should also place a positive duty on all employees to comply with the policy and to ensure that their colleagues are treated with respect and dignity.

In addition, it is recommended that the statement explains the procedure which should be followed by employees subjected to sexual harassment at work in order to obtain assistance and to whom they should complain; that it contain an undertaking that allegations of sexual harassment will be dealt with seriously, expeditiously and confidentially; and that employees will be protected against victimisation or retaliation for bringing a complaint of sexual harassment.

It should also specify that appropriate disciplinary measures will be taken against employees found guilty of sexual harassment.

(ii) Communicating the policy

Once the policy has been developed, it is important to ensure that it is communicated effectively to all employees, so that they are aware that they have a right to complain and to whom they should complain; that their complaint will be dealt with promptly and fairly; and so that employees are made aware of the likely consequences of engaging in sexual harassment. Such communication will highlight management's commitment to eliminating sexual harassment, thus enhancing a climate in which it will not occur.

(iii) Responsibility

All employees have a responsibility to help ensure a working environment in which the dignity of employees is respected and managers (including supervisors) have a particular duty to ensure that sexual harassment does not occur in work areas for which they are responsible. It is recommended that managers should explain the organisation's policy to their staff and take steps to positively promote the policy. Managers should also be responsive and supportive to any member of staff who complains about sexual harassment; provide full and clear advice on the procedure to be adopted; maintain confidentiality in any cases of sexual harassment; and ensure that there is no further problem of sexual harassment or any victimisation after a complaint has been resolved.

(iv) Training

An important means of ensuring that sexual harassment does not occur and that, if it does occur, the problem is resolved efficiently is through the provision of training for managers and supervisors. Such training should aim to identify the factors which contribute to a working environment free of sexual harassment and to familiarise participants with their responsibilities under the employer's policy and any problems they are likely to encounter.

In addition, those playing an official role in any formal complaints procedure in respect of sexual harassment should receive specialist training, such as that outlined above.

It is also good practice to include information as to the organisation's policy on sexual harassment and procedures for dealing with it as part of appropriate induction and training programmes.

[3813]

B Procedures

The development of clear and precise procedures to deal with sexual harassment once it has occurred is of great importance. The procedures should ensure the resolution of problems in an efficient and effective manner. Practical guidance for employees on how to deal with sexual harassment when it occurs and with its aftermath will make it more likely that it will be dealt with at an early stage. Such guidance should of course draw attention to an employee's legal rights and to any time limits within which they must be exercised.

(i) Resolving problems informally

Most recipients of harassment simply want the harassment to stop. Both informal and formal methods of resolving problems should be available.

Employees should be advised that, if possible, they should attempt to resolve the problem informally in the first instance. In some cases, it may be possible and sufficient for the employee to explain clearly to the person engaging in the unwanted conduct that the behaviour in question is not welcome, that it offends them or makes them uncomfortable, and that it interferes with their work.

In circumstances where it is too difficult or embarrassing for an individual to do this on their own behalf, an alternative approach would be to seek support from, or for an initial approach to be made by, a sympathetic friend or confidential counsellor.

If the conduct continues or if it is not appropriate to resolve the problem informally, it should be raised through the formal complaints procedure.

(ii) Advice and assistance

It is recommended that employers should designate someone to provide advice and assistance to employees subjected to sexual harassment, where possible, with responsibilities to assist in the resolution of any problems, whether through informal or formal means. It may be helpful if the officer is designated with the agreement of the trade unions or employees, as this is likely to enhance their acceptability. Such officers could be selected from personnel departments or equal opportunities departments for example. In some organisations they are designated as 'confidential counsellors' or 'sympathetic friends'. Often such a role may be played by someone from the employee's trade union or by women's support groups.

Whatever the location of this responsibility in the organisation, it is recommended that the designated officer receives appropriate training in the best means of resolving problems and in the detail of the organisation's policy and procedures, so that they can perform their role effectively. It is also important that they are given adequate resources to carry out their function, and protection against victimisation for assisting any recipient of sexual harassment.

(iii) Complaints procedure

It is recommended that, where the complainant regards attempts at informal resolution as inappropriate, where informal attempts at resolution have been refused, or where the outcome has been unsatisfactory, a formal procedure for resolving the complaint should be provided. The procedure should give employees confidence that the organisation will take allegations of sexual harassment seriously.

By its nature sexual harassment may make the normal channels of complaint difficult to use because of embarrassment, fears of not being taken seriously, fears of damage to reputation, fears of reprisal or the prospect of damaging the working environment. Therefore, a formal procedure should specify to whom the employee should bring a complaint, and it should also provide an alternative if in the particular circumstances the normal grievance procedure may not be suitable, for example because the alleged harasser is the employee's line manager. It is also advisable to make provision for employees to bring a complaint in the first instance to someone of their own sex, should they so choose.

It is good practice for employers to monitor and review complaints of sexual harassment and how they have been resolved, in order to ensure that their procedures are working effectively.

(iv) Investigations

It is important to ensure that internal investigations of any complaints are handled with sensitivity and with due respect for the rights of both the complainant and the alleged harasser. The investigation should be seen to be independent and objective. Those carrying out the investigation should not be connected with the allegation in any way, and every effort should be made to resolve complaints speedily—grievances should be handled promptly and the procedure should set a time limit within which complaints will be processed, with due regard for any time limits set by national legislation for initiating a complaint through the legal system.

It is recommended as good practice that both the complainant and the alleged harasser have the right to be accompanied and/or represented, perhaps by a representative of their trade union or a friend or colleague; that the alleged harasser be given full details of the nature of the complaint and the opportunity to respond; and that strict confidentiality be maintained throughout any investigation into an allegation. Where it is necessary to interview witnesses, the importance of confidentiality should be emphasised.

It must be recognised that recounting the experience of sexual harassment is difficult and can damage the employee's dignity. Therefore, a complainant should not be required to repeatedly recount the events complained of where this is unnecessary.

The investigation should focus on the facts of the complaint and it is advisable for the employer to keep a complete record of all meetings and investigations.

(v) Disciplinary offence

It is recommended that violations of the organisation's policy protecting the dignity of employees at work should be treated as a disciplinary offence; and the disciplinary rules should make clear what is regarded as inappropriate behaviour at work. It is also good practice to ensure that the range of penalties to which offenders will be liable for violating the rule is clearly stated and also to make it clear that it will be considered a disciplinary offence to victimise or retaliate against an employee for bringing a complaint of sexual harassment in good faith.

Where a complaint is upheld and it is determined that it is necessary to relocate or transfer one party, consideration should be given, wherever practicable, to allowing the complainant to choose whether he or she wishes to remain in their post or be transferred to another location. No element of penalty should be seen to attach to a complainant whose complaint is upheld and in addition, where a complaint is upheld, the employer should monitor the situation to ensure that the harassment has stopped.

Even where a complaint is not upheld, for example because the evidence is regarded as inconclusive, consideration should be given to transferring or rescheduling the work of one of the employees concerned rather than requiring them to continue to work together against the wishes of either party.

[3814]

6. Recommendations to trade unions

Sexual harassment is a trade union issue as well as an issue for employers. It is recommended as good practice that trade unions should formulate and issue clear policy statements on sexual harassment and take steps to raise awareness of the problem of sexual harassment in the workplace, in order to help create a climate in which it is neither condoned nor ignored. For example, trade unions could aim to give all officers and representatives training on equality issues, including dealing with sexual harassment and include such information in union-sponsored or approved training courses, as well as information on the union's policy. Trade unions should consider declaring that sexual harassment is inappropriate behaviour and educating members and officials about its consequences is recommended as good practice.

Trade unions should also raise the issue of sexual harassment with employers and encourage the adoption of adequate policies and procedures to protect the dignity of women and men at work in the organisation. It is advisable for trade unions to inform members of their right not to be sexually harassed at work and provide members with clear guidance as to what to do if they are sexually harassed, including guidance on any relevant legal rights.

Where complaints arise, it is important for trade unions to treat them seriously and sympathetically and ensure that the complainant has the opportunity of representation if a complaint is to be pursued. It is important to create an environment in which members feel able to raise such complaints knowing they will receive a sympathetic and supportive response from local union representatives. Trade unions could consider designating specially-trained officials to advise and counsel members with complaints of sexual harassment and act on their behalf if required. This will provide a focal point for support. It is also a good idea to ensure that there are sufficient female representatives to support women subjected to sexual harassment.

It is recommended too, where the trade union is representing both the complainant and the alleged harasser for the purpose of the complaints procedure, that it be made clear that the union is not condoning offensive behaviour by providing representation. In any event, the same official should not represent both parties.

It is good practice to advise members that keeping a record of incidents by the harassed worker will assist in bringing any formal or informal action to a more effective conclusion; and that the union wishes to be informed of any incident of sexual harassment and that such information will be kept confidential. It is also good practice for the union to monitor and review the union's record in responding to complaints and in representing alleged harassers and the harassed, in order to ensure its responses are effective.

[3815]

7. Employees' responsibilities

Employees have a clear role to play in helping to create a climate at work in which sexual harassment is unacceptable. They can contribute to preventing sexual harassment through an awareness and sensitivity towards the issue and by ensuring that standards of conduct for themselves and for colleagues do not cause offence.

Employees can do much to discourage sexual harassment by making it clear that they find such behaviour unacceptable and by supporting colleagues who suffer such treatment and are considering making a complaint.

PART 3

Employees who are themselves recipients of harassment should, where practicable, tell the harasser that the behaviour is unwanted and unacceptable. Once the offender understands clearly that the behaviour is unwelcome, this may be enough to put an end to it. If the behaviour is persisted in, employees should inform management and/or their employee representative through the appropriate channels and request assistance in stopping the harassment, whether through informal or formal means.

[3816]

COUNCIL DIRECTIVE

of 19 October 1992

on the introduction of measures to encourage improvements in the safety and health of pregnant workers and workers who have recently given birth or are breastfeeding (tenth individual Directive within the meaning of Article 16(1) of Directive 89/391)

(92/85/EEC)

NOTES

Date of publication in OJ: OJ L348, 28.11.92, p 1.

For the domestic implementation of this Directive see now the Employment Rights Act 1996, ss 71–75 at **[1102]–[1106]** (as substituted by the Employment Relations Act 1999, s 7, Sch 4, Pt I); the Management of Health and Safety at Work Regulations 1999, SI 1999/3242, regs 16–18 at **[2541]–[2543]**; and the Social Security Contributions and Benefits Act 1992, Pt XII, at **[433]** et seq, and Regulations made thereunder.

THE COUNCIL OF THE EUROPEAN COMMUNITIES,

Having regard to the Treaty establishing the European Economic Community, and in particular Article 118a thereof,

Having regard to the proposal from the Commission, drawn up after consultation with the Advisory Committee on Safety, Hygiene and Health Protection at work,[1]

In cooperation with the European Parliament,[2]

Having regard to the opinion of the Economic and Social Committee,[3]

Whereas Article 118a of the Treaty provides that the Council shall adopt, by means of directives, minimum requirements for encouraging improvements, especially in the working environment, to protect the safety and health of workers;

Whereas this Directive does not justify any reduction in levels of protection already achieved in individual Member States, the Member States being committed, under the Treaty, to encouraging improvements in conditions in this area and to harmonizing conditions while maintaining the improvements made;

Whereas, under the terms of Article 118a of the Treaty, the said directives are to avoid imposing administrative, financial and legal constraints in a way which would hold back the creation and development of small and medium-sized undertakings;

Whereas, pursuant to Decision 74/325/EEC,[4] as last amended by the 1985 Act of Accession, the Advisory Committee on Safety, Hygiene and Health Protection at Work is consulted by the Commission on the drafting of proposals in this field;

Whereas the Community Charter of the fundamental social rights of workers, adopted at the Strasbourg European Council on 9 December 1989 by the Heads of State or Government of 11 Member States, lays down, in paragraph 19 in particular, that—

'Every worker must enjoy satisfactory health and safety conditions in his working environment. Appropriate measures must be taken in order to achieve further harmonization of conditions in this area while maintaining the improvements made';

Whereas the Commission, in its action programme for the implementation of the Community Charter of the fundamental social rights of workers, has included among its aims the adoption by the Council of a Directive on the protection of pregnant women at work;

Whereas Article 15 of Council Directive 89/391/EEC of 12 June 1989 on the introduction of measures to encourage improvements in the safety and health of workers at work[5] provides that particularly sensitive risk groups must be protected against the dangers which specifically affect them;

Whereas pregnant workers, workers who have been recently given birth or who are breastfeeding must be considered a specific risk group in many respects, and measures must be taken with regard to their safety and health;

Whereas the protection of the safety and health of pregnant workers, workers who have recently given birth or workers who are breastfeeding should not treat women on the labour market unfavourably nor work to the detriment of directives concerning equal treatment for men and women;

Whereas some types of activities may pose a specific risk, for pregnant workers, workers who have recently given birth or workers who are breastfeeding, of exposure to dangerous agents, processes or working conditions; whereas such risks must therefore be assessed and the result of such assessment communicated to female workers and/or their representatives;

Whereas, further, should the result of this assessment reveal the existence of a risk to the safety or health of the female worker, provision must be made for such worker to be protected;

Whereas pregnant workers and workers who are breastfeeding must not engage in activities which have been assessed as revealing a risk of exposure, jeopardising safety and health, to certain particularly dangerous agents or working conditions;

Whereas provision should be made for pregnant workers, workers who have recently given birth or workers who are breastfeeding not to be required to work at night where such provision is necessary from the point of view of their safety and health;

Whereas the vulnerability of pregnant workers, workers who have recently given birth or who are breastfeeding makes it necessary for them to be granted the right to maternity leave of at least 14 continuous weeks, allocated before and/or after confinement, and renders necessary the compulsory nature of maternity leave of at least two weeks, allocated before and/or after confinement;

Whereas the risk of dismissal for reasons associated with their condition may have harmful effects on the physical and mental state of pregnant workers, workers who have recently given birth or who are breastfeeding; whereas provision should be made for such dismissal to be prohibited;

Whereas measures for the organization of work concerning the protection of the health of pregnant workers, workers who have recently given birth or workers who are breastfeeding would serve no purpose unless accompanied by the maintenance of rights linked to the employment contract, including maintenance of payment and/or entitlement to an adequate allowance;

Whereas, moreover, provision concerning maternity leave would also serve no purpose unless accompanied by the maintenance of rights linked to the employment contract and/or entitlement to an adequate allowance;

Whereas the concept of an adequate allowance in the case of maternity leave must be regarded as a technical point of reference with a view to fixing the minimum level of protection and should in no circumstances be interpreted as suggesting an analogy between pregnancy and illness,

NOTES

1 OJ C281, 9.11.90, p 3; and OJ C25, 1.2.91, p 9.
2 OJ C19, 28.1.91, p 177; and OJ C150, 15.6.92, p 99.
3 OJ C41, 18.2.91, p 29.
4 OJ L185, 9.7.74, p 15.
5 OJ L183, 29.6.89, p 1.

HAS ADOPTED THIS DIRECTIVE—

SECTION I
PURPOSE AND DEFINITIONS

Article 1

Purpose

1. The purpose of this Directive, which is the tenth individual Directive within the meaning of Article 16(1) of Directive 89/391/EEC, is to implement measures to encourage improvements in the safety and health at work of pregnant workers and workers who have recently given birth or who are breastfeeding.

2. The provisions of Directive 89/391/EEC, except for Article 2(2) thereof, shall apply in full to the whole area covered by paragraph 1, without prejudice to any more stringent and/or specific provisions contained in this Directive.

3. This Directive may not have the effect of reducing the level of protection afforded to pregnant workers, workers who have recently given birth or who are breastfeeding as compared with the situation which exists in each Member State on the date on which this Directive is adopted.

[3817]

Article 2

Definitions

For the purposes of this Directive—

(a) *pregnant worker* shall mean a pregnant worker who informs her employer of her condition, in accordance with national legislation and/or national practice;

(b) *worker who has recently given birth* shall mean a worker who has recently given birth within the meaning of national legislation and/or national practice and who informs her employer of her condition, in accordance with that legislation and/or practice;

(c) *worker who is breastfeeding* shall mean a worker who is breastfeeding within the meaning of national legislation and/or national practice and who informs her employer of her condition, in accordance with that legislation and/or practice.

[3818]

SECTION II
GENERAL PROVISIONS

Article 3

Guidelines

1. In consultation with the Member States and assisted by the Advisory Committee on Safety, Hygiene and Health Protection at Work, the Commission shall draw up guidelines on the assessment of the chemical, physical and biological agents and industrial process considered hazardous for the safety or health of workers within the meaning of Article 2.

The guidelines referred to in the first subparagraph shall also cover movements and postures, mental and physical fatigue and other types of physical and mental stress connected with the work done by workers within the meaning of Article 2.

2. The purpose of the guidelines referred to in paragraph 1 is to serve as a basis for the assessment referred to in Article 4(1).

To this end, Member States shall bring these guidelines to the attention of all employers and all female workers and/or their representatives in the respective Member State.

[3819]

Article 4

Assessment and information

1. For all activities liable to involve a specific risk of exposure to the agents, processes or working conditions of which a non-exhaustive list is given in Annex 1, the employer shall assess the nature, degree and duration of exposure, in the undertaking and/or establishment concerned, or workers within the meaning of Article 2, either directly or by way of the protective and preventative services referred to in Article 7 of Directive 89/391/EEC, in order to—

— assess any risks to the safety or health and any possible effect on the pregnancies or breastfeeding of workers within the meaning of Article 2,

— decide what measures should be taken.

2. Without prejudice to Article 10 of Directive 89/391/EEC, workers within the meaning of Article 2 and workers likely to be in one of the situations referred to in Article 2 in the undertaking and/or establishment concerned and/or their representatives shall be informed of the results of the assessment referred to in paragraph 1 and of all measures to be taken concerning health and safety at work.

[3820]

Article 5

Action further to the results of the assessment

1. Without prejudice to Article 6 of Directive 89/391/EEC, if the results of the assessment referred to in Article 4(1) reveal a risk to the safety or health or an effect on the

pregnancy or breastfeeding of a worker within the meaning of Article 2, the employer shall take the necessary measures to ensure that, by temporarily adjusting the working conditions and/or the working hours of the worker concerned, the exposure of that worker to such risks is avoided.

2. If the adjustment of her working conditions and/or working hours is not technically and/or objectively feasible, or cannot reasonably be required on duly substantiated grounds, the employer shall take the necessary measures to move the worker concerned to another job.

3. If moving her to another job is not technically and/or objectively feasible or cannot reasonably be required on duly substantiated grounds, the worker concerned shall be granted leave in accordance with national legislation and/or national practice for the whole of the period necessary to protect her safety or health.

4. The provisions of this Article shall apply *mutatis mutandis* to the case where a worker pursuing an activity which is forbidden pursuant to Article 6 becomes pregnant or starts breastfeeding and informs her employer thereof.

[3821]

Article 6

Cases in which exposure is prohibited

In addition to the general provisions concerning the protection of workers, in particular those relating to the limit values for occupational exposure—

1. pregnant workers within the meaning of Article 2(a) may under no circumstances be obliged to perform duties for which the assessment has revealed a risk of exposure, which would jeopardize safety or health, to the agents and working conditions listed in Annex II, Section A;
2. workers who are breastfeeding, within the meaning of Article 2(c), may under no circumstances be obliged to perform duties for which the assessment has revealed a risk of exposure, which would jeopardize safety or health, to the agents and working conditions listed in Annex II, Section B.

[3822]

Article 7

Night work

1. Member States shall take the necessary measures to ensure that workers referred to in Article 2 are not obliged to perform night work during their pregnancy and for a period following childbirth which shall be determined by the national authority competent for safety and health, subject to submission, in accordance with the procedures laid down by the Member States, of a medical certificate stating that this is necessary for the safety or health of the worker concerned.

2. The measures referred to in paragraph 1 must entail the possibility, in accordance with national legislation and/or national practice, of—

(a) transfer to daytime work; or

(b) leave from work or extension of maternity leave where such a transfer is not technically and/or objectively feasible or cannot reasonably be required on duly substantiated grounds.

[3823]

Article 8

Maternity leave

1. Member States shall take the necessary measures to ensure that workers within the meaning of Article 2 are entitled to a continuous period of maternity leave of at least 14 weeks allocated before and/or after confinement in accordance with national legislation and/or practice.

2. The maternity leave stipulated in paragraph 1 must include compulsory maternity leave of at least two weeks allocated before and/or after confinement in accordance with national legislation and/or practice.

[3824]

Article 9

Time off for ante-natal examinations

Member States shall take the necessary measures to ensure that pregnant workers within the meaning of Article 2(a) are entitled to, in accordance with national legislation and/or practice, time off, without loss of pay, in order to attend ante-natal examinations, if such examinations have to take place during working hours.

[3825]

Article 10

Prohibition of dismissal

In order to guarantee workers, within the meaning of Article 2, the exercise of their health and safety protection rights as recognized under this Article, it shall be provided that—

1. Member States shall take the necessary measures to prohibit the dismissal of workers, within the meaning of Article 2, during the period from the beginning of their pregnancy to the end of the maternity leave referred to in Article 8(1) save in exceptional cases not connected with their condition which are permitted under national legislation and/or practice and, where applicable, provided that the competent authority has given its consent;
2. if a worker, within the meaning of Article 2, is dismissed during the period referred to in point 1, the employer must cite duly substantiated grounds for her dismissal in writing;
3. Member States shall take the necessary measures to protect workers, within the meaning of Article 2, from consequences of dismissal which is unlawful by virtue of point 1.

[3826]

Article 11

Employment rights

In order to guarantee workers within the meaning of Article 2 the exercise of their health and safety protection rights as recognized in this Article, it shall be provided that—

1. in the cases referred to in Articles 5, 6 and 7, the employment rights relating to the employment contract, including the maintenance of a payment to, and/or entitlement to an adequate allowance for, workers within the meaning of Article 2, must be ensured in accordance with national legislation and/or national practice;
2. in the case referred to in Article 8, the following must be ensured—
   (a) the rights connected with the employment contract of workers within the meaning of Article 2, other than those referred to in point (b) below;
   (b) maintenance of a payment to, and/or entitlement to an adequate allowance for, workers within the meaning of Article 2;
3. the allowance referred to in point 2(b) shall be deemed adequate if it guarantees income at least equivalent to that which the worker concerned would receive in the event of a break in her activities on grounds connected with her state of health, subject to any ceiling laid down under national legislation;
4. Member States may make entitlement to pay or the allowance referred to in points 1 and 2(b) conditional upon the worker concerned fulfilling the conditions of eligibility for such benefits laid down under national legislation.

These conditions may under no circumstances provide for periods of previous employment in excess of 12 months immediately prior to the presumed date of confinement.

[3827]

NOTES

The Council and Commission issued the following formal statement at the 1608th meeting of the Council on 19 October 1992 (OJ L348/92, p 8)—

THE COUNCIL AND THE COMMISSION stated that—

"In determining the level of the allowances referred to in Article 11(2)(b) and (3), reference shall be made, for purely technical reasons, to the allowance which a worker would receive in the event of a break in her activities on grounds connected with her state of health. Such a reference is not intended in any way to imply that pregnancy and childbirth be equated with sickness. The national social security legislation of all Member States provides for an allowance to be paid during an absence from work due to sickness. The link with such allowance in the chosen formulation is simply intended to serve as a concrete, fixed reference amount in all Member States for the determination of the minimum amount of maternity allowance payable. In so far as allowances are paid in individual Member States which exceed those provided for in the Directive, such allowances are, of course, retained. This is clear from Article 1(3) of the Directive.".

Article 12

Defence of rights

Member States shall introduce into their national legal systems such measures as are necessary to enable all workers who should themselves wronged by failure to comply with the obligations arising from this Directive to pursue their claims by judicial process (and/or, in accordance with national laws and/or practices) by recourse to other competent authorities.

[3828]

NOTE

This Article is printed as in the *Official Journal*: presumably the word "consider" ought to have been inserted after the word "should".

Article 13

Amendments to the Annexes

1. Strictly technical adjustments to Annex I as a result of technical progress, changes in international regulations or specifications and new findings in the area covered by this Directive shall be adopted in accordance with the procedure laid down in Article 17 of Directive 89/391/EEC.

2. Annex II may be amended only in accordance with the procedure laid down in Article 118a of the Treaty.

[3829]

NOTES

Article 118a: see now Art 138 at **[3522]**.

Article 14

Final provisions

1. Member States shall bring into force the laws, regulations and administrative provisions necessary to comply with this Directive not later than two years after the adoption thereof or ensure, at the latest two years after the adoption of this Directive, that the two sides of industry introduce the requisite provisions by means of collective agreements, with Member States being required to make all the necessary provisions to enable them at all times to guarantee the results laid down by this Directive. They shall forthwith inform the Commission thereof.

2. When Member States adopt the measure referred to in paragraph 1, they shall contain a reference of this Directive or shall be accompanied by such reference on the occasion of their official publication. The methods of making such a reference shall be laid down by the Member States.

3. Member States shall communicate to the Commission the texts of the essential provisions of national law which they have already adopted or adopt in the field governed by this Directive.

4.–6. …

[3830]

NOTES

Paras 4–6: repealed by European Parliament and Council Directive 2007/30/EC, Art 3(11), as from 27 June 2007. Note that the 2007 Directive has a transposition date of 31 December 2012, and paras 4–6 originally read as follows:

"4. Member States shall report to the Commission every five years on the practical implementation of the provisions of this Directive, indicating the points of view of the two sides of industry.

However, Member States shall report for the first time to the Commission on the practical implementation of the provisions of this Directive, indicating the points of view of the two sides of industry, four years after its adoption.

The Commission shall inform the European Parliament, the Council, the Economic and Social Committee and the Advisory Committee on Safety, Hygiene and Health Protection at Work.

5. The Commission shall periodically submit to the European Parliament, the Council and the Economic and Social Committee a report on the implementation of this Directive, taking into account paragraphs 1, 2 and 3.

6. The Council will re-examine this Directive, on the basis of an assessment carried out on the basis of the reports referred to in the second subparagraph of paragraph 4 and, should the need arise, of a proposal, to be submitted by the Commission at the latest five years after adoption of the Directive.".

Article 15

The Directive is addressed to the Member States.

[3831]

ANNEX I
NON-EXHAUSTIVE LIST OF AGENTS, PROCESSES AND WORKING CONDITIONS

(*referred to in Article 4(1)*)

A. AGENTS

1. Physical agents where these are regarded as agents causing foetal lesions and/or likely to disrupt placental attachment, and in particular—

(a) shocks, vibration or movement;
(b) handling of loads entailing risks, particularly of a dorsolumbar nature;
(c) noise;
(d) ionising radiation;[1]
(e) non-ionising radiation;
(f) extremes of cold or heat;
(g) movements and postures, travelling—either inside or outside the establishment—mental and physical fatigue and other physical burdens connected with the activity of the worker within the meaning of Article 2 of the Directive.

2. Biological agents

Biological agents of risk groups 2, 3 and 3 [*] within the meaning of Article 2(d) numbers 2, 3 and 4 of Directive 90/679/EEC,[2] in so far as it is known that these agents or the therapeutic measures necessitated by such agents endanger the health of pregnant women and the unborn child and in so far as they do not yet appear in Annex II.

3. Chemical agents

The following chemical agents in so far as it is known that they endanger the health of pregnant women and the unborn child and in so far as they do not yet appear in Annex II—

(a) substances labelled R 40, R 45, R 46, and R 47 under Directive 67/548/EEC[3] in so far as they do not yet appear in Annex II;
(b) chemical agents in Annex I to Directive 90/394/EEC;[4]
(c) mercury and mercury derivatives;
(d) antimitotic drugs;
(e) carbon monoxide;
(f) chemical agents of known and dangerous percutaneous absorption.

B. PROCESSES

Industrial processes listed in Annex I to Directive 90/394/EEC.

C. WORKING CONDITIONS

Underground mining work.

[3832]

NOTES

1 See Directive 80/836/Euratom (OJ L246, 17.9.80, p 1).
2 OJ L374, 31.12.90, p 1.
3 OJ L196, 16.8.67, p 1. Directive as last amended by Directive 90/517/EEC (OJ L287, 19.10.90, p 37).
4 OJ L196, 26.7.90, p 1.
* Text printed as in the Official Journal.

ANNEX II
NON-EXHAUSTIVE LIST OF AGENTS AND WORKING CONDITIONS

(*referred to in Article 6*)

A. PREGNANT WORKERS WITHIN THE MEANING OF ARTICLE 2(A)

1. *Agents*

(a) Physical agents
Work in hyperbaric atmosphere, e g pressurized enclosures and underwater diving.

(b) Biological agents
The following biological agents—
— toxoplasma,
— rubella virus,
unless the pregnant workers are proved to be adequately protected against such agents by immunization.

(c) Chemical agents
Lead and lead derivatives in so far as these agents are capable of being absorbed by the human organism.

2. *Working conditions*

Underground mining work.

B. WORKERS WHO ARE BREASTFEEDING WITHIN THE MEANING OF ARTICLE 2(C)

1. *Agents*

(a) Chemical agents
Lead and lead derivatives in so far as these agents are capable of being absorbed by the human organism.

2. *Working conditions*

Underground mining work.

[3833]

COUNCIL DIRECTIVE

of 23 November 1993

concerning certain aspects of the organisation of working time (Note)

(93/104/EC)

NOTES

This Directive (as subsequently amended by Directive 2000/34/EC) was repealed by the consolidating European Parliament and Council Directive of 4 November 2003 concerning certain aspects of the organisation of working time (2003/88/EC) at **[4090]** et seq. The 2003 Directive came into force on 2 August 2004 (see Art 28). Annex II to Directive 2003/88 is a table correlating provisions of this Directive with those of the consolidating Directive.

[3834]

COUNCIL DIRECTIVE

of 22 June 1994

on the protection of young people at work

(94/33/EC)

NOTES

Date of publication in OJ: OJ L 216, 20.8.94, p 12.

For the domestic implementation of those parts of this Directive within the scope of this work, see in particular the Working Time Regulations 1998 SI 1998/1833, at **[2411]** et seq.

THE COUNCIL OF THE EUROPEAN UNION,

Having regard to the Treaty establishing the European Community, and in particular Article 118a thereof,

Having regard to the proposal from the Commission,[1]

Having regard to the opinion, of the Economic and Social Committee,[2]

Acting in accordance with the procedure referred to in Article 189c of the Treaty,[3]

Whereas Article 118a of the Treaty provides that the Council shall adopt, by means of directives, minimum requirements to encourage improvements, especially in the working environment, as regards the health and safety of workers;

Whereas, under that Article, such directives must avoid imposing administrative, financial and legal constraints in a way which would hold back the creation and development of small and medium-sized undertakings;

Whereas points 20 and 22 of the Community Charter of the Fundamental Social Rights of Workers, adopted by the European Council in Strasbourg on 9 December 1989, state that—

'20. Without prejudice to such rules as may be more favourable to young people, in particular those ensuring their preparation for work through vocational training, and subject to derogations limited to certain light work, the minimum employment age must not be lower than the minimum school-leaving age and, in any case, not lower than 15 years;

22. Appropriate measures must be taken to adjust labour regulations applicable to young workers so that their specific development and vocational training and access to employment needs are met.

The duration of work must, in particular, be limited—without it being possible to circumvent this limitation through recourse to overtime—and night work prohibited in the case of workers of under eighteen years of age, save in the case of certain jobs laid down in national legislation or regulations.';

Whereas account should be taken of the principles of the International Labour Organisation regarding the protection of young people at work, including those relating to the minimum age for access to employment or work;

Whereas, in its Resolution on child labour,[4] the European Parliament summarised the various aspects of work by young people and stressed its effects on their health, safety and physical and intellectual development, and pointed to the need to adopt a Directive harmonising national legislation in the field;

Whereas Article 15 of Council Directive 89/391/EEC of 12 June 1989 on the introduction of measures to encourage improvements in the safety and health of workers at work[5] provides that particularly sensitive risk groups must be protected against the dangers which specifically affect them;

Whereas children and adolescents must be considered specific risk groups, and measures must be taken with regard to their safety and health;

Whereas the vulnerability of children calls for Member States to prohibit their employment and ensure that the minimum working or employment age is not lower than the minimum age at which compulsory schooling as imposed by national law ends or 15 years in any event; whereas derogations from the prohibition on child labour may be admitted only in special cases and under the conditions stipulated in this Directive; whereas, under no circumstances, may such derogations be detrimental to regular school attendance or prevent children benefiting fully from their education;

Whereas, in view of the nature of the transition from childhood to adult life, work by adolescents should be strictly regulated and protected;

Whereas every employer should guarantee young people working conditions appropriate to their age;

Whereas employers should implement the measures necessary to protect the safety and health of young people on the basis on an assessment of work-related hazards to the young;

Whereas Member States should protect young people against any specific risks arising from their lack of experience, absence of awareness of existing or potential risks, or from their immaturity;

Whereas Member States should therefore prohibit the employment of young people for the work specified by this Directive;

Whereas the adoption of specific minimal requirements in respect of the organisation of working time is likely to improve working conditions for young people;

Whereas the maximum working time of young people should be strictly limited and night work by young people should be prohibited, with the exception of certain jobs specified by national legislation or rules;

Whereas Member States should take the appropriate measures to ensure that the working time of adolescents receiving school education does not adversely affect their ability to benefit from that education;

Whereas time spent on training by young persons working under a theoretical and/or practical combined work/training scheme or an in-plant work-experience should be counted as working time;

Whereas, in order to ensure the safety and health of young people, the latter should be granted minimum daily, weekly and annual periods of rest and adequate breaks;

Whereas, with respect to the weekly rest period, due account should be taken of the diversity of cultural, ethnic, religious and other factors prevailing in the Member States; whereas in particular, it is ultimately for each Member State to decide whether Sunday should be included in the weekly rest period, and if so to what extent;

Whereas appropriate work experience may contribute to the aim of preparing young people for adult working and social life, provided it is ensured that any harm to their safety, health and development is avoided;

Whereas, although derogations from the bans and limitations imposed by this Directive would appear indispensable for certain activities or particular situations, applications thereof must not prejudice the principles underlying the established protection system;

Whereas this Directive constitutes a tangible step towards developing the social dimension of the internal market;

Whereas the application in practice of the system of protection laid down by this Directive will require that Member States implement a system of effective and proportionate measures;

Whereas the implementation of some provisions of this Directive poses particular problems for one Member State with regard to its system of protection for young people at work; whereas that Member State should therefore be allowed to refrain from implementing the relevant provisions for a suitable period,

NOTES

1 OJ C84, 4.4.92, p 7.
2 OJ C313, 30.11.92, p 70.
3 Opinion of the European Parliament of 17 December 1992 (OJ C21, 25.1.93, p 167). Council Common Position of 23 November 1993 (not yet published in the Official Journal) and Decision of the European Parliament of 9 March 1994 (OJ C 91, 28.3.94, p 89).
4 OJ C190, 20.7.87, p 44.
5 OJ L183, 29.6.89, p 1.

HAS ADOPTED THIS DIRECTIVE—

SECTION I

Article 1

Purpose

1. Member States shall take the necessary measures to prohibit work by children.

They shall ensure, under the conditions laid down by this Directive, that the minimum working or employment age is not lower than the minimum age at which compulsory full-time schooling as imposed by national law ends or 15 years in any event.

2. Member States ensure that work by adolescents is strictly regulated and protected under the conditions laid down in this Directive.

3. Member States shall ensure in general that employers guarantee that young people have working conditions which suit their age.

They shall ensure that young people are protected against economic exploitation and against any work likely to harm their safety, health or physical, mental, moral or social development or to jeopardise their education.

[3835]

Article 2

Scope

1. This Directive shall apply to any person under 18 years of age having an employment contract or an employment relationship defined by the law in force in a Member State and/or governed by the law in force in a Member State.

2. Member States may make legislative or regulatory provision for this Directive not to apply, within the limits and under the conditions which they set by legislative or regulatory provision, to occasional work or short-term work involving—

(a) domestic service in a private household, or
(b) work regarded as not being harmful, damaging or dangerous to young people in a family undertaking.

[3836]

Article 3

Definitions

For the purposes of this Directive—

(a) 'young person' shall mean any person under 18 years of age referred to in Article 2(1);
(b) 'child' shall mean any young person of less than 15 years of age or who is still subject to compulsory full-time schooling under national law;
(c) 'adolescent' shall mean any young person of at least 15 years of age but less than 18 years of age who is no longer subject to compulsory full-time schooling under national law;
(d) 'light work' shall mean all work which, on account of the inherent nature of the tasks which it involves and the particular conditions under which they are performed—
  (i) is not likely to be harmful to the safety, health or development of children, and
  (ii) is not such as to be harmful to their attendance at school, their participation in vocational guidance or training programmes approved by the competent authority or their capacity to benefit from the instruction received;
(e) 'working time' shall mean any period during which the young person is at work, at the employer's disposal and carrying out his activity or duties in accordance with national legislation and/or practice;
(f) 'rest period' shall mean any period which is not working time.

[3837]

Article 4

Prohibition of work by children

1. Member States shall adopt the measures necessary to prohibit work by children.

2. Taking into account the objectives set out in Article 1, Member States may make legislative or regulatory provision for the prohibition of work by children not to apply to—

(a) children pursuing the activities set out in Article 5;
(b) children of at least 14 years of age working under a combined work/ training scheme or an in-plant work-experience scheme, provided that such work is done in accordance with the conditions laid down by the competent authority;
(c) children of at least 14 years of age performing light work other than that covered by Article 5; light work other than that covered by Article 5 may, however, be performed by children of 13 years of age for a limited number of hours per week in the case of categories of work determined by national legislation.

3. Member States that make use of the opinion referred to in paragraph 2(c) shall determine, subject to the provisions of this Directive, the working conditions relating to the light work in question.

[3838]

Article 5

Cultural or similar activities

1. The employment of children for the purposes of performance in cultural, artistic, sports or advertising activities shall be subject to prior authorisation to be given by the competent authority in individual cases.

2. Member States shall by legislative or regulatory provision lay down the working conditions for children in the cases referred to in paragraph 1 and the details of the prior authorisation procedure, on condition that the activities—

(i) are not likely to be harmful to the safety, health or development of children, and

(ii) are not such as to be harmful to their attendance at school, their participation in vocational guidance or training programmes approved by the competent authority or their capacity to benefit from the instruction received.

3. By way of derogation from the procedure laid down in paragraph 1, in the case of children of at least 13 years of age, Member States may authorise, by legislative or regulatory provision, in accordance with conditions which they shall determine, the employment of children for the purposes of performance in cultural, artistic, sports or advertising activities.

4. The Member States which have a specific authorisation system for modelling agencies with regard to the activities of children may retain that system.

[3839]

SECTION II

Article 6

General obligations on employers

1. Without prejudice to Article 4 (1), the employer shall adopt the measures necessary to protect the safety and health of young people, taking particular account of the specific risks referred to in Article 7(1).

2. The employer shall implement the measures provided for in paragraph 1 on the basis of an assessment of the hazards to young people in connection with their work.

The assessment must be made before young people begin work and when there is any major change in working conditions and must pay particular attention to the following points—

(a) the fitting-out and layout of the workplace and the workstation;

(b) the nature, degree and duration of exposure to physical, biological and chemical agents;

(c) the form, range and use of work equipment, in particular agents, machines, apparatus and devices, and the way in which they are handled;

(d) the arrangement of work processes and operations and the way in which these are combined (organisation of work);

(e) the level of training and instruction given to young people.

Where this assessment shows that there is a risk to the safety, the physical or mental health or development of young people, an appropriate free assessment and monitoring of their health shall be provided at regular intervals without prejudice to Directive 89/391/EEC.

The free health assessment and monitoring may form part of a national health system.

3. The employer shall inform young people of possible risks and of all measures adopted concerning their safety and health.

Furthermore, he shall inform the legal representatives of children of possible risks and of all measures adopted concerning children's safety and health.

4. The employer shall involve the protective and preventive services referred to in Article 7 of Directive 89/391/EEC in the planning, implementation and monitoring of the safety and health conditions applicable to young people.

[3840]

Article 7

Vulnerability of young people—Prohibition of work

1. Member States shall ensure that young people are protected from any specific risks to their safety, health and development which are a consequence of their lack of experience, of absence of awareness of existing or potential risks or of the fact that young people have not yet fully matured.

2. Without prejudice to Article 4(1), Member States shall to this end prohibit the employment of young people for—

(a) work which is objectively beyond their physical or psychological capacity;

(b) work involving harmful exposure to agents which are toxic, carcinogenic, cause heritable genetic damage, or harm to the unborn child or which in any other way chronically affect human health;

(c) work involving harmful exposure to radiation;

(d) work involving the risk of accidents which it may be assumed cannot be recognised or avoided by young persons owing to their insufficient attention to safety or lack of experience or training; or

(e) work in which there is a risk to health from extreme cold or heat, or from noise or vibration.

Work which is likely to entail specific risks for young people within the meaning of paragraph l includes—

— work involving harmful exposure to the physical, biological and chemical agents referred to in point I of the Annex, and

— processes and work referred to in point II of the Annex.

3. Member States may, by legislative or regulatory provision, authorise derogations from paragraph 2 in the case of adolescents where such derogations are indispensable for their vocational training, provided that protection of their safety and health is ensured by the fact that the work is performed under the supervision of a competent person within the meaning of Article 7 of Directive 89/391/EEC and provided that the protection afforded by that Directive is guaranteed.

[3841]

SECTION III

Article 8

Working time

1. Member States which make use of the option in Article 4(2)(b) or (c) shall adopt the measures necessary to limit the working time of children to—

(a) eight hours a day and 40 hours a week for work performed under a combined work/training scheme or an in-plant work-experience scheme;

(b) two hours on a school day and 12 hours a week for work performed in term-time outside the hours fixed for school attendance, provided that this is not prohibited by national legislation and/or practice;

in no circumstances may the daily working time exceed seven hours; this limit may be raised to eight hours in the case of children who have reached the age of 15;

(c) seven hours a day and 35 hours a week for work performed during a period of at least a week when school is not operating; these limits may be raised to eight hours a day and 40 hours a week in the case of children who have reached the age of 15;

(d) seven hours a day and 35 hours a week for light work performed by children no longer subject to compulsory full-time schooling under national law.

2. Member States shall adopt the measures necessary to limit the working time of adolescents to eight hours a day and 40 hours a week.

3. The time spent on training by a young person working under a theoretical and/or practical combined work/training scheme or an in-plant work-experience scheme shall be counted as working time.

4. Where a young person is employed by more than one employer, working days and working time shall be cumulative.

5. Member States may, by legislative or regulatory provision, authorise derogations from paragraph 1(a) and paragraph 2 either by way of exception or where there are objective grounds for so doing.

Member States shall, by legislative or regulatory provision, determine the conditions, limits and procedure for implementing such derogations.

[3842]

Article 9

Night work

1.

(a) Member States which make use of the option in Article 4(2)(b) or (c) shall adopt the measures necessary to prohibit work by children between 8 pm and 6 am.

(b) Member States shall adopt the measures necessary to prohibit work by adolescents either between 10 pm and 6 am or between 11 pm and 7 am.

2.

(a) Member States may, by legislative or regulatory provision, authorise work by adolescents in specific areas of activity during the period in which night work is prohibited as referred to in paragraph 1(b).

In that event, Member States shall take appropriate measures to ensure that the adolescent is supervised by an adult where such supervision is necessary for the adolescent's protection.

(b) If point (a) is applied, work shall continue to be prohibited between midnight and 4 am.

However, Member States may, by legislative or regulatory provision, authorise work by adolescents during the period in which night work is prohibited in the following cases, where there are objective grounds for so doing and provided that adolescents are allowed suitable compensatory rest time and that the objectives set out in Article 1 are not called into question—

— work performed in the shipping or fisheries sectors;
— work performed in the context of the armed forces or the police;
— work performed in hospitals or similar establishments;
— cultural, artistic, sports or advertising activities.

3. Prior to any assignment to night work and at regular intervals thereafter, adolescents shall be entitled to a free assessment of their health and capacities, unless the work they do during the period during which work is prohibited is of an exceptional nature.

[3843]

Article 10

Rest period

1.

(a) Member States which make use of the option in Article 4(2), (b) or (c) shall adopt the measures necessary to ensure that, for each 24 hour period, children are entitled to a minimum rest period of 14 consecutive hours.

(b) Member States shall adopt the measures necessary to ensure that, for each 24-hour period, adolescents are entitled to a minimum rest period of 12 consecutive hours.

2. Member States shall adopt the measures necessary to ensure that, for each seven-day period—

— children in respect of whom they have made use of the option in Article 4(2)(b) or (c), and
— adolescents

are entitled to a minimum rest period of two days, which shall be consecutive if possible.

Where justified by technical or organisation reasons, the minimum rest period may be reduced, but may in no circumstances be less than 36 consecutive hours.

The minimum rest period referred to in the first and second subparagraphs shall in principle include Sunday.

3. Member States may, by legislative or regulatory provision, provide for the minimum rest periods referred to in paragraphs 1 and 2 to be interrupted in the case of activities involving periods of work that are split up over the day or are of short duration.

4. Member States may make legislative or regulatory provision for derogations from paragraph 1(b) and paragraph 2 in respect of adolescents in the following cases, where there are objective grounds for so doing and provided that they are granted appropriate compensatory rest time and that the objectives set out in Article 1 are not called into question—

(a) work performed in the shipping or fisheries sectors;
(b) work performed in the context of the armed forces or the police;
(c) work performed in hospitals or similar establishments;

(d) work performed in agriculture;
(e) work performed in the tourism industry or in the hotel, restaurant and café sector;
(f) activities involving periods of work split up over the day.

[3844]

Article 11

Annual rest

Member States which make use of the option referred to in Article 4(2)(b) or (c) shall see to it that a period free of any work is included, as far as possible, in the school holidays of children subject to compulsory full-time schooling under national law.

[3845]

Article 12

Breaks

Member States shall adopt the measures necessary to ensure that, where daily working time is more than four and a half hours, young people are entitled to a break of at least 30 minutes, which shall be consecutive if possible.

[3846]

Article 13

Work by adolescents in the event of *force majeure*

Member States may, by legislative or regulatory provision, authorise derogations from Article 8(2), Article 9(l)(b), Article 10(1)(b) and, in the case of adolescents, Article 12, for work in the circumstances referred to in Article 5(4) of Directive 89/391/EEC, provided that such work is of a temporary nature and must be performed immediately, that adult workers are not available and that the adolescents are allowed equivalent compensatory rest time within the following three weeks.

[3847]

SECTION IV

Article 14

Measures

Each Member State shall lay down any necessary measures to be applied in the event of failure to comply with the provisions adopted in order to implement this Directive; such measures must be effective and proportionate.

[3848]

Article 15

Adaptation of the Annex

Adaptations of a strictly technical nature to the Annex in the light of technical progress, changes in international rules or specifications and advances in knowledge in the field covered by this Directive shall be adopted in accordance with the procedure provided for in Article 17 of Directive 89/391/EEC.

[3849]

Article 16

Non-reducing clause

Without prejudice to the right of Member States to develop, in the light of changing circumstances, different provisions on the protection of young people, as long as the minimum requirements provided for by this Directive are complied with, the implementation of this Directive shall not constitute valid grounds for reducing the general level of protection afforded to young people.

[3850]

Article 17

Final provisions

1.

(a) Member States shall bring into force the laws, regulations and administrative provisions necessary to comply with this Directive not later than 22 June 1996 or ensure, by that date at the latest, that the two sides of industry introduce the requisite provisions by means of collective agreements, with Member States being required to make all the necessary provisions to enable them at all times to guarantee the results laid down by this Directive.

(b) The United Kingdom may refrain from implementing the first subparagraph of Article 8(1)(b) with regard to the provision relating to the maximum weekly working time, and also Article 8(2) and Article 9(1)(b) and (2) for a period of four years from the date specified in subparagraph (a).
The Commission shall submit a report on the effects of this provision.
The Council, acting in accordance with the conditions laid down by the Treaty, shall decide whether this period should be extended.

(c) Member States shall forthwith inform the Commission thereof.

2. When Member States adopt the measures referred to in paragraph 1, such measures shall contain a reference to this Directive or shall be accompanied by such reference on the occasion of their official publication. The methods of making such reference shall be laid down by Member States.

3. Member States shall communicate to the Commission the texts of the main provisions of national law which they have already adopted or adopt in the field governed by this Directive.

4, 5. …

[3851]

NOTES

Paras 4, 5: repealed by European Parliament and Council Directive 2007/30/EC, Art 3(15), as from 27 June 2007. Note that the 2007 Directive has a transposition date of 31 December 2012, and paras 4, 5 originally read as follows:

"4. Member States shall report to the Commission every five years on the practical implementation of the provisions of this Directive, indicating the viewpoints of the two sides of industry.

The Commission shall inform the European Parliament, the Council and the Economic and Social Committee thereof.

5. The Commission shall periodically submit to the European Parliament, the Council and the Economic and Social Committee a report on the application of this Directive taking into account paragraphs 1, 2, 3 and 4.".

[Article 17a

Implementation report

Every five years, the Member States shall submit to the Commission a report on the practical implementation of this Directive in the form of a specific chapter of the single report referred to in Article 17a(1), (2) and (3) of Directive 89/391/EEC, which serves as a basis for the Commission's evaluation, in accordance with Article 17a(4) of that Directive.]

[3851A]

NOTES

Inserted by European Parliament and Council Directive 2007/30/EC, Art 2(4), as from 28 June 2007. Note that the 2007 Directive has a transposition date of 31 December 2012.

Article 18

This Directive is addressed to the Member States.

[3852]

ANNEX
NON-EXHAUSTIVE LIST OF AGENTS, PROCESSES AND WORK (ARTICLE 7(2), SECOND SUBPARAGRAPH)

I. Agents

1. *Physical agents*

(a) Ionising radiation;

(b) Work in a high-pressure atmosphere, e g in pressurised containers, diving.

2. *Biological agents*

(a) Biological agents belonging to groups 3 and 4 within the meaning of Article 2(d) of Council Directive 90/679/EEC of 26 November 1990 on the protection of workers from risks related to exposure to biological agents at work (Seventh individual Directive within the meaning of Article 16(1) of Directive 89/391/EEC).[1]

3. *Chemical agents*

(a) Substances and preparations classified according to Council Directive 67/548/EEC of 27 June 1967 on the approximation of laws, regulations and administrative provisions relating to the classification, packaging and labelling of dangerous substances[2] with amendments and Council Directive 88/379/EEC of 7 June 1988 on the approximation of the laws, regulations and administrative provisions of the Member States relating to the classification, packaging and labelling of dangerous preparations[3] as toxic (T), very toxic (Tx), corrosive (C) or explosive (E);

(b) Substances and preparations classified according to Directives 67/548/EEC and 88/379/EEC as harmful (Xn) and with one or more of the following risk phrases—

— danger of very serious irreversible effects (R39),

— possible risk of irreversible effects (R40),

— may cause sensitisation by inhalation (R42),

— may cause sensitisation by skin contact (R43),

— may cause cancer (R45),

— may cause heritable genetic damage (R46),

— danger of serious damage to health by prolonged exposure (R48),

— may impair fertility (R60),

— may cause harm to the unborn child (R61);

(c) Substances and preparations classified according to Directives 67/548/EEC and 88/379/EEC as irritant (Xi) and with one or more of the following risk phrases—

— highly flammable (R12);

— may cause sensitisation by inhalation (R42),

— may cause sensitisation by skin contact (R43);

(d) Substances and preparations referred to Article 2(c) of Council Directive 90/394/EEC of 28 June 1990 on the protection of workers from the risks related to exposure to carcinogens at work (Sixth individual Directive within the meaning of Article 16(1) of Directive 89/391/EEC);[4]

(e) Lead and compounds thereof, inasmuch as the agents in question are absorbable by the human organism;

(f) Asbestos.

II. Processes and work

1. Processes at work referred to in Annex I to Directive 90/394/EEC.

2. Manufacture and handling of devices, fireworks or other objects containing explosives.

3. Work with fierce or poisonous animals.

4. Animal slaughtering on an industrial scale.

5. Work involving the handling of equipment for the production, storage or application of compressed, liquefied or dissolved gases.

6. Work with vats, tanks, reservoirs or carboys containing chemical agents referred to in 1.3.

7. Work involving a risk of structural collapse.

8. Work involving high-voltage electrical hazards.

9. Work the pace of which is determined by machinery and involving payment by results.
[3853]

NOTES

[1] OJ L374, 31.12.90, p 1.
[2] OJ L196, 16.8.67, p 1. Directive as last amended by Directive 93/679/EEC (OJ L268, 29.10.93, p 71).
[3] OJ L187, 16.7.88, p 14. Directive as last amended by Directive 93/18/EEC (OJ L104, 29.4.93, p 46).
[4] OJ L196, 26.7.90, p 1.

COUNCIL DIRECTIVE

of 22 September 1994

on the establishment of a European Works Council or a procedure in Community-scale undertakings and Community-scale groups of undertakings for the purposes of informing and consulting employees

(94/45/EC)

NOTES

Date of publication in OJ: OJ L254, 30.9.94, p 64.

This Directive was adopted under the Agreement on Social Policy 1992, so that by virtue of Protocol 14 to the Treaty on European Union on Social Policy it did not bind the United Kingdom. It was extended to the UK by Directive 97/74/EC at **[3919]**, with a required date of transposition of 15 December 1999. For the domestic implementation of this Directive as applied by Directive 97/74/EC, see the Transnational Information and Consultation of Employees Regulations 1999, SI 1999/3323 at **[2577]**.

THE COUNCIL OF THE EUROPEAN UNION,

Having regard to the Agreement on social policy annexed to Protocol 14 on social policy annexed to the Treaty establishing the European Community, and in particular Article 2(2) thereof,

Having regard to the proposal from the Commission,[1]

Having regard to the opinion of the Economic and Social Committee,[2]

Acting in accordance with the procedure referred to in Article 189c of the Treaty,[3]

Whereas, on the basis of the Protocol on Social Policy annexed to the Treaty establishing the European Community, the Kingdom of Belgium, the Kingdom of Denmark, the Federal Republic of Germany, the Hellenic Republic, the Kingdom of Spain, the French Republic, Ireland, the Italian Republic, the Grand Duchy of Luxembourg, the Kingdom of the Netherlands and the Portuguese Republic (hereinafter referred to as 'the Member States'), desirous of implementing the Social Charter of 1989, have adopted an Agreement on Social Policy;

Whereas Article 2(2) of the said Agreement authorizes the Council to adopt minimum requirements by means of directives;

Whereas, pursuant to Article 1 of the Agreement, one particular objective of the Community and the Member States is to promote dialogue between management and labour;

Whereas point 17 of the Community Charter of Fundamental Social Rights of Workers provides, *inter alia*, that information, consultation and participation for workers must be developed along appropriate lines, taking account of the practices in force in different Member States; whereas the Charter states that this shall apply especially in companies or groups of companies having establishments or companies in two or more Member States';

Whereas the Council, despite the existence of a broad consensus among the majority of Member States, was unable to act on the proposal for a Council Directive on the establishment of a European Works Council in Community-scale undertakings or groups of undertakings for the purposes of informing and consulting employees,[4] as amended on 3 December 1991;[5]

Whereas the Commission, pursuant to Article 3(2) of the Agreement on Social Policy, has consulted management and labour at Community level on the possible direction of

Community action on the information and consultation of workers in Community-scale undertakings and Community-scale groups of undertakings;

Whereas the Commission, considering after this consultation that Community action was advisable, has again consulted management and labour on the content of the planned proposal, pursuant to Article 3(3) of the said Agreement, and management and labour have presented their opinions to the Commission;

Whereas, following this second phase of consultation, management and labour have not informed the Commission of their wish to initiate the process which might lead to the conclusion of an agreement, as provided for in Article 4 of the Agreement;

Whereas the functioning of the internal market involves a process of concentrations of undertakings, cross-border mergers, take-overs, joint ventures and, consequently, a transnationalisation of undertakings and groups of undertakings; whereas, if economic activities are to develop in a harmonious fashion, undertakings and groups of undertakings operating in two or more Member States must inform and consult the representatives of those of their employees that are affected by their decisions;

Whereas procedures for informing and consulting employees as embodied in legislation or practice in the Member States are often not geared to the transnational structure of the entity which takes the decisions affecting those employees; whereas this may lead to the unequal treatment of employees affected by decisions within one and the same undertaking or group of undertakings;

Whereas appropriate provisions must be adopted to ensure that the employees of Community-scale undertakings are properly informed and consulted when decisions which affect them are taken in a Member State other than that in which they are employed;

Whereas, in order to guarantee that the employees of undertakings or groups of undertakings operating in two or more Member States are properly informed and consulted, it is necessary to set up European Works Councils or to create other suitable procedures for the transnational information and consultation of employees;

Whereas it is accordingly necessary to have a definition of the concept of controlling undertaking relating solely to this Directive and not prejudging definitions of the concepts of group or control which might be adopted in texts to be drafted in the future;

Whereas the mechanisms for informing and consulting employees in such undertakings or groups must encompass all of the establishments or, as the case may be, the group's undertakings located within the Member States, regardless of whether the undertaking or the group's controlling undertaking has its central management inside or outside the territory of the Member States;

Whereas, in accordance with the principle of autonomy of the parties, it is for the representatives of employees and the management of the undertaking or the group's controlling undertaking to determine by agreement the nature, composition, the function, mode of operation, procedures and financial resources of European Works Councils or other information and consultation procedures so as to suit their own particular circumstances;

Whereas, in accordance with the principle of subsidiarity, it is for the Member States to determine who the employees' representatives are and in particular to provide, if they consider appropriate, for a balanced representation of different categories of employees;

Whereas, however, provision should be made for certain subsidiary requirements to apply should the parties so decide or in the event of the central management refusing to initiate negotiations or in the absence of agreement subsequent to such negotiations;

Whereas, moreover, employees' representatives may decide not to seek the setting-up of a European Works Council or the parties concerned may decide on other procedures for the transnational information and consultation of employees;

Whereas, without prejudice to the possibility of the parties deciding otherwise, the European Works Council set up in the absence of agreement between the parties must, in order to fulfil the objective of this Directive, be kept informed and consulted on the activities of the undertaking or group of undertakings so that it may assess the possible impact on employees' interests in at least two different Member States; whereas, to that end, the undertaking or controlling undertaking must be required to communicate to the employees' appointed representatives general information concerning the interests of employees and information relating more specifically to those aspects of the activities of the undertaking or group of undertakings which affect employees' interests; whereas the European Works Council must be able to deliver an opinion at the end of that meeting;

Whereas certain decisions having a significant effect on the interests of employees must be the subject of information and consultation of the employees' appointed representatives as soon as possible;

Whereas provision should be made for the employees' representatives acting within the framework of the Directive to enjoy, when exercising their functions, the same protection and guarantees similar to those provided to employees' representatives by the legislation and/or practice of the country of employment; whereas they must not be subject to any discrimination as a result of the lawful exercise of their activities and must enjoy adequate protection as regards dismissal and other sanctions;

Whereas the information and consultation provisions laid down in this Directive must be implemented in the case of an undertaking or a group's controlling undertaking which has its central management outside the territory of the Member States by its representative agent, to be designated if necessary, in one of the Member States or, in the absence of such an agent, by the establishment or controlled undertaking employing the greatest number of employees in the Member States;

Whereas special treatment should be accorded to Community-scale undertakings and groups of undertakings in which there exists, at the time when this Directive is brought into effect, an agreement, covering the entire workforce, providing for the transnational information and consultation of employees;

Whereas the Member States must take appropriate measures in the event of failure to comply with the obligations laid down in this Directive,

NOTES

1 OJ C135, 18.5.94, p 8 and OJ C199, 21.7.94, p 10.
2 Opinion delivered on 1 June 1994 (not yet published in the Official Journal).
3 Opinion of the European Parliament of 4 May 1994 (OJ C205, 25.7.94) and Council common position of 18 July 1994 (OJ C244, 31.8.94, p 37).
4 OJ C39, 15.2.91, p 10.
5 OJ C336, 31.12.91, p 11.

HAS ADOPTED THIS DIRECTIVE—

SECTION I
GENERAL

Article 1

Objective

1. The purpose of this Directive is to improve the right to information and to consultation of employees in Community-scale undertakings and Community-scale groups of undertakings.

2. To that end, a European Works Council or a procedure for informing and consulting employees shall be established in every Community-scale undertaking and every Community-scale group of undertakings, where requested in the manner laid down in Article 5(l), with the purpose of informing and consulting employees under the terms, in the manner and with the effects laid down in this Directive.

3. Notwithstanding paragraph 2, where a Community-scale group of undertakings within the meaning of Article 2(1)(c) comprises one or more undertakings or groups of undertakings which are Community-scale undertakings or Community-scale groups of undertakings within the meaning of Article 2(1)(a) or (c), a European Works Council shall be established at the level of the group unless the agreements referred to in Article 6 provide otherwise.

4. Unless a wider scope is provided for in the agreements referred to in Article 6, the powers and competence of European Works Councils and the scope of information and consultation procedures established to achieve the purpose specified in paragraph 1 shall, in the case of a Community-scale undertaking, cover all the establishments located within the Member States and, in the case of a Community-scale group of undertakings, all group undertakings located within the Member States.

5. Member States may provide that this Directive shall not apply to merchant navy crews.

[3854]

Article 2

Definitions

For the purposes of this Directive—

(a) 'Community-scale undertaking' means any undertaking with at least 1 000 employees within the Member States and at least 150 employees in each of at least two Member States;

(b) 'group of undertakings' means a controlling undertaking and its controlled undertakings;

(c) 'Community-scale group of undertakings' means a group of undertakings with the following characteristics—
- at least 1 000 employees within the Member States,
- at least two group undertakings in different Member States, and
- at least one group undertaking with at least 150 employees in one Member State and at least one other group undertaking with at least 150 employees in another Member State;

(d) 'employees' representatives' means the employees' representatives provided for by national law and/or practice;

(e) 'central management' means the central management of the Community-scale undertaking or, in the case of a Community-scale group of undertakings, of the controlling undertaking;

(f) 'consultation' means the exchange of views and establishment of dialogue between employees' representatives and central management or any more appropriate level of management;

(g) 'European Works Council' means the council established in accordance with Article 1(2) or the provisions of the Annex, with the purpose of informing and consulting employees;

(h) 'special negotiating body' means the body established in accordance with Article 5(2) to negotiate with the central management regarding the establishment of a European Works Council or a procedure for informing and consulting employees in accordance with Article 1(2).

2. For the purposes of this Directive, the prescribed thresholds for the size of the workforce shall be based on the average number of employees, including part-time employees, employed during the previous two years calculated according to national legislation and/or practice.

[3855]

Article 3

Definition of 'controlling undertaking'

1. For the purposes of this Directive, 'controlling undertaking' means an undertaking which can exercise a dominant influence over another undertaking ('the controlled undertaking') by virtue, for example, of ownership, financial participation or the rules which govern it.

2. The ability to exercise a dominant influence shall be presumed, without prejudice to proof to the contrary, when, in relation to another undertaking directly or indirectly—

(a) holds a majority of that undertaking's subscribed capital; or

(b) controls a majority of the votes attached to that undertaking's issued share capital; or

(c) can appoint more than half of the members of that undertaking's administrative, management or supervisory body.

3. For the purposes of paragraph 2, a controlling undertaking's rights as regards voting and appointment shall include the rights of any other controlled undertaking and those of any person or body acting in his or its own name but on behalf of the controlling undertaking or of any other controlled undertaking.

4. Notwithstanding paragraphs 1 and 2, an undertaking shall not be deemed to be a 'controlling undertaking' with respect to another undertaking in which it has holdings where the former undertaking is a company referred to in Article 3(5)(a) or (c) of Council Regulation (EEC) No 4064/89 of 21 December 1989 on the control of concentrations between undertakings.[1]

5. A dominant influence shall not be presumed to be exercised solely by virtue of the fact that an office holder is exercising his functions, according to the law of a Member State relating to liquidation, winding up, insolvency, cessation of payments, compositions or analogous proceedings.

6. The law applicable in order to determine whether an undertaking is a 'controlling undertaking' shall be the law of the Member State which governs that undertaking.

Where the law governing that undertaking is not that of a Member State, the law applicable shall be the law of the Member State within whose territory the representative of the undertaking or, in the absence of such a representative, the central management of the group undertaking which employs the greatest number of employees is situated.

7. Where, in the case of a conflict of laws in the application of paragraph 2, two or more undertakings from a group satisfy one or more of the criteria laid down in that paragraph, the undertaking which satisfies the criterion laid down in point (c) thereof shall be regarded as the controlling undertaking, without prejudice to proof that another undertaking is able to exercise a dominant influence.

[3856]

NOTES

[1] OJ L395, 30.12.89, p 1.

SECTION II
ESTABLISHMENT OF A EUROPEAN WORKS COUNCIL OR AN EMPLOYEE INFORMATION AND CONSULTATION PROCEDURE

Article 4

Responsibility for the establishment of a European Works Council or an employee information and consultation procedure

1. The central management shall be responsible for creating the conditions and means necessary for the setting up of a European Works Council or an information and consultation procedure, as provided for in Article 1(2), in a Community-scale undertaking and a Community-scale group of undertakings.

2. Where the central management is not situated in a Member State, the central management's representative agent in a Member State, to be designated if necessary, shall take on the responsibility referred to in paragraph 1.

In the absence of such a representative, the management of the establishment or group undertaking employing the greatest number of employees in any one Member State shall take on the responsibility referred to in paragraph 1.

3. For the purposes of this Directive, the representative or representatives or, in the absence of any such representatives, the management referred to in the second subparagraph of paragraph 2, shall be regarded as the central management.

[3857]

Article 5

Special negotiating body

1. In order to achieve the objective in Article 1(1), the central management shall initiate negotiations for the establishment of a European Works Council or an information and consultation procedure on its own initiative or at the written request of at least 100 employees or their representatives in at least two undertakings or establishments in at least two different Member States.

2. For this purpose, a special negotiating body shall be established in accordance with the following guidelines—

(a) The Member States shall determine the method to be used for the election or appointment of the members of the special negotiating body who are to be elected or appointed in their territories.

Member States shall provide that employees in undertakings and/or establishments in which there are no employees' representatives through no fault of their own, have the right to elect or appoint members of the special negotiating body.

The second subparagraph shall be without prejudice to national legislation and/or practice laying down thresholds for the establishment of employee representation bodies.

[(b) The special negotiating body shall have a minimum of three members and a maximum of members equal to the number of Member States.]

(c) In these elections or appointments, it must be ensured—

— firstly, that each Member State in which the Community-scale undertaking has one or more establishments or in which the Community-scale group of undertakings has the controlling undertaking or one or more controlled undertakings is represented by one member,

— secondly, that there are supplementary members in proportion to the number of employees working in the establishments, the controlling undertaking or the controlled undertakings as laid down by the legislation of the Member State within the territory of which the central management is situated.

(d) The central management and local management shall be informed of the composition of the special negotiating body.

3. The special negotiating body shall have the task of determining, with the central management, by written agreement, the scope, composition, functions, and term of office of the European Works Council(s) or the arrangements for implementing a procedure for the information and consultation of employees.

4. With a view to the conclusion of an agreement in accordance with Article 6, the central management shall convene a meeting with the special negotiating body. It shall inform the local managements accordingly.

For the purpose of the negotiations, the special negotiating body may be assisted by experts of its choice.

5. The special negotiating body may decide, by at least two-thirds of the votes, not to open negotiations in accordance with paragraph 4, or to terminate the negotiations already opened.

Such a decision shall stop the procedure to conclude the agreement referred to in Article 6. Where such a decision has been taken, the provisions in the Annex shall not apply.

A new request to convene the special negotiating body may be made at the earliest two years after the abovementioned decision unless the parties concerned lay down a shorter period.

6. Any expenses relating to the negotiations referred to in paragraphs 3 and 4 shall be borne by the central management so as to enable the special negotiating body to carry out its task in an appropriate manner.

In compliance with this principle, Member States may lay down budgetary rules regarding the operation of the special negotiating body. They may in particular limit the funding to cover one expert only.

[3858]

NOTES

Para 2: sub-para (b) substituted by Council Directive 2006/109/EC, Art 1, Annex, as from 1 January 2007.

Article 6

Content of the agreement

1. The central management and the special negotiating body must negotiate in a spirit of cooperation with a view to reaching an agreement on the detailed arrangements for implementing the information and consultation of employees provided for in Article 1(1).

2. Without prejudice to the autonomy of the parties, the agreement referred to in paragraph 1 between the central management and the special negotiating body shall determine—

(a) the undertakings of the Community-scale group of undertakings or the establishments of the Community-scale undertaking which are covered by the agreement;

(b) the composition of the European Works Council, the number of members, the allocation of seats and the term of office;

(c) the functions and the procedure for information and consultation of the European Works Council;

(d) the venue, frequency and duration of meetings of the European Works Council;

(e) the financial and material resources to be allocated to the European Works Council;

(f) the duration of the agreement and the procedure for its renegotiation.

3. The central management and the special negotiating body may decide, in writing, to establish one or more information and consultation procedures instead of a European Works Council.

The agreement must stipulate by what method the employees' representatives shall have the right to meet to discuss the information conveyed to them.

This information shall relate in particular to transnational questions which significantly affect workers' interests.

4. The agreements referred to in paragraphs 2 and 3 shall not, unless provision is made otherwise therein, be subject to the subsidiary requirements of the Annex.

5. For the purposes of concluding the agreements referred to in paragraphs 2 and 3, the special negotiating body shall act by a majority of its members.

[3859]

Article 7

Subsidiary requirements

1. In order to achieve the objective in Article 1(1), the subsidiary requirements laid down by the legislation of the Member State in which the central management is situated shall apply—

— where the central management and the special negotiating body so decide, or
— where the central management refuses to commence negotiations within six months of the request referred to in Article 5(1), or
— where, after three years from the date of this request, they are unable to conclude an agreement as laid down in Article 6 and the special negotiating body has not taken the decision provided for in Article 5(5).

2. The subsidiary requirements referred to in paragraph 1 as adopted in the legislation of the Member States must satisfy the provisions set out in the Annex.

[3860]

SECTION III
MISCELLANEOUS PROVISIONS

Article 8

Confidential information

1. Member States shall provide that members of special negotiating bodies or of European Works Councils and any experts who assist them are not authorised to reveal any information which has expressly been provided to them in confidence.

The same shall apply to employees' representatives in the framework of an information and consultation procedure.

This obligation shall continue to apply, wherever the persons referred to in the first and second subparagraphs are, even after the expiry of their terms of office.

2. Each Member State shall provide, in specific cases and under the conditions and limits laid down by national legislation, that the central management situated in its territory is not obliged to transmit information when its nature is such that, according to objective criteria, it would seriously harm the functioning of the undertakings concerned or would be prejudicial to them.

A Member State may make such dispensation subject to prior administrative or judicial authorisation.

3. Each Member State may lay down particular provisions for the central management of undertakings in its territory which pursue directly and essentially the aim of ideological guidance with respect to information and the expression of opinions, on condition that, at the date of adoption of this Directive such particular provisions already exist in the national legislation.

[3861]

Article 9

Operation of European Works Council and information and consultation procedure for workers

The central management and the European Works Council shall work in a spirit of cooperation with due regard to their reciprocal rights and obligations.

The same shall apply to cooperation between the central management and employees' representatives in the framework of an information and consultation procedure for workers.

[3862]

Article 10

Protection of employees' representatives

Members of special negotiating bodies, members of European Works Councils and employees' representatives exercising their functions under the procedure referred to in Article 6(3) shall, in the exercise of their functions, enjoy the same protection and guarantees provided for employees' representatives by the national legislation and/or practice in force in their country of employment.

This shall apply in particular to attendance at meetings of special negotiating bodies or European Works Councils or any other meetings within the framework of the agreement referred to in Article 6(3), and the payment of wages for members who are on the staff of the Community-scale undertaking or the Community-scale group of undertakings for the period of absence necessary for the performance of their duties.

[3863]

Article 11

Compliance with this Directive

1. Each Member State shall ensure that the management of establishments of a Community-scale undertaking and the management of undertakings which form part of a Community-scale group of undertakings which are situated within its territory and their employees' representatives or, as the case may be, employees abide by the obligations laid down by this Directive, regardless of whether or not the central management is situated within its territory.

2. Member States shall ensure that the information on the number of employees referred to in Article 2(1)(a) and (c) is made available by undertakings at the request of the parties concerned by the application of this Directive.

3. Member States shall provide for appropriate measures in the event of failure to comply with this Directive; in particular, they shall ensure that adequate administrative or judicial procedures are available to enable the obligations deriving from this Directive to be enforced.

4. Where Member States apply Article 8, they shall make provision for administrative or judicial appeal procedures which the employees' representatives may initiate when the central management requires confidentiality or does not give information in accordance with that Article.

Such procedures may include procedures designed to protect the confidentiality of the information in question.

[3864]

Article 12

Link between this Directive and other provisions

1. This Directive shall apply without prejudice to measures taken pursuant to Council Directive 75/129/EEC of 17 February 1975 on the approximation of the laws of the Member States relating to collective redundancies,[1] and to Council Directive 77/187/EEC of 14 February 1977 on the approximation of the laws of the Member States relating to the safeguarding of employees' rights in the event of transfers of undertakings, businesses or parts of businesses.[2]

2. This Directive shall be without prejudice to employees' existing rights to information and consultation under national law.

[3865]

NOTES

1 OJ L48, 22.2.75, p 29. Regulation as last amended by Directive 92/56/EEC (OJ L245, 26.8.92, p 3).

2 OJ L61, 5.3.77, p 26.

Article 13

Agreements in force

1. Without prejudice to paragraph 2, the obligations arising from this Directive shall not apply to Community-scale undertakings or Community-scale groups of undertakings in which, on the date laid down in Article 14(1) for the implementation of this Directive or the date of its transposition in the Member State in question, where this is earlier than the abovementioned date, there is already an agreement, covering the entire workforce, providing for the transitional information and consultation of employees.

2. When the agreements referred to in paragraph l expire, the parties to those agreements may decide jointly to renew them.

Where this is not the case, the provisions of this Directive shall apply.

[3866]

Article 14

Final provisions

1. Member States shall bring into force the laws, regulations and administrative provisions necessary to comply with this Directive no later than 22 September 1996 or shall ensure by that date at the latest that management and labour introduce the required provisions by way of agreement, the Member States being obliged to take all necessary steps enabling them at all times to guarantee the results imposed by this Directive. They shall forthwith inform the Commission thereof.

2. When Member States adopt these measures, they shall contain a reference to this Directive or shall be accompanied by such reference on the occasion of their official publication. The methods of making such reference shall be laid down by Member States.

[3867]

Article 15

Review by the Commission

Not later than 22 September 1999, the Commission shall, in consultation with the Member States and with management and labour at European level, review its operation and, in particular examine whether the workforce size thresholds are appropriate with a view to proposing suitable amendments to the Council, where necessary.

[3868]

Article 16

This Directive is addressed to the Member States.

[3869]

ANNEX
SUBSIDIARY REQUIREMENTS

referred to in Article 7 of the Directive

1. In order to achieve the objective in Article 1(1) of the Directive and in the cases provided for in Article 7(l) of the Directive, the establishment, composition and competence of a European Works Council shall be governed by the following rules—

(a) The competence of the European Works Council shall be limited to information and consultation on the matters which concern the Community-scale undertaking or Community-scale group of undertakings as a whole or at least two of its establishments or group undertakings situated in different Member States.
In the case of undertakings or groups of undertakings referred to in Article 4(2), the competence of the European Works Council shall be limited to those matters concerning all their establishments or group undertakings situated within the Member States or concerning at least two of their establishments or group undertakings situated in different Member States.

(b) The European Works Council shall be composed of employees of the Community-scale undertaking or Community-scale group of undertakings elected or appointed from their number by the employees' representatives or, in the absence thereof, by the entire body of employees.

The election or appointment of members of the European Works Council shall be carried out in accordance with national legislation and/or practice.

(c) The European Works Council shall have a minimum of three members and a maximum of 30.

Where its size so warrants, it shall elect a select committee from among its members, comprising at most three members.

It shall adopt its own rules of procedure.

(d) In the election or appointment of members of the European Works Council, it must be ensured—

— firstly, that each Member State in which the Community-scale undertaking has one or more establishments or in which the Community-scale group of undertakings has the controlling undertaking or one or more controlled undertakings is represented by one member,

— secondly, that there are supplementary members in proportion to the number of employees working in the establishments, the controlling undertaking or the controlled undertakings as laid down by the legislation of the Member State within the territory of which the central management is situated.

(e) The central management and any other more appropriate level of management shall be informed of the composition of the European Works Council.

(f) Four years after the European Works Council is established it shall examine whether to open negotiations for the conclusion of the agreement referred to in Article 6 of the Directive or to continue to apply the subsidiary requirements adopted in accordance with this Annex.

Articles 6 and 7 of the Directive shall apply, *mutatis mutandis*, if a decision has been taken to negotiate an agreement according to Article 6 of the Directive, in which case 'special negotiating body' shall be replaced by 'European Works Council'.

2. The European Works Council shall have the right to meet with the central management once a year, to be informed and consulted, on the basis of a report drawn up by the central management, on the progress of the business of the Community-scale undertaking or Community-scale group of undertakings and its prospects. The local managements shall be informed accordingly.

The meeting shall relate in particular to the structure, economic and financial situation, the probable development of the business and of production and sales, the situation and probable trend of employment, investments, and substantial changes concerning organisation, introduction of new working methods or production processes, transfers of production, mergers, cut-backs or closures of undertakings, establishments or important parts thereof, and collective redundancies.

3. Where there are exceptional circumstances affecting the employees' interests to a considerable extent, particularly in the event of relocations, the closure of establishments or undertakings or collective redundancies, the select committee or, where no such committee exists, the European Works Council shall have the right to be informed. It shall have the right to meet, at its request, the central management, or any other more appropriate level of management within the Community-scale undertaking or group of undertakings having its own powers of decision, so as to be informed and consulted on measures significantly affecting employees' interests.

Those members of the European Works Council who have been elected or appointed by the establishments and/or undertakings which are directly concerned by the measures in question shall also have the right to participate in the meeting organised with the select committee.

This information and consultation meeting shall take place as soon as possible on the basis of a report drawn up by the central management or any other appropriate level of management of the Community-scale undertaking or group of undertakings, on which an opinion may be delivered at the end of the meeting or within a reasonable time.

This meeting shall not affect the prerogatives of the central management.

4. The Member States may lay down rules on the chairing of information and consultation meetings.

Before any meeting with the central management, the European Works Council or the select committee, where necessary enlarged in accordance with the second paragraph of point 3, shall be entitled to meet without the management concerned being present.

5. Without prejudice to Article 8 of the Directive, the members of the European Works Council shall inform the representatives of the employees of the establishments or of the

undertakings of a Community-scale group of undertakings or, in the absence of representatives, the workforce as a whole, of the content and outcome of the information and consultation procedure carried out in accordance with this Annex.

6. The European Works Council or the select committee may be assisted by experts of its choice, in so far as this is necessary for it to carry out its tasks.

7. The operating expenses of the European Works Council shall be borne by the central management.

The central management concerned shall provide the members of the European Works Council with such financial and material resources as enable them to perform their duties in an appropriate manner.

In particular, the cost of organising meetings and arranging for interpretation facilities and the accommodation and travelling expenses of members of the European Works Council and its select committee shall be met by the central management unless otherwise agreed.

In compliance with these principles, the Member States may lay down budgetary rules regarding the operation of the European Works Council. They may in particular limit funding to cover one expert only.

[3870]

DIRECTIVE OF THE EUROPEAN PARLIAMENT AND OF THE COUNCIL

of 24 October 1995

on the protection of individuals with regard to the processing of personal data and on the free movement of such data

(95/46/EC)

NOTES

Date of publication in OJ: OJ L281, 23.11.95, p 31.

For the domestic implementation of this Directive, see the Data Protection Act 1998 at **[1311]**.

THE EUROPEAN PARLIAMENT AND THE COUNCIL OF THE EUROPEAN UNION,

Having regard to the Treaty establishing the European Community, and in particular Article 100a thereof,

Having regard to the proposal from the Commission,[1]

Having regard to the opinion of the Economic and Social Committee,[2]

Acting in accordance with the procedure referred to in Article 189b of the Treaty,

(1) Whereas the objectives of the Community, as laid down in the Treaty, as amended by the Treaty on European Union, include creating an ever closer union among the peoples of Europe, fostering closer relations between the States belonging to the Community, ensuring economic and social progress by common action to eliminate the barriers which divide Europe, encouraging the constant improvement of the living conditions of its peoples, preserving and strengthening peace and liberty and promoting democracy on the basis of the fundamental rights recognised in the constitution and laws of the Member States and in the European Convention for the Protection of Human Rights and Fundamental Freedoms;

(2) Whereas data-processing systems are designed to serve man; whereas they must, whatever the nationality or residence of natural persons, respect their fundamental rights and freedoms, notably the right to privacy, and contribute to economic and social progress, trade expansion and the well-being of individuals;

(3) Whereas the establishment and functioning of an internal market in which, in accordance with Article 7a of the Treaty, the free movement of goods, persons, services and capital is ensured require not only that personal data should be able to flow freely from one Member State to another, but also that the fundamental rights of individuals should be safeguarded;

(4) Whereas increasingly frequent recourse is being had in the Community to the processing of personal data in the various spheres of economic and social activity; whereas the progress made in information technology is making the processing and exchange of such data considerably easier;

(5) Whereas the economic and social integration resulting from the establishment and functioning of the internal market within the meaning of Article 7a of the Treaty will necessarily lead to a substantial increase in cross-border flows of personal data between all those involved in a private or public capacity in economic and social activity in the Member States; whereas the exchange of personal data between undertakings in different Member States is set to increase; whereas the national authorities in the various Member States are being called upon by virtue of Community law to collaborate and exchange personal data so as to be able to perform their duties or carry out tasks on behalf of an authority in another Member State within the context of the area without internal frontiers as constituted by the internal market;

(6) Whereas, furthermore, the increase in scientific and technical cooperation and the coordinated introduction of new telecommunications networks in the Community necessitate and facilitate cross-border flows of personal data;

(7) Whereas the difference in levels of protection of the rights and freedoms of individuals, notably the right to privacy, with regard to the processing of personal data afforded in the Member States may prevent the transmission of such data from the territory of one Member State to that of another Member State; whereas this difference may therefore constitute an obstacle to the pursuit of a number of economic activities at Community level, distort competition and impede authorities in the discharge of their responsibilities under Community law; whereas this difference in levels of protection is due to the existence of a wide variety of national laws, regulations and administrative provisions;

(8) Whereas, in order to remove the obstacles to flows of personal data, the level of protection of the rights and freedoms of individuals with regard to the processing of such data must be equivalent in all Member States; whereas this objective is vital to the internal market but cannot be achieved by the Member States alone, especially in view of the scale of the divergences which currently exist between the relevant laws in the Member States and the need to coordinate the laws of the Member States so as to ensure that the cross-border flow of personal data is regulated in a consistent manner that is in keeping with the objective of the internal market as provided for in Article 7a of the Treaty; whereas Community action to approximate those laws is therefore needed;

(9) Whereas, given the equivalent protection resulting from the approximation of national laws, the Member States will no longer be able to inhibit the free movement between them of personal data on grounds relating to protection of the rights and freedoms of individuals, and in particular the right to privacy; whereas Member States will be left a margin for manoeuvre, which may, in the context of implementation of the Directive, also be exercised by the business and social partners; whereas Member States will therefore be able to specify in their national law the general conditions governing the lawfulness of data processing; whereas in doing so the Member States shall strive to improve the protection currently provided by their legislation; whereas, within the limits of this margin for manoeuvre and in accordance with Community law, disparities could arise in the implementation of the Directive, and this could have an effect on the movement of data within a Member State as well as within the Community;

(10) Whereas the object of the national laws on the processing of personal data is to protect fundamental rights and freedoms, notably the right to privacy, which is recognised both in Article 8 of the European Convention for the Protection of Human Rights and Fundamental Freedoms and in the general principles of Community law; whereas, for that reason, the approximation of those laws must not result in any lessening of the protection they afford but must, on the contrary, seek to ensure a high level of protection in the Community;

(11) Whereas the principles of the protection of the rights and freedoms of individuals, notably the right to privacy, which are contained in this Directive, give substance to and amplify those contained in the Council of Europe Convention of 28 January 1981 for the Protection of Individuals with regard to Automatic Processing of Personal Data;

(12) Whereas the protection principles must apply to all processing of personal data by any person whose activities are governed by Community law; whereas there should be excluded the processing of data carried out by a natural person in the exercise of activities which are exclusively personal or domestic, such as correspondence and the holding of records of addresses;

(13) Whereas the activities referred to in Titles V and VI of the Treaty on European Union regarding public safety, defence, State security or the activities of the State in the area of criminal laws fall outside the scope of Community law, without prejudice to the obligations incumbent upon Member States under Article 56(2), Article 57 or Article 100a of the Treaty establishing the European Community; whereas the processing of personal data that is necessary to safeguard the economic well-being of the State does not fall within the scope of this Directive where such processing relates to State security matters;

(14) Whereas, given the importance of the developments under way, in the framework of the information society, of the techniques used to capture, transmit, manipulate, record, store or communicate sound and image data relating to natural persons, this Directive should be applicable to processing involving such data;

(15) Whereas the processing of such data is covered by this Directive only if it is automated or if the data processed are contained or are intended to be contained in a filing system structured according to specific criteria relating to individuals, so as to permit easy access to the personal data in question;

(16) Whereas the processing of sound and image data, such as in cases of video surveillance, does not come within the scope of this Directive if it is carried out for the purposes of public security, defence, national security or in the course of State activities relating to the area of criminal law or of other activities which do not come within the scope of Community law;

(17) Whereas, as far as the processing of sound and image data carried out for purposes of journalism or the purposes of literary or artistic expression is concerned, in particular in the audiovisual field, the principles of the Directive are to apply in a restricted manner according to the provisions laid down in Article 9;

(18) Whereas, in order to ensure that individuals are not deprived of the protection to which they are entitled under this Directive, any processing of personal data in the Community must be carried out in accordance with the law of one of the Member States; whereas, in this connection, processing carried out under the responsibility of a controller who is established in a Member State should be governed by the law of that State;

(19) Whereas establishment on the territory of a Member State implies the effective and real exercise of activity through stable arrangements; whereas the legal form of such an establishment, whether simply branch or a subsidiary with a legal personality, is not the determining factor in this respect; whereas, when a single controller is established on the territory of several Member States, particularly by means of subsidiaries, he must ensure, in order to avoid any circumvention of national rules, that each of the establishments fulfils the obligations imposed by the national law applicable to its activities;

(20) Whereas the fact that the processing of data is carried out by a person established in a third country must not stand in the way of the protection of individuals provided for in this Directive; whereas in these cases, the processing should be governed by the law of the Member State in which the means used are located, and there should be guarantees to ensure that the rights and obligations provided for in this Directive are respected in practice;

(21) Whereas this Directive is without prejudice to the rules of territoriality applicable in criminal matters;

(22) Whereas Member States shall more precisely define in the laws they enact or when bringing into force the measures taken under this Directive the general circumstances in which processing is lawful; whereas in particular Article 5, in conjunction with Articles 7 and 8, allows Member States, independently of general rules, to provide for special processing conditions for specific sectors and for the various categories of data covered by Article 8;

(23) Whereas Member States are empowered to ensure the implementation of the protection of individuals both by means of a general law on the protection of individuals as regards the processing of personal data and by sectorial laws such as those relating, for example, to statistical institutes;

(24) Whereas the legislation concerning the protection of legal persons with regard to the processing data which concerns them is not affected by this Directive;

(25) Whereas the principles of protection must be reflected, on the one hand, in the obligations imposed on persons, public authorities, enterprises, agencies or other bodies responsible for processing, in particular regarding data quality, technical security, notification to the supervisory authority, and the circumstances under which processing can be carried out, and, on the other hand, in the right conferred on individuals, the data on whom are the subject of processing, to be informed that processing is taking place, to consult the data, to request corrections and even to object to processing in certain circumstances;

(26) Whereas the principles of protection must apply to any information concerning an identified or identifiable person; whereas, to determine whether a person is identifiable, account should be taken of all the means likely reasonably to be used either by the controller or by any other person to identify the said person; whereas the principles of protection shall not apply to data rendered anonymous in such a way that the data subject is no longer identifiable; whereas codes of conduct within the meaning of Article 27 may be a useful instrument for providing guidance as to the ways in which data may be rendered anonymous and retained in a form in which identification of the data subject is no longer possible;

(27) Whereas the protection of individuals must apply as much to automatic processing of data as to manual processing; whereas the scope of this protection must not in effect depend on the techniques used, otherwise this would create a serious risk of circumvention; whereas, nonetheless, as regards manual processing, this Directive covers only filing systems,

not unstructured files; whereas, in particular, the content of a filing system must be structured according to specific criteria relating to individuals allowing easy access to the personal data; whereas, in line with the definition in Article 2(c), the different criteria for determining the constituents of a structured set of personal data, and the different criteria governing access to such a set, may be laid down by each Member State; whereas files or sets of files as well as their cover pages, which are not structured according to specific criteria, shall under no circumstances fall within the scope of this Directive;

(28) Whereas any processing of personal data must be lawful and fair to the individuals concerned; whereas, in particular, the data must be adequate, relevant and not excessive in relation to the purposes for which they are processed; whereas such purposes must be explicit and legitimate and must be determined at the time of collection of the data; whereas the purposes of processing further to collection shall not be incompatible with the purposes as they were originally specified;

(29) Whereas the further processing of personal data for historical, statistical or scientific purposes is not generally to be considered incompatible with the purposes for which the data have previously been collected provided that Member States furnish suitable safeguards; whereas these safeguards must in particular rule out the use of the data in support of measures or decisions regarding any particular individual;

(30) Whereas, in order to be lawful, the processing of personal data must in addition be carried out with the consent of the data subject or be necessary for the conclusion or performance of a contract binding on the data subject, or as a legal requirement, or for the performance of a task carried out in the public interest or in the exercise of official authority, or in the legitimate interests of a natural or legal person, provided that the interests or the rights and freedoms of the data subject are not overriding; whereas, in particular, in order to maintain a balance between the interests involved while guaranteeing effective competition, Member States may determine the circumstances in which personal data may be used or disclosed to a third party in the context of the legitimate ordinary business activities of companies and other bodies; whereas Member States may similarly specify the conditions under which personal data may be disclosed to a third party for the purposes of marketing whether carried out commercially or by a charitable organisation or by any other association or foundation, of a political nature for example, subject to the provisions allowing a data subject to object to the processing of data regarding him, at no cost and without having to state his reasons;

(31) Whereas the processing of personal data must equally be regarded as lawful where it is carried out in order to protect an interest which is essential for the data subject's life;

(32) Whereas it is for national legislation to determine whether the controller performing a task carried out in the public interest or in the exercise of official authority should be a public administration or another natural or legal person governed by public law, or by private law such as a professional association;

(33) Whereas data which are capable by their nature of infringing fundamental freedoms or privacy should not be processed unless the data subject gives his explicit consent; whereas, however, derogations from this prohibition must be explicitly provided for in respect of specific needs, in particular where the processing of these data is carried out for certain health-related purposes by persons subject to a legal obligation of professional secrecy or in the course of legitimate activities by certain associations or foundations the purpose of which is to permit the exercise of fundamental freedoms;

(34) Whereas Member States must also be authorised, when justified by grounds of important public interest, to derogate from the prohibition on processing sensitive categories of data where important reasons of public interest so justify in areas such as public health and social protection—especially in order to ensure the quality and cost-effectiveness of the procedures used for settling claims for benefits and services in the health insurance system—scientific research and government statistics; whereas it is incumbent on them, however, to provide specific and suitable safeguards so as to protect the fundamental rights and the privacy of individuals;

(35) Whereas, moreover, the processing of personal data by official authorities for achieving aims, laid down in constitutional law or international public law, of officially recognised religious associations is carried out on important grounds of public interest;

(36) Whereas where, in the course of electoral activities, the operation of the democratic system requires in certain Member States that political parties compile data on people's political opinion, the processing of such data may be permitted for reasons of important public interest, provided that appropriate safeguards are established;

(37) Whereas the processing of personal data for purposes of journalism or for purposes of literary of artistic expression, in particular in the audiovisual field, should qualify for exemption from the requirements of certain provisions of this Directive in so far as this is necessary to reconcile the fundamental rights of individuals with freedom of information and notably the right to receive and impart information, as guaranteed in particular in Article 10 of

the European Convention for the Protection of Human Rights and Fundamental Freedoms; whereas Member States should therefore lay down exemptions and derogations necessary for the purpose of balance between fundamental rights as regards general measures on the legitimacy of data processing, measures on the transfer of data to third countries and the power of the supervisory authority; whereas this should not, however, lead Member States to lay down exemptions from the measures to ensure security of processing; whereas at least the supervisory authority responsible for this sector should also be provided with certain ex-post powers, e g to publish a regular report or to refer matters to the judicial authorities;

(38) Whereas, if the processing of data is to be fair, the data subject must be in a position to learn of the existence of a processing operation and, where data are collected from him, must be given accurate and full information, bearing in mind the circumstances of the collection;

(39) Whereas certain processing operations involve data which the controller has not collected directly from the data subject; whereas, furthermore, data can be legitimately disclosed to a third party, even if the disclosure was not anticipated at the time the data were collected from the data subject; whereas, in all these cases, the data subject should be informed when the data are recorded or at the latest when the data are first disclosed to a third party;

(40) Whereas, however, it is not necessary to impose this obligation of the data subject already has the information; whereas, moreover, there will be no such obligation if the recording or disclosure are expressly provided for by law or if the provision of information to the data subject proves impossible or would involve disproportionate efforts, which could be the case where processing is for historical, statistical or scientific purposes; whereas, in this regard, the number of data subjects, the age of the data, and any compensatory measures adopted may be taken into consideration;

(41) Whereas any person must be able to exercise the right of access to data relating to him which are being processed, in order to verify in particular the accuracy of the data and the lawfulness of the processing; whereas, for the same reasons, every data subject must also have the right to know the logic involved in the automatic processing of data concerning him, at least in the case of the automated decisions referred to in Article 15(1); whereas this right must not adversely affect trade secrets or intellectual property and in particular the copyright protecting the software; whereas these considerations must not, however, result in the data subject being refused all information;

(42) Whereas Member States may, in the interest of the data subject or so as to protect the rights and freedoms of others, restrict rights of access and information; whereas they may, for example, specify that access to medical data may be obtained only through a health professional;

(43) Whereas restrictions on the rights of access and information and on certain obligations of the controller may similarly be imposed by Member States in so far as they are necessary to safeguard, for example, national security, defence, public safety, or important economic or financial interests of a Member State or the Union, as well as criminal investigations and prosecutions and action in respect of breaches of ethics in the regulated professions; whereas the list of exceptions and limitations should include the tasks of monitoring, inspection or regulation necessary in the three last-mentioned areas concerning public security, economic or financial interests and crime prevention; whereas the listing of tasks in these three areas does not affect the legitimacy of exceptions or restrictions for reasons of State security or defence;

(44) Whereas Member States may also be led, by virtue of the provisions of Community law, to derogate from the provisions of this Directive concerning the right of access, the obligation to inform individuals, and the quality of data, in order to secure certain of the purposes referred to above;

(45) Whereas, in cases where data might lawfully be processed on grounds of public interest, official authority or the legitimate interests of a natural or legal person, any data subject should nevertheless be entitled, on legitimate and compelling grounds relating to his particular situation, to object to the processing of any data relating to himself; whereas Member States may nevertheless lay down national provisions to the contrary;

(46) Whereas the protection of the rights and freedoms of data subjects with regard to the processing of personal data requires that appropriate technical and organisational measures be taken, both at the time of the design of the processing system and at the time of the processing itself, particularly in order to maintain security and thereby to prevent any unauthorised processing; whereas it is incumbent on the Member States to ensure that controllers comply with these measures; whereas these measures must ensure an appropriate level of security, taking into account the state of the art and the costs of their implementation in relation to the risks inherent in the processing and the nature of the data to be protected;

(47) Whereas where a message containing personal data is transmitted by means of a telecommunications or electronic mail service, the sole purpose of which is the transmission of such messages, the controller in respect of the personal data contained in the message will normally be considered to be the person from whom the message originates, rather than the person offering the transmission services; whereas, nevertheless, those offering such services will normally be considered controllers in respect of the processing of the additional personal data necessary for the operation of the service;

(48) Whereas the procedures for notifying the supervisory authority are designed to ensure disclosure of the purposes and main features of any processing operation for the purpose of verification that the operation is in accordance with the national measures taken under this Directive;

(49) Whereas, in order to avoid unsuitable administrative formalities, exemptions from the obligation to notify and simplification of the notification required may be provided for by Member States in cases where processing is unlikely adversely to affect the rights and freedoms of data subjects, provided that it is in accordance with a measure taken by a Member State specifying its limits; whereas exemption or simplification may similarly be provided for by Member States where a person appointed by the controller ensures that the processing carried out is not likely adversely to affect the rights and freedoms of data subjects; whereas such a data protection official, whether or not an employee of the controller, must be in a position to exercise his functions in complete independence;

(50) Whereas exemption or simplification could be provided for in cases of processing operations whose sole purpose is the keeping of a register intended, according to national law, to provide information to the public and open to consultation by the public or by any person demonstrating a legitimate interest;

(51) Whereas, nevertheless, simplification or exemption from the obligation to notify shall not release the controller from any of the other obligations resulting from this Directive;

(52) Whereas, in this context, *ex post facto* verification by the competent authorities must in general be considered a sufficient measure;

(53) Whereas, however, certain processing operation are likely to pose specific risks to the rights and freedoms of data subjects by virtue of their nature, their scope or their purposes, such as that of excluding individuals from a right, benefit or a contract, or by virtue of the specific use of new technologies; whereas it is for Member States, if they so wish, to specify such risks in their legislation;

(54) Whereas with regard to all the processing undertaken in society, the amount posing such specific risks should be very limited; whereas Member States must provide that the supervisory authority, or the data protection official in cooperation with the authority, check such processing prior to it being carried out; whereas following this prior check, the supervisory authority may, according to its national law, give an opinion or an authorisation regarding the processing; whereas such checking may equally take place in the course of the preparation either of a measure of the national parliament or of a measure based on such a legislative measure, which defines the nature of the processing and lays down appropriate safeguards;

(55) Whereas, if the controller fails to respect the rights of data subjects, national legislation must provide for a judicial remedy; whereas any damage which a person may suffer as a result of unlawful processing must be compensated for by the controller, who may be exempted from liability if he proves that he is not responsible for the damage, in particular in cases where he establishes fault on the part of the data subject or in case of *force majeure*; whereas sanctions must be imposed on any person, whether governed by private of public law, who fails to comply with the national measures taken under this Directive;

(56) Whereas cross-border flows of personal data are necessary to the expansion of international trade; whereas the protection of individuals guaranteed in the Community by this Directive does not stand in the way of transfers of personal data to third countries which ensure an adequate level of protection; whereas the adequacy of the level of protection afforded by a third country must be assessed in the light of all the circumstances surrounding the transfer operation or set of transfer operations;

(57) Whereas, on the other hand, the transfer of personal data to a third country which does not ensure an adequate level of protection must be prohibited;

(58) Whereas provisions should be made for exemptions from this prohibition in certain circumstances where the data subject has given his consent, where the transfer is necessary in relation to a contract or a legal claim, where protection of an important public interest so requires, for example in cases of international transfers of data between tax or customs administrations or between services competent for social security matters, or where the transfer is made from a register established by law and intended for consultation by the public or persons having a legitimate interest; whereas in this case such a transfer should not involve the entirety of the data or entire categories of the data contained in the register and, when the

register is intended for consultation by persons having a legitimate interest, the transfer should be made only at the request of those persons or if they are to be the recipients;

(59) Whereas particular measures may be taken to compensate for the lack of protection in a third country in cases where the controller offers appropriate safeguards; whereas, moreover, provision must be made for procedures for negotiations between the Community and such third countries;

(60) Whereas, in any event, transfers to third countries may be effected only in full compliance with the provisions adopted by the Member States pursuant to this Directive, and in particular Article 8 thereof;

(61) Whereas Member States and the Commission, in their respective spheres of competence, must encourage the trade associations and other representative organisations concerned to draw up codes of conduct so as to facilitate the application of this Directive, taking account of the specific characteristics of the processing carried out in certain sectors, and respecting the national provisions adopted for its implementation;

(62) Whereas the establishment in Member States of supervisory authorities, exercising their functions with complete independence, is an essential component of the protection of individuals with regard to the processing of personal data;

(63) Whereas such authorities must have the necessary means to perform their duties, including powers of investigation and intervention, particularly in cases of complaints from individuals, and powers to engage in legal proceedings; whereas such authorities must help to ensure transparency of processing in the Member States within whose jurisdiction they fall;

(64) Whereas the authorities in the different Member States will need to assist one another in performing their duties so as to ensure that the rules of protection are properly respected throughout the European Union;

(65) Whereas, at Community level, a Working Party on the Protection of Individuals with regard to the Processing of Personal Data must be set up and be completely independent in the performance of its functions; whereas, having regard to its specific nature, it must advise the Commission and, in particular, contribute to the uniform application of the national rules adopted pursuant to this Directive;

(66) Whereas, with regard to the transfer of data to third countries, the application of this Directive calls for the conferment of powers of implementation on the Commission and the establishment of a procedure as laid down in Council Decision 87/373/EEC;[3]

(67) Whereas an agreement on a *modus vivendi* between the European Parliament, the Council and the Commission concerning the implementing measures for acts adopted in accordance with the procedure laid down in Article 189b of the EC Treaty was reached on 20 December 1994;

(68) Whereas the principles set out in this Directive regarding the protection of the rights and freedoms of individuals, notably their right to privacy, with regard to the processing of personal data may be supplemented or clarified, in particular as far as certain sectors are concerned, by specific rules based on those principles;

(69) Whereas Member States should be allowed a period of not more than three years from the entry into force of the national measures transposing this Directive in which to apply such new national rules progressively to all processing operations already under way; whereas, in order to facilitate their cost-effective implementation, a further period expiring 12 years after the date on which this Directive is adopted will be allowed to Member States to ensure the conformity of existing manual filing systems with certain of the Directive's provisions; whereas, where data contained in such filing systems are manually processed during this extended transition period, those systems must be brought into conformity with these provisions at the time of such processing;

(70) Whereas it is not necessary for the data subject to give his consent again so as to allow the controller to continue to process, after the national provisions taken pursuant to this Directive enter into force, any sensitive data necessary for the performance of a contract concluded on the basis of free and informed consent before the entry into force of these provisions;

(71) Whereas this Directive does not stand in the way of a Member State's regulating marketing activities aimed at consumers residing in territory in so far as such regulation does not concern the protection of individuals with regard to the processing of personal data;

(72) Whereas this Directive allows the principle of public access to official documents to be taken into account when implementing the principles set out in this Directive,

NOTES

[1] OJ C277, 5.11.90, p 3 and OJ C311, 27.11.92, p 30.
[2] OJ C159, 17.6.91, p 38.
[3] OJ L197, 18.7.87, p 33.

HAVE ADOPTED THIS DIRECTIVE—

CHAPTER I
GENERAL PROVISIONS

Article 1

Object of the Directive

1. In accordance with this Directive, Member States shall protect the fundamental rights and freedoms of natural persons, and in particular their right to privacy with respect to the processing of personal data.

2. Member States shall neither restrict nor prohibit the free flow of personal data between Member States for reasons connected with the protection afforded under paragraph 1.

[3871]

Article 2

Definitions

For the purposes of this Directive—

(a) "personal data" shall mean any information relating to an identified or identifiable natural person ("data subject"); an identifiable person is one who can be identified, directly or indirectly, in particular by reference to an identification number or to one or more factors specific to his physical, physiological, mental, economic, cultural or social identity;

(b) "processing of personal data" ("processing") shall mean any operation or set of operations which is performed upon personal data, whether or not by automatic means, such as collection, recording, organisation, storage, adaptation or alteration, retrieval, consultation, use, disclosure by transmission, dissemination or otherwise making available, alignment or combination, blocking, erasure or destruction;

(c) "personal data filing system" ("filing system") shall mean any structured set of personal data which are accessible according to specific criteria, whether centralised, decentralised or dispersed on a functional or geographical basis;

(d) "controller" shall mean the natural or legal person, public authority, agency or any other body which alone or jointly with others determines the purposes and means of the processing of personal data; where the purposes and means of processing are determined by national or Community laws or regulations, the controller or the specific criteria for his nomination may be designated by national or Community law;

(e) "processor" shall mean a natural or legal person, public authority, agency or any other body which processes personal data on behalf of the controller;

(f) "third party" shall mean any natural or legal person, public authority, agency or any other body other than the data subject, the controller, the processor and the persons who, under the direct authority of the controller or the processor, are authorised to process the data;

(g) "recipient" shall mean a natural or legal person, public authority, agency or any other body to whom data are disclosed, whether a third party or not; however, authorities which may receive data in the framework of a particular inquiry shall not be regarded as recipients;

(h) "the data subject's consent" shall mean any freely given specific and informed indication of his wishes by which the data subject signifies his agreement to personal data relating to him being processed.

[3872]

Article 3

Scope

1. This Directive shall apply to the processing of personal data wholly or partly by automatic means, and to the processing otherwise than by automatic means of personal data which form part of a filing system or are intended to form part of a filing system.

2. This Directive shall not apply to the processing of personal data—

— in the course of an activity which falls outside the scope of Community law, such as those provided for by Titles V and VI of the Treaty on European Union and in any case to processing operations concerning public security, defence, State security (including the economic well-being of the State when the processing operation relates to State security matters) and the activities of the State in areas of criminal law,

— by a natural person in the course of a purely personal or household activity.

[3873]

Article 4

National law applicable

1. Each Member State shall apply the national provisions it adopts pursuant to this Directive to the processing of personal data where—

(a) the processing is carried out in the context of the activities of an establishment of the controller on the territory of the Member State; when the same controller is established on the territory of several Member States, he must take the necessary measures to ensure that each of these establishments complies with the obligations laid down by the national law applicable;

(b) the controller is not established on the Member State's territory, but in a place where its national law applies by virtue of international public law;

(c) the controller is not established on Community territory and, for purposes of processing personal data makes use of equipment, automated or otherwise, situated on the territory of the said Member State, unless such equipment is used only for purposes of transit through the territory of the Community.

2. In the circumstances referred to in paragraph 1(c), the controller must designate a representative established in the territory of that Member State, without prejudice to legal actions which could be initiated against the controller himself.

[3874]

CHAPTER II

GENERAL RULES ON THE LAWFULNESS OF THE PROCESSING OF PERSONAL DATA

Article 5

Member States shall, within the limits of the provisions of this Chapter, determine more precisely the conditions under which the processing of personal data is lawful.

[3875]

SECTION I

PRINCIPLES RELATING TO DATA QUALITY

Article 6

1. Member States shall provide that personal data must be—

(a) processed fairly and lawfully;

(b) collected for specified, explicit and legitimate purposes and not further processed in a way incompatible with those purposes. Further processing of data for historical, statistical or scientific purposes shall not be considered as incompatible provided that Member States provide appropriate safeguards;

(c) adequate, relevant and not excessive in relation to the purposes for which they are collected and/or further processed;

(d) accurate and, where necessary, kept up to date; every reasonable step must be taken to ensure that data which are inaccurate or incomplete, having regard to the purposes for which they were collected or for which they are further processed, are erased or rectified;

(e) kept in a form which permits identification of data subjects for no longer than is necessary for the purposes for which the data were collected or for which they are further processed. Member States shall lay down appropriate safeguards for personal data stored for longer periods for historical, statistical or scientific use.

2. It shall be for the controller to ensure that paragraph 1 is complied with.

[3876]

SECTION II
CRITERIA FOR MAKING DATA PROCESSING LEGITIMATE

Article 7

Member States shall provide that personal data may be processed only if—

(a) the data subject has unambiguously given his consent; or

(b) processing is necessary for the performance of a contract to which the data subject is party or in order to take steps at the request of the data subject prior to entering into a contract; or

(c) processing is necessary for compliance with a legal obligation to which the controller is subject; or

(d) processing is necessary in order to protect the vital interests of the data subject; or

(e) processing is necessary for the performance of a task carried out in the public interest or in the exercise of official authority vested in the controller or in a third party to whom the data are disclosed; or

(f) processing is necessary for the purposes of the legitimate interests pursued by the controller or by the third party or parties to whom the data are disclosed, except where such interests are overridden by the interests for fundamental rights and freedoms of the data subject which require protection under Article 1(1).

[3877]

SECTION III
SPECIAL CATEGORIES OF PROCESSING

Article 8

The processing of special categories of data

1. Member States shall prohibit the processing of personal data revealing racial or ethnic origin, political opinions, religious or philosophical beliefs, trade-union membership, and the processing of data concerning health or sex life.

2. Paragraph 1 shall not apply where—

(a) the data subject has given his explicit consent to the processing of those data, except where the laws of the Member State provide that the prohibition referred to in paragraph 1 may not be lifted by the data subject's giving his consent; or

(b) processing is necessary for the purposes of carrying out the obligations and specific rights of the controller in the field of employment law in so far as it is authorised by national law providing for adequate safeguards; or

(c) processing is necessary to protect the vital interests of the data subject or of another person where the data subject is physically or legally incapable of giving his consent; or

(d) processing is carried out in the course of its legitimate activities with appropriate guarantees by a foundation, association or any other non-profit-seeking body with a political, philosophical, religious or trade-union aim and on condition that the processing relates solely to the members of the body or to persons who have regular contact with it in connection with its purposes and that the data are not disclosed to a third party without the consent of the data subjects; or

(e) the processing relates to data which are manifestly made public by the data subject or is necessary for the establishment, exercise or defence of legal claims.

3. Paragraph 1 shall not apply where processing of the data is required for the purposes of preventive medicine, medical diagnosis, the provision of care or treatment or the management of health-care services, and where those data are processed by a health professional subject under national law or rules established by national competent bodies to the obligation of professional secrecy or by another person also subject to an equivalent obligation of secrecy.

4. Subject to the provision of suitable safeguards, Member States may, for reasons of substantial public interest, lay down exemptions in addition to those laid down in paragraph 2 either by national law or by decision of the supervisory authority.

5. Processing of data relating to offences, criminal convictions or security measures may be carried out only under the control of official authority, or if suitable specific safeguards are provided under national law, subject to derogations which may be granted by the Member State under national provisions providing suitable specific safeguards. However, a complete register of criminal convictions may be kept only under the control of official authority.

Member States may provide that data relating to administrative sanctions or judgements in civil cases shall also be processed under the control of official authority.

6. Derogations from paragraph 1 provided for in paragraphs 4 and 5 shall be notified to the Commission.

7. Member States shall determine the conditions under which a national identification number or any other identifier of general application may be processed.

[3878]

Article 9

Processing of personal data and freedom of expression

Member States shall provide for exemptions or derogations from the provisions of this Chapter, Chapter IV and Chapter VI for the processing of personal data carried out solely for journalistic purposes or the purpose of artistic or literary expression only if they are necessary to reconcile the right to privacy with the rules governing freedom of expression.

[3879]

SECTION IV
INFORMATION TO BE GIVEN TO THE DATA SUBJECT

Article 10

Information in cases of collection of data from the data subject

Member States shall provide that the controller or his representative must provide a data subject from whom data relating to himself are collected with at least the following information, except where he already has it—

(a) the identity of the controller and of his representative, if any;
(b) the purposes of the processing for which the data are intended;
(c) any further information such as
 — the recipients or categories of recipients of the data,
 — whether replies to the questions are obligatory or voluntary, as well as the possible consequences of failure to reply,
 — the existence of the right of access to and the right to rectify the data concerning him

in so far as such further information is necessary, having regard to the specific circumstances in which the data are collected, to guarantee fair processing in respect of the data subject.

[3880]

Article 11

Information where the data have not been obtained from the data subject

1. Where the data have not been obtained from the data subject, Member States shall provide that the controller or his representative must at the time of undertaking the recording of personal data or if a disclosure to a third party is envisaged, no later than the time when the data are first disclosed provide the data subject with at least the following information, except where he already has it—

(a) the identity of the controller and of his representative, if any;
(b) the purposes of the processing;
(c) any further information such as
 — the categories of data concerned,
 — the recipients or categories of recipients,
 — the existence of the right of access to and the right to rectify the data concerning him

in so far as such further information is necessary, having regard to the specific circumstances in which the data are processed, to guarantee fair processing in respect of the data subject.

2. Paragraph 1 shall not apply where, in particular for processing for statistical purposes or for the purposes of historical or scientific research, the provision of such information proves impossible or would involve a disproportionate effort or if recording or disclosure is expressly laid down by law. In these cases Member States shall provide appropriate safeguards.

[3881]

SECTION V
THE DATA SUBJECT'S RIGHT OF ACCESS TO DATA

Article 12
Right of access

Member States shall guarantee every data subject the right to obtain from the controller—

(a) without constraint at reasonable intervals and without excessive delay or expense—
- — confirmation as to whether or not data relating to him are being processed and information at least as to the purposes of the processing, the categories of data concerned, and the recipients or categories of recipients to whom the data are disclosed,
- — communication to him in an intelligible form of the data undergoing processing and of any available information as to their source,
- — knowledge of the logic involved in any automatic processing of data concerning him at least in the case of the automated decisions referred to in Article 15(1);

(b) as appropriate the rectification, erasure or blocking of data the processing of which does not comply with the provisions of this Directive, in particular because of the incomplete or inaccurate nature of the data;

(c) notification to third parties to whom the data have been disclosed of any rectification, erasure or blocking carried out in compliance with (b), unless this proves impossible or involves a disproportionate effort.

[3882]

SECTION VI
EXEMPTIONS AND RESTRICTIONS

Article 13

Exemptions and restrictions

1. Member States may adopt legislative measures to restrict the scope of the obligations and rights provided for in Articles 6(1), 10, 11(1), 12 and 21 when such a restriction constitutes a necessary measures to safeguard—

(a) national security;

(b) defence;

(c) public security;

(d) the prevention, investigation, detection and prosecution of criminal offences, or of breaches of ethics for regulated professions;

(e) an important economic or financial interest of a Member State or of the European Union, including monetary, budgetary and taxation matters;

(f) a monitoring, inspection or regulatory function connected, even occasionally, with the exercise of official authority in cases referred to in (c), (d) and (e);

(g) the protection of the data subject or of the rights and freedoms of others.

2. Subject to adequate legal safeguards, in particular that the data are not used for taking measures or decisions regarding any particular individual, Member States may, where there is clearly no risk of breaching the privacy of the data subject, restrict by a legislative measure the rights provided for in Article 12 when data are processed solely for purposes of scientific research or are kept in personal form for a period which does not exceed the period necessary for the sole purpose of creating statistics.

[3883]

SECTION VII
THE DATA SUBJECT'S RIGHT TO OBJECT

Article 14

The data subject's right to object

Member States shall grant the data subject the right—

(a) at least in the cases referred to in Article 7(e) and (f), to object at any time on compelling legitimate grounds relating to his particular situation to the processing of data relating to him, save where otherwise provided by national legislation. Where there is a justified objection, the processing instigated by the controller may no longer involve those data;

(b) to object, on request and free of charge, to the processing of personal data relating to him which the controller anticipates being processed for the purposes of direct marketing, or to be informed before personal data are disclosed for the first time to third parties or used on their behalf for the purposes of direct marketing, and to be expressly offered the right to object free of charge to such disclosures or uses.

Member States shall take the necessary measures to ensure that data subjects are aware of the existence of the right referred to in the first subparagraph of (b).

[3884]

Article 15

Automated individual decisions

1. Member States shall grant the right to every person not to be subject to a decision which produces legal effects concerning him or significantly affects him and which is based solely on automated processing of data intended to evaluate certain personal aspects relating to him, such as his performance at work, creditworthiness, reliability, conduct, etc.

2. Subject to the other Articles of this Directive, Member States shall provide that a person may be subjected to a decision of the kind referred to in paragraph 1 if that decision—

(a) is taken in the course of the entering into or performance of a contract, provided the request for the entering into or the performance of the contract, lodged by the data subject, has been satisfied or that there are suitable measures to safeguard his legitimate interests, such as arrangements allowing him to put his point of view; or

(b) is authorised by a law which also lays down measures to safeguard the data subject's legitimate interests.

[3885]

SECTION VII
CONFIDENTIALITY AND SECURITY OF PROCESSING

Article 16

Confidentiality of processing

Any person acting under the authority of the controller or of the processor, including the processor himself, who has access to personal data must not process them except on instructions from the controller, unless he is required to do so by law.

[3886]

Article 17

Security of processing

1. Member States shall provide that the controller must implement appropriate technical and organisational measures to protect personal data against accidental or unlawful destruction or accidental loss, alteration, unauthorised disclosure or access, in particular where the processing involves the transmission of data over a network, and against all other unlawful forms of processing.

Having regard to the state of the art and the cost of their implementation, such measures shall ensure a level of security appropriate to the risks represented by the processing and the nature of the data to be protected.

2. The Member States shall provide that the controller must, where processing is carried out on his behalf, choose a processor providing sufficient guarantees in respect of the

technical security measures and organisational measures governing the processing to be carried out, and must ensure compliance with those measures.

3. The carrying out of processing by way of a processor must be governed by a contract or legal act binding the processor to the controller and stipulating in particular that—

- the processor shall act only on instructions from the controller,
- the obligations set out in paragraph 1, as defined by the law of the Member State in which the processor is established, shall also be incumbent on the processor.

4. For the purposes of keeping proof, the parts of the contract or the legal act relating to data protection and the requirements relating to the measures referred to in paragraph 1 shall be in writing or in another equivalent form.

[3887]

SECTION IX
NOTIFICATION

Article 18

Obligation to notify the supervisory authority

1. Member States shall provide that the controller or his representative, if any, must notify the supervisory authority referred to in Article 28 before carrying out any wholly or partly automatic processing operation or set of such operations intended to serve a single purpose or several related purposes.

2. Member States may provide for the simplification of or exemption from notification only in the following cases and under the following conditions—

- where, for categories of processing operations which are unlikely, taking account of the data to be processed, to affect adversely the rights and freedoms of data subjects, they specify the purposes of the processing, the data or categories of data undergoing processing, the category or categories of data subject, the recipients or categories of recipient to whom the data are to be disclosed and the length of time the data are to be stored, and/or
- where the controller, in compliance with the national law which governs him, appoints a personal data protection official, responsible in particular—
  - for ensuring in an independent manner the internal application of the national provisions taken pursuant to this Directive
  - for keeping the register of processing operations carried out by the controller, containing the items of information referred to in Article 21(2),

  thereby ensuring that the rights and freedoms of the data subjects are unlikely to be adversely affected by the processing operations.

3. Member States may provide that paragraph 1 does not apply to processing whose sole purpose is the keeping of a register which according to laws or regulations is intended to provide information to the public and which is open to consultation either by the public in general or by any person demonstrating a legitimate interest.

4. Member States may provide for an exemption from the obligation to notify or a simplification of the notification in the case of processing operations referred to in Article 8(2)(d).

5. Member States may stipulate that certain or all non-automatic processing operations involving personal data shall be notified, or provide for these processing operations to be subject to simplified notification.

[3888]

Article 19

Contents of notification

1. Member States shall specify the information to be given in the notification. It shall include at least—

(a) the name and address of the controller and of his representative, if any;
(b) the purpose or purposes of the processing;
(c) a description of the category or categories of data subject and of the data or categories of data relating to them;
(d) the recipients or categories of recipient to whom the data might be disclosed;
(e) proposed transfers of data to third countries;

(f) a general description allowing a preliminary assessment to be made of the appropriateness of the measures taken pursuant to Article 17 to ensure security of processing.

2. Member States shall specify the procedures under which any change affecting the information referred to in paragraph 1 must be notified to the supervisory authority.

[3889]

Article 20

Prior checking

1. Member States shall determine the processing operations likely to present specific risks to the rights and freedoms of data subjects and shall check that these processing operations are examined prior to the start thereof.

2. Such prior checks shall be carried out by the supervisory authority following receipt of a notification from the controller or by the data protection official, who, in cases of doubt, must consult the supervisory authority.

3. Member States may also carry out such checks in the context of preparation either of a measure of the national parliament or of a measure based on such a legislative measure, which define the nature of the processing and lay down appropriate safeguards.

[3890]

Article 21

Publicising of processing operations

1. Member States shall take measures to ensure that processing operations are publicised.

2. Member States shall provide that a register of processing operations notified in accordance with Article 18 shall be kept by the supervisory authority.

The register shall contain at least the information listed in Article 19(1)(a) to (e).

The register may be inspected by any person.

3. Member States shall provide, in relation to processing operations not subject to notification, that controllers or another body appointed by the Member States make available at least the information referred to in Article 19(1)(a) to (e) in an appropriate form to any person on request.

Member States may provide that this provision does not apply to processing whose sole purpose is the keeping of a register which according to laws or regulations is intended to provide information to the public and which is open to consultation either by the public in general or by any person who can provide proof of a legitimate interest.

[3891]

CHAPTER III
JUDICIAL REMEDIES, LIABILITY AND SANCTIONS

Article 22

Remedies

Without prejudice to any administrative remedy for which provision may be made, *inter alia* before the supervisory authority referred to in Article 28, prior to referral to the judicial authority, Member States shall provide for the right of every person to a judicial remedy for any breach of the rights guaranteed him by the national law applicable to the processing in question.

[3892]

Article 23

Liability

1. Member States shall provide that any person who has suffered damage as a result of an unlawful processing operation or of any act incompatible with the national provisions adopted pursuant to this Directive is entitled to receive compensation from the controller for the damage suffered.

PART 3

2. The controller may be exempted from this liability, in whole or in part, if he proves that he is not responsible for the event giving rise to the damage.

[3893]

Article 24

Sanctions

The Member States shall adopt suitable measures to ensure the full implementation of the provisions of this Directive and shall in particular lay down the sanctions to be imposed in case of infringement of the provisions adopted pursuant to this Directive.

[3894]

CHAPTER IV
TRANSFER OF PERSONAL DATA TO THIRD COUNTRIES

Article 25

Principles

1. The Member States shall provide that the transfer to a third country of personal data which are undergoing processing or are intended for processing after transfer may take place only if, without prejudice to compliance with the national provisions adopted pursuant to the other provisions of this Directive, the third country in question ensures an adequate level of protection.

2. The adequacy of the level of protection afforded by a third country shall be assessed in the light of all the circumstances surrounding a data transfer operation or set of data transfer operations; particular consideration shall be given to the nature of the data, the purpose and duration of the proposed processing operation or operations, the country of origin and country of final destination, the rules of law, both general and sectoral, in force in the third country in question and the professional rules and security measures which are complied with in that country.

3. The Member States and the Commission shall inform each other of cases where they consider that a third country does not ensure an adequate level of protection within the meaning of paragraph 2.

4. Where the Commission finds, under the procedure provided for in Article 31(2), that a third country does not ensure an adequate level of protection within the meaning of paragraph 2 of this Article, Member States shall take the measures necessary to prevent any transfer of data of the same type to the third country in question.

5. At the appropriate time, the Commission shall enter into negotiations with a view to remedying the situation resulting from the finding made pursuant to paragraph 4.

6. The Commission may find, in accordance with the procedure referred to in Article 31(2), that a third country ensures an adequate level of protection within the meaning of paragraph 2 of this Article, by reason of its domestic law or of the international commitments it has entered into, particularly upon conclusion of the negotiations referred to in paragraph 5, for the protection of the private lives and basic freedoms and rights of individuals.

Member States shall take the measures necessary to comply with the Commission's decision.

[3895]

Article 26

Derogations

1. By way of derogation from Article 25 and save where otherwise provided by domestic law governing particular cases, Member States shall provide that a transfer or a set of transfers of personal data to a third country which does not ensure an adequate level of protection within the meaning of Article 25(2) may take place on condition that—

(a) the data subject has given his consent unambiguously to the proposed transfer; or
(b) the transfer is necessary for the performance of a contract between the data subject and the controller or the implementation of precontractual measures taken in response to the data subject's request; or

(c) the transfer is necessary for the conclusion or performance of a contract concluded in the interest of the data subject between the controller and a third party; or

(d) the transfer is necessary or legally required on important public interest grounds, or for the establishment, exercise or defence of legal claims; or

(e) the transfer is necessary in order to protect the vital interests of the data subject; or

(f) the transfer is made from a register which according to laws or regulations is intended to provide information to the public and which is open to consultation either by the public in general or by any person who can demonstrate legitimate interest, to the extent that the conditions laid down in law for consultation are fulfilled in the particular case.

2. Without prejudice to paragraph 1, a Member State may authorise a transfer or a set of transfers of personal data to a third country which does not ensure an adequate level of protection within the meaning of Article 25(2), where the controller adduces adequate safeguards with respect to the protection of the privacy and fundamental rights and freedoms of individuals and as regards the exercise of the corresponding rights; such safeguards may in particular result from appropriate contractual clauses.

3. The Member State shall inform the Commission and the other Member States of the authorisations it grants pursuant to paragraph 2.

If a Member State or the Commission objects on justified grounds involving the protection of the privacy and fundamental rights and freedoms of individuals, the Commission shall take appropriate measures in accordance with the procedure laid down in Article 31(2).

Member States shall take the necessary measures to comply with the Commission's decision.

4. Where the Commission decides, in accordance with the procedure referred to in Article 31(2), that certain standard contractual clauses offer sufficient safeguards as required by paragraph 2, Member States shall take the necessary measures to comply with the Commission's decision.

[3896]

CHAPTER V
CODES OF CONDUCT

Article 27

1. The Member States and the Commission shall encourage the drawing up of codes of conduct intended to contribute to the proper implementation of the national provisions adopted by the Member States pursuant to this Directive, taking account of the specific features of the various sectors.

2. Member States shall make provision for trade associations and other bodies representing other categories of controllers which have drawn up draft national codes or which have the intention of amending or extending existing national codes to be able to submit them to the opinion of the national authority.

Member States shall make provision for this authority to ascertain, among other things, whether the drafts submitted to it are in accordance with the national provisions adopted pursuant to this Directive. If it sees fit, the authority shall seek the views of data subjects or their representatives.

3. Draft Community codes, and amendments or extensions to existing Community codes, may be submitted to the Working Party referred to in Article 29. This Working Party shall determine, among other things, whether the drafts submitted to it are in accordance with the national provisions adopted pursuant to this Directive. If it sees fit, the authority shall seek the views of data subjects or their representatives. The Commission may ensure appropriate publicity for the codes which have been approved by the Working Party.

[3897]

CHAPTER VI
SUPERVISORY AUTHORITY AND WORKING PARTY ON THE PROTECTION OF INDIVIDUALS WITH REGARD TO THE PROCESSING OF PERSONAL DATA

Article 28

Supervisory authority

1. Each Member State shall provide that one or more public authorities are responsible for monitoring the application within its territory of the provisions adopted by the Member States pursuant to this Directive.

These authorities shall act with complete independence in exercising the functions entrusted to them.

2. Each Member State shall provide that the supervisory authorities are consulted when drawing up administrative measures or regulations relating to the protection of individuals' rights and freedoms with regard to the processing of personal data.

3. Each authority shall in particular be endowed with—

— investigative powers, such as powers of access to data forming the subject-matter of processing operations and powers to collect all the information necessary for the performance of its supervisory duties,

— effective powers of intervention, such as, for example, that of delivering opinions before processing operations are carried out, in accordance with Article 20, and ensuring appropriate publication of such opinions, of ordering the blocking, erasure or destruction of data, of imposing a temporary or definitive ban on processing, of warning or admonishing the controller, or that of referring the matter to national parliaments or other political institutions,

— the power to engage in legal proceedings where the national provisions adopted pursuant to this Directive have been violated or to bring these violations to the attention of the judicial authorities.

Decisions by the supervisory authority which give rise to complaints may be appealed against through the courts.

4. Each supervisory authority shall hear claims lodged by any person, or by an association representing that person, concerning the protection of his rights and freedoms in regard to the processing of personal data. The person concerned shall be informed of the outcome of the claim.

Each supervisory authority shall, in particular, hear claims for checks on the lawfulness of data processing lodged by any person when the national provisions adopted pursuant to Article 13 of this Directive apply. The person shall at any rate be informed that a check has taken place.

5. Each supervisory authority shall draw up a report on its activities at regular intervals. The report shall be made public.

6. Each supervisory authority is competent, whatever the national law applicable to the processing in question, to exercise, on the territory of its own Member State, the powers conferred on it in accordance with paragraph 3. Each authority may be requested to exercise its powers by an authority of another Member State.

The supervisory authorities shall cooperate with one another to the extent necessary for the performance of their duties, in particular by exchanging all useful information.

7. Member States shall provide that the members and staff of the supervisory authority, even after their employment has ended, are to be subject to a duty of professional secrecy with regard to confidential information to which they have access.

[3898]

Article 29

Working Party on the Protection of Individuals with regard to the Processing of Personal Data

1. A Working Party on the Protection of Individuals with regard to the Processing of Personal Data, hereinafter referred to as "the Working Party", is hereby set up.

It shall have advisory status and act independently.

2. The Working Party shall be composed of a representative of the supervisory authority or authorities designated by each Member State and of a representative of the authority or authorities established for the Community institutions and bodies, and of a representative of the Commission.

Each member of the Working Party shall be designated by the institution, authority or authorities which he represents. Where a Member State has designated more than one supervisory authority, they shall nominate a joint representative. The same shall apply to the authorities established for Community institutions and bodies.

3. The Working Party shall take decisions by a simple majority of the representatives of the supervisory authorities.

4. The Working Party shall elect its chairman. The chairman's term of office shall be two years. His appointment shall be renewable.

5. The Working Party's secretariat shall be provided by the Commission.

6. The Working Party shall adopt its own rules of procedure.

7. The Working Party shall consider items placed on its agenda by its chairman, either on his own initiative or at the request of a representative of the supervisory authorities or at the Commission's request.

[3899]

Article 30

1. The Working Party shall—
   (a) examine any question covering the application of the national measures adopted under this Directive in order to contribute to the uniform application of such measures;
   (b) give the Commission an opinion on the level of protection in the Community and in third countries;
   (c) advise the Commission on any proposed amendment of this Directive, on any additional or specific measures to safeguard the rights and freedoms of natural persons with regard to the processing of personal data and on any other proposed Community measures affecting such rights and freedoms;
   (d) give an opinion on codes of conduct drawn up at Community level.

2. If the Working Party finds that divergences likely to affect the equivalence of protection for persons with regard to the processing of personal data in the Community are arising between the laws or practices of Member States, it shall inform the Commission accordingly.

3. The Working Party may, on its own initiative, make recommendations on all matters relating to the protection of persons with regard to the processing of personal data in the Community.

4. The Working Party's opinions and recommendations shall be forwarded to the Commission and to the committee referred to in Article 31.

5. The Commission shall inform the Working Party of the action it has taken in response to its opinions and recommendations. It shall do so in a report which shall also be forwarded to the European Parliament and the Council. The report shall be made public.

6. The Working Party shall draw up an annual report on the situation regarding the protection of natural persons with regard to the processing of personal data in the Community and in third countries, which it shall transmit to the Commission, the European Parliament and the Council. The report shall be made public.

[3900]

CHAPTER VII
COMMUNITY IMPLEMENTING MEASURES

[Article 31

The Committee

1. The Commission shall be assisted by a committee.

2. Where reference is made to this Article, Articles 4 and 7 of Decision 1999/468/EC(36) shall apply, having regard to the provisions of Article 8 thereof.

The period laid down in Article 4(3) of Decision 1999/468/EC shall be set at three months.

3. The Committee shall adopt its rules of procedure.]

[3901]

NOTES

Substituted by European Parliament and Council Regulation 1882/2003/EC, Art 2, Annex II, para 18, as from 20 November 2003.

FINAL PROVISIONS

Article 32

1. Member States shall bring into force the laws, regulations and administrative provisions necessary to comply with this Directive at the latest at the end of a period of three years from the date of its adoption.

When Member States adopt these measures, they shall contain a reference to this Directive or be accompanied by such reference on the occasion of their official publication. The methods of making such reference shall be laid down by the Member States.

2. Member States shall ensure that processing already under way on the date the national provisions adopted pursuant to this Directive enter into force, is brought into conformity with these provisions within three years of this date.

By way of derogation from the preceding subparagraph, Member States may provide that the processing of data already held in manual filing systems on the date of entry into force of the national provisions adopted in implementation of this Directive shall be brought into conformity with Articles 6, 7 and 8 of this Directive within 12 years of the date on which it is adopted. Member States shall, however, grant the data subject the right to obtain, at his request and in particular at the time of exercising his right of access, the rectification, erasure or blocking of data which are incomplete, inaccurate or stored in a way incompatible with the legitimate purposes pursued by the controller.

3. By way of derogation from paragraph 2, Member States may provide, subject to suitable safeguards, that data kept for the sole purpose of historical research need not be brought into conformity with Articles 6, 7 and 8 of this Directive.

4. Member States shall communicate to the Commission the text of the provisions of domestic law which they adopt in the field covered by this Directive.

[3902]

Article 33

The Commission shall report to the Council and the European Parliament at regular intervals, starting not later than three years after the date referred to in Article 32(1), on the implementation of this Directive, attaching to its report, if necessary, suitable proposals for amendments. The report shall be made public.

The Commission shall examine, in particular, the application of this Directive to the data processing of sound and image data relating to natural persons and shall submit any appropriate proposals which prove to be necessary, taking account of developments in information technology and in the light of the state of progress in the information society.

[3903]

Article 34

This Directive is addressed to the Member States.

[3904]

COUNCIL DIRECTIVE

of 3 June 1996

on the framework agreement on parental leave concluded by UNICE, CEEP and the ETUC

(96/34/EC)

NOTES

Date of publication in OJ: OJ L145, 19.6.96, p 4.

This Directive implements a Framework Agreement made by the Social Partners (the Union of Industrial and Employers' Confederations of Europe (UNICE), the European Centre of Enterprises with Public Participation (CEEP) and the European Trade Union Confederation (ETUC) in accordance with Art 4 to the Agreement on Social Policy annexed to Protocol 14 to the Treaty of Union 1992, and therefore did not bind the United Kingdom. It was subsequently extended to the UK by Directive 97/75/EC at **[3923]**, with a required date of transposition of 15 December 1999; see Art 2(1a) below at **[3906]**.

For the domestic implementation of this Directive see the Employment Rights Act 1996, ss 57A, 57B (as inserted by the Employment Relations Act 1999, ss 7, 8, Sch 4, Pts I, II), 76–80, at **[1084]**, **[1085]**, **[1111]–[1115]**.

THE COUNCIL OF THE EUROPEAN UNION,

Having regard to the Agreement on social policy, annexed to the Protocol (No 14) on social policy, annexed to the Treaty establishing the European Community, and in particular Article 4(2) thereof,

Having regard to the proposal from the Commission,

(1) Whereas on the basis of the Protocol on social policy, the Member States, with the exception of the United Kingdom of Great Britain and Northern Ireland, (hereinafter referred to as 'the Member States'), wishing to pursue the course mapped out by the 1989 Social Charter have concluded an Agreement on social policy amongst themselves;

(2) Whereas management and labour may, in accordance with Article 4(2) of the Agreement on social policy, request jointly that agreements at Community level be implemented by a Council decision on a proposal from the Commission;

(3) Whereas paragraph 16 of the Community Charter of the Fundamental Social Rights of Workers on equal treatment for men and women provides, *inter alia*, that 'measures should also be developed enabling men and women to reconcile their occupational and family obligations';

(4) Whereas the Council, despite the existence of a broad consensus, has not been able to act on the proposal for a Directive on parental leave for family reasons,[1] as amended[2] on 15 November 1984;

(5) Whereas the Commission, in accordance with Article 3(2) of the Agreement on social policy, consulted management and labour on the possible direction of Community action with regard to reconciling working and family life;

(6) Whereas the Commission, considering after such consultation that Community action was desirable, once again consulted management and labour on the substance of the envisaged proposal in accordance with Article 3(3) of the said Agreement;

(7) Whereas the general cross-industry organisations (UNICE, CEEP and the ETUC) informed the Commission in their joint letter of 5 July 1995 of their desire to initiate the procedure provided for by Article 4 of the said Agreement;

(8) Whereas the said cross-industry organisations concluded, on 14 December 1995, a framework agreement on parental leave; whereas they have forwarded to the Commission their joint request to implement this framework agreement by a Council Decision on a proposal from the Commission in accordance with Article 4(2) of the said Agreement;

(9) Whereas the Council, in its Resolution of 6 December 1994 on certain aspects for a European Union social policy; a contribution to economic and social convergence in the Union,[3] asked the two sides of industry to make use of the possibilities for concluding agreements, since they are as a rule closer to social reality and to social problems; whereas in Madrid, the members of the European Council from those States which have signed the Agreement on social policy welcomed the conclusion of this framework agreement;

(10) Whereas the signatory parties wanted to conclude a framework agreement setting out minimum requirements on parental leave and time off from work on grounds of *force majeure* and referring back to the Member States and/or management and labour for the definition of the conditions under which parental leave would be implemented, in order to take account of the situation, including the situation with regard to family policy, existing in each Member State, particularly as regards the conditions for granting parental leave and exercise of the right to parental leave;

(11) Whereas the proper instrument for implementing this framework agreement is a Directive within the meaning of Article 189 of the Treaty; whereas it is therefore binding on the Member States as to the result to be achieved, but leaves them the choice of form and methods;

(12) Whereas, in keeping with the principle of subsidiarity and the principle of proportionality as set out in Article 3b of the Treaty, the objectives of this Directive cannot be sufficiently achieved by the Member States and can therefore be better achieved by the Community; whereas this Directive is confined to the minimum required to achieve these objectives and does not go beyond what is necessary to achieve that purpose;

(13) Whereas the Commission has drafted its proposal for a Directive, taking into account the representative status of the signatory parties, their mandate and the legality of the clauses of the framework agreement and compliance with the relevant provisions concerning small and medium-sized undertakings;

(14) Whereas the Commission, in accordance with its Communication of 14 December 1993 concerning the implementation of the Protocol on social policy, informed the European Parliament by sending it the text of the framework agreement, accompanied by its proposal for a Directive and the explanatory memorandum;

(15) Whereas the Commission also informed the Economic and Social Committee by sending it the text of the framework agreement, accompanied by its proposal for a Directive and the explanatory memorandum;

(16) Whereas clause 4 point 2 of the framework agreement states that the implementation of the provisions of this agreement does not constitute valid grounds for reducing the general level of protection afforded to workers in the field of this agreement. This does not prejudice the right of Member States and/or management and labour to develop different legislative, regulatory or contractual provisions, in the light of changing circumstances (including the introduction of non-transferability), as long as the minimum requirements provided for in the present agreement are complied with;

(17) Whereas the Community Charter of the Fundamental Social Rights of Workers recognises the importance of the fight against all forms of discrimination, especially based on sex, colour, race, opinions and creeds;

(18) Whereas Article F(2) of the Treaty on European Union provides that 'the Union shall respect fundamental rights, as guaranteed by the European Convention for the Protection of Human Rights and Fundamental Freedoms signed in Rome on 4 November 1950 and as they result from the constitutional traditions common to the Member States, as general principles of Community law';

(19) Whereas the Member States can entrust management and labour, at their joint request, with the implementation of this Directive, as long as they take all the necessary steps to ensure that they can at all times guarantee the results imposed by this Directive;

(20) Whereas the implementation of the framework agreement contributes to achieving the objectives under Article 1 of the Agreement on social policy,

NOTES

[1] OJ C333, 9.12.83, p 6.
[2] OJ C316, 27.11.84, p 7.
[3] OJ C368, 23.12.94, p 6.

HAS ADOPTED THIS DIRECTIVE—

Article 1

Implementation of the framework agreement

The purpose of this Directive is to put into effect the annexed framework agreement on parental leave concluded on 14 December 1995 between the general cross-industry organisations (UNICE, CEEP and the ETUC).

[3905]

Article 2

Final provisions

1. The Member States shall bring into force the laws, regulations and administrative provisions necessary to comply with this Directive by 3 June 1998 at the latest or shall ensure by that date at the latest that management and labour have introduced the necessary measures by agreement, the Member States being required to take any necessary measure enabling them at any time to be in a position to guarantee the results imposed by this Directive. They shall forthwith inform the Commission thereof.

[1a. As regards the United Kingdom of Great Britain and Northern Ireland, the date of 3 June 1998 in paragraph 1 shall be replaced by 15 December 1999.]

2. The Member States may have a maximum additional period of one year, if this is necessary to take account of special difficulties or implementation by a collective agreement.

They must forthwith inform the Commission of such circumstances.

3. When Member States adopt the measures referred to in paragraph 1, they shall contain a reference to this Directive or be accompanied by such reference on the occasion of their official publication. The methods of making such reference shall be laid down by Member States.

[3906]

NOTES

Para 1a: inserted by Council Directive 97/75/EC, Art 2.

Article 3

This Directive is addressed to the Member States.

[3907]

ANNEX

FRAMEWORK AGREEMENT ON PARENTAL LEAVE

Preamble

The enclosed framework agreement represents an undertaking by UNICE, CEEP and the ETUC to set out minimum requirements on parental leave and time off from work on grounds of *force majeure*, as an important means of reconciling work and family life and promoting equal opportunities and treatment between men and women.

ETUC, UNICE and CEEP request the Commission to submit this framework agreement to the Council for a Council Decision making these minimum requirements binding in the Member States of the European Community, with the exception of the United Kingdom of Great Britain and Northern Ireland.

I. General considerations

1. Having regard to the Agreement on social policy annexed to the Protocol on social policy, annexed to the Treaty establishing the European Community, and in particular Articles 3(4) and 4(2) thereof;

2. Whereas Article 4(2) of the Agreement on social policy provides that agreements concluded at Community level shall be implemented, at the joint request of the signatory parties, by a Council decision on a proposal from the Commission;

3. Whereas the Commission has announced its intention to propose a Community measure on the reconciliation of work and family life;

4. Whereas the Community Charter of Fundamental Social Rights stipulates at point 16 dealing with equal treatment that measures should be developed to enable men and women to reconcile their occupational and family obligations;

5. Whereas the Council Resolution of 6 December 1994 recognises that an effective policy of equal opportunities presupposes an integrated overall strategy allowing for better organisation of working hours and greater flexibility, and for an easier return to working life, and notes the important role of the two sides of industry in this area and in offering both men and women an opportunity to reconcile their work responsibilities with family obligations;

6. Whereas measures to reconcile work and family life should encourage the introduction of new flexible ways of organising work and time which are better suited to the changing needs of society and which should take the needs of both undertakings and workers into account;

7. Whereas family policy should be looked at in the context of demographic changes, the effects of the ageing population, closing the generation gap and promoting women's participation in the labour force;

8. Whereas men should be encouraged to assume an equal share of family responsibilities, for example they should be encouraged to take parental leave by means such as awareness programmes;

9. Whereas the present agreement is a framework agreement setting out minimum requirements and provisions for parental leave, distinct from maternity leave, and for time off from work on grounds of *force majeure*, and refers back to Member States and social partners for the establishment of the conditions of access and detailed rules of application in order to take account of the situation in each Member State;

10. Whereas Member States should provide for the maintenance of entitlements to benefits in kind under sickness insurance during the minimum period of parental leave;

11. Whereas Member States should also, where appropriate under national conditions and taking into account the budgetary situation, consider the maintenance of entitlements to relevant social security benefits as they stand during the minimum period of parental leave;

12. Whereas this agreement takes into consideration the need to improve social policy requirements, to enhance the competitiveness of the Community economy and to avoid imposing administrative, financial and legal constraints in a way which would impede the creation and development of small and medium-sized undertakings;

13. Whereas management and labour are best placed to find solutions that correspond to the needs of both employers and workers and must therefore have conferred on them a special role in the implementation and application of the present agreement,

The signatory parties have agreed the following—

II. Content

Clause 1. Purpose and scope

1. This agreement lays down minimum requirements designed to facilitate the reconciliation of parental and professional responsibilities for working parents.

2. This agreement applies to all workers, men and women, who have an employment contract or employment relationship as defined by the law, collective agreements or practices in force in each Member State.

Clause 2. Parental leave

1. This agreement grants, subject to clause 2.2, men and women workers an individual right to parental leave on the grounds of the birth or adoption of a child to enable them to take care of that child, for at least three months, until a given age up to 8 years to be defined by Member States and/or management and labour.

2. To promote equal opportunities and equal treatment between men and women, the parties to this agreement consider that the right to parental leave provided for under clause 2.1 should, in principle, be granted on a non-transferable basis.

3. The conditions of access and detailed rules for applying parental leave shall be defined by law and/or collective agreement in the Member States, as long as the minimum requirements of this agreement are respected. Member States and/or management and labour may, in particular:

(a) decide whether parental leave is granted on a full-time or part-time basis, in a piecemeal way or in the form of a time-credit system;

(b) make entitlement to parental leave subject to a period of work qualification and/or a length of service qualification which shall not exceed one year;

(c) adjust conditions of access and detailed rules for applying parental leave to the special circumstances of adoption;

(d) establish notice periods to be given by the worker to the employer when exercising the right to parental leave, specifying the beginning and the end of the period of leave;

(e) define the circumstances in which an employer, following consultation in accordance with national law, collective agreements and practices, is allowed to postpone the granting of parental leave for justifiable reasons related to the operation of the undertaking (eg where work is of a seasonal nature, where a replacement cannot be found within the notice period, where a significant proportion of the workforce applies for parental leave at the same time, where a specific function is of strategic importance). Any problem arising from the application of this provision should be dealt with in accordance with national law, collective agreements and practices;

(f) in addition to (e), authorise special arrangements to meet the operational and organisational requirements of small undertakings.

4. In order to ensure that workers can exercise their right to parental leave, Member States and/or management and labour shall take the necessary measures to protect workers against dismissal on the grounds of an application for, or the taking of, parental leave in accordance with national law, collective agreements or practices.

5. At the end of parental leave, workers shall have the right to return to the same job or, if that is not possible, to an equivalent or similar job consistent with their employment contract or employment relationship.

6. Rights acquired or in the process of being acquired by the worker on the date on which parental leave starts shall be maintained as they stand until the end of parental leave. At the end of parental leave, these rights, including any changes arising from national law, collective agreements or practice, shall apply.

7. Member States and/or management and labour shall define the status of the employment contract or employment relationship for the period of parental leave.

8. All matters relating to social security in relation to this agreement are for consideration and determination by Member States according to national law, taking into account the importance of the continuity of the entitlements to social security cover under the different schemes, in particular health care.

Clause 3. Time off from work on grounds of force majeure

1. Member States and/or management and labour shall take the necessary measures to entitle workers to time off from work, in accordance with national legislation, collective agreements and/or practice, on grounds of *force majeure* for urgent family reasons in cases of sickness or accident making the immediate presence of the worker indispensable.

2. Member States and/or management and labour may specify the conditions of access and detailed rules for applying clause 3.1 and limit this entitlement to a certain amount of time per year and/or per case.

Clause 4. Final provisions

1. Member States may apply or introduce more favourable provisions than those set out in this agreement.

2. Implementation of the provisions of this agreement shall not constitute valid grounds for reducing the general level of protection afforded to workers in the field covered by this agreement. This shall not prejudice the right of Member States and/or management and labour to develop different legislative, regulatory or contractual provisions, in the light of changing circumstances (including the introduction of non-transferability), as long as the minimum requirements provided for in the present agreement are complied with.

3. The present agreement shall not prejudice the right of management and labour to conclude, at the appropriate level including European level, agreements adapting and/or complementing the provisions of this agreement in order to take into account particular circumstances.

4. Member States shall adopt the laws, regulations and administrative provisions necessary to comply with the Council decision within a period of two years from its adoption or shall ensure that management and labour[1] introduce the necessary measures by way of agreement by the end of this period. Member States may, if necessary to take account of particular difficulties or implementation by collective agreement, have up to a maximum of one additional year to comply with this decision.

5. The prevention and settlement of disputes and grievances arising from the application of this agreement shall be dealt with in accordance with national law, collective agreements and practices.

6. Without prejudice to the respective role of the Commission, national courts and the Court of Justice, any matter relating to the interpretation of this agreement at European level should, in the first instance, be referred by the Commission to the signatory parties who will give an opinion.

7. The signatory parties shall review the application of this agreement five years after the date of the Council decision if requested by one of the parties to this agreement.

[3908]

NOTES

[1] Within the meaning of Article 2(4) of the Agreement on social policy.

DIRECTIVE OF THE EUROPEAN PARLIAMENT AND OF THE COUNCIL

of 16 December 1996

concerning the posting of workers in the framework of the provision of services

(96/71/EC)

NOTES

Date of publication in OJ: OJ L18, 21.1.97, p 1.

For the domestic implementation of this Directive, see, inter alia, the Equal Opportunities (Employment Legislation) (Territorial Limits) Regulations 1999, SI 1999/3163 which amends the Sex Discrimination Act 1975, s 10 at **[112]**, the Race Relations Act 1976, s 8 at **[216]**, and amended the Disability Discrimination Act 1995, s 68 at **[942]**.

THE EUROPEAN PARLIAMENT AND THE COUNCIL OF THE EUROPEAN UNION,

Having regard to the Treaty establishing the European Community, and in particular Articles 57(2) and 66 thereof,

Having regard to the proposal from the Commission,[1]

Having regard to the opinion of the Economic and Social Committee,[2]

Acting in accordance with the procedure laid down in Article 189b of the Treaty,[3]

(1) Whereas, pursuant to Article 3(c) of the Treaty, the abolition, as between Member States, of obstacles to the free movement of persons and services constitutes one of the objectives of the Community;

(2) Whereas, for the provision of services, any restrictions based on nationality or residence requirements are prohibited under the Treaty with effect from the end of the transitional period;

(3) Whereas the completion of the internal market offers a dynamic environment for the transnational provision of services, prompting a growing number of undertakings to post employees abroad temporarily to perform work in the territory of a Member State other than the State in which they are habitually employed;

(4) Whereas the provision of services may take the form either of performance of work by an undertaking on its account and under its direction, under a contract concluded between that undertaking and the party for whom the services are intended, or of the hiring-out of workers for use by an undertaking in the framework of a public or a private contract;

(5) Whereas any such promotion of the transnational provision of services requires a climate of fair competition and measures guaranteeing respect for the rights of workers;

(6) Whereas the transnationalization of the employment relationship raises problems with regard to the legislation applicable to the employment relationship; whereas it is in the interests of the parties to lay down the terms and conditions governing the employment relationship envisaged;

(7) Whereas the Rome Convention of 19 June 1980 on the law applicable to contractual obligations,[4] signed by 12 Member States, entered into force on 1 April 1991 in the majority of Member States;

(8) Whereas Article 3 of that Convention provides, as a general rule, for the free choice of law made by the parties; whereas, in the absence of choice, the contract is to be governed, according to Article 6(2), by the law of the country, in which the employee habitually carries out his work in performance of the contract, even if he is temporarily employed in another country, or, if the employee does not habitually carry out his work in any one country, by the law of the country in which the place of business through which he was engaged is situated, unless it appears from the circumstances as a whole that the contract is more closely connected with another country, in which case the contract is to be governed by the law of that country;

(9) Whereas, according to Article 6(1) of the said Convention, the choice of law made by the parties is not to have the result of depriving the employee of the protection afforded to him by the mandatory rules of the law which would be applicable under paragraph 2 of that Article in the absence of choice;

(10) Whereas Article 7 of the said Convention lays down, subject to certain conditions, that effect may be given, concurrently with the law declared applicable, to the mandatory rules of the law of another country, in particular the law of the Member State within whose territory the worker is temporarily posted;

(11) Whereas, according to the principle of precedence of Community law laid down in its Article 20, the said Convention does not affect the application of provisions which, in

relation to a particular matter, lay down choice-of-law rules relating to contractual obligations and which are or will be contained in acts of the institutions of the European Communities or in national laws harmonized in implementation of such acts;

(12) Whereas Community law does not preclude Member States from applying their legislation, or collective agreements entered into by employers and labour, to any person who is employed, even temporarily, within their territory, although his employer is established in another Member State; whereas Community law does not forbid Member Stares to guarantee the observance of those rules by the appropriate means;

(13) Whereas the laws of the Member States must be coordinated in order to lay down a nucleus of mandatory rules for minimum protection to be observed in the host country by employers who post workers to perform temporary work in the territory of a Member State where the services are provided; whereas such coordination can be achieved only by means of Community law;

(14) Whereas a 'hard core' of clearly defined protective rules should be observed by the provider of the services notwithstanding the duration of the worker's posting;

(15) Whereas it should be laid down that, in certain clearly defined cases of assembly and/or installation of goods, the provisions on minimum rates of pay and minimum paid annual holidays do nor apply;

(16) Whereas there should also be some flexibility in application of the provisions concerning minimum rates of pay and the minimum length of paid annual holidays; whereas, when the length of the posting is not more than one month, Member States may, under certain conditions, derogate from the provisions concerning minimum rates of pay or provide for the possibility of derogation by means of collective agreements; whereas, where the amount of work to be done is not significant, Member States may derogate from the provisions concerning minimum rates of pay and the minimum length of paid annual holidays;

(17) Whereas the mandatory rules for minimum protection in force in the host country must not prevent the application of terms and conditions of employment which are more favourable to workers;

(18) Whereas the principle that undertakings established outside the Community must not receive more favourable treatment than undertakings established in the territory of a Member State should be upheld;

(19) Whereas, without prejudice to other provisions of Community law, this Directive does not entail the obligation to give legal recognition to the existence of temporary employment undertakings, nor does it prejudice the application by Member States of their laws concerning the hiring-out of workers and temporary employment undertakings to undertakings not established in their territory but operating therein in the framework of the provision of services;

(20) Whereas this Directive does not affect either the agreements concluded by the Community with third countries or the laws of Member States concerning the access to their territory of third-country providers of services; whereas this Directive is also without prejudice to national laws relating to the entry, residence and access to employment of third-country workers;

(21) Whereas Council Regulation (EEC) No 1408/71 of 14 June 1971 on the application of social security schemes to employed persons and their families moving within the Community[5] lays down the provisions applicable with regard to social security benefits and contributions;

(22) Whereas this Directive is without prejudice to the law of the Member States concerning collective action to defend the interests of trades and professions;

(23) Whereas competent bodies in different Member States must cooperate with each other in the application of this Directive; whereas Member States must provide for appropriate remedies in the event of failure to comply with this Directive;

(24) Whereas it is necessary to guarantee proper application of this Directive and to that end to make provision for close collaboration between the Commission and the Member States;

(25) Whereas five years after adoption of this Directive at the latest the Commission must review the detailed rules for implementing this Directive with a view to proposing, where appropriate, the necessary amendments,

NOTES

1 OJ C225, 30.8.91, p 6 and OJ C187, 9.7.93, p 5.

2 OJ C49, 24.2.92, p 41.

3 Opinion of the European Parliament of 10 February 1993 (OJ C72, 15.3.93, p 78), Council common position of 3 June 1996 (OJ C220, 29.7.96, p 1) and Decision of the European Parliament of 18 September 1996 (not yet published in the Official Journal). Council Decision of 24 September 1996.

4 OJ L266, 9.10.80, p 1.

[5] OJ L149, 5.7.71, p 2; Special Edition 1971 (II), p 416. Regulation as last amended by Regulation 3096/95/EC (OJ L335, 30.12.95, p 10).

HAVE ADOPTED THIS DIRECTIVE—

Article 1

Scope

1. This Directive shall apply to undertakings established in a Member State which, in the framework of the transnational provision of services, post workers, in accordance with paragraph 3, to the territory of a Member State.

2. This Directive shall not apply to merchant navy undertakings as regards seagoing personnel.

3. This Directive shall apply to the extent that the undertakings referred to in paragraph 1 take one of the following transnational measures—

(a) post workers to the territory of a Member State on their account and under their direction, under a contract concluded between the undertaking making the posting and the party for whom the services are intended, operating in that Member State, provided there is an employment relationship between the undertaking making the posting and the worker during the period of posting; or

(b) post workers to an establishment or to an undertaking owned by the group in the territory of a Member State, provided there is an employment relationship between the undertaking making the posting and the worker during the period of posting; or

(c) being a temporary employment undertaking or placement agency, hire out a worker to a user undertaking established or operating in the territory of a Member State, provided there is an employment relationship between the temporary employment undertaking or placement agency and the worker during the period of posting.

4. Undertakings established in a non-member State must not be given more favourable treatment than undertakings established in a Member State.

[3909]

Article 2

Definition

1. For the purposes of this Directive, 'posted worker' means a worker who, for a limited period, carries out his work in the territory of a Member State other than the State in which he normally works.

2. For the purposes of this Directive, the definition of a worker is that which applies in the law of the Member State to whose territory the worker is posted.

[3910]

Article 3

Terms and conditions of employment

1. Member States shall ensure that, whatever the law applicable to the employment relationship, the undertakings referred to in Article 1(1) guarantee workers posted to their territory the terms and conditions of employment covering the following matters which, in the Member State where the work is carried out, are laid down—

— by law, regulation or administrative provision, and/or

— by collective agreements or arbitration awards which have been declared universally applicable within the meaning of paragraph 8, insofar as they concern the activities referred to in the Annex—

(a) maximum work periods and minimum rest periods;

(b) minimum paid annual holidays;

(c) the minimum rates of pay, including overtime rates; this point does not apply to supplementary occupational retirement pension schemes;

(d) the conditions of hiring-out of workers, in particular the supply of workers by temporary employment undertakings;

(e) health, safety and hygiene at work;

(f) protective measures with regard to the terms and conditions of employment of pregnant women or women who have recently given birth, of children and of young people;

(g) equality of treatment between men and women and other provisions on non-discrimination.

For the purposes of this Directive, the concept of minimum rates of pay referred to in paragraph 1(c) is defined by the national law and/or practice of the Member State to whose territory the worker is posted.

2. In the case of initial assembly and/or first installation of goods where this is an integral part of a contract for the supply of goods and necessary for taking the goods supplied into use and carried out by the skilled and/or specialist workers of the supplying undertaking, the first subparagraph of paragraph 1(b) and (c) shall not apply, if the period of posting does not exceed eight days.

This provision shall not apply to activities in the field of building work listed in the Annex.

3. Member States may, after consulting employers and labour, in accordance with the traditions and practices of each Member State, decide not to apply the first subparagraph of paragraph 1(c) in the cases referred to in Article 1(3)(a) and (b) when the length of the posting does not exceed one month.

4. Member States may, in accordance with national laws and/or practices, provide that exemptions may be made from the first subparagraph of paragraph 1(c) in the cases referred to in Article 1(3)(a) and (b) and from a decision by a Member State within the meaning of paragraph 3 of this Article, by means of collective agreements within the meaning of paragraph 8 of this Article, concerning one or more sectors of activity, where the length of the posting does not exceed one month.

5. Member States may provide for exemptions to be granted from the first subparagraph of paragraph 1(b) and (c) in the cases referred to in Article 1(3)(a) and (b) on the grounds that the amount of work to be done is not significant.

Member States availing themselves of the option referred to in the first subparagraph shall lay down the criteria which the work to be performed must meet in order to be considered as 'non-significant'.

6. The length of the posting shall be calculated on the basis of a reference period of one year from the beginning of the posting.

For the purpose of such calculations, account shall be taken of any previous periods for which the post has been filled by a posted worker.

7. Paragraphs 1 to 6 shall not prevent application of terms and conditions of employment which are more favourable to workers.

Allowances specific to the posting shall be considered to be part of the minimum wage, unless they are paid in reimbursement of expenditure actually incurred on account of the posting, such as expenditure on travel, board and lodging.

8. 'Collective agreements or arbitration awards which have been declared universally applicable' means collective agreements or arbitration awards which must be observed by all undertakings in the geographical area and in the profession or industry concerned.

In the absence of a system for declaring collective agreements or arbitration awards to be of universal application within the meaning of the first subparagraph, Member States may, if they so decide, base themselves on—

— collective agreements or arbitration awards which are generally applicable to all similar undertakings in the geographical area and in the profession or industry concerned, and/or
— collective agreements which have been concluded by the most representative employers' and labour organizations at national level and which are applied throughout national territory,

provided that their application to the undertakings referred to in Article 1(1) ensures equality of treatment on matters listed in the first subparagraph of paragraph 1 of this Article between those undertakings and the other undertakings referred to in this subparagraph which are in a similar position.

Equality of treatment, within the meaning of this Article, shall be deemed to exist where national undertakings in a similar position—

— are subject, in the place in question or in the sector concerned, to the same obligations as posting undertakings as regards the matters listed in the first subparagraph of paragraph 1, and

— are required to fulfil such obligations with the same effects.

9. Member States may provide that the undertakings referred to in Article 1(1) must guarantee workers referred to in Article 1(3)(c) the terms and conditions which apply to temporary workers in the Member State where the work is carried out.

10. This Directive shall not preclude the application by Member States, in compliance with the Treaty, to national undertakings and to the undertakings of other States, on a basis of equality of treatment, of—

- — terms and conditions of employment on matters other than those referred to in the first subparagraph of paragraph 1 in the case of public policy provisions,
- — terms and conditions of employment laid down in the collective agreements or arbitration awards within the meaning of paragraph 8 and concerning activities other than those referred to in the Annex.

[3911]

Article 4

Cooperation on information

1. For the purposes of implementing this Directive, Member States shall, in accordance with national legislation and/or practice, designate one or more liaison offices or one or more competent national bodies.

2. Member States shall make provision for cooperation between the public authorities which, in accordance with national legislation, are responsible for monitoring the terms and conditions of employment referred to in Article 3. Such cooperation shall in particular consist in replying to reasoned requests from those authorities for information on the transnational hiring-out of workers, including manifest abuses or possible cases of unlawful transnational activities.

The Commission and the public authorities referred to in the first subparagraph shall cooperate closely in order to examine any difficulties which might arise in the application of Article 3(10).

Mutual administrative assistance shall be provided free of charge.

3. Each Member State shall take the appropriate measures to make the information on the terms and conditions of employment referred to in Article 3 generally available.

4. Each Member State shall notify the other Member States and the Commission of the liaison offices and/or competent bodies referred to in paragraph 1.

[3912]

Article 5

Measures

Member States shall take appropriate measures in the event of failure to comply with this Directive.

They shall in particular ensure that adequate procedures are available to workers and/or their representatives for the enforcement of obligations under this Directive.

[3913]

Article 6

Jurisdiction

In order to enforce the right to the terms and conditions of employment guaranteed in Article 3, judicial proceedings may be instituted in the Member State in whose territory the worker is or was posted, without prejudice, where applicable, to the right, under existing international conventions on jurisdiction, to institute proceedings in another State.

[3914]

Article 7

Implementation

Member States shall adopt the laws, regulations and administrative provisions necessary to comply with this Directive by 16 December 1999 at the latest. They shall forthwith inform the Commission thereof.

When Member States adopt these provisions, they shall contain a reference to this Directive or shall be accompanied by such reference on the occasion of their official publication. The methods of making such reference shall be laid down by Member States.

[3915]

Article 8

Commission review

By 16 December 2001 at the latest, the Commission shall review the operation of this Directive with a view to proposing the necessary amendments to the Council where appropriate.

[3916]

Article 9

This Directive is addressed to the Member States.

[3917]

ANNEX

The activities mentioned in Article 3(1), second indent, include all building work relating to the construction, repair, upkeep, alteration or demolition of buildings, and in particular the following work—

1. excavation
2. earthmoving
3. actual building work
4. assembly and dismantling of prefabricated elements
5. fitting out or installation
6. alterations
7. renovation
8. repairs
9. dismantling
10. demolition
11. maintenance
12. upkeep, painting and cleaning work
13. improvements.

[3918]

COUNCIL DIRECTIVE

of 15 December 1997

extending, to the United Kingdom of Great Britain and Northern Ireland, Directive 94/45/EC on the establishment of a European Works Council or a procedure in Community-scale undertakings and Community-scale groups of undertakings for the purposes of informing and consulting employees

(97/74/EC)

NOTES

Date of publication in OJ: OJ L10, 16.1.98, p 22.

For the domestic implementation of this Directive see the Transnational Information and Consultation of Employees Regulations 1999, SI 1999/3323 at **[2577]**. Council Directive 94/45/EC is at **[3854]**.

THE COUNCIL OF THE EUROPEAN UNION,

Having regard to the Treaty establishing the European Community, and in particular Article 100 thereof,

Having regard to the proposal from the Commission,[1]

Having regard to the opinion of the European Parliament,[2]

Having regard to the opinion of the Economic and Social Committee,[3]

Whereas the Council, acting in accordance with the Agreement on social policy annexed to Protocol 14 to the Treaty, and in particular Article 2(2) thereof, adopted Directive 94/45/EC;[4] whereas, as a result, the said Directive does not apply to the United Kingdom of Great Britain and Northern Ireland;

Whereas the Amsterdam European Council held on 16 and 17 June 1997 noted with approval the agreement of the Intergovernmental Conference to incorporate the Agreement on social policy in the Treaty and also noted that a means should be found to give legal effect to the wish of the United Kingdom of Great Britain and Northern Ireland to accept the Directives already adopted on the basis of that Agreement before the signature of the Amsterdam Treaty; whereas this Directive seeks to achieve this aim by extending Directive 94/45/EC to the United Kingdom;

Whereas the fact that Directive 94/45/EC is not applicable in the United Kingdom directly affects the functioning of the internal market; whereas implementation of the said Directive in all the Member States will improve the functioning of the internal market;

Whereas Directive 94/45/EC provides for a maximum of 17 members of the special negotiating body; whereas such a number corresponds to the 14 Member States which are party to the Agreement on social policy plus the three remaining Contracting Parties of the European Economic Area; whereas the adoption of this Directive will bring the total number of States covered by Directive 94/45/EC to 18; whereas, therefore, the abovementioned maximum should be increased to 18 so that each Member State in which the Community-scale undertaking has one or more establishments or in which the Community-scale group of undertakings has the controlling undertaking or one or more controlled undertakings is represented;

Whereas Directive 94/45/EC provides for special treatment to be accorded to Community-scale undertakings and groups of undertakings in which there is, at 22 September 1996, an agreement covering the entire workforce providing for the transnational information and consultation of employees; whereas, accordingly, Community-scale undertakings and groups of undertakings falling within the scope of that Directive solely as a result of its application to the United Kingdom should be granted similar treatment;

Whereas the adoption of this Directive will make Directive 94/45/EC applicable in all Member States including the United Kingdom; whereas, from the date on which this Directive enters into force, the term 'Member States' in Directive 94/45/EC should be construed as including, where appropriate, the United Kingdom;

Whereas Member States were required to bring into force the laws, regulations and administrative provisions to comply with Directive 94/45/EC no later than two years after its adoption; whereas a similar period should be granted to the United Kingdom, as well as to the other Member States, to bring into force the necessary measures to comply with this Directive,

NOTES

1 OJ C335, 6.11.97.
2 OJ C371, 8.12.97.
3 OJ C355, 21.11.97.
4 OJ L254, 30.9.94, p 64.

HAS ADOPTED THIS DIRECTIVE—

Article 1

Without prejudice to Article 3, Directive 94/45/EC shall apply to the United Kingdom of Great Britain and Northern Ireland.

[3919]

Article 2

(Amended Council Directive 94/45/EC, Art 5(2)(b), and is now spent following the substitution of that sub-paragraph by Council Directive 2006/109/EC (see **[3858]***).)*

Article 3

1. The obligations resulting from this Directive shall not apply to Community-scale undertakings or Community-scale groups of undertakings, which, solely by virtue of

Article 1, fall within the scope of this Directive, provided that, on the date laid down in Article 4(1) or the date of its transposition in the Member State in question, where this is earlier than the said date, there is already an agreement covering the entire workforce providing for the transnational information and consultation of employees.

2. When the agreements referred to in paragraph 1 expire, the parties to those agreements may decide jointly to renew them. Where this is not the case, Directive 94/45/EC, as extended by this Directive, shall apply.

[3920]

Article 4

1. Member States shall bring into force the laws, regulations and administrative provisions necessary to comply with this Directive no later than 15 December 1999 or shall ensure, by that date at the latest, that management and labour introduce the required provisions by way of agreement, the Member States being obliged to take all necessary steps enabling them at all times to guarantee the results imposed by this Directive. They shall forthwith inform the Commission thereof.

2. When Member States adopt these measures, they shall contain a reference to this Directive or shall be accompanied by such reference on the occasion of their official publication. The methods of making such reference shall be laid down by the Member States.

[3921]

Article 5

This Directive is addressed to the Member States.

[3922]

COUNCIL DIRECTIVE

of 15 December 1997

amending and extending, to the United Kingdom of Great Britain and Northern Ireland, Directive 96/34/EC on the framework agreement on parental leave concluded by UNICE, CEEP and the ETUC

(97/75/EC)

NOTES

Date of publication in OJ: OJ L10, 16.1.98, p 24.

The date by which domestic implementation of Council Directive 96/34/EC in the UK was required was 15 December 1999: see Art 2(1A) of Directive 96/34/EC, as inserted by Art 2 below. For the domestic implementation of this Directive, see the Employment Rights Act 1996, ss 57A, 57B (as inserted by the Employment Relations Act 1999, ss 7, 8, Sch 4, Pts I, II), and 76–80, at **[1084]**, **[1085]**, and **[1111]**–**[1115]**. Directive 96/34/EC is at **[3905]**.

THE COUNCIL OF THE EUROPEAN UNION,

Having regard to the Treaty establishing the European Community, and in particular Article 100 thereof,

Having regard to the proposal from the Commission,[1]

Having regard to the opinion of the European Parliament,[2]

Having regard to the opinion of the Economic and Social Committee,[3]

Whereas the Council, acting in accordance with the Agreement on social policy annexed to Protocol 14 to the Treaty, and in particular Article 4(2) thereof, adopted Directive 96/34/EC;[4] whereas, as a result, the said Directive does not apply to the United Kingdom of Great Britain and Northern Ireland;

Whereas the Amsterdam European Council, held on 16 and 17 June 1997, noted with approval the agreement of the Intergovernmental Conference to incorporate the Agreement on social policy in the Treaty and also noted that a means had to be found to give legal effect to the wish of the United Kingdom of Great Britain and Northern Ireland to accept the Directives already adopted on the basis of that Agreement before the signature of the Amsterdam Treaty; whereas this Directive seeks to achieve this aim by extending Directive 96/34/EC to the United Kingdom;

Whereas the fact that Directive 96/34/EC is not applicable in the United Kingdom directly affects the functioning of the internal market; whereas implementation of the framework agreement annexed to the said Directive and, in particular, the principle of reconciliation of parental and professional responsibilities for working parents, in all the Member States will improve the functioning of the internal market;

Whereas implementation of the framework agreement aims, in particular, at achieving the objective of equal treatment between men and women with regard to labour opportunities and treatment at work, and the reconciliation of working and family life;

Whereas the adoption of this Directive will make Directive 96/34/EC applicable in the United Kingdom; whereas, from the date on which this Directive enters into force, the term 'Member States' in Directive 96/34/EC should be construed as including the United Kingdom,

NOTES

[1] OJ C335, 6.11.97.
[2] OJ C371, 8.12.97.
[3] OJ C355, 21.11.97.
[4] OJ L145, 19.6.96, p 4.

HAS ADOPTED THIS DIRECTIVE—

Article 1

Without prejudice to Article 2, Directive 96/34/EC shall apply to the United Kingdom of Great Britain and Northern Ireland.

[3923]

Article 2

(*Amends Council Directive 96/34/EC, Art 2 at* **[3906]**.)

Article 3

This Directive is addressed to the Member States.

[3924]

COUNCIL DIRECTIVE

of 15 December 1997

on the burden of proof in cases of discrimination based on sex

(97/80/EC)

NOTES

Date of publication in OJ: OJ L14, 20.1.98, p 6.

This Directive is repealed, with effect from 15 August 2009, by the Directive of the European Parliament and of the Council on the implementation of the principle of equal opportunities and equal treatment of men and women in matters of employment and occupation (recast) (Directive 2006/54/EC at **[4122]** et seq). The 2006 Directive consolidates and updates the four major Directives on gender equality; ie, this Directive, the Equal Pay Directive (75/117/EEC), the Equal Treatment Directive (76/207/EEC), and the Directive on Equal Treatment in Occupational Social Security Schemes (86/378/EEC). These Directives are repealed by Art 34 of, and Annex I, Pt A to, the 2006 Directive, with effect from 15 August 2009 (see **[4155]** and **[4158]**).

This Directive was extended to the UK by Directive 98/52/EC at **[3954A]**; see Art 7 at **[3931]**. For the domestic implementation of this Directive, see the Sex Discrimination Act 1975, ss 1, 3, 63A, 66A, at **[100]**, **[103]**, **[178]**, **[180A]**, as substituted or inserted by the Sex Discrimination (Indirect Discrimination and Burden of Proof) Regulations 2001, SI 2001/2660.

THE COUNCIL OF THE EUROPEAN UNION,

Having regard to the Agreement on social policy annexed to the Protocol (*No 14*) *on social policy annexed to the Treaty establishing the European Community, and in particular Article* 2(2) *thereof,*

Having regard to the proposal from the Commission,[1]

Having regard to the opinion of the Economic and Social Committee,[2]

Acting, in accordance with the procedure laid down in Article 189c of the Treaty, in cooperation with the European Parliament,[3]

(1) Whereas, on the basis of the Protocol on social policy annexed to the Treaty, the Member States, with the exception of the United Kingdom of Great Britain and Northern Ireland (hereinafter called 'the Member States'), wishing to implement the 1989 Social Charter, have concluded an Agreement on social policy;

(2) Whereas the Community Charter of the Fundamental Social Rights of Workers recognizes the importance of combating every form of discrimination, including discrimination on grounds of sex, colour, race, opinions and beliefs;

(3) Whereas paragraph 16 of the Community Charter of the Fundamental Social Rights of Workers on equal treatment for men and women, provides, inter alia, that 'action should be intensified to ensure the implementation of the principle of equality for men and women as regards, in particular, access to employment, remuneration, working conditions, social protection, education, vocational training and career development';

(4) Whereas, in accordance with Article 3(2) of the Agreement on social policy, the Commission has consulted management and labour at Community level on the possible direction of Community action on the burden of proof in cases of discrimination based on sex;

(5) Whereas the Commission, considering Community action advisable after such consultation, once again consulted management and labour on the content of the proposal contemplated in accordance with Article 3(3) of the same Agreement; whereas the latter have sent their opinions to the Commission;

(6) Whereas, after the second round of consultation, neither management nor labour have informed the Commission of their wish to initiate the process—possibly leading to an agreement—provided for in Article 4 of the same Agreement;

(7) Whereas, in accordance with Article 1 of the Agreement, the Community and the Member States have set themselves the objective, inter alia, of improving living and working conditions; whereas effective implementation of the principle of equal treatment for men and women would contribute to the achievement of that aim;

(8) Whereas the principle of equal treatment was stated in Article 119 of the Treaty, in Council Directive 75/117/EEC of 10 February 1975 on the approximation of the laws of the Member States relating to the application of the principle of equal pay for men and women[4] *and in Council Directive 76/207/EEC of 9 February 1976 on the implementation of the principle of equal treatment for men and women as regards access to employment, vocational training and promotion and working conditions;*[5]

(9) Whereas Council Directive 92/85/EEC of 19 October 1992 on the introduction of measures to encourage improvements in the safety and health at work of pregnant workers and workers who have recently given birth or are breastfeeding[6] *also contributes to the effective implementation of the principle of equal treatment for men and women; whereas that Directive should not work to the detriment of the aforementioned Directives on equal treatment; whereas, therefore, female workers covered by that Directive should likewise benefit from the adaptation of the rules on the burden of proof;*

(10) Whereas Council Directive 96/34/EC of 3 June 1996 on the framework agreement on parental leave concluded by UNICE, CEEP and the ETUC,[7] *is also based on the principle of equal treatment for men and women;*

(11) Whereas the references to 'judicial process' and 'court' cover mechanisms by means of which disputes may be submitted for examination and decision to independent bodies which may hand down decisions that are binding on the parties to those disputes;

(12) Whereas the expression 'out-of-court procedures' means in particular procedures such as conciliation and mediation;

(13) Whereas the appreciation of the facts from which it may be presumed that there has been direct or indirect discrimination is a matter for national judicial or other competent bodies, in accordance with national law or practice;

(14) Whereas it is for the Member States to introduce, at any appropriate stage of the proceedings, rules of evidence which are more favourable to plaintiffs;

(15) Whereas it is necessary to take account of the specific features of certain Member States' legal systems, inter alia where an inference of discrimination is drawn if the respondent fails to produce evidence that satisfies the court or other competent authority that there has been no breach of the principle of equal treatment;

(16) Whereas Member States need not apply the rules on the burden of proof to proceedings in which it is for the court or other competent body to investigate the facts of the case; whereas the procedures thus referred to are those in which the plaintiff is not required to prove the facts, which it is for the court or competent body to investigate;

(17) Whereas plaintiffs could be deprived of any effective means of enforcing the principle of equal treatment before the national courts if the effect of introducing evidence of an apparent discrimination were not to impose upon the respondent the burden of proving that his practice is not in fact discriminatory;

(18) Whereas the Court of Justice of the European Communities has therefore held that the rules on the burden of proof must be adapted when there is a prima facie case of discrimination and that, for the principle of equal treatment to be applied effectively, the burden of proof must shift back to the respondent when evidence of such discrimination is brought;

(19) Whereas it is all the more difficult to prove discrimination when it is indirect; whereas it is therefore important to define indirect discrimination;

(20) Whereas the aim of adequately adapting the rules on the burden of proof has not been achieved satisfactorily in all Member States and, in accordance with the principle of subsidiarity stated in Article 3b of the Treaty and with that of proportionality, that aim must be attained at Community level; whereas this Directive confines itself to the minimum action required and does not go beyond what is necessary for that purpose,

NOTES

Repealed as noted at the beginning of this Directive.

1 OJ C332, 7.11.96, p 11 and OJ C185, 18.6.97, p 21.
2 OJ C133, 28.4.97, p 34.
3 Opinion of the European Parliament of 10 April 1997 (OJ C132, 28.4.97, p 215), Common Position of the Council of 24 July 1997 (OJ C307, 8.10.97, p 6) and Decision of the European Parliament of 6 November 1997 (OJ C358, 24.11.97).
4 OJ L45, 19.2.75, p 19.
5 OJ L39, 14.2.76, p 40.
6 OJ L348, 28.11.92, p 1.
7 OJ L145, 19.6.96, p 4.

HAS ADOPTED THIS DIRECTIVE—

Article 1

Aim

The aim of this Directive shall be to ensure that the measures taken by the Member States to implement the principle of equal treatment are made more effective, in order to enable all persons who consider themselves wronged because the principle of equal treatment has not been applied to them to have their rights asserted by judicial process after possible recourse to other competent bodies.

[3925]

NOTES

Repealed as noted at the beginning of this Directive.

Article 2

Definitions

1. For the purposes of this Directive, the principle of equal treatment shall mean that there shall be no discrimination whatsoever based on sex, either directly or indirectly.

2. For purposes of the principle of equal treatment referred to in paragraph 1, indirect discrimination shall exist where an apparently neutral provision, criterion or practice disadvantages a substantially higher proportion of the members of one sex unless that provision, criterion or practice is appropriate and necessary and can be justified by objective factors unrelated to sex.

[3926]

NOTES

Repealed as noted at the beginning of this Directive.

Article 3

Scope

1. This Directive shall apply to—

(*a*) *the situations covered by Article 119 of the Treaty and by Directives 75/117/EEC, 76/207/EEC and, insofar as discrimination based on sex is concerned, 92/85/EEC and 96/34/EC;*

(*b*) *any civil or administrative procedure concerning the public or private sector which provides for means of redress under national law pursuant to the measures referred to in (a) with the exception of out-of-court procedures of a voluntary nature or provided for in national law.*

2. This Directive shall not apply to criminal procedures, unless otherwise provided by the Member States.

[3927]

NOTES

Repealed as noted at the beginning of this Directive.
Article 119: see now Art 141 at **[3525]**.

Article 4

Burden of proof

1. Member States shall take such measures as are necessary, in accordance with their national judicial systems, to ensure that, when persons who consider themselves wronged because the principle of equal treatment has not been applied to them establish, before a court or other competent authority, facts from which it may be presumed that there has been direct or indirect discrimination, it shall be for the respondent to prove that there has been no breach of the principle of equal treatment.

2. This Directive shall not prevent Member States from introducing rules of evidence which are more favourable to plaintiffs.

3. Member States need not apply paragraph 1 to proceedings in which it is for the court or competent body to investigate the facts of the case.

[3928]

NOTES

Repealed as noted at the beginning of this Directive.

Article 5

Information

Member States shall ensure that measures taken pursuant to this Directive, together with the provisions already in force, are brought to the attention of all the persons concerned by all appropriate means.

[3929]

NOTES

Repealed as noted at the beginning of this Directive.

Article 6

Non-regression

Implementation of this Directive shall under no circumstances be sufficient grounds for a reduction in the general level of protection of workers in the areas to which it applies, without prejudice to the Member States' right to respond to changes in the situation by introducing laws, regulations and administrative provisions which differ from those in force on the notification of this Directive, provided that the minimum requirements of this Directive are complied with.

[3930]

NOTES

Repealed as noted at the beginning of this Directive.

PART 3

Article 7

Implementation

The Member States shall bring into force the laws, regulations and administrative provisions necessary for them to comply with this Directive by 1 January 2001. They shall immediately inform the Commission thereof.

[As regards the United Kingdom of Great Britain and Northern Ireland, the date of 1 January 2001 in paragraph 1 shall be replaced by 22 July 2001.]

When the Member States adopt those measures they shall contain a reference to this Directive or shall be accompanied by such a reference on the occasion of their official publication. The methods of making such references shall be laid down by the Member States.

The Member States shall communicate to the Commission, within two years of the entry into force of this Directive, all the information necessary for the Commission to draw up a report to the European Parliament and the Council on the application of this Directive.

[3931]

NOTES

Repealed as noted at the beginning of this Directive.
Words in square brackets inserted by Council Directive 98/52/EC, Art 2.

Article 8

This Directive is addressed to the Member States.

[3932]

NOTES

Repealed as noted at the beginning of this Directive.

COUNCIL DIRECTIVE

of 15 December 1997

concerning the Framework Agreement on part-time work concluded by UNICE, CEEP and the ETUC

(97/81/EC)

NOTES

Date of publication in OJ: OJ L14, 20.1.98, p 9.

This Directive implements a Framework Agreement made by the Social Partners (the Union of Industrial and Employers' Confederations of Europe (UNICE)), the European Centre of Enterprises with Public Participation (CEEP), and the European Trade Union Confederation (ETUC) in accordance with Art 4 of the Agreement on Social Policy annexed to Protocol 14 to the Treaty of Union 1992 and, therefore, did not bind the United Kingdom. It was subsequently extended to the UK by Directive 98/23/EC at **[3940]** with a required date of transposition of 7 April 2000 (see Art 2(1A) of this Directive at **[3934]**). For the domestic implementation of this Directive as extended to the UK by Directive 98/23/EC, see the Employment Relations Act 1999, ss 19–21 at **[1439]**–**[1441]** and the Part-time Workers (Prevention of Less Favourable Treatment) Regulations 2000, SI 2000/1551 at **[2637]**.

THE COUNCIL OF THE EUROPEAN UNION,

Having regard to the Agreement on social policy annexed to the Protocol (No 14) on social policy, annexed to the Treaty establishing the European Community, and in particular Article 4(2) thereof,

Having regard to the proposal from the Commission,

(1) Whereas on the basis of the Protocol on social policy annexed to the Treaty establishing the European Community, the Member States, with the exception of the United Kingdom of Great Britain and Northern Ireland (hereinafter referred to as 'the Member States'), wishing to continue along the path laid down in the 1989 Social Charter, have concluded an agreement on social policy;

(2) Whereas management and labour (the social partners) may, in accordance with Article 4(2) of the Agreement on social policy, request jointly that agreements at Community level be implemented by a Council decision on a proposal from the Commission;

(3) Whereas point 7 of the Community Charter of the Fundamental Social Rights of Workers provides, *inter alia*, that 'the completion of the internal market must lead to an improvement in the living and working conditions of workers in the European Community. This process must result from an approximation of these conditions while the improvement is being maintained, as regards in particular (...) forms of employment other than open-ended contracts, such as fixed-term contracts, part-time working, temporary work and seasonal work';

(4) Whereas the Council has not reached a decision on the proposal for a Directive on certain employment relationships with regard to distortions of competition,[1] as amended,[2] nor on the proposal for a Directive on certain employment relationships with regard to working conditions;[3]

(5) Whereas the conclusions of the Essen European Council stressed the need to take measures to promote employment and equal opportunities for women and men, and called for measures with a view to increasing the employment-intensiveness of growth, in particular by a more flexible organization of work in a way which fulfils both the wishes of employees and the requirements of competition;

(6) Whereas the Commission, in accordance with Article 3(2) of the Agreement on social policy, has consulted management and labour on the possible direction of Community action with regard to flexible working time and job security;

(7) Whereas the Commission, considering after such consultation that Community action was desirable, once again consulted management and labour at Community level on the substance of the envisaged proposal in accordance with Article 3(3) of the said Agreement;

(8) Whereas the general cross-industry organizations, the Union of Industrial and Employer's Confederations of Europe (UNICE), the European Centre of Enterprises with Public Participation (CEEP) and the European Trade Union Confederation (ETUC) informed the Commission in their joint letter of 19 June 1996 of their desire to initiate the procedure provided for in Article 4 of the Agreement on social policy; whereas they asked the Commission, in a joint letter dated 12 March 1997, for a further three months; whereas the Commission complied with this request;

(9) Whereas the said cross-industry organizations concluded, on 6 June 1997, a Framework Agreement on part-time work; whereas they forwarded to the Commission their joint request to implement this Framework Agreement by a Council decision on a proposal from the Commission, in accordance with Article 4(2) of the said Agreement;

(10) Whereas the Council, in its Resolution of 6 December 1994 on prospects for a European Union social policy: contribution to economic and social convergence in the Union,[4] asked management and labour to make use of the opportunities for concluding agreements, since they are as a rule closer to social reality and to social problems;

(11) Whereas the signatory parties wished to conclude a framework agreement on part-time work setting out the general principles and minimum requirements for part-time working; whereas they have demonstrated their desire to establish a general framework for eliminating discrimination against part-time workers and to contribute to developing the potential for part-time work on a basis which is acceptable for employers and workers alike;

(12) Whereas the social partners wished to give particular attention to part-time work, while at the same time indicating that it was their intention to consider the need for similar agreements for other flexible forms of work;

(13) Whereas, in the conclusions of the Amsterdam European Council, the Heads of State and Government of the European Union strongly welcomed the agreement concluded by the social partners on part-time work;

(14) Whereas the proper instrument for implementing the Framework Agreement is a Directive within the meaning of Article 189 of the Treaty; whereas it therefore binds the Member States as to the result to be achieved, whilst leaving national authorities the choice of form and methods;

(15) Whereas, in accordance with the principles of subsidiarity and proportionality as set out in Article 3(b) of the Treaty, the objectives of this Directive cannot be sufficiently achieved by the Member States and can therefore be better achieved by the Community; whereas this Directive does not go beyond what is necessary for the attainment of those objectives;

(16) Whereas, with regard to terms used in the Framework Agreement which are not specifically defined therein, this Directive leaves Member States free to define those terms in accordance with national law and practice, as is the case for other social policy Directives using similar terms, providing that the said definitions respect the content of the Frame-work Agreement;

(17) Whereas the Commission has drafted its proposal for a Directive, in accordance with its Communication of 14 December 1993 concerning the application of the Protocol (No 14) on social policy and its Communication of 18 September 1996 concerning the development of the social dialogue at Community level, taking into account the representative status of the signatory parties and the legality of each clause of the Framework Agreement;

(18) Whereas the Commission has drafted its proposal for a Directive in compliance with Article 2(2) of the Agreement on social policy which provides that Directives in the social policy domain 'shall avoid imposing administrative, financial and legal constraints in a way which would hold back the creation and development of small and medium-sized undertakings';

(19) Whereas the Commission, in accordance with its Communication of 14 December 1993 concerning the application of the Protocol (No 14) on social policy, informed the European Parliament by sending it the text of its proposal for a Directive containing the Framework Agreement;

(20) Whereas the Commission also informed the Economic and Social Committee;

(21) Whereas Clause 6.1 of the Framework Agreement provides that Member States and/or the social partners may maintain or introduce more favourable provisions;

(22) Whereas Clause 6.2 of the Framework Agreement provides that implementation of this Directive may not serve to justify any regression in relation to the situation which already exists in each Member State;

(23) Whereas the Community Charter of the Fundamental Social Rights of Workers recognizes the importance of the fight against all forms of discrimination, especially based on sex, colour, race, opinion and creed;

(24) Whereas Article F(2) of the Treaty on European Union states that the Union shall respect fundamental rights, as guaranteed by the European Convention for the Protection of Human Rights and Fundamental Freedoms and as they result from the constitutional traditions common to the Member States, as general principles of Community law;

(25) Whereas the Member States may entrust the social partners, at their joint request, with the implementation of this Directive, provided that the Member States take all the necessary steps to ensure that they can at all times guarantee the results imposed by this Directive;

(26) Whereas the implementation of the Framework Agreement contributes to achieving the objectives under Article 1 of the Agreement on social policy,

NOTES

1 OJ C224, 8.9.90, p 6.
2 OJ C305, 5.12.90, p 8.
3 OJ C224, 8.9.90, p 4.
4 OJ C368, 23.12.94, p 6.

HAS ADOPTED THIS DIRECTIVE—

Article 1

The purpose of this Directive is to implement the Framework Agreement on part-time work concluded on 6 June 1997 between the general cross-industry organizations (UNICE, CEEP and the ETUC) annexed hereto.

[3933]

Article 2

1. Member States shall bring into force the laws, regulations and administrative provisions necessary to comply with this Directive not later than 20 January 2000, or shall ensure that, by that date at the latest, the social partners have introduced the necessary measures by agreement, the Member States being required to take any necessary measures to enable them at any time to be in a position to guarantee the results imposed by this Directive. They shall forthwith inform the Commission thereof.

Member States may have a maximum of one more year, if necessary, to take account of special difficulties or implementation by a collective agreement.

They shall inform the Commission forthwith in such circumstances.

When Member States adopt the measures referred to in the first subparagraph, they shall contain a reference to this Directive or shall be accompanied by such reference on the occasion of their official publication. The methods of making such a reference shall be laid down by the Member States.

[1A. As regards the United Kingdom of Great Britain and Northern Ireland, the date of 20 January 2000 in paragraph 1 shall be replaced by the date of 7 April 2000.]

2. Member States shall communicate to the Commission the text of the main provisions of domestic law which they have adopted or which they adopt in the field governed by this Directive.

[3934]

NOTES

Para 1A: inserted by Council Directive 98/23/EC, Art 2.

Article 3

This Directive shall enter into force on the day of its publication in the *Official Journal of the European Communities*.

[3935]

Article 4

This Directive is addressed to the Member States.

[3936]

ANNEX

UNION OF INDUSTRIAL AND EMPLOYERS' CONFEDERATIONS OF EUROPE
EUROPEAN TRADE UNION CONFEDERATION
EUROPEAN CENTRE OF ENTERPRISES WITH PUBLIC PARTICIPATION
FRAMEWORK AGREEMENT ON PART-TIME WORK

Preamble

This Framework Agreement is a contribution to the overall European strategy on employment. Part-time work has had an important impact on employment in recent years. For this reason, the parties to this agreement have given priority attention to this form of work. It is the intention of the parties to consider the need for similar agreements relating to other forms of flexible work.

Recognizing the diversity of situations in Member States and acknowledging that part-time work is a feature of employment in certain sectors and activities, this Agreement sets out the general principles and minimum requirements relating to part-time work. It illustrates the willingness of the social partners to establish a general framework for the elimination of discrimination against part-time workers and to assist the development of opportunities for part-time working on a basis acceptable to employers and workers.

This Agreement relates to employment conditions of part-time workers recognizing that matters concerning statutory social security are for decision by the Member States. In the context of the principle of non-discrimination, the parties to this Agreement have noted the Employment Declaration of the Dublin European Council of December 1996, wherein the Council inter alia emphasized the need to make social security systems more employment-friendly by 'developing social protection systems capable of adapting to new patterns of work and of providing appropriate protection to people engaged in such work'. The parties to this Agreement consider that effect should be given to this Declaration.

ETUC, UNICE and CEEP request the Commission to submit this Framework Agreement to the Council for a decision making these requirements binding in the Member States which are party to the Agreement on social policy annexed to the Protocol (No 14) on social policy annexed to the Treaty establishing the European Community.

The parties to this Agreement ask the Commission, in its proposal to implement this Agreement, to request that Member States adopt the laws, regulations and administrative provisions necessary to comply with the Council decision within a period of two years from its adoption or ensure[1] that the social partners establish the necessary measures by way of agreement by the end of this period. Member States may, if necessary to take account of particular difficulties or implementation by collective agreement, have up to a maximum of one additional year to comply with this provision.

Without prejudice to the role of national courts and the Court of Justice, the parties to this agreement request that any matter relating to the interpretation of this agreement at European level should, in the first instance, be referred by the Commission to them for an opinion.

[3937]

PART 3

NOTES

[1] Within the meaning of Article 2(4) of the agreement on social policy of the Treaty establishing the European Community.

General considerations

1. Having regard to the Agreement on social policy annexed to the Protocol (No 14) on social policy annexed to the Treaty establishing the European Community, and in particular Articles 3(4) and 4(2) thereof;

2. Whereas Article 4(2) of the Agreement on social policy provides that agreements concluded at Community level may be implemented, at the joint request of the signatory parties, by a Council decision on a proposal from the Commission.

3. Whereas, in its second consultation document on flexibility of working time and security for workers, the Commission announced its intention to propose a legally binding Community measure;

4. Whereas the conclusions of the European Council meeting in Essen emphasized the need for measures to promote both employment and equal opportunities for women and men, and called for measures aimed at 'increasing the employment intensiveness of growth, in particular by more flexible organization of work in a way which fulfils both the wishes of employees and the requirements of competition';

5. Whereas the parties to this agreement attach importance to measures which would facilitate access to part-time work for men and women in order to prepare for retirement, reconcile professional and family life, and take up education and training opportunities to improve their skills and career opportunities for the mutual benefit of employers and workers and in a manner which would assist the development of enterprises;

6. Whereas this Agreement refers back to Member States and social partners for the arrangements for the application of these general principles, minimum requirements and provisions, in order to take account of the situation in each Member State;

7. Whereas this Agreement takes into consideration the need to improve social policy requirements, to enhance the competitiveness of the Community economy and to avoid imposing administrative, financial and legal constraints in a way which would hold back the creation and development of small and medium-sized undertakings;

8. Whereas the social partners are best placed to find solutions that correspond to the needs of both employers and workers and must therefore be given a special role in the implementation and application of this Agreement.

[3938]

THE SIGNATORY PARTIES HAVE AGREED THE FOLLOWING:

Clause 1: Purpose

The purpose of this Framework Agreement is—

(a) to provide for the removal of discrimination against part-time workers and to improve the quality of part-time work;

(b) to facilitate the development of part-time work on a voluntary basis and to contribute to the flexible organization of working time in a manner which takes into account the needs of employers and workers.

Clause 2: Scope

1. This Agreement applies to part-time workers who have an employment contract or employment relationship as defined by the law, collective agreement or practice in force in each Member State.

2. Member States, after consultation with the social partners in accordance with national law, collective agreements or practice, and/or the social partners at the appropriate level in conformity with national industrial relations practice may, for objective reasons, exclude wholly or partly from the terms of this Agreement part-time workers who work on a casual basis. Such exclusions should be reviewed periodically to establish if the objective reasons for making them remain valid.

Clause 3: Definitions

For the purpose of this agreement—

1. The term 'part-time worker' refers to an employee whose normal hours of work, calculated on a weekly basis or on average over a period of employment of up to one year, are less than the normal hours of work of a comparable full-time worker.
2. The term 'comparable full-time worker' means a full-time worker in the same establishment having the same type of employment contract or relationship, who is engaged in the same or a similar work/occupation, due regard being given to other considerations which may include seniority and qualification/skills.

Where there is no comparable full-time worker in the same establishment, the comparison shall be made by reference to the applicable collective agreement or, where there is no applicable collective agreement, in accordance with national law, collective agreements or practice.

Clause 4: Principle of non-discrimination

1. In respect of employment conditions, part-time workers shall not be treated in a less favourable manner than comparable full-time workers solely because they work part time unless different treatment is justified on objective grounds.

2. Where appropriate, the principle of *pro rata temporis* shall apply.

3. The arrangements for the application of this clause shall be defined by the Member States and/or social partners, having regard to European legislation, national law, collective agreements and practice.

4. Where justified by objective reasons, Member States after consultation of the social partners in accordance with national law, collective agreements or practice and/or social partners may, where appropriate, make access to particular conditions of employment subject to a period of service, time worked or earnings qualification. Qualifications relating to access by part-time workers to particular conditions of employment should be reviewed periodically having regard to the principle of non-discrimination as expressed in Clause 4.1.

Clause 5: Opportunities for part-time work

1. In the context of Clause 1 of this Agreement and of the principle of non-discrimination between part-time and full-time workers—

(a) Member States, following consultations with the social partners in accordance with national law or practice, should identify and review obstacles of a legal or administrative nature which may limit the opportunities for part-time work and, where appropriate, eliminate them;

(b) the social partners, acting within their sphere of competence and through the procedures set out in collective agreements, should identify and review obstacles which may limit opportunities for part-time work and, where appropriate, eliminate them.

2. A worker's refusal to transfer from full-time to part-time work or vice-versa should not in itself constitute a valid reason for termination of employment, without prejudice to termination in accordance with national law, collective agreements and practice, for other reasons such as may arise from the operational requirements of the establishment concerned.

3. As far as possible, employers should give consideration to—

(a) requests by workers to transfer from full-time to part-time work that becomes available in the establishment;

(b) requests by workers to transfer from part-time to full-time work or to increase their working time should the opportunity arise;

(c) the provision of timely information on the availability of part-time and full-time positions in the establishment in order to facilitate transfers from full-time to part-time or vice versa;

(d) measures to facilitate access to part-time work at all levels of the enterprise, including skilled and managerial positions, and where appropriate, to facilitate access by part-time workers to vocational training to enhance career opportunities and occupational mobility;

(e) the provision of appropriate information to existing bodies representing workers about part-time working in the enterprise.

Clause 6: Provisions on implementation

1. Member States and/or social partners may maintain or introduce more favourable provisions than set out in this agreement.

2. Implementation of the provisions of this Agreement shall not constitute valid grounds for reducing the general level of protection afforded to workers in the field of this agreement. This does not prejudice the right of Member States and/or social partners to develop different legislative, regulatory or contractual provisions, in the light of changing circumstances, and does not prejudice the application of Clause 5.1 as long as the principle of non-discrimination as expressed in Clause 4.1 is complied with.

3. This Agreement does not prejudice the right of the social partners to conclude, at the appropriate level, including European level, agreements adapting and/or complementing the provisions of this Agreement in a manner which will take account of the specific needs of the social partners concerned.

4. This Agreement shall be without prejudice to any more specific Community provisions, and in particular Community provisions concerning equal treatment or opportunities for men and women.

5. The prevention and settlement of disputes and grievances arising from the application of this Agreement shall be dealt with in accordance with national law, collective agreements and practice.

6. The signatory parties shall review this Agreement, five years after the date of the Council decision, if requested by one of the parties to this Agreement. **[3939]**

COUNCIL DIRECTIVE

of 7 April 1998

on the extension of Directive 97/81/EC on the framework agreement on part-time work concluded by UNICE, CEEP and the ETUC to the United Kingdom of Great Britain and Northern Ireland

(98/23/EC)

NOTES

Date of publication in OJ: OJ L131, 5.5.98, p 10.

The date given for the transposition of the principal Directive (97/81/EC) which this Directive extends to the United Kingdom is 7 April 2000 (see Art 2(1A) of the 1997 Directive at **[3934]**). For the domestic implementation of Directive 97/81/EC, as extended to the UK by this Directive, see the Employment Relations Act 1999, ss 19–21 at **[1439]**–**[1441]** and the Part-time Workers (Prevention of Less Favourable Treatment) Regulations 2000, SI 2000/1551 at **[2637]**.

THE COUNCIL OF THE EUROPEAN UNION,

Having regard to the Treaty establishing the European Community, and in particular Article 100 thereof,

Having regard to the proposal from the Commission,

Having regard to the opinion of the European Parliament,[1]

Having regard to the opinion of the Economic and Social Committee,[2]

Whereas the Council, acting in accordance with the Agreement on Social Policy annexed to Protocol (No 14) on Social Policy annexed to the EC Treaty, and in particular Article 4(2) thereof, adopted Directive 97/81/EC,[3] whereas, as a result, the said Directive does not apply to the United Kingdom of Great Britain and Northern Ireland;

Whereas the Amsterdam European Council held on 16 and 17 June 1997, noted with approval the agreement of the Intergovernmental Conference to incorporate the Agreement on Social Policy in the EC Treaty; whereas it pointed out that a means had to be found to give legal effect to the wish of the United Kingdom to accept the Directives already adopted on the basis of that agreement and those which might be adopted before the entry into force of the new treaty;

Whereas at the Council of 24 July 1997, the Council and the Commission agreed to put into effect the conclusions adopted at the Amsterdam European Council; whereas they also agreed to apply the same procedure, *mutatis mutandis*, to future Directives adopted on the basis of the Agreement on Social Policy; whereas this Directive seeks to achieve this aim by extending Directive 97/81/EC to the United Kingdom;

Whereas the fact that Directive 97/81/EC is not applicable in the United Kingdom of Great Britain and Northern Ireland directly affects the functioning of the internal market; whereas the implementation of the framework agreement annexed to the said Directive, and in particular the principle of non-discrimination between part-time and full-time workers in all the Member States, will improve the functioning of the internal market;

Whereas the adoption of this Directive will make Directive 97/81/EC applicable in the United Kingdom; whereas, from the date on which this Directive enters into force, the term 'Member States' in Directive 97/81/EC should be construed as including the United Kingdom;

Whereas the United Kingdom should benefit from the same period of two years that was granted to other Member States to bring into force the necessary provisions to comply with Directive 97/81/EC,

NOTES

[1] Opinion delivered on 1 April 1998 (not yet published in the Official Journal).
[2] Opinion delivered on 25 March 1998 (not yet published in the Official Journal).
[3] OJ L14, 20.1.98, p 9.

HAS ADOPTED THIS DIRECTIVE—

Article 1

Without prejudice to Article 2, Directive 97/81/EC shall apply to the United Kingdom of Great Britain and Northern Ireland.

[3940]

Article 2

(*Amends Directive 97/81/EC, Art 2 at* **[3934]**.)

Article 3

This Directive is addressed to the Member States.

[3941]

COUNCIL DIRECTIVE

of 29 June 1998

on safeguarding the supplementary pension rights of employed and self-employed persons moving within the Community

(98/49/EC)

NOTES

Date of publication in OJ: OJ L209, 25.7.98, p 46.

For the domestic implementation of this Directive see the Occupational Pension Schemes (Preservation of Benefit) Regulations 1991, SI 1991/167.

THE COUNCIL OF THE EUROPEAN UNION,

Having regard to the Treaty establishing the European Community, and in particular Articles 51 and 235 thereof,

Having regard to the proposal from the Commission,[1]

Having regard to the opinion of the European Parliament,[2]

Having regard to the opinion of the Economic and Social Committee,[3]

(1) Whereas one of the fundamental freedoms of the Community is the free movement of persons; whereas the Treaty provides that the Council shall, acting unanimously, adopt such measures in the field of social security as are necessary to provide freedom of movement of workers;

PART 3

(2) Whereas the social protection of workers is ensured by statutory social security schemes complemented by supplementary social security schemes;

(3) Whereas the legislation already adopted by the Council with a view to protecting the social security rights of workers moving within the Community and of members of their family, namely Council Regulations (EEC) No 1408/71 of 14 June 1971 on the application of social security schemes to employed persons, to self-employed persons and to members of their families moving within the Community[4] and (EEC) No 574/72 of 21 March 1972 laying down the procedure for implementing Regulation (EEC) No 1408/71 on the application of social security schemes to employed persons, to self-employed persons and to members of their families moving within the Community,[5] concern only statutory pension schemes; whereas the system of coordination provided for in those Regulations does not extend to supplementary pension schemes, except for schemes which are covered by the term 'legislation' as defined by the first subparagraph of Article 1(j) of Regulation (EEC) No 1408/71 or in respect of which a Member State makes a declaration under that Article;

(4) Whereas the Council has a wide discretion regarding the choice of the most appropriate measures for attaining the objective of Article 51 of the Treaty; and whereas the system of coordination provided for in Regulations (EEC) No 1408/71 and (EEC) No 574/72, and in particular the rules of aggregation, are not appropriate to supplementary pension schemes, except for schemes which are covered by the term 'legislation' as defined by the first subparagraph of Article 1(j) of Regulation (EEC) No 1408/71 or in respect of which a Member State makes a declaration under that Article, and should therefore be subject to specific measures, of which this Directive is the first, in order to take account of their special nature and characteristics and the diversity of such schemes within and between Member States;

(5) Whereas no pension or benefit should be subject to both the provisions of this Directive and those of Regulations (EEC) No 1408/71 and (EEC) No 574/72, and therefore any supplementary pension scheme which comes within the scope of those Regulations, because a Member State has made a declaration to that effect under Article 1(j) of Regulation (EEC) No 1408/71, cannot be subject to the provisions of this Directive;

(6) Whereas in its Recommendation 92/442/EEC of 27 July 1992 on the convergence of social protection objectives and policies[6] the Council recommended that Member States should 'promote, where necessary, changes to the conditions governing the acquisition of pension and, especially, supplementary pension rights with a view to eliminating obstacles to the mobility of employed workers';

(7) Whereas a contribution to this objective can be made if workers who move or whose place of employment moves from one Member State to another are guaranteed equal treatment as regards the protection of their supplementary pension rights with workers who remain or whose place of employment changes but remains within the same Member State;

(8) Whereas freedom of movement for persons, which is one of the basic rights enshrined in the Treaty, is not confined to employed persons but also extends to self-employed persons;

(9) Whereas the Treaty does not provide powers other than those of Article 235 to take appropriate measures within the field of social security for self-employed persons;

(10) Whereas, in order to enable the right of free movement to be exercised effectively, workers and others holding entitlement should have certain guarantees for equal treatment regarding the preservation of their vested pension rights deriving from supplementary pension schemes;

(11) Whereas the Member States should take the necessary measures to ensure that benefits under supplementary pension schemes are paid to members and former members thereof as well as others holding entitlement under such schemes in all Member States, given that all restrictions on the free movement of payments and capital are prohibited under Article 73b of the Treaty;

(12) Whereas in order to facilitate the exercise of the right to free movement, national regulations should, where necessary, be adjusted in order to enable contributions to continue to be made to a supplementary pension scheme established in one Member State by or on behalf of workers who are posted to another Member State in accordance with Title II of Regulation (EEC) No 1408/71;

(13) Whereas in this regard the Treaty requires not only the abolition of any discrimination based on nationality between workers of the Member States but also the elimination of any national measure likely to impede or render less attractive for those workers the exercise of the fundamental freedoms guaranteed by the Treaty as interpreted by the Court of Justice of the European Communities in successive judgments;

(14) Whereas workers exercising their right to free movement should be adequately informed by employers, trustees or others responsible for the management of supplementary pension schemes, particularly with regard to the choices and alternatives available to them;

(15) Whereas this Directive is without prejudice to the laws of the Member States concerning collective action to defend the interests of trades and professions;

(16) Whereas, by reason of the diversity of supplementary social security schemes, the Community should lay down only a general framework of objectives and therefore a Directive is the appropriate legal instrument;

(17) Whereas, in accordance with the principles of subsidiarity and proportionality as set out in Article 3b of the Treaty, the objectives of this Directive cannot be sufficiently achieved by the Member States and can therefore be better achieved by the Community; whereas this Directive does not go beyond what is necessary to achieve those objectives,

NOTES

1 OJ C5, 9.1.98, p 4.
2 OJ C152, 18.5.98.
3 OJ C57, 25.5.98, p 26.
4 OJ L149, 5.7.71, p 2. Regulation as last amended by Regulation 1223/98/EC (OJ L168, 13.6.98, p 1).
5 OJ L74, 27.3.72, p 1. Regulation as last amended by Regulation 1223/98/EC (OJ L168, 13.6.98, p 1).
6 OJ L245, 26.8.92, p 49.

HAS ADOPTED THIS DIRECTIVE—

CHAPTER I
OBJECTIVE AND SCOPE

Article 1

The aim of this Directive is to protect the rights of members of supplementary pension schemes who move from one Member State to another, thereby contributing to the removal of obstacles to the free movement of employed and self-employed persons within the Community. Such protection refers to pension rights under both voluntary and compulsory supplementary pension schemes, with the exception of schemes covered by Regulation (EEC) No 1408/71.

[3942]

Article 2

This Directive shall apply to members of supplementary pension schemes and others holding entitlement under such schemes who have acquired or are in the process of acquiring rights in one or more Member States.

[3943]

CHAPTER II
DEFINITIONS

Article 3

For the purpose of this Directive—

(a) 'supplementary pension' means retirement pensions and, where provided for by the rules of a supplementary pension scheme established in conformity with national legislation and practice, invalidity and survivors' benefits, intended to supplement or replace those provided in respect of the same contingencies by statutory social security schemes;

(b) 'supplementary pension scheme' means any occupational pension scheme established in conformity with national legislation and practice such as a group insurance contract or pay-as-you-go scheme agreed by one or more branches or sectors, funded scheme or pension promise backed by book reserves, or any collective or other comparable arrangement intended to provide a supplementary pension for employed or self-employed persons;

(c) 'pension rights' means any benefits to which scheme members and others holding entitlement are entitled under the rules of a supplementary pension scheme and, where applicable, under national legislation;

(d) 'vested pension rights' means any entitlement to benefits obtained after fulfilment of the conditions required by the rules of a supplementary pension scheme and, where applicable, under national legislation;

(e) 'posted worker' means a person who is posted to work in another Member State

PART 3

and who under the terms of Title II of Regulation (EEC) No 1408/71 continues to be subject to the legislation of the Member State of origin, and 'posting' shall be construed accordingly;

(f) 'contribution' means any payment made or deemed to have been made to a supplementary pension scheme.

[3944]

CHAPTER III
MEASURES FOR SAFEGUARDING THE SUPPLEMENTARY PENSION RIGHTS OF WORKERS MOVING WITHIN THE COMMUNITY

Article 4

Equality of treatment as regards preservation of pension rights

Member States shall take the necessary measures to ensure the preservation of vested pension rights for members of a supplementary pension scheme in respect of whom contributions are no longer being made to that scheme as a consequence of their moving from one Member State to another, to the same extent as for members in respect of whom contributions are no longer being made but who remain within the same Member State. This Article shall also apply to other persons holding entitlement under the rules of the supplementary pension scheme in question.

[3945]

Article 5

Cross border payments

Member States shall ensure that, in respect of members of supplementary pension schemes, as well as others holding entitlement under such schemes, supplementary pension schemes make payment in other Member States, net of any taxes and transaction charges which may be applicable, of all benefits due under such schemes.

[3946]

Article 6

Contributions to supplementary pension schemes by and on behalf of posted workers

1. Member States shall adopt such measures as are necessary to enable contributions to continue to be made to a supplementary pension scheme established in a Member State by or on behalf of a posted worker who is a member of such a scheme during the period of his or her posting in another Member State.

2. Where, pursuant to paragraph 1, contributions continue to be made to a supplementary pension scheme in one Member State, the posted worker and, where applicable, his employer shall be exempted from any obligation to make contributions to a supplementary pension scheme in another Member State.

[3947]

Article 7

Information to scheme members

Member States shall take measures to ensure that employers, trustees or others responsible for the management of supplementary pension schemes provide adequate information to scheme members, when they move to another Member State, as to their pension rights and the choices which are available to them under the scheme. Such information shall at least correspond to information given to scheme members in respect of whom contributions cease to be made but who remain within the same Member State.

[3948]

CHAPTER IV
FINAL PROVISIONS

Article 8

Member States may provide that the provisions of Article 6 shall apply only to postings that commence on or after 25 July 2001.

[3949]

Article 9

Member States shall introduce into their national legal systems such measures as are necessary to enable all persons who consider themselves wronged by failure to apply the provisions of this Directive to pursue their claims by judicial process after possible recourse to other competent authorities.

[3950]

Article 10

1. Member States shall bring into force the laws, regulations and administrative provisions necessary to comply with this Directive not later than 36 months following the date of its entry into force, or shall ensure by that date at the latest that management and labour introduce the requisite provisions by way of agreement. Member States shall take all necessary steps to enable themselves at all times to guarantee the results imposed by this Directive. They shall immediately inform the Commission thereof.

When Member States adopt these provisions, these shall contain a reference to this Directive or shall be accompanied by such reference at the time of their official publication. The procedure for such reference shall be adopted by Member States.

They shall inform the Commission of the national authorities to be contacted regarding the application of this Directive.

2. Not later than 25 January 2002 Member States shall communicate to the Commission the text of the provisions of national law which they adopt in the field covered by this Directive.

3. On the basis of the information supplied by Member States, the Commission shall submit a report to the European Parliament, the Council and the Economic and Social Committee, within six years of the entry into force of this Directive.

The report shall deal with the application of this Directive and shall, where appropriate, propose any amendments that may prove necessary.

[3951]

Article 11

This Directive shall enter into force on the day of its publication in the *Official Journal of the European Communities*.

[3952]

Article 12

This Directive is addressed to the Member States.

[3953]

COUNCIL DIRECTIVE

of 29 June 1998

amending Directive 77/187/EEC on the approximation of the laws of the Member States relating to the safeguarding of employees' rights in the event of transfers of undertakings, businesses or parts of businesses (Note)

(98/50/EC)

NOTES

Date of publication in OJ: OJ L201 17.7.98, p 88.
Repealed and replaced by Council Directive 2001/23/EC at **[4015]**.

[3954]

COUNCIL DIRECTIVE

of 13 July 1998

on the extension of Directive 97/80/EC on the burden of proof in cases of discrimination based on sex to the United Kingdom of Great Britain and Northern Ireland

(98/52/EC)

NOTES

Date of publication in OJ: OJ L205, 22.7.1998, p 66.

This Directive is superseded by the Directive of the European Parliament and of the Council on the implementation of the principle of equal opportunities and equal treatment of men and women in matters of employment and occupation (recast) (Directive 2006/54/EC at **[4122]** et seq). The 2006 Directive consolidates and updates the four major Directives on gender equality; ie, the Equal Pay Directive (75/117/EEC), the Equal Treatment Directive (76/207/EEC), the Directive on Equal Treatment in Occupational Social Security Schemes (86/378/EEC), and the Burden of Proof Directive (97/80/EC). These Directives are repealed by Art 34 of, and Annex I, Pt A to, the 2006 Directive, with effect from 15 August 2009 (see **[4155]** and **[4158]**). This Directive, however, is not specifically repealed by those provisions; this appears to be an oversight.

For the domestic implementation of this Directive, see the Sex Discrimination Act 1975, ss 1, 3, 63A, 66A at **[100]**, **[103]**, **[178]**, **[180A]**, as substituted or inserted by the Sex Discrimination (Indirect Discrimination and Burden of Proof) Regulations 2001, SI 2001/2660. Directive 97/80/EC is at **[3925]**.

THE COUNCIL OF THE EUROPEAN UNION,

Having regard to the Treaty establishing the European Community, and in particular Article 100 thereof,

Having regard to the proposal from the Commission,[1]

Having regard to the opinion of the European Parliament,[2]

Having regard to the opinion of the Economic and Social Committee,[3]

Whereas the Council, acting in accordance with the Agreement on social policy annexed to Protocol 14 on social policy annexed to the EC Treaty, and in particular Article 2(2) thereof, adopted Directive 97/80/EC;[4] *whereas, as a result, the said Directive does not apply to the United Kingdom;*

Whereas the Amsterdam European Council, held on 16 and 17 June 1997, noted with approval the agreement of the Intergovernmental Conference to incorporate the Agreement on social policy in the Treaty and also noted that a means had to be found to give legal effect to the wish of the United Kingdom to accept the Directives already adopted on the basis of that Agreement and those which may be adopted before the entry into force of the Treaty of Amsterdam;

Whereas, at the Council of 24 July 1997, the Council and the Commission agreed to put into effect the conclusions adopted at the Amsterdam European Council; whereas they also agreed to apply the same procedure, mutatis mutandis, to future Directives adopted on the basis of the Agreement on social policy; whereas this Directive seeks to achieve this aim by extending Directive 97/80/EC to the United Kingdom;

Whereas the fact that Directive 97/80/EC is not applicable in the United Kingdom directly affects the functioning of the common market; whereas an effective implementation of the principle of equal treatment for men and women, in particular as regards the rules organizing the burden of proof in cases of discrimination based on sex, in all the Member States will improve the functioning of the common market;

Whereas the adoption of this Directive will make Directive 97/80/EC applicable in the United Kingdom; whereas, from the date on which this Directive enters into force, the term 'Member States' in Directive 97/80/EC should be construed as including the United Kingdom;

Whereas the United Kingdom should benefit from the same period of three years that was granted to other Member States to bring into force the necessary provisions to comply with Directive 97/80/EC,

NOTES

Superseded as noted at the beginning of this Directive.

1 OJ C332, 7.11.1996, p 11.
2 OJ C167, 1.6.1998.
3 OJ C157, 25.5.1998, p 64.
4 OJ L14, 20.1.1998, p 6.

HAS ADOPTED THIS DIRECTIVE:

Article 1

Without prejudice to Article 2, Directive 97/80/EC shall apply to the United Kingdom of Great Britain and Northern Ireland.

[3954A]

NOTES

Superseded as noted at the beginning of this Directive.

Article 2

(*Amends Directive 97/80/EC, Art 7 at* **[3931]***, and is superseded as noted at the beginning of this Directive*)

Article 3

This Directive shall enter into force on the day of its publication.

[3954B]

NOTES

Superseded as noted at the beginning of this Directive.

Article 4

This Directive is addressed to the Member States.

[3954C]

NOTES

Superseded as noted at the beginning of this Directive.

COUNCIL DIRECTIVE

of 20 July 1998

on the approximation of the laws of the Member States relating to collective redundancies

(98/59/EC)

NOTES

Date of publication in OJ: OJ L225, 12.8.98, p 16. The text of this Directive incorporates the corrigendum published in OJ L59, 27.2.2007, p 84.

This Directive is essentially a consolidation of Directive 75/129/EEC as amended by Directive 92/56/EEC. For the domestic implementation of those Directives, see the Trade Union and Labour Relations (Consolidation) Act 1992, ss 188–198 at **[672]–[683]**.

THE COUNCIL OF THE EUROPEAN UNION,

Having regard to the Treaty establishing the European Community, and in particular Article 100 thereof,

Having regard to the proposal from the Commission,

Having regard to the opinion of the European Parliament,[1]

Having regard to the opinion of the Economic and Social Committee,[2]

(1) Whereas for reasons of clarity and rationality Council Directive 75/129/EEC of 17 February 1975 on the approximation of the laws of the Member States relating to collective redundancies[3] should be consolidated;

(2) Whereas it is important that greater protection should be afforded to workers in the event of collective redundancies while taking into account the need for balanced economic and social development within the Community;

(3) Whereas, despite increasing convergence, differences still remain between the provisions in force in the Member States concerning the practical arrangements and procedures for such redundancies and the measures designed to alleviate the consequences of redundancy for workers;

(4) Whereas these differences can have a direct effect on the functioning of the internal market;

(5) Whereas the Council resolution of 21 January 1974 concerning a social action programme[4] made provision for a directive on the approximation of Member States' legislation on collective redundancies;

(6) Whereas the Community Charter of the fundamental social rights of workers, adopted at the European Council meeting held in Strasbourg on 9 December 1989 by the Heads of State or Government of 11 Member States, states, *inter alia*, in point 7, first paragraph, first sentence, and second paragraph; in point 17, first paragraph; and in point 18, third indent—

"7. The completion of the internal market must lead to an improvement in the living and working conditions of workers in the European Community (…).

The improvement must cover, where necessary, the development of certain aspects of employment regulations such as procedures for collective redundancies and those regarding bankruptcies.

(…)

17. Information, consultation and participation for workers must be developed along appropriate lines, taking account of the practices in force in the various Member States.

(…)

18. Such information, consultation and participation must be implemented in due time, particularly in the following cases—

(…)

(…)

— in cases of collective redundancy procedures;

(…)";

(7) Whereas this approximation must therefore be promoted while the improvement is being maintained within the meaning of Article 117 of the Treaty;

(8) Whereas, in order to calculate the number of redundancies provided for in the definition of collective redundancies within the meaning of this Directive, other forms of termination of employment contracts on the initiative of the employer should be equated to redundancies, provided that there are at least five redundancies;

(9) Whereas it should be stipulated that this Directive applies in principle also to collective redundancies resulting where the establishment's activities are terminated as a result of a judicial decision;

(10) Whereas the Member States should be given the option of stipulating that workers' representatives may call on experts on grounds of the technical complexity of the matters which are likely to be the subject of the informing and consulting;

(11) Whereas it is necessary to ensure that employers' obligations as regards information, consultation and notification apply independently of whether the decision on collective redundancies emanates from the employer or from an undertaking which controls that employer;

(12) Whereas Member States should ensure that workers' representatives and/or workers have at their disposal administrative and/or judicial procedures in order to ensure that the obligations laid down in this Directive are fulfilled;

(13) Whereas this Directive must not affect the obligations of the Member States concerning the deadlines for transposition of the Directives set out in Annex I, Part B,

NOTES

1 OJ C210, 6.7.98.

2 OJ C158, 26.5.97, p 11.

3 OJ L48, 22.2.75, p 29. Directive as amended by Directive 92/56/EEC (OJ L245, 26.8.92, p 3).

4 OJ C13, 12.2.74, p 1.

HAS ADOPTED THIS DIRECTIVE—

SECTION I
DEFINITIONS AND SCOPE

Article 1

1. For the purposes of this Directive—

(a) 'collective redundancies' means dismissals effected by an employer for one or more reasons not related to the individual workers concerned where, according to the choice of the Member States, the number of redundancies is—

(i) either, over a period of 30 days—

— at least 10 in establishments normally employing more than 20 and less than 100 workers,

— at least 10% of the number of workers in establishments normally employing at least 100 but less than 300 workers,

— at least 30 in establishments normally employing 300 workers or more,

(ii) or, over a period of 90 days, at least 20, whatever the number of workers normally employed in the establishments in question;

(b) 'workers' representatives' means the workers' representatives provided for by the laws or practices of the Member States.

For the purpose of calculating the number of redundancies provided for in the first subparagraph of point (a), terminations of an employment contract which occur on the employer's initiative for one or more reasons not related to the individual workers concerned shall be assimilated to redundancies, provided that there are at least five redundancies.

2. This Directive shall not apply to—

(a) collective redundancies effected under contracts of employment concluded for limited periods of time or for specific tasks except where such redundancies take place prior to the date of expiry or the completion of such contracts;

(b) workers employed by public administrative bodies or by establishments governed by public law (or, in Member States where this concept is unknown, by equivalent bodies);

(c) the crews of seagoing vessels.

[3955]

SECTION II
INFORMATION AND CONSULTATION

Article 2

1. Where an employer is contemplating collective redundancies, he shall begin consultations with the workers' representatives in good time with a view to reaching an agreement.

2. These consultations shall, at least, cover ways and means of avoiding collective redundancies or reducing the number of workers affected, and of mitigating the consequences by recourse to accompanying social measures aimed, *inter alia*, at aid for redeploying or retraining workers made redundant.

Member States may provide that the workers' representatives may call on the services of experts in accordance with national legislation and/or practice.

3. To enable workers' representatives to make constructive proposals, the employers shall in good time during the course of the consultations—

(a) supply them with all relevant information and

(b) in any event notify them in writing of—

(i) the reasons for the projected redundancies;

(ii) the number and categories of workers to be made redundant;

(iii) the number and categories of workers normally employed;

(iv) the period over which the projected redundancies are to be effected;

(v) the criteria proposed for the selection of the workers to be made redundant in so far as national legislation and/or practice confers the power therefor upon the employer;

(vi) the method for calculating any redundancy payments other than those arising out of national legislation and/or practice.

The employer shall forward to the competent public authority a copy of, at least, the elements of the written communication which are provided for in the first subparagraph, point (b), sub-points (i) to (v).

4. The obligations laid down in paragraphs 1, 2 and 3 shall apply irrespective of whether the decision regarding collective redundancies is being taken by the employer or by an undertaking controlling the employer.

In considering alleged breaches of the information, consultation and notification requirements laid down by this Directive, account shall not be taken of any defence on the

part of the employer on the ground that the necessary information has not been provided to the employer by the undertaking which took the decision leading to collective redundancies.
[3956]

SECTION III
PROCEDURE FOR COLLECTIVE REDUNDANCIES

Article 3

1. Employers shall notify the competent public authority in writing of any projected collective redundancies.

However, Member States may provide that in the case of planned collective redundancies arising from termination of the establishment's activities as a result of a judicial decision, the employer shall be obliged to notify the competent public authority in writing only if the latter so requests.

This notification shall contain all relevant information concerning the projected collective redundancies and the consultations with workers' representatives provided for in Article 2, and particularly the reasons for the redundancies, the number of workers to be made redundant, the number of workers normally employed and the period over which the redundancies are to be effected.

2. Employers shall forward to the workers' representatives a copy of the notification provided for in paragraph 1.

The workers' representatives may send any comments they may have to the competent public authority.
[3957]

Article 4

1. Projected collective redundancies notified to the competent public authority shall take effect not earlier than 30 days after the notification referred to in Article 3(1) without prejudice to any provisions governing individual rights with regard to notice of dismissal.

Member States may grant the competent public authority the power to reduce the period provided for in the preceding subparagraph.

2. The period provided for in paragraph 1 shall be used by the competent public authority to seek solutions to the problems raised by the projected collective redundancies.

3. Where the initial period provided for in paragraph 1 is shorter than 60 days, Member States may grant the competent public authority the power to extend the initial period to 60 days following notification where the problems raised by the projected collective redundancies are not likely to be solved within the initial period.

Member States may grant the competent public authority wider powers of extension.

The employer must be informed of the extension and the grounds for it before expiry of the initial period provided for in paragraph 1.

4. Member States need not apply this Article to collective redundancies arising from termination of the establishment's activities where this is the result of a judicial decision.
[3958]

SECTION IV
FINAL PROVISIONS

Article 5

This Directive shall not affect the right of Member States to apply or to introduce laws, regulations or administrative provisions which are more favourable to workers or to promote or to allow the application of collective agreements more favourable to workers.
[3959]

Article 6

Member States shall ensure that judicial and/or administrative procedures for the enforcement of obligations under this Directive are available to the workers' representatives and/or workers.
[3960]

Article 7

Member States shall forward to the Commission the text of any fundamental provisions of national law already adopted or being adopted in the area governed by this Directive.

[3961]

Article 8

1. The Directives listed in Annex I, Part A, are hereby repealed without prejudice to the obligations of the Member States concerning the deadlines for transposition of the said Directive set out in Annex I, Part B.

2. References to the repealed Directives shall be construed as references to this Directive and shall be read in accordance with the correlation table in Annex II.

[3962]

Article 9

This Directive shall enter into force on the 20th day following its publication in the *Official Journal of the European Communities.*

[3963]

Article 10

This Directive is addressed to the Member States.

[3964]

ANNEX I

PART A

REPEALED DIRECTIVES
(REFERRED TO BY ARTICLE 8)

Council Directive 75/129/EEC and its following amendment:

Council Directive 92/56/EEC.

[3965]

PART B

DEADLINES FOR TRANSPOSITION INTO NATIONAL LAW
(REFERRED TO BY ARTICLE 8)

Directive	*Deadline for transposition*
75/129/EEC (OJ L48, 22.2.1975, p 29)	19 February 1977
92/56/EEC (OJ L245, 26.8.1992, p 3)	24 June 1994

[3966]

ANNEX II

CORRELATION TABLE

Directive 75/129/EEC	*This Directive*
Article 1(1), first subparagraph, point (a), first indent, point 1	Article 1(1), first subparagraph, point (a)(i), first indent
Article 1(1), first subparagraph, point (a), first indent, point 2	Article 1(1), first subparagraph, point (a)(i), second indent

Directive 75/129/EEC	*This Directive*
Article 1(1), first subparagraph, point (a), first indent, point 3	Article 1(1), first subparagraph, point (a)(i), third indent
Article 1(1), first subparagraph, point (a), second indent	Article 1(1), first subparagraph, point (a)(ii)
Article 1(1), first subparagraph, point (b)	Article 1(1), first subparagraph, point (b)
Article 1(1), second subparagraph	Article 1(1), second subparagraph
Article 1(2)	Article 1(2)
Article 2	Article 2
Article 3	Article 3
Article 4	Article 4
Article 5	Article 5
Article 5a	Article 6
Article 6(1)	—
Article 6(2)	Article 7
Article 7	—
—	Article 8
—	Article 9
—	Article 10
—	Annex I
—	Annex II

[3967]

COUNCIL DIRECTIVE

of 28 June 1999

concerning the framework agreement on fixed-term work concluded by ETUC, UNICE and CEEP

(99/70/EC)

NOTES

Date of publication in OJ: OJ L175, 10.7.99, p 43.

For the domestic implementation of this Directive, see the Fixed-term Employees (Prevention of Less Favourable Treatment) Regulations 2002, SI 2002/2034 at **[2730]**.

THE COUNCIL OF THE EUROPEAN UNION,

Having regard to the Treaty establishing the European Community, and in particular Article 139(2) thereof,

Having regard to the proposal from the Commission,

Whereas:

(1) Following the entry into force of the Treaty of Amsterdam the provisions of the Agreement on social policy annexed to the Protocol on social policy, annexed to the Treaty establishing the European Community have been incorporated into Articles 136 to 139 of the Treaty establishing the European Community;

(2) Management and labour (the social partners) may, in accordance with Article 139(2) of the Treaty, request jointly that agreements at Community level be implemented by a Council decision on a proposal from the Commission;

(3) Point 7 of the Community Charter of the Fundamental Social Rights of Workers provides, *inter alia*, that 'the completion of the internal market must lead to an improvement

in the living and working conditions of workers in the European Community. This process must result from an approximation of these conditions while the improvement is being maintained, as regards in particular forms of employment other than open-ended contracts, such as fixed-term contracts, part-time working, temporary work and seasonal work';

(4) The Council has been unable to reach a decision on the proposal for a Directive on certain employment relationships with regard to distortions of competition,[1] nor on the proposal for a Directive on certain employment relationships with regard to working conditions;[2]

(5) The conclusions of the Essen European Council stressed the need to take measures with a view to 'increasing the employment-intensiveness of growth, in particular by a more flexible organisation of work in a way which fulfils both the wishes of employees and the requirements of competition';

(6) The Council Resolution of 9 February 1999 on the 1999 Employment Guidelines invites the social partners at all appropriate levels to negotiate agreements to modernise the organisation of work, including flexible working arrangements, with the aim of making undertakings productive and competitive and achieving the required balance between flexibility and security;

(7) The Commission, in accordance with Article 3(2) of the Agreement on social policy, has consulted management and labour on the possible direction of Community action with regard to flexible working time and job security;

(8) The Commission, considering after such consultation that Community action was desirable, once again consulted management and labour on the substance of the envisaged proposal in accordance with Article 3(3) of the said Agreement;

(9) The general cross-industry organisations, namely the Union of Industrial and Employers' Confederations of Europe (UNICE), the European Centre of Enterprises with Public Participation (CEEP) and the European Trade Union Confederation (ETUC), informed the Commission in a joint letter dated 23 March 1998 of their desire to initiate the procedure provided for in Article 4 of the said Agreement; they asked the Commission, in a joint letter, for a further period of three months; the Commission complied with this request extending the negotiation period to 30 March 1999;

(10) The said cross-industry organisations on 18 March 1999 concluded a framework agreement on fixed-term work; they forwarded to the Commission their joint request to implement the framework agreement by a Council Decision on a proposal from the Commission, in accordance with Article 4(2) of the Agreement on social policy;

(11) The Council, in its Resolution of 6 December 1994 on 'certain aspects for a European Union social policy: a contribution to economic and social convergence in the Union',[3] asked management and labour to make use of the opportunities for concluding agreements, since they are as a rule closer to social reality and to social problems;

(12) The signatory parties, in the preamble to the framework agreement on part-time work concluded on 6 June 1997, announced their intention to consider the need for similar agreements relating to other forms of flexible work;

(13) Management and labour wished to give particular attention to fixed-term work, while at the same time indicating that it was their intention to consider the need for a similar agreement relating to temporary agency work;

(14) The signatory parties wished to conclude a framework agreement on fixed-term work setting out the general principles and minimum requirements for fixed-term employment contracts and employment relationships; they have demonstrated their desire to improve the quality of fixed-term work by ensuring the application of the principle of non-discrimination, and to establish a framework to prevent abuse arising from the use of successive fixed-term employment contracts or relationships;

(15) The proper instrument for implementing the framework agreement is a directive within the meaning of Article 249 of the Treaty; it therefore binds the Member States as to the result to be achieved, whilst leaving them the choice of form and methods;

(16) In accordance with the principles of subsidiarity and proportionality as set out in Article 5 of the Treaty, the objectives of this Directive cannot be sufficiently achieved by the Member States and can therefore be better achieved by the Community; this Directive limits itself to the minimum required for the attainment of those objectives and does not go beyond what is necessary for that purpose;

(17) As regards terms used in the framework agreement but not specifically defined therein, this Directive allows Member States to define such terms in conformity with national law or practice as is the case for other Directives on social matters using similar terms, provided that the definitions in question respect the content of the framework agreement;

(18) The Commission has drafted its proposal for a Directive, in accordance with its Communication of 14 December 1993 concerning the application of the agreement on social policy and its Communication of 20 May 1998 on adapting and promoting the social dialogue at Community level, taking into account the representative status of the contracting parties,

their mandate and the legality of each clause of the framework agreement; the contracting parties together have a sufficiently representative status;

(19) The Commission informed the European Parliament and the Economic and Social Committee by sending them the text of the agreement, accompanied by its proposal for a Directive and the explanatory memorandum, in accordance with its communication concerning the implementation of the Protocol on social policy;

(20) On 6 May 1999 the European Parliament adopted a Resolution on the framework agreement between the social partners;

(21) The implementation of the framework agreement contributes to achieving the objectives in Article 136 of Treaty,

NOTES

1 OJ C224, 8.9.90, p 6 and OJ C305, 5.12.90, p 8.
2 OJ C224, 8.9.90, p 4.
3 OJ C368, 23.12.94, p 6.

HAS ADOPTED THIS DIRECTIVE—

Article 1

The purpose of the Directive is to put into effect the framework agreement on fixed-term contracts concluded on 18 March 1999 between the general cross-industry organisations (ETUC, UNICE and CEEP) annexed hereto.

[3968]

Article 2

Member States shall bring into force the laws, regulations and administrative provisions necessary to comply with this Directive by 10 July 2001, or shall ensure that, by that date at the latest, management and labour have introduced the necessary measures by agreement, the Member States being required to take any necessary measures to enable them at any time to be in a position to guarantee the results imposed by this Directive. They shall forthwith inform the Commission thereof.

Member States may have a maximum of one more year, if necessary, and following consultation with management and labour, to take account of special difficulties or implementation by a collective agreement. They shall inform the Commission forthwith in such circumstances.

When Member States adopt the provisions referred to in the first paragraph, these shall contain a reference to this Directive or shall be accompanied by such reference at the time of their official publication. The procedure for such reference shall be adopted by the Member States.

[3969]

NOTES

The date of 10 July 2001 in the first paragraph is by virtue of the Corrigendum to Council Directive 1999/70/EC of 28 June 1999 concerning the framework agreement on fixed-term work concluded by ETUC, UNICE and CEEP (OJ L175, 10.7.1999). The original date (as published in the Official Journal) was 10 July 1999.

Article 3

This Directive shall enter into force on the day of its publication in the *Official Journal of the European Communities*.

[3970]

Article 4

This Directive is addressed to the Member States.

[3971]

ANNEX
ETUC-UNICE-CEEP
FRAMEWORK AGREEMENT ON FIXED-TERM WORK

Preamble

This framework agreement illustrates the role that the social partners can play in the European employment strategy agreed at the 1997 Luxembourg extra-ordinary summit and, following the framework agreement on part-time work, represents a further contribution towards achieving a better balance between "flexibility in working time and security for workers".

The parties to this agreement recognise that contracts of an indefinite duration are, and will continue to be, the general form of employment relationship between employers and workers. They also recognise that fixed-term employment contracts respond, in certain circumstances, to the needs of both employers and workers.

This agreement sets out the general principles and minimum requirements relating to fixed-term work, recognising that their detailed application needs to take account of the realities of specific national, sectoral and seasonal situations. It illustrates the willingness of the Social Partners to establish a general framework for ensuring equal treatment for fixed-term workers by protecting them against discrimination and for using fixed-term employment contracts on a basis acceptable to employers and workers.

This agreement applies to fixed-term workers with the exception of those placed by a temporary work agency at the disposition of a user enterprise. It is the intention of the parties to consider the need for a similar agreement relating to temporary agency work.

This agreement relates to the employment conditions of fixed-term workers, recognising that matters relating to statutory social security are for decision by the Member States. In this respect the Social Partners note the Employment Declaration of the Dublin European Council in 1996 which emphasised *inter alia*, the need to develop more employment-friendly social security systems by "developing social protection systems capable of adapting to new patterns of work and providing appropriate protection to those engaged in such work". The parties to this agreement reiterate the view expressed in the 1997 part-time agreement that Member States should give effect to this Declaration without delay.

In addition, it is also recognised that innovations in occupational social protection systems are necessary in order to adapt them to current conditions, and in particular to provide for the transferability of rights.

The ETUC, UNICE and CEEP request the Commission to submit this framework agreement to the Council for a decision making these requirements binding in the Member States which are party to the Agreement on social policy annexed to the Protocol (No 14) on social policy annexed to the Treaty establishing the European Community.

The parties to this agreement ask the Commission, in its proposal to implement the agreement, to request Member States to adopt the laws, regulations and administrative provisions necessary to comply with the Council decision within two years from its adoption or ensure[1] that the social partners establish the necessary measures by way of agreement by the end of this period. Member States may, if necessary and following consultation with the social partners, and in order to take account of particular difficulties or implementation by collective agreement have up to a maximum of one additional year to comply with this provision.

The parties to this agreement request that the social partners are consulted prior to any legislative, regulatory or administrative initiative taken by a Member State to conform to the present agreement.

Without prejudice to the role of national courts and the Court of Justice, the parties to this agreement request that any matter relating to the interpretation of this agreement at European level, should in the first instance, be referred by the Commission to them for an opinion.

[3972]

NOTES

[1] Within the meaning of Article 2.4 of the Agreement on social policy annexed to the Protocol (No 14) on social policy annexed to the Treaty establishing the European Community.

General considerations

1. Having regard to the Agreement on social policy annexed to the Protocol (No 14) on social policy annexed to the Treaty establishing the European Community, and in particular Article 3.4 and 4.2 thereof;

2. Whereas Article 4.2 of the Agreement on social policy provides that agreements concluded at Community level may be implemented, at the joint request of the signatory parties, by a Council decision on a proposal from the Commission;

3. Whereas, in its second consultation document on flexibility in working time and security for workers, the Commission announced its intention to propose a legally-binding Community measure;

4. Whereas in its opinion on the proposal for a directive on part-time work, the European Parliament invited the Commission to submit immediately proposals for directives on other forms of flexible work, such as fixed-term work and temporary agency work;

5. Whereas in the conclusions of the extraordinary summit on employment adopted in Luxembourg, the European Council invited the social partners to negotiate agreements to "modernise the organisation of work, including flexible working arrangements, with the aim of making undertakings productive and competitive and achieving the required balance between flexibility and security";

6. Whereas employment contracts of an indefinite duration are the general form of employment relationships and contribute to quality of life of the workers concerned and improve performance;

7. Whereas the use of fixed-term employment contracts based on objective reasons is a way to prevent abuse;

8. Whereas fixed-term employment contracts are a feature of employment in certain sectors, occupations and activities which can suit both employers and workers;

9. Whereas more than half of fixed-term workers in the European Union are women and this agreement can therefore contribute to improving equality of opportunities between women and men;

10. Whereas this agreement refers back to Member States and social partners for the arrangements for the application of its general principles, minimum requirements and provisions, in order to take account of the situation in each Member State and the circumstances of particular sectors and occupations, including the activities of a seasonal nature;

11. Whereas this agreement takes into consideration the need to improve social policy requirements, to enhance the competitiveness of the Community economy and to avoid imposing administrative, financial and legal constraints in a way which would hold back the creation and development of small and medium-sized undertakings;

12. Whereas the social partners are best placed to find solutions that correspond to the needs of both employers and workers and shall therefore be given a special role in the implementation and application of this agreement.

[3973]

THE SIGNATORY PARTIES HAVE AGREED THE FOLLOWING

Purpose (clause 1)

The purpose of this framework agreement is to—

(1) improve the quality of fixed-term work by ensuring the application of the principle of non-discrimination;

(2) establish a framework to prevent abuse arising from the use of successive fixed-term employment contracts or relationships.

Scope (clause 2)

1. This agreement applies to fixed-term workers who have an employment contract or employment relationship as defined in law, collective agreements or practice in each Member State.

2. Member States after consultation with the social partners and/or the social partners may provide that this agreement does not apply to—

(a) initial vocational training relationships and apprenticeship schemes;

(b) employment contracts and relationships which have been concluded within the framework of a specific public or publicly-supported training, integration and vocational retraining programme.

Definitions (clause 3)

1. For the purpose of this agreement the term "fixed-term worker" means a person having an employment contract or relationship entered into directly between an employer and a worker where the end of the employment contract or relationship is determined by objective conditions such as reaching a specific date, completing a specific task, or the occurrence of a specific event.

2. For the purpose of this agreement, the term "comparable permanent worker" means a worker with an employment contract or relationship of an indefinite duration, in the same establishment, engaged in the same or similar work/occupation, due regard being given to qualifications/skills.

Where there is no comparable permanent worker in the same establishment, the comparison shall be made by reference to the applicable collective agreement, or where there is no applicable collective agreement, in accordance with national law, collective agreements or practice.

Principle of non-discrimination (clause 4)

1. In respect of employment conditions, fixed-term workers shall not be treated in a less favourable manner than comparable permanent workers solely because they have a fixed-term contract or relation unless justified on objective grounds.

2. Where appropriate, the principle of *pro rata temporis* shall apply.

3. The arrangements for the application of this clause shall be defined by the Member States after consultation with the social partners and/or the social partners, having regard to Community law, national law, collective agreements and practice.

4. Period of service qualifications relating to particular conditions of employment shall be the same for fixed-term workers as for permanent workers except where different length of service qualifications are justified on objective grounds.

Measures to prevent abuse (clause 5)

1. To prevent abuse arising from the use of successive fixed-term employment contracts or relationships, Member States, after consultation with social partners in accordance with national law, collective agreements or practice, and/or the social partners, shall, where there are no equivalent legal measures to prevent abuse, introduce in a manner which takes account of the needs of specific sectors and/or categories of workers, one or more of the following measures—

(a) objective reasons justifying the renewal of such contracts or relationships;
(b) the maximum total duration of successive fixed-term employment contracts or relationships;
(c) the number of renewals of such contracts or relationships.

2. Member States after consultation with the social partners and/or the social partners, shall, where appropriate, determine under what conditions fixed-term employment contracts or relationships—

(a) shall be regarded as "successive";
(b) shall be deemed to be contracts or relationships of indefinite duration.

Information and employment opportunities (clause 6)

1. Employers shall inform fixed-term workers about vacancies which become available in the undertaking or establishment to ensure that they have the same opportunity to secure permanent positions as other workers. Such information may be provided by way of a general announcement at a suitable place in the undertaking or establishment.

2. As far as possible, employers should facilitate access by fixed-term workers to appropriate training opportunities to enhance their skills, career development and occupational mobility.

Information and consultation (clause 7)

1. Fixed-term workers shall be taken into consideration in calculating the threshold above which workers' representative bodies provided for in national and Community law may be constituted in the undertaking as required by national provisions.

2. The arrangements for the application of clause 7.1 shall be defined by Member States after consultation with the social partners and/or the social partners in accordance with national law, collective agreements or practice and having regard to clause 4.1.

3. As far as possible, employers should give consideration to the provision of appropriate information to existing workers' representative bodies about fixed-term work in the undertaking.

Provisions on implementation (clause 8)

1. Member States and/or the social partners can maintain or introduce more favourable provisions for workers than set out in this agreement.

2. This agreement shall be without prejudice to any more specific Community provisions, and in particular Community provisions concerning equal treatment or opportunities for men and women.

3. Implementation of this agreement shall not constitute valid grounds for reducing the general level of protection afforded to workers in the field of the agreement.

4. The present agreement does not prejudice the right of the social partners to conclude at the appropriate level, including European level, agreements adapting and/or complementing the provisions of this agreement in a manner which will take account of the specific needs of the social partners concerned.

5. The prevention and settlement of disputes and grievances arising from the application of this agreement shall be dealt with in accordance with national law, collective agreements and practice.

6. The signatory parties shall review the application of this agreement five years after the date of the Council decision if requested by one of the parties to this agreement.

18 March 1999

[3974]

COUNCIL DIRECTIVE

of 29 June 2000

implementing the principle of equal treatment between persons irrespective of racial or ethnic origin

(2000/43/EC)

NOTES

Date of publication in OJ: OJ L180, 19.7.2000, p 22.

For the domestic implementation of this Directive, see the Race Relations Act 1976 at **[207]** et seq, as amended by the Race Relations Act 1976 (Amendment) Regulations 2003, SI 2003/1626.

THE COUNCIL OF THE EUROPEAN UNION,

Having regard to the Treaty establishing the European Community and in particular Article 13 thereof,

Having regard to the proposal from the Commission,[1]

Having regard to the opinion of the European Parliament,[2]

Having regard to the opinion of the Economic and Social Committee,[3]

Having regard to the opinion of the Committee of the Regions,[4]

Whereas:

(1) The Treaty on European Union marks a new stage in the process of creating an ever closer union among the peoples of Europe.

(2) In accordance with Article 6 of the Treaty on European Union, the European Union is founded on the principles of liberty, democracy, respect for human rights and fundamental freedoms, and the rule of law, principles which are common to the Member States, and should respect fundamental rights as guaranteed by the European Convention for the protection of Human Rights and Fundamental Freedoms and as they result from the constitutional traditions common to the Member States, as general principles of Community Law.

(3) The right to equality before the law and protection against discrimination for all persons constitutes a universal right recognised by the Universal Declaration of Human Rights, the United Nations Convention on the Elimination of all forms of Discrimination Against Women, the International Convention on the Elimination of all forms of Racial Discrimination and the United Nations Covenants on Civil and Political Rights and on Economic, Social and Cultural Rights and by the European Convention for the Protection of Human Rights and Fundamental Freedoms, to which all Member States are signatories.

(4) It is important to respect such fundamental rights and freedoms, including the right to freedom of association. It is also important, in the context of the access to and provision of goods and services, to respect the protection of private and family life and transactions carried out in this context.

(5) The European Parliament has adopted a number of Resolutions on the fight against racism in the European Union.

(6) The European Union rejects theories which attempt to determine the existence of separate human races. The use of the term "racial origin" in this Directive does not imply an acceptance of such theories.

(7) The European Council in Tampere, on 15 and 16 October 1999, invited the Commission to come forward as soon as possible with proposals implementing Article 13 of the EC Treaty as regards the fight against racism and xenophobia.

(8) The Employment Guidelines 2000 agreed by the European Council in Helsinki, on 10 and 11 December 1999, stress the need to foster conditions for a socially inclusive labour market by formulating a coherent set of policies aimed at combating discrimination against groups such as ethnic minorities.

(9) Discrimination based on racial or ethnic origin may undermine the achievement of the objectives of the EC Treaty, in particular the attainment of a high level of employment and of social protection, the raising of the standard of living and quality of life, economic and social cohesion and solidarity. It may also undermine the objective of developing the European Union as an area of freedom, security and justice.

(10) The Commission presented a communication on racism, xenophobia and anti-Semitism in December 1995.

(11) The Council adopted on 15 July 1996 Joint Action (96/443/JHA) concerning action to combat racism and xenophobia[5] under which the Member States undertake to ensure effective judicial cooperation in respect of offences based on racist or xenophobic behaviour.

(12) To ensure the development of democratic and tolerant societies which allow the participation of all persons irrespective of racial or ethnic origin, specific action in the field of discrimination based on racial or ethnic origin should go beyond access to employed and self-employed activities and cover areas such as education, social protection including social security and healthcare, social advantages and access to and supply of goods and services.

(13) To this end, any direct or indirect discrimination based on racial or ethnic origin as regards the areas covered by this Directive should be prohibited throughout the Community. This prohibition of discrimination should also apply to nationals of third countries, but does not cover differences of treatment based on nationality and is without prejudice to provisions governing the entry and residence of third-country nationals and their access to employment and to occupation.

(14) In implementing the principle of equal treatment irrespective of racial or ethnic origin, the Community should, in accordance with Article 3(2) of the EC Treaty, aim to eliminate inequalities, and to promote equality between men and women, especially since women are often the victims of multiple discrimination.

(15) The appreciation of the facts from which it may be inferred that there has been direct or indirect discrimination is a matter for national judicial or other competent bodies, in accordance with rules of national law or practice. Such rules may provide in particular for indirect discrimination to be established by any means including on the basis of statistical evidence.

(16) It is important to protect all natural persons against discrimination on grounds of racial or ethnic origin. Member States should also provide, where appropriate and in accordance with their national traditions and practice, protection for legal persons where they suffer discrimination on grounds of the racial or ethnic origin of their members.

(17) The prohibition of discrimination should be without prejudice to the maintenance or adoption of measures intended to prevent or compensate for disadvantages suffered by a group of persons of a particular racial or ethnic origin, and such measures may permit organisations of persons of a particular racial or ethnic origin where their main object is the promotion of the special needs of those persons.

(18) In very limited circumstances, a difference of treatment may be justified where a characteristic related to racial or ethnic origin constitutes a genuine and determining occupational requirement, when the objective is legitimate and the requirement is proportionate. Such circumstances should be included in the information provided by the Member States to the Commission.

(19) Persons who have been subject to discrimination based on racial and ethnic origin should have adequate means of legal protection. To provide a more effective level of protection, associations or legal entities should also be empowered to engage, as the Member States so determine, either on behalf or in support of any victim, in proceedings, without prejudice to national rules of procedure concerning representation and defence before the courts.

(20) The effective implementation of the principle of equality requires adequate judicial protection against victimisation.

(21) The rules on the burden of proof must be adapted when there is a prima facie case of discrimination and, for the principle of equal treatment to be applied effectively, the burden of proof must shift back to the respondent when evidence of such discrimination is brought.

(22) Member States need not apply the rules on the burden of proof to proceedings in which it is for the court or other competent body to investigate the facts of the case. The procedures thus referred to are those in which the plaintiff is not required to prove the facts, which it is for the court or competent body to investigate.

(23) Member States should promote dialogue between the social partners and with non-governmental organisations to address different forms of discrimination and to combat them.

(24) Protection against discrimination based on racial or ethnic origin would itself be strengthened by the existence of a body or bodies in each Member State, with competence to analyse the problems involved, to study possible solutions and to provide concrete assistance for the victims.

(25) This Directive lays down minimum requirements, thus giving the Member States the option of introducing or maintaining more favourable provisions. The implementation of this Directive should not serve to justify any regression in relation to the situation which already prevails in each Member State.

(26) Member States should provide for effective, proportionate and dissuasive sanctions in case of breaches of the obligations under this Directive.

(27) The Member States may entrust management and labour, at their joint request, with the implementation of this Directive as regards provisions falling within the scope of collective agreements, provided that the Member States take all the necessary steps to ensure that they can at all times guarantee the results imposed by this Directive.

(28) In accordance with the principles of subsidiarity and proportionality as set out in Article 5 of the EC Treaty, the objective of this Directive, namely ensuring a common high level of protection against discrimination in all the Member States, cannot be sufficiently achieved by the Member States and can therefore, by reason of the scale and impact of the proposed action, be better achieved by the Community. This Directive does not go beyond what is necessary in order to achieve those objectives,

NOTES

1 Not yet published in the Official Journal.
2 Opinion delivered on 18.5.2000 (not yet published in the Official Journal).
3 Opinion delivered on 12.4.2000 (not yet published in the Official Journal).
4 Opinion delivered on 31.5.2000 (not yet published in the Official Journal).
5 OJ L185, 24.7.96, p 5.

HAS ADOPTED THIS DIRECTIVE—

CHAPTER I
GENERAL PROVISIONS

Article 1

Purpose

The purpose of this Directive is to lay down a framework for combating discrimination on the grounds of racial or ethnic origin, with a view to putting into effect in the Member States the principle of equal treatment.

[3975]

Article 2

Concept of discrimination

1. For the purposes of this Directive, the principle of equal treatment shall mean that there shall be no direct or indirect discrimination based on racial or ethnic origin.

2. For the purposes of paragraph 1—

(a) direct discrimination shall be taken to occur where one person is treated less favourably than another is, has been or would be treated in a comparable situation on grounds of racial or ethnic origin;

(b) indirect discrimination shall be taken to occur where an apparently neutral provision, criterion or practice would put persons of a racial or ethnic origin at a particular disadvantage compared with other persons, unless that provision, criterion or practice is objectively justified by a legitimate aim and the means of achieving that aim are appropriate and necessary.

3. Harassment shall be deemed to be discrimination within the meaning of paragraph 1, when an unwanted conduct related to racial or ethnic origin takes place with the purpose or effect of violating the dignity of a person and of creating an intimidating, hostile, degrading, humiliating or offensive environment. In this context, the concept of harassment may be defined in accordance with the national laws and practice of the Member States.

4. An instruction to discriminate against persons on grounds of racial or ethnic origin shall be deemed to be discrimination within the meaning of paragraph 1.

[3976]

Article 3

Scope

1. Within the limits of the powers conferred upon the Community, this Directive shall apply to all persons, as regards both the public and private sectors, including public bodies, in relation to—

(a) conditions for access to employment, to self-employment and to occupation, including selection criteria and recruitment conditions, whatever the branch of activity and at all levels of the professional hierarchy, including promotion;
(b) access to all types and to all levels of vocational guidance, vocational training, advanced vocational training and retraining, including practical work experience;
(c) employment and working conditions, including dismissals and pay;
(d) membership of and involvement in an organisation of workers or employers, or any organisation whose members carry on a particular profession, including the benefits provided for by such organisations;
(e) social protection, including social security and healthcare;
(f) social advantages;
(g) education;
(h) access to and supply of goods and services which are available to the public, including housing.

2. This Directive does not cover difference of treatment based on nationality and is without prejudice to provisions and conditions relating to the entry into and residence of third-country nationals and stateless persons on the territory of Member States, and to any treatment which arises from the legal status of the third-country nationals and stateless persons concerned.

[3977]

Article 4

Genuine and determining occupational requirements

Notwithstanding Article 2(1) and (2), Member States may provide that a difference of treatment which is based on a characteristic related to racial or ethnic origin shall not constitute discrimination where, by reason of the nature of the particular occupational activities concerned or of the context in which they are carried out, such a characteristic constitutes a genuine and determining occupational requirement, provided that the objective is legitimate and the requirement is proportionate.

[3978]

Article 5

Positive action

With a view to ensuring full equality in practice, the principle of equal treatment shall not prevent any Member State from maintaining or adopting specific measures to prevent or compensate for disadvantages linked to racial or ethnic origin.

[3979]

Article 6

Minimum requirements

1. Member States may introduce or maintain provisions which are more favourable to the protection of the principle of equal treatment than those laid down in this Directive.

2. The implementation of this Directive shall under no circumstances constitute grounds for a reduction in the level of protection against discrimination already afforded by Member States in the fields covered by this Directive.

[3980]

CHAPTER II
REMEDIES AND ENFORCEMENT

Article 7

Defence of rights

1. Member States shall ensure that judicial and/or administrative procedures, including where they deem it appropriate conciliation procedures, for the enforcement of obligations under this Directive are available to all persons who consider themselves wronged by failure to apply the principle of equal treatment to them, even after the relationship in which the discrimination is alleged to have occurred has ended.

2. Member States shall ensure that associations, organisations or other legal entities, which have, in accordance with the criteria laid down by their national law, a legitimate interest in ensuring that the provisions of this Directive are complied with, may engage, either on behalf or in support of the complainant, with his or her approval, in any judicial and/or administrative procedure provided for the enforcement of obligations under this Directive.

3. Paragraphs 1 and 2 are without prejudice to national rules relating to time limits for bringing actions as regards the principle of equality of treatment.

[3981]

Article 8

Burden of proof

1. Member States shall take such measures as are necessary, in accordance with their national judicial systems, to ensure that, when persons who consider themselves wronged because the principle of equal treatment has not been applied to them establish, before a court or other competent authority, facts from which it may be presumed that there has been direct or indirect discrimination, it shall be for the respondent to prove that there has been no breach of the principle of equal treatment.

2. Paragraph 1 shall not prevent Member States from introducing rules of evidence which are more favourable to plaintiffs.

3. Paragraph 1 shall not apply to criminal procedures.

4. Paragraphs 1, 2 and 3 shall also apply to any proceedings brought in accordance with Article 7(2).

5. Member States need not apply paragraph 1 to proceedings in which it is for the court or competent body to investigate the facts of the case.

[3982]

Article 9

Victimisation

Member States shall introduce into their national legal systems such measures as are necessary to protect individuals from any adverse treatment or adverse consequence as a reaction to a complaint or to proceedings aimed at enforcing compliance with the principle of equal treatment.

[3983]

Article 10

Dissemination of information

Member States shall take care that the provisions adopted pursuant to this Directive, together with the relevant provisions already in force, are brought to the attention of the persons concerned by all appropriate means throughout their territory.

[3984]

Article 11

Social dialogue

1. Member States shall, in accordance with national traditions and practice, take adequate measures to promote the social dialogue between the two sides of industry with a view to fostering equal treatment, including through the monitoring of workplace practices, collective agreements, codes of conduct, research or exchange of experiences and good practices.

2. Where consistent with national traditions and practice, Member States shall encourage the two sides of the industry without prejudice to their autonomy to conclude, at the appropriate level, agreements laying down anti-discrimination rules in the fields referred to in Article 3 which fall within the scope of collective bargaining. These agreements shall respect the minimum requirements laid down by this Directive and the relevant national implementing measures.

[3985]

Article 12

Dialogue with non-governmental organisations

Member States shall encourage dialogue with appropriate non-governmental organisations which have, in accordance with their national law and practice, a legitimate interest in contributing to the fight against discrimination on grounds of racial and ethnic origin with a view to promoting the principle of equal treatment.

[3986]

CHAPTER III
BODIES FOR THE PROMOTION OF EQUAL TREATMENT

Article 13

1. Member States shall designate a body or bodies for the promotion of equal treatment of all persons without discrimination on the grounds of racial or ethnic origin. These bodies may form part of agencies charged at national level with the defence of human rights or the safeguard of individuals' rights.

2. Member States shall ensure that the competences of these bodies include—

— without prejudice to the right of victims and of associations, organisations or other legal entities referred to in Article 7(2), providing independent assistance to victims of discrimination in pursuing their complaints about discrimination,
— conducting independent surveys concerning discrimination,
— publishing independent reports and making recommendations on any issue relating to such discrimination.

[3987]

CHAPTER IV
FINAL PROVISIONS

Article 14

Compliance

Member States shall take the necessary measures to ensure that—

(a) any laws, regulations and administrative provisions contrary to the principle of equal treatment are abolished;
(b) any provisions contrary to the principle of equal treatment which are included in individual or collective contracts or agreements, internal rules of undertakings, rules governing profit-making or non-profit-making associations, and rules governing the independent professions and workers' and employers' organisations, are or may be declared, null and void or are amended.

[3988]

Article 15

Sanctions

Member States shall lay down the rules on sanctions applicable to infringements of the national provisions adopted pursuant to this Directive and shall take all measures necessary to ensure that they are applied. The sanctions, which may comprise the payment of compensation to the victim, must be effective, proportionate and dissuasive. The Member States shall notify those provisions to the Commission by 19 July 2003 at the latest and shall notify it without delay of any subsequent amendment affecting them.

[3989]

Article 16

Implementation

Member States shall adopt the laws, regulations and administrative provisions necessary to comply with this Directive by 19 July 2003 or may entrust management and labour, at their joint request, with the implementation of this Directive as regards provisions falling within the scope of collective agreements. In such cases, Member States shall ensure that by 19 July 2003, management and labour introduce the necessary measures by agreement, Member States being required to take any necessary measures to enable them at any time to be in a position to guarantee the results imposed by this Directive. They shall forthwith inform the Commission thereof.

When Member States adopt these measures, they shall contain a reference to this Directive or be accompanied by such a reference on the occasion of their official publication. The methods of making such a reference shall be laid down by the Member States.

[3990]

Article 17

Report

1. Member States shall communicate to the Commission by 19 July 2005, and every five years thereafter, all the information necessary for the Commission to draw up a report to the European Parliament and the Council on the application of this Directive.

2. The Commission's report shall take into account, as appropriate, the views of the European Monitoring Centre on Racism and Xenophobia, as well as the viewpoints of the social partners and relevant non-governmental organisations. In accordance with the principle of gender mainstreaming, this report shall, inter alia, provide an assessment of the impact of the measures taken on women and men. In the light of the information received, this report shall include, if necessary, proposals to revise and update this Directive.

[3991]

Article 18

Entry into force

This Directive shall enter into force on the day of its publication in the Official Journal of the European Communities.

[3992]

Article 19

Addressees

This Directive is addressed to the Member States.

[3993]

COUNCIL DIRECTIVE

of 27 November 2000

establishing a general framework for equal treatment in employment and occupation

(2000/78/EC)

NOTES

Date of publication in OJ: OJ L303, 2.12.2000, p 16.

For the domestic implementation of this Directive, see the Disability Discrimination Act 1995 at **[900]** et seq (as amended, with effect from 1 October 2004, by the Disability Discrimination Act 1995 (Amendment) Regulations 2003, SI 2003/1673 and the Disability Discrimination Act 1995 (Pensions) Regulations 2003, SI 2003/2770 at **[3032]** and **[3036]** respectively), the Employment Equality (Religion or Belief) Regulations 2003, SI 2003/1660 at **[2941]**, the Employment Equality (Sexual Orientation) Regulations 2003, SI 2003/1661 at **[2987]**, and the Employment Equality (Age) Regulations 2006, SI 2006/1031 at **[3403]**.

THE COUNCIL OF THE EUROPEAN UNION,

Having regard to the Treaty establishing the European Community, and in particular Article 13 thereof,

Having regard to the proposal from the Commission,[1]

Having regard to the Opinion of the European Parliament,[2]

Having regard to the Opinion of the Economic and Social Committee,[3]

Having regard to the Opinion of the Committee of the Regions,[4]

Whereas—

(1) In accordance with Article 6 of the Treaty on European Union, the European Union is founded on the principles of liberty, democracy, respect for human rights and fundamental freedoms, and the rule of law, principles which are common to all Member States and it respects fundamental rights, as guaranteed by the European Convention for the Protection of Human Rights and Fundamental Freedoms and as they result from the constitutional traditions common to the Member States, as general principles of Community law.

(2) The principle of equal treatment between women and men is well established by an important body of Community law, in particular in Council Directive 76/207/EEC of 9 February 1976 on the implementation of the principle of equal treatment for men and women as regards access to employment, vocational training and promotion, and working conditions.[5]

(3) In implementing the principle of equal treatment, the Community should, in accordance with Article 3(2) of the EC Treaty, aim to eliminate inequalities, and to promote equality between men and women, especially since women are often the victims of multiple discrimination.

(4) The right of all persons to equality before the law and protection against discrimination constitutes a universal right recognised by the Universal Declaration of Human Rights, the United Nations Convention on the Elimination of All Forms of Discrimination against Women, United Nations Covenants on Civil and Political Rights and on Economic, Social and Cultural Rights and by the European Convention for the Protection of Human Rights and Fundamental Freedoms, to which all Member States are signatories. Convention No 111 of the International Labour Organisation (ILO) prohibits discrimination in the field of employment and occupation.

(5) It is important to respect such fundamental rights and freedoms. This Directive does not prejudice freedom of association, including the right to establish unions with others and to join unions to defend one's interests.

(6) The Community Charter of the Fundamental Social Rights of Workers recognises the importance of combating every form of discrimination, including the need to take appropriate action for the social and economic integration of elderly and disabled people.

(7) The EC Treaty includes among its objectives the promotion of coordination between employment policies of the Member States. To this end, a new employment chapter was incorporated in the EC Treaty as a means of developing a coordinated European strategy for employment to promote a skilled, trained and adaptable workforce.

(8) The Employment Guidelines for 2000 agreed by the European Council at Helsinki on 10 and 11 December 1999 stress the need to foster a labour market favourable to social integration by formulating a coherent set of policies aimed at combating discrimination against groups such as persons with disability. They also emphasise the need to pay particular attention to supporting older workers, in order to increase their participation in the labour force.

(9) Employment and occupation are key elements in guaranteeing equal opportunities for all and contribute strongly to the full participation of citizens in economic, cultural and social life and to realising their potential.

(10) On 29 June 2000 the Council adopted Directive 2000/43/EC[6] implementing the principle of equal treatment between persons irrespective of racial or ethnic origin. That Directive already provides protection against such discrimination in the field of employment and occupation.

(11) Discrimination based on religion or belief, disability, age or sexual orientation may undermine the achievement of the objectives of the EC Treaty, in particular the attainment of a high level of employment and social protection, raising the standard of living and the quality of life, economic and social cohesion and solidarity, and the free movement of persons.

PART 2

(12) To this end, any direct or indirect discrimination based on religion or belief, disability, age or sexual orientation as regards the areas covered by this Directive should be prohibited throughout the Community. This prohibition of discrimination should also apply to nationals of third countries but does not cover differences of treatment based on nationality and is without prejudice to provisions governing the entry and residence of third-country nationals and their access to employment and occupation.

(13) This Directive does not apply to social security and social protection schemes whose benefits are not treated as income within the meaning given to that term for the purpose of applying Article 141 of the EC Treaty, nor to any kind of payment by the State aimed at providing access to employment or maintaining employment.

(14) This Directive shall be without prejudice to national provisions laying down retirement ages.

(15) The appreciation of the facts from which it may be inferred that there has been direct or indirect discrimination is a matter for national judicial or other competent bodies, in accordance with rules of national law or practice. Such rules may provide, in particular, for indirect discrimination to be established by any means including on the basis of statistical evidence.

(16) The provision of measures to accommodate the needs of disabled people at the workplace plays an important role in combating discrimination on grounds of disability.

(17) This Directive does not require the recruitment, promotion, maintenance in employment or training of an individual who is not competent, capable and available to perform the essential functions of the post concerned or to undergo the relevant training, without prejudice to the obligation to provide reasonable accommodation for people with disabilities.

(18) This Directive does not require, in particular, the armed forces and the police, prison or emergency services to recruit or maintain in employment persons who do not have the required capacity to carry out the range of functions that they may be called upon to perform with regard to the legitimate objective of preserving the operational capacity of those services.

(19) Moreover, in order that the Member States may continue to safeguard the combat effectiveness of their armed forces, they may choose not to apply the provisions of this Directive concerning disability and age to all or part of their armed forces. The Member States which make that choice must define the scope of that derogation.

(20) Appropriate measures should be provided, ie effective and practical measures to adapt the workplace to the disability, for example adapting premises and equipment, patterns of working time, the distribution of tasks or the provision of training or integration resources.

(21) To determine whether the measures in question give rise to a disproportionate burden, account should be taken in particular of the financial and other costs entailed, the scale and financial resources of the organisation or undertaking and the possibility of obtaining public funding or any other assistance.

(22) This Directive is without prejudice to national laws on marital status and the benefits dependent thereon.

(23) In very limited circumstances, a difference of treatment may be justified where a characteristic related to religion or belief, disability, age or sexual orientation constitutes a genuine and determining occupational requirement, when the objective is legitimate and the requirement is proportionate. Such circumstances should be included in the information provided by the Member States to the Commission.

(24) The European Union in its Declaration No 11 on the status of churches and non-confessional organisations, annexed to the Final Act of the Amsterdam Treaty, has explicitly recognised that it respects and does not prejudice the status under national law of churches and religious associations or communities in the Member States and that it equally respects the status of philosophical and non-confessional organisations. With this in view, Member States may maintain or lay down specific provisions on genuine, legitimate and justified occupational requirements which might be required for carrying out an occupational activity.

(25) The prohibition of age discrimination is an essential part of meeting the aims set out in the Employment Guidelines and encouraging diversity in the workforce. However, differences in treatment in connection with age may be justified under certain circumstances and therefore require specific provisions which may vary in accordance with the situation in Member States. It is therefore essential to distinguish between differences in treatment which are justified, in particular by legitimate employment policy, labour market and vocational training objectives, and discrimination which must be prohibited.

(26) The prohibition of discrimination should be without prejudice to the maintenance or adoption of measures intended to prevent or compensate for disadvantages suffered by a group of persons of a particular religion or belief, disability, age or sexual orientation, and

such measures may permit organisations of persons of a particular religion or belief, disability, age or sexual orientation where their main object is the promotion of the special needs of those persons.

(27) In its Recommendation 86/379/EEC of 24 July 1986 on the employment of disabled people in the Community,[7] the Council established a guideline framework setting out examples of positive action to promote the employment and training of disabled people, and in its Resolution of 17 June 1999 on equal employment opportunities for people with disabilities,[8] affirmed the importance of giving specific attention inter alia to recruitment, retention, training and lifelong learning with regard to disabled persons.

(28) This Directive lays down minimum requirements, thus giving the Member States the option of introducing or maintaining more favourable provisions. The implementation of this Directive should not serve to justify any regression in relation to the situation which already prevails in each Member State.

(29) Persons who have been subject to discrimination based on religion or belief, disability, age or sexual orientation should have adequate means of legal protection. To provide a more effective level of protection, associations or legal entities should also be empowered to engage in proceedings, as the Member States so determine, either on behalf or in support of any victim, without prejudice to national rules of procedure concerning representation and defence before the courts.

(30) The effective implementation of the principle of equality requires adequate judicial protection against victimisation.

(31) The rules on the burden of proof must be adapted when there is a prima facie case of discrimination and, for the principle of equal treatment to be applied effectively, the burden of proof must shift back to the respondent when evidence of such discrimination is brought. However, it is not for the respondent to prove that the plaintiff adheres to a particular religion or belief, has a particular disability, is of a particular age or has a particular sexual orientation.

(32) Member States need not apply the rules on the burden of proof to proceedings in which it is for the court or other competent body to investigate the facts of the case. The procedures thus referred to are those in which the plaintiff is not required to prove the facts, which it is for the court or competent body to investigate.

(33) Member States should promote dialogue between the social partners and, within the framework of national practice, with non-governmental organisations to address different forms of discrimination at the workplace and to combat them.

(34) The need to promote peace and reconciliation between the major communities in Northern Ireland necessitates the incorporation of particular provisions into this Directive.

(35) Member States should provide for effective, proportionate and dissuasive sanctions in case of breaches of the obligations under this Directive.

(36) Member States may entrust the social partners, at their joint request, with the implementation of this Directive, as regards the provisions concerning collective agreements, provided they take any necessary steps to ensure that they are at all times able to guarantee the results required by this Directive.

(37) In accordance with the principle of subsidiarity set out in Article 5 of the EC Treaty, the objective of this Directive, namely the creation within the Community of a level playing-field as regards equality in employment and occupation, cannot be sufficiently achieved by the Member States and can therefore, by reason of the scale and impact of the action, be better achieved at Community level. In accordance with the principle of proportionality, as set out in that Article, this Directive does not go beyond what is necessary in order to achieve that objective.

NOTES

1 OJ C177 E, 27.6.2000, p 42.
2 Opinion delivered on 12 October 2000 (not yet published in the Official Journal).
3 OJ C204, 18.7.2000, p 82.
4 OJ C226, 8.8.2000, p 1.
5 OJ L9, 14.2.1976, p 40.
6 OJ L180, 19.7.2000, p 22.
7 OJ L225, 12.8.1986, p 43.
8 OJ C186, 2.7.1999, p 3.

HAS ADOPTED THIS DIRECTIVE—

CHAPTER I
GENERAL PROVISIONS

Article 1

Purpose

The purpose of this Directive is to lay down a general framework for combating discrimination on the grounds of religion or belief, disability, age or sexual orientation as regards employment and occupation, with a view to putting into effect in the Member States the principle of equal treatment.

[3994]

Article 2

Concept of discrimination

1. For the purposes of this Directive, the "principle of equal treatment" shall mean that there shall be no direct or indirect discrimination whatsoever on any of the grounds referred to in Article 1.

2. For the purposes of paragraph 1—

(a) direct discrimination shall be taken to occur where one person is treated less favourably than another is, has been or would be treated in a comparable situation, on any of the grounds referred to in Article 1;

(b) indirect discrimination shall be taken to occur where an apparently neutral provision, criterion or practice would put persons having a particular religion or belief, a particular disability, a particular age, or a particular sexual orientation at a particular disadvantage compared with other persons unless—

(i) that provision, criterion or practice is objectively justified by a legitimate aim and the means of achieving that aim are appropriate and necessary, or

(ii) as regards persons with a particular disability, the employer or any person or organisation to whom this Directive applies, is obliged, under national legislation, to take appropriate measures in line with the principles contained in Article 5 in order to eliminate disadvantages entailed by such provision, criterion or practice.

3. Harassment shall be deemed to be a form of discrimination within the meaning of paragraph 1, when unwanted conduct related to any of the grounds referred to in Article 1 takes place with the purpose or effect of violating the dignity of a person and of creating an intimidating, hostile, degrading, humiliating or offensive environment. In this context, the concept of harassment may be defined in accordance with the national laws and practice of the Member States.

4. An instruction to discriminate against persons on any of the grounds referred to in Article 1 shall be deemed to be discrimination within the meaning of paragraph 1.

5. This Directive shall be without prejudice to measures laid down by national law which, in a democratic society, are necessary for public security, for the maintenance of public order and the prevention of criminal offences, for the protection of health and for the protection of the rights and freedoms of others.

[3995]

Article 3

Scope

1. Within the limits of the areas of competence conferred on the Community, this Directive shall apply to all persons, as regards both the public and private sectors, including public bodies, in relation to—

(a) conditions for access to employment, to self-employment or to occupation, including selection criteria and recruitment conditions, whatever the branch of activity and at all levels of the professional hierarchy, including promotion;

(b) access to all types and to all levels of vocational guidance, vocational training, advanced vocational training and retraining, including practical work experience;

(c) employment and working conditions, including dismissals and pay;

(d) membership of, and involvement in, an organisation of workers or employers, or any organisation whose members carry on a particular profession, including the benefits provided for by such organisations.

2. This Directive does not cover differences of treatment based on nationality and is without prejudice to provisions and conditions relating to the entry into and residence of third-country nationals and stateless persons in the territory of Member States, and to any treatment which arises from the legal status of the third-country nationals and stateless persons concerned.

3. This Directive does not apply to payments of any kind made by state schemes or similar, including state social security or social protection schemes.

4. Member States may provide that this Directive, in so far as it relates to discrimination on the grounds of disability and age, shall not apply to the armed forces.

[3996]

Article 4

Occupational requirements

1. Notwithstanding Article 2(1) and (2), Member States may provide that a difference of treatment which is based on a characteristic related to any of the grounds referred to in Article 1 shall not constitute discrimination where, by reason of the nature of the particular occupational activities concerned or of the context in which they are carried out, such a characteristic constitutes a genuine and determining occupational requirement, provided that the objective is legitimate and the requirement is proportionate.

2. Member States may maintain national legislation in force at the date of adoption of this Directive or provide for future legislation incorporating national practices existing at the date of adoption of this Directive pursuant to which, in the case of occupational activities within churches and other public or private organisations the ethos of which is based on religion or belief, a difference of treatment based on a person's religion or belief shall not constitute discrimination where, by reason of the nature of these activities or of the context in which they are carried out, a person's religion or belief constitute a genuine, legitimate and justified occupational requirement, having regard to the organisation's ethos. This difference of treatment shall be implemented taking account of Member States' constitutional provisions and principles, as well as the general principles of Community law, and should not justify discrimination on another ground.

Provided that its provisions are otherwise complied with, this Directive shall thus not prejudice the right of churches and other public or private organisations, the ethos of which is based on religion or belief, acting in conformity with national constitutions and laws, to require individuals working for them to act in good faith and with loyalty to the organisation's ethos.

[3997]

Article 5

Reasonable accommodation for disabled persons

In order to guarantee compliance with the principle of equal treatment in relation to persons with disabilities, reasonable accommodation shall be provided. This means that employers shall take appropriate measures, where needed in a particular case, to enable a person with a disability to have access to, participate in, or advance in employment, or to undergo training, unless such measures would impose a disproportionate burden on the employer. This burden shall not be disproportionate when it is sufficiently remedied by measures existing within the framework of the disability policy of the Member State concerned.

[3998]

Article 6

Justification of differences of treatment on grounds of age

1. Notwithstanding Article 2(2), Member States may provide that differences of treatment on grounds of age shall not constitute discrimination, if, within the context of national law, they are objectively and reasonably justified by a legitimate aim, including legitimate employment policy, labour market and vocational training objectives, and if the means of achieving that aim are appropriate and necessary.

Such differences of treatment may include, among others—

(a) the setting of special conditions on access to employment and vocational training, employment and occupation, including dismissal and remuneration conditions, for young people, older workers and persons with caring responsibilities in order to promote their vocational integration or ensure their protection;

(b) the fixing of minimum conditions of age, professional experience or seniority in service for access to employment or to certain advantages linked to employment;

(c) the fixing of a maximum age for recruitment which is based on the training requirements of the post in question or the need for a reasonable period of employment before retirement.

2. Notwithstanding Article 2(2), Member States may provide that the fixing for occupational social security schemes of ages for admission or entitlement to retirement or invalidity benefits, including the fixing under those schemes of different ages for employees or groups or categories of employees, and the use, in the context of such schemes, of age criteria in actuarial calculations, does not constitute discrimination on the grounds of age, provided this does not result in discrimination on the grounds of sex.

[3999]

Article 7

Positive action

1. With a view to ensuring full equality in practice, the principle of equal treatment shall not prevent any Member State from maintaining or adopting specific measures to prevent or compensate for disadvantages linked to any of the grounds referred to in Article 1.

2. With regard to disabled persons, the principle of equal treatment shall be without prejudice to the right of Member States to maintain or adopt provisions on the protection of health and safety at work or to measures aimed at creating or maintaining provisions or facilities for safeguarding or promoting their integration into the working environment.

[4000]

Article 8

Minimum requirements

1. Member States may introduce or maintain provisions which are more favourable to the protection of the principle of equal treatment than those laid down in this Directive.

2. The implementation of this Directive shall under no circumstances constitute grounds for a reduction in the level of protection against discrimination already afforded by Member States in the fields covered by this Directive.

[4001]

CHAPTER II
REMEDIES AND ENFORCEMENT

Article 9

Defence of rights

1. Member States shall ensure that judicial and/or administrative procedures, including where they deem it appropriate conciliation procedures, for the enforcement of obligations under this Directive are available to all persons who consider themselves wronged by failure to apply the principle of equal treatment to them, even after the relationship in which the discrimination is alleged to have occurred has ended.

2. Member States shall ensure that associations, organisations or other legal entities which have, in accordance with the criteria laid down by their national law, a legitimate interest in ensuring that the provisions of this Directive are complied with, may engage, either on behalf or in support of the complainant, with his or her approval, in any judicial and/or administrative procedure provided for the enforcement of obligations under this Directive.

3. Paragraphs 1 and 2 are without prejudice to national rules relating to time limits for bringing actions as regards the principle of equality of treatment.

[4002]

Article 10

Burden of proof

1. Member States shall take such measures as are necessary, in accordance with their national judicial systems, to ensure that, when persons who consider themselves wronged

because the principle of equal treatment has not been applied to them establish, before a court or other competent authority, facts from which it may be presumed that there has been direct or indirect discrimination, it shall be for the respondent to prove that there has been no breach of the principle of equal treatment.

2. Paragraph 1 shall not prevent Member States from introducing rules of evidence which are more favourable to plaintiffs.

3. Paragraph 1 shall not apply to criminal procedures.

4. Paragraphs 1, 2 and 3 shall also apply to any legal proceedings commenced in accordance with Article 9(2).

5. Member States need not apply paragraph 1 to proceedings in which it is for the court or competent body to investigate the facts of the case.

[4003]

Article 11

Victimisation

Member States shall introduce into their national legal systems such measures as are necessary to protect employees against dismissal or other adverse treatment by the employer as a reaction to a complaint within the undertaking or to any legal proceedings aimed at enforcing compliance with the principle of equal treatment.

[4004]

Article 12

Dissemination of information

Member States shall take care that the provisions adopted pursuant to this Directive, together with the relevant provisions already in force in this field, are brought to the attention of the persons concerned by all appropriate means, for example at the workplace, throughout their territory.

[4005]

Article 13

Social dialogue

1. Member States shall, in accordance with their national traditions and practice, take adequate measures to promote dialogue between the social partners with a view to fostering equal treatment, including through the monitoring of workplace practices, collective agreements, codes of conduct and through research or exchange of experiences and good practices.

2. Where consistent with their national traditions and practice, Member States shall encourage the social partners, without prejudice to their autonomy, to conclude at the appropriate level agreements laying down anti-discrimination rules in the fields referred to in Article 3 which fall within the scope of collective bargaining. These agreements shall respect the minimum requirements laid down by this Directive and by the relevant national implementing measures.

[4006]

Article 14

Dialogue with non-governmental organisations

Member States shall encourage dialogue with appropriate non-governmental organisations which have, in accordance with their national law and practice, a legitimate interest in contributing to the fight against discrimination on any of the grounds referred to in Article 1 with a view to promoting the principle of equal treatment.

[4007]

CHAPTER III
PARTICULAR PROVISIONS

Article 15

Northern Ireland

1. In order to tackle the under-representation of one of the major religious communities in the police service of Northern Ireland, differences in treatment regarding recruitment into

that service, including its support staff, shall not constitute discrimination insofar as those differences in treatment are expressly authorised by national legislation.

2. In order to maintain a balance of opportunity in employment for teachers in Northern Ireland while furthering the reconciliation of historical divisions between the major religious communities there, the provisions on religion or belief in this Directive shall not apply to the recruitment of teachers in schools in Northern Ireland in so far as this is expressly authorised by national legislation.

[4008]

CHAPTER IV
FINAL PROVISIONS

Article 16

Compliance

Member States shall take the necessary measures to ensure that—

(a) any laws, regulations and administrative provisions contrary to the principle of equal treatment are abolished;

(b) any provisions contrary to the principle of equal treatment which are included in contracts or collective agreements, internal rules of undertakings or rules governing the independent occupations and professions and workers' and employers' organisations are, or may be, declared null and void or are amended.

[4009]

Article 17

Sanctions

Member States shall lay down the rules on sanctions applicable to infringements of the national provisions adopted pursuant to this Directive and shall take all measures necessary to ensure that they are applied. The sanctions, which may comprise the payment of compensation to the victim, must be effective, proportionate and dissuasive. Member States shall notify those provisions to the Commission by 2 December 2003 at the latest and shall notify it without delay of any subsequent amendment affecting them.

[4010]

Article 18

Implementation

Member States shall adopt the laws, regulations and administrative provisions necessary to comply with this Directive by 2 December 2003 at the latest or may entrust the social partners, at their joint request, with the implementation of this Directive as regards provisions concerning collective agreements. In such cases, Member States shall ensure that, no later than 2 December 2003, the social partners introduce the necessary measures by agreement, the Member States concerned being required to take any necessary measures to enable them at any time to be in a position to guarantee the results imposed by this Directive. They shall forthwith inform the Commission thereof.

In order to take account of particular conditions, Member States may, if necessary, have an additional period of 3 years from 2 December 2003, that is to say a total of 6 years, to implement the provisions of this Directive on age and disability discrimination. In that event they shall inform the Commission forthwith. Any Member State which chooses to use this additional period shall report annually to the Commission on the steps it is taking to tackle age and disability discrimination and on the progress it is making towards implementation. The Commission shall report annually to the Council.

When Member States adopt these measures, they shall contain a reference to this Directive or be accompanied by such reference on the occasion of their official publication. The methods of making such reference shall be laid down by Member States.

[4011]

Article 19

Report

1. Member States shall communicate to the Commission, by 2 December 2005 at the latest and every five years thereafter, all the information necessary for the Commission to draw up a report to the European Parliament and the Council on the application of this Directive.

2. The Commission's report shall take into account, as appropriate, the viewpoints of the social partners and relevant non-governmental organisations. In accordance with the principle of gender mainstreaming, this report shall, inter alia, provide an assessment of the impact of the measures taken on women and men. In the light of the information received, this report shall include, if necessary, proposals to revise and update this Directive.

[4012]

Article 20

Entry into force

This Directive shall enter into force on the day of its publication in the Official Journal of the European Communities.

[4013]

Article 21

Addressees

This Directive is addressed to the Member States.

[4014]

COUNCIL DIRECTIVE

of 12 March 2001

on the approximation of the laws of the Member States relating to the safeguarding of employees' rights in the event of transfers of undertakings, businesses or parts of undertakings or businesses

(2001/23/EC)

NOTES

Date of publication in OJ: OJ L82, 22.03.2001, p 16.

This Directive consolidates Directive 77/187/EC ('the Acquired Rights Directive') as amended by Directive 98/50/EC. Annex II at **[4031]** is a table correlating the provisions in the former and current Directives. For the domestic implementation of this Directive, see the Transfer of Undertakings (Protection of Employment) Regulations 2006, SI 2006/246 at **[3376]**.

THE COUNCIL OF THE EUROPEAN UNION,

Having regard to the Treaty establishing the European Community, and in particular Article 94 thereof,

Having regard to the proposal from the Commission,

Having regard to the opinion of the European Parliament,[1]

Having regard to the opinion of the Economic and Social Committee,[2]

Whereas:

(1) Council Directive 77/187/EEC of 14 February 1977 on the approximation of the laws of the Member States relating to the safeguarding of employees' rights in the event of transfers of undertakings, businesses or parts of undertakings or businesses[3] has been substantially amended.[4] In the interests of clarity and rationality, it should therefore be codified.

(2) Economic trends are bringing in their wake, at both national and Community level, changes in the structure of undertakings, through transfers of undertakings, businesses or parts of undertakings or businesses to other employers as a result of legal transfers or mergers.

(3) It is necessary to provide for the protection of employees in the event of a change of employer, in particular, to ensure that their rights are safeguarded.

(4) Differences still remain in the Member States as regards the extent of the protection of employees in this respect and these differences should be reduced.

(5) The Community Charter of the Fundamental Social Rights of Workers adopted on 9 December 1989 ("Social Charter") states, in points 7, 17 and 18 in particular that: "The completion of the internal market must lead to an improvement in the living and working conditions of workers in the European Community. The improvement must cover, where necessary, the development of certain aspects of employment regulations such as procedures for collective redundancies and those regarding bankruptcies. Information, consultation and

participation for workers must be developed along appropriate lines, taking account of the practice in force in the various Member States. Such information, consultation and participation must be implemented in due time, particularly in connection with restructuring operations in undertakings or in cases of mergers having an impact on the employment of workers".

(6) In 1977 the Council adopted Directive 77/187/EEC to promote the harmonisation of the relevant national laws ensuring the safeguarding of the rights of employees and requiring transferors and transferees to inform and consult employees' representatives in good time.

(7) That Directive was subsequently amended in the light of the impact of the internal market, the legislative tendencies of the Member States with regard to the rescue of undertakings in economic difficulties, the case-law of the Court of Justice of the European Communities, Council Directive 75/129/EEC of 17 February 1975 on the approximation of the laws of the Member States relating to collective redundancies[5] and the legislation already in force in most Member States.

(8) Considerations of legal security and transparency required that the legal concept of transfer be clarified in the light of the case-law of the Court of Justice. Such clarification has not altered the scope of Directive 77/187/EEC as interpreted by the Court of Justice.

(9) The Social Charter recognises the importance of the fight against all forms of discrimination, especially based on sex, colour, race, opinion and creed.

(10) This Directive should be without prejudice to the time limits set out in Annex I Part B within which the Member States are to comply with Directive 77/187/EEC, and the act amending it,

NOTES

1 Opinion delivered on 25 October 2000 (not yet published in the Official Journal).
2 OJ C367, 20.12.2000, p 21.
3 OJ L61, 5.3.1977, p 26.
4 See Annex I, Part A.
5 OJ L48, 22.2.1975, p 29. Directive replaced by Directive 98/59/EC (OJ L225, 12.8.1998, p 16).

HAS ADOPTED THIS DIRECTIVE—

CHAPTER I
SCOPE AND DEFINITIONS

Article 1

1.

(a) This Directive shall apply to any transfer of an undertaking, business, or part of an undertaking or business to another employer as a result of a legal transfer or merger.

(b) Subject to subparagraph (a) and the following provisions of this Article, there is a transfer within the meaning of this Directive where there is a transfer of an economic entity which retains its identity, meaning an organised grouping of resources which has the objective of pursuing an economic activity, whether or not that activity is central or ancillary.

(c) This Directive shall apply to public and private undertakings engaged in economic activities whether or not they are operating for gain. An administrative reorganisation of public administrative authorities, or the transfer of administrative functions between public administrative authorities, is not a transfer within the meaning of this Directive.

2. This Directive shall apply where and in so far as the undertaking, business or part of the undertaking or business to be transferred is situated within the territorial scope of the Treaty.

3. This Directive shall not apply to seagoing vessels.

[4015]

Article 2

1. For the purposes of this Directive—

(a) "transferor" shall mean any natural or legal person who, by reason of a transfer within the meaning of Article 1(1), ceases to be the employer in respect of the undertaking, business or part of the undertaking or business;

(b) "transferee" shall mean any natural or legal person who, by reason of a transfer within the meaning of Article 1(1), becomes the employer in respect of the undertaking, business or part of the undertaking or business;

(c) "representatives of employees" and related expressions shall mean the representatives of the employees provided for by the laws or practices of the Member States;

(d) "employee" shall mean any person who, in the Member State concerned, is protected as an employee under national employment law.

2. This Directive shall be without prejudice to national law as regards the definition of contract of employment or employment relationship.

However, Member States shall not exclude from the scope of this Directive contracts of employment or employment relationships solely because—

(a) of the number of working hours performed or to be performed,

(b) they are employment relationships governed by a fixed-duration contract of employment within the meaning of Article 1(1) of Council Directive 91/383/EEC of 25 June 1991 supplementing the measures to encourage improvements in the safety and health at work of workers with a fixed-duration employment relationship or a temporary employment relationship, or

they are temporary employment relationships within the meaning of Article 1(2) of Directive 91/383/EEC, and the undertaking, business or part of the undertaking or business transferred is, or is part of, the temporary employment business which is the employer.

[4016]

CHAPTER II
SAFEGUARDING OF EMPLOYEES' RIGHTS

Article 3

1. The transferor's rights and obligations arising from a contract of employment or from an employment relationship existing on the date of a transfer shall, by reason of such transfer, be transferred to the transferee.

Member States may provide that, after the date of transfer, the transferor and the transferee shall be jointly and severally liable in respect of obligations which arose before the date of transfer from a contract of employment or an employment relationship existing on the date of the transfer.

2. Member States may adopt appropriate measures to ensure that the transferor notifies the transferee of all the rights and obligations which will be transferred to the transferee under this Article, so far as those rights and obligations are or ought to have been known to the transferor at the time of the transfer. A failure by the transferor to notify the transferee of any such right or obligation shall not affect the transfer of that right or obligation and the rights of any employees against the transferee and/or transferor in respect of that right or obligation.

3. Following the transfer, the transferee shall continue to observe the terms and conditions agreed in any collective agreement on the same terms applicable to the transferor under that agreement, until the date of termination or expiry of the collective agreement or the entry into force or application of another collective agreement.

Member States may limit the period for observing such terms and conditions with the proviso that it shall not be less than one year.

4.

(a) Unless Member States provide otherwise, paragraphs 1 and 3 shall not apply in relation to employees' rights to old-age, invalidity or survivors' benefits under supplementary company or intercompany pension schemes outside the statutory social security schemes in Member States.

(b) Even where they do not provide in accordance with subparagraph (a) that paragraphs 1 and 3 apply in relation to such rights, Member States shall adopt the measures necessary to protect the interests of employees and of persons no longer employed in the transferor's business at the time of the transfer in respect of rights conferring on them immediate or prospective entitlement to old age benefits, including survivors' benefits, under supplementary schemes referred to in subparagraph (a).

[4017]

Article 4

1. The transfer of the undertaking, business or part of the undertaking or business shall not in itself constitute grounds for dismissal by the transferor or the transferee. This provision

shall not stand in the way of dismissals that may take place for economic, technical or organisational reasons entailing changes in the workforce.

Member States may provide that the first subparagraph shall not apply to certain specific categories of employees who are not covered by the laws or practice of the Member States in respect of protection against dismissal.

2. If the contract of employment or the employment relationship is terminated because the transfer involves a substantial change in working conditions to the detriment of the employee, the employer shall be regarded as having been responsible for termination of the contract of employment or of the employment relationship.

[4018]

Article 5

1. Unless Member States provide otherwise, Articles 3 and 4 shall not apply to any transfer of an undertaking, business or part of an undertaking or business where the transferor is the subject of bankruptcy proceedings or any analogous insolvency proceedings which have been instituted with a view to the liquidation of the assets of the transferor and are under the supervision of a competent public authority (which may be an insolvency practitioner authorised by a competent public authority).

2. Where Articles 3 and 4 apply to a transfer during insolvency proceedings which have been opened in relation to a transferor (whether or not those proceedings have been instituted with a view to the liquidation of the assets of the transferor) and provided that such proceedings are under the supervision of a competent public authority (which may be an insolvency practitioner determined by national law) a Member State may provide that—

(a) notwithstanding Article 3(1), the transferor's debts arising from any contracts of employment or employment relationships and payable before the transfer or before the opening of the insolvency proceedings shall not be transferred to the transferee, provided that such proceedings give rise, under the law of that Member State, to protection at least equivalent to that provided for in situations covered by Council Directive 80/987/EEC of 20 October 1980 on the approximation of the laws of the Member States relating to the protection of employees in the event of the insolvency of their employer, and, or alternatively, that,

(b) the transferee, transferor or person or persons exercising the transferor's functions, on the one hand, and the representatives of the employees on the other hand may agree alterations, in so far as current law or practice permits, to the employees' terms and conditions of employment designed to safeguard employment opportunities by ensuring the survival of the undertaking, business or part of the undertaking or business.

3. A Member State may apply paragraph 20(b) to any transfers where the transferor is in a situation of serious economic crisis, as defined by national law, provided that the situation is declared by a competent public authority and open to judicial supervision, on condition that such provisions already existed in national law on 17 July 1998.

The Commission shall present a report on the effects of this provision before 17 July 2003 and shall submit any appropriate proposals to the Council.

4. Member States shall take appropriate measures with a view to preventing misuse of insolvency proceedings in such a way as to deprive employees of the rights provided for in this Directive.

[4019]

Article 6

1. If the undertaking, business or part of an undertaking or business preserves its autonomy, the status and function of the representatives or of the representation of the employees affected by the transfer shall be preserved on the same terms and subject to the same conditions as existed before the date of the transfer by virtue of law, regulation, administrative provision or agreement, provided that the conditions necessary for the constitution of the employee's representation are fulfilled.

The first subparagraph shall not supply if, under the laws, regulations, administrative provisions or practice in the Member States, or by agreement with the representatives of the employees, the conditions necessary for the reappointment of the representatives of the employees or for the reconstitution of the representation of the employees are fulfilled.

Where the transferor is the subject of bankruptcy proceedings or any analogous insolvency proceedings which have been instituted with a view to the liquidation of the assets of the transferor and are under the supervision of a competent public authority (which may be an insolvency practitioner authorised by a competent public authority), Member States may take the necessary measures to ensure that the transferred employees are properly represented until the new election or designation of representatives of the employees.

If the undertaking, business or part of an undertaking or business does not preserve its autonomy, the Member States shall take the necessary measures to ensure that the employees transferred who were represented before the transfer continue to be properly represented during the period necessary for the reconstitution or reappointment of the representation of employees in accordance with national law or practice.

2. If the term of office of the representatives of the employees affected by the transfer expires as a result of the transfer, the representatives shall continue to enjoy the protection provided by the laws, regulations, administrative provisions or practice of the Member States.

[4020]

CHAPTER III
INFORMATION AND CONSULTATION

Article 7

1. The transferor and transferee shall be required to inform the representatives of their respective employees affected by the transfer of the following—

— the date or proposed date of the transfer,
— the reasons for the transfer,
— the legal, economic and social implications of the transfer for the employees,
— any measures envisaged in relation to the employees.

The transferor must give such information to the representatives of his employees in good time, before the transfer is carried out.

The transferee must give such information to the representatives of his employees in good time, and in any event before his employees are directly affected by the transfer as regards their conditions of work and employment.

2. Where the transferor or the transferee envisages measures in relation to his employees, he shall consult the representatives of this employees in good time on such measures with a view to reaching an agreement.

3. Member States whose laws, regulations or administrative provisions provide that representatives of the employees may have recourse to an arbitration board to obtain a decision on the measures to be taken in relation to employees may limit the obligations laid down in paragraphs 1 and 2 to cases where the transfer carried out gives rise to a change in the business likely to entail serious disadvantages for a considerable number of the employees.

The information and consultations shall cover at least the measures envisaged in relation to the employees.

The information must be provided and consultations take place in good time before the change in the business as referred to in the first subparagraph is effected.

4. The obligations laid down in this Article shall apply irrespective of whether the decision resulting in the transfer is taken by the employer or an undertaking controlling the employer.

In considering alleged breaches of the information and consultation requirements laid down by this Directive, the argument that such a breach occurred because the information was not provided by an undertaking controlling the employer shall not be accepted as an excuse.

5. Member States may limit the obligations laid down in paragraphs 1, 2 and 3 to undertakings or businesses which, in terms of the number of employees, meet the conditions for the election or nomination of a collegiate body representing the employees.

6. Member States shall provide that, where there are no representatives of the employees in an undertaking or business through no fault of their own, the employees concerned must be informed in advance of—

— the date or proposed date of the transfer,
— the reason for the transfer,
— the legal, economic and social implications of the transfer for the employees,
— any measures envisaged in relation to the employees.

[4021]

CHAPTER IV
FINAL PROVISIONS

Article 8

This Directive shall not affect the right of Member States to apply or introduce laws, regulations or administrative provisions which are more favourable to employees or to promote or permit collective agreements or agreements between social partners more favourable to employees.

[4022]

Article 9

Member States shall introduce into their national legal systems such measures as are necessary to enable all employees and representatives of employees who consider themselves wronged by failure to comply with the obligations arising from this Directive to pursue their claims by judicial process after possible recourse to other competent authorities.

[4023]

Article 10

The Commission shall submit to the Council an analysis of the effect of the provisions of this Directive before 17 July 2006. It shall propose any amendment which may seem necessary.

[4024]

Article 11

Member States shall communicate to the Commission the texts of the laws, regulations and administrative provisions which they adopt in the field covered by this Directive.

[4025]

Article 12

Directive 77/187/EEC, as amended by the Directive referred to in Annex I, Part A, is repealed, without prejudice to the obligations of the Member States concerning the time limits for implementation set out in Annex I, Part B.

References to the repealed Directive shall be construed as references to this Directive and shall be read in accordance with the correlation table in Annex II.

[4026]

Article 13

This Directive shall enter into force on the 20th day following its publication in the Official Journal of the European Communities.

[4027]

Article 14

This Directive is addressed to the Member States.

[4028]

ANNEX I

PART A
REPEALED DIRECTIVE AND ITS AMENDING DIRECTIVE

(*referred to in Article 12*)

Council Directive 77/187/EEC (OJ L 61, 5.3.1977, p. 26)

Council Directive 98/50/EC (OJ L 201, 17.7.1998, p. 88)

[4029]

PART B
DEADLINES FOR TRANSPOSITION INTO NATIONAL LAW

(*referred to in Article 12*)

Directive	*Deadline for transposition*
77/187/EEC	16 February 1979
98/50/EC	17 July 2001

[4030]

ANNEX II
CORRELATION TABLE

Directive 77/187/EEC	*This Directive*
Article 1	Article 1
Article 2	Article 2
Article 3	Article 3
Article 4	Article 4
Article 4a	Article 5
Article 5	Article 6
Article 6	Article 7
Article 7	Article 8
Article 7a	Article 9
Article 7b	Article 10
Article 8	Article 11
—	Article 12
—	Article 13
—	Article 14
—	Annex I
—	Annex II

[4031]

COUNCIL DIRECTIVE

of 8 October 2001

supplementing the Statute for a European company with regard to the involvement of employees

(2001/86/EC)

NOTES

Date of publication in OJ: OJ L294, 10.11.2001, p 22.

For the domestic implementation of this Directive see the European Public Limited-Liability Company Regulations 2004, SI 2004/2326 at **[3177]**.

THE COUNCIL OF THE EUROPEAN UNION,

Having regard to the Treaty establishing the European Community, and in particular Article 308 thereof,

Having regard to the amended proposal from the Commission,[1]

Having regard to the opinion of the European Parliament,[2]

Having regard to the opinion of the Economic and Social Committee,[3]

Whereas:

(1) In order to attain the objectives of the Treaty, Council Regulation (EC) No 2157/2001[4] establishes a Statute for a European company (SE).

(2) That Regulation aims at creating a uniform legal framework within which companies from different Member States should be able to plan and carry out the reorganisation of their business on a Community scale.

(3) In order to promote the social objectives of the Community, special provisions have to be set, notably in the field of employee involvement, aimed at ensuring that the establishment of an SE does not entail the disappearance or reduction of practices of employee involvement existing within the companies participating in the establishment of an SE. This objective should be pursued through the establishment of a set of rules in this field, supplementing the provisions of the Regulation.

(4) Since the objectives of the proposed action, as outlined above, cannot be sufficiently achieved by the Member States, in that the object is to establish a set of rules on employee involvement applicable to the SE, and can therefore, by reason of the scale and impact of the proposed action, be better achieved at Community level, the Community may adopt measures, in accordance with the principle of subsidiarity as set out in Article 5 of the Treaty. In accordance with the principle of proportionality, as set out in that Article, this Directive does not go beyond what is necessary to achieve these objectives.

(5) The great diversity of rules and practices existing in the Member States as regards the manner in which employees' representatives are involved in decision-making within companies makes it inadvisable to set up a single European model of employee involvement applicable to the SE.

(6) Information and consultation procedures at transnational level should nevertheless be ensured in all cases of creation of an SE.

(7) If and when participation rights exist within one or more companies establishing an SE, they should be preserved through their transfer to the SE, once established, unless the parties decide otherwise.

(8) The concrete procedures of employee transnational information and consultation, as well as, if applicable, participation, to apply to each SE should be defined primarily by means of an agreement between the parties concerned or, in the absence thereof, through the application of a set of subsidiary rules.

(9) Member States should still have the option of not applying the standard rules relating to participation in the case of a merger, given the diversity of national systems for employee involvement. Existing systems and practices of participation where appropriate at the level of participating companies must in that case be maintained by adapting registration rules.

(10) The voting rules within the special body representing the employees for negotiation purposes, in particular when concluding agreements providing for a level of participation lower than the one existing within one or more of the participating companies, should be proportionate to the risk of disappearance or reduction of existing systems and practices of participation. That risk is greater in the case of an SE established by way of transformation or merger than by way of creating a holding company or a common subsidiary.

(11) In the absence of an agreement subsequent to the negotiation between employees' representatives and the competent organs of the participating companies, provision should be made for certain standard requirements to apply to the SE, once it is established. These standard requirements should ensure effective practices of transnational information and consultation of employees, as well as their participation in the relevant organs of the SE if and when such participation existed before its establishment within the participating companies.

(12) Provision should be made for the employees' representatives acting within the framework of the Directive to enjoy, when exercising their functions, protection and guarantees which are similar to those provided to employees' representatives by the legislation and/or practice of the country of employment. They should not be subject to any discrimination as a result of the lawful exercise of their activities and should enjoy adequate protection as regards dismissal and other sanctions.

(13) The confidentiality of sensitive information should be preserved even after the expiry of the employees' representatives terms of office and provision should be made to allow the competent organ of the SE to withhold information which would seriously harm, if subject to public disclosure, the functioning of the SE.

(14) Where an SE and its subsidiaries and establishments are subject to Council Directive 94/45/EC of 22 September 1994 on the establishment of a European Works Council or a

procedure in Community-scale undertakings and Community-scale groups of undertakings for the purposes of informing and consulting employees,[5] the provisions of that Directive and the provision transposing it into national legislation should not apply to it nor to its subsidiaries and establishments, unless the special negotiating body decides not to open negotiations or to terminate negotiations already opened.

(15) This Directive should not affect other existing rights regarding involvement and need not affect other existing representation structures, provided for by Community and national laws and practices.

(16) Member States should take appropriate measures in the event of failure to comply with the obligations laid down in this Directive.

(17) The Treaty has not provided the necessary powers for the Community to adopt the proposed Directive, other than those provided for in Article 308.

(18) It is a fundamental principle and stated aim of this Directive to secure employees' acquired rights as regards involvement in company decisions. Employee rights in force before the establishment of SEs should provide the basis for employee rights of involvement in the SE (the "before and after" principle). Consequently, that approach should apply not only to the initial establishment of an SE but also to structural changes in an existing SE and to the companies affected by structural change processes.

(19) Member States should be able to provide that representatives of trade unions may be members of a special negotiating body regardless of whether they are employees of a company participating in the establishment of an SE. Member States should in this context in particular be able to introduce this right in cases where trade union representatives have the right to be members of, and to vote in, supervisory or administrative company organs in accordance with national legislation.

(20) In several Member States, employee involvement and other areas of industrial relations are based on both national legislation and practice which in this context is understood also to cover collective agreements at various national, sectoral and/or company levels,

NOTES

1 OJ C138, 29.5.1991, p 8.
2 OJ C342, 20.12.1993, p 15.
3 OJ C124, 21.5.1990, p 34.
4 See page 1 of this Official Journal.
5 OJ L254, 30.9.1994, p 64. Directive as last amended by Directive 97/74/EC (OJ L10, 16.1.1998, p 22).

HAS ADOPTED THIS DIRECTIVE—

SECTION I
GENERAL

Article 1

Objective

1. This Directive governs the involvement of employees in the affairs of European public limited-liability companies (Societas Europaea, hereinafter referred to as "SE"), as referred to in Regulation (EC) No 2157/2001.

2. To this end, arrangements for the involvement of employees shall be established in every SE in accordance with the negotiating procedure referred to in Articles 3 to 6 or, under the circumstances specified in Article 7, in accordance with the Annex.

[4032]

Article 2

Definitions

For the purposes of this Directive—

(a) "SE" means any company established in accordance with Regulation (EC) No 2157/2001;
(b) "participating companies" means the companies directly participating in the establishing of an SE;
(c) "subsidiary" of a company means an undertaking over which that company exercises a dominant influence defined in accordance with Article 3(2) to (7) of Directive 94/45/EC;

(d) "concerned subsidiary or establishment" means a subsidiary or establishment of a participating company which is proposed to become a subsidiary or establishment of the SE upon its formation;

(e) "employees' representatives" means the employees' representatives provided for by national law and/or practice;

(f) "representative body" means the body representative of the employees set up by the agreements referred to in Article 4 or in accordance with the provisions of the Annex, with the purpose of informing and consulting the employees of an SE and its subsidiaries and establishments situated in the Community and, where applicable, of exercising participation rights in relation to the SE;

(g) "special negotiating body" means the body established in accordance with Article 3 to negotiate with the competent body of the participating companies regarding the establishment of arrangements for the involvement of employees within the SE;

(h) "involvement of employees" means any mechanism, including information, consultation and participation, through which employees' representatives may exercise an influence on decisions to be taken within the company;

(i) "information" means the informing of the body representative of the employees and/or employees' representatives by the competent organ of the SE on questions which concern the SE itself and any of its subsidiaries or establishments situated in another Member State or which exceed the powers of the decision-making organs in a single Member State at a time, in a manner and with a content which allows the employees' representatives to undertake an in-depth assessment of the possible impact and, where appropriate, prepare consultations with the competent organ of the SE;

(j) "consultation" means the establishment of dialogue and exchange of views between the body representative of the employees and/or the employees' representatives and the competent organ of the SE, at a time, in a manner, and with a content which allows the employees' representatives, on the basis of information provided, to express an opinion on measures envisaged by the competent organ which may be taken into account in the decision-making process within the SE;

(k) "participation" means the influence of the body representative of the employees and/or the employees' representatives in the affairs of a company by way of—

— the right to elect or appoint some of the members of the company's supervisory or administrative organ, or

— the right to recommend and/or oppose the appointment of some or all of the members of the company's supervisory or administrative organ.

[4033]

SECTION II
NEGOTIATING PROCEDURE

Article 3

Creation of a special negotiating body

1. Where the management or administrative organs of the participating companies draw up a plan for the establishment of an SE, they shall as soon as possible after publishing the draft terms of merger or creating a holding company or after agreeing a plan to form a subsidiary or to transform into an SE, take the necessary steps, including providing information about the identity of the participating companies, concerned subsidiaries or establishments, and the number of their employees, to start negotiations with the representatives of the companies' employees on arrangements for the involvement of employees in the SE.

2. For this purpose, a special negotiating body representative of the employees of the participating companies and concerned subsidiaries or establishments shall be created in accordance with the following provisions—

(a) in electing or appointing members of the special negotiating body, it must be ensured—

(i) that these members are elected or appointed in proportion to the number of employees employed in each Member State by the participating companies and concerned subsidiaries or establishments, by allocating in respect of a Member State one seat per portion of employees employed in that Member State which equals 10%, or a fraction thereof, of the number of employees employed by the participating companies and concerned subsidiaries or establishments in all the Member States taken together;

(ii) that in the case of an SE formed by way of merger, there are such further additional members from each Member State as may be necessary in order to ensure that the special negotiating body includes at least one member representing each participating company which is registered and has employees in that Member State and which it is proposed will cease to exist as a separate legal entity following the registration of the SE, in so far as—

— the number of such additional members does not exceed 20% of the number of members designated by virtue of point (i), and

— the composition of the special negotiating body does not entail a double representation of the employees concerned.

If the number of such companies is higher than the number of additional seats available pursuant to the first subparagraph, these additional seats shall be allocated to companies in different Member States by decreasing order of the number of employees they employ;

(b) Member States shall determine the method to be used for the election or appointment of the members of the special negotiating body who are to be elected or appointed in their territories. They shall take the necessary measures to ensure that, as far as possible, such members shall include at least one member representing each participating company which has employees in the Member State concerned. Such measures must not increase the overall number of members.

Member States may provide that such members may include representatives of trade unions whether or not they are employees of a participating company or concerned subsidiary or establishment.

Without prejudice to national legislation and/or practice laying down thresholds for the establishing of a representative body, Member States shall provide that employees in undertakings or establishments in which there are no employees' representatives through no fault of their own have the right to elect or appoint members of the special negotiating body.

3. The special negotiating body and the competent organs of the participating companies shall determine, by written agreement, arrangements for the involvement of employees within the SE.

To this end, the competent organs of the participating companies shall inform the special negotiating body of the plan and the actual process of establishing the SE, up to its registration.

4. Subject to paragraph 6, the special negotiating body shall take decisions by an absolute majority of its members, provided that such a majority also represents an absolute majority of the employees. Each member shall have one vote. However, should the result of the negotiations lead to a reduction of participation rights, the majority required for a decision to approve such an agreement shall be the votes of two thirds of the members of the special negotiating body representing at least two thirds of the employees, including the votes of members representing employees employed in at least two Member States—

— in the case of an SE to be established by way of merger, if participation covers at least 25% of the overall number of employees of the participating companies, or

— in the case of an SE to be established by way of creating a holding company or forming a subsidiary, if participation covers at least 50% of the overall number of employees of the participating companies.

Reduction of participation rights means a proportion of members of the organs of the SE within the meaning of Article 2(k), which is lower than the highest proportion existing within the participating companies.

5. For the purpose of the negotiations, the special negotiating body may request experts of its choice, for example representatives of appropriate Community level trade union organisations, to assist it with its work. Such experts may be present at negotiation meetings in an advisory capacity at the request of the special negotiating body, where appropriate to promote coherence and consistency at Community level. The special negotiating body may decide to inform the representatives of appropriate external organisations, including trade unions, of the start of the negotiations.

6. The special negotiating body may decide by the majority set out below not to open negotiations or to terminate negotiations already opened, and to rely on the rules on information and consultation of employees in force in the Member States where the SE has

employees. Such a decision shall stop the procedure to conclude the agreement referred to in Article 4. Where such a decision has been taken, none of the provisions of the Annex shall apply.

The majority required to decide not to open or to terminate negotiations shall be the votes of two thirds of the members representing at least two thirds of the employees, including the votes of members representing employees employed in at least two Member States.

In the case of an SE established by way of transformation, this paragraph shall not apply if there is participation in the company to be transformed.

The special negotiating body shall be reconvened on the written request of at least 10% of the employees of the SE, its subsidiaries and establishments, or their representatives, at the earliest two years after the abovementioned decision, unless the parties agree to negotiations being reopened sooner. If the special negotiating body decides to reopen negotiations with the management but no agreement is reached as a result of those negotiations, none of the provisions of the Annex shall apply.

7. Any expenses relating to the functioning of the special negotiating body and, in general, to negotiations shall be borne by the participating companies so as to enable the special negotiating body to carry out its task in an appropriate manner.

In compliance with this principle, Member States may lay down budgetary rules regarding the operation of the special negotiating body. They may in particular limit the funding to cover one expert only.

[4034]

Article 4

Content of the agreement

1. The competent organs of the participating companies and the special negotiating body shall negotiate in a spirit of cooperation with a view to reaching an agreement on arrangements for the involvement of the employees within the SE.

2. Without prejudice to the autonomy of the parties, and subject to paragraph 4, the agreement referred to in paragraph 1 between the competent organs of the participating companies and the special negotiating body shall specify—

(a) the scope of the agreement;

(b) the composition, number of members and allocation of seats on the representative body which will be the discussion partner of the competent organ of the SE in connection with arrangements for the information and consultation of the employees of the SE and its subsidiaries and establishments;

(c) the functions and the procedure for the information and consultation of the representative body;

(d) the frequency of meetings of the representative body;

(e) the financial and material resources to be allocated to the representative body;

(f) if, during negotiations, the parties decide to establish one or more information and consultation procedures instead of a representative body, the arrangements for implementing those procedures;

(g) if, during negotiations, the parties decide to establish arrangements for participation, the substance of those arrangements including (if applicable) the number of members in the SE's administrative or supervisory body which the employees will be entitled to elect, appoint, recommend or oppose, the procedures as to how these members may be elected, appointed, recommended or opposed by the employees, and their rights;

(h) the date of entry into force of the agreement and its duration, cases where the agreement should be renegotiated and the procedure for its renegotiation.

3. The agreement shall not, unless provision is made otherwise therein, be subject to the standard rules referred to in the Annex.

4. Without prejudice to Article 13(3)(a), in the case of an SE established by means of transformation, the agreement shall provide for at least the same level of all elements of employee involvement as the ones existing within the company to be transformed into an SE.

[4035]

Article 5

Duration of negotiations

1. Negotiations shall commence as soon as the special negotiating body is established and may continue for six months thereafter.

2. The parties may decide, by joint agreement, to extend negotiations beyond the period referred to in paragraph 1, up the total of one year from the establishment of the special negotiating body.

[4036]

Article 6

Legislation applicable to the negotiation procedure

Except where otherwise provided in this Directive, the legislation applicable to the negotiation procedure provided for in Articles 3 to 5 shall be the legislation of the Member State in which the registered office of the SE is to be situated.

[4037]

Article 7

Standard rules

1. In order to achieve the objective described in Article 1, Member States shall, without prejudice to paragraph 3 below, lay down standard rules on employee involvement which must satisfy the provisions set out in the Annex.

The standard rules as laid down by the legislation of the Member State in which the registered office of the SE is to be situated shall apply from the date of the registration of the SE where either—

(a) the parties so agree; or

(b) by the deadline laid down in Article 5, no agreement has been concluded, and—

— the competent organ of each of the participating companies decides to accept the application of the standard rules in relation to the SE and so to continue with its registration of the SE, and

— the special negotiating body has not taken the decision provided in Article 3(6).

2. Moreover, the standard rules fixed by the national legislation of the Member State of registration in accordance with part 3 of the Annex shall apply only—

(a) in the case of an SE established by transformation, if the rules of a Member State relating to employee participation in the administrative or supervisory body applied to a company transformed into an SE;

(b) in the case of an SE established by merger—

— if, before registration of the SE, one or more forms of participation applied in one or more of the participating companies covering at least 25% of the total number of employees in all the participating companies, or

— if, before registration of the SE, one or more forms of participation applied in one or more of the participating companies covering less than 25% of the total number of employees in all the participating companies and if the special negotiating body so decides,

(c) in the case of an SE established by setting up a holding company or establishing a subsidiary—

— if, before registration of the SE, one or more forms of participation applied in one or more of the participating companies covering at least 50% of the total number of employees in all the participating companies; or

— if, before registration of the SE, one or more forms of participation applied in one or more of the participating companies covering less than 50% of the total number of employees in all the participating companies and if the special negotiating body so decides.

If there was more than one form of participation within the various participating companies, the special negotiating body shall decide which of those forms must be established in the SE. Member States may fix the rules which are applicable in the absence of any decision on the matter for an SE registered in their territory. The special negotiating body shall inform the competent organs of the participating companies of any decisions taken pursuant to this paragraph.

3. Member States may provide that the reference provisions in part 3 of the Annex shall not apply in the case provided for in point (b) of paragraph 2.

[4038]

SECTION III
MISCELLANEOUS PROVISIONS

Article 8

Reservation and confidentiality

1. Member States shall provide that members of the special negotiating body or the representative body, and experts who assist them, are not authorised to reveal any information which has been given to them in confidence.

The same shall apply to employees' representatives in the context of an information and consultation procedure.

This obligation shall continue to apply, wherever the persons referred to may be, even after the expiry of their terms of office.

2. Each Member State shall provide, in specific cases and under the conditions and limits laid down by national legislation, that the supervisory or administrative organ of an SE or of a participating company established in its territory is not obliged to transmit information where its nature is such that, according to objective criteria, to do so would seriously harm the functioning of the SE (or, as the case may be, the participating company) or its subsidiaries and establishments or would be prejudicial to them.

A Member State may make such dispensation subject to prior administrative or judicial authorisation.

3. Each Member State may lay down particular provisions for SEs in its territory which pursue directly and essentially the aim of ideological guidance with respect to information and the expression of opinions, on condition that, on the date of adoption of this Directive, such provisions already exist in the national legislation.

4. In applying paragraphs 1, 2 and 3, Member States shall make provision for administrative or judicial appeal procedures which the employees' representatives may initiate when the supervisory or administrative organ of an SE or participating company demands confidentiality or does not give information.

Such procedures may include arrangements designed to protect the confidentiality of the information in question.

[4039]

Article 9

Operation of the representative body and procedure for the information and consultation of employees

The competent organ of the SE and the representative body shall work together in a spirit of cooperation with due regard for their reciprocal rights and obligations.

The same shall apply to cooperation between the supervisory or administrative organ of the SE and the employees' representatives in conjunction with a procedure for the information and consultation of employees.

[4040]

Article 10

Protection of employees' representatives

The members of the special negotiating body, the members of the representative body, any employees' representatives exercising functions under the information and consultation procedure and any employees' representatives in the supervisory or administrative organ of an SE who are employees of the SE, its subsidiaries or establishments or of a participating company shall, in the exercise of their functions, enjoy the same protection and guarantees provided for employees' representatives by the national legislation and/or practice in force in their country of employment.

This shall apply in particular to attendance at meetings of the special negotiating body or representative body, any other meeting under the agreement referred to in Article 4(2)(f) or any meeting of the administrative or supervisory organ, and to the payment of wages for members employed by a participating company or the SE or its subsidiaries or establishments during a period of absence necessary for the performance of their duties.

[4041]

Article 11

Misuse of procedures

Member States shall take appropriate measures in conformity with Community law with a view to preventing the misuse of an SE for the purpose of depriving employees of rights to employee involvement or withholding such rights.

[4042]

Article 12

Compliance with this Directive

1. Each Member State shall ensure that the management of establishments of an SE and the supervisory or administrative organs of subsidiaries and of participating companies which are situated within its territory and the employees' representatives or, as the case may be, the employees themselves abide by the obligations laid down by this Directive, regardless of whether or not the SE has its registered office within its territory.

2. Member States shall provide for appropriate measures in the event of failure to comply with this Directive; in particular they shall ensure that administrative or legal procedures are available to enable the obligations deriving from this Directive to be enforced.

[4043]

Article 13

Link between this Directive and other provisions

1. Where an SE is a Community-scale undertaking or a controlling undertaking of a Community-scale group of undertakings within the meaning of Directive 94/45/EC or of Directive 97/74/EC[1] extending the said Directive to the United Kingdom, the provisions of these Directives and the provisions transposing them into national legislation shall not apply to them or to their subsidiaries.

However, where the special negotiating body decides in accordance with Article 3(6) not to open negotiations or to terminate negotiations already opened, Directive 94/45/EC or Directive 97/74/EC and the provisions transposing them into national legislation shall apply.

2. Provisions on the participation of employees in company bodies provided for by national legislation and/or practice, other than those implementing this Directive, shall not apply to companies established in accordance with Regulation (EC) No 2157/2001 and covered by this Directive.

3. This Directive shall not prejudice—
   (a) the existing rights to involvement of employees provided for by national legislation and/or practice in the Member States as enjoyed by employees of the SE and its subsidiaries and establishments, other than participation in the bodies of the SE;
   (b) the provisions on participation in the bodies laid down by national legislation and/or practice applicable to the subsidiaries of the SE.

4. In order to preserve the rights referred to in paragraph 3, Member States may take the necessary measures to guarantee that the structures of employee representation in participating companies which will cease to exist as separate legal entities are maintained after the registration of the SE.

[4044]

NOTES

1 OJ L10, 16.1.1998, p 22.

Article 14

Final provisions

1. Member States shall adopt the laws, regulations and administrative provisions necessary to comply with this Directive no later than 8 October 2004, or shall ensure by that date at the latest that management and labour introduce the required provisions by way of agreement, the Member States being obliged to take all necessary steps enabling them at all times to guarantee the results imposed by this Directive. They shall forthwith inform the Commission thereof.

2. When Member States adopt these measures, they shall contain a reference to this Directive or shall be accompanied by such reference on the occasion of their official publication. The methods of making such reference shall be laid down by the Member States.

[4045]

Article 15

Review by the Commission

No later than 8 October 2007, the Commission shall, in consultation with the Member States and with management and labour at Community level, review the procedures for applying this Directive, with a view to proposing suitable amendments to the Council where necessary.

[4046]

Article 16

Entry into force

This Directive shall enter into force on the day of its publication in the Official Journal of the European Communities.

[4047]

Article 17

Addressees

This Directive is addressed to the Member States.

[4048]

ANNEX
STANDARD RULES

(referred to in Article 7)

Part 1: Composition of the body representative of the employees

In order to achieve the objective described in Article 1, and in the cases referred to in Article 7, a representative body shall be set up in accordance with the following rules.

(a) The representative body shall be composed of employees of the SE and its subsidiaries and establishments elected or appointed from their number by the employees' representatives or, in the absence thereof, by the entire body of employees.

(b) The election or appointment of members of the representative body shall be carried out in accordance with national legislation and/or practice.

Member States shall lay down rules to ensure that the number of members of, and allocation of seats on, the representative body shall be adapted to take account of changes occurring within the SE and its subsidiaries and establishments.

(c) Where its size so warrants, the representative body shall elect a select committee from among its members, comprising at most three members.

(d) The representative body shall adopt its rules of procedure.

(e) The members of the representative body are elected or appointed in proportion to the number of employees employed in each Member State by the participating companies and concerned subsidiaries or establishments, by allocating in respect of a Member State one seat per portion of employees employed in that Member State which equals 10%, or a fraction thereof, of the number of employees employed by the participating companies and concerned subsidiaries or establishments in all the Member States taken together.

(f) The competent organ of the SE shall be informed of the composition of the representative body.

(g) Four years after the representative body is established, it shall examine whether to open negotiations for the conclusion of the agreement referred to in Articles 4 and 7 or to continue to apply the standard rules adopted in accordance with this Annex.

Articles 3(4) to (7) and 4 to 6 shall apply, mutatis mutandis, if a decision has been taken to negotiate an agreement according to Article 4, in which case the term "special negotiating body" shall be replaced by "representative body". Where, by the deadline by which the negotiations come to an end, no agreement has been concluded, the arrangements initially adopted in accordance with the standard rules shall continue to apply.

[4049]

Part 2: Standard rules for information and consultation

The competence and powers of the representative body set up in an SE shall be governed by the following rules.

(a) The competence of the representative body shall be limited to questions which concern the SE itself and any of its subsidiaries or establishments situated in another Member State or which exceed the powers of the decision-making organs in a single Member State.

(b) Without prejudice to meetings held pursuant to point (c), the representative body shall have the right to be informed and consulted and, for that purpose, to meet with the competent organ of the SE at least once a year, on the basis of regular reports drawn up by the competent organ, on the progress of the business of the SE and its prospects. The local managements shall be informed accordingly.
The competent organ of the SE shall provide the representative body with the agenda for meetings of the administrative, or, where appropriate, the management and supervisory organ, and with copies of all documents submitted to the general meeting of its shareholders.
The meeting shall relate in particular to the structure, economic and financial situation, the probable development of the business and of production and sales, the situation and probable trend of employment, investments, and substantial changes concerning organisation, introduction of new working methods or production processes, transfers of production, mergers, cut-backs or closures of undertakings, establishments or important parts thereof, and collective redundancies.

(c) Where there are exceptional circumstances affecting the employees' interests to a considerable extent, particularly in the event of relocations, transfers, the closure of establishments or undertakings or collective redundancies, the representative body shall have the right to be informed. The representative body or, where it so decides, in particular for reasons of urgency, the select committee, shall have the right to meet at its request the competent organ of the SE or any more appropriate level of management within the SE having its own powers of decision, so as to be informed and consulted on measures significantly affecting employees' interests.
Where the competent organ decides not to act in accordance with the opinion expressed by the representative body, this body shall have the right to a further meeting with the competent organ of the SE with a view to seeking agreement.
In the case of a meeting organised with the select committee, those members of the representative body who represent employees who are directly concerned by the measures in question shall also have the right to participate.
The meetings referred to above shall not affect the prerogatives of the competent organ.

(d) Member States may lay down rules on the chairing of information and consultation meetings.
Before any meeting with the competent organ of the SE, the representative body or the select committee, where necessary enlarged in accordance with the third subparagraph of paragraph (c), shall be entitled to meet without the representatives of the competent organ being present.

(e) Without prejudice to Article 8, the members of the representative body shall inform the representatives of the employees of the SE and of its subsidiaries and establishments of the content and outcome of the information and consultation procedures.

(f) The representative body or the select committee may be assisted by experts of its choice.

(g) In so far as this is necessary for the fulfilment of their tasks, the members of the representative body shall be entitled to time off for training without loss of wages.

(h) The costs of the representative body shall be borne by the SE, which shall provide the body's members with the financial and material resources needed to enable them to perform their duties in an appropriate manner.
In particular, the SE shall, unless otherwise agreed, bear the cost of organising meetings and providing interpretation facilities and the accommodation and travelling expenses of members of the representative body and the select committee.

In compliance with these principles, the Member States may lay down budgetary rules regarding the operation of the representative body. They may in particular limit funding to cover one expert only.

[4050]

Part 3: Standard rules for participation

Employee participation in an SE shall be governed by the following provisions.

(a) In the case of an SE established by transformation, if the rules of a Member State relating to employee participation in the administrative or supervisory body applied before registration, all aspects of employee participation shall continue to apply to the SE. Point (b) shall apply mutatis mutandis to that end.

(b) In other cases of the establishing of an SE, the employees of the SE, its subsidiaries and establishments and/or their representative body shall have the right to elect, appoint, recommend or oppose the appointment of a number of members of the administrative or supervisory body of the SE equal to the highest proportion in force in the participating companies concerned before registration of the SE.

If none of the participating companies was governed by participation rules before registration of the SE, the latter shall not be required to establish provisions for employee participation.

The representative body shall decide on the allocation of seats within the administrative or supervisory body among the members representing the employees from the various Member States or on the way in which the SE's employees may recommend or oppose the appointment of the members of these bodies according to the proportion of the SE's employees in each Member State. If the employees of one or more Member States are not covered by this proportional criterion, the representative body shall appoint a member from one of those Member States, in particular the Member State of the SE's registered office where that is appropriate. Each Member State may determine the allocation of the seats it is given within the administrative or supervisory body.

Every member of the administrative body or, where appropriate, the supervisory body of the SE who has been elected, appointed or recommended by the representative body or, depending on the circumstances, by the employees shall be a full member with the same rights and obligations as the members representing the shareholders, including the right to vote.

[4051]

DIRECTIVE OF THE EUROPEAN PARLIAMENT AND OF THE COUNCIL

of 11 March 2002

establishing a general framework for informing and consulting employees in the European Community

(2002/14/EC)

NOTES

Date of publication in OJ: OJ L80, 23.3.2002, p 29.

For the domestic implementation of this Directive, see the Information and Consultation of Employees Regulations 2004, SI 2004/3426 at **[3254]**.

THE EUROPEAN PARLIAMENT AND THE COUNCIL OF THE EUROPEAN UNION,

Having regard to the Treaty establishing the European Community, and in particular Article 137(2) thereof,

Having regard to the proposal from the Commission,[1]

Having regard to the opinion of the Economic and Social Committee,[2]

Having regard to the opinion of the Committee of the Regions,[3]

Acting in accordance with the procedure referred to in Article 251,[4] and in the light of the joint text approved by the Conciliation Committee on 23 January 2002,

Whereas—

(1) Pursuant to Article 136 of the Treaty, a particular objective of the Community and the Member States is to promote social dialogue between management and labour.

(2) Point 17 of the Community Charter of Fundamental Social Rights of Workers provides, inter alia, that information, consultation and participation for workers must be developed along appropriate lines, taking account of the practices in force in different Member States.

(3) The Commission consulted management and labour at Community level on the possible direction of Community action on the information and consultation of employees in undertakings within the Community.

(4) Following this consultation, the Commission considered that Community action was advisable and again consulted management and labour on the contents of the planned proposal; management and labour have presented their opinions to the Commission.

(5) Having completed this second stage of consultation, management and labour have not informed the Commission of their wish to initiate the process potentially leading to the conclusion of an agreement.

(6) The existence of legal frameworks at national and Community level intended to ensure that employees are involved in the affairs of the undertaking employing them and in decisions which affect them has not always prevented serious decisions affecting employees from being taken and made public without adequate procedures having been implemented beforehand to inform and consult them.

(7) There is a need to strengthen dialogue and promote mutual trust within undertakings in order to improve risk anticipation, make work organisation more flexible and facilitate employee access to training within the undertaking while maintaining security, make employees aware of adaptation needs, increase employees' availability to undertake measures and activities to increase their employability, promote employee involvement in the operation and future of the undertaking and increase its competitiveness.

(8) There is a need, in particular, to promote and enhance information and consultation on the situation and likely development of employment within the undertaking and, where the employer's evaluation suggests that employment within the undertaking may be under threat, the possible anticipatory measures envisaged, in particular in terms of employee training and skill development, with a view to offsetting the negative developments or their consequences and increasing the employability and adaptability of the employees likely to be affected.

(9) Timely information and consultation is a prerequisite for the success of the restructuring and adaptation of undertakings to the new conditions created by globalisation of the economy, particularly through the development of new forms of organisation of work.

(10) The Community has drawn up and implemented an employment strategy based on the concepts of "anticipation", "prevention" and "employability", which are to be incorporated as key elements into all public policies likely to benefit employment, including the policies of individual undertakings, by strengthening the social dialogue with a view to promoting change compatible with preserving the priority objective of employment.

(11) Further development of the internal market must be properly balanced, maintaining the essential values on which our societies are based and ensuring that all citizens benefit from economic development.

(12) Entry into the third stage of economic and monetary union has extended and accelerated the competitive pressures at European level. This means that more supportive measures are needed at national level.

(13) The existing legal frameworks for employee information and consultation at Community and national level tend to adopt an excessively a posteriori approach to the process of change, neglect the economic aspects of decisions taken and do not contribute either to genuine anticipation of employment developments within the undertaking or to risk prevention.

(14) All of these political, economic, social and legal developments call for changes to the existing legal framework providing for the legal and practical instruments enabling the right to be informed and consulted to be exercised.

(15) This Directive is without prejudice to national systems regarding the exercise of this right in practice where those entitled to exercise it are required to indicate their wishes collectively.

(16) This Directive is without prejudice to those systems which provide for the direct involvement of employees, as long as they are always free to exercise the right to be informed and consulted through their representatives.

(17) Since the objectives of the proposed action, as outlined above, cannot be adequately achieved by the Member States, in that the object is to establish a framework for employee information and consultation appropriate for the new European context described above, and can therefore, in view of the scale and impact of the proposed action, be better achieved at Community level, the Community may adopt measures in accordance with the principle of

subsidiarity as set out in Article 5 of the Treaty. In accordance with the principle of proportionality, as set out in that Article, this Directive does not go beyond what is necessary in order to achieve these objectives.

(18) The purpose of this general framework is to establish minimum requirements applicable throughout the Community while not preventing Member States from laying down provisions more favourable to employees.

(19) The purpose of this general framework is also to avoid any administrative, financial or legal constraints which would hinder the creation and development of small and medium-sized undertakings. To this end, the scope of this Directive should be restricted, according to the choice made by Member States, to undertakings with at least 50 employees or establishments employing at least 20 employees.

(20) This takes into account and is without prejudice to other national measures and practices aimed at fostering social dialogue within companies not covered by this Directive and within public administrations.

(21) However, on a transitional basis, Member States in which there is no established statutory system of information and consultation of employees or employee representation should have the possibility of further restricting the scope of the Directive as regards the numbers of employees.

(22) A Community framework for informing and consulting employees should keep to a minimum the burden on undertakings or establishments while ensuring the effective exercise of the rights granted.

(23) The objective of this Directive is to be achieved through the establishment of a general framework comprising the principles, definitions and arrangements for information and consultation, which it will be for the Member States to comply with and adapt to their own national situation, ensuring, where appropriate, that management and labour have a leading role by allowing them to define freely, by agreement, the arrangements for informing and consulting employees which they consider to be best suited to their needs and wishes.

(24) Care should be taken to avoid affecting some specific rules in the field of employee information and consultation existing in some national laws, addressed to undertakings or establishments which pursue political, professional, organisational, religious, charitable, educational, scientific or artistic aims, as well as aims involving information and the expression of opinions.

(25) Undertakings and establishments should be protected against disclosure of certain particularly sensitive information.

(26) The employer should be allowed not to inform and consult where this would seriously damage the undertaking or the establishment or where he has to comply immediately with an order issued to him by a regulatory or supervisory body.

(27) Information and consultation imply both rights and obligations for management and labour at undertaking or establishment level.

(28) Administrative or judicial procedures, as well as sanctions that are effective, dissuasive and proportionate in relation to the seriousness of the offence, should be applicable in cases of infringement of the obligations based on this Directive.

(29) This Directive should not affect the provisions, where these are more specific, of Council Directive 98/59/EC of 20 July 1998 on the approximation of the laws of the Member States relating to collective redundancies[5] and of Council Directive 2001/23/EC of 12 March 2001 on the approximation of the laws of the Member States relating to the safeguarding of employees' rights in the event of transfers of undertakings, businesses or parts of undertakings or businesses.[6]

(30) Other rights of information and consultation, including those arising from Council Directive 94/45/EEC of 22 September 1994 on the establishment of a European Works Council or a procedure in Community-scale undertakings and Community-scale groups of undertakings for the purposes of informing and consulting employees,[7] should not be affected by this Directive.

(31) Implementation of this Directive should not be sufficient grounds for a reduction in the general level of protection of workers in the areas to which it applies,

NOTES

1 OJ C2, 5.1.1999, p 3.
2 OJ C258, 10.9.1999, p 24.
3 OJ C144, 16.5.2001, p 58.
4 Opinion of the European Parliament of 14 April 1999 (OJ C219, 30.7.1999, p 223), confirmed on 16 September 1999 (OJ C54, 25.2.2000, p 55), Council Common Position of 27 July 2001 (OJ C307, 31.10.2001, p 16) and Decision of the European Parliament of 23 October 2001 (not yet published in the Official Journal). Decision of the European Parliament of 5 February 2002 and Decision of the Council of 18 February 2002.
5 OJ L225, 12.8.1998, p 16.

[6] OJ L82, 22.3.2001, p 16.
[7] OJ L254, 30.9.1994, p 64. Directive as amended by Directive 97/74/EC (OJ L10, 16.1.1998, p 22.

HAVE ADOPTED THIS DIRECTIVE—

Article 1

Object and principles

1. The purpose of this Directive is to establish a general framework setting out minimum requirements for the right to information and consultation of employees in undertakings or establishments within the Community.

2. The practical arrangements for information and consultation shall be defined and implemented in accordance with national law and industrial relations practices in individual Member States in such a way as to ensure their effectiveness.

3. When defining or implementing practical arrangements for information and consultation, the employer and the employees' representatives shall work in a spirit of cooperation and with due regard for their reciprocal rights and obligations, taking into account the interests both of the undertaking or establishment and of the employees.

[4052]

Article 2

Definitions

For the purposes of this Directive—

(a) "undertaking" means a public or private undertaking carrying out an economic activity, whether or not operating for gain, which is located within the territory of the Member States;
(b) "establishment" means a unit of business defined in accordance with national law and practice, and located within the territory of a Member State, where an economic activity is carried out on an ongoing basis with human and material resources;
(c) "employer" means the natural or legal person party to employment contracts or employment relationships with employees, in accordance with national law and practice;
(d) "employee" means any person who, in the Member State concerned, is protected as an employee under national employment law and in accordance with national practice;
(e) "employees' representatives" means the employees' representatives provided for by national laws and/or practices;
(f) "information" means transmission by the employer to the employees' representatives of data in order to enable them to acquaint themselves with the subject matter and to examine it;
(g) "consultation" means the exchange of views and establishment of dialogue between the employees' representatives and the employer.

[4053]

Article 3

Scope

1. This Directive shall apply, according to the choice made by Member States, to—

(a) undertakings employing at least 50 employees in any one Member State, or
(b) establishments employing at least 20 employees in any one Member State.

Member States shall determine the method for calculating the thresholds of employees employed.

2. In conformity with the principles and objectives of this Directive, Member States may lay down particular provisions applicable to undertakings or establishments which pursue directly and essentially political, professional organisational, religious, charitable, educational, scientific or artistic aims, as well as aims involving information and the expression of opinions, on condition that, at the date of entry into force of this Directive, provisions of that nature already exist in national legislation.

3. Member States may derogate from this Directive through particular provisions applicable to the crews of vessels plying the high seas.

[4054]

Article 4

Practical arrangements for information and consultation

1. In accordance with the principles set out in Article 1 and without prejudice to any provisions and/or practices in force more favourable to employees, the Member States shall determine the practical arrangements for exercising the right to information and consultation at the appropriate level in accordance with this Article.

2. Information and consultation shall cover—
   (a) information on the recent and probable development of the undertaking's or the establishment's activities and economic situation;
   (b) information and consultation on the situation, structure and probable development of employment within the undertaking or establishment and on any anticipatory measures envisaged, in particular where there is a threat to employment;
   (c) information and consultation on decisions likely to lead to substantial changes in work organisation or in contractual relations, including those covered by the Community provisions referred to in Article 9(1).

3. Information shall be given at such time, in such fashion and with such content as are appropriate to enable, in particular, employees' representatives to conduct an adequate study and, where necessary, prepare for consultation.

4. Consultation shall take place—
   (a) while ensuring that the timing, method and content thereof are appropriate;
   (b) at the relevant level of management and representation, depending on the subject under discussion;
   (c) on the basis of information supplied by the employer in accordance with Article 2(f) and of the opinion which the employees' representatives are entitled to formulate;
   (d) in such a way as to enable employees' representatives to meet the employer and obtain a response, and the reasons for that response, to any opinion they might formulate;
   (e) with a view to reaching an agreement on decisions within the scope of the employer's powers referred to in paragraph 2(c).

[4055]

Article 5

Information and consultation deriving from an agreement

Member States may entrust management and labour at the appropriate level, including at undertaking or establishment level, with defining freely and at any time through negotiated agreement the practical arrangements for informing and consulting employees. These agreements, and agreements existing on the date laid down in Article 11, as well as any subsequent renewals of such agreements, may establish, while respecting the principles set out in Article 1 and subject to conditions and limitations laid down by the Member States, provisions which are different from those referred to in Article 4.

[4056]

Article 6

Confidential information

1. Member States shall provide that, within the conditions and limits laid down by national legislation, the employees' representatives, and any experts who assist them, are not authorised to reveal to employees or to third parties, any information which, in the legitimate interest of the undertaking or establishment, has expressly been provided to them in confidence. This obligation shall continue to apply, wherever the said representatives or experts are, even after expiry of their terms of office. However, a Member State may authorise the employees' representatives and anyone assisting them to pass on confidential information to employees and to third parties bound by an obligation of confidentiality.

2. Member States shall provide, in specific cases and within the conditions and limits laid down by national legislation, that the employer is not obliged to communicate

information or undertake consultation when the nature of that information or consultation is such that, according to objective criteria, it would seriously harm the functioning of the undertaking or establishment or would be prejudicial to it.

3. Without prejudice to existing national procedures, Member States shall provide for administrative or judicial review procedures for the case where the employer requires confidentiality or does not provide the information in accordance with paragraphs 1 and 2. They may also provide for procedures intended to safeguard the confidentiality of the information in question.

[4057]

Article 7

Protection of employees' representatives

Member States shall ensure that employees' representatives, when carrying out their functions, enjoy adequate protection and guarantees to enable them to perform properly the duties which have been assigned to them.

[4058]

Article 8

Protection of rights

1. Member States shall provide for appropriate measures in the event of non-compliance with this Directive by the employer or the employees' representatives. In particular, they shall ensure that adequate administrative or judicial procedures are available to enable the obligations deriving from this Directive to be enforced.

2. Member States shall provide for adequate sanctions to be applicable in the event of infringement of this Directive by the employer or the employees' representatives. These sanctions must be effective, proportionate and dissuasive.

[4059]

Article 9

Link between this Directive and other Community and national provisions

1. This Directive shall be without prejudice to the specific information and consultation procedures set out in Article 2 of Directive 98/59/EC and Article 7 of Directive 2001/23/EC.

2. This Directive shall be without prejudice to provisions adopted in accordance with Directives 94/45/EC and 97/74/EC.

3. This Directive shall be without prejudice to other rights to information, consultation and participation under national law.

4. Implementation of this Directive shall not be sufficient grounds for any regression in relation to the situation which already prevails in each Member State and in relation to the general level of protection of workers in the areas to which it applies.

[4060]

Article 10

Transitional provisions

Notwithstanding Article 3, a Member State in which there is, at the date of entry into force of this Directive, no general, permanent and statutory system of information and consultation of employees, nor a general, permanent and statutory system of employee representation at the workplace allowing employees to be represented for that purpose, may limit the application of the national provisions implementing this Directive to—

(a) undertakings employing at least 150 employees or establishments employing at least 100 employees until 23 March 2007, and

(b) undertakings employing at least 100 employees or establishments employing at least 50 employees during the year following the date in point (a).

[4061]

Article 11

Transposition

1. Member States shall adopt the laws, regulations and administrative provisions necessary to comply with this Directive not later than 23 March 2005 or shall ensure that

management and labour introduce by that date the required provisions by way of agreement, the Member States being obliged to take all necessary steps enabling them to guarantee the results imposed by this Directive at all times. They shall forthwith inform the Commission thereof.

2. Where Member States adopt these measures, they shall contain a reference to this Directive or shall be accompanied by such reference on the occasion of their official publication. The methods of making such reference shall be laid down by the Member States.

[4062]

Article 12

Review by the Commission

Not later than 23 March 2007, the Commission shall, in consultation with the Member States and the social partners at Community level, review the application of this Directive with a view to proposing any necessary amendments.

[4063]

Article 13

Entry into force

This Directive shall enter into force on the day of its publication in the *Official Journal of the European Communities*.

[4064]

Article 14

Addresses

This Directive is addressed to the Member States.

[4065]

DIRECTIVE OF THE EUROPEAN PARLIAMENT AND OF THE COUNCIL

of 11 March 2002

on the organisation of the working time of persons performing mobile road transport activities

(2002/15/EC)

NOTES

Date of publication in OJ: OJ L80, 23.3.2002, p 35.

For the domestic implementation of this Directive, see the Road Transport (Working Time) Regulations 2005, SI 2005/639 at **[3294A]**.

THE EUROPEAN PARLIAMENT AND THE COUNCIL OF THE EUROPEAN UNION,

Having regard to the Treaty establishing the European Community, and in particular Article 71 and Article 137(2) thereof,

Having regard to the proposal from the Commission,[1]

Having regard to the opinion of the Economic and Social Committee,[2]

Following consultation of the Committee of the Regions,

Acting in accordance with the procedure laid down in Article 251 of the Treaty,[3] and in the light of the joint text approved by the Conciliation Committee on 16 January 2002,

Whereas:

(1) Council Regulation (EEC) No 3820/85 of 20 December 1985 on the harmonisation of certain social legislation relating to road transport[4] laid down common rules on driving times and rest periods for drivers; that Regulation does not cover other aspects of working time for road transport.

(2) Council Directive 93/104/EC of 23 November 1993 concerning certain aspects of the organisation of working time[5] makes it possible to adopt more specific requirements for the

organisation of working time. Bearing in mind the sectoral nature of this Directive, the provisions thereof take precedence over Directive 93/104/EC by virtue of Article 14 thereof.

(3) Despite intensive negotiations between the social partners, it has not been possible to reach agreement on the subject of mobile workers in road transport.

(4) It is therefore necessary to lay down a series of more specific provisions concerning the hours of work in road transport intended to ensure the safety of transport and the health and safety of the persons involved.

(5) Since the objectives of the proposed action cannot be sufficiently achieved by the Member States and can therefore, by reason of the scale and effects of the proposed action, be better achieved at Community level, the Community may adopt measures, in accordance with the principle of subsidiarity as set out in Article 5 of the Treaty. In accordance with the principle of proportionality, as set out in that Article, this Directive does not go beyond what is necessary in order to achieve those objectives.

(6) The scope of this Directive covers only mobile workers employed by transport undertakings established in a Member State participating in mobile road transport activities covered by Regulation (EEC) No 3820/85 or, failing that, by the European agreement concerning the work of crews of vehicles engaged in international road transport (AETR).

(7) It should be made clear that mobile workers excluded from the scope of this Directive, other than self-employed drivers, benefit from the basic protection provided for in Directive 93/104/EC. That basic protection includes the existing rules on adequate rest, the maximum average working week, annual leave and certain basic provisions for night workers including health assessment.

(8) As self-employed drivers are included within the scope of Regulation (EEC) No 3820/85 but excluded from that of Directive 93/104/EC, they should be excluded temporarily from the scope of this Directive in accordance with the provisions of Article 2(1).

(9) The definitions used in this Directive are not to constitute a precedent for other Community regulations on working time.

(10) In order to improve road safety, prevent the distortion of competition and guarantee the safety and health of the mobile workers covered by this Directive, the latter should know exactly which periods devoted to road transport activities constitute working time and which do not and are thus deemed to be break times, rest times or periods of availability. These workers should be granted minimum daily and weekly periods of rest, and adequate breaks. It is also necessary to place a maximum limit on the number of weekly working hours.

(11) Research has shown that the human body is more sensitive at night to environmental disturbances and also to certain burdensome forms of organisation and that long periods of night work can be detrimental to the health of workers and can endanger their safety and also road safety in general.

(12) As a consequence, there is a need to limit the duration of periods of night work and to provide that professional drivers who work at night should receive appropriate compensation for their activity and should not be disadvantaged as regards training opportunities.

(13) Employers should keep records of instances when the maximum average working week applicable to mobile workers is exceeded.

(14) The provisions of Regulation (EEC) No 3820/85 on driving time in international and national passenger transport, other than regular services, should continue to apply.

(15) The Commission should monitor the implementation of this Directive and developments in this field in the Member States and submit to the European Parliament, the Council, the Economic and Social Committee and the Committee of the Regions a report on the application of the rules and the consequences of the provisions on night work.

(16) It is necessary to provide that certain provisions may be subject to derogations adopted, according to the circumstances, by the Member States or the two sides of industry. As a general rule, in the event of a derogation, the workers concerned must be given compensatory rest periods,

NOTES

1. OJ C43, 17.2.1999, p 4.
2. OJ C138, 18.5.1999, p 33.
3. Opinion of the European Parliament of 14 April 1999 (OJ C219, 30.7.1999, p 235), as confirmed on 6 May 1999 (OJ C279, 1.10.1999, p 270), Council Common Position of 23 March 2001 (OJ C142, 15.5.2001, p 24) and Decision of the European Parliament of 14 June 2001 (not yet published in the Official Journal). Decision of the European Parliament of 5 February 2002 and Council Decision of 18 February 2002.
4. OJ L370, 31.12.1985, p 1.
5. OJ L307, 13.12.1993, p 18. Directive as last amended by Directive 2000/34/EC of the European Parliament and of the Council (OJ L195, 1.8.2000, p 41).

HAVE ADOPTED THIS DIRECTIVE:

Article 1

Purpose

The purpose of this Directive shall be to establish minimum requirements in relation to the organisation of working time in order to improve the health and safety protection of persons performing mobile road transport activities and to improve road safety and align conditions of competition.

[4065A]

Article 2

Scope

1. This Directive shall apply to mobile workers employed by undertakings established in a Member State, participating in road transport activities covered by Regulation (EEC) No 3820/85 or, failing that, by the AETR Agreement.

Without prejudice to the provisions of following subparagraph, this Directive shall apply to self-employed drivers from 23 March 2009.

At the latest two years before this date, the Commission shall present a report to the European Parliament and the Council. This report shall analyse the consequences of the exclusion of self-employed drivers from the scope of the Directive in respect of road safety, conditions of competition, the structure of the profession as well as social aspects. The circumstances in each Member State relating to the structure of the transport industry and to the working environment of the road transport profession shall be taken into account. On the basis of this report, the Commission shall submit a proposal, the aim of which may be either, as appropriate

— to set out the modalities for the inclusion of the self-employed drivers within the scope of the Directive in respect of certain self-employed drivers who are not participating in road transport activities in other Member States and who are subject to local constraints for objective reasons, such as peripheral location, long internal distances and a particular competitive environment, or
— not to include self-employed drivers within the scope of the Directive.

2. The provisions of Directive 93/104/EC shall apply to mobile workers excluded from the scope of this Directive.

3. In so far as this Directive contains more specific provisions as regards mobile workers performing road transport activities it shall, pursuant to Article 14 of Directive 93/104/EC, take precedence over the relevant provisions of that Directive.

4. This Directive shall supplement the provisions of Regulation (EEC) No 3820/85 and, where necessary, of the AETR Agreement, which take precedence over the provisions of this Directive.

[4065B]

Article 3

Definitions

For the purposes of this Directive:

(a) "working time" shall mean:

1. in the case of mobile workers: the time from the beginning to the end of work, during which the mobile worker is at his workstation, at the disposal of the employer and exercising his functions or activities, that is to say:
   — the time devoted to all road transport activities. These activities are, in particular, the following:
     (i) driving;
     (ii) loading and unloading;
     (iii) assisting passengers boarding and disembarking from the vehicle;
     (iv) cleaning and technical maintenance;
     (v) all other work intended to ensure the safety of the vehicle, its cargo and passengers or to fulfil the legal or regulatory obligations directly linked to the specific transport operation under way, including

monitoring of loading and unloading, administrative formalities with police, customs, immigration officers etc,

— the times during which he cannot dispose freely of his time and is required to be at his workstation, ready to take up normal work, with certain tasks associated with being on duty, in particular during periods awaiting loading or unloading where their foreseeable duration is not known in advance, that is to say either before departure or just before the actual start of the period in question, or under the general conditions negotiated between the social partners and/or under the terms of the legislation of the Member States;

2. in the case of self-employed drivers, the same definition shall apply to the time from the beginning to the end of work, during which the self employed driver is at his workstation, at the disposal of the client and exercising his functions or activities other than general administrative work that is not directly linked to the specific transport operation under way.

The break times referred to in Article 5, the rest times referred to in Article 6 and, without prejudice to the legislation of Member States or agreements between the social partners providing that such periods should be compensated or limited, the periods of availability referred to in (b) of this Article, shall be excluded from working time;

(b) "periods of availability" shall mean:

— periods other than those relating to break times and rest times during which the mobile worker is not required to remain at his workstation, but must be available to answer any calls to start or resume driving or to carry out other work. In particular such periods of availability shall include periods during which the mobile worker is accompanying a vehicle being transported by ferryboat or by train as well as periods of waiting at frontiers and those due to traffic prohibitions.

These periods and their foreseeable duration shall be known in advance by the mobile worker, that is to say either before departure or just before the actual start of the period in question, or under the general conditions negotiated between the social partners and/or under the terms of the legislation of the Member States,

— for mobile workers driving in a team, the time spent sitting next to the driver or on the couchette while the vehicle is in motion;

(c) "workstation" shall mean:

— the location of the main place of business of the undertaking for which the person performing mobile road transport activities carries out duties, together with its various subsidiary places of business, regardless of whether they are located in the same place as its head office or main place of business,

— the vehicle which the person performing mobile road transport activities uses when he carries out duties, and

— any other place in which activities connected with transportation are carried out;

(d) "mobile worker" shall mean any worker forming part of the travelling staff, including trainees and apprentices, who is in the service of an undertaking which operates transport services for passengers or goods by road for hire or reward or on its own account;

(e) "self-employed driver" shall mean anyone whose main occupation is to transport passengers or goods by road for hire or reward within the meaning of Community legislation under cover of a Community licence or any other professional authorisation to carry out the aforementioned transport, who is entitled to work for himself and who is not tied to an employer by an employment contract or by any other type of working hierarchical relationship, who is free to organise the relevant working activities, whose income depends directly on the profits made and who has the freedom to, individually or through a cooperation between self-employed drivers, have commercial relations with several customers.

For the purposes of this Directive, those drivers who do not satisfy these criteria shall be subject to the same obligations and benefit from the same rights as those provided for mobile workers by this Directive;

(f) "person performing mobile road transport activities" shall mean any mobile worker or self-employed driver who performs such activities;

(g) "week" shall mean the period between 00.00 hours on Monday and 24.00 hours on Sunday;

(h) "night time" shall mean a period of at least four hours, as defined by national law, between 00.00 hours and 07.00 hours;

(i) "night work" shall mean any work performed during night time.

[4065C]

Article 4

Maximum weekly working time

Member States shall take the measures necessary to ensure that:

(a) the average weekly working time may not exceed 48 hours. The maximum weekly working time may be extended to 60 hours only if, over four months, an average of 48 hours a week is not exceeded. The fourth and fifth subparagraphs of Article 6(1) of Regulation (EEC) No 3820/85 or, where necessary, the fourth subparagraph of Article 6(1) of the AETR Agreement shall take precedence over this Directive, in so far as the drivers concerned do not exceed an average working time of 48 hours a week over four months;

(b) working time for different employers is the sum of the working hours. The employer shall ask the mobile worker concerned in writing for an account of time worked for another employer. The mobile worker shall provide such information in writing.

[4065D]

Article 5

Breaks

1. Member States shall take the measures necessary to ensure that, without prejudice to the level of protection provided by Regulation (EEC) No 3820/85 or, failing that, by the AETR Agreement, persons performing mobile road transport activities, without prejudice to Article 2(1), in no circumstances work for more than six consecutive hours without a break. Working time shall be interrupted by a break of at least 30 minutes, if working hours total between six and nine hours, and of at least 45 minutes, if working hours total more than nine hours.

2. Breaks may be subdivided into periods of at least 15 minutes each.

[4065E]

Article 6

Rest periods

For the purposes of this Directive, apprentices and trainees shall be covered by the same provisions on rest time as other mobile workers in pursuance of Regulation (EEC) No 3820/85 or, failing that, of the AETR Agreement.

[4065F]

Article 7

Night work

1. Member States shall take the measures necessary to ensure that:

— if night work is performed, the daily working time does not exceed ten hours in each 24 period,

— compensation for night work is given in accordance with national legislative measures, collective agreements, agreements between the two sides of industry and/or national practice, on condition that such compensation is not liable to endanger road safety.

2. By 23 March 2007, the Commission shall, within the framework of the report which it draws up in accordance with Article 13(2), assess the consequences of the provisions laid down in paragraph 1 above. The Commission shall, if necessary, submit appropriate proposals along with that report.

3. The Commission shall present a proposal for a Directive containing provisions relating to the training of professional drivers, including those who perform night work, and laying down the general principles of such training.

[4065G]

Article 8

Derogations

1. Derogations from Articles 4 and 7 may, for objective or technical reasons or reasons concerning the organisation of work, be adopted by means of collective agreements,

agreements between the social partners, or if this is not possible, by laws, regulations or administrative provisions provided there is consultation of the representatives of the employers and workers concerned and efforts are made to encourage all relevant forms of social dialogue.

2. The option to derogate from Article 4 may not result in the establishment of a reference period exceeding six months, for calculation of the average maximum weekly working time of forty-eight hours.

[4065H]

Article 9

Information and records

Member States shall ensure that:

(a) mobile workers are informed of the relevant national requirements, the internal rules of the undertaking and agreements between the two sides of industry, in particular collective agreements and any company agreements, reached on the basis of this Directive, without prejudice to Council Directive 91/533/EEC of 14 October 1991 on an employer's obligation to inform employees of the conditions applicable to the contract or employment relationship;[1]

(b) without prejudice to Article 2(1), the working time of persons performing mobile road transport activities is recorded. Records shall be kept for at least two years after the end of the period covered. Employers shall be responsible for recording the working time of mobile workers. Employers shall upon request provide mobile workers with copies of the records of hours worked.

[4065I]

NOTES

[1] OJ L288, 18.10.1991, p 32.

Article 10

More favourable provisions

This Directive shall not affect Member States' right to apply or introduce laws, regulations or administrative provisions more favourable to the protection of the health and safety of persons performing mobile road transport activities, or their right to facilitate or permit the application of collective agreements or other agreements concluded between the two sides of industry which are more favourable to the protection of the health and safety of mobile workers. Implementation of this Directive shall not constitute valid grounds for reducing the general level of protection afforded to workers referred to in Article 2(1).

[4065J]

Article 11

Penalties

Member States shall lay down a system of penalties for breaches of the national provisions adopted pursuant to this Directive and shall take all the measures necessary to ensure that these penalties are applied. The penalties thus provided for shall be effective, proportional and dissuasive.

[4065K]

Article 12

Negotiations with third countries

Once this Directive has entered into force, the Community shall begin negotiations with the relevant third countries with a view to the application of rules equivalent to those laid down in this Directive to mobile workers employed by undertakings established in a third country.

[4065L]

Article 13

Reports

1. Member States shall report to the Commission every two years on the implementation of this Directive, indicating the views of the two sides of industry. The report must reach the

Commission no later than 30 September following the date on which the two-year period covered by the report expires. The two-year period shall be the same as that referred to in Article 16(2) of Regulation (EEC) No 3820/85.

2. The Commission shall produce a report every two years on the implementation of this Directive by Member States and developments in the field in question. The Commission shall forward this report to the European Parliament, the Council, the Economic and Social Committee and the Committee of the Regions.

[4065M]

Article 14

Final provisions

1. Member States shall adopt the laws, regulations and administrative provisions necessary to comply with this Directive by 23 March 2005 or shall ensure by that date that the two sides of industry have established the necessary measures by agreement, the Member States being obliged to take any steps to allow them to be able at any time to guarantee the results required by this Directive. When Member States adopt the measures referred to in the first subparagraph, they shall contain a reference to this Directive or shall be accompanied by such reference on the occasion of their official publication. The methods of making such reference shall be laid down by Member States.

2. Member States shall communicate to the Commission the provisions of national law which they have already adopted or which they adopt in the field covered by this Directive.

3. Member States shall take care that consignors, freight forwarders, prime contractors, subcontractors and enterprises which employ mobile workers comply with the relevant provisions of this Directive.

[4065N]

Article 15

Entry into force

This Directive shall enter into force on the day of its publication in the Official Journal of the European Communities.

[4065O]

Article 16

Addressees

This Directive is addressed to the Member States.

[4065P]

Done at Brussels, 11 March 2002.

DIRECTIVE OF THE EUROPEAN PARLIAMENT AND OF THE COUNCIL

of 23 September 2002

amending Council Directive 76/207/EEC on the implementation of the principle of equal treatment for men and women as regards access to employment, vocational training and promotion and working conditions

(2002/73/EC)

NOTES

Date of publication in OJ: OJ L269, 5.10.2002, p 15.

This Directive is superseded by the Directive of the European Parliament and of the Council on the implementation of the principle of equal opportunities and equal treatment of men and women in matters of employment and occupation (recast) (Directive 2006/54/EC at **[4122]** et seq). The 2006 Directive consolidates and updates the four major Directives on gender equality; ie, the Equal Pay Directive (75/117/EEC), the Equal Treatment Directive (76/207/EEC), the Directive on Equal Treatment in

Occupational Social Security Schemes (86/378/EEC), and the Burden of Proof Directive (97/80/EC). These Directives are repealed by Art 34 of, and Annex I, Pt A to, the 2006 Directive, with effect from 15 August 2009 (see **[4155]** and **[4158]**). This Directive, however, is not specifically repealed by those provisions; this appears to be an oversight.

This Directive amends the operative provisions of the Equal Treatment Directive 76/207 at **[3713]** et seq.

For the domestic implementation of this Directive, see the Sex Discrimination Act 1975 at **[100]** et seq, and the amendments made to that Act by the Employment Equality (Sex Discrimination) Regulations 2005, SI 2005/2467 at **[3338]**.

THE EUROPEAN PARLIAMENT AND THE COUNCIL OF THE EUROPEAN UNION,

Having regard to the Treaty establishing the European Community and, in particular, Article 141(3) thereof,

Having regard to the proposal from the Commission,[1]

Having regard to the Opinion of the Economic and Social Committee,[2]

Acting in accordance with the procedure laid down in Article 251 of the Treaty,[3] *in the light of the joint text approved by the Conciliation Committee on 19 April 2002,*

Whereas—

(*1*) *In accordance with Article 6 of the Treaty on European Union, the European Union is founded on the principles of liberty, democracy, respect for human rights and fundamental freedoms, and the rule of law, principles which are common to the Member States, and shall respect fundamental rights as guaranteed by the European Convention for the Protection of Human Rights and Fundamental Freedoms and as they result from the constitutional traditions common to the Member States, as general principles of Community law.*

(*2*) *The right to equality before the law and protection against discrimination for all persons constitutes a universal right recognised by the Universal Declaration of Human Rights, the United Nations Convention on the Elimination of all forms of Discrimination Against Women, the International Convention on the Elimination of all Forms of Racial Discrimination and the United Nations Covenants on Civil and Political Rights and on Economic, Social and Cultural Rights and by the Convention for the Protection of Human Rights and Fundamental Freedoms, to which all Member States are signatories.*

(*3*) *This Directive respects the fundamental rights and observes the principles recognised in particular by the Charter of Fundamental Rights of the European Union.*

(*4*) *Equality between women and men is a fundamental principle, under Article 2 and Article 3(2) of the EC Treaty and the case-law of the Court of Justice. These Treaty provisions proclaim equality between women and men as a "task" and an "aim" of the Community and impose a positive obligation to "promote" it in all its activities.*

(*5*) *Article 141 of the Treaty, and in particular paragraph 3, addresses specifically equal opportunities and equal treatment of men and women in matters of employment and occupation.*

(*6*) *Council Directive 76/207/EEC*[4] *does not define the concepts of direct or indirect discrimination. On the basis of Article 13 of the Treaty, the Council has adopted Directive 2000/43/EC of 29 June 2000 implementing the principle of equal treatment between persons irrespective of racial or ethnic origin*[5] *and Directive 2000/78/EC of 27 November 2000 establishing a general framework for equal treatment in employment and occupation*[6] *which define direct and indirect discrimination. Thus it is appropriate to insert definitions consistent with these Directives in respect of sex.*

(*7*) *This Directive does not prejudice freedom of association, including the right to establish unions with others and to join unions to defend one's interests. Measures within the meaning of Article 141(4) of the Treaty may include membership or the continuation of the activity of organisations or unions whose main objective is the promotion, in practice, of the principle of equal treatment between women and men.*

(*8*) *Harassment related to the sex of a person and sexual harassment are contrary to the principle of equal treatment between women and men; it is therefore appropriate to define such concepts and to prohibit such forms of discrimination. To this end it must be emphasised that these forms of discrimination occur not only in the workplace, but also in the context of access to employment and vocational training, during employment and occupation.*

(*9*) *In this context, employers and those responsible for vocational training should be encouraged to take measures to combat all forms of sexual discrimination and, in particular, to take preventive measures against harassment and sexual harassment in the workplace, in accordance with national legislation and practice.*

(*10*) *The appreciation of the facts from which it may be inferred that there has been direct or indirect discrimination is a matter for national judicial or other competent bodies, in accordance with rules of national law or practice. Such rules may provide in particular for indirect discrimination to be established by any means including on the basis of statistical*

PART 2

evidence. According to the case-law of the Court of Justice,[7] *discrimination involves the application of different rules to a comparable situation or the application of the same rule to different situations.*

(11) The occupational activities that Member States may exclude from the scope of Directive 76/207/EEC should be restricted to those which necessitate the employment of a person of one sex by reason of the nature of the particular occupational activities concerned, provided that the objective sought is legitimate, and subject to the principle of proportionality as laid down by the case-law of the Court of Justice.[8]

(12) The Court of Justice has consistently recognised the legitimacy, in terms of the principle of equal treatment, of protecting a woman's biological condition during and after pregnancy. It has moreover consistently ruled that any unfavourable treatment of women related to pregnancy or maternity constitutes direct sex discrimination. This Directive is therefore without prejudice to Council Directive 92/85/EEC of 19 October 1992 on the introduction of measures to encourage improvements in the safety and health at work of pregnant workers and workers who have recently given birth or are breastfeeding[9] *(tenth individual Directive within the meaning of Article 16(1) of Directive 89/391/EEC), which aims to ensure the protection of the physical and mental state of women who are pregnant, women who have recently given birth or women who are breastfeeding. The preamble to Directive 92/85/EEC provides that the protection of the safety and health of pregnant workers, workers who have recently given birth or workers who are breastfeeding should not involve treating women who are on the labour market unfavourably nor work to the detriment of Directives concerning equal treatment for men and women. The Court of Justice has recognised the protection of employment rights of women, in particular their right to return to the same or an equivalent job, with no less favourable working conditions, as well as to benefit from any improvement in working conditions to which they would be entitled during their absence.*

(13) In the Resolution of the Council and of the Ministers for Employment and Social Policy meeting within the Council of 29 June 2000 on the balanced participation of women and men in family and working life,[10] *Member States were encouraged to consider examining the scope for their respective legal systems to grant working men an individual and untransferable right to paternity leave, while maintaining their rights relating to employment. In this context, it is important to stress that it is for the Member States to determine whether or not to grant such a right and also to determine any conditions, other than dismissal and return to work, which are outside the scope of this Directive.*

(14) Member States may, under Article 141(4) of the Treaty, maintain or adopt measures providing for specific advantages, in order to make it easier for the under-represented sex to pursue a vocational activity or to prevent or compensate for disadvantages in professional careers. Given the current situation, and bearing in mind Declaration No 28 to the Amsterdam Treaty, Members States should, in the first instance, aim at improving the situation of women in working life.

(15) The prohibition of discrimination should be without prejudice to the maintenance or adoption of measures intended to prevent or compensate for disadvantages suffered by a group of persons of one sex. Such measures permit organisations of persons of one sex where their main object is the promotion of the special needs of those persons and the promotion of equality between women and men.

(16) The principle of equal pay for men and women is already firmly established by Article 141 of the Treaty and Council Directive 75/117/EEC of 10 February 1975 on the approximation of the laws of the Member States relating to the application of the principle of equal pay for men and women[11] *and is consistently upheld by the case-law of the Court of Justice; the principle constitutes an essential and indispensable part of the acquis communautaire concerning sex discrimination.*

(17) The Court of Justice has ruled that, having regard to the fundamental nature of the right to effective judicial protection, employees enjoy such protection even after the employment relationship has ended.[12] *An employee defending or giving evidence on behalf of a person protected under this Directive should be entitled to the same protection.*

(18) The Court of Justice has ruled that, in order to be effective, the principle of equal treatment implies that, whenever it is breached, the compensation awarded to the employee discriminated against must be adequate in relation to the damage sustained. It has furthermore specified that fixing a prior upper limit may preclude effective compensation and that excluding an award of interest to compensate for the loss sustained is not allowed.[13]

(19) According to the case-law of the Court of Justice, national rules relating to time limits for bringing actions are admissible provided that they are not less favourable than time limits for similar actions of a domestic nature and that they do not render the exercise of rights conferred by the Community law impossible in practice.

(20) Persons who have been subject to discrimination based on sex should have adequate means of legal protection. To provide a more effective level of protection, associations,

organisations and other legal entities should also be empowered to engage in proceedings, as the Member States so determine, either on behalf or in support of any victim, without prejudice to national rules of procedure concerning representation and defence before the courts.

(21) Member States should promote dialogue between the social partners and, within the framework of national practice, with non-governmental organisations to address different forms of discrimination based on sex in the workplace and to combat them.

(22) Member States should provide for effective, proportionate and dissuasive sanctions in case of breaches of the obligations under Directive 76/207/EEC.

(23) In accordance with the principle of subsidiarity as set out in Article 5 of the Treaty, the objectives of the proposed action cannot be sufficiently achieved by the Member States and can therefore be better achieved by the Community. In accordance with the principle of proportionality, as set out in that Article, this Directive does not go beyond what is necessary for that purpose.

(24) Directive 76/207/EEC should therefore be amended accordingly,

NOTES

Superseded as noted at the beginning of this Directive.

1 OJ C337 E, 28.11.2000, p 204 and OJ C270 E, 25.9.2001, p 9.
2 OJ C123, 25.4.2001, p 81.
3 Opinion of the European Parliament of 31 May 2001 (OJ C47, 21.2.2002, p 19), Council Common Position of 23 July 2001 (OJ C307, 31.10.2001, p 5) and Decision of the European Parliament of 24 October 2001 (OJ C112E, 9.5.2002, p 14). Decision of the European Parliament of 12 June 2002 and Council Decision of 13 June 2002.
4 OJ L39, 14.2.1976, p 40.
5 OJ L180, 19.7.2000, p 22.
6 OJ L303, 2.12.2000, p 16.
7 *Case C-394/96 Brown*, [1998] ECR I-4185, Case C-342/93 *Gillespie*, [1996] ECR I-475.
8 *Case C-222/84 Johnston*, [1986] ECR 1651, *Case C-273/97 Sirdar* [1999] ECR I-7403 and *Case C-285/98 Kreil* [2000] ECR I-69.
9 OJ L348, 28.11.1992, p 1.
10 OJ C218, 31.7.2000, p 5.
11 OJ L45, 19.2.1975, p 19.
12 *Case C-185/97 Coote* [1998] ECR I-5199.
13 *Case C-180/95, Draehmpaehl*, [1997] ECR I-2195, *Case C-271/91, Marshall* [1993] ECR I-4367.

HAVE ADOPTED THIS DIRECTIVE—

Article 1

(*This Article amends Directive 76/207/EEC, Art 1, at* **[3713]**, *substitutes Arts 2, 3, 6, 7 of that Directive, at* **[3714]**, **[3715]**, **[3718]**, **[3719]**, *inserts Arts 8a–8e, at* **[3721]**–**[3725]**, *and repeals Arts 4, 5, and is superseded as noted at the beginning of this Directive.*)

Article 2

1. Member States shall bring into force the laws, regulations and administrative provisions necessary to comply with this Directive by 5 October 2005 at the latest or shall ensure, by that date at the latest, that management and labour introduce the requisite provisions by way of agreement. Member States shall take all necessary steps to enable them at all times to guarantee the results imposed by this Directive. They shall immediately inform the Commission thereof.

When Member States adopt those measures, they shall contain a reference to this Directive or be accompanied by such reference on the occasion of their official publication. Member States shall determine how such reference is to be made.

2. The Member States shall communicate to the Commission, within three years of the entry into force of this Directive, all the information necessary for the Commission to draw up a report to the European Parliament and the Council on the application of this Directive.

3. Without prejudice to paragraph 2, Member States shall communicate to the Commission, every four years, the texts of laws, regulations and administrative provisions of any measures adopted pursuant to Article 141(4) of the Treaty, as well as reports on these measures and their implementation. On the basis of that information, the Commission will adopt and publish every four years a report establishing a comparative assessment of any measures in the light of Declaration No 28 annexed to the Final Act of the Treaty of Amsterdam.

[4066]

NOTES
Superseded as noted at the beginning of this Directive.

Article 3

This Directive shall enter into force on the day of its publication in the Official Journal of the European Communities.

[4067]

NOTES
Superseded as noted at the beginning of this Directive.

Article 4

This Directive is addressed to the Member States.

[4068]

NOTES
Superseded as noted at the beginning of this Directive.

DIRECTIVE OF THE EUROPEAN PARLIAMENT AND OF THE COUNCIL

of 23 September 2002

amending Council Directive 80/987/EEC on the approximation of the laws of the Member States relating to the protection of employees in the event of the insolvency of their employer

(2002/74/EC)

NOTES
Date of publication in OJ: OJ L270, 8.10.2002, p 10.
This Directive amends the operative provisions of Council Directive 80/987/EEC at **[3740]** et seq.
For the domestic implementation of Council Directive 80/987/EEC, see the Employment Rights Act 1996, ss 166–170 at **[1210]**–**[1214]** and Part XII at **[1226]** et seq, as amended to implement the amendments made to the 1980 Directive by this Directive.

THE EUROPEAN PARLIAMENT AND THE COUNCIL OF THE EUROPEAN UNION,

Having regard to the Treaty establishing the European Community, and in particular Article 137(2) thereof,

Having regard to the proposal from the Commission,[1]

Having regard to the opinion of the Economic and Social Committee,[2]

Having consulted the Committee of the Regions,

Acting in accordance with the procedure laid down in Article 251 of the Treaty,[3]

Whereas:

(1) The Community Charter of Fundamental Social Rights for Workers adopted on 9 December 1989 states, in point 7, that the completion of the internal market must lead to an improvement in the living and working conditions of workers in the European Community and that this improvement must cover, where necessary, the development of certain aspects of employment regulations such as procedures for collective redundancies and those regarding bankruptcies.

(2) Directive 80/987/EEC[4] aims to provide a minimum degree of protection for employees in the event of the insolvency of their employer. To this end, it obliges the Member States to establish a body which guarantees payment of the outstanding claims of the employees concerned.

(3) Changes in insolvency law in the Member States and the development of the internal market mean that certain provisions of that Directive must be adapted.

(4) Legal certainty and transparency also require clarification with regard to the scope and certain definitions of Directive 80/987/EEC. In particular the possible exclusions granted

to the Member States should be indicated in the enacting provisions of the Directive and consequently the Annex thereto should be deleted.

(5) In order to ensure equitable protection for the employees concerned, the definition of the state of insolvency should be adapted to new legislative trends in the Member States and should also include within this concept insolvency proceedings other than liquidation. In this context, Member States should, in order to determine the liability of the guarantee institution, be able to lay down that where an insolvency situation results in several insolvency proceedings, the situation be treated as a single insolvency procedure.

(6) It should be ensured that the employees referred to in Directive 97/81/EC of 15 December 1997 concerning the Framework Agreement on part-time work concluded by UNICE, CEEP and the ETUC,[5] Council Directive 1999/70/EC of 28 June 1999 concerning the framework agreement on fixed-term work concluded by the ETUC, UNICE and CEEP[6] and Council Directive 91/383/EEC of 25 June 1991 supplementing the measures to encourage improvements in the safety and health at work of workers with a fixed-duration employment relationship or a temporary employment relationship[7] are not excluded from the scope of this Directive.

(7) In order to ensure legal certainty for employees in the event of insolvency of undertakings pursuing their activities in a number of Member States, and to strengthen workers' rights in line with the established case law of the Court of Justice, provisions should be introduced which expressly state which institution is responsible for meeting pay claims in these cases and establishes as the aim of cooperation between the competent administrative authorities of the Member States the early settlement of employees' outstanding claims. Furthermore it is necessary to ensure that the relevant arrangements are properly implemented by making provision for collaboration between the competent administrative authorities in the Member States.

(8) Member States may set limitations on the responsibility of the guarantee institutions which should be compatible with the social objective of the Directive and may take into account the different levels of claims.

(9) In order to make it easier to identify insolvency proceedings in particular in situations with a cross-border dimension, provision should be made for the Member States to notify the Commission and the other Member States about the types of insolvency proceedings which give rise to intervention by the guarantee institution.

(10) Directive 80/987/EEC should be amended accordingly.

(11) Since the objectives of the proposed action, namely the amendment of certain provisions of Directive 80/987/EEC to take account of changes in the activities of undertakings in the Community, cannot be sufficiently achieved by the Member States and can therefore be better achieved at Community level, the Community may adopt measures, in accordance with the principle of subsidiarity as set out in Article 5 of the Treaty. In accordance with the principle of proportionality, as set out in that Article, this Directive does not go beyond what is necessary in order to achieve that objective.

(12) The Commission should submit to the European Parliament and the Council a report on the implementation and application of this Directive in particular as regards the new forms of employment emerging in the Member States,

NOTES

1 OJ C154E, 29.5.2001, p 109.
2 OJ C221, 7.8.2001, p 110.
3 Opinion of the European Parliament of 29 November 2001 (not yet published in the Official Journal), Council Common Position of 18 February 2002 (OJ C119E, 22.5.2002, p 1) (not yet published in the Official Journal) and European Parliament Decision of 14 May 2002 (not yet published in the Official Journal). Council Decision of 27 June 2002.
4 OJ L283, 28.10.1980, p 23. Directive as last amended by the 1994 Act of Accession.
5 OJ L14, 20.1.1998, p. 9. Directive as last amended by Directive 98/23/EC (OJ L131, 5.5.1998, p 10).
6 OJ L175, 10.7.1999, p 43.
7 OJ L206, 29.7.1991, p 19.

HAVE ADOPTED THIS DIRECTIVE:

Article 1

(*Amends the title of Directive 80/987/EEC, and substitutes Arts 1–4, at* **[3740]–[3743]**, *inserts Arts 8a, 8b, 10a, at* **[3748]**, **[3749]**, **[3752]**, *amends Arts 9, 10, at* **[3750]**, **[3751]**, *and repeals the Annex.*)

Article 2

1. Member States shall bring into force the laws, regulations and administrative provisions necessary to comply with this Directive before 8 October 2005. They shall forthwith inform the Commission thereof.

They shall apply the provisions referred to in the first subparagraph to any state of insolvency of an employer occurring after the date of entry into force of those provisions.

When Member States adopt these measures, they shall contain a reference to this Directive or be accompanied by such reference on the occasion of their official publication. The methods of making such a reference shall be laid down by the Member States.

2. Member States shall communicate to the Commission the text of the provisions of national law which they adopt in the field covered by this Directive.

[4069]

Article 3

This Directive shall enter into force on the day of its publication in the Official Journal of the European Communities.

[4070]

Article 4

By 8 October 2010 at the latest, the Commission shall submit to the European Parliament and the Council a report on the implementation and application of this Directive in the Member States.

[4071]

Article 5

This Directive is addressed to the Member States.

[4072]

DIRECTIVE OF THE EUROPEAN PARLIAMENT AND OF THE COUNCIL

of 3 June 2003

on the activities and supervision of institutions for occupational retirement provision

(2003/41/EC)

NOTES

Date of publication in OJ: OJ L235, 23.9.2003, p 10.

For the domestic implementation of this Directive, see the Occupational Pension Schemes (Administration and Audited Accounts) (Amendment) Regulations 2005, SI 2005/1426, the Occupational Pension Schemes (Scheme Funding) Regulations 2005, SI 2005/3377, the Occupational Pension Schemes (Investment) Regulations 2005, SI 2005/3348, and the Occupational Pension Schemes (Regulatory Own Funds) Regulations 2005, SI 2005/3380.

THE EUROPEAN PARLIAMENT AND THE COUNCIL OF THE EUROPEAN UNION,

Having regard to the Treaty establishing the European Community, and in particular Article 47(2), Article 55 and Article 95(1) thereof,

Having regard to the proposal from the Commission,[1]

Having regard to the opinion of the European Economic and Social Committee,[2]

Acting in accordance with the procedure laid down in Article 251 of the Treaty,[3]

Whereas:

(1) A genuine internal market for financial services is crucial for economic growth and job creation in the Community.

(2) Major achievements have already been made in the establishment of this internal market, allowing financial institutions to operate in other Member States and ensuring a high level of protection for the consumers of financial services.

(3) The communication from the Commission 'Implementing the framework for financial markets: action plan' identifies a series of actions that are needed in order to

complete the internal market for financial services, and the European Council, at its meeting in Lisbon on 23 and 24 March 2000, called for the implementation of this action plan by 2005.

(4) The action plan for financial services stresses as an urgent priority the need to draw up a directive on the prudential supervision of institutions for occupational retirement provision, as these institutions are major financial institutions which have a key role to play in ensuring the integration, efficiency and liquidity of the financial markets, but they are not subject to a coherent Community legislative framework allowing them to benefit fully from the advantages of the internal market.

(5) Since social-security systems are coming under increasing pressure, occupational retirement pensions will increasingly be relied on as a complement in future. Occupational retirement pensions should therefore be developed, without, however, calling into question the importance of social-security pension systems in terms of secure, durable and effective social protection, which should guarantee a decent standard of living in old age and should therefore be at the centre of the objective of strengthening the European social model.

(6) This Directive thus represents a first step on the way to an internal market for occupational retirement provision organised on a European scale. By setting the 'prudent person' rule as the underlying principle for capital investment and making it possible for institutions to operate across borders, the redirection of savings into the sector of occupational retirement provision is encouraged, thus contributing to economic and social progress.

(7) The prudential rules laid down in this Directive are intended both to guarantee a high degree of security for future pensioners through the imposition of stringent supervisory standards, and to clear the way for the efficient management of occupational pension schemes.

(8) Institutions which are completely separated from any sponsoring undertaking and which operate on a funded basis for the sole purpose of providing retirement benefits should have freedom to provide services and freedom of investment, subject only to coordinated prudential requirements, regardless of whether these institutions are considered as legal entities.

(9) In accordance with the principle of subsidiarity, Member States should retain full responsibility for the organisation of their pension systems as well as for the decision on the role of each of the three 'pillars' of the retirement system in individual Member States. In the context of the second pillar, they should also retain full responsibility for the role and functions of the various institutions providing occupational retirement benefits, such as industry-wide pension funds, company pension funds and life-assurance companies. This Directive is not intended to call this prerogative into question.

(10) National rules concerning the participation of self-employed persons in institutions for occupational retirement provision differ. In some Member States, institutions for occupational retirement provision can operate on the basis of agreements with trade or trade groups whose members act in a self-employed capacity or directly with self-employed and employed persons. In some Member States a self-employed person can also become a member of an institution when the self-employed person acts as employer or provides his professional services to an undertaking. In some Member States self-employed persons cannot join an institution for occupational retirement provision unless certain requirements, including those imposed by social and labour law, are met.

(11) Institutions managing social-security schemes, which are already coordinated at Community level, should be excluded from the scope of this Directive. Account should nevertheless be taken of the specificity of institutions which, in a single Member State, manage both social-security schemes and occupational pension schemes.

(12) Financial institutions which already benefit from a Community legislative framework should in general be excluded from the scope of this Directive. However, as these institutions may also in some cases offer occupational pension services, it is important to ensure that this Directive does not lead to distortions of competition. Such distortions may be avoided by applying the prudential requirements of this Directive to the occupational pension business of life-assurance companies. The Commission should also carefully monitor the situation in the occupational pensions market and assess the possibility of extending the optional application of this Directive to other regulated financial institutions.

(13) When aiming at ensuring financial security in retirement, the benefits paid by institutions for occupational retirement provision should generally provide for the payment of a lifelong pension. Payments for a temporary period or a lump sum should also be possible.

(14) It is important to ensure that older and disabled people are not placed at risk of poverty and can enjoy a decent standard of living. Appropriate cover for biometrical risks in occupational pension arrangements is an important aspect of the fight against poverty and insecurity among elderly people. When setting up a pension scheme, employers and employees, or their respective representatives, should consider the possibility of the pension

scheme including provisions for the coverage of the longevity risk and occupational disability risks as well as provision for surviving dependants.

(15) Giving Member States the possibility to exclude from the scope of national implementing legislation institutions managing schemes which together have less than 100 members in total can facilitate supervision in some Member States, without undermining the proper functioning of the internal market in this field. However, this should not undermine the right of such institutions to appoint for the management of their investment portfolio and the custody of their assets investment managers and custodians established in another Member State and duly authorised.

(16) Institutions such as 'Unterstützungskassen' in Germany, where the members have no legal rights to benefits of a certain amount and where their interests are protected by a compulsory statutory insolvency insurance, should be excluded from the scope of the Directive.

(17) In order to protect members and beneficiaries, institutions for occupational retirement provision should limit their activities to the activities, and those arising therefrom, referred to in this Directive.

(18) In the event of the bankruptcy of a sponsoring undertaking, a member faces the risk of losing both his/her job and his/her acquired pension rights. This makes it necessary to ensure that there is a clear separation between that undertaking and the institution and that minimum prudential standards are laid down to protect members.

(19) Institutions for occupational retirement provision operate and are supervised with significant differences in Member States. In some Member States, supervision can be exercised not only over the institution itself but also over the entities or companies which are authorised to manage these institutions. Member States should be able to take such specificity into account as long as all the requirements laid down in this Directive are effectively met. Member States should also be able to allow insurance entities and other financial entities to manage institutions for occupational retirement provision.

(20) Institutions for occupational retirement provision are financial service providers which bear a heavy responsibility for the provision of occupational retirement benefits and therefore should meet certain minimum prudential standards with respect to their activities and conditions of operation.

(21) The huge number of institutions in certain Member States means a pragmatic solution is necessary as regards prior authorisation of institutions. However, if an institution wishes to manage a scheme in another Member State, a prior authorisation granted by the competent authority of the home Member State should be required.

(22) Each Member State should require that every institution located in its territory draw up annual accounts and annual reports taking into account each pension scheme operated by the institution and, where applicable, annual accounts and annual reports for each pension scheme. The annual accounts and annual reports, reflecting a true and fair view of the institution's assets, liabilities and financial position, taking into account each pension scheme operated by an institution, and duly approved by an authorised person, are an essential source of information for members and beneficiaries of a scheme and the competent authorities. In particular, they enable the competent authorities to monitor the financial soundness of an institution and assess whether the institution is able to meet all its contractual obligations.

(23) Proper information for members and beneficiaries of a pension scheme is crucial. This is of particular relevance for requests for information concerning the financial soundness of the institution, the contractual rules, the benefits and the actual financing of accrued pension entitlements, the investment policy and the management of risks and costs.

(24) The investment policy of an institution is a decisive factor for both security and affordability of occupational pensions. The institutions should therefore draw up and, at least every three years, review a statement of investment principles. It should be made available to the competent authorities and on request also to members and beneficiaries of each pension scheme.

(25) To fulfil their statutory function, the competent authorities should be provided with adequate rights to information and powers of intervention with respect to institutions and the persons who effectively run them. Where an institution for occupational retirement provision has transferred functions of material importance such as investment management, information technology or accounting to other companies (outsourcing), it should be possible for the rights to information and powers of intervention to be enlarged so as to cover these outsourced functions in order to check whether those activities are carried out in accordance with the supervisory rules.

(26) A prudent calculation of technical provisions is an essential condition to ensure that obligations to pay retirement benefits can be met. Technical provisions should be calculated on the basis of recognised actuarial methods and certified by qualified persons. The maximum interest rates should be chosen prudently according to any relevant national rules. The

minimum amount of technical provisions should both be sufficient for benefits already in payment to beneficiaries to continue to be paid and reflect the commitments that arise out of members' accrued pension rights.

(27) Risks covered by institutions vary significantly from one Member State to another. Home Member States should therefore have the possibility of making the calculation of technical provisions subject to additional and more detailed rules than those laid down in this Directive.

(28) Sufficient and appropriate assets to cover the technical provisions protect the interests of members and beneficiaries of the pension scheme if the sponsoring undertaking becomes insolvent. In particular in cases of cross-border activity, the mutual recognition of supervisory principles applied in Member States requires that the technical provisions be fully funded at all times.

(29) If the institution does not work on a cross-border basis, Member States should be able to permit underfunding provided that a proper plan is established to restore full funding and without prejudice to the requirements of Council Directive 80/987/EEC of 20 October 1980 on the approximation of the laws of the Member States relating to the protection of employees in the event of the insolvency of their employer.[4]

(30) In many cases, it could be the sponsoring undertaking and not the institution itself that either covers any biometric risk or guarantees certain benefits or investment performance. However, in some cases, it is the institution itself which provides such cover or guarantees and the sponsor's obligations are generally exhausted by paying the necessary contributions. In these circumstances, the products offered are similar to those of life-assurance companies and the institutions concerned should hold at least the same additional own funds as life-assurance companies.

(31) Institutions are very long-term investors. Redemption of the assets held by these institutions cannot, in general, be made for any purpose other than providing retirement benefits. Furthermore, in order to protect adequately the rights of members and beneficiaries, institutions should be able to opt for an asset allocation that suits the precise nature and duration of their liabilities. These aspects call for efficient supervision and an approach towards investment rules allowing institutions sufficient flexibility to decide on the most secure and efficient investment policy and obliging them to act prudently. Compliance with the 'prudent person' rule therefore requires an investment policy geared to the membership structure of the individual institution for occupational retirement provision.

(32) Supervisory methods and practices vary among Member States. Therefore, Member States should be given some discretion on the precise investment rules that they wish to impose on the institutions located in their territories. However, these rules must not restrict the free movement of capital, unless justified on prudential grounds.

(33) As very long-term investors with low liquidity risks, institutions for occupational retirement provision are in a position to invest in non-liquid assets such as shares as well as in risk capital markets within prudent limits. They can also benefit from the advantages of international diversification. Investments in shares, risk capital markets and currencies other than those of the liabilities should therefore not be restricted except on prudential grounds.

(34) However, if the institution works on a cross-border basis, it may be asked by the competent authorities of the host Member State to apply limits for investment in shares and similar assets not admitted to trading on a regulated market, in shares and other instruments issued by the same undertaking or in assets denominated in non-matching currencies provided such rules also apply to institutions located in the host Member State.

(35) Restrictions regarding the free choice by institutions of approved asset managers and custodians limit competition in the internal market and should therefore be eliminated.

(36) Without prejudice to national social and labour legislation on the organisation of pension systems, including compulsory membership and the outcomes of collective bargaining agreements, institutions should have the possibility of providing their services in other Member States. They should be allowed to accept sponsorship from undertakings located in other Member States and to operate pension schemes with members in more than one Member State. This would potentially lead to significant economies of scale for these institutions, improve the competitiveness of the Community industry and facilitate labour mobility. This requires mutual recognition of prudential standards. Proper enforcement of these prudential standards should be supervised by the competent authorities of the home Member State, unless specified otherwise.

(37) The exercise of the right of an institution in one Member State to manage an occupational pension scheme contracted in another Member State should fully respect the provisions of the social and labour law in force in the host Member State insofar as it is relevant to occupational pensions, for example the definition and payment of retirement benefits and the conditions for transferability of pension rights.

(38) When a scheme is ring-fenced, the provisions of this Directive apply individually to that scheme.

(39) It is important to make provision for cooperation between the competent authorities of the Member States for supervisory purposes and between those authorities and the Commission for other purposes. For the purposes of carrying out their duties and of contributing to the consistent and timely implementation of this Directive, competent authorities should provide each other with the information necessary to apply the provisions of the Directive. The Commission has indicated its intention to set up a committee of supervisors in order to encourage cooperation, coordination and exchanges of views between national competent authorities, and to promote the consistent implementation of this Directive.

(40) Since the objective of the proposed action, namely to create a Community legal framework covering institutions for occupational retirement provision, cannot be sufficiently achieved by the Member States and can therefore, by reason of the scale and effects of the action, be better achieved by the Community, the Community may adopt measures, in accordance with the principle of subsidiarity as set out in Article 5 of the Treaty. In accordance with the principle of proportionality as set out in that Article, this Directive does not go beyond what is necessary in order to achieve that objective,

NOTES

1 OJ C96E, 27.3.2001, p 136.

2 OJ C155, 29.5.2001, p 26.

3 Opinion of the European Parliament of 4 July 2001 (OJ C65E, 14.3.2002, p 135), Council common position of 5 November 2002 (not yet published in the Official Journal) and decision of the European Parliament of 12 March 2003 (not yet published in the Official Journal) and decision of the Council of 13 May 2003.

4 OJ L283, 28.10.1980, p 23. Directive as last amended by Directive 2002/74/EC of the European Parliament and of the Council (OJ L270, 8.10.2002, p 10).

HAVE ADOPTED THE FOLLOWING DIRECTIVE:

Article 1

Subject

This Directive lays down rules for the taking-up and pursuit of activities carried out by institutions for occupational retirement provision.

[4073]

Article 2

Scope

1. This Directive shall apply to institutions for occupational retirement provision. Where, in accordance with national law, institutions for occupational retirement provision do not have legal personality, Member States shall apply this Directive either to those institutions or, subject to paragraph 2, to those authorised entities responsible for managing them and acting on their behalf.

2. This Directive shall not apply to:

(a) institutions managing social-security schemes which are covered by Regulation (EEC) No 1408/71[1] and Regulation (EEC) No 574/72;[2]

(b) institutions which are covered by Directive 73/239/EEC,[3] Directive 85/611/EEC,[4] Directive 93/22/EEC,[5] Directive 2000/12/EC[6] and Directive 2002/83/EC;[7]

(c) institutions which operate on a pay-as-you-go basis;

(d) institutions where employees of the sponsoring undertakings have no legal rights to benefits and where the sponsoring undertaking can redeem the assets at any time and not necessarily meet its obligations for payment of retirement benefits;

(e) companies using book-reserve schemes with a view to paying out retirement benefits to their employees.

[4074]

NOTES

1 Council Regulation (EEC) No 1408/71 of 14 June 1971 on the application of social-security schemes to employed persons, to self-employed persons and to members of their families moving within the Community (OJ L149, 5.7.1971, p 2). Regulation as last amended by Regulation (EC) No 1386/2001 of the European Parliament and of the Council (OJ L187, 10.7.2001, p 1).

2 Council Regulation (EEC) No 574/72 of 21 March 1972 fixing the procedure for implementing Regulation (EEC) No 1408/71 on the application of social-security schemes to employed persons,

to self-employed persons and to members of their families moving within the Community (OJ L74, 27.3.1972, p 1). Regulation as last amended by Commission Regulation (EC) No 410/2002 (OJ L62, 5.3.2002, p 17).

3 First Council Directive 73/239/EEC of 24 July 1973 on the coordination of laws, regulations and administrative provisions relating to the taking-up and pursuit of the business of direct insurance other than life assurance (OJ L228, 16.8.1973, p 3). Directive as last amended by Directive 2002/13/EC of the European Parliament and of the Council (OJ L77, 20.3.2002, p 17).

4 Council Directive 85/611/EEC of 20 December 1985 on the coordination of laws, regulations and administrative provisions relating to undertakings for collective investment in transferable securities (UCITS) (OJ L375, 31.12.1985, p 3). Directive as last amended by Directive 2001/108/EC of the European Parliament and of the Council (OJ L41, 13.2.2002, p 35).

5 Council Directive 93/22/EEC of 10 May 1993 on investment services in the securities field (OJ L141, 11.6.1993, p 27). Directive as last amended by Directive 2000/64/EC of the European Parliament and of the Council (OJ L290, 17.11.2000, p 27).

6 Directive 2000/12/EC of the European Parliament and of the Council of 20 March 2000 relating to the taking-up and pursuit of the business of credit institutions (OJ L126, 26.5.2000, p 1). Directive as amended by Directive 2000/28/EC (OJ L275, 27.10.2000, p 37).

7 Directive 2002/83/EC of the European Parliament and of the Council of 5 November 2002 concerning life assurance (OJ L345, 19.12.2002, p 1).

Article 3

Application to institutions operating social-security schemes

Institutions for occupational retirement provision which also operate compulsory employment-related pension schemes which are considered to be social-security schemes covered by Regulations (EEC) No 1408/71 and (EEC) No 574/72 shall be covered by this Directive in respect of their non-compulsory occupational retirement provision business. In that case, the liabilities and the corresponding assets shall be ring-fenced and it shall not be possible to transfer them to the compulsory pension schemes which are considered as social-security schemes or vice versa.

[4075]

Article 4

Optional application to institutions covered by Directive 2002/83/EC

Home Member States may choose to apply the provisions of Articles 9 to 16 and Articles 18 to 20 of this Directive to the occupational-retirement-provision business of insurance undertakings which are covered by Directive 2002/83/EC. In that case, all assets and liabilities corresponding to the said business shall be ring-fenced, managed and organised separately from the other activities of the insurance undertakings, without any possibility of transfer.

In such case, and only as far as their occupational retirement provision business is concerned, insurance undertakings shall not be subject to Articles 20 to 26, 31 and 36 of Directive 2002/83/EC.

The home Member State shall ensure that either the competent authorities, or the authorities responsible for supervision of insurance undertakings covered by Directive 2002/83/EC, as part of their supervisory work, verify the strict separation of the relevant occupational retirement provision business.

[4076]

Article 5

Small pension institutions and statutory schemes

With the exception of Article 19, Member States may choose not to apply this Directive, in whole or in part, to any institution located in their territories which operates pension schemes which together have less than 100 members in total. Subject to Article 2(2), such institutions should nevertheless be given the right to apply this Directive on a voluntary basis. Article 20 may be applied only if all the other provisions of this Directive apply.

Member States may choose not to apply Articles 9 to 17 to institutions where occupational retirement provision is made under statute, pursuant to legislation, and is guaranteed by a public authority. Article 20 may be applied only if all the other provisions of this Directive apply.

[4077]

Article 6

Definitions

For the purposes of this Directive:

(a) 'institution for occupational retirement provision', or 'institution', means an institution, irrespective of its legal form, operating on a funded basis, established separately from any sponsoring undertaking or trade for the purpose of providing retirement benefits in the context of an occupational activity on the basis of an agreement or a contract agreed:
 — individually or collectively between the employer(s) and the employee(s) or their respective representatives, or
 — with self-employed persons, in compliance with the legislation of the home and host Member States,

and which carries out activities directly arising therefrom;

(b) 'pension scheme' means a contract, an agreement, a trust deed or rules stipulating which retirement benefits are granted and under which conditions;

(c) 'sponsoring undertaking' means any undertaking or other body, regardless of whether it includes or consists of one or more legal or natural persons, which acts as an employer or in a self-employed capacity or any combination thereof and which pays contributions into an institution for occupational retirement provision;

(d) 'retirement benefits' means benefits paid by reference to reaching, or the expectation of reaching, retirement or, where they are supplementary to those benefits and provided on an ancillary basis, in the form of payments on death, disability, or cessation of employment or in the form of support payments or services in case of sickness, indigence or death. In order to facilitate financial security in retirement, these benefits usually take the form of payments for life. They may, however, also be payments made for a temporary period or as a lump sum;

(e) 'member' means a person whose occupational activities entitle or will entitle him/her to retirement benefits in accordance with the provisions of a pension scheme;

(f) 'beneficiary' means a person receiving retirement benefits;

(g) 'competent authorities' means the national authorities designated to carry out the duties provided for in this Directive;

(h) 'biometrical risks' mean risks linked to death, disability and longevity;

(i) 'home Member State' means the Member State in which the institution has its registered office and its main administration or, if it does not have a registered office, its main administration;

(j) 'host Member State' means the Member State whose social and labour law relevant to the field of occupational pension schemes is applicable to the relationship between the sponsoring undertaking and members.

[4078]

Article 7

Activities of an institution

Each Member State shall require institutions located within its territory to limit their activities to retirement-benefit related operations and activities arising therefrom.

When, in accordance with Article 4, an insurance undertaking manages its occupational retirement provision business by ring-fencing its assets and liabilities, the ring-fenced assets and liabilities shall be restricted to retirement-benefit related operations and activities directly arising therefrom.

[4079]

Article 8

Legal separation between sponsoring undertakings and institutions for occupational retirement provision

Each Member State shall ensure that there is a legal separation between a sponsoring undertaking and an institution for occupational retirement provision in order that the assets of the institution are safeguarded in the interests of members and beneficiaries in the event of bankruptcy of the sponsoring undertaking.

[4080]

Article 9

Conditions of operation

1. Each Member State shall, in respect of every institution located in its territory, ensure that:

(a) the institution is registered in a national register by the competent supervisory authority or authorised; in the case of cross-border activities referred to in Article 20, the register shall also indicate the Member States in which the institution is operating;

(b) the institution is effectively run by persons of good repute who must themselves have appropriate professional qualifications and experience or employ advisers with appropriate professional qualifications and experience;

(c) properly constituted rules regarding the functioning of any pension scheme operated by the institution have been implemented and members have been adequately informed of these rules;

(d) all technical provisions are computed and certified by an actuary or, if not by an actuary, by another specialist in this field, including an auditor, according to national legislation, on the basis of actuarial methods recognised by the competent authorities of the home Member State;

(e) where the sponsoring undertaking guarantees the payment of the retirement benefits, it is committed to regular financing;

(f) the members are sufficiently informed of the conditions of the pension scheme, in particular concerning:

(i) the rights and obligations of the parties involved in the pension scheme;

(ii) the financial, technical and other risks associated with the pension scheme;

(iii) the nature and distribution of those risks.

2. In accordance with the principle of subsidiarity and taking due account of the scale of pension benefits offered by the social-security regimes, Member States may provide that the option of longevity and disability cover, provision for surviving dependants and a guarantee of repayment of contributions as additional benefits be offered to members if employers and employees, or their respective representatives, so agree.

3. A Member State may make the conditions of operation of an institution located in its territory subject to other requirements, with a view to ensuring that the interests of members and beneficiaries are adequately protected.

4. A Member State may permit or require institutions located in its territory to entrust management of these institutions, in whole or in part, to other entities operating on behalf of those institutions.

5. In the case of cross-border activity as referred to in Article 20, the conditions of operation of the institution shall be subject to a prior authorisation by the competent authorities of the home Member State.

[4081]

Article 10

Annual accounts and annual reports

Each Member State shall require that every institution located in its territory draw up annual accounts and annual reports taking into account each pension scheme operated by the institution and, where applicable, annual accounts and annual reports for each pension scheme. The annual accounts and the annual reports shall give a true and fair view of the institution's assets, liabilities and financial position. The annual accounts and information in the reports shall be consistent, comprehensive, fairly presented and duly approved by authorised persons, according to national law.

[4082]

Article 11

Information to be given to the members and beneficiaries

1. Depending on the nature of the pension scheme established, each Member State shall ensure that every institution located in its territory provides at least the information set out in this Article.

2. Members and beneficiaries and/or, where applicable, their representatives shall receive:

(a) on request, the annual accounts and the annual reports referred to in Article 10, and, where an institution is responsible for more than one scheme, those relating to their particular pension scheme;

(b) within a reasonable time, any relevant information regarding changes to the pension-scheme rules.

3. The statement of investment policy principles, referred to in Article 12, shall be made available to members and beneficiaries and/or, where applicable, to their representatives on request.

4. Each member shall also receive, on request, detailed and substantial information on:

(a) the target level of the retirement benefits, if applicable;

(b) the level of benefits in case of cessation of employment;

(c) where the member bears the investment risk, the range of investment options, if applicable, and the actual investment portfolio as well as information on risk exposure and costs related to the investments;

(d) the arrangements relating to the transfer of pension rights to another institution for occupational retirement provision in the event of termination of the employment relationship.

Members shall receive every year brief particulars of the situation of the institution as well as the current level of financing of their accrued individual entitlements.

5. Each beneficiary shall receive, on retirement or when other benefits become due, the appropriate information on the benefits which are due and the corresponding payment options.

[4083]

Article 12

Statement of investment policy principles

Each Member State shall ensure that every institution located in its territory prepares and, at least every three years, reviews a written statement of investment-policy principles. This statement is to be revised without delay after any significant change in the investment policy. Member States shall provide that this statement contains, at least, such matters as the investment risk measurement methods, the risk-management processes implemented and the strategic asset allocation with respect to the nature and duration of pension liabilities.

[4084]

Article 13

Information to be provided to the competent authorities

Each Member State shall ensure that the competent authorities, in respect of any institution located in its territory, have the necessary powers and means:

(a) to require the institution, the members of its board of directors and other managers or directors or persons controlling the institution to supply information about all business matters or forward all business documents;

(b) to supervise relationships between the institution and other companies or between institutions, when institutions transfer functions to those other companies or institutions (outsourcing), influencing the financial situation of the institution or being in a material way relevant for effective supervision;

(c) to obtain regularly the statement of investment-policy principles, the annual accounts and the annual reports, and all the documents necessary for the purposes of supervision. These may include documents such as:

- (i) internal interim reports;
- (ii) actuarial valuations and detailed assumptions;
- (iii) asset-liability studies;
- (iv) evidence of consistency with the investment-policy principles;
- (v) evidence that contributions have been paid in as planned;
- (vi) reports by the persons responsible for auditing the annual accounts referred to in Article 10;

(d) to carry out on-site inspections at the institution's premises and, where appropriate, on outsourced functions to check if activities are carried out in accordance with the supervisory rules.

[4085]

Article 14

Powers of intervention and duties of the competent authorities

1. The competent authorities shall require every institution located in their territories to have sound administrative and accounting procedures and adequate internal control mechanisms.

2. The competent authorities shall have the power to take any measures including, where appropriate, those of an administrative or financial nature, either with regard to any institution located in their territories or against the persons running the institution, which are appropriate and necessary to prevent or remedy any irregularities prejudicial to the interests of the members and beneficiaries.

They may also restrict or prohibit the free disposal of the institution's assets when, in particular:

(a) the institution has failed to establish sufficient technical provisions in respect of the entire business or has insufficient assets to cover the technical provisions;

(b) the institution has failed to hold the regulatory own funds.

3. In order to safeguard the interests of members and beneficiaries, the competent authorities may transfer the powers which the persons running an institution located in their territories hold in accordance with the law of the home Member State wholly or partly to a special representative who is fit to exercise these powers.

4. The competent authorities may prohibit or restrict the activities of an institution located in their territories in particular if:

(a) the institution fails to protect adequately the interests of members and beneficiaries;

(b) the institution no longer fulfils the conditions of operation;

(c) the institution fails seriously in its obligations under the rules to which it is subject;

(d) in the case of cross-border activity, the institution does not respect the requirements of social and labour law of the host Member State relevant to the field of occupational pensions.

Any decision to prohibit the activities of an institution shall be supported by precise reasons and notified to the institution in question.

5. Member States shall ensure that decisions taken in respect of an institution under laws, regulations and administrative provisions adopted in accordance with this Directive are subject to the right to apply to the courts.

[4086]

Articles 15–21

(*Outside the scope of this work.*)

Article 22

Implementation

1. Member States shall bring into force the laws, regulations and administrative provisions necessary to comply with this Directive before 23 September 2005. They shall forthwith inform the Commission thereof.

When Member States adopt these measures, they shall contain a reference to this Directive or shall be accompanied by such reference on the occasion of their official publication. The methods of making such reference shall be laid down by Member States.

2. Member States shall communicate to the Commission the text of the main provisions of national law which they adopt in the field governed by this Directive.

3. Member States may postpone until 23 September 2010 the application of Article 17(1) and (2) to institutions located in their territory which at the date specified in paragraph 1 of this Article do not have the minimum level of regulatory own funds required pursuant to Article 17(1) and (2). However, institutions wishing to operate pension schemes on a cross-border basis, within the meaning of Article 20, may not do so until they comply with the rules of this Directive.

4. Member States may postpone until 23 September 2010 the application of Article 18(1)(f) to institutions located in their territory. However, institutions wishing to

operate pension schemes on a cross-border basis, within the meaning of Article 20, may not do so until they comply with the rules of this Directive.

[4087]

Article 23

Entry in force

This Directive shall enter into force on the day of its publication in the *Official Journal of the European Union*.

[4088]

Article 24

Addressees

This Directive is addressed to the Member States.

[4089]

COUNCIL DIRECTIVE

of 22 July 2003

supplementing the Statute for a European Cooperative Society with regard to the involvement of employees

(2003/72/EC)

NOTES

Date of publication in OJ: OJ L207, 18.8.2003, p 25.

For the domestic implementation of this Directive see the European Cooperative Society (Involvement of Employees) Regulations 2006, SI 2006/2059 at **[3463B]**.

THE COUNCIL OF THE EUROPEAN UNION,

Having regard to the Treaty establishing the European Community, and in particular Article 308 thereof,

Having regard to the proposal from the Commission,[1]

Having regard to the opinion of the European Parliament,[2]

Having regard to the opinion of the European Economic and Social Committee,[3]

Whereas:

(1) In order to attain the objectives of the Treaty, Council Regulation (EC) No 1435/2003[4] establishes a Statute for a European Cooperative Society (SCE).

(2) That Regulation aims at creating a uniform legal framework within which cooperatives and other entities and natural persons from different Member States should be able to plan and carry out the reorganisation of their business in cooperative form on a Community scale.

(3) In order to promote the social objectives of the Community, special provisions have to be set, notably in the field of employee involvement, aimed at ensuring that the establishment of an SCE does not entail the disappearance or reduction of practices of employee involvement existing within the entities participating in the establishment of an SCE. This objective should be pursued through the establishment of a set of rules in this field, supplementing the provisions of Regulation (EC) No 1435/2003.

(4) Since the objectives of the proposed action, as outlined above, cannot be sufficiently achieved by the Member States, in that the object is to establish a set of rules on employee-involvement applicable to the SCE, and can therefore, by reason of the scale and impact of the proposed action, be better achieved at Community level, the Community may adopt measures, in accordance with the principle of subsidiarity as set out in Article 5 of the Treaty. In accordance with the principle of proportionality, as set out in that Article, this Directive does not go beyond what is necessary to achieve these objectives.

(5) The great diversity of rules and practices existing in the Member States as regards the manner in which employees' representatives are involved in decision-making within cooperatives makes it inadvisable to set up a single European model of employee involvement applicable to the SCE.

(6) Information and consultation procedures at transnational level should be ensured in all cases of creation of an SCE, with the necessary adaptation for SCEs formed *ex novo* where this is justified by their size, as measured in terms of employment.

(7) If participation rights exist within one or more entities establishing an SCE, they should in principle be preserved through their transfer to the SCE, once established, unless the parties decide otherwise.

(8) The concrete procedures of employee transnational information and consultation, as well as, if applicable, participation, to apply to each SCE should be defined primarily by means of an agreement between the parties concerned or, in the absence thereof, through the application of a set of subsidiary rules.

(9) Member States should still have the option of not applying the standard rules relating to participation in the case of a merger, given the diversity of national systems for employee involvement. Existing systems and practices of participation where appropriate at the level of participating entities must in that case be maintained by adapting registration rules.

(10) The voting rules within the special body representing the employees for negotiation purposes, in particular when concluding agreements providing for a level of participation lower than the one existing within one or more of the participating entities, should be proportionate to the risk of disappearance or reduction of existing systems and practices of participation. That risk is greater in the case of an SCE established by way of transformation or merger than by way of creating an *ex novo* SCE.

(11) In the absence of an agreement subsequent to the negotiation between employees' representatives and the competent organs of the participating entities, provision should be made for certain standard rules to apply to the SCE, once it is established. These standard rules should ensure effective practices of transnational information and consultation of employees, as well as their participation in the relevant organs of the SCE if such participation existed before its establishment within the participating entities.

(12) When application of the abovementioned procedures to the entities participating in the *ex novo* SCE cannot be justified because of their small size as measured in terms of employment, the SCE should be subject to the national rules on the involvement of employees in force in the Member State where it establishes its registered office, or in the Member States where it has subsidiaries or establishments. This should be without prejudice to the obligation placed on an SCE already established to implement these procedures if a significant number of employees so requests.

(13) Specific provisions should apply to employee participation in general meetings, in so far as national laws so allow. The application of these provisions does not preclude the application of other forms of participation, as provided for in this Directive.

(14) Member States should ensure through appropriate provisions that, in the case of structural changes following the creation of an SCE, the arrangements for the involvement of employees can, where appropriate, be renegotiated.

(15) Provision should be made for the employees' representatives acting within the framework of this Directive to enjoy, when exercising their functions, the same protection and guarantees as those provided for employees' representatives by the legislation and/or practice of the country of employment. They should not be subject to any discrimination, including harassment, as a result of the lawful exercise of their activities and should enjoy adequate protection as regards dismissal and other sanctions.

(16) The confidentiality of sensitive information should be preserved even after the expiry of the terms of office of the employees' representatives, and provision should be made to allow the competent organ of the SCE to withhold information which would seriously harm, if subject to public disclosure, the functioning of the SCE.

(17) Where an SCE and its subsidiaries and establishments are subject to Council Directive 94/45/EC of 22 September 1994 on the establishment of a European Works Council or a procedure in Community-scale undertakings and Community-scale groups of undertakings for the purposes of informing and consulting employees,[5] the provisions of that Directive and the provisions transposing it into national legislation should not apply to it nor to its subsidiaries and establishments, unless the special negotiating body decides not to open negotiations or to terminate negotiations already opened.

(18) This Directive should not affect other existing rights regarding involvement and need not affect other existing representation structures, provided for by Community and national laws and practices.

(19) Member States should take appropriate measures in the event of failure to comply with the obligations laid down in this Directive.

(20) The Treaty has not provided the necessary powers for the Community to adopt this Directive, other than those provided for in Article 308.

(21) It is a fundamental principle and stated aim of this Directive to secure employees' acquired rights as regards involvement in company decisions. Employee rights in force before the establishment of SCEs should provide the basis for employee rights of involvement in the

SCE (the "before and after" principle). Consequently, that approach should apply not only to the initial establishment of an SCE but also to structural changes in an existing SCE and to the entities affected by structural change processes. Therefore, where the registered office of an SCE is transferred from one Member State to another, at least the same level of employee involvement rights should continue to apply. Further, if the threshold concerning employee involvement is reached or exceeded after the registration of an SCE, these rights should apply in the same manner in which they would have applied, had the threshold been reached or exceeded before registration.

(22) Member States may provide that representatives of trade unions may be members of a special negotiating body regardless of whether they are employees of an entity participating in the establishment of an SCE. Member States should in this context in particular be able to introduce this right in cases where trade union representatives have the right to be members of, and to vote in, supervisory or administrative company organs in accordance with national legislation.

(23) In several Member States, employee involvement and other areas of industrial relations are based on both national legislation and practice which in this context is understood also to cover collective agreements at various national, sectorial and/or company levels,

NOTES

[1] OJ C236, 31.8.1993, p 36.
[2] OJ C42, 15.2.1993, p 75.
[3] OJ C223, 31.8.1992, p 42.
[4] See page 1 of this Official Journal.
[5] OJ L254, 30.9.1994, p 64. Directive as amended by Directive 97/74/EC (OJ L10, 16.1.1998, p 22).

HAS ADOPTED THIS DIRECTIVE:

SECTION I
GENERAL

Article 1

Objective

1. This Directive governs the involvement of employees in the affairs of European Cooperative Societies (hereinafter referred to as SCEs), as referred to in Regulation (EC) No 1435/2003.

2. To this end, arrangements for the involvement of employees shall be established in every SCE in accordance with the negotiating procedure referred to in Articles 3 to 6 or, under the circumstances specified in Articles 7 and 8, in accordance with the Annex.

[4089A]

Article 2

Definitions

For the purposes of this Directive:

(a) "SCE" means any cooperative society established in accordance with Regulation (EC) No 1435/2003;
(b) "participating legal entities" means companies and firms within the meaning of the second paragraph of Article 48 of the Treaty, including cooperatives, as well as legal bodies formed under, and governed by, the law of a Member State, directly participating in the establishing of an SCE;
(c) "subsidiary" of a participating legal entity or of an SCE means an undertaking over which that legal entity or SCE exercises a dominant influence defined in accordance with Article 3(2) to (7) of Directive 94/45/EC;
(d) "concerned subsidiary or establishment" means a subsidiary or establishment of a participating legal entity which is proposed to become a subsidiary or establishment of the SCE upon its formation;
(e) "employees' representatives" means the employees' representatives provided for by national law and/or practice;
(f) "representative body" means the body representative of the employees set up by the agreements referred to in Article 4 or in accordance with the provisions of the

Annex, with the purpose of informing and consulting the employees of an SCE and its subsidiaries and establishments situated in the Community and, where applicable, of exercising participation rights in relation to the SCE;

(g) "special negotiating body" means the body established in accordance with Article 3 to negotiate with the competent organ of the participating legal entities regarding the establishment of arrangements for the involvement of employees within the SCE;

(h) "involvement of employees" means any mechanism, including information, consultation and participation, through which employees' representatives may exercise an influence on decisions to be taken within an undertaking;

(i) "information" means the informing of the body representative of the employees and/or the employees' representatives by the competent organ of the SCE on questions which concern the SCE itself and any of its subsidiaries or establishments situated in another Member State or which exceed the powers of the decision-making organs in a single Member State at a time, in a manner and with a content which allows the employees' representatives to undertake an in-depth assessment of the possible impact and, where appropriate, prepare consultations with the competent organ of the SCE;

(j) "consultation" means the establishment of dialogue and exchange of views between the body representative of the employees and/or the employees' representatives and the competent organ of the SCE, at a time, in a manner and with a content which allows the employees' representatives, on the basis of information provided, to express an opinion on measures envisaged by the competent organ which may be taken into account in the decision-making process within the SCE;

(k) "participation" means the influence of the body representative of the employees and/or the employees' representatives in the affairs of a legal entity by way of:

— the right to elect or appoint some of the members of the legal entity's supervisory or administrative organ, or

— the right to recommend and/or oppose the appointment of some or all of the members of the legal entity's supervisory or administrative organ.

[4089B]

SECTION II

NEGOTIATING PROCEDURE APPLICABLE TO SCES ESTABLISHED BY AT LEAST TWO LEGAL ENTITIES OR BY TRANSFORMATION

Article 3

Creation of a special negotiating body

1. Where the management or administrative organs of participating legal entities draw up a plan for the establishment of an SCE, they shall as soon as possible take the necessary steps, including providing information on the identity of the participating legal entities and subsidiaries or establishments, as well as the number of their employees, to start negotiations with the representatives of the legal entities' employees on arrangements for the involvement of employees in the SCE.

2. For this purpose, a special negotiating body representative of the employees of the participating legal entities and concerned subsidiaries or establishments shall be created in accordance with the following provisions:

(a) in electing or appointing members of the special negotiating body, it shall be ensured:

(i) that such members are elected or appointed in proportion to the number of employees employed in each Member State by the participating legal entities and concerned subsidiaries or establishments, by allocating in respect of a Member State one seat per each portion of employees employed in that Member State which equals 10%, or a fraction thereof, of the number of employees employed in all the Member States taken together;

(ii) that in the case of an SCE formed by way of merger, there are such further additional members from each Member State as may be necessary in order to ensure that the special negotiating body includes at least one member representing each participating cooperative which is registered and has employees in that Member State and which it is proposed will cease to exist as a separate legal entity following the registration of the SCE, insofar as:

— the number of such additional members does not exceed 20% of the number of members designated by virtue of point (i); and
— the composition of the special negotiating body does not entail a double representation of the employees concerned.

If the number of such cooperatives is higher than the number of additional seats available pursuant to the first subparagraph, these additional seats shall be allocated to cooperatives in different Member States by decreasing order of the number of employees they employ.

(b) Member States shall determine the method to be used for the election or appointment of the members of the special negotiating body who are to be elected or appointed in their territories. They shall take the necessary measures to ensure that, as far as possible, such members shall include at least one member representing each participating legal entity which has employees in the Member State concerned. Such measures must not increase the overall number of members. The methods used to nominate, appoint or elect employee representatives should seek to promote gender balance.

Member States may provide that such members may include representatives of trade unions whether or not they are employees of a participating legal entity or concerned subsidiary or establishment.

Without prejudice to national legislation and/or practice laying down thresholds for the establishing of a representative body, Member States shall provide that employees in undertakings or establishments in which there are no employees' representatives through no fault of their own have the right to elect or appoint members of the special negotiating body.

3. The special negotiating body and the competent organs of the participating legal entities shall determine, by written agreement, arrangements for the involvement of employees within the SCE.

To this end, the competent organs of the participating legal entities shall inform the special negotiating body of the plan and the actual process of establishing the SCE, up to its registration.

4. Subject to paragraph 6, the special negotiating body shall take decisions by an absolute majority of its members, provided that such a majority also represents an absolute majority of the employees. Each member shall have one vote. However, should the result of the negotiations lead to a reduction of participation rights, the majority required for a decision to approve such an agreement shall be the votes of two thirds of the members of the special negotiating body representing at least two thirds of the employees, including the votes of members representing employees employed in at least two Member States,

— in the case of an SCE to be established by way of merger, if participation covers at least 25% of the overall number of employees of the participating cooperatives, or
— in the case of an SCE to be established by any other way, if participation covers at least 50% of the overall number of employees of the participating legal entities.

Reduction of participation rights means a proportion of members of the organs of the SCE within the meaning of Article 2(k), which is lower than the highest proportion existing within the participating legal entities.

5. For the purpose of the negotiations, the special negotiating body may request experts of its choice, for example representatives of appropriate Community level trade union organisations, to assist it with its work. Such experts may be present at negotiation meetings in an advisory capacity at the request of the special negotiating body, where appropriate to promote coherence and consistency at Community level. The special negotiating body may decide to inform the representatives of appropriate external organisations, including trade unions, of the start of the negotiations.

6. The special negotiating body may decide by the majority set out in the second subparagraph not to open negotiations or to terminate negotiations already opened, and to rely on the rules on information and consultation of employees in force in the Member States where the SCE has employees. Such a decision shall stop the procedure to conclude the agreement referred to in Article 4. Where such a decision has been taken, none of the provisions of the Annex shall apply.

The majority required to decide not to open or to terminate negotiations shall be the votes of two thirds of the members representing at least two thirds of the employees, including the votes of members representing employees employed in at least two Member States.

In the case of an SCE established by way of transformation, this paragraph shall not apply if there is participation in the cooperative to be transformed.

The special negotiating body shall be reconvened at the written request of at least 10% of the employees of the SCE, its subsidiaries and establishments, or their representatives, at the earliest two years after the abovementioned decision, unless the parties agree to negotiations being reopened sooner. If the special negotiating body decides to reopen negotiations with the management but no agreement is reached as a result of those negotiations, none of the provisions of the Annex shall apply.

7. Any expenses relating to the functioning of the special negotiating body and, in general, to negotiations shall be borne by the participating legal entities so as to enable the special negotiating body to carry out its task in an appropriate manner.

In compliance with this principle, Member States may lay down budgetary rules regarding the operation of the special negotiating body. They may in particular limit the funding to cover one expert only.

[4089C]

Article 4

Content of the agreement

1. The competent organs of the participating legal entities and the special negotiating body shall negotiate in a spirit of cooperation with a view to reaching an agreement on arrangements for the involvement of the employees within the SCE.

2. Without prejudice to the autonomy of the parties, and subject to paragraph 4, the agreement referred to in paragraph 1 between the competent organs of the participating legal entities and the special negotiating body shall specify:

(a) the scope of the agreement;
(b) the composition, number of members and allocation of seats on the representative body which will be the discussion partner of the competent organ of the SCE in connection with arrangements for the information and consultation of the employees of the SCE and its subsidiaries and establishments;
(c) the functions and the procedure for the information and consultation of the representative body;
(d) the frequency of meetings of the representative body;
(e) the financial and material resources to be allocated to the representative body;
(f) if, during negotiations, the parties decide to establish one or more information and consultation procedures instead of a representative body, the arrangements for implementing those procedures;
(g) if, during negotiations, the parties decide to establish arrangements for participation, the substance of those arrangements including (if applicable) the number of members in the SCE's administrative or supervisory body which the employees will be entitled to elect, appoint, recommend or oppose, the procedures as to how these members may be elected, appointed, recommended or opposed by the employees, and their rights;
(h) the date of entry into force of the agreement and its duration, cases where the agreement should be renegotiated and the procedure for its renegotiation, including, where appropriate, in the event of structural changes in the SCE and its subsidiaries and establishments which occur after the creation of the SCE.

3. The agreement shall not, unless provision is made otherwise therein, be subject to the standard rules referred to in the Annex.

4. Without prejudice to Article 15(3)(a), in the case of an SCE established by means of transformation, the agreement shall provide for at least the same level of all elements of employee involvement as the ones existing within the cooperative to be transformed into an SCE.

5. The agreement may specify the arrangements for the entitlement of employees to participate in the general meetings or in the section or sectorial meetings in accordance with Article 9 of this Directive and Article 59(4) of Regulation (EC) No 1435/2003.

[4089D]

Article 5

Duration of negotiations

1. Negotiations shall commence as soon as the special negotiating body is established and may continue for six months thereafter.

2. The parties may decide, by joint agreement, to extend negotiations beyond the period referred to in paragraph 1, up to a total of one year from the establishment of the special negotiating body.

[4089E]

Article 6

Legislation applicable to the negotiation procedure

Except where otherwise provided in this Directive, the legislation applicable to the negotiation procedure provided for in Articles 3, 4 and 5 shall be the legislation of the Member State in which the registered office of the SCE is to be situated.

[4089F]

Article 7

Standard rules

1. In order to achieve the objective described in Article 1, Member States shall lay down standard rules on employee involvement which must satisfy the provisions set out in the Annex.

The standard rules as laid down by the legislation of the Member State in which the registered office of the SCE is to be situated shall apply from the date of the registration of the SCE where either:

(a) the parties so agree; or

(b) by the deadline laid down in Article 5, no agreement has been concluded, and:
- — the competent organ of each of the participating legal entities decides to accept the application of the standard rules in relation to the SCE and so to continue with its registration of the SCE, and
- — the special negotiating body has not taken the decision provided in Article 3(6).

2. Moreover, the standard rules fixed by the national legislation of the Member State of registration in accordance with part 3 of the Annex shall apply only:

(a) in the case of an SCE established by transformation, if the rules of a Member State relating to employee participation in the administrative or supervisory body applied to a cooperative transformed into an SCE;

(b) in the case of an SCE established by merger:
- — if, before registration of the SCE, one or more forms of participation applied in one or more of the participating cooperatives covering at least 25% of the total number of employees employed by them, or
- — if, before registration of the SCE, one or more forms of participation applied in one or more of the participating cooperatives covering less than 25% of the total number of employees employed by them and if the special negotiating body so decides;

(c) in the case of an SCE established by any other way;
- — if, before registration of the SCE, one or more forms of participation applied in one or more of the participating legal entities covering at least 50% of the total number of employees employed by them; or
- — if, before registration of the SCE, one or more forms of participation applied in one or more of the participating legal entities covering less than 50% of the total number of employees employed by them and if the special negotiating body so decides.

If there was more than one form of participation within the various participating legal entities, the special negotiating body shall decide which of those forms must be established in the SCE. Member States may fix the rules which are applicable in the absence of any decision on the matter for an SCE registered in their territory. The special negotiating body shall inform the competent organs of the participating legal entities of any decisions taken pursuant to this paragraph.

3. Member States may lay down that the standard rules referred to in Part 3 of the Annex shall not apply in the case provided for in paragraph 2(b).

[4089G]

SECTION III
RULES APPLICABLE TO SCES ESTABLISHED EXCLUSIVELY BY NATURAL PERSONS OR BY A SINGLE LEGAL ENTITY AND NATURAL PERSONS

Article 8

1. In the case of an SCE established exclusively by natural persons or by a single legal entity and natural persons, which together employ at least 50 employees in at least two Member States, the provisions of Articles 3 to 7 shall apply.

2. In the case of an SCE established exclusively by natural persons or by a single legal entity and natural persons, which together employ fewer than 50 employees, or employ 50 or more employees in only one Member State, employee involvement shall be governed by the following:

— in the SCE itself, the provisions of the Member State of the SCE's registered office, which are applicable to other entities of the same type, shall apply,

— in its subsidiaries and establishments, the provisions of the Member State where they are situated, and which are applicable to other entities of the same type, shall apply.

In the case of transfer from one Member State to another of the registered office of an SCE governed by participation, at least the same level of employee participation rights shall continue to apply.

3. If, after the registration of an SCE referred to in paragraph 2, at least one third of the total number of employees of the SCE and its subsidiaries and establishments in at least two different Member States so requests, or if the total number of employees reaches or exceeds 50 employees in at least two Member States, the provisions of Articles 3 to 7 shall be applied, *mutatis mutandis*. In this case, the words "participating legal entities" and "concerned subsidiaries or establishments" shall be replaced by the words "SCE" and "subsidiaries or establishments of the SCE" respectively.

[4089H]

SECTION IV

PARTICIPATION IN THE GENERAL MEETING OR SECTION OR SECTORIAL MEETING

Article 9

Subject to the limits laid down in Article 59(4) of Regulation (EC) No 1435/2003, the employees of the SCE and/or their representatives will be entitled to participate in the general meeting or, if it exists, in the section or sectorial meeting, with the right to vote, in the following circumstances:

1. when the parties so decide in the agreement referred to in Article 4, or
2. when a cooperative governed by such a system transforms itself into an SCE, or
3. when, in the case of an SCE established by means other than transformation, a participating cooperative was governed by such a system and:
   (i) the parties cannot reach agreement, as referred to in Article 4, by the deadline laid down in Article 5; and
   (ii) Article 7(1)(b) and Part 3 of the Annex apply; and
   (iii) the participating cooperative governed by such a system has the highest proportion of participation, within the meaning of Article 2(k), in force in the participating cooperatives concerned before registration of the SCE.

[4089I]

SECTION V

MISCELLANEOUS PROVISIONS

Article 10

Reservation and confidentiality

1. Member States shall provide that members of the special negotiating body or the representative body, and experts who assist them, are not authorised to reveal any information which as been given to them in confidence.

The same shall apply to employees' representatives in the context of an information and consultation procedure.

This obligation shall continue to apply, wherever the persons referred to may be, even after the expiry of their terms of office.

2. Each Member State shall provide, in specific cases and under the conditions and limits laid down by national legislation, that the supervisory or administrative organ of an SCE or of a participating legal entity established in its territory is not obliged to transmit information where its nature is such that, according to objective criteria, to do so would seriously harm the functioning of the SCE (or, as the case may be, a participating legal entity) or its subsidiaries and establishments or would be prejudicial to them.

A Member State may make such dispensation subject to prior administrative or judicial authorisation.

3. Each Member State may lay down particular provisions for SCEs in its territory which pursue directly and essentially the aim of ideological guidance with respect to information and the expression of opinions, on condition that, on the date of adoption of this Directive, such provisions already exist in the national legislation.

4. In applying paragraphs 1, 2 and 3, Member States shall make provision for administrative or judicial appeal procedures which the employees' representatives may initiate when the supervisory or administrative organ of an SCE or of a participating legal entity demands confidentiality or does not give information.

Such procedures may include arrangements designed to protect the confidentiality of the information in question.

[4089J]

Article 11

Operation of the representative body and procedure for the information and consultation of employees

The competent organ of the SCE and the representative body shall work together in a spirit of cooperation with due regard for their reciprocal rights and obligations.

The same shall apply to cooperation between the supervisory or administrative organ of the SCE and the employees' representatives in conjunction with a procedure for the information and consultation of employees.

[4089K]

Article 12

Protection of employees' representatives

The members of the special negotiating body, the members of the representative body, any employees' representatives exercising functions under the information and consultation procedure and any employees' representatives in the supervisory or administrative organ of an SCE who are employees of the SCE, its subsidiaries or establishments or of a participating legal entity shall, in the exercise of their functions, enjoy the same protection and guarantees provided for employees' representatives by the national legislation and/or practice in force in their country of employment.

This shall apply in particular to attendance at meetings of the special negotiating body or representative body, any other meeting under the agreement referred to in Article 4(2)(f) or any meeting of the administrative or supervisory organ, and to the payment of wages for members employed by a participating legal entity or the SCE or its subsidiaries or establishments during a period of absence necessary for the performance of their duties.

[4089L]

Article 13

Misuse of procedures

Member States shall take appropriate measures in conformity with Community law with a view to preventing the misuse of an SCE for the purpose of depriving employees of rights to employee involvement or withholding such rights.

[4089M]

Article 14

Compliance with this Directive

1. Each Member State shall ensure that the management of establishments of an SCE and the supervisory or administrative organs of subsidiaries and of participating legal entities which are situated within its territory and the employees' representatives or, as the case may be, the employees themselves abide by the obligations laid down by this Directive, regardless of whether or not the SCE has its registered office within its territory.

2. Member States shall provide for appropriate measures in the event of failure to comply with this Directive; in particular they shall ensure that administrative or legal procedures are available to enable the obligations deriving from this Directive to be enforced.

[4089N]

Article 15

Link between this Directive and other provisions

1. Where an SCE is a Community-scale undertaking or a controlling undertaking of a Community-scale group of undertakings within the meaning of Directive 94/45/EC or of Council Directive 97/74/EC of 15 December 1997 extending the said Directive to the United Kingdom,[1] the provisions of these Directives and the provisions transposing them into national legislation shall not apply to them or to their subsidiaries.

However, where the special negotiating body decides in accordance with Article 3(6) not to open negotiations or to terminate negotiations already opened, Directive 94/45/EC or Directive 97/74/EC and the provisions transposing them into national legislation shall apply.

2. Provisions on the participation of employees in company bodies provided for by national legislation and/or practice, other than those implementing this Directive, shall not apply to the SCEs to which Articles 3 to 7 apply.

3. This Directive shall not prejudice:

(a) the existing rights to involvement of employees provided for by national legislation and/or practice in the Member States as enjoyed by employees of the SCE and its subsidiaries and establishments, other than participation in the bodies of the SCE;

(b) the provisions on participation in the bodies laid down by national legislation and/or practice applicable to the subsidiaries of the SCE or to SCEs to which Articles 3 to 7 do not apply.

4. In order to preserve the rights referred to in paragraph 3, Member States may take the necessary measures to guarantee that the structures of employee representation in participating legal entities which will cease to exist as separate legal entities are maintained after the registration of the SCE.

[4089O]

NOTES

1 OJ L10, 16.1.1998, p 22.

Article 16

Final provisions

1. Member States shall adopt the laws, regulations and administrative provisions necessary to comply with this Directive no later than 18 August 2006, or shall ensure by that

date at the latest that management and labour introduce the required provisions by way of agreement, the Member States being obliged to take all necessary steps enabling them at all times to guarantee the results imposed by this Directive. They shall forthwith inform the Commission thereof.

2. When Member States adopt these measures, they shall contain a reference to this Directive or shall be accompanied by such reference on the occasion of their official publication. The methods of making such reference shall be laid down by the Member States.

[4089P]

Article 17

Review by the Commission

Not later than 18 August 2009, the Commission shall, in consultation with the Member States and with management and labour at Community level, review the application of applying this Directive, with a view to proposing suitable amendments to the Council where necessary.

[4089Q]

Article 18

Entry into force

This Directive shall enter into force on the date of its publication in the *Official Journal of the European Union*.

[4089R]

Article 19

Addressees

This Directive is addressed to the Member States.

[4089S]

Done at Brussels, 22 July 2003.

ANNEX

STANDARD RULES

(*referred to in Articles 7 and 8*)

Part 1: Composition of the body representative of the employees

In order to achieve the objective described in Article 1, and in the cases referred to in Article 7, a representative body shall be set up in accordance with the following rules:

(a) The representative body shall be composed of employees of the SCE and its subsidiaries and establishments elected or appointed from their number by the employees' representatives or, in the absence thereof, by the entire body of employees.

(b) The election or appointment of members of the representative body shall be carried out in accordance with national legislation and/or practice.

Member States shall lay down rules to ensure that the number of members of, and allocation of seats on, the representative body shall be adapted to take account of changes occurring within the SCE and its subsidiaries and establishments. The methods used to nominate, appoint or elect employee representatives should seek to promote gender balance.

(c) Where its size so warrants, the representative body shall elect a select committee from among its members, comprising at most three members.

(d) The representative body shall adopt its rules of procedure.

(e) The members of the representative body are elected or appointed in proportion to the number of employees employed in each Member State by the SCE and its subsidiaries or establishments, by allocating in respect of a Member State one seat per each portion of employees employed in that Member State which equals 10%, or a fraction thereof, of the number of employees employed by them in all the Member States taken together.

(f) The competent organ of the SCE shall be informed of the composition of the representative body.

(g) Not later than four years after its establishment, the representative body shall examine whether to open negotiations for the conclusion of the agreement referred to in Articles 4 and 7 or to continue to apply the standard rules adopted in accordance with this Annex.

Article 3(4) to (7) and Articles 4, 5 and 6 shall apply, *mutatis mutandis*, if a decision has been taken to negotiate an agreement according to Article 4, in which case the term "special negotiating body" shall be replaced by "representative body". Where, by the deadline by which the negotiations come to an end, no agreement has been concluded, the arrangements initially adopted in accordance with the standard rules shall continue to apply.

[4089T]

Part 2: Standard rules for information and consultation

The competence and powers of the representative body set up in an SCE shall be governed by the following rules:

(a) The competence of the representative body shall be limited to questions which concern the SCE itself and any of its subsidiaries or establishments situated in another Member State or which exceed the powers of the decision-making organs in a single Member State.

(b) Without prejudice to meetings held pursuant to paragraph (c), the representative body shall have the right to be informed and consulted and, for that purpose, to meet with the competent organ of the SCE at least once a year, on the basis of regular reports drawn up by the competent organ, on the progress of the business of the SCE and its prospects. The local managements shall be informed accordingly.

The competent organ of the SCE shall provide the representative body with the agenda for meetings of the administrative, or, where appropriate, the management and supervisory organ, and with copies of all documents submitted to the general meeting of its members.

The meeting shall relate in particular to the structure, economic and financial situation, the probable development of the business and of production and sales, initiatives with regard to corporate social responsibility, the situation and probable trend of employment, investments, and substantial changes concerning organisation, the introduction of new working methods or production processes, transfers of production, mergers, cut-backs or closures of undertakings, establishments or important parts thereof, and collective redundancies.

(c) Where there are exceptional circumstances affecting the employees' interests to a considerable extent, particularly in the event of relocations, transfers, the closure of establishments or undertakings or collective redundancies, the representative body shall have the right to be informed. The representative body or, where it so decides, in particular for reasons of urgency, the select committee, shall have the right to meet at its request, the competent organ of the SCE or any more appropriate level of management within the SCE having its own powers of decision, so as to be informed and consulted on measures significantly affecting employees' interests.

Where the competent organ decides not to act in accordance with the opinion expressed by the representative body, this body shall have the right to a further meeting with the competent organ of the SCE with a view to seeking agreement.

In the case of a meeting organised with the select committee, those members of the representative body who represent employees who are directly concerned by the measures in question shall also have the right to participate.

The meetings referred to above shall not affect the prerogatives of the competent organ.

(d) Member States may lay down rules on the chairing of information and consultation meetings.

Before any meeting with the competent organ of the SCE, the representative body or the select committee, where necessary enlarged in accordance with the third subparagraph of paragraph (c), shall be entitled to meet without the representatives of the competent organ being present.

(e) Without prejudice to Article 10, the members of the representative body shall inform the representatives of the employees of the SCE and of its subsidiaries and establishments of the content and outcome of the information and consultation procedures.

(f) The representative body or the select committee may be assisted by experts of its choice.

(g) In so far as this is necessary for the fulfilment of their tasks, the members of the representative body shall be entitled to time off for training without loss of wages.

(h) The costs of the representative body shall be borne by the SCE, which shall provide the body's members with the financial and material resources needed to enable them to perform their duties in an appropriate manner.

In particular, the SCE shall, unless otherwise agreed, bear the cost of organising meetings and providing interpretation facilities and the accommodation and travelling expenses of members of the representative body and the select committee.

In compliance with these principles, the Member States may lay down budgetary rules regarding the operation of the representative body. They may in particular limit funding to cover one expert only.

[4089U]

Part 3: Standard rules for participation

Employee participation in an SCE shall be governed by the following provisions:

(a) In the case of an SCE established by transformation, if the rules of a Member State relating to employee participation in the administrative or supervisory body applied before registration, all aspects of employee participation shall continue to apply to the SCE. Paragraph (b) shall apply mutatis mutandis to that end.

(b) In other cases where an SCE is established, the employees of the SCE, its subsidiaries and establishments and/or their representative body shall have the right to elect, appoint, recommend or oppose the appointment of a number of members of the administrative or supervisory body of the SCE equal to the highest proportion in force in the participating companies concerned before registration of the SCE.

(c) If none of the participating legal entities was governed by participation rules before registration of the SCE, the latter shall not be required to establish provisions for employee participation.

(d) The representative body shall decide on the allocation of seats within the administrative or supervisory body among the members representing the employees from the various Member States or on the way in which the SCE's employees may recommend or oppose the appointment of the members of these bodies according to the proportion of the SCE's employees in each Member State. If the employees of one or more Member States are not covered by this proportional criterion, the representative body shall appoint a member from one of those Member States, in particular the Member State of the SCE's registered office where that is appropriate. Each Member State may determine the allocation of the seats it is given within the administrative or supervisory body.

(e) Every member of the administrative body or, where appropriate, the supervisory body of the SCE who has been elected, appointed or recommended by the representative body or, depending on the circumstances, by the employees shall be a full member with the same rights and obligations as the members representing the members of the cooperative, including the right to vote.

[4089V]

DIRECTIVE OF THE EUROPEAN PARLIAMENT AND OF THE COUNCIL

of 4 November 2003

concerning certain aspects of the organisation of working time

(2003/88/EC)

NOTES

Date of publication in OJ: OJ L229, 18.11.2003, p 9.

This Directive is a consolidation of Directive 93/104/EEC, as amended by Council Directive 2000/34/EC ('the Working Time Directive' and 'the 'Horizontal Amending Directive'). A correlation table is in Annex II at **[4121]**. For the domestic implementation of this Directive and its predecessor in the United Kingdom, see the Working Time Regulations 1998, SI 1998/1833 at **[2411]**.

THE EUROPEAN PARLIAMENT AND THE COUNCIL OF THE EUROPEAN UNION,

Having regard to the Treaty establishing the European Community, and in particular Article 137(2) thereof,

Having regard to the proposal from the Commission,

Having regard to the opinion of the European Economic and Social Committee,[1]

Having consulted the Committee of the Regions,

Acting in accordance with the procedure referred to in Article 251 of the Treaty,[2]

Whereas:

(1) Council Directive 93/104/EC of 23 November 1993, concerning certain aspects of the organisation of working time,[3] which lays down minimum safety and health requirements for the organisation of working time, in respect of periods of daily rest, breaks, weekly rest, maximum weekly working time, annual leave and aspects of night work, shift work and patterns of work, has been significantly amended. In order to clarify matters, a codification of the provisions in question should be drawn up.

(2) Article 137 of the Treaty provides that the Community is to support and complement the activities of the Member States with a view to improving the working environment to protect workers' health and safety. Directives adopted on the basis of that Article are to avoid imposing administrative, financial and legal constraints in a way which would hold back the creation and development of small and medium-sized undertakings.

(3) The provisions of Council Directive 89/391/EEC of 12 June 1989 on the introduction of measures to encourage improvements in the safety and health of workers at work[4] remain fully applicable to the areas covered by this Directive without prejudice to more stringent and/or specific provisions contained herein.

(4) The improvement of workers' safety, hygiene and health at work is an objective which should not be subordinated to purely economic considerations.

(5) All workers should have adequate rest periods. The concept of "rest" must be expressed in units of time, ie in days, hours and/or fractions thereof. Community workers must be granted minimum daily, weekly and annual periods of rest and adequate breaks. It is also necessary in this context to place a maximum limit on weekly working hours.

(6) Account should be taken of the principles of the International Labour Organisation with regard to the organisation of working time, including those relating to night work.

(7) Research has shown that the human body is more sensitive at night to environmental disturbances and also to certain burdensome forms of work organisation and that long periods of night work can be detrimental to the health of workers and can endanger safety at the workplace.

(8) There is a need to limit the duration of periods of night work, including overtime, and to provide for employers who regularly use night workers to bring this information to the attention of the competent authorities if they so request.

(9) It is important that night workers should be entitled to a free health assessment prior to their assignment and thereafter at regular intervals and that whenever possible they should be transferred to day work for which they are suited if they suffer from health problems.

(10) The situation of night and shift workers requires that the level of safety and health protection should be adapted to the nature of their work and that the organisation and functioning of protection and prevention services and resources should be efficient.

(11) Specific working conditions may have detrimental effects on the safety and health of workers. The organisation of work according to a certain pattern must take account of the general principle of adapting work to the worker.

(12) A European Agreement in respect of the working time of seafarers has been put into effect by means of Council Directive 1999/63/EC of 21 June 1999 concerning the Agreement on the organisation of working time of seafarers concluded by the European Community Shipowners' Association (ECSA) and the Federation of Transport Workers' Unions in the European Union (FST)[5] based on Article 139(2) of the Treaty. Accordingly, the provisions of this Directive should not apply to seafarers.

(13) In the case of those "share-fishermen" who are employees, it is for the Member States to determine, pursuant to this Directive, the conditions for entitlement to, and granting of, annual leave, including the arrangements for payments.

(14) Specific standards laid down in other Community instruments relating, for example, to rest periods, working time, annual leave and night work for certain categories of workers should take precedence over the provisions of this Directive.

(15) In view of the question likely to be raised by the organisation of working time within an undertaking, it appears desirable to provide for flexibility in the application of certain provisions of this Directive, whilst ensuring compliance with the principles of protecting the safety and health of workers.

(16) It is necessary to provide that certain provisions may be subject to derogations implemented, according to the case, by the Member States or the two sides of industry. As a general rule, in the event of a derogation, the workers concerned must be given equivalent compensatory rest periods.

(17) This Directive should not affect the obligations of the Member States concerning the deadlines for transposition of the Directives set out in Annex I, part B,

NOTES

1 OJ C61, 14.3.2003, p 123.

2 Opinion of the European Parliament of 17 December 2002 (not yet published in the Official Journal) and Council Decision of 22 September 2003.

3 OJ L307, 13.12.1993, p 18. Directive as amended by Directive 2000/34/EC of the European Parliament and of the Council (OJ L195, 1.8.2000, p 41).

4 OJ L183, 29.6.1989, p 1.

5 OJ L167, 2.7.1999, p 33.

HAVE ADOPTED THIS DIRECTIVE:

CHAPTER 1
SCOPE AND DEFINITIONS

Article 1
Purpose and scope

1. This Directive lays down minimum safety and health requirements for the organisation of working time.

2. This Directive applies to:
   (a) minimum periods of daily rest, weekly rest and annual leave, to breaks and maximum weekly working time; and
   (b) certain aspects of night work, shift work and patterns of work.

3. This Directive shall apply to all sectors of activity, both public and private, within the meaning of Article 2 of Directive 89/391/EEC, without prejudice to Articles 14, 17, 18 and 19 of this Directive.

This Directive shall not apply to seafarers, as defined in Directive 1999/63/EC without prejudice to Article 2(8) of this Directive.

4. The provisions of Directive 89/391/EEC are fully applicable to the matters referred to in paragraph 2, without prejudice to more stringent and/or specific provisions contained in this Directive.

[4090]

Article 2
Definitions

For the purposes of this Directive, the following definitions shall apply:

1. "working time" means any period during which the worker is working, at the employer's disposal and carrying out his activity or duties, in accordance with national laws and/or practice;
2. "rest period" means any period which is not working time;
3. "night time" means any period of not less than seven hours, as defined by national law, and which must include, in any case, the period between midnight and 5.00;
4. "night worker" means:
   (a) on the one hand, any worker, who, during night time, works at least three hours of his daily working time as a normal course; and
   (b) on the other hand, any worker who is likely during night time to work a certain proportion of his annual working time, as defined at the choice of the Member State concerned:
      (i) by national legislation, following consultation with the two sides of industry; or
      (ii) by collective agreements or agreements concluded between the two sides of industry at national or regional level;
5. "shift work" means any method of organising work in shifts whereby workers

succeed each other at the same work stations according to a certain pattern, including a rotating pattern, and which may be continuous or discontinuous, entailing the need for workers to work at different times over a given period of days or weeks;

6. "shift worker" means any worker whose work schedule is part of shift work;
7. "mobile worker" means any worker employed as a member of travelling or flying personnel by an undertaking which operates transport services for passengers or goods by road, air or inland waterway;
8. "offshore work" means work performed mainly on or from offshore installations (including drilling rigs), directly or indirectly in connection with the exploration, extraction or exploitation of mineral resources, including hydrocarbons, and diving in connection with such activities, whether performed from an offshore installation or a vessel;
9. "adequate rest" means that workers have regular rest periods, the duration of which is expressed in units of time and which are sufficiently long and continuous to ensure that, as a result of fatigue or other irregular working patterns, they do not cause injury to themselves, to fellow workers or to others and that they do not damage their health, either in the short term or in the longer term.

[4091]

CHAPTER 2
MINIMUM REST PERIODS—OTHER ASPECTS OF THE ORGANISATION OF WORKING TIME

Article 3

Daily rest

Member States shall take the measures necessary to ensure that every worker is entitled to a minimum daily rest period of 11 consecutive hours per 24-hour period.

[4092]

Article 4

Breaks

Member States shall take the measures necessary to ensure that, where the working day is longer than six hours, every worker is entitled to a rest break, the details of which, including duration and the terms on which it is granted, shall be laid down in collective agreements or agreements between the two sides of industry or, failing that, by national legislation.

[4093]

Article 5

Weekly rest period

Member States shall take the measures necessary to ensure that, per each seven-day period, every worker is entitled to a minimum uninterrupted rest period of 24 hours plus the 11 hours' daily rest referred to in Article 3.

If objective, technical or work organisation conditions so justify, a minimum rest period of 24 hours may be applied.

[4094]

Article 6

Maximum weekly working time

Member States shall take the measures necessary to ensure that, in keeping with the need to protect the safety and health of workers:

(a) the period of weekly working time is limited by means of laws, regulations or administrative provisions or by collective agreements or agreements between the two sides of industry;

(b) the average working time for each seven-day period, including overtime, does not exceed 48 hours.

[4095]

Article 7

Annual leave

1. Member States shall take the measures necessary to ensure that every worker is entitled to paid annual leave of at least four weeks in accordance with the conditions for entitlement to, and granting of, such leave laid down by national legislation and/or practice.

2. The minimum period of paid annual leave may not be replaced by an allowance in lieu, except where the employment relationship is terminated.

[4096]

CHAPTER 3
NIGHT WORK—SHIFT WORK—PATTERNS OF WORK

Article 8

Length of night work

Member States shall take the measures necessary to ensure that:

(a) normal hours of work for night workers do not exceed an average of eight hours in any 24-hour period;

(b) night workers whose work involves special hazards or heavy physical or mental strain do not work more than eight hours in any period of 24 hours during which they perform night work.

For the purposes of point (b), work involving special hazards or heavy physical or mental strain shall be defined by national legislation and/or practice or by collective agreements or agreements concluded between the two sides of industry, taking account of the specific effects and hazards of night work.

[4097]

Article 9

Health assessment and transfer of night workers to day work

1. Member States shall take the measures necessary to ensure that:

(a) night workers are entitled to a free health assessment before their assignment and thereafter at regular intervals;

(b) night workers suffering from health problems recognised as being connected with the fact that they perform night work are transferred whenever possible to day work to which they are suited.

2. The free health assessment referred to in paragraph 1(a) must comply with medical confidentiality.

3. The free health assessment referred to in paragraph 1(a) may be conducted within the national health system.

[4098]

Article 10

Guarantees for night-time working

Member States may make the work of certain categories of night workers subject to certain guarantees, under conditions laid down by national legislation and/or practice, in the case of workers who incur risks to their safety or health linked to night-time working.

[4099]

Article 11

Notification of regular use of night workers

Member States shall take the measures necessary to ensure that an employer who regularly uses night workers brings this information to the attention of the competent authorities if they so request.

[4100]

Article 12

Safety and health protection

Member States shall take the measures necessary to ensure that:

(a) night workers and shift workers have safety and health protection appropriate to the nature of their work;

(b) appropriate protection and prevention services or facilities with regard to the safety and health of night workers and shift workers are equivalent to those applicable to other workers and are available at all times.

[4101]

Article 13

Pattern of work

Member States shall take the measures necessary to ensure that an employer who intends to organise work according to a certain pattern takes account of the general principle of adapting work to the worker, with a view, in particular, to alleviating monotonous work and work at a predetermined work-rate, depending on the type of activity, and of safety and health requirements, especially as regards breaks during working time.

[4102]

CHAPTER 4
MISCELLANEOUS PROVISIONS

Article 14

More specific Community provisions

This Directive shall not apply where other Community instruments contain more specific requirements relating to the organisation of working time for certain occupations or occupational activities.

[4103]

Article 15

More favourable provisions

This Directive shall not affect Member States' right to apply or introduce laws, regulations or administrative provisions more favourable to the protection of the safety and health of workers or to facilitate or permit the application of collective agreements or agreements concluded between the two sides of industry which are more favourable to the protection of the safety and health of workers.

[4104]

Article 16

Reference periods

Member States may lay down:

(a) for the application of Article 5 (weekly rest period), a reference period not exceeding 14 days;

(b) for the application of Article 6 (maximum weekly working time), a reference period not exceeding four months.

The periods of paid annual leave, granted in accordance with Article 7, and the periods of sick leave shall not be included or shall be neutral in the calculation of the average;

(c) for the application of Article 8 (length of night work), a reference period defined after consultation of the two sides of industry or by collective agreements or agreements concluded between the two sides of industry at national or regional level.

If the minimum weekly rest period of 24 hours required by Article 5 falls within that reference period, it shall not be included in the calculation of the average.

[4105]

CHAPTER 5
DEROGATIONS AND EXCEPTIONS

Article 17

Derogations

1. With due regard for the general principles of the protection of the safety and health of workers, Member States may derogate from Articles 3 to 6, 8 and 16 when, on account of the

specific characteristics of the activity concerned, the duration of the working time is not measured and/or predetermined or can be determined by the workers themselves, and particularly in the case of:

(a) managing executives or other persons with autonomous decision-taking powers;

(b) family workers; or

(c) workers officiating at religious ceremonies in churches and religious communities.

2. Derogations provided for in paragraphs 3, 4 and 5 may be adopted by means of laws, regulations or administrative provisions or by means of collective agreements or agreements between the two sides of industry provided that the workers concerned are afforded equivalent periods of compensatory rest or that, in exceptional cases in which it is not possible, for objective reasons, to grant such equivalent periods of compensatory rest, the workers concerned are afforded appropriate protection.

3. In accordance with paragraph 2 of this Article derogations may be made from Articles 3, 4, 5, 8 and 16:

(a) in the case of activities where the worker's place of work and his place of residence are distant from one another, including offshore work, or where the worker's different places of work are distant from one another;

(b) in the case of security and surveillance activities requiring a permanent presence in order to protect property and persons, particularly security guards and caretakers or security firms;

(c) in the case of activities involving the need for continuity of service or production, particularly:

(i) services relating to the reception, treatment and/or care provided by hospitals or similar establishments, including the activities of doctors in training, residential institutions and prisons;

(ii) dock or airport workers;

(iii) press, radio, television, cinematographic production, postal and telecommunications services, ambulance, fire and civil protection services;

(iv) gas, water and electricity production, transmission and distribution, household refuse collection and incineration plants;

(v) industries in which work cannot be interrupted on technical grounds;

(vi) research and development activities;

(vii) agriculture;

(viii) workers concerned with the carriage of passengers on regular urban transport services;

(d) where there is a foreseeable surge of activity, particularly in:

(i) agriculture;

(ii) tourism;

(iii) postal services;

(e) in the case of persons working in railway transport:

(i) whose activities are intermittent;

(ii) who spend their working time on board trains; or

(iii) whose activities are linked to transport timetables and to ensuring the continuity and regularity of traffic;

(f) in the circumstances described in Article 5(4) of Directive 89/391/EEC;

(g) in cases of accident or imminent risk of accident.

4. In accordance with paragraph 2 of this Article derogations may be made from Articles 3 and 5:

(a) in the case of shift work activities, each time the worker changes shift and cannot take daily and/or weekly rest periods between the end of one shift and the start of the next one;

(b) in the case of activities involving periods of work split up over the day, particularly those of cleaning staff.

5. In accordance with paragraph 2 of this Article, derogations may be made from Article 6 and Article 16(b), in the case of doctors in training, in accordance with the provisions set out in the second to the seventh subparagraphs of this paragraph.

With respect to Article 6 derogations referred to in the first subparagraph shall be permitted for a transitional period of five years from 1 August 2004.

Member States may have up to two more years, if necessary, to take account of difficulties in meeting the working time provisions with respect to their responsibilities for the organisation and delivery of health services and medical care. At least six months before the end of the transitional period, the Member State concerned shall inform the Commission giving its reasons, so that the Commission can give an opinion, after appropriate consultations, within the three months following receipt of such information. If the Member State does not follow the opinion of the Commission, it will justify its decision. The notification and justification of the Member State and the opinion of the Commission shall be published in the *Official Journal of the European Union* and forwarded to the European Parliament.

Member States may have an additional period of up to one year, if necessary, to take account of special difficulties in meeting the responsibilities referred to in the third subparagraph. They shall follow the procedure set out in that subparagraph.

Member States shall ensure that in no case will the number of weekly working hours exceed an average of 58 during the first three years of the transitional period, an average of 56 for the following two years and an average of 52 for any remaining period.

The employer shall consult the representatives of the employees in good time with a view to reaching an agreement, wherever possible, on the arrangements applying to the transitional period. Within the limits set out in the fifth subparagraph, such an agreement may cover:

(a) the average number of weekly hours of work during the transitional period; and
(b) the measures to be adopted to reduce weekly working hours to an average of 48 by the end of the transitional period.

With respect to Article 16(b) derogations referred to in the first subparagraph shall be permitted provided that the reference period does not exceed 12 months, during the first part of the transitional period specified in the fifth subparagraph, and six months thereafter.

[4106]

Article 18

Derogations by collective agreements

Derogations may be made from Articles 3, 4, 5, 8 and 16 by means of collective agreements or agreements concluded between the two sides of industry at national or regional level or, in conformity with the rules laid down by them, by means of collective agreements or agreements concluded between the two sides of industry at a lower level.

Member States in which there is no statutory system ensuring the conclusion of collective agreements or agreements concluded between the two sides of industry at national or regional level, on the matters covered by this Directive, or those Member States in which there is a specific legislative framework for this purpose and within the limits thereof, may, in accordance with national legislation and/or practice, allow derogations from Articles 3, 4, 5, 8 and 16 by way of collective agreements or agreements concluded between the two sides of industry at the appropriate collective level.

The derogations provided for in the first and second subparagraphs shall be allowed on condition that equivalent compensating rest periods are granted to the workers concerned or, in exceptional cases where it is not possible for objective reasons to grant such periods, the workers concerned are afforded appropriate protection.

Member States may lay down rules:

(a) for the application of this Article by the two sides of industry; and
(b) for the extension of the provisions of collective agreements or agreements concluded in conformity with this Article to other workers in accordance with national legislation and/or practice.

[4107]

Article 19

Limitations to derogations from reference periods

The option to derogate from Article 16(b), provided for in Article 17(3) and in Article 18, may not result in the establishment of a reference period exceeding six months.

However, Member States shall have the option, subject to compliance with the general principles relating to the protection of the safety and health of workers, of allowing, for objective or technical reasons or reasons concerning the organisation of work, collective agreements or agreements concluded between the two sides of industry to set reference periods in no event exceeding 12 months.

Before 23 November 2003, the Council shall, on the basis of a Commission proposal accompanied by an appraisal report, re-examine the provisions of this Article and decide what action to take.

[4108]

Article 20

Mobile workers and offshore work

1. Articles 3, 4, 5 and 8 shall not apply to mobile workers.

Member States shall, however, take the necessary measures to ensure that such mobile workers are entitled to adequate rest, except in the circumstances laid down in Article 17(3)(f) and (g).

2. Subject to compliance with the general principles relating to the protection of the safety and health of workers, and provided that there is consultation of representatives of the employer and employees concerned and efforts to encourage all relevant forms of social dialogue, including negotiation if the parties so wish, Member States may, for objective or technical reasons or reasons concerning the organisation of work, extend the reference period referred to in Article 16(b) to 12 months in respect of workers who mainly perform offshore work.

3. Not later than 1 August 2005 the Commission shall, after consulting the Member States and management and labour at European level, review the operation of the provisions with regard to offshore workers from a health and safety perspective with a view to presenting, if need be, the appropriate modifications.

[4109]

Article 21

Workers on board seagoing fishing vessels

1. Articles 3 to 6 and 8 shall not apply to any worker on board a seagoing fishing vessel flying the flag of a Member State.

Member States shall, however, take the necessary measures to ensure that any worker on board a seagoing fishing vessel flying the flag of a Member State is entitled to adequate rest and to limit the number of hours of work to 48 hours a week on average calculated over a reference period not exceeding 12 months.

2. Within the limits set out in paragraph 1, second subparagraph, and paragraphs 3 and 4 Member States shall take the necessary measures to ensure that, in keeping with the need to protect the safety and health of such workers:

(a) the working hours are limited to a maximum number of hours which shall not be exceeded in a given period of time; or

(b) a minimum number of hours of rest are provided within a given period of time.

The maximum number of hours of work or minimum number of hours of rest shall be specified by law, regulations, administrative provisions or by collective agreements or agreements between the two sides of the industry.

3. The limits on hours of work or rest shall be either:

(a) maximum hours of work which shall not exceed:
  (i) 14 hours in any 24-hour period; and
  (ii) 72 hours in any seven-day period; or

(b) minimum hours of rest which shall not be less than:
  (i) 10 hours in any 24-hour period; and
  (ii) 77 hours in any seven-day period.

4. Hours of rest may be divided into no more than two periods, one of which shall be at least six hours in length, and the interval between consecutive periods of rest shall not exceed 14 hours.

5. In accordance with the general principles of the protection of the health and safety of workers, and for objective or technical reasons or reasons concerning the organisation of work, Member States may allow exceptions, including the establishment of reference periods, to the limits laid down in paragraph 1, second subparagraph, and paragraphs 3 and 4. Such exceptions shall, as far as possible, comply with the standards laid down but may take account of more frequent or longer leave periods or the granting of compensatory leave for the workers. These exceptions may be laid down by means of:

(a) laws, regulations or administrative provisions provided there is consultation, where possible, of the representatives of the employers and workers concerned and efforts are made to encourage all relevant forms of social dialogue; or

(b) collective agreements or agreements between the two sides of industry.

6. The master of a seagoing fishing vessel shall have the right to require workers on board to perform any hours of work necessary for the immediate safety of the vessel, persons on board or cargo, or for the purpose of giving assistance to other vessels or persons in distress at sea.

7. Members States may provide that workers on board seagoing fishing vessels for which national legislation or practice determines that these vessels are not allowed to operate in a specific period of the calendar year exceeding one month, shall take annual leave in accordance with Article 7 within that period.

[4110]

Article 22

Miscellaneous provisions

1. A Member State shall have the option not to apply Article 6, while respecting the general principles of the protection of the safety and health of workers, and provided it takes the necessary measures to ensure that:

(a) no employer requires a worker to work more than 48 hours over a seven-day period, calculated as an average for the reference period referred to in Article 16(b), unless he has first obtained the worker's agreement to perform such work;

(b) no worker is subjected to any detriment by his employer because he is not willing to give his agreement to perform such work;

(c) the employer keeps up-to-date records of all workers who carry out such work;

(d) the records are placed at the disposal of the competent authorities, which may, for reasons connected with the safety and/or health of workers, prohibit or restrict the possibility of exceeding the maximum weekly working hours;

(e) the employer provides the competent authorities at their request with information on cases in which agreement has been given by workers to perform work exceeding 48 hours over a period of seven days, calculated as an average for the reference period referred to in Article 16(b).

Before 23 November 2003, the Council shall, on the basis of a Commission proposal accompanied by an appraisal report, re-examine the provisions of this paragraph and decide on what action to take.

2. Member States shall have the option, as regards the application of Article 7, of making use of a transitional period of not more than three years from 23 November 1996, provided that during that transitional period:

(a) every worker receives three weeks' paid annual leave in accordance with the conditions for the entitlement to, and granting of, such leave laid down by national legislation and/or practice; and

(b) the three-week period of paid annual leave may not be replaced by an allowance in lieu, except where the employment relationship is terminated.

3. If Member States avail themselves of the options provided for in this Article, they shall forthwith inform the Commission thereof.

[4111]

CHAPTER 6
FINAL PROVISIONS

Article 23

Level of Protection

Without prejudice to the right of Member States to develop, in the light of changing circumstances, different legislative, regulatory or contractual provisions in the field of working time, as long as the minimum requirements provided for in this Directive are complied with, implementation of this Directive shall not constitute valid grounds for reducing the general level of protection afforded to workers.

[4112]

Article 24

Reports

1. Member States shall communicate to the Commission the texts of the provisions of national law already adopted or being adopted in the field governed by this Directive.

2. Member States shall report to the Commission every five years on the practical implementation of the provisions of this Directive, indicating the viewpoints of the two sides of industry.

The Commission shall inform the European Parliament, the Council, the European Economic and Social Committee and the Advisory Committee on Safety, Hygiene and Health Protection at Work thereof.

3. Every five years from 23 November 1996 the Commission shall submit to the European Parliament, the Council and the European Economic and Social Committee a report on the application of this Directive taking into account Articles 22 and 23 and paragraphs 1 and 2 of this Article.

[4113]

Article 25

Review of the operation of the provisions with regard to workers on board seagoing fishing vessels

Not later than 1 August 2009 the Commission shall, after consulting the Member States and management and labour at European level, review the operation of the provisions with regard to workers on board seagoing fishing vessels, and, in particular examine whether these provisions remain appropriate, in particular, as far as health and safety are concerned with a view to proposing suitable amendments, if necessary.

[4114]

Article 26

Review of the operation of the provisions with regard to workers concerned with the carriage of passengers

Not later than 1 August 2005 the Commission shall, after consulting the Member States and management and labour at European level, review the operation of the provisions with regard to workers concerned with the carriage of passengers on regular urban transport services, with a view to presenting, if need be, the appropriate modifications to ensure a coherent and suitable approach in the sector.

[4115]

Article 27

Repeal

1. Directive 93/104/EC, as amended by the Directive referred to in Annex I, part A, shall be repealed, without prejudice to the obligations of the Member States in respect of the deadlines for transposition laid down in Annex I, part B.

2. The references made to the said repealed Directive shall be construed as references to this Directive and shall be read in accordance with the correlation table set out in Annex II.

[4116]

Article 28

Entry into force

This Directive shall enter into force on 2 August 2004.

[4117]

Article 29

Addressees

This Directive is addressed to the Member States.

[4118]

ANNEX I

PART A
REPEALED DIRECTIVE AND ITS AMENDMENT

(*Article 27*)

Council Directive 93/104/EC	(OJ L307, 13.12.1993, p 18)
Directive 2000/34/EC of the European Parliament and of the Council	(OJ L195, 1.8.2000, p 41)

[4119]

PART B
DEADLINES FOR TRANSPOSITION INTO NATIONAL LAW

(*Article 27*)

Directive	*Deadline for transposition*
93/104/EC	23 November 1996
2000/34/EC	1 August 2003[1]

[4120]

NOTES

[1] 1 August 2004 in the case of doctors in training. See Article 2 of Directive 2000/34/EC.

ANNEX II

CORRELATION TABLE

Directive 93/104/EC	*This Directive*
Articles 1 to 5	Articles 1 to 5
Article 6, introductory words	Article 6, introductory words
Article 6(1)	Article 6(a)
Article 6(2)	Article 6(b)
Article 7	Article 7
Article 8, introductory words	Article 8, introductory words
Article 8(1)	Article 8(a)
Article 8(2)	Article 8(b)
Articles 9, 10 and 11	Articles 9, 10 and 11
Article 12, introductory words	Article 12, introductory words
Article 12(1)	Article 12(a)
Article 12(2)	Article 12(b)
Articles 13, 14 and 15	Articles 13, 14 and 15
Article 16, introductory words	Article 16, introductory words
Article 16(1)	Article 16(a)

Directive 93/104/EC	*This Directive*
Article 16(2)	Article 16(b)
Article 16(3)	Article 16(c)
Article 17(1)	Article 17(1)
Article 17(2), introductory words	Article 17(2)
Article 17(2)(1)	Article 17(3)(a) to (e)
Article 17(2)(2)	Article 17(3)(f) to (g)
Article 17(2)(3)	Article 17(4)
Article 17(2)(4)	Article 17(5)
Article 17(3)	Article 18
Article 17(4)	Article 19
Article 17a(1)	Article 20(1), first subparagraph
Article 17a(2)	Article 20(1), second subparagraph
Article 17a(3)	Article 20(2)
Article 17a(4)	Article 20(3)
Article 17b(1)	Article 21(1), first subparagraph
Article 17b(2)	Article 21(1), second subparagraph
Article 17b(3)	Article 21(2)
Article 17b(4)	Article 21(3)
Article 17b(5)	Article 21(4)
Article 17b(6)	Article 21(5)
Article 17b(7)	Article 21(6)
Article 17b(8)	Article 21(7)
Article 18(1)(a)	—
Article 18(1)(b)(i)	Article 22(1)
Article 18(1)(b)(ii)	Article 22(2)
Article 18(1)(c)	Article 22(3)
Article 18(2)	—
Article 18(3)	Article 23
Article 18(4)	Article 24(1)
Article 18(5)	Article 24(2)
Article 18(6)	Article 24(3)
—	Article 25[1]
—	Article 26[2]
—	Article 27
—	Article 28
Article 19	Article 29
—	Annex I
—	Annex II

[4121]

NOTES

[1] Directive 2000/34/EC, Article 3.
[2] Directive 2000/34/EC, Article 4.

COUNCIL DIRECTIVE

of 13 December 2004

implementing the principle of equal treatment between men and women in the access to and supply of goods and services

(2004/113/EC)

NOTES

Date of publication in OJ: OJ L373, 21.12.2004, p 37.

For the domestic implementation of this Directive see the Sex Discrimination Act 1975, Pt III at **[123A]** et seq, as amended by the Sex Discrimination (Amendment of Legislation) Regulations 2008, SI 2008/963 at **[3474P]**.

THE COUNCIL OF THE EUROPEAN UNION,

Having regard to the Treaty establishing the European Community and in particular Article 13(1) thereof,

Having regard to the proposal from the Commission,

Having regard to the Opinion of the European Parliament,[1]

Having regard to the Opinion of the European Economic and Social Committee,[2]

Having regard to the opinion of the Committee of the Regions,[3]

Whereas:

(1) In accordance with Article 6 of the Treaty on European Union, the Union is founded on the principles of liberty, democracy, respect for human rights and fundamental freedoms and the rule of law, principles which are common to the Member States, and respects fundamental rights as guaranteed by the European Convention for the Protection of Human Rights and Fundamental Freedoms and as they result from the constitutional traditions common to the Member States as general principles of Community law.

(2) The right to equality before the law and protection against discrimination for all persons constitutes a universal right recognised by the Universal Declaration of Human Rights, the United Nations Convention on the Elimination of all forms of Discrimination Against Women, the International Convention on the Elimination of all forms of Racial Discrimination and the United Nations Covenants on Civil and Political Rights and on Economic, Social and Cultural Rights and by the European Convention for the Protection of Human Rights and Fundamental Freedoms, to which all Member States are signatories.

(3) While prohibiting discrimination, it is important to respect other fundamental rights and freedoms, including the protection of private and family life and transactions carried out in that context and the freedom of religion.

(4) Equality between men and women is a fundamental principle of the European Union. Articles 21 and 23 of the Charter of Fundamental Rights of the European Union prohibit any discrimination on grounds of sex and require equality between men and women to be ensured in all areas.

(5) Article 2 of the Treaty establishing the European Community provides that promoting such equality is one of the Community's essential tasks. Similarly, Article 3(2) of the Treaty requires the Community to aim to eliminate inequalities and to promote equality between men and women in all its activities.

(6) The Commission announced its intention of proposing a directive on sex discrimination outside of the labour market in its Communication on the Social Policy Agenda. Such a proposal is fully consistent with Council Decision 2001/51/EC of 20 December 2000 establishing a Programme relating to the Community framework strategy on gender equality (2001–2005)[4] covering all Community policies and aimed at promoting equality for men and women by adjusting these policies and implementing practical measures to improve the situation of men and women in society.

(7) At its meeting in Nice of 7 and 9 December 2000, the European Council called on the Commission to reinforce equality-related rights by adopting a proposal for a directive on promoting gender equality in areas other than employment and professional life.

(8) The Community has adopted a range of legal instruments to prevent and combat sex discrimination in the labour market. These instruments have demonstrated the value of legislation in the fight against discrimination.

(9) Discrimination based on sex, including harassment and sexual harassment, also takes place in areas outside of the labour market. Such discrimination can be equally damaging, acting as a barrier to the full and successful integration of men and women into economic and social life.

(10) Problems are particularly apparent in the area of the access to and supply of goods and services. Discrimination based on sex, should therefore be prevented and eliminated in this area. As in the case of Council Directive 2000/43/EC of 29 June 2000 implementing the principle of equal treatment between persons irrespective of racial and ethnic origin,[5] this objective can be better achieved by means of Community legislation.

(11) Such legislation should prohibit discrimination based on sex in the access to and supply of goods and services. Goods should be taken to be those within the meaning of the provisions of the Treaty establishing the European Community relating to the free movement of goods. Services should be taken to be those within the meaning of Article 50 of that Treaty.

(12) To prevent discrimination based on sex, this Directive should apply to both direct discrimination and indirect discrimination. Direct discrimination occurs only when one person is treated less favourably, on grounds of sex, than another person in a comparable situation. Accordingly, for example, differences between men and women in the provision of healthcare services, which result from the physical differences between men and women, do not relate to comparable situations and therefore, do not constitute discrimination.

(13) The prohibition of discrimination should apply to persons providing goods and services, which are available to the public and which are offered outside the area of private and family life and the transactions carried out in this context. It should not apply to the content of media or advertising nor to public or private education.

(14) All individuals enjoy the freedom to contract, including the freedom to choose a contractual partner for a transaction. An individual who provides goods or services may have a number of subjective reasons for his or her choice of contractual partner. As long as the choice of partner is not based on that person's sex, this Directive should not prejudice the individual's freedom to choose a contractual partner.

(15) There are already a number of existing legal instruments for the implementation of the principle of equal treatment between men and women in matters of employment and occupation. Therefore, this Directive should not apply in this field. The same reasoning applies to matters of self-employment insofar as they are covered by existing legal instruments. The Directive should apply only to insurance and pensions which are private, voluntary and separate from the employment relationship.

(16) Differences in treatment may be accepted only if they are justified by a legitimate aim. A legitimate aim may, for example, be the protection of victims of sex-related violence (in cases such as the establishment of single-sex shelters), reasons of privacy and decency (in cases such as the provision of accommodation by a person in a part of that person's home), the promotion of gender equality or of the interests of men or women (for example single-sex voluntary bodies), the freedom of association (in cases of membership of single-sex private clubs), and the organisation of sporting activities (for example single-sex sports events). Any limitation should nevertheless be appropriate and necessary in accordance with the criteria derived from case law of the Court of Justice of the European Communities.

(17) The principle of equal treatment in the access to goods and services does not require that facilities should always be provided to men and women on a shared basis, as long as they are not provided more favourably to members of one sex.

(18) The use of actuarial factors related to sex is widespread in the provision of insurance and other related financial services. In order to ensure equal treatment between men and women, the use of sex as an actuarial factor should not result in differences in individuals' premiums and benefits. To avoid a sudden readjustment of the market, the implementation of this rule should apply only to new contracts concluded after the date of transposition of this Directive.

(19) Certain categories of risks may vary between the sexes. In some cases, sex is one but not necessarily the only determining factor in the assessment of risks insured. For contracts insuring those types of risks, Member States may decide to permit exemptions from the rule of unisex premiums and benefits, as long as they can ensure that underlying actuarial and statistical data on which the calculations are based, are reliable, regularly up-dated and available to the public. Exemptions are allowed only where national legislation has not already applied the unisex rule. Five years after transposition of this Directive, Member States should re-examine the justification for these exemptions, taking into account the most recent actuarial and statistical data and a report by the Commission three years after the date of transposition of this Directive.

(20) Less favourable treatment of women for reasons of pregnancy and maternity should be considered a form of direct discrimination based on sex and therefore prohibited in insurance and related financial services. Costs related to risks of pregnancy and maternity should therefore not be attributed to the members of one sex only.

(21) Persons who have been subject to discrimination based on sex should have adequate means of legal protection. To provide a more effective level of protection, associations, organisations and other legal entities should also be empowered to engage in proceedings, as the Member States so determine, either on behalf or in support of any victim, without prejudice to national rules of procedure concerning representation and defence before the courts.

(22) The rules on the burden of proof should be adapted when there is a prima facie case of discrimination and for the principle of equal treatment to be applied effectively, the burden of proof should shift back to the defendant when evidence of such discrimination is brought.

(23) The effective implementation of the principle of equal treatment requires adequate judicial protection against victimisation.

(24) With a view to promoting the principle of equal treatment, Member States should encourage dialogue with relevant stakeholders, which have, in accordance with national law and practice, a legitimate interest in contributing to the fight against discrimination on grounds of sex in the area of access to and supply of goods and services.

(25) Protection against discrimination based on sex should itself be strengthened by the existence of a body or bodies in each Member State, with competence to analyse the problems involved, to study possible solutions and to provide concrete assistance for the victims. The body or bodies may be the same as those with responsibility at national level for the defence of human rights or the safeguarding of individuals' rights, or the implementation of the principle of equal treatment.

(26) This Directive lays down minimum requirements, thus giving the Member States the option of introducing or maintaining more favourable provisions. The implementation of this Directive should not serve to justify any regression in relation to the situation, which already prevails in each Member State.

(27) Member States should provide for effective, proportionate and dissuasive penalties in cases of breaches of the obligations under this Directive.

(28) Since the objectives of this Directive, namely to ensure a common high level of protection against discrimination in all the Member States, cannot be sufficiently achieved by the Member States and can, therefore, by reason of the scale and effects of the action, be better achieved at Community level, the Community may adopt measures, in accordance with the principle of subsidiarity as set out in Article 5 of the Treaty. In accordance with the principle of proportionality, as set out in that Article, this Directive does not go beyond what is necessary in order to achieve those objectives.

(29) In accordance with paragraph 34 of the interinstitutional agreement on better law-making,[6] Member States are encouraged to draw up, for themselves and in the interest of the Community, their own tables, which will, as far as possible, illustrate the correlation between the Directive and the transposition measures and to make them public,

NOTES

[1] Opinion delivered on 30 March 2004 (not yet published in the Official Journal).
[2] OJ C241, 28.9.2004, p 44.
[3] OJ C121, 30.4.2004, p 27.
[4] OJ L17, 19.1.2001, p 22.
[5] OJ L180, 19.7.2000, p 22.
[6] OJ C321, 31.12.2003, p 1.

HAS ADOPTED THIS DIRECTIVE:

CHAPTER I
GENERAL PROVISIONS

Article 1

Purpose

The purpose of this Directive is to lay down a framework for combating discrimination based on sex in access to and supply of goods and services, with a view to putting into effect in the Member States the principle of equal treatment between men and women.

[4121A]

Article 2

Definitions

For the purposes of this Directive, the following definitions shall apply:

(a) direct discrimination: where one person is treated less favourably, on grounds of sex, than another is, has been or would be treated in a comparable situation;

(b) indirect discrimination: where an apparently neutral provision, criterion or practice would put persons of one sex at a particular disadvantage compared with persons of the other sex, unless that provision, criterion or practice is objectively justified by a legitimate aim and the means of achieving that aim are appropriate and necessary;

(c) harassment: where an unwanted conduct related to the sex of a person occurs with the purpose or effect of violating the dignity of a person and of creating an intimidating, hostile, degrading, humiliating or offensive environment;

(d) sexual harassment: where any form of unwanted physical, verbal, non-verbal or physical conduct of a sexual nature occurs, with the purpose or effect of violating the dignity of a person, in particular when creating an intimidating, hostile, degrading, humiliating or offensive environment.

[4121B]

Article 3

Scope

1. Within the limits of the powers conferred upon the Community, this Directive shall apply to all persons who provide goods and services, which are available to the public irrespective of the person concerned as regards both the public and private sectors, including public bodies, and which are offered outside the area of private and family life and the transactions carried out in this context.

2. This Directive does not prejudice the individual's freedom to choose a contractual partner as long as an individual's choice of contractual partner is not based on that person's sex.

3. This Directive shall not apply to the content of media and advertising nor to education.

4. This Directive shall not apply to matters of employment and occupation. This Directive shall not apply to matters of self-employment, insofar as these matters are covered by other Community legislative acts.

[4121C]

Article 4

Principle of equal treatment

1. For the purposes of this Directive, the principle of equal treatment between men and women shall mean that

(a) there shall be no direct discrimination based on sex, including less favourable treatment of women for reasons of pregnancy and maternity;

(b) there shall be no indirect discrimination based on sex.

2. This Directive shall be without prejudice to more favourable provisions concerning the protection of women as regards pregnancy and maternity.

3. Harassment and sexual harassment within the meaning of this Directive shall be deemed to be discrimination on the grounds of sex and therefore prohibited. A person's rejection of, or submission to, such conduct may not be used as a basis for a decision affecting that person.

4. Instruction to direct or indirect discrimination on the grounds of sex shall be deemed to be discrimination within the meaning of this Directive.

5. This Directive shall not preclude differences in treatment, if the provision of the goods and services exclusively or primarily to members of one sex is justified by a legitimate aim and the means of achieving that aim are appropriate and necessary.

[4121D]

Article 5

Actuarial factors

1. Member States shall ensure that in all new contracts concluded after 21 December 2007 at the latest, the use of sex as a factor in the calculation of premiums and benefits for the purposes of insurance and related financial services shall not result in differences in individuals' premiums and benefits.

2. Notwithstanding paragraph 1, Member States may decide before 21 December 2007 to permit proportionate differences in individuals' premiums and benefits where the use of sex is a determining factor in the assessment of risk based on relevant and accurate actuarial and statistical data. The Member States concerned shall inform the Commission and ensure that accurate data relevant to the use of sex as a determining actuarial factor are compiled, published and regularly updated. These Member States shall review their decision five years after 21 December 2007, taking into account the Commission report referred to in Article 16, and shall forward the results of this review to the Commission.

3. In any event, costs related to pregnancy and maternity shall not result in differences in individuals' premiums and benefits.

Member States may defer implementation of the measures necessary to comply with this paragraph until two years after 21 December 2007 at the latest. In that case the Member States concerned shall immediately inform the Commission.

[4121E]

Article 6

Positive action

With a view to ensuring full equality in practice between men and women, the principle of equal treatment shall not prevent any Member State from maintaining or adopting specific measures to prevent or compensate for disadvantages linked to sex.

[4121F]

Article 7

Minimum requirements

1. Member States may introduce or maintain provisions which are more favourable to the protection of the principle of equal treatment between men and women than those laid down in this Directive.

2. The implementation of this Directive shall in no circumstances constitute grounds for a reduction in the level of protection against discrimination already afforded by Member States in the fields covered by this Directive.

[4121G]

CHAPTER II
REMEDIES AND ENFORCEMENT

Article 8

Defence of rights

1. Member States shall ensure that judicial and/or administrative procedures, including where they deem it appropriate conciliation procedures, for the enforcement of the obligations under this Directive are available to all persons who consider themselves wronged by failure to apply the principle of equal treatment to them, even after the relationship in which the discrimination is alleged to have occurred has ended.

2. Member States shall introduce into their national legal systems such measures as are necessary to ensure real and effective compensation or reparation, as the Member States so determine, for the loss and damage sustained by a person injured as a result of discrimination within the meaning of this Directive, in a way which is dissuasive and proportionate to the damage suffered. The fixing of a prior upper limit shall not restrict such compensation or reparation.

3. Member States shall ensure that associations, organisations or other legal entities, which have, in accordance with the criteria laid down by their national law, a legitimate interest in ensuring that the provisions of this Directive are complied with, may engage, on behalf or in support of the complainant, with his or her approval, in any judicial and/or administrative procedure provided for the enforcement of obligations under this Directive.

4. Paragraphs 1 and 3 shall be without prejudice to national rules on time limits for bringing actions relating to the principle of equal treatment.

[4121H]

Article 9

Burden of proof

1. Member States shall take such measures as are necessary, in accordance with their national judicial systems, to ensure that, when persons who consider themselves wronged because the principle of equal treatment has not been applied to them establish, before a court or other competent authority, facts from which it may be presumed that there has been direct or indirect discrimination, it shall be for the respondent to prove that there has been no breach of the principle of equal treatment.

2. Paragraph 1 shall not prevent Member States from introducing rules of evidence, which are more favourable to plaintiffs.

3. Paragraph 1 shall not apply to criminal procedures.

4. Paragraphs 1, 2 and 3 shall also apply to any proceedings brought in accordance with Article 8(3).

5. Member States need not apply paragraph 1 to proceedings in which it is for the court or other competent authority to investigate the facts of the case.

[4121I]

Article 10

Victimisation

Member States shall introduce into their national legal systems such measures as are necessary to protect persons from any adverse treatment or adverse consequence as a reaction to a complaint or to legal proceedings aimed at enforcing compliance with the principle of equal treatment.

[4121J]

Article 11

Dialogue with relevant stakeholders

With a view to promoting the principle of equal treatment, Member States shall encourage dialogue with relevant stakeholders which have, in accordance with national law and practice, a legitimate interest in contributing to the fight against discrimination on grounds of sex in the area of access to and supply of goods and services.

[4121K]

CHAPTER III
BODIES FOR THE PROMOTION OF EQUAL TREATMENT

Article 12

1. Member States shall designate and make the necessary arrangements for a body or bodies for the promotion, analysis, monitoring and support of equal treatment of all persons without discrimination on the grounds of sex. These bodies may form part of agencies

charged at national level with the defence of human rights or the safeguard of individuals' rights, or the implementation of the principle of equal treatment.

2. Member States shall ensure that the competencies of the bodies referred to in paragraph 1 include:

(a) without prejudice to the rights of victims and of associations, organisations or other legal entities referred to in Article 8(3), providing independent assistance to victims of discrimination in pursuing their complaints about discrimination;

(b) conducting independent surveys concerning discrimination;

(c) publishing independent reports and making recommendations on any issue relating to such discrimination.

[4121L]

CHAPTER IV
FINAL PROVISIONS

Article 13

Compliance

Member States shall take the necessary measures to ensure that the principle of equal treatment is respected in relation to the access to and supply of goods and services within the scope of this Directive, and in particular that:

(a) any laws, regulations and administrative provisions contrary to the principle of equal treatment are abolished;

(b) any contractual provisions, internal rules of undertakings, and rules governing profit-making or non-profit-making associations contrary to the principle of equal treatment are, or may be, declared null and void or are amended.

[4121M]

Article 14

Penalties

Member States shall lay down the rules on penalties applicable to infringements of the national provisions adopted pursuant to this Directive and shall take all measures necessary to ensure that they are applied. The penalties, which may comprise the payment of compensation to the victim, shall be effective, proportionate and dissuasive. Member States shall notify those provisions to the Commission by 21 December 2007 at the latest and shall notify it without delay of any subsequent amendment affecting them.

[4121N]

Article 15

Dissemination of information

Member States shall take care that the provisions adopted pursuant to this Directive, together with the relevant provisions already in force, are brought to the attention of the persons concerned by all appropriate means throughout their territory.

[4121O]

Article 16

Reports

1. Member States shall communicate all available information concerning the application of this Directive to the Commission, by 21 December 2009. and every five years thereafter.

The Commission shall draw up a summary report, which shall include a review of the current practices of Member States in relation to Article 5 with regard to the use of sex as a factor in the calculation of premiums and benefits. It shall submit this report to the European Parliament and to the Council no later 21 December 2010. Where appropriate, the Commission shall accompany its report with proposals to modify the Directive.

2. The Commission's report shall take into account the viewpoints of relevant stakeholders.

[4121P]

Article 17

Transposition

1. Member States shall bring into force the laws, regulations and administrative provisions necessary to comply with this Directive by 21 December 2007 at the latest. They shall forthwith communicate to the Commission the text of those provisions.

When Member States adopt these measures, they shall contain a reference to this Directive or be accompanied by such a reference on the occasion of their official publication. The methods of making such publication of reference shall be laid down by the Member States.

2. Member States shall communicate to the Commission the text of the main provisions of national law which they adopt in the field covered by this Directive.

[4121Q]

Article 18

Entry into force

This Directive shall enter into force on the day of its publication in the Official Journal of the European Union.

[4121R]

Article 19

Addressees

This Directive is addressed to the Member States.

[4121S]

Done at Brussels, 13 December 2004.

DIRECTIVE OF THE EUROPEAN PARLIAMENT AND OF THE COUNCIL

of 5 July 2006

on the implementation of the principle of equal opportunities and equal treatment of men and women in matters of employment and occupation (recast)

(2006/54/EC)

NOTES

Date of publication in OJ: OJ L204, 26.7.2006, p 23.

This Directive consolidates and updates the four major directives on gender equality, the Equal Pay Directive (75/117/EEC at **[3702]**), the Equal Treatment Directive (76/207/EEC at **[3713]**), the Directive on Equal Treatment in Occupational Social Security Schemes (86/378/EEC at **[3758]**), and the Burden of Proof Directive (97/80/EC at **[3925]**), in each case as subsequently amended. These Directives are repealed by Art 34 of, and Annex I, Pt A to, this Directive, with effect from 15 August 2009 (see **[4155]** and **[4158]**). From that date, references in other Community legislation are to be read as references to the corresponding provisions in this Directive. Note that, apparently by oversight, Art 34 of this Directive does not list the amending Directives 96/97/EC, 98/52/EC (at **[3954A]**), or 2002/73/EC (at **[4066]**). However, it appears from Annex I, Pt A of this Directive that the amending Directives are also intended to be repealed.

Although this Directive came into force on 15 August 2006 (20 days after its publication in the Official Journal on 26 July 2006), the deadline for transposition is not until 15 August 2008. Article 33 (at **[4154]**) makes it clear that the obligations for transposition of provisions that are contained in the original Directives on the dates provided for in those Directives are not affected by this. The original dates for transposition are set out in a table in Annex I, Pt B (at **[4160]**). The new obligation to transpose only applies to 'those provisions which represent a substantive change compared with the earlier Directives'. These are not specifically identified within the Directive. No proposals for amendments to the relevant domestic legislation to take account of the new Directive have been made public by the UK Government as at 6 April 2008.

For the domestic implementation of the Directives consolidated by this Directive, see the Equal pay Act 1970 at **[5]** et seq, the Sex Discrimination Act 1975 at **[100]** et seq, the Social Security Act 1989, Sch 5 at **[401]**, and the Pensions Act 1995, ss 62–66 at **[890]**–**[894]**.

THE EUROPEAN PARLIAMENT AND THE COUNCIL OF THE EUROPEAN UNION,

Having regard to the Treaty establishing the European Community, and in particular Article 141(3) thereof,

Having regard to the proposal from the Commission,

Having regard to the opinion of the European Economic and Social Committee,[1]

Acting in accordance with the procedure laid down in Article 251 of the Treaty,[2]

Whereas:

(1) Council Directive 76/207/EEC of 9 February 1976 on the implementation of the principle of equal treatment for men and women as regards access to employment, vocational training and promotion, and working conditions[3] and Council Directive 86/378/EEC of 24 July 1986 on the implementation of the principle of equal treatment for men and women in occupational social security schemes[4] have been significantly amended.[5] Council Directive 75/117/EEC of 10 February 1975 on the approximation of the laws of the Member States relating to the application of the principle of equal pay for men and women[6] and Council Directive 97/80/EC of 15 December 1997 on the burden of proof in cases of discrimination based on sex[7] also contain provisions which have as their purpose the implementation of the principle of equal treatment between men and women. Now that new amendments are being made to the said Directives, it is desirable, for reasons of clarity, that the provisions in question should be recast by bringing together in a single text the main provisions existing in this field as well as certain developments arising out of the case-law of the Court of Justice of the European Communities (hereinafter referred to as the Court of Justice).

(2) Equality between men and women is a fundamental principle of Community law under Article 2 and Article 3(2) of the Treaty and the case-law of the Court of Justice. Those Treaty provisions proclaim equality between men and women as a "task" and an "aim" of the Community and impose a positive obligation to promote it in all its activities.

(3) The Court of Justice has held that the scope of the principle of equal treatment for men and women cannot be confined to the prohibition of discrimination based on the fact that a person is of one or other sex. In view of its purpose and the nature of the rights which it seeks to safeguard, it also applies to discrimination arising from the gender reassignment of a person.

(4) Article 141(3) of the Treaty now provides a specific legal basis for the adoption of Community measures to ensure the application of the principle of equal opportunities and equal treatment in matters of employment and occupation, including the principle of equal pay for equal work or work of equal value.

(5) Articles 21 and 23 of the Charter of Fundamental Rights of the European Union also prohibit any discrimination on grounds of sex and enshrine the right to equal treatment between men and women in all areas, including employment, work and pay.

(6) Harassment and sexual harassment are contrary to the principle of equal treatment between men and women and constitute discrimination on grounds of sex for the purposes of this Directive. These forms of discrimination occur not only in the workplace, but also in the context of access to employment, vocational training and promotion. They should therefore be prohibited and should be subject to effective, proportionate and dissuasive penalties.

(7) In this context, employers and those responsible for vocational training should be encouraged to take measures to combat all forms of discrimination on grounds of sex and, in particular, to take preventive measures against harassment and sexual harassment in the workplace and in access to employment, vocational training and promotion, in accordance with national law and practice.

(8) The principle of equal pay for equal work or work of equal value as laid down by Article 141 of the Treaty and consistently upheld in the case-law of the Court of Justice constitutes an important aspect of the principle of equal treatment between men and women and an essential and indispensable part of the *acquis communautaire*, including the case-law of the Court concerning sex discrimination. It is therefore appropriate to make further provision for its implementation.

(9) In accordance with settled case-law of the Court of Justice, in order to assess whether workers are performing the same work or work of equal value, it should be determined whether, having regard to a range of factors including the nature of the work and training and working conditions, those workers may be considered to be in a comparable situation.

(10) The Court of Justice has established that, in certain circumstances, the principle of equal pay is not limited to situations in which men and women work for the same employer.

(11) The Member States, in collaboration with the social partners, should continue to address the problem of the continuing gender-based wage differentials and marked gender segregation on the labour market by means such as flexible working time arrangements which enable both men and women to combine family and work commitments more successfully. This could also include appropriate parental leave arrangements which could be taken up by either parent as well as the provision of accessible and affordable child-care facilities and care for dependent persons.

(12) Specific measures should be adopted to ensure the implementation of the principle of equal treatment in occupational social security schemes and to define its scope more clearly.

(13) In its judgment of 17 May 1990 in Case C-262/88,[8] the Court of Justice determined that all forms of occupational pension constitute an element of pay within the meaning of Article 141 of the Treaty.

(14) Although the concept of pay within the meaning of Article 141 of the Treaty does not encompass social security benefits, it is now clearly established that a pension scheme for public servants falls within the scope of the principle of equal pay if the benefits payable under the scheme are paid to the worker by reason of his/her employment relationship with the public employer, notwithstanding the fact that such scheme forms part of a general statutory scheme. According to the judgments of the Court of Justice in Cases C-7/93[9] and C-351/00,[10] that condition will be satisfied if the pension scheme concerns a particular category of workers and its benefits are directly related to the period of service and calculated by reference to the public servant's final salary. For reasons of clarity, it is therefore appropriate to make specific provision to that effect.

(15) The Court of Justice has confirmed that whilst the contributions of male and female workers to a defined-benefit pension scheme are covered by Article 141 of the Treaty, any inequality in employers' contributions paid under funded defined-benefit schemes which is due to the use of actuarial factors differing according to sex is not to be assessed in the light of that same provision.

(16) By way of example, in the case of funded defined-benefit schemes, certain elements, such as conversion into a capital sum of part of a periodic pension, transfer of pension rights, a reversionary pension payable to a dependant in return for the surrender of part of a pension or a reduced pension where the worker opts to take earlier retirement, may be unequal where the inequality of the amounts results from the effects of the use of actuarial factors differing according to sex at the time when the scheme's funding is implemented.

(17) It is well established that benefits payable under occupational social security schemes are not to be considered as remuneration insofar as they are attributable to periods of employment prior to 17 May 1990, except in the case of workers or those claiming under them who initiated legal proceedings or brought an equivalent claim under the applicable national law before that date. It is therefore necessary to limit the implementation of the principle of equal treatment accordingly.

(18) The Court of Justice has consistently held that the Barber Protocol[11] does not affect the right to join an occupational pension scheme and that the limitation of the effects in time of the judgment in Case C-262/88 does not apply to the right to join an occupational pension scheme. The Court of Justice also ruled that the national rules relating to time limits for bringing actions under national law may be relied on against workers who assert their right to join an occupational pension scheme, provided that they are not less favourable for that type of action than for similar actions of a domestic nature and that they do not render the exercise of rights conferred by Community law impossible in practice. The Court of Justice has also pointed out that the fact that a worker can claim retroactively to join an occupational pension scheme does not allow the worker to avoid paying the contributions relating to the period of membership concerned.

(19) Ensuring equal access to employment and the vocational training leading thereto is fundamental to the application of the principle of equal treatment of men and women in matters of employment and occupation. Any exception to this principle should therefore be limited to those occupational activities which necessitate the employment of a person of a particular sex by reason of their nature or the context in which they are carried out, provided that the objective sought is legitimate and complies with the principle of proportionality.

(20) This Directive does not prejudice freedom of association, including the right to establish unions with others and to join unions to defend one's interests. Measures within the meaning of Article 141(4) of the Treaty may include membership or the continuation of the activity of organisations or unions whose main objective is the promotion, in practice, of the principle of equal treatment between men and women.

(21) The prohibition of discrimination should be without prejudice to the maintenance or adoption of measures intended to prevent or compensate for disadvantages suffered by a group of persons of one sex. Such measures permit organisations of persons of one sex where their main object is the promotion of the special needs of those persons and the promotion of equality between men and women.

(22) In accordance with Article 141(4) of the Treaty, with a view to ensuring full equality in practice between men and women in working life, the principle of equal treatment does not prevent Member States from maintaining or adopting measures providing for specific advantages in order to make it easier for the under-represented sex to pursue a vocational activity or to prevent or compensate for disadvantages in professional careers. Given the

current situation and bearing in mind Declaration No 28 to the Amsterdam Treaty, Member States should, in the first instance, aim at improving the situation of women in working life.

(23) It is clear from the case-law of the Court of Justice that unfavourable treatment of a woman related to pregnancy or maternity constitutes direct discrimination on grounds of sex. Such treatment should therefore be expressly covered by this Directive.

(24) The Court of Justice has consistently recognised the legitimacy, as regards the principle of equal treatment, of protecting a woman's biological condition during pregnancy and maternity and of introducing maternity protection measures as a means to achieve substantive equality. This Directive should therefore be without prejudice to Council Directive 92/85/EEC of 19 October 1992 on the introduction of measures to encourage improvements in the safety and health at work of pregnant workers and workers who have recently given birth or are breastfeeding.[12] This Directive should further be without prejudice to Council Directive 96/34/EC of 3 June 1996 on the framework agreement on parental leave concluded by UNICE, CEEP and the ETUC.[13]

(25) For reasons of clarity, it is also appropriate to make express provision for the protection of the employment rights of women on maternity leave and in particular their right to return to the same or an equivalent post, to suffer no detriment in their terms and conditions as a result of taking such leave and to benefit from any improvement in working conditions to which they would have been entitled during their absence.

(26) In the Resolution of the Council and of the Ministers for Employment and Social Policy, meeting within the Council, of 29 June 2000 on the balanced participation of women and men in family and working life,[14] Member States were encouraged to consider examining the scope for their respective legal systems to grant working men an individual and non-transferable right to paternity leave, while maintaining their rights relating to employment.

(27) Similar considerations apply to the granting by Member States to men and women of an individual and non-transferable right to leave subsequent to the adoption of a child. It is for the Member States to determine whether or not to grant such a right to paternity and/or adoption leave and also to determine any conditions, other than dismissal and return to work, which are outside the scope of this Directive.

(28) The effective implementation of the principle of equal treatment requires appropriate procedures to be put in place by the Member States.

(29) The provision of adequate judicial or administrative procedures for the enforcement of the obligations imposed by this Directive is essential to the effective implementation of the principle of equal treatment.

(30) The adoption of rules on the burden of proof plays a significant role in ensuring that the principle of equal treatment can be effectively enforced. As the Court of Justice has held, provision should therefore be made to ensure that the burden of proof shifts to the respondent when there is a prima facie case of discrimination, except in relation to proceedings in which it is for the court or other competent national body to investigate the facts. It is however necessary to clarify that the appreciation of the facts from which it may be presumed that there has been direct or indirect discrimination remains a matter for the relevant national body in accordance with national law or practice. Further, it is for the Member States to introduce, at any appropriate stage of the proceedings, rules of evidence which are more favourable to plaintiffs.

(31) With a view to further improving the level of protection offered by this Directive, associations, organisations and other legal entities should also be empowered to engage in proceedings, as the Member States so determine, either on behalf or in support of a complainant, without prejudice to national rules of procedure concerning representation and defence.

(32) Having regard to the fundamental nature of the right to effective legal protection, it is appropriate to ensure that workers continue to enjoy such protection even after the relationship giving rise to an alleged breach of the principle of equal treatment has ended. An employee defending or giving evidence on behalf of a person protected under this Directive should be entitled to the same protection.

(33) It has been clearly established by the Court of Justice that in order to be effective, the principle of equal treatment implies that the compensation awarded for any breach must be adequate in relation to the damage sustained. It is therefore appropriate to exclude the fixing of any prior upper limit for such compensation, except where the employer can prove that the only damage suffered by an applicant as a result of discrimination within the meaning of this Directive was the refusal to take his/her job application into consideration.

(34) In order to enhance the effective implementation of the principle of equal treatment, Member States should promote dialogue between the social partners and, within the framework of national practice, with non-governmental organisations.

(35) Member States should provide for effective, proportionate and dissuasive penalties for breaches of the obligations under this Directive.

(36) Since the objectives of this Directive cannot be sufficiently achieved by the Member States and can therefore be better achieved at Community level, the Community may adopt measures in accordance with the principle of subsidiarity as set out in Article 5 of the Treaty. In accordance with the principle of proportionality, as set out in that Article, this Directive does not go beyond what is necessary in order to achieve those objectives.

(37) For the sake of a better understanding of the different treatment of men and women in matters of employment and occupation, comparable statistics disaggregated by sex should continue to be developed, analysed and made available at the appropriate levels.

(38) Equal treatment of men and women in matters of employment and occupation cannot be restricted to legislative measures. Instead, the European Union and the Member States should continue to promote the raising of public awareness of wage discrimination and the changing of public attitudes, involving all parties concerned at public and private level to the greatest possible extent. The dialogue between the social partners could play an important role in this process.

(39) The obligation to transpose this Directive into national law should be confined to those provisions which represent a substantive change as compared with the earlier Directives. The obligation to transpose the provisions which are substantially unchanged arises under the earlier Directives.

(40) This Directive should be without prejudice to the obligations of the Member States relating to the time limits for transposition into national law and application of the Directives set out in Annex I, Part B.

(41) In accordance with paragraph 34 of the Inter-institutional agreement on better law-making,[15] Member States are encouraged to draw up, for themselves and in the interest of the Community, their own tables, which will, as far as possible, illustrate the correlation between this Directive and the transposition measures and to make them public,

NOTES

1 OJ C157, 28.6.2005, p 83.

2 Opinion of the European Parliament of 6 July 2005 (not yet published in the Official Journal), Council Common Position of 10 March 2006 (OJ C126E, 30.5.2006, p 33) and Position of the European Parliament of 1 June 2006 (not yet published in the Official Journal).

3 OJ L39, 14.2.1976, p 40. Directive as amended by Directive 2002/73/EC of the European Parliament and of the Council (OJ L269, 5.10.2002, p 15).

4 OJ L225, 12.8.1986, p 40. Directive as amended by Directive 96/97/EC (OJ L46, 17.2.1997, p 20).

5 See Annex I Part A.

6 OJ L45, 19.2.1975, p 19.

7 OJ L14, 20.1.1998, p 6. Directive as amended by Directive 98/52/EC (OJ L205, 22.7.1998, p 66).

8 C-262/88: *Barber v Guardian Royal Exchange Assurance Group* (1990 ECR I-1889).

9 C-7/93: *Bestuur van het Algemeen Burgerlijk Pensioenfonds v G. A. Beune* (1994 ECR I-4471).

10 C-351/00: *Pirkko Niemi* (2002 ECR I-7007).

11 Protocol 17 concerning Article 141 of the Treaty establishing the European Community (1992).

12 OJ L348, 28.11.1992, p 1.

13 OJ L145, 19.6.1996, p 4. Directive as amended by Directive 97/75/EC (OJ L10, 16.1.1998, p 24).

14 OJ C218, 31.7.2000, p 5.

15 OJ C321, 31.12.2003, p 1.

HAVE ADOPTED THIS DIRECTIVE:

TITLE I
GENERAL PROVISIONS

Article 1
Purpose

The purpose of this Directive is to ensure the implementation of the principle of equal opportunities and equal treatment of men and women in matters of employment and occupation.

To that end, it contains provisions to implement the principle of equal treatment in relation to:

(a) access to employment, including promotion, and to vocational training;
(b) working conditions, including pay;
(c) occupational social security schemes.

It also contains provisions to ensure that such implementation is made more effective by the establishment of appropriate procedures.

[4122]

Article 2

Definitions

1. For the purposes of this Directive, the following definitions shall apply:
   (a) 'direct discrimination': where one person is treated less favourably on grounds of sex than another is, has been or would be treated in a comparable situation;
   (b) 'indirect discrimination': where an apparently neutral provision, criterion or practice would put persons of one sex at a particular disadvantage compared with persons of the other sex, unless that provision, criterion or practice is objectively justified by a legitimate aim, and the means of achieving that aim are appropriate and necessary;
   (c) 'harassment': where unwanted conduct related to the sex of a person occurs with the purpose or effect of violating the dignity of a person, and of creating an intimidating, hostile, degrading, humiliating or offensive environment;
   (d) 'sexual harassment': where any form of unwanted verbal, non-verbal or physical conduct of a sexual nature occurs, with the purpose or effect of violating the dignity of a person, in particular when creating an intimidating, hostile, degrading, humiliating or offensive environment;
   (e) 'pay': the ordinary basic or minimum wage or salary and any other consideration, whether in cash or in kind, which the worker receives directly or indirectly, in respect of his/her employment from his/her employer;
   (f) 'occupational social security schemes': schemes not governed by Council Directive 79/7/EEC of 19 December 1978 on the progressive implementation of the principle of equal treatment for men and women in matters of social security[1] whose purpose is to provide workers, whether employees or self-employed, in an undertaking or group of undertakings, area of economic activity, occupational sector or group of sectors with benefits intended to supplement the benefits provided by statutory social security schemes or to replace them, whether membership of such schemes is compulsory or optional.

2. For the purposes of this Directive, discrimination includes:
   (a) harassment and sexual harassment, as well as any less favourable treatment based on a person's rejection of or submission to such conduct;
   (b) instruction to discriminate against persons on grounds of sex;
   (c) any less favourable treatment of a woman related to pregnancy or maternity leave within the meaning of Directive 92/85/EEC.

[4123]

NOTES

[1] OJ L6, 10.1.1979, p 24.

Article 3

Positive action

Member States may maintain or adopt measures within the meaning of Article 141(4) of the Treaty with a view to ensuring full equality in practice between men and women in working life.

[4124]

TITLE II
SPECIFIC PROVISIONS

CHAPTER 1
EQUAL PAY

Article 4

Prohibition of discrimination

For the same work or for work to which equal value is attributed, direct and indirect discrimination on grounds of sex with regard to all aspects and conditions of remuneration shall be eliminated.

In particular, where a job classification system is used for determining pay, it shall be based on the same criteria for both men and women and so drawn up as to exclude any discrimination on grounds of sex.

[4125]

CHAPTER 2
EQUAL TREATMENT IN OCCUPATIONAL SOCIAL SECURITY SCHEMES

Article 5

Prohibition of discrimination

Without prejudice to Article 4, there shall be no direct or indirect discrimination on grounds of sex in occupational social security schemes, in particular as regards:

(a) the scope of such schemes and the conditions of access to them;
(b) the obligation to contribute and the calculation of contributions;
(c) the calculation of benefits, including supplementary benefits due in respect of a spouse or dependants, and the conditions governing the duration and retention of entitlement to benefits.

[4126]

Article 6

Personal scope

This Chapter shall apply to members of the working population, including self-employed persons, persons whose activity is interrupted by illness, maternity, accident or involuntary unemployment and persons seeking employment and to retired and disabled workers, and to those claiming under them, in accordance with national law and/or practice.

[4127]

Article 7

Material scope

1. This Chapter applies to:
   (a) occupational social security schemes which provide protection against the following risks:
      (i) sickness,
      (ii) invalidity,
      (iii) old age, including early retirement,
      (iv) industrial accidents and occupational diseases,
      (v) unemployment;
   (b) occupational social security schemes which provide for other social benefits, in cash or in kind, and in particular survivors' benefits and family allowances, if such benefits constitute a consideration paid by the employer to the worker by reason of the latter's employment.

2. This Chapter also applies to pension schemes for a particular category of worker such as that of public servants if the benefits payable under the scheme are paid by reason of the employment relationship with the public employer. The fact that such a scheme forms part of a general statutory scheme shall be without prejudice in that respect.

[4128]

Article 8

Exclusions from the material scope

1. This Chapter does not apply to:
   (a) individual contracts for self-employed persons;
   (b) single-member schemes for self-employed persons;
   (c) insurance contracts to which the employer is not a party, in the case of workers;
   (d) optional provisions of occupational social security schemes offered to participants individually to guarantee them:
      (i) either additional benefits,
      (ii) or a choice of date on which the normal benefits for self-employed persons will start, or a choice between several benefits;

(e) occupational social security schemes in so far as benefits are financed by contributions paid by workers on a voluntary basis.

2. This Chapter does not preclude an employer granting to persons who have already reached the retirement age for the purposes of granting a pension by virtue of an occupational social security scheme, but who have not yet reached the retirement age for the purposes of granting a statutory retirement pension, a pension supplement, the aim of which is to make equal or more nearly equal the overall amount of benefit paid to these persons in relation to the amount paid to persons of the other sex in the same situation who have already reached the statutory retirement age, until the persons benefiting from the supplement reach the statutory retirement age.

[4129]

Article 9

Examples of discrimination

1. Provisions contrary to the principle of equal treatment shall include those based on sex, either directly or indirectly, for:

(a) determining the persons who may participate in an occupational social security scheme;
(b) fixing the compulsory or optional nature of participation in an occupational social security scheme;
(c) laying down different rules as regards the age of entry into the scheme or the minimum period of employment or membership of the scheme required to obtain the benefits thereof;
(d) laying down different rules, except as provided for in points (h) and (j), for the reimbursement of contributions when a worker leaves a scheme without having fulfilled the conditions guaranteeing a deferred right to long-term benefits;
(e) setting different conditions for the granting of benefits or restricting such benefits to workers of one or other of the sexes;
(f) fixing different retirement ages;
(g) suspending the retention or acquisition of rights during periods of maternity leave or leave for family reasons which are granted by law or agreement and are paid by the employer;
(h) setting different levels of benefit, except in so far as may be necessary to take account of actuarial calculation factors which differ according to sex in the case of defined-contribution schemes; in the case of funded defined-benefit schemes, certain elements may be unequal where the inequality of the amounts results from the effects of the use of actuarial factors differing according to sex at the time when the scheme's funding is implemented;
(i) setting different levels for workers' contributions;
(j) setting different levels for employers' contributions, except:
  (i) in the case of defined-contribution schemes if the aim is to equalise the amount of the final benefits or to make them more nearly equal for both sexes,
  (ii) in the case of funded defined-benefit schemes where the employer's contributions are intended to ensure the adequacy of the funds necessary to cover the cost of the benefits defined;
(k) laying down different standards or standards applicable only to workers of a specified sex, except as provided for in points (h) and (j), as regards the guarantee or retention of entitlement to deferred benefits when a worker leaves a scheme.

2. Where the granting of benefits within the scope of this Chapter is left to the discretion of the scheme's management bodies, the latter shall comply with the principle of equal treatment.

[4130]

Article 10

Implementation as regards self-employed persons

1. Member States shall take the necessary steps to ensure that the provisions of occupational social security schemes for self-employed persons contrary to the principle of equal treatment are revised with effect from 1 January 1993 at the latest or for Member States whose accession took place after that date, at the date that Directive 86/378/EEC became applicable in their territory.

2. This Chapter shall not preclude rights and obligations relating to a period of membership of an occupational social security scheme for self-employed persons prior to revision of that scheme from remaining subject to the provisions of the scheme in force during that period.

[4131]

Article 11

Possibility of deferral as regards self-employed persons

As regards occupational social security schemes for self-employed persons, Member States may defer compulsory application of the principle of equal treatment with regard to:

(a) determination of pensionable age for the granting of old-age or retirement pensions, and the possible implications for other benefits:
   (i) either until the date on which such equality is achieved in statutory schemes,
   (ii) or, at the latest, until such equality is prescribed by a directive;

(b) survivors' pensions until Community law establishes the principle of equal treatment in statutory social security schemes in that regard;

(c) the application of Article 9(1)(i) in relation to the use of actuarial calculation factors, until 1 January 1999 or for Member States whose accession took place after that date until the date that Directive 86/378/EEC became applicable in their territory.

[4132]

Article 12

Retroactive effect

1. Any measure implementing this Chapter, as regards workers, shall cover all benefits under occupational social security schemes derived from periods of employment subsequent to 17 May 1990 and shall apply retroactively to that date, without prejudice to workers or those claiming under them who have, before that date, initiated legal proceedings or raised an equivalent claim under national law. In that event, the implementation measures shall apply retroactively to 8 April 1976 and shall cover all the benefits derived from periods of employment after that date. For Member States which acceded to the Community after 8 April 1976, and before 17 May 1990, that date shall be replaced by the date on which Article 141 of the Treaty became applicable in their territory.

2. The second sentence of paragraph 1 shall not prevent national rules relating to time limits for bringing actions under national law from being relied on against workers or those claiming under them who initiated legal proceedings or raised an equivalent claim under national law before 17 May 1990, provided that they are not less favourable for that type of action than for similar actions of a domestic nature and that they do not render the exercise of rights conferred by Community law impossible in practice.

3. For Member States whose accession took place after 17 May 1990 and which were on 1 January 1994 Contracting Parties to the Agreement on the European Economic Area, the date of 17 May 1990 in the first sentence of paragraph 1 shall be replaced by 1 January 1994.

4. For other Member States whose accession took place after 17 May 1990, the date of 17 May 1990 in paragraphs 1 and 2 shall be replaced by the date on which Article 141 of the Treaty became applicable in their territory.

[4133]

Article 13

Flexible pensionable age

Where men and women may claim a flexible pensionable age under the same conditions, this shall not be deemed to be incompatible with this Chapter.

[4134]

CHAPTER 3
EQUAL TREATMENT AS REGARDS ACCESS TO EMPLOYMENT, VOCATIONAL TRAINING AND PROMOTION AND WORKING CONDITIONS

Article 14

Prohibition of discrimination

1. There shall be no direct or indirect discrimination on grounds of sex in the public or private sectors, including public bodies, in relation to:

(a) conditions for access to employment, to self-employment or to occupation, including selection criteria and recruitment conditions, whatever the branch of activity and at all levels of the professional hierarchy, including promotion;

(b) access to all types and to all levels of vocational guidance, vocational training, advanced vocational training and retraining, including practical work experience;

(c) employment and working conditions, including dismissals, as well as pay as provided for in Article 141 of the Treaty;

(d) membership of, and involvement in, an organisation of workers or employers, or any organisation whose members carry on a particular profession, including the benefits provided for by such organisations.

2. Member States may provide, as regards access to employment including the training leading thereto, that a difference of treatment which is based on a characteristic related to sex shall not constitute discrimination where, by reason of the nature of the particular occupational activities concerned or of the context in which they are carried out, such a characteristic constitutes a genuine and determining occupational requirement, provided that its objective is legitimate and the requirement is proportionate.

[4135]

Article 15

Return from maternity leave

A woman on maternity leave shall be entitled, after the end of her period of maternity leave, to return to her job or to an equivalent post on terms and conditions which are no less favourable to her and to benefit from any improvement in working conditions to which she would have been entitled during her absence.

[4136]

Article 16

Paternity and adoption leave

This Directive is without prejudice to the right of Member States to recognise distinct rights to paternity and/or adoption leave. Those Member States which recognise such rights shall take the necessary measures to protect working men and women against dismissal due to exercising those rights and ensure that, at the end of such leave, they are entitled to return to their jobs or to equivalent posts on terms and conditions which are no less favourable to them, and to benefit from any improvement in working conditions to which they would have been entitled during their absence.

[4137]

TITLE III
HORIZONTAL PROVISIONS

CHAPTER 1
REMEDIES AND ENFORCEMENT

SECTION 1
REMEDIES

Article 17

Defence of rights

1. Member States shall ensure that, after possible recourse to other competent authorities including where they deem it appropriate conciliation procedures, judicial procedures for the enforcement of obligations under this Directive are available to all persons who consider themselves wronged by failure to apply the principle of equal treatment to them, even after the relationship in which the discrimination is alleged to have occurred has ended.

2. Member States shall ensure that associations, organisations or other legal entities which have, in accordance with the criteria laid down by their national law, a legitimate interest in ensuring that the provisions of this Directive are complied with, may engage, either on behalf or in support of the complainant, with his/her approval, in any judicial and/or administrative procedure provided for the enforcement of obligations under this Directive.

3. Paragraphs 1 and 2 are without prejudice to national rules relating to time limits for bringing actions as regards the principle of equal treatment.

[4138]

Article 18

Compensation or reparation

Member States shall introduce into their national legal systems such measures as are necessary to ensure real and effective compensation or reparation as the Member States so determine for the loss and damage sustained by a person injured as a result of discrimination on grounds of sex, in a way which is dissuasive and proportionate to the damage suffered. Such compensation or reparation may not be restricted by the fixing of a prior upper limit, except in cases where the employer can prove that the only damage suffered by an applicant as a result of discrimination within the meaning of this Directive is the refusal to take his/her job application into consideration.

[4139]

SECTION 2
BURDEN OF PROOF

Article 19

Burden of proof

1. Member States shall take such measures as are necessary, in accordance with their national judicial systems, to ensure that, when persons who consider themselves wronged because the principle of equal treatment has not been applied to them establish, before a court or other competent authority, facts from which it may be presumed that there has been direct or indirect discrimination, it shall be for the respondent to prove that there has been no breach of the principle of equal treatment.

2. Paragraph 1 shall not prevent Member States from introducing rules of evidence which are more favourable to plaintiffs.

3. Member States need not apply paragraph 1 to proceedings in which it is for the court or competent body to investigate the facts of the case.

4. Paragraphs 1, 2 and 3 shall also apply to:
(a) the situations covered by Article 141 of the Treaty and, insofar as discrimination based on sex is concerned, by Directives 92/85/EEC and 96/34/EC;
(b) any civil or administrative procedure concerning the public or private sector which provides for means of redress under national law pursuant to the measures referred to in (a) with the exception of out-of-court procedures of a voluntary nature or provided for in national law.

5. This Article shall not apply to criminal procedures, unless otherwise provided by the Member States.

[4140]

CHAPTER 2
PROMOTION OF EQUAL TREATMENT—DIALOGUE

Article 20

Equality bodies

1. Member States shall designate and make the necessary arrangements for a body or bodies for the promotion, analysis, monitoring and support of equal treatment of all persons without discrimination on grounds of sex. These bodies may form part of agencies with responsibility at national level for the defence of human rights or the safeguard of individuals' rights.

2. Member States shall ensure that the competences of these bodies include:
(a) without prejudice to the right of victims and of associations, organisations or other legal entities referred to in Article 17(2), providing independent assistance to victims of discrimination in pursuing their complaints about discrimination;
(b) conducting independent surveys concerning discrimination;

(c) publishing independent reports and making recommendations on any issue relating to such discrimination;

(d) at the appropriate level exchanging available information with corresponding European bodies such as any future European Institute for Gender Equality.

[4141]

Article 21

Social dialogue

1. Member States shall, in accordance with national traditions and practice, take adequate measures to promote social dialogue between the social partners with a view to fostering equal treatment, including, for example, through the monitoring of practices in the workplace, in access to employment, vocational training and promotion, as well as through the monitoring of collective agreements, codes of conduct, research or exchange of experience and good practice.

2. Where consistent with national traditions and practice, Member States shall encourage the social partners, without prejudice to their autonomy, to promote equality between men and women, and flexible working arrangements, with the aim of facilitating the reconciliation of work and private life, and to conclude, at the appropriate level, agreements laying down anti-discrimination rules in the fields referred to in Article 1 which fall within the scope of collective bargaining. These agreements shall respect the provisions of this Directive and the relevant national implementing measures.

3. Member States shall, in accordance with national law, collective agreements or practice, encourage employers to promote equal treatment for men and women in a planned and systematic way in the workplace, in access to employment, vocational training and promotion.

4. To this end, employers shall be encouraged to provide at appropriate regular intervals employees and/or their representatives with appropriate information on equal treatment for men and women in the undertaking.

Such information may include an overview of the proportions of men and women at different levels of the organisation; their pay and pay differentials; and possible measures to improve the situation in cooperation with employees' representatives.

[4142]

Article 22

Dialogue with non-governmental organisations

Member States shall encourage dialogue with appropriate non-governmental organisations which have, in accordance with their national law and practice, a legitimate interest in contributing to the fight against discrimination on grounds of sex with a view to promoting the principle of equal treatment.

[4143]

CHAPTER 3
GENERAL HORIZONTAL PROVISIONS

Article 23

Compliance

Member States shall take all necessary measures to ensure that:

(a) any laws, regulations and administrative provisions contrary to the principle of equal treatment are abolished;

(b) provisions contrary to the principle of equal treatment in individual or collective contracts or agreements, internal rules of undertakings or rules governing the independent occupations and professions and workers' and employers' organisations or any other arrangements shall be, or may be, declared null and void or are amended;

(c) occupational social security schemes containing such provisions may not be approved or extended by administrative measures.

[4144]

Article 24

Victimisation

Member States shall introduce into their national legal systems such measures as are necessary to protect employees, including those who are employees' representatives provided for by national laws and/or practices, against dismissal or other adverse treatment by the employer as a reaction to a complaint within the undertaking or to any legal proceedings aimed at enforcing compliance with the principle of equal treatment.

[4145]

Article 25

Penalties

Member States shall lay down the rules on penalties applicable to infringements of the national provisions adopted pursuant to this Directive, and shall take all measures necessary to ensure that they are applied. The penalties, which may comprise the payment of compensation to the victim, must be effective, proportionate and dissuasive. The Member States shall notify those provisions to the Commission by 5 October 2005 at the latest and shall notify it without delay of any subsequent amendment affecting them.

[4146]

Article 26

Prevention of discrimination

Member States shall encourage, in accordance with national law, collective agreements or practice, employers and those responsible for access to vocational training to take effective measures to prevent all forms of discrimination on grounds of sex, in particular harassment and sexual harassment in the workplace, in access to employment, vocational training and promotion.

[4147]

Article 27

Minimum requirements

1. Member States may introduce or maintain provisions which are more favourable to the protection of the principle of equal treatment than those laid down in this Directive.

2. Implementation of this Directive shall under no circumstances be sufficient grounds for a reduction in the level of protection of workers in the areas to which it applies, without prejudice to the Member States' right to respond to changes in the situation by introducing laws, regulations and administrative provisions which differ from those in force on the notification of this Directive, provided that the provisions of this Directive are complied with.

[4148]

Article 28

Relationship to Community and national provisions

1. This Directive shall be without prejudice to provisions concerning the protection of women, particularly as regards pregnancy and maternity.

2. This Directive shall be without prejudice to the provisions of Directive 96/34/EC and Directive 92/85/EEC.

[4149]

Article 29

Gender mainstreaming

Member States shall actively take into account the objective of equality between men and women when formulating and implementing laws, regulations, administrative provisions, policies and activities in the areas referred to in this Directive.

[4150]

Article 30

Dissemination of information

Member States shall ensure that measures taken pursuant to this Directive, together with the provisions already in force, are brought to the attention of all the persons concerned by all suitable means and, where appropriate, at the workplace.

[4151]

TITLE IV
FINAL PROVISIONS

Article 31

Reports

1. By 15 February 2011, the Member States shall communicate to the Commission all the information necessary for the Commission to draw up a report to the European Parliament and the Council on the application of this Directive.

2. Without prejudice to paragraph 1, Member States shall communicate to the Commission, every four years, the texts of any measures adopted pursuant to Article 141(4) of the Treaty, as well as reports on these measures and their implementation. On the basis of that information, the Commission will adopt and publish every four years a report establishing a comparative assessment of any measures in the light of Declaration No 28 annexed to the Final Act of the Treaty of Amsterdam.

3. Member States shall assess the occupational activities referred to in Article 14(2), in order to decide, in the light of social developments, whether there is justification for maintaining the exclusions concerned. They shall notify the Commission of the results of this assessment periodically, but at least every 8 years.

[4152]

Article 32

Review

By 15 February 2011 at the latest, the Commission shall review the operation of this Directive and if appropriate, propose any amendments it deems necessary.

[4153]

Article 33

Implementation

Member States shall bring into force the laws, regulations and administrative provisions necessary to comply with this Directive by 15 August 2008 at the latest or shall ensure, by that date, that management and labour introduce the requisite provisions by way of agreement. Member States may, if necessary to take account of particular difficulties, have up to one additional year to comply with this Directive. Member States shall take all necessary steps to be able to guarantee the results imposed by this Directive. They shall forthwith communicate to the Commission the texts of those measures.

When Member States adopt these measures, they shall contain a reference to this Directive or be accompanied by such reference on the occasion of their official publication. They shall also include a statement that references in existing laws, regulations and administrative provisions to the Directives repealed by this Directive shall be construed as references to this Directive. Member States shall determine how such reference is to be made and how that statement is to be formulated.

The obligation to transpose this Directive into national law shall be confined to those provisions which represent a substantive change as compared with the earlier Directives. The obligation to transpose the provisions which are substantially unchanged arises under the earlier Directives.

Member States shall communicate to the Commission the text of the main provisions of national law which they adopt in the field covered by this Directive.

[4154]

Article 34

Repeal

1. With effect from 15 August 2009 Directives 75/117/EEC, 76/207/EEC, 86/378/EEC and 97/80/EC shall be repealed without prejudice to the obligations of the Member States relating to the time-limits for transposition into national law and application of the Directives set out in Annex I, Part B.

2. References made to the repealed Directives shall be construed as being made to this Directive and should be read in accordance with the correlation table in Annex II.

[4155]

Article 35

Entry into force

This Directive shall enter into force on the 20th day following its publication in the Official Journal of the European Union.

[4156]

Article 36

Addressees

This Directive is addressed to the Member States.

[4157]

Done at Strasbourg, 5 July 2006.

ANNEX I

PART A
REPEALED DIRECTIVES WITH THEIR SUCCESSIVE AMENDMENTS

Council Directive 75/117/EEC	OJ L45, 19.2.1975, p 19
Council Directive 76/207/EEC	OJ L39, 14.2.1976, p 40
Directive 2002/73/EC of the European Parliament and of the Council	OJ L269, 5.10.2002, p 15
Council Directive 86/378/EEC	OJ L225, 12.8.1986, p 40
Council Directive 96/97/EC	OJ L46, 17.2.1997, p 20
Council Directive 97/80/EC	OJ L14, 20.1.1998, p 6
Council Directive 98/52/EC	OJ L205, 22.7.1998, p 66

[4158]

PART B
LIST OF TIME LIMITS FOR TRANSPOSITION INTO NATIONAL LAW AND APPLICATION DATES

(*referred to in Article 34(1)*)

Directive	Time-limit for transposition	Date of application
Directive 75/117/EEC	19.2.1976	
Directive 76/207/EEC	14.8.1978	
Directive 86/378/EEC	1.1.1993	

Directive	Time-limit for transposition	Date of application
Directive 96/97/EC	1.7.1997	17.5.1990 in relation to workers, except for those workers or those claiming under them who had before that date initiated legal proceedings or raised an equivalent claim under national law. Article 8 of Directive 86/378/EEC – 1.1.1993 at the latest. Article 6(1)(i), first indent of Directive 86/378/EEC – 1.1.1999 at the latest.
Directive 97/80/EC	1.1.2001	As regards the United Kingdom of Great Britain and Northern Ireland 22.7.2001
Directive 98/52/EC	22.7.2001	
Directive 2002/73/EC	5.10.2005	

[4159]

ANNEX II
CORRELATION TABLE

Directive 75/117/EEC	Directive 76/207/EEC	Directive 86/378/EEC	Directive 97/80/EC	This Directive
—	Article 1(1)	Article 1	Article 1	Article 1
—	Article 1(2)	—	—	—
—	Article 2(2), first indent	—	—	Article 2(1)(a)
—	Article 2(2), second indent	—	Article 2(2)	Article 2(1)(b)
—	Article 2(2), third and fourth indents	—	—	Article 2(1)(c) and (d)
—	—	—	—	Article 2(1)(e)
—	—	Article 2(1)	—	Article 2(1)(f)
—	Article 2(3) and (4) and Article 2(7) third subparagraph	—	—	Article 2(2)
—	Article 2(8)	—	—	Article 3
Article 1	—	—	—	Article 4
—	—	Article 5(1)	—	Article 5
—	—	Article 3	—	Article 6
—	—	Article 4	—	Article 7(1)
—	—	—	—	Article 7(2)
—	—	Article 2(2)	—	Article 8(1)
—	—	Article 2(3)	—	Article 8(2)
—	—	Article 6	—	Article 9

PART 3

Directive 75/117/EEC	Directive 76/207/EEC	Directive 86/378/EEC	Directive 97/80/EC	This Directive
—	—	Article 8	—	Article 10
—	—	Article 9	—	Article 11
—	—	(Article 2 of Directive 96/97/EC)	—	Article 12
—	—	Article 9a	—	Article 13
—	Articles 2(1) and 3(1)	—	Article 2(1)	Article 14(1)
—	Article 2(6)	—	—	Article 14(2)
—	Article 2(7), second subparagraph	—	—	Article 15
—	Article 2(7), fourth subparagraph, second and third sentence	—	—	Article 16
Article 2	Article 6(1)	Article 10	—	Article 17(1)
—	Article 6(3)	—	—	Article 17(2)
—	Article 6(4)	—	—	Article 17(3)
—	Article 6(2)	—	—	Article 18
—	—	—	Articles 3 and 4	Article 19
—	Article 8a	—	—	Article 20
—	Article 8b	—	—	Article 21
—	Article 8c	—	—	Article 22
Articles 3 and 6	Article 3(2)(a)	—	—	Article 23(a)
Article 4	Article 3(2)(b)	Article 7(a)	—	Article 23(b)
—	—	Article 7(b)	—	Article 23(c)
Article 5	Article 7	Article 11	—	Article 24
Article 6	—	—	—	—
—	Article 8d	—	—	Article 25
	Article 2(5)			Article 26
—	Article 8e(1)	—	Article 4(2)	Article 27(1)
—	Article 8e(2)	—	Article 6	Article 27(2)
—	Article 2(7) first subparagraph	Article 5(2)	—	Article 28(1)
—	Article 2(7) fourth subparagraph first sentence			Article 28(2)
—	Article 1(1a)			Article 29
Article 7	Article 8	—	Article 5	Article 30
Article 9	Article 10	Article 12(2)	Article 7, fourth subparagraph	Article 31(1) and (2)

Directive 75/117/EEC	Directive 76/207/EEC	Directive 86/378/EEC	Directive 97/80/EC	This Directive
—	Article 9(2)	—	—	Article 31(3)
—	—	—	—	Article 32
Article 8	Article 9(1), first subparagraph and 9(2) and (3)	Article 12(1)	Article 7, first, second and third subparagraphs	Article 33
—	Article 9(1), second subparagraph	—	—	—
—	—	—	—	Article 34
—	—	—	—	Article 35
—	—	—	—	Article 36
—	—	Annex	—	—

[4160]–[4500]

PART 3

PART 4
STATUTORY CODES OF PRACTICE

HEALTH AND SAFETY COMMISSION CODE OF PRACTICE: SAFETY REPRESENTATIVES AND SAFETY COMMITTEES (1978)

NOTES

This Code of Practice was issued under the Health and Safety at Work etc Act 1974, s 16 at **[44]**, and came into force on 1 October 1978. It has the legal effect indicated in that section. For the Safety Representatives and Safety Committees Regulations 1977, SI 1977/500, see **[2034]**.

The Health and Safety Commission is abolished and replaced by a new Health and Safety Executive, as from 1 April 2008, by the Legislative Reform (Health and Safety Executive) Order 2008, SI 2008/960, art 2. Para 8 of Sch 2 to the 2008 Order provides that codes of practice issued by the Commission under the Health and Safety at Work etc Act 1974, s 16, before 1 April 2008, have effect on or after that date as though they had been issued by the new Executive.

1. The Safety Representatives and Safety Committees Regulations 1977 concern safety representatives appointed in accordance with Section 2(4) of the Act and cover:

(a) prescribed cases in which recognised trade unions may appoint safety representatives from amongst the employees;

(b) prescribed functions of safety representatives.

Section 2(6) of the Act requires an employer to consult with safety representatives with a view to the making and maintenance of arrangements which will enable him and his employees to cooperate effectively in promoting and developing measures to ensure the health and safety at work of the employees, and in checking the effectiveness of such measures. Under section 2(4) safety representatives are required to represent the employees in those consultations.

2. This Code of Practice has been approved by the Health and Safety Commission with the consent of the Secretary of State. It relates to the requirements placed on safety representatives by section 2(4) of the Act and on employers by the Regulations and takes effect on the date the Regulations come into operation.

3. The employer, the recognised trade unions concerned and safety representatives should make full and proper use of the existing agreed industrial relations machinery to reach the degree of agreement necessary to achieve the purpose of the Regulations and in order to resolve any differences.

Interpretation

4.—(a) In this Code, "the 1974 Act" means the Health and Safety at Work etc Act 1974 and "the Regulations" mean the Safety Representatives and Safety Committees Regulations 1977;

(b) words and expressions which are defined in the Act or in the Regulations have the same meaning in this Code unless the context requires otherwise.

Functions of safety representatives

5. In order to fulfil their functions under section 2(4) of the Act safety representatives should:

(a) take all reasonably practical steps to keep themselves informed of:

- (i) the legal requirements relating to the health and safety of persons at work, particularly the group or groups of persons they directly represent,
- (ii) the particular hazards of the workplace and the measures deemed necessary to eliminate or minimise the risk deriving from these hazards, and
- (iii) the health and safety policy of their employer and the organisation and arrangements for fulfilling that policy;

(b) encourage cooperation between their employer and his employees in promoting and developing essential measures to ensure the health and safety of employees and in checking the effectiveness of these measures;

(c) bring to the employer's notice normally in writing any unsafe or unhealthy conditions or working practices or unsatisfactory arrangements for welfare at work which come to their attention whether on an inspection or day to day observation. The report does not imply that all other conditions and working practices are safe and healthy or that the welfare arrangements are satisfactory in all other respects.

Making a written report does not preclude the bringing of such matters to the attention of the employer or his representative by a direct oral approach in the first instance, particularly in

PART 4

situations where speedy remedial action is necessary. It will also be appropriate for minor matters to be the subject of direct oral discussion without the need for a formal written approach.

Information to be provided by employers

6. The Regulations require employers to make information within their knowledge available to safety representatives necessary to enable them to fulfil their functions. Such information should include:

(a) information about the plans and performance of their undertaking and any changes proposed insofar as they affect the health and safety at work of their employees;

(b) information of a technical nature about hazards to health and safety and precautions deemed necessary to eliminate or minimise them, in respect of machinery, plant, equipment, processes, systems of work and substances in use at work, including any relevant information provided by consultants or designers or by the manufacturer, importer or supplier of any article or substance used, or proposed to be used, at work by their employees;

(c) information which the employer keeps relating to the occurrence of any accident, dangerous occurrence or notifiable industrial disease and any statistical records relating to such accidents, dangerous occurrences or cases of notifiable industrial disease;

(d) any other information specifically related to matters affecting the health and safety at work of his employees, including the results of any measurements taken by the employer or persons acting on his behalf in the course of checking the effectiveness of his health and safety arrangements;

(e) information on articles or substances which an employer issues to home-workers.

[4501]

HEALTH AND SAFETY COMMISSION CODE OF PRACTICE: TIME OFF FOR THE TRAINING OF SAFETY REPRESENTATIVES (1978)

NOTES

This Code of Practice was issued under the Health and Safety at Work etc Act 1974, s 16, at **[44]**, and came into force on 1 October 1978. It has the legal effect indicated in that section. For the Safety Representatives and Safety Committees Regulations 1977, SI 1977/500, see **[2034]**.

The Health and Safety Commission is abolished and replaced by a new Health and Safety Executive, as from 1 April 2008, by the Legislative Reform (Health and Safety Executive) Order 2008, SI 2008/960, art 2. Para 8 of Sch 2 to the 2008 Order provides that codes of practice issued by the Commission under the Health and Safety at Work etc Act 1974, s 16, before 1 April 2008, have effect on or after that date as though they had been issued by the new Executive.

Preface

This document sets out a Code of Practice, which has been approved by the Health and Safety Commission, relating to the time off with pay which a safety representative is to be permitted to take during his working hours for the purpose of undergoing training approved by the TUC or by independent unions. It should be read in conjunction with the Safety Representatives and Safety Committees Regulations 1977, with particular reference to Regulation 4, which sets out the functions of a safety representative and the time off for training necessary to perform these functions.

The Advisory, Conciliation and Arbitration Service has also prepared a Code of Practice on Time Off for trade union duties and activities generally under Section 57 of the Employment Protection Act. However, this Code, approved by the Health and Safety Commission, is concerned with time off for training of safety representatives appointed under the Regulations.

Issues which may arise are covered by paragraph 3 of the Code of Practice on Safety Representatives approved by the Health and Safety Commission. The Schedule to the Regulations deals with the computation of pay for the time off allowed. Regulation 11 contains provisions as to reference of complaints to industrial tribunals about time off and the payment to be made.

To complement training approved by the TUC or by independent unions for safety representatives, an employer should make such arrangements as are necessary to provide training in the technical hazards of the workplace and relevant precautions on safe methods of work, and on his organisation and arrangements for health and safety.

Code of Practice

1. The function of safety representatives appointed by recognised trade unions as set out in Section 2(4) of the Health and Safety at Work etc Act 1974 is to represent employees in consultations with employers about health and safety matters. Regulations 4(1) of the Safety Representatives and Safety Committees Regulations (SI 1977/500) prescribes other functions of safety representatives appointed under those Regulations.

2. Under Regulations 4(2)(b) of those Regulations the employer has a duty to permit those safety representatives such time off with pay during the employee's working hours as shall be necessary for the purpose of "undergoing such training in aspects of those functions as may be reasonable in all the circumstances".

3. As soon as possible after their appointment safety representatives should be permitted time off with pay to attend basic training facilities approved by the TUC or by the independent union or unions which appointed the safety representatives. Further training, similarly approved, should be undertaken where the safety representative has special responsibilities or where such training is necessary to meet changes in circumstances or relevant legislation.

4. With regard to the length of training required, this cannot be rigidly prescribed, but basic training should take into account the function of safety representatives placed on them by the Regulations. In particular, basic training should provide an understanding of the role of safety representatives, of safety committees, and of trade union policies and practices in relation to:

- (a) the legal requirements relating to the health and safety of persons at work, particularly the group or class of persons they directly represent;
- (b) the nature and extent of workplace hazards, and the measures necessary to eliminate or minimise them,
- (c) the health and safety policy of employers, and organisation and arrangements for fulfilling those policies.

Additionally, safety representatives will need to acquire new skills in order to carry out their functions, including safety inspections, and in using basic sources of legal and official information and information provided by or through the employer on health and safety matters.

5. Trade unions are responsible for appointing safety representatives and when the trade union wishes a safety representative to receive training relevant to his functions it should inform management of the course it has approved and supply a copy of the syllabus, indicating its contents, if the employer asks for it. It should normally give at least a few weeks' notice of the safety representatives it has nominated for attendance. The number of safety representatives attending training courses at any one time should be that which is reasonable in the circumstances, bearing in mind such factors as the availability of relevant courses and the operational requirements of the employer. Unions and management should endeavour to reach agreement on the appropriate numbers and arrangements and refer any problems which may arise to the relevant agreed procedures.

[4502]

COMMISSION FOR RACIAL EQUALITY: CODE OF PRACTICE FOR THE ELIMINATION OF RACIAL DISCRIMINATION AND THE PROMOTION OF EQUALITY OF OPPORTUNITY IN EMPLOYMENT (1983) (NOTE)

NOTES

This Code of Practice was issued by the Commission for Racial Equality under the Race Relations Act 1976, s 47 (now repealed), in July 1983 and came into effect on 1 April 1984 (see the Race Relations Code of Practice Order 1983, SI 1983/1081). It was replaced by the Commission for Racial Equality Code Of Practice on Racial Equality in Employment (2005) at **[4745]**, which was issued in November 2005, and came into effect on 6 April 2006 (see the Race Relations Code of Practice relating to Employment (Appointed Day) Order 2006, SI 2006/630, art 2). The 2006 Order revokes SI 1983/1081 (see art 4). Art 3 of the 2006 Order further provides that where a court or tribunal is hearing any proceedings arising from a complaint (whenever presented) alleging that a person has, before 6 April

2006, committed an act which is unlawful discrimination for the purposes of any provision of the 1976 Act the revised Code of Practice shall not have effect for the purpose of s 47(10) of the 1976 Act, and instead, the 1983 Code of Practice will continue to have effect for that purpose.

As to the dissolution of the Commission for Racial Equality and the transfer of its property, rights and liabilities etc to the Commission for Equality and Human Rights, see the Equality Act 2006, ss 36–38 at **[1679]–[1681]**.

[4503]–[4507]

EQUAL OPPORTUNITIES COMMISSION: CODE OF PRACTICE ON SEX DISCRIMINATION EQUAL OPPORTUNITY POLICIES, PROCEDURES AND PRACTICES IN EMPLOYMENT (1985)

NOTES

This Code of Practice was issued by the Equal Opportunities Commission under the Sex Discrimination Act 1975, s 56A (repealed as noted below), and was brought into effect on 30 April 1985 by the Sex Discrimination Code of Practice Order 1985, SI 1985/387. The Annex, which summarises the relevant provisions of the 1975 Act, is omitted. Unless otherwise specified, notes are as in the Code.

The statutory provision under which this Code was made was repealed by the Equality Act 2006, ss 40, 91, Sch 3, paras 6, 11, Sch 4; however the Code is continued in force by s 42(3) of the 2006 Act (see **[1685]**). As to the dissolution of the Equal Opportunities Commission and the transfer of its property, rights and liabilities etc to the Commission for Equality and Human Rights, see the Equality Act 2006, ss 36–38 at **[1679]–[1681]**.

Introduction

1. The EOC issues this Code of Practice for the following purposes:

(a) for the elimination of discrimination in employment;

(b) to give guidance as to what steps it is reasonably practicable for employers to take to ensure that their employees do not in the course of their employment act unlawfully contrary to the Sex Discrimination Act (SDA);

(c) for the promotion of equality of opportunity between men and women in employment.

The SDA prohibits discrimination against men, as well as against women. It also requires that married people should not be treated less favourably than single people of the same sex.

It should be noted that the provisions of the SDA—and therefore of this Code— apply to the UK-based subsidiaries of foreign companies.

2. The Code gives guidance to employers, trade unions and employment agencies on measures which can be taken to achieve equality. The chances of success of any organisation will clearly be improved if it seeks to develop the abilities of all employees, and the Code shows the close link which exists between equal opportunity and good employment practice. In some cases, an initial cost may be involved, but this should be more than compensated for by better relationships and better use of human resources.

Small businesses

3. The Code has to deal in general terms and it will be necessary for employers to adapt it in a way appropriate to the size and structure of their organisations. Small businesses, for example, will require much simpler procedures than organisations with complex structures and it may not always be reasonable for them to carry out all the Code's detailed recommendations. In adapting the Code's recommendations, small firms should, however, ensure that their practices comply with the Sex Discrimination Act.

Employers' responsibility

4. The primary responsibility at law rests with each employer to ensure that there is no unlawful discrimination. It is important, however, that measures to eliminate discrimination or promote equality of opportunity should be understood and supported by all employees. Employers are therefore recommended to involve their employees in equal opportunity policies.

Individual employees' responsibility

5. While the main responsibility for eliminating discrimination and providing equal opportunity is that of the employer, individual employees at all levels have responsibilities too. They must not discriminate or knowingly aid their employer to do so.

Trade union responsibility

6. The full commitment of trade unions is essential for the elimination of discrimination and for the successful operation of an equal opportunities policy. Much can be achieved by collective bargaining and throughout the Code it is assumed that all the normal procedures will be followed.

7. It is recommended that unions should co-operate in the introduction and implementation of equal opportunities policies where employers have decided to introduce them, and should urge that such policies be adopted where they have not yet been introduced.

8. Trade Unions have a responsibility to ensure that their representatives and members do not unlawfully discriminate on grounds of sex or marriage in the admission or treatment of members. The guidance in this Code also applies to trade unions in their role as employers.

Employment agencies

9. Employment agencies have a responsibility as suppliers of job applicants to avoid unlawful discrimination on the grounds of sex or marriage in providing services to clients. The guidance in this Code also applies to employment agencies in their role as employers.

Definitions

10. For ease of reference, the main employment provisions of the Sex Discrimination Act, including definitions of direct and indirect sex and marriage discrimination, are provided in a Legal Annex to this Code.

[4508]

PART 1
THE ROLE OF GOOD EMPLOYMENT PRACTICES IN ELIMINATING SEX AND MARRIAGE DISCRIMINATION

11. This section of the Code describes those good employment practices which will help to eliminate unlawful discrimination. It recommends the establishment and use of consistent criteria for selection, training, promotion, redundancy and dismissal which are made known to all employees. Without this consistency, decisions can be subjective and leave the way open for unlawful discrimination to occur.

Recruitment

12. It is unlawful: UNLESS THE JOB IS COVERED BY AN EXCEPTION:[1] TO DISCRIMINATE DIRECTLY OR INDIRECTLY ON THE GROUNDS OF SEX OR MARRIAGE

— IN THE ARRANGEMENTS MADE FOR DECIDING WHO SHOULD BE OFFERED A JOB
— IN ANY TERMS OF EMPLOYMENT
— BY REFUSING OR OMITTING TO OFFER A PERSON EMPLOYMENT

[Section 6(1)(a); 6(1)(b); 6(1)(c)]

NOTES

[1] There are a number of exceptions to the requirements of the SDA, that employers must not discriminate against their employees or against potential employees.

13. It is therefore recommended that:

(a) each individual should be assessed according to his or her personal capability to carry out a given job. It should not be assumed that men only or women only will be able to perform certain kinds of work;

(b) any qualifications or requirements applied to a job which effectively inhibit applications from one sex or from married people should be retained only if they are justifiable in terms of the job to be done;
[Section 6(1)(a) together with section 1(1)(b) or 3(1)(b)]

(c) any age limits should be retained only if they are necessary for the job. An unjustifiable age limit could constitute unlawful indirect discrimination, for example, against women who have taken time out of employment for child-rearing;

(d) where trade unions uphold such qualifications or requirements as union policy, they should amend that policy in the light of any potentially unlawful effect.

Genuine Occupational Qualifications (GOQs)

14. It is unlawful: EXCEPT FOR CERTAIN JOBS WHEN A PERSON'S SEX IS A GENUINE OCCUPATIONAL QUALIFICATION (GOQ) FOR THAT JOB to select candidates on the ground of sex.
[Section 7(2); 7(3) and 7(4)]

15. There are very few instances in which a job will qualify for a GOQ on the ground of sex. However, exceptions may arise for example, where considerations of privacy and decency or authenticity are involved. The SDA expressly states that the need of the job for strength and stamina does not justify restricting it to men. When a GOQ exists for a job, it applies also to promotion, transfer or training for that job, but cannot be used to justify a dismissal.

16. In some instances, the GOQ will apply to some of the duties only. A GOQ will not be valid, however, where members of the appropriate sex are already employed in sufficient numbers to meet the employer's likely requirements without undue inconvenience. For example, in a job where sales assistants may be required to undertake changing room duties, it might not be lawful to claim a GOQ in respect of *all* the assistants on the grounds that any of them might be required to undertake changing room duties from time to time.

17. It is therefore recommended that:

— A job for which a GOQ was used in the past should be re-examined if the post falls vacant to see whether the GOQ still applies. Circumstances may well have changed, rendering the GOQ inapplicable.

Sources of Recruitment

18. It is unlawful: UNLESS THE JOB IS COVERED BY AN EXCEPTION:

— TO DISCRIMINATE ON GROUNDS OF SEX OR MARRIAGE IN THE ARRANGEMENTS MADE FOR DETERMINING WHO SHOULD BE OFFERED EMPLOYMENT WHETHER RECRUITING BY ADVERTISEMENTS, THROUGH EMPLOYMENT AGENCIES, JOBCENTRES, OR CAREER OFFICES.

— TO IMPLY THAT APPLICATIONS FROM ONE SEX OR FROM MARRIED PEOPLE WILL NOT BE CONSIDERED.
[Section 6(1)(a)]

— TO INSTRUCT OR PUT PRESSURE ON OTHERS TO OMIT TO REFER FOR EMPLOYMENT PEOPLE OF ONE SEX OR MARRIED PEOPLE UNLESS THE JOB IS COVERED BY AN EXCEPTION.
[Sections 39 and 40]

It is also unlawful WHEN ADVERTISING JOB VACANCIES,

— TO PUBLISH OR CAUSE TO BE PUBLISHED AN ADVERTISEMENT WHICH INDICATES OR MIGHT REASONABLY BE UNDERSTOOD AS INDICATING AN INTENTION TO DISCRIMINATE UNLAWFULLY ON GROUNDS OF SEX OR MARRIAGE.

Advertising

19. It is therefore recommended that:

(a) job advertising should be carried out in such a way as to encourage applications from suitable candidates of both sexes. This can be achieved both by wording of the advertisements and, for example, by placing advertisements in publications likely to reach both sexes. All advertising material and accompanying literature relating to employment or training issues should be reviewed to ensure that it avoids presenting men and women in stereotyped roles. Such stereotyping tends to perpetuate sex segregation in jobs and can also lead people of the opposite sex to believe that they would be unsuccessful in applying for particular jobs;

(b) where vacancies are filled by promotion or transfer, they should be published to all eligible employees in such a way that they do not restrict applications from either sex;

(c) recruitment solely or primarily by word of mouth may unnecessarily restrict the choice of applicants available. The method should be avoided in a workforce predominantly of one sex, if in practice it prevents members of the opposite sex from applying;

(d) where applicants are supplied through trade unions and members of one sex only come forward, this should be discussed with the unions and an alternative approach adopted.

Careers service schools

20. When notifying vacancies to the Careers Service, employers should specify that these are open to both boys and girls. This is especially important when a job has traditionally been done exclusively or mainly by one sex. If dealing with single sex schools, they should ensure, where possible, that both boys' and girls' schools are approached; it is also a good idea to remind mixed schools that jobs are open to boys and girls.

Selection methods

Tests

21.—(a) If selection tests are used, they should be specifically related to job and/or career requirements and should measure an individual's actual or inherent ability to do or train for the work or career.

(b) Tests should be reviewed regularly to ensure that they remain relevant and free from any unjustifiable bias, either in content or in scoring mechanism.

Application and Interviewing

22. It is unlawful: UNLESS THE JOB IS COVERED BY AN EXCEPTION:

— TO DISCRIMINATE ON GROUNDS OF SEX OR MARRIAGE BY REFUSING OR DELIBERATELY OMITTING TO OFFER EMPLOYMENT.
[Section 6(1)(c)]

23. It is therefore recommended that:

(a) employers should ensure that personnel staff, line managers and all other employees who may come into contact with job applicants, should be trained in the provisions of the SDA, including the fact that it is unlawful to instruct or put pressure on others to discriminate;

(b) applications from men and women should be processed in exactly the same way. For example, there should not be separate lists of male and female or married and single applicants. All those handling applications and conducting interviews should be trained in the avoidance of unlawful discrimination and records of interviews kept, where practicable, showing why applicants were or were not appointed;

(c) questions should relate to the requirements of the job. Where it is necessary to assess whether personal circumstances will affect performance of the job (for example, where it involves unsocial hours or extensive travel) this should be discussed objectively without detailed questions based on assumptions about marital status, children and domestic obligations. Questions about marriage plans or family intentions should not be asked, as they could be construed as showing bias against women. Information necessary for personnel records can be collected after a job offer has been made.

Promotion, transfer and training

24. It is unlawful: UNLESS THE JOB IS COVERED BY AN EXCEPTION, FOR EMPLOYERS TO DISCRIMINATE DIRECTLY OR INDIRECTLY ON THE GROUNDS OF SEX OR MARRIAGE IN THE WAY THEY AFFORD ACCESS TO OPPORTUNITIES FOR PROMOTION, TRANSFER OR TRAINING.
[Section 6(2)(a)]

25. It is therefore recommended that:

(a) where an appraisal system is in operation, the assessment criteria should be examined to ensure that they are not unlawfully discriminatory and the scheme monitored to assess how it is working in practice;

(b) when a group of workers predominantly of one sex is excluded from an appraisal scheme, access to promotion, transfer and training and to other benefits should be reviewed, to ensure that there is no unlawful indirect discrimination;

(c) promotion and career development patterns are reviewed to ensure that the traditional qualifications are justifiable requirements for the job to be done. In some circumstances, for example, promotion on the basis of length of service could amount to unlawful indirect discrimination, as it may unjustifiably affect more women than men;

(d) when general ability and personal qualities are the main requirements for promotion

PART 4

to a post, care should be taken to consider favourably candidates of both sexes with differing career patterns and general experience;

(e) rules which restrict or preclude transfer between certain jobs should be questioned and changed if they are found to be unlawfully discriminatory. Employees of one sex may be concentrated in sections from which transfers are traditionally restricted without real justification;

(f) policies and practices regarding selection for training, day release and personal development should be examined for unlawful direct and indirect discrimination. Where there is found to be an imbalance in training as between sexes, the cause should be identified to ensure that it is not discriminatory;

(g) age limits for access to training and promotion should be questioned.

Health and safety legislation

26. Equal treatment of men and women may be limited by statutory provisions which require men and women to be treated differently. For example, the Factories Act 1961 places restrictions on the hours of work of female manual employees, although the Health and Safety Executive can exempt employers from these restrictions, subject to certain conditions. The Mines and Quarries Act 1954 imposes limitations on women's work and there are restrictions where there is special concern for the unborn child (e g lead and ionising radiation). However the broad duties placed on employers by the Health and Safety at Work, etc, Act 1974 makes no distinctions between men and women. Section 2(1) requires employers to ensure, so far as is reasonably practicable, the health and safety and welfare at work of *all* employees.

SPECIFIC HEALTH AND SAFETY REQUIREMENTS UNDER EARLIER LEGISLATION ARE UNAFFECTED BY THE ACT.

It is therefore recommended that

— company policy should be reviewed and serious consideration given to any significant differences in treatment between men and women, and there should be well-founded reasons if such differences are maintained or introduced.

NOTES

Some statutory restrictions placed on adult women's hours of work were repealed on February 1987 and others in February 1988. They now no longer apply. Paragraph 26 of the code is still relevant, however, to other health and safety legislation which requires men and women to be treated differently, and which has not been repealed.

Terms of employment, benefits, facilities and services

27. It is unlawful: UNLESS THE JOB IS COVERED BY AN EXCEPTION: TO DISCRIMINATE ON THE GROUNDS OF SEX OR MARRIAGE, DIRECTLY OR INDIRECTLY, IN THE TERMS ON WHICH EMPLOYMENT IS OFFERED OR IN AFFORDING ACCESS TO ANY BENEFITS,[1] FACILITIES OR SERVICES.

[Sections 6(1)(b); 6(2)(a); 29]

NOTES

1 Certain provisions relating to death and retirement are exempt from the Act. [This is now subject to the amendments made by the Sex Discrimination Act 1986, s 2: Ed.]

28. It is therefore recommended that:

(a) all terms of employment, benefits, facilities and services are reviewed to ensure that there is no unlawful discrimination on grounds of sex or marriage. For example, part-time work, domestic leave, company cars and benefits for dependants should be available to both male and female employees in the same or not materially different circumstances.

29. In an establishment where part-timers are solely or mainly women, unlawful indirect discrimination may arise if, as a group, they are treated less favourably than other employees without justification.

It is therefore recommended that:

(b) where part-time workers do not enjoy pro-rata pay or benefits with full-time workers, the arrangements should be reviewed to ensure that they are justified without regard to sex.

Grievances, disciplinary procedures and victimisation

30. It is unlawful: TO VICTIMISE AN INDIVIDUAL FOR A COMPLAINT MADE IN GOOD FAITH ABOUT SEX OR MARRIAGE DISCRIMINATION OR FOR GIVING EVIDENCE ABOUT SUCH A COMPLAINT.

[Section 4(1); 4(2); and 4(3)]

31. It is therefore recommended that:

(a) particular care is taken to ensure that an employee who has in good faith taken action under the Sex Discrimination Act or the Equal Pay Act does not receive less favourable treatment than other employees, for example by being disciplined or dismissed;

(b) employees should be advised to use the internal procedures, where appropriate, but this is without prejudice to the individual's right to apply to an industrial tribunal within the statutory time limit, ie before the end of the period of three months beginning when the act complained of was done. (There is no time limit if the victimisation is continuing);

(c) particular care is taken to deal effectively with all complaints of discrimination, victimisation or harassment. It should not be assumed that they are made by those who are over-sensitive.

Dismissals, redundancies and other unfavourable treatment of employees

32. It is unlawful: TO DISCRIMINATE DIRECTLY OR INDIRECTLY ON GROUNDS OF SEX OR MARRIAGE IN DISMISSALS OR BY TREATING AN EMPLOYEE UNFAVOURABLY IN ANY OTHER WAY.
[Section 6(2)(b)]

It is therefore recommended that:

(a) care is taken that members of one sex are not disciplined or dismissed for performance or behaviour which would be overlooked or condoned in the other sex;

(b) redundancy procedures affecting a group of employees predominantly of one sex should be reviewed, so as to remove any effects which could be disproportionate and unjustifiable;

(c) conditions of access to voluntary redundancy benefit[1] should be made available on equal terms to male and female employees in the same or not materially different circumstances;

(d) where there is down-grading or short-time working (for example, owing to a change in the nature or volume of an employer's business) the arrangements should not unlawfully discriminate on the ground of sex;

(e) all reasonably practical steps should be taken to ensure that a standard of conduct or behaviour is observed which prevents members of either sex from being intimidated, harassed or otherwise subjected to unfavourable treatment on the ground of their sex.

[4509]

NOTES

[1] Certain provisions relating to death and retirement are exempt from the Act. [See note to para 27 of the Code: Ed.]

PART 2
THE ROLE OF GOOD EMPLOYMENT PRACTICES IN PROMOTING EQUALITY OF OPPORTUNITY

33. This section of the Code describes those employment practices which help to promote equality of opportunity. It gives information about the formulation and implementation of equal opportunities policies. While such policies are not required by law, their value has been recognised by a number of employers who have voluntarily adopted them. Others may wish to follow this example.

Formulating an equal opportunities policy

34. An equal opportunities policy will ensure the effective use of human resources in the best interests of both the organisation and its employees. It is a commitment by an employer to the development and use of employment procedures and practices which do not discriminate on grounds of sex or marriage and which provide genuine equality of opportunity for all employees. The detail of the policy will vary according to size of the organisation.

Implementing the policy

35. An equal opportunities policy must be seen to have the active support of management at the highest level. To ensure that the policy is fully effective, the following procedure is recommended:

(a) the policy should be clearly stated and, where appropriate, included in a collective agreement;
(b) overall responsibility for implementing the policy should rest with senior management;
(c) the policy should be made known to all employees and, where reasonably practicable, to all job applicants.

36. Trade unions have a very important part to play in implementing genuine equality of opportunity and they will obviously be involved in the review of established procedures to ensure that these are consistent with the law.

Monitoring

37. It is recommended that the policy is monitored regularly to ensure that it is working in practice. Consideration could be given to setting up a joint Management/Trade Union Review Committee.

38. In a small firm with a simple structure it may be quite adequate to assess the distribution and payment of employees from personal knowledge.

39. In a large and complex organisation a more formal analysis will be necessary, for example, by sex, grade and payment in each unit. This may need to be introduced by stages as resources permit. Any formal analysis should be regularly updated and available to Management and Trade Unions to enable any necessary action to be taken.

40. Sensible monitoring will show, for example, whether members of one sex:
(a) do not apply for employment or promotion, or that fewer apply than might be expected;
(b) are not recruited, promoted or selected for training and development or are appointed/selected in a significantly lower proportion than their rate of application;
(c) are concentrated in certain jobs, sections or departments.

Positive action

Recruitment, training and promotion

41. Selection for recruitment or promotion must be on merit, irrespective of sex. However, the Sex Discrimination Act does allow certain steps to redress the effects of previous unequal opportunities. Where there have been few or no members of one sex in particular work in their employment for the previous 12 months, the Act allows employers to give special encouragement to, and provide specific training for, the minority sex. Such measures are usually described as Positive Action.

[Section 48]

42. Employers may wish to consider positive measures such as:
(a) training their own employees (male or female) for work which is traditionally the preserve of the other sex, for example, training women for skilled manual or technical work;
(b) positive encouragement to women to apply for management posts— special courses may be needed;
(c) advertisements which encourage application from the minority sex but make it clear that selection will be on merit without reference to sex;
(d) notifying job agencies, as part of a Positive Action Programme that they wish to encourage members of one sex to apply for vacancies, where few or no members of that sex are doing the work in question. In these circumstances, job agencies should tell both men and women about the posts and, in addition, let the under-represented sex know that applications from them are particularly welcome. Withholding information from one sex in an attempt to encourage applications from the opposite sex would be unlawful.

NOTES

Section 47 of the SDA 1975 allowed training bodies to run single-sex courses. Since November 1986, this has applied also to other persons including employers. Single-sex training need therefore no longer be confined to an organisation's own employees, as indicated in paragraph 42(a) of the Code, but may be extended to other groups—for example, job applicants or school leavers. Positive Action in recruitment for employment, however, is still not allowed. [Ed.]

Other working arrangements

43. There are other forms of action which could assist both employer and employee by helping to provide continuity of employment to working parents, many of whom will have valuable experience or skills.

Employers may wish to consider with their employees whether:

(a) certain jobs can be carried out on a part-time or flexi-time basis;

(b) personal leave arrangements are adequate and available to both sexes. It should not be assumed that men may not need to undertake domestic responsibilities on occasion, especially at the time of childbirth;

(c) child-care facilities are available locally or whether it would be feasible to establish nursery facilities on the premises or combine with other employers to provide them;

(d) residential training could be facilitated for employees with young children. For example, where this type of training is necessary, by informing staff who are selected well in advance to enable them to make childcare and other personal arrangements; employers with their own residential training centres could also consider whether childcare facilities might be provided;

(e) the statutory maternity leave provisions could be enhanced, for example, by reducing the qualifying service period, extending the leave period, or giving access to part-time arrangements on return.

These arrangements, and others, are helpful to both sexes but are of particular benefit to women in helping them to remain in gainful employment during the years of child-rearing.

[4510]

CODE OF PRACTICE: PICKETING (1992)

NOTES

This Code was originally made under the Employment Act 1980, s 3 (as amended by the Employment Act 1988, s 18). See now the Trade Union and Labour Relations (Consolidation) Act 1992, ss 201, 202 at **[686]**, **[687]**.

This Code was made by the Secretary of State for Employment, and came into force on 1 May 1992 (see the Employment Code of Practice (Picketing) Order 1992, SI 1992/476). It replaces the previous Code issued in 1980. For the legal status of the Code, see now the Trade Union and Labour Relations (Consolidation) Act 1992, s 207 at **[692]**.

Text and notes printed in green bold in the original Code are reproduced in italics in this work (see the preamble below). Notes are as in the Code.

Preamble

The legal framework within which the Code will operate is explained in its text. While every effort has been made to ensure that explanations included in the Code are accurate, only the courts can give authoritative interpretations of the law.

The Code's provisions apply equally to men and to women, but for simplicity the masculine pronoun is used throughout. Wherever it appears in the Code, the word "court" is used to mean the High Court in England and Wales and the Court of Session in Scotland, but without prejudice to the Code's relevance to any proceedings before any other court.

Passages in this Code which are printed [*in italics*] outline or re-state provisions in primary legislation.

On the day on which this Code of Practice comes into operation in pursuance of an order under section 3(5) of the Employment Act 1980, the Code of Practice "Picketing" which came into effect on 17 December 1980 ceases to have effect subject to any transitional provisions or savings made by the order.

[4511]

Section A. Introduction

1. The purpose of this Code is to provide practical guidance on picketing in trade disputes for those:

— contemplating, organising or taking part in a picket or activities associated with picketing, such as assemblies of demonstrations; and/or

— employers, workers or members of the general public who may be affected by a picket or any associated activities.

2. There is no legal "right to picket" as such, but attendance for the purpose of peaceful picketing has long been recognised to be a lawful activity. However, the law imposes certain limits on how, where and for what purpose such picketing can be undertaken. These limits help ensure proper protection for those who may be affected by picketing—including those who wish to cross a picket line and go to work.

3. It is a **civil** wrong, actionable in the civil courts, to persuade someone to break his contract of employment, or to secure the breaking of a commercial contract. But the law exempts from this liability those acting in contemplation or furtherance of a trade dispute, including—in certain circumstances—pickets themselves.

4. This exemption is provided by means of special "statutory immunities" to prevent liability arising to such **civil law** proceedings. These immunities—which are explained in more detail in Section B of this Code—have the effect that trade unions and individuals can, in certain circumstances, organise or conduct a picket without fear of being successfully sued in the courts. However, this protection applies only to acts of inducing breach, or interference with the performance, of contracts, or threatening to do either of these things.

5. These "statutory immunities" afford no protection for a picket, anyone involved in activities associated with picketing, or anyone organising a picket who commits some other kind of civil wrong—such as trespass or nuisance.[1] Nor do they protect anyone—whether a picket, an employee who decides to take industrial action or to break his contract of employment because he is persuaded to do so by a picket, or anyone else—from the consequences which may follow if they choose to take industrial action or break their contracts of employment. These could include, for example, loss of wages, or other disciplinary action or dismissal from employment.

NOTES

[1] See the further explanation in paragraph 27 in Section B of the Code.

---

6. The **criminal** law applies to pickets just as it applies to everyone else. No picket, person involved in activities associated with picketing or person organising a picket, has any exemption from the provisions of the criminal law as this applies, for example, to prevent obstruction, preserve public order, or regulate assemblies or demonstrations.

7. This Code outlines aspects of the law on picketing—although it is, of course, for the courts and industrial tribunals to interpret and apply the law in particular cases. Sections B and C, respectively, outline provisions of the civil and criminal law and, where relevant, give guidance on good practice. Section D describes the role of the police in enforcing the law. Sections E, F and G also give guidance on good practice in relation to the conduct of particular aspects of picketing and of certain activities associated with picketing.

8. *The Code itself imposes no legal obligations and failure to observe it does not by itself render anyone liable to proceedings. But statute law provides that any provisions of the Code are to be admissible in evidence and taken into account in proceedings before any court, industrial tribunal or the Central Arbitration Committee where they consider them relevant.*

[4512]

Section B. Picketing and the Civil Law

9. *The law sets out the basic rules which must be observed if picketing is to be carried out, or organised, lawfully. To keep to these rules, attendance for the purpose of picketing may only:*

(*i*) *be taken in contemplation or furtherance of a trade dispute;*

(*ii*) *be carried out by a person attending at or near his own place of work; a trade union official, in addition to attending at or near his own place of work, may also attend at or near the place of work of a member of his trade union whom he is accompanying on the picket line and whom he represents.*

Furthermore, the only purpose involved must be peacefully to obtain or communicate information, or peacefully to persuade a person to work or not to work.

10. Picketing commonly involves persuading workers to break, or interfere with the performance of, their contracts of employment by not going into work. Picketing can also disrupt the business of the employer who is being picketed by interfering with the performance of a commercial contract which the employer has with a customer or supplier. If pickets follow the rules outlined in paragraph 9, however, they may have the protection against civil proceedings afforded by the "statutory immunities". These rules, and immunities, are explained more fully in paragraphs 11 to 30 below.

In contemplation or furtherance of a trade dispute

11. *Picketing is lawful only if it is carried out in contemplation or furtherance of a "trade dispute". A "trade dispute" is defined in law so as to cover the matters which normally occasion disputes between employers and workers—such as terms and conditions of employment, the allocation of work, matters of discipline, trade union recognition.*

"Secondary" action

12. *The "statutory immunities" do not apply to protect a threat of, or call for or other inducement of "secondary" industrial action. The law defines "secondary" action—which is sometimes referred to as "sympathy" or "solidarity" action—as that by workers whose employer is not a party to the trade dispute to which the action relates.*

13. However, a worker employed by a party to a trade dispute, picketing at his own place of work may try to persuade another worker, not employed by that employer, to break, or interfere with the performance of, the second worker's contract of employment, and/or to interfere with the performance of a commercial contract. This could happen, for example, if a picket persuaded a lorry driver employed by another employer not to cross the picket line and deliver goods to be supplied, under a commercial contract, to the employer in dispute. Such an act by a picket would be an unlawful inducement to take secondary action unless provision was made to the contrary.

14. *Accordingly, the law contains provisions which make it lawful for a peaceful picket, at the picket's own place of work, to seek to persuade workers other than those employed by the picket's own employer not to work, or not to work normally. To have such protection, the peaceful picketing must be done:*
(*a*) *by a worker employed by the employer who is party to the dispute;*[2] *or*
(*b*) *by a trade union official whose attendance is lawful* (*see paragraphs 22–23 below*).

NOTES

2 *However, the peaceful picketing may be done by a worker who is not in employment but was last employed by the employer in dispute in certain circumstances—see paragraph 20.*

15. Where an entrance or exit is used jointly by the workers of more than one employer, the workers who are not involved in the dispute to which a picket relates should not be interfered with by picketing activities. Particular care should be taken to ensure that picketing does not involve calls for a breach, or interference with the performance, of contracts by employees of other employer(s) who are not involved in the dispute. Observing this principle will help avoid consequences which might otherwise be damaging and disruptive to good industrial relations.

Attendance at or near a picket's own place of work

16. *It is lawful for a person to induce breach, or interference with the performance, of a contract in the course of attendance for the purpose of picketing only if he pickets at or near his own place of work.*

17. The expression "at or near his own place of work" is not further defined in statute law. The provisions means that, except for those covered by paragraphs 22 and 23 below, lawful picketing must be limited to attendance at, or near, an entrance to or exit from the factory, site or office at which the picket works. Picketing should be confined to a location, or locations, as near as practicable to the place of work.

18. The law does not enable a picket to attend lawfully at an entrance to, or exit from, *any* place of work other than his own. This applies even, for example, if those working at the other place of work are employed by the same employer, or are covered by the same collective bargaining arrangements as the picket.

19. *The law identifies two specific groups in respect of which particular arrangements apply. These groups are:*
— *those* (*e g mobile workers*) *who work at more than one place; and*
— *those for whom it is impracticable to picket at their own place of work because of its location.*

The law provides that it is lawful for such workers to picket those premises of their employer from which they work, or those from which their work is administered. In the case of lorry drivers, for example, this will usually mean, in practice, the premises of their employer from which their vehicles operate.

20. Special provisions also apply to people who are not in work, and who have lost their jobs for reasons connected with the dispute which has occasioned the picketing. This might arise, for example, where the dismissal of a group of employees has led directly to the organisation of a picket, or where an employer has dismissed employees because they refuse to work normally, and some or all of those dismissed then wish to set up a picket. *In such cases the law provides that it is lawful for a worker to picket at his former place of work. This special arrangement ceases to apply, however, to any worker who subsequently takes a job at another place of work.*

21. The law does not protect anyone who pickets without permission on or inside any part of premises which are private property. The law will not, therefore, protect pickets who trespass, or those who organise such trespass, from being sued in the civil courts.

Trade union officials

22. For the reasons described in Section F of this Code, it may be helpful to the orderly organisation and conduct of picketing for a trade union official[3] to be present on a picket line where his members are picketing. *The law provides that it is lawful for a trade union official to picket at any place of work provided that:*

(i) *he is accompanying members of his trade union who are picketing lawfully at or near their own place of work; and*

(ii) *he personally represents those members.*

NOTES

3 *The law defines an "official of the union" as a person who is an officer of the union (or of a branch or section of the union), or who, not being such an officer, is a person elected or appointed in accordance with the rules of the union to be a representative of its members (or some of them), including any person so elected or appointed who is an employee of the same employer as the members, or one or more of the members, whom he is elected to represent.* This could include, for example, a shop steward.

23. If these conditions are satisfied, then a trade union official has the same legal protection as other pickets who picket lawfully at or near their own place of work. *However, the law provides that an official—whether a lay official or an employee of the union—is regarded for this purpose as representing only those members of his union whom he has been specifically* appointed or elected to represent. An official cannot, therefore, claim that he represents a group of members simply because they belong to his trade union. He must represent and be responsible for them in the normal course of his trade union duties. For example, it is lawful for an official—such as a shop steward—who represents members at a particular place of work to be present on a picket line where those members are picketing lawfully; for a branch official to be present only where members of his branch are lawfully picketing; for a national official who represents a particular trade group or section within the union, to be present wherever members of that trade group or section are lawfully picketing; for a regional official to be present only where members of his region are lawfully picketing; and for a national official such as a general secretary or president who represents the whole union to be present wherever any members of his union are picketing lawfully.

Lawful purposes of picketing

24. In no circumstances does a picket have power, under the law, to require other people to stop, or to compel them to listen or to do what he asks them to do. A person who decides to cross a picket line must be allowed to do so. *In addition, the law provides a remedy for any union member who is disciplined by his union because he has crossed a picket line.*[4]

NOTES

4 *A member disciplined for crossing a picket line is "unjustifiably disciplined"; the remedy for unjustifiable discipline is by complaint to an industrial tribunal.* (See also paragraphs 60–61 in Section F of this Code.)

25. *The **only** purposes of picketing declared lawful in statute are:*

— *peacefully obtaining and communicating information: and*

— *peacefully persuading a person to work or not to work.*

26. The law allows pickets to seek to explain their case to those entering or leaving the picketed premises, and/or to ask them not to enter or leave the premises where the dispute is taking place. This may be done by speaking to people, or it may involve the distribution of leaflets or the carrying of banners or placards putting the pickets' case. **In all cases, however, any such activity must by carried out *peacefully*.**

27. The law protects peaceful communication and persuasion. It does not give pickets, anyone organising or participating in any activity associated with picketing, or anyone organising a picket, protection against civil proceedings being brought against them for any conduct occurring during the picketing, or associated activity, which amounts to a separate civil wrong such as:

— unlawful threat or assault;

— harassment (i e threatening or unreasonable behaviour causing fear or apprehension to those in the vicinity);

— obstruction of a path, road, entrance or exit to premises;
— interference (e g because of noise or crowds) in the rights of those in neighbouring properties (i e "private nuisance");
— trespassing on private property.

28. Both individual pickets, and anyone—including a union—organising a picket or associated activity, should be careful not to commit such civil wrongs. It is possible, for example, that material on placards carried by pickets—or, for that matter, by those involved in activities associated with picketing—could be defamatory or amount to a threat or harassment. Pickets will also have no legal protection if they do or say things, or make offensive gestures at people, which amount to unlawful threat or harassment. Section C of this Code explains that such actions may also give rise to prosecution under the criminal law.

29. Similarly, if the noise or other disturbance caused to residents of an area by pickets, or by those associated with picketing activity, amounts to a civil wrong, those involved or responsible are not protected by the law from proceedings being brought against them.

30. Similar principles apply in respect of any breach of the criminal law by pickets, or their organiser. As explained in Section C of this Code, a picket, or anyone involved in an associated activity, who threatens or intimidates someone, or obstructs an entrance to a workplace, or causes a breach of the peace, commits a criminal offence. Where pickets commit a criminal offence, then in many circumstances they will not be acting peacefully; consequently, any immunity under the civil law will be lost.

Seeking redress

31. An employer, a worker, or anyone else who is party to a contract which is, or may be, broken or interfered with by unlawful picketing has a civil law remedy. He may apply to the court for an order[5] preventing, or stopping the unlawful picketing, or its organisation. Such a person may also claim damages from those responsible where the activities of the unlawful picket have caused him loss. An order can be sought against the person—which could include a particular trade union or unions—on whose instructions or advice the unlawful picketing is taking place, or will take place.

NOTES

[5] An injunction in England and Wales; an interdict in Scotland.

32. In making an order, the court has authority to require a trade union which has acted unlawfully to take such steps as are considered necessary to ensure that there is no further call for, or other organisation of, unlawful picketing. An order may be granted by the court on an interim basis, pending a full hearing of the case.

33. If a court order is made, it can apply not only to the person or union named in the order, but to anyone else acting on his behalf or on his instructions. Thus an organiser of unlawful picketing cannot avoid liability, for example, merely by changing the people on the unlawful picket line from time to time.

34. Similarly, anyone who is wronged in any other way by a picket can seek an order from the court to get the unlawful act stopped or prevented, and/or for damages. Thus, for example, if picketing, or associated activities, give rise to unlawful disturbance to residents in the vicinity, one or more of the residents so affected can apply to the court for such an order and/or for damages. Such proceedings might be taken against individual pickets, or the person—including a union where applicable—responsible for the unlawful act.

35. If a court is not obeyed, or is ignored, those who sought it can go back to court and ask to have those concerned declared in contempt of court. Anyone who is found to be in contempt of court may face heavy fines, or other penalties, which the court may consider appropriate. For example, a union may be deprived of its assets through sequestration, where the union's funds are placed in the control of a person appointed by the court who may, in particular, pay any fines or legal costs arising from the court proceedings. Similarly, if a person knows that such an order had been made against someone, or some union, and yet aids and abets that person to disobey or ignore the order, he may also be found to be acting in contempt of court and liable to be punished by the court.

Determining whether a union is responsible

36. Pickets will usually attend at a place of work for the purpose of persuading others not to work, or not to work normally, and may thereby be inducing them to breach, or interfere with the performance of, contracts. The law lays down rules which determine whether a union will be held liable for any such acts of inducement which are unlawful.

37. *The law provides that a union will be held responsible for such an unlawful act if it is done, authorised or endorsed by:*

(*a*) *the union's principal executive committee, president, or general secretary;*

(*b*) *any person given power under the union's own rules to do, authorise or endorse acts of the kind in question; or*

(*c*) *any other committee of the union, or any official of the union*[6]*—including those who are employed by the union, and those, like shop stewards, who are not.*[7]

A union will be held responsible for such an act by such a body or person regardless of any provisions to the contrary in its own rules, or anything in any other contract or rule of law.

NOTES

[6] See footnote at paragraph 22 for the relevant definition of "official". *In this case, however, an act will also be taken to have been done by an "official of the union" if it was done (or authorised or endorsed) by a group of persons, or any member of a group, to which such an official belonged at the relevant time if the group's purposes included organising or co-ordinating industrial action.*

[7] *However, if an act which is done (or authorised or endorsed) by a union committee or official is "effectively repudiated" by the union's principal executive committee, president or general secretary, the union will not be held responsible in law. In order to avoid liability in this way, the act concerned must be repudiated by any of these as soon as reasonably practicable after it has come to their knowledge. In addition, the union must, without delay:*

(*a*) *give written notice of the repudiation to the committee or official in question; and*

(*b*) *do its best to give individual written notice of the fact and date of the repudiation to: (i) every member of the union who it has reason to believe is taking part – or might otherwise take part – in industrial action as a result of the act; and (ii) the employer of every such member.*

38. Pickets may, of course, commit civil wrongs other than inducing breach, or interference with the performance, of contracts. The question of whether a union will be held responsible for those wrongs will be determined according to common law principles of liability, rather than by reference to the rules described in paragraph 37 above.

The need for a ballot

39. If what is done in the course of picketing amounts to a call for industrial action, and is an act for which the union is responsible in law, the union can only have the protection of statutory immunity if it has first held a properly-conducted secret ballot.

40. *The law requires that entitlement to vote in such a ballot must be given to all the union members who it is reasonable at the time of the ballot for the union to believe will be called upon to take part in, or continue with, the industrial action, and to no other member. The ballot must produce a majority of those voting which is in favour of taking, or continuing with, industrial action.* These, and other requirements of the law in respect of such ballots, are restated in the statutory Code of Practice "Trade Union Ballots on Industrial Action (1st Revision)".

[4513]

Section C. Picketing and the Criminal Law

41. If a picket commits a criminal offence he is just as liable to be prosecuted as any other member of the public who breaks the law. The immunity provided under the civil law does not protect him in any way.

42. The criminal law protects the rights of every person to go about his lawful daily business free from interference by others. No one is under any obligation to stop when a picket asks him to do so, or, if he does stop, to comply with a request, for example, not to go into work. Everyone has the right, if he wishes to do so, to cross a picket line in order to go into his place of work or to deliver or collect goods. A picket may exercise peaceful persuasion, but if he goes beyond that and tries by means other than peaceful persuasion to deter another person from exercising those rights he may commit a criminal offence.

43. *Among other matters, it is a criminal offence for pickets (as for others):*

— *to use threatening, abusive or insulting words or behaviour, or disorderly behaviour within the sight or hearing of any person—whether a worker seeking to cross a picket line, an employer, an ordinary member of the public, or the police—likely to be caused harassment, alarm or distress by such conduct;*

— *to use threatening, abusive or insulting words or behaviour towards any person with intent to cause fear of violence or to provoke violence;*

— *to use or threaten unlawful violence;*

— *to obstruct the highway or the entrance to premises or to seek physically to bar the passage of vehicles or persons by lying down in the road, linking arms across or circling in the road, or jostling or physically restraining those entering or leaving the premises;*

— *to be in possession of an offensive weapon;*
— *intentionally or recklessly to damage property;*
— *to engage in violent, disorderly or unruly behaviour or to take any action which is likely to lead to a breach of the peace;*
— *to obstruct a police officer in the execution of his duty.*

44. A picket has no right under the law to require a vehicle to stop or to be stopped. The law allows him only to ask a driver to stop by words or signals. A picket may not physically obstruct a vehicle if the driver decides to drive on or, indeed, in any other circumstances. A driver must—as on all other occasions—exercise due care and attention when approaching or driving past a picket line, and may not drive in such a manner as to give rise to a reasonable foreseeable risk of injury.

[4514]

Section D. Role of the Police

45. It is not the function of the police to take a view of the merits of a particular trade dispute. They have a general duty to uphold the law and keep the peace, whether on the picket line or elsewhere. The law gives the police discretion to take whatever measures may reasonable be considered necessary to ensure that picketing remains peaceful and orderly.

46. The police have no responsibility for enforcing the civil law. An employer cannot require the police to help in identifying the pickets against whom he wishes to seek an order from the civil court. Nor is it the job of the police to enforce the terms of an order. Enforcement of an order on the application of a plaintiff is a matter for the court and its officer. The police may, however, decide to assist the officers of the court if they think there may be a breach of the peace.

47. As regards the **criminal law** the police have considerable discretionary powers to limit the numbers of pickets at any one place where they have reasonable cause to fear disorder.[8] The law does not impose a specific limit on the number of people who may picket at any one place; nor does this Code affect in any way the discretion of the police to limit the number of people on a particular picket line. It is for the police to decide, taking into account all the circumstances, whether the number of pickets at any particular place provides reasonable grounds for the belief that a breach of the peace is likely to occur. If a picket does not leave the picket line when asked to do so by the police, he is liable to be arrested for obstruction either of the highway or of a police officer in the execution of his duty if the obstruction is such as to cause, or be likely to cause, a breach of the peace.

[4515]

NOTES

[8] In *Piddington v Bates (1960)* the High Court upheld the decision of a police constable in the circumstances of that case to limit the number of pickets to two.

Section E. Limiting Numbers of Pickets

48. Violence and disorder on the picket line is more likely to occur if there are excessive numbers of pickets. Wherever large numbers of people with strong feelings are involved there is danger that the situation will get out of control, and that those concerned will run the risk of committing an offence, with consequent arrest and prosecution, or of committing a civil wrong which exposes them, or anyone organising them, to civil proceedings.

49. This is particularly so wherever people seek by sheer weight of numbers to stop others going into work or delivering or collecting goods. In such cases, what is intended is not peaceful persuasion, but obstruction or harassment—if not intimidation. Such a situation is often described as "mass picketing". In fact, it is not picketing in its lawful sense of an attempt at peaceful persuasion, and may well result in a breach of the peace or other criminal offences.

50. Moreover, anyone seeking to demonstrate support for those in dispute should keep well away from any picket line so as not to create a risk of a breach of the peace or other criminal offence being committed on that picket line. Just as with a picket itself, the numbers involved is any such demonstration should not be excessive, and the demonstration should be conducted lawfully. *Section 14 of the Public Order Act 1986 provides the police with the power to impose conditions (for example, as to numbers, location and duration) on public* *assemblies of 20 or more people where the assembly is likely to result in serious public disorder; or serious damage to property; or serious disruption to the life of the community; or if its purpose is to coerce.*

51. Large numbers on a picket line are also likely to give rise to fear and resentment amongst those seeking to cross that picket line, even where no criminal offence is committed. They exacerbate disputes and sour relations not only between management and employees but between the pickets and their fellow employees. Accordingly pickets and their organisers should ensure that in general the number of pickets does not exceed six at any entrance to, or exit from, a workplace; frequently a smaller number will be appropriate.

[4516]

Section F. Organisation of Picketing

52. Sections B and C of this Code outline aspects of the civil law and the criminal law, as they may apply to pickets, and to anyone, including a trade union, who organises a picket. While it is possible that a picket may be entirely "spontaneous", it is much more likely that it will be organised by an identifiable individual or group.

53. Paragraphs 36–38 in Section B of this Code describe how to identify whether a trade union is, in fact, responsible in terms of civil law liability, for certain acts. As explained in these paragraphs, the law means, for example, that if such an act takes place in the course of picketing, and if a trade union official has done, authorised or endorsed the act, then the official's union will be responsible in law unless the act is "effectively repudiated" by the union's national leadership.

Functions of the picket organiser

54. Wherever picketing is "official" (ie organised by a trade union), an experienced person, preferably a trade union official who represents those picketing, should always be in charge of the picket line. He should have a letter of authority from his union which he can show to the police officers or to people who want to cross the picket line. Even when he is not on the picket line himself he should be available to give the pickets advice if a problem arises.

55. A picket should not be designated as an "official" picket unless it is actually organised by a trade union. Nor should pickets claim the authority and support of a union unless the union is prepared to accept the consequent responsibility. In particular, union authority and support should not be claimed by the pickets if the union has, in fact, repudiated calls to take industrial action made, or being made, in the course of the picketing.

56. Whether a picket is "official" or "unofficial", an organiser of pickets should maintain close contact with the police. Advance consultation with the police is always in the best interests of all concerned. In particular the organiser and the pickets should seek directions from the police on the number of people who should be present on the picket line at any one time and on where they should stand in order to avoid obstructing the highway.

57. The other main functions of the picket organiser should include ensuring that:

— the pickets understand the law and are aware of the provisions of this Code, and that the picketing is conducted peacefully and lawfully;

— badges or armbands, which authorised pickets should wear so that they are clearly identified, are distributed to such pickets and are worn while they are picketing;

— workers from other places of work do not join the picket line, and that any offers of support on the picket line from outsiders are refused;

— the number of pickets at any entrance to, or exit from, a place of work is not so great as to give rise to fear and resentment amongst those seeking to cross that picket line (see paragraph 51 in Section E of this Code);

— close contact with his own union office (if any), and with the officers of other unions if they are involved in the picketing, is established and maintained;

— such special arrangements as may be necessary for essential supplies, services or operations (see paragraphs 62–64 in Section G of this Code) are understood and observed by the pickets.

Consultations with other trade unions

58. Where several unions are involved in a dispute, they should consult each other about the organisation of any picketing. It is important that they should agree how the picketing is to be carried out, how many pickets there should be from each union, and who should have overall responsibility for organising them.

Right to cross picket lines

59. Everyone has the right to decide for himself whether he will cross a picket line. Disciplinary action should not be taken or threatened by a union against a member on the grounds that he has crossed a picket line.

60. *If a union disciplines any member for crossing a picket line, the member will have been "unjustifiably disciplined". In such a case, the individual can make a complaint to an industrial tribunal. If the tribunal finds the complaint well-founded, it will make a declaration to that effect.*

61. *If the union has not lifted the penalty imposed on the member, or if it has not taken all necessary steps to reverse anything done in giving effect to the penalty, an application for compensation should be made to the Employment Appeal Tribunal (EAT). In any other case, the individual can apply to an industrial tribunal for compensation. The EAT or tribunal will award whatever compensation it considers just and equitable in all the circumstances, subject to a specified maximum amount. Where the application is made to the EAT, there will normally be a specified minimum award.*

[4517]

Section G. Essential Supplies, Services and Operations

62. Pickets, and anyone organising a picket should take very great care to ensure that their activities do not cause distress, hardship or inconvenience to members of the public who are not involved in the dispute. Particular care should be taken to ensure that the movement of essential goods and supplies, the carrying out of essential maintenance of plant and equipment, and the provision of services essential to the life of the community are not impeded, still less prevented.

63. The following list of essential supplies and services is provided as an illustration of the kind of activity which requires special protection to comply with the recommendations in paragraph 62 above. However, **the list is not intended to be comprehensive**. The supplies and services which may need to be protected in accordance with these recommendations could cover different activities in different circumstances. Subject to this *caveat*, "essential supplies, services and operations" include:

— the production, packaging, marketing and/or distribution of medical and pharmaceutical products;

— the provision of supplies and services essential to health and welfare institutions, e g hospitals, old people's homes;

— the provision of heating fuel for schools, residential institutions, medical institutions and private residential accommodation;

— the production and provision of other supplies for which there is a crucial need during a crisis in the interests of public health and safety (e g chlorine, lime and other agents for water purification; industrial and medical gases; sand and salt for road gritting purposes);

— activities necessary to the maintenance of plant and machinery;

— the proper care of livestock;

— necessary safety procedures (including such procedures as are necessary to maintain plant and machinery);

— the production, packaging, marketing and/or distribution of food and animal feeding stuffs;

— the operation of essential services, such as police, fire, ambulance, medical and nursing services, air safety, coastguard and air sea rescue services, and services provided by voluntary bodies (e g Red Cross and St John's ambulances, meals on wheels, hospital car service), and mortuaries, burial and cremation services.

64. Arrangements to ensure these safeguards for essential supplies, services and operations should be agreed in advance between the pickets, or anyone organising the picket, and the employer, or employers, concerned.

[4518]–[4528]

ACAS CODE OF PRACTICE 2
DISCLOSURE OF INFORMATION TO TRADE UNIONS FOR COLLECTIVE BARGAINING PURPOSES (1998)

NOTES

This revised Code was issued on 28 October 1997, and was brought into force on 5 February 1998 by the Employment Protection Code of Practice (Disclosure of Information) Order 1998, SI 1998/45. It replaces the similarly named Code of 1977.

Authority: Trade Union and Labour Relations (Consolidation) Act 1992, s 201. For the legal status of this Code, see s 207 of the 1992 Act at **[692]**.

Text in bold type summarises statutory provisions on the disclosure of information, while practical guidance is set out in ordinary type. Notes are as in the Code.

Introduction

1. Under the Trade Union and Labour Relations (Consolidation) Act 1992 the Advisory, Conciliation and Arbitration Service (ACAS) may issue Codes of Practice containing such practical guidance as the Service thinks fit for the purpose of promoting the improvement of industrial relations. In particular, the Service has a duty to provide practical guidance on the information to be disclosed by employers to trade union representatives in accordance with sections 181 and 182 of that Act, for the purposes of collective bargaining.

2. The Act and the Code apply to employers operating in both the public and private sectors of industry. They do not apply to collective bargaining between employers' associations and trade unions, although the parties concerned may wish to follow the guidelines contained in the Code.

3. **The information which employers may have a duty to disclose under section 181 is information which it would be in accordance with good industrial relations practice to disclose. In determining what would be in accordance with good industrial relations practice, regard is to be had to any relevant provisions of the Code.** However, the Code imposes no legal obligations on an employer to disclose any specific item of information. Failure to observe the Code does not by itself render anyone liable to proceedings, but the Act requires any relevant provisions to be taken into account in proceedings before the Central Arbitration Committee.[1]

[4529]

NOTES

[1] Trade Union and Labour Relations (Consolidation) Act 1992, sections 181(2)(b), 181(4) and 207(1) and (2).

This Code replaces the Code of Practice on Disclosure of Information to Trade Unions for Collective Bargaining Purposes, issued by the Service in 1977.

Provisions of the Act

4. **The Act places a general duty on an employer who recognises an independent trade union to disclose, for the purposes of all stages of collective bargaining about matters, and in relation to descriptions of workers, in respect of which the union is recognised by him, information requested by representatives of the union. The representative of the union is an official or other person authorised by the union to carry on such collective bargaining.**

5. **The information requested has to be in the employer's possession, or in the possession of any associated employer, and must relate to the employer's undertaking. The information to be disclosed is that without which a trade union representative would be impeded to a material extent in bargaining and which it would be in accordance with good industrial relations practice to disclose for the purpose of collective bargaining. In determining what is in accordance with good industrial relations practice, any relevant provisions of this Code are to be taken into account.**

6. **No employer is required to disclose any information which: would be against the interests of national security; would contravene a prohibition imposed by or under an enactment; was given to an employer in confidence, or was obtained by the employer in consequence of the confidence reposed in him by another person; relates to an individual unless he has consented to its disclosure; would cause substantial injury to the undertaking (or national interest in respect of Crown employment) for reasons other than its effect on collective bargaining; or was obtained for the purpose of any legal proceedings.**

7. **In providing information the employer is not required to produce original documents for inspection or copying. Nor is he required to compile or assemble information which would entail work or expenditure out of reasonable proportion to the value of the information in the conduct of collective bargaining. The union representative can request that the information be given in writing by the employer or be confirmed in writing. Similarly, an employer can ask the trade union representative to make the request for information in writing or confirm it in writing.**

8. If the trade union considers that an employer has failed to disclose to its representatives information which he was required to disclose by section 181 of the Act, or to confirm such information in writing in accordance with that section, it may make a complaint to the Central Arbitration Committee. The Committee may ask the Advisory, Conciliation and Arbitration Service to conciliate. If conciliation does not lead to a settlement of the complaint, the Service shall inform the Committee accordingly who shall proceed to hear and determine the complaint. If the complaint is upheld by the Committee, it is required to specify the information that should have been disclosed or confirmed in writing, the date the employer failed to disclose, or confirm in writing, any of the information and a period of time within which the employer ought to disclose the information, or confirm it in writing. If the employer does not disclose the information, or confirm it in writing, within the specified time, the union (except in relation to Crown employment and Parliamentary staff) may present a further complaint to the Committee and may also present a claim for improved terms and conditions. If the further complaint is upheld by the Committee, an award, which would have effect as part of the contract of employment, may be made against the employer on the terms and conditions specified in the claim, or other terms and conditions which the Committee considers appropriate.

[4530]

Providing information

9. The absence of relevant information about an employer's undertaking may to a material extent impede trade unions in collective bargaining, particularly if the information would influence the formulation, presentation or pursuance of a claim, or the conclusion of an agreement. The provision of relevant information in such circumstances would be in accordance with good industrial relations practice.

10. To determine what information will be relevant, negotiators should take account of the subject-matter of the negotiations and the issues raised during them; the level at which negotiations take place (department, plant, division, or company level); the size of the company; and the type of business the company is engaged in.

11. Collective bargaining within an undertaking can range from negotiations on specific matters arising daily at the workplace affecting particular sections of the workforce, to extensive periodic negotiations on terms and conditions of employment affecting the whole workforce in multi-plant companies. The relevant information and the depth, detail and form in which it could be presented to negotiators will vary accordingly. Consequently, it is not possible to compile a list of items that should be disclosed in all circumstances. Some examples of information relating to the undertaking which could be relevant in certain collective bargaining situations are given below:

(i) *Pay and benefits*: principles and structure of payment systems; job evaluation systems and grading criteria; earnings and hours analysed according to work-group, grade, plant, sex, out-workers and homeworkers, department or division, giving, where appropriate, distributions and make-up of pay showing any additions to basic rate or salary; total pay bill; details of fringe benefits and non-wage labour costs.

(ii) *Conditions of service*: policies on recruitment, redeployment, redundancy, training, equal opportunity, and promotion; appraisal systems; health, welfare and safety matters.

(iii) *Manpower*: numbers employed analysed according to grade, department, location, age and sex; labour turnover; absenteeism; overtime and short-time; manning standards; planned changes in work methods, materials, equipment or organisation; available manpower plans; investment plans.

(iv) *Performance*: productivity and efficiency data; savings from increased productivity and output, return on capital invested; sales and state of order book.

(v) *Financial*: cost structures; gross and net profits; sources of earnings; assets; liabilities; allocation of profits; details of government financial assistance; transfer prices; loans to parent or subsidiary companies and interest charged.

12. These examples are not intended to represent a check list of information that should be provided for all negotiations. Nor are they meant to be an exhaustive list of types of information as other items may be relevant in particular negotiations.

[4531]

Restrictions on the duty to disclose

13. Trade unions and employers should be aware of the restrictions on the general duty to disclose information for collective bargaining.[2]

14. Some examples of information which if disclosed in particular circumstances might cause substantial injury are: cost information on individual products; detailed analysis of proposed investment, marketing or pricing policies; and price quotas or the make-up of tender prices. Information which has to be made available publicly, for example under the Companies Acts, would not fall into this category.

15. Substantial injury may occur if, for example, certain customers would be lost to competitors, or suppliers would refuse to supply necessary materials, or the ability to raise funds to finance the company would be seriously impaired as a result of disclosing certain information. The burden of establishing a claim that disclosure of certain information would cause substantial injury lies with the employer.

[4532]

NOTES

[2] Trade Union and Labour Relations (Consolidation) Act 1992, section 182. See paragraphs 6 and 7 of this Code.

Trade unions' responsibilities

16. Trade unions should identify and request the information they require for collective bargaining in advance of negotiations whenever practicable. Misunderstandings can be avoided, costs reduced, and time saved, if requests state as precisely as possible all the information required, and the reasons why the information is considered relevant. Requests should conform to an agreed procedure. A reasonable period of time should be allowed for employers to consider a request and to reply.

17. Trade unions should keep employers informed of the names of the representatives authorised to carry on collective bargaining on their behalf.

18. Where two or more trade unions are recognised by an employer for collective bargaining purposes they should co-ordinate their requests for information whenever possible.

19. Trade unions should review existing training programmes or establish new ones to ensure negotiators are equipped to understand and use information effectively.

[4533]

Employers' responsibilities[3]

20. Employers should aim to be as open and helpful as possible in meeting trade union requests for information. Where a request is refused, the reasons for the refusal should be explained as far as possible to the trade union representatives concerned and be capable of being substantiated should the matter be taken to the Central Arbitration Committee.

21. Information agreed as relevant to collective bargaining should be made available as soon as possible once a request for the information has been made by an authorised trade union representative. Employers should present information in a form and style which recipients can reasonably be expected to understand.

[4534]

NOTES

[3] The Stock Exchange has drawn attention to the need for employers to consider any obligations which they may have under their Listing Agreement.

Joint arrangements for disclosure of information

22. Employers and trade unions should endeavour to arrive at a joint understanding on how the provisions on the disclosure of information can be implemented most effectively. They should consider what information is likely to be required, what is available, and what could reasonably be made available. Consideration should also be given to the form in which the information will be presented, when it should be presented and to whom. In particular, the parties should endeavour to reach an understanding on what information could most appropriately be provided on a regular basis.

23. Procedures for resolving possible disputes concerning any issues associated with the disclosure of information should be agreed. Where possible such procedures should normally be related to any existing arrangements within the undertaking or industry and the complaint, conciliation and arbitration procedure described in the Act.[4]

[4535]–[4561]

NOTES

[4] Trade Union and Labour Relations (Consolidation) Act 1992, sections 183 to 185. See paragraph 8 of this Code.

CODE OF PRACTICE: FOR ALL EMPLOYERS ON THE AVOIDANCE OF RACE DISCRIMINATION IN RECRUITMENT PRACTICE WHILE SEEKING TO PREVENT ILLEGAL WORKING (2001) (NOTE)

NOTES

This Code was made under the Asylum and Immigration Act 1996, s 8A (repealed by the Immigration, Asylum and Nationality Act 2006, ss 26, 61, Sch 3, as from 29 February 2008) and came into force on 2 May 2001 (see the Immigration (Restrictions on Employment) (Code of Practice) Order 2001, SI 2001/1436). At 6 April 2008, no Order revoking SI 2001/1436 had been made, but the 2001 Code is effectively superseded by the Border and Immigration Agency Code of Practice: Guidance for Employers on the Avoidance of Unlawful Discrimination in Employment Practice while seeking to prevent Illegal Working at **[4772]**.

[4562]–[4631]

COMMISSION FOR RACIAL EQUALITY CODE OF PRACTICE ON THE DUTY TO PROMOTE RACIAL EQUALITY (2002)

NOTES

This Code was issued by the Commission for Racial Equality under the Race Relations Act 1976, s 71C (as inserted by the Race Relations (Amendment) Act 2000 and repealed as noted below). Following Parliamentary approval, the Code was brought into effect by the Race Relations Act 1976 (General Statutory Duty: Code of Practice) Order 2002 (SI 2002/1435) with effect from 30 May 2002.

The statutory provision under which this Code was made was repealed by the Equality Act 2006, ss 40, 91, Sch 3, paras 21, 30, Sch 4; however the Code is continued in force by s 42(3) of the 2006 Act (see **[1685]**). As to the dissolution of the Commission for Racial Equality and the transfer of its property, rights and liabilities etc to the Commission for Equality and Human Rights, see the Equality Act 2006, ss 36–38 at **[1679]–[1681]**.

Much of the Code relates to the application of the general statutory duty to the provision of public services and in particular education; Section 4 (in Part II) and much of Section 6 (in Part III) have been omitted as outside the scope of this work. The bodies subject to the general statutory duty are listed in Appendix 1; as this reproduces Sch 1A to the 1976 Act (at **[314]** et seq) it is omitted. Similarly Appendix 2 (Bodies required to publish a race equality scheme) reproduces Sch 1 to the Race Relations Act 1976 (Statutory Duties) Order 2001, SI 2001/3458 (at **[2711]**) and is accordingly omitted. Appendix 3 is included; it lists the bodies subject to the duty to undertake ethnic monitoring of employees, comprising the bodies listed in Sch 1 to the Act *other than* those listed in Sch 3 to the 2001 Order. Appendices 4 and 6 are omitted as outside the scope of this work; Appendix 5, which lists those bodies within Sch 1A to the Act which are Scottish public authorities, is also omitted.

The equivalent Code for Scotland 'The Duty to Promote Racial Equality in Scotland' (2003) (applicable to those bodies subject to the authority of the Scottish Parliament) is omitted for reasons of space.

Permission to reproduce this Code was kindly granted by the Commission for Racial Equality.

GLOSSARY

IN THIS CODE, THE WORDS BELOW HAVE THE MEANINGS SHOWN BENEATH THEM.

action plan

a practical and realistic plan, with an agreed timetable, showing how an authority is planning to meet its duties.

PART 4

assessing impact

a systematic way of finding out whether a policy (or proposed policy) affects different racial groups differently. This may include obtaining and analysing data, and consulting people, including staff, on the policy.

complementary

this refers to the fact that the three parts of the general duty support each other and may, in practice, overlap. However, they are different, and public authorities should consider each one individually.

consultation

asking for views on policies or services from staff, colleagues, service-users, or the general public. Different circumstances call for different types of consultation. For example, consultation includes meetings, focus groups, reference groups, citizens' juries, surveys, and questionnaires.

direct discrimination

treating one person less favourably than another on racial grounds (see page 5). Direct discrimination is unlawful under the Race Relations Act.

disciplinary procedures

the arrangements and procedures used to discipline staff. These may include informal and formal disciplinary measures.

duty to promote race equality

the general duty, unless the context suggests otherwise.

ethnic monitoring

the process you use to collect, store and analyse data about people's ethnic backgrounds.

focus groups, reference groups and citizens' juries

various forms of face-to-face consultation with members of the public, service-users, or others.

formal investigation

an investigation by the CRE under sections 49–52 of the Race Relations Act. The investigation can be either a "named person" investigation or a general investigation.

- A "named person" investigation can be carried out if the CRE suspects that an organisation is discriminating on racial grounds. The CRE can ask the organisation for documents and information. If the CRE is satisfied that unlawful discrimination has taken place, or is taking place, the CRE can issue a "non-discrimination notice".
- A general investigation can be carried out, without suspicion of discrimination, to examine practice within an area of activity. At the end of the investigation, the CRE can make recommendations.

functions

the full range of a public authority's duties and powers.

further and higher education institution

the governing body of an institution in the further and higher education sectors (as defined in sections 91(3) and 91(5) of the Further and Higher Education Act).

general duty

the duty as given in section 71(1) of the Race Relations Act (see chapter 3, paragraph 3.1).

grievance procedures

arrangements or procedures for dealing with grievances, such as complaints about bullying, harassment or discrimination; or appeals against decisions on promotion or appraisal marks.

indirect racial discrimination

occurs when a rule or condition which is applied equally to everyone—

- can be met by a considerably smaller proportion of people from a particular racial group;
- is to the disadvantage of that group; and
- cannot be justified on non-racial grounds.

All three conditions must apply.

judicial review

a claim to the High Court or the Scottish Court of Sessions asking the court to review the way a public authority or certain other bodies made a decision. The court will not decide the merits of the decision, only whether it is legal. The court can ask the authority to reconsider the matter.

monitoring

the process of collecting, analysing and evaluating information, to measure performance, progress or change.

non-devolved authorities

public authorities in Scotland whose functions and powers remain the responsibility of the Westminster Parliament rather than the Scottish Parliament.

obligatory

this refers to the fact that public authorities are legally bound to meet the general duty, and must make race equality a central part of their functions.

orders

ministerial directions to apply the law, or to change the way it applies.

performance assessment procedures

formal and informal staff appraisals that are likely to affect career development, pay and benefits.

policies

the formal and informal decisions about how a public authority carries out its duties and uses its powers.

positive action

action permitted by the Race Relations Act that allows a person to—

- provide facilities to meet the special needs of people from particular racial groups in relation to their training, education or welfare (section 35); and
- target job training at people from racial groups that are under-represented in a particular area of work, or encourage them to apply for such work (sections 37 and 38).

promoting race equality

public authorities should have "due regard to the need", in carrying out their functions, to—

- tackle unlawful racial discrimination;
- promote equality of opportunity; and
- promote good relations between people from different racial groups.

proportionate

this refers to the fact that the weight given to race equality should be proportionate to its relevance to a particular function. This approach may mean giving greater consideration and resources to functions or policies that have most effect on the public, or on the authority's employees.

PART 4

public appointments

appointments to the boards of public bodies. These are bodies that have a role in the processes of national government, but operate at arm's length from government.

public authority

a body named, defined or described in schedule 1A to the Race Relations Act or, depending on the context, a body named, defined or described in one of the schedules to the Race Relations Act 1976 (Statutory Duties) Order 2001.

public functions

functions that affect, or are likely to affect, the public or a section of the public. While only the courts can decide this, public functions would normally not include internal management or contractual matters such as employing staff; purchasing goods, works or services; or buying or selling premises. This term is used to refer to those authorities that are bound by the duties only in relation to their public functions (for example professional representative organisations, such as the Royal College of Surgeons, or broadcasting authorities).

public procurement

the contractual or other arrangements that a public authority makes to obtain goods, works or services from an outside organisation.

publish

making publicly available; for example by producing a written document for distribution.

race equality policy

a written statement of an educational establishment's policy on race equality, which is put into practice and monitored.

race equality scheme

a timetabled and realistic plan, setting out an authority's arrangements for meeting the general and specific duties.

Race Relations Act

the Race Relations Act 1976, as amended by the Race Relations (Amendment) Act 2000.

racial group

a group of people defined by their race, colour, nationality (including citizenship), ethnic or national origins.

racial grounds

reasons of race, colour, nationality (including citizenship), ethnic or national origins.

relevance

this refers to the fact that race equality will be more relevant to some public functions than others. Relevance is about how far a function or policy affects people, as members of the public, and as employees of the authority.

schedule

an appendix to legislation, such as schedule 1A to the Race Relations Act. This schedule lists the public authorities to which the general duty applies.

school

the governing body of an educational establishment maintained by local education authorities in England and Wales, or of a city technology college, a city college for technology of the arts, or a city academy.

Scottish public authority

a public authority whose functions can only be carried out in, or in relation to, Scotland.

specific duty

a duty imposed by the Race Relations Act 1976 (Statutory Duties) Order 2001.

statutory code of practice

a document such as this one, which offers practical guidance on the law, has been approved by Parliament, and is admissible in evidence in a court of law.

statutory duties

duties, either general or specific, which an authority is legally bound to meet.

training

a wide range of career development opportunities, which could include informal in-house training as well as more formal courses.

victimisation

punishing or treating someone unfairly because they have made a complaint of racial discrimination, or are thought to have done so; or because they have supported someone else who has made a complaint of racial discrimination. Victimisation is defined as unlawful discrimination under the Race Relations Act.

[4632]

PART I
PROMOTING RACE EQUALITY IN ALL LISTED PUBLIC AUTHORITIES

1—PROMOTING RACE EQUALITY

Introduction

1.1. The Race Relations Act (see the glossary) places a general duty on a wide range of public authorities to promote race equality. This duty means that authorities (listed in appendix 1 of this code) must have due regard to the need to—

(a) eliminate unlawful racial discrimination;
(b) promote equality of opportunity; and
(c) promote good relations between people of different racial groups.

1.2. Most public authorities are bound by this duty. Many of them provide major public services, such as education or health. Some of them (for example professional representative organisations, such as the Royal College of Surgeons, or broadcasting authorities) are bound by this duty only so far as their public functions (see the glossary) are concerned.

1.3. The duty aims to make the promotion of race equality central to the way public authorities work. Promoting race equality will improve the way public services are delivered for everyone. In most cases, these authorities should be able to use their existing arrangements – such as those for policy making – to meet the duty's requirements. This should help to avoid any unnecessary or duplicated work.

Benefits of the duty

1.4. The duty will help public authorities to make steady progress in achieving race equality. In relation to policy development and service delivery, the duty will—

(a) encourage policy makers to be more aware of possible problems;
(b) contribute to more informed decision making;
(c) make sure that policies are properly targeted;
(d) improve the authority's ability to deliver suitable and accessible services that meet varied needs;
(e) encourage greater openness about policy making;
(f) increase confidence in public services, especially among ethnic minority communities;
(g) help to develop good practice; and
(h) help to avoid claims of unlawful racial discrimination.

1.5. The duty of public authorities to promote race equality in *employment* will—
(a) help to make the authority's workforce more representative of the communities it serves;
(b) attract able staff;
(c) avoid losing or undervaluing able staff;
(d) improve staff morale and productivity;
(e) improve the way staff are managed;
(f) help to develop good practice; and
(g) help to avoid claims of unlawful racial discrimination.

Purpose of the Code

1.6. Public authorities can decide how they will meet their duty to promote race equality. The Race Relations Act gives the CRE the power to issue codes of practice, with the approval of Parliament.

1.7. This code offers practical guidance to public authorities on how to meet their duty to promote race equality. It includes guidance on both the general duty (see 1.1) and specific duties imposed by the Home Secretary. The code's aim is to help public authorities to adopt good practice and to eliminate racial discrimination. The code should also help the public understand what public authorities have to do, and the role that the public can play.

1.8. The specific duties imposed by order of the Home Secretary came into effect on **3 December 2001**. Public authorities bound by these duties (see appendices 2, 3 and 4) were required to have properly timetabled and realistic plans for meeting these duties in place by **31 May 2002**.

1.9. This code applies to public authorities in England and Wales (see appendix 1) and to "non-devolved" public authorities in Scotland (see the glossary and appendix 1). Chapter 6 of this code applies only to the governing bodies of educational institutions in England and Wales. The Code of Practice for Scotland will apply to devolved public authorities in Scotland (see the glossary).

Nature of the Code

1.10. This code of practice is a "statutory" code. This means that it has been approved by Parliament. It also means that the code is admissible in evidence in any legal action, and a court or tribunal should take the code's recommendations into account. On its own, the code does not place any legal obligations on public authorities. It is not a complete statement of the law, as only the courts can give this. If a public authority does not follow the code's guidance, it may need to be able to show how it has otherwise met its legal obligations under the general duty and any specific duties.

How to use this Code

1.11. The code is divided into five parts, seven chapters and six appendices.
(a) Part I (chapters 2 and 3) applies to all listed public authorities, including schools, and further and higher education institutions.
(b) Part II (chapters 4 and 5) deals with promoting race equality in certain public authorities other than educational institutions.
(c) Part III (chapter 6) deals with promoting race equality in educational institutions.
(d) Part IV (chapter 7) deals with the CRE's role, including enforcing this code.
(e) Part V (appendices 1 to 6) lists the public authorities that are bound by the general duty (appendix 1), the public authorities that are required to publish a race equality scheme (appendix 2), the public authorities bound by the employment duty (appendix 3), the public authorities bound by the duties for educational institutions (appendix 4), Scottish public authorities (appendix 5), and other guidance published by the CRE (appendix 6).

[4633]

2—PROMOTING RACE EQUALITY

The legal framework

2.1. The Race Relations Act (see the glossary) defines direct and indirect discrimination, and victimisation (see the glossary for each of these terms). It outlaws racial discrimination in employment, training, education, housing, public appointments, and the provision of goods, facilities and services. The Race Relations (Amendment) Act 2000 came into force on 2 April 2001 and since then the Race Relations Act (the Act) has covered all the functions of public authorities (with just a few exceptions).

2.2. Section 71(1) of the Act places a general duty on listed public authorities (see appendix 1). The Act also gives the Home Secretary power to make orders placing specific duties on all or some of these authorities (section 71(2)). Scottish ministers have a similar power over Scottish public authorities (section 71B(1); see the glossary). Under the Race Relations Act 1976 (Statutory Duties) Order 2001, the specific duties discussed in this code came into force on **3 December 2001**.

2.3. The Act gives the CRE enforcement powers over the specific duties imposed by the Home Secretary and Scottish ministers. The Act also gives the CRE power to issue codes of practice containing practical guidance on how public authorities can meet the general duty (see chapter 3) and specific duties (see chapters 4, 5 and 6). This is a statutory code, issued for this purpose.

The general duty to promote race equality

2.4. This general duty applies to all public authorities listed in schedule 1A to the Act (see appendix 1). The duty's aim is to make the promotion of race equality central to the work of the listed public authorities.

Specific duties to promote race equality

2.5. Specific duties have been placed on some public authorities responsible for delivering important public services. The duties involve making arrangements that will help these authorities to meet the general duty to promote race equality.

(a) The public authorities listed in appendix 2 must prepare and publish a race equality scheme. This scheme should set out the "functions" or "policies" (see the glossary for both terms) that are relevant to meeting the general duty, and the arrangements that will help to meet the duty in the areas of policy and service delivery (see chapter 4).

(b) The public authorities listed in appendix 3 must monitor their employment procedures and practice (see chapter 5). Some of these authorities have to produce a race equality scheme. They may find it useful to include the arrangements they make to meet their employment duties in their race equality schemes.

(c) The educational institutions listed in appendix 4 have to prepare a race equality policy and put in place arrangements for meeting their specific duties on policy and employment (see chapter 6).

2.6. Public authorities that introduce effective arrangements, as required under the specific duties, should be able to show that they are meeting the general duty to promote race equality. Taking action to promote race equality should give authorities the evidence they need to show that they are meeting the general duty.

2.7. Chapters 4, 5, and 6 give guidance on the specific duties.

Liability under the Race Relations Act

2.8. Public authorities are responsible for meeting their general and specific duties. Within each public authority, this responsibility will rest with the groups or individuals who are liable (legally responsible) for the authority's acts or failure to act.

Private or voluntary organisations carrying out a public authority's functions

2.9. When a public authority has a contract or other agreement with a private company or voluntary organisation to carry out any of its functions (see the glossary), and the duty to promote race equality applies to those functions, the public authority remains responsible for meeting the general duty and any specific duties that apply to those functions. The authority should therefore consider the arrangements it will need. If the authority's race equality duties are relevant to the functions it is contracting out, it may be appropriate to incorporate those duties among the performance requirements for delivery of the service. For example, a contractor could be required to monitor service users by their racial group, to make sure the authority is meeting its duties. This would not involve requirements concerning the contractor's internal practices. Whatever action the authority takes, it must be consistent with the policy and legal framework for public procurement.

2.10. In addition to specifications for the general duty and any specific duties, public authorities may promote race equality by encouraging contractors to draw up policies that will help them (contractors) to avoid unlawful discrimination, and promote equality of opportunity. Such encouragement should only be within a voluntary framework, once contracts have been awarded, rather than by making specific criteria or conditions part of the selection process. Public authorities should bear in mind that the general duty does not override other laws or regulations on public procurement. In particular, as above, whatever action the authority takes must be consistent with the policy and legal framework for public procurement.

Partnership

2.11. Public authorities should take account of their general duty to promote race equality – and any specific duties – when they work with other public, private or voluntary organisations. There is no similar obligation on private or voluntary-sector partners.

2.12. Public authorities that are involved in partnership work with other public authorities, or with private or voluntary-sector organisations, are still responsible for meeting their general duty to promote race equality, and any specific duties.

2.13. In practice, this will mean that a public authority working within a partnership will need to seek agreement from its partners to arrangements for planning, funding and managing joint work that will allow it to meet its statutory race equality duties. Public authorities should reflect their partnership work in their race equality schemes.

Inspecting and auditing public authorities

2.14. Agencies that audit or inspect public authorities are bound by the duty to promote race equality. These agencies need to consider how the duty fits with their inspection or audit obligations. In most cases, inspection and audit bodies should be able to use their existing inspection arrangements to promote race equality.

[4634]

3—PROMOTING RACE EQUALITY

The general duty

3.1. This chapter explains what public authorities can do to meet the general duty to promote race equality. The duty is set out in section 71(1) of the Race Relations Act (the Act) and it applies to every public authority listed in schedule 1A to the Act (see appendix 1 of this code). Section 71(1) says—

(1) Every body or other person specified in Schedule 1A or of a description falling within that Schedule shall, in carrying out its functions, have due regard to the need

(a) to eliminate unlawful racial discrimination; and

(b) to promote equality of opportunity and good relations between persons of different racial groups.*

* For immigration and nationality functions, the general duty does not include the words "equality of opportunity and" (section 71A(1)).

Guiding principles

3.2. Four principles should govern public authorities' efforts to meet their duty to promote race equality.

(a) Promoting race equality is obligatory for all public authorities listed in schedule 1A to the Act (see appendix 1).

(b) Public authorities must meet the duty to promote race equality in all relevant functions.

(c) The weight given to race equality should be proportionate to its relevance.

(d) The elements of the duty are complementary (which means they are all necessary to meet the whole duty).

"Obligatory"

3.3. Public authorities listed in schedule 1A to the Act must make race equality a central part of their functions (such as planning, policy making, service delivery, regulation, inspection, enforcement, and employment). The general duty does not tell public authorities how to do their work, but it expects them to assess whether race equality is relevant to their functions. If it is, the authority should do everything it can to meet the general duty. The duty should underpin all policy and practice, and it should encourage improvement. It is not necessarily a new responsibility for the authority, just a more effective way of doing what it already does.

"Relevant"

3.4. Race equality will be more relevant to some functions than others. Relevance is about how much a function affects people, as members of the public or as employees of the authority. For example, a local authority may decide that race equality is more relevant to raising educational standards than to its work on highway maintenance. Public authorities should therefore assess whether, and how, race equality is relevant to each of their functions. A public authority may decide that the general duty does not apply to some of its functions; for example those that are purely technical, such as traffic control or weather forecasting.

"Proportionate"

3.5. Under section 71(1) of the Act, public authorities are expected to have "due regard" to the three parts of the duty to promote race equality (see 1.1). This means that the weight given to race equality should be proportionate to its relevance to a particular function. In practice, this approach may mean giving greater consideration and resources to functions or policies that have most effect on the public, or on the authority's employees. The authority's concern should be to ask whether particular policies could affect different racial groups in different ways, and whether the policies will promote good race relations.

3.6. "Due regard" does not mean that race equality is less important when the ethnic minority population is small. It is also not acceptable for a public authority to claim that it does not have enough resources to meet the duty. This is because meeting the general duty is a statutory requirement. In practice, this means that public authorities should draw on work they already do to promote race equality, and build on it, using their existing administrative systems and processes and adjusting their plans and priorities, where necessary.

3.7. The general duty is a continuing duty. What a public authority has to do to meet it may change over time as its functions or policies change, or as the communities it serves change.

"Complementary"

3.8. The general duty has three parts—
(a) eliminating unlawful racial discrimination;
(b) promoting equality of opportunity; and
(c) promoting good relations between people of different racial groups.

3.9. These three parts support each other. And, in practice, they may overlap (for example, promoting equality of opportunity may also eliminate or prevent unlawful racial discrimination, *and* promote good race relations). However, it is important to remember that the three parts are different, and that achieving one of them may not lead to achieving all three. For example, a new equal opportunities policy that is not clearly explained when it is introduced may improve equality of opportunity, but it may also damage race relations and create resentment if staff do not understand how it benefits everyone.

3.10. Public authorities should consider and deal with all three parts of the general duty.

How to meet the general duty

3.11. Public authorities should consider the following four steps to meet the general duty.
(a) Identify which of their functions and policies are relevant to the duty, or, in other words, affect most people.
(b) Put the functions and policies in order of priority, based on how relevant they are to race equality.
(c) Assess whether the way these 'relevant' functions and policies are being carried out meets the three parts of the duty.
(d) Consider whether any changes need to be made to meet the duty, and make the changes.

Identifying relevant functions

3.12. To identify relevant functions, a public authority will find it useful, first, to make a list of all its functions, including employment. It should then assess how relevant each function is to each part of the general duty. As shown in paragraph 3.4, some functions may, by their nature, have little or no relevance.

3.13. A public authority should consider setting priorities, and giving priority to those functions that are most relevant to race equality.

Assessing impact and considering change

3.14. To assess the impact its functions and policies have on race equality, the authority may find it useful to draw up a clear statement of the aims of each function or policy. It should then consider whether it has information about how different racial groups are affected by the function or policy, as employees or users (or possible users) of services. The authority should also consider whether its functions and policies are promoting good race relations. The authority could get this information from various sources; for example previous research, records of complaints, surveys, or local meetings. These methods should help public authorities to assess which of their services are used by which racial groups, or what people think of their services, and whether they are being provided fairly to people from different racial groups. This kind of evidence should help public authorities to decide what they might need to do to meet all three parts of the general duty.

3.15. Public authorities may also need to consider adapting their existing information systems, so that they can provide information about different racial groups and show what progress the authority is making on race equality.

3.16. To assess the effects of a policy, or the way a function is being carried out, public authorities could ask themselves the following questions.

(a) Could the policy or the way the function is carried out have an adverse impact on equality of opportunity for some racial groups? In other words, does it put some racial groups at a disadvantage?
(b) Could the policy or the way the function is carried out have an adverse impact on relations between different racial groups?
(c) Is the adverse impact, if any, unavoidable? Could it be considered to be unlawful racial discrimination? Can it be justified by the aims and importance of the policy or function? Are there other ways in which the authority's aims can be achieved without causing an adverse impact on some racial groups?
(d) Could the adverse impact be reduced by taking particular measures?
(e) Is further research or consultation necessary? Would this research be proportionate to the importance of the policy or function? Is it likely to lead to a different outcome?

3.17. If the assessment suggests that the policy, or the way the function is carried out, should be modified, the authority should do this to meet the general duty.

[4635]

PART II
PROMOTING RACE EQUALITY IN LISTED PUBLIC AUTHORITIES OTHER THAN EDUCATIONAL INSTITUTIONS

4—PROMOTING RACE EQUALITY

Specific duties: policy and service delivery

(*Outside the scope of this work.*)

5—PROMOTING RACE EQUALITY

Specific duties: employment

5.1. The specific duty on employment applies to most of the public authorities bound by the general duty (see appendix 3). Schools and further and higher education institutions are not bound by the employment duty, as they have separate employment responsibilities (see chapter 6). A few, mainly advisory, agencies are also not bound by the employment duty.

5.2. Articles 5(1), 5(2), and 5(3) of the Race Relations Act 1976 (Statutory Duties) Order 2001 say the following—

5.—(1) A person to which this article applies shall,

(a) before 31st May 2002, have in place arrangements for fulfilling, as soon as is reasonably practicable, its duties under paragraph (2); and
(b) fulfil those duties in accordance with such arrangements.

(2) It shall be the duty of such a person to monitor, by reference to the racial groups to which they belong,

(a) the numbers of—

(i) staff in post, and

(ii) applicants for employment, training and promotion, from each such group, and

(b) where that person has 150 or more full-time staff, the numbers of staff from each such group who—

(i) receive training;

(ii) benefit or suffer detriment as a result of its performance assessment procedures;

(iii) are involved in grievance procedures;

(iv) are the subject of disciplinary procedures; or

(v) cease employment with that person.

(3) Such a person shall publish annually the results of its monitoring under paragraph (2).

5.3. Public authorities that have to produce race equality schemes may find it useful to include their arrangements for meeting their employment duty in their race equality schemes.

5.4. The specific duties on employment are designed to provide a framework for measuring progress in equality of opportunity in public-sector employment. The specific duties are also aimed at providing monitoring information to guide initiatives that could lead to a more representative public-sector workforce. For example, these initiatives could include setting recruitment targets for under-represented racial groups, or targeting management development courses at racial groups that are under-represented at certain levels. The specific duties on employment set minimum standards. Other issues may also be relevant for good employment practice. This will depend on local circumstances.

5.5. Ethnic monitoring (see the glossary) is central to providing a clear picture of what is happening during the authority's employment cycle – from applying for a job and joining the authority to leaving it. Monitoring helps to measure overall progress and to show whether the authority's equal opportunities policies are effective. Monitoring is the essential tool to assess progress – or lack of it – in removing barriers to equality of opportunity in the public services.

5.6. It is important that the authority explains to applicants and existing staff why they are monitoring employment. People will normally only have to give information about their racial group voluntarily, and the authority should explain the conditions of the Data Protection Act 1998 (about processing this information) to them.

5.7. Wherever possible, the authority should build monitoring information into the information systems it already uses. The authority may be able to publish its monitoring results each year through its existing reporting systems. In its published results, the authority should explain how it is dealing with trends or problems highlighted by its monitoring. The authority may also find it useful to combine and analyse ethnic monitoring data with other data; for example on sex and disability.

5.8. To help meet the specific duty on employment, public authorities should—

(a) collect ethnic monitoring data; and

(b) publish the results of the monitoring each year.

5.9. To check that they are meeting the general duty, public authorities may want to—

(a) analyse the data to find any patterns of inequality; and

(b) take whatever steps are needed to remove barriers and promote equality of opportunity.

5.10. If the monitoring shows that current employment policies, procedures and practice are leading to unlawful racial discrimination, the authority should take steps to end the discrimination. As a first step, the authority should examine each of its procedures closely to find out where and how discrimination might be happening, and then consider what changes to introduce.

5.11. On the other hand, the monitoring may show that current policies, procedures and practice have an adverse impact on equality of opportunity or good race relations (even though they are not causing unlawful discrimination). If this is the case, the authority should consider changing its policies or procedures so that they still meet the same aims, but do not harm equality of opportunity or race relations.

Positive action

5.12. If monitoring reveals that some racial groups are under-represented in the workforce, the authority could consider using "positive action" (see the glossary). This allows employers and others to target their job training and recruitment efforts at those groups that are under-represented in a particular area of work. However, positive action does not allow discrimination when deciding who will be offered a job.

Ethnic categories and the 2001 census

5.13. Public authorities are encouraged to use the same ethnic classification system as the one used in the 2001 census. Some authorities already have systems in place. If an authority chooses to collect more detailed information, it should make sure that the categories are the same as, or similar to, those used in the 2001 census. Any extra ethnic categories it adds to reflect its particular circumstances should fit in with the 2001 census categories.

5.14. Public authorities should make realistic and timetabled plans to adapt their ethnic monitoring systems to meet the specific duties.

5.15. The 2001 census used different ethnic classifications for England and Wales, and Scotland.

[4636]

PART III
PROMOTING RACE EQUALITY IN EDUCATIONAL INSTITUTIONS

6—PROMOTING RACE EQUALITY

Specific duties: educational institutions

Introduction

6.1. This part of the code is written mainly for education providers. They are as follows.

(a) The governing bodies of maintained schools (see the glossary) and other educational institutions maintained by a local education authority (LEA) – in other words, all community, foundation and voluntary schools, and special schools maintained by the LEA.

(b) The governing bodies of City Technology Colleges, City Colleges for Technology or the Arts, and City Academies.

(c) The governing bodies of further education institutions (see the glossary).

(d) The governing bodies of higher education institutions (see the glossary).

6.2. Schools and further and higher education institutions must all meet the general duty. Chapter 3 explains what they need to do to meet the duty. The Home Secretary has also placed specific duties on schools (see 6.7–6.22), and on further and higher education institutions (see 6.23–6.44), to help them to meet the general duty.

6.3. The specific duties on employment, described in chapter 5, do not apply directly to schools. The main responsibility for monitoring employment rests with LEAs. All schools are expected to give their LEA ethnic monitoring data on their staff from their regular returns, so that the LEA can meet the duty.

6.4. Further and higher education institutions have other employment duties, which are described in paragraphs 6.39 to 6.41. As well as these duties, further and higher education institutions will have to give bodies such as the higher education funding councils (see 6.45 – 6.48 for details of the specific duties placed on these bodies), monitoring information about their teaching staff.

6.5. The aim of the general duty is to make race equality central to the way public authorities carry out their functions (see the glossary). Promoting race equality should be a central part of all policy development, service delivery and employment practice.

6.6–6.22. (*Outside the scope of this work.*)

Further and higher education institutions

6.23–6.34. (*Outside the scope of this work.*)

Monitoring admission, recruitment and progress

6.35. Under the duty, further and higher education institutions must monitor, by racial group, student admission and progress, and staff recruitment and career progress (see 6.23).

6.36. Monitoring involves collecting information to measure an institution's performance and effectiveness. The results may suggest how the institution can improve.

6.37. The institution should monitor all stages of the student admissions process, from applications to outcomes. To help interpret the information, the institution might also consider monitoring other areas that could have an adverse impact on students from some racial groups, such as—

(a) choice of subject;
(b) home or international status; and
(c) selection methods.

6.38. The institution should monitor all students' achievements and progress. To help interpret the information, the institution might also consider monitoring other areas that could have an adverse impact on students from some racial groups, such as—
(a) student numbers, transfers and drop-outs;
(b) different methods of assessing students;
(c) work placements;
(d) the results of programmes targeted at people from specific racial groups; and
(e) bullying and racial harassment.

6.39. The institution should monitor all activities that relate to staff recruitment and selection, and to career development and opportunities for promotion. It might consider monitoring for each department as well as the whole institution. This is likely to include—
(a) selecting and training panel members;
(b) applications and appointments;
(c) success rates for the different selection methods;
(d) permanent, temporary or fixed-term appointments; and
(e) home or international status (for institutions that recruit internationally).

6.40. The institution should identify areas where career progress could be affected and monitor those. They might include—
(a) staff, by their grade and type of post;
(b) staff, by their length of service;
(c) staff training and development, including applications and selection, if appropriate;
(d) the results of training and career-development programmes or strategies that target staff from particular racial groups;
(e) staff appraisals; and
(f) staff promotion, including recruitment methods and criteria for choosing candidates.

6.41. The institution will find it useful to assess its monitoring information regularly. This will allow it to evaluate the progress it is making in meeting its race equality targets and aims. These assessments will help the institution to—
(a) highlight any differences between staff and students from different racial groups;
(b) ask why these differences exist;
(c) review how effective its current targets and aims are;
(d) decide what more it can do to improve the performance of students from different racial groups (including positive action as allowed in section 35 of the Race Relations Act; see the glossary) and to improve the recruitment and progression of staff from different racial groups (again including positive action as allowed in sections 37 and 38 of the Race Relations Act; see the glossary); and
(e) decide what further action it may need to take to meet the three parts of the general duty.

6.42–6.44. (*Outside the scope of this work.*)

Employment duties of bodies with specific responsibilities for education

6.45. Local education authorities (LEAs) have a duty to monitor by racial group, for all the maintained schools in their area, the following—
(a) staff in post; and
(b) applicants for employment, training and promotion;
(c) for schools with 150 or more full-time staff, or equivalent, the number of staff—
  (i) receiving training;
  (ii) benefiting, or suffering a detriment, as a result of performance assessment procedures;
  (iii) involved in grievance procedures;
  (iv) subject to disciplinary procedures; and
  (v) ending employment with these schools.

6.46. LEAs have a duty to take reasonably practicable steps to publish, each year, the results of this monitoring.

6.47. The Department for Education and Skills has a duty to—
(a) monitor, by racial group, the number of teaching staff from each racial group at all maintained schools;
(b) take reasonably practicable steps to use information provided by LEAs for that purpose; and

(c) take reasonably practicable steps to publish, each year, the results of this monitoring.

6.48. The Learning and Skills Council for England, the Higher Education Funding Councils for England and Wales, and the National Council for Education and Training for Wales have a duty to—

(a) monitor, by racial group, the number of teaching staff at all the establishments for which they are responsible; and
(b) take reasonably practicable steps to publish, each year, the results of this monitoring.

[4637]

PART IV
ROLE OF THE COMMISSION FOR RACIAL EQUALITY

7—PARTNERSHIP AND ENFORCEMENT

Role of the Commission for Racial Equality

7.1. The Commission for Racial Equality (CRE) was set up under the Race Relations Act as an independent statutory agency. The CRE reports every year to the Home Secretary, but it is not formally part of the Home Office. The duties of the CRE, as set out in the Act, are to—

(a) work towards eliminating discrimination;
(b) promote equality of opportunity and good relations between persons of different racial groups; and
(c) review the workings of the Act.

7.2. The CRE has both promotional and enforcement powers, and both apply to its work on the duty to promote race equality. This chapter explains how the CRE will use both these powers to help promote race equality.

Partnership

Helping public authorities to meet their duty

7.3. The CRE will—

(a) give practical advice;
(b) work with main parts of the public sector, including the inspectorates, to develop good practice; and
(c) monitor and spread good practice.

Providing practical guidance

7.4. The CRE has issued non-statutory supplementary guides to this code, for public authorities, schools and further and higher education institutions (see appendix 6).

7.5. The CRE will continue to work with public authorities to help them to meet their general and specific duties.

Developing and monitoring good practice

7.6. The CRE works with public authorities to develop and share good practice in a number of ways, for example by—

(a) sharing and demonstrating good practice;
(b) supporting training;
(c) giving information and advice;
(d) updating guidance and publishing other material;
(e) promoting good practice; and
(f) identifying poor practice.

Enforcement

7.7. The CRE is committed to using the full range of its enforcement powers appropriately. The CRE has a new power under the Act to enforce the specific duties to promote race equality.

The general duty

7.8. If a public authority does not meet the general duty, its actions (or failure to act) can be challenged by a claim to the High Court for judicial review (see the glossary). A claim for judicial review can be made by a person or group of people with an interest in the matter, or by the CRE.

Specific duties

7.9. If a public authority does not meet any of its specific duties, it could face enforcement action by the CRE under section 71D of the Race Relations Act.

7.10. If the CRE is satisfied that a public authority has failed (or is failing) to meet any of its specific duties, the CRE can serve a "compliance notice" on that authority. This notice will state that the authority must meet its duty and tell the CRE, within 28 days, what it has done, or is doing, to meet its duty.

7.11. In the compliance notice, the CRE can also ask the authority to give it written information showing that it has met its duty. The notice will state the time by which the CRE should receive the information. The CRE cannot ask for more information than a public authority would have to provide during High Court proceedings in England, or in the Scottish Court of Session.

7.12. If, three months after a compliance notice has been served, the CRE considers that the authority has still not met one or more of its specific duties referred to in the notice, the CRE can apply to the county court (in England) or sheriff court (in Scotland) for an order to obey the notice.

7.13. If the compliance notice says that the authority must provide information, and it has not done so within the given time – or the CRE believes that the authority will not provide the information – the CRE can apply to the county court (in England) or sheriff court (in Scotland) for an order saying that the authority must provide the relevant information.

7.14. The county court or sheriff court may grant the order in the terms that the CRE applied for, or in more limited terms. If the court makes an order and the authority does not keep to it, the authority may be found in contempt of court.

Unlawful discrimination

7.15. The Act gives individuals the right to take legal action against unlawful racial discrimination. The Act also gives the CRE the power to take legal action against certain acts of unlawful discrimination. This power includes the power to carry out formal investigations (see the glossary).

CRE codes of practice

7.16. This and other statutory codes of practice that the CRE issues under the Act are admissible in evidence in court. A court will be expected to take the code of practice into account if it seems relevant to any matter the court is ruling on. Public authorities do not have to follow the guidance in this code of practice. However, they are expected to meet the general duty and any specific duties by which they are bound.

[4638]

(*Appendix 1* (*Public authorities bound by the general duty*), *Appendix 2* (*Public authorities required to publish a race equality scheme*) *omitted: see the introductory notes to this Code.*)

APPENDIX 3
PUBLIC AUTHORITIES BOUND BY THE EMPLOYMENT DUTY

Ministers of the Crown and government departments

(1) A Minister of the Crown or government department

(2) Sub-paragraph (1) does not include the Security Service, the Intelligence Service or the Government Communications Headquarters

Scottish Administration

(1) An office-holder in the Scottish Administration (within the meaning given by section 126(7)(a) of the Scotland Act 1998)

(2) Members of the staff of the Scottish Administration (within the meaning given by section 126(7)(b) of that Act)

National Assembly for Wales

(1) The National Assembly for Wales

(2) An Assembly subsidiary as defined by section 99(4) of the Government of Wales Act 1998

Armed Forces

Any of the naval, military or air forces of the Crown

National Health Service: England and Wales

A health authority established under section 8 of the National Health Service Act 1977

A National Health Service trust established under section 5 of the National Health Service and Community Care Act 1990

A primary care trust established under section 16A of that Act

A special health authority established under section 11 of that Act

Local government

A body corporate established pursuant to an order under section 67 of the Local Government Act 1985 (transfer of functions to successors of residuary bodies, etc)

A body corporate established pursuant to an order under section 22 of the Local Government Act 1992 (residuary bodies)

The Broads Authority established by section 1 of the Norfolk and Suffolk Broads Act 1988

Any charter trustees constituted under section 246 of that Act

The Common Council of the City of London in its capacity as a local authority or port health authority

The Council of the Isles of Scilly

A fire authority constituted by a combination scheme under section 5 or 6 of the Fire Services Act 1947

The Greater London Authority

An internal drainage board which is continued in being by virtue of section 1 of the Land Drainage Act 1991

A joint authority established under Part IV of the Local Government Act 1985 (fire services, civil defence and transport)

A joint authority established under section 21 of the Local Government Act 1992

A joint board which is continued in being by virtue of section 263(1) of that Act

A joint committee constituted in accordance with section 102(1)(b) of the Local Government Act 1972

A joint planning board constituted for an area in Wales outside a National Park by an order under section 2(1B) of the Town and Country Planning Act 1990

A local authority (within the meaning of the Local Government Act 1972), namely
- (a) in England, a county council, a London borough council, a district council;
- (b) in Wales, a county council, a county borough council

A local probation board established under section 4 of the Criminal Justice and Court Services Act 2000

The London Development Agency

The London Fire and Emergency Planning Authority

A magistrates' courts committee established under section 27 of the Justices of the Peace Act 1997

A national park authority established by an order under section 63 of the Environment Act 1995

A passenger transport executive for a passenger transport area (within the meaning of Part II of the Transport Act 1968)

A port health authority constituted by an order under section 2 of the Public Health (Control of Disease) Act 1984

A regional development agency established under the Regional Development Agencies Act 1998 (other than the London Development Agency)

The Sub-Treasurer of the Inner Temple or the Under-Treasurer of the Middle Temple, in his capacity as a local authority

Transport for London

A waste disposal authority established by virtue of an order under section 10(1) of the Local Government Act 1985

Education

The Adult Learning Inspectorate

The British Educational Communication and Technology Agency

The Construction Industry Training Board

The Engineering Construction Industry Training Board

The General Teaching Council for Scotland

The General Teaching Council for Wales

The Higher Education Funding Council for England

The Higher Education Funding Council for Wales

The Learning and Skills Council for England

The managers of a grant-aided school (within the meaning of section 135 of the Education (Scotland) Act 1980)

The National Council for Education and Training for Wales

The Qualifications and Curriculum Authority

The Qualifications, Curriculum and Assessment Authority for Wales

The Student Loans Company

The Teacher Training Agency

Housing bodies

A housing action trust established under Part III of the Housing Act 1988

The Housing Corporation

Police

The British Transport Police

A chief constable of a police force maintained under section 2 of the Police Act 1996

The Chief Constable for the Ministry of Defence Police appointed by the Secretary of State under section 1(3) of the Ministry of Defence Police Act 1987

The Commissioner of Police for the City of London

The Commissioner of Police of the Metropolis

The Common Council of the City of London in its capacity as a police authority

The Metropolitan Police Authority established under section 5B of the Police Act 1996

A police authority established under section 3 of the Police Act 1996

The Police Complaints Authority

The Police Information Technology Organisation

A selection panel for independent members of police authorities

The Service Authority for the National Crime Squad

The Service Authority for the National Criminal Intelligence Service

Health

The Commission for Health Improvement

The Council for Professions Supplementary to Medicine, in respect of its public functions

The Dental Practice Board
The English National Board for Nursing, Midwifery and Health Visiting
The Human Fertilisation and Embryology Authority
The Joint Committee on Postgraduate Training for General Practice
The National Biological Standards Board
The Public Health Laboratory Service Board
The Royal College of Anaesthetists, in respect of its public functions
The Royal College of General Practitioners, in respect of its public functions
The Royal College of Midwives, in respect of its public functions
The Royal College of Nursing, in respect of its public functions
The Royal College of Obstetricians and Gynaecologists, in respect of its public functions
The Royal College of Ophthalmologists, in respect of its public functions
The Royal College of Paediatrics and Child Health, in respect of its public functions
The Royal College of Pathologists, in respect of its public functions
The Royal College of Physicians, in respect of its public functions
The Royal College of Psychiatrists, in respect of its public functions
The Royal College of Radiologists, in respect of its public functions
The Royal College of Speech and Language Therapists, in respect of its public functions
The Royal College of Surgeons of England, in respect of its public functions
The Specialist Training Authority of the Medical Royal Colleges
The Welsh National Board for Nursing, Midwifery and Health Visiting

Libraries, museums and arts

The Arts Council of England
The Arts Council of Wales
The British Library
The British Museum
The British Tourist Authority
The Commission for Architecture and the Built Environment
The Countryside Council for Wales The Design Council
English Nature
The English Tourist Board
The Film Council
The Geffrye Museum
The Historic Buildings and Monuments Commission for England
The Historic Royal Palaces Trust
The Horniman Museum
The Imperial War Museum
The Library and Information Services Council (Wales)
The Millennium Commission
The Museum of London
The Museum of Science and Industry in Manchester
The National Endowment for Science, Technology and the Arts
The National Gallery

The National Heritage Memorial Fund

The National Library of Wales

The National Lottery Charities Board

The National Maritime Museum

National Museums and Galleries on Merseyside

National Museums and Galleries of Wales

The National Portrait Gallery

The Natural History Museum

The Registrar of Public Lending Right Resource: The Council for Museums, Archives and Libraries

The Royal Armouries

The Royal Botanic Gardens, Kew

The Royal Commission on Ancient and Historical Monuments of Wales

The Royal Commission on Historical Manuscripts

The Science Museum

Sir John Soane's Museum

Sport England

The Sports Council for Wales

The Tate Gallery

The UK Sports Council

The Victoria and Albert Museum

The Wales Tourist Board

The Wallace Collection

Public corporations and nationalised industries

The Bank of England, in respect of its public functions

The British Broadcasting Corporation, in respect of its public functions

The Broadcasting Standards Commission, in respect of its public functions

The Channel Four Television Corporation, in respect of its public functions

The Civil Aviation Authority

The Coal Authority

The Covent Garden Market Authority

A Customer Service Committee maintained under section 28 of the Water Industry Act 1991

The Independent Television Commission, in respect of its public functions

The Radio Authority, in respect of its public functions

Sianel Pedwar Cymru (Welsh Fourth Channel Authority), in respect of its public functions

The United Kingdom Atomic Energy Authority, in respect of its public functions

Regulatory, audit and inspection

The Advisory, Conciliation and Arbitration Service (ACAS)

The Association of Authorised Public Accountants

The Association of Certified Chartered Accountants

The Association of Child Psychotherapy

The Audit Commission for Local Authorities and the National Health Service in England and Wales

The British Hallmarking Council

The British Standards Institute

The Chartered Institute of Patent Agents, in respect of its public functions

The Council for Licensed Conveyancers, in respect of its public functions

The Engineering Council

The Financial Services Authority

The General Chiropractic Council

The General Council of the Bar of England and Wales, in respect of its public functions

The General Dental Council

The General Medical Council

The General Optical Council

The General Osteopathic Council

The General Social Care Council

The Insolvency Practitioners Association

The Institute of Chartered Accountants in England and Wales

The Institute of Legal Executives, in respect of its public functions

The Institute of Trade Mark Attorneys

The Law Society of England and Wales, in respect of its public functions

Her Majesty's Magistrates' Courts Service Inspectorate

The Master of the Court of the Faculties of the Archbishop of Canterbury, in respect of its public functions

The National Audit Office

The Royal Pharmaceutical Society of Great Britain, in respect of its statutory functions and the regulation of the pharmacy profession

The United Kingdom Central Council for Nursing, Midwifery and Health Visiting, in respect of its public functions

Research

The Alcohol Education and Research Council

The Apple and Pear Research Council

The Biotechnology and Biological Sciences Research Council

The Council for the Central Laboratory of the Research Councils

The Economic and Social Research Council

The Engineering and Physical Sciences Research Council

The Fire Service Research and Training Trust

The Horticultural Development Council

The Medical Research Council

The Natural Environment Research Council

The Particle Physics and Astronomy Research Council

Other bodies, etc

A board of visitors established under section 6(2) of the Prison Act 1952

The Britain-Russia Centre

The British Association for Central and Eastern Europe

The British Council

The British Potato Council

The British Waterways Board

The British Wool Marketing Board

The Children and Family Court Advisory and Support Service

The Commission for Racial Equality

The Community Development Foundation

The Criminal Injuries Compensation Authority

The Disability Rights Commission

The Electoral Commission

English Partnerships

The Environment Agency

The Equal Opportunities Commission

Food From Britain

The Gaming Board for Great Britain

The Gas and Electricity Consumer Council

The Great Britain-China Centre

The Health and Safety Commission

The Health and Safety Executive

The Home-Grown Cereals Authority

The Horserace Betting Levy Board

The Horserace Totalisator Board

The Information Commissioner

Investors in People UK

The Joint Nature Conservation Committee

The Legal Services Commission

The Local Government Commission for England

The Marshall Aid Commemoration Commission

The Meat and Livestock Commission

The Milk Development Council

The National Consumer Council

The National Forest Company

The National Radiological Protection Board

The New Opportunities Fund

The Northern Lighthouse Board

The Oil and Pipelines Agency

The Sea Fish Industry Authority

The Strategic Rail Authority

The Trinity House Lighthouse Service

A visiting committee appointed under section 152 of the Immigration and Asylum Act 1999 for an immigration detention centre

The Welsh Development Agency

The Welsh Language Board

The Westminster Foundation for Democracy

The Wine Standards Board of the Vintners' Company

The Youth Justice Board for England and Wales.

[4639]

(*Appendix 4* (*Public authorities bound by the duties for educational institutions*), *Appendix 5* (*Scottish public authorities*), *Appendix 6* (*Other guidance published by the CRE*) *omitted: see the introductory notes to this Code.*)

ACAS CODE OF PRACTICE 3
TIME OFF FOR TRADE UNION DUTIES AND ACTIVITIES (INCLUDING GUIDANCE ON TIME OFF FOR UNION LEARNING REPRESENTATIVES) (2003)

NOTES

This Code was originally issued by ACAS under the Employment Protection Act 1975, s 6 (repealed) and was brought into effect on 1 April 1978 (by SI 1977/2076). The present Code is the third reissue; earlier revisions came into effect on 13 May 1991 (by SI 1991/968) and 5 February 1998 (by SI 1998/46). The statutory authority for the making of the Code and its revision is TULR(C)A 1992, ss 199, 201 at **[684]**, **[686]**, and its legal status is, as for the other ACAS Codes, as set out in s 207 at **[692]**. This Code came into effect on 27 April 2003 (see the Employment Protection Code of Practice (Time Off) Order 2003, SI 2003/1191).

INTRODUCTION

1. Under section 199 of the Trade Union and Labour Relations (Consolidation) Act 1992 the Advisory, Conciliation and Arbitration Service (ACAS) has a duty to provide practical guidance on the time off to be permitted by an employer:

(a) to a trade union official in accordance with section 168 of the Trade Union and Labour Relations (Consolidation) Act 1992; and

(b) to a trade union member in accordance with section 170 of the Trade Union and Labour Relations (Consolidation) Act 1992.

Section 199 of the Act, as amended by the Employment Act 2002, also provides for ACAS to issue practical guidance on time off and training for Union Learning Representatives.

This Code, which replaces the Code of Practice issued by ACAS in 1998, is intended to provide such guidance.

The background

2. Since the Employment Protection Act 1975, trade union officials have had a statutory right to reasonable paid time off from employment to carry out trade union duties and to undertake trade union training. Union officials and members were also given a statutory right to reasonable unpaid time off when taking part in trade union activities. In 1989 restrictions were introduced on the range of issues for which paid time off for trade union duties could be claimed to those covered by recognition agreements between employers and trade unions. Additionally union duties must relate to the official's own employer and not, for example, to any associated employer. All the time off provisions were brought together in sections 168–170 of the Trade Union and Labour Relations (Consolidation) Act 1992. Section 43 of the Employment Act 2002 added a new right for Union Learning Representatives to take paid time off during working hours to undertake their duties and to undertake relevant training.

General purpose of the Code

3. The general purpose of the statutory provisions and this Code of Practice is to aid and improve the effectiveness of relationships between employers and trade unions. Employers and unions have a joint responsibility to ensure that agreed arrangements work to mutual advantage by specifying how reasonable time off for union duties and activities and for training will work. This may be particularly important in the case of Union Learning Representatives where the lack of such an understanding may result in duplication of functions concerning employees' training needs.

Structure of the Code

4. Section 1 of this Code provides guidance on time off for trade union duties. Section 2 deals with time off for training of trade union officials and offers guidance on sufficient training for Union Learning Representatives. Section 3 considers time off for trade union activities. In each case the amount and frequency of time off, and the purposes for which and any conditions subject to which time off may be taken, are to be those that are reasonable in all the circumstances. Section 4 describes the responsibilities which employers and trade unions share in considering reasonable time off. Section 5 notes the advantages of reaching formal agreements on time off. Section 6 deals with industrial action and Section 7 with methods of appeal.

5. The annex to this Code reproduces the relevant statutory provisions on time off. To help differentiate between these and practical guidance, the summary of statutory provisions relating to time off which appears in the main text of the Code is in **bold type**. Practical guidance is in ordinary type. While every effort has been made to ensure that the summary of the statutory provisions included in this Code is accurate, only the courts can interpret the law authoritatively.

Status of the Code

6. The provisions of this Code are admissible in evidence and may be taken into account in determining any question arising during employment tribunal proceedings relating to time off for trade union duties and activities. However, failure to observe any provision of the Code does not of itself render a person liable to any proceedings.

[4640]

SECTION 1
TIME OFF FOR TRADE UNION DUTIES

Entitlement

7. **Employees who are officials of an independent trade union recognised by their employer are to be permitted reasonable time off during working hours to carry out certain trade union duties.**

8. **An official is an employee who has been elected or appointed in accordance with the rules of the union to be a representative of all or some of the union's members in the particular company or workplace.**

9. **Officials are entitled to time off where the duties are concerned with:**

- **negotiations with the employer about matters which fall within section 178(2) of the Trade Union and Labour Relations (Consolidation) Act 1992 (TULR(C)A) and for which the union is recognised for the purposes of collective bargaining by the employer; or**
- **any other functions on behalf of employees of the employer which are related to matters falling within section 178(2) TULR(C)A and which the employer has agreed the union may perform.**

Matters falling within section 178(2) TULR(C)A are listed in the sub-headings of paragraph 11 below.

10. **An independent trade union is recognised by an employer when it is recognised to any extent for the purposes of collective bargaining. Where a trade union is not so recognised by an employer, employees have no statutory right to time off to undertake any duties except that of accompanying a worker at a disciplinary or grievance hearing** (see para 16).

Examples of trade union duties

11. **Subject to the recognition or other agreement, trade union officials should be allowed to take reasonable time off for duties concerned with negotiations or, where their employer has agreed, for duties concerned with other functions related to or connected with:**

(a) **terms and conditions of employment, or the physical conditions in which workers are required to work.** Examples could include:
- pay
- hours of work
- holidays and holiday pay
- sick pay arrangements

— pensions
— learning and training needs
— equal opportunities
— notice periods
— the working environment
— operation of digital equipment and other machinery;

(b) **engagement or non-engagement, or termination or suspension of employment or the duties of employment, of one or more workers.** Examples could include:
— recruitment and selection policies
— human resource planning
— redundancy and dismissal arrangements;

(c) **allocation of work or the duties of employment as between workers or groups of workers.** Examples could include:
— job grading
— job evaluation
— job descriptions
— flexible working practices
— family friendly policies;

(d) **matters of discipline.** Examples could include:
— disciplinary procedures
— arrangements for representing trade union members at internal interviews
— arrangements for appearing on behalf of trade union members, or as witnesses, before agreed outside appeal bodies or employment tribunals;

(e) **trade union membership or non-membership.** Examples could include:
— representational arrangements
— any union involvement in the induction of new workers;

(f) **facilities for officials of trade unions.** Examples could include any agreed arrangements for the provision of:
— accommodation
— equipment
— names of new workers to the union;

(g) **machinery for negotiation or consultation and other procedures.** Examples could include arrangements for:
— collective bargaining
— grievance procedures
— joint consultation
— communicating with members
— communicating with other union officials also concerned with collective bargaining with the employer.

12. The duties of an official of a recognised trade union must be connected with or related to negotiations or the performance of functions both in time and subject matter. Reasonable time off may be sought, for example, to:
— prepare for negotiations
— inform members of progress
— explain outcomes to members
— prepare for meetings with the employer about matters for which the trade union has only representational rights.

Union Learning Representatives

13. **Employees who are members of an independent trade union recognised by the employer can take reasonable time off to undertake the duties of a Union Learning Representative, provided that the union has given the employer notice in writing that the employee is a learning representative of the trade union and the training condition is met.** (See paras 22–27 for further information on the training condition.) **The functions for which time off as a Union Learning Representative is allowed are:**
— **analysing learning or training needs**
— **providing information and advice about learning or training matters**
— **arranging learning or training**
— **promoting the value of learning or training**
— **consulting the employer about carrying on any such activities**
— **preparation to carry out any of the above activities**
— **undergoing relevant training**

In practice, the roles and responsibilities of Union Learning Representatives will often vary by union and by workplace but will include one or more of these functions.

14. Many employers have in place well established training and development programmes for their employees. Union Learning Representatives should liaise with their employers to ensure that their respective training activities complement one another and that the scope for duplication is minimised.

Payment for time off for trade union duties

15. **An employer who permits officials time off for trade union duties must pay them for the time off taken. The employer must pay either the amount that the officials would have earned had they worked during the time off taken or, where earnings vary with the work done, an amount calculated by reference to the average hourly earnings for the work they are employed to do. There is no statutory requirement to pay for time off where the duty is carried out at a time when the official would not otherwise have been at work, but staff who work part time will be entitled to be paid if staff who work full time would be entitled to be paid. In all cases the amount of time off must be reasonable.**

Time off to accompany workers at disciplinary or grievance hearings

16. **Trade union officials are statutorily entitled to take a reasonable amount of paid time off to accompany a worker at a disciplinary or grievance hearing so long as they have been certified by their union as being capable of acting as a workers companion. The right to time off in these situations applies regardless of whether the certified person belongs to a recognised union or not although the worker being accompanied must be employed by the same employer.** Time off for an official or a certified person to accompany a worker of another employer is a matter for voluntary agreement between the parties concerned.

[4641]

SECTION 2
TRAINING OF OFFICIALS IN ASPECTS OF EMPLOYMENT RELATIONS AND EMPLOYEE DEVELOPMENT

Entitlement

17. **Employees who are officials of an independent trade union recognised by their employer are to be permitted reasonable time off during working hours to undergo training relevant to the carrying out of their trade union duties.[1] These duties must be concerned with:**

— **negotiations with the employer about matters which fall within section 178(2) TULR(C)A and for which the union is recognised to any extent for the purposes of collective bargaining by the employer; or**

— **any other functions on behalf of employees of the employer which are related to matters falling within section 178(2) TULR(C)A and which the employer has agreed the union may perform.**

Matters falling within section 178(2) TULR(C)A are set out in paragraph 11 above.

NOTES

[1] Section 1 of this Code gives a more complete summary of the statutory entitlement of officials to time off to undertake trade union duties.

18. **Employees who are Trade Union Learning Representatives are also permitted reasonable time off during working hours to undergo training relevant to their functions as a Union Learning Representative.**

What is relevant employment relations training?

19. **Training should be in aspects of employment relations relevant to the duties of an official.** There is no one recommended syllabus for training as an official's duties will vary according to:

— the collective bargaining arrangements at the place of work, particularly the scope of the recognition or other agreement

— the structure of the union

— the role of the official.

20. **The training must also be approved by the Trades Union Congress or by the independent trade union of which the employee is an official.**

21. Trade union officials are more likely to carry out their duties effectively if they possess skills and knowledge relevant to their duties. In particular, employers should be prepared to consider releasing trade union officials for initial training in basic representational skills as soon as possible after their election or appointment, bearing in mind that suitable courses may be infrequent. Reasonable time off could also be considered, for example:

— for further training particularly where the official has special responsibilities
— for training courses to develop the official's skills in representation and negotiation
— where there are proposals to change the structure and topics of negotiation about matters for which the union is recognised; or where significant changes in the organisation of work are being contemplated
— where legislative change may affect the conduct of employment relations at the place of work and may require the reconsideration of existing agreements.

Training for Union Learning Representatives

22. **Employees who are members of an independent trade union recognised by the employer are entitled to reasonable paid time off to undertake the functions of a Union Learning Representative. To qualify for paid time off the member must be sufficiently trained to carry out duties as a learning representative:**

— either at the time when their trade union gives notice to their employer in writing that they are a learning representative of the trade union
— or within six months of that date

23. In the latter case, the trade union is required to give the employer notice in writing that the employee will be undergoing such training and when the employee has done so to give the employer notice of that fact. It should be confirmed by the union in a letter that the training undertaken is sufficient to allow the Learning Representative to undertake their role and it is good practice for the union to give details of the training which has been completed and any previous training that has been taken into account. In the interests of good practice, the six month qualifying period during which an untrained Union Learning Representative must receive sufficient training to continue operating as a learning representative may be extended, with agreement, to take into account any significant unforeseen circumstances such as prolonged absence from work due to ill health, pregnancy or bereavement.

24. To satisfy this training requirement an employee will need to be able to demonstrate to their trade union that they have received sufficient training to enable them to operate competently in one or more of the following areas of activity relevant to their duties as a Union Learning Representative:

analysing learning or training needs;

— this could for example include understanding the different methods for identifying learning interests or needs, being able to effectively identify and record individual learning needs or being able to draw up a plan to meet identified learning requirements.

providing information and advice about learning or training matters;

— including, for example, the development of communication and interviewing skills
— knowledge of available opportunities, in order to be able to provide accurate information to members about learning opportunities within and outside the workplace
— the ability to 'signpost' members to other sources of advice and guidance where additional support is needed, for example, basic skills tutors or fuller in depth professional career guidance.

arranging and supporting learning and training;

— for example, obtaining and providing information on learning opportunities, supporting and encouraging members to access learning opportunities and helping to develop and improve local learning opportunities.

promoting the value of learning and training;

— some examples of this activity could be, understanding current initiatives for the development of learning and skills in the workplace, promoting the value of learning to members and within trade union networks and structures and working with employers to meet the learning and skill needs of both individuals and the organisation.

25. An employee could demonstrate to their trade union that they have received sufficient training to enable them to operate competently in one or more of these areas of activity by:

- completing a training course approved by the Trades Union Congress or by the independent trade union of which the employee is a Union Learning Representative, or by
- showing that they have previously gained the relevant expertise and experience to operate effectively as a learning representative.

In the latter case, previous experience and expertise gained in areas such as teaching, training, counselling, providing careers advice and guidance or human resource development, may well be relevant, as may periods of extensive on-the-job training and experience gained in shadowing an experienced Union Learning Representative.

26. Reasonable time off should also be considered for further training to help Union Learning Representatives develop their skills and competencies.

27. Although not required by law it is recognised that there would be clear advantages both to the individual and the organisation if training undertaken leads to a recognised qualification standard.

Payment for time off for training

28. **An employer who permits time off for officials or Union Learning Representatives to attend training relevant to their duties at the workplace must pay them for the time off taken. The employer must pay either the amount that the officials or Union Learning Representatives would have earned had they worked during the time off taken or, where earnings vary with the work done, an amount calculated by reference to the average hourly earnings for the work that they are employed to do. There is no statutory requirement to pay for time off where training is undertaken at a time when the official would not otherwise have been at work, but staff who work part time will be entitled to be paid if staff who work full time would be entitled to be paid. In all cases, the amount of time off must be reasonable.**

[4642]

SECTION 3
TIME OFF FOR TRADE UNION ACTIVITIES

Entitlement

29. To operate effectively and democratically, trade unions need the active participation of members. It can also be very much in employers' interests that such participation is assured. **An employee who is a member of an independent trade union recognised by the employer in respect of that description of employee is to be permitted reasonable time off during working hours to take part in any trade union activity. An employee who is a member of an independent and recognised trade union is also permitted to take reasonable time off during working hours for the purposes of accessing the services of a Union Learning Representative.**

What are examples of trade union activities?

30. The activities of a trade union member can be, for example:
- attending workplace meetings to discuss and vote on the outcome of negotiations with the employer
- meeting full-time officials to discuss issues relevant to the workplace
- voting in union elections.

31. Where the member is acting as a representative of a recognised union, activities can be, for example, taking part in:
- branch, area or regional meetings of the union where the business of the union is under discussion
- meetings of official policy making bodies such as the executive committee or annual conference
- meetings with full-time officials to discuss issues relevant to the workplace.

32. **There is no right to time off for trade union activities which themselves consist of industrial action.**

Payment for time off for trade union activities

33. Para 15 sets out the statutory entitlement to payment for time off to undertake trade union <u>duties</u>.

34. **There is no statutory requirement that union members or representatives be paid for time off taken on trade union activities.** Nevertheless employers may want to consider payment in certain circumstances, for example to ensure that workplace meetings are fully representative or to ensure that employees can make use of the services of a Union Learning Representative.

[4643]

SECTION 4
THE RESPONSIBILITIES OF EMPLOYERS AND TRADE UNIONS

General considerations

35. **The amount and frequency of time off should be reasonable in all the circumstances.** Although the statutory provisions apply to all employers without exception as to size and type of business or service, trade unions should be aware of the wide variety of difficulties and operational requirements to be taken into account when seeking or agreeing arrangements for time off, for example:

— the size of the organisation and the number of workers
— the production process
— the need to maintain a service to the public
— the need for safety and security at all times.

36. Employers in turn should have in mind the difficulties for trade union officials and members in ensuring effective representation and communications with, for example:

— shift workers
— part-time workers
— home workers
— those employed at dispersed locations
— workers with particular domestic commitments.

37. For time off arrangements to work satisfactorily trade unions should:

— ensure that officials are aware of their role, responsibilities and functions
— inform management, in writing, as soon as possible of appointments or resignations of officials
— ensure that officials receive any appropriate written credentials promptly
— ensure that employers receive details of the functions of union officials where they carry out special duties or functions.

38. Employers should consider making available to officials the facilities necessary for them to perform their duties efficiently and communicate effectively with their members, colleague lay officials and full-time officers. Where resources permit the facilities could include:

— accommodation for meetings which could include provision for Union Learning Representatives and a union member(s) to meet to discuss relevant training matters
— access to a telephone and other office equipment
— the use of notice boards which could include other forms of electronic communications such as e-mail and intranet/internet
— where the volume of the official's work justifies it, the use of dedicated office space.

Requesting time off

39. Trade union officials and members requesting time off to pursue their duties or activities or to access the services of a Union Learning Representative should provide management with as much notice as possible and give details of:

— the purpose of such time off
— the intended location
— the timing and duration of time off required.

40. In addition, officials who request paid time off to undergo relevant training should:

— give at least a few weeks' notice to management of nominations for training courses
— provide a copy of the syllabus or prospectus indicating the contents of the training course.

41. When deciding whether requests for paid time off should be granted, consideration would need to be given as to their reasonableness, for example to ensure adequate cover for safety or to safeguard the production process or the provision of service. Consideration could also be given to allowing Union Learning Representatives access to a room in which they can discuss training in a confidential manner with an employee. Similarly, managers and unions

should seek to agree a mutually convenient time which minimises the effect on production or services. Where workplace meetings are requested, consideration should be given to holding them, for example:
— towards the end of a shift or the working week
— before or after a meal break.

42. Employers need to consider each application for time off on its merits; they might also need to consider the reasonableness of the request in relation to agreed time off already taken or in prospect.

[4644]

SECTION 5
AGREEMENTS ON TIME OFF

43. To take account of the wide variety of circumstances and problems which can arise, there can be positive advantages for employers and trade unions in establishing agreements on time off in ways which reflect their own situations. A formal agreement can help to:
— provide clear guidelines against which applications for time off can be determined
— avoid misunderstanding
— facilitate better planning
— ensure fair and reasonable treatment.

44. Agreements should specify:
— the amount of time off permitted
— the occasions on which time off can be taken
— in what circumstances time off will be paid
— to whom time off will be paid
— the procedure for requesting time off
— the procedure for resolving grievances about time off.

45. In addition, it would be sensible for agreements to make clear:
— arrangements for the appropriate payment to be made when time off relates in part to union duties and in part to union activities
— whether payment (to which there would be no legal entitlement) might be made to shift and part-time employees undertaking trade union duties outside their normal working hours.

46. Agreements for time off and other facilities for union representation should be consistent with wider agreements which deal with such matters as constituencies, number of representatives and the election of officials.

47. In smaller organisations, it might be thought more appropriate for employers and unions to reach understandings about how requests for time off are to be made; and more broadly to agree flexible arrangements which can accommodate their particular circumstances.

48. The absence of a formal agreement on time off, however, does not in itself deny an individual any statutory entitlement. Nor does any agreement supersede statutory entitlement to time off.

[4645]

SECTION 6
INDUSTRIAL ACTION

49. Employers and unions have a responsibility to use agreed procedures to settle problems and avoid industrial action. Time off may therefore be permitted for this purpose particularly where there is a dispute. **There is no right to time off for trade union activities which themselves consist of industrial action.** However, where an official is not taking part in industrial action but represents members involved, normal arrangements for time off with pay for the official should apply.

[4646]

SECTION 7
RESOLVING DISPUTES

50. Every effort should be made to resolve any dispute or grievance in relation to time off work for union duties or activities. There is advantage in agreeing ways in which such disputes can be settled and any appropriate procedures to resolve disputes should be followed. **Where the grievance remains unresolved, trade union officials, Union Learning Representatives or members have a right to complain to an employment tribunal that**

their employer has failed to allow reasonable time off or, in the case of a Union Learning Representative or official, has failed to pay for all or part of the time off taken. Such complaints may be resolved by conciliation by ACAS or through a compromise agreement and, if this is successful, no tribunal hearing will be necessary. ACAS assistance may also be sought without the need for a formal complaint to a tribunal.

[4647]

(*The Annex sets out the law on time off for trade union duties and activities, ie, TULR(C)A 1992, ss 168, 168A, 169, 170, 178(1)–(3) and 173(1) and the definition of 'official' in s 119. The 1992 Act is set out at* **[469]** *et seq.*)

EQUAL OPPORTUNITIES COMMISSION CODE OF PRACTICE ON EQUAL PAY (2003)

NOTES

This Code is a re-issue, significantly expanded and rewritten, of the Equal Opportunities Commission's 1997 Code of Practice on Equal Pay. It came into effect on 1 December 2003 (see the Code of Practice on Equal Pay Order 2003, SI 2003/2865) and is issued under the Sex Discrimination Act 1975, s 56A (repealed as noted below). Notes are as in the Code.

The statutory provision under which this Code was made was repealed by the Equality Act 2006, ss 40, 91, Sch 3, paras 6, 11, Sch 4; however the Code is continued in force by s 42(3) of the 2006 Act (see **[1685]**). As to the dissolution of the Equal Opportunities Commission and the transfer of its property, rights and liabilities etc to the Commission for Equality and Human Rights, see the Equality Act 2006, ss 36–38 at **[1679]**–**[1681]**.

INTRODUCTION

1. The Equal Pay Act gives women (or men) a right to equal pay for equal work. An employer can only pay a man more than a woman for doing equal work if there is a genuine and material reason for doing so which is not related to sex. The Equal Opportunities Commission (EOC) has issued this revised Code of Practice on Equal Pay in order to provide practical guidance on how to ensure pay is determined without sex discrimination. The revised Code (the Code) is aimed at employers, but employees and their representatives or advisers—for example, from a trade union, or Citizens Advice Bureau, may also find it useful.[1]

2. The Act applies to both men and women but to avoid repetition the Code is written as though the claimant is a woman comparing her work and pay with those of a man. The Equal Pay Act specifically deals with the pay of women compared to men, (or vice versa), and not to comparisons between people of the same sex.

3. The Code is admissible in evidence in any proceedings under the Sex Discrimination Act 1975 or the Equal Pay Act 1970 (each as amended), before the Employment Tribunal. This means that, while the Code is not binding, the Employment Tribunal may take into account an employer's failure to act on its provisions.

4. Despite the fact that it is over 30 years since the Equal Pay Act became law, women working full-time earn on average 81 per cent of the hourly earnings of male full-time employees.[2] Part-time working further accentuates the gender pay gap with women working part-time earning on average only 41% of the hourly earnings of male full-time employees. Both the Government and the EOC regard this as unacceptable. By helping employers to check the pay gap in their organisation and by encouraging good equal pay practice, this Code reinforces the Government's commitment to closing the gap between men's and women's pay.

5. Depending on the particular circumstances a number of other pieces of legislation can give rise to claims related to pay discrimination. They include the Race Relations Act, the Disability Discrimination Act, the Pensions Act 1995, the Part-Time (Prevention of Less Favourable Treatment) Regulations 2000 and the Fixed-Term Employees (Prevention of Less Favourable Treatment) Regulations 2002. A female part-time cleaner, for example, could claim equal pay under the Equal Pay Act with a male part-time cleaner, but she could also claim under the Part-Time Workers Regulations, that she was being treated less favourably than a female full-time cleaner. These other pieces of legislation are dealt with in Annex A, but employers should be aware of the need to pay particular attention to the situation in respect of part-time, black and minority ethnic employees and employees with a disability.

6. It is in everyone's interest to avoid litigation, and the Code recommends equal pay reviews as the best means of ensuring that a pay system delivers equal pay. Employers can

avoid equal pay claims by regularly reviewing and monitoring their pay practices, in consultation with their workforce. Consultation is likely to increase understanding and acceptance of any changes required. Involving recognised trade unions or other employee representatives also helps to ensure that pay systems meet the legal requirement for transparency.

7. The Code includes, as good equal pay practice, a summary of EOC guidance on how to carry out an equal pay review. The full guidance is in the EOC's Equal Pay Review Kit.[3] The EOC has also produced a separate kit for smaller organisations without specialist personnel expertise.[4] Both are available on the EOC website www.eoc.org.uk or from the EOC Helpline 0845 601 5901.

8. Whilst every effort has been made to ensure that the explanations given in the Code are accurate, only the Courts or Tribunals can give authoritative interpretations of the law.

[4648]

NOTES

1 For ease of communication the word 'employee' is used throughout this document, but it is not used as a legal term. 'Employee' should be read as referring to all people who work in your organisation.

2 *New Earnings Survey 2002*, Office for National Statistics.

3 The EOC Equal Pay Review Kit.

4 EOC Equal Pay, Fair Pay: a guide to effective pay practices in small businesses.

SECTION ONE
EQUAL PAY LEGISLATION

The Treaty of Rome and the Equal Pay Directive

9. The principle that a woman is entitled to equal pay for equal work is set out in European Union and British legislation.[5] The British Courts take into account the decisions of the European Court of Justice in interpreting the Equal Pay Act and the Sex Discrimination Act. A woman bringing an equal pay claim will usually do so under the domestic British legislation, but in some circumstances she can claim under European law.

10. **Article 141 of the Treaty of Amsterdam** (previously Article 119 of the Treaty of Rome) requires Member States to ensure that the principle of equal pay for male and female workers for equal work or work of equal value is applied. The **Equal Pay Directive**[6] explains the practical application of the principle of equal pay, namely the elimination of sex discrimination in pay systems. European law defines pay as:

> *'The ordinary basic or minimum wage or salary and any other consideration, whether in cash or kind, which the worker receives directly or indirectly, in respect of his employer or employment.'*

Pensions are treated as pay.

The Equal Pay Act 1970

11. The Equal Pay Act 1970, as amended, entitles a woman doing equal work with a man in the same employment to equality in pay and terms and conditions. The meaning of 'same employment' is considered in paragraph 21. The Act does so by giving her the right to equality in the terms of her contract of employment. The man with whom she is claiming equal pay is known as her comparator. Equal work is work that is the same or broadly similar, work that has been rated as equivalent, or work that is of equal value (see paragraphs 27–32).

12. Claims for equal pay are taken through the Employment Tribunal. If a woman succeeds in a claim:

- Her pay, including any occupational pension rights, must be raised to that of her male comparator
- Any beneficial term in the man's contract but not in hers must be inserted into her contract
- Any term in her contract that is less favourable than the same term in the man's contract must be made as good as it is in his
- Compensation consisting of arrears of pay (if the claim is about pay) and/or damages (if the complaint is about some other contractual term).

13. The woman can compare any term in her contract with the equivalent term in her comparator's contract. This means that each element of the pay package has to be considered

separately and it is not sufficient to compare total pay. For example, a woman can claim equal pay with a male comparator who earns a higher rate of basic pay than she does, even if other elements of her pay package are more favourable than his.

14. Once a woman establishes that she and her comparator are doing equal work it is up to her employer to show that the explanation for the pay difference is genuinely due to a 'material factor' that is not tainted by sex discrimination. This defence is known as the 'genuine material factor' defence. In practice, an employer may identify more than one factor. For example, an employer may argue that the man is paid more because he is better qualified than the woman *and* because it is difficult to recruit people with his particular skills.

The Sex Discrimination Act 1975

15. The Equal Pay Act applies to pay or benefits provided under the contract of employment. The Sex Discrimination Act 1975, as amended, complements the Equal Pay Act. It covers non-contractual issues such as recruitment, training, promotion, dismissal and the allocation of benefits, for example, flexible working arrangements or access to a workplace nursery.

16. The Sex Discrimination Act also covers non-contractual pay matters, such as promotion and discretionary bonuses. Decisions about performance markings in a performance-related pay scheme are aspects of treatment which could be challenged under the Sex Discrimination Act if discriminatory. By contrast, where those decisions result in different levels of pay, that difference and the terms of the scheme could be challenged under the Equal Pay Act. This means that if a woman wishes to make a claim in respect of non-contractual or discretionary payments her claim will be made under the Sex Discrimination Act.[7] If there is any doubt as to which Act a payment falls under, legal advice should be sought.

Protection against victimisation

17. The Sex Discrimination Act also protects employees from being victimised for making a complaint (unless this is both untrue and made in bad faith) about equal pay or sex discrimination, or for giving evidence about such a complaint. Victimisation because a woman intends to bring a claim is also unlawful. The 'complaint' does not have to be by way of filing a claim with the Employment Tribunal, but includes any discussion or correspondence about the matter between the woman and her employer. The protection against victimisation also includes not only the woman bringing the claim, but also anyone who assists her, for example, her comparator and any trade union or employee representatives.

THE SCOPE OF THE EQUAL PAY ACT

Employers

18. The Equal Pay Act applies to all employers irrespective of their size and whether they are in the public or the private sector.

Employees

19. The Equal Pay Act applies to:

— All employees (including apprentices and those working from home), whether on full-time, part-time, casual or temporary contracts, regardless of length of service

— Other workers (e g self employed) whose contracts require personal performance of the work

— Employment carried out for a British employer unless the employee works wholly outside Great Britain[8]

— Employment carried out on British registered ships or UK registered aircraft operated by someone based in Great Britain unless the employee works wholly outside Great Britain.

20. The Equal Pay Act also applies to Armed Services personnel, but there is a requirement to first make a complaint to an officer under the relevant service redress procedures and submit a complaint to the Defence Council under those procedures before presenting a claim to the Employment Tribunal.[9]

Same employment

21. A woman can claim equal pay with a man working:

— For the same employer at the same workplace

— For the same employer but at a different workplace where common terms and conditions apply, for example at another branch of a store
— For an associated employer; for example, at her employer's parent company
— European law also allows a comparison to be made between employees who do not work for the same employer, but who are *'in the same establishment or service'*. As there is no clear definition of *'in the same establishment or service'* this is an area of law on which specific legal advice should be sought. However, European law as it currently stands suggests a comparison can only be made where the differences in pay are attributable to a 'common source' and there is a single body, responsible for and capable of remedying the pay inequality, for example where pay differences arise from a sector-wide collective agreement or from legislation.

The pay package

22. The Equal Pay Act covers all aspects of the pay and benefits package, including:
— Basic pay
— Non-discretionary bonuses
— Overtime rates and allowances
— Performance related benefits
— Severance and redundancy pay
— Access to pension schemes
— Benefits under pension schemes
— Hours of work
— Company cars
— Sick pay
— Fringe benefits such as travel allowances.

Comparators

23. A woman can claim equal pay for equal work with a man, or men, in the same employment. It is for the woman to select the man or men with whom she wishes to be compared, and her employer cannot interfere with her choice of comparator(s). She can claim equal pay with more than one comparator, but to avoid repetition the Code (and the law) is written as though there is only one comparator.

24. The comparator can be:
— Someone with whom she is working at the present time, subject to the usual time limits (see paragraphs 47–48)
— Her predecessor, however long ago he did the job, or her successor.

25. The comparator does not have to give his consent to being named. If the woman's equal pay claim is successful, the result will be that her pay is raised to the same level as his. There will not be any reduction in the comparator's pay and benefits.

26. There are a number of ways in which a woman may be able to select a comparator. These include:
— Her own knowledge and experience
— The internal grievance procedure (see paragraph 36)
— The Equal Pay Questionnaire (see paragraph 37)
— Discovery (asking for documents through the Employment Tribunal). Once a woman has filed her claim with the Employment Tribunal, provided that she has shown that her contractual terms are less favourable than those of male colleagues, she can apply for discovery to enable her to name appropriate comparators.

Equal pay for equal work

27. The comparator may be doing the *same* job as the woman, or he may be doing a *different* job. She can claim equal pay for equal work with a comparator doing work that is:
— The *same*, or broadly similar (known as **like work**)
— *Different*, but which is rated under the same job evaluation scheme as equivalent to hers (known as **work rated as equivalent**)
— *Different*, but of equal value in terms of demands such as effort, skill and decision-making (known as **work of equal value**).

Like work

28. Like work means the woman and her comparator are doing the same or broadly similar work. Job titles could be different, yet the work being done could be broadly similar—the nature of the work actually being done needs to be considered. Where

PART 4

differences exist the Employment Tribunal will look at the nature and extent of the differences, how frequently they occur, and whether they are of practical importance in relation to the terms and conditions of the job.

Like work comparisons that have succeeded, in the particular circumstances of the case, include:
— Male and female cleaners doing 'wet' and 'dry' cleaning in different locations on the same site
— A woman cook preparing lunches for directors and a male chef cooking breakfast, lunch and tea for employees.

Work rated as equivalent

29. Work rated as equivalent means that the jobs being done by the woman and her comparator have been assessed under the same job evaluation scheme as being equivalent, that is, they have been assessed as having the same number of points, or as falling within the same job evaluation grade.

Work rated as equivalent comparisons that have succeeded in the particular circumstances of the case, include:
— Where a woman and a man had been placed in the same job evaluation grade but the employer had refused to pay the woman (who had been evaluated as having fewer points) the rate for the grade.

Work of equal value

30. Work of equal value means that the jobs done by the woman and her comparator are different, but can be regarded as being of equal value or worth. This can be measured by comparing the jobs under headings such as effort, skill and decision-making.

31. Comparing jobs on the basis of equal value means jobs that are entirely different in their nature can be used as the basis for equal pay claims. Job comparisons can be made both within a particular pay/grading structure and between different structures or departments, for example, in a printing firm, between a bindery and a press room. Equal value is likely to be relevant where men and women are in the same employment but do different types of work.

Equal value comparisons that have succeeded in the particular circumstances of the case, include:
— Cooks and carpenters
— Speech therapists and clinical psychologists
— Kitchen assistants and refuse workers.

32. A woman can claim equal pay under more than one heading. For example, a woman working as an administrator in a garage could claim 'like work' with a male administrator working alongside her and 'equal value' with a mechanic.

Pregnant women and women on maternity leave

33. During the period of Ordinary Maternity Leave a woman's contract remains in place and all of her contractual terms and conditions must continue, with the exception of her normal pay (i e wages or salary).[10] The position with regard to bonuses, occupational pension rights, and the provision of maternity benefits over and above those required by the statutory scheme is unclear, and specific legal advice will be needed.

34. When a woman is on Additional Maternity Leave,[11] even though her contract remains in place, her contractual terms cease to apply, except for some limited exceptions not relevant to pay. However, her entitlement to paid leave under the Working Time Regulations continues to accrue, and in some circumstances it may be unlawful under either the Equal Pay Act or the Sex Discrimination Act to treat a woman on maternity leave differently from other workers,

e g by failing to pay her a bonus. The situation will vary according to the facts and again, this is an area where detailed legal advice should be sought.

35. Pay increases continue to accrue while a woman is on maternity leave and she is entitled to the benefit of any pay increases that she would have received had she been at work.[12]

RAISING THE MATTER WITH THE EMPLOYER

Using the grievance procedure

36. Before making a complaint to the Employment Tribunal, a woman should try to resolve the issue of equal pay by mutual agreement with her employer, perhaps through the employer's own grievance procedure. Employers and employees can also seek advice from an ACAS conciliator. ACAS can be contacted at www.acas.org.uk. However, the time limit for making a complaint to the Employment Tribunal will still apply and will not be extended to take account of the time taken to complete the grievance procedure.[13] Although there is no legal requirement to do so it is good practice for the employer, the employee, and/or her union representative, to keep records of any meetings.

The Equal Pay Questionnaire

37. A woman is entitled to write to her employer asking for information that will help her establish whether she has received equal pay and if not, what the reasons for the pay difference are. There is a standard questionnaire form which can be used to do this. The focus of the questionnaire is on establishing whether she is receiving less favourable pay and contractual terms and conditions than a colleague or colleagues of the opposite sex, and whether the employer agrees that she and her comparator are doing 'equal work'. The woman can send the questionnaire to her employer either before she files her claim with the Employment Tribunal or within 21 days of doing so. Copies of the questionnaire can be obtained from the Women and Equality Unit website www.womenandequalityunit.gov.uk.

38. If the woman takes a case to the Employment Tribunal, the information provided by her employer should enable her to present her claim in the most effective way and the proceedings should be simpler because the key facts will have been identified in advance. If her employer fails, without reasonable excuse, to reply within 8 weeks, or responds with an evasive or equivocal reply, the Employment Tribunal may take this into account at the hearing. The Employment Tribunal may then draw an inference unfavourable to the employer, for example, that the employer has no genuine reason for the difference in pay.

RESPONDING TO REQUESTS FROM AN EMPLOYEE FOR INFORMATION

Transparency

39. The European Court of Justice has held that pay systems must be transparent. Transparency means that pay and benefit systems should be capable of being understood by everyone (employers, employees and their trade unions). Employees should be able to understand how each element of their pay packet contributes to total earnings in a pay period. Where the pay structure is not transparent, and a woman is able to show some indication of sex discrimination, the burden of proof switches to the employer who then has to demonstrate that the pay system does not discriminate.

40. It is advisable for an employer to keep records that will allow him or her to explain why he or she did something, showing clearly what factors he or she relied on at the time that the decision on pay was made. Employers should be aware that employees may bring complaints or make enquiries about pay decisions which were taken many years previously, since when the person who took the decision may have left the organisation. For this reason it is advisable for employers to keep records that may, in the future, help them to explain why pay decisions were made.

41. Bearing in mind the guidance given in the preceding paragraphs, when responding either to a grievance or to the questionnaire employers need to:

- Decide whether or not they agree that the woman is doing equal work
- Consider the reasons for any difference in pay
- If they do not agree that the woman's work is equal to that of her comparator, they should explain in what way the work is not equal

— Explain the reasons for any difference in pay.

Further guidance is given in the notes accompanying the questionnaire.

Confidentiality

42. The principle of transparency set out above does not mean that an individual has the automatic right to know what another individual earns. The principle of transparency means that a woman has the right to know how the calculations are made, not the content of the calculation. It is necessary to balance the ideal of transparency with the rights of individual privacy. The equal pay questionnaire cannot be used to require an employer to disclose confidential information, unless the Employment Tribunal orders the employer to do so. A woman can use the questionnaire to request key information and it is likely that in many cases an employer will be able to answer detailed questions in general terms, while still preserving the anonymity and confidentiality of employees.

The Data Protection Act

43. Much of the information requested will not be confidential but some information, such as the exact details of a comparator's pay package, may be confidential to that person. Personal data is protected by the Data Protection Act 1998 and can only be disclosed in accordance with data protection principles. Pay records will usually be personal data covered by the Data Protection Act. Moreover, other issues such as ethnic origin and medical details are sensitive personal data to which particular safeguards apply. The disclosure of confidential information in the employment context is also protected by the implied duty of trust and confidence owed by an employer to an employee.

44. The EOC has produced a guidance note that explains an employer's legal obligations when responding to an equal pay questionnaire or to a request for information during the course of tribunal proceedings.[14] However, this is a developing area of law and, if in doubt, an employer should seek specific advice from the Information Commissioner www.informationcommissioner.gov.uk and/or take legal advice.

Disclosure of information to trade unions or employee representatives

45. Under the Trade Union and Labour Relations (Consolidation) Act 1992 an employer is under a duty, on request, to disclose to a recognised trade union, information to enable constructive collective bargaining. Information about pay and terms and conditions of employment usually comes within the duty to disclose, but it is important to note that the duty applies only to information for collective bargaining.

46. It also represents good practice for employers who do not recognise trade unions to communicate regularly with their workforce and, where appropriate, their representatives.

BRINGING AN EQUAL PAY CLAIM

The time limits for applying to an Employment Tribunal

47. If a woman wishes to lodge a claim with the Employment Tribunal she must do so within the prescribed time limits. **It is her responsibility to ensure that she does so.** The woman bringing the claim and her representatives should be alert to the importance of lodging the equal pay claim with the Employment Tribunal within the time limits. Using the internal grievance procedure does not extend the time limits set for lodging a claim, nor does serving the questionnaire.[15]

48. The Equal Pay Act and the Sex Discrimination Act have different time limits.

— Claims under the Equal Pay Act can be taken at any time up to six months after leaving the employment with the employer (as opposed to leaving the particular post about which the equal pay claim is made, but remaining in the same employment). This time limit also applies to equal pay claims taken where a stable relationship with an employer has come to an end. The time limit can be extended only where the employer deliberately conceals the existence of pay inequality from the complainant, or the complainant is a minor or of unsound mind[16]

— In contracting out situations the time limit runs from the date of the contracting out in respect of periods of service up to that date

— Claims under the Sex Discrimination Act can be taken within three months of the alleged act of discrimination, subject to the tribunal's discretion to extend the time limit where it is just and equitable to do so

— Because of the requirement on Armed Services personnel to use the relevant Service

Redress Procedure referred to in paragraph 20 different rules apply. In the case of the Equal Pay Act, the time limit is nine months from the end of the period of service, and in the case of the Sex Discrimination Act, the time limit is six months from the date of the act complained of. The time limits can be extended only as described above.

The burden of proof

49. The woman bringing an equal pay claim has to show the Employment Tribunal that on the face of it she is receiving less pay than a man in the same employment who is doing equal work. Her employer must then either accept her claim or prove to the Employment Tribunal that the difference in pay was for a genuine and material reason, which was not the difference of sex.

The Employment Tribunal procedure

50. The fact that a woman is paid less than a man doing equal work does not necessarily mean that she is suffering sex discrimination in pay. In making a decision about a case the Employment Tribunal has to assess the evidence about:

— The work done by the woman and her comparator
— The value placed on the work (sometimes with the advice of an Independent Expert), in terms of the demands of the jobs
— The pay of the woman and her comparator and how it is arrived at
— The reasons for the difference in pay.

51. In *like work* and *work rated as equivalent* claims the procedure is the same as in any other employment case. There are special tribunal procedures for *work of equal value* claims.[17]

Assessing equal value

52. The concept of equal pay for work of equal value means that a woman can claim equal pay with a man doing a completely different job. In comparing such jobs the Employment Tribunal will apply techniques akin to analytical job evaluation, whereby the demands on the jobholders and the skills required of them are assessed using objective criteria. The Employment Tribunal may also appoint an Independent Expert to assess the value of the jobs. The Employment Tribunal-appointed Independent Expert may make a detailed study of an employer's pay system and the employer would be expected to co-operate with any such exercise.

53. Employers should be aware that they, and the woman bringing the claim, might also appoint someone with equal pay expertise to act as an expert on their behalf. It is important when dealing with experts to be clear who is the Independent Expert appointed by the Employment Tribunal and who is acting for the parties to the claim.

The employer's defence

54. The possible defences against an equal pay claim are as follows:

— The woman and the man are not doing equal work
— For equal value claims only—the jobs being done by the woman and the man have been evaluated and rated differently under an analytical job evaluation scheme that is free of sex bias. An analytical job evaluation scheme evaluates jobs according to the demands made on the jobholders. **A non-analytical job evaluation scheme does not provide a defence to a claim**
— The difference in pay is genuinely due to a material factor, which is not the difference of sex.

The job evaluation defence

55. Where employers use analytical job evaluation schemes they need to check that the scheme has been designed and implemented in such a way that it does not discriminate on grounds of sex. An analytical evaluation discriminates on the grounds of sex where values have been attributed to the different demands against which it has measured the jobs, and these values cannot be justified irrespective of the sex of the person on whom these demands are made.

56. A job evaluation scheme will be discriminatory if it fails to include, or properly take into account, a factor, or job demand, that is an important element in the woman's job (eg caring demands in a job involving looking after elderly people), or if it gives an

PART 4

unjustifiably heavy weighting to factors that are more typical of the man's job (e g the physical demands of being employed as a gardener).

57. A woman may also challenge a job evaluation scheme on the basis that instead of a factor, say, 'mental concentration' (in her job) being awarded fewer points than 'physical effort' (in her comparator's job), it should have received the same or more points. Similarly, she may argue that 'physical effort' (in his job) has been overrated compared with the skill her job requires for 'manual dexterity'. Even where she has received the same or more points than a man for a particular factor, she may still argue that the demands of her job under this factor have been underrated, that is, that the difference in points under the factor should have been bigger.

58. Employers also need to check the outcomes of the job evaluation for sex bias. This means checking what impact the scheme has had on women and men, that is, how many women and how many men have moved up or down the grades? Any ensuing pay protection (red-circling) should also be free of sex bias and should be phased out as soon as is practicable.[18]

59. The EOC has produced a guidance note recommending that matters, such as the following, should be considered as a matter of good practice.[19] In order to check that a scheme is non-discriminatory, an employer needs to look at matters such as:

— Whether statistics recorded on pay are broken down by gender
— Whether the scheme is appropriate to the jobs it will cover
— If a proprietary scheme is used does the supplier have equal opportunities guidelines?
— If any groups of workers are excluded from the scheme, are there clear and justifiable reasons for their exclusion?
— Is the composition of the job evaluation panel/steering committee representative of the jobs covered by the scheme and are the members trained in job evaluation and avoiding sex bias?
— Are the job descriptions written to an agreed format and assessed to a common standard? Are trained job analysts used and have the jobholders been involved in writing their own job descriptions?
— Where the scheme uses generic/bench mark jobs are these free from sex bias?
— Are the factor definitions and levels exact and are detailed descriptions provided for each factor? Do the factors cover **all** the important job demands?

If a job evaluation scheme is to remain free of sex bias it should be monitored. The employer (and not the job evaluation supplier or consultant) will need to show that the scheme is non-discriminatory.

The 'genuine material factor defence'—testing for sex discrimination

60. The Employment Tribunal tests for sex discrimination by first establishing a difference in pay or terms between the woman bringing the claim and a man doing equal work, and then asking whether the difference is due to discrimination or some other factor that does not amount to sex discrimination. This means that an employer can pay a man more than a woman for doing equal work, but only if the reason for doing so—the factor which the employer regards as the reason for the difference in pay—is not related to the sex of the jobholders.

61. The employer will have to show that the factor, or factors, on which he or she relies is free from both direct and indirect sex discrimination:

— Direct sex discrimination occurs when the difference in pay or terms is directly related to the difference of sex
— Indirect sex discrimination arises when the pay difference is due to a provision, criterion or practice which:
  — Applies to both men and women, but
  — Adversely affects a considerably larger proportion of women than men, and
  — Is not objectively justified irrespective of the sex of the jobholders.

62. Whether a defence succeeds or fails will always depend on the circumstances of the case and there is no such thing as an automatic or blanket defence. The defences that are likely to succeed include allowances such as London weighting and night-shift payments. Factors such as different market rates of pay for different specialisms or different levels of skills and experience have been successful in some cases but not in others.

63. The factor put forward to explain the difference in pay has to be significant; it has to be the real reason for the difference and it must not be connected with the sex of the people doing the job. For example, if the employer considers that the reason for paying the comparator more than the woman bringing the claim is that people will not do the work for

the lower rate of pay, then the employer would have to bring evidence of actual difficulties in recruiting and retaining people to do the job being done by the male comparator.

64. Where a woman is claiming equal pay on the basis that the two jobs are work of equal value, indirect discrimination may arise where one of the jobs is done by a much higher proportion of women than the other job. The onus lies on the employee to provide evidence of significant disparate impact.[20]

65. In such a case, if the Employment Tribunal accepts that the jobs are of equal value, the employer will need to provide objective justification for the pay difference between the two kinds of job. This is a higher standard of justification than that of the material factor defence.

66. The employer must show that:

— The purpose of the provision or practice is to meet a real business need
— The provision or practice is appropriate and necessary as a means of meeting that need.

An example of objective justification is:

— A pay system that makes an additional payment to employees working unsocial hours, in which most of the employees getting the bonus are men. Here the employer would have to show that:
  — There is a real business need to create a system to encourage a particular group of employees to work unsociable hours, and
  — The additional payments meet that need, and
  — The payments are an effective way of meeting that need, and do not go beyond what is necessary to achieve it (ie without the payment, the extra work would not be done, and the payment is only made when the workers actually do the work).

Awards of equal pay

67. If the woman succeeds in her claim she is entitled to:

— An order from the Employment Tribunal declaring her rights
— Equalisation of contractual terms for the future (if she is still in employment)
— Compensation consisting of arrears of pay (if the claim is about pay) and/or damages (if the complaint is about some other contractual term).

Back pay can be awarded up to a maximum of six years (five years in Scotland) from the date that proceedings were filed with the Employment Tribunal.[21] In addition, the Employment Tribunal may award interest on the award of compensation. With up to six year's worth of back pay being awarded, the interest element of any award is likely to be considerable.

[4649]

NOTES

5 This Code applies to Great Britain. Northern Ireland has its own equivalent equal pay and sex discrimination legislation and Equality Commission.

6 European Council Directive 75/117/EEC. [See now European Parliament and Council Directive 2006/54/EC at **[4122]**: Ed.]

7 Also, if a woman considers that a term in a collective agreement, or an employer's rule, provides for the doing of an unlawful discriminatory act, and that the term or rule may at some time have effect in relation to her, she can challenge that term or rule under the Sex Discrimination Act 1986 as amended by section 32 of the Trade Union Reform and Employment Rights Act 1993.

8 Great Britain includes such of the territorial waters of the UK as are adjacent to Great Britain and certain areas designated in relation to employment in the offshore oil and gas industry.

9 S 7A(5) of the Equal Pay Act read with the Service Redress Procedures.

10 Under the Employment Rights Act 1996, and the Maternity and Parental Leave Regulations 1999, as amended by the Maternity and Parental Leave (Amendment) Regulations 2002, Ordinary Maternity Leave is 26 weeks for all mothers whose expected week of childbirth is after 6 April 2003.

11 Under the Employment Rights Act 1996, as amended by the Employment Relations Act 1999, women who have at least 26 weeks service at the beginning of the 14th week before the expected week of childbirth are entitled to 26 weeks Additional Maternity Leave starting after their Ordinary Maternity Leave. [This service qualification has since been removed: Ed.]

12 *Gillespie & others v Northern Health and Social Services Board* (1996 ECJ).

PART 4

13 A woman will be obliged to use the grievance procedure once the relevant provisions of the Employment Act 2002 have come into effect in October 2004. Time limits will be amended to allow the grievance procedure to be used.
14 EOC practical tips: responding to an equal pay questionnaire and requests for information during tribunal proceedings in accordance with Data Protection Act principles.
15 See footnote 13.
16 The Equal Pay Act 1970 (Amendment) Regulations 2003 (SI 2003/1656).
17 These are to be found in the Employment Tribunals (Constitution and Rules of Procedure) Regulations 2001 (SI 2001/1171) and the Employment Tribunals (Constitution and Rules of Procedure) (Scotland) Regulations 2001 (SI 2001/1170) and S 2A of the Equal Pay Act itself.
18 The EOC Equal Pay Review Kit Guidance Note 4: Job Evaluation Schemes Free of Sex Bias.
19 The EOC Equal Pay Review Kit Guidance Note 4: Job Evaluation Schemes Free of Sex Bias.
20 The advice given here is based on *Nelson v Carillion Services Ltd*, Court of Appeal decision 15 April 2003. Specific legal advice should be sought.
21 Special rules apply where the woman is under a disability or the employer has concealed a breach of the Equal Pay Act.

SECTION TWO
GOOD EQUAL PAY PRACTICE

Introduction

68. The loss to women arising out of the gender pay gap is well documented, but organisations also lose out by failing to properly reward the range of skills and experience that women bring to the workforce. The most commonly recognised risk of failing to ensure that pay is determined without sex discrimination is equal pay cases being taken against the organisation. The direct costs of a claim can include not only any eventual equal pay award to the woman bringing the claim (see paragraph 67) but also the costs of time spent at a hearing, and the costs of legal representation. The indirect costs are harder to quantify, but include lower productivity on the part of those employees who consider that they are not getting equal pay and on the part of managers whose time is taken up in dealing with the claim.

69. Tackling the gender pay gap reduces the risk of litigation. It can also increase efficiency by attracting the best employees, reducing staff turnover, increasing commitment, and reducing absenteeism. Pay is one of the key factors affecting motivation and relationships at work. It is therefore important to develop pay arrangements that are right for the organisation and that reward employees fairly. Providing equal pay for equal work is central to the concept of rewarding people fairly for what they do.

The essential features of an equal pay review

70. Employers are responsible for providing equal pay and for ensuring that pay systems are transparent. Pay arrangements are frequently complicated and the features that can give rise to sex discrimination are not always obvious. A structured pay system is more likely to provide equal pay and is easier to check than a system that relies primarily on managerial discretion. ACAS, the employment relations' experts, provide basic advice on the various different types of pay systems and on job evaluation.

71. The advice given in paragraphs 39–46 on striking a balance between transparency and confidentiality are also relevant to equal pay reviews. The EOC has produced a guidance note that explains an employer's legal obligations when carrying out an equal pay review.[22]

72. While employers are not required, by law, to carry out an equal pay review, this Code recommends equal pay reviews as the most appropriate method of ensuring that a pay system delivers equal pay free from sex bias. Whatever kind of equal pay review process is used, it should include:

- Comparing the pay of men and women doing equal work. Here employers need to check for one or more of the following: like work; work rated as equivalent; work of equal value. ***These checks are the foundation of an equal pay review***
- Identifying any equal pay gaps
- Eliminating those pay gaps that cannot satisfactorily be explained on grounds other than sex.

These features are the same whatever the size of the organisation and they are essential. **A pay review process that does not include these features cannot claim to be an equal pay review.** Moreover, an equal pay review is not simply a data collection exercise. It entails a commitment to put right any sex based pay inequalities and this means that the review must have the involvement and support of managers with the authority to deliver the necessary changes.

73. The validity of the review and success of subsequent action taken will be enhanced if the pay system is understood and accepted by the managers who operate the system, by the employees and by their unions. Employers should therefore aim to secure the involvement of employees and, where possible, trade union representatives, when carrying out an equal pay review.

VOLUNTARY EQUAL PAY REVIEWS

A model for carrying out an equal pay review

74. The EOC recommends a five-step equal pay review model:

STEP 1: Deciding the scope of the review and identifying the data required

STEP 2: Determining where men and women are doing equal work

STEP 3: Collecting pay data to identify equal pay gaps

STEP 4: Establishing the causes of any significant pay gaps and assessing the reasons for these

STEP 5: Developing an equal pay action plan and/or reviewing and monitoring.

The EOC Equal Pay Review Kit sets out the detail of the model recommended here and provides supporting guidance notes.

STEP 1: Deciding the scope of the review and identifying the data required

75. In scoping the review employers need to decide:

— Which employees are going to be included? It is advisable to include all employees who are deemed to be in the same establishment or service (see paragraph 21)

— What information will be needed? Employers will need to collect and compare broad types of information about:

  — All the various elements of pay, including pensions and other benefits

  — The personal characteristics of each employee, that is, gender; full-time or part-time; qualifications relevant to the job; hours worked and when and where they work these; length of service; role and time in grade and performance related pay ratings[23]

  — It is particularly important to ensure that information is collected about part-time employees.

The information will vary depending upon the type of organisation, its pay policies and practices and the scope of the review.

— Who should be involved in carrying out the review? An equal pay review requires different types of input from people with different perspectives. There will be a need for knowledge and understanding of the pay and grading arrangements; of any job evaluation schemes; and of the payroll and human resource systems. It can also be helpful to have someone with an understanding of equality issues, particularly the effects of indirect discrimination in pay systems

— When to involve the workforce? Employers need to consider when to involve the trade unions or other employee representatives

— Whether expert advice is needed? Employers may also wish to consider whether to bring in outside expertise. ACAS can provide practical, independent and impartial advice on the employee relations aspects of equal pay reviews.

The scope of the Equal Pay Review[24]

In nearly three quarters of organisations, the review applied (or applies) to the whole workforce. In over half of all the cases it involved an examination of a job evaluation system to ensure that it was free of sex bias. Moreover, just under half of organisations had extended the review beyond pay and gender, to include other processes such as recruitment and selection; two-fifths had covered pay differences by ethnicity; more than a third had covered age and nearly a third had covered disability.

The scope of the Equal Pay Review	Percentage of organisations covering
Whole workforce	73
Examination of job evaluation system	55
Other HR processes	49

PART 4

The scope of the Equal Pay Review[24]	
Pay differences by ethnic origin	40
Pay differences by age	36
Pay differences by disability	31
N = number of organisations	67

Include ethnicity and disability in the review

76. This Code is concerned with an important, but narrow, aspect of sex discrimination in employment—the pay of women compared to men doing equal work, (or vice versa). It does not deal with comparisons on the grounds of ethnicity or disability. However, as a matter of good practice employers may also want to look at ethnicity and disability, or age. Before deciding to do so it may be helpful to consider the quality of the information available to the employer, and whether it is adequate for the purposes of carrying out a wider review. To ensure the relevant provisions of race and disability legislation are taken into account, it would be appropriate to seek advice from the Commission for Racial Equality and/or the Disability Rights Commission.

77. Public Sector organisations obliged by the Race Relations (Amendment) Act 2000 to adopt an Equality Scheme should ensure that their pay review deals with any pay gaps between workers from different ethnic groups as well as the gaps between men's and women's pay. Here too, advice can be obtained from the Commission for Racial Equality.

STEP 2: Determining where men and women are doing equal work

78. In Step 2 employers need to do one or more of the following checks:
— Like work
— Work rated as equivalent
— Work of equal value.

These checks determine where men and women are doing equal work. They are the foundation of an equal pay review.

Example[25]—determining where men and women are doing equal work

Human Resources and the unions met to agree which areas to examine. According to the HR manager, 'we already had an idea of where the discrepancies were'. Data collection was on the basis of figures from: the personnel database, the pay database, the performance pay database and the starters and leavers database. A small local consultancy had helped to introduce a new job evaluation scheme; however, the basis for making equal work comparisons was predominantly by existing grade. The organisation looked at global differences, differences by grade and differences by components of pay (basic pay, overtime and allowances).

79. Employers who do not have analytical job evaluation schemes designed with equal value in mind will need to find an alternative means of estimating whether men and women are doing equal work. The EOC Equal Pay Review Kit includes suggestions as to how this can be done.[26] Employers who do use analytical job evaluation schemes need to check that their scheme has been designed and implemented in such a way and at all times so as not to discriminate on grounds of sex.[27]

STEP 3: Collecting pay data to identify equal pay gaps

80. In Step 3 employers need to collect and compare pay information for men and women doing equal work by:

— Calculating average basic pay and total earnings
— Comparing access to and amounts received of each element of the pay package.

To ensure comparisons are consistent, when calculating average basic pay and average total earnings for men and women separately, employers should do this either on an hourly basis or on a full-time salary basis (grossing up or down for those who work fewer, or more, hours—excluding overtime—per week than the norm).

81. Employers then need to review the pay comparisons to identify any gender pay gaps and decide if any are significant enough to warrant further investigation. It is advisable to record all the significant or patterned pay gaps that have been identified.

Example[28]—data collection and analysis

The organisation had a well-established process for undertaking equal pay audits. Data were brought together and presented in tabular form by the data analysis section of the human resources department. The data were then reviewed, analysed and commented on by the head of employee relations, who shared the data with trade union representatives. Union and management worked together to develop action points arising from the data.

STEP 4: Establishing the causes of any significant pay gaps and assessing the reasons for these

82. In Step 4 employers need to:

— Find out if there is a genuine and material reason for the difference in pay that has nothing to do with the sex of the jobholders
— Examine their pay systems to find out which pay policies and practices are contributing to any gender pay gaps.

Example[29]—finding out which policies and practices are contributing to the gender pay gap

The review showed a 23 per cent gap in the average basic pay of men and women across the organisation. In grades with a large enough number of staff to make a comparison, 50 per cent had variances of five per cent or greater in favour of either men or women. Starting pay was not found to be an issue, nor was performance pay. The key factor in grade inequalities was identified as long pay ranges and the impact of past restructuring. There was a body of staff (largely male), who had reached the upper quartile of their current pay range prior to the most recent restructuring. However, new appointees, who were increasingly female, and those who had taken career breaks, had little chance of progressing to this level.

The other area of concern identified by the review was premium payments for working unsocial hours. These were paid at the rate of 20 per cent of basic salary to some grades. However, in 1998 these payments were restricted to existing staff. The period since 1998 had seen an increase in the number of female recruits into what were traditionally male areas. Due to the change in the rules they were not eligible for the premium payments. The result was that overall in the eligible grades, men received on average two and a half times the amount of earnings from premium pay that women received.

83. Pay systems vary considerably. Pay systems that group jobs into pay grades or bands have traditionally treated jobs in the same grade or band as being of broadly equal value, either because they have been evaluated with similar scores under a job evaluation scheme, or because they are simply regarded as equivalent. However, recent years have seen a trend towards structures with fewer, broader grades or bands and greater use of performance pay and market factors. A single broad band or grade may contain jobs or roles of significantly different value because it encompasses a wide range of job evaluation scores. This, coupled with a wider use of other determinants of pay and more complex methods of pay progression, means that it is important for employers to check all aspects of the pay system from a variety of standpoints: design, implementation, and impact on men and women.[30]

STEP 5: Developing an equal pay action plan and/or reviewing and monitoring

84. Where the reason for the pay difference is connected with sex, employers will need to provide equal pay for current and future employees.

PART 4

85. Employers who find no gaps between men's and women's pay, or who find gaps for which there are genuinely non-discriminatory reasons, should nevertheless keep their pay systems under review by introducing regular monitoring undertaken jointly with trade unions. This will ensure that the pay system remains free of sex bias.

> **Example[31]—developing an action plan**
>
> Following the review, an Action Plan looking at internal processes was developed. This is ongoing and is reviewed through partnership processes. The aim is to integrate equal pay issues into employee relations' work.
>
> Early action has been in relation to internal recruitment processes. This included looking at whether people were encouraged (or not) to apply for particular jobs. This lack of recognition of potential opportunities was closing off progression routes to some groups, and impacting on the organisational gender pay gap. The organisation also found that it had a body of staff (mainly women) that did not seek promotion. A challenge for the organisation was to encourage more women to aim for promotion, especially once they had fewer family responsibilities.
>
> The remuneration manager anticipated that the gender pay gap in the main staff would fall from the 13 per cent identified in the pay review to under five per cent over the following five years. A recent repeat of the review had already shown a fall, however, the decline in the gap might not always be maintained. This is because the company's pay system is highly market sensitive and a tightening of the labour market in areas in which men are in the majority (such as Information Technology) would have a negative impact on the downward trend.

[4650]

NOTES

22 EOC practical tips: conducting an equal pay review in accordance with Data Protection Act principles.

23 The EOC Equal Pay Review Kit Guidance Note 2: Data collection provides detailed guidance on the information required to carry out an equal pay review.

24 Case study taken from *Monitoring Progress Towards Pay Equality*, Neathey, Dench & Thomson, Institute for Employment Studies, EOC 2003.

25 Case study taken from *Monitoring Progress Towards Pay Equality*, Neathey, Dench & Thomson, Institute for Employment Studies, EOC 2003.

26 The EOC Equal Pay Review Kit Guidance Note 5: Assessing Equal Value.

27 The EOC Equal Pay Review Kit Guidance Note 4: Job Evaluation Schemes Free of Sex Bias.

28 Case study taken from *Monitoring Progress Towards Pay Equality*, Neathey, Dench & Thomson, Institute for Employment Studies, EOC 2003.

29 Case study taken from *Monitoring Progress Towards Pay Equality*, Neathey, Dench & Thomson, Institute for Employment Studies, EOC 2003.

30 The EOC Equal Pay Review Kit Guidance Note 6: Reviewing your payment systems, policies and practices.

31 Case study taken from *Monitoring Progress Towards Pay Equality*, Neathey, Dench & Thomson, Institute for Employment Studies, EOC 2003.

SECTION THREE: AN EQUAL PAY POLICY

The organisation's intentions in respect of equal pay

86. It is good equal pay practice to provide employees with a clear statement of the organisation's intentions in respect of equal pay. Evidence of an equal pay policy may assist an employer's defence against an equal pay claim.

87. It is recommended that an equal pay policy should:

— Commit the organisation to carry out an equal pay review and to monitor pay regularly in partnership with trade union/employee representatives
— Set objectives
— Identify the action to be taken
— Implement that action in a planned programme in partnership with the workforce
— Assign responsibility and accountability for the policy to a senior manager
— Commit the organisation to set aside the resources necessary to achieve equal pay.

88. Everyone involved in setting the pay of staff should be committed to and, if possible, trained in the identification of sex discrimination in the pay process.

A model equal pay policy

We are committed to the principle of equal pay for all our employees. We aim to eliminate any sex bias in our pay systems.

We understand that equal pay between men and women is a legal right under both domestic and European law.

It is in the interest of the organisation to ensure that we have a fair and just pay system. It is important that employees have confidence in the process of eliminating sex bias and we are therefore committed to working in partnership with the recognised trade unions. As good business practice we are committed to working with trade union/ employee representatives to take action to ensure that we provide equal pay.

We believe that in eliminating sex bias in our pay system we are sending a positive message to our staff and customers. It makes good business sense to have a fair, transparent reward system and it helps us to control costs. We recognise that avoiding unfair discrimination will improve morale and enhance efficiency.

Our objectives are to:

— Eliminate any unfair, unjust or unlawful practices that impact on pay
— Take appropriate remedial action.

We will:

— Implement an equal pay review in line with EOC guidance for all current staff and starting pay for new staff (including those on maternity leave, career breaks, or non-standard contracts)
— Plan and implement actions in partnership with trade union/employee representatives
— Provide training and guidance for those involved in determining pay
— Inform employees of how these practices work and how their own pay is determined
— Respond to grievances on equal pay as a priority
— In conjunction with trade union/employee representatives, monitor pay statistics annually.

[4651]

ANNEX A
OTHER LEGISLATION THAT MAY IMPACT ON PAY

The Race Relations Act 1976 & the Race Relations (Amendment) Act 2000 require employers not to discriminate on grounds of race or ethnicity. This means that a black or minority ethnic employee could bring a discrimination claim seeking the same rate of pay as a white colleague in the same circumstances, who is either of the same or the opposite sex. The Race Relations (Amendment) Act 2000 imposes a duty on public bodies to promote race equality. The Commission for Racial Equality can provide advice on specific issues relating to race or ethnicity.

The Transfer of Undertakings (Protection of Employment) Regulations 1981 protects the rights of workers in the event of a relevant transfer of an undertaking to a new employer. All contracts of employment and employment relationships automatically transfer to the new employer at the date of transfer. The Regulations prohibit changes in contract terms connected with a relevant transfer. (At present, terms relating to pensions do not transfer (except for some enhanced redundancy rights). The Government is consulting on this and may introduce a requirement that a transferee provides an equivalent pension to that provided by the transferor).

The Pregnant Workers Directive 1992 states that all women are entitled to a minimum of 14 weeks maternity leave. However, United Kingdom law provides for more than this. (See under Employment Rights Act 1996, as amended by the Employment Relations Act 1999 and the Maternity and Parental Leave (Amendment) Regulations 2002).

The Trade Union Labour Relations (Consolidation) Act 1992 and the ACAS codes of practice on the disclosure of information and on disciplinary practice set out the regulations on the sharing of information for the purposes of collective bargaining between the employer and recognised trade unions.

PART 4

The Disability Discrimination Act 1995 requires an employer with 15 or more employees not to discriminate against disabled employees. Discrimination, which includes discrimination in relation to pay, means, without justification, treating a person less favourably for a reason related to his disability or failing to make a reasonable adjustment to a physical feature of premises or to working arrangements, which place the disabled employee at a substantial disadvantage.

Currently, the Disability Discrimination Act does not, in certain circumstances, make unlawful differences in pay linked to performance (cf. The Disability Discrimination (Employment) Regulations 1996, Reg 3). However, legislation being implemented from 1 October 2004 will end both that limitation and the exemption of smaller employers. Also from 1 October 2004, direct discrimination, for example actions based purely on prejudice against disabled people, will no longer be capable of justification, and nor will a failure to make reasonable adjustments. The Disability Rights Commission can provide advice on specific issues relating to disability.

The Pensions Act 1995 provides for equal treatment in occupational pension schemes. It does so by incorporating an equal treatment rule into every occupational pension scheme. The Occupational Pension Schemes (Equal Treatment) Regulations 1995 set out the procedural rules for enforcing any rights under the equal treatment rule. The Regulations adopt the procedural structures contained in the Equal Pay Act, with some modifications, such as removing the power to grant compensation for breach of the equal treatment rule.

The Employment Rights Act 1996 requires employers to issue a written statement of terms and conditions of employment. The Act also provides the framework for maternity rights the detail of which is set out in the Maternity and Parental Leave Regulations 1999.

The Data Protection Act 1998 does not list pay as sensitive information although it is personal data. Information about ethnic origin and medical data is listed as sensitive. The DPA does allow information about ethnic origin to be processed *'If it is necessary for the purpose of identifying or keeping under review the existence or absence of equality of opportunity of treatment between persons of different racial or ethnic origins, with a view to enabling such equality to be promoted or maintained, and is carried out with appropriate safeguards for the rights and freedoms of the data subjects'* (Sch 3 paragraph 9 of the DPA).

The Working Time Regulations 1998 set a maximum limit on how many hours people can work and provides a statutory entitlement to 20 days paid holiday per annum.

The National Minimum Wage Act 1998 and the National Minimum Wage Regulations 1999 set minimum hourly wage for all workers aged 18 and over. There is a separate lower rate for workers under the age of 18.

The Maternity and Parental Leave Regulations 1999, as amended by the Maternity and Parental Leave (Amendment) Regulations 2002, provide for Ordinary Maternity Leave of 26 weeks for all mothers whose expected week of childbirth is after 6 April 2003, and Additional Maternity Leave of a further 26 weeks for employees with sufficient length of service.

The Part-Time (Prevention of Less Favourable Treatment) Regulations 2000 give part-time male and female workers a right not to be treated less favourably than full-time workers unless any difference in treatment can be objectively justified. The regulations apply to all aspects of pay and conditions of employment (contractual and non-contractual) and will usually require that the part-time worker should be paid and receive other benefits on a pro-rata basis.

The part-timer can make comparison with a full-timer of the same sex, but otherwise, the range of comparators is more restricted than under the Equal Pay Act. Although the regulations apply to both employees and workers, a part-time worker has to name a full-time worker (not a full-time employee) as a comparator. Likewise, a part-time employee has to name a full-time employee (not a full-time worker) as comparator. In either case, the comparator has to be doing the same or broadly similar work, so there is no scope for an 'equal value' claim under the regulations.

There is also no scope for a part-timer to name a comparator working for a different employer (even an associated employer) and there are restrictions on naming a comparator based at a different site even if they are working for the same employer. Where a full-time worker or employee becomes part-time the appropriate comparison is with their own previous full-time terms and conditions.

The Fixed-Term Employees (Prevention of Less Favourable Treatment) Regulations 2002 give fixed-term employees the right to the same pay and terms and conditions of employment as permanent employees on broadly similar work, unless their less favourable treatment can be objectively justified. An employee can make a comparison with employees of the same sex, but the range of comparators is more restrictive than under the Equal Pay Act, for example, a fixed-term employee cannot select a predecessor as a comparator, nor can she/he make a comparison with someone working for an associated employer. The Fixed-term Employees Regulations do not apply to agency workers or apprentices.

The Regulations adopt a 'package approach', whereby an employer can justify the difference in treatment by showing that the value of the fixed-term employee's package of terms and conditions is at least equal to that of the permanent employee. This approach is not permissible under the Equal Pay Act.

The Employment Act 2002 empowers the Secretary of State to make regulations to enable workers on short term contracts to enjoy the rights and benefits of permanent workers, including pay. From October 2004 the Act will make it compulsory for employers and employees to use a three-stage grievance procedure. This should assist internal resolution of disputes. The Act also introduces the equal pay questionnaire procedure and improves maternity rights.

[4652]

(*Annex B has been omitted; see useful addresses at* **[5046]**.)

ACAS CODE OF PRACTICE 1
DISCIPLINARY AND GRIEVANCE PROCEDURES (2004)

NOTES

This is the fourth version of the Code originally produced by ACAS in 1977, and reissued in 1998 and 2000. This version was produced under the authority given to ACAS by TULR(C)A 1992, s 199 at **[684]** and approved by the Secretary of State and by Parliament in accordance with s 200(2) and (4) at **[685]** (see the Employment Code of Practice (Disciplinary and Grievance Procedures) Order 2004, SI 2004/2356). It came into effect on 1 October 2004. The statutory status of the Code is specified in TULR(C)A, s 207 at **[692]**.

INTRODUCTION

This Code of Practice provides practical guidance to employers, workers and their representatives on:

- The statutory requirements relating to disciplinary and grievance issues;
- What constitutes reasonable behaviour when dealing with disciplinary and grievance issues;
- Producing and using disciplinary and grievance procedures; and
- A worker's right to bring a companion to grievance and disciplinary hearings.

The statutory dismissal, disciplinary and grievance procedures, as set out in the Employment Act 2002, apply only to employees as defined in the 2002 Act and this term is used throughout sections 1 and 2 of the Code. However, it is good practice to allow all workers access to disciplinary and grievance procedures. The right to be accompanied applies to all workers (which includes employees) and this term is used in section 3 of the Code.

A failure to follow any part of this Code does not, in itself, make a person or organisation liable to proceedings. However, employment tribunals will take the Code into account when considering relevant cases. Similarly, arbitrators appointed by Acas to determine relevant cases under the Acas Arbitration Scheme will take the Code into account.

A failure to follow the statutory disciplinary and grievance procedures where they apply may have a number of legal implications which are described in the Code.

The Code (from sections 1 to 3) is issued under section 199 of the Trade Union and Labour Relations (Consolidation) Act 1992 and was laid before both Houses of Parliament on [date to be inserted]. The Code comes into effect by order of the Secretary of State on [date to be inserted].

More comprehensive, practical, advice and guidance on disciplinary and grievance procedures is contained in the Acas Handbook 'Discipline and Grievances at Work' which also includes information on the Disability Discrimination Act 1995 and the Data Protection Act 1998. The Handbook can be obtained from the Acas website at **www.acas.org.uk**. Further information on the detailed provisions of the statutory disciplinary and grievance procedures can be found on the Department of Trade and Industry's website at **www.dti.gov.uk/er**.

[4653]

SECTION 1
DISCIPLINARY RULES AND PROCEDURES

AT A GLANCE

Drawing up disciplinary rules and procedures

- Involve management, employees and their representatives where appropriate (Paragraph 52).
- Make rules clear and brief and explain their purpose (Paragraph 53).
- Explain rules and procedures to employees and make sure they have a copy or ready access to a copy of them (Paragraph 55).

Operating disciplinary procedures

- Establish facts before taking action (Paragraph 8).
- Deal with cases of minor misconduct or unsatisfactory performance informally (Paragraphs 11–12).
- For more serious cases, follow formal procedures, including informing the employee of the alleged misconduct or unsatisfactory performance (Paragraph 13).
- Invite the employee to a meeting and inform them of the right to be accompanied. (Paragraph 14–16).
- Where performance is unsatisfactory explain to the employee the improvement required, the support that will be given and when and how performance will be reviewed. (Paragraphs 19–20).
- If giving a warning, tell the employee why and how they need to change, the consequences of failing to improve and that they have a right to appeal (Paragraphs 21–22).
- If dismissing an employee, tell them why, when their contract will end and that they can appeal (Paragraph 25).
- Before dismissing or taking disciplinary action other than issuing a warning, always follow the statutory dismissal and disciplinary procedure (Paragraphs 26–32).
- When dealing with absences from work, find out the reasons for the absence before deciding on what action to take (Paragraph 37).

Holding appeals

- If the employee wishes to appeal invite them to a meeting and inform the employee of their right to be accompanied (Paragraphs 44–48).
- Where possible, arrange for the appeal to be dealt with by a more senior manager not involved with the earlier decision (Paragraph 46).
- Inform the employee about the appeal decision and the reasons for it (Paragraph 48).

Records

- Keep written records for future reference (Paragraph 49).

GUIDANCE

Why have disciplinary rules and procedures?

1. Disciplinary rules and procedures help to promote orderly employment relations as well as fairness and consistency in the treatment of individuals. Disciplinary procedures are also a legal requirement in certain circumstances (see paragraph 6).

2. Disciplinary rules tell employees what behaviour employers expect from them. If an employee breaks specific rules about behaviour, this is often called misconduct. Employers use disciplinary procedures and actions to deal with situations where employees allegedly break disciplinary rules. Disciplinary procedures may also be used where employees don't meet their employer's expectations in the way they do their job. These cases, often known as

unsatisfactory performance (or capability), may require different treatment from misconduct, and disciplinary procedures should allow for this.

3. Guidance on how to draw up disciplinary rules and procedures is contained in paragraphs 52–62.

4. When dealing with disciplinary cases, employers need to be aware both of the law on unfair dismissal and the statutory minimum procedure contained in the Employment Act 2002 for dismissing or taking disciplinary action against an employee. Employers must also be careful not to discriminate on the grounds of gender, race (including colour, nationality and ethnic or national origins), disability, age, sexual orientation or religion.

The law on unfair dismissal

5. The law on unfair dismissal requires employers to act reasonably when dealing with disciplinary issues. What is classed as reasonable behaviour will depend on the circumstances of each case, and is ultimately a matter for employment tribunals to decide. However, the core principles employers should work to are set out in the box overleaf. Drawing up and referring to a procedure can help employers deal with disciplinary issues in a fair and consistent manner.

Core principles of reasonable behaviour

- Use procedures primarily to help and encourage employees to improve rather than just as a way of imposing a punishment.
- Inform the employee of the complaint against them, and provide them with an opportunity to state their case before decisions are reached.
- Allow employees to be accompanied at disciplinary meetings.
- Make sure that disciplinary action is not taken until the facts of the case have been established and that the action is reasonable in the circumstances.
- Never dismiss an employee for a first disciplinary offence, unless it is a case of gross misconduct.
- Give the employee a written explanation for any disciplinary action taken and make sure they know what improvement is expected.
- Give the employee an opportunity to appeal.
- Deal with issues as thoroughly and promptly as possible.
- Act consistently.

The statutory minimum procedure

6. Employers are also required to follow a specific statutory minimum procedure if they are contemplating dismissing an employee or imposing some other disciplinary penalty that isn't suspension on full pay or a warning. Guidance on this statutory procedure is provided in paragraphs 26–32. If an employee is dismissed without the employer following this statutory procedure, and makes a claim to an employment tribunal, providing they have the necessary qualifying service and providing they are not prevented from claiming unfair dismissal by virtue of their age, the dismissal will automatically be ruled unfair. The statutory procedure is a minimum requirement and even where the relevant procedure is followed the dismissal may still be unfair if the employer has not acted reasonably in all the circumstances.

What about small businesses?

7. In small organisations it may not be practicable to adopt all the detailed good practice guidance set out in this Code. Employment tribunals will take account of an employer's size and administrative resources when deciding if it acted reasonably. However, all organisations regardless of size must follow the minimum statutory dismissal and disciplinary procedures.

Dealing with disciplinary issues in the workplace

8. When a potential disciplinary matter arises, the employer should make necessary investigations to establish the facts promptly before memories of events fade. It is important to keep a written record for later reference. Having established the facts, the employer should decide whether to drop the matter, deal with it informally or arrange for it to be handled formally. Where an investigatory meeting is held solely to establish the facts of a case, it should be made clear to the employee involved that it is not a disciplinary meeting.

9. In certain cases, for example in cases involving gross misconduct, where relationships have broken down or there are risks to an employer's property or responsibilities to other

parties, consideration should be given to a brief period of suspension with full pay whilst unhindered investigation is conducted. Such a suspension should only be imposed after careful consideration and should be reviewed to ensure it is not unnecessarily protracted. It should be made clear that the suspension is not considered a disciplinary action.

10. When dealing with disciplinary issues in the workplace employers should bear in mind that they are required under the Disability Discrimination Act 1995 to make reasonable adjustments to cater for employees who have a disability, for example providing for wheelchair access if necessary.

Informal action

11. Cases of minor misconduct or unsatisfactory performance are usually best dealt with informally. A quiet word is often all that is required to improve an employee's conduct or performance. The informal approach may be particularly helpful in small firms, where problems can be dealt with quickly and confidentially. There will, however, be situations where matters are more serious or where an informal approach has been tried but isn't working.

12. If informal action doesn't bring about an improvement, or the misconduct or unsatisfactory performance is considered to be too serious to be classed as minor, employers should provide employees with a clear signal of their dissatisfaction by taking formal action.

Formal action

Inform the employee of the problem

13. The first step in any formal process is to let the employee know in writing what it is they are alleged to have done wrong. The letter or note should contain enough information for the individual to be able to understand both what it is they are alleged to have done wrong and the reasons why this is not acceptable. If the employee has difficulty reading, or if English is not their first language, the employer should explain the content of the letter or note to them orally. The letter or note should also invite the individual to a meeting at which the problem can be discussed, and it should inform the individual of their right to be accompanied at the meeting (see section three). The employee should be given copies of any documents that will be produced at the meeting.

Hold a meeting to discuss the problem

14. Where possible, the timing and location of the meeting should be agreed with the employee. The length of time between the written notification and the meeting should be long enough to allow the employee to prepare but not so long that memories fade. The employer should hold the meeting in a private location and ensure there will be no interruptions.

15. At the meeting, the employer should explain the complaint against the employee and go through the evidence that has been gathered. The employee should be allowed to set out their case and answer any allegations that have been made. The employee should also be allowed to ask questions, present evidence, call witnesses and be given an opportunity to raise points about any information provided by witnesses.

16. An employee who cannot attend a meeting should inform the employer in advance whenever possible. If the employee fails to attend through circumstances outside their control and unforeseeable at the time the meeting was arranged (eg illness) the employer should arrange another meeting. A decision may be taken in the employee's absence if they fail to attend the re-arranged meeting without good reason. If an employee's companion cannot attend on a proposed date, the employee can suggest another date so long as it is reasonable and is not more than five working days after the date originally proposed by the employer. This five day time limit may be extended by mutual agreement.

Decide on outcome and action

17. Following the meeting the employer must decide whether disciplinary action is justified or not. Where it is decided that no action is justified the employee should be informed. Where it is decided that disciplinary action is justified the employer will need to consider what form this should take. Before making any decision the employer should take account of the employee's disciplinary and general record, length of service, actions taken in any previous similar case, the explanations given by the employee and – most important of all – whether the intended disciplinary action is reasonable under the circumstances.

18. Examples of actions the employer might choose to take are set out in paragraphs 19–25. It is normally good practice to give employees at least one chance to improve their

conduct or performance before they are issued with a final written warning. However, if an employee's misconduct or unsatisfactory performance – or its continuance – is sufficiently serious, for example because it is having, or is likely to have, a serious harmful effect on the organisation, it may be appropriate to move directly to a final written warning. In cases of gross misconduct, the employer may decide to dismiss even though the employee has not previously received a warning for misconduct. (Further guidance on dealing with gross misconduct is set out at paragraphs 35, 36).

First formal action – unsatisfactory performance

19. Following the meeting, an employee who is found to be performing unsatisfactorily should be given a written note setting out:

- the performance problem;
- the improvement that is required;
- the timescale for achieving this improvement;
- a review date; and
- any support the employer will provide to assist the employee.

20. The employee should be informed that the note represents the first stage of a formal procedure and that failure to improve could lead to a final written warning and, ultimately, dismissal. A copy of the note should be kept and used as the basis for monitoring and reviewing performance over a specified period (e g six months).

First formal action–misconduct

21. Where, following a disciplinary meeting, an employee is found guilty of misconduct, the usual first step would be to give them a written warning setting out the nature of the misconduct and the change in behaviour required.

22. The employee should be informed that the warning is part of the formal disciplinary process and what the consequences will be of a failure to change behaviour. The consequences could be a final written warning and ultimately, dismissal. The employee should also be informed that they may appeal against the decision. A record of the warning should be kept, but it should be disregarded for disciplinary purposes after a specified period (e g six months).

23. Guidance on dealing with cases of gross misconduct is provided in paragraphs 35, 36.

Final written warning

24. Where there is a failure to improve or change behaviour in the timescale set at the first formal stage, or where the offence is sufficiently serious, the employee should normally be issued with a final written warning—but only after they have been given a chance to present their case at a meeting. The final written warning should give details of, and grounds for, the complaint. It should warn the employee that failure to improve or modify behaviour may lead to dismissal or to some other penalty, and refer to the right of appeal. The final written warning should normally be disregarded for disciplinary purposes after a specified period (for example 12 months).

Dismissal or other penalty

25. If the employee's conduct or performance still fails to improve, the final stage in the disciplinary process might be dismissal or (if the employee's contract allows it or it is mutually agreed) some other penalty such as demotion, disciplinary transfer, or loss of seniority/pay. A decision to dismiss should only be taken by a manager who has the authority to do so. The employee should be informed as soon as possible of the reasons for the dismissal, the date on which the employment contract will terminate, the appropriate period of notice and their right of appeal.

26. It is important for employers to bear in mind that before they dismiss an employee or impose a sanction such as demotion, loss of seniority or loss of pay, they must as a minimum have followed the statutory dismissal and disciplinary procedures. The standard statutory procedure to be used in almost all cases requires the employer to:

Step 1

Write to the employee notifying them of the allegations against them and the basis of the allegations and invite them to a meeting to discuss the matter;

Step 2

Hold a meeting to discuss the allegations–at which the employee has the right to be accompanied–and notify the employee of the decision;

Step 3

If the employee wishes to appeal, hold an appeal meeting at which the employee has the right to be accompanied–and inform the employee of the final decision.

27. More detail on the statutory standard procedure is set out at Annex A. There is a modified two step procedure for use in special circumstances involving gross misconduct and details of this are set out at Annex B. Guidance on the modified procedure is contained in paragraph 36. There are a number of situations in which it is not necessary for employers to use the statutory procedures or where they will have been deemed to be completed and these are described in Annex E.

28. If the employer fails to follow this statutory procedure (where it applies), and an employee who is qualified to do so makes a claim for unfair dismissal, the employment tribunal will automatically find the dismissal unfair. The tribunal will normally increase the compensation awarded by 10 per cent, or, where it feels it is just and equitable to do so, up to 50 per cent. Equally, if the employment tribunal finds that an employee has been dismissed unfairly but has failed to follow the procedure (for instance they have failed to attend the disciplinary meeting without good cause), compensation will be reduced by, normally, 10 per cent, or, if the tribunal considers it just and equitable to do so, up to 50 per cent.

29. If the tribunal considers there are exceptional circumstances, compensation may be adjusted (up or down) by less than 10 per cent or not at all.

30. Employers and employees will normally be expected to go through the statutory dismissal and disciplinary procedure unless they have reasonable grounds to believe that by doing so they might be exposed to a significant threat, such as violent, abusive or intimidating behaviour, or they will be harassed. There will always be a certain amount of stress and anxiety for both parties when dealing with any disciplinary case, but this exemption will only apply where the employer or employee reasonably believes that they would come to some serious physical or mental harm; their property or some third party is threatened or the other party has harassed them and this may continue.

31. Equally, the statutory procedure does not need to be followed if circumstances beyond the control of either party prevent one or more steps being followed within a reasonable period. This will sometimes be the case where there is a long-term illness or a long period of absence abroad but, in the case of employers, wherever possible they should consider appointing another manager to deal with the procedure.

32. Where an employee fails to attend a meeting held as part of the statutory discipline procedure without good reason the statutory procedure comes to an end. In those circumstances the employee's compensation may be reduced if they bring a successful complaint before an employment tribunal. If the employee does have a good reason for non-attendance, the employer must re-arrange the meeting. If the employee does not attend the second meeting for good reason the employer need not arrange a third meeting but there will be no adjustment of compensation.

What if a grievance is raised during a disciplinary case?

33. In the course of a disciplinary process, an employee might raise a grievance that is related to the case. If this happens, the employer should consider suspending the disciplinary procedure for a short period while the grievance is dealt with. Depending on the nature of the grievance, the employer may need to consider bringing in another manager to deal with the disciplinary process. In small organisations this may not be possible, and the existing manager should deal with the case as impartially as possible.

34. Where the action taken or contemplated by the employer is dismissal the statutory grievance procedure does not apply. Where the action taken or contemplated is paid suspension or a warning the statutory grievance procedure and not the dismissal and disciplinary procedure applies to any grievance. However, where the employer takes, or is contemplating other action short of dismissal and asserts that the reason for the action is conduct or capability related, the statutory grievance procedure does not apply unless the grievance is that the action amounts, or would amount, to unlawful discrimination, or that the true reason for the action is not the reason given by the employer. In those cases the employee must have raised a written grievance in accordance with the statutory grievance procedure before presenting any complaint to an employment tribunal about the issue raised by the

grievance. However, if the written grievance is raised before any disciplinary appeal meeting, the rest of the grievance procedure does not have to be followed, although the employer may use the appeal meeting to discuss the grievance. .

Dealing with gross misconduct

35. If an employer considers an employee guilty of gross misconduct, and thus potentially liable for summary dismissal, it is still important to establish the facts before taking any action. A short period of suspension with full pay may be helpful or necessary, although it should only be imposed after careful consideration and should be kept under review. It should be made clear to the employee that the suspension is not a disciplinary action and does not involve any prejudgement.

36. It is a core principle of reasonable behaviour that employers should give employees the opportunity of putting their case at a disciplinary meeting before deciding whether to take action. This principle applies as much to cases of gross misconduct as it does to ordinary cases of misconduct or unsatisfactory performance. There may however be some very limited cases where despite the fact that an employer has dismissed an employee immediately without a meeting an employment tribunal will, very exceptionally, find the dismissal to be fair To allow for these cases there is a statutory modified procedure under which the employer is required to write to the employee after the dismissal setting out the reasons for the dismissal and to hold an appeal meeting, if the employee wants one. The statutory procedure that must be followed by employers in such cases is set out in Annex B. If an employer fails to follow this procedure and the case goes to tribunal, the dismissal will be found to be automatically unfair.

Dealing with absence from work

37. When dealing with absence from work, it is important to determine the reasons why the employee has not been at work. If there is no acceptable reason, the matter should be treated as a conduct issue and dealt with as a disciplinary matter.

38. If the absence is due to genuine (including medically certified) illness, the issue becomes one of capability, and the employer should take a sympathetic and considerate approach. When thinking about how to handle these cases, it is helpful to consider:

- how soon the employee's health and attendance will improve;
- whether alternative work is available;
- the effect of the absence on the organisation;
- how similar situations have been handled in the past; and
- whether the illness is a result of disability in which case the provisions of the Disability Discrimination Act 1995 will apply.

39. The impact of long-term absences will nearly always be greater on small organisations, and they may be entitled to act at an earlier stage than large organisations.

40. In cases of extended sick leave both statutory and contractual issues will need to be addressed and specialist advice may be necessary.

Dealing with special situations

If the full procedure is not immediately available

41. Special arrangements might be required for handling disciplinary matters among nightshift employees, employees in isolated locations or depots, or others who may be difficult to reach. Nevertheless the appropriate statutory procedure must be followed where it applies.

Trade union representatives

42. Disciplinary action against a trade union representative can lead to a serious dispute if it is seen as an attack on the union's functions. Normal standards apply but, if disciplinary action is considered, the case should be discussed, after obtaining the employee's agreement, with a senior trade union representative or permanent union official.

Criminal charges or convictions not related to employment

43. If an employee is charged with, or convicted of, a criminal offence not related to work, this is not in itself reason for disciplinary action. The employer should establish the facts of the case and consider whether the matter is serious enough to warrant starting the disciplinary procedure. The main consideration should be whether the offence, or alleged

offence, is one that makes the employee unsuitable for their type of work. Similarly, an employee should not be dismissed solely because they are absent from work as a result of being remanded in custody.

Appeals

44. Employees who have had disciplinary action taken against them should be given the opportunity to appeal. It is useful to set a time limit for asking for an appeal—five working days is usually enough.

45. An employee may choose to appeal for example because:
- they think a finding or penalty is unfair;
- new evidence comes to light; or
- they think the disciplinary procedure wasn't used correctly.

It should be noted that the appeal stage is part of the statutory procedure and if the employee pursues an employment tribunal claim the tribunal may reduce any award of compensation if the employee did not exercise the right of appeal

46. As far as is reasonably practicable a more senior manager not involved with the case should hear the appeal. In small organisations, even if a more senior manager is not available, another manager should hear the appeal, if possible. If that is not an option, the person overseeing the case should act as impartially as possible. Records and notes of the original disciplinary meeting should be made available to the person hearing the appeal.

47. The employers should contact the employee with appeal arrangements as soon as possible, and inform them of their statutory right to be accompanied at the appeal meeting.

48. The manager must inform the employee about the appeal decision, and the reasons for it, as soon as possible. They should also confirm the decision in writing. If the decision is the final stage of the organisation's appeals procedure, the manager should make this clear to the employee.

Keeping records

49. It is important, and in the interests of both employers and employees, to keep written records during the disciplinary process. Records should include:
- the complaint against the employee;
- the employee's defence;
- findings made and actions taken;
- the reason for actions taken;
- whether an appeal was lodged;
- the outcome of the appeal;
- any grievances raised during the disciplinary procedure; and
- subsequent developments.

50. Records should be treated as confidential and be kept no longer than necessary in accordance with the Data Protection Act 1998. This Act gives individuals the right to request and have access to certain personal data.

51. Copies of meeting records should be given to the employee including copies of any formal minutes that may have been taken. In certain circumstances (for example to protect a witness) the employer might withhold some information.

Drawing up disciplinary rules and procedures

52. Management is responsible for maintaining and setting standards of performance in an organisation and for ensuring that disciplinary rules and procedures are in place. Employers are legally required to have disciplinary procedures. It is good practice to involve employees (and, where appropriate, their representatives) when making or changing rules and procedures, so that everyone affected by them understands them.

Rules

53. When making rules, the aim should be to specify those that are necessary for ensuring a safe and efficient workplace and for maintaining good employment relations.

54. It is unlikely that any set of rules will cover all possible disciplinary issues, but rules normally cover:
- bad behaviour, such as fighting or drunkenness;
- unsatisfactory work performance;
- harassment or victimisation;

- misuse of company facilities (for example e-mail and internet);
- poor timekeeping;
- unauthorised absences; and
- repeated or serious failure to follow instructions.

55. Rules should be specific, clear and recorded in writing. They also need to be readily available to employees, for instance on a noticeboard or, in larger organisations, in a staff handbook or on the Intranet. Management should do all they can to ensure that every employee knows and understands the rules, including those employees whose first language is not English or who have trouble reading. This is often best done as part of an induction process.

56. Employers should inform employees of the likely consequences of breaking disciplinary rules. In particular, they should list examples of acts of gross misconduct that may warrant summary dismissal.

57. Acts which constitute gross misconduct are those resulting in a serious breach of contractual terms and are best decided by organisations in the light of their own particular circumstances. However, examples of gross misconduct might include:

- theft or fraud;
- physical violence or bullying;
- deliberate and serious damage to property;
- serious misuse of an organisation's property or name;
- deliberately accessing internet sites containing pornographic, offensive or obscene material;
- serious insubordination;
- unlawful discrimination or harassment;
- bringing the organisation into serious disrepute;
- serious incapability at work brought on by alcohol or illegal drugs;
- causing loss, damage or injury through serious negligence;
- a serious breach of health and safety rules; and
- a serious breach of confidence.

Procedures

58. Disciplinary procedures should not be seen primarily as a means of imposing sanctions but rather as a way of encouraging improvement amongst employees whose conduct or performance is unsatisfactory. Some organisations may prefer to have separate procedures for dealing with issues of conduct and capability. Large organisations may also have separate procedures to deal with other issues such as harassment and bullying.

59. When drawing up and applying procedures employers should always bear in mind the requirements of natural justice. This means that employees should be given the opportunity of a meeting with someone who has not been involved in the matter. They should be informed of the allegations against them, together with the supporting evidence, in advance of the meeting. Employees should be given the opportunity to challenge the allegations before decisions are reached and should be provided with a right of appeal.

60. Good disciplinary procedures should:

- be put in writing;
- say to whom they apply;
- be non-discriminatory;
- allow for matters to be dealt without undue delay;
- allow for information to be kept confidential;
- tell employees what disciplinary action might be taken;
- say what levels of management have the authority to take disciplinary action;
- require employees to be informed of the complaints against them and supporting evidence, before a meeting;
- give employees a chance to have their say before management reaches a decision;
- provide employees with the right to be accompanied;
- provide that no employee is dismissed for a first breach of discipline, except in cases of gross misconduct;
- require management to investigate fully before any disciplinary action is taken;
- ensure that employees are given an explanation for any sanction; and
- allow employees to appeal against a decision.

61. It is important to ensure that everyone in an organisation understands the disciplinary procedures including the statutory requirements. In small firms this is best done by making sure all employees have access to a copy of the procedures, for instance on a noticeboard, and

by taking a few moments to run through the procedures with the employee. In large organisations formal training for those who use and operate the procedures may be appropriate.

Further action

62. It is sensible to keep rules and procedures under review to make sure they are always relevant and effective. New or additional rules should only be introduced after reasonable notice has been given to all employees and any employee representatives have been consulted. **[4654]**

SECTION 2
GRIEVANCE PROCEDURES

AT A GLANCE

Drawing up grievance procedures

- Involve management, employees and their representatives where appropriate. (Paragraph 90).
- Explain procedures to employees and make sure they have a copy or ready access to a copy of them. (Paragraph 94).

Operating grievance procedures

- Many grievances can be settled informally with line managers (Paragraph 67).
- Employees should raise formal grievances with management (Paragraph 73).
- Invite the employee to a meeting and inform them about the right to be accompanied (Paragraph 77).
- Give the employee an opportunity to have their say at the meeting (Paragraph 78).
- Write with a response within a reasonable time and inform the employee of their right to appeal (Paragraph 81).

Appeals

- If possible, a more senior manager should handle the appeal (Paragraph 82).
- Tell the employee they have the right to be accompanied (Paragraph 82).
- The senior manager should respond to the grievance in writing after the appeal and tell the employee if it is the final stage in the grievance procedure (Paragraph 83).

Records

- Written records should be kept for future reference (Paragraph 87).

GUIDANCE

Why have grievance procedures?

63. Grievances are concerns, problems or complaints that employees raise with their employers.

64. Grievance procedures are used by employers to deal with employees' grievances.

65. Grievance procedures allow employers to deal with grievances fairly, consistently and speedily. Employers must have procedures available to employees so that their grievances can be properly considered.

66. Guidance on drawing up grievance procedures is set out in paragraphs 90–95.

Dealing with grievances in the workplace

67. Employees should aim to resolve most grievances informally with their line manager. This has advantages for all workplaces, particularly where there might be a close personal relationship between a manager and an employee. It also allows for problems to be resolved quickly.

68. If a grievance cannot be settled informally, the employee should raise it formally with management. There is a statutory grievance procedure that employees must invoke if they wish subsequently to use the grievance as the basis of certain applications to an employment tribunal.

69. Under the standard statutory procedure, employees must:

Step 1

Inform the employer of their grievance in writing.

Step 2

Be invited by the employer to a meeting to discuss the grievance where the right to be accompanied will apply and be notified in writing of the decision. The employee must take all reasonable steps to attend this meeting.

Step 3

Be given the right to an appeal meeting if they feel the grievance has not been satisfactorily resolved and be notified of the final decision.

More detail on the standard statutory procedure is set out in Annex C.

70. There are certain occasions when it is not necessary to follow the statutory procedure for example, if the employee is raising a concern in compliance with the Public Interest Disclosure Act or a grievance is raised on behalf of at least two employees by an appropriate representative such as an official of an independent trade union. A full list of exemptions is set out in Annex E.

71. It is important that employers and employees follow the statutory grievance procedure where it applies. The employee should (subject to the exemptions described in Annex E) at least have raised the grievance in writing and waited 28 days before presenting any tribunal claim relating to the matter. A premature claim will be automatically rejected by the tribunal although (subject to special time limit rules) it may be presented again once the written grievance has been raised. Furthermore if a grievance comes before an employment tribunal and either party has failed to follow the procedure then the tribunal will normally adjust any award by 10 per cent or, where it feels it just and equitable to do so, by up to 50 per cent, depending on which party has failed to follow the procedure. In exceptional cases compensation can be adjusted by less than 10 per cent or not at all.

72. Wherever possible a grievance should be dealt with before an employee leaves employment. A statutory grievance procedure ('the modified grievance procedure' described in Annex D), however, applies where an employee has already left employment, the standard procedure has not been commenced or completed before the employee left employment and both parties agree in writing that it should be used instead of the standard statutory procedure. Under the modified procedure the employee should write to the employer setting out the grievance as soon as possible after leaving employment and the employer must write back setting out its response.

Raising a grievance

73. Employees should normally raise a grievance with their line manager unless someone else is specified in the organisation's procedure. If the complaint is against the person with whom the grievance would normally be raised the employee can approach that person's manager or another manager in the organisation. In small businesses where this isn't possible, the line manager should hear the grievance and deal with it as impartially as possible.

74. Managers should deal with all grievances raised, whether or not the grievance is presented in writing. However, employees need to be aware that if the statutory procedure applies, they will not subsequently be able to take the case to an employment tribunal unless they have first raised a grievance in writing and waited a further 28 days before presenting the tribunal claim.

75. Setting out a grievance in writing is not easy—especially for those employees whose first language is not English or who have difficulty expressing themselves on paper. In these circumstances the employee should be encouraged to seek help for example from a work colleague, a trade union or other employee representative. Under the Disability Discrimination Act 1995 employers are required to make reasonable adjustments which may include assisting employees to formulate a written grievance if they are unable to do so themselves because of a disability.

76. In circumstances where a grievance may apply to more than one person and where a trade union is recognised it may be appropriate for the problem to be resolved through collective agreements between the trade union(s) and the employer.

Grievance meetings

77. On receiving a formal grievance, a manager should invite the employee to a meeting as soon as possible and inform them that they have the right to be accompanied. It is good practice to agree a time and place for the meeting with the employee. Small organisations might not have private meeting rooms, but it is important that the meeting is not interrupted and that the employee feels their grievance is being treated confidentially. If an employee's companion cannot attend on a proposed date, the employee can suggest another date so long as it is reasonable and is not more than five working days after the date originally proposed by the employer. This five day time limit may be extended by mutual agreement.

78. The employee should be allowed to explain their complaint and say how they think it should be settled. If the employer reaches a point in the meeting where they are not sure how to deal with the grievance or feel that further investigation is necessary the meeting should be adjourned to get advice or make further investigation. This might be particularly useful in small organisations that lack experience of dealing with formal grievances. The employer should give the grievance careful consideration before responding.

79. Employers and employees will normally be expected to go through the statutory grievance procedures unless they have reasonable grounds to believe that by doing so they might be exposed to a significant threat, such as violent, abusive or intimidating behaviour, or they will be harassed. There will always be a certain amount of stress and anxiety for both parties when dealing with grievance cases, but this exemption will only apply where the employer or employee reasonably believes that they would come to some serious physical or mental harm; their property or some third party is threatened or the other party has harassed them and this may continue.

80. Equally, the statutory procedure does not need to be followed if circumstances beyond the control of either party prevent one or more steps being followed within a reasonable period. This will sometimes be the case where there is a long-term illness or a long period of absence abroad but wherever possible the employer should consider appointing another manager to deal with the procedure.

81. The employer should respond in writing to the employee's grievance within a reasonable time and should let the employee know that they can appeal against the employer's decision if they are not satisfied with it. What is considered reasonable will vary from organisation to organisation, but five working days is normally long enough. If it is not possible to respond within five working days the employee should be given an explanation for the delay and told when a response can be expected.

Appeals

82. If an employee informs the employer that they are unhappy with the decision after a grievance meeting, the employer should arrange an appeal. It should be noted that the appeal stage is part of the statutory procedure and if the employee pursues an employment tribunal claim the tribunal may reduce any award of compensation if the employee did not exercise the right of appeal. As far as is reasonably practicable the appeal should be with a more senior manager than the one who dealt with the original grievance. In small organisations, even if there is no more senior manager available, another manager should, if possible, hear the appeal. If that is not an option, the person overseeing the case should act as impartially as possible. At the same time as inviting the employee to attend the appeal, the employer should remind them of their right to be accompanied at the appeal meeting.

83. As with the first meeting, the employer should write to the employee with a decision on their grievance as soon as possible. They should also tell the employee if the appeal meeting is the final stage of the grievance procedure.

84. In large organisations it is good practice to allow a further appeal to a higher level of management, such as a director. However, in smaller firms the first appeal will usually mark the end of the grievance procedure.

Special considerations

85. Complaints about discrimination, bullying and harassment in the workplace are sensitive issues, and large organisations often have separate grievance procedures for dealing with these. It is important that these procedures meet the statutory minimum requirements.

86. Organisations may also wish to consider whether they need a whistleblowing procedure in the light of the Public Interest Disclosure Act 1998. This Act provides protection to employees who raise concerns about certain kinds of wrongdoing in accordance with its procedures.

Keeping records

87. It is important, and in the interests of both employer and employee, to keep written records during the grievance process. Records should include:

- the nature of the grievance raised;
- a copy of the written grievance
- the employer's response;
- action taken;
- reasons for action taken;
- whether there was an appeal and, if so, the outcome; and
- subsequent developments.

88. Records should be treated as confidential and kept in accordance with the Data Protection Act 1998, which gives individuals the right to request and have access to certain personal data.

89. Copies of meeting records should be given to the employee including any formal minutes that may have been taken. In certain circumstances (for example to protect a witness) the employer might withhold some information.

Drawing up grievance procedures

90. When employers draw up grievance procedures, it pays to involve everybody they will affect, including managers, employees and, where appropriate, their representatives.

91. Grievance procedures should make it easy for employees to raise issues with management and should:
- be simple and put in writing;
- enable an employee's line manager to deal informally with a grievance, if possible;
- keep proceedings confidential; and
- allow the employee to have a companion at meetings.

92. Issues that may cause grievances include:
- terms and conditions of employment;
- health and safety;
- work relations;
- bullying and harassment;
- new working practices;
- working environment;
- organisational change; and
- equal opportunities.

93. Where separate procedures exist for dealing with grievances on particular issues (for example, harassment and bullying) these should be used instead of the normal grievance procedure.

94. It's important to ensure that everyone in the organisation understands the grievance procedures including the statutory requirements and that, if necessary, supervisors, managers and employee representatives are trained in their use. Employees must be given a copy of the procedures or have ready access to them, for instance on a noticeboard. Large organisations can include them with disciplinary procedures as part of an induction process.

95. Take the time to explain the detail of grievance procedures to employees. This is particularly useful for people who don't speak English very well or who have difficulty with reading.

[4655]

SECTION 3
A WORKER'S RIGHT TO BE ACCOMPANIED

AT A GLANCE

The right to be accompanied
- All workers have the right to be accompanied at a disciplinary or grievance hearing (Paragraph 96).

- Workers must make a reasonable request to the employer if they want to be accompanied (Paragraph 96).
- Disciplinary hearings, for these purposes, include meetings where either disciplinary actions or some other actions might be taken against the worker. Appeal hearings are also covered (Paragraphs 97–99).
- Grievance hearings are defined as meetings where an employer deals with a worker's complaint about a duty owed to them by the employer (Paragraphs 100–102).

The companion
- The companion can be a fellow worker or a union official (Paragraph 104).
- Nobody has to accept an invitation to act as a companion (Paragraph 107).
- Fellow workers who are acting as companions can take paid time off to prepare for and go to a hearing (Paragraph 109).

Applying the right
- Agree a suitable date with the worker and the companion (Paragraph 110).
- The worker should tell the employer who the chosen companion is (Paragraph 112).
- The companion can have a say at the hearing but can't answer questions for the worker (Paragraph 113–114).
- Don't disadvantage workers who have applied the right, or their companions (Paragraph 116).

GUIDANCE

What is the right to be accompanied?

96. Workers have a statutory right to be accompanied by a fellow worker or trade union official where they are required or invited by their employer to attend certain disciplinary or grievance hearings. They must make a reasonable request to their employer to be accompanied. Further guidance on what is a reasonable request and who can accompany a worker appears at paragraphs 103–109.

What is a disciplinary hearing?

97. For the purposes of this right, disciplinary hearings are defined as meetings that could result in:

- a formal warning being issued to a worker (ie a warning that will be placed on the worker's record);
- the taking of some other disciplinary action (such as suspension without pay, demotion or dismissal) or other action; or
- the confirmation of a warning or some other disciplinary action (such as an appeal hearing).

98. The right to be accompanied will also apply to any disciplinary meetings held as part of the statutory dismissal and disciplinary procedures. This includes any meetings held after an employee has left employment.

99. Informal discussions or counselling sessions do not attract the right to be accompanied unless they could result in formal warnings or other actions. Meetings to investigate an issue are not disciplinary hearings. If it becomes clear during the course of such a meeting that disciplinary action is called for, the meeting should be ended and a formal hearing arranged at which the worker will have the right to be accompanied.

What is a grievance hearing?

100. For the purposes of this right, a grievance hearing is a meeting at which an employer deals with a complaint about a duty owed by them to a worker, whether the duty arises from statute or common law (for example contractual commitments).

101. For instance, an individual's request for a pay rise is unlikely to fall within the definition, unless a right to an increase is specifically provided for in the contract or the request raises an issue about equal pay. Equally, most employers will be under no legal duty to provide their workers with car parking facilities, and a grievance about such facilities would carry no right to be accompanied at a hearing by a companion. However, if a worker

were disabled and needed a car to get to and from work, they probably would be entitled to a companion at a grievance hearing, as an issue might arise as to whether the employer was meeting its obligations under the Disability Discrimination Act 1995.

102. The right to be accompanied will also apply to any meetings held as part of the statutory grievance procedures. This includes any meetings after the employee has left employment.

What is a reasonable request?

103. Whether a request for a companion is reasonable will depend on the circumstances of the individual case and, ultimately, it is a matter for the courts and tribunals to decide. However, when workers are choosing a companion, they should bear in mind that it would not be reasonable to insist on being accompanied by a colleague whose presence would prejudice the hearing or who might have a conflict of interest. Nor would it be reasonable for a worker to ask to be accompanied by a colleague from a geographically remote location when someone suitably qualified was available on site. The request to be accompanied does not have to be in writing.

The companion

104. The companion may be:

- a fellow worker (ie another of the employer's workers);
- an official employed by a trade union, or a lay trade union official, as long as they have been reasonably certified in writing by their union as having experience of, or having received training in, acting as a worker's companion at disciplinary or grievance hearings. Certification may take the form of a card or letter.

105. Some workers may, however, have additional contractual rights to be accompanied by persons other than those listed above (for instance a partner, spouse or legal representative). If workers are disabled, employers should consider whether it might be reasonable to allow them to be accompanied because of their disability.

106. Workers may ask an official from any trade union to accompany them at a disciplinary or grievance hearing, regardless of whether the union is recognised or not. However, where a union is recognised in a workplace, it is good practice for workers to ask an official from that union to accompany them.

107. Fellow workers or trade union officials do not have to accept a request to accompany a worker, and they should not be pressurised to do so.

108. Trade unions should ensure that their officials are trained in the role of acting as a worker's companion. Even when a trade union official has experience of acting in the role, there may still be a need for periodic refresher training.

109. A worker who has agreed to accompany a colleague employed by the same employer is entitled to take a reasonable amount of paid time off to fulfil that responsibility. This should cover the hearing and it is also good practice to allow time for the companion to familiarise themselves with the case and confer with the worker before and after the hearing. A lay trade union official is permitted to take a reasonable amount of paid time off to accompany a worker at a hearing, as long as the worker is employed by the same employer. In cases where a lay official agrees to accompany a worker employed by another organisation, time off is a matter for agreement by the parties concerned.

Applying the right

110. Where possible, the employer should allow a companion to have a say in the date and time of a hearing. If the companion can't attend on a proposed date, the worker can suggest an alternative time and date so long as it is reasonable and it is not more than five working days after the original date.

111. In the same way that employers should cater for a worker's disability at a disciplinary or grievance hearing, they should also cater for a companion's disability, for example providing for wheelchair access if necessary.

112. Before the hearing takes place, the worker should tell the employer who they have chosen as a companion. In certain circumstances (for instance when the companion is an official of a non-recognised trade union) it can be helpful for the companion and employer to make contact before the hearing.

113. The companion should be allowed to address the hearing in order to:

- put the worker's case

- sum up the worker's case
- respond on the worker's behalf to any view expressed at the hearing.

114. The companion can also confer with the worker during the hearing. It is good practice to allow the companion to participate as fully as possible in the hearing, including asking witnesses questions. The companion has no right to answer questions on the worker's behalf, or to address the hearing if the worker does not wish it, or to prevent the employer from explaining their case.

115. Workers whose employers fail to comply with a reasonable request to be accompanied may present a complaint to an employment tribunal. Workers may also complain to a tribunal if employers fail to re-arrange a hearing to a reasonable date proposed by the worker when a companion cannot attend on the date originally proposed. The tribunal may order compensation of up to two weeks' pay. This could be increased if, in addition, the tribunal finds that the worker has been unfairly dismissed.

116. Employers should be careful not to disadvantage workers for using their right to be accompanied or for being companions, as this is against the law and could lead to a claim to an employment tribunal.

[4656]

SECTION 4
ANNEXES

ANNEX A
STANDARD STATUTORY DISMISSAL AND DISCIPLINARY PROCEDURE

(This is a summary of the statutory procedure which is set out in full in Schedule 2 to the Employment Act 2002)

This procedure applies to disciplinary action short of dismissal (excluding oral and written warnings and suspension on full pay) based on either conduct or capability. It also applies to dismissals (except for constructive dismissals) including dismissals on the basis of conduct, capability, expiry of a fixed term contract, redundancy and retirement. However, it does not apply in certain kinds of excepted cases that are described in Annex E.

Step 1
Statement of grounds for action and invitation to meeting

- The employer must set out in writing the employee's alleged conduct or characteristics, or other circumstances, which lead them to contemplate dismissing or taking disciplinary action against the employee.
- The employer must send the statement or a copy of it to the employee and invite the employee to attend a meeting to discuss the matter.

Step 2
The meeting

- The meeting must take place before action is taken, except in the case where the disciplinary action consists of suspension.
- The meeting must not take place unless:
  - (i) the employer has informed the employee what the basis was for including in the statement under Step 1 the ground or grounds given in it; and
  - (ii) the employee has had a reasonable opportunity to consider their response to that information.
- The employee must take all reasonable steps to attend the meeting.
- After the meeting, the employer must inform the employee of their decision and notify them of the right to appeal against the decision if they are not satisfied with it.
- Employees have the right to be accompanied at the meeting (see section 3).

Step 3
Appeal

- If the employee wishes to appeal, they must inform the employer.
- If the employee informs the employer of their wish to appeal, the employer must invite them to attend a further meeting.
- The employee must take all reasonable steps to attend the meeting.
- The appeal meeting need not take place before the dismissal or disciplinary action takes effect.

- Where reasonably practicable, the appeal should be dealt with by a more senior manager than attended the first meeting (unless the most senior manager attended that meeting).
- After the appeal meeting, the employer must inform the employee of their final decision.
- Employees have the right to be accompanied at the appeal meeting (see section 3).

[4657]

ANNEX B
MODIFIED STATUTORY DISMISSAL AND DISCIPLINARY PROCEDURE

(This is a summary of the statutory procedure which is set out in full in Schedule 2 to the Employment Act 2002)

Step 1
Statement of grounds for action

- The employer must set out in writing:
  - (i) the employee's alleged misconduct which has led to the dismissal;
  - (ii) the reasons for thinking at the time of the dismissal that the employee was guilty of the alleged misconduct; and
  - (iii) the employee's right of appeal against dismissal.
- The employer must send the statement or a copy of it to the employee.

Step 2
Appeal

- If the employee does wish to appeal, they must inform the employer.
- If the employee informs the employer of their wish to appeal, the employer must invite them to attend a meeting.
- The employee must take all reasonable steps to attend the meeting
- After the appeal meeting, the employer must inform the employee of their final decision.
- Where reasonably practicable the appeal should be dealt with by a more senior manager not involved in the earlier decision to dismiss.
- Employees have the right to be accompanied at the appeal meeting (see section 3).

[4658]

ANNEX C
STANDARD STATUTORY GRIEVANCE PROCEDURE

(This is a summary of the statutory procedure which is set out in full in Schedule 2 to the Employment Act 2002)

Step 1
Statement of grievance

- The employee must set out the grievance in writing and send the statement or a copy of it to the employer.

Step 2
Meeting

- The employer must invite the employee to attend a meeting to discuss the grievance.
- The meeting must not take place unless:
  - (i) the employee has informed the employer what the basis for the grievance was when they made the statement under Step 1; and
  - (ii) the employer has had a reasonable opportunity to consider their response to that information.
- The employee must take all reasonable steps to attend the meeting.
- After the meeting, the employer must inform the employee of their decision as to their response to the grievance and notify them of the right of appeal against the decision if they are not satisfied with it.
- Employees have the right to be accompanied at the meeting (see section 3).

Step 3
Appeal

- If the employee does wish to appeal, they must inform the employer.

- If the employee informs the employer of their wish to appeal, the employer must invite them to attend a further meeting.
- The employee must take all reasonable steps to attend the meeting.
- After the appeal meeting, the employer must inform the employee of their final decision.
- Where reasonably practicable, the appeal should be dealt with by a more senior manager than attended the first meeting (unless the most senior manager attended that meeting).
- Employees have the right to be accompanied at the appeal meeting (see section 3).

[4659]

ANNEX D
MODIFIED STATUTORY GRIEVANCE PROCEDURE

(This is a summary of the statutory procedure which is set out in full in Schedule 2 to the Employment Act 2002)

Step 1
Statement of grievance

- The employee must set out in writing:
  - (i) the grievance; and
  - (ii) the basis for it.
- The employee must send the statement or a copy of it to the employer.

Step 2
Response

- The employer must set out their response in writing and send the statement or a copy of it to the employee.

[4660]

ANNEX E
STATUTORY PROCEDURES: EXEMPTIONS AND DEEMED COMPLIANCE

The Employment Act 2002 (Dispute Resolution) Regulations 2004 contain detailed provisions about the application of the Statutory Dispute Resolution Procedures. This Annex summarises the particular provisions of the 2004 Regulations which describe:

(*a*) certain situations in which the statutory procedures will not apply at all; and
(*b*) other situations in which a party who has not completed the applicable procedure will nevertheless be treated as though they had done so.

Where a statutory procedure applies *and* one of the conditions for extending time limits contained in the 2004 Regulations has been met, then the normal time limit for presenting an employment tribunal claim will be extended by three months. The guidance notes accompanying tribunal application forms describe those conditions. However, in cases where the procedures do not apply at all, there can be *no* such extension.

(a) Situations in which the Statutory Procedures do not apply at all

The Disciplinary and Dismissal Procedures do not apply where:

- Factors beyond the control of either party make it impracticable to carry out or complete the procedure for the foreseeable future; or
- The employee is dismissed in circumstances covered by the modified dismissal procedure and presents a tribunal complaint before the employer has taken step 1; or
- All of the employees of the same description or category are dismissed and offered re-engagement either before or upon termination of their contract; or
- The dismissal is one of a group of redundancies covered by the duty of collective consultation of worker representatives under the Trade Union and Labour Relations (Consolidation) Act 1992; or
- The employee is dismissed while taking part in unofficial industrial action, or other industrial action which is not 'protected action' under the 1992 Act, unless the employment tribunal has jurisdiction to hear a claim of unfair dismissal; or
- The employee is unfairly dismissed for taking part in industrial action which is 'protected action' under the 1992 Act; or
- The employer's business suddenly and unexpectedly ceases to function and it becomes impractical to employee any employees; or
- The employee cannot continue in the particular position without contravening a statutory requirement; or

- The employee is one to whom a dismissal procedure agreement designated under section 110 of the Employment Relations Act 1996 applies.

The Grievance Procedures do not apply where:

- The employee is no longer employed, and it is no longer practicable for the employee to take step 1 of the procedure; or
- The employee wishes to complain about an actual or threatened dismissal; or
- The employee raises a concern as a 'protected disclosure' in compliance with the public interest disclosure provisions of the 1996 Act;
- The employee wishes to complain about (actual or threatened) action short of dismissal to which the standard disciplinary procedure applies, unless the grievance is that this involves unlawful discrimination (including under the Equal Pay Act) or is not genuinely on grounds of capability or conduct.

In addition, neither party need comply with an applicable statutory procedure where to do so would be contrary to the interests of national security.

(b) Situations in which the Statutory Procedures have not been completed but are treated as having been complied with.

The Disciplinary and Dismissal Procedures are treated as having been complied with where all stages of the procedure have been completed, other than the right of appeal, and:

- The employee then applies to the employment tribunal for interim relief; or
- A collective agreement provides for a right of appeal, which the employee exercises.

The Grievance Procedures are treated as having been complied with where:

- The employee is complaining that action short of dismissal to which the standard disciplinary procedure applies is not genuinely on grounds of conduct or capability, or involves unlawful discrimination, and the employee has raised that complaint as a written grievance before any appeal hearing under a statutory procedure or, if none is being followed, before presenting a tribunal complaint; or
- The employment has ended and the employee has raised a written grievance, but it has become not reasonably practical to have a meeting or an appeal. However, the employer must still give the employee a written answer to the grievance; or
- An official of a recognised independent union or other appropriate representative has raised the grievance on behalf of two or more named employees. Employees sharing the grievance may choose one of their number to act as a representative; or
- The employee pursues the grievance using a procedure available under an industry-level collective agreement.

(c) Other Special Circumstances in which the Statutory Procedures need not be begun or completed

In addition, neither the employer nor employee need begin a procedure (which will then be treated as not applying), or comply with a particular requirement of it (but will still be deemed to have complied) if the reason for not beginning or not complying is:

- The reasonable belief that doing so would result in a significant threat to themselves, any other person, or their or any other persons' property;
- Because they have been subjected to harassment and reasonably believe that doing so would result in further harassment; or
- Because it is not practicable to do so within a reasonable period.

[4661]

DISABILITY RIGHTS COMMISSION CODE OF PRACTICE: EMPLOYMENT AND OCCUPATION (2004)

NOTES

This Code of Practice is the first of two new Codes prepared by the Disability Rights Commission in 2004, under the powers conferred on it by the Disability Discrimination Act 1995, s 53A (inserted by the Disability Rights Commission Act 1999 and repealed as noted below). It replaces the former (1996) Code produced by the then Department for Education and Employment, which has been revoked by SI 2004/2300. The Code was approved by the Secretary of State and by Parliament in accordance with s 53A (see the Disability Discrimination Codes of Practice (Employment and Occupation, and Trade Organisations and Qualifications Bodies) Appointed Day Order 2004, SI 2004/2302) and came into effect on 1 October 2004.

The statutory provision under which this Code was made was repealed by the Equality Act 2006, ss 40, 91, Sch 3, paras 41, 52, Sch 4; however the Code is continued in force by s 42(3) of the 2006 Act (see

[1685]). As to the dissolution of the Disability Rights Commission and the transfer of its property, rights and liabilities etc to the Commission for Equality and Human Rights, see the Equality Act 2006, ss 36–38 at **[1679]–[1681]**.

The Code was prepared to coincide with the coming into force of major amendments to Part II of the DDA 1995 as well as to reflect the developments in the interpretation and application of the DDA 1995 in the eight years since Part II first came into force. As such it represents a significant restatement of guiding principles which, if only by virtue of its length, is likely to contain material of use to advocates in most tribunal claims under Part II, and to the tribunals themselves in determining issues of interpretation, application and scope of the law. It also contains much practical advice for employers, with examples of good practice, and a useful index (at **[4677A]**). The Code is reproduced here in full save for the Foreword and Contents. Section references that appeared in the margin of the original Code are reproduced at the start of the relevant paragraph in bold.

1. INTRODUCTION

PURPOSE OF PART 2 OF THE ACT

1.1 The Disability Discrimination Act 1995 (the Act) brought in measures to prevent discrimination against disabled people. Part 2 of the Act is based on the principle that disabled people should not be discriminated against in employment or when seeking employment. It also protects disabled people engaged in a range of occupations. Employers must comply with the duties set out in Part 2, as must others to whom those duties apply (see paragraphs 3.8 to 3.14).

1.2 Except for the Armed Forces, these duties now apply to all employers no matter how many (or how few) people they employ. The law changed in this regard on 1 October 2004. Other major changes in the law which took effect on that date, including the extension of the duties to some people or bodies who are not employers, are summarised in Appendix A.

PURPOSE OF THE CODE

1.3 This Code of Practice (the Code) gives practical guidance on how to prevent discrimination against disabled people in employment or when seeking employment. It describes the duties of employers and others in this regard. The Code helps disabled people to understand the law and what they can do if they feel that they have been discriminated against. By encouraging good practice, the Code assists employers to avoid workplace disputes and to work towards the elimination of discrimination against disabled people.

1.4 The Code also gives guidance on the law which is intended to help lawyers when advising their clients, and to assist courts and tribunals when interpreting new legal concepts. The Code explains the operation and effect of technical statutory provisions – some of which only came into force on 1 October 2004, and many of which have a complex legal effect. Because of this, the Code is necessarily comprehensive and detailed. However, the Disability Rights Commission (DRC) also produces a range of other publications about the Act, and about the rights of disabled people under it, which are intended to be of use to a range of audiences and for a variety of purposes. Details of how to obtain these publications are included in Appendix C.

1.5 **[s 53A]** The DRC has prepared and issued this Code under the Act on the basis of a request by the Secretary of State. It applies to England, Wales and Scotland. A similar but separate Code applies to Northern Ireland.

STATUS OF THE CODE

1.6 **[s 53A(8)]** The Code does not impose legal obligations. Nor is it an authoritative statement of the law – that is a matter for the courts and tribunals. However, the Code can be used in evidence in legal proceedings under the Act. Courts and employment tribunals must take into account any part of the Code that appears to them relevant to any question arising in those proceedings. If employers (and others who have duties under the Act's provisions on employment and occupation) follow the guidance in the Code, it may help to avoid an adverse decision by a court or tribunal in such proceedings.

HOW TO USE THE CODE

1.7 This chapter gives an introduction to the Code. Chapter 2 sets out some general guidance on how to avoid discrimination. Chapter 3 contains an overview of the Act's provisions on employment and occupation, and those provisions are examined in more detail in subsequent chapters.

1.8 Chapter 4 details what is meant by discrimination and harassment, and Chapter 5 explains the duty to make reasonable adjustments for disabled people. Chapter 6 examines the relevance of justification under Part 2. Chapters 7 and 8 consider the application of these principles in the context of recruitment processes and of subsequent employment, and Chapter 9 examines their application to certain occupations.

1.9 Chapter 10 explains how the Act's provisions on employment and occupation operate in the particular context of occupational pension schemes and group insurance services.

1.10 Chapter 11 describes how the Act deals with discrimination in providing employment services. Such services include vocational guidance and training.

1.11 Chapter 12 looks at particular issues concerning adjustments to premises, and Chapter 13 deals with various other points and explains what happens if discrimination is alleged.

1.12 Appendix A summarises some recent changes in the Act's provisions on employment and occupation. Appendix B gives more information on what is meant by 'disability' and by 'disabled person'. Separate statutory guidance relating to the definition of disability has been issued under the Act (see paragraph 3.6). Appendix C lists other sources of relevant information about matters referred to in the Code.

1.13 Each chapter of the Code should be viewed as part of an overall explanation of the Act's provisions on employment and occupation and the regulations made under them. In order to understand the law properly it is necessary to read the Code as a whole. The Code should not be read too narrowly or literally. It is intended to explain the principles of the law, to illustrate how the Act might operate in certain situations and to provide general guidance on good practice. There are some questions which the Code cannot resolve and which must await the authoritative interpretation of the courts and tribunals. The Code is not intended to be a substitute for taking appropriate advice on the legal consequences of particular situations.

EXAMPLES IN THE CODE

1.14 Examples of good practice and how the Act is likely to work are given in boxes. They are intended simply to illustrate the principles and concepts used in the legislation and should be read in that light. The examples should not be treated as complete or authoritative statements of the law.

1.15 As stated in paragraph 1.2, the Act's provisions on employment and occupation now apply to small employers as well as to larger ones. The size of an employer is sometimes relevant to the way in which the Act applies. Where this is the case, examples in the Code show how the application of the Act could be affected by the size of the employer.

1.16 While the examples refer to particular situations, they should be understood more widely as demonstrating how the law is likely to be applied generally. They can often be used to test how the law might apply in similar circumstances involving different disabilities or situations. Some of the examples are based on real cases which have been decided by the courts. In general, however, the examples attempt to use as many different varieties of disabilities and situations as possible to demonstrate the breadth and scope of the Act. Examples relating to men or women are given for realism and could, of course, apply to people of either gender.

REFERENCES TO 'EMPLOYERS' IN THE CODE

1.17 Throughout the Code, references are made to 'employers' for convenience. However, as explained in paragraphs 3.11 and 3.12, the Act's provisions on employment and occupation impose obligations on persons who might not ordinarily be described as employers – such as partners in firms, barristers and people providing practical work experience. References in the Code need to be read in this light.

OTHER REFERENCES IN THE CODE

1.18 References to the Act are shown in the margins. For example, s 1(1) means section 1(1) of the Act and Sch 1 means Schedule 1 to the Act. References to Part 2, 3 or 4 refer to the relevant Part of the Act. Where reference is made to regulations, the appropriate Statutory Instrument (SI) number is shown in the margin.

CHANGES TO THE LEGISLATION

1.19 The Code refers to the Disability Discrimination Act as of 1 October 2004. There may be changes to the Act or to other legislation, for example, to the range of people who are considered to be 'disabled' under the Act, which may have an effect on the duties explained in this Code. You will need to ensure that you keep up to date with any developments that affect the Act's provisions. You can get relevant information from the DRC (see below for contact details).

FURTHER INFORMATION

1.20 Copies of the Act and regulations made under it can be purchased from the Stationery Office (see inside the front of the Code for details). Separate codes covering other aspects of the Act, and guidance relating to the definition of disability are also available from the Stationery Office. The text of all the DRC's codes (including this Code) can also be downloaded free of charge from the DRC website (see paragraph 1.21).

1.21 Free information about the Act is available on the DRC website. It can also be obtained by contacting the DRC Helpline. This information is available in accessible formats. Calls to the Helpline are charged at local rate.

Website: www.drc-gb.org

Telephone: 08457 622 633

Textphone: 08457 622 644

Fax: 08457 778 878

Post: DRC Helpline

FREEPOST MID02164

Stratford upon Avon

CV37 9BR

[4662]

2. HOW CAN DISCRIMINATION BE AVOIDED?

INTRODUCTION

2.1 Prevention is better than cure. There are various actions which employers can take in order to avoid discriminating against disabled people. By doing so, employers are not only likely to minimise the incidence of expensive and time-consuming litigation, but will also improve their general performance and the quality of their business operations. This chapter sets out some guidance on ways to help ensure that disabled people are not discriminated against.

UNDERSTANDING THE SOCIAL DIMENSION OF DISABILITY

2.2 The concept of discrimination in the Act reflects an understanding that functional limitations arising from disabled people's impairments do not inevitably restrict their ability to participate fully in society. Rather than the limitations of an impairment, it is often environmental factors (such as the structure of a building, or an employer's working practices) which unnecessarily lead to these social restrictions. This principle underpins the duty to make reasonable adjustments described in Chapter 5. Understanding this will assist employers and others to avoid discrimination. It is as important to consider which aspects of employment and occupation create difficulties for a disabled person as it is to understand the particular nature of an individual's disability.

RECOGNISING THE DIVERSE NATURE OF DISABILITY

2.3 There are around ten million disabled adults in our society. The nature and extent of their disabilities vary widely, as do their requirements for overcoming any difficulties they may face. If employers are to avoid discriminating, they need to understand this, and to be aware of the effects their decisions and actions – and those of their agents and employees – may have on disabled people. The evidence shows that many of the steps that can be taken to avoid discrimination cost little or nothing and are easy to implement.

AVOIDING MAKING ASSUMPTIONS

2.4 It is advisable to avoid making assumptions about disabled people. Disabilities will often affect different people in different ways and their needs may be different as well. The following suggestions may help to avoid discrimination:

- Do not assume that because a person does not look disabled, he is not disabled.
- Do not assume that because you do not know of any disabled people working within an organisation there are none.
- Do not assume that most disabled people use wheelchairs.
- Do not assume that people with learning disabilities cannot be valuable employees, or that they can only do low status jobs.
- Do not assume that a person with a mental health problem cannot do a demanding job.
- Do not assume that all blind people read Braille or have guide dogs.
- Do not assume that all deaf people use sign language.
- Do not assume that because a disabled person may have less employment experience (in paid employment) than a non-disabled person, he has less to offer.

FINDING OUT ABOUT DISABLED PEOPLE'S NEEDS

2.5 As explained later in the Code (see paragraphs 7.22 and 8.16 for example), the Act requires employers to think about ways of complying with their legal duties. Listening carefully to disabled people and finding out what they want will help employers to meet their obligations by identifying the best way of meeting disabled people's needs. There is a better chance of reaching the best outcome if discussions are held with disabled people at an early stage.

2.6 Often, discussing with disabled people what is required to meet their needs will reassure an employer that suitable adjustments can be carried out cheaply and with very little inconvenience.

2.7 Evidence shows that in meeting the needs of disabled employees an organisation learns how to meet the needs of disabled customers, and vice versa. By consulting with disabled employees, an organisation can therefore improve the service it provides to its disabled customers and enhance its business.

2.8 There are various ways in which the views of disabled people can be obtained. Many larger employers have established formal structures for seeking and representing the views of disabled people. Small employers can also consult with disabled employees, although the methods may be less formal.

> A large employer sets up a network through which disabled employees can discuss their concerns and make recommendations to management, either directly or via a recognised trade union.
>
> A small employer asks a disabled employee if he has any concerns about how a reorganisation of the business will impact upon him.

SEEKING EXPERT ADVICE

2.9 It may be possible to avoid discrimination by using personal or in-house knowledge and expertise – particularly if information or views are obtained from the disabled person concerned. However, although the Act does not specifically require anyone to obtain expert advice about meeting the needs of disabled people with regard to employment, in practice it may sometimes be necessary to do so in order to comply with the principal duties set out in the Act. Expert advice might be especially useful if a person is newly disabled or if the effects of a person's disability become more marked. Expert advice about meeting the needs of disabled people may be available from local Jobcentre Plus offices, or from local and national disability organisations.

PLANNING AHEAD

2.10 The duties which the Act places on employers are owed to the individual disabled people with whom they have dealings. There is no duty owed to disabled people in general. Nevertheless, it is likely to be cost effective for employers to plan ahead. Considering the needs of a range of disabled people when planning for change (such as when planning a building refurbishment, a new IT system, or the design of a website) is likely to make it easier to implement adjustments for individuals when the need arises.

2.11 It is good practice for employers to have access audits carried out to identify any improvements which can be made to a building to make it more accessible. Access audits should be carried out by suitably qualified people, such as those listed in the National Register of Access Consultants (see Appendix C for details). Websites and intranet sites can also be reviewed to see how accessible they are to disabled people using access software.

> The owner of a small shop is planning a refit of her premises. As part of the refit she asks the designers to comply with British Standard 8300 to ensure that the shop has a good standard of access for a variety of disabled people, whether customers or employees. BS 8300 is a code of practice on the design of buildings and their approaches to meet the needs of disabled people (see Appendix C for details).

> An employer is re-designing its website, which it uses to promote the company as well as to advertise vacancies. The employer ensures that the new design for the website is easy to read for people with a variety of access software; has the website checked for accessibility; and invites disabled readers of the website to let the employer know if they find any part of it inaccessible.

IMPLEMENTING ANTI-DISCRIMINATORY POLICIES AND PRACTICES

2.12 Employers are more likely to comply with their duties under the Act, and to avoid the risk of legal action being taken against them, if they implement anti-discriminatory policies and practices. These are often referred to as equality policies or diversity policies. Additionally, in the event that legal action is taken, employers may be asked to demonstrate to an employment tribunal that they have effective policies and procedures in place to minimise the risk of discrimination. Although large and small employers are likely to have different kinds of anti-discriminatory policies and practices, it is advisable for all employers to take the following steps:

- Establish a policy which aims to prevent discrimination against disabled people and which is communicated to all employees and agents of the employer.
- Provide disability awareness and equality training to all employees. In addition, train employees and agents so that they understand the employer's policy on disability, their obligations under the Act and the practice of reasonable adjustments. People within the organisation who have responsibility for managing, recruiting or training employees are likely to need more specialist training.
- Inform all employees and agents that conduct which breaches the policy will not be tolerated, and respond quickly and effectively to any such breaches.
- Monitor the implementation and effectiveness of such a policy.
- Address acts of disability discrimination by employees as part of disciplinary rules and procedures.
- Have complaints and grievance procedures which are easy for disabled people to use and which are designed to resolve issues effectively.
- Have clear procedures to prevent and deal with harassment for a reason related to a person's disability.
- Establish a policy in relation to disability-related leave, and monitor the implementation and effectiveness of such a policy.
- Consult with disabled employees about their experiences of working for the organisation.
- Regularly review the effectiveness of reasonable adjustments made for disabled people in accordance with the Act, and act on the findings of those reviews.
- Keep clear records of decisions taken in respect of each of these matters.

> When a large company introduces a new disability policy, it might ask an external training company to run training sessions for all staff, or it might ask a human resources manager to deliver training to staff on this policy. The external training company might be one run by disabled people.
>
> A small employer introducing a similar policy asks the managing director to devote a team meeting to explaining the policy to her staff and to discuss why it is important and how it will operate.

A large employer trains all its employees in disability equality, the organisation's disability policy and the Disability Discrimination Act. It also trains all occupational health advisers with whom it works to ensure that they have the necessary expertise about the Act and the organisation's disability policy.

A small employer only uses occupational health advisers who can demonstrate that they have knowledge of the Act.

A large employer issues a questionnaire to employees about the organisation's attitude to disability, inviting suggestions for improvements.

A small employer asks disabled employees to feed back views on the employer's approach to disability issues.

AUDITING POLICIES AND PROCEDURES

2.13 Although there is no duty under Part 2 to anticipate the needs of disabled people in general, it is a good idea for employers to keep all their policies under review, and to consider the needs of disabled people as part of this process. It is advisable for employers to do this in addition to having a specific policy to prevent discrimination. Employers are likely to have policies about matters such as:

- flexible working arrangements
- appraisal and performance-related pay systems
- sickness absence
- redundancy selection criteria
- emergency evacuation procedures
- procurement of equipment, IT systems, software and websites
- information provision
- employee training and development
- employee assistance schemes offering financial or emotional support.

An organisation has a policy to ensure that all employees are kept informed about the organisation's activities through an intranet site. The policy says that the intranet site should be accessible to all employees, including those who use access software (such as synthetic speech output) because of their disabilities.

An employer has a policy of having annual appraisal interviews for all employees. The policy says that during the interviews, disabled employees should be asked whether they need any (further) reasonable adjustments. This could equally apply to a large or small employer.

An employer introduces a system for performance-related pay. It takes advice on performance-related pay systems from an employers' organisation, to ensure that the system it introduces is an effective tool for improving performance and is fair to all employees. It also ensures that every year the system is monitored to ensure that disabled people do not, on average, get lower awards.

A redundancy policy that has sickness absence as a selection criterion is amended to exclude disability-related absence. The sickness absence policy is also changed so that disability-related sickness is recorded separately.

A new procurement policy requires a number of factors to be taken into account in procuring equipment and IT systems. These factors include cost and energy efficiency. It is good practice for such factors to include accessibility for disabled people as well.

Emergency evacuation policies and procedures are reviewed to ensure that there are individual evacuation plans for any disabled people who need them.

MONITORING

2.14 Monitoring of employees is an important way of determining whether anti-discrimination measures taken by an organisation are effective, and ensuring that disability equality is a reality within that organisation. Information must be gathered sensitively, with appropriately worded questions, and confidentiality must be ensured. Knowing the proportion of disabled people at various levels of the organisation, and at various stages in relation to the recruitment process, can help an organisation determine where practices and policies need to be improved. The extent to which formal monitoring can be carried out will depend on the size of the organisation.

2.15 Monitoring will be more effective if employees (or job applicants) feel comfortable about disclosing information about their disabilities. This is more likely to be the case if the employer explains the purpose of the monitoring and if employees or job applicants believe that the employer genuinely values disabled employees and is using the information gathered to create positive change.

Through monitoring of candidates at the recruitment stage an employer becomes aware that, although several disabled people applied for a post, none was short-listed for interview. It uses this information to review the essential requirements for the post.

2.16 Some organisations, especially large ones, choose to monitor by broad type of disability to understand the barriers faced by people with different types of impairment.

A large employer notices through monitoring that the organisation has been successful at retaining most groups of disabled people, but not people with mental health problems. It acts on this information by contacting a specialist organisation for advice about good practice in retaining people with mental health problems.

ENSURING GOOD PRACTICE IN RECRUITMENT

Attracting disabled applicants

2.17 An organisation which recognises that suitably qualified disabled people have not applied to work for it may want to make contact with local employment services, including Jobcentre Plus and specialist disability employment services, to encourage disabled people to apply. It is normally lawful for an employer to advertise a vacancy as open only to disabled people (see paragraph 7.5).

By monitoring the recruitment process a small employer notices that very few disabled people apply to work for it. In the light of this information, it decides to notify local disability employment projects of its vacancies.

A retailer has a number of vacancies to fill. It contacts Jobcentre Plus and arranges an open morning for local disabled people to find out more about working for this employer.

Through its monitoring process, a medium-sized employer becomes aware of the fact that disabled people are under-represented in its workforce. It is looking for people to fill 3 work experience placements and decides to offer these placements to disabled people only.

A museum wants to understand the needs of its disabled visitors better. It decides to change its person specifications for posts in the visitor services department to include a requirement to have knowledge of disability access issues. It notifies local employment services for disabled people of these posts.

2.18 It is good practice to consider carefully what information should be included in advertisements and where they should be placed.

An advertisement which specifies that flexible working is available may encourage more disabled applicants to apply.

An advertisement that appears in the disability press and a local talking newspaper may encourage disabled applicants to apply.

Promoting a positive image

2.19 It is good practice for an employer to consider its image to ensure that it gives an impression of itself as an organisation that is aware of the needs of disabled people and is striving to create a more diverse workforce.

A large employer ensures that its recruitment brochure includes images of disabled employees, and contains information about its disability policy.

A small employer advertises in a local newspaper. The advertisement states that disabled people are encouraged to apply.

Use of the Disability Symbol

2.20 The Disability Symbol is a recognition given to employers by Jobcentre Plus. An employer displaying the Disability Symbol must commit itself to a number of measures concerning the recruitment, development and retention of disabled people, including offering a guaranteed interview to any disabled person who meets the essential requirements of the job. It is important that employers make clear what those essential requirements are. For more information about the Disability Symbol see Appendix C.

RESOLVING DISPUTES

2.21 Having policies and practices to combat discrimination, together with regular consultation with employees, is likely to minimise disputes about disability discrimination. But when such disputes do occur, it is in the interests of employers to attempt wherever possible to resolve them as they arise. Grievance procedures can provide an open and fair way for employees to make their concerns known, and can enable grievances to be resolved quickly before they become major problems. Use of the procedures may highlight areas in which the duty to make reasonable adjustments has not been observed, and can prevent misunderstandings leading to complaints to tribunals. It is important to ensure that grievance procedures are accessible to disabled people.

2.22 In certain circumstances, employers and employees are required by law to comply with internal dispute resolution procedures before making a complaint to a tribunal. Chapter 13 contains further information about grievance procedures and about resolving disputes under the Act. Whether or not an attempt at internal resolution of a dispute is made as a result of a legal requirement, it should be carried out in a non-discriminatory way to comply with the Act.

[4663]

3. THE ACT'S PROVISIONS ON EMPLOYMENT AND OCCUPATION – AN OVERVIEW

INTRODUCTION

3.1 This chapter gives an overview of the provisions of the Act relating to employment and occupation. It explains who has rights and duties under those provisions and outlines what is made unlawful by them. Later chapters explain the provisions in greater detail.

WHO HAS RIGHTS UNDER THE ACT?

Disabled people

3.2 **[ss 1 & 2, Schs 1& 2]** The Act gives protection from discrimination to a 'disabled' person within the meaning of the Act. A disabled person is someone who has a physical or mental impairment which has an effect on his or her ability to carry out normal day-to-day activities. That effect must be:

- substantial (that is, more than minor or trivial), and
- adverse, and
- long term (that is, it has lasted or is likely to last for at least a year or for the rest of the life of the person affected).

3.3 Physical or mental impairment includes sensory impairment. Hidden impairments are also covered (for example, mental illness or mental health problems, learning disabilities, dyslexia, diabetes and epilepsy).

3.4 In considering its duties under the Act, an employer should not use any definition of 'disabled person' which is narrower than that in the Act. An employer who is requested to make a disability-related adjustment may ask the person requesting it for evidence that the impairment is one which meets the definition of disability in the Act. It may be appropriate to do so where the disability is not obvious. However, employers should not ask for more information about the impairment than is necessary for this purpose. Nor should they ask for evidence of disability where it ought to be obvious that the Act will apply.

> A woman with ME (chronic fatigue syndrome) asks for time off to attend regular hospital appointments. The employer could legitimately ask to see a letter from the doctor or an appointment card. However, the employer then asks her questions about the likely progress of the illness so that he can bear this in mind when thinking about restructuring the department. This is likely to be unlawful.

People who have had a disability in the past

3.5 People who have had a disability within the meaning of the Act in the past are protected from discrimination even if they no longer have the disability.

> A job applicant discloses on her application form that while at university from 1992 to 1993 she had long-term clinical depression after her father died. It would be discrimination to refuse to interview or recruit her because she has had a disability in the past. The fact that the disability preceded the Disability Discrimination Act 1995 is irrelevant.

More information about the meaning of disability

3.6 For a fuller understanding of the concept of disability under the Act, reference should be made to Appendix B. A government publication, **Guidance on matters to be taken into account in determining questions relating to the definition of disability**, provides additional help in understanding the concept of disability and in identifying who is a disabled person. Where relevant, the Guidance must be taken into account in any legal proceedings.

People who have been victimised

3.7 The Act also gives rights to people who have been victimised, whether or not they have a disability or have had one in the past. (see paragraphs 4.33 to 4.36).

WHO HAS OBLIGATIONS UNDER THE ACT?

Employers

3.8 **[s 68(1)]** Later chapters explain in detail the duties which the Act imposes upon employers. The Act defines 'employment' as employment under a contract of service or of apprenticeship or a contract personally to do any work. Anyone who works under a contract falling within this definition is an employee, whether or not, for example, he works full-time.

3.9 **[s 68(1), s 64(7), s 4(6), s 68(2)–(2D)]** Members of the Armed Forces are excluded from protection under the Act's provisions on employment and occupation. Otherwise, those provisions now apply to all employers in respect of people they employ wholly or partly at an establishment in Great Britain. Protection under the Act extends to employment wholly outside Great Britain, provided that the employment has a sufficiently close connection with Great Britain – and the Act sets out the circumstances in which this will be the case. Certain employment on board ships, hovercraft and aircraft is also covered.

3.10 A person who is recruiting an employee has duties under the Act even if he is not yet an employer (because the new recruit will be his first employee).

People or bodies concerned with certain occupations

3.11 The Act's definition of employment is wide enough to include people who are self-employed but who agree to perform work personally. The provisions of Part 2 also extend to the following occupations which do not fall within the definition of employment:

- contract workers
- office holders
- police officers
- partners in firms
- barristers and advocates
- people undertaking practical work experience for a limited period for the purposes of vocational training.

Many of the principles which apply to employers under Part 2 are equally applicable in respect of these occupations. Further details about the application of the Act's provisions on employment and occupation in this regard are set out in Chapter 9.

Others to whom Part 2 applies

3.12 In addition, the Act's provisions on employment and occupation may also impose obligations upon the following people and organisations:

- trustees and managers of occupational pension schemes (see Chapter 10)
- insurers who provide group insurance services for an employer's employees (see Chapter 10)
- landlords of premises occupied by an employer or other person to whom Part 2 applies (see Chapter 12)
- employees and agents of a person to whom Part 2 applies
- Ministers of the Crown, government departments and agencies.

Providers of employment services

3.13 **[s 21A]** The Act also contains provisions to prevent discrimination by people or organisations who provide employment services – such as employment agencies and careers guidance services (see Chapter 11).

Trade organisations and qualifications bodies

3.14 **[ss 12–14B]** Finally, Part 2 makes special provision in respect of discrimination against disabled people by trade organisations and qualifications bodies. The nature and effect of the provisions in question is explained in a separate code of practice issued by the DRC (see Appendix C for details).

WHAT DOES THE ACT SAY ABOUT DISCRIMINATION IN RELATION TO EMPLOYMENT AND OCCUPATION?

Effect of the Act

3.15 The Act makes it unlawful for an employer to **discriminate** against a disabled person in relation to the recruitment or retention of staff.

3.16 However, the Act does not prohibit an employer from appointing the best person for the job. Nor does it prevent employers from treating disabled people more favourably than those who are not disabled.

Forms of discrimination

3.17 The four forms of discrimination which are unlawful under Part 2 are:

- direct discrimination (the meaning of which is explained at paragraphs 4.5 to 4.23)
- failure to comply with a duty to make reasonable adjustments (explained in Chapter 5)
- 'disability-related discrimination' (see paragraphs 4.27 to 4.32), and
- victimisation of a person (whether or not he is disabled) – what the Act says about victimisation is explained at paragraphs 4.33 to 4.36.

Aspects of employment in respect of which discrimination is unlawful

3.18 **[s 4(1)]** In relation to recruitment, the Act says that it is unlawful for an employer to discriminate against a disabled person:

- in the arrangements made for determining who should be offered employment
- in the terms on which the disabled person is offered employment, or
- by refusing to offer, or deliberately not offering, the disabled person employment.

What this means in practice is explained in Chapter 7.

3.19 **[s 4(2)]** In relation to the retention of staff, the Act says that it is unlawful for an employer to discriminate against a disabled person whom it employs:

- in the terms of employment which it affords him
- in the opportunities which it affords him for promotion, a transfer, training or receiving any other benefit
- by refusing to afford him, or deliberately not affording him, any such opportunity, or
- by dismissing him, or subjecting him to any other detriment.

What this means in practice is explained in Chapter 8.

3.20 **[s 16A(3)]** The Act also makes it unlawful for an employer to discriminate against a disabled person after that person's employment has come to an end (see paragraph 8.28).

WHAT ELSE IS UNLAWFUL UNDER THE ACT'S PROVISIONS ON EMPLOYMENT AND OCCUPATION?

Harassment

3.21 **[s 3B]** In addition to what it says about discrimination, Part 2 makes it unlawful, in relation to the recruitment or retention of staff, for an employer to subject a disabled person to **harassment** for a reason which relates to his disability. What the Act says about harassment is explained in more detail at paragraphs 4.38 and 4.39.

Instructions and pressure to discriminate

3.22 **[s 16C, s 17B(1)]** It is also unlawful for a person who has authority or influence over another to instruct him, or put pressure on him, to act unlawfully under the provisions of Part 2 (or, insofar as they relate to employment services, Part 3). This covers pressure to discriminate, whether applied directly to the person concerned, or indirectly but in a way in which he is likely to hear of it. However, the Act does not give individual disabled people the right to take legal action in respect of unlawful instructions or pressure to discriminate. Such action may only be taken by the DRC (see paragraphs 13.28 to 13.30).

WHO IS LIABLE FOR UNLAWFUL ACTS?

Responsibility for the acts of others

3.23 **[s 58]** Employers who act through agents (such as occupational health advisers or recruitment agencies) are liable for the actions of their agents done with the employer's express or implied authority. The Act also says that employers are responsible for the actions of their employees in the course of their employment. However, in legal proceedings against an employer based on the actions of an employee, it is a defence that the employer took 'such steps as were reasonably practicable' to prevent such actions. It is not a defence for the employer simply to show that the action took place without its knowledge or approval. Chapter 2 gives guidance on the steps which it might be appropriate to take for this purpose.

> A shopkeeper goes abroad for 3 months and leaves his son in charge of the shop. While he is away his son picks on a shop assistant with a learning disability, by constantly criticising her work unfairly. The shop assistant leaves her job as a result of this bullying. The shopkeeper is responsible for the actions of his son.

Aiding an unlawful act

3.24 **[s 57]** A person who knowingly helps another to do something made unlawful by the Act will be treated as having done the same kind of unlawful act. This means that, where an employer is liable for an unlawful act of its employee or agent, that employee or agent will be liable for aiding the unlawful act of the employer.

> A recruitment consultant engaged by an engineering company refuses to consider a disabled applicant for a vacancy, because the company has told the consultant that it does not want the post filled by someone who is 'handicapped'. Under the Act the consultant could be liable for aiding the company to discriminate, in addition to the company's own liability for its unlawful act.

3.25 Where an employee discriminates against or harasses a disabled employee, it is the employer who will be liable for that unlawful act – unless it can show that it took such steps as were reasonable to prevent the unlawful act in question. But the employee who committed the discrimination or harassment will be liable for aiding the unlawful act – and this will be the case even if the employer is able to show that it took reasonable steps to prevent the act.

> An employer has policies relating to harassment and disability. It ensures that all employees are aware of the policies and of the fact that harassment of disabled employees is subject to disciplinary action. It also ensures that managers receive training in applying the policies. A woman with a learning disability is humiliated by a colleague and disciplinary action is taken against the colleague. In these circumstances the colleague would be liable for aiding the unlawful act of the employer (the harassment) even though the employer would itself avoid liability because it had taken reasonably practicable steps to prevent the unlawful act.

Enforcing rights under Part 2

3.26 **[s 17A]** Enforcement of rights under Part 2 takes place in the employment tribunals. Enforcement of rights under the Act in relation to the provision of employment services also takes place in the employment tribunals. More information about enforcement is given in Chapter 13.

[4664]

4. WHAT IS DISCRIMINATION AND HARASSMENT?

INTRODUCTION

4.1 As noted at paragraph 3.17, the forms of discrimination which the Act makes unlawful in relation to employment are:

- direct discrimination
- failure to comply with a duty to make reasonable adjustments
- disability-related discrimination, and
- victimisation.

4.2 This chapter describes these four forms of discrimination in more detail, and explains the differences between them. It explores, in particular, the distinction between direct discrimination and disability-related discrimination (see paragraphs 4.28 to 4.31). These two forms of discrimination both depend on the way in which the employer treats the disabled person concerned – both require the disabled person to have been treated less favourably than other people are (or would be) treated. However, whether such treatment amounts to one of these forms of discrimination or the other (and, indeed, whether the treatment is unlawful in the first place) depends on the circumstances in which it arose.

4.3 The chapter examines the four forms of discrimination in the order in which they are listed in paragraph 4.1. This is because less favourable treatment which does not amount to direct discrimination can sometimes be justified. (In contrast, neither direct discrimination nor a failure to comply with a duty to make a reasonable adjustment is justifiable. Victimisation cannot be justified either.) In deciding whether the treatment is justified, and therefore whether there has been disability-related discrimination, the Act requires the question of reasonable adjustments to be taken into account (see paragraphs 6.4 and 6.5 where this is explained in more detail). Consequently, although the chapter describes direct discrimination first, it touches on the subject of reasonable adjustments before moving on to disability-related discrimination.

4.4 This chapter also explains what the Act means by 'harassment'. The concepts of discrimination and harassment are relevant not only in relation to employment but also to the application of Part 2 in other situations – for example, in relation to the occupations mentioned in Chapter 9. The provisions about discrimination and harassment in Part 2 are also relevant to what the Act says about employment services in Part 3. This is described in Chapter 11.

WHAT DOES THE ACT MEAN BY 'DIRECT DISCRIMINATION'?

What does the Act say?

4.5 **[s 3A(5)]** The Act says that an employer's treatment of a disabled person amounts to direct discrimination if:

- it is on the ground of his disability
- the treatment is less favourable than the way in which a person not having that particular disability is (or would be) treated, and
- the relevant circumstances, including the abilities, of the person with whom the comparison is made are the same as, or not materially different from, those of the disabled person.

4.6 It follows that direct discrimination depends on an employer's treatment of a disabled person being on the ground of his disability. It also depends on a comparison of that treatment with the way in which the employer treats (or would treat) an appropriate comparator. If, on the ground of his disability, the disabled person is treated less favourably than the comparator is (or would be) treated, the treatment amounts to direct discrimination.

When is direct discrimination likely to occur?

4.7 Treatment of a disabled person is 'on the ground of' his disability if it is caused by the fact that he is disabled or has the disability in question. In general, this means that treatment is on the ground of disability if a disabled person would not have received it but for his disability. However, disability does not have to be the only (or even the main) cause of the treatment complained of – provided that it is an effective cause, determined objectively from all the circumstances.

4.8 Consequently, if the less favourable treatment occurs because of the employer's generalised, or stereotypical, assumptions about the disability or its effects, it is likely to be direct discrimination. This is because an employer would not normally make such assumptions about a non-disabled person, but would instead consider his individual abilities.

> A blind woman is not short-listed for a job involving computers because the employer wrongly assumes that blind people cannot use them. The employer makes no attempt to look at the individual circumstances. The employer has treated the woman less

favourably than other people by not short-listing her for the job. The treatment was on the ground of the woman's disability (because assumptions would not have been made about a non-disabled person).

4.9 In addition, less favourable treatment which is disability-specific, or which arises out of prejudice about disability (or about a particular type of disability), is also likely to amount to direct discrimination.

An employer seeking a shop assistant turns down a disabled applicant with a severe facial disfigurement solely on the ground that other employees would be uncomfortable working alongside him. This would amount to direct discrimination and would be unlawful.

A disabled woman who uses a wheelchair applies for a job. She can do the job just as well as any other applicant, but the employer wrongly assumes that the wheelchair will cause an obstruction in the office. He therefore gives the job to a person who is no more suitable for the job but who is not a wheelchair-user. This would amount to direct discrimination and would be unlawful.

4.10 In some cases, an apparently neutral reason for less favourable treatment of a disabled person may, on investigation, turn out to be a pretext for direct discrimination.

4.11 Direct discrimination will often occur where the employer is aware that the disabled person has a disability, and this is the reason for the employer's treatment of him. Direct discrimination need not be conscious – people may hold prejudices that they do not admit, even to themselves. Thus, a person may behave in a discriminatory way while believing that he would never do so. Moreover, direct discrimination may sometimes occur even though the employer is unaware of a person's disability.

An employer advertises a promotion internally to its workforce. The job description states that people with a history of mental illness would not be suitable for the post. An employee who would otherwise be eligible for the promotion has a history of schizophrenia, but the employer is unaware of this. The employee would, nevertheless, have a good claim for unlawful direct discrimination in relation to the promotion opportunities afforded to him by his employer. The act of direct discrimination in this case is the blanket ban on anyone who has had a mental illness, effectively rejecting whole categories of people with no consideration of their individual abilities.

4.12 In situations such as those described in the above examples, it will often be readily apparent that the disabled person concerned has been treated less favourably on the ground of his disability. In other cases, however, this may be less obvious. Whether or not the basis for the treatment in question appears to be clear, a useful way of telling whether or not it is discriminatory, (and of establishing what kind of discrimination it is), is to focus on the person with whom the disabled person should be compared. That person may be real or hypothetical (see paragraph 4.18).

Identifying comparators in respect of direct discrimination

4.13 In determining whether a disabled person has been treated less favourably in the context of direct discrimination, his treatment must be compared with that of an appropriate comparator. This must be someone who does not have the same disability. It could be a non-disabled person or a person with other disabilities.

A person who becomes disabled takes six months' sick leave because of his disability, and is dismissed by his employer. A non-disabled fellow employee also takes six months' sick leave (because he has broken his leg) but is not dismissed. The difference in treatment is attributable to the employer's unwillingness to employ disabled staff and

PART 4

> the treatment is therefore on the ground of disability. The non-disabled employee is an appropriate comparator in the context of direct discrimination because his relevant circumstances are the same as those of the disabled person. It is the fact of having taken six months' sick leave which is relevant in these circumstances. As the disabled person has been treated less favourably than the comparator, this is direct discrimination.

4.14 It follows that, in the great majority of cases, some difference will exist between the circumstances (including the abilities) of the comparator and those of the disabled person – there is no need to find a comparator whose circumstances are the same as those of the disabled person in every respect. What matters is that the comparator's **relevant** circumstances (including his abilities) must be the same as, or not materially different from, those of the disabled person.

> In the previous example, the position would be different if it were the employer's policy to dismiss any member of staff who has been off sick for six months, and that policy were applied equally to disabled and non-disabled staff. In this case there would be no direct discrimination because the disabled person would not have been treated less favourably than the comparator – both would have been dismissed. Nevertheless, there may be a claim for failure to make reasonable adjustments to the policy, for example by allowing disability leave (see paragraph 4.25). In addition, the employer's policy may give rise to a claim for disability-related discrimination (see paragraph 4.27).

4.15 Once an appropriate comparator is identified, it is clear that the situation described in the example at paragraph 4.8 amounts to direct discrimination:

> In the example about the blind woman who is not short-listed for a job involving computers, there is direct discrimination because the woman was treated less favourably on the ground of her disability than an appropriate comparator (that is, a person who is not blind but who has the same abilities to do the job as the blind applicant): such a person would not have been rejected out of hand without consideration of her individual abilities.

4.16 The examples of direct discrimination in paragraph 4.9 also become clearer when the appropriate comparator is identified in each case:

> In the example about the disabled person with a severe facial disfigurement who applies to be a shop assistant, there is direct discrimination because the man was treated less favourably on the ground of his disability than an appropriate comparator (that is, a person who does not have such a disfigurement but who does have the same abilities to do the job): such a person would not have been rejected in the same way.

> In the example about the disabled woman who is not offered a job because she uses a wheelchair, there is direct discrimination because the woman was treated less favourably on the ground of her disability than an appropriate comparator (that is, a person who does not use a wheelchair but who does have the same abilities to do the job): such a person would not have been rejected in the same way.

4.17 The comparator used in relation to direct discrimination under the Act is the same as it is for other types of direct discrimination – such as direct sex discrimination. It is, however, made explicit in the Act that the comparator must have the same relevant abilities as the disabled person.

4.18 It may not be possible to identify an actual comparator whose relevant circumstances are the same as (or not materially different from) those of the disabled person in question. In such cases a hypothetical comparator may be used. Evidence which helps to establish how a hypothetical comparator would have been treated is likely to include details of how other people (not satisfying the statutory comparison test) were treated in circumstances which were broadly similar.

> A disabled person works in a restaurant. She makes a mistake on the till and this results in a small financial loss to her employer. She is dismissed because of this. The situation has not arisen before, and so there is no actual comparator. Nevertheless, six months earlier a non-disabled fellow employee was disciplined for taking home items of food without permission and received a written warning. The treatment of that person might be used as evidence that a hypothetical non-disabled member of staff who makes an error on the till would not have been dismissed for that reason.

4.19 It should be noted that the type of comparator described in the preceding paragraphs is only relevant to disability discrimination when assessing whether there has been **direct** discrimination. A different comparison falls to be made when assessing whether there has been a failure to comply with a duty to make reasonable adjustments (see paragraphs 5.3 and 5.4) or when considering disability-related discrimination (see paragraph 4.30).

Focusing on relevant circumstances

4.20 As stated in paragraph 4.14, direct discrimination only occurs where the **relevant** circumstances of the comparator, including his abilities, are the same as, or not materially different from, those of the disabled person himself. It is therefore important to focus on those circumstances which are, in fact, relevant to the matter to which the less favourable treatment relates. Although, in some cases, the effects of the disability may be relevant, the fact of the disability itself is not a relevant circumstance for these purposes. This is because the comparison must be with a person **not** having that particular disability.

> A disabled person with arthritis who can type at 30 words per minute (wpm) applies for an administrative job which includes typing, but is rejected on the ground that her typing speed is too slow. The correct comparator in a claim for direct discrimination would be a person not having arthritis who also has a typing speed of 30 wpm (with the same accuracy rate).

> A disabled person with a severe visual impairment applies for a job as a bus driver and is refused the job because he fails to meet the minimum level of visual acuity which is essential to the safe performance of the job. The correct comparator is a person not having that particular disability (for example, a person who merely has poorer than average eyesight) also failing to meet that minimum standard.

> A disabled person with schizophrenia applies for a job as an administrative assistant with his local authority, and declares his history of mental illness. The local authority refuses him employment, relying on a negative medical report from the authority's occupational health adviser which is based on assumptions about the effects of schizophrenia, without adequate consideration of the individual's abilities and the impact of the impairment in his particular case. This is likely to amount to direct discrimination and to be unlawful. The comparator here is a person who does not have schizophrenia, but who has the same abilities to do the job (including relevant qualifications and experience) as the disabled applicant: such a person would not have been rejected without adequate consideration of his individual abilities.

4.21 If (as in the above examples) a disabled person alleges that he has been refused the offer of a job on the ground of his disability, it is only appropriate to compare those of his circumstances which are relevant to his ability to do the job. It is not appropriate to compare other circumstances which are not relevant to this issue. The need to focus on relevant circumstances applies not only to recruitment cases of this kind, but also to any other situation where direct discrimination may have occurred.

> A disabled man with arthritis applies for an administrative job which includes typing, but is rejected in favour of a non-disabled candidate. Because of his arthritis, the man has a slow typing speed and has difficulty walking. The job is entirely desk-based, and does not require the person doing it to be able to walk further than a few metres within the office. The comparator in a claim of direct discrimination would be a non-disabled applicant with the same slow typing speed (and with the same abilities to do the job – eg, the same typing accuracy rate, and the same knowledge of word-processing packages) – but it would not be necessary for the comparator to have mobility problems (because the ability to walk further than a few metres is not relevant to the candidates' ability to do the job).

Relevance of reasonable adjustments to comparison

4.22 In making the comparison in respect of a claim of direct discrimination, the disabled person's abilities must be considered **as they in fact are**. In some cases, there will be particular reasonable adjustments which an employer was required by the Act to make, but in fact failed to make. It may be that those adjustments would have had an effect on the disabled person's abilities to do the job. But in making the comparison, the disabled person's abilities should be considered as they **in fact** were, and not as they would or might have been had those adjustments been made. On the other hand, if adjustments have **in fact** been made which have had the effect of enhancing the disabled person's abilities, then it is those enhanced abilities which should be considered. The disabled person's abilities are being considered as they in fact are (and not as they might have been if the adjustments had not been made).

> A disabled person who applies for an administrative job which includes typing is not allowed to use her own adapted keyboard (even though it would have been reasonable for the employer to allow this) and types a test document at 30 wpm. Her speed with the adapted keyboard would have been 50 wpm. A non-disabled candidate is given the job because her typing speed on the test was 45 wpm with the same accuracy rate. This is not direct discrimination, as the comparator is a non-disabled person typing at 30 wpm. (But the disabled person would be likely to have good claims in respect of two other forms of discrimination-failure to make reasonable adjustments and disability-related discrimination-see paragraph 4.37.)

> A disabled person with arthritis who applies for a similar job is allowed to use an adapted keyboard and types a test document at 50 wpm. A non-disabled candidate types at 30 wpm with the same accuracy rate. However, the disabled candidate is rejected because of prejudice and the other candidate is offered the job instead. This is direct discrimination, as the comparator would be a person not having arthritis who could type at 50 wpm.

Can direct discrimination be justified?

4.23 **[s 3A(4)]** Treatment of a disabled person which amounts to direct discrimination under the Act's provisions on employment and occupation is unlawful. It can never be justified.

FAILURE TO MAKE REASONABLE ADJUSTMENTS – RELATIONSHIP TO DISCRIMINATION

4.24 **[s 3A(2)]** For the reason given in paragraph 4.3, it may be necessary to consider whether an employer has failed to comply with a duty to make a reasonable adjustment in order to determine whether disability-related discrimination has occurred.

4.25 Irrespective of its relevance to disability-related discrimination, however, a failure to comply with a duty to make a reasonable adjustment in respect of a disabled person amounts to discrimination in its own right. Such a failure is therefore unlawful. Chapter 5 explains the circumstances in which an employer has such a duty, and gives guidance as to what employers need to do when the duty arises.

4.26 As with direct discrimination, the Act does not permit an employer to justify a failure to comply with a duty to make a reasonable adjustment (see paragraphs 5.43 and 5.44).

WHAT IS DISABILITY-RELATED DISCRIMINATION?

What does the Act say?

4.27 **[s 3A(1)]** The Act says that an employer's treatment of a disabled person amounts to discrimination if:

- it is for a reason related to his disability
- the treatment is less favourable than the way in which the employer treats (or would treat) others to whom that reason does not (or would not) apply, and
- the employer cannot show that the treatment is justified.

4.28 Although the Act itself does not use the term 'disability-related discrimination', this expression is used in the Code when referring to treatment of a disabled person which:

- is unlawful because each of the conditions listed in paragraph 4.27 is satisfied, but
- does not amount to direct discrimination under the Act.

4.29 In general, direct discrimination occurs when the reason for the less favourable treatment in question is the disability, while disability-related discrimination occurs when the reason relates to the disability but is not the disability itself. The expression 'disability-related discrimination' therefore distinguishes less favourable treatment which amounts to direct discrimination from a wider class of less favourable treatment which, although not amounting to direct discrimination, is nevertheless unlawful.

When does disability-related discrimination occur?

4.30 In determining whether disability-related discrimination has occurred, the employer's treatment of the disabled person must be compared with that of a person **to whom the disability-related reason does not apply**. This contrasts with direct discrimination, which requires a comparison to be made with a person without the disability in question but whose relevant circumstances are the same. The comparator may be non-disabled or disabled – but the key point is that the disability-related reason for the less favourable treatment must not apply to him.

> A disabled man is dismissed for taking six months' sick leave which is disability-related. The employer's policy, which has been applied equally to all staff (whether disabled or not) is to dismiss all employees who have taken this amount of sick leave. The disability-related reason for the less favourable treatment of the disabled person is the fact of having taken six months' sick leave, and the correct comparator is a person to whom that reason does not apply – that is, someone who has not taken six months' sick leave. Consequently, unless the employer can show that the treatment is justified, it will amount to disability-related discrimination because the comparator would not have been dismissed. However, the reason for the treatment is not the disability itself (it is only a matter related thereto, namely the amount of sick leave taken). So there is no direct discrimination.

> A disabled woman is refused an administrative job because she cannot type. She cannot type because she has arthritis. A non-disabled person who was unable to type would also have been turned down. The disability-related reason for the less favourable treatment is the woman's inability to type, and the correct comparator is a person to whom that reason does not apply – that is, someone who can type. Such a person would not have been refused the job. Nevertheless, the disabled woman has been treated less favourably for a disability-related reason and this will be unlawful unless it can be justified. There is no direct discrimination, however, because the comparator for direct discrimination is a person who does not have arthritis, but who is also unable to type.

4.31 The relationship between a disabled person's disability and the employer's treatment of him must be judged objectively. The reason for any less favourable treatment may well relate to the disability even if the employer does not have knowledge of the disability as such, or of whether its salient features are such that it meets the definition of disability in the Act. Less favourable treatment which is not itself direct discrimination will still be unlawful (subject to justification) if, in fact, the reason for it relates to the person's disability.

> A woman takes three periods of sickness absence in a two month period because of her disability, which is multiple sclerosis (MS). Her employer is unaware that she has MS and dismisses her, in the same way that it would dismiss any employee for a similar attendance record. Nevertheless, this is less favourable treatment for a disability-related reason (namely, the woman's record of sickness absence) and would be unlawful unless it can be justified.

4.32 The circumstances in which justification may be possible are explained in Chapter 6. However, it is worth noting that the possibility of justifying potential discrimination only arises at all when the form of discrimination being considered is disability-related discrimination, rather than direct discrimination or failure to make reasonable adjustments.

WHAT DOES THE ACT SAY ABOUT VICTIMISATION?

4.33 **[s 55(1) & (2)]** Victimisation is a special form of discrimination which is made unlawful by the Act. It is unlawful for one person to treat another ('the victim') less favourably than he treats or would treat other people in the same circumstances because the victim has:

- brought, or given evidence or information in connection with, proceedings under the Act (whether or not proceedings are later withdrawn)
- done anything else under or by reference to the Act, or
- alleged someone has contravened the Act (whether or not the allegation is later dropped),

or because the person believes or suspects that the victim has done or intends to do any of these things.

> A disabled employee complains of discrimination, having been refused promotion at work. A colleague gives evidence at the tribunal hearing on his behalf. The employer makes the disabled person's colleague redundant because of this. This amounts to victimisation. It would also be unlawful to subject a colleague to any detriment where he attends the tribunal not to give evidence but purely to offer support to the claimant – because this would be something which is done by reference to the Act.

4.34 **[s 55(4)]** It is not victimisation to treat a person less favourably because that person has made an allegation which was false and not made in good faith.

4.35 However, the fact that a person has given evidence on behalf of an applicant in a claim which was unsuccessful does not, of itself, prove that his evidence was false or that it was not given in good faith.

4.36 **[s 55(5)]** Unlike the other forms of discrimination which are made unlawful by the Act, victimisation may be claimed by people who are not disabled as well as by those who are.

HOW DO THE DIFFERENT FORMS OF DISCRIMINATION COMPARE IN PRACTICE?

4.37 The way in which the different forms of discrimination which are unlawful under the Act's provisions on employment and occupation may operate in practice can be demonstrated by the following series of examples.

> A woman with arthritis applies for a secretarial job in a local business. There is a question on the application form about disability, and she indicates that she has arthritis

but that it does not affect her typing. The employer rejects her application because it nevertheless wrongly assumes that she will not be able to carry out the job due to her arthritis. This is direct discrimination.

In the situation described above, the woman instead declares on the application form that her arthritis does affect her ability to type. She is called for an interview and is told that a typing test forms part of the selection process. She tells the employer that she will need to use an adapted keyboard in order to take the test, but this is not provided on the day of the interview, and the woman fails the test as a result. As a consequence of failing the test, she is turned down for the job. This is not direct discrimination, as the reason for the employer's rejection of the woman was not her disability, but was the fact that she failed the typing test.

However, in such circumstances the employer has a duty to make reasonable adjustments to its selection arrangements. Depending on the circumstances, it may be a reasonable adjustment for the employer to provide the adapted keyboard or allow the woman to use her own keyboard in order that she is not placed at a substantial disadvantage by the test. If this is the case, then the employer will be unlawfully discriminating against her by failing to make the adjustment.

Although there is no direct discrimination, the employer has still treated the woman less favourably for a reason relating to her disability (namely the fact that she failed the typing test). This will be disability-related discrimination unless the employer can show that it is justified – and the employer will be unable to show this if it would have been reasonable for it to provide her with an adapted keyboard or allow her to use her own in order to take the typing test.

Because of the way in which she has been treated, the disabled woman makes a claim against the employer under Part 2 of the Act. Some time later, however, the same employer advertises a further secretarial vacancy. The woman applies again, but the employer rejects her application because she has previously made a claim under the Act. This is victimisation.

WHAT DOES THE ACT SAY ABOUT HARASSMENT?

4.38 **[s 3B(1)]** The Act says that harassment occurs where, for a reason which relates to a person's disability, another person engages in unwanted conduct which has the purpose or effect of:

- violating the disabled person's dignity, or
- creating an intimidating, hostile, degrading, humiliating or offensive environment for him.

4.39 **[s 3B(2)]** If the conduct in question was engaged in with the intention that it should have either of these effects, then it amounts to harassment irrespective of its actual effect on the disabled person. In the absence of such intention, however, the conduct will only amount to harassment if it should reasonably be considered as having either of these effects. Regard must be had to all the circumstances in order to determine whether this is the case. Those circumstances include, in particular, the perception of the disabled person.

A man with a learning disability is often called 'stupid' and 'slow' by a colleague at work. This is harassment, whether or not the disabled man was present when these comments were made, because they were said with the intention of humiliating him.

A man with a stammer feels he is being harassed because his manager makes constant jokes about people with speech impairments. He asks his manager to stop doing this, but the manager says he is being 'oversensitive' as he habitually makes jokes in the office about many different sorts of people. This is likely to amount to harassment because making remarks of this kind should reasonably be considered as having either of the effects mentioned above.

An employee with HIV uses a colleague's mug. The colleague then makes a point of being seen washing the mug with bleach, which is not something she would do if anyone else used her mug. She also makes offensive comments about having her mug used by someone with HIV. This is likely to amount to harassment.

An employee circulates by email a joke about people with autism. A colleague with autism receives the email and finds the joke offensive. This is likely to amount to harassment.

A woman with depression considers that she is being harassed by her manager who constantly asks her if she is feeling all right, despite the fact that she has asked him not to do so in front of the rest of the team. This could amount to harassment.

WHAT DOES THE ACT SAY ABOUT STATUTORY OBLIGATIONS?

4.40 **[s 59]** Nothing is made unlawful by the Act if it is required by an express statutory obligation. However, it is only in cases where a statutory obligation is specific in its requirements, leaving an employer with no choice other than to act in a particular way, that the provisions of the Act may be overridden. The provision in section 59 of the Act is thus of narrow application, and it is likely to permit disability discrimination only in rare circumstances.

WHAT EVIDENCE IS NEEDED TO PROVE THAT DISCRIMINATION OR HARASSMENT HAS OCCURRED?

4.41 As stated in paragraph 3.26, enforcement of rights under the Act's provisions on employment and occupation takes place in the employment tribunals. A person who brings a claim for unlawful discrimination or harassment must show that discrimination has occurred. He must prove this on the balance of probabilities in order to succeed with a claim in an employment tribunal.

4.42 **[s 17A(1C)]** However, the Act says that, when such a claim is heard by an employment tribunal, the tribunal must uphold the claim if:

- the claimant proves facts from which the tribunal could conclude in the absence of an adequate explanation that the person against whom the claim is made (the respondent) has acted unlawfully, and
- the respondent fails to prove that he did not act in that way.

A disabled employee scores very poorly in a redundancy selection process in comparison with other employees in the same position as himself, getting low marks for skill and performance in his job. The employee has always had good appraisals in comparison with other employees and no action has ever been taken against him in respect of competence. Unless the employer demonstrates a non-discriminatory reason for the low scores, unlawful discrimination will be inferred in these circumstances.

4.43 Consequently, where a disabled person is able to prove on the balance of probabilities facts from which an inference of unlawful discrimination or harassment could be drawn, the burden of proof shifts to the respondent – for example, the disabled person's employer. This means that the employer must show that it is more likely than not that its conduct was not unlawful. This principle applies to allegations in respect of all forms of discrimination, including victimisation, and to harassment. Its practical effect in relation to the three principal forms of disability discrimination can be summarised as follows:

- To prove an allegation of **direct discrimination**, an employee must prove facts from which it could be inferred in the absence of an adequate explanation that he has been treated less favourably on the ground of his disability than an appropriate comparator has been, or would be, treated. If the employee does this, the claim will succeed unless the employer can show that disability was not any part of the reason for the treatment in question.
- To prove an allegation that there has been a **failure to comply with a duty to make reasonable adjustments**, an employee must prove facts from which it could be inferred in the absence of an adequate explanation that such a duty has arisen, and that it has been breached. If the employee does this, the claim will succeed unless the employer can show that it did not fail to comply with its duty in this regard.
- To prove an allegation of **disability-related discrimination**, an employee must prove facts from which it could be inferred in the absence of an adequate explanation that, for a reason relating to his disability, he has been treated less favourably than a person

to whom that reason does not apply has been, or would be, treated. If the employee does this, the burden of proof shifts, and it is for the employer to show that the employee has not received less favourable treatment for a disability-related reason. Even if the employer cannot show this, however, the employee's claim will not succeed if the employer shows that the treatment was justified.

4.44 **[s 56]** The Act provides a means by which a disabled person can seek evidence about whether he has been discriminated against, or subjected to harassment, under the Act's provisions on employment and occupation. He may do this by using a questionnaire to obtain further information from a person he thinks has acted unlawfully in relation to him (see paragraph 13.13). If there has been a failure to provide a satisfactory response to questions asked by the disabled person in this way, inferences may be drawn from that failure.

4.45 In addition, the fact that there has been a failure to comply with a relevant provision of the Code must be taken into account by a court or tribunal, where it considers it relevant, in determining whether there has been discrimination or harassment (see paragraph 1.6).

[4665]

5. WHAT IS THE DUTY TO MAKE REASONABLE ADJUSTMENTS?

INTRODUCTION

5.1 In Chapter 4 it was noted that one of the ways in which discrimination occurs under Part 2 of the Act is when an employer fails to comply with a duty imposed on it to make 'reasonable adjustments' in relation to the disabled person. This chapter examines the circumstances in which a duty to make reasonable adjustments arises and outlines what an employer needs to do in order to discharge such a duty.

5.2 The concept of a duty to make reasonable adjustments is also relevant to the application of Part 2 in other situations – for example, in relation to the occupations mentioned in Chapter 9, and to the provision of occupational pensions, as explained in Chapter 10.

WHEN DOES AN EMPLOYER'S DUTY TO MAKE REASONABLE ADJUSTMENTS ARISE?

5.3 **[s 4A(1)]** The duty to make reasonable adjustments arises where a provision, criterion or practice applied by or on behalf of the employer, or any physical feature of premises occupied by the employer, places a disabled person at a substantial disadvantage compared with people who are not disabled. An employer has to take such steps as it is reasonable for it to have to take in all the circumstances to prevent that disadvantage – in other words the employer has to make a 'reasonable adjustment'. Where the duty arises, an employer cannot justify a failure to make a reasonable adjustment.

> A man who is disabled because he has dyslexia applies for a job which involves writing letters. The employer gives all applicants a test of their letter-writing ability. The man can generally write letters very well but finds it difficult to do so in stressful situations and within short deadlines. He is given longer to take the test. This adjustment is likely to be a reasonable one for the employer to make.

5.4 It does not matter if a disabled person cannot point to an actual non-disabled person compared with whom he is at a substantial disadvantage. The fact that a non-disabled person, or even another disabled person, would not be substantially disadvantaged by the provision, criterion or practice or by the physical feature in question is irrelevant. The duty is owed specifically to the individual disabled person.

WHICH DISABLED PEOPLE DOES THE DUTY PROTECT?

5.5 **[s 4A(2)]** The duty to make reasonable adjustments applies in recruitment and during all stages of employment, including dismissal. It may also apply after employment has ended. The duty relates to all disabled employees of an employer and to any disabled applicant for employment. In the case of a provision, criterion or practice for determining to whom employment should be offered, the duty also applies in respect of any disabled person who has notified the employer that he may be an applicant for that employment.

5.6 The extent of the duty to make reasonable adjustments depends on the employment circumstances of the disabled person in question. For example, more extensive duties are owed to employees than to people who are merely thinking about applying for a job. More extensive duties are also owed to current employees than to former employees. The extent to which employers have knowledge of relevant circumstances is also a factor (see paragraphs 5.12 to 5.16).

5.7 In order to avoid discrimination, it would be prudent for employers not to attempt to make a fine judgement as to whether a particular individual falls within the statutory definition of disability, but to focus instead on meeting the needs of each employee and job applicant.

WHAT ARE 'PROVISIONS, CRITERIA AND PRACTICES'?

5.8 **[s 18D(2)]** Provisions, criteria and practices include arrangements, for example for determining to whom employment should be offered, and terms, conditions or arrangements on which employment, promotion, a transfer, training or any other benefit is offered or afforded. The duty to make reasonable adjustments applies, for example, to selection and interview procedures and the premises used for such procedures, as well as to job offers, contractual arrangements and working conditions.

> A call centre normally employs supervisors on a full-time basis. A woman with sickle cell anaemia applies for a job as a supervisor. Because of pain and fatigue relating to her condition she asks to be able to do the job on a part-time basis. The call centre agrees. The hours of work which are offered amount to an adjustment to a working practice. This is likely to be a reasonable adjustment to the call centre's working practice.

> An employer has a policy that designated car parking spaces are only offered to senior managers. A woman who is not a manager, but who has a mobility impairment and needs to park very close to the office, is given a designated car parking space. This is likely to be a reasonable adjustment to the employer's car parking policy.

WHAT IS A 'PHYSICAL FEATURE'?

5.9 The Act says that the following are to be treated as a physical feature:

- any feature arising from the design or construction of a building on the premises occupied by the employer
- any feature on the premises of any approach to, exit from, or access to such a building
- any fixtures, fittings, furnishings, furniture, equipment or materials in or on the premises, and
- any other physical element or quality of any land comprised in the premises occupied by the employer.

All these features are covered, whether temporary or permanent. Considerations which need to be taken into account when making adjustments to premises are explained in Chapter 12.

> The design of a particular workplace makes it difficult for someone with a hearing impairment to hear, because the main office is open plan and has hard flooring. That is a substantial disadvantage caused by the physical features of the workplace.

> Clear glass doors at the end of a corridor in a particular workplace present a hazard for a visually impaired employee. This is a substantial disadvantage caused by the physical features of the workplace.

5.10 Physical features will include steps, stairways, kerbs, exterior surfaces and paving, parking areas, building entrances and exits (including emergency escape routes), internal and external doors, gates, toilet and washing facilities, lighting and ventilation, lifts and escalators, floor coverings, signs, furniture, and temporary or movable items. This is not an exhaustive list.

WHAT DISADVANTAGES GIVE RISE TO THE DUTY?

5.11 The Act says that only substantial disadvantages give rise to the duty. Substantial disadvantages are those which are not minor or trivial. Whether or not such a disadvantage exists in a particular case is a question of fact. What matters is not that a provision, criterion or practice or a physical feature is capable of causing a substantial disadvantage to the disabled person in question, but that it actually has this effect on him, or (where applicable) that it would have this effect if he were doing the job at the time.

WHAT IF THE EMPLOYER DOES NOT KNOW THAT THE PERSON IS DISABLED OR IS AN ACTUAL OR POTENTIAL JOB APPLICANT?

5.12 **[s 4A(3)(b)]** Although (as explained in paragraphs 4.11 and 4.31) less favourable treatment can occur even if the employer does not know that an employee is disabled, the employer only has a duty to make an adjustment if it knows, or could reasonably be expected to know, that the employee has a disability and is likely to be placed at a substantial disadvantage. The employer must, however, do all it can reasonably be expected to do to find out whether this is the case.

> An employee has depression which sometimes causes her to cry at work, but the reason for her behaviour is not known to her employer. The employer makes no effort to find out if the employee is disabled and whether a reasonable adjustment could be made to her working arrangements. The employee is disciplined without being given any opportunity to explain that the problem arises from a disability. The employer may be in breach of the duty to make reasonable adjustments because it failed to do all it could reasonably be expected to do to establish if the employee was disabled and substantially disadvantaged.

> An employer has an annual appraisal system which specifically provides an opportunity for employees to notify the employer in confidence if they are disabled and are put at a substantial disadvantage by the working arrangements or premises. This gives the employer the opportunity to find out if an employee requires reasonable adjustments, although it would not mean that the employer should not consider reasonable adjustments for an employee at other times of the year.

5.13 **[s 4A(3)]** The principle stated in paragraph 5.12 applies equally to a disabled person who is an actual or potential applicant for employment.

> An applicant is not short-listed for interview for the position of administrative assistant, a post which mainly involves typing, because he states on his application form that he cannot type. The reason he cannot type is that he has severe arthritis, but this is not stated anywhere on the form. The employer would not be expected to make an adjustment to the typing requirement in these circumstances as it had no knowledge of the disability and could not reasonably be expected to know of it.

5.14 In addition, an employer only has a duty to make an adjustment if it knows, or could reasonably be expected to know, that the disabled person is, or may be, an applicant.

5.15 If an employer's agent or employee (such as an occupational health adviser, a personnel officer or line manager or recruitment agent) knows, in that capacity, of an employee's disability, the employer will not usually be able to claim that it does not know of the disability, and that it therefore has no obligation to make a reasonable adjustment. The same applies in respect of actual or potential applicants for employment. Employers therefore need to ensure that where information about disabled people may come through different channels, there is a means—suitably confidential—for bringing the information together, to make it easier for the employer to fulfil its duties under the Act.

> An occupational health adviser is engaged by a large employer to provide it with information about its employees' health. The occupational health adviser becomes aware of an employee's disability, which the employee's line manager does not know about. The employer's working arrangements put the employee at a substantial disadvantage because of the effects of her disability and she claims that a reasonable adjustment should have been made. It will not be a defence for the employer to claim that it did not know of her disability. This is because the information gained by the occupational health adviser on the employer's behalf is imputed to the employer. The occupational health adviser's knowledge means that the employer's duty under the Act applies. If the employee did not give consent for the occupational health adviser to pass on personal information to the line manager, it might be necessary for the line manager to implement the reasonable adjustment without knowing precisely why it has to do so.

5.16 Information will not be imputed to the employer if it is gained by a person providing services to employees independently of the employer. This is the case even if the employer has arranged for those services to be provided.

> An employer contracts with an agency to provide an independent counselling service to employees. The contract says that the counsellors are not acting on the employer's behalf while in the counselling role. Any information about a person's disability obtained by a counsellor during such counselling would not be imputed to the employer and so would not trigger the employer's duty to make reasonable adjustments.

DOES THE DUTY TO MAKE REASONABLE ADJUSTMENTS APPLY IN OTHER SITUATIONS RELATED TO EMPLOYMENT AND OCCUPATION?

5.17 Paragraphs 5.3 to 5.16 explain when it may be necessary to make an adjustment in relation to employment. Part 2 imposes similar requirements in relation to the occupations it covers, subject to certain differences explained in Chapter 9. Reasonable adjustments may also be required in relation to occupational pension schemes and group insurance services, as explained in Chapter 10.

WHAT ADJUSTMENTS MIGHT AN EMPLOYER HAVE TO MAKE?

5.18 **[s 18B(2)]** The Act gives a number of examples of adjustments, or 'steps', which employers may have to take, if it is reasonable for them to have to do so (see paragraphs 5.24 to 5.42). Any necessary adjustments should be implemented in a timely fashion, and it may also be necessary for an employer to make more than one adjustment. It is advisable to agree any proposed adjustments with the disabled person in question before they are made. The Act does not give an exhaustive list of the steps which may have to be taken to discharge the duty. Steps other than those listed here, or a combination of steps, will sometimes have to be taken. However, the steps in the Act are:

- making adjustments to premises

> An employer makes structural or other physical changes such as widening a doorway, providing a ramp or moving furniture for a wheelchair user; relocates light switches, door handles or shelves for someone who has difficulty in reaching; or provides appropriate contrast in decor to help the safe mobility of a visually impaired person.

- allocating some of the disabled person's duties to another person

> An employer reallocates minor or subsidiary duties to another employee as a disabled person has difficulty doing them because of his disability. For example, the job

> involves occasionally going onto the open roof of a building but the employer transfers this work away from an employee whose disability involves severe vertigo.

- transferring the person to fill an existing vacancy

> An employer should consider whether a suitable alternative post is available for an employee who becomes disabled (or whose disability worsens), where no reasonable adjustment would enable the employee to continue doing the current job. Such a post might also involve retraining or other reasonable adjustments such as equipment for the new post.

- altering the person's hours of working or training

> This could include allowing a disabled person to work flexible hours to enable him to have additional breaks to overcome fatigue arising from his disability. It could also include permitting part time working, or different working hours to avoid the need to travel in the rush hour if this is a problem related to an impairment. A phased return to work with a gradual build-up of hours might also be appropriate in some circumstances.

- assigning the person to a different place of work or training

> An employer relocates the work station of a newly disabled employee (who now uses a wheelchair) from an inaccessible third floor office to an accessible one on the ground floor. It would be reasonable to move his place of work to other premises of the same employer if the first building is inaccessible.

- allowing the person to be absent during working or training hours for rehabilitation, assessment or treatment

> An employer allows a person who has become disabled more time off during work than would be allowed to non-disabled employees to enable him to have rehabilitation training. A similar adjustment would be appropriate if a disability worsens or if a disabled person needs occasional treatment anyway.

- giving, or arranging for, training or mentoring (whether for the disabled person or any other person)

> This could be training in particular pieces of equipment which the disabled person uses, or an alteration to the standard employee training to reflect the employee's particular disability. For example, all employees are trained in the use of a particular machine but an employer provides slightly different or longer training for an employee with restricted hand or arm movements, or training in additional software for a visually impaired person so that he can use a computer with speech output.

> An employer provides training for employees on conducting meetings in a way that enables a deaf staff member to participate effectively.

A disabled man returns to work after a six-month period of absence due to a stroke. His employer pays for him to see a work mentor, and allows time off to see the mentor, to help with his loss of confidence following the onset of his disability.

- acquiring or modifying equipment

An employer might have to provide special equipment (such as an adapted keyboard for someone with arthritis or a large screen for a visually impaired person), an adapted telephone for someone with a hearing impairment, or other modified equipment for disabled employees (such as longer handles on a machine). There is no requirement to provide or modify equipment for personal purposes unconnected with an employee's work, such as providing a wheelchair if a person needs one in any event but does not have one. The disadvantage in such a case does not flow from the employer's arrangements or premises.

- modifying instructions or reference manuals

The format of instructions and manuals might need to be modified for some disabled people (eg produced in Braille or on audio tape) and instructions for people with learning disabilities might need to be conveyed orally with individual demonstration.

- modifying procedures for testing or assessment

A person with restricted manual dexterity would be disadvantaged by a written test, so the employer gives that person an oral test instead.

- providing a reader or interpreter

A colleague reads mail to a person with a visual impairment at particular times during the working day. Alternatively, the employer might hire a reader.

- providing supervision or other support

An employer provides a support worker, or arranges help from a colleague, in appropriate circumstances, for someone whose disability leads to uncertainty or lack of confidence.

5.19 It may sometimes be necessary for an employer to take a combination of steps.

A woman who is deafblind is given a new job with her employer in an unfamiliar part of the building. The employer (i) arranges facilities for her guide dog in the new area, (ii) arranges for her new instructions to be in Braille and (iii) trains colleagues to communicate with her, and provides disability equality training to all staff.

5.20 As mentioned above, it might be reasonable for employers to have to take other steps, which are not given as examples in the Act. These steps could include:

- conducting a proper assessment of what reasonable adjustments may be required
- permitting flexible working
- allowing a disabled employee to take a period of disability leave

> An employee who has cancer needs to undergo treatment and rehabilitation. His employer allows a period of disability leave and permits him to return to his job at the end of this period.

- participating in supported employment schemes, such as Workstep

> A man applies for a job as an office assistant after several years of not working because of depression. He has been participating in a supported employment scheme where he saw the post advertised. As a reasonable adjustment he asks the employer to let him make private phone calls during the working day to a support worker at the scheme.

- employing a support worker to assist a disabled employee

> An adviser with a visual impairment is sometimes required to make home visits. The employer employs a support worker to assist her on these visits.

- modifying disciplinary or grievance procedures

> A woman with a learning disability is allowed to take a friend (who does not work with her) to act as an advocate at a meeting with her employer about a grievance. The employer also ensures that the meeting is conducted in a way that does not disadvantage or patronise the disabled woman.

- adjusting redundancy selection criteria

> A woman with an autoimmune disease has taken several short periods of absence during the year because of the condition. When her employer is taking absences into account as a criterion for selecting people for redundancy, he discounts these periods of disability-related absence.

- modifying performance-related pay arrangements.

> A disabled woman who is paid purely on her output needs frequent short additional breaks during her working day – something her employer agrees to as a reasonable adjustment. It is likely to be a reasonable adjustment for her employer to pay her at an agreed rate (e g her average hourly rate) for these breaks.

5.21 Advice and assistance (which may include financial assistance) in relation to making adjustments may be available from the Access to Work scheme (see paragraphs 8.19 and 8.20).

5.22 In some cases a reasonable adjustment will not work without the co-operation of other employees. Employees may therefore have an important role in helping to ensure that a reasonable adjustment is carried out in practice. Subject to considerations about confidentiality (explained at paragraphs 8.21 to 8.23), employers must ensure that this happens. It is unlikely to be a valid defence to a claim under the Act that staff were obstructive or unhelpful when the employer tried to make reasonable adjustments. An employer would at least need to be able to show that it took such behaviour seriously and dealt with it appropriately. Employers will be more likely to be able to do this if they establish and implement the type of policies and practices described at paragraph 2.12.

> An employer ensures that an employee with autism has a structured working day as a reasonable adjustment. As part of the reasonable adjustment it is the responsibility of the employer to ensure that other employees co-operate with this arrangement.

5.23 Further examples of the way in which reasonable adjustments work in practice are given in Chapters 7 and 8, which deal with recruitment and retention.

WHEN IS IT 'REASONABLE' FOR AN EMPLOYER TO HAVE TO MAKE ADJUSTMENTS?

5.24 Whether it is reasonable for an employer to make any particular adjustment will depend on a number of things, such as its cost and effectiveness. However, if an adjustment is one which it is reasonable to make, then the employer must do so. Where a disabled person is placed at a substantial disadvantage by a provision, criterion or practice of the employer, or by a physical feature of the premises it occupies, the employer must consider whether any reasonable adjustments can be made to overcome that disadvantage. There is no onus on the disabled person to suggest what adjustments should be made (although it is good practice for employers to ask) but, where the disabled person does so, the employer must consider whether such adjustments would help overcome the disadvantage, and whether they are reasonable.

> A disabled employee has been absent from work as a result of depression. Neither the employee nor his doctor is able to suggest any adjustments that could be made. Nevertheless the employer should still consider whether any adjustments, such as working from home for a time, would be reasonable.

5.25 Effective and practicable adjustments for disabled people often involve little or no cost or disruption and are therefore very likely to be reasonable for an employer to have to make. Even if an adjustment has a significant cost associated with it, it may still be cost-effective in overall terms – and so may be a reasonable adjustment to make. Many adjustments do not involve making physical changes to premises. However, where such changes do need to be made, employers may need to take account of the considerations explained in Chapter 12 which deals with issues about making alterations to premises.

5.26 **[SI 1999/3242]** If making a particular adjustment would increase the risks to the health and safety of any person (including the disabled person in question) then this is a relevant factor in deciding whether it is reasonable to make that adjustment. Suitable and sufficient risk assessments, such as those carried out for the purposes of the Management of Health and Safety at Work Regulations 1999, should be used to help determine whether such risks are likely to arise.

5.27 **[s 18B(1)]** The Act lists a number of factors which may, in particular, have a bearing on whether it will be reasonable for the employer to have to make a particular adjustment. These factors make a useful checklist, particularly when considering more substantial adjustments. The effectiveness and practicability of a particular adjustment might be considered first. If it is practicable and effective, the financial aspects might be looked at as a whole – the cost of the adjustment and resources available to fund it. Other factors might also have a bearing. The factors in the Act are listed below.

The effectiveness of the step in preventing the disadvantage

5.28 It is unlikely to be reasonable for an employer to have to make an adjustment involving little benefit to the disabled person.

> A disabled employee cannot physically access the stationery cupboard at work. It is unlikely to be reasonable for the employer to have to make the cupboard accessible, unless distribution of stationery was a significant part of the employee's job.

5.29 However, an adjustment which, taken alone, is of marginal benefit, may be one of several adjustments which, when looked at together, would be effective. In that case, it is likely to be reasonable to have to make it.

The practicability of the step

5.30 It is more likely to be reasonable for an employer to have to take a step which is easy to take than one which is difficult. In some circumstances it may be reasonable to have to take a step, even though it is difficult.

> It might be impracticable for an employer who needs to appoint an employee urgently to have to wait for an adjustment to be made to an entrance. How long it might be reasonable for the employer to have to wait would depend on the circumstances. However, it might be possible to make a temporary adjustment in the meantime, such as using another, less convenient entrance.

The financial and other costs of the adjustment and the extent of any disruption caused

5.31 If an adjustment costs little or nothing and is not disruptive, it would be reasonable unless some other factor (such as practicability or effectiveness) made it unreasonable. The costs to be taken into account include those for staff and other resources. The significance of the cost of a step may depend in part on what the employer might otherwise spend in the circumstances. In assessing the likely costs of making an adjustment, the availability of external funding (such as funding by Access to Work) should be taken into account.

> It would be reasonable for an employer to have to spend at least as much on an adjustment to enable the retention of a disabled person-including any retraining-as might be spent on recruiting and training a replacement.

5.32 The significance of the cost of a step may also depend in part on the value of the employee's experience and expertise to the employer.

5.33 Examples of the factors that might be considered as relating to the value of an employee would include:

- the amount of resources (such as training) invested in the individual by the employer
- the employee's length of service
- the employee's level of skill and knowledge
- the employee's quality of relationships with clients
- the level of the employee's pay.

5.34 It is more likely to be reasonable for an employer to have to make an adjustment with significant costs for an employee who is likely to be in the job for some time than for a temporary employee.

5.35 An employer is more likely to have to make an adjustment which might cause only minor inconvenience to other employees or the employer than one which might unavoidably prevent other employees from doing their job, or cause other significant disruption.

The extent of the employer's financial or other resources

5.36 It is more likely to be reasonable for an employer with substantial financial resources to have to make an adjustment with a significant cost, than for an employer with fewer resources. The resources in practice available to the employer as a whole should be taken into account as well as other calls on those resources. For larger employers, it is good practice to have a specific budget for reasonable adjustments – but limitations on the size of any such budget will not affect the existence of the employer's duties to disabled employees. The reasonableness of an adjustment will depend not only on the resources in practice available for the adjustment but also on all other relevant factors (such as effectiveness and practicability).

> If a shop is part of a retail chain, the total resources of that business would be taken into account when assessing whether an adjustment is reasonable. Competing demands on those resources will also be taken into account.

5.37 It is more likely to be reasonable for an employer with a substantial number of staff to have to make certain adjustments, than for a smaller employer.

> It would generally be reasonable for an employer with a large staff to make significant efforts to reallocate duties or identify a suitable alternative post or provide supervision from existing staff. It may also be reasonable for a small company to make these adjustments but not if it involved disproportionate effort.

The availability to the employer of financial or other assistance to help make an adjustment

5.38 The availability of outside help (such as advice and assistance from Access to Work) may well be a relevant factor.

> A small employer, in recruiting a disabled person, finds that the only feasible adjustment is too costly for it alone. However, if assistance is available e g from the Access to Work scheme or a voluntary body, it may well be reasonable for the employer to make the adjustment.

5.39 A disabled person is not required to contribute to the cost of a reasonable adjustment. However, if a disabled person has a particular piece of special or adapted equipment which he is prepared to use for work, this might make it reasonable for the employer to have to take some other step (as well as allowing the use of the equipment).

> An employer requires its employees to use company cars for all business travel. One employee's disability means she would have to use an adapted car or an alternative form of transport. If she has an adapted car of her own which she is willing to use on business, it might well be reasonable for the employer to allow this and pay her an allowance to cover the cost of doing so, even if it might not have been reasonable for it to provide an adapted company car (because of the additional expense), or to pay an allowance to cover alternative travel arrangements in the absence of an adapted car. This would be a reasonable step to take because it would be cost-effective for the employer, easy to implement and would remove the disadvantage to the disabled employee immediately.

> A disabled woman employed as a computer engineer uses a piece of communications equipment that she obtained through the Access to Work scheme. Her employer pays the cost of repair when it breaks down.

The nature of the employer's activities, and the size of its undertaking

5.40 As explained in paragraphs 3.9 and 3.10, Part 2 now applies to all employers (except for the Armed Forces), irrespective of their size. However, the size of an employer's undertaking and the nature of its activities may be relevant in determining the reasonableness of a particular step.

> A small manufacturing company making chairs employs a craftswoman who becomes disabled and can no longer carry out her job, even after adjustments have been considered. The only jobs available in the company are production-based as the company owner herself carries out all other functions, such as marketing and running the office. Given the nature of the business, it is not likely to be reasonable for the employer to provide an alternative job for the employee.

In contrast, a business of the same size which designs, manufactures and retails games is likely to have a wide range of jobs. In these circumstances, if an employee were no longer able to work in a production role it might be reasonable for the employer to provide an alternative job.

A sales assistant in a small shop who has a mental health problem requests time off each week to attend a psychotherapy appointment. It would be more likely to be reasonable for her employer to agree to this if there were other sales assistants who could cover for her absence.

In relation to private households, the extent to which taking the step would disrupt the household or disturb any person residing there

5.41 The duty to make reasonable adjustments may apply in respect of disabled people who work in private households. However, even if the financial cost would be minimal, it might not be reasonable to take a particular step if doing so would entail disruption to the household or disturbance to people who live there.

A man employs a deaf cleaner in his house. They communicate with each other by writing notes. It is likely to be a reasonable adjustment for him to communicate with her in this way.

A person with a severe dust allergy applies for the position of nanny. When she is interviewed it becomes apparent that she can only work in an environment which is dust free. The prospective employers take the view that this would be too disruptive to their home life. It is unlikely to be reasonable for them to have to make the adjustments needed to employ this person.

Other factors

5.42 Although the Act does not mention any further factors, others may be relevant depending on the circumstances. For example:

- effect on other employees

A disabled person wants to work in a cold office as heat aggravates his skin condition. This is not reasonable in the open plan office where he works because it would be uncomfortable for other employees to have to work in these conditions. Moving him to a small office on his own may be a reasonable adjustment in these circumstances.

A disabled woman working as a baker in a small bakery wants to avoid night shifts because disturbances to her sleep patterns trigger her migraines. Other employees would also like to avoid night shifts, for reasons unrelated to disability. This is unlikely to be a relevant factor for the employer in considering whether it is reasonable to allow the disabled employee's request.

- adjustments made for other disabled employees

If an employer has a number of staff with mobility problems this may mean that it would be reasonable to make significant structural changes to their workplace.

- the extent to which the disabled person is willing to co-operate

An employee with a mobility impairment works in a team located on an upper floor to which there is no access by lift. Getting there is very tiring for the employee, and the employer could easily make a more accessible location available for him. Following a workplace assessment the employer decides to move the employee to the alternative location, but the employee refuses to co-operate. If there is no other adjustment that the employer can reasonably make, it does not have to do any more.

CAN FAILURE TO MAKE A REASONABLE ADJUSTMENT EVER BE JUSTIFIED?

5.43 **[s 3A(2)]** The Act does not permit an employer to justify a failure to comply with a duty to make a reasonable adjustment. This is a change in the law (see Appendix A).

5.44 Clearly, however, an employer will only breach such a duty if the adjustment in question is one which it is reasonable for it to have to make. So, where the duty applies, it is the question of 'reasonableness' which alone determines whether the adjustment has to be made.

[4666]

6. JUSTIFICATION

INTRODUCTION

6.1 Most conduct which is potentially unlawful under Part 2 of the Act cannot be justified. Conduct which amounts to:

- direct discrimination
- failure to comply with a duty to make a reasonable adjustment
- victimisation
- harassment
- instructions or pressure to discriminate, or
- aiding an unlawful act

is unlawful irrespective of the reason or motive for it.

When does the Act permit justification?

6.2 Paragraph 4.27 explains that one of the forms of discrimination which is unlawful under Part 2 is disability-related discrimination. However, an employer's conduct towards a disabled person does not amount to disability-related discrimination if it can be justified. This chapter explains the limited circumstances in which this may happen.

6.3 **[s 3A(3) & (4)]** Where less favourable treatment of a disabled person is capable of being justified (that is, where it is **not** direct discrimination), the Act says that it will, in fact, be justified if, but only if, the reason for the treatment is both material to the circumstances of the particular case and substantial. This is an objective test. 'Material' means that there must be a reasonably strong connection between the reason given for the treatment and the circumstances of the particular case. 'Substantial' means, in the context of justification, that the reason must carry real weight and be of substance.

A man who has severe back pain and is unable to bend is rejected for a job as a carpet fitter as he cannot carry out the essential requirement of the job, which is to fit carpets. This would be lawful as the reason he is rejected is a substantial one and is clearly material to the circumstances.

6.4 In certain circumstances, the existence of a material and substantial reason for disability-related less favourable treatment is not enough to justify that treatment. This is the case where an employer is also under a duty to make reasonable adjustments in relation to the disabled person but fails to comply with that duty.

6.5 **[s 3A(6)]** In those circumstances, it is necessary to consider not only whether there is a material and substantial reason for the less favourable treatment, but also whether the treatment would still have been justified even if the employer had complied with its duty to make reasonable adjustments. In effect, it is necessary to ask the question 'would a reasonable adjustment have made any difference?' If a reasonable adjustment would have made a difference to the reason that is being used to justify the treatment, then the less favourable treatment cannot be justified.

> An applicant for an administrative job appears not to be the best person for the job, but only because her typing speed is too slow as a result of arthritis in her hands. If a reasonable adjustment-perhaps an adapted keyboard-would overcome this, her typing speed would not in itself be a substantial reason for not employing her. Therefore the employer would be unlawfully discriminating if, on account of her typing speed, he did not employ her or provide that adjustment.

6.6 In relation to disability-related discrimination, the fact that an employer has failed to comply with a duty to make a reasonable adjustment means that the sequence of events for justifying disability-related less favourable treatment is as follows:

- The disabled person proves facts from which it could be inferred in the absence of an adequate explanation that:
  a. for a reason related to his disability, he has been treated less favourably than a person to whom that reason does not apply has been, or would be, treated, and
  b. a duty to make a reasonable adjustment has arisen in respect of him and the employer has failed to comply with it.
- The employer will be found to have discriminated unless it proves that:
  a. the reason for the treatment is both material to the circumstances of the particular case and substantial, and
  b. the reason would still have applied if the reasonable adjustment had been made.

CAN HEALTH AND SAFETY CONCERNS JUSTIFY LESS FAVOURABLE TREATMENT?

6.7 Stereotypical assumptions about the health and safety implications of disability should be avoided, both in general terms and in relation to particular types of disability. Indeed, less favourable treatment which is based on such assumptions may itself amount to direct discrimination – which is incapable of justification (see paragraph 4.5). The fact that a person has a disability does not necessarily mean that he represents an additional risk to health and safety.

> An employer has a policy of not employing anyone with diabetes because it believes that people with this condition are a health and safety risk. A person with diabetes applies to work for this employer and is turned down on the basis of her disability, without regard to her personal circumstances. A stereotypical assumption has been made which is likely to amount to direct discrimination and is therefore unlawful.

6.8 Under health and safety law it is the duty of every employer to ensure, so far as is reasonably practicable, the health, safety and welfare at work of all employees. Part of this duty is a requirement for all employers to assess the risks to the health and safety of all employees in the workplace and then to put in place measures that reduce the risks to as low a level as can reasonably be achieved. Genuine concerns about the health and safety of anybody (including a disabled employee) may be relevant when seeking to establish that disability-related less favourable treatment of a disabled person is justified. However, it is important to remember that health and safety law does not require employers to remove all conceivable risk, but to ensure that risk is properly appreciated, understood and managed. Further information can be obtained from the Health and Safety Executive (see Appendix C for details).

PART 4

6.9 It is the employer who must decide what action to take in response to concerns about health and safety. However, when an employer has reason to think that the effects of a person's disability may give rise to an issue about health and safety, it is prudent for it to have a new risk assessment carried out by a suitably qualified person. This is because:

- If an employer treats a disabled person less favourably merely on the basis of generalised assumptions about the health and safety implications of having a disability, such treatment may itself amount to direct discrimination – which is incapable of justification.
- Even where there is no direct discrimination, an employer which treats a disabled person less favourably without having a suitable and sufficient risk assessment carried out is unlikely to be able to show that its concerns about health and safety justify the less favourable treatment.

> A pilot develops a heart condition, and his employer asks him to undertake a risk assessment to be carried out by an appropriate consultant. This is likely to be justifiable.

6.10 Nevertheless, an employer should not subject a disabled person to a risk assessment if this is not merited by the particular circumstances of the case.

> A person with a learning disability has been working in a shop for many years, stocking shelves without any problems. A new manager is appointed who insists that a risk assessment is carried out for her but not for all the other shelf stackers. This is unlikely to be warranted – and indeed it is likely to amount to direct discrimination.

6.11 A risk assessment must be suitable and sufficient. It should identify the risks associated with a work activity, taking account of any reasonable adjustments put in place for the disabled person, and should be specific for the individual carrying out a particular task. It is therefore unlikely that an employer which has a **general** policy of treating people with certain disabilities (such as epilepsy, diabetes or mental health problems) less favourably than other people will be able to justify doing so – even if that policy is in accordance with the advice of an occupational health adviser.

6.12 A 'blanket' policy of this nature will usually be unlawful. This is because it is likely to amount to direct discrimination (which cannot ever be justified) or to disability-related less favourable treatment which is not justifiable in the circumstances-i e disability-related discrimination (see paragraphs 7.8 and 7.9).

6.13 Reasonable adjustments made by an employer may remove or reduce health and safety risks related to a person's disability. A suitable and sufficient assessment of such risks therefore needs to take account of the impact which making any reasonable adjustments would have. If a risk assessment is not conducted on this basis, then an employer is unlikely to be able to show that its concerns about health and safety justify less favourable treatment of the disabled person.

CAN MEDICAL INFORMATION JUSTIFY LESS FAVOURABLE TREATMENT?

6.14 Consideration of medical information (such as a doctor's report or the answers to a medical questionnaire) is likely to form part of an assessment of health and safety risks. In most cases, however, having a disability does not adversely affect a person's general health. In other cases, its effect on a person's health may fluctuate. Although medical information about a disability may justify an adverse employment decision (such as a decision to dismiss or not to promote), it will not do so if there is no effect on the person's ability to do the job (or if any effect is less than substantial), no matter how great the effects of the disability are in other ways. Indeed, less favourable treatment of a disabled person in a case where his disability has no effect on his ability to do the job may well amount to direct discrimination – which is incapable of being justified.

> An employer requires all candidates for a job as a technician in a chemical plant to complete a medical questionnaire. Medical information about one candidate shows that

she has a degenerative condition which is likely to affect her ability to walk. This is not relevant to her ability to do the sedentary job in question. It would be unlawful for the employer to reject her on the ground of her disability as her disability is irrelevant to her ability to do the job. This would amount to direct discrimination.

The same employer is looking for a technician to work on a specific project for two years. A medical questionnaire shows that a candidate has a degenerative condition which could mean that he would not be able to work for that long. Because of this, further medical evidence is requested from his doctor and this confirms that he would not be able to work for two years. It is likely to be lawful to reject this candidate if the two-year requirement is justified in terms of the work and if there are no reasonable adjustments that could be made.

6.15 In addition, where medical information is available, employers must weigh it up in the context of the actual job, and the capabilities of the individual. An employer should also consider whether reasonable adjustments could be made in order to overcome any problems which may have been identified as a result of the medical information. It should not be taken for granted that the person who provides the medical information will be aware that employers have a duty to make reasonable adjustments, what these adjustments might be, or of the relevant working arrangements. It is good practice, therefore, to ensure that medical advisers are made aware of these matters. Information provided by a medical adviser should only be relied on if the adviser has the appropriate knowledge and expertise.

An occupational health adviser recommends that an administrative assistant cannot carry on in her current job because she has been diagnosed with Repetitive Strain Injury. The employer has another member of staff who uses voice recognition software, and considers this technology may be of relevance. The employer asks the adviser to review his conclusion taking this into account. The adviser revises his opinion and concludes that, with appropriate software, she can continue in her role.

6.16 In any event, although medical evidence may generally be considered as an 'expert contribution', it should not ordinarily be the sole factor influencing an employer's decision on employment related matters. The views of the disabled person (about his own capabilities and possible adjustments) should also be sought. In addition, and subject to the considerations about confidentiality explained in paragraphs 8.21 and 8.22, other contributions could come from the disabled person's line manager (about the nature of the job and possible adjustments). It may also be possible to seek help from disability organisations or from Jobcentre Plus, who have staff trained to advise about disability issues in the workplace. Ultimately, it is for the employer—and not the medical adviser—to take decisions as to whether, for example, to reject a job applicant or to maintain a disabled person's employment.

An employer receives advice from an occupational health adviser stating simply that an employee is 'unfit for work'. In spite of this the employer must consider whether there are reasonable adjustments which should be made.

[4667]

7. DISCRIMINATION IN THE RECRUITMENT OF EMPLOYEES

INTRODUCTION

7.1 **[s 4(1)]** It has already been explained (at paragraph 3.18) that it is unlawful for an employer to discriminate against a disabled person:

- in the arrangements made for determining who should be offered employment
- in the terms on which the disabled person is offered employment, or
- by refusing to offer, or deliberately not offering, the disabled person employment.

PART 4

7.2 This chapter examines these principles in more detail. In order to do so, it is necessary to look at the various stages of the recruitment process, from specifying the job and advertising the vacancy, to the process of assessing candidates, interview and selection.

7.3 Although the following paragraphs refer only to the recruitment of employees, it should be remembered that the same principles apply to the recruitment of people to occupations covered by the Act's provisions on employment and occupation. Any variations in the way the Act applies to such occupations are explained in Chapter 9.

GENERAL CONSIDERATIONS

Recruiting the best person for the job

7.4 Before considering the recruitment process itself it should be noted that, although an employer must not discriminate against a disabled candidate, there is no requirement (aside from the duty to make reasonable adjustments) to treat a disabled person more favourably than it treats or would treat others. An employer will have to assess an applicant's merits as they would be if any reasonable adjustments required under the Act had been made. If, after allowing for those adjustments, a disabled person would not be the best person for the job, the employer does not have to recruit that person.

7.5 On the other hand, the Act does not prevent posts being advertised as open only to disabled applicants, or to an applicant being preferred for the job because of his disability. Special rules apply to local authority employers, however, as explained in paragraph 13.25.

A note about 'arrangements' for determining who should be offered employment

7.6 Although the statutory provisions specifically deal with recruitment in relation to employment as defined by the Act (see paragraph 3.8), the meaning of 'arrangements'—that is, arrangements for determining who should be offered employment—is wide. Such arrangements are not confined to those which an employer makes in deciding who should be offered a specific job, but also include arrangements for deciding who should be offered employment more generally. Thus, for example, participation in a pre-employment training programme could be 'an arrangement' if its completion is a necessary step along the road to gaining an offer of employment.

SPECIFYING THE JOB

How does the Act affect the way in which a job description or person specification should be prepared?

7.7 The inclusion of unnecessary or marginal requirements in a job description or person specification can lead to discrimination.

> An employer stipulates that employees must be 'active and energetic', when in fact the job in question is largely sedentary in nature. This requirement could unjustifiably exclude some people whose disabilities result in them getting tired more easily than others.

> An employer specifies that a driving licence is required for a job which involves limited travel. An applicant for the job has no driving licence because of the particular effects in his case of cerebral palsy. He is otherwise the best candidate for that job, he could easily and cheaply do the travelling involved other than by driving and it is likely to be a reasonable adjustment for the employer to let him do so. It would be discriminatory to insist on the specification and reject his application solely because he has no driving licence.

> An employer stipulates that employees must be 'good team players', when in fact the job in question does not involve working in a team. This requirement could unjustifiably exclude some people who have difficulty communicating, such as some people with autism.

7.8 Blanket exclusions (ie exclusions which do not take account of individual circumstances) can also lead to discrimination. Indeed, such exclusions are likely to amount to direct discrimination, and so be incapable of justification (see paragraph 4.5).

An employer excludes people with epilepsy from all driving jobs. One of the jobs, in practice, only requires a standard licence and standard insurance cover. If, as a result, someone with epilepsy, who has such a licence and can obtain such insurance cover, is turned down for the job, the employer will have discriminated unlawfully in excluding her from consideration.

An employer stipulates that candidates for a job must not have a history of mental illness, believing that such candidates will have poor attendance. The employer rejects an applicant solely because he has had a mental illness, without checking the individual's actual attendance record. This will amount to discrimination – and will be unlawful.

An employer stipulates that anyone with an infectious disease cannot work in the food preparation area. It refuses to employ someone with AIDS in this area, believing him to be a health and safety risk. Whether or not the employer has a written policy to this effect, this action will amount to discrimination, as the employer has not considered the actual circumstances of the case.

7.9 In addition, stating that a certain personal, medical or health-related characteristic is essential or desirable can lead to discrimination if the characteristic is not necessary for the performance of the job. An employer would therefore need to ensure that any such requirements were genuinely essential to the job, and that it would not be reasonable to waive them in any individual case.

A television company requires all television engineers to have a high standard of hearing and vision. A woman with a hearing impairment is turned down for a job in the graphic design department because she does not pass a hearing test. If this standard of hearing is not necessary in order to do the particular job she applied for, the employer will have unlawfully discriminated against her by failing to make a reasonable adjustment to its policy of requiring job applicants to pass the test.

7.10 Likewise, although an employer is entitled to specify that applicants for a job must have certain qualifications, it will have to justify rejecting a disabled person for lacking a qualification if the reason why the disabled person lacks it is related to his disability. Justification will involve showing that the qualification is relevant and significant in terms of the particular job and the particular applicant, and that there is no reasonable adjustment which would change this. In some circumstances it might be feasible to reassign the duties to which the qualification relates, or to waive the requirement for the qualification if this particular applicant has alternative evidence of the necessary level of competence.

An employer seeking someone to work in an administrative post specifies that candidates must have the relevant NVQ Level 4 qualification. If Level 4 fairly reflects the complex and varied nature and substantial personal responsibility of the work, and these aspects of the job cannot reasonably be altered, the employer will be able to justify rejecting a disabled applicant who has only been able to reach Level 3 because of his disability and who cannot show the relevant level of competence by other means.

An employer specifies that two GCSEs are required for a certain post. This is to show that a candidate has the general level of ability required. No particular subjects are

> specified. An applicant whose dyslexia prevented her from passing written examinations cannot meet this requirement. The employer would be unable to justify rejecting her on this account alone if she could show in some other way that she had the expertise called for in the post.

ADVERTISING THE VACANCY

Can a job advertisement encourage applications from disabled people?

7.11 The Act does not prevent a job advertisement saying that the employer would welcome applications from disabled people. This would be a positive and public statement of the employer's policy. More information about good practice in relation to attracting disabled job applicants is given at paragraphs 2.17 and 2.18.

What about discriminatory job advertisements?

7.12 **[s 16B(1)]** The Act says that, when advertising a job vacancy, it is unlawful for the person offering the job to publish an advertisement (or cause it to be published) which indicates, or might reasonably be understood to indicate:

- that the success of a person's application for the job may depend to any extent on his not having any disability, or any particular disability, or
- that the person determining the application is reluctant to make reasonable adjustments.

> An employer advertises a work placement for an office worker, stating 'We are sorry but because our offices are on the first floor, they are not accessible to disabled people'. This is likely to be unlawful. It would be better for the advertisement to state 'although our offices are on the first floor, we welcome applications from disabled people and are willing to make reasonable adjustments.'

> An advertisement for an assistant in office supplies stipulates that a driving licence is required. The post itself does not involve significant amounts of driving, and reasonable adjustments to this element of the job would be possible. However, the advertisement implies that the employer is unwilling to make such reasonable adjustments, for example by allowing travel by taxi or allocating the driving to someone else. This is likely to be unlawful.

7.13 **[s 16B(2)–(4)]** This applies to every form of advertisement or notice, whether to the public or not, for any employment, promotion or transfer of employment. However, an advertisement may still be lawful even if it does indicate that having a particular disability will adversely affect an applicant's prospects of success. This will be the case where, for example, because of the nature of the job in question, the employer is entitled to take the effects of the disability into account when assessing the suitability of applicants.

> It would be lawful for a company specialising in inner city bicycle courier services to advertise for couriers who 'must be able to ride a bicycle.'

7.14 **[s 17B(1)]** The Act does not give individual job applicants the right to take legal action in respect of discriminatory advertisements. Such action may only be taken by the DRC (see paragraphs 13.28 to 13.30).

> An employer states in an advertisement for an office worker, 'Sorry but gaining access to our building can be difficult for some people.' The DRC could take proceedings on the grounds that this constitutes a discriminatory advertisement.

7.15 In addition, it should be noted that the content of the advertisement could be taken into account by an employment tribunal in determining a claim brought by a disabled person under the Act.

> A disabled person who walks with the aid of crutches applies for the job mentioned in the previous example and is turned down. He could ask the employment tribunal to take the content of the advertisement into account when determining whether he did not get the job for a disability-related reason.

APPLICATION FORMS AND INFORMATION

Does an employer have to provide information about jobs in accessible formats?

7.16 Where an employer provides information about a job, it is likely to be a reasonable adjustment for it to provide on request information in a format that is accessible to a disabled applicant – particularly if the employer's information systems, and the time available before the new employee is needed, mean it can easily be done. Accessible formats include email, Braille, Easy Read, large print, audio tape and computer disc. A disabled person's requirements will depend upon his impairment, but on other factors too. For example, many blind people do not read Braille but prefer to receive information by email or on audio tape.

> A person whom the employer knows to be disabled asks to be given information about a job in a format that is accessible to her. It is likely to be a reasonable adjustment for the employer to provide the information in an accessible format.

> An employer advertises vacancies on its website. The website is not accessible to disabled people who use particular types of software on their computers. A man with a visual impairment, who uses 'screen reader' software on his computer and has notified the employer that he would like to work for it, cannot read the job vacancies on the employer's website. It is likely to be unlawful for the employer to refuse to make its website accessible to the disabled man, unless it is prepared to provide him with the same information in an accessible format.

Does an employer have to accept applications in accessible formats?

7.17 Where an employer invites applications by completing and returning an application form, it is likely to be a reasonable adjustment for it to accept applications which contain the necessary information in accessible formats. However, a disabled person might not have a right to submit an application in his preferred format (such as Braille) if he would not be substantially disadvantaged by submitting it in some other format (such as email) which the employer would find easier to access. Where applications are invited by completing and returning a form on-line, that form should be accessible to disabled people (or an accessible alternative should be provided).

> Because of his disability, a candidate asks to submit an application in a particular format, different from the one specified for candidates in general (eg on tape). It is likely to be a reasonable adjustment for the employer to allow this.

7.18 Whether or not an application is submitted in an accessible format, employers and their staff or agents must not discriminate against disabled people in the way that they deal with their applications.

SELECTION, ASSESSMENT AND INTERVIEW ARRANGEMENTS

When must an employer make adjustments to its selection, assessment and interview arrangements?

7.19 An employer is not required to make changes in anticipation of applications from disabled people in general – although it would obviously be good practice to do so. It is only

PART 4

if the employer knows or could be reasonably expected to know that a particular disabled person is, or may be, applying and is likely to be substantially disadvantaged by the employer's premises or arrangements, that the employer may have to make changes.

When should an employer short-list a disabled person for interview?

7.20 Many employers operate a guaranteed interview scheme, under which a disabled candidate who wishes to use the scheme will be short-listed for interview automatically if he demonstrates that he meets the minimum criteria for getting the job.

7.21 Regardless of whether an employer operates a guaranteed interview scheme, it will need to consider whether it should make reasonable adjustments when short-listing for interview. This will be the case if an employer knows or ought to know that an applicant has a disability and is likely to be at a substantial disadvantage because of its recruitment arrangements or the premises in which any interviews are held. In these circumstances, the employer should consider whether there is any reasonable adjustment which would remove the disadvantage. Any such adjustment should be taken into account when short-listing applicants. If the employer cannot make this judgment without more information it would be discriminatory for it not to put the disabled person on the short-list for interview if that is how it would normally seek additional information about candidates.

What adjustments might an employer have to make when arranging or conducting interviews?

7.22 Employers should think ahead for interviews. Depending upon the circumstances, changes may need to be made to arrangements for interviews or to the way in which interviews are carried out.

> A hearing impaired candidate informs a potential employer that he can lip read but will need to be able to see the interviewer's face clearly. The interviewer ensures that her face is well lit, that she faces the applicant when speaking, that she speaks clearly and is prepared to repeat questions if the candidate does not understand her. These are likely to be reasonable adjustments for the employer to make.

> An employer arranges a British Sign Language (BSL) interpreter to attend an interview with a deaf candidate who uses BSL to communicate. The interviewer also allows extra time for the interview. (Communication support for interviews such as sign language interpreters may also be available through the Access to Work scheme). These are likely to be reasonable adjustments for the employer to make.

> An employer pays expenses to candidates who come for interview. A disabled candidate brings his support worker with him to the interview. The employer pays the expenses of the support worker as well. This is likely to be a reasonable adjustment to the usual policy of paying only the candidate's own expenses.

> An employer allows a candidate who has a learning disability to bring a supportive person to an interview to assist when answering questions that are not part of the assessment itself. This is likely to be a reasonable adjustment to the selection process.

7.23 It is a good idea to give applicants the opportunity to indicate any relevant effects of a disability and to suggest adjustments to help overcome any disadvantage the disability may cause at interview. This could help the employer avoid discrimination in the interview and in considering the application, by clarifying whether any reasonable adjustments may be required. However, an employer must not assume that no adjustments need to be made simply because the applicant has not requested any (see paragraph 5.24).

7.24 The practical effects of an employer's duties may be different if a person whom the employer previously did not know, and could not reasonably be expected to have known, to be disabled arrives for interview and is substantially disadvantaged because of the arrangements. The employer may still be under a duty to make a reasonable adjustment from the time that it first learns of the disability and the disadvantage. However, the employer might not be required to do as much as might have been the case if it had known (or if it ought to have known) in advance about the disability and its effects.

> A job applicant does not tell an employer in advance that she uses a wheelchair and the employer does not know of her disability. On arriving for the interview she discovers that the room is not accessible. Although the employer could not have been expected to make the necessary changes in advance, it would be a reasonable adjustment to hold the interview in an alternative, accessible room if one was available without too much disruption or cost. Alternatively, it might be a reasonable adjustment to reschedule the interview if this was practicable.

What about aptitude or other tests in the recruitment process?

7.25 The Act does not prevent employers carrying out aptitude or other tests, including psychological tests. However, routine testing of all candidates may still discriminate against particular individuals or substantially disadvantage them. In those cases, the employer would need to revise the tests – or the way the results are assessed – to take account of a disabled candidate. This does not apply, however, where the nature and form of the test is necessary to assess a matter relevant to the job. The following are examples of adjustments which may be reasonable:

- allowing a disabled person extra time to complete the test
- permitting a disabled person the assistance of a reader or scribe during the test
- accepting a lower 'pass rate' for a person whose disability inhibits performance in such a test.

The extent to which such adjustments might be required would depend on how closely the test is related to the job in question and what adjustments the employer might have to make if the applicant were given the job.

> An employer sets a word processing test for candidates for a position as administrative officer. A person with repetitive strain injury (RSI) takes the test using voice-activated software, as this is how she would carry out the job if she were appointed. Permitting her to take the test in this way is likely to be a reasonable adjustment for the employer to make.

> An employer sets candidates a short oral test. An applicant is disabled by a severe stammer, but only under stress. It is likely to be a reasonable adjustment to allow her more time to complete the test. Alternatively, it may be a reasonable adjustment to give the test in written form instead – though not if excellent oral communication skills are necessary for the job and assessing those skills was the purpose of the test.

7.26 However, employers would be well advised to seek professional advice in the light of individual circumstances before making adjustments to psychological or aptitude tests.

When can an employer ask questions about a disability?

7.27 The Act does not prohibit an employer from seeking information about a disability. However, the Data Protection Code of Practice on Employment and Recruitment (see Appendix C for details) states that information should not be sought from applicants unless necessary to enable the recruitment decision to be made, or for a related purpose such as equal opportunities monitoring. Disability-related questions must not be used to discriminate against a disabled person. An employer should only ask such questions if they are, or may be, relevant to the person's ability to do the job – after a reasonable adjustment, if necessary.

> An applicant with a visual impairment is asked at interview whether or not she was born with that condition. This is irrelevant to her ability to do the job and may upset the applicant, potentially preventing her from performing as well as she would otherwise have done. This is likely to be unlawful.

> An applicant who is a wheelchair user is asked whether any changes may be needed to the workplace to accommodate him. This would not be unlawful.

7.28 Asking a basic question as to whether or not a person is disabled is unlikely to yield any useful information for the employer and may simply lead to confusion. The fact that such a question was asked might subsequently be used as evidence of discrimination. In addition, short-listing on the basis of an applicant's responses to a medical questionnaire may be discriminatory if the employer has not ascertained the likely effects of a disability or medical condition on the applicant's ability to do the job, or whether reasonable adjustments would overcome any disadvantage it causes. Even where there are medical requirements which must be met, it is good practice for employers not to require job applicants to answer a medical questionnaire until after a conditional job offer has been made.

7.29 On the other hand, when inviting a job applicant to attend an interview, it is good practice for an employer to ask whether any adjustments might be needed to enable him to participate fully in the process, and what those adjustments might be.

> An application form includes the statement 'Please let us know if you require any reasonable adjustments, due to disability, to enable you to attend an interview, or which you wish us to take into account when considering your application. Reasonable adjustments are things like sign language interpreters, altering the time of the interview, or making the interview room accessible for you. If you would like to discuss your disability requirements further, please contact the Human Resources manager'. This will not be discriminatory and is likely to help an employer comply with its duties under the Act.

7.30 In addition, once a decision has been made to appoint a disabled person, it is good practice for an employer to discuss reasonable adjustments with him before he starts work. An employer may also wish to monitor disabled applicants, as part of an overall monitoring policy, although this information should be kept separately from an application form. More information about good practice in relation to monitoring is given in paragraphs 2.14 to 2.16.

Can a disabled person be required to have a medical examination?

7.31 Although the Act does not prevent an employer from asking a disabled person to have a medical examination, an employer will probably be discriminating unlawfully if, without justification, it insists on a medical check for a disabled person but not for others. The fact that a person has a disability is, in itself, unlikely to justify singling out that person to have a health check – although this might be justified in relation to some jobs. Paragraphs 6.14 to 6.16 explain the circumstances in which medical information may legitimately influence an employer's decision as to whether to offer a job to a disabled person.

> An employer requires all candidates for employment to have a medical examination. The employer would be entitled to apply that requirement to a disabled person who applies for employment.

> An employer issues a health questionnaire to all job applicants and requires any successful job applicant who states they are disabled to undergo a medical examination. This is likely to be unlawful.

> An employer issues a health questionnaire to all successful job applicants but does not require them to undergo a medical examination unless they have a condition which may be relevant to the job, or the working environment. A successful job applicant indicates that he has a disabling heart condition. It is likely that the employer would be justified in asking him to have a medical examination provided it is restricted to assessing the implications for the particular job in question.

OFFERS OF EMPLOYMENT

7.32 Terms and conditions of service should not discriminate against a disabled person. In general, an employer should not offer a job to a disabled person on terms which are less favourable than those which would be offered to other people.

> A person with a history of depression is offered employment with a six month probationary period, even though other employees are only required to serve a three month probationary period. This will amount to direct discrimination and will be unlawful.

[4668]

8. DISCRIMINATION AGAINST EMPLOYEES

INTRODUCTION

8.1 **[s 4(2)]** It has already been explained (at paragraph 3.19) that it is unlawful for an employer to discriminate against a disabled person whom it employs:

- in the terms of employment which it affords him
- in the opportunities which it affords him for promotion, a transfer, training or receiving any other benefit
- by refusing to afford him, or deliberately not affording him, any such opportunity, or
- by dismissing him, or subjecting him to any other detriment.

8.2 This chapter examines these principles in more detail. In order to do so, it is necessary to look at various aspects of the employment relationship and its associated conditions and benefits, from terms and conditions of service to arrangements for induction and training, and from opportunities for promotion or transfer to arrangements for managing disability or ill health, and terminating employment.

8.3 Although the following paragraphs refer only to the treatment of employees, it should be remembered that the same principles apply to people in occupations covered by the Act's provisions on employment and occupation. Any variations in the way the Act applies to such occupations are explained in Chapter 9. In addition, particular issues about discrimination in providing occupational pensions and group insurance services are considered in Chapter 10.

TERMS AND CONDITIONS OF SERVICE

8.4 As stated at paragraph 7.32, terms and conditions of service should not discriminate against a disabled person. The employer should consider whether any reasonable adjustments need to be made to the terms and conditions which would otherwise apply.

> An employer's terms and conditions state the hours an employee has to be in work. It might be a reasonable adjustment to change these hours for someone whose disability means that she has difficulty using public transport during rush hours.

8.5 Where the terms and conditions of employment include an element of performance-related pay, the employer must ensure that the way such pay arrangements operate does not discriminate against a disabled employee. If, on the ground of disability, an employee is denied the opportunity to receive performance-related pay, this is likely to be direct

PART 4

discrimination. Even if less favourable treatment of an employee in relation to performance-related pay is not directly discriminatory, it will amount to disability-related discrimination unless the employer can show that it is justified.

8.6 If an employee has a disability which adversely affects his rate of output, the effect may be that he receives less under a performance-related pay scheme than other employees. The employer must consider whether there are reasonable adjustments which would overcome this substantial disadvantage.

> A disabled man with arthritis works in telephone sales and is paid commission on the value of his sales. Because of a worsening of his impairment he is advised to switch to new computer equipment. This equipment slows his work down for a period of time while he gets used to it and consequently the value of his sales falls. It is likely to be a reasonable adjustment for his employer to continue to pay him his previous level of commission for the period in which he adjusts to the new equipment.

> A disabled home-worker, who is paid a fixed rate for each item he produces, has a reduced output rate because he does not have the right equipment to do the job to the best of his ability. It is likely to be a reasonable adjustment for the employer to provide that equipment, possibly with funding or advice from the Access to Work scheme, to improve the disabled worker's output and consequently his pay.

> A woman who has recently become disabled because of diabetes works for an employer that operates a performance related bonus scheme. When she has her annual appraisal, the woman is unable to demonstrate that she has met all her objectives for the year, unlike in previous years when she had in fact exceeded her objectives. The reason why the woman has not met her objectives this year is that she has been adjusting to her disability (attending hospital appointments, paying careful attention to her diet, taking regular breaks etc). The disabled woman's employer is likely to be discriminating against her if, because she has not met her objectives for the year, it refuses to pay her a bonus.

INDUCTION, TRAINING AND DEVELOPMENT

8.7 **[s 4(2) & s 4A(1)]** Employers must not discriminate in their induction procedures. The employer may have to make adjustments to ensure a disabled person is introduced into a new working environment in a clearly structured and supported way, with an individually tailored induction programme if necessary.

> A small manufacturing company usually hands out written copies of all its policies by way of induction to new employees and gives them half a day to read the documentation and to raise any questions with their line manager. A new employee has dyslexia and the employer arranges for her supervisor to spend a morning with her talking through the relevant policies. This is likely to be a reasonable adjustment.

> An employer runs a one day induction course for new recruits. A recruit with a learning disability is put at a substantial disadvantage by the way the course is normally run. The employer is likely to have to make an alternative arrangement such as permitting the person to attend a longer course, or allowing someone to sit in on the course to provide support, assistance or encouragement to the disabled person.

8.8 In addition, employers must not discriminate in selection for training and must make reasonable adjustments in order to avoid disabled people being placed at a substantial disadvantage.

Instead of taking an informed decision, an employer wrongly assumes that a disabled person will be unwilling or unable to undertake demanding training or attend a residential training course. This is likely to amount to direct discrimination.

An employer may need to alter the time or the location of the training for someone with a mobility problem, make training manuals, slides or other visual media accessible to a visually impaired employee (perhaps by providing Braille versions or having them read out), or ensure that an induction loop is available for someone with a hearing impairment.

An employee with a hearing impairment is selected for a post as a TV engineer. He attends the induction course which consists of a video and discussion. The video is not subtitled and thus the employee cannot participate fully in the induction. This is likely to be unlawful.

An employer refuses to allow a disabled employee to be coached for a theory examination relating to practical work which the employee is unable to do because of his disability. This is likely to be justified because the employee would never be suited for the area of work for which the coaching was designed, and a reasonable adjustment could not alter that position.

However, if the disabled employee required coaching to enable him to understand the requirements of the practical work because he would be managing staff carrying out the work, a decision not to provide coaching would be unlikely to be justified.

BENEFITS PROVIDED BY EMPLOYERS

8.9 **[s 4(2) & s 4A(1)]** Employers often provide a range of benefits to their staff. 'Benefits' include 'facilities' and 'services'. An employer must not discriminate in the way that it makes benefits available to disabled employees where those benefits are available to other employees. The employer must make any necessary reasonable adjustment to the way the benefits are provided. As explained in Chapter 10, an employer's duty to make reasonable adjustments now extends to the way it provides any benefits relating to occupational pension schemes or group insurance services.

8.10 Benefits might include canteens, meal vouchers, social clubs and other recreational activities, dedicated car parking spaces, discounts on products, bonuses, share options, hairdressing, clothes allowances, financial services, healthcare, medical assistance/insurance, transport to work, company car, education assistance, workplace nurseries, and rights to special leave. This is not an exhaustive list.

If physical features of a company's social club would inhibit a disabled person's access it might be a reasonable adjustment for the employer to make suitable modifications.

An employer provides dedicated car parking spaces close to the workplace. A disabled employee finds it very difficult to get from the public car parks further away. It is likely to be a reasonable adjustment for the employer to allocate one of the dedicated spaces to that employee.

8.11 **[s 16A]** Some benefits may continue after employment has ended. An employer's duties under the Act extend to its former employees in respect of such benefits.

8.12 **[s 4(2) & (4)]** The provisions on employment and occupation in Part 2 do not normally apply to benefits which an employer provides to the public, or to a section of the public which includes the disabled employee. This is because the provision of those benefits relates to the employer's activities as a service provider rather than as an employer. Such activities are usually subject to the duties in Part 3 instead. However, the Act's provisions on employment and occupation will apply if the benefit to employees is materially different (for example, at a discount) or is governed by the contract of employment, or relates to training.

> A disabled employee of a supermarket chain is discriminated against for a reason related to his disability when buying goods as a customer of the supermarket. Even though he is an employee, he would have no claim under the Act's provisions on employment and occupation, because he is merely buying goods as a customer. However, if the discrimination related to the use of his employee's discount card, that would relate to his employment benefits and the Act's provisions on employment and occupation would apply.

PROMOTION AND TRANSFER

8.13 **[s 4(2) & s 4A(1)]** Employers must ensure that arrangements for promoting staff, or for transferring staff between jobs, do not discriminate against disabled people. It is likely to be direct discrimination if a disabled employee is treated less favourably in this regard on the ground of disability (see paragraph 4.5). If the treatment is not directly discriminatory, but is for a reason related to the disability, it will amount to disability-related discrimination unless the employer can show that it is justified. Employers must not discriminate in the practical arrangements necessary to enable the promotion or transfer to take place or, of course, in the new job itself. Reasonable adjustments may need to be made to the various stages in the promotion or transfer process.

> A garage owner does not consider a clerk, who has lost the use of her right arm, for promotion to assistant manager because he wrongly and unreasonably believes that her disability might prevent her performing competently in a managerial post. This is likely to be discrimination.

> An employer interviewing a number of people for promotion is aware that one of the candidates has a hearing impairment, but does not find out whether he needs any special arrangements. The candidate requires a sign language interpreter. It is likely to be a reasonable adjustment to arrange for an interpreter.

> A woman who has a disability resulting from a back injury is seeking a transfer to a different department. A minor aspect of the role she seeks involves assisting with unloading the weekly delivery van – but she is unable to do this because of her disability. In assessing her suitability for transfer, the employer should consider whether reallocating this duty to someone else would be a reasonable step to take.

> A disabled teacher who has depression applies for a promotion to be a Head of Department in her school. The Head Teacher responsible for filling this post says that the woman would be unsuitable because she would not be able to cope with the stress of the job. He has no evidence that this would be the case, and is merely making an assumption about her disability. This is likely to be unlawful.

8.14 As with other aspects of employment, employers will be better placed to ensure that promotion and transfer arrangements do not discriminate against disabled people if they have established and implemented policies and practices to counter discrimination generally (see paragraph 2.12). These will help employers to check, for example, that qualifications required for promotion or transfer are justified for the job to be done, and to monitor other arrangements – such as systems for determining criteria for a particular job – so that they do not exclude disabled people who may have been unable to meet those criteria because of their disability but who would be capable of performing well in the job.

MANAGING DISABILITY OR ILL HEALTH

Retention of disabled employees

8.15 **[s 4(2)]** An employer must not discriminate against an employee who becomes disabled, or who has a disability which worsens. Employers will often find that it is of benefit to their organisation to retain a disabled employee as this will prevent their knowledge and skills from being lost to the enterprise. In addition, the cost of retaining such an employee will frequently be less than the cost of recruiting and training a new member of staff.

8.16 If as a result of the disability an employer's arrangements or a physical feature of the employer's premises place the employee at a substantial disadvantage in doing his existing job, the employer must consider any reasonable adjustment that would resolve the difficulty. The nature of the adjustments which an employer may have to consider will depend on the circumstances of the case, but the following considerations will always be relevant:

- The first consideration in making reasonable adjustments should be to enable the disabled employee to continue in his present job if at all possible.
- The employer should consult the disabled person at appropriate stages about what his needs are and, where the employee has a progressive condition, what effect the disability might have on future employment, so that reasonable adjustments may be planned.
- In appropriate cases, the employer should also consider seeking expert advice on the extent of a disabled person's capabilities and on what might be done to change premises or working arrangements. Where an employee has been off work, a phased return might be appropriate.
- If there are no reasonable adjustments which would enable the disabled employee to continue in his present job, the employer must consider whether there are suitable alternative positions to which he could be redeployed.

> A nurse becomes disabled after a back injury. After talking to her and taking specialist advice, the employer decides that there are no reasonable adjustments that could be made to her present role. The employer then considers whether there is another role that would be suitable and offers an alternative post to the employee, at roughly the same level of seniority. However, if after considering these steps, it is apparent that there is no alternative position on a similar salary and with similar conditions, a position on a lower salary or with worse conditions could be offered as a reasonable adjustment.

8.17 It may be possible to modify a job to accommodate an employee's changing needs. This might be by rearranging working methods or giving another employee certain minor tasks that the disabled person can no longer do, or by providing practical aids or adaptations to premises or equipment, or allowing the disabled person to work at different times or places from those with equivalent jobs. It may be that a reduction in working hours is appropriate.

> A newly disabled employee may need time to readjust. In those circumstances, an employer might allow a trial period to assess whether the employee is able to cope with the current job, with or without modifications; the employee may initially be permitted to work from home, or with a gradual build-up to full time hours.

> It may be a reasonable adjustment for an employer to move a newly disabled person to a different post within the organisation if a suitable vacancy exists or is expected shortly.

> Additional job coaching may be necessary to enable a disabled person to take on a new job.

8.18 The issue of job retention might also arise when an employee has a stable impairment but the nature of his job changes. In these circumstances an employer may also have a duty to make reasonable adjustments.

> A woman with a learning disability is allocated to a new department because of a business reorganisation. She is given extra training to enable her to carry out her new role. This is likely to be a reasonable adjustment for the employer to make.

> An employer installs a new software system for all computer users in the office. A disabled man who uses voice-activated software finds that this software is not compatible with the new office computer software. The employer provides him with new voice-activated software which is compatible with the office system. It also offers him appropriate training in the use of the two new software systems. These are likely to be reasonable adjustments for the employer to make.

Access to Work Scheme

8.19 In determining what adjustments to make to facilitate the employment of a disabled person, employers should have regard to the range of advice and assistance which is available from Jobcentre Plus through the Access to Work scheme. The purpose of the scheme is to provide practical support to disabled people in, or entering, paid employment to help overcome work related obstacles resulting from disability. Access to Work provides a grant towards these additional employment costs. However, there is no automatic right to support from the Access to Work scheme – this is subject to an assessment when an application for support is made by the disabled person.

8.20 The Access to Work scheme may assist an employer to decide what steps to take. If financial assistance is available from the scheme, it may also make it reasonable for an employer to take certain steps which would otherwise be unreasonably expensive. However, Access to Work does not diminish any of an employer's duties under the Act. In particular:

- the responsibility for making a reasonable adjustment is the responsibility of the employer – even where Access to Work is involved in the provision of advice or funding in relation to the adjustment
- it is likely to be a reasonable step for the employer to assist a disabled person in making an application for assistance from Access to Work and to provide ongoing administrative support (by completing claim forms, for example), and
- it may be unreasonable for an employer to decide not to make an adjustment if the decision is based on the cost of the adjustment but before it is known if financial assistance for it is available from Access to Work or another source.

Further information about what the Access to Work scheme can offer, the scheme's eligibility requirements, and how to apply, is set out in Appendix C.

Confidential information

8.21 The extent to which an employer is entitled to let other staff know about an employee's disability will depend partly on the terms of employment. An employer could be discriminating against the employee by revealing such information if the employer would not reveal similar information about another person for an equally legitimate management purpose; or if the employer revealed such information without consulting the individual, instead of adopting the usual practice of talking to an employee before revealing personal information about him. Employers also need to be aware that they have obligations under the Data Protection Act in respect of personal data.

8.22 However, as noted at paragraph 5.22, sometimes a reasonable adjustment will not work without the co-operation of other employees. In order to secure such co-operation, it may be necessary for the employer to tell one or more of a disabled person's colleagues (in confidence) about a disability which is not obvious. This may be limited to the disabled person's supervisor, or it may be appropriate to involve other colleagues, depending on the nature of the disability and the reason they need to know about it. In any event, an employer must not disclose confidential details about an employee without his consent. A disabled person's refusal to give such consent may impact upon the effectiveness of the adjustments which the employer is able to make or its ability to make adjustments at all.

> In order for a person with epilepsy to work safely in a particular factory, it may be necessary to advise fellow workers about how they can assist the disabled worker to manage her condition.

> An office worker with cancer says that he does not want colleagues to know of his condition. As an adjustment he needs extra time away from work to receive treatment and to rest. Neither his colleagues nor the line manager need to be told the precise reasons for the extra leave but the latter will need to know that the adjustment is required in order to implement it effectively.

8.23 The Act does not prevent a disabled person keeping a disability confidential from an employer. But keeping a disability confidential is likely to mean that unless the employer could reasonably be expected to know about it anyway, the employer will not be under a duty to make a reasonable adjustment. If a disabled person expects an employer to make a reasonable adjustment, he will need to provide the employer – or someone acting on its behalf-with sufficient information to carry out that adjustment.

> An employee has symptomatic HIV. He prefers not to tell his employer of the condition. However, as the condition progresses, he finds it increasingly difficult to work the required number of hours in a week. Until he tells his employer of his condition – or the employer becomes aware of it (or could reasonably be expected to be aware of it) – the employer does not have to make a reasonable adjustment by changing his working hours to overcome the difficulty. However, once the employer is informed he may then have to make a reasonable adjustment.

TERMINATION OF EMPLOYMENT

8.24 Where a disabled person is dismissed or is selected for redundancy or for compulsory early retirement (including compulsory ill-health retirement), the employer must ensure that the disabled person is not being discriminated against. It is likely to be direct discrimination if the dismissal or selection is made on the ground of disability (see paragraph 4.5). If the dismissal or selection is not directly discriminatory, but is made for a reason related to the disability, it will amount to disability-related discrimination unless the employer can show that it is justified. The reason would also have to be one which could not be removed by any reasonable adjustment.

> It would be justifiable to terminate the employment of an employee whose disability makes it impossible for him to perform the main functions of his job any longer, if an adjustment such as a move to a vacant post elsewhere in the business is not practicable or otherwise not reasonable for the employer to have to make.

8.25 When setting criteria for redundancy selection, employers should consider whether any proposed criterion would adversely impact upon a disabled employee. If so, it may be necessary for the employer to make reasonable adjustments. For example, it is likely to be a reasonable adjustment to discount disability-related sickness absence when assessing attendance as part of a redundancy selection scheme. Some employers use 'flexibility' as a selection criterion for redundancy (for example, willingness to re-locate or to work unpopular hours, or ability to carry out a wide variety of tasks). An employer should carefully consider how to apply this criterion to a disabled employee as it might be discriminatory.

8.26 Where the dismissal of a disabled person is being considered for a reason relating to that person's conduct, the employer should consider whether any reasonable adjustments need to be made to the disciplinary or dismissal process. In addition, if the conduct in question is related to the employee's disability, that may be relevant in determining the sanction which it is appropriate to impose.

> A young man with learning disabilities asks if he can bring a friend to a disciplinary hearing, rather than a work colleague. It is likely to be a reasonable adjustment for his employer to allow this.

> A woman shouts at her line manager in front of work colleagues and uses inappropriate language. The employer would usually consider dismissal as a sanction for such behaviour, but takes into account the fact that she was in great pain on the day in question because of her disability and instead issues a warning. This is likely to be a reasonable adjustment to make.

8.27 **[s 4(5)]** A disabled person will be taken to have been dismissed for the purposes of the Act if:

- he is expressly dismissed, or
- the period for which he is employed expires without his employment being immediately renewed on the same terms, or
- he gives notice, or does some other act to bring his employment to an end in circumstances in which he is entitled to terminate it without notice by reason of the employer's conduct (this is known as 'constructive dismissal').

AFTER THE TERMINATION OF EMPLOYMENT

8.28 **[s 16A(3)]** Where a disabled person's employment has come to an end, the Act says that it will still be unlawful for his former employer:

- to discriminate against him by subjecting him to a detriment, or
- to subject him to harassment

if the discrimination or harassment arises out of the employment which has come to an end and is closely connected to it.

> A disabled person working as a sales consultant has to go back to his former workplace for a meeting to finalise handover of his customer files to his replacement. On arrival, he is verbally abused by one of his former colleagues. The abuse relates to his disability. This is unlawful.

8.29 **[s 55]** It is also unlawful to victimise a person (whether or not he is disabled) after his employment has come to an end (see paragraphs 4.33 to 4.36).

> A disabled person gives the name of his former employer as a referee for a new job. The employer gives him a poor reference, referring to his disability as being a hindrance. This poor reference is an untrue reflection of the standard of work carried out by the disabled person. The poor reference was given because he brought a claim of disability discrimination against his former employer. Consequently it is unlawful.

8.30 **[s 16A(4)–(6)]** An employer's duty to make reasonable adjustments may also apply in respect of a former employee who is a disabled person. This will be the case where:

- the disabled person is placed at a substantial disadvantage in comparison with other former employees:
  a. by a provision, practice or criterion applied by the employer to the disabled person in relation to any matter arising out of his former employment, or
  b. by a physical feature of premises occupied by the employer, and
- the employer either knows, or could reasonably be expected to know, that the former employee in question has a disability and is likely to be affected in this way.

> A former employee with life-time membership of the works social club is no longer able to access the club because of a mobility impairment. Once the employer becomes aware of the problem, it will need to consider making reasonable adjustments.

8.31 The former employees with whom the position of the disabled person should be compared must be people who are not disabled, but who are former employees of the same employer. If it is not possible to identify an actual comparator for this purpose, then a hypothetical comparator may be used (see paragraph 4.18).

8.32 The principles relating to post-termination discrimination also apply to other relationships covered by Part 2, and to the relationship between a provider of employment services and its former clients. These relationships are considered in the following chapters.

[4669]

9. DISCRIMINATION IN OCCUPATION

INTRODUCTION

9.1 The preceding chapters focus on discrimination against employees. However, as noted at paragraph 3.11, Part 2 of the Act also applies to certain occupations. This chapter explains the relevant provisions.

9.2 The following paragraphs explain the provisions of Part 2 which focus specifically on the occupations in question. In other respects, however, the employment provisions of the Act apply in the usual way. So, where appropriate, regard should be had to the matters concerning recruitment and retention which are explained in Chapters 7 and 8; occupational pension schemes and group insurance services (Chapter 10); adjustments to premises (Chapter 12); and to the other relevant issues (Chapter 13).

DISCRIMINATION AGAINST CONTRACT WORKERS

What does the Act say about contract workers?

9.3 **[s 4B(1)]** The Act says that it is unlawful for a 'principal' to discriminate against a disabled contract worker:

- in the terms on which he is allowed to do 'contract work'
- by not allowing him to do, or continue to do, contract work
- in the way it affords him access to, or by failing to afford him access to, benefits in relation to contract work, or
- by subjecting him to any other detriment.

9.4 **[s 4B(2) & s 55]** The Act also says that it is unlawful for a principal to subject a disabled contract worker to harassment or to victimise any contract worker, whether or not he is disabled.

9.5 **[s 4B(9)]** For this purpose, 'contract work' is work which an individual carries out for a person (a 'principal') who hires him under a contract made with his employer. Usually, that contract is made directly between the principal and the contract worker's employer, (which is generally an employment business), but this is not always the case. Provided that there is an unbroken chain of contracts between the individual and the end-user of his services, that end-user is a principal for the purposes of the Act, and so the individual is a contract worker.

> A disabled person works for a computer software company which sometimes uses an employment business to deploy staff to work on projects for other companies. The

employment business arranges for the disabled person to work on a project for a large supermarket chain. In this case the 'principal' is the supermarket chain.

9.6 The effect of the Act is that, where a person is a principal for the purposes of the Act, he is treated as if he were, or would be, the actual employer of the disabled contract worker. Therefore, the same principles relating to discrimination apply to a principal as to an employer.

The employer of a labourer, who some years ago was disabled by clinical depression but has since recovered, proposes to supply him to a contractor to work on a building site. Although his past disability is covered by the Act, the contractor's site manager refuses to accept him because of his medical history. The contractor is likely to be acting unlawfully.

How does the duty to make reasonable adjustments apply in respect of disabled contract workers?

9.7 **[s 4B(6)]** The duty to make reasonable adjustments applies to a principal in the same way as it applies to an employer.

9.8 However, in deciding whether any, and if so, what, adjustments would be reasonable for a principal to make, the period for which the disabled contract worker will work for the principal is important. It might well be unreasonable for a principal to have to make certain adjustments if the worker will be with the principal for only a short time.

An employment business enters into a contract with a firm of accountants to provide an assistant for two weeks to cover an unexpected absence. The employment business proposes a name. The person concerned finds it difficult, because of his disability, to travel during the rush hour and would like his working hours to be modified accordingly. It might not be reasonable for the firm to have to agree, given the short time in which to negotiate and implement the new hours.

Does this mean that a principal has the same duties to make adjustments as the employer of a disabled contract worker?

9.9 In the case of a disabled contract worker, both his employer and the principal to whom he is supplied may separately be under a duty to make reasonable adjustments.

A travel agency hires a clerical worker from an employment business to fulfil a three month contract to file travel invoices during the busy summer holiday period. The contract worker is a wheelchair user, and is quite capable of doing the job if a few minor, temporary changes are made to the arrangement of furniture in the office. It is likely to be reasonable for the travel agency to make these adjustments.

9.10 **[s 4A(1) & s 4B(4) & (5)]** A disabled contract worker's employer will have to make reasonable adjustments if the contract worker is substantially disadvantaged by the employer's own premises – or by a provision, criterion or practice applied by it. The Act says that the employer will also have to make reasonable adjustments where the contract worker is likely to be substantially disadvantaged by the premises – or by a provision criterion or practice – of all or most of the principals to whom he might be supplied. This duty only arises if the contract worker is likely to be affected in this way each time he is supplied for work. The employer would have to make reasonable adjustments to overcome the disadvantage wherever it might arise, rather than taking separate steps in relation to each principal.

A blind secretary is employed by an employment business which supplies her to other organisations for secretarial work. Her ability to access standard computer equipment places her at a substantial disadvantage at the offices of all or most of the principals to whom she might be supplied. The employment business provides her with a specially adapted portable computer and Braille keyboard.

9.11 **[s 4A(1) applied by s 4B(6) & (7)]** A principal has the same duties to make reasonable adjustments as a disabled contract worker's employer, but does not have to make any adjustment which the employer should make. So, in effect, the principal is responsible for any additional reasonable adjustments which are necessary solely because of its own arrangements or premises.

In the preceding example, a bank which hired the blind secretary may have to make changes which are necessary to ensure that the computer provided by the employment business is compatible with the system which the bank is already using.

9.12 It would be reasonable for a principal and the employer of a contract worker to co-operate with any steps taken by the other to assist the contract worker. It is good practice for the principal and the employer to discuss what adjustments should be made – and who should make them.

The bank and the employment business in the preceding examples would need to co-operate with each other so that, for example, the employment business allows the bank to make any necessary adaptations to the equipment which the employment business provided to ensure its compatibility with the bank's existing systems.

What about Workstep?

9.13 These arrangements also apply to the Workstep scheme (formerly known as the Supported Placement Scheme) operated by Jobcentre Plus for severely disabled people. The 'contractor' under the scheme (usually a local authority or voluntary body) is the equivalent of the contract worker's own employer, and the 'host employer' is the equivalent of the principal. A local authority can even be both the contractor and the host employer at the same time (as can a voluntary body).

DISCRIMINATION AGAINST OFFICE HOLDERS

Who are office holders?

9.14 **[s 4C]** Examples of office holders include some company directors, judges, and chairmen or members of non-departmental public bodies. What the holders of such offices or posts have in common is that they are not regarded as 'employees' by the law, even though they may be similar to employees in providing services personally under the direction of another in return for remuneration. The Act gives specific protection to such office holders against discrimination if they are not otherwise protected under Part 2. This protection extends to applicants for such appointments and applies also to office holders appointed by, or on the recommendation of, the Government (including the devolved administrations for Scotland and Wales), or subject to its approval. However, it does not extend to the holders of political office.

What does the Act say about office holders?

9.15 **[s 4D(1)]** The Act says that, in relation to an appointment to such an office or post, it is unlawful to discriminate against a disabled person:

- in the arrangements which are made to determine who should be offered the appointment
- in the terms on which the appointment is offered, or
- by refusing to offer him the appointment.

9.16 **[s 4D(2)]** In addition, where the appointment is made on the Government's recommendation (or is subject to its approval) the Act says that it is unlawful to discriminate against a disabled person:

- in the arrangements which are made to determine who should be recommended or approved, or
- in making or refusing to make a recommendation, or in giving or refusing to give approval.

> A deaf woman who communicates using British Sign Language applies for appointment as a member of a public body. Without interviewing her, the public body making the appointments writes to her saying that she would not be suitable as good communication skills are a requirement. This is likely to be unlawful.

9.17 **[s 4D(3)]** The Act also says that it is unlawful, in relation to a disabled person who has been appointed to such an office or post, to discriminate against him:

- in the terms of the appointment
- in the opportunities which are afforded (or refused) for promotion, a transfer, training or receiving any other benefit
- by terminating the appointment, or
- by subjecting him to any other detriment in relation to the appointment.

9.18 **[s 4D(4) & s 55]** In addition, the Act says that it is unlawful to subject a disabled person to harassment if he is an office holder, or if he is seeking or being considered for an appointment (or a related Government recommendation or approval). It is also unlawful to victimise such a person, whether he is disabled or not.

9.19 **[s 4D(5)]** As far as benefits are concerned, the Act mirrors the position in respect of benefits to employees (see paragraphs 8.9 to 8.12).

9.20 **[s 16B]** The Act gives the DRC power to take action in respect of a discriminatory advertisement for appointment to an office or post (see paragraphs 13.28 to 13.30). This mirrors the DRC's power in respect of advertisements for employment (see paragraphs 7.12 and 7.13).

How does the duty to make reasonable adjustments apply in respect of office holders?

9.21 **[s 4E(1)]** Part 2 also requires reasonable adjustments to be made for disabled people holding relevant offices or posts, or seeking such appointments. The duty relates to any provision, criterion or practice applied by or on behalf of the relevant person (see paragraph 9.22), and to any physical feature of premises under the control of such a person where the functions of the office or post are performed.

> A selection process is carried out to appoint the chair of a public health body. The best candidate is found to be a disabled person with a progressive condition who is not able to work full-time because of her disability. Whoever makes or recommends the appointment should consider whether it would be a reasonable adjustment to appoint the disabled person on a job-share or part-time basis.

Who needs to avoid discriminating against office holders?

9.22 **[s 4F(2)]** The effect of the Act is to give a disabled person holding a relevant office or post, or seeking or being considered for appointment, similar rights to those of an employee or job applicant. In the employment context, it is clearly the employer who has the obligations under the Act. However, in relation to office holders, the person on whom the duties are imposed ('the relevant person') depends on the circumstances. It may be:

- the person with power to make the appointment
- the person or body with power to recommend or approve the appointment
- the person with power to determine the terms or working conditions of the appointment (including any benefit or physical feature), or
- the person with power to terminate the appointment.

DISCRIMINATION AGAINST POLICE OFFICERS

9.23 **[s 64A]** Not all police officers are regarded as 'employees' in law. However, the Act says that all police officers and police cadets count as employees for the purposes of Part 2.

As a result, disabled police officers and police cadets (and disabled people applying to join the police service) have the same rights as other employees and job applicants under Part 2. These include rights in respect of harassment and victimisation (the latter extending to non-disabled people as well as to those who are disabled).

9.24 These rights—which also apply in respect of special constables and small police forces such as the British Transport Police—are enforceable against the relevant chief officer of police or police authority (or the relevant chief constable in the case of Scottish police forces). In addition, a chief officer of police (or chief constable) is liable under the Act for the discriminatory acts of one police officer (or cadet) committed against another.

DISCRIMINATION AGAINST PARTNERS IN FIRMS

What does the Act say about partners in firms?

9.25 **[s 6A(1)]** The Act says that it is unlawful for a firm, in relation to a position as a partner in the firm, to discriminate against a disabled person:

- in the arrangements it makes to determine who should be offered that position
- in the terms on which it offers him that position
- by refusing or deliberately omitting to offer him that position, or
- where the disabled person is already a partner in the firm:
  a. in the way it affords him access to any benefits, or by refusing or deliberately omitting to afford him access to them, or
  b. by expelling him from the partnership, or subjecting him to any other detriment.

9.26 **[s 6A(2) & s 55]** The Act also says that it is unlawful for a firm to subject a disabled person who is an existing or prospective partner to harassment, or to victimise any existing or prospective partner, whether or not he is disabled.

9.27 **[s 6C]** The effect of the Act is to give a partner or applicant for partnership similar rights against the firm to those of an employee or job applicant against an employer. The same applies where people are proposing to form themselves into a partnership and a disabled person is a prospective partner. Limited liability partnerships are also covered.

> A group of self-employed accountants decide to go into partnership. One of them discloses that he is disabled because of cancer. The others decide to go ahead and form a partnership without the disabled person because they are worried about him being absent from work for medical treatment. This is likely to be unlawful.

9.28 **[s 6A(3)]** As far as benefits are concerned, (and in common with the rules which apply to office holders), the Act mirrors the position in respect of benefits to employees (see paragraphs 8.9 to 8.12).

9.29 **[s 16B]** The Act gives the DRC power to take action in respect of a discriminatory advertisement for any partnership in a firm (see paragraphs 13.28 to 13.30). This mirrors the DRC's power in respect of advertisements for employment (see paragraphs 7.12 and 7.13).

How does the duty to make reasonable adjustments apply in respect of partners in firms?

9.30 **[s 6B(1)]** The duty to make reasonable adjustments applies to a firm in the same way as it applies to an employer. It relates to any provision, criterion or practice applied by or on behalf of the firm and to any physical feature of premises occupied by the firm.

9.31 **[s 6B(4)]** Although, in general, the cost of making a reasonable adjustment cannot be passed on to the disabled person concerned, where a firm is required to make adjustments in respect of a disabled partner or prospective partner, the cost of doing so is an expense of the firm. Provided that the disabled person is, or becomes, a partner in the firm, he may be required to make a reasonable contribution towards this expense. In assessing the reasonableness of any such contribution, particular regard should be had to the proportion in which the disabled partner is entitled to share in the firm's profits.

> A disabled person who uses a wheelchair as a result of a mobility impairment joins a firm of architects as a partner, receiving 20% of the firm's profits. He is asked to pay 20% towards the cost of a lift which must be installed so that he can work on the premises. This is likely to be reasonable.

DISCRIMINATION AGAINST BARRISTERS AND ADVOCATES

What does the Act say about barristers and advocates?

9.32 **[s 7A(1)]** The Act says that, in England and Wales, it is unlawful for a barrister or a barrister's clerk, in relation to any offer of a pupillage or tenancy, to discriminate against a disabled person:

- in the arrangements which are made to determine to whom it should be offered
- in respect of any terms on which it is offered, or
- by refusing or deliberately omitting to offer it to him.

9.33 **[s 7A(2)]** The Act also says that it is unlawful for a barrister or barrister's clerk, in relation to a disabled pupil or tenant in the set of chambers in question, to discriminate against him:

- in respect of any terms applicable to him as a pupil or tenant
- in the opportunities for training, or gaining experience, which are afforded or denied to him
- in the benefits which are afforded or denied to him
- by terminating his pupillage or by subjecting him to any pressure to leave the chambers, or
- by subjecting him to any other detriment.

> A solicitor telephones chambers to instruct a particular barrister, who is disabled, to appear in a particular Crown Court case. The clerk assumes that the court is not accessible and passes the brief to another barrister. This is likely to be unlawful.

9.34 **[s 7A(3) & s 55]** In addition, the Act says that it is unlawful for a barrister or barrister's clerk to subject a disabled person who is a pupil or tenant in a set of chambers (or who has applied to be a pupil or tenant) to harassment, or to victimise such a person, whether he is disabled or not. In effect, therefore, barristers and pupils have rights under Part 2 which are similar to the rights of employees.

9.35 **[s 7A(5)]** Barristers who are permitted to practise from a set of chambers, but who are not tenants (barristers who do this are colloquially known as 'squatters'), have the same rights under Part 2 as barristers who are tenants.

9.36 **[s 7C & s 55]** In Scotland, advocates do not practise in sets of chambers. However, the Act makes it unlawful for a Scottish advocate to discriminate against a disabled pupil or to subject him to harassment. It is also unlawful to victimise a pupil, whether or not he is disabled. Disabled pupils (and prospective pupils) in Scotland have rights under Part 2 which are equivalent to those of their counterparts in England and Wales.

9.37 **[s 7A(4) & s 7C(4)]** The Act also says that it is unlawful to discriminate against a disabled person in relation to the giving, withholding or acceptance of instructions to a barrister or an advocate. It would therefore be unlawful for a solicitor to refuse to instruct a barrister or an advocate merely because they have a disability.

9.38 **[s 16B]** The Act gives the DRC power to take action in respect of a discriminatory advertisement for any tenancy or pupillage (see paragraphs 13.28 to 13.30). This mirrors the DRC's power in respect of advertisements for employment (see paragraphs 7.12 and 7.13).

How does the duty to make reasonable adjustments apply in respect of barristers and advocates?

9.39 **[s 7B(1)]** In England and Wales, the duty to make reasonable adjustments applies to barristers and barrister's clerks in the same way as it applies to an employer. It relates to any provision, criterion or practice applied by or on behalf of a barrister or barrister's clerk and to any physical feature of premises occupied by a barrister or by a barrister's clerk. Nevertheless, although it is unlawful to discriminate against a disabled barrister or pupil in relation to the giving, withholding or acceptance of instructions, it should be noted that a solicitor is under no duty to make a reasonable adjustment in relation to a disabled barrister whom he instructs.

9.40 **[s 7B(2)]** Where a group of barristers practise together in a set of chambers, the duty to make reasonable adjustments applies to each individual barrister who has responsibility for any disadvantage to the disabled person if the adjustment is not made. Chambers need to consider whether their practices could disadvantage disabled pupils and tenant barristers. For example, the practice of writing messages on scrap paper is likely to disadvantage visually impaired members of chambers, and may need to be altered for individual disabled tenants and pupils.

9.41 **[s 7D]** The application of the duty to Scottish advocates is slightly more restricted, in recognition of the fact that Scottish advocates do not practise in sets of chambers, but tend to practise from home. Disabled pupils (and prospective pupils) in Scotland do have rights in respect of reasonable adjustments which are equivalent to those of their counterparts in England and Wales. However, where a disabled pupil is engaged by an advocate who practises from home, that may affect the extent of the adjustments which it is reasonable for the advocate to make (see paragraph 5.41).

DISCRIMINATION IN RELATION TO PRACTICAL WORK EXPERIENCE

What does the Act say about practical work experience?

9.42 **[s 14C(1)]** The Act says that it is unlawful for a 'placement provider' to discriminate against a disabled person who is seeking or undertaking a work placement:

- in the arrangements he makes for determining who should be offered a work placement
- in the terms on which he affords him access to any work placement or any facilities concerned with such placement

> A bank offers three month placements in its accounts department to students on a business studies course. A disabled student is offered a placement on the basis that it lasts for only two weeks as it is believed – without asking the student herself – that she will not be able to cope with a three month placement. This is likely to be unlawful.

- by refusing or deliberately omitting to afford him such access

> A student with ME is refused a work placement at a primary school, as it is believed that she will not be 'up to the job' because of her disability. This is likely to be unlawful.

- by terminating his placement

> A person with a mental health problem on a four week placement has to take a morning off to attend a hospital appointment related to her disability. The placement is terminated as a result of this. This is likely to be unlawful.

- by subjecting him to any other detriment during the placement

> A design company offers work placements in its creative department. People on placement do a range of things, including research and design. A person with a hearing impairment is given only photocopying to do on his placement because the supervisor does not think that he can do anything else. This would be subjecting the disabled person to a detriment and is likely to be unlawful.

9.43 **[s 14C(2) & s 55]** The Act also says that it is unlawful for a placement provider to subject a disabled person to harassment if he is providing a work placement to that person, or if that person has applied to him for a work placement, or to victimise such a person, whether he is disabled or not.

An employee at a company gives evidence in a tribunal case on behalf of a disabled person who was refused a work placement because of his disability and who has brought a claim of discrimination. The employee is dismissed because of this. This is likely to be unlawful.

9.44 **[s 14C(4)]** For these purposes, a work placement is practical work experience undertaken for a limited period for the purposes of a person's vocational training. A placement provider is any person who provides a work placement to a person whom he does not employ.

9.45 **[s 14C(3)]** The above applies only to the extent that discrimination in relation to practical work experience is not the subject of other provisions of the Act, such as those relating to discrimination in the provision of goods, facilities and services, or to discrimination in education. The DRC has issued separate codes of practice giving guidance on the operation of Part 3 and Part 4 of the Act (see Appendix C for details).

A university arranges work placements in industry for its students. The placement provider in this case is the company offering the work experience and is covered by the provisions of Part 2. The university itself is not covered by these provisions, but is instead subject to the provisions on education in Part 4.

A sixth form college offers work placements for trainee teachers. In this case the college is a placement provider and is covered by the provisions of Part 2.

9.46 **[s 16B]** The Act gives the DRC power to take action in respect of a discriminatory advertisement for any work placement (see paragraphs 13.28 to 13.30). This mirrors the DRC's powers in respect of advertisements for employment (see paragraphs 7.12 and 7.13).

How does the duty to make reasonable adjustments apply in respect of work placements?

9.47 **[s 14D]** The duty to make reasonable adjustments applies to a placement provider in the same way as it applies to an employer. The duty applies in respect of any provision, criterion or practice applied by or on behalf of the placement provider and to any physical feature of premises occupied by the provider.

A disabled person who has a heart condition obtains a six week placement at a computer company. Such placements are normally offered only on a full-time basis. However, because this would be too tiring for the disabled person, the placement provider allows him to work mornings only.

A disabled student needs to be accompanied by her support worker whilst on work placement. The placement provider facilitates this by providing an additional work station for the support worker.

While on a work placement, a student with learning disabilities is given personal instruction in health and safety procedures in the workplace, rather than written information.

9.48 The considerations outlined in Chapter 5 apply in determining what adjustments it is reasonable for a placement provider to make. However, the length of the placement will also be a relevant factor. Although many adjustments cost little or nothing to make, it is unlikely to be reasonable for a placement provider to spend significant sums on individually-tailored adjustments in respect of short placements. Nevertheless, some disabled students undertaking work placements may be able to fund adjustments out of their Disabled Students Allowance. Alternatively, some disabled people may already have equipment which they are prepared to use in the workplace. In that case, the placement provider may have to make reasonable adjustments in order to facilitate the use of that equipment (for example, by ensuring that it is transported and stored safely, and is adequately insured whilst at the workplace).

> A person with a hearing impairment on a business studies course has a six week placement with a bank. As he requires an induction loop to participate in meetings, the bank obtains a temporary induction loop as a reasonable adjustment.

> A disabled person who uses voice activated software is assisted by the placement provider's IT department to install her own software onto a workplace computer. She is also provided with a headset and microphone to use with it.

> A placement provider arranges to transport a disabled person's ergonomic chair to the workplace so that she can use it during a three week work placement.

9.49 An organisation which sends a disabled person on a work placement may also have a duty under the Act to make reasonable adjustments in respect of that person.

> Where a course provider supplies a laptop computer for a visually impaired person to complete work, it would also be reasonable for it to supply the computer for that person to use during a related work placement.

9.50 It would be reasonable to expect the sending organisation and the placement provider to co-operate to ensure that appropriate adjustments are identified and made. It is good practice for a placement provider to ask a disabled person about reasonable adjustments before the placement begins, and to allow him to visit the workplace in advance to see how his needs can be addressed. Once a particular adjustment has been identified, it would be reasonable for the sending organisation and the placement provider to discuss its implementation in the light of their respective obligations under the Act.

[4670]

10. DISCRIMINATION IN PROVIDING OCCUPATIONAL PENSIONS AND GROUP INSURANCE SERVICES

INTRODUCTION

10.1 Chapter 8 explains how the Act protects disabled people from discrimination in employment. In particular, paragraph 8.9 makes the point that employers must not discriminate in the way that they make benefits available to disabled employees where those benefits are available to other employees. Some of the most significant benefits which employers commonly make available to their employees relate to occupational pensions and group insurance schemes. This chapter explains what the Act says about discrimination in providing these particular types of benefit. This includes discrimination by the employer and by others concerned with providing the benefit in question.

OCCUPATIONAL PENSION SCHEMES

What does the Act say about employers?

10.2 As far as employers are concerned, Part 2 does not distinguish between discrimination in providing pensions and discrimination in relation to other benefits. This is subject to one qualification (explained at paragraphs 10.13 and 10.14) concerning the remedies available for discrimination under Part 2.

10.3 **[s 4(2) & s 4A(1)]** Thus, an employer must not discriminate against a disabled person in the opportunities it affords him for receiving pension benefits, or by refusing him, or deliberately not affording him, any such opportunity. The duty to make reasonable adjustments applies to the manner in which employers make pensions available to a disabled employee.

10.4 To the extent that an employer has control over matters relating to pension benefits afforded to employees, the usual principles about discrimination will apply under Part 2. As explained in Chapter 4, less favourable treatment of a disabled person in relation to such benefits may amount to direct discrimination or to disability-related discrimination. Discrimination may also occur because of a failure to comply with a duty to make a reasonable adjustment to any provision, criterion or practice in relation to pension benefits in respect of a disabled person.

> A person with MS completes the first six months of her employment. After this period the employer usually writes to employees inviting them to join the pension scheme. The employer is worried, however, that the disabled employee may draw early on the pension scheme and so does not invite her to join. This is likely to be unlawful.

10.5 In relation to a well established pension scheme, the application of provisions, criteria and practices relating to pension benefits is likely to be controlled by the trustees or managers of the pension scheme. However, when new schemes are set up, employers are likely to have substantial input in relation to such matters (for example, setting scheme rules), and in doing so they must not discriminate against disabled people.

What does the Act say about pension scheme trustees and managers?

10.6 **[s 4G(3)]** Part 2 contains provisions which relate specifically to discrimination against disabled people by the trustees or managers of occupational pension schemes. The principal effect of these provisions is to make it unlawful for pension scheme trustees or managers to contravene a 'non-discrimination rule' which is deemed to be included in every occupational pension scheme.

10.7 This non-discrimination rule effectively makes the trustees and managers of the scheme subject to the general provisions of Part 2 by doing two things:

- **[s 4G(1)]** First, the non-discrimination rule prohibits pension scheme trustees or managers from discriminating against a disabled person who is a member or prospective member of the scheme in carrying out any of their functions in relation to the scheme. This includes functions relating to the admission and treatment of members of the scheme.
- Second, the rule prohibits the trustees or managers from subjecting such a person to harassment in relation to the scheme.

[s 4K(2)] The Act sets out the circumstances in which a person counts as a prospective member of a pension scheme.

> A disabled person applies to join an occupational pension scheme. The trustees say that he can join but as he has diabetes, he will not be able to take early retirement on health grounds. This decision is reached with no consideration of the individual circumstances and is likely to be unlawful.

10.8 **[s 4G(2) & (5)]** The Act says that the other provisions of a pension scheme have effect subject to the non-discrimination rule explained above. This means that where there is a conflict between the non-discrimination rule and a rule of the pension scheme, the non-discrimination rule prevails. Thus, pension scheme trustees and managers do not have to act in accordance with a scheme rule which would produce a discriminatory result. The Act also ensures that pension scheme trustees and managers have power to make alterations to the scheme in order to make the scheme conform with the non-discrimination rule.

> The rules of an employer's final salary scheme provide that the maximum pension receivable by a member is equivalent to 2/3 of salary in the last year of work. An employee becomes disabled and as a result has to reduce her working hours for the remainder of her working life, which will amount to two years. She has worked for twenty years full time prior to this. The scheme's rules put the disabled person at a substantial disadvantage because, regardless of her previous twenty years' service, her pension will only be calculated on her part-time salary as a result of her disability. The trustees decide in her case to average out her salary over a period of years prior to her retirement date, which will enable her full-time earnings to be taken into account. This is likely to be a reasonable adjustment to make.

10.9 **[s 4H]** The duty to make reasonable adjustments applies to pension scheme trustees and managers in the same way as it applies to an employer. The duty is owed to disabled people who are members or prospective members of the scheme, and relates to any provision, criterion or practice (including a scheme rule) applied by or on behalf of the trustees or managers and any physical feature of premises which they occupy. The Act refers to making alterations to the rules of the pension scheme as an example of a reasonable adjustment.

10.10 **[s 4G(4) & s 4K]** Although the statutory non-discrimination rule does not apply in relation to rights accrued and benefits payable in respect of periods of service prior to 1 October 2004, it does apply to communications about such rights or benefits with members or prospective members of the scheme. So far as communications generally are concerned, both the non-discrimination rule and the duty to make reasonable adjustments apply in relation to disabled people who are entitled to, and currently receiving, dependants' or survivors' benefits under a pension scheme as they do in relation to disabled pensioner members of the scheme. The same applies in respect of pension credit members of the scheme. Communications include the provision of information and the operation of a dispute resolution procedure, and reasonable adjustments could involve providing information in accessible formats (such as large print, Braille, tape or disc), or providing a sign language interpreter for a meeting.

> A blind woman whose partner dies and who is in receipt of a survivor's pension asks for and receives information about the pension scheme on tape. The information relates to the period before October 2004 but nevertheless this is likely to be a reasonable adjustment to make.

How can disabled people complain about discrimination in relation to occupational pension schemes?

10.11 **[s 17A(1)]** The Act says that if a disabled person believes that he has been unlawfully discriminated against in relation to an occupational pension scheme, he may make an application to an employment tribunal. This is the case whether the allegation of discrimination is made against the employer or against the trustees or managers of the pension scheme. Chapter 13 gives more information about making a claim under Part 2. However, the Act contains additional provisions which apply specifically to complaints relating to occupational pension schemes. These provisions are explained in the following paragraphs.

10.12 **[s 4I]** When a disabled member or prospective member of an occupational pension scheme complains to an employment tribunal that he has been treated unlawfully under Part 2 by the trustees or managers of the scheme, the employer is treated as a party to the proceedings. The employer is therefore entitled to appear at the tribunal hearing and to make representations to the tribunal. This is because the employer may be required (as a matter of obligation or practice) to fund any award made against the trustees or managers of the scheme.

10.13 **[s 4J(1)]** In addition, special rules may apply in respect of the remedies available when a complaint brought by a disabled person against the trustees or managers (or a complaint against the employer itself) is successful. Provided that the complainant is not a pensioner member of the scheme, these rules will apply to such a complaint if it relates to:

- the terms on which people become members of an occupational pension scheme, or
- the terms on which members of the scheme are treated.

10.14 **[s 4J(2)–(4)]** In such circumstances, the Act modifies the usual rules governing the remedies which may be granted by an employment tribunal when it upholds a complaint (see paragraphs 13.14 to 13.16). In particular:

- the tribunal may make a declaration that the complainant has a right to be admitted to the scheme or to membership of the scheme without discrimination in respect of a specified period, but
- the only compensation which the tribunal may award is compensation for injury to feelings and compensation of the kind described in paragraph 13.16.

10.15 A complaint about discrimination by pension scheme trustees or managers may also be made through the pensions dispute resolution mechanism which every occupational pension scheme is required to have for resolving disputes between individual pension scheme members and the trustees or managers. Information about the scheme should give details about this. The Pensions Ombudsman also has power to investigate complaints in certain circumstances. Details about the Pensions Ombudsman, and about the Pensions Advisory Service (which can provide an advice and conciliation service for members of the public who have problems with their occupational pensions), are given in Appendix C.

GROUP INSURANCE SERVICES

What does the Act say about employers?

10.16 **[s 4(2) & s 4A(1)]** As far as employers are concerned, Part 2 does not distinguish between discrimination in providing benefits relating to insurance and discrimination in relation to other benefits. Thus, an employer must not discriminate against a disabled person in the opportunities it affords him for receiving insurance-related benefits, or by refusing him, or deliberately not affording him, any such opportunity. The duty to make reasonable adjustments applies to the manner in which employers make insurance services available to a disabled employee. However, it should be noted that the employer's role is often limited to explaining the availability of group insurance services and to proposing employees to the insurer for cover under a group policy.

What does the Act say about group insurers?

10.17 **[s 18]** The Act says that, where an insurer agrees with an employer to provide insurance services to its employees, or to give its employees an opportunity to receive such services, it is unlawful for the insurer to discriminate against a disabled person:

- who is an employee of that employer and who, by virtue of his employment, would ordinarily be eligible to receive such services, or
- who has applied for, or is contemplating applying for, such employment.

10.18 **[s 18(3)]** The insurance services to which these principles apply are those for the provision of benefits in respect of:

- termination of service
- retirement, old age or death, or
- accident, injury, sickness or invalidity.

When does a group insurer discriminate against a disabled person?

10.19 **[s 18(2)]** Although discrimination by **employers** in providing insurance-related benefits is defined in the usual way for the purposes of Part 2 (as explained in Chapter 4), the circumstances in which **insurers** will be in breach of Part 2 are defined differently. For the purposes of Part 2, an insurer is only taken to discriminate against a disabled person if it acts in a way which would amount to discrimination under Part 3 (which deals with discrimination by the providers of goods, facilities or services). For this purpose, the insurer's actions have to be assessed as if the insurer were providing the service in question to members of the public, and as if the disabled person were receiving the service (or trying to secure its provision) as a member of the public.

10.20 Part 3 makes it unlawful to discriminate against a disabled person for a disability-related reason in respect of the provision of goods, facilities or services to members of the public unless the conduct can be justified: for example, by reference to actuarial evidence. However, within the confines of the Code it is not possible to explain the operation of Part 3 in detail. The DRC has issued a separate code of practice giving guidance in this regard (see Appendix C for details).

What does the Act say about bringing claims for discrimination in relation to group insurance services?

10.21 **[s 17A(1)]** The Act says that if a disabled person believes that he has been unlawfully discriminated against in relation to group insurance services, he may make an application to an employment tribunal. This is the case whether the allegation of discrimination is made against the employer or against the group insurer. Chapter 13 gives more information about making a claim under Part 2.

[4671]

11. DISCRIMINATION IN PROVIDING EMPLOYMENT SERVICES

INTRODUCTION

11.1 Although the operation of Part 3 of the Act is mentioned in Chapter 10 (in the context of group insurance services), the explanation of the law in other chapters of the Code is confined to the Act's provisions on employment and occupation – which are in Part 2. However, as the purpose of the Code is to give practical guidance on how to prevent discrimination against disabled people in employment or when seeking employment, it is also necessary to look at what the Act says about the provision of employment services. Such services are covered by Part 3, which relates to discrimination in the provision of goods, facilities or services.

11.2 It is not the purpose of this chapter to give a detailed explanation of how the provisions of Part 3 work—but simply to summarise their application to employment services. For a full explanation of the operation of Part 3, reference should be made to the separate code of practice (the Part 3 Code) issued by the DRC in this regard (see Appendix C for details).

WHAT ARE EMPLOYMENT SERVICES?

11.3 **[s 21A(1)]** For the purposes of Part 3, 'employment services' are:

- vocational guidance or training services, or
- services designed to assist people to find or keep jobs, or to establish themselves in an occupation in a self-employed capacity.

11.4 Employment services therefore include services provided by an employment agency or employment business. This includes employment services provided by Jobcentre Plus and other schemes that assist people to find work. Many people who receive employment services (or who seek the provision of such services) are engaged in, or seeking, contract work. This is particularly true of people who look for work by using the services of employment businesses. The Act gives rights to disabled contract workers not only in relation to the provision of employment services, but also in relation to the contract work itself. What the Act says about contract workers is explained in paragraphs 9.3 to 9.13.

WHAT IS UNLAWFUL UNDER THE ACT?

Discrimination in providing employment services

11.5 **[s 19 applied by s 21A(4)]** Where a person or body is concerned with the provision of employment services to the public, or a section of the public, the Act says that it is unlawful for it to discriminate against a disabled person:

- by refusing to provide (or deliberately not providing) to the disabled person any such service which it provides (or is prepared to provide) to members of the public

> An employment agency refuses to allow a disabled person with a mobility impairment to register with the agency as it says that it does not have any posts which would be 'suitable' and on the ground floor. This is likely to be unlawful.

- in the standard of service which it provides to the disabled person or the manner in which it provides the service

> A temp agency which has a person with a hearing impairment on its books, does not contact him with any work, despite the fact that there is plenty of suitable work for him to do. This is likely to be unlawful.

PART 4

> A woman who has cerebral palsy visits a careers guidance service. The advisor is dismissive of various professions that the woman expresses an interest in, saying that they would be too difficult for her to get into because of her disability. This is likely to be unlawful.

- in the terms on which it provides the service to the disabled person.

> A disabled person with a speech impairment requests job advice from his local careers guidance service. He is asked to return next week when there is more time available to meet his needs, although other people, who do not have speech impairments, are being seen there and then. This is likely to be unlawful.

11.6 It is irrelevant whether or not a charge is made for the provision of the service. More detailed guidance on the kinds of treatment which are unlawful in relation to the provision of services is set out in Chapter 3 of the Part 3 Code.

11.7 It is also unlawful for a provider of employment services to discriminate against a disabled person:

- in failing to comply with a duty to make reasonable adjustments (under section 21 of the Act) to a practice, policy or procedure in circumstances in which the effect of that failure is to place the disabled person at a substantial disadvantage in comparison with people who are not disabled in relation to the provision of the service
- in failing to comply with a duty to make reasonable adjustments (under section 21 of the Act) in relation to a physical feature in circumstances in which the effect of that failure is to make it impossible or unreasonably difficult for the disabled person to make use of any such service, or
- in failing to comply with a duty under that section to provide an auxiliary aid or service in the same circumstances.

The duties to make reasonable adjustments under section 21 are explained in paragraphs 11.15 to 11.19.

Harassment

11.8 **[s 21A(2)]** It is unlawful for a provider of employment services to subject a disabled person to harassment if that person is someone to whom such services are being provided, or who has requested such services from the provider.

> A disabled man who has autism visits a careers guidance service. The advisor makes offensive comments about the man's communication skills. This is likely to amount to harassment whether or not the advisor knows that the man has autism.

Victimisation

11.9 **[s 55]** It is also unlawful for a provider of employment services to victimise a person (whether or not he is disabled).

Other unlawful acts

11.10 **[ss 16A–16C]** The provisions which apply under Part 2 in respect of relationships which have come to an end apply equally in respect of employment services, as do the provisions in respect of discriminatory advertisements. In addition, the sanctions which apply under Part 2 in respect of unlawful instructions or pressure to discriminate apply in respect of similar conduct relating to employment services.

WHAT AMOUNTS TO DISCRIMINATION?

11.11 **[s 20 applied by s 21A(5)]** The Act says that, in the circumstances described in paragraphs 11.5 and 11.7, discrimination can occur in different ways.

11.12 One way in which discrimination occurs is when treatment of a disabled person by a provider of employment services:

- is for a reason related to his disability
- the treatment is less favourable than the way in which the service provider treats (or would treat) others to whom that reason does not (or would not) apply, and
- the service provider cannot show that the treatment is justified.

11.13 Discrimination also occurs when a provider of such services fails to comply with a duty to make reasonable adjustments to a practice, policy or procedure.

11.14 In addition, discrimination occurs when a provider of employment services:
- fails to comply with a duty to make reasonable adjustments in relation to a physical feature or a duty to provide an auxiliary aid or service, and
- cannot show that the failure is justified.

WHAT IS THE DUTY TO MAKE REASONABLE ADJUSTMENTS?

11.15 **[s 21]** The duty to make reasonable adjustments under Part 3 requires service providers to take positive steps to make their services accessible to disabled people. What is required is set out in section 21, and comprises a series of duties falling into three main areas:
- changing practices, policies and procedures (such as a policy of not admitting assistance dogs)
- providing auxiliary aids and services (such as information in accessible formats)
- overcoming a physical feature (such as stairs) by
- removing the feature, or
- altering it, or
- avoiding it, or
- providing services by alternative methods.

11.16 **[s 21 applied by s 21A(6)]** Where employment services are offered to the public, the provider of those services may have to make a reasonable adjustment if:
- it has a practice, policy or procedure (including a provision or criterion) which places disabled people at a substantial disadvantage in comparison with people who are not disabled in relation to the provision of the service, or
- a physical feature makes it impossible or unreasonably difficult for disabled people to make use of such a service, or
- an auxiliary aid or service (such as information on tape or a sign language interpreter) would enable (or make it easier for) disabled people to make use of any such service.

11.17 To comply with the duty in these circumstances, the steps which the service provider has to take are those which it is reasonable, in all the circumstances of the case, for it to take in order to:
- change the practice, policy or procedure so that it no longer places disabled people at a substantial disadvantage

> A vocational guidance organisation has a policy of not allowing dogs in its building. It would be reasonable to waive this policy so that disabled people with assistance dogs can enter the building.

- overcome the physical feature

> A building from which an employment agency operates has no colour contrast on the entrance steps, making it unreasonably difficult for blind and partially sighted people to use them. It is likely to be reasonable to apply colour contrast to the steps.

- provide the auxiliary aid or service.

> A woman who has dyslexia finds it difficult to fill in an employment agency's registration form. An employee of the agency helps her to fill it in.

11.18 In contrast to the position under Part 2, a service provider's duty to make reasonable adjustments under Part 3 is a duty owed to disabled people at large. It is not simply a duty that is weighed up in relation to each individual disabled person who wants to access a service provider's services. Providers of employment services should therefore consider the need for reasonable adjustments in advance of being approached by a disabled person. Carrying out an access audit of their premises and services (including websites) is likely to assist service providers in this regard. More information about access audits and website accessibility is given in Appendix C.

> A recruitment agency advertises job vacancies on its website. The agency has its website checked for accessibility, and makes changes to enable disabled people using a variety of access software to use it.

11.19 More detailed guidance on the application of the duty to service providers is set out in Chapters 4 and 5 of the Part 3 Code. Chapter 6 of that Code gives guidance on how leases, building regulations and other statutory requirements affect a service provider's duty to make reasonable adjustments to premises. The issues are similar to (but not exactly the same as) those explained in the following chapter of this Code.

CAN ACTS WHICH ARE POTENTIALLY DISCRIMINATORY EVER BE JUSTIFIED?

11.20 **[s 20(3A) applied by s 21A(5)]** Most conduct which is potentially unlawful under the Act is incapable of being justified. Treatment of a disabled person by a provider of employment services can never be justified if it amounts to direct discrimination (see paragraph 4.5), and the same applies to a failure to comply with a duty to make reasonable adjustments to a practice, policy or procedure. However, as noted at paragraphs 11.12 and 11.14, a provider of such services may in limited circumstances be permitted to justify certain other failures to make a reasonable adjustment as well as treatment which would otherwise amount to disability-related discrimination (see paragraph 11.21).

11.21 **[s 20 applied by s 21A(5)]** Where a claim of discrimination against a provider of employment services is based on a failure to comply with a duty to make reasonable adjustments in relation to a physical feature or a duty to provide an auxiliary aid or service, or on less favourable treatment which does not amount to direct discrimination, that failure or treatment (as the case may be) may be justified if:

- the service provider holds the opinion that one or more of the conditions listed in section 20 of the Act are satisfied, and
- it is reasonable in all the circumstances of the case for it to hold that opinion.

11.22 The conditions listed in section 20 of the Act relate to:

- health or safety
- the disabled person being incapable of entering into a contract
- the service provider being otherwise unable to provide the service to the public
- enabling the service provider to provide the service to the disabled person or other members of the public, and
- the greater cost of providing a tailor-made service.

These conditions are explained in more detail in Chapter 7 of the Part 3 Code.

BRINGING CLAIMS FOR DISCRIMINATION RELATING TO EMPLOYMENT SERVICES

11.23 **[s 25(8)]** The Act says that if a disabled person believes that he has been unlawfully discriminated against in respect of employment services, he may make an application to an employment tribunal. Discrimination includes victimisation, and employment tribunals also deal with claims of harassment in relation to employment services. This is an exception to the usual practice for claims brought under Part 3 – which are otherwise brought in a county court or, in Scotland, a sheriff court. Claims of discrimination in respect of employment services are therefore heard in the same venue as other employment-related discrimination claims.

[4672]

12. MAKING REASONABLE ADJUSTMENTS TO PREMISES – LEGAL CONSIDERATIONS

INTRODUCTION

12.1 In Chapter 5 it was explained that one of the situations in which there is a duty to make reasonable adjustments arises where a physical feature of premises occupied by an employer places a disabled person at a substantial disadvantage compared with people who are not disabled. In such circumstances the employer must consider whether any reasonable steps can be taken to overcome that disadvantage. Making adjustments to premises may be a reasonable step for an employer to have to take. This applies equally to people or bodies other than employers who have duties under Part 2 of the Act. This chapter addresses the issues of how leases, building regulations and other statutory requirements affect the duty to make reasonable adjustments to premises.

12.2 The issues dealt with in this chapter largely concern the need to obtain consent to the making of reasonable adjustments where an employer occupies premises under a lease or other binding obligation. However, employers should remember that even where consent is not given for altering a physical feature, they still have a duty to make reasonable adjustments—which will involve them considering taking other steps to overcome the disadvantage which the feature causes in respect of the disabled person.

WHAT ABOUT THE NEED TO OBTAIN STATUTORY CONSENT FOR SOME BUILDING CHANGES?

12.3 **[s 59]** An employer might have to obtain statutory consent before making adjustments involving changes to premises. Such consents include planning permission, building regulations approval or a building warrant in Scotland, listed building consent, scheduled monument consent and fire regulations approval. The Act does not override the need to obtain such consents.

12.4 Employers should plan for and anticipate the need to obtain consent to make a particular adjustment. It might take time to obtain such consent, but it could be reasonable to make an interim or other adjustment—one that does not require consent—in the meantime.

> An employee who uses a wheelchair requires a ramp in order to access the building. The employer provides a temporary ramp, pending the outcome of an application for consent to install a permanent ramp. This is likely to be a reasonable step to take.

12.5 Where consent has been refused, there is likely to be a means of appeal. Whether or not the employer's duty to take such steps as it is reasonable to take includes pursuing an appeal will depend on the circumstances of the case.

BUILDING REGULATIONS AND BUILDING DESIGN

12.6 **[SI 2000/2531]** The design and construction of a new building, or the material alteration of an existing one, must comply with Building Regulations. For buildings in England or Wales, Part M of the Building Regulations (access to and use of buildings) is intended to ensure that reasonable provision is made for people to gain access to and use buildings. A similar provision applies in Scotland under the Technical Standards for compliance with the Building Standards (Scotland) Regulations 1990 and, from May 2005, under the Building (Scotland) Regulations 2004 and associated Technical Handbooks.

12.7 Nevertheless, the fact that the design and construction of a building (or a physical feature of a building) which an employer occupies meets the requirements of the Building Regulations does not diminish the employer's duty to make reasonable adjustments in respect of the building's physical features. In particular, it should be noted that the partial exemption from the duty to remove or alter physical features which applies to service providers under Part 3 of the Act does not apply to employers under Part 2.

12.8 The Building Regulations building standards provide only a baseline standard of accessibility, which is not intended to address the specific needs of individual employees. It is therefore good practice for employers to carry out an assessment of the access needs of each disabled employee, and to consider what alterations can be made to the features of its buildings in order to meet those needs. It is also good practice to anticipate the needs of disabled people when planning building or refurbishment works.

12.9 When assessing the access requirements of disabled people, it is likely to be helpful to refer to British Standard 8300:2001, *Design of buildings and their approaches to meet the needs of disabled people*—Code of Practice. Indeed, it is unlikely to be reasonable for an employer to have to make an adjustment to a physical feature of a building which it occupies if the design and construction of the physical features of the building is in accordance with BS8300. Further information about BS8300 can be found in Appendix C.

12.10 In addition, although less comprehensive than BS8300, guidance accompanying the Building Regulations (known as 'Approved Document M') sets out a number of 'provisions' as suggested ways in which the requirements of the Regulations might be met. It is unlikely to be reasonable for an employer to have to make an adjustment to a physical feature of a building which it occupies if that feature accords with the relevant provisions of the most up to date version of Approved Document M.

12.11 Financial assistance may be available from Access to Work to help meet the cost of making reasonable adjustments to the physical features of a building which an employer occupies (see paragraph 8.19).

WHAT IF A BINDING OBLIGATION OTHER THAN A LEASE PREVENTS A BUILDING BEING ALTERED?

12.12 **[s 18B(3)]** The employer may be bound by the terms of an agreement or other legally binding obligation (for example, a mortgage, charge or restrictive covenant or, in Scotland, a feu disposition) under which it cannot alter the premises without someone else's consent. In these circumstances, the Act provides that it is always reasonable for the employer to have to request that consent, but that it is never reasonable for the employer to have to make an alteration before having obtained that consent.

> A retailer builds his shop with the assistance of a bank loan. The loan is secured by way of a charge on the shop under which the bank's consent is required for any changes. It is reasonable for the retailer to seek the bank's consent for changes (such as the installation of a lift) but it is not reasonable for the retailer to have to make any alterations if the bank does not give its consent.

WHAT HAPPENS IF A LEASE SAYS THAT CERTAIN CHANGES TO PREMISES CANNOT BE MADE?

12.13 **[s 18A(2)]** Special provisions apply where an employer occupies premises under a lease, the terms of which prevent it from making an alteration to the premises. In such circumstances, if the alteration is one which the employer proposes to make in order to comply with a duty of reasonable adjustment, the Act overrides the terms of the lease so as to entitle the employer to make the alteration with the consent of its landlord ('the lessor'). In such a case the employer must first write to the lessor asking for consent to make the alteration. The lessor cannot unreasonably withhold consent but may attach reasonable conditions to the consent.

12.14 **[Sch 4, Part I, para 1]** If the employer fails to make a written application to the lessor for consent to the alteration, the employer will not be able to rely upon the fact that the lease has a term preventing it from making alterations to the premises to defend its failure to make an alteration. In these circumstances, anything in the lease which prevents that alteration being made must be ignored in deciding whether it was reasonable for the employer to have made the alteration.

> An employer occupies premises under a lease a term of which says that the employer cannot make alterations to a staircase. When deciding whether or not it was reasonable for the employer to make an alteration to the staircase to overcome a disadvantage experienced by a disabled employee, a tribunal will ignore the term of the lease unless the employer has written to the lessor to ask for permission to make the alteration.

WHAT HAPPENS IF THE LESSOR HAS A 'SUPERIOR' LESSOR?

12.15 The employer's lessor may itself hold a lease the terms of which prevent it from consenting to the alteration without the consent of its landlord ('the superior lessor'). In such circumstances the effect of the superior lease is modified so as to require the lessee of that lease to apply in writing to its lessor (the 'superior lessor' in this context) if it wishes to consent to the alteration. As with the employer's lessor, the superior lessor must not withhold such consent unreasonably but may attach reasonable conditions to the consent.

> A bank occupies its premises under a lease, the terms of which prevent it from making alterations without the consent of the landlord. The landlord holds the premises under a lease which has a similar term. The landlord receives an application from the bank for consent to alter the premises. The landlord is entitled to consent to the application if it receives the consent of its landlord. The bank's landlord writes to the superior lessor asking for this consent. The superior lessor cannot unreasonably refuse to give consent but may consent subject to reasonable conditions.

12.16 Where a superior lessor receives an application from its lessee, the provisions described in paragraphs 12.17 to 12.30 apply as if its lessee were the employer.

HOW DO ARRANGEMENTS FOR GAINING CONSENT WORK?

12.17 **[SI 2004/153]** Regulations made under the Act govern the procedure for obtaining consent. These Regulations (the Disability Discrimination (Employment Field) (Leasehold Premises) Regulations 2004) are referred to in this Chapter as the 'Leasehold Premises Regulations'.

12.18 **[reg 4]** The Leasehold Premises Regulations say that, once the application has been made, the lessor has 21 days, beginning with the day on which it receives the application, to reply in writing to the employer (or the person who made the application on its behalf). If it fails to do so it is taken to have unreasonably withheld its consent to the alteration. However, where it is reasonable to do so, the lessor is permitted to take more than 21 days to reply to the request.

12.19 If the lessor replies consenting to the application subject to obtaining the consent of another person (required under a superior lease or because of a binding obligation), but fails to seek the consent of the other person within 21 days of receiving the application (or such longer period as may be reasonable), it will also be taken to have withheld its consent.

12.20 The Leasehold Premises Regulations provide that a lessor will be treated as not having sought the consent of another person unless the lessor has applied in writing to the other person indicating that the occupier has asked for consent for an alteration in order to comply with a duty to make reasonable adjustments, and that the lessor has given its consent conditionally upon obtaining the other person's consent.

12.21 **[reg 6]** If the lessor replies refusing consent to the alteration, the employer must inform the disabled person of this, but has no further obligation to make the alteration (but see paragraph 12.2).

WHEN IS IT UNREASONABLE FOR A LESSOR TO WITHHOLD CONSENT?

12.22 Whether withholding consent will be reasonable or not will depend on the specific circumstances. For example, if a particular adjustment is likely to result in a substantial permanent reduction in the value of the lessor's interest in the premises, the lessor is likely to be acting reasonably in withholding consent. The lessor is also likely to be acting reasonably if it withholds consent because an adjustment would cause significant disruption or inconvenience to other tenants (for example, where the premises consist of multiple adjoining units).

> A particular adjustment helps make a public building more accessible generally and is therefore likely to benefit the landlord. It is likely to be unreasonable for consent to be withheld in these circumstances.

> A particular adjustment is likely to result in a substantial permanent reduction in the value of the landlord's interest in the premises. The landlord is likely to be acting reasonably in withholding consent.

PART 4

> A particular adjustment would cause significant disruption or major inconvenience to other tenants (for example, where the premises consist of multiple adjoining units). The landlord is likely to be acting reasonably in withholding consent.

12.23 A trivial or arbitrary reason would almost certainly be unreasonable. Many reasonable adjustments to premises will not harm the lessor's interests and so it would generally be unreasonable to withhold consent for them.

12.24 **[reg 5]** The Leasehold Premises Regulations say that, provided the consent has been sought in the way required by the lease, it is unreasonable for a lessor to withhold consent in circumstances where the lease says that consent will be given to alterations of the kind for which consent has been sought.

12.25 **[reg 6]** The Leasehold Premises Regulations provide that withholding consent will be reasonable where:

- there is a binding obligation requiring the consent of any person to the alteration
- the lessor has taken steps to seek consent, and
- consent has not been given or has been given subject to a condition making it reasonable for the lessor to withhold its consent.

It will also be reasonable for a lessor to withhold consent where it is bound by an agreement under which it would have to make a payment in order to give the consent, but which prevents it from recovering the cost from the employer.

WHAT CONDITIONS WOULD IT BE REASONABLE FOR A LESSOR TO MAKE WHEN GIVING CONSENT?

12.26 The Leasehold Premises Regulations set out some conditions which it is reasonable for a lessor to make. Depending on the circumstances of the case there may be other conditions which it would also be reasonable for a lessor to require the employer to meet. Where a lessor imposes other conditions, their reasonableness may be challenged in the course of subsequent employment tribunal proceedings (see paragraph 12.28).

12.27 **[reg 7]** The conditions set out in the Leasehold Premises Regulations as ones which a lessor may reasonably require an employer to meet are that it:

- obtains any necessary planning permission and other statutory consents
- submits plans and specifications for the lessor's approval (provided that such approval will not be unreasonably withheld) and thereafter carries out the work in accordance with them
- allows the lessor a reasonable opportunity to inspect the work after it is completed, or
- reimburses the lessor's reasonable costs incurred in connection with the giving of consent.

In addition, in a case where it would be reasonable for the lessor to withhold consent, the lessor may give such consent subject to a condition that the premises are reinstated to their original condition at the end of the lease.

WHAT HAPPENS IF THE LESSOR REFUSES CONSENT OR ATTACHES CONDITIONS TO CONSENT?

12.28 **[Sch 4, Part I, para 2]** Where a disabled person brings legal proceedings against his employer under Part 2 – and those proceedings involve a failure to make an alteration to premises – he may ask the employment tribunal hearing the case to bring in the lessor as an additional party to the proceedings. The employer may also make such a request. The tribunal will grant that request if it is made before the hearing of the case begins. It may refuse the request if it is made after the hearing of the claim begins. The request will not be granted if it is made after the tribunal has determined the claim.

12.29 Where the lessor has been made a party to the proceedings, the employment tribunal may determine whether the lessor has unreasonably refused consent to the alteration or has consented subject to unreasonable conditions. In either case, the tribunal can:

- make an appropriate declaration
- make an order authorising the employer to make a specified alteration
- order the lessor to pay compensation to the disabled person.

12.30 The tribunal may require the employer to comply with any conditions specified in the order. If the tribunal orders the lessor to pay compensation, it cannot also order the employer to do so.

COMPARISON WITH THE PROCEDURE FOR OBTAINING CONSENT UNDER PART 3

12.31 There are similar provisions which govern the procedure by which a service provider may obtain consent to an alteration which it proposes to make in order to comply with a duty of reasonable adjustment under Part 3 of the Act. These provisions – which are explained in Chapter 6 of the Part 3 Code – apply where a provider of employment services needs to obtain consent in order to make a reasonable adjustment (see paragraphs 11.16 and 11.17). However, it should be noted that the procedures for obtaining consent under Parts 2 and 3 differ in certain ways. In particular:

- The periods within which the lessor must respond to an application for consent are not the same—under Part 3 the relevant period is 42 days beginning with the day on which the application is received
- Under Part 3 the lessor may require plans and specifications to be submitted **before** it decides whether to give consent
- Under Part 3 it is possible to make a free-standing reference to the court if the lessor has either refused consent or attached conditions to it. Under Part 2, the question of consent to alterations can only be considered by an employment tribunal in the course of a complaint of discrimination.

[4673]

13. OTHER RELEVANT PROVISIONS

13.1 Additional provisions of the Act (and provisions of other legislation) are relevant to understanding the protection from discrimination afforded to disabled people in respect of employment. This chapter describes those provisions, and focuses in particular on the way in which disputes should be resolved.

RESOLVING DISPUTES

When is it necessary to try to resolve disputes within the workplace?

13.2 It is good practice to attempt to resolve disputes within the workplace and without resorting to legal proceedings. In addition, legislation **requires** employers and employees to try to do this in certain circumstances. The requirement may apply where an employer has dismissed an employee, or is contemplating dismissing him, or taking disciplinary action against him, or where an employee has a grievance against his employer. In broad terms, the statutory procedures—which are set out in the Employment Act 2002 (the 2002 Act)—require:

- the grounds for the employer's action, or details of the employee's grievance, to be set out in writing and sent to the other party
- a meeting to take place between the employer and employee in order to discuss the matter, and for the employer to inform the employee of its decision afterwards, and
- an internal appeal against that decision to take place if the employee is not satisfied with it.

13.3 Employers must make reasonable adjustments in respect of the way in which the statutory procedures are implemented to prevent a disabled person from being placed at a substantial disadvantage in comparison with people who are not disabled. Failure to do so will itself amount to a breach of the 1995 Act.

13.4 So, for example, it is likely to be a reasonable adjustment for an employer to allow a disabled employee who has communication difficulties some assistance to make a written statement of a grievance he wishes to make (such as by providing him with assistance via a non-interested party). Depending on the circumstances, it may be reasonable to allow a disabled person with learning disabilities to be accompanied to a meeting by a family member or friend, or to send written communications to a blind or visually impaired person in a format which is accessible to him.

13.5 The effect of what the 2002 Act says about dispute resolution is that, where an employee has a grievance against his employer (including an allegation that the employer has breached Part 2 of the 1995 Act), he may not commence employment tribunal proceedings without first giving the employer a written statement of the reasons for the grievance.

13.6 In addition, in any employment tribunal proceedings where it appears to the tribunal that the statutory procedures apply, any award which the tribunal makes will be either reduced or increased if the procedures were not fully complied with before the proceedings were begun. The award will be reduced if the tribunal concludes that the failure to comply is wholly or mainly attributable to the employee. It will be increased if the tribunal concludes that the employer is wholly or mainly at fault. Save in exceptional circumstances, the amount by which any award will be reduced or increased will be between 10% and 50%.

When are attempts at internal dispute resolution unnecessary?

13.7 Although, as stated above, it is good practice to try to resolve disputes within the workplace wherever possible, there are occasions where internal dispute resolution will not be practical or appropriate. The legislation recognises this, and the statutory procedures mentioned in paragraph 13.2 do not have to be complied with in respect of every claim which arises under Part 2.

13.8 Compliance with those procedures is only **required** in respect of disputes involving employers and employees who work (or have worked) under a contract of service or apprenticeship. People who fall within the wider definition of 'employment' set out at paragraph 3.8 do not need to use the statutory procedures before bringing a claim in the employment tribunal. Neither do those procedures apply to disputes under the Act involving partners in firms, barristers or advocates, or office holders, for example. Equally, they do not apply in respect of disputes between employees and pension scheme trustees or managers, or to disputes involving providers of employment services.

13.9 **[SI 2004/752, reg 11]** As indicated above, however, there are also cases where, because of the circumstances surrounding the dispute, it may be inappropriate for the parties to be required to seek a resolution within the workplace. The Employment Act 2002 (Dispute Resolution) Regulations 2004 (the 2004 Regulations) provide that the statutory procedures do not need to be followed if:

- one of the parties to the dispute has reasonable grounds to believe that compliance with the procedure would result in a significant threat to himself, his property or another person, or
- one of the parties has been subjected to harassment and has reasonable grounds to believe that complying with the procedure would result in his being subjected to further harassment, or
- it is not practicable to comply with the procedure within a reasonable period.

13.10 **[reg 7]** In addition, the 2004 Regulations say that, where an employee's grievance is that disciplinary action taken against him itself amounts to discrimination by the employer, the parties are not required to meet to discuss the matter. However, an employee must still send the employer written details of his grievance before commencing employment tribunal proceedings.

What if a dispute cannot be resolved by using an employer's grievance procedure?

13.11 **[s 17A(1) & s 55 & Sch 3, para 3]** The Act says that a person who believes that someone has unlawfully discriminated against him (which includes victimising him or failing to make a reasonable adjustment) or has subjected him to harassment, may make an application to an employment tribunal. Such an application must normally be made within three months of the date when the incident complained about occurred. Before making an application to a tribunal, however, it is necessary to ensure that any requirement under the 2002 Act relating to internal dispute resolution procedures has been complied with (see paragraphs 13.2 to 13.10).

13.12 **[reg 15]** In cases where such a procedure applies, the 2004 Regulations say that the usual time limit is extended by three months (so that the time limit for making a claim becomes six months in total). However, this only applies to those people who are **required** to use such a procedure. It does not apply to people who do not have to do so (see paragraph 13.8).

13.13 Before making an application to an employment tribunal (or within 28 days of lodging it), a disabled person can request information relevant to his claim from the person against whom the claim is made. This is known as the 'questionnaire procedure'. There is a standard form of questionnaire (DL56) and accompanying booklet which explains how the procedure works (see Appendix C for details).

13.14 When an application to an employment tribunal has been made, a conciliation officer from the Advisory, Conciliation and Arbitration Service (ACAS) will try to promote settlement of the dispute without a tribunal hearing. However, if a hearing becomes necessary—and if the application is upheld—the tribunal may:

- **[s 17A(2)]** declare the rights of the disabled person (the applicant), and the other person (the respondent) in relation to the application
- order the respondent to pay the applicant compensation, and
- recommend that, within a specified time, the respondent takes reasonable action to prevent or reduce the adverse effect in question.

13.15 **[s 17A(4)]** The Act allows compensation for injury to feelings to be awarded whether or not other compensation is awarded.

13.16 **[s 17A(5)]** The Act also says that if a respondent fails, without reasonable justification, to comply with an employment tribunal's recommendation, the tribunal may:

- increase the amount of compensation to be paid, or
- order the respondent to pay compensation if it did not make such an order earlier.

13.17 **[s 4J]** It should be noted that in relation to certain claims of discrimination concerning occupational pension schemes, the Act modifies the remedies available (see paragraphs 10.13 and 10.14).

13.18 Sources of information about how to make an application to an employment tribunal are listed in Appendix C.

OTHER PROVISIONS

Anti-avoidance provisions

13.19 **[Sch 3A, Part 1]** Generally speaking, a disabled person cannot waive his rights (or an employer's duties) under the Act. The Act says that any term in a contract of employment or other agreement is 'void' (ie not valid) where:

- making the contract is unlawful under Part 2 because of the inclusion of the term
- the term is included in furtherance of an act which is itself unlawful under Part 2, or
- the term provides for the doing of an act which is unlawful under Part 2.

13.20 An employer should not include in an agreement any provision intended to avoid obligations under the Act, or to prevent someone from fulfilling obligations. An agreement should not, therefore, be used to try to justify less favourable treatment or deem an adjustment unreasonable. Even parts of agreements which unintentionally have such an effect are unenforceable if they would restrict the working of the Act's provisions on employment and occupation. However, as explained in Chapter 12, special arrangements cover leases and other agreements which might restrict the making of adjustments to premises.

Compromise agreements

13.21 **[Sch 3A, Part 1]** The effect of the Act's provisions is also to make a contract term unenforceable if it would prevent anyone from making an application to an employment tribunal under Part 2, or would force them to discontinue an application (see paragraph 13.11). There is a limited exception to this principle relating to settlement agreements which have either been brokered by an ACAS conciliation officer, or which are made in circumstances where the following conditions are satisfied:

- the disabled person has received advice from a relevant independent adviser about the terms and effects of the agreement, particularly its effect on his ability to apply to a tribunal
- the adviser has a contract of insurance or an indemnity provided for members of a profession or professional body, and
- the agreement is in writing, relates to the application, identifies the adviser and says that these conditions are satisfied.

[Sch 3A, Part 1] The Act defines the circumstances in which a person is a 'relevant independent adviser' for this purpose.

Variation of contracts

13.22 **[Sch 3A, para 3]** A disabled person interested in a contract of employment or other agreement which contains a term of the kind mentioned in paragraph 13.19 may apply to a county court or, in Scotland, a sheriff court, for an order removing or modifying that term.

Collective agreements and rules of undertakings

13.23 **[Sch 3A, Part 2]** There are also anti-avoidance provisions in the Act relating to the terms of collective agreements, and to rules made by employers in relation to working practices or recruitment. The Act says that any such term or rule is void where:

- making the collective agreement is unlawful under Part 2 because of the inclusion of the term
- the term or rule is included in furtherance of an act which is itself unlawful under Part 2, or
- the term or rule provides for the doing of an act which is unlawful under Part 2.

13.24 It does not matter whether the collective agreement was entered into, or the rule was made, before or after these provisions became law – the term or rule in question can still be challenged under the Act. In addition, where these provisions apply, certain disabled people may ask an employment tribunal to make a declaration that a discriminatory term or rule is void if they believe that it may affect them in the future. The Act specifies which disabled people may make such an application.

Local authority employers

13.25 Although the Act does not prevent posts being advertised as open only to disabled candidates, there is a requirement under section 7 of the Local Government and Housing Act 1989 that every appointment to local authorities must be made on merit. This means that a post cannot be advertised by a local authority employer as open only to disabled people. Applications from disabled people can nevertheless be encouraged. In addition, this requirement to appoint 'on merit' does not exclude the duty under the 1995 Act to make reasonable adjustments. A disabled person's 'merit' must therefore be assessed after taking into account any such adjustments.

Provision for certain charities

13.26 **[s 18C]** The Act says that some charities (and government-funded supported employment – such as Workstep) are allowed to treat some groups of disabled people more favourably than others. But they can do this only if two conditions are met. First, the group being treated more favourably must be connected with the charitable purposes of the charity. Second, the more favourable treatment of that group must be in pursuance of those charitable purposes. In the case of supported employment, those treated more favourably must be disabled people whom the programme aims to help.

DISABILITY RIGHTS COMMISSION

General functions

13.27 **[Disability Rights Commission Act 1999]** The DRC has statutory powers to work towards the elimination of discrimination and to promote the equalisation of opportunity for disabled people. In particular, the DRC:

- keeps the Act under review
- supplies assistance and support to disabled litigants under the Act
- provides information and advice to anyone with rights or obligations under the Act
- carries out formal investigations, and
- prepares new or revised Codes of Practice.

Enforcement of certain provisions under Part 2

13.28 In addition, the DRC has a direct involvement in the enforcement of the provisions of Part 2 relating to:

- instructing or pressurising other people to act unlawfully (see paragraph 3.22), and
- discriminatory advertisements (see paragraphs 7.12 and 7.13).

13.29 **[s 17B]** Only the DRC may bring proceedings in respect of these matters. Where it does so, the DRC may seek:

- a declaration from an employment tribunal that a contravention has occurred, and
- an injunction from a county court (or, in Scotland, an order from a sheriff court) restraining further contraventions.

13.30 The DRC may only apply for an injunction or order if it has first obtained a declaration from an employment tribunal that an unlawful act has occurred, and then only if it appears to the DRC that a further unlawful act is likely to occur unless the person concerned is restrained.

Further information

13.31 The Commission may be contacted at:
DRC Information, Freepost, MID 02164, Stratford upon Avon, CV37 9BR.

For other contact details, please see paragraph 1.21.

[4674]

APPENDIX A: CHANGES TO THE ACT

The table below summarises the main changes to the Act's provisions on employment and occupation taking effect on 1 October 2004. It does not include all the changes occurring on that date, and is not a full explanation of the law.

	Position before 1st October 2004	Position after 1st October 2004
Scope	• DDA covered employers with 15 or more employees. • Some occupations (e g police & firefighters) were not covered.	• All employers are covered by the DDA except for the Armed Forces. • New occupations such as police and partners in firms are covered. • Practical work experience, whether paid or unpaid, is covered. • There are new provisions on discriminatory advertisements. • Employment services are covered.
Types of Discrimination	Three kinds of discrimination: • Less favourable treatment • Failure to make reasonable adjustments. • Victimisation.	Four kinds of discrimination: • Direct discrimination. • Failure to make reasonable adjustments. • 'Disability-related discrimination'. • Victimisation.
When is Justification relevant?	Justification was of relevance in cases about: • Less favourable treatment. • Failure to make reasonable adjustments.	Justification is NOT relevant in cases about: • Direct discrimination. • Failure to make reasonable adjustments. Justification is relevant in cases about: • Disability-related discrimination.
Harassment	Covered, but no separate provisions on this.	New provisions on harassment.
Claims	Most claims covered by the Code were brought in the employment tribunal apart from those involving trustees and managers of occupational pension schemes and claims about employment services.	All claims covered by this Code are brought in the employment tribunal

[4675]

APPENDIX B: THE MEANING OF DISABILITY

This appendix is included to aid understanding about who is covered by the Act and should provide sufficient information on the definition of disability to cover the large majority of cases. The definition of disability in the Act is designed to cover only people who would generally be considered to be disabled. A Government publication 'Guidance on matters to be taken into account in determining questions relating to the definition of disability', is also available.

WHEN IS A PERSON DISABLED?

A person has a disability if he has a physical or mental impairment, which has a substantial and long-term adverse effect on his ability to carry out normal day-to-day activities.

WHAT ABOUT PEOPLE WHO HAVE RECOVERED FROM A DISABILITY?

People who have had a disability within the definition are protected from discrimination even if they have since recovered.

WHAT DOES 'IMPAIRMENT' COVER?

It covers physical or mental impairments; this includes sensory impairments, such as those affecting sight or hearing.

ARE ALL MENTAL IMPAIRMENTS COVERED?

The term 'mental impairment' is intended to cover a wide range of impairments relating to mental functioning, including what are often known as learning disabilities. The Act says that a mental illness must be a clinically well-recognised illness in order to amount to a mental impairment. A clinically well-recognised illness is one that is recognised by a respected body of medical opinion.

WHAT IS A 'SUBSTANTIAL' ADVERSE EFFECT?

A substantial adverse effect is something which is more than a minor or trivial effect. The requirement that an effect must be substantial reflects the general understanding of disability as a limitation going beyond the normal differences in ability which might exist among people.

WHAT IS A 'LONG-TERM' EFFECT?

A long-term effect of an impairment is one:

- which has lasted at least 12 months, or
- where the total period for which it lasts is likely to be at least 12 months, or
- which is likely to last for the rest of the life of the person affected.

Effects which are not long-term would therefore include loss of mobility due to a broken limb which is likely to heal within 12 months and the effects of temporary infections, from which a person would be likely to recover within 12 months.

WHAT IF THE EFFECTS COME AND GO OVER A PERIOD OF TIME?

If an impairment has had a substantial adverse effect on normal day-to-day activities but that effect ceases, the substantial effect is treated as continuing if it is likely to recur; that is if it is more probable than not that the effect will recur.

WHAT ARE 'NORMAL DAY-TO-DAY ACTIVITIES'?

They are activities which are carried out by most people on a fairly regular and frequent basis. The term is not intended to include activities which are normal only for a particular person or group of people, such as playing a musical instrument, or a sport, to a professional standard or performing a skilled or specialised task at work. However, someone who is affected in such a specialised way but is also affected in normal day-to-day activities would be covered by this part of the definition. The test of whether an impairment affects normal day-to-day activities is whether it affects one of the broad categories of capacity listed in Schedule 1 to the Act. They are:

- mobility
- manual dexterity
- physical co-ordination
- continence
- ability to lift, carry or otherwise move everyday objects
- speech, hearing or eyesight
- memory or ability to concentrate, learn or understand, or
- perception of the risk of physical danger.

WHAT ABOUT TREATMENT?

Someone with an impairment may be receiving medical or other treatment which alleviates or removes the effects (though not the impairment). In such cases, the treatment is ignored and the impairment is taken to have the effect it would have had without such treatment. This does not apply if substantial adverse effects are not likely to recur even if the treatment stops (i e the impairment has been cured).

DOES THIS INCLUDE PEOPLE WHO WEAR SPECTACLES?

No. The sole exception to the rule about ignoring the effects of treatment is the wearing of spectacles or contact lenses. In this case, the effect while the person is wearing spectacles or contact lenses should be considered.

ARE PEOPLE WHO HAVE DISFIGUREMENTS COVERED?

People with severe disfigurements are covered by the Act. They do not need to demonstrate that the impairment has a substantial adverse effect on their ability to carry out normal day-to-day activities.

WHAT ABOUT PEOPLE WHO KNOW THEIR CONDITION IS GOING TO GET WORSE OVER TIME?

Progressive conditions are conditions which are likely to change and develop over time. Examples given in the Act are cancer, multiple sclerosis, muscular dystrophy and HIV infection. Where a person has a progressive condition he will be covered by the Act from the moment the condition leads to an impairment which has some effect on ability to carry out normal day-to-day activities, even though not a substantial effect, if that impairment is likely eventually to have a substantial adverse effect on such ability.

WHAT ABOUT PEOPLE WHO ARE BLIND OR PARTIALLY SIGHTED?

[SI 2003/712] People who are registered as blind or partially sighted, or who are certified as being blind or partially sighted by a consultant ophthalmologist are automatically treated under the Act as being disabled. People who are not registered or certified as blind or partially sighted will be covered by the Act if they can establish that they meet the Act's definition of disability.

ARE PEOPLE WITH GENETIC CONDITIONS COVERED?

If a genetic condition has no effect on ability to carry out normal day-to-day activities, the person is not covered. Diagnosis does not in itself bring someone within the definition. If the condition is progressive, then the rule about progressive conditions applies.

ARE ANY CONDITIONS SPECIFICALLY EXCLUDED FROM THE COVERAGE OF THE ACT?

Yes. Certain conditions are to be regarded as not amounting to impairments for the purposes of the Act. These are:

- addiction to or dependency on alcohol, nicotine, or any other substance (other than as a result of the substance being medically prescribed)
- seasonal allergic rhinitis (e g hayfever), except where it aggravates the effect of another condition
- tendency to set fires
- tendency to steal
- tendency to physical or sexual abuse of other persons
- exhibitionism
- voyeurism.

Also, disfigurements which consist of a tattoo (which has not been removed), non-medical body piercing, or something attached through such piercing, are to be treated as not having a substantial adverse effect on the person's ability to carry out normal day-to-day activities.

[4676]

APPENDIX C: FURTHER INFORMATION

ONLINE INFORMATION

There is a wide range of practical information about employing disabled people and about the Disability Discrimination Act available free of charge on the DRC website.

Website: www.drc-gb.org

LEAFLETS ABOUT THE ACT

A range of leaflets about the Act is available online and can also be obtained free of charge from the DRC Helpline. Calls to the Helpline are charged at local rate.

Telephone: 08457 622 633

Textphone: 08457 622 644

Fax: 08457 778 878

Website: www.drc-gb.org

Post: DRC Helpline,

FREEPOST,
MID 02164,

Stratford Upon Avon,
CV37 9BR

The leaflets produced by the DRC include practical guides to the Act designed for disabled people and for employers. There is also a practical guide which is specifically intended to assist small employers.

CODES OF PRACTICE

Codes of Practice and accompanying guidance for Part 2 (this Code as well as the Code of Practice for Trade Organisations and Qualifications Bodies), Part 3 (Rights of access-Goods, facilities, services and premises) and Part 4 (Codes of practice for schools and post-16 education) are available through the DRC website (in electronic form) and through the Stationery Office on:

Telephone: 0870 600 5522

Fax: 0870 600 5533

Email: book.orders@tso.co.uk

Website: www.tso.co.uk

GUIDANCE ABOUT MAKING A CLAIM

Employment tribunal application forms can be obtained from Jobcentre Plus offices and from Citizens' Advice Bureaux. The DRC also produces a self-help pack about making a claim in an employment tribunal. Information about the Questions Procedure is also available from the DRC. The forms DL56 and accompanying guidance can be obtained either through the DRC website or from the DRC Helpline.

GUIDANCE ON BUILDING DESIGN

Copies of BS8300 'Designing Buildings and their approaches to meet the access needs of disabled people' can be obtained from the British Standards Institute:

Telephone: 020 8996 9002

Fax: 020 8996 7001

Website: www.bsi-global.com

ACCESS AUDITS

The National Register of Access Consultants provides a database of registered access auditors.

Telephone: 020 7234 0434

Fax: 020 7357 8183

Minicom: 020 7357 8182

Email: info@nrac.org.uk

Website: www.nrac.org.uk

MAKING WEBSITES ACCESSIBLE

Disabled people use a wide range of specialist hardware and software to access computers. It is important that websites are designed to be compatible with this. Websites can also have 'access features' built into their design, such as a choice of font sizes or colour schemes.

RNIB's online Web Access Centre can provide more information on designing and evaluating websites.

Telephone: 020 7391 2178

Email: webaccess@rnib.org.uk

Website: www.rnib.org.uk

HEALTH AND SAFETY

The Health and Safety Commission (HSC) and the Health and Safety Executive (HSE) are responsible for the regulation of almost all the risks to health and safety arising from work activity in Britain.

Telephone: 08701 545500
Fax: 02920 859260

Minicom: 02920 808537

Email: hseinformationservices@natbrit.com
Website: www.hse.gov.uk

JOBCENTRE PLUS (INCLUDING ACCESS TO WORK AND THE DISABILITY SYMBOL)

There is a wide range of practical help and advice to assist employers in the recruitment and employment of disabled people available from Jobcentre Plus. Telephone numbers and addresses of local Jobcentre Plus offices can be found in local telephone directories or through the Jobcentre Plus website www.jobcentreplus.gov.uk

Jobcentre Plus also provides information and advice to disabled people in work or looking for work. It is a first point of contact for people wishing to get help from the Access to Work scheme. Disabled people should contact a Disability Employment Advisor at their local Jobcentre Plus office about Access to Work or about any other employment issues, whether they are in work or looking for work. Information about Access to Work can also be obtained from Access to Work business centres. Your local Access to Work business centre can be found through the Jobcentre Plus website www.jobcentreplus.gov.uk or by talking to a member of staff at a local Jobcentre Plus office. Jobcentre Plus can also provide employers with information about the Disability Symbol.

WHAT DOES THE ACCESS TO WORK SCHEME OFFER?

Access to Work may be able to offer advice and help on the following:

Adaptations to premises and equipment

Modification of an employer's or self-employed person's premises or equipment, to enable them to employ or retain a disabled employee. Employers will be expected to contribute if adaptations bring general benefits to the business, firm, other employees or customers.

Communication support at interview

Help with the costs of employing an interpreter or communicator to accompany a hearing impaired person, where there might be communication difficulties at a job interview with an employer.

Miscellaneous assistance

Provision under this element is predominantly in the form of one-off items of support that do not fit elsewhere, such as a grant towards the costs of deaf awareness training for close colleagues of a deaf person. Cost of travel **within** work is also placed in this element.

Special aids and equipment

Provision of aids and equipment to a disabled person which a non-disabled person doing the same job would not need. Leasing equipment can also be considered when it offers the most cost-effective solution. Employers will be expected to contribute if aids bring general benefits to the business, firm, other employees or customers.

Support workers

Help with the costs of employing personal support for a person with a disability at a job interview (e g advocacy support); on their journey to and from work (e g escort or driver) and help in the workplace including Personal Readers.

Travel to work

Support when a disabled person incurs extra costs in travelling to and from work because of their disability. Beneficiaries are expected to contribute the usual costs of travelling to work by public transport (or mileage costs where there is no public transport).

WHAT IS THE DISABILITY SYMBOL?

The Disability Symbol is a recognition given by Jobcentre Plus to employers who have agreed to take action to meet five commitments regarding the employment, retention, training and career development of disabled employees.

Employers who use the symbol have agreed with Jobcentre Plus that they will take action on these five commitments:

- to interview all disabled applicants who meet the minimum criteria for a job vacancy and consider them on their abilities
- to ensure there is a mechanism in place to discuss, at any time, but at least once a year, with disabled employees what can be done to make sure they can develop and use their abilities
- to make every effort when employees become disabled to make sure they stay in employment
- to take action to ensure that all employees develop the appropriate level of disability awareness needed to make these commitments work
- each year, to review the five commitments and what has been achieved, plan ways to improve on them and let employees and Jobcentre Plus know about progress and future plans.

OTHER SOURCES OF INFORMATION

ACAS, the Advisory, Conciliation and Arbitration Service can help employers and individuals with information on legislation and on industrial relations practices and procedures. ACAS has a Helpline service which can be contacted on:

Telephone: 08457 47 47 47

Textphone: 08456 06 16 00

Website: www.acas.org.uk

Equality Direct also gives advice to employers across a range of equality issues (available in England only).

Telephone/Textphone: 08457 600 3444

Website: www.equalitydirect.org.uk

The Information Commissioner's Office provides information and guidance about the Data Protection Act and the Codes of Practice which relate to it.

Telephone: 01625 545 745

Fax: 01625 524510

Email: mail@ico.gsi.gov.uk

Website: www.informationcommissioner.gov.uk

The Pensions Ombudsman investigates and makes decisions about complaints and disputes about the way that occupational pension schemes are run.

Telephone: 020 7834 9144

Fax: 020 7821 0065

Email: enquiries@pensions-ombudsman.org.uk

Website: www.pensions-ombudsman.org.uk

OPAS, The Pensions Advisory Service, is an independent organisation that provides information and guidance on the whole spectrum of pensions, including State, company, personal and stakeholder schemes. It can help any member of the public who has a problem, complaint or dispute with their occupational or private pension provider.

Telephone: 0845 6012923

Fax: 020 7233 8016

Email: enquiries@opas.org.uk

Website: www.opas.org.uk

[4677]

INDEX

[4677A]

DISABILITY RIGHTS COMMISSION CODE OF PRACTICE: TRADE ORGANISATIONS AND QUALIFICATIONS BODIES (2004)

NOTES

Note: a new code of practice was issued by the Commission for Equality and Human Rights on 16 May 2008 entitled "Disability Discrimination Act 1995 Code of Practice for Trade Organisations, Qualifications Bodies and General Qualifications Bodies". It comes into force on 23 June 2008 (see the Disability Discrimination Code of Practice (Trade Organisations, Qualifications Bodies and General Qualifications Bodies) (Commencement) Order 2008, SI 2008/1335). This code is revoked (as from the same date) by the Disability Discrimination Code of Practice (Trade Organisations and Qualifications Bodies) (Revocation) Order 2008, SI 2008/1336, subject to transitional provisions in relation to proceedings under Part 2 of the 1995 Act to the extent they relate to events taking place before 23 June 2008 and have not been determined by that date. The new code is available on the Equality and Human Rights Commission's website at: www.equalityhumanrights.com.

This Code of Practice is the second of two new Codes prepared by the Disability Rights Commission in 2004, under the powers conferred on it by the Disability Discrimination Act 1995 s 53A (inserted by the Disability Rights Commission Act 1999 and repealed as noted below). It replaces the former (1999) Code of Practice on the Duties of Trade Organisations to their Disabled Members and Applicants produced by the then Department for Education and Employment, which has been revoked by SI 2004/2300. The Code was approved by the Secretary of State and by Parliament in accordance with s 53A and came into effect on 1 October 2004 (see the Disability Discrimination Codes of Practice (Employment and Occupation, and Trade Organisations and Qualifications Bodies) Appointed Day Order 2004, SI 2004/2302). The statutory provision under which this Code was made was repealed by the Equality Act 2006, ss 40, 91, Sch 3, paras 41, 52, Sch 4; however the Code is continued in force by s 42(3) of the 2006 Act (see **[1685]**). As to the dissolution of the Disability Rights Commission and the transfer of its property, rights and liabilities etc to the Commission for Equality and Human Rights, see the Equality Act 2006, ss 36–38 at **[1679]**–**[1681]**. The Code is reproduced here in full save for the Foreword and Contents, and Appendices B and C. The equivalent Appendices to the DRC's Code of Practice on Employment and Occupation (at **[4676]** and **[4677]**) contain all the information in the Appendices to this Code, and should be consulted accordingly. Section references that appeared in the margin of the original Code are reproduced at the start of the relevant paragraph in bold.

1. INTRODUCTION

PURPOSE OF PART 2 OF THE ACT

1.1 The Disability Discrimination Act 1995 (the Act) brought in measures to prevent discrimination against disabled people. Part 2 of the Act is based on the principle that disabled people should not be discriminated against in employment or when seeking employment. A person's prospects of gaining employment, or of progressing in or retaining employment, may be affected by his ability to become a member of a trade organisation or to take advantage of its membership services. A person's employment prospects may also be affected by his ability to obtain a professional or trade qualification.

1.2 It is for this reason that, in addition to imposing duties on employers which are intended to prevent discrimination against disabled people, Part 2 sets out a number of duties with which trade organisations and bodies which confer professional or trade qualifications must comply for the same purpose. The extension of Part 2 to cover qualifications bodies as from 1 October 2004 represents a change in the law. Other major changes in the law which took effect on that date are summarised in Appendix A.

PURPOSE OF THE CODE

1.3 This Code of Practice (the Code) gives practical guidance on how to prevent discrimination against disabled people by trade organisations and qualifications bodies. It describes the duties on such organisations and bodies in this regard. The Code helps disabled people to understand the law and what they can do if they feel that they have been discriminated against. By encouraging good practice, the Code assists trade organisations and qualifications bodies to avoid complaints being made against them and to work towards the elimination of discrimination against disabled people.

1.4 The Code also gives guidance on the law which is intended to help lawyers when advising their clients, and to assist courts and tribunals when interpreting new legal concepts. The Code explains the operation and effect of technical statutory provisions – some of which only came into force on 1 October 2004, and many of which have a complex legal effect. Because of this, the Code is necessarily comprehensive and detailed. However, the Disability Rights Commission (DRC) also produces a range of other publications about the Act, and about the rights of disabled people under it, which are intended to be of use to a range of audiences and for a variety of purposes. Details of how to obtain these publications are included in Appendix C.

1.5 **[s 53A]** The DRC has prepared and issued this Code under the Act on the basis of a request by the Secretary of State. It applies to England, Wales and Scotland. A similar but separate Code applies to Northern Ireland.

1.6 As employers themselves, trade organisations and qualifications bodies have duties under Part 2 in respect of disabled people whom they employ, or who apply to them for employment. However, these matters are not considered in the Code – which is concerned only with the duties of trade organisations and qualifications bodies acting in their capacity as such. Guidance on the application of the Act to employers is given in a separate code of practice issued by the DRC (see Appendix C for details).

STATUS OF THE CODE

1.7 **[s 53A(8)]** The Code does not impose legal obligations. Nor is it an authoritative statement of the law—that is a matter for the courts and tribunals. However, the Code can be used in evidence in legal proceedings under the Act. Courts and employment tribunals must take into account any part of the Code that appears to them relevant to any question arising in those proceedings. If trade organisations and qualifications bodies follow the guidance in the Code, it may help to avoid an adverse decision by a court or tribunal in such proceedings.

HOW TO USE THE CODE

1.8 This chapter gives an introduction to the Code. Chapter 2 sets out some general guidance on how to avoid discrimination. Chapter 3 contains an overview of the relevant provisions of the Act, and those provisions are examined in more detail in subsequent chapters.

1.9 Chapter 4 details what is meant by discrimination and harassment, and Chapter 5 explains the duty to make reasonable adjustments for disabled people. Chapter 6 examines the relevance of justification under Part 2. Chapters 7 and 8 focus on particular issues relating to discrimination by trade organisations and qualifications bodies respectively.

1.10 Chapter 9 looks at issues concerning adjustments to premises, and Chapter 10 deals with various other points and explains what happens if discrimination is alleged.

1.11 Appendix A summarises some recent changes in the Act's provisions on trade organisations and qualifications bodies. Appendix B gives more information on what is meant by 'disability' and by 'disabled person'. Separate statutory guidance relating to the definition of disability has been issued under the Act (see paragraph 3.6). Appendix C lists other sources of relevant information about matters referred to in the Code.

1.12 Each chapter of the Code should be viewed as part of an overall explanation of the relevant provisions of the Act and the regulations made under them. In order to understand the law properly it is necessary to read the Code as a whole. The Code should not be read too narrowly or literally. It is intended to explain the principles of the law, to illustrate how the Act might operate in certain situations and to provide general guidance on good practice. There are some questions which the Code cannot resolve and which must await the authoritative interpretation of the courts and tribunals. The Code is not intended to be a substitute for taking appropriate advice on the legal consequences of particular situations.

EXAMPLES IN THE CODE

1.13 Examples of good practice and how the Act is likely to work are given in boxes. They are intended simply to illustrate the principles and concepts used in the legislation and should be read in that light. The examples should not be treated as complete or authoritative statements of the law.

1.14 While the examples refer to particular situations, they should be understood more widely as demonstrating how the law is likely to be applied generally. They can often be used to test how the law might apply in similar circumstances involving different disabilities or situations. The examples attempt to use as many different varieties of disabilities and situations as possible to demonstrate the breadth and scope of the Act. Examples relating to men or women are given for realism and could, of course, apply to people of either gender.

REFERENCES IN THE CODE

1.15 References to the Act are shown in the margins. For example, s 1(1) means section 1(1) of the Act and Sch 1 means Schedule 1 to the Act. References to Part 2, 3 or 4 refer to the relevant Part of the Act. Where reference is made to regulations, the appropriate Statutory Instrument (SI) number is shown in the margin.

CHANGES TO THE LEGISLATION

1.16 The Code refers to the Disability Discrimination Act as of 1 October 2004. There may be changes to the Act or to other legislation, for example, to the range of people who are considered to be disabled under the Act, which may have an effect on the duties explained in the Code. You will need to ensure that you keep up to date with any developments that affect the Act's provisions. You can get relevant information from the DRC (see paragraph 1.18 for contact details).

FURTHER INFORMATION

1.17 Copies of the Act and regulations made under it can be purchased from the Stationery Office (see inside the front cover of the Code for details). Separate codes covering other aspects of the Act, and guidance relating to the definition of disability are also available from the Stationery Office. The text of all the DRC's codes (including this Code) can also be downloaded free of charge from the DRC website (see paragraph 1.18).

1.18 Free information about the Act is available on the DRC website. It can also be obtained by contacting the DRC Helpline. This information is available in accessible formats. Calls to the Helpline are charged at local rate.

Website: www.drc-gb.org

Telephone: 08457 622 633
Textphone: 08457 622 644

Fax: 08457 778 878

Post: DRC Helpline,

FREEPOST
MID02164,

Stratford upon Avon,

CV37 9BR

[4678]

2. HOW CAN DISCRIMINATION BE AVOIDED?

INTRODUCTION

2.1 Prevention is better than cure. There are various actions which trade organisations and qualifications bodies can take in order to avoid discriminating against disabled people. By doing so, organisations and bodies are not only likely to minimise the incidence of expensive and time-consuming litigation, but will also improve their general performance and the quality of the services they provide. This chapter sets out some guidance on ways to help ensure that disabled people are not discriminated against.

UNDERSTANDING THE SOCIAL DIMENSION OF DISABILITY

2.2 The concept of discrimination in the Act reflects an understanding that functional limitations arising from disabled people's impairments do not inevitably restrict their ability to participate fully in society. Rather than the limitations of an impairment, it is often environmental factors (such as the structure of a building, or an organisation's practices) which unnecessarily lead to these social restrictions. This principle underpins the duty to make reasonable adjustments described in Chapter 5. Understanding this will assist trade organisations and qualifications bodies to avoid discrimination. It is as important to consider which aspects of an organisation or body's activities create difficulties for a disabled person as it is to understand the particular nature of an individual's disability.

RECOGNISING THE DIVERSE NATURE OF DISABILITY

2.3 There are more than eight million disabled adults in our society. The nature and extent of their disabilities vary widely, as do their requirements for overcoming any difficulties they may face. If trade organisations and qualifications bodies are to avoid discriminating, they need to understand this, and to be aware of the effects their decisions and actions – and those of their agents and employees – may have on disabled people. The evidence shows that many of the steps that can be taken to avoid discrimination cost little or nothing and are easy to implement.

AVOIDING MAKING ASSUMPTIONS

2.4 It is advisable to avoid making assumptions about disabled people. Disabilities will often affect different people in different ways and their needs may be different as well. The following suggestions may help to avoid discrimination:

- Do not assume that because a person does not look disabled, he is not disabled.
- Do not assume that most disabled people use wheelchairs.
- Do not assume that all blind people read Braille or have guide dogs.
- Do not assume that all deaf people use sign language.
- Do not assume that disabled people have lesser career aspirations than non-disabled people.
- Do not assume that people with certain types of disability (such as mental health problems or epilepsy) present a health and safety risk.
- Do not assume that because you are unaware of any disabled members of an organisation there are none.
- Do not assume that because you are unaware of any disabled people who are engaged in a particular profession or trade there are none.

FINDING OUT ABOUT DISABLED PEOPLE'S NEEDS

2.5 As explained later in the Code (see paragraphs 5.14 and 8.22 for example), the Act requires trade organisations and qualifications bodies to think about ways of complying with their legal duties. Listening carefully to disabled people and finding out what they want will help organisations and bodies to meet their obligations by identifying the best way of meeting disabled people's needs. There is a better chance of reaching the best outcome if discussions are held with disabled people at an early stage.

2.6 Often, discussing with disabled people what is required to meet their needs will reassure a trade organisation or qualifications body that suitable adjustments can be carried out cheaply and with very little inconvenience.

2.7 There are various ways in which the views of disabled people can be obtained. Many trade unions and professional bodies have established formal structures for seeking and representing the views of disabled people. These may take the form of an advisory committee, perhaps a sub-committee of the equal opportunities committee or national governing body. Some organisations have a standing national forum for disabled members as well as arranging periodic conferences.

SEEKING EXPERT ADVICE

2.8 It may be possible to avoid discrimination by using personal or in-house knowledge and expertise—particularly if information or views are obtained from the disabled person concerned. However, although the Act does not specifically require anyone to obtain expert advice about meeting the needs of disabled people, in practice it may sometimes be necessary to do so in order to comply with the principal duties set out in the Act. Expert advice might be especially useful if a person is newly disabled or if the effects of a person's disability become more marked. Local and national disability organisations in particular may be able to give useful advice about the needs of disabled people and steps that can be taken to meet those needs.

PLANNING AHEAD

2.9 The duties which the Act places on trade organisations and qualifications bodies are owed to the individual disabled people with whom those organisations and bodies have dealings. There is no duty owed to disabled people in general. Nevertheless, it is likely to be cost effective for trade organisations and qualifications bodies to plan ahead. Considering the needs of a range of disabled people when planning for change (such as when planning a building refurbishment, a new IT system, or the design of a website) is likely to make it easier to implement adjustments for individuals when the need arises.

2.10 It is good practice for trade organisations and qualifications bodies to have access audits carried out to identify any improvements which can be made to a building to make it more accessible. Access audits should be carried out by suitably qualified people, such as those listed in the National Register of Access Consultants (see Appendix C for details). Websites and intranet sites can also be reviewed to see how accessible they are to disabled people using access software.

> A trade organisation is re-fitting its premises including its facilities for members. The architects are asked to comply with British Standard 8300 to ensure that facilities such as the entrance, reception, meeting rooms, lecture theatre and toilets are accessible to a wide range of disabled visitors. BS 8300 is a code of practice on the design of buildings and their approaches to meet the needs of disabled people (see Appendix C for details).

> A qualifications body is re-designing its website. In doing so it ensures that the new website is easy to read for people with a variety of access software; has the website checked for accessibility; and invites disabled readers of the website to let the qualifications body know if they find any part of it inaccessible.

IMPLEMENTING ANTI-DISCRIMINATORY POLICIES AND PRACTICES

2.11 Trade organisations and qualifications bodies are more likely to comply with their duties under the Act, and to avoid the risk of legal action being taken against them, if they implement anti-discriminatory policies and practices. These are often referred to as equality policies or diversity policies. Additionally, in the event that legal action is taken, trade organisations and qualifications bodies may be asked to demonstrate to an employment tribunal that they have effective policies and procedures in place to minimise the risk of discrimination.

RECOMMENDED STEPS FOR ALL TRADE ORGANISATIONS AND QUALIFICATIONS BODIES

2.12 Anti-discriminatory policies and practices will vary depending on the nature of the organisation (for example, on whether it is a trade organisation or qualifications body and on the size and nature of its membership). However, it is advisable for all trade organisations and qualifications bodies to take the following steps:

- Establish a policy which aims to prevent discrimination against disabled people and which is communicated to all employees and agents of the organisation or body.
- Provide disability awareness and equality training to all employees. In addition, train employees and agents so that they understand the organisation or body's policy on disability, their obligations under the Act and the practice of reasonable adjustments.
- Ensure that members and potential members of the organisation (or, in the case of a qualifications body, people who wish to have a qualification conferred on them and people who already hold a qualification) are informed about the organisation or body's disability policy.

- Ensure that people within the organisation or body who have responsibility for liaising with members or applicants have more in-depth training about the organisation's duties under the Act.
- Inform all employees and agents that conduct which breaches the anti-discrimination policy will not be tolerated, and respond quickly and effectively to any such breaches.
- Monitor the implementation and effectiveness of such a policy.
- Address acts of disability discrimination by employees as part of disciplinary rules and procedures.
- Have complaints and grievance procedures which are easy for disabled people to use and which are designed to resolve issues effectively.
- Regularly review the effectiveness of reasonable adjustments made for disabled people in accordance with the Act, and act on the findings of those reviews.
- Keep clear records of decisions taken in respect of each of these matters.

ADDITIONAL RECOMMENDED STEPS FOR TRADE UNIONS

2.13 Trade unions are a particular kind of trade organisation. In addition to taking the general steps outlined in paragraph 2.12, it is advisable for trade unions to:

- Have (and inform local branches about) a central budget or 'access fund' to pay for adjustments for disabled members in circumstances where it would be too expensive for the adjustments to be funded by local branches.
- Ensure that union representatives understand the Act's provisions on employment and occupation so that they are able to support union members who encounter disability discrimination at work.
- Ensure that health and safety representatives have a proper understanding of the principles of risk assessment and reasonable adjustments, so that health and safety issues are not used to discriminate against disabled people in the workplace or when participating in union activities.

The above considerations apply just as much to unpaid union representatives in the workplace as to salaried employees of a union.

2.14 Trade unions should not enter into collective agreements containing terms which discriminate against disabled people (see paragraphs 10.14 to 10.16). In addition, European law encourages trade unions to enter into collective agreements at national and local level in respect of anti-discriminatory policies and practices. It is advisable for trade unions to monitor the effectiveness of any such agreements.

ADDITIONAL RECOMMENDED STEPS FOR QUALIFICATIONS BODIES

2.15 The general steps outlined in paragraph 2.12 are recommended for trade organisations and qualifications bodies alike. However, there are additional steps which it is advisable for qualifications bodies to take. These are to:

- Ensure that there are effective systems in place for disabled people to request reasonable adjustments for examinations or practical tests, so that qualifications bodies are in a position to respond quickly and effectively to individual requests for specific adjustments. This may involve establishing procedures with educational institutions to ensure that institutions request relevant information from their students and then pass this on to the qualifications bodies (see paragraph 8.23).
- Regularly review any competence standards which relate to particular professional or trade qualifications to ensure that they are framed in a way which does not unnecessarily exclude disabled people from being able to meet them. This will involve carefully scrutinising each competence standard to check that it is not discriminatory. Consideration should be given to whether each standard can be objectively justified. Disabled people who work in the relevant profession or trade could be consulted to learn from their experiences, and factors such as changes in technology, which can enable people to do jobs in different ways, should be taken into account.

Further advice about how to avoid discrimination in relation to competence standards is given at paragraph 8.41.

AUDITING POLICIES AND PROCEDURES

2.16 Although there is no duty under Part 2 to anticipate the needs of disabled people in general, it is a good idea for trade organisations and qualifications bodies to keep all their policies under review, and to consider the needs of disabled people as part of this process. It is advisable for organisations and bodies to do this in addition to having a specific policy to prevent discrimination. Trade organisations and qualifications bodies are likely to have policies about matters such as:

- emergency evacuation procedures
- procurement of equipment, IT systems and websites
- information provision
- service standards for members

> A trade organisation has a policy to ensure that all members are kept informed about the organisation's activities through a website. The policy states that the website should be accessible to disabled people, including those who use access software (such as speech synthesis). The website editor is given additional training in accessible website design.

> A trade organisation has a policy outlining the level of service that all members and potential members should receive. It includes standards of service for disabled members and potential members, such as provision of application forms in accessible formats.

> A new procurement policy requires a number of factors to be taken into account in procuring equipment and IT systems. These factors include cost and energy efficiency. It is good practice for such factors to include accessibility for disabled people as well.

> A trade union reviews its procedures for organising conferences to ensure that access for disabled members is taken into account at all stages.

MONITORING

2.17 Monitoring of members (or, in the case of qualifications bodies, people applying for a qualification or people who hold qualifications) is an important way of determining whether anti-discrimination measures taken by an organisation or body are effective, and ensuring that disability equality is a reality. Information must be gathered sensitively, with appropriately worded questions, and confidentiality must be ensured. Knowing the proportion of disabled people and their status in respect of an organisation or body can help it determine where practices and policies need to be improved.

2.18 Monitoring will be more effective if disabled people feel comfortable about disclosing information about their disabilities. This is more likely to be the case if the trade organisation or qualifications body explains the purpose of the monitoring and if members and applicants believe that it genuinely supports equality for disabled people and is using the information gathered to create positive change.

> By monitoring of its membership, a professional association becomes aware that disabled people are under-represented at fellowship level. The association uses this information to review its criteria for awarding fellowships, and carries out research into the barriers facing disabled people at senior levels of the profession.

> A trade union becomes aware, through monitoring, that disabled people are under-represented as conference delegates. It uses this information to find out from disabled members how arrangements for conferences can be improved to enable fuller participation.

2.19 Some organisations choose to monitor by broad type of disability to understand the barriers faced by people with different types of impairment.

Through monitoring of people applying for and achieving registration, a qualifications body becomes aware that people with certain disabilities are significantly under-represented as applicants for, and holders of, a particular qualification. The qualifications body uses this information to review its competence standards to ensure that they do not present unnecessary barriers to disabled people.

PROMOTING EQUALITY

2.20 In order to enhance disabled people's opportunities for gaining, retaining and progressing in employment, trade organisations and qualifications bodies need to consider equality of opportunity for disabled people from two perspectives. First, such organisations and bodies should ensure that disabled people have equal access to membership, and to the benefits of membership, or (as the case may be) to opportunities for gaining and retaining a professional or trade qualification. Secondly, it is good practice for a trade organisation or qualifications body to seek to promote equality for disabled people within the trade, profession or employment sector in which it operates.

> A trade organisation in the tourism sector holds a conference in association with employers in that sector and disability organisations to promote opportunities for disabled people within the tourism industry.

> A trade union representing people in the broadcasting trades ensures that its promotional literature and its website show positive images of disabled people carrying out a variety of jobs within this industry.

> A qualifications body in the health sector promotes a scheme through which disabled people are encouraged to apply to train as health professionals.

RESOLVING DISPUTES

2.21 Although the Act does not require trade organisations or qualifications bodies to resolve disputes within the organisation or body, it is in the interests of such an organisation or body wherever possible to resolve problems as they arise. This should be done in a non-discriminatory way to comply with the requirements of the Act.

2.22 Grievance procedures can provide an open and fair way for concerns to be made known. Such procedures may be particularly appropriate for use by members of trade organisations, and can enable grievances to be resolved quickly before they become major problems. Use of the procedures may highlight areas in which the duty to make reasonable adjustments has not been observed, and can prevent misunderstandings leading to complaints to tribunals.

2.23 Chapter 10 contains further information about grievance procedures and about resolving disputes under the Act.

[4679]

3. DISCRIMINATION BY TRADE ORGANISATIONS AND QUALIFICATIONS BODIES – AN OVERVIEW

INTRODUCTION

3.1 This chapter gives an overview of those provisions of the Act which are relevant to trade organisations and qualifications bodies. It explains who has rights and duties under those provisions and outlines what is made unlawful by them. Later chapters explain the provisions in greater detail.

WHO HAS RIGHTS UNDER THE ACT?

Disabled people

3.2 **[ss 1 & 2 & Sch 1 & 2]** The Act gives protection from discrimination to a 'disabled' person within the meaning of the Act.

A disabled person is someone who has a physical or mental impairment which has an effect on his or her ability to carry out normal day-to-day activities. That effect must be:

- substantial (that is, more than minor or trivial), and
- adverse, and
- long term (that is, it has lasted or is likely to last for at least a year or for the rest of the life of the person affected).

3.3 Physical or mental impairment includes sensory impairment. Hidden impairments are also covered (for example, mental illness or mental health problems, learning disabilities, dyslexia, diabetes and epilepsy).

3.4 In considering its duties under the Act, a trade organisation or a qualifications body should not use any definition of 'disabled person' which is narrower than that in the Act. If such an organisation or body is asked to make a disability-related adjustment, it may ask the person requesting it for evidence that the impairment is one which meets the definition of disability in the Act. It may be appropriate to do so where the disability is not obvious. However, it is not appropriate to ask for more information about the impairment than is necessary for this purpose. Nor should evidence of disability be asked for where it ought to be obvious that the Act will apply.

People who have had a disability in the past

3.5 People who have had a disability within the meaning of the Act in the past are protected from discrimination even if they no longer have the disability.

More information about the meaning of disability

3.6 For a fuller understanding of the concept of disability under the Act, reference should be made to Appendix B. A government publication, Guidance on matters to be taken into account in determining questions relating to the definition of disability, provides additional help in understanding the concept of disability and in identifying who is a disabled person. Where relevant, the Guidance must be taken into account in any legal proceedings.

People who have been victimised

3.7 The Act also gives rights to people who have been victimised, whether or not they have a disability or have had one in the past. (see paragraphs 4.32 to 4.35).

WHO HAS OBLIGATIONS UNDER THE ACT?

Trade organisations

3.8 **[s 13(4)]** The Act defines a trade organisation as an organisation of workers or of employers, or any other organisation whose members carry on a particular profession or trade for the purposes of which the organisation exists. Bodies like trade unions, employers' associations, chartered professional institutions are all trade organisations because they exist for the purposes of the profession or trade which their members carry on. Examples of trade organisations include the Law Society, the Royal College of Nursing, the Swimming Teachers' Association, the Society of Floristry, the British Computer Society, and the Institute of Carpenters. The Act applies to all trade organisations, no matter how many (or how few) members they may have.

Qualifications bodies

3.9 **[s 14A(5)]** The Act defines a qualifications body as an authority or body which can confer, renew or extend a professional or trade qualification. For this purpose a professional or trade qualification is an authorisation, qualification, recognition, registration, enrolment, approval or certification which is needed for, or which facilitates engagement in, a particular profession or trade. What this means in practice is considered in paragraphs 8.5 to 8.7. Qualifications bodies include examination boards, the General Medical Council, the Nursing and Midwifery Council, and the Driving Standards Agency. Other examples are City and Guilds, the Institute of the Motor Industry, the Hospitality Awarding Body and the Guild of Cleaners and Launderers.

3.10 **[s 14A(5)]** Nevertheless, certain bodies are not regarded as qualifications bodies for the purposes of Part 2, even though they may perform some of the functions mentioned in paragraph 3.9. These are listed in the Act. Broadly speaking, they comprise local education authorities in England and Wales, education authorities in Scotland, and other bodies having responsibility for schools and colleges. This is because discrimination by such bodies is the concern of Part 4 of the Act, which relates to discrimination in the provision of education. The DRC has issued two separate codes of practice giving guidance on the operation of Part 4 (see Appendix C for details).

3.11 Clearly, certain trade organisations (such as the Law Society) also confer professional or trade qualifications. Consequently, the same organisation or body can be both a trade organisation and a qualifications body. Where this is the case, the application of the Act's provisions depends upon the capacity in which the organisation or body is acting at the time in question. For example, if an alleged act of discrimination relates to conferring, renewing or extending a professional or trade qualification, the relevant provisions are those relating to discrimination by qualifications bodies – the fact that the body is also a trade organisation is irrelevant in this context.

Employers and others to whom Part 2 applies

3.12 The primary focus of Part 2 is, of course, on the duties of employers to disabled people. As mentioned at paragraph 1.6, however, that is not the subject of this Code. Guidance on the application of the Act to employers (as well as its application to people and bodies concerned with certain occupations and to persons such as the trustees or managers of occupational pension schemes and the providers of group insurance services) is given in a separate code of practice issued by the DRC (see Appendix C for details). It has already been noted that, as employers themselves, trade organisations and qualifications bodies have duties under Part 2 in respect of disabled people whom they employ, or who apply to them for employment. Those duties are governed by the employment provisions of the Act.

WHAT DOES THE ACT SAY ABOUT DISCRIMINATION BY TRADE ORGANISATIONS AND QUALIFICATIONS BODIES?

Effect of the Act

3.13 The Act makes it unlawful for a trade organisation to **discriminate** against a disabled person in relation to membership of the organisation or access to membership benefits. The Act also makes it unlawful for a qualifications body to **discriminate** against a disabled person in relation to conferring professional or trade qualifications.

3.14 However, the Act does not prevent organisations or bodies from treating disabled people more favourably than those who are not disabled.

Forms of discrimination

3.15 The four forms of discrimination which are unlawful under Part 2 are:

- direct discrimination (the meaning of which is explained at paragraphs 4.5 to 4.22)
- failure to comply with a duty to make reasonable adjustments (explained in Chapter 5)
- 'disability-related discrimination' (see paragraphs 4.26 to 4.31), and
- victimisation of a person (whether or not he is disabled) – what the Act says about victimisation is explained at paragraphs 4.32 to 4.35.

Discrimination by trade organisations

3.16 **[s 13(1)]** The Act says that it is unlawful for a trade organisation to discriminate against a disabled person:

- in the arrangements it makes for the purpose of determining who should be offered membership of the organisation, or
- in the terms on which it is prepared to admit him to membership, or
- by refusing to accept, or deliberately not accepting, his application for membership.

3.17 **[s 13(2)]** The Act also says that it is unlawful for a trade organisation to discriminate against a disabled member:

- in the way it affords the member access to any benefits or by refusing or deliberately omitting to afford access to them, or
- by depriving the member of membership, or varying the terms of his membership, or
- by subjecting the member to any other detriment.

What this means in practice is explained in Chapter 7.

3.18 It should be noted that the Act does not protect corporate members of trade organisations, even if a disabled person is a representative of a corporate member.

> A trade organisation in the building industry has both individual and corporate members. A disabled employee of a company which is a member of this trade organisation would not have protection from discrimination by the trade organisation under Part 2, whereas an individual member of the organisation would have such protection.

Discrimination by qualifications bodies

3.19 **[s 14A(1)]** In relation to conferring, renewing, or extending professional or trade qualifications (abbreviated to 'conferring'), the Act says that it is unlawful for a qualifications body to discriminate against a disabled person:

- in the arrangements it makes for the purpose of determining upon whom to confer a professional or trade qualification, or
- in the terms on which it is prepared to confer such a qualification, or
- by refusing or deliberately omitting to grant any application by him for a professional or trade qualification, or
- by withdrawing such a qualification from him or varying the terms on which he holds it.

What this means in practice is explained in Chapter 8.

WHAT ELSE IS UNLAWFUL UNDER THE RELEVANT PROVISIONS OF THE ACT?

Harassment

3.20 **[s 13(3) & s 14A(2)]** In addition to what it says about discrimination, Part 2 makes it unlawful for either a trade organisation or a qualifications body to subject a disabled person to **harassment** for a reason which relates to his disability. What the Act says about harassment is explained in more detail at paragraphs 4.37 and 4.38.

Instructions and pressure to discriminate

3.21 **[s 16C & s 17B(1)]** It is also unlawful for a person who has authority or influence over another to instruct him, or put pressure on him, to act unlawfully under the provisions of Part 2. This covers pressure to discriminate, whether applied directly to the person concerned, or indirectly but in a way in which he is likely to hear of it. However, the Act does not give individual disabled people the right to take legal action in respect of unlawful instructions or pressure to discriminate. Such action may only be taken by the DRC (see paragraphs 10.18 to 10.20).

> A trade union is holding a conference. The conference organiser, who is a paid employee of the union working in the events department, instructs the branch representatives not to send any wheelchair users to the conference as the venue is not wheelchair accessible. This is likely to be unlawful as it is an instruction to discriminate.

Discriminatory advertisements

3.22 **[s 16B]** The Act does not prevent advertisements for membership of trade organisations or for professional or trade qualifications from saying that applications from disabled people are welcome. However, it does say that it is unlawful for those seeking members for an organisation (or seeking candidates for qualifications) to publish an advertisement (or cause it to be published) which indicates, or might reasonably be understood to indicate:

- that the success of a person's application may depend to any extent on his not having any disability, or any particular disability, or
- that the person determining the application is reluctant to make reasonable adjustments.

3.23 This applies to every form of advertisement or notice, whether to the public or not. However, an advertisement may still be lawful even if it does indicate that having a particular disability will adversely affect an applicant's prospects of success. This will be the case where, for example, the particular circumstances are such that the trade organisation or qualifications body is entitled to take the effects of the disability into account when assessing the suitability of applicants.

> A qualifications body in the tourism industry advertises in a trade publication, inviting readers to apply to take a course leading to a qualification accredited by that body. The advertisement says that candidates 'must have excellent written and spoken English'. This would exclude people who used British Sign Language as their first language, or people who had dyslexia, and may be unlawful.

> However a qualifications body advertising a course in tree surgery, would not be discriminating by stipulating that candidates 'must not be afraid of heights', even if this would exclude people who had vertigo as a result of their disability.

3.24 It is good practice to consider carefully what information should be included in advertisements and where they should be placed.

3.25 **[s 17B(1)]** The Act does not give individual applicants for membership of trade organisations or applicants for professional or trade qualifications the right to take legal action in respect of discriminatory advertisements. Such action may only be taken by the DRC (see paragraphs 10.18 to 10.20).

WHO IS LIABLE FOR UNLAWFUL ACTS?

Responsibility for the acts of others

3.26 **[s 58]** Trade organisations and qualifications bodies who act through agents are liable for the actions of their agents done with the express or implied authority of the organisation or body in question – this can include the actions of unpaid union representatives in the workplace. The Act also says that trade organisations and qualifications bodies are responsible for the actions of their employees in the course of their employment. For example, a trade union is responsible for the actions of its salaried officials in the course of their employment.

3.27 However, in legal proceedings against a trade organisation or qualifications body based on the actions of an employee, it is a defence that the organisation or body took 'such steps as were reasonably practicable' to prevent such actions. It is not a defence simply to show that the action took place without the knowledge or approval of the organisation or body. Chapter 2 gives guidance on the steps which it might be appropriate to take for this purpose.

> A trade union has a disability policy which states that it will pay for sign language interpreters to interpret at branch meetings, should the need arise, from a central union fund. This policy, and the arrangements available for paying for sign language interpreters (and for other adjustments), is explained to all branch representatives and new members. In addition all branch representatives are required to undergo basic training in the policy. A deaf union member requests a sign language interpreter for a branch meeting, but the branch representative who has undergone this training says that this is not possible as there are insufficient funds in the branch to pay for this adjustment. In this case the union could demonstrate that it had taken 'such steps as were reasonably practicable' to prevent such actions and it is likely that it has not acted unlawfully. The branch representative, however, is likely to be acting unlawfully (see paragraphs 3.28 and 3.29).

Aiding an unlawful act

3.28 **[s 57]** A person who knowingly helps another to do something made unlawful by the Act will be treated as having done the same kind of unlawful act. This means that, where a trade organisation or qualifications body is liable for an unlawful act of its employee or agent, that employee or agent will be liable for aiding the unlawful act of the organisation or body.

3.29 Where an employee of a trade organisation or qualifications body discriminates against or harasses a disabled person, it is the employing organisation or body which will be liable for that unlawful act – unless it can show that it took such steps as were reasonable to prevent the unlawful act in question. But the employee who committed the discrimination or harassment will be liable for aiding the unlawful act – and this will be the case even if the trade organisation or qualifications body is able to show that it took reasonable steps to prevent the act.

> In the previous example, where the union has taken steps to ensure that disabled members can participate in branch meetings, it is likely that the branch representative would be acting unlawfully in aiding an unlawful act by the union, even though the union itself has avoided liability by taking reasonably practicable steps.

Enforcing rights under Part 2

3.30 **[s 17A]** Enforcement of rights under Part 2 takes place in the employment tribunals. More information about enforcement is given in Chapter 10.

[4680]

4. WHAT IS DISCRIMINATION AND HARASSMENT?

INTRODUCTION

4.1 As noted at paragraph 3.15, the forms of discrimination by trade organisations and qualifications bodies which the Act makes unlawful are:

- direct discrimination
- failure to comply with a duty to make reasonable adjustments
- disability-related discrimination, and
- victimisation.

4.2 This chapter describes these four forms of discrimination in more detail, and explains the differences between them. It explores, in particular, the distinction between direct discrimination and disability-related discrimination (see paragraphs 4.27 to 4.30). These two forms of discrimination both depend on the way in which the disabled person concerned is treated – both require the disabled person to have been treated less favourably than other people are (or would be) treated. However, whether such treatment amounts to one of these forms of discrimination or the other (and, indeed, whether the treatment is unlawful in the first place) depends on the circumstances in which it arose.

4.3 The chapter examines the four forms of discrimination in the order in which they are listed in paragraph 4.1. This is because less favourable treatment which does not amount to direct discrimination can sometimes be justified. (In contrast, neither direct discrimination nor a failure to comply with a duty to make a reasonable adjustment is justifiable. Victimisation cannot be justified either.) In deciding whether the treatment is justified, and therefore whether there has been disability-related discrimination, the Act requires the question of reasonable adjustments to be taken into account (see paragraphs 6.5 and 6.6 where this is explained in more detail). Consequently, although the chapter describes direct discrimination first, it touches on the subject of reasonable adjustments before moving on to disability-related discrimination.

4.4 This chapter also explains what the Act means by 'harassment'. The concepts of discrimination and harassment (and those relating to reasonable adjustments explained in Chapter 5) are also relevant to the application of the Act's provisions on employment and occupation more generally. As explained at paragraph 1.6, the Code focuses only on the duties of trade organisations and qualifications bodies acting in their capacity as such. However, in their capacity as employers, trade organisations and qualifications bodies also have duties under the Act's provisions on employment, which are the subject of a separate code of practice issued by the DRC (see Appendix C for details).

WHAT DOES THE ACT MEAN BY 'DIRECT DISCRIMINATION'?

What does the Act say?

4.5 **[s 3A(5)]** The Act says that treatment of a disabled person by a trade organisation or qualifications body amounts to direct discrimination if:

- it is on the ground of his disability
- the treatment is less favourable than the way in which a person not having that particular disability is (or would be) treated, and
- the relevant circumstances, including the abilities, of the person with whom the comparison is made are the same as, or not materially different from, those of the disabled person.

4.6 It follows that direct discrimination depends on treatment of a disabled person by a trade organisation or qualifications body being on the ground of his disability. It also depends on a comparison of that treatment with the way in which the organisation or body treats (or would treat) an appropriate comparator. If, on the ground of his disability, the disabled person is treated less favourably than the comparator is (or would be) treated, the treatment amounts to direct discrimination.

When is direct discrimination likely to occur?

4.7 Treatment of a disabled person is 'on the ground of' his disability if it is caused by the fact that he is disabled or has the disability in question. In general, this means that treatment is on the ground of disability if a disabled person would not have received it but for his disability. However, disability does not have to be the only (or even the main) cause of the treatment complained of – provided that it is an effective cause, determined objectively from all the circumstances.

4.8 Consequently, if the less favourable treatment occurs because of generalised, or stereotypical, assumptions about the disability or its effects, it is likely to be direct discrimination. This is because a trade organisation or qualifications body would not normally make such assumptions about a non-disabled person, but would instead consider his individual abilities.

> A trade union member who has a mental health problem – which her branch secretary is aware of – is refused admission to a meeting because the branch secretary wrongly assumes that she would seriously disrupt the meeting with loud interjections. The branch secretary has treated her less favourably than other members by refusing her entry to the meeting. The treatment was on the ground of the woman's disability (because assumptions would not have been made about a non-disabled person).

4.9 In addition, less favourable treatment which is disability-specific, or which arises out of prejudice about disability (or about a particular type of disability), is also likely to amount to direct discrimination.

> An applicant for a professional hairdressing qualification is told that he would not be suitable for the qualification because he has a disability and thus the qualifications body refuses to confer the qualification upon him. This refusal is unrelated to any competence standard which is applied by the body when conferring the qualification, but arises instead from prejudice about the applicant's disability. This amounts to direct discrimination.

4.10 In some cases, an apparently neutral reason for less favourable treatment of a disabled person may, on investigation, turn out to be a pretext for direct discrimination.

> A disabled member of a professional body wishes to represent the body publicly by giving a television interview but is told that only people who have been members for at least three years are permitted to do this. However, she discovers that another member, who is not disabled, has given a public presentation on behalf of the professional body even though he had only been a member for two years at the time. Although the reason given to the disabled member (that she had not been a member of the body for long

enough to represent it publicly) appeared to be a neutral one, it would seem that the reason was actually a pretext for direct discrimination, and is therefore unlawful.

4.11 Direct discrimination will often occur where the trade organisation or qualifications body is aware that the disabled person has a disability, and this is the reason for its treatment of him. Direct discrimination need not be conscious – people may hold prejudices that they do not admit, even to themselves. Thus, a person may behave in a discriminatory way while believing that he would never do so. Moreover, direct discrimination may sometimes occur even though the trade organisation or qualifications body is unaware of a person's disability.

4.12 In situations such as those described in the above examples, it will often be readily apparent that the disabled person concerned has been treated less favourably on the ground of his disability. In other cases, however, this may be less obvious. Whether or not the basis for the treatment in question appears to be clear, a useful way of telling whether or not it is discriminatory, (and of establishing what kind of discrimination it is), is to focus on the person with whom the disabled person should be compared. That person may be real or hypothetical (see paragraph 4.18).

Identifying comparators in respect of direct discrimination

4.13 In determining whether a disabled person has been treated less favourably in the context of direct discrimination, his treatment must be compared with that of an appropriate comparator. This must be someone who does not have the same disability. It could be a non-disabled person or a person with other disabilities.

4.14 It follows that, in the great majority of cases, some difference will exist between the circumstances (including the abilities) of the comparator and those of the disabled person – there is no need to find a comparator whose circumstances are the same as those of the disabled person in every respect. What matters is that the comparator's **relevant** circumstances (including his abilities) must be the same as, or not materially different from, those of the disabled person.

4.15 Once an appropriate comparator is identified, it is clear that the situation described in the example at paragraph 4.8 amounts to direct discrimination:

In the example about the trade union member who is refused admission to a meeting because she has a mental health problem, there is direct discrimination because the woman was treated less favourably on the ground of her disability than an appropriate comparator (that is, a person who does not have a mental health problem but whose relevant circumstances (including abilities) are otherwise the same): such a person would not have been refused admission to the meeting in the same circumstances.

4.16 The example of direct discrimination in paragraph 4.9 also becomes clearer when the appropriate comparator is identified:

In the example about the applicant for a professional hairdressing qualification who is told that he would not be suitable for the qualification because he has a disability, there is direct discrimination because the man was treated less favourably on the ground of his disability than an appropriate comparator (that is, a person who does not have the same disability, but whose relevant abilities in respect of the qualification are the same): such a person would not have been treated in this way.

4.17 The comparator used in relation to direct discrimination under the Act is the same as it is for other types of direct discrimination – such as direct sex discrimination. It is, however, made explicit in the Act that the comparator must have the same relevant abilities as the disabled person.

4.18 It may not be possible to identify an actual comparator whose relevant circumstances are the same as (or not materially different from) those of the disabled person in question. In such cases a hypothetical comparator may be used. Evidence which helps to establish how a hypothetical comparator would have been treated is likely to include details of how other people (not satisfying the statutory comparison test) were treated in circumstances which were broadly similar.

In the example at paragraph 4.10, there is nobody who has represented the professional body in television interviews with whom the disabled person can be compared. Nevertheless, the treatment of the member who had only two years' membership but was able to give a public presentation on behalf of the body might be evidence of discrimination: it might be used as evidence that a hypothetical non-disabled member who wanted to participate in a television interview would not have been treated in the same way as the disabled member was treated.

4.19 It should be noted that the type of comparator described in the preceding paragraphs is only relevant to disability discrimination when assessing whether there has been **direct** discrimination. A different comparison falls to be made when assessing whether there has been a failure to comply with a duty to make reasonable adjustments (see paragraphs 5.2 and 5.3) or when considering disability-related discrimination (see paragraph 4.29).

Focusing on relevant circumstances

4.20 As stated in paragraph 4.14, direct discrimination only occurs where the **relevant** circumstances of the comparator, including his abilities, are the same as, or not materially different from, those of the disabled person himself. It is therefore important to focus on those circumstances which are, in fact, relevant to the matter to which the less favourable treatment relates. Although, in some cases, the effects of the disability may be relevant, the fact of the disability itself is not a relevant circumstance for these purposes. This is because the comparison must be with a person **not** having that particular disability.

A woman who has a severe facial disfigurement applies for membership of a professional association in the tourism industry. Despite meeting the formal requirements for membership, she is told that her disability would not create a good impression and her application is rejected. The correct comparator in a claim for direct discrimination would be a person who does not have a facial disfigurement but who meets the formal requirements for membership of the professional association.

Relevance of reasonable adjustments to comparison

4.21 In making the comparison in respect of a claim of direct discrimination, the disabled person's abilities must be considered **as they in fact are**. In some cases, there will be particular reasonable adjustments which a trade organisation or qualifications body was required by the Act to make, but in fact failed to make. It may be that those adjustments would have had an effect on the disabled person's relevant abilities. But in making the comparison, the disabled person's abilities should be considered as they **in fact** were, and not as they would or might have been had those adjustments been made. On the other hand, if adjustments have **in fact** been made which have had the effect of enhancing the disabled person's abilities, then it is those enhanced abilities which should be considered. The disabled person's abilities are being considered as they in fact are (and not as they might have been if the adjustments had not been made).

A disabled person has to sit an examination in order to obtain a professional or trade qualification. Because of her disability she has difficulty writing, and asks to be allowed to type her answers. The qualifications body does not permit this (even though it would have been reasonable for it to do so) and, as a result, the woman is unable to complete the examination in time. This is not direct discrimination, as the comparator is a non-disabled person who fails to complete the examination in time. (But the woman would be likely to have good claims in respect of two other forms of discrimination – failure to make reasonable adjustments and disability-related discrimination – see paragraph 4.36).

Can direct discrimination be justified?

4.22 **[s 3A(4)]** Treatment of a disabled person which amounts to direct discrimination under Part 2 is unlawful. It can never be justified.

FAILURE TO MAKE REASONABLE ADJUSTMENTS—RELATIONSHIP TO DISCRIMINATION

4.23 For the reason given in paragraph 4.3, it may be necessary to consider whether a trade organisation or qualifications body has failed to comply with a duty to make a reasonable adjustment in order to determine whether disability-related discrimination has occurred.

4.24 **[s 3A(2)]** Irrespective of its relevance to disability-related discrimination, however, a failure to comply with a duty to make a reasonable adjustment in respect of a disabled person amounts to discrimination in its own right. Such a failure is therefore unlawful. Chapter 5 explains the circumstances in which a trade organisation or qualifications body has such a duty, and gives guidance as to what they need to do when the duty arises.

4.25 As with direct discrimination, the Act does not permit an organisation or body to justify a failure to comply with a duty to make a reasonable adjustment (see paragraphs 5.26 and 5.27).

WHAT IS DISABILITY-RELATED DISCRIMINATION?

What does the Act say?

4.26 **[s 3A(1)]** The Act says that treatment of a disabled person by a trade organisation or qualifications body amounts to discrimination if:

- it is for a reason related to his disability
- the treatment is less favourable than the way in which the trade organisation or qualifications body treats (or would treat) others to whom that reason does not (or would not) apply, and
- the organisation or body cannot show that the treatment is justified.

4.27 Although the Act itself does not use the term 'disability-related discrimination', this expression is used in the Code when referring to treatment of a disabled person which:

- is unlawful because each of the conditions listed in paragraph 4.26 is satisfied, but
- does **not** amount to direct discrimination under the Act.

4.28 In general, direct discrimination occurs when the reason for the less favourable treatment in question is the disability, while disability-related discrimination occurs when the reason relates to the disability but is not the disability itself. The expression 'disability-related discrimination' therefore distinguishes less favourable treatment which amounts to direct discrimination from a wider class of less favourable treatment which, although not amounting to direct discrimination, is nevertheless unlawful.

When does disability-related discrimination occur?

4.29 In determining whether disability-related discrimination has occurred, the treatment of the disabled person must be compared with that of a person **to whom the disability-related reason does not apply**. This contrasts with direct discrimination, which requires a comparison to be made with a person without the disability in question but whose relevant circumstances are the same. The comparator may be non-disabled or disabled – but the key point is that the disability-related reason for the less favourable treatment must not apply to him.

> A trade union refuses to allow a disabled person, who has a severe back condition and has been unable to carry out branch activities for the past couple of months due to her disability, to go on a training course. The union says that anyone who had not been carrying out their branch activities for this amount of time would have been refused training. The disability-related reason for the less favourable treatment is the fact that the woman has not been carrying out branch activities, and the correct comparator is a person to whom that reason does not apply – that is, someone who had been carrying out branch activities. Consequently, unless the trade union can show that the treatment is justified, it will amount to disability-related discrimination because the comparator would **not** have been refused the opportunity to go on the training course. However, the reason for the treatment is not the disability itself (it is only a matter related thereto, namely not carrying out branch activities). So there is no direct discrimination.

PART 4

4.30 The relationship between a disabled person's disability and the treatment of him by the organisation or body in question must be judged objectively. The reason for any less favourable treatment may well relate to the disability even if the organisation or body does not have knowledge of the disability as such, or of whether its salient features are such that it meets the definition of disability in the Act. Less favourable treatment which is not itself direct discrimination will still be unlawful (subject to justification) if, in fact, the reason for it relates to the person's disability.

> In the example at paragraph 4.29, the trade union did not know that the reason why the woman had not been carrying out branch activities was disability-related. Nevertheless, its refusal to allow her to attend the training course is less favourable treatment for a disability-related reason, and would be unlawful unless it can be justified.

4.31 The circumstances in which justification may be possible are explained in Chapter 6. However, it is worth noting that the possibility of justifying potential discrimination only arises at all when the form of discrimination being considered is disability-related discrimination, rather than direct discrimination or failure to make reasonable adjustments.

WHAT DOES THE ACT SAY ABOUT VICTIMISATION?

4.32 **[s 55(1) & (2)]** Victimisation is a special form of discrimination which is made unlawful by the Act. It is unlawful for one person to treat another ('the victim') less favourably than he treats or would treat other people in the same circumstances because the victim has:

- brought, or given evidence or information in connection with, proceedings under the Act (whether or not proceedings are later withdrawn)
- done anything else under or by reference to the Act, or
- alleged someone has contravened the Act (whether or not the allegation is later dropped),
- or because the person believes or suspects that the victim has done or intends to do any of these things.

> A member of a trade organisation brings a claim of discrimination against the organisation. He is accompanied to the hearing of the claim by a friend who is also a member of the organisation. This person is subsequently refused a place on a course run by the organisation because he accompanied the claimant to the hearing. This amounts to victimisation.

4.33 **[s 55(4)]** It is not victimisation to treat a person less favourably because that person has made an allegation which was false and not made in good faith.

4.34 However, the fact that a person has given evidence on behalf of an applicant in a claim which was unsuccessful does not, of itself, prove that his evidence was false or that it was not given in good faith.

4.35 **[s 55(5)]** Unlike the other forms of discrimination which are made unlawful by the Act, victimisation may be claimed by people who are not disabled as well as by those who are.

HOW DO THE DIFFERENT FORMS OF DISCRIMINATION COMPARE IN PRACTICE?

4.36 The way in which the different forms of discrimination which are unlawful under Part 2 may operate in practice can be demonstrated by the following series of examples.

> A disabled person who has multiple sclerosis applies to go to a union conference which lasts for one week. She mentions her disability on the booking form, but says that it would not affect her ability to attend. Nevertheless, the conference organiser wrongly assumes that the woman's disability will prevent her from participating at the conference and she is refused a place. This is direct discrimination.

In the situation described above, the woman states on the booking form that she will have to miss one day of the conference in order to have hospital treatment in relation to her disability. Because full attendance is required of all conference participants, she is refused a place. This is not direct discrimination, as the reason for the refusal of a place was not the woman's disability, but the fact that she would not be able to attend the conference in full.

However, the trade union has a duty to make reasonable adjustments. In order to prevent the disabled woman being substantially disadvantaged by the union's policy of only allowing people to attend the conference if they can attend it in full, it may be a reasonable adjustment for the union to waive this requirement. If so, the union will be unlawfully discriminating against the woman by refusing to do this.

Although there is no direct discrimination, the union has still treated the woman less favourably for a reason relating to her disability (namely, the fact that she cannot attend the conference in full). This will be disability-related discrimination unless the union can show that it is justified – and the union will be unable to show this if it would have been reasonable for it to have waived the requirement for full attendance.

Because of the way in which she has been treated, the woman makes a claim against the trade union under Part 2 of the Act. Some time later, however, she asks for union representation in relation to a grievance at work. Her request is rejected because she has previously made a claim against the union. This is victimisation.

WHAT DOES THE ACT SAY ABOUT HARASSMENT?

4.37 **[s 3B(1)]** The Act says that harassment occurs where, for a reason which relates to a person's disability, another person engages in unwanted conduct which has the purpose or effect of:

- violating the disabled person's dignity, or
- creating an intimidating, hostile, degrading, humiliating or offensive environment for him.

4.38 **[s 3B(2)]** If the conduct in question was engaged in with the intention that it should have either of these effects, then it amounts to harassment irrespective of its actual effect on the disabled person. In the absence of such intention, however, the conduct will only amount to harassment if it should reasonably be considered as having either of these effects. Regard must be had to all the circumstances in order to determine whether this is the case. Those circumstances include, in particular, the perception of the disabled person.

An assessor from a motor mechanics qualifications body is judging a number of practical tasks performed in the workplace by a trainee motor mechanic who has a speech impairment. The assessor imitates the mechanic's manner of speech and makes offensive remarks about him to the trainee's line manager. This is harassment, whether or not the disabled man was present when the comments were made, because they were made with the intention of humiliating him.

At an awards ceremony of a trade organisation, a member of the organisation makes a speech including derogatory remarks about people with schizophrenia. A woman with schizophrenia who is a member of the trade organisation and who is present in the audience complains about the speech but is told that the comments were made as a joke and that the speaker did not have any intention of causing offence. Nevertheless the experience of the woman is likely to amount to harassment because the comments made by the speaker could reasonably be considered as having either of the effects mentioned above.

A trade union member with HIV uses another member's mug at a union meeting. The other member then makes a point of being seen washing the mug with bleach, which is

PART 4

not something she would do if anyone else used her mug. She also makes offensive comments about having her mug used by someone with HIV. This is likely to amount to harassment.

A trade union branch representative circulates a joke about people with autism by email to branch members. A member with autism receives the email and finds the joke offensive. This is likely to amount to harassment.

WHAT DOES THE ACT SAY ABOUT STATUTORY OBLIGATIONS?

4.39 **[s 59]** Nothing is made unlawful by the Act if it is required by an express statutory obligation. However, it is only in cases where a statutory obligation is specific in its requirements, leaving a trade organisation or qualifications body with no choice other than to act in a particular way, that the provisions of the Act may be overridden. The provision in section 59 of the Act is thus of narrow application, and it is likely to permit disability discrimination only in rare circumstances.

WHAT EVIDENCE IS NEEDED TO PROVE THAT DISCRIMINATION OR HARASSMENT HAS OCCURRED?

4.40 As stated in paragraph 3.30, enforcement of rights under Part 2 takes place in the employment tribunals. A person who brings a claim for unlawful discrimination or harassment must show that discrimination has occurred. He must prove this on the balance of probabilities in order to succeed with a claim in an employment tribunal.

4.41 **[s 17A(1C)]** However, the Act says that, when such a claim is heard by an employment tribunal, the tribunal must uphold the claim if:

- the claimant proves facts from which the tribunal could conclude in the absence of an adequate explanation that the person against whom the claim is made (the respondent) has acted unlawfully, and
- the respondent fails to prove that he did not act in that way.

A disabled man with autism is the only trade union branch member in the workplace not to be sent an email inviting him to stand for election as a branch representative. Unless the union demonstrates a non-discriminatory reason for this omission, unlawful discrimination will be inferred in these circumstances.

4.42 Consequently, where a disabled person is able to prove on the balance of probabilities facts from which an inference of unlawful discrimination or harassment could be drawn, the burden of proof shifts to the respondent, who must then show that it is more likely than not that its conduct was not unlawful. This principle applies to allegations in respect of all forms of discrimination, including victimisation, and to harassment. Its practical effect in relation to the three principal forms of disability discrimination can be summarised as follows:

- To prove an allegation of **direct discrimination**, a claimant must prove facts from which it could be inferred in the absence of an adequate explanation that he has been treated less favourably on the ground of his disability than an appropriate comparator has been, or would be, treated. If the claimant does this, the claim will succeed unless the respondent can show that disability was not any part of the reason for the treatment in question.
- To prove an allegation that there has been a **failure to comply with a duty to make reasonable adjustments**, a claimant must prove facts from which it could be inferred in the absence of an adequate explanation that such a duty has arisen, and that it has been breached. If the claimant does this, the claim will succeed unless the respondent can show that it did not fail to comply with its duty in this regard.
- To prove an allegation of **disability-related discrimination**, a claimant must prove facts from which it could be inferred in the absence of an adequate explanation that, for a reason relating to his disability, he has been treated less favourably than a person

to whom that reason does not apply has been, or would be, treated. If the claimant does this, the burden of proof shifts, and it is for the respondent to show that the claimant has not received less favourable treatment for a disability-related reason. Even if the respondent cannot show this, however, the claim will not succeed if the respondent shows that the treatment was justified.

4.43 **[s 56]** The Act provides a means by which a disabled person can seek evidence about whether he has been discriminated against, or subjected to harassment, under Part 2. He may do this by using a questionnaire to obtain further information from a person he thinks has acted unlawfully in relation to him (see paragraph 10.5). If there has been a failure to provide a satisfactory response to questions asked by the disabled person in this way, inferences may be drawn from that failure.

4.44 In addition, the fact that there has been a failure to comply with a relevant provision of the Code must be taken into account by a court or tribunal, where it considers it relevant, in determining whether there has been discrimination or harassment (see paragraph 1.7).

[4681]

5. WHAT IS THE DUTY TO MAKE REASONABLE ADJUSTMENTS?

INTRODUCTION

5.1 In Chapter 4 it was noted that one of the ways in which discrimination occurs under Part 2 of the Act is when a trade organisation or a qualifications body fails to comply with a duty imposed on it to make 'reasonable adjustments' in relation to the disabled person. This chapter examines the circumstances in which a duty to make reasonable adjustments arises and outlines what a trade organisation or qualifications body needs to do in order to discharge such a duty.

WHEN DOES THE DUTY TO MAKE REASONABLE ADJUSTMENTS ARISE?

5.2 **[s 14(1) & s 14B(1)]** Subject to what is said in paragraph 5.7, the duty to make reasonable adjustments arises where a provision, criterion or practice applied by or on behalf of a trade organisation or a qualifications body, or any physical feature of premises which it occupies, places a disabled person at a substantial disadvantage compared with people who are not disabled. The trade organisation or qualifications body has to take such steps as it is reasonable for it to have to take in all the circumstances to prevent that disadvantage – in other words it has to make a 'reasonable adjustment'. Where the duty arises, an organisation or body cannot justify a failure to make a reasonable adjustment.

> A trade organisation for hairdressers arranges a one-day training course in colouring techniques for its members. A disabled member wishes to attend this course, but the programme for the day does not allow him sufficient rest breaks. He would therefore be at a substantial disadvantage because of his disability. The trade organisation rearranges the programme for the day to include more breaks. This is likely to be a reasonable adjustment for it to make.

> A trade organisation for carpenters has an application form with several paragraphs in small print. A partially sighted carpenter cannot read the whole form and is therefore at a substantial disadvantage because he cannot fill it in correctly. The trade organisation provides him with an application form in large print. This is likely to be a reasonable adjustment for it to make.

> A qualifications body holds an awards ceremony at its headquarters. A newly qualified woman who uses a wheelchair wants to attend the ceremony but is at a substantial disadvantage because the stage where the awards are presented is only accessible by stairs. The qualifications body provides a ramp up to the stage. This is likely to be a reasonable adjustment for the qualifications body to make.

> A disabled woman who is unable to use public transport wishes to attend a trade fair in central London, organised by a trade organisation of which she is a member. There is very little parking in the area and the information brochure suggests that 'visitors to the trade fair are advised to come by public transport'. The woman asks the trade organisation if it can arrange a parking space and it does so. This is likely to be a reasonable adjustment for the trade organisation to make.

5.3 It does not matter if a disabled person cannot point to an actual non-disabled person compared with whom he is at a substantial disadvantage. The fact that a non-disabled person, or even another disabled person, would not be substantially disadvantaged by the provision, criterion or practice or by the physical feature in question is irrelevant. The duty is owed specifically to the individual disabled person.

WHICH DISABLED PEOPLE DOES THE DUTY PROTECT?

5.4 In order to avoid discrimination, it is prudent not to attempt to make a fine judgement as to whether a particular individual falls within the statutory definition of disability, but to focus instead on meeting the needs of each individual with whom a trade organisation or qualifications body has dealings. However, the Act says that the duties are owed to the following people:

- **[s 14(2)]** disabled people who are members of trade organisations, or who are applicants, or potential applicants, for membership of such organisations, and
- **[s 14B(2)]** disabled people who are holders of professional or trade qualifications, or who are applicants, or potential applicants, for such qualifications.

5.5 The extent of the duty to make reasonable adjustments depends on the circumstances of the disabled person in question. For example, more extensive duties are owed to members of trade organisations and holders of professional or trade qualifications than to people who are merely thinking about applying. More extensive duties are also owed to current members and qualification holders than to past members or to people who no longer hold a qualification. The extent to which trade organisations and qualifications bodies have knowledge of relevant circumstances is also a factor. These issues are explained in more detail in Chapters 7 and 8.

WHAT ARE 'PROVISIONS, CRITERIA AND PRACTICES'?

5.6 **[s 18D(2)]** Provisions, criteria and practices include arrangements, for example for determining who to accept as a member of a trade organisation, or upon whom to confer a professional or trade qualification, as well as the rules of membership of an organisation. The duty to make reasonable adjustments applies, for example, to selection and interview procedures for trade organisations and to examination and assessment procedures used by qualifications bodies. In addition, the duty applies to premises used for such procedures.

> A trade union requires its members to be either employed or seeking employment in a specific sector. A woman with a spinal injury as a result of an accident is not in work or looking for work, because she is adjusting to her newly acquired disability, but nevertheless would like to remain a member of the union, as it would help her to maintain contact with the sector in which she worked prior to her accident. The union agrees that she can retain her membership. This is likely to be a reasonable adjustment for the trade union to make to a criterion (in this case a membership criterion).

5.7 **[s 14B(1)]** It should be noted that, in relation to qualifications bodies, there is no duty to make any adjustment to a provision, criterion or practice of a kind which the Act defines as a 'competence standard'. What the Act says about competence standards is considered in more detail in paragraphs 8.27 to 8.40.

WHAT IS A 'PHYSICAL FEATURE'?

5.8 **[s 18D(2)]** The Act says that the following are to be treated as a physical feature:

- any feature arising from the design or construction of a building on the premises occupied by the trade organisation or qualifications body
- any feature on the premises of any approach to, exit from, or access to such a building
- any fixtures, fittings, furnishings, furniture, equipment or materials in or on the premises, and
- any other physical element or quality of any land comprised in the premises occupied by the trade organisation or qualifications body.

All these features are covered, whether temporary or permanent. Considerations which need to be taken into account when making adjustments to premises are explained in Chapter 9.

> The design of a professional association's training facility makes it difficult for a person with a visual impairment to find his way around, as there are glass doors, glass panels and reflecting surfaces. That is a substantial disadvantage caused by the physical features of the professional association's premises.

5.9 Physical features will include steps, stairways, kerbs, exterior surfaces and paving, parking areas, building entrances and exits (including emergency escape routes), internal and external doors, gates, toilet and washing facilities, lighting and ventilation, lifts and escalators, floor coverings, signs, furniture, and temporary or movable items. This is not an exhaustive list.

WHAT DISADVANTAGES GIVE RISE TO THE DUTY?

5.10 The Act says that only substantial disadvantages give rise to the duty. Substantial disadvantages are those which are not minor or trivial. Whether or not such a disadvantage exists in a particular case is a question of fact. What matters is not that a provision, criterion or practice or a physical feature is capable of causing a substantial disadvantage to the disabled person in question, but that it actually has (or would have) this effect on him.

IS KNOWLEDGE OF THE DISABILITY A FACTOR?

5.11 **[s 14(3) & s 14B(3)]** Although (as explained in paragraphs 4.11 and 4.30) less favourable treatment can occur even if a trade organisation or qualifications body does not know that the person is disabled, the organisation or body only has a duty to make an adjustment if it knows, or could reasonably be expected to know, that the person has a disability and is likely to be placed at a substantial disadvantage. A trade organisation or qualifications body must, however, do all it can reasonably be expected to do to find out whether this is the case. More information is given in Chapters 7 and 8 about the relationship between the knowledge of a trade organisation or qualifications body and its duties under the Act.

WHAT ADJUSTMENTS MIGHT HAVE TO BE MADE?

5.12 **[s 18B(2)]** The Act gives a number of examples of adjustments, or 'steps', which persons who are subject to the duty may have to take, if it is reasonable for them to have to do so (see paragraphs 5.14 to 5.25). Any necessary adjustments should be implemented in a timely fashion, and it may also be necessary to make more than one adjustment. It is advisable to agree any proposed adjustments with the disabled person in question before they are made. The Act does not give an exhaustive list of the steps which may have to be taken to discharge the duty. Not all of the steps listed in the Act are likely to be relevant to trade organisations and qualifications bodies. By the same token, steps other than those listed, or a combination of steps, will sometimes have to be taken. However, the steps in the Act which it is likely to be reasonable for trade organisations and qualifications bodies to have to take are:

- making adjustments to premises

> A trade organisation or qualifications body might have to make structural or other physical changes such as: widening a doorway, providing a ramp or moving furniture for a wheelchair user; relocating light switches, door handles or shelves for someone who has difficulty in reaching; providing appropriate contrast in décor to help the safe mobility of a visually impaired person.

PART 4

- giving, or arranging for, training or mentoring (whether for the disabled person or any other person)

This could be training in the use of particular pieces of equipment which the disabled person uses while participating in activities as a benefit of their membership of the trade organisation, or training which any member can take part in but which needs altering for the disabled person because of their disability. For example, all members might have the opportunity to be trained to use the trade organisation's library computer system but the trade organisation might have to provide longer or different training for a disabled person.

A trade union provides training for a branch in conducting meetings in a way that enables a deaf branch member to participate.

A disabled member of a professional association wishes to become a fellow of the organisation but has concerns about the requirement to pass an assessment – an oral presentation to fellows of the association with questions and answers – as she has a speech impairment. The professional association arranges for her to see a mentor (in this case a disabled fellow of the same organisation) to support her in achieving fellowship status.

- acquiring or modifying equipment

A trade organisation or qualifications body might have to provide special equipment for a disabled person to enable him to take part in activities or benefit from services provided by the organisation or body. There is no requirement to provide or modify equipment for personal purposes unconnected with the person's dealings with the trade organisation or qualifications body, for example to provide a wheelchair if a person needs one in any event but does not have one.

- modifying instructions or reference manuals

The way instructions are normally given might need to be revised when telling a disabled person how to do a task. The format of instructions or reference manuals may need to be modified (eg produced in Braille or on audio tape) and instructions for people with learning disabilities may need to be conveyed orally with individual demonstration.

- modifying procedures for testing or assessment

This could involve ensuring that particular testing methods do not adversely affect particular disabled people. For example, a person with restricted manual dexterity might be disadvantaged by a hand written test and would need to have an alternative arrangement such as an oral test or to be permitted to use a computer with voice recognition software. More information about how the Act affects testing and examinations is set out in Chapter 8.

- providing a reader or interpreter

> This could involve the provision of a sign language interpreter for meetings, talks or training; or could involve provision of a reader for a visually impaired person.

- providing supervision or other support

> This could involve the provision of a support worker to enable a disabled person to participate in a conference, meeting, training session, interview, examination, assessment or social event; or extra support for a disabled trade union representative to enable that person to fulfil their role on an on-going basis.

5.13 As mentioned above, it may be reasonable for a trade organisation or qualifications body to take steps which are not given as examples in the Act. Such steps might include:

- conducting a proper assessment of what reasonable adjustments may be required
- modifying the arrangements for meetings, and
- making adjustments to the way in which information is provided.

Further examples of the way in which reasonable adjustments work in practice are given in Chapters 7 and 8.

WHEN IS IT 'REASONABLE' FOR A TRADE ORGANISATION OR QUALIFICATIONS BODY TO HAVE TO MAKE ADJUSTMENTS?

5.14 Whether it is reasonable for a trade organisation or qualifications body to make any particular adjustment will depend on a number of things, such as its cost and effectiveness. However, if an adjustment is one which it is reasonable to make, then the organisation or body must do so. Where a disabled person is placed at a substantial disadvantage by a provision, criterion or practice of the organisation or body, or by a physical feature of the premises it occupies, the organisation or body must consider whether any reasonable adjustments can be made to overcome that disadvantage. There is no onus on the disabled person to suggest what adjustments should be made but, where the disabled person does so, the organisation or body must consider whether such adjustments would help overcome the disadvantage, and whether they are reasonable.

5.15 Nevertheless, an organisation or body may not know enough about the disabled person to determine what adjustments are appropriate. It is therefore good practice to ask a disabled person whether he requires any adjustments to be made. It is also a good idea for a disabled person to make suggestions about adjustments which would be helpful.

5.16 Effective and practicable adjustments for disabled people often involve little or no cost or disruption and are therefore very likely to be reasonable for a trade organisation or qualifications body to have to make. Many adjustments do not involve making physical changes to premises. However, where such changes do need to be made, trade organisations and qualifications bodies may need to take account of the considerations explained in Chapter 9, which deals with issues about making alterations to premises.

> A qualifications body allows a student to have extra time to take a written test because the student has dyslexia. This adjustment only involves the cost of paying an invigilator for the extra time in question, and is likely to be a reasonable one to make.

> A trade union member with a hearing impairment requests a seat at the front of the conference hall, so that she can lip read. This is likely to be a reasonable adjustment for the trade union to make and would involve no additional cost and no disruption to the union.

> A member of a professional association attending a meeting at that association asks for a mug half full of tea, rather than a china tea cup and saucer, because she has a hand tremor due to a neurological condition. This would involve very little cost or disruption to the professional association and is likely to be a reasonable adjustment to make.

5.17 **[SI 1999/3242]** If making a particular adjustment would increase the risks to the health and safety of any person (including the disabled person in question) then this is a relevant factor in deciding whether it is reasonable to make that adjustment. Suitable and sufficient risk assessments, such as those carried out for the purposes of the Management of Health and Safety at Work Regulations 1999, should be used to help determine whether such risks are likely to arise.

5.18 **[s 18B(1)]** The Act lists a number of factors which may, in particular, have a bearing on whether it will be reasonable to have to make a particular adjustment. These factors make a useful checklist, particularly when considering more substantial adjustments. The effectiveness and practicability of a particular adjustment might be considered first. If it is practicable and effective, the financial aspects might be looked at as a whole – cost of the adjustment and resources available to fund it. Other factors might also have a bearing. The factors in the Act include the following:

The effectiveness of the step in preventing the disadvantage

5.19 It is unlikely to be reasonable to have to make an adjustment involving little benefit to the disabled person. However, such an adjustment may be one of several adjustments which, when looked at together, would be effective and, in that case, it is likely to be reasonable to have to make it.

The practicability of the step

5.20 It is more likely to be reasonable to have to take a step which is easy to take than one which is difficult. In some circumstances it may be reasonable to have to take a step, even though it is difficult.

> A trade organisation is asked by a woman with a severe allergy to many commonly found substances (such as latex) to ensure that a venue for a lecture is free of all these substances. This is likely to be an impractical step to take. However, it may instead be reasonable for the trade organisation to provide the woman with a video of the lecture.

The financial and other costs of the adjustment and the extent of any disruption caused

5.21 If an adjustment costs little or nothing and is not disruptive, it would be reasonable unless some other factor (such as practicability or effectiveness) made it unreasonable. It may, of course, be reasonable to have to make more expensive adjustments in some circumstances. The costs to be taken into account include those for staff and other resources. The significance of the cost of a step may depend in part on what the trade organisation or qualifications body might otherwise spend in the circumstances. In assessing the likely costs of making an adjustment, the availability of external funding should be taken into account.

The extent of the financial or other resources available to the trade organisation or qualifications body

5.22 It is more likely to be reasonable for a trade organisation or qualifications body with substantial financial resources to have to make an adjustment with a significant cost, than for one with fewer resources. The resources in practice available to the organisation or body as a whole should be taken into account as well as other calls on those resources. It is good practice for organisations and bodies to have a specific budget for reasonable adjustments – but limitations on the size of any such budget will not affect the existence of the duties owed to disabled people. The reasonableness of an adjustment will depend not only on the resources in practice available for the adjustment but also on all other relevant factors (such as effectiveness and practicability).

> A large professional association with 300,000 members and considerable funds would be expected to make more substantial changes to its premises, in order to make them accessible for a member, than would a small trade organisation with only fifty members and very limited funds.

> A union branch is sending a disabled representative to a regional 3-day conference. The disabled person, who has cerebral palsy, requires a support worker to accompany her to the conference. Although the cost of providing this support would be relatively high compared to the resources available to the branch, the cost is unlikely to be seen as unreasonably high when assessed against the overall funds of the union.

The availability of financial or other assistance to help make an adjustment

5.23 The availability of outside help may well be a relevant factor. This help may be financial or practical. Disability organisations and bodies like the DRC may be able to provide further information or assistance.

5.24 A disabled person is not required to contribute to the cost of a reasonable adjustment. However, if a disabled person has a particular piece of special or adapted equipment which he is prepared to use, this might make it reasonable for a trade organisation or qualifications body to have to take some other step (as well as allowing the use of the equipment).

> A blind person wishes to go to an event organised by a trade organisation of which she is a member. She wishes to take notes at this event using a laptop computer. The trade organisation provides her with a table to put the computer on while she takes notes. This is likely to be a reasonable adjustment for the organisation to make.

The nature of the activities of the organisation or body, and the size of its undertaking

5.25 The size of an organisation or body's undertaking and the nature of its activities may be relevant in determining the reasonableness of a particular step.

CAN FAILURE TO MAKE A REASONABLE ADJUSTMENT EVER BE JUSTIFIED?

5.26 **[s 3A(2)]** The Act does not permit a trade organisation or qualifications body to justify a failure to comply with a duty to make a reasonable adjustment. This is a change in the law (see Appendix A).

5.27 Clearly, however, an organisation or body will only breach such a duty if the adjustment in question is one which it is reasonable for it to have to make. So, where the duty applies, it is the question of 'reasonableness' which alone determines whether the adjustment has to be made.

> A woman with severe back pain wishes to attend a trade union conference. The only adjustment she needs is for a space to be made available for her to set up a portable couch on which she can lie down during the conference proceedings. This is likely to be a reasonable adjustment for the trade union to make. It involves no cost and little disruption for the union. Nevertheless, the union does not allow this as it says "nobody has ever needed this adjustment before and there may be health and safety implications". The trade union will be acting unlawfully.

6. JUSTIFICATION

INTRODUCTION

6.1 Most conduct which is potentially unlawful under Part 2 of the Act cannot be justified. Conduct which amounts to:

- direct discrimination
- failure to comply with a duty to make a reasonable adjustment
- victimisation
- harassment
- instructions or pressure to discriminate, or
- aiding an unlawful act

is unlawful irrespective of the reason or motive for it.

WHEN DOES THE ACT PERMIT JUSTIFICATION?

6.2 Paragraph 4.26 explains that one of the forms of discrimination which is unlawful under Part 2 is disability-related discrimination. However, the conduct of a trade organisation or qualifications body towards a disabled person does not amount to disability-related discrimination if it can be justified. This chapter explains the limited circumstances in which this may happen.

6.3 **[s 3A(3) & (4)]** Where less favourable treatment of a disabled person is capable of being justified (that is, where it is **not** direct discrimination), the Act says that it will, in fact, be justified if, but only if, the reason for the treatment is both material to the circumstances of the particular case **and** substantial. This is an objective test. 'Material' means that there must be a reasonably strong connection between the reason given for the treatment and the circumstances of the particular case. 'Substantial' means, in the context of justification, that the reason must carry real weight and be of substance.

6.4 **[s 14A(3)]** This general principle is subject to one exception – which relates to the application of a 'competence standard' to a disabled person by a qualifications body. The Act says that less favourable treatment of a disabled person in this regard will be justified only if the qualifications body can show that the standard is (or would be) applied equally to people who do not have the disabled person's disability, and that its application is a proportionate means of achieving a legitimate aim. What the Act says about competence standards is considered in more detail in paragraphs 8.27 to 8.40.

6.5 In certain circumstances, the existence of a material and substantial reason for less favourable treatment is not enough to justify that treatment. This is the case where a trade organisation or qualifications body is also under a duty to make reasonable adjustments in relation to the disabled person but fails to comply with that duty.

6.6 **[s 3A(6)]** In those circumstances, it is necessary to consider not only whether there is a material and substantial reason for the less favourable treatment, but also whether the treatment would still have been justified even if the organisation or body had complied with its duty to make reasonable adjustments. In effect, it is necessary to ask the question "would a reasonable adjustment have made any difference?" If a reasonable adjustment would have made a difference to the reason that is being used to justify the treatment, then the less favourable treatment cannot be justified.

6.7 In relation to disability-related discrimination, the fact that a trade organisation or qualifications body has failed to comply with a duty to make a reasonable adjustment means that the sequence of events for justifying disability-related less favourable treatment is as follows:

- The disabled person proves facts from which it could be inferred in the absence of an adequate explanation that:
  a. for a reason related to his disability, he has been treated less favourably than a person to whom that reason does not apply has been, or would be, treated, and
  b. a duty to make a reasonable adjustment has arisen in respect of him and the organisation or body has failed to comply with it.
- The trade organisation or qualifications body will be found to have discriminated unless it proves that:
  a. the reason for the treatment is both material to the circumstances of the particular case and substantial, and
  b. the reason would still have applied if the reasonable adjustment had been made.

CAN HEALTH AND SAFETY CONCERNS JUSTIFY LESS FAVOURABLE TREATMENT?

6.8 Stereotypical assumptions about the health and safety implications of disability should be avoided, both in general terms and in relation to particular types of disability.

Indeed, less favourable treatment which is based on such assumptions may itself amount to direct discrimination – which is incapable of justification (see paragraph 4.5). The fact that a person has a disability does not necessarily mean that he represents an additional risk to health and safety.

> A person with bi-polar affective disorder applies for registration as a health professional with a professional association. The association refuses to register her, simply on the basis that she has mentioned her disability on a health questionnaire. The association makes an assumption that her disability would present a health and safety risk, without making any attempt to find out whether or how it would present such a risk, or indeed whether she had made a recovery. This is likely to be direct discrimination and therefore to be unlawful.

6.9 Genuine concerns about the health and safety of anybody (including a disabled person) may be relevant when seeking to establish that disability-related less favourable treatment of a disabled person is justified. However, it is important to remember that health and safety legislation does not require the removal of all conceivable risk but that risk is properly appreciated, understood and managed. Further information can be obtained from the Health and Safety Executive (see Appendix C for details).

6.10 Paragraphs 6.11 to 6.15 examine the circumstances in which concerns about health and safety may justify less favourable treatment of a disabled person, and this is followed by a consideration of the relevance of medical information in this context. As noted in paragraph 6.4, however, the basis upon which a qualifications body may justify less favourable treatment of a disabled person in the application of a competence standard differs from that which usually applies under the Act. The following principles do not have the same relevance to justification in those circumstances, but regard should instead be had to paragraphs 8.35 to 8.40.

6.11 It is the trade organisation or qualifications body which must decide what action to take in response to concerns about health and safety. However, leaving aside the question of competence standards, it is prudent for a trade organisation or qualifications body to have a risk assessment carried out by a suitably qualified person in circumstances where it has reason to think that the effects of a person's disability may give rise to an issue about health and safety. This is because:

- If a trade organisation or qualifications body treats a disabled person less favourably merely on the basis of generalised assumptions about the health and safety implications of having a disability, such treatment may itself amount to direct discrimination – which is incapable of justification.

> A qualifications body refuses to issue a certificate to operate heavy machinery to a man with epilepsy. No attempt is made to find out the actual circumstances of the individual through a risk assessment. The qualifications body merely makes an assumption that it would be a health and safety risk to let someone with epilepsy operate heavy machinery. This is likely to be direct discrimination and therefore to be unlawful.

- Even where there is no direct discrimination, an organisation or body which treats a disabled person less favourably without having a suitable and sufficient risk assessment carried out is unlikely to be able to show that its concerns about health and safety justify the less favourable treatment.

6.12 Nevertheless, a trade organisation or qualifications body should not subject a disabled person to a risk assessment if this is not merited by the particular circumstances of the case.

> A man who has diabetes applies to go on a residential training course in accounting provided by a professional association of which he is a member. The man's condition is stable and he has successfully managed it for many years. Nevertheless, the association says that it has health and safety concerns; that it wants to undertake a risk assessment;

> and that it needs further medical evidence from the man's doctor. This is likely to be unlawful, as the circumstances of the case do not indicate that there would be any health and safety risk.

6.13 A risk assessment must be suitable and sufficient. It should identify the risks associated with a particular activity, taking account of any reasonable adjustments put in place for the disabled person, and should be specific for the individual carrying out a particular task. It is therefore unlikely that a trade organisation or qualifications body which has a **general** policy of treating people with certain disabilities (such as epilepsy, diabetes or mental health problems) less favourably than other people will be able to justify doing so – even if that policy is in accordance with the advice of an occupational health adviser.

6.14 A 'blanket' policy of this nature will usually be unlawful. This is because it is likely to amount to direct discrimination (which cannot ever be justified) or to disability-related less favourable treatment which is not justifiable in the circumstances – ie, disability-related discrimination.

> A qualifications body for social care professionals has a policy of asking applicants for registration to fill out a health questionnaire. Any applicant who states that they have had treatment for a mental health problem is refused registration without any investigation into their individual circumstances. The qualifications body is applying a blanket policy, which is likely to amount to direct discrimination.

6.15 Reasonable adjustments made by a trade organisation or qualifications body may remove or reduce health and safety risks related to a person's disability. A suitable and sufficient assessment of such risks therefore needs to take account of the impact which making any reasonable adjustments would have. If a risk assessment is not conducted on this basis, then an organisation or body is unlikely to be able to show that its concerns about health and safety justify less favourable treatment of the disabled person.

CAN MEDICAL INFORMATION JUSTIFY LESS FAVOURABLE TREATMENT?

6.16 Consideration of medical information (such as a doctor's report or the answers to a medical questionnaire) is likely to form part of an assessment of health and safety risks. In most cases, however, having a disability does not adversely affect a person's general health. In other cases, its effect on a person's health may fluctuate. Although medical information about a disability may justify an adverse decision, it will not do so if there is no effect on the person's relevant skills and abilities (or if any effect is less than substantial), no matter how great the effects of the disability are in other ways. Indeed, less favourable treatment of a disabled person in a case where his disability has no effect on his relevant skills and abilities may well amount to direct discrimination – which is incapable of being justified.

6.17 In addition, where medical information is available, trade organisations and qualifications bodies must weigh it up in the context of the relevant circumstances, and the capabilities of the individual. An organisation or body should also consider whether reasonable adjustments could be made in order to overcome any problems which may have been identified as a result of the medical information. It should not be taken for granted that the person who provides the medical information will be aware that trade organisations and qualifications bodies have a duty to make reasonable adjustments, or what these adjustments might be. It is good practice, therefore, to ensure that medical advisers are made aware of these matters. Information provided by a medical adviser should only be relied on if the adviser has the appropriate knowledge and expertise.

6.18 In any event, although medical evidence may generally be considered as an 'expert contribution', it should not ordinarily be the sole factor influencing a decision by a trade organisation or qualifications body. The views of the disabled person (about his own capabilities and possible adjustments) should also be sought. It may also be possible to seek help from disability organisations. Ultimately, it is for the trade organisation or qualifications body – and not the medical adviser – to take decisions.

[4683]

7. DISCRIMINATION BY TRADE ORGANISATIONS

INTRODUCTION

7.1 Chapter 3 explains what the Act means by 'trade organisation', and that the Act makes it unlawful for a trade organisation to discriminate against a disabled person who is a member of the organisation or an applicant for membership. Chapter 3 also explains that the Act says it is unlawful for a trade organisation to subject such a person to harassment, or to victimise any person – whether disabled or not.

7.2 This chapter looks at discrimination by trade organisations in more detail. In order to do so, (and after considering an important point about the relationship of trade organisations to qualifications bodies), it is necessary to look at the different aspects of a trade organisation's functions, from those which relate to becoming a member of the organisation to those which concern the benefits of membership once achieved. It is also necessary to consider issues relating to the variation and withdrawal of membership.

TRADE ORGANISATIONS AS QUALIFICATIONS BODIES

7.3 It has already been noted (at paragraph 3.11) that some trade organisations confer professional or trade qualifications and that, as a consequence, such organisations can be subject to the Act's provisions about trade organisations or, depending upon the context, to those about qualifications bodies.

7.4 However, it should also be noted that membership of certain trade organisations (for example, the Institute of Linguists or the Chartered Institute of Personnel and Development) itself amounts to a professional or trade qualification for the reasons explained at paragraph 8.6. Where this is the case, decisions about granting, varying or withdrawing membership of the trade organisation will also be subject to the rules about conferring professional or trade qualifications. This fact is likely to be of particular significance where such decisions result from the application of a 'competence standard' (see paragraphs 8.27 to 8.40).

BECOMING A MEMBER

What does the Act say?

7.5 **[s 13(1)]** The Act says that it is unlawful for a trade organisation to discriminate against a disabled person:

- in the arrangements it makes for the purpose of determining who should be offered membership of the organisation

> A trade organisation asks a woman with a learning disability to take an additional test before allowing her membership, even though she already meets the entry criteria for that organisation. This is likely to be unlawful.

- in the terms on which it is prepared to admit him to membership

> A trade organisation for journalists asks a partially sighted woman to pay an extra fee for membership because of the cost of putting information onto audio tape. This is likely to be unlawful.

- by refusing to accept, or deliberately not accepting, his application for membership.

> A nursing organisation refuses to admit a woman with a history of mental health problems – without further enquiry. This is likely to be unlawful.

7.6 **[s 16B]** As explained at paragraphs 3.22 to 3.25, the Act also makes it unlawful in certain circumstances to publish a discriminatory advertisement for membership of a trade organisation.

What amounts to direct discrimination?

7.7 **[s 3A(5)]** A trade organisation may wish to differentiate between individuals when dealing with applications for membership of the organisation. However, in doing so, it should avoid discriminating against disabled applicants or potential applicants. As explained in Chapter 4, treating a disabled person in a different way from the way in which other people are (or would be) treated amounts to discrimination in certain circumstances. In particular, such treatment is unlawful if it amounts to direct discrimination under Part 2. As explained at paragraph 4.5, treatment of a disabled person amounts to direct discrimination if:

- it is on the ground of his disability
- the treatment is less favourable than the way in which a person not having that particular disability is (or would be) treated, and
- the relevant circumstances, including the abilities, of the person with whom the comparison is made are the same as, or not materially different from, those of the disabled person.

> A trade organisation refuses to let a woman who has schizophrenia become a member, even though the woman has shown that she has sufficient qualifications and experience to gain membership. This is likely to amount to direct discrimination, because she is being treated less favourably on the ground of her disability. The treatment is less favourable than the way in which someone who does not have schizophrenia would be treated; the relevant circumstances of the woman (in this case her qualifications and experience) are the same as those of other candidates who do not have schizophrenia.

What amounts to disability-related discrimination?

7.8 **[s 3A(1)]** Less favourable treatment of a disabled person may be unlawful under the Act even if it does not amount to direct discrimination. This will be the case if it amounts to disability-related discrimination instead. As explained at paragraph 4.26, this is less favourable treatment which is for a reason related to the person's disability. However, unlike treatment which amounts to direct discrimination (and which is therefore incapable of justification), a trade organisation's treatment of a disabled person does not amount to disability-related discrimination if the organisation can show that it is justified. The circumstances in which this may be possible are explained in Chapter 6.

7.9 In summary, less favourable treatment of a disabled person will be unlawful if it amounts either to direct discrimination or to disability-related discrimination, and involves:

- a trade organisation's arrangements for selecting new members
- the terms on which membership is offered, or
- the rejection or non-acceptance of an application for membership.

When does the duty to make reasonable adjustments apply to applicants and potential applicants for membership?

7.10 **[s 14]** The duty of a trade organisation to make reasonable adjustments obviously applies in respect of its disabled members. However, the duty also applies in respect of any disabled person who is, or has notified the organisation that he may be, an applicant for membership.

> A disabled man, who is unable to write because of his disability, requests an electronic application form from a trade organisation so that he can fill it in on his computer. The organisation may have a duty to make this reasonable adjustment because it knows that this man is a potential applicant for membership.

7.11 **[s 14(3)]** The duty only applies in respect of a disabled person if the trade organisation knows that the person is, or may be, an applicant for membership. 'Knowledge', in this context, means that the organisation knows, or could reasonably be expected to know, about this. Likewise, the duty applies only if the organisation knows that the person has a disability which is likely to place him at a substantial disadvantage in comparison with people who are not disabled.

7.12 Where a trade organisation has knowledge that a person **may be** an applicant for membership, the duty to make reasonable adjustments applies to provisions, criteria or practices for determining to whom membership should be offered. However, reasonable adjustments to premises are only required in respect of existing members and **actual** applicants for membership of whom the organisation has knowledge.

7.13 Where it applies, the duty to make reasonable adjustments is likely to affect arrangements in relation to, for example, advertisements, application forms and interviews for membership of the organisation. This is not a complete list of everything which could be covered by the duty (and which would be relevant in connection with becoming a member of a trade organisation), but it is intended as an indication of the likely relevant areas.

> A man with a speech impairment applies for membership of a professional association. The association normally conducts a short interview for its potential members. Because the man has difficulty with verbal communication he asks if he can have the interview in the form of written questions and answers. This is likely to be a reasonable adjustment to the organisation's membership arrangements.

7.14 As explained in paragraphs 5.26 and 5.27, a trade organisation is never able to justify a failure to comply with a duty to make a reasonable adjustment under the Act.

MEMBERSHIP BENEFITS

What does the Act say?

7.15 **[s 13(2)]** The Act says that it is unlawful for a trade organisation to discriminate against a disabled person who is a member of the organisation:

- in the way it affords him access to any benefits or by refusing or deliberately omitting to afford him access to them, or
- by subjecting him to any other detriment.

> An employee of a trade organisation deliberately fails to invite a member with schizophrenia to an annual dinner, because she thinks that other members may be offended by this person's behaviour, even though she has never met the member and knows nothing about his behaviour. This is likely to be unlawful.

7.16 The Act does not define what a benefit is (although it does say that benefits include facilities and services). Whether something is a benefit will depend on all the relevant circumstances, including an organisation's rules and practices. However, the following are likely to amount to benefits: training facilities, welfare or insurance services, participation at meetings and other events and invitations to attend those events, information about the organisation's activities, and assistance to members in employers' disciplinary or dismissal procedures.

When does less favourable treatment in relation to membership benefits amount to discrimination?

7.17 **[s 3A]** A trade organisation needs to take care if it differentiates between members in relation to the provision of membership benefits. For example, if the organisation's treatment of a disabled member in this regard amounts to direct discrimination under the Act (see paragraph 7.7) it will be unlawful.

7.18 Even where it is not directly discriminatory, treatment of a disabled person will be unlawful if it amounts to disability-related discrimination (see paragraph 4.26).

When does the duty to make reasonable adjustments apply in respect of membership benefits?

7.19 **[s 14]** A trade organisation has a duty to make reasonable adjustments in respect of the way it makes benefits available to its members. It owes this duty to a disabled member of the organisation if it has knowledge of the fact that he has a disability and is likely to be placed at a substantial disadvantage in comparison with people who are not disabled. The duty is likely to apply, for example, in respect of the provision of the benefits mentioned in paragraph 7.16. Where the duty does apply, the trade organisation must take such steps as are reasonable to prevent the provision, criterion or practice, or the physical feature, (as the case may be) from placing the disabled member at a substantial disadvantage.

> A trade union has a website through which it informs members about its services. A member with a learning disability requests that a summary of the information on the website is provided in a format that is easy for her to understand (Easy Read). This is likely to be a reasonable adjustment for the union to make.

> A trade organisation organises a trade fair. A blind member requests assistance at the trade fair to find his way around. This is likely to be a reasonable adjustment for the trade organisation to make.

> A deaf woman, who is a union member, has a problem at work which she wants to discuss in depth with a trade union representative. The trade union pays for and arranges a sign language interpreter for the meeting. This is likely to be a reasonable adjustment for the union to make.

7.20 For many members, the manner in which a trade organisation makes information available to them is likely to be an important issue. If this information is not provided in forms accessible to disabled people they are likely to be placed at a substantial disadvantage. However, recent technological developments have meant that it is increasingly practicable to produce material in alternative formats quickly and cheaply. Disability organisations and bodies like the DRC are able to advise trade organisations about practicable methods of providing information in an accessible way. What is reasonable will depend on the individual circumstances of the case.

> A trade organisation provides a magazine for its members. A blind member of the organisation asks for the magazine to be sent to him electronically as an email attachment so that he can read it using access software on his home computer. This is likely to be a reasonable adjustment for the trade organisation to make.

7.21 In some cases a reasonable adjustment will not work without the co-operation of other members of the organisation. Members may therefore have an important role in helping to ensure that a reasonable adjustment is carried out in practice. Subject to considerations about confidentiality (explained at paragraphs 7.34 to 7.36), trade organisations must ensure that this happens. It is unlikely to be a valid defence to a claim under the Act that members were obstructive or unhelpful when the trade organisation tried to make reasonable adjustments. A trade organisation would at least need to be able to show that it took such behaviour seriously and dealt with it appropriately. Trade organisations will be more likely to be able to do this if they establish and implement the type of policies and practices described at paragraph 2.12 (and, in the case of trade unions, 2.13).

> A professional association organises a question and answer session with a panel of experts, to which it invites members. The event is organised at a venue with an induction loop to enable a deaf member who uses a hearing aid to participate. The Chair of the event reminds all contributors to speak in turn, and only when they are holding the microphone to enable everyone present to follow the proceedings. When a member persistently speaks out of turn, without the microphone, she is reminded that the organisation has a disability policy and that contributions will not be taken from her if she continues to ignore the rules laid down for the session which were designed to enable disabled people to participate.

VARIATION AND WITHDRAWAL OF MEMBERSHIP

What does the Act say?

7.22 **[s 13(2)]** The Act says that it is unlawful for a trade organisation to discriminate against a disabled person who is a member of the organisation:

- by depriving him of membership, or varying the terms on which he is a member, or
- by subjecting him to any other detriment.

> A man who is a member of a trade organisation becomes disabled after a spinal injury. His membership is withdrawn without any consideration or consultation with him about whether or how he can still meet the membership requirements. This is likely to be direct discrimination and therefore to be unlawful.

7.23 **[s 16A]** The Act also says that, where a disabled person's membership of a trade organisation has come to an end, it is still unlawful for the trade organisation:

- to discriminate against him by subjecting him to a detriment, or
- to subject him to harassment

if the discrimination or harassment arises out of his former membership of the organisation and is closely connected to it.

7.24 **[s 55]** It is also unlawful to victimise a person (whether or not he is disabled) after he has ceased to be a member of a trade organisation (see paragraphs 4.32 to 4.35).

When does less favourable treatment in relation to variation or withdrawal of membership amount to discrimination?

7.25 **[s 3A]** If a trade organisation varies the terms on which a disabled person is a member of the organisation, or withdraws his membership, it may be treating him less favourably than it treats other members. Depending upon the circumstances, the organisation may be discriminating against the disabled person by treating him in this way. For example, if the organisation's treatment of a disabled member amounts to direct discrimination under the Act (see paragraph 7.7) it will be unlawful.

7.26 Even where it does not amount to direct discrimination, treatment of a disabled person will be unlawful if it amounts to disability-related discrimination (see paragraph 4.26).

> A member of a trade union complains about another member who has Asperger's syndrome (a form of autism) after a conference, saying that the fellow member behaved in an inappropriate way whilst at the conference hotel. The man's behaviour was related to his disability but she was not aware of this at the time. The trade union disciplines the disabled man and his membership is withdrawn, even though the union knows about his disability. This is likely to be less favourable treatment for a disability-related reason and is therefore likely to be unlawful, unless the trade union can show that the treatment was justified.

When does the duty to make reasonable adjustments apply in respect of the variation or withdrawal of membership?

7.27 **[s 14]** The duty of a trade organisation to make reasonable adjustments for a member who it knows to have a disability extends to the way in which it operates grievance and disciplinary procedures, or procedures for the variation or withdrawal of membership. Where a provision, criterion or practice, or a physical feature, places a disabled member at a substantial disadvantage in this regard, the trade organisation must take such steps as are reasonable to prevent this.

> A disabled doctor has a meeting to discuss his continued membership of a professional association. The venue is changed to one that is accessible to the doctor, who has a mobility impairment. This is likely to be a reasonable adjustment for the association to make.

> A disabled woman has a grievance hearing at the offices of a trade union. She is provided with a car parking space at the venue because her disability makes it impossible for her to use public transport. This is likely to be a reasonable adjustment for the union to make, whether or not the grievance was related to her disability.

7.28 **[s 16A(4)–(6)]** A trade organisation's duty to make reasonable adjustments may also apply in respect of a former member who is a disabled person. This will be the case where:

- the disabled person is placed at a substantial disadvantage in comparison with other former members:
  a. by a provision, practice or criterion applied by the trade organisation to the disabled person in relation to any matter arising out of his former membership, or
  b. by a physical feature of premises occupied by the organisation, and
- the organisation either knows, or could reasonably be expected to know, that the former member in question has a disability and is likely to be affected in this way.

> A newly disabled person wishes to attend a conference of a trade organisation of which he is a former member. This conference is open to former members. He explains to the conference organisers that he is now partially sighted. They arrange for a guide to accompany him at the conference and produce conference papers in large print. These are likely to be reasonable adjustments for the trade organisation to make.

7.29 The former members with whom the position of the disabled person should be compared must be people who are not disabled, but who are former members of the same organisation. If it is not possible to identify an actual comparator for this purpose, then a hypothetical comparator may be used (see paragraph 4.18).

KNOWLEDGE OF DISABILITY

7.30 **[s 14(3)]** The point has been made a number of times in this chapter that a trade organisation only has a duty to make a reasonable adjustment if it knows, or could reasonably be expected to know, that a person is, or may be, an applicant for membership or has a disability and is likely to be placed at a substantial disadvantage in comparison with people who are not disabled. However, a trade organisation will be deemed to have that knowledge in certain circumstances.

Obtaining information

7.31 It is good practice for a trade organisation to invite its members to tell it about their disability-related needs. In any event, where information which should alert a trade organisation to the circumstances mentioned in paragraph 7.30 is available to it, or would be if it were reasonably alert, the organisation cannot simply ignore it. It is therefore in the interests of a trade organisation to be aware of the possibility that people it is dealing with may have a disability and to make reasonable enquiries if circumstances suggest this may be the case. It also means that it is a good idea for disabled people, if they wish to take full advantage of the provisions of the Act, to let trade organisations know of their disability and of substantial disadvantages at which they are likely to be placed. The earlier a trade organisation is told about a disability and its effects, the more likely it is to be able to make effective adjustments.

> A trade union has questions on its membership application form asking if the applicant is disabled or needs information in an accessible format (such as large print, Braille, tape or email). It also asks if the applicant has any additional disability-related needs.

> A professional association sends its members invitations to a conference. The invitation contains general details about access for disabled people, and the booking form asks

> about access requirements – such as whether delegate information is required in an accessible format, and whether delegates have any specific dietary requirements.

7.32 If a trade organisation's agent or employee (such as a trade union representative) knows, in that capacity, of a member's disability, the organisation will not usually be able to claim that it does not know of the disability. The same applies in respect of actual or potential applicants for membership of the organisation. Trade organisations therefore need to ensure that where information about disabled people may come through different channels, there is a means – suitably confidential – for bringing the information together, to make it easier for the organisation to fulfil its duties under the Act.

> A trade union member tells her branch secretary that she is unable to climb stairs due to her mobility impairment. The branch secretary arranges for the member to go on a training course organised by the union's education department. When the member arrives at the training session, she is unable to gain access to the building because of a flight of stairs. The union would be unable to claim that it did not know about the member's disability.

7.33 Information will not be imputed to a trade organisation if it is gained by a person providing services to members independently of the organisation. This is the case even if the organisation has arranged for those services to be provided.

> A trade organisation member uses a counselling Helpline which is independent of the organisation but which is provided as a benefit of membership. During his conversation with the counsellor the member discusses his worries about his worsening sight problem. The trade organisation itself should not be assumed to know about his need for the organisation's magazine to be in an accessible format, on the basis of this conversation.

Confidential information

7.34 The extent to which a trade organisation is entitled to let other members know about a fellow member's disability will depend partly on the terms of membership. An organisation could be discriminating against the member by revealing such information if it would not reveal similar information about another person for an equally legitimate purpose; or if the organisation revealed such information without consulting the individual, instead of adopting the usual practice of talking to a member before revealing personal information about him. Trade organisations also need to be aware that they have obligations under the Data Protection Act in respect of personal data.

> A member of a trade union wishes to go on a residential weekend conference, travelling there on a coach arranged by the union. The union member has to take dialysis equipment with her because she has had kidney failure. Another member needs to be informed, in order to help her load and unload the equipment. The disabled member gives her permission for another union member to be told that she is taking medical equipment with her, so that she can be helped with the equipment.

7.35 However, as noted at paragraph 7.21, sometimes a reasonable adjustment will not work without the co-operation of other members. In order to secure such co-operation, it may be necessary for a trade organisation to tell one or more of a disabled person's fellow members (in confidence) about a disability which is not obvious. Who it might be appropriate to tell will depend on the nature of the disability and the reason they need to know about it. In any event, a trade organisation must not disclose confidential details about a member without his consent. A disabled person's refusal to give such consent may impact upon the effectiveness of the adjustments which the trade organisation is able to make or its ability to make adjustments at all.

7.36 The Act does not prevent a disabled person keeping a disability confidential from a trade organisation. But this is likely to mean that unless the organisation could reasonably be expected to know about the person's disability anyway, it will not be under a duty to make a reasonable adjustment. If a disabled person expects a trade organisation to make a reasonable adjustment, he will need to provide the organisation – or someone acting on its behalf – with sufficient information to carry out that adjustment.

THE ROLE OF TRADE UNIONS

7.37 Trade unions are obvious examples of what the Act means by trade organisations. Representing the interests of their members in the workplace is one of the most important functions of trade unions, and so union representatives need to be familiar with the Act's provisions on employment and occupation. They need to be able to recognise potential claims under the Act and to know how to respond appropriately. Union representatives should also understand the need to make reasonable adjustments at branch meetings, for example, and that the reasonableness of the cost of making an adjustment should be assessed having regard to the union's overall resources, and to any access funds which may be available (see paragraph 2.13).

7.38 It is important for trade unions to ensure that union representatives receive proper training on the Act and that they are aware of the DRC's code of practice on the Act's provisions on employment and occupation (see Appendix C). It is also advisable for trade unions to have arrangements in place so that appropriate cases are referred to the union's solicitors.

[4684]

8. DISCRIMINATION BY QUALIFICATIONS BODIES

INTRODUCTION

8.1 Chapter 3 describes the meaning of 'qualifications body', and explains that it is unlawful for such a body to discriminate against a disabled person in relation to conferring professional or trade qualifications, or to subject him to harassment, or to victimise any person – whether disabled or not.

8.2 This chapter looks at the provisions about qualifications bodies in more detail. It explains what the definition of 'professional or trade qualification' covers in practice. It considers when less favourable treatment of a disabled person by a qualifications body is unlawful, and when the duty to make reasonable adjustments arises. Finally, it examines the meaning and significance of 'competence standards'.

8.3 **[s 17A(1A)]** It should be noted that a disabled person is not permitted to bring a claim in an employment tribunal about alleged discrimination or harassment by a qualifications body if a statutory appeal is available in respect of the matter in question. For example, the Medical Act 1983 sets out specific mechanisms for appealing decisions of the General Medical Council or its committees regarding the registration of medical practitioners. A complaint to which these appeal mechanisms applied could not, therefore, be brought instead in an employment tribunal.

8.4 It should also be noted that the provisions of the Act which relate specifically to qualifications bodies focus only on the functions of conferring professional or trade qualifications. The performance of other functions by such bodies may be subject to other provisions of the Act. For example, where a qualifications body is also a trade organisation, regard must also be had to what the Act says about trade organisations – and to Chapter 7 of the Code in particular.

WHAT IS A PROFESSIONAL OR TRADE QUALIFICATION?

8.5 **[s 14A(5)]** As noted at paragraph 3.9, the key feature of a qualifications body is that it confers professional or trade qualifications. The Act says that such a qualification is an authorisation, qualification, recognition, registration, enrolment, approval or certification which is needed for, or which facilitates engagement in, a particular profession or trade. Clearly, therefore, the expression includes those qualifications etc, which are conferred solely in anticipation of furthering a particular career. However, it is also capable of including more general qualifications if attaining them facilitates engagement in a particular profession or trade. In order to decide whether a particular qualification is a professional or trade qualification for the purposes of the Act, it is necessary to address the following three questions:

- What is the profession or trade?
- What is the qualification?

- Does possession of that particular qualification make it easier to work in that particular profession or trade (rather than merely assisting general advancement in that or any other career)?

8.6 The word 'qualification' should not be interpreted narrowly—attaining a professional or trade qualification need not involve passing formal examinations or tests. In some cases, simply being a member of an organisation or body may amount to such a qualification if membership itself facilitates engagement in a particular profession or trade.

8.7 The following list (which is not intended to be exhaustive) gives examples of qualifications which would or could count as professional or trade qualifications under the Act provided that the criteria set out in paragraph 8.5 are met:

- Registration with the Nursing and Midwifery Council
- A certificate to practise as a solicitor issued by the Law Society
- Registration with the Council for Registered Gas Installers (CORGI)
- NVQs
- BTECs
- City and Guilds
- Scottish Vocational Qualifications
- HGV driving licences
- Membership, registration or fellowship of trade or professional bodies (e g Fellow of the Institute of Linguists).

8.8 In relation to certain professions or trades, educational institutions or other bodies may devise, run and examine their own courses, although approval for entry into the profession or trade is controlled by an external body. Because of the wide definition of 'professional or trade qualification', such external bodies are likely to be qualifications bodies if they perform any of the following functions:

- maintaining a register of people who are qualified to practice in the profession or trade
- Conducting additional tests for people who have qualified, or who wish to qualify, into the profession or trade, such as basic skills tests or medical checks, or
- giving approval for a person's qualification to his course provider.

WHAT AMOUNTS TO DIRECT DISCRIMINATION?

8.9 **[s 14A(1)]** It is obvious that a qualifications body will differentiate between individuals when conferring, renewing or extending professional or trade qualifications. However, in doing so, it should avoid discriminating against disabled people – it is unlawful for a qualifications body to discriminate against a disabled person in respect of a number of matters which are specified in the Act (and listed in paragraph 3.19).

8.10 **[s 3A(5)]** As explained in Chapter 4, treating a disabled person in a different way from the way in which other people are (or would be) treated amounts to discrimination in certain circumstances. In particular, such treatment is unlawful if it amounts to direct discrimination under Part 2. As explained at paragraph 4.5, treatment of a disabled person amounts to direct discrimination if:

- it is on the ground of his disability
- the treatment is less favourable than the way in which a person not having that particular disability is (or would be) treated, and
- the relevant circumstances, including the abilities, of the person with whom the comparison is made are the same as, or not materially different from, those of the disabled person.

> A qualifications body recommends to a college of higher education that a man with a mobility impairment should not be allowed on to a social work course, as they wrongly assume that he may have difficulty visiting the homes of clients. This is likely to amount to direct discrimination.

WHAT AMOUNTS TO DISABILITY-RELATED DISCRIMINATION?

8.11 **[s 3A(1)]** Less favourable treatment of a disabled person may be unlawful under the Act even if it does not amount to direct discrimination. This will be the case if it amounts to disability-related discrimination instead. As explained at paragraph 4.26, this is less favourable treatment which is for a reason related to the person's disability. However, unlike treatment which amounts to direct discrimination (and which is therefore incapable of justification), a qualifications body's treatment of a disabled person does not amount to disability-related discrimination if the body can show that it is justified. The general circumstances in which this may be possible are explained in Chapter 6. However, special rules apply in respect of justification of less favourable treatment in the application of a competence standard (see paragraphs 8.35 to 8.40).

8.12 In summary, less favourable treatment of a disabled person will be unlawful if it amounts to either direct discrimination or disability-related discrimination, and involves:

- the arrangements for determining upon whom to confer a professional or trade qualification
- the terms upon which a qualifications body confers, renews or extends such a qualification
- a refusal or deliberate omission by such a body to grant his application for a qualification, or
- the withdrawal of a qualification from him or a variation of the terms on which he holds it.

> A professional association which maintains a register of approved acupuncturists withdraws registration from a woman who, because of treatment for cancer, has not been able to work for a year. The association has a policy of withdrawing registration from anyone who has not practised for this length of time. The treatment of the woman is for a disability-related reason (her lack of recent practice is due to her disability). The treatment is less favourable than the way in which someone who had practised recently would have been treated. It would therefore amount to disability-related discrimination unless the association (acting as a qualifications body) can justify it.

8.13 **[s 16A]** The Act also says that, where a disabled person ceases to hold a professional or trade qualification, it is still unlawful for the qualifications body which conferred it:

- to discriminate against him by subjecting him to a detriment, or
- to subject him to harassment

if the discrimination or harassment arises out of his having formerly held the qualification and is closely connected to it.

8.14 It is also unlawful to victimise a person (whether or not he is disabled) after he has ceased to hold such a qualification (see paragraphs 4.32 to 4.35).

HOW DOES THE DUTY TO MAKE REASONABLE ADJUSTMENTS APPLY TO QUALIFICATIONS BODIES?

In respect of which disabled people is the duty owed?

8.15 **[s 14B(1)]** A qualifications body has a duty to make reasonable adjustments to the way it confers, renews or extends professional or trade qualifications (except in respect of competence standards). It owes this duty to a disabled person who holds a qualification conferred by it and to a disabled applicant or potential applicant for such a qualification.

8.16 **[s 14B(2)]** The duty extends to holders of a qualification conferred by the body and to applicants for such a qualification. However, in the case of a provision, criterion or practice for determining on whom a qualification is to be conferred, the duty only applies to a disabled person who has either applied for the qualification or has notified the body that he may apply.

8.17 **[s 14B(3)]** The duty only applies if the qualifications body knows, or could reasonably be expected to know, that the disabled person concerned is, or may be, an applicant for a professional or trade qualification. Likewise, the duty only applies if the body knows or should know that the person has a disability and is likely to be placed at a substantial disadvantage compared with people who are not disabled.

8.18 **[s 16A(4)–(6)]** The duty of a qualifications body to make reasonable adjustments may also extend to a disabled person who formerly held a professional or trade qualification. This is the case where a provision, practice or criterion, or a physical feature of premises occupied by the qualifications body, places the disabled person at a substantial disadvantage compared with others in the same position. The duty only applies, however, if the qualifications body knows, or could reasonably be expected to know, that the person concerned has a disability and is likely to be affected in this way.

8.19 The people with whom the position of the disabled person should be compared must be people who are not disabled, but who also formerly held the same professional or trade qualification conferred by the qualifications body in question. If it is not possible to identify an actual comparator for this purpose, then a hypothetical comparator may be used (see paragraph 4.18).

What is the effect of the duty?

8.20 Where it applies, the duty to make reasonable adjustments is likely to affect arrangements in relation to, for example, taking tests and examinations, and renewing qualifications where it is necessary to do so. However, there is no duty to make adjustments to competence standards applied to a disabled person by a qualifications body. Where the duty does apply, however, the qualifications body must take such steps as are reasonable to prevent the provision, criterion or practice, or the physical feature, (as the case may be) from placing the disabled person in question at a substantial disadvantage.

A woman with a mental health problem is informed that an oral examination for a diploma in interpreting and translation has been arranged for 8:30 am. The timing of the examination would substantially disadvantage the woman, because a side effect of her medication is extreme drowsiness for several hours after taking her morning dose – which prevents her from concentrating well. The qualifications body agrees to her request to take the examination later in the day.

A man who lip-reads because of his hearing impairment is due to have a practical test as part of his beauty therapy course. The qualifications body instructs an assessor working on its behalf to face the man when she issues instructions during the assessment and to talk clearly.

An advanced craft test for carpentry consists of a seven hour practical examination. A woman with arthritis who is only able to work part-time as a result of her disability wishes to take this test as two sessions of three and a half hours on two consecutive days. The qualifications body awarding the qualification allows the test to be taken in this way.

A candidate for a written examination as part of a jewellery-making course has dyslexia. The qualifications body allows her extra time to sit the examination, and also permits the use of a reader and an amanuensis (someone to write on her behalf) as the candidate is not able to read and write well because of her dyslexia.

A woman with a learning disability is allowed extra time by a qualifications body to take a written examination. This is likely to be a reasonable adjustment for the qualifications body to make, because the trade which the woman wants to enter would not require written work to be done in a short amount of time, so the ability to write quickly is not a competence standard.

A disabled man asks for twice as much time for a test in shorthand because his disability makes it impossible for him to write quickly. This is unlikely to be a reasonable adjustment for the qualifications body to make, because speed is an essential element of the shorthand qualification – in other words, it is likely to be a competence standard, and thus the duty to make reasonable adjustments does not apply.

What are the practical implications of the duty?

8.21 Although there is no duty on a qualifications body to make a reasonable adjustment if it does not have the requisite knowledge (see paragraph 8.17), it will be deemed to have that knowledge in certain circumstances.

8.22 Where information is available which should alert a qualifications body to the circumstances mentioned in paragraph 8.17, or would be if it were reasonably alert, the body cannot simply ignore it. It is thus a good idea for disabled people, if they wish to take full advantage of the provisions of the Act, to let educational institutions and qualifications bodies know of their disability and of substantial disadvantages that are likely to arise. The earlier a qualifications body is told about a disability and its effects, the more likely it is to be able to make effective adjustments.

8.23 As mentioned at paragraph 2.15, it is also advisable for qualifications bodies to set up systems for working with educational institutions and other bodies with whom they work to ensure that qualifications bodies obtain the information they need to make adjustments for disabled students who are taking examinations or other assessments in order to obtain a professional or trade qualification. For example, such a system could comprise the following steps:

- Well in advance of the examination or assessment in question, the qualifications body asks educational institutions to seek information from candidates about whether they have disabilities which make reasonable adjustments necessary.
- Each educational institution requests this information from its students, together with their individual consent to inform the qualifications body. The information is then passed on to the qualifications body.
- Students may be given a contact at the qualifications body with whom they can discuss their requirements further.
- The qualifications body uses the information it obtains to decide what adjustments should be made. It then notifies educational institutions of its decision, and discusses with them how such adjustments will be implemented.

> A body which confers qualifications in accountancy asks a college for information about students who may require reasonable adjustments. The college seeks this information from its students. A student with cerebral palsy has difficulty writing, and therefore asks to be allowed to take the examinations using a computer. The colleges relays this request to the qualifications body, which gives its consent and liaises with the college to ensure that the college can provide him with appropriate facilities to take the examinations.

8.24 Educational institutions or other bodies often provide education, training or other services (such as facilities for taking examinations or assessments) which lead to the attainment of a professional or trade qualification, even though they do not themselves confer the qualification. Such institutions or bodies are likely to have separate duties under Part 3 or Part 4 in respect of the education, training or other services they provide. To ensure full compliance with the Act, it is advisable for such institutions or bodies to inform qualifications bodies at an early stage about an applicant's disability and its relevant implications – subject, of course, to obtaining the applicant's consent first.

8.25 In practice, the needs of a disabled person who is taking an examination, test or assessment can only be met fully if the educational institution or body and the qualifications body concerned work together to achieve an appropriate outcome.

> A partially-sighted man requests a test paper in large print and a desk light. The qualifications body provides a large print test paper and liaises with the college where the man is sitting the test to ensure that it provides a desk light.

> A partially sighted man on another course has always had course information provided to him in large print by the college as a reasonable adjustment (under Part 4 of the Act), and has used a desk light when taking internal tests as part of his course. With the man's consent, the college informs the qualifications body that the man needs an

> examination paper in large print for examinations set by the qualifications body. The college provides him with a desk light for such examinations.

8.26 The Act does not prevent a disabled person keeping a disability confidential from a qualifications body (although other legislation may require its disclosure – in relation to an application for a driving licence, for example). But this is likely to mean that unless the qualifications body could reasonably be expected to know about the person's disability anyway, it will not be under a duty to make a reasonable adjustment. If a disabled person expects a qualifications body to make a reasonable adjustment, he will need to provide it with sufficient information to carry out that adjustment.

WHAT DOES THE ACT SAY ABOUT COMPETENCE STANDARDS?

What is a competence standard?

8.27 **[s 14A(5)]** The Act says that a competence standard is an academic, medical, or other standard applied by or on behalf of a qualifications body for the purpose of determining whether or not a person has a particular level of competence or ability. So, for example, having a certain standard of eyesight is a competence standard required for a pilot's qualification. Having a certain level of knowledge of the UK taxation system is a competence standard for an accountancy qualification.

8.28 Qualifications bodies are likely to impose various requirements and conditions upon the conferment of a professional or trade qualification. However, any such requirement or condition only amounts to a competence standard if its purpose is to demonstrate a particular level of competence or ability. A requirement that a person has a particular level of knowledge of a subject, for example, or has the strength or ability to carry out a particular task or activity within a set period of time, would probably be a competence standard.

8.29 On the other hand, a condition that a person has, for example, a certain length of experience of doing something will not be a competence standard if it does not determine a particular level of competence or ability. The following are examples of requirements which are therefore unlikely to amount to competence standards:

- a requirement that a candidate must have at least ten years continuous experience (a person who has two periods of experience which total ten years may have equivalent ability and experience)
- a requirement that a candidate must complete twelve qualifying sessions (for qualification as a barrister)
- a requirement that a candidate must be currently professionally employed in a particular field.

8.30 Generally, there is a difference between a competence standard and the process by which attainment of the standard is determined. For example, the conferment of many qualifications is dependent upon passing an academic examination. Having the requisite level of knowledge to pass the examination is a competence standard. However, the examination itself (as opposed to performance in it) may not involve a competence standard – because the mechanical process of sitting the examination is unlikely to be relevant to the determination of a relevant competence or ability.

8.31 Sometimes, of course, the process of assessing whether a competence standard has been achieved is inextricably linked to the standard itself. The conferment of some qualifications is conditional upon having a practical skill or ability which must be demonstrated by completing a practical test. The ability to take the test may itself amount to a competence standard.

> An oral examination for a person training to be a Russian interpreter cannot be done in an alternative way, e g as a written examination, because the examination is to ascertain whether someone can speak Russian.

> A driving test for a heavy goods vehicle licence cannot be done solely as a written test because the purpose of the test is to ascertain whether someone can actually drive a heavy goods vehicle.

> A practical test in tree surgery cannot be taken on the ground because the test is to ascertain whether someone can actually cut the branches of trees, including the high branches.

What is the significance of this distinction?

8.32 Special rules apply in relation to the application of a competence standard to a disabled person by or on behalf of a qualifications body. The effect of the Act is that:

- there is no duty to make reasonable adjustments in respect of the application of a competence standard, and
- in the limited circumstances in which less favourable treatment of a disabled person in the application of such a standard may be justified, justification is assessed by reference to a special statutory test (see paragraph 8.36).

8.33 It follows that it is very important to ascertain whether a particular provision, criterion or practice of a qualifications body is a competence standard and, if so, whether the matter at issue concerns the application of that standard to the disabled person concerned. Although there is no duty to make reasonable adjustments in respect of the application of a competence standard, such a duty is likely to apply in respect of the process by which competence is assessed.

> A woman taking a written test for a qualification in office administration asks the relevant qualifications body for extra time for the test because she has dyslexia. This is likely to be a reasonable adjustment for the qualifications body to make. She also asks if she can leave out the questions asking her to write a business letter and to précis a document, because she feels these questions would substantially disadvantage her because of her dyslexia. The qualifications body would not have to make this adjustment because these questions are there to determine her competence at writing and précising, so are part of the competence standard being tested.

8.34 As noted in paragraphs 8.23 and 8.24, it is advisable for qualifications bodies and, where relevant, educational institutions to ensure that they have adequate information to assess their responsibilities to disabled people. Even though a qualifications body has no duty to alter a competence standard, it needs to obtain enough information about a person's disability to decide whether a reasonable adjustment should be made to some other aspect of the process by which it confers the qualification in question. A qualifications body must ascertain whether a person's disability impacts upon a competence standard in the first place. However, as noted at paragraph 8.31, there may be an overlap between a competence standard and any process by which an individual is assessed against that standard.

When can less favourable treatment be justified in relation to competence standards?

8.35 **[s 3A(4) applied by s 14A(4)]** Less favourable treatment of a disabled person can never be justified if it amounts to direct discrimination under Part 2 (see paragraph 8.10) – as where the treatment is based on generalised, or stereotypical, assumptions about the disability or its effects. This principle applies to the way that a disabled person is treated in the application of a competence standard in the same way that it applies to treatment of him in other respects.

8.36 **[s 14A(3)]** To the extent that it does **not** amount to direct discrimination, the Act says that, where the application of a competence standard to a disabled person amounts to less favourable treatment of him for a reason which relates to his disability, that treatment is justified if, but only if, the qualifications body can show that:

- the standard is (or would be) applied equally to people who do not have his particular disability, and
- its application is a proportionate means of achieving a legitimate aim.

> A qualifications body refuses to grant a qualification to a man who fails a fitness test. This does not amount to direct discrimination because anyone, disabled or non-disabled, failing the fitness test would be treated in the same way. But it is less

favourable treatment for a reason related to the man's disability. The treatment could be justified if the fitness test was applied equally to all candidates **and** the fitness test was a proportionate way of showing that the person was fit enough to carry out the essential requirements of the job to which the qualification relates.

In the above situation the qualifications body had not reviewed the fitness standards to see if they were proportionate to the requirements of the job. If it had done so, it would have found that the fitness standard demanded was much higher than many people actually working in that job could now achieve (even though these people achieved that standard at the time of qualification). The qualifications body would therefore be unlikely to be able to justify this competence standard.

8.37 The effect of these provisions is that, in the limited circumstances in which justification may be possible, less favourable treatment which is disability-related and which arises from the application of a competence standard is capable of justification on an objective basis. Justification does not depend on an individual assessment of the disabled person's circumstances, but depends instead on an assessment of the purpose and effect of the competence standard itself.

8.38 These special rules about justification are only relevant to the actual application of a competence standard. If a qualifications body applies a competence standard incorrectly, then it is not, in fact, applying the standard and these rules do not operate. Instead, the more usual test of justification operates (assuming, of course, that the incorrect application of the standard is not directly discriminatory, but that it is disability-related less favourable treatment).

8.39 The application of a competence standard concerning a medical requirement may, depending on the circumstances, result in less favourable treatment of a disabled person. Medical requirements which are based on stereotypical assumptions about the health and safety implications of disability generally, or about particular types of disability, are likely to be directly discriminatory – less favourable treatment of a disabled person resulting from the application of such a requirement will therefore be unlawful.

A man studying to become a social care professional has epilepsy. His condition is controlled by medication and he has not had a seizure for two years. Nevertheless the relevant qualifications body prevents him from carrying on with his training for the qualification on health and safety grounds. It does this without first undertaking a risk assessment. This is likely to be unlawful.

8.40 Nevertheless, genuine concerns about health and safety may be relevant to the justification of a competence standard concerning a medical requirement. Assuming that it does not amount to direct discrimination, the application of such a requirement to a disabled person will be justified only if the body can show that the requirement applies (or would apply) equally to people who do not have that disability. It would also be necessary to show that the requirement serves a valid purpose and is a legitimate means of achieving that purpose. The qualifications body would have to provide cogent evidence that the standard is genuinely fundamental to the needs of the profession or trade in order to ensure the competence of practitioners.

How can qualifications bodies avoid discrimination in relation to competence standards?

8.41 If unlawful discrimination is to be avoided when the application of a competence standard results in less favourable treatment of a disabled person, the qualifications body concerned will have to show two things. First, it will have to show that the application of the standard does not amount to direct discrimination. Second, it will be necessary to show that the standard can be objectively justified. This is more likely to be possible where a qualifications body has considered the nature and effects of its competence standards in advance of an issue arising in practice. It would be advisable for qualifications bodies to review and evaluate competence standards. This process might involve:

- identifying the specific purpose of each competence standard which is applied, and examining the manner in which the standard achieves that purpose
- considering the impact which each competence standard may have on disabled people and, in the case of a standard which may have an adverse impact, asking whether the application of the standard is absolutely necessary

- reviewing the purpose and effect of each competence standard in the light of changing circumstances—such as developments in technology
- examining whether the purpose for which any competence standard is applied could be achieved in a way which does not have an adverse impact on disabled people, and
- documenting the manner in which these issues have been addressed, the conclusions which have been arrived at, and the reasons for those conclusions.

[4685]

9. MAKING REASONABLE ADJUSTMENTS TO PREMISES – LEGAL CONSIDERATIONS

INTRODUCTION

9.1 In Chapter 5 it was explained that one of the situations in which there is a duty to make reasonable adjustments arises where a physical feature of premises occupied by a trade organisation or a qualifications body places a disabled person at a substantial disadvantage compared with people who are not disabled. In such circumstances the organisation or body must consider whether any reasonable steps can be taken to overcome that disadvantage. Making adjustments to premises may be a reasonable step to have to take. This chapter addresses the issues of how leases, building regulations and other statutory requirements affect the duty to make reasonable adjustments to premises.

9.2 The issues dealt with in this chapter largely concern the need to obtain consent to the making of reasonable adjustments where a trade organisation or qualifications body occupies premises under a lease or other binding obligation. However, such organisations and bodies should remember that even where consent is not given for altering a physical feature, they still have a duty to consider taking other steps to overcome the disadvantage which the feature causes in respect of the disabled person.

WHAT ABOUT THE NEED TO OBTAIN STATUTORY CONSENT FOR SOME BUILDING CHANGES?

9.3 **[s 59]** A trade organisation or qualifications body might have to obtain statutory consent before making adjustments involving changes to premises. Such consents include planning permission, building regulations approval or a building warrant in Scotland, listed building consent, scheduled monument consent and fire regulations approval. The Act does not override the need to obtain such consents.

9.4 Organisations and bodies should plan for and anticipate the need to obtain consent to make a particular adjustment. It might take time to obtain such consent, but it could be reasonable to make an interim or other adjustment – one that does not require consent – in the meantime.

> A trade organisation occupies premises with steps up to the main entrance. These premises have facilities for members, such as a conference room and a library. The trade organisation is not aware of any members who have a mobility impairment and does not do anything to make its premises more accessible. When a new member notifies the organisation that she walks with crutches and wishes to use the premises, the organisation tries to obtain statutory consent to install a ramp with a handrail. It takes several months to obtain such permission. Because it cannot make this adjustment in time, it decides to make a temporary adjustment – making an existing side entrance, without steps, available for the disabled member to use. If the trade organisation had anticipated that this need was very likely to arise (through carrying out an access audit, for example), it would have been able to make this adjustment sooner.

9.5 Where consent has been refused, there is likely to be a means of appeal. Whether or not the duty to take such steps as it is reasonable to take includes pursuing an appeal will depend on the circumstances of the case.

BUILDING REGULATIONS AND BUILDING DESIGN

9.6 **[SI 2000/2531]** The design and construction of a new building, or the material alteration of an existing one, must comply with Building Regulations. For buildings in England or Wales, Part M of the Building Regulations (access to and use of buildings) is intended to ensure that reasonable provision is made for people to gain access to and use buildings. A similar provision applies in Scotland under the Technical Standards for compliance with the Building Standards (Scotland) Regulations 1990 and, from May 2005, under the Building (Scotland) Regulations 2004 and associated Technical Handbooks.

9.7 Nevertheless, the fact that the design and construction of a building (or a physical feature of a building) which a trade organisation or qualifications body occupies meets the requirements of the Building Regulations does not diminish its duty to make reasonable adjustments in respect of the building's physical features. In particular, it should be noted that the partial exemption from the duty to remove or alter physical features which applies to service providers under Part 3 of the Act does not apply to trade organisations or qualifications bodies under Part 2.

9.8 The Building Regulations building standards provide only a baseline standard of accessibility, which is not intended to address the specific needs of individual disabled people. It is therefore good practice for trade organisations and qualifications bodies to carry out an assessment of the access needs of each disabled person with whom it has dealings, and to consider what alterations can be made to the features of its buildings in order to meet those needs. It is also good practice to anticipate the needs of disabled people when planning building or refurbishment works.

9.9 When assessing the access requirements of disabled people, it is likely to be helpful to refer to British Standard 8300:2001, **Design of buildings and their approaches to meet the needs of disabled people – Code of Practice**. Indeed, it is unlikely to be reasonable for a trade organisation or qualifications body to have to make an adjustment to a physical feature of a building which it occupies if the design and construction of the physical features of the building is in accordance with BS8300. Further information about BS8300 can be found in Appendix C.

9.10 In addition, although less comprehensive than BS8300, guidance accompanying the Building Regulations (known as 'Approved Document M') sets out a number of 'provisions' as suggested ways in which the requirements of the Regulations might be met. It is unlikely to be reasonable for a trade organisation or qualifications body to have to make an adjustment to a physical feature of a building which it occupies if that feature accords with the relevant provisions of the most up to date version of Approved Document M.

WHAT IF A BINDING OBLIGATION OTHER THAN A LEASE PREVENTS A BUILDING BEING ALTERED?

9.11 **[s 18B(3)]** A trade organisation or qualifications body may be bound by the terms of an agreement or other legally binding obligation (for example, a mortgage, charge or restrictive covenant or, in Scotland, a feu disposition) under which it cannot alter the premises without someone else's consent. In these circumstances, the Act provides that it is always reasonable for the organisation or body to have to request that consent, but that it is never reasonable for it to have to make an alteration before having obtained that consent.

WHAT HAPPENS IF A LEASE SAYS THAT CERTAIN CHANGES TO PREMISES CANNOT BE MADE?

9.12 **[s 18A(2)]** Special provisions apply where a trade organisation or qualifications body occupies premises under a lease, the terms of which prevent it from making an alteration to the premises. In such circumstances, if the alteration is one which the organisation or body proposes to make in order to comply with a duty of reasonable adjustment, the Act overrides the terms of the lease so as to entitle it to make the alteration with the consent of its landlord ('the lessor'). In such a case the organisation or body must first write to the lessor asking for consent to make the alteration. The lessor cannot unreasonably withhold consent but may attach reasonable conditions to the consent.

9.13 **[Sch 4, Part I, para 1]** If a trade organisation or qualifications body fails to make a written application to the lessor for consent to the alteration, it will not be able to rely upon the fact that the lease has a term preventing it from making alterations to the premises to defend its failure to make an alteration. In these circumstances, anything in the lease which prevents that alteration being made must be ignored in deciding whether it was reasonable for the organisation or body to have made the alteration.

WHAT HAPPENS IF THE LESSOR HAS A 'SUPERIOR' LESSOR?

9.14 The lessor may itself hold a lease the terms of which prevent it from consenting to the alteration without the consent of its landlord ('the superior lessor'). In such circumstances

PART 4

the effect of the superior lease is modified so as to require the lessee of that lease to apply in writing to its lessor (the 'superior lessor' in this context) if it wishes to consent to the alteration. As with the lessor of the trade organisation or qualifications body, the superior lessor must not withhold such consent unreasonably but may attach reasonable conditions to the consent.

9.15 Where a superior lessor receives an application from its lessee, the provisions described in paragraphs 9.16 to 9.29 apply as if its lessee were the trade organisation or qualifications body.

HOW DO ARRANGEMENTS FOR GAINING CONSENT WORK?

9.16 **[SI 2004/153]** Regulations made under the Act govern the procedure for obtaining consent. These Regulations (the Disability Discrimination (Employment Field) (Leasehold Premises) Regulations 2004) are referred to in this Chapter as the 'Leasehold Premises Regulations'.

9.17 **[reg 4]** The Leasehold Premises Regulations say that, once the application has been made, the lessor has 21 days, beginning with the day on which it receives the application, to reply in writing to the trade organisation or qualifications body (or the person who made the application on its behalf). If it fails to do so it is taken to have unreasonably withheld its consent to the alteration. However, where it is reasonable to do so, the lessor is permitted to take more than 21 days to reply to the request.

9.18 If the lessor replies consenting to the application subject to obtaining the consent of another person (required under a superior lease or because of a binding obligation), but fails to seek the consent of the other person within 21 days of receiving the application (or such longer period as may be reasonable), it will also be taken to have withheld its consent.

9.19 The Leasehold Premises Regulations provide that a lessor will be treated as not having sought the consent of another person unless the lessor has applied in writing to the other person indicating that the occupier has asked for consent for an alteration in order to comply with a duty to make reasonable adjustments, and that the lessor has given its consent conditionally upon obtaining the other person's consent.

9.20 **[reg 6]** If the lessor replies refusing consent to the alteration, the trade organisation or qualifications body must inform the disabled person of this, but has no further obligation to make the alteration (but see paragraph 9.2).

WHEN IS IT UNREASONABLE FOR A LESSOR TO WITHHOLD CONSENT?

9.21 Whether withholding consent will be reasonable or not will depend on the specific circumstances. For example, if a particular adjustment is likely to result in a substantial permanent reduction in the value of the lessor's interest in the premises, the lessor is likely to be acting reasonably in withholding consent. The lessor is also likely to be acting reasonably if it withholds consent because an adjustment would cause significant disruption or inconvenience to other tenants (for example, where the premises consist of multiple adjoining units).

> A particular adjustment helps make a public building more accessible generally and is therefore likely to benefit the landlord. It is likely to be unreasonable for consent to be withheld in these circumstances.

> A particular adjustment is likely to result in a substantial permanent reduction in the value of the landlord's interest in the premises. The landlord is likely to be acting reasonably in withholding consent.

> A particular adjustment would cause significant disruption or major inconvenience to other tenants (for example, where the premises consist of multiple adjoining units). The landlord is likely to be acting reasonably in withholding consent.

9.22 A trivial or arbitrary reason would almost certainly be unreasonable. Many reasonable adjustments to premises will not harm the lessor's interests and so it would generally be unreasonable to withhold consent for them.

9.23 **[reg 5]** The Leasehold Premises Regulations say that, provided the consent has been sought in the way required by the lease, it is unreasonable for a lessor to withhold consent in circumstances where the lease says that consent will be given to alterations of the kind for which consent has been sought.

9.24 **[reg 6]** The Leasehold Premises Regulations provide that withholding consent will be reasonable where:

- there is a binding obligation requiring the consent of any person to the alteration
- the lessor has taken steps to seek consent, and
- consent has not been given or has been given subject to a condition making it reasonable for the lessor to withhold its consent.

It will also be reasonable for a lessor to withhold consent where it is bound by an agreement under which it would have to make a payment in order to give the consent, but which prevents it from recovering the cost from the trade organisation or qualifications body.

WHAT CONDITIONS WOULD IT BE REASONABLE FOR A LESSOR TO MAKE WHEN GIVING CONSENT?

9.25 The Leasehold Premises Regulations set out some conditions which it is reasonable for a lessor to make. Depending on the circumstances of the case there may be other conditions which it would also be reasonable for a lessor to require a trade organisation or qualifications body to meet. Where a lessor imposes other conditions, their reasonableness may be challenged in the course of subsequent employment tribunal proceedings (see paragraph 9.27).

9.26 **[reg 7]** The conditions set out in the Leasehold Premises Regulations as ones which a lessor may reasonably require a trade organisation or qualifications body to meet are that it:

- obtains any necessary planning permission and other statutory consents
- submits plans and specifications for the lessor's approval (provided that such approval will not be unreasonably withheld) and thereafter carries out the work in accordance with them
- allows the lessor a reasonable opportunity to inspect the work after it is completed, or
- reimburses the lessor's reasonable costs incurred in connection with the giving of consent.

In addition, in a case where it would be reasonable for the lessor to withhold consent, the lessor may give such consent subject to a condition that the premises are reinstated to their original condition at the end of the lease.

WHAT HAPPENS IF THE LESSOR REFUSES CONSENT OR ATTACHES CONDITIONS TO CONSENT?

9.27 **[Sch 4, Part I, para 2]** Where a disabled person brings legal proceedings against a trade organisation or qualifications body under Part 2 – and those proceedings involve a failure to make an alteration to premises – he may ask the employment tribunal hearing the case to bring in the lessor as an additional party to the proceedings. The organisation or body may also make such a request. The tribunal will grant that request if it is made before the hearing of the case begins. It may refuse the request if it is made after the hearing of the claim begins. The request will not be granted if it is made after the tribunal has determined the claim.

9.28 Where the lessor has been made a party to the proceedings, the employment tribunal may determine whether the lessor has unreasonably refused consent to the alteration or has consented subject to unreasonable conditions. In either case, the tribunal can:

- make an appropriate declaration
- make an order authorising the organisation or body to make a specified alteration
- order the lessor to pay compensation to the disabled person.

9.29 The tribunal may require the organisation or body to comply with any conditions specified in the order. If the tribunal orders the lessor to pay compensation, it cannot also order the organisation or body to do so.

COMPARISON WITH THE PROCEDURE FOR OBTAINING CONSENT UNDER PART 3

9.30 There are similar provisions which govern the procedure by which a service provider may obtain consent to an alteration which it proposes to make in order to comply with a duty

PART 4

of reasonable adjustment under Part 3 of the Act. However, it should be noted that the procedures for obtaining consent under Parts 2 and 3 respectively differ in certain ways. In particular:

- the periods within which the lessor must respond to an application for consent are not the same – under Part 3 the relevant period is 42 days beginning with the day on which the application is received
- Under Part 3 the lessor may require plans and specifications to be submitted **before** it decides whether to give consent
- Under Part 3 it is possible to make a free-standing reference to the court if the lessor has either refused consent or attached conditions to it. Under Part 2, the question of consent to alterations can only be considered by an employment tribunal in the course of a complaint of discrimination.

[4686]

10. OTHER RELEVANT PROVISIONS

10.1 Additional provisions of the Act (and provisions of other legislation) are relevant to understanding the protection from discrimination afforded to disabled people in relation to trade organisations and qualifications bodies. This chapter describes those provisions, and focuses in particular on the way in which disputes under the Act should be resolved.

RESOLVING DISPUTES UNDER THE ACT

10.2 Chapter 2 explained that, broadly speaking, the Act does not require the internal resolution of disputes by trade organisations and qualifications bodies, but that it is desirable for grievance procedures to be used where possible. Where grievance or disciplinary procedures exist, they must not discriminate against disabled people. Trade organisations and qualifications bodies may have to make reasonable adjustments to enable disabled people to use such procedures effectively, or to ensure that they do not place disabled people at a substantial disadvantage compared with others.

10.3 **[s 17A(1) & s 55 & Sch 3, para 3]** The Act says that a person who believes that someone has unlawfully discriminated against him (which includes victimising him or failing to make a reasonable adjustment) or has subjected him to harassment, may make an application to an employment tribunal. Such an application must normally be made within three months of the date when the incident complained about occurred.

10.4 **[s 17A(1A)]** This is subject to one proviso. In cases of alleged discrimination or harassment by a qualifications body, the Act says that no application may be made to an employment tribunal if a statutory appeal is available in respect of the matter in question.

10.5 Before making an application to an employment tribunal (or within 28 days of lodging it), a disabled person can request information relevant to his claim from the person against whom the claim is made. This is known as the 'questionnaire procedure'. There is a standard form of questionnaire (DL56) and accompanying booklet which explains how the procedure works (see Appendix C for details).

10.6 When an application to an employment tribunal has been made, a conciliation officer from the Advisory, Conciliation and Arbitration Service (ACAS) will try to promote settlement of the dispute without a tribunal hearing. However, if a hearing becomes necessary—and if the application is upheld—the tribunal may:

- **[s 17A(2)]** declare the rights of the disabled person (the applicant), and the other person (the respondent) in relation to the application
- order the respondent to pay the applicant compensation, and
- recommend that, within a specified time, the respondent takes reasonable action to prevent or reduce the adverse effect in question.

10.7 **[s 17A(4)]** The Act allows compensation for injury to feelings to be awarded whether or not other compensation is awarded.

10.8 **[s 17A(5)]** The Act also says that if a respondent fails, without reasonable justification, to comply with an employment tribunal's recommendation, the tribunal may:

- increase the amount of compensation to be paid, or
- order the respondent to pay compensation if it did not make such an order earlier.

10.9 Sources of information about how to make an application to an employment tribunal are listed in Appendix C.

OTHER PROVISIONS

Anti-avoidance provisions

10.10 **[Sch 3A, Part 1]** Generally speaking, a disabled person cannot waive his rights (or the duties of a trade organisation or qualifications body) under the Act. The Act says that any term of a contract is 'void' (i e not valid) where:

- making the contract is unlawful under Part 2 because of the inclusion of the term
- the term is included in furtherance of an act which is itself unlawful under Part 2, or
- the term provides for the doing of an act which is unlawful under Part 2.

10.11 Trade organisations and qualifications bodies should not include in an agreement any provision intended to avoid obligations under the Act, or to prevent someone from fulfilling obligations. An agreement should not, therefore, be used to try to justify less favourable treatment or deem an adjustment unreasonable. Even parts of agreements which unintentionally have such an effect are unenforceable if they would restrict the working of Part 2. However, as explained in Chapter 9, special arrangements cover leases and other agreements which might restrict the making of adjustments to premises.

Compromise agreements

10.12 **[Sch 3A, Part 1]** The effect of the Act's provisions is also to make a contract term unenforceable if it would prevent anyone from making an application to an employment tribunal under Part 2, or would force them to discontinue an application (see paragraph 10.3). There is a limited exception to this principle relating to settlement agreements which have either been brokered by an ACAS conciliation officer, or which are made in circumstances where the following conditions are satisfied:

- the disabled person has received advice from a relevant independent adviser about the terms and effects of the agreement, particularly its effect on his ability to apply to a tribunal
- the adviser has a contract of insurance or an indemnity provided for members of a profession or professional body, and
- the agreement is in writing, relates to the application, identifies the adviser and says that these conditions are satisfied.

[Sch 3A, Part 1] The Act defines the circumstances in which a person is a 'relevant independent adviser' for this purpose.

Variation of contracts

10.13 **[Sch 3A, para 3]** A disabled person interested in a contract which contains a term of the kind mentioned in paragraph 10.10 may apply to a county court or, in Scotland, a sheriff court, for an order removing or modifying that term.

Collective agreements and rules of undertakings

10.14 **[Sch 3A, Part 2]** There are also anti-avoidance provisions in the Act relating to the terms of collective agreements, and to rules made by trade organisations or qualifications bodies which apply to all or any of an organisation's members or prospective members, or (as the case may be), to all or any of the people on whom a body has conferred qualifications, or who are seeking qualifications from it.

10.15 The Act says that any such term or rule is void where:

- making the collective agreement is unlawful under Part 2 because of the inclusion of the term
- the term or rule is included in furtherance of an act which is itself unlawful under Part 2, or
- the term or rule provides for the doing of an act which is unlawful under Part 2.

10.16 It does not matter whether the collective agreement was entered into, or the rule was made, before or after these provisions became law – the term or rule in question can still be challenged under the Act. In addition, where these provisions apply, certain disabled people may ask an employment tribunal to make a declaration that a discriminatory term or rule is void if they believe that it may affect them in the future. The Act specifies which disabled people may make such an application.

DISABILITY RIGHTS COMMISSION

General functions

10.17 **[Disability Rights Commission Act 1999]** The DRC has statutory powers to work towards the elimination of discrimination and to promote the equalisation of opportunity for disabled people. In particular, the DRC:

- keeps the Act under review
- supplies assistance and support to disabled litigants under the Act
- provides information and advice to anyone with rights or obligations under the Act

- carries out formal investigations, and
- prepares new or revised Codes of Practice.

Enforcement of certain provisions under Part 2

10.18 In addition, the DRC has a direct involvement in the enforcement of the provisions of Part 2 relating to:

- instructing or pressurising other people to act unlawfully (see paragraph 3.21), and
- discriminatory advertisements (see paragraphs 3.22 and 3.23).

10.19 **[s 17B]** Only the DRC may bring proceedings in respect of these matters. Where it does so, the DRC may seek:

- a declaration from an employment tribunal as to whether a contravention has occurred, and
- an injunction from a county court (or, in Scotland, an order from a sheriff court) restraining further contraventions.

10.20 The DRC may only apply for an injunction or order if it has first obtained a declaration from an employment tribunal that an unlawful act has occurred, and then only if it appears to the DRC that a further unlawful act is likely to occur unless the person concerned is restrained.

Further information

10.21 The Commission may be contacted at:

DRC Information, Freepost, MID 02164, Stratford upon Avon, CV37 9BR.

For other contact details, please see paragraph 1.18.

[4687]

APPENDIX A: CHANGES TO THE ACT

The table below summarises the main changes to the Act's provisions on trade organisations and qualifications bodies taking effect on 1 October 2004. It does not include all the changes occurring on that date, and is not a full explanation of the law.

	Position before 1st October 2004	Position after 1st October 2004
Scope	• DDA covered by trade organisations	• DDA covers trade organisations and qualifications bodies
Types of Discrimination	Three kinds of discrimination: • Less favourable treatment • Failure to make reasonable adjustments. • Victimisation.	Four kinds of discrimination: • Direct discrimination. • Failure to make reasonable adjustments. • 'Disability-related discrimination'. • Victimisation.
When is Justification relevant?	*Justification was of relevance in cases about:* • Less favourable treatment. • Failure to make reasonable adjustments.	*Justification is NOT relevant in cases about:* • Direct discrimination. • Failure to make reasonable adjustments. *Justification is relevant in cases about:* • Disability-related discrimination. • Competence standards – where a different test of justification is used
Harassment	Covered, but no separate provisions on this.	New provisions on harassment.

	Position before 1st October 2004	Position after 1st October 2004
Reasonable adjustments to physical features of premises	No requirement to make reasonable adjustments to physical features, simply to prevent the feature causing substantial disadvantage.	Reasonable adjustments include adjustments to physical features.

[4688]

(*Appendix B* (*The meaning of disability*) *and Appendix C* (*Further information*) *are omitted; see the equivalent Appendices in the DRC's Code of Practice on Employment and Occupation at* **[4676]** *and* **[4677]**.)

INDEX

PART 4

[4689]

CODE OF PRACTICE: ACCESS AND UNFAIR PRACTICES DURING RECOGNITION AND DERECOGNITION BALLOTS (2005)

NOTES

This Code is issued under the power given to the Secretary of State by the Trade Union and Labour Relations (Consolidation) Act 1992, s 203 (at **[688]**), with the authority of Parliament. It came into effect on 1 October 2005 (see the Employment Code of Practice (Access and Unfair Practices during Recognition and Derecognition Ballots) Order 2005, SI 2005/2421). The statutory status of the Code is as stated in s 207 of the 1992 Act (at **[692]**).

This Code replaces the Code of Practice on Access to Workers during Recognition and Derecognition Ballots (2000). Notes are as in the original.

PREAMBLE

This document revises the Code of Practice on Access to Workers during Recognition and Derecognition Ballots, which came into effect on 6 June 2000. It also contains practical guidance on unfair practices during recognition and derecognition ballots, for which the law provides a separate power for the Secretary of State to issue a Code of Practice. These two Codes on access and unfair practices are therefore combined within this single document. For simplicity and ease of reference, the text refers to there being just one Code of Practice dealing with both topics.

This Code supersedes the Code of Practice on Access to Workers during Recognition and Derecognition Ballots, which came into effect on 6 June 2000. Pursuant to section 208(2) of the Trade Union and Labour Relations (Consolidation) Act 1992, that Code shall cease to have effect on the date on which this Code of Practice comes in force.

The legal framework within which this Code will operate is explained in its text. While every effort has been made to ensure that explanations included in the Code are accurate, only the courts can give authoritative interpretations of the law.

The Code's provisions apply equally to men and to women, but for simplicity the masculine pronoun is used throughout.

Unless the text specifies otherwise, (i) the term "union" should be read to mean "unions" in cases where two or more unions are seeking to be jointly recognised; (ii) the term "workplace" should be read to mean "workplaces" in cases where a recognition application covers more than one workplace; and (iii) the term "working day" should be read to mean any day other than a Saturday or a Sunday, Christmas Day or Good Friday, or a day which is a bank holiday.

Passages in this Code which appear in italics are extracts from, or re-statements of, provisions in primary legislation.

[4690]

SECTION A
INTRODUCTION

Background

1. Schedule A1 of the Trade Union and Labour Relations (Consolidation) Act 1992, inserted by the Employment Relations Act 1999 and subsequently amended by the Employment Relations Act 2004, sets out the statutory procedure for the recognition and derecognition of trade unions for the purpose of collective bargaining.

Recognition

2. Where an employer and a trade union fail to reach agreement on recognition voluntarily, the statute provides for the union to apply to the Central Arbitration Committee (CAC) to decide whether it should be recognised for collective bargaining purposes. In certain cases, the CAC may award recognition, or dismiss the application, without a ballot. In other cases, the CAC will be obliged to hold a secret ballot of members of the bargaining unit to determine the issue. If a ballot takes place, the CAC will decide whether it should be held at the workplace, by post, or, if special factors make it appropriate, by a combination of the two methods. The ballot must be conducted by a qualified independent person appointed by the CAC.

3. Schedule A1 places various duties and obligations on parties during the period of a recognition ballot including the following:

(a) Paragraph 26(2) of Schedule A1 places a duty on the employer *to co-operate generally, in connection with the ballot, with the union and the independent person appointed to conduct the ballot;*

(b) Paragraph 26(3) of Schedule A1 places a duty on the employer to give a union applying for recognition *such access to the workers constituting the bargaining unit as is reasonable to enable the union to inform the workers of the object of the ballot and to seek their support and their opinions on the issues involved;*

(c) Paragraph 26(4A) of Schedule A1 places a duty on the employer *to refrain from making any offer to any or all of the workers constituting the bargaining unit which (i) has or is likely to have the effect of inducing any or all of them not to attend a relevant meeting between the union and the workers constituting the bargaining unit and (ii) is not reasonable in the circumstances.* A "relevant meeting" is defined as a meeting arranged in accordance with the duty to provide reasonable access to which the employer has agreed, or is required, to permit the worker to attend;

(d) Paragraph 26(4B) of Schedule A1 places a duty on the employer *to refrain from taking or threatening to take any action against a worker solely or mainly on the grounds that he attended or took part in any relevant meeting between the union and the workers in the bargaining unit, or on the grounds that he indicated his intention to attend or take part in such a meeting.* The definition of a "relevant meeting" is the same as at (c);

(e) *Paragraph 27A(1) of Schedule A1 places an obligation on both the employer and the union to refrain from using an unfair practice with a view to influencing the result of a recognition ballot. The unfair practices are defined by paragraph 27A(2) of Schedule A1.*

4. Section 203(1)(a) of the Trade Union and Labour Relations (Consolidation) Act 1992 gives a general power to the Secretary of State to issue Codes of Practice containing practical guidance for the purpose of promoting the improvement of industrial relations. Paragraphs 26(8) and 26(9) of Schedule A1 specify that this general power includes the particular power to issue a Code of Practice giving practical guidance about reasonable access during recognition ballots and about the employer's duty to refrain from making offers to workers not to attend access meetings. In addition, paragraph 27A(5) of Schedule A1 specifies that the general power includes the particular power to issue a Code of Practice about unfair practices for the purposes of paragraph 27A.

Derecognition

5. The CAC can also call a derecognition ballot in cases where an employer, or his workers, are seeking to end recognition arrangements with a union. In general, the duties and obligations on the parties are the same in both recognition and derecognition ballots. Paragraph 118(3) of Schedule A1 contains identical wording to paragraph 26(3) of Schedule A1, placing a duty on the employer to give the recognised union reasonable access to the workers comprising the bargaining unit where the CAC is holding a ballot on derecognition. Similarly, paragraph 118(4A) places a duty on the employer to refrain from making offers to workers not to attend access meetings. And paragraph 119A(1) requires both the employer, the union and, in cases where workers are applying to derecognise the union, those workers to refrain from using an unfair practice during the period of a derecognition ballot. Paragraphs 118(8) and 119(9) and paragraph 119A(5) contain similar provisions to paragraphs 26(8) and 26(9) and 27A(5) enabling the Secretary of State to issue a Code of Practice giving practical guidance about reasonable access and unfair practices during derecognition ballots.

6. For simplicity, most examples and explanations in this Code relate to the case where the union is seeking recognition. However, the guidance contained in this Code applies equally to cases where the ballot is about recognition or derecognition.

General purpose of the Code

7. This Code covers two related issues: the union's access to workers during the period of recognition or derecognition ballots and the avoidance of unfair practices when campaigning during that period. As regards the first topic of **access**, this Code gives practical guidance about the issues which arise when an employer receives a request by a union to be granted access to his workers at their workplace and/or during their working time. Of course, the union does not need the employer's consent or assistance to arrange access outside the workplace and outside working hours – say, when hiring a public hall to hold a meeting or when using local newspapers and media to put across its case. The Code does not therefore

PART 4

deal with the issues that arise when arranging such access, though those parts of the Code which concern the conduct of parties when campaigning are relevant. This Code deals with the specific circumstances of access during the period of recognition or derecognition ballots. It does not provide guidance on access at other times.

8. Access can take many and varied forms depending largely on the type of workplace involved and the characteristics of the balloted workforce. The overall aim is to ensure that the union can reach the workers involved, but local circumstances will need to be taken into account when deciding what form the access should take. Each case should be looked at on the facts. This Code therefore aims to help the employer and the union arrive at agreed arrangements for access, which can take full account of the circumstances of each individual case.

9. The second purpose of this Code is to help parties avoid committing **unfair practices**. Recognition and derecognition ballots usually occur because the employer and the union cannot agree the way ahead. In some cases a party will wish to communicate its views to the workers concerned through active campaigning once the CAC has informed it that a ballot will be held. This Code aims to encourage reasonable and responsible behaviour by both the employer and the union when undertaking campaigning activity in this period. A failure to follow the Code's guidance on responsible behaviour may not necessarily mean that an unfair practice has occurred. However, responsible campaigning should help ensure that acrimony between the parties is avoided and it greatly reduces the risk that individual workers are exposed to intimidation, threat or other unfair practices when deciding which way to cast their vote. As regards the treatment of individuals, both parties should note that the law provides protections against dismissal or detriment for workers who campaign either for or against recognition. The Code does not cover campaigning activity which occurs before the CAC decides that a ballot should be held. However, parties are still advised to act responsibly when undertaking early campaigning and they may benefit by drawing on the guidance provided by this Code.

10. In order for a ballot to take place, the union must have satisfied the CAC that at least 10% of the proposed bargaining unit are already members of the union, and that a majority of the workers in the proposed bargaining unit would be likely to favour recognition. There is therefore a good chance that recognition will be granted to the union, and that a working relationship between the parties will have to be sustained after the ballot. This longer term perspective should encourage both the employer and the union to behave responsibly and in a co-operative spirit during the balloting period.

Structure of the Code

11. This Code deals mainly with issues concerning access and unfair practices. These are distinct, though related, matters and all sections of the Code should therefore be read in conjunction. Sections B–D contain guidance on access, whilst Section E provides guidance on conduct to avoid committing an unfair practice. Finally, Section F provides guidance on the resolution of any disputes which might arise about the arrangement of access to the union or to the conduct of either the employer or the union when campaigning during the balloting period.

Legal Status of the Code

12. *Under paragraphs 27 and 119 of Schedule A1, the CAC may order employers who are breaching their duty to allow reasonable access to take specified, reasonable steps to do so, and can award recognition without a ballot, or can refuse to award derecognition where applied for by the employer, if an employer fails to abide by its orders to remedy a breach. Paragraphs 27C–27F of Schedule A1 provide a number of actions which the CAC may take when it concludes that a party has committed an unfair practice during a recognition or derecognition ballot. For example, the CAC may order a further ballot and it may order a party to take specified actions to help remedy the effects of the unfair practice. In addition, the CAC may award recognition or derecognition (or dismiss an application for recognition or derecognition) where an unfair practice has involved the use of violence or the dismissal of a union official, or where the CAC has found that a party has committed a second unfair practice or failed to comply with a remedial order.*

13. *This Code itself imposes no legal obligations and failure to observe it does not in itself render anyone liable to proceedings. But section 207 of the Trade Union and Labour Relations (Consolidation) Act 1992 provides that any provisions of this Code are to be admissible in evidence and are to be taken into account in proceedings before any court, tribunal or the CAC where they consider them relevant.*

[4691]

SECTION B
PREPARING FOR ACCESS

When should preparations for access begin?

14. Preparations for access should begin as soon as possible. The CAC is required to give notice to the employer and the union that it intends to arrange for the holding of a ballot. There then follows a period of ten working days before the CAC proceeds with arrangements for the ballot. The parties should make full use of this notification period to prepare for access. The union should request an early meeting with the employer in this period to discuss access arrangements. The employer should agree to arrange the meeting on an early date and at a mutually convenient time. The employer and the union should ensure that the individual or individuals representing them at the meeting are expressly authorised by them to take all relevant decisions regarding access, or are authorised to make recommendations directly to those who take such decisions.

Joint applications by two or more unions

15. Where there is a joint application for recognition by two or more unions acting together, the unions should act jointly in preparing and implementing the access arrangements. Therefore, unless the employer and the unions agree otherwise, the unions should have common access arrangements. The amount of time needed for access would normally be the same for single or joint applications.

Establishing an access agreement

16. It would be reasonable for the employer to want to give his prior permission before allowing a full time union official to enter his workplace and talk to his workers. In particular, the employer may have security and health and safety issues to consider. The parties should discuss practical arrangements for the union's activities at the workplace, in advance of the period of access actually beginning.

17. Consideration should be given to establishing an agreement, preferably in written form, on access arrangements. Such an agreement could include:

- the union's programme for where, when and how it will access the workers on site and/or during their working time; and
- a mechanism for resolving disagreements, if any arise, about implementing the agreed programme of access.

When discussions about access arrangements are taking place, parties should also seek to reach understandings about the standards of conduct expected of those individuals who campaign on their behalf (see paragraph 52 below for more guidance on this point).

18. In seeking to reach an agreement, the union should put its proposals for accessing the workers to the employer. The employer should not dismiss the proposals unless he considers the union's requirements to be unreasonable in the circumstances. If the employer rejects the proposals, he should offer alternative arrangements to the union at the earliest opportunity, preferably within three working days of receiving the union's initial proposals. In the course of this dialogue the union will need to reveal its plans for on-site access.

19. It is reasonable for the union to request information from the employer to help it formulate and refine its access proposals. In particular, the employer should disclose to the union information about his typical methods of communicating with his workforce and provide such other practical information as may be needed about, say, workplace premises or patterns of work. Where relevant to the union in framing its plans, the employer should also disclose information about his own plans to put across his views, directly or indirectly, to the workers about the recognition (or derecognition) of the union. The employer should not, however, disclose to the union the names or addresses (postal or e-mail) of the workers who will be balloted, unless the workers concerned have authorised the disclosure.

Amending the access agreement

20. Every effort should be made to ensure access agreements are faithfully implemented. To avoid misunderstanding on the ground, the employer should seek to draw the attention of relevant managers to the agreement and the commitments to release workers to attend access meetings. Likewise, the union should take steps to ensure that the relevant union officials and representatives are made aware of the agreed arrangements. However, in some cases, the agreement may need to be changed if circumstances alter. For example, a union official selected to enter the workplace may be unexpectedly called away by his union on other urgent

business. Likewise, the employer might wish to re-arrange an event if the selected meeting-room is unexpectedly and unavoidably needed for other important business purposes. If such circumstances arise, the union, or the employer if his situation changes, should notify the other party at the earliest opportunity that a change will need to be made to the agreed access arrangements, and offer alternative suggestions. The other party should generally accept the alternative arrangements, if they are of an equivalent nature to those already agreed.

Resolving differences about agreeing access arrangements

21. Where the employer and the union fail to agree access arrangements voluntarily, either party, acting separately or together, may ask the Advisory, Conciliation and Arbitration Service (Acas) to conciliate. Given the limited time available, Acas will respond to the conciliation request as soon as possible, and preferably within one working day of receiving the request. Both parties should give all reasonable assistance to Acas to enable it to help the parties overcome their difficulties through conciliation.

22. Every effort should be made to resolve any procedural difficulties remaining, but, ultimately, where it remains deadlocked, the CAC may be asked to assist. The CAC could, in appropriate circumstances, consider delaying the arrangement of the ballot for a limited period to give extra time for the parties to settle their differences. However, where no agreement is forthcoming, the CAC may be asked to adjudicate and to make an order.

[4692]

SECTION C
ACCESS IN OPERATION

What is the access period?

23. *Following the notification period, and providing it does not receive a contrary request from the trade union, the CAC will be required to arrange the holding of the ballot. As soon as is reasonably practicable, the CAC must inform the parties of the fact that it is arranging the ballot, the name of the qualified independent person appointed to conduct the ballot, and the period within which the ballot must be conducted. The ballot must be held within 20 working days from the day after the appointment of the independent person, or longer if the CAC should so decide.*

24. The period of access will begin as soon as the parties have been informed of the arrangements for the ballot as in paragraph 23 above. The CAC will endeavour to inform both parties as soon as the independent person has been appointed. This may be achieved by a telephone call to both parties, followed by a letter of confirmation.

25. If the ballot is to be conducted by post, the period of access will come to an end on the closing date of the balloting period. If the ballot is to be conducted at the workplace, access will continue until the ballot has closed. However, where the ballot is to be conducted at the workplace, and where the union has already had adequate access opportunities, both the employer and the union should largely confine their activities during the actual hours of balloting to the encouragement of workers to vote. They should reduce or cease other campaigning activity at this time. For example, both the employer and the union should avoid scheduling large meetings at such times. This should ensure that the ballot is conducted in a calm and orderly fashion, with minimum disruption to the normal functioning of the workplace.

Who may be granted access?

26. The access agreement should specify who should be given access to the workers who will be balloted. Employers should be prepared to give access to:

- (a) individual union members employed by the employer, who are nominated by the union as the lead representative of their members at workplaces where the bargaining unit is situated;
- (b) individual union members employed by the employer, who are nominated by the union as the lead representative of their members at other workplaces in the employer's business, provided that it is practicable for them to attend events at workplaces where the bargaining unit is situated. The costs of travelling from other workplaces should be met by the individuals or the union; and
- (c) "full-time" union officials. (That is, individuals employed by the union, who are officials of the union within the meaning of the Sections 1 and 119 of the Trade Union and Labour Relations (Consolidation) Act 1992).

The number of union representatives entitled to gain access should be proportionate to the scale and nature of the activities or events organised within the agreed access programme.

Where will the access take place?

27. Where practicable in the circumstances, a union should be granted access to the workers at their actual workplace. However, each case will depend largely on the type of workplace concerned, and the union will need to take account of the wide variety of circumstances and operational requirements that are likely to be involved. In particular, consideration will need to be given to the employer's responsibility for health and safety and security issues. In other words, access arrangements should reflect local circumstances and each case should be examined on the facts.

28. Where they are suitable for the purpose, the employer's typical methods of communicating with his workforce should be used as a benchmark for determining how the union should communicate with members of the same workforce during the access period. If the employer follows the custom and practice of holding large workforce meetings in, for example, a meeting room or a canteen, then the employer should make the same facilities available to the union. However, in cases where the workplace is more confined, and it is therefore the employer's custom and practice to hold only small meetings at the workplace, then the union will also be limited to holding similar small meetings at that workplace. In exceptional circumstances, due to the nature of the business or severe space limitations, access may need to be restricted to meetings away from the workplace premises, and the union will need to consider finding facilities off-site at its own expense unless it agrees otherwise with the employer. In these circumstances, the employer should give all reasonable assistance to the union in notifying the workers in advance of where and when such off-site events are to take place. Where such exceptional circumstances exist, it would normally be expected that the employer would not hold similar events at the workplace.

When will the access take place?

29. The union should ensure that disruption to the business is minimised, especially for small businesses which might find it more difficult to organise cover for absent workers. The union's access to the workers should usually take place during normal working hours but at times which minimise any possible disruption to the activities of the employer. This will ensure that the union is able to communicate with as large a number of the workers as possible. Again, the arrangements should reflect the circumstances of each individual case. Consideration should be given to holding events, particularly those involving a large proportion of the workers in the bargaining unit, during rest periods or towards the end of a shift. In deciding the timing of meetings and other events, the union and the employer should be guided by the employer's custom and practice when communicating with his workforce. If, due to exceptional circumstances, access must be arranged away from the workplace, it might be practicable to arrange events in work time if they are held nearby, within easy walking distance. Otherwise, off-site events should normally occur outside work time.

The frequency and duration of union activities

30. The parties will need to establish agreed limits on the duration and frequency of the union's activities during the access period. Subject to the circumstances discussed in paragraphs 27–29 above, the employer should allow the union to hold one meeting of at least 30 minutes in duration for every 10 days of the access period, or part thereof, which all workers or a substantial proportion of them are given the opportunity to attend. In circumstances where the employer or others organise similar large-scale meetings in work time against the recognition application (or in favour of derecognition), then it would be reasonable for the union to hold additional meetings, if necessary, to ensure that in total it has the same number of large-scale meetings as the employer and his supporters.

31. Where they would be appropriate having regard to all the circumstances, union "surgeries" could be organised at the workplace during working hours at which each worker would have the opportunity, if they wish, to meet a union representative for fifteen minutes on an individual basis or in small groups of two or three. The circumstances would include whether there was a demand from the workforce for surgeries, whether the surgeries could be arranged off-site as effectively, whether the holding of surgeries would lead to an unacceptable increase in tension at the workplace and whether the employer, line managers or others use similar one-to-one or small meetings to put across the employer's case. The union should organise surgeries in a systematic way, ensuring that workers attend meetings at pre-determined times, thereby avoiding delays before workers are seen and ensuring that they promptly return to their work stations afterwards. Wherever practicable, the union should seek

to arrange surgeries during periods of down-time such as rest or meal breaks. Where surgeries do not take place, the minimum time allowed for each larger scale meeting should be 45 minutes.

32. An employer should ensure that workers who attend a meeting or a "surgery" organised by the union with his agreement during work time, should be paid, in full, for the duration of their absence from work. The employer will not be expected to pay the worker if the meeting or surgery takes place when the worker would not otherwise have been at work, and would not have been receiving payment from the employer.

33. Where the union wishes one of the employer's workers within the meaning of paragraphs 26(a) and 26(b) above to conduct a surgery, the employer should normally give time off with pay to the worker concerned. The worker should ensure that he provides the employer with as much notice as possible, giving details about the timing and location of the surgery. Exceptionally, it may be reasonable for the employer to refuse time off. This will apply if unavoidable situations arise where there is no adequate cover for the worker's absence from the workplace and the production process, or the provision of a service cannot otherwise be maintained. Before refusing permission, the employer should discuss the matter with the union and the worker to explore alternative arrangements.

What about written communication?

34. The union may want to display written material at the place of work. Employers, where practicable, should provide a notice board for the union's use. This notice board should be in a prominent location in the workplace and the union should be able to display material, including references to off-site meetings, without interference from the employer. Often, an existing notice-board could be used for this purpose. The union should also be able to place additional material near to the noticeboard including, for example, copies of explanatory leaflets, which the workers may read or take away with them. If there are no union representatives within the meaning of paragraphs 26(a) and 26(b) above present at the workplace, the employer should allow access to a full time official of the union to display the material.

35. The union may also wish to make use of its web-site pages on the internet for campaigning purposes. An employer should allow his workers access to the union's material in the same way that he explicitly, or tacitly, allows his workers to down-load information in connection with activities not directly related to the performance of their job. If an employer generally disallows all such internet use, he should consider giving permission to one of his workers nominated by the union to down-load the material, and it would be this person's responsibility to disseminate it more widely among other workers.

36. A nominated union representative employed by the employer may also want to make use of internal electronic communication, such as electronic mail or intranets, for campaigning purposes. For example, he may want to remind workers of forthcoming union meetings or surgeries. The employer should allow the representative to make reasonable use of these systems if the employer explicitly, or tacitly, allows his workers to use them for matters which are not directly related to the performance of their job. In cases where such use is disallowed, it would still be reasonable for the representative to use them, if the employer uses such forms of communication to send to the workers information against the union's case. When sending messages in this capacity, the representative should make it clear that the advice comes from the union and not the employer.

What about small businesses?

37. Access arrangements for small businesses need not necessarily create difficulties. For example, it may be easier to arrange for a smaller number of workers to meet together. On the other hand, there may be difficulties providing cover for workers in smaller organisations, or in finding accommodation for meetings. In such cases, the employer and the union should try to reach an understanding about how access arrangements can be organised to ensure minimum disruption. Agreements may need to be flexible to accommodate any particular needs of the employer.

Arrangements for non-typical workers

38. Many, or sometimes most, workers in a bargaining unit may not work full time in a standard Monday-Friday working week. Others might rarely visit the employer's premises. The employer should bear in mind the difficulties faced by unions in communicating with:

- shift workers
- part-time workers

- homeworkers
- a dispersed or peripatetic workforce
- those on maternity or parental leave
- those on sick leave.

39. The employer should be receptive to a union's suggestions for securing reasonable access to such "non-typical workers", and allow them, where practicable, to achieve a broadly equivalent level of access to those workers as to typical workers. It would be reasonable for the union to organise its meetings or surgery arrangements on a more flexible basis to cover shift workers or part-time workers. An employer should agree to the maximum flexibility of arrangements, where reasonable in the circumstances. This would not extend to an employer being obliged to meet the travel costs of his workers attending meetings arranged by the union.

40. In addition, the union will be able to make use of the independent person to distribute information to home addresses via the postal service. This will ensure that literature will be received by any workers who are not likely to attend the workplace during the access period, for example those on maternity or sick leave. The CAC will supply the name, address and telephone number of the independent person to both the union and the employer.

What about joint employer/union activities?

41. There may be scope for the union and the employer to undertake joint activities where they both put across their respective views about recognition or derecognition in a non-confrontational way. Such joint activities can be an efficient method of providing information, minimising business disruption and costs. For example, the parties may wish to consider:

- the arrangement of joint meetings with each party allocated a period of thirty minutes to address the workers; and
- the use of a joint notice-board where an equal amount of space is devoted to the employer and the union.

[4693]

SECTION D
OTHER ACCESS ISSUES

Observing an access agreement

42. Both parties should ensure they keep to agreements about access arrangements. For example, if the parties agree to hold a meeting lasting 30 minutes in duration, every effort should be made to ensure that the meeting does not over-run its allocated time. Likewise, neither party should remove, or tamper, with material placed on a notice board by the other party, unless they are obliged to do so for legal reasons.

Privacy of meetings

43. Employers should respect the privacy of access meetings. *Paragraph 26(4D) of Schedule A1 of the Trade Union and Labour Relations (Consolidation) Act 1992 therefore provides that the employer or any representative of his must not attend an access meeting unless invited to do so. Likewise, the employer must not use the union's unwillingness to allow him or his representative to attend as a reason to refuse an access meeting unless it is reasonable to do so. The employer must not record or otherwise be informed of the proceedings of a meeting unless it is reasonable for him to do so.*

44. Supervisors or managers may attend an access meeting, even though they may be seen as representatives of the employer, provided they have been invited to attend by the union. In general, it should be expected that such workers would be invited by the union to attend access meetings where they fall within the bargaining unit and are therefore entitled to vote. However, there may be circumstances – for example, where the attendance of supervisors would deter other workers from expressing their opinions, or where managers are campaigning on behalf of the employer – where it is reasonable for the union not to invite them. In such circumstances, consideration should be given to arranging separate access meetings for the supervisors and managers concerned. In situations where they are not invited to attend meetings with other workers, supervisors or other managers should not insist on attending simply because they are part of the bargaining unit. To avoid uncertainty and the disruption of meetings, the union should consider in advance whether it wishes to exclude such individuals from meetings, taking steps where possible to inform the individuals concerned before the meeting occurs. The union should avoid issuing generalised or loosely drafted invitations to attend access meetings, if its intention is to prevent certain individuals from attending.

45. In small workplaces or in workplaces with no dedicated meeting rooms, it may be difficult to find suitable accommodation on site which can be set aside for the exclusive use of the union to hold a meeting. Achieving privacy in such circumstances may be difficult, but solutions might be found by holding meetings during lunch breaks or at other times when business would not be significantly affected if managers or other work colleagues were required to vacate the premises or meeting area in question. In extreme cases, for example where continuous working is necessary, privacy may be achieved only by holding meetings away from the workplace.

46. Many employers have security cameras or other recording equipment permanently positioned on site to monitor or record workplace activity. Most are installed for reasons of security, health and safety or quality control. Where such equipment is used, and could record meetings, the employer should inform the union accordingly unless key security considerations prevent such disclosure. The employer and the union should then discuss ways to ensure the privacy of meetings. It may be possible, for example, to turn off the equipment in question for the short period of meetings. Alternatively, the employer may wish to ensure that any transmissions from the surveillance equipment during the period of the meeting are not viewed live or recorded. The scope for such measures may be limited in rare cases where security or health and safety may be significantly and unavoidably jeopardised as a result.

47. The employer should not eavesdrop on access meetings or pressurise any of those attending to disclose what occurred at them. Generally, the employer should not seek to question attendees about the proceedings of meetings but, in exceptional cases of, say, alleged harassment or damage to property, there may be a need for the employer to investigate the conduct of meetings. However, it must be recognised that information often circulates quite widely within workplaces and the employer may therefore learn what took place even though he took no specific steps to discover what had occurred. In some cases, individual workers may disclose without prompting what took place at meetings in their ordinary exchanges with line managers or other work colleagues.

Behaving responsibly

48. Both parties should endeavour to ensure that, wherever possible, potentially acrimonious situations are avoided. For access arrangements to work satisfactorily, the employer and the union should behave responsibly, and give due consideration to the requirements of the other party throughout the access period. For example, neither the union nor the employer should seek to disrupt or interfere with meetings being held by the other party. So, if the union is holding a meeting, the employer should avoid the scheduling of other conflicting meetings or events which would draw workers away from the union's meeting. Unless special factors apply, the employer should not offer inducements to workers not to attend access meetings. For example, where an access meeting is held towards the end of the working day, the employer should not tell workers that they could go home early if they do not attend the union's meeting. However, unforeseen events may arise – an urgent order, for example – where the employer may need to require workers not to attend an access meeting, paying them overtime, or some other additional payment or fringe benefit, for any extra work involved. The offer of additional pay for extra work in such circumstances is reasonable. Where such exceptional events occur, the employer should explain the position to the union as soon as practicable, and offer alternative but comparable access arrangements for the workers involved.

49. Where it is practicable to hold meetings or surgeries at the workplace, the employer should provide appropriate accommodation, fit for the purpose, which should include adequate heating and lighting, and arrangements to ensure that the meeting is held in private. In turn, the union should ensure that business costs and business disruption are minimised. Unions should be aware of the needs of the employer to maintain the production process, to maintain a level of service, and to ensure safety and security at all times.

[4694]

SECTION E
RESPONSIBLE CAMPAIGNING AND UNFAIR PRACTICES

50. This Section of the Code provides guidance on those standards of behaviour which are likely to prevent undue influence or other unfair practices from occurring. In places, it also refers to behaviour which, if pursued, may constitute an unfair practice. However, given the range of possible behaviours involved, it is unrealistic for the Code to identify every circumstance which might give rise to undue influence or other unfair practice. In any event, as Section F discusses, it is the task of the Central Arbitration Committee to judge whether an unfair practice has been committed, basing its judgment on the particular facts of a case.

Responsible campaigning

51. Recognition and derecognition ballots concern important, and sometimes complex, issues. It may help those workers entitled to vote in these ballots to receive information from the employer and the union setting out their views on the implications of recognition and non-recognition. Parties are not required to undertake any campaigning activity during this period. Indeed, a party might choose to desist from campaigning altogether because it wishes to avoid unnecessary acrimony or because it sees an advantage in employment relations terms in leaving the issue to the workers to decide. This Code should not therefore be read as discouraging such behaviour. That said, there will be other cases where parties will wish to campaign and such activity can benefit the balloting process in helping the workers make informed decisions. But active campaigning needs to be responsible or it can lead to the use of unfair practices which distort the balloting process, increase workplace friction and can sour employment relations.

52. Campaigning can expose sharp divisions of opinion, and ill-judged activity can damage trust and long-term employment relations. Parties should therefore discuss with each other at an early stage how they would wish campaigning to be undertaken. This discussion could take place at the same time the parties seek to reach access agreements. There are advantages in parties exchanging information about their approach to campaigning, indicating for example those persons or organisations which are likely to undertake the activity on their behalf. Prior discussion should focus in particular on the standards of conduct expected of campaigners to minimise the risk of intimidation occurring. One way to structure such joint discussions might be for the parties to discuss how they think the guidance in this section of the Code could best be applied to their particular situation. Where they agree standards of conduct, parties should take steps to ensure that those who campaign on their behalf are fully aware of them.

What are unfair practices?

53. *Parties must refrain from using an unfair practice during recognition or derecognition ballots. A party uses an unfair practice if, with a view to influencing the result of the ballot, the party:*

(*a*) *offers to pay money or give money's worth to a worker entitled to vote in a ballot in return for the worker's agreement to vote in a particular way or to abstain from voting;*

(*b*) *makes an "outcome-specific" offer to a worker entitled to vote in a ballot. (An "outcome-specific" offer is an offer to pay money or give money's worth which is conditional on the issuing by the CAC of a declaration that the union is entitled to be recognised or is not entitled to be recognised, and such an offer is not conditional on anything which is done or occurs as a result of the declaration in question).* Thus, an offer by either a union (or an employer) to pay each worker £100, provided the ballot does (or does not) result in recognition would be categorised as an unfair practice. In contrast, an undertaking by a union to secure an increase of £1,000 in the annual pay of workers through the collective bargaining process following a vote for recognition would not be captured because the offer clearly depends on other circumstances – in this case, the negotiation of a collective agreement – which is contingent on recognition being awarded;

(*c*) *coerces or attempts to coerce a worker entitled to vote in a ballot to disclose whether he intends to vote or abstain from voting in the ballot, or how he intends to vote, or how he has voted, in the ballot;*

(*d*) *dismisses or threatens to dismiss a worker;*

(*e*) *takes or threatens to take disciplinary action against a worker;*

(*f*) *subjects or threatens to subject a worker to any other detriment by, for example, threatening to give a worker a lower performance mark or a worse promotional assessment if he supports recognition or non-recognition; or*

(*g*) *uses or attempts to use undue influence on a worker entitled to vote in a ballot.*[1]

54. The statute refers to the term "money's worth" when defining an unfair offer to a worker. The term covers the making of non-cash offers to workers. Such non-cash offers usually involve the provision of goods and services, for which workers would otherwise need to pay if they procured the goods or services for themselves. Most fringe benefits – say, a better company car, subsidised health insurance or free legal services – would normally fall into this category. In addition, offers to provide additional paid holiday or other paid leave are likely to constitute "money's worth". Of course, providing such "money's worth" for permissible reasons – for example, as a normal inducement to join a union or as a typical bonus for meeting a work target – would not be categorised as an unfair practice.

55. Unfair practices can involve the taking of disciplinary action against workers, where such disciplinary action has the purpose of influencing the result of the ballot. The period of

ballots is relatively short and this lessens the scope for disciplinary matters to arise. However, it is worth noting that this unfair practice is not limited just to disciplinary action taken against workers entitled to vote in a ballot. It is possible that an unfair practice could be committed if, say, disciplinary action were taken against a union activist involved in the union's campaign who was not entitled to vote in the ballot. Equally, the employer is not prevented from taking any disciplinary action just because a ballot is occurring. There may be sound grounds for the employer to discipline a worker, which are totally unconnected with the ballot. Likewise, it is possible that a worker's campaigning activity – say, the use of threatening behaviour against other workers or the unauthorised use of work time for campaigning – may itself give rise to disciplinary action which would not constitute an unfair practice. When contemplating disciplinary action, the employer should in addition take note of the guidance provided in the *Acas Code of Practice on Disciplinary and Grievance Procedures*, especially its advice on the disciplining of union officials.

56. The statutory list of unfair practices highlights actions to bribe, pressurise or exert other undue influence on workers to vote in particular ways or not to vote at all. Such conduct, especially the exertion of undue influence, can take many forms. At one extreme, undue influence may take the obvious form of actual or threatened physical violence against workers. It may also take other, and more subtle, forms of behaviour to influence the outcome of the ballot. For example, the introduction of higher pay or better conditions in the ballot period may constitute undue influence if the ballot period is not the normal time for reviewing pay or if there is not some other pressing reason unconnected with the ballot for raising pay.

Who should campaign?

57. Transparency is an important feature of normal campaigning activity and reduces the risk that a worker might be unduly influenced through subterfuge or misrepresentation. So, those authorised by the employer or a union to campaign on their behalf should take steps to inform the workers involved that they are so authorised and are therefore acting under instruction or at the behest of the party involved. Where there is reason to believe that workers do not understand their role, supervisors and line managers who undertake such work on behalf of the employer should state that they are acting in that capacity when communicating campaign messages to the workforce. In similar circumstances, union members who act as officials of the union or who are otherwise authorised to represent the union in its campaigning work should also explain their role when speaking to other workers in their capacity as campaigners.

58. Sometimes, a party might employ or hire a paid consultant to assist its campaigning work. Such consultants are therefore acting as agents of the party involved. If their behaviour constitutes an unfair practice, then the party who hired their services is also committing an unfair practice where the party expressly or by implication authorised the behaviour. A failure by a party to repudiate and correct misconduct by a consultant can be taken as implying that such conduct is authorised. Parties should therefore monitor the activities of the consultants they hire. Where outside consultants are used by either party, and undertake active campaigning by speaking to the workforce, then they should inform the workers that they have been hired by that party. They should also take steps to inform the workers accurately about the general purpose of their engagement. Whilst there is no need to divulge commercial confidences or to detail the precise contractual remit, if a consultant has been hired to advance the case of the union or the employer in the campaign then that essential fact should be divulged to the workforce when the consultant is communicating with them. It follows that consultants should not present themselves as independent or impartial third parties when undertaking their campaigning work.

59. The employer and the union are usually responsible for the actions of those whom they authorise or hire to campaign on their behalf. They should therefore take steps to brief their representatives or agents accordingly in advance of undertaking such activity. The briefing should not be limited to just the messages or information which the union or employer wish to convey. It should also provide clear advice to representatives or agents on the behavioural standards expected of them and the need to avoid actions which could constitute an unfair practice.

60. The employer and the union should also dissociate themselves from material containing personal attacks or allegations which is circulated on an anonymous basis. The party whose case appears to be favoured by the anonymous material should usually repudiate it, informing all workers in the bargaining unit accordingly.

What are the main forms of campaigning?

61. All campaigning involves communication with workers in the bargaining unit. Sometimes, that communication can take the form of face-to-face discussion with a worker or

workers. Such encounters can perform useful functions as many workers may feel nervous about asking questions at mass meetings and small scale gatherings may encourage more open debate. Section C therefore refers to the option for unions to access the workforce by holding "surgeries" which individual workers or small groups of workers can attend if they wish. That said, the employer or the union must take particular care when handling one-to-one meetings or encounters with small groups, because a worker may feel more vulnerable in those situations and undue influence may arise if a worker feels threatened as a result. Workers should not normally be required to attend small meetings organised by either the employer or the union for campaigning purposes, and they should not be threatened with sanctions if they fail to attend. Workers who voluntarily attend should be informed that they are under no obligation to answer any direct questions which are put to them. In particular, they should not be required to disclose the way they have voted or their voting intentions.

62. Most small or one-to-one meetings occur at the place of work. But a party might also try to arrange similar encounters outside the workplace to canvass opinion by visiting a worker's home or by ringing a home telephone. When undertaking such activity, unions should note that neither the CAC nor the qualified independent person it employs to run the ballot will disclose to the union the names, addresses or telephone numbers of the workers involved. Whereas canvassing at a worker's home may be an acceptable practice, reflecting perhaps restricted access at work, considerable care needs to be taken by the party involved to avoid possible intimidation, however unintended, which could give rise to undue influence. Where practicable, a party should seek and obtain a worker's permission in advance before visiting him at home. In particular, the number of people visiting a worker's home to campaign or canvass, even where prior permission is obtained, should be limited to one or, perhaps, two people. If a worker does not wish to open or continue a discussion with the campaigners, then that wish must be completely respected. A failure to leave a worker's premises on request would almost certainly be seen as an intimidatory practice. Also, if a worker indicates he does not wish to be revisited at home, or rung again by telephone, then that wish should be respected.

63. The holding of one or two face-to-face meetings, either on site or off it, may not in itself be perceived as placing unwelcome pressure on the worker involved. Indeed, a worker might request further meetings himself to cover the issues fully or to follow up a discussion. However, the frequency of meetings, or frequent requests to attend meetings, can be perceived as potentially threatening by some workers. There may come a point where persistent approaches to workers will be construed as harassment. Parties must therefore be aware that the intensity of their campaigning activity can give rise to problems.

64. Campaigning can also be undertaken by circulating information by e-mails, videos or other mediums. There is nothing intrinsically wrong with communication of that nature. Indeed, because such communication does not require the physical presence of the campaigner, they may well be seen as having less potential to threaten the worker. That said, the content of such communications can still intimidate or threaten the voter, and care should therefore be taken to avoid such effects when drafting written communication or producing videos.

How should campaigners put across their message?

65. Campaigning is inherently a partisan activity. Each party is therefore unlikely to put across a completely balanced message to the workforce, and some overstatement or exaggeration may well occur. In general, workers will expect such behaviour and can deal with it. Also, by listening to both sides, they will be able to question and evaluate the material presented to them.

66. Campaigning should focus on the issues at stake. These will mostly concern the workplace, the performance of the union or the running of the employer's business. Sometimes, it will be legitimate to focus on the work behaviours and previous work histories of key individuals. For example, it may be pertinent to refer to the way a proprietor or a senior manager has responded to workplace grievances in the past or to the way a key union official has handled negotiations elsewhere. But campaigning about the personal lives of senior managers or union leaders usually adds nothing beneficial to the discussion of the issues and should be avoided. Personalised attacks and the denigration of individuals may also harm the long-term health of employment relations.

67. Parties, especially the employer, should take particular care if they discuss job losses or the relocation of business activity. Such statements can be seen as directly threatening the livelihoods of the workers involved, and can give rise to undue influence by implicitly threatening to harm the workers concerned. It is a fine line, therefore, to distinguish between fair comment about job prospects and intimidatory behaviour designed primarily to scare the

workers to vote against recognition. In general, references to job prospects are more likely to constitute fair comment if they can be clearly linked to the future economic performance of the employer with or without union recognition, and are expressed in measured terms. Unsubstantiated assertions on this particularly sensitive issue should therefore be avoided. So, it might be fair comment to argue that the employer's business may run less successfully if recognition is awarded, and employment may be less secure as a result, because pay levels would rise or work would be organised less flexibly. On the other hand, statements that the employer will make redundancies or relocate simply because a union is recognised should be avoided.

68. Part of a party's normal campaigning is to engage with the arguments put forward by others. That can be helpful and can assist workers in understanding the issues at stake. Each party will therefore try to obtain the campaigning literature of the other party to enable them to discuss the points raised. This should not normally present a problem as literature tends to be widely available either on websites, notice boards or elsewhere. Indeed, parties may often find it mutually advantageous to exchange these materials.

69. Campaigning meetings should be treated as far as possible as private affairs, and there are legislative requirements covering the privacy of access meetings at work (see paragraphs 43–47 in Section D). Meetings or other campaigning activities which occur off-site are generally not covered by the access provisions, but the privacy of those gatherings should be respected. A party should not infiltrate meetings or use other covert methods to monitor another party's campaign. It is also likely to constitute an intimidatory practice for parties to photograph, record or otherwise place workers under surveillance without permission whilst they are undertaking campaigning or attending campaigning events off-site, unless such activity takes place at a location (for example, the entrance to a workplace) where surveillance equipment normally operates for other legitimate reasons. Parties should also not penalise workers, or threaten to penalise them, if they attend or take part in those off-site activities.

[4695]

SECTION F
RESOLVING DISPUTES

Intervention by the CAC

Access

70. Disputes may arise between the parties during the access period about the failure to allow reasonable access or to implement access agreements. If these disputes cannot be resolved, the union may ask the CAC to decide whether the employer has failed to perform his statutory duties in relation to the ballot.

71. *If the CAC is satisfied that the employer has failed to perform one or more of his five duties:*

a) *to co-operate generally with the union and the independent person on the ballot;*
b) to give the union such access to the workers constituting the bargaining unit as is reasonable to inform them of the object of the ballot and to seek their support and opinions;
c) *to provide the CAC with the names and home addresses of those workers;*
d) to refrain from making any offer to any or all of the workers constituting the bargaining unit which (i) has or is likely to have the effect of inducing any or all of them not to attend any relevant meeting between the union and the workers constituting the bargaining unit and (ii) is not reasonable in the circumstances; and
e) to refrain from taking or threatening to take any action against a worker solely or mainly on the grounds that he (i) attended or took part in any relevant meeting between the union and the workers constituting the bargaining unit, or (ii) indicated his intention to attend or take part in such a meeting.

and the ballot has not been held, the CAC may order the employer to take such steps to remedy the failure as the CAC considers reasonable, and within a time that the CAC considers reasonable. Where the CAC is asked to make an order very shortly before the end of the access period, it may be impracticable for the CAC to consider the request and for the employer and the union to remedy any failure in the short time before the ballot is held. In such circumstances, the CAC may extend the access period by ordering the ballot to be rescheduled for a later date to ensure that access is achieved.

72. *If the employer fails to comply with the CAC's order within the time specified, and the ballot has still not been held, the CAC may issue a declaration that the union is recognised, or that the union is not derecognised.*

73. It is the employer's duty to provide reasonable access, and complaints about a failure to provide such access can be made by unions only. However, in deciding whether the employer has complied with his duty to give the union access, the CAC may take into account all relevant circumstances. This may include the behaviour of the union. The CAC may therefore decide that the employer has complied with the duty in circumstances where, because the union has acted unreasonably, he denies the union access or refuses to implement agreed access arrangements.

Unfair Practices

74. Complaints may also surface that a party has committed an unfair practice during the balloting period. Such complaints may be referred by the employer or the union to the CAC to adjudicate though any complaints must be made either before the ballot closes or on the first working day after that. Where time permits, it is a good practice for the parties to try to resolve them locally in the first instance.

75. The CAC must decide that a complaint is well-founded if the party complained against used an unfair practice and the CAC is satisfied that the practice changed or was likely to change, in the case of a worker entitled to vote in a ballot either (i) his intention to vote or to abstain from voting or (ii) his intention to vote in a particular way or (iii) how he voted.

76. Where it considers a complaint is well-founded, the CAC must issue a declaration to that effect, and it may

- *issue a remedial order to the party concerned to take such action as it specifies and within a timetable it specifies to mitigate the effect of the unfair practice, and /or*
- *give notice to the parties that it intends to hold a fresh secret ballot* (and thereby replace any which may have been contaminated by the unfair practice).

77. Where a party either (i) fails to comply with a remedial order or (ii) has committed a second unfair practice in relation to the ballot (or a re-run ballot) or (iii) has committed an unfair practice involving the use of violence or the dismissal of a union official, the CAC may take other sanctions against that party. Where that party is the union, the CAC may declare that the union is not entitled to be recognised. Where that party is the employer, the CAC may declare that the union is entitled to be recognised.[2]

Minor disputes

78. Some disputes about access may be minor by nature. For example, the employer may be aggrieved that an access meeting has over-run somewhat. Or a union might have cause to complain if it regards the meeting room provided by the employer as being too small to accommodate everyone in comfort. In such cases, both parties should avoid taking hasty action which might prejudice the implementation of other access arrangements. The union should generally avoid taking minor complaints about access to the CAC as a first course of action.

79. Instead, the parties should make every effort to resolve the dispute between themselves. They should make full use of any mechanism to resolve such disputes which they may have established in the access agreement, and consider the use of Acas's conciliation services. It would generally be a good practice if both the employer and the union nominated a person to act as their lead contact if disagreements or questions arose about the implementation of access arrangements.

80. The period of access will be limited in duration, given that the balloting period will normally be a maximum of 20 working days, and the parties should therefore ensure that disputes are swiftly resolved. The parties should endeavour to inform each other immediately if a dispute arises, and should seek to resolve any disputes as a matter of priority, preferably within one working day of their occurrence.

81. It is also a good practice to follow similar procedures in cases where there are complaints about a person's conduct whilst campaigning. For example, some complaints will be based on a misunderstanding which can be resolved quickly between the parties. And in cases where minor offence has been caused as a result of a careless or unintended remark, then the matter may be simply remedied by the issuing of an apology. Regular and early communication between the parties about the poor behaviour by individual campaigners may also ensure that senior figures on the union and employer sides can prevent repetitions of such behaviour and thereby ensure that unnecessary disputes are avoided.

82. It should be noted that a complaint to the CAC about an unfair practice is unlikely to succeed if it relates to minor aberrations in conduct because such matters are very unlikely to have influenced voting behaviours or intentions. So, for example, a campaigner's use of

strong language or swearing (which, perhaps regrettably, is commonplace inside many workplaces and outside them as well) may not in itself constitute the basis for a well-founded complaint.

The independent person

83. The prime duties of the independent person are to ensure that:

- the names and addresses of the workers comprising the balloting constituency are accurate;
- the ballot is conducted properly and in secret; and
- the CAC is promptly informed of the ballot result.

It is not the function of the independent person to adjudicate disputes about access or unfair practices. That is the CAC's role. However, the independent person may have wide experience and knowledge of balloting arrangements in different settings. The parties might consider informing the independent person about their problems and draw on his experience to identify possible options to resolve their difficulties.

[4696]

NOTES

[1] See paragraphs 27A(2) and 119A(2) of Schedule A1 of the Trade Union and Labour Relations (Consolidation) Act 1992.

[2] There are other sanctions which apply in the special case where a worker has applied to the CAC to derecognise a union.

CODE OF PRACTICE: INDUSTRIAL ACTION BALLOTS AND NOTICE TO EMPLOYERS (2005)

NOTES

This Code is issued under the power given to the Secretary of State by the Trade Union and Labour Relations (Consolidation) Act 1992, s 203 (at **[688]**), with the authority of Parliament. It came into effect on 1 October 2005 (see the Employment Code of Practice (Industrial Action Ballots and Notice to Employers) Order 2005, SI 2005/2420). This Code replaces the similarly named Code issued in 2000. The statutory status of the Code is as stated in s 207 of the 1992 Act (at **[692]**). Notes are as in the original.

PREAMBLE

This document revises and supersedes the Code of Practice on Industrial Action Ballots and Notice to Employers [PL962 (Rev1)], which came into effect on 18 September 2000. Pursuant to section 208(2) of the Trade Union and Labour Relations (Consolidation) Act 1992, that Code shall cease to have effect on the date on which this Code of Practice comes in force.

The legal framework for the operation of this Code is explained in Annex 1 and in its main text. While every effort has been made to ensure that explanations included in the Code are accurate, only the courts can give authoritative interpretations of the law.

The Code's provisions apply equally to men and to women, but for simplicity the masculine pronoun is used throughout. Wherever it appears in the Code the word "court" is used to mean the High Court in England and Wales and the Court of Session in Scotland, but without prejudice to the Code's relevance to any proceedings before any other court.

Passages in this Code which are printed in italic are re-statements of provisions in primary legislation.

[4697]

SECTION A
INTRODUCTION

1. This Code provides practical guidance to trade unions and employers to promote the improvement of industrial relations and good practice in the conduct of trade union industrial action ballots.

2. A union is legally responsible for organising industrial action only if it "authorises or endorses" the action. Authorisation would take place before the industrial action starts, and endorsement after it has previously started as unofficial action.[1]

3. Apart from certain small accidental failures that are unlikely to affect the result, a failure to satisfy the statutory requirements[2] relating to the ballot or giving employers notice of industrial action will give grounds for proceedings against a union by an employer, a customer or supplier of an employer, or an individual member of the public claiming that an effect or likely effect of the industrial action would be to prevent or delay the supply of goods or services to him or to reduce the quality of goods or services so supplied. With the exception of failures to comply with the requirements to give notice to employers, these will also give grounds for action by the union's members.

4. The Code does not deal with other matters which may affect a union's liability in respect of industrial action. For example, the law will give no protection against proceedings to a union which organises secondary action, intimidatory or violent picketing, industrial action which is not "in contemplation or furtherance of a trade dispute",[3] industrial action to establish or maintain any closed shop practice or in support of a worker dismissed while taking part in unofficial industrial action. Nor does it apply to union election ballots, ballots on union political funds or ballots on union recognition or derecognition arranged for by the Central Arbitration Committee under section 70A of and Schedule A1 to the Trade Union and Labour Relations (Consolidation) Act 1992 ("the 1992 Act").[4] These are subject to separate statutory requirements.

Legal status

5. *The Code itself imposes no legal obligations and failure to observe it does not by itself render anyone liable to proceedings. But section 207 of the 1992 Act provides that any provisions of the Code are to be admissible in evidence and are to be taken into account in proceedings before any court where it considers them relevant.*

[4698]

NOTES

1 A note on trade union legal liability for the organisation of industrial action is set out in Annex 1 to this Code.

2 Set out in sections 226–232A and section 234A of the Trade Union and Labour Relations (Consolidation) Act 1992 as amended by the Trade Union Reform and Employment Rights Act 1993, the Employment Relations Act 1999 and the Employment Relations Act 2004.

3 *The term "trade dispute" is defined in section 244 of the 1992 Act.*

4 Inserted by the Employment Relations Act 1999.

SECTION B
WHETHER A BALLOT IS APPROPRIATE

Observing procedural agreements

6. An industrial action ballot should not take place until any agreed procedures, whether formal or otherwise, which might lead to the resolution of a dispute without the need for industrial action have been completed and consideration has been given to resolving the dispute by other means, including seeking assistance from the Advisory, Conciliation and Arbitration Service (Acas).[5] A union should hold a ballot on industrial action only if it is contemplating the organisation of industrial action.

Balloting by more than one union

7. Where more than one union decides that it wishes to ballot members working for the same employer in connection with the same dispute, the arrangements for the different ballots should be co-ordinated so that, as far as practicable, they are held at the same time and the results are announced simultaneously.

[4699]

NOTES

5 Acas can provide assistance after the ballot stage as well. Parties should therefore consider using its services at other times during the course of a dispute to avoid industrial action altogether or to bring that action to an end through a negotiated resolution of the issues at dispute.

SECTION C
PREPARING FOR AN INDUSTRIAL ACTION BALLOT

Arranging for independent scrutiny of the ballot

8. *For a ballot where more than 50 members are given entitlement to vote (see paragraph 21 below), the union must appoint a qualified person as the scrutineer of the ballot.*[6] *For a person to be qualified for appointment as scrutineer of an industrial action ballot, he must be among those specified in an order made by the Secretary of State*[7] *and the union must not have grounds for believing that he will carry out the functions which the law requires other than competently or that his independence in relation to the union might reasonably be called into question.*

9. *The scrutineer's terms of appointment must require him to take such steps as appear appropriate to him for the purpose of enabling him to make a report to the union as soon as reasonably practicable after the date of the ballot (i e the last day on which votes may be cast, if they may be cast on more than one day), and in any event not later than four weeks after that date.*

10. *The union must ensure that the scrutineer carries out the functions required to be part of his terms of appointment, and that there is no interference with this from the union, or any of its members, officials or employees; and comply with all reasonable requests made by the scrutineer for the purpose of carrying out those functions.*

11. It may be desirable to appoint the scrutineer before steps are taken to satisfy any of the other requirements of the law to make it easier for the scrutineer to satisfy himself whether what is done conforms to the legal requirements.

12. In some circumstances, it may help ensure adequate standards for the conduct of the ballot or simplify the balloting process if a union gives the scrutineer additional tasks to carry out on the union's behalf, such as:—

- supervising the production and distribution of voting papers;
- being the person to whom the voting papers are returned by those voting in the ballot; and
- retaining custody of all returned voting papers for a set period after the ballot.

13. Although the scrutiny requirement does not apply to ballots where 50 or fewer members are entitled to vote, a union may want to consider whether the appointment of a scrutineer would still be of benefit in enabling it to demonstrate compliance with the statutory requirements more easily.

Providing ballot notice to employers

14. *The union must take such steps as are reasonably necessary to ensure that any employer who it is reasonable for the union to believe will be the employer of any of its members who will be given entitlement to vote receives written notice of the ballot not later than the seventh day before the intended opening day of the ballot (i e the first day on which a voting paper is sent to any person entitled to vote). That notice must:—*

- *state that the union intends to hold the ballot;*
- *specify the date which the union reasonably believes will be the opening day of the ballot; and*
- *contain either:*
  - (*a*) *a list of the categories of employee to which the employees concerned belong, a list of the workplaces at which they work and figures (together with an explanation of how they were arrived at) showing the total number of employees concerned, the number of them in each of the categories listed and the number of them that work at each of the workplaces listed; or*
  - (*b*) *where some or all of the employees concerned are employees from whose wages the employer makes deductions representing payments to the union,* a practice commonly known as "check off" or "DOCAS", other alternatives apply. In such circumstances, the notice must contain either:
    - (*i*) *those same lists, figures and explanations as set out in* (*a*); *or*
    - (*ii*) *such information as will enable the employer to readily deduce the total number of employees concerned, the categories of employee to which they belong, the number of employees concerned in each of those categories, the workplaces at which the employees concerned work and the number of them at each of these workplaces.*

  Where only some of the employees concerned pay their union contributions by the "check off", the union's notice may include both types of information. That is, the lists, figures and explanations should be provided for those who do not pay their subscriptions through the check off whilst information relating to check off payments may suffice for those who do.

The "employees concerned" are those whom the union reasonably believes will be entitled to vote in the ballot.

The lists and figures or information supplied should be as accurate as is reasonably practicable in the light of the information in the union's possession at the time when it complied with subsection 226A(1)(a). Information is "in the union's possession" provided it is held for union purposes in a document (either in electronic or other form) and provided it is in the possession or under the control of an officer or employee of the union. Dependent on the precise status of the individuals concerned, information held by shop stewards or other lay representatives would probably not qualify for these purposes as being "in the union's possession".

But a notice will not fail to satisfy the requirements simply because it does not name any employees.

15. There are many ways to categorise a group of employees. When deciding which categories it should list in the notice, the union should consider choosing a categorisation which relates to the nature of the employees' work. For example, the appropriate categorisation might be based on the occupation, grade or pay band of the employees involved. The decision might also be informed by the categorisations of the employees typically used by the employer in his dealings with the union. The availability of data to the union is also a legitimate factor in determining the union's choice.

16. When providing an explanation of how the figures in the written notice were arrived at, unions should consider describing the sources of the data used (for example, membership lists held centrally or information held at regional offices, or data collected from surveys or other sources). It is not reasonable to expect union records to be perfectly accurate and to contain detailed information on all members. Where the union's data are known to be incomplete or to contain other inaccuracies, it is a desirable practice for unions to describe in the notices the main deficiencies. In some cases, the figures will be estimates based on assumptions and the notice should therefore describe the main assumptions used when making estimates.

17. To reduce the risk of legal action, the union should allow sufficient time for delivery, use a suitable means of transmission (such as first class post, courier, fax, email or hand delivery) and consider obtaining confirmation that the employer has received the notice, by using recorded delivery or otherwise.

18. It may also reduce the risk of litigation for a union to check that an employer accepts that the information provided complies with the requirements of section 226A(2)(c) of the 1992 Act. Similarly, it would be in the interests of good industrial relations for an employer who believes the notice he has received does not contain sufficient information to comply with the statutory requirements to raise that with the union promptly before pursuing the matter in the court.

Providing sample voting paper(s) to employers

19. *The union must take such steps as are reasonably necessary to ensure that any employer who it is reasonable for the union to believe will be the employer of any of its members who will be given entitlement to vote receives a sample voting paper (and a sample of any variant of that voting paper) not later than the third day before the opening day of the ballot. Where more than one employer's workers are being balloted, it is sufficient to send each employer only the voting paper or papers which will be sent to his employees.*

20. If the sample voting paper is available in time, the union may wish to include it with the notice of intention to ballot. As with the ballot notice, the risk of non-compliance can be reduced by allowing enough time, using appropriate means of transmission and, possibly, by obtaining confirmation of receipt.

Establishing entitlement to vote (the "balloting constituency")

21. *Entitlement to vote in the ballot must be given to all the union's members who it is reasonable at the time of the ballot for the union to believe will be induced by the union (whether that inducement will be successful or not) to take part in or continue with the industrial action, and to no other members.*[8]

22. *The validity of the ballot will not however be affected if the union subsequently induces members to take part in or continue with industrial action who at the time of the ballot:—*

- *were not members; or*
- *were members but who it was not reasonable to expect would be induced to take action* (for example because they changed jobs after the ballot).

23. *It should also be noted that accidental failures to comply with the requirements on:*
- *in particular, who is given entitlement to vote,*
- *the dispatch of voting papers,*
- *giving members the opportunity to vote conveniently by post, and*
- *balloting merchant seamen employed in a ship at sea or outside Great Britain at some time during the voting period*

will be disregarded if, taken together, they are on a scale unlikely to affect the ballot's result.

Balloting members at more than one workplace

24. *Where the members of a union with different workplaces are to be balloted, a separate ballot will be necessary for each workplace unless one of the conditions set out below is met. Where separate ballots are held, it will be unlawful for the union to organise industrial action at any such workplace where a majority of those voting in the ballot for that workplace have not voted "Yes" in response to the relevant required question (or questions) (see paragraph 30 below). (If an employee works at or from a single set of premises, his workplace is those premises. If not, it is the premises with which his employment has the closest connection.)*

25. *In summary, the conditions for holding a single ballot for more than one workplace are:—*
- *at each of the workplaces covered by the single ballot there is at least one member of the union affected*[9] *by the dispute; or*
- *entitlement to vote in the single ballot is given, and limited, to all of a union's members who, according to the union's reasonable belief, are employed in a particular occupation or occupations by one employer or any of a number of employers with whom the union is in dispute; or*
- *entitlement to vote in the single ballot is given, and limited, to all of a union's members who are employed by a particular employer or any of a number of employers with whom the union is in dispute.*

Where a single ballot across a number of workplaces is held and the majority is in favour of industrial action, it is lawful for the union to organise industrial action at any such workplace.

It is possible for a union to hold more than one ballot on a dispute at a single workplace. If the conditions above are met, some or all of those ballots may also cover members in other workplaces.

The balloting method

26. *Votes must be recorded by the individual voter marking a voting paper. Voting papers must be sent out by post and members must be enabled conveniently to return them by post at no direct expense to themselves.*[10] In practice, this means that those properly entitled to vote should be supplied with pre-paid reply envelopes in which to return the voting paper.

27. The period between sending out voting papers (i e the opening day of the ballot) and the date by which completed voting papers should be returned should be long enough for the voting papers to be distributed and returned and for the members concerned to consider their vote. The appropriate period may vary according to such factors as the geographical dispersion of the workforce, their familiarity or otherwise with the issues in the dispute, the class of post used and whether the ballot is being held at a time of year when members are more than usually likely to be away from home or the workplace, for example during the summer holidays. Generally, seven days should be the minimum period where voting papers are sent out and returned by first class post and fourteen days where second class post is used, although – very exceptionally – shorter periods may be possible for ballots with very small, concentrated constituencies who can be expected to be familiar with the terms of the dispute.

28. In order to reduce the likelihood of dispute over whether or not sufficient time has been allowed, the union may wish to consider obtaining one or more certificates of posting to confirm the date when voting papers were actually put into the post, and the number sent out.

Voting papers

29. *The voting paper must:—*
- *where applicable, state the name of the independent scrutineer;*
- *clearly specify the address to which, and the date by which, it is to be returned;*

- *be marked with a number, which is one of series of consecutive numbers used to give a different number to each voting paper;*
- *make clear whether voters are being asked if they are prepared to take part in, or to continue to take part in, industrial action which consists of a strike, or in industrial action short of a strike, which for this purpose includes overtime bans and call-out bans; and*
- *specify the person or persons (and/or class or classes of person/s) who the union intends to have authority to make the first call for industrial action to which the ballot relates, in the event of a vote in favour of industrial action.*[11]

30. *While the question (or questions) may be framed in different ways, the voter must be asked to say by answering "Yes" or "No" whether he is willing to take part in or continue with the industrial action. If the union has not decided whether the industrial action would consist of a strike or action short of a strike (including overtime bans or call-out bans), separate questions in respect of each type of action must appear on the voting paper.*

31. The relevant required question (or questions) should be simply expressed. Neither they, nor anything else which appears on the voting paper, should be presented in such a way as to encourage a voter to answer one way rather than another as a result of that presentation. It is not in general good practice for the union to include additional questions on the voting paper (for example, asking if voters agree with the union's opinion on the merits of the dispute or are prepared to "support" industrial action), but if it chooses to do so they should be clearly separate from the required question(s).

32. *The following words must appear on every voting paper:—*

> *"If you take part in a strike or other industrial action, you may be in breach of your contract of employment. However, if you are dismissed for taking part in strike or other industrial action which is called officially and is otherwise lawful, the dismissal will be unfair if it takes place fewer than twelve weeks after you started taking part in the action, and depending on the circumstances may be unfair if it takes place later."*

This statement must not be qualified or commented upon by anything else on the voting paper.

33. An example voting paper containing the information required by law and other useful information is set out in Annex 2 to this Code. Factual information as indicated would appear in the square brackets and either or both questions could be used as appropriate.

Printing and distribution of the voting papers

34. The union will wish to ensure that arrangements for producing and distributing voting papers will prevent mistakes which might invalidate the ballot. If in doubt, the independent scrutineer may be able to provide useful advice.

35. If there is no independent scrutineer, or if a union decides that it cannot follow the advice offered by the scrutineer, it should consider:—

- printing the voting papers on a security background to prevent duplication;
- whether the arrangements proposed for printing (or otherwise producing) the voting papers, and for their distribution to those entitled to vote in the ballot, offer all concerned sufficient assurance of security.

Communication with members

36. A union should give relevant information to its members entitled to vote in the ballot, including (so far as practicable):-

- the background to the ballot and the issues to which the dispute relates;
- the nature and timing of the industrial action the union proposes to organise if a majority vote "Yes";
- any considerations in respect of turnout or size of the majority vote in the ballot that will be taken into account in deciding whether to call for industrial action; and
- the possible consequences for workers if they take industrial action.

In doing so, the union should ensure that any information it gives to members in connection with the ballot is accurate and not misleading.

[4700]

NOTES

6 *Where separate workplace ballots are required, the scrutiny procedures must be followed in respect of each separate ballot if the number of members given entitlement to vote aggregated across all of the ballots is more than 50.*

7 *In broad terms, the current order (SI 1993/1909) covers practising solicitors, qualified*

accountants and four named bodies (Election.com Limited; Electoral Reform (Ballot Services) Limited; The Involvement and Participation Association; and Popularis Limited)).

8 *The union may choose whether or not to give a vote to any "overseas member", ie any member (other than a merchant seaman or offshore worker) who is outside Great Britain for the whole of the voting period. However, members who may be called upon to take part in or continue with the industrial action, and will be in Northern Ireland for the whole of the voting period, must be given entitlement to vote in a ballot where: (i) the ballot is a workplace ballot at their workplace in Great Britain; or (ii) they work in Northern Ireland but it is intended that they should be called upon to take part in the industrial action alongside their counterparts in Britain, and the ballot is a general ballot covering places of work in both Northern Ireland and Great Britain.*

9 Section 228A(5) of the 1992 Act defines for this purpose which members are affected by a dispute.

10 *There is a limited exception for the balloting of union members who are merchant seamen, where the union reasonably believes that they will be employed in a ship at sea (or outside Great Britain) at some time in the period during which votes may be cast and that it will be convenient for them to vote while on the ship or where the ship is. So far as reasonably practicable, the union must ensure that, in these circumstances, those members get a voting paper while on board ship (or at the place where the ship is located), and an opportunity to vote on board ship (or at that place). The recommendations in this Code should be applied to such ballots, however, save to the extent that they are irrelevant because the dispatch of voting papers is not by post.*

11 Where a person who has not been not specified on the voting paper calls industrial action before it is first called by a specified person, then – in order to be certain that the ballot will give protection against legal proceedings – the union should if possible ensure that the call by the unspecified person is effectively repudiated.

SECTION D
HOLDING AN INDUSTRIAL ACTION BALLOT

37. *In an industrial action ballot:—*

- *every person entitled to vote must be allowed to do so without interference from, or constraint imposed by, the union or any of its members, officials or employees;*
- *as far as reasonably practicable, every person entitled to vote must be:-*
  - *sent a voting paper by post to his home address, or another address which he has asked the union (in writing) to treat as his postal address;*
  - *given a convenient opportunity to vote by post; and*
  - *allowed to do so without incurring any direct cost to himself (see also paragraph 26); and*
- *as far as reasonably practicable, the ballot must be conducted in such a way as to ensure that those voting do so in secret.*

Checks on number of voting papers for return

38. In order to reduce the risk of failures to satisfy the statutory requirements and invalidating the ballot, the union should establish an appropriate checking system so that:—

- no-one properly entitled to vote is accidentally disenfranchised, for example through the use of an out of date or otherwise inaccurate membership list; and
- votes from anyone not properly entitled to vote are excluded.

The independent scrutineer may provide advice on this.

Ensuring secrecy of voting

39. Any list of those entitled to vote should be compiled, and the voting papers themselves handled, so as to preserve the anonymity of the voter so far as this is consistent with the proper conduct of the ballot.

40. Steps should be taken to ensure that a voter's anonymity is preserved when a voting paper is returned. This means, for example, that:—

- envelopes in which voting papers are to be posted should have no distinguishing marks from which the identity of the voter could be established; and
- the procedures for counting voting papers should not prejudice the statutory requirement for secret voting.

[4701]

SECTION E
FOLLOWING AN INDUSTRIAL ACTION BALLOT

41. *The union must:—*

- *ensure that the votes given in an industrial action ballot are fairly and accurately counted;*

- *observe its obligations in connection with the notification of details of the result of an industrial action ballot to all those entitled to vote in the ballot and their employers; and*
- *provide a copy of the scrutineer's report on the ballot to anyone entitled to receive it.*

An inaccuracy in the counting of the votes is to be disregarded if it is both accidental and on a scale which could not affect the result of the ballot. Whether an accidental inaccuracy meets this test in practice will depend on the closeness of the ballot result.

Counting votes accurately and fairly

42. Where the union itself is conducting the ballot, it may wish to apply some or all of the following procedures to secure that the statutory requirements have been complied with:—

- ensuring all unused or unissued voting papers are retained only for so long as is necessary after the time allowed for voting has passed to allow the necessary information for checking the number of voting papers issued and used to be prepared, and that a record is kept of such voting papers when they are destroyed;
- rejection of completed voting papers received after the official close of voting or the time set for receipt of voting papers;
- settlement well in advance of the actual ballot of the organisational arrangements for conducting the count of votes cast, and making available equipment or facilities needed in the conduct of the count to those concerned;
- storage of all voting papers received at the counting location under secure conditions from when they arrive until they are counted;
- setting clear criteria to enable those counting the votes to decide which voting papers are to be rejected as "spoiled", and designating someone who is neither directly affected by the dispute to which the ballot relates nor a union official who regularly represents any of those entitled to vote in the ballot to adjudicate on any borderline cases;
- locking and securing the counting room during the period during which votes are to be counted whenever counting staff are not actually at work; and
- storage of voting papers, once counted, under secure conditions (ie so that they cannot be tampered with in any way and are available for checking if necessary) for at least 6 months after the ballot.

The union may wish to consider putting the counting exercise as a whole into the hands of the independent scrutineer.

Announcing details of the result of a ballot

43. *A union must, as soon as reasonably practicable after holding an industrial action ballot, take steps to inform all those entitled to vote,*[12] *and their employer(s), of the number of:—*

- *votes cast in the ballot;*
- *individuals answering "Yes" to the required question (or questions);*
- *individuals answering "No" to the required question (or questions); and*
- *spoiled voting papers.*

Where separate workplace ballots are required (see paragraphs 24 and 25 above), these details must be notified separately for each such workplace to those entitled to vote there.

44. To help ensure that its result can be notified as required, the union may wish to consider, for example:—

- designating a "Returning Officer" for the centralised count of votes cast in the ballot (or separate "Returning Officers" for counts conducted at different locations) to whom the results will be notified in the form required prior to their announcement;
- organising the counting of votes in such a way that the information required to satisfy the relevant statutory requirements can be easily obtained after the counting process is over;
- using its own journals, local communications news-sheets, company or union branch notice boards to publicise the details of the ballot result to its members; and
- checking with relevant employers that the ballot result details notified to them have arrived.

45. *Before giving the seven-day notice to employers of intended industrial action, the union must have taken the required steps to notify the relevant employer(s) of the ballot result details. Where the employees of more than one employer have been balloted, a failure to provide the required ballot result details to a particular employer or employers will mean that if the union organises industrial action by the workers of that employer or those employers it will not have the support of a ballot. In cases where it is lawful to hold a single ballot across*

PART 4

the workplaces of several or many employers (see paragraph 25 above), the "ballot result" refers to the result aggregated across all the employers and workplaces involved.

46. *If the inducement of industrial action to which the ballot relates is to be capable of being protected by the law, some part of the action must be induced and start to take place within four weeks from the date of the ballot (i e the last day on which votes may be cast in the ballot) or such longer period not exceeding eight weeks as the union and employer may agree.*[13] (To reduce the risk of misunderstanding, both parties may find it helpful for such agreements to be in writing.) *If a ballot results in a "Yes" vote for both a strike and action short of a strike and action short of a strike is induced and starts to take place within the relevant period, the ballot would also continue to protect strike action subsequently, and vice versa.*

Obtaining, and providing copies of, the scrutineer's report

47. *Where more than 50 members are given entitlement to vote, a union must appoint an independent scrutineer, whose terms of appointment must include the production of a report on the conduct of the ballot. This report must be produced as soon as reasonably practicable after the date of the ballot, and in any event not later than four weeks after that date.*

48. *The union must provide a copy of the scrutineer's report to any union member who was entitled to vote in the ballot, or any employer of such a member, who requests one within six months of the date of the ballot. The copy must be supplied as soon as reasonably practicable, and free of charge (or on payment of a reasonable fee specified by the union).*

49. In order to reduce the risk of challenge to a ballot's compliance with the statutory requirements, a union may wish to delay any call for industrial action, following a ballot, until it has obtained the scrutineer's report on the ballot.

If the union decides to authorise or endorse industrial action

50. *If the union decides to authorise or endorse industrial action following a ballot, it must take such steps as are reasonably necessary to ensure that any employer who it is reasonable for the union to believe employs workers who will be, or have been, called upon to take part in the action receives no less than seven days before the day specified in the notice as the date on which workers are intended to begin to take part in continuous action or as the first date on which they are intended to take part in discontinuous action a written notice from the union which:—*

- *is given by any officer, official or committee of the union for whose act of inducing industrial action the union is responsible in law* (an indication of whom this might cover is given in *Annex 1* to this Code);
- *specifies: (i) whether the union intends the action to be "continuous" or "discontinuous";*[14] and *(ii) the date on which any of the affected employees are intended to begin to take part in the action (where it is continuous action), or all the dates on which any of them are intended to take part (where it is discontinuous action);*
- *states that it is a notice given for the purposes of section 234A of the 1992 Act; and*
- *contains either:—*

  (a) *a list of the categories of employee to which the affected employees belong, a list of the workplaces at which they work and figures (together with an explanation of how they were arrived at) showing the total number of affected employees, the number of them in each of the categories listed and the number of them that work at each of the workplaces listed; or*

  (b) *where some or all of the employees are employees from whose wages the employer makes deductions representing payments to the union,* a practice commonly known as "check off" or "DOCAS", *other alternatives apply. In such circumstances the notice must contain either:—*

  (i) *those same lists, figures and explanations as set out in (a); or*

  (ii) *such information as will enable the employer to readily deduce the total number of affected employees, the categories of employee to which they belong, the number of employees concerned in each of those categories, the workplaces at which the affected employees work and the number of them at each of these workplaces.*

  Where only some of the affected employees pay their union contributions by the "check off", the union's notice may include both types of information. That is, the lists, figures and explanations should be provided for those who do not pay their subscriptions through the check off whilst information relating to check off payments may suffice for those who do.

The "affected employees " are those whom the union reasonably believes will be induced by the union or have been so induced to take part in or continue to take part in the industrial action.

The lists and figures or information supplied should be as accurate as is reasonably practicable in the light of the information in the union's possession at the time when it complied with subsection 234A(1). Information is "in the union's possession" if it is held for union purposes in a document (either in electronic or other form) and it is in the possession or under the control of an officer or employee of the union. Dependent on the precise status of the individuals concerned, information held by shop stewards or other lay representatives would probably not qualify for these purposes as being "in the union's possession".

But a notice will not fail to satisfy the requirements simply because it does not name any employees.

Changes in the union's intentions, for example as to the dates on which action is to be taken, require further notices to be given accordingly.

51. With the exception of the requirements relating to continuous and discontinuous action and to the need to give further notices in the event of changes in the union's intentions, the statutory requirements applying to notice of industrial action are for the most part the same as those applying to notice of industrial action ballots and the guidance in paragraphs 15–18 will be of relevance, taking account of the different circumstances.

52. *Where continuous industrial action is suspended,* for example for further negotiations between the employer and union, *the union must normally give the employer a further notice as in paragraphs 50 and 51 above before resuming the action. There is an exception to this requirement to give further notice, however, where the union agrees with the employer that the industrial action will cease to be authorised or endorsed with effect from a date specified in the agreement but may be authorised or endorsed again on or after another date specified in the agreement and the union:—*

- *ceases to authorise or endorse the action with effect from the specified date; and*
- *subsequently re-authorises or re-endorses the action from a date on or after the originally specified date or such later date as may be agreed with the employer.*

For this exception to apply, the resumed industrial action must be of the same kind as covered in the original notice. That will not be so if, for example, the later action is taken by different or additional descriptions of workers. In order to avoid misunderstanding, both parties may find it helpful for such agreements to be in writing.

Seeking union members' views after a union has authorised or endorsed industrial action

53. There is no statutory obligation on a union to ballot, or otherwise consult, its members before it decides to call off industrial action. However, if a union decides to seek its members' views about continuing with industrial action, it may wish to apply the same standards to the process of seeking their views as are set out in this Code.

[4702]

NOTES

12 *If overseas members of a trade union have been given entitlement to vote in an industrial action ballot the detailed information about its result need not be sent to them, but the information supplied to non-overseas members in accordance with the statutory requirements must distinguish between votes cast, individuals voting, and spoiled ballot papers to show which details relate to overseas, and which to non-overseas, members.* (*For these purposes members in Northern Ireland given entitlement to vote do not count as "overseas" members.*)

13 *A union may be allowed to make its first call for industrial action more than four weeks after the date of the ballot if either* (a) *the employer and union agree on an extension, for example to enable talks which are making progress to continue, of up to eight weeks after the date of the ballot or* (b) *an injunction granted by a court or an undertaking given by the union to the court prohibits the union from calling for industrial action during some part, or the whole, of the four weeks following the date of the ballot, and the injunction subsequently lapses or is set aside or the union is released from its undertaking. In the latter case, a union may forthwith apply to the court for an order which, if granted, would provide that the period during which the prohibition had effect would not count towards the four week period for which ballots are normally effective. However, if the court believes that the result of a ballot no longer represents the views of union members, or that something has happened or is likely to happen which would result in union members voting against taking, or continuing with, action if there were a fresh ballot, it may not make such an order. In any case, a ballot can never be effective if a union's first call for industrial action is made more than twelve weeks after the date of the ballot.*

14 *For these purposes, industrial action is "discontinuous" if it is to involve action other than on all the days when action might be taken by those concerned.* An indefinite strike would, therefore, be

PART 4

"continuous"; an overtime ban might be "continuous" or "discontinuous", depending on whether the ban applied to overtime working on all the days on which overtime would otherwise be worked or to overtime working on only some of those days.

ANNEX 1
TRADE UNION LIABILITY

1. *Section 20 of the Trade Union and Labour Relations (Consolidation) Act 1992 lays down when a union is to be held responsible for the act of inducing, or threatening, a breach or interference with a contract in circumstances where there is no immunity. The union will be held liable for any such act which is done, authorised or endorsed by:—*

- *its Executive Committee, General Secretary, President;*
- *any person given power under the union's rules to do, authorise or endorse acts of the kind in question; or*
- *any committee or official of the union (whether employed by it or not).*

A union will be held responsible for such an act by such a body or person regardless of any term or condition to the contrary in its own rules, or in any other contractual provision or rule of law.

2. *For these purposes:—*

- *a "committee of the union" is any group of persons constituted in accordance with the rules of the union;*
- *an "official of the union" is any person who is an officer of the union or of a branch or section of the union or any person who is elected or appointed in accordance with the union's own rules to be a representative of its members, including any person so elected or appointed who is an employee of the same employer as the members, or one or more of the members, he is elected to represent* (e g a shop steward)*; and*
- *an act will be treated to have been done (or authorised or endorsed) by an official if it was so done (or authorised or endorsed) by a group of persons, or any member of a group, to which an official belonged at the relevant time if the group's purposes included organising or co-ordinating industrial action.*

3. *A union will not be held liable for such an act of any of its committees or officials, however, if its Executive Committee, President or General Secretary repudiates the act as soon as reasonably practicable after it has come to the attention of any of them, and the union takes the steps which the law requires to make that repudiation effective. But the union will not be considered to have "effectively repudiated" an act if the Executive Committee, President or General Secretary subsequently behave in a manner which is inconsistent with the repudiation.*

4. The fact that a union is responsible for organising industrial action to which immunity does not apply does not prevent legal action also being taken against the individual organisers of that action.

"Immunity"

5. A trade union which organises (ie authorises or endorses) industrial action without satisfying the requirements of section 226 (for balloting on industrial action), or 234A (for notice to employers of official industrial action), of the 1992 Act will have no "immunity". Without immunity the trade union will be at risk of legal action by (i) an employer (and/or a customer or supplier of such an employer) who suffers (or may suffer) damage as a consequence of the trade union's unlawful inducement to his workers to break or interfere with the performance of contracts; and/or (ii) any individual who is (or is likely to be) deprived of goods or services because of the industrial action. Such legal proceedings might result in a court order requiring the trade union not to proceed with, and/or desist from, the unlawful inducement of its members to take part or continue with the action, and that no member does anything after the order is made as a result of unlawful inducement prior to the making of the order.

6. Under section 62 of the 1992 Act, a member of a trade union who claims that members of the union, including himself, are likely to be or have been induced by the union to take industrial action which does not have the support of a ballot may apply to the court for an order, which may require the trade union to take steps to ensure that there is no, or no further, unlawful inducement to members to take part or continue to take part in the action, and that no member does anything after the order is made as a result of unlawful inducement prior to the making of the order.

Contempt and other proceedings

7. If a court order issued following legal proceedings as described in paragraphs 5 and 6 above is not obeyed, anyone who sought it can go back to court and ask that those concerned

be declared in contempt of court. A union found in contempt of court may face heavy fines, or other penalties which the court may consider appropriate.

8. In addition, any member of the union may have grounds for legal action against the union's trustees if they have caused or permitted the unlawful application of union funds or property.

[4703]

ANNEX 2
EXAMPLE OF VOTING PAPER FOR BALLOT ON TAKING INDUSTRIAL ACTION

[VOTING PAPER NUMBER]

[NAME OF THE TRADE UNION]

ARE YOU PREPARED TO TAKE PART IN INDUSTRIAL ACTION CONSISTING OF A STRIKE?[15]

YES.. NO ....

ARE YOU PREPARED TO TAKE PART IN INDUSTRIAL ACTION SHORT OF A STRIKE (*which for this purpose is defined to include overtime and call-out bans*)?[15]

YES.. NO ....

Your union intends the following to have authority to make the call for industrial action to which this ballot relates: *[DETAILS OF RELEVANT PERSON, PERSONS, AND/OR CLASS OR CLASSES OF PERSONS]*

If your vote is to count, this voting paper must be returned to *[FULL ADDRESS OF LOCATION TO WHICH THE VOTING PAPER IS TO BE RETURNED]* by *[FULL DATE AND TIME AS APPROPRIATE]*. Please use the enclosed pre-paid envelope provided for this purpose.

The independent scrutineer for this ballot is *[DETAILS OF RELEVANT PERSON]*.

The law requires your union to ensure that your vote is accurately and fairly counted and that you are able to vote without interference from the union or any of its members, officials or employees and, so far as is reasonably practicable, in secret.

If you take part in a strike or other industrial action, you may be in breach of your contract of employment. However, if you are dismissed for taking part in a strike or other industrial action which is called officially and is otherwise lawful, the dismissal will be unfair if it takes place fewer than twelve weeks after you started taking part in the action, and depending on the circumstances may be unfair if it takes place later.

[4704]

NOTES

15 Either question or both should be included as appropriate.

ANNEX 3
INFORMATION TO BE GIVEN TO EMPLOYERS

The following paragraphs of the Code deal with requirements to provide information to employers:—

	Paragraphs
Ballot notice	14–18
Sample voting papers	19–20
Results of the ballot	43–45
Scrutineer's report on the conduct of the ballot	48
Notice of intention to authorise or endorse industrial action or resume suspended industrial action	50–51

[4705]

PART 4

EMPLOYMENT PRACTICES DATA PROTECTION CODE (2005)

NOTES

This consolidated Code of Practice was issued by the Information Commissioner in June 2005 and replaces the four separate Parts originally issued between 2002 and 2004. The Code is issued under the authority conferred by the Data Protection Act 1998, s 51(3)(b) (at **[1335]**). That Act does not confer any specific legal status on the Code, and does not require either ministerial or Parliamentary approval. The Code came into effect on its issue by the Commissioner. The Supplementary Guidance referred to in the Code is not reproduced for reasons of space; it is available on the Commissioner's website (www.ico.gov.uk).

Note that where the text of this Code originally cross-referred to a page number within the hardcopy version of the Code, the appropriate paragraph number has been substituted in its place.

ABOUT THE CODE

Our aim:

This Code is intended to help employers comply with the Data Protection Act and to encourage them to adopt good practice. The Code aims to strike a balance between the legitimate expectations of workers that personal information about them will be handled properly and the legitimate interests of employers in deciding how best, within the law, to run their own businesses. It does not impose new legal obligations.

Who is the Code for?

The Employment Practices Data Protection Code deals with the impact of data protection laws on the employment relationship. It covers such issues as the obtaining of information about workers, the retention of records, access to records and disclosure of them. Not every aspect of the Code will be relevant to every organisation – this will vary according to size and the nature of its business. Some of the issues addressed may arise only rarely – particularly for small businesses. Here the Code is intended to serve as a reference document to be called on when necessary.

The benefits of the Code

The Data Protection Act 1998 places responsibilities on any organisation to process personal information that it holds in a fair and proper way. Failure to do so can ultimately lead to a criminal offence being committed.

The effect of the Act on how an organisation processes information on its workers is generally straightforward. But in some areas it can be complex and difficult to understand, especially if your organisation has only limited experience of dealing with data protection issues. The Code therefore covers the points you need to check, and what action, if any, you may need to take. Following the Code should produce other benefits in terms of relationships with your workers, compliance with other legislation and efficiencies in storing and managing information.

Following the Code will:

- increase trust in the workplace – there will be transparency about information held on individuals, thus helping to create an open atmosphere where workers have trust and confidence in employment practices.
- encourage good housekeeping – following the Code encourages organisations to dispose of out-of-date information, freeing up both physical and computerised filing systems and making valuable information easier to find.
- protect organisations from legal action – adhering to the Code will help employers to protect themselves from challenges against their data protection practices.
- encourage workers to treat customers' personal data with respect – following the Code will create a general level of awareness of personal data issues, helping to ensure that information about customers is treated properly.
- help organisations to meet other legal requirements – the Code is intended to be consistent with other legislation such as the Human Rights Act 1998 and the Regulation of Investigatory Powers Act 2000 (RIPA).
- assist global businesses to adopt policies and practices which are consistent with similar legislation in other countries – the Code is produced in the light of EC Directive 95/46/EC and ought to be in line with data protection law in other European Union member states.

- help to prevent the illicit use of information by workers – informing them of the principles of data protection, and the consequences of not complying with the Act, should discourage them from misusing information held by the organisation.

What is the legal status of the Code?

The Code has been issued by the Information Commissioner under section 51 of the Data Protection Act. This requires him to promote the following of good practice, including compliance with the Act's requirements, by data controllers and empowers him, after consultation, to prepare Codes of Practice giving guidance on good practice.

The basic legal requirement on each employer is to comply with the Act itself. The Code is designed to help. It sets out the Information Commissioner's recommendations as to how the legal requirements of the Act can be met. Employers may have alternative ways of meeting these requirements but if they do nothing they risk breaking the law.

Any enforcement action would be based on a failure to meet the requirements of the Act itself. However, relevant parts of the Code are likely to be cited by the Commissioner in connection with any enforcement action that arises in relation to the processing of personal information in the employment context.

Who does data protection cover in the workplace?

The Code is concerned with information that employers might collect and keep on any individual who might wish to work, work, or have worked for them. In the Code the term 'worker' includes:

- applicants (successful and unsuccessful)
- former applicants (successful and unsuccessful)
- employees (current and former)
- agency staff (current and former)
- casual staff (current and former)
- contract staff (current and former)

Some of this Code will also apply to others in the workplace, such as volunteers and those on work experience placements.

What information is covered by the Code?

Information about individuals, that is kept by an organisation on computer in the employment context, will fall within the scope of the Data Protection Act and therefore, within the scope of this Code. However, information that is kept in simple manual files will often fall outside the Act. Where information falls outside the Act, this Code can do no more than offer advice on good information handling practice.

Personal information

The Code is concerned with 'personal information'. That is, information which:

- is about a living person and affects that person's privacy (whether in his/her personal or family life, business or professional capacity) in the sense that the information has the person as its focus or is otherwise biographical in nature, and
- identifies a person, whether by itself, or together with other information in the organisation's possession or that is likely to come into its possession.

This means that automated and computerised personal information kept about workers by employers is covered by the Act. It also covers personal information put on paper or microfiche and held in any 'relevant filing system'. In addition, information recorded with the intention that it will be put in a relevant filing system or held on computer is covered.

Only a well structured manual system will qualify as a relevant filing system. This means that the system must amount to more than a bundle of documents about each worker filed in date order. There must be some sort of system to guide a searcher to where specific information about a named worker can be found readily. This might take the form of topic dividers within individually named personnel files or name dividers within a file on a particular topic, such as 'Training Applications'.

Processing

The Act applies to personal information that is subject to 'processing'. For the purposes of the Act, the term 'processing' applies to a comprehensive range of activities. It includes the initial obtaining of personal information, the retention and use of it, access and disclosure and final disposal.

Examples of personal information **likely** to be covered by the Act include:

- details of a worker's salary and bank account held on an organisation's computer system
- an e-mail about an incident involving a named worker
- a supervisor's notebook containing information on a worker where there is an intention to put that information in that worker's computerised personnel file
- an individual worker's personnel file where the documents are filed in date order but there is an index to the documents at the front of the file
- an individual worker's personnel file where at least some of the documents are filed behind sub dividers with headings such as application details, leave record and performance reviews
- a set of leave cards where each worker has an individual card and the cards are kept in alphabetical order
- a set of completed application forms, filed in alphabetical order within a file of application forms for a particular vacancy.

Examples of information **unlikely** to be covered by the Act include:

- information on the entire workforce's salary structure, given by grade, where individuals are not named and are not identifiable
- a report on the comparative success of different recruitment campaigns where no details regarding individuals are held
- a report on the results of "exit interviews" where all responses are anonymised and where the results are impossible to trace back to individuals
- a personnel file that contains information about a named worker but where the information is simply filed in date order with nothing to guide a searcher to where specific information, such as the worker's leave entitlement, can be found.

Sensitive personal information

What are sensitive data?

Sensitive data are information concerning an individual's;

- racial or ethnic origin
- political opinions
- religious beliefs or other beliefs of a similar nature
- trade union membership (within the meaning of the Trade Union and Labour Relations (Consolidation) Act 1992)
- physical or mental health or condition
- sexual life
- commission or alleged commission of any offence, or
- proceedings for any offence committed or alleged to have been committed, the disposal of such proceedings or the sentence of any court in such proceedings

Sensitive data processed by an employer might typically be about a worker's;

- physical or mental health
  - — as a part of sickness records revealed through monitoring e-mails sent by a worker to his or her manager or to an occupational health advisor
  - — obtained as part of a pre-employment medical questionnaire or examination.
  - — drug or alcohol test results
- criminal convictions
  - — to assess suitability for certain types of employment
- disabilities
  - — to facilitate adaptations in the workplace
  - — to ensure special needs are catered for at interview or selection testing
  - — in monitoring equality of opportunity
- racial origin
  - — to ensure that recruitment processes do not discriminate against particular racial groups
  - — to ensure equality of opportunity
- trade union membership
  - — to enable deduction of subscriptions from payroll
  - — revealed by internet access logs which show that a worker routinely accesses a particular trade union website.

The Act sets out a series of conditions, at least one of which has to apply before an employer can collect, store, use, disclose or otherwise process sensitive data.

See Supplementary Guidance page 72 which explains more about the conditions for processing sensitive data.

What responsibilities do workers have under the Act?

Workers – as well as employers – have responsibilities for data protection under the Act. Line managers have responsibility for the type of personal information they collect and how they use it. No-one at any level should disclose personal information outside the organisation's procedures, or use personal information held on others for their own purposes. Anyone disclosing personal information without the authority of the organisation may commit a criminal offence, unless there is some other legal justification, for example under 'whistle-blowing' legislation.

Of course, applicants for jobs ought to provide accurate information and may breach other laws if they do not. However, the Act does not create any new legal obligation for them to do so.

Managing Data Protection (post) explains more about allocating responsibility.

Parts of the Code

The Employment Practices Data Protection Code starts with a section on managing data protection in employment practices. It is then split into four parts;

- **recruitment and selection** – is about job applications and pre-employment vetting
- **employment records** – is about collecting, storing, disclosing and deleting records
- **monitoring at work** – is about monitoring workers' use of telephones, the internet, e-mail systems and vehicles
- **workers' health** – is about occupational health, medical testing, drug and genetic screening.

Each part of the Code has been designed to stand alone. Which parts of the Code you choose to use will depend on the relevance to your organisation of each area covered.

The Good Practice Recommendations

Each part of the Code consists of a series of good practice recommendations. These good practice recommendations may be relevant to either large or small employers, but some of them address activities that are of a more specialist nature than others or may occur only rarely, particularly in a small business, These recommendations are most likely to be relevant to larger organisations. However, how far they are applicable and what is needed to achieve them will, of course, depend very much not just on size but also on the nature of each organisation.

Supplementary Guidance

Supporting guidance, aimed mainly at those in larger organisations who are responsible for ensuring that employment policies and practices comply with data protection law, includes more detailed notes and examples. These notes and examples, do not form part of this Code.

[4706]

MANAGING DATA PROTECTION

Good Practice Recommendations – Managing Data Protection

Data protection compliance should be seen as an integral part of employment practice. It is important to develop a culture in which respect for private life, data protection, security and confidentiality of personal information is seen as the norm.

0.1 Identify the person within the organisation responsible for ensuring that employment policies and procedures comply with the Act and for ensuring that they continue to do so. Put in place a mechanism for checking that procedures are followed in practice.

Key points and possible actions

- The nature and size of the organisation will influence where responsibility should rest.
- Ensure the person responsible reads all relevant parts of the Code.
- Check employment policies and procedures, including unwritten practices, against the relevant parts of the Code.
- Eliminate areas of non-compliance.
- Inform those who need to know why certain procedures have changed.
- Introduce a mechanism for checking that procedures are followed in practice, for example, occasional audits and spot checks and/or a requirement for managers to sign a compliance statement.

0.2 Ensure that business areas and individual line managers who process information about workers understand their own responsibility for data protection compliance and if necessary amend their working practices in the light of this.

Key points and possible actions

- Prepare a briefing to departmental heads and line managers about their responsibilities.

0.3 Assess what personal information about workers is in existence and who is responsible for it.

Key points and possible actions

- Use the various parts of this Code as the framework to assess what personal information your organisation keeps and where responsibility for it lies.
- Remember that personal information may be held in different departments as well as within the personnel/human resource function.

0.4 Eliminate the collection of personal information that is irrelevant or excessive to the employment relationship. If sensitive data are collected ensure that a sensitive data condition is satisfied.

Key points and possible actions

- Consider each type of personal information that is held and decide whether any information could be deleted or not collected in the first place.
- Check that the collection and use of any sensitive personal data satisfies at least one of the sensitive data conditions.

See Supplementary Guidance page 72 which explains more about the conditions for processing sensitive data.

0.5 Ensure that all workers are aware how they can be criminally liable if they knowingly or recklessly disclose personal information outside their employer's policies and procedures. Make serious breaches of data protection rules a disciplinary matter.

Key points and possible actions

- Prepare a guide explaining to workers the consequences of their actions in this area.
- Make sure that the serious infringement of data protection rules is clearly indicated as a disciplinary matter.
- Ensure that the guide is brought to the attention of new workers.
- Ensure that workers can ask questions about the guide.

0.6 Ensure that your organisation has a valid notification in the register of data controllers that relates to the processing of personal information about workers, unless it is exempt from notification.

Key points and possible actions

- Consult the Data Protection Register website – www.dpr.gov.uk – to check the notification status of your organisation.
- Check whether your organisation is exempt from notification using the website.
- Check whether all your processing of information about workers is correctly described there – unless your organisation is exempt.
- Allocate responsibility for checking and updating this information on a regular basis, for example every 6 months.

0.7 Consult workers, and/or trade unions or other representatives, about the development and implementation of employment practices and procedures that involve the processing of personal information about workers.

Key points and possible actions

- Consultation is only mandatory under employment law, in limited circumstances and for larger employers but it should nevertheless help to ensure that processing of personal information is fair.
- When formulating new employment practices and procedures, assess the impact on collection and use of personal information.

[4707]

PART 1: RECRUITMENT AND SELECTION

ABOUT PART 1 OF THE CODE

Data protection in recruitment and selection

The recruitment and selection process necessarily involves an employer in collecting and using information about workers. Much of this information is personal in nature and can affect a worker's privacy. The Act does not prevent an employer from carrying out an effective recruitment exercise but helps to strike a balance between the employer's needs and the applicant's right to respect for his or her private life.

What does this part of the Code cover?

This part of the Code covers all aspects of the recruitment and selection process from the advertising of vacancies through to the deletion of information on unsuccessful applicants. It does not though deal in detail with the collection and use of health information on job applicants. This is covered in Part 4. Nor does it deal in detail with the right of applicants to access to the information that an employer keeps about them. This is essentially no different from the right of access that a worker has once employed or engaged. This is covered in Part 2.

Some recommendations in the Code are only likely to be of relevance to those using sophisticated selection methods such as psychometric testing or to those employing workers with responsibilities that mean that special checks are justified, for example, criminal record checks on those working with children. For this reason some sub sections are likely to be of relevance mainly to larger or specialist organisations.

Verification and vetting

The terms "verification" and "vetting" are both used in this part of the Code. Verification covers the process of checking that details supplied by applicants (e g qualifications) are accurate and complete. Verification, therefore, is limited to checking of information that is sought in the application or supplied later in the recruitment process. As used here the term also includes the taking up of references provided by the applicant. Where an employer is justified in asking an applicant about any criminal convictions the Criminal Records Bureau provides a verification service covering certain, high risk areas of employment.

Vetting covers the employer actively making its own enquiries from third parties about an applicant's background and circumstances. It goes beyond the verification of details addressed above. As such it is particularly intrusive and should be confined to areas of special risk. It is for example used for some government workers who have regular access to highly classified information.

In some sectors vetting may be a necessary and accepted practice. Limited vetting may be a legal requirement for some jobs, for example, child care jobs under the Protection of Children Act 1999. The Department of Health has developed a Protection of Vulnerable Adults list which employers intending to recruit certain types of care workers are required to consult. Such vetting usually takes place through the Criminal Records Bureau.

See Supplementary Guidance, page 17 for background information on the Criminal Records Bureau.

[4708]

GOOD PRACTICE RECOMMENDATIONS – PART 1

The parts of the Code in this section are:

1.1 Advertising

1.2 Applications

1.3 Verification

1.4 Short-listing

1.5 Interviews

1.6 Pre-employment vetting

1.7 Retention of recruitment records

1.1 Advertising

This sub-section covers any method used to notify potential applicants of job vacancies, using such media as notices, newspapers, radio, television and the internet.

1.1.1 Inform individuals responding to job advertisements of the name of the organisation to which they will be providing their information and how it will be used unless this is self-evident.

Key points and possible actions

- Ensure that the name of your organisation appears in all recruitment advertisements.

- Ensure that your organisation is named on the answerphone message which invites potential applicants to leave details.
- Ensure that your organisation is named on your website before personal information is collected on an online application form.
- To the extent that it is not self evident describe in the advertisement the purposes for which you may use personal information, for example, to market your organisations products and service.

1.1.2 Recruitment agencies, used on behalf of an employer, should identify themselves and explain how personal information they receive will be used and disclosed unless this is self-evident.

Key points and possible actions

- If you use a recruitment agency check that it identifies itself in any advertisement, and that it informs applicants if the information requested is to be used for any purpose of which the applicant is unlikely to be aware.

1.1.3 On receiving identifiable particulars of applicants from an agency ensure, as soon as you can, that the applicants are aware of the name of the organisation holding their information.

Key points and possible actions

- Inform the applicant as soon as you can of the employer's identity and of any uses that the employer might make of the information received that are not self-evident.

OR

- If the employer does not wish to be identified at an early stage in the recruitment process, ensure the agency only sends anonymised information about applicants. Ensure the employer is identified to individuals whose applications are to be pursued further.

[4709]

1.2 Applications

This sub-section covers CVs sent 'on spec' as well as more formal responses to job advertisements.

1.2.1 State, on any application form, to whom the information is being provided and how it will be used if this is not self-evident.

Key points and possible actions

- Ensure the name of your organisation is stated on the application form.
- If information from the application form will be used for any other purpose than to recruit for a specific job or passed to anyone else, make sure that this purpose is stated on the application form.

1.2.2 Only seek personal information that is relevant to the recruitment decision to be made.

Key points and possible actions

- Determine whether all questions are relevant for all applicants.
- Consider customising application forms where posts justify the collection of more intrusive personal information.
- Remove or amend any questions which require the applicant to provide information extraneous to the recruitment decision.
- Remove questions that are only relevant to people your organisation goes on to employ (e g banking details) but are not relevant to unsuccessful applicants.

1.2.3 Only request information about an applicant's criminal convictions if and to the extent that the information can be justified in terms of the role offered. If this information is justified, make it clear that spent convictions do not have to be declared, unless the job being filled is covered by the Exceptions Order to the Rehabilitation of Offenders Act 1974.

Key points and possible actions

- Consider whether the collection of information about criminal convictions can be justified for each job for which it is sought.
- Check that it is stated that spent convictions do not have to be declared (unless the job is one covered by the Exceptions Order).
- In any case limit the collection of information to offences that have a direct bearing on suitability for the job in question.

See Supplementary Guidance, page 19 for more information on the Exceptions Order.

1.2.4 Explain the nature of and sources from which information might be obtained about the applicant in addition to the information supplied directly by the applicant.

Key points and possible actions

- Ensure there is a clear statement on the application form or surrounding documents, explaining what information will be sought and from whom.

1.2.5 If sensitive data are collected ensure a sensitive data condition is satisfied.

Key points and possible actions

- Assess whether the collection of sensitive data is relevant to the recruitment process.
- Remove any questions about sensitive data that do not have to be asked at the initial application stage.
- Ensure that the purpose of collecting any relevant sensitive data is explained on the application form or surrounding documentation.
- Ensure the purpose of collection satisfies one of the sensitive data conditions.
- If health information is to be collected, refer to Part 4 of the Code: Information About Workers' Health.

See Supplementary Guidance, page 72 which explains more about the conditions for processing sensitive data.

1.2.6 Provide a secure method for sending applications.

Key points and possible actions

- Ensure that a secure method of transmission is used for sending applications online. (Eg encryption-based software).
- Ensure that once electronic applications are received, they are saved in a directory or drive which has access limited to those involved in the recruitment process.
- Ensure that postal applications are given directly to the person or people processing the applications and that these are stored in a locked drawer.
- Ensure that faxed applications are given directly to the person or people processing the applications and that these are stored in a locked drawer.
- If applications are processed by line managers, make sure line managers are aware of how to gather and store applications.

[4710]

1.3 Verification

1.3.1 Explain to applicants as early as is reasonably practicable in the recruitment process the nature of the verification process and the methods used to carry it out.

Key points and possible actions

- Ensure that information provided to applicants for example on an application form or associated documents explains what information will be verified and how, including in particular any external sources that will be used.
- Do not force applicants to use their subject access rights to obtain records from another organisation (ie by making such a requirement a condition of getting a job).

1.3.2 Where the need to protect the employer's business, customers, clients or others warrants the collection and verification of details of an applicant's criminal convictions use only a disclosure from the Criminal Records Bureau (CRB) or Disclosure Scotland for this verification.

Key points and possible actions

- Do not attempt to obtain information about criminal convictions by forcing an applicant to use his/her subject access right or from sources other than the CRB, Disclosure Scotland or the applicant.
- Confine the obtaining of a disclosure, as far as practicable, to an applicant it is intended to appoint. Avoid requiring all short-listed applicants to obtain a disclosure.
- Do not share with other employers the information obtained through a "disclosure".
- Abide by the CRB or Disclosure Scotland's Code of Practice in obtaining and handling disclosure information.

1.3.3 If it is necessary to secure the release of documents or information from another organisation or person, obtain a signed consent form from the applicant unless consent to their release has been indicated in some other way.

Key points and possible actions

- Ensure applicants provide signed consent if this is required to secure the release of documents to you from another organisation or person.
- Remember that if you mislead another person or organisation into giving you personal information about an applicant you may be committing a criminal offence.

1.3.4 Give the applicant an opportunity to make representations should any of the checks produce discrepancies.

Key points and possible actions

- Ensure that those staff who are involved in verification in your organisation are aware

PART 4

what to do should inconsistencies emerge between what the applicant said in the application and what your checks have discovered.

- Make sure that in this situation, staff inform the applicant and allow them the opportunity to provide an explanation of the inconsistencies.
- Ensure this feedback to the applicant is incorporated into any recruitment procedures.

[4711]

1.4 Short-listing

1.4.1 Be consistent in the way personal information is used in the process of short-listing candidates for a particular position.

Key points and possible actions

- Check shortlist methods with sources of good practice such as the Equal Opportunities Commission or Commission for Racial Equality.

See Supplementary Guidance page 83 for contact details.

1.4.2 Inform applicants if an automated short-listing system will be used as the sole basis of making a decision. Make provisions to consider representations from applicants about this and to take these into account before making the final decision.

Key points and possible actions

- Ensure all the applicants are informed that an automated system is used as the sole basis of short-listing and of how to make representations against any adverse decision.
- Test and keep the results produced by the system under review to ensure they properly and fairly apply your short-listing criteria to all applicants.

1.4.3 Ensure that tests based on the interpretation of scientific evidence, such as psychological tests, are only used and interpreted by those who have received appropriate training.

Key points and possible actions

- Determine which such tests are used within your organisation.
- Ensure all tests are assessed by properly qualified persons.

[4712]

1.5 Interviews

1.5.1 Ensure that personal information that is recorded and retained following interview can be justified as relevant to, and necessary for, the recruitment process itself, or for defending the process against challenge.

Key points and possible actions

- Ensure that all interviewers are aware that interviewees may have a right to request access to their interview notes.
- Ensure that all interviewers are given instructions on how to store interview notes.
- Make provisions for interview notes to be destroyed after a reasonable time, allowing the organisation to protect itself from any potential claims such as those for race or sex discrimination.
- Explain to interviewers or those in contact with applicants, how to deal with a request for access to interview notes.

[4713]

1.6 Pre-employment vetting

1.6.1 Only use vetting where there are particular and significant risks involved to the employer, clients, customers or others, and where there is no less intrusive and reasonably practicable alternative.

Key points and possible actions

- Find out for which jobs, if any, pre-employment vetting takes place.
- Consider whether pre-employment vetting is justified for each of these jobs and whether the information could be obtained in a less intrusive way.
- Wherever practicable obtain relevant information directly from the applicant and, if necessary, verify it rather than undertake pre-employment vetting.
- Do not vet workers just because a customer for your products or services imposes a condition requiring you to do so, unless you can satisfy yourself that the condition is justified.

1.6.2 Only carry out pre-employment vetting on an applicant as at late a stage as is practicable in the recruitment process.

Key points and possible actions

- Ascertain at which point pre-employment vetting takes place and who is subject to it. Eliminate any comprehensive pre-employment vetting that takes place for all shortlisted applicants (only the people selected for the job should be submitted to comprehensive pre-employment vetting).

1.6.3 Make it clear early in the recruitment process that vetting will take place and how it will be conducted.

Key points and possible actions

- Provide information about any vetting that might take place on application forms or other recruitment material. This should explain the nature, extent and range of sources to be used to carry out the vetting.
- Make clear the extent to which you will release information about the applicant to the sources you use.

1.6.4 Only use vetting as a means of obtaining specific information, not as a means of general intelligence gathering. Ensure that the extent and nature of information sought is justified.

Key points and possible actions

- Ensure that there are clearly stated objectives in any vetting process.
- Consider the extent and nature of information that is sought against these objectives.
- Eliminate any vetting that consists of general intelligence-gathering. Ensure that it is clearly focussed information that will have a significant bearing on the employment decision.

1.6.5 Only seek information from sources where it is likely that relevant information will be revealed. Only approach the applicant's family or close associates in exceptional cases.

Key points and possible actions

- Ensure that those who will seek the information are briefed about which sources to use, ensuring that those sources are likely to produce relevant information.
- Ensure that if family members or close associates are approached it can be justified by the special nature of the job.

1.6.6 Do not place reliance on information collected from possibly unreliable sources. Allow the applicant to make representations regarding information that will affect the decision to finally appoint.

Key points and possible actions

- Ensure that information that has been collected from a vetting process is evaluated in the light of the reliability of the sources.
- Ensure that no recruitment decision is made solely on the basis of information obtained from a source that may be unreliable.
- Ensure that if information received will lead to the applicant not being appointed, then this will be made known to the applicant.
- Put in place a mechanism for providing this feedback, allowing the applicant to respond and obliging those involved in the recruitment decision to take this response into account.

1.6.7 Where information is collected about a person other than the applicant that affects the other person's privacy, ensure so far as practicable that the other person is made aware of this.

Key points and possible actions

- Ensure that those conducting a vetting process are briefed to avoid discovering information about other people unnecessarily.
- Where substantial personal information has been collected about another person and is to be retained, ensure there is a process in place to inform the other person of this and of how the information will be used.

1.6.8 If it is necessary to secure the release of documents or information from a third party, obtain a signed consent from the applicant.

Key points and possible actions

- If you are asking a third party, such as a previous employer, to disclose confidential personal information to you the third party will need the applicant's permission before doing so.
- It may be easier for you to obtain this permission from the applicant and pass it on to the third party than for the third party to obtain permission directly.

[4714]

1.7 Retention of recruitment records

1.7.1 Establish and adhere to retention periods for recruitment records that are based on a clear business need.

Key points and possible actions

- Assess who in your organisation retains recruitment records (eg are they held centrally, at departmental level or in the line).
- Ensure that no recruitment record is held beyond the statutory period in which a claim arising from the recruitment process may be brought unless there is a clear business reason for exceeding this period.
- Consider anonymising any recruitment information that is to be held longer than the period necessary for responding to claims.

1.7.2 Destroy information obtained by a vetting exercise as soon as possible, or in any case within 6 months. A record of the result of vetting or verification can be retained.

Key points and possible actions

- Check who in your organisation retains information from vetting. Ensure that vetting records are destroyed after 6 months. Manual records should be shredded and electronic files permanently deleted from the system.
- Inform those responsible for the destruction of this information that they may keep a record that vetting was carried out, the result and the recruitment decision taken.

1.7.3 Consider carefully which information contained on an application form is to be transferred to the worker's employment record. Do not retain information that has no bearing on the on-going employment relationship.

Key points and possible actions

- Check how information is transferred from recruitment records to employment records.
- Ensure those responsible for such transfers only move information relevant to on-going employment to employment files.

1.7.4 Delete information about criminal convictions collected in the course of the recruitment process once it has been verified through a Criminal Records Bureau disclosure unless, in exceptional circumstances, the information is clearly relevant to the on-going employment relationship.

Key points and possible actions

- Make sure it is only recorded whether a check has yielded a satisfactory or an unsatisfactory result. Delete other information.

1.7.5 If it is your practice to do so advise unsuccessful applicants that there is an intention to keep their names on file for future vacancies (if appropriate) and give them the opportunity to have their details removed from the file.

Key points and possible actions

- Ensure that application forms or surrounding documentation tell applicants that, should they be unsuccessful, their details will be kept on file unless they specifically request that this should not be the case.

1.7.6 Ensure that personal information received during the recruitment process are securely stored or are destroyed.

Key points and possible actions

- Assess who in your organisation presently processes recruitment information.
- Inform them that manual records should be kept securely, for example in a locked filing cabinet.
- Make sure that electronic files are kept securely, for example by using passwords and other technical security measures.

[4715]

PART 2: EMPLOYMENT RECORDS

ABOUT PART 2 OF THE CODE

Data protection in employment records

Running a business necessarily involves keeping records about workers. Such records will contain information that is personal in nature and can affect a worker's privacy. The Act does not prevent an employer from collecting, maintaining and using records about workers but helps to strike a balance between the employer's need to keep records and the worker's right to respect for his or her private life. This part of the Code will assist employers not only to comply with the law but also to follow good records management practice.

What does this part of the code cover?

This part of the Code covers all aspects of the collection, holding and use of employment records from the initial obtaining of information once a worker has been employed or engaged through to the ultimate deletion of the former worker's record. It also deals with the rights of job applicants as well as workers to access to information the employer keeps about them. It does not though deal in detail with the collection and use of health information. This is covered in Part 4.

Some recommendations in the Code are only likely to be of relevance to those involved in particular activities such as marketing to their workers or to those who find themselves in particular situations such as a business merger or acquisition. For this reason some sub sections are likely to be of relevance mainly to larger organisations.

Sickness and injury records

For the purposes of this Code it is necessary to distinguish between records that include "sensitive data" and those that do not. The term 'sickness record' is therefore used to describe a record which contains details of the illness or condition responsible for a worker's absence. Similarly, an injury record is a record which contains details of the injury suffered. The term 'absence record' is used to describe a record that may give the reason for absence as 'sickness' or 'accident' but does not include any reference to specific medical conditions.

Many employers keep accident records. Such a record will only be an "injury record" if it includes details of the injury suffered by an identifiable worker.

Sickness and injury records include information about workers' physical or mental health. The holding of sickness or injury records will therefore involve the processing of sensitive personal data. This means one of the conditions for processing sensitive personal data must be satisfied.

Employers are advised as far as practicable to restrict their record keeping to absence records rather than sickness or injury records.

See Supplementary Guidance page 72 which explains more about the conditions for processing sensitive data.

Workers' access to information about themselves

Workers, like any other individuals, have a right to gain access to information that is kept about them. This right is known as subject access. The right applies, for example, to sickness records, disciplinary or training records, appraisal or performance review notes, e-mails, word-processed documents, e-mail logs, audit trails, information held in general personnel files and interview notes, whether held as computerised files, or as structured paper records. A fee of up to £10 can be charged by the employer for giving access.

Responding to a subject access request involves:

- telling the worker if the organisation keeps any personal information about him or her;
- giving the worker a description of the type of information the organisation keeps, the purposes it is used for and the types of organisations which it may be passed on to, if any;
- showing the worker all the information the organisation keeps about him or her, explaining any codes or other unintelligible terms used;
- providing this information in a hard copy or in readily readable, permanent electronic form unless providing it in that way would involve disproportionate effort or the worker agrees to receive it in some other way;
- providing the worker with any additional information the organisation has as to the source of the information kept about him or her.

There are a number of exemptions from the right of subject access which can be relevant in an employment context.

See Supplementary Guidance – Exemptions from the subject access right page 42 for details.

References

The provision of a reference about a worker from one party, such as a present employer, to another, such as a prospective employer, will generally involve the disclosure of personal data. In considering how the Act applies to such disclosure it is important to establish who the reference is being given by or on behalf of.

The Code therefore distinguishes between a reference given in a personal capacity and one given in a corporate capacity. A corporate reference is one given on behalf of the employer by one of its staff. Many employers have rules about who can give such a reference and what it can include. The employer remains legally responsible for compliance with the Data Protection Act.

A personal reference is one given by a member of staff in an individual capacity. It may refer to work done but it is not given on behalf of the employer. References that are given in a personal capacity do not, at least in data protection terms, incur a liability for the employer.

Under a specific exemption in the Act, a worker does not have the right to gain access to a confidential job reference from the organisation which has given it. However, once the reference is with the organisation to which it was sent then no such specific exemption from the right of access exists. That organisation is though entitled to take steps to protect the identity of third parties such as the author of the reference.

Disclosure requests

Employers regularly receive requests for information about individual workers that come from outside the employer's organisation. An employer has a responsibility to its workers to be cautious in responding to such requests. It risks a breach of the Act if it does not take sufficient care to ensure the interests of its workers are safeguarded. In some cases though the employer has no choice but to respond positively to a request for disclosure. This is where there is a legal obligation to disclose. It is not the Data Protection Act but other laws that create such obligations. Where they do so the Act does not stand in the way of disclosure.

In some other cases the employer will have a choice whether or not to disclose but provided sensitive data are not involved it is clear that the Act will not stand in the way of disclosure. This is where the circumstances of the disclosure are covered by one of the exemptions from the 'non-disclosure provisions' of the Act.

See Supplementary Guidance: Exemptions from non-disclosure page 43 for details.

[4716]

GOOD PRACTICE RECOMMENDATIONS – PART 2

The parts of the Code referred to in this section are:

2.1 Collecting and keeping general records

2.2 Security

2.3 Sickness and injury records

2.4 Pension and insurance schemes

2.5 Equal opportunities monitoring

2.6 Marketing

2.7 Fraud detection

2.8 Workers' access to information about themselves

2.9 References

2.10 Disclosure requests

2.11 Publication and other disclosures

2.12 Merger, acquisition, and business re-organisation

2.13 Discipline, grievance and dismissal

2.14 Outsourcing data processing

2.15 Retention of records

2.1 Collecting and keeping general records

2.2.1 Ensure that newly appointed workers are aware of the nature and source of any information stored about them, how it will be used and who it will be disclosed to.

Key points and possible actions

- It is not generally necessary to seek a worker's consent to keep employment records.

It will usually be sufficient to ensure that the worker is aware that records are being kept and is given an explanation of the purposes they are kept for and the nature of any intended disclosures.

- It is only if sensitive data are collected that consent may be necessary.
- Decide on how best to inform new workers about how information about them will be held, used and disclosed.
- If your organisation has not done so previously, distribute this information to existing workers.
- In large organisations, randomly check with a sample of workers, that they did in fact receive this information. Rectify any communication gaps.

2.1.2 Inform new workers and remind existing workers about their rights under the Act, including their right of access to the information kept upon them.

Key points and possible actions

- Ensure that information given to new workers includes information about their rights under the Act.
- Set up a system to remind existing workers of their rights.

2.1.3 Ensure that there is a clear and foreseeable need for any information collected from workers and that the information collected actually meets that need.

Key points and possible actions

- Review all forms where information is requested from workers.
- Remove or amend any questions which require the worker to provide information extraneous to your needs.

2.1.4 Provide each worker with a copy of information that may be subject to change, e g personal details such as home address, annually or allow workers to view this on-line. Ask workers to check their records for accuracy and ensure any necessary amendments are made to bring records up-to-date.

Key points and possible actions

- Determine the different types of personal data kept about workers and whether they are likely to be subject to change.
- Decide whether data that change could easily be viewed electronically and make any changes to systems necessary to enable this.
- Ensure that the system restricts access to individuals' records so that each worker can only get access to his or her own record.
- If it is only possible for workers to view data manually, consider how this can best be done.
- Make provision to amend any details that are incorrect on individual workers' files.

2.1.5 Incorporate accuracy, consistency and validity checks into systems.

Key points and possible actions

- Review computerised systems to see if accuracy checks can be easily built in.
- Put in place arrangements to ensure that when systems are updated or new systems purchased they facilitate data protection compliance.
- Remember that legal responsibility for data protection compliance rests with users rather than suppliers of systems.

[4717]

2.2 Security

2.2.1 Apply security standards that take account of the risks of unauthorised access to, accidental loss of, destruction of, or damage to employment records.

Key points and possible actions

- BS 7799: 1995 (Code of Practice for Information Security Management) provides guidance which, if followed, should address the main security risks.
- Obtain a copy of BS7799 if you do not have one already and compare its recommendations to your own existing procedures.
- Put in place measures to rectify any shortfalls, bearing in mind that not all controls will be relevant to all organisations.

2.2.2 Institute a system of secure cabinets, access controls and passwords to ensure that staff can only gain access to employment records where they have a legitimate business need to do so.

Key points and possible actions

- Review who in your organisation has access to employment records and determine whether it is necessary for everyone who currently has access to retain it.
- Remove access rights from those who have unnecessary or over-extensive access to personal information about others.

- Make sure manual files that hold personal information are securely held with locks and only those who should have access retain the key.
- In the case of computerised records, ensure that passwords or similar controls are set up to limit unauthorised access.

2.2.3 Use the audit trail capabilities of automated systems to track who accesses and amends personal information.

Key points and possible actions

- Check whether computerised systems that retain personal information currently have audit trail capabilities. If they do, check that the audit trail is enabled.
- If they do not, see if it would be possible to create audit trails of who accesses and amends personal information.
- If you have a system with audit trails, ensure that regular checks occur to detect unauthorised or suspicious use. Set up a procedure to investigate patterns of unusual or unauthorised access of personal information.

2.2.4 Take steps to ensure the reliability of staff that have access to workers' records.

Key points and possible actions

- Carry out background checks on staff that will have access to workers' records, for example by taking up references.
- Review the contracts of workers who deal with personal information to ensure they include confidentiality clauses concerning the unauthorised disclosure and use of personal information.
- Set up induction training for these staff that contains explanation about their responsibilities. Organise refresher training as and when necessary.

2.2.5 Ensure that if employment records are taken off-site, e g on laptop computers, this is controlled. Make sure only the necessary information is taken and there are security rules for staff to follow.

Key points and possible actions

- Formulate a procedure for taking laptop computers off-site (or review the existing procedure). Include points regarding the information that may be taken off-site, security of passwords and keeping the laptop in view or secured at all times.
- Inform all workers, including senior staff, of the procedure.

2.2.6 Take account of the risks of transmitting confidential worker information by fax or e-mail. Only transmit information between locations if a secure network or comparable arrangements are in place.

Key points and possible actions

- Check that your security policy properly addresses the risk of sending and receiving worker information by e-mail or fax and review the relevant procedures.
- Ensure that all managers use a secure system if workers' records are to be transmitted by fax.
- In the case of e-mail deploy some technical means of ensuring security, such as effective password protection and encryption.
- Advise all managers about permanently deleting e-mails that contain personal information about workers from their work-stations.
- Check whether deleted e-mails will still be kept on a server. Wherever possible ensure these too can be permanently deleted. In any case, restrict access to them.

[4718]

2.3 Sickness and injury records

2.3.1 Where possible keep sickness and injury records separate from absence and accident records. Do not use sickness records for a particular purpose when records of absence could be used instead.

Key points and possible actions

- Review how sickness and accident records are currently kept.
- If necessary, change the way information on sickness and accidents is kept so that information on workers' health is not accessed when only information on absence or the circumstances of an accident at work is needed.
- Inform those accessing both sickness/injury and absence records of when it is and is not necessary to access the full sickness or injury records.

2.3.2 Ensure that the holding and use of sickness and injury records satisfies a sensitive data condition.

Key points and possible actions

- Check current practices on the use of sickness and injury records against the sensitive data conditions in the Code.

- Take any remedial action necessary including restricting the purposes for which records can be used and/or deleting records if no condition can be satisfied.
- Inform those handling sickness and injury records of any changes in procedures or practices.

See Supplementary Guidance page 72 which explains more about the sensitive data conditions.

2.3.3 Only disclose information from sickness or injury records about an identifiable worker's illness, medical condition or injury where there is a legal obligation to do so, where it is necessary for legal proceedings or where the worker has given explicit consent to the disclosure.

Key points and possible actions

- Ensure that all those who deal with workers' sickness or injury records are aware in which circumstances there may be a legal obligation to disclose.
- Ensure when appropriate, written consent is obtained from the worker.

2.3.4 Do not make the sickness, injury or absence records of individual workers available to other workers unless it is necessary for them to do their jobs.

Key points and possible actions

- Managers can be provided with information about those who work for them in so far as this is necessary for them to carry out their managerial roles.
- No 'league tables' of individual records should be published.
- Ensure that managers are aware of the sensitive nature of sickness and injury records.

[4719]

2.4 Pension and insurance schemes

Pension or insurance-based schemes such as those offering private medical care are usually controlled by a third party but can be administered in-house. Some employers also insure their business against sickness by key workers. These recommendations are directed at employers who are party to such schemes rather than at insurance companies or pensions providers.

2.4.1 Do not access personal information required by a third party to administer a scheme, in order to use it for general employment purposes.

Key points and possible actions

- Identify and review schemes currently in operation in your business.
- Identify where information could possibly 'leak' from a scheme to be used for other employment purposes.
- Identify ways of stopping this occurring, for example by passing information in sealed envelopes.

2.4.2 Limit your exchange of information with a scheme provider to the minimum necessary for operation of the scheme bearing in mind the scheme's funding obligations.

Key points and possible actions

- Remember that if information on a worker's sickness, injury or other sensitive data is exchanged a sensitive data condition must be satisfied.
- Bear in mind that your funding of a scheme does not give you a right to receive information about individual scheme members beyond that necessary for the operation of the scheme.
- Review the exchange of information with any scheme providers.
- Identify and eliminate any personal information passed to you by the scheme provider that is not essential to the operation of the scheme.

2.4.3 Do not use information gained from the internal trustees or administrators of pension schemes for general employment purposes.

Key points and possible actions

- Inform trustees and administrators of their general data protection responsibilities. In particular make sure they know they must not use personal information acquired in their capacity as trustee or administrator in their capacity as employer.

2.4.4 If your business takes on the role of broker or your staff act as group secretary for a private medical insurance scheme, ensure that personal information gathered is kept to minimum, limit access to the information and do not use it for general employment purposes.

Key points and possible actions

- Consider carefully what information is actually needed to administer the scheme.
- Limit access to personal data arising from the administration of the scheme and ensure that information gathered in this context is not used for any other purposes.

2.4.5 Ensure that when a worker joins a health or insurance scheme it is made clear what, if any, information is passed between the scheme controller and the employer and how it will be used.

Key points and possible actions

- Assess the information given to workers when they join a health or insurance scheme.
- If no specific mention is made about the transfer of information, amend the documentation about the scheme accordingly.

[4720]

2.5 Equal opportunities monitoring

2.5.1 Information about a worker's ethnic origin, disability, religion or sexual orientation is sensitive personal data. Ensure that equal opportunities monitoring of these characteristics satisfies a sensitive data condition.

Key points and possible actions

- Check your organisation's current equal opportunities monitoring against the sensitive data conditions in the Code.
- Make any necessary changes to the monitoring procedure to ensure that a sensitive data condition can always be satisfied.

See Supplementary Guidance page 72 for conditions to be satisfied.

2.5.2 Only use information that identifies individual workers where this is necessary to carry out meaningful equal opportunities monitoring. Where practicable, keep the information collected in an anonymised form.

Key points and possible actions

- Review current practices. Check whether any monitoring form gives the impression that information is anonymous, when in fact, it can be traced back to individuals.
- If identifiable information is held but it can be anonymised, do this.
- When there is no reasonable alternative but to be able to identify individuals, check whether the monitoring form states this and explains how the information is to be used.
- Ensure that identifiable information collected for equal opportunities monitoring is not used for any other purposes.
- Make any necessary changes to procedures and ensure that staff involved in monitoring understand why these changes have been made.

2.5.3 Ensure questions are designed so that the personal information collected through them is accurate and not excessive.

Key points and possible actions

- Check that questions allow people to identify themselves accurately. For example, in ethnic origin monitoring, do not limit the range of choices given so that workers are forced to make a choice that does not properly describe them.
- If you assign workers to categories ensure the record is clear that it is your assumption and not a matter of fact.

[4721]

2.6 Marketing

2.6.1 Inform new workers if your organisation intends to use their personal information to deliver advertising or marketing messages to them. Give workers a clear opportunity to object (an 'opt-out') and respect any objections whenever received.

Key points and possible actions

- Review whether your business markets its, or anyone else's, products or services to current or former workers.
- Ensure that any new worker who will receive marketing information from your company has been informed that this will happen.
- Ensure that a clear procedure for 'opting-out' is made known to all workers.

2.6.2 Do not disclose workers' details to other organisations for their marketing unless individual workers have positively and freely indicated their agreement (an 'opt-in').

Key points and possible actions

- Review whether your business discloses workers' details. If so, put in place a procedure to ensure that a worker's details are not passed on until you have received a positive indication of agreement from him or her.

2.6.3 If you intend to use details of existing workers for marketing for the first time either in ways that were not explained when they first joined or that they would not expect, do not proceed until individual workers have positively and freely indicated their agreement (an 'opt-in').

Key points and possible actions

- When considering this type of campaign, construct an approval form to send to workers. Only direct material to those workers who have given a positive indication of agreement.
- Enclosing details of particular offers within a communication that workers will receive anyway, for example in a pay-slip, is acceptable as long as the offer includes an explanation of how to object.

[4722]

2.7 Fraud detection

Public sector employers, in particular, use workers' records in the prevention and detection of fraud, for example, in order to check that they are not paying state benefits to those who by virtue of their employment are not entitled to receive them. Such exercises involve the electronic comparison of data sets held for different purposes in order to identify inconsistencies or discrepancies which may indicate fraud. This is known as data matching.

2.7.1 Consult workers, and/or trade unions or other representatives before starting a data matching exercise.

Key points and possible actions

- Inform trade unions and other workers' representatives of any proposed data matching exercise.
- Discuss how the plan will work in detail and take account of legitimate concerns raised before starting the exercise.

2.7.2 Inform new workers of the use of payroll or other information in fraud prevention exercises and remind them of this periodically.

Key points and possible actions

- Explain how fraud prevention exercises operate to new workers as part of information given about data protection.
- Set up regular reminders to workers on how the data matching exercise works – e g prior to the start of each new exercise.

2.7.3 Do not disclose worker information to other organisations for the prevention or detection of fraud unless:-

- **you are required by law to make the disclosure, or**
- **you believe that failure to disclose, in a particular instance, is likely to prejudice the prevention or detection of crime, or**
- **the disclosure is provided for in workers' contracts of employment.**

Key points and possible actions

- Ensure staff who would be approached by outside agencies for this type of information, understand the rules of disclosure.

[4723]

2.8 Workers' access to information about themselves

Workers, like any other individuals, have a right to gain access to information that is kept about them. This right is known as subject access.

2.8.1 Establish a system that enables your organisation to recognise a subject access request and to locate all the information about a worker in order to be able to respond promptly and in any case within 40 calendar days of receiving a request.

Key points and possible actions

- Assess what personal information about workers is in existence and who is responsible for it (**See recommendation 0.3 *ante*.**)
- Ensure that the information is accessible.
- Establish who in the organisation is responsible for responding to subject access requests.
- Ensure that all workers who are likely to receive subject access requests can recognise them and know who to pass them to.
- Have a checklist in place listing all places where personal information might be held that should be checked.
- Use the checklist to gather all personal information in time to enable a response within 40 days.

2.8.2 Check the identity of anyone making a subject access request to ensure information is only given to the person entitled to it.

Key points and possible actions

- In smaller organisations where workers make access requests in person, identity checks may not be necessary, but in large organisations it should not simply be assumed all requests are genuine.

- Brief anyone responsible for responding to a subject access request on how to check the identity of the person making it.

2.8.3 Provide the worker with a hard copy of the information kept, making clear any codes used and the sources of the information.

Key points and possible actions

- In the checklist used to gather all personal information include a check to ensure that the information supplied is intelligible, that it includes sources and that if at all possible it is in hard copy form.
- Although a hard copy of the subject access information does not have to be provided if this would involve "disproportionate effort" some form of access to the information still has to be given.

2.8.4 Make a judgement as to what information it is reasonable to withhold concerning the identities of third parties.

Key points and possible actions

- Information released to a worker could include information that enables a third party such as another worker to be identified. The employer has to balance the worker's right to know against an expectation of privacy that the third party might have.
- You can use the guidance on Access when Information about Third Parties is involved on page 40 of the Supplementary Guidance to help you make the necessary judgement.
- Brief those handling subject access requests on how to make decisions concerning third party information.

2.8.5 Inform managers and other relevant people in the organisation of the nature of information that will be released to individuals who make subject access requests.

Key points and possible actions

- Managers should be made aware of the extent to which information relating to them might be released to workers.
- If managers and others are aware of the extent and nature of the information that an individual could gain access to it should encourage them to record only what is truly relevant and useful.

2.8.6 Ensure that on request, promptly and in any event within 40 calendar days, workers are provided with a statement of how any automated decision-making process, to which they are subject, is used, and how it works.

Key points and possible actions

- Determine whether your organisation has any automated systems which are used as the sole basis for decision-making, for example during short-listing.
- If so, document how the system works and the basis of its decisions.
- Make this information available to those who are responsible for responding to requests about the process and make sure that they are aware of the requirement to respond within 40 calendar days.

2.8.7 When purchasing a computerised system ensure that the system enables you to retrieve all the information relating to an individual worker without difficulty.

Key points and possible actions

- Ensure that the supplier of a system that you will use to take automated decisions about workers provides the information needed to enable you to respond fully to requests for information about how the system works.
- Put in place arrangements to ensure that when systems are updated or new systems purchased they facilitate responses to subject access requests.

[4724]

2.9 References

The provision of a reference about a worker from one party, such as a present employer, to another, such as a prospective employer, will generally involve the disclosure of personal data. This sub section of the Code applies not only to references given to prospective employers, but also references given in other circumstances, for example character references given in connection with legal proceedings or financial references given in connection with a worker's application for a mortgage.

References Given:

2.9.1 Set out a clear company policy stating who can give corporate references, in what circumstances, and the policy that applies to the granting of access to them. Make anyone who is likely to become a referee aware of this policy.

Key points and possible actions

- Determine who is allowed to give corporate references, this may, for example, be done by grade. Check whether your organisation distinguishes between corporate and personal references. If not, consider doing so.
- Draw up a policy explaining how reference requests should be handled, outlining the types of information that can be provided and the extent to which workers are given access. Ensure the policy is brought to the attention of anyone who is likely to receive a reference request.

2.9.2 Do not provide confidential references about a worker unless you are sure that this is the worker's wish.

Key points and possible actions

- As part of the policy, include a requirement that all those giving corporate references must be satisfied that the worker wishes the reference to be provided.
- As part of an Exit Policy, include on file a record of whether the worker wishes references to be provided after he/she has left.

References received:

2.9.3 When responding to a request from a worker to see his or her own reference and the reference enables a third party to be identified, make a judgement as to what information it is reasonable to withhold.

Key points and possible actions

- You can use the guidance on Access when Information about Third Parties is Involved on page 40 of the Supplementary Guidance to help you make this judgement.
- Brief those responsible for responding to requests for access to references received on how to make decisions concerning third party information.

[4725]

2.10 Disclosure requests

This is concerned with requests for information about individual workers that come from outside the employer's organisation.

2.10.1 Establish a disclosure policy to tell staff who are likely to receive requests for information about workers how to respond, and to where they should refer requests that fall outside the policy rules.

Key points and possible actions

- Distribute information, based on this Code, on how to handle disclosure requests and ensure that all those likely to handle such requests receive the information.
- Give examples of situations where a member of staff might need to refer a request to a higher authority within the organisation.
- Provide contact details of whom staff should contact, should they be unsure of how to deal with a disclosure request.

2.10.2 Ensure that disclosure decisions that are not covered by clear policy rules are only taken by staff who are familiar with the Act and this Code, and who are able to give the decision proper consideration.

Key points and possible actions

- Determine who will be responsible for dealing with disclosure requests not covered by the policy.
- Organise any necessary training for those who will take on this role.

2.10.3 Unless you are under a legal obligation to do so, only disclose information about a worker where you conclude that in all the circumstances it is right to do so.

Key points and possible actions

- In some cases you will be under a legal obligation to disclose. Where this is the case you have no choice but to disclose. The Act does not stand in your way provided that you disclose no more than you are obliged to.
- In some cases you will not be under an obligation to disclose but you will be able to rely on an exemption in the Act if you choose to do so. This is most likely to arise in the case of criminal or tax investigations or where legal action is involved.
- Where you can relay on an exemption in the Act you still need to take care with the disclosure of confidential or sensitive information.
- In other cases you could breach the Act if you disclose. Only disclose, if in all the circumstances you are satisfied that it is fair to do so. Bear in mind that the duty of fairness is owed primarily to the worker. Where possible seek and take account of the workers' views.

- Only disclose confidential information if the worker has clearly agreed or you are satisfied that despite the duty of confidence the worker's interest or the wider public interest justifies disclosure.
- Ensure that if you intend to disclose sensitive personal data a sensitive data condition is satisfied.

2.10.4 Where a disclosure is requested in an emergency, make a careful decision as to whether to disclose, considering the nature of the information being requested and the likely impact on the individual of not providing it.

Key points and possible actions

- Make sure staff who are likely to receive such requests know whether they can handle them themselves or if not, who to refer them to. If they handle them themselves make them aware of their responsibility to assess the nature of the emergency and determine whether the request could be submitted in writing.

2.10.5 Make staff aware that those seeking information sometimes use deception to gain access to it. Ensure that they check the legitimacy of any request and the identity and authority of the person making it.

Key points and possible actions

- As part of the disclosure policy, make it a requirement that staff check the identity of any person making a request, the authority of the individual concerned and the basis for the request.
- Ensure that when a request is made on the basis of a stated legal obligation, that it is received in writing, spelling out the legal obligation on which it is based. If the stated legal obligation is in doubt check it against the law.

2.10.6 Where the disclosure involves a transfer of information about a worker to a country outside the European Economic Area (EEA), ensure that there is a proper legal basis for making the transfer.

Key points and possible actions

- The Act restricts the transfer of personal information outside the EEA.
- Review the Information Commissioner's guidance at *www.informationcommissioner.gov.uk: Data Protection: Your Legal Obligations: International Transfers*, if you intend to pass workers' information outside the EEA.
- Keep a record of the legal basis on which you make the transfer.

2.10.7 Inform the worker before or as soon as is practicable after a request has been received that a non-regular disclosure is to be made, unless prevented by law from doing so, or unless this would constitute a "tip off" prejudicing a criminal or tax investigation.

Key points and possible actions

- For each non-regular disclosure, make a judgment as to whether the worker can be informed and whether a copy of the information can be provided to him or her. (A reminder of this could be placed in any system for handling non-regular disclosures.)
- In cases where the information can be provided to the worker do so as soon as possible.

2.10.8 Keep a record of non-regular disclosures. Regularly check and review this record to ensure that the requirements of the Act are being satisfied.

Key points and possible actions

- Set up a system for non-regular disclosures recording the details of the person who made the disclosure, the person who authorised it, the person requesting the disclosure, the reasons for the disclosure, the information disclosed and the date and time.
- Also set up a system to regularly check and review this record.

[4726]

2.11 Publication and other disclosures

2.11.1 If publishing information about workers ensure that:

- **there is a legal obligation to do so, or**
- **the information is clearly not intrusive, or**
- **the worker has consented to disclosure, or**
- **the information is in a form that does not identify individual workers.**

Key points and possible actions

- An employer must balance the benefits of publishing information about workers with the reasonable expectations of its workers that their employer will respect the privacy of their personal information.
- Assess the current information published about named workers (eg in annual reports or on the website or in other publications) and the basis on which this takes place.

- Determine whether it is necessary to obtain consent from workers who are named and if so, set up an arrangement for obtaining consent from workers who are named in publications in the future.

2.11.2 Where information about workers is published on the basis of consent, ensure that when the worker gives consent he or she is made aware of the extent of information that will be published, how it will be published and the implications of this.

Key points and possible actions

- In any arrangement for obtaining consent for the publication of information on named workers, ensure that the worker is made aware of the full extent of any information to be published and where it is to be published. This is particularly important if information is to be published on the internet.

2.11.3 Personal information about workers should only be supplied to a trade union for its recruitment purposes if;

- **the trade union is recognised by the employer,**
- **the information is limited to that necessary to enable a recruitment approach, and**
- **each worker has been previously told that this will happen and has been given a clear opportunity to object.**

Key points and possible actions

- If your organisation has a recognised trade union that is requesting personal information about workers for a recruitment drive, inform all workers and give them an opportunity to object if they so wish.

2.11.4 Where staffing information is supplied to trade unions in the course of collective bargaining, ensure the information is such that individual workers cannot be identified.

Key points and possible actions

- Review your arrangements for the supply of information in connection with collective bargaining to ensure that in future all information on workers is supplied in an anonymised form.

[4727]

2.12 Merger, acquisition, and business re-organisation

Business mergers and acquisitions will generally involve the disclosure of information about workers. This may take place during evaluation of assets and liabilities prior to the final merger or acquisition decision. Once a decision has been made disclosure is also likely to take place either in the run-up to or at the time of the actual merger or acquisition. A similar situation arises in business re-organisations that involve the transfer of workers' employment from one legal entity to another. This sub-section of the Code will be relevant to such situations.

2.12.1 Ensure, wherever practicable, that information handed over to another organisation in connection with a prospective acquisition, merger or business re-organisation is anonymised.

Key points and possible actions

- Ensure that in any merger or acquisition situation, those responsible for negotiation are aware of the Code, including its provisions on sensitive data.
- Assess any request for personal information from the other organisation. If at all possible, limit the information given to anonymised details.

2.12.2 Only hand over personal information prior to a final merger or acquisition decision after securing assurances that it will be used solely for the evaluation of assets and liabilities, it will be treated in confidence and will not be disclosed to other parties, and it will be destroyed or returned after use.

Key points and possible actions

- Remind those negotiating that they must receive strict assurances about how personal information will be used and what will happen to it should discussions end.
- Consider setting up a "data room" with accompanying rules of access.

2.12.3 Unless it is impractical to do so, tell workers if their employment records are to be disclosed to another organisation before an acquisition, merger or re-organisation takes place. If the acquisition, merger or re-organisation proceeds make sure workers are aware of the extent to which their records are to be transferred to the new employer.

Key points and possible actions

- In some circumstances "insider trading" or similar restrictions will apply. An example is where providing an explanation to workers would alert them to the possibility of a takeover of which they would otherwise be unaware and could thereby affect the price of a company's shares. The obligation to provide an explanation to workers is lifted in such circumstances.

2.12.4 Where a merger, acquisition or re-organisation involves a transfer of information about a worker to a country outside the European Economic Area (EEA) ensure that there is a proper basis for making the transfer.

Key points and possible actions

- Review the Information Commissioner's guidance at *www.informationcommissioner.gov.uk: Data Protection: Your Legal Obligations: International Transfers* if you intend to pass workers' information outside the EEA.
- Check that there is a legal basis for the transfer that you intend to make.

2.12.5 New employers should ensure that the records they hold as a result of a merger, acquisition or re-organisation do not include excessive information, and are accurate and relevant.

Key points and possible actions

- Remember that a new employer's use of workers' information acquired as the result of a merger, acquisition or re-organisation is constrained by the expectations the workers will have from their former employer's use of information.
- When taking over an organisation assess what personal information you now hold as outlined in 0.3 and 0.4 (*ante*).

[4728]

2.13 Discipline, grievance and dismissal

2.13.1 Remember that the Data Protection Act applies to personal information processed in relation to discipline, grievance and dismissal proceedings.

Key points and possible actions

- Assess your organisation's disciplinary procedures and grievance procedures. Consider whether they need to be amended in the light of the Code.
- Ensure that managers are aware that subject access rights apply even if responding to a request might impact on a disciplinary or grievance investigation or on forthcoming proceedings, unless responding would be likely to prejudice a criminal investigation.
- Ensure that those involved in investigating disciplinary matters or grievances are aware that they must not gather information by deception.
- Ensure that records used in the course of proceedings are of good enough quality to support any conclusion drawn from them.
- Ensure that all records are kept securely.
- Check that unsubstantiated allegations have been removed unless there are exceptional reasons for retaining some record.

2.13.2 Do not access or use information you keep about workers merely because it might have some relevance to a disciplinary or grievance investigation if access or use would be either:

- **incompatible with the purpose(s) you obtained the information for, or**
- **disproportionate to the seriousness of the matter under investigation.**

Key points and possible actions

- Make those in the organisation who are likely to carry out investigations aware that they do not have an unrestricted right of access to all information held about workers under investigation.
- Put in place a system to ensure that decisions on whether access is justified take into account the provisions of this Code and the Act.

2.13.3 Ensure that there are clear procedures on how "spent" disciplinary warnings are handled.

Key points and possible actions

- Determine what is meant by a "spent" warning in your organisation. Assess the disciplinary procedure and decide whether it needs to be amended to clarify what happens once a warning period has expired.
- Set up a diary system, either manual or computerised, to remove spent warnings from individual's records, if this is a requirement of your procedure.

2.13.4 Ensure that when employment is terminated the reason for this is accurately recorded, and that the record reflects properly what the worker has been told about the termination.

Key points and possible actions

- Ensure that if a worker has resigned, even if asked to do so, that this is recorded on his or her record, as "resigned" rather than "dismissed".

[4729]

2.14 Outsourcing data processing

Frequently, organisations do not process all the information they hold on workers themselves but outsource this to other organisations. Such organisations are termed 'data processors' in the Data Protection Act.

2.14.1 Satisfy yourself that any data processor you choose adopts appropriate security measures both in terms of the technology it uses and how it is managed.

Key points and possible actions

- Check whether the data processor has in place appropriate security measures. Is it, for example, certified to BS7799?
- Check that the processor actually puts their security measures into practice.

2.14.2 Have in place a written contract with any data processor you choose that requires it to process personal information only on your instructions, and to maintain appropriate security.

Key points and possible actions

- If there is no contract, put one in place.
- Check that any contract you have with a data processor includes clauses ensuring proper data security measures.

2.14.3 Where the use of a data processor would involve a transfer of information about a worker to a country outside the European Economic Area (EEA), ensure that there is a proper basis for making the transfer.

Key points and possible actions

- Review the Information Commissioner guidelines at *www.informationcommissioner.gov.uk: Data Protection: Your Legal Obligations: International transfers* if you intend to pass workers' information outside the EEA.
- Check that there is a legal basis for the transfer that you intend to make.

[4730]

2.15 Retention of records

See Part 1: Recruitment and Selection, para 1.7, for specific recommendations on retention of recruitment records.

2.15.1 Establish and adhere to standard retention times for the various categories of information to be held on the records of workers and former workers. Base the retention times on business need taking into account relevant professional guidelines.

Key points and possible actions

- Remember that the Act does not override any statutory requirement to retain records, for example, in relation to income tax or certain aspects of health and safety.
- Only retain information on records that is still needed; eliminate personal information that is no longer of any relevance, once the employment relationship has ended.
- As far as possible set standard retention times for categories of information held in employment records. Consider basing these on a risk analysis approach.
- Assess who in your organisation retains employment records (see 0.3 *ante*). Make sure no one retains information beyond the standard retention times unless there is a sound business reason for doing so.
- If possible, set up a computerised system which flags information retained for more than a certain time as due for review or deletion.

2.15.2 Anonymise any information about workers and former workers where practicable.

Key points and possible actions

- Where statistical information only is required, anonymised records should be sufficient.

2.15.3 If the holding of any information on criminal convictions of workers is justified, ensure that the information is deleted once the conviction is 'spent' under the Rehabilitation of Offenders Act.

Key points and possible actions

- Use a computerised or manual system to ensure spent convictions are deleted from the system.
- Identify if your organisation may be justified in making exceptions to this, for example, certain convictions held in connection with workers who work with children.

2.15.4 Ensure that records which are to be disposed of are securely and effectively destroyed.

Key points and possible actions

- Review arrangements for dealing with old records to ensure they are securely disposed of and advise anyone holding employment records of these arrangements for disposal.
- Do not assume that pressing the "delete" key on a computer based system necessarily removes a record completely from the system. Check that computer records that are to be deleted are in practice removed completely.
- Make sure that computer equipment that has held employment records is never sold on unless you are sure the records have been fully removed.

[4731]

PART 3: MONITORING AT WORK

ABOUT PART 3 OF THE CODE

Data protection and monitoring at work

A number of the requirements of the Data Protection Act will come into play whenever an employer wishes to monitor workers. The Act does not prevent an employer from monitoring workers, but such monitoring must be done in a way which is consistent with the Act. Employers – especially in the public sector – must also bear in mind Article 8 of the European Convention on Human Rights which creates a right to respect for private and family life and for correspondence.

How does the Data Protection Act regulate monitoring?

Monitoring is a recognised component of the employment relationship. Most employers will make some checks on the quantity and quality of work produced by their workers. Workers will generally expect this. Many employers carry out monitoring to safeguard workers, as well as to protect their own interests or those of their customers. For example, monitoring may take place to ensure that those in hazardous environments are not being put at risk through the adoption of unsafe working practices. Monitoring arrangements may equally be part of the security mechanisms used to protect personal datapersonal information. In other cases, for example in the context of some financial services, the employer may be under legal or regulatory obligations which it can only realistically fulfil if it undertakes some monitoring. However where monitoring goes beyond one individual simply watching another and involves the manual recording or any automated processing of personal information, it must be done in a way that is both lawful and fair to workers.

Monitoring may, to varying degrees, have an adverse impact on workers. It may intrude into their private lives, undermine respect for their correspondence or interfere with the relationship of mutual trust and confidence that should exist between them and their employer. The extent to which it does this may not always be immediately obvious. It is not always easy to draw a distinction between work-place and private information. For example monitoring e-mail messages from a worker to an occupational health advisor, or messages between workers and their trade union representatives, can give rise to concern.

In broad terms, what the Act requires is that any adverse impact on workers is justified by the benefits to the employer and others. This Code is designed to help employers determine when this might be the case.

What does this part of the Code cover?

This part of the Code applies where activities that are commonly referred to as "monitoring" are taking place or are planned. This means activities that set out to collect information about workers by keeping them under some form of observation, normally with a view to checking their performance or conduct. This could be done either directly, indirectly, perhaps by examining their work output, or by electronic means.

This part of Code is primarily directed at employers – especially larger organisations – using or planning some form of **systematic monitoring**. This is where the employer monitors all workers or particular groups of workers as a matter of routine, perhaps by using an electronic system to scan all e-mail messages or by installing monitoring devices in all company vehicles.

The Act still applies to **occasional monitoring**. This is where the employer introduces monitoring as a short term measure in response to a particular problem or need, for example by keeping a watch on the e-mails sent by a worker suspected of racial harassment or by installing a hidden camera when workers are suspected of drug dealing on the employer's premises.

This part of the Code deals with both types of monitoring, but it is likely to be of most relevance to employers involved in systematic monitoring, which will generally be larger organisations.

Examples of monitoring

There is no hard-and-fast definition of 'Monitoring' to which this part of the Code applies. Examples of activities addressed in this part of the Code include:

- gathering information through point of sale terminals, to check the efficiency of individual supermarket check-out operators
- recording the activities of workers by means of CCTV cameras, either so that the recordings can be viewed routinely to ensure that health and safety rules are being complied with, or so that they are available to check on workers in the event of a health and safety breach coming to light
- randomly opening up individual workers' e-mails or listening to their voice-mails to look for evidence of malpractice
- using automated checking software to collect information about workers, for example to find out whether particular workers are sending or receiving inappropriate e-mails
- examining logs of websites visited to check that individual workers are not downloading pornography
- keeping recordings of telephone calls made to or from a call centre, either to listen to as part of workers training, or simply to have a record to refer to in the event of a customer complaint about a worker
- systematically checking logs of telephone numbers called to detect use of premium-rate lines
- videoing workers outside the workplace, to collect evidence that they are not in fact sick
- obtaining information through credit reference agencies to check that workers are not in financial difficulties.

Outside this part of the Code

There are other activities that this part of the Code does not specifically address. Most employers will keep some business records that contain information about workers but are not collected primarily to keep a watch on their performance or conduct. An example could be records of customer transactions – including paper records, computer records or recordings of telephone calls. This part of the Code is **not** concerned with occasional access to records of this type in the course of an investigation into a specific problem, such as a complaint from a customer.

See Part 2: Employment Records, para 2.13, for guidance relating to grievance and disciplinary investigations.

Examples of activities not directly addressed in this part of the Code include;

- looking back through customer records in the event of a complaint, to check that the customer was given the correct advice
- checking a collection of e-mails sent by a particular worker which is stored as a record of transactions, in order to ensure the security of the system or to investigate an allegation of malpractice
- looking back through a log of telephone calls made that is kept for billing purposes, to establish whether a worker suspected of disclosing trade secrets has been contacting a competitor.

Impact assessments

The Data Protection Act does not prevent monitoring. Indeed in some cases monitoring might be necessary to satisfy its requirements. However, any adverse impact of monitoring on individuals must be justified by the benefits to the employer and others. We use the term "impact assessment" to describe the process of deciding whether this is the case.

In all but the most straightforward cases, employers are likely to find it helpful to carry out a formal or informal 'impact assessment' to decide if and how to carry out monitoring. This is the means by which employers can judge whether a monitoring arrangement is a proportionate response to the problem it seeks to address. This Code does not prejudge the outcome of the impact assessment. Each will necessarily depend on the particular circumstances of the employer. Nor does the Code attempt to set out for employers the benefits they might gain from monitoring. What it does do is assist employers in identifying and giving appropriate weight to the other factors they should take into account.

An impact assessment involves;

- identifying clearly the **purpose(s)** behind the monitoring arrangement and the benefits it is likely to deliver
- identifying any likely **adverse impact** of the monitoring arrangement
- considering **alternatives** to monitoring or different ways in which it might be carried out
- taking into account the **obligations** that arise from monitoring
- judging whether monitoring is **justified**.

Adverse impact

Identifying any likely adverse impact means taking into account the consequences of monitoring, not only for workers, but also for others who might be affected by it, such as customers. Consider:

- what intrusion, if any, will there be into the private lives of workers and others, or interference with their private e-mails, telephone calls or other correspondence? Bear in mind that the private lives of workers can, and usually will, extend into the workplace.
- to what extent will workers and others know when either they, or information about them, are being monitored and then be in a position to act to limit any intrusion or other adverse impact on themselves?
- whether information that is confidential, private or otherwise sensitive will be seen by those who do not have a business need to know, e g IT workers involved in monitoring e-mail content
- what impact, if any, will there be on the relationship of mutual trust and confidence that should exist between workers and their employer?
- what impact, if any, will there be on other legitimate relationships, e g between trades union members and their representatives?
- what impact, if any, will there be on individuals with professional obligations of confidentiality or secrecy, e g solicitors or doctors?
- whether the monitoring will be oppressive or demeaning.

Alternatives

Considering alternatives, or different methods of monitoring, means asking questions such as:

- can established or new methods of supervision, effective training and/or clear communication from managers, rather than electronic or other systemic monitoring, deliver acceptable results?
- can the investigation of specific incidents or problems be relied on, for example accessing stored e-mails to follow up an allegation of malpractice, rather than undertaking continuous monitoring?
- can monitoring be limited to workers about whom complaints have been received, or about whom there are other grounds to suspect of wrong-doing?
- can monitoring be targeted at areas of highest risk, e g can it be directed at a few individuals whose jobs mean they pose a particular risk to the business rather than at everyone?
- can monitoring be automated? If so, will it be less intrusive, e g does it mean that private information will be 'seen' only by a machine rather than by other workers?
- can spot-checks or audit be undertaken instead of using continuous monitoring? Remember though that continuous automated monitoring could be less intrusive than spot-check or audit that involves human intervention.

Obligations

Taking into account the obligations that arise from monitoring means considering such matters as:

- whether and how workers will be notified about the monitoring arrangements
- how information about workers collected through monitoring will be kept securely and handled in accordance with the Act.

See Part 2 – Employment Records, para 2.2, for more information on security requirements.

- the implications of the rights that individuals have to obtain a copy of information about them that has been collected through monitoring.

See Part 2 – Employment Records, para 2.8, which explains more about rights to access.

Is monitoring justified?

Making a conscious decision as to whether the current or proposed method of monitoring is justified involves;

- establishing the benefits of the method of monitoring
- considering any alternative method of monitoring
- weighing these benefits against any adverse impact
- placing particular emphasis on the need to be fair to individual workers
- ensuring, particularly where monitoring electronic communications is involved, that any intrusion is no more than absolutely necessary
- bearing in mind that significant intrusion into the private lives of individuals will not normally be justified unless the employer's business is at real risk of serious damage
- taking into account the results of consultation with trade unions or other representatives, if any, or with workers themselves.

See Supplementary Guidance page 57 for a chart to help assess the degree of intrusiveness involved in monitoring the content of various types of communication

Making an impact assessment need not be a complicated or onerous process. It will often be enough for an employer to make a simple mental evaluation of the risks faced by his or her business and to assess whether the carrying out of monitoring would reduce or eradicate those risks. In other cases the impact assessment will be more complicated, for example where an employer faces a number of different risks of varying degrees of seriousness. In such cases appropriate documentation would be advisable.

Is a worker's consent needed?

There are limitations as to how far consent can be relied on in the employment context to justify the processing of personal information. To be valid, for the purposes of the Data Protection Act, consent must be "freely given", which may not be the case in the employment environment. Once given, consent can be withdrawn. In any case, employers who can justify monitoring on the basis of an impact assessment will not generally need the consent of individual workers.

Are there special rules for electronic communications?

Electronic communications are broadly telephone calls, fax messages, e-mails and internet access. Monitoring can involve the 'interception' of such communications. The Regulation of Investigatory Powers Act, and the Lawful Business Practice Regulations made under it, set out when interception can take place despite the general rule that interception without consent is against the law. It should be remembered that – whilst the Regulations deal only with interception – the Data Protection Act is concerned more generally with the processing of personal information. Therefore when monitoring involves an interception which results in the recording of personal information an employer will need to satisfy both the Regulations and the requirements of the Data Protection Act.

See Supplementary Guidance page 58, for more details on The Lawful Business Practice Regulations.

[4732]

GOOD PRACTICE RECOMMENDATIONS – PART 3

The parts of the Code in this section are:

3.1 The general approach to monitoring

3.2 Monitoring electronic communications

3.3 Video and audio monitoring

3.4 Covert monitoring

3.5 In-vehicle monitoring

3.6 Monitoring through information from third parties

3.1 The general approach to monitoring

Core Principles

- It will usually be intrusive to monitor your workers.

PART 4

- Workers have legitimate expectations that they can keep their personal lives private and that they are also entitled to a degree of privacy in the work environment.
- If employers wish to monitor their workers, they should be clear about the purpose and satisfied that the particular monitoring arrangement is justified by real benefits that will be delivered.
- Workers should be aware of the nature, extent and reasons for any monitoring, unless (exceptionally) covert monitoring is justified.
- In any event, workers' awareness will influence their expectations.

3.1.1 Identify who within the organisation can authorise the monitoring of workers and ensure they are aware of the employer's responsibilities under the Act.

Key points and possible actions

- There are non-compliance risks if line mangers introduce monitoring arrangements without due authority.
- Those who monitor workers, or who can authorise such monitoring, should be briefed on the Act and this Code.

3.1.2 Before monitoring, identify clearly the purpose(s) behind the monitoring and the specific benefits it is likely to bring. Determine – preferably using an impact assessment – whether the likely benefits justify any adverse impact.

Key points and possible actions

- Identify the monitoring that currently takes place in your organisation.
- Identify any monitoring that you plan to implement.
- Consider conducting an impact assessment on either current or planned monitoring based on the guidance ante.

3.1.3 If monitoring is to be used to enforce the organisation's rules and standards make sure that the rules and standards are clearly set out in a policy which also refers to the nature and extent of any associated monitoring. Ensure workers are aware of the policy.

Key points and possible actions

- Identify which of your organisation's rules and standards are enforced partly or wholly through the use of monitoring.
- Ensure that these rules and standards are set out in policies that are clearly communicated to workers.

3.1.4 Tell workers what monitoring is taking place and why, and keep them aware of this, unless covert monitoring is justified.

Key points and possible actions

- Ensure that workers are aware of the nature and extent of any monitoring.
- Set up a system (for example by using the workers handbook or via an intranet) to ensure workers remain aware that monitoring is being conducted.
- Tell workers when significant changes are introduced.

3.1.5 If sensitive information is collected in the course of monitoring, ensure that a sensitive data condition is satisfied.

Key points and possible actions

- If monitoring workers' performance or conduct results in the collection of information on such matters as health, racial origin, trade union activities or sex life, check that at least one of the sensitive data conditions is met. See Supplementary Guidance page 72 which explains more about the conditions for processing sensitive data.

3.1.6 Keep to a minimum those who have access to personal information obtained through monitoring. Subject them to confidentiality and security requirements and ensure that they are properly trained where the nature of the information requires this.

Key points and possible actions

- Assess whether the organisation could reduce the number of staff involved in monitoring workers.
- Consider whether monitoring is more appropriately carried out by security or personnel functions rather than by line managers.
- Ensure that the training for workers who may come across personal information whilst monitoring makes them aware of data protection obligations.

3.1.7 Do not use personal information collected through monitoring for purposes other than those for which the monitoring was introduced unless:

(a) it is clearly in the individual's interest to do so; or
(b) it reveals activity that no employer could reasonably be expected to ignore.

Key points and possible actions

- Ensure that only senior management can authorise the use of personal information obtained through monitoring for new or different purposes.
- Ensure that they are familiar with the Act and the relevant parts of this Code.

3.1.8 If information gathered from monitoring might have an adverse impact on workers, present them with the information and allow them to make representations before taking action.

Key points and possible actions

- Equipment or systems malfunction can cause information collected through monitoring to be misleading or inaccurate. Information can also be misinterpreted or even deliberately falsified.
- Ensure that, within or alongside disciplinary or grievance procedures, workers can see, and if necessary explain or challenge, the results of any monitoring.

3.1.9 Ensure that the right of access of workers to information about them which is kept for, or obtained through, monitoring is not compromised. Monitoring systems must be capable of meeting this and other data protection requirements.

Key points and possible actions

- Assess whether monitoring systems collect information in a way that enables you to respond readily to access requests.
- If they do not, ensure that a mechanism that will allow you to do so is built into the system.
- Check that any electronic monitoring system, bought 'off-the-shelf', has the capability to enable you to meet access requests.

3.1.10 Do not monitor workers just because a customer for your products or services imposes a condition requiring you to do so, unless you can satisfy yourself that the condition is justified.

Key points and possible actions

- Monitoring is not justified simply because it is a condition of business. Such a condition cannot over-ride the employer's obligations to comply with the Act.
- Consider carrying out an impact assessment to assess whether meeting any external stipulation means that your organisation is in breach of the Act. If so, cease monitoring on this basis.

[4733]

3.2 Monitoring electronic communications

This sub-section deals with the monitoring of telephone, fax, e-mail, voice-mail, internet access and other forms of electronic communication.

3.2.1 If you wish to monitor electronic communications, establish a policy on their use and communicate it to workers – see 'Policy for the use of electronic communications' below.

Key points and possible actions

- If your organisation does not have a policy on the use of electronic communications, decide whether you should establish one.
- Review any existing policy to ensure that it reflects data protection principles.
- Review any existing policies and actual practices to ensure that they are not out of line, eg whether private calls are banned in the policy but generally accepted in practice.
- Check that workers are aware of the policy and if not bring it to their attention.

Policy for the use of electronic communications

Employers should consider integrating the following data protection features into a policy for the use of electronic communications:

- Set out clearly to workers the circumstances in which they may or may not use the employer's telephone systems (including mobile phones), the e-mail system and internet access for private communications.
- Make clear the extent and type of private use that is allowed, for example restrictions on overseas phone calls or limits on the size and/or type of e-mail attachments that they can send or receive.
- In the case of internet access, specify clearly any restrictions on material that can be viewed or copied. A simple ban on 'offensive material' is unlikely to be sufficiently clear for people to know what is and is not allowed. Employers may wish to consider giving examples of the sort of material that is considered offensive, for example material containing racist terminology or nudity.

- Advise workers about the general need to exercise care, about any relevant rules, and about what personal information they are allowed to include in particular types of communication.
- Make clear what alternatives can be used, e g the confidentiality of communications with the company doctor can only be ensured if they are sent by internal post, rather than by e-mail, and are suitably marked.
- Lay down clear rules for private use of the employer's communication equipment when used from home or away from the workplace, e g the use of facilities that enable external dialling into company networks
- Explain the purposes for which any monitoring is conducted, the extent of the monitoring and the means used.
- Outline how the policy is enforced and penalties which exist for a breach of policy.

There may, of course, be other matters that an employer also wants to address in its policy.

3.2.2 Ensure that where monitoring involves the interception of a communication it is not outlawed by the Regulation of Investigatory Powers Act 2000.

Key points and possible actions

- Interception occurs when, in the course of its transmission, the contents of a communication are made available to someone other than the sender or intended recipient. It does not include access to stored e-mails that have been opened.
- The intended recipient may be the business, but it could be a specified individual.
- Check whether any interception is allowed under the Lawful Business Practice Regulations.
- Take any necessary action to bring such monitoring in line with RIPA and these Regulations. See Supplementary Guidance page 58 for more information about the Lawful Business Practice Regulations.

3.2.3 Consider – preferably using an impact assessment – whether any monitoring of electronic communications can be limited to that necessary to ensure the security of the system and whether it can be automated.

Key points and possible actions

- Automated systems can be used to provide protection from intrusion, malicious code such as viruses and Trojans, and to prevent password misuse. Such systems may be less intrusive than monitoring of communications to or from workers.

3.2.4 If telephone calls or voice-mails are, or are likely to be, monitored, consider – preferably using an impact assessment – whether the benefits justify the adverse impact. If so, inform workers about the nature and extent of such monitoring.

Key points and possible actions

- If telephone calls or voice-mails are monitored, or will be monitored in the future, consider carrying out an impact assessment.
- If voice-mails need to be checked for business calls when workers are away, make sure they know this may happen and that it may be unavoidable that some personal messages are heard.
- In other cases, assess whether it is essential to monitor the content of calls and consider the use of itemised call records instead.
- Ensure that workers are aware of the nature and extent of telephone monitoring.

3.2.5 Ensure that those making calls to, or receiving calls from, workers are aware of any monitoring and the purpose behind it, unless this is obvious.

Key points and possible actions

- Consider the use of recorded messages, informing external callers that calls may be monitored.
- If this is not feasible, encourage workers to tell callers that their conversations may be monitored.

3.2.6 Ensure that workers are aware of the extent to which you receive information about the use of telephone lines in their homes, or mobile phones provided for their personal use, for which your business pays partly or fully. Do not make use of information about private calls for monitoring, unless they reveal activity that no employer could reasonably be expected to ignore.

Key points and possible actions

- Remember that expectations of privacy are likely to be significantly greater at home than in the workplace.
- If any workers using mobiles or home telephone lines, for which you pay, are currently subjected to monitoring ensure that they are aware of the nature and the reasons for monitoring.

3.2.7 If e-mails and/or internet access are, or are likely to be, monitored, consider, preferably using an impact assessment, whether the benefits justify the adverse impact. If so, inform workers about the nature and extent of all e-mail and internet access monitoring.

Key points and possible actions

- If e-mails and/or internet access are presently monitored, or will be monitored in the future, consider carrying out an impact assessment.
- Check that workers are aware of the nature and extent of e-mail and internet access monitoring.

3.2.8 Wherever possible avoid opening e-mails, especially ones that clearly show they are private or personal.

Key points and possible actions

- Ensure that e-mail monitoring is confined to address/heading unless it is essential for a valid and defined reason to examine content.
- Encourage workers to mark any personal e-mails as such and encourage them to tell those who write to them to do the same.
- If workers are allowed to access personal e-mail accounts from the workplace, such e-mails should only be monitored in exceptional circumstances.

3.2.9 Where practicable, and unless this is obvious, ensure that those sending e-mails to workers, as well as workers themselves, are aware of any monitoring and the purpose behind it.

Key points and possible actions

- It may be practicable – for example when soliciting e-mail job applications – to provide information about the nature and extent of monitoring.
- In some cases, those sending e-mails to a work-place address will be aware that monitoring takes place without the need for specific information.

3.2.10 If it is necessary to check the e-mail accounts of workers in their absence, make sure that they are aware that this will happen.

Key points and possible actions

- If e-mail accounts need to be checked in the absence of workers, make sure they know this will happen.
- Encourage the use of a marking system to help protect private or personal communications.
- Avoid, where possible, opening e-mails that clearly show they are private or personal communications.

3.2.11 Inform workers of the extent to which information about their internet access and e-mails is retained in the system and for how long.

Key points and possible actions

- Check whether workers are currently aware of the retention period of e-mail and internet usage.
- If it is not already in place, set up a system (e g displaying information online or in a communication pack) that informs workers of retention periods.

[4734]

3.3. Video and audio monitoring

Some – though not all – of the data protection issues that arise when carrying out video monitoring in public places will arise in the workplace. Employers carrying out video monitoring of workers will therefore find the guidance in the Information Commissioner's CCTV Code useful. Audio monitoring means the recording of face-to-face conversations, not recording telephone calls.

See www.informationcommissioner.gov.uk and search for the CCTV Code of Practice.

3.3.1 If video or audio monitoring is (or is likely) to be used, consider – preferably using an impact assessment – whether the benefits justify the adverse impact.

Key points and possible actions

- Where possible, any video or audio monitoring should be targeted at areas of particular risk and confined to areas where expectations of privacy are low.
- Continuous video or audio monitoring of particular individuals is only likely to be justified in rare circumstances.

3.3.2 Give workers a clear notification that video or audio monitoring is being carried out and where and why it is being carried out.

Key points and possible actions

- Unless covert monitoring is justified, ensure that workers are informed of the extent and nature of any monitoring that is taking place and the reasons for it.

3.3.3 Ensure that people other than workers, such as visitors or customers, who may inadvertently be caught by monitoring, are made aware of its operation and why it is being carried out.

Key points and possible actions

- Ensure that there are adequate notices, or other means, to inform such people about the monitoring and its purpose(s).

[4735]

3.4. Covert monitoring

Covert monitoring means monitoring carried out in a manner calculated to ensure those subject to it are unaware that it is taking place. This sub-section is largely directed at covert video or audio monitoring, but will also be relevant where electronic communications are monitored when workers would not expect it.

3.4.1 Senior management should normally authorise any covert monitoring. They should satisfy themselves that there are grounds for suspecting criminal activity or equivalent malpractice and that notifying individuals about the monitoring would prejudice its prevention or detection.

Key points and possible actions

- Covert monitoring should not normally be considered. It will be rare for covert monitoring of workers to be justified. It should therefore only be used in exceptional circumstances.

3.4.2 Ensure that any covert monitoring is strictly targeted at obtaining evidence within a set timeframe and that the covert monitoring does not continue after the investigation is complete.

Key points and possible actions

- Deploy covert monitoring only as part of a specific investigation and cease once the investigation has been completed.

3.4.3 Do not use covert audio or video monitoring in areas which workers would genuinely and reasonably expect to be private.

Key points and possible actions

- If embarking on covert monitoring with audio or video equipment, ensure that this is not used in places such as toilets or private offices.
- There may be exceptions to this in cases of suspicion of serious crime but there should be an intention to involve the police.

3.4.4 If a private investigator is employed to collect information on workers covertly make sure there is a contract in place that requires the private investigator to only collect information in a way that satisfies the employer's obligations under the Act.

Key points and possible actions

- Check any arrangements for employing private investigators to ensure your contracts with them impose requirements on the investigator to only collect and use information on workers in accordance with your instructions and to keep the information secure.

3.4.5 Ensure that information obtained through covert monitoring is used only for the prevention or detection of criminal activity or equivalent malpractice. Disregard and, where feasible, delete other information collected in the course of monitoring unless it reveals information that no employer could reasonably be expected to ignore.

Key points and possible actions

- In a covert monitoring exercise, limit the number of people involved in the investigation.
- Prior to the investigation, set up clear rules limiting the disclosure and access to information obtained.
- If information is revealed in the course of covert monitoring that is tangential to the original investigation, delete it from the records unless it concerns other criminal activity or equivalent malpractice.

[4736]

3.5 In-vehicle monitoring

Devices can record or transmit information such as the location of a vehicle, the distance it has covered and information about the user's driving habits. Monitoring of vehicle movements, where the vehicle is allocated to a specific driver, and information about the performance of the vehicle can therefore be linked to a specific individual, will fall within the scope of the Data Protection Act.

3.5.1 If in-vehicle monitoring is or will be used, consider – preferably using an impact assessment – whether the benefits justify the adverse impact.

Key points and possible actions

- Where private use of a vehicle is allowed, monitoring its movements when used privately, without the freely given consent of the user, will rarely be justified.
- If the vehicle is for both private and business use, it ought to be possible to provide a 'privacy button' or similar arrangement to enable the monitoring to be disabled.
- Where an employer is under a legal obligation to monitor the use of vehicles, even if used privately, for example by fitting a tachograph to a lorry, then the legal obligation will take precedence.

3.5.2 Set out a policy that states what private use can be made of vehicles provided by, or on behalf of, the employer, and any conditions attached to use.

Key points and possible actions

- Make sure, either in the policy or separately, that details of the nature and extent of monitoring are set out.
- Check that workers using vehicles are aware of the policy.

[4737]

3.6 Monitoring through information from third parties

Employers need to take special care when wishing to make use of information held by third parties, such as credit reference or electoral roll information. This section also applies to information held by employers in a non-employment capacity, such as when a bank monitors its workers' bank accounts. Where an employer wishes to obtain information about a worker's criminal convictions, a disclosure must be obtained via the Criminal Records Bureau.

See Part 1 – Recruitment and Selection, para 1.3.2, for more information about the Criminal Records Bureau.

3.6.1 Before undertaking any monitoring which uses information from third parties, ensure – preferably using an impact assessment – that the benefits justify the adverse impact.

Key points and possible actions

- A worker's financial circumstances should not be monitored unless there are firm grounds to conclude that financial difficulties would pose a significant risk to the employer.

3.6.2 Tell workers what information sources are to be used to carry out checks on them and why the checks are to be carried out.

Key points and possible actions

- Set up a system to tell workers the nature and extent of any monitoring which uses information from third parties. (This could be via a workers handbook, notice board or on-line.)
- Where a specific check is to be carried out, the workers should be directly informed, unless to do so would be likely to prejudice the prevention or detection of crime.

3.6.3 Ensure that, if workers are monitored through the use of information held by a credit reference agency, the agency is aware of the use to which the information is put. Do not use a facility provided to conduct credit checks on customers to monitor or vet workers.

Key points and possible actions

- If your organisation uses a credit reference agency to check customers, make sure this facility is not being used to monitor or vet workers. If such practices are in place, stop them immediately.

3.6.4 Take particular care with information about workers which you have as a result of a non-employment relationship with them.

Key points and possible actions

- Check whether your organisation routinely uses information about workers that has been obtained from them because they are also (or have been) your customers, clients or suppliers. If such practices are in place, stop them unless they are justified by a risk you face.

3.6.5 Ensure that workers carrying out monitoring which involves information from third parties are properly trained. Put in place rules preventing the disclosure or inappropriate use of information obtained through such monitoring.

Key points and possible actions

- Identify who may carry out monitoring using information from third parties.
- Assess whether the organisation could reduce the number of workers involved in this activity without compromising necessary monitoring.
- Set up instructions or training for workers involved in this monitoring, making them aware of the data protection principles involved.
- Consider placing confidentiality clauses in the contracts of relevant staff.

3.6.6 Do not retain all the information obtained through such monitoring. Simply record that a check has taken place and the result of this.

Key points and possible actions

- Review procedures on retaining information. Unless there is a legal or regulatory obligation, check that information is not normally retained for more than 6 months.

[4738]

PART 4: INFORMATION ABOUT WORKERS' HEALTH

ABOUT PART 4 OF THE CODE

Data protection and information about workers' health

The Data Protection Act's sensitive data rules come into play whenever an employer wishes to process information about workers' health. These rules do not prevent the processing of such information but limit the circumstances in which it can take place. The processing must also be consistent with the other requirements of the Act. Employers, especially in the public sector, need to bear in mind Article 8 of the European Convention on Human Rights which creates a right to respect for private and family life.

What does this part of the Code cover?

This part of the Code addresses the collection and subsequent use of information about a worker's physical or mental health or condition. Collection will often be done by some form of medical examination or test, but may involve other means such as health questionnaires.

The issues addressed in this part of the Code will arise typically from the carrying out of medical examination and testing or from the operation of an occupational health scheme. This part of the Code is therefore most likely to be of relevance to larger organisations and those with specific health and safety obligations.

Examples of information about workers' health

This part of the Code applies to information such as:

- a questionnaire completed by workers to detect problems with their health
- information about a worker's disabilities or special needs
- the results of an eye-test taken by a worker using display screens
- records of blood tests carried out to ensure a worker has not been exposed to hazardous substances
- the results of a test carried out to check a worker's exposure to alcohol or drugs
- the results of genetic tests carried out on workers
- an assessment of fitness for work to determine entitlement to benefits or suitability for continued employment
- records of vaccination and immunisation status and history.

Outside the Code

The Data Protection Act only comes into play when personal information is or will be held electronically or recorded in a structured filing system. This will often be the case but sometimes it may not, for example where a line-manager enquires about a worker's health but does not keep, or intend to keep, any record of the conversation, or only keeps a note in a general notebook.

Where samples are taken, as might be the case with drug or alcohol testing, the Code only applies from the point at which samples yield personal information about a worker. This Code does not address consent for any physical intervention involved in taking a sample from a worker in the course of medical testing.

Sensitive data rules

Where information about workers' health is to be processed, one of the Act's sensitive data conditions must be satisfied. There are various conditions. Below we have listed the ones likely to be of most relevance to employers. Employers holding information about workers' health ought to be able to answer 'yes' to one or more of these questions:

- Is the processing necessary to enable the employer to meet its legal obligations, for example to ensure health and safety at work, or to comply with the requirement not to discriminate against workers on the grounds of sex, age, race or disability?
- Is the processing for medical purposes, e g the provision of care or treatment, and undertaken by a health professional or someone working under an equivalent duty of confidentiality, e g an occupational health doctor?
- Is the processing in connection with actual or prospective legal proceedings?
- Has the worker given consent explicitly to the processing of his or her medical information?

This is not an exhaustive list of all the conditions.

See Supplementary Guidance, page 72 for more information on these and other sensitive data conditions.

Relying on the worker's consent

There are limitations as to how far consent can be relied on as a basis for the processing of information about workers' health. To be valid, consent must be:

- **explicit.** This means the worker must have been told clearly what personal data are involved and have been properly informed about the use that will be made of them. The worker must have given a positive indication of agreement, e g a signature.
- **freely given.** This means the worker must have a real choice whether or not to consent and there must be no penalty imposed for refusing to give consent.

See Supplementary Guidance page 75 for further explanation of what this means in practice.

Impact assessments

Once a sensitive data condition is satisfied, an employer then needs to be clear that either:

- it is under a legal duty to process information about workers' health, e g the duty to monitor workers' possible exposure to hazardous materials under the Control of Substances Hazardous to Health Regulations 2002, or
- the benefits gained from processing information about workers' health justify the privacy intrusion or any other adverse impact on them. In other words, the collection and use of information about workers' health must be a proportionate response to a particular problem.

An 'impact assessment' is a useful tool for employers to use to help them to judge whether the second of the above options applies.

Particularly where medical testing is involved, employers are likely to find it helpful to carry out a formal or informal 'impact assessment' to decide how or whether to collect information about workers' health. This Code does not prejudge the outcome of the impact assessment. Each will necessarily depend on the particular circumstances of the employer. Nor does the Code attempt to set out for employers the benefits they might gain from holding information about workers' health. What it does do is assist employers in identifying and giving appropriate weight to the other factors they should take into account.

An impact assessment involves:

- identifying clearly the **purpose**(s) for which health information is to be collected and held and the benefits this is likely to deliver
- identifying any likely **adverse impact** of collecting and holding the information
- considering **alternatives** to collecting and holding such information
- taking into account the **obligations** that arise from collecting and holding health information
- judging whether collecting and holding health information is **justified**.

Purpose(s)

It is important that a realistic assessment is made of the extent to which the collection of health information will actually address the risks it is directed at. Decisions based on, for example, the effect of particular medical conditions on a worker's future employability or the effect of particular drugs on safety should be based on relevant and reputable scientific evidence.

Adverse impact

Identifying any likely adverse impact means taking into account the consequences of collecting and holding health information, not only for workers, but also for others who might be affected by it, such as a worker's family. Consider:

PART 4

- how extensive will the intrusion into the private lives of workers and others be as a result of collecting information about their health?
- whether health information will be seen by those who do not have a business need to know, e g IT workers involved in maintaining electronic files about workers
- what impact, if any, will the collection of health information have on the relationship of mutual trust and confidence that should exist between workers and their employer?
- whether the collection of health information will be oppressive or demeaning.

Alternatives

Considering whether it is necessary to collect information about workers' health, and if so how to do this in the least intrusive manner, means asking questions such as:

- can health questionnaires rather than tests be used to obtain the information the employer requires?
- can changes in the workplace, for example eliminating exposure to a hazardous substance, remove the need to obtain information through testing?
- can medical testing be targeted at individuals who have exhibited behavioural problems that may be drink or drug related, rather than at all workers?
- can the collection of health information be confined to areas of highest risk, e g can it be directed at a few individuals the nature of whose jobs mean they pose a particular risk rather than at everyone?
- can medical testing be designed to reveal only a narrow range of information that is directly relevant to the purpose for which it is undertaken?
- can access to health information be limited so that it will only be seen by medically qualified staff or those working under specific confidentiality agreements?

Obligations

Taking into account the obligations that arise from collecting information about workers' health means considering such matters as:

- whether and how workers will be notified about the collection of their health information
- how information about workers' health will be kept securely and handled in accordance with the Act.

See Part 2 – Employment Records, para 2.2, for more information on security requirements.

- the implications of the rights that individuals have to obtain a copy of information that has been collected about their health.

See Part 2 – Employment Records, para 2.8, which explains more about rights to access.

Is health information justified?

Making a conscious decision as to whether the current or proposed collection and use of health information is justified involves:

- establishing the benefits the collection and use of health information will bring
- considering any alternative method of obtaining these benefits and/or the information needed
- weighing these benefits against the adverse impact
- placing particular emphasis on the need to be fair to individual workers
- ensuring that the intrusion is no more than absolutely necessary
- bearing in mind that health information can be particularly sensitive, that its obtaining can be particularly intrusive and that significant intrusion will not normally be justified unless the employer's business is at real risk of serious damage
- taking into account the results of consultation with trade unions or other representatives, if any, or with workers themselves.

Making an impact assessment need not be a complicated or onerous process. Even in the context of health information it may sometimes be enough for an employer to make a simple mental evaluation of the risks faced by his or her business and to assess whether the collection and use of information about workers' health would reduce or eradicate those risks or would bring particular benefits. In other cases the impact assessment will be more complicated, for example where an employer faces a number of different risks of varying degrees of seriousness. In such cases appropriate documentation would be advisable.

[4739]

GOOD PRACTICE RECOMMENDATIONS – PART 4

The parts of the Code in this section are:

4.1 Information about workers' health: general considerations

Sickness and Injury records are dealt with in Part 2 of the Code. See para 2.3.

4.1 Information about workers' health: general considerations

Core Principles

- **It will be intrusive and may be highly intrusive to obtain information about your workers' health.**
- **Workers have legitimate expectations that they can keep their personal health information private and that employers will respect their privacy.**
- **If employers wish to collect and hold information on their workers' health, they should be clear about the purpose and satisfied that this is justified by real benefits that will be delivered.**
- **One of the sensitive data conditions must be satisfied.**
- **Workers should be aware of the extent to which information about their health is held and the reasons for which it is held.**
- **Decisions on a worker's suitability for particular work are properly management decisions but the interpretation of medical information should be left to a suitably qualified health professional.**

4.1.1 Identify who within the organisation can authorise or carry out the collection of information about workers' health on behalf of the organisation and ensure they are aware of their employer's responsibilities under the Act.

Key points and possible actions

- Those who handle information about workers' health, or who can authorise the collection of such information, should be briefed on the Act and this Code.
- There are non-compliance risks if those lacking proper authority and any necessary training introduce the collection of health information and in particular medical testing.
- Leave the interpretation of medical information to those who are qualified to do this.

4.1.2 If health information is to be collected ensure a sensitive data condition can be satisfied.

Key points and possible actions

- The collection and use of information about workers' health is against the law unless a sensitive data condition is satisfied.
- In general employers should only collect health information where this is necessary for the protection of health and safety, to prevent discrimination on the grounds of disability, to satisfy other legal obligations or if each worker affected has given his or her explicit consent.
- If consent is to be relied on, it must be freely given. That means a worker must be able to say 'no' without penalty and must be able to withdraw consent once given. Blanket consent obtained at the outset of employment cannot always be relied on.
- Consent should not be confined to the testing itself, it should also cover the subsequent recording, use and disclosure of the test results.

See Supplementary Guidance, page 72 which explains more about the conditions for processing sensitive data.

4.1.3 Identify clearly the purposes behind the collection of information about workers' health and the specific business benefits which it is likely to bring.

Key points and possible actions

- Identify the collection and use of information about workers' health that currently takes place in your organisation.
- Identify any collection or use of information about workers' health that you plan to implement.
- Consider conducting an impact assessment on current or planned collection and use of health information.

See Part 4 *post* for information on how to carry out an impact assessment.

4.1.4 Protect information about workers' health with appropriate security measures. Ensure that wherever practicable only suitably qualified health professionals have access to medical details.

Key points and possible actions

- Managers should not have access to more information about a worker's health than is necessary for them to carry out their management responsibilities. As far as possible the information should be confined to that necessary to establish fitness to work, rather than consist of more general medical details.
- Safety representatives should be provided with anonymised information unless any workers concerned have consented to the provision of information in an identifiable form.
- Unless the general standard of information security in your organisation is sufficiently high, medical information about workers should be separated from other personnel information, for example by keeping it in a sealed envelope, or subject to additional access controls on an electronic system.
- Information about workers' health collected to run a pension or insurance scheme should not be available to the employer unless this is necessary for the employer's role in administering the scheme.

4.1.5 Do not collect more information about workers' health than is necessary for the purpose(s) behind its collection.

Key points and possible actions

- Review any health questionnaires to ensure that only information that is really needed is collected.
- If commissioning a medical report on a sick employee, seek information on the worker's fitness for continued employment rather than medical details.
- Do not ask workers to consent to the disclosure of their entire general practitioner record as a matter of expediency. Only seek the disclosure of the whole record, or substantial parts of it, where this is genuinely necessary.
- If seeking a report from a worker's general practitioner or other medical practitioner who has been responsible for the care of the worker, ensure that you meet the requirements of the Access to Medical Reports Act 1988. This includes obtaining the worker's consent to your application for a report.

[4740]

4.2 Occupational health schemes

This sub-section gives good practice recommendations for employers with occupational health schemes. It does not provide detailed professional guidance to doctors, nurses and others involved in such schemes.

4.2.1 Ensure workers are aware of how information about their health will be used and who will have access to it.

Key points and possible actions

- Unless told otherwise workers are entitled to assume that information they give to a doctor, nurse or other health professional will be treated in confidence and not passed to others.
- Set out clearly to workers, preferably in writing, how information they supply in the context of an occupational health scheme will be used, who it might be made available to and why.

4.2.2 Do not compromise any confidentiality of communications between workers and health professionals in an occupational health service.

Key points and possible actions

- If workers are allowed to use telephone or e-mail for confidential communication with their occupational health service, do not compromise this confidentiality by monitoring the contents of these communications.

4.2.3 Act in a way that is consistent with the Guidance on Ethics for Occupational Physicians published by the Faculty of Occupational Medicine.

Key points and possible actions

- Although this is guidance for occupational physicians rather than employers, it should give you a clear understanding of the legal and ethical constraints that apply to the exchange of information when working with occupational health professionals.

[4741]

4.3 Information from medical examination and testing

This sub-section gives good practice recommendations specific to the collection and handling of information derived from medical examination and testing. The general recommendations in section 4.1 should also be taken into account.

Employers should bear in mind that obtaining a worker's consent or satisfying another sensitive data condition is not, on its own, sufficient to ensure data protection compliance. There is still an obligation to ensure that information obtained through medical examination is relevant, is accurate, is up to date and is kept secure.

See Supplementary Guidance page 72 for more Information on the Sensitive Data Conditions.

4.3.1 Where information obtained from medical testing is used to enforce the organisation's rules and standards make sure that the rules and standards are clearly set out in a policy which workers are aware of.

Key points and possible actions

- Ensure workers understand these rules and standards.
- Set out the circumstances in which medical testing may take place, the nature of the testing, how information obtained through testing will be used, and the safeguards that are in place for the workers that are subject to it.

4.3.2 Only obtain information through medical examination or testing of applicants or other potential workers at an appropriate point in the recruitment process, i e where there is a likelihood of appointing them. You must also be satisfied that the testing is a necessary and justified measure to:

- **Determine whether the potential worker is fit or likely to remain fit to carry out the job in question, or**
- **Meet any legal requirements for testing, or**
- **Determine the terms on which a potential worker is eligible to join a pension or insurance scheme.**

Key points and possible actions

- Record the business purpose for which examination or testing is to be introduced and the sensitive data condition that can be satisfied.
- Consider less intrusive ways of meeting the objectives, for example using a health questionnaire as an alternative to a medical examination or as a means to select those required to undergo a full examination.
- Only carry out a pre-employment medical examination or medical testing where there is a real likelihood that the individual will be appointed.
- Make it clear early on in the recruitment process that individuals may be subjected to medical examination or testing once there is a likelihood that they will be appointed.

4.3.3 Only obtain information through a medical examination or medical testing of current workers if the testing is part of a occupational health and safety programme that workers have a free choice to participate in, or you are satisfied that it is a necessary and justified measure to:

- **Prevent a significant risk to the health and safety of the worker, or others, or**
- **Determine a particular worker's fitness for carrying out his or her job, or**
- **Determine whether a worker is fit to return to work after a period of sickness absence, or when this might be the case, or**
- **Determine the worker's entitlement to health related benefits e g sick pay, or**
- **Prevent discrimination against workers on the grounds of disability or assess the need to make reasonable adjustments to the working environment, or**
- **Comply with other legal obligations.**

Key points and possible actions

- Record the business purpose for which the programme of examination or testing of workers is to be introduced and the sensitive data condition that can be satisfied.
- Establish and document who will be tested, what precisely are they being tested for, the frequency of testing, and the consequences of a positive or negative test.
- Consider less intrusive ways of meeting the employer's objectives, for example collecting information via a health questionnaire either as a first stage or as an alternative to a medical examination.

4.3.4 Do not obtain a sample covertly or use an existing sample, test result or other information obtained through a medical examination for a purpose other than that for which it was originally obtained.

Key points and possible actions

- Be clear about the purpose(s) for which any testing is being carried out and communicate this to workers.
- The covert obtaining of bodily samples for testing is most unlikely ever to be justified.
- If there is a wish to carry out a different test on an existing sample, this can only be done if the worker has been told about it and has freely consented.

4.3.5 Permanently delete information obtained in the course of medical examination or testing that is not relevant for the purpose(s) for which the examination or testing is undertaken.

Key points and possible actions

- Health information that is excessive, irrelevant or out of date should not be retained by an employer.
- If the retention of medical information is necessary only for the operation of an occupational health service, it should be kept in a confidential occupational health file.

[4742]

4.4 Information from drug and alcohol testing

This part of the Code gives good practice recommendations specific to the collection and handling of information derived from drug and alcohol testing. The recommendations in sub-sections 4.1 and 4.3 should also be taken into account.

4.4.1 Before obtaining information through drug or alcohol testing ensure that the benefits justify any adverse impact, unless the testing is required by law.

Key points and possible actions

- The collection of information through drug and alcohol testing is unlikely to be justified unless it is for health and safety reasons.
- Post-incident testing where there is a reasonable suspicion that drug or alcohol use is a factor is more likely to be justified than random testing.
- Given the intrusive nature of testing employers would be well advised to undertake and document an impact assessment.

See Part 4 *post* for information about how to carry out an impact assessment.

4.4.2 Minimise the amount of personal information obtained through drug and alcohol testing.

Key points and possible actions

- Only use drug or alcohol testing where it provides significantly better evidence of impairment than other less intrusive means.
- Use the least intrusive forms of testing practicable to deliver the benefits to the business that the testing is intended to bring.
- Tell workers what drugs they are being tested for.
- Base any testing on reliable scientific evidence of the effect of particular substances on workers.
- Limit testing to those substances and the extent of exposure that will have a significant bearing on the purpose(s) for which the testing is conducted.

4.4.3 Ensure the criteria used for selecting workers for testing are justified, properly documented, adhered to and are communicated to workers.

Key points and possible actions

- It is unfair and deceptive to lead workers to believe that testing is being carried out randomly if, in fact, other criteria are being used.
- If random testing is to be used, ensure that it is carried out in a genuinely random way.
- If other criteria are used to trigger testing, for example suspicion that a worker's performance is impaired as a result of drug or alcohol use, the employer should ensure workers are aware of the true criteria that are used.

4.4.4 Confine the obtaining of information through random testing to those workers who are employed to work in safety critical activities.

Key points and possible actions

- Collecting personal information by testing all workers in a business will not be justified if in fact it is only workers engaged in particular activities that pose a risk.
- Even in safety-critical businesses such as public transport or heavy industry, workers in different jobs will pose different safety risks. Therefore collecting information through the random testing of all workers will rarely be justified.

4.4.5 Gather information through testing designed to ensure safety at work rather than to reveal the illegal use of substances in a worker's private life.

Key points and possible actions

- Very few employers will be justified in testing to detect illegal use rather than on safety grounds. Testing to detect illegal use may, exceptionally, be justified where illegal use would:
  - breach the worker's contract of employment, conditions of employment or disciplinary rules, and

- cause serious damage to the employer's business, e g by substantially undermining public confidence in the integrity of a law enforcement agency.

4.4.6 Ensure that workers are fully aware that drug or alcohol testing is taking place, and of the possible consequences of being tested.

Key points and possible actions

- Explain your drug or alcohol policy in a staff handbook.
- Explain the consequences for workers of breaching the policy.
- Ensure workers are aware of the blood-alcohol level at which they may be disciplined when being tested for alcohol.
- Do not conduct testing on samples collected without the worker's knowledge.

4.4.7 Ensure that information is only obtained through drug and alcohol testing that is;

- **of sufficient technical quality to support any decisions or opinions that are derived from it and,**
- **subject to rigorous integrity and quality control procedures and,**
- **conducted under the direction of, and positive test results interpreted by, a person who is suitably qualified and competent in the field of drug testing.**

Key points and possible actions

- Use a professional service with qualified staff and that meets appropriate standards.
- Ensure workers have access to a duplicate of any sample taken to enable them to have it independently analysed as a check on the accuracy of the employer's results.
- Do not assume that the tests are infallible and be prepared to deal properly with disputes arising from their use.

[4743]

4.5 Information from genetic testing

Genetic testing has the potential to provide employers with information predictive of the likely future general health of workers or with information about their genetic susceptibility to occupational diseases. Genetic testing is, though, still under development and in most cases has an uncertain predictive value. It is rarely, if ever, used in the employment context. The Human Genetics Commission advises that employers should not demand that an individual take a genetic test as a condition of employment. It should therefore only be introduced after very careful consideration, if at all. This sub-section supplements sub-sections 4.1 and 4.3.

4.5.1 Do not use genetic testing in an effort to obtain information that is predictive of a worker's future general health.

Key points and possible actions

- Obtaining information through genetic testing is too intrusive and the information's predictive value is insufficiently certain to be relied on to provide information about a worker's future health.

4.5.2 Do not insist that a worker discloses the results of a previous genetic test.

Key points and possible actions

- It is important that workers are not put off taking genetic tests that may be beneficial for their health care by the fear that they may have to disclose the results to a current or future employer.
- You can ask for information that is relevant to your health and safety or other legal duties but the provision of the information should be voluntary.

4.5.3 Only use genetic testing to obtain information where it is clear that a worker with a particular, detectable genetic condition is likely to pose a serious safety risk to others or where it is known that a specific working environment or practice might pose specific risks to workers with particular genetic variations.

Key points and possible actions

- Only seek information through genetic testing as a last resort, where:
  - it is not practicable to make changes to the working environment or practices so as to reduce risks to all workers and
  - it is the only reasonable method to obtain the required information.
- Inform the Human Genetics Commission of any proposals to use genetic testing for employment purposes.

4.5.4 If a genetic test is used to obtain information for employment purposes ensure that it is valid and is subject to assured levels of accuracy and reliability.

Key points and possible actions

- There should be scientific evidence that any genetic test is valid for the purpose for which it is used.

- Ensure the results of any test undertaken are always communicated to the person tested and professional advice is available.
- Ensure test results are carefully interpreted, taking account of how they might be affected by environmental conditions.

[4744]

(*Contact details—omitted; see Useful addresses at* **[5046]**.)

COMMISSION FOR RACIAL EQUALITY: CODE OF PRACTICE ON RACIAL EQUALITY IN EMPLOYMENT (2005)

NOTES

This Code of Practice was issued by the Commission for Racial Equality under the Race Relations Act 1976, s 47 (repealed as noted below) in November 2005 and came into effect on 6 April 2006 (see the Race Relations Code of Practice relating to Employment (Appointed Day) Order 2006, SI 2006/630). It replaces the 1983 Code (at **[4503]**) subject to savings in that where a court or tribunal is hearing any proceedings arising from a complaint (whenever presented) alleging that a person has, before 6 April 2006, committed an act which is unlawful discrimination for the purposes of any provision of the 1976 Act, the 1983 Code continues to apply.

The statutory provision under which this Code was made was repealed by the Equality Act 2006, ss 40, 91, Sch 3, paras 21, 26, Sch 4; however the Code is continued in force by s 42(3) of the 2006 Act (see **[1685]**). As to the dissolution of the Commission for Racial Equality and the transfer of its property, rights and liabilities etc to the Commission for Equality and Human Rights, see the Equality Act 2006, ss 36–38 at **[1679]–[1681]**.

Permission to reproduce this Code was kindly granted by the Commission for Racial Equality.

1. INTRODUCTION

1.1 This code replaces the statutory *Code of Practice For the Elimination of Racial Discrimination and the Promotion of Equality of Opportunity in Employment,* issued by the Commission for Racial Equality (CRE) in 1984 under the Race Relations Act 1976 (RRA).

1.2 References in this code to the RRA include all subsequent amending legislation.

1.3 The RRA gives the CRE a legal duty to:

a. work towards the elimination of racial discrimination and harassment;

b. promote equality of opportunity and good relations between people from different racial groups; and

c. keep under review the way the RRA is working, and, if necessary, make proposals to the secretary of state for amending it.

1.4 Section 47 of the RRA gives the CRE the power to issue codes of practice in the field of employment (see the glossary at Appendix 7), and to give such practical guidance as it sees fit.

Purpose of the code

1.5 The purpose of this code is to:

a. give employers and principals (referred to in this code as employers; see the glossary at Appendix 7) practical guidance on how to prevent unlawful racial discrimination, and achieve equality of opportunity in the field of employment;

b. help employers and others who have duties under the employment provisions of the RRA to understand their responsibilities and rights;

c. help lawyers and other advisers to advise their clients;

d. give employment tribunals and courts clear guidelines on good equal opportunities practice in employment; and

e. make sure anyone who is considering bringing legal proceedings under the RRA, or attempting to negotiate in the workplace, understands the legislation and is aware of good practice in the field of employment.

Status of the code

1.6 This code is a statutory code. This means it has been approved by the secretary of state and laid before parliament. The code does not impose any legal obligations. Nor is it an authoritative statement of the law; only the courts and employment tribunals can provide this. However, the code can be used in evidence in legal proceedings brought under the RRA. Courts and tribunals must take account of any part of the code that might be relevant to a question arising during those proceedings.

1.7 Employers are liable for acts of unlawful racial discrimination or harassment by their workers (see the glossary at Appendix 7). However, employers should be able to defend themselves better in any case of alleged racial discrimination brought against the organisation, if they can show they have taken the steps recommended in this code.

Application of the code

1.8 The RRA and this code apply to:

a. all employers in England, Scotland and Wales, whatever their size, resources or number of workers; Northern Ireland is covered by separate legislation;
b. certain organisations, such as employment and recruitment agencies, (including online agencies), trade unions, professional associations, partnerships, accrediting bodies and vocational training organisations, in relation to their role as providers of services specifically covered by the RRA; and
c. applicants for employment, workers and former workers.

Public authorities

1.9 While the RRA applies to all employers, section 71(1) gives public authorities additional statutory duties (see paras 2.28–2.29). The aim is to make the promotion of racial equality central to their work. However, it should be emphasised that much of the guidance and good practice associated with these duties is relevant to all employers.

Smaller organisations

1.10 Some employers in smaller organisations may not need detailed procedures, such as some of those recommended in this code; for example, in the arrangements they make to monitor workers and applicants by racial group. The guidance may therefore need to be adapted, occasionally, to suit an organisations individual circumstances. However, smaller organisations should note that employment tribunals have dismissed the argument that they should make allowance for the size or nature of a business in considering its liability for acts of unlawful racial discrimination or harassment by its workers. It is recommended that smaller organisations make sure their policies and practices are consistent with the RRA, and that they follow the general spirit and intentions of this code.

1.11 The CRE has produced a practical guide for this sector: *Racial Equality and the Smaller Business: A practical guide* (see Appendix 6). This guide recognises the heavy demands on the time and resources of smaller organisations, and suggests simple but effective procedures that should help ensure that everyone is treated fairly and equally.

Benefits of the code

1.12 This code should help employers to:

a. understand and meet their legal obligations;
b. adopt and put into practice effective policies, designed to prevent unlawful racial discrimination or harassment, and ensure equality of opportunity for all;
c. draw on the talents, skills, experience, networks and different cultural perspectives of a diverse workforce;
d. create a working environment where people feel they are respected and valued;
e. reduce the risks of legal liability, costly and time-consuming grievances and damage to productivity, staff morale and the organisation's reputation; and
f. foster good race relations in the workplace.

1.13 The code should also help workers and their representatives understand their rights under the RRA, and what constitutes good practice in the field of employment.

Other areas of equality

1.14 This code is restricted by the terms of the RRA to matters concerning racial discrimination, and equality of opportunity in employment, between people from different racial groups. However, the principles of good practice may also be useful when promoting equality of opportunity generally, though the statutory requirements differ in other areas of equality.

1.15 Discrimination in employment on grounds of religion or belief is unlawful under the Employment Equality (Religion or Belief) Regulations 2003. However, if people affected by religious discrimination are from a particular racial group (see the glossary at Appendix 7), the discrimination might also amount to indirect racial discrimination (see para 2.9 and Example 20, para 4.72).

How to use the code

1.16 The code has six chapters and seven appendices, as described below.

a. Following this introduction, Chapter 2 looks at the legal context and explains briefly the basic legal concepts used in the RRA.

b. Chapter 3 recommends a framework for action, based on drawing up an equal opportunities policy, and putting it into practice. The chapter concludes with advice for employers on promoting equality of opportunity in their roles as purchasers and suppliers of goods, facilities and services.

c. Chapter 4 makes recommendations on good employment practice in the main areas of employment, from recruitment to employers' responsibilities to former workers.

d. Chapter 5 considers the additional responsibilities that certain organisations, including trade unions, professional associations, employment and recruitment agencies, partnerships, accrediting bodies and vocational training organisations, have under the RRA in relation to the services they provide for their members, and for the public.

e. Chapter 6 is aimed at workers and draws together the corresponding rights and responsibilities they have under the RRA.

1.17 The seven appendices contain:

a. more detailed explanation of positive action and genuine occupational requirements and qualifications;

b. a sample policy on equal opportunities in employment;

c. a sample anti-harassment policy;

d. guidelines on job application forms;

e. a list of relevant organisations and websites;

f. a list of CRE publications; and

g. a glossary.

1.18 The examples in text boxes refer to cases that have been heard in employment tribunals or courts. The cases have been chosen because they illustrate a point, not because they have been won or lost. Other examples illustrate how a concept or policy is likely to be applied in practice, and should not be treated as complete or authoritative statements of the law.

1.19 Each chapter of the code forms part of an overall explanation of the RRA's provisions on employment. It is therefore important to read the code as a whole, in order to understand the law properly. The code should not be read too narrowly or literally. It is intended to explain the principles of the law, to illustrate how the RRA might operate in certain situations and to provide general guidance on good practice. The code should also not be seen as a substitute for seeking specialist advice on the possible legal consequences of particular situations.

[4745]

2. THE LEGAL CONTEXT

2.1 The Race Relations Act 1976 (RRA) makes it unlawful to discriminate against, or harass, applicants for employment, workers (see the glossary at Appendix 7) and former workers, on racial grounds.

Racial grounds and racial groups

2.2 The RRA defines racial grounds as including race, colour, nationality (including citizenship) or ethnic or national origins. Racial groups (see the glossary at Appendix 7) are groups defined by those grounds. All racial groups are protected from unlawful racial discrimination or harassment under the RRA (see Example 1).

Example 1: Racial groups

BBC v Souster [2001] IRLR 150

Mr Souster, a presenter for BBC Scotland's Rugby Special, complained that he had lost his job because he was English and the BBC wanted a Scottish person. Mr Souster claimed that being English was a matter of national origins, while the BBC argued that, since both the Scots and the English share a British passport, there could be no unlawful discrimination between different parts of the one nation. The Scottish Court of Session, which had to decide whether the RRA applies to discrimination between the Scots and the English, ruled that national origins should be interpreted more broadly and flexibly than just by reference to a passport. As England and Scotland were once separate nations, the English and the Scots have separate national origins and therefore the RRA does cover discrimination between them.

On the question of whether the English and Scots are part of a 'racial group', the Court of Session followed the House of Lords' ruling in an earlier case (*Mandla v Dowell-Lee*, 1983 IRLR 209), to the effect that '… it is possible for a person to fall into a particular racial group either by birth or by adherence'. The court also observed that, if the way the discriminator treats someone is based on her or his perception of that persons national or ethnic origins, then their actual origins, let alone their passport nationality, are irrelevant.

This definition of racial grounds clearly takes into account the complex reality of national identity, where a person may change their nationality by marriage or geographical migration or indeed simply by association, as well as the complexity of racial prejudice, where a person who discriminates may do so in complete ignorance of the victim's actual nationality or national background.

2.3 To comply with the EC Race Directive (2000/43/EC), the government introduced the Race Relations Act (Amendment) Regulations 2003, which give legal protection from racial discrimination and harassment on grounds of race or ethnic or national origins. Since the grounds protected under the original RRA (see para 2.2) differ from those protected under the Regulations, the amended RRA contains disparities in certain definitions and standards, such as indirect discrimination and harassment. However, this does not substantially affect the practical guidance given in this code.

Types of discrimination

2.4 The RRA defines four main types of unlawful discrimination:

a. direct discrimination;
b. indirect discrimination;
c. victimisation; and
d. harassment.

Direct discrimination [Section 1(1)(a) of the RRA]

2.5 Direct discrimination occurs when a person is treated less favourably, on racial grounds, than another person is or would be treated in the same or similar circumstances (see Example 2). Apart from limited exceptions (see paras 2.33–2.36) to the general prohibition of discrimination in the RRA, direct discrimination is automatically unlawful, whatever the reason for it. There can be no justification for the difference in treatment.

Example 2: Direct discrimination

Hussain v Alfred Brown (Worsted Mills) Ltd, Case No 1805479/98
An Asian with 15 years' experience in textile work applied, for the fourth time, for a job as a warper at a textile mill, close to where he lived in Bradford. As before, he did not receive a reply to his application. However, his son, who had applied at the same time, in the name of J A Taylor, and as someone with ten years' experience, was called in for a trial. The employment tribunal upheld his fathers claim that he had been discriminated against on racial grounds. The tribunal took account of the fact that, in four years, not one of the company's 70 workers had been from an ethnic minority group, even though the mill was very near Bradford, with its large ethnic minority population, many of whom had considerable skills in the textile trade. The complainant was awarded a total of around £7,000 in compensation, including £2,500 for injury to feelings.

2.6 In considering whether there has been less favourable treatment, the employment tribunal will examine evidence of any disadvantage the complainant has suffered as a result of the alleged act of discrimination. This may include evidence that the person has been disciplined or dismissed, or any other evidence that shows that the circumstances in which the complainant has to continue to work are to her or his disadvantage (see Example 3).

Example 3: Proving less favourable treatment

Shamoon v Chief Constable of the Royal Ulster Constabulary (RUC) [2003] IRLR 285

When complaints were made about the appraisal reports written by a chief inspector at the RUC, her appraisal duties were withdrawn. Meanwhile, the other two chief inspectors at her grade continued to carry out appraisals. The RUC argued that carrying out appraisals was not a right, but, at most, a practice; that it was a small part of the complainant's duties; and that she did not suffer loss of rank or any financial disadvantage when the function was removed from her. The chief inspector brought legal proceedings under the Sex Discrimination Act 1975.

In an important case for all discrimination law, the House of Lords held that a reasonable employee might well feel demeaned, both in the eyes of those whom she managed and in the eyes of her colleagues, once it was known that a part of her normal duties had been taken away from her following a complaint. The House of Lords concluded that, if an employee reasonably believes that the circumstances in which they would have to continue to work would put them at a disadvantage, this would be sufficient to prove they had suffered a detriment.

2.7 In cases alleging direct racial discrimination, the way a person has been treated will be compared with the way a person from a different racial group has been, or would be, treated in the same or similar circumstances. The courts have recognised that it may not always be possible to compare the alleged treatment with the treatment of an actual other person, and that a hypothetical comparison might have to be made with a person from a different racial group in a similar situation. The question to be asked is: 'how would a person from a different racial group be treated, in circumstances that are not identical, but not too dissimilar?' (see Example 4).

Example 4: a hypothetical comparator

Balamoody v UK Central Council for Nursing, Midwifery and Health Visiting [2002] IRLR 288

The complainant, a Mauritian, was the owner of a nursing home. He was convicted in a magistrates' court of failures in relation to the administration of drugs and staffing at the home. As a result, the UK Central Council for Nursing, Midwifery and Health Visiting found him guilty of professional misconduct and struck him off its register. The complainant blamed his matron, a white woman, for the offences he had been convicted for. He complained that the disparity in their treatment – she had not faced disciplinary proceedings – was due to his race.

Example 4: a hypothetical comparator

In a case of direct discrimination, one has to compare like with like (section 3(4) of the RRA). If the complainant can point to an actual person whose circumstances are sufficiently similar to his or her own, so much the better. In this case, the employment tribunal found that the matron was not an appropriate comparator, and dismissed the claim. The Employment Appeals Tribunal went on to uphold the tribunal's decision. However, the Court of Appeal held that both tribunals had made an error of principle: in those circumstances where it was not possible to find an actual comparator who had been treated less favourably, the tribunal would have to construct a hypothetical comparator, as a benchmark, to show how a person from other racial groups would have been treated. In this case, the court felt there was evidence to allow an inference that the council's refusal to reinstate the applicant on the register was racially discriminatory.

Segregation [Section 1 (2) of the RRA]

2.8 Segregating a person from others, on racial grounds, automatically means treating her or him less favourably, and constitutes unlawful direct discrimination. The segregation of workers, by racial group, will be unlawful even if they have the same access to promotion, training or pay and conditions as other workers.

Indirect discrimination [Sections 1 (1) (b) and 1 (1A) of the RRA]

2.9 The RRA contains two definitions of indirect discrimination, depending on the grounds of discrimination. The definition of indirect discrimination introduced under section 1(1A) to comply with the EC Race Directive applies when the discrimination is on grounds of race or ethnic or national origins, but not colour or nationality. When the discrimination is on grounds of colour or nationality, the original definition under section 1(1)(b) applies (see Example 5).

Example 5: Indirect discrimination

Aina v Employment Service [2002] DCLD 103D
A Black African employee applied for the post of equal opportunities manager in his organisation. He was assessed as having the skills and ability for the job. However, his application was rejected because, unknown to him, the post was open only to permanent staff at higher grades than his. Monitoring data showed that the organisation had no permanent Black African employees at the grades in question. The employment tribunal held that there was no justification for the requirement, and that it amounted to indirect discrimination on racial grounds.

a. *Grounds of race or ethnic or national origins [section 1(1A) of the RRA]*
This occurs when a provision, criterion or practice which, on the face of it has nothing to do with race or ethnic or national origin, and is applied equally to everyone—
   i. puts or would put people of a certain race or ethnic or national origins at a particular disadvantage when compared with others; *and*
   ii. puts a person of that race or ethnic or national origins at that disadvantage; *and*
   iii. cannot be shown to be a 'proportionate means of achieving a legitimate aim'.

b. *Grounds of colour or nationality [section 1(1)(b) of the RRA]*
This occurs when an apparently non-discriminatory requirement or condition which applies equally to everyone—
   i. can only be met by a considerably smaller proportion of people from a particular racial group than the proportion not from that group who can meet it; *and*
   ii. cannot be justified on non-racial grounds; *and*
   iii. puts a person from that group at a disadvantage because he or she cannot meet it.

2.10 Although the definition of indirect discrimination introduced to meet the EC Race Directive does not apply to grounds of colour or nationality, in practice, a criterion that disadvantaged someone because of his or her colour would also be likely to disadvantage that person because of his or her race or ethnic or national origins.

- **Example A**. A prohibition on workers wearing their hair in locks would disproportionately disadvantage black people, compared with white people, but this prohibition could also be challenged on grounds of ethnic or national origins, for example, Jamaican.

2.11 'Proportionate means' may be defined as means that are appropriate and necessary to achieve a legitimate business or other objective, such as meeting health and safety requirements (see also para 2.12).

- **Example B**. A blanket ban on beards in a food packaging factory might not be a proportionate means of meeting health and safety requirements, if face masks could be used satisfactorily instead.
- **Example C**. Y, a white English woman, applies for a job as a receptionist with a hospital trust in Wales. Under the Welsh Language Act 1993, the trust has drawn up a Welsh Language Scheme, which permits the trust to require applicants for posts involving the provision of services to the public to be able to speak Welsh, or to be prepared to learn it to an acceptable degree within six months. Y does not speak Welsh and is not prepared to learn it. She does not get the job and her complaint that she has been discriminated against on grounds of national origins fails, because the requirement is considered to be a reasonable means of achieving a legitimate aim. It should be noted that Y might have had a stronger case if the post she had applied for had been one of many receptionist posts at the hospital trust, or, if the trust had had enough Welsh-speaking receptionists to do the work. Meanwhile, W, a man of Pakistani origin, who also does not speak Welsh, successfully applies for a post in the trust's finance department; as the post does not involve contact with the public, it carries no Welsh language requirement.

2.12 The test of indirect discrimination is the same under both definitions; it involves drawing an objective balance between the discriminatory effects of the provision, criterion, practice, requirement or condition and the employer's reasonable need to apply it. When assessing the justification for policies and practices that could have a disproportionate effect on some racial groups, it would be useful to consider the following questions:

a. Does the provision, criterion, practice, requirement or condition correspond to a real need?
b. Does the need pursue a legitimate aim, for example health and safety?
c. Are the means used to achieve the aim appropriate and necessary?
d. Is there any other way of achieving the aim in question?
e. Is there a way of reducing any potentially unlawful discriminatory effect?

2.13 The concept of 'provision, criterion or practice', which was introduced to comply with the EC Race Directive, is broader and less restrictive than the concept of 'requirement or condition' in the original definition of indirect discrimination in the RRA. The concept of 'provision, criterion or practice' covers the full breadth of formal and informal practices in employment.

- **Example D**. M, who is of Nigerian origin, is informed of a vacancy for a managing director. M phones and is told that the company's normal practice is to use head-hunters for recruitment to senior management posts. If M can show that this practice makes it more difficult for people of Nigerian origin than others to get senior management jobs in this company, and that this puts her at a disadvantage, the practice could amount to unlawful indirect discrimination.

<u>*Victimisation*</u> *[Section 2 of the RRA]*

2.14 It is unlawful to treat a person less favourably on racial grounds because he or she has:

a. brought proceedings under the RRA; or
b. given evidence or information in connection with any proceedings under the RRA; or
c. alleged that an act of unlawful discrimination has been committed; or
d. done anything under the RRA in relation to someone, or intends to do so, or is suspected of having done or intending to do so.

Example 6: Victimisation

Mann v Gloucester County Council Fire and Rescue Services (1) and Gibb (2) [1997] Case No 1400859/96

A complaint by an Asian fire fighter that the sub-officer in charge of the station had made racially derogatory remarks was initially upheld during the informal stage of an investigation, but later dismissed. The fire station's divisional officer made recommendations, to make sure there were no recriminations. However, almost immediately, the Asian fire fighter was 'sent to Coventry' and his colleagues refused to speak to him. The tribunal upheld his claim of unlawful victimisation, rejecting the fire authority's claim that it had taken all reasonably practicable steps to prevent this. The tribunal thought it was unrealistic of the authority to expect either of the parties, and everybody else concerned, to rise above the situation before a good deal of skilled counselling had been given to them all.

2.15 For a claim of victimisation under the RRA to succeed, a complainant would also have to show that:

a. he or she has been or would have been treated less favourably, on racial grounds, than others in those circumstances; and
b. the treatment was a result of his or her action in relation to allegations or proceedings under the RRA.

Harassment [Section 3A(1) of the RRA]

2.16 The definition of harassment introduced by the 2003 Race Regulations applies when the conduct in question is on grounds of race or ethnic or national origins, but not colour or nationality. Harassment on grounds of colour or nationality involves less favourable treatment and may constitute unlawful direct discrimination (see Example 7, and Examples 19 and 20).

2.17 A person harasses another on grounds of race or ethnic or national origins when he or she engages in unwanted conduct that has the purpose or effect of:

a. violating the other person's dignity; or
b. creating an intimidating, hostile, degrading, humiliating or offensive environment for that person.

Harassment on grounds of colour or nationality may be recognisable by the same type of behaviour.

Example 7: Harassment

Anisetti v Tokyo-Mitsubishi International plc Case No 6002429/98

The Indian-born head of credit derivatives at an international Japanese bank in London resigned, claiming he had been made to feel like a 'second-class citizen' by his Japanese employers. He said he had been humiliated, excluded by workers speaking Japanese and underpaid, simply because he was not Japanese. The bank argued that it was 'natural' for Japanese staff to use their own language among themselves.

An employment tribunal upheld the complainant's claim that he had been discriminated against unlawfully, not because of his Indian national origins, but because he was not Japanese. The tribunal noted that the bank had maintained a practice which had effectively excluded the complainant from various activities, and treated him less favourably than others. The complainant was awarded around £1 million in compensation.

2.18 The definition of what is intimidating, hostile, degrading, humiliating or offensive is mainly a subjective one. In considering a claim of harassment, unless the conduct was intentionally hostile, it would only be considered to have the effects described above (see para 2.17) if, after considering all the circumstances, including, especially, the perceptions of the person affected, it was reasonable to do so. This means a court could decide that a complainant was oversensitive and had unreasonably taken offence.

2.19 While the statutory definition of harassment in the RRA applies only to grounds of race or ethnic or national origins, and not to those of colour and nationality, in cases where abuse is overtly directed at a person's skin colour, employment tribunals and courts may interpret 'race' widely, to include colour.

2.20 Similarly, offensive behaviour in relation to a person's nationality may also be regarded as offensive on the grounds of that person's actual or perceived national origins (see Example 1), and would therefore be covered by the statutory definition of harassment in the RRA.

2.21 Employers should note that a single incident, for example a racist joke, on any racial grounds, could be sufficient to cause a person to feel harassed.

Discriminatory advertisements [Section 29 of the RRA]

2.22 It is unlawful to publish, or to be responsible for publishing, any advertisement (see the glossary at Appendix 7) that indicates, or may reasonably be understood to indicate, an intention to discriminate, even if the act of discrimination were lawful.

- **Example E**. An advertisement in a local newspaper for a Turkish machinist for a dress manufacturing company would be unlawful.

2.23 The test for deciding whether an advertisement indicates an intention to discriminate is whether a reasonable person would consider it to be discriminatory. The definition of advertisement is very wide and includes any form of advertisement or notice, whether public or not; for example, internal circulars or newsletters announcing staff vacancies, emails, displays on notice boards or shop windows, and job advertisements, banners and pop-up windows on websites.

2.24 The RRA allows a small number of limited exceptions, where the advertisement refers to a situation where discrimination is not unlawful; for example, a lawful positive action training measure (see paras 2.33 and 3.43–3.45 and Appendix 1) or a genuine occupational qualification (see para 2.36 and Appendix 1). The advertisement should make it clear that the employer is making use of the exception.

Pressure to discriminate [Section 31 of the RRA]

2.25 It is unlawful to induce, or attempt to induce, a person to discriminate against, or harass, someone on racial grounds. The pressure may amount to no more than persuasion, and need not necessarily involve a benefit or loss. Nor does the pressure have to be applied directly; it is unlawful if it is applied in such a way that the other person is likely to hear of it. And it is unlawful in itself, even if the person who was put under pressure does not go on to commit an unlawful act of discrimination.

Instructions to discriminate [Section 30 of the RRA]

2.26 It is unlawful for a person who has authority over another person, or whose wishes that person normally follows, to instruct him or her to discriminate against, or harass, someone on racial grounds (see Example 8).

Example 8: Instructions to discriminate

Weatherfield Ltd t/a Van and Truck Rentals v Sargent [1999] IRLR 94
A white woman was told as part of an induction course for her new job as a receptionist that the company, a van and truck rental firm, had a special policy on ethnic minority customers. She was instructed to identify 'coloured or Asian callers' by the sound of their voice and to tell them there were no vehicles available. The woman was so upset by this that she resigned, giving her reasons in a letter. The Court of Appeal ruled that she had been discriminated against on racial grounds when she resigned in response to being given an instruction to discriminate against black and Asian customers.

Aiding unlawful acts [Section 33 of the RRA]

2.27 A person who knowingly helps another person to discriminate against, or harass, someone unlawfully, on racial grounds, will be treated as having discriminated similarly themselves. Their only defence would be that they had been told the act would not be unlawful, and it was reasonable for them to believe that statement – it is an offence to make a reckless statement on such matters. In an employment situation, anything a worker does in the course of his or her employment is treated as having been done by his or her employer as well, whether or not the employer knew about it or approved of it. A person who knowingly takes part in an act of unlawful discrimination or harassment will therefore be deemed to have helped his or her employer in acting unlawfully.

Public authorities [Section 71 of the RRA]

2.28 Section 71(1) of the RRA gives public authorities listed in schedule 1A of the RRA a statutory general duty to have 'due regard' to the need to eliminate unlawful racial discrimination, and to promote equality of opportunity and good relations between people from different racial groups, in carrying out all their functions.

2.29 Most public authorities bound by the general duty must also meet certain specific duties:

a. to prepare and publish a race equality scheme or policy, which states how they will meet the general duty in the areas of policy and service delivery; and

b. to monitor specified employment procedures and practices, by racial group (see paras 3.32–3.35).

2.30 The duty to promote race equality also applies to the procurement (see the glossary at Appendix 7) of goods, facilities and services. Where a public authority's function is carried out, wholly or in part, by an external supplier on its behalf, the authority remains responsible for meeting the duty. Contractors themselves must not discriminate unlawfully on racial grounds, but they do not have the same legal duty to promote equality of opportunity. This means public authorities should build racial equality considerations into the procurement process, to make sure any function that is relevant to the duty meets the requirements of the RRA, regardless of who is carrying out the function.

2.31 A statutory *Code of Practice on the Duty to Promote Race Equality* was laid before parliament, and came into effect in May 2002 (see Appendix 6).

Burden of proof [Section 54A of the RRA]

2.32 As a result of the amendments required by the EC Race Directive, the burden of proof used by employment tribunals and courts will vary according to the grounds of the discrimination.

a. *Grounds of race or ethnic or national origins [section 54A of the RRA]*
If a complainant can establish the facts from which an employment tribunal can conclude that an act of racial discrimination or harassment on grounds of race or ethnic or national origins has occurred, the employer will have to prove that any difference in treatment was not due in any way to discrimination or harassment. If the explanation is inadequate or unsatisfactory, the tribunal *must* find that unlawful discrimination or harassment has occurred.

b. *Grounds of colour or nationality*
In cases where the discrimination is on grounds of colour or nationality, and section 54A does not therefore apply, if the complainant establishes facts from which an employment tribunal could conclude that he or she has suffered racial discrimination, the tribunal will ask the employer for an explanation. If the explanation is unsatisfactory, the tribunal *may* find that discrimination has occurred.

When racial discrimination is not unlawful

Positive action [Sections 35, 37 and 38 of the RRA]

2.33 The term 'positive action' refers to the measures that employers may lawfully take to provide access to facilities that meet special needs in relation to education and training or welfare, or to train or encourage people from a particular racial group that is under-represented in particular work (see also paras 3.43–3.45, Appendix 1 and Example 10).

National security [Section 42 of the RRA]

2.34 An act of discrimination in employment, on racial grounds, may be permitted if it is done to safeguard national security, and if it can be justified.

Employment for training in skills to be used outside Britain [Section 6 of the RRA]

2.35 Employers may discriminate on grounds of colour or nationality, but not race or ethnic or national origins, in employing a person who does not normally live in Britain for work at an establishment in Britain (see the glossary at Appendix 7), in order to train him or her in skills that will only be used outside Britain.

Genuine occupational requirement and genuine occupational qualification [Sections 4A and 5 of the RRA]

2.36 It is lawful for an employer to discriminate on racial grounds in recruiting people for jobs where being of a particular race or ethnic or national origin is a 'genuine occupational requirement' (GOR), or being of a particular colour or nationality is a 'genuine occupational qualification' (GOQ) (see Appendix 1).

[4746]

3. THE RESPONSIBILITIES OF EMPLOYERS: A FRAMEWORK FOR ACTION

3.1 The Race Relations Act 1976 (RRA) gives employers a legal duty not to discriminate against or harass applicants for employment, workers (see the glossary at Appendix 7) and former workers, on racial grounds.

What the law says [Sections 4 and 4A of the RRA]

3.2 Employers must not discriminate on racial grounds or subject a person to harassment in:

a. the arrangements they make to decide who should be offered employment; or
b. the terms on which they offer to employ a person; or
c. by refusing or deliberately failing to offer employment.

3.3 It is also unlawful for employers to discriminate on racial grounds against a worker, or to subject him or her to harassment:

a. in the terms of employment provided; or
b. in the way they make opportunities for training, promotion or transfer, or other benefits, facilities or services, available; or
c. by refusing access to such opportunities or benefits, facilities or services; or
d. by dismissing the worker or subjecting him or her to some other detriment.

Legal responsibility for discrimination [Sections 32 and 33 of the RRA]

3.4 Legal responsibility for unlawful racial discrimination rests with employers. Discriminatory acts or conduct by workers or agents (for example, contractors) 'in the course of their employment' are treated as having been done by their employer (see also para 2.27), unless the employer can show he or she has taken all reasonably practicable steps to prevent such acts. Employers may be held liable whether or not those acts were done with their knowledge or approval. An employer's liability for racial discrimination may extend to a worker's behaviour when 'off duty', but in a work-related situation, such as a social event for staff, for example a Christmas party. In relation to the police, chief officers will be liable for acts of unlawful racial discrimination or harassment by police officers.

3.5 A worker who discriminates against, or harasses, someone, on racial grounds, in the course of his or her employment may be personally liable for his or her actions. Under the RRA, the employer will also be liable, unless he or she can show that all reasonably practical steps were taken to prevent unlawful racial discrimination or harassment. In this case, the worker may be solely liable for the unlawful act.

3.6 It is unlawful to discriminate against a former worker, on racial grounds, or to subject him or her to harassment, after the employment relationship has come to an end, if the discrimination or harassment has arisen from, or is closely connected with, the employment.

A FRAMEWORK FOR ACTION

3.7 Good employment practice is the key to employers meeting their legal responsibilities, and avoiding claims of racial discrimination or harassment. Employers need to make sure no worker (past, present or future) is treated less favourably than others, on racial grounds.

3.8 A systematic approach to developing and maintaining good practice is the best way of showing that an organisation is taking its legal responsibilities seriously. To help employers and others meet their legal obligations, it is recommended that they:

a. draw up an equal opportunities policy in employment; and
b. put the equal opportunities policy in employment into practice.

3.9 The policy may apply to all types of equality of opportunity covered by legislation, but it needs to make explicit reference to racial equality and consider all the ways in which employers are likely to be affected by the provisions of the RRA.

A. Draw up an equal opportunities policy on employment

3.10 The aim of an equal opportunities policy in employment is to make sure that:

a. no job applicant or worker receives less favourable treatment than another, on racial grounds;
b. no job applicant or worker is placed at a disadvantage by requirements, provisions, criteria, conditions or practices, unless they can be justified as a necessary and appropriate means of achieving a legitimate aim; and
c. people from under-represented racial groups are given training and encouragement to take equal advantage of opportunities in the organisation.

3.11 An equal opportunities policy in employment should be a written policy, which sets out:

a. the employer's commitment to the principle of equality;
b. the organisation's ethos and values;
c. how the policy applies to the organisations procedures and practice;
d. what is and what is not acceptable behaviour at work;
e. how to use the organisation's complaints procedure to raise any concerns or complaints workers might have about discrimination or harassment;
f. the rights and responsibilities of all; and
g. how the organisation will deal with any breaches of the policy.

3.12 The policy should cover all aspects of employment, including recruitment, terms and conditions of work, training and development, promotion, performance, grievance, discipline and treatment of workers when their contract of employment ends.

3.13 As far as possible, the equal opportunities policy should be drawn up and agreed in consultation with workers and any recognised trade unions or other workplace representatives.

3.14 Appendix 2 contains a sample equal opportunities policy in employment. It sets standards of good practice for all employers. Smaller organisations may only need a simple policy, and procedures and practices that are appropriate to their size and resources.

B. Put the equal opportunities policy into practice

3.15 Employment tribunals have made it clear that statements of intent or paper policies and procedures alone are unlikely to provide employers with a defence in legal proceedings under the RRA. This means employers need to be able to show that they take their equal opportunities policy seriously, and put it into operation in all aspects of employment in the organisation (see Examples 9 and 10).

Example 9: Putting policy into practice

Baptiste v Westminster Press Ltd t/a Bradford and District Newspapers, Case No 35945/96 [1996] DCLD 30

An unsuccessful black applicant for a post in the advertising department of a newspaper was told at the interview for the job that the phrase 'black bastard' was commonly used in the organisation. The tribunal dismissed the company's two-page equal opportunities policy and one-page code of practice as a classic example of employers believing that the preparation of such documents alone, without any supporting advice or instructions to managers on implementing or monitoring them, was sufficient to meet their legal obligations. The complainant was awarded a total of around £12,000 in compensation.

Example 10: Interview

Umerji v Blackburn Borough Council, Case No 29273/94 [1995] DCLD 47

An Asian part-time worker on a short-term contract with a local council was one of six candidates interviewed by a panel for the full-time post of welfare officer with the council. He performed better than any of the other candidates, scoring higher than a white council worker. The panel agreed to offer the Asian applicant the job. The panel subsequently reversed its decision and decided to offer the post to the white worker. According to the council, the Asian applicant was not selected because he had failed to meet the criterion of 'written communication' skills, which only became apparent when the application forms were considered after the interview process.

The tribunal upheld the Asian worker's claim of unlawful racial discrimination. It found that he had not only achieved the highest score in both the test of his technical ability and in the interview as a whole, but had also overcome the 'hurdle' of the application form, by being put on the shortlist in the first place. Further, as a council worker, his written communication skills were well known to his employer. The tribunal found the councils replies to the race relations questionnaire (see the glossary at Appendix 7) to be 'evasive and/or equivocal', and rejected its explanations as 'a cover-up'.

Example 10: Interview

The tribunal criticised the council for failing to follow its own equal opportunities and selection procedures: 'It is quite pointless for the respondent to go to the trouble and expense of creating an elaborate selection procedure and an elaborate equal opportunities policy, if it then breaches that procedure and the policy by following an entirely separate procedure, directed apparently by events, and by the personal whim of individual officers.' The tribunal awarded compensation of around £14,000.

3.16 The most systematic, practical and effective way of approaching this is to draw up an equal opportunities action plan. Its aims should be to:

a. promote the equal opportunities policy;
b. make sure all workers understand the policy, and provide training for those who have particular responsibilities under it;
c. monitor workers and applicants for employment, promotion and training, by racial group, and review all employment policies, procedures and practices, to see if they are potentially discriminatory or obstruct equality of opportunity; and
d. take steps to remove potentially unlawful discrimination, and reduce any significant disparities between racial groups.

Promote the equal opportunities policy

3.17 The equal opportunities policy in employment should be publicised as widely as possible, for example through office notice boards, circulars, email bulletins, contracts of employment, training on equality, induction, internal and external websites, annual reports and staff newsletters and handbooks.

3.18 The policy should be a priority for the organisation, and an essential part of its business or corporate plan. The policy will carry greater force if it has the explicit backing of the chair or director or proprietor, and the board and senior management (where applicable).

3.19 Overall responsibility for the policy, and for reporting regularly on its effectiveness, should rest with a senior manager (where applicable).

Train workers on the equal opportunities policy

3.20 Employers should make sure all their workers understand the organisation's equal opportunities policy, and how it affects them, and that they are aware of any plans for putting it into practice. This could be done by providing basic training and providing written information and guidance on the policy and plan. Some workers may need more advanced training, depending on their jobs. Equal opportunities should also be a standard component of other training courses, at all levels.

3.21 The training will benefit from consulting workers and their representatives about their needs, and incorporating feedback from any training into future courses.

3.22 Employers should make sure in-house trainers are themselves trained before running courses for other staff. External trainers also need to be fully informed about the organisations policies, including its equal opportunities policy.

3.23 Employers will find it helpful to give a named manager responsibility for equal opportunities training in the organisation.

3.24 In the event of legal proceedings being brought against them under the RRA, employers may find it easier to defend themselves if they are able to show that the basic equal opportunities training all workers receive includes the following:

a. the law against racial discrimination and harassment;
b. the organisation's equal opportunities policy, why it has been introduced and how it will be put into practice;
c. what is acceptable and unacceptable conduct in the workplace;
d. workers' responsibilities under the equal opportunities policy to maintain and promote a workplace free of unlawful racial discrimination and harassment; and
e. how prejudice can affect the way an organisation functions, and the effects that generalisations about racial groups, and bias in day-to-day operations, can have on peoples chances of obtaining work, promotion, recognition and respect.

Monitor workers and applicants by racial group, and review all employment policies, procedures and practices

3.25 Monitoring, by racial group, gives employers the information they need to understand how their policies, practices and procedures in the field of employment affect people from different racial groups.

3.26 Monitoring is a process that involves collecting, analysing and evaluating information, to measure performance, progress and change. It can be done in several ways, including questionnaires, surveys, consultation and feedback. Monitoring, by racial group, will allow employers to:

a. determine the composition of their workforce, by racial group, and compare this information with benchmarks, such as census data;
b. know how their workforce is distributed across the organisation, by location, type of job and grade;
c. uncover any disparities between racial groups, in the workforce as a whole and at different levels of the organisation, and investigate the underlying causes;
d. find out whether people from certain racial groups are typically taking longer to obtain promotion;
e. examine whether the practices, provisions, criteria, requirements or conditions used to select candidates for employment, training and promotion might be indirectly discriminatory, and why, and consider how they might be changed to avoid any negative effects on candidates from a particular racial group (or groups);
f. set realistic targets and timetables for reducing any significant racial disparities, both within the workforce as a whole, and at different levels of the organisation;
g. send a clear message to its workers, and to job seekers, that the organisation is serious about achieving fair and equitable participation, and encourage them to cooperate fully; and
h. judge whether the equal opportunities policy is achieving its aims.

Example 11: Monitoring

Richards v Brighton Borough Council [1992] Case No 14213/91 and EAT 431/92 [1993] DCLD 19

A black woman, who had been turned down for the post of information officer in a council's housing department, in favour of a white woman with much less relevant work experience, won her claim of racial discrimination against the council. The tribunal noted the council's failure to monitor its equal opportunities policy.

3.27 Monitoring, by racial group, should cover the following:

a. applications for jobs, temporary and permanent, advertised and non-advertised, and success rates at each stage of the process;
b. distribution of workers in the organisation, by type of job, location, and grade;
c. applications for promotion, transfer and training, and success rates for each;
d. results of performance appraisals;
e. grievances and disciplinary action, including the results, and tribunal decisions involving claims of racial discrimination or harassment; and
f. terminations of contract (for whatever reason).

3.28 Section 8 of the RRA gives the meaning of employment at an establishment in Great Britain (see 'employment' in the glossary at Appendix 7). Employers who have operations or subsidiaries in other countries, or who have outsourced functions to other countries, need to make arrangements to keep their monitoring data for workers at establishments in Great Britain separate (or in a form that is readily identifiable).

- **Example F**. A bank outsources its payroll function to a company in Manila. It transfers a senior manager to Manila from its office in London, to oversee the work. The bank would include the senior manager, but not the payroll workers in Manila, in the monitoring data it keeps to meet the recommendations of this code.

3.29 The information needed for effective monitoring may be obtained in a number of ways. The best course is to ask workers and applicants for jobs, training and promotion to select the racial group they want to be associated with from a list of categories. The 2001 census provides the most comprehensive and reliable data about the population in England, Scotland and Wales, increasingly supplemented by the Labour Force Survey and other survey statistics (see the Office for National Statistics in Appendix 5). Employers should therefore use categories that are compatible with those used in the 2001 census. Employers who wish to include a group that is not separately listed in the census classification should add the group as a sub-group of the appropriate main group in the census classification system. For example, Somali would be a sub-group of Other in the broad Black or Black British category, Sikh a sub-group of Indian in the Asian or Asian British category, and Roma/Gypsy a sub-group of Other in the White category. In response to increasing national consciousness in England, Scotland and Wales, employers may also want to consider offering workers and applicants the opportunity to classify themselves in terms of a national identity. It is important to remember that any aggregation of data, especially when the numbers are small, risks masking significant disparities between sub-groups, for example between Indian and Bangladeshi, if they are considered only as part of the broad Asian group.

3.30 Smaller organisations may only need a simple method of collecting information about workers' and job applicants' racial groups, such as a questionnaire. Larger organisations are likely to need more sophisticated procedures and computerised systems as well, to capture the full picture across their subsidiaries and branches in Britain.

3.31 To ensure the integrity of their monitoring systems, employers should consider the following steps:

a. consult workers, trade unions and other representatives in the workplace, and make sure they understand the reasons for introducing monitoring, before asking workers for information about their racial group;
b. assure everyone concerned that information about ethnic or racial background will be treated in the strictest confidence;
c. analyse the information regularly, preferably together with other available information, for example, on sex, sexual orientation, disability, religion or belief, or age;
d. review the information periodically, and make sure it is current; and
e. make sure managers responsible for monitoring, and anyone else involved in the process, are properly trained in data protection and sensitive data processing.

Public authorities and monitoring

3.32 Most of the public authorities bound by the statutory general duty to promote race equality (see paras 2.28–2.29) also have a specific duty to monitor, by racial group, all their workers, and all applicants for jobs, promotion and training. Public authorities with 150 or more full-time-equivalent workers must also monitor the number of workers from each racial group who:

a. receive training;
b. benefit or suffer detriment from performance assessment;
c. are involved in grievances;
d. are subject to disciplinary action; and
e. end employment with the organisation (for whatever reason).

3.33 Public authorities must publish the results of this monitoring each year.

3.34 Educational institutions are not bound by the specific duty for public authorities as employers. However, schools do have to give their local education authorities (education authorities in Scotland) information about staff, so that the authorities can meet their duty to monitor, by racial group, employment in the schools they manage, and publish a report on it each year. Further and higher education institutions have a specific duty to monitor, by racial group, the recruitment of staff and their career progress. They are also expected to take reasonable and practicable steps to publish the results of their monitoring each year.

3.35 A statutory *Code of Practice on the Duty to Promote Race Equality* was laid before parliament and came into effect in May 2002. The CRE has also produced non-statutory guidance for public authorities on different aspects of the duty (see Appendix 6).

Take steps to prevent unlawful discrimination, and reduce any significant disparities between racial groups

3.36 If the monitoring data show significant disparities between racial groups, employers should investigate the possible causes, and examine all the arrangements, procedures and practices that give effect to their policies in the field of employment, including recruitment, training, promotion, grievance and discipline, performance assessment and dismissal. The absence of disparities for ethnic minorities as a whole, or for one racial group in particular (see para 3.29), should not be taken as evidence that 'discrimination is not a problem'. The aim should be to make sure none of the rules, requirements, procedures or practices used, formally or informally, put *any* racial groups at a significant disadvantage; for example, indirectly discriminatory eligibility rules for promotion, or restrictive advertising techniques. It is recommended that employers approach this as systematically as possible, taking the following steps:

a. review the selection criteria used, to make sure they are strictly related to the job or training opportunity, and do not have an unjustifiable adverse effect on any racial groups;
b. examine all decision-making processes, to make sure they are fair, and are followed consistently across the full range of recruitment and assessment exercises;
c. review the policy on advertising jobs, and training and promotion opportunities, to

make sure the information is reaching any underrepresented groups, and that people from these groups feel encouraged to apply;

d. reassess the labour markets from which they traditionally recruit;

e. set targets (see paras 3.38–3.42) for employment, training and promotion, as part of a programme of action to reduce any significant disparities between racial groups, and regularly review progress; and

f. consider whether lawful positive action (see Appendix 1) might be appropriate.

3.37 Larger employers may find it useful to:

a. nominate a person with specialist knowledge of discrimination and equality to monitor the effectiveness of the organisation's equal opportunities policy, conduct independent investigations of complaints of discrimination and harassment, and advise on, and coordinate, action; and

b. encourage their branches or subsidiaries to draw up and implement their own equal opportunities action plan, against standards set and controlled centrally.

Racial equality targets

3.38 Employers could consider setting racial equality targets as a means of planning the reduction of any significant disparities between racial groups. A racial equality target could represent improvements in representation for particular racial groups or progress towards equality of treatment. For example, it could show the percentage of workers from a particular racial group (or groups) that an organisation is aiming to have in particular areas or types of work within a certain period of time; or a reduction or elimination of any unfavourable disparity in assessment ratings between racial groups over a certain period of time.

3.39 Racial equality targets are *not* quotas. Restricting recruitment to people from particular racial groups, in order to improve their representation in the workforce, would be positive discrimination. This is unlawful in Britain. All selection for employment must be, and be seen to be, fair, and based solely on merit.

3.40 Racial equality targets for recruitment, promotion and training should be based on the ethnic and racial composition of the area from which an organisation decides to recruit for particular jobs, and on the ethnic and racial composition of its own workforce. Progress towards racial equality targets can then be monitored against the steps being taken, including positive action training and encouragement (see paras 3.43–3.45 and Appendix 1), to make recruitment and other employment policies and practices fairer and more equal.

3.41 Employers should consider publishing their racial equality targets, for example, in their annual reports, to show how their organisation is working towards fair participation.

3.42 Employers should base their corporate priorities, objectives, approaches and any racial equality targets on the outcomes listed below.

a. The ethnic and racial composition of the workforce, at each location and level, reflects the composition of the labour markets used for different types of work.

b. Vacancies attract applications from the full range of qualified candidates in the relevant labour markets, including candidates from ethnic minorities.

c. The ratio of appointments to applications is proportionate across all racial groups.

d. The organisation's board and senior management team (where applicable) reflect the ethnic and racial backgrounds of all potential candidates, both internally and externally.

e. Workers from all racial groups are equally likely to apply for, and be offered, training.

f. Applications for promotion and deputising are received from across the full spectrum of workers, irrespective of racial group.

g. Workers spend the same length of time at a particular grade, on average, irrespective of racial group.

h. Progress from one grade to another is unaffected by workers' racial groups.

i. Workers are not disproportionately subject to disciplinary proceedings, because of their racial group.

j. Workers from all racial groups benefit equally from bonuses or performance pay.

k. Grievances are not more likely to be brought by workers from particular racial groups.

l. The number of complaints alleging racial discrimination or harassment is negligible.

m. There are no significant disparities between racial groups among staff leaving the organisation, for whatever reason.

Positive action [Sections 35, 37 and 38 of the RRA]

3.43 The RRA recognises that, due to past discrimination or other disadvantages, people from particular racial groups may not have fully realised their potential, and may not have the

PART 4

qualifications or experience to make them eligible for particular jobs. The aim of positive action, as permitted under the RRA, is to give people from a particular racial group (or groups) the opportunity to compete for work in which they have been under-represented or absent. The RRA also allows action to be taken to make facilities or services, such as language classes or training or education in basic work skills, available for people from a particular racial group (or groups) who would otherwise be excluded from opportunities.

3.44 If the results of monitoring show under-representation, or the complete absence of a racial group (or groups) in particular work (see Appendix 1), for example among senior managers or shop floor supervisors, it is recommended that employers take the following steps:

a. consider positive action training or encouragement;
b. make sure the positive action scheme offers only training or encouragement, and not employment – employers making use of the positive action provisions of the RRA should be especially careful that the training or encouragement provided as a form of positive action does not constitute employment, or lead automatically to employment; for example, 'on-the-job' training or apprenticeships, which are defined as employment, and not training, cannot form part of a positive action programme (see Example 12); and
c. inform workers, trade unions and other workplace representatives about their plans, explaining that the aim of positive action training or encouragement is to help create a level playing field, not to favour any particular racial group.

Example 12: Positive action

Hughes and others v London Borough of Hackney (unreported) [1986]
A local authority included a statement in an advertisement for gardening apprentices encouraging young people from 'black and ethnic minorities' to apply, and referring to section 38 of the RRA. Three white people applied for the jobs and were told they were open only to people from ethnic minorities. The employment tribunal upheld their claims that they had been unlawfully discriminated against on racial grounds, pointing out that 'encouragement' under the positive action provisions of the RRA did not extend to providing job opportunities for any section of the community.

■ **Example G**. A national broadcaster used section 37 of the RRA to set up a mentoring scheme for would-be sports journalists. The scheme gave 12 young people from ethnic minorities a year's training and work placements in the sports broadcasting department, leading to a postgraduate certificate in broadcast journalism from a leading institution. Twelve specially selected and trained senior managers from the sports department were matched with the trainees.

3.45 Positive action may, and should, be used to encourage or train workers to compete for jobs where they are under-represented (section 38 of the RRA).

Equal opportunities conditions in contracts

3.46 Employers should encourage companies and other organisations, with whom they have, or propose to enter into, contracts for goods, facilities or services, to take practical steps to promote equality of opportunity in their employment practices. Employers should therefore:

a. make acceptance on tender lists, and the award or renewal of a contract, conditional on the organisation's providing information about any findings of racial discrimination or harassment, and adopting the recommendations of this code;
b. include terms and conditions in contracts that require contractors to follow the recommendations of this code; and
c. encourage individuals and organisations from under-represented racial groups to tender or compete for contracts.

3.47 Most public authorities have a legal duty to promote race equality when carrying out their functions (see also paras 2.28–2.31). The duty applies whether they carry out these functions themselves or contract them out to private businesses or voluntary organisations. While bound by the RRA's general prohibition of unlawful racial discrimination, private businesses and voluntary organisations are not bound by the duty. Public authorities therefore need to make arrangements during the tendering process, and through the contract itself, to make sure contractors are able to meet the duty on their behalf, if it applies to the goods, works, facilities or services being contracted out. The CRE has produced guides to procurement for local authorities and other public authorities (see Appendix 6).
[4747]

4. THE RESPONSIBILITIES OF EMPLOYERS: EQUALITY OF OPPORTUNITY AND GOOD EMPLOYMENT PRACTICE

What the law says [Sections 4 and 4A of the RRA]

4.1 The Race Relations Act 1976 (RRA) makes it unlawful for employers to discriminate against a person on racial grounds, or subject them to harassment, in the arrangements they make for recruitment and selection, and in the terms and conditions on which they offer employment, training or promotion.

4.2 Employers must therefore make sure their policies, procedures and practices in the field of employment are not potentially discriminatory, and that they promote equality of opportunity, not obstruct it.

4.3 The framework for action (see Chapter 3) emphasises the importance of applying the organisations equal opportunities policy to all aspects of employment, from recruitment to termination of the employment contract. This chapter of the code makes recommendations on good equal opportunities procedures and practice in key areas of employment.

RECRUITMENT

Principles of good practice

4.4 The following principles apply to all aspects of recruitment for employment, including promotion, and training.

a. Recruitment policies, procedures and practices should meet all the terms and objectives of the organisation's equal opportunities policy and action plan.
b. All staff responsible for recruitment should receive training in the equal opportunities policy.
c. Opportunities for employment, including promotion, and training should be equally open to all eligible candidates, and selection should be based solely on merit (except where the positive action exception applies to training; see Appendix 1).
d. No applicant or worker should be placed at a disadvantage by rules, requirements, conditions or practices that have a disproportionately adverse effect on his or her racial group.

Planning

Job descriptions

4.5 It is recommended that employers prepare a job description for any vacant post they decide to fill.

4.6 To avoid claims that a job description includes a requirement that might be indirectly discriminatory on racial grounds, employers need to make sure that:

a. they are able to justify each duty or task as being necessary;
b. the job description does not overstate a duty, or the responsibilities attached to it; and
c. the job description is written in plain English (or Welsh in Wales), and is free of jargon.

4.7 A helpful way of drawing up a job description might be to describe the duties and the tasks a person would be expected to carry out over a certain period of time, for example an average working day or week, in order to get a clear picture of what the job actually entails.

Person specifications

4.8 A person specification describes the skills, knowledge, abilities, qualifications, experience and qualities that are considered necessary or desirable in a candidate, in order to perform all the duties in the job description satisfactorily. It is recommended that employers prepare a written person specification to accompany the job description.

4.9 To avoid claims that a person specification includes potentially discriminatory requirements, criteria or conditions, employers need to make sure of the following.

a. The person specification includes only the criteria needed to perform the duties in the job description satisfactorily.
b. The person specification does not overstate the requirements; for example, by calling for 'excellent knowledge of English' (or Welsh in Wales) when 'good understanding' is more appropriate, or by asking for higher qualifications than are actually needed to do the job satisfactorily.
c. The person specification makes clear the relative importance placed on each criterion, and whether it is necessary or desirable.

PART 4

d. As far as possible, all the criteria are capable of being tested objectively. This means avoiding vague or subjective qualities. Attributes such as 'leadership', which are widely used in the selection process, need to be precisely and objectively defined in terms of the measurable skills and qualities that contribute to it; for example, fairness, knowledge, diplomacy, imagination and decisiveness.

e. The person specification makes clear that degrees or diplomas obtained abroad are acceptable, if they are of an equivalent standard to UK qualifications (see Appendix 5 for details of UK National Academic Recognition Information Centre).

f. To reduce the risk of including criteria that reflect personal preferences rather than justifiable requirements, as far as possible, the manager responsible for the post obtains approval of the person specification from the person responsible for equal opportunities in the organisation (in smaller organisations, this might be the director or proprietor).

4.10 Employers should consider reviewing the person specifications they have used over a period of time, or a representative sample of them, as part of their equal opportunities review of the recruitment process, to make sure the requirements and criteria applied do not contribute to any significant disparities between the success rates for different racial groups.

Job advertisements

4.11 It is recommended that employers take the following steps, to make sure all opportunities for employment or training are advertised widely, fairly and openly.

a. Employers should avoid recruitment, solely or in the first instance, on the basis of recommendations by existing staff, particularly when the workforce is wholly or predominantly from one racial group.

b. The advertisement, in all its forms (including signs in shop windows, and on notice boards and recruitment websites), must not indicate an intention to discriminate unlawfully (see paras 2.22–2.24). Nor should it be possible for an ordinary member of the public to understand the advertisement as discriminating against people from a particular racial group (or groups), unless a statutory exception to discriminate applies (see paras 2.33–2.36), and this is clearly stated in the advertisement.

c. Employers should consider including a reference to the organisation's equal opportunities policy in the advertisement. However, statements encouraging applicants from particular racial groups to apply should not be used, unless the job in question meets the conditions for taking positive action (see paras 3.43–3.45 and Appendix 1). Advertisements for a job relying on a genuine occupational requirement or qualification should make clear how the exception applies to the duties of the job (see Appendix 1).

d. Every effort should be made to ensure that the advertisement accurately reflects the job description and the requirements listed in the person specification.

e. Employers should remember, when recruiting through recruitment agencies, job centres, careers offices, schools or online agencies, that it is unlawful to:

   i. instruct them to discriminate, for example by suggesting that certain groups would (or would not) be preferred; or

   ii. put pressure on them to discriminate against people from a particular racial group (or groups).

f. Recruitment and other agencies should be made aware of the employer's equal opportunities policy, as well as other relevant policies. They should also be given copies of the job descriptions and person specifications for posts they are helping the employer to fill.

g. To avoid indirect discrimination, employers should not unjustifiably restrict job advertisements or information about vacant posts to areas, publications, recruitment agencies, job centres, careers offices and schools that would result in excluding or disproportionately reducing the number of applicants from a particular racial group (or groups). All staff should be informed of any opportunities for promotion or career development (see Example 13).

h. Employers should consider reviewing the job advertisements they have placed over a period of time, or a representative sample of advertisements, as part of their equal opportunities review of the recruitment process, to make sure the advertisements, and where they were placed, did not contribute to any significant disparities between the success rates for different racial groups.

Example 13: Job advertisements

Gulsher v Gateway Foodmarkets Ltd, Case No 17036/92 [1994] DCLD 19
An employer promoted a worker to a new post without advertising the vacancy internally. As a result, no one in the organisation was given the opportunity to apply. The tribunal ruled that the employer had unlawfully discriminated against a black worker who was qualified for the post, and would have applied for it if he had known about it. The complainant was awarded £500 for injury to feelings.

Application forms

4.12 It is recommended that, where practicable, all employers should use a standard application form (see Appendix 4). This has the following advantages.

a. It reduces the time spent in sifting through a great deal of information that is not relevant to the job, which is usually the case with CVs and application letters.
b. It helps employers obtain the information they need, and in the form in which they need it, to make an objective assessment of the applicant's ability to do the job.
c. It makes it easier to obtain information about applicants' racial groups; this is mandatory for public authorities under their legal duty to monitor various aspects of employment, by racial group (see paras 3.32–3.34).
d. It provides employers with evidence that they have tried to meet their legal obligations, should they face legal proceedings under the RRA.
e. It gives all applicants the opportunity to compete on equal terms.

4.13 To reduce the risk of unlawful racial discrimination, employers should follow the guidelines below; smaller organisations may adapt these to their particular circumstances.

a. The section of the application form requesting personal information (including information about racial group) should be detachable from the rest of the form, and not made known to members of the selection panel before the interview.
b. The question about an applicant's racial group should include a clear explanation as to why this information is needed, and an assurance that the information will be treated in strictest confidence, and will not be used to assess suitability for the job, or in the selection decision.
c. Information about eligibility to work in the UK, which employers are required to obtain under the Asylum and Immigration Act 1996, should preferably be verified in the final stages of the selection process, to make sure the appointment is based on merit alone, and is not influenced by other factors. Employers can apply for work permits and should not exclude potentially suitable candidates from the selection process. Depending on the employer's recruitment process, and the type of job being filled, candidates might be asked for the relevant documents when they are invited to an interview, or when an offer of employment is made. It is important to carry out these checks before the persons employment begins. The Home Office (see Appendix 5) has published a code of practice for employers on how to avoid unlawful racial discrimination when complying with this requirement.
d. Only information that is relevant to the job, and to the skills and qualifications listed in the person specification, should be requested in the application form (apart from the questions in the personal details section of the form).
e. Applicants should not be asked to provide photographs, unless a genuine occupational requirement or qualification applies (see Appendix 1).
f. Applicants should be assured that their referees will not be approached unless they are offered the job.
g. Recruitment and employment agencies acting on behalf of an organisation should have copies of its equal opportunities policy, and understand its recruitment policies, and the role of the application form in the selection process.

4.14 Employers who accept CVs might consider publishing guidance on their websites, to help applicants organise their CVs as closely as possible to the organisation's job application form (if they use one), or the form in which employers would prefer to receive the information.

4.15 Employers should review their job application form periodically, as part of their equal opportunities review of the recruitment process, to make sure it does not contribute to any significant disparities between the success rates for different racial groups.

The selection process

4.16 Employers are responsible for making sure their selection procedures are fair, and operate consistently, to ensure the appointment of the best person for the job, irrespective of race, colour, nationality (including citizenship) or ethnic or national origins.

4.17 Every selection decision, from short-listing to appointment, is equally important and it is recommended that employers keep records that will allow them to justify each decision, and the process by which it was reached. Employers need to be able to show that:

a. each selection decision was based on objective evidence of the candidate's ability to do the job satisfactorily, and not on assumptions or prejudices about the capabilities of people from certain racial groups; and
b. all staff involved in the selection process had received training on the equal opportunities policy, and its application to recruitment.

4.18 Actual selection procedures will vary from one organisation to another, depending on size and administrative resources – for example, some organisations may be able to ensure that a member of staff with expertise in personnel matters is involved in the selection process – but the principles of fair selection apply to all.

4.19 As far as possible, to ensure consistency, it would be best if the same staff were responsible for selection decisions at all stages of the recruitment process for each vacancy.

4.20 Employers should make sure the arrangements they make for holding tests or interviews, or using assessment centres, do not put any candidates at a disadvantage, on racial grounds; for example, because the dates or times coincide with religious festivals or observance, or because they fail to take account of dietary needs or cultural norms.

Shortlisting

4.21 It is recommended that employers build the following guidelines for good practice into their selection procedures and practice.

a. Wherever possible, more than one person should be involved in shortlisting candidates, to reduce the chance of one individual's bias prejudicing an applicant's chances of being selected.
b. The marking system, including the cut-off score for selection, should be agreed before the applications are assessed, and applied consistently to all applications.
c. Each person involved in the selection should mark the applications separately, before meeting to agree a final mark.
d. Assumptions about candidates as members of particular racial groups, and the type of work they would be able or willing to do, should play no part in the process. Selection should be based only on information provided in the application form (where one is used), or in any formal performance assessment reports, in the case of internal applicants.
e. The weight given to each item in the person specification should not be changed during shortlisting; for example, in order to include someone who would otherwise not be shortlisted.

4.22 As part of their equal opportunities review of the recruitment process, employers should use the information they have collected about applicants' racial groups to see whether decisions at the shortlisting stage might have contributed to any significant disparities between the success rates for different racial groups. If so, they should investigate further, and take steps to remove any barriers.

Selection tests and assessment centres

4.23 It is recommended that ability tests and personality questionnaires should only be used as one of several assessment methods.

4.24 Well-designed, properly administered and professionally validated ability tests can be a useful method of predicting candidates' performance in a particular job. However, this depends critically on the design of the test; its validation (see the glossary at Appendix 7) as a reliable predictor of performance, irrespective of racial group; and its fair administration by professionals trained in assessment and in the organisations equal opportunities policy. (See Appendix 5 for details of the British Psychological Centre, the representative body for psychologists and psychology in the UK, and its online Psychological Testing Centre.)

4.25 If tests and assessment centres are used as part of the selection process, it is recommended that employers take account of the following guidelines.

a. Tests should correspond to the job in question, and measure as closely as possible the appropriate levels of the skills and abilities included in the person specification.
b. Special care should be taken to make sure candidates whose first language is not

English (or Welsh in Wales) understand the instructions. Tests that are fair for speakers of English (or Welsh) as a first language may present problems for people who are less proficient in the language. The Welsh Language Act 1993 puts Welsh and English on an equal basis in the delivery of public services in Wales and bilingual tests may need to be used for recruitment to some public sector jobs, where the ability to speak Welsh is deemed to be essential or desirable.

c. All the candidates, without exception, should take the same test (see Example 14).

d. Test papers, assessment notes and records of decisions should be kept on file for at least 12 months.

Example 14: Selection tests

Mallidi v The Post Office, Case No 2403719/98 [2001] DCLD 47

An Asian woman who had worked for the Post Office on a casual basis for a number of years was asked to take a written aptitude test in order to remain in employment on a contractual basis. She failed the test, and her employment was terminated. Her complaint, when she found that white workers in the same situation had been given temporary or permanent contracts without having to take a test, was not investigated, and she brought legal proceedings claiming racial discrimination.

The tribunal found that whole batches of casual workers were given contracts without passing a test. Nor was the Post Office able to explain why workers had to sit the test at certain times, and in certain cases but not in others. The tribunal inferred that the only explanation for the Asian woman's dismissal was her race (the tribunal also found that the aptitude test was indirectly discriminatory). It also found no evidence that the Post Office's 'intention to operate an equal opportunities policy … was actually implemented on a day-to-day basis'. The tribunal awarded compensation of nearly £20,000, including £10,000 for injury to feelings.

4.26 As part of their equal opportunities review of the recruitment process, employers should use the information they have received about applicants' racial groups to see whether the tests and assessment methods used might have contributed to any significant disparities between the success rates for different racial groups. If so, they should investigate further and take steps to remove any barriers.

Interviews

4.27 For many employers, the interview is the decisive stage of the selection process. It is also the stage when it is easiest to make judgements about a candidate based on instant, subjective and, sometimes, wholly irrelevant impressions. If assumptions about the capabilities or characteristics of people from a particular racial group contribute to an unfavourable impression, this could lead to an unlawful, racially discriminatory selection decision.

4.28 To strengthen their legal defence in any proceedings alleging unlawful racial discrimination, it is recommended that employers take steps to make sure all job interviews are conducted strictly on the basis of the application form, the job description, the person specification, the agreed weight given to each criterion, and the results of any selection tests, so that all applicants are assessed objectively, and solely on their ability to do the job satisfactorily.

4.29 Staff involved in selection panels would benefit especially from equal opportunities training in interviewing techniques, to help them:

a. recognise when they are making stereotyped assumptions about people;

b. apply a scoring method objectively;

c. prepare questions based on the person specification, and the information in the application form; and

d. avoid questions about hobbies, social activities or religious or cultural beliefs or practices, unless these are demonstrably relevant to the job.

4.30 Employers need to make arrangements to keep application forms, and documents relating to each stage of the recruitment process, for 12 months, in case of any complaints about decisions or procedures, or requests for the information under the Data Protection Act 1998, or, where appropriate, the Freedom of Information Act 2000. The documentation should include:

a. records of discussions and decisions by members of the selection panel; for example, on marking standards or interview questions;

PART 4

b. notes taken by each member of the panel during the interviews; and
c. each panel members marks at each stage of the process; for example, on the application form, any selection tests and each interview question.

4.31 Employers should remind gate, reception and personnel staff that it would be unlawful to treat people from a particular racial group (or groups) less favourably than others, and should consider issuing written guidance to this effect.

4.32 Evidence of good practice throughout the recruitment process will help avoid litigation, or end it at an early stage. Employers will be in a better position to show that they took reasonably practicable steps to prevent unlawful racial discrimination or harassment, should the matter reach an employment tribunal.

4.33 As part of their equal opportunities review of the recruitment process, employers should use the information they have received about applicants' racial groups to see whether selection decisions at the interview stage might have contributed to any significant disparities between the success rates for different racial groups. If so, they should investigate further and take steps to remove any barriers.

References

4.34 To make sure the selection decision is based strictly on the application form, the job description, the person specification, any selection tests and interviews, and is not influenced by other factors, such as potentially subjective judgements about a candidate by referees, employers should avoid making references part of the selection process. It is recommended that references should only be obtained, and circulated to members of the selection panel, after a selection decision has been reached.

4.35 Employers will find it more useful to avoid asking for general character references, and to send referees copies of the job description and person specification instead, requesting evidence of the candidate's ability to meet the specific requirements of the job. This is more likely to ensure that the reference focuses on information that is relevant to the job.

Eligibility to work in the UK

4.36 Under the Asylum and Immigration Act 1996, employers have to carry out checks of a job applicant's eligibility to work in the UK. Employers should preferably do this in the final stages of the selection process, to ensure appointment on the basis of merit alone (see para 4.13c).

Terms and conditions

4.37 It is unlawful for employers to discriminate, on racial grounds, in the terms and conditions of work they offer, including pay, hours of work, overtime, bonuses, holiday entitlement, sickness leave, and maternity and paternity leave.

4.38 It is recommended that employers make sure their rules and requirements on access to any benefits, facilities or services, such as luncheon vouchers, discount travel services or membership of a gym, do not unlawfully discriminate against a particular racial group (or groups) (see paras 2.9–2.13).

4.39 When employees' cultural or religious practices, such as those expressed in dress codes, conflict with an employers policies or workplace requirements, it is recommended that the employer consider whether it is practicable to vary or adapt these requirements. Employers should consult staff, trades unions and other workplace representatives on practical ways in which they can accommodate workers' needs. Discrimination in the field of employment on grounds of religion or belief is unlawful under the Employment Equality (Religion or Belief) Regulations 2003. If the policy or requirement affects people from a particular racial group (or groups), it might also amount to unlawful indirect racial discrimination (see paras 2.9–2.13).

Induction

4.40 Induction is an opportunity for employers to make sure all new staff understand the organisation's commitment to equality of opportunity. Employers might consider providing translations or interpreters, if necessary.

4.41 As a minimum, good employment practice would see employers using the induction process to make new recruits familiar with:
a. equal opportunities principles and workers' legal rights and responsibilities under the RRA;
b. what is acceptable and unacceptable conduct in the workplace, in the light of the organisation's policies on harassment, discipline and grievances; and

c. the organisation's procedures for bringing complaints of racial discrimination or harassment against colleagues or managers.

4.42 For permanent or long-term workers, it is recommended that employers include training on the organisation's equal opportunities policy and action plan (see para 3.20). Employers might consider asking new recruits to sign a statement, affirming that they have read and understood all the policies covered during the induction. This may serve as evidence that they have taken reasonably practicable steps to prevent unlawful racial discrimination or harassment, should they face legal proceedings under the RRA.

4.43 Staff responsible for induction will need to be trained on the organisation's equal opportunities policy, and on how assumptions about new recruits, based on their racial group, can affect the degree to which they are informed, for example, about their rights at work, access to staff facilities and benefits, and the complaints procedure.

Probation

4.44 The RRA protects all workers from unlawful discrimination or harassment on racial grounds during any probationary period.

4.45 To strengthen their legal defence in any proceedings alleging unlawful racial discrimination or harassment, employers are advised to make sure that:

a. any job plan agreed with the probationer includes:
   i. what the probationer is expected to achieve during the probation period; and
   ii. the standards by which performance will be assessed – as far as possible, these should be objectively measurable;

b. managers carry out regular supervision and keep written records of all supervision meetings held during the probation period;

c. any concerns about performance are put in writing, following discussions with the probationer, and a copy sent to the probationer and the personnel office (if the organisation has one); and

d. training on the equal opportunities policy includes guidance for managers on how to avoid judgements about a new worker based on fixed ideas of what it means to 'get on' with other members of staff, or 'fit in'.

IN THE COURSE OF EMPLOYMENT

Language in the workplace

4.46 There is a clear business interest in having a common language in the workplace, to avoid misunderstandings, with all the risks these can entail, whether legal, financial or in relation to health and safety. It is also a matter of courtesy, conducive to good working relations, not to exclude people from conversations that might concern them, when they are present. In the main, English is the language of business in Britain and is likely to be the preferred language of communication in most workplaces (see Example 15), unless other languages are specifically required.

Example 15: Language
Shah v George Grassic t/a The Suite Factory [1995] DCLD 24 An Asian worker in a furniture factory (where there were eight Asians in a workforce of 40) came out of a disciplinary meeting onto the shop floor and, in the owner's presence, began to speak to other Asian workers in their own language. The owner instructed him to speak English, so that he knew what was being said. The worker refused and was warned that if he did not do as he had been instructed he would be dismissed immediately. The worker said he could speak in any language he wished and continued to ignore the instruction. He was then summarily dismissed. The tribunal dismissed the worker's complaint that he had been discriminated against on racial grounds, and ruled that, whether or not it is discriminatory to forbid people to speak in their native language depends on the circumstances: 'If the worker had been told not to speak in his native tongue at all on any occasion at work, in any circumstances, then that, in our view, would clearly be a discriminatory instruction. … [but in these circumstances] It was not unreasonable for [the owner] to expect the common courtesy of being spoken to, or about, in a way in which he could understand.'

4.47 The situation is different in Wales, where Welsh, as an indigenous language, is protected by the Welsh Language Act 1993, and promoted by *Iaith Pawb* (*Everyone's*

PART 4

Language), the Welsh Assembly Government's *Action Plan for a Bilingual Wales.* Many organisations in the public, private and voluntary sectors in Wales operate through the medium of Welsh, or bilingually in Welsh and English. It is therefore recommended that employers in Wales seek advice from the Welsh Language Board in relation to the use of Welsh in the workplace, as well as following the recommendations of this code.

4.48 However, employers should make sure that any rules, requirements, conditions, policies or practices involving the use of a particular language during or outside working hours, for example during work breaks, do not amount to unlawful racial discrimination or harassment against a worker or job applicant (see Example 7). Employers should be able to justify these as being a reasonable means of achieving a legitimate business end. Blanket rules, requirements or practices involving the use of a particular language are often unlikely to be justifiable. Even during working hours, most types of work permit casual conversation at the same time, for example while picking fruit, or filing papers. An employer who prohibits workers from talking casually to each other in a language they do not share with all colleagues, or uses occasions when this happens to trigger disciplinary or capability procedures or impede progress, may be considered to be acting unreasonably.

4.49 Employers should always consult workers, trade unions and other workplace representatives before drawing up any proposals on the use of language in the workplace.

4.50 Where the workforce includes people who are not proficient in the language of the workplace, employers should consider taking reasonable steps to improve communication (see Example I at para 4.58). These might include providing:

a. interpreting and translation facilities; for example, multilingual safety signs and notices, to make sure workers understand health and safety requirements;
b. training in language and communication skills; and
c. training for managers and supervisors on the various populations and cultures that make up Britain today.

Language requirements for a job

4.51 A language requirement for a job may be indirectly discriminatory and unlawful unless it is necessary for the satisfactory performance of the job.

4.52 Under the Welsh Language Act 1993, public bodies providing services to the public in Wales must make their services available in Welsh as well as English. This means a wide range of posts in public bodies in Wales, and some in public bodies outside Wales, will need workers who can speak, write and read Welsh sufficiently well for the post in question. In some cases, this may make Welsh language skills an essential requirement for appointment, in others it may require the applicant to agree to learn the language to the required level within a reasonable period of time after appointment (see Example C, para 2.11).

Performance assessment

4.53 It is unlawful to discriminate against, or harass, a worker, on racial grounds in assessing his or her performance.

4.54 To strengthen their legal defence in any proceedings alleging unlawful racial discrimination, employers need to make sure that performance assessments are not used to pass judgements about the person, based on assumptions about their capabilities as members of certain racial groups. Employers will find it helpful to base all assessments on actual performance of specific tasks, measured by impartial and objective standards. This is particularly important when performance is linked to promotion or a benefit, such as pay or bonuses (see Example 16).

Example 16: Performance assessment

Nasr v Salisbury Health Care NHS Trust, Case No 3102492/99
A consultant of Egyptian origin was not awarded a discretionary point to take his salary above the standard, whereas his 12 colleagues, who were white and of British origin, had each been awarded at least one point. The tribunal upheld his claim of unlawful direct discrimination. It found that the members of the discretionary points committee did not independently record their assessment of each of the candidates against the appropriate criteria and guidelines. Nor were any notes kept of the discussions or the assessment process. The tribunal concluded that 'such a high level of subjectivity is anathema to the successful application of equal opportunity guidelines, since it works to the disadvantage of ethnic minorities, both in operation and perception'. The complainant was awarded £18,000 in exemplary damages.

4.55 It is recommended that training courses for managers on the equal opportunities policy (see para 3.20) should include guidance on objective performance assessment. Equally, any training on assessment methods should take the organisation's equal opportunities policy fully into account.

4.56 To be sure workers are being assessed fairly, and consistently, employers will find it helpful to monitor the results of performance assessments, by racial group (see paras 3.25–3.31), and use the data to inform their review of the organisation's policies, procedures and practices in this area. Any significant disparities in assessment marks between racial groups should be investigated, and steps taken to deal with possible causes.

- **Example H**. A large-scale study of appraisal in 13 civil service departments in 2000 found that staff from white racial groups were consistently awarded higher marks than staff from other racial groups. This was true across grades, age groups, and length-of-service bands. The researchers found no evidence of significant differences in education or training between the groups that were likely to affect performance. Interviews with staff from all racial groups revealed common concerns about the appraisal system itself. Staff from 'non-white' groups were concerned that their performance reviews and appraisal markings reflected stereotyped attitudes about their racial groups. The researchers produced reports and made recommendations for each department. Departments are now acting on these and are themselves monitoring appraisal results and carrying out further investigations and analyses, for example of the language used in appraisal reports, depending on the racial groups concerned.

Training and development

4.57 It is unlawful for employers to discriminate against, or harass, a person, on racial grounds, in the arrangements they make for training, transfer and other development opportunities, or by deliberately refusing to make these available to all workers (see Example 17). The RRA permits some exceptions, including an exception for training provided as part of a positive action initiative (see paras 3.43–3.45 and Appendix 1).

Example 17: Training and development

Bath v Bedfordshire County Council, Case No 36632/91 [1993] DCLD 17
An Asian careers officer found that, although he had been employed to spend one-third of his time counselling pupils about careers, the council refused to let him do this, because he did not have a diploma in careers guidance. No qualifications had been specified in either the job advertisement or the job description. Three years later, five candidates – two white, and three Asian or African Caribbean – were interviewed for one place on a diploma course. The Asian officer was the best qualified academically and the successful white candidate the least qualified. The tribunal ruled that the interviews had been conducted 'for the sake of form' and that the result was a foregone conclusion that amounted to unlawful racial discrimination.

4.58 Employers should consider adopting a policy on training, transfer and development, linked to the organisations business plan (if it has one), and based on regularly updated audits of workers' skills and training needs. The policy should describe the range of development opportunities open to all staff, such as mentoring and shadowing schemes, and to any support its staff will receive.

- **Example I**. Employers might consider providing language training for workers whose language skills are weak. Even when their skills are adequate for the job they are doing, a better command of the language will open the door to better career prospects. Good communication in the workplace also improves overall efficiency, and health and safety, and contributes to better understanding between workers from all racial groups as well as between managers and workers and their representatives.

4.59 To help avoid claims of unlawful discrimination or harassment on racial grounds, it is recommended that employers ensure that managers and supervisors responsible for selecting workers for training and other development opportunities are themselves trained to:

a. understand their legal responsibilities under the RRA, and how the organisation's equal opportunities policy applies to matters of training and career development;
b. recognise workers' training needs, regardless of racial group;
c. encourage all workers to apply for training and other development opportunities, so that no one is overlooked as a result of subjective judgements about their abilities as members of particular racial groups;

d. monitor the take-up of training and other development opportunities, by racial group, and take steps to deal with any significant disparities in take-up between racial groups;

e. regularly review the selection criteria for training and other development opportunities, to make sure they are not potentially discriminatory on racial grounds; and

f. advertise all training and other development opportunities as widely as possible throughout the organisation, for example, through notice boards, and internal websites and bulletins.

Promotion

4.60 It is unlawful for employers to discriminate against, or harass, workers on racial grounds in the way they make opportunities for promotion available, or by refusing or deliberately failing to make them available (see Example 18).

Example 18: Promotion

Dr Halim v Moray College, Case No S/200267/02

The complainant, who was a lecturer at a college in Scotland, was twice overlooked for promotion, even though he was better qualified than those who were promoted. He believed this was because he had complained to the college principal that his line manager was racist and that he had given him unfair appraisals. The principal had advised the complainant to raise the matter directly with his line manager.

There were nine applicants for the first post, including the complainant and his line manager, and the panel included the principal. The principal's sole comment on the complainant was 'This man's not for shortlisting'. At the tribunal hearing, he said he did not consider the application to be 'a serious one' and thought it was all 'part of a sad ruse'. The complainant's line manager was appointed to the post. The panel for the second promotion included the complainant's line manager and the principal and deputy principal. This time he was rejected because the panel said he did not meet some of the essential criteria. The principal also told the tribunal that the complainant 'did not understand what the job was about'.

The tribunal found the college's explanations unconvincing. In upholding the complainant's claim, it took into account the following: unlike the shortlisted candidates, the complainant had met some of the essential criteria; the panel members had been aware of the complainant's grievance; and the person who was the subject of the grievance had been a member of the panel. The tribunal awarded £14,000 in damages.

4.61 It is recommended that all promotion opportunities, including development opportunities that could lead to permanent promotion, should be advertised widely throughout the organisation, and filled in line with the organisation's equal opportunities and recruitment policies and procedures. This would mean using the organisations standard job application form (if it has one) to fill all promotion and development opportunities, and making sure that selection is based strictly on demonstrable merit.

4.62 Employers should avoid by-passing their recruitment procedures, unless a temporary promotion is absolutely necessary. In this case, the promotion should last no longer than the time needed to fill the post permanently, and openly, through the organisation's recruitment procedures.

4.63 Employers will find it helpful to build the following guidelines into their policies and procedures for promotion and career development.

a. Where posts are advertised internally and externally, the same selection procedures and criteria should apply to both internal and external candidates. Discussions about candidates, particularly internal candidates, should not be based on rumours or unsubstantiated opinions.

b. As far as possible, selection decisions based on performance assessments should be endorsed by the organisation's personnel department (if it has one).

c. No assumptions should be made about the eligibility of staff, based on their grade, current post or racial group, and information about all promotion and other development opportunities that could lead to permanent promotion, such as deputising and secondments, should be communicated to all staff; restricting applications for promotion and other development opportunities to staff at a particular grade or level could indirectly discriminate against some racial groups.

d. Records should be kept, by racial group, of who is taking up different types of opportunities, and who is not (see paras 3.25–3.31); who is successful, and who is not.

4.64 As part of their equal opportunities review of the recruitment process, employers should use the monitoring data on promotions to see if there are significant disparities between racial groups in the take-up of promotion and other development opportunities, success rates and length of time spent at a particular grade. If disparities are found, employers should investigate the possible causes in each case and take steps to remove any barriers.

Discipline and grievance

4.65 Employers must not discriminate on racial grounds in the way they respond to grievances, or invoke disciplinary measures. Disciplinary action is an extreme measure and should be taken fairly and consistently, regardless of the workers racial group. Equally, allegations of racial discrimination or harassment must always be taken seriously and investigated promptly, not dismissed as 'over-sensitivity' on a worker's part.

4.66 All employers (irrespective of their size) must now have minimum statutory procedures in place for dealing with dismissal, disciplinary action and grievances in the workplace (section 3 of the Employment Rights Act 1996, as amended by the Employment Act 2002) (see 'disciplinary procedure' and 'grievance procedure' in the glossary at Appendix 7, and ACAS in Appendix 5). These provisions apply only to employees (see the glossary at Appendix 7).

4.67 It is in the interests of employers to attempt, wherever possible, to resolve grievances as they arise, and before they become major problems, through mediation. Grievance procedures can provide an open and fair way for complainants to make their concerns known, and for their grievances to be resolved quickly, without having to bring legal proceedings.

4.68 It is recommended that employers monitor, by racial group, the number of workers who have brought grievances or been subjected to disciplinary action (public authorities with at least 150 full-time-equivalent workers have a legal duty to do this; see paras 3.32–3.34), and the outcomes of each case. It will also be useful to be able to match the data with information about the workers' grades, their managers and the areas of the organisation where they work.

4.69 If an investigation into a grievance or disciplinary matter finds evidence that the grievance was brought in bad faith, for example, to get another worker into trouble, the employer should take steps to make sure this does not happen again, either by recommending training or taking disciplinary action against the worker in question, as appropriate. However, employers must be careful not to punish someone for having made a complaint that proves to have been unfounded, but that was made in good faith, as that could amount to unlawful victimisation (see paras 2.14–2.15).

4.70 It is recommended that, before taking disciplinary action, employers should consider the possible effect on a workers behaviour of the following:

a. racist abuse or other provocation on racial grounds;
b. difficulty in communicating with, or understanding, colleagues; and
c. different cultural norms.

4.71 As part of their equal opportunities review, employers should use the monitoring data on grievances and disciplinary action to see if there are significant disparities between racial groups, investigate the possible causes in each case, and take steps to deal with them.

Harassment

4.72 It is unlawful for employers to engage in, or condone, unwanted conduct that will violate the dignity of workers or job applicants, or create an intimidating, hostile, degrading, offensive or humiliating atmosphere for that person (see Example 7, and Examples 19 and 20).

PART 4

Example 19: Harassment

Milovanovic v Hebden Dyeing and Finishing Co Ltd, Case No 29691/94 [1995] DCLD No 24
A Serbian worker, who had lived in Britain for over 40 years, was one of 25 workers in a dyeing company. He complained in vain of persistent harassment based on his ethnic background, especially after the war in Bosnia began. He faced comments such as 'Go back to Bosnia or wherever you belong, and fight and die like a dog instead of our lads'; and 'If all foreigners and blacks go back to their own country, we will have a better environment in this country'. He handed in his notice and brought a successful claim of direct racial discrimination against the company (see para 2.16). The complainant was awarded around £4,000 in damages.

Example 20: Harassment

Mohammed Wahid Zia v Killermont Polo Club (Scotland) Ltd, Case No S/105430/2001
A Muslim of Pakistani origin, who was employed as a part-time waiter in Glasgow, claimed that his employers, who were Indian Sikhs, harassed, humiliated and demeaned him on racial grounds, and that they also made derogatory remarks about his religion. The tribunal upheld his claims of direct racial discrimination (see para 2.16), victimisation and unfair dismissal. The application was made before 19 July 2003, when it became unlawful to treat a worker or a job applicant less favourably on grounds of religion or belief. Since then, in similar circumstances, the case could have been brought on religious as well as racial grounds. The complainant was awarded a total of around £33,000 in compensation, including £22,000 for injury to feelings.

4.73 It is recommended that employers introduce a policy for dealing with racial harassment. The policy could be part of a wider anti-harassment policy or the organisation's policies on discipline and grievance, or a policy covering dignity in the workplace. Whatever form the policy takes, it should make clear what is and what is not acceptable behaviour in the organisation (see the sample policy at Appendix 3).

4.74 To make sure the policy is effective, it is recommended that employers:

a. publicise the policy through the organisation's websites, notice boards and other forms of communication, so that all staff know about it and understand why it has been adopted, how it will work and how it affects them;
b. make both the policy for dealing with racial harassment and the equal opportunities policy standard components of all training, including induction and specialist courses; and
c. offer an informal route to resolving a grievance as well as the formal one of an investigation.

4.75 If an allegation of racial harassment or discrimination is upheld, it is in the interest of good workplace relations for the employer to make sure that:

a. the harassment has actually stopped, particularly if the parties continue to work together, and
b. the complainant is not victimised for having brought the grievance.

<u>*Dismissal and termination of employment*</u>

4.76 It is unlawful for employers to discriminate against, or harass, workers on racial grounds, by dismissing them or subjecting them to any other detriment (see Example 21 and Example 22). Dismissal includes termination of a contract by the employer (with or without notice), and non-renewal or expiry of a fixed-term contract, unless a genuine occupational requirement applies (see para 2.36 and Appendix 1).

Example 21: Dismissal
Birdi v Waites (1) and Waites Architecture (2), Case No 37708/95 [1996] DCLD 30 A tribunal found that a firm of architects had a record of dismissing black and Asian professional staff after short service, and that this amounted to unlawful racial discrimination. It found that an Asian architect had been criticised without reason during his employment with the firm, marginalised and then dismissed after nine months, for poor performance. He was the third consecutive ethnic minority worker to be dismissed in under 12 months.

Example 22: Redundancy
Sahota and ORS v Shareporter Ltd, [1983] COIT 1414/148 Three sewing machinists, each with less than a year's service, claimed compensation for their selection for redundancy. Two were of Indian origin and the third was an Italian. The machine room supervisor, whose views of black and Asian workers were known to be both strong and derogatory, had made the selection. The tribunal did not accept the company's claim that the machinists had been selected objectively, on the grounds of skill, as one of the machinists was a high bonus earner of some speed and reliability. The tribunal ruled that all three complainants had been dismissed in a redundancy situation because of their race.

4.77 It is recommended that employers make sure the criteria they use for dismissal (including redundancies) are not indirectly discriminatory, and that their procedures are fair and objective, and are followed consistently.

4.78 Dismissal, or any other detriment – such as demotion or compulsory transfer – must always be fair and reasonable. Employers should make sure such decisions are based on a worker's actual performance or conduct during his or her employment, as reflected in any performance assessments. Any aptitude tests designed to select people for redundancy should be objective, and fairly and consistently administered (see paras 4.23–4.26). Wherever possible, employers should consult their workers, and trade unions and other workplace representatives, about proposed redundancies, and the criteria for selection.

4.79 Staff responsible for selecting workers for dismissal should be instructed not to discriminate on racial grounds, and trained in the organisation's equal opportunities policy, and how it might apply to dismissal and redundancy.

4.80 Workers who are eligible for redeployment should be given the chance to show they have the skills or abilities required in alternative jobs. Employers should use their normal recruitment policy to fill these jobs.

4.81 It is recommended that employers monitor all dismissals, by racial group (see also paras 3.25 and 3.31). They will find it useful to be able to match this data with information about the workers' grades, the areas of the organisation where they work, and their managers.

4.82 As well as the guidelines proposed in relation to disciplinary action (see paras 4.65–4.71), employers will find it helpful to:

a. make sure the decision to dismiss is not made by one individual, but, as far as possible, in discussion with a senior member of staff in the personnel department (if the organisation has one);
b. keep written records of all decisions to dismiss; and
c. encourage leavers to give feedback about their employment.

4.83 Employers should use the monitoring data to see if policies, procedures or practices that might have been criticised in the feedback could be contributing to any significant disparities between racial groups, for example in performance ratings or promotion.

RESPONSIBILITIES TO FORMER EMPLOYEES [SECTION 27A OF THE RRA]

4.84 It is unlawful for employers to discriminate against, or harass, former workers, on racial grounds.

- **Example J**. Employers will find themselves in a stronger position, should they face legal proceedings under the RRA, if they can show that they gave their staff clear

PART 4

guidance on supplying references to former workers. References need to be true and accurate, and give a fair representation of the worker's performance, based on evidence of the work they actually did, and not on rumours or assumptions based on their racial group. Best practice would consist of giving the worker a copy of the reference.

[4748]

5. ADDITIONAL RESPONSIBILITIES OF TRADE UNIONS, EMPLOYERS' ASSOCIATIONS, PROFESSIONAL AND TRADE ASSOCIATIONS AND EMPLOYMENT AND RECRUITMENT AGENCIES

TRADE UNIONS, EMPLOYERS ASSOCIATIONS AND PROFESSIONAL AND TRADE ASSOCIATIONS [SECTION 11 OF THE RRA]

5.1 For the purposes of the Race Relations Act (RRA), trade unions, employers' associations and professional and trade associations (referred to as trade unions and other membership organisations) are both employers (see the glossary at Appendix 7) and providers of services specifically covered by the RRA. In their role as employers, these organisations have all the responsibilities outlined in Chapters 3 and 4 of this code. They are also responsible for making sure their representatives do not discriminate unlawfully on racial grounds.

5.2 National, regional and local trade union officials and shop floor representatives have an important role to play on behalf of their members in preventing unlawful racial discrimination or harassment in the workplace, and in promoting equality of opportunity and good relations between people from different racial groups. Trade unions are in a strong position to negotiate changes in policies, procedures and practices, when needed, and to support measures that will prevent unlawful racial discrimination or harassment in the workplace, and promote equality of opportunity. It is recommended that trade unions and other membership organisations also make their members aware of the importance of racial equality, and of their responsibilities under the RRA.

5.3 As providers of services for their members, trade unions and other membership organisations must make sure services are provided without unlawful racial discrimination or harassment.

What the law says

<u>*Admission of members*</u>

5.4 It is unlawful for trade unions and other membership organisations to discriminate against a person, on racial grounds, in the terms on which they offer membership, or by refusing membership.

<u>*Treatment of members*</u>

5.5 It is unlawful for trade unions and other membership organisations to discriminate against members, on racial grounds:

a. in the way they make benefits, facilities or services available, or by refusing or deliberately failing to make them available; these may include:
   i. training facilities;
   ii. welfare and insurance schemes;
   iii. entertainment and social events;
   iv. being involved in negotiations; and
   v. advice, representation and assistance in grievance, disciplinary or dismissal procedures (see Examples 23 and 24).

b. by depriving them of membership, or varying the terms on which they are a member;

c. by subjecting them to some other detriment.

Example 23: Providing services to members
Oliver v Unison, Case No 2800830/00 A black trade union member claimed at a tribunal that the branch secretary had discriminated against her by refusing to represent her in a formal grievance she had brought against two of her colleagues for bullying and racial harassment, having said that he was too busy. When she later found that he was representing the alleged harassers, also union members, she made a formal complaint to the union, which failed to investigate it properly and dismissed it. The tribunal unanimously decided that the union had discriminated against her in its provision of services, as well as by dismissing her complaint against one of its officials.

Example 24: Providing services to members
Short v Greater London Unison, Case No 2301192/98 [2000] DCLD 46 A tribunal found that a trade union had discriminated on grounds of race and sex when it refused to support one of its members, a white man, in his discrimination action against his council employer. The claim against the council arose when the man failed to get the only remaining job in his section following a restructuring. He claimed discrimination when three black women on the interview panel appointed a black woman to the post. The branch secretary refused to support his discrimination claim against the council because he could not see the relevance of an interview panel being made up entirely of black women to any complaint of either race or sex discrimination. The tribunal said there was not the slightest doubt that had the request come from a black woman complaining of rejection by an all white, all male panel, she would have received representation.

5.6 Trade unions and other membership organisations must not harass members or potential members on racial grounds.

Preventing unlawful racial discrimination and harassment

5.7 It is recommended that trade unions and other membership organisations adopt the following guidelines.

a. Make it clear that unlawful discrimination or harassment by members, on racial grounds, brings the organisation into disrepute, and will be dealt with through sanctions ranging from training and counselling to disciplinary action, and possibly even expulsion.

b. Make it clear to members that they may be personally liable for acts or deliberate omissions amounting to unlawful racial discrimination or harassment in the course of their employment.

c. Remind members involved in selection decisions on recruitment, promotion, training or transfer:
   i. not to discriminate against, or harass, someone, on racial grounds; and
   ii. to examine their procedures and joint agreements for any indirectly discriminatory requirements, conditions, criteria, provisions or practices, such as unjustifiable restrictions on transfers between departments, or irrelevant or subjective selection criteria that could exclude or disadvantage applicants from some racial groups.

d. Encourage members to cooperate with management in measures such as monitoring, and positive action (see Appendix 1).

e. Make sure members observe the organisation's equal opportunities policy.

f. Monitor membership, by racial group.

g. Represent members, irrespective of race, colour, nationality (including citizenship) or ethnic or national origins.

h. Consider positive action measures (see Appendix 1), to encourage and train members from racial groups that have been under-represented.

i. Provide training, information and literature (in different languages and formats (when needed) for officers, shop stewards, representatives and members. The training and information could cover the following:
   i. the RRA, and the nature and causes of unlawful racial discrimination and harassment;

ii. the cultural and historical backgrounds of the diverse racial groups in Britain;
iii. the effects of racial prejudice;
iv. the organisation's equal opportunities policy;
v. how to play a full part in the organisation, and stand for election; and
vi. how to avoid unlawful racial discrimination or harassment when representing members.

Pressure or instructions to discriminate

5.8 It is unlawful for members of trade unions and other membership organisations, or their representatives, to put pressure on workers or employers (see the glossary at Appendix 7) or to induce or instruct them to discriminate against, or harass, someone, on racial grounds, in the decisions they make:

a. when recruiting, promoting, transferring, training or dismissing staff; for example, by resisting an employer's attempts to stop the practice of using internal trawls for promotions at a local office where workers from some racial groups are in a minority; or
b. in the terms of employment, benefits, facilities or services; for example, by restricting the numbers of workers from a particular racial group in a section, grade or department; or
c. by resisting changes to practices that are designed to remove indirect discrimination, such as mobility between departments, or rights of seniority.

5.9 It is unlawful to discriminate against, or harass, a person because he or she has complained of unlawful racial discrimination or brought legal proceedings under the RRA, or provided information or evidence in connection with such proceedings, or has otherwise done (or intended to do) anything else under the RRA (see also paras 2.14–2.15).

Promoting equal opportunities

5.10 It is recommended that trade unions and other membership organisations consider the following guidelines, to help them play a full part in achieving equality of opportunity in employment.

a. Cooperate with management in introducing equal opportunities and anti-harassment policies, and putting them into practice.
b. Negotiate the adoption of these policies, if they have not been introduced, or their extension, if they are too narrow.
c. Use their influence to press for changes, if there is evidence that particular procedures and practices might be leading to unlawful racial discrimination; for example, practices such as:
   i. rights of seniority in promotion, especially when all senior posts are occupied by people from a particular racial group;
   ii. unjustifiable restrictions on transfers between areas of an organisation;
   iii. use of transfers as a penalty;
   iv. arbitrary changes to job descriptions, without consultation;
   v. failure to advertise opportunities internally; and
   vi. disregard of policies, in order to favour friends or favourites.
d. Encourage management to take steps to ensure that all workers understand their rights and responsibilities under the organisation's equal opportunities policy, for example, by providing written guidance and training on good equal opportunities practice in different aspects of employment.
e. Cooperate with measures to monitor and ensure the effectiveness of the equal opportunities policy, or encourage the organisation to take them if they have not already.
f. Encourage members to fill out monitoring questionnaires accurately.
g. Encourage employers to review their policies, procedures and practices in the light of the results of monitoring, assess their effects on workers from different racial groups, and take action to reduce or eliminate any significant racial disparities.
h. Make sure employers consult workers before introducing policies or making changes to procedures and practice.
i. Cooperate with employers in finding ways of reducing any significant disparities between racial groups, as revealed through monitoring, assessments and reviews.
j. Encourage employers to tackle under-representation of a particular racial group (or groups) in the workforce as a whole, or in particular work, and support any positive action training or encouragement (see Appendix 1).

EMPLOYMENT AND RECRUITMENT AGENCIES [SECTIONS 14 AND 29 OF THE RRA]

What the law says

5.11 In their role as employers, employment and recruitment agencies, including online recruitment agencies, have all the responsibilities outlined in Chapters 3 and 4 of this code. They also have responsibilities as suppliers of job applicants and workers to other employers.

5.12 It is unlawful for employment and recruitment agencies to:

a. discriminate against, or harass, a person, on racial grounds, in the way they provide any of their services;

- **Example K**. An employment agency put forward white job seekers for managerial jobs and black job seekers for cleaning and security jobs.

b. publish job advertisements that suggest or could be taken to suggest that applications from certain racial groups will not be considered, or will be treated more favourably or less favourably than others;

- **Example L**. An unlawful advertisement reads: 'Admin worker required. Must be a German national'.

c. act on instructions or pressure from employers, to reject, prefer or restrict the numbers of applicants from certain racial groups, unless a statutory exception applies (see para 2.24, Appendix 1 and Example 25);

- **Example M**. A recruitment agency followed an employer's instruction to recommend only Scottish candidates for telesales vacancies.

d. act on indirectly discriminatory instructions from employers, so that applicants have to meet requirements or conditions that could unreasonably exclude or significantly reduce the number of applicants from a particular racial group (or groups);

- **Example N**. An employment agency received a potentially discriminatory instruction from one of its clients to send only applicants who had been resident in the UK for five years. In another case, the employer wanted the agency to give preference to candidates with qualifications from Oxford or Cambridge; this could have disproportionately and adversely affected any ethnic minority job applicant who was eligible in all other respects, as statistics show that people from ethnic minorities are less likely to have studied at 'traditional' universities.

e. knowingly aid an employer in an act of unlawful racial discrimination or harassment (see paras 2.27 and 3.4).

Example 25: Pressure to discriminate

Britannia Products Ltd, Brook Street Bureau (Bradford), and Network Industrial Recruitment, CRE Formal Investigation [1994]

A CRE formal investigation of an employment agency and one of its clients found evidence of pressure having been brought on the agency to discriminate unlawfully. The investigation also found that the company was more likely to lay off ethnic minority than white workers, and that the agency's records showed that Asian job applicants received lower marks for appearance, speech and personality than other applicants. The CRE issued a non-discrimination notice (see the glossary at Appendix 7) against both the organisation and the agency.

5.13 To avoid unlawful racial discrimination, or harassment, employment and recruitment agencies are advised to ensure that they are not:

a. making assumptions about the type of work some racial groups do better than others, and screening applicants on that basis;

b. making 'business' assumptions about their clients' racial preferences; and

c. treating clients from certain racial groups less favourably than others.

Pressure or instructions to discriminate

5.14 Employment and recruitment agencies, or their representatives, should not put pressure on workers or clients or employers (see the glossary at Appendix 7), or induce or instruct them, to discriminate unlawfully against, or harass, someone, on racial grounds.

5.15 It is unlawful for employment and recruitment agencies, or their representatives, to discriminate against, or harass, a person because he or she has complained of unlawful racial discrimination or brought legal proceedings under the RRA, or provided information or evidence in connection with such proceedings, or has otherwise done (or intended to do) anything else under the RRA (see also paras 2.14–2.15).

Promoting equal opportunities

5.16 It is recommended that employment and recruitment agencies:

a. adopt an equal opportunities policy that makes it clear that no job applicant will be treated less favourably on racial grounds; in addition, no job applicant will be placed at a disadvantage by requirements, provisions, criteria, conditions or practices, unless they can be justified as a necessary and appropriate means of achieving a legitimate objective;

b. give anyone registering with the agency a copy of the policy, and include the policy in the terms of business sent to clients, suppliers and subcontractors;

c. make sure all staff understand that it is against the law to discriminate on racial grounds, or harass clients, and that stereotypes and generalisations about racial groups can affect the way they treat people from these groups; and

d. keep records of applicants' racial groups, and monitor the effectiveness of any measures they take to prevent unlawful racial discrimination and harassment; for example, by checking periodically that qualified applicants from ethnic minority groups are being referred for suitable jobs at a similar rate to qualified applicants from other groups.

5.17 It is also recommended that agencies instruct their staff:

a. not to ask clients for racial preferences;

b. to follow the agency's equal opportunities policy;

c. to report to a supervisor any employer who gives them instructions to discriminate on racial grounds, or who tries to persuade them to discriminate in this way;

d. to explain to employers the requirements of the law, and the agency's obligations, and to send them a copy of the agency's equal opportunities policy;

e. not to draw attention to job applicants' racial groups when recommending them for a vacancy, unless the employer is properly relying on a statutory exception to the RRA (see paras 2.33–2.36), and has given a written statement to this effect;

f. to report to a manager or supervisor any employer's refusal to interview an applicant, on racial grounds, or any evidence that an applicant has been rejected for a job on racial grounds; the manager or supervisor should inform the employer that his or her refusal could be unlawfully discriminatory; if the employer does not cooperate, the agency should inform the applicant of his or her right to take a complaint to an employment tribunal; and

g. to inform a manager or supervisor if they believe that a job applicant, although interviewed, has been rejected on racial grounds. If the manager or supervisor is satisfied that there are grounds for this belief, the applicant should be informed of his or her right to make a complaint before an employment tribunal. Agencies should keep written records of such cases.

5.18 Employment or recruitment agencies should also consider the following guidelines.

a. Make it clear to all job applicants, employers and other clients, subcontractors or franchises that the agency is committed to equality of opportunity.

b. As part of the duty to promote race equality (see paras 2.28–2.31), public authorities that recruit workers through an agency may make it a term of the contract between them that the agency has an equal opportunities policy, and that it should monitor the selection process by applicants' racial groups.

c. Issue all staff with written instructions that they must treat all job seekers equally, irrespective of race, colour, nationality (including citizenship), or ethnic or national origins.

d. Inform employers of the agency's equal opportunities policy, and remind them that it is unlawful to discriminate against, or harass, someone on racial grounds in the selection process.

5.19 Although organisations in the private and voluntary sectors are not bound by the duty placed on public authorities to promote race equality (see paras 2.28–2.31), the CRE would recommend that they encourage the organisations with whom they have (or propose to enter into) contracts for work to take practical steps to ensure equality of opportunity in their employment practices.

[4749]

6. RIGHTS AND RESPONSIBILITIES OF WORKERS

Rights

6.1 All workers (see the glossary at Appendix 7) have the right to work free from unlawful racial discrimination and harassment. They have the right not to be treated less favourably on racial grounds than a worker from another racial group:

a. in access to job opportunities;
b. in the terms and conditions on which they are employed;
c. in the opportunities they have for promotion, transfer or training; or in the access they have to benefits, facilities or services; and
d. in matters of dismissal or redundancy, or through exposure to any other detriment.

6.2 Workers also have other rights, including the following:
a. not to be subjected to unwanted behaviour that violates their dignity or creates an intimidating, hostile, degrading, humiliating or offensive environment for them;
b. not to be victimised for claiming unlawful racial discrimination or harassment, or for backing someone else's complaint under the Race Relations Act 1976 (RRA);
c. not to be instructed to discriminate unlawfully against, or harass, someone, on racial grounds, or to be put under any pressure, or inducement, to do so; and
d. to take their complaint to an employment tribunal, if they are not satisfied with the way their employer has dealt with it; employees have the right to have their complaint considered under statutory grievance and disciplinary procedures (see para 4.66).

6.3 Workers who believe their employer or a colleague is harassing or discriminating unlawfully against them, on racial grounds, have several options. They can:
a. consult their trade union (if there is one where they work and they are a member of it) or workplace representative;
b. report the matter to their manager (unless this person is the alleged discriminator) and/or to someone in the personnel department (if there is one);
c. use informal procedures, such as mediation, and, if unsuccessful, the employer's grievance procedure, which must be followed if the employee is considering taking the matter to an employment tribunal (see paras 4.65–4.71); and
d. seek legal advice about pursuing their claim in an employment tribunal, if they are not satisfied with the result of the grievance procedure.

6.4 Employment tribunals have wide powers to order compensation, following a finding of unlawful racial discrimination. Awards of compensation may include:
a. past loss of earnings or other financial loss, including future loss;
b. injury to feelings;
c. personal injury, physical or psychological, caused by the discrimination or harassment; and
d. a further award for injury to feelings, in exceptional circumstances, to reflect the way in which the person bringing the claim of discrimination or harassment has been treated.

6.5 Employment tribunals can also make a declaration about the rights of the parties, or recommend that the employer take steps to reduce the effects of the discrimination on the complainant.

Responsibilities

6.6 Responsibility for preventing unlawful racial discrimination or harassment and promoting equality of opportunity between people of different racial groups rests principally with employers. Employers are also liable for any unlawful acts of racial discrimination or harassment by their workers, unless they can show they have taken reasonably practicable steps to prevent such acts (see para 3.4 and Example 26) However, individual workers do not escape responsibility: a worker, whatever his or her grade or racial group, may be held personally liable for his or her actions, if they are proved to be unlawful, even if the employer has a strong defence against liability (see paras 2.27 and 3.4).

■ **Example O**. A manager, who discriminates unlawfully on racial grounds against another worker, may be held personally liable and made to pay compensation to that worker, especially if the employer can persuade an employment tribunal that the organisation took reasonable steps to prevent the manager from discriminating unlawfully.

Example 26: Worker's liability

Hussain v Westcroft Castings Ltd (1), Mr A Scotson (2) and Mr H Irvine (3), Case No 21858/94

A Pakistani worker at a small metal castings foundry, unable to cope any longer with the vicious abuse and harassment directed at him, brought racial discrimination claims against the company, one of the workers and his manager. His manager, having promised when he first complained that he would sort things out, responded the next time by asking him what he had done 'to stir this up'. He took no action whatever against the culprit. The tribunal found the manager's responses 'deplorably inadequate' and dismissed the company's defence that what had happened was merely 'jocular banter'. The tribunal also made clear that the size of the company has no bearing on 'the standards expected of reasonable employers when handling disciplinary matters'. Findings of unlawful direct discrimination were made against the company and the two named individuals.

6.7 Workers are responsible for respecting the rights of their fellow workers, including their right to work free from unlawful racial discrimination or harassment.

6.8 The following actions by individual workers would be unlawful:

a. discriminating on racial grounds against colleagues, junior staff, agency staff, contractors, or job applicants in the course of their employment;

■ **Example P**. A manager prefers to work with people whom he has worked with before on other jobs. Most of them are Asian. This could be indirectly discriminatory if teams are regularly put together on this basis and suitable workers from other racial groups are excluded as a result.

b. harassing someone at work because of their racial group, by behaving in a way that violates their dignity, or creates a hostile, humiliating, offensive, degrading or intimidating environment;

c. attempting to induce, pressurise or persuade other workers to discriminate unlawfully on racial grounds;

■ **Example Q**. A worker refused to be part of a team that included workers from particular racial groups, and induced other workers to refuse as well.

d. helping someone to plan or carry out an act of unlawful racial discrimination or harassment;

■ **Example R**. A manager gave one of her workers advice on getting a colleague from a particular racial group demoted.

e. victimising a worker who has complained in good faith about racial discrimination or harassment, or taken legal action about it, or given evidence or information in a case of racial discrimination, even if the complaint is not upheld.

6.9 It is recommended that workers:

a. cooperate with measures taken by management to promote equal opportunities and prevent unlawful racial discrimination and harassment, such as monitoring or positive action training; or work through their trade union or other workplace representatives to encourage management to take such measures;
b. take part in training on the organisation's equal opportunities policy;
c. follow the organisation's equal opportunities and anti-harassment policies;
d. alert management, and trade unions or other workplace representatives, to incidents of racial discrimination or harassment;
e. avoid infringing workers' rights to work in an environment free of unlawful racial discrimination or harassment; and
f. be alert to the possibility that apparently non-discriminatory rules, requirements, conditions, practices, provisions and criteria could put people from some racial groups at a particular disadvantage.

6.10 As recruitment becomes more competitive, it is in the interests of *all* workers to take advantage of any training programmes their employers or trade unions provide, such as language training schemes, communication courses, courses on industrial relations and courses designed to improve negotiation skills. Effective communication, and the ability to be flexible and accommodating about the different ways in which people may need to balance the conflicting demands of their personal life, cultural background and work, lie at the heart of good relations at work.

[4750]

7. APPENDICES

APPENDIX 1
POSITIVE ACTION AND GENUINE OCCUPATIONAL REQUIREMENTS OR QUALIFICATIONS

Positive action [Sections 35, 37 and 38 of the RRA]

The term 'positive action' refers to measures that may lawfully be taken to meet special needs or to train or encourage people from a racial group that is under-represented in particular work, or among the post-holders of membership organisations (see also paras 3.43–3.46).

Section 35

This section of the Race Relations Act 1976 (RRA) makes it lawful to provide people from a particular racial group with access to facilities or services, in order to meet any special needs they might have in respect of education, training or welfare, or to any ancillary benefits. Schemes with an industrial language training component, language courses and access courses designed to meet special needs have all been developed under this section.

Section 37

Section 37 allows training or encouragement to be provided for a particular racial group that is under-represented in particular work – that is, in one of the following situations.

1. ***Where there is national under-representation*** – that is, where, during the previous 12 months, no one from a particular racial group has done the work in question in Great Britain, or where the proportion of people from that group doing that work was small compared to its proportion of the population of Great Britain. In this case, training or encouragement can be provided exclusively for the racial group (or groups) in question.

2. ***Where there is local under-representation*** – that is, during the previous 12 months, no one from a particular racial group has done the work in question in that area, or where the proportion of people from that group doing that work was small compared to its proportion of the population of that area. In this case, training or encouragement cannot be provided exclusively for the racial group in question but:

- posts or places on training courses may be reserved for that group; or
- as long as an opportunity is made available and known to all, applications may be encouraged from the under-represented group.

Section 38

Section 38 allows training or encouragement to be provided for a particular racial group that is under-represented in a particular type of work in a workplace, or among the post-holders of a membership organisation – that is, in one of the following situations:

1. ***Workplace*** – where, during the previous 12 months, no one from a particular racial group was doing a particular type of work in a workplace, or where the proportion of employees from that racial group doing that work there was small, compared to its proportion in the workforce or in the population of the area from which the employer recruits for that type of work. In this case, employers may:

- provide training exclusively for employees (but not non-employees) from that racial group; or
- encourage people from that group alone (whether or not they are employees), to take advantage of opportunities for doing that work there.

2. ***Membership organisation*** – where, during the previous 12 months, no one from a particular racial group has held a post in that organisation, or where the proportion of people from that racial group holding such a post was small, compared to the proportion of people from that racial group. In this case, the organisation may:

- provide training for people from that racial group that will help equip them to hold such a post; or
- encourage people from that racial group alone to take advantage of opportunities to hold such a post.

Encouragement means making it easier for people from a racial group underrepresented in particular work to take advantage of job opportunities. It can take the form of explicit encouragement to apply; for example, in advertisements for jobs, mentoring opportunities, shadowing schemes, open days, and career fairs; and in information about careers and vacancies provided to schools in areas with large ethnic minority populations.

The RRA also allows employers, trade unions, employers' associations and trade or professional organisations (but not other organisations) to provide training or encouragement *exclusively* for employees or members from a particular racial group (or groups), to equip them to do particular work or hold particular posts.

Genuine occupational requirements and genuine occupational qualifications [Sections 4A and 5 of the RRA]

Discrimination on racial grounds is allowed in certain limited circumstances, when being from a particular racial group is a 'genuine occupational requirement' (GOR) or a 'genuine occupational qualification' (GOQ).

GOR and GOQ exceptions are very restrictively defined and it is for the employer to justify selecting or promoting or (in the case of GORs only) dismissing in a way that would otherwise be unlawfully discriminatory.

Employers are strongly advised to seek legal advice on using a GOR or GOQ exception, before advertising the post. All advertisements indicating an intention to discriminate are unlawful, unless a statutory exception applies.

Genuine occupational requirements (GOR)

Any job may be restricted to a person from a particular race or ethnic or national origin, if one of these characteristics is a GOR for the job or the context within which the job is to be carried out. This means an employer may lawfully discriminate on these grounds in recruitment, and in training for promotion or transfer to that job, if he or she can show that the use of a GOR is a reasonable means of achieving a legitimate aim.

The RRA also permits dismissal, in order to meet a GOR. In other words, if an employer reasonably believes a person does not meet the GOR that applies to the post, he or she may then be dismissed. If a person were appointed to meet a GOR and the job came to an end, then normal redundancy rules would apply.

- **Example S**. A local council has a health project worker of Bangladeshi origin who is responsible for encouraging people of Bangladeshi origin to make more use of the council's health services. The project has been a success, with marked improvements in the use of health services by Bangladeshis. The council now wants to repeat the exercise for its growing local Somali community and to recruit a person of Somali national origin for the post, as the person best equipped for the duties of the post. Some of these involve visiting the homes of elderly people and people with disabilities and the worker will therefore need to have a good knowledge of the culture and language of the Somali community. The council does not have the resources for two posts and has decided, following a review of the Bengali project, that it is now less necessary than the Somali project. The council does not have other Somali workers who can do the job. The council could rely on the GOR exception when advertising the vacancy to recruit a person of Somali national origin, and to redeploy the Bangladeshi worker or end her or his contract. If the contract has lasted for two years or more, the council would need to take into account the statutory redundancy payment due for non-renewal of the contract, which amounts to a dismissal in law.

Genuine occupational qualifications (GOQ)

The GOR exception may not be used to discriminate on grounds of colour or nationality. Discrimination on grounds of colour or nationality is only possible for specific types of jobs.

a. To achieve authenticity in a dramatic performance or similar entertainment or in modelling or photographic or artistic work.

- **Example T**. A theatre director may decide that only a black person can convincingly play the part of Dr Martin Luther King, while a painter working on a scene from the Mahabharata may ask an employment agency to send only Indian models.

b. To achieve authenticity in bars and restaurants.

c. To provide personal services to people from a particular racial group, defined by colour or nationality, in order to promote their welfare, which only a person of the same colour or nationality can do 'most effectively'.

Genuine occupational qualifications and requirements		
Nature of exception	**GOR**	**GOQ**
Discrimination on grounds of race or ethnic or national origins	✔	
Discrimination on grounds of colour or nationality		✔
Purpose of exception		
Promotion	✔	✔
Transfer	✔	✔
Recruitment	✔	✔
Termination of contract	✔	
Any job	✔	
Certain types of jobs		✔

[4751]

APPENDIX 2
SAMPLE POLICY ON EQUAL OPPORTUNITIES IN EMPLOYMENT

.... [organisation's name] is committed to building an organisation that makes full use of the talents, skills, experience, and different cultural perspectives available in a multi-ethnic society, and where people feel they are respected and valued, and can achieve their potential regardless of race, colour, nationality, national or ethnic origins.

.... will follow the recommendations of the CRE's statutory *Code of Practice on Racial Equality in Employment* in all its employment policies, procedures and practices.

The aims of this policy are to ensure that:

- no one receives less favourable treatment, on grounds of race, colour, nationality, or ethnic or national origins, or is disadvantaged by any conditions, requirements, provisions, criteria, procedures or practices that cannot be justified on non-racial grounds, or victimised for taking action against racial discrimination or harassment, or instructed or put under pressure to discriminate against, or harass, someone on racial grounds;
- the organisation is free of unwanted conduct that violates the dignity of workers or creates an intimidating, hostile, degrading, offensive or humiliating environment;
- opportunities for employment, training and promotion are equally open to candidates from all racial groups; and
- selection for employment, promotion, transfer and training, and access to benefits, facilities and services, will be fair and equitable, and based solely on merit.

This policy applies to all aspects of employment, from recruitment to dismissal and former workers' rights.

We will take the following steps to put the policy into practice and make sure it is achieving its ends.

- The policy will be a priority for the organisation.
- .... (named senior manager and job title) will be responsible for the day-to-day operation of the policy.
- The policy will be communicated to all workers and job applicants, and will be placed on the organisation's intranet and website.
- Workers and their representatives and trade unions will be consulted regularly about the policy, and about related action plans and strategies.
- All workers will be trained on the policy; on their rights and responsibilities under the policy, and on how the policy will affect the way they carry out their duties. No one will be in any doubt about what constitutes acceptable and unacceptable conduct in the organisation.
- Managers and workers in key decision-making areas will be trained on the discriminatory effects that provisions, practices, requirements, conditions, and criteria can have on some racial groups, and the importance of being able to justify decisions to apply them.
- Complaints about racial discrimination or harassment in the course of employment

will be regarded seriously, and may result in disciplinary sanctions, and even dismissal. The complaints procedure will be published in a form that is easily accessible.

- Opportunities for employment, promotion, transfer and training will be advertised widely, internally and externally, and all applicants will be welcomed, irrespective of race, colour, nationality or ethnic or national origins.
- All workers will be encouraged to develop their skills and qualifications, and to take advantage of promotion and development opportunities in the organisation.
- Selection criteria will be entirely related to the job or training opportunity.
- Information on the ethnic and racial backgrounds of workers and applicants for employment, promotion and training will be collected and analysed, to monitor each stage of the recruitment process. The information will be held in strictest confidence and will only be used to promote equality of opportunity and prevent unlawful racial discrimination.
- If the data show that people from a particular racial group are under-represented in particular areas of work, lawful positive action training and encouragement will be considered for workers and others from that group, to improve their chances of applying successfully for vacancies in these areas.
- Grievances, disciplinary action, performance assessment, and terminations of employment, for whatever reason, will also be monitored by racial group
- Requirements, conditions, provisions, criteria and practices will be reviewed regularly, in the light of the monitoring results, and revised, if they are found to, or might, discriminate unlawfully on racial grounds.
- All contracts between .... and contractors to supply goods, materials or services will include a clause prohibiting unlawful racial discrimination or harassment by contractors and their staff, and by any sub-contractors and their staff. The clause will also encourage contractors and potential contractors to provide equality of opportunity in their employment practices.
- An equal opportunities action plan will be drawn up, with racial equality targets and timetables, to show what steps the organisation plans to take to achieve equality of opportunity.
- The effectiveness of the policy and the plan will be monitored regularly. A report on progress will be produced each year, and published via the intranet, the website, the staff newsletter, notice boards, and the annual report.
- Customers and clients will be made aware of the policy, and of their right to fair and equal treatment, irrespective of race, colour, nationality or ethnic or national origins.

This policy has been endorsed by .... [an appropriate senior person] *and has the full support of the management/board.*

The policy was approved on .... [insert date], *following consultation with senior managers, workers, workers representatives and trade unions.*

Overall responsibility for the effectiveness of this policy lies with .... [an appropriate senior person].

All staff are responsible for familiarising themselves with this policy. Managers must also make sure their workers know about, and follow, the policy.

For further information, please contact [insert name and details].

[4752]

APPENDIX 3
SAMPLE ANTI-HARASSMENT POLICY

As part of its equal opportunities policy, the company is committed to promoting a harmonious working environment, where every worker is treated with respect and dignity. No one should feel threatened, intimidated or degraded on grounds of race, colour, nationality, ethnic or national origins, sex, married status, sexual orientation, disability, physical characteristics, health, age, or religion or belief.

The policy also covers harassment that falls outside the categories referred to above, and that can be classed as bullying. Harassment at work is unacceptable and will not be permitted or condoned. Examples might include:

- racially derogatory remarks or insults;
- graffiti or slogans;
- racist 'jokes', banter, ridicule or taunts;
- using a disparaging or offensive tone when communicating with people from certain racial groups;

- avoiding people because of their racial group;
- having unrealistic expectations of performance or imposing excessive workloads on people, based on their racial group; and
- unnecessarily picking on individuals from particular racial groups.

All workers have a right to work in an environment that:

- is free from abuse or insults;
- is safe;
- promotes dignity at work;
- encourages individuals to treat each other with respect;
- values politeness;
- is open and fair; and
- encourages individuals to support each other.

All workers should:

- encourage a person who says they have been bullied or harassed to seek help, and be sensitive to their feelings; and
- refrain from taking part in, or encouraging or condoning, gossip about cases of alleged or actual harassment or bullying.

All complaints of harassment or racial discrimination will be treated seriously and dealt with promptly through the complaints procedure.

Disciplinary action, including dismissal, may be taken against any worker found responsible for unlawful racial discrimination or harassment.

All workers must follow this policy.

[4753]

APPENDIX 4
GUIDELINES ON JOB APPLICATION FORMS

Personal details

- First name(s) and surname.
- Address and contact number.
- Racial group (select from categories).
- Other equality information being sought, for example, on sex, disability, sexual orientation, religion or belief, or age.

Education and training

- Details of qualifications, wherever they were obtained (only if relevant).

Employment

- Job history or other related experience.

Suitability for the job

- How the applicant meets the requirements of the job description and person specification. To make it easier to evaluate and compare applications, candidates should be asked to consider each requirement of the person specification, in turn, and to relate their answers to the duties listed in the job description.

References

- Names and contact details of two referees, one of whom should be the current or most recent employer (where applicable). Applicants should be assured that referees will only be approached if they are offered the job.

All the personal details in the relevant section of the application form (including information about racial group and other equality characteristics) should be detachable from the rest of the form, and not made known to members of the selection panel before the interview.

The request for information about an applicants racial group should be accompanied by a clear explanation of the reasons for requesting this and how the information will be used, with an assurance that it will be treated in strictest confidence, and will not be used to assess suitability for the job or in the selection decision.

The application form should state clearly that candidates will be offered the job on the understanding that they are eligible to work in the UK (see also para 4.13c).

[4754]

(*Appendix 5* (*Relevant organisations*) *and Appendix 6* (*CRE publications*) *are omitted. See Useful addresses at* **[5046]**.)

APPENDIX 7
GLOSSARY

IN THIS CODE, THE WORDS BELOW HAVE THE MEANINGS GIVEN BENEATH THEM.

Adverse impact
A significant difference in patterns of representation or outcomes between racial groups, with the difference amounting to a detriment for one or more racial groups.

Advertisement
Any form of advertisement or notice, including signs, labels, show cards or goods, samples, circulars, catalogues, price lists or other material and exhibitions of pictures, models or films, whether public or not, and disseminated through means such as the internet, newspapers or other publications, television or radio, displays, or in any other way.

Citizenship
See 'nationality' below. In general, the rights, duties and responsibilities of a good citizen, of any state.

Commission for Racial Equality
A non-departmental public body, set up under the RRA to work towards the elimination of unlawful racial discrimination, to promote equality of opportunity and good relations between people from different racial groups, and to keep under review the working of the RRA and make proposals for amending it.

Complainant
A person with a complaint of racial discrimination or harassment under the RRA.

Contract of employment
A contract of employment, like any other contract, is an agreement enforceable by law reached between two parties.

Contract worker
An individual who does work for a person (known as a principal), but is employed by another person, who supplies the individual under a contract made with the principal.

Data use
Data can be lawfully processed, with appropriate safeguards for the rights and freedoms of data subjects, in order to identify or keep under review the existence or absence of equality of opportunity or treatment between people from different racial groups.

Direct discrimination
Less favourable treatment of a person on racial grounds compared with the treatment or likely treatment of a person from another racial group in the same or similar circumstances.

Disciplinary procedure
An arrangement or procedure for disciplining workers. This may include informal and formal disciplinary measures. Under the Employment Act 2002, employers must have a written disciplinary procedure. The statutory procedure is implied in contracts of employment and amounts to a minimum standard required of employers. The ACAS *Code of Practice on Disciplinary and Grievance Procedures* provides detailed guidance for employers.

Dispute resolution
Minimum statutory procedures under the Employment Act 2002 for dealing with dismissal, disciplinary action and grievances in the workplace.

Employee
An individual who carries out work for a person at an establishment in Great Britain under a contract of service or of apprenticeship or a contract personally to execute any work or labour. The contract may be written down or agreed orally or implied by the nature of the relationship. Many casual workers are likely to be employees with short-term contracts.

Employer / Principal
A person who makes work available to an individual under a contract of service or of apprenticeship, or, for the purposes of this code, to a contract worker.

Employment
Being employed under a contract of service or of apprenticeship, or a contract personally to carry out any work or labour.

Employment at an establishment in Great Britain

For the purposes of the RRA, employment is to be regarded as being at an establishment in Great Britain if a worker:

a. does his or her work wholly or partly in Great Britain; or
b. does his or her work wholly outside Great Britain, and
   1. the case involves discrimination on grounds of race or ethnic or national origins);
   2. the employer has a place of business at an establishment in Great Britain;
   3. the work is for the purposes of the business carried on at that establishment; and
   4. the worker is ordinarily resident in Great Britain—
      i. at the time he or she applies for or is offered employment; or
      ii. at any time during the course of the employment.

Employment agency
A person or organisation (including employment businesses, as defined by the Employment Agencies Act 1973 and Regulations) who, for profit or not, provides services for the purpose of finding employment for job seekers or supplying employers with workers. Employment agencies have specific provisions under section 14 of the RRA.

Equal opportunities action plan
A practical and realistic plan, with an agreed timetable and targets, showing how an employer is planning to achieve the aims of an equal opportunities policy.

Equal opportunities policy in employment
A statement of an organisation's commitment to the principle of equality of opportunity in employment. The policy should include what the organisation intends to do to prevent unlawful discrimination and promote equality of opportunity between people from different racial groups in the field of employment.

Ethnic group
Defined by the House of Lords as a group that regards itself or is regarded by others as a distinct community by virtue of certain characteristics that will help to distinguish the group from the surrounding community. Two of these characteristics are essential:

1. a long shared history, of which the group is conscious as distinguishing it from other groups, and the memory of which it keeps alive; and
2. a cultural tradition of its own, including family and social customs and manners, often but not necessarily associated with religious observance.

Other relevant characteristics (one or more of which will commonly be found) are:

a. either a common geographical origin or descent from a small number of common ancestors;
b. a common language, not necessarily peculiar to the group;
c. a common literature peculiar to the group;
d. a common religion different from that of neighbouring groups or from the general community surrounding it; and
e. being a minority or being an oppressed or a dominant group within a larger community. Both a conquered people (say, the inhabitants of England shortly after the Norman conquest) and their conquerors might be ethnic groups.

Although the House of Lords emphasised the need to interpret the word 'ethnic' 'relatively widely, in a broad, cultural/historic sense', it also observed that 'the word "ethnic" still retains a racial flavour'. On this basis, tribunals and courts have proceeded to rule that the English, Scots and Welsh, among others, are not racial groups by virtue of distinct 'ethnic origins' (see also 'national origins' below and Example 1).

Formal investigation
An investigation by the CRE under sections 49–52 of the RRA. The investigation may be of a 'named person', who the CRE suspects might be discriminating unlawfully on racial grounds, or a general investigation to examine practice in an area of activity. The CRE can make recommendations and, in the case of a named investigation, issue a non-discrimination notice (see below) for five years.

Functions
The full range of a public authority's duties and powers.

General duty
The duty given to public authorities, under section 71(1) of the Race Relations Act 1976, to have due regard to the need to eliminate unlawful racial discrimination and to promote equality of opportunity and good relations between people from different racial groups.

Genuine occupational qualification (GOQ)
An employer may discriminate on grounds of colour or nationality only in respect of certain types of work, where being from a particular racial group is a GOQ for the job.

Genuine occupational requirement (GOR)
An employer may discriminate on grounds of race or ethnic or national origins only in situations where, because of the nature of the employment or the context in which it is carried out, being of a particular race or ethnic or national origin is a genuine and determining occupational requirement.

Grievance procedure
An arrangement or procedure for dealing with grievances about practice or conduct in the workplace, such as bullying or harassment or racial discrimination, or appeals against decisions on promotion or, in some cases, appraisal marks. From October 2004, under the Employment Act 2002, employees must invoke a statutory grievance procedure if they wish subsequently to use the grievance as the basis of certain applications to an employment tribunal. The new statutory procedure will not be implied in contracts of employment until further notification from the Department of Trade and Industry). The ACAS *Code of Practice on Disciplinary and Grievance Procedures* provides detailed guidance for employers.

Harassment
Unwanted behaviour that has the purpose or effect of violating a person's dignity or creates a degrading, humiliating, hostile, intimidating or offensive working environment. Harassment on grounds of race or ethnic or national origins is a specific unlawful act under the RRA. Harassment on other grounds may involve less favourable treatment and may be unlawful direct discrimination.

Indirect discrimination
Grounds of race or ethnic or national origins – the use of an apparently non-discriminatory 'provision, criterion or practice' which puts people from a particular race or ethnic or national origin at a particular disadvantage compared with others, unless it can be shown that the provision, criterion or practice is a proportionate means of achieving a legitimate end.

All racial grounds (but effectively grounds of colour or nationality) – the use of an apparently non-discriminatory requirement or condition which applies equally to everyone, but can only be met by a considerably smaller proportion of people from a particular racial group, is to the detriment of someone from that group, and cannot be objectively justified.

Large business
A business with over 250 employees.

Monitoring
A process that involves collecting, storing, analysing and evaluating information, to measure performance, progress or change. Monitoring racial equality involves collecting, storing, analysing and evaluating information about the racial groups to which people say they belong.

National origins
National origins are not limited to 'nationality' in the legal sense of citizenship of a nation state, which an individual acquires at birth or through naturalisation. The Scottish Court of Session defined 'national origins' as 'identifiable elements, both historically and geographically, which at least at some point in time reveals the existence of a nation' (see Example 1). National origins may include origins in a nation that no longer exists (Czechoslovakia, for example), or in a 'nation' that was never a nation state in the modern sense, such as 'the Basque nation' or 'the Iroquois nation'.

Nationality
An aspect of a person's identity (see 'citizenship' above), conveying rights and duties, and defined by a specific legal relationship between an individual and a state, through birth or naturalisation, which is recognised by that state. Article 2 of the European Convention on Nationality defines 'nationality' as 'the legal bond between a person and a state' which 'does not indicate the person's ethnic origin'.

Non-discrimination notice
A notice which the CRE may serve on an organisation in the course of a 'named person' formal investigation (see 'Formal investigation'), if it finds evidence of unlawful racial discrimination or harassment.

Performance assessment
Formal and informal staff appraisals that are likely to affect career development, pay and benefits.

Policies
The sets of principles or criteria that define the different ways in which an organisation carries out its role or functions and meets its duties. Policies also include formal and informal decisions made in the course of their implementation.

Positive action
Measures that employers may lawfully take under the RRA to meet special needs or to train or encourage people from a racial group that is under-represented in particular work. See also Appendix 1.

Procurement
The process by which a person enters into a contract with an external supplier to carry out work or provide goods or services. The term encompasses the full range of contracts including private finance initiative (PFI) projects and public private partnerships (PPP). It does not include the decision to 'buy' from an external supplier.

Proportionate means
Means that are appropriate and necessary to achieve a legitimate business or other objective, such as meeting health and safety requirements.

Practices
The customary ways in which intentions or policies are actually carried out. They include attitudes and behaviour that could amount to unlawful racial discrimination through unwitting prejudice, ignorance, thoughtlessness and racist stereotyping.

Probation
A trial period before a person's employment position is confirmed.

Public authority
For the purposes of this code, a body named, defined or described in schedule 1A to the Race Relations Act 1976 or, depending on the context, a body named, defined or described in one of the schedules to the Race Relations Act 1976 (Statutory Duties) Order 2001 or the Race Relations Act 1976 (General Statutory Duty) Order 2003. The term includes all central government departments and their executive agencies and non-departmental public bodies, all NHS institutions, the governing bodies of schools and of further and higher education institutions, the Scottish Executive and the Welsh Assembly Government.

Race
The Race Relations Act uses 'race' both to describe the catch-all class that receives protection under the Act, that is, 'racial group', and as one of five sub-classes that fall within it. The courts and employment tribunals have not so far been called on to define the term.

Race relations questionnaire
A procedure involving a questionnaire (better known as the RR65 form) which workers who believe they have been discriminated against unlawfully, or harassed, on racial grounds, can use to ask their employer questions, before deciding whether to bring a claim in an employment tribunal.

Race equality scheme
A timetabled plan setting out how a public authority intends to meet its statutory general duty to eliminate unlawful racial discrimination and promote equality of opportunity and good relations between different racial groups. The scheme should indicate the functions and policies that have been assessed as being relevant to meeting the duty, and the arrangements that have been made to assess, consult on and monitor present and proposed policies for any implications they might have for promoting racial equality.

Race Relations Act (RRA)
The Race Relations Act 1976 as amended by the Race Relations (Amendment) Act 2000 and the Race Relations Act 1976 (Amendment) Regulations 2003.

Racial grounds
Grounds of race, colour, nationality (including citizenship) or ethnic or national origins.

Racial group

- Racial groups are groups defined by racial grounds i e race, colour, nationality (including citizenship) or ethnic or national origins. All racial groups are protected from unlawful racial discrimination under the RRA. Romany Gypsies, Irish Travellers, Jews and Sikhs have been explicitly recognised by the courts as constituting racial groups for the purposes of the RRA.
- A person may fall into more than one racial group; for example, a 'Nigerian' may be defined by 'race', 'colour', 'ethnic or national origins' and 'nationality'. See also 'ethnic group' above.

- The courts have held that a person's actual racial group may be irrelevant to the way they are treated, and that their racial group may be defined by a discriminator's perception of, or (incorrect) assumptions about, their ethnic or national origins (see also Example 1).

Religious discrimination
The RRA does not apply to discrimination on grounds of religion or belief, unless a person who has been discriminated against on grounds of religion or belief has also been discriminated against on racial grounds. Religious discrimination in employment and training is unlawful under the Employment Equality (Religion or Belief) Regulations 2003.

Secondment
The temporary transfer, on loan, of an employee to another department or (host) organisation for a fixed period, to complete an agreed assignment for the benefit of all parties. The secondee remains an employee of the lending organisation, and a contract worker (see above) with the host organisation.

Segregation
Segregation on racial grounds is automatically regarded as treating the segregated person less favourably than others. It constitutes unlawful direct racial discrimination.

Small business
A business with 1–49 employees.

Specific duties
Duties placed on selected public authorities bound by the general duty (see above) under the Race Relations Act 1976 (Statutory Duties) Order 2001 or the Race Relations Act 1976 (Statutory Duties) Order 2003. In Scotland, additional public authorities are listed in the Race Relations Act 1976 (Statutory Duties)(Scotland) Order 2002 (SSI No 62) and the Race Relations Act 1976 (Statutory Duties)(Scotland) Amendment Order 2003 (SSI No 566). The current list of authorities is available on the Home Office and CRE websites. The duties include the production and publication of a 'race equality scheme' (see above), and the monitoring, by racial group, of specified aspects of employment.

Statutory code of practice
Practical guidance which has been approved by the secretary of state and laid before parliament. A statutory code of practice is admissible in evidence in a tribunal or court of law, and must be taken into account when it is relevant to any question arising in proceedings under the relevant legislation, in this case the RRA.

Targets
Numerical benchmarks for planning progress towards a goal. Racial equality targets measure progress towards eliminating under-representation of a particular racial group (or groups) in an organisation.

Training
A wide range of career development opportunities, which could include informal in-house training as well as more formal courses.

Validation
A process used to check the relationship between scores produced by a test or other assessment method and scores produced by other measures. In the case of psychometric tests, the other measures may be other tests of the same attribute, or the performance assessment measures used for the job in question.

Victimisation
Less favourable treatment of a person because they have brought legal proceedings under the Race Relations Act 1976, or are suspected of having done so; or because they have alleged that a person has committed an act which would amount to unlawful discrimination; or because they have given evidence or information in connection with proceedings brought under the RRA; or because they have otherwise done anything under the RRA in relation to any person, or because they have intended or intend to do any of these acts.

Worker
For the purposes of this code, the term 'worker' includes employees, contract workers (see above) and police constables.

[4755]

GUIDANCE ON MATTERS TO BE TAKEN INTO ACCOUNT IN DETERMINING QUESTIONS RELATING TO THE DEFINITION OF DISABILITY (2006)

NOTES

This Guidance was issued by the Secretary of State for Work and Pensions on 29 March 2006 under the Disability Discrimination Act 1995, s 3(8) and has effect from 1 May 2006 (see the Disability Discrimination (Guidance on the Definition of Disability) Appointed Day Order 2006, SI 2006/1005); it applies to proceedings arising from a complaint alleging that a person has, after 1 May 2006, committed an act which is unlawful discrimination for the purposes of the 1995 Act. It replaces the 1996 Guidance save that the 1996 Guidance continues to have effect after 30 April 2006 for the purposes of s 3(3) of the 1995 Act in relation to any proceedings arising from a complaint (whenever presented) alleging that a person has, before 1 May 2006, committed an act which is unlawful discrimination for the purposes of the 1995 Act (see the Disability Discrimination (Guidance on the Definition of Disability) Revocation Order 2006, SI 2006/1007).

For the legal status of the Code see s 3 of the 1995 Act (at **[902]**). Notes are as in the original.

STATUS AND PURPOSE OF THE GUIDANCE

This guidance is issued by the Secretary of State under section 3 of the Disability Discrimination Act 1995, as amended.[1] In this document, any reference to 'the Act' means the Disability Discrimination Act 1995 (as amended).

This guidance concerns the definition of disability in the Act. Section 3 of the Act enables the Secretary of State to issue guidance about matters to be taken into account in determining whether a person is a disabled person. The guidance gives examples.

This guidance does not impose any legal obligations in itself, nor is it an authoritative statement of the law. However, section 3(3) of the Act requires that an adjudicating body[2] which is determining for any purpose of the Act whether a person is a disabled person, must take into account any aspect of this guidance which appears to it to be relevant.

This guidance applies to England, Wales and Scotland. Similar, but separate, guidance applies to Northern Ireland.

[4756]

NOTES

1 Including by the Special Educational Needs and Disability Act 2001, the Disability Discrimination Act 1995 (Amendment) Regulations 2003, and the Disability Discrimination Act 2005.

2 Section 3(3A) defines an 'adjudicating body' as a court, tribunal, or any other person who, or body which, may decide a claim under Part 4 of the Act.

PART 1
INTRODUCTION

The Disability Discrimination Act 1995

1. The Act prohibits discrimination against disabled people in a range of circumstances, covering employment and occupation, education, transport, and the provision of goods, facilities, services, premises and the exercise of public functions. Only those people who are defined as disabled in accordance with section 1 of the Act, and the associated schedules and Regulations made thereunder, will be entitled to the protection that the Act provides.

Using the guidance

2. This guidance is primarily designed for adjudicating bodies which determine cases brought under the Act. The definition of who is a disabled person for the purposes of the Act is a legal definition and it is only adjudicating bodies which can determine whether a person meets that definition. However, the guidance is also likely to be of value to a range of people and organisations as an explanation of how the definition operates.

3. **In the vast majority of cases there is unlikely to be any doubt whether or not a person has or has had a disability, but this guidance should prove helpful in cases where the matter is not entirely clear**.

4. The definition of disability has a number of elements. The guidance covers each of these elements in turn. Each section contains an explanation of the relevant provisions of the

Act which supplement the basic definition. Guidance and examples are provided where relevant. Those using this guidance for the first time should read it all, as each part of the guidance builds upon the part(s) preceding it.

5. Throughout the guidance, descriptions of statutory provisions in the legislation are immediately preceded by bold underlined text and followed by a reference to the relevant provision of the Act or to Regulations made under the Act. References to sections of the Act are marked **'S'**; references to schedules are marked **'Sch'**; and references to paragraphs in schedules are marked **'Para'**.

Other references to 'disability'

6. The definition of disability set out in the Act and described in this guidance is the only definition relevant to determining whether someone is a disabled person for the purposes of the Act. References to 'disability' or to mental or physical impairments in the context of other legislation are not relevant to determining whether someone is a disabled person under this Act and should be disregarded.

7. There is a range of services, concessions, schemes and financial benefits for which disabled people may qualify. These include, for example: local authority services for disabled people; the Blue Badge parking scheme; tax concessions for people who are blind; and disability-related social security benefits. However, each of these has its own individual eligibility criteria and qualification for any one of them does not automatically confer entitlement to protection under the Act, nor does entitlement to the protection of the Act confer eligibility for benefits, or concessions. Similarly, a child who has been identified as having special educational needs is not necessarily disabled for the purposes of the Act.

8. **In order to be protected by the Act, a person must meet the Act's definition of disability as explained below**.

[4757]

PART 2
GUIDANCE ON MATTERS TO BE TAKEN INTO ACCOUNT IN DETERMINING QUESTIONS RELATING TO THE DEFINITION OF DISABILITY

Section A: General

Main elements of the definition of disability

A1. **The Act defines** a disabled person as a person with 'a physical or mental impairment which has a substantial and long-term adverse effect on his ability to carry out normal day-to-day activities' (**S 1**).

A2. This means that, in general:

- the person must have an impairment that is either physical or mental (**see paragraphs A3 to A8 below**);
- the impairment must have adverse effects which are substantial (**see Section B**);
- the substantial adverse effects must be long-term (**see Section C**); and
- the long-term substantial adverse effects must be effects on normal day-to-day activities (**see Section D**).

This definition is subject to the provisions in **Schedule 1** (**Sch 1**) and **Schedule 2** (**Sch 2**).

Meaning of 'impairment'

A3. The definition requires that the effects which a person may experience must arise from a physical or mental impairment. The term mental or physical impairment should be given its ordinary meaning. In many cases, there will be no dispute whether a person has an impairment. Any disagreement is more likely to be about whether the effects of the impairment are sufficient to fall within the definition. Even so, it may sometimes be necessary to decide whether a person has an impairment so as to be able to deal with the issues about its effects.

A4. Whether a person is disabled for the purposes of the Act is generally determined by reference to the **effect** that an impairment has on that person's ability to carry out normal day-to-day activities. It is not possible to provide an exhaustive list of conditions that qualify as impairments for the purposes of the Act. Any attempt to do so would inevitably become out of date as medical knowledge advanced.

A5. It is important to remember that not all impairments are readily identifiable. While some impairments, particularly visible ones, are easy to identify, there are many which are not so immediately obvious.

A6. A disability can arise from a wide range of impairments which can be:

- sensory impairments, such as those affecting sight or hearing;
- impairments with fluctuating or recurring effects such as rheumatoid arthritis, myalgic encephalitis (ME)/chronic fatigue syndrome (CFS), fibromyalgia, depression and epilepsy;
- progressive, such as motor neurone disease, muscular dystrophy, forms of dementia and lupus (SLE);
- organ specific, including respiratory conditions, such as asthma, and cardiovascular diseases, including thrombosis, stroke and heart disease;
- developmental, such as autistic spectrum disorders (ASD), dyslexia and dyspraxia;
- learning difficulties;
- mental health conditions and mental illnesses, such as depression, schizophrenia, eating disorders, bipolar affective disorders, obsessive compulsive disorders, as well as personality disorders and some self-harming behaviour;
- produced by injury to the body or brain.

A7. It may not always be possible, nor is it necessary, to categorise a condition as either a physical or a mental impairment. The underlying cause of the impairment may be hard to establish. There may be adverse effects which are both physical and mental in nature. Furthermore, effects of a mainly physical nature may stem from an underlying mental impairment, and vice versa.

A8. It is not necessary to consider how an impairment is caused, even if the cause is a consequence of a condition which is excluded. For example, liver disease as a result of alcohol dependency would count as an impairment, although alcoholism itself is expressly excluded from the scope of the definition of disability in the Act. What it is important to consider is the effect of an impairment not its cause – provided that it is not an excluded condition. **See also paragraph A12 below (exclusions from the definition)**.

A woman has obesity which gives rise to impairments such as mobility restrictions and breathing difficulties. She is unable to walk more than 50 yards without having to rest.

A man has borderline moderate learning difficulties which have an adverse impact on his short-term memory and his levels of literacy and numeracy. For example, he cannot write any original material, as opposed to slowly copying existing text, and he cannot write his address from memory.

It is the effects of these impairments that need to be considered, rather than the underlying conditions themselves.

Mental illness

A9. The Act previously required that where an impairment arose from, or consisted of, a mental illness, that illness had to be clinically well-recognised in order for it to be regarded as a mental impairment for the purposes of the Act. The Disability Discrimination Act 2005 amended the original Act to remove this requirement with effect from 5 December 2005. However, anyone who has an impairment **including one resulting from a mental illness** will still need to meet the requirements of the definition as set out in paragraph A1, in order to demonstrate that they have a disability under the Act.

Persons deemed to be disabled

A10. The following people are deemed to meet the definition of disability without having to show that they have an impairment that has (or is likely to have) a substantial, adverse, long-term effect on the ability to carry out normal day-to-day activities:

- A person who has cancer, HIV infection or multiple sclerosis (MS) (**Sch 1, Para 6A**). **See also paragraphs B16 to B19 below (progressive conditions)**.
- A person who is certified as blind or partially sighted by a consultant ophthalmologist, or is registered as such with a local authority.[3]

A11. Anyone who has an impairment which is not listed in A10 above will need to meet the requirements of the definition as set out in paragraph A1 in order to demonstrate that they have a disability under the Act.

PART 4

Exclusions from the definition

A12. Certain conditions are not to be regarded as impairments for the purposes of the Act. These are:

- addiction to, or dependency on, alcohol, nicotine, or any other substance (other than in consequence of the substance being medically prescribed);
- the condition known as seasonal allergic rhinitis (e g hayfever), except where it aggravates the effect of another condition;
- tendency to set fires;
- tendency to steal;
- tendency to physical or sexual abuse of other persons;
- exhibitionism;
- voyeurism.

A13. Also, disfigurements which consist of a tattoo (which has not been removed), non-medical body piercing, or something attached through such piercing, are to be treated as not having a substantial adverse effect on the person's ability to carry-out normal day-to-day activities.[4]

A14. A person with an excluded condition may nevertheless be protected as a disabled person if he or she has an accompanying impairment which meets the requirements of the definition. For example, a person who is addicted to a substance such as alcohol may also have depression, or a physical impairment such as liver damage, arising from the alcohol addiction. While this person would not meet the definition simply on the basis of having an addiction, he or she may still meet the definition as a result of the effects of the depression or the liver damage.

People who have had a disability in the past

A15. **The Act says** that Part 1 of the Act (disability), Part 2 (the employment field and members of locally-electable authorities), Part 3 (discrimination in other areas),[5] Part 4 (education), and Part 5A (public authorities)[6] also apply in relation to a person who previously has had a disability as defined in paragraphs A1 and A2 above. For this purpose, those Parts of the Act are subject to the provisions in Schedule 2 to the Act (**S 2, Sch 2**). This means that someone who is no longer disabled, but who met the requirements of the definition in the past, will still be covered by those Parts of the Act listed above. For example, a woman who, four years ago, experienced a mental illness that had a substantial and long-term adverse effect on her ability to carry out normal day-to-day activities, but who has experienced no recurrence of the condition, is still entitled to the protection afforded by the Act, as a person with a past disability.

A16. A particular instance of someone who is treated under the Act as having had a disability in the past is someone whose name was on the register of disabled persons under provisions in the Disabled Persons (Employment) Act 1944.

A17. The introduction of the employment provisions in the Disability Discrimination Act 1995 coincided with the abolition of the Quota scheme which had operated under the Disabled Persons (Employment) Act 1944. Special provisions still apply, however, to any person who was registered under the Disabled Persons (Employment) Act 1944. **The Disability Discrimination Act 1995 says** that anyone who was registered as a disabled person under the Disabled Persons (Employment) Act 1944 and whose name appeared on the register both on 12 January 1995 and on 2 December 1996 (the date on which the employment provisions came into force) was to be treated as having a disability for the purposes of the Disability Discrimination Act 1995 during the period of three years starting on 2 December 1996. This applied regardless of whether the person otherwise met the definition of a 'disabled person' during that period. As the three-year transitional period has ended, those people who were treated by this provision as being disabled are now treated as having had a disability in the past (**Sch 1, Para 7**).

[4758]

NOTES

3 The Disability Discrimination (Blind and Partially Sighted Persons) Regulations 2003. Note: these may be subject to amendment in 2006.

4 The Disability Discrimination (Meaning of Disability) Regulations 1996.

5 Part 3 covers goods, facilities, and services; public authorities; private clubs; and premises.

6 Part 5A covers the *duties* of a public authority, as opposed to the *functions* of a public authority, which are dealt with in Part 3.

Section B: Substantial

Meaning of 'substantial adverse effect'

B1. The requirement that an adverse effect on normal day-to-day activities should be a substantial one reflects the general understanding of disability as a limitation going beyond the normal differences in ability which may exist among people. A substantial effect is one that is greater than the effect which would be produced by the sort of physical or mental conditions experienced by many people which have only 'minor' or 'trivial' effects. This section looks in more detail at what 'substantial' means. It should be read in conjunction with Section D which considers what is meant by 'normal day-to-day activities'.

The time taken to carry out an activity

B2. The time taken by a person with an impairment to carry out a normal day-to-day activity should be considered when assessing whether the effect of that impairment is substantial. It should be compared with the time it might take a person who did not have the impairment to complete an activity.

A ten-year old child has cerebral palsy. The effects include muscle stiffness, poor balance and uncoordinated movements. The child is still able to do most things for himself, but he gets tired very easily and it is harder for him to accomplish tasks like eating and drinking, washing, and getting dressed. Although he has the ability to carry out everyday activities such as these, everything takes longer compared to a child of a similar age who does not have cerebral palsy. This amounts to a substantial adverse effect.

The way in which an activity is carried out

B3. Another factor to be considered when assessing whether the effect of an impairment is substantial is the way in which a person with that impairment carries out a normal day-to-day activity. The comparison should be with the way that the person might be expected to carry out the activity if he or she did not have the impairment.

A person who has obsessive compulsive disorder follows a complicated ritual of hand washing. When preparing a simple meal, he washes his hands carefully after handling each ingredient and each utensil. A person without the disorder might wash his or her hands at appropriate points in preparing the meal, for example after handling raw meat, but would not normally do this after every stage in the process of preparation.

Cumulative effects of an impairment

B4. An impairment might not have a substantial adverse effect on a person's ability to undertake a particular day-to-day activity in isolation, but its effects on more than one activity, taken together, could result in an overall substantial adverse effect.

B5. For example, a person whose impairment causes breathing difficulties may, as a result, experience minor effects on the ability to carry out a number of activities such as getting washed and dressed, preparing a meal, or travelling on public transport. But taken together, the cumulative result would amount to a substantial adverse effect on his or her ability to carry out these normal day-to-day activities.

A man with depression experiences a range of symptoms that include a loss of energy and motivation that makes even the simplest of tasks or decisions seem quite difficult. For example, he finds it difficult to get up in the morning, get washed and dressed, and prepare breakfast. He is forgetful and cannot plan ahead. As a result he has often run out of food before he thinks of going shopping again. Household tasks are frequently left undone, or take much longer to complete than normal. Together, the effects amount to a substantial adverse effect.

B6. A person may have more than one impairment, any one of which alone would not have a substantial effect. In such a case, account should be taken of whether the impairments together have a substantial effect overall on the person's ability to carry out normal day-to-day activities. For example, a minor impairment which affects physical co-ordination and an irreversible but minor injury to a leg which affects mobility, when taken together, might have a substantial effect on the person's ability to carry out certain normal day-to-day activities.

Effects of behaviour

B7. Account should be taken of how far a person can reasonably be expected to modify his or her behaviour to prevent or reduce the effects of an impairment on normal day-to-day activities. If a person can reasonably be expected to behave in such a way that the impairment ceases to have a substantial adverse effect on his or her ability to carry out normal day-to-day activities the person would no longer meet the definition of disability. For example, when considering modification of behaviour, it would be reasonable to expect a person who has back pain to avoid extreme activities such as parachuting. It would not be reasonable to expect him or her to give up, or modify, more normal activities that might exacerbate the symptoms; such as moderate gardening, shopping, or using public transport.

B8. Account should also be taken of where a person avoids doing things which, for example, cause pain, fatigue or substantial social embarrassment; because of a loss of energy and motivation. It would not be reasonable to conclude that a person who employed an avoidance strategy was not a disabled person. In determining a question as to whether a person meets the definition of disability it is important to consider the things that a person cannot do, or can only do with difficulty, rather than focussing on those things that a person can do.

In order to manage her condition, a woman with a persistent stammer uses coping strategies, such as avoiding using the telephone, not giving verbal instructions at work, limiting social contact outside her immediate family, and avoiding challenging situations with service providers. As a consequence, it may not be readily obvious that she has an impairment which adversely affects her ability to carry out normal day-to-day activities.
In determining whether she meets the definition of disability, consideration should be given to the extent to which it is reasonable to expect her to place such restrictions on her working and domestic life.

B9. In some cases, people have coping strategies which cease to work in certain circumstances (for example, where someone who has dyslexia is placed under stress). If it is possible that a person's ability to manage the effects of an impairment will break down so that effects will sometimes still occur, this possibility must be taken into account when assessing the effects of the impairment.

See also paragraphs B11 to B15 below (effects of treatment), paragraph C8 (likelihood of recurrence) and D11 (indirect effects).

Effects of environment

B10. Environmental conditions may exacerbate the effect of an impairment. Factors such as temperature, humidity, lighting, the time of day or night, how tired the person is, or how much stress he or she is under, may have an impact on the effects. When assessing whether adverse effects are substantial, the extent to which such environmental factors are likely to exacerbate the effects should, therefore, also be considered. **See also paragraphs C4 to C7 below, meaning of 'long-term' (recurring or fluctuating effects).**

A woman has had rheumatoid arthritis for the last three years and has difficulty carrying out day-to-day activities such as walking, undertaking household tasks, and getting washed and dressed. The effects are particularly bad during autumn and winter months when the weather is cold and damp. Symptoms are mild during the summer months. The effect on ability to carry out normal day-to-day activities fluctuates according to the weather conditions, but because the effect of the impairment is likely to recur, this person meets the definition of disability requirement on the meaning of 'long-term'(Sch 1, Para 2(2)).

Effects of treatment

B11. **The Act provides** that, where an impairment is subject to treatment or correction, the impairment is to be treated as having the effect that it would have without the measures in question (**Sch 1, Para 6(1)**). **The Act states** that the treatment or correction measures which are to be disregarded for these purposes include, in particular, medical treatment and the use of a prosthesis or other aid (**Sch 1, Para 6(2)**).

B12. This provision applies even if the measures result in the effects being completely under control or not at all apparent. Where treatment is continuing it may be having the effect of masking or ameliorating a disability so that it does not have a substantial adverse effect. If the final outcome of such treatment cannot be determined or if it is known that removal of the medical treatment would result in either a relapse or a worsened condition, it would be reasonable to disregard the medical treatment in accordance with paragraph 6 of Schedule 1.

B13. For example, if a person with a hearing impairment wears a hearing aid the question as to whether his or her impairment has a substantial adverse effect is to be decided by reference to what the hearing level would be without the hearing aid. Similarly, in the case of someone with diabetes which is being controlled by medication or diet, or the case of a person with depression which is being treated by counselling, whether or not the effect is substantial should be decided by reference to what the effects of the condition would be if he or she were not taking that medication or following the required diet, or were not receiving counselling (the so-called "deduced effects").

B14. **The Act states** that this provision does not apply to sight impairments to the extent that they are capable of correction by spectacles or contact lenses. In other words, the only effects on the ability to carry out normal day-to-day activities which are to be considered are those which remain when spectacles or contact lenses are used (or would remain if they were used). This does not include the use of devices to correct sight which are not spectacles or contact lenses (**Sch 1, Para 6(3)**).

B15. Account should be taken of where the effect of the continuing medical treatment is to create a permanent improvement rather than a temporary improvement. For example, a person who develops pneumonia may be admitted to hospital for treatment including a course of antibiotics. This cures the impairment and no effects remain. **See also paragraph C9 below, regarding medical or other treatment that permanently reduces or removes the effects of an impairment**.

Progressive conditions

B16. A progressive condition is one which is likely to change and develop over time. **The Act gives** examples of progressive conditions, including cancer, multiple sclerosis, and HIV infection. It should be noted that, following the amendments made by the Disability Discrimination Act 2005 (**see paragraph A10**), persons with cancer, multiple sclerosis or HIV infection are all now deemed to be disabled persons, for the purposes of the Act, from the point at which they have that condition: thus effectively from diagnosis.

B17. Progressive conditions are subject to the special provisions set out in **Sch 1, Para 8**. These provisions provide that a person with a progressive condition is to be regarded as having an impairment which has a substantial adverse effect on his or her ability to carry out normal day-to-day activities *before* it does so. A person who has a progressive condition, will be treated as having an impairment which has a **substantial** adverse effect from the moment any impairment resulting from that condition first has **some** adverse effect on his or her ability to carry out normal day-to-day activities, provided that in the future the adverse effect is **more likely than not** to become substantial. Medical prognosis of the likely impact of the condition will be the normal route to establishing protection under this provision. The effect need not be continuous and need not be substantial. (**See also paragraphs C4 to C7 on recurring or fluctuating effects**). The person will still need to show that the impairment meets the requirements of **Sch 1, Para 2** (meaning of long-term).

B18. Further examples of progressive conditions to which the special provisions apply include systemic lupus erythematosis (SLE), various types of dementia, rheumatoid arthritis, and motor neurone disease. This list, however, is not exhaustive.

A young boy aged 8 has been experiencing muscle cramps and some weakness. The effects are quite minor at present, but he has been diagnosed as having muscular dystrophy. Eventually it is expected that the resulting muscle weakness will cause substantial adverse effects on his ability to walk, run and climb stairs. Although there is no substantial adverse effect at present, muscular dystrophy is a progressive condition, and this child will still be entitled to the protection of the Act under the special provisions in Sch 1, Para 8 of the Act if it can be shown that the effects are likely to become substantial.

A woman has been diagnosed with lupus (SLE) following complaints to her GP that she is experiencing mild aches and pains in her joints. She has also been feeling generally unwell, with some flu-like symptoms. The initial symptoms do not have a substantial adverse effect on her ability to carry out normal day-to-day activities. However, SLE is a progressive condition, with fluctuating effects. She has been advised that the condition may come and go over many years, and in the future the effects may become substantial, including severe joint pain, inflammation, stiffness, and skin rashes. Providing it can be shown that the effects are likely to become substantial, she will be covered by the special provisions in Sch 1, Para 8. She will, however, still need to meet the 'long-term' condition of the definition in order to be protected by the Act.

B19. A person with a progressive condition which has no effect on day-to-day activities because it is successfully treated (for example by surgery) may still be covered by **Sch 1, Para 8** where the effects of that treatment give rise to a further impairment which does have an effect on normal day-to-day activities. For example, treatment for the condition may result in an impairment which has some effect on normal day-to-day activities and the effects of that impairment are likely to become substantial in the future.

A man has an operation to remove the colon because of progressing and uncontrollable ulcerative colitis. This is a treatment that is fairly routine for severe colitis. The operation results in his no longer experiencing adverse effects from the colitis. He requires a colostomy, however, which means that his bowel actions can only be controlled by a sanitary appliance. The effect of the incontinence should be taken into account as an effect arising from the original impairment.

Whether the effects of any treatment can qualify for the purposes of the Sch 1, Para 8 will depend on the circumstances of the individual case.

Severe disfigurements

B20. The Act provides that where an impairment consists of a severe disfigurement, it is to be treated as having a substantial adverse effect on the person's ability to carry out normal day-to-day activities. There is no need to demonstrate such an effect (**Sch 1, Para 3**). Regulations provide that a disfigurement which consists of a tattoo (which has not been removed) is not to be considered as a severe disfigurement. Also excluded is a piercing of the body for decorative purposes including anything attached through the piercing.[7]

B21. Examples of disfigurements include scars, birthmarks, limb or postural deformation (including restricted bodily development), or diseases of the skin. Assessing severity will be mainly a matter of the degree of the disfigurement. However, it may be necessary to take account of where the disfigurement in question is (e g on the back as opposed to the face).

[4759]

NOTES

[7] The Disability Discrimination (Meaning of Disability) Regulations 1996.

Section C: Long term

Meaning of 'long-term effects'

C1. The Act states that, for the purpose of deciding whether a person is disabled, a long-term effect of an impairment is one:

- which has lasted at least 12 months; or

- where the total period for which it lasts, from the time of the first onset, is likely to be at least 12 months; or
- which is likely to last for the rest of the life of the person affected (**Sch 1, Para 2**).

For the purpose of deciding whether a person has had a disability in the past, a long-term effect of an impairment is one which has lasted at least 12 months (**Sch 2, Para 5**).

Meaning of 'likely'

C2. It is likely that an event will happen if it is more probable than not that it will happen.

C3. In assessing the likelihood of an effect lasting for 12 months, account should be taken of the total period for which the effect exists. This includes any time before the point at which the alleged incident of discriminatory behaviour which is being considered by the adjudicating body occurred. Account should also be taken of both the typical length of such an effect on an individual, and any relevant factors specific to this individual (for example, general state of health or age).

Recurring or fluctuating effects

C4. **The Act states** that, if an impairment has had a substantial adverse effect on a person's ability to carry out normal day-to-day activities but that effect ceases, the substantial effect is treated as continuing if it is likely to recur. In other words, it is more likely than not that the effect will recur. (In deciding whether a person has had a disability in the past, the question is whether a substantial adverse effect has in fact recurred.) Conditions with effects which recur only sporadically or for short periods can still qualify as impairments for the purposes of the Act, in respect of the meaning of 'long-term'(**Sch 1, Para 2(2); Sch 2, Para 5**).

C5. For example, a person with rheumatoid arthritis may experience substantial adverse effects for a few weeks after the first occurrence and then have a period of remission. **See also example at B10 above**. If the substantial adverse effects are likely to recur, they are to be treated as if they were continuing. If the effects are likely to recur beyond 12 months after the first occurrence, they are to be treated as long-term. Other impairments with effects which can recur, or where effects can be sporadic, include Menière's disease and epilepsy as well as mental health conditions such as schizophrenia, bipolar affective disorder, and certain types of depression, though this is not an exhaustive list. It should be noted that some impairments with recurring or fluctuating effects may be less obvious in their impact on the individual concerned than is the case with other impairments where the effects are more constant.

A young man has bipolar affective disorder, a recurring form of depression. The first episode occurred in months one and two of a 13-month period. The second episode took place in month 13. This man will satisfy the requirements of the definition in respect of the meaning of long-term, because the adverse effects have recurred beyond 12 months after the first occurrence and are therefore treated as having continued for the whole period (in this case, a period of 13 months).
A woman has two discrete episodes of depression within a ten-month period. In month one she loses her job and has a period of depression lasting six weeks. In month nine she suffers a bereavement and has a further episode of depression lasting eight weeks. Even though she has experienced two episodes of depression she will not be covered by the Act. This is because, as at this stage, the effects of his impairment have not yet lasted more than 12 months after the first occurrence, and there is no evidence that these episodes are part of an underlying condition of depression which is likely to recur beyond the 12-month period.

C6. It is not necessary for the effect to be the same throughout the period which is being considered in relation to determining whether the "long-term" element of the definition is met. A person may still satisfy the long-term element of the definition even if the effect is not the same throughout the period. It may change: for example activities which are initially very difficult may become possible to a much greater extent. The effect might even disappear temporarily. Or other effects on the ability to carry out normal day-to-day activities may develop and the initial effect may disappear altogether.

C7. Regulations specifically exclude seasonal allergic rhinitis (eg hayfever) except where it aggravates the effects of an existing condition.[8] For example, this may occur in some cases of asthma. **See also paragraph A12 (exclusions)**.

Likelihood of recurrence

C8. Likelihood of recurrence should be considered taking all the circumstances of the case into account. This should include what the person could reasonably be expected to do to prevent the recurrence. For example, the person might reasonably be expected to take action which prevents the impairment from having such effects (e g avoiding substances to which he or she is allergic). This may be unreasonably difficult with some substances. In addition, it is possible that the way in which a person can control or cope with the effects of an impairment may not always be successful: for example, because a routine is not followed or the person is in an unfamiliar environment. If there is an increased likelihood that the control will break down, it will be more likely that there will be a recurrence. That possibility should be taken into account when assessing the likelihood of a recurrence. **See also paragraphs B7 to B9 above (effects of behaviour, including coping strategies and medical advice), paragraph B10 (environmental effects); and paragraphs B11 to B15 (effect of treatment).**

A woman experiences stress-related anxiety. She is able to manage her workload and meet normal deadlines provided that she avoids too much responsibility. She achieves this through careful monitoring of her workload and regular supervision by her manager. She can cope with the symptoms of her condition most of the time, provided that she is not exposed to stressful situations.
The possibility that she might be exposed to stressful situations should be taken into account when deciding whether there is a likelihood of recurrence.

C9. If medical or other treatment is likely to permanently cure a condition and therefore remove the impairment, so that recurrence of its effects would then be unlikely even if there were no further treatment, this should be taken into consideration when looking at the likelihood of recurrence of those effects. However, if the treatment simply delays or prevents a recurrence, and a recurrence would be likely if the treatment stopped, as is the case with most medication, then the treatment is to be ignored and the effect is to be regarded as likely to recur.

Assessing whether a past disability was long-term

C10. **The Act provides** that a person who has had a disability within the definition is protected from some forms of discrimination even if he or she has since recovered or the effects have become less than substantial. In deciding whether a past condition was a disability, its effects count as long-term if they lasted 12 months or more after the first occurrence, or if a recurrence happened or continued until more than 12 months after the first occurrence (**S 2, Sch 2, Para 5**). **For the forms of discrimination covered by this provision see paragraph A15 above. For examples of how this provision works, see above at C5.**

NOTES

[8] The Disability Discrimination (Meaning of Disability) Regulations 1996.

Section D : Normal day-to-day activities

List of 'capacities'

D1. **The Act states** that an impairment is to be taken to affect the ability of a person to carry out normal day-to-day activities **only** if it affects that person in respect of one or more of the following (**Sch 1, Para 4**):

- mobility;
- manual dexterity;
- physical co-ordination;
- continence;
- ability to lift, carry or otherwise move everyday objects;
- speech, hearing or eyesight;
- memory or ability to concentrate, learn or understand; or
- perception of the risk of physical danger.

For the purposes of this guidance, the above list will be referred to as a list of 'capacities'.

D2. The list of capacities should be looked at in a broad sense, and applied equally to both physical and mental impairments. For example, it is often assumed that for people with a mental impairment the relevant capacity will be 'memory or ability to concentrate, learn or understand'. The capacities of mobility and physical co-ordination, for example, are often seen as relevant only where there is a physical impairment. However, in many instances this will not be the case. A person with a mental impairment may also have difficulties carrying out activities that involve mobility or other 'physical' skills, and people with a physical impairment may also have effects that involve mental processes such as the ability to concentrate (for example, as a result of pain or fatigue).

D3. **An impairment will only be treated as affecting a normal day-to-day activity if it involves at least one of the capacities set out at D1 above**. The substantial effect is determined by looking at the effect on the particular day-to-day activity, not the relevant capacity. So, for example, an inability to go shopping because of restricted mobility is in itself a substantial effect on a normal day-to-day activity: it is not necessary to show that all or any other aspects of the capacity of mobility are substantially affected.

Meaning of 'normal day-to-day activities'

D4. **It should be noted that the list of capacities set out in D1 above is not a list of day-to-day activities**. It is not possible to provide an exhaustive list of day-to-day activities, although guidance on this matter is given here. In general, day-to-day activities are things people do on a regular or daily basis, and examples include shopping, reading and writing, having a conversation or using the telephone, watching television, getting washed and dressed, preparing and eating food, carrying out household tasks, walking and travelling by various forms of transport, and taking part in social activities.

D5. The term 'normal day-to-day activities' is not intended to include activities which are normal only for a particular person, or a small group of people. In deciding whether an activity is a normal day-to-day activity, account should be taken of how far it is normal for a large number of people, and carried out by people on a daily or frequent and fairly regular basis. In this context, 'normal' should be given its ordinary, everyday meaning.

D6. A normal day-to-day activity is not necessarily one that is carried out by a majority of people. For example, it is possible that some activities might be carried out only, or more predominantly, by people of a particular gender, such as applying make-up or using hair curling equipment, and cannot therefore be said to be normal for *most* people. They would nevertheless be considered to be normal day-to-day activities.

Work-related and other specialised activities

D7. Normal day-to-day activities do not include work of any particular form because no particular form of work is 'normal' for most people. In any individual case, the activities carried out might be highly specialised. For example, carrying out delicate work with specialised tools may be a normal working activity for a watch repairer, whereas it would not be normal for a person who is employed as semi-skilled worker. The Act only covers effects which go beyond the normal differences in skill or ability.

D8. The same is true of other specialised activities such as playing a musical instrument to a high standard of achievement; taking part in a particular game or hobby where very specific skills or level of ability are required; or playing a particular sport to a high level of ability, such as would be required for a professional footballer or athlete.

D9. However, many types of work or specialised hobby, sport or pastime may still involve normal day-to-day activities. For example; sitting down, standing up, walking, running, verbal interaction, writing, making a cup of tea, using everyday objects such as a keyboard, and lifting, moving or carrying everyday objects such as chairs.

> **A woman plays the piano to a high standard, and often takes part in public performances. She has developed carpal tunnel syndrome in her wrists, an impairment that adversely affects manual dexterity. She can continue to play the piano, but not to such a high standard, and she has to take frequent breaks to rest her arms. This would not of itself be an adverse effect on a normal day-to-day activity. However, as a result of her impairment she also finds it difficult to operate a computer keyboard and cannot use her PC to send emails or write letters. This is an adverse effect on a normal day-to-day activity.**

A man works in a warehouse, loading and unloading heavy stock. He develops heart problems and no longer has the ability to lift or move heavy items of stock at work. Lifting and moving such unusually heavy types of item is not a normal day-to-day activity. However, he is also unable to lift, carry or move moderately heavy everyday objects such as chairs, either at work or around the home. This is an adverse effect on a normal day-to-day activity.

D10. The effects experienced by a person as a result of environmental conditions, either in the workplace or in another location where a specialised activity is being carried out, should not be discounted simply because there may be a work-related or other specialised activity involved. It is important to consider whether there may also be an adverse effect on the ability to carry out a normal day-to-day activity.

A middle-aged man works in a factory where chemical fumes cause him to have breathing difficulties, and this has made it impossible for him to continue to do his job. He has been diagnosed with occupational asthma, which has a substantial adverse effect while he is at work. As a result he is no longer able to work where he would continue to be exposed to the fumes. Even in a non-work situation he finds any general exertion difficult and this adversely affects activities which involve the capacities of mobility and ability to lift and carry everyday objects. The effects fluctuate, and when he is not at work his asthma attacks are very infrequent. Although the substantial effect is only apparent while at work, the man is able to demonstrate that his impairment has an adverse effect on normal day-to-day activities and at least one capacity in the list in D1.

Indirect effects

D11. An impairment may not directly **prevent** someone from carrying out one or more normal day-to-day activities, but it may still have a substantial adverse long-term effect on how he or she carries out those activities. For example:

- pain or fatigue: where an impairment causes pain or fatigue in performing normal day-to-day activities the person may have the capacity to do something but suffer pain in doing so; or the impairment might make the activity more than usually fatiguing so that the person might not be able to repeat the task over a sustained period of time. **See also paragraphs B7 and B9 above (effects of behaviour)**;

A man has had chronic fatigue syndrome for several years and although he has the physical capability to walk and to stand, he finds these very difficult to sustain for any length of time because of the overwhelming fatigue he experiences. As a consequence, he is restricted in his ability to take part in normal day-to-day activities such as travelling, so he avoids going out socially, and works from home several days a week. Therefore there is a substantial adverse effect on normal day-to-day activities.

- medical advice: where a person has been advised by a medical practitioner or other health professional, as part of a treatment plan, to change, limit or refrain from a normal day-to-day activity on account of an impairment or only do it in a certain way or under certain conditions. **See also paragraphs B11 to B15 above (effects of treatment)**.

A woman who works as a teacher develops sciatic pain which is attributed to a prolapsed inter-vertebral disc. Despite physiotherapy and traction her pain became worse. As part of her treatment plan her doctor prescribes daily pain relief medication and advises her to avoid repetitive bending or lifting, and to avoid carrying heavy items. This prevents her from carrying out a range of normal day-to-day activities such as shopping.

Children with a disability

D12. The effects of impairments may not be apparent in babies and young children because they are too young to have developed the ability to act in a way which falls within the capacities listed in D1. Regulations provide that where an impairment to a child under six years old does not have an effect in respect of any of the capacities, it is to be treated as having a substantial and long-term adverse effect on the ability of that child to carry out normal day-to-day activities where it would normally have a substantial and long-term adverse effect on the ability of a person aged six years or over to carry out normal day-to-day activities.[9]

D13. Children aged six and older are subject to the normal requirements of the definition.

A six-year-old child has been diagnosed as having autism. He has difficulty communicating through speech and in recognising when someone is happy or sad. Without a parent or carer with him he will often try to run out of the front door and on to the road to look at the wheels of parked or sometimes passing cars, and he has no sense of danger at all. When going somewhere new or taking a different route he can become very anxious. This amounts to a substantial adverse effect on his ability to carry out normal day-to-day activities, even for such a young child. The capacities of mobility, speech, and perception of risk are all affected.

D14. Since September 2002, provisions in the Special Educational Needs and Disability Act 2001 have extended Part 4 of the Disability Discrimination Act 1995 to cover every aspect of education.[10] These provisions provide protection for disabled pupils and students by preventing discrimination against them at school or in post-16 education for a reason related to their disability. A pupil or student must satisfy the definition of disability as described in this guidance in order to be protected by Part 4 of the Act. The duties for schools in the Act are designed to dovetail with duties under the Special Educational Needs (SEN) framework which are based on a separate definition of special educational needs. Further information on these duties can be found in the SEN Code of Practice[11] and the Code of Practice for Schools.[12]

Examples of children in an educational setting where their impairment has a substantial and long-term adverse effect on ability to carry out normal day-to-day activities:

A 10-year-old girl has learning difficulties. She has a short attention span and has difficulties remembering facts from one day to the next. She can read only a few familiar words and has some early mathematical skills. To record her work in class she needs to use a tape recorder, pictures and symbols.

A 14-year-old boy has been diagnosed as having attention deficit hyperactivity disorder (ADHD). He often forgets his books, worksheets or homework. In class he finds it difficult to concentrate and skips from task to task forgetting instructions. He often fidgets and makes inappropriate remarks in class or in the playground. Sometimes there can be outbursts of temper.

In both of these examples reading, writing and participating in activities in class and/or in the playground, which are all normal day-to-day activities, are adversely affected to a substantial degree. The capacity affected is 'memory, or ability to concentrate, learn or understand.'

List of capacities, with examples of normal day-to-day activities

D15. The following section looks at the **list of capacities**, and provides examples of normal day-to-day activities which might affect those capacities. The examples given are purely illustrative and should not in any way be considered as a prescriptive list of activities related to a specific capacity.

D16. Examples are given of circumstances where it **would be reasonable** to regard the effect as substantial. In addition, examples are given of circumstances where it would **not be reasonable** to regard the effect as substantial. In these examples, the effect described should be thought of as if it were the **only** effect of the impairment.

D17. The examples of what it would, and what it would not, be reasonable to regard as substantial adverse effects on normal day-to-day activities are indicators and not tests. They do not mean that if a person can do an activity listed then he or she does not experience any substantial adverse effects: the person may be affected in relation to other activities, and this instead may indicate a substantial effect. Or the person may be affected in a minor way in a number of different activities, and the cumulative effect could amount to a substantial adverse effect. **See also paragraphs B4 to B6 (cumulative effects).**

D18. The examples describe the effect which would occur when the various factors described in Sections A, B and C above have been allowed for, including for example the effects of a person making such modifications of behaviour as might reasonably be expected, or of disregarding the impact of medical or other treatment.

D19. Some of the examples show how an adverse effect may arise from either a physical or a mental impairment. Where illustrations of both types of impairment have not been given, this does not mean that only one type of impairment could result in that particular effect. **Regard should be given to the fact that physical impairments can result in mental effects, and mental impairments can have physical manifestations.**

Mobility

D20. This covers moving or changing position in a wide sense. Account should be taken of the extent to which, because of either a physical or a mental impairment, a person finds difficult such day-to-day activities as: getting around unaided or using a normal means of transport; leaving home with or without assistance; walking a short distance; climbing stairs; travelling in a car or completing a journey on public transport; sitting, standing, bending, or reaching; or getting around in an unfamiliar place.

Examples

It would be reasonable to regard as having a substantial adverse effect:

- difficulty in travelling a short journey as a passenger in a vehicle, because, for example, it would be painful getting in and out of a car, or sitting in a car for even a short time; the person has a frequent need for a lavatory; or perhaps, as a result of a mental impairment, the person would become distressed while in the car;
- total inability to walk, or difficulty walking other than at a slow pace or with unsteady or jerky movements;
- difficulty in going up or down steps, stairs or gradients; for example, because movements are painful, uncomfortable or restricted in some way;
- difficulty using one or more forms of public transport; for example, as a result of physical restrictions, pain or fatigue, or as a result of a mental impairment;
- difficulty going out of doors unaccompanied; for example, because the person has a phobia;

A young man with severe anxiety and symptoms of agoraphobia is unable to go out because he fears being outside in open spaces and gets panic attacks in stressful situations such as shopping or travelling on a route that is less than familiar.

A woman with Downs Syndrome has learning difficulties, and finds difficulty in travelling unaccompanied because she often gets lost in areas that are slightly unfamiliar.

A man with Menière's disease experiences dizziness and nausea. This restricts his ability to move around within his home without some form of support.

In these cases, the restricted ability to travel and move around affects the capacity of mobility and has a substantial adverse effect on the ability to carry out normal day-to-day activities.

It would not be reasonable to regard as having a substantial adverse effect:

- experiencing some discomfort as a result of travelling in a car for a journey lasting more than two hours;
- experiencing some tiredness or minor discomfort as a result of walking unaided for a distance of about 1.5 kilometres or one mile.

Manual dexterity

D21. This covers the ability to use hands and fingers with precision. Account should be taken of the extent to which a person can manipulate the fingers on each hand or co-ordinate the use of both hands together to do a task. This includes the ability to carry out normal day-to-day activities that involve things like picking up or manipulating small objects, operating a range of equipment manually, or communicating through writing or typing on standard machinery. Loss of function in the dominant hand would be expected to have a greater effect than equivalent loss in the non-dominant hand.

Examples

It would be reasonable to regard as having a substantial adverse effect:

- difficulty co-ordinating the use of a knife and fork at the same time;
- difficulty preparing a meal because of problems doing things like opening cans or other packages; peeling vegetables; lifting saucepans; and opening the oven door;
- difficulty opening doors which have door knobs rather than lever handles, or gripping handrails on steps or gradients;
- difficulty pressing the buttons on keyboards or keypads at the same speed as someone who does not have an impairment;
- difficulty in dealing with buttons and fasteners when dressing and activities associated with toileting.

> **A man with tenosynovitis experiences significant pain in his hands and lower arms when undertaking repetitive tasks such as using a keyboard at home or work, peeling vegetables, and writing. The impairment substantially adversely affects these normal day-to-day activities and it has an impact on the capacity of manual dexterity.**

It would not be reasonable to regard as having a substantial adverse effect:

- inability to undertake activities requiring delicate hand movements, such as threading a small needle;
- inability to reach typing speeds standardised for secretarial work;
- inability to pick up a single small item, such as a pin.

Physical co-ordination

D22. This covers balanced and effective interaction of body movement, including hand and eye co-ordination. In the case of a child, it is necessary to take account of the level of achievement which would be normal for a person of a similar age. In any case, account should be taken of the ability to carry out 'composite' activities such as walking and using hands at the same time.

Examples

It would be reasonable to regard as having a substantial adverse effect:

- ability to pour hot water into a cup to make a cup of tea only with unusual slowness or concentration;
- difficulty placing food into one's own mouth with a fork or spoon, without unusual concentration or assistance;
- inability to place a key in a lock without unusual concentration or requiring assistance.

> **A young man who has dyspraxia experiences a range of effects which include difficulty co-ordinating physical movements. He is frequently knocking over cups and bottles of drink and cannot combine two activities at the same time, such as walking while holding a plate of food upright, without spilling the food. It would be reasonable to regard this as a substantial adverse effect on normal day-to-day activities affecting manual dexterity.**

It would not be reasonable to regard as having a substantial adverse effect:

- simple clumsiness;
- inability to catch a tennis ball.

Continence

D23. This covers the ability to control urination and/or defecation. Account should be taken of the frequency and extent of the loss of control.

Examples

It would be reasonable to regard as having a substantial adverse effect:

- infrequent loss of control of the bowels, if it is entirely unpredictable and leads to immediate major soiling;
- loss of control of the bladder while asleep at least once a month;

PART 4

- frequent minor faecal incontinence or frequent minor leakage from the bladder, particularly if it is unpredictable.

> **A young woman has developed colitis, an inflammatory bowel disease. The condition is a chronic one which is subject to periods of remission and flare-ups. During a flare-up she experiences severe abdominal pain and bouts of diarrhoea. This makes it very difficult for her to travel or go to work as she must ensure she is always close to a lavatory. This has a substantial adverse effect on her ability to carry out normal day-to-day activities.**

It would <u>not be reasonable</u> to regard as having a substantial adverse effect:

- infrequent (less than once a month) loss of control of the bladder while asleep;
- infrequent and minor leakage from the bladder;
- incontinence in a very young child who would not be expected to be able to control urination and/or defecation.

<u>Ability to lift, carry or otherwise move everyday objects</u>

D24. Account should be taken of a person's ability to repeat such functions or, for example, to bear weights over a reasonable period of time. Everyday objects might include such items as books, a kettle of water, bags of shopping, a briefcase, an overnight bag, a chair or other piece of light furniture.

Examples

It would be reasonable to regard as having a substantial adverse effect:

- difficulty picking up objects of moderate weight with one hand;
- difficulty opening a moderately heavy door;
- difficulty carrying a moderately loaded tray steadily.

> **A man with achondroplasia has unusually short stature, and arms which are disproportionate in size to the rest of his body. He has difficulty lifting or manipulating everyday items like a vacuum cleaner, or bulky items of household furniture, and has difficulty opening moderately heavy doors, and operating revolving barriers at the entrance to some stations and buildings. It would be reasonable to regard this as a substantial adverse effect on normal day-to-day activities.**

It would <u>not be reasonable</u> to regard as having a substantial adverse effect:

- inability to carry heavy luggage without assistance;
- inability to move heavy objects without a mechanical aid, such as moving a heavy piece of furniture without a trolley.

<u>Speech, hearing or eyesight</u>

D25. This covers the ability to speak, hear or see and includes face-to-face, telephone and written communication. Account should be taken of the extent to which, as a result of either a physical or mental impairment, a person may have the capacity to speak, hear or see, but may nevertheless be substantially adversely affected in a range of activities involving one of these capacities as a result of the effects of his or her impairment.

(i) Speech

Account should be taken of how far a person is able to speak clearly at a normal pace and rhythm and to understand someone else speaking normally in the person's native language. It is necessary to consider any effects on speech patterns or which impede the acquisition or processing of a person's native language, for example by someone who has had a stroke.

Examples

It would be reasonable to regard as having a substantial adverse effect:

- difficulty giving clear basic instructions orally to colleagues or providers of a service;
- difficulty asking specific questions to clarify instructions;
- taking longer than someone who does not have an impairment to say things.

A man has had a stammer since childhood. He does not stammer all the time, but his stammer can appear, particularly in telephone calls, to go beyond the occasional lapses in fluency found in the speech of people who do not have the impairment. However, this effect can often be hidden by his coping strategy. He may try to avoid telephone calls where he believes he will stammer, or he may not speak as much during telephone calls. He may sometimes try to avoid stammering by substituting words, or by inserting extra words or phrases.

A 6-year-old boy has verbal dyspraxia which adversely affects his ability to speak. He is unable to make himself clear to other people, including his friends and teachers at school.

A woman has bipolar disorder. Her speech may sometimes become over-excited and irrational, making it difficult for others to understand what she is saying.

In these cases it would be reasonable to regard these effects as substantial adverse effects.

It would not be reasonable to regard as having a substantial adverse effect:

- inability to articulate fluently due to a lisp or other minor speech impediment;
- inability to speak in front of an audience simply as a result of nervousness;
- inability to be understood because of having a strong accent;
- inability to converse in a language which is not the speaker's native language.

(ii) Hearing

Account should be taken of effects where the level of background noise is within such a range and of such a type that most people would be able to hear adequately. If a person uses a hearing aid or similar device, what needs to be considered is the effect that would be experienced if the person were not using the hearing aid or device.

Examples

It would be reasonable to regard as having a substantial adverse effect:

- difficulty hearing someone talking at a sound level which is normal for everyday conversations, and in a moderately noisy environment;
- difficulty hearing and understanding another person speaking clearly over the voice telephone (where the telephone is not affected by bad reception);
- difficulty hearing or understanding normal conversations because of interference caused by auditory hallucinations as a result of a mental impairment.

A woman has tinnitus which interferes with, and makes difficult, the ability to hear or understand normal conversation, to the extent that she cannot hear and respond to what a supermarket checkout assistant is saying if the two people behind her in the queue are holding a conversation at the same time. This has a substantial adverse effect on her ability to carry out the normal day-to-day activity of shopping.

It would not be reasonable to regard as having a substantial adverse effect:

- inability to hold a conversation in a very noisy place, such as a factory floor, a pop concert or alongside a busy main road;
- inability to sing in tune.

(iii) Eyesight

If a person's sight is corrected by spectacles or contact lenses, or could be corrected by them, what needs to be considered is the effect remaining while he or she is wearing such spectacles or lenses.

If a person's eyesight is impaired sufficiently to lead to registration or certification as a blind or partially sighted person he or she is deemed to be a disabled person[13], and does not need to prove that he or she has an impairment which has a substantial and long-term adverse effect on his or her ability to carry out normal day-to-day activities.

Account should be taken of the possible effects on a person who has monocular vision, particularly if the sight in the remaining eye

is compromised in any way.

Examples

It would be reasonable to regard as having a substantial adverse effect:

- inability to see to pass the eyesight test for a standard driving test (however where this is corrected by glasses, this is not a substantial adverse effect);
- difficulty recognising by sight a known person across a moderately-sized room (unless this can be corrected by glasses);
- inability to distinguish any colours at all;
- difficulty reading ordinary newsprint (unless this can be corrected by reading glasses);
- difficulty walking safely without bumping into things (unless this can be corrected by glasses).

> **A man has retinitis pigmentosa (RP), a heredity eye disorder which affects the retina. In RP sight loss is gradual but progressive. It is unusual for people with RP to become totally blind – most retain some useful vision well into old age. In this case the man has difficulty seeing in poor light and a marked reduction in his field of vision (referred to as tunnel vision). As a result he often bumps into furniture and doors when he is in an unfamiliar environment, and can only read when he is in a very a well-lit area. It would be reasonable to conclude that the adverse effects of this impairment on normal day-to-day activities are substantial.**

It would not be reasonable to regard as having a substantial adverse effect:

- inability to read very small or indistinct print without the aid of a magnifying glass;
- inability to distinguish a known person across a substantial distance (eg across the width of a football pitch);
- simple inability to distinguish between red and green, which is not accompanied by any other effect such as blurring of vision.

Memory or ability to concentrate, learn or understand

D26. Account should be taken of the person's ability to remember, organise his or her thoughts, plan a course of action and carry it out, take in new knowledge, and to understand spoken or written information. This includes considering whether the person has cognitive difficulties or learns to do things significantly more slowly than a person who does not have an impairment. Account should be taken of whether the person has persistent and significant difficulty in reading and understanding text in his or her native language despite adequate educational opportunities or in reading and understanding straightforward numbers. The ability to learn or understand covers human non-factual information and non-verbal communication such as body language and facial expressions. Account should be taken of whether the inability to understand communication leads to difficulties in understanding and following verbal instructions.

Examples

It would be reasonable to regard as having a substantial adverse effect:

- intermittent loss of consciousness and associated confused behaviour;
- persistent difficulty in remembering the names of familiar people such as family or friends;
- difficulty in adapting after a reasonable period to minor changes in work routine;
- persistent and significant difficulty with reading;
- persistent difficulty in remembering the spelling and meaning of words in common usage;
- considerable difficulty in following a short sequence such as a simple recipe or a brief list of domestic tasks;
- significant difficulty taking part in normal social interaction or forming social relationships;
- disordered perception of reality.

A man has Asperger's Syndrome, a form of autism, and this causes him to have difficulty communicating with people. He finds it hard to understand non-verbal communications such as facial expressions, and non-factual communication such as jokes. He takes everything that is said very literally, and therefore has difficulty in making or keeping friends or developing close relationships. He is given verbal instructions during office banter with his manager, but his ability to understand the instruction is impaired because he is unable to isolate the instruction from the social conversation.

A woman with bipolar affective disorder is easily distracted. This results in her frequently not being able to concentrate on performing an activity like making a sandwich without being distracted from the task. Consequently, it takes her significantly longer than a person without the disorder to complete the task.

It would be reasonable to regard these impairments as having a substantial adverse effect on normal day-to-day activities, which involve the capacity of 'memory or ability to concentrate, learn or understand'.

It would not be reasonable to regard as having a substantial adverse effect:
- occasionally forgetting the name of a familiar person, such as a colleague;
- inability to concentrate on a task requiring application over several hours;
- inability to fill in a long, detailed, technical document without assistance;
- inability to read at faster than normal speed;
- some shyness or timidity;
- minor problems with writing or spelling.

Perception of the risk of physical danger

D27. This includes both the underestimation and overestimation of physical danger, including danger to well-being. Account should be taken, for example, of whether the person is inclined to neglect basic functions such as eating, drinking, sleeping, keeping warm or personal hygiene; reckless behaviour which puts the person or others at risk; or excessive avoidance behaviour without a good cause.

Examples

It would be reasonable to regard as having a substantial adverse effect:
- difficulty in safely operating properly-maintained equipment;
- persistent difficulty crossing a road safely;
- persistent failure to nourish oneself (where nourishment is available);
- inability to recognise the physical dangers of touching an object which is very hot or cold.

A man has had paranoid schizophrenia for five years, and one of the effects of this impairment is an inability to make proper judgements about activities that may result in a risk to his personal safety. For example, he will walk into roads without checking if cars are coming. This makes normal day-to-day activities such as shopping very difficult.

A woman has had anorexia, an eating disorder, for two years. She fails to eat properly, and this results in a risk to her well-being. She has no regard for self-preservation, so her perception of physical danger is compromised.

In both cases, these people have an impaired appreciation of danger which results in a substantial adverse effect on their ability to carry out normal day-to-day activities.

It would not be reasonable to regard as having a substantial adverse effect:
- fear of significant heights;
- underestimating the risk associated with dangerous hobbies, such as mountain climbing;
- a person consciously taking a higher than normal risk on their own initiative, such as persistently crossing a road when the signals are adverse, or driving fast on highways for own pleasure.
- underestimating risks – other than obvious ones – in unfamiliar workplaces.

[4760]

NOTES

9 The Disability Discrimination (Meaning of Disability) Regulations 1996.

10 The Special Educational Needs and Disability Act 2001 amends Part 4 of the Disability Discrimination Act 1995 to prevent discrimination against disabled people in their access to education.

11 The Special Educational Needs Code of Practice (November 2001), Department for Education and Skills.

12 Code of Practice for Schools: Disability Discrimination Act 1995: Part 4 (July 2002), Disability Rights Commission.

13 The Disability Discrimination (Blind and Partially Sighted Persons) Regulations 2003. Note: these may be subject to amendment in 2006.

EQUAL OPPORTUNITIES COMMISSION: GENDER EQUALITY DUTY CODE OF PRACTICE ENGLAND AND WALES

NOTES

This Code of Practice was issued by the Equal Opportunities Commission under the Sex Discrimination Act 1975, s 76E(1) (repealed as noted below), and was brought into effect, on 6 April 2007, by the Sex Discrimination Code of Practice (Public Authorities) (Duty to Promote Equality) (Appointed Day) Order 2007, SI 2007/741.

The statutory provision under which this Code was made was repealed by the Equality Act 2006, ss 40, 91, Sch 3, paras 6, 16, Sch 4; however the Code is continued in force by s 42(3) of the 2006 Act (see **[1685]**). As to the dissolution of the Equal Opportunities Commission and the transfer of its property, rights and liabilities etc to the Commission for Equality and Human Rights, see the Equality Act 2006, ss 36–38 at **[1679]**–**[1681]**.

Only those parts of the Code of particular relevance to employment law are reproduced. The following are omitted: Foreword; paras 2.53–2.61; paras 3.57–3.74; Chapters 4–6; Appendices C–G.

The equivalent Code for Scotland ('Gender Equality Duty Code of Practice for Scotland') is omitted for reasons of space. It applies to those bodies subject to the authority of the Scottish Parliament.

CHAPTER 1: OVERVIEW OF THE GENDER EQUALITY DUTY

What this code is and how to use it

1.1. This Code of Practice (the Code) gives practical guidance to public authorities on how to meet the legal requirements of the gender equality duty. The Equal Opportunities Commission (EOC) has prepared and issued this Code under the Sex Discrimination Act 1975, as amended by the Equality Act 2006. The Code is expected to come into effect on April 6 2007.

1.2. Those parts of the Code which deal with the general gender equality duty in section 76A of the Sex Discrimination Act 1975 apply (subject to the exceptions set out in Appendix B) to all public authorities in England and Wales and to reserved functions of public authorities in Scotland. A similar but separate code applies to Scotland. Those parts of the Code (primarily Chapter 3) which deal with the specific duties imposed by the Sex Discrimination Act 1975 (Public Authorities) (Statutory Duties) Order 2006 (the Order) apply only to the public authorities listed in the Schedule to that Order. This does not include authorities all of whose functions are public functions in relation to Wales.

1.3. This Code of Practice is a 'statutory' code and has been laid before Parliament before taking effect. This means that the Code is admissible in evidence in any legal action under the Sex Discrimination Act 1975 or the Equal Pay Act 1970, in criminal or civil proceedings before any court or tribunal.

1.4. A court or tribunal must take into account any part of the Code that appears to them to be relevant to any question arising in the proceedings. This includes the question of whether public authorities have breached the law. A tribunal or court may draw an adverse inference that a breach of the law has occurred if a public authority has failed to follow relevant provisions in the Code. If a public authority does not follow the Code's provisions, it will need to show how it has otherwise met its legal obligations under the general duty and any specific duties.

1.5. On its own, the Code does not impose any legal obligations on public authorities. The Code is not a complete statement of the law – only the courts can give this.

1.6. References to the Sex Discrimination Act 1975 (SDA), the Equal Pay Act 1970 (EqPA) and the Equality Act 2006 are shown in the margins.

1.7. Where examples are used, they are intended to illustrate the ways in which different types of public authorities can comply with the duty. They should be read in that light, and not as authoritative statements of the law. Where examples are taken from the voluntary sector, they are intended to illustrate gender equality issues and possible means of addressing them, not to imply that those bodies are covered by the gender duty.

1.8. The EOC will be issuing non-statutory guidance to supplement this Code, to cover particular parts of the public sector, aspects of the duty such as gender impact assessment and how the duty applies to procurement.

What is the gender equality duty?

1.9. The Equality Act 2006 amends the SDA to place a statutory duty on all public authorities, when carrying out their functions, to have due regard to the need:

- to eliminate unlawful discrimination and harassment
- to promote equality of opportunity between men and women.

1.10. This is known as the 'general duty' and will come into effect on 6 April 2007.

1.11. The duty applies to all public authorities in respect of all of their functions (with limited exceptions described in Appendix B). This means it applies to policy-making, service provision, employment matters, and in relation to enforcement or any statutory discretion and decision-making. It also applies to a public authority in relation to services and functions which are contracted out. In addition, it applies to private and voluntary bodies which are carrying out public functions, but only in respect of those functions. For examples of the kind of public authorities which are covered, see Appendix A.

1.12. Public authorities are expected to have 'due regard' to the need to eliminate unlawful discrimination and harassment and promote equality of opportunity between men and women in all of their functions. Due regard comprises two linked elements: proportionality and relevance. The weight which public authorities give to gender equality should therefore be proportionate to its relevance to a particular function. The greater the relevance of a function to gender equality, the greater regard which should be paid to it. For more detail on due regard and the component parts of the duty, see Chapter 2, paragraphs 2.1–2.16 and 2.21–2.32.

1.13. As part of the duty, public authorities are required to have due regard to the need to eliminate unlawful discrimination and harassment in employment and vocational training (including further and higher education), for people who intend to undergo, are undergoing or have undergone gender reassignment. For the purposes of this Code, the expression 'transsexual people' is used to refer to the people who are covered by those provisions. For more detail, see Chapter 2, paragraphs 2.17–2.20.

1.14. To support progress in delivering the general duty, there is also a series of 'specific duties' which apply to listed public authorities as laid out in the Order in Appendix C. The Order sets out steps those authorities must take to help them meet the general duty.

1.15. Those specific duties, in brief, are:

- **To prepare and publish a gender equality scheme**, showing how it will meet its general and specific duties and setting out its gender equality objectives.
- In formulating its overall objectives, **to consider the need to include objectives to address the causes of any gender pay gap.**
- **To gather and use information** on how the public authority's policies and practices affect gender equality in the workforce and in the delivery of services.
- **To consult stakeholders (i e employees, service users and others, including trade unions) and take account of relevant information** in order to determine its gender equality objectives.
- **To assess the impact of its current and proposed policies and practices** on gender equality.
- **To implement the actions set out in its scheme** within three years, unless it is unreasonable or impracticable to do so.
- **To report** against the scheme every year and **review** the scheme at least every three years.

1.16. The first scheme must be published by 30 April 2007. For more detail on these specific duties and how to meet them, see Chapter 3.

1.17. This document contains guidance on how to meet both the general and the specific duties in Chapters 2 and 3. Even if a public authority is not subject to the specific duties (such as public authorities operating solely in Wales), it will still be expected to provide clear evidence of meeting the general duty. The specific duties laid out in Chapter 3 can act as a framework to assist authorities in complying with the general duty.

Why has the gender equality duty been introduced?

1.18. The gender equality duty aims to make gender equality central to the way that public authorities work, in order to create:

- better-informed decision-making and policy development
- a clearer understanding of the needs of service users
- better-quality services which meet varied needs
- more effective targeting of policy and resources
- better results and greater confidence in public services
- a more effective use of talent in the workforce.

1.19. The duty is intended to address the fact that, despite 30 years of individual legal rights to sex equality, there is still widespread discrimination – sometimes intentional, sometimes unintentional – and persistent gender inequality. Policies and practices that seem neutral can have a significantly different effect on women and on men, often contributing to greater gender inequality and poor policy outcomes. Individual legal rights have not been enough by themselves to change this.

1.20. The duty is intended to improve this situation, both for men and for women, for boys and for girls. Gender roles and relationships structure men's and women's lives. Women are frequently disadvantaged by policies and practices that do not recognise their greater caring responsibilities, the different pattern of their working lives, their more limited access to resources and their greater vulnerability to domestic violence and sexual assault. Men are also disadvantaged by workplace cultures that do not support their family or childcare responsibilities, by family services that assume they have little or no role in parenting, or by health services which do not recognise their different needs. Both sexes suffer from stereotyping of their roles and needs. The duty should help the public sector, and those working with it, to identify and respond to stereotyping, sex discrimination and sexism, resulting in improvements for all.

1.21. The duty requires public authorities to identify and tackle discrimination, to prevent harassment, and to ensure that their work promotes equality of opportunity between men and women. It is a form of legally enforceable 'gender mainstreaming' – building gender equality into the core business thinking and processes of an organisation. It is different from previous sex equality legislation in two crucial respects:

- public authorities have to be proactive in eliminating discrimination and harassment, rather than waiting for individuals to take cases against them.
- public authorities have to be proactive in promoting equality of opportunity, and not just avoiding discrimination.

Outcomes – the changes to which the gender equality duty should lead

1.22. The aim of the duty is not to establish processes but to make visible and faster progress towards gender equality. Indicators of progress might include:

- Service-users notice that services are more accessible and better tailored to their needs, and service outcomes by gender begin to improve.
- Women and men are making greater use of services that their sex had previously under-used.
- Service-users with caring responsibilities are receiving appropriate support, such as better pushchair access on public transport and crèche facilities for trainees.
- Fathers receive greater support for their childcare responsibilities from public services and employers.
- Girls have higher aspirations for their future careers.
- Women and men from all groups feel effectively engaged in decision and policy-making around issues that have a direct effect on them.
- Women and men are represented at all levels of the workforce and in all areas of work.
- Harassment and sexual harassment of staff, service users and others is dealt with promptly and systematically, according to agreed procedures, and tolerance of harassment drops within the organisation as a whole.

- The reported level of discrimination experienced by pregnant staff and staff returning from maternity leave reduces significantly and is eventually eliminated.
- The gap between women and men's pay narrows and is eventually eliminated.
- Employees with caring responsibilities are receiving greater support from the public authority, including flexible and part-time working opportunities at all levels of work.
- Transsexual people feel supported and valued as staff and potential staff.
- Barriers to the recruitment and retention of transsexual staff have been identified and removed.
- Employees are aware of the gender equality duty, understand how it will affect their work, and have the skills to implement the duty in their work.
- Gender equality issues, and their budgetary implications, are considered at the beginning of policy-making.
- It is easy to find a wide variety of data and information to assess effectively how certain actions will affect women and men.

How the gender equality duty fits into the broader equality picture

1.23. Women and men, including transsexual women and men, will experience different forms of disadvantage depending on their age, ethnicity, religion or belief, sexual orientation, marital or civil partnership status, and whether or not they have a disability. In order to understand and address questions of gender equality under the duty, public authorities may need to consider that complexity and whether particular groups of women or men are experiencing particular disadvantages.

> Only 47% of disabled women are in employment, compared with 53% of disabled men. Of the disabled women in employment, only 52% work full-time. This compares with an employment rate of 75% for non-disabled women and 86% for non-disabled men. (EOC Facts about women and men in Great Britain 2005)

1.24. The gender equality duty is similar to the existing duties on race and disability equality and all three have the same spirit and intention behind them, requiring public authorities to take action to tackle discrimination, to prevent harassment, and to ensure that their work promotes equality of opportunity across all their functions. The gender equality duty has fewer requirements to set up processes than the race duty, however, in order to ensure that public authorities focus on the achievement of outcomes.

1.25. The gender equality scheme, which is a requirement for listed public authorities under the specific duties, can be published as part of an overall equality scheme, covering the requirements of all three duties. There are, however, slight differences in the requirements of the three duties. Public authorities which choose to take the overall equality scheme approach must ensure that they clearly meet the requirements of the gender equality duty, including specific objectives on gender equality. The scheme should show clearly and specifically which elements of the overall equality scheme refer to gender equality.

Which organisations have to take action on the general duty?

S76A Sex Discrimination Act (margin note)

1.26. The general duty applies to all functions of every public authority (bar the exceptions listed in Appendix B). The definition of a public authority is 'any person who has functions of a public nature'. Despite a slight difference in the wording, this is the same approach as the definition of public authorities covered by the Disability Discrimination Act 2005 and the Human Rights Act 1998.

1.27. Because the duty is based on this definition, public authorities covered by the general gender duty are not individually listed. The duty would apply to all of the authorities listed in Schedule 1A to the amended Race Relations Act 1976. Further details on the definition of a public authority are contained in Appendix A.

1.28. The gender duty can also apply directly to certain private or voluntary sector bodies when they are carrying out public functions (the private functions of such bodies being excluded). Further details of who is affected by this are contained in Appendix A.

Which public authorities have to take action on the specific duties?

1.29. To find out whether a public authority is covered, check the list at Appendix D. The list will be subject to periodic updating by Government, the relevant order being available on the Stationery Office website.

How will the gender equality duty be enforced?

1.30. The general duty is enforceable by judicial review. Any person or body affected by a failure to comply with the general duty by a public authority may take action through judicial review proceedings.

S32 Equality Act (margin note)

1.31. From late 2007, the Commission for Equality and Human Rights (CEHR) will have the power to conduct formal assessments and to issue compliance notices in connection with a breach of the general duty which will be enforceable in the courts.

S76D SDA (margin note)

1.32. The CEHR and EOC will have the power to issue compliance notices in respect of the specific duties. For more detail see Chapter 4.

1.33. In addition it is likely that relevant inspection bodies will require evidence of compliance with the general and specific duties.

Future changes in the legislation

1.34. There may be changes in the future to the sex equality legislation which will affect the definition of unlawful discrimination and harassment under the duty. Public authorities will need to ensure that they keep up-to-date with any developments which affect the duties explained in this Code. Relevant information will be publicised by the EOC on the gender duty section of their website, and will be available from the CEHR in the future. This Code will remain in force after the dissolution of the EOC, however, until the CEHR updates it.

Where to obtain further information now and in the future

1.35. Copies of the Sex Discrimination Act, the Equal Pay Act, the Equality Act and the orders or regulations made under them can be obtained from the Stationery Office. The text of this Code and of the Equal Pay Code of Practice can be downloaded free of charge from the EOC's website on www.eoc.org.uk. There is also supporting guidance available on the EOC website.

1.36. Free information on the duty is available through the EOC Helpline on 0845 601 5901 or by email on info@eoc.org.uk.

1.37. The Equality Act also provides for the dissolution of the EOC and the passing of its functions to the CEHR. This is currently expected to happen in late 2007. Once this transition has occurred, promotion and enforcement of the gender equality duty will pass to the CEHR. **[4761]**

CHAPTER 2: HOW TO MEET THE GENERAL DUTY

Introduction

2.1. All public authorities and private and voluntary bodies carrying out public functions on behalf of a public authority are subject to the general duty, and this Chapter explains how to meet it.

2.2. All public authorities are legally required, when exercising their functions, to have due regard to the need:

- to eliminate discrimination and harassment that is unlawful under the Sex Discrimination Act 1975 (SDA) and discrimination that is unlawful under the Equal Pay Act 1970 (EqPA)
- to promote equality of opportunity between men and women.

2.3. This means that the duty is not a negative or passive one, but requires public authorities to adopt a proactive approach to meeting the duty. When the EOC (and subsequently the CEHR) and public sector inspectorates are monitoring and evaluating compliance with this duty, they will be looking for evidence of action and positive change. Without such evidence, it will be difficult to establish that the authority is meeting the gender equality duty.

2.4. Smaller public authorities will have fewer resources and this will affect the steps which they take to ensure compliance with the general duty.

How the different parts of the duty work together

2.5. As stated above the general duty has three parts:

- eliminating unlawful discrimination
- eliminating harassment
- promoting equality of opportunity between men and women

2.6. These three parts support each other, and in practice may overlap. For example, promoting equality of opportunity may also eliminate or prevent unlawful discrimination and harassment. It is important to remember, however, that the three parts are different, and that achieving on one may not lead to achieving all three. Public authorities should consider and deal with all three parts of the gender duty.

Unlawful discrimination

2.7. Unlawful discrimination includes discrimination as defined by the SDA, and discrimination that is unlawful under the EqPA. Public authorities are legally required to have due regard to the need to eliminate both forms of discrimination.

2.8. In the SDA, unlawful discrimination is defined as:

- direct and indirect discrimination on grounds of sex
- discrimination on the grounds of pregnancy and maternity leave
- discrimination on the grounds of gender reassignment
- direct and indirect discrimination against married persons and civil partners
- victimisation
- harassment and sexual harassment.

Further details of the above definitions and where they apply can be found in Appendix E.

In the employment field, the SDA prohibits discrimination in non-contractual pay and benefits, such as discretionary bonuses. Sex discrimination related to contractual pay and benefits is dealt with under the EqPA.

2.9. The EqPA (read in the light of article 141 of the Treaty of Rome) gives an individual a right to the same contractual pay and benefits as a person of the opposite sex in the same employment, or where the source of the pay is the same, where the man and the woman are doing:

- the same or broadly similar work
- work which has been rated as equivalent under an analytical job evaluation study
- work that is of equal value (work of equal value is where the work done is different but considered to be of equal value or worth in terms of demands such as effort, skill and decision-making).

A public authority can pay a man more than a woman (or vice versa) in such circumstances if there is a genuine and material factor for doing so which is not attributable to direct or indirect sex discrimination.

Harassment and sexual harassment

2.10. Harassment and sexual harassment are unlawful under the SDA and the duty requires public authorities to have due regard to the need to eliminate them. The duty to have due regard to the need to promote equality of opportunity between men and women is also relevant to ensuring that harassment is prevented before it occurs.

2.11. Different legal definitions apply, depending on whether the harassment occurs in:

- employment and related fields, vocational training (including further and higher education) and in the exercise of public functions; or
- schools, the provision of goods, facilities or services, or in the disposal or management of premises.

Appendix E explains the definitions of harassment. Paragraphs 2.69–2.77 provide information on how to meet the duty to have due regard to the need to eliminate harassment.

The promotion of equality of opportunity between men and women

2.12. The term 'sex' is used to describe biological differences between women and men. The term 'gender' refers to the wider social roles and relationships which structure men's and women's lives. Gender inequality exists in all aspects of society and refers to lasting and embedded patterns of advantage and disadvantage.

2.13. The duty on public authorities to have due regard to the need to promote equality of opportunity between men and women is a new aspect of the SDA. In order to achieve actual equality of opportunity, it is necessary to recognise that in certain circumstances women and men, because of their sex or gender roles, are not in the same position. In some circumstances it may therefore be appropriate for public authorities to treat women and men differently, if that action is aimed at overcoming previous disadvantage.

2.14. For example, where one sex is under-represented in particular work, a public authority could promote equality of opportunity by taking positive action to encourage members of the under-represented sex to apply for such work, or to provide training to equip the under-represented sex for such work. It would not, however, be lawful to discriminate in favour of one sex in the actual appointments procedure. See Chapter 6 for more detail.

2.15. As another example, women make up the substantial majority of victims of domestic violence and rape. It would not be appropriate, therefore, for a local council to seek to fund refuge services on a numerically equal basis for men and for women. The promotion of equal opportunities between men and women requires public authorities to recognise that the two groups are not starting from an equal footing and identical treatment would not be appropriate.

2.16. In some instances, promoting equality of opportunity may require separate provision to be offered, as an alternative approach to improve take-up of services by the under-represented sex, where this is permitted under the SDA. An example of this might be to encourage men to increase their low take-up of primary health care services. For more detail, see Chapter 6 on single-sex activities.

The gender equality duty and gender reassignment

2.17. The gender equality duty requires public authorities to have due regard to the need to eliminate unlawful discrimination and harassment against transsexual people in the fields of employment and vocational training (including further and higher education). This section gives further details on issues relating to the gender duty and gender reassignment.

S2A SDA (margin note)

2.18. The SDA provides that people who intend to undergo, are undergoing or have undergone gender reassignment are protected against discrimination and harassment in the fields of employment and related areas and in vocational training (including further and higher education). This means that public authorities must have due regard to the need to eliminate unlawful discrimination and harassment in those fields against transsexual people when discharging their gender duty.

2.19. The scope of legal protection against discrimination on grounds of gender reassignment will be extended in the SDA, by 21 December 2007, by the implementation of the Goods and Services Directive 2004/113. As a matter of domestic law, as a consequence, by that date (or the date of implementation if earlier), public authorities will be under a duty to have due regard to the need to eliminate unlawful discrimination and harassment on grounds of gender reassignment in the provision of goods and services.

2.20. Public authorities may wish to take the need to have due regard to the need to eliminate gender reassignment discrimination and harassment into account when discharging their gender equality duty in relation to the provision of goods and services, before they are required to do so following the implementation of the Goods and Services Directive.

What does the general duty mean? Due regard, proportionality and relevance

S76A SDA (margin note)

2.21. Public authorities will be expected to have due regard to the need to eliminate unlawful discrimination and harassment and promote equality of opportunity between women and men in relation to all their functions and to provide evidence that they have done so. This includes their core functions of policy development, service design and delivery, decision-making and employment, the exercise of statutory discretion, enforcement and any services and functions which have been contracted out. For details on contracted-out services see Chapter 5 on procurement.

2.22. Having due regard means that the weight given to the need to promote gender equality is **proportionate** to its **relevance** to a particular function. In practice, this principle will mean public authorities should prioritise action to address the most significant gender inequalities within their remit, and take actions which are likely to deliver the best gender equality outcomes. This is likely to mean focussing on functions or policies that have most effect on the public, or on the authority's employees, or on a section of the public or on a section of the authority's employees. The authority should ask whether particular functions could affect women and men in different ways, and whether functions can be carried out in a way which promotes equality of opportunity between men and women.

2.23. The general duty applies to public authorities whatever their size, but the way in which it is implemented should be appropriate to the size of the authority and its functions. For example, a primary school may wish to train its staff in gender equality in order to meet the duty, but does not have sufficient budget to meet this training need alongside other competing needs. It decides to meet the duty by arranging gender equality training for the head teacher, who then runs a feedback session for staff and governors at the next in-service training day. This could be a proportionate means of meeting the duty.

2.24. Gender equality will be more relevant to some functions than others. Relevance is about how much a function affects people's gender equality, as members of the public or as employees of the authority. For example, a school may decide that gender equality is more relevant to the way that it designs its teaching methods than to its building maintenance work. Public authorities should therefore assess whether, and how, gender equality is relevant to each of their functions. A public authority may decide that little or no action is required to discharge the gender equality duty in some of its services, for example those which are purely technical, such as traffic control or weather forecasting. Gender equality will always be relevant, however, to the employment side of any of a public authority's functions.

2.25. The requirement for proportionality and relevance should not be interpreted, however, as a simple question of the numbers of people affected. Public authorities should also take into account the seriousness or extent of the discrimination, harassment or gender inequality, even if the number of people affected is small. This would often be the case where, for example, transsexual people were affected, as their numbers would be likely to be small but the seriousness or extent of discrimination and harassment might be significant.

2.26. Where changing a function or proposed policy would lead to significant benefits to the gender equality of men and women, (or, in employment and vocational training – including further and higher education – for transsexual men and women), public authorities should give greater weight to the case for change and take steps accordingly.

2.27. For example, a Regional Development Agency has a target of increasing employment rates in a particular district. When developing this policy, it discovers that women are less economically active than men in that district but the employment services and training opportunities which they are providing are not being accessed by women, because of lack of childcare support. They decide to adjust their policy and resource allocations to provide childcare advice and support.

2.28. It will not be acceptable for a public authority to claim that it does not have enough resources to meet the duty. This is because meeting the general duty is a statutory requirement. Existing resources may therefore need to be reprioritised to meet the duty. In practice this may mean that public authorities will use their existing administrative systems and processes, adjusting their plans and priorities where necessary.

2.29. The general duty does not only require authorities to have due regard to gender equality when making decisions about the future. It also requires them to take action to tackle the ongoing consequences of decisions made in the past which failed to give due regard to gender equality. This will entail identifying and addressing any significant inequalities resulting from policies currently in place.

2.30. For example, previous organisational policy may have given training allowances to full-time staff but not to part-time staff, resulting in more men than women taking up the benefit and improving their qualifications. The public authority may need to consider what action it can take to redress this balance, in order to meet the duty.

2.31. Public authorities are not likely to be able to take action to improve all of their functions in a single cycle, for example during the three year life of a gender equality scheme. They have, however, a continuing duty which requires them to prioritise for review functions with the most relevance to gender equality. Consulting male and female employees and service users will be helpful to this process of prioritisation and review, and is a legal requirement under the specific duties.

2.32. The technique of impact assessment, discussed in detail in Chapter 3, is designed to assist authorities in ensuring that they have due regard to gender equality in all their decisions and functions.

How to meet the general duty

2.33. The steps which will assist a public authority to comply with the duty are as follows:

- gathering and analysing information
- consulting stakeholders

- carrying out impact assessments
- prioritising and implementing gender equality objectives
- reporting and reviewing.

These steps are covered in more detail in Chapter 3. Although they are a legal requirement for listed public authorities, they can also assist those authorities which are only covered by the general duty.

2.34. Other important mechanisms for successful compliance with the duty include:

- accountability and leadership
- mainstreaming the duty into core functions
- ensuring implementation through clear staff roles
- staff expertise and training.

Accountability and leadership

2.35. Public authorities are responsible for meeting their general and specific duties. Within each public authority, this responsibility will rest with the groups or individuals who are liable (legally responsible) for the authority's acts or failure to act.

2.36. As well as being legally liable for meeting the duty, these individuals and senior staff have an important leadership role to play in ensuring the success of the duty. As a matter of good practice, it is recommended that all such individuals should be briefed on their responsibilities under the duty and given regular reports on progress. They should be encouraged to build the duty into strategic planning, keynote speeches and organisational development work, so that a consistent message is given to staff and stakeholders that gender equality is integral to the core business of the authority.

2.37. Senior management will be responsible for ensuring that the necessary resources and expertise to meet the duty are made available within the organisation.

Mainstreaming the duty into the core functions of a public authority

2.38. The duty requires public authorities to have due regard to the need to eliminate unlawful discrimination and harassment and to promote equality of opportunity in all their functions. This includes the high-level functions of a public authority such as business planning, budget allocation, annual reporting and organisational development. These will be particularly important in ensuring that the duty is mainstreamed into the day-to-day workings of the public authority, is not marginalised, and results in changes in the most relevant areas of the authority's work.

2.39. Reflecting the duty in the mainstream business plan will also have practical benefits, through bringing together the planning processes of the public authority as a whole with those required under the duty. Having clear gender equality objectives in the organisational business plan, and reporting against them in the annual report could also improve staff ownership, and transparency and accountability to stakeholders.

Ensuring implementation through clear staff roles

2.40. It is recommended as a matter of good practice that a senior member of staff should be given strategic responsibility for ensuring the duty is implemented. In larger authorities, they will need to work with a group of colleagues from policy development, service delivery, employment and, where contracted-out services form a part of the authority's functions, procurement staff. This working group may also be working on the wider equality agenda, including the race and disability duties, but will need to pay specific attention to meeting gender equality goals. The working group will need to develop and drive forward a specific action plan, which allows for effective monitoring and review of progress.

2.41. Smaller authorities will also need to ensure one person is given responsibility for ensuring the duty is implemented, that all functions of the authority are appropriately dealt with, and that there is an action plan.

2.42. Many larger authorities employ specialist equality staff to steer the process of implementing equality; smaller ones may make it part of a person's responsibilities. It is recommended that specialist equality posts should be located in a strategic part of the public authority such as policy, performance management, planning or strategy. The human resources function will have to play a crucial role in the employment aspects but is not best placed to lead overall, as the duty requires due regard in all functions of a public authority, including service delivery and policy-making.

2.43. Wherever they are situated, equality staff or lead individuals cannot be expected to bear all responsibility for the successful implementation of the duty. That will require ownership, action and culture change across the organisation as a whole. Designating a senior person with significant strategic or management responsibilities, supported by designated key staff, should contribute to change across the organisation.

2.44. Reporting on progress to senior management team meetings should help increase their understanding that gender equality can and should be a core part of their business and of their policy development and service delivery objectives, not just a marginal issue or a small part of human resources work.

Staff expertise and training

2.45. In addition to any specialist equality staff, it will also be necessary to build the skills and understanding of relevant staff within the public authority, for example policy and service managers, procurement staff, and human resource managers. Where an authority is subject to the specific duties, relevant staff throughout the organisation will have to have the skills to collect and analyse gender data, to ensure that stakeholders are consulted effectively and to undertake gender impact assessments. These skills will also be useful for authorities which are subject to the general duty only. In some specialist areas, such as understanding the needs of transsexual people, public authorities may wish to obtain external assistance.

2.46. It is recommended that all relevant staff in the public authority should have some understanding of the duty, its meaning for their work and the authority's priority goals in gender equality. This can be achieved by staff briefing, and where relevant, training programmes, and by building goals and targets relevant to the duty into individual personal development plans across the organisation. It can also be supported by recognising progress in achieving gender equality when rewarding individual and team performance.

Success factors in gender mainstreaming

2.47. When planning for implementation of the duty, and reviewing progress, public authorities may wish to consider the factors commonly associated with successful gender mainstreaming in organisations:

- ongoing top-level commitment and willingness to commit resources to achieving gender equality
- developing a shared understanding of the problem, and a shared vision of what gender equality would look like for the authority, which links directly to organisational objectives
- board-level leadership and accountability (with engagement of elected representatives where applicable)
- senior management support and accountability
- specialist staff to steer the process and support staff capacity
- good systems for disaggregating new and existing data by gender
- developing staff understanding of gender equality and skills in analysing the gender impact of policy
- involving staff, service users, unions and voluntary sector organisations
- building gender equality standards and objectives into routine organisational procedures such as policy and budget approval documentation, organisational and departmental targets and objectives, and individual job descriptions, objectives and appraisals.

2.48. These processes are needed to make the duty work, but they are not an end in themselves. The purpose of the duty is to eliminate unlawful discrimination and harassment and promote equality of opportunity between women and men. Ultimately, the key to the success of the duty is achieving culture change in public authorities, a process which will take time and commitment. An authority which makes the effort to meet the needs of women and of men will see the benefits, however, through delivering better quality services and having a more productive workforce.

Meeting the gender equality duty in policy development

2.49. To meet the duty effectively, public authorities must ensure that they have due regard to the need to eliminate unlawful discrimination and harassment against either women or men, (and, in employment and vocational training – including further and higher education – against transsexual men and women) and that their policies are not maintaining or leading to gender inequality. To assist public authorities to do this, it is recommended that they should:

- collect evidence on the impact of core policies on women and men
- when new policies are being developed, assess their likely consequences for women and men

- alter or amend proposed policies so that they have due regard to the need to promote gender equality and eliminate unlawful discrimination and harassment
- resource the above changes appropriately.

2.50. Conducting impact assessments on policies is a useful way of demonstrating that public authorities have had due regard to the need to eliminate unlawful discrimination and harassment and to promote equality of opportunity when developing policy. It is also a legal requirement if a public authority is subject to the specific duties. Even for those public authorities which are not, however, it can be a useful tool for meeting the duty. For more detail on conducting gender impact assessments, see Chapter 3.

2.51. The best way to find out if a policy is likely to have a negative or a positive impact on gender equality is to:

- find out if research or data already exist, and if so, analyse and apply it
- take action to develop relevant information if it does not exist
- ask and involve external and internal stakeholders, such as women's and men's voluntary sector groups, service user and consumer groups, trade unions and employee or staff networks.

2.52. Going through this process brings significant benefits to the effectiveness of policymaking. Developing a good base of evidence about differences in the impact of policies on women and men will avoid resources being misdirected and potentially wasted.

Women's current and future entitlement to pensions is significantly lower than men's. The DWP produced a report 'Women and Pensions – The Evidence' that specifically investigated the gender differences in pension provision between men and women. It showed that only 24% of recently retired women were entitled to a full Basic State Pension in their own right. Even when looking at working-age women, 2.2 million women are not building up rights to even the Basic State Pension.

Women's greater likelihood of undertaking unpaid parenting and caring commitments, and the subsequent impact on their ability to engage in paid employment, were identified as the key causes of the gender differences.

The subsequent DWP White Paper 'Security in retirement: towards a new pensions system' put forward several changes to the recognition of unpaid caring work within the state pension system that will mean for the first time paid work and unpaid care will be equally recognised within the state pension system.

This will benefit not just women, but also the increasing number of men undertaking unpaid care and help produce a pensions system that fully reflects working lives both now and in the future.

2.53–2.61 (*omitted: outside the scope of this work.*)

Meeting the gender equality duty in employment

2.62. To meet the gender equality duty as an employer, a public authority will need to ensure that it has due regard to the need to eliminate unlawful discrimination and harassment in its employment practices and actively promotes gender equality within its workforce. This includes discrimination and harassment of transsexual people on grounds of their gender reassignment.

2.63. In practice this will involve a cyclical process of: data collection, analysis of data, developing an action plan, implementing the plan and monitoring the outcomes to inform further action. It is recommended that the public authority involves the workforce in the process and agrees a timescale over which it will take action. Doing this will not only enable that authority to meet its obligations under the duty, but will also improve its ability to recruit and retain staff and improve service delivery. For more detail on data collection, see Chapter 3.

2.64. The following issues are usually the most common ones to be considered when a public authority is deciding employment priorities for action:

- ensuring fair recruitment processes
- avoiding concentration of women and men into particular areas of work and addressing it where it already exists ('occupational segregation')
- promoting and managing flexible working
- ensuring high-level part-time work and supporting part-time workers

- managing leave for parents and carers
- managing pregnancy and return from maternity leave
- eliminating harassment including sexual harassment
- eliminating discrimination against, and harassment of, transsexual staff and potential staff
- grievance and disciplinary procedures
- redundancy
- retirement
- equal pay
- work-based training opportunities.

London Underground has targeted women in its recruitment of train drivers as part of a strategy that identified the lack of gender balance in the workforce as a central factor affecting its ability to move from being an asset-based organisation to a customer-focused organisation. In an 18-month campaign, it increased the number of female tube drivers from 75 to 167. It broadened its recruitment advertising by placing an advertisement in Cosmopolitan magazine, which produced 6,000 applications. The strategy also tackled ongoing workplace issues that were discouraging women:

— sexual harassment and a culture that was unwelcoming to women
— the lack of adequate physical facilities such as women's toilets and showers and difficulties accessing the facilities that did exist
— inflexibility in working time and rostering

A central feature of the work was the implementation of a Managing Equality and Diversity competence programme, which was rolled out to all managers, the introduction of a managing diversity competence statement and the development of personal diversity goals and measures for managers.

IDS Diversity at Work No 4, October 2004

Transsexual employees and potential employees

2.65. Discrimination on the grounds of sex includes discrimination on the grounds of gender reassignment in employment and vocational training (including further and higher education). Public authorities should review all employment policies and procedures to ensure that they adequately cover transsexual employees – especially those dealing with recruitment, confidentiality, harassment, access to training and development, occupational pensions and insurance.

2.66. It is important to remember that the legal obligation to prevent discrimination against transsexual people in employment and vocational training (including further and higher education) covers not only those who have undergone gender reassignment in the past but also those who intend to undergo gender reassignment and those who are undergoing it.

Meeting the gender equality duty for equal pay

2.67. Public authorities are required to comply with the EqPA. The requirement to have due regard to the need to eliminate unlawful discrimination includes discrimination that is unlawful under the EqPA.

2.68. The right of an individual under the EqPA is set out in paragraph 2.9 above. 'Like work' means work which is the same or broadly similar. Work rated as equivalent means work that has been rated using a non-discriminatory job evaluation scheme as equivalent. Work of equal value is where the work done is different but considered to be of equal value or worth in terms of demands such as effort, skill and decision-making. More detail on this can be found in the Code of Practice on Equal Pay and the EOC website, at www.eoc.org.uk

A public sector organisation based in Wales, with over five hundred staff undertook an equal pay review (EPR). Just under half the workforce was female. Part-time work was fairly common and this group was slightly more likely to be female than male. Prior to the review, the organisation had a fairly complicated pay structure which was felt to have too many grades for the number of staff. There were also several people outside of the pay structure. The organisation began a pay and grading exercise in 1999 and this eventually evolved into a full EPR. There was significant union involvement throughout the process and members of each staff grade were also involved in the working group. The working group used consultants to help them draft the job evaluation system and set up the EPR. The review was thorough and included data on every aspect of recruitment, pay and progression. The review found that women were earning 81% of men's basic hourly wages, but only 71% once additional allowances were taken into account. Since action was taken, the pay gap has reduced to 13% for total pay – i e women are now earning 87% of men's total hourly pay.

Equal Pay Reviews in Practice, IES for EOC 2005

Meeting the duty to eliminate harassment

2.69. Having due regard to the need to eliminate harassment, including sexual harassment, is a legal requirement under the general duty. The duty to have due regard to the need to promote equality of opportunity between men and women is also relevant here as this may help eliminate harassment. A public authority should consider the steps it needs to take to ensure that harassment is prevented across all its activities before it occurs.

2.70. In order to discharge this duty, it is recommended that public authorities develop and regularly review a clear policy for preventing and tackling harassment across all of its functions where relevant. This would include, for example:

- in employment, education and service delivery
- in relation to those not traditionally thought of as receiving a service, such as those who are subject to state powers, for example prisoners or asylum seekers
- in regulatory and enforcement functions
- in management of premises.

2.71. It is recommended that public authorities actively promote the policy to ensure that everyone is aware of and understands it. It is also recommended that public authorities provide training so that their managers and staff are equipped to deal with instances of harassment should they occur.

2.72. Public authorities should also adopt and communicate complaints and investigations procedures for dealing both formally and informally (as appropriate) with harassment, in a supportive manner. In the employment context, it is recommended that procedures for investigating harassment complaints should be linked to grievance and disciplinary procedures and should conform to the accepted standards for disciplinary action in the Acas Code of Practice on Disciplinary and Grievance Procedures.

2.73. Public authorities will need to determine the effectiveness of their policy and procedures. They can do this by monitoring the number of complaints of harassment and their outcome, and by reviewing policies and procedures periodically to ensure they are working effectively and that those who have made complaints are not victimised.

2.74. Where complaints of harassment are upheld, there should be a consistent and proportionate relationship between the severity of the harassment and the penalty imposed on the harasser. In the case of harassment by an employee, this may include disciplinary action and, in severe cases, dismissal. In the case of harassment by service users, tenants, pupils etc, public authorities should ensure that they deal with complaints of harassment by male and female employees consistently to avoid any direct discrimination. Appropriate action may involve warnings as to the consequences of repeated acts of harassment and, in serious cases, the withdrawal of services or the withdrawal of normal services.

2.75. 'Sexual Harassment: Guidance for Managers and Supervisors' explains how to prevent harassment taking place and how to handle complaints. It is available, along with other information and guidance on harassment, on the EOC website www.eoc.org.uk

2.76. A public authority is liable for any acts of harassment carried out by its employees in the course of their employment, or by any other person over whom the public authority has direct control and therefore for whose conduct it could reasonably be held responsible. This is the case, in most circumstances, even where those acts are carried out without either the knowledge or approval of the public authority. Public authorities will have a defence to claims of harassment which has been committed by their employees or agents if they have taken such prior measures as are reasonably practicable to prevent harassment taking place.

2.77. The harassment provisions in the employment and vocational training sections of the SDA do not expressly extend to harassment of employees by someone who is not under the direct control of the employer. An employee who has been subjected to serious harassment, however, which the employer could have prevented but did not, may be entitled to resign and claim constructive unfair dismissal.

[4762]

CHAPTER 3: HOW TO MEET THE SPECIFIC DUTIES

Introduction

3.1. All the public authorities listed in Appendix D are subject to the specific duties described in this chapter. Further orders may be made by government from time to time to update the list of authorities.

3.2. The duties set out a framework to assist listed public authorities in planning, delivering and evaluating action to meet the general duty and to report on those activities. At the heart of this framework is the Gender Equality Scheme (the scheme), which is explained below. When developing and implementing the scheme, however, public authorities should bear in mind the scheme is a means of meeting the three elements of the general duty, not an end in itself. When public authorities are being assessed on whether or not they have met the duty, the existence of the scheme will not in itself be enough. They will have to demonstrate what action they have taken and the outcomes they have achieved.

3.3. The duties apply to all listed authorities whatever their size, but the way in which they are implemented should be appropriate to the size of the authority and its functions. A large NHS trust, for example, may have the capacity to undertake a significant change project to implement the duty. A small school, while still obliged to implement the specific duties, will do so on a scale appropriate to its size and resources.

What do the specific duties require public authorities to do?

3.4. The full text of the specific duties Order is set out at Appendix C, but in summary it provides that the public authority should:

- **prepare and publish a Gender Equality Scheme** showing how it intends to fulfil the general and specific duties and setting out its gender equality objectives
- **in preparing a scheme:**
  - **consult employees, service users and others** (including trade unions)
  - **take into account any information it has gathered or considers relevant** as to how its policies and practices affect gender equality in the workplace and in the delivery of its services
  - in formulating its overall gender equality objectives, **consider the need to have objectives to address the causes of any gender pay gap**
- **ensure that the scheme sets out the actions** the authority has taken or intends to take to —
  - gather information on the effect of its policies and practices on men and women, in employment, services and performance of its functions
  - use the information to review the implementation of the scheme objectives
  - assess the impact of its current and future policies and practices on gender equality
  - consult relevant employees, service users and others (including trade unions)
  - ensure implementation of the scheme objectives
- **implement the scheme and their actions for gathering and using information** within three years of publication of the scheme, unless it is unreasonable or impracticable to do so
- **review and revise the scheme** at least every three years
- **report on progress annually**.

3.5. All listed public authorities must publish their schemes no later than 30 April 2007.

3.6. All listed public authorities are required to comply with the same specific duties. This contrasts with the specific duties under the Race Relations Act 1976 (as amended), which have different requirements for different sectors, and the specific duties under the Disability Discrimination Act 1995 (as amended) which have different requirements in relation to information gathering.

PART 4

Preparing and publishing a gender equality scheme

3.7. In order to prepare a scheme identifying gender equality objectives, and setting out the actions it intends to carry out to achieve them, each public authority will have to develop an understanding of the major gender equality issues in its functions. This should be based on a good evidence base and developed through consultation with stakeholders, and the specific duties set out these elements of the process as a legal requirement. Public authorities are then required to commit to a set of priority objectives, selected according to the principles of proportionality and relevance. Public authorities have discretion to decide those priorities themselves, but the priorities which they select should reflect the evidence. The general duty requires public authorities to focus on the issues within their remit which have the greatest importance and impact on gender equality.

3.8. The scheme should be published in a readily accessible format, for example, in a clearly signposted part of the public authority's website. It can be published as part of another published document or within a number of other published documents, for example within the business plan of a public authority or within a general equality scheme. Public authorities will have to ensure, however, that the individual elements of the scheme are easily identifiable, in order to show evidence of meeting the gender duty. This is also recommended in order to assure accountability to stakeholders.

What should be in a gender equality scheme and action plan?

3.9. The gender equality scheme is legally required to contain the public authority's overall objectives for meeting the duty (see paragraphs 3.34–3.39) including any pay objectives (paragraphs 3.40–3.52). To demonstrate that the public authority is meeting the duty in full, it is recommended that the scheme should also contain a rationale for the choice of those objectives, based on:

- an overview of the remit and functions of the authority, including functions carried out through partnership and procurement
- the major findings of the information-gathering exercise
- the major findings of the consultation exercise.

3.10. Schemes are legally required to contain information on how the public authority will take action to:

- collect information (paras 3.12–3.23)
- use this information, and any other relevant information, to meet the general and specific duties
- use the information to review the effectiveness of its implementation of the duty and to prepare subsequent schemes (paras 3.22–3.23)
- assess the impact on gender equality of its existing and new policies and practices (paras 3.57–3.74)
- consult relevant employees, service users and others (including trade unions) (paras 3.24–3.33)
- achieve fulfilment of the objectives (paras 3.75–3.78)

3.11. Although not a formal legal requirement, evidence of effective practice which could usefully be included in the scheme might be:

- evidence of commitment from senior leaders
- evidence of the link to the authority's priorities and business plans
- the identification of individuals with clear responsibilities for taking action on the scheme or elements of the scheme
- the allocation of specific budgets, for example, for consultation or information gathering
- measurable and time bound indicators of progress towards the objectives
- measures to strengthen the capacity of the authority to meet the duty
- separate action plans for individual identifiable departments
- details of how impact assessment will be incorporated into the authority's decision-making process
- details of how the public authority will ensure the duty is met in procurement and partnerships.

Gathering and using information

3.12. In order to understand which of its functions have the greatest relevance to gender equality, a public authority will need to gather and use information on how women and men are affected by its activities. A public authority may already have this information, disaggregated by gender. This information will have a crucial role in helping the public authority to determine its gender equality priorities, conduct effective gender impact assessments of policies and practices, and monitor progress towards its gender equality objectives. Information can be both quantitative and qualitative, and from a variety of sources.

3.13. The specific duties require each listed public authority to gather information on the effect of its policies and practices on men and women, and in particular:

- the extent to which they promote equality between male and female staff
- the extent to which the services it provides and the functions it performs take account of the needs of women and men.

3.14. Policies and practices are very broad terms, and cover every aspect of a public authority's activities and functions.

3.15. The specific duties also require the public authority to take into account any other information which it considers relevant. This might include, for example, the national level gender equality policies and documents which relate to their business – for example, Public Service Agreements, national policy frameworks in their sector, or existing research which indicates the major gender issues in their area of work.

3.16. In order to meet the gender equality duty, public authorities will have to set up systems, or adapt existing systems, to ensure they obtain and monitor the relevant information. In many cases this should involve disaggregating existing information; in some cases this may require the collection of new information. Information should be collected on the gender profile of service users, on staff, and on any other people, such as tenants, who may be affected by decision-making and policy functions.

3.17. Information may also need to be collected to compare the profile of potential staff or service users with actual staff or service users. For example, to analyse the gender aspects of an employment scheme, a public authority would have to compare the percentage of women in the scheme with the pool of economically inactive or unemployed women relative to men.

3.18. Setting up these systems or adapting existing systems may be a significant task initially, in order to develop the evidence base for the initial scheme. It will, however, have major benefits in improving the performance management of the organisation overall. It is recommended that public authorities ensure their systems allow them to cross-reference information by ethnicity, disability, age and other categories, so that there is evidence of any issues for different groups of women and men.

3.19. Public authorities which do not already have data might look at collecting information in the following areas:

- gender differences in service use – needs, expectations, barriers, satisfaction rates, outcomes
- balance of women and men in key decision-making bodies, including public appointments
- the gender profile of their staff, including analysis of patterns for part-time staff and those with caring responsibilities
- the extent and causes of the gender pay gap in the authority for full-time and part-time staff – including data on pay systems, the impact of caring responsibilities and occupational segregation (see paras 3.40–3.56)
- the prevalence of harassment and sexual harassment of staff and service users, the number of formal complaints and the outcome of complaints
- return rates of women on maternity leave and whether they are returning to jobs at the same level of responsibility and pay
- issues and barriers affecting transsexual staff and potential staff.

3.20. Quantitative monitoring is likely to be difficult in relation to transsexual staff or job applicants because of very low numbers and privacy concerns. Staff and job applicants should be told why the information is being collected and what it will be used for and be assured of confidentiality and genuine anonymity. They should also be told that they are under no obligation to give such information. Further advice can be sought from Acas and transsexual groups.

3.21. Quantitative data can be supplemented by qualitative information from consultation with stakeholders, including voluntary sector groups and trade unions, and from focus groups or other sources.

3.22. The duty is not just about collecting information, however, but analysing and using it, so that public authorities know where they are being successful and where they need to take action. For example, information may indicate that very few men are accessing flexible working policies, relative to the proportion of women staff who do so, so a public authority may want to take steps to support more men to work on a flexible basis.

3.23. Once enough information has been collected to give a picture of gender equality priorities across the public authority, priority indicators in key areas should be identified for annual monitoring to allow the public authority to meet the specific duty to review progress.

Using data to develop the Women's Offending Reduction Programme – Home Office

Women make up 6% of the prison population and just one in five of known offenders[1] and are therefore often forgotten in debates around criminal justice policy. However, between 1992 and 2002 the male prison population increased by 50%, while the female prison population increased by 173%.[2] 71% of women sentenced to prison in 2002 received a sentence of less than 12 months.[3] 55% of women in prison have at least one child under 16.[4] In 1993 there was one female suicide in custody, in 2003 there were 14.[5] Half of women in prison have experienced domestic violence compared with 25% of the female population.[6] Women are twice as likely as men to have received help for mental or emotional problems in the twelve months prior to custody and more likely to have a serious mental illness.[7]

The Women's Offending Reduction Programme seeks to co-ordinate work across government departments and agencies to ensure that policies, services, programmes and other interventions respond more appropriately to the particular needs and characteristics of women offenders. A number of government departments, agencies and organisations are 'stakeholders' in the Programme. By ensuring the delivery of a co-ordinated multi-agency response to women's offending, the Programme seeks to tackle the variety of factors which can affect why women offend, including poor housing, mental health problems, substance misuse, abuse, child care, education and employment.

By gathering data on the patterns and trends in women's offending, sentencing and the characteristics of women offenders, they are better able to identify issues and to track the progress of their work. The ultimate measure of success of the Programme will be a reduction in offending by women and fewer women held in custody.

1 www.homeoffice.gov.uk/rds/pdfs2/s95women03
2 www.homeoffice.gov.uk/rds/pdfs2/s95women03
3 www.homeoffice.gov.uk/rds/pdfs2/s95women03
4 Social Exclusion Unit Report (July 2002): Reducing Re-offending by Ex-prisoners.
5 www.homeoffice.gov.uk/rds/pdfs2/s95women03
6 Home Office & Prison Service, *Abuse, Interventions and Women in Prison: A Literature Review* (London, Home Office, 2003).
7 Department of Health, *Mainstreaming Gender and Women's Mental Health* (London, Department of Health, 2003).

Consultation

3.24. The specific duties require listed public authorities to consult stakeholders when preparing a scheme. The requirement is to consult employees, service users and others (including trade unions) who appear to the authority to have an interest in the way the authority carries out its functions.

3.25. In addition, the scheme itself must include an outline of the actions which the authority intends to take or has taken in order to consult.

3.26. By consulting stakeholders, public authorities will be able to:
- build up a better picture of the most important gender issues in their work
- gather evidence to use in determining priorities and in the gender impact assessment process
- get feedback on their initial draft objectives
- develop greater ownership and understanding of their gender equality objectives
- improve accountability to their staff, service users and the general public.

3.27. Consultation will be especially important where one sex is under-represented in the formal decision-making processes of the public authority.

3.28. Using the information gathered during consultation will also be beneficial in conducting impact assessments, gathering evidence and monitoring progress. Public authorities may choose to consult stakeholders again at any relevant stages of the implementation or review process, although there is no legal requirement to do so.

3.29. The extent of consultation should be appropriate to the size, remit and resources of the authority and there is no prescribed means of carrying it out. Public authorities are free to adapt their existing processes of public consultation. It is important to remember, however, that the duty is to consult on gender equality. Women and men (and, where appropriate, girls and boys) should both be consulted, but public authorities will have to ensure that the consultation process gives adequate attention to issues of gender equality, and any questions are structured in such a way as to bring out any potential differences in views between women and men, or between groups of women and men.

3.30. It is also important that women and men are enabled to participate fully in a consultation process, in order to get a full picture of their concerns. Some women may be less likely to attend, or to speak out at a traditional public meeting if they do not feel sufficiently confident, if their community discourages women taking up public roles, or if there are language barriers.

3.31. Where one sex has been under-represented or disadvantaged in a policy area, service or employment issue, public authorities may need to make special efforts to encourage participation. For example, women have rarely been involved in decision-making on regeneration. Similarly, men may not have been previously included in discussions on childcare services. There may also be particular barriers to participation where a minority group has experienced multiple disadvantages, for example, on the grounds of ethnicity and sexual orientation. Public authorities may wish to consult such groups in a single-sex or group-specific environment.

3.32. It is recommended that consultation on employment issues with the transsexual community is conducted separately, although they should also be actively encouraged to participate in mainstream consultation processes.

3.33. Voluntary sector organisations, such as women's groups and men's groups, are likely to be useful sources of information through consultation. Public authorities should bear in mind, however, that such organisations may have limited capacity and resources and may need support to develop their capacity to engage with the process.

Overcoming consultation fatigue

One problem that has been faced in the implementation of positive equality duties in Northern Ireland is 'consultation fatigue', with community and voluntary groups being overloaded with lengthy consultation documents. In its review of the implementation of the duties, the Equality Commission for Northern Ireland (ECNI) stated that there was "consensus that blanket mail shots to everyone on a public authority's consultation list are rarely appropriate and should not be routinely advocated".

One means of tackling 'consultation fatigue' is to ensure that consultation is 'joined-up' within organisations, so that there can be one consultation exercise on related policies with affected groups. The ECNI has also recommended that "a number of public authorities should consolidate consultation exercises where possible on the same, or similar, policies". Health authorities in Northern Ireland undertake a region-wide equality impact assessment (EQIA) timetable so that each policy area is subject to equality impact assessment by all health authorities at the same time. This joined-up approach enables one consultation exercise for each EQIA.

Prioritising and setting gender equality objectives

3.34. The purpose of producing the scheme is to bring about change. It is therefore important that public authorities focus on achieving outcomes – specific identifiable improvements in policies, in the way services and functions are delivered and in the gender equality outcomes for employees. Focussing on outcomes rather than processes will be of benefit to smaller public authorities, which may not necessarily have the resources to undertake large-scale processes.

3.35. The specific duties require listed public authorities to ensure that their schemes set out overall objectives that the authority has identified for meeting the duty.

3.36. The duty does not prescribe which objectives should be chosen and it is up to the authority to select the priorities for action, in consultation with service users and employees, and taking into account all relevant information.

3.37. In deciding priorities for action, public authorities will also need to consider the resource implications – a major deep-seated inequality may take significant staff and cash resource to correct. It may be, however, that it is so clearly a significant gender inequality issue that not to address it could lay the public authority open to enforcement action by the EOC or CEHR.

3.38. The priorities are intended to cover a three-year period. It will clearly not be possible to address and resolve all issues of gender inequality in that 3 year period, but the requirement to have due regard means that public authorities are expected to begin to address the most significant problems.

3.39. Appropriate weight must be given to the three elements of the duty, as set out in Chapter 2, across all of the authority's functions. In determining priorities, therefore, public authorities must review questions of harassment, discrimination and the promotion of gender equality across employment, service provision, public functions and any other functions. In addition, they must take into account services and functions that are contracted out.

Objectives to address the gender pay gap

3.40. The general duty includes a requirement to have due regard to the need to eliminate discrimination that is unlawful under the EqPA. The specific duties require listed public authorities, when setting their overall objectives, to 'consider the need to have objectives that address the causes of any differences between the pay of men and women that are related to their sex'.

3.41. These requirements, taken together with the specific duty to collect and make use of information on gender equality in the workforce and the duty to assess the impact of policies and practices, mean that listed public authorities have to undertake a process of determining whether their policies and practices are contributing to the causes of the gender pay gap. This should be done in consultation with employees and others, including trade unions.

3.42. The gender pay gap is determined by calculating women's overall average pay as a percentage of men's. The main factors which contribute to this gap are:

- discrimination, including pay discrimination (which is often inadvertent, but nonetheless unlawful)
- the impact of women's disproportionate share of caring responsibilities (which often results in women undertaking part-time work which is often poorly paid and often restricts career continuity and progression)
- the concentration of women in particular occupations ('occupational segregation'), usually characterised by lower levels of pay than in those numerically dominated by men.

3.43. The first step for a public authority considering the need for pay objectives should be to gather information to ascertain if there is a gender pay gap in its workforce. If there is, the authority should gather the information needed to identify the main cause or causes of that gap. These steps will enable it to give proper consideration to whether pay objectives are needed, and help it identify the causes those objectives may need to address. The size of the pay gap and the relative significance of each of the three causes will vary between different public authorities.

3.44. If a public authority fails to demonstrate that it has adequately collected and analysed information to establish whether or not there is a gender pay gap in its workforce, or fails to take action if there is a problem, it risks non-compliance with the duty, and subsequent enforcement action. Public authorities that do not set their own pay systems will still be expected to gather information and take appropriate action on any causes of the gender pay gap within their organisation which remain within their control.

3.45. Public authorities must be able to demonstrate that they have considered the need to have objectives that address the gender pay gap. For this reason, if a public authority does not include such objectives it should give reasons for that decision in its scheme. This might include providing evidence that there is no gender pay gap within its workforce, or within any wider group of women and men who are affected by its functions as an organisation, or that the alternative objectives which it has chosen have greater significance for gender equality. Public authorities should bear in mind, however, that pay discrimination is unlawful, and the general duty requires them to have due regard to the need to eliminate unlawful discrimination.

Pay discrimination

3.46. In order to fulfil the general duty to have due regard to the need to eliminate discrimination that is unlawful under the EqPA, a public authority must be able to demonstrate that it has considered the need to take action on pay discrimination.

3.47. The gender equality duty does not require public authorities to undertake equal pay reviews. No specific course of action is prescribed to tackle pay discrimination. The statutory Code of Practice on Equal Pay recommends, however, that the most effective way of establishing whether a public authority's pay policies and pay systems are discriminatory is to undertake an equal pay review.

The fundamental components of an equal pay review are:

- comparing the pay of women and men doing equal work. Here employers need to check for one or more of the following: like work; work rated as equivalent; work of equal value – these checks are the foundation of an equal pay review
- identifying any equal pay gaps, including by differences between part-time and full-time workers' pay
- eliminating those pay gaps that cannot satisfactorily be explained on grounds other than sex.

The Code of Practice on Equal Pay and supporting toolkits are the recommended tools for undertaking this process. These can be found at www.eoc.org.uk

3.48. A public authority that has undertaken a pay review, containing the elements described above, in the preceding four years may not need to repeat it, unless it has undergone significant changes to its workforce, as it should already have evidence of the situation in its organisation and should be taking action.

3.49. Public authorities may also choose to collect pay information across a selected sample of their staff, for example administrators, manual workers, or departments or units such as IT or physiotherapy, to see if women and men carrying out the same jobs or jobs of equal value are receiving equal pay. Given the requirement to consult, any such approach should be discussed with the relevant trade union. Sampling may indicate a problem which suggests the need to proceed to a full pay review.

3.50. If a public authority decides not to undertake a full pay review, it may be appropriate for it to carry out a screening process, for example, to address areas known to pose a high risk of pay discrimination. These will include:

- starting salaries: checking whether women and men who have been recruited to the same jobs or jobs of equal value are being appointed on the same starting salary and whether any patterns are related to sex-based factors
- progression: whether unjustifiably long pay scales are inadvertently discriminating against women (who may be less likely to have continuous service)
- bonus payments: whether bonuses are paid, or higher bonuses are paid, in jobs where men predominate.

3.51. Many public authorities, such as schools, do not set their own pay systems. They are legally liable, however, under the EqPA, for the implementation of those pay systems. Some are likely to find the screening of high-risk factors, as set out above, which they, as employers, have control over, particularly useful in complying with the duty. Schools should ensure that decisions made within the school, which have an impact on an individual's pay (such as the allocation of Teaching and Learning Responsibility payments) are free of discrimination. Where a public authority does not set its own pay system, any pay review of that system would often be more appropriately carried out at a higher level (for example Local Education Authorities for schools).

3.52. Where public authorities do not set their own pay systems, but an authority becomes aware that there are elements in that system which are causing, or risk causing, pay discrimination, it is recommended that the public authority should alert the relevant pay body. The remit of pay review bodies in Great Britain includes a requirement to seek to ensure non-discriminatory pay systems, and to develop systems that support diversity.

Caring responsibilities and occupational segregation

3.53. Public authorities should also gather evidence on the impact of caring responsibilities on their workforces. Based on that evidence and on consultation with employees and trade unions, they should consider whether it is appropriate to set objectives to address any relevant issues. Women are significantly more likely than men to work part-time, often because of childcare and other caring responsibilities. Part-time work in Britain is characterised by particularly low rates of hourly pay and reduced access to promotion and development opportunities. In addition, lack of availability of suitable childcare restricts women's employment choices. Support to female and male employees with childcare responsibilities, through providing more flexible working and training opportunities or childcare provision or subsidy, will also contribute to the promotion of equality of opportunity between women and men.

3.54. Public authorities should also collect evidence on the extent of occupational segregation in their workforces. Based on that evidence and on consultation with employees and trade unions, they should consider whether it is appropriate to set objectives to address it. Employers who have strongly segregated workforces may be at higher risk of having equal pay claims taken against them. In a highly segregated workforce it can be easy for pay arrangements to evolve in which women are paid less than men when they are doing work of equal value, giving rise to equal pay tribunal claims.

3.55. Public authorities can check which issues are relevant to any gender pay gap in their organisation by:

- monitoring where women and men work in their organisation, what hours they work and at what grade. This will map any segregation by seniority and by types of work and will alert public authorities to the possible impact of caring responsibilities.
- using any annual staff monitoring exercise to ask staff if they have caring responsibilities, and whether this is for children or for older people.

Closing the gender pay gap within the wider remit of a public authority

3.56. In addition to its functions as an employer, a public authority may have functions which have the potential to address the gender pay gap in a wider policy sense. This would be the case, for example, for a Regional Development Agency, a Learning and Skills Council or a local authority in its education functions. If this is the case, the public authority should also be considering whether it can address the causes of the gender pay gap within that wider remit where appropriate. This might include reviewing the high-level policy priorities of the authority overall, for example setting regional economic objectives that address the under-utilisation of the skills of part-time women workers. It might also include specific measures such as improving school careers advice so that boys and girls consider a wider range of career options, training women to fill areas of skills shortage in traditionally male-dominated areas and vice versa, or providing childcare support for male and female students in vocational training.

3.57–3.74 (*omitted: outside the scope of this work.*)

Implementing the scheme

3.75. Listed public authorities are expected, within the three year period, to implement:

- their actions for gathering and using information
- the objectives in their scheme.

3.76. If a public authority does not comply with any specific duty imposed by the Order, including implementing the elements indicated above, the EOC or CEHR may issue a compliance notice (see Chapter 4 for further information about enforcement).

3.77. The public authority will not be under an obligation to implement their actions for gathering or using information or to implement the scheme objectives if, in all the circumstances of the case, it would be unreasonable or impracticable for it to do so. The words 'unreasonable' and 'impracticable' are intended to relate to particular and unforeseen circumstances. For example:

- where there are particular difficulties with implementing objectives in the scheme but these difficulties could not have been foreseen, then it is likely to be unreasonable to have to implement them
- where costs associated with an action unexpectedly escalate so as to be out of proportion to the duty, then it is unlikely to be practicable to implement the duty.

3.78. It is important, however, that public authorities consider other solutions where it is not reasonable or practicable for them to carry out a particular part of the scheme. Once barriers to equality have been identified, an authority will need to address them, considering alternative methods of overcoming them if those proposed originally are not practicable or reasonable.

Annual reports

3.79. Listed public authorities must take such steps as are reasonably practicable to publish annually a report, summarising the actions they have taken to implement their scheme objectives. This report can be published as a separate document or within another published document, for example, the public authority's main annual report.

Reviewing and revising the scheme

3.80. Listed public authorities have an obligation to review and revise the scheme every three years. It is recommended that this should involve a review of progress to date and of the appropriateness of the previous scheme objectives, with a view to continuous improvement in the implementation of the duty. Evidence for this process would include the information gathered to date, the results of impact assessments, and any feedback from stakeholders on the effectiveness of the preceding scheme.

3.81. In preparing the new scheme, public authorities are required to collect and make use of information, and to consult stakeholders as before. Stakeholders can also usefully be involved in the review of the previous scheme, although this is not a legal requirement.

[4763]

Chapters 4, 5, 6 (*omitted: outside the scope of this work.*)

APPENDIX A: WHAT IS THE DEFINITION OF A PUBLIC AUTHORITY FOR THE PURPOSES OF THE GENERAL DUTY?

For the purposes of the gender duty, public authorities are bodies whose functions are those of a public nature. The most obvious examples of this are government departments, local authorities, the police and the armed forces. They will generally possess special powers, be democratically accountable, be publicly funded in whole or in part, be under an obligation to act only in the public interest and have a statutory constitution. These bodies are sometimes referred to as 'pure public authorities'. The gender duty will therefore apply for example to:

- Ministers, government departments and executive agencies (such as the Home Office and its executive agencies, including the Prison Service, and the Immigration and Nationality Directorate).
- The National Assembly for Wales.
- Army, Navy and Air Forces of the Crown (subject to a limited exception relating to work with the Government Communications Headquarters).
- Local government including local authorities, fire authorities, local probation boards, regional development agencies, magistrates courts committees, passenger transport executives and licensing boards.
- Governing bodies of further and higher education institutions, colleges and universities.
- Governing bodies of educational establishments maintained by local education authorities (including schools).
- The National Health Service including NHS Trusts, Health Authorities and primary care trusts, Local Health Boards (Wales).
- Police, including Chief Officers of Police, police authorities and the Independent Police Complaints Commission.
- Inspection and audit agencies such as the National Audit Office, Wales Audit Office, Audit Commissions, Her Majesty's Inspectorate of Constabulary (HMIC), the Healthcare Commission, the Health and Safety Executive.
- Some publicly-funded cultural bodies or institutions such as Sports Councils and Big Lottery Fund.
- Other bodies such as the Criminal Injuries Compensation Authority, the Crown Prosecution Service, Courts and tribunals (though not for judicial acts), Prison Boards of Visitors, the Children and Family Court Advisory and Support Service, the Community Development Foundation, Visiting Committees for Immigration Detention Centres, the Youth Justice Board for England and Wales, the Sentencing Advisory Panel.

This is not an exhaustive list.

Equivalent public authorities in Scotland are also covered by the general duty. Further detail is provided in the Scottish Code of Practice.

Private bodies carrying out public functions

The Equality Act 2006 is designed to ensure that a wide number of authorities are subject to the gender duty in relation to the performance of public functions. 'Public authority' therefore includes any person who has functions of a public nature. This will include private bodies or voluntary organisations who are carrying out public functions on behalf of a public authority. An organisation will be exercising a public function where it is in effect exercising a function which would otherwise be exercised by the state – and where individuals have to rely upon that person for the exercise of that function. These bodies are sometimes referred to as 'functional public bodies'. Whether or not an organisation is exercising a function of a public nature will ultimately be a matter for the courts. As the law presently stands, a private body may be held to be performing public functions and thus subject to the gender equality duty in relation to those functions if:

- it is publicly funded

- it is exercising powers of a public nature directly assigned to it by statute; or
- it is taking the place of central or local government
- it is providing a public service
- its structures and work are closely linked with the delegating or contracting-out state body
- there is a close relationship between the private body and any public authority.

Additional factors which may be relevant in determining whether or not a body is carrying out a function of a public nature include:

- the extent to which the private body is supervised by a state regulatory body
- the fact of supervision by a state regulatory body.

For example, the following bodies are likely to be deemed to be performing 'functions of a public nature' in relation to their public functions, and therefore subject to the gender equality duty in relation to those functions:

- the privatised utilities
- private security firms managing contracted-out prisons
- GPs when providing services under contract to a Primary Care Trust.

In relation to a particular act, a person is not a public authority if the nature of the act is private (for example, a private company running a prison will not be covered by the duty in relation to its private activities such as providing security guards for supermarkets).

A pure public authority contracting out services will always remain subject to the duty. It is possible that a 'pure' public authority which is subject to the duty could also be contracting out services to a 'functional' public authority (ie a private organisation providing a service of a public nature). In this case, both bodies will be subject to the duty in their own right. If there is a breach of the general duty, the legal responsibility for this could rest, depending on the circumstances, with either body. Actual responsibility would depend on the act which is the subject of the complaint, who was responsible for it and who was in breach of the general duty in respect of it. For example, a private prison might close down its childcare facilities for use by visitors, contrary to the terms of its contract with the Home Office. Whilst both the prison and the Home Office could be challenged in judicial review proceedings, the likelihood is that the Home Office would establish they had discharged their duty if they had included a requirement for childcare facilities in the contractual specifications. The private prison would be more likely to have difficulty in establishing that it had discharged the duty.

It is recommended that those authorities who may be carrying out functions of a public nature, but who are unsure whether they fall within the definition of a 'public authority' should safeguard their position by ensuring that they comply with the general duty in relation to those functions. It may also be advisable to seek legal advice on whether or not the gender equality duty applies in such a situation.

[4764]

APPENDIX B: PUBLIC BODIES AND FUNCTIONS WHICH ARE EXEMPT FROM THE GENDER DUTY

S76A(3) SDA 1975

The Act currently exempts the following public authorities from the gender duty:

- both Houses of Parliament
- the Scottish Parliament
- the General Synod of the Church of England
- the Security Service
- the Secret Intelligence Service
- the Government Communications Headquarters
- a part of the armed forces of the Crown which is, in accordance with a requirement of the Secretary of State, assisting the Government Communications Headquarters, or
- a person specified by order of the Secretary of State.

S76A(4) SDA 1975

In addition there are certain functions of public authorities which the Act excludes from being subject to the duty. The general duty does not apply to the exercise of:

- a function in connection with proceedings in the House of Commons or the House of Lords
- a function in connection with proceedings in the Scottish Parliament (other than a function of the Scottish Parliamentary Corporate Body)
- a judicial function (whether in connection with a court or tribunal)

- a function exercised on behalf of or on the instructions of a person exercising a judicial function (whether in connection with a court or a tribunal)
- a function specified by order of the Secretary of State.

[4765]

Appendices C–G (*omitted: outside the scope of this work.*)

BORDER & IMMIGRATION AGENCY CODE OF PRACTICE: CIVIL PENALTIES FOR EMPLOYERS (FEBRUARY 2008)

PREVENTION OF ILLEGAL WORKING

IMMIGRATION, ASYLUM AND NATIONALITY ACT 2006

NOTES

This Code of Practice, and the Code immediately following at **[4772]**, were issued by the Border and Immigration Agency (part of the Home Office). This Code is made under the authority of s 19 of the Immigration, Asylum and Nationality Act 2006; the Parliamentary authority for the Codes is SI 2007/3290, regs 11 and 12 respectively at **[3474B]** and **[3474C]**. The Codes came into force on 29 February 2008. The Codes have no specific statutory status. They replace the previous Code issued by the Home Office under the Asylum and Immigration Act 1996 at **[4562]**. The new Codes do not apply in respect of those employees continuously employed since a date prior to 29 February 2008.

1. INTRODUCTION

1.1 The Government is introducing civil penalties for employers of illegal migrant workers as part of a fundamental reform of our immigration system, in which the rights and responsibilities of employers are clearly set out and penalties are proportionate to the level of non-compliance or illegal behaviour.

1.2 As an employer, you have a responsibility to prevent illegal working in the United Kingdom. The illegal working provisions of the Immigration, Asylum and Nationality Act 2006 ('the 2006 Act') came into effect on 29 February 2008 and replaced the previous offence under section 8 of the Asylum and Immigration Act 1996,[1] ('the 1996 Act'), **which has now been repealed**. Section 15 of the 2006 Act allows the Secretary of State to serve an employer with a notice requiring the payment of a penalty of a specified amount where they have employed a person aged 16 or over, who is subject to immigration control unless:

- that person has been given valid and subsisting leave to be in the United Kingdom by the Government, and that leave does not restrict them from taking the job in question; **or**
- the person comes into a category where employment is also allowed.

1.3 For the purposes of the 2006 Act, an 'employer' is defined as a person who employs an individual under a contract of employment. This can be a contract of service or apprenticeship, whether express or implied. If the contract is expressed, this can be either orally or in writing. In most cases, it should be clear when you are entering into such a contract of service with an employee.

1.4 This Code of practice has been issued under section 19 of the 2006 Act. The Code has been prepared to set out the factors that may be considered when determining the level of penalty to be imposed in each case. This Code has been produced alongside other guidance documents and sources of information. You may wish to refer to this Code alongside that guidance and information.

1. 5 This is a statutory Code. This means that it has been approved by the Secretary of State and laid before Parliament. The Code does not impose any legal obligations on employers, nor is it an authoritative statement of the law; only the courts can provide that. However, the Code can be used as evidence in legal proceedings and courts must take account of any part of the Code that might be relevant.

[4766]

NOTES

1 As amended by section 22 of the Immigration and Asylum Act 1999, section 147 of the Nationality, Immigration and Asylum Act 2002 and section 6 of the Asylum and Immigration (Treatment of Claimants, etc.) Act 2004).

2. HOW THE LEVEL OF PENALTY MAY BE DETERMINED

2.1 If we find you to be employing illegal migrant workers, we may look at certain factors when deciding the level of your civil penalty.

2.2 Table 1 is a framework designed to assist the Border and Immigration Agency with the assessment of whether to issue a penalty notice to an employer, and if so, at what level. It provides a sliding scale with minimum and maximum penalties, but the actual amount will be decided by the Border and Immigration Agency on a case by case basis. The framework is provided for guidance purposes (explanatory flow charts are also attached at Appendix 2). The level of penalty to be imposed per worker may be increased or reduced according to different criteria. For example, the penalty can be increased according to the number of times you are found with illegal migrant workers in your workforce and have failed to establish a statutory excuse.

Table 1- framework for assessment of level of civil penalty

OCCASION ON WHICH WARNING/PENALTY ISSUED		NATURE OF CHECKS COMPLETED				
		FULL	PARTIAL		NO	
	3RD+	No penalty	Maximum penalty of **£10,000** per worker		Maximum penalty of **£10,000** per worker	
			Reduced by up to **£1,250** per worker reported	Reduced by up to **£1,250** per worker, with co-operation		
			Minimum penalty of **£7,500** per worker			
	2ND	No penalty	Maximum penalty of **£7,500** per worker		Maximum penalty of **£10,000** per worker	
			Reduced by up to **£1,250** per worker reported	Reduced by up to **£1,250** per worker, with co-operation	Reduced by up to **£1,250** per worker reported	Reduced by up to **£1,250** per worker, with co-operation
			Minimum penalty of **£5,000** per worker		Minimum penalty of **£7,500** per worker	
	1ST	No penalty	Maximum penalty of **£5,000** per worker		Maximum penalty of **£7,500** per worker	
			Reduced by up to **£2,500** per worker reported	Reduced by up to **£2,500** per worker, with co-operation	Reduced by up to **£2,500** per worker reported	Reduced by up to **£2,500** per worker, with co-operation
			No penalty warning letter issued		Minimum penalty of **£2,500** per worker	

2.3 Where an objection is made against the imposition of a civil penalty, reference will be made to this framework, in addition to factors listed at Appendix 4. The factors we will take into account are:

A) the nature of checks that you have conducted; **and**
B) reporting suspected illegal workers to the Border and Immigration Agency; **and**
C) your co-operation with the Border and Immigration Agency; **and**
D) the number of offences you have committed in the past.

A. The Nature of Checks Conducted

2.4 The system of civil penalties is designed to encourage employers to comply with their legal obligations, without criminalising those who are less than diligent in operating their recruitment and employment practices. Under the 2006 Act, an employer may establish a statutory excuse by checking original documents presented by a potential or existing employee. Details of what documents are acceptable and how to do this are provided in Appendix 1.

2.5 In all cases, you must undertake these steps **before** a person begins employment to establish the statutory excuse and, where a document or documents from List B are provided, you must also carry out a follow-up check at least once every **12 months** after the initial check to retain the statutory excuse.

2.6 The Government is soon to begin introducing identity cards for foreign nationals on a compulsory basis. However, before full roll-out of the cards, if you are presented with a false travel document or visa, you will only be subject to legal action if the falsity is reasonably apparent. The falsity would be considered to be 'reasonably apparent' if an individual who is untrained in the identification of false documents, examining it carefully, but briefly and without the use of technological aids, could reasonably be expected to realise that the document in question is not genuine.

2.7 Equally, where a potential employee presents a document and it is reasonably apparent that the person presenting the document is not the rightful holder of that document, then you may also be subject to enforcement action, even if the document itself is genuine. Therefore, you should examine the photograph and personal details in the document and compare these with the holder in order to detect any impersonation.

Full and partial checks

2.8 A **full check** shall be considered to have been conducted where you can provide copies of certain documents, as described in Appendix 1, for all relevant employees and the official is satisfied that the specified steps were taken when checking these documents. If a full check has been conducted, then the employer will be entitled to a statutory excuse and no penalty may be payable, even if illegal migrant workers are found to be working.

2.9 However, the provision of such records **does not** provide a statutory excuse if you **knew** that the employee was not permitted to take the work in question. You may receive a penalty or be prosecuted for a criminal offence, including the offence of knowingly employing an illegal migrant worker, or facilitating a breach of UK immigration law. Action will be taken against any employer where there is sufficient evidence available and where prosecution would be in the public interest.

2.10 Where only a partial check has been carried out for migrant workers who are found to be working illegally, the employer may be subject to a civil penalty. A **partial check** shall be considered to have been conducted where, for example, you have only checked and copied one of a specified combination of two original documents that are required to establish the statutory excuse, or failed to conduct a follow-up check on a worker with temporary immigration status, after having conducted a full document check at the point of recruitment.

2.11 If you cannot provide a record of having conducted the prescribed document checks prior to recruitment, or you have accepted a document which clearly does not belong to the holder, or it is reasonably apparent that the document is false, or shows that the person does not have a current entitlement to work in this country, you shall be considered to have conducted no check for the purpose of imposing a penalty. Where **no check** has been conducted, the employer may be subject to the maximum level of penalty.

2.12 In each case, it is for you to show that you have complied with the requirements to establish a statutory excuse.

B. Reporting Suspected Illegal Workers to the Border and Immigration Agency

2.13 As shown in Table 1, the civil penalty may be reduced at the discretion of the Border and Immigration Agency, having regard to the suggested minimum and maximum penalties. If more than one employee is found working illegally, you may be penalised for each worker found, but any reduction made may be applied proportionately for each illegal migrant worker detected.

2.14 If you report any suspicions about your employees' entitlement to work in the UK, or to undertake the work in question to the Border and Immigration Agency, a sum may be deducted from the amount of penalty due for each worker. This information must have been reported to the Employers' Helpline on **0845 010 6677**[2] **before** any immigration visit is made to the employer. When reporting, you will be given a call reference and this must be referred to when applying a reduction in penalty.

C. Co-Operation with the Border and Immigration Agency in Conducting an Operation

2.15 The penalty due for each worker can also be reduced where you have co-operated with the Border and Immigration Agency in any investigation, or in any consequent operation to detect and detain illegal migrant workers within your workforce.

PART 4

2.16 The level of any reduction made will depend on whether you have been found to be employing illegal migrant workers within the previous three years. The sliding scale also allows for a warning letter to be issued instead of a civil penalty in cases where:

- It is the first occasion on which you are found with illegal migrant workers in your workforce; **and**
- You have conducted partial checks on the workers; **and**
- You have reported suspected illegal workers; **and**
- There is no evidence of deliberate wrong doing by you; **and**
- You have co-operated with the Border and Immigration Agency.

2.17 Where it can be established that you have conducted full checks and did not knowingly employ an illegal worker, you will receive no penalty or warning.

D. Previous Offences

2.18 When considering whether a higher level of penalty should apply to an employer who has been visited before, previous penalties or warnings will not be considered if they were issued more than three years before the date of the new visit. Where an employer is revisited, and has received a penalty or warning within three years of the current visit, those penalties and warnings will be counted.

Multiple premises

2.19 A company with multiple premises where recruitment is devolved to each site, will not be liable to a cumulative penalty if illegal workers are detected at different sites, unless this can be attributed to a general failure in the company's centrally set recruitment practices.

Transfer Of Undertakings

2.20 Employers who acquire staff as a result of a Transfer of Undertakings (Protection of Employment) transfer are provided with a period of 28 days grace to undertake the appropriate document checks.

[4767]

NOTES

[2] For current information, please visit www.bia.homeoffice.gov.uk

APPENDIX 1: DOCUMENTS REQUIRED FOR THE PURPOSE OF ESTABLISHING THE STATUTORY EXCUSE

Any one of the documents, or combination of documents described in **List A** or **List B** will provide you with a statutory excuse if you take reasonable steps to check the validity of the original document and that the person presenting the document is the rightful holder, then make a copy of the relevant page, or pages before employing an individual.

For identity cards, passports and travel documents, a copy should be taken of:

- the document's front cover; **and**
- any page containing the holder's personal details including nationality, his or her photograph, date of birth and/or signature; **and**
- any biometric details; **and**
- the date of expiry; **and**
- any relevant UK immigration endorsements.

Other documents should be copied in their entirety.

All copies of documents should be kept securely. If your potential employee gives you two documents which have different names, ask them for a further document to explain the reason for this. The further document could be a marriage certificate, a divorce decree, or a deed poll document.

By doing this, the Border and Immigration Agency will be able to examine your right to the statutory excuse if they detect any illegal migrants working for you.

If reasonable steps are taken to check the validity of a document or documents from **List A**, the statutory excuse will have been established for the duration of the employment **and no further checks will be required**.

Each time that a document or combination of documents from **List B** is provided, you must note the date on which you carried out the original document check. In order to retain your excuse against a penalty for employing that individual, you must carry out a follow-up check at least once every **12 months** after the initial check. Again, this will involve asking the employee to produce a valid original document, or documents either from **List A**, or from **List B** and copying it for your records. If a document, or documents, from **List A** are subsequently presented and reasonable steps are taken to check the validity of the document or documents, the statutory excuse will have been established for the remainder of the employment and **no further checks will be required**.

Please note the references to the provision of a National Insurance number in Lists A and B. **The provision of a National Insurance number in isolation is never sufficient for the purpose of establishing a statutory excuse**. The National Insurance number can only be used for this purpose when presented in combination with one of the documents, as appropriate, specified in Lists A and B.

All references to the documents issued by the Home Office in Lists A and B, also include documents issued by the former Immigration and Nationality Directorate (IND) and Work Permits (UK).

List A Documents

1. A passport showing that the holder, or a person named in the passport as the child of the holder, is a British citizen or a citizen of the United Kingdom and Colonies having the right of abode in the United Kingdom; **or**

2. A passport or national identity card showing that the holder, or a person named in the passport as the child of the holder, is a national of a European Economic Area country or Switzerland; **or**

3. A residence permit, registration certificate or document certifying or indicating permanent residence issued by the Home Office or the Border and Immigration Agency to a national of a European Economic Area country or Switzerland; **or**

4. A permanent residence card issued by the Home Office or the Border and Immigration Agency to the family member of a national of a European Economic Area country or Switzerland; **or**

5. A Biometric Immigration Document issued by the Border and Immigration Agency to the holder which indicates that the person named in it is allowed to stay indefinitely in the United Kingdom, or has no time limit on their stay in the United Kingdom; **or**

6. A passport or other travel document endorsed to show that the holder is exempt from immigration control, is allowed to stay indefinitely in the United Kingdom, has the right of abode in the United Kingdom, or has no time limit on their stay in the United Kingdom; **or**

7. An Immigration Status Document issued by the Home Office or the Border and Immigration Agency to the holder with an endorsement indicating that the person named in it is allowed to stay indefinitely in the United Kingdom, or has no time limit on their stay in the United Kingdom, **when produced in combination with** an official document giving the person's permanent National Insurance Number and their name issued by a Government agency or a previous employer (e g P45, P60, National Insurance Card); **or**

8. A full birth certificate issued in the United Kingdom which includes the name(s) of at least one of the holder's parents, **when produced in combination with** an official document giving the person's permanent National Insurance Number and their name issued by a Government agency or a previous employer (e g P45, P60, National Insurance Card); **or**

9. A full adoption certificate issued in the United Kingdom which includes the name(s) of at least one of the holder's adoptive parents, **when produced in combination with** an official document giving the person's permanent National Insurance Number and their name issued by a Government agency or a previous employer (e g P45, P60, National Insurance Card); **or**

10. A birth certificate issued in the Channel Islands, the Isle of Man, or Ireland, **when produced in combination with** an official document giving the person's permanent National Insurance Number and their name issued by a Government agency or a previous employer (e g P45, P60, National Insurance Card); **or**

11. An adoption certificate issued in the Channel Islands, the Isle of Man, or Ireland, **when produced in combination with** an official document giving the person's permanent National Insurance Number and their name issued by a Government agency or a previous employer (e g P45, P60, National Insurance Card); **or**

12. A certificate of registration or naturalisation as a British citizen, **when produced in combination with** an official document giving the person's permanent National Insurance Number and their name issued by a Government agency or a previous employer (e g P45, P60, National Insurance Card); **or**

13. A letter issued by the Home Office or the Border and Immigration Agency to the holder which indicates that the person named in it is allowed to stay indefinitely in the United Kingdom, or has no time limit on their stay, **when produced in combination with** an official document giving the person's permanent National Insurance Number and their name issued by a Government agency or a previous employer (e g P45, P60, National Insurance Card).

List B Documents

1. A passport or other travel document endorsed to show that the holder is allowed to stay in the United Kingdom and is allowed to do the work in question, provided that it does not require the issue of a work permit; **or**

2. A Biometric Immigration Document, issued by the Border and Immigration Agency to the holder which indicates that the person named in it can stay in the United Kingdom and is allowed to do the work in question; **or**

3. A work permit or other approval to take employment issued by the Home Office or the Border and Immigration Agency, **when produced in combination with** either a passport or another travel document endorsed to show that the holder is allowed to stay in the United Kingdom and is allowed to do the work in question, or a letter issued by the Home Office or the Border and Immigration Agency to the holder, or the employer or prospective employer confirming the same; **or**

4. A certificate of application issued by the Home Office or the Border and Immigration Agency to or for a family member of a national of a European Economic Area country or Switzerland, stating that the holder is permitted to take employment, which is less than 6 months old, when produced in combination with evidence of verification by the Border and Immigration Agency Employer Checking Service; **or**

5. A residence card or document issued by the Home Office or the Border and Immigration Agency to a family member of a national of a European Economic Area country or Switzerland; **or**

6. An Application Registration Card (ARC) issued by the Home Office or the Border and Immigration Agency stating that the holder is permitted to take employment, **when produced in combination with** evidence of verification by the Border and Immigration Agency Employer Checking Service; **or**

7. An Immigration Status Document issued by the Home Office or the Border and Immigration Agency to the holder with an endorsement indicating that the person named in it can stay in the United Kingdom, and is allowed to do the work in question, **when produced in combination with** an official document giving the person's permanent National Insurance Number and their name issued by a Government agency or previous employer (e g P45, P60, National Insurance Card); **or**

8. A letter issued by the Home Office or the Border and Immigration Agency to the holder or the employer or prospective employer, which indicates that the person named in it can stay in the United Kingdom and is allowed to do the work in question, **when produced in combination with** an official document giving the person's permanent National Insurance Number and their name issued by a Government agency or previous employer (e g P45, P60, National Insurance Card).

[4768]

APPENDIX 2: FLOWCHARTS FOR DETERMINATION OF THE CIVIL PENALTY

FIRST VISIT TO EMPLOYER

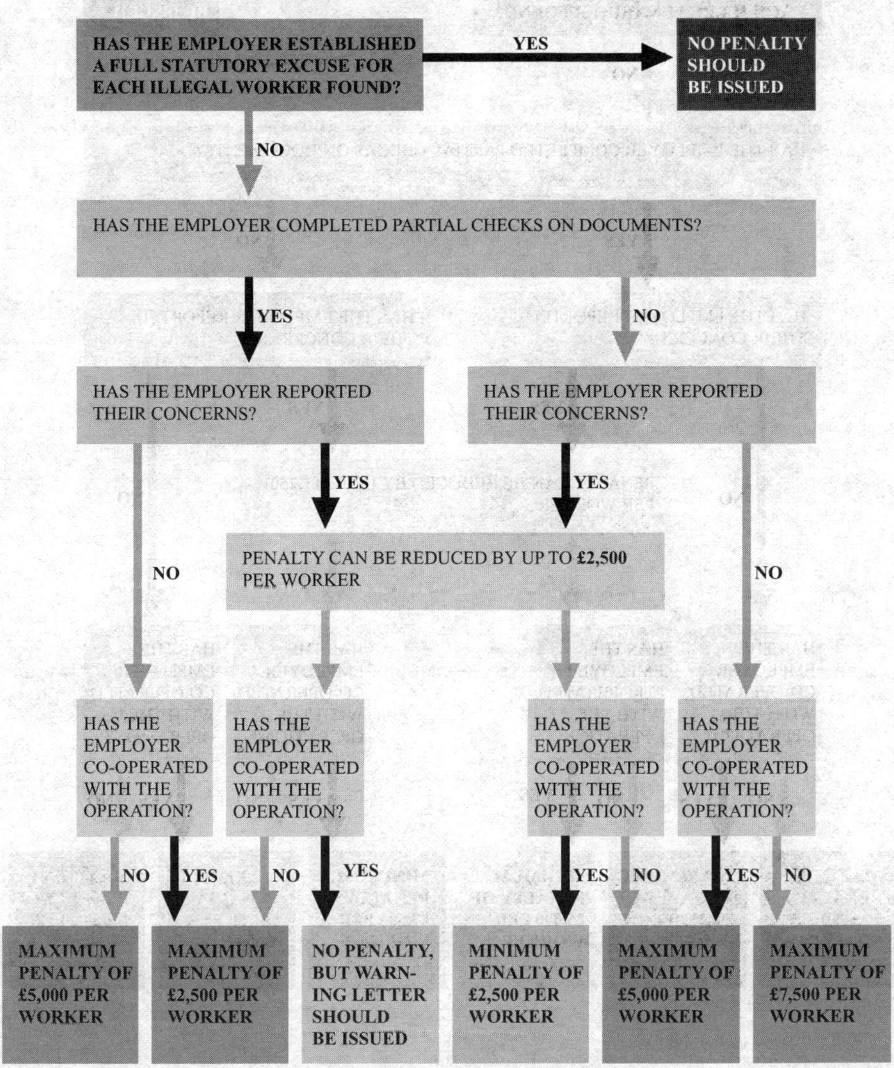

SECOND VISIT TO EMPLOYER (WITHIN THREE YEARS OF FIRST VISIT)

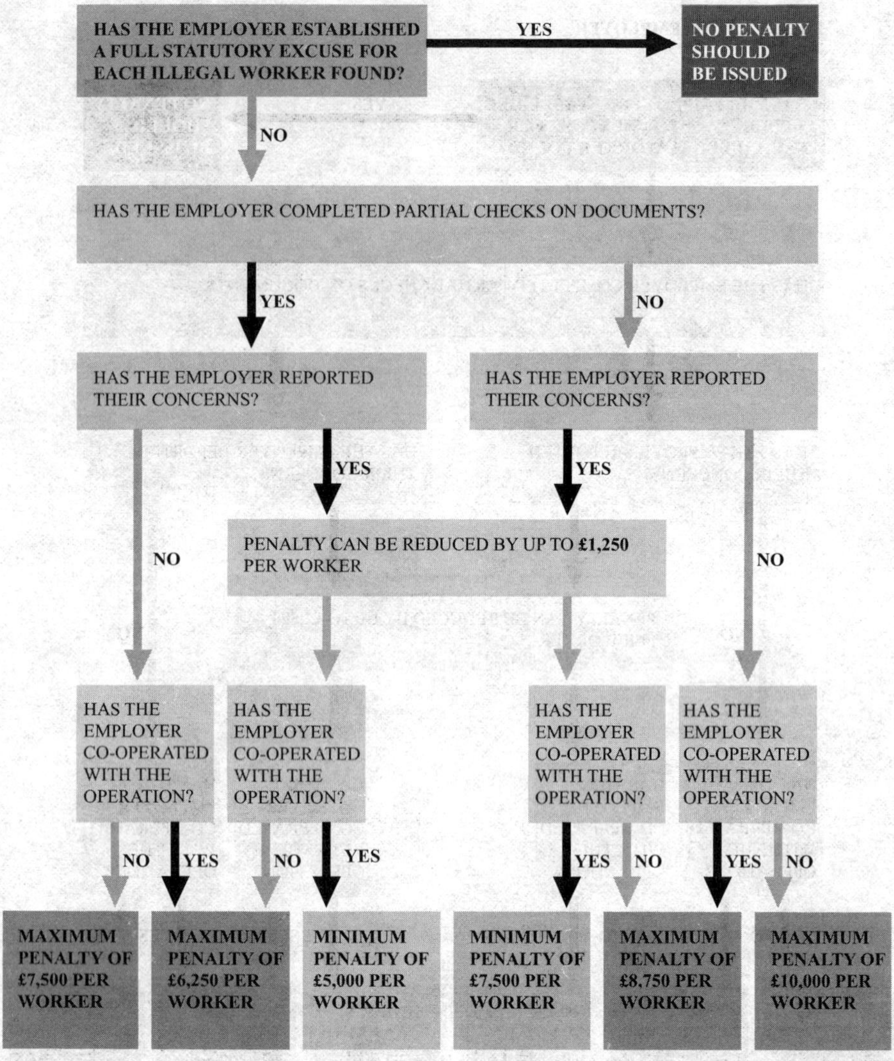

THIRD AND EVERY SUBSEQUENT VISIT TO EMPLOYER (WITHIN THREE YEARS OF FIRST VISIT)

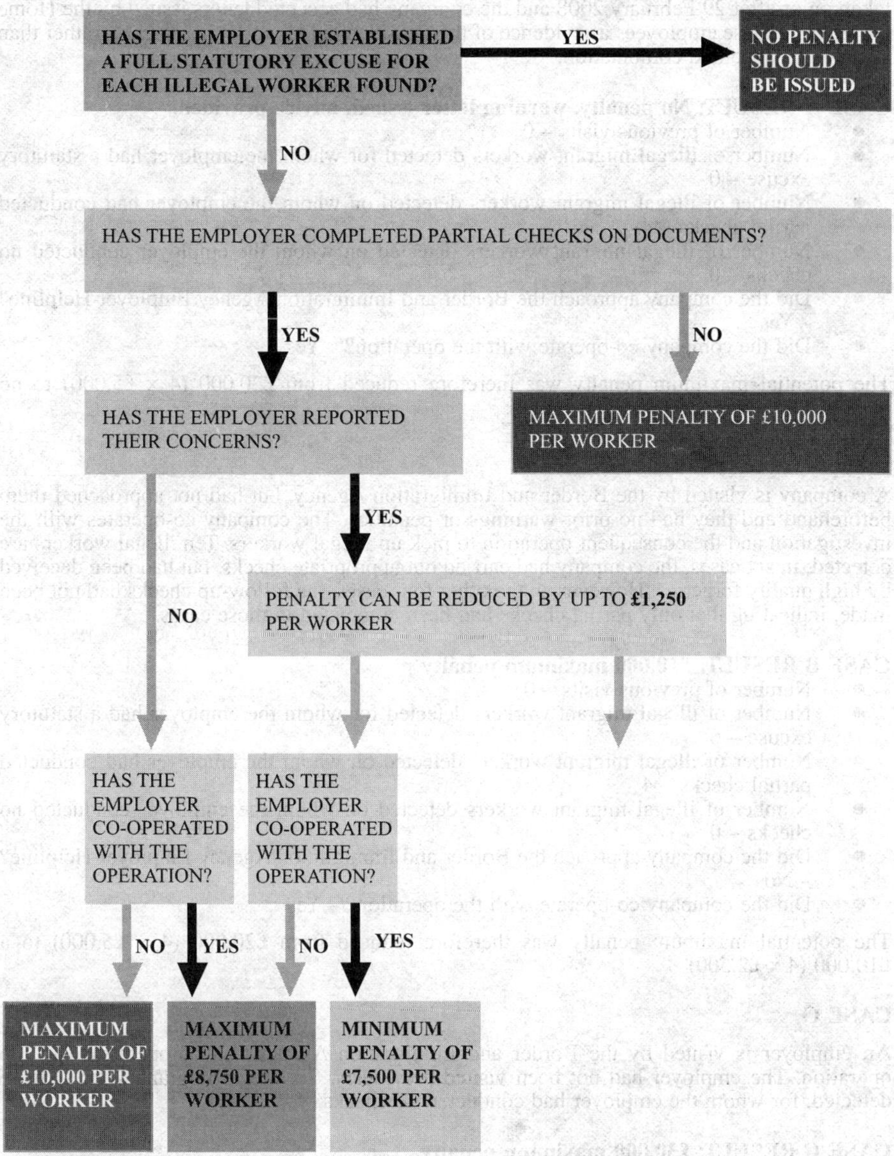

[4769]

APPENDIX 3: CASE SCENARIOS

In any scenario where the full checks have been completed and the employer did not knowingly employ an illegal migrant worker, the employer will not be liable to a civil penalty. The following scenarios provide examples of potential maximum penalty amounts, however, the penalties set out in these scenarios are only intended as guidelines and each case will be considered on its merits.

CASE A

A company contacts the Border and Immigration Agency Employers' Helpline with concerns that a number of its employees may be working illegally. In co-operation with the employer, the Border and Immigration Agency find that four workers on the staff lists are illegal migrant workers and mount an operation to collect these individuals for removal. The company had not been visited previously by the Border and Immigration Agency. All these employees were taken on or after 29 February 2008 and the company had accepted letters issued by the Home Office from these employees as evidence of their entitlement to work in each case, rather than as part of a specified combination.

CASE A RESULT: No penalty, warning letter issued, advice provided.

- Number of previous visits – 0
- Number of illegal migrant workers detected for whom the employer had a statutory excuse – 0
- Number of illegal migrant workers detected on whom the employer had conducted partial checks – 4
- Number of illegal migrant workers detected on whom the employer conducted no checks – 0
- Did the company approach the Border and Immigration Agency Employer Helpline? – Yes
- Did the company co-operate with the operation? – Yes

The potential maximum penalty was therefore reduced from £20,000 (4 x £5,000) to no penalty, but a warning letter was issued.

CASE B

A company is visited by the Border and Immigration Agency, but had not approached them beforehand and they had no prior warnings or penalties. The company co-operates with the investigation and the consequent operation to pick up illegal workers. Ten illegal workers are detected; in six cases, the company had carried out appropriate checks, but had been deceived by high quality forgeries. However, in the other four cases, the follow-up checks had not been made, indicating that only partial checks had been completed in those cases.

CASE B RESULT: £10,000 maximum penalty

- Number of previous visits – 0
- Number of illegal migrant workers detected for whom the employer had a statutory excuse – 6
- Number of illegal migrant workers detected on whom the employer had conducted partial checks – 4
- Number of illegal migrant workers detected on whom the employer conducted no checks – 0
- Did the company approach the Border and Immigration Agency Employer Helpline? – No
- Did the company co-operate with the operation? – Yes

The potential maximum penalty was therefore reduced from £20,000 (4 x £5,000) to a £10,000 (4 x £2,500)

CASE C

An employer is visited by the Border and Immigration Agency and co-operates with the operation. The employer had not been visited previously. Six illegal migrant workers were detected, for whom the employer had conducted no checks.

CASE C RESULT: £30,000 maximum penalty

- Number of previous visits – 0
- Number of illegal migrant workers detected for whom the employer had a statutory excuse – 0
- Number of illegal migrant workers detected on whom the employer had conducted partial checks – 0
- Number of illegal migrant workers detected on whom the employer conducted no checks – 6
- Did the company approach the Border and Immigration Agency Employer Helpline? – No
- Did the company co-operate with the operation? – Yes

The potential maximum penalty was therefore reduced from £45,000 (6 x £7,500) to a £30,000 penalty (6 x £5,000).

CASE D

The same employer as case C contacts the Border and Immigration Agency six months later to report suspicions about some members of staff. The employer co-operates with the subsequent operation, which results in the detection of three illegal migrant workers. The employer provides evidence of checks for these workers, having improved their processes, but the checks had only been partial.

CASE D RESULT: £15,000 maximum penalty

- Number of previous visits – 1
- Number of illegal migrant workers detected for whom the employer had a statutory excuse – 0
- Number of illegal migrant workers detected on whom the employer had conducted partial checks – 3
- Number of illegal migrant workers detected on whom the employer conducted no checks – 0
- Did the company approach the Border and Immigration Agency Employer Helpline? – Yes
- Did the company co-operate with the operation? – Yes

The potential maximum penalty was therefore reduced from £22,500 (3 x £7,500) to a £15,000 penalty (3 x £5,000).

CASE E

The same employer as in cases C and D is visited again six months later. The employer did not approach the Border and Immigration Agency this time, but co-operates with the enforcement operation. Two illegal workers are detected and the checks made were only partial.

CASE E RESULT: £17,500 maximum penalty

- Number of previous visits – 2
- Number of illegal migrant workers detected for whom the employer had a statutory excuse – 0
- Number of illegal migrant workers detected on whom the employer had conducted partial checks – 2
- Number of illegal migrant workers detected on whom the employer conducted no checks – 0
- Did the company approach the Border and Immigration Agency Employer Helpline? – No
- Did the company co-operate with the operation? – Yes

The potential maximum penalty was therefore reduced from £20,000 (2 x £10,000) to a £17,500 penalty (2 x £8,750).

CASE F

An employer is visited by the Border and Immigration Agency and co-operates. Two illegal migrant workers are detected whose leave expired over a year ago and began their employment after the Immigration (Restrictions on Employment) Order 2007 came into force. The employer can provide evidence of full checks at the point of recruitment, but has carried out no follow-up checks within the past 12 months. The employer has not been visited previously.

CASE F RESULT: £5,000 maximum penalty

- Number of previous visits – 0
- Number of illegal migrant workers detected for whom the employer had a statutory excuse – 0
- Number of illegal migrant workers detected on whom the employer had conducted partial checks – 2
- Number of illegal migrant workers detected on whom the employer conducted no checks – 0
- Did the company approach the Border and Immigration Agency Employer Helpline? – No
- Did the company co-operate with the operation? – Yes

The potential maximum penalty was therefore reduced from £10,000 (2 x £5,000) to a £5,000 penalty (2 x £2,500).

[4770]

APPENDIX 4: ADDITIONAL FACTORS TO BE CONSIDERED WHEN DETERMINING THE LEVEL OF A CIVIL PENALTY

Each case will be examined in context, and consideration must be given to the fairness of the financial penalty to be imposed on the employer. Therefore, the following factors may be considered by an official when determining the level of penalty appropriate for each illegal migrant worker detected:

- whether full or partial document checks have been completed by the employer;
- whether any previous penalties or warnings have been issued to the employer within the previous three years, and if there has been any subsequent improvement in their procedures;
- whether the Civil Penalty Code of practice has been adhered to;
- if the employer reported any suspected illegal workers;
- if the employer has not obstructed the Border and Immigration Agency in conducting any operation to apprehend the illegal workers in question;
- whether the migrant worker is living and working in the UK illegally;
- whether the migrant worker is legally resident in the UK, but has been found to be working in breach of their employment restrictions;
- the proportionality of the level of penalty given;
- whether previous civil penalties have been paid in full;
- the ability of the employer to pay; and
- the thoroughness and/or consistency of the employers' existing employment processes.

[4771]

BORDER & IMMIGRATION AGENCY CODE OF PRACTICE: GUIDANCE FOR EMPLOYERS ON THE AVOIDANCE OF UNLAWFUL DISCRIMINATION IN EMPLOYMENT PRACTICE WHILE SEEKING TO PREVENT ILLEGAL WORKING (FEBRUARY 2008)

PREVENTION OF ILLEGAL WORKING

IMMIGRATION, ASYLUM AND NATIONALITY ACT 2006

NOTES

This Code of Practice was issued under section 23 of the Immigration, Asylum and Nationality Act 2006. For further details see the notes to the preceding Code of Practice at **[4766]**.

1. INTRODUCTION

1.1 This Code has been issued by the Border and Immigration Agency and aims to provide employers with guidance on how to avoid a civil penalty for employing an illegal migrant worker, in a way that **does not result in unlawful race discrimination**.[1]

1.2 Failing to carry out identity checks on potential employees is not a criminal offence, but those employers who only carry out checks on workers who they believe are not British citizens, for example, on the basis of race or ethnicity, could find that this is used against them as evidence in any proceedings brought under the Race Relations Act 1976. This is why we recommend that employers obtain a statutory excuse for all potential employees; this not only protects the employer from liability for a civil penalty, but also demonstrates consistent, transparent and non-discriminatory recruitment practices.

1.3 Legal migrant workers make a substantial contribution to this country's economy. However, those who use illegal migrant workers are often guilty of breaking other laws relating to health and safety, exploitation and tax evasion. The United Kingdom, like many other countries around the world, has laws to deal with illegal migrant working.

1.4 It is important to remember that the population of the UK is ethnically diverse. Many people from ethnic minorities in this country are British citizens and many non-British citizens from black and minority ethnic communities are entitled to work here. Therefore, it must not be assumed that someone from an ethnic minority is an immigrant, or that someone born abroad is not entitled to work in the UK.

[4772]

NOTES

1 This Code draws on the previous Code, entitled 'Immigration and Asylum Act 1999 – Section 22 Code of Practice: For all employers on the avoidance of race discrimination in recruitment practice while seeking to prevent illegal working'. This document was issued by the Home Office in June 2001. This Code also draws on the 'Statutory Code of Practice on Racial Equality in Employment', which was published by the CRE in April 2006. Further information and details are contained in Appendix 2.

2. PURPOSE AND STATUS OF THIS CODE

2.1 The purpose of this Code is to give you practical guidance on how to avoid unlawful racial discrimination whilst also complying with the law to prevent illegal migrant working.

2.2 This is a statutory Code. This means that it has been approved by the Secretary of State and laid before Parliament. The Code does not impose any legal obligations on employers, nor is it an authoritative statement of the law; only the courts and Employment Tribunals can provide that. However, the Code can be used as evidence in legal proceedings. Courts and Employment Tribunals must take account of any part of the Code that might be relevant on matters of racial discrimination in employment practices.

2.3 This Code, which is issued under section 23 of the Immigration, Asylum and Nationality Act 2006 ('the 2006 Act'), is intended to strengthen the safeguards against unlawful discrimination by re-emphasising your statutory duty to avoid discrimination in your employment practices.

2.4 The Equality and Human Rights Commission (EHRC), also known as the Commission for Equality and Human Rights,[2] the Equality Commission for Northern Ireland and the members of the Illegal Working Group (IWG),[3] which is comprised of representatives from a range of business sectors, government departments and voluntary organisations, have been consulted on the contents of this Code, as required by section 23 of the 2006 Act. Their comments and recommendations have been incorporated, where appropriate.

2.5 This Code applies to all employers in England, Scotland, Wales and Northern Ireland. It also applies to certain organisations, such as employment businesses, employment and recruitment agencies (including on-line agencies). An employment agency or business practising unlawful discrimination will be liable, even if it is acting on the instructions of an employer.

2.6 Whilst some smaller organisations may wish to adapt the guidance to suit their particular circumstances, it should be noted that no allowances can be made for smaller companies when considering their liability under the law. We recommend that smaller organisations ensure that their employment practices do not discriminate on grounds of race and that they follow the advice given in this Code.

2.7 Public authorities are also subject to the requirements of this Code. They also have a general statutory duty to promote equality of opportunity and good race relations, which includes a requirement to monitor specified employment procedures and practices.

2.8 This Code outlines your legal obligations under the Race Relations Act 1976 ("the 1976 Act"),[4] Race Relations (Northern Ireland) Order 1997, the 2006 Act and the Immigration (Restrictions on Employment) Order 2007. However, it is not intended to be a comprehensive statement of the law.

2.9 This Code has been produced alongside other guidance documents and sources of information, details of which are provided in Appendix 2. You may wish to refer to this Code alongside that guidance and information.

[4773]

NOTES

2 Formerly known as the Commission for Racial Equality (CRE).

3 Formerly known as the Illegal Working Steering Group and the Illegal Working Stakeholder Group.

4 Any reference in this Code to the Race Relations Act includes all subsequent amending legislation.

3. YOUR RESPONSIBILITY AS AN EMPLOYER UNDER THE LAW: THE RACE RELATIONS ACT 1976 AND RACE RELATIONS (NORTHERN IRELAND) ORDER 1997

3.1 Under section 4 of the 1976 Act, and section 6 of the 1997 Order, **it is unlawful** to discriminate in employment practices on racial grounds. That means that an employer cannot discriminate against a potential or existing employee on the following grounds:

- race;
- colour;
- nationality (including citizenship);
- ethnic origin;
- national origin.

Race discrimination may be either **direct** or **indirect**.

3.2 **Direct discrimination** means treating a person less favourably on racial grounds, for example by rejecting all job applicants who do not have British nationality, or by refusing to consider any non-European job applicants. Treatment based on racial or national stereotypes can also constitute direct discrimination. Examples include:

- where the assumption is made that people from certain nationalities or ethnic groups cannot work as a team;
- where individuals are only recruited from one nationality or ethnic group;
- where all refugees are automatically rejected;
- where an employee with limited leave to remain in the UK is given a more degrading form of work to do in comparison with workers with unlimited leave;
- where it is assumed that overseas qualifications and experience are inferior to those gained in the UK.[5]

3.3 **Indirect discrimination** means imposing a condition or requirement which applies equally to everyone, but is harder for people from particular racial groups to satisfy and which cannot be justified. For example, it would be discriminatory to ask for a very high standard of English when the job does not require this, or to reject an applicant who has an unfamiliar accent.

3.4 **It is unlawful** to victimise or harass a person because he or she has made or supported a complaint of racial discrimination. **It is also unlawful** to instruct or induce another person to discriminate, or to publish an advertisement or notice that indicates an intention to discriminate.

3.5 Employers must not discriminate on racial grounds or subject a person to harassment in:

a) the arrangements they make to decide who should be offered employment; or
b) the terms on which they offer to employ a person; or
c) by refusing or deliberately failing to offer employment.

3.6 It is also unlawful for employers to discriminate on racial grounds against a worker, or to subject him or her to harassment:

a) in the terms of employment provided; or
b) in the way they make opportunities for training, promotion, transfer, facilities, services or other benefits available; or
c) by refusing access to such opportunities, benefits, facilities or services; or
d) by dismissing the worker, or subjecting him to some other detriment.

3.7 Under the 1976 Act and the 1997 Order, discrimination committed by an **employee** in the course of his or her employment, is treated as having been committed by the **employer** as well as by the individual employee, **whether or not the employer knew or approved the acts of discrimination**. You can avoid this liability if you can prove that you took sufficient and reasonable steps to prevent such discrimination, for example, by applying consistent checks to all potential employees. A complaint to an Employment Tribunal may be made against both the employer and the individual employee who is alleged to have discriminated.

3.8 Separate legislation similarly outlaws discrimination on grounds of religious affiliation, gender, sexual orientation, disability and age[6] in employment practices. Although this Code only addresses racial discrimination, you should be mindful of other forms of discrimination, particularly religious discrimination, when applying the provisions of the 2006 Act. If people affected by religious discrimination are from a particular racial group, the discrimination might also amount to indirect racial discrimination.

[4774]

NOTES

5 If you are unsure about the UK equivalent of an overseas qualification, you could consult the National Recognition Information Centre (NARIC) website at: www.naric.org.uk, which provides useful information.

6 Regulations on age discrimination came into force on 1 October 2006. See the Equality Act 2006 for further details.

4. RIGHT OF COMPLAINT

4.1 Anyone who believes that he or she has been discriminated against, either directly or indirectly, by an employer, a prospective employer, or an employment agency, may bring a complaint before an Employment Tribunal, or an Industrial Tribunal in Northern Ireland. If the complaint is upheld, the Tribunal will normally order the employer to pay compensation, for which there is no upper limit.

4.2 The EHRC and the Northern Ireland Equality Commission can also bring proceedings against an employer who publishes a discriminatory advertisement, or who instructs or induces another person to discriminate.

4.3 Where an employer has been found to have committed an act of unlawful racial discrimination, the Public Procurement Regulations 2006 provide that public authorities may disqualify the organisation from entering into public procurement contracts.

[4775]

5. YOUR RESPONSIBILITY AS AN EMPLOYER UNDER THE LAW: SECTION 15 AND SECTION 21 OF THE IMMIGRATION, ASYLUM AND NATIONALITY ACT 2006 EXPLAINED

5.1 The 2006 Act has strengthened the law on the prevention of illegal migrant working by replacing the previous controls under section 8 of the Asylum and Immigration Act 1996 ('the 1996 Act'). There is now a system of civil penalties for employers who employ an illegal migrant worker (section 15) without having obtained a statutory excuse, and a separate criminal offence of knowingly employing an illegal migrant worker (section 21).

The 2006 Act sets out the changes to the law on the prevention of illegal migrant working. You will be committing an offence if you are found to be employing a person aged 16 or over who is subject to immigration control[7] unless:

- that person has current and valid permission to be in the United Kingdom, **and**
- the person has valid permission to do the type of work offered.

Under section 15, you may be liable for a civil penalty in respect of each illegal migrant worker employed.[8]

5.2 Section 15 can also provide you with a statutory excuse against liability for a civil penalty. This can be done by checking and copying one of the original documents, or a specified combination of original documents from **List A** or **Lists B** (provided in Appendix 1), **before** employing that person. Those people who have restrictions on their time in the UK may be subject to repeat checks. If you can show that you complied with the requirements, you may be excused from liability for the penalty, even if it turns out that the person being employed is subject to immigration control and is working without the necessary permission.

5.3 However, the excuse is not available if you knew, at any time during the period of employment, that the employment was not allowed. **If you know that you are employing a person without the required permission to work, you could be served with a civil penalty or prosecuted under section 21 for the offence of knowingly employing an illegal migrant worker, for which there is a maximum prison sentence of two years and an unlimited fine**.

5.4 Section 21 deals with cases involving the intentional use of illegal workers, which are often linked to exploitation, or other forms of illegal activity. The offence is committed by a person where he or she employed an individual knowing that they did not have current leave to enter or remain, or that their conditions of stay prevented them from undertaking the employment offered.

5.5 There is a difference between the entitlement of asylum seekers and refugees to work in the United Kingdom. The term asylum seeker is used to describe those who have made a claim for asylum under the Refugee Convention or under Article 3 of the European Convention on Human Rights.

5.6 For the purposes of sections 15 and 21, a person who has been granted temporary admission to the United Kingdom, or temporary release from immigration detention, such as an asylum seeker, may only be employed if the Home Office or the Border and Immigration Agency has lifted restrictions on their taking employment.[9]

5.7 In the case of the minority of asylum seekers who enjoy permission to work, this will be clearly indicated on their Application Registration Card (ARC). As part of the checks required to obtain or retain a statutory excuse under section 15, you should contact the Employer Checking Service to verify whether the employee continues to be entitled to work in the United Kingdom.[10] You must inform your employee that you are undertaking this check before doing so.

5.8 Since 1 May 2004, neither the Standard Acknowledgement Letter (SAL), nor the form entitled IS96(W) have been acceptable as evidence that an asylum seeker has permission to work in the UK. If a potential, or current employee, presents one of these documents to you, please refer them to the Border and Immigration Agency on **0151 237 6375** for further advice on how they can obtain an appropriate ARC.

5.9 Those who have been granted refugee status, or have been allowed to remain exceptionally on humanitarian grounds, will have no restriction on the type of work that they can do, whilst their leave remains valid.

[4776]

NOTES

7 A person subject to immigration control is a person who, under the Immigration Act 1971, requires leave to enter or remain in the UK.

8 Further information on the civil penalty scheme is available in the *'Prevention of illegal working. Immigration, Asylum and Nationality Act 2006: Civil Penalties for Employers Code of Practice* – Border and Immigration Agency, 2008.' See Appendix 2.

9 An asylum applicant may apply to the Secretary of State for permission to take up employment (which shall not include permission to become self-employed, or to engage in a business or professional activity) only in exceptional circumstances, for example, if a decision has not been taken on the applicant's asylum application within one year of the date on which it was recorded. The Secretary of State shall only consider such an application if, in his opinion, any delay in reaching a decision at first instance cannot be attributed to the applicant.

10 The Border and Immigration Agency will issue separate guidance to employers detailing the procedure to be followed.

6. MAKING THE DOCUMENT CHECKS

6.1 In order to establish the statutory excuse against liability for a civil penalty, you must check the original document(s) presented from **List A**, or **Lists B** (see Appendix 1) before the person starts their employment and make a paper copy, or electronic record of the document(s) and store it securely. In certain circumstances, you may retain the document(s).[11] Further details are provided in the Immigration (Restrictions on Employment) Order 2007.

6.2 You should undertake basic visual checks to ensure that the document or documents, relate to the applicant by comparing any photographs in the document or documents, and dates of birth against the appearance and apparent age of the applicant. You should check for any obvious discrepancy in age. You should also check that any United Kingdom Government endorsements (stamps, vignettes etc.) entitle the potential employee to do the type of work offered and that any expiry date has not passed.

6.3 Where a job applicant has produced an original document or documents from **List A**, you have checked and copied the relevant parts of the document or documents, and you are satisfied that the person is entitled to take the job offered, you will have established an excuse in relation to your employment of that person and will not need to carry out any subsequent document checks. This is because the documents from **List A** show that there are no time restrictions on the individual's ability to take up employment in the UK.

6.4 Where an employee produces an original document or documents from **Lists B**, you must note the date on which you carry out the original document check. In order to retain your excuse against a penalty for employing that individual, you must carry out a follow-up check at least once every **12 months** after the initial check. Again, this will involve asking the employee to produce an original document or documents either from **List A**, or **Lists B**. This is because the documents from **Lists B** show that there are restrictions on the length of time the individual can stay in the UK and you will need to ensure that your employee has retained their entitlement to work.

6.5 The same visual checks should be carried out to ensure that each document is not false and that it relates to the holder. You should take another copy of the document, recording the date on which the check was made. These follow-up checks must be repeated:

- no later than **12 months** after the previous check, **or**
- until the employee produces a document on **List A**, **or**
- until the employee leaves your employment.

6.6 There may be occasions when an employee is unable to produce a document from **List A** or **Lists B** when requested to as part of a follow-up check, and claims that this is due to having an outstanding application for leave to remain with the Border and Immigration Agency. If this happens you can use the Employer Checking Service to verify whether the employee continues to enjoy the right to work in the United Kingdom. It is the employers' responsibility to inform the employee, or potential employee, that they may be making the checks.

6.7 The checks you need to make to claim the statutory excuse are in most cases straightforward and can be built into your normal employment procedures. **These document checks are not compulsory, but they are advisable as part of good employment practice. If you do not make these checks at the point of recruitment, you will not have the benefit of the statutory excuse if you are later found to be employing illegal migrant workers.**

When you make pre-recruitment checks, you should ensure that they are made in a non-discriminatory manner by applying them to all applicants and at the same point of the recruitment process.

6.8 We don't expect employers to act as Immigration Officers. Responsibility for immigration control lies firmly with the Border and Immigration Agency. If you are worried that a document you have been shown does not relate to the holder, you do not have to employ that person. The Employer Checking Service is available to employers who may wish to clarify an individual's right to work.

6.9 Further details on obtaining a statutory excuse are available in guidance produced by the Home Office and the Border and Immigration Agency. Details are contained in Appendix 2.

[4777]

NOTES

[11] It is not appropriate to retain a person's original documents indefinitely. The only exception to this is when an individual provides a P45 as part of a combination of documents. In these circumstances, the employer may retain part 2 of the P45 for their records, otherwise, an employer may only obtain a person's documents for the purpose of copying them. The employer must also have facilities for keeping the documents and copies of documents safe. A job applicant's original documents must not be kept for longer than a day. If an employer deliberately appropriates a person's passport or other original documents belonging to them, or retains these without their consent, then they may be guilty of an offence under the Theft Act 1968, or under section 25(5) of the Identity Cards Act 2006.

7. HOW TO AVOID RACIAL DISCRIMINATION

7.1 As a matter of good employment practice, you should have clear written procedures for the recruitment and selection of all staff, based on equal and fair treatment for all applicants. Copies of these procedures should be made available to all relevant staff.

7.2 All job selections should be on the basis of suitability for the post. You should ensure that no prospective job applicants are discouraged or excluded, either directly or indirectly, because of their personal appearance or accent. You should not make assumptions about a person's right to work or immigration status on the basis of their colour, race, nationality, or ethnic or national origins, or the length of time they have been resident in the UK.

7.3 **The best way to ensure that you do not discriminate is to treat all applicants in the same way at each stage of the recruitment process**. For example, if you provide information to prospective applicants, or if you supply an application form, you could also include a reminder that the successful applicant, or short-listed applicants, will be required to produce an original document or documents included in **List A** or **Lists B**.

7.4 You may ask applicants to provide the specified document(s) to obtain a statutory excuse at any stage **before** they start work. Depending on your recruitment processes, you may find it most convenient to request documents from all those called to a first interview, or just from those called to a second interview, or only from persons short-listed to fill the vacancy. Original documents should be checked before employment commences. If you ask for documents from one applicant, you should make sure you ask for documents from all applicants being considered at that stage.

7.5 Job applicants should not be treated less favourably if they produce a document or documents from **Lists B** rather than **List A**. A person producing document(s) from **Lists B** will have a time limit on their legal ability to stay and work in the UK, but it is possible for certain categories of entrant to obtain an extension to their entitlement to remain and work in this country.

7.6 Once a person who has limited leave to remain has established their initial and ongoing entitlement to work, they should not be treated less favourably during their employment, including the terms of employment provided, opportunities for training, promotion or transfer, benefits, facilities or services, or by dismissing the worker or subjecting them to some other detriment, other than the repeat checks.

7.7 You should only ask questions about an applicant's or employee's immigration status, where necessary, to determine whether their status imposes limitations on the number of hours they are entitled to work each week, or on the length of time they are permitted to work within their overall period or type of leave given. For example, those granted leave as students undertaking full-time undergraduate study in the UK should not work for more than 20 hours per week during term time, except where the placement is a necessary part of their studies and is undertaken with the educational institution's express agreement.

7.8 If a person is not able to produce the appropriate listed document(s), you should not assume that he or she is living or working in the UK illegally. You should instead refer the person to the Border and Immigration Agency through the Immigration Enquiry Bureau on **0870 606 7766**, or a Citizens Advice Bureau for advice. You should try to keep the job open for as long as possible, but you are not obliged to do so if you need to recruit someone urgently. **It is ultimately the decision of the employer whether or not to employ an individual**.

[4778]

8. MONITORING APPLICATIONS

8.1 As a matter of good practice, you should monitor the ethnicity of applications during the recruitment and selection process of job applicants. This will help you to know whether you are reaching a wide range of potential job applicants. This can then be used in reviewing recruitment procedures. It is also good practice to take measures to encourage an integrated and diverse workforce and provide English language teaching for those who need it.

[4779]–[5000]

(*Appendix 1* (*Documents required for the purpose of establishing the statutory excuse*) *is identical to the Appendix 1 in the Code of Practice on Civil Penalties for Employers* (*see that Appendix at* **[4768]**). *Appendix 2* (*Other sources of information*) *omitted for reasons of space.*)

PART 5
MISCELLANEOUS MATERIALS

A. INTERNATIONAL LAW MATERIALS

INTERNATIONAL LABOUR ORGANISATION CONVENTION (NO 87) ON FREEDOM OF ASSOCIATION AND PROTECTION OF THE RIGHT TO ORGANISE (1948)

[Adopted, 9 July 1948; in force 4 July 1950.]

NOTES
The Preamble, and Articles 12, 13 and 17–21, which deal with ancillary and procedural matters, are omitted.

PART I
FREEDOM OF ASSOCIATION

Article 1

Each Member of the International Labour Organisation for which this Convention is in force undertakes to give effect to the following provisions.

Article 2

Workers and employers, without distinction whatsoever, shall have the right to establish and, subject only to the rules of the organisation concerned, to join organisations of their own choosing without previous authorisation.

Article 3

1. Workers' and employers' organisations shall have the right to draw up their constitutions and rules, to elect their representatives in full freedom, to organise their administration and activities and to formulate their programmes.

2. The public authorities shall refrain from any interference which would restrict this right or impede the lawful exercise thereof.

Article 4
Workers' and employers' organisations shall not be liable to be dissolved or suspended by administrative authority.

Article 5

Workers' and employers' organisations shall have the right to establish and join federations and confederations and any such organisation, federation or confederation shall have the right to affiliate with international organisations of workers and employers.

Article 6
The provisions of Articles 2, 3 and 4 hereof apply to federations and confederations of workers' and employers' organisations.

Article 7
The acquisition of legal personality by workers' and employers' organisations, federations and confederations shall not be made subject to conditions of such a character as to restrict the application of the provisions of Articles 2, 3 and 4 hereof.

Article 8

1. In exercising the rights provided for in this Convention workers and employers and their respective organisations, like other persons or organised collectivities, shall respect the law of the land.

2. The law of the land shall not be such as to impair, nor shall it be so applied as to impair, the guarantees provided for in this Convention.

Article 9

1. The extent to which the guarantees provided for in this Convention shall apply to the armed forces and the police shall be determined by national laws or regulations.

2. In accordance with the principle set forth in paragraph 8 of Article 19 of the Constitution of the International Labour Organisation the ratification of this Convention by any Member shall not be deemed to affect any existing law, award, custom or agreement in virtue of which members of the armed forces or the police enjoy any right guaranteed by this Convention.

Article 10

In this Convention the term 'organisation' means any organisation of workers or of employers for furthering and defending the interests of workers or of employers.

[5001]

PART II
PROTECTION OF THE RIGHT TO ORGANISE

Article 11

Each Member of the International Labour Organisation for which this Convention is in force undertakes to take all necessary and appropriate measures to ensure that workers and employers may exercise freely the right to organise.

[5002]

PART IV
FINAL PROVISIONS

Article 14

The formal ratifications of this Convention shall be communicated to the Director-General of the International Labour Office for registration.

Article 15

1. This Convention shall be binding only upon those Members of the International Labour Organisation whose ratifications have been registered with the Director-General.

2. It shall come into force twelve months after the date on which the ratifications of two Members have been registered with the Director-General.

3. Thereafter, this Convention shall come into force for any Member twelve months after the date on which its ratification has been registered.

Article 16

1. A Member which has ratified this Convention may denounce it after the expiration of ten years from the date on which the Convention first comes into force, by an act communicated to the Director-General of the International Labour Office for registration. Such denunciation shall not take effect until one year after the date on which it is registered.

2. Each Member which has ratified this Convention and which does not, within the year following the expiration of the period of ten years mentioned in the preceding paragraph, exercise the right of denunciation provided for in this article, will be bound for another period of ten years and, thereafter, may denounce this Convention at the expiration of each period of ten years under the terms provided for in this article.

[5003]

INTERNATIONAL LABOUR ORGANISATION CONVENTION (NO 98) ON THE RIGHT TO ORGANISE AND COLLECTIVE BARGAINING (1949)

[Adopted, 1 July 1949; in force 18 July 1951.]

NOTES

The Preamble, and Articles 9, 10 and 12–16, which deal with ancillary and procedural matters, are omitted.

Article 1

1. Workers shall enjoy adequate protection against acts of anti-union discrimination in respect of their employment.

2. Such protection shall apply more particularly in respect of acts calculated to:
   (a) Make the employment of a worker subject to the condition that he shall not join a union or shall relinquish trade union membership
   (b) Cause the dismissal of or otherwise prejudice a worker by reason of union membership or because of participation in union activities outside working hours or, with the consent of the employer, within working hours.

Article 2

1. Workers' and employers' organisations shall enjoy adequate protection against any acts of interference by each other or each others' agents or members in their establishment functioning or administration.

2. In particular, acts which are designed to promote the establishment of workers' organisations under the domination of employers or employers' organisations, or to support workers' organisations by financial or other means, with the object of placing such organisations under the control of employers or employers' organisations, shall be deemed to constitute acts of interference within the meaning of this article.

Article 3

Machinery appropriate to national conditions shall be established, where necessary, for the purpose of ensuring respect for the right to organise as defined in the preceding articles.

Article 4

Measures appropriate to national conditions shall be taken where necessary, to encourage and promote the full development and utilisation of machinery for voluntary negotiation between employers or employers' organisations and workers' organisations, with a view to the regulation of terms and conditions of employment by means of collective agreements.

Article 5

1. The extent to which the guarantees provided for in this Convention shall apply to the armed forces and the police shall be determined by national laws or regulations.

2. In accordance with the principle set forth in paragraph 8 of Article 19 of the Constitution of the International Labour Organisation the ratification of this Convention by any Member shall not be deemed to affect any existing law, award, custom or agreement in virtue of which members of the armed forces or the police enjoy any right guaranteed by this Convention.

Article 6

This Convention does not deal with the position of public servants engaged in the administration of the State, nor shall it be construed as prejudicing their rights or status in any way.

Article 7

The formal ratifications of this Convention shall be communicated to the Director-General of the International Labour Office for registration.

Article 8

1. This Convention shall be binding only upon those Members of the International Labour Organisation whose ratifications have been registered with the Director-General.

2. It shall come into force twelve months after the date on which the ratifications of two Members have been registered with the Director-General.

3 Thereafter, this Convention shall come into force for any Member twelve months after the date on which its ratification has been registered.

Article 11

1. A Member which has ratified this Convention may denounce it after the expiration of ten years from the date on which the Convention first comes into force, by an act communicated to the Director-General of the International Labour Office for registration. Such denunciation shall not take effect until one year after the date on which it is registered.

2. Each Member which has ratified this Convention and which does not, within the year following the expiration of the period of ten years mentioned in the preceding paragraph, exercise the right of denunciation provided for in this article, will be bound for another period of ten years and, thereafter, may denounce this Convention at the expiration of each period of ten years under the terms provided for in this Article.

[5004]

THE EUROPEAN CONVENTION FOR THE PROTECTION OF HUMAN RIGHTS AND FUNDAMENTAL FREEDOMS (1950) (NOTE)

[Signed 4 November 1950; in force 3 September 1953.]

NOTES

The European Convention is given domestic legal status by the Human Rights Act 1998. Sch 1 to that Act at **[1408]** et seq sets out the operative provisions of the Convention relevant to this work, except for Article 13, which is as follows:

"Everyone whose rights and freedoms as set forth in this Convention are violated shall have an effective remedy before a national authority notwithstanding that the violation has been committed by persons acting in an official capacity.".

[5005]

EUROPEAN SOCIAL CHARTER (1996)

(*Revised*)

Strasbourg, 3.V.1996

NOTES

The European Social Charter was adopted by the Council of Ministers of the Council of Europe on 3 May 1996 and is intended to be a replacement for the 1961 Social Charter. It was signed by the United Kingdom on 7 November 1997 but has not yet been ratified, and is not yet in force (as at 6 April 2008). For provisions as to commencement see Art K at **[5012]**.

PREAMBLE

The governments signatory hereto, being members of the Council of Europe,

Considering that the aim of the Council of Europe is the achievement of greater unity between its members for the purpose of safeguarding and realising the ideals and principles which are their common heritage and of facilitating their economic and social progress, in particular by the maintenance and further realisation of human rights and fundamental freedoms;

Considering that in the European Convention for the Protection of Human Rights and Fundamental Freedoms signed at Rome on 4 November 1950, and the Protocols thereto, the member States of the Council of Europe agreed to secure to their populations the civil and political rights and freedoms therein specified;

Considering that in the European Social Charter opened for signature in Turin on 18 October 1961 and the Protocols thereto, the member States of the Council of Europe agreed to secure to their populations the social rights specified therein in order to improve their standard of living and their social well-being;

Recalling that the Ministerial Conference on Human Rights held in Rome on 5 November 1990 stressed the need, on the one hand, to preserve the indivisible nature of all human rights, be they civil, political, economic, social or cultural and, on the other hand, to give the European Social Charter fresh impetus;

Resolved, as was decided during the Ministerial Conference held in Turin on 21 and 22 October 1991, to update and adapt the substantive contents of the Charter in order to take account in particular of the fundamental social changes which have occurred since the text was adopted;

Recognising the advantage of embodying in a Revised Charter, designed progressively to take the place of the European Social Charter, the rights guaranteed by the Charter as amended, the rights guaranteed by the Additional Protocol of 1988 and to add new rights,

Have agreed as follows—

[5006]

PART I

The Parties accept as the aim of their policy, to be pursued by all appropriate means both national and international in character, the attainment of conditions in which the following rights and principles may be effectively realised—

1. Everyone shall have the opportunity to earn his living in an occupation freely entered upon.
2. All workers have the right to just conditions of work.
3. All workers have the right to safe and healthy working conditions.
4. All workers have the right to a fair remuneration sufficient for a decent standard of living for themselves and their families.
5. All workers and employers have the right to freedom of association in national or international organisations for the protection of their economic and social interests.
6. All workers and employers have the right to bargain collectively.
7. Children and young persons have the right to a special protection against the physical and moral hazards to which they are exposed.
8. Employed women, in case of maternity, have the right to a special protection.
9. Everyone has the right to appropriate facilities for vocational guidance with a view to helping him choose an occupation suited to his personal aptitude and interests.
10. Everyone has the right to appropriate facilities for vocational training.
11. Everyone has the right to benefit from any measures enabling him to enjoy the highest possible standard of health attainable.
12. All workers and their dependents have the right to social security.
13. Anyone without adequate resources has the right to social and medical assistance.
14. Everyone has the right to benefit from social welfare services.
15. Disabled persons have the right to independence, social integration and participation in the life of the community.
16. The family as a fundamental unit of society has the right to appropriate social, legal and economic protection to ensure its full development.
17. Children and young persons have the right to appropriate social, legal and economic protection.
18. The nationals of any one of the Parties have the right to engage in any gainful occupation in the territory of any one of the others on a footing of equality with the nationals of the latter, subject to restrictions based on cogent economic or social reasons.
19. Migrant workers who are nationals of a Party and their families have the right to protection and assistance in the territory of any other Party.
20. All workers have the right to equal opportunities and equal treatment in matters of employment and occupation without discrimination on the grounds of sex.
21. Workers have the right to be informed and to be consulted within the undertaking.
22. Workers have the right to take part in the determination and improvement of the working conditions and working environment in the undertaking.
23. Every elderly person has the right to social protection.
24. All workers have the right to protection in cases of termination of employment.

25. All workers have the right to protection of their claims in the event of the insolvency of their employer.
26. All workers have the right to dignity at work.
27. All persons with family responsibilities and who are engaged or wish to engage in employment have a right to do so without being subject to discrimination and as far as possible without conflict between their employment and family responsibilities.
28. Workers' representatives in undertakings have the right to protection against acts prejudicial to them and should be afforded appropriate facilities to carry out their functions.
29. All workers have the right to be informed and consulted in collective redundancy procedures.
30. Everyone has the right to protection against poverty and social exclusion.
31. Everyone has the right to housing.

[5007]

PART II

The Parties undertake, as provided for in Part III, to consider themselves bound by the obligations laid down in the following articles and paragraphs.

Article 1—The right to work

With a view to ensuring the effective exercise of the right to work, the Parties undertake—

1. to accept as one of their primary aims and responsibilities the achievement and maintenance of as high and stable a level of employment as possible, with a view to the attainment of full employment;
2. to protect effectively the right of the worker to earn his living in an occupation freely entered upon;
3. to establish or maintain free employment services for all workers;
4. to provide or promote appropriate vocational guidance, training and rehabilitation.

Article 2—The right to just conditions of work

With a view to ensuring the effective exercise of the right to just conditions of work, the Parties undertake—

1. to provide for reasonable daily and weekly working hours, the working week to be progressively reduced to the extent that the increase of productivity and other relevant factors permit;
2. to provide for public holidays with pay;
3. to provide for a minimum of four weeks' annual holiday with pay;
4. to eliminate risks in inherently dangerous or unhealthy occupations, and where it has not yet been possible to eliminate or reduce sufficiently these risks, to provide for either a reduction of working hours or additional paid holidays for workers engaged in such occupations;
5. to ensure a weekly rest period which shall, as far as possible, coincide with the day recognised by tradition or custom in the country or region concerned as a day of rest;
6. to ensure that workers are informed in written form, as soon as possible, and in any event not later than two months after the date of commencing their employment, of the essential aspects of the contract or employment relationship;
7. to ensure that workers performing night work benefit from measures which take account of the special nature of the work.

Article 3—The right to safe and healthy working conditions

With a view to ensuring the effective exercise of the right to safe and healthy working conditions, the Parties undertake, in consultation with employers' and workers' organisations—

1. to formulate, implement and periodically review a coherent national policy on occupational safety, occupational health and the working environment. The primary aim of this policy shall be to improve occupational safety and health and to prevent accidents and injury to health arising out of, linked with or occurring in the course of work, particularly by minimising the causes of hazards inherent in the working environment;
2. to issue safety and health regulations;
3. to provide for the enforcement of such regulations by measures of supervision;

4. to promote the progressive development of occupational health services for all workers with essentially preventive and advisory functions.

Article 4—The right to a fair remuneration

With a view to ensuring the effective exercise of the right to a fair remuneration, the Parties undertake—

1. to recognise the right of workers to a remuneration such as will give them and their families a decent standard of living;
2. to recognise the right of workers to an increased rate of remuneration for overtime work, subject to exceptions in particular cases;
3. to recognise the right of men and women workers to equal pay for work of equal value;
4. to recognise the right of all workers to a reasonable period of notice for termination of employment;
5. to permit deductions from wages only under conditions and to the extent prescribed by national laws or regulations or fixed by collective agreements or arbitration awards.

The exercise of these rights shall be achieved by freely concluded collective agreements, by statutory wage-fixing machinery, or by other means appropriate to national conditions.

Article 5—The right to organise

With a view to ensuring or promoting the freedom of workers and employers to form local, national or international organisations for the protection of their economic and social interests and to join those organisations, the Parties undertake that national law shall not be such as to impair, nor shall it be so applied as to impair, this freedom. The extent to which the guarantees provided for in this article shall apply to the police shall be determined by national laws or regulations. The principle governing the application to the members of the armed forces of these guarantees and the extent to which they shall apply to persons in this category shall equally be determined by national laws or regulations.

Article 6—The right to bargain collectively

With a view to ensuring the effective exercise of the right to bargain collectively, the Parties undertake—

1. to promote joint consultation between workers and employers;
2. to promote, where necessary and appropriate, machinery for voluntary negotiations between employers or employers' organisations and workers' organisations, with a view to the regulation of terms and conditions of employment by means of collective agreements;
3. to promote the establishment and use of appropriate machinery for conciliation and voluntary arbitration for the settlement of labour disputes;

and recognise—

4. the right of workers and employers to collective action in cases of conflicts of interest, including the right to strike, subject to obligations that might arise out of collective agreements previously entered into.

Article 7—The right of children and young persons to protection

With a view to ensuring the effective exercise of the right of children and young persons to protection, the Parties undertake—

1. to provide that the minimum age of admission to employment shall be 15 years, subject to exceptions for children employed in prescribed light work without harm to their health, morals or education;
2. to provide that the minimum age of admission to employment shall be 18 years with respect to prescribed occupations regarded as dangerous or unhealthy;
3. to provide that persons who are still subject to compulsory education shall not be employed in such work as would deprive them of the full benefit of their education;
4. to provide that the working hours of persons under 18 years of age shall be limited in accordance with the needs of their development, and particularly with their need for vocational training;
5. to recognise the right of young workers and apprentices to a fair wage or other appropriate allowances;

6. to provide that the time spent by young persons in vocational training during the normal working hours with the consent of the employer shall be treated as forming part of the working day;
7. to provide that employed persons of under 18 years of age shall be entitled to a minimum of four weeks' annual holiday with pay;
8. to provide that persons under 18 years of age shall not be employed in night work with the exception of certain occupations provided for by national laws or regulations;
9. to provide that persons under 18 years of age employed in occupations prescribed by national laws or regulations shall be subject to regular medical control;
10. to ensure special protection against physical and moral dangers to which children and young persons are exposed, and particularly against those resulting directly or indirectly from their work.

Article 8—The right of employed women to protection of maternity

With a view to ensuring the effective exercise of the right of employed women to the protection of maternity, the Parties undertake—

1. to provide either by paid leave, by adequate social security benefits or by benefits from public funds for employed women to take leave before and after childbirth up to a total of at least fourteen weeks;
2. to consider it as unlawful for an employer to give a woman notice of dismissal during the period from the time she notifies her employer that she is pregnant until the end of her maternity leave, or to give her notice of dismissal at such a time that the notice would expire during such a period;
3. to provide that mothers who are nursing their infants shall be entitled to sufficient time off for this purpose;
4. to regulate the employment in night work of pregnant women, women who have recently given birth and women nursing their infants;
5. to prohibit the employment of pregnant women, women who have recently given birth or who are nursing their infants in underground mining and all other work which is unsuitable by reason of its dangerous, unhealthy or arduous nature and to take appropriate measures to protect the employment rights of these women.

Article 9—The right to vocational guidance

With a view to ensuring the effective exercise of the right to vocational guidance, the Parties undertake to provide or promote, as necessary, a service which will assist all persons, including the handicapped, to solve problems related to occupational choice and progress, with due regard to the individual's characteristics and their relation to occupational opportunity: this assistance should be available free of charge, both to young persons, including schoolchildren, and to adults.

Article 10—The right to vocational training

With a view to ensuring the effective exercise of the right to vocational training, the Parties undertake—

1. to provide or promote, as necessary, the technical and vocational training of all persons, including the handicapped, in consultation with employers' and workers' organisations, and to grant facilities for access to higher technical and university education, based solely on individual aptitude;
2. to provide or promote a system of apprenticeship and other systematic arrangements for training young boys and girls in their various employments;
3. to provide or promote, as necessary—
   (a) adequate and readily available training facilities for adult workers;
   (b) special facilities for the retraining of adult workers needed as a result of technological development or new trends in employment;
4. to provide or promote, as necessary, special measures for the retraining and reintegration of the long-term unemployed;
5. to encourage the full utilisation of the facilities provided by appropriate measures such as—
   (a) reducing or abolishing any fees or charges;
   (b) granting financial assistance in appropriate cases;
   (c) including in the normal working hours time spent on supplementary training taken by the worker, at the request of his employer, during employment;
   (d) ensuring, through adequate supervision, in consultation with the

employers' and workers' organisations, the efficiency of apprenticeship and other training arrangements for young workers, and the adequate protection of young workers generally.

Article 11—The right to protection of health

With a view to ensuring the effective exercise of the right to protection of health, the Parties undertake, either directly or in co-operation with public or private organisations, to take appropriate measures designed *inter alia*—

1. to remove as far as possible the causes of ill-health;
2. to provide advisory and educational facilities for the promotion of health and the encouragement of individual responsibility in matters of health;
3. to prevent as far as possible epidemic, endemic and other diseases, as well as accidents.

Article 12—The right to social security

With a view to ensuring the effective exercise of the right to social security, the Parties undertake—

1. to establish or maintain a system of social security;
2. to maintain the social security system at a satisfactory level at least equal to that necessary for the ratification of the European Code of Social Security;
3. to endeavour to raise progressively the system of social security to a higher level;
4. to take steps, by the conclusion of appropriate bilateral and multilateral agreements or by other means, and subject to the conditions laid down in such agreements, in order to ensure—
   (a) equal treatment with their own nationals of the nationals of other Parties in respect of social security rights, including the retention of benefits arising out of social security legislation, whatever movements the persons protected may undertake between the territories of the Parties;
   (b) the granting, maintenance and resumption of social security rights by such means as the accumulation of insurance or employment periods completed under the legislation of each of the Parties.

Article 13—The right to social and medical assistance

With a view to ensuring the effective exercise of the right to social and medical assistance, the Parties undertake—

1. to ensure that any person who is without adequate resources and who is unable to secure such resources either by his own efforts or from other sources, in particular by benefits under a social security scheme, be granted adequate assistance, and, in case of sickness, the care necessitated by his condition;
2. to ensure that persons receiving such assistance shall not, for that reason, suffer from a diminution of their political or social rights;
3. to provide that everyone may receive by appropriate public or private services such advice and personal help as may be required to prevent, to remove, or to alleviate personal or family want;
4. to apply the provisions referred to in paragraphs 1, 2 and 3 of this article on an equal footing with their nationals to nationals of other Parties lawfully within their territories, in accordance with their obligations under the European Convention on Social and Medical Assistance, signed at Paris on 11 December 1953.

Article 14—The right to benefit from social welfare services

With a view to ensuring the effective exercise of the right to benefit from social welfare services, the Parties undertake—

1. to promote or provide services which, by using methods of social work, would contribute to the welfare and development of both individuals and groups in the community, and to their adjustment to the social environment;
2. to encourage the participation of individuals and voluntary or other organisations in the establishment and maintenance of such services.

Article 15—The right of persons with disabilities to independence, social integration and participation in the life of the community

With a view to ensuring to persons with disabilities, irrespective of age and the nature and origin of their disabilities, the effective exercise of the right to independence, social integration and participation in the life of the community, the Parties undertake, in particular—

1. to take the necessary measures to provide persons with disabilities with guidance, education and vocational training in the framework of general schemes wherever possible or, where this is not possible, through specialised bodies, public or private;
2. to promote their access to employment through all measures tending to encourage employers to hire and keep in employment persons with disabilities in the ordinary working environment and to adjust the working conditions to the needs of the disabled or, where this is not possible by reason of the disability, by arranging for or creating sheltered employment according to the level of disability. In certain cases, such measures may require recourse to specialised placement and support services;
3. to promote their full social integration and participation in the life of the community in particular through measures, including technical aids, aiming to overcome barriers to communication and mobility and enabling access to transport, housing, cultural activities and leisure.

Article 16—The right of the family to social, legal and economic protection

With a view to ensuring the necessary conditions for the full development of the family, which is a fundamental unit of society, the Parties undertake to promote the economic, legal and social protection of family life by such means as social and family benefits, fiscal arrangements, provision of family housing, benefits for the newly married and other appropriate means.

Article 17—The right of children and young persons to social, legal and economic protection

With a view to ensuring the effective exercise of the right of children and young persons to grow up in an environment which encourages the full development of their personality and of their physical and mental capacities, the Parties undertake, either directly or in co-operation with public and private organisations, to take all appropriate and necessary measures designed—

(a) to ensure that children and young persons, taking account of the rights and duties of their parents, have the care, the assistance, the education and the training they need, in particular by providing for the establishment or maintenance of institutions and services sufficient and adequate for this purpose;
(b) to protect children and young persons against negligence, violence or exploitation;
(c) to provide protection and special aid from the state for children and young persons temporarily or definitively deprived of their family's support;

to provide to children and young persons a free primary and secondary education as well as to encourage regular attendance at schools.

Article 18—The right to engage in a gainful occupation in the territory of other Parties

With a view to ensuring the effective exercise of the right to engage in a gainful occupation in the territory of any other Party, the Parties undertake—

1. to apply existing regulations in a spirit of liberality;
2. to simplify existing formalities and to reduce or abolish chancery dues and other charges payable by foreign workers or their employers;
3. to liberalise, individually or collectively, regulations governing the employment of foreign workers;

and recognise—

4. the right of their nationals to leave the country to engage in a gainful occupation in the territories of the other Parties.

Article 19—The right of migrant workers and their families to protection and assistance

With a view to ensuring the effective exercise of the right of migrant workers and their families to protection and assistance in the territory of any other Party, the Parties undertake—

1. to maintain or to satisfy themselves that there are maintained adequate and free services to assist such workers, particularly in obtaining accurate information, and to take all appropriate steps, so far as national laws and regulations permit, against misleading propaganda relating to emigration and immigration;
2. to adopt appropriate measures within their own jurisdiction to facilitate the departure, journey and reception of such workers and their families, and to provide, within their own jurisdiction, appropriate services for health, medical attention and good hygienic conditions during the journey;

3. to promote co-operation, as appropriate, between social services, public and private, in emigration and immigration countries;
4. to secure for such workers lawfully within their territories, insofar as such matters are regulated by law or regulations or are subject to the control of administrative authorities, treatment not less favourable than that of their own nationals in respect of the following matters—
   (a) remuneration and other employment and working conditions;
   (b) membership of trade unions and enjoyment of the benefits of collective bargaining;
   (c) accommodation;
5. to secure for such workers lawfully within their territories treatment not less favourable than that of their own nationals with regard to employment taxes, dues or contributions payable in respect of employed persons;
6. to facilitate as far as possible the reunion of the family of a foreign worker permitted to establish himself in the territory;
7. to secure for such workers lawfully within their territories treatment not less favourable than that of their own nationals in respect of legal proceedings relating to matters referred to in this article;
8. to secure that such workers lawfully residing within their territories are not expelled unless they endanger national security or offend against public interest or morality;
9. to permit, within legal limits, the transfer of such parts of the earnings and savings of such workers as they may desire;
10. to extend the protection and assistance provided for in this article to self-employed migrants insofar as such measures apply;
11. to promote and facilitate the teaching of the national language of the receiving state or, if there are several, one of these languages, to migrant workers and members of their families;
12. to promote and facilitate, as far as practicable, the teaching of the migrant worker's mother tongue to the children of the migrant worker.

Article 20—The right to equal opportunities and equal treatment in matters of employment and occupation without discrimination on the grounds of sex

With a view to ensuring the effective exercise of the right to equal opportunities and equal treatment in matters of employment and occupation without discrimination on the grounds of sex, the Parties undertake to recognise that right and to take appropriate measures to ensure or promote its application in the following fields—

(a) access to employment, protection against dismissal and occupational reintegration;
(b) vocational guidance, training, retraining and rehabilitation;
(c) terms of employment and working conditions, including remuneration;
(d) career development, including promotion.

Article 21—The right to information and consultation

With a view to ensuring the effective exercise of the right of workers to be informed and consulted within the undertaking, the Parties undertake to adopt or encourage measures enabling workers or their representatives, in accordance with national legislation and practice—

(a) to be informed regularly or at the appropriate time and in a comprehensible way about the economic and financial situation of the undertaking employing them, on the understanding that the disclosure of certain information which could be prejudicial to the undertaking may be refused or subject to confidentiality; and
(b) to be consulted in good time on proposed decisions which could substantially affect the interests of workers, particularly on those decisions which could have an important impact on the employment situation in the undertaking.

Article 22—The right to take part in the determination and improvement of the working conditions and working environment

With a view to ensuring the effective exercise of the right of workers to take part in the determination and improvement of the working conditions and working environment in the undertaking, the Parties undertake to adopt or encourage measures enabling workers or their representatives, in accordance with national legislation and practice, to contribute—

(a) to the determination and the improvement of the working conditions, work organisation and working environment;

(b) to the protection of health and safety within the undertaking;
(c) to the organisation of social and socio-cultural services and facilities within the undertaking;
(d) to the supervision of the observance of regulations on these matters.

Article 23—The right of elderly persons to social protection

With a view to ensuring the effective exercise of the right of elderly persons to social protection, the Parties undertake to adopt or encourage, either directly or in co-operation with public or private organisations, appropriate measures designed in particular—

to enable elderly persons to remain full members of society for as long as possible, by means of—
- (a) adequate resources enabling them to lead a decent life and play an active part in public, social and cultural life;
- (b) provision of information about services and facilities available for elderly persons and their opportunities to make use of them;

to enable elderly persons to choose their life-style freely and to lead independent lives in their familiar surroundings for as long as they wish and are able, by means of—
- (a) provision of housing suited to their needs and their state of health or of adequate support for adapting their housing;
- (b) the health care and the services necessitated by their state;

to guarantee elderly persons living in institutions appropriate support, while respecting their privacy, and participation in decisions concerning living conditions in the institution.

Article 24—The right to protection in cases of termination of employment

With a view to ensuring the effective exercise of the right of workers to protection in cases of termination of employment, the Parties undertake to recognise—

(a) the right of all workers not to have their employment terminated without valid reasons for such termination connected with their capacity or conduct or based on the operational requirements of the undertaking, establishment or service;
(b) the right of workers whose employment is terminated without a valid reason to adequate compensation or other appropriate relief.

To this end the Parties undertake to ensure that a worker who considers that his employment has been terminated without a valid reason shall have the right to appeal to an impartial body.

Article 25—The right of workers to the protection of their claims in the event of the insolvency of their employer

With a view to ensuring the effective exercise of the right of workers to the protection of their claims in the event of the insolvency of their employer, the Parties undertake to provide that workers' claims arising from contracts of employment or employment relationships be guaranteed by a guarantee institution or by any other effective form of protection.

Article 26—The right to dignity at work

With a view to ensuring the effective exercise of the right of all workers to protection of their dignity at work, the Parties undertake, in consultation with employers' and workers' organisations—

1. to promote awareness, information and prevention of sexual harassment in the workplace or in relation to work and to take all appropriate measures to protect workers from such conduct;
2. to promote awareness, information and prevention of recurrent reprehensible or distinctly negative and offensive actions directed against individual workers in the workplace or in relation to work and to take all appropriate measures to protect workers from such conduct.

Article 27—The right of workers with family responsibilities to equal opportunities and equal treatment

With a view to ensuring the exercise of the right to equality of opportunity and treatment for men and women workers with family responsibilities and between such workers and other workers, the Parties undertake—

1. to take appropriate measures—
   (a) to enable workers with family responsibilities to enter and remain in

employment, as well as to re-enter employment after an absence due to those responsibilities, including measures in the field of vocational guidance and training;

(b) to take account of their needs in terms of conditions of employment and social security;

(c) to develop or promote services, public or private, in particular child daycare services and other childcare arrangements;

2. to provide a possibility for either parent to obtain, during a period after maternity leave, parental leave to take care of a child, the duration and conditions of which should be determined by national legislation, collective agreements or practice;
3. to ensure that family responsibilities shall not, as such, constitute a valid reason for termination of employment.

Article 28—The right of workers' representatives to protection in the undertaking and facilities to be accorded to them

With a view to ensuring the effective exercise of the right of workers' representatives to carry out their functions, the Parties undertake to ensure that in the undertaking—

(a) they enjoy effective protection against acts prejudicial to them, including dismissal, based on their status or activities as workers' representatives within the undertaking;

(b) they are afforded such facilities as may be appropriate in order to enable them to carry out their functions promptly and efficiently, account being taken of the industrial relations system of the country and the needs, size and capabilities of the undertaking concerned.

Article 29—The right to information and consultation in collective redundancy procedures

With a view to ensuring the effective exercise of the right of workers to be informed and consulted in situations of collective redundancies, the Parties undertake to ensure that employers shall inform and consult workers' representatives, in good time prior to such collective redundancies, on ways and means of avoiding collective redundancies or limiting their occurrence and mitigating their consequences, for example by recourse to accompanying social measures aimed, in particular, at aid for the redeployment or retraining of the workers concerned.

Article 30—The right to protection against poverty and social exclusion

With a view to ensuring the effective exercise of the right to protection against poverty and social exclusion, the Parties undertake—

(a) to take measures within the framework of an overall and co-ordinated approach to promote the effective access of persons who live or risk living in a situation of social exclusion or poverty, as well as their families, to, in particular, employment, housing, training, education, culture and social and medical assistance;

(b) to review these measures with a view to their adaptation if necessary.

Article 31—The right to housing

With a view to ensuring the effective exercise of the right to housing, the Parties undertake to take measures designed—

1. to promote access to housing of an adequate standard;
2. to prevent and reduce homelessness with a view to its gradual elimination;
3. to make the price of housing accessible to those without adequate resources.

[5008]

PART III

Article A—Undertakings

1. Subject to the provisions of Article B below, each of the Parties undertakes—

(a) to consider Part I of this Charter as a declaration of the aims which it will pursue by all appropriate means, as stated in the introductory paragraph of that part;

(b) to consider itself bound by at least six of the following nine articles of Part II of this Charter: Articles 1, 5, 6, 7, 12, 13, 16, 19 and 20;

(c) to consider itself bound by an additional number of articles or numbered paragraphs of Part II of the Charter which it may select, provided that the total number of articles or numbered paragraphs by which it is bound is not less than sixteen articles or sixty-three numbered paragraphs.

2. The articles or paragraphs selected in accordance with sub-paragraphs b and c of paragraph 1 of this article shall be notified to the Secretary General of the Council of Europe at the time when the instrument of ratification, acceptance or approval is deposited.

3. Any Party may, at a later date, declare by notification addressed to the Secretary General that it considers itself bound by any articles or any numbered paragraphs of Part II of the Charter which it has not already accepted under the terms of paragraph 1 of this article. Such undertakings subsequently given shall be deemed to be an integral part of the ratification, acceptance or approval and shall have the same effect as from the first day of the month following the expiration of a period of one month after the date of the notification.

4. Each Party shall maintain a system of labour inspection appropriate to national conditions.

Article B—Links with the European Social Charter and the 1988 Additional Protocol

No Contracting Party to the European Social Charter or Party to the Additional Protocol of 5 May 1988 may ratify, accept or approve this Charter without considering itself bound by at least the provisions corresponding to the provisions of the European Social Charter and, where appropriate, of the Additional Protocol, to which it was bound.

Acceptance of the obligations of any provision of this Charter shall, from the date of entry into force of those obligations for the Party concerned, result in the corresponding provision of the European Social Charter and, where appropriate, of its Additional Protocol of 1988 ceasing to apply to the Party concerned in the event of that Party being bound by the first of those instruments or by both instruments.

[5009]

PART IV

Article C—Supervision of the implementation of the undertakings contained in this Charter

The implementation of the legal obligations contained in this Charter shall be submitted to the same supervision as the European Social Charter.

Article D—Collective complaints

1. The provisions of the Additional Protocol to the European Social Charter providing for a system of collective complaints shall apply to the undertakings given in this Charter for the States which have ratified the said Protocol.

2. Any State which is not bound by the Additional Protocol to the European Social Charter providing for a system of collective complaints may when depositing its instrument of ratification, acceptance or approval of this Charter or at any time thereafter, declare by notification addressed to the Secretary General of the Council of Europe, that it accepts the supervision of its obligations under this Charter following the procedure provided for in the said Protocol.

[5010]

PART V

Article E—Non-discrimination

The enjoyment of the rights set forth in this Charter shall be secured without discrimination on any ground such as race, colour, sex, language, religion, political or other opinion, national extraction or social origin, health, association with a national minority, birth or other status.

Article F—Derogations in time of war or public emergency

1. In time of war or other public emergency threatening the life of the nation any Party may take measures derogating from its obligations under this Charter to the extent strictly

required by the exigencies of the situation, provided that such measures are not inconsistent with its other obligations under international law.

2. Any Party which has availed itself of this right of derogation shall, within a reasonable lapse of time, keep the Secretary General of the Council of Europe fully informed of the measures taken and of the reasons therefor. It shall likewise inform the Secretary General when such measures have ceased to operate and the provisions of the Charter which it has accepted are again being fully executed.

Article G—Restrictions

1. The rights and principles set forth in Part I when effectively realised, and their effective exercise as provided for in Part II, shall not be subject to any restrictions or limitations not specified in those parts, except such as are prescribed by law and are necessary in a democratic society for the protection of the rights and freedoms of others or for the protection of public interest, national security, public health, or morals.

2. The restrictions permitted under this Charter to the rights and obligations set forth herein shall not be applied for any purpose other than that for which they have been prescribed.

Article H—Relations between the Charter and domestic law or international agreements

The provisions of this Charter shall not prejudice the provisions of domestic law or of any bilateral or multilateral treaties, conventions or agreements which are already in force, or may come into force, under which more favourable treatment would be accorded to the persons protected.

Article I—Implementation of the undertakings given

1. Without prejudice to the methods of implementation foreseen in these articles the relevant provisions of Articles 1 to 31 of Part II of this Charter shall be implemented by—

(a) laws or regulations;

(b) agreements between employers or employers' organisations and workers' organisations;

(c) a combination of those two methods;

(d) other appropriate means.

2. Compliance with the undertakings deriving from the provisions of paragraphs 1, 2, 3, 4, 5 and 7 of Article 2, paragraphs 4, 6 and 7 of Article 7, paragraphs 1, 2, 3 and 5 of Article 10 and Articles 21 and 22 of Part II of this Charter shall be regarded as effective if the provisions are applied, in accordance with paragraph 1 of this article, to the great majority of the workers concerned.

Article J—Amendments

1. Any amendment to Parts I and II of this Charter with the purpose of extending the rights guaranteed in this Charter as well as any amendment to Parts III to VI, proposed by a Party or by the Governmental Committee, shall be communicated to the Secretary General of the Council of Europe and forwarded by the Secretary General to the Parties to this Charter.

2. Any amendment proposed in accordance with the provisions of the preceding paragraph shall be examined by the Governmental Committee which shall submit the text adopted to the Committee of Ministers for approval after consultation with the Parliamentary Assembly. After its approval by the Committee of Ministers this text shall be forwarded to the Parties for acceptance.

3. Any amendment to Part I and to Part II of this Charter shall enter into force, in respect of those Parties which have accepted it, on the first day of the month following the expiration of a period of one month after the date on which three Parties have informed the Secretary General that they have accepted it.

In respect of any Party which subsequently accepts it, the amendment shall enter into force on the first day of the month following the expiration of a period of one month after the date on which that Party has informed the Secretary General of its acceptance.

4. Any amendment to Parts III to VI of this Charter shall enter into force on the first day of the month following the expiration of a period of one month after the date on which all Parties have informed the Secretary General that they have accepted it.

PART VI

Article K—Signature, ratification and entry into force

1. This Charter shall be open for signature by the member States of the Council of Europe. It shall be subject to ratification, acceptance or approval. Instruments of ratification, acceptance or approval shall be deposited with the Secretary General of the Council of Europe.

2. This Charter shall enter into force on the first day of the month following the expiration of a period of one month after the date on which three member States of the Council of Europe have expressed their consent to be bound by this Charter in accordance with the preceding paragraph.

3. In respect of any member State which subsequently expresses its consent to be bound by this Charter, it shall enter into force on the first day of the month following the expiration of a period of one month after the date of the deposit of the instrument of ratification, acceptance or approval.

Article L—Territorial application

1. This Charter shall apply to the metropolitan territory of each Party. Each signatory may, at the time of signature or of the deposit of its instrument of ratification, acceptance or approval, specify, by declaration addressed to the Secretary General of the Council of Europe, the territory which shall be considered to be its metropolitan territory for this purpose.

2. Any signatory may, at the time of signature or of the deposit of its instrument of ratification, acceptance or approval, or at any time thereafter, declare by notification addressed to the Secretary General of the Council of Europe, that the Charter shall extend in whole or in part to a non-metropolitan territory or territories specified in the said declaration for whose international relations it is responsible or for which it assumes international responsibility. It shall specify in the declaration the articles or paragraphs of Part II of the Charter which it accepts as binding in respect of the territories named in the declaration.

3. The Charter shall extend its application to the territory or territories named in the aforesaid declaration as from the first day of the month following the expiration of a period of one month after the date of receipt of the notification of such declaration by the Secretary General.

4. Any Party may declare at a later date by notification addressed to the Secretary General of the Council of Europe that, in respect of one or more of the territories to which the Charter has been applied in accordance with paragraph 2 of this article, it accepts as binding any articles or any numbered paragraphs which it has not already accepted in respect of that territory or territories. Such undertakings subsequently given shall be deemed to be an integral part of the original declaration in respect of the territory concerned, and shall have the same effect as from the first day of the month following the expiration of a period of one month after the date of receipt of such notification by the Secretary General.

Article M—Denunciation

1. Any Party may denounce this Charter only at the end of a period of five years from the date on which the Charter entered into force for it, or at the end of any subsequent period of two years, and in either case after giving six months' notice to the Secretary General of the Council of Europe who shall inform the other Parties accordingly.

2. Any Party may, in accordance with the provisions set out in the preceding paragraph, denounce any article or paragraph of Part II of the Charter accepted by it provided that the number of articles or paragraphs by which this Party is bound shall never be less than sixteen in the former case and sixty-three in the latter and that this number of articles or paragraphs shall continue to include the articles selected by the Party among those to which special reference is made in Article A, paragraph 1, sub-paragraph b.

3. Any Party may denounce the present Charter or any of the articles or paragraphs of Part II of the Charter under the conditions specified in paragraph 1 of this article in respect of any territory to which the said Charter is applicable, by virtue of a declaration made in accordance with paragraph 2 of Article L.

Article N—Appendix

The appendix to this Charter shall form an integral part of it.

Article O—Notifications

The Secretary General of the Council of Europe shall notify the member States of the Council and the Director General of the International Labour Office of—

(a) any signature;
(b) the deposit of any instrument of ratification, acceptance or approval;
(c) any date of entry into force of this Charter in accordance with Article K;
(d) any declaration made in application of Articles A, paragraphs 2 and 3, D, paragraphs 1 and 2, F, paragraph 2, L, paragraphs 1, 2, 3 and 4;
(e) any amendment in accordance with Article J;
(f) any denunciation in accordance with Article M;
(g) any other act, notification or communication relating to this Charter.

[5012]

In witness whereof, the undersigned, being duly authorised thereto, have signed this revised Charter.

Done at Strasbourg, this 3rd day of May 1996, in English and French, both texts being equally authentic, in a single copy which shall be deposited in the archives of the Council of Europe. The Secretary General of the Council of Europe shall transmit certified copies to each member State of the Council of Europe and to the Director General of the International Labour Office.

APPENDIX TO THE REVISED EUROPEAN SOCIAL CHARTER

Scope of the Revised European Social Charter in terms of persons protected

1. Without prejudice to Article 12, paragraph 4, and Article 13, paragraph 4, the persons covered by Articles 1 to 17 and 20 to 31 include foreigners only in so far as they are nationals of other Parties lawfully resident or working regularly within the territory of the Party concerned, subject to the understanding that these articles are to be interpreted in the light of the provisions of Articles 18 and 19.

This interpretation would not prejudice the extension of similar facilities to other persons by any of the Parties.

2. Each Party will grant to refugees as defined in the Convention relating to the Status of Refugees, signed in Geneva on 28 July 1951 and in the Protocol of 31 January 1967, and lawfully staying in its territory, treatment as favourable as possible, and in any case not less favourable than under the obligations accepted by the Party under the said convention and under any other existing international instruments applicable to those refugees.

3. Each Party will grant to stateless persons as defined in the Convention on the Status of Stateless Persons done in New York on 28 September 1954 and lawfully staying in its territory, treatment as favourable as possible and in any case not less favourable than under the obligations accepted by the Party under the said instrument and under any other existing international instruments applicable to those stateless persons.

Part I, paragraph 18, and Part II, Article 18, paragraph 1

It is understood that these provisions are not concerned with the question of entry into the territories of the Parties and do not prejudice the provisions of the European Convention on Establishment, signed in Paris on 13 December 1955.

Part II

Article 1, paragraph 2

This provision shall not be interpreted as prohibiting or authorising any union security clause or practice.

Article 2, paragraph 6

Parties may provide that this provision shall not apply—

(a) to workers having a contract or employment relationship with a total duration not exceeding one month and/or with a working week not exceeding eight hours;
(b) where the contract or employment relationship is of a casual and/or specific nature, provided, in these cases, that its non-application is justified by objective considerations.

Article 3, paragraph 4

It is understood that for the purposes of this provision the functions, organisation and conditions of operation of these services shall be determined by national laws or regulations, collective agreements or other means appropriate to national conditions.

Article 4, paragraph 4

This provision shall be so understood as not to prohibit immediate dismissal for any serious offence.

Article 4, paragraph 5

It is understood that a Party may give the undertaking required in this paragraph if the great majority of workers are not permitted to suffer deductions from wages either by law or through collective agreements or arbitration awards, the exceptions being those persons not so covered.

Article 6, paragraph 4

It is understood that each Party may, insofar as it is concerned, regulate the exercise of the right to strike by law, provided that any further restriction that this might place on the right can be justified under the terms of Article G.

Article 7, paragraph 2

This provision does not prevent Parties from providing in their legislation that young persons not having reached the minimum age laid down may perform work in so far as it is absolutely necessary for their vocational training where such work is carried out in accordance with conditions prescribed by the competent authority and measures are taken to protect the health and safety of these young persons.

Article 7, paragraph 8

It is understood that a Party may give the undertaking required in this paragraph if it fulfils the spirit of the undertaking by providing by law that the great majority of persons under eighteen years of age shall not be employed in night work.

Article 8, paragraph 2

This provision shall not be interpreted as laying down an absolute prohibition. Exceptions could be made, for instance, in the following cases—

(a) if an employed woman has been guilty of misconduct which justifies breaking off the employment relationship;
(b) if the undertaking concerned ceases to operate;
(c) if the period prescribed in the employment contract has expired.

Article 12, paragraph 4

The words "and subject to the conditions laid down in such agreements" in the introduction to this paragraph are taken to imply *inter alia* that with regard to benefits which are available independently of any insurance contribution, a Party may require the completion of a prescribed period of residence before granting such benefits to nationals of other Parties.

Article 13, paragraph 4

Governments not Parties to the European Convention on Social and Medical Assistance may ratify the Charter in respect of this paragraph provided that they grant to nationals of other Parties a treatment which is in conformity with the provisions of the said convention.

Article 16

It is understood that the protection afforded in this provision covers single-parent families.

Article 17

It is understood that this provision covers all persons below the age of 18 years, unless under the law applicable to the child majority is attained earlier, without prejudice to the other specific provisions provided by the Charter, particularly Article 7.

This does not imply an obligation to provide compulsory education up to the above-mentioned age.

Article 19, paragraph 6

For the purpose of applying this provision, the term "family of a foreign worker" is understood to mean at least the worker's spouse and unmarried children, as long as the latter are considered to be minors by the receiving State and are dependent on the migrant worker.

Article 20

1. It is understood that social security matters, as well as other provisions relating to unemployment benefit, old age benefit and survivor's benefit, may be excluded from the scope of this article.

2. Provisions concerning the protection of women, particularly as regards pregnancy, confinement and the post-natal period, shall not be deemed to be discrimination as referred to in this article.

3. This article shall not prevent the adoption of specific measures aimed at removing *de facto* inequalities.

4. Occupational activities which, by reason of their nature or the context in which they are carried out, can be entrusted only to persons of a particular sex may be excluded from the scope of this article or some of its provisions. This provision is not to be interpreted as requiring the Parties to embody in laws or regulations a list of occupations which, by reason of their nature or the context in which they are carried out, may be reserved to persons of a particular sex.

Articles 21 and 22

1. For the purpose of the application of these articles, the term "workers' representatives" means persons who are recognised as such under national legislation or practice.

2. The terms "national legislation and practice" embrace as the case may be, in addition to laws and regulations, collective agreements, other agreements between employers and workers' representatives, customs as well as relevant case law.

3. For the purpose of the application of these articles, the term "undertaking" is understood as referring to a set of tangible and intangible components, with or without legal personality, formed to produce goods or provide services for financial gain and with power to determine its own market policy.

4. It is understood that religious communities and their institutions may be excluded from the application of these articles, even if these institutions are "undertakings" within the meaning of paragraph 3. Establishments pursuing activities which are inspired by certain ideals or guided by certain moral concepts, ideals and concepts which are protected by national legislation, may be excluded from the application of these articles to such an extent as is necessary to protect the orientation of the undertaking.

5. It is understood that where in a state the rights set out in these articles are exercised in the various establishments of the undertaking, the Party concerned is to be considered as fulfilling the obligations deriving from these provisions.

6. The Parties may exclude from the field of application of these articles, those undertakings employing less than a certain number of workers, to be determined by national legislation or practice.

Article 22

1. This provision affects neither the powers and obligations of states as regards the adoption of health and safety regulations for workplaces, nor the powers and responsibilities of the bodies in charge of monitoring their application.

2. The terms "social and socio-cultural services and facilities" are understood as referring to the social and/or cultural facilities for workers provided by some undertakings such as welfare assistance, sports fields, rooms for nursing mothers, libraries, children's holiday camps, etc.

Article 23, paragraph 1

For the purpose of the application of this paragraph, the term "for as long as possible" refers to the elderly person's physical, psychological and intellectual capacities.

Article 24

1. It is understood that for the purposes of this article the terms "termination of employment" and "terminated" mean termination of employment at the initiative of the employer.

2. It is understood that this article covers all workers but that a Party may exclude from some or all of its protection the following categories of employed persons—
   (a) workers engaged under a contract of employment for a specified period of time or a specified task;
   (b) workers undergoing a period of probation or a qualifying period of employment, provided that this is determined in advance and is of a reasonable duration;
   (c) workers engaged on a casual basis for a short period.

3. For the purpose of this article the following, in particular, shall not constitute valid reasons for termination of employment—
   (a) trade union membership or participation in union activities outside working hours, or, with the consent of the employer, within working hours;
   (b) seeking office as, acting or having acted in the capacity of a workers' representative;
   (c) the filing of a complaint or the participation in proceedings against an employer involving alleged violation of laws or regulations or recourse to competent administrative authorities;
   (d) race, colour, sex, marital status, family responsibilities, pregnancy, religion, political opinion, national extraction or social origin;
   (e) maternity or parental leave;
   (f) temporary absence from work due to illness or injury.

4. It is understood that compensation or other appropriate relief in case of termination of employment without valid reasons shall be determined by national laws or regulations, collective agreements or other means appropriate to national conditions.

Article 25

1. It is understood that the competent national authority may, by way of exemption and after consulting organisations of employers and workers, exclude certain categories of workers from the protection provided in this provision by reason of the special nature of their employment relationship.

2. It is understood that the definition of the term "insolvency" must be determined by national law and practice.

3. The workers' claims covered by this provision shall include at least—
   (a) the workers' claims for wages relating to a prescribed period, which shall not be less than three months under a privilege system and eight weeks under a guarantee system, prior to the insolvency or to the termination of employment;
   (b) the workers' claims for holiday pay due as a result of work performed during the year in which the insolvency or the termination of employment occurred;
   (c) the workers' claims for amounts due in respect of other types of paid absence relating to a prescribed period, which shall not be less than three months under a privilege system and eight weeks under a guarantee system, prior to the insolvency or the termination of the employment.

4. National laws or regulations may limit the protection of workers' claims to a prescribed amount, which shall be of a socially acceptable level.

Article 26

It is understood that this article does not require that legislation be enacted by the Parties.

It is understood that paragraph 2 does not cover sexual harassment.

Article 27

It is understood that this article applies to men and women workers with family responsibilities in relation to their dependent children as well as in relation to other members of their immediate family who clearly need their care or support where such responsibilities restrict their possibilities of preparing for, entering, participating in or advancing in economic activity. The terms "dependent children" and "other members of their immediate family who clearly need their care and support" mean persons defined as such by the national legislation of the Party concerned.

Articles 28 and 29

For the purpose of the application of this article, the term "workers' representatives" means persons who are recognised as such under national legislation or practice.

Part III

It is understood that the Charter contains legal obligations of an international character, the application of which is submitted solely to the supervision provided for in Part IV thereof.

Article A, paragraph 1

It is understood that the numbered paragraphs may include articles consisting of only one paragraph.

Article B, paragraph 2

For the purpose of paragraph 2 of Article B, the provisions of the revised Charter correspond to the provisions of the Charter with the same article or paragraph number with the exception of—

(a) Article 3, paragraph 2, of the revised Charter which corresponds to Article 3, paragraphs 1 and 3, of the Charter;

(b) Article 3, paragraph 3, of the revised Charter which corresponds to Article 3, paragraphs 2 and 3, of the Charter;

(c) Article 10, paragraph 5, of the revised Charter which corresponds to Article 10, paragraph 4, of the Charter;

(d) Article 17, paragraph 1, of the revised Charter which corresponds to Article 17 of the Charter.

Part V

Article E

A differential treatment based on an objective and reasonable justification shall not be deemed discriminatory.

Article F

The terms "in time of war or other public emergency" shall be so understood as to cover also the *threat* of war.

Article I

It is understood that workers excluded in accordance with the appendix to Articles 21 and 22 are not taken into account in establishing the number of workers concerned.

Article J

The term "amendment" shall be extended so as to cover also the addition of new articles to the Charter.

[5013]

B. EMPLOYMENT APPEAL TRIBUNAL PRACTICE DIRECTION AND PRACTICE STATEMENT, ETC

PRACTICE DIRECTION (EMPLOYMENT APPEAL TRIBUNAL – PROCEDURE) 2008

NOTES

Commencement: 22 May 2008 (see para 1.1).

1. INTRODUCTION AND OBJECTIVE

1.1 This Practice Direction ("PD") supersedes all previous Practice Directions. It comes into force on 22 May 2008.

1.2 The Employment Appeal Tribunal Rules 1993 (SI 1993/2854) as amended by the Employment Appeal Tribunal (Amendment) Rules 2001 (SI 2001/1128 and 2001/1476) and the Employment Appeal Tribunal (Amendment) Rules 2004 (SI 2004/2526) ("the Rules") apply to all proceedings irrespective of when those proceedings were commenced.

1.3 By s 30(3) of the Employment Tribunals Act 1996 ("ETA 1996") the Employment Appeal Tribunal ("the EAT") has power, subject to the Rules, to regulate its own procedure. In so doing, the EAT regards itself as subject in all its actions to the duties imposed by Rule 2A. It will seek to apply the overriding objective when it exercises any power given to it by the Rules or interprets any Rule.

1.4 The overriding objective of this PD is to enable the EAT to deal with cases justly. Dealing with a case justly includes, so far as is practicable:

1.4.1 ensuring that the parties are on an equal footing;
1.4.2 dealing with the case in ways which are proportionate to the importance and complexity of the issues;
1.4.3 ensuring that it is dealt with expeditiously and fairly;
1.4.4 saving expense.

1.5 The parties are required to help the EAT to further the overriding objective.

1.6 Where the Rules do not otherwise provide, the following procedure will apply to all appeals to the EAT.

1.7 The provisions of this PD are subject to any specific directions which the EAT may make in any particular case. Otherwise, the directions set out below must be complied with in all appeals from Employment Tribunals. In national security appeals, and appeals from the Certification Officer and the Central Arbitration Committee, the Rules set out the separate procedures to be followed and the EAT will normally give specific directions.

1.8 Where it is appropriate to the EAT's jurisdiction, procedure, unrestricted rights of representation and restricted costs regime, the EAT is guided by the Civil Procedure Rules. So, for example:

1.8.1 For the purpose of serving a valid Notice of Appeal under Rule 3 and para 3 below, when an Employment Tribunal decision is sent to parties on a Wednesday, that day does not count and the Notice of Appeal must arrive at the EAT by 4.00 pm on or before the Wednesday 6 weeks (i e 42 days) later.
1.8.2 When a date is given for serving of a document or for doing some other act, the complete document must be received by the EAT or the relevant party by 4.00pm on that date. Any document received after 4.00 pm will be deemed to be lodged on the next working day.
1.8.3 Except as provided in 1.8.4 below, all days count, but if a time limit expires on a day when the central office of the EAT, or the EAT office in Edinburgh (as appropriate), is closed, it is extended to the next working day.
1.8.4 Where the time limit is 5 days (e g an appeal against a Registrar's order or direction), Saturdays, Sundays, Christmas Day, Good Friday and Bank Holidays do not count. For example an appeal against an order made on a Wednesday must arrive at the EAT on or before the following Wednesday.

1.9 In this PD any reference to the date of an order shall mean the date stamped upon the relevant order by the EAT ("the seal date").

1.10 The parties can expect the EAT normally to have read the documents (or the documents indicated in any essential reading list if permission is granted under para 6.3 below for an enlarged appeal bundle) in advance of any hearing.

[5014]

2. INSTITUTION OF APPEAL

2.1 The Notice of Appeal must be, or be substantially, in accordance with Form 1 (in the amended form annexed to this Practice Direction) or Forms 1A or 2 of the Schedule to the Rules and must identify the date of the judgment, decision or order being appealed. Copies of the judgment, decision or order appealed against and of the Employment Tribunal's written reasons, together with a copy of the Claim (ET1) and the Response (ET3) must be attached, or if not, a written explanation must be given. A Notice of Appeal without such documentation will not be validly lodged.

2.2 If the appellant has made an application to the Employment Tribunal for a review of its judgment or decision, a copy of such application should accompany the Notice of Appeal together with the judgment and written reasons of the Employment Tribunal in respect of that review application, or a statement, if such be the case, that a judgment is awaited. If any of these documents cannot be included, a written explanation must be given. The appellant should also attach (where they are relevant to the appeal) copies of any orders including case management orders made by the Employment Tribunal.

2.3 Where written reasons of the Employment Tribunal are not attached to the Notice of Appeal, either (as set out in the written explanation) because a request for written reasons has been refused by the Employment Tribunal or for some other reason, an appellant must, when lodging the Notice of Appeal, apply in writing to the EAT to exercise its discretion to hear the appeal without written reasons or to exercise its power to request written reasons from the Employment Tribunal, setting out the full grounds of that application.

2.4 The Notice of Appeal must clearly identify the point(s) of law which form(s) the ground(s) of appeal from the judgment, decision or order of the Employment Tribunal to the EAT. It should also state the order which the appellant will ask the EAT to make at the hearing.

2.5 Rules 3(7)–(10) give a judge or the Registrar power to decide that no further action shall be taken in certain cases where it appears that the Notice of Appeal or any part of it (a) discloses no reasonable grounds for bringing the appeal, or (b) is an abuse of the Employment Appeal Tribunal's process or is otherwise likely to obstruct the just disposal of proceedings. The Rules specify the rights of the appellant and the procedure to be followed. The appellant can request an oral hearing before a judge to challenge the decision. If it appears to the judge or Registrar that a Notice of Appeal or an application gives insufficient grounds of, or lacks clarity in identifying, a point of law, the judge or Registrar may postpone any decision under Rule 3(7) pending the appellant's amplification or clarification of the Notice of Appeal or further information from the Employment Tribunal.

2.6 **Perversity Appeals**: an appellant may not state as a ground of appeal simply words to the effect that "the judgment or order was contrary to the evidence," or that "there was no evidence to support the judgment or order", or that "the judgment or order was one which no reasonable Tribunal could have reached and was perverse" unless the Notice of Appeal also sets out full particulars of the matters relied on in support of those general grounds.

2.7 A party cannot reserve a right to amend, alter or add, to a Notice of Appeal or a respondent's Answer. Any application for permission to amend must be made as soon as practicable and must be accompanied by a draft of the amended Notice of Appeal or amended Answer which makes clear the precise amendments for which permission is sought.

2.8 A respondent to the appeal who wishes to resist the appeal and/or to cross-appeal, but who has not delivered a respondent's Answer as directed by the Registrar, or otherwise ordered, may be precluded from taking part in the appeal unless permission is granted to serve an Answer out of time.

2.9 Where an application is made for permission to institute or continue relevant proceedings by a person who has been made the subject of a Restriction of Proceedings Order pursuant to s 33 of ETA 1996, that application will be considered on paper by a judge, who may make an order granting, refusing or otherwise dealing with such application on paper.

[5015]

3. TIME FOR INSTITUTING APPEALS

3.1 The time within which an appeal must be instituted depends on whether the appeal is against a judgment or against an order or decision of the Employment Tribunal.

3.2 If the appeal is against an order or decision, the appeal must be instituted within 42 days of the date of the order or decision. The EAT will treat a Tribunal's refusal to make an order or decision as itself constituting an order or decision. The date of an order or decision is the date when the order or decision was sent to the parties, which is normally recorded on or in the order or decision.

3.3 If the appeal is against a judgment, the appeal must be instituted within 42 days from the date on which the written record of the judgment was sent to the parties. However in three situations the time for appealing against a judgment will be 42 days from the date when written reasons were sent to the parties. This will be the case only if (1) written reasons were requested orally at the hearing before the Tribunal or (2) written reasons were requested in writing within 14 days of the date on which the written record of the judgment was sent to the parties or (3) the Tribunal itself reserved its reasons and gave them subsequently in writing: such exception will not apply if the request to the Tribunal for written reasons is made out of time (whether or not such request is granted). The date of the written record and of the written reasons is the date when they are sent to the parties, which is normally recorded on or in the written record and the written reasons.

3.4 The time limit referred to in paras 3.1 to 3.3 above apply even though the question of remedy and assessment of compensation by the Employment Tribunal has been adjourned or has not been dealt with and even though an application has been made to the Employment Tribunal for a review.

3.5 An application for an extension of time for appealing cannot be considered until a Notice of Appeal in accordance with para 2(1) above has been lodged with the EAT.

3.6 Any application for an extension of time for appealing must be made as an interim application to the Registrar, who will normally determine the application after inviting and considering written representations from each side. An interim appeal lies from the Registrar's decision to a judge. Such an appeal must be notified to the EAT within 5 days of the date when the Registrar's decision was sent to the parties. [See para 4.3 below.]

3.7 In determining whether to extend the time for appealing, particular attention will be paid to whether any good excuse for the delay has been shown and to the guidance contained in the decisions of the EAT and the Court of Appeal, as summarised in ***United Arab Emirates v Abdelghafar*** [1995] ICR 65, ***Aziz v Bethnal Green City Challenge Co Ltd*** [2000] IRLR 111 and ***Jurkowska v HI Mad*** [2008] EWCA Civ 231.

3.8 It is not usually a good reason for late lodgment of a Notice of Appeal that an application for litigation support from public funds has been made, but not yet determined; or that support is being sought from, but has not yet been provided by, some other body, such as a trade union, employers' association or the Equality and Human Rights Commission.

3.9 In any case of doubt or difficulty, a Notice of Appeal should be lodged in time and an application made to the Registrar for directions.

[5016]

4. INTERIM APPLICATIONS

4.1 Interim applications should be made in writing (no particular form is required) and will be initially referred to the Registrar who after considering the papers may deal with the case or refer it to a judge. The judge may dispose of it himself or refer it to a full EAT hearing. Parties are encouraged to make any such applications at a Preliminary Hearing ("PH") or an Appointment for Directions if one is ordered (see paras 9.7–9.18 and 11.2 below).

4.2 Unless otherwise ordered, any application for extension of time will be considered and determined as though it were an interim application to the Registrar, who will normally determine the application after inviting and considering written representations from each side.

4.3 An interim appeal lies from the Registrar's decision to a judge. Such an appeal must be notified to the EAT within 5 days of the date when the Registrar's decision was sent to the parties.

[5017]

5. THE RIGHT TO INSPECT THE REGISTER AND CERTAIN DOCUMENTS AND TO TAKE COPIES

5.1 Any document lodged in the Central Office of the EAT in London or in the EAT office in Edinburgh in any proceedings before the EAT shall be sealed with the seal of the EAT showing the date (and time, if received after 4.00 pm) on which the document was lodged.

5.2 Particulars of the date of delivery at the Central Office of the EAT or in the EAT office in Edinburgh of any document for filing or lodgment together with the time, if received after 4.00 pm, the date of the document and the title of the appeal of which the document forms part of the record shall be entered in the Register of Cases kept in the Central Office and in Edinburgh or in the file which forms part of the Register of Cases.

5.3 Any person shall be entitled during office hours by appointment to inspect and request a copy of any of the following documents filed or lodged in the Central Office or the EAT office in Edinburgh, namely:

5.3.1 any Notice of Appeal or respondent's Answer or any copy thereof;
5.3.2 any judgment or order given or made in court or any copy of such judgment or order; and
5.3.3 with the permission of the EAT, which may be granted on an application, any other document.

5.4 A copying charge per page will be payable for those documents mentioned in para 5.3 above.

5.5 Nothing in this Direction shall be taken as preventing any party to an appeal from inspecting and requesting a copy of any document filed or lodged in the Central Office or the EAT office in Edinburgh before the commencement of the appeal, but made with a view to its commencement.

[5018]

6. PAPERS FOR USE AT THE HEARING

6.1 It is the responsibility of the parties or their advisers (see paras 6.5 and 6.6 below) to prepare a core bundle of papers for use at any hearing. Ultimate responsibility lies with the appellant, following consultation with other parties. The bundle must include only those exhibits (productions in Scotland) and documents used before the Employment Tribunal which are considered to be necessary for the appeal. It is the duty of the parties or their advisers to ensure that only those documents are included which are (a) relevant to the point(s) of law raised in the appeal and (b) likely to be referred to at the hearing. It is also the responsibility of parties to retain copies of all documents and correspondence, including hearing bundles, sent to EAT. Bundles (see para 6.2 below) used at one EAT hearing will not be retained by the EAT for a subsequent hearing.

6.2 The documents in the core bundle should be numbered by item, then paginated continuously and indexed, in the following order:

6.2.1 Judgment, decision or order appealed from and written reasons
6.2.2 Sealed Notice of Appeal
6.2.3 Respondent's Answer if a Full Hearing ("FH"), respondent's Submissions if a PH
6.2.4 ET1 claim (and any Additional Information or Written Answers)
6.2.5 ET3 response (and any Additional Information or Written Answers)
6.2.6 Questionnaire and Replies (discrimination and equal pay cases)
6.2.7 Relevant orders, judgments and written reasons of the Employment Tribunal
6.2.8 Relevant orders and judgments of the EAT
6.2.9 Affidavits and Employment Tribunal comments (where ordered)
6.2.10 Any documents agreed or ordered pursuant to para 7 below.

6.3 Other documents relevant to the particular hearing (for example the particulars or contract of employment and any procedures) referred to at the Employment Tribunal may follow in the core bundle, if the total pages do not exceed 100. No bundle containing more than 100 pages should be agreed or lodged without the permission of the Registrar or order of a judge which will not be granted without the provision of an essential reading list as soon as practicable thereafter. If permitted or ordered, further pages should follow, with consecutive pagination, in an additional bundle or bundles if appropriate.

6.4 All documents must be legible and unmarked.

6.5 **PH cases** (see para 9.5.2 below)**, Appeals from Registrar's Order, Rule 3(10) hearings, Appointments for Directions**: the appellant must prepare and lodge 4 copies (2 copies if judge sitting alone) of the bundle as soon as possible after service of the Notice of Appeal and no later than 28 days from the seal date of the relevant order unless otherwise directed.

6.6 **FH cases** (see para 9.5.3 below): the parties must co-operate in agreeing a bundle of papers for the hearing. By no later than 28 days from the seal date of the relevant order, unless otherwise directed, the appellant is responsible for ensuring that 4 copies (2 copies if judge sitting alone) of a bundle agreed by the parties is lodged at the EAT.

6.7 **Warned List and Fast Track FH cases**: the bundles should be lodged as soon as possible and (unless the hearing date is within seven days) in any event within seven days after the parties have been notified that the case is expedited or in the Warned List.

6.8 In the event of disagreement between the parties or difficulty in preparing the bundles, the Registrar may give appropriate directions, whether on application in writing (on notice) by one or more of the parties or of his/her own initiative.

[5019]

7. EVIDENCE BEFORE THE EMPLOYMENT TRIBUNAL

7.1 An appellant who considers that a point of law raised in the Notice of Appeal cannot be argued without reference to evidence given (or not given) at the Employment Tribunal, the nature or substance of which does not, or does not sufficiently, appear from the written reasons, must ordinarily submit an application with the Notice of Appeal. The application is for the nature of such evidence (or lack of it) to be admitted, or if necessary for the relevant parts of the employment judge's notes of evidence to be produced. If such application is not so made, then it should be made:

7.1.1 if a PH is ordered, in the skeleton or written submissions lodged prior to such PH; or

7.1.2 if the case is listed for FH without a PH, then within 14 days of the seal date of the order so providing.

Any such application by a respondent to an appeal, must, if not made earlier, accompany the respondent's Answer.

7.2 The application must explain why such a matter is considered necessary in order to argue the point of law raised in the Notice of Appeal or respondent's Answer. The application must identify:

7.2.1 the issue(s) in the Notice of Appeal or respondent's Answer to which the matter is relevant;

7.2.2 the names of the witnesses whose evidence is considered relevant, alternatively the nature of the evidence the absence of which is considered relevant;

7.2.3 (if applicable) the part of the hearing when the evidence was given;

7.2.4 the gist of the evidence (or absence of evidence) alleged to be relevant; and

7.2.5 (if the party has a record), saying so and by whom and when it was made, or producing an extract from a witness statement given in writing at the hearing.

7.3 The application will be considered on the papers, or if appropriate at a PH, by the Registrar or a judge. The Registrar or a judge may give directions for written representations (if they have not already been lodged), or may determine the application, but will ordinarily make an order requiring the party who seeks to raise such a matter to give notice to the other party(ies) to the appeal/cross-appeal. The notice will require the other party(ies) to co-operate in agreeing, within 21 days (unless a shorter period is ordered), a statement or note of the relevant evidence, alternatively a statement that there was no such evidence. All parties are required to use their best endeavours to agree such a statement or note.

7.4 In the absence of such agreement within 21 days (or such shorter period as may be ordered) of the requirement, any party may make an application within seven days thereafter to the EAT, for directions. The party must enclose all relevant correspondence and give notice to the other parties. The directions may include: the resolution of the disagreement on the papers or at a hearing; the administration by one party to the others of, or a request to the employment judge to respond to, a questionnaire; or, if the EAT is satisfied that such notes are necessary, a request that the employment judge produce his/her notes of evidence either in whole or in part.

7.5 If the EAT requests any documents from the employment judge, it will supply copies to the parties upon receipt.

7.6 In an appeal from an Employment Tribunal which ordered its proceedings to be tape recorded, the EAT will apply the principles above to any application for a transcript.

7.7 A note of evidence is not to be produced and supplied to the parties to enable the parties to embark on a "fishing expedition" to establish grounds or additional grounds of appeal or because they have not kept their own notes of the evidence. If an application for such a note is found by the EAT to have been unreasonably made or if there is unreasonable lack of co-operation in agreeing a relevant note or statement, the party behaving unreasonably is at risk of being ordered to pay costs.

[5020]

8. FRESH EVIDENCE AND NEW POINTS OF LAW

8.1 Where an application is made by a party to an appeal to put in, at the hearing of the appeal, any document which was not before the Employment Tribunal, and which has not been agreed in writing by the other parties, the application and a copy of the documents sought to be admitted should be lodged at the EAT with the Notice of Appeal or the respondent's Answer, as appropriate. The application and copy should be served on the other parties. The same principle applies to any oral evidence not given at the Employment Tribunal which is sought to be adduced on the appeal. The nature and substance of such evidence together with the date when the party first became aware of its existence must be disclosed in a document, where appropriate a witness statement from the relevant witness with signed statement of truth, which must be similarly lodged and served.

8.2 In exercising its discretion to admit any fresh evidence or new document, the EAT will apply the principles set out in ***Ladd v Marshall*** [1954] 1WLR 1489, having regard to the overriding objective, ie:

8.2.1 the evidence could not have been obtained with reasonable diligence for use at the Employment Tribunal hearing;
8.2.2 it is relevant and would probably have had an important influence on the hearing;
8.2.3 it is apparently credible.

Accordingly the evidence and representations in support of the application must address these principles.

8.3 A party wishing to resist the application must, within 14 days of its being sent, submit any representations in response to the EAT and other parties.

8.4 The application will be considered by the Registrar or a judge on the papers (or, if appropriate, at a PH) who may determine the issue or give directions for a hearing or may seek comments from the employment judge. A copy of any comments received from the employment judge will be sent to all parties.

8.5 If a respondent intends to contend at the FH that the appellant has raised a point which was not argued below, the respondent shall so state:

8.5.1 if a PH has been ordered, in writing to the EAT and all parties, within 14 days of receiving the Notice of Appeal;
8.5.2 if the case is listed for a FH without a PH, in a respondent's Answer.

In the event of dispute the employment judge should be asked for his/her comments as to whether a particular legal argument was deployed.

[5021]

9. CASE TRACKS AND DIRECTIONS: THE SIFT OF APPEALS

9.1 Consistent with the overriding objective, the EAT will seek to give directions for case management so that the case can be dealt with quickly, or better considered, and in the most effective and just way.

9.2 Applications and directions for case management will usually be dealt with on the papers ("the sift") by a judge, or by the Registrar with an appeal to a judge. Any party seeking directions must serve a copy on all parties. Directions may be given at any stage, before or after the registration of a Notice of Appeal. An order made will contain a time for compliance, which must be observed or be the subject of an application by any party to vary or discharge it, or to seek an extension of time. Otherwise, failure to comply with an order in time or at all may result in the EAT exercising its power under Rule 26 to strike out the appeal, cross-appeal or respondent's Answer or debar the party from taking any further part in the proceedings or to make any other order it thinks fit, including an award of costs.

9.3 Any application to vary or discharge an order, or to seek an extension of time, must be lodged at the EAT and served on the other parties within the time fixed for compliance. Such other parties must, if opposing the application and within 14 days (or such shorter period as may be ordered) of receiving it, submit their representations to the EAT and the other parties.

9.4 An application to amend a Notice of Appeal or respondent's Answer must include the text of the original document with any changes clearly marked and identifiable, for example with deletions struck through in red and the text of the amendment either written or underlined in red. Any subsequent amendments will have to be in a different identifiable colour.

9.5 Notices of Appeal are sifted by a judge or the Registrar so as to determine the most effective case management of the appeal. The sift will result in a decision as to which track the appeal will occupy, and directions will be given. There are 4 tracks:

9.5.1 Rule 3(7) cases [see para 9.6 below].
9.5.2 Preliminary Hearing (PH) cases [see paras 9.7 – 9.18 below].
9.5.3 Full Hearing (FH) cases [see para 9.19 below].

9.5.4 Fast Track Full Hearing ("FTFH") cases [see paras 9.20 – 9.21 below].

The judge or Registrar may also stay (or sist in Scotland) the appeal for a period, normally 21 days pending the making or the conclusion of an application by the appellant to the Employment Tribunal (if necessary out of time) for a review or pending the response by the Employment Tribunal to an invitation from the judge or Registrar to clarify, supplement or give its written reasons.

Rule 3(7) cases (9.5.1)

9.6 The judge or Registrar, having considered the Notice of Appeal and, if appropriate, having obtained any additional information, may decide that it or any of the grounds contained in it discloses no reasonable grounds for bringing the appeal or is an abuse of the process or otherwise likely to obstruct the just disposal of the proceedings. Reasons will be sent and within 28 days the appellant may submit a fresh Notice of Appeal for further consideration or request an oral hearing before a judge. At that hearing the judge may confirm the earlier decision or order that the appeal proceeds to a Preliminary or Full Hearing. A hearing under Rule 3(10), including judgment and any directions, will normally last not more than one and a half hours. A judge or Registrar may also follow the Rule 3(7) procedure, of his or her own initiative, or on application, at any later stage of the proceedings, if appropriate.

Preliminary Hearing cases (9.5.2)

9.7 The purpose of a PH is to determine whether:

9.7.1 the grounds in the Notice of Appeal raise a point of law which gives the appeal a reasonable prospect of success at a FH; or

9.7.2 for some other compelling reason the appeal should be heard e g that the appellant seeks a declaration of incompatibility under the Human Rights Act 1998; or to argue that a decision binding on the EAT should be considered by a higher court.

9.8 Prior to the PH there will be automatic directions. These include sending the Notice of Appeal to the respondent(s) to the appeal. The direction may order or in any event will enable the respondent(s) to lodge and serve, within 14 days of the seal date of the order (unless otherwise directed), concise written submissions in response to the Notice of Appeal, dedicated to showing that there is no reasonable prospect of success for all or any grounds of any appeal. Such submissions will be considered at the PH.

9.9 If the respondent to the appeal intends to serve a cross-appeal this must be accompanied by written submissions and must be lodged and served within 14 days of service of the Notice of Appeal. The respondent to the appeal must make clear whether it is intended to advance the cross-appeal:

9.9.1 in any event (an unconditional cross-appeal); or

9.9.2 only if the Appellant succeeds (a conditional cross-appeal).

In either case the respondent is entitled to attend the PH, which will also amount to a PH of the cross-appeal, and make submissions.

9.10 All parties will be notified of the date fixed for the PH. In the normal case, unless ordered otherwise, only the appellant and/or a representative should attend to make submissions to the EAT on the issue whether the Notice of Appeal raises a point of law with a reasonable prospect of success:

9.10.1 Except where the respondent to the appeal makes a cross-appeal, or the EAT orders a hearing with all parties present, the respondent to the appeal is not required to attend the hearing and is not usually permitted to take part in it. But any written submissions as referred to in (8) above will be considered at the PH.

9.10.2 If the appellant does not attend, the appeal may nevertheless be dealt with as above on written submissions, and be wholly or in part dismissed or allowed to proceed.

9.11 The PH, including judgment and directions, will normally last no more than one hour.

9.12 The sift procedure will be applied to cross-appeals as well as appeals. If an appeal has been assigned to the FH track, without a PH, and the respondent includes a cross-appeal in the respondent's Answer, the respondent must immediately apply to the EAT in writing on notice to the appellant for directions on the papers as to whether the EAT considers that there should be a PH of the cross-appeal.

9.13 If satisfied that the appeal (and/or the cross-appeal) should be heard at a FH on all or some of the grounds of appeal, the EAT will give directions relating to, for example, a time estimate, any application for fresh evidence, a procedure in respect of matters of evidence before the Employment Tribunal not sufficiently appearing from the written reasons, the exchange and lodging of skeleton arguments and an appellant's Chronology, and bundles of documents and authorities.

9.14 Permission to amend a Notice of Appeal (or cross-appeal) may be granted:

9.14.1 **If the proposed amendment is produced at the hearing**, then, if such amendment has not previously been notified to the other parties, and the appeal (or cross-appeal) might not have been permitted to proceed but for the amendment, the opposing party(ies) will have the opportunity to apply on notice to vary or discharge the permission to proceed, and for consequential directions as to the hearing or disposal of the appeal or cross-appeal.

9.14.2 **If a draft amendment is not available at the PH**, an application for permission to amend, in writing on notice to the other party(ies) in accordance with para 9.4 above, will be permitted to be made within 14 days. Where, but for such proposed amendment, the appeal (or cross-appeal) may not have been permitted to proceed to a FH, provision may be made in the order on the PH for the appeal (or cross-appeal) to be dismissed if the application for permission to amend is not made. Where such an application is made and refused, provision will be made for any party to have liberty to apply, in writing on notice to the other party(ies), as to the hearing or disposal of the appeal.

9.15 If not satisfied that the appeal, or any particular ground of it, should go forward to a FH, the EAT at the PH will dismiss the appeal, wholly or in part, and give a judgment setting out the reasons for doing so.

9.16 If an appeal is permitted to go forward to an FH on all grounds, a reasoned judgment will not normally be given.

9.17 Parties who become aware that a similar point is raised in other proceedings at an Employment Tribunal or the EAT are encouraged to co-operate in bringing this to the attention of the Registrar so that consideration can be given to the most expedient way of dealing with the cases, in particular to the possibility of having two or more appeals heard together.

9.18 If an appeal is permitted to go forward to an FH, a listing category will be assigned ie:

P (recommended to be heard in the President's list);
A (complex, and raising point(s) of law of public importance);
B (any other case);

The President reserves the discretion to alter any relevant category as circumstances require.

Full Hearing cases (9.5.3)

9.19 If a judge or the Registrar decides to list the case for an FH without a PH s/he will consider appropriate directions, relating for example to amendment, further information, any application for fresh evidence, a procedure in respect of matters of evidence at the Employment Tribunal not sufficiently appearing from the written reasons, allegations of bias, apparent bias or improper conduct, provisions for skeleton arguments, appellant's Chronology and bundles of documents and of authorities, time estimates and listing category (as set out in para 9.18 above).

Fast Track Full Hearing cases (9.5.4)

9.20 FH cases are normally heard in the order in which they are received. However, there are times when it is expedient to hear an appeal as soon as it can be fitted into the list. Appeals placed in this Fast Track, at the discretion of a judge or the Registrar, will normally fall into the following cases:

9.20.1 appeals where the parties have made a reasoned case on the merits for an expedited hearing;

9.20.2 appeals against interim orders or decisions of an Employment Tribunal, particularly those which involve the taking of a step in the proceedings within a specified period, for example adjournments, further information, amendments, disclosure, witness orders;

9.20.3 appeals on the outcome of which other applications to the Employment Tribunal or the EAT or the civil courts depend;

9.20.4 appeals in which a reference to the European Court of Justice (ECJ), or a declaration of incompatibility under the Human Rights Act 1998, is sought;

9.20.5 appeals involving reinstatement, re-engagement, interim relief or a recommendation for action (discrimination cases).

9.21 Category B cases estimated to take two hours or less may also be allocated to the Fast Track.

[5022]

10. RESPONDENT'S ANSWER AND DIRECTIONS

10.1 After the sift stage or a PH, at which a decision is made to permit the appeal to go forward to an FH, the EAT will send the Notice of Appeal, with any amendments which have been permitted, and any submissions or skeleton argument lodged by the appellant, to all parties who are respondents to the appeal. Within 14 days of the seal date of the order (unless otherwise directed), respondents must lodge at the EAT and serve on the other parties a respondent's Answer. If it contains a cross-appeal, the appellant must within 14 days of service (unless otherwise directed), lodge and serve a Reply.

10.2 After lodgment and service of the respondent's Answer and of any Reply to a cross-appeal, the Registrar may, where necessary, invite applications from the parties in writing, on notice to all other parties, for directions, and may give any appropriate directions on the papers or may fix a day when the parties should attend on an Appointment for Directions.

10.3 A judge may at any time, upon consideration of the papers or at a hearing, make an order requiring or recommending consideration by the parties or any of them of compromise, conciliation, mediation or, in particular, reference to ACAS.

[5023]

11. COMPLAINTS ABOUT THE CONDUCT OF THE EMPLOYMENT TRIBUNAL HEARING

11.1 An appellant who intends to complain about the conduct of the Employment Tribunal (for example bias, apparent bias or improper conduct by the employment judge or lay members or any procedural irregularity at the hearing) must include in the Notice of Appeal full particulars of each complaint made.

11.2 An appeal which is wholly or in part based on such a complaint will be sifted by a judge or the Registrar as set out in para 9.5 above and this may result in a decision as to the appropriate track which the appeal will occupy. At the sift stage or before, the judge or Registrar may postpone a decision as to track, and direct that the appellant or a representative provide an affidavit setting out full particulars of all allegations of bias or misconduct relied upon. At the sift stage the Registrar may enquire of the party making the complaint whether it is intended to proceed with it and may draw attention to para 11.6 below.

11.3 If the appeal is allocated to the PH or FH track, the EAT may take the following steps prior to such hearing within a time-limit set out in the relevant order:

11.3.1 require the appellant or a representative to provide, if not already provided, an affidavit as set out in para 11.2 above;

11.3.2 require any party to give an affidavit or to obtain a witness statement from any person who has represented any of the parties at the Tribunal hearing, and any other person present at the Tribunal hearing or a relevant part of it, giving their account of the events set out in the affidavit of the appellant or the appellant's representative. For the above purpose, the EAT will provide copies of any affidavits received from or on behalf of the appellant to any other person from whom an account is sought;

11.3.3 seek comments, upon all affidavits or witness statements received, from the employment judge of the Employment Tribunal from which the appeal is brought and may seek such comments from the lay members of the Tribunal. For the above purpose, copies of all relevant documents will be provided by the EAT to the employment judge and, if appropriate, the lay members; such documents will include any affidavits and witness statements received, the Notice of Appeal and other relevant documents.

11.3.4 the EAT will on receipt supply to the parties copies of all affidavits, statements and comments received.

11.4 A respondent who intends to make such a complaint must include such particulars as set out in paras 11.1 and 11.2 above:

11.4.1 (in the event of a PH being ordered in respect of the appellant's appeal, in accordance with para 9.5.2 above) in the cross-appeal referred to in para 9.9 above, or, in the absence of a cross-appeal, in written submissions, as referred to in para 9.8 above;

11.4.2 (in the event of no PH being ordered, in accordance with para 9.5.3 above) in his respondent's Answer.

A similar procedure will then be followed as in para 11.3 above.

11.5 In every case which is permitted to go forward to an FH the EAT will give appropriate directions, ordinarily on the papers after notice to the appellant and respondent, as to the procedure to be adopted at, and material to be provided to, the FH; but such directions may be given at the sift stage or at a PH.

11.6 Parties should note the following:

11.6.1 The EAT will not permit complaints of the kind mentioned above to be raised or developed at the hearing of the appeal unless this procedure has been followed.

11.6.2 The EAT recognises that employment judges and Employment Tribunals are themselves obliged to observe the overriding objective and are given wide powers and duties of case management (see Employment Tribunal (Constitution and Rules of Procedure) Regulations 2004 (SI No 1861)), so appeals in respect of the conduct of Employment Tribunals, which is in exercise of those powers and duties, are the less likely to succeed.

11.6.3 Unsuccessful pursuit of an allegation of bias or improper conduct, particularly in respect of case management decisions, may put the party raising it at risk of an order for costs.

[5024]

12. LISTING OF APPEALS

12.1 **Estimate of Length of Hearing**: the lay members of the EAT are part-time members. They attend when available on pre-arranged dates. They do not sit for continuous periods. Consequently appeals which run beyond their estimated length have to be adjourned part-heard (often with substantial delay) until a day on which the judge and members are all available. To avoid inconvenience to the parties and to the EAT, and to avoid additional delay and costs suffered as a result of adjournment of part-heard appeals, all parties are required to ensure that the estimates of length of hearing (allowing for the fact that the parties can expect the EAT to have pre-read the papers and for deliberation and the giving of a judgment) are accurate when first given. Any change in such estimate, or disagreement with an estimate made by the EAT on a sift or at a PH, is to be notified immediately to the Listing Officer.

12.2 If the EAT concludes that the hearing is likely to exceed the estimate, or if for other reasons the hearing may not be concluded within the time available, it may seek to avoid such adjournment by placing the parties under appropriate time limits in order to complete the presentation of the submissions within the estimated or available time.

12.3 Subject to para 12.6 below a date will be fixed for a PH as soon as practicable after the sift (referred to in para 9.5 above) and for an FH as soon as practicable after the sift if no PH is ordered, or otherwise after the PH.

12.4 The Listing Officer will normally consult the parties on dates, and will accommodate reasonable requests if practicable, but is not bound to do so. Once the date is fixed, the appeal will be set down in the list. A party finding that the date which has been fixed causes serious difficulties may apply to the Listing Officer for it to be changed, having first notified all other parties entitled to appear on the date, of their application and the reasons for it.

12.5 Parties receiving such an application must, as soon as possible and within seven days, notify the Listing Officer of their views.

12.6 In addition to this fixed date procedure, a list ("the warned list") may be drawn up. Cases will be placed in such warned list at the discretion of the Listing Officer or may be so placed by the direction of a judge or the Registrar. These will ordinarily be short cases, or cases where expedition has been ordered. Parties or their representatives will be notified that their case has been included in this list, and as much notice as possible will be given of the intention to list a case for hearing, when representations by way of objection from the parties will be considered by the Listing Officer and if necessary on appeal to the Registrar or a judge. The parties may apply on notice to all other parties for a fixed date for hearing.

12.7 Other cases may be put in the list by the Listing Officer with the consent of the parties at shorter notice: for example, where other cases have been settled or withdrawn or where it appears that they will take less time than originally estimated. Parties who wish their cases to be taken as soon as possible and at short notice should notify the Listing Officer. Representations by way of objection may be made by the parties to the Listing Officer and if necessary by appeal to a judge or the Registrar.

12.8 Each week an up-to-date list for the following week will be prepared, including any changes which have been made, in particular specifying cases which by then have been given fixed dates. The list appears on the EAT website.

[5025]

13. SKELETON ARGUMENTS

(This part of the Practice Direction does not apply to an appeal heard in Scotland, unless otherwise directed in relation to that appeal by the EAT)

13.1 Skeleton arguments must be provided by all parties in all hearings, unless the EAT is notified by a party or representative in writing that the Notice of Appeal or respondent's Answer or relevant application contains the full argument, or the EAT otherwise directs in a particular case. It is the practice of the EAT for all the members to read the papers in advance. A well-structured skeleton argument helps the members and the parties to focus on the point(s) of law required to be decided and so make the oral hearing more effective.

13.2 The skeleton argument should be concise and should identify and summarise the point(s) of law, the steps in the legal argument and the statutory provisions and authorities to be relied upon, identifying them by name, page and paragraph and stating the legal proposition sought to be derived from them. It is not, however, the purpose of the skeleton argument to argue the case on paper in detail. The parties can be referred to by name or as they appeared at the Employment Tribunal i e claimant (C) and respondent (R).

13.3 The skeleton argument should state the form of order which the party will ask the EAT to make at the hearing: for example, in the case of an appellant, whether the EAT will be asked to remit the whole or part of the case to the same or to a different Employment Tribunal, or whether the EAT will be asked to substitute a different decision for that of the Employment Tribunal.

13.4 The appellant's skeleton argument must be accompanied by a Chronology of events relevant to the appeal which, if possible, should be agreed by the parties. That will normally be taken as an uncontroversial document, unless corrected by another party or the EAT.

13.5 Unless impracticable, the skeleton argument should be prepared using the pagination in the index to the appeal bundle. In a case where a note of the evidence at the Employment Tribunal has been produced, the skeleton argument should identify the parts of the record to which that party wishes to refer.

13.6 Represented parties should give the instructions necessary for their representative to comply with this procedure within the time limits.

13.7 The fact that conciliation or settlement negotiations are in progress in relation to the appeal does not excuse delay in lodging and exchanging skeleton arguments.

13.8 A skeleton argument may be lodged by the appellant with the Notice of Appeal or by the respondent with the respondent's Answer.

13.9 Skeleton arguments must (if not already so lodged):

13.9.1 be lodged at the EAT not less than 10 days (unless otherwise ordered) before the date fixed for the PH, appeal against Registrar's Order, Rule 3 (10) hearing or Appointment for Directions; or, if the hearing is fixed at less than seven days' notice, as soon as possible after the hearing date has been notified. In the event that the hearing has been ordered to be heard with all parties present, the skeleton arguments must also then be exchanged between the parties;

13.9.2 be lodged at the EAT, *and* exchanged between the parties, not less than 14 days before the FH;

13.9.3 in the case of warned list and fast track FH cases be lodged at the EAT and exchanged between the parties as soon as possible and (unless the hearing date is less than seven days later) in any event within seven days after the parties have been notified that the case is expedited or in the warned list.

13.10 Failure to follow this procedure may lead to an adjournment of an appeal or to dismissal for non-compliance with the PD pursuant to Rule 26, and to an award of costs. The party in default may also be required to attend before the EAT to explain their failure. It will always mean that the defaulting party must immediately despatch any delayed skeleton argument to the EAT by hand or by fax or by email to londoneat@tribunals.gsi.gov.uk or, as appropriate, edinburgheat@tribunals.gsi.gov.uk and (unless notified by the EAT to the contrary) bring to the hearing sufficient copies (a minimum of 6) of the skeleton argument and any authorities referred to. The EAT staff will not be responsible for supplying or copying these on the morning of the hearing.

[5026]

14. CITATION OF AUTHORITIES

General

14.1 It is undesirable for parties to cite the same case from different sets of reports. The parties should, if practicable, agree which report will be used at the hearing. Where the Employment Tribunal has cited from a report it may be convenient to cite from the same report.

14.2 It is the responsibility of a party wishing to cite any authority to provide photocopies for the use of each member of the Tribunal and photocopies or at least a list for the other parties. All authorities should be indexed and incorporated in an agreed bundle.

14.3 Parties are advised not to cite an unnecessary number of authorities either in skeleton arguments or in oral argument at the hearing. It is of assistance to the EAT if parties could highlight or sideline passages relied on within the bundle of authorities.

14.4 It is unnecessary for a party citing a case in oral argument to read it in full to the EAT. Whenever a case is cited in a skeleton argument or in an oral argument it is helpful if the legal proposition for which it is cited is stated. References need only be made to the relevant passages in the report. If the formulation of the legal proposition based on the authority cited is not in dispute, further examination of the authority will often be unnecessary.

14.5 For decisions of the ECJ, the official report should be used where possible.

PH cases

14.6 If it is thought necessary to cite any authority at a PH, appeal against Registrar's Order, Rule 3(10) hearing or Appointment for Directions, three copies should be provided for the EAT (one copy if a judge is sitting alone) no less than 10 days before the hearing, unless otherwise ordered: and additional copies for any other parties notified. All authorities should be bundled, indexed and incorporated in one agreed bundle.

FH cases

14.7 The parties must co-operate in agreeing a list of authorities and must jointly or severally lodge a list and three bundles of copies (one copy if judge sitting alone) of such authorities at the EAT not less than seven days before the FH, unless otherwise ordered.

[5027]

15. DISPOSAL OF APPEALS BY CONSENT

15.1 An appellant who wishes to abandon or withdraw an appeal should notify the other parties and the EAT immediately. If a settlement is reached, the parties should inform the EAT as soon as possible. The appellant should submit to the EAT a letter signed by or on behalf of the appellant and signed also by or on behalf of the respondent, asking the EAT for permission to withdraw the appeal and to make a consent order in the form of an attached draft signed by or for both parties dismissing the appeal, together with any other agreed order.

15.2 If the other parties do not agree to the proposed order the EAT should be informed. Written submissions should be lodged at the EAT and served on the parties. Any outstanding issue may be determined on the papers by the EAT, particularly if it relates to costs, but the EAT may fix an oral hearing to determine the outstanding matters in dispute between the parties.

15.3 If the parties reach an agreement that the appeal should be allowed by consent, and that an order made by the Employment Tribunal should be reversed or varied or the matter remitted to the Employment Tribunal on the ground that the decision contains an error of law, it is usually necessary for the matter to be heard by the EAT to determine whether there is a good reason for making the proposed order. On notification by the parties, the EAT will decide whether the appeal can be dealt with on the papers or by a hearing at which one or more parties or their representatives should attend to argue the case for allowing the appeal and making the order that the parties wish the EAT to make.

15.4 If the application for permission to withdraw an appeal is made close to the hearing date the EAT may require the attendance of the Appellant and/or a representative to explain the reasons for delay in making a decision not to pursue the appeal.

[5028]

16. APPELLANT'S FAILURE TO PRESENT A RESPONSE

16.1 If the appellant in a case did not present a Response (ET3) to the Employment Tribunal and did not apply to the Employment Tribunal for an extension of time for doing so, or applied for such an extension and was refused, the Notice of Appeal must include particulars directed to the following issues, namely whether:

16.1.1 there is a good excuse for failing to present a Response (ET3) and (if that be the case) for failing to apply for such an extension of time; and

16.1.2 there is a reasonably arguable defence to the Claim (ET1).

16.2 In order to satisfy the EAT on these issues, the appellant must lodge at the EAT, together with the Notice of Appeal, a witness statement explaining in detail the circumstances in which there has been a failure to serve a Response (ET3) in time or apply for such an extension of time, the reason for that failure and the facts and matters relied upon for contesting the Claim (ET1) on the merits. There should be exhibited to the witness statement all relevant documents and a completed draft Response (ET3).

[5029]

17. HEARINGS

17.1 Where consent is to be obtained from the parties pursuant to s 28(3) of the ETA 1996 to an appeal commencing or continuing to be heard by a judge together with only one lay member, the parties must, prior to the commencement or continuation of such hearing in front of a two-member court, themselves or by their representatives each sign a form containing the name of the one member remaining, and stating whether the member is a person falling within s 28(1)(a) or (b) of the ETA 1996.

17.2 **Video and Telephone Hearings**. Facilities can be arranged for the purpose of holding short PHs or short Appointments for Directions by video or telephone link, upon the application (in writing) of an appellant or respondent who, or whose representative, has a relevant disability (supported by appropriate medical evidence). Such facilities will only be made available for a hearing at which the party or, if more than one party will take part, both or all parties is or are legally represented. An application that a hearing should be so held will be determined by a judge or the Registrar, and must be made well in advance of the date intended for the hearing, so that arrangements may be made. So far as concerns video conferencing facilities, they may not always be available, dependent on the location of the parties: as for telephone hearings or, especially, telephone conferencing facilities, consideration may need to be given as to payment by a party or parties of any additional expenditure resulting.

[5030]

18. HANDING DOWN OF JUDGMENTS

(England and Wales)

18.1 When the EAT reserves judgment to a later date, the parties will be notified of the date when it is ready to be handed down. It is not necessary for a party or representative to attend.

18.2 Copies of the judgment will be available to the parties or their representatives on the morning on which it is handed down or, if so directed by a judge, earlier to the parties' representatives in draft subject to terms as to confidentiality.

18.3 The judgment will be pronounced without being read aloud, by the judge who presided or by another judge, on behalf of the EAT. The judge may deal with any application or may refer it to the judge and/or the Tribunal who heard the appeal, whether to deal with on the papers or at a further oral hearing on notice. Applications for permission to appeal should be made pursuant to para 21 below. Applications for costs should be made pursuant to para 19 below.

18.4 Transcripts of unreserved judgments at a PH, appeal against Registrar's Order, Appointment for Directions and Rule 3(10) hearing will not (save as below) be produced and provided to the parties:

18.4.1 Where an appeal, or any ground of appeal, is dismissed in the presence of the appellant, no transcript of the judgment is produced unless, within 14 days of the seal date of the order, either party applies to the EAT for a transcript, or the EAT of its own initiative directs that a judgment be transcribed (in circumstances such as those set out in para 18.5.2 below).

18.4.2 Where an appeal or any ground of appeal is dismissed in the absence of the appellant, a transcript will be supplied to the appellant.

18.4.3 Where an appeal is allowed to go forward to a PH or an FH, a judgment will not normally be delivered, but, if it is, the judge may order it to be transcribed, in which case a transcript is provided to the parties.

18.5 Transcripts of unreserved judgments at an FH. Where judgment is delivered at the hearing, no transcript will be produced and provided to the parties unless:

18.5.1 either party applies for it to the EAT within 14 days of that hearing; or

18.5.2 the EAT of its own initiative directs that the judgment be transcribed, e g where it is considered that a point of general importance arises or that the matter is to be remitted to, or otherwise continued before, the Employment Tribunal.

18.6 Where judgment at either a PH or an FH is reserved, and later handed down in writing, a copy is provided to all parties, and to recognised law reporters.

(Scotland)

18.7 Judgments are normally reserved in Scotland and will be handed down as soon as practicable thereafter on a provisional basis to both parties who will thereafter have a period of 14 days to make any representations with regard to expenses, leave to appeal or any other relevant matter. At the expiry of that period or after such representations have been dealt with, whichever shall be the later, an order will be issued to conform to the original judgment.

EAT Website

18.8 All FH judgments which are transcribed or handed down will be posted on the EAT website. Any other judgment may be posted on the EAT website if so directed by the Registrar or a Judge.

[5031]

19. COSTS (REFERRED TO AS EXPENSES IN SCOTLAND)

19.1 In this PD "costs" includes legal costs, expenses, allowances paid by the Secretary of State and payment in respect of time spent in preparing a case. Such costs may relate to interim applications or hearings or to a PH or FH.

19.2 An application for costs must be made either during or at the end of a relevant hearing, or in writing to the Registrar within 14 days of the seal date of the relevant order of the EAT or, in the case of a reserved judgment, as provided for in paragraph 18.3 above, copied to all parties.

19.3 The party seeking the order must state the legal ground on which the application is based and the facts on which it is based and, by a schedule or otherwise, show how the costs have been incurred. If the application is made in respect of only part of the proceedings, particulars must be given showing how the costs have been incurred on that specific part. If the party against whom the order is sought wishes the EAT to have regard to means and/or an alleged inability to pay, a witness statement giving particulars and exhibiting any documents must be served on the other party(ies) and lodged with the EAT. Further directions may be required to be given by the EAT in such cases.

19.4 Such application may be resolved by the EAT on the papers, provided that the opportunity has been given for representations in writing by all relevant parties, or the EAT may refer the matter for an oral hearing, and may assess the costs either on the papers or at an oral hearing, or refer the matter for detailed assessment.

19.5 **Wasted Costs**: An application for a wasted costs order must be made in writing, setting out the nature of the case upon which the application is based and the best particulars of the costs sought to be recovered. Such application must be lodged with the EAT and served upon the party(ies) sought to be charged. Further directions may be required to be given by the EAT in such cases.

19.6 Where the EAT makes any costs order it shall provide written reasons for so doing if such order is made by decision on the papers. If such order is made at a hearing, then written reasons will be provided if a request is made at the hearing or within 21 days of the seal date of the costs order. The Registrar shall send a copy of the written reasons to all the parties to the proceedings.

[5032]

20. REVIEW

Where an application is made for a review of a judgment or order of the EAT, it can be considered on paper by a judge who may, if he or she heard the original appeal or made the original order alone, without lay members, make such order, granting, refusing, adjourning or otherwise dealing with such application, as he or she may think fit. If the original judgment or order was made by the judge together with lay members, then the judge may, pursuant to Rule 33, consider and refuse such application for review on the papers. If the judge does not refuse such application, he or she may make any relevant further order, but would not grant such application without notice to the opposing party and reference to the lay members, for consideration with them, either on paper or in open court. A request to review a judgment or order of the EAT must be made within 14 days of the seal date of the order, or must include an application, with reasons for an extension of time copied to all parties.

[5032A]

21. APPEALS FROM THE EAT

Appeals heard in England and Wales

21.1 An application to the EAT for permission to appeal to the Court of Appeal must be made (unless the EAT otherwise orders) at the hearing or when a reserved judgment is handed down or in writing within 7 days thereafter as provided in para 18.3 above. If not made then, or if refused, or unless the EAT otherwise orders, any such applications must be made to the Court of Appeal within 21 days of the sealed order. An application for an extension of time for permission to appeal may be entertained by the EAT where a case is made out to the satisfaction of a judge or Registrar that there is a need to delay until after a transcript is received (expedited if appropriate). Applications for an extension of time for permission to appeal should however normally be made to the Court of Appeal.

21.2 The party seeking permission must state the point of law to be advanced and the grounds.

Appeals heard in Scotland

21.3 An application to the EAT for permission to appeal to the Court of Session must be made within 42 days of the date of the hearing where judgment is delivered at that hearing: if judgment is reserved, within 42 days of the date the transcript was sent to parties.

21.4 The party seeking permission must state the point of law to be advanced and the grounds.

[5032B]

22. CONCILIATION

22.1 Pursuant to Rule 36 and the overriding objective, the EAT encourages alternative dispute resolution. To this end it has agreed a pilot scheme with ACAS for ACAS to provide conciliation in certain cases. See 2007 Protocol.

22.2 In all cases the parties should, and when so directed must, consider conciliation of their appeals. The Registrar or a Judge may at any stage make such a direction and require the parties to report on steps taken, but not the substance, to effect a conciliated settlement with the assistance of an ACAS officer notified by ACAS to the EAT.

[5032C]

EAT FORM 1
NOTICE OF APPEAL FROM DECISION OF EMPLOYMENT TRIBUNAL

1. The Appellant is (*name and address of the Appellant*):—

....

....

2. Any communication relating to this appeal may be sent to the Appellant at (*Appellant's address for service, including telephone number if any*):—

....

....

3. The Appellant appeals from (*here give particulars of the judgment, decision or order of the Employment Tribunal from which the appeal is brought including the location of the Employment Tribunal and the date*):—

....

....

4. The parties to the proceedings before the Employment Tribunal, other than the Appellant, were (*names and addresses of other parties to the proceedings resulting in judgment, decision or order appealed from*):—

....

....

5. Copies of—
- (a) the written record of the employment tribunal's judgment, decision or order and the written reasons of the employment tribunal;
- (b) the claim (ET1);
- (c) the response (ET3);
- (d) an explanation as to why any of these documents are not included;

are attached to this Notice.

6. If the appellant has made an application to the employment tribunal for a review of its judgment or decision, copies of—
- (a) the review application;
- (b) the judgment;
- (c) the written reasons of the employment tribunal in respect of that review application; and/or
- (d) a statement by or on behalf of the applicant, if such be the case, that a judgment is awaited;

are attached to this Notice. If any of these documents exist but cannot be included, then a written explanation must be given.

7. The grounds upon which this appeal is brought are that the employment tribunal erred in law in that (here set out in paragraphs the various grounds of appeal):—

....

....

....

....

....

....

....

....

Signed .... Date: ....

N.B. The details entered on your Notice of Appeal must be legible and suitable for photocopying or electronic scanning. The use of black ink or typescript is recommended

[5032D]

EAT PRACTICE STATEMENT (2005)

This is a Practice Statement handed down by the President of the Employment Appeal Tribunal on 3 February 2005.

1. The attention of litigants and practitioners in the Employment Appeal Tribunal is expressly drawn to the wording and effect of Rules 3(1)(b) and 3(3) of the Employment Appeal Tribunal Rules (1993) (as amended). As is quite clear from the terms of paragraph 2.1 of the Employment Appeal Tribunal Practice Direction 2004 handed down on 9 December 2004, a Notice of Appeal without the specified documentation will not be validly lodged. The documentation required to accompany the Notice of Appeal in order for it to be valid now includes a copy of the Claim (ET1) and the Response (ET3) in the Employment Tribunal proceedings appealed from, if such be available to the appellant, and in any event if such not be available for whatever reason then a written explanation as to why they are not provided. Paragraph 2.1 of the Practice Direction makes this entirely clear:

> "2.1 … Copies of the judgment, decision or order appealed against and of the Employment Tribunal's written reasons, together with a copy of the Claim (ET1) and the Response (ET3) must be attached, or if not, a written explanation must be given. A Notice of Appeal without such documentation will not be validly lodged."

2. The reported decision of the Employment Appeal Tribunal in ***Kanapathiar v London Borough of Harrow*** [2003] IRLR 571 made quite clear that the effect of failure to lodge documents required by the Rules with the Notice of Appeal within the time limit specified for lodging of a Notice of Appeal would mean that the Notice of Appeal had not been validly lodged in time. The same now applies to the additional documents required by the amended Rule, namely the Claim and the Response.

3. It is apparent that both practitioners and litigants in person are not complying with the new Rules and Practice Direction, and not appreciating the consequences of their non-compliance. Between 2 and 26 January 2005, 20 Notices of Appeal were received by the Employment Appeal Tribunal and returned as invalid (compared with 4 during the similar period in 2004). Of those 20 Notices of Appeal, 7 would have been invalid in any event under the old Rules. 13 however were only invalid because they were neither accompanied by the Claim nor the Response nor by any explanation as to their absence or unavailability. If the Notices of Appeal are relodged well within the very generous 42-day time limit, there may still be time for the missing documents to be supplied and the time limit to be complied with. If however, as is very often the case, such Notices of Appeal are delivered either at, or only immediately before, the expiry of the time limit, the absence of the relevant documents is, even if speedily pointed out by the Employment Appeal Tribunal, likely to lead to the Notice of Appeal being out of time.

4. Of the 20 Notices of Appeal which were invalidly lodged during the period above referred to, only 10 were lodged by litigants in person and 10 by solicitors or other representatives: and it is plain that the latter ought certainly to have known of the requirements, although, given the wide publication both of the Rules and the Practice Direction, together with the guidance given by the Employment Tribunals, both at the Tribunal and sent with their judgments, there can be no excuse for litigants in person either.

5. The reason for this Statement in open court is to re-emphasise these requirements and the consequence of failure to comply with them, namely that an appeal not lodged within the 42 days validly constituted, ie accompanied by the required documents, will be out of time, and extensions of time are only exceptionally granted (see paragraph 3.7 of the Practice Direction).

6. From the date of this Practice Statement, ignorance or misunderstanding of the requirements as to service of the documents required to make a Notice of Appeal within the 42 days valid will not be accepted by the Registrar as an excuse.

The Hon Mr Justice Burton

President of the Employment Appeal Tribunal

3 February 2005

[5032E]

EMPLOYMENT TRIBUNALS (SCOTLAND) PRACTICE DIRECTION NO 1 (2006)

In consequence of the power given to me under Regulation 13 of the Employment Tribunals (Constitution and Rules of Procedure) Regulations 2004 I make the following Practice Direction:—

Intimation of List of Documents 14 days before a Hearing

When a party is legally represented their representative will intimate a list of the documents to be relied upon at any Hearing on the merits of the claim to the other party (or parties) or their representative (if represented) not later than 14 days before any such Hearing.

COLIN M MILNE
President of Employment Tribunals, Scotland
14 December 2006

Notes

Many cases before the Employment Tribunal are subject to extensive case management by the judiciary, an element of which may involve orders being made regarding the identification and disclosure of documents. There is currently less opportunity to undertake in-depth case management of cases that might be regarded as more straightforward. Nevertheless, in keeping with one of the principal objectives identified in the Report of the Employment Tribunal System Taskforce, it is generally agreed that there is merit in each side having as much notice of the other side's case as possible in advance of the Hearing. The Rules of Procedure generally assist this objective but users have expressed concern about the lack of direction regarding the lodging of documents. There is no provision in the rules requiring the lodging of documents within a certain time span. It is not uncommon for a party to wait until the day of the Hearing to reveal the documents upon which they intend to rely to the other party (or parties, as the case may be). That on occasion leads to delay as the implications of that documentation are considered by the other side.

Following extensive consultation with Scottish users, I have agreed to make a Practice Direction requiring parties who are legally represented to provide a list of the documents they are going to rely upon to the other party/parties no later than 14 days before a Hearing on the merits of the case. It is expected that this list will be sufficiently detailed to enable the other party/parties to understand the nature of each of the documents which is to be produced. However, this direction is without prejudice to the right of any Employment Tribunal Chairman to impose a more onerous direction in respect of the provision of information about documents to be relied upon at any Hearing.

Consideration was given to the idea of actually requiring copies of the documents themselves to be provided to the other party/parties at least 14 days before the Hearing but that was considered to place too heavy a cost burden on parties, given the number of cases which settle in the 14 day period before the Hearing. Requiring a simple list however should at least put the other side on notice as to the documents which are going to be relied upon, thereby minimising the risk of delay arising from last minute surprises.

With regard to the general need for Employment Tribunals to be accessible to all users, it was felt unduly onerous to apply this Practice Direction to parties who are not legally represented. The imposition of a requirement, as here, which applies only to those who are legally represented finds a parallel in the provisions of the Rules themselves (see, for example, the obligations imposed when a party is legally represented under Rule 11).

[5032F]

NOTES

This Practice Direction applies to Scotland only.

EMPLOYMENT TRIBUNALS (SCOTLAND) PRACTICE DIRECTION NO 2 (2006)

In consequence of the power given to me under Regulation 13 of the Employment Tribunals (Constitution and Rules of Procedure) Regulations 2004 I make the following Practice Direction:—

Sist for Mediation

Where both (or, as the case may be, all) parties to a claim agree that it should be sisted for mediation a Chairman of Employment Tribunals shall sist it for that purpose. The Chairman shall nevertheless review the need for that sist within such timescale as he or she thinks necessary having regard to the interests of justice.

COLIN M MILNE
President of Employment Tribunals, Scotland
14 December 2006

Notes

The sole purpose of this Practice Direction is to focus parties' minds on mediation as an option for the resolution of employment disputes. The role of Acas in providing a conciliation service is well known and highly valued but in certain circumstances Acas may also provide mediation. In recent times an employment dispute meditation service has also become more widely available from other providers. However, while mediation is on the increase in employment cases there is some evidence to suggest that not all parties are aware of this as an option which might be utilised.

While the direction directs that, where parties agree, a Chairman will sist the case, it must be borne in mind that Chairmen still have to consider the overriding objective, which involves taking account of what is in the interests of justice overall. It is therefore appropriate that any sist granted to allow for mediation to take place should be kept under regular review. The timing and circumstances of the review process are a matter for judicial discretion in each individual case in light of the interests of justice in that case.

This Practice Direction in relation to mediation clearly envisages what might be described as external mediation. It is without prejudice to the pilot being carried out in England and Wales (which pilot has not been extended to Scotland) in relation to judicial mediation.

[5032G]

NOTES

This Practice Direction applies to Scotland only.

EMPLOYMENT TRIBUNALS (SCOTLAND) PRACTICE DIRECTION NO 3 (2006)

In consequence of the power given to me under Regulation 13 of the Employment Tribunals (Constitution and Rules of Procedure) Regulations 2004 I make the following Practice Direction:—

Counter Claims

(a) When a respondent wishes to present a claim against the claimant ("a counter claim") in accordance with Article 4 of the Employment Tribunals (Extension of Jurisdiction) (Scotland) Order 1994 they should, (if reasonably practicable) specify the amount claimed as part of the detail of the counter claim along with the other information provided for in Regulation 7 of the Employment Tribunals (Rules of Procedure) Regulations 2004.

(b) When a claimant receives notice of a counter claim the claimant will indicate to the Tribunal Office if it is intended to resist the counter claim and the reasons for so resisting within a period of 28 days from the date on which he or she was sent a copy of the counter claim, unless an order of the Tribunal is granted extending that period.

COLIN M MILNE
President of Employment Tribunals, Scotland
14 December 2006

Notes

Consultation with Scottish users has established a desire to revert to the earlier Scottish practice in relation to counter claims. Rule 7 of Schedule 1 of the Employment Tribunals (Constitution and Rules of Procedure) Regulations 2004 does envisage the possibility of a Practice Direction being made in relation to counter claims.

The issues addressed in my Practice Direction concern the two items that users feel should be included so that parties have basic information available about the counterclaim and any response to it. The 28 day period referred to in paragraph (b) of the direction is without prejudice to the right of a party to seek an order from the Tribunal, in terms of rule 10(2)(e), extending the time limit for the lodging of a response to a counterclaim.

I also gave consideration to formally prescribing forms for use in making a counterclaim and responding to such a claim. In Scotland forms were in use under the Employment Tribunals (Constitution and Rules of Procedure) (Scotland) Regulations 1993, being issued by the employment tribunal office to respondents in every case in which a breach of contract claim was made and, in turn, issued to the claimant in every case in which a counterclaim was made. However, these forms are no longer issued. They were very basic in format and it seems to me that it is unnecessary to stipulate the use of a specific form, although parties may note that the old forms are still produced, by way of guidance, in Appendix 4 and Appendix 5 of Leslie's Employment Tribunal Practice in Scotland. Parties' representatives may find it convenient to use something similar to these forms although what matters, irrespective of the exact format used, is clear presentation of the information required to set out the basis of the counterclaim and any response to it.

[5032H]

NOTES

This Practice Direction applies to Scotland only.

C. CLAIM AND RESPONSE FORMS FOR TRIBUNAL CLAIMS

NOTES

The Forms reproduced below are the current versions (as at 6 April 2008) of the Claim Form and Response Form prescribed for use in Employment Tribunal proceedings in individual claims. They are obtainable from Employment Tribunal offices and the Employment Tribunals website (www.employmenttribunals.gov.uk), where they can either be downloaded or completed online.

CLAIM TO AN EMPLOYMENT TRIBUNAL (ET1)

Claim to an Employment Tribunal

Please read the **guidance notes** and the notes on this page carefully **before** filling in this form.

By law, your claim **must** be on an approved form provided by the Employment Tribunals Service and you must provide the information marked with ✻ and, if it is relevant, the information marked with ● (see 'Information needed before a claim can be accepted').

You may find it helpful to take advice **before** filling in the form, particularly if your claim involves discrimination.

How to fill in this form

All claimants **must** fill in **sections 1, 2 and 3**. Y ou then only need to fill in those sections of the form that apply to your case. For example:

For **unpaid wages**, fill in **sections 4 and 8**.

For **unfair dismissal**, fill in **sections 4 and 5**.

For **discrimination**, fill in **sections 4 and 6**.

For a **redundancy payment**, fill in **sections 4 and 7**.

For **unfair dismissal** and **discrimination**, fill in **sections 4, 5 and 6**.

For **unfair dismissal** and **unpaid wages**, fill in **sections 4, 5 and 8**.

Fill in **section 10** only if there is some information you wish to draw to the tribunal's attention and **section 12** only if you have appointed a representative to act on your behalf in dealing with your claim.

If this claim is one of a number of claims arising out of the same or similar circumstances, you can obtain a Multiple Claim Form from the ETS Public Enquiry Line on 08457 959775 or from www.employmenttribunals.gov.uk. Alternatively you can give the names and addresses of additional claimants on a separate sheet or sheets of paper. If you do this you must make it clear that the relevant required information for all the additional claimants is the same as stated in the main claim.

Please make sure that all the information you give is as accurate as possible.

Where there a retick boxes, please tick the one that applies.

Please write clearly in black ink using CAPITAL LETTERS.

If you fax the form, do not send a copy in the post.

ET1 v02 ET1 v02

1 Your details

1.1 Title: Mr ☐ Mrs ☐ Miss ☐ Ms ☐ Other ☐

1.2 ✱ First name (or names):

1.3 ✱ Surname or family name:

1.4 Date of birth (date/month/year): Are you: male? ☐ female? ☐

1.5 ✱ Address: Number or Name
Street
\+ Town/City
County
Postcode

1.6 Phone number **(where we can contact you during normal working hours):**

1.7 How would you prefer us to communicate with you? E-mail ☐ Post ☐ Fax ☐
(Please tick only one box)

E-mail address:

Fax number:

2 Respondent's details

2.1 ✱ Give the name of your employer or the organisation you are claiming against.

2.2 ✱ Address: Number or Name
Street
Town/City
\+ County
Postcode

Phone number:

2.3 If you worked at an address different from the one you have given at 2.2, please give the full address and postcode.

Postcode

Phone number:

2.4 ● If your complaint is against more than one respondent please give the names, addresses and postcodes of additional respondents.

ET1 v02 001 1 ET1 v02 001

3 Action before making a claim

3.1✻ Are you, or were you, an employee of the respondent? Yes ☐ No ☐
If 'Yes', please now go straight to section 3.3.

3.2 Are you, or were you, a worker providing services to the respondent? Yes ☐ No ☐
If 'Yes', please now go straight to section 4.
If 'No', please now go straight to section 6.

3.3● Is your claim, or part of it, about a dismissal by the respondent? Yes ☐ No ☐
If 'No', please now go straight to section 3.5.
If your claim is about constructive dismissal, i.e. you resigned because of something your employer did or failed to do which made you feel you could no longer continue to work for them, tick the box here and the 'Yes' box in section 3.4. ☐

3.4● Is your claim about anything else, in addition to the dismissal? Yes ☐ No ☐
If 'No', please now go straight to section 4.
If 'Yes', please answer questions 3.5 to 3.7 about the non-dismissal aspects of your claim.

3.5● Have you put your complaint(s) in writing to the respondent?

Yes ☐ Please give the date you put it to them in writing. ☐☐ ☐☐ ☐☐☐☐

No ☐

If 'No', please now go straight to section 3.7.

3.6● Did you allow at least 28 days between the date you put your complaint in writing to the respondent and the date you sent us this claim? Yes ☐ No ☐
If 'Yes', please now go straight to section 4.

3.7● Please explain why you did not put your complaint in writing to the respondent or, if you did, why you did not allow at least 28 days before sending us your claim.
(In most cases, it is a legal requirement to take these procedural steps. Your claim will not be accepted unless you give a valid reason why you did not have to meet the requirement in your case. If you are not sure, you may want to get legal advice.)

ET1 v02 002 2 ET1 v02 002

4 Employment details

4.1 Please give the following information if possible.

When did your employment start?

When did or will it end?

Is your employment continuing? Yes No

4.2 Please say what job you do or did.

4.3 How many hours do or did you work each week? hours each week

4.4 How much are or were you paid?

Pay before tax £

Normal take-home pay (including overtime, commission, bonuses and so on) £

Hourly
Weekly
Monthly
Yearly

4.5 If your employment has ended, did you work (or were you paid for) a period of notice? Yes No

If 'Yes', how many weeks or months did you work or were you paid for? weeks months

5 Unfair dismissal or constructive dismissal

Please fill in this section only if you believe you have been unfairly or constructively dismissed.

5.1 • If you were dismissed by your employer, you should explain why you think your dismissal was unfair. If you resigned because of something your employer did or failed to do which made you feel you could no longer continue to work for them (constructive dismissal) you should explain what happened.

ET1 v02 003 3 ET1 v02 003

5 Unfair dismissal or constructive dismissal continued

5.1 continued

5.2 Were you in your employer's pension scheme? Yes ☐ No ☐

5.3 If you received any other benefits from your employer, please give details.

5.4 Since leaving your employment have you got another job? Yes ☐ No ☐
If 'No', please now go straight to section 5.7.

5.5 Please say when you started (or will start) work.

5.6 Please say how much you are now earning (or will earn). £ each

5.7 Please tick the box to say what you want if your case is successful:

a To get your old job back and compensation (reinstatement) ☐

b To get another job with the same employer and compensation (re-engagement) ☐

c Compensation only ☐

6 Discrimination

Please fill in this section only if you believe you have been discriminated against.

6.1 • Please tick the box or boxes to indicate what discrimination (including victimisation) you are complaining about:

Sex (including equal pay)	☐	Race	☐
Disability	☐	Religion or belief	☐
Sexual orientation	☐	Age	☐

6.2 • Please describe the incidents which you believe amounted to discrimination, the dates of these incidents and the people involved.

7 Redundancy payments

Please fill in this section only if you believe you are owed a redundancy payment.

7.1• Please explain why you believe you are entitled to this payment and set out the steps you have taken to get it.

8 Other payments you are owed

Please fill in this section only if you believe you are owed other payments.

8.1• Please tick the box or boxes to indicate that money is owed to you for:

unpaid wages?

holiday pay?

notice pay?

other unpaid amounts?

8.2 How much are you claiming? £

Is this: before tax? after tax?

8.3• Please explain why you believe you are entitled to this payment. If you have specified an amount, please set out how you have worked this out.

ET1 v02 006 6 ET1 v02 006

9 Other complaints

Please fill in this section only if you believe you have a complaint that is not covered elsewhere.

9.1• Please explain what you are complaining about and why.
Please include any relevant dates.

10 Other information

10.1 Please do not send a covering letter with this form.
You should add any extra information you want us to know here.

ET1 v02 007 7 ET1 v02 007

11 Disability

11.1 Please tick this box if you consider yourself to have a disability Yes ☐ No ☐
If 'Yes', please say what this disability is and tell us what assistance, if any, you will need as your claim progresses through the system.

12 Your representative

Please fill in this section only if you have appointed a representative. If you do fill this section in, we will in future only send correspondence to your representative and not to you.

12.1 Representative's name:

12.2 Name of the representative's organisation:

12.3 Address: Number or Name
Street
Town/City
County
Postcode

12.4 Phone number:

12.5 Reference:

12.6 How would you prefer us to communicate with them? (Please tick only one box) Post ☐ Fax ☐ E-mail ☐
Fax number:
E-mail address:

13 Multiple cases

13.1 To your knowledge, is your claim one of a number of claims arising from the same or similar circumstances? Yes ☐ No ☐

Please sign and date here

Signature: Date:

Data Protection Act 1998. We will send a copy of this form to the respondent(s) and Acas. We will put some of the information you give us on this form onto a computer. This helps us to monitor progress and produce statistics. Information provided on this form is passed to the Department of Trade and Industry to assist research into the use and effectiveness of Employment Tribunals.

ET1 v02 008 8 ET1 v02 008

Additional space for notes.

Equal Opportunities Monitoring Form

You are not obliged to fill in this section but, if you do so, it will enable us to monitor our processes and ensure that we provide equality of opportunity to all. The information you give here will be treated in strict confidence and this page will not form part of your case. It will be used only for monitoring and research purposes without identifying you.

1. What is your country of birth?

- England
- Wales
- Scotland
- Northern Ireland
- Republic of Ireland
- Elsewhere, *please write in the present name of the country*

2. What is your ethnic group? Choose ONE section from A to E, then ✓ the appropriate box to indicate your cultural background.

A White

- British
- Irish
- Any other White background *please write in*

B Mixed

- White and Black Caribbean
- White and Black African
- White and Asian
- Any other Mixed background *please write in*

C Asian or Asian British

- Indian
- Pakistani
- Bangladeshi
- Any other Asian background *please write in*

D: Black or Black British

- Caribbean
- African
- Any other Black background *please write in*

E Chinese or other ethnic group

- Chinese
- Any other, *please write in*

3. What is your religion? ✓ box only

- None
- Christian (including Church of England, Catholic, Protestant and all other Christian denominations)
- Buddhist
- Hindu
- Jewish
- Muslim
- Sikh
- Any other religion, *please write in*

Employment Tribunals - Multiple Claim Form

Please use this form if you wish to present two or more claims which arise from the same set of facts. Use additional sheets if necessary.

The following claimants are represented by (if applicable) and the relevant required information for all the additional claimants is the same as stated in the main claim of

V

Title
First name (or names)
Surname or family name
Date of birth
Number or Name
Street
Town/City
County
Postcode

Title
First name (or names)
Surname or family name
Date of birth
Number or Name
Street
Town/City
County
Postcode

Title
First name (or names)
Surname or family name
Date of birth
Number or Name
Street
Town/City
County
Postcode

ET1a v01 ET1a v01

Title
First name (or names)
Surname or family name
Date of birth
Number or Name
Street
Town/City
County
Postcode

Title
First name (or names)
Surname or family name
Date of birth
Number or Name
Street
Town/City
County
Postcode

Title
First name (or names)
Surname or family name
Date of birth
Number or Name
Street
Town/City
County
Postcode

Title
First name (or names)
Surname or family name
Date of birth
Number or Name
Street
Town/City
County
Postcode

ET1a v01 ET1a v01

RESPONSE TO AN EMPLOYMENT TRIBUNAL CLAIM (ET3)

Case number:

1 Name of respondent company or organisation

1.1* Name of your organisation:

Contact name:

1.2* Address Number or Name

Street

Town/City

\+ County

Postcode

1.3 Phone number:

1.4 How would you prefer us to communicate with you? (Please tick only one box) E-mail Post Fax

E-mail address:

Fax number:

1.5 What does this organisation mainly make or do?

1.6 How many people does this organisation employ in Great Britain?

1.7 Does this organisation have more than one site in Great Britain? Yes No

1.8 If 'Yes', how many people are employed at the place where the claimant worked?

2 Action before a claim

2.1 Is, or was, the claimant an employee? Yes No
If 'Yes', please now go straight to section 2.3.

2.2 Is, or was, the claimant a worker providing services to you? Yes No
If 'Yes', please now go straight to section 3.
If 'No', please now go straight to section 5.

2.3 If the claim, or part of it, is about a dismissal, do you agree that the claimant was dismissed? Yes No
If 'Yes', please now go straight to section 2.6.

2.4 If the claim includes something **other than** dismissal, does it relate to an action you took on grounds of the claimant's conduct or capability? Yes No
If 'Yes', please now go straight to section 2.6.

2.5 Has the substance of this claim been raised by the claimant in writing under a grievance procedure? Yes No

2.6 If 'Yes', please explain below what stage you have reached in the dismissal and disciplinary procedure or grievance procedure (whichever is applicable).
If 'No' and the claimant says they have raised a grievance with you in writing, please say whether you received it and explain why you did not accept this as a grievance.

ET3 v02 001 1 ET3 v02 001

3 Employment details

3.1 Are the dates of employment given by the claimant correct? Yes ☐ No ☐
If 'Yes', please now go straight to section 3.3.

3.2 If 'No', please give dates and say why you disagree with the dates given by the claimant.

When their employment started

When their employment ended or will end

Is their employment continuing? Yes ☐ No ☐

I disagree with the dates for the following reasons.

3.3 Is the claimant's description of their job or job title correct? Yes ☐ No ☐
If 'Yes', please now go straight to section 3.5.

3.4 If 'No', please give the details you believe to be correct below.

3.5 Is the information given by the claimant correct about being paid for, or working, a period of notice? Yes ☐ No ☐
If 'Yes', please now go straight to section 3.7.

3.6 If 'No', please give the details you believe to be correct below. If you gave them no notice or didn't pay them instead of letting them work their notice, please explain what happened and why.

3.7 Are the claimant's hours of work correct? Yes ☐ No ☐
If 'Yes', please now go straight to section 3.9.

3.8 If 'No', please enter the details you believe to be correct. hours each week

3.9 Are the earnings details given by the claimant correct? Yes ☐ No ☐
If 'Yes', please now go straight to section 4.

3.10 If 'No', please give the details you believe to be correct below.

Pay before tax £

Normal take-home pay (including overtime, commission, bonuses and so on) £

Hourly ☐
Weekly ☐
Monthly ☐
Yearly ☐

ET3 v02 002 2 ET3 v02 002

4 Unfair dismissal or constructive dismissal

4.1 Are the details about pension and other benefits given by the claimant correct? Yes ☐ No ☐
If 'Yes', please now go straight to section 5.

4.2 If 'No', please give the details you believe to be correct below.

5 Response

5.1* Do you resist the claim? Yes ☐ No ☐
If 'No', please now go straight to section 6.

5.2• If 'Yes', please set out in full the grounds on which you resist the claim.

6 Other information

6.1 Please do not send a covering letter with this form. You should add any extra information you want us to know here.

7 Your representative

If you have a representative, please fill in the following.

7.1 Representative's name:

7.2 Name of the representative's organisation:

7.3 Address
Number or Name
Street
Town/City
County
Postcode

7.4 Phone number:

7.5 Reference:

7.6 How would you prefer us to communicate with them? (Please tick only one box) E-mail Post Fax

E-mail address:

Fax number:

Please sign and date here

Signature: Date:

Data Protection Act 1998. We will send a copy of this form to the claimant and Acas. We will put some of the information you give us on this form onto a computer. This helps us to monitor progress and produce statistics. Information provided on this form is passed to the Department of Trade and Industry to assist research into the use and effectiveness of Employment Tribunals.

ET3 v02 004 URN 05/1442 4 ET3 v02 004 URN 05/1442

[5034]–[5042]

D. CODES OF PRACTICE, ETC

AGE DIVERSITY AT WORK
A PRACTICAL GUIDE FOR BUSINESS (2006)

NOTES

The Code of Practice on Age Diversity at Work was originally issued by the Department for Education and Employment in 1999, and was revised and reissued by the Department for Work and Pensions in 2002. The 2002 Code was replaced by the current 'Practical Guide for Business' in 2006. The purpose of the Guide is to promote good employment practice and there is no statutory authority for the Guide which, therefore, has no specific legal status.

INTRODUCTION

This handy guide is to help employers think about what they can do to remove age discrimination from employment practices – to make decisions that do not discriminate against someone because of their age.

It's time to bring ageism to an end – to stamp out misguided attitudes that people are past it after 50 or incapable of doing a responsible job when they are young.

Being positive about age is about building an effective workforce of different ages. Businesses of all sizes are reporting the benefits of employing an age-diverse workforce – higher retention rates, lower absenteeism, increased motivation, greater flexibility and a wider pool of skills.

RECRUITMENT

Advertising

Remove age limits from job adverts, so no-one is discouraged from applying because of their age.

Use language and pictures to appeal to wide age groups.

Avoid phrases like 'applicants should be 25–35 years of age', 'young graduates', 'mature person' – they are discriminatory.

Publicise your vacancies in ways most likely to attract people of a variety of ages – consider national and local newspapers, free papers, internet, jobcentres, community and business networks.

Be aware that older people increasingly make up a bigger proportion of the population. Ignoring this will reduce your choice of potential candidates.

Experience and qualifications

Avoid specifying a minimum length of experience such as 10 years, as this disadvantages younger workers. The quality and relevance of experience is important – not the number of years.

Avoid phrases like 'only people with GCSEs need apply'. That would rule out many older people who left school before GCSEs were introduced, even though they may have the necessary skills.

Application forms

Remove date of birth and put it on a separate monitoring form that interviewers don't see.

Monitoring

Check how effective your recruitment process is. Count the number of candidates of different age groups who applied; were short-listed; interviewed; appointed.

Graduate and specialist recruitment

If you have special recruitment programmes for graduates or managers, make them open to all ages.

Recruitment agencies

If you use a recruitment agency, check that they don't exclude people because of their age.

SELECTION

Focus on skills, not on stereotypes. For example, a manager can potentially be a younger or older person.

Make sure you're not making assumptions about the capability or medical fitness of someone based purely on their age.

If the staff responsible for selecting and interviewing candidates are not trained in equal opportunities, they may be discriminating unwittingly and leave you open for prosecution.

Interviewing

Use people of different ages on the interview panel, to reduce the possibility of bias towards one age group.

Ask job-related questions and be careful not to base decisions on prejudice and stereotypes.

Use selection criteria to mark candidates against. This can help with decision-making and record the fairness of the process.

Monitoring

Check the number of candidates of different age groups who applied, were short-listed, were interviewed and were appointed.

PROMOTION

Avoid having a minimum or maximum cut-off age for promotion.

Make your promotion opportunities open to all employees. Let your staff know that age is not a barrier and that they will not be regarded as 'too young' or 'too old'.

Promote on the basis of performance that you can measure and potential that is demonstrated – rather than on age or length of service.

TRAINING & DEVELOPMENT

Make sure training is open to all, for example not overlooking an older person, thinking they may not be interested in career development. Training can be worthwhile for all ages of employees – they could be working with you longer than assumed.

Awareness of individual learning styles

A worker who has been away from formal learning for a few years might take a bit longer to adjust to training and may need some reassurance. Someone used to a formal learning environment might take a bit longer to adjust to on-the-job training.

Ask employees who have benefited from training to be role models to inspire others.

REDUNDANCY

Beware of losing the skills your business needs. If you target older workers when selecting for redundancy, you may discover later that vital skills and company knowledge are lost.

Base your redundancy decisions on job-related criteria and the needs of your business – don't use age as a factor.

Consider alternatives to redundancy – like part-time working, natural wastage, redeployment to other parts of the company, job-sharing, career breaks.

Voluntary redundancy

Be aware that asking for volunteers might have a less demoralising effect on the workforce – but it could leave you with an imbalance in the remaining skills and experience in the company.

Last in – first out

'Last in – first out' is not necessarily the best approach, as the 'last in' could be crucial to your business.

Be careful not to lose the balance of skills and experience that comes from employing a workforce of various ages.

RETIREMENT

From October 2006, compulsory retirement below age 65 is unlawful – you would need to justify any enforced retirements below that age.

You don't have to set a compulsory retirement age – it isn't required by law. In fact, compulsory retirement could mean you lose skilled people and affect your business productivity. Why train new staff or pay higher rates for agency workers, when an existing employee, who knows your business, could do the job.

Flexible retirement

Flexible retirement can be a useful way of preparing employees to handle the change between full-time work and full retirement.

There are alternatives to stopping work altogether – for example reduced hours, job-sharing, part-time working.

See if employees who have retired are seeking employment again. This could involve short-term contracts, re-employment as an advisor, temporary cover during holidays, sickness absence or busy periods.

Being flexible about retirement can mean reducing capacity without losing valuable workers and their expertise.

Mentoring

As older workers get near to retirement, involve them in mentoring other staff to pass on skills and experience.

Performance

Use performance standards – they don't have to be complex but they are essential when dealing with poor performers. Don't use retirement as an easy alternative for poor performance – it is not cost effective.

[5043]

CODE OF PRACTICE ON WORKFORCE MATTERS IN LOCAL AUTHORITY SERVICE CONTRACTS

NOTES

This Code was issued by the Office of the Deputy Prime Minister in February 2003 and is reproduced from an ODPM circular of March 2003. Note that the functions of the Office of the Deputy Prime Minister have been transferred to the Department for Communities and Local Government (see: www.communities.gov.uk).

The Code at the time of its issue in February 2003 had no formal legal basis; it is framed accordingly as essentially an instruction to local authorities as to the terms to be included in those contracts for which tendering processes began after the issue of the Code.

Subsequently, partial statutory authority has been given to the Code by the Local Government Act 2003, ss 101, 102 and 124 (at **[1584]**, **[1585]** and **[1585A]**). The operative sections, 101 and 102, deal respectively with terms of employment and pension rights; s 124 defines the 'appropriate person' empowered to issue directions to best value authorities (for England, this is the Secretary of State, for Wales either the Secretary of State or the Welsh Assembly, depending on the category of authority concerned). It should however be noted that the matters as to which directions can be given under ss 101 and 102 are limited in scope to staff transferring on the contracting out of a service (or a contract returning in-house); the powers do not give statutory support to the provisions of the Code requiring authorities to stipulate that contractors must afford equivalent terms to subsequently engaged staff.

Workforce matters under best value

1. This document sets out an approach to workforce matters in local authority service contracts which involve a transfer of staff from the local authority to the service provider, or in which staff originally transferred out from the local authority as a result of an outsourcing are TUPE transferred to a new provider under a retender of a contract. This Code will form part of the service specification and conditions for all such contracts.

2. The Code recognises that there is no conflict between good employment practice, value for money and quality of service. On the contrary, quality and good value will not be provided by organisations who do not manage workforce issues well. The intention of the authority is therefore to select only those providers who offer staff a package of terms and conditions which will secure high quality service delivery throughout the life of the contract. These must be sufficient to recruit and motivate high quality staff to work on the contract and designed to prevent the emergence of a 'two-tier workforce', dividing transferees and new joiners working beside each other on the same contracts.

3. Service providers who intend to cut costs by driving down the terms and conditions for staff, whether for transferees or for new joiners taken on to work beside them, will not provide best value and will not be selected to provide services for the council. However, nothing in this Code should discourage local authorities or service providers from addressing productivity issues by working with their workforces in a positive manner to achieve continuous improvement in the services they deliver.

Treatment of transferees

4. In its contracting-out of services, the local authority will apply the principles set out in the Cabinet Office Statement of Practice on Staff Transfers in the Public Sector and the annex to it, A Fair Deal for Staff Pensions. The service provider will be required to demonstrate its support for these principles and its willingness to work with the local authority fully to implement them.

5. The intention of the Statement is that staff will transfer and that TUPE should apply, and that in circumstances where TUPE does not apply in strict legal terms, the principles of TUPE should be followed and the staff involved should be treated no less favourably than had the Regulations applied. The Government has now indicated an intention to legislate to make statutory within local government the provisions in the Cabinet Office Statement.

6. The annex to the Statement requires the terms of a business transfer specifically to protect the pensions of transferees. Staff must have ongoing access to the Local Government Pension Scheme or be offered an alternative good quality occupational pension scheme, as defined in the annex to the Cabinet Office Statement, under which they can continue to earn pension benefits through their future service. There must also be arrangements for handling the accrued benefits which staff have already earned.

Treatment of new joiners to an outsourced workforce

7. Where the service provider recruits new staff to work on a local authority contract alongside staff transferred from the local authority, it will offer employment on fair and reasonable terms and conditions which are, overall, no less favourable than those of transferred employees. The service provider will also offer reasonable pension arrangements (as described at paragraph 10 below).

8. The principle underpinning the provisions of paragraph 7 is to consider employees' terms and conditions (other than pensions arrangements which are dealt with in paragraph 10) in the round – as a 'package'. This Code does not prevent service providers from offering new recruits a package of non-pension terms and conditions which differs from that of transferred staff, so long as the overall impact of the changes to this package meets the conditions in paragraph 7. The aim is to provide a flexible framework under which the provider can design a package best suited to the delivery of the service, but which will exclude changes which would undermine the integrated nature of the team or the quality of the workforce.

9. The service provider will consult representatives of a trade union where one is recognised, or other elected representatives of the employees where there is no recognised trade union, on the terms and conditions to be offered to such new recruits. [References to 'trade unions' throughout this code should be read to refer to other elected representatives of the employees where there is no recognised trade union.] The arrangements for consultation will involve a genuine dialogue. The precise nature of the arrangements for consultation is for agreement between the service provider and the recognised trade unions. The intention is that contractors

and recognised trade unions should be able to agree on a particular package of terms and conditions, in keeping with the terms of this Code, to be offered to new joiners.

Pension arrangements for new joiners to an outsourced workforce

10. The service provider will be required to offer new recruits taken on to work on the contract beside transferees one of the following pension provision arrangements:

- membership of the local government pension scheme, where the employer has admitted body status within the scheme and makes the requisite contributions;
- membership of a good quality employer pension scheme, either being a contracted out, final-salary based defined benefit scheme, or a defined contribution scheme. For defined contribution schemes the employer must match employee contributions up to 6%, although either could pay more if they wished;
- a stakeholder pension scheme, under which the employer will match employee contributions up to 6%, although either could pay more if they wished.

On a retender of a contract to which this Code applies the new service provider will be required to offer one of these pensions options to any staff who transfer to it and who had prior to the transfer a right under the Code to one of these pension options.

Monitoring arrangements

11. Throughout the length of the contract, the service provider will provide the local authority with information as requested which is necessary to allow the local authority to monitor compliance with the conditions set out in this Code. This information will include the terms and conditions for transferred staff and the terms and conditions for employees recruited to work on the contract after the transfer.

12. Such requests for information will be restricted to that required for the purpose of monitoring compliance, will be designed to place the minimum burden on the service provider commensurate with this, and will respect commercial confidentiality. The service provider and the local authority will also support a central Government-sponsored review and monitoring programme on the impact of the Code, drawn up in consultation with representatives of local government, contractors, trade unions and the Audit Commission and will provide information as requested for this purpose. Such requests will follow the same principles of proportionality and confidentiality.

Enforcement

13. The local authority will enforce the obligations on the service provider created under this Code. Employees and recognised trade unions should in the first instance seek to resolve any complaints they have about how the obligations under this Code are being met, directly with the service provider. Where it appears to the local authority that the service provider is not meeting its obligations, or where an employee of the service provider or a recognised trade union writes to the authority to say that it has been unable to resolve a complaint directly with the service provider, the local authority will first seek an explanation from the service provider. If the service provider's response satisfies the local authority that the Code is being followed, the local authority will inform any complainant of this. If the response does not satisfy the local authority, it will ask the service provider to take immediate action to remedy this. If, following such a request, the service provider still appears to the local authority not to be complying with the Code, the local authority will seek to enforce the terms of the contract, which will incorporate this Code. In addition, where a service provider has not complied with this Code, the local authority will not be bound to consider that provider for future work.

14. The contract shall include a provision for resolving disputes about the application of this Code in a fast, efficient and cost-effective way as an alternative to litigation, and which is designed to achieve a resolution to which all the parties are committed. The service provider, local authority and recognised trade unions or other staff representatives, shall all have access to this 'alternative dispute resolution' (ADR) process. The Government has asked local authorities, trade unions and contractors to come forward with an ADR mechanism which is consistent with this Code, for inclusion in contracts. In the event that within a specified timescale the parties are unable to agree, the government will publish as an annex to this Code its proposed ADR mechanism.

15. Local authorities will be required to certify in their Performance Plans that individual contracts comply with best value requirements, including workforce requirements in this Code and the accompanying statutory guidance. The Audit Commission's appointed auditor will through the audit of the Performance Plan:

- provide assurance that local authorities are meeting their statutory duty of certifying their compliance with the Code and that they have put in place adequate arrangements to ensure compliance;
- receive information from third parties about any concerns with the authority's compliance;
- consider the information received and decide how to deal with those concerns;
- where the subject of any concern is of material significance (eg large contracts or a major breach of this Code is alleged) the auditor will decide on a proportionate response to investigate the concerns.

16. If, as a result of investigations, the auditor has concerns about an authority's compliance with this Code, they may exercise their appropriate statutory powers, which include:

- requiring the authority to respond publicly to a written recommendation;
- recommending that the Secretary of State should give a direction under Section 15 of the Local Government Act 1999.

The Audit Commission will issue guidance to local authorities and auditors on how these matters will be dealt with.

Sub-contractors

17. This Code sets out procedures for handling matters between the local authority and a primary service provider. Where the primary service provider transfers staff originally in the employ of the local authority to a sub-contractor in consequence of the terms of the primary service provider's obligations to the local authority, the primary service provider will be responsible for the observance of this Code by the sub-contractor.

Operation of this Code

18. The Government will monitor the operation of this Code and consult with representatives of local government, trade unions, service providers and the Audit Commission to assist in this process.

[5044]

E. CABINET OFFICE STATEMENT OF PRACTICE

STAFF TRANSFERS IN THE PUBLIC SECTOR

Statement of Practice
January 2000 (Revised November 2007)

NOTES

This Statement of Practice was issued in January 2000 by the Cabinet Office. It has no statutory basis or force, but represents the policy which Government departments are required to follow and provides guidance for the rest of the public service, as to the application of the principles of TUPE in the contracting out or market testing of public service activities. The Statement was reissued in November 2007 with detailed revisions to reflect legislative changes (principally but not only the revision of the TUPE Regulations in 2006) and is reproduced here in its revised form. Both Annex A and Annex B are omitted for reasons of space. The full document can be accessed at www.hm-treasury.gov.uk. Annex A is also reproduced in *Harvey*.

Guiding Principles

- The Government is committed to ensuring that the public sector is a good employer and model contractor and client. The people employed in the public sector, directly and indirectly, are its biggest asset and critical in developing modern, high quality, efficient, responsive, customer focused and environmentally friendly public services.

- The Government's approach to modernising public services is a pragmatic one, based on finding the best supplier who can deliver quality services and value for money for the taxpayer. This involves some services or functions being provided by, or in partnership with, the private or voluntary sector, or restructured and organised in a new way within the public sector. The involvement, commitment and motivation of staff are vital for achieving smooth and seamless transition during such organisational change.

- Public Private Partnerships and the process of modernisation through organisational change in the public sector will be best achieved by clarity and certainty about the treatment of staff involved. The Government is committed to ensuring that staff involved in all such transfers are treated fairly and consistently and their rights respected. This will encourage a co-operative, partnership approach to the modernisation of the public sector with consequential benefits for all citizens.

Introduction

1. In order to meet these guiding principles the Government believes that there must be a clear and consistent policy for the treatment of staff, founded upon the provisions of the Transfer of Undertaking (Protection of Employment) Regulations 2006 (TUPE), which replaces the Transfer of Undertaking (Protection of Employment) Regulations 1981. This Statement of Practice[1] sets out the framework that the Government expects all public sector organisations to work within to achieve this aim (see paragraph 6 for the coverage of this Statement).

2. TUPE implements the 2001 European Council Acquired Rights Directive. In broad terms, TUPE protects employees' terms and conditions (except certain occupational pension arrangements) when the business or service in which they work is transferred from one employer to another. Employment with the new employer is treated as continuous from the date of the employee's start with the first employer. Terms and conditions cannot be changed where the operative reason for the change is the transfer although changes for other reasons may be negotiated, subject to certain conditions.

3. The Government takes a positive attitude towards TUPE, regarding it as an important aspect of employment rights legislation with the potential to promote a co-operative, partnership approach towards business restructuring and change in the public sector.

4. The Government's strategy in revising this legislation is based on the principle that it must be made to work effectively for all those whose interests depend upon it. This mirrors the Government's approach to employment relations issues generally.

5. In the area of Public Private Partnerships and change in the public sector, the consultations that the Government has undertaken and the representations which have been made, have showed a strong consensus between private sector employers, the voluntary

sector, employee representatives and public sector organisations for the application of TUPE to situations where a service or function is contracted out, then retendered, brought back into the public sector, transferred within the public sector, or restructured and organised in a new way in a different part of the public sector. In any event, the TUPE Regulations 2006 have expanded the previous definition of what constitutes a transfer. It is accepted that there will still be some genuinely exceptional circumstances where TUPE will not apply but it is anticipated that there will be fewer than under the 1981 Regulations. Attempts to orchestrate a non-TUPE situation in other circumstances should not be tolerated. The policy in this Statement of Practice is therefore based on the following principles:

- contracting-out exercises with the private sector and voluntary organisations and transfers between different parts of the public sector, will be conducted on the basis that staff will transfer and TUPE should apply, unless there are genuinely exceptional reasons not to do so. Further guidance in relation to transferring staff from the public sector to a service provider and any subsequent re-tendering is provided at Annex B, 'Code of Practice on Workforce Matters in Public Sector Service Contracts' (issued in March 2003 and revised in March 2005);
- this includes second and subsequent round contracts that result in a new contractor and where a function is brought back into a public sector organisation where, in both cases, when the contract was first awarded staff transferred from the public sector;
- in circumstances where TUPE does not apply in strict legal terms to certain types of transfer between different parts of the public sector, the principles of TUPE should be followed (where possible using legislation to effect the transfer) and the staff involved should be treated no less favourably than had the Regulations applied; and
- there should be appropriate arrangements to protect occupational pensions, redundancy and severance terms of staff in all these types of transfer. Attached at Annex A is HM Treasury's Statement of Practice on Staff Transfers from Central Government "A fair deal for Staff Pensions" which sets out the policy on staff pensions announced by the Chief Secretary on 14 June 1999 that must be followed by Central Government Departments and Agencies, and which Ministers expect to be adopted by other public sector employers. This has been supplemented by further guidance issued in June 2004 'Fair deal for Staff Pensions: Procurement of Bulk Transfer Agreements and related issues', also attached at Annex A.

NOTES

[1] Further copies of this Statement can be obtained from Phillip Jones tel. 020 7276 1519 or by email to Phillip.Jones@cabinet-office.x.gsi.gov.uk

Coverage

6. This Statement of Practice sets out a framework to be followed by public sector organisations to implement the Government's policy on the treatment of staff transfers where the public sector is the employer when contracting out or the client in a subsequent retendering situation. It applies directly to Central Government Departments and Agencies and to the NHS. The Government expects other public sector organisations to follow this Statement of Practice. Local government is subject to some different considerations particularly the current restrictions in legislation contained in Parts I and II of the Local Government Act 1988. However abolition of CCT from January 2000 and proposals to modify Section 17 of the 1988 Act, as part of the introduction of Best Value, will remove in part obstacles to local authorities following this Statement of Practice. However, in doing so, they must have regard to the need to comply with their best value duties. The Personnel and Human Resources panel of the Local Government Association support the principles set out in this Statement of Practice and have encouraged their adoption by individual local authorities.

7. The Statement of Practice covers the following types of situation that may involve transfers of staff:

- Public Private Partnerships (e g following Better Quality Service reviews). This includes contracting-out; market testing; PFI; privatisation and other outsourcing and contracting exercises, (paragraphs 10–16);
- Second and subsequent generation contracting where, when the contract was first awarded, staff transferred from the public sector, (paragraph 12);
- Reorganisations and transfers from one part of the public sector to another, (paragraphs 17–20); and
- Reorganisations and transfers within the Civil Service (where TUPE cannot apply because there is no change in employer but TUPE principles should be followed), (paragraphs 21 and 22).

8. This Statement deals only with the policy framework for the treatment of staff involved in such transfers. It does not offer policy advice or guidance on:

- assessing the options for a particular service or function;
- project appraisal or procurement (except on the application of TUPE);
- managing a contracting exercise;
- how to discharge the obligations when TUPE applies or not;
- or how to secure appropriate pension provision, redundancy or severance terms.

Nor does it remove the need to seek legal advice in each individual case.

9. Detailed guidance on these aspects is provided separately, often tailored for different parts of the public sector to reflect their different needs, and for different types of Public Private Partnership. A list of relevant guidance for these aspects is at Annex B.

Transfers as a Result of Public Private Partnerships

10. This section of the Statement deals with the policy that should be adopted for the transfer of staff from the public sector to a private sector employer or a voluntary sector body. This will be as a result of a Public Private Partnership where a service or function currently performed by the public sector will in future be carried out by a private sector organisation. This may, for example, be a result of a PFI initiative, strategic contracting out or market testing exercises. All will involve some sort of contracting exercise where the public sector organisation (not necessarily the one in which the staff are employed) is the contracting authority.

11. In such transfers the application of TUPE will always be a matter of law based on the individual circumstances of the particular transfer. However, the policy adopted in defining the terms of the contracting exercise can help ensure that staff should be protected by TUPE and that all parties have a clear understanding that TUPE should apply and will be followed. In such transfers, therefore, the public sector contracting authority should, except in genuinely exceptional circumstances (see paragraph 14), ensure that:

- at the earliest appropriate stage in the contracting exercise, it states that staff are to transfer and this should normally have the effect of causing TUPE to apply, although legal advice should always be taken to confirm the applicability of TUPE in individual cases;
- at the earliest appropriate stage staff and recognised unions (or, if none, other independent staff representatives) are informed in writing of the intention that staff will transfer (and where possible when the transfer will take place) and that TUPE should apply;
- potential bidders are then invited to tender, drawing their attention in the Invitation to Tender letter to the intention that staff will transfer and TUPE should apply. The public sector contracting authority should also be aware of the new requirement in the 2006 TUPE Regulations in relation to notification of employee liability information, and legal advice should be taken as necessary. Potential bidders should be also advised that they can, if they wish, submit bids on the basis that staff do not transfer and TUPE does not apply, but that these will only be accepted if they fall within the genuinely exceptional circumstances ie unless the bid falls within one of the exceptions at paragraph 14 it must comply with the condition that staff transfer and TUPE should apply;
- the contracting exercise is then operated on the basis that the intention is that staff will transfer and TUPE should apply. Public sector contracting authorities should however consider all bids received. If a tenderer considers that staff should not transfer, they should be asked to give their reasons for this. Tenderers should be reminded if they do not consider that staff should transfer and the contract does not fall within the exceptions in paragraph 14, the contracting authority reserves the right not to accept the tender;
- in a very few cases bids made on the basis staff will not transfer and TUPE not apply will fall within the genuinely exceptional circumstances set out in paragraph 14 and cause the authority to accept the bid. The costs of redeploying staff and redundancies costs to the public sector employer must be taken into account when assessing such a bid. In all other cases the bid should not be accepted as it will not conform to the contracting authority's view that staff should transfer and TUPE apply; and
- where there is then a contractual requirement that staff should transfer, the requirements of TUPE should be scrupulously followed by the public sector contracting authority who should also ensure that it is satisfied that bidders' proposals fully meet the requirements of TUPE.

Second and subsequent transfers

12. This part of the Statement also extends to the retendering of contracts where, when the contract was first awarded staff transferred from the public sector (irrespective of whether TUPE applied at the time). Where a public contracting authority retenders such a contract then, except in exceptional circumstances (and where the incumbent contractor is successful), TUPE should apply and staff working on the contract should usually transfer. Views should be sought from the current contractor as to whether, from their point of view, there are any exceptional circumstances why staff should not transfer (by reference to paragraph 14). The retendering exercise should then be conducted as described above in paragraph 11.

Transfer of services or functions back into the public sector

13. There may also be circumstances that require a function contracted-out to a private sector contractor or voluntary sector body to be brought back into the public sector on the termination of the contract. If, when the contract was first awarded staff transferred from the public sector (irrespective of whether TUPE applied at the time), then the public sector organisation should ensure that staff working on the contract transfer (and TUPE should therefore apply) into its organisation unless there are genuinely exceptional reasons not to do so. Views should be sought from the current contractor as to whether, from their point of view, there are any exceptional circumstances why staff should not transfer (by reference to paragraph 14). For transfers into the Civil Service, where TUPE applies, then the recruitment provisions of the Civil Service Order in Council and Civil Service Commissioners Recruitment Code are not relevant.[2] The Civil Service Nationality rules, which are statutorily based, will continue to apply.

NOTES

[2] Civil Service Management Code.

Exceptions

14. There may be a small number of cases where the policy set out in paragraphs 11–13 may not be followed and TUPE may not apply. There must be genuinely exceptional reasons why this should be the case. Circumstances that may qualify for such exceptions are, broadly:

- where a contract is for the provision of both goods and services, but the provision of services is ancillary in purpose to the provision of the goods; or
- where the activity for which the public sector organisation is contracting is essentially new or a one off project; or
- where services or goods are essentially a commodity bought 'off the shelf' and no grouping of staff are specifically and permanently assigned to a common task.

15. Where a public sector organisation believes such genuinely exceptional circumstances exist then it should be prepared to justify this, and the departure from the Government's policy (paras 11–13), publicly, if challenged. In central government, the agreement of the relevant departmental Ministers may need to be obtained before such an exception is made.

16. In such exceptional cases where staff do not transfer and TUPE does not apply, the public sector organisation should, in the case of first generation contracts, seek to identify as soon as possible with the contractor any staff that will be taken on voluntarily by the contractor,[3] and then, where possible, to redeploy those members of staff remaining within the public sector organisation (the costs of such redeployments and possible resulting redundancy payments must be taken into account when evaluating the bid).

NOTES

[3] Public Sector organisations should be aware that the transfer of a major part of the workforce, in terms of numbers or skills, may cause TUPE to apply.

Transfers and Reorganisations within the public sector

17. TUPE can apply to the transfers of a function from one part of the public sector to another where there is a change of employer. This, for example, can include:[4]

- Transfers between local government and civil service Departments and agencies
- Transfers between local government and NDPBs
- Transfers between local government and the NHS
- Transfers between the NHS and Civil Service Departments and Agencies
- Transfers between the NHS and NDPBs

- Transfers between NDPBs and civil service departments and agencies

18. The application of TUPE will, again, always be a matter of law based on the individual circumstances of the particular transfer. The amended Acquired Rights Directive directly legislates the *Henke* judgement of the European Court of Justice that: an administrative reorganisation of public administrative authorities or the transfer of administrative function is not a transfer and, therefore, as a matter of law, does not fall within the Directive. This provision in the Directive has been incorporated into the 2006 TUPE Regulations at 3(5). Case law[5] suggests that it excludes from the legislation's application only a relatively limited range of situations involving the transfer of entities pursuing non-economic objectives within the public sector. Nevertheless the issue has still to be tested fully in the tribunals and courts. The *Henke* exception has been thought to apply where: the reason for a transfer is only because there is a change of geographical boundaries and the type of public sector body carrying out the function does not change (e g the transfer of administrative staff as a result of changes to police authority boundaries); or where the main function is a judicial, quasi-judicial or quasi-judicial regulatory function (e g the creation of the Financial Services Authority) and incapable of being performed other than by a public sector authority. Officeholders who are not workers are also excluded from the scope of the Directive.

19. However, transfers at the instigation and under the control of Central Government will usually be effected through legislation, in particular those involving Officeholders. Provision can then be made for staff to transfer on TUPE terms, irrespective of whether the transfer is excluded from the scope of the Directive implemented by TUPE. Departments must therefore ensure that legislation effecting transfers of functions between public sector bodies makes provision for staff to transfer and on a basis that follows the principles of TUPE along with appropriate arrangements to protect occupational pension, redundancy and severance terms.

20. Section 38 of the Employment Relations Act also includes a power that can be used to apply the requirements of TUPE specifically to transfers outside the scope of the Directive e g Transfer of Undertakings (Protection of Employment) (Rent Officer Service) Regulations 1999 (SI 1999/2511). The DTI should be consulted about any proposal to exercise this power. Where, for whatever reason, this power or other legislation is not used there will be no legal requirement or obligation in such cases for staff to transfer to another part of the public sector where the function is to be performed (as to attempt to compel them would, in effect, constitute a unilateral change in their employment contract by imposing a change of employer). In such cases, as a matter of policy, public sector bodies should ensure that the principles underpinning TUPE are followed, so staff are offered the opportunity to transfer on terms that are, overall, no less favourable than had TUPE applied. They should also ensure appropriate pension provision and redundancy and severance terms. Staff who choose not to transfer should, where possible, be redeployed within the transferring public sector organisation.

NOTES

4 This list is not exhaustive.

5 *Mayeur v Association Promotion de l'Information Messine*: C-175/99 2000 IRLR 783, ECJ and *Collino v Telecom Italia SpA*: C-343/98 2000 IRLR 788, ECJ. These cases limit the application of the Henke exception to cases involving simply a re-organisation of public administrative structures or the transfer of administrative functions between public administrative authorities.

Transfers and Reorganisations within the Civil Service

21. Reorganisation and transfers between Central Government Departments and agencies (i e within the Civil Service) do not involve a change in employer and TUPE therefore cannot apply. However, terms and conditions of employment do vary between different departments and many of the considerations addressed in the Statement for other types of transfer may also apply.

22. As a matter of policy, therefore, such reorganisations and transfers between Central Government Departments will be conducted on the basis that:

- as a general rule, when functions are transferred from one department to another staff will be transferred with the work;
- departments should, however, make every effort to provide an opportunity for those who wish to stay with or return to their original department to do so, having regard to ensuring consistent treatment of staff affected and the needs of the work;
- departments should ensure that wherever possible the principles of TUPE are followed. The existing terms and conditions of staff cannot be changed unilaterally,

over time; the receiving department may aim to move, through negotiation with staff, towards fuller alignment of the terms of transferred staff to those of the main body of staff.

- staff and their recognised unions are informed at the earliest appropriate stage of the reorganisation and transfer.

Cabinet Office

January 2000

(Revised November 2007)

[5045]

(*Annexes A and B omitted for reasons of space; see the note at the beginning of this Statement of Practice.*)

F. USEFUL ADDRESSES

USEFUL ADDRESSES

1. ADVISORY, CONCILIATION AND ARBITRATION SERVICE

NOTES

Further information is available on the ACAS website at www.acas.org.uk.

ACAS National Helpline	Tel: 08457 47 47 47 Textphone: 08456 06 16 00
Head Office	Brandon House, 180 Borough High Street, London SE1 1LW Tel: 020 7210 3613
Regional offices	
London	Euston Tower, 286 Euston Road, London NW1 3JJ Tel: 020 7396 0022
East of England	Acas House, Kempson Way, Suffolk Business Park, Bury St Edmunds, Suffolk IP32 7AR Tel: 01284 774500
East Midlands	Lancaster House, 10 Sherwood Rise, Nottingham NG7 6JE Tel: 0115 985 8253
West Midlands	Apex House, 3 Embassy Drive, Calthorpe Road, Edgbaston, Birmingham B15 1TR Tel: 0121 345 1410
North West	Commercial Union House, 2–10 Albert Square, Manchester M60 8AD Tel: 0161 833 8500 Pavilion 1, The Matchworks, Speke Road, Speke, Liverpool L19 2PH Tel: 0151 728 5600
North East	Cross House, Westgate Road, Newcastle upon Tyne NE1 4XX Tel: 0191 269 6000
Scotland	151 West George Street, Glasgow G2 7JJ Tel: 0141 248 1400
South West	The Waterfront, Welshback, Bristol BS1 4SB Tel: 0117 906 5200
South East	Suites 3–5, Business Centre, 1–7 Commercial Road, Paddock Wood, Kent TN12 6EN Tel: 01892 837273 Cygnus House, Ground Floor, Waterfront Business Park, Fleet, Hampshire GU51 3QT Tel: 01252 816 650
Wales	3 Purbeck House, Lambourne Crescent, Llanishen, Cardiff CF14 5GJ Tel: 02920 762636
Yorkshire & Humber	The Cube, 123 Albion Street, Leeds, LS2 8ER 0113 205 3800

2. BORDER AND IMMIGRATION AGENCY (EMPLOYMENT MATTERS)

Website: www.bia.homeoffice.gov.uk

Sponsor and employers' helpline
Tel: 0845 010 6677

Work permits customer contact centre
Customer Contact Centre, UK Border Agency, PO Box 3468, Sheffield S3 8WA
Tel: 0114 207 4074 Fax: 0114 207 4000
Email: wpcustomers@ind.homeoffice.gsi.gov.uk

3. BRITISH PSYCHOLOGICAL SOCIETY
St Andrews House, 48 Princess Road East, Leicester LE1 7DR
Tel: 0116 254 9568 Fax: 0116 227 1314
Website: www.bps.org.uk
Email: enquiries@bps.org.uk

4. CENTRAL ARBITRATION COMMITTEE
PO Box 51547, London, SE1 1ZG
Tel: 020 7904 2300 Fax: 020 7904 2301
Website: www.cac.gov.uk
Email: enquiries@cac.gov.uk

5. CHARTERED INSTITUTE OF PERSONNEL AND DEVELOPMENT
151 The Broadway, London, SW19 1JQ
Tel: 020 8612 6200 Fax: 020 8612 6201
Website: www.cipd.co.uk

6. CERTIFICATION OFFICE FOR TRADE UNIONS AND EMPLOYERS' ASSOCIATIONS
Brandon House, 180 Borough High Street, London SE1 1LW
Tel: 020 7210 3734 Fax: 020 7210 3612
Website: www.certoffice.org
Email: info@certoffice.org

7. COMMISSION FOR EQUALITY AND HUMAN RIGHTS
See EQUALITY AND HUMAN RIGHTS COMMISSION

8. CRIMINAL RECORDS BUREAU
PO Box 110, Liverpool L69 3EF
Tel: 0870 909 0811
Website: www.crb.gov.uk

9. DEPARTMENT FOR BUSINESS, ENTERPRISE & REGULATORY REFORM (BERR) EMPLOYMENT MATTERS
Ministerial Correspondence Unit
Department for Business, Enterprise & Regulatory Reform
1 Victoria Street, London, SW1H 0ET
Tel: 020 7215 5000 Fax: 020 7215 0105
Email: enquiries@berr.gsi.gov.uk
Website: www.berr.gov.uk/employment/

10. DISCLOSURE SCOTLAND
PO Box 250, Glasgow G51 1YU
Tel: 0870 609 6006 Fax: 0870 609 6996
Website: www.disclosurescotland.co.uk
Email: info@disclosurescotland.co.uk

11. EMPLOYMENT APPEAL TRIBUNAL
England & Wales
Audit House, 58 Victoria Embankment, London EC4Y 0DS
Tel: 020 7273 1041 Fax: 020 7273 1045
Website: www.employmentappeals.gov.uk
Email: londoneat@tribunals.gsi.gov.uk

Scotland
52 Melville Street, Edinburgh EH3 7HS
Tel: 0131 225 3963 Fax: 0131 220 6694
Email: edinburgheat@tribunals.gsi.gov.uk

12. EMPLOYMENT TRIBUNALS
NOTE: the Employment Tribunals Service has, since 9 May 2007, been part of the Tribunals Service, an executive agency of the Ministry of Justice. For contact details of the Tribunals Service see below. This section contains the contact details for employment tribunals, which remain unchanged.
Customer Services Team, 3rd Floor, Alexandra House, 14–22 The Parsonage,
Manchester M3 2JA
Tel: 0161 833 6314 Fax: 0161 833 6310
Website: www.employmenttribunals.gov.uk
Email: customer.services@tribunals.gsi.gov.uk

Enquiry Line
Tel: 0845 795 9775 Minicom: 0845 757 3722

Public Register of ET judgments

England & Wales
Tribunals Service, Field Support Unit, 1st Floor, 100 Southgate Street, Bury St Edmunds IP33 2AQ
Tel: 0845 7959775 Fax: 01284 766334
Email: buryet@tribunals.gsi.gov.uk

Scotland
Tribunals Service, Eagle Building, 215 Bothwell Street, Glasgow G2 7TS
Tel: 0141 204 0730 Fax: 0141 204 0732
Email: glasgowet@tribunals.gsi.gov.uk

Employment Tribunals Offices in England, Wales and Scotland

Aberdeen
Mezzanine Floor, Atholl House, 84–88 Guild Street, Aberdeen AB11 6LT
Tel: 01224 593137 Fax: 01224 593138
Email: aberdeenet@tribunals.gsi.gov.uk

Ashford
1st Floor, Ashford House, County Square Shopping Centre, Ashford, Kent TN23 1YB
Tel: 01233 621346 Fax: 01233 624423
Email: ashfordet@tribunals.gsi.gov.uk

Bedford
8–10 Howard Street, Bedford MK40 3HS
Tel: 01234 351306 Fax: 01234 352315
Email: bedfordet@tribunals.gsi.gov.uk

Birmingham
Phoenix House, 1–3 Newhall Street, Birmingham B3 3NH
Tel: 0121 236 6051 Fax: 0121 236 6029
Email: birminghamet@tribunals.gsi.gov.uk

Bristol
Ground Floor, The Crescent Centre, Temple Back, Bristol BS1 6EZ
Tel: 0117 929 8261 Fax: 0117 925 3452
Email: bristolet@tribunals.gsi.gov.uk

Bury St Edmunds
100 Southgate Street, Bury St Edmunds IP33 2AQ
Tel: 01284 762171 Fax: 01284 706064
Email: buryet@tribunals.gsi.gov.uk

Cardiff
Caradog House, 1–6 St Andrews Place, Cardiff CF10 3BE
Tel: 02920 678100 Fax: 02920 225906
Email: cardiffet@tribunals.gsi.gov.uk

Dundee
Ground Floor, Block C, Caledonian House, Greenmarket, Dundee DD1 4QX
Tel: 01382 221578 Fax: 01382 227136
Email: dundeeet@tribunals.gsi.gov.uk

Edinburgh
54–56 Melville Street, Edinburgh EH3 7HF
Tel: 0131 226 5584 Fax: 0131 220 6847
Email: edinburghet@tribunals.gsi.gov.uk

Exeter
2nd Floor, Keble House, Southernhay Gardens, Exeter EX1 1NT
Tel: 01392 279665 Fax: 01392 430063
Email: exeteret@tribunals.gsi.gov.uk

Glasgow
Eagle Building, 215 Bothwell Street, Glasgow G2 7TS
Tel: 0141 204 0730 Fax: 0141 204 0732
Email: glasgowet@tribunals.gsi.gov.uk

Leeds
4th Floor, City Exchange, 11 Albion Street, Leeds LS1 5ES
Tel: 0113 245 9741 Fax: 0113 242 8843
Email: leedset@tribunals.gsi.gov.uk

Leicester
5a New Walk, Leicester LE1 6TE
Tel: 0116 255 0099 Fax: 0116 255 6099
Email: leicesteret@tribunals.gsi.gov.uk

Liverpool
1st Floor, Cunard Building, Pier Head, Liverpool L3 1TS
Tel: 0151 236 9397 Fax: 0151 231 1484
Email: liverpoolet@tribunals.gsi.gov.uk

London Central
Victory House, 30–34 Kingsway, London WC2B 6EX
Tel: 020 7273 8603 Fax: 020 7273 8686
Email: londoncentralet@tribunals.gsi.gov.uk

London South
Montague Court, 101 London Road, West Croydon CR0 2RF
Tel: 020 8667 9131 Fax: 020 8649 9470
Email: londonsouthet@tribunals.gsi.gov.uk

Manchester
Alexandra House, 14–22 The Parsonage, Manchester M3 2JA
Tel: 0161 833 0581 Fax: 0161 832 0249
Email: manchesteret@tribunals.gsi.gov.uk

Newcastle
Quayside House, 110 Quayside, Newcastle upon Tyne NE1 3DX
Tel: 0191 260 6900 Fax: 0191 222 1680
Email: newcastleet@tribunals.gsi.gov.uk

Nottingham
3rd Floor, Byron House, 2a Maid Marian Way, Nottingham NG1 6HS
Tel: 0115 947 5701 Fax: 0115 950 7612
Email: nottinghamet@tribunals.gsi.gov.uk

Reading
5th Floor, 30–31 Friar Street, Reading RG1 1DY
Tel: 0118 959 4917 Fax: 0118 956 8066
Email: readinget@tribunals.gsi.gov.uk

Sheffield
14 East Parade, Sheffield S1 2ET
Tel: 0114 276 0348 Fax: 0114 276 2551
Email: sheffieldet@tribunals.gsi.gov.uk

Shrewsbury
Prospect House, Belle Vue Road, Shrewsbury SY3 7NR
Tel: 01743 358341 Fax: 01743 244186
Email: shrewsburyet@tribunals.gsi.gov.uk

Southampton
3rd Floor, Duke's Keep, Marsh Lane, Southampton SO14 3EX
Tel: 023 8071 6400 Fax: 023 8063 5506
Email: southamptonet@tribunals.gsi.gov.uk

Stratford
44 The Broadway, Stratford, London E15 1XH
Tel: 020 8221 0921 Fax: 020 8221 0398
Email: stratfordet@tribunals.gsi.gov.uk

Watford
3rd Floor, Radius House, 51 Clarendon Road, Watford, WD17 1HU
Tel: 01923 281750 Fax: 01923 281781
Email: watfordet@tribunals.gsi.gov.uk

13. EQUALITY AND HUMAN RIGHTS COMMISSION

NOTE: successor to the Equal Opportunities Commission, the Commission for Racial Equality, and the Disability Rights Commission.

Website: www.equalityhumanrights.com

Equality and Human Rights Commission Helpline
Freepost RRLL-GHUX-CTRX
Arndale House, The Arndale Centre, Manchester, M4 3EQ
England: 0845 604 6610
Wales: 0845 604 8810
Scotland: 0845 604 5510

Equality and Human Rights Commission Offices in England, Wales and Scotland

London
3 More London, Riverside Tooley Street, London, SE1 2RG
Tel: 020 3117 0235 Fax: 0207 407 7557
Email: info@equalityhumanrights.com

Manchester
Arndale House, The Arndale Centre, Manchester, M4 3AQ
Tel: 0161 829 8100 Fax: 01925 884 000
Email: info@equalityhumanrights.com

Cardiff
3rd floor, 3 Callaghan Square, Cardiff, CF10 5BT
Tel: 02920 447710 Fax: 02920 447712
Email: wales@equalityhumanrights.com

Glasgow
The Optima Building, 58 Robertson Street, Glasgow, G2 8DU
Tel: 0141 228 5910 Fax: 0141 228 5912
Email: scotland@equalityhumanrights.com

14. EQUALITY COMMISSION FOR NORTHERN IRELAND

Equality House, 7–9 Shaftesbury Square, Belfast BT2 7DP
Tel: 02890 500600 Fax: 02890 248687
Website: www.equalityni.org
Email: information@equalityni.org

15. HEALTH AND SAFETY EXECUTIVE

NOTE: successor since 1 April 2008 to the Health and Safety Commission and the Health and Safety Executive
HSE, Rose Court, 2 Southwark Bridge, London SE1 9HS
Tel: 0845 345 0055 Fax: 0845 408 9566 Minicom: 0845 408 9577
Website: www.hse.gov.uk
Email: hse.infoline@natbrit.com

16. INFORMATION COMMISSIONER

(*Formerly* **Data Protection Commissioner**)
Information Commissioner's Office
Wycliffe House, Water Lane, Wilmslow, Cheshire SK9 5AF
Tel: 01625 545745 or
Tel: 08456 306060
Fax: 01625 524510
Website: www.ico.gov.uk
Email: mail@ico.gsi.gov.uk

Regional Offices
Northern Ireland
Information Commissioner's Office – Northern Ireland
51 Adelaide Street,
Belfast, BT2 8FE, Northern Ireland
Telephone: 028 9026 9380
Fax: 028 9026 9388
Email: ni@ico.gsi.gov.uk

Scotland
Information Commissioner's Office – Scotland
28 Thistle Street, Edinburgh, EH2 1EN
Tel: 0131 225 6341   Fax: 0131225 6989
Email: scotland@ico.gsi.gov.uk

Wales
Information Commissioner's Office – Wales
Cambrian Buildings, Mount Stuart Square, Cardiff, CF10 5FL
Telephone: 029 2044 8044
Fax: 029 204 8045
Email: wales@ico.gsi.gov.uk

17. NORTHERN IRELAND COUNCIL FOR ETHNIC MINORITIES (NICEM)
3rd Floor, Ascot House, 24–31 Shaftesbury Square, Belfast BT2 7DB
Tel: 028 9023 8645   Fax: 028 9031 9485
Website: www.nicem.org.uk
Email: info@nicem.org.uk

18. OPAS (PENSIONS ADVISORY SERVICE)
11 Belgrave Road, London SW1V 1RB
Tel: 0845 601 2923   Fax: 020 7592 7000
Website: www.pensionsadvisoryservice.org.uk
Email: enquiries@pensionsadvisoryservice.org.uk

19. PENSIONS OMBUDSMAN
11 Belgrave Road, London SW1V 1RB
Tel: 020 7834 9144   Fax: 020 7821 0065
Website: www.pensions-ombudsman.org.uk
Email: enquiries@pensions-ombudsman.org.uk

20. PENSIONS REGULATOR
Napier House, Trafalgar Square, Brighton BN1 4DW
Tel 0870 6063636   Fax: 0870 2411144
Website: www.pensionregulator.gov.uk
Email: customersupport@thepensionsregulator.gov.uk

21. TSO (THE STATIONERY OFFICE)
To place an order or make an enquiry:
Tel: 0870 600 5522   Fax: 0870 600 5533
Email: customer.services@tso.co.uk
Website: www.tso.co.uk

22. TRIBUNALS SERVICE
Head of Communications
Tribunals Service
1st Floor, 4 Abbey Orchard Street, London SW1P 2BS
Tel: 020 7340 6589
Website: www.tribunals.gov.uk
Email: ts.webmaster@tribunals.gsi.gov.uk

[5046]

Index

A

E

J

L

P

T